standard catalog of WORLD COINS 1801-1900

second edition

by Chester L. Krause and Clifford Mishler

Colin R. Bruce II
Senior Editor

Thomas Michael
Market Analyst

Elizabeth A. Burgert
Coordinating Editor

Randy Thern
Numismatic Cataloging Supervisor

Fred J. Borgmann
Technical Editor

Sherry Dopp
Illustration Coordinator

Robert Wilhite
U.S. Market Analyst

Dana Roberts, Paul Montz, Georg H. Förster
Special Contributors

UNCIRCULATED VALUATIONS

The uncirculated valuations represented in this edition are for typical quality specimens, for some of the more popularly collected series. Brilliant uncirculated (BU), or superior quality examples may easily command 10% to 50% premiums, or even greater where particularly popular or rare types or dates are concerned.

BULLION VALUE (BV) MARKET VALUATIONS

Valuations for all platinum, gold, palladium or silver coins of the more common, basically bullion types, or those possessing only modest numismatic premiums are presented in this edition based on market levels of $350 per ounce for platinum, $285 for gold, $265 for palladium and $5.20 per ounce for silver. Wherever the letters "BV" – Bullion Value – appear in a value column, that particular issue in the condition indicated generally trades at or near the bullion value of its precious metal content. Further information on using this catalog to evaluate platinum, gold, palladium or silver coins amid fluctuating precious metal market conditions is presented in the introduction.

When I was young I thought that money was the most important thing in life; now that I am old I know that it is. – Oscar Wilde

standard catalog of WORLD COINS 1801-1900

second edition

by Chester L. Krause and Clifford Mishler

Published in the United States by

700 E. State Street, Iola, WI 54990-0001
Phone: 715-445-2214 • FAX: 715-445-4087

Library of Congress Catalog Card Number: 79-640940
International Standard Book Number: 0-87341-652-X

Printed in the United States of America

Table of Contents

Advertiser Index

INTRODUCTION

Nearly a quarter century has passed since the *Standard Catalog of World Coins* was nurtured to life in its first edition, compiled in 1971 and released to the collecting public in March, 1972. Within its pages were listings organized in a logical format by denomination, date and mint of issue. Thus was our initial coverage presentation of the world's coinage from the mid-1800's through the 1960s. The collecting of world coins has never been the same since.

Prior to the release of that first *Standard Catalog of World Coins*, detailed world coin collecting information was available only to those who pursued their interests with the aid of specialized country catalogs, in whatever scope they existed. Generally speaking, they were available in English only for the most popular countries, with coverage restricted to the 19th and 20th centuries.

The *Standard Catalog of World Coins* changed all that. True to its stated objective of providing users a comprehensive one volume catalog, it literally replaces a shelf of often elusive specialized references, many of which were obscure, long out-of-print, non-English works. That original compilation listed the issues of all but a few countries in orderly, detailed arrangements. Several of those compilations were pioneering listings, just the first of a multitude to follow from edition to edition.

Research conducted by contributors and staff editors through the years gradually expanded the scope of the listings, embracing earlier eras and somewhat esoteric issues. Thus, the data base from which annual editions of the *Standard Catalog of World Coins* have been drawn grew to include the first half of the 19th century, then the 18th and 17 centuries, successively, on a selective basis as useful and reliable listings could be generated.

Also folded into the listings were the more esoteric categories; patterns, pieforts, trial strikes, medallic and pretender issues, related token issues, NCLTs, collector sets, and presentation sets — any "coins" an individual pursuing an interest in a given country might logically be expected to encounter -- which related to the circulation issue coinage of the respective countries. Early on, the resulting mass of the annual *Standard Catalog of World Coins* editions caused the volume to be reckoned as the "telephone book" or "bible" of the world coin field, be it the individual pursuit from the collector or dealer perspective.

The *Standard Catalog* quickly developed growing pains. As its distribution broadened, more suggestions and demands were visited upon the editors; the addressing of those needs and desires taxed the capability of the editors to incorporate the information in a manageable package. The editors welcomed and listened attentively to these appeals. There was no question, the additional information merited inclusion in the listings, and the annual edition progressively grew more voluminous and unwieldy.

Something had to give. As page counts continued to climb, effective with the 1984 edition, the editors began to systematically condense the listings, overlay large coin photos, and selectively eliminate esoteric categories. Effective with the 1988 edition, the scope of coverage was limited to issues of the 19th and 20th centuries. In response to demand for reincorporation of the pre-1801 issues, and the listings of those esoteric categories that had been removed from the annual *Standard Catalog of World Coins* volumes in the early 1980s, the 1986 and 1992 editions were published as hardbound, double volume sets. With the 1997 edition a lighter-weight paper was incorporated.

Krause Publications has determined to best suit the needs of collectors and dealers alike, individual century volumes are the logical answer. The *Standard Catalog of World Coins-19th Century,* 2nd edition is a result of that decision. This volume provides comprehensive, detailed coverage limited to the 19th century world coinage realm.

This newly revised 19th century edition is introduced shortly after the release of the 26th edition *Standard Catalog of World Coins-20th Century* and the *18th Century Standard Catalog.* In the fall of 1999, a newly updated 17th century volume will be introduced. These new releases represent months of research by our staff and many outside contributors to provide the most accurate and complete numismatic references in the world.

Welcome to the complete, one volume reference for 19th century world coins collecting information... "basically a compilation of the digested knowledge," as stated in the introduction to the first edition, "which students of the numismatic science have contributed to the coin collection hobby through the years," enhanced through the incorporation of original contributions that have substantially expanded the realm of awareness...a worthy successor to the ideals embodied in the publication of the first *Standard Catalog of World Coins* in 1972.

Clifford Mishler
President
Krause Publications

ACKNOWLEDGMENTS

Many individuals have contributed countless changes which have been incorporated into previous titles and now this new 19th Century edition. While all can not be acknowledged, special appreciation is extended to the following who have exhibited a special enthusiasm — for this edition.

Dr. Lawrence A. Adams
Esko Ahlroth
Stephen Album
Antonio Alessandrini
Robert Archer (deceased)
Don Bailey
Dr. Bernd Becker
Allen G. Berman
Wolfgang Bertsch
Joseph Boling
Al Boulanger
B.F. Brekke
Larry Briggs
Michael Broome
Ferrán Calicó
Xavier Calicó (deceased)
Ralph A. Cannito
Peter A. Chase
Scott E. Cordry
Jerry Crain
Jed Crump
A.J. Cunietti-Ferrando
John S. Davenport
George D. Dean
Jean-Paul Divo
Sheridan Downey
Frederic Droulers
Graham P. Dyer
Dr. Jan M. Dyroff
Wilhelm Eglseer
Esko Ekman
Jack Erb
George Falcke
John Ferm
George A. Fisher
Horace P. Flatt
Georg H. Förster
Wayne Freese
Arthur Friedberg
Tom Galway
Vladimir Gamboa
Gary P. Ganguillet
Edward J. Ganister
Dennis Gill
Ronald J. Gillio
Lawrence S. Goldberg
Alberto Gomes
Ralph C. Gordan (deceased)
Brian Greer
Bruce Griffith
Marcel Häberling
Hakim Hamidi
Brian Hannon
Hans Herrli
Joe Hollingsworth
Nicolae Hridan
Serge Huard
Clyde Hubbard
Louis Hudson
John G. Humphris
Dr. Norman Jacobs
Ton Jacobs
Uno Jensen
Robert Johnston
Roberto Jovel
William M. Judd
Robert W. Julian
Craig Keplinger
John M. Kleeberg
Peter Kraneveld
Prashant P. Kulkarni
Joseph E. Lang
Nirat Lertchitvikul
George Lill III
Jan Lingen
Mike Locke
Jim Long
Rudi Lotter
Alan Luedeking
Ma Tak Wo
Kenneth MacKenzie
Ranko Mandic
Harrington Manville
John B. McCaugherty
Don Medcalf
Sewall H. Menzel
Jurgen Mikeska
Dr. William J.D. Mira
Dr. Richard Montrey
Paul Montz
Steve Musil
R. Paul Nadin-Davis
Hitoshi Nagai
N. Douglas Nicol
Frank Olrog (deceased)
Wayne N. Palmer
Gus A. Pappas
Duwayne A. Perry
Jens Pilegaard
Rick Ponterio
Tom Reynolds
Dana Roberts
Arnaldo Russo
John Sacher
Dr. Wolfgang Schuster
David E. Seelye
Dale Seppa
Ladislav Sin
Larry Sheppard
Lester D. Snell
Richard Snow
Jørgen Sømod
William F. Spengler
Richard Stuart
Alim A. Sumana
Erwin Schäffer
J. L. Van der Schueren
Robert van Bebber
Erik J. Van Loon
Edmundo Fadon Vicente
Fredric R. Wachter
Brian Wagner
Justin C. Wang
William B. Warden, Jr.
John Wells
Paul Welz
Stewart Westdal
J. Hugh Witherow
Joseph Zaffern

AUCTION HOUSES AND DISTRIBUTORS

Leu Numismatik AG
Baldwin's Auctions Ltd.
Bonhams
Bowers & Merena, Inc.
Frankfurter Münzhandlung GmbH
Giessener Münzhandlung
Hess-Divo Ltd.
Gerhard Hirsch
Fritz Rudolf Künker
Müzhandlung Möller
Noble Numismatics Pty. Ltd.
Ponterio & Associates
Laurens Schulman
Sotheby's
Spink America
Stack's
Superior Stamp & Coin
Swiss Bank Corp.
Taisei Stamps & Coins, (S) Pte. Ltd.
World Wide Coins of California

SOCIETIES and INSTITUTIONS

American Numismatic Association
American Numismatic Society
Numismatics International
British Museum
Smithsonian Institution
Johns Hopkins University
Russian Numismatic Society

PUBLICATIONS

The Statesman's Year-Book, 1998-99. 135th Edition

by Barry Turner, editor, The Statesman's Year-Book Office, The Macmillan Press Ltd., 25 Eccleston Place, London SW1W 9NF, England. (Statistical and Historical Annual of the States of the World)

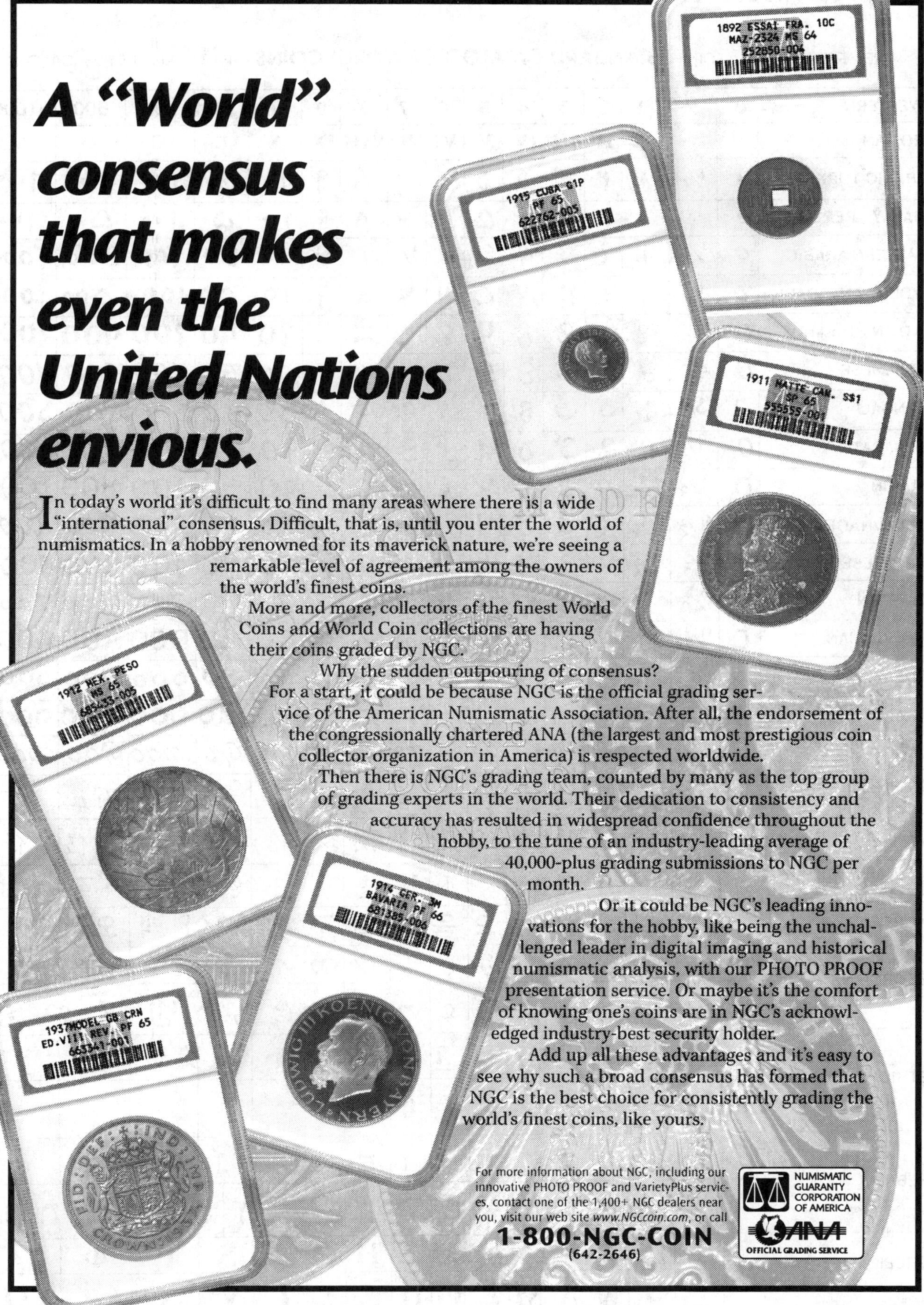
A "World" consensus that makes even the United Nations envious.
In today's world it's difficult to find many areas where there is a wide "international" consensus. Difficult, that is, until you enter the world of numismatics. In a hobby renowned for its maverick nature, we're seeing a remarkable level of agreement among the owners of the world's finest coins.
More and more, collectors of the finest World Coins and World Coin collections are having their coins graded by NGC.
Why the sudden outpouring of consensus? For a start, it could be because NGC is the official grading service of the American Numismatic Association. After all, the endorsement of the congressionally chartered ANA (the largest and most prestigious coin collector organization in America) is respected worldwide.
Then there is NGC's grading team, counted by many as the top group of grading experts in the world. Their dedication to consistency and accuracy has resulted in widespread confidence throughout the hobby, to the tune of an industry-leading average of 40,000-plus grading submissions to NGC per month.
Or it could be NGC's leading innovations for the hobby, like being the unchallenged leader in digital imaging and historical numismatic analysis, with our PHOTO PROOF presentation service. Or maybe it's the comfort of knowing one's coins are in NGC's acknowledged industry-best security holder.
Add up all these advantages and it's easy to see why such a broad consensus has formed that NGC is the best choice for consistently grading the world's finest coins, like yours.
For more information about NGC, including our innovative PHOTO PROOF and VarietyPlus services, contact one of the 1,400+ NGC dealers near you, visit our web site www.NGCcoin.com, or call
1-800-NGC-COIN
(642-2646)
NUMISMATIC GUARANTY CORPORATION OF AMERICA
ANA
OFFICIAL GRADING SERVICE

STANDARD INTERNATIONAL NUMERAL SYSTEMS

WESTERN	0	½	1	2	3	4	5	6	7	8	9	10	50	100	500	1000
ROMAN			I	II	III	IV	V	VI	VII	VIII	IX	X	L	C	D	M
ARABIC-TURKISH	٠	١/٢	١	٢	٣	٤	٥	٦	٧	٨	٩	١٠	٥٠	١٠٠	٥٠٠	١٠٠٠
MALAY—PERSIAN	۰	۱/۲	۱	۲	۳	۴	۵	۶ or ۶	۷	۸	۹	۱۰	۵۰	۱۰۰	۵۰۰	۱۰۰۰
EASTERN ARABIC	0	1/2	۱	۲	۳	۴	۵	۶	۷	۸	۹	۱0	۵0	۱00	۵00	۱000
HYDERABAD ARABIC	0	١/٢	١	٢	٣	٤	٥	٦	٧	٨	٩	١0	٥0	١00	٥00	١000
INDIAN (Sanskrit)	०	१/२	१	२	३	४	५	६	७	८	९	१०	५०	१००	५००	१०००
ASSAMESE	০	১/২	১	২	৩	৪	৫	৬	৭	৮	৯	১০	৫০	১০০	৫০০	১০০০
BENGALI	০	১/২	১	২	৩	৪	৫	৬	৭	৮	৯	১০	৫০	১০০	৫০০	১০০০
GUJARATI	૦	૧/૨	૧	૨	૩	૪	૫	૬	૭	૮	૯	૧૦	૫૦	૧૦૦	૫૦૦	૧૦૦૦
KUTCH	0	1/२	1	२	३	४	५	६	७	८	९	10	५0	100	५00	1000
DEVAVNAGRI	०	९/२	९	२	३	४	५	६ or ६	७	८	९ or ९	९०	५०	९००	५००	९०००
NEPALESE	०	१/२	१ or १	२	३	४	५ or ५	६	७	८ or ८	९ or ९ or ९	१०	४०	१००	४००	१०००
TIBETAN	༠	༡/༢	༡	༢	༣	༤	༥	༦	༧	༨	༩	༡༠	༥༠	༡༠༠	༥༠༠	༡༠༠༠
MONGOLIAN	᠐	᠑/᠒	᠑	᠒	᠓	᠔	᠕	᠖	᠗	᠘	᠙	᠑᠐	᠕᠐	᠑᠐᠐	᠕᠐᠐	᠑᠐᠐᠐
BURMESE	၀	၁/၂	၁	၂	၃	၄	၅	၆	၇	၈	၉	၁၀	၅၀	၁၀၀	၅၀၀	၁၀၀၀
THAI-LAO	๐	๑/๒	๑	๒	๓	๔	๕	๖	๗	๘	๙	๑๐	๕๐	๑๐๐	๕๐๐	๑๐๐๐
JAVANESE	꧐		꧑	꧒	꧓	꧔	꧕	꧖	꧗	꧘	꧙	꧑꧐	꧕꧐	꧑꧐꧐	꧕꧐꧐	꧑꧐꧐꧐
ORDINARY CHINESE JAPANESE-KOREAN	零	半	一	二	三	四	五	六	七	八	九	十	十五	百	百五	千
OFFICIAL CHINESE			壹	貳	叁	肆	伍	陸	柒	捌	玖	拾	拾伍	佰	佰伍	仟
COMMERCIAL CHINESE			〡	〢	〣	〤	〥	〦	〧	〨	〩	十	〥十	〡百	〥百	〡千
KOREAN		반	일	이	삼	사	오	육	칠	팔	구	십	오십	백	오백	천
GEORGIAN			ა	ბ	გ	დ	ე	ვ	ზ	ჱ	თ	ი	ნ	რ	ფ	ჩ
			11 ია	20 კ	30 ლ	40 მ	50 ნ	60 ჲ	70 ო	80 პ	90 ჟ	100 რ	200 ს 300 ტ	400 უ	600 ქ	700 ღ 800 ყ
ETHIOPIAN	◆		፩	፪	፫	፬	፭	፮	፯	፰	፱	፲	፶	፻	፭፻	፲፻
				20 ፳	30 ፴	40 ፵		60 ፷	70 ፸	80 ፹	90 ፺					
HEBREW			א	ב	ג	ד	ה	ו	ז	ח	ט	י	נ	ק	תק	
				20 כ	30 ל	40 מ		60 ס	70 ע	80 פ	90 צ	200 ר	300 ש	400 ת	600 תר 700 תש	800 תת
GREEK			Α	Β	Γ	Δ	Ε	ΣΤ	Ζ	Η	Θ	Ι	Ν	Ρ	Φ	Α
				20 Κ	30 Λ	40 Μ	60 Ξ	70 Ο	80 Π		200 Σ	300 Τ	400 Υ	600 Χ	700 Ψ	800 Ω

HOW TO USE THIS CATALOG

This catalog is designed to serve the needs of both the novice and advanced collectors. It provides a comprehensive guide to 100 years of world coinage. It is generally arranged so that persons with no more than a basic knowledge of world history after 1800 and a casual acquaintance with coin collecting can consult it with confidence and ease. The following explanations summarize the general practices used in preparing this catalog's listings. However, because of specialized requirements which may vary by country and era, these must not be considered ironclad. Where these standards have been set aside, appropriate notations of the variations are incorporated in that particular listing.

ARRANGEMENT

All coin listings are alphabetically arranged in a historical-geographic approach according to the current identity of the sovereign government concerned. Thus, the coins of Persia can be located by referring to the listings for Iran, or the now defunct Union of Soviet Socialist Republics (U.S.S.R.) by turning to Russia. This approach has also resulted in combining the coin listings for such issuing entities as Annam, French Cochin China, Tonkin, North and South Viet Nam as subgroupings under the identity of Viet Nam. Likewise, coins of North and South Korea will be found under Korea, and those of the Congo Free State, Belgian Congo, Congo Democratic Republic, Katanga and Zaire, under the latter identity.

Coins of each country are generally arranged by denomination from lowest to highest, except where arrangement by ruler, mint of issue, type or period makes a series easier to understand. Exceptions which are not readily adaptable to this traditional North American cataloging style are generally found in the more complicated series, most notably those encompassing the early issues of Afghanistan, Mughal issues of India, Indian Princely States, Iran, Nepal and the areas under the influence of the late Ottoman Empire, which are listed by ruler or by mint.

Strict date sequence of listings is also interrupted in a number of countries which have been subjected to major monetary reforms or conversion to decimal or other new currency systems. Where these considerations apply, appropriate headings are incorporated to introduce the change from one standard to another.

IDENTIFICATION

The most important step in the identification of a coin is the determination of the nation of origin. This is generally easily accomplished where English-speaking lands are concerned, however, use of the country index is sometimes required. The coins of Great Britain provide an interesting challenge. For hundreds of years the only indication of the country of origin was in the abbreviated Latin legends. In recent times there have been occasions when there has been no indication of origin. Only through the familiarity of the monarchical portraits, symbols and legends or indication of currency system are they identifiable.

The coins of many countries beyond the English-language realm, such as those of French, Italian or Spanish heritage, are also quite easy to identify through reference to their legends, which appear in the national languages based on Western alphabets. In many instances the name is spelled exactly the same in English as in the national language, such as France; while in other cases it varies only slightly, like Italia for Italy, Belgique or Belgie for Belgium, Brasil for Brazil and Danmark for Denmark.

This is not always the case, however, as in Norge for Norway, Espana for Spain, Sverige for Sweden and Helvetia for Switzerland. Some other examples include:

DEUTSCHES REICH - Germany 1873-1945

BUNDESREPUBLIC DEUTSCHLAND - Federal Republic of Germany.

DEUTSCHE DEMOKRATISCHE REPUBLIK - German Democratic Republic.

EMPIRE CHERIFIEN MAROC - Morocco.

ESTADOS UNIDOS MEXICANOS - United Mexican States (Mexico).

ETAT DU GRAND LIBAN - State of Great Lebanon (Lebanon).

Thus it can be seen there are instances in which a little schooling in the rudiments of foreign languages can be most helpful. In general, colonial possessions of countries using the Western alphabet are similarly identifiable as they often carry portraits of their current rulers, the familiar lettering, sometimes in combination with a companion designation in the local language.

Collectors have the greatest difficulty with coins that do not bear legends or dates in the Western systems. These include coins bearing Cyrillic lettering, attributable to Bulgaria, Russia, the Slavic states and Mongolia, the Greek script peculiar to Greece, Crete and the Ionian Islands; The Amharic characters of Ethiopia, or Hebrew in the case of Israel. Dragons and sunbursts along with the distinctive word characters, attribute a coin to the Oriental countries of China, Japan, Korea, Tibet, Viet Nam and their component parts.

The most difficult coins to identify are those bearing only Persian or Arabic script and its derivatives, found on the issues of nations stretching in a wide swath across North Africa and East Asia, from Morocco to Indonesia, and the Indian subcontinent coinages which surely are more confusing in their vast array of Nagari, Sanskrit, Ahom, Assamese and other local dialects found on the local issues of the Indian Princely States. Although the task of identification on the more modern issues of these lands is often eased by the added presence of Western alphabet legends, a feature sometimes adopted as early as the late 19th Century, for the earlier pieces it is often necessary for the uninitiated to laboriously seek and find.

Except for the cruder issues, however, it will be found that certain characteristics and symbols featured in addition to the predominant legends are typical on coins from a given country or group of countries. The toughra monogram, for instance, occurs on some of the coins of Afghanistan, Egypt, the Sudan, Pakistan, Turkey and other areas of the late Ottoman Empire. A predominant design feature on the coins of Nepal is the trident; while neighboring Tibet features a lotus blossom or lion on many of their issues.

To assist in identification of the more difficult coins, we have assembled the *Instant Identifier* and *Monogram* sections presented on the following pages. They are designed to provide a point of beginning for collectors by allowing them to compare unidentified coins with photographic details from typical issues.

We also suggest reference to the *Index of Coin Denominations* presented here and also the comprehensive *Country Index*, where the inscription will be found listed just as it appears on the coin for nations using the Western alphabet.

DATING

Coin dating is the final basic attribution consideration. Here, the problem can be more difficult because the reading of a coin date is subject not only to the vagaries of numeric styling, but to calendar variations caused by the observance of various religious eras or regal periods from country to country, or even within a country. Here again with the exception of the sphere from North Africa through the Orient, it will be found that most countries rely on Western date numerals and Christian (AD) era reckoning, although in a few instances, coin dating has been tied to the year of a reign or government. The Vatican, for example dates its coinage according to the year of reign of the current pope, in addition to the Christian-era date.

Silver Bullion Chart

Oz.	3.000	3.500	4.000	4.500	5.000	5.500	6.000	6.500	7.000	7.500	8.000	8.500	9.000	9.500	10.000	10.500	Oz.
0.001	0.003	0.004	0.004	0.005	0.005	0.006	0.006	0.007	0.007	0.008	0.008	0.009	0.009	0.010	0.010	0.011	0.001
0.002	0.006	0.007	0.008	0.009	0.010	0.011	0.012	0.013	0.014	0.015	0.016	0.017	0.018	0.019	0.020	0.021	0.002
0.003	0.009	0.011	0.012	0.014	0.015	0.017	0.018	0.020	0.021	0.023	0.024	0.026	0.027	0.029	0.030	0.032	0.003
0.004	0.012	0.014	0.016	0.018	0.020	0.022	0.024	0.026	0.028	0.030	0.032	0.034	0.036	0.038	0.040	0.042	0.004
0.005	0.015	0.018	0.020	0.023	0.025	0.028	0.030	0.033	0.035	0.038	0.040	0.043	0.045	0.048	0.050	0.052	0.005
0.006	0.018	0.021	0.024	0.027	0.030	0.033	0.036	0.039	0.042	0.045	0.048	0.051	0.054	0.057	0.060	0.063	0.006
0.007	0.021	0.025	0.028	0.032	0.035	0.039	0.042	0.046	0.049	0.053	0.056	0.060	0.063	0.067	0.070	0.074	0.007
0.008	0.024	0.028	0.032	0.036	0.040	0.044	0.048	0.052	0.056	0.060	0.064	0.068	0.072	0.076	0.080	0.084	0.008
0.009	0.027	0.032	0.036	0.041	0.045	0.050	0.054	0.059	0.063	0.068	0.072	0.077	0.081	0.086	0.090	0.095	0.009
0.010	0.030	0.035	0.040	0.045	0.050	0.055	0.060	0.065	0.070	0.075	0.080	0.085	0.090	0.095	0.100	0.105	0.010
0.020	0.060	0.070	0.080	0.090	0.100	0.110	0.120	0.130	0.140	0.150	0.160	0.170	0.180	0.190	0.200	0.210	0.020
0.030	0.090	0.105	0.120	0.135	0.150	0.165	0.180	0.195	0.210	0.225	0.240	0.255	0.270	0.285	0.300	0.315	0.030
0.040	0.120	0.140	0.160	0.180	0.200	0.220	0.240	0.260	0.280	0.300	0.320	0.340	0.360	0.380	0.400	0.420	0.040
0.050	0.150	0.175	0.200	0.225	0.250	0.275	0.300	0.325	0.350	0.375	0.400	0.425	0.450	0.475	0.500	0.525	0.050
0.060	0.180	0.210	0.240	0.270	0.300	0.330	0.360	0.390	0.420	0.450	0.480	0.510	0.540	0.570	0.600	0.630	0.060
0.070	0.210	0.245	0.280	0.315	0.350	0.385	0.420	0.455	0.490	0.525	0.560	0.595	0.630	0.665	0.700	0.735	0.070
0.080	0.240	0.280	0.320	0.360	0.400	0.440	0.480	0.520	0.560	0.600	0.640	0.680	0.720	0.760	0.800	0.840	0.080
0.090	0.270	0.315	0.360	0.405	0.450	0.495	0.540	0.585	0.630	0.675	0.720	0.765	0.810	0.855	0.900	0.945	0.090
0.100	0.300	0.350	0.400	0.450	0.500	0.550	0.600	0.650	0.700	0.750	0.800	0.850	0.900	0.950	1.000	1.050	0.100
0.110	0.330	0.385	0.440	0.495	0.550	0.605	0.660	0.715	0.770	0.825	0.880	0.935	0.990	1.045	1.100	1.155	0.110
0.120	0.360	0.420	0.480	0.540	0.600	0.660	0.720	0.780	0.840	0.900	0.960	1.020	1.080	1.140	1.200	1.260	0.120
0.130	0.390	0.455	0.520	0.585	0.650	0.715	0.780	0.845	0.910	0.975	1.040	1.105	1.170	1.235	1.300	1.365	0.130
0.140	0.420	0.490	0.560	0.630	0.700	0.770	0.840	0.910	0.980	1.050	1.120	1.190	1.260	1.330	1.400	1.470	0.140
0.150	0.450	0.525	0.600	0.675	0.750	0.825	0.900	0.975	1.050	1.125	1.200	1.275	1.350	1.425	1.500	1.575	0.150
0.160	0.480	0.560	0.640	0.720	0.800	0.880	0.960	1.040	1.120	1.200	1.280	1.360	1.440	1.520	1.600	1.680	0.160
0.170	0.510	0.595	0.680	0.765	0.850	0.935	1.020	1.105	1.190	1.275	1.360	1.445	1.530	1.615	1.700	1.785	0.170
0.180	0.540	0.630	0.720	0.810	0.900	0.990	1.080	1.170	1.260	1.350	1.440	1.530	1.620	1.710	1.800	1.890	0.180
0.190	0.570	0.665	0.760	0.855	0.950	1.045	1.140	1.235	1.330	1.425	1.520	1.615	1.710	1.805	1.900	1.995	0.190
0.200	0.600	0.700	0.800	0.900	1.000	1.100	1.200	1.300	1.400	1.500	1.600	1.700	1.800	1.900	2.000	2.100	0.200
0.210	0.630	0.735	0.840	0.945	1.050	1.155	1.260	1.365	1.470	1.575	1.680	1.785	1.890	1.995	2.100	2.205	0.210
0.220	0.660	0.770	0.880	0.990	1.100	1.210	1.320	1.430	1.540	1.650	1.760	1.870	1.980	2.090	2.200	2.310	0.220
0.230	0.690	0.805	0.920	1.035	1.150	1.265	1.380	1.495	1.610	1.725	1.840	1.955	2.070	2.185	2.300	2.415	0.230
0.240	0.720	0.840	0.960	1.080	1.200	1.320	1.440	1.560	1.680	1.800	1.920	2.040	2.160	2.280	2.400	2.520	0.240
0.250	0.750	0.875	1.000	1.125	1.250	1.375	1.500	1.625	1.750	1.875	2.000	2.125	2.250	2.375	2.500	2.625	0.250
0.260	0.780	0.910	1.040	1.170	1.300	1.430	1.560	1.690	1.820	1.950	2.080	2.210	2.340	2.470	2.600	2.730	0.260
0.270	0.810	0.945	1.080	1.215	1.350	1.485	1.620	1.755	1.890	2.025	2.160	2.295	2.430	2.565	2.700	2.835	0.270
0.280	0.840	0.980	1.120	1.260	1.400	1.540	1.680	1.820	1.960	2.100	2.240	2.380	2.520	2.660	2.800	2.940	0.280
0.290	0.870	1.015	1.160	1.305	1.450	1.595	1.740	1.885	2.030	2.175	2.320	2.465	2.610	2.755	2.900	3.045	0.290
0.300	0.900	1.050	1.200	1.350	1.500	1.650	1.800	1.950	2.100	2.250	2.400	2.550	2.700	2.850	3.000	3.150	0.300
0.310	0.930	1.085	1.240	1.395	1.550	1.705	1.860	2.015	2.170	2.325	2.480	2.635	2.790	2.945	3.100	3.255	0.310
0.320	0.960	1.120	1.280	1.440	1.600	1.760	1.920	2.080	2.240	2.400	2.560	2.720	2.880	3.040	3.200	3.360	0.320
0.330	0.990	1.155	1.320	1.485	1.650	1.815	1.980	2.145	2.310	2.475	2.640	2.805	2.970	3.135	3.300	3.465	0.330
0.340	1.020	1.190	1.360	1.530	1.700	1.870	2.040	2.210	2.380	2.550	2.720	2.890	3.060	3.230	3.400	3.570	0.340
0.350	1.050	1.225	1.400	1.575	1.750	1.925	2.100	2.275	2.450	2.625	2.800	2.975	3.150	3.325	3.500	3.675	0.350
0.360	1.080	1.260	1.440	1.620	1.800	1.980	2.160	2.340	2.520	2.700	2.880	3.060	3.240	3.420	3.600	3.780	0.360
0.370	1.110	1.295	1.480	1.665	1.850	2.035	2.220	2.405	2.590	2.775	2.960	3.145	3.330	3.515	3.700	3.885	0.370
0.380	1.140	1.330	1.520	1.710	1.900	2.090	2.280	2.470	2.660	2.850	3.040	3.230	3.420	3.610	3.800	3.990	0.380
0.390	1.170	1.365	1.560	1.755	1.950	2.145	2.340	2.535	2.730	2.925	3.120	3.315	3.510	3.705	3.900	4.095	0.390
0.400	1.200	1.400	1.600	1.800	2.000	2.200	2.400	2.600	2.800	3.000	3.200	3.400	3.600	3.800	4.000	4.200	0.400
0.410	1.230	1.435	1.640	1.845	2.050	2.255	2.460	2.665	2.870	3.075	3.280	3.485	3.690	3.895	4.100	4.305	0.410
0.420	1.260	1.470	1.680	1.890	2.100	2.310	2.520	2.730	2.940	3.150	3.360	3.570	3.780	3.990	4.200	4.410	0.420
0.430	1.290	1.505	1.720	1.935	2.150	2.365	2.580	2.795	3.010	3.225	3.440	3.655	3.870	4.085	4.300	4.515	0.430
0.440	1.320	1.540	1.760	1.980	2.200	2.420	2.640	2.860	3.080	3.300	3.520	3.740	3.960	4.180	4.400	4.620	0.440
0.450	1.350	1.575	1.800	2.025	2.250	2.475	2.700	2.925	3.150	3.375	3.600	3.825	4.050	4.275	4.500	4.725	0.450
0.460	1.380	1.610	1.840	2.070	2.300	2.530	2.760	2.990	3.220	3.450	3.680	3.910	4.140	4.370	4.600	4.830	0.460
0.470	1.410	1.645	1.880	2.115	2.350	2.585	2.820	3.055	3.290	3.525	3.760	3.995	4.230	4.465	4.700	4.935	0.470
0.480	1.440	1.680	1.920	2.160	2.400	2.640	2.880	3.120	3.360	3.600	3.840	4.080	4.320	4.560	4.800	5.040	0.480
0.490	1.470	1.715	1.960	2.205	2.450	2.695	2.940	3.185	3.430	3.675	3.920	4.165	4.410	4.655	4.900	5.145	0.490
0.500	1.500	1.750	2.000	2.250	2.500	2.750	3.000	3.250	3.500	3.750	4.000	4.250	4.500	4.750	5.000	5.250	0.500
0.510	1.530	1.785	2.040	2.295	2.550	2.805	3.060	3.315	3.570	3.825	4.080	4.335	4.590	4.845	5.100	5.355	0.510
0.520	1.560	1.820	2.080	2.340	2.600	2.860	3.120	3.380	3.640	3.900	4.160	4.420	4.680	4.940	5.200	5.460	0.520
0.530	1.590	1.855	2.120	2.385	2.650	2.915	3.180	3.445	3.710	3.975	4.240	4.505	4.770	5.035	5.300	5.565	0.530
0.540	1.620	1.890	2.160	2.430	2.700	2.970	3.240	3.510	3.780	4.050	4.320	4.590	4.860	5.130	5.400	5.670	0.540
0.550	1.650	1.925	2.200	2.475	2.750	3.025	3.300	3.575	3.850	4.125	4.400	4.675	4.950	5.225	5.500	5.775	0.550
0.560	1.680	1.960	2.240	2.520	2.800	3.080	3.360	3.640	3.920	4.200	4.480	4.760	5.040	5.320	5.600	5.880	0.560
0.570	1.710	1.995	2.280	2.565	2.850	3.135	3.420	3.705	3.990	4.275	4.560	4.845	5.130	5.415	5.700	5.985	0.570
0.580	1.740	2.030	2.320	2.610	2.900	3.190	3.480	3.770	4.060	4.350	4.640	4.930	5.220	5.510	5.800	6.090	0.580
0.590	1.770	2.065	2.360	2.655	2.950	3.245	3.540	3.835	4.130	4.425	4.720	5.015	5.310	5.605	5.900	6.195	0.590
0.600	1.800	2.100	2.400	2.700	3.000	3.300	3.600	3.900	4.200	4.500	4.800	5.100	5.400	5.700	6.000	6.300	0.600
0.610	1.830	2.135	2.440	2.745	3.050	3.355	3.660	3.965	4.270	4.575	4.880	5.185	5.490	5.795	6.100	6.405	0.610
0.620	1.860	2.170	2.480	2.790	3.100	3.410	3.720	4.030	4.340	4.650	4.960	5.270	5.580	5.890	6.200	6.510	0.620
0.630	1.890	2.205	2.520	2.835	3.150	3.465	3.780	4.095	4.410	4.725	5.040	5.355	5.670	5.985	6.300	6.615	0.630
0.640	1.920	2.240	2.560	2.880	3.200	3.520	3.840	4.160	4.480	4.800	5.120	5.440	5.760	6.080	6.400	6.720	0.640
0.650	1.950	2.275	2.600	2.925	3.250	3.575	3.900	4.225	4.550	4.875	5.200	5.525	5.850	6.175	6.500	6.825	0.650
0.660	1.980	2.310	2.640	2.970	3.300	3.630	3.960	4.290	4.620	4.950	5.280	5.610	5.940	6.270	6.600	6.930	0.660
0.670	2.010	2.345	2.680	3.015	3.350	3.685	4.020	4.355	4.690	5.025	5.360	5.695	6.030	6.365	6.700	7.035	0.670
0.680	2.040	2.380	2.720	3.060	3.400	3.740	4.080	4.420	4.760	5.100	5.440	5.780	6.120	6.460	6.800	7.140	0.680
0.690	2.070	2.415	2.760	3.105	3.450	3.795	4.140	4.485	4.830	5.175	5.520	5.865	6.210	6.555	6.900	7.245	0.690
0.700	2.100	2.450	2.800	3.150	3.500	3.850	4.200	4.550	4.900	5.250	5.600	5.950	6.300	6.650	7.000	7.350	0.700
0.710	2.130	2.485	2.840	3.195	3.550	3.905	4.260	4.615	4.970	5.325	5.680	6.035	6.390	6.745	7.100	7.455	0.710
0.720	2.160	2.520	2.880	3.240	3.600	3.960	4.320	4.680	5.040	5.400	5.760	6.120	6.480	6.840	7.200	7.560	0.720
0.730	2.190	2.555	2.920	3.285	3.650	4.015	4.380	4.745	5.110	5.475	5.840	6.205	6.570	6.935	7.300	7.665	0.730
0.740	2.220	2.590	2.960	3.330	3.700	4.070	4.440	4.810	5.180	5.550	5.920	6.290	6.660	7.030	7.400	7.770	0.740
0.750	2.250	2.625	3.000	3.375	3.750	4.125	4.500	4.875	5.250	5.625	6.000	6.375	6.750	7.125	7.500	7.875	0.750
0.760	2.280	2.660	3.040	3.420	3.800	4.180	4.560	4.940	5.320	5.700	6.080	6.460	6.840	7.220	7.600	7.980	0.760
0.770	2.310	2.695	3.080	3.465	3.850	4.235	4.620	5.005	5.390	5.775	6.160	6.545	6.930	7.315	7.700	8.085	0.770
0.780	2.340	2.730	3.120	3.510	3.900	4.290	4.680	5.070	5.460	5.850	6.240	6.630	7.020	7.410	7.800	8.190	0.780
0.790	2.370	2.765	3.160	3.555	3.950	4.345	4.740	5.135	5.530	5.925	6.320	6.715	7.110	7.505	7.900	8.295	0.790
0.800	2.400	2.800	3.200	3.600	4.000	4.400	4.800	5.200	5.600	6.000	6.400	6.800	7.200	7.600	8.000	8.400	0.800
0.810	2.430	2.835	3.240	3.645	4.050	4.455	4.860	5.265	5.670	6.075	6.480	6.885	7.290	7.695	8.100	8.505	0.810
0.820	2.460	2.870	3.280	3.690	4.100	4.510	4.920	5.330	5.740	6.150	6.560	6.970	7.380	7.790	8.200	8.610	0.820
0.830	2.490	2.905	3.320	3.735	4.150	4.565	4.980	5.395	5.810	6.225	6.640	7.055	7.470	7.885	8.300	8.715	0.830
0.840	2.520	2.940	3.360	3.780	4.200	4.620	5.040	5.460	5.880	6.300	6.720	7.140	7.560	7.980	8.400	8.820	0.840
0.850	2.550	2.975	3.400	3.825	4.250	4.675	5.100	5.525	5.950	6.375	6.800	7.225	7.650	8.075	8.500	8.925	0.850
0.860	2.580	3.010	3.440	3.870	4.300	4.730	5.160	5.590	6.020	6.450	6.880	7.310	7.740	8.170	8.600	9.030	0.860
0.870	2.610	3.045	3.480	3.915	4.350	4.785	5.220	5.655	6.090	6.525	6.960	7.395	7.830	8.265	8.700	9.135	0.870
0.880	2.640	3.080	3.520	3.960	4.400	4.840	5.280	5.720	6.160	6.600	7.040	7.480	7.920	8.360	8.800	9.240	0.880
0.890	2.670	3.115	3.560	4.005	4.450	4.895	5.340	5.785	6.230	6.675	7.120	7.565	8.010	8.455	8.900	9.345	0.890
0.900	2.700	3.150	3.600	4.050	4.500	4.950	5.400	5.850	6.300	6.750	7.200	7.650	8.100	8.550	9.000	9.450	0.900
0.910	2.730	3.185	3.640	4.095	4.550	5.005	5.460	5.915	6.370	6.825	7.280	7.735	8.190	8.645	9.100	9.555	0.910
0.920	2.760	3.220	3.680	4.140	4.600	5.060	5.520	5.980	6.440	6.900	7.360	7.820	8.280	8.740	9.200	9.660	0.920
0.930	2.790	3.255	3.720	4.185	4.650	5.115	5.580	6.045	6.510	6.975	7.440	7.905	8.370	8.835	9.300	9.765	0.930
0.940	2.820	3.290	3.760	4.230	4.700	5.170	5.640	6.110	6.580	7.050	7.520	7.990	8.460	8.930	9.400	9.870	0.940
0.950	2.850	3.325	3.800	4.275	4.750	5.225	5.700	6.175	6.650	7.125	7.600	8.075	8.550	9.025	9.500	9.975	0.950
0.960	2.880	3.360	3.840	4.320	4.800	5.280	5.760	6.240	6.720	7.200	7.680	8.160	8.640	9.120	9.600	10.080	0.960
0.970	2.910	3.395	3.880	4.365	4.850	5.335	5.820	6.305	6.790	7.275	7.760	8.245	8.730	9.215	9.700	10.185	0.970
0.980	2.940	3.430	3.920	4.410	4.900	5.390	5.880	6.370	6.860	7.350	7.840	8.330	8.820	9.310	9.800	10.290	0.980
0.990	2.970	3.465	3.960	4.455	4.950	5.445	5.940	6.435	6.930	7.425	7.920	8.415	8.910	9.405	9.900	10.395	0.990
1.000	3.000	3.500	4.000	4.500	5.000	5.500	6.000	6.500	7.000	7.500	8.000	8.500	9.000	9.500	10.000	10.500	1.000

11
ADVERTISEMENT

GOLD BULLION CHART

Oz.	270.00	280.00	290.00	300.00	310.00	320.00	330.00	340.00	350.00	360.00	370.00	380.00	390.00	400.00	410.00	Oz.
0.001	0.27	0.28	0.29	0.30	0.31	0.32	0.33	0.34	0.35	0.36	0.37	0.38	0.39	0.40	0.41	0.001
0.002	0.54	0.56	0.58	0.60	0.62	0.64	0.66	0.68	0.70	0.72	0.74	0.76	0.78	0.80	0.82	0.002
0.003	0.81	0.84	0.87	0.90	0.93	0.96	0.99	1.02	1.05	1.08	1.11	1.14	1.17	1.20	1.23	0.003
0.004	1.08	1.12	1.16	1.20	1.24	1.28	1.32	1.36	1.40	1.44	1.48	1.52	1.56	1.60	1.64	0.004
0.005	1.35	1.40	1.45	1.50	1.55	1.60	1.65	1.70	1.75	1.80	1.85	1.90	1.95	2.00	2.05	0.005
0.006	1.62	1.68	1.74	1.80	1.86	1.92	1.98	2.04	2.10	2.16	2.22	2.28	2.34	2.40	2.46	0.006
0.007	1.89	1.96	2.03	2.10	2.17	2.24	2.31	2.38	2.45	2.52	2.59	2.66	2.73	2.80	2.87	0.007
0.008	2.16	2.24	2.32	2.40	2.48	2.56	2.64	2.72	2.80	2.88	2.96	3.04	3.12	3.20	3.28	0.008
0.009	2.43	2.52	2.61	2.70	2.79	2.88	2.97	3.06	3.15	3.24	3.33	3.42	3.51	3.60	3.69	0.009
0.010	2.70	2.80	2.90	3.00	3.10	3.20	3.30	3.40	3.50	3.60	3.70	3.80	3.90	4.00	4.10	0.010
0.020	5.40	5.60	5.80	6.00	6.20	6.40	6.60	6.80	7.00	7.20	7.40	7.60	7.80	8.00	8.20	0.020
0.030	8.10	8.40	8.70	9.00	9.30	9.60	9.90	10.20	10.50	10.80	11.10	11.40	11.70	12.00	12.30	0.030
0.040	10.80	11.20	11.60	12.00	12.40	12.80	13.20	13.60	14.00	14.40	14.80	15.20	15.60	16.00	16.40	0.040
0.050	13.50	14.00	14.50	15.00	15.50	16.00	16.50	17.00	17.50	18.00	18.50	19.00	19.50	20.00	20.50	0.050
0.060	16.20	16.80	17.40	18.00	18.60	19.20	19.80	20.40	21.00	21.60	22.20	22.80	23.40	24.00	24.60	0.060
0.070	18.90	19.60	20.30	21.00	21.70	22.40	23.10	23.80	24.50	25.20	25.90	26.60	27.30	28.00	28.70	0.070
0.080	21.60	22.40	23.20	24.00	24.80	25.60	26.40	27.20	28.00	28.80	29.60	30.40	31.20	32.00	32.80	0.080
0.090	24.30	25.20	26.10	27.00	27.90	28.80	29.70	30.60	31.50	32.40	33.30	34.20	35.10	36.00	36.90	0.090
0.100	27.00	28.00	29.00	30.00	31.00	32.00	33.00	34.00	35.00	36.00	37.00	38.00	39.00	40.00	41.00	0.100
0.110	29.70	30.80	31.90	33.00	34.10	35.20	36.30	37.40	38.50	39.60	40.70	41.80	42.90	44.00	45.10	0.110
0.120	32.40	33.60	34.80	36.00	37.20	38.40	39.60	40.80	42.00	43.20	44.40	45.60	46.80	48.00	49.20	0.120
0.130	35.10	36.40	37.70	39.00	40.30	41.60	42.90	44.20	45.50	46.80	48.10	49.40	50.70	52.00	53.30	0.130
0.140	37.80	39.20	40.60	42.00	43.40	44.80	46.20	47.60	49.00	50.40	51.80	53.20	54.60	56.00	57.40	0.140
0.150	40.50	42.00	43.50	45.00	46.50	48.00	49.50	51.00	52.50	54.00	55.50	57.00	58.50	60.00	61.50	0.150
0.160	43.20	44.80	46.40	48.00	49.60	51.20	52.80	54.40	56.00	57.60	59.20	60.80	62.40	64.00	65.60	0.160
0.170	45.90	47.60	49.30	51.00	52.70	54.40	56.10	57.80	59.50	61.20	62.90	64.60	66.30	68.00	69.70	0.170
0.180	48.60	50.40	52.20	54.00	55.80	57.60	59.40	61.20	63.00	64.80	66.60	68.40	70.20	72.00	73.80	0.180
0.190	51.30	53.20	55.10	57.00	58.90	60.80	62.70	64.60	66.50	68.40	70.30	72.20	74.10	76.00	77.90	0.190
0.200	54.00	56.00	58.00	60.00	62.00	64.00	66.00	68.00	70.00	72.00	74.00	76.00	78.00	80.00	82.00	0.200
0.210	56.70	58.80	60.90	63.00	65.10	67.20	69.30	71.40	73.50	75.60	77.70	79.80	81.90	84.00	86.10	0.210
0.220	59.40	61.60	63.80	66.00	68.20	70.40	72.60	74.80	77.00	79.20	81.40	83.60	85.80	88.00	90.20	0.220
0.230	62.10	64.40	66.70	69.00	71.30	73.60	75.90	78.20	80.50	82.80	85.10	87.40	89.70	92.00	94.30	0.230
0.240	64.80	67.20	69.60	72.00	74.40	76.80	79.20	81.60	84.00	86.40	88.80	91.20	93.60	96.00	98.40	0.240
0.250	67.50	70.00	72.50	75.00	77.50	80.00	82.50	85.00	87.50	90.00	92.50	95.00	97.50	100.00	102.50	0.250
0.260	70.20	72.80	75.40	78.00	80.60	83.20	85.80	88.40	91.00	93.60	96.20	98.80	101.40	104.00	106.60	0.260
0.270	72.90	75.60	78.30	81.00	83.70	86.40	89.10	91.80	94.50	97.20	99.90	102.60	105.30	108.00	110.70	0.270
0.280	75.60	78.40	81.20	84.00	86.80	89.60	92.40	95.20	98.00	100.80	103.60	106.40	109.20	112.00	114.80	0.280
0.290	78.30	81.20	84.10	87.00	89.90	92.80	95.70	98.60	101.50	104.40	107.30	110.20	113.10	116.00	118.90	0.290
0.300	81.00	84.00	87.00	90.00	93.00	96.00	99.00	102.00	105.00	108.00	111.00	114.00	117.00	120.00	123.00	0.300
0.310	83.70	86.80	89.90	93.00	96.10	99.20	102.30	105.40	108.50	111.60	114.70	117.80	120.90	124.00	127.10	0.310
0.320	86.40	89.60	92.80	96.00	99.20	102.40	105.60	108.80	112.00	115.20	118.40	121.60	124.80	128.00	131.20	0.320
0.330	89.10	92.40	95.70	99.00	102.30	105.60	108.90	112.20	115.50	118.80	122.10	125.40	128.70	132.00	135.30	0.330
0.340	91.80	95.20	98.60	102.00	105.40	108.80	112.20	115.60	119.00	122.40	125.80	129.20	132.60	136.00	139.40	0.340
0.350	94.50	98.00	101.50	105.00	108.50	112.00	115.50	119.00	122.50	126.00	129.50	133.00	136.50	140.00	143.50	0.350
0.360	97.20	100.80	104.40	108.00	111.60	115.20	118.80	122.40	126.00	129.60	133.20	136.80	140.40	144.00	147.60	0.360
0.370	99.90	103.60	107.30	111.00	114.70	118.40	122.10	125.80	129.50	133.20	136.90	140.60	144.30	148.00	151.70	0.370
0.380	102.60	106.40	110.20	114.00	117.80	121.60	125.40	129.20	133.00	136.80	140.60	144.40	148.20	152.00	155.80	0.380
0.390	105.30	109.20	113.10	117.00	120.90	124.80	128.70	132.60	136.50	140.40	144.30	148.20	152.10	156.00	159.90	0.390
0.400	108.00	112.00	116.00	120.00	124.00	128.00	132.00	136.00	140.00	144.00	148.00	152.00	156.00	160.00	164.00	0.400
0.410	110.70	114.80	118.90	123.00	127.10	131.20	135.30	139.40	143.50	147.60	151.70	155.80	159.90	164.00	168.10	0.410
0.420	113.40	117.60	121.80	126.00	130.20	134.40	138.60	142.80	147.00	151.20	155.40	159.60	163.80	168.00	172.20	0.420
0.430	116.10	120.40	124.70	129.00	133.30	137.60	141.90	146.20	150.50	154.80	159.10	163.40	167.70	172.00	176.30	0.430
0.440	118.80	123.20	127.60	132.00	136.40	140.80	145.20	149.60	154.00	158.40	162.80	167.20	171.60	176.00	180.40	0.440
0.450	121.50	126.00	130.50	135.00	139.50	144.00	148.50	153.00	157.50	162.00	166.50	171.00	175.50	180.00	184.50	0.450
0.460	124.20	128.80	133.40	138.00	142.60	147.20	151.80	156.40	161.00	165.60	170.20	174.80	179.40	184.00	188.60	0.460

GOLD BULLION CHART

Oz.	270.00	280.00	290.00	300.00	310.00	320.00	330.00	340.00	350.00	360.00	370.00	380.00	390.00	400.00	410.00	Oz.
0.470	126.90	131.60	136.30	141.00	145.70	150.40	155.10	159.80	164.50	169.20	173.90	178.60	183.30	188.00	192.70	0.470
0.480	129.60	134.40	139.20	144.00	148.80	153.60	158.40	163.20	168.00	172.80	177.60	182.40	187.20	192.00	196.80	0.480
0.490	132.30	137.20	142.10	147.00	151.90	156.80	161.70	166.60	171.50	176.40	181.30	186.20	191.10	196.00	200.90	0.490
0.500	135.00	140.00	145.00	150.00	155.00	160.00	165.00	170.00	175.00	180.00	185.00	190.00	195.00	200.00	205.00	0.500
0.510	137.70	142.80	147.90	153.00	158.10	163.20	168.30	173.40	178.50	183.60	188.70	193.80	198.90	204.00	209.10	0.510
0.520	140.40	145.60	150.80	156.00	161.20	166.40	171.60	176.80	182.00	187.20	192.40	197.60	202.80	208.00	213.20	0.520
0.530	143.10	148.40	153.70	159.00	164.30	169.60	174.90	180.20	185.50	190.80	196.10	201.40	206.70	212.00	217.30	0.530
0.540	145.80	151.20	156.60	162.00	167.40	172.80	178.20	183.60	189.00	194.40	199.80	205.20	210.60	216.00	221.40	0.540
0.550	148.50	154.00	159.50	165.00	170.50	176.00	181.50	187.00	192.50	198.00	203.50	209.00	214.50	220.00	225.50	0.550
0.560	151.20	156.80	162.40	168.00	173.60	179.20	184.80	190.40	196.00	201.60	207.20	212.80	218.40	224.00	229.60	0.560
0.570	153.90	159.60	165.30	171.00	176.70	182.40	188.10	193.80	199.50	205.20	210.90	216.60	222.30	228.00	233.70	0.570
0.580	156.60	162.40	168.20	174.00	179.80	185.60	191.40	197.20	203.00	208.80	214.60	220.40	226.20	232.00	237.80	0.580
0.590	159.30	165.20	171.10	177.00	182.90	188.80	194.70	200.60	206.50	212.40	218.30	224.20	230.10	236.00	241.90	0.590
0.600	162.00	168.00	174.00	180.00	186.00	192.00	198.00	204.00	210.00	216.00	222.00	228.00	234.00	240.00	246.00	0.600
0.610	164.70	170.80	176.90	183.00	189.10	195.20	201.30	207.40	213.50	219.60	225.70	231.80	237.90	244.00	250.10	0.610
0.620	167.40	173.60	179.80	186.00	192.20	198.40	204.60	210.80	217.00	223.20	229.40	235.60	241.80	248.00	254.20	0.620
0.630	170.10	176.40	182.70	189.00	195.30	201.60	207.90	214.20	220.50	226.80	233.10	239.40	245.70	252.00	258.30	0.630
0.640	172.80	179.20	185.60	192.00	198.40	204.80	211.20	217.60	224.00	230.40	236.80	243.20	249.60	256.00	262.40	0.640
0.650	175.50	182.00	188.50	195.00	201.50	208.00	214.50	221.00	227.50	234.00	240.50	247.00	253.50	260.00	266.50	0.650
0.660	178.20	184.80	191.40	198.00	204.60	211.20	217.80	224.40	231.00	237.60	244.20	250.80	257.40	264.00	270.60	0.660
0.670	180.90	187.60	194.30	201.00	207.70	214.40	221.10	227.80	234.50	241.20	247.90	254.60	261.30	268.00	274.70	0.670
0.680	183.60	190.40	197.20	204.00	210.80	217.60	224.40	231.20	238.00	244.80	251.60	258.40	265.20	272.00	278.80	0.680
0.690	186.30	193.20	200.10	207.00	213.90	220.80	227.70	234.60	241.50	248.40	255.30	262.20	269.10	276.00	282.90	0.690
0.700	189.00	196.00	203.00	210.00	217.00	224.00	231.00	238.00	245.00	252.00	259.00	266.00	273.00	280.00	287.00	0.700
0.710	191.70	198.80	205.90	213.00	220.10	227.20	234.30	241.40	248.50	255.60	262.70	269.80	276.90	284.00	291.10	0.710
0.720	194.40	201.60	208.80	216.00	223.20	230.40	237.60	244.80	252.00	259.20	266.40	273.60	280.80	288.00	295.20	0.720
0.730	197.10	204.40	211.70	219.00	226.30	233.60	240.90	248.20	255.50	262.80	270.10	277.40	284.70	292.00	299.30	0.730
0.740	199.80	207.20	214.60	222.00	229.40	236.80	244.20	251.60	259.00	266.40	273.80	281.20	288.60	296.00	303.40	0.740
0.750	202.50	210.00	217.50	225.00	232.50	240.00	247.50	255.00	262.50	270.00	277.50	285.00	292.50	300.00	307.50	0.750
0.760	205.20	212.80	220.40	228.00	235.60	243.20	250.80	258.40	266.00	273.60	281.20	288.80	296.40	304.00	311.60	0.760
0.770	207.90	215.60	223.30	231.00	238.70	246.40	254.10	261.80	269.50	277.20	284.90	292.60	300.30	308.00	315.70	0.770
0.780	210.60	218.40	226.20	234.00	241.80	249.60	257.40	265.20	273.00	280.80	288.60	296.40	304.20	312.00	319.80	0.780
0.790	213.30	221.20	229.10	237.00	244.90	252.80	260.70	268.60	276.50	284.40	292.30	300.20	308.10	316.00	323.90	0.790
0.800	216.00	224.00	232.00	240.00	248.00	256.00	264.00	272.00	280.00	288.00	296.00	304.00	312.00	320.00	328.00	0.800
0.810	218.70	226.80	234.90	243.00	251.10	259.20	267.30	275.40	283.50	291.60	299.70	307.80	315.90	324.00	332.10	0.810
0.820	221.40	229.60	237.80	246.00	254.20	262.40	270.60	278.80	287.00	295.20	303.40	311.60	319.80	328.00	336.20	0.820
0.830	224.10	232.40	240.70	249.00	257.30	265.60	273.90	282.20	290.50	298.80	307.10	315.40	323.70	332.00	340.30	0.830
0.840	226.80	235.20	243.60	252.00	260.40	268.80	277.20	285.60	294.00	302.40	310.80	319.20	327.60	336.00	344.40	0.840
0.850	229.50	238.00	246.50	255.00	263.50	272.00	280.50	289.00	297.50	306.00	314.50	323.00	331.50	340.00	348.50	0.850
0.860	232.20	240.80	249.40	258.00	266.60	275.20	283.80	292.40	301.00	309.60	318.20	326.80	335.40	344.00	352.60	0.860
0.870	234.90	243.60	252.30	261.00	269.70	278.40	287.10	295.80	304.50	313.20	321.90	330.60	339.30	348.00	356.70	0.870
0.880	237.60	246.40	255.20	264.00	272.80	281.60	290.40	299.20	308.00	316.80	325.60	334.40	343.20	352.00	360.80	0.880
0.890	240.30	249.20	258.10	267.00	275.90	284.80	293.70	302.60	311.50	320.40	329.30	338.20	347.10	356.00	364.90	0.890
0.900	243.00	252.00	261.00	270.00	279.00	288.00	297.00	306.00	315.00	324.00	333.00	342.00	351.00	360.00	369.00	0.900
0.910	245.70	254.80	263.90	273.00	282.10	291.20	300.30	309.40	318.50	327.60	336.70	345.80	354.90	364.00	373.10	0.910
0.920	248.40	257.60	266.80	276.00	285.20	294.40	303.60	312.80	322.00	331.20	340.40	349.60	358.80	368.00	377.20	0.920
0.930	251.10	260.40	269.70	279.00	288.30	297.60	306.90	316.20	325.50	334.80	344.10	353.40	362.70	372.00	381.30	0.930
0.940	253.80	263.20	272.60	282.00	291.40	300.80	310.20	319.60	329.00	338.40	347.80	357.20	366.60	376.00	385.40	0.940
0.950	256.50	266.00	275.50	285.00	294.50	304.00	313.50	323.00	332.50	342.00	351.50	361.00	370.50	380.00	389.50	0.950
0.960	259.20	268.80	278.40	288.00	297.60	307.20	316.80	326.40	336.00	345.60	355.20	364.80	374.40	384.00	393.60	0.960
0.970	261.90	271.60	281.30	291.00	300.70	310.40	320.10	329.80	339.50	349.20	358.90	368.60	378.30	388.00	397.70	0.970
0.980	264.60	274.40	284.20	294.00	303.80	313.60	323.40	333.20	343.00	352.80	362.60	372.40	382.20	392.00	401.80	0.980
0.990	267.30	277.20	287.10	297.00	306.90	316.80	326.70	336.60	346.50	356.40	366.30	376.20	386.10	396.00	405.90	0.990
1.000	270.00	280.00	290.00	300.00	310.00	320.00	330.00	340 00	350.00	360.00	370.00	380.00	390.00	400.00	410.00	1.000

Countries in the Arabic sphere generally date their coins to the Mohammedan era (AH), which commenced on July 16, 622 AD (Julian calendar), when the prophet Mohammed fled from Mecca to Medina. As their calendar is reckoned by the lunar year of 354 days, which is about three percent (precisely 2.98%) shorter than the Christian year, a formula is required to convert AH dating to its Western equivalent. To convert an AH date to the approximate AD date, subtract three percent of the AH date (round to the closest whole number) from the AH date, then add 622. A chart for converting all AH years from 1010 (July 2, 1601) to 1421 (April 6, 2000) is presented on the last page of this volume.

The Mohammedan calendar is not always based on the lunar year (AH), however, causing some confusion, particularly in Afghanistan and Iran, where a calendar based on the solar year (SH) was introduced around 1920. These dates can be converted to AD by simply adding 621. In 1976 the government of Iran implemented a new solar calendar based on the foundation of the Iranian monarchy in 559 BC. The first year observed on the new calendar was 2535 (MS), which commenced March 20, 1976. A reversion to the traditional SH dating standard occurred a few years later.

Several different eras of reckoning, including Christian and Mohammedan (AH), have been used to date coins of the Indian subcontinent. The two basic systems are the Vikrama Samvat (VS), which dates from Oct. 18, 58 BC, and the Saka era, the origin of which is reckoned from March 3, 78 AD. Dating according to both eras appears on various coins of the area.

Coins of Thailand (Siam) are found dated by three different eras. The most predominant is the Buddhist era (BE) which originated in 543 BC. Next is the Bangkok or Ratanakosindsok (RS) era, dating from 1781 AD; followed by the Chula-Sakarat (CS) era, dating from 638 AD. The latter era originated in Burma and is used on that country's coins.

Other calendars include that of the Ethiopian era (EE) which commenced seven years, eight months after AD dating; and that of the Jewish people, which commenced on Oct. 7, 3761 BC. Korea claims a legendary dating from 2333 BC, which is acknowledged in some of its coin dating. Some coin issues of the Indonesian area carry dates determined by the Javanese Aji Saka era (AS), a calendar of 354 days (100 Javanese years equal 97 Christian or Gregorian calendar years) which can be matched to AD dating by comparing it to AH dating.

The following table indicates the year dating for the various eras which correspond to 1998 in Christian calendar reckoning, but it must be remembered that there are overlaps between the eras in some instances.

Christian era (AD)	—	1998
Mohammedan era (AH)	—	AH1419
Solar year (SH)	—	SH1377
Monarchic Solar era (MS)	—	MS2557
Vikrama Samvat (VS)	—	VS2055
Saka era (SE)	—	SE1920
Buddhist era (BE)	—	BE2541
Bangkok era (RS)	—	RS217
Chula-Sakarat era (CS)	—	CS1360
Ethiopian era (EE)	—	EE1990
Jewish era	—	5758
Korean era	—	4331
Javanese Aji Saka era (AS)	—	AS1931
Fasli era (FE)	—	FE1408

Coins of Oriental origin — principally Japan, Korea, China, Turkestan and Tibet and some modern gold issues of Turkey — are generally dated to the year of the government, dynasty, reign or cyclic eras, with the dates indicated in Oriental characters which usually read from right to left. In recent years, however, some dating has been according to the Christian calendar and in Western numerals. In Japan, Oriental character dating was reversed to read from left to right in Showa year 23 (1948 AD).

More detailed guides to less prevalent coin dating systems which are strictly local in nature are presented with the appropriate listings.

Some coins carry dates according to both locally observed and Christian eras. This is particularly true in the Arabic world, where the Hejira date may be indicated in Arabic numerals and the Christian date in Western numerals, or both dates in either form.

The date actually carried on a given coin is generally cataloged here in the first column (Date) to the right of the catalog number. If the date is not by AD reckoning, the next column (Year) indicates the date by the conventional calendar which applies, generally Christian. If an AD date appears in either column, the AD is not necessarily indicated. Era abbreviations in the dating table in this section are generally shown in conjunction with the listings of coins dated in those eras.

Dates listed in either column which does not actually appear on a given coin is generally enclosed by parentheses. Undated coins are indicated by the letters ND in the date column and the estimated year of issue in parentheses.

Timing differentials between some era of reckoning particularly the 354-day Mohammedan and 365-day Christian years, cause situations whereby coins which carry dates for both eras exist bearing two year dates from one calendar combined with a single date from another.

NUMBERING SYSTEM

Some catalog numbers assigned in this volume are based on established references. This practice has been observed for two reasons: First, when world coins are listed chronologically they are basically self-cataloging; second, there was no need to confuse collectors with totally new numeric designations where appropriate systems already existed. As time progressed we found many of these established systems incomplete and inadequate and are now replaced with new KM numbers with appropriate cross-referencing.

Some of the coins listed in this catalog are identified or cross-referenced by numbers assigned by R.S. Yeoman (Y#), or slight adaptations thereof, in his *Modern World Coins,* and *Current Coins of the World.* For the pre-Yeoman dated issues, the numbers assigned by William D. Craig (C#) in his *Coins of the World* (1750-1850 period), 3rd edition, have generally been applied.

In some countries, listings are cross-referenced to Robert Friedberg's (FR#) *Gold Coins of the World* or *Coins of the British World.* Major Fred Pridmore's (P#) studies of British colonial coinage are also referenced, as are W.H. Valentine's (V#) references on the *Modern Copper Coins of the Muhammadan States.* Coins issued under the Chinese sphere of influence are assigned numbers from E. Kann's (K#) *Illustrated Catalog of Chinese Coins* and T.K. Hsu's (Su) work of similar title.

DENOMINATIONS

The second basic consideration to be met in the attribution of a coin is the determination of denomination. Since denominations are usually expressed in numeric, rather than word form on a coin, this is usually quite easily accomplished on coins from nations which use Western numerals, except in those instances where issues are devoid of any mention of face value, and denomination must be attributed by size, metallic composition or weight. Coins listed in this volume are generally illustrated in actual size. Where size is critical to proper attribution, the coin's millimeter size is indicated.

The sphere of countries stretching from North Africa through the Orient, on which numeric symbols generally unfamiliar to Westerners are employed, often provide the collector with a much greater challenge. This is particularly true on nearly all pre-20th Century issues. On some of the more modern issues, and increasingly so as the years progress, Western style numerals, usually presented in combination with the local numeric system, are becoming more commonplace on these coins.

Determination of a coin's currency system can also be valuable in attributing the issue to its country of origin. A comprehensive alphabetical index of currency names, applicable to the countries as cataloged in this volume, with all individual nations of use for each, is presented in this section.

The included table of *Standard International Numeral Systems* presents charts of the basic numeric designations found on coins of non-Western origin. Although denomination numerals are generally prominently displayed on coins, it must be remembered that these are general representations of characters which individual coin engravers may have rendered in widely varying styles. Where numeric or script denominations designation forms peculiar to a given coin or country apply, such as the script used on some Persian (Iranian) issues, they are so indicated or illustrated in conjunction with the appropriate listings.

MINTAGES

Quantities minted of each date are indicated where that information is available, generally stated in millions, rounded off to the nearest 10,000 pieces. On quantities of a few thousand or less, actual mintages are generally indicated, a fact that can be determined by the presence of a comma, rather than a decimal point, in the stated figure. The following mintage conversion formulas have been observed:

10,000,000 - 10.000
1,000,000 - 1.000
100,000 - .100
10,000 - .010
9,999 - 9,999
1,000 - 1,000
842 - 842 pcs. (Pieces)
27 - 27 pcs.

The abbreviation "Inc. Ab." or "I.A." means Included Above, while "Inc. Be." or "I.B." means Included Below. An "*" beside a mintage figure indicates the number given is an estimate or mintage limit.

MINT AND PRIVY MARKS

The presence of distinctive, but frequently inconspicuously placed, mint marks indicates the mint of issue for many of the coins listed in this catalog. An appropriate designation in the date listings notes the presence, if any, of a mint mark on a particular coin type by incorporating the letter or letters of the mint mark adjoining the date, i.e., 1883CC or 1890H.

The presence of mint and/or mintmaster's privy marks on a coin in non-letter form is indicated by incorporating the mint letter in lower case within parentheses adjoining the date; i.e. 1827(a). The corresponding mark is illustrated or identified in the introduction of the country.

A listing format by mints of issue has been adopted for some countries — including France, Spain and Mexico — to allow for a more logical arrangement. In these instances, the name of the mint and its mint mark letter or letters is presented at the beginning of each series.

Where listings incorporate mintmaster initials, they are always presented in capital letters separated from the date; i.e., 1850 MF. The different mint mark and mintmaster letters found on the coins of any country, state or city of issue are always shown at the beginning of listings.

METALS

At the beginning of each date listing, the metallic composition of each coin denomination is listed, and thereafter, whenever a change in metal occurs. The traditional coinage metals and their symbolic chemical abbreviations used in this catalog are:

Platinum - (PT)	Copper - (Cu)
Gold - (Au)	Brass -
Silver - (Ag)	Copper-nickel - (CN)
Billion -	Lead - (Pb)
Nickel - (Ni)	Steel -
Zinc - (Zn)	Tin - (Sn)
Bronze - (Ae)	Aluminum - (Al)

During the 18th and 19th centuries, most of the worlds coins were struck of copper or bronze, silver and gold. Commencing in the early years of the 20th century, however, numerous new coinage metals, primarily non-precious metal alloys, were introduced. Gold has not been widely used for circulation coinages since World War I, although silver remained a popular coinage metal in most parts of the world until after World War II. With the disappearance of silver for circulation coinage, numerous additional compositions were introduced to coinage applications.

Coin Alignment

Medal Alignment

COIN vs MEDAL ALIGNMENT

Coins are traditionally struck with obverse and reverse aligned at a rotation of 180 degrees from each other. When a coin is held for vertical viewing with the obverse design aligned upright and the index finger and thumb at the top and bottom, upon rotation from left to right for viewing the reverse, the latter will be upside down. Such alignment is called "coin rotation." Some coins are struck with the obverse and reverse designs mated on an alignment of zero or 360 degrees. If such a piece is held and rotated as described, the reverse will appear upright. This is the alignment which is generally observed in the striking of medals, and for that reason coins produced in this manner are termed to have been struck in "medal rotation." In some instances, usually through error, certain coin issues have been struck to both alignment standards, creating interesting collectible varieties which will be found noted in some listing.

OFF-METAL STRIKES

Off-metal strikes previously designated by "(OMS)" which also included the wide range of error coinage struck in other than their officially authorized compositions have been incorporated into Pattern listings along with special issues which were struck for presentation or other reasons.

Collectors of Germanic coinage may be familiar with the term "Abschlag" which quickly identifies similar types of coinage.

PRECIOUS METAL WEIGHTS

Listings of weight, fineness and actual silver (ASW), gold (AGW), platinum or palladium (APW) content of most machine-struck silver, gold, platinum and palladium coins are provided in this edition. These designations will be found incorporated in the listings immediately beneath illustrations or in conjunction with type changes wherever these factors could be determined.

The ASW, AGW and APW figures were determined by multiplying the gross weight of a given coin by its known or tested fineness and converting the resulting gram or grain weight to troy ounces, rounded to the nearest ten-thousandth of an ounce. A silver coin with a 24.25 gram weight and .875 fineness, for example, would have a fine weight of approximately 21.2188 grams, or a .6822 ASW, a factor that can be used to accurately determine the intrinsic value for multiple examples.

The ASW, AGW or APW figure can be multiplied by the spot price of each precious metal to determine the current intrinsic value of any coin accompanied by these designations.

WEIGHTS AND FINENESSES

Coin weights are indicated in grams (abbreviated "g") along with fineness where the information is of value in differentiating between types. These weights are based on 31.103 grams per troy (scientific) ounce, as opposed to the avoirdupois (commercial) standard of 28.35 grams. Actual coin weights are generally shown in hundredths or thousands of a gram; i.e., .500 SILVER 2.9200g.

As the silver and gold bullion markets have advanced and declined sharply in recent years, the fineness and total precious metal content of coins has become especially significant where bullion coins — issues which trade on the basis of their intrinsic metallic content rather than numismatic value — are concerned. In many instances, such issues have become worth more in bullion form than their nominal collector values or denominations indicate.

Establishing the weight of a coin can also be valuable for determining its denomination. Actual weight is also necessary to ascertain the specific gravity of the coin's metallic content, an important factor in determining authenticity.

TROY WEIGHT STANDARDS

24 Grains = 1 Pennyweight
480 Grains = 1 Ounce
31.103 Grams = 1 Ounce

UNIFORM WEIGHTS

15.432 Grains = 1 Gram
0.0648 Gram = 1 Grain

AVOIRDUPOIS STANDARDS

27-11/32 Grains = 11 Dram
437-1/2 Grains = 1 Ounce
28.350 Grams = 1 Ounce

BULLION VALUE CHARTS

Universal silver, gold, and platinum bullion value charts are provided for use in combination with the ASW, AGW and APW factors to determine approximate intrinsic values of listed coins. By adding the component weights as shown in troy ounces on each chart, the approximate intrinsic value of any silver, gold or platinum coin's precious metal content can be determined.

Again referring to the examples presented in the above section, the intrinsic value of a silver coin with a .6822 ASW would be indicated as $4.43 + based on the application of the silver bullion chart. This result is obtained by moving across the top to the $6.50 column, then moving down to the line indicated .680 in the far left hand corner which reveals a bullion value of $4.420. To determine the value of the remaining .0022 of ASW, return up the same column to the .002 line, the closest factor available, where a $ .0130 value is indicted. The two factors total to $4.433, which would be slightly less than actual value.

The silver bullion chart provides silver values in thousandths from .001 to .009 troy ounce, and in hundredths from .01 to 1.00 in 50¢ value increments from $3.00 to $10.50. If the market value of silver exceeds $10.50, doubling the increments presented will provide valuations in $1 steps from $6.00 to $21.00.

The gold/platinum bullion chart is similarly arranged in $10 increments from $350 to $490, and by doubling the increments presented, $20 steps from $700 to $980 can be determined.

Valuations for most of the silver, gold, platinum and palladium coins listed in this edition are based on assumed market values of $4.70 per troy ounce for silver, $378. for gold, $383. for platinum, and $116. for palladium. To arrive at accurate current market indications for these issues, increase or decrease the valuations appropriately based on any variations in these indicated levels.

HOMELAND TYPES

Homeland types are coins which colonial powers used in a colony, but do not bear that location's name. In some cases they were legal tender in the homeland, in others not. They are listed under the homeland and cross-referenced at the colony listing.

COUNTERMARKS/COUNTERSTAMPS

There is some confusion among collectors over the terms "countermark" and "counterstamp" when applied to a coin bearing an additional mark or change of design and/or denomination.

To clarify, a countermark might be considered similar to the "hall mark" applied to a piece of silverware, by which a silversmith assured the quality of the piece. In the same way, a countermark assures the quality of the coin on which it is placed, as, for example, when the royal crown of England was countermarked (punched into) on segmented Spanish reales, allowing them to circulate in commerce in the British West Indies. An additional countermark indicating the new denomination may also be encountered on these coins.

Countermarks are generally applied singularly and in most cases indiscriminately on either side of the "host" coin.

Counterstamped coins are more extensively altered. The counterstamping is done with a set of dies, rather than a hand punch. The coin being counterstamped is placed between the new dies and struck as if it were a blank planchet as found with the Manila 8 reales issue of the Philippines.

PHOTOGRAPHS

To assist the reader in coin identification, every effort has been made to present actual size photographs of every coinage type listed. Obverse and reverse are illustrated, except when a change in design is restricted to one side, and the coin has a diameter of 39mm or larger, in which case only the side required for identification of the type is generally illustrated. All coins up to 60mm are illustrated actual size, to the nearest

1/2mm up to 25mm, and to the nearest 1mm thereafter. Coins larger than 60mm diameter are illustrated in reduced size, with the actual size noted thereunder. Where slight change in size is important to coin type identification, actual millimeter measurements are stated.

TRADE COINS

From approximately 1750-1940, a number of nations, particularly European colonial powers and commercial traders, minted trade coins to facilitate commerce with the local populace of Africa, the Arab countries, the Indian subcontinental, Southeast Asia and the Far East. Such coins generally circulated at a value based on the weight and fineness of their silver or gold content, rather than their stated denomination. Examples include the sovereigns of Great Britain and the gold ducat issues of Austria, Hungary and the Netherlands. Trade coinage will be found listed at the end of the domestic issues.

VALUATIONS

Values quoted in this catalog represent the current market and are compiled from recommendations provided and verified through various source documents and specialized consultants. **It should be stressed, however, that this book is intended to serve only as a guide for evaluating coins, actual market conditions are constantly changing and additional influences,** such as particularly strong local demand for certain coin series, fluctuation of international exchange rates and worldwide collection patterns must also be considered. Publication of this catalog is not intended as a solicitation by the publisher, editors or contributors to buy or sell the listed coins at the prices indicated.

All valuations are stated in U.S. dollars, based on careful assessment of the varied international collector market. Valuations for coins priced below $1,000.00 are generally stated in full amounts — i.e. 37.50 or 950.00 — while valuations at or above that figure are rounded off in even dollars — i.e. $1250.00 is expressed 1250. A comma is added to indicate tens of thousands of dollars in value.

For the convenience of overseas collectors and for U.S. collectors doing business with overseas dealers, the base exchange rate for the national currencies of approximately 180 countries are presented in the Foreign Exchange Table.

It should be noted that when particularly select uncirculated or proof-like examples of uncirculated coins become available they can be expected to command proportionately high premiums. Such examples in reference to choice Germanic Thalers are referred to as "erst schlage" or first strikes.

TOKEN COINAGE

At times local economic conditions have forced regular coinage from circulation or found mints unable to cope with the demand for coinage, giving rise to privately-issued token coinage substitutes. British tokens of the late 1700s and early 1880s, and the German and French and French Colonial emergency emissions of the World War I era are examples of such tokens being freely accepted in monetary transactions over wide areas. Tokens were likewise introduced to satisfy specific restricted needs, such as the leper colony issues of Brazil, Colombia and the Philippines.

This catalog includes introductory or detailed listings with "Tn" prefixes of many token coinage issues, particularly those which enjoyed wide circulation and where the series was limited in diversity. More complex series, and those more restricted in scope of circulation are generally not listed, although a representative sample may be illustrated and reference provided to more specialized catalogs.

MEDALLIC ISSUES

Medallic issues are segregated following the regular issue listings. Grouped there are coin-type issues which can generally be identified as commemoratives produced to the country's established coinage standards but without the usual indicator of denomination. These pieces may or may not feature designs adapted from the country's regular issue or commemorative coinage, and may or may not have been issued in conjunction with related coinage issues.

RESTRIKES, COUNTERFEITS

Deceptive restrike and counterfeit (both contemporary and modern) examples exist of some coin issues. Where possible, the existence of restrikes is noted. Warnings are also incorporated in instances where particularly deceptive counterfeits are known to exist. Collectors who are uncertain about the authenticity of a coin held in their collection, or being offered for sale, should take the precaution of having it authenticated by the American Numismatic Association Authentication Bureau, 818 N. Cascade, Colorado Springs, CO 80903. Their reasonably-priced certification tests are widely accepted by collectors and dealers alike.

NON-CIRCULATING LEGAL TENDER COINS

Coins of non-circulating legal tender (NCLT) origin are individually listed and integrated by denomination into the regular listings for each country. These coins fall outside the customary definitions of coin-of-the-realm issues, but where created and sold by, or under authorization of, agencies of sovereign governments expressly for collectors. These are primarily individual coins and sets of a commemorative nature, marketed at prices substantially in excess of face value, and usually do not have counterparts released for circulation.

EDGE VARIETIES

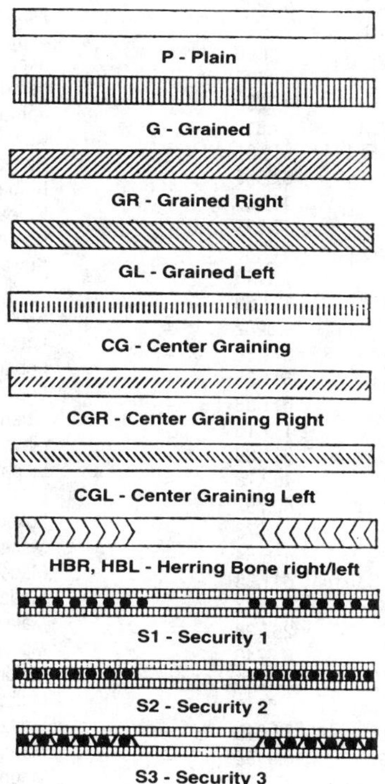

krause publications

700 E. State Street • Iola, WI 54990-0001

Foreign Exchange Table

The latest foreign exchange fixed rates below apply to trade with banks in the country of origin. The left column shows the number of units per U.S. dollar at the official rate. The right column shows the number of units per dollar at the free market rate.

Country	Official #/$	Market #/$
Afghanistan (Afghan)	4,750	20,200
Albania (Lek)	151.50	–
Algeria (Dinar)	59.152	75.00
Andorra uses French Franc and Spanish Peseta		
Angola (Readjust Kwanza)	257,128	–
Anguilla uses E.C. Dollar	2.70	–
Antigua uses E.C. Dollar	2.70	–
Argentina (New Peso)	1.00	–
Armenia (Dram)	420.0	–
Aruba (Florin)	1.79	–
Australia (Dollar)	1.6246	–
Austria (Schilling)	12.8295	–
Azerbaijan (Manat)	3,950	–
Bahamas (Dollar)	1.00	–
Bahrain Is. (Dinar)	.38	–
Bangladesh (Taka)	47.10	–
Barbados (Dollar)	2.0113	–
Belarus (Ruble)	11,500	–
Belgium (Franc)	37.605	–
Belize (Dollar)	2.00	–
Benin uses CFA Franc West	611.38	–
Bermuda (Dollar)	1.00	–
Bhutan (Ngultrum)	42.53	–
Bolivia (Boliviano)	5.54	–
Bosnia-Herzegovina (New Dinar)	141.00	195.0
Botswana (Pula)	4.7226	–
British Virgin Islands uses U.S. Dollar	1.00	–
Brazil (Real)	1.1615	–
Brunei (Ringgit)	1.7258	–
Bulgaria (Lev)	1,816	–
Burkina Faso uses CFA Fr. West	611.38	–
Burma (Kyat)	6.5955	–
Burundi (Franc)	423.33	–
Cambodia (Riel)	3,590	–
Cameron uses CFA Franc	611.38	–
Canada (Dollar)	1.4743	–
Cape Verde (Escudo)	101.68	–
Cayman Is. (Dollar)	0.8282	–
Central African Rep.	611.38	–
CFA Franc Central	611.38	–
CFA Franc West	611.38	–
CFP Franc	111.16	–
Chad uses CFA Franc Central	611.38	–
Chile (Peso)	462.78	–
China, P.R. (Renminbi Yuan)	8.2797	–
Colombia (Peso)	1,373	–
Comoros (Franc)	458.54	–
Congo uses CFA Franc Central	611.38	–
Cook Islands (Dollar)	1.47	–
Costa Rica (Colon)	257.38	–
Croatia (Kuna)	6.6745	–
Cuba (Peso)	23.00	35.00
Cyprus (Pound)	.5340	–
Czech Republic (Koruna)	32.615	–
Denmark (Danish Krone)	6.9488	–
Djibouti (Franc)	177.72	–
Dominica uses E.C. Dollar	2.70	–
Dominican Republic (Peso)	15.28	–
East Caribbean (Dollar)	2.70	–
Ecuador (Sucre)	5,300	–
Egypt (Pound)	3.4137	–
El Salvador (Colon)	8.755	–
England (Sterling Pound)	.6132	–
Equatorial Guinea uses CFA Franc Central	611.38	–
Eritrea, see Ethiopia		
Estonia (Kroon)	14.589	–
Ethiopia (Birr)	6.9189	7.25
European Currency Unit	1.0883	–
Falkland Is. (Pound)	.6132	–
Faroe Islands (Krona)	6.9488	–
Fiji Islands (Dollar)	2.0424	–
Finland (Markka)	5.5439	–
France (Franc)	6.1138	–
French Polynesia uses CFP Franc	111.16	–
Gabon (CFA Franc)	611.38	–
Gambia (Dalasi)	10.628	–
Georgia (Lari)	1.30	–
Germany (D. Mark)	1.8242	–
Ghana (Cedi)	2,331.5	–
Gibraltar (Pound)	.6132	–
Greece (Drachma)	303.2	–
Greenland uses Denmark Krone	6.9488	–
Grenada uses E.C. Dollar	2.70	–
Guatemala (Quetzal)	6.3239	–
Guernsey uses Sterling Pound	.6132	–
Guinea Bissau (CFA Franc)	611.38	–
Guinea Conakry (Franc)	1,238	–
Guyana (Dollar)	144.30	–
Haiti (Gourde)	16.047	–
Honduras (Lempira)	13.29	–
Hong Kong (Dollar)	7.749	–
Hungary (Forint)	220.5	–
Iceland (Krona)	71.12	–
India (Rupee)	42.525	–
Indonesia (Rupiah)	15,290	–
Iran (Rial)	3,000	4,800
Iraq (Dinar)	1,200	1,690
Ireland (Punt)	.7245	–
Isle of Man uses Sterling Pound	.6132	–
Israel (New Sheqalim)	3.6657	–
Italy (Lira)	1,798	–
Ivory Coast uses CFA Franc West	611.38	–
Jamaica (Dollar)	35.75	–
Japan (Yen)	141.13	–
Jersey uses Sterling Pound	.6132	–
Jordan (Dinar)	.709	–
Kazakhstan (Tenge)	65.00	–
Kenya (Shilling)	59.50	–
Kiribati uses Australian Dollar	1.6246	–
Korea-PDR (Won)	2.20	170.0
Korea-Rep. (Won)	1,313	–
Kuwait (Dinar)	.3076	–
Kyrgyzstan (Som)	11.05	–
Laos (Kip)	2,009	–
Latvia (Lat)	.5995	–
Lebanon (Pound)	1,516	–
Lesotho (Maloti)	6.335	–
Liberia (Dollar)	1.00	30.00
Libya (Dinar)	.3835	2.00
Liechtenstein uses Swiss Franc	1.5415	–
Lithuania (Litas)	4.00	–
Luxembourg (Franc)	37.605	–
Macao (Pataca)	8.0047	–
Macedonia (New Denar)	56.236	–
Madagascar (Franc)	5,400	–
Malawi (Kwacha)	26.45	–
Malaysia (Ringgit)	4.26	–
Maldives (Rufiya)	11.77	–
Mali uses CFA Franc West	611.38	–
Malta (Lira)	.3984	–
Marshall Islands uses U.S. Dollar	1.00	–
Mauritania (Ouguiya)	200.27	–
Mauritius (Rupee)	24.40	–
Mexico (Peso)	8.965	–
Moldova (Leu)	4.55	–
Monaco uses French Franc	6.1138	–
Mongolia (Tugrik)	800.32	–
Montenegro uses Yugoslavia	10.9447	–
Montserrat uses E.C. Dollar	2.70	–
Morocco (Dirham)	9.8507	10.50
Mozambique (Metical)	11,495	12,100
Myanmar (Burma) (Kyat)	6.4734	202.0
Namibia (Rand)	6.335	–
Nauru uses Australian Dollar	1.6246	–
Nepal (Rupee)	63.40	–
Netherlands (Gulden)	2.056	–
Netherlands Antilles (Gulden)	1.79	–
New Caledonia uses CFP Franc	111.16	–
New Zealand (Dollar)	1.9397	–
Nicaragua (Cordoba Oro)	10.6018	–
Niger uses CFA Franc West	611.38	–
Nigeria (Naira)	86.50	–
Northern Ireland uses Sterling Pound	.6132	–
Norway (Krone)	7.7316	–
Oman (Rial)	.385	–
Pakistan (Rupee)	46.44	–
Palau uses U.S. Dollar	1.00	–
Panama (Balboa) uses U.S. Dollar	1.00	–
Papua New Guinea (Kina)	2.2297	–
Paraguay (Guarani)	2,775	–
Peru (Nuevo Sol)	2.9225	–
Philippines (Peso)	42.00	–
Poland (Zloty)	3.495	–
Portugal (Escudo)	186.57	–
Qatar (Riyal)	3.6403	–
Romania (Leu)	8,692	–
Russia (Ruble)	5,634	–
Rwanda (Franc)	308.87	370.0
St. Helena (Pound)	.6132	–
St. Kitts uses E.C. Dollar	2.70	–
St. Lucia uses E.C. Dollar	2.70	–
St. Vincent uses E.C. Dollar	2.70	–
San Marino uses Italian Lira	1,798	–
Sao Tome e Principe (Dobra)	2,390	–
Saudi Arabia (Riyal)	3.7509	–
Scotland uses Sterling Pound	.6132	–
Senegal uses CFA Franc West	611.38	–
Seychelles (Rupee)	5.31	–
Sierra Leone (Leone)	1,470	–
Singapore (Dollar)	1.7258	–
Slovakia (Sk. Koruna)	35.272	–
Slovenia (Tolar)	172.22	–
Solomon Is. (Dollar)	4.805	–
Somalia (Shilling)	2,620	–
Somaliland (Somali Shilling)	1,800	3,000
South Africa (Rand)	6.335	–
Spain (Peseta)	154.74	–
Sri Lanka (Rupee)	65.475	–
Sudan (Dinar)	161.3	165.0
Surinam (Guilder)	401	–
Swaziland (Lilangeni)	6.335	–
Sweden (Krona)	8.10	–
Switzerland (Franc)	1.5415	–
Syria (Pound)	41.85	–
Taiwan (NT Dollar)	34.41	–
Tajikistan uses Russian Ruble	5,634	–
Tanzania (Shilling)	663	–
Thailand (Baht)	41.75	–
Togo uses CFA Franc West	611.38	–
Tonga (Pa'anga)	1.5073	–
Transdniestra (New Ruble)	630,000	675,000
Trinidad & Tobago (Dollar)	6.24	–
Tunisia (Dinar)	1.1737	–
Turkey (Lira)	271,395	–
Turkmenistan (Manat)	195	6,500
Turks & Caicos uses U.S. Dollar	1.00	–
Tuvalu uses Australian Dollar	1.6246	–
Uganda (Shilling)	1,233	–
Ukraine (Hryvnia)	2.115	–
United Arab Emirates (Dirham)	3.6729	–
Uruguay (Peso Uruguayo)	10.505	–
Uzbekistan (Som)	24.00	–
Vanuatu (Vatu)	131	–
Vatican City uses Italian Lira	1,798	–
Venezuela (Bolivar)	555.25	–
Vietnam (Dong)	12,986	–
Western Samoa (Tala)	3.003	–
Yemen (Riyal)	130.99	–
Yugoslavia (Novikh Dinar)	10.9447	6.50
Zaire (Noveaux Zaire)	140,500	–
Zambia (Kwacha)	1,973	–
Zimbabwe (Dollar)	18.46	–

STANDARD INTERNATIONAL GRADING TERMINOLOGY AND ABBREVIATIONS

	PROOF	UNCIRCULATED	EXTREMELY FINE	VERY FINE	FINE	VERY GOOD	GOOD	POOR
U.S. and ENGLISH SPEAKING LANDS	PRF	UNC	EF or XF	VF	F	VG	G	PR
BRAZIL	—	(1)FDC or FC	(3) S	(5) MBC	(7) BC	(8) BC/R	(9) R	UT GeG
DENMARK	M	0	01	1+	1	1÷	2	3
FINLAND	00	0	01	1+	1	1?	2	3
FRANCE	FB Flan Bruni	FDC Fleur de Coin	SUP Superbe	TTB Très très beau	TB Très beau	B Beau	TBC Très Bien Conservée	BC Bien Conservée
GERMANY	PP Polierte Platte	STG Stempelglanz	VZ Vorzüglich	SS Sehr schön	S Schön	S.G.E. Sehr gut erhalten	G.E. Gut erhalten	Gering erhalten
ITALY	FS Fondo Specchio	FDC Fior di Conio	SPL Splendido	BB Bellissimo	MB Molto Bello	B Bello	M	—
JAPAN	—	未使用	極美品	美品	並品	—	—	—
NETHERLANDS	— Proef	FDC Fleur de Coin	Pr. Prachtig	Z.f. Zeer fraai	Fr. Fraai	Z.g. Zeer goed	G	—
NORWAY	M	0	01	1+	1	1÷	2	3
PORTUGAL	—	Soberba	Bela	MBC	BC	MREG	REG	MC
SPAIN	Prueba	SC	EBC	MBC	BC+	BC	RC	MC
SWEDEN	Polerad	0	01	1+	1	1?	2	—

CONDITIONS/GRADING

Wherever possible, coin valuations are given in four grades of preservation. The following standards have been observed to provide continuity in grouping grade ranges in this catalog. However, because they cannot be universally applied, appropriate variations have been incorporated and noted: 1) Good, Very Good, Fine and Very Fine — used for crude "dump" or similar issues: 2) Very Good, Very Fine and Extremely Fine — used for early machine-minted issues of Europe (early 1800s), Latin America (up to the mid-1800s), the present. Listings in three grades of preservation will also be found, usually in cases of modern issues.

There are almost no grading guides for world coins. What follows is an attempt to help bridge that gap until a detailed, illustrated guide becomes available.

In grading world coins, there are two elements to look for: 1) Overall wear, and 2) loss of design details, such as strands of hair, feathers on eagles, designs on coats of arms, etc.

The age, rarity or type of a coin should not be a consideration in grading.

Grade each coin by the weaker of the two sides. This method appears to give results most nearly consistent with conservative American Numismatic Association standards for U.S. coins. Split grades, i.e., F/VF for obverse and reverse, respectively, are normally no more than one grade apart. If the two sides are more than one grade apart, the series of coins probably wears differently on each side and should then be graded by the weaker side alone.

Grade by the amount of overall wear and loss of detail evident in the main design on each side. On coins with a moderately small design element which is prone to early wear, grade by that design alone. For example, the 5-ore (KM#554) of Sweden has a crown above the monogram on which the beads on the arches show wear most clearly. So, grade by the crown alone.

For **Uncirculated** (Unc.) grades there will be no visible signs of wear or handling, even under a 30-power microscope. Bag marks may be present.

For **Almost Uncirculated** (AU), all detail will be visible. There will be wear only on the highest point of the coin. There will often be half or more of the original mint luster present.

On the **Extremely Fine** (XF or EF) coin, there will be about 95% of the original detail visible. Or, on a coin with a design with no inner detail to wear down, there will be a light wear over nearly all the coin. If a small design is used as the grading area, about 90% of the original detail will be visible. This latter rule stems from the logic that a smaller amount of detail needs to be present because a small area is being used to grade the whole coin.

The **Very Fine** (VF) coin will have about 75% of the original detail visible. Or, on a coin with no inner detail, there will be moderate wear over the entire coin. Corners of letters and numbers may be weak. A small grading area will have about 66% of the original detail.

For **Fine** (F), there will be about 50% of the original detail visible. Or, on a coin with no inner detail, there will be fairly heavy wear over all of the coin. Sides of letters will be weak. A typically uncleaned coin will often appear as dirty or dull. A small grading area will have just under 50% of the original detail.

On the **Very Good** (VG) coin, there will be about 25% of the original detail visible. There will be heavy wear on all of the coin.

The **Good** (G) coin's design will be clearly outlined but with substantial wear. Some of the larger detail may be visible. The rim may have a few weak spots of wear.

On the **About Good** (AG) coin, there will typically be only a silhouette of a large design. The rim will be worn down into the letters if any.

Strong or weak strikes, partially weak strikes, damage, corrosion, attractive or unattractive toning, dipping or cleaning should be described along with the above grades. These factors affect the quality of the coin just as do wear and loss of detail, but are easier to describe.

In the case of countermarked/counterstamped coins, the condition of the host coin will have a bearing on the end valuation. The important factor in determining the grade is the condition, clarity and completeness of the countermark itself. This is in reference to countermarks/counterstamps having raised design while being struck in a depression.

Incuse countermarks cannot be graded for wear. They are graded by the clarity and completeness including the condition of the host coin which will also have more bearing on the final grade/valuation determined.

CHART OF COIN SIZES BY MILLIMETERS

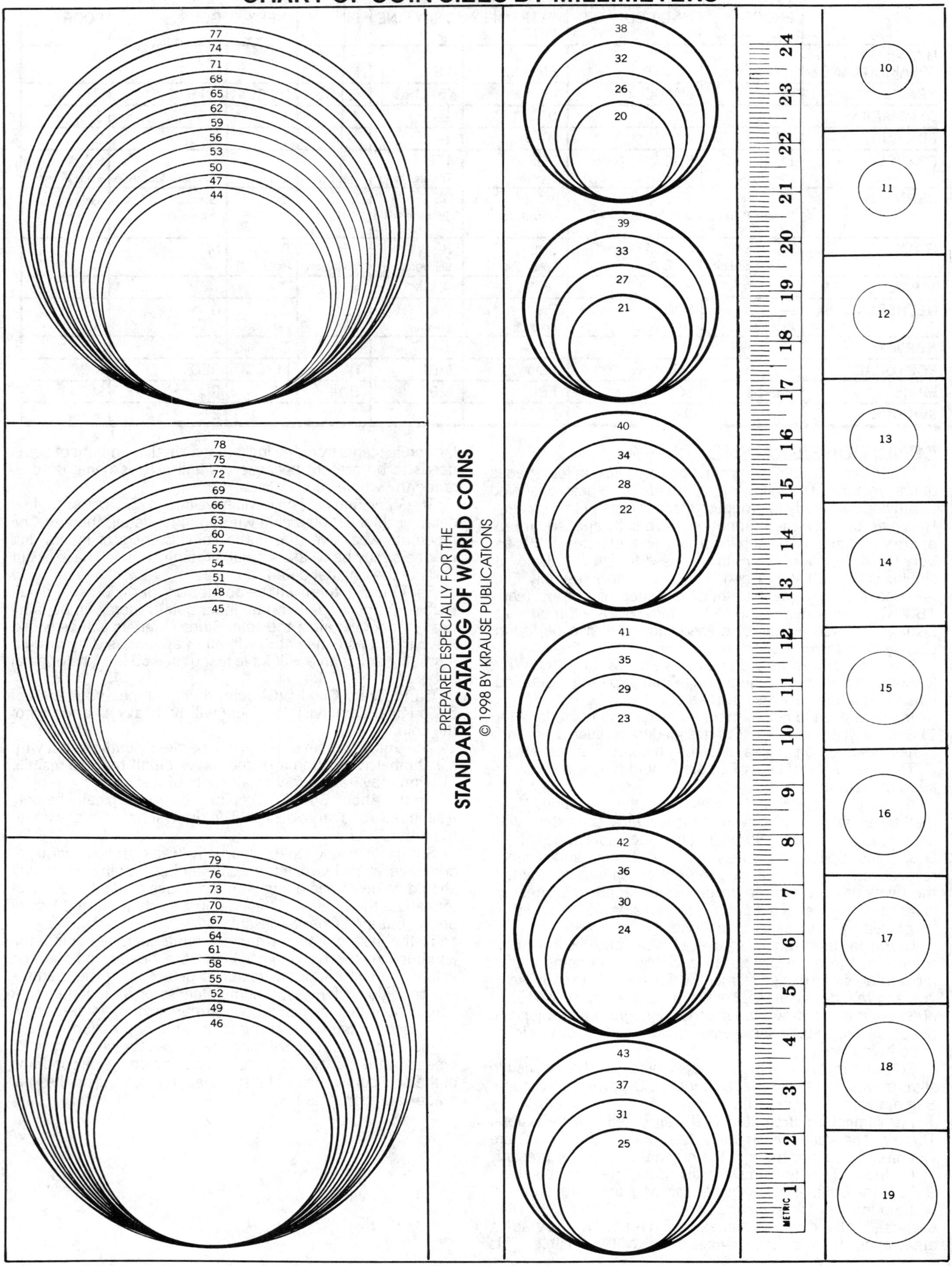
77
74
71
68
65
62
59
56
53
50
47
44
78
75
72
69
66
63
60
57
54
51
48
45
79
76
73
70
67
64
61
58
55
52
49
46
PREPARED ESPECIALLY FOR THE
STANDARD CATALOG OF WORLD COINS
© 1998 BY KRAUSE PUBLICATIONS
38
32
26
20
39
33
27
21
40
34
28
22
41
35
29
23
42
36
30
24
43
37
31
25
METRIC
1
2
3
4
5
6
7
8
9
10
11
12
13
14
15
16
17
18
19
20
21
22
23
24
10
11
12
13
14
15
16
17
18
19

INSTANT IDENTIFIER

Aachen
(German States)

Albania

Austria

Baden
(German States)

Bradenburg-
Ansbach
(German States)

Finland

Jever
(German States)

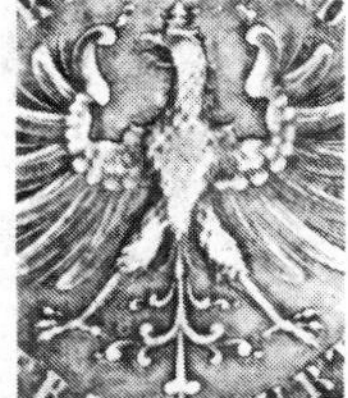

Frankfurt
(German States)

Furstenberg
(German States)

Geneva
(Swiss Cantons)

German Empire

Montenegro
(Yugoslavia)

Nurnberg
(German States)

Milan
(Italian States)

Prussia
(German States)

Russia (Czarist)
Russian Poland

Schwarzburg-
Rudolstadt
(German States)

Schwarzburg-
Sondershausen
(German States)

Serbia
(Yugoslavia)

Teutonic Order
(German States)

Genoa
(Italian States)

Syrian Arab
Republic

United Arab
Republic
(Egypt, Syria)

Arab Republic
of Egypt
Libya

Yemen
Arab Republic

Bulgaria

Burma
(Myanmar)

Ethiopia

Finland

Norway

Gorizia
(Italian States)

Hannover
(German States)

Hesse-
Darmstadt
(German States)

Hohenlohe-
Neuenstein-
Oehringen
(German States)

Iran
(Persia)

Morocco

Siberia

Tibet
(China)

Nepal

Morocco
(AH1371 = 1951AD)

Manchukuo
(China)

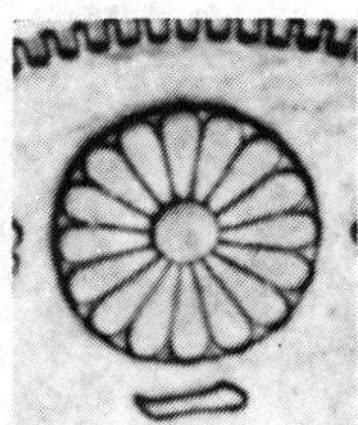

Japan

INSTANT IDENTIFIER

Hanau-Munzenberg (German States)

Nassau (German States)

Hesse-Cassel (German States)

Sri Lanka (Ceylon)

Tibet (China)

Utrecht (Netherlands)

Venice (Italian States)

Neuchatel (Swiss Cantons)

China (Empire-Provincial)

China (Empire-Provincial)

Japan

Japan

African States

Bretzenheim (German States)

Hall in Swabia (German States)

Greenland

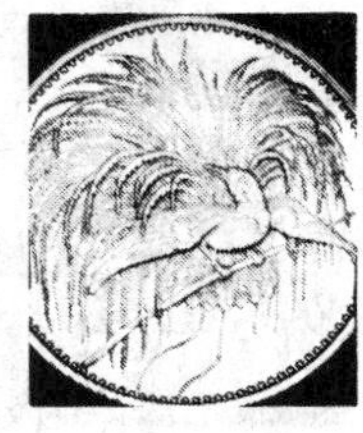

German New Guinea (Papua New Guinea)

Lithuania

Mongolia

Sudan

Algeria

Lowenstein-Wertheim (German States)

Maldive Islands

Afghanistan

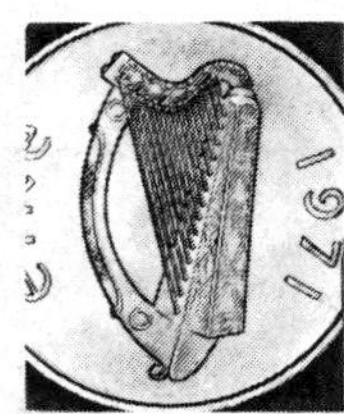

Ireland

Israel

Lebanon

Papal States (Vatican)

Regensburg (German States)

Sweden

North Korea

CCCP-Russia

CCCP-Russia

Yugoslavia

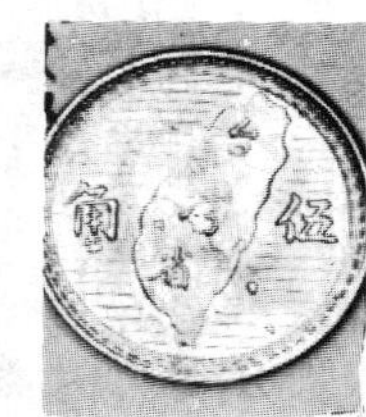

Formosa (Rep. of China)

Mainz (German States)

Solms-Laubach (German States)

Ticino (Swiss Cantons)

Fugger (German States)

Naples & Sicily (Italian States)

Saxe-Saalfield (German States)

Stolberg-Stolberg (German States)

INSTANT IDENTIFIER

French Colonial

French Colonial

French Colonial

Bangladesh

Isle Of Man
Sicily

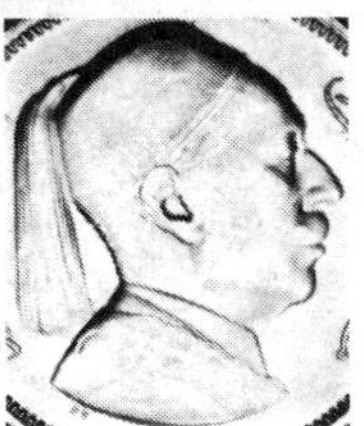
Libya

Anhalt-Bernberg
(German States)

Aargau
(Swiss Cantons)

Augsburg
(German States)

Basel
(Swiss Cantons)

Bavaria
(German States)

Brazil

Bremen
(German States)

Luzern
(Swiss Cantons)

Chur Pfalz
(German States)

Fulda
(German States)

Glarus
(Swiss Cantons)

Grand Duchy
Of Warsaw
(Poland)

Graubunden
(Swiss Cantons)

Hamburg
(German States)

Lucca
(Italian States)

Hesse-Cassel
(German States)

Hesse-Homburg
(German States)

Hildesheim
(German States)

Hohenzollern-
Hechingen
(German States)

Hungary

Julich-Berg
(German States)

Gelderland
(Netherlands)

Lippe-Detmold
(German States)

Lubeck
(German States)

Mecklenburg-
Strelitz
(German States)

Oldenburg
(German States)

Passau
(German States)

Portugal

Vaud
(Swiss Cantons)

Anhalt
(Joint Coinage)
(German States)

Oldenburg
(German States)

Schwarzenberg
(German States)

Schaffhausen
(Swiss Cantons)

Paderborn
(German States)

Thurgau
(Swiss Cantons)

Westfrisia
(Netherlands)

INSTANT IDENTIFIER

Arenberg (German States)

Rhenish Confederation (German States)

Reuss-Greiz (German States)

Sardinia (Italian States)

Saxony (German States)

Schaumburg-Lippe (German States)

Schleswig-Holstein (German States)

St. Gall (Swiss Cantons)

Slovakia

Solothurn (Swiss Cantons)

Unterwalden (Nidwalden) (Swiss Cantons)

Wurttemberg (German States)

Wurzburg (German States)

Zurich (Swiss Cantons)

Waldeck-Pyrmont (German States)

Iraq

Pakistan

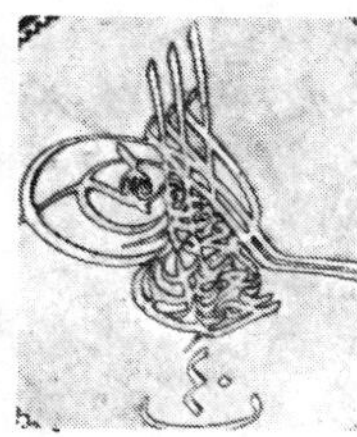
Turkey-Egypt Sudan, Algeria (Ottoman Empire)

Muscat & Oman, Oman

Saudi Arabia

Tunisia

Wismar (German States)

Order of Malta

Bamberg (German States)

Brunswick-Wolfenbuttel (German States)

Brunswick-Luneburg (German States)

Erfurt Mainz (German States)

Hannover (German States)

Eichstadt (German States)

Greece

Serbia

Switzerland

Albania

Thailand (Siam)

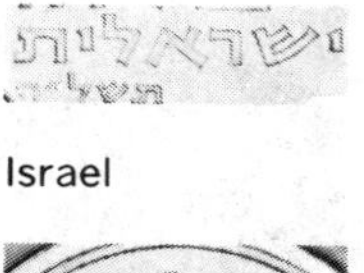
Israel

Japan (Dai Nippon)

South Korea

Sitten (Swiss Cantons)

Rostock (German States)

Saint Alban (German States)

English East India Co. (Sumatra)

China, Japan, Annam, Korea
(All holed 'cash' coins look quite similar.)

Japan

Korea

COUNTRY INDEX

A

B

C

D

E

F

COIN DENOMINATIONS

A

ABAZI - Georgia
ABBASI - Afghanistan, Azerbaijan, Iran
ACKEY - Ghana-Gold Coast
ADELAIDE POUND - South Australia
ADLI ALTIN - Turkey
AKAHI DALA - Hawaii
AKCE - Egypt, Turkey
AKCHEH - Egypt
ALBUS - German States
ALTIN - Turkey
AMMAN CASH - India-Independent Kingdoms
ANANTARAYA - India-IPS
ANGSTER - Swiss Cantons
ANNA - India-British, Independent Kingdoms, IPS; Kenya, Muscat & Oman, Yemen Republic
ARGENTINO - Argentina
ASHRAFI - Afghanistan, Egypt, India-IPS
ASPER - Algiers, Egypt
ATRIBUO - German States
ATT - Cambodia, Thailand
AURAR - Iceland

B

BAHT - Thailand
BAIOCCHI - Vatican-Papal City States; Papal States
BAIOCCO - Vatican-Papal City States; Papal States
BAIZA - Kuwait, Yemen Republic
BAN - Romania
BANI - Romania
BANU - Romania
BATZEN - Swiss Cantons, Switzerland
BAZARUCOS - India-Portuguese
BENDUQI - Morocco
BIRR - Ethiopia
BISTI - Georgia, Azerbaijan
BIT - Dominica, Essequibo & Demerary, Grenada, St. Vincent, Torola
BLACK DOG - Nevis, St. Vincent, Tortola
BOLIVAR - Venezuela
BOLIVIANO - Bolivia
BOLOGNINO - Italian States
BRACTEATE - Hungary
BU - Japan
BUDJU - Algiers
BUQSHA - Yemen Republic
BURBEN - Tunis

C

CACHE - India-French
CAGLIARESE - Italian States
CARLINI - Italian States
CAROLIN - Sweden
CASH - China; India-British, Independent Kingdom, IPS; Vietnam-Annam
CASSEN - German States
CASSENGELD - German States
CAVALLI - Italian States
CEDID MAHMUDIYE - Turkey
CENT - British Honduras, Canada, China, Danish West Indies, French Cochin China, French Indo-China, Hawaii, Hong Kong, Indonesia, Liberia, Malaysia, Mauritius, Netherlands, Sierra Leone, Sarawak, Sri Lanka, United States of America
CENTAVO - Argentina, Bolivia, Chile, Colombia, Costa Rica, Cuba, Dominican Republic, Ecuador, El Salvador, Guatemala, Honduras, Mexico, Nicaragua, Paraguay, Peru, Puerto Rico, Venezuela
CENTECIMO - Bolivia
CENTESIMI - Eritrea, Italian States, Italy, San Marino
CENTESIMO - Dominican Republic, Italian States, Italy, Paraguay, Uruguay, Vatican Papal States
CENTIME - Belgium, Cambodia, Comoros, Croatia, Egypt, France, French Colonies, French Guiana, German States, Guadeloupe, Haiti, Isle De Bourbon, Luxembourg, Martinique, Monaco, Reunion, Swiss Cantons, Tunisia, Zara, Zaire
CENTIMO - Guatemala, Philippines, Puerto Rico, Spain, Peru
CHI'EN - China
CHIFTE RUMI - Egypt
CHO GIN - Japan
CHON - Korea
CHRISTIAN D'OR - Denmark
CHUKCRAM - India-IPS
COLON - Costa Rica
COLONES - Costa Rica
CONVENTION KREUZER - German States
CONVENTION THALER - Austrian States
CORONA - Austria
CROWN - Great Britain

D

DALER - Denmark
DAM - Nepal
DECIME - Monaco
DECIMO - Argentina, Chile, Colombia, Ecuador
DENAR - Hungary
DENARI - Swiss Cantons, Italian States
DENGA - Russia
DENIERS - Haiti, Swiss Cantons
DHINGLA - India-IPS
DHINGLO - India-IPS
DI FIORINO - Italian States
DIME - Nicaragua-Mercado De Leon; Hawaii, United States of America
DINAR - Afghanistan, Iran, Serbia, Yugoslavia
DINERO - Balearic Islands, Peru
DIRHAM - Morocco
DODICI - Italian States
DOKDA - India-IPS
DOKDO - India-IPS
DOLLAR - British West Indies, Canada, China, Great Britain, Hong Kong, Japan, New South Wales, Newfoundland, Puerto Rico, St. Kitts, Sierra Leone, Thailand, United States of America
DOLYA - Russia
DOPPIA - Italian States, Vatican Papal States
DOUBLE - Guernsey
DOUBLE FLORIN - Great Britain
DOUBLE MOHUR - India-Independent Kingdoms
DOUBLE PAISA - India-Independent Kingdoms
DOUDOU - India-French
DRACHMAI - Greece
DREILING - German States
DUB - India-British
DUCAT - Austria, Austrian States, Batavian Republic, German States, Hungary, Kingdom of Holland, Netherlands, Poland, Sweden, Swiss Cantons
DUCAT SPECIA - Denmark
DUCATI - Italian States
DUDU - India-British
DUENG - Thailand
DUIT - Netherlands East Indies, Indonesia
DUPLONE - Swiss Cantons
DURO - Gerona, Tortosa

E

ESCALIN - Guadeloupe, Haiti, St. Lucia
ESCUDO - Argentina, Bolivia, Central American Republic, Chile, Colombia, Costa Rica, Ecuador, Guatemala, Mexico, Peru, Philippines, Portugal, Spain

F

FALUS - Afghanistan, China, India-Independent Kingdoms, IPS; Morocco; Uzbekistan
FANAM - India-British, Independent Kingdoms, IPS
FANO - India-Danish
FARTHING - Antigua, Great Britain, Ireland, Isle of Man, Jamaica, Malta, Sri Lanka, Trinidad
FELS - Algeria
FEN - China
FILLER - Hungary
FIORINI - Italian States
FIORINO - Italian States
FLORIN - Austria, Great Britain, Ireland, Kingdom of Holland
FORINT - Hungary
FRACTIONAL FALUS - Afghanistan
FRANC - Austria, Belgium, Cambodia, Cattaro, Comoros, Croatia, Egypt, France, French West Africa, Hungary, Italian States, Martinique, Monaco, Montenegro, Reunion, Swiss Cantons, Switzerland, Tunisia, Zara, Zaire
FRANCESCONE - Italian States
FRANCHI - Italian States, Swiss Cantons
FRANCO - Dominican Republic, Ecuador, Italian States, Swiss Cantons
FRANK - German States, Swiss Cantons
FRANKEN - German States, Swiss Cantons, Switzerland
FREDERICK D'OR - German States
FREDERIK D'OR - Denmark
FUANG - Cambodia, Thailand
FUN - Japan, Korea

G

GAZETTA - Ionian Islands
GAZETTAE - Ionian Islands
GERSH - Ethiopia
GIULIO - Vatican Papal States
GOLD BAHT - Thailand
GOLD KORI - India-IPS
GOLD RUPEE - India-Independent Kingdoms, Indonesia
GOLD SALUNG - Thailand
GOLDGULDEN - German States, Hungary
GORYOBAN - Japan
GOURDE - Haiti
GRAMO - Argentina
GRANA - Italian States
GRANO - Italian States, Mexico
GRANI - Italian States
GROAT - Great Britain
GROSCHEL - German States
GROSCHEN - German States, Hungary, Posen, Poland
GROSETTI - Ragusa
GROSSO - Vatican Papal States
GROSZ - Poland
GROSZE - Poland
GROSZY - Poland, Zamosc
GROTE - German States
GROTEN - German States
GUILDER - Guyana, Netherlands Antilles
GUINEA - Great Britain
GULDEN - Austria, Batavian Republic, German States, Indonesia, Kingdom of Holland, Netherlands, Philippines
GUTE GROSHEN - German States

H

HALBAG - German States
HALF CENT - United States of America
HALF DOLLAR - United States of America
HALFPENNY - St. Helena
HALLER - Swiss Cantons
HAPAHA - Hawaii
HAPA HANERI - Hawaii
HAPALUA - Hawaii
HARF - Yemen Republic
HAYRIYE ALTIN - Iraq, Turkey
HEAVY AMMAN CASH - India-Independent Kingdoms
HEAVY PAISA - India-Independent Kingdoms
HEAVY RUPEE - Afghanistan, India-IPS
HELLER - Austria, German States

I

J

JA'U - India Princely States
JOKOH - Straits Settlements

K

KABIR - Yemen Republic
KALI FANAM - India-IPS
KAROLIN - German States
KAS - India-Danish
KEPING - Indonesia, Thailand
KHARUB - Algeria, Tunis, Tunisia
KHARUBA - Algeria
KHUMSI - Yemen Republic
KIN, ICHI-BU - Japan
KIN, ICHI-BU ISSHU - Japan
KIN, ICHI-BU NISSAU - Japan
KIN, ISSHU - Japan
KIN, KAKU SHU-NAKA - Japan
KIN, NI-BU - Japan
KIN, NI-BU ISSHU - Japan
KIN, NISSHU - Japan
KIN, RYO - Japan
KIN, SHU-NAKA - Japan
KOBAN - Japan
KOPEK - Poland, Russia
KORI - India-IPS
KORONA - Hungary
KRAJCZAR - Hungary
KRAN - Iran
KREUTZER - German States
KREUZER - Austria, Austrian States, German States, Swiss Cantons
KRONA - Sweden
KRONE - Austria, Denmark, German States, Liechtenstein, Norway
KRONEN - Liechtenstein
KRONER - Denmark, Norway
KRONOR - Sweden
KUPANG - Thailand
KURUSH - Turkey
KWAN PING - China-Foreign Enclaves
KYAT - Myanmar

L

LAIRD - Nigeria
LANG - Vietnam-Annam
LARI - Maldive Islands
LARIAT - Maldive Islands
LARIN - Maldive Islands
LEI - Romania
LEPTA - Greece
LEPTON - Greece
LEU - Romania
LEV - Bulgaria
LEVA - Bulgaria
LI - China
LIANG - China
LIBRA - Peru
LIGHT PAISA - India-Independent Kingdoms
LIGHT RUPEE - Afghanistan
LIRA - Eritrea, Italian States, Italy, San Marino, Vatican Papal States
LIRE - Eritrea, Italian States, Italy, San Marino, Vatican Papal States
LIVRE - Guadeloupe, Martinique, Mauritius & Reunion, St. Lucia

M

MACE - China
MACUTA - Angola
MAHALLAK - Harar, Ethiopia
MAHBUB - Egypt
MAHMUDI - Mecca
MANGIR - Libya
MARIENGROSCHEN - German States
MARK - German New Guinea, Germany, German States
MARAVEDI - Navarre, Spain, Venezuela
MARKKA - Finland
MARKKAA - Finland
MAT - Myanmar
MATICAES - Mozambique
MAZUNA - Morocco
MELGAREJO - Bolivia
MEMDUHIYE ALTIN - Turkey
MIL - Hong Kong
MISCAL - China
MISRIYA - Egypt
MOHAR - Nepal
MOHUR - Afghanistan; India: British, Independent Kingdoms, IPS, Mughal Empire; Indonesia
MOMME - Japan
MON - Japan, Korea
MU - Myanmar
MUDRA - India-IPS
MUN - Korea

N

NAN RYO - Japan
NASRI - Tunis
NAZARANA ANNA - India-IPS
NAZARANA KORI - India-IPS
NAZARANA MOHUR - India-IPS, Mughal Empire
NAZARANA NEW PAISA - India-IPS
NAZARANA OLD PAISA - India-IPS
NAZARANA PAISA - India-IPS

NAZARANA RUPEE - Afghanistan, India-Independent Kingdoms, IPS, Mughal Empire
NAZARANA TAKKA - India-IPS
NEU-GROSCHEN - German States
NEW ALTIN - Turkey
NEW PAISA - India-IPS
NOUSF - Egypt

O

OBAN - Japan
OBOL - Greece, Hungary
OBOLI - Greece
OCHAVO - Catalonia
OCTAVO - Mexico, Philippines
ONCA - Mozambique
ONCIE - Italian States
ONZA - Bolivia, Costa Rica
ORE - Denmark, Greenland, Norway, Sweden
OTTANTA - Italian States

P

PAGODA - India-British, IPS
PAI - India-IPS
PAISA - Afghanistan; India-Independent Kingdoms, IPS, Mughal Empire; Nepal
PAISE - India-Independent Kingdoms
PANA - Mughal Empire
PANCHIA - India-British
PAOLI - Italian States
PAOLO - Italian States
PARA - Egypt, Greece, Iraq, Libya, Sudan, Turkey, Yugoslavia
PARALE - Romania
PARAS - Greece
PARDAO - India-Portuguese
PAVALI - India-IPS
PE - Cambodia, Myanmar
PECA - Portugal
PENCE - Australia, British Guiana & West Indies, British Honduras, Dominica, El Salvador, Great Britain, Ireland, Isle of Man, Jamaica, Jersey, Mozambique, New South Wales, St. Helena, St. Kitts, Scotland, South Africa, Sri Lanka, Trinidad
PENCE TOKEN - Ireland
PENNI - Finland
PENNIA - Finland
PENNY - Australia, Bahamas, Canada, Cape of Good Hope, Great Britain, Griqua Town, Ireland, Isle of Man, Jamaica, Jersey, New Brunswick, New Zealand, Nova Scotia, Orange Free State, St. Helena, Sierra Leone, South Africa, Trinidad
PERPERO - Ragusa
PESA - German East Africa
PESETA - Balearic Islands, Barcelona, Catalonia, Peru, Spain
PESO - Argentina, Cambodia, Chile, Colombia, Costa Rica, Cuba, Dominican Republic, El Salvador, Guatemala, Honduras, Mexico, Netherlands Antilles, Paraguay, Philippines, Puerto Rico, Uruguay
PESO FUERTES - Paraguay
PFENNIG - German New Guinea, German States, Germany, Swiss Cantons
PFENNIGE - German States
PFENNING - Austrian States, German States
PHAN - Vietnam-Annam
PHOENIX - Greece
PIASTRE - Cambodia, Cyprus, Darfur, Egypt, French Cochin China, French Indo-China, Iraq, Sudan, Tunis, Turkey
PICE - East Africa; India-British, IPS; Kenya, Sri Lanka
PIE - India-British, IPS
PILON - Mexico
PISTOLE - German States
PIT - Thailand
PITIS - Indonesia, Malaysia, Thailand
POLTINA - Russia
POLUPOLTINNIK - Russia
POLUSHKA - Russia
POND - South Africa
POT DUENG - Thailand
POUND - Australia, Great Britain, Peru, St. Vincent
PUL - Uzbekistan
PULI - Georgia
PYA - Myanmar
PYSA - Zanzibar

Q

QIRSH - Egypt
QUART - Gibraltar
QUAN - Vietnam-Annam
QUARTER DOLLAR - United States of America
QUARTILLA - Mexico
QUARTO - Gibraltar, Mexico, Philippines, Spain
QUATTRINI - Italian States
QUATTRINO - Italian States, Vatican Papal States

R

RAPPEN - Swiss Cantons, Switzerland
REAAL - Netherlands Antilles
REAL - Argentina, Bolivia, Central American Republic, Chile, Colombia, Costa Rica, Dominican Republic, Ecuador, El Salvador, Guatemala, Honduras, Mexico, Mozambique, Nicaragua, Paraguay, Peru, Philippines, Spain, Venezuela
REAL BATU - Indonesia
REALE - Italian States
REALES - Argentina, Bolivia, Central American Republic, Chile, Colombia, Costa Rica, Cuba, Dominican Republic, Ecuador, El Salvador, Mexico, Nicaragua, Peru, Philippines, Spain, Venezuela
REALES DE VELLON - Valencia
REIS - Angola, Azores, Brazil, India-Portuguese, Madeira Islands, Mozambique, Portugal, St. Thomas & Prince
RIGSBANKDALER - Denmark
RIGSBANKSKILLING - Denmark
RIGSDALER - Denmark
RIGSMONTSKILLING - Denmark
RIJKSDAALER - Batavian Republic, Kingdom of Holland, Netherlands
RIKSDALER - Norway, Sweden
RIKSDALER RIKSMYNT - Sweden
RIKSDALER SPECIE - Sweden
RIN - Japan
RIXDOLLAR - Ceylon
RIYAL (or RIAL) - British Honduras, Iran, Yemen Republic
ROPELL - German States
ROUBLE - Russia
ROYALIN - India-Danish
ROYALINE - India-Danish
RUBLE - Poland
RUBIYA - Egypt
RUMI ALTIN - Turkey
RUPEE - Afghanistan, Bhutan, India: Andaman Islands, British, Independent Kingdoms, IPS, Mughal Empire; Indonesia, Madura Island, Kenya, Mozambique, Nepal, Yemen Republic
RUPEE SIZE - Djibouti
RUPI - Iran
RUPIA - India-Portuguese
RUPIE - German East Africa
RUPIEN - German East Africa
RUSPONE - Italian States
RYAL - Zanzibar, Yemen Republic
RYAL SIZE - Djibouti

S

SALUNG - Thailand
SANAR - Afghanistan
SAPEQUE - French Cochin China, French Indo-China
SAR - China
SATANG - Thailand
SATIMI - Romania
SCHILLING - German States, Poland, Swiss Cantons
SCHWAREN - German States
SCUDI - Italian States, Vatican Papal States
SCUDO - Bolivia, Italian States, Mexico, Vatican Papal States
SECHSLING - German States
SEER - British India
SEL - India-Independent Kingdoms
SEN - Japan
SHAHI - Afghanistan, Iran
SHAHI SEFID - Iran
SHILLING - Australia, British Honduras, Canada, Dominica, El Salvador, Great Britain, Guernsey, Ireland, Isle of Man, Jersey, Mozambique, St. Vincent, South Africa, Scotland, Tortola, Trinidad
SHILLINGS TOKEN - Ireland
SHO - Tibet
SHU - Japan
SIK - Thailand
SILBER GROSCHEN - German States
SIO - Thailand
SIXPENCE - Great Britain
SKILDINGAR - Iceland
SKILLING - Danish West Indies, Denmark, Norway, Sweden
SOL - Argentina, Bolivia, Haiti, Peru, Swiss Cantons
SOLDI - Italian States, Vatican Papal States, Swiss Cantons
SOLDO - Italian States, Vatican Papal States
SOLES - Argentina, Bolivia, Peru
SOU - St. Bartholomew, Canada
SOUS - French Guiana, Guadeloupe, Mauritius, St. Lucia, St. Martin
SOVEREIGN - Australia, Great Britain, India-IPS, Yemen Republic
SOVRANO - Italian States
SPECIE DALER - Norway
STAMPEE - St. Lucia, St. Vincent, Trinidad
STIVER - British Guiana & West Indies, Ceylon, Essequibo & Demerary, Indonesia, St. Bartholomew
STOTINKI - Bulgaria
STUBER - German States
STUIVER - Indonesia, Kingdom of Holland, Netherlands Antilles, St. Martin
SUCRE - Ecuador
SUELDO - Balearic Islands
SULTANI - Algiers, Libya
SURRE ALTIN - Turkey

T

TAEL - China-Foreign Enclaves
TAKKA - India-IPS
TALAR - Poland
TALARA - Poland
TALLERO - Eritrea
TAMLUNG - Thailand
TANGA - India-Portuguese
TANGKA - Tibet
TARI - Italian States
TEK RUMI - Egypt
TENGA - China, Uzbekistan
TESTONE - Vatican Papal States
THALER - Austria, Austrian States, German States, Hungary, Liechtenstein, Mozambique
THELER - German States
TICAL - Cambodia
TIEN - Vietnam-Annam
TILLA - Afghanistan, China, Uzbekistan
TIMASHA - India-Independent Kingdoms
TLACO - Mexico
TOKA CASH - India-IPS
TOLA - Nepal
TOMAN - Afghanistan, Iran
TORNESE - Italian States
TORNESI - Italian States
TOT - Thailand
TRA - Kedah, Malaysia
TRADE DOLLAR - Japan, United States of America
TRAMBIYO - India-IPS

U

UMI KENETA - Hawaii
UNIT - French West Africa, Mecca

V

VAN - Vietnam-Annam
VELLI FANAM - India-IPS
VENEZOLANO - Venezuela
VIRARAYA FANAM - India-IPS

W

WARN - Korea
WERK - Ethiopia
WHAN - Korea

X

XERAFIM - India-Portuguese
XERAFIN - India-Portuguese

Y

YANG - Korea
YEN - Japan
YUAN - Cambodia

Z

ZECCHINI - Vatican Papal States
ZECCHINO - Italian States
ZERI MAHBUB - Egypt, Libya, Turkey
ZLOTE - Poland
ZLOTY - Poland, Zamosc
ZLOTYCH - Poland, Russia
ZOLOTA - Turkey
ZOLOTNIKS - Russia

MINT INDEX

A

A - Ackroyd & Best
A - Alamos (Mexico)
A - Antioquia
A - Berlin (Germany)
A - Clausthal (German States)
A - Medellin
A - Paris (France)
A - Vienna (Austria)
AARGAU - Swiss Cantons
AB - Geneva (Swiss Canton)
AB - Graubunden
AB - Strassburg (France)
ACKROYD & BEST - East Africa
ADELAIDE - Australia
AEGINA - Greece
AI - Karlsburg (Transylvania)
AL-IV - Karlsburg (Transylvania)
ALAMOS - Mexico
ALTONA - Danish West Indies, Denmark
ALTENA - Venezuela
AM - Bogota
AMSTERDAM - Netherlands East Indies
ANCONA - Vatican Papal City States
ANHWEI - China
ANTIOQUIA - Colombia
AREQ - Arequipa, Peru
AREQUIPA - Peru
AS - Alamos (Mexico)
ATHENS - Greece
AURICH - German States
AVIGNON - Vatican Papal City States
AYACUCHO - Peru

B

B - Bahia (Brazil)
B - Barcelona
B - Basel (Swiss Cantons)
B - Bayreuth (German States)
B - Beaumont-le-Roger (France)
B - Bern (Switzerland)
B - Bologna (Italy)
B - Bombay (India-British)
B - Breslau (Poland)
B - Brunswick (German States)
B - Bucharest (Romania)
B - Budapest (Hungary)
B - Burgos
B - Dieppe (France)
B - Dresden (Germany)
B - Freiburg (Swiss Cantons)
B - Glarus
B - Hamburg (Germany)
B - Hannover (German States)
B - Kormoczbanya (Kremnitz, Hungary)
B - Kremnitz (Hungary)
B - Luzern (Swiss Cantons)
B - Nuevo Reino (Bogota)
B - Regensburg (German States)
B - Rouen (France)
B - Santa Fe de Bogota
B - Schwyz (Swiss Cantons)
B - Vienna (Austria)
B - Zurich (Swiss Cantons)
BA - Barcelona (Spain)
BA - (ligate) Basel (Switzerland)
BA - Buenos Aires (Argentina)
BA - Santa Fe de Bogota
BAHIA - Brazil
BAMBERG - German States
BANGKO SENTRAL PILIPINAS - Philippines
BARCELONA - Spain
BASEL - Swiss Cantons, Switzerland
BAYONNE - France
BAYREUTH - German States
BB - Strasbourg (France)
BD - Pau (France)
BEAUMONT-LE-ROGER - French Indo-China
BEI - Basel (Swiss Cantons)
BEL - Freiburg (Swiss Cantons)
BEL - Lausanne (Swiss Cantons)
BEL - Vaud
BERGA - Spain
BERLIN - Dominican Republic, German East Africa, German New Guinea, German States, Germany, Italy, Morocco, Papua New Guinea, Poland, Uruguay, Venezuela
BERN - Liberia, Liechtenstein, Swiss Cantons, Switzerland
BGA - Berga
B.H. - Frankfurt (German States)
B (rosette) H - Regensburg (German States)
BI - (ligate) Birmingham (Great Britain)
BILBAO - Spain
BIRm - Costa Rica, Ecuador
BIRMINGHAM - Italian States, Kenya, Morocco
BIRMINGHAM H - Belize, Cyprus, Italy, Uruguay
BO - Bilbao
BOARD OF PUBLIC WORKS - China
BOARD OF REVENUE - China
BOGOTA - Colombia (Santa Fe de Bogota)
BOLOGNA - Italian States, Italy, Vatican Papal City States, Vatican Papal States
BOMBAY - Ceylon, India-British
BOMBAY B - India-Republic, Straits Settlements
BOMBAY I - East Africa, Great Britain, India
BORDEAUX - France, French Cochin China, Greece
BP - Budapest (Hungary)
BRESLAU - Austria, German States, Poland
BRUNSWICK - German States
BRUSSELS - Belgium, Luxembourg, Netherlands, Peru, Philippines, Romania, Russia, Spain, Switzerland, Venezuela
BSP - Bangko Sentral Pilipinas
BUCHAREST - Romania
BUDAPEST - Egypt, Hungary
BUENOS AIRES - Argentina
BURGOS - Spain

C

C - Calcutta (India-British)
C - Cartagena (Colombia)
C - Cassel (Germany)
C - Castelsarrasin (France)
C - Catalonia (Spain)
C - Charlotte (U.S.A.)
C - Chihuahua
C - Christophstal (German States)
C - Clausthal (German States)
C - Cuiaba (Brazil)
C - Culiacan (Mexico)
C - Dresden (Germany)
C - Frankfurt am Main (German States)
C - Prague (Bohemia)
C crowned - Cadiz (Spain)
C-A - Karlsburg (Transylvania)
CA - Chihuahua (Mexico)
CA - Cuenca (Spain)
CA - Vienna (Austria)
CADIZ - Spain
CALCUTTA - India-British, Kenya
C.A.M. - San Salvador
CARACAS - Venezuela
CARSON CITY - United States of America
CARTAGENA - Colombia
CASSEL - German States
CASTLESARRASIN - France
CATALONIA - Spain
CB - Hermannstadt (Transylvania)
CC - Carson City (U.S.A.)
CC - Genoa (Italy)
CE - Real del Catorce (Mexico)
CENTRAL AMERICAN MINT - El Salvador
CH - Chalons (France)
CH - Chihuahua (Mexico)
CH - Pressburg (Hungary)
CHALONS - France
CHARLOTTE - United States of America
CHEKIANG - China
CHI - Valcambi (Switzerland)
CHICHOW - China
CHIHUAHUA - Mexico
CHIHLI - China
CHINGCHOW - China
CHING-KIANG - China
CHRISTOPHSTAL - German States
CI or CI BI - Hermannstadt (Transylvania)
CL - Genoa (Italy)
CLAUSTHAL - German States
C/M - Calcutta (India)
CM - Kaschau
CM - St. Petersburg (Russia)
Cn - Culiacan (Mexico)
Co. - Cuzco (Peru)
COMAYAGUA - (Honduras)
COPENHAGEN - Danish West Indies, Denmark, Greenland
CORDOBA - Argentina
CORDOVA - Argentina
CR - San Jose (Costa Rica)
CT - Christophstal (German States)
CUENCA - Spain
CUIABA - Brazil
CULIACAN - Mexico
CUZ or CUZO plain - Cuzco (Peru)
CV - Klausenburg (Transylvania)
CUZO monogram - Cuzco (Peru)
CUZCO - Peru

D

D - Aurich (German States)
D - Daloghena (U.S.A.)
D - Denver (USA)
D - Durango (Mexico)
D - Dusseldorf (German States)
D - Graz (Styria)
D - Lyon (France)
D - Munich (Germany)
D - Salzburg (Austria)
D - Stuttgart (Germany)
D - Zurich
DALOGHENA - United States of America
DARMSTADT - German States, Germany
DB - Schwyz (Swiss Cantons)
DENVER - Ecuador
DIEPPE - France
Do - Durango (Mexico)
DORDRECHT - Netherlands, Netherlands East Indies
DRESDEN - German States, Germany
DT - Dordrecht (Netherlands)
DURANGO - Mexico
DUSSELDORF - German States

E

E - Dresden (Germany)
E - Einkhuizen (Netherlands)
E - Evora (Portugal)
E - Karlsburg (Transylvania)
E - Konigsberg (German States)
E - Muldenhutten (Germany)
EKATERINBURG - Russia
ENKHUIZEN - Netherlands, Netherlands East Indies
EoMo - Estado de Mexico (Mexico)
ESTADO DE MEXICO - Mexico
EVORA - Portugal

F

F - Cassel (German States)
F - Dresden (Germany)
F - Freudenstadt (German States)
F - Glarus
F - Hall (Austria)
F - Magdeburg (German States)
F - Nuevo Reino (Bogota, Colombia)
F - Stuttgart (Germany)
FENGTIEN - China
FH - Hall (Austria)
FIRENZE - Italian States, Italy
FLORENCE - Italian States, Italy
FRANKFURT - German States, Germany
FREIBOURG - Swiss Cantons
FREUDENSTADT - German States
FS - Santa Fe-Nuevo Reino (Colombia)
FT - Klausenburg (Transylvania)
FUCHOU - China
FUCHOW - China
FUKIEN - China

G

G - Dresden (Germany)
G - Geneva (Switzerland)
G - Glatz (Poland)
G - Goias (Brazil)
G - Granada
G - Graz (Styria)
G - Guanajuato (Mexico)
G - Guatemala
G - Gunzburg (Austria)
G - Hall (Austria)
G - Karlsruhe (Germany)
G - Nagybanya (Hungary)
G - Schwerin (German State)
G - Stettin (German State)
GA - Karlsburg (Transylvania)
GA - Guadalajara (Mexico)
GC - Gualalupe y Calvo (Mexico)
GC - Pressburg
GENEVA - France, Swiss Cantons
GENOA - France
GLARUS - Swiss Cantons
GLATZ - German States, Poland
G.M. - Mantua (Italian States)
GN - Culiacan (Mexico)
GN Nagybanya
GN-BW - Bamberg (German States)
GO - Guanajuato (Mexico)
GOIAS - Brazil
GR - Graz (Styria)
GRANADA - Spain
GRAUBUNDEN - Swiss Cantons
GRAZ - Austria, Italian States
GUADALAJARA - Mexico
GUADALUPE Y CALVO - Mexico
GUANAJUATO - Mexico
GUATEMALA - Central American Republic, Guatemala
GUNZBURG - Austria, Italian States
GYF - Karlsburg (Romania)

H

H - Amsterdam (Netherlands)
H - Birmingham (Great Britain)
H - Darmstadt (Germany)
H - Dresden (Germany)
H - Geneva (Swiss Cantons)
H - Gunzburg (Austria)
H - Hall (Austria)
H - Heaton (England)
H - Hermosillo (Mexico)
H - La Rochelle (France)
H - Schwyz (Swiss Cantons)
HA - Hall (Austria)
HALL - Austria, Austrian States, Hungary, Italian States
HAMBURG - German East Africa, German States, Germany, Romania
HANCHENG - China
HANNOVER - German States, Germany
HANOI - French Indo-China
HARDERWIJK - Netherlands, Netherlands East Indies
HAVANA - Cuba
HB - Graubunden
HEATON - Bolivia, British North Borneo, Canada, Ceylon, Colombia, Costa Rica, Dominican Republic, East Africa, Ecuador, El Salvador, French Indo-China, Great Britain, Greece, Guatemala, Guernsey, Haiti, Hong Kong, India-British, Jamaica, Jersey, Kenya, Mauritius, Nicaragua, Romania, Straits Settlements
HEILUNGKIANG - China
HELSINKI - Finland
HERMOSILLO - Mexico
HF - Huguenin Freres (Le Locle, Switzerland)
HK - Harderwijk (Netherlands)
H.K. - Rostock (German States)
HN - Hoorn (Netherlands)
Ho - Hermosillo (Mexico)
HONG KONG - China-Foreign Enclaves
HONAN - China
HOORN - Netherlands, Netherlands East Indies
HOPEH - China
HS - Hermannstadt (Transylvania)
HU PU - China
HUGUENIN FRERES, LE LOCLE - Nicaragua, Romania
HUNAN - China
HUPEH - China

I

I - Bombay
I - Hamburg (Germany)
I - Limoges (France)
ICB - Pressburg
I/P - Potosi (Mexico)
IZHORA - Russia

J

J - Hamburg (Germany)
J - Jubia (Spain)
J - Paris
JA - Jubia (Spain)
JUBIA - Spain

K

K - Bordeaux (France)
K - Kampen (Netherlands)
K - Kormoczbanya (Kremnitz, Hungary)
K - Kremnitz (Hungary)
K - St. Gall (Swiss Cantons)
KAMPEN - Netherlands, Netherlands East Indies
KANSU - China
KARLSBURG - Austria, Hungary
KARLSRUHE - German States, Germany
KASCHAU - Hungary
KB - Berlin (Germany)
KB - Kremnitz (Hungary)
KB - Kormoczbanya (Bulgaria)
KIANGNAN - China
KIANGSI - China
KIANGSU - China
KING'S NORTON - Angola, Bolivia, East Africa, Egypt, Great Britain, Greece, Hong Kong, Romania
KIRIN - China
KLAUSENBURG - Austria
KM - Copenhagen (Denmark)
KN - King's Norton (Great Britain)
KOLPINO - Russia
KOLYVAN - Russia
KONGSBERG - Danish West Indies, Norway
KONIGSBERG - German States, Poland
KORMOCZBANYA - Bulgaria, Hungary
KREMNITZ - Austria, Hungary, Italian States, Transylvania
KUCHE - China
KV - Klausenburg (Transylvania)
KWANGSI - China
KWANGTUNG - China
KWEICHOW - China
KYF - Hungary

L

L - Bayonne (France)
L - Leipzig (German States)
L - Lima (Peru)
L - Lisbon (Portugal)
LA PAZ - Bolivia
LA PLATA - Bolivia
LA ROCHELLE - France
LAUSANNE - Swiss Cantons
LEGHORN - Italian States
LEIPZIG - German States
LE LOCLE - Ecuador (Switzerland)
LILLE - France
LIMA - Ecuador, Peru
LIMAE monogram - Lima (Peru)
LIMOGES - France
LISBON - Brazil, Portugal
LIVORNO - Italian States
LLANTRISANT - London, Philippines
LONDON - France, Great Britain, Liberia, Peru
LUZERN - Swiss Cantons
LYON - France, Uruguay

M

M - Aargau (Swiss Cantons)
M - Madras (India)
M - Madrid
M - Manila (Philippines)
M - Medellin (Colombia)
M - Melbourne (Australia)
M - Mexico City (Mexico)
M - Milan (Italy)
M - Minas Gerais (Brazil)
M - Monaco
M - Moscow (Russia)
M - Munich (Germany)
M - Schwyz (Swiss Cantons)
M - Toulouse (France)
M crowned - Madrid (Spain)
MA - (ligate) Marseille (France)
MA - Manila (Philippines)
MADRAS - India-British
MADRID - Morocco, Philippines, Spain
MAGDEBURG - German States
MANILA - Philippines
MANTUA - Austria
MARSEILLE - France
MATO GROSSO - Brazil
MC - Brunswick
MD - Madrid (Spain)
MEDELLIN - Colombia
MELBOURNE - Australia
MEXICO CITY - Colombia, Dominican Republic, Ecuador, El Salvador, Mexico, Nicaragua, Uruguay
MILAN - Austria, Eritrea, Italian States, Italy, San Marino
MINAS GERAIS - Brazil
MO - Mexico City (Mexico)
MOSCOW - Russia
MULDENHUTTEN - German States, Germany
MUNICH - German States, Germany, Leichtenstein
MV or MW - Warsaw (Poland)
MX - Mexico

N

N - Graubunden
N - Nagybanya (Romania)
N - Naples (Italy)
N - Nuevo Reino (Bogota, Colombia)
NAGYBANYA - Austria, Hungary, Italian States
NANTES - France
NAPLES - Italy
N-B or N.B. - Nagybanya (Hungary)
NER - Cartagena (Colombia)
NEW ORLEANS - United States of America
NG - Guatemala
NR - Cartagena (Colombia)
NR - Nuevo Reino (Bogota)
NRE - Cartagena (Colombia)
NUEVA GUATEMALA - Guatemala
NUEVO REINO - Bogota (Colombia)

O

O - New Orleans (U.S.A.)
O - Oaxaca (Mexico)
O - Oravicza (Hungary)
OA - Oaxaca (Mexico)
OAXACA - Mexico
OESCHGER MESDACH & Co. - Spain
OM - Oeschger Mesdach & Co.
OM - Strasbourg (France)
OR monogram - Oruro (Bolivia)
ORAVICZA - Austria
ORAVITZA - Italian States
ORURO - Bolivia
OSAKA - French Indo-China

P

P - Pamplona (Spain)
P - Pernambuco (Brazil)
P - Perth (Australia)
P - Popayan (Colombia)
P - Porto
P - Prague (Bohemia)
P - San Luis Potosi
PA - Pamplona (Spain)
PALERMO - Italian States
PAMPLONA - Spain
PAOTING - China
PARIS - Bolivia, Brazil, Comoros, Dominican Republic, Ethiopia, France, French Colonies, French Guiana, French Indo-China, German States, Greece, Haiti, Honduras, Italy, Luxembourg, Monaco, Morocco, Portugal, Romania, Russia, Switzerland, Tunis, Tunisia, Uruguay
PASCO - Peru
PAU - France
PAZ - Bolivia, Peru
PEIYANG ARSENAL - China
PEKING - China
PERNAMBUCO - Brazil
PERPIGNAN - France
PERTH - Australia
PHILADELPHIA - Colombia, Ecuador, Peru, United States of America
PI - San Luis Potosi (Mexico)
PISIS - Italian States
PISA - Italy
PN or Pn - Popayan (Colombia)
PO - Pasco (Peru)
POISSY - France, French Indo-China, Greece, Morocco, Romania, Uruguay
POPAYAN - Colombia
PORTO - Portugal
POTOSI - Argentina, Bolivia
P.P. - Pamplona
P.R. - Dusseldorf (Germany)
P-R - Gunzburg (Austria)
PRAGUE - Austria
PRESSBURG - Austria, Hungary
PRETORIA - East Africa, Mauritius (Great Britain)
PROVINCIA YORO - Honduras
PTA monogram - La Plata
PTS monogram - Potosi
P-Y - Provincia Yoro (Honduras)

Q

Q - Perpignan (France)
QUITO - Quito (Ecuador)

R

R - London (Great Britain)
R - Rio de Janeiro
R - Rioja (Argentina)
R - Rome (Italy)
R - Saint Andre (France)
R crowned - Rome (Italy)
RA - Rioja (Argentina)
REAL DE CATORCE - Mexico
REGENSBURG - German States
RIO DE JANEIRO - Brazil, St. Thomas & Prince
RIOJA - Argentina
RIOXA - Argentina
RN - Cartagena (Colombia)
ROME - Eritrea, France, Italy, San Marino, Vatican Papal States.
ROSTOCK - German States
ROUEN - France
ROYAL CANADIAN MINT - Dominican Republic
ROYAL MINT (London) - Belize, British Honduras, Cyprus, East Africa, Great Britain, Jamaica, Romania
RS - Rio de Janeiro (Brazil)

S

S - Cartagena (Colombia)
S - Dresden (Germany)
S - Hannover (Germany)
S - Nuevo Reino (Bogota, Colombia)
S - San Francisco (U.S.A.)
S - Schmollnitz (Hungary)
S - Schwabach (German States)
S - Seville (Spain)
S - Solothurn (Switzerland)
S - Sydney (Australia)
S - Stuttgart (German States)
S Utrecht (Netherlands)
SA - Pretoria (South Africa)
Sa - Soerabaja
SAINT ANDRE - France
ST. GAUL - Swiss Cantons
ST. PETERSBURG - Russia
SALZBURG - Austria
SAN FRANCISCO - El Salvador, French Indo-China, Liberia, Peru, United States of America
SAN JOSE - Central American Republic
SAN LUIS POTOSI - Mexico
SANTANDER - Spain
SANTIAGO - Bolivia, Chile, Ecuador, Uruguay
SANTIAGO del ESTERO - Argentina
SAO PAULO - Brazil
SCHMOLLNITZ - Austria, Hungary, Italian States
SCHWABACH - German States
SCHWERIN - German States
SCHWYZ - Swiss Cantons
SE - Santiago del Estero (Argentina)
SEGOVIA - Spain
SEVILLE - Spain
SF - Santa Fe-Nuevo Reino (Colombia)
SGV - Madrid
SHANSI - China
SHANTUNG - China
SHENSI - China
SHERRITT - Philippines
SIBER - Lausanne (Swiss Cantons)
SINKIANG - China
S/L - Seville
SLP - San Luis Potosi (Mexico)
So - (O and S) Santiago (Chile)
SOERABAJA - Netherlands, Netherlands East Indies
SOHO - Straits Settlements
SOLOTHURN - Switzerland
SOUZAN - Russia
SP - Sao Paulo (Brazil)
SR - Santander (Spain)
STETTIN - German States
ST. GALL - Swiss Cantons
STRASBOURG - France, Greece, Italy, Switzerland
STUTTGART - German States, Germany
SY - Sydney (Australia)
SYDNEY - Australia
SZECHUAN - China

T

T - Nantes (France)
T - Tabora (Tanzania)
T - Tegucigalpa (Honduras)
T - Toledo (Spain)
T - Tubingen (German States)
T - Tucuman (Argentina)
T - Turin (Italy)
TABORA - German East Africa
TAIWAN - China
T'AI P'ING - China
TAKU - China
TEGUCIGALPA - Central American Republic, Honduras
T.G. - Yoro (Honduras)
TIERRA DEL FUEGO - Argentina
TIFLIS - Georgia
TL - Comayagua (Honduras)
TM - Tucuman (Argentina)
TN - Tucaman (Argentina)
TO - Toledo (Spain)
TOLE - Toledo (Spain)
TOLEDO - Spain
TOULOUSE - France
TOWER MINT - Dominican Republic (London)
TUBINGEN - German States
TUCUMAN - Argentina
TUNG CH'UAN - China
TUNG SAN SHENG - China
TURIN - France, Italy

U

U - Turin (Italy)
URUMCHI - China
USHI - China
UTRECHT - France, Luxembourg, Netherlands, Netherlands East Indies, Uruguay

V

V - Valencia (Spain)
V - Venice (Italy)
V - Vienna (Austria)
VA - Valencia (Spain)
VAL - Valencia (Spain)
VALCAMBIA - Bolivia, Dominican Republic
VALENCIA - Spain
VENICE - Austria, Italian States
VIENNA - Austria, Greece, Hungary, Italian States, Liechtenstein, Romania, Uruguay

W

W - Breslau (Poland)
W - Lille (France)
W - Soho (Malaysia)
W - Vienna (Austria)
W - Watt & Co.
W - J. Watt & Sons (Birmingham, Great Britain)
WARSAW - Poland, Russia
WATERBURY - Colombia, Haiti (Scoville, CT, USA)

SYMBOLS

ESSENTIAL BOOKS FOR SERIOUS COLLECTORS

1999 North American Coins & Prices

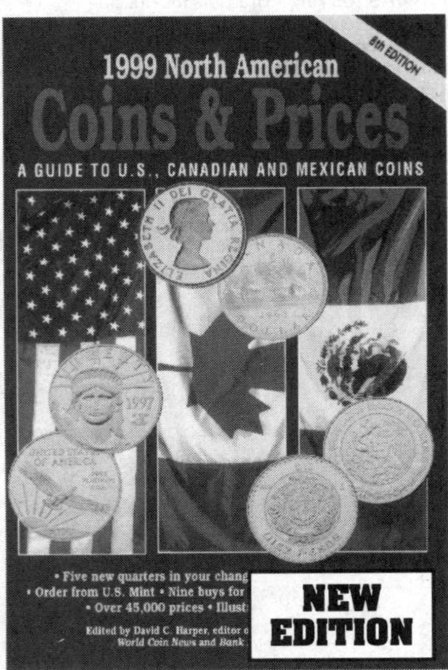

8th Edition
Edited by
David C. Harper

You'll find updated coin prices, commemoratives, varieties and errors, and the latest hot coin topics and controversies. More than 45,000 updated values help you know instantly the current value of a coin and more than 1,500 photos help you identify with certainty your treasures, rarities, and varieties.

Softcover • 6 x 9
544 pages
1,500 b&w photos
NA08 • $16.95

Standard Guide to Small Size U.S. Paper Money

2nd Edition

by Dean Oakes & John Schwartz

This new updated edition provides you with the most complete listings ever published for small-size U.S. paper money from 1928-1988, including higher denomination notes and the new $100 bill. Updated serial number information and a complete overhaul of web notes coverage make it essential for serious collectors.

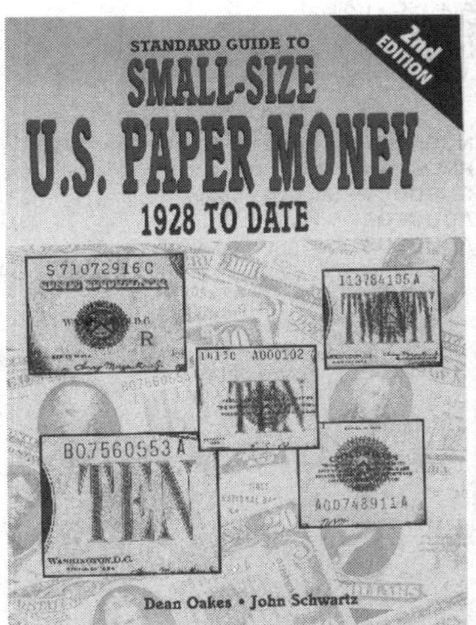

Softcover • 6 x 9
400 pages
250 b&w photos
HP04 • $24.95

Early Paper Money of America

4th Edition
by Eric P. Newman

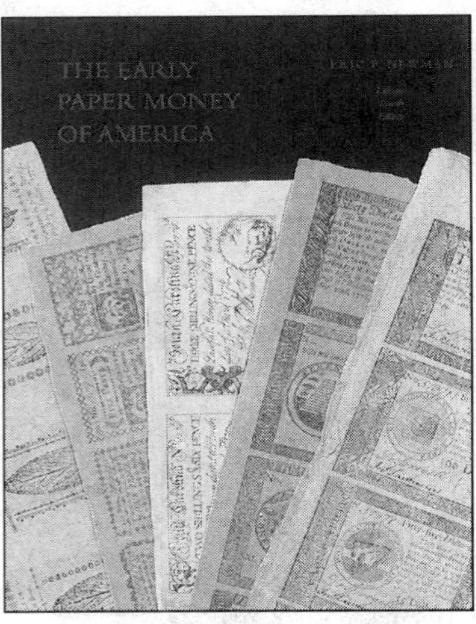

Compile historical and descriptive data on American paper currency from 1686 to 1800. Eric P. Newman has completely revised and updated his popular book to include current values of all available bills.

Hardcover • 8-1/2 x 11
480 pages
930 b&w photos
100 color photos
EP04 • $75.00

America's Money-America's Story

by Richard Doty

The most comprehensive chronicle of American money ever published. This exhaustively researched volume traces American money's evolution from pre-European settlement to the present day. Included are chapters on the Revolutionary War, the California Gold Rush, America's Gilded Age, and more.

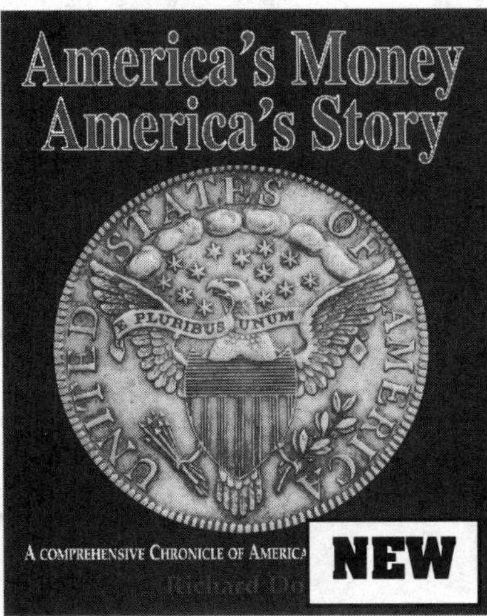

Softcover • 8-1/2 x 11
248 pages • 250+ b&w photos
TPAN • 34.95

To order by credit card or to receive a FREE catalog,
call 800-258-0929 Dept. NRB1
Mon-Fri, 7 a.m. - 8 p.m. • Sat, 8 a.m. - 2 p.m., CST

To order by mail, send a selection list and quantity with payment to:
Krause Publications Book Dept. NRB1• 700 E. State Street • Iola, WI 54990-0001
web site: www.krause.com

Shipping & Handling: Book Post - $3.25 1st book; $2 ea. add'l. Call for Overnight or UPS delivery rates. Foreign addresses $15 per shipment plus $5.95 per book. **Sales tax:** WI res. 5.5%; IL res. 6.5%.

Dealers call 888-457-2873 ext. 880
8 a.m. - 5 p.m. M-F

GERMAN STATES INSTANT IDENTIFIER

Aachen

Anhalt
(Joint Coinage)

Anhalt-Bernberg

Arenberg

Augsburg

Augsburg

Baden

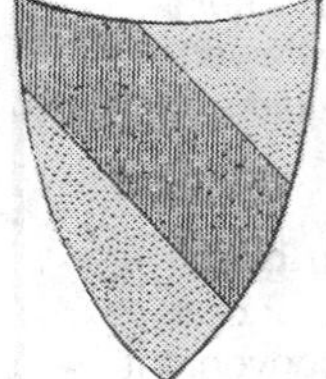
Baden

Bamberg

Bamberg

Bavaria

Bentheim

Berlin

Biberach

Brandenburg
Old City

Brandenburg
New City

Brandenburg
Ansbach

Bremen

Bretzenheim

Brunswick

Brunswick-
Luneburg

Brunswick-
Wolfenbuttel

Chur Pfalz

Cologne

Constance

Dessau

Dortmund

Eichstadt

Emden

Erfurt
Mainz

Erfurt

Essen

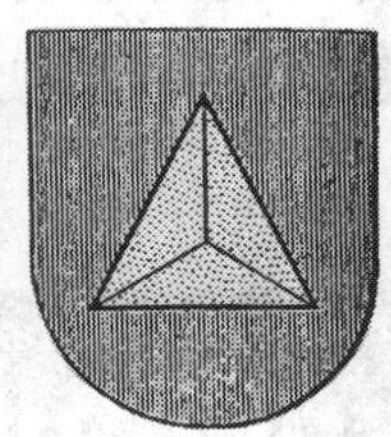
Frankenthal

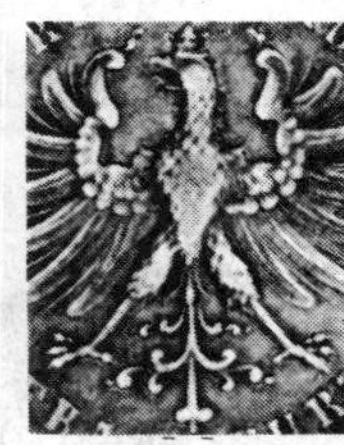
Frankfurt am Main

Frankfurt am Main

Frankfurt
am Oder

Friedberg

Fugger

Fulda

Fulda

Furstenberg

Furth

GERMAN STATES INSTANT IDENTIFIER

German Empire

German New Guinea

Glogau

Gorlitz

Goslar

Gottingen

Greifswald

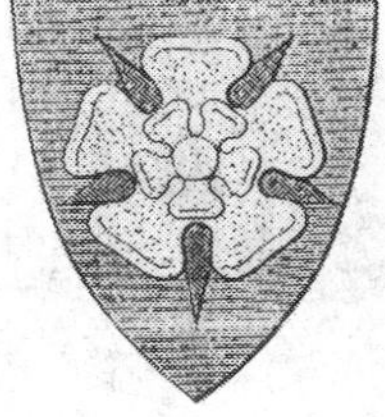
Hagenau

Hall in Swabia

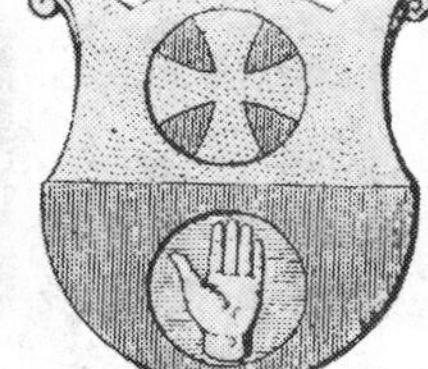
Hall in Swabia

Hamburg

Hamburg

Hamm

Hanau

Hanau-Munzenberg

Hannover

Hannover

Hannover

Heilbronn

Herford

Hersfeld

Hesse-Cassel

Hesse-Cassel

Hesse-Darmstadt

Hesse-Homburg

Hildesheim

Hildesheim

Hohenlohe-Neuenstein-Oehringen

Hohenzollern

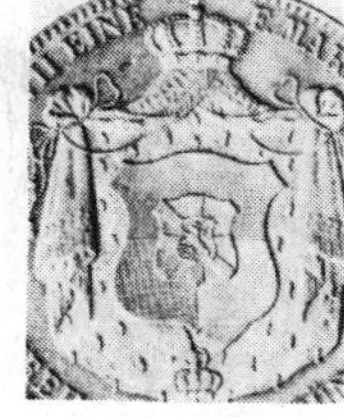
Hohenzollern-Hechingen

Jever

Julich-Berg

Kaufbeuren

Kempten

Landau

Liegnitz

Lindau

Lippe-Detmold

Lowenstein-Wertheim

Lubeck

Lubeck

Luneburg

GERMAN STATES INSTANT IDENTIFIER

Magdeburg

Mainz

Mainz

Mecklenburg-Strelitz

Memmingen

Muhlhausen

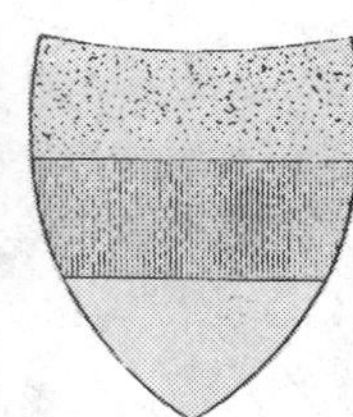
Munster

Munsterberg

Nassau

Nordhausen

Nurnberg

Oldenburg

Oldenburg

Oldenburg

Osnabruck

Paderborn

Paderborn

Passau

Passau

Prussia

Quedlinburg

Regensburg

Reuss-Greiz

Rhenish Confederation

Rostock

Rostock

Rothenburg

Rottweil

Saint Alban

Saxe-Altenburg

Saxe-Coburg-Gotha

Saxe-Meiningen

Saxe-Saalfield

Saxe-Weimar

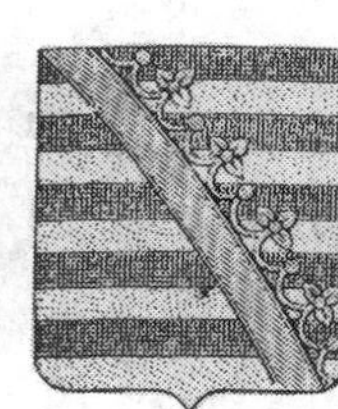
Saxony

Saxony

Schaumburg-Lippe

Schmalkalden

Schwarzburg

Schwarzburg-Rudolstadt

Schwarzburg-Sondershausen

Schwarzenberg

GERMAN STATES INSTANT IDENTIFIER

Solms-Laubach

Speyer

Stade

Stolberg-Stolberg

Stralsund

Teutonic Order

Trier

Waldeck-Pyrmont

Wismar

Wismar

Worms

Wurttemberg

Wurzburg

Wurzburg

NUMISMATIC SOCIETIES

A great many numismatic organizations exist today. They offer their members a wide variety of services and benefits. Formeost among these are their publications which present information often previously unpublished. Many sponsor major educational programs at large conventions, maintain extensive libraries, and prepare regular auctions for their membership. Assistance with research is an important hallmark of some societies. Locating other collectors with similar interests may also be easily achieved through membership in such groups.

Listed here are some of the national and international organizations and societies active at this time:

American Israel Numismatic Association
5150 W. Copand Rd., Ste. 1193
Margate, Florida 33063 , U.S.A.

American Numismatic Association
818 North Cascade Ave.
Colorado Springs, Colorado 80903, U.S.A.

American Numismatic Society
Broadway at 155th Street
New York, New York 10032, U.S.A.

Asociacion Numismatica Espanola
Gra via de las Corts
Catalanes, 627, pra. la.
08010 Barcelona, Spain

Canadian Numismatic Association
Box 226
Barrie, Ontario, Canada L4M 4T2

Centro Numismatico Buenos Aires
Av. San Juan 2630
(1232) Buenos Aires, Argentina

Clube Numismatic Association Numismatique (C.I.N.)
Rua Angelina Vidal, 40
1100 Lisbon - Portugal

Commission Internationale Numismatique (C.I.N.)
Rutimeyer Strasse 12
CH-4054 Basel
Switzerland

Czech & Slovak Numismatic Society
P.O. Box 36206
San Jose, California 65158, U.S.A.

Deutsche Numismatische Gesellschaft
Dr. R. Albert
Hans-Purrman-Allee 26
D-6720 Speyer, Germany

Hellenic Numismatic Society
Didotou 45
10680 Anthens, Greece

La Societe Americaine Pour L'Etude De La Numismatique Francaise
5140 East Boulevard N.W.
Canton, Ohio 44718, U.S.A.

Lithuania Numismatic Association
(The Knight)
P.O. Box 612
Columbia, Maryland 21045, U.S.A.

Malaysia Numismatic Society
P.O. Box 12367
Kuala Lumpur, 50776
Malaysia

Nordisk Numis Union
Kgl Mont - OG
Medaillesamling
National Musset
Kopenhagen, Denmark

Numismatic Association of Australia
Box 1920R
GPO Melbourne
Victoria 3001, Australia

Numismatic Association of Thailand
Royal Mint
11017 Pradipat Road
Bangkok, Thailand

Numismatics International
P.O. Box 670013
Dallas, Texas 75367, U.S.A.

Numismatic Society of India
P.O. Box Hindu University
Varanasi, india 221-005

Numismatischer Verein Zurich
Postfach 4584
8022 Zurich, Switzerland

Oriental Numismatic Society
30 Warren Road
Woodley, Reading, Berks.
United Kingdom RG5 3AR
American Section
P.O. Box 356
New Hope, Pennsylvania 18938, U.S.A.

Royal Numismatic Society
Dept. Coins/Medals
British Museum
London, England WC1B 3DG

Royal Numismatic Soceity of New Zealand
G.P.O. Box 2023
Wellington, New Zealand

Russian Numismatic Society
P.O. Box 3013
Alexandria, Virginia 22302, U.S.A.

Sodiedade Portuguesa De Numismatica
Rua De Costa Cabral, 664
4200 Porto, Portugal

Societe Royale de Numimatique de Belgique
Ave. Leopold 28A
B1330 Rixensart, Belgium

South Africa Numismatic Society
P.O. Box 1689
Capt Town 8000, South Africa

Turkish Numismatic Society
P.K. 258 Osmanbey
Istanbul, Turkey

Verband Der Deutschen Munzvereine
(Association of German Numismatic Societies)
Reisenbergstr. 58A
8000 Munich 60, Germany

MONOGRAMS

MJ
Maximilian IV Joseph
Berg

CC99
Christian IX
Danish West Indies

V OC
Dutch East India
Co. (Indonesia)

CVII
Christian VII
Danish West Indies

CCX
Christian X
Danish West Indies

G
Georg
Mecklenburg-Strelitz

CWF
Carl Wilhelm
Ferdinand
Brunswick-
Wolfenbuttel

H7
Haakon VII
Norway

A
Albert I
Belgium

GRI
Georgius Rex
Imperator
New Guinea

L
Leopold II
Belgium

EAR
Ernest August Rex
Hannover

FRVI
Frederik VI Rex
Denmark

CX
Christian X
Denmark

A
Albert I
Belgium

AF
Adolph Friederich IV
Mecklenburg-Strelitz

B
Baudouin I
Belgium

C
Cayenne
French Guiana

CL
Carl & Louise
Saxe-Meiningen

CR
Christian VIII (Denmark)
Tranquebar

FW
Friedrich Wilhelm
Mecklenburg-Strelitz

C7
Christian VII
Tranquebar

C7
Christian VII
Denmark

CIX
Christian IX
Denmark

CCX
Christian X
Denmark

CCXIII
Charles XIII
Sweden

CLXIV
Carl XIV Johann
Norway

CXIV
Carl XIV Johann
Sweden

EP
Elizabeth-Philip
Great Britain

ERI
Edward Rex
Imperator
New Guinea

EIIR
Elizabeth II Regina
Cook Isl.

FA
Friedrich August
Lubeck Bishopric

FF
Friedrich Franz
Mecklenburg-
Schwerin

FJI
Franz Joseph I
Austria

O
Oscar I
Sweden

AFC
Alexius Friedrich
Christian
Anhalt-Bernburg

NII
Nicholas II
Russia

FRVII
Frederik VII Rex
Danish West Indies
Denmark

FC
Friedrich Christian
Brandenburg-
Bayreuth

AIII
Alexander III
Russia

W
William I
Netherlands

LLX
Ludwig X
Hesse-Darmstadt

MONOGRAMS

MJ
Maximilian IV Joseph
Berg

FI
Frederick IX & Ingrid
Denmark

F VI R
Fred. VI Denmark
Tranquebar

FVII
Frederick VII
Denmark

FF8
Frederick VIII
Denmark

F IX R
Frederick IX
Denmark

FVII
Ferdinand VII
Mexico

PI
Paul I
Russia

FVII
Ferdinand VII
Mexico

FW
Friedrich Wilhelm III
Prussia

GA IV
Gustav Adolf IV
Sweden

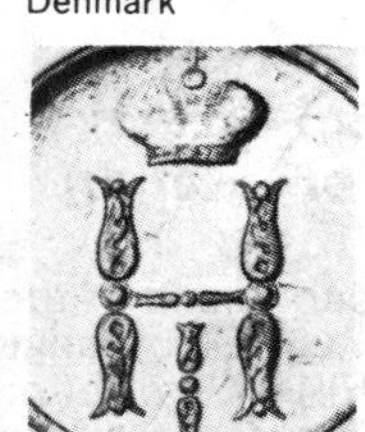
HI
Nicholas I
Russia

HC
Henri Christophe
Haiti

HVII
Haakon VII
Norway

HN
Hieronymus
Napoleon
Westphalia

J
Joachim (Murat)
Berg

E(K)I II
Katherine II
Russia

L
Ludwig
Hesse-Darmstadt

L
Leopold
Belgium

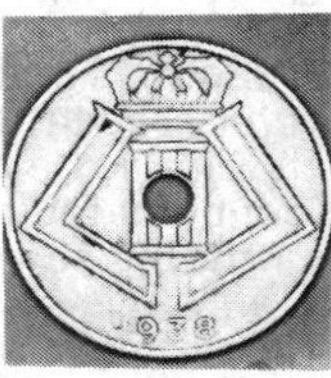
LL III
Leopold III
Belgium

LL
Louis XVIII
Antwerp

C XIVJ
Carl XIV Johann
Norway

M
Morelos
Revolutionary
Mexico

M 2 R
Margrethe II Regina
Denmark

NII
Nicholas II
Russia

NI
Nicholas I
Russia

NFP
Nicholas Friedrich
Peter
Oldenburg

OII
Oscar II
Norway

E
Ernest I
Saxe-Coburg-Gotha

O V
Olav V
Norway

P I
Paul I
Russia

P III
Peter III
Russia

R
Rainier III
Monaco

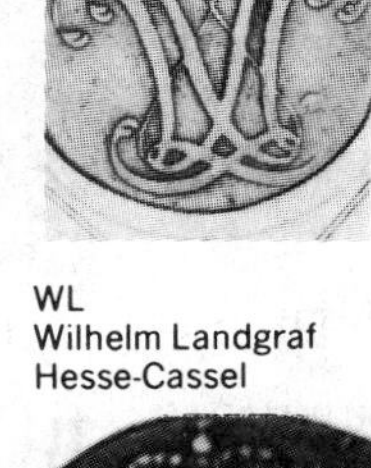
WL
Wilhelm Landgraf
Hesse-Cassel

WR
William Rex
Hannover

PFA
Peter Friedrich
August
Oldenburg

OII
Oscar II
Sweden

GR
Georgius Rex
Hannover

FRVI
Frederik VI Rex
Tranquebar

PF
Paul Friedrich
Mecklenburg-
Schwerin

FII
Friedrich II
Wurttemberg

FER VII
Ferdinand VII
(Spain) Gerona

ILLUSTRATED GUIDE TO EASTERN MINT NAMES

PREPARED ESPECIALLY FOR THE **STANDARD CATALOG OF WORLD COINS**

Compiled by Harry S. Scherzer.
Scrip typeset by Ketab Corporation

Eastern mint names are basically composed of the Arabic alphabet which in fact covers a number of languages — Arabic is Semitic: Persian is Indo-European; and Malayan is in the Malayo-Polynesian group. Differences are not just of dialect, they are of basic structure. However, Arabic itself is the really important one, bearing a relationship to other Oriental languages not unlike that of Latin to the languages of Europe. Just as medieval European coins are inscribed in Latin, so are the majority of the coins of North African, Turkish, Persian, and Indian origin inscribed until very recent times in Arabic. A limited knowledge of Persian will also be necessary for unravelling the Persian poetic couplets found on Indian and Persian coins particularly during the seventeenth and eighteenth centuries A.D.

(Courtesy of Richard J. Plant)

Mint name	Arabic
ANKARA Turkey	انقره
AL-'ARAISH "Larache", Morocco	العرايش
AL-'ARAISHAN "Larache", Morocco	العرايشة
ABUSHAHR "Bushire", Iran	ابو شهر
ADRANAH "Edirne", Turkey	ادرنة
AFGHANISTAN	افغانستان
AHMADABAD Bombay, India-British	احمد اباد
AHMADNAGAR-FARRUKHABAD Afghanistan	احمدنكر فرخ اباد
AHMADPUR See "Bahawalpur", Afghanistan	احمد پور
AHMADSHAHI See "Ashraf Al-Bilad" and "Qandahar", Afghanistan	احمد شاهى
AJMAN See "United Arab Emirates"	اجمان
AKSU China-Sinkiang	اقصو
ALGERIA See "Al-Jaza 'Iriyat"	—
BI-ANGLAND "In England" (Birmingham) For Morocco	بانكلند
BI-ANGLAND "In England" (London) For Morocco	بانكلند
DAULAT ANJAZANCHIYAH "The State of Anjazanchiyah" See Comoros	دولة انجزنجية
ANWALA "Aonla," Afghanistan	انوله
AL-ARABIYAT AS-SA'UDIYAT "Saudi-Arabian", Saudi Arabia	العربية السعودية
ARDEBIL Iran	اردبيل
ARKAT "Arcot", India-French	اركات
ASHRAF AL-BILAD "Most Noble of Cities" See "Ahmadshahi", Afghanistan	اشرف البلاد

ILLUSTRATED GUIDE TO EASTERN MINT NAMES

ASTARABAD
Iran
استراباد

ATCHEH
Indonesia
اجه

ATTOCK
Afghanistan
اتك

AZIMABAD
See "Patna", Bengal, India-British
عظيم اباد

BACAIM (no legends)
See "India-Portuguese"
—

BADAKHSHAN
See Afghanistan
بد خشان

BAGCHIH-SERAI
See "Krim"
باغجه سراي

BAGHDAD
Iraq
بغداد

BAHAWALPUR
See "Ahmadpur" and "Dar Es-Surur", Afghanistan
بها ولپور

BAHRAIN
See "El-Bahrain"
بحرين

EL-BAHRAIN
"Of the Two Seas", Bahrain
البحرين

BALKH
See "Umm Al-Bilad", Afghanistan
بلخ

BANARAS
"Awadh", Bengal, India-British
بنارس

BANDAR ABBAS
Iran
بندر عباس

BANJARMASIN
Indonesia
بنجرمسن

BARELI
Afghanistan
بريلي

BI BARIZ
"In Paris"
For Morocco
بباريز

BEHBEHAN
Iran
بهبهان

BERLIN
For Morocco
برلين

BHAKHAR
Afghanistan
بهكر

BOMBAY
See "Munbai", Bombay, India-British
—

BORUJERD
Iran
بروجرد

NEGRI BRUNEI
"State of Brunei", Brunei
نكري بروني

BRUSAH
"Bursa", Turkey
بروسة

BUKHARA
See Russian Turkestan
بخارا

BUSHIRE
See "Abushahr", Iran
—

CALCUTTA
See "Kalkatah", Bengal, India-British
كلكته

COCHIN
See India-Dutch and "V.O.C.", India-Dutch
—

COMOROS
See "Anjazanchiyah",
"The Largest of the Islands", Comoros
كموز

DACCA
See "Jahangirnagar", Bengal, India-British
—

DAMAO (no legends)
See India-Portuguese
—

DAR AL-AMAN
"Abode of Security" (honorific)
See "Multan"
دار الامان

DAR AL-ISLAM
See Bahawalpur, India Princely States
دار الاسلام

DAR AL-MULK
"Abode of the King" (honorific)
See "Kabul"
دارالملك

DAR AL-NUSRAT
"Abode of the New (Town?)" (honorific)
See "Herat"
دارالنصرت

DAR AL-KHILAFAT
"Abode of the Caliphate" (honorific)
See "Tehran" and "Yemen"
دار الخلافة

DAR AS-SALAM
"Abode of Peace" (honorific)
See "Ligkeh", Thailand
دار السلام

DAR AS-SULTANAT
"Abode of the Sultanate" (honorific)
See "Herat" and "Kabul", Afghanistan
دار السلطنة

DAR AS-SURUR
"Abode of Happiness" (honorific)
See "Bahawalpur", Afghanistan
دار السرور

DARBAND
Iran
دربند

ILLUSTRATED GUIDE TO EASTERN MINT NAMES

DARFUR See "Al-Fasher", Sudan	الفشير
DEHLI See "Shajahanabad", Afghanistan	دهلي
DELI Indonesia	دلي
DERA "Dera Ghazi Khan", Afghanistan	ديره
DERAJAT "Dera Ishmael Khan", Afghanistan	ديره جات
DEZFUL Iran	دزفول
DIU (no legends) See India-Portuguese	—
DJIBOUTI See "Jaibuti"	—
EDIRNE See "Adranah", Turkey	—
EGYPT See "Misr" and "Al-Misriyat"	—
ERAVAN Iran	ايروان
FARRUKHABAD Bengal, India-British	فرخ اباد
AL-FASHER See "Darfur", Sudan	الفشير
FES "Fez", Morocco	فاس
FERGANA See "Khoqand", Russian Turkestan	فرغانة
FILASTIN "Palestine", Israel	فلسطين
AL-FUJAIRAH See "United Arab Emirates"	الفجيره
GANJAH Iran	كنجه
GERMAN EAST AFRICA See "Sharakat Almaniyah", Tanzania	شراكة المانيا
GHAZNI Afghanistan	غزني
GOA (no legends) See India-Portuguese	—
HAIDARABAD SIND MINT Afghanistan	حيدرآباد سند
HALEB "Allepo", Syria	حلب
HAMADAN Iran	همدان
AL-HARAR Ethiopia-Eritrea	الهرر
AL-HEJAZ Saudi Arabia-Hejaz	الحجاز
HERAT See "Dar Al-Nushat" and "Dar As-Sultanat", Afghanistan	هرات
HERAT Iran	هرات
ILI China-Sinkiang	الي
IRAN	ايران
AL-IRAQ "Iraque"	العراق
AL-IRAQIYAT "Iraqi," Iraq	العراقية
ISFAHAN Iran	اصفهان
ISLAMBUL Turkey	اسلامبول
ITALIAN SOMALILAND See "Al-Somal Al-Italianiah", Somalia	الصومال الايطليانية
JAHANGIRNAGAR See "Dacca", Bengal, India-British	جهانكيرنكر
BI-JAIBUTI "In Djibouti", Djibouti	بجيبوتي
JAVA Indonesia	جاوا
JAZA'IR Algeria-Algiers	جزاير
AL-JAZA'IRIYAT Algeria-Algiers	الجزايرة
JERING "Jaring", Thailand	جريج
AL-JOMHURIYAT EL-IRAQIYAT "The Iraqi Republic" Iraq	الجمهورية العرقية
AL-JOMHURIYAT EL-LUBNANIYAT "The Lebanese Republic", Lebanon	الجمهورية البنانية

ILLUSTRATED GUIDE TO EASTERN MINT NAMES

AL-JOMHURIYAT AL-MUTTAHIDAH AL-ARABIYAT
"United Arab Republic"
See "Egypt, Syria, Yemen"
الجمهورية المتحدة العربية

AL-JOMHURIYAT AS-SUDAN
"The Sudanese Republic", Sudan
الجمهورية السودان

AL-JOMHURIYAT AS-SURIYAT
"The Syrian Republic", Syria
الجمهورية السورية

AL-JOMHURIYAT AL-TUNISIAT
"The Tunisian Republic", Tunisia
الجمهورية التونسية

AL-JOMHURIYAT AL-TURKIYAH
"The Turkish Republic", Turkey
الجمهورية توركية

JORDAN
See "Al-Urduniyat" and "Al-Mamlakat, etc.," Jordan
—

KABUL
See "Dar Al-Mulk" > AH1163 and "Dar As-Sultanat" >AH1164, Afghanistan
كابل

KAFFA
Krim, Russian Caucasia
كفه

KALKATAH
"Calcutta", Bengal, India-British
كلكته

KASHAN
Iran
كاشان

KASHMIR
Afghanistan
كشمير

KASHQUAR
China-Sinkiang
كشقر

KEDAH
See "Bilad Kedah" and "Bilad Al-Perlis Kedah", Malaysia
كداه

KELANTAN
See "Khalifat Al-Mu'Minin" and "Negri Kelantin", Malaysia
كلنتن

KEMASIN
Malaysia
كماسن

KERMAN
Iran
كرمان

KERMANSHAHAN
See "Kermanshah", Iran
كرمانشاهان

KHALIFAT AL-MU'MININ
"Commander of the Faithful" (honorific)
See "Kelantin" and "Trengganu"
خليفة المؤمنين

KHALIFAT AL-KARAM
"Noble Caliph" (honorific)
See "Patani"
خليفة الكرم

KHANABAD
Afghanistan
خان اباد

KHOQAND
See Russian Turkestan
خوقند

KHUI
See "Khoy", Iran
خوى

AL-KHURFAH
See "Yemen"
الخرفاه

KHUTAN
China-Sinkiang
ختن

KHWAREZM
Russian Turkestan-Khiva
خوارزم

KOSOVAH
Turkey
قوصوه

KOTSHA
China-Sinkiang
كوتشر

AL-KUWAIT
Kuwait
الكويت

LADAKH
Afghanistan
لداخ

LAHEJ
See "Yemen"
لحج

LAHIJAN
See "Gilan", Iran
لاهيجان

LAHORE
Afghanistan
لاهور

LEBANON
See "Al-Lubnaniyat" and "Jomhuriyat, etc."
—

AL-LIBIYAT
"Libyan", Libya
الليبية

LIBYA
See "Al-Libyat" and "Mamlakat, etc."
ليبيا

NEGRI LIGKEH
"State of Ligeh (or Ligor)"
See "Dar As-Salam", Thialand
نكري لغكه

ILLUSTRATED GUIDE TO EASTERN MINT NAMES

Mint name	Arabic
AL-LUBNANIYAT "Lebanese", Lebanon	النلنية
MACHHLIPATAN See "Mazulipatam", India-French "Masulipatam", India-Madras	مچهلي پتن
MACHHLIPATAN-BANDAR See "Machhlipatan", India-Madras	مچهلي پتن بندر
AL-MAGHRIBIYAT "Moroccan", Morocco	المغربية
TANAH MALAYU "Land of the Malays" See "Sumatra", Indonesia and "Malacca", Malaysia	تانه ملايو
PULU MALAYU "Island of the Malays" See "Sumatra", Indonesia	فولو ملايو
MALUKA Indonesia	ملوکی
AL-MAMLAKAT AL-ARABIYAT AL-SA'UDIYAT "The Kingdom of Saudi Arabia"	المملكة العربية السعودية
AL-MAMLAKAT AL-LIBIYAT "The Kingdom of Libya"	المملكة الليبية
AL-MAMLAKAT AL-MAGHRIBIYAT "The Kingdom of Morocco"	المملكة المغربية
AL-MAMLAKAT AL-MUTAWAKELIYAT AL-YEMENIAT "The Mutawakelite Kingdom of Yemen"	المملكة المتوكلية اليمنية
AL-MAMLAKAT AL-MISRIYAT "The Kingdom of Egypt"	المملكة المصرية
AL-MAMLAKAT AL-URDUNIYAT AL-HASHEMIYAT "The Hashemite Kingdom of Jordan"	المملكة الاردنية الهاشمية
MANASTIR Turkey	مناستر
MARAGHEH Iran	مراغه
MARAKESH "Marrakech", Morocco	مراكش
AL-MASCARA Algeria-Algiers	المعسكر
MASH'HAD Afghanistan	مشهد
MASH'HAD Iran	مشهد
MASULIPATAM See "Machhlipatan", India-Madras	—
MAZANDARAN Iran	مازندران
MAZULIPATAM See "Machhlipatan", India-French	—
MEDEA Algeria-Algiers	مديه
MEKHA "Mecca", Saudi-Arabia	مكة
MENANGKABAU Indonesia	منفكابو
MIKNAS "Meknes", Morocco	مكناس
MIKNASAH "Meknes", Morocco	مكناسة
MISR Egypt	مصر
AL-MISRIYAT "Egptian", Egypt	المصرية
AL-MOHAMMEDIYAT ASH-SHERIFATE "The Mohammedan Sherifate" or "Empire Cherifien" (French), Morocco	المحمدية الشريفة
MOMBASA Kenya	ممباسه
MOROCCO See "Al-Maghribyat" and "Al-Mohammediyat Ash-Sherifate"	—
MOXOUDABAT See "Murshidabad", India-French	—
MUBARAK "Auspicious" (honorific) See "Rikab"	مبارک
AL-MAKALA "Mukalla" See "Yemen"	المكلا
MULTAN See "Dar Al-Aman", Afghanistan	ملتان

ILLUSTRATED GUIDE TO EASTERN MINT NAMES

Mint	Legend
MUNBAI See "Bombay", India-British	منبي
MURADABAD Afghanistan	مراد اباد
MURSHIDABAD See "Moxoudabat", India-French	مرشد اباد
MURSHIDABAD Bengal, India-British	مرشد اباد
MUSCAT Oman	مسقط
NAJIBABAD Afghanistan	نجيب اباد
NAKAPATTANAM (Tamil legends) "Negapatnam", India-Dutch	[illegible]
NAKHCHAWAN Iran	نخجوان
NEGAPATNAM See "Nakappattanam"	—
NEJD Saudi Arabia	نجد
NIHAWAND Iran	نهاوند
NUKHWI "Sheki", Iran	نخوى
NUKHWI See "Sheki", Russian Caucasia	نخوي
OMAN	عمان
OMDURMAN Sudan	ام درمان
PAHANG "Pahang Company", Malaysia	فاحغ
PAKISTAN	پاكستان
PALEMBANG Indonesia	فلمبغ
PALESTINE See "Filastin", Israel	—
PANA'HABAD "Shusha" See "Karabagh", Russian Caucasia	پناه باد
AL-PATANI See "Khalifat Al-Karam", "Khalifat Al-Mu'Minin" and "Bilad Al-Patani", Thailand	الفطاني
PATNA See "Azimabad", Bengal, India-British	پتنه
PULU PENANG "Prince of Wales Island", Malaysia	فولو فنيغ
NEGRI PERAQ "State of Perak", Malaysia	نكري فيرق
PULU PERCHA "Island of Sumatra", Indonesia	فولو فرج
PERLIS See "Kedah", Malaysia	—
PESHAWAR Afghanistan	پشاور
PHALICHERY SEE "Pondichery", India-French	پهلجري
PONDICHERY See "Phalichery", India-French	—
PONTIANAQ (no legends) Indonesia	—
PULICAT (no legends) See "India-Dutch"	—
QANDAHAR See "Ashraf Al-Bilad" and "Ahmadshahi", Afghanistan	قندهار
QATAR WA DUBAI "Qatar and Dubai", Qatar	قطرودبي
DAULAT QATAR "State of Qatar", Qatar	—
QAZWIN Iran	قزوين
QUAITI Yemen	قيطي
QUM Iran	قم
QUSANTINAT "Constantine", Algeria-Algiers	قسنطينة
QUSTINTINIYAH "Constantinople", Turkey	قسطنطنية
RA'NASH Iran	رعنش

ILLUSTRATED GUIDE TO EASTERN MINT NAMES

RABAT
See "Rabat Al-Fath", Morocco
رباط

RABAT AL-FATH
"Rabat", Morocco
رباط الفتح

RAS AL-KHAIMA
See "United Arab Emirates"
راس الخيمه

RASHT
Iran
رشت

REHMAN
Thailand
رحمن

REZA'IYEH
See "Urumi", Iran
رظاعيه

RIKAB
See "Mubarak", Afghanistan
ركاب

RIKAB
Iran
ركاب

SA'UJBALAQ
Iran
ساوج بلاق

SAGAR
Bengal, India-British
ساكر

SAHRIND
Afghanistan
شهرند

AL-SAIWI
See "Bilad Al-Saiwi",
"Sai", "Saiburi" and
"Teluban", Thailand
السيوي

SAN'A
See "Yemen", Yemen
Republic
سنة

SARAKHS
Iran
سرخس

SARHIND
See "Sahrind", Afghanistan
——

SARI
Iran
ساري

SARI POL
Afghanistan
سربل

SAUDI ARABIA
"See "Al-Hejaz", "Nejd"
and "Al-Arabiyat As-Sa'udiya",
Saudi Arabia
——

NEGRI SELANGHUR
"State of Selangor", Malaysia
نكري سلاغور

SELANIK
"Salonika", Turkey
سلانيك

SHAJAHANABAD
See "Dehli", Afghanistan
شاجهان اباد

SHAMAKHI
Russian Caucasia
شماخ

SHAMAKHA
Russian Caucasia
شماخه

SHARAKAT ALMANIYAH
"German Company" or
"German East Africa", Tanzania
شراكتة المانيا

ES-SHARJAH
See "United Arab Emirates"
الشارجة

SHIRAZ
Iran
شيراز

SHUSHTAR
Iran
شوشتر

NEGRI SIAK
"State of Siak", Indonesia
نكري سيك

SIMNAN
Iran
سمنان

SIND
Afghanistan
سند

AL-SOMAL AL-ITALIANIYAH
"Italian Somaliland", Somalia
الصومال الايطليانية

SULTANABAD
Iran
سلطاناباد

SUMENEP
Indonesia
سمنف

SURAT
See "Surate", India-French
سورت

SURAT
Bombay, India-British
سورت

AS-SURIYAT
"Syrian", Syria
السورية

AL-SUWAIR
"Essaouira Mogador", Morocco
الصوير

AL-SUWAIRAH
"Essaouira Mogador", Morocco
الصويرة

SYRIA
See "Haleb", As-Suriyat",
"Jomhuriyat, etc.", Syria
——

TABARISTAN
Iran
طبرستان

TABRIZ
Iran
تبريز

ILLUSTRATED GUIDE TO EASTERN MINT NAMES

TANGIER
See "Tanjah", Morocco —

TANJAH
"Tangier", Morocco طنجة

TAQIDEMT
Algeria-Algiers تاقدمت

TARABALUS GHARB
"Tripoli West", Libya طرابلس غرب

TARIM
See "Yemen" تريم

NEGRI TARUMON
"State of Tarumon", Indonesia نكري ترومن

TASHQURGHAN
Afghanistan تاش قورغان

TATTA
Afghanistan تته

TEGNAPATAM (no legends)
"Fort St. David", Madras, India-British —

TEHRAN
See "Dar Al-Khilafat", Iran طهران

TELLICHERY
Bombay, India-British تلچري

TETUAN
Morocco تطوان

TIFLIS
See Russia, Georgia تفليس

TRANQUEBAR (no legends)
See "India-Danish" —

TRENGKANU
See "Khalifat Al-Mu'Minin", Malaysia ترغكانو

TUNIS
Tunisia تونس

TUNISIA
See "Tunis", "Al-Tunisiyat", "Jomhuriyat, etc." —

AL-TUNISIYAT
"Tunisian," Tunisia التونسية

TURKEY
See "Turkiyah", "Jomhuriyat, etc." —

AL-TURKIYAH
"Turkish", Turkey التوركية

TUTICORIN (degenerate Nagari legends)
See "India-Dutch" —

TUYSERKAN
Iran توى سركان

TANAH UGI
"Land of the Bugis", Indonesia تانه اغيسى

UMM AL-BILAD
"Mother of Cities"
See "Balkh", Afghanistan ام البلاد

UMM AL-QAIWAIN
See "United Arab Emirates" ام القوين

UNITED ARAB EMIRATES —

UNITED ARAB REPUBLIC
See "Al-Jomhuriyat Al-Arabiyat AL-Muttahidah الامارات العربية المتحدة

AL-URDUNIYAT
"Jordanian", Jordan الاردنية

URUMCHI
China-Sinkiang ارومجي

URUMI
See "Reza'iyeh", Iran ارومى

USHI
China-Sinkiang اوش

WAN
"Van", Turkey وان

YARKHAND
China-Sinkiang يارقند

YARKHISSARMARAN
"Yanghissar"
China-Sinkiang يارکسارمرن

YAZD
Iran يزد

YEMEN
See "Sana", "Dar Al-Khilafat", Al-Yemeniyat", Mamlakat, etc." —

AL-YEMENIYAT
"The Yemen" اليمنية

ZANJAN
Iran زنجان

ZANJIBARA
"Zanzibar", Tanzania زنجباراه

A Guide To International Numerics

	ENGLISH	CZECH	DANISH	DUTCH	ESPERANTO	FRENCH
¼	one-quarter	jeden-ctvrt	én-fjerdedel	een-kwart	unu-kvar'ono	un-quart
½	one-half	jeden-polovicni or pul	én-halv	een-half	unu-du'one	un-demi
1	one	jeden	én	een	unu	un
2	two	dve	to	twee	du	deux
3	three	tri	tre	drie	tri	trois
4	four	ctyri	fire	vier	kvar	quatre
5	five	pet	fem	vijf	kvin	cinq
6	six	sest	seks	zes	ses	six
7	seven	sedm	syv	zeven	sep	sept
8	eight	osm	otte	acht	ok	huit
9	nine	devet	ni	negen	nau	neuf
10	ten	deset	ti	tien	dek	dix
12	twelve	dvanáct	tolv	twaalf	dek du	douze
15	fifteen	patnáct	femten	vijftien	dek kvin	quinze
20	twenty	dvacet	tyve	twintig	du'dek	vingt
24	twenty-four	dvacet-ctyri	tyve-fire	twintig-vier	du'dek-kvar	vingt-quatre
25	twenty-five	dvacet-pet	tyve-fem	twintig-vijf	du'dek-kvin	vingt-cinq
30	thirty	tricet	tredive	dertig	tri'dek	trente
40	forty	ctyricet	fyrre	veertig	kvar'dek	quarante
50	fifty	padesát	halvtreds	vijftig	kvin'dek	cinquante
60	sixty	sedesát	tres	zestig	ses'dek	soixante
70	seventy	sedmdesát	halvfjerds	zeventig	sep'dek	soixante-dix
80	eighty	osemdesát	firs	tachtig	ok'dek	quatre-vingt
90	ninety	devadesát	halvfems	negentig	nau'dek	quatre-vingt-dix
100	one hundred	jedno sto	én-hundrede	een-honderd	unu-cento	un-cent
1000	thousand	tisíc	tusind	duizend	mil	mille

	GERMAN	HUNGARIAN	INDONESIAN	ITALIAN	NORWEGIAN	POLISH
¼	einviertel	egy-negyed	satu-suku	uno-quarto	en-fjerdedel	jeden-ćwierć
½	einhalb	egy-fél	satu-setengah	uno-mezzo	en-halv	jeden-polowa
1	ein	egy	satu	uno	en	jeden
2	zwei	kettö	dud	due	to	dwa
3	drei	három	tiga	tre	tre	trzy
4	vier	négy	empot	quattro	fire	cztery
5	fünf	öt	lima	cinque	fem	pięć
6	sechs	hat	enam	sei	seks	sześć
7	sieben	hét	tudjuh	sette	sju	siedem
8	acht	nyolc	delapan	otto	atte	osiem
9	neun	kilenc	sembilan	nove	ni	dziewięć
10	zehn	tíz	sepuluh	dieci	ti	dziesięć
12	zwolf	tizenkettő	dua belas	dodici	tolv	dwanaście
15	fünfzehn	tizenöt	lima belas	quindici	femten	pietnaście
20	zwanzig	húsz	dua pulah	venti	tjue or tyve	dwadzieścia
24	vierundzwanzig	húsz-négy	dua pulah-empot	venti-quattro	tjue-fire or tyve-fire	dwadzieścia-cztery
25	fünfundzwanzig	húsz-öt	dua pulah-lima	venti-cinque	tjue-fem or tyve-fem	dwadzieścia-pięć
30	dreissig	harminc	tigapulah	trenta	tredve	trzydzieści
40	vierzig	negyven	empat pulah	quaranta	forti	czterdrieści
50	fünfzig	otven	lima pulah	cinquanta	femti	pięćdziesiat
60	sechzig	hatvan	enam pulah	sessanta	seksti	sześćdziesiat
70	siebzig	hetven	tudjuh pulu	settanta	sytti	siedemdziesiat
80	achtzig	nyolcvan	delapan puluh	ottanta	atti	osiemdziesiat
90	neunzig	kilencven	sembilan puluh	novanta	nitty	dziewięćdziesiat
100	ein hundert	egy-száz	satu-seratus	uno-cento	en-hundre	jeden-sto
1000	tausend	ezer	seribu	mille	tusen	tysiac

	PORTUGUESE	RUMANIAN	SERBO-CROATIAN	SPANISH	SWEDISH	TURKISH
¼	um-quarto	un-sfert	jedan-ceturtina	uno-cuarto	en-fjärdedel	bir-ceyrek
½	um-meio	o-jumatate	jedan-polovina	uno-medio	en-hälft	bir-yarim
1	um	un	jedan	uno	en	bir
2	dois	doi	dva	dos	tva	iki
3	três	trei	tri	tres	tre	üc
4	quatro	patru	cetiri	cuatro	fyra	dört
5	cinco	cinci	pet	cinco	fem	bes
6	seis	sase	sest	seis	sex	alti
7	sete	sapte	sedam	siete	sju	yedi
8	oito	opt	osam	ocho	atta	sekiz
9	nove	noua	devet	nueve	nio	dokuz
10	dez	zece	deset	diez	tio	on
12	doze	doisprezece	dvanaest	doce	tolv	on iki
15	quinze	cincisprezece	petnaest	quince	femton	on bes
20	vinte	douazeci	dvadeset	veinte	tjugu	yirmi
24	vinte-quatro	douazeci-patru	dvadeset-cetiri	veinte-cuarto	tjugu-fyra	yirmi-dört
25	vinte-cinco	douazeci-cinci	dvadeset-pet	veinte-cinco	tjugu-fem	yirmi-bes
30	trinta	treizeci	trideset	treinta	trettio	otuz
40	quarenta	patruzeci	cetrdeset	cuarenta	fyrtio	kirk
50	cinqüenta	cincizeci	padeset	cincuenta	femtio	elli
60	sessenta	saizeci	sezdeset	sesenta	sextio	altmis
70	setenta	saptezeci	sedamdeset	setenta	sjuttio	yetmis
80	oitenta	optzeci	osamdeset	ochenta	attio	seksen
90	noventa	nouazeci	devedeset	noventa	nittio	doksan
100	um-cem	o-suta	jedan-sto	uno-ciento	en-hundra	bir-yüz
1000	mil	mie	hiljada	mil	tusen	bin

AFGHANISTAN

The Islamic State of Afghanistan, which occupies a mountainous region of Southwest Asia, has an area of 251,773 sq. mi. (652,090 sq. km.) and a population of 21.3 million. Presently about a fifth of the total population lives (mostly in Pakistan) in exile as refugees. Capital: Kabul. It is bordered by Iran, Pakistan, Turkmenistan, Uzbekistan, Tajikistan, and China's Sinkiang Province. Agriculture and herding are the principal industries; textile mills and cement factories add to the industrial sector. Cotton, wool, fruits, nuts, oil, sheepskin coats and hand-woven carpets are normally exported but foreign trade has been interrupted since 1979.

Because of its strategic position astride the ancient land route to India, Afghanistan (formerly known as Aryana and Khorasan) was invaded by Darius I, Alexander the Great, various Scythian tribes, the White Huns, the Arabs, the Turks, Genghis Khan, Tamerlane, the Mughals, the Persians, and in more recent times by Great Britain. It was a powerful empire under the Kushans, Hephthalites, Ghaznavids and Ghorids. The name Afghanistan, "Land of the Afghans," came into use in the eighteenth and nineteenth centuries to describe the realm of the Afghan kings. For a short period, this mountainous region was the easternmost frontier of the Iranian world, with strong cultural influences from the Turks and Mongols to the north and India to the south.

Previous to 1747, Afghan Kings ruled not only in Afghanistan, but also in India, of which Sher Shah Suri was one. Ahmad Shah Abdali, founder of the Durrani dynasty, established his rule at Qandahar in 1747. His clan was known as Saddozai.He conquered large territories in India and eastern Iran, which were lost by his grandson Shah Zaman. A new family, the Barakzai, drove the Durrani king out of Kabul, the capital, in 1819, but the Durranis were not eliminated completely until 1858. Further conflicts among the Barakzai prevented full unity until the reign of Abdur Rahman in 1880. In 1929, King Amanullah, grandson of Abdul Rahman, was driven out of the country by a commoner known as Baccha-i-Saqao, "Son of the Water-Carrier," who ruled as Habibullah for less than a year before he was defeated by Muhammad Nadir Shah, a relative of the Barakzai. The last king, Muhammad Zahir Shah, became a constitutional, though still autocratic, monarch in 1964. In 1973 a coup d'etat displaced him and created the Republic of Afghanistan. A subsequent military coup established the pro-Soviet Democratic Republic of Afghanistan in 1978. Mounting resistance in the countryside and violence within the government led to the Soviet invasion of late 1979 and the installation of Babrak Karmal as prime minister. A brutal civil war ensued, which continues to the present, even after Soviet forces withdrew in 1989 and Karmal's government was defeated. An unstable coalition of former *Mujahideen* (Freedom Fighters) factions is currently trying to govern.

Afghanistan's traditional coinage was much like that of its neighbors Iran and India. There were four major mints: Kabul, Qandahar, Balkh and Herat. The early Durranis also controlled mints in Iran and India. On gold and silver coins, the inscriptions in Persian (called *Dari* in Afghanistan) included the name of the mint city and, normally, of the ruler recognized there, but some issues are anonymous. The arrangement of the inscriptions, and frequently the name of the ruler, was different at each mint. Copper coins were controlled locally and usually did not name any ruler. For these reasons the coinage of each mint is treated separately. The relative values of gold, silver, and copper coins were not fixed but were determined in the marketplace.

In 1890 Abdur Rahman had a modern mint set up in Kabul using British minting machinery and the help of British advisors. The other mints were closed down, except for the issue of local coppers. The new system had sixty paisa to the rupee; intermediate denominations also had special names.

Until 1919, coins were dated by the lunar Islamic Hijri calendar (AH), often with the king's regnal year as a second date. The solar Hijri (SH) calendar was introduced in 1919 (1337 AH, 1298 SH). The rebel Habibullah reinstated lunar Hijri dating (AH 1347-50), but the solar calendar was used thereafter. The solar Hijri year begins on the first day of spring, about March 21. Adding 621 to the SH year yields the AD year in which it begins.

RULERS

Names of rulers are shown in Perso-Arabic script in the style usually found on their coins; they are not always in a straight line.

DURRANI OR SADDOZAI DYNASTY

Shah Shuja al-Mulk, 1st reign,
شاه شجاع الملک
AH1216/1801AD (no coins)

Mahmud Shah, 1st reign,
محمود شاه
AH1216-1218/1801-1803AD

Qaisar Shah,
قیصر شاه
AH1218/1803AD

Shah Shuja al-Mulk, 2nd reign,
AH1218-1224/1803-1808AD

Mahmud Shah, 2nd reign,
AH1224-1233/1808-1817AD

Ayyub Shah, Puppet of Dost Muhammad,
ایوب شاه
AH1233-1239/1817-1823AD

Sherdil Khan
AH1240-1242/1824-1826AD

Purdil Khan
AH1242-1245/1826-1829AD

Sultan Muhammad, at Peshawar
سلطان محمد
AH1247-1250/1831-1834AD

Kohandil Khan, 1st reign, at Qandahar
کهندل خان
AH1245-1254/1829-1838AD

Shah Shuja al-Mulk, as nominee of British East India Co., 3rd reign,
AH1255-1258/1839-1842AD

Fath Jang
فتح جنگ
AH1258/1842AD

Shahpur Shah
شاپور شاه
AH1258/1842AD

Kohandil Khan, 2nd reign
AH1259-1272/1843-1855AD

Rahmolil Khan
AH1272/1855AD

Succession at Kashmir, AH1221-1234

Qaisar Shah,
AH1221-1223/1806-1808AD

Ata Muhammad, called Shah Nur al Din on coins,
شاه نور الدین
AH1223-1228/1808-1813AD

Azim Khan, coins in name of Mahmud Shah,
AH1228-1234/1813-1818AD

Succession at Herat, AH1216-1298

Mahmud Shah,
AH1216-1245/1801-1829AD

Kamran Shah,
کامران شاه
AH1245-1258/1829-1842AD

Yar Muhammad Khan Barakzai,
یار محمد خان بارکزای
AH1258-1267/1842-1851AD

Muhammad Yusuf Khan Sadozai,
محمد یوسف خان سادوزای
AH1267-1272/1851-1856AD

Iranian Occupation of Herat (coins in name of Nasir al-Din Shah):
AH1272-1280/1856-1863AD

Sher Ali, AH1280-1296/1863-1879AD

Muhammad Yaqub,
محمد یعقوب
AH1296-1298/1879-1881AD

thereafter, as in the rest of Afghanistan

BARAKZAI DYNASTY

Dost Muhammad, 1st reign, anonymous coinage
دوست محمد
AH1239-1255/1824-1839AD

British Occupation
AH1255-1258/1839-1842AD

Dost Muhammad, at Qandahar, 2nd reign,
"Akbar Amir" (Great King) in center of obv.
اکبر امیر
AH1272-1280/1855-1863AD

Sher Ali, 1st reign,
شیر علی
AH1280-1283/1863-1866AD

Muhammad Afzal,
محمد افضل
AH1283-1284/1866-1867AD

Muhammad A'zam,
محمد اعظم
AH1283-1285/1866-1868AD

Sher Ali, 2nd reign,
AH1285-1296/1868-1879AD

Muhammad Yaqub,
AH1296-1297/1879-1880AD

Wali Muhammad, at Kabul
والی محمد
AH1297/1880AD

Woli Sher Ali, at Qandahar
والی شیر علی
AH1297/1880AD

Abdur Rahman,
عبد الرحمن
AH1297-1319/1880-1901AD

Muhammad Ishaq, rebel at Balkh,
محمد اسحاق
AH1305-1306/1889AD

MINTNAMES

Hammered coins were struck at numerous mints in Afghanistan and adjacent lands. These are listed below, together with their honorific titles, and shown in the style ordinarily found on the coins.

Afghanistan — افغانستان

Ahmadpur, See Bahawalpur — احمد پور

Ahmadshahi, See Qandahar — احمد شاهی

'Ashraf al-Bilad', Most Noble of Cities — اشرف البلاد

Badakhshan — بدخشان

Bahawalpur — بهاولپور

'Dar as-Surur', Abode of Happiness — دار السرور

Balkh — بلخ

'Umm al-Bilad', Mother of Cities — ام البلاد

Bhakkar — بهکر

Dera, Dera Ghazi Khan — دیره

Mint	
Derajat	ديره جات
Dera Isma'il Khan	
Ghazni	غزني
Herat	هرات
Dar al-Nusrat Seat of Victory	دارالنصرت
'Dar as-Sultanat' Abode of the Sultanate	دار السلطنة
Jalalabad	جلا ل ا باد
Kabul	كابل
'Dar al-Mulk' Abode of the King	دارالملك
'Dar as-Sultanat' (see Herat)	
Kashmir	كشمير
Khanabad	خان اباد
Ladakh (Not usually clear on coins)	لداخ
Mashhad	مشهد
Multan	ملتان
'Dar al-Aman' Abode of Security	دار الامان
Peshawar	پشاور
Qandahar See Ahmadshahi	قندهار
Sar-i Pol	سرّپل
Tashqurghan	تاش قورغان

ANONYMOUS HAMMERED COPPER COINAGE

Afghan copper coins, prior to the beginning of machine-struck coinage in 1891, were not regulated by the central authorities. Mintmasters produced many types of hand-struck coinage including the use of old Afghan coins as blanks. Consequently, weights are quite random, and there are no denominations in the true sense of the term. All were known as 'Falus', and lots of mixed sizes were accounted by weight. Every few years, sometimes every year, coppers were recalled and recoined, at a fee, often substantial, which was paid to the mintmaster and formed his salary. This accounts for the large number of overstruck pieces, which are generally less desirable than clear singly struck specimens.

Hundreds of varieties were issued at the principal mints of Kabul and Ahmadshahi/Qandahar, and the following listing is only a representation of what exists. It is arranged chronologically by mint, to the extent that coins bear dates. A more detailed, but still very fragmentary listing is given by W.H. Valentine, in 'Modern Copper Coins of the Muhammadan States'. No attempt at a complete listing has ever been undertaken.

Prices are for well-struck specimens with clear design and date. Partial or overstruck coins are worth considerably less. Unrepresented types are worth about the same as listed pieces of the same mint.

IMPORTANT: Most types were used at one time or other at all mints. The type cannot therefore be used to determine the mint, which can ordinarily only be ascertained by reading the Persian inscription.

NOTE: Copper coins bearing the name of the issuing ruler are included under "Named Hammered Coinage", below, by mint. For later anonymous issues, see the local coppers listed after the milled coinage.

Ahmadshahi Mint

(See also Qandahar)

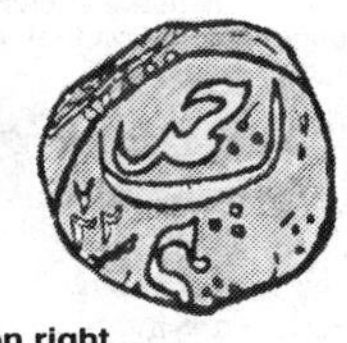

Obv: Lion right.

KM#	Date	Good	VG	Fine	VF
11	AH1227	2.50	4.00	7.00	12.00

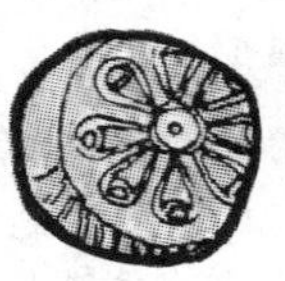

Obv: 8-petalled flower.

KM#	Date	Good	VG	Fine	VF
14	AH1240	3.00	6.00	10.00	17.00

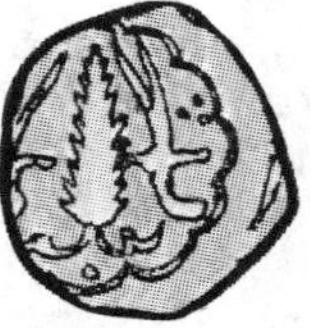

Obv: Leaf between swords.

KM#	Date	Good	VG	Fine	VF
15	AH1240	3.50	7.00	12.00	20.00

Obv: Flower between swords.

KM#	Date	Good	VG	Fine	VF
16	AH1241	3.50	7.00	12.00	20.00

Obv: 3 flowers on 1 stem.

KM#	Date	Good	VG	Fine	VF
18	AH1245	3.50	7.00	12.00	20.00

Obv: 3 swords.

KM#	Date	Good	VG	Fine	VF
20	AH1249	4.50	9.00	15.00	25.00

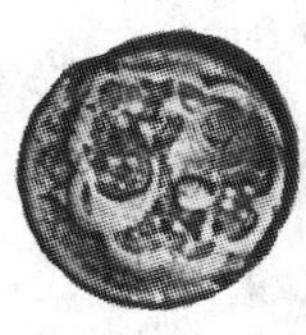

Obv: *Falus*. Rev: Mintname and date in toughra.

KM#	Date	Good	VG	Fine	VF
A21	AH1251	4.50	9.00	15.00	25.00

Obv: Flower.

KM#	Date	Good	VG	Fine	VF
21	AH1252	2.00	4.00	7.00	12.00

Obv: Sunface.

KM#	Date	Good	VG	Fine	VF
22	AH1253	2.00	4.00	7.00	12.00

Obv: Crossed swords.

KM#	Date	Good	VG	Fine	VF
23	ND	2.50	5.00	8.00	13.00
	AH1253	3.00	6.00	10.00	17.00

Obv: Leaf between 2 swords.

KM#	Date	Good	VG	Fine	VF
24	AH1254	3.00	6.00	10.00	17.00

Obv: Ornate borders.

KM#	Date	Good	VG	Fine	VF
25	AH1255	4.50	9.00	15.00	25.00

Obv: 2 bladed sword.

KM#	Date	Good	VG	Fine	VF
26	AH1255	2.50	5.00	8.00	13.00

Obv: Sword between 2 leaves.

KM#	Date	Good	VG	Fine	VF
27	AH1256	2.50	5.00	8.00	13.00
	1257	2.50	5.00	8.00	13.00

Obv: Sword between two flowers.

KM#	Date	Good	VG	Fine	VF
A28	AH1262	4.50	9.00	15.00	25.00

Obv: Bird.

KM#	Date	Good	VG	Fine	VF
28	ND	2.00	4.00	7.00	12.00

KM#	Date	Good	VG	Fine	VF
29	AH1264	3.00	6.00	10.00	17.00

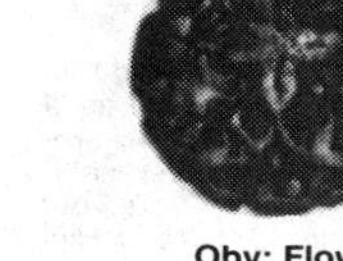

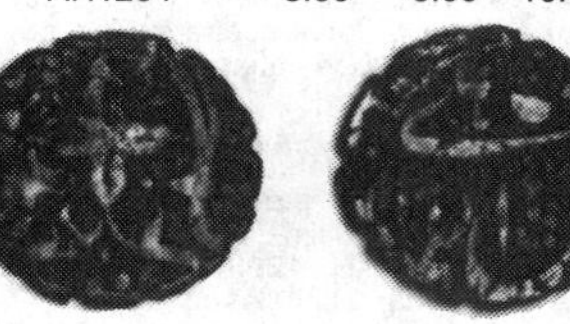
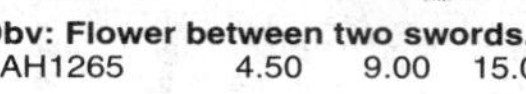

Obv: Flower between two swords.

KM#	Date	Good	VG	Fine	VF
29A	AH1265	4.50	9.00	15.00	25.00

Badakhshan Mint

Rev. leg: ***Badakhshan.***

KM#	Date	Good	VG	Fine	VF
30	ND	7.50	15.00	25.00	40.00

Balkh Mint

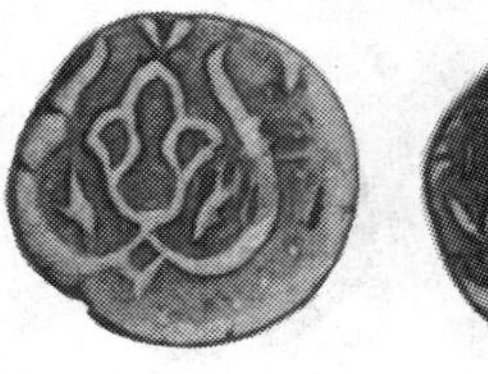

Obv: Small flower within flower bulb.

KM#	Date	Good	VG	Fine	VF
31	AH1221	5.00	7.00	10.00	15.00

Obv: Flower between 2 swords.
Rev: ***Umm al-Bilad.***

KM#	Date	Good	VG	Fine	VF
32	AH1228	2.00	4.00	7.00	12.00
	1233	2.00	4.00	7.00	12.00
	1234	2.00	4.00	7.00	12.00
	1238	2.00	4.00	7.00	12.00

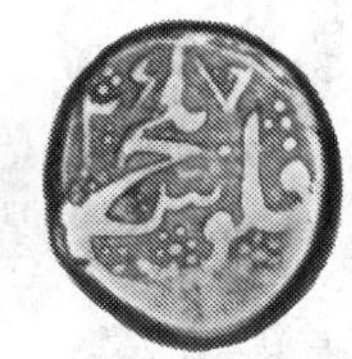

Obv: Tiger right.

KM#	Date	Good	VG	Fine	VF
35	AH1267	2.50	5.00	8.00	13.00

Obv: Tiger right.

KM#	Date	Good	VG	Fine	VF
36	AH1276	5.00	10.00	18.00	27.50

Obv: Plant between 2 swords.

KM#	Date	Good	VG	Fine	VF
37	AH1274	3.00	6.00	10.00	16.00
	1275	4.50	9.00	15.00	25.00
	1277	4.50	9.00	15.00	25.00

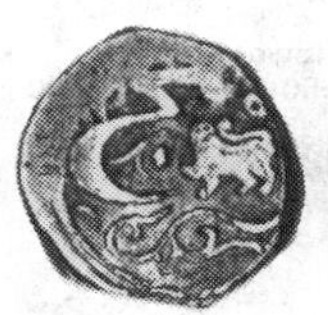

Crude, irregular flan.

KM#	Date	Good	VG	Fine	VF
38.1	AH1295	2.50	5.00	8.00	13.00

Obv: Small lion and inscriptions.

KM#	Date	Good	VG	Fine	VF
38.2	AH1295	1.75	3.50	6.00	10.00

NOTE: This type struck by machine over a number of years without change of date. Lion usually faces right, rarely left.

Ghazni Mint

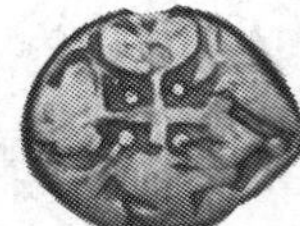
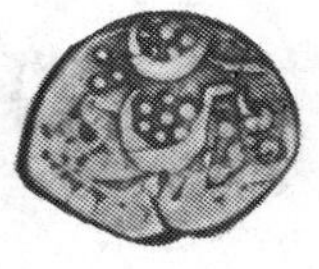

KM#	Date	Good	VG	Fine	VF
39	ND(ca 1860-80)	3.50	7.00	12.00	20.00

Obv: Floral design.

KM#	Date	Good	VG	Fine	VF
40	ND	3.00	6.00	10.00	17.00

Herat Mint

Obv: Leaf and 2 swords.

KM#	Date	Good	VG	Fine	VF
43	AH1224	2.00	4.00	7.00	12.00
	1226	2.00	4.00	7.00	12.00

Obv: Sunface.

KM#	Date	Good	VG	Fine	VF
44	AH1227	2.00	4.00	7.00	12.00

Obv: Crab.

KM#	Date	Good	VG	Fine	VF
45	AH(12)95	2.00	4.00	7.00	12.00

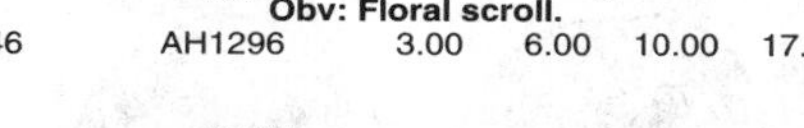

Obv: Floral scroll.

KM#	Date	Good	VG	Fine	VF
46	AH1296	3.00	6.00	10.00	17.00

Obv: Fish ?

KM#	Date	Good	VG	Fine	VF
47	AH1297	2.00	4.00	7.00	12.00

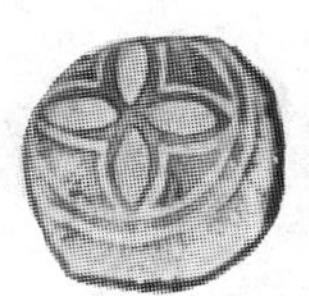

Obv: 4 ovals in the shape of a cross within double circle.

KM#	Date	Good	VG	Fine	VF
50	AH1305	5.00	9.00	15.00	25.00

Jalalabad Mint

Obv: Large flower.
Rev. leg: ***Falus*** **above mintname.**

KM#	Date	Good	VG	Fine	VF
52	AH—	13.00	26.00	45.00	75.00

NOTE: Crudely overstruck on earlier types.

Kabul Mint

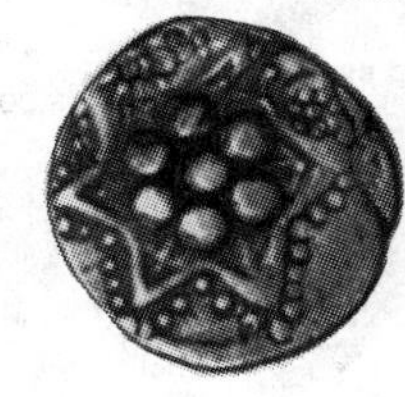

Obv: Lily blossom.

KM#	Date	Good	VG	Fine	VF
53	AH(1)222	3.50	7.00	12.00	20.00

Obv: Leaf and 2 swords.

KM#	Date	Good	VG	Fine	VF
A54	AH1227	3.00	6.00	10.00	17.00

Obv: Leaf and swords, *J* in center, large size.

KM#	Date	Good	VG	Fine	VF
54	AH1229	2.50	5.00	8.00	13.00

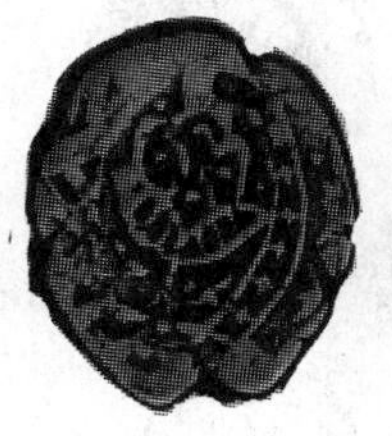

Obv: Flower.

KM#	Date	Good	VG	Fine	VF
55.1	AH1232	3.00	6.50	12.00	20.00

Obv: 2 leaves between swords.

KM#	Date	Good	VG	Fine	VF
55.2	AH1232	12.00	17.00	25.00	35.00

Obv: Two ducks, necks intertwined within leaf.

KM#	Date	Good	VG	Fine	VF
55.3	AH123x	20.00	25.00	35.00	40.00

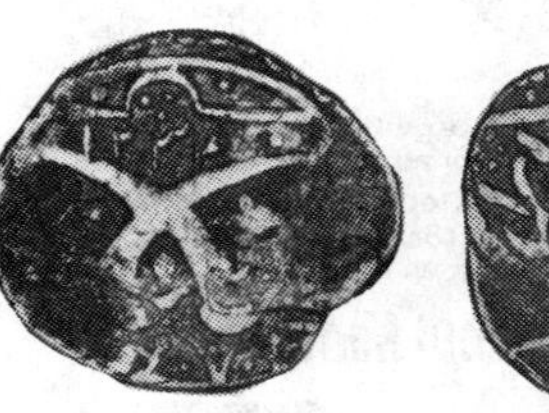

Obv: Crossed swords.

KM#	Date	Good	VG	Fine	VF
56	AH1234	2.50	5.00	8.00	13.00

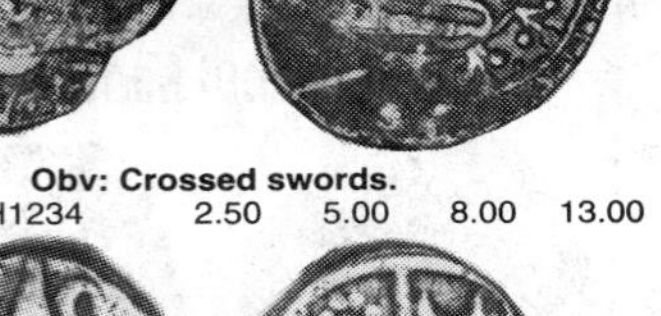
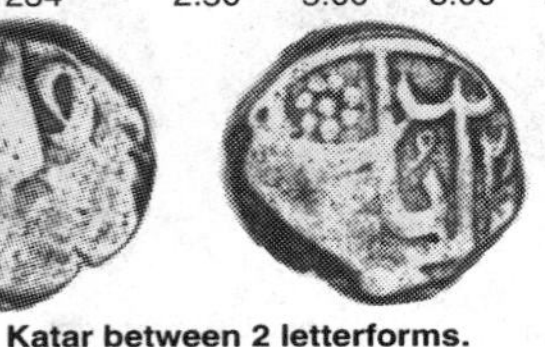

Obv: Katar between 2 letterforms.

KM#	Date	Good	VG	Fine	VF
57	AH1235	3.00	6.00	10.00	16.00

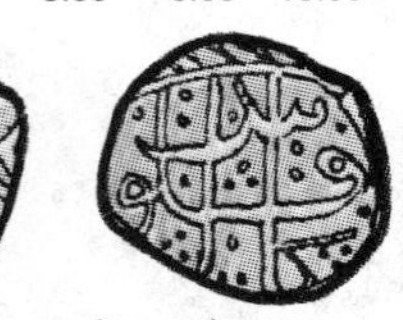

Obv: Crossed swords.

KM#	Date	Good	VG	Fine	VF
58	AH1236	3.00	6.00	10.00	16.00

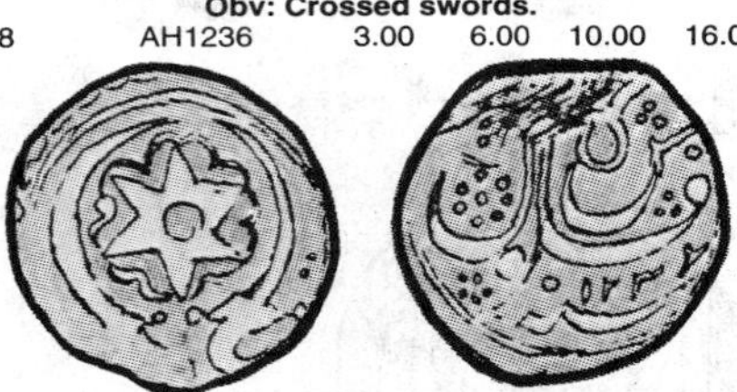

Obv: Star between 2 swords.

KM#	Date	Good	VG	Fine	VF
59	AH1236	3.50	7.00	12.00	20.00
	ND	3.00	6.00	10.00	16.00

Obv: Flower between 2 leaves.

KM#	Date	Good	VG	Fine	VF
60	AH1236	4.00	7.00	12.00	20.00

Obv: Two ducks, necks intertwined.

KM#	Date	Good	VG	Fine	VF
62	AH1238	10.00	15.00	30.00	50.00

Obv: Floral pattern.

KM#	Date	Good	VG	Fine	VF
66	AH12xx	2.00	4.00	7.00	12.00
	ND	2.00	4.00	7.00	12.00

Obv: Flower between two swords.

KM#	Date	Good	VG	Fine	VF
67	AH1249	5.00	10.00	18.00	25.00

Obv: Sword and stars.

KM#	Date	Good	VG	Fine	VF
68	AH1252	2.00	4.00	7.00	12.00
	126x	2.00	4.00	7.00	12.00
	ND	2.00	4.00	7.00	12.00

Obv: Sword right.

KM#	Date	Good	VG	Fine	VF
69	AH1258	3.00	6.00	10.00	16.00

Obv: Sword and floral ornaments.

KM#	Date	Good	VG	Fine	VF
70	AH1254	2.00	4.00	7.00	12.00
	1258	3.00	6.00	10.00	16.00

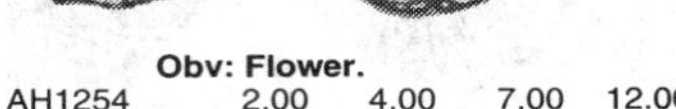

Obv: Flower.

KM#	Date	Good	VG	Fine	VF
71	AH1254	2.00	4.00	7.00	12.00

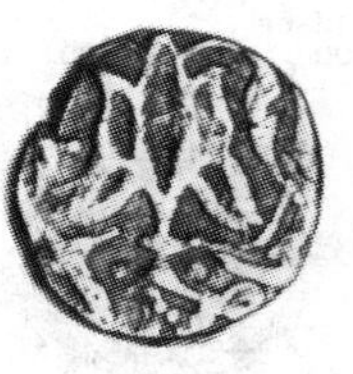

Obv: Flower and swords.

KM#	Date	Good	VG	Fine	VF
72	AH1254-58	2.00	4.00	7.00	12.00
	1256	2.00	4.00	7.00	12.00

Obv: Sword.

KM#	Date	Good	VG	Fine	VF
73	AH1254	2.50	5.00	8.00	13.00

Obv: Flower and swords.

KM#	Date	Good	VG	Fine	VF
75	AH1261	2.50	5.00	8.00	13.00
	1265	2.50	5.00	8.00	13.00

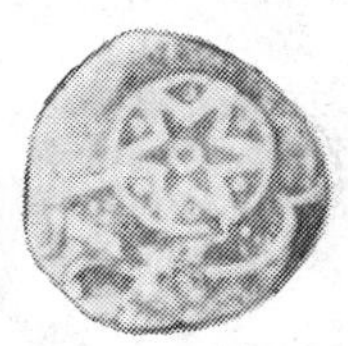

Obv: Star within circle.

KM#	Date	Good	VG	Fine	VF
A76	AH—	2.75	5.50	9.00	15.00

Obv: Flower within chevron border.

KM#	Date	Good	VG	Fine	VF
76	AH1261	4.00	8.00	13.00	22.00

Obv: Flower within star.

KM#	Date	Good	VG	Fine	VF
A77	AH1262	4.00	8.00	13.00	22.00

Obv: Floral spray.

KM#	Date	Good	VG	Fine	VF
77	AH1267	4.50	9.00	15.00	25.00

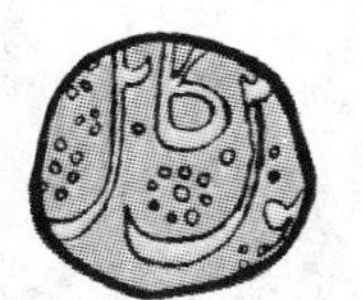

Obv: Flower.

KM#	Date	Good	VG	Fine	VF
78	AH1268	2.00	4.00	7.00	12.00

Obv: *Mihrabi* square.

KM#	Date	Good	VG	Fine	VF
A79	AH1285	4.00	8.00	15.00	25.00

Obv: Flower.

KM#	Date	Good	VG	Fine	VF
79	ND	3.50	7.00	12.00	20.00

Khanabad Mint

KM#	Date	Good	VG	Fine	VF
80	AH1301	8.00	16.00	27.00	45.00
	1302	8.00	16.00	27.00	45.00

KM#	Date	Good	VG	Fine	VF
81	AH(1)302	—	—	—	—

Peshawar Mint

KM#	Date	Good	VG	Fine	VF
83	AH1249	4.50	9.00	15.00	25.00

Obv: *Sahih* (Valid).

KM#	Date	Good	VG	Fine	VF
84	ND	4.50	9.00	15.00	25.00

Obv: *Ma'mur* (Prosperous).

KM#	Date	Good	VG	Fine	VF
84A	ND	4.50	9.00	15.00	25.00

Qandahar Mint

(See also Ahmadshahi)

Obv: Flower between 2 swords.

KM#	Date	Good	VG	Fine	VF
A85	AH1202	9.50	9.00	15.00	25.00

Obv: Large date and legend.

KM#	Date	Good	VG	Fine	VF
85	AH1228	2.00	4.00	7.00	12.00

Obv: 4-petaled flower within 4 swords.

KM#	Date	Good	VG	Fine	VF
87	ND	2.00	4.00	7.00	12.00

Obv: 3 flowers on 1 stem. Rev: Sword.

KM#	Date	Good	VG	Fine	VF
88	ND	4.00	7.00	12.00	20.00

Obv: Sword.

KM#	Date	Good	VG	Fine	VF
A89	AH1282	5.00	9.00	15.00	25.00

Obv: Flower w/fancy border.

KM#	Date	Good	VG	Fine	VF
89	AH1289	8.00	16.00	27.00	45.00

NOTE: This type evidently served as the prototype for the British occupation issue dated AH1296, KM#94.

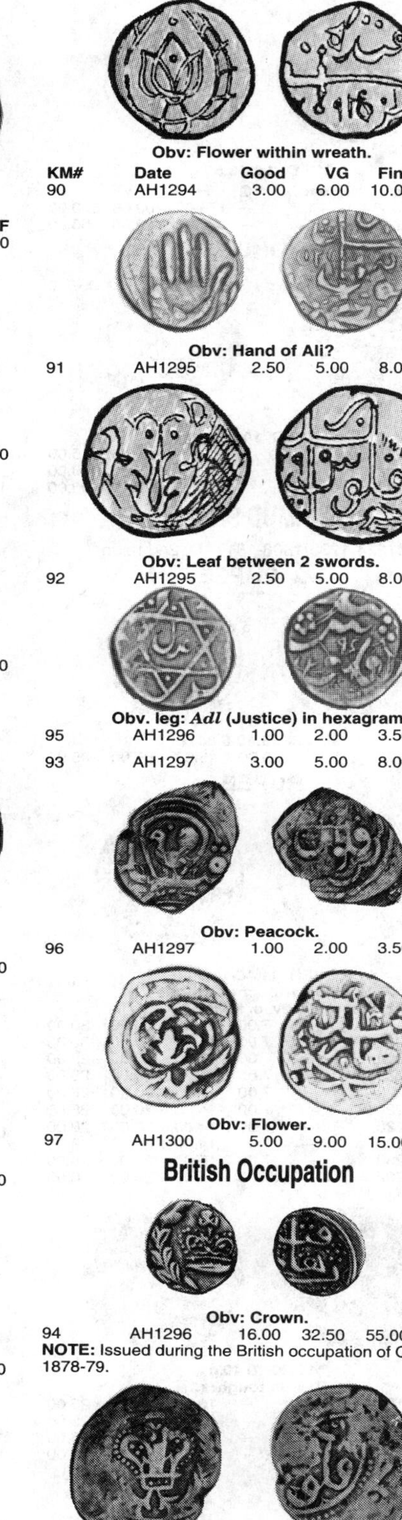

Obv: Flower within wreath.

KM#	Date	Good	VG	Fine	VF
90	AH1294	3.00	6.00	10.00	17.00

Obv: Hand of Ali?

KM#	Date	Good	VG	Fine	VF
91	AH1295	2.50	5.00	8.00	13.00

Obv: Leaf between 2 swords.

KM#	Date	Good	VG	Fine	VF
92	AH1295	2.50	5.00	8.00	13.00

Obv. leg: *Adl* (Justice) in hexagram.

KM#	Date	Good	VG	Fine	VF
95	AH1296	1.00	2.00	3.50	6.00
93	AH1297	3.00	5.00	8.00	15.00

Obv: Peacock.

KM#	Date	Good	VG	Fine	VF
96	AH1297	1.00	2.00	3.50	6.00

Obv: Flower.

KM#	Date	Good	VG	Fine	VF
97	AH1300	5.00	9.00	15.00	25.00

British Occupation

Obv: Crown.

KM#	Date	Good	VG	Fine	VF
94	AH1296	16.00	32.50	55.00	90.00

NOTE: Issued during the British occupation of Qandahar 1878-79.

Crude large flan.

KM#	Date	Good	VG	Fine	VF
A101.1	AH1296	17.50	35.00	60.00	100.00
	130x	—	—	—	—

Crude small flan.

KM#	Date	Good	VG	Fine	VF
A101.2	(AH1296)	20.00	40.00	65.00	110.00

Qandahar Mint (resumed)

Obv: 4 leaves joined.

KM#	Date	Good	VG	Fine	VF
B101 (102)	AH1307	2.50	5.00	8.00	13.00

Obv: 5-pointed star.

KM#	Date	Good	VG	Fine	VF
C101 (102A)	AH1308	3.50	6.50	10.00	15.00

NOTE: Several varieties exist.

Sar-i Pol Mint

Obv: Lion.

KM#	Date	Good	VG	Fine	VF
98	AH1297	7.50	15.00	25.00	40.00
	ND	7.50	15.00	25.00	40.00

Tashqurghan Mint

Obv: Stem with leaves.

KM#	Date	Good	VG	Fine	VF
99	AH1300	8.00	16.00	28.00	45.00

Obv: Flower.

KM#	Date	Good	VG	Fine	VF
100	AH1300	10.00	20.00	35.00	60.00

NAMED HAMMERED COINAGE

Unlike the anonymous copper coinage, which was purely local, the silver and gold coins, as well as some of the early copper coins, bear the name or characteristic type of the ruler. Because the sequence of rulers often varied at different mint cities, each ruled by different princes, the coins are best organized according to mint. Each mint employed characteristic types and calligraphy, which continued from one ruler to the next. It is hoped that this system will facilitate identification of these coins.

The following listings include not only the mints situated in contiguous territories under Durrani and Barakzai rule for extended periods of time, but also mints in Kashmir or in other parts of India which the Afghans occupied for relatively brief intervals.

Ahmadpur Mint

(In Bahawalpur)

MAHMUD SHAH

AH1216-1218/1801-1803AD

LIGHT RUPEE

SILVER, 8.20-8.40 g

KM#	Date	Year	VG	Fine	VF	XF
108	AH1217	48	22.00	40.00	50.00	60.00
	—	49	22.00	40.00	50.00	60.00

NOTE: Posthumous issue. Reverse only shown.

Ahmadshahi/Qandahar Mint

Ashraf-al-Bilad

Until AH1273, this mint was almost always given on the coins as *Ahmadshahi*, a name given it by Ahmad Shah in honor of himself in AH1171, often with the honorific *Ashraf al-Bilad* (meaning 'Most Noble of Cities'). On later issues, after AH1271, the traditional name *Qandahar* is generally used.

MAHMUD SHAH

AH1216-1218/1801-1803AD, 1st reign

RUPEE

SILVER, 11.40-11.60 g

KM#	Date	Year	VG	Fine	VF	XF
143	AH1216	—	15.00	30.00	45.00	60.00
	1217	2	15.00	30.00	45.00	60.00
	1217	3	15.00	30.00	45.00	60.00
	1218	3	15.00	30.00	45.00	60.00

ASHRAFI

GOLD, 25mm, 3.50 g

KM#	Date	Year	VG	Fine	VF	XF
144	AH1218	3	—	275.00	400.00	500.00

MOHUR

GOLD, 10.90 g

KM#	Date	Year	VG	Fine	VF	XF
145	AH1218	2	—	275.00	350.00	400.00
	1218	3	—	275.00	350.00	400.00

QAISAR SHAH

AH1218/1803AD

RUPEE

SILVER, 11.50-11.60 g

KM#	Date	Year	VG	Fine	VF	XF
148	AH1218	1	20.00	50.00	70.00	85.00

MOHUR

GOLD, 10.90 g

KM#	Date	Year	VG	Fine	VF	XF
149	AH1218	—	—	350.00	475.00	600.00

SHAH SHUJA AL-MULK

AH1218-1224/1803-1808AD, 2nd reign

1/4 RUPEE

SILVER, 2.80-3.00 g

KM#	Date	Year	VG	Fine	VF	XF
151	AH1218	2	20.00	40.00	60.00	90.00

RUPEE

SILVER, 11.40-11.60 g

KM#	Date	Year	VG	Fine	VF	XF
153	AH1218	3	7.50	15.00	20.00	27.50
	1219	1	7.50	15.00	20.00	27.50
	1220	2	7.50	15.00	20.00	27.50
	1221	3	7.50	15.00	20.00	27.50
	1222	—	7.50	15.00	20.00	27.50
	1223	—	7.50	15.00	20.00	27.50
	1224	—	7.50	15.00	20.00	27.50

NOTE: Varieties of the obverse exist.

ASHRAFI

GOLD, 3.00-3.50 g

KM#	Date	Year	VG	Fine	VF	XF
154	AH1220	3	—	175.00	200.00	350.00
	1222	—	—	175.00	200.00	350.00

MOHUR

GOLD, 10.90 g

KM#	Date	Year	VG	Fine	VF	XF
155	AH—	2	—	—	300.00	375.00
	AH1220	3	—	—	325.00	400.00
	1222	—	—	—	325.00	400.00

MAHMUD SHAH

AH1224-1233/1808-1817AD, 2nd reign

1/2 RUPEE

SILVER, 5.40-5.80 g

KM#	Date	Year	VG	Fine	VF	XF
156	AH1224	—	20.00	45.00	65.00	85.00

RUPEE

SILVER, 11.40-11.60 g
Rev: In cartouche or circle.

KM#	Date	Year	VG	Fine	VF	XF
157	AH1222 (mule w/rev. of KM#153)					
		—	7.00	14.00	20.00	30.00
	1223	—	7.00	14.00	20.00	30.00
	1224	—	7.00	14.00	20.00	28.00
	1225	—	7.00	14.00	20.00	28.00
	1226	—	7.00	14.00	20.00	28.00
	1227	—	7.00	14.00	20.00	28.00
	1228	—	7.00	14.00	20.00	28.00
	1229	—	7.00	14.00	20.00	28.00
	1230	—	7.00	14.00	20.00	28.00
	1232	—	7.00	14.00	20.00	28.00

10.20-10.40 g
Rev: In toughra.

KM#	Date	Year	VG	Fine	VF	XF
158.1	AH1229	—	—	10.00	16.00	25.00
	1230	—	—	10.00	16.00	25.00
	1231	—	—	10.00	16.00	25.00
	1232	—	—	10.00	16.00	25.00

Rev: Legend in a circle.

KM#	Date	Year	VG	Fine	VF	XF
158.2	AH1232	—	8.00	15.00	25.00	35.00
	1233	—	8.00	15.00	25.00	35.00
	1234	—	8.00	15.00	25.00	35.00

ASHRAFI

GOLD, 28mm, 2.40 g

KM#	Date	Year	VG	Fine	VF	XF
159	AH1224	—	—	—	Rare	—
	1226	—	—	—	Rare	—

AYYUB SHAH

AH1233-1245/1817-1829AD

RUPEE

SILVER
Rev: Mint in center circled by Kalimah.

KM#	Date	Year	VG	Fine	VF	XF
162	AH1234	—	—	—	—	—
	1235	—	—	—	—	—

SILVER, 11.20-11.60 g

KM#	Date	Year	VG	Fine	VF	XF
163	AH1235	—	15.00	30.00	40.00	50.00
	1236	—	—	Reported, not confirmed		
	1237	—	15.00	30.00	40.00	50.00
	1239	—	15.00	30.00	40.00	50.00

NOTE: Reverses differ each year. Coins dated AH1239 are struck in debased silver.

KM#	Date	Year	VG	Fine	VF	XF
164	AH1237	—	25.00	50.00	—	—

ANONYMOUS COINAGE

During the reign of Ayyub Shah

AH1233-1245/1817-1826AD

FALUS

BRONZE
Rev. leg: *Ya Ghaus al Azam.*

KM#	Date	Year	VG	Fine	VF	XF
165	AH1240	—	50.00	65.00	90.00	120.00
	1241	—	50.00	65.00	90.00	120.00

During the reign of Dost Muhammad, 1st reign

AH1239-1255/1824-1839AD

RUPEE

SILVER
Obv: Kalimah. Rev: Mintname in circle.

KM#	Date	Year	VG	Fine	VF	XF
160	AH1234	—	—	—	Rare	—

Obv: Kalimah. Rev: Mint name.

KM#	Date	Year	VG	Fine	VF	XF
168	AH1243	—	10.00	20.00	30.00	40.00
	1244		7.00	15.00	20.00	30.00
	1245	—	—	10.00	15.00	25.00
	1246	—	—	10.00	15.00	25.00
	1247	—	—	10.00	15.00	25.00
	1248	—	—	10.00	15.00	25.00
	1249	—	—	9.00	14.00	23.00
	1250	—	—	9.00	14.00	23.00
	1251	—	—	9.00	14.00	23.00
	1252	—	7.00	13.00	20.00	30.00
	1253	—	7.00	13.00	20.00	30.00
	1254	—	7.00	13.00	20.00	30.00

NOTE: Minor variations exist on both sides.

SHAH SHUJA AL-MULK

AH1255-1258/1839-1842AD, 3rd reign

1/4 RUPEE

SILVER, 2.30 g

KM#	Date	Year	VG	Fine	VF	XF
171	AH1255	—	25.00	32.50	45.00	60.00

1/2 RUPEE

SILVER

KM#	Date	Year	VG	Fine	VF	XF
172	AH1255	—	25.00	32.50	45.00	60.00

RUPEE

SILVER, 9.00-9.20 g

KM#	Date	Year	VG	Fine	VF	XF
173	AH1255	—	10.00	20.00	25.00	35.00
	1256	—	12.50	30.00	40.00	50.00
	1257	—	—	—	Rare	—
	1258	—	15.00	30.00	50.00	75.00

FATH JANG

AH1258/1842AD

RUPEE

SILVER, 9.15-9.35 g

KM#	Date	Year	VG	Fine	VF	XF
178	AH1258	—	20.00	50.00	75.00	100.00

ANONYMOUS COINAGE

During the reign of Kohandil Khan

AH1256-1271/1840-1855AD

1/2 RUPEE

SILVER

KM#	Date	Year	VG	Fine	VF	XF
182.1	AH1260	—	4.00	10.00	14.00	20.00
	1261	—	4.00	10.00	14.00	20.00
	1262	—	4.00	10.00	14.00	20.00
	1263	—	4.00	10.00	14.00	20.00
	1264	—	4.00	10.00	14.00	20.00
	1265	—	4.00	10.00	14.00	20.00
	1267	—	5.00	12.00	19.00	25.00
	1268	—	6.50	16.00	25.00	35.00
	1269	—	6.50	16.00	25.00	35.00
	1270	—	6.50	16.00	25.00	35.00
	1271	—	6.50	16.00	25.00	35.00
	1272	—	6.50	16.00	25.00	35.00

NOTE: Both obverse and reverse have legends differently arranged in different years.

Obv. and rev: Similar to 1 Rupee, KM#183.

KM#	Date	Year	VG	Fine	VF	XF
182.2	AH1264	—	25.00	45.00	70.00	100.00
	1267	—	25.00	45.00	70.00	100.00
	1269	—	15.00	25.00	45.00	70.00
	1270		10.00	20.00	35.00	55.00

RUPEE

SILVER

KM#	Date	Year	VG	Fine	VF	XF
183	AH1259	—	12.50	27.50	35.00	50.00

RAHAMDIL KHAN

AH1271-1272/1855-1856AD

1/2 RUPEE

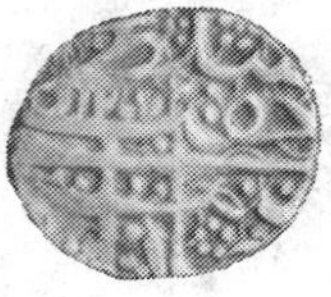

SILVER

Mintname: ***Ahmadshahi***

KM#	Date	Year	VG	Fine	VF	XF
184	AH1271	—	15.00	35.00	50.00	70.00
	1272	—	15.00	35.00	50.00	70.00

DOST MUHAMMAD

AH1258-1280/1842-1863AD, 2nd reign

In the names of Amir Kabir and his late son Akbar Khan

1/2 RUPEE

SILVER

Mintname: ***Ahmadshahi***

Dated on both sides.

KM#	Date	Year	VG	Fine	VF	XF
186	AH1272	—	3.00	6.00	10.00	15.00
	1273	—	3.00	6.00	10.00	15.00

Mintname: ***Qandahar***

Obv: AH1273. Rev: AH1274. Dated on both sides.

KM#	Date	Year	VG	Fine	VF	XF
187.1	AH1272	—	3.00	6.00	8.50	13.50
	1273	—	3.00	6.00	8.50	13.50
	1274	—	3.00	6.00	8.50	13.50
	1275	—	3.00	6.00	8.50	13.50
	1276	—	3.00	6.00	9.00	15.00
	1277	—	3.00	6.00	9.00	15.00
	1278	—	3.00	6.00	9.00	15.00
	1279	—	— Reported, not confirmed			

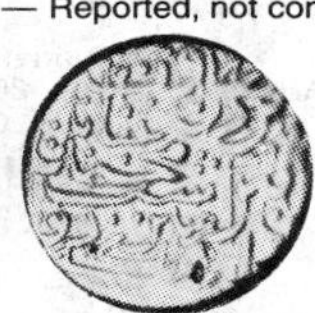

Posthumous Issue

Rev: ***Qandahar*** above, ***Duriba*** below.

KM#	Date	Year	VG	Fine	VF	XF
187.2	AH1281	—	15.00	35.00	50.00	—

RUPEE

SILVER

Mintname: ***Ahmadshahi***

Dated on both sides.

KM#	Date	Year	VG	Fine	VF	XF
188	AH1272	—	10.00	25.00	35.00	50.00
	1273	—	10.00	25.00	35.00	50.00

SHER ALI

AH1280-1283/1863-1866AD, 1st reign

1/2 RUPEE

SILVER

Obv: Couplet. Rev: Title of ruler and mint.

KM#	Date	Year	VG	Fine	VF	XF
191	AH1280	—	5.00	10.00	17.00	30.00
	1281	—	6.00	13.00	20.00	30.00
	1282	—	5.00	8.00	15.00	30.00
	1283	—	—	—	Rare	—
	1285	—	9.00	15.00	25.00	45.00

Obv: Couplet. Rev: Mint only.

KM#	Date	Year	VG	Fine	VF	XF
192	AH1282	—	—	—	—	—
	1283	—	10.00	20.00	30.00	40.00

NOTE: Arrangement of rev. legend varies.

TILLA

GOLD

KM#	Date	Year	VG	Fine	VF	XF
194	AH1283	—	—	150.00	200.00	250.00
	1284	—	—	150.00	200.00	250.00
	1285	—	—	150.00	200.00	250.00

MUHAMMAD AFZAL

AH1283-1284/1866-1867AD

1/2 RUPEE

SILVER

KM#	Date	Year	VG	Fine	VF	XF
196	AH1283	—	25.00	50.00	75.00	100.00

Obv: KM#196. Rev: KM#201.

KM#	Date	Year	VG	Fine	VF	XF
197	AH1283	—	30.00	60.00	95.00	110.00
	1284	—	30.00	60.00	95.00	110.00

MUHAMMAD A'ZAM

AH1283-1285/1866-1868AD

1/2 RUPEE

SILVER

KM#	Date	Year	VG	Fine	VF	XF
201	AH1283	—	25.00	50.00	75.00	100.00
	1284	—	25.00	50.00	75.00	100.00

SHER ALI

AH1285-1296/1868-1879AD, 2nd reign

1/2 RUPEE

SILVER

KM#	Date	Year	VG	Fine	VF	XF
205.1	AH1284	—	6.00	13.00	20.00	30.00
	1285	—	6.00	13.00	20.00	30.00

NOTE: Resumption of type identical to KM#191 of first reign.

Rev: Legend within wreath.

KM#	Date	Year	VG	Fine	VF	XF
205.3	AH1285	—	15.00	25.00	40.00	60.00

KM#	Date	Year	VG	Fine	VF	XF
205.2	AH1287	—	12.50	20.00	30.00	40.00

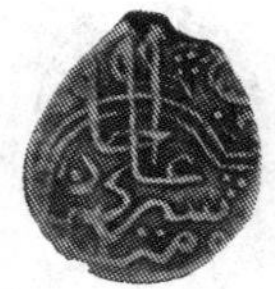

KM#	Date	Year	VG	Fine	VF	XF
206	AH1277 (error) for 1288					
		—	5.50	12.50	20.00	30.00
	1288	—	4.00	7.00	10.00	15.00
	1289	—	5.00	12.50	20.00	30.00

KM#	Date	Year	VG	Fine	VF	XF
207.1	AH1290	—	3.00	6.00	10.00	15.00
	1291	—	3.00	6.00	10.00	15.00
	1292	—	3.00	6.00	10.00	15.00
	1293	—	3.00	6.00	10.00	15.00

NOTE: Variety of 1293 exists with double leaf at bottom of obverse.

Obv: Teardrop design.

KM#	Date	Year	VG	Fine	VF	XF
207.2	AH1294	—	3.00	6.00	10.00	15.00
	1295	—	3.00	6.00	10.00	15.00

KM#	Date	Year	VG	Fine	VF	XF
208	AH1295	—	3.50	13.50	22.50	37.50

MUHAMMAD YAQUB

AH1296-1297/1879-1880AD

1/2 RUPEE

SILVER

KM#	Date	Year	VG	Fine	VF	XF
212	AH1296	—	6.00	16.00	25.00	35.00
	1297	—	12.00	25.00	35.00	45.00

NOTE: Mules exist bearing both dates.

RUPEE

SILVER

KM#	Date	Year	VG	Fine	VF	XF
213	AH1298	—	— Reported, not confirmed			

WALI SHER ALI

AH1297/1880AD

1/2 RUPEE

SILVER
Dated on both sides.

KM#	Date	Year	VG	Fine	VF	XF
217	AH1297	—	8.50	17.50	25.00	35.00

RUPEE

SILVER
Type of 1/2 Rupee

KM#	Date	Year	VG	Fine	VF	XF
218	AH1297	—	15.00	30.00	40.00	60.00

TILLA

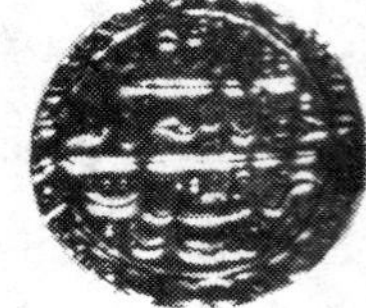

GOLD

KM#	Date	Year	VG	Fine	VF	XF
219	AH1297	—	—	—	Rare	—

ANONYMOUS COINAGE

1/2 RUPEE

SILVER
Dated on both sides.
Obv. leg: *Al-Mulk Lillah*.

KM#	Date	Year	VG	Fine	VF	XF
221	AH1297	—	10.00	20.00	30.00	40.00

NOTE: It is not known under whose authority this type was struck.

ABDUR RAHMAN

AH1297-1319/1880-1901AD

1/2 RUPEE

SILVER
Mintname: *Ahmadshahi*

KM#	Date	Year	VG	Fine	VF	XF
222	AH1298	—	15.00	30.00	40.00	50.00

Mintname: *Qandahar*

KM#	Date	Year	VG	Fine	VF	XF
225	AH1298	—	20.00	35.00	50.00	70.00
	1304	—	20.00	35.00	50.00	70.00

RUPEE

SILVER
Mintname: *Ahmadshahi*
Obv: 2 leaves, date. Rev: Mintname.

KM#	Date	Year	VG	Fine	VF	XF
223.1	AH1298	—	—	—	—	—

Mintname: *Qandahar*
Obv: 2 leaves, date. Rev: Mintname, date.

KM#	Date	Year	VG	Fine	VF	XF
223.2	AH1298	—	35.00	65.00	85.00	120.00
	1299	—	35.00	65.00	85.00	120.00

NOTE: Variety with only 1 leaf on obverse exists.

KM#	Date	Year	VG	Fine	VF	XF
224	AH1298	—	7.50	12.50	20.00	30.00
	1299	3	10.00	16.00	25.00	40.00
	1300	—	10.00	16.00	25.00	40.00
	1301	—	10.00	16.00	25.00	40.00
	1302	—	10.00	16.00	25.00	40.00
	1303	—	6.00	10.00	15.00	25.00
	1304	—	—	6.00	10.00	17.50
	1305	—	—	6.00	10.00	17.50
	1306	—	—	6.00	10.00	17.50
	1307	—	—	6.00	10.00	17.50
	1308	—	—	6.00	10.00	17.50

TILLA

GOLD

KM#	Date	Year	VG	Fine	VF	XF
226	AH1298	—	—	—	Rare	—

Bahawalpur Mint

Dar as-Surur

Most Bahawalpur coins have crude oblique milling on the edge.

MAHMUD SHAH

AH1216-1218/1801-1803AD, 1st reign

RUPEE

SILVER, 11.40-11.60 g
Rev: Mint and epithet.

KM#	Date	Year	VG	Fine	VF	XF
242	AH1217	—	30.00	65.00	80.00	100.00

Rev: Mint and *Julus* formula.

KM#	Date	Year	VG	Fine	VF	XF
243	AH1217	1	—	30.00	50.00	65.00
	1217	2	—	30.00	50.00	65.00
	1218	2	—	30.00	50.00	65.00

2 RUPEES

SILVER, 23.00-23.20 g

KM#	Date	Year	VG	Fine	VF	XF
244	AH1217	1	85.00	140.00	200.00	275.00

NOTE: Regnal year written as numeral, not *Ahad*.

MOHUR

GOLD, 11.00 g

KM#	Date	Year	VG	Fine	VF	XF
245	AH1218	2	—	—	400.00	500.00

2 MOHURS

GOLD, 22.00-22.20 g

KM#	Date	Year	VG	Fine	VF	XF
246	AH1217	1	—	—	750.00	1000.
	1217	2	—	—	750.00	1000.
	1218	2	—	—	750.00	1000.

SHAH SHUJA AL-MULK

AH1218-1224/1803-1808AD, 2nd reign

RUPEE

SILVER, 11.20-11.60 g

KM#	Date	Year	VG	Fine	VF	XF
253	AH1218	1	—	30.00	50.00	65.00
	1218	2	—	30.00	50.00	65.00
	1219	1	—	30.00	50.00	65.00
	1220	—	—	30.00	50.00	65.00
	1221	—	—	30.00	50.00	65.00
	1222	—	—	30.00	50.00	65.00
	1212 (error for 1221 ?)	—	—	35.00	55.00	75.00

2 RUPEES

SILVER, 23.00 g

KM#	Date	Year	VG	Fine	VF	XF
254	AH1218	1	50.00	100.00	200.00	275.00
	1219	—	—	—	Unique	—

MOHUR

GOLD, 11.00-11.10 g

KM#	Date	Year	VG	Fine	VF	XF
255	AH1218	1	—	—	350.00	450.00

2 MOHURS

GOLD, 22.00 g

KM#	Date	Year	VG	Fine	VF	XF
256	AH1218	1	—	—	850.00	1100.

MAHMUD SHAH

AH1224-1233/1808-1817AD, 2nd reign

RUPEE

SILVER, 21.5-26mm, 11.00-11.20 g

KM#	Date	Year	VG	Fine	VF	XF
263	AH1224	1	25.00	55.00	75.00	110.00
	1239	—	15.00	30.00	40.00	60.00
	1240	—	15.00	30.00	40.00	60.00
	1241	—	15.00	30.00	40.00	60.00
	1242	—	15.00	30.00	40.00	60.00
	1244	—	15.00	30.00	40.00	60.00
	1244//1245	—	15.00	30.00	40.00	60.00
	1249	—	15.00	30.00	40.00	60.00
	1249//1250	—	15.00	30.00	40.00	60.00
	1250	—	15.00	30.00	40.00	60.00

NOTE: Coins dated after AH1233 are struck in Mahmud's name by the virtually independent Nawabs of Bahawalpur.

MOHUR

GOLD, 21.5mm, 11.00 g

KM#	Date	Year	VG	Fine	VF	XF
265	AH1225	1	—	—	Rare	—

Balkh Mint

Umm al-Bilad

Located in northern Afghanistan, Balkh bore the honorary epithet of *Umm al-Bilad*, 'Mother of Cities', because of its great age. It was taken by Ahmad Shah from the Amir of Bukhara in AH1180 (1765AD) and lost by Taimur Shah to the Uzbeks in AH1206 (1792AD).

SHAH SHUJA AL-MULK

AH1218-1224/1803-1808AD, 2nd reign

FALUS

Copper, 24mm
Obv: Mint, date and sword.

KM#	Date	Year	VG	Fine	VF	XF
266	AH1218	—	10.00	20.00	35.00	55.00

Bhakhar Mint

The mint is found variously spelled, as *Bhakhar* (most common), *Bakhar*, and *Bakkar*.

MAHMUD SHAH

AH1216-1218/1801-1803AD, 1st reign

RUPEE

SILVER, 11.40-11.60 g
Broad flan, nazarana style.

KM#	Date	Year	VG	Fine	VF	XF
308	ND	—	40.00	90.00	150.00	200.00

SHAH SHUJA AL-MULK

AH1218-1224/1803-1808AD, 2nd reign

FALUS

COPPER

KM#	Date	Year	VG	Fine	VF	XF
308a	AH1218	—	4.50	10.00	15.00	25.00
	1222	—	4.50	10.00	15.00	25.00

RUPEE

SILVER, 11.40-11.60 g

KM#	Date	Year	VG	Fine	VF	XF
309.1	AH1218	—	15.00	25.00	35.00	50.00
	1219	—	15.00	25.00	35.00	50.00
	1220	—	15.00	25.00	35.00	50.00
	1221	12	15.00	25.00	35.00	50.00
	1222	—	15.00	25.00	35.00	50.00
	1223	—	15.00	25.00	35.00	50.00
	1224	—	15.00	25.00	35.00	50.00
	ND	—	6.00	12.00	18.00	25.00

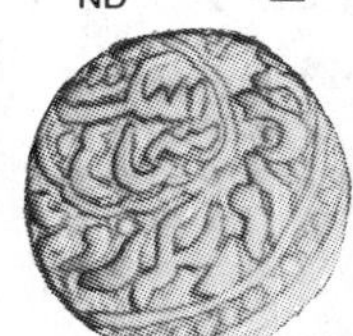
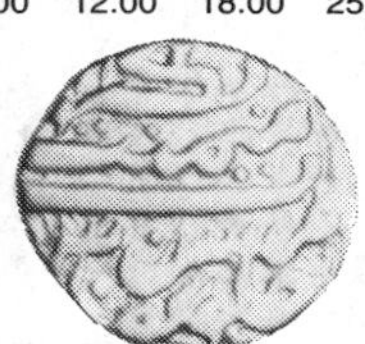

Obv: King's name circled within couplet.

KM#	Date	Year	VG	Fine	VF	XF
309.2	AH1223	—	50.00	100.00	150.00	180.00

MAHMUD SHAH

AH1224-1233/1809-1817AD, 2nd reign

RUPEE

SILVER, 11.40-11.60 g

KM#	Date	Year	VG	Fine	VF	XF
307	AH1228	—	15.00	25.00	35.00	50.00
	1229	—	15.00	25.00	35.00	50.00
	ND	—	6.00	10.00	18.00	25.00

SHAH SHUJA AL-MULK

AH1233-1234/1817-1818AD, 3rd reign in Peshawar

RUPEE

SILVER, 11.40-11.60 g

KM#	Date	Year	VG	Fine	VF	XF
A310	AH1234	—	—	—	—	—

Dera Mint

Dera Ghazi Khan

The mint of Dera was located at Dera Ghazi Khan, taken by the Sikhs in AH1235 (1819AD), and now within Pakistan.

MAHMUD SHAH

AH1216-1218/1801-1803AD, 1st reign

RUPEE

SILVER, 11.40-11.60 g

KM#	Date	Year	VG	Fine	VF	XF
338	AH1216	1	12.50	32.50	45.00	60.00
	1217	2	12.50	32.50	45.00	60.00

SHAH SHUJA AL-MULK

AH1218-1224/1803-1808AD, 2nd reign

RUPEE

SILVER, 11.40-11.60 g

KM#	Date	Year	VG	Fine	VF	XF
343	—	1	12.50	32.50	45.00	60.00
	—	4	12.50	32.50	45.00	60.00
	—	5	12.50	32.50	45.00	60.00

MOHUR

GOLD

KM#	Date	Year	VG	Fine	VF	XF
345	AH1218	1	—	—	400.00	450.00

Derajat Mint

Dera Ismail Khan

The mint of Derajat was located at Dera Ismail Khan, which fell to the Sikhs in (AH1236) 1820-21AD. Issues in the name of Mahmud Shah dated AH1236 and later are actually Sikh issues. The Sikhs formally annexed Derajat in 1835AD (AH1281).

MAHMUD SHAH

AH1216-1218/1801-1803AD, 1st reign

RUPEE

SILVER, 11.00-11.20 g

KM#	Date	Year	VG	Fine	VF	XF
363	AH1216	1	18.00	38.00	50.00	70.00
	1217	2	18.00	38.00	50.00	70.00

SHAH SHUJA AL-MULK

AH1218-1224/1803-1808AD, 2nd reign

RUPEE

SILVER, 20-21.5mm, 10.80-11.20 g

KM#	Date	Year	VG	Fine	VF	XF
368	AH1218	1	12.50	20.00	30.00	40.00
	1218	2	12.50	20.00	30.00	40.00
	1219	2	12.50	20.00	30.00	40.00
	1220	2	12.50	20.00	30.00	40.00
	1220	3	12.50	20.00	30.00	40.00
	1221	3	12.50	20.00	30.00	40.00
	1221	4	12.50	20.00	30.00	40.00
	1221	5	12.50	20.00	30.00	40.00
	—	6	12.50	20.00	30.00	40.00
	1223	—	12.50	20.00	30.00	40.00
	—	8	—	—	—	—

MAHMUD SHAH

AH1224-1233/1808-1817AD, 2nd reign

FALUS

COPPER

KM#	Date	Year	Good	VG	Fine	VF
370	AH124(9)	—	5.00	8.00	12.00	18.00

RUPEE

SILVER, 10.60-11.20 g

KM#	Date	Year	VG	Fine	VF	XF
373	AH1224	1	12.50	30.00	40.00	50.00
	1226	3	12.50	30.00	40.00	50.00
	1227	3	12.50	30.00	40.00	50.00
	1228	4	12.50	30.00	40.00	50.00
	1229	—	12.50	30.00	40.00	50.00
	1230	—	12.50	30.00	40.00	50.00
	1231	4	7.50	15.00	25.00	35.00
	1232	—	7.50	15.00	25.00	35.00
	1233	—	7.50	15.00	25.00	35.00
	1234	—	7.50	15.00	25.00	35.00
	1236	—	7.50	15.00	25.00	35.00
	1237	—	7.50	15.00	25.00	35.00
	1238	14	7.50	15.00	25.00	35.00
	1239	—	7.50	15.00	25.00	35.00
	1240	—	7.50	15.00	25.00	35.00
	1241	—	7.50	15.00	25.00	35.00
	1242	—	7.50	15.00	25.00	35.00
	1243	—	7.50	15.00	25.00	35.00
	1244	—	7.50	15.00	25.00	35.00
	1245	—	7.50	15.00	25.00	35.00
	1246	—	7.50	15.00	25.00	35.00
	1247	—	7.50	15.00	25.00	35.00
	1248	—	7.50	15.00	25.00	35.00
	1249	—	7.50	15.00	25.00	35.00
	1250	—	7.50	15.00	25.00	35.00
	1251	—	7.50	15.00	25.00	35.00
	1252	—	7.50	15.00	25.00	35.00

NOTE: Coins after AH1235 were issued under Sikh protectorate.

Herat Mint

Dar as-Sultanat

After AH1254, rupees ceased to be coined at Herat. Later emissions, beginning with anonymous issues of Yar Muhammad Khan, were 1/2 rupees. From AH1272-80 (1856-63AD), Herat was occupied by the Persians, who struck coins there in the name of Nasir al-Din Shah. The mint was closed in AH1308 (1891AD), except for a few later coins in copper.

MAHMUD SHAH

AH1216-1245/1801-1829AD

1/12 RUPEE

SILVER, 0.90 g

KM#	Date	Year	VG	Fine	VF	XF
392	AH1230	—	15.00	35.00	50.00	65.00

1/6 RUPEE

SILVER, 1.80 g

KM#	Date	Year	VG	Fine	VF	XF
393	AH1225	—	15.00	35.00	50.00	70.00
	1238	—	15.00	35.00	50.00	70.00

1/4 RUPEE

SILVER, 11.5mm, 2.80 g

KM#	Date	Year	VG	Fine	VF	XF
395	AH1225	—	25.00	55.00	75.00	100.00
	1242	—	25.00	55.00	75.00	100.00

1/2 RUPEE

SILVER, 5.00-5.60 g
Rev: Mintname and date in small circle.

KM#	Date	Year	VG	Fine	VF	XF
A396	AH1230	—	—	—	Rare	—

KM#	Date	Year	VG	Fine	VF	XF
396	AH1242	—	25.00	45.00	60.00	85.00
	1243	—	25.00	45.00	60.00	85.00

RUPEE

SILVER, 11.00-11.60 g

KM#	Date	Year	VG	Fine	VF	XF
398.1	AH1216	—	6.00	9.00	15.00	25.00
	1217	—	6.00	9.00	15.00	25.00
	1218	—	6.00	9.00	15.00	25.00

KM#	Date	Year	VG	Fine	VF	XF
398.2	AH1219	—	6.00	9.00	15.00	25.00
	1220	—	6.00	9.00	15.00	25.00
	1221	—	6.00	9.00	15.00	25.00
	1222	—	6.00	9.00	15.00	25.00
	1223	—	6.00	9.00	15.00	25.00
	1224	—	6.00	9.00	15.00	25.00
	1225	—	6.00	9.00	15.00	25.00
	1226	—	6.00	9.00	15.00	25.00
	1227	—	6.00	9.00	15.00	25.00
	1228	—	6.00	9.00	15.00	25.00
	1229	—	6.00	9.00	15.00	25.00
	1230	—	6.00	10.00	16.50	27.00
	1231	—	6.00	11.50	18.00	28.00
	1232	—	6.00	11.50	18.00	28.00
	1233	—	6.00	11.50	18.00	28.00
	1234	—	6.00	11.50	18.00	28.00
	1235	—	6.00	11.50	18.00	28.00
	1236	—	6.00	11.50	18.00	28.00
	1237	—	6.00	11.50	18.00	28.00
	1238	—	6.00	11.50	18.00	28.00
	1240	—	6.00	11.50	18.00	28.00

KM#	Date	Year	VG	Fine	VF	XF
398.3	AH1242	—	8.00	14.00	20.00	30.00
	1243	—	8.00	14.00	20.00	30.00
	1244	—	8.00	14.00	20.00	30.00
	1254 (error date)	—	8.00	14.00	20.00	30.00

KAMRAN SHAH

AH1245-1258/1829-1842AD

1/6 RUPEE

SILVER, 1.80 g

KM#	Date	Year	VG	Fine	VF	XF
400	AH1257	—	30.00	60.00	100.00	150.00

1/4 RUPEE

SILVER, 2.60-2.80 g

KM#	Date	Year	VG	Fine	VF	XF
401	AH1248	—	35.00	75.00	100.00	135.00

1/2 RUPEE

SILVER, 5.20-5.60 g

KM#	Date	Year	VG	Fine	VF	XF
402	AH125x	—	20.00	30.00	45.00	75.00

RUPEE

SILVER, 10.20-11.00 g

KM#	Date	Year	VG	Fine	VF	XF
403	AH1244	—	30.00	65.00	90.00	125.00
	1245	—	30.00	65.00	90.00	125.00
	1246	—	30.00	65.00	90.00	125.00
	1248	—	30.00	65.00	90.00	125.00
	1249	—	30.00	65.00	90.00	125.00
	1251	—	30.00	65.00	90.00	125.00
	1252	—	30.00	65.00	90.00	125.00
	1254	—	30.00	65.00	90.00	125.00
	1255	—	30.00	65.00	90.00	125.00

YAR MUHAMMAD KHAN SADOZAI

AH1258-1267/1842-1851AD

Anonymous coinage struck with the Kalimah on obv., mint and date on rev.

1/6 RUPEE

SILVER

KM#	Date	Year	VG	Fine	VF	XF
404	AH1258	—	25.00	35.00	50.00	75.00
	1259	—	25.00	35.00	50.00	75.00
	1260	—	25.00	35.00	50.00	75.00

1/2 RUPEE

SILVER

KM#	Date	Year	VG	Fine	VF	XF
405.1	AH1261	—	10.00	25.00	35.00	50.00
	1262	—	10.00	25.00	35.00	50.00
	1263	—	10.00	25.00	35.00	50.00
	1264	—	10.00	25.00	40.00	60.00
	1265	—	10.00	25.00	40.00	60.00
	1266	—	10.00	25.00	40.00	60.00

Rev: Legend in circle.

KM#	Date	Year	VG	Fine	VF	XF
405.2	AH1269(sic)	—	12.50	30.00	50.00	70.00

Obv: Kalimah in small double circle.

KM#	Date	Year	VG	Fine	VF	XF
405.3	AH1267	—	25.00	40.00	60.00	80.00

MUHAMMAD YUSUF KHAN SADOZAI

AH1267-1272/1851-1856AD

1/2 RUPEE

SILVER
Obv: Kalimah in circle.

KM#	Date	Year	VG	Fine	VF	XF
A406	AH1270	—	35.00	60.00	80.00	100.00

Rev: Mint in circular area.

KM#	Date	Year	VG	Fine	VF	XF
406	AH1271	—	35.00	60.00	80.00	100.00

Rev: Mint in square.

KM#	Date	Year	VG	Fine	VF	XF
407	AH1271	—	40.00	70.00	90.00	125.00

Obv: Kalimah.

KM#	Date	Year	VG	Fine	VF	XF
408	AH1272	—	20.00	50.00	90.00	120.00

TILLA

GOLD

KM#	Date	Year	VG	Fine	VF	XF
409	AH1272	—	—	—	450.00	500.00

SHER ALI

AH1280-1296/1863-1879AD

1/2 RUPEE

SILVER
Rev: Legend in square.

KM#	Date	Year	VG	Fine	VF	XF
410	AH1280	—	—	—	—	—

Obv: *Amir* at top. Rev: Date.

KM#	Date	Year	VG	Fine	VF	XF
411	AH1280	—	10.00	20.00	35.00	50.00
	1281	—	10.00	20.00	35.00	50.00

Obv: *Amir* at bottom, date both sides.

KM#	Date	Year	VG	Fine	VF	XF
412	AH1281	—	8.00	15.00	25.00	40.00
	1282	—	8.00	15.00	25.00	40.00
	1283	—	8.00	15.00	25.00	40.00
	1284	—	8.00	15.00	25.00	40.00
	1287	—	8.00	15.00	25.00	40.00

NOTE: Mules exist bearing various combinations of these dates.

Obv: *Amir* at top, legend rearranged.

KM#	Date	Year	VG	Fine	VF	XF
414	AH1287	—	15.00	30.00	45.00	65.00
	1288	—	10.00	23.00	40.00	55.00
	1290	—	10.00	23.00	40.00	55.00

Obv: Shorter inscription (ruler's name only).

KM#	Date	Year	VG	Fine	VF	XF
413	AH1292	—	12.50	20.00	30.00	40.00
	1295	—	—	5.00	10.00	16.00

NOTE: Several varieties exist.

NOTE: A tilla dated AH1284 of Sher Ali has been reported.

MUHAMMAD YAQUB

AH1296-1298/1879-1881AD

1/6 RUPEE

SILVER, 11mm, 1.80 g

KM#	Date	Year	VG	Fine	VF	XF
415	AH1297	—	—	—	Rare	—

1/2 RUPEE

SILVER

KM#	Date	Year	VG	Fine	VF	XF
417	AH1296	—	3.00	5.00	7.00	13.50
	1297	—	3.00	5.00	7.00	13.50
	1298	—	3.00	5.00	7.00	13.50

Obv: Date below.
Rev: Date in *b* of *Zarb*.

KM#	Date	Year	VG	Fine	VF	XF
416	AH1298	—	—	—	—	—

ABDUR RAHMAN

AH1297-1319/1880-1901AD

1/8 RUPEE

SILVER, 13mm

KM#	Date	Year	VG	Fine	VF	XF
418	AH1307	—	—	—	Rare	—

1/2 RUPEE

SILVER

KM#	Date	Year	VG	Fine	VF	XF
419	AH1297	—	3.00	5.00	8.00	14.00
	1298	—	5.00	10.00	15.00	25.00
	1299	—	8.00	14.00	20.00	30.00
	1300	—	2.50	5.00	8.00	14.00
	1301	—	2.50	5.00	8.00	14.00
	1302	—	2.50	5.00	8.00	14.00
	1303	—	1.50	3.00	6.00	12.00
	1304	—	1.50	3.00	6.00	12.00
	1305	—	1.50	3.00	6.00	12.00
	1306	—	1.50	3.00	6.00	12.00
	1307	—	1.50	3.00	6.00	12.00
	1308	—	1.50	3.00	6.00	12.00

NOTE: Many coins of this type KM#419 are found with blundered dates. Such coins are worth the same as normal dates. Mulings of dates exist.

Kabul Mint

Dar al-Mulk (until AH1163)
Dar as-Sultanat (after AH1164)
GOLD

MAHMUD SHAH

AH1216-1218/1801-1803AD, 1st reign

RUPEE

SILVER, 11.40-11.60 g

KM#	Date	Year	VG	Fine	VF	XF
448	AH1216	1	11.00	25.00	35.00	45.00
	1217	1	11.00	25.00	35.00	45.00
	1217	2	11.00	25.00	35.00	45.00
	1218	2	11.00	25.00	35.00	45.00

MOHUR

GOLD, 10.80-11.00 g

KM#	Date	Year	VG	Fine	VF	XF
450	AH(1216)	1	—	—	400.00	450.00
	1218	3	—	—	350.00	400.00

QAISAR SHAH

AH1218/1803AD

Rebel issue

RUPEE

SILVER, 11.65 g

KM#	Date	Year	VG	Fine	VF	XF
453	AH1222	1	45.00	100.00	150.00	200.00

MOHUR

GOLD, 11.00 g

KM#	Date	Year	VG	Fine	VF	XF
455	AH1222	—	—	—	Rare	—

SHAH SHUJA AL-MULK

AH1218-1224/1803-1808AD, 2nd reign

RUPEE

SILVER, 11.50-11.60 g

KM#	Date	Year	VG	Fine	VF	XF
457	AH1218	1	13.50	30.00	40.00	55.00
	1219	2	13.50	30.00	40.00	55.00
	1220	—	13.50	30.00	40.00	55.00
	1222	—	13.50	30.00	40.00	55.00
	1223	—	13.50	30.00	40.00	55.00

MOHUR

GOLD, 10.95 g

KM#	Date	Year	VG	Fine	VF	XF
459	AH1222	4	—	—	350.00	400.00
	1223	—	—	—	350.00	400.00

MAHMUD SHAH

AH1224-1233/1808-1817AD, 2nd reign

RUPEE

SILVER, 10.75-11.60 g
Rev: Mintname as on previous reign, KM#457.

KM#	Date	Year	VG	Fine	VF	XF
461.1	AH1225	2	10.00	20.00	30.00	40.00
	1226	3	10.00	20.00	30.00	40.00
	1227	4	10.00	20.00	30.00	40.00

KM#	Date	Year	VG	Fine	VF	XF
461.2	AH122x	6	10.00	20.00	30.00	40.00

Rev: Mintname in small circle.

KM#	Date	Year	VG	Fine	VF	XF
462	AH1228	5	9.00	18.00	25.00	35.00

Rev: Mintname in toughra form.

KM#	Date	Year	VG	Fine	VF	XF
463	AH(122)6	—	10.00	20.00	30.00	40.00
	1228	—	10.00	20.00	30.00	40.00
	1230	—	10.00	20.00	30.00	40.00
	1231	8	10.00	20.00	30.00	40.00
	1233	—	10.00	20.00	30.00	40.00

2 RUPEES

SILVER, 23.00-23.20 g

KM#	Date	Year	VG	Fine	VF	XF
464	AH1225	1	65.00	115.00	150.00	200.00

MOHUR

GOLD, 10.90-11.00 g

KM#	Date	Year	VG	Fine	VF	XF
465	AH1224	2	—	—	300.00	375.00
	122x	8	—	—	300.00	375.00

AYYUB SHAH

AH1233-1239/1817-1826AD

RUPEE

SILVER, 10.70-11.40 g

KM#	Date	Year	VG	Fine	VF	XF
468	AH1234	1	12.50	30.00	40.00	55.00
	1234	2	12.50	30.00	40.00	55.00
	1235	2	12.50	30.00	40.00	55.00
	1236	2	12.50	30.00	40.00	55.00
	1236	3	12.50	30.00	40.00	50.00
	1237	2	12.50	30.00	40.00	55.00
	1237	3	12.50	30.00	40.00	50.00
	1238	3	12.50	30.00	40.00	50.00
	1239	4	12.50	30.00	40.00	55.00

NOTE: Various arrangements of obverse legend.

MOHUR

GOLD, 10.79 g

KM#	Date	Year	VG	Fine	VF	XF
469	AH1237	3	—	—	—	2000.

ANONYMOUS COINAGE

RUPEE

SILVER, 11.00-11.40 g
Obv: Kalimah.

KM#	Date	Year	VG	Fine	VF	XF
473	AH1239	4	15.00	35.00	50.00	70.00

DOST MUHAMMAD

AH1239-1255/1824-1839AD, 1st reign

In the name of Mahmud Shah Durrani

RUPEE

SILVER

KM#	Date	Year	VG	Fine	VF	XF
475	AH1239	—	20.00	50.00	75.00	100.00

Anonymous, with title Sultan al-Zaman

KM#	Date	Year	VG	Fine	VF	XF
476	AH1239	1	20.00	50.00	75.00	100.00

Anonymous, with title Sahib al-Zaman

Rev: Mintname in toughra form.

KM#	Date	Year	VG	Fine	VF	XF
477	AH1240	1	8.50	12.50	20.00	30.00
	1241	2	8.50	12.50	20.00	30.00

Obv: Cartouche in center.

KM#	Date	Year	VG	Fine	VF	XF
478	AH1241	—	6.00	10.00	15.00	22.50
	1242	—	6.00	10.00	15.00	22.50
	1243	—	6.00	10.00	15.00	22.50
	1244	—	6.00	10.00	15.00	22,50

Rev: Mintname in ordinary form.

KM#	Date	Year	VG	Fine	VF	XF
479	AH1244	—	8.00	15.00	22.50	35.00
	1245	—	8.00	15.00	22.50	35.00

In the name of his father, Payinda Khan.

KM#	Date	Year	VG	Fine	VF	XF
480.1	AH1245	—	5.00	8.00	12.00	20.00
	1246	—	5.00	8.00	12.00	20.00
	1247	—	5.00	8.00	12.00	20.00
	1248	—	5.00	8.00	12.00	20.00
	1249	—	5.00	8.00	12.00	20.00
	1250	—	5.00	8.00	12.00	20.00

NOTE: Various arrangements of obverse couplet and various borders on reverse.

KM#	Date	Year	VG	Fine	VF	XF
480.2	AH1247	—	5.00	8.00	12.00	20.00
	1248	—	5.00	8.00	12.00	20.00

In his own name

KM#	Date	Year	VG	Fine	VF	XF
481	AH1250	—	4.50	8.00	12.00	20.00
	1251	—	4.50	8.00	12.00	20.00
	1252	—	4.50	8.00	12.00	20.00
	1253	—	4.50	8.00	12.00	20.00
	1254	—	4.50	8.00	12.00	20.00
	1255	—	4.50	8.00	12.00	20.00

SHAH SHUJA AL-MULK

AH1255-1258/1839-1842AD, 3rd reign

RUPEE

SILVER, 11.50 g
Obv: Short inscription, title *Sultan*. Broad flan.

KM#	Date	Year	VG	Fine	VF	XF
482	AH1255	—	—	—	Rare	—

9.20 g
Obv: Long inscription.

KM#	Date	Year	VG	Fine	VF	XF
483	AH1255	1	10.00	18.00	25.00	35.00

9.20-9.50 g
Obv: Short inscription, title *Sultan*.

KM#	Date	Year	VG	Fine	VF	XF
484.1	AH1255	—	6.50	10.00	17.00	27.00
	1256	—	6.50	10.00	17.00	27.00
	1257	—	7.00	12.00	18.00	28.00
	1258	—	7.00	12.00	18.00	28.00

NOTE: Varieties exist, some on broad planchets.

Obv: *Dur-e-Duran* above *Sultan*.

KM#	Date	Year	VG	Fine	VF	XF
484.2	AH1255	—	6.00	12.00	18.00	28.00

Anonymous in name of Sahib al-Zaman

KM#	Date	Year	VG	Fine	VF	XF
485	AH1257	—	12.50	25.00	36.00	50.00

In the name of Shah Zaman

KM#	Date	Year	VG	Fine	VF	XF
486	AH1258	—	16.00	35.00	50.00	70.00

MOHUR

GOLD, 10.70-10.80 g

KM#	Date	Year	VG	Fine	VF	XF
487	AH1255	—	—	—	285.00	350.00
	1258	—	—	—	285.00	350.00

FATH JANG

AH1258/1842AD

RUPEE

SILVER, 9.30-9.40 g
Obv: Couplet, name *Fath Jung* at top.

KM#	Date	Year	VG	Fine	VF	XF
488.1	AH1258	—	18.00	38.00	60.00	80.00

Obv: Couplet, name *Fath Jung* in center.

KM#	Date	Year	VG	Fine	VF	XF
488.2	AH1258	—	25.00	50.00	70.00	100.00

Obv: Name only w/title *Dur-e-Duran*.

KM#	Date	Year	VG	Fine	VF	XF
488.3	AH1258	—	18.00	38.00	60.00	80.00

Obv: Name only w/title *Padshah-i Ghazi*.

KM#	Date	Year	VG	Fine	VF	XF
488.4	AH1258	—	18.00	38.00	60.00	80.00

SHAHPUR SHAH

AH1258/1842AD

RUPEE

SILVER, 9.40 g

KM#	Date	Year	VG	Fine	VF	XF
489	AH1258	—	35.00	65.00	100.00	150.00

DOST MUHAMMAD

AH1258-1280/1842-1863AD, 2nd reign

Anonymous

RUPEE

SILVER
Obv: Kalimah

KM#	Date	Year	VG	Fine	VF	XF
493	AH1258	—	9.00	16.00	25.00	35.00

In his own name

Obv: Long couplet.

KM#	Date	Year	VG	Fine	VF	XF
496	AH1259	—	13.50	30.00	40.00	55.00

Obv: Couplet ending *Khaliq-i-Akbar*, many varieties.

KM#	Date	Year	VG	Fine	VF	XF
497	AH1259	—	10.00	15.00	22.50	40.00
	1262	—	7.00	11.00	15.00	25.00
	1263	—	4.50	7.00	10.00	18.00
	1264	—	4.50	7.00	10.00	18.00
	1265	—	4.50	7.00	10.00	18.00
	1266 obverse 5-pointed star					
		—	4.50	7.00	10.00	18.00
	1266 obverse and reverse 5-pointed star					
		—	4.50	7.00	10.00	18.00
	1267	—	4.50	7.00	10.00	18.00
	1268	—	4.50	7.00	12.00	20.00
	1269	—	4.50	7.00	10.00	18.00
	1270	—	4.50	7.00	10.00	18.00
	1271	—	4.50	7.00	10.00	18.00
	1272	—	4.50	7.00	10.00	18.00
	1273	—	4.50	7.00	10.00	18.00
	1274	—	4.50	7.00	10.00	18.00
	1275	—	4.50	7.00	10.00	18.00
	1276	—	4.50	7.00	10.00	18.00
	1277	—	4.50	7.00	10.00	18.00
	1278	—	4.50	7.00	10.00	18.00
	1279	—	4.50	7.00	10.00	18.00
	1280	—	12.50	20.00	30.00	40.00

NOTE: Mulings exist with different dates on obverse and reverse.

Obv: 1 leaf in field in 2-4 o'clock margin.
Rev: 2 leaves facing each other at bottom.

KM#	Date	Year	VG	Fine	VF	XF
498	AH1271	—	4.00	7.00	10.00	18.00
	1272	—	4.00	7.00	10.00	18.00
	1273	—	4.00	7.00	10.00	18.00
	1274	—	4.00	7.00	10.00	18.00
	1277	—	4.00	7.00	10.00	18.00

TILLA

GOLD

KM#	Date	Year	VG	Fine	VF	XF
499	AH1269	—	—	235.00	275.00	325.00

SHER ALI

AH1280-1283/1863-1866AD, 1st reign

RUPEE

SILVER
Obv: New couplet, *Bi-Valayi Amir*.

KM#	Date	Year	VG	Fine	VF	XF
502	AH1280	—	—	—	Rare	—

Obv: Couplet starting *Za Aini Marhamat. . .*

KM#	Date	Year	VG	Fine	VF	XF
503	AH1280	—	5.00	9.00	13.00	20.00
	1281	—	5.00	9.00	13.00	20.00
	1282	—	5.00	9.00	13.00	20.00

NOTE: Two varieties of obv. exist.

Anonymous, with title Sahib al-Zaman

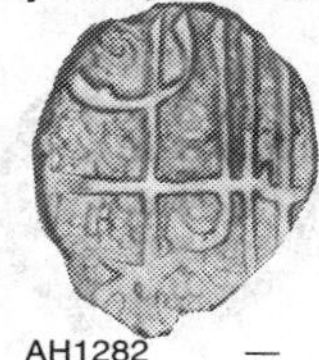 

KM#	Date	Year	VG	Fine	VF	XF
504	AH1282	—	12.50	25.00	35.00	50.00

MUHAMMAD AFZAL

AH1283-1284/1866-1867AD

RUPEE

SILVER

KM#	Date	Year	VG	Fine	VF	XF
507	AH1283	—	9.00	15.00	20.00	30.00
	1284	—	15.00	25.00	40.00	55.00

NOTE: 2 varieties are known dated AH1283.

MUHAMMAD A'ZAM

AH1283-1285/1866-1868AD

RUPEE

SILVER
Obv: *A'zam* above *Amir*.

KM#	Date	Year	VG	Fine	VF	XF
508.1	AH1284	—	10.00	15.00	20.00	30.00
	1285	—	10.00	15.00	20.00	30.00

Obv: *A'zam* above *Muhammad*.

KM#	Date	Year	VG	Fine	VF	XF
508.2	AH1284	—	15.00	30.00	45.00	60.00

KM#	Date	Year	VG	Fine	VF	XF
509	AH1285	—	13.00	25.00	35.00	45.00

SHER ALI

AH1285-1296/1868-1879AD, 2nd reign

1/6 RUPEE

SILVER, 1.50 g

KM#	Date	Year	VG	Fine	VF	XF
511	AH1287	—	25.00	50.00	65.00	85.00

1/2 RUPEE

NOTE: KM#512, which was reported for AH1288, 1292, 1293 and 1294, is a misreading of the Qandahar Mint.

SILVER
Large, thin planchet; fine engraving.

KM#	Date	Year	VG	Fine	VF	XF
513	AH1292	—	—	5.00	10.00	18.00

 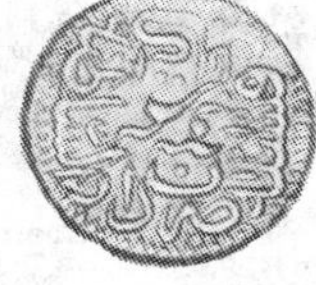

Small, thick planchet; coarse engraving.

KM#	Date	Year	VG	Fine	VF	XF
514	AH1295	—	—	4.00	8.00	15.00

RUPEE

SILVER

Obv: Couplet starting *Za Iltifat-i. . .*

KM#	Date	Year	VG	Fine	VF	XF
516	AH1285	—	7.50	12.50	20.00	30.00

Obv: 3-stem toughra.

KM#	Date	Year	VG	Fine	VF	XF
517	AH1285	—	8.00	15.00	25.00	40.00
	1286	—	3.00	6.00	10.00	20.00
	1286/87	—	6.00	10.00	15.00	25.00
	1287	—	6.00	10.00	15.00	25.00

Obv: 5-stem toughra.

KM#	Date	Year	VG	Fine	VF	XF
518	AH1285	—	40.00	60.00	90.00	140.00
	1286	—	30.00	50.00	80.00	125.00

KM#	Date	Year	VG	Fine	VF	XF
519	AH1287	—	3.50	6.00	10.00	18.00
	1288	—	—	5.00	7.50	15.00
	1289	—	—	5.00	7.50	15.00
	1290	—	—	5.00	7.50	15.00
	1291	—	—	5.00	7.50	15.00
	1292	—	—	5.00	7.50	15.00
	1293	—	—	5.00	7.50	15.00
	1294	—	—	5.00	7.50	15.00
	1295	—	—	5.00	7.50	15.00
	1295//1296	—	—	5.00	7.50	15.00
	1296	—	5.00	7.50	12.50	20.00

NOTE: Other examples bearing different obverse and reverse dates exist.

Fine style

KM#	Date	Year	VG	Fine	VF	XF
520	AH1292	—	4.50	9.00	15.00	25.00
	1293	—	4.50	9.00	15.00	25.00

Coarse style

KM#	Date	Year	VG	Fine	VF	XF
521	AH1293	—	3.50	6.00	10.00	18.00
	1294	—	3.50	6.00	10.00	18.00
	1295	—	3.50	6.00	10.00	18.00

TOMAN

GOLD, 3.45 g

KM#	Date	Year	VG	Fine	VF	XF
524	AH1294	—	—	180.00	225.00	275.00
	1295	—	—	165.00	200.00	250.00
	1296	—	—	165.00	200.00	250.00

MOHUR

GOLD, 10.90 g

KM#	Date	Year	VG	Fine	VF	XF
525	AH1288	—	—	225.00	300.00	400.00

MUHAMMAD YAQUB

AH1296-1297/1879-1880AD

1/3 RUPEE

SILVER

KM#	Date	Year	VG	Fine	VF	XF
531	AH1296	—	25.00	55.00	75.00	100.00

RUPEE

SILVER

KM#	Date	Year	VG	Fine	VF	XF
533	AH1296	—	—	5.00	8.00	16.00
	1297	—	— Reported, not confirmed			

WALI MUHAMMAD

AH1297/1880AD

RUPEE

SILVER

KM#	Date	Year	VG	Fine	VF	XF
538	AH1297	—	10.00	16.00	25.00	40.00

ABDUR RAHMAN

AH1297-1319/1880-1901AD

1/3 RUPEE

SILVER, 15mm

KM#	Date	Year	VG	Fine	VF	XF
541	AH1297	—	40.00	70.00	90.00	110.00
	1298	—	30.00	60.00	75.00	100.00

RUPEE

SILVER

Obv: Rudimentary toughra.

KM#	Date	Year	VG	Fine	VF	XF
543	AH1297	—	25.00	45.00	60.00	85.00

Obv: Name of ruler in fancy border.

KM#	Date	Year	VG	Fine	VF	XF
A544	AH1297	—	20.00	40.00	55.00	75.00

Obv: Ornate toughra.

KM#	Date	Year	VG	Fine	VF	XF
B544	AH1298	—	30.00	60.00	90.00	120.00

Obv: Name of ruler within dotted circle.

KM#	Date	Year	VG	Fine	VF	XF
C544	AH1297	—	30.00	60.00	90.00	120.00

Obv: Date above. Rev: Date in "b" of *Zarb.*

KM#	Date	Year	VG	Fine	VF	XF
D544	AH1297	—	35.00	65.00	100.00	140.00

Obv: Name of ruler in plain border.

KM#	Date	Year	VG	Fine	VF	XF
544.1	AH1297	—	4.00	6.00	10.00	18.00
	1298	—	7.50	10.00	13.00	22.50
	1299	—	12.50	20.00	30.00	45.00
	1300	—	12.50	18.00	25.00	35.00
	1301	—	3.00	6.00	10.00	18.00
	1302	—	3.00	6.00	10.00	18.00
	1303	—	3.00	6.00	10.00	18.00
	1304	—	3.00	6.00	10.00	18.00
	1305	—	3.00	6.00	10.00	18.00
	1306	—	3.00	6.00	10.00	18.00
	1307	—	3.00	6.00	10.00	18.00
	1308	—	7.00	10.00	15.00	25.00

NOTE: Obverses are often muled with reverses bearing a different date. For machine struck coins dated AH1303//1304 and 1304//1304 see KM#805.

NOTE: The year AH1297 has been observed struck over an 1876 British India 1/4 rupee, probably a mint sport.

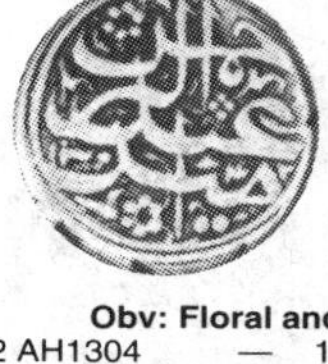

Obv: Floral and legend varieties

KM#	Date	Year	VG	Fine	VF	XF
544.2	AH1304	—	15.00	22.50	35.00	50.00

NAZARANA RUPEE

SILVER

KM#	Date	Year	VG	Fine	VF	XF
545	AH1303	—	25.00	50.00	75.00	100.00

MUHAMMAD ISHAQ

AH1305-1306/1889AD

RUPEE

SILVER
Struck at Balkh, but inscribed *Kabul*.
Obv: W/o *Alif* before *Ishaq*.
Rev: Mint name across center.

KM#	Date	Year	VG	Fine	VF	XF
548	AH1305	—	35.00	70.00	100.00	125.00
	1306	—	30.00	55.00	75.00	100.00

Obv: *Alif* before *Ishaq*.
Rev: Mint name at top, date at bottom.

KM#	Date	Year	VG	Fine	VF	XF
549	AH1305	—	35.00	70.00	100.00	125.00
	1306	—	35.00	70.00	100.00	125.00

NOTE: Mules of KM#548 obverse and KM#549 reverse exist.

Kashmir Mint

MAHMUD SHAH

AH1216-1218/1801-1803AD, 1st reign
AH1223-1233/1808-1818AD, 2nd reign

FRACTIONAL FALUS

COPPER, 3.80-4.40 g
First Reign

KM#	Date	Year	Good	VG	Fine	VF
580	AH1217	2	3.00	4.00	5.00	7.00

20mm, 7.20-7.80 g
Second Reign
Obv: King's name in toughra style.

KM#	Date	Year	Good	VG	Fine	VF
581	AH—	1	3.00	4.00	5.00	7.00

FALUS

COPPER, 25.5mm, 10.20 g
First Reign

KM#	Date	Year	Good	VG	Fine	VF
583	AH1216	1	4.00	7.00	10.00	16.00

20mm, 9.40-9.80 g
Second Reign
Obv: Toughra style. Rev: Legend.

KM#	Date	Year	Good	VG	Fine	VF
584	AH—	1	3.00	4.50	7.00	10.00
	1229	—	3.00	4.50	7.00	10.00
	1230	6	3.00	4.50	7.00	10.00

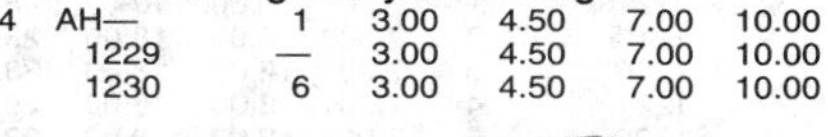

10.00 g
Rev: Swords and plume.

KM#	Date	Year	Good	VG	Fine	VF
585	AH1233	11	4.00	6.00	10.00	15.00

1/4 RUPEE

SILVER, 2.50-2.60 g

KM#	Date	Year	VG	Fine	VF	XF
586	AH1217	2	18.50	40.00	60.00	80.00

RUPEE

SILVER, 10.80-11.00 g

1st Reign

KM#	Date	Year	VG	Fine	VF	XF
588	AH1216	1	8.50	15.00	25.00	35.00
	1217	2	8.50	15.00	25.00	35.00
	1218	3	8.50	15.00	25.00	35.00

KM#	Date	Year	VG	Fine	VF	XF
589	AH1218	3	10.00	20.00	30.00	45.00

KM#	Date	Year	VG	Fine	VF	XF
591	AH1228	6	4.50	9.00	14.00	20.00
	1229	6	4.50	9.00	14.00	20.00
	1229	7	4.50	9.00	14.00	20.00
	1230	7	4.50	9.00	14.00	20.00
	1230	8	4.50	9.00	14.00	20.00
	1230	10	4.50	9.00	14.00	20.00
	1232	10	4.50	9.00	14.00	20.00
	1233	10	6.50	12.50	20.00	30.00
	1233	11	6.50	12.50	20.00	30.00

NOTE: The sequence of regnal years at Kashmir is very confused.

SHAH SHUJA AL-MULK

AH1218-1223/1803-1808AD, 2nd reign

FALUS

COPPER, 7.40-9.00 g
Rev: Sword.

KM#	Date	Year	Good	VG	Fine	VF
594	AH1218	1	2.50	3.50	5.00	7.00
	—	2	3.00	4.50	6.50	9.00

Rev: 2 swords.

KM#	Date	Year	Good	VG	Fine	VF
A595	AH1219	—	5.00	8.50	15.00	22.50

Rev: Crossed swords.

KM#	Date	Year	Good	VG	Fine	VF
595	AH(12)19	—	3.00	4.00	6.00	8.50
596	AH1220	3	3.00	4.00	6.00	8.50

Rev: Sword.

KM#	Date	Year	Good	VG	Fine	VF
597	AH1221	4	3.50	5.00	7.50	10.00

Reign in Kashmir

AH1227-1228/1812-1813AD

RUPEE

SILVER, 10.80-11.20 g

KM#	Date	Year	VG	Fine	VF	XF
598	AH1218	1	—	6.00	10.00	17.50
	1219	2	—	6.00	10.00	17.50
	1220	3	—	6.00	10.00	17.50
	1221	4	—	6.00	10.00	17.50
	1222	5	—	6.00	10.00	17.50
	1223	6	4.50	7.50	12.50	20.00

QAISAR SHAH

AH1222-1223/1807-1808AD

RUPEE

SILVER, 11.00-11.20 g

KM#	Date	Year	VG	Fine	VF	XF
600	AH1222	1	20.00	40.00	60.00	80.00
	1223	1	20.00	40.00	60.00	80.00
	1223	2	20.00	40.00	60.00	80.00

ATA MUHAMMAD BAMIZAI KHAN

Rebel governor of Kashmir
AH1223-1228/1808-1813AD

In the name of Shah Nur al-Din, the patron saint of Kashmir.

FALUS

COPPER, 16.5mm, 7.50 g

KM#	Date	Year	Good	VG	Fine	VF
601	AH1225	3	8.00	15.00	22.50	35.00
	1228	—	8.00	15.00	22.50	35.00

RUPEE

SILVER, 10.70-11.10 g

KM#	Date	Year	VG	Fine	VF	XF
603	AH1223	1	6.50	12.50	20.00	30.00
	1224	1	6.50	12.50	20.00	30.00
	1224	2	6.50	12.50	20.00	30.00
	1225	2	6.50	12.50	20.00	30.00
	1225	3	6.50	12.50	20.00	30.00
	1226	4	6.50	12.50	20.00	30.00
	1227	4	6.50	12.50	20.00	30.00
	1227	5	6.50	12.50	20.00	30.00
	1228	5	6.50	12.50	20.00	30.00

HEAVY RUPEE

(1-1/4 Rupee)

SILVER, 14.50 g

KM#	Date	Year	VG	Fine	VF	XF
604	AH1223	1	—	200.00	250.00	300.00
	1225	—	—	—	Rare	—

2 MOHURS

GOLD, 21.60-21.80 g

KM#	Date	Year	VG	Fine	VF	XF
607	AH1225	2	—	—	5000.	6500.

KM#	Date	Year	VG	Fine	VF	XF
608	AH1225	3	—	—	Rare	—

MUHAMMAD A'ZIM

(Governor for Ayub Shah)
AH1228-1234/1813-1819AD

FALUS

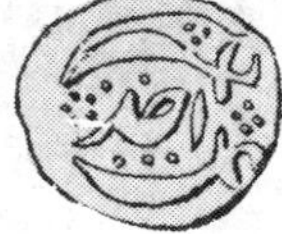

COPPER, 7.50 g

KM#	Date	Year	Good	VG	Fine	VF
609	AH1228	1	5.00	9.00	16.00	25.00

AYYUB SHAH

AH1233-1245/1818-1829AD

FALUS

COPPER, 7.00-8.00 g

KM#	Date	Year	Good	VG	Fine	VF
610	AH1233	—	7.00	12.00	18.00	27.50

RUPEE

SILVER, 11.00-11.20 g
Rev: Mint name and regnal year.

KM#	Date	Year	VG	Fine	VF	XF
613	AH1233	1	15.00	30.00	50.00	75.00
	1234	1	12.50	25.00	40.00	60.00

Rev: Mint, regnal year and *Julus* formula.

KM#	Date	Year	VG	Fine	VF	XF
614	AH1234	2	15.00	30.00	50.00	75.00

NOTE: Kashmir fell to the Sikhs in AH1234 (1819AD), ending the Durrani dominion in India.

Mashhad Mint

Mashhad, entitled Muqaddas (holy), was the chief city of Iranian Khorasan. From AH1161/1748AD until AH1218/1803AD, it was the capital of the Afsharid principality, which remained under nominal Durrani suzerainty from AH1163/1750AD onwards. Coins were struck in the name of Durrani rulers in AH1163, 1168-1186, 1198-1218. Issues in the name of Iranian rulers will be listed in a future edition of this catalog under Iran.

MAHMUD SHAH

AH1216-1218/1801-1803AD, First Reign

RUPEE

SILVER, 11.00-11.50 g

KM#	Date	Year	VG	Fine	VF	XF
G640	AH1218	—	60.00	125.00	160.00	200.00

NOTE: In AH1218/1803AD, Mashhad was seized by Fath Ali Shah and permanently annexed to Iran.

Multan Mint

Dar al-Aman

Multan was annexed by Ahmad Shah in AH1165/1752AD, and held under Afghan rule until lost to the Sikhs in AH1233/1818AD, except for an interval of Maratha control in AH1173/1759AD and Sikh control from AH1185-1194/1771-1780AD.

MAHMUD SHAH

AH1216-1218/1801-1803AD, 1st reign

RUPEE

SILVER, 11.50-11.60 g

KM#	Date	Year	VG	Fine	VF	XF
668	AH1216	1	20.00	40.00	60.00	85.00
	1218	1	20.00	40.00	60.00	85.00

SHAH SHUJA AL-MULK

AH1218-1224/1803-1808AD, 2nd reign

RUPEE

SILVER, 20.5mm, 11.40-11.60 g

KM#	Date	Year	VG	Fine	VF	XF
673	AH1218	1	20.00	40.00	60.00	85.00
	1219	—	20.00	40.00	60.00	85.00

MOHUR

GOLD, 10.90-11.00 g

KM#	Date	Year	VG	Fine	VF	XF
675	AH1218	1	—	—	Rare	—
	1224	8	—	—	Rare	—

NOTE: Multan fell to the Sikhs in AH1233/1818AD.

MAHMUD SHAH

AH1224-1233/1808-1817AD, 2nd reign

FALUS

COPPER, 11.60-12.80 g

KM#	Date	Year	Good	VG	Fine	VF
677	AH1226	1	3.75	7.50	10.00	16.50
	1227	1	3.75	7.50	10.00	16.50
	1227	2	3.75	7.50	10.00	16.50
	1228	3	3.75	7.50	10.00	16.50
	1228	5	3.75	7.50	10.00	16.50
	1229	—	3.75	7.50	10.00	16.50
	1230	7	3.75	7.50	10.00	16.50
	1231	7	3.75	7.50	10.00	16.50
	1235	—	3.75	7.50	10.00	16.50
	1253	—	3.75	7.50	10.00	16.50
	1254	—	3.75	7.50	10.00	16.50
	1257	—	3.75	7.50	10.00	16.50
	1260	—	3.75	7.50	10.00	16.50
	1263	—	3.75	7.50	10.00	16.50
	1264	—	3.75	7.50	10.00	16.50
	1267	—	3.75	7.50	10.00	16.50
	1270	—	3.75	7.50	10.00	16.50

NOTE: Issues dated after AH1233 are posthumous issues struck by the Sikhs.

AYYUB SHAH

AH1233-1245/1817-1826AD

RUPEE

SILVER, 11.20-11.40 g
Obv: Kalima, mint and date.

KM#	Date	Year	VG	Fine	VF	XF
680	AH1239	—	—	—	Rare	—

Peshawar Mint

Peshawar passed to Ahmad Shah after the death of Nadir Shah Afshar, who had seized it from the Mughals in AH1151/1738AD. It was lost to the Sikhs in AH1250/1834AD. Although the winter capital of the Durranis, it was never granted an honorific epithet.

MAHMUD SHAH

AH1216-1218/1801-1803AD, 1st reign

RUPEE

SILVER, 11.40-11.60 g
Rev: Mint name w/*Julus* formula.

KM#	Date	Year	VG	Fine	VF	XF
718	AH1216	1	10.00	13.50	20.00	30.00

Rev: Mint name.

KM#	Date	Year	VG	Fine	VF	XF
719	AH1217	2	10.00	13.50	20.00	30.00
	1218	3	10.00	13.50	20.00	30.00

SHAH SHUJA AL-MULK

AH1218-1224/1803-1808AD, 2nd reign

As local ruler at Peshawar

1/10 RUPEE

SILVER, 1.00 g

KM#	Date	Year	VG	Fine	VF	XF
720	AH1227	7	—	—	Rare	—

RUPEE

SILVER, 11.40-11.60 g

KM#	Date	Year	VG	Fine	VF	XF
722	AH1218	1	7.00	12.00	18.00	28.00
	1219	2	7.00	12.00	18.00	28.00
	1220	3	7.00	12.00	18.00	28.00
	1221	4	7.00	12.00	18.00	28.00
	1222	5	7.00	12.00	18.00	28.00
	1223	6	7.00	12.00	18.00	28.00
	1224	7	7.00	12.00	18.00	28.00

As local ruler at Peshawar

KM#	Date	Year	VG	Fine	VF	XF
723	AH1227	1	40.00	70.00	100.00	130.00

Briefly at Peshawar in AH1233/1818AD.

KM#	Date	Year	VG	Fine	VF	XF
724	AH1233	1	40.00	70.00	100.00	130.00
	1234	1	40.00	70.00	100.00	130.00

NOTE: This coin may be distinguished from KM#722 and 723 by the octagon and calligraphy of the rev. and by the date.

MAHMUD SHAH

AH1224-1233/1808-1817AD, 2nd reign

FALUS

COPPER, 11.40 g

KM#	Date	Year	VG	Fine	VF	XF
726	AH1232	8	—	—	Rare	—

RUPEE

SILVER, 10.60-11.50 g
Rev: Legend w/beaded circle.

KM#	Date	Year	VG	Fine	VF	XF
A727	AH1224	1	—	20.00	45.00	80.00

Obv: Linear legends. Rev: Legend in octagon.

KM#	Date	Year	VG	Fine	VF	XF
727.1	AH1225	1	—	11.00	18.00	26.00
	1226	2	—	11.00	18.00	26.00
	1227	2	—	11.00	18.00	26.00
	(122)7	3	—	11.00	18.00	26.00

KM#	Date	Year	VG	Fine	VF	XF
727.2	AH1224	1	—	—	—	—
	1227	3	—	11.00	18.00	26.00
	1227	4	—	11.00	18.00	26.00
	1228	4	—	11.00	18.00	26.00
	1228	5	—	11.00	18.00	26.00
	1229	5	—	11.00	18.00	26.00
	1229	6	—	11.00	18.00	26.00
	1230	6	—	11.00	18.00	26.00
	1230	7	—	11.00	18.00	26.00
	1231	7	—	11.00	18.00	26.00
	1231	8	—	11.00	18.00	26.00

Rev: Legend within square.

KM#	Date	Year	VG	Fine	VF	XF
727.3	AH1227	7	—	25.00	35.00	50.00

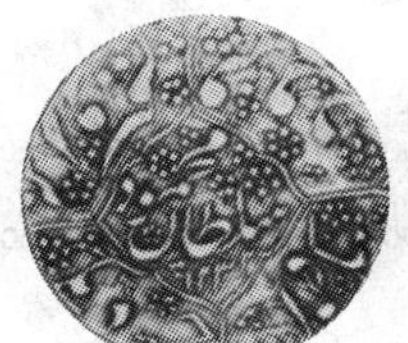

Obv: Circular legend around central cartouche.

KM#	Date	Year	VG	Fine	VF	XF
728	AH1231	8	10.00	20.00	30.00	40.00
	1232	8	10.00	20.00	30.00	40.00
	1232	9	10.00	20.00	30.00	40.00
	1233 6 (error for 9)					
		—	12.50	25.00	35.00	45.00
	1233	9	10.00	20.00	30.00	40.00
	1233	10	10.00	20.00	30.00	40.00

AYYUB SHAH

AH1233-1245/1817-1829AD

FALUS

COPPER, 10.40-12.20 g

KM#	Date	Year	Good	VG	Fine	VF
730	AH1234	2	6.00	10.00	17.50	30.00
	123x	3	6.00	10.00	17.50	30.00
	1236	4	6.00	10.00	17.50	30.00
	1237	—	5.00	8.50	15.00	25.00
	1238	6	5.00	8.50	15.00	25.00
	1239	—	5.00	8.50	15.00	25.00
	1240	—	6.50	11.00	18.00	32.50

RUPEE

SILVER, 10.40-10.60 g
Obv: Ruler's name in fancy diamond.

KM#	Date	Year	VG	Fine	VF	XF
732	AH1233	1	23.00	45.00	65.00	85.00

Obv: Couplet in 3 lines.

KM#	Date	Year	VG	Fine	VF	XF
733	AH1233	1	8.00	13.00	20.00	30.00
	1233	2	8.00	13.00	20.00	30.00
	1234	2	8.00	13.00	20.00	30.00
	(123)4	6	8.00	13.00	20.00	30.00
	1235	2	8.00	13.00	20.00	30.00
	1235	3	8.00	13.00	20.00	30.00
	1236	3	8.00	13.00	20.00	30.00
	1236	4	8.00	13.00	20.00	30.00
	1237	4	8.00	13.00	20.00	30.00
	1237	5	8.00	13.00	20.00	30.00
	1238	5	8.00	13.00	20.00	30.00
	1238	6	8.00	13.00	20.00	30.00
	1239	6	8.00	13.00	20.00	30.00
	1239	7	8.00	13.00	20.00	30.00
	1240	6	8.00	13.00	20.00	30.00
	1240	7	8.00	13.00	20.00	30.00
	1240	8	8.00	13.00	20.00	30.00
	1241	7	8.00	13.00	20.00	30.00
	1242	9	8.00	13.00	20.00	30.00
	1243	9	8.00	13.00	20.00	30.00
	1243	10	8.00	13.00	20.00	30.00
	1244	11	8.00	13.00	20.00	30.00
	1245	11	5.00	8.50	14.00	20.00

Obv: Name in foliated diamond.

KM#	Date	Year	VG	Fine	VF	XF
734	AH124x	12	25.00	45.00	65.00	85.00

MOHUR

GOLD, 21.5mm, 10.50-10.60 g

KM#	Date	Year	VG	Fine	VF	XF
735	AH—	6	—	—	325.00	375.00
	—	7	—	—	325.00	375.00

DOST MUHAMMAD

AH1239-1255/1824-1839AD, 1st reign

RUPEE

SILVER, 23mm, 10.40 g
Dated on both sides.

KM#	Date	Year	VG	Fine	VF	XF
738	AH1246	—	22.50	50.00	75.00	120.00
	1249	—	22.50	50.00	75.00	120.00

SULTAN MUHAMMAD

AH1247-1250/1831-1834AD at Peshawar

Anonymous couplet type

RUPEE

SILVER

KM#	Date	Year	VG	Fine	VF	XF
739	AH1247	—	12.50	25.00	35.00	60.00
	1248	—	12.50	25.00	35.00	60.00
	1249	—	12.50	25.00	35.00	60.00

NOTE: Peshawar fell to the Sikhs in AH1250/1834AD. For later issues, see India, Sikhs.

Qandahar Mint

Issues of this mint are listed together with those of Ahmadshahi, which was a name of Qandahar granted in honor of Ahmad Shah, founder of the Durrani Kingdom.

Rikab Mint

The Camp mint brought *Mubarak* with the royal entourage while traveling.

SHAH SHUJA AL-MULK

AH1218-1224/1803-1808AD, 2nd reign

MOHUR

GOLD, 10.80-10.90 g

KM#	Date	Year	VG	Fine	VF	XF
749	AH1219	—	—	—	Rare	—

MILLED COINAGE

MONETARY SYSTEM

10 Dinar = 1 Paisa
5 Paise = 1 Shahi
2 Shahi = 1 Sanar
2 Sanar = 1 Abbasi
1-1/2 Abbasi = 1 Qiran
2 Qiran = 1 Kabuli Rupee

PAISA

BRONZE, 25mm

KM#	Date	Mintage	VG	Fine	VF	XF
800	AH1309	—	25.00	40.00	120.00	225.00

Thicker variety of KM#802.

KM#	Date	Mintage	VG	Fine	VF	XF
801	AH1309	—	20.00	30.00	50.00	70.00

BRONZE or BRASS, 20mm

KM#	Date	Mintage	VG	Fine	VF	XF
802	AH1309	—	2.50	5.00	7.50	20.00
	1312	—	2.00	4.00	6.50	15.00
	1313	—	2.50	5.00	7.50	20.00
	1314	—	2.00	4.00	6.50	15.00
	1316	—	3.00	5.00	7.50	20.00
	1317	—	4.00	6.00	10.00	30.00

NOTE: Coins dated AH1313 and 1317 are known in two varieties. 3 varieties are known for AH1314.

KM#	Date	Mintage	VG	Fine	VF	XF
827	AH1317	—	3.50	6.00	12.00	35.00

NOTE: 2 varieties are known.

Mule. Obv: KM#827. Rev: KM#802.

KM#	Date	Mintage	VG	Fine	VF	XF
828	AH1317	—	10.00	15.00	30.00	50.00

SHAHI

(5 Paisa)

COPPER or BRASS

KM#	Date	Mintage	VG	Fine	VF	XF
803	AH1309	—	15.00	25.00	55.00	140.00

100 DINARS

(10 Paisa)

COPPER

KM#	Date	Mintage	VG	Fine	VF	XF
809	AH1311	—	125.00	200.00	350.00	600.00

SANAR

(10 Paisa)

1.5500 g, .500 SILVER, .0249 oz ASW
Obv: Date in loop of toughra.

KM#	Date	Mintage	VG	Fine	VF	XF
823	AH1315	—	7.00	10.00	20.00	40.00
	ND	—	8.50	13.00	25.00	45.00

Rev: Date below mosque.

KM#	Date	Mintage	VG	Fine	VF	XF
824	AH1315	—	9.00	14.00	25.00	45.00
	ND	—	8.50	13.50	25.00	45.00

ABBASI

(20 Paisa)

3.1100 g, .500 SILVER, .0499 oz ASW
Obv: Date above toughra.

KM#	Date	Mintage	VG	Fine	VF	XF
810	AH1313	—	3.00	5.00	8.00	14.00

Rev: Date below mosque.

KM#	Date	Mintage	VG	Fine	VF	XF
811	AH1313	—	10.00	17.50	27.50	50.00

Rev: New style mosque.

KM#	Date	Mintage	VG	Fine	VF	XF
816	AH1314	—	4.00	8.00	15.00	25.00

1/2 RUPEE

(Qiran)

4.6500 g, .500 SILVER, .0747 oz ASW
Rev: Star above mosque.

KM#	Date	Mintage	VG	Fine	VF	XF
804	AH1308	—	5.00	7.50	10.00	20.00
	1309	—	5.00	8.00	12.00	25.00
	1310	—	5.00	8.00	12.00	25.00

Rev: *Kabul* above mosque.

KM#	Date	Mintage	VG	Fine	VF	XF
812	AH1313	—	6.00	8.50	12.50	27.50

Rev: *Yak Mesqhal* above mosque.

KM#	Date	Mintage	VG	Fine	VF	XF
817	AH1314	—	7.50	13.50	28.00	60.00

NOTE: The half rupee dated AH1314 bears the denomination of 1 Qiran; all others have Half Rupee.

Rev: Crossed swords and cannons below mosque.

KM#	Date	Mintage	VG	Fine	VF	XF
825	AH1316	—	4.50	8.50	15.00	30.00
	1317	—	— Reported, not confirmed			
	1318	—	— Reported, not confirmed			

RUPEE

SILVER

KM#	Date	Mintage	VG	Fine	VF	XF
805	AH1304/1303	—	25.00	35.00	55.00	115.00
	1304	—	25.00	35.00	55.00	115.00

NOTE: Similar to KM#544.1, these machine struck Rupees were produced by the Birmingham Mint as patterns.

9.2000 g, .900 SILVER, .2662 oz ASW
Obv: Star above toughra.
Rev: Star above, *Kabul* below mosque.

KM#	Date	Mintage	VG	Fine	VF	XF
806	AH1308	—	5.00	8.00	14.00	25.00
	1309	—	4.00	6.00	10.00	20.00
	1310/09	—	4.00	6.00	10.00	25.00
	1310	—	5.00	8.00	14.00	25.00
	1311	—	4.00	6.00	10.00	20.00
	1311/09	—	4.00	6.00	10.00	20.00
	1312/1/9	—	4.00	7.00	14.00	25.00
	1312/1	—	4.00	6.00	10.00	20.00
	1312	—	4.00	6.00	10.00	20.00
	1313	—	4.00	6.00	10.00	20.00
	1391(error)		12.00	15.00	17.50	25.00

NOTE: 2 varieties each are known for dates AH1311-13.

Rev: *Kabul* to right of mosque.

KM#	Date	Mintage	VG	Fine	VF	XF
813	AH1313	—	5.00	7.50	10.00	20.00

Rev: *Kabul* above mosque.

KM#	Date	Mintage	VG	Fine	VF	XF
814	AH1312	—	10.00	20.00	50.00	75.00
	1313	—	5.00	7.00	9.00	20.00

Rev: *Du Mesqal* above mosque.

KM#	Date	Mintage	VG	Fine	VF	XF
818	AH1314	—	6.00	10.00	20.00	40.00

Obv: *Kabul* above toughra, undivided dates.

KM#	Date	Mintage	VG	Fine	VF	XF
819.1	AH1314	—	4.00	10.00	17.50	35.00
	1315	—	4.00	5.50	9.00	20.00

Obv: Divided dates, last 2 digits right of toughra.

KM#	Date	Mintage	VG	Fine	VF	XF
819.2	AH1315	—	20.00	50.00	100.00	150.00
	1316	—	5.00	8.00	15.00	30.00

Obv: Divided dates, "17" below toughra.

KM#	Date	Mintage	VG	Fine	VF	XF
819.4	AH1317	—	20.00	50.00	100.00	150.00

Obv: Date at right of toughra.

KM#	Date	Mintage	VG	Fine	VF	XF
819.3	AH1317	—	15.00	40.00	60.00	110.00

Obv: 3 stars above toughra, date in toughra.

KM#	Date	Mintage	VG	Fine	VF	XF
829	AH1317	—	6.00	10.00	25.00	50.00

Obv: Date at right of toughra.
Rev: New style mosque.

KM#	Date	Mintage	VG	Fine	VF	XF
830	AH1318	—	5.00	8.00	12.50	25.00

5 RUPEES

46.0500 g, .900 SILVER, 1.3325 oz ASW

KM#	Date	Mintage	VG	Fine	VF	XF
820	AH1314	—	20.00	30.00	60.00	115.00

45.6000 g, .900 SILVER, 1.3194 oz ASW
Obv: Similar to KM#820.

KM#	Date	Mintage	VG	Fine	VF	XF
826	AH1316	—	17.50	27.50	50.00	110.00

TILLA

(10 Rupees)

4.6000 g, .900 GOLD, 22mm, .1331 oz AGW
Rev. leg: *Allah Akbar* above mosque.

KM#	Date	Mintage	VG	Fine	VF	XF
807	AH1309	—	BV	70.00	110.00	210.00

19mm
Rev. leg: *Allah Akbar* above.

KM#	Date	Mintage	VG	Fine	VF	XF
815	AH1313	—	70.00	90.00	140.00	280.00

Rev: Date below mosque.

KM#	Date	Mintage	VG	Fine	VF	XF
821	AH1314	—	BV	70.00	100.00	150.00
	1316	—	BV	85.00	110.00	175.00

Obv: Date below toughra.

KM#	Date	Mintage	VG	Fine	VF	XF
822	AH1314	—	BV	75.00	100.00	165.00
	1316	—	BV	70.00	100.00	165.00

2 TILLAS

(20 Rupees)

9.2000 g, .900 GOLD, 22mm, .2661 oz AGW

KM#	Date	Mintage	VG	Fine	VF	XF
808	AH1309	—	BV	140.00	210.00	265.00

ALGERIA

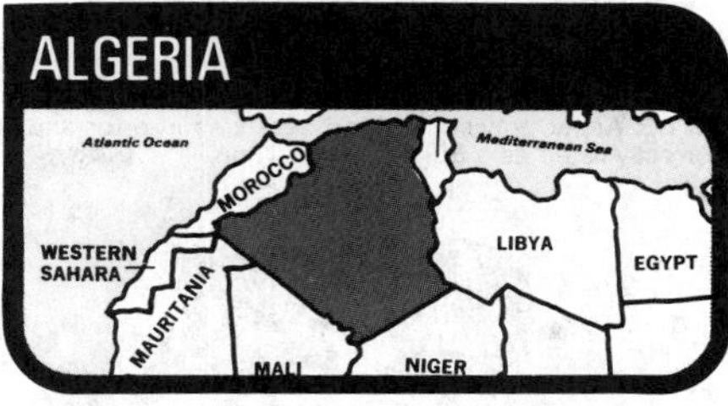

The Democratic and Popular Republic of Algeria, a North African country fronting on the Mediterranean Sea between Tunisia and Morocco, has an area of 919,595 sq. mi. (2,381,740 sq. km.) and a population of 28.5 million. Capital: Algiers (Alger). Most of the country's working population is engaged in agriculture although a recent industrial diversification, financed by oil revenues, is making steady progress. Wines, fruits, iron and zinc ores, phosphates, tobacco products, liquified natural gas, and petroleum are exported.

Algiers, the capital and chief seaport of Algeria, was the site of Phoenician and Roman settlements before the present Moslem city was founded about 950. Nominally part of the sultanate of Tilimsan, Algiers had a large measure of independence under the amirs of its own. In 1492 the Jews and Moors who had been expelled from Spain settled in Algiers and enjoyed an increasing influence until the imposition of Turkish control in 1518. For the following three centuries Algiers was the headquarters of the notorious Barbary pirates as Turkish control became more and more nominal. The French took Algiers in 1830, and after a long and wearisome war completed the conquest of Algeria and annexed it to France, 1848.Following the armistice signed by France and Nazi Germany on June 22, 1940, Algeria fell under Vichy Government control until liberated by the Allied invasion forces under the command of Gen. D.D. Eisenhower on Nov. 8, 1942. The inability to obtain equal rights with Frenchmen led to an organized revolt which began on Nov. 1, 1954 and lasted until a ceasefire was signed on July l, 1962. Independence was proclaimed on July 5, 1962, following a self-determination referendum, and the Republic was declared on September 25, 1962.

RULERS

Ottoman, until 1830
Abd-el-Kader (rebel)
AH1250-1264/1834-1847AD

ALGIERS

MINTNAMES

Jaza'ir جزاير

al-Mascara المعسكر

During revolt of Abd-el-Kader
AH1250-1264/1834-1847AD

Medea مديه

AH1246/1830AD

Qusantinah
Constantine قسنطينة

AH1245-1254/1830-1837AD

Taqidemt تاقدمت

During revolt of Abd-el-Kader
AH1250-1264/1834-1847AD

NOTE: The dots above and below the letters are integral parts of the letters, but for stylistic reasons, are occasionally omitted.

MONETARY SYSTEM
(Until 1847)

14-1/2 Asper (Akche, Dirham Saghir)
= 1 Kharub
2 Kharuba = 1 Muzuna
24 Muzuna = 3 Batlaka (Pataka) = 1 Budju

NOTE: Coin denominations are not expressed on the coins, and are best determined by size and weight. The silver Budju weighed about 13.5 g until AH1236/1821AD, when it was reduced to about 10.0 g. The fractional pieces varied in proportion to the Budju. They had secondary names, which are given in the text. In 1829 three new silver coins were introduced and Budju became Tugrali-rial, Tugrali-batlaka = 1/3 Rial = 8 Muzuna and Tugrali-nessflik = 1/2 Batlaka = 4 Muzuna. The gold Sultani was officially valued at 108 Muzuna, but varied in accordance with the market price of gold expressed in silver. It weighed 3.20-3.40 g. The Zer-i Mahbub was valued at 80 Muzuna and weighed 2.38-3.10 g.

OTTOMAN COINAGE
SELIM III

AH1203-1222/1789-1807AD

FELS

COPPER, 1.73 g
Obv. leg: *Sultan Selim.*
Rev: Mintname: *Jaza'ir* within octagram.

KM#	Date	Mintage	Good	VG	Fine	VF
52	AH122x	—	45.00	90.00	150.00	—

NOTE: Some experts believe this strike to be a contemporary counterfeit of KM#47.

1/8 BUDJU

(3 Mazuna)

SILVER, 1.65-1.70 g
Mintname: *Jaza'ir*

KM#	Date	Mintage	VG	Fine	VF	XF
40	AH1216	—	20.00	40.00	60.00	100.00
	1218	—	20.00	40.00	60.00	100.00
	1220	—	20.00	40.00	60.00	100.00

NOTE: Earlier dates (AH1200-1215) exist for this type.

Rev: Mintname within octagram.

KM#	Date	Mintage	VG	Fine	VF	XF
47	AH1221	—	40.00	60.00	125.00	175.00
	1222	—	40.00	60.00	125.00	175.00

1/4 BUDJU

SILVER, 2.90-3.40 g, 19-20mm
Mintname: *Jaza'ir*

KM#	Date	Mintage	VG	Fine	VF	XF
42	AH1216	—	20.00	35.00	60.00	100.00
	1217	—	20.00	35.00	60.00	100.00
	1218	—	20.00	35.00	60.00	100.00
	1219	—	20.00	35.00	60.00	100.00
	1220	—	20.00	35.00	60.00	100.00

NOTE: Earlier dates (AH1205-1215) exist for this type.

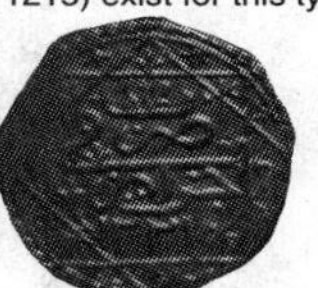

Rev: Mintname within octagram.

KM#	Date	Mintage	VG	Fine	VF	XF
48	AH1221	—	40.00	75.00	125.00	175.00
	1222	—	40.00	75.00	125.00	175.00
	1223	—	40.00	75.00	125.00	175.00

1/2 BUDJU

SILVER, 5.80-6.80 g
Mintname: *Jaza'ir*

KM#	Date	Mintage	VG	Fine	VF	XF
45	AH1216	—	60.00	100.00	150.00	225.00
	1217	—	60.00	100.00	150.00	225.00
	1218	—	60.00	100.00	150.00	225.00
	1219	—	60.00	100.00	150.00	225.00
	1220	—	60.00	100.00	150.00	225.00

NOTE: Earlier dates (AH1213-1215) exist for this type.

1/4 SULTANI

GOLD, 15-16mm, 0.85 g
Mintname: *Jaza'ir*
Obv. leg: 2 lines. Rev: Mintname above date.

KM#	Date	Mintage	VG	Fine	VF	XF
44	AH1217	—	65.00	100.00	200.00	250.00
	1219	—	65.00	100.00	200.00	250.00

NOTE: Earlier dates (AH1209-1214) exist for this type.

Rev: Mintname within octagram.

KM#	Date	Mintage	VG	Fine	VF	XF
49	AH1221	—	150.00	225.00	300.00	375.00
	1222	—	150.00	225.00	300.00	375.00

1/2 SULTANI

GOLD, 1.54-1.70 g, 18-19mm
Mintname: *Jaza'ir*

KM#	Date	Mintage	VG	Fine	VF	XF
46	AH1216	—	100.00	150.00	200.00	275.00
	1217	—	100.00	150.00	200.00	275.00
	1218	—	100.00	150.00	200.00	275.00
	1219	—	100.00	150.00	200.00	275.00

NOTE: Earlier date (AH1215) exists for this type.

Rev: Mintname within octagram.

KM#	Date	Mintage	VG	Fine	VF	XF
50	AH1221	—	200.00	275.00	375.00	500.00
	1222	—	200.00	275.00	375.00	500.00

SULTANI

GOLD, 3.25-3.40 g, 22-25mm
Mintname: *Jaza'ir*
Obv: Star of Solomon.

KM#	Date	Mintage	VG	Fine	VF	XF
41	AH1216	—	200.00	275.00	375.00	500.00
	1217	—	200.00	275.00	375.00	500.00
	1218	—	200.00	275.00	375.00	500.00
	1219	—	200.00	275.00	375.00	500.00
	1220	—	200.00	275.00	375.00	500.00
	1221	—	200.00	275.00	375.00	500.00

NOTE: Earlier dates (AH1204-1215) exist for this type.

3.10 g
Rev: Mintname within octagram.

KM#	Date	Mintage	VG	Fine	VF	XF
51	AH1221	—	—	—	Rare	—
	1222	—	—	—	Rare	—

MUSTAFA IV

AH1222-1223/1807-1808AD

1/8 BUDJU

SILVER, 16mm, 1.48 g
Mintname: *Jaza'ir* in octagram.

KM#	Date	Mintage	VG	Fine	VF	XF
53	AH1222	—	100.00	150.00	250.00	350.00
	1223	—	100.00	150.00	250.00	350.00

1/4 BUDJU

SILVER, 2.88-3.40 g
Mintname: *Jaza'ir* in octagram.

KM#	Date	Mintage	VG	Fine	VF	XF
54	AH1222	—	100.00	150.00	250.00	350.00
	1223	—	100.00	150.00	250.00	350.00

1/4 SULTANI

GOLD, 0.80 g
Mintname: *Jaza'ir* in octagram.

KM#	Date	Mintage	VG	Fine	VF	XF
55	AH1222	—	—	—	Rare	—
	1223	—	—	—	Rare	—

1/2 SULTANI

GOLD, 1.60-1.73 g
Mintname: *Jaza'ir* in octagram.

KM#	Date	Mintage	VG	Fine	VF	XF
56	AH1222	—	—	—	Rare	—
	1223	—	—	—	Rare	—

SULTANI

GOLD, 3.15-3.40 g
Mintname: *Jaza'ir* in octagram.

KM#	Date	Mintage	VG	Fine	VF	XF
57	AH1222	—	—	—	Rare	—
	1223	—	—	—	Rare	—

MAHMUD II

AH1223-1252/1808-1839AD

NOTE: Asper previously listed here was in error and is correctly listed as a Burben under Tunis.

2 ASPERS

COPPER, 0.80 g
Mintname: *Jaza'ir*

KM#	Date	Mintage	VG	Fine	VF	XF
70	AH1237	—	15.00	25.00	36.50	70.00
	1238	—	15.00	25.00	36.50	70.00
	1240	—	15.00	25.00	36.50	70.00
	1242	—	15.00	25.00	36.50	70.00
	1243	—	15.00	25.00	36.50	70.00
	1244	—	15.00	25.00	36.50	70.00

Mintname: *Constantine*

KM#	Date	Mintage	Good	VG	Fine	VF
81	AH1247	—	40.00	60.00	90.00	135.00
	1250	—	40.00	60.00	90.00	135.00

NOTE: Varieties exist.

5 ASPERS

(Valued at 1/3 Kharuba)

COPPER, 1.80-2.20 g
Mintname: *Jaza'ir*

KM#	Date	Mintage	VG	Fine	VF	XF
71	AH1237	—	12.50	22.50	35.00	50.00
	1238	—	12.50	22.50	35.00	50.00
	1239	—	12.50	22.50	35.00	50.00
	1240	—	15.00	25.00	40.00	60.00
	1244	—	10.00	20.00	30.00	45.00

NOTE: The 5 Aspers formerly listed as C#140 is probably an example of the 1/8 Budju, KM#74, of very base metal.

10 ASPERS

COPPER

KM#	Date	Mintage	Good	VG	Fine	VF
72	AH1237					
		1 known	—	—	Unc.	2500.

NOTE: Possibly a pattern issue.

KHARUB

BILLON, 14mm, 0.70-0.80 g
Mintname: *Jaza'ir*

KM#	Date	Mintage	VG	Fine	VF	XF
73	AH1237	—	10.00	15.00	30.00	75.00
	1238	—	10.00	15.00	30.00	75.00
	1240	—	10.00	15.00	30.00	75.00
	1242	—	10.00	15.00	30.00	75.00

0.70-0.90 g
Mintname: *Constantine*

KM#	Date	Mintage	VG	Fine	VF	XF
76	AH1245	—	50.00	100.00	175.00	275.00
	1246	—	50.00	100.00	175.00	275.00
	1247	—	50.00	100.00	175.00	275.00
	1250	—	50.00	100.00	175.00	275.00
	1252	—	50.00	100.00	175.00	275.00

1/8 BUDJU

(Sumun Budju = 3 Muzuna)

SILVER, 1.61 g
Mintname: *Jaza'ir* in octagram.
Similar to 1/4 Budju, KM#54, but w/Mahmud's name.

KM#	Date	Mintage	VG	Fine	VF	XF
A61	AH1223	—	150.00	200.00	225.00	250.00

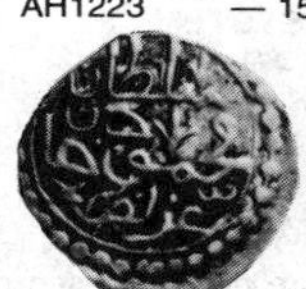

SILVER, 1.65-1.70 g
Mintname: *Jaza'ir*

KM#	Date	Mintage	VG	Fine	VF	XF
61	AH1225	—	25.00	45.00	75.00	125.00
	1226	—	25.00	45.00	75.00	125.00
	1227	—	25.00	45.00	75.00	125.00
	1228	—	25.00	45.00	75.00	125.00
	1229	—	25.00	45.00	75.00	125.00
	1230	—	25.00	45.00	75.00	125.00
	1231	—	25.00	45.00	75.00	125.00
	1232	—	25.00	45.00	75.00	125.00
	1233	—	25.00	45.00	75.00	125.00

KM#	Date	Mintage	VG	Fine	VF	XF
61	1234	—	25.00	45.00	75.00	125.00
	1235	—	25.00	45.00	75.00	125.00

Reduced standard, 1.20-1.30 g

KM#	Date	Mintage	VG	Fine	VF	XF
74	AH1229	—	10.00	15.00	30.00	65.00
	1237	—	10.00	15.00	30.00	65.00
	1238	—	10.00	15.00	30.00	65.00
	1239	—	10.00	15.00	30.00	65.00
	1240	—	10.00	15.00	30.00	65.00
	1242	—	10.00	15.00	30.00	65.00
	1243	—	10.00	15.00	30.00	65.00
	1244	—	10.00	15.00	30.00	65.00
	1245	—	10.00	15.00	30.00	65.00

1/6 BUDJU

(Tugrali-ness-flik)
(4 Muzuna = 1/2 Batlaka)

SILVER, 1.50 g

KM#	Date	Mintage	Fine	VF	XF	Unc
77	AH1245	—	35.00	70.00	120.00	200.00

SILVER or BILLON, 18-19mm, 1.40-1.50 g
Mintname: *Constantine*

KM#	Date	Mintage	VG	Fine	VF	XF
82	AH1247	—	50.00	100.00	175.00	250.00
	1248	—	50.00	100.00	175.00	250.00
	1252	—	50.00	100.00	175.00	250.00

1/4 BUDJU

(6 Muzuna = Rebi Budju)

SILVER, 21mm, 2.40 g

KM#	Date	Mintage	Fine	VF	XF	Unc
67	AH1229	—	15.00	30.00	55.00	90.00
	1231	—	15.00	30.00	55.00	90.00
	1234	—	15.00	30.00	55.00	90.00
	1235	—	15.00	30.00	55.00	90.00
	1236	—	15.00	30.00	55.00	90.00
	1237	—	12.50	22.00	35.00	60.00
	1238	—	12.50	22.00	35.00	60.00
	1239	—	12.50	22.00	35.00	60.00
	1240	—	12.50	22.00	35.00	60.00
	1241	—	12.50	22.00	35.00	60.00
	1242	—	12.50	22.00	35.00	60.00
	1243	—	12.50	22.00	35.00	60.00
	1244	—	12.50	22.00	35.00	60.00
	1245	—	15.00	27.50	50.00	85.00
	1246	—	20.00	35.00	60.00	100.00

Mintname: *Medea*
21mm, 2.03 g

KM#	Date	Mintage	VG	Fine	VF	XF
80.1	AH1246	—	—	—	Rare	—

Mintname: *Constantine*
21mm, 2.00 g
Obv: Ornament and Sultan's name around.

Rev: Similar to KM#67.

KM#	Date	Mintage	VG	Fine	VF	XF
80.2	AH1246	—	—	—	Rare	—

1/3 BUDJU

(Tugrali-batlaka)

SILVER, 20mm, 3.25-3.80 g
Mintname: *Jaza'ir*
Octagram type

KM#	Date	Mintage	VG	Fine	VF	XF
59	AH1223	—	40.00	75.00	125.00	200.00
	1224	—	75.00	90.00	125.00	200.00
	1225	—	75.00	90.00	125.00	200.00
	1226	—	35.00	60.00	100.00	150.00
	1227	—	35.00	60.00	100.00	150.00
	1228	—	35.00	60.00	100.00	150.00
	1229	—	35.00	60.00	100.00	150.00

Mintname not in octagram.

KM#	Date	Mintage	VG	Fine	VF	XF
62	AH1228	—	35.00	60.00	100.00	150.00
	1230	—	35.00	60.00	100.00	150.00
	1231	—	35.00	60.00	100.00	150.00
	1232	—	35.00	60.00	100.00	150.00
	1233	—	35.00	60.00	100.00	150.00
	1234	—	35.00	60.00	100.00	150.00
	1235	—	75.00	90.00	125.00	200.00

SILVER, 3.10 g
Toughra type

KM#	Date	Mintage	Fine	VF	XF	Unc
78	AH1245	—	45.00	75.00	135.00	245.00

NOTE: Varieties exist.

BUDJU

SILVER, 9.80-10.10 g
Mintname: *Jaza'ir*

KM#	Date	Mintage	VG	Fine	VF	XF
68	AH1236	—	20.00	45.00	100.00	175.00
	1237	—	16.00	30.00	65.00	110.00
	1238	—	16.00	30.00	65.00	110.00
	1239	—	16.00	30.00	65.00	110.00
	1240	—	16.00	30.00	65.00	110.00
	1241	—	16.00	30.00	65.00	110.00
	1242	—	20.00	30.00	65.00	110.00
	1243	—	25.00	45.00	100.00	175.00
	1244	—	40.00	45.00	100.00	175.00
	1245	—	45.00	100.00	200.00	350.00

(Tugrali-rial)

10.020 g
Mintname: *Jaza'ir*

KM#	Date	Mintage	VG	Fine	VF	XF
79	AH1245	—	70.00	175.00	350.00	750.00

SILVER or BILLON, 7.90-9.80 g
Mintname: *Constantine*

KM#	Date	Mintage	VG	Fine	VF	XF
83	AH1247	—	100.00	150.00	350.00	750.00
	1248	—	100.00	150.00	350.00	750.00
	1249	—	100.00	170.00	380.00	900.00
	1250	—	100.00	170.00	380.00	900.00
	1251	—	200.00	500.00	600.00	900.00
	1253	—	100.00	150.00	350.00	750.00

2 BUDJU

(Zudj Budju)

SILVER, 19.50-20.00 g
Mintname: *Jaza'ir*

KM#	Date	Mintage	VG	Fine	VF	XF
75	AH1236	—	30.00	50.00	80.00	120.00
	1237	—	30.00	50.00	80.00	120.00
	1238	—	30.00	50.00	80.00	120.00
	1239	—	30.00	50.00	80.00	120.00
	1240	—	35.00	60.00	90.00	130.00
	1241	—	30.00	50.00	80.00	120.00
	1242	—	30.00	50.00	80.00	120.00
	1243	—	40.00	60.00	100.00	175.00
	1244	—	65.00	95.00	170.00	275.00

NOTE: Varieties exist.

1/4 SULTANI

GOLD, 14-15mm, 0.78-0.85 g
Mintname: *Jaza'ir*
Obv. leg: *Sultan Mahmud.*

KM#	Date	Mintage	VG	Fine	VF	XF
63.1	AH1224	—	—	—	Rare	—
	1228	—	—	—	Rare	—
	1234	—	—	—	Rare	—

Obv. leg: *Sultan Mahmud Han.*

KM#	Date	Mintage	VG	Fine	VF	XF
63.2	AH1231	—	85.00	125.00	175.00	250.00
	1232	—	85.00	125.00	175.00	250.00
	1238	—	85.00	125.00	175.00	250.00
	1240	—	85.00	125.00	175.00	250.00
	1243	—	85.00	125.00	175.00	250.00

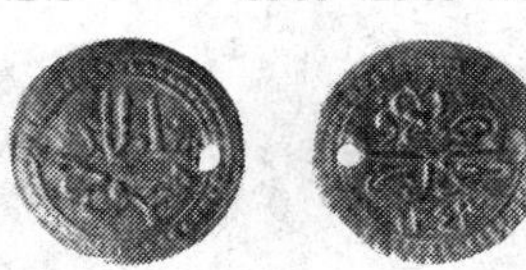

GOLD, 0.705 g

KM#	Date	Mintage	VG	Fine	VF	XF
64.1	AH1246 1 known	—	—	—	2500.	—

Mintname: *Medea*

KM#	Date	Mintage	VG	Fine	VF	XF
64.2	AH1246	—	—	—	Rare	—

1/2 SULTANI

GOLD, 1.15-1.60 g
Mintname: *Jaza'ir*

KM#	Date	Mintage	VG	Fine	VF	XF
65	AH1231	—	100.00	140.00	200.00	275.00
	1232	—	100.00	140.00	200.00	275.00
	1234	—	100.00	140.00	200.00	275.00
	1236	—	100.00	140.00	200.00	275.00
	1237	—	100.00	140.00	200.00	275.00
	1238	—	100.00	140.00	200.00	275.00
	1239	—	100.00	140.00	200.00	275.00
	1240	—	100.00	140.00	200.00	275.00

NOTE: Varieties exist.

Different type.

KM#	Date	Mintage	VG	Fine	VF	XF
84	AH1236	—	—	—	—	—

SULTANI

GOLD, 22-24mm, 3.20 g
Mintname: *Jaza'ir*
Rev: Year in fourth line.

KM#	Date	Mintage	VG	Fine	VF	XF
60	AH1223	—	250.00	350.00	450.00	575.00
	1224	—	250.00	350.00	450.00	575.00
	1225	—	250.00	350.00	450.00	575.00
	1226	—	250.00	350.00	450.00	575.00
	1228	—	250.00	350.00	450.00	575.00
	1231	—	250.00	350.00	450.00	575.00
	1232	—	250.00	350.00	450.00	575.00
	1234	—	250.00	350.00	450.00	575.00

Rev: Year in third line.

KM#	Date	Mintage	VG	Fine	VF	XF
66	AH1235	—	165.00	225.00	300.00	400.00
	1236	—	165.00	225.00	300.00	400.00
	1237	—	165.00	225.00	300.00	400.00
	1238	—	165.00	225.00	300.00	400.00
	1239	—	165.00	225.00	300.00	400.00
	1240	—	165.00	225.00	300.00	400.00
	1241	—	165.00	225.00	300.00	400.00
	1243	—	165.00	225.00	300.00	400.00
	3421(error)	—	165.00	225.00	300.00	400.00
	1244	—	165.00	225.00	300.00	400.00
	1245	—	275.00	400.00	550.00	750.00

GOLD, 2.50-3.20 g
Rev: Year in second line.

KM#	Date	Mintage	VG	Fine	VF	XF
A69	AH1230	—	200.00	300.00	400.00	550.00

GOLD, 2.38 g
Mintname: *Constantine*
Obv: Toughra. Rev: 4-line leg. w/20 above *ibn*.

KM#	Date	Mintage	VG	Fine	VF	XF
69	AH1246	—	—	—	Rare	—

NOTE: The regnal year 20 is probably an error for 23.

REVOLUTIONARY COINAGE

ABDEL KADER

AH1250-1264/1834-1847AD

5 ASPERS/KHARUBA

(Mohammadiya)

COPPER-BILLON, 0.73-1.30 g
Mintname: *Taqidemt*
12-18mm

KM#	Date	Mintage	VG	Fine	VF	XF
85	AH1250	—	25.00	40.00	60.00	120.00
	1252	—	25.00	40.00	60.00	120.00
	1253	—	25.00	40.00	60.00	120.00
	1254, Arabic '4'	—	22.50	35.00	45.00	90.00
	1254, Persian '4'	—	22.50	35.00	45.00	90.00
	1255	—	22.50	35.00	45.00	90.00
	1256	—	22.50	35.00	45.00	90.00
	1257	—	25.00	40.00	60.00	120.00

KHARUBA

BILLON
Mintname: *Al Mascara*

KM#	Date	Mintage	VG	Fine	VF	XF
87	AH1254	—	70.00	100.00	150.00	250.00

BILLON, 8mm, 0.40-0.70 g
Mintname: *Taqidemt*
Obv: Different legend.

KM#	Date	Mintage	VG	Fine	VF	XF
86	AH1254	—	7.50	25.00	55.00	110.00
	1258	—	17.50	35.00	55.00	110.00

1/6 BUDJU

(3 Muzuna-Nasfia)

BILLON, 1.00 g
Mintname: *Taqidemt*

KM#	Date	Mintage	VG	Fine	VF	XF
88	AH1254	—	100.00	160.00	285.00	465.00
	1255	—	—	—	—	—

1/2 BUDJU

Silver, 2.88 g
Mintname: *Taqidemt*
Obv. inscription: *Nasr min/Allah wa fath/garib* translated *Victory of God and Conquest is Near.*

KM#	Date	Mintage	VG	Fine	VF	XF
90	AH1256	—	—	—	Rare	—

BUDJU

SILVER, 27-28mm, 5.57-6.03 g
Mintname: *Taqidemt*
Denomination uncertain
Obv: 3 lines. Rev: 4 lines.

KM#	Date	Mintage	VG	Fine	VF	XF
89	AH1256	—	150.00	300.00	600.00	900.00

NOTE: This coin has also been considered to be a 1/2 Budju, but its weight apparently indicates a reduced Budju in debased metal. Varieties exist.

PATTERNS (Pn)

(Including off metal strikes)

KM#	Date	Mintage	Identification	Mkt.Val.
Pn1	AH1223	—	1/2 Budju	—

KM#	Date	Mintage	Identification	Mkt.Val.
Pn2	AH1223 R.Y.13	—	1/2 Sultani, White metal	175.00

KM#	Date	Mintage	Identification	Mkt.Val.
Pn3	AH1223 R.Y.13	—	2 Sultani, White metal	450.00

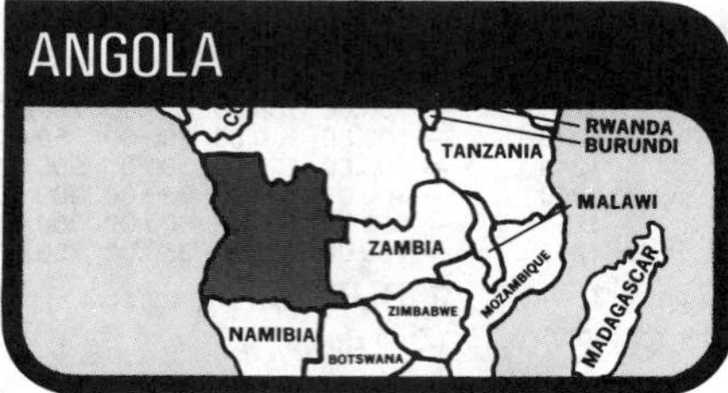

The Republic of Angola, a country on the west coast of southern Africa bounded by Zaire, Zambia, and Namibia (South-West Africa), has an area of 481,354 sq. mi. (1,246,700 sq. km.) and a population of 10.1 million, predominantly Bantu in origin. Capital: Luanda. Most of the people are engaged in subsistence agriculture. However, important oil and mineral deposits make Angola potentially one of the richest countries in Africa. Iron and diamonds are exported.

Angola was discovered by Portuguese navigator Diogo Cao in 1482. Portuguese settlers arrived in 1491, and established Angola as a major slaving center which sent about 3 million slaves to the New World.

A revolt, characterized by guerrilla warfare, against Portuguese rule began in 1961 and continued until 1974, when a new regime in Portugal offered independence. The independence movement was actively supported by three groups, the National Front, based in Zaire, the Soviet-backed Popular Movement, and the moderate National Union. Independence was proclaimed on Nov. 11, 1975, and the Portuguese departed, leaving the Angolan people to work out their own political destiny. Within hours, each of the independence groups proclaimed itself Angola's sole ruler. A bloody intertribal civil war erupted in which the Communist Popular Movement, assisted by Soviet arms and Cuban mercenaries, was the eventual victor.

RULERS

Portuguese until 1975
KN - King's Norton

MONETARY SYSTEM

(Until 1860)

50 Reis = 1 Macuta

1/4 MACUTA

COPPER

KM#	Date	Mintage	VG	Fine	VF	XF
44	1814	—	10.00	25.00	45.00	85.00
(38)	1815	—	200.00	300.00	500.00	850.00
	1816	—	—	Reported, not confirmed		

1/2 MACUTA

COPPER

KM#	Date	Mintage	VG	Fine	VF	XF
45	1814	—	12.00	28.00	48.00	90.00
(39)	1815	.018	150.00	250.00	400.00	750.00
	1819	—	—	—	Rare	—

KM#	Date	Mintage	VG	Fine	VF	XF
56	1848	.417	8.00	16.00	45.00	135.00
(42)	1851	.104	5.00	10.00	25.00	65.00
	1853	.143	5.00	10.00	25.00	65.00

Obv. leg: PETRUS V D.G. . . .

KM#	Date	Mintage	VG	Fine	VF	XF
58	1858	.226	4.00	8.00	20.00	55.00
(43)	1860	.398	4.00	8.00	20.00	55.00

MACUTA

COPPER

KM#	Date	Mintage	VG	Fine	VF	XF
46	1814	*	7.00	15.00	30.00	75.00
(40)	1816	6,110	35.00	75.00	175.00	300.00
	1819	—	—	—	Rare	—

***NOTE:** Lightweight coins exist weighing 10.96 g.

Similar to 1/2 Macuta, KM#42.

KM#	Date	Mintage	VG	Fine	VF	XF
59	1860	.194	7.00	15.00	30.00	65.00
(44)						

2 MACUTAS

COPPER
Similar to 1 Macuta, KM#40.

KM#	Date	Mintage	VG	Fine	VF	XF
47	1815	—	25.00	55.00	120.00	225.00
(41)	1816	3,175	35.00	75.00	175.00	300.00
	1819	—	—	—	Rare	—

COUNTERMARKED COINAGE

(1809)

An order of April 18, 1809 provided for the use of an arms countermark to be applied to various circulating coinage. The mark doubled the host coin's face value.

10 REIS

COPPER
c/m: Arms on V Reis, KM#7.

KM#	Date	Year	Good	VG	Fine	VF
38	ND(1809)	1752	25.00	50.00	125.00	250.00
(45)		1753	6.00	12.00	28.00	55.00
		1757	10.00	22.00	45.00	85.00

20 REIS

COPPER
c/m: Arms on X Reis, KM#2.

KM#	Date	Year	Good	VG	Fine	VF
39	ND(1809)	1694	12.00	25.00	50.00	100.00
		1696	10.00	20.00	40.00	80.00
		1697	7.00	15.00	30.00	60.00
		1699	7.00	15.00	30.00	60.00

c/m: Arms on X Reis, KM#8.

KM#	Date	Year	Good	VG	Fine	VF
40	ND(1809)	1752	25.00	50.00	125.00	250.00
(46)		1753	6.00	12.00	28.00	55.00
		1757	6.00	12.00	28.00	55.00

40 REIS

COPPER

c/m: Arms on XX Reis, KM#1.

KM#	Date	Year	Good	VG	Fine	VF
41	ND(1809)	1693	12.00	25.00	50.00	100.00
		1694	9.00	17.00	35.00	70.00
		1695	9.00	17.00	35.00	70.00
		1697	7.00	15.00	30.00	60.00
		1698	7.00	15.00	30.00	60.00
		1699	7.00	15.00	30.00	60.00

c/m: Arms on XX Reis, KM#6.

KM#	Date	Year	Good	VG	Fine	VF
42	ND(1809)	1752	15.00	30.00	65.00	150.00
(47)		1753	5.00	10.00	25.00	85.00
		1757	4.00	8.00	20.00	70.00

80 REIS

COPPER

c/m: Arms on XL Reis, KM#9.

KM#	Date	Year	Good	VG	Fine	VF
43	ND(1809)	1753	9.00	17.00	35.00	70.00
(48)		1757	9.00	17.00	35.00	70.00

(1837;1853)

The Edict of March 21, 1837 initiated the use of crowned arms countermarks on various circulating coinage. The mark doubled the host coin's face value. A second edict was issued March 1, 1853 extending the use of these marks for the same purpose of doubling face value.

10 REIS

COPPER

c/m: Crowned arms on 5 Reis, KM#19.

KM#	Date	Year	Good	VG	Fine	VF
48	ND(1837)	1770	25.00	45.00	85.00	150.00
		1771	25.00	45.00	85.00	150.00

1/2 MACUTA

COPPER

c/m: Crowned arms on 1/4 Macuta, KM#10.

KM#	Date	Year	Good	VG	Fine	VF
49.1	ND(1837)	1762	3.50	7.00	16.00	35.00
(49)		1763	2.50	5.00	12.00	25.00
		1770	2.50	5.00	12.00	25.00
		1771	7.00	15.00	30.00	60.00

c/m: Crowned arms on 1/4 Macuta, KM#27.

KM#	Date	Year	Good	VG	Fine	VF
49.2	ND(1837)	1785	3.50	7.00	16.00	35.00
(53)						

c/m: Crowned arms on 1/4 Macuta, KM#29.

KM#	Date	Year	Good	VG	Fine	VF
49.3	ND(1837)	1789	4.00	8.00	17.00	35.00
(55)						

MACUTA

COPPER

c/m: Crowned arms on 1/2 Macuta, KM#11.

KM#	Date	Year	Good	VG	Fine	VF
50.1	ND(1837)	1762	15.00	25.00	40.00	80.00
(50)		1763	4.00	8.00	17.00	35.00
		1770	4.00	8.00	17.00	35.00

c/m: Crowned arms on 1/2 Macuta, KM#28.

KM#	Date	Year	Good	VG	Fine	VF
50.2	ND(1837)	1785	5.00	9.00	18.00	37.00
(54)		1786	5.00	9.00	18.00	37.00

c/m: Crowned arms on 1/2 Macuta, KM#30.

KM#	Date	Year	Good	VG	Fine	VF
50.3	ND(1837)	1789	5.00	9.00	18.00	38.00
(56)						

c/m: Crowned arms on 1/2 Macuta, KM#39.

KM#	Date	Year	Good	VG	Fine	VF
53	ND(1853)	1814	50.00	100.00	175.00	350.00

2 MACUTAS

COPPER

c/m: Crowned arms on 1 Macuta, KM#12.

KM#	Date	Year	Good	VG	Fine	VF
51.1	ND(1837)	1762	35.00	75.00	125.00	250.00
(51)		1763	6.00	12.00	22.00	45.00
		1770	5.00	10.00	20.00	40.00

c/m: Crowned arms on 1 Macuta, KM#20.

KM#	Date	Year	Good	VG	Fine	VF
51.2	ND(1837)	1783	50.00	100.00	175.00	350.00
(52)		1785	6.00	12.00	22.00	45.00
		1786	7.50	15.00	28.00	55.00

c/m: Crowned arms on 1 Macuta, KM#31.

KM#	Date	Year	Good	VG	Fine	VF
51.3	ND(1837)	1789	6.00	12.00	22.00	45.00
(57)						

c/m: Crowned arms on 1 Macuta, KM#40.

KM#	Date	Year	Good	VG	Fine	VF
54	ND(1853)	1814	30.00	60.00	100.00	200.00
(58)		1816	30.00	60.00	100.00	200.00

4 MACUTAS

COPPER

c/m: Crowned arms on 2 Macutas, KM#41.

KM#	Date	Year	Good	VG	Fine	VF
55	ND(1853)	1815	40.00	80.00	150.00	300.00
(59)		1816	40.00	80.00	150.00	300.00

PATTERNS (Pn)

(Including off metal strikes)

KM#	Date	Mintage	Identification	Mkt.Val.
Pn1	1831	—	1/4 Macuta, Copper, rev: 54 beads in circle	850.00
Pn2	1831	—	1/4 Macuta, Copper, rev: 64 beads in circle	850.00
Pn3	1831	—	1/2 Macuta, Copper	Rare
Pn4	1831	—	1 Macuta, Copper	Rare
Pn5	1831	—	2 Macutas, Copper	Rare

KM#	Date	Mintage	Identification	Mkt.Val.
Pn6	1886	—	20 Reis, Bronze	700.00

Listings For

ANNAM: refer to Vietnam-Annam

ANTWERP: refer to France

ANVERS: refer to France

ANTIGUA & BARBUDA

The Independent State of Antigua and Barbuda, located on the eastern edge of the Leeward Islands in the Caribbean Sea, has an area of 171 sq. mi. (440 sq. km.) and a population of *65,176. Capital: St. John's. Prior to 1967 Antigua and its dependencies, Barbuda and Redonda, comprised a presidency of the Leeward Islands. The mountainous island produces sugar, molasses, rum, cotton and fruit. Tourism is making an increasingly valuable contribution to the economy.

Antigua was discovered by Columbus in 1493, settled by British colonists from St. Kitts in 1632, occupied by the French in 1666, and ceded to Britain in 1667. It became an associated state with internal self-government on February 27, 1967. On November 1, 1981 it became independent as Antigua and Barbuda.

Spanish silver coinage and French colonial "Black Dogs" were used throughout the islands' early history; however, late in the seventeeth century the introduction of British tin farthings was attempted with complete lack of success. In 1822, British colonial Anchor Money was introduced.

From 1825 to 1955, Antigua was on the sterling standard and used British coins. Coins of the British Caribbean Territories (Eastern Group) and East Caribbean States circulated from 1955, and banknotes of East Caribbean Currency Authority are now used on the island. The earlier coinage was augmented in 1981 by that of the East Caribbean States.

RULERS

British

ANTIGUA

TOKEN ISSUES (Tn)

FARTHING

COPPER

KM#	Date	Mintage	Fine	VF	XF	Unc
Tn1	1836	—	20.00	40.00	70.00	135.00
	1836	—	—	—	Proof	225.00

NOTE: Although dated 1836, this was issued about 1850 by Hannay and Coltart, merchants of St. John. Five die varieties exist. Occasionally found countermarked with incuse 3 or 4.

ARGENTINA

The Argentine Republic, located in southern South America, has an area of 1,073,518 sq. mi. (3,761,274 sq. km.) and a population of 35 million. Capital: Buenos Aires. Its varied topography ranges from the subtropical lowlands of the north to the towering Andean Mountains in the west and the wind-swept Patagonian steppe in the south. The rolling, fertile pampas of central Argentina are ideal for agriculture and grazing, and support most of the republic's population. Meat packing, flour milling, textiles, sugar refining and dairy products are the principal industries. Oil is found in Patagonia, but most mineral requirements must be imported.

Argentina was discovered in 1516 by the Spanish navigator Juan de Solis. A permanent Spanish colony was established at Buenos Aires in 1580, but the colony developed slowly. When Napoleon conquered Spain, the Argentines set up their own government on May 25, 1810. Independence was formally declared on July 9, 1816. A strong tendency toward local autonomy, fostered by difficult transportation, resulted in a federalized union with much authority left to the states or provinces, which resulted in the coinage of 1817-1867.

Internal conflict through the first half century of Argentine independence resulted in a provisional national coinage, chiefly of crown-sized silver. This was supplemented by provincial issues, mainly of minor denominations.

RULERS

Spanish until 1810

MINT MARKS

BA = Buenos Aires
CORDOBA, CORDOVA
PTS=Potosi monogram (Bolivia)
R, RA, RIOJA, RIOXA
SE = Santiago del Estero
T, TM = Tucuman
TIERRA DEL FUEGO

In the Colonial era, Potosi-struck coinage was used in Argentina (see Bolivia for these issues). During the war for Independence Potosi was held and used to strike coinage by both the Royalist and Independence forces. The mint was captured in 1813 by Independence forces who held it for eight months, using the facilities and some remaining workers to strike their new coinage until it was retaken in 1814 by Royalist forces. The Royalists set about recalling the Independence coinage and using the mint to strike coins of the old type with the King's portrait. Royalists abandoned the mint in April 1815 with the reappearance of Independent forces who again occupied and made use of the mint until it was retaken by the Spanish army in November 1815. The Royalists held the mint and used it to strike the King's coinage until 1824 when Independence was finally secured.

MONETARY SYSTEM

8 Reales = 8 Soles = 1/2 Escudo
16 Reales or Soles = 1 Escudo
10 Decimos = 1 Real
100 Centavos = 1 Peso
10 Pesos = 1 Argentino

PROVINCIAS DEL RIO DE LA PLATA

1/4 REAL

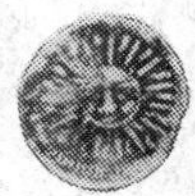

SILVER
1/4 Real of Rondeau

KM#	Date	Mintage	VG	Fine	VF	XF
A1	ND(1815-16)	4-6 pcs.	—	—	Rare	—

1/2 REAL

1.6915 g, .896 SILVER, .0487 oz ASW
Mint mark: Potosi monogram
Obv: Flame tips end counter clockwise.

KM#	Date	Mintage	VG	Fine	VF	XF
1.1	1813 J	—	10.00	15.00	30.00	65.00

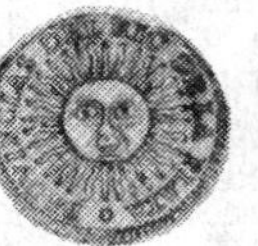

Obv: Flame tips end clockwise.

KM#	Date	Mintage	VG	Fine	VF	XF
1.2	1815 F	—	12.50	17.50	35.00	70.00

1/2 SOL

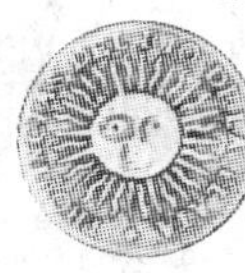

SILVER
Mint mark: Potosi monogram

KM#	Date	Mintage	VG	Fine	VF	XF
10	1815 FL	—	15.00	25.00	60.00	125.00

REAL

3.3830 g, .896 SILVER, .0974 oz ASW
Mint mark: Potosi monogram

KM#	Date	Mintage	VG	Fine	VF	XF
2	1813 J	—	10.00	15.00	30.00	70.00
	1815 F	—	10.00	15.00	30.00	70.00

Mint mark: RA
Similar to 2 Soles, KM#18.

KM#	Date	Mintage	VG	Fine	VF	XF
17	1824 DS	—	10.00	17.00	35.00	80.00
	1825 CA	—	—	—	Rare	—

SOL

SILVER
Mint mark: Potosi monogram
Similar to 1/2 Sol, KM#10.

KM#	Date	Mintage	VG	Fine	VF	XF
11	1815 FL	—	17.50	37.50	85.00	175.00

2 REALES

6.766 g, .896 SILVER, .1949 oz ASW
Mint mark: Potosi monogram

KM#	Date	Mintage	VG	Fine	VF	XF
3	1813 J	—	15.00	25.00	55.00	100.00
	1815 F	—	15.00	25.00	55.00	100.00

2 SOLES

SILVER
Mint mark: Potosi monogram
Similar to 2 Reales, KM#3.

KM#	Date	Mintage	VG	Fine	VF	XF
12	1815 FL	—	30.00	50.00	100.00	200.00

Mint mark: RA

KM#	Date	Mintage	VG	Fine	VF	XF
18	1824 DS	—	12.00	16.50	25.00	45.00
	1825 CA	—	25.00	45.00	75.00	155.00
	1825 CA. DE B. AS.	—	14.00	25.00	45.00	85.00
	1826/5 P	—	15.00	27.50	60.00	120.00
	1826 'P' omitted from rev. leg.	—	9.00	14.00	25.00	45.00
	1826 P medal alignment	—	14.00	25.00	50.00	90.00
	1826 P coin alignment	—	20.00	40.00	75.00	150.00

4 REALES

13.5320 g, .896 SILVER, .3898 oz ASW
Mint mark: Potosi monogram

KM#	Date	Mintage	VG	Fine	VF	XF
4	1813 J	—	30.00	50.00	85.00	160.00
	1815 F	—	30.00	55.00	90.00	180.00

NOTE: Size of sunface varies for 1815 dated coins.

4 SOLES

SILVER
Mint mark: Potosi monogram

KM#	Date	Mintage	VG	Fine	VF	XF
13	1815 FL	—	40.00	75.00	140.00	275.00

Mint mark: RA

KM#	Date	Mintage	VG	Fine	VF	XF
22	1828 P coin alignment					
		—	20.00	30.00	50.00	90.00
	1828 P medal alignment					
		—	25.00	35.00	55.00	100.00
	1832 P	—	20.00	30.00	50.00	90.00

8 REALES

27.0640 g, .896 SILVER, .7795 oz ASW
Mint mark: Potosi monogram
Obv: Flame tips end clockwise.

KM#	Date	Mintage	VG	Fine	VF	XF
5	1813 J	—	50.00	75.00	125.00	250.00
	1813 J PRORVINCIAS (error)					
		—	—	—	Rare	—

NOTE: Traces of earlier Spanish colonial edge designs are occasionally encountered and are considered rare.

Obv: Flame tips end counterclockwise.

KM#	Date	Mintage	VG	Fine	VF	XF
14	1815 F	—	50.00	75.00	125.00	250.00
	1815 F PROVICIAS (error)					
		—	75.00	125.00	200.00	350.00

Mint mark: RA

KM#	Date	Mintage	VG	Fine	VF	XF
20	1826 P	—	40.00	80.00	165.00	300.00
	1827 P	—	45.00	90.00	240.00	375.00
	1828 P	—	35.00	75.00	125.00	235.00
	1830 P	—	70.00	160.00	450.00	900.00
	1831/0 P	—	50.00	140.00	390.00	750.00
	1831 P	—	50.00	130.00	360.00	650.00
	1832 P	—	35.00	80.00	165.00	330.00
	1833 P	—	35.00	75.00	125.00	235.00
	1834 P	—	35.00	75.00	125.00	235.00
	1835 P	—	35.00	75.00	125.00	235.00
	1836 P	—	35.00	75.00	125.00	235.00
	1837 P	—	35.00	75.00	125.00	250.00

8 SOLES

SILVER
Mint mark: Potosi monogram

KM#	Date	Mintage	VG	Fine	VF	XF
15	1815 FL	—	50.00	100.00	150.00	275.00
	1815 FL S/R	—	60.00	120.00	180.00	350.00

ESCUDO

3.3750 g, .875 GOLD, .0949 oz AGW
Mint mark: Potosi monogram

KM#	Date	Mintage	VG	Fine	VF	XF
6	1813 J	—	—	—	Rare	—

2 ESCUDOS

6.7500 g, .875 GOLD, .1899 oz AGW
Mint mark: Potosi monogram

KM#	Date	Mintage	VG	Fine	VF	XF
7	1813 J	—	—	—	Unique	—

Mint mark: RA

KM#	Date	Mintage	VG	Fine	VF	XF
19.1	1824 DS	—	175.00	275.00	450.00	750.00
	1825 CA. DE B. AS..					
		—	175.00	275.00	450.00	750.00
	1826 P	—	175.00	275.00	450.00	750.00

Rev: P omitted from legend.

KM#	Date	Mintage	VG	Fine	VF	XF
19.2	1826	—	175.00	275.00	450.00	750.00

NOTE: Struck in medal and coin alignment.

4 ESCUDOS

13.5000 g, .875 GOLD, .3798 oz AGW
Mint mark: Potosi monogram

KM#	Date	Mintage	VG	Fine	VF	XF
8	1813 J	—	—	Reported, not confirmed		

8 ESCUDOS

27.0000 g, .875 GOLD, .7596 oz AGW
Mint mark: Potosi monogram

KM#	Date	Mintage	VG	Fine	VF	XF
9	1813 J	—	4000.	6000.	10,000.	20,000.

NOTE: Superior Casterline sale 5-89 choice VF realized $11,000.

Mint mark: RA

KM#	Date	Mintage	VG	Fine	VF	XF
21	1826 P	—	650.00	1250.	1950.	2750.
	1828 P	—	650.00	1250.	1950.	2750.
	1829 P	2 known	—	—	Rare	—
	1830 P	—	1500.	3000.	4500.	6000.
	1831/0	—	—	—	Rare	—
	1831 P	—	600.00	1200.	1850.	2700.
	1832 P	—	600.00	1200.	1850.	2700.
	1833 P	—	700.00	1350.	2000.	3000.
	1834 P	—	700.00	1350.	2000.	3000.
	1835 P	—	700.00	1350.	2000.	3000.

CONFEDERACION ARGENTINA

CENTAVO

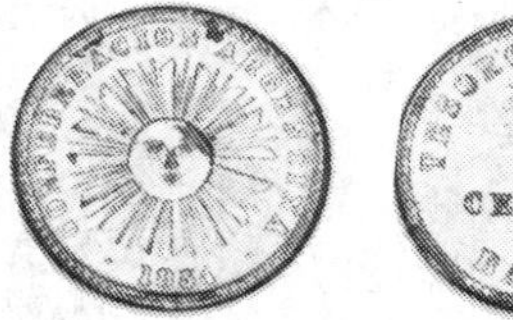

COPPER

KM#	Date	Mintage	VG	Fine	VF	XF
23	1854	—	2.50	5.00	15.00	40.00

2 CENTAVOS

COPPER

KM#	Date	Mintage	VG	Fine	VF	XF
24	1854	—	3.00	7.50	20.00	50.00

NOTE: Struck in medal and coin alignment.

4 CENTAVOS

COPPER

KM#	Date	Mintage	VG	Fine	VF	XF
25	1854	—	5.00	12.50	27.50	75.00

NOTE: Struck in medal and coin alignment.

PROVINCIAL COINAGE

BUENOS AIRES

Buenos Aires, a city and province in eastern Argentina, was the first province to have coins made outside the country. Governor Martin Rodriguez initiated negotiations with Boulton & Watt (Soho Mint) in 1821. The Banco Nacional was dissolved in 1836 and the Casa de Moneda took its place.

NOTE: National Bank 5/10 reales are frequently struck over Soho decimos of 1822-1823.

MONETARY SYSTEM

10 Decimos = 1 Real

DECIMO

COPPER

KM#	Date	Mintage	VG	Fine	VF	XF
1	1822	—	1.25	4.00	15.00	35.00
	1823	—	1.00	3.00	12.00	25.00

NOTE: Officially retired in 1827, in favor of Banco Nacional issues, KM#2-5.

1/4 REAL

COPPER

Obv: Fraction in shaded circle.
Rev: BUENOS AYRES 1827 within branches.

KM#	Date	Mintage	VG	Fine	VF	XF
2	1827	—	15.00	25.00	45.00	100.00

5/10 REAL

COPPER

KM#	Date	Mintage	VG	Fine	VF	XF
3	1827	—	2.00	4.00	10.00	25.00
	1828	—	2.00	4.00	10.00	25.00
	1830	—	3.00	5.00	12.50	30.00
	1831/27	—	—	—	—	—
	1831	—	2.00	4.00	10.00	25.00

NOTE: Struck in medal and coin alignment.

KM#	Date	Mintage	VG	Fine	VF	XF
6	1840	—	6.00	12.00	25.00	55.00

10 DECIMOS

COPPER

KM#	Date	Mintage	VG	Fine	VF	XF
4	1827	—	5.00	10.00	22.00	50.00
	1828	—	10.00	22.50	45.00	75.00
	1830	—	5.00	10.00	22.00	50.00

REAL

COPPER

KM#	Date	Mintage	VG	Fine	VF	XF
7	1840	—	2.00	4.00	10.00	22.00

KM#	Date	Mintage	VG	Fine	VF	XF
10	1854	—	4.00	10.00	15.00	35.00

20 DECIMOS

COPPER

KM#	Date	Mintage	VG	Fine	VF	XF
5	1827	—	4.00	9.00	22.00	55.00
	1830	—	3.00	5.00	20.00	50.00
	1831	—	12.50	30.00	50.00	100.00

NOTE: Struck in medal and coin alignment.

2 REALES

COPPER

KM#	Date	Mintage	VG	Fine	VF	XF
8	1840	—	2.00	4.00	11.50	25.00
	1844	—	2.00	4.00	11.50	25.00

KM#	Date	Mintage	VG	Fine	VF	XF
9	1853	—	1.00	2.50	7.50	20.00
	1854	—	1.00	2.75	10.00	22.50
	1855	—	1.00	2.50	7.50	20.00
	1856	—	2.00	4.00	12.50	30.00

KM#	Date	Mintage	VG	Fine	VF	XF
11	1860	—	2.00	5.00	11.50	25.00
	1861	—	2.00	5.00	10.00	25.00

CORDOBA

Cordoba, a city and province in central Argentina, was the most prolific of the provincial issuers. The provincial government contracted with concessionaires to make coins. The contractors for 1833 are not known, but all the private makers' coinage is relatively crude and replete with variations, die-sinking incongruities and minor errors. On many pieces it is almost impossible to find the same pairing of dies, i.e., 1/4 Reales, 1/2 Reales and 1 Reales of the 1839-41 type.

On February 2, 1844 a provincial mint was authorized by Governor Manuel Lopez. It operated from 1844 to 1852.

CONCESSIONAIRES

Letter	Date	Name
PP, PNP	1839-41	Pedro Nolasco Pizarro
JPP	1841-44	Jose Policarpo Patino

1/4 REAL

SILVER

Obv: Castle, date below.
Rev: Sun face.

KM#	Date	Mintage	VG	Fine	VF	XF
1.1	1833	—	25.00	40.00	65.00	100.00
	1838	—	25.00	40.00	65.00	100.00

Obv: Wide castle, w/o date.

KM#	Date	Mintage	VG	Fine	VF	XF
1.2	ND	—	2250.	3750.	—	—

Obv: Castle flanked by Prize Cup.

KM#	Date	Mintage	VG	Fine	VF	XF
2.1	1839 lg. eight/small sun face	—	1000.	—	—	—
	1839 sm. eight/small sun face	—	—	—	Rare	—

Obv: Castle flanked by P-P, date below.

KM#	Date	Mintage	VG	Fine	VF	XF
2.2	1839 PP	—	10.00	20.00	35.00	65.00
	1840 PP	—	15.00	30.00	60.00	100.00
	1841 PP	—	25.00	40.00	85.00	140.00

NOTE: Many legend and die varieties exist.

Obv: Fraction.

KM#	Date	Mintage	VG	Fine	VF	XF
33	ND(1853-54)	—	15.00	25.00	40.00	75.00

NOTE: Die varieties exist.

1/2 REAL

SILVER

Obv: Arms in wreath, leg: EN UNION Y LIBERTAD.
Rev: Sun face, leg: PROVINCIA DE CORDOVA.

KM#	Date	Mintage	VG	Fine	VF	XF
3	1839 PNP	—	22.50	50.00	65.00	125.00
	1839 PNP LIVERTAD	—	25.00	55.00	75.00	150.00

KM#	Date	Mintage	VG	Fine	VF	XF
3	1839 PNP CORDOBA on rev.	—	25.00	55.00	75.00	150.00
	1840 PNP LIVERTAD	—	15.00	37.50	60.00	115.00
	1840 PNP LIVEITAD	—	—	—	Rare	—

Obv. leg: EN UNION Y LIVERTAD.
Rev. leg: CONFEDERADA.

KM#	Date	Mintage	VG	Fine	VF	XF
4	1839 PNP	—	22.50	50.00	70.00	125.00

Obv. leg: CONFEDERADA.
Rev. leg: PROVINCIA DE CORDOVA.

KM#	Date	Mintage	VG	Fine	VF	XF
5	1840 PNP	—	25.00	50.00	70.00	125.00

Obv. leg: PROVINCIA DE CORDOV.
Rev. leg: PROVINCIA DE CORDOV.

KM#	Date	Mintage	VG	Fine	VF	XF
15	1841 PNP	—	22.50	50.00	70.00	125.00
	1841	—	22.50	50.00	70.00	125.00

Obv: Banner above castle; date below, leg: CORDOVA.
Rev: Sun face, leg: CONFEDERADA.

KM#	Date	Mintage	VG	Fine	VF	XF
6	1840 PNP crossed lances below castle	—	25.00	55.00	75.00	—

Obv. leg: CONFEDERADA.
Rev. leg: PROVINCIA DE CORDOVA.

KM#	Date	Mintage	VG	Fine	VF	XF
16	1841 PNP	—	22.50	50.00	70.00	—
	1841	—	22.50	50.00	70.00	—

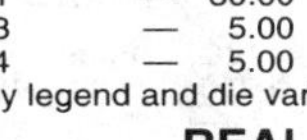

Obv: Denomination. Rev: Sun face.

KM#	Date	Mintage	VG	Fine	VF	XF
29	1850	—	5.00	10.00	20.00	45.00
	1850 error: CONFEDRRADA	—	5.00	10.00	20.00	45.00
	1851	—	30.00	75.00	120.00	225.00
	1853	—	5.00	10.00	20.00	45.00
	1854	—	5.00	10.00	20.00	45.00

NOTE: Many legend and die varieties exist.

REAL

SILVER
Obv: Arms (shaded) in wreath; date below, leg: PROVINCIA DE CORDOVA.
Rev: Sun face, leg: CONFEDERADA.

KM#	Date	Mintage	VG	Fine	VF	XF
7	1840 PNP	—	5.00	10.00	20.00	40.00
	1841/0 PNP	—	—	—	—	—
	1841 PNP	—	5.00	10.00	20.00	40.00
	1841 PNP CORDOBA	—	35.00	60.00	100.00	200.00
	1841 PNP CORDOBA & inverted 4	—	45.00	75.00	120.00	220.00
	1841 JPP	—	5.00	10.00	20.00	40.00
	1842 JPP	—	5.00	10.00	20.00	40.00
	1842 JPP PROVINCI	—	7.50	15.00	30.00	65.00
	1842 JPP PROVINCA	—	7.50	15.00	25.00	60.00
	1843 JPP	—	5.00	10.00	20.00	40.00
	1843 JPP inverted 3	—	6.50	12.50	22.00	50.00
	3481 JPP (error for 1843)	—	10.00	22.00	40.00	85.00
	1843 JPP PROVICIA	—	7.50	15.00	25.00	60.00
	1843 JPP CORDOV	—	5.00	10.00	20.00	40.00
	4481 JPP (error for 1844)	—	40.00	70.00	100.00	200.00

NOTE: Many legend and die varieties exist.

Obv. leg: PROVINCIA DE CORDOVA.
Rev. leg: PROVINCIA DE CORDOVA.

KM#	Date	Mintage	VG	Fine	VF	XF
8	1840 PNP	—	15.00	35.00	65.00	120.00
	1841 PNP	—	15.00	35.00	65.00	120.00

Obv. leg: PROVINCIA DE CORDOVA.
Rev. leg: EN UNION Y LIBERTAD.

KM#	Date	Mintage	VG	Fine	VF	XF
9	1840 PNP	—	5.00	10.00	20.00	45.00
	1841 PNP	—	5.00	10.00	20.00	45.00
	1841 PNP CORDOBA	—	30.00	50.00	80.00	125.00

Obv. leg: CONFEDERADA.
Rev. leg: CONFEDERADA.

KM#	Date	Mintage	VG	Fine	VF	XF
10	1840 PNP	—	30.00	50.00	80.00	120.00

Obv. leg: CONFEDERADA.
Rev. leg: PROVINCIA DE CORDOVA.

KM#	Date	Mintage	VG	Fine	VF	XF
11	1840 PNP	—	30.00	50.00	80.00	125.00

Obv. leg: EN UNION Y LIBERTAD.
Rev. leg: PROVINCIA DE CORDOVA.

KM#	Date	Mintage	VG	Fine	VF	XF
12	1840 PNP	—	30.00	50.00	80.00	125.00

Obv. leg: EN UNION Y LIVERTAD.
Rev. leg: CONFEDERADA.

KM#	Date	Mintage	VG	Fine	VF	XF
13	1840 PNP	—	30.00	50.00	80.00	125.00

Obv. leg: PROVINCIA DE CORDOVA, arms w/o shading and 2 rosettes.
Rev. leg: CONFEDERADA, sun face.

KM#	Date	Mintage	VG	Fine	VF	XF
17	1841 PNP	—	5.00	10.00	20.00	40.00
	1843 JPP	—	5.00	10.00	20.00	40.00
	1843 JPP PROVINCI	—	5.00	10.00	20.00	40.00
	1843 JPP CONFEDERDA	—	5.00	10.00	20.00	40.00
	1843 JPP CORDOV	—	5.00	10.00	20.00	40.00

Rev. leg: LIBRE YNDEPENDIENTE.

KM#	Date	Mintage	VG	Fine	VF	XF
20	1843 JPP	—	8.00	16.00	30.00	60.00

Obv. leg: PROVINCIA DE CORDOVA; banner above castle. Rev. leg: CONFEDERADA, sun face.

KM#	Date	Mintage	VG	Fine	VF	XF
14	1840 PNP	—	50.00	80.00	120.00	200.00
	1841 PNP	—	8.00	16.00	30.00	60.00
	1841 PNP CORDOBA	—	35.00	60.00	100.00	150.00
	1841 PNP CORDOV, inverted 4	—	6.00	12.00	25.00	45.00
	1841 PNP inverted 4	—	6.00	12.00	25.00	45.00
	1841 PNP CORDOV	—	10.00	20.00	35.00	70.00

NOTE: Many legend and die varieties exist.

Obv. leg: PROVINCIA DE CORDOVA.
Rev. leg: EN UNION Y LIBERTAD.

KM#	Date	Mintage	VG	Fine	VF	XF
18	1841 PNP	—	15.00	25.00	45.00	90.00

Obv. leg: PROVINCIA DE CORDOVA.
Rev. leg: PROVINCIA DE CORDOVA.

KM#	Date	Mintage	VG	Fine	VF	XF
19	1841 PNP rosette below castle	—	22.50	45.00	75.00	150.00

Obv. leg: PROVINCIA DE CORDOVA, arms w/o shading; date below.
Rev. leg: CONFEDERADA, sun face.

KM#	Date	Mintage	VG	Fine	VF	XF
21	1843 JPP	—	5.00	10.00	20.00	40.00
	1843 JPP CONFEDERDA	—	5.00	10.00	20.00	40.00
	1843 JPP CORDOV	—	5.00	10.00	20.00	40.00
	1843 JPP CORDOV & CONFEDERDA	—	5.00	10.00	20.00	40.00
	1843 JPP CORDOV & PROVINCI	—	6.50	12.50	25.00	50.00
	1843 JPP CORDO	—	5.00	10.00	20.00	40.00
	1843 JPP CORDO & CONFEDERDA	—	5.00	10.00	20.00	40.00
	1844 JPP	—	5.00	10.00	20.00	40.00
	1844 JPP CORDOV	—	22.50	45.00	80.00	130.00

NOTE: Many legend and die varieties exist.

Obv. leg: PROVINCIA DE CORDOVA.
Rev. leg: LIBRE YNDEPENDIENTE.

KM#	Date	Mintage	VG	Fine	VF	XF
22	1843 JPP	—	7.50	15.00	30.00	55.00

NOTE: Many legend and die varieties exist.

Obv. leg: PROVINCIA DE CORDOBA, denomination.
Rev. leg: CONFEDERADA, sun face, date below.

KM#	Date	Mintage	VG	Fine	VF	XF
26	1848	—	6.50	12.50	25.00	50.00

NOTE: Many legend and die varieties exist.

2 REALES

.750 SILVER
Obv: Castle among flags in sprays, leg: PROVINCIA DE CORDOBA.
Rev: Sun face in sprays, date below, leg: CONFEDERADA.

KM#	Date	Mintage	VG	Fine	VF	XF
23	1844	—	8.00	16.00	30.00	60.00
	1844 CONFEDRADA	—	20.00	40.00	80.00	150.00
	1845	—	8.00	16.00	30.00	55.00

NOTE: Many legend and die varieties exist.

KM#	Date	Mintage	VG	Fine	VF	XF
25	1846	—	9.00	18.00	35.00	65.00
	1848	—	—	—	Rare	—

NOTE: Many legend and die varieties exist.

KM#	Date	Mintage	VG	Fine	VF	XF
27	1849	—	8.00	16.00	30.00	55.00

KM#	Date	Mintage	VG	Fine	VF	XF
28	1849	—	8.00	16.00	30.00	55.00
	1850	—	8.00	16.00	30.00	55.00

NOTE: Many legend and die varieties exist.

Similar to 4 Reales, KM#31.

KM#	Date	Mintage	VG	Fine	VF	XF
30	1852	—	15.00	30.00	45.00	85.00
	1854	—	15.00	30.00	45.00	85.00

4 REALES

.750 SILVER
Rev. weight: 9 Ds.

KM#	Date	Mintage	VG	Fine	VF	XF
24.1	1844	—	100.00	200.00	325.00	575.00

Larger dies.

KM#	Date	Mintage	VG	Fine	VF	XF
24.2	1845 obv. w/portcullis	—	30.00	55.00	85.00	160.00
	1845 obv. w/o portcullis	—	22.50	40.00	70.00	100.00
	1846 die of 1845	—	80.00	120.00	160.00	300.00

KM#	Date	Mintage	VG	Fine	VF	XF
24.3	1846 milled edge	—	47.50	85.00	125.00	175.00
	1846 laureate edge	—	30.00	55.00	85.00	160.00
	1847	—	20.00	30.00	55.00	90.00
	1850	—	20.00	30.00	55.00	90.00
	1851 sm. 5mm sunface, wgt: 9.D.	—	20.00	30.00	55.00	90.00
	1851 lg. 6.5mm sunface, wgt: 9.D.	—	20.00	30.00	55.00	90.00

Rev: Flatter sunface w/even length sunburst.

KM#	Date	Mintage	VG	Fine	VF	XF
24.4	1852	—	—	—	—	—

NOTE: Die and edge varieties exist.

KM#	Date	Mintage	VG	Fine	VF	XF
31	1852	—	30.00	50.00	80.00	150.00

8 REALES

.750 SILVER
Obv: High spear tips at left.

KM#	Date	Mintage	VG	Fine	VF	XF
32	1852	—	50.00	80.00	150.00	300.00

NOTE: 9 known varieties of obverses w/differences in width of base, size of and distance between leaves and positions of flag poles in relation to letters in inscription. Spelling differences are known w/CORDOBA the common one and Cordova the rare one.

ENTRE RIOS

Entre Rios (Colonia San Jose) was a settlement of Swiss and Italian families in northeast Argentina on the Uruguayan border. General Urquiza (deposer of Rosas) was a political power in the province. As governor, during the war with Paraguay, he authorized an Italian, Pablo Cataldi, to make coins for the settlement during a coin shortage in 1867.

1/2 REAL

SILVER

KM#	Date	Mintage	VG	Fine	VF	XF
1	1867	—	60.00	90.00	150.00	275.00

LA RIOJA

La Rioja (Rioxa), a city and province in northwest Argentina, was the source of rich mineral wealth. Governor Nicolas Davila, authorized a mint at Chilecito to take advantage of the rich mines at Famatina in 1820. The mint made "cob" types, with and without the name RIOXA from 1821 to 1823. The cobs were officially recalled in 1824.

In Chilecito, another city in La Rioja province, gold 1 Escudos and silver 1 Reales were struck in 1823. This mint was transferred to La Rioja in 1824, where coins were struck until 1860.

***NOTE:** Virtually all of the early pieces are false. All pieces dated between 1820 and 1824 should only be bought with certification of two or more authorities.

1/2 REAL

SILVER
Cob type w/RIOXA.

KM#	Date	Mintage	Good	VG	Fine	VF
3	1822	—	—	—	Rare	—

Obv: Arms in branches. Rev: Sun above mountain.

KM#	Date	Mintage	Good	VG	Fine	VF
18	1844 B	—	3.50	6.50	15.00	25.00

Obv. leg: REPUB. ARGENT. CONFEDERADA.
Rev. leg: PROV. DE LA. RIOJA.

KM#	Date	Mintage	Good	VG	Fine	VF
22	1854 B	.017	2.00	3.00	7.50	15.00

Rev. leg: CRED. PUB. DE LA RIOJA.

KM#	Date	Mintage	Good	VG	Fine	VF
23	1854 B	5,940	2.00	4.00	10.00	20.00

Obv. leg: CONFEDERACION ARGENTINA.
Rev. leg: PROV. DE LA. RIOJA.

KM#	Date	Mintage	Good	VG	Fine	VF
24	1854 B	.024	2.00	3.00	7.50	15.00

Rev. leg: CRED. PUB. DE LA RIOJA.

KM#	Date	Mintage	Good	VG	Fine	VF
25	1854 B	.071	2.00	3.00	7.50	15.00
	1860 B	—	2.50	5.00	12.50	25.00

REAL

SILVER
Mint: Chilecito
Cob type w/RIOXA.

KM#	Date	Mintage	Good	VG	Fine	VF
4	1822	—	—	—	Rare	—

NOTE: 1821 dated coins are counterfeit.

Mint: La Rioja
Obv: Sun above arms.
Rev. leg: SVR AMERICA RIOXA.

KM#	Date	Mintage	Good	VG	Fine	VF
5	ND (1823)	—	—	—	Rare	—

Rev. leg: SUD AMERICA 1823 RIOXA

KM#	Date	Mintage	Good	VG	Fine	VF
6	1823	—	—	—	Rare	—

2 REALES

SILVER
Cob Type

KM#	Date	Mintage	Good	VG	Fine	VF
1	(1)821	—	—	—	Rare	—
	(1)822	—	—	—	Rare	—
	(1)823	—	—	—	Rare	—

General Rosas

KM#	Date	Mintage	Good	VG	Fine	VF
12	1842	—	25.00	40.00	65.00	125.00

Mountain type

KM#	Date	Mintage	Good	VG	Fine	VF
15	1843 RB	—	8.00	16.00	30.00	55.00

Mountain and sun type

KM#	Date	Mintage	Good	VG	Fine	VF
16	1843 RB	—	8.00	16.00	32.00	65.00
	1844 RB	—	6.00	12.00	25.00	50.00

NOTE: Struck in coin and medal rotation.

KM#	Date	Mintage	Good	VG	Fine	VF
26	1859 B	—	20.00	35.00	60.00	90.00
	1860 B	—	6.00	12.00	20.00	45.00

4 REALES

SILVER
Cob Type
Obv: Pillars, RIOXA, date. Rev: Castles & lions.

KM#	Date	Mintage	Good	VG	Fine	VF
2.1	(1)821	—	100.00	200.00	350.00	500.00
	(1)822	—	—	—	Rare	—

Obv: W/o RIOXA

KM#	Date	Mintage	Good	VG	Fine	VF
2.2	(1)823	—	125.00	250.00	400.00	600.00

KM#	Date	Mintage	VG	Fine	VF	XF
20	1846 RV	—	15.00	25.00	45.00	75.00
	1849 RV	—	—	—	—	—
	1849 RB	—	15.00	25.00	45.00	75.00
	1850 RB	—	20.00	35.00	60.00	100.00

KM#	Date	Mintage	VG	Fine	VF	XF
21	1852 B	—	60.00	90.00	150.00	250.00

8 REALES

SILVER

KM#	Date	Mintage	VG	Fine	VF	XF
8	1838 R	—	35.00	70.00	150.00	285.00
	1839 R	—	35.00	70.00	150.00	285.00
	1840 R	—	45.00	85.00	175.00	350.00

NOTE: Struck in coin and medal rotation.

Obv. leg: REPUBLICA ARGENTINA.

KM#	Date	Mintage	VG	Fine	VF	XF
10	1840 R	—	550.00	1000.	2000.	3500.

ESCUDO

3.3750 g, .875 GOLD, .0949 oz AGW
Obv: Sun above arms in branches.
Rev. leg: SUD AMERICA 1823 RIOXA in wreath.

KM#	Date	Mintage	VG	Fine	VF	XF
7	1823	—	—	—	Unique	—

2 ESCUDOS

6.7500 g, .875 GOLD, .1899 oz AGW
General Rosas

KM#	Date	Mintage	VG	Fine	VF	XF
13	1842 R	—	250.00	500.00	800.00	1500.

KM#	Date	Mintage	VG	Fine	VF	XF
17	1843 RB	—	200.00	400.00	600.00	1000.

8 ESCUDOS

27.0000 g, .875 GOLD, .7596 oz AGW
General Rosas

KM#	Date	Mintage	VG	Fine	VF	XF
A9	1836 R	—	—	—	Rare	—

KM#	Date	Mintage	VG	Fine	VF	XF
9	1838 R	—	650.00	1150.	2000.	3500.
	1840 R	—	750.00	1250.	2150.	3750.

Obv. leg: REPUBLICA ARGENTINA.

KM#	Date	Mintage	VG	Fine	VF	XF
11	1840 R	—	850.00	1350.	2250.	4000.

General Rosas

KM#	Date	Mintage	VG	Fine	VF	XF
14	1842 R	—	—	—	*Rare	—

***NOTE:** Superior Heifetz sale 12-89 VF realized $18,700.

KM#	Date	Mintage	VG	Fine	VF	XF
19	1845 B	—	1250.	1850.	2750.	5000.

MENDOZA

Mendoza, a province in western Argentina, was one of the first to make coins designed to resemble the Spanish Colonial cobs of Potosi. The mint was established in 1822, under Governor Pedro Molina. These local cobs were put in circulation in December 1823 and retired from circulation less than a year later.

In 1835 Molina again saw that coins were needed, and decided to award contracts for production rather than have the provincial mint make them. Abel Bucci and Manuel Espeys, who had the contract failed to supply any volume of coinage for circulation and were retired in 1836.

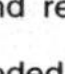

DECIMO

COPPER
Obv: Date and denomination within wreath.
Rev: Arms within branches.

KM#	Date	Mintage	Good	VG	Fine	VF
4	1823	—	—	—	Unique	—

1/8 REAL

COPPER

KM#	Date	Mintage	Good	VG	Fine	VF
5	1835	—	—	—	Rare	—

1/4 REAL

SILVER
Obv: Arms divide value.
Rev: Small animal.

KM#	Date	Mintage	Good	VG	Fine	VF
6	1836	—	—	—	Unique	—

SALTA

Salta, a province in northwest Argentina, was a frequent battleground during the War of Independence. Governor Martin Guemes fought the Spaniards without help from the patriotic forces in Buenos Aires. There was no money with which to pay the troops and what was circulating was counterfeit. Low morale and frequent desertions were one result. In desperation, Guemes decided to countermark the false coins with the word PATRIA and to guarantee them as genuine.

When this action became known to the patriot government in Buenos Aires, it was declared to be a violation of national laws and all the pieces were to be withdrawn.

Meanwhile, Guemes had gained valuable time, culminating with a victory at Castanares which finally rid the north of Spanish influence.

All genuine Salta countermarks are only found on counterfeit Potosi cobs.

c/m: PATRIA monogram in wreath.

2 REALES

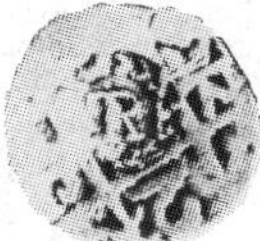

SILVER
c/m: PATRIA monogram in wreath on Potosi Mint cobs.

KM#	Date	Mintage	Good	VG	Fine	VF
2	ND(1817)	—	50.00	100.00	150.00	—

4 REALES

SILVER
c/m: PATRIA monogram in wreath on Potosi Mint cobs.

KM#	Date	Mintage	Good	VG	Fine	VF
3	ND(1817)	—	—	—	Rare	—

8 REALES

All known specimens are considered fantasies.

SANTIAGO DEL ESTERO

Santiago del Estero is a province in north central Argentina. In 1823, during the governorship of Felipe Ibarra, coinage began in an effort to replace the fast-disappearing cob coins of the Potosi mint. The pieces were not well received and coining was soon halted. Another effort, in 1836, faired no better.

1/2 REAL

SILVER
Obv: SoEo in angles of crossed arrows, date below. Rev: Sun in branches.

KM#	Date	Mintage	Good	VG	Fine	VF
1	(1)823 So Eo	—	—	—	Unique	—

Obv: S E in angles of crossed arrows, date below.

KM#	Date	Mintage	Good	VG	Fine	VF
2	(1)823	—	75.00	150.00	225.00	300.00

REAL

SILVER
Obv: SoEo in angles of crossed arrows, date below. Rev: Cross.

KM#	Date	Mintage	Good	VG	Fine	VF
3	(1)823	—	—	—	Unique	—

Rev: Sun in branches.

KM#	Date	Mintage	Good	VG	Fine	VF
4	(1)823	—	100.00	200.00	350.00	600.00

Obv: S E in angles of crossed arrows, date below.

KM#	Date	Mintage	Good	VG	Fine	VF
5	(1)823	—	50.00	100.00	150.00	250.00

Rev: Sun above Liberty cap in branches.

KM#	Date	Mintage	Good	VG	Fine	VF
6	(1)836	—	35.00	75.00	125.00	200.00

TUCUMAN

Tucuman is a province in northwestern Argentina. Due to the large quantity of false Potosi cobs circulating in the province, Governor Bernabe Araoz established a mint in 1823 to make cobs that would be distinctive to the area. Their circulation was brief due to the introduction of Confederation coins.

2 REALES

SILVER
Mint mark: TN
Similar to Potosi Cob 2 Reales.

KM#	Date	Mintage	Good	VG	Fine	VF
1	ND(1823)	—	35.00	75.00	100.00	125.00

NOTE: Most coins exist without the TN mint mark. Coins with the T discernable are generally worth two times the above values, with TN visable four times. Those with fictitious dates are attributed to Venezuela. Virtually all have the date 752 but there are 2 known pieces dated 753. These are similar to Potosi coins but can be easily distinguished by the Pillars of Hercules on the obverse.

REPUBLIC

Decimal Coinage

100 Centavos = 1 Peso
5 Pesos = 1 Argentino

CENTAVO

BRONZE

KM#	Date	Mintage	Fine	VF	XF	Unc
7	1882	.108	6.50	13.50	25.00	50.00
	1883	.786	.75	1.75	4.50	25.00
	1884	4.604	.50	1.00	2.50	9.00
	1885	1.314	.50	1.00	3.50	12.00
	1886	.444	.75	1.75	4.50	28.00
	1888	.413	.75	2.25	5.50	30.00
	1889	.568	.75	2.25	5.50	30.00
	1890	2.137	.50	1.00	2.50	9.00
7	1891	.605	.75	1.75	4.50	25.00
	1892	.205	1.00	2.25	5.50	30.00
	1893	.754	.50	1.75	4.50	25.00
	1894	.532	1.00	1.75	4.50	25.00
	1895	.423	.75	2.25	5.50	25.00
	1896	.174	4.50	11.00	16.00	40.00

2 CENTAVOS

BRONZE

KM#	Date	Mintage	Fine	VF	XF	Unc
8	1882	.088	7.00	15.00	30.00	70.00
	1883	1.389	1.00	2.00	4.50	20.00
	1884	5.667	.75	1.75	3.00	10.00
	1885	3.065	.75	1.75	3.50	12.00
	1887	.363	4.50	11.50	18.00	45.00
	1888	.659	1.75	3.50	8.50	30.00
	1889	2.391	.75	1.75	3.50	12.00
	1890	3.609	.75	1.75	3.50	12.00
	1891	8.050	.50	1.75	3.00	10.00
	1892	3.497	.75	1.75	3.50	12.00
	1893	5.473	.75	1.75	3.50	12.00
	1894	2.233	.75	1.75	3.50	12.00
	1895	.593	1.25	3.50	8.50	30.00
	1896	.596	1.75	4.50	12.50	35.00

5 CENTAVOS

COPPER-NICKEL

KM#	Date	Mintage	Fine	VF	XF	Unc
9	1896	1.499	1.50	4.00	8.00	30.00
	1897	3.981	.50	1.00	4.00	15.00
	1898	2.661	.50	1.00	4.00	15.00
	1899	2.835	.25	.50	3.00	12.00

NOTE: Later dates (1903-1942) exist for this type.

10 CENTAVOS

2.5000 g, .900 SILVER, .0723 oz ASW

KM#	Date	Mintage	Fine	VF	XF	Unc
1	1881	1,020	75.00	150.00	225.00	375.00
	1882	.778	5.00	10.00	20.00	50.00
	1883	2.786	2.00	4.00	10.00	25.00

COPPER-NICKEL

KM#	Date	Mintage	Fine	VF	XF	Unc
10	1896	1.877	2.00	4.50	12.50	40.00
	1897	8.582	.50	1.50	6.50	20.00
	1898	8.534	.50	1.50	6.50	20.00
	1899	8.889	.50	1.50	6.50	20.00

NOTE: Later dates (1905-1950) exist for this type.

20 CENTAVOS

5.0000 g, .900 SILVER, .1446 oz ASW

KM#	Date	Mintage	Fine	VF	XF	Unc
2	1881	2,018	50.00	80.00	130.00	200.00
	1882	.762	8.00	15.00	30.00	60.00
	1883/2 inverted 2					
		1.511	10.00	20.00	40.00	85.00
	1883	Inc. Ab.	5.00	10.00	20.00	45.00

COPPER-NICKEL

KM#	Date	Mintage	Fine	VF	XF	Unc
11	1896	2.030	1.00	3.00	7.00	25.00
	1897	5.263	1.00	3.00	7.00	25.00
	1898	1.264	2.00	5.00	10.00	40.00
	1899	.840	3.00	8.00	15.00	55.00

NOTE: Later dates (1905-1942) exist for this type.

50 CENTAVOS

12.5000 g, .900 SILVER, .3617 oz ASW

KM#	Date	Mintage	Fine	VF	XF	Unc
3	1881	1,020	125.00	225.00	375.00	650.00
	1882	.476	25.00	40.00	75.00	165.00
	1883	2.273	10.00	20.00	40.00	85.00

PESO

25.0000 g, .900 SILVER, .7234 oz ASW

KM#	Date	Mintage	Fine	VF	XF	Unc
4	1881	.062	100.00	150.00	225.00	365.00
	1882	.414	50.00	85.00	150.00	285.00
	1883	.098	100.00	150.00	225.00	365.00

1/2 ARGENTINO

4.0322 g, .900 GOLD, .1167 oz AGW

KM#	Date	Mintage	Fine	VF	XF	Unc
5	1881	9 pcs.	—	—	Rare	—
	1884	421 pcs.	550.00	900.00	1250.	1850.

ARGENTINO

8.0645 g, .900 GOLD, .2334 oz AGW

KM#	Date	Mintage	Fine	VF	XF	Unc
6	1881	.037	125.00	150.00	200.00	275.00
	1882	.252	100.00	125.00	150.00	225.00
	1883	.906	100.00	125.00	150.00	225.00
	1884	.448	100.00	125.00	150.00	225.00
	1885	.204	100.00	125.00	150.00	225.00
	1886	.398	100.00	125.00	150.00	225.00
	1887	1.835	100.00	120.00	140.00	200.00
	1888	1.663	100.00	120.00	140.00	200.00
	1889	.404	175.00	275.00	400.00	550.00
	1896	.197	100.00	125.00	150.00	225.00

ESSAIS (E)

KM#	Date	Mintage	Identification	Mkt.Val.
E1	1878	—	1 Centavo, Copper	70.00
E2	1878	—	2 Centavo, Copper	80.00
E3	1879	—	20 Centavos Fuertes, Silver	275.00
E3a	1879	—	20 Centavos Fuertes, Bronze	225.00
E4	1879	—	40 Centavos Fuertes, Silver	500.00
E4a	1879	—	40 Centavos Fuertes, Bronze	350.00
E5	1879	—	80 Centavos Fuertes, Silver	650.00
E4	1879	—	40 Centavos Fuertes, Silver	450.00
E5b	1879	—	80 Centavos Fuertes, Copper	450.00

KM#	Date	Mintage	Identification	Mkt.Val.
E6	1879	—	1 Patacon, Silver	2750.
E6a	1879	—	1 Patacon, Copper	1250.

PATTERNS (Pn)

(Including off metal strikes)

KM#	Date	Mintage	Identification	Mkt.Val.
Pn1	1822	—	1 Decimo, Copper, Province of Buenos Aires, medallic rev.	—
Pn2	1823	—	1 Octavo, Copper	—
Pn3	1824	—	1 Quinto, Copper	—
Pn4	1826	—	1 Real, Silver	—
Pn4a	1826	—	1 Real, Copper	—

KM#	Date	Mintage	Identification	Mkt.Val.
Pn5	1827	—	1 Real, Silver	250.00
Pn5a	1827	—	1 Real, Copper	—
PnA6	1827	—	20 Decimos, Silver, KM5	—
PnB6	1840	—	5/10 Real, Silver, KM6	—
PnC6	1852	—	4 Reales, Copper, Cordoba KM31	—
PnD6	1852	—	8 Reales, Copper, Cordoba KM32	—

KM#	Date	Mintage	Identification	Mkt.Val.
Pn6	1876	—	1 Peso, Silver	—
Pn6a	1876	—	1 Peso, Copper	—

KM#	Date	Mintage	Identification	Mkt.Val.
Pn13	1879	—	1 Peso, Silver	—
Pn13a	1879	—	1 Peso, Copper	—
Pn13b	1879	—	1 Peso, Tin	—

KM#	Date	Mintage	Identification	Mkt.Val.
Pn14	1880	—	1 Centavo, Copper, w/E, KM7	120.00
Pn15	1880	—	2 Centavos, Copper, w/E, KM8	130.00
Pn16	1880	—	50 Centavos, Silver, KM3	—
Pn17	1880	—	1 Peso, Silver, KM4	—
Pn18	1880	—	1 Peso, Silver, UN PESO PLATA	—
Pn19	18xx	—	1 Centavo, Copper	—
Pn20	18xx	—	1 Centavo, Silver	—
Pn21	18xx	—	1 Centavo, Gold	—
Pn22	18xx	—	20 Centavos, Silver	—
Pn23	188x	—	50 Centavos, Silver	—
Pn24	1881	9 pcs.	1/2 Argentino, Gold	—
Pn25	1887	—	20 Centavos, Nickel, w/E	150.00
Pn26	1892	—	1 Centavo, Aluminum, UN CENTAVO	125.00
Pn27	1892	—	1 Centavo, Aluminum, 1 CENTAVO	125.00
Pn28	1892	—	1 Centavo, Nickel	125.00
Pn28a	1892	—	1 Centavo, Copper-Nickel	—

PIEFORTS (P)

KM#	Date	Mintage	Identification	Mkt.Val.
P1	1892	—	1 (UN) Centavo, Copper, rev: plain field	—
P2	1892	—	1 Centavo, Nickel, rev: wreath	—

PIEFORTS WITH ESSAI (PE)

KM#	Date	Mintage	Identification	Mkt.Val.
PE1	1879	—	20 Centavos, Fuertes, Silver	—
PE2	1879	—	40 Centavos, Fuertes, Silver	—
PE3	1879	—	80 Centavos, Fuertes, Silver	—
PE4	1879	—	1 Patacon, Silver	—

MINT SETS (MS)

KM#	Date	Mintage	Identification	Issue Price	Mkt. Val.
MS1	1879(4)	—	KM Pn9-12	—	3375.

TIERRA DEL FUEGO

An archipelago located south off the tip of South America. The main island is divided between Chile and Argentina. Julius Popper was a South American adventurer who was given permission to mine ore on that island and strike coins. He was quite vehement in carrying out his perceived duties and protecting his mining rights. He summarily executed anyone who he thought to be encroaching on his mining rights. This became so notorious that the government finally had the Popper dies transferred to Buenos Aires, where the coins were struck under better conditions. As a result, both coins come in 2 different types - somewhat rusted or mottled die strikes which were produced locally in Tierra Del Fuego and the type which usually comes BU and proof-like.

TOKEN ISSUES (Tn)

Julius Popper Series

GRAMO

GOLD

KM#	Date	Mintage	Fine	VF	XF	Unc
Tn1	1889	—	—	—	650.00	1000.

5 GRAMOS

GOLD

KM#	Date	Mintage	Fine	VF	XF	Unc
Tn2	1889	—	—	—	3000.	4750.

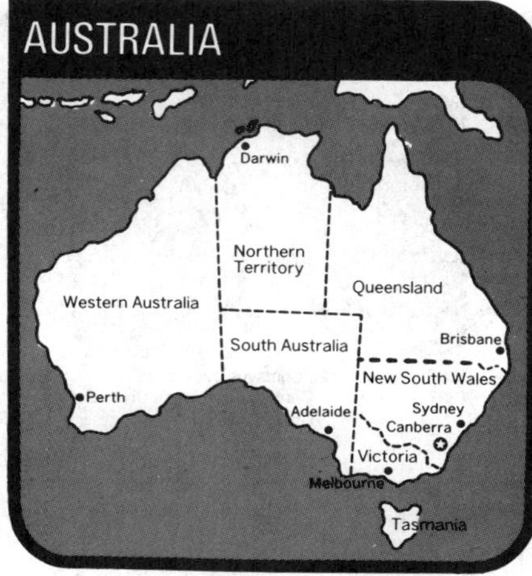

The Commonwealth of Australia, the smallest continent and largest island in the world, is located south of Indonesia between the Indian and Pacific oceans. It has an area of 2,966,200 sq. mi. (7,686,850 sq. km.) and a population of 18.3 million. Capital: Canberra. Due to its early and sustained isolation, Australia is the habitat of such curious and unique fauna as the kangaroo, koala, platypus, wombat, echidna and frilled-necked lizard. The continent possesses extensive mineral deposits, the most important of which are iron ore, coal, gold, silver, nickel, uranium, lead and zinc. Livestock raising, mining and manufacturing are the principal industries. Chief exports are wool, meat, wheat, iron ore, coal and nonferrous metals.

The first caucasians to see Australia probably were Portuguese and Spanish navigators of the late 16th century. In 1770, Captain James Cook explored the east coast and annexed it for Great Britain. New South Wales was founded as a penal colony, following the loss of British North America, by Capt. Arthur Phillip on January 26, 1788, a date now celebrated as Australia Day. Dates of creation of the six colonies that now comprise the states of the Australian Commonwealth are: New South Wales, 1823; Tasmania, 1825; Western Australia, 1838; South Australia, 1842; Victoria, 1851; Queensland, 1859. A constitution providing for federation of the colonies was approved by the British Parliament in 1900; the Commonwealth of Australia came into being in 1901. Australia passed the Statute of Westminster Adoption Act on October 9, 1942, which officially established Australia's complete autonomy in external and internal affairs, thereby formalizing a situation that had existed for years. Australia is a member of the Commonwealth of Nations. Elizabeth II is Head of State.

Australia's currency system was changed from Pounds-Shillings-Pence to a decimal system of Dollars and Cents on Feb. 14, 1966.

RULERS

British

MONETARY SYSTEM

(Until 1966)

12 Pence = 1 Shilling
2 Shillings = 1 Florin
5 Shillings = 1 Crown
20 Shillings = 1 Pound

NEW SOUTH WALES

CUT AND COUNTERSTAMPED COINAGE

15 PENCE

Struck over center plugs of cut Spanish or Spanish Colonial 8 Reales.
.903 SILVER

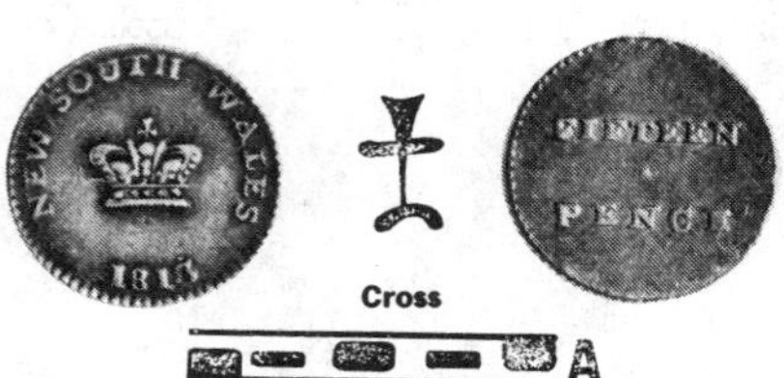

Cross

A

Crown band
Mira type A/1. Rev: FIFTEEN/4.5mm/PENCE.

KM#	Date	Mintage	Good	VG	Fine	VF
1.1	1813	*.026	450.00	950.00	2150.	4750.

Cross

C

Crown band
Mira type C/4. Rev: FIFTEEN/4.0mm/PENCE.

KM#	Date	Mintage	Good	VG	Fine	VF
1.2	1813	*1,600	1000.	3500.	4500.	7500.

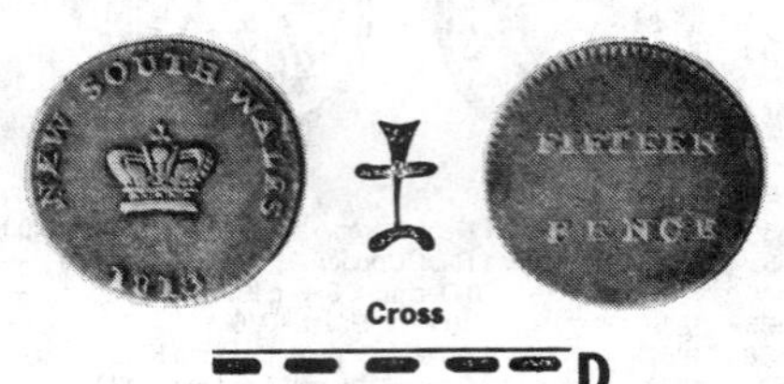

Cross

D

Crown band
Mira type D/2. Rev: FIFTEEN/5.0mm/PENCE.

KM#	Date	Mintage	Good	VG	Fine	VF
1.3	1813	*8,000	750.00	1500.	3000.	5250.

Cross

E

Crown band
Mira type E/3. Rev: FIFTEEN/5.0mm/PENCE.

KM#	Date	Mintage	Good	VG	Fine	VF
1.4	1813	*4,400	1200.	2500.	4000.	6500.

***NOTE:** Estimated original mintage.
REFERENCE: "A Classification of the New South Wales Dumps", 1977 by Dr. W. J. D. Mira.

'HOLEY DOLLAR'

(5 Shillings)

.903 SILVER
c/s: NEW SOUTH WALES-1813/FIVE SHILLINGS on holed Bolivia, Potosi 8 Reales KM#55.

KM#	Date	Mintage	Good	VG	Fine	VF
2.1	1813(1773-89)	*.040	3000.	6500.	13,500.	26,500.

c/s: On holed Bolivia, Potosi 8 Reales KM#73.

KM#	Date	Mintage	Good	VG	Fine	VF
2.3	1813(1791-1808)	—	2500.	4500.	11,000.	20,000.

c/s: On holed Mexico City 8 Reales, KM#104.

KM#	Date	Mintage	Good	VG	Fine	VF
2.5	1813(1757)	1 known	—	—	Rare	—

M. R. Roberts 1988 sale, unique, realized A $45,000.

c/s: On holed Mexico City 8 Reales, KM#106.

KM#	Date	Mintage	Good	VG	Fine	VF
2.6	1813(1772-89)	Inc. Ab.	2500.	4500.	11,000.	20,000.

c/s: On holed Mexico City 8 Reales, KM#107.

KM#	Date	Mintage	Good	VG	Fine	VF
2.7	1813(1789-90)	Inc. Ab.	2500.	4500.	11,000.	20,000.

c/s: On holed Mexico City 8 Reales, KM#109.

KM#	Date	Mintage	Good	VG	Fine	VF
2.9	1813(1791-1808)	Inc. Ab.	2250.	3750.	7500.	16,000.

c/s: On holed Mexico City 8 Reales, KM#110.

KM#	Date	Mintage	Good	VG	Fine	VF
2.10	1813(1809-10)	Inc. Ab.	2500.	4500.	11,000.	20,000.

c/s: On holed Peru, Lima 8 Reales, KM#117.1.

KM#	Date	Mintage	Good	VG	Fine	VF
2.11	1813(1772-89)	Inc. Ab.	3000.	6000.	12,500.	23,000.

c/s: On holed Peru, Lima 8 Reales, KM#117.1.

KM#	Date	Mintage	Good	VG	Fine	VF
2.13	1813(1791-1808)	Inc. Ab.	3000.	6000.	12,500.	23,000.

c/s: On holed Peru, Lima 8 Reales, KM#117.1.

KM#	Date	Mintage	Good	VG	Fine	VF
2.14	1813(1810)	2 known	—	—	Rare	—

M. R. Roberts 1988 sale, AEF realized A $50,000.

c/s: On holed Spain, Madrid 8 Reales C#71.1.

KM#	Date	Mintage	Good	VG	Fine	VF
2.15	1813(1788-1808)	Inc. Ab.	7500.	12,500.	25,000.	32,000.

c/s: On holed Spain, Seville 8 Reales, C#71.2.

KM#	Date	Mintage	Good	VG	Fine	VF
2.16	1813(1788-1803)	Inc. Ab.	7500.	12,500.	25,000.	32,000.

SOUTH AUSTRALIA

ADELAIDE POUND

8.7500 g, .917 GOLD, .2579 oz AGW

KM#	Date	Mintage	Fine	VF	XF	Unc
1	1852	*20-50 pcs.	—	25,000.	40,000.	56,500.

Rev: Dentilated inner circle.

KM#	Date	Mintage	Fine	VF	XF	Unc
2	1852	.025	2500.	4000.	7500.	12,500.

INGOTS

GOLD

The Bullion Act of 1852 allowed for ingots to be stamped in two weights of 5 dwt. 11 grs., and 5 dwt. 1 gr. Only two examples, one of each type, are known. Other ingots were issued with a circular stamp showing the weight; two known 5 dwt. 5 grs., ,and 4 dwt. 19 grs.

PATTERNS (Pn)

(Including off metal strikes)

KM#	Date	Mintage	Identification	Mkt.Val.
Pn1	1852	7 known	5 Pounds, .917 Gold, restrike	55,000.
Pn1a	1852	2 known	5 Pounds, .917 Silver, restrike	Rare

NOTE: The above gold restrikes were produced at the Melbourne branch of the Royal Mint in 1921. The origin of the silver restrikes is undocumented.

VICTORIA

PATTERNS (Pn)

Port Phillip, Kangaroo Office

These extremely rare gold patterns originated from a commercial venture set up by Messrs. Hodgkin, Taylor and Tyndall of England. Their idea was to buy up gold dust and use it to strike their own gold of 1/4, 1/2, 1 and 2 ounces which they proposed to pass on as bullion currency from their store in Melbourne. The dies were cut by W. J. Taylor and the machinery provided. This equipment arrived at Hobson's Bay on October 23, 1853, but before it could be removed and set up at the store, known as the Kangaroo Office, the availability of the British sovereign pre-empted the venture.

KM#	Date	Mintage	Identification	Mkt.Val.
Pn1	1853	—	1/4 Ounce, Gold	*30,000.

***NOTE:** P.J. Downie Sale 5-87 AXF realized $23,100.

KM#	Date	Mintage	Identification	Mkt.Val.
Pn1b	1853	—	1/4 Ounce, Copper, milled edge	900.00

KM#	Date	Mintage	Identification	Mkt.Val.
Pn2	1853	—	1/2 Ounce, Gold	*Rare

***NOTE:** Spink Australia Sale 10-77 XF realized $27,100.

KM#	Date	Mintage	Identification	Mkt.Val.
Pn2b	1853	—	1/2 Ounce, Gilt (?), 6.33 g (restrike)	Rare
Pn2c	1853	—	1/2 Ounce, Copper, milled edge	1250.

KM#	Date	Mintage	Identification	Mkt.Val.
Pn3	1853	—	1 Ounce, Gold	Rare
Pn3b	1853	—	1 Ounce, Gilt Lead, 24.08 g	350.00
Pn3c	1853	—	1 Ounce, Brass, milled edge	2150.
Pn3d	1853	—	1 Ounce, Copper, milled edge	1250.

KM#	Date	Mintage	Identification	Mkt.Val.
Pn4	1853	—	2 Ounces, Gold	Rare
Pn4a	1853	—	2 Ounces, Gilt Copper	2150.
Pn4b	1853	—	2 Ounces, Copper	2000.
Pn4c	1853	—	2 Ounces, Pewter, milled edge	3200.
Pn4d	1854	—	2 Ounces, Copper, milled edge	5250.
Pn4e	1854	—	2 Ounces, Lead, plain edge	2650.

NOTE: Uniface gilt copper electrotypes of both obverses and reverses of all denominations, with the exception of the 1/2 Ounce obverse, are know to exist. Values range from $125. to $200. Bonded pairs have been noted.

KM#	Date	Mintage	Identification	Mkt.Val.
Pn5	ND(1855)	—	4 Pence, Copper	7500.

KM#	Date	Mintage	Identification	Mkt.Val.
Pn6	ND(1855)	—	6 Pence, Copper, milled edge	1700.
Pn6a	ND(1855)	—	6 Pence, Copper, plain edge	1250.
Pn6b	ND(1855)	—	6 Pence, Copper, silvered,	

KM#	Date	Mintage	Identification	Mkt.Val.
Pn6b			milled edge	1350.
Pn6c	ND(1855)	—	6 Pence, Aluminum, milled edge	1200.
Pn6d	ND(1855)	—	6 Pence, Silver, milled edge	2150.
Pn6e	ND(1855)	—	6 Pence, Silver, plain edge	1850.
Pn6f	ND(1855)	—	6 Pence, Gold, milled edge	15,000.
Pn6g	ND(1855)	—	6 Pence, Gold, plain edge	13,500.

KM#	Date	Mintage	Identification	Mkt.Val.
Pn7	ND(1855)	—	1 Shilling, Copper, milled edge	2100.
Pn7a	ND(1855)	—	1 Shilling, Copper, plain edge	1650.
Pn7b	ND(1855)	—	1 Shilling, Tin, Silver plated, milled edge	1350.
Pn7c	ND(1855)	—	1 Shilling, Aluminum, milled edge	1100.
Pn7d	ND(1855)	—	1 Shilling, Silver, milled edge	4000.
Pn7e	ND(1855)	—	1 Shilling, Silver, plain edge	2350.
Pn7f	ND(1855)	—	1 Shilling, Gold, milled edge	15,000.
Pn7g	ND(1855)	—	1 Shilling, Gold, plain edge	R,NC

KM#	Date	Mintage	Identification	Mkt.Val.
Pn8	ND(1860)	—	1 Shilling, Copper, milled edge, DEI GRATIA, coronet bust	1850.
Pn8a	ND(1860)	—	1 Shilling, Copper, plain edge, DEI GRATIA, coronet bust	1450.
Pn8b	ND(1860)	—	1 Shilling, Silver, milled edge, DEI GRATIA, coronet bust	2300.
Pn8c	ND(1860)	—	1 Shilling, Silver, plain edge, DEI GRATIA, coronet bust	1800.
Pn8d	ND(1860)	—	1 Shilling, Gold, milled edge, DEI GRATIA, coronet bust	R,NC
Pn8e	ND(1860)	—	1 Shilling, Gold, plain edge, DEI GRATIA, coronet bust	R,NC

KM#	Date	Mintage	Identification	Mkt.Val.
Pn9	ND(1860)	—	1 Shilling, Copper, milled edge, DEI GRATIA, laureate bust	1650.
Pn9a	ND(1860)	—	1 Shilling, Copper, plain edge, DEI GRATIA, laureate bust	1300.
Pn9b	ND(1860)	—	1 Shilling, Silver, milled edge, DEI GRATIA, laureate bust	2100.
Pn9c	ND(1860)	—	1 Shilling, Silver, plain edge, DEI GRATIA, laureate bust	1650.
Pn9d	ND(1860)	—	1 Shilling, Gold, DEI GRATIA, laureate bust	R,NC

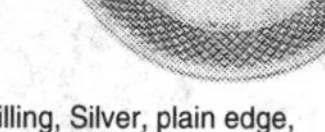

KM#	Date	Mintage	Identification	Mkt.Val.
Pn10	ND(1860)	—	1 Shilling, Silver, plain edge, REGINA, coronet bust	2000.

PRIVATE TOKEN ISSUES (Tn)

Port Phillip, Kangaroo Office

1/2 PENNY

BRONZE

KM#	Date	Mintage	VG	Fine	VF	XF
Tn1	ND	—	—	—	1650.	2750.

TRIAL STRIKES (TS)

KM#	Date	Mintage	Identification	Mkt.Val.
TS1	1853	—	1 Ounce, Bronze, obv., milled edge, 6.48 g	2000.
TS2	1853	—	2 Ounces, Copper, rev., milled edge, 15.18 g	4000.
TS3	1853	—	2 Ounces, Lead, rev., 20.29 g	1500.
TS4	1853	—	2 Ounces, Lead, rev., 22.32 g	1500.

COMMONWEALTH OF AUSTRALIA

TRADE COINAGE

MINT MARKS

M - Melbourne
P - Perth
S - Sydney
(sy) - Sydney

1/2 SOVEREIGN

3.9940 g, .917 GOLD, .1177 oz AGW
Obv: Fillet head.

KM#	Date	Mintage	Fine	VF	XF	Unc
1	1855(sy)	.021	7000.	15,000.	40,000.	90,000.
	1856(sy)	.478	400.00	1500.	4000.	10,000.

Obv: Hair tied with banksia wreath.

KM#	Date	Mintage	Fine	VF	XF	Unc
3	1857(sy)	.537	200.00	600.00	1500.	5000.
	1857(sy)	—	—	—	Proof	27,500.
	1858(sy)	.483	200.00	600.00	1750.	7000.
	1858(sy) SOVRREIGN (error)	—	—	—	—	—
	1859(sy)	.341	200.00	600.00	2000.	9000.
	1860(sy)	.156	350.00	1500.	5000.	14,250.
	1861(sy)	.186	200.00	600.00	1750.	6000.
	1862(sy)	.210	175.00	700.00	2000.	7000.
	1863(sy)	.348	155.00	600.00	2000.	7000.
	1864(sy)	.141	175.00	750.00	2200.	9200.
	1865(sy)	.062	300.00	700.00	2000.	9000.
	1866(sy)	.154	250.00	700.00	2000.	9000.
	1866(sy)	—	—	—	Proof	20,000.

Obv: Young head, date below.
Rev: Mintmark below shield.

KM#	Date	Mintage	Fine	VF	XF	Unc
5	1871S	.180	80.00	160.00	750.00	2250.
	1871S	—	—	—	Proof	13,500.
	1872S	.356	80.00	160.00	750.00	2250.
	1873M	.165	80.00	160.00	850.00	2500.
	1875S	.252	80.00	160.00	750.00	2250.
	1877M	.140	120.00	200.00	850.00	2500.
	1879S	.220	80.00	160.00	600.00	1850.
	1880S	.080	80.00	200.00	1000.	2750.
	1880S	—	—	—	Proof	12,000.
	1881S	.062	80.00	220.00	1100.	3000.
	1881M	.042	90.00	250.00	1250.	3500.
	1881M	—	—	—	Proof	12,000.
	1882S	.052	145.00	275.00	1750.	6000.
	1882M	.106	90.00	220.00	800.00	2250.
	1883S	.220	80.00	165.00	500.00	1500.
	1883S	—	—	—	Proof	12,000.
	1884M	.048	90.00	250.00	1500.	4500.
	1884M	—	—	—	Proof	12,000.
	1885M	.011	250.00	550.00	2500.	8000.
	1886S	.082	80.00	165.00	650.00	2250.
	1886M	.038	90.00	200.00	1000.	2750.
	1886M	—	—	—	Proof	12,000.
	1887S	.134	80.00	165.00	700.00	2500.
	1887S	—	—	—	Proof	12,000.
	1887M	.064	145.00	275.00	1750.	6000.

Obv: Jubilee head.
Rev: Date and mintmark below shield.

KM#	Date	Mintage	Fine	VF	XF	Unc
9	1887S	Inc. Ab.	70.00	110.00	250.00	750.00
	1887S	—	—	—	Proof	10,000.
	1887M	Inc. Ab.	80.00	120.00	300.00	850.00
	1887M	—	—	—	Proof	10,000.
	1888M	—	—	—	Proof	11,500.
	1889S	.064	80.00	120.00	500.00	1450.
9	1889M	—	—	—	Proof	11,500.
	1890M	—	—	—	Proof	11,500.
	1891S w/J.E.B.	.154	90.00	150.00	650.00	2000.
	1891S w/o J.E.B.	Inc. Ab.	80.00	120.00	500.00	1450.
	1891M	—	—	—	Proof	11,500.
	1892S	—	—	—	Proof	11,500.
	1892M	—	—	—	Proof	11,500.
	1893S	—	—	—	Proof	11,500.
	1893M	.110	70.00	115.00	450.00	1400.
	1893M	—	—	—	Proof	10,000.

Obv: Older veiled head. Rev: Mintmark above date.

KM#	Date	Mintage	Fine	VF	XF	Unc
12	1893S	.250	65.00	100.00	300.00	1250.
	1893S	—	—	—	Proof	10,000.
	1893M	2 known	1000.	—	—	—
	1893M	—	—	—	Proof	11,500.
	1894M	—	—	—	Proof	11,500.
	1895M	—	—	—	Proof	11,500.
	1896M	.218	70.00	125.00	350.00	1500.
	1896M	—	—	—	Proof	10,000.
	1897S	.230	65.00	100.00	300.00	1350.
	1897M	—	—	—	Proof	11,500.
	1898M	—	—	—	Proof	11,500.
	1899M	.090	70.00	125.00	450.00	1500.
	1899M	—	—	—	Proof	10,000.
	1899P	1 known	—	—	Proof	—
	1900S	.260	65.00	100.00	300.00	1350.
	1900M	.113	70.00	125.00	450.00	1500.
	1900M	—	—	—	Proof	10,000.
	1900P	.119	70.00	125.00	450.00	1500.

NOTE: Later date (1901) exists for this type.

SOVEREIGN

7.9881 g, .917 GOLD, .2354 oz AGW
Obv: Fillet head.

KM#	Date	Mintage	Fine	VF	XF	Unc
2	1855(sy)	.502	1250.	3500.	9000.	25,000.
	1856(sy)	.981	1250.	3500.	9000.	25,000.

Obv: Hair tied with banksia wreath.

KM#	Date	Mintage	Fine	VF	XF	Unc
4	1857(sy)	.499	250.00	500.00	1750.	4500.
	1857(sy) (plain or milled edge)				Proof	30,000.
	1858(sy)	1.101	250.00	600.00	1850.	7000.
	1859(sy)	1.050	250.00	600.00	1850.	4500.
	1860(sy)	1.573	350.00	850.00	2500.	7500.
	1861(sy)	1.626	200.00	400.00	1200.	3000.
	1862(sy)	2.477	225.00	475.00	1750.	4500.
	1863(sy)	1.255	175.00	425.00	1400.	3500.
	1864(sy)	2.698	125.00	275.00	1100.	2750.
	1865(sy)	2.130	150.00	375.00	1350.	3500.
	1866(sy)	2.911	125.00	275.00	1000.	1850.
	1866(sy)	—	—	—	Proof	25,000.
	1867/6(sy)	I.A.	—	—	—	—
	1867(sy)	2.370	135.00	325.00	1000.	1850.
	1868(sy)	3.522	125.00	275.00	1000.	1850.
	1870(sy)	1.220	125.00	275.00	650.00	1600.
	1870(sy)	—	—	—	Proof	50,000.

NOTE: 1,202,600 pcs. reported in 1869 are dated 1868.

Obv: Young head, date below.
Rev: Mintmark below shield.

NOTE: Mintage figures include St. George and shield types. No separate mintage figures are known.

KM#	Date	Mintage	Fine	VF	XF	Unc
6	1871S incuse ww	2.814	BV	100.00	250.00	700.00
6	1871S raised ww	Inc. Ab.	BV	100.00	250.00	700.00
	1871S	—	—	—	Proof	13,500.
	1872S	1.815	BV	100.00	250.00	750.00

KM#	Date	Mintage	Fine	VF	XF	Unc
6	1872/1M	.748	200.00	350.00	600.00	2000.
	1872M	Inc. Ab.	BV	100.00	225.00	675.00
	1873S	1.478	BV	100.00	225.00	675.00
	1873M	3 pcs.	—	Reported, not confirmed		
	1874M	1.373	BV	100.00	250.00	750.00
	1875S	2.122	BV	100.00	200.00	625.00
	1875S	—	—	—	Proof	13,000.
	1877S	1.590	BV	95.00	200.00	625.00
	1878S	1.259	BV	95.00	200.00	625.00
	1879S	1.366	BV	95.00	200.00	625.00
	1879M	1 pc.	—	Reported, not confirmed		
	1880S	1.459	BV	95.00	200.00	625.00
	1880S	—	—	—	Proof	13,000.
	1880M	3.053	500.00	1000.	2500.	7000.
	1880M	—	—	—	Proof	12,500.
	1881S	1.360	BV	95.00	175.00	450.00
	1881M	2.324	BV	135.00	300.00	1200.
	1882S	1.298	BV	95.00	175.00	450.00
	1882M	2.466	BV	95.00	175.00	450.00
	1883S	1.108	BV	95.00	175.00	450.00
	1883S	—	—	—	Proof	12,500.
	1883M	2.050	150.00	350.00	1000.	2500.
	1883M	—	—	—	Proof	12,500.
	1884S	1.595	BV	95.00	175.00	420.00
	1884M	2.942	BV	95.00	175.00	420.00
	1884M	—	—	—	Proof	12,500.
	1885S	1.486	BV	95.00	175.00	420.00
	1885M	2.957	BV	95.00	175.00	420.00
	1885M	—	—	—	Proof	12,500.
	1886S	1.677	BV	95.00	175.00	450.00
	1886S	—	—	—	Proof	12,500.
	1886M	2.902	1500.	3000.	6000.	9000.
	1886M	—	—	—	Proof	14,000.
	1887S	1.000	BV	100.00	300.00	550.00
	1887S	—	—	—	Proof	12,500.
	1887M	1.915	600.00	1200.	3000.	6000.
	1887M	—	—	—	Proof	12,500.

NOTE: Mintmark placement varies.

Obv: Young head, mintmark below.
Rev: St. George slaying dragon, date below.

NOTE: Mintage figures include St. George and shield types. No separate mintage figures are known.

KM#	Date	Mintage	Fine	VF	XF	Unc
7	1871S	2.814	—	BV	300.00	900.00
	1871S	—	—	—	Proof	13,500.
	1872S	1.815	—	BV	250.00	800.00
	1872M	.748	—	200.00	500.00	1750.
	1873S	1.478	—	BV	300.00	1000.
	1873M	.752	—	BV	250.00	700.00
	1873M	—	—	—	Proof	12,000.
	1874S	1.899	—	BV	200.00	600.00
	1874M	1.373	—	BV	200.00	600.00
	1874M	—	—	—	Proof	12,000.
	1875S	2.122	—	BV	165.00	550.00
	1875M	1.888	—	BV	165.00	550.00
	1875M	—	—	—	Proof	12,000.
	1876S	1.613	—	BV	150.00	500.00
	1876M	2.124	—	BV	150.00	500.00
	1877S	2 pcs.	—		Rare	—
	1877M	1.487	—	BV	150.00	500.00
	1878M	2.171	—	BV	150.00	475.00
	1879S	1.366	—	BV	350.00	1200.
	1879M	2.740	—	BV	150.00	450.00
	1880S	1.459	—	BV	200.00	600.00
	1880S	—	—	—	Proof	12,000.
	1880M	3.053	—	BV	150.00	400.00
	1881S	1.360	—	BV	200.00	600.00
	1881M	2.324	—	BV	150.00	475.00
	1881M	—	—	—	Proof	12,000.
	1882S	1.298	—	BV	150.00	400.00
	1882M	2.466	—	BV	150.00	475.00
	1883S	1.108	—	BV	150.00	475.00
	1883M	2.050	—	BV	150.00	475.00
	1883M	—	—	—	Proof	12,000.
	1884S	1.595	—	BV	150.00	425.00
	1884M	2.942	—	BV	150.00	425.00
	1884M	—	—	—	Proof	12,000.
	1885S	1.486	—	BV	150.00	425.00
	1885M	2.957	—	BV	150.00	425.00
	1885M	—	—	—	Proof	12,000.
	1886S	1.677	—	BV	150.00	425.00
	1886M	2.902	—	BV	150.00	425.00
	1886M	—	—	—	Proof	12,000.
	1887S	1.000	—	BV	190.00	600.00
	1887M	1.915	—	BV	190.00	600.00
	1887M	—	—	—	Proof	12,000.

NOTE: Designers initials on reverse omitted on some pieces 1880S-1882S and 1881M-1882M. Mintmark placement varies.

Obv: Jubilee head. Rev: Mintmark above date.

KM#	Date	Mintage	Fine	VF	XF	Unc
10	1887S	1.002	BV	175.00	375.00	850.00
10	1887S	—	—	—	Proof	11,000.
	1887M	.940	—	BV	125.00	225.00
	1887M	—	—	—	Proof	10,000.
	1888S	2.187	—	BV	125.00	225.00
	1888M	2.830	—	BV	120.00	210.00
	1888M	—	—	—	Proof	10,000.
	1889S	3.262	—	BV	120.00	210.00
	1889M	2.732	—	BV	120.00	210.00
	1889M	—	—	—	Proof	10,000.
	1890S	2.808	—	BV	120.00	210.00
	1890M	2.473	—	BV	120.00	210.00
	1890M	—	—	—	Proof	10,000.
	1891S	2.596	—	BV	120.00	210.00
	1891M	2.749	—	BV	120.00	210.00
	1892S	2.837	—	BV	120.00	210.00
	1892M	3.488	—	BV	120.00	210.00
	1893S	1.498	—	BV	120.00	210.00
	1893S	—	—	—	Proof	10,000.
	1893M	1.649	—	BV	120.00	210.00
	1893M	—	—	—	Proof	10,000.

Obv: Older veiled head.

KM#	Date	Mintage	Fine	VF	XF	Unc
13	1893S	1.346	—	BV	100.00	180.00
	1893S	—	—	—	Proof	10,000.
	1893M	1.914	—	BV	100.00	180.00
	1893M	—	—	—	Proof	10,000.
	1894S	3.067	—	BV	100.00	160.00
	1894S	—	—	—	Proof	10,000.
	1894M	4.166	—	BV	100.00	160.00
	1894M	—	—	—	Proof	10,000.
	1895S	2.758	—	BV	100.00	170.00
	1895M	4.165	—	BV	100.00	160.00
	1895M	—	—	—	Proof	10,000.
	1896S	2.544	—	BV	100.00	170.00
	1896M	4.456	—	BV	100.00	170.00
	1896M	—	—	—	Proof	10,000.
	1897S	2.532	—	BV	100.00	190.00
	1897M	5.130	—	BV	100.00	170.00
	1897M	—	—	—	Proof	10,000.
	1898S	2.548	—	BV	100.00	190.00
	1898M	5.509	—	BV	100.00	170.00
	1898M	—	—	—	Proof	10,000.
	1899S	3.259	—	BV	100.00	130.00
	1899M	5.579	—	BV	100.00	130.00
	1899M	—	—	—	Proof	10,000.
	1899P	.690	BV	120.00	160.00	375.00
	1899P	—	—	—	Proof	12,500.
	1900S	3.586	—	BV	100.00	130.00
	1900M	4.305	—	BV	100.00	130.00
	1900M	—	—	—	Proof	10,000.
	1900P	1.886	—	BV	100.00	160.00

NOTE: Later date (1901) exists for this type.

2 POUNDS

15.9761 g, .917 GOLD, .4707 oz AGW
50th Anniversary of Reign

KM#	Date	Mintage	Fine	VF	XF	Unc
8	1887S	*11 pcs.	—	—	Proof	27,500.

***NOTE:** Spink Australia Sale #30 11-89 nearly FDC realized $16,940.

5 POUNDS

39.9403 g, .917 GOLD, 1.1771 oz AGW
50th Anniversary of Reign

KM#	Date	Mintage	Fine	VF	XF	Unc
11	1887S	*3 pcs.	—	—	Proof	Rare

***NOTE:** Spink Australia Sale #30 11-89 nearly FDC realized $62,370.

PATTERNS (Pn)

(Including off metal strikes)

KM#	Date	Mintage	Identification	Mkt.Val.
Pn1	1853	—	1/2 Sovereign, Gold T.1	60,000.

KM#	Date	Mintage	Identification	Mkt.Val.
Pn2	1853	—	1 Sovereign, Gold T.1	75,000.

KM#	Date	Mintage	Identification	Mkt.Val.
Pn3	1855	—	1/2 Sovereign, Gold, T.2, milled edge	60,000.
Pn4	1855	—	1 Sovereign, Gold, T.2, milled edge	60,000.

KM#	Date	Mintage	Identification	Mkt.Val.
Pn5	1856	—	1/2 Sovereign, Gold, T.2, plain edge	50,000.

KM#	Date	Mintage	Identification	Mkt.Val.
Pn6	1856	—	1 Sovereign, Gold, T.2, plain edge	60,000.

PRIVATE TOKEN ISSUES (Tn)

The first copper token of penny value was issued in Melbourne in 1849. With the increase in population following the discovery of gold in the early 1850's a large number of traders tokens were used in the colonies. Most of these were of copper and were valued as pennies or halfpennies. A few were of silver and valued at a higher rate. The greatest number appeared between 1857 and 1863. The total number exceeded 530 and they were issued by some 126 firms. About 1860 British bronze coins began to arrive in the colonies in quantity and with their use the tokens became unpopular. Victoria declared tokens illegal in 1863 and the other colonies took similar action in the following years, the last being Tasmania in 1876. These are listed in "The Coins and Tokens of British Oceania" by Robert L. Clarke.

Other references are Dr. Andrews "Australasian Coins and Tokens" and "Unofficial Coins of Colonial Australia & New Zealand by G.C. Heyde.

NOTE: An F designation indicates a fabrication. Most of these pieces show major die deterioration such as cracks and flaws, unlike restrikes which show only minor die deterioration from surface rust. Restrikes were made using original die combinations. Fabrications were made using die combinations that are not known on original pieces.

Lewis Abrahams

Hobart, Tasmania

1/2 PENNY

COPPER, 27.5mm
Obv. leg: LEWIS ABRAHAMS. . .
Rev. leg: TASMANIA above emu and kangaroo.

KM#	Date	Mintage	VG	Fine	VF	XF
Tn6	1855	—	2.50	5.00	20.00	45.00

PENNY

COPPER, 34mm
Obv. & rev: Similar to KM#Tn6.

KM#	Date	Mintage	VG	Fine	VF	XF
Tn7	1855	—	4.00	8.00	30.00	60.00

Adamson, Watts, McKechnie & Co.

Melbourne, Victoria

1/2 PENNY

COPPER, 28mm

KM#	Date	Mintage	VG	Fine	VF	XF
Tn8.1	ND	—	5.00	10.00	50.00	300.00

Thick flan

KM#	Date	Mintage	VG	Fine	VF	XF
Tn8.2	ND (restrike)	—	—	—	—	300.00

John Allen

Kaima, New South Wales

PENNY

COPPER, 34mm

KM#	Date	Mintage	Good	VG	Fine	VF
Tn9	1855	5 known	3000.	5000.	6500.	10,000.

William Allen

Jamberoo, New South Wales

PENNY

COPPER, 34mm

KM#	Date	Mintage	VG	Fine	VF	XF
Tn10	1855	25 known	400.00	800.00	1500.	2500.

John Andrew & Co.

Melbourne, Victoria

1/2 PENNY

COPPER, 27.5mm
Obv. leg: JOHN ANDREW & CO. . . around crowned lion. Rev. leg: MELBOURNE VICTORIA above seated Justice.

KM#	Date	Mintage	VG	Fine	VF	XF
Tn-A11	1860	—	3.00	7.50	20.00	75.00

PENNY

COPPER, 34mm

KM#	Date	Mintage	VG	Fine	VF	XF
Tn11	1860	—	3.00	7.50	20.00	75.00

Jno Andrew & Co.

Melbourne, Victoria

1/2 PENNY

COPPER, 27.5mm

KM#	Date	Mintage	VG	Fine	VF	XF
Tn12	1860	—	300.00	500.00	900.00	1500.

KM#	Date	Mintage	VG	Fine	VF	XF
Tn13	1862	—	3.00	7.50	20.00	75.00

PENNY

COPPER, 34mm

KM#	Date	Mintage	VG	Fine	VF	XF
Tn14	1860	—	300.00	500.00	900.00	1500.

KM#	Date	Mintage	VG	Fine	VF	XF
Tn15	1862	—	3.00	7.50	20.00	75.00

Annand, Smith & Co.

Melbourne, Victoria

PENNY

COPPER, 34mm
Rev: 11 leaves to branch, H + S on rock.

KM#	Date	Mintage	VG	Fine	VF	XF
Tn16.1	ND	—	10.00	30.00	45.00	100.00

Rev: 14 leaves to branch.

KM#	Date	Mintage	VG	Fine	VF	XF
Tn16.2	ND	—	10.00	30.00	45.00	100.00

Barraclough

Richmond, Victoria

PENNY

COPPER, 35mm
Rev: Vertical leaf point between E and S in STOKES.

KM#	Date	Mintage	VG	Fine	VF	XF
Tn19.1	1862	—	35.00	75.00	200.00	300.00

Rev: Vertical leaf point above last S in STOKES.

KM#	Date	Mintage	VG	Fine	VF	XF
Tn19.2	1862	—	17.50	35.00	125.00	200.00

William Bateman Junr. & Co.

Warnambool, Victoria

PENNY

BRONZE

KM#	Date	Mintage	VG	Fine	VF	XF
Tn20	1855	—	12.50	25.00	80.00	200.00

Battle & Weight

Sydney, New South Wales

PENNY

COPPER, 34mm
Obv. leg: SOUTH HEAD ROAD. . .
Rev: Standing Justice.

Tn21	ND	—	4.00	10.00	30.00	125.00

Bell & Gardner

Rockhampton, Queensland

PENNY

COPPER, 34mm

Tn22	ND	—	125.00	250.00	900.00	1500.

I. Booth

Melbourne, Victoria

PENNY

COPPER, 34mm
Obv. leg: I. BOOTH. . .
Rev. leg: BRITANNIA above seated Britannia.

Tn23	ND	—	4.00	10.00	25.00	75.00

Joseph Brickhill

Campbelltown, Tasmania

PENNY

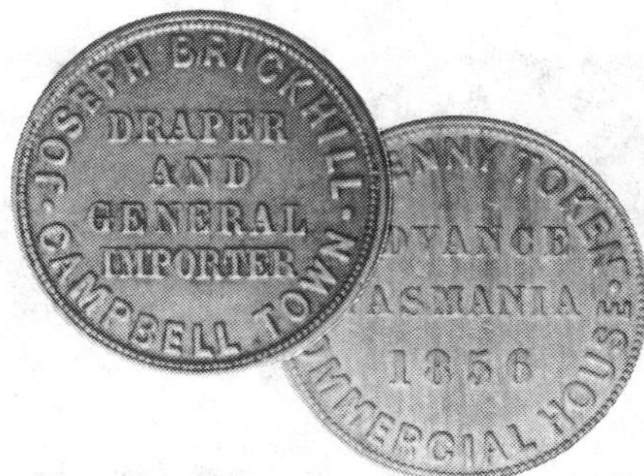

COPPER, 34mm
Obv. leg: JOSEPH BRICKHILL. . .
Rev. leg: ONE PENNY TOKEN. . .

KM#	Date	Mintage	VG	Fine	VF	XF
Tn24	1856	—	3.00	7.50	15.00	75.00

Brookes

Brisbane, Queensland

PENNY

COPPER, 34mm
Obv. & rev. leg: IRONMONGERS BROOKES BRISBANE in fancy lettering.

Tn25.1	ND	—	25.00	50.00	100.00	250.00

Obv. & rev: Similar to KM#Tn25.1 but plain lettering.

Tn25.2	ND	—	3.00	6.00	35.00	100.00

NOTE: 2 varieties exist.

W & B Brookes

Brisbane, Queensland

PENNY

COPPER, 34mm
Obv. leg: W & B BROOKES. . .
Rev. leg: QUEENSLAND above Australian arms.

Tn26	1863	—	2.00	4.00	30.00	100.00

T. Butterworth & Co.

Castlemaine, Victoria

PENNY

COPPER, 34mm
Obv. leg: T. BUTTERWORTH & CO. . .
Rev. leg: WHOLESALE & RETAIL. . .

KM#	Date	Mintage	VG	Fine	VF	XF
Tn28	ND	—	3.00	7.50	30.00	125.00

NOTE: 3 varieties exist.

Obv. leg: T. BUTTERWORTH & CO. . .
Rev: Seated Justice.

Tn29	1859	—	3.00	6.00	20.00	75.00

J. W. Buxton

Brisbane, Queensland

PENNY

BRONZE

Tn30	ND	—	15.00	30.00	100.00	200.00

R. Calder

Castlemaine, Victoria

PENNY

COPPER, 34mm
Rev. leg: M in MAKER above T in EAST.

Tn31	1862	—	37.50	75.00	125.00	250.00

Rev. leg: M in MAKER above AS in EAST.

TnF31	(fabrication)	—	as struck	300.00

James Campbell

Morpeth, New South Wales

1/2 PENNY

COPPER, 27mm
Obv. leg: JAMES CAMPBELL. . .

Rev. leg: TASMANIA above standing Justice.

KM#	Date	Mintage	VG	Fine	VF	XF
Tn32	ND	—	5.00	12.50	40.00	100.00

PENNY

COPPER, 34mm
Obv. & rev: Similar to KM#Tn32.

KM#	Date	Mintage	VG	Fine	VF	XF
Tn33	ND	—	3.00	7.50	20.00	100.00

3 PENCE

SILVER

KM#	Date	Mintage	VG	Fine	VF	XF
Tn34	ND	—	500.00	1000.	1750.	3000.

Collins & Co.

Bathurst, New South Wales

PENNY

COPPER, 34mm

KM#	Date	Mintage	VG	Fine	VF	XF
Tn35	1864	—	17.50	35.00	150.00	300.00

W. C. Cook

Sandridge, Melbourne, Victoria

PENNY

COPPER, 34mm

KM#	Date	Mintage	VG	Fine	VF	XF
Tn36	1862	—	15.00	30.00	100.00	275.00

Obv. & rev. leg. c/m:
SUGAR WORKS BY W. COOK. . .

KM#	Date	Mintage	VG	Fine	VF	XF
Tn37	ND	—	12.50	25.00	85.00	150.00

Thomas H. Cope

South Yarra, Victoria

PENNY

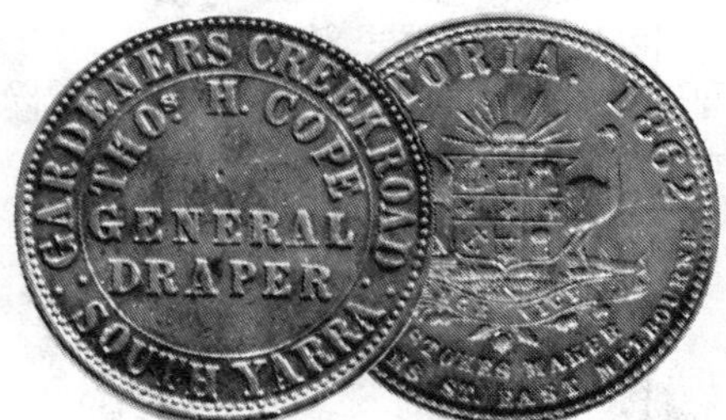

COPPER, 34mm
Rev. leg: R in MAKER above E in MELBOURNE.

KM#	Date	Mintage	VG	Fine	VF	XF
Tn38.1	1862	—	14.00	35.00	125.00	200.00

Rev. leg: R in MAKER above L in MELBOURNE.

KM#	Date	Mintage	VG	Fine	VF	XF
Tn38.2	1862	—	14.00	35.00	125.00	200.00

Crocker & Hamilton

Adelaide, South Australia

1/2 PENNY

COPPER, 28mm

KM#	Date	Mintage	VG	Fine	VF	XF
Tn39	1857	—	5.00	12.50	30.00	125.00

PENNY

COPPER, 34mm
Obv. leg: CROCKER & HAMILTON. . .
Rev. leg: DRAPERS. . .

KM#	Date	Mintage	VG	Fine	VF	XF
Tn40	ND	—	3.00	7.50	30.00	125.00

Crombie, Clapperton & Findlay

Melbourne, Victoria

1/2 PENNY

COPPER, 28mm
Obv. leg: CROMBIE, CLAPPERTON & FINDLAY. . .
Rev. leg: MELBOURNE above kangaroo.

KM#	Date	Mintage	VG	Fine	VF	XF
Tn41	ND	—	7.50	15.00	75.00	150.00

NOTE: 2 varieties exist.

Crothers & Co.

Stawell, Victoria

1/2 PENNY

COPPER, 24mm
Obv. & rev: Similar to KM#Tn43.

KM#	Date	Mintage	VG	Fine	VF	XF
Tn42	ND	—	7.50	15.00	75.00	150.00

PENNY

COPPER, 31mm

KM#	Date	Mintage	VG	Fine	VF	XF
Tn43	ND	—	7.50	15.00	75.00	150.00

NOTE: 2 varieties exist.
NOTE: KM#Tn42 and Tn43 are known also in brass.

Jas. Davey & Co.

Sale, Victoria

PENNY

COPPER, 34mm

KM#	Date	Mintage	VG	Fine	VF	XF
Tn44	1862	—	100.00	200.00	325.00	500.00

A. Davidson

Melbourne, Victoria

PENNY

COPPER, 34mm
Rev: Lower right leaf touches R in MAKER.

KM#	Date	Mintage	VG	Fine	VF	XF
Tn45.1	1862	—	25.00	50.00	100.00	250.00

Rev: Lower right leaf doesn't touch R in MAKER.

KM#	Date	Mintage	VG	Fine	VF	XF
Tn45.2	1862	—	50.00	175.00	350.00	500.00

Obv: Similar to KM#Tn45.
Rev: VICTORIA 1862 above Australian arms.

KM#	Date	Mintage	Fine	VF	XF	Unc
TnF46	1862 (fabrication)	—	—		as struck	300.00

Alfred Davies

Fremantle, Western Australia

PENNY

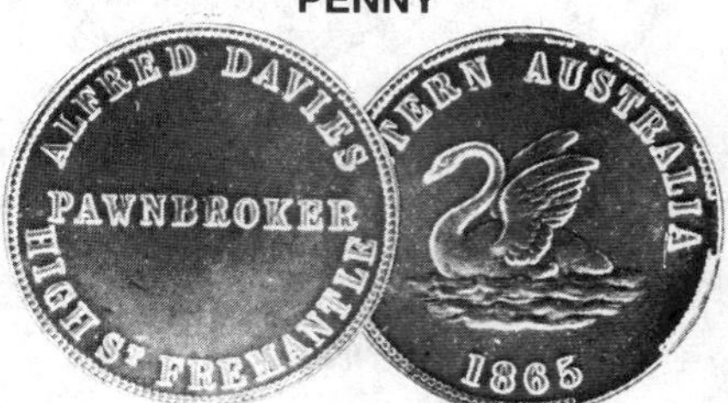

COPPER, 31mm

KM#	Date	Mintage	VG	Fine	VF	XF
Tn47	1865	—	7.50	15.00	75.00	125.00

Davies, Alexander & Co.

Goulbourn, New South Wales

PENNY

COPPER, 34mm

Obv. leg: DAVIES, ALEXANDER & CO. . . above golden fleece. Rev. leg: AUSTRALIAN STORES. . . above arm.

KM#	Date	Mintage	VG	Fine	VF	XF
Tn48	ND	—	5.00	10.00	60.00	150.00

NOTE: 3 varieties exist.

E. F. Dease

Launceston, Tasmania

1/2 PENNY

COPPER, 28mm
Similar to 1 Penny, KM#Tn25.

KM#	Date	Mintage	VG	Fine	VF	XF
Tn50	ND	—	17.50	35.00	75.00	200.00

Mule. Obv: KM#Tn50. Rev: New Zealand H. J. Hall 1/2 Penny, KM#Tn25.

KM#	Date	Mintage	Fine	VF	XF	Unc
Tn51	ND	—	—	—	800.00	1200.

PENNY

COPPER, 36mm
Rev: 6 spikes on pineapple.

KM#	Date	Mintage	VG	Fine	VF	XF
Tn52.1	ND	—	5.00	10.00	35.00	125.00

Rev: 7 spikes on pineapple.

KM#	Date	Mintage	VG	Fine	VF	XF
Tn52.2	ND	2 known	—	800.00	1200.	1500.

Edwd. De Carle & Co.

Melbourne, Victoria

PENNY

COPPER, 33mm
Obv. leg: EDWD. DE'CARLE & CO. . .
Rev. leg: TASMANIA above seated Justice.

KM#	Date	Mintage	VG	Fine	VF	XF
Tn53	1855	—	3.00	7.50	25.00	75.00

COPPER, 34mm
Obv. leg: E. DE CARLE & CO. . .
Rev. leg: BRITANNIA above seated Britannia.

KM#	Date	Mintage	VG	Fine	VF	XF
Tn54	ND	—	3.00	7.50	20.00	100.00

Obv: Lion. Rev: Seated justice, leg: MELBOURNE VICTORIA.

KM#	Date	Mintage	VG	Fine	VF	XF
Tn55	1855	—	3.00	7.50	25.00	75.00

COPPER, 33mm
Obv: Head of Lord Raglan left.

Rev: Similar to KM#Tn53.

KM#	Date	Mintage	VG	Fine	VF	XF
Tn56	1855	2 known	—	—	22,000.	—

NOTE: Believed to be pattern.

S. Deeble

Melbourne, Victoria

PENNY

COPPER, 34mm
Rev. leg: M in MAKER above S in EAST.

KM#	Date	Mintage	VG	Fine	VF	XF
Tn57.1	1862	—	17.50	35.00	125.00	200.00

Rev. leg: M in MAKER above AS in EAST.

KM#	Date	Mintage	VG	Fine	VF	XF
Tn57.2	1862	—	7.50	15.00	75.00	150.00

Obv: Similar to KM#Tn57.
Rev. leg: ADVANCE AUSTRALIA above wheat sheaf.

KM#	Date	Mintage	VG	Fine	VF	XF
Tn58	1862	—	7.50	15.00	75.00	150.00

Obv: Similar to KM#Tn57.
Rev. leg: VICTORIA 1862 above emu.

KM#	Date	Mintage	VG	Fine	VF	XF
Tn59	1862	—	35.00	100.00	250.00	500.00

James Dixon

Wangaratta, Victoria

PENNY

COPPER, 34mm
Obv: Similar to KM#Tn61. Rev. leg: Large VICTORIA, M of MAKER above AS in EAST.

KM#	Date	Mintage	VG	Fine	VF	XF
TnF60	1862 (fabrication)		—	—	as struck	600.00

Rev. leg: Small VICTORIA.

KM#	Date	Mintage	VG	Fine	VF	XF
TnF61	1855 (fabrication)		—	—	as struck	1000.

Rev. leg: T. STOKES MAKER below vine.

KM#	Date	Mintage	VG	Fine	VF	XF
TnF62	1862 (fabrication)		—	—	as struck	600.00

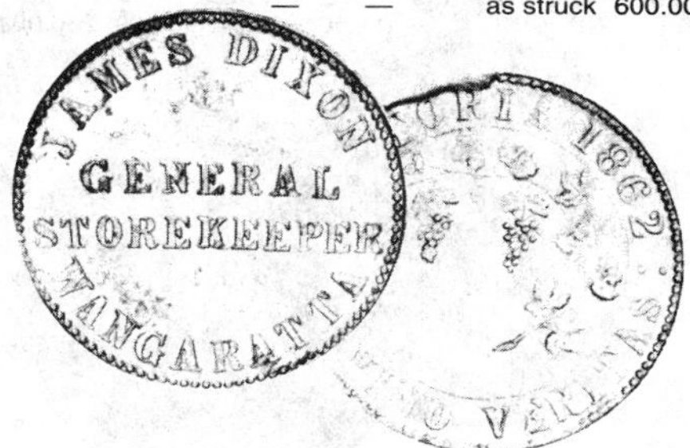

Rev: Stem of vine at right points down.

KM#	Date	Mintage	VG	Fine	VF	XF
TnF63.1	1862 (fabrication)		—	—	as struck	600.00

Rev: Stem of vine at right points up.

KM#	Date	Mintage	VG	Fine	VF	XF
TnF63.2	1862 (fabrication)		—	—	as struck	600.00

Rev. leg: VICTORIA 1862 above emu.

KM#	Date	Mintage	VG	Fine	VF	XF
TnF64	1862 (fabrication)		—	—	as struck	600.00

Evans & Foster

Wangaratta, Victoria

PENNY

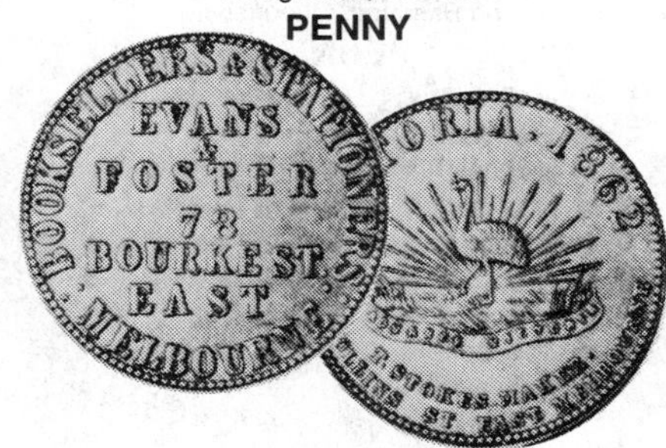

COPPER, 34mm
Rev. leg: VICTORIA.1862 (w/dot).

KM#	Date	Mintage	VG	Fine	VF	XF
Tn65	1862	—	62.50	125.00	250.00	450.00

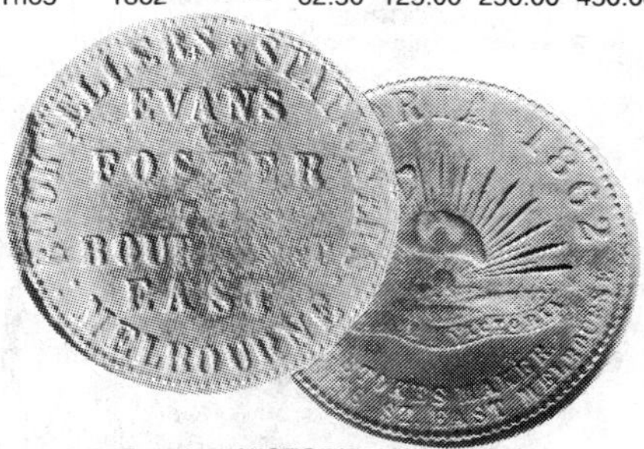

Rev. leg: VICTORIA 1862 (w/dot).

KM#	Date	Mintage	VG	Fine	VF	XF
TnF65	1862 (fabrication)		—	—	as struck	300.00

Fenwick Brothers

Melbourne, Victoria

PENNY

BRONZE, 34mm

KM#	Date	Mintage	VG	Fine	VF	XF
Tn66	ND	—	17.50	35.00	125.00	250.00

KM#	Date	Mintage	VG	Fine	VF	XF
Tn67	ND	—	15.00	30.00	100.00	200.00

NOTE: KM#Tn66 and Tn67 are known also in brass.

Fisher

South Yarra, Melbourne, Victoria

1/2 PENNY

COPPER, 28mm

KM#	Date	Mintage	VG	Fine	VF	XF
Tn68	1857	—	3.50	7.50	25.00	75.00

Flavelle Bros. & Co.

Sydney, New South Wales
and Brisbane, Queensland

PENNY

COPPER, 33mm
Rev: Thick foliage behind kangaroo's tail.

KM#	Date	Mintage	VG	Fine	VF	XF
Tn69.1	ND	—	3.00	7.50	25.00	75.00

Rev: Thin foliage behind kangaroo's tail.

KM#	Date	Mintage	Fine	VF	XF	Unc
Tn69.2	ND	—	—	—	350.00	500.00

Obv. leg: OPTICIANS & JEWELERS below ONE PENNY.
Rev: Similar to KM#Tn69.

KM#	Date	Mintage	VG	Fine	VF	XF
Tn70	ND	—	3.00	7.50	25.00	75.00

J. G. Fleming

Hobart, Tasmania

PENNY

COPPER, 31mm
Obv. leg: J. G. FLEMING. . ., scroll at right points to dot.
Rev. leg: SUGAR LOAF. . ., top of loaf points to right of R of SUGAR.

KM#	Date	Mintage	VG	Fine	VF	XF
Tn71.1	1874	—	3.00	7.50	15.00	50.00

Obv: Scroll at right points to R of DEALER.
Rev: Top of loaf points to R of SUGAR.

KM#	Date	Mintage	VG	Fine	VF	XF
Tn71.2	1874	—	25.00	62.50	125.00	250.00

I. Friedman

Hobart, Tasmania

1/2 PENNY

COPPER, 27mm
Obv. leg: I. FRIEDMAN. . .
Rev. leg: TASMANIA above seated Justice.

KM#	Date	Mintage	VG	Fine	VF	XF
Tn72	1857	—	3.00	7.50	15.00	75.00

NOTE: 3 varieties exist.

PENNY

COPPER, 34mm
Similar to 1/2 Penny, KM#Tn72.

KM#	Date	Mintage	VG	Fine	VF	XF
Tn73	1857	—	3.00	7.50	15.00	75.00

NOTE: 4 varieties exist.

W. Froomes

Castlemaine, Victoria

PENNY

COPPER, 34mm

KM#	Date	Mintage	VG	Fine	VF	XF
Tn74	1862	—	4.00	8.00	50.00	125.00

Gipps Land Hardware Company

Port Albert & Sale, Victoria

PENNY

COPPER, 34mm

KM#	Date	Mintage	VG	Fine	VF	XF
Tn75	1862	—	4.00	8.00	50.00	125.00

Obv: Gippsland all one word.

KM#	Date	Mintage	VG	Fine	VF	XF
TnF75	1862 (fabrication)	—	—		as struck	800.00

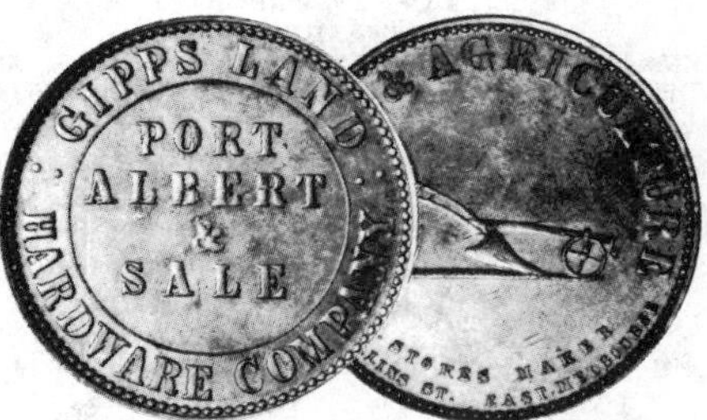

KM#	Date	Mintage	VG	Fine	VF	XF
Tn76	ND	—	4.00	8.00	50.00	125.00

R. Grieve

Eagle Hawk, Victoria

PENNY

COPPER, 34mm
Rev. leg: M of MAKER above T of EAST.

KM#	Date	Mintage	VG	Fine	VF	XF
Tn77	1862	—	4.00	8.00	50.00	175.00

Rev. leg: M of MAKER above AS of EAST.

KM#	Date	Mintage	VG	Fine	VF	XF
TnF77	1862 (fabrication)	—	—		as struck	300.00

J. R. Grundy

Ballarat, Victoria

PENNY

COPPER, 34mm
Rev. leg: 7mm between I of INDUSTRIA and V of VICTORIA.

KM#	Date	Mintage	VG	Fine	VF	XF
Tn78.1	1861	—	4.00	12.00	30.00	100.00

Rev. leg: 5.5mm between I of INDUSTRIA and V of VICTORIA.

KM#	Date	Mintage	VG	Fine	VF	XF
Tn78.2	1861	—	4.00	12.00	30.00	100.00

Obv: Top petal to R.
Rev: Raised rim.

KM#	Date	Mintage	VG	Fine	VF	XF
Tn79.1	1861	—	5.00	15.00	50.00	125.00

Obv: Top petal to C.
Rev: Raised rim.

KM#	Date	Mintage	VG	Fine	VF	XF
Tn79.2	1861	—	32.50	65.00	125.00	225.00

Hanks and Compy.

Sydney, New South Wales

1/2 PENNY

COPPER, 28mm
Obv. leg: AUSTRALIAN TEA MART. . .
Rev. leg: PEACE & PLENTY above Australian arms.

KM#	Date	Mintage	VG	Fine	VF	XF
Tn80	1857	—	3.50	8.00	25.00	75.00

PENNY

COPPER, 34mm
Similar to 1/2 Penny, KM#Tn80.

KM#	Date	Mintage	VG	Fine	VF	XF
Tn81	1857	—	3.00	7.00	25.00	75.00

Hanks and Lloyd

Sydney, New South Wales

1/2 PENNY

COPPER, 28mm
Obv. leg: AUSTRALIA TEA MART. . .
Rev. leg: TO COMMEMORATE. . .

KM#	Date	Mintage	VG	Fine	VF	XF
Tn82	1855	—	3.00	7.50	25.00	75.00

Obv. leg: Similar to 1/2 Penny, KM#Tn82, AND (5.5mm long). Rev. leg: PEACE & LIBERTY above Australian arms.

KM#	Date	Mintage	VG	Fine	VF	XF
Tn83.1	1857	—	3.00	7.00	25.00	75.00

Obv. leg: . . . AND (7mm long).

KM#	Date	Mintage	VG	Fine	VF	XF
Tn83.2	1857	—	3.00	7.00	25.00	75.00

PENNY

COPPER, 34mm
Similar to 1/2 Penny, KM#Tn82.

KM#	Date	Mintage	VG	Fine	VF	XF
Tn84	1855	—	3.00	7.50	25.00	75.00

Similar to 1/2 Penny, KM#Tn83.
Obv. leg: 1.0mm between LL of LLOYD, SYDNEY 2.5mm high.

KM#	Date	Mintage	VG	Fine	VF	XF
Tn85.1	1857	—	3.00	7.50	25.00	75.00

Obv. leg: 0.5mm between LL of LLOYD, SYDNEY 3mm high.

KM#	Date	Mintage	VG	Fine	VF	XF
Tn85.2	1857	—	4.00	10.00	35.00	80.00

Obv. leg: 1.0mm between LL of LLOYD, SYDNEY 3mm high.

KM#	Date	Mintage	VG	Fine	VF	XF
Tn85.3	1857	—	8.00	20.00	50.00	150.00

Harrold Brothers

Adelaide, South Australia

PENNY

COPPER, 34mm

KM#	Date	Mintage	VG	Fine	VF	XF
Tn86	1858	—	17.50	35.00	125.00	250.00

O. H. Hedberg

Hobart, Tasmania

1/2 PENNY

COPPER, 28mm

KM#	Date	Mintage	VG	Fine	VF	XF
Tn87	ND	—	4.00	10.00	30.00	125.00

NOTE: 6 varieties exist.

Mule. Obv. & rev: Similar to obv., KM#Tn87.

KM#	Date	Mintage	VG	Fine	VF	XF
Tn88	ND	—	25.00	50.00	100.00	250.00

Mule. Obv: KM#Tn87. Rev: New Zealand Lipman Levy 1/2 Penny, KM#Tn38.

KM#	Date	Mintage	Fine	VF	XF	Unc
Tn89	ND	—	—	—	600.00	800.00

Mule. Obv: Similar to rev. 1/2 Penny, KM#Tn87. Rev: Golden fleece, E.F. Dease, KM#Tn50.

KM#	Date	Mintage	Fine	VF	XF	Unc
Tn90	ND	—	—	—	750.00	1000.

PENNY

COPPER, 34mm

KM#	Date	Mintage	VG	Fine	VF	XF
Tn91	ND	—	4.00	12.00	30.00	125.00

NOTE: 4 varieties exist.

KM#	Date	Mintage	Fine	VF	XF	Unc
Tn93	ND	—	—	—	1500.	3000.

KM#	Date	Mintage	Fine	VF	XF	Unc
Tn94	1860	—	—	175.00	350.00	500.00

Rev: Britannia's staff points to I.

KM#	Date	Mintage	Fine	VF	XF	Unc
Tn96.1	ND	—	—	400.00	800.00	1200.

NOTE: 3 varieties exist.

Rev: Waves across baseline.

KM#	Date	Mintage	Fine	VF	XF	Unc
Tn96.2	ND	—	—	900.00	1200.	1500.

2 PENCE

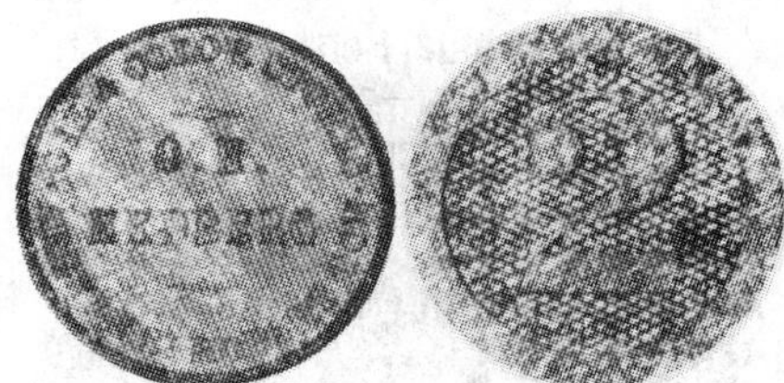

WHITE METAL, 28mm

KM#	Date	Mintage	Fine	VF	XF	Unc
Tn97	ND	2 known	—	—	3500.	—

4 PENCE

WHITE METAL, 34mm
Mule. Obv: Similar to Penny, KM#Tn93.
Rev. leg: FOUR PENCE on raised rim above large 4.

KM#	Date	Mintage	Fine	VF	XF	Unc
Tn98	ND	2 known	—	—	3500.	—

John Henderson

Fremantle, Western Australia

PENNY

BRONZE, 34mm
Rev: N of TOKEN on roof.

KM#	Date	Mintage	VG	Fine	VF	XF
Tn99.1	1874	—	7.50	15.00	75.00	125.00

Rev: N of TOKEN above roof.

KM#	Date	Mintage	VG	Fine	VF	XF
Tn99.2	1874	—	7.50	15.00	75.00	125.00

Obv. leg: N of JOHN below kangaroo's ear.

KM#	Date	Mintage	VG	Fine	VF	XF
Tn100.1	ND	—	7.50	15.00	75.00	125.00

Obv. leg: N of JOHN ends on kangaroo's ear.

KM#	Date	Mintage	VG	Fine	VF	XF
Tn100.2	ND	—	7.50	15.00	75.00	125.00

Obv. leg: N of JOHN begins on kangaroo's ear.

KM#	Date	Mintage	VG	Fine	VF	XF
Tn100.3	ND	—	11.50	22.50	110.00	175.00

NOTE: KM#Tn99.1 through Tn100.3 are know also in brass.

R. Henry

Hobart, Tasmania

PENNY

COPPER, 33mm
Obv. leg: R. HENRY. . .
Rev. leg: ONE PENNY TOKEN above tools.

KM#	Date	Mintage	VG	Fine	VF	XF
Tn101	ND	—	17.50	35.00	100.00	300.00

Samuel Henry

Deloraine, Tasmania

PENNY

COPPER, 34mm

KM#	Date	Mintage	VG	Fine	VF	XF
Tn102	1857	—	20.00	40.00	150.00	350.00

Hide & De Carle

Melbourne, Victoria

1/2 PENNY

COPPER, 28mm
Obv. leg: HIDE & DE CARLE above crowned lion in center. Rev. leg: MELBOURNE VICTORIA above seated Justice.

KM#	Date	Mintage	VG	Fine	VF	XF
Tn103	1857	—	3.50	7.50	15.00	75.00
	1858	—	3.50	7.50	15.00	75.00

NOTE: 3 varieties exist for 1857.

PENNY

COPPER, 34mm
Similar to 1/2 Penny, KM#Tn103.

KM#	Date	Mintage	VG	Fine	VF	XF
Tn104	1857	—	3.00	7.00	12.00	50.00
	1858	—	3.00	7.00	12.00	50.00

NOTE: 5 varieties exist for 1857, 7 varieties exist for 1858.

A. G. Hodgson

Melbourne, Victoria

1/2 PENNY

COPPER, 28mm

KM#	Date	Mintage	VG	Fine	VF	XF
Tn107	1866	—	10.00	20.00	40.00	125.00

Obv. leg: MELBOURNE above A. G. HODGSON, as Tn112. Rev: Similar to 1/2 Penny, KM#Tn107.

KM#	Date	Mintage	VG	Fine	VF	XF
Tn108	1860	3 known	—	—	1500.	2250.

NOTE: Possible pattern.

Obv: Similar to Penny, KM#Tn112.
Rev: Similar to Penny, KM#Tn112.

KM#	Date	Mintage	VG	Fine	VF	XF
Tn109	1862	—	5.00	10.00	75.00	250.00

PENNY

COPPER, 34mm
Obv. inner leg: LONSDALE STREET WEST.

KM#	Date	Mintage	VG	Fine	VF	XF
Tn110	1860	—	5.00	12.50	50.00	100.00

Obv. inner leg: LONSDALE STREET.

KM#	Date	Mintage	VG	Fine	VF	XF
Tn111	1860	—	37.50	75.00	250.00	750.00

KM#	Date	Mintage	VG	Fine	VF	XF
Tn112	1862	—	5.00	15.00	75.00	250.00

Obv: Similar to KM#Tn112.
Rev: Similar to KM#Tn111.

KM#	Date	Mintage	VG	Fine	VF	XF
Tn113	1860	—	—	—	750.00	1250.

Hodgson Bros.

Bendigo, Victoria

PENNY

COPPER, 34mm
Obv. leg: 5mm gap at bottom.

KM#	Date	Mintage	VG	Fine	VF	XF
Tn114.1	1862	—	18.50	37.50	150.00	425.00

Obv. leg: 9mm gap at bottom.

KM#	Date	Mintage	VG	Fine	VF	XF
Tn114.2	1862	—	15.00	30.00	125.00	350.00

Obv: Similar to KM#Tn114.1.
Rev: VICTORIA 1862 above Australian arms.

TnF115.1
1862 (fabrication) — — as struck 300.00

Obv: Similar to KM#Tn114.2.
Rev: Similar to KM#Tn115.1.

TnF115.2
1862 (fabrication) — — as struck 300.00

Hogarth, Erichsen & Co.

Sydney (New South Wales)

3 PENCE

SILVER, 16mm
Obv: Curved groundline above curved SYDNEY.
Rev: 3 (7mm high).

KM#	Date	Mintage	VG	Fine	VF	XF
Tn116.1	1858	—	150.00	300.00	750.00	1500.

Obv: Curved groundline above curved SYDNEY.
Rev: 3 (8mm high).

KM#	Date	Mintage	VG	Fine	VF	XF
Tn116.2	1858	—	125.00	250.00	500.00	1000.

Obv: Straight "low" groundline above curved SYDNEY.

KM#	Date	Mintage	VG	Fine	VF	XF
Tn116.3	1858	—	125.00	250.00	500.00	1000.

Obv: Straight "high" groundline above curved SYDNEY. Rev: 3 (7mm high).

KM#	Date	Mintage	VG	Fine	VF	XF
Tn117.1	1858	—	90.00	200.00	400.00	1200.

Obv: Straight "high" groundline above straight SYDNEY. Emu at left, kangaroo at right.

KM#	Date	Mintage	VG	Fine	VF	XF
Tn117.2	1858	—	125.00	250.00	500.00	1000.

Obv: Small 3. Rev: Kangaroos at left, emu at right.

KM#	Date	Mintage	VG	Fine	VF	XF
Tn118	1860	—	75.00	125.00	200.00	500.00

4 PENCE

SILVER, 16mm

KM#	Date	Mintage	VG	Fine	VF	XF
Tn119	1860	—	2500.	4000.	7500.	12,500.

J. Hosie

Melbourne, Victoria

PENNY

COPPER, 34mm
Obv: W/bars before 10 & after 12.
Rev. leg: M of MAKER above AS of EAST.

KM#	Date	Mintage	VG	Fine	VF	XF
Tn121.1	1862	—	4.00	8.00	50.00	125.00

Obv: W/bars before 10 & after 12.
Rev. leg: M of MAKER above S of EAST.

KM#	Date	Mintage	VG	Fine	VF	XF
Tn121.2	1862	—	4.00	8.00	50.00	125.00

NOTE: 2 varieties exist.

Rev: Vine branch.

KM#	Date	Mintage	VG	Fine	VF	XF
Tn122	1862	—	7.50	15.00	75.00	200.00

Obv: W/o bars before 10 & after 12.
Rev. leg: VICTORIA 1862 above Australian arms.
M of MAKER above ST of EAST.

KM#	Date	Mintage	VG	Fine	VF	XF
Tn123.1	1862	—	7.50	15.00	75.00	200.00

Rev. leg: M of MAKER above S of EAST.

KM#	Date	Mintage	VG	Fine	VF	XF
Tn123.2	1862	—	7.50	15.00	75.00	200.00

John Howell

Adelaide, South Australia

PENNY

COPPER, 34mm
Obv. leg: RUNDLE ST w/dash below T of ST.

KM#	Date	Mintage	VG	Fine	VF	XF
Tn128.1	ND	—	3.50	7.50	45.00	175.00

Obv. leg: RUNDLE ST w/dot below T of ST.

KM#	Date	Mintage	VG	Fine	VF	XF
Tn128.2	ND	—	3.50	7.50	45.00	175.00

Obv. leg: HINDLEY ST.

KM#	Date	Mintage	VG	Fine	VF	XF
Tn129	ND	—	3.50	7.50	45.00	175.00

J. Hutton

Hobart, Tasmania

1/2 PENNY

COPPER, 28mm
Similar to Penny, KM#Tn131.

KM#	Date	Mintage	VG	Fine	VF	XF
Tn130	ND	—	3.00	7.50	12.50	50.00

COPPER, 34mm

KM#	Date	Mintage	VG	Fine	VF	XF
Tn131	ND	—	3.00	9.00	15.00	75.00

Robert Hyde & Co.

Melbourne, Victoria

1/2 PENNY

COPPER, 28mm

KM#	Date	Mintage	VG	Fine	VF	XF
Tn132	1857	—	4.00	8.00	25.00	75.00
	1861	—	4.00	8.00	25.00	75.00

NOTE: 3 varieties exist for 1857, 4 varieties exist for 1861.

PENNY

COPPER, 34mm

KM#	Date	Mintage	VG	Fine	VF	XF
Tn133	1857	—	3.00	7.50	15.00	50.00
	1861	—	3.00	7.50	15.00	50.00

NOTE: 2 varieties exist for 1861.

Iredale & Co.

Sydney, New South Wales

PENNY

COPPER, 34mm
Rev: Seated figure, leg: BRITANNIA.

KM#	Date	Mintage	VG	Fine	VF	XF
Tn134	ND	—	7.50	35.00	125.00	250.00

Obv: Similar to Penny, KM#Tn134.
Rev. leg: AUSTRALIA above standing Justice.

KM#	Date	Mintage	VG	Fine	VF	XF
Tn135	ND	—	3.75	7.50	15.00	75.00

NOTE: 6 varieties exist.

W. W. Jamieson & Co.

Warrnambool, Victoria

PENNY

COPPER, 34mm

KM#	Date	Mintage	VG	Fine	VF	XF
Tn136	1862	—	10.00	20.00	100.00	250.00

William Andrew Jarvey

Hobart, Tasmania

PENNY

COPPER, 33mm
Rev: Bar points to OK of TOKEN.

KM#	Date	Mintage	VG	Fine	VF	XF
Tn137.1	ND	—	4.00	8.00	35.00	100.00

Rev: Bar points to TO of TOKEN.

KM#	Date	Mintage	VG	Fine	VF	XF
Tn137.2	ND	—	15.00	30.00	125.00	350.00

Rev: Balls supported on bars.

KM#	Date	Mintage	VG	Fine	VF	XF
Tn137.3	ND	—	4.00	8.00	25.00	75.00

David Jones

Ballarat, Victoria

PENNY

COPPER, 32mm

KM#	Date	Mintage	VG	Fine	VF	XF
Tn138	1862	—	5.00	10.00	75.00	250.00

NOTE: Replicas exist in copper and silver piedforts. Authenticity can be verified by rev. roof supports and struts.

T. H. Jones & Co.

Ipswich, Queensland

PENNY

COPPER, 34mm
Obv. leg: IRONMONGERS & GENERAL IMPORTERS. . .

KM#	Date	Mintage	VG	Fine	VF	XF
Tn139	ND	—	12.50	25.00	75.00	150.00

NOTE: 3 varieties exist.

R. Josephs

New Town, Tasmania

1/2 PENNY

COPPER, 28mm

KM#	Date	Mintage	VG	Fine	VF	XF
Tn140	1855	—	3.00	7.00	15.00	75.00

PENNY

COPPER, 34mm

Similar to 1/2 Penny, KM#Tn140.

KM#	Date	Mintage	VG	Fine	VF	XF
Tn141	1855	—	3.00	7.00	15.00	75.00

Larcombe & Compy.

Brisbane, Queensland

PENNY

COPPER, 33mm

KM#	Date	Mintage	VG	Fine	VF	XF
Tn142	ND	—	5.00	15.00	45.00	150.00

Rev: Emu similar to Tn143.

KM#	Date	Mintage	Fine	VF	XF	Unc
Tn143	ND	—	—	1500.	2000.	2500.

S. & S. Lazarus

Melbourne, Victoria

PENNY

COPPER, 35mm
Obv. leg: E of WHOLESALE above I of RETAIL, S of QUEENS below 7 of 70.

KM#	Date	Mintage	VG	Fine	VF	XF
Tn144.1	ND	—	75.00	150.00	350.00	750.00

Obv. leg: E of WHOLESALE above L of RETAIL, S of QUEENS to right of 7 of 70.

KM#	Date	Mintage	VG	Fine	VF	XF
Tn144.2	ND	—	100.00	200.00	400.00	850.00

Obv. leg: E of WHOLESALE above I of RETAIL, S of QUEENS below left of 7 of 70.

KM#	Date	Mintage	VG	Fine	VF	XF
Tn144.3	ND	—	75.00	150.00	300.00	650.00

J. D. Leeson

Sale, Victoria

PENNY

COPPER, 34mm

KM#	Date	Mintage	VG	Fine	VF	XF
Tn145	1862	—	37.50	75.00	250.00	750.00

J. M. Leigh

Sydney, New South Wales

PENNY

COPPER, 33mm
Obv. leg: J. M. LEIGH. . .
Rev. leg: BRITANNIA above seated Britannia.

KM#	Date	Mintage	VG	Fine	VF	XF
Tn146	ND	—	3.50	7.50	35.00	100.00

Levy Brothers

Melbourne, Victoria

PENNY

COPPER, 34mm

KM#	Date	Mintage	VG	Fine	VF	XF
Tn147	1855	—	25.00	50.00	200.00	500.00

H. Lipscombe

Hobart, Tasmania

PENNY

COPPER, 33mm
Obv. leg: H. LIPSCOMBE. MURRAY STREET. . . around fruit. Rev. leg: SHIPPING SUPPLIED. . .

KM#	Date	Mintage	VG	Fine	VF	XF
Tn148	ND	—	5.00	10.00	50.00	250.00

NOTE: 2 varieties exist.

W. F. & D. L. Lloyd

Wollongong, New South Wales

1/2 PENNY

COPPER, 28mm

KM#	Date	Mintage	Good	VG	Fine	VF
Tn149	1859	—	30.00	75.00	200.00	500.00

PENNY

COPPER, 34mm

KM#	Date	Mintage	Good	VG	Fine	VF
Tn150	1859	—	30.00	75.00	225.00	400.00

Love & Roberts

Waga Waga, New South Wales

PENNY

COPPER, 34mm
Obv. leg: V of LOVE at center of S of STOREKEEPERS.
Rev: Plough handles point to N of FARMING.

KM#	Date	Mintage	VG	Fine	VF	XF
Tn151.1	1865	—	50.00	100.00	200.00	425.00

Rev: Plough handles point to NG of FARMING.

KM#	Date	Mintage	VG	Fine	VF	XF
Tn151.2	1865	—	35.00	70.00	140.00	300.00

Obv. leg: V of LOVE at top of S of STOREKEEPERS.
Rev: Similar to Penny, KM#Tn151.1.

TnF151 1865 (fabrication) — — as struck 300.00

KM#	Date	Mintage	VG	Fine	VF	XF
Tn151.3	1865	—	70.00	140.00	280.00	600.00

J. MacGregor

Sydney, New South Wales

1/2 PENNY

BRONZE, 25mm
Obv. leg: THE CITY TEA WAREHOUSE. . .
Rev. leg: THE SULTAN'S STEAM COFFEE WORKS. . . above Australian arms.

KM#	Date	Mintage	VG	Fine	VF	XF
Tn152	ND	—	—	7.00	15.00	75.00

PENNY

BRONZE, 31mm
Similar to 1/2 Penny, KM#Tn149.

KM#	Date	Mintage	VG	Fine	VF	XF
Tn153	ND	—	—	7.00	15.00	75.00

Macintosh & Degraves

Hobart, Tasmania

SHILLING

SILVER, 22mm

KM#	Date	Mintage	VG	Fine	VF	XF
Tn154	1823	—	800.00	1500.	2500.	4500.

H. J. Marsh & Brother

Hobart, Tasmania

1/2 PENNY

COPPER, 27mm
Obv. leg: H.J. MARSH & BROTHER. . .
Rev. leg: HALFPENNY TOKEN above sailing ship.

KM#	Date	Mintage	VG	Fine	VF	XF
Tn155	ND	—	5.00	10.00	50.00	250.00

PENNY

COPPER, 34mm

KM#	Date	Mintage	VG	Fine	VF	XF
Tn156	ND	—	12.50	25.00	50.00	100.00

COPPER, 33mm

KM#	Date	Mintage	VG	Fine	VF	XF
Tn157	ND	—	12.50	25.00	50.00	100.00

Obv: Similar to Penny, KM#Tn157 w/I of IRONMONGERS above bottom of J of H.J.
Rev: Modified tool design, spade handle to right.

KM#	Date	Mintage	VG	Fine	VF	XF
Tn158.1	ND	—	5.00	10.00	50.00	300.00

Obv: Similar to Penny, KM#Tn158 w/I of IRONMONGERS below bottom of J of H.J.

KM#	Date	Mintage	VG	Fine	VF	XF
Tn158.2	ND	—	18.50	37.50	75.00	150.00

John Martin

Adelaide, South Australia

PENNY

COPPER, 34mm

KM#	Date	Mintage	VG	Fine	VF	XF
Tn159	ND	—	5.00	12.50	30.00	125.00

Martin & Sach

Adelaide, South Australia

PENNY

COPPER, 34mm
Obv. leg: MARTIN & SACH. . .
Rev. leg: AUSTRALIA above standing Justice w/scales in right hand.

KM#	Date	Mintage	VG	Fine	VF	XF
Tn160	ND	—	4.00	10.00	25.00	100.00

NOTE: 3 varieties exist.

Mason & Culley

Williamstown, Victoria

PENNY

COPPER, 34mm

Tn162 ND Approx. 12 known 1250. 2000. 3000. 4000.

R. Andrew Mather

Hobart, Tasmania

PENNY

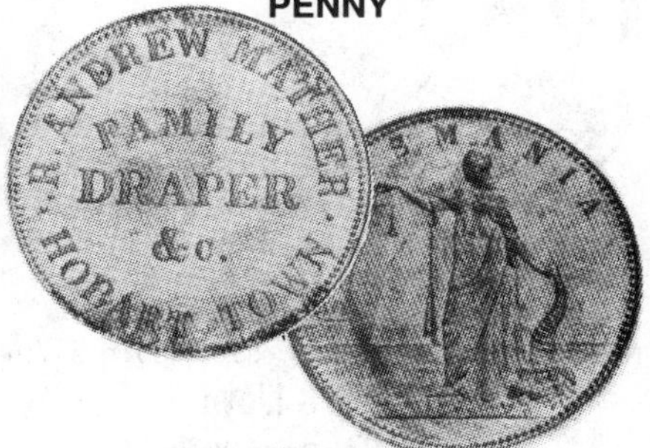

COPPER, 34mm

KM#	Date	Mintage	VG	Fine	VF	XF
Tn163	ND	—	3.00	7.50	20.00	75.00

NOTE: 3 varieties exist.

J. McFarlane

Melbourne, Victoria

PENNY

COPPER, 34mm
Obv. leg: CORNER OF ELIZABETH &. . .
Rev. leg: PEACE AND PLENTY. . . above standing Peace, lion and sheep.

KM#	Date	Mintage	VG	Fine	VF	XF
Tn164	ND	—	3.50	10.00	35.00	100.00

Merry & Bush

Brisbane, Queensland

PENNY

COPPER, 34mm

KM#	Date	Mintage	VG	Fine	VF	XF
Tn165	ND(1863)	—	12.50	25.00	100.00	200.00

T. F. Merry & Co.

Toowoomba, Queensland

1/2 PENNY

COPPER, 28mm
Similar to 1 Penny, KM#Tn167.

KM#	Date	Mintage	VG	Fine	VF	XF
Tn166	ND	—	15.00	30.00	150.00	350.00

PENNY

COPPER, 34mm
Obv. leg: A of TOOWOOMBA slightly below S of MERCHANTS.

KM#	Date	Mintage	VG	Fine	VF	XF
Tn167.1	ND	—	3.00	6.00	30.00	75.00

Obv. leg: A of TOOWOOMBA beyond S of MERCHANTS.

KM#	Date	Mintage	VG	Fine	VF	XF
Tn167.2	ND	—	15.00	30.00	150.00	350.00

Metcalfe & Lloyd

Sydney, New South Wales

1/2 PENNY

COPPER, 28mm
Obv. leg: SHIPPING AND FAMILY GROCERS. . .
Rev. leg: PURVEYORS OF THE. . .

KM#	Date	Mintage	VG	Fine	VF	XF
Tn168	1863	—	3.00	7.00	15.00	75.00

PENNY

COPPER, 34mm
Similar to 1/2 Penny, KM#Tn168.

KM#	Date	Mintage	VG	Fine	VF	XF
Tn169	1863	—	3.00	7.00	15.00	75.00

Miller Brothers

Melbourne, Victoria

PENNY

COPPER, 34mm
Rev. leg: R of MAKER touches leaf.

KM#	Date	Mintage	VG	Fine	VF	XF
Tn170.1	1862	—	10.00	40.00	75.00	250.00

Rev. leg: R of MAKER away from leaf.

KM#	Date	Mintage	VG	Fine	VF	XF
Tn170.2	1862	—	10.00	60.00	100.00	200.00

Obv: Similar to Penny, KM#Tn170.
Rev. leg: VICTORIA 1862 above Australian arms.

KM#	Date	Mintage	VG	Fine	VF	XF
Tn171	1862	—	10.00	40.00	75.00	250.00

KM#	Date	Mintage	VG	Fine	VF	XF
Tn172	1862	—	10.00	60.00	100.00	200.00

Miller & Dismorr

Melbourne, Victoria

PENNY

COPPER, 34mm

KM#	Date	Mintage	VG	Fine	VF	XF
Tn173	ND	—	10.00	20.00	100.00	250.00

Joseph Moir

Hobart, Tasmania

PENNY

COPPER, 34mm

KM#	Date	Mintage	VG	Fine	VF	XF
Tn174	ND	—	17.50	35.00	125.00	200.00

William Morgan

Adelaide, South Australia

PENNY

COPPER, 34mm

KM#	Date	Mintage	VG	Fine	VF	XF
Tn175	1858	—	10.00	20.00	100.00	250.00

NOTE: Two varieties exist.

Moubray, Lush & Co.

Melbourne, Victoria

PENNY

COPPER, 34mm

KM#	Date	Mintage	VG	Fine	VF	XF
Tn176	ND	—	10.00	20.00	100.00	250.00

D. T. Mulligan

Rockhampton, Queensland

1/2 PENNY

COPPER, 28mm
Obv. leg: QUEENSLAND STORES. . .
Rev. leg: QUEENSLAND above Australian arms.

KM#	Date	Mintage	VG	Fine	VF	XF
Tn177	1863	—	12.50	25.00	80.00	200.00

NOTE: 2 varieties exist.

PENNY

COPPER, 34mm
Similar to 1/2 Penny, KM#Tn177.

KM#	Date	Mintage	VG	Fine	VF	XF
Tn178	1863	—	3.50	7.00	30.00	100.00

Murray and Christie

Castlemaine, Victoria

PENNY

COPPER, 34mm

KM#	Date	Mintage	VG	Fine	VF	XF
Tn179	ND	—	4.00	8.00	50.00	200.00

NOTE: 2 varieties exist.

Mule. W/rev. of 1 Penny, KM#Tn179 and rev. leg: AUSTRALIA 1862 above Australian arms.

KM#	Date	Mintage	VG	Fine	VF	XF
Tn180	1862	—	4.00	8.00	50.00	200.00

A. Nicholas

Hobart, Tasmania

PENNY

COPPER, 33mm

KM#	Date	Mintage	VG	Fine	VF	XF
Tn183	ND	—	750.00	1500.	3000.	—

Alfred Nicholas

Hobart, Tasmania

1/2 PENNY

COPPER, 26mm
Obv. leg: ALFRED NICHOLAS. . .
Rev. leg: BRITANNIA above seated Britannia.

KM#	Date	Mintage	VG	Fine	VF	XF
Tn181	ND	—	5.00	10.00	50.00	200.00

PENNY

COPPER, 33mm
Similar to 1/2 Penny, KM#Tn181.
Rev: Center prong of trident inside N of BRITANNIA.

KM#	Date	Mintage	VG	Fine	VF	XF
Tn182.1	ND	—	2.50	5.00	35.00	150.00

Rev: Center prong of trident below N of BRITANNIA.

KM#	Date	Mintage	VG	Fine	VF	XF
Tn182.2	ND	—	2.50	5.00	35.00	150.00

George Nichols

Melbourne, Victoria

PENNY

COPPER, 35mm
Obv. leg: BOOKSELLER & STATIONER. . .
Rev. leg: VICTORIA 1862 above Australian arms w/ear of kangaroo below T of VICTORIA.

KM#	Date	Mintage	VG	Fine	VF	XF
Tn184.1	1862	—	5.00	10.00	75.00	250.00

Rev: Ear of kangaroo above T of VICTORIA.

KM#	Date	Mintage	VG	Fine	VF	XF
Tn184.2	1862	—	3.00	6.00	45.00	150.00

James Nokes

Melbourne, Victoria

1/2 PENNY

COPPER, 28mm
Obv. leg: JAMES NOKES GROCER. . .
Rev. leg: IN COMMEMORATION OF. . .

KM#	Date	Mintage	VG	Fine	VF	XF
Tn185	ND	—	3.00	7.50	25.00	75.00

Obv: Similar to 1/2 Penny, KM#Tn185.
Rev. leg: BRITANNIA above seated Britannia.

KM#	Date	Mintage	VG	Fine	VF	XF
Tn186	ND	—	4.00	8.00	50.00	125.00

B. Palmer

Sydney, New South Wales

PENNY

COPPER, 34mm
Obv. leg: WHOLESALE WINE &. . .
Rev. leg: LIVERPOOL ARMS around dove.

KM#	Date	Mintage	VG	Fine	VF	XF
Tn187	ND	—	3.00	5.00	15.00	75.00

R. Parker

Geelong, Victoria

PENNY

COPPER, 34mm

KM#	Date	Mintage	VG	Fine	VF	XF
Tn188	ND	—	3.00	7.50	25.00	125.00

NOTE: 7 varieties exist at 34mm, 4 varieties exist at 35mm.

Hugh Peck

Melbourne, Victoria

PENNY

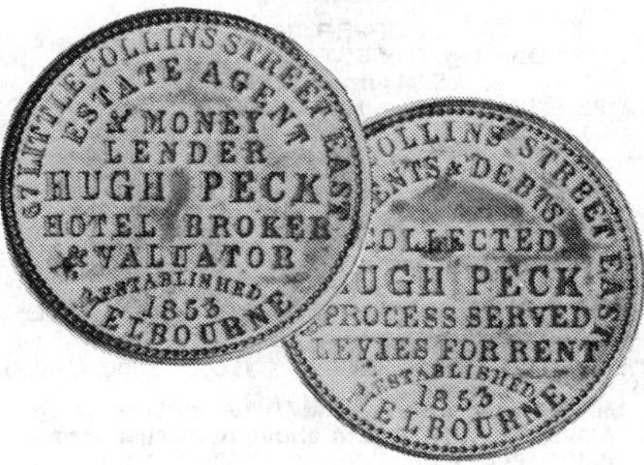

COPPER, 34mm

KM#	Date	Mintage	VG	Fine	VF	XF
Tn189	ND	—	4.00	8.00	40.00	100.00

Obv: Similar to 1 Penny, KM#Tn189.
Rev. leg: VICTORIA 1862 above Australian arms.

KM#	Date	Mintage	VG	Fine	VF	XF
Tn190	1862	—	4.00	8.00	50.00	125.00

Peek & Campbell

Sydney, New South Wales

1/2 PENNY

COPPER, 29mm
Obv: Left side of building w/horizontal bricks raised and joints sunken.

KM#	Date	Mintage	VG	Fine	VF	XF
Tn191.1	1852	—	40.00	80.00	200.00	1000.

Obv: Lower left side of building as KM#Tn191.1 except brick courses in perspective.

KM#	Date	Mintage	VG	Fine	VF	XF
Tn191.2	1852	—	50.00	100.00	250.00	1250.

Obv: Smaller bricks and sunken joints raised.

KM#	Date	Mintage	VG	Fine	VF	XF
Tn191.3	1852	—	40.00	80.00	200.00	1000.

PENNY

COPPER, 34mm
Obv. leg: S of ESTABLISHED above S of large SYDNEY.

KM#	Date	Mintage	VG	Fine	VF	XF
Tn192.1	1852	—	100.00	200.00	350.00	1750.
	1853	—	50.00	100.00	250.00	750.00

Obv. leg: E of ESTABLISHED above S of small SYDNEY.

KM#	Date	Mintage	VG	Fine	VF	XF
Tn192.2	1853	—	600.00	1500.	2500.	—

Obv: Similar to 1 Penny, KM#Tn192 but lower leg. in 2 lines. Rev. leg: BRITANNIA above seated BRITANNIA.

KM#	Date	Mintage	Good	VG	Fine	VF
Tn193	1852	—	600.00	1500.	3000.	6000.

Mule. W/obv. 1 Penny, KM#Tn192 and rev. w/leg: ADVANCE AUSTRALIA above Australian arms.

KM#	Date	Mintage	Good	VG	Fine	VF
Tn194	1854	—	600.00	1500.	2500.	—

John Pettigrew & Co.

Ipswich, Queensland

1/2 PENNY

BRONZE, 26mm

KM#	Date	Mintage	VG	Fine	VF	XF
Tn195	1865	—	5.00	15.00	45.00	150.00

PENNY

BRONZE, 31mm
Similar to 1/2 Penny, KM#Tn195.

KM#	Date	Mintage	VG	Fine	VF	XF
Tn196	1865	—	5.00	12.50	30.00	100.00

Geo. Petty

Melbourne, Victoria

PENNY

COPPER, 35mm
Rev. leg: Bottom of V of VICTORIA above scale bar.

KM#	Date	Mintage	VG	Fine	VF	XF
Tn197.1	ND	—	4.00	8.00	50.00	125.00

Rev. leg: Bottom of V of VICTORIA below scale bar.

KM#	Date	Mintage	VG	Fine	VF	XF
Tn197.2	ND	—	8.00	20.00	100.00	200.00

Obv: Similar to 1 Penny, KM#Tn197. Rev. leg: MELBOURNE VICTORIA above seated Justice.

KM#	Date	Mintage	Fine	VF	XF	Unc
Tn198	1860	—	—	1250.	1750.	2500.

Obv: Similar to 1 Penny, KM#Tn197. Rev. leg: SIC VOS NON. . . around golden fleece.

KM#	Date	Mintage	Fine	VF	XF	Unc
Tn199	ND	—	—	1250.	1750.	2500.

R. B. Ridler

Richmond, Victoria

PENNY

COPPER, 34mm
Rev. leg: VICTORIA.1862 (w/dot).

KM#	Date	Mintage	VG	Fine	VF	XF
Tn200	1862	—	4.00	8.00	50.00	125.00

Mule. W/rev. leg: VICTORIA 1862 (w/o dot).

KM#	Date	Mintage	VG	Fine	VF	XF
TnF200	1862 (fabrication)	—	—		as struck	300.00

Obv: Similar to Penny, KM#Tn200. Rev. leg: VICTORIA 1862 around grape vine.

KM#	Date	Mintage	Fine	VF	XF	Unc
TnF201	1862 (fabrication)	—	—		as struck	300.00

KM#	Date	Mintage	VG	Fine	VF	XF
Tn202	1862	—	10.00	20.00	100.00	250.00
TnF2021862 (fabrication)		—	—		as struck	300.00

KM#	Date	Mintage	VG	Fine	VF	XF
Tn209 (292)	1862	—	10.00	20.00	100.00	250.00

Robison Bros. & Co.

Melbourne, Victoria

PENNY

COPPER, 34mm
Obv. leg: VICTORIA COPPER WORKS. . . Rev: Similar to 1 Penny, KM#Tn200.

KM#	Date	Mintage	VG	Fine	VF	XF
Tn203	1862	—	4.00	8.00	50.00	125.00

NOTE: 4 varieties exist.

Obv: Similar to 1 Penny, KM#Tn203. Rev: Similar to 1 Penny, KM#Tn202.

KM#	Date	Mintage	VG	Fine	VF	XF
Tn204	1862	—	5.00	10.00	75.00	200.00

Obv: Similar to 1 Penny, KM#Tn203. Rev. leg: VICTORIA 1862 around grape vine.

KM#	Date	Mintage	VG	Fine	VF	XF
Tn205	1862	—	4.00	8.00	50.00	125.00

G. & W. H. Rocke

Melbourne, Victoria

PENNY

COPPER, 34mm
Obv. leg: G. & W. H. Rocke. . . w/crowned lion in center. Rev. leg: MELBOURNE VICTORIA above seated Justice.

KM#	Date	Mintage	VG	Fine	VF	XF
Tn206	1859	—	4.00	8.00	50.00	125.00

NOTE: 4 varieties exist.

G. Ryland

Castlemaine, Victoria

PENNY

COPPER, 34mm

KM#	Date	Mintage	VG	Fine	VF	XF
Tn207	1862	—	12.50	25.00	150.00	300.00

J. Sawyer

Brisbane, Queensland

PENNY

COPPER, 35mm

KM#	Date	Mintage	VG	Fine	VF	XF
Tn208	1864	—	3.50	7.50	30.00	100.00

Smith, Peate & Co.

Sydney, New South Wales

1/2 PENNY

COPPER, 28mm
Obv. leg: SMITH, PEATE & CO. . .
Rev. leg: ESTABLISHED above standing Justice.

KM#	Date	Mintage	VG	Fine	VF	XF
Tn210	1856	—	3.00	7.50	15.00	75.00

NOTE: 7 varieties exist.

PENNY

COPPER, 34mm
Similar to 1/2 Penny, KM#Tn210.

KM#	Date	Mintage	VG	Fine	VF	XF
Tn211	1856	—	3.50	7.50	15.00	75.00

NOTE: 4 varieties confirmed.

Southward & Sumpton

Ballarat, Victoria

PENNY

COPPER, 34mm

KM#	Date	Mintage	VG	Fine	VF	XF
Tn212	ND	—	4.00	8.00	50.00	200.00

Stead Brothers

Sandhurst, Victoria

PENNY

COPPER, 34mm

KM#	Date	Mintage	VG	Fine	VF	XF
Tn213	1862	—	25.00	50.00	250.00	750.00
	1862(restrike)		—	—	—	300.00

KM#	Date	Mintage	VG	Fine	VF	XF
Tn214	1862	—	62.50	125.00	500.00	1250.
	1862(restrike)		—	—	—	350.00

Stewart & Hemmant

Brisbane & Rockhampton, Queensland

PENNY

COPPER, 33mm
Obv. leg: STEWART & HEMMANT. . .
Rev. leg: CRITERION. . . above emu.

KM#	Date	Mintage	VG	Fine	VF	XF
Tn215	ND	—	5.00	10.00	30.00	100.00

NOTE: 2 varieties exist.

Brisbane, Queensland

30mm
Obv. leg: STEWART & HEMMANT around CRITERION.

KM#	Date	Mintage	VG	Fine	VF	XF
Tn216	ND	—	37.50	75.00	200.00	300.00

T. Stokes

Melbourne, Victoria

1/2 PENNY

COPPER, 28mm
Obv. leg: MILITARY ORNAMENTS & BUTTON. . .
Rev. leg: T. STOKES DIE SINKERS. . .

KM#	Date	Mintage	VG	Fine	VF	XF
Tn217	ND	—	15.00	30.00	200.00	500.00

PENNY

COPPER, 34mm
Obv: CHECK & TOKEN MAKER. . .

KM#	Date	Mintage	VG	Fine	VF	XF
TnF219	1862 (fabrication)		—	—	as struck	300.00

Obv. leg: THOMAS STOKES MAKER.
Rev. leg: VICTORIA.1862 above Australian arms w/rose leaf pointing left of S of STOKES.

KM#	Date	Mintage	VG	Fine	VF	XF
Tn221.1	1862	—	5.00	10.00	25.00	60.00

Rev: Large letters, w/tendrill pointing to E of MAKER.

KM#	Date	Mintage	VG	Fine	VF	XF
Tn221.2	1862	—	5.00	10.00	25.00	60.00

Obv: Similar to 1 Penny, KM#Tn221.
Rev. leg: VICTORIA.1862 above emu.

KM#	Date	Mintage	VG	Fine	VF	XF
Tn222	1862	—	5.00	10.00	25.00	60.00

Obv: Similar to 1 Penny, KM#Tn221, but H of Thomas above C of Collins.
Rev. leg: DIE SINKER SEAL ENGRAVER. . .

KM#	Date	Mintage	VG	Fine	VF	XF
Tn223	ND	3 known	—	—	5000.	8000.

NOTE: Considered a pattern.

Obv. leg: LETTER CUTTER BUTTON CHECK &. . .
Rev. leg: VICTORIA 1862 above grape vine.

KM#	Date	Mintage	VG	Fine	VF	XF
Tn224	1862	—	5.00	10.00	25.00	60.00

Obv: Similar to 1 Penny, KM#Tn224.
Rev. leg: VICTORIA.1862 above emu.

KM#	Date	Mintage	VG	Fine	VF	XF
Tn225.1	1862	—	15.00	37.50	75.00	150.00

Obv. leg: LETTER CUTTER - BUTTON CHECK & . . .
Rev: Emu.

KM#	Date	Mintage	VG	Fine	VF	XF
Tn225.2	1862	—	62.50	125.00	250.00	500.00

Obv. leg: LETTER CUTTER SEAL ENGRAVER. . .
Rev. leg: VICTORIA 1862 above grape vine.

KM#	Date	Mintage	VG	Fine	VF	XF
Tn226	1862	—	5.00	10.00	25.00	60.00

Obv: Similar to 1 Penny, KM#Tn226.
Rev: Emu-A.

KM#	Date	Mintage	VG	Fine	VF	XF
Tn227	1862	—	5.00	10.00	25.00	60.00

Obv. leg: LETTER CUTTER.SEAL ENGRAVER. TOKEN MAKER

KM#	Date	Mintage	VG	Fine	VF	XF
Tn228	1862	—	7.00	25.00	60.00	120.00

NOTE: 3 varieties exist.

Obv. leg: . . . ENGRAVER.TOKEN MAKER
Rev. leg: VICTORIA 1862 above Australian arms.

KM#	Date	Mintage	VG	Fine	VF	XF
TnF229	1862 (fabrication)	—	—	as struck		300.00

Obv. leg: . . . ENGRAVER - TOKEN MAKER.
Rev: Arms.

KM#	Date	Mintage	VG	Fine	VF	XF
TnF230	1862 (fabrication)	—	—	as struck		300.00

Obv: Similar to 1 Penny, KM#Tn229.
Rev. leg: VICTORIA 1862 above grape vine, leaf does not touch R in MAKER.

KM#	Date	Mintage	VG	Fine	VF	XF
Tn231	1862	—	5.00	15.00	35.00	75.00

Obv. leg: . . . ENGRAVER-TOKEN MAKER.
Rev. leg: VICTORIA 1862 above Australian arms.

KM#	Date	Mintage	VG	Fine	VF	XF
TnF232	1862 (fabrication)	—	—	as struck		300.00

Obv. leg: MILITARY ORNAMENT BUTTON &. . .

KM#	Date	Mintage	VG	Fine	VF	XF
Tn233	1862	—	5.00	10.00	25.00	60.00

NOTE: Two varieties exist.

KM#	Date	Mintage	VG	Fine	VF	XF
Tn234	1862	—	50.00	100.00	200.00	300.00

KM#	Date	Mintage	VG	Fine	VF	XF
Tn235	1862	—	7.00	25.00	60.00	120.00

KM#	Date	Mintage	VG	Fine	VF	XF
Tn236.1	1862	—	5.00	10.00	25.00	60.00

NOTE: 8 varieties exist.

KM#	Date	Mintage	VG	Fine	VF	XF
Tn236.2	1862	—	5.00	10.00	25.00	60.00

NOTE: 3 varieties exist.

Mule. W/obv. leg: ADVANCE AUSTRALIA above wheat sheaf.
Rev: Similar to 1 Penny rev., KM#Tn236.1.

KM#	Date	Mintage	VG	Fine	VF	XF
Tn237	1862	—	5.00	10.00	25.00	60.00

NOTE: 6 varieties exist.

Stokes & Martin

Melbourne, Victoria

PENNY

COPPER, 31mm

KM#	Date	Mintage	VG	Fine	VF	XF
Tn238	ND	—	20.00	40.00	80.00	175.00

Alfred Taylor

Adelaide, South Australia

PENNY

COPPER, 34mm

KM#	Date	Mintage	VG	Fine	VF	XF
Tn239	ND	—	3.50	7.50	30.00	125.00

J. Taylor

Ballarat, Victoria

PENNY

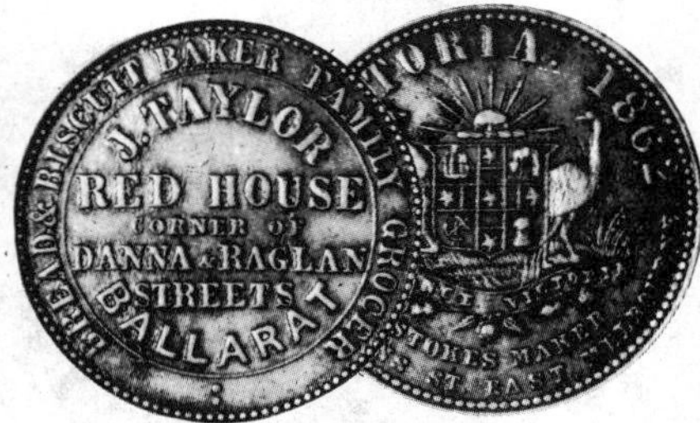

COPPER, 34mm

KM#	Date	Mintage	VG	Fine	VF	XF
Tn240	1862	—	10.00	15.00	75.00	250.00

Obv: As KM#Tn240. Rev: Wheat sheaf.

KM#	Date	Mintage	VG	Fine	VF	XF
Tn241	1862	—	10.00	15.00	75.00	250.00

Obv: Similar to 1 Penny, KM#Tn240.
Rev. leg: VICTORIA 1862 above grape vines.

KM#	Date	Mintage	VG	Fine	VF	XF
Tn242	1862	—	10.00	15.00	75.00	250.00

W. J. Taylor

Melbourne, Victoria

PATTERNS

1/2 PENNY

COPPER, 28mm
Obv. leg. below kangaroo: W.J.TAYLOR, MEDALLIST TO THE GREAT EXHIBITION.

KM#	Date	Mintage	VG	Fine	VF	XF
Tn243	1851	—	—	—	Rare	—

NOTE: Spink Australia Sale Nov. 1979, lot #279, good VF realized A$2600.
NOTE: Restrikes known.

KM#	Date	Mintage	VG	Fine	VF	XF
Tn244	1851	—	3.00	7.50	15.00	75.00

Mule: Rev. similar to Tn#244 w/leg: UNITED STATES.

KM#	Date	Mintage	VG	Fine	VF	XF
Tn245	1857	—	25.00	50.00	300.00	650.00

2 PENCE

COPPER, 28mm

KM#	Date	Mintage	VG	Fine	VF	XF
Tn246	1851	—	—	—	Rare	—

NOTE: Spink Australia sale Nov. 1979, lot #277, nearly FDC realized A$2400.

Obv: Like KM#Tn243. Rev: Similar to KM#Tn246 but w/large 2 in relief on plain field.

KM#	Date	Mintage	VG	Fine	VF	XF
Tn247	1851	—	—	—	Rare	—

NOTE: Spink Australia sale, Nov. 1979, lot #278, nearly FDC realized A$1700.

T. W. Thomas & Co.

Melbourne, Victoria

1/2 PENNY

COPPER
Obv. leg: T. W. THOMAS & CO. . .
Rev. leg: IN COMMEMORATION OF THE. . .

KM#	Date	Mintage	VG	Fine	VF	XF
Tn248	ND	—	5.00	10.00	30.00	75.00

J. C. Thornthwaite

Sydney, New South Wales

1/2 PENNY

COPPER, 28mm

KM#	Date	Mintage	Good	VG	Fine	VF
Tn249.1	1854	—	50.00	100.00	250.00	600.00

Obv. leg: . . . MEDALLISIT (error).

KM#	Date	Mintage	Good	VG	Fine	VF
Tn249.2	1854	—	100.00	150.00	300.00	750.00

33mm
c/s on 1 Penny, KM#Tn250.

KM#	Date	Mintage	VG	Fine	VF	XF
Tn249.3	1854	Unique	—	—	—	7000.

NOTE: A pattern using 1/2 penny die on obverse.

PENNY

COPPER, 35mm

KM#	Date	Mintage	VG	Fine	VF	XF
Tn250	1854	—	200.00	350.00	1000.	1500.

3 PENCE

SILVER, 16mm
Rev: Large sunburst above 3.

KM#	Date	Mintage	VG	Fine	VF	XF
Tn251	1854	—	250.00	500.00	800.00	1500.

Obv: Similar to 3 Pence, KM#Tn251.
Rev: Small sunburst above floral 3.

KM#	Date	Mintage	VG	Fine	VF	XF
Tn252	1854	—	1250.	2500.	4500.	7500.

Obv: Similar to 3 Pence, KM#Tn251.
Rev:W/o sun date or J.C.T. leg: SILVER 3 TOKEN.

KM#	Date	Mintage	VG	Fine	VF	XF
Tn253	1854	—	1000.	2000.	4000.	—

Thrale & Cross

Melbourne, Victoria

1/2 PENNY

COPPER, 28mm

KM#	Date	Mintage	VG	Fine	VF	XF
Tn254	ND	—	25.00	75.00	200.00	400.00

Obv: Similar to 1/2 Penny, KM#Tn254.
Rev. leg: AUSTRALIA above seated woman.

KM#	Date	Mintage	VG	Fine	VF	XF
Tn255	ND	—	25.00	100.00	250.00	500.00

Thick flan variety.

A. Toogood

Sydney, New South Wales

PENNY

COPPER, 34mm
Obv. leg: A. TOOGOOD MERCHANT. . .
Rev. leg: AUSTRALIA above seated Justice.

KM#	Date	Mintage	VG	Fine	VF	XF
Tn256	1855	—	3.00	7.50	15.00	75.00

NOTE: 2 varieties exist.

T. Warburton

Melbourne, Victoria

PENNY

COPPER
Obv. leg: IRON & ZINC SPOUTING. . .
Rev. leg: VICTORIA 1862 above emu.

KM#	Date	Mintage	VG	Fine	VF	XF
Tn257	1862	—	4.00	8.00	25.00	125.00

NOTE: 2 varieties exist.

Obv: Similar to 1 Penny, KM#Tn257.
Rev. leg: VICTORIA 1862 above grape vine.

KM#	Date	Mintage	VG	Fine	VF	XF
Tn258	1862	—	4.00	8.00	25.00	125.00

NOTE: 2 varieties exist.

Obv: Similar to 1 Penny, KM#Tn257.
Rev. leg: VICTORIA 1862 above Australian arms.

KM#	Date	Mintage	VG	Fine	VF	XF
Tn259	1862	—	3.50	7.50	20.00	75.00

Obv: Similar to 1 Penny, KM#Tn257. Rev. leg: ADVANCE AUSTRALIA above wheat sheaf.

KM#	Date	Mintage	VG	Fine	VF	XF
Tn260	1862	—	4.00	8.00	50.00	175.00

NOTE: 2 varieties exist.

Warnock Bros.

Melbourne and Maldon, Victoria

1/2 PENNY

COPPER, 28mm
Similar to 1 Penny, KM#Tn263.

KM#	Date	Mintage	VG	Fine	VF	XF
Tn261	1861	—	3.00	7.50	15.00	75.00

PENNY

COPPER, 34mm
Similar to 1 Penny, KM#Tn263.

KM#	Date	Mintage	VG	Fine	VF	XF
Tn262	1861	—	3.00	7.50	17.50	80.00

BRONZE, 31mm

KM#	Date	Mintage	VG	Fine	VF	XF
Tn263	1863	—	4.00	8.00	25.00	125.00

NOTE: 2 varieties exist.

R. S. Waterhouse

Hobart, Tasmania

1/2 PENNY

COPPER, 26mm
Obv. leg: R. S. WATERHOUSE DRAPERY. . .
Rev. leg: FOR READY MONEY. . . around baby ski jumper.

KM#	Date	Mintage	VG	Fine	VF	XF
Tn264	ND	—	3.50	7.50	35.00	150.00

NOTE: 2 varieties exist.

PENNY

COPPER, 33mm
Similar to 1/2 Penny, KM#Tn264.

KM#	Date	Mintage	VG	Fine	VF	XF
Tn265	ND	—	3.50	7.50	35.00	150.00

W. R. Watson & Co.

Ballarat, Victoria

PENNY

COPPER, 34mm
Rev: Vine leaf touches R of MAKER.

KM#	Date	Mintage	VG	Fine	VF	XF
Tn266	1862	—	3.00	6.00	45.00	150.00

Rev: Vine leaf does not touch R of MAKER.

KM#	Date	Mintage	VG	Fine	VF	XF
Tn267	1862	—	5.00	10.00	50.00	175.00

W. Watson & Co.

Ballarat, Victoria

PENNY

COPPER, 34mm

Rev: Coat of arms.

KM#	Date	Mintage	VG	Fine	VF	XF
TnF293	1862 (fabrication)	—	—		as struck	500.00

Rev: Vine and branch.

KM#	Date	Mintage	VG	Fine	VF	XF
TnF294	1862 (fabrication)	—	—		as struck	500.00

Weight & Johnson

Sydney, New South Wales

1/2 PENNY

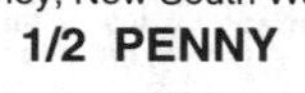

COPPER, 28mm
Obv. leg: LIVERPOOL & LONDON. . .
Rev: Standing Justice.

KM#	Date	Mintage	VG	Fine	VF	XF
Tn-A268	ND	—	5.00	30.00	100.00	200.00

NOTE: 4 varieties exist.

PENNY

COPPER, 34mm

KM#	Date	Mintage	VG	Fine	VF	XF
Tn268	ND	—	5.00	30.00	100.00	200.00

Thomas White and Son

Westbury, Tasmania

1/2 PENNY

COPPER, 28mm
Obv. leg: THOMAS WHITE AND SON. . .
Rev. leg: TASMANIA above emu and kangaroo.

KM#	Date	Mintage	VG	Fine	VF	XF
Tn269	1855	—	7.50	15.00	75.00	300.00

PENNY

COPPER, 34mm

KM#	Date	Mintage	VG	Fine	VF	XF
Tn270	1855	—	5.00	10.00	50.00	250.00
	1857	—	5.00	10.00	50.00	250.00

NOTE: Beware of modern replicas in bright copper of KM#Tn269 and Tn270 dated 1855.

Whitty & Brown

Sydney, New South Wales

PENNY

COPPER, 33mm

KM#	Date	Mintage	VG	Fine	VF	XF
Tn271	ND	—	7.50	15.00	50.00	125.00

NOTE: Varieties exist.

J. W. & G. Williams

Eaglehawk, Victoria

PENNY

COPPER, 34mm

KM#	Date	Mintage	VG	Fine	VF	XF
Tn272	ND	—	4.00	8.00	50.00	175.00

W. D. Wood

Hobart, Tasmania

1/2 PENNY

COPPER, 28mm

KM#	Date	Mintage	VG	Fine	VF	XF
Tn273	ND	—	7.50	15.00	75.00	200.00

PENNY

COPPER, 34mm

KM#	Date	Mintage	VG	Fine	VF	XF
Tn274	ND	—	7.50	15.00	75.00	200.00

Obv. leg: MONTPELIER RETREAT. . .
Rev. leg: HOBART TOWN above building w/date below.

KM#	Date	Mintage	VG	Fine	VF	XF
Tn275	1855	—	7.50	15.00	75.00	200.00

FOREIGN TOKEN ISSUES

The following tokens although struck abroad were circulated in Australia.

Charles Harrold & Co.

Birmingham, England

1/2 PENNY

COPPER, 29mm

KM#	Date	Mintage	VG	Fine	VF	XF
Tn290	ND	—	—	—	—	1150.

KM#	Date	Mintage	VG	Fine	VF	XF
Tn291	ND	—	—	—	—	1000.

William Hodgins

Clochjordan, Ireland

PENNY

COPPER

KM#	Date	Mintage	VG	Fine	VF	XF
Tn276	1858	—	7.50	15.00	50.00	85.00

Professor Holloway

London, England

1/2 PENNY

COPPER, 28mm
Obv: J. MOORE incuse on truncation of neck.
Rev: J.M. on base, border on dress.

KM#	Date	Mintage	VG	Fine	VF	XF
Tn277.1	1857	—	3.00	6.00	25.00	125.00
	1858	—	3.00	6.00	25.00	125.00

Obv: J. MOORE in raised letters on truncation of neck. Rev: W/o J.M. on base.

KM#	Date	Mintage	Fine	VF	XF	Unc
Tn277.2	1857	—	—	—	200.00	300.00

PENNY

COPPER, 34mm
Obv: J. MOORE incuse on truncation of neck.
Rev: J.M. on base, border on dress.

KM#	Date	Mintage	VG	Fine	VF	XF
Tn278.1	1857	—	3.00	6.00	25.00	125.00
	1858	—	3.00	6.00	25.00	125.00

NOTE: 5 varieties exist for 1857. 4 varieties exist for 1858.

Obv: J. MOORE in raised letters on truncation of neck. Rev: W/o J.M. on base.

KM#	Date	Mintage	Fine	VF	XF	Unc
Tn278.2	1857	—	—	—	200.00	300.00

Joseph Lane & Son

Birmingham, England

1/2 PENNY

COPPER, 29mm

KM#	Date	Mintage	VG	Fine	VF	XF
Tn279	ND	—	—	—	100.00	200.00

NOTE: Known in 3 thicknesses.

T. Pope & Co.

Birmingham, England

PENNY

COPPER, 34mm

KM#	Date	Mintage	VG	Fine	VF	XF
Tn280	ND	—	7.50	15.00	75.00	125.00

UNNAMED TOKEN ISSUES

Advance Australia

PENNY

COPPER, uniface
Obv: Australian arms.

KM#	Date	Mintage	VG	Fine	VF	XF
Tn281	1850 (as crudely struck)	1 known	—	—	—	—

COPPER, 34mm
(W.J. Taylor)
Obv. leg: ADVANCE AUSTRALIA around ONE PENNY, large crosses below.
Rev: Emu and kangaroo w/tall thin foliage behind tail.

KM#	Date	Mintage	VG	Fine	VF	XF
Tn282.1	ND	—	7.50	15.00	75.00	125.00

Rev: Thick foliage behind kangaroos tail.

KM#	Date	Mintage	VG	Fine	VF	XF
Tn282.2	ND	—	150.00	300.00	900.00	1500.

COPPER, 33mm
(Whittey & Brown, Sydney)
Obv: Small crosses below.
Rev: Revised design, w/o W.J. TAYLOR.LONDON at exergue.

KM#	Date	Mintage	VG	Fine	VF	XF
Tn282.3	ND	—	20.00	50.00	125.00	175.00

NOTE: 2 varieties exist.

COPPER, 33mm
(Whittey & Brown, Sydney)
Rev: Drapery extends to right elbow and hangs below horizon.

KM#	Date	Mintage	VG	Fine	VF	XF
Tn283	ND	—	7.50	15.00	35.00	80.00

NOTE: Varieties exist.

Rev: Drapery ends before right elbow and hangs above horizon.

KM#	Date	Mintage	VG	Fine	VF	XF
Tn284	ND	—	4.50	9.00	30.00	75.00

NOTE: Varieties exist. Numerous degrees of die rotation.

Peace & Plenty

Melbourne, Victoria

PENNY

COPPER, 34mm

KM#	Date	Mintage	VG	Fine	VF	XF
Tn285	1858	—	3.00	7.00	12.00	75.00
	1859	—	3.00	7.00	12.00	75.00

NOTE: 4 varieties exist for 1858, 3 varieties exist for 1859.

Peace and Plenty

Sydney, New South Wales

PENNY

BRONZE
Obv: No projections from base.

KM#	Date	Mintage	VG	Fine	VF	XF
Tn286.1	ND	1 known	—	—	500.00	—

Obv: 1 diagonal projection from lower right of base.

KM#	Date	Mintage	VG	Fine	VF	XF
Tn286.2	ND	—	7.50	15.00	50.00	125.00

Obv: 2 diagonal projections from base, 1 at center and 1 at right.

KM#	Date	Mintage	VG	Fine	VF	XF
Tn286.3	ND	—	7.50	15.00	50.00	125.00

Obv: 3 or more diagonal projections from base, 1 at center and 1 at right, etc.

KM#	Date	Mintage	VG	Fine	VF	XF
Tn286.4	ND	—	7.50	15.00	50.00	125.00

PROOF SETS (PS)

KM#	Date	Mintage	Identification	Issue Price	Mkt. Val.
PSA1	1887S(4)	2 known	KM8-11	—	Rare

AUSTRIA

The Republic of Austria, a parliamentary democracy located in mountainous central Europe, has an area of 32,378 sq. mi. (83,850 sq. km.) and a population of 8 million. Capital: Vienna. Austria is primarily an industrial country. Machinery, iron, steel, textiles, yarns and timber are exported.

The territories later to be known as Austria were overrun in pre-Roman times by various tribes, including the Celts. Upon the fall of the Roman Empire, the country became a margravate of Charlemagne's Empire. Premysl Otaker, King of Bohemia, gained possession in 1252, only to lose the territory to Rudolf of Habsburg in 1276. Thereafter, until World War I, the story of Austria was conducted by the ruling Habsburgs.

During World War I, the Austro-Hungarian Empire was one of the Central Powers with Germany, Bulgaria and Turkey. At the end of the war, the Empire was dismembered and Austria was established as an independent republic. In March, 1938, Austria was incorporated into Hitler's short-lived Greater German Reich. Allied forces of both East and West occupied Austria in April 1945, and subsequently divided it into 4 zones of military occupation. On May 15, 1955, the 4 powers formally recognized Austria as a 'sovereign independent democratic state.'

A number of coin-issuing entities that were or are a part of Austria continue to be of interest to collectors of world coins.

RULERS

Franz II (I), 1792-1835
(as Franz II, Holy Roman Emperor, 1792-1806)
(as Franz I, Austrian Emperor, 1806-1835)
Ferdinand I, 1835-1848
Franz Joseph I, 1848-1916

MINT MARKS

A, W, WI - Vienna
(a) - Vienna
AI,AL-IV,C-A,E,GA - Karlsburg (Transylvania)
B,K,KB - Kremnitz (Hungary)
C - Prague (Bohemia)
CB,CI,CI-BI(NI),HS - Hermannstadt (Transylvania)
CV,FT,KV - Klausenburg (Transylvania)
D - Salzburg
D,G,GR - Graz (Styria)
F, HA - Hall
G,H,P-R - Gunzburg
GM - Mantua
(h) Shield - Vienna
M - Milan (Lombardy)
NB - Nagybanya (Hungary)
O - Oravicza (Hungary)
P - Prague (Bohemia)
S - Schmollnitz (Hungary)
V - Venice (Venetia)
(v) Eagle - Hall
W - Breslau (Poland)

MINT IDENTIFICATION

To aid in determining an Austrian coin's mint it is necessary to first check for the provincial coat of arms for the province in which the mint is located. In some cases the coat of arms will dominate the reverse. The Hungarian Madonna and child is a prime example. On more traditional Austrian design types the provincial coat of arms will be the only one on the imperial eagle's breast. When a more complicated coat of arms is used the provincial arms will usually be found in the center or at the top center usually overlapping neighboring arms.

Legend endings frequently reflect the various provincial coats of arms. Sometimes mint marks appear on coins such as the letter W for Breslau. Mintmaster's and mint officials' initials or symbols also appear and can be used to confirm the mint identity.

The following pages will present the mint name, illustrate or describe the provincial coats of arms, legend endings, mint marks, and mint officials' initials or symbols with which the mint identity can be determined.

KARLSBURG MINT

(in Transylvania)

For coat of arms and legend endings, see Hermannstadt.

MINT MARKS

E - 1797, 1819-1824, 1830-1833, 1857-1868

NAGYBANYA MINT

(Hungary)

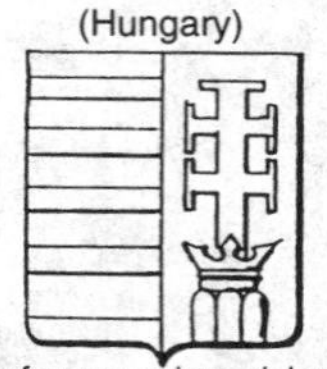

Hungarian coat of arms on imperial eagle's breast.

MINT MARKS

G - 1797, 1813-1814, 1819-1826
NB

SALZBURG MINT

Initials	Years	Mintmaster
M	1803-1806	Franz Xaver Matzenkopf

MONETARY SYSTEM

Before 1857

8 Heller = 4 Pfennig = 1 Kreuzer
60 Kreuzer = 1 Florin (Gulden)
2 Florin = 1 Species or Convention Thaler

1857-1892

100 Kreuzer = 1 Florin (Gulden)
1-1/2 Florin = 1 Vereinsthaler

UNIFORM COINAGE

1/4 KREUZER

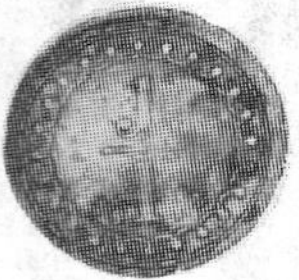

COPPER

KM#	Date	Mintage	Fine	VF	XF	Unc
2106	1812A	—	2.00	4.00	8.00	25.00
	1812B	1.725	3.00	6.00	12.50	35.00
	1812S	—	— Reported, not confirmed			

KM#	Date	Mintage	Fine	VF	XF	Unc
2107	1816A	—	1.50	2.50	5.00	30.00
	1816B	6.652	1.50	2.50	5.00	30.00
	1816E	—	—	—	Rare	—
	1816G	—	—	—	Rare	—
	1816O	—	3.00	6.00	12.00	35.00
	1816S	—	1.00	2.00	4.00	25.00

NOTE: The above 6 issues struck until 1852 w/1816 date.

KM#	Date	Mintage	Fine	VF	XF	Unc
2180	1851A	—	.50	1.00	2.00	7.50
	1851B	9.637	1.00	3.50	6.00	10.00
	1851G	—	10.00	30.00	60.00	120.00

1/2 KREUZER

COPPER

KM#	Date	Mintage	Fine	VF	XF	Unc
2109	1812A	—	2.00	6.00	12.00	40.00
	1812B	—	—	—	Rare	—
	1812S	—	3.00	8.00	20.00	50.00

KM#	Date	Mintage	Fine	VF	XF	Unc
2110	1816A	—	1.00	2.00	4.00	25.00
	1816B	6.652	1.50	5.00	10.00	40.00
	1816E	—	—	—	Rare	—
	1816G	—	—	—	Rare	—
	1816O	—	2.00	8.00	20.00	50.00
	1816S	—	2.00	6.00	12.50	40.00

NOTE: The above 6 issues were struck until 1852 w/1816 date.

KM#	Date	Mintage	Fine	VF	XF	Unc
2181	1851A	—	1.00	2.00	4.00	10.00
	1851B	27.733	1.00	2.00	5.00	11.00
	1851C	—	100.00	150.00	300.00	600.00
	1851G	—	10.00	20.00	40.00	100.00

5/10 KREUZER

COPPER, 1.67 g
Obv: Small eagle.

KM#	Date	Mintage	Fine	VF	XF	Unc
2182	1858A	—	1.50	3.00	6.00	9.00
	1858B	11.058	2.00	3.00	6.50	10.00
	1858E	—	15.00	35.00	60.00	130.00
	1858M	—	3.50	8.00	20.00	35.00
	1858V	—	5.00	10.00	20.00	40.00
	1859A	—	.75	1.50	3.00	7.00
	1859B	13.397	3.50	6.50	10.00	20.00
	1859E	—	15.00	30.00	60.00	120.00
	1859M	—	8.00	16.00	24.00	40.00
	1859V	—	15.00	30.00	60.00	100.00
	1860A	—	1.00	3.00	7.50	15.00
	1860E	—	15.00	30.00	60.00	120.00
	1860V	—	5.00	7.50	18.00	40.00
	1861A	—	5.00	10.00	25.00	50.00
	1861B	3.474	3.50	7.50	15.00	30.00
	1863B	—	6.00	12.00	20.00	40.00
	1864A	—	2.00	5.00	10.00	25.00
	1864B	7.598	2.50	5.00	10.00	20.00
	1864V	—	15.00	30.00	60.00	100.00
	1865A	—	2.00	5.00	10.00	20.00
	1865B	7.182	6.50	13.50	22.50	50.00
	1866A	—	2.00	5.00	10.00	20.00

Reduced weight, 1.60 g

KM#	Date	Mintage	Fine	VF	XF	Unc
2183	1877	—	5.00	10.00	15.00	25.00
	1881	4.200	2.00	4.00	6.00	10.00
	1885	2.000	.75	1.50	3.00	7.00

Obv: Large eagle.

KM#	Date	Mintage	Fine	VF	XF	Unc
2184	1885	Inc. Ab.	.50	1.00	2.00	5.00
	1891	2.000	3.00	6.00	12.50	15.00

KREUZER

COPPER

KM#	Date	Mintage	Fine	VF	XF	Unc
2112	1812A	—	3.00	6.00	15.00	40.00
	1812B	92.163	2.00	4.00	10.00	30.00
	1812C	—	— Reported, not confirmed			
	1812E	—	2.50	5.00	12.00	35.00
	1812G	—	3.00	8.00	20.00	42.00
	1812O	—	6.00	20.00	35.00	65.00
	1812S	—	2.00	4.00	12.00	35.00

KM#	Date	Mintage	Fine	VF	XF	Unc
2113	1816A	—	1.00	2.00	4.00	25.00
	1816B	54.516	1.00	2.00	5.00	25.00
	1816E	—	7.50	15.00	25.00	55.00
	1816G	—	2.00	6.00	12.00	32.00
	1816O	—	2.00	6.00	12.00	35.00
	1816S	—	2.00	6.00	12.00	35.00
	1816S.	—	2.00	6.00	12.00	35.00

NOTE: The above 6 issues were struck until 1852 w/1816 date.

KM#	Date	Mintage	Fine	VF	XF	Unc
2185	1851A	—	.50	.75	1.50	5.00
	1851B	106.458	1.00	1.50	3.00	6.00
	1851C	—	40.00	60.00	120.00	250.00
	1851E	—	8.00	15.00	30.00	80.00
	1851 sm.G	—	2.00	5.00	20.00	60.00
	1851 lg.G	—	2.00	5.00	20.00	60.00

Obv: Small eagle

KM#	Date	Mintage	Fine	VF	XF	Unc
2186	1858A	—	.50	1.00	2.00	4.00
	1858B	23.497	1.00	2.00	3.00	5.00
	1858E	—	5.00	10.00	20.00	45.00
	1858M	—	4.00	7.00	15.00	40.00
	1858V	—	11.00	20.00	40.00	75.00
	1859A	—	.50	1.00	2.00	4.00
	1859B	93.406	1.00	2.00	3.50	6.00
	1859E	—	2.50	5.00	10.00	17.50
	1859M	—	2.50	5.00	12.00	20.00
	1859V	—	7.00	14.00	25.00	45.00
	1860A	—	.50	1.00	2.00	4.00
	1860B	87.955	.50	1.00	2.00	4.00
	1860E	—	5.00	10.00	20.00	45.00
	1860V	—	4.00	9.00	20.00	35.00
	1861A	—	.75	1.50	2.50	5.00
	1861B	54.201	.50	1.00	3.00	5.00
	1861E	—	2.50	6.00	12.50	27.50
	1862B	11.599	5.00	10.00	25.00	50.00
	1862E	—	10.00	20.00	40.00	90.00
	1863E	—	15.00	35.00	75.00	160.00
	1873A	—	2.00	4.00	7.00	15.00
	1878	—	.50	1.00	2.00	3.00
	1879	—	.50	1.00	2.00	4.00
	1881	37.900	.25	.50	1.50	3.00

Obv: Large eagle.

KM#	Date	Mintage	Fine	VF	XF	Unc
2187	1885	29.000	.25	.50	1.25	3.00
	1891	23.800	.25	.50	1.25	3.00

2 KREUZER

COPPER
Revolution 1848-1849

KM#	Date	Mintage	Fine	VF	XF	Unc
2188	1848A	7.755	5.00	10.00	17.50	45.00

KM#	Date	Mintage	Fine	VF	XF	Unc
2189	1851A	—	3.00	7.50	15.00	30.00
	1851B	22.419	3.50	8.00	16.00	32.50
	1851C	—	300.00	500.00	700.00	1000.
	1851 lg. G	—	8.00	15.00	30.00	85.00
	1851 sm. G	—	8.00	15.00	30.00	85.00

3 KREUZER

.346 SILVER
Obv: Bust of Franz I right.
Rev: Crowned imperial eagle.

KM#	Date	Mintage	Fine	VF	XF	Unc
2114	1801E	—	30.00	60.00	120.00	225.00
	1810A	—	—	Reported, not confirmed		

NOTE: Earlier dates (1792-1799) exist for this type.

COPPER, 8.75 g
Obv: Bust of Franz I right.
Rev: Crowned imperial eagle.

KM#	Date	Mintage	Fine	VF	XF	Unc
2115.3	1801E	—	15.00	30.00	75.00	150.00
	1801F	2.762	10.00	15.00	35.00	100.00
	1803F	—	20.00	40.00	60.00	140.00

NOTE: Varieties of tail feathers and heads exist.
NOTE: Earlier date (1800) exists for this type.

COPPER

KM#	Date	Mintage	Fine	VF	XF	Unc
2116	1812A	—	15.00	25.00	40.00	150.00
	1812B	13.594	2.00	4.00	8.00	25.00
	1812B(error)UH	—	5.00	10.00	20.00	40.00
	1812E	—	9.00	15.00	30.00	75.00
	1812G	—	6.00	12.50	20.00	65.00
	1812O	—	6.00	12.50	25.00	70.00
	1812S	—	3.00	6.00	12.00	35.00

1.7000 g, .344 SILVER, .0188 oz ASW

KM#	Date	Mintage	Fine	VF	XF	Unc
2117	1814A	—	—	—	Rare	—
	1815A	—	7.50	15.00	30.00	60.00
	1815B	—	10.00	20.00	40.00	90.00
	1815V	—	7.50	15.00	30.00	60.00

.346 SILVER

KM#	Date	Mintage	Fine	VF	XF	Unc
2118	1817A	—	50.00	80.00	150.00	300.00
	1818B	.538	12.00	25.00	40.00	90.00
	1818V	—	—	—	Rare	—
	1819A	—	12.00	25.00	50.00	100.00
	1820A	—	7.50	15.00	30.00	55.00
	1820B	1.457	7.50	15.00	30.00	55.00
	1820G	—	—	—	Rare	—
	1820V	—	—	—	—	—
	1821A	—	7.50	15.00	30.00	60.00
	1821B	4.894	7.50	15.00	30.00	60.00
	1821E	—	25.00	50.00	75.00	200.00
	1821G	—	25.00	50.00	75.00	175.00
	1822A	.079	12.00	25.00	50.00	100.00
	1823A	.035	25.00	45.00	75.00	150.00
	1823B	I.A.	—	—	Rare	—
	1824A	.037	—	—	Rare	—
	1824G	I.A.	25.00	50.00	75.00	175.00

KM#	Date	Mintage	Fine	VF	XF	Unc
2119	1825A	.051	25.00	50.00	75.00	175.00
	1826A	—	8.00	15.00	30.00	50.00
	1826B	.375	8.00	15.00	30.00	60.00
	1826E	—	25.00	40.00	75.00	175.00
	1827A	.118	40.00	80.00	150.00	250.00
	1827B	—	45.00	75.00	150.00	250.00
	1828A	—	8.00	15.00	30.00	50.00
	1828B	.965	8.00	15.00	30.00	60.00
	1828E	—	35.00	60.00	120.00	200.00
	1828G	—	40.00	70.00	140.00	225.00
	1829A	—	8.00	15.00	30.00	50.00

KM#	Date	Mintage	Fine	VF	XF	Unc
2119	1829B	.133	22.50	40.00	75.00	160.00
	1829E	—	17.50	30.00	60.00	140.00
	1829G	—	40.00	70.00	140.00	225.00
	1830A	—	8.00	15.00	30.00	55.00
	1830B	.076	40.00	80.00	150.00	250.00
	1830E	—	40.00	70.00	140.00	225.00
	1831A	—	—	Reported, not confirmed		

Struck in a collar, short braids.

KM#	Date	Mintage	Fine	VF	XF	Unc
2120	1831A	—	40.00	75.00	130.00	225.00

Obv: Larger head.

KM#	Date	Mintage	Fine	VF	XF	Unc
2121	1831A	—	—	Reported, not confirmed		
	1832A	—	5.00	10.00	20.00	50.00
	1833A	—	5.00	10.00	20.00	50.00
	1833C	—	8.00	15.00	30.00	60.00
	1834A	—	20.00	40.00	70.00	130.00
	1834C	—	30.00	50.00	80.00	175.00
	1835A	—	20.00	40.00	70.00	130.00

Obv: Head of Ferdinand I right.
Rev: Eagle, value on chest.

KM#	Date	Mintage	Fine	VF	XF	Unc
2190	1835A	—	20.00	30.00	65.00	140.00
	1835E	—	30.00	50.00	100.00	250.00
	1836A	—	10.00	20.00	40.00	80.00
	1836E	—	25.00	40.00	90.00	240.00

KM#	Date	Mintage	Fine	VF	XF	Unc
2191	1837A	—	3.50	7.50	15.00	40.00
	1837C	—	25.00	40.00	75.00	150.00
	1837E	—	25.00	40.00	75.00	150.00
	1838A	—	3.50	7.50	15.00	45.00
	1838B	.130	15.00	25.00	40.00	100.00
	1838C	—	10.00	20.00	35.00	75.00
	1838E	—	15.00	25.00	50.00	110.00
	1839A	—	4.00	8.00	15.00	40.00
	1839C	—	12.50	25.00	50.00	100.00
	1839E	—	12.50	25.00	50.00	100.00
	1840A	—	2.50	5.00	10.00	30.00
	1840E	—	12.50	25.00	45.00	90.00
	1841A	—	15.00	25.00	50.00	110.00
	1841E	—	35.00	60.00	100.00	175.00
	1842A	—	6.00	12.00	20.00	50.00
	1842E	—	15.00	25.00	50.00	110.00
	1843A	—	10.00	15.00	30.00	80.00
	1843E	—	15.00	25.00	50.00	110.00
	1844A	—	6.00	10.00	20.00	50.00
	1844E	—	15.00	25.00	50.00	110.00
	1845A	—	3.00	7.50	15.00	35.00
	1845E	—	15.00	30.00	55.00	120.00
	1846A	—	2.50	5.00	12.50	30.00
	1846E	—	15.00	30.00	55.00	120.00
	1847A	—	2.50	5.00	12.50	30.00
	1847C	—	5.00	10.00	20.00	45.00
	1847E	—	15.00	30.00	55.00	120.00
	1848/5A	—	3.50	7.00	15.00	35.00
	1848A	—	2.50	5.00	12.50	30.00
	1848E	—	22.50	40.00	75.00	150.00
2192	1848GM swan above mint mark	—	200.00	350.00	700.00	1200.
	1848GM w/o swan above mint mark	—	200.00	350.00	700.00	1200.

NOTE: The above issue was struck in Mantua by the Austrian garrison under General Josef Radetzky during the siege of March 18-22, 1848 by Italian rebels.

COPPER

KM#	Date	Mintage	Fine	VF	XF	Unc
2193	1851A	—	6.0	12.00	25.00	100.00
	1851B	7.173	5.00	10.00	20.00	90.00
	1851C	36 pcs.	350.00	650.00	1200.	2000.
	1851G	—	10.00	20.00	55.00	160.00

NOTE: Varieties of size of mint mark exist.

4 KREUZER

COPPER

KM#	Date	Mintage	Fine	VF	XF	Unc
2194	1860A	—	2.00	6.00	12.00	40.00
	1860B	—	2.00	6.00	12.00	35.00
	1860E	—	10.00	25.00	60.00	160.00

KM#	Date	Mintage	Fine	VF	XF	Unc
2194	1861A	—	2.00	6.00	12.00	35.00
	1861B	18.470	2.00	6.00	12.00	35.00
	1861E	—	7.00	20.00	50.00	140.00
	1862B	.383	3.00	9.00	16.00	40.00
	1864B	6.666	2.00	6.00	12.00	35.00
	1865B	.224	3.00	9.00	16.00	45.00

5 KREUZER

.438 SILVER

KM#	Date	Mintage	Fine	VF	XF	Unc
2122	1815A	—	7.50	15.00	25.00	55.00
2123	1817A	—	25.00	40.00	75.00	175.00
	1818A	—	10.00	20.00	30.00	75.00
	1818B	.538	10.00	20.00	30.00	75.00
	1819A	—	—	—	Rare	—
	1820A	—	10.00	20.00	30.00	75.00
	1820B	1.457	10.00	20.00	30.00	75.00
	1820G	—	—	—	Rare	—
	1820V	—	15.00	35.00	60.00	125.00
	1821A	—	10.00	20.00	30.00	75.00
	1821B	4.894	10.00	25.00	40.00	90.00
	1821E	—	25.00	50.00	75.00	175.00
	1821G	—	20.00	40.00	70.00	140.00
	1822E	5,791	—	—	Rare	—
	1822G	1 known		—	Rare	—
	1823A	—	30.00	50.00	75.00	125.00
	1824A	—	—	—	Rare	—
	1824G	1 known		—	Rare	—

Obv: Bust w/short hair, 1 ribbon on neck.

KM#	Date	Mintage	Fine	VF	XF	Unc
2124	1825A	.015	75.00	100.00	200.00	400.00
	1826A	.053	60.00	90.00	175.00	350.00
	1826E	I.A.	—	—	Rare	—
	1827A	.018	—	—	Rare	—
	1828A	.044	60.00	90.00	175.00	350.00
	1830A	—	—	—	—	—

Obv: Bust w/short hair, both ribbons on neck.

KM#	Date	Mintage	Fine	VF	XF	Unc
2125	1831A	—	—	—	—	—

Obv: Larger head.

KM#	Date	Mintage	Fine	VF	XF	Unc
2126	1832A	—	20.00	35.00	60.00	125.00
	1833A	.029	20.00	40.00	70.00	150.00
	1834A	.031	20.00	35.00	60.00	125.00
	1835A	—	15.00	25.00	50.00	100.00
2195	1835A	—	25.00	50.00	100.00	185.00
	1836A	—	12.50	25.00	50.00	110.00
2196	1837A	—	5.00	10.00	20.00	45.00
	1838A	—	5.00	10.00	20.00	45.00
	1838B	.130	— Reported, not confirmed			
	1839A	—	5.00	10.00	20.00	45.00
	1839C	—	7.50	15.00	30.00	60.00
	1840A	—	5.00	12.50	25.00	60.00
	1840C	—	5.00	10.00	20.00	45.00
	1842A	—	15.00	30.00	60.00	125.00
	1844A	—	10.00	20.00	40.00	80.00
	1846A	—	5.00	12.50	30.00	60.00
	1847A	—	7.50	15.00	30.00	70.00
	1848A	90.472	5.00	10.00	20.00	50.00

1.3333 g, .375 SILVER, .0161 oz ASW

KM#	Date	Mintage	Fine	VF	XF	Unc
2197	1858A	—	2.00	3.50	7.50	15.00
	1858B	851 pcs.	250.00	350.00	600.00	1100.
	1858V	—	200.00	300.00	450.00	750.00

KM#	Date	Mintage	Fine	VF	XF	Unc
2197	1859A	—	1.00	2.00	4.00	10.00
	1859M	—	10.00	15.00	25.00	40.00
	1859V	—	10.00	15.00	25.00	40.00
	1860A	—	—	—	—	—
	1860B	851 pcs.	250.00	350.00	600.00	1100.
	1860V	—	50.00	75.00	100.00	175.00
	1863A	1.013	5.00	8.00	16.00	40.00
	1864A	1.922	1.50	3.00	6.00	12.50

Obv: Head w/heavier whiskers.

KM#	Date	Mintage	Fine	VF	XF	Unc
2198	1867A	.069	90.00	125.00	200.00	500.00

6 KREUZER

COPPER
Obv: Bust of Franz I right.

KM#	Date	Mintage	Fine	VF	XF	Unc
2128	1803F	—	—	—	Rare	—

NOTE: Earlier date (1800) exists for this issue.

2.2300 g, .428 SILVER, .0306 oz ASW
Revolution 1848-1849

KM#	Date	Mintage	Fine	VF	XF	Unc
2199	1848A	90.400	3.00	5.00	10.00	20.00
	1848B	—	20.00	30.00	50.00	90.00
	1848C	—	4.00	7.50	15.00	40.00

1.9100 g, .438 SILVER, .0268 oz ASW

KM#	Date	Mintage	Fine	VF	XF	Unc
2200	1849A	—	1.00	2.00	3.00	10.00
	1849B	—	15.00	25.00	40.00	90.00
	1849C	—	4.00	7.50	15.00	40.00

NOTE: The above 1849 dated issues were struck from 1849-1852 and restruck again in 1859-1870.

7 KREUZER

4.6800 g, .250 SILVER, .0376 oz ASW

KM#	Date	Mintage	Fine	VF	XF	Unc
2129	1802A	—	5.00	10.00	20.00	60.00
	1802B	102.034	5.00	10.00	20.00	60.00
	1802C	—	5.00	10.00	25.00	75.00
	1802E	—	20.00	40.00	65.00	200.00
	1802F	—	25.00	50.00	80.00	225.00
	1802G	—	17.50	35.00	60.00	130.00

NOTE: The above 6 issues were overstruck on 1795 dated 12 Kreuzer pieces, KM#2137.

10 KREUZER

.500 SILVER
Obv: Crowned bust in wreath. Rev: Eagle, leg:. . . D. LO. SAL. WIRC.

KM#	Date	Mintage	Fine	VF	XF	Unc
2131	1809A	—	40.00	75.00	160.00	275.00
	1810A	—	35.00	70.00	140.00	225.00

Rev. leg:. . . LO: WI: ET IN FR: D:

KM#	Date	Mintage	Fine	VF	XF	Unc
2132	1814A	—	—	—	Rare	—
	1815A	—	15.00	30.00	60.00	120.00
	1815B	1.800	15.00	30.00	60.00	120.00
	1815C	—	20.00	40.00	75.00	160.00

Rev. leg:. . . GAL. LOD. IL. REX. A. A.

KM#	Date	Mintage	Fine	VF	XF	Unc
2133	1817A	—	45.00	80.00	150.00	275.00
	1818A	—	—	—	Rare	—
	1818B	—	—	—	Rare	—
	1818G	—	—	—	Rare	—
	1818V	—	25.00	50.00	100.00	175.00
	1819A	.012	—	—	Rare	—
	1820A	—	—	—	Rare	—
	1820B	—	—	—	Rare	—
	1820G	—	—	—	Rare	—
	1821B	—	—	—	Rare	—
	1821G	—	50.00	90.00	150.00	275.00
	1821V	—	—	—	Rare	—
	1822G	—	—	—	Rare	—
	1823A	—	30.00	50.00	80.00	175.00
	1823G	—	30.00	60.00	120.00	225.00
	1824A	—	30.00	60.00	100.00	200.00
	1824G	—	—	—	Rare	—

Obv: Older head of Franz I right, 1 ribbon on neck.
Rev: Eagle, value below.

KM#	Date	Mintage	Fine	VF	XF	Unc
2134	1825A	—	—	—	Rare	—
	1826A	—	35.00	70.00	140.00	225.00
	1827A	—	35.00	70.00	140.00	225.00
	1828A	—	35.00	70.00	140.00	200.00
	1828E	—	45.00	90.00	175.00	300.00
	1829A	.020	—	—	Rare	—
	1829E	I.A.	35.00	75.00	150.00	250.00
	1830A	—	35.00	75.00	150.00	250.00
	1830B	.045	150.00	275.00	350.00	450.00
	1830E	—	40.00	80.00	160.00	265.00

Obv: Both ribbons on neck.

KM#	Date	Mintage	Fine	VF	XF	Unc
2135	1831A	—	— Reported, not confirmed			

Obv: Larger head

KM#	Date	Mintage	Fine	VF	XF	Unc
2136	1832A	—	20.00	30.00	60.00	135.00
	1833A	—	20.00	30.00	65.00	150.00
	1834A	—	20.00	30.00	70.00	160.00
	1835A	—	35.00	60.00	120.00	250.00

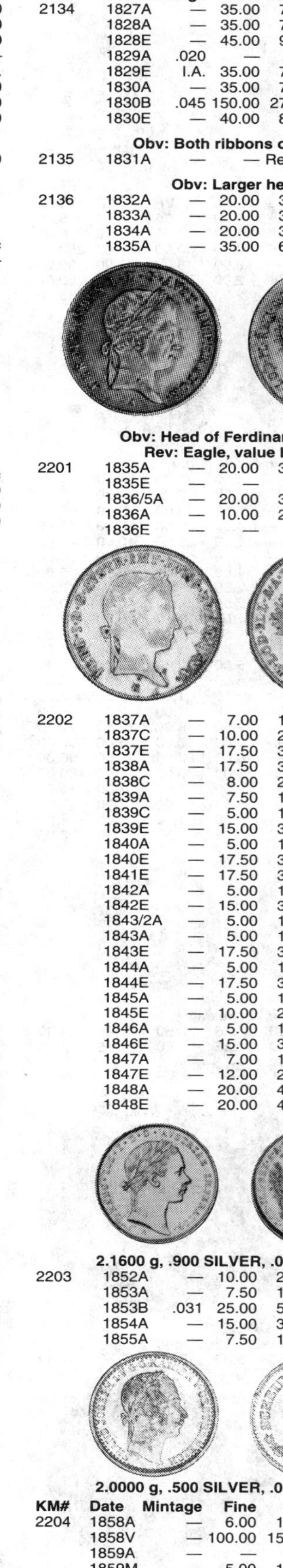

Obv: Head of Ferdinand I right.
Rev: Eagle, value below.

KM#	Date	Mintage	Fine	VF	XF	Unc
2201	1835A	—	20.00	35.00	70.00	175.00
	1835E	—	—	—	Rare	—
	1836/5A	—	20.00	30.00	60.00	160.00
	1836A	—	10.00	20.00	40.00	120.00
	1836E	—	—	—	Rare	—
2202	1837A	—	7.00	15.00	30.00	60.00
	1837C	—	10.00	20.00	40.00	80.00
	1837E	—	17.50	35.00	65.00	150.00
	1838A	—	17.50	35.00	65.00	150.00
	1838C	—	8.00	20.00	40.00	70.00
	1839A	—	7.50	15.00	30.00	60.00
	1839C	—	5.00	10.00	20.00	50.00
	1839E	—	15.00	30.00	50.00	120.00
	1840A	—	5.00	12.50	25.00	60.00
	1840E	—	17.50	35.00	65.00	150.00
	1841E	—	17.50	35.00	65.00	150.00
	1842A	—	5.00	12.50	25.00	60.00
	1842E	—	15.00	30.00	50.00	120.00
	1843/2A	—	5.00	10.00	20.00	50.00
	1843A	—	5.00	10.00	20.00	50.00
	1843E	—	17.50	35.00	65.00	150.00
	1844A	—	5.00	10.00	20.00	50.00
	1844E	—	17.50	35.00	65.00	150.00
	1845A	—	5.00	10.00	20.00	50.00
	1845E	—	10.00	25.00	50.00	100.00
	1846A	—	5.00	10.00	20.00	50.00
	1846E	—	15.00	30.00	50.00	120.00
	1847A	—	7.00	15.00	30.00	60.00
	1847E	—	12.00	25.00	50.00	100.00
	1848A	—	20.00	40.00	70.00	160.00
	1848E	—	20.00	40.00	70.00	160.00

2.1600 g, .900 SILVER, .0625 oz ASW

KM#	Date	Mintage	Fine	VF	XF	Unc
2203	1852A	—	10.00	20.00	40.00	60.00
	1853A	—	7.50	15.00	30.00	50.00
	1853B	.031	25.00	50.00	100.00	160.00
	1854A	—	15.00	30.00	50.00	120.00
	1855A	—	7.50	15.00	25.00	50.00

2.0000 g, .500 SILVER, .0322 oz ASW

KM#	Date	Mintage	Fine	VF	XF	Unc
2204	1858A	—	6.00	12.00	25.00	37.50
	1858V	—	100.00	150.00	250.00	500.00
	1859A	—	—	—	—	—
	1859M	—	5.00	10.00	20.00	40.00
	1859V	—	8.00	16.00	30.00	60.00
	1860V	—	9.00	18.00	40.00	75.00
	1861V	—	15.00	30.00	50.00	110.00
	1862V	—	30.00	50.00	80.00	180.00
	1863A	—	7.00	15.00	30.00	45.00
	1864A	1.050	10.00	20.00	30.00	65.00
	1864V	.036	150.00	250.00	400.00	650.00
	1865V	1.198	10.00	20.00	30.00	80.00

Obv: Head of Franz Joseph I right

w/heavier whiskers.

KM#	Date	Mintage	Fine	VF	XF	Unc
2205	1867A	.059	100.00	200.00	300.00	550.00

1.6667 g, .400 SILVER, .0214 oz ASW

KM#	Date	Mintage	Fine	VF	XF	Unc
2206	1868	12.000	.75	1.00	3.00	8.00
	1869	30.000	.75	1.00	3.00	10.00
	1870	35.000	.75	1.00	2.50	8.00
	1871	2.000	10.00	20.00	40.00	90.00
	1872	70.000	.25	.50	1.00	6.00

15 KREUZER

COPPER

KM#	Date	Mintage	Fine	VF	XF	Unc
2138	1807A	—	3.00	5.00	10.00	50.00
	1807B	22.007	3.00	5.00	10.00	50.00
	1087B (error for 1807)	—	45.00	90.00	150.00	350.00
	1807E	—	10.00	20.00	45.00	150.00
	1807G	—	15.00	30.00	75.00	275.00
	1807S	—	3.00	5.00	10.00	55.00

20 KREUZER

6.6800 g, .583 SILVER, .1252 oz ASW

KM#	Date	Mintage	Fine	VF	XF	Unc
2139	1802A	—	9.00	20.00	40.00	90.00
	1802B	1.359	7.00	15.00	27.50	60.00
	1802C	—	7.00	15.00	27.50	60.00
	1802E	—	15.00	35.00	60.00	120.00
	1802G	—	12.00	25.00	50.00	90.00
	1802H	—	9.00	20.00	40.00	85.00
	1803A	—	7.00	15.00	27.50	55.00
	1803B	8.469	7.00	15.00	27.50	60.00
	1803C	5.925	7.00	15.00	30.00	70.00
	1803E	—	7.00	15.00	30.00	75.00
	1803F	—	7.00	15.00	30.00	70.00
	1803G	—	9.00	20.00	40.00	80.00
	1803H	—	12.00	25.00	50.00	100.00
	1804A	—	9.00	20.00	40.00	80.00
	1804B	5.693	7.00	15.00	27.50	60.00
	1804C	.566	7.00	15.00	30.00	70.00
	1804E	—	7.00	15.00	27.50	65.00
	1804F	.651	7.00	15.00	30.00	70.00
	1804G	—	7.00	15.00	30.00	60.00

NOTE: Earlier dates (1792-1797) exist for this type.

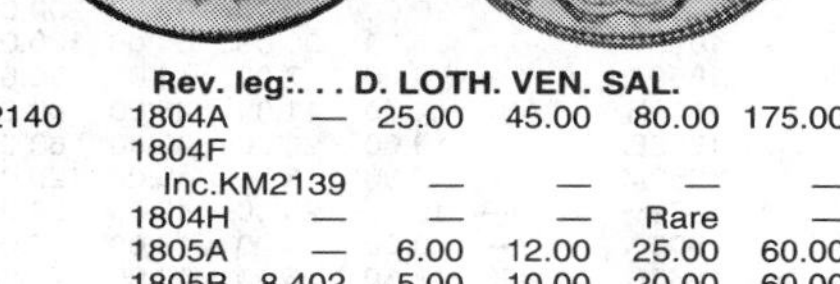

Rev. leg:. . . D. LOTH. VEN. SAL.

KM#	Date	Mintage	Fine	VF	XF	Unc
2140	1804A	—	25.00	45.00	80.00	175.00
	1804F Inc.KM2139		—	—	—	—
	1804H	—	—	—	Rare	—
	1805A	—	6.00	12.00	25.00	60.00
	1805B	8.402	5.00	10.00	20.00	60.00
	1805C	1.993	7.00	15.00	30.00	80.00
	1805E	—	7.00	15.00	25.00	60.00
	1805G	—	10.00	20.00	40.00	90.00
	1806A	—	5.00	10.00	20.00	55.00
	1806B	19.090	5.00	10.00	20.00	60.00
	1806C	2.977	6.00	12.00	25.00	60.00
	1806D	—	10.00	20.00	40.00	85.00
	1806E	—	—	—	Rare	—
	1806G	—	10.00	20.00	40.00	90.00

Rev. leg:. . . D. LO. SAL. WIRC.

KM#	Date	Mintage	Fine	VF	XF	Unc
2141	1806A	—	7.00	15.00	30.00	75.00
	1806B Inc.KM2140		15.00	30.00	60.00	120.00
	1806C	—	25.00	55.00	100.00	175.00
	1807A	—	7.00	15.00	30.00	75.00
	1807B	6.723	12.00	25.00	45.00	95.00
	1807C	2.421	12.00	25.00	45.00	95.00
	1807D	—	12.00	25.00	45.00	100.00
	1808A	—	5.00	10.00	20.00	50.00
	1808B	3.235	7.00	15.00	30.00	75.00
	1808C	1.188	5.00	10.00	20.00	55.00
	1808D	—	10.00	20.00	40.00	80.00
	1808E	—	7.00	15.00	35.00	80.00
	1808G	—	7.00	15.00	30.00	70.00
	1809A	—	5.00	10.00	20.00	55.00
	1809B	7.239	7.00	15.00	27.50	65.00
	1809C	2.381	7.00	15.00	27.50	60.00
	1809D	—	12.00	25.00	50.00	100.00
	1809E	—	7.00	15.00	35.00	80.00
	1809G	—	5.00	10.00	20.00	50.00
	1810A	—	5.00	10.00	20.00	50.00
	1810C	.714	—	—	—	—
	1810E	—	50.00	100.00	150.00	200.00
	1810G	—	12.00	25.00	50.00	100.00
	1812C	.092	—	—	—	—
	1813C	.055	—	—	—	—
	1814C	—	12.00	25.00	50.00	100.00

Rev. leg:. . . LO WI: ET IN FR D.

KM#	Date	Mintage	Fine	VF	XF	Unc
2142	1811A	—	5.00	10.00	20.00	45.00
	1811B	.580	9.00	20.00	40.00	80.00
	1811E	—	12.00	25.00	50.00	100.00
	1812A	—	5.00	10.00	20.00	45.00
	1812B	.774	20.00	40.00	80.00	120.00
	1812E	—	10.00	20.00	40.00	80.00
	1812G	—	10.00	20.00	40.00	80.00
	1813A	—	5.00	10.00	20.00	50.00
	1813B	1.103	6.00	12.00	25.00	50.00
	1813E	—	6.00	12.00	25.00	55.00
	1813G	—	100.00	150.00	200.00	300.00
	1814A	—	5.00	10.00	20.00	45.00
	1814B	1.021	7.00	15.00	35.00	70.00
	1814C	—	7.00	15.00	30.00	60.00
	1814E	—	10.00	20.00	40.00	80.00
	1814G	—	7.00	15.00	35.00	70.00
	1815A	—	5.00	10.00	20.00	45.00
	1815B	1.043	4.00	8.00	15.00	45.00
	1815C	.128	6.00	12.00	25.00	50.00
	1815E	—	7.00	15.00	30.00	65.00
	1815G	—	6.00	12.00	25.00	50.00
	1815	—	15.00	30.00	60.00	120.00
	1816B	5.773	10.00	20.00	40.00	80.00
	1816C	.785	— Reported, not confirmed			

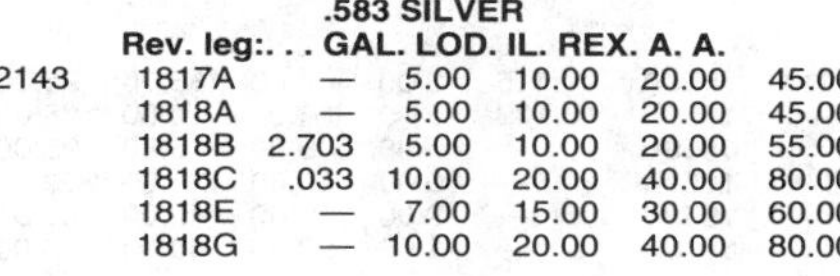

.583 SILVER

Rev. leg:. . . GAL. LOD. IL. REX. A. A.

KM#	Date	Mintage	Fine	VF	XF	Unc
2143	1817A	—	5.00	10.00	20.00	45.00
	1818A	—	5.00	10.00	20.00	45.00
	1818B	2.703	5.00	10.00	20.00	55.00
	1818C	.033	10.00	20.00	40.00	80.00
	1818E	—	7.00	15.00	30.00	60.00
	1818G	—	10.00	20.00	40.00	80.00
	1818V	—	6.00	12.00	25.00	55.00
	1818V FNANCISCUS (error)	—	60.00	100.00	150.00	375.00
	1819A	—	5.00	10.00	20.00	45.00
	1819C	.081	25.00	45.00	75.00	140.00
	1819E	—	8.00	15.00	30.00	60.00
	1819M	—	7.00	15.00	25.00	50.00
	1820A	—	5.00	10.00	20.00	45.00
	1820B	1.118	12.00	25.00	50.00	100.00
	1820C	.028	10.00	20.00	40.00	80.00
	1820E	—	7.00	15.00	30.00	65.00
	1820G	—	25.00	45.00	75.00	140.00
	1821A	—	6.00	12.00	25.00	55.00
	1821B	1.075	10.00	20.00	40.00	80.00
	1821C	.116	20.00	40.00	70.00	130.00
	1821E	—	7.00	15.00	30.00	70.00
	1821G	—	25.00	45.00	75.00	140.00
	1822A	—	6.00	12.00	25.00	55.00
	1822B	.269	10.00	20.00	40.00	80.00
	1822C	.165	20.00	40.00	70.00	130.00
	1822E	—	7.00	15.00	30.00	75.00
	1822G	—	12.00	25.00	45.00	85.00
	1823A	—	5.00	10.00	20.00	45.00
	1823B	.324	25.00	45.00	75.00	140.00
	1823C	.096	30.00	50.00	90.00	150.00
	1823E	—	6.00	12.00	25.00	55.00
	1823G	—	12.00	25.00	50.00	100.00
	1824A	—	5.00	10.00	20.00	45.00
	1824B	.014	40.00	60.00	90.00	175.00
	1824E	—	6.00	12.00	25.00	60.00
	1824G	—	6.00	12.00	25.00	55.00

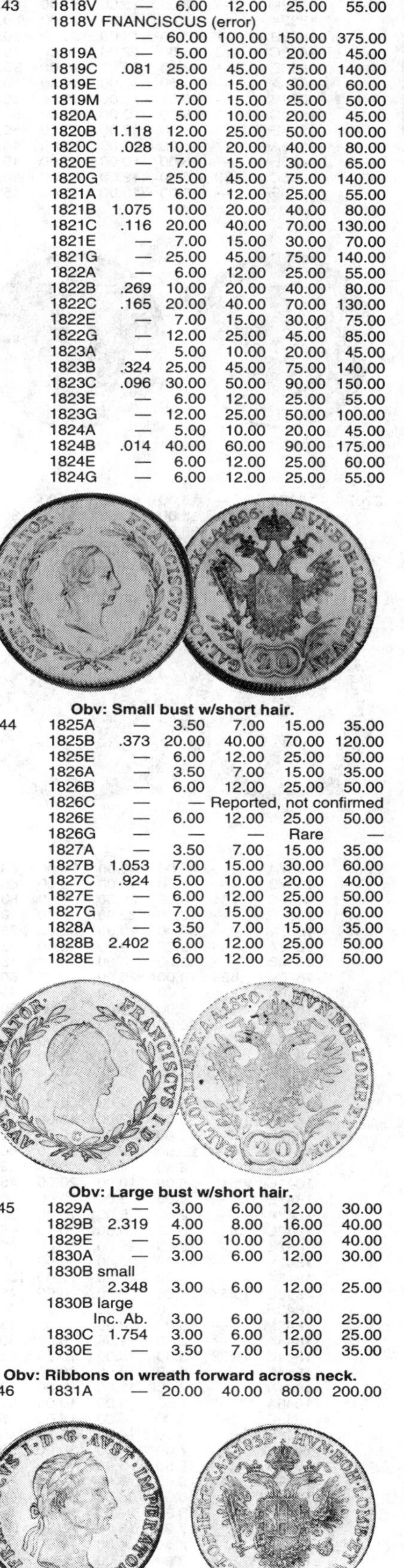

Obv: Small bust w/short hair.

KM#	Date	Mintage	Fine	VF	XF	Unc
2144	1825A	—	3.50	7.00	15.00	35.00
	1825B	.373	20.00	40.00	70.00	120.00
	1825E	—	6.00	12.00	25.00	50.00
	1826A	—	3.50	7.00	15.00	35.00
	1826B	—	6.00	12.00	25.00	50.00
	1826C	—	— Reported, not confirmed			
	1826E	—	6.00	12.00	25.00	50.00
	1826G	—	—	—	Rare	—
	1827A	—	3.50	7.00	15.00	35.00
	1827B	1.053	7.00	15.00	30.00	60.00
	1827C	.924	5.00	10.00	20.00	40.00
	1827E	—	6.00	12.00	25.00	50.00
	1827G	—	7.00	15.00	30.00	60.00
	1828A	—	3.50	7.00	15.00	35.00
	1828B	2.402	6.00	12.00	25.00	50.00
	1828E	—	6.00	12.00	25.00	50.00

Obv: Large bust w/short hair.

KM#	Date	Mintage	Fine	VF	XF	Unc
2145	1829A	—	3.00	6.00	12.00	30.00
	1829B	2.319	4.00	8.00	16.00	40.00
	1829E	—	5.00	10.00	20.00	40.00
	1830A	—	3.00	6.00	12.00	30.00
	1830B small	2.348	3.00	6.00	12.00	25.00
	1830B large	Inc. Ab.	3.00	6.00	12.00	25.00
	1830C	1.754	3.00	6.00	12.00	25.00
	1830E	—	3.50	7.00	15.00	35.00

Obv: Ribbons on wreath forward across neck.

KM#	Date	Mintage	Fine	VF	XF	Unc
2146	1831A	—	20.00	40.00	80.00	200.00

Obv: Ribbons on wreath behind neck.

KM#	Date	Mintage	Fine	VF	XF	Unc
2147	1831A	—	3.00	6.00	12.00	30.00
	1831C	—	10.00	20.00	40.00	80.00
	1831M	—	6.00	12.00	25.00	50.00
	1831V	—	7.00	15.00	30.00	55.00
	1832A	—	3.00	6.00	12.00	25.00
	1832B	—	100.00	150.00	250.00	400.00
	1832C	5.122	5.00	10.00	20.00	45.00

KM#	Date	Mintage	Fine	VF	XF	Unc
2147	1832M	—	7.00	15.00	30.00	60.00
	1833A	—	6.00	12.00	25.00	50.00
	1833B	—	7.00	15.00	30.00	60.00
	1833C	1.818	6.00	12.00	25.00	50.00
	1833E	—	12.00	25.00	45.00	90.00
	1834A	—	3.50	7.00	15.00	40.00
	1834B	—	6.00	12.00	25.00	50.00
	1834C	1.517	6.00	12.00	25.00	50.00
	1834E	—	6.00	12.00	25.00	50.00
	1835A	—	5.00	10.00	20.00	45.00
	1835B	—	5.00	10.00	20.00	45.00
	1835C	1.489	6.00	12.00	25.00	50.00
	1835E	—	5.00	10.00	20.00	45.00

KM#	Date	Mintage	Fine	VF	XF	Unc
2207	1835A	—	15.00	30.00	60.00	120.00
	1835C	.295	15.00	30.00	60.00	130.00
	1835E	—	35.00	75.00	125.00	250.00
	1836A	—	10.00	20.00	45.00	90.00
	1836E	—	25.00	50.00	100.00	225.00

KM#	Date	Mintage	Fine	VF	XF	Unc
2208	1837A	—	5.00	10.00	20.00	45.00
	1837B	—	7.50	15.00	30.00	60.00
	1837C	.484	10.00	20.00	40.00	80.00
	1837E	—	10.00	22.00	45.00	100.00
	1837M	—	30.00	60.00	100.00	225.00
	1838A	—	5.00	10.00	20.00	45.00
	1838B	—	5.00	10.00	20.00	45.00
	1838C	.625	10.00	20.00	40.00	80.00
	1838/7E	—	8.00	16.50	35.00	80.00
	1838E	—	6.00	12.00	25.00	60.00
	1838M	—	30.00	60.00	100.00	225.00
	1839A	—	5.00	10.00	20.00	45.00
	1839B	—	8.00	18.00	35.00	70.00
	1839C	.220	15.00	30.00	60.00	120.00
	1839E	—	4.00	9.00	20.00	60.00
	1840A	—	2.50	4.00	8.00	30.00
	1840C	1.122	3.00	7.00	15.00	35.00
	1840E	—	10.00	20.00	40.00	80.00
	1840M	—	25.00	50.00	90.00	160.00
	1841A	—	2.50	4.00	8.00	30.00
	1841C	2.543	5.00	10.00	20.00	45.00
	1841E	—	4.00	9.00	20.00	60.00
	1842A	—	2.50	5.00	10.00	35.00
	1842C	.644	5.00	10.00	20.00	45.00
	1842E	—	12.00	25.00	50.00	100.00
	1842M	—	10.00	20.00	40.00	80.00
	1843A	—	20.00	40.00	70.00	130.00
	1843C	1.257	5.00	10.00	20.00	45.00
	1843E	—	5.00	15.00	30.00	80.00
	1843M	—	5.00	10.00	20.00	45.00
	1844A	—	2.50	4.00	8.00	30.00
	1844C	1.492	5.00	10.00	20.00	45.00
	1844E	—	4.00	9.00	20.00	80.00
	1844M	—	7.00	15.00	30.00	60.00
	1845A	—	2.50	5.00	10.00	35.00
	1845C	1.461	3.00	6.00	14.00	35.00
	1845E	—	9.00	18.00	35.00	90.00
	1845M	—	7.00	15.00	30.00	60.00
	1846A	—	2.50	5.00	10.00	35.00
	1846C	1.549	3.00	6.00	14.00	35.00
	1846/5E	—	15.00	35.00	60.00	135.00
	1846E	—	13.50	27.50	50.00	120.00
	1846M	—	7.00	15.00	35.00	70.00
	1847A	—	2.50	4.00	8.00	30.00
	1847C	1.528	3.00	6.00	15.00	35.00
	1847E	—	7.00	15.00	30.00	70.00
	1847M	—	14.00	30.00	60.00	100.00
	1848A	13.632	2.50	4.00	8.00	30.00
	1848C	2.241	3.00	6.00	10.00	30.00
	1848E	—	12.00	25.00	45.00	100.00
2209	1848GM					
		7,799	125.00	250.00	350.00	800.00

NOTE: The above issue was struck in Mantua by the Austrian garrison under General Josef Radetzky during the siege of March 18-22, 1848 by Italian rebels.

KM#	Date	Mintage	Fine	VF	XF	Unc
2210	1852A	—	25.00	50.00	100.00	200.00
	1852C	.114	60.00	100.00	200.00	400.00

4.3200 g, .900 SILVER, .1250 oz ASW

KM#	Date	Mintage	Fine	VF	XF	Unc
2211	1852A	—	4.00	8.00	18.00	30.00
	1852B	4.926	5.00	8.00	15.00	32.00
	1852C	1.687	50.00	100.00	150.00	325.00
	1852E	—	75.00	150.00	275.00	650.00
	1853A	—	4.00	8.00	18.00	35.00
	1853C	1.590	5.50	11.00	22.00	45.00
	1853E	—	12.50	25.00	50.00	90.00
	1854A	—	4.00	8.00	18.00	30.00
	1854B	2.287	5.00	8.00	18.00	40.00
	1854C	2.098	6.50	13.00	25.00	50.00
	1854E	—	10.00	20.00	40.00	75.00
	1855A	—	4.00	8.00	18.00	35.00
	1855B	2.198	5.00	8.00	15.00	30.00
	1855C	1.904	10.00	20.00	30.00	47.50
	1855E	—	10.00	20.00	35.00	65.00
	1856A	—	20.00	35.00	50.00	100.00
	1856B	3.654	5.00	8.00	15.00	30.00
	1856C	.048	35.00	75.00	115.00	225.00
	1856E	—	10.00	20.00	37.50	65.00
	1869B	3.224	5.00	8.00	15.00	30.00
	1870B	9.487	5.00	8.00	15.00	30.00
	1871B	4.092	5.00	8.00	15.00	30.00
	1872B	.335	5.00	8.00	15.00	30.00
	1873B	1.286	5.00	8.00	15.00	30.00

2.6667 g, .500 SILVER, .0429 oz ASW

KM#	Date	Mintage	Fine	VF	XF	Unc
2212	1868	30.000	1.00	2.00	5.00	16.00
	1869	30.000	1.00	2.00	4.00	14.00
	1870	30.000	1.00	2.00	4.00	12.00
	1872	.576	15.00	30.00	55.00	125.00

1/4 FLORIN

5.3450 g, .520 SILVER, .0893 oz ASW

KM#	Date	Mintage	Fine	VF	XF	Unc
2213	1857A	—	7.50	15.00	25.00	40.00
	1857B	—	12.00	22.50	37.50	60.00
	1857E	—	35.00	70.00	100.00	140.00
	1857M	—	50.00	75.00	125.00	250.00
	1857V	—	22.00	40.00	60.00	140.00
	1858A	31.197	4.50	9.00	15.00	25.00
	1858B	2.982	6.50	13.00	25.00	50.00
	1858E					
		Inc. Ab.	6.50	13.00	20.00	35.00
	1858M					
		Inc. Ab.	25.00	45.00	80.00	160.00
	1859M	27.415	45.00	75.00	115.00	200.00

KM#	Date	Mintage	Fine	VF	XF	Unc
2214	1859A	27.415	3.00	7.00	15.00	25.00
	1859B	13.109	3.00	6.00	10.00	25.00
	1859E	—	4.00	8.00	15.00	25.00
	1859M	—	30.00	60.00	125.00	300.00
	1859V	—	9.00	20.00	40.00	80.00
	1860A	—	11.50	23.00	40.00	55.00
2214	1860B	21.247	2.00	4.00	6.50	20.00
	1860E	—	35.00	60.00	90.00	180.00
	1860V	—	10.00	20.00	40.00	80.00
	1861A	—	3.00	7.00	15.00	40.00
	1861B	1.656	30.00	50.00	80.00	120.00
	1861E	—	90.00	180.00	250.00	425.00
	1861V	—	15.00	40.00	70.00	150.00
	1862A	—	3.00	7.00	15.00	40.00
	1862B	2.796	7.50	15.00	25.00	75.00
	1862E	—	8.00	16.00	30.00	75.00
	1862V	—	10.00	20.00	40.00	90.00
	1863A	—	15.00	35.00	60.00	120.00
	1863V	.800	17.50	35.00	60.00	140.00
	1864A	4.843	3.00	7.00	15.00	30.00
	1864V	.165	17.50	30.00	50.00	120.00
	1865A	.080	27.50	50.00	80.00	135.00

Obv: Head of Franz Joseph I right w/heavier side whiskers. Rev: Eagle, value below.

KM#	Date	Mintage	Fine	VF	XF	Unc
2215	1866A	—	150.00	250.00	400.00	850.00
	1866V	—	120.00	225.00	400.00	950.00

Rev. leg: HUNGAR, BOHEM. GAL. - LOD. ILL. . .

KM#	Date	Mintage	Fine	VF	XF	Unc
2216	1867A	—	75.00	150.00	250.00	500.00
	1868A	—	65.00	110.00	200.00	315.00
	1869A	—	55.00	90.00	150.00	250.00
	1870A	7,956	120.00	200.00	400.00	700.00
	1871A	—	100.00	175.00	300.00	600.00
2217	1872	.100	50.00	100.00	200.00	375.00
	1873	.050	40.00	75.00	150.00	300.00
	1874	.100	80.00	150.00	250.00	425.00
	1875	.020	100.00	250.00	350.00	550.00

30 KREUZER

COPPER

KM#	Date	Mintage	Fine	VF	XF	Unc
2149	1807A	—	4.00	8.00	16.00	45.00
	1807B	15.787	5.00	10.00	25.00	70.00
	1807B (error) inverted C in ERBLAENDISCH					
		—	40.00	70.00	120.00	250.00
	1807E	—	15.00	30.00	60.00	175.00
	1807G	—	12.00	25.00	50.00	150.00
	1807S	—	4.00	8.00	16.00	45.00

NOTE: The above 5 issues struck until 1811.

FLORIN

12.3400 g, .900 SILVER, .3571 oz ASW

KM#	Date	Mintage	Fine	VF	XF	Unc
2219	1857A	—	20.00	35.00	70.00	150.00
	1857B	—	100.00	210.00	350.00	600.00
	1857E	—	100.00	225.00	375.00	675.00
	1857V	—	135.00	240.00	400.00	775.00
	1858A	—	7.50	15.00	22.50	35.00
	1858B	1.920	9.00	18.00	27.50	45.00
	1858E	—	15.00	25.00	40.00	75.00
	1858M	—	20.00	45.00	90.00	200.00
	1858V	—	14.00	30.00	60.00	120.00
	1859A	—	5.00	7.00	14.00	30.00
	1859B	7.537	6.00	11.00	25.00	40.00
	1859E	—	10.00	20.00	35.00	60.00
	1859M	—	12.00	18.00	45.00	125.00
	1859V	—	12.50	25.00	45.00	90.00
	1860A	—	3.00	5.00	10.00	25.00
	1860B	1.883	12.50	25.00	40.00	70.00

KM#	Date	Mintage	Fine	VF	XF	Unc
2219	1860E	—	10.00	20.00	35.00	50.00
	1860V	—	17.50	30.00	60.00	120.00
	1861A	—	3.00	5.00	10.00	25.00
	1861B	.815	75.00	150.00	300.00	500.00
	1861E	—	15.00	30.00	60.00	120.00
	1861V	—	20.00	35.00	75.00	150.00
	1862A	—	6.00	10.00	15.00	27.50
	1862B	.314	11.00	25.00	50.00	90.00
	1862E	—	60.00	150.00	225.00	450.00
	1862V	—	25.00	60.00	95.00	190.00
	1863A	—	7.00	12.00	17.50	35.00
	1863B	.287	17.50	35.00	60.00	100.00
	1863E	—	17.50	32.50	65.00	95.00
	1863V	—	17.50	37.50	65.00	130.00
	1864A	—	15.00	30.00	50.00	120.00
	1864B	.340	40.00	75.00	140.00	350.00
	1864E	.150	40.00	100.00	175.00	275.00
	1864V	.130	55.00	110.00	200.00	400.00
	1865A	—	15.00	30.00	50.00	120.00
	1865B	.291	20.00	35.00	65.00	110.00
	1865E	—	15.00	32.50	70.00	100.00
	1865V	.031	120.00	240.00	400.00	675.00

NOTE: Varieties exist.

Obv: Head of Franz Joseph I right w/heavier side whiskers. Rev: Eagle, value below.

KM#	Date	Mintage	Fine	VF	XF	Unc
2220	1866A	—	25.00	50.00	85.00	150.00
	1866B	.359	27.50	60.00	90.00	150.00
	1866E	—	70.00	150.00	250.00	450.00
	1866V	—	80.00	150.00	250.00	450.00

Rev. leg: HUNGAR, BOHEN. GAL. - LOD. ILL. . .

KM#	Date	Mintage	Fine	VF	XF	Unc
2221	1867A	—	25.00	40.00	80.00	150.00
	1867B	.714	15.00	30.00	50.00	85.00
	1867E	—	150.00	250.00	400.00	650.00
	1868A	—	30.00	50.00	90.00	160.00
	1869A	—	22.50	35.00	70.00	150.00
	1870A	—	15.00	30.00	50.00	90.00
	1871A	—	12.50	25.00	40.00	70.00
	1872A	—	150.00	250.00	400.00	800.00

KM#	Date	Mintage	Fine	VF	XF	Unc
2222	1872	4.725	12.50	25.00	40.00	100.00
	1873	7.880	8.00	16.00	30.00	75.00
	1874	2.479	22.50	40.00	70.00	100.00
	1875/3	5.053	—	—	—	—
	1875	Inc. Ab.	6.00	10.00	15.00	30.00
	1876	7.283	6.00	9.00	14.00	27.50
	1877	13.963	5.00	8.00	13.00	25.00
	1878	18.963	5.00	8.00	13.00	25.00
	1878 plain edge	—	—	—	—	—
	1879	37.485	5.00	8.00	13.00	25.00
	1880	6.505	7.50	12.00	20.00	35.00
	1881	6.128	7.50	12.00	20.00	35.00
	1882	5.476	9.00	15.00	25.00	45.00
	1883	6.036	7.00	10.00	14.00	25.00
	1884	4.303	7.00	10.00	14.00	25.00
	1885	3.395	7.00	12.00	16.00	25.00
	1886	6.710	6.00	10.00	14.00	25.00
	1887	5.692	6.00	10.00	14.00	25.00
	1888	6.572	6.00	10.00	14.00	25.00
	1889	5.053	6.00	10.00	14.00	25.00
	1890	4.164	6.00	10.00	14.00	25.00
	1891	4.235	6.00	10.00	14.00	25.00
	1892	2.504	10.00	15.00	25.00	50.00

1/2 THALER

14.0300 g, .833 SILVER, .3757 oz ASW
Obv. leg: FRANCISCVS II. D. G. R. IMP. . .

KM#	Date	Mintage	Fine	VF	XF	Unc
2149	1801A	—	60.00	100.00	150.00	225.00
	1802A	—	60.00	100.00	150.00	225.00
	1803A	—	100.00	175.00	275.00	350.00
	1804A	—	60.00	100.00	150.00	225.00

NOTE: Earlier dates (1792-1800) exist for this type.

Obv. leg: FRANCISCVS II. D. G. ROM ET. . .

KM#	Date	Mintage	Fine	VF	XF	Unc
2150	1804A	—	—	—	Rare	—
	1805A	—	150.00	250.00	400.00	750.00
	1805V	—	—	—	—	—
	1806A	—	120.00	225.00	375.00	700.00

Obv. leg: FRANCISCVS I. D. G. AVSTRIAE. . .
Rev. leg:. . . D. LO. SAL. WIRC.

KM#	Date	Mintage	Fine	VF	XF	Unc
2151	1807A	—	—	—	Rare	—
	1808A	—	125.00	200.00	400.00	675.00
	1809A	—	125.00	200.00	400.00	675.00
	1809C	—	150.00	225.00	450.00	750.00
	1810A	—	150.00	225.00	450.00	750.00

Rev. leg:. . . LO: WI: ET IN. FR: DVX

KM#	Date	Mintage	Fine	VF	XF	Unc
2152	1811A	2,186	60.00	100.00	150.00	250.00
	1812A	1,930	65.00	110.00	175.00	275.00
	1813A	1,718	65.00	110.00	175.00	275.00
	1814A	1,533	50.00	80.00	125.00	225.00
	1815A	7,849	30.00	50.00	90.00	150.00
	1815B	.057	40.00	70.00	130.00	200.00

Rev. leg:. . . GAL. LOD. IL. REX. A. A.

KM#	Date	Mintage	Fine	VF	XF	Unc
2153	1817A	.012	40.00	70.00	115.00	175.00
	1818A	3,695	50.00	80.00	125.00	185.00
	1818B	—	50.00	80.00	125.00	185.00
	1818V	—	35.00	60.00	100.00	150.00
	1819A	—	40.00	65.00	110.00	165.00
	1819B	.015	—	—	Rare	—
	1819C	—	45.00	75.00	125.00	185.00
	1819E	—	—	—	Rare	—
	1819G	—	50.00	80.00	135.00	200.00
	1820A	—	40.00	70.00	115.00	175.00
	1820B	.023	—	—	Rare	—
	1820C	—	40.00	70.00	115.00	175.00
	1820E	—	50.00	80.00	125.00	185.00
	1820G	—	—	—	Rare	—
	1821A	—	40.00	70.00	115.00	175.00
	1821B	9,650	40.00	70.00	115.00	175.00
	1821C	—	35.00	60.00	100.00	150.00
	1821E	—	50.00	80.00	125.00	185.00
	1821G	—	50.00	80.00	125.00	185.00
	1821V	—	—	—	Rare	—
	1822A	—	35.00	60.00	100.00	150.00
	1822B	.013	—	—	Rare	—
	1822C	—	40.00	70.00	115.00	175.00
	1822E	—	50.00	80.00	125.00	185.00
	1822G	—	50.00	80.00	125.00	185.00
	1823A	—	35.00	60.00	100.00	150.00
	1823B	.015	50.00	80.00	125.00	185.00
	1823C	—	50.00	80.00	125.00	185.00
	1823E	—	50.00	80.00	125.00	185.00
	1823G	—	35.00	65.00	110.00	165.00
	1824A	—	35.00	60.00	100.00	150.00
	1824B	.013	40.00	70.00	115.00	175.00
	1824C	—	30.00	55.00	100.00	135.00
	1824G	—	65.00	115.00	150.00	225.00

Obv: Bust w/short hair.

KM#	Date	Mintage	Fine	VF	XF	Unc
2154	1825A	—	50.00	80.00	125.00	185.00
	1825B	.015	50.00	80.00	125.00	185.00
	1825C	—	50.00	80.00	125.00	185.00
	1826A	—	30.00	50.00	80.00	125.00
	1826B	.013	40.00	70.00	115.00	175.00
	1826C	—	35.00	60.00	100.00	150.00
	1826G	—	80.00	150.00	250.00	450.00
	1827A	—	25.00	40.00	60.00	120.00
	1827B	5,230	—	—	Rare	—
	1827C	—	60.00	100.00	175.00	250.00
	1828A	—	30.00	55.00	85.00	130.00
	1829A	—	30.00	50.00	80.00	125.00
	1830A	—	25.00	45.00	75.00	112.00
	1830E	—	—	—	Rare	—

Obv: Ribbons on wreath forward across neck.

KM#	Date	Mintage	Fine	VF	XF	Unc
2155	1831A	—	60.00	100.00	165.00	225.00

KM#	Date	Mintage	Fine	VF	XF	Unc
2156	1832A	—	40.00	75.00	125.00	200.00
	1832A plain edge	—	—	—	—	—
	1833A	—	40.00	75.00	125.00	200.00
	1833A plain edge	—	—	—	—	—
	1833E	—	—	—	Rare	—
	1834A	—	40.00	75.00	125.00	200.00
	1835A	—	35.00	60.00	100.00	175.00

Obv: Head of Ferdinand I right. Rev: Eagle.

KM#	Date	Mintage	Fine	VF	XF	Unc
2224	1835A	—	250.00	400.00	600.00	1200.
	1835C	—	—	—	Rare	—
	1836A	—	250.00	400.00	600.00	1200.
	1836C	—	275.00	550.00	1100.	1700.

KM#	Date	Mintage	Fine	VF	XF	Unc
2225	1837A	—	50.00	100.00	200.00	400.00
	1838A	—	50.00	100.00	200.00	400.00
	1839A	—	45.00	90.00	175.00	350.00
	1840A	—	30.00	65.00	135.00	275.00
	1841A	—	45.00	90.00	175.00	350.00
	1842A	—	40.00	80.00	160.00	300.00
	1843A	—	40.00	80.00	160.00	300.00
	1844A	—	45.00	90.00	175.00	350.00
	1845A	—	40.00	80.00	160.00	300.00
	1846A	—	30.00	65.00	135.00	275.00
	1847A	—	30.00	65.00	135.00	275.00
	1848A	3,964	50.00	100.00	225.00	500.00

KM#	Date	Mintage	Fine	VF	XF	Unc
2226	1848GM	3,947	275.00	450.00	750.00	1500.

NOTE: The above issue was struck in Mantua by the Austrian garrison under General Josef Radetzky during the siege of March 18-22, 1848 by Italian rebels.

Obv: Young head of Franz Joseph I left.

KM#	Date	Mintage	Fine	VF	XF	Unc
2227	1848A	—	700.00	1450.	2000.	3250.
	1849A	—	700.00	1450.	2000.	3250.
	1850A	—	850.00	1750.	2250.	3750.
	1851A	—	650.00	1250.	1800.	3000.

.900 SILVER
Obv: Young head of Franz Joseph I right.
Edge lettering: VIRIBVS VNITIS.

KM#	Date	Mintage	Fine	VF	XF	Unc
2228.1	1852A	—	125.00	250.00	400.00	800.00
	1853A	—	200.00	375.00	500.00	1000.
	1854A	—	200.00	375.00	500.00	1000.
	1855A	—	150.00	325.00	450.00	950.00
	1856A	—	150.00	325.00	425.00	900.00

Edge lettering: VIRIBUS-VIRIBUS

KM#	Date	Mintage	Fine	VF	XF	Unc
2228.2	1856A	—	150.00	275.00	450.00	750.00

2 FLORINS

24.6900 g, .900 SILVER, .7145 oz ASW

KM#	Date	Mintage	Fine	VF	XF	Unc
2230	1859A	—	75.00	125.00	175.00	275.00
	1859B	.511	40.00	70.00	120.00	200.00
	1860A	—	550.00	950.00	1500.	2250.
	1860V	—	175.00	350.00	700.00	1100.
	1861A	—	—	—	—	—
	1862A	.015	100.00	180.00	300.00	450.00
	1863A	.024	50.00	90.00	150.00	250.00
	1864A	.031	50.00	90.00	150.00	250.00
	1865A	.072	50.00	90.00	150.00	250.00
	1866A	—	— Reported, not confirmed			

KM#	Date	Mintage	Fine	VF	XF	Unc
2231	1866A	.011	175.00	350.00	700.00	1100.

KM#	Date	Mintage	Fine	VF	XF	Unc
2232	1867A	.045	50.00	100.00	150.00	250.00
	1868A	—	50.00	100.00	150.00	250.00
	1869A	—	40.00	75.00	125.00	200.00
	1870A	—	40.00	75.00	125.00	200.00
	1871A	—	50.00	100.00	150.00	250.00
	1872A	—	75.00	150.00	250.00	375.00

KM#	Date	Mintage	Fine	VF	XF	Unc
2233	1872	.045	35.00	65.00	110.00	200.00
	1873	.099	35.00	65.00	120.00	225.00
	1874	.079	25.00	50.00	80.00	150.00
	1875	.106	30.00	60.00	85.00	150.00
	1876	.092	35.00	65.00	90.00	170.00
	1877	.105	25.00	55.00	80.00	150.00
	1878	.147	30.00	60.00	80.00	150.00
	1879	.501	25.00	50.00	70.00	150.00
	1880	.083	30.00	60.00	80.00	140.00
	1881	.104	30.00	60.00	80.00	140.00
	1882	.121	25.00	50.00	70.00	130.00
	1883	.070	35.00	65.00	95.00	160.00
	1884	.087	25.00	50.00	70.00	130.00
	1885	.078	25.00	50.00	70.00	140.00
	1886	.093	25.00	50.00	70.00	140.00
	1887	.117	25.00	50.00	70.00	140.00
	1888	.073	25.00	50.00	70.00	140.00
	1889	.147	35.00	65.00	90.00	170.00
	1890	.104	35.00	65.00	90.00	150.00
	1891	.117	35.00	65.00	90.00	150.00
	1892	.032	30.00	60.00	70.00	140.00

THALER

28.0600 g, .833 SILVER, .7514 oz ASW
Obv. leg: FRANCISCVS II. D.G.R. IMP. S.A. . .

KM#	Date	Mintage	Fine	VF	XF	Unc
2158	1801A	—	85.00	175.00	325.00	650.00
	1802A	—	110.00	225.00	450.00	850.00
	1803A	—	125.00	250.00	475.00	950.00
	1804A	—	75.00	150.00	275.00	550.00

NOTE: Earlier dates (1792-1800) exist for this type.

Obv. leg: FRANCISCVS II D.G. ROM. ET. . .

KM#	Date	Mintage	Fine	VF	XF	Unc
2159	1804A	—	60.00	125.00	250.00	475.00
2159	1805A	—	60.00	125.00	250.00	475.00
	1806A	—	60.00	125.00	250.00	475.00

Obv. leg: FRANCISCVS I.D.G. AVSTRIAE. . .
Rev. leg:. . . D. LO. SAL. WIRC.

KM#	Date	Mintage	Fine	VF	XF	Unc
2160	1806A	—	—	—	Rare	—
	1807A	—	40.00	80.00	160.00	325.00
	1808A	—	40.00	80.00	160.00	325.00
	1809A	—	40.00	80.00	160.00	325.00
	1809B (restrike 1841)					
	1809C	—	35.00	70.00	140.00	275.00
	1810A	—	30.00	60.00	120.00	150.00

NOTE: 1810A exists as a klippe.

Rev. leg:. . . LO: WI: ET IN. FR: DVX.

KM#	Date	Mintage	Fine	VF	XF	Unc
2161	1811A	—	30.00	65.00	130.00	250.00
	1811C	—	30.00	65.00	130.00	250.00
	1812A	—	175.00	350.00	725.00	1100.
	1812C	—	50.00	100.00	200.00	400.00
	1813A	—	50.00	100.00	200.00	400.00
	1813C	—	50.00	100.00	200.00	400.00
	1813G	—	55.00	100.00	200.00	325.00
	1814A	—	25.00	50.00	100.00	200.00
	1814B	—	—	—	Rare	—
	1814C	—	40.00	80.00	160.00	325.00
	1814G	—	55.00	100.00	200.00	325.00
	1815A	—	25.00	50.00	100.00	200.00
	1815B	—	50.00	110.00	225.00	325.00
	1815C	—	35.00	75.00	150.00	250.00

Rev. leg:. . . GAL. LOD. IL. REX. A. A.

KM#	Date	Mintage	Fine	VF	XF	Unc
2162	1817A	—	25.00	50.00	100.00	250.00
	1818A	—	25.00	50.00	100.00	250.00
	1818B	—	30.00	55.00	110.00	200.00
	1818V	—	35.00	70.00	150.00	275.00
	1819A	—	35.00	70.00	135.00	300.00
	1819B	.153	—	—	Rare	—
	1819C	—	35.00	70.00	150.00	275.00
	1819E	—	35.00	70.00	150.00	275.00
	1819G	—	30.00	60.00	125.00	250.00
	1819M	—	45.00	90.00	180.00	300.00
	1820A	—	20.00	40.00	80.00	200.00
	1820B	.250	—	—	Rare	—
	1820C	—	30.00	55.00	100.00	200.00
	1820E	—	50.00	100.00	200.00	325.00
	1820G	—	65.00	130.00	250.00	375.00
	1820M	—	30.00	60.00	125.00	250.00
	1821A	—	25.00	50.00	100.00	250.00
	1821B	.150	20.00	40.00	85.00	150.00
	1821C	—	20.00	40.00	85.00	150.00
	1821E	—	27.50	55.00	125.00	225.00
	1821G	—	25.00	50.00	100.00	200.00
	1821M	—	50.00	100.00	200.00	300.00
	1821V	—	45.00	80.00	175.00	275.00

KM#	Date	Mintage	Fine	VF	XF	Unc
2162	1822A	—	20.00	40.00	80.00	200.00
	1822B	.215	25.00	50.00	100.00	200.00
	1822C	—	25.00	50.00	100.00	200.00
	1822E	—	30.00	60.00	125.00	250.00
	1822G	—	25.00	50.00	100.00	200.00
	1822M	—	50.00	100.00	200.00	400.00
	1822V	—	—	—	Rare	—
	1823A	—	20.00	40.00	80.00	200.00
	1823B	.201	25.00	50.00	100.00	200.00
	1823C	—	35.00	70.00	150.00	275.00
	1823E	—	30.00	60.00	125.00	250.00
	1823G	—	30.00	60.00	125.00	250.00
	1824A	—	25.00	50.00	100.00	250.00
	1824B	.282	25.00	50.00	100.00	200.00
	1824C	—	30.00	60.00	125.00	250.00
	1824E	—	35.00	70.00	150.00	275.00
	1824G	—	30.00	60.00	125.00	250.00

Obv: Bust w/short hair.

KM#	Date	Mintage	Fine	VF	XF	Unc
2163	1824A	—	40.00	80.00	155.00	250.00
	1824C	—	—	—	—	—
	1825A	—	30.00	60.00	125.00	250.00
	1825B	.336	30.00	60.00	125.00	250.00
	1825C	—	35.00	70.00	145.00	270.00
	1825G	—	30.00	60.00	125.00	250.00
	1826A	—	25.00	55.00	100.00	225.00
	1826B	.269	30.00	60.00	125.00	250.00
	1826C	—	30.00	60.00	125.00	250.00
	1826G	—	35.00	70.00	145.00	275.00
	1827A	—	30.00	60.00	125.00	250.00
	1827B	.089	80.00	175.00	325.00	475.00
	1827C	—	25.00	50.00	100.00	200.00
	1828A	—	25.00	50.00	100.00	225.00
	1829A	—	25.00	50.00	100.00	225.00
	1830A	—	20.00	40.00	80.00	175.00
	1830E	—	75.00	150.00	275.00	425.00

Obv: Ribbons on wreath forward across neck.

KM#	Date	Mintage	Fine	VF	XF	Unc
2164	1831A	—	40.00	80.00	175.00	325.00

Obv: Ribbons on wreath hang behind neck.

KM#	Date	Mintage	Fine	VF	XF	Unc
2165	1831A	—	400.00	800.00	1200.	1600.
	1832A	—	40.00	80.00	175.00	325.00
	1833A	—	50.00	100.00	200.00	350.00
	1833A (error) Edge: FUNDAMENIVM	—	100.00	200.00	325.00	525.00
	1833B	—	75.00	150.00	325.00	650.00
	1833E	—	50.00	100.00	200.00	350.00
	1834A	—	42.50	85.00	175.00	325.00
	1835A	—	50.00	100.00	200.00	350.00

Ferdinandus I

Obv: Oval loop in knot of wreath.

KM#	Date	Mintage	Fine	VF	XF	Unc
2238	1835A	—	125.00	250.00	400.00	800.00
	1835C	—	—	—	Rare	—
	1836A	—	75.00	150.00	250.00	500.00
	1836C	—	250.00	400.00	800.00	1500.

Obv: Sharp cornered loop in knot of wreath.

KM#	Date	Mintage	Fine	VF	XF	Unc
2239	1835A	—	375.00	600.00	1100.	1700.

KM#	Date	Mintage	Fine	VF	XF	Unc
2240	1837A	—	50.00	100.00	200.00	350.00
	1837M	—	275.00	500.00	1000.	1700.
	1838A	—	50.00	100.00	200.00	350.00
	1838M	—	550.00	1150.	1750.	2400.
	1839A	—	50.00	100.00	200.00	350.00
	1840A	—	45.00	90.00	175.00	325.00
	1841A	—	40.00	80.00	150.00	275.00
	1842A	—	40.00	80.00	150.00	275.00
	1843A	—	40.00	80.00	150.00	275.00
	1844A	—	40.00	80.00	150.00	275.00
	1845A	—	40.00	80.00	150.00	275.00
	1846A	—	40.00	80.00	150.00	275.00
	1847A	—	40.00	80.00	150.00	275.00
	1848A	.119	30.00	60.00	100.00	225.00

Obv. leg: FRANC.IOS.I.D.G.AVSTR. IMP.HVNG.BOH.REX.
Rev: Similar to KM#2240.

KM#	Date	Mintage	Fine	VF	XF	Unc
2241	1848A	—	500.00	1000.	1500.	2250.
	1849A	—	500.00	1000.	1500.	2250.
	1850A	—	700.00	1350.	1950.	2650.
	1851A	—	500.00	1000.	1500.	2250.

Obv. leg:. . . AVSTRIAE.IMPERATOR.
Rev: Similar to KM#2240.

KM#	Date	Mintage	Fine	VF	XF	Unc
2242	1852A	—	600.00	1250.	2250.	3000.

25.9900 g, .900 SILVER, .7520 oz ASW
Edge lettering: VIRIBVS VNITIS.

KM#	Date	Mintage	Fine	VF	XF	Unc
2243.1	1852A	—	60.00	120.00	225.00	350.00
	1853A	—	45.00	100.00	200.00	300.00
	1853B	—	160.00	275.00	450.00	700.00
	1854A	—	45.00	100.00	200.00	375.00
	1855A	—	40.00	90.00	175.00	325.00
	1856A	—	40.00	90.00	175.00	325.00

Edge lettering: VIRIBUS-VIRIBUS.

KM#	Date	Mintage	Fine	VF	XF	Unc
2243.2	1856A	—	—	—	—	—

(Vereins)

18.5186 g, .900 SILVER, .5359 oz ASW

KM#	Date	Mintage	Fine	VF	XF	Unc
2244	1857A	9.154	15.00	30.00	60.00	100.00
	1857A (restrike 1994-1996 Jablonec Mint)	—	—	—	—	—
	1857B	—	50.00	100.00	200.00	425.00
	1857E	—	40.00	80.00	165.00	325.00
	1857V	—	75.00	150.00	300.00	550.00
	1858A	Inc. Ab.	15.00	30.00	60.00	100.00
	1858B	—	20.00	40.00	80.00	150.00
	1858E	—	50.00	100.00	200.00	425.00
	1858M	—	37.50	75.00	150.00	300.00
	1858V	—	37.50	75.00	150.00	300.00
	1859A	4.949	20.00	40.00	70.00	125.00
	1859B	—	20.00	40.00	80.00	150.00
	1859E	—	40.00	80.00	160.00	350.00
	1859M	—	37.50	75.00	150.00	300.00
	1860A	1.620	20.00	40.00	70.00	150.00
	1860V	.043	37.50	75.00	150.00	300.00
	1861A	3.140	20.00	40.00	70.00	150.00
	1861B	—	20.00	40.00	75.00	150.00
	1861E	—	20.00	40.00	75.00	150.00
	1861V	—	25.00	50.00	100.00	175.00
	1862A	.998	25.00	50.00	90.00	175.00
	1862B	—	25.00	50.00	85.00	175.00
	1862V	—	25.00	50.00	100.00	175.00
	1863A	2.209	20.00	40.00	70.00	125.00
	1863B	—	25.00	50.00	85.00	175.00
	1863E	—	25.00	50.00	90.00	175.00
	1863V	—	25.00	50.00	100.00	175.00
	1864A	2.636	17.50	35.00	65.00	110.00

KM#	Date	Mintage	Fine	VF	XF	Unc
2244	1864B	—	27.50	55.00	100.00	200.00
	1864E	.556	17.50	35.00	65.00	125.00
	1864V	.107	62.50	125.00	250.00	450.00
	1865A	2.085	17.50	35.00	65.00	110.00
	1865B	—	20.00	40.00	75.00	125.00
	1865E	—	17.50	35.00	60.00	100.00
	1865V	—	75.00	150.00	275.00	525.00

NOTE: Varieties in asterisk size on edge exist on 1863 and 1864 dated coins.

Obv: Head w/heavier whiskers.

KM#	Date	Mintage	Fine	VF	XF	Unc
2245	1866A	1.236	25.00	50.00	90.00	150.00
	1866B	Inc. Ab.	35.00	60.00	100.00	175.00
	1866E	Inc. Ab.	40.00	80.00	150.00	275.00
	1867A	.850	30.00	60.00	110.00	200.00
	1867B	Inc. Ab.	40.00	85.00	150.00	275.00
	1867E	Inc. Ab.	40.00	80.00	150.00	275.00
	1868E	.168	— Reported, not confirmed			

2 THALER

37.0371 g, .900 SILVER, 1.0718 oz ASW
Opening of Vienna-Trieste Railway
Obv: Wreath tips point between "KA" of "KAISER."

KM#	Date	Mintage	Fine	VF	XF	Unc
2246.1 (M10.1)	1857A	1,644	400.00	800.00	1500.	2250.

NOTE: Varieties exist.

Obv: Wreath tips point between "AI" of "KAISER."

KM#	Date	Mintage	Fine	VF	XF	Unc
2246.2 (M10.2)	1857A	Inc.Ab.	400.00	800.00	1500.	2250.

KM#	Date	Mintage	Fine	VF	XF	Unc
2249	1865A	7,425	350.00	600.00	1000.	1800.

KM#	Date	Mintage	Fine	VF	XF	Unc
2250	1866A	.010	175.00	350.00	500.00	850.00
	1867A	8,300	175.00	350.00	500.00	850.00

1/2 KRONE

5.5555 g, .900 GOLD, .1608 oz AGW

KM#	Date	Mintage	Fine	VF	XF	Unc
2251	1858A	.020	350.00	650.00	950.00	1400.
	1858E	.025	300.00	525.00	800.00	1200.
	1858V	947 pcs.	1300.	1800.	2250.	3000.
	1859A	.402	275.00	600.00	800.00	1300.
	1859B	4,376	350.00	700.00	1100.	1600.
	1859E	.017	350.00	700.00	1100.	1600.
	1860A	.201	175.00	325.00	575.00	850.00
	1860B	.043	325.00	600.00	875.00	1400.
	1861A	2,868	525.00	875.00	1250.	1800.
	1861B	.018	350.00	700.00	1100.	1600.
	1861E	.055	275.00	500.00	700.00	1150.
	1863A	40 pcs.	2000.	4000.	8000.	10,000.
	1864A	980 pcs.	1000.	1500.	2000.	2500.
	1865A	2,690	750.00	1250.	1750.	2250.

KM#	Date	Mintage	Fine	VF	XF	Unc
2252	1866A	4,000	425.00	700.00	1100.	1600.

KRONE

11.1111 g, .900 GOLD, .3215 oz AGW

KM#	Date	Mintage	Fine	VF	XF	Unc
2253	1858A	.047	450.00	800.00	1150.	2250.
	1858E	.031	350.00	575.00	850.00	1500.
	1858V	600 pcs.	1750.	2500.	3500.	4500.
	1859A	.010	350.00	650.00	825.00	1750.
	1859M	3,974	650.00	1250.	1750.	3000.
	1859V	1,885	1250.	2000.	2750.	3500.
	1860A	557 pcs.	875.00	1400.	1750.	3000.
	1861A	2,010	650.00	1100.	1500.	2750.
	1863A	1,000	700.00	1250.	1750.	3000.
	1864A	1,530	650.00	1100.	1400.	2750.
	1865A	2,800	650.00	1100.	1400.	2750.

Obv: Large bust.

KM#	Date	Mintage	Fine	VF	XF	Unc
2255	1866A	3,000	875.00	1500.	2000.	3500.

TRADE COINAGE

4 FLORIN-10 FRANCS

3.2258 g, .900 GOLD, .0933 oz AGW

KM#	Date	Mintage	Fine	VF	XF	Unc
2260	1870	7,440	60.00	100.00	160.00	250.00
	1871	6,665	60.00	100.00	160.00	250.00
	1872	4,960	60.00	90.00	140.00	225.00
	1877	3,004	80.00	160.00	250.00	350.00
	1878	6,820	55.00	90.00	140.00	225.00
	1881	8,370	55.00	90.00	140.00	200.00
	1883	3,720	65.00	120.00	180.00	325.00
	1884	7,518	55.00	90.00	115.00	200.00
	1885	.038	55.00	60.00	110.00	165.00
	1888	4,145	55.00	100.00	140.00	250.00
	1889	5,707	55.00	90.00	135.00	225.00
	1890	2,947	65.00	120.00	180.00	300.00
	1891	.011	55.00	65.00	90.00	175.00
	1892	(restrike)	—	—	BV	55.00

DUCAT

3.4909 g, .986 GOLD, .1106 oz AGW
Obv: Bust right, leg: FRANC. II. D. G. R. . .
Rev: Crowned imperial eagle.

KM#	Date	Mintage	Fine	VF	XF	Unc
2166	1801A	—	120.00	200.00	290.00	450.00
	1802A	—	110.00	180.00	260.00	400.00
	1802B	—	100.00	160.00	250.00	375.00
	1802G	—	110.00	170.00	250.00	375.00
	1803A	—	120.00	200.00	290.00	450.00
	1804A	—	110.00	180.00	260.00	400.00
	1804E	—	100.00	160.00	250.00	375.00

NOTE: Earlier dates (1792-1800) exist for this type.

Obv. leg: FRANCISCVS II D. G. ROM. . .
Rev. leg:. . . D. LOTH. VEN. SAL.

KM#	Date	Mintage	Fine	VF	XF	Unc
2167	1804A	—	325.00	650.00	1000.	1750.
	1805A	—	325.00	650.00	1000.	1750.
	1806A	—	300.00	600.00	900.	1600.
	1806B	—	325.00	650.00	1000.	1750.
	1806C	—	750.00	1500.	2250.	3000.
	1806D	—	325.00	650.00	1000.	1750.

Rev. leg:. . . D. LO. SAL. WIRC.

KM#	Date	Mintage	Fine	VF	XF	Unc
2168	1806A	—	160.00	250.00	375.00	550.00
	1806D	—	750.00	1250.	1500.	2000.
	1807A	—	125.00	200.00	275.00	450.00
	1807C	—	180.00	275.00	425.00	650.00
	1808A	—	125.00	200.00	275.00	450.00
	1808D	—	—	—	Rare	—
	1809A	—	125.00	200.00	275.00	450.00
	1809B	—	160.00	250.00	375.00	575.00
	1809D	—	500.00	700.00	950.00	1200.
	1810A	—	125.00	200.00	275.00	450.00

Rev. leg:. . . LO: WI: ET IN. FR: DVX.

KM#	Date	Mintage	Fine	VF	XF	Unc
2169	1811A	—	80.00	120.00	200.00	300.00
	1811B	—	80.00	120.00	200.00	300.00
	1812A	—	80.00	120.00	200.00	300.00
	1812B	—	80.00	120.00	200.00	300.00
	1812G	—	—	—	Rare	—
	1813A	—	100.00	140.00	225.00	325.00
	1813B	—	80.00	120.00	200.00	300.00
	1813E	—	100.00	140.00	225.00	325.00
	1813G	—	—	—	Rare	—
	1814A	—	80.00	120.00	200.00	300.00
	1814B	—	100.00	140.00	225.00	325.00
	1814E	—	100.00	140.00	225.00	325.00
	1814G	—	—	—	Rare	—
	1815A	—	80.00	120.00	200.00	300.00
	1815B	—	80.00	120.00	200.00	300.00
	1815E	—	80.00	120.00	200.00	300.00
	1815G	—	100.00	140.00	225.00	325.00

Rev. leg:. . . GAL. LOB. IL. REX. A. A.

KM#	Date	Mintage	Fine	VF	XF	Unc
2170	1816A	—	80.00	120.00	200.00	300.00
	1817A	—	80.00	120.00	200.00	300.00
	1818A	—	80.00	120.00	200.00	300.00
	1818B	—	80.00	120.00	200.00	300.00
	1818E	—	80.00	120.00	200.00	300.00
	1818G	—	100.00	140.00	225.00	325.00
	1819A	—	80.00	120.00	200.00	300.00
	1819B	—	100.00	140.00	225.00	325.00
	1819E	—	80.00	120.00	200.00	300.00
	1819G	—	100.00	140.00	225.00	325.00
	1819V	—	350.00	525.00	700.00	1050.
	1820A	—	80.00	120.00	200.00	300.00
	1820B	—	80.00	120.00	200.00	300.00
	1820E	—	80.00	120.00	200.00	300.00
	1820G	—	80.00	120.00	200.00	300.00
	1821A	—	80.00	120.00	200.00	300.00
	1821B	—	80.00	120.00	200.00	300.00
	1821E	—	80.00	120.00	200.00	300.00
	1821G	—	80.00	120.00	200.00	300.00
	1822A	—	80.00	120.00	200.00	300.00
	1822B	—	80.00	120.00	200.00	300.00
	1822E	—	80.00	120.00	200.00	300.00
	1822G	—	80.00	120.00	200.00	300.00
	1823A	—	80.00	120.00	200.00	300.00
	1823B	—	80.00	120.00	200.00	300.00
	1823E	—	80.00	120.00	200.00	300.00
	1823G	—	80.00	120.00	200.00	300.00
	1824A	—	80.00	120.00	200.00	300.00
	1824B	—	80.00	120.00	200.00	300.00
	1824E	—	80.00	120.00	200.00	300.00
	1824G	—	100.00	140.00	225.00	325.00
	1824V	—	250.00	375.00	550.00	800.00

Obv: Ribbons on wreath forward across neck.

KM#	Date	Mintage	Fine	VF	XF	Unc
2171	1825A	—	80.00	120.00	200.00	300.00
	1825B	—	100.00	130.00	225.00	325.00
	1825E	—	110.00	160.00	250.00	375.00
	1825G	—	—	—	—	—
	1826A	—	80.00	120.00	200.00	300.00
	1826B	—	110.00	160.00	250.00	375.00
	1826E	—	90.00	130.00	200.00	300.00
	1826G	—	—	—	Rare	—
	1827A	—	80.00	120.00	200.00	300.00
	1827B	—	110.00	160.00	250.00	375.00
	1827E	—	110.00	160.00	250.00	375.00
	1828A	—	100.00	140.00	225.00	325.00
	1828B	—	80.00	120.00	200.00	300.00
	1828E	—	80.00	120.00	200.00	300.00
	1829A	—	80.00	120.00	180.00	275.00
	1829B	—	80.00	120.00	200.00	300.00
	1829E	—	80.00	120.00	200.00	300.00
	1830A	—	80.00	120.00	180.00	275.00
	1830B	—	100.00	130.00	200.00	300.00
	1830E	—	90.00	130.00	200.00	300.00
	1831A	—	1100.	1600.	2400.	3200.

Obv: Ribbons on wreath behind neck.

KM#	Date	Mintage	Fine	VF	XF	Unc
2172	1831A	—	110.00	160.00	250.00	375.00
	1832A	—	100.00	120.00	200.00	300.00
	1832B	—	100.00	120.00	200.00	300.00
	1833A	—	100.00	120.00	200.00	300.00
	1833B	—	100.00	120.00	200.00	300.00
	1833E	—	110.00	160.00	250.00	375.00
	1834A	—	100.00	120.00	200.00	300.00
	1834B	—	100.00	120.00	200.00	300.00
	1834E	—	110.00	160.00	250.00	375.00
	1835A	—	100.00	120.00	200.00	300.00
	1835B	—	100.00	120.00	200.00	300.00
	1835E	—	110.00	160.00	250.00	375.00

Obv. leg:. . . AVSTRIAE IMPERATOR.

KM#	Date	Mintage	Fine	VF	XF	Unc
2261	1835A	—	275.00	500.00	800.00	1200.
	1835E	—	275.00	500.00	800.00	1200.
	1836A	—	160.00	275.00	450.00	650.00
	1836E	—	200.00	325.00	525.00	800.00

Obv. leg: . . . AVSTRI. IMP.

KM#	Date	Mintage	Fine	VF	XF	Unc
2262	1837A	—	60.00	80.00	130.00	200.00
	1837B	—	80.00	115.00	190.00	275.00
	1837E	—	80.00	115.00	190.00	275.00
	1838A	—	60.00	80.00	180.00	275.00
	1838B	—	80.00	115.00	190.00	275.00
	1838E	—	80.00	115.00	190.00	275.00
	1839A	—	60.00	80.00	130.00	200.00
	1839B	—	80.00	115.00	200.00	275.00
	1839E	—	80.00	115.00	200.00	275.00
	1840A	—	60.00	80.00	130.00	200.00
	1840B	—	60.00	80.00	130.00	200.00
	1840E	—	60.00	80.00	140.00	225.00
	1840V	—	475.00	650.00	975.00	1275.
	1841A	—	60.00	80.00	130.00	200.00
	1841B	—	60.00	80.00	110.00	180.00
	1841E	—	60.00	80.00	110.00	180.00
	1841V	—	250.00	350.00	525.00	725.00
	1842A	—	65.00	100.00	160.00	250.00
	1842B	—	100.00	130.00	200.00	350.00
	1842E	—	60.00	80.00	110.00	180.00
	1842V	—	200.00	275.00	700.00	1000.
	1843A	—	60.00	80.00	110.00	180.00
	1843B	—	60.00	80.00	130.00	200.00
	1843E	—	60.00	80.00	130.00	200.00
	1843V	—	200.00	275.00	700.00	1350.
	1844A	—	60.00	80.00	110.00	180.00
	1844B	—	60.00	80.00	110.00	180.00
	1844E	—	60.00	80.00	110.00	180.00
	1844V	—	200.00	275.00	700.00	1350.
	1845A	—	60.00	80.00	110.00	180.00
	1845B	—	60.00	80.00	110.00	180.00
	1845E	—	60.00	80.00	130.00	200.00
	1845V	—	200.00	275.00	700.00	1200.
	1846A	—	60.00	80.00	130.00	200.00
	1846B	—	60.00	80.00	130.00	200.00
	1846E	—	60.00	80.00	130.00	200.00
	1846V	—	200.00	275.00	700.00	1000.
	1847A	—	60.00	80.00	110.00	180.00
	1847B	—	60.00	80.00	110.00	180.00
	1847E	—	80.00	100.00	180.00	250.00
	1847V	—	250.00	350.00	550.00	775.00
	1848A	—	60.00	80.00	110.00	180.00
	1848B	—	60.00	80.00	110.00	180.00
	1848E	—	60.00	80.00	110.00	180.00
	1848V	—	60.00	80.00	110.00	180.00

KM#	Date	Mintage	Fine	VF	XF	Unc
2263	1852A	—	80.00	100.00	160.00	225.00
	1853A	—	90.00	120.00	180.00	250.00
	1853B	.114	90.00	110.00	180.00	250.00
	1853E	—	100.00	130.00	200.00	250.00
	1854A	—	60.00	80.00	120.00	180.00
	1854B	.087	110.00	135.00	225.00	350.00
	1854E	—	100.00	130.00	200.00	250.00
2263	1854V	—	250.00	450.00	800.00	1200.
	1855A	—	60.00	80.00	120.00	180.00
	1855B	.133	160.00	225.00	350.00	550.00
	1855E	—	90.00	110.00	180.00	250.00
	1855V	—	250.00	450.00	800.00	1200.
	1856A	—	60.00	80.00	140.00	200.00
	1856B	.121	80.00	110.00	180.00	250.00
	1856E	—	60.00	80.00	140.00	200.00
	1856V	—	250.00	450.00	800.00	1200.
	1857A	—	60.00	80.00	130.00	180.00
	1857B	.086	60.00	80.00	130.00	200.00
	1857E	—	100.00	140.00	225.00	350.00
	1857V	—	250.00	450.00	800.00	1200.
	1858A	—	60.00	80.00	110.00	160.00
	1858B	.071	100.00	130.00	180.00	250.00
	1858E	—	90.00	110.00	180.00	250.00
	1858M	—	275.00	800.00	1750.	2500.
	1858V	—	250.00	450.00	800.00	1200.
	1859A	—	60.00	80.00	110.00	160.00
	1859B	.034	60.00	80.00	140.00	200.00
	1859E	—	60.00	80.00	110.00	180.00
	1859V	—	250.00	450.00	800.00	1200.

KM#	Date	Mintage	Fine	VF	XF	Unc
2264	1860A	—	70.00	100.00	140.00	225.00
	1860B	.056	80.00	120.00	180.00	275.00
	1860E	—	100.00	140.00	200.00	325.00
	1860V	—	250.00	400.00	800.00	1200.
	1861A	—	60.00	80.00	120.00	200.00
	1861B	.121	60.00	100.00	160.00	250.00
	1861E	—	90.00	120.00	200.00	325.00
	1861V	—	325.00	800.00	1750.	2500.
	1862A	—	60.00	80.00	120.00	225.00
	1862B	.068	60.00	90.00	140.00	225.00
	1862E	—	60.00	100.00	160.00	225.00
	1862V	—	200.00	400.00	800.00	1200.
	1863A	—	60.00	80.00	120.00	225.00
	1863B	.058	60.00	80.00	120.00	225.00
	1863E	—	60.00	80.00	120.00	225.00
	1863V	—	175.00	375.00	600.00	1000.
	1864A	—	60.00	100.00	160.00	250.00
	1864B	.099	75.00	120.00	180.00	275.00
	1864E	—	60.00	100.00	160.00	250.00
	1864V	—	275.00	800.00	1750.	2500.
	1865A	—	60.00	100.00	160.00	250.00
	1865B	.081	60.00	100.00	160.00	250.00
	1865E	—	60.00	100.00	160.00	250.00
	1865V	—	250.00	475.00	800.00	1200.

Obv: Head of Franz Joseph I right w/heavier side whiskers.

KM#	Date	Mintage	Fine	VF	XF	Unc
2265	1866A	—	75.00	115.00	200.00	350.00
	1866B	.076	75.00	140.00	225.00	400.00
	1866E	—	75.00	115.00	200.00	350.00
	1866V	—	275.00	575.00	1100.	1700.

KM#	Date	Mintage	Fine	VF	XF	Unc
2266	1867A	—	60.00	90.00	130.00	180.00
	1867B	.112	60.00	100.00	140.00	200.00
	1867E	—	70.00	110.00	160.00	225.00
	1868A	—	60.00	90.00	130.00	180.00
	1869A	—	60.00	90.00	130.00	180.00
	1870A	—	60.00	90.00	130.00	180.00
	1871A	—	60.00	90.00	130.00	180.00
	1872A	—	60.00	90.00	130.00	180.00

KM#	Date	Mintage	Fine	VF	XF	Unc
2267	1872	.460	60.00	100.00	125.00	175.00
	1873	.516	60.00	100.00	125.00	175.00
	1874	.353	60.00	100.00	125.00	175.00
	1875	.184	60.00	100.00	125.00	175.00
	1876	.680	60.00	80.00	125.00	150.00
	1877	.823	60.00	80.00	125.00	175.00
	1878	.281	60.00	80.00	125.00	175.00
	1879	.362	60.00	80.00	125.00	175.00

KM#	Date	Mintage	Fine	VF	XF	Unc
2267	1880	.341	60.00	100.00	150.00	225.00
	1881	.477	60.00	80.00	125.00	175.00
	1882	.390	60.00	100.00	125.00	175.00
	1883	.409	60.00	100.00	125.00	175.00
	1884	.238	60.00	80.00	125.00	175.00
	1885	.257	60.00	80.00	125.00	150.00
	1886	.291	60.00	80.00	125.00	150.00
	1887	.223	60.00	80.00	100.00	150.00
	1888	.309	60.00	80.00	100.00	150.00
	1889	.335	60.00	80.00	100.00	150.00
	1890	.374	60.00	80.00	100.00	150.00
	1891	.325	60.00	80.00	100.00	150.00
	1892	.361	60.00	80.00	100.00	150.00
	1893	.285	60.00	80.00	100.00	150.00
	1894	.293	60.00	80.00	100.00	150.00
	1895	.330	60.00	80.00	100.00	150.00
	1896	.414	60.00	80.00	100.00	150.00
	1897	.256	60.00	80.00	100.00	150.00
	1898	.350	60.00	80.00	100.00	150.00
	1899	.412	60.00	80.00	100.00	150.00
	1900	.356	60.00	100.00	125.00	175.00

NOTE: Later dates (1901-1915 & 1951) exist for this type.

50th Jubilee
Rev: Second date below eagle.

KM#	Date	Mintage	Fine	VF	XF	Unc
2268	1848/1898A	.027	150.00	250.00	350.00	500.00
	1849/1898A	2,292	500.00	1000.	1300.	1800.
	1850/1898A	2,292	500.00	1000.	1300.	1800.
	1851/1898A	2,292	500.00	1000.	1300.	1800.

8 FLORIN-20 FRANCS

6.4516 g, .900 GOLD, .1867 oz AGW
Obv: Joseph I, value below.

KM#	Date	Mintage	Fine	VF	XF	Unc
2269	1870	.025	BV	100.00	175.00	250.00
	1871	.034	BV	100.00	150.00	200.00
	1872	5,185	100.00	175.00	275.00	375.00
	1873	.023	BV	100.00	175.00	250.00
	1874	.042	BV	100.00	150.00	200.00
	1875	.086	BV	100.00	150.00	200.00
	1876	.146	BV	100.00	150.00	200.00
	1877	.125	BV	100.00	150.00	200.00
	1878	.125	BV	100.00	150.00	200.00
	1879	.043	BV	100.00	175.00	250.00
	1880	.062	BV	100.00	150.00	200.00
	1881	.062	BV	100.00	150.00	200.00
	1882	.115	BV	100.00	150.00	200.00
	1883	.031	BV	100.00	150.00	200.00
	1884	.091	BV	100.00	150.00	200.00
	1885	.178	BV	100.00	150.00	200.00
	1886	.140	BV	100.00	150.00	200.00
	1887	.174	BV	100.00	150.00	200.00
	1888	.114	BV	100.00	150.00	200.00
	1889	.208	BV	100.00	150.00	175.00
	1890	.043	BV	100.00	150.00	200.00
	1891	.019	100.00	150.00	225.00	325.00
	1892	(restrike)	—	—	BV	110.00

2 DUCAT

7.0000 g, .986 GOLD, .2219 oz AGW
Obv: Head right.
Rev: Crowned imperial eagle.

KM#	Date	Mintage	Fine	VF	XF	Unc
2173	1803A	—	—	—	Rare	—

NOTE: Earlier date (1799) exists for this type.

Similar to 1 Ducat, KM#2167.

KM#	Date	Mintage	Fine	VF	XF	Unc
2179	1804A	—	—	—	Rare	—

4 DUCAT

14.0000 g, .986 GOLD, .4438 oz AGW
Obv. leg: FRANCISCVS II. D. G. R. IMP. . .
Rev. leg: . . .LOTH. M. D. HET.

KM#	Date	Mintage	Fine	VF	XF	Unc
2174	1801A	—	300.00	750.00	1800.	2500.
	1802A	—	300.00	800.00	2000.	3000.
	1803A	—	300.00	750.00	1800.	2500.
	1804A	—	300.00	750.00	1800.	2500.

NOTE: Earlier dates (1793-1800) exist for this date.

Obv. leg: FRANCISCVS II. D. G. ROM. ET. . .
Rev. leg:. . . D. LOTH. VEN. SAL.

KM#	Date	Mintage	Fine	VF	XF	Unc
2175	1804A	—	325.00	900.00	2200.	3000.
	1805A	—	325.00	900.00	2200.	3000.
	1806A	—	300.00	750.00	1800.	2500.

Obv. leg:. . . AVSTRIAE IMPERATOR.
Rev. leg:. . . D. LO. SAL. WIRC.

KM#	Date	Mintage	Fine	VF	XF	Unc
2176	1807A	—	350.00	1000.	2250.	3200.
	1808A	—	325.00	900.00	2200.	3000.
	1809A	—	300.00	750.00	1800.	2500.
	1810A	—	350.00	1000.	2250.	3200.

Rev. leg:. . . LO: WI: ET IN. FR: DVX.

KM#	Date	Mintage	Fine	VF	XF	Unc
2177	1811A	—	300.00	750.00	1600.	2200.
	1812A	—	350.00	800.00	1800.	2500.
	1813A	—	300.00	750.00	1600.	2200.
	1814A	—	350.00	800.00	1800.	2500.
	1815A	—	300.00	750.00	1600.	2200.

Rev. leg:. . . GAL. LOD. IL. REX. A. A.

KM#	Date	Mintage	Fine	VF	XF	Unc
2178	1816A	—	300.00	550.00	1500.	2500.
	1817A	—	300.00	550.00	1500.	2500.
	1818A	—	325.00	675.00	1800.	2750.
	1819A	—	300.00	550.00	1500.	2500.
	1820A	—	300.00	550.00	1500.	2500.
	1821A	—	300.00	550.00	1500.	2500.
	1822A	—	300.00	550.00	1500.	2500.
	1823A	—	300.00	550.00	1500.	2500.
	1824A	—	300.00	550.00	1500.	2500.
	1825A	—	250.00	500.00	1200.	2000.
	1826A	—	300.00	550.00	1500.	2500.
	1827A	—	300.00	550.00	1500.	2500.
	1828A	—	250.00	500.00	1275.	2000.
	1829A	—	250.00	500.00	1275.	2000.
	1830A	—	250.00	500.00	1275.	2000.

13.9636 g, .986 GOLD, .4430 oz AGW

KM#	Date	Mintage	Fine	VF	XF	Unc
2270	1835A	—	—	—	Rare	—
	1837A	—	250.00	400.00	1000.	2000.
	1838A	—	250.00	400.00	1000.	2000.
	1839A	—	250.00	400.00	1000.	2000.
	1840A	—	250.00	400.00	1000.	2000.
	1841A	—	250.00	400.00	1000.	2000.
	1842A	—	250.00	400.00	1000.	2000.
	1843A	—	250.00	400.00	1000.	2000.
	1844A	—	250.00	400.00	1000.	2000.
	1845A	—	250.00	400.00	1000.	2000.
	1846A	—	250.00	400.00	1000.	2000.
	1847A	—	250.00	400.00	1000.	2000.
	1848A	4,411	250.00	400.00	1000.	2000.
	1848E	—	250.00	500.00	1250.	2500.

KM#	Date	Mintage	Fine	VF	XF	Unc
2271.1	1852A	—	—	No specimens known		
	1853A	—	—	No specimens known		
	1854A	—	250.00	500.00	1250.	2500.
	1855A	—	250.00	500.00	1250.	2500.
	1856A	—	250.00	500.00	1250.	2500.
	1857A	—	250.00	400.00	1000.	2000.
	1858A	—	250.00	400.00	1000.	2000.
	1859A	.013	250.00	400.00	1000.	2000.

Obv: Laurel wreath w/o berries.

KM#	Date	Mintage	Fine	VF	XF	Unc
2271.2	1854A	—	350.00	850.00	1750.	2100.
	1855A	—	—	—	Rare	—
	1857V	—	800.00	1600.	3000.	4000.

KM#	Date	Mintage	Fine	VF	XF	Unc
2272	1860A	6,303	250.00	600.00	1500.	2750.
	1861A	7,664	250.00	600.00	1500.	2750.
	1862A	8,944	250.00	500.00	1250.	2250.
	1863A	.022	250.00	400.00	1000.	2000.

KM#	Date	Mintage	Fine	VF	XF	Unc
2272	1864A	.045	250.00	400.00	1000.	2000.
	1864V	4,463	400.00	800.00	1750.	2750.
	1865A	.013	250.00	400.00	1000.	2000.
	1865V	.010	250.00	400.00	1000.	2000.

Obv: Laureate bust w/heavier side whiskers.

KM#	Date	Mintage	Fine	VF	XF	Unc
2273	1866A	8,463	250.00	500.00	1250.	2250.

KM#	Date	Mintage	Fine	VF	XF	Unc
2274	1867A	.016	250.00	400.00	1000.	2000.
	1868A	.017	250.00	400.00	1000.	2000.
	1869A	.019	250.00	400.00	1000.	2000.
	1870A	.012	250.00	400.00	1000.	2000.
	1871A	.019	250.00	400.00	1000.	2000.
	1872A	*.012	250.00	400.00	1000.	2000.

Obv: Similar to 4 Ducat, KM#2272, but w/o mint mark.

KM#	Date	Mintage	Fine	VF	XF	Unc
2276	1872	*.012	250.00	525.00	725.00	1200.
	1873	.024	225.00	400.00	600.00	1000.
	1874	.015	225.00	325.00	600.00	1000.
	1875	.012	225.00	325.00	600.00	1000.
	1876	5,243	250.00	450.00	800.00	1300.
	1877	5,970	250.00	450.00	800.00	1300.
	1878	.023	225.00	325.00	550.00	800.00
	1879	.029	225.00	325.00	550.00	800.00
	1880	.023	225.00	325.00	550.00	800.00
	1881	.035	225.00	325.00	550.00	800.00
	1882	.029	225.00	325.00	550.00	800.00
	1883	.037	225.00	325.00	550.00	800.00
	1884	.035	225.00	325.00	550.00	800.00
	1885	.028	225.00	325.00	550.00	800.00
	1886	.018	225.00	300.00	525.00	800.00
	1887	.027	225.00	300.00	525.00	800.00
	1888	.036	225.00	300.00	525.00	800.00
	1889	.031	225.00	300.00	525.00	800.00
	1890	.047	225.00	300.00	525.00	750.00
	1891	.054	225.00	300.00	525.00	750.00
	1892	.058	225.00	300.00	525.00	750.00
	1893	.054	225.00	275.00	550.00	800.00
	1894	.035	225.00	275.00	550.00	800.00
	1895	.040	225.00	275.00	550.00	800.00
	1896	.049	225.00	250.00	500.00	800.00
	1897	.035	225.00	275.00	550.00	800.00
	1898	.054	225.00	250.00	500.00	800.00
	1899	.054	225.00	250.00	500.00	600.00
	1900	.047	225.00	250.00	500.00	600.00

NOTE: Later dates (1901-1915) exist for this type.

TRADE COINAGE

THALER

28.0668 g, .833 SILVER, .7517 oz ASW

KM#	Date	Mintage	Fine	VF	XF	Unc
T1	1780 SF (restrike-1853-present)					
			—	—	—	7.00
	1780 SF	(restrike)		—	Proof	9.00

An unofficial trade dollar, the final date of the famous Maria Theresa Thaler has been restruck intermittently since 1781 to modern times at many world mints. It has been used in many areas that lacked a firm local coinage, particularly in north and east Africa and the Near East. Gunzburg Mint was where the original talers were struck. (Listings for these can be found in volume 2 under Burgau-Austrian States, KM#23). Since then the thalers have been restruck at the following mints: Vienna, Prague, Milan, Venice, Gunzburg, London, Paris, Brussels, Kremnitz, Karlsburg, Rome, Bombay and Florence with an estimated 800 million struck to date. For original Thaler listings refer to BURGAU.

MONETARY REFORM

1892-1918

100 Heller = 1 Corona

HELLER

BRONZE

KM#	Date	Mintage	Fine	VF	XF	Unc
2800	1892	—	35.00	75.00	150.00	350.00
	1893	29.000	.20	.35	.50	4.00
	1894	30.100	.20	.35	.50	4.00
	1895	49.500	.20	.35	.50	3.00
	1896	15.600	.35	1.50	3.00	8.00
	1897	12.400	.35	2.00	4.00	10.00
	1898	6.780	5.00	10.00	20.00	35.00
	1899	1.901	3.00	12.00	25.00	60.00
	1900	26.981	.20	.50	1.50	4.00

NOTE: Later dates (1901-1916) exist for this type.

2 HELLER

BRONZE

KM#	Date	Mintage	Fine	VF	XF	Unc
2801	1892	.260	50.00	100.00	200.00	450.00
	1893	41.507	.20	.50	1.75	5.00
	1894	78.036	.15	.25	.75	3.00
	1895	25.610	.20	.50	2.25	6.25
	1896	43.080	.15	.25	.75	3.50
	1897	98.000	.15	.25	.75	3.00
	1898	10.720	.75	1.50	4.00	12.00
	1899	42.734	.15	.25	1.00	4.00
	1900	7.942	.50	1.00	3.00	9.00

NOTE: Later dates (1901-1915) exist for this type.

10 HELLER

NICKEL

KM#	Date	Mintage	Fine	VF	XF	Unc
2802	1892	—	125.00	250.00	450.00	1150.
	1892	—	—	—	Proof	1500.
	1893	43.524	.25	.50	1.50	4.00
	1894	45.558	.25	.50	1.25	4.00
	1895	79.918	.25	.50	1.00	3.00

NOTE: Later dates (1907-1911) exist for this type.

20 HELLER

NICKEL

KM#	Date	Mintage	Fine	VF	XF	Unc
2803	1892	1.500	7.50	15.00	35.00	75.00
	1892	—	—	—	Proof	250.00
	1893	41.457	.25	.65	1.50	6.00
	1894	50.116	.25	.65	1.50	6.00
	1895	32.927	.25	.65	1.50	6.00

NOTE: Later dates (1907-1914) exist for this type.

CORONA

5.0000 g, .835 SILVER, .1342 oz ASW

KM#	Date	Mintage	Fine	VF	XF	Unc
2804	1892	.235	80.00	160.00	275.00	700.00
	1893	50.124	1.75	3.00	5.00	10.00
	1894	28.003	1.75	3.00	5.00	12.00
	1895	15.115	3.75	6.00	15.00	35.00
	1896	3.068	7.50	15.00	25.00	55.00
	1897	2.142	20.00	30.00	60.00	150.00
	1898	5.855	2.50	5.00	8.00	25.00
	1899	11.820	1.75	2.75	5.00	10.00
	1900	3.745	2.50	5.00	8.00	14.00

NOTE: Later dates (1901-1907) exist for this type.

5 CORONA

24.0000 g, .900 SILVER, .6945 oz ASW

KM#	Date	Mintage	Fine	VF	XF	Unc
2807	1900	8.525	8.00	12.50	30.00	75.00

NOTE: Later date (1907) exists for this type.

10 CORONA

3.3875 g, .900 GOLD, .0980 oz AGW

Obv: Laureate head of Franz Joseph I right.

Rev: Eagle w/value and date below.

KM#	Date	Mintage	Fine	VF	XF	Unc
2805	1892	—	1000.	1500.	2500.	3500.
	1893	—	—	—	Rare	—
	1896	.211	BV	55.00	60.00	80.00
	1897	1.803	BV	55.00	60.00	90.00

NOTE: Later dates (1905-1906) exist for this type.

20 CORONA

6.7751 g, .900 GOLD, .1960 oz AGW

KM#	Date	Mintage	Fine	VF	XF	Unc
2806	1892	.653	—	BV	125.00	150.00
	1893	7.872	—	BV	100.00	115.00
	1894	6.714	—	BV	100.00	115.00
	1895	2.266	—	BV	100.00	115.00
	1896	6.868	—	BV	100.00	115.00
	1897	5.133	—	BV	100.00	115.00
	1898	1.874	—	BV	100.00	115.00
	1899	.098	100.00	110.00	130.00	150.00
	1900	.027	200.00	400.00	600.00	800.00

NOTE: Later dates (1901-1905) exist for this type.

MEDALLIC ISSUES (M)

GULDEN

12.9900 g, .900 SILVER, .3758 oz ASW
Wedding of Emperor Franz Joseph

KM#	Date	Mintage	Fine	VF	XF	Unc
M1	1854A	—	20.00	30.00	60.00	150.00

Pribram Mine

KM#	Date	Mintage	Fine	VF	XF	Unc
M2	1875	8,000	150.00	200.00	300.00	500.00

ZWEI (2) GULDEN

25.9900 g, .900 SILVER, .7520 oz ASW
Wedding of Emperor Franz Joseph
Denomination on edge

KM#	Date	Mintage	Fine	VF	XF	Unc
M3	1854A	—	50.00	100.00	175.00	300.00

2 FLORINS

22.0000 g, .900 SILVER, .6366 oz ASW
Vienna Shooting Fest
Rev: F. GAUL below eagle.

KM#	Date	Mintage	Fine	VF	XF	Unc
M4	1873	—	500.00	800.00	1250.	2000.
	1873	—	—	—	Proof	2250.

NOTE: The Kremnica Mint struck reproductions with 'R.1973-KOLARSKY' below eagle, 24.31 g.

24.6900 g, .900 SILVER, .7145 oz ASW
Silver Wedding Anniversary

KM#	Date	Mintage	Fine	VF	XF	Unc
M5	1879	.275	18.00	25.00	45.00	110.00

NOTE: Varieties exist w/and w/o dots in legend.

First Federal Shooting Festival

KM#	Date	Mintage	Fine	VF	XF	Unc
M6	1880	—	50.00	100.00	150.00	235.00

Reopening of Kuttenberg Mines

KM#	Date	Mintage	Fine	VF	XF	Unc
M7	1887	400 pcs.	1500.	2150.	2900.	4500.
	1887	—	—	—	Proof	4800.

NOTE: The Kremnica Mint struck reproductions with "R74" below church left of shield.

THALER

(Fein)

SILVER
Mint: Vienna - w/o mint mark.
3rd German Shooting Festival

KM#	Date	Mintage	Fine	VF	XF	Unc
M8	1868	—	30.00	60.00	125.00	220.00

(Gedenk)

Opening of Mt. Raxalpe Inn

KM#	Date	Mintage	Fine	VF	XF	Unc
M9	1877	100 pcs.	1500.	2250.	3500.	5500.

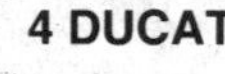

4 DUCAT

14.0000 g, .986 GOLD, .4438 oz AGW
Vienna Shooting Festival

KM#	Date	Mintage	Fine	VF	XF	Unc
M12	1873	—	600.00	1200.	2500.	3500.
	1873	—	—	—	Proof	7000.

PATTERNS (Pn)

(Including off metal strikes)

KM#	Date	Mintage	Identification	Mkt.Val.
Pn37	1851C	—	1/4 Kreuzer, KM2180	—

KM#	Date	Mintage	Identification	Mkt.Val.
Pn38	1851C	—	2 Kreuzer, KM2189	2150.
Pn39	1851C	—	3 Kreuzer, KM2193	2750.
Pn40	1851E	—	1/4 Kreuzer, KM2180	1400.
Pn41	1851E	—	1/2 Kreuzer, KM2181	2250.
Pn42	1851E	—	2 Kreuzer, KM2189	2500.
Pn43	1851E	—	3 Kreuzer, KM2193	2150.
Pn44	1852E	—	20 Kreuzer, KM2210	1750.
Pn45	1853B	—	1/2 Thaler, KM2228	5500.
Pn46	1854	—	1 Gulden, Aluminum, KM2218	1200.
Pn47	1855A	—	5 Gulden, Gold	—
Pn48	1855A	—	10 Gulden, Gold	—
Pn49	1855A	—	20 Gulden, Gold	—
Pn50	1855M	—	1 Ducat, Gold, KM2263	—
Pn51	1857B	—	1/4 Gulden, Aluminum	—
Pn52	1858A	—	3 Kreuzer	—
Pn53	1858B	—	3 Kreuzer, Lead	—
Pn54	1858E	—	3 Kreuzer, Lead	—
Pn55	1858B	—	10 Kreuzer	950.00
Pn56	1858M	—	2 Florins, KM2230	—
Pn57	1859E	—	5 Kreuzer, Aluminum, KM2197	—
Pn58	1859B	—	1 Krone, Gold, KM2253	—
Pn59	1866	—	2 Florin, Copper, w/o mm, KM2230	700.00
Pn60	1867B	—	10 Kreuzer, KM2205	1600.
Pn61	1868B	—	10 Kreuzer, Copper, KM2206	—
Pn62	1868	—	1 Thaler, KM2246	—
Pn63	1870A	—	20 Kreuzer, Copper, KM2212	—
Pn64	1871	—	1 Florin, Aluminum, w/o mm, KM2221	750.00
Pn65	1875	—	1 Florin, Copper, KM2223	160.00
Pn66	1887	—	2 Florins, Copper, KM2237	2200.
Pn67	1887	—	2 Florins, Bronze, KM2237	2000.

AUSTRIAN STATES

AUERSPERG

Auersberg

The Auersperg princes were princes of estates in Austrian Carniola, a former duchy with estates in Laibach and Silesia, a former province in southwestern Poland and Swabia, one of the stem-duchies of medieval Germany. They were elevated to princely rank in 1653, and the following year were made dukes of Muensterberg, which they ultimately sold to Prussia.

RULERS

Wilhelm, 1800-1822

MONETARY SYSTEM

120 Kreuzer = 1 Convention Thaler

THALER

(Convention)

SILVER

KM#	Date	Mintage	VG	Fine	VF	XF
5	1805	—	80.00	175.00	275.00	500.00

GURK

A bishopric in the Austrian Alpine province of Carinthia, was founded in 1071. In 1806 it was mediatized and assigned to Austria.

RULERS

Franz Xavier V, Count Salm-Reifferscheid, (later Prince), 1783-1822

20 KREUZER

SILVER

KM#	Date	Mintage	VG	Fine	VF	XF
1	1806	—	37.50	75.00	90.00	125.00

THALER

(Convention)

SILVER

KM#	Date	Mintage	VG	Fine	VF	XF
2	1801	—	100.00	200.00	325.00	500.00

TRADE COINAGE

DUCAT

3.5000 g, .986 GOLD, .1109 oz AGW
Obv: Bust of Franz Xavier right.
Rev: Crowned and mantled arms.

KM#	Date	Mintage	VG	Fine	VF	XF
3	1806	—	250.00	450.00	850.00	2000.

OLMUTZ

In Moravia

Olmutz (Olomouc), a bishopric in the eastern part of the Czech Republic which was, until 1640, the recognized capital of Moravia, obtained the right to mint a coinage in 1144, but exercised it sparingly until the 17th century, when it became an archbishopric.

RULERS

Anton Theodor, Count von Colloredo, 1777-1811
Maria Thaddaus, Count von Trauttmansdorf, 1811-1819
Rudolph Johann, Archduke of Austria, 1819-1831

RUDOLPH JOHANN

Archduke of Austria

1819-1831

20 KREUZER

SILVER

KM#	Date	Mintage	VG	Fine	VF	XF
195	1820	—	20.00	35.00	60.00	100.00

1/2 CONVENTION THALER

SILVER

KM#	Date	Mintage	VG	Fine	VF	XF
196	1820	—	50.00	90.00	150.00	220.00

THALER

SILVER

KM#	Date	Mintage	VG	Fine	VF	XF
197	1820	—	100.00	200.00	400.00	700.00

TRADE COINAGE

DUCAT

3.5000 g, .986 GOLD, .1109 oz AGW

KM#	Date	Mintage	VG	Fine	VF	XF
198	1820	—	175.00	275.00	650.00	1400.

SALZBURG

A town on the Austro-Bavarian frontier which grew up around a monastery and bishopric that was founded circa 700. It was raised to the rank of archbishopric in 798. In 1803 Salzburg was secularized and given to an archduke of Austria. In 1803 it was annexed to Austria but years later passed to Bavaria, returning to Austria in 1813. It became a crownland in 1849, remaining so until becoming part of the Austrian Republic in 1918.

RULERS

Hieronymus, 1772-1803
Ferdinand, Elector, 1803-1805

ENGRAVERS INITIALS

FM, M - Franz Xavier Matzenkopf, Jr. 1755-1805

MONETARY SYSTEM

4 Pfenning = 1 Kreutzer
120 Kreutzer = 1 Convention Thaler

HIERONYMUS

1772-1803

EIN (1) PFENNING

COPPER

KM#	Date	Mintage	VG	Fine	VF	XF
474	1801	—	3.00	5.00	9.00	18.00
	1802	—	3.00	5.00	9.00	18.00

NOTE: Earlier dates (1792-1800) exist for this type.

KM#	Date	Mintage	VG	Fine	VF	XF
480	1802	—	5.00	7.00	10.00	20.00

ZWEI (2) PFENNING

COPPER

KM#	Date	Mintage	VG	Fine	VF	XF
472	1801	—	3.00	6.00	12.00	25.00

NOTE: Earlier dates (1791-1800) exist for this type.

KM#	Date	Mintage	VG	Fine	VF	XF
481	1802	—	5.00	8.50	17.00	38.00

EIN (1) KREUZER

COPPER

KM#	Date	Mintage	VG	Fine	VF	XF
470	1801	—	2.00	3.00	5.00	16.00
	1802	—	2.00	3.00	5.00	16.00

NOTE: Earlier dates (1790-1800) exist for this type.

KM#	Date	Mintage	VG	Fine	VF	XF
482	1802	—	5.00	10.00	20.00	42.00

5 KREUZER

BILLON

KM#	Date	Mintage	VG	Fine	VF	XF
477	1801	—	7.50	20.00	50.00	130.00
	1802	—	7.50	20.00	50.00	130.00

NOTE: Earlier dates (1793-1800) exist for this type.

10 KREUZER

3.8900 g, .500 SILVER, .0625 oz ASW

KM#	Date	Mintage	VG	Fine	VF	XF
464	1801 M	—	15.00	30.00	55.00	110.00
	1802 M	—	15.00	30.00	55.00	110.00

NOTE: Earlier dates (1788-1800) exist for this type.

20 KREUZER

6.6800 g, .583 SILVER, .1252 oz ASW

KM#	Date	Mintage	VG	Fine	VF	XF
460	1801 M	—	3.00	6.00	15.00	40.00
	1802 M	—	3.00	6.00	15.00	40.00
	1803 M	—	5.00	15.00	20.00	55.00

NOTE: Varieties exist.
NOTE: Earlier dates (1787-1800) exist for this type.

1/2 THALER

14.0300 g, .833 SILVER, .3757 oz ASW

KM#	Date	Mintage	VG	Fine	VF	XF
461	1802 M	—	50.00	100.00	175.00	325.00

NOTE: Earlier dates (1787-1797) exist for this type.

THALER

28.0600 g, .833 SILVER, .7515 oz ASW

KM#	Date	Mintage	Fine	VF	XF	Unc
465	1801 M	—	65.00	110.00	150.00	325.00
	1802 M	—	75.00	120.00	165.00	350.00
	1803 M	—	100.00	150.00	250.00	550.00

NOTE: Varieties exist.
NOTE: Earlier dates (1789-1800) exist for this type.

TRADE COINAGE

DUCAT

3.5000 g, .986 GOLD, .1109 oz AGW
Obv: Bust right. Rev: Crowned, mantled arms.

KM#	Date	Mintage	VG	Fine	VF	XF
463	1801 M	—	80.00	125.00	250.00	450.00
	1802 M	—	80.00	125.00	250.00	450.00

NOTE: Earlier dates (1787-1800) exist for this type.

Similar to KM#463.

KM#	Date	Mintage	VG	Fine	VF	XF
486	1803 M	—	350.00	750.00	2250.	4000.

NOTE: Varieties exist.

FERDINAND

1803-1805

EIN (1) PFENNING

COPPER
Rev: 1 PFENNING.

KM#	Date	Mintage	VG	Fine	VF	XF
488	1804	—	5.00	7.00	12.00	30.00

Rev: EIN PFENNING.

KM#	Date	Mintage	VG	Fine	VF	XF
489	1804	—	1.50	3.00	7.00	22.00
	1805	—	1.50	3.00	7.00	22.00

NOTE: Varieties exist.

ZWEI (2) PFENNING

COPPER
Rev: II PFENNING.

KM#	Date	Mintage	VG	Fine	VF	XF
490	1804	—	5.00	9.00	20.00	45.00

Rev: ZWEI PFENNING.

KM#	Date	Mintage	VG	Fine	VF	XF
493	1805	—	3.50	7.50	16.50	40.00
(C116a)	1806	—	3.50	7.50	16.50	40.00

EIN (1) KREUZER

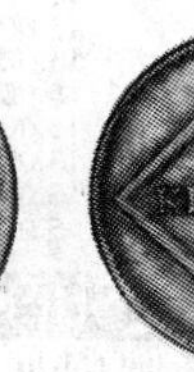

COPPER

KM#	Date	Mintage	VG	Fine	VF	XF
491	1804	—	3.00	6.00	12.00	30.00
	1805	—	1.50	4.00	10.00	25.00
	1806	—	1.50	4.00	10.00	25.00

3 KREUZER

BILLON

KM#	Date	Mintage	VG	Fine	VF	XF
483	1803	—	10.00	20.00	40.00	80.00
	1804	—	10.00	20.00	40.00	80.00

Rev: Date in lozenge.

KM#	Date	Mintage	VG	Fine	VF	XF
494	1805	—	10.00	20.00	40.00	85.00

NOTE: Varieties exist with and without mint mark.

6 KREUZER

BILLON

KM#	Date	Mintage	VG	Fine	VF	XF
484	1803	—	10.00	30.00	65.00	140.00
	1804	—	10.00	30.00	60.00	130.00
	1805	—	10.00	25.00	50.00	115.00

Rev: Date in lozenge.

KM#	Date	Mintage	VG	Fine	VF	XF
495	1805	—	10.00	30.00	60.00	130.00
	1806	—	10.00	30.00	60.00	130.00

20 KREUZER

6.6800 g, .583 SILVER, .1252 oz ASW

KM#	Date	Mintage	VG	Fine	VF	XF
492	1804 M	—	10.00	20.00	40.00	90.00

KM#	Date	Mintage	VG	Fine	VF	XF
496	1805 M	—	10.00	25.00	50.00	100.00
	1806 M	—	10.00	25.00	50.00	100.00

THALER

28.0600 g, .833 SILVER, .7515 oz ASW

KM#	Date	Mintage	Fine	VF	XF	Unc
485	1803	—	100.00	175.00	400.00	750.00

KM#	Date	Mintage	Fine	VF	XF	Unc
497	1805 M	—	150.00	250.00	450.00	850.00

Rev. leg: . . . PAS ETBER S R IP ELECTOR.

KM#	Date	Mintage	Fine	VF	XF	Unc
499	1806 M	—	200.00	300.00	550.00	1000.

TRADE COINAGE

DUCAT

3.5000 g, .986 GOLD, .1109 oz AGW

KM#	Date	Mintage	VG	Fine	VF	XF
487	1803 M	—	100.00	250.00	700.00	1200.
	1804 M	—	125.00	275.00	800.00	1350.

KM#	Date	Mintage	VG	Fine	VF	XF
498	1805 M	—	100.00	250.00	750.00	1250.
	1806 M	—	100.00	250.00	750.00	1250.

TYROL

Tirol

A princely county situated in Austria between Germany and Italy. In 1363 Margaret Maultasch, countess of Tyrol, handed over Tyrol to Rudolph, Duke of Austria. Except for a period of Bavarian occupation, 1805-14, Tyrol remained a Hapsburg possession until the breakup of the Austrian Empire at the end of World War I. The world's first dollar-size silver crown was struck at Hall, Tyrol, in 1486.

RULERS

Napoleon, (France) 1805-1809
Maximilian Joseph I, (Bavaria) 1805-1814
Andreas Hofer, Rebellion, 1809
Franz I, (Austria), 1814-1835
Ferdinand, (Austria), 1835-1848
Franz Joseph, (Austria), 1848-1916

MINT MARKS

F, FH, G, H, HA - Hall

MONETARY SYSTEM

120 Kreuzer = 1 Convention Thaler

INSURRECTION COINAGE

1809

EIN (1) KREUZER

COPPER
Issue of Andreas Hofer

KM#	Date	Mintage	VG	Fine	VF	XF
148	1809	—	10.00	15.00	35.00	85.00

NOTE: Varieties exist.

20 KREUZER

SILVER
Issue of Andreas Hofer

KM#	Date	Mintage	VG	Fine	VF	XF
149	1809	—	15.00	25.00	50.00	100.00

NOTE: Three varieties exist.

AZERBAIJAN

The Republic of Azerbaijan (formerly Azerbaijan S.S.R.) includes the Nakhichevan Autonomous Republic and Nagomo-Karabakh Autonomous Region (which was abolished in 1991). Situated in the eastern area of Transcaucasia, it is bordered in the west by Armenia, in the north by Georgia and Dagestan, to the east by the Caspian Sea and to the south by Iran. It has an area of 33,430 sq. mi. (86,600 sq. km.) and a population of 7.8 million. Capital: Baku. The area is rich in mineral deposits of aluminum, copper, iron, lead, salt and zinc, with oil as its leading industry. Agriculture and livestock follow in importance.

Ancient home of Scythian tribes and known under the Romans as Albania and to the Arabs as Arran, the country of Azerbaijan was formed at the time of its invasion by Seliuk Turks and grew into a prosperous state under Persian suzerainty. From the 16th century the country was a theatre of fighting and political rivaltry between Turkey, Persia and later Russia. Baku was first annexed to Russia by Czar Peter I in 1723 and remained under Russian rule for 12 years. After the Russian retreat the whole of Azerbaijan north of the Aras River became a khanate under Persian control. Czar Alexander I, after an eight-year war with Persia, annexed it in 1813 to the Russian empire.

Until the Russian Revolution of 1905, there was no political life in Azerbaijan. A Mussavat (Equality) party was formed in 1911 by Mohammed Emin, Rasulzade, a former Social Democrat. After the Russian Revolution of March 1917, the party started a campaign for independence. Baku, however, the capital with its mixed population, constituted an alien enclave in the country While a national Azerbaijani government was established at Gandzha (Elizavetpol), a Communist-controlled council assumed power at Baku with Stepan Shaumian, an Armenian, at its head. The Gandzha government joined first, on Sept. 20, 1917, a Transcaucasian federal republic, but on May 28, 1918, proclaimed the independence of Azerbaijan. On June 4, 1918, at Batum, a peace treaty was signed with Turkey. Turko-Azerbaijani forces started an offensive against Baku, occupied since Aug. 17, 1918 by 1,400 British troops coming by sea from Anzali, Persia. On Sept. 14 the Briish evacuated Baku, returning to Anzali, and three days later the Azerbaijan government, headed by Fath Khoysky, established itself at Baku.

After the collapse of the Ottoman empire, the British returned to Baku, at first ignoring the Azerbaijan government. A general election with universal suffrage for the Azerbaijan constituent assembly took place on Dec. 7, 1918 and out of 120 members there were 84 Mussavat supporters. On Jan. 15, 1920, the Allied powers recognized Azerbaijan de facto, but on April 27 of the same year the Red army invaded the country, and a Soviet republic of Azerbaijan was proclaimed the next day. Later it became a member of the Transcaucasian Federation joining the U.S.S.R. on Dec. 30, 1922, it became a self-constituent republic in 1936.

KARABAGH

Karabagh, a former Khanate in Azerbaijan was under the control of the Ottomans until 996AD when Persia regained control. The principal mint was located in Panahabad, now the town of Shusha. The hereditary Jewanshir family then broke away from Persia in the second half of the 1700's and abandoned their principality to the Russians in 1822. For the remainder of the Czarist period it formed part of the Muslim governorship of Baker until 1868, when it was transfered to Elizabetpol.

It now forms part of The Nagorno-Karabakh-Oblast which was established as an autonomous region with Azerbaijan in 1923. They elected for independence in the C.I.S. in 1991.

RULERS

Ibrahim Khalil Khan,
AH1177-1221/1763-1806AD
Mahdi Quli Khan Muzatfar,
AH1221-1235/1806-1822AD

MINTNAME

Panahabad (Shusha) بناه باد

MONETARY SYSTEM
Derived from the Safavid Persian System

1 Bisti = 20 Dinars
1 Abbasi = 200 Dinars

All coins are anonymous except KM#5, which is in the name of Fath'ali Shah of Iran.

The silver abbasi of Karabagh circulated widely in Iran, where it came to be known as a "Panabadi", a term later used for the half Kran in Iran.

Ibrahim Khalil Khan

AH1177-1221/1763-1806AD

ABBASI

SILVER
In the name of Fath'ali Shah

KM#	Date	Good	VG	Fine	VF
5	AH1216	15.00	20.00	40.00	75.00

MAHDI QULI KHAN MUZATFAR

AH1221-1235/1806-1822AD

ABBASI

SILVER
Obv: Russian crown and branches. Rev: Mintname.

KM#	Date	Good	VG	Fine	VF
6	AH1222	15.00	20.00	45.00	80.00

Obv: Kalimah. Rev: Mintname and date.

KM#	Date	Good	VG	Fine	VF
7	AH1221	12.00	18.00	40.00	65.00

Obv: Date and unread inscription. Rev: Mintname. (Date sometimes also on reverse.)

KM#	Date	Good	VG	Fine	VF
8	AH1228	10.00	15.00	30.00	55.00
	1229	10.00	15.00	30.00	55.00
	1230	10.00	15.00	30.00	55.00
	1231	10.00	15.00	30.00	55.00
	1232	10.00	15.00	30.00	55.00
	1233	10.00	15.00	30.00	55.00
	1234	10.00	15.00	30.00	55.00
	1235	10.00	15.00	30.00	55.00
	1236	10.00	15.00	30.00	55.00
	1237	10.00	15.00	30.00	55.00

NOTE: The above listing of types is incomplete. In addition, more dates of the listed type likely exist.

NOTE: AH1236 and 1237 dates were struck posthumously.

SCHEMAKHI

Schemakhi, later the capital of Shirwan, is a former khanate located in Azerbaijan. It was taken by the Ottomans in 1578. Restored to Persian rule in 1607, it remained so throughout much of its later history until the Khan Mustafa submitted to the Russians in 1805 and later occupied by the Russians who annexed the khanate in 1813. After destruction in 1859 by earthquake, it came under the government of Baker. Presently is part of Azerbaijan, C.I.S.

RULERS

Persian until annexed to Russia in 1813 by the Peace of Gulistan

MINTNAME

Shamakha شماخه

Shamakhi شماخ

MONETARY SYSTEM

20 Dinars = 1 Bisti
10 Bisti = 1 Abbasi

ABBASI

SILVER, 2.00-2.30 g

KM#	Date	Good	VG	Fine	VF
20	AH1223	16.50	35.00	75.00	110.00
	1227	15.00	32.50	70.00	100.00
	1228	15.00	32.50	70.00	100.00
	1229	15.00	32.50	70.00	100.00
	1230	15.00	32.50	70.00	100.00
	1231	15.00	32.50	70.00	100.00
	1232	15.00	32.50	70.00	100.00
	1233	15.00	32.50	70.00	100.00
	1234	15.00	32.50	70.00	100.00
	1235	15.00	32.50	70.00	100.00

SHEKI

Sheki, with its capital Nukha was a former khanate in Russian Caucasia, and in 1578 was part of Shirwan (under Ottoman rule). It was occupied in 1806 when the Russians invested Ja'far Quli Khan as governor and then annexed by Russia in 1819. Sheki is now part of Azerbaijan, which joined the Commonwealth of Independent States in December 1991.

RULERS

Muhammad Hasan,
AH1198-1221/1783-1806AD
Ja'far Quli Khan,
AH1221-1230/1806-1815AD
Ismail Khan,
AH1230-1234/1815-1819AD
Annexed to Russia in 1819

MONETARY SYSTEM

200 Dinars = 1 Abbasi
20 Dinars = 1 Bisti

MINTNAME

Nukha 

JA'FAR QULI KHAN

AH1221-1230/1806-1815AD

BISTI

COPPER, 22-24mm
Obv: Russian crown above date, 6-pointed star below. Rev. leg: *Duriba Nukha Falus*..

KM#	Date	Good	VG	Fine	VF
10	AH1221	35.00	50.00	90.00	160.00
	1222	35.00	50.00	90.00	160.00
	1229	35.00	50.00	90.00	160.00

Obv: Rosette and sprig below date.

KM#	Date	Good	VG	Fine	VF
11	1223	35.00	50.00	90.00	160.00
	1226	35.00	50.00	90.00	160.00

30-32mm
Obv: Large crown above date in cartouche.

KM#	Date	Good	VG	Fine	VF
12	AH1228	35.00	50.00	90.00	160.00
	1233	35.00	50.00	90.00	160.00

MUHAMMAD HASAN

AH1198-1221/1783-1806AD

ABBASI

SILVER, 2.10-2.30 g

KM#	Date	Good	VG	Fine	VF
5	AH1218	35.00	60.00	115.00	185.00

ISMAIL KHAN

AH1230-1234/1815-1819AD

1/2 ABBASI

SILVER, 1.10-1.20 g
Obv: Crown and stars at side, date below inner circle. Rev: Mintname and falus.

KM#	Date	Good	VG	Fine	VF
15	AH1231	35.00	60.00	115.00	185.00
	1232	35.00	60.00	115.00	185.00

ABBASI

SILVER, 2.10-2.30 g

KM#	Date	Good	VG	Fine	VF
16	AH1232	35.00	60.00	115.00	185.00
	1233	35.00	60.00	115.00	185.00

The Azores, an archipelago of nine islands of volcanic origin, are located in the Atlantic Ocean 740 miles (1,190 km.) west of Cape de Roca, Portugal. They are the westernmost region of Europe under the administration of Portugal and have an area of 902 sq. mi. (2,305 sq. km.) and a population of 236,000. Principal city: Ponta Delgada. The natives are mainly of Portuguese descent and earn their livelihood by fishing, wine making, basket weaving and the growing of fruit, grains and sugar cane. Pineapples are the chief item of export. The climate is particularly temperate, making the islands a favorite winter resort.

The Azores were discovered about 1427 by the Portuguese navigator Diogo de Sevill. Portugal secured the islands in the 15th century and established the first settlement, on Santa Maria, about 1439. From 1580 to 1640 the Azores were subject to Spain.

The Azores' first provincial coinage was ordered by law of August 19, 1750. Copper coins were struck for circulation in both the Azores and Madeira Islands. Keeping the same technical specifications, but with different designs. In 1795 a second provincial coinage was introduced but the weight was reduced by 50 percent.

Angra on Terceira Island became the capital of the captaincy-general of the Azores in 1766 and it was here in 1826 that the constitutionalists set up a pro-Pedro government in opposition to King Miguel in Lisbon. The whole Portuguese fleet attacked Terceira and was repelled at Praia, after which Azoreans, Brazilians and British mercenaries defeated Miguel in Portugal. Maria de Gloria, Pedro's daughter, was proclaimed queen of Portugal on Terceira in 1828.

A U.S. naval base was established at Ponta Delgada in 1917.

After World War II, the islands acquired a renewed importance as a refueling stop for transatlantic air transport. The United States maintains defense bases in the Azores as part of the collective security program of NATO.

In 1976 the archipelago became the Autonomous Region of Azores.

RULERS

Portuguese

MONETARY SYSTEM

1000 Reis (Insulanos) = 1 Milreis

TERCEIRA ISLAND

INSURRECTION OF 1826

On the death of John VI in 1826 the constitutionalists on Terceira supported Pedro, the Brazilian emperor and oldest son of John VI, for the Portuguese throne in opposition to Miguel, Pedro's younger brother who was proclaimed king in 1828.

After repelling the attack of the entire Portuguese fleet at Praia, the constitutionalists with their British mercenaries invaded Portugal and defeated Miguel in 1834. Maria da Gloria, daughter of Pedro, was then proclaimed Queen of Portugal.

TOKEN ISSUES (Tn)

LXXX (80) REIS

COPPER
Obv: AZORES INDEPENDEN. ILHA TERCEIRA

KM#	Date	Mintage	Good	VG	Fine	VF
Tn1	1826	4 known	750.00	1250.	2000.	3000.

MARIA II IN EXILE

1828-1833

In 1828 Pedro declined the Portuguese throne in favor of his daughter, Maria da Gloria, who was therefore forced to live in exile 1828-1834 until Miguel was completely defeated.

For similar 5 and 10 Reis coins with titles of Michael I, see Portugal.

5 REIS

COPPER

KM#	Date	Mintage	VG	Fine	VF	XF
5	1830	—	2.50	6.00	15.00	35.00

10 REIS

COPPER

KM#	Date	Mintage	VG	Fine	VF	XF
6	1830	—	3.50	7.50	18.00	45.00

80 REIS

BRONZE

KM#	Date	Mintage	VG	Fine	VF	XF
			Rev: Large leg. and large stars.			
4.1	1829	—	30.00	50.00	80.00	140.00
			Rev: Small leg. and small stars.			
4.2	1829	—	15.00	30.00	45.00	75.00

NOTE: Cast from gun or bell metal with varying degrees of planchet thickness and porosity.

PATTERNS (Pn)

(Including off metal strikes)

KM#	Date	Mintage	Identification	Mkt.Val.
Pn1	1829	—	40 Reis, Copper	1700.
Pn2	1829	—	40 Reis, Lead	350.00

KM#	Date	Mintage	Identification	Mkt.Val.
Pn3	1829	—	80 Reis, Bronze, cast	175.00
Pn4	1829	—	80 Reis, Bronze, struck	1750.
Pn5	1829	—	600 Reis, Copper	1400.
Pn6	1829	—	800 Reis, Silver, cast	2500.

KM#	Date	Mintage	Identification	Mkt.Val.
Pn7	1833	—	20 Reis, Copper	3500.
Pn8	1833	—	50 Reis, Copper	2200.

NOTE: Pn3 and Pn4 were cast and struck from gun or bell metal.

AZORES

PROVINCIAL COINAGE

5 REIS

COPPER
Maria II

KM#	Date	Mintage	VG	Fine	VF	XF
10	1843	—	2.50	6.00	12.00	40.00

Luiz I

KM#	Date	Mintage	Fine	VF	XF	Unc
13	1865	.090	8.00	20.00	45.00	110.00
	1866	.100	18.00	30.00	60.00	180.00
	1880	.040	3.00	6.00	15.00	35.00

10 REIS

COPPER
Maria II

KM#	Date	Mintage	VG	Fine	VF	XF
11	1843	—	2.50	6.00	15.00	45.00

Luiz I

KM#	Date	Mintage	Fine	VF	XF	Unc
14	1865	.350	3.00	7.00	18.00	50.00
	1866	.175	30.00	50.00	80.00	200.00

20 REIS

COPPER
Maria II

KM#	Date	Mintage	VG	Fine	VF	XF
12	1843	—	2.50	6.00	15.00	45.00

Luiz I

KM#	Date	Mintage	Fine	VF	XF	Unc
15	1865	.178	5.00	10.00	20.00	50.00
	1866	.150	6.00	12.00	25.00	60.00

COUNTERMARKED COINAGE

Decree of June 14, 1871

This first decree ordained that the circulating Brazilian Patacas of 2000 Reis, including the fractions of 1000, 500 and 200 Reis, which at the time locally had a value of 1200, 600, 300 and 120 Reis (Portuguese) respectively, were to be countermarked with a royal crown. These were eventually to be replaced or exchanged by current Portuguese coinage upon their entry into the public treasury. This countermark is also known on copper coins and on various silver coins of other nations that were circulating at the time. The following list is a basic guide with samples of known examples. Grades noted are for the basic coin as the countermark is normally found in better condition.

10 REIS

COPPER
c/m: Crown on Azores 5 Reis, KM#9.

KM#	Date	Good	VG	Fine	VF
30	ND(1795)	10.00	18.00	35.00	65.00

20 REIS

COPPER
c/m: Crown on Azores X Reis, KM#6.

KM#	Date	Good	VG	Fine	VF
18.1	ND(1830)	10.00	20.00	40.00	80.00

c/m: Crown on Mozambique X Reis, KM#482 (Portugal)

KM#	Date	Good	VG	Fine	VF
18.2	ND(1852)	10.00	20.00	40.00	80.00

c/m: Crown on St. Thomas 20 Reis, KM#D1.

KM#	Date	Good	VG	Fine	VF
18.3	ND(1819)	10.00	20.00	40.00	80.00

40 REIS

COPPER
c/m: Crown on St. Thomas 40 Reis, KM#E1.

KM#	Date	Good	VG	Fine	VF
22.1	ND(1819)	10.00	20.00	40.00	80.00
	ND(1825)	10.00	20.00	40.00	80.00

c/m: Crown on Mozambique 40 Reis, KM#22.

KM#	Date	Good	VG	Fine	VF
22.2	ND(1840)	10.00	20.00	40.00	80.00

120 REIS

COPPER

c/m: Crown on Angola Macuta, KM#12.

KM#	Date	Good	VG	Fine	VF
19.3	ND(1770)	20.00	30.00	60.00	100.00

c/m: Crown on Azores 80 Reis, KM#4.2.

KM#	Date	Good	VG	Fine	VF
19.4	ND(1829)	20.00	30.00	60.00	100.00

SILVER

c/m: Crown on Brazilian 200 Reis, KM#469.

KM#	Date	Good	VG	Fine	VF
19.1	ND(1854-67)	10.00	20.00	30.00	50.00

c/m: Crown on Brazilian 200 Reis, KM#471.

KM#	Date	Good	VG	Fine	VF
19.2	ND(1867-69)	10.00	20.00	30.00	50.00

300 REIS

SILVER

c/m: Crown on Brazilian 500 Reis, KM#458.

KM#	Date	Good	VG	Fine	VF
20.1	ND(1848-52)	12.50	25.00	40.00	60.00

c/m: Crown on Brazilian 500 Reis, KM#464.

KM#	Date	Good	VG	Fine	VF
20.2	ND(1853-67)	12.50	25.00	40.00	60.00

c/m: Crown on Brazilian 500 Reis, KM#472.

KM#	Date	Good	VG	Fine	VF
20.3	ND(1867-68)	12.50	25.00	40.00	60.00

600 REIS

SILVER

c/m: Crown on Brazilian 1000 Reis, KM#459.

KM#	Date	Good	VG	Fine	VF
28.1	ND(1849-52)	15.00	27.50	45.00	65.00

c/m: Crown on Brazilian 1000 Reis, KM#465.

KM#	Date	Good	VG	Fine	VF
28.2	ND(1853-66)	15.00	27.50	45.00	65.00

c/m: Crown on Brazilian 1000 Reis, KM#476.

KM#	Date	Good	VG	Fine	VF
28.3	ND(1869)	17.50	30.00	50.00	75.00

c/m: Crown on East India Co. Bengal Rupee, KM#108.

KM#	Date	Good	VG	Fine	VF
28.4	ND(1819-32)	12.00	30.00	60.00	100.00

1200 REIS

SILVER

c/m: Crown on Austria-Burgau Thaler, KM#23.

KM#	Date	Good	VG	Fine	VF
21.1	ND(1780*SF)	25.00	45.00	85.00	165.00

c/m: Crown on Brazilian 1200 Reis, KM#454.

KM#	Date	Good	VG	Fine	VF
21.4	ND(1834)	100.00	165.00	275.00	450.00

c/m: Crown on Brazilian 2000 Reis, KM#462.

KM#	Date	Good	VG	Fine	VF
21.2	ND(1851-52)	30.00	55.00	110.00	200.00

c/m: Crown on Brazilian 2000 Reis, KM#466.

KM#	Date	Good	VG	Fine	VF
21.3	ND(1853-67)	30.00	55.00	110.00	200.00

Decree of March 31, 1887

Countermark crowned G.P., 8mm. Illustration is twice normal size.

This second decree ordained that all foreign silver and copper coinage circulating in the Azores was to be countermarked with a crowned G.P. (Governo Portugues) within a circle. These also were eventually to be replaced or exchanged by current Portuguese coinage upon their entry into the public treasury. This countermark for general use is found on a profusion of Portuguese Brazilian, and foreign issues. The largest crown or dollar size includes the Portuguese 1000 Reis, Brazilian 2000 Reis, obsolete 960 Reis, 1200 Reis, Austrian Thaler, English 5 Shilling or Crown, Spanish American 8 Reales and Spanish 2 Escudos for comparison to the United States dollar. This countermark has been heavily counterfeited and should be approached with caution. The following list is a basic guide with samples of known examples. Grades noted are for the basic coin and the countermark is normally found in better condition than the coin bearing it.

15 REIS

COPPER

c/m: Crowned G.P. on Portuguese India (Goa) 15 Reis, KM#263.

KM#	Date	Good	VG	Fine	VF
23	ND	10.00	20.00	30.00	60.00

120 REIS

SILVER

c/m: Crowned G.P. on Portuguese 80 Reis, KM#238.

KM#	Date	Good	VG	Fine	VF
24	ND	15.00	25.00	40.00	70.00

300 REIS

SILVER

c/m: Crowned G.P. on Spanish or Spanish Colonial 2 Reales.

KM#	Date	Good	VG	Fine	VF
25	ND	20.00	30.00	50.00	80.00

600 REIS

SILVER

c/m: Crowned G.P. on Bolivia 4 Reales, KM#54.

KM#	Date	Good	VG	Fine	VF
26.1	ND(1773-89)	30.00	50.00	85.00	145.00

c/m: Crowned G.P. on Portuguese 400 Reis, KM#331.

KM#	Date	Good	VG	Fine	VF
26.2	ND(1802-16)	25.00	45.00	75.00	125.00

c/m: Crowned G.P. on Portuguese 400 Reis, KM#386.

KM#	Date	Good	VG	Fine	VF
26.3	ND(1828-34)	35.00	60.00	110.00	165.00

1200 REIS

SILVER

c/m: Crowned G.P. on Brazilian (Minas Gerais) 960 Reis, KM#242.

KM#	Date	Good	VG	Fine	VF
29.1	ND(1791-1808)	55.00	90.00	145.00	225.00

c/m: Crowned G.P. on Brazilian 960 Reis, KM#307.1.

KM#	Date	VG	Fine	VF	XF
29.2	ND(1809-18)	40.00	60.00	110.00	165.00

c/m: Crowned G.P. on Brazilian 960 Reis, KM326.1.

KM#	Date	VG	Fine	VF	XF
29.5	ND(1818-22)	40.00	60.00	110.00	165.00

c/m: Crowned G.P. on Peru 8 Reales, KM#142.3.

KM#	Date	VG	Fine	VF	XF
29.3	ND(1828-40)	40.00	60.00	110.00	165.00

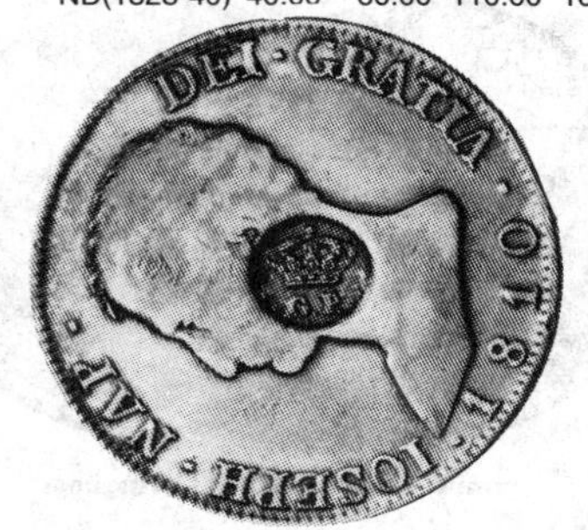

c/m: Crowned G.P. on Spain 20 Reales, C#92.

KM#	Date	Good	VG	Fine	VF
29.4	ND(1808-13)	65.00	100.00	185.00	325.00

NOTE: The above examples as noted are listed only to determine relative size and do not reflect a current price for other foreign types found with genuine countermarks.

PATTERNS (Pn)

KM#	Date	Mintage	Identification	Mkt.Val.
Pn3	1865	—	20 Reis, Copper	Rare

KM#	Date	Mintage	Identification	Mkt.Val.
Pn4	ND(1900)	—	5 Reis, Copper, similar to KM16 but no obv. legend	500.00

TRIAL STRIKES (TS)

KM#	Date	Mintage	Identification	Mkt.Val.
TS2	1843	—	10 Reis, Copper, uniface, reverse	500.00

BAHAMAS

The Commonwealth of the Bahamas is an archipelago of about 3,000 islands, cays and rocks located in the Atlantic Ocean east of Florida and north of Cuba. The total land area of the 800 mile (1,287 km.) long chain of islands is 5,382 sq. mi. (13,935 sq. km.). They have a population of 256,616. Capital: Nassau. The Bahamas import most of their food and manufactured products and export cement, refined oil, pulpwood and lobsters. Tourism is the principal industry.

The Bahamas were discovered by Columbus in October, 1492, upon his sighting of the island of San Salvador, but Spain made no attempt to settle them. British influence began in 1626 when Charles I granted them to the lord proprietors of Carolina, with settlements in 1629 at New Providence by colonists from the northern territory. Although the Bahamas were temporarily under Spanish control in 1641 and 1703, they continued under British proprietors until 1717, when, as the result of political and economic mismanagement, the civil and military governments were surrendered to the King and the islands designated a British Crown Colony. Full international agreement on British possession of the islands resulted from the Treaty of Versailles in 1783. The Bahamas obtained complete internal self-government under the constitution of Jan. 7, 1964. Full independence was achieved on July 10, 1973. The Bahamas is a member of the Commonwealth of Nations. The Queen of the United Kingdom is Head of State.

The coinage of Great Britain was legal tender in the Bahamas from 1825 to the issuing of a definitive coinage in 1966.

RULERS

British

MONETARY SYSTEM

12 Pence = 1 Shilling

PENNY

COPPER

KM#	Date	Mintage	Fine	VF	XF	Unc
1	1806 engrailed edge	.120	35.00	70.00	165.00	275.00
	1806 engrailed edge	—			Proof	300.00
	1806 plain edge	(restrike)			Proof	175.00
	1807 engrailed edge	—			Proof	3000.

GILT

KM#	Date	Mintage	Fine	VF	XF	Unc
1a	1806 engrailed edge	(restrike)			Proof	350.00

BELGIUM

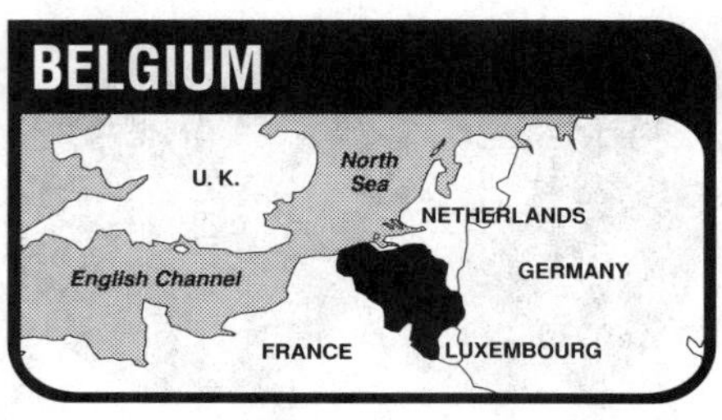

The Kingdom of Belgium, a constitutional monarchy in northwest Europe, has an area of 11,787 sq. mi. (30,519 sq. km.) and a population of 10.1 million, chiefly Dutch-speaking Flemish and French-speaking Walloons. Capital: Brussels. Agriculture, dairy farming, and the processing of raw materials for re-export are the principal industries. Beurs voor Diamant in Antwerp is the world's largest diamond trading center. Iron and steel, machinery motor vehicles, chemicals, textile yarns and fabrics comprise the principal exports.

The Celtic tribe called 'Belgae', from which Belgium derived its name, was described by Caesar as the most courageous of all the tribes of Gaul. The Belgae eventually capitulated to Rome and the area remained for centuries as a part of the Roman Empire known as Belgica.

As Rome began its decline Frankish tribes migrated westward and established the Merovingian, and subsequently, the Carolingian empires. At the death of Charlemagne Europe was divided among his three sons Karl, Lothar and Ludwig. The eastern part of today's Belgium lies in the Duchy of Lower Lorraine while much of the western parts eventually became the County of Flanders. After further divisions the area came under the control of the Duke of Burgundy from whence it passed under Hapsburg control when Marie of Burgundy married Maximilian of Austria. Phillip I (the Fair), son of Maximilian and Marie then added Spain to the Hapsburg empire by marrying Johanna, daughter of Ferdinand and Isabella. Charles and Ferdinand, sons of Phillip and Johanna, began the separate Spanish and Austrian lines of the Hapsburg family. The Burgundian lands, along with the northern provinces which make up present day Netherlands, became the Spanish Netherlands. The northern provinces successfully rebelled and broke away from Hapsburg rule in the late 16th century and early 17th century. The southern provinces along with the Duchy of Luxembourg remained under the influence of Spain until the year 1700 when Charles II, last of the Spanish Hapsburg line, died without leaving an heir and the Spanish crown went to the Bourbon family of France. The Spanish Netherlands then reverted to the control of the Austrian line of Hapsburgs and became the Austrian Netherlands. The Austrian Netherlands along with the Bishopric of Liege fell to the French Republic in 1794.

At the Congress of Vienna in 1815 the area was reunited with the Netherlands, but in 1830 independence was gained and the constitutional monarchy of Belgium was established. A large part of the Duchy of Luxembourg was incorporated into Belgium and the first king was Leopold I of Saxe-Coburg-Gotha. It was invaded by the German Army in August, 1914 and the German forces carried on a devastating occupation of most of the territory until the Armistice. Belgium joined the League of Nations. On May 10, 1940 it was invaded again by Nazi German armies. The Belgian and Allied forces were quickly overwhelmed and were evacuated through Dunkirk. Allied troops reached Belgium again in Sept. 1944. Prince Charles, Count of Flanders, assumed King Leopold's responsibilities until liberation by the U.S. Army in Austria on May 8, 1945. As of January 1, 1989, Belgium became a federal kingdom.

RULERS

Leopold I, 1831-1865
Leopold II, 1865-1909

MINT MARKS

Angel head - Brussels

MINTMASTERS INITIALS & PRIVY MARKS

(b) - bird - Vogelier
Lamb head - Lambret

MONETARY SYSTEM

100 Centimes = 1 Franc
43 Francs = 1 Ecu

LEGENDS

Belgian coins are usually inscribed either in Dutch, French or both. However some modern coins are being inscribed in Latin and German. The language used is best told by noting the spelling of the name of the country.

(Fr) French: BELGIQUE or BELGES
(Du) Dutch: BELGIE or BELGEN

Many Belgian coins are collected by what is known as Position A and Position B edges. Some dates command a premium depending on the position which are as follows:

Position A: Coins with portrait side down having upright edge lettering.
Position B: Coins with portrait side up having upright edge lettering.

CENTIME

COPPER
Wide rims.

KM#	Date	Mintage	VG	Fine	VF	XF
1.1	1832	—	20.00	60.00	225.00	450.00
	1833/2	5.007	2.50	20.00	125.00	180.00
	1833	Inc. Ab.	2.00	10.00	55.00	120.00
	1835/2	4.367	2.50	20.00	125.00	180.00
	1835	Inc. Ab.	2.50	10.00	65.00	140.00
	Narrow rims.					
1.2	1835/2	I.A.	3.00	14.00	120.00	180.00
	1835	Inc. Ab.	1.25	4.00	35.00	65.00
	1836/2	4.256	1.25	4.50	40.00	75.00
	1836	Inc. Ab.	1.25	4.50	30.00	60.00
	1837	—	22.50	90.00	400.00	700.00
	1838	—	22.50	90.00	400.00	700.00
	1841	—	22.50	90.00	400.00	700.00
	1844	1.822	2.75	10.00	65.00	130.00
	1845	8.324	.75	3.00	12.00	35.00
	1846/1	8.241	— Reported, not confirmed			
	1846	Inc. Ab.	.75	3.50	12.50	35.00
	1847	5.138	.75	3.50	12.50	35.00
	1848/1	.383	70.00	175.00	400.00	700.00
	1848	Inc. Ab.	70.00	175.00	400.00	700.00
	1849	1.218	1.50	12.50	45.00	100.00
	1850	2.309	1.50	8.00	30.00	60.00
	1855	2.428	50.00	120.00	300.00	500.00
	1856	Inc. Ab.	.75	7.50	30.00	60.00
	1857	.948	3.00	12.00	45.00	90.00
	1858	.916	3.00	12.00	45.00	90.00
	1859	.982	3.00	12.00	45.00	90.00
	1860	1.581	1.00	3.00	12.00	40.00
	1861	1.696	1.00	3.00	12.00	40.00
	1862	11.907	.50	1.50	5.00	20.00
	1863	Inc. Ab.	40.00	100.00	300.00	650.00
	Rev: W/o dash below CENT.					
1.3	1857	Inc. Ab.	10.00	30.00	100.00	200.00
	1858	Inc. Ab.	10.00	30.00	100.00	200.00
	1859	Inc. Ab.	25.00	70.00	120.00	270.00
	1860	Inc. Ab.	8.00	12.00	40.00	120.00
	Rev: W/o stop in signature.					
1.4	1862	Inc. Ab.	2.00	3.00	10.00	25.00

NOTE: Until 1838 these were often struck over Netherlands 1/2 Cent, KM#51. If the date of the Netherlands coin is still visible, add up to 50 percent to the value, except for the date 1838 which is extremely rare.

Obv. French leg: DES BELGES.

KM#	Date	Mintage	Fine	VF	XF	Unc
33.1	1869	5.064	1.00	2.50	12.00	30.00
	1870	3.930	1.00	2.50	12.00	30.00
	1873	2.036	1.00	2.50	12.00	30.00
	1874	3.907	1.00	2.50	12.00	30.00
	1875	2.970	1.00	2.50	12.00	30.00
	1876	2.966	1.00	2.50	12.00	30.00
	1882	5.000	.25	1.00	5.00	20.00
	1883	—	60.00	300.00	600.00	1200.
	1899	2.500	1.00	1.00	3.50	10.00

NOTE: Later dates (1901-1907) exist for this type

Thin flan.

KM#	Date	Mintage	Fine	VF	XF	Unc
33.2	1882	Inc. Ab.	1.00	1.50	4.00	12.50

NOTE: Later dates (1901-1902) exist for this type

Obv. Dutch leg: DER BELGEN.

KM#	Date	Mintage	Fine	VF	XF	Unc
34.1	1882	Inc. Ab.	50.00	150.00	325.00	550.00
	1887	5.000	1.00	2.50	4.50	12.00
	1892	—	50.00	150.00	300.00	500.00
	1894	5.000	.50	1.75	3.00	10.00
	1899	2.500	.50	2.00	3.50	10.00

NOTE: Later dates (1901-1907) exist for this type.

Thin flan.

KM#	Date	Mintage	Fine	VF	XF	Unc
34.2	1887	Inc. Ab.	3.00	4.50	12.00	35.00

NOTE: Later dates (1901-1902) exist for this type.

2 CENTIMES

COPPER
Wide rims.

KM#	Date	Mintage	VG	Fine	VF	XF
4.1	1833	16.748	2.50	5.00	35.00	65.00
	1834	3.268	3.00	8.00	65.00	150.00
	1835	26.774	2.50	6.00	22.50	45.00

Medal alignment.

KM#	Date	Mintage	VG	Fine	VF	XF
4.3	1833	Inc. Ab.	10.00	30.00	140.00	300.00
	1834	Inc. Ab.	20.00	45.00	225.00	500.00
	Narrow rims.					
4.2	1835/3	Inc. Ab.	10.00	20.00	60.00	100.00
	1835	Inc. Ab.	.75	3.00	12.00	18.00
	.1835.	Inc. Ab.	6.50	15.00	50.00	90.00
	1836/3	27.539	5.00	10.00	45.00	100.00
	1836	Inc. Ab.	.75	3.00	12.00	15.00
	1837	—	30.00	65.00	300.00	500.00
	1838/7	—	70.00	130.00	600.00	1200.
	1838	—	30.00	65.00	300.00	500.00
	1841	2.226	1.50	10.00	25.00	50.00
	1842	2.824	1.50	10.00	25.00	50.00
	1844	1.802	1.00	6.00	20.00	40.00
	1845 lg.dt.	8.324	.75	2.50	10.00	20.00
	1845 sm.dt.	I.A.	.75	2.50	10.00	20.00
	1846	8.008	.75	2.50	10.00	20.00
	1847	3.432	1.00	3.50	12.00	25.00
	1848	.420	12.00	30.00	110.00	200.00
	1849	3.690	1.00	3.50	12.00	25.00
	1850	.404	8.00	30.00	125.00	275.00
	1851	2.407	1.00	5.00	20.00	40.00
	1852 lg.dt.	.731	5.00	15.00	50.00	100.00
	1852 sm.dt.	I.A.	5.00	15.00	50.00	100.00
	1853	.466	12.00	30.00	90.00	200.00
	1855	.172	22.00	50.00	225.00	500.00
	1856 lg. dt.	6.255	.75	2.00	8.00	15.00
	1856 sm. dt.	I.A.	.75	2.00	8.00	15.00
	1857	4.612	.75	3.00	10.00	20.00
	1857 w/o signature	Inc. Ab.	5.00	10.00	50.00	120.00
	1858/47	3.177	1.50	3.00	15.00	35.00
	1858/57	I.A.	1.50	8.00	40.00	90.00
	1858	Inc. Ab.	.75	3.00	10.00	27.50
	1859	4.074	.75	3.00	10.00	27.50
	1860 lg. dt.	3.070	.75	2.00	8.00	27.50
	1860 sm. dt.	I.A.	.75	2.00	8.00	27.50
	1861	2.924	.75	2.00	8.00	25.00
	1862 lg.dt.	6.586	.50	2.00	8.00	15.00
	1862 sm.dt.	I.A.	.50	2.00	8.00	15.00
	1863/2	18.621	.75	2.50	12.00	20.00
	1863	Inc. Ab.	.50	1.00	4.00	6.00
	1864/1	16.840	3.00	8.00	25.00	45.00
	1864	Inc. Ab.	.50	1.00	4.00	6.00
	1865	2.447	.50	2.00	8.00	15.00

NOTE: Until 1836 these were commonly struck over Netherlands 1 Cent, KM#47. If the date of the Netherlands coin is still visible, add up to 50 percent to the value.

Rev: W/o stop in signature.

KM#	Date	Mintage	VG	Fine	VF	XF
4.4	1844	Inc. Ab.	1.00	10.00	25.00	45.00
	1845	Inc. Ab.	.75	2.50	10.00	17.50
	1851	Inc. Ab.	.75	3.00	20.00	40.00
	1861	Inc. Ab.	.75	2.00	8.00	15.00
	BRONZE					
4.2a	1845	Inc. Ab.	40.00	70.00	300.00	600.00
	1859	Inc. Ab.	40.00	70.00	300.00	600.00

COPPER
c/s: Script L monogram on Netherlands, 1 Cent, KM#47.

KM#	Date	Mintage	VG	Fine	VF	XF
84	ND	—	120.00	450.00	900.00	1400.

Obv. French leg: DES BELGES.

KM#	Date	Mintage	Fine	VF	XF	Unc
35.1	1869	2.972	4.00	15.00	60.00	150.00
	1869 plain edge (restrike)		—	—	—	—
	1870	5.654	.75	1.00	5.00	12.00
	1870/1	I.A.	1.25	2.00	12.50	30.00
	1871	Inc.1870	1.25	5.00	20.00	45.00
	1873	7.491	.75	1.00	5.00	12.00
	1874 sm. wide date	7.876	.75	1.00	5.00	12.00
	1874 lg. narrow date	Inc. Ab.	.75	1.00	5.00	12.00
	1875	7.932	.75	1.00	5.00	12.00
	1876	10.472	.50	.75	3.00	10.00

NOTE: Later dates (1902-1909) exist for this type.

5 CENTIMES

COPPER

KM#	Date	Mintage	VG	Fine	VF	XF
5.1	1811 (error)	—	60.00	120.00	350.00	800.00
	1833	4.437	2.50	8.00	27.50	55.00
	1834	2.515	3.00	7.00	25.00	50.00
	1835	—	60.00	120.00	500.00	1500.
	1837	12.038	1.00	3.00	10.00	25.00
	1838	Inc. Ab.	60.00	175.00	450.00	800.00
	1841 narrow 1	2.509	2.50	7.00	25.00	45.00
	1841 wide 1	Inc. Ab.	2.50	7.00	25.00	45.00
	1842	5.536	1.00	4.00	15.00	30.00
	1847	1.131	4.00	10.00	40.00	90.00
	1848	1.845	2.50	7.00	25.00	45.00
	1849 lg. 9	1.447	2.50	12.00	35.00	70.00
	1849 sm. 9	I.A.	2.50	12.00	35.00	70.00
	1850 5 w/ball top, round 0 w/wide center	2.689	1.50	5.00	15.00	30.00
	1850 5 w/less curved top, 0 tall w/narrow center	Inc. Ab.	1.50	5.00	15.00	30.00
	1851	2.381	1.50	5.00	15.00	30.00
	1852	1.943	1.50	5.00	15.00	30.00
	1853	.705	10.00	40.00	120.00	250.00
	1855 lg. 5	.265	40.00	85.00	250.00	450.00
	1855 sm. 5	I.A.	40.00	85.00	250.00	450.00
	1856	5.656	1.00	2.00	10.00	30.00
	1857	2.299	1.50	4.00	12.50	35.00
	1858	2.712	1.50	4.00	12.50	35.00
	1858 w/o cross on crown	Inc. Ab.	5.00	15.00	45.00	100.00
	1859	2.591	1.50	4.00	12.50	35.00
	1860	.199	60.00	175.00	400.00	750.00
	1861	Inc. Ab.	70.00	200.00	450.00	900.00
	BRONZE					
5.1a	1833	Inc. Ab.	100.00	200.00	600.00	900.00
	1834	—	— Reported, not confirmed			
	1837	—	— Reported, not confirmed			
	1848	Inc. Ab.	75.00	120.00	400.00	600.00
	1850	Inc. Ab.	100.00	200.00	600.00	900.00
	1858	Inc. Ab.	90.00	150.00	500.00	800.00
	1859	Inc. Ab.	75.00	120.00	400.00	600.00
	COPPER **Rev: W/o stop in signature.**					
5.2	1833	Inc. Ab.	5.00	12.00	45.00	150.00
	1834	Inc. Ab.	8.00	20.00	60.00	190.00
	1837	Inc. Ab.	3.00	5.00	20.00	90.00
	1841	Inc. Ab.	4.50	9.00	30.00	125.00
	1842	Inc. Ab.	4.00	7.00	25.00	75.00
	1847	Inc. Ab.	10.00	20.00	65.00	200.00
	1848	Inc. Ab.	3.00	10.00	30.00	120.00
	1849	Inc. Ab.	8.00	15.00	50.00	140.00
	1850	Inc. Ab.	3.00	6.00	30.00	90.00
	1851	Inc. Ab.	4.00	8.00	35.00	100.00
	1852	Inc. Ab.	3.00	10.00	30.00	120.00
	Rev: Large S in CENTS.					
5.3	1858	Inc. Ab.	2.00	5.00	30.00	90.00
	1859	Inc. Ab.	3.00	6.00	40.00	120.00

COPPER-NICKEL

KM#	Date	Mintage	Fine	VF	XF	Unc
21	1861	8.259	.15	.35	1.50	8.00
	1862/1	14.149	.25	2.00	6.00	20.00
	1862	Inc. Ab.	.15	.25	1.25	7.00
	1863/2	16.055	.25	3.00	8.00	25.00
	1863	Inc. Ab.	.25	.40	2.00	9.00
	1864	2.513	4.00	10.00	20.00	80.00

NOTE: Varieties exist.

Obv. French leg: DES BELGES.

KM#	Date	Mintage	Fine	VF	XF	Unc
40	1894	3.111	1.00	3.50	7.00	17.50
	1895	3.693	1.00	3.50	8.00	20.00
	1898	1.004	7.00	12.00	55.00	110.00
	1900/891	1.666	7.00	12.00	55.00	125.00
	1900	Inc. Ab.	5.00	10.00	40.00	85.00

NOTE: Later date (1901) exists for this type.

Obv. Dutch leg: DER BELGEN.

KM#	Date	Mintage	Fine	VF	XF	Unc
41	1894	1.658	1.00	3.50	8.00	20.00
	1895/4	—	2.00	5.00	15.00	25.00
	1895	4.957	1.00	3.50	7.00	17.50
	1898	.985	8.00	15.00	60.00	120.00
	1900	1.670	5.00	10.00	40.00	85.00

10 CENTIMES

COPPER

KM#	Date	Mintage	VG	Fine	VF	XF
2.1	1832	.993	9.00	30.00	100.00	200.00
	1833	.994	9.00	30.00	100.00	200.00
	1835	—	125.00	250.00	850.00	1800.
	1838	—	125.00	250.00	900.00	1900.
	1841	—	125.00	250.00	850.00	1800.
	1847/37	.135	16.00	50.00	115.00	250.00
	1847	Inc. Ab.	16.00	50.00	115.00	250.00
	1848/38	.777	20.00	55.00	120.00	200.00
	1848	Inc. Ab.	20.00	55.00	120.00	200.00
	1849/39	I.A.	—	—	—	—
	1849	Inc. Ab.	125.00	150.00	850.00	1800.
	1855	.191	50.00	100.00	300.00	700.00
	1856	Inc. Ab.	100.00	200.00	750.00	1500.

Medal alignment.

KM#	Date	Mintage	VG	Fine	VF	XF
2.2	1832	Inc. Ab.	125.00	300.00	1000.	2000.

COPPER-NICKEL

KM#	Date	Mintage	VG	Fine	VF	XF
22	1861	9.080	.25	.75	2.50	7.00
	1862/61					
		15.129	.35	1.00	3.00	10.00
	1862	Inc. Ab.	.10	.50	2.50	6.00
	1862 dot after PREMIER					
		Inc. Ab.	5.00	15.00	60.00	100.00
	1863	14.482	.10	.50	3.00	8.00
	1864	3.202	2.50	5.00	10.00	25.00

Obv. French leg: DES BELGES.

KM#	Date	Mintage	Fine	VF	XF	Unc
42	1894	11.886	.75	2.50	7.00	18.00
	1895/4	.736	7.00	30.00	100.00	200.00
	1895	Inc. Ab.	30.00	50.00	110.00	160.00
	1898	3.499	3.00	6.00	12.00	35.00

NOTE: Later date (1901) exists for this type.

Obv. Dutch leg: DER BELGEN.

KM#	Date	Mintage	Fine	VF	XF	Unc
43	1894	9.209	.75	3.00	7.00	18.00
	1895/4	3.529	9.00	35.00	120.00	225.00
	1895	Inc. Ab.	1.00	4.50	7.50	30.00
	1898	3.500	3.00	6.00	15.00	35.00

NOTE: Later date (1901) exists for this type.

20 CENTIMES

1.0000 g, .900 SILVER, 0289 oz ASW

KM#	Date	Mintage	VG	Fine	VF	XF
19	1852 w/periods					
		.301	8.00	20.00	75.00	125.00
	1852 w/o periods					
		Inc. Ab.	10.00	25.00	90.00	150.00
	1853 w/periods					
		1.965	3.00	8.00	30.00	80.00
	1853 w/o periods					
		Inc. Ab.	5.00	12.00	40.00	110.00
	1858	.865	40.00	125.00	350.00	600.00

COPPER-NICKEL

KM#	Date	Mintage	VG	Fine	VF	XF
20	1860	1.804	10.00	20.00	50.00	130.00
	1860 l.	I.A.	90.00	250.00	500.00	700.00
	1861	Inc. Ab.	1.00	3.00	8.00	32.00

1/4 FRANC

1.2500 g, .900 SILVER, .0362 oz ASW

KM#	Date	Mintage	VG	Fine	VF	XF
8	1834 signature					
		.762	15.00	30.00	120.00	220.00
	1834 w/o signature					
		Inc. Ab.	20.00	50.00	220.00	325.00
	1835 signature					
		.640	15.00	35.00	150.00	250.00
	1835 w/o signature					
		Inc. Ab.	20.00	50.00	220.00	325.00
	1841	8,000	175.00	300.00	1000.	1800.
	1843	Inc. Ab.	50.00	115.00	300.00	800.00
	1844	.966	8.00	20.00	120.00	200.00

KM#	Date	Mintage	VG	Fine	VF	XF
14	1849	.101	200.00	500.00	1250.	2200.
	1850	Inc. Ab.	85.00	250.00	750.00	1700.

NOTE: Varieties exist w/and w/o periods in signature.

1/2 FRANC

2.5000 g, .900 SILVER, .0723 oz ASW

KM#	Date	Mintage	VG	Fine	VF	XF
6	1833	.058	50.00	150.00	450.00	1200.
	1834	1.578	15.00	40.00	175.00	300.00
	1835	.805	20.00	50.00	200.00	450.00
	1838	.550	30.00	60.00	275.00	700.00
	1840	.347	30.00	60.00	275.00	750.00
	1841	Inc. Ab.	200.00	350.00	1200.	2200.
	1843	.366	30.00	65.00	300.00	800.00
	1844	1.584	15.00	35.00	130.00	275.00.

NOTE: Varieties exist.

KM#	Date	Mintage	VG	Fine	VF	XF
15	1847	(restrike)	—	—	—	—
	1849	.210	150.00	500.00	1500.	2500.
	1850	Inc. Ab.	125.00	325.00	1000.	1800.

50 CENTIMES

2.5000 g, .835 SILVER, .0671 oz ASW

Obv. French leg: DES BELGES.

KM#	Date	Mintage	Fine	VF	XF	Unc
26	1866	6.806	4.00	20.00	85.00	160.00
	1867	1.014	12.00	40.00	165.00	275.00
	1868	1.076	50.00	100.00	450.00	900.00
	1881/61	.200	90.00	300.00	850.00	1400.
	1881	Inc. Ab.	70.00	225.00	750.00	1100.
	1886/61					
		1.250	12.00	30.00	90.00	150.00
	1886	Inc. Ab.	2.00	15.00	50.00	120.00
	1898	.499	2.00	25.00	85.00	145.00
	1899	.500	2.00	25.00	85.00	145.00

Obv. Dutch leg: DER BELGEN.

KM#	Date	Mintage	Fine	VF	XF	Unc
27	1866 (restrike)	—	—	—	—	—
	1886	3.750	2.00	14.00	40.00	120.00
	1898	.501	2.50	22.00	85.00	145.00
	1899	.500	2.50	22.00	85.00	145.00

FRANC

5.0000 g, .900 SILVER, .1447 oz ASW

KM#	Date	Mintage	VG	Fine	VF	XF
7.1	1833	.061	110.00	150.00	400.00	1200.
	1834	.482	30.00	60.00	175.00	400.00
	1835	.861	35.00	70.00	280.00	500.00
	1838	.525	35.00	90.00	300.00	700.00
	1838 lg.star	I.A.	110.00	650.00	1500.	2200.
	1840	.261	40.00	90.00	310.00	800.00
	1841	Inc. Ab.	135.00	375.00	1100.	2000.
	1843	2.196	65.00	225.00	700.00	1500.
	1844	Inc. Ab.	20.00	40.00	140.00	300.00

Medal alignment.

KM#	Date	Mintage	VG	Fine	VF	XF
7.2	1833	Inc. Ab.	200.00	1200.	2800.	4000.

KM#	Date	Mintage	VG	Fine	VF	XF
16.1	1849	.041	150.00	350.00	1200.	2200.
	1850	.162	125.00	300.00	1100.	2000.

NOTE: Edge varieties exist.

Obv: W/o period in signature.

KM#	Date	Mintage	VG	Fine	VF	XF
16.2	1850	Inc. Ab.	225.00	1300.	3300.	4200.

5.0000 g, .835 SILVER, .1342 oz ASW

Obv. French leg: DES BELGES.

KM#	Date	Mintage	Fine	VF	XF	Unc
28.1	1866	3.041	5.00	25.00	85.00	175.00
	1867	6.652	3.00	20.00	80.00	140.00
	1868	.675	— Reported, not confirmed			
	1869	1.394	6.00	35.00	135.00	350.00
	1881/67	.119	100.00	250.00	950.00	1500.
	1881	Inc. Ab.	50.00	250.00	800.00	1400.
	1886/66					
		1.250	4.00	20.00	100.00	175.00
	1886	Inc. Ab.	3.00	15.00	65.00	120.00

Obv: W/o period in signature.

KM#	Date	Mintage	Fine	VF	XF	Unc
28.2	1886	Inc. Ab.	7.00	30.00	75.00	175.00

Obv. Dutch leg: DER BELGEN.

KM#	Date	Mintage	Fine	VF	XF	Unc
29.1	1886	1.026	4.00	20.00	65.00	130.00
	1887	2.724	3.00	15.00	75.00	135.00

Obv: W/o period in signature.

KM#	Date	Mintage	Fine	VF	XF	Unc
29.2	1886	Inc. Ab.	12.50	35.00	75.00	150.00
	1887	Inc. Ab.	12.50	35.00	75.00	150.00

50th Anniversary Independence

KM#	Date	Mintage	Fine	VF	XF	Unc
38	1880	.545	8.00	30.00	65.00	120.00

2 FRANCS/2 FRANK

10.0000 g, .900 SILVER, .2894 oz ASW
Edge inscription inclined to left.

KM#	Date	Mintage	VG	Fine	VF	XF
9.1	1834 Pos. A	.276	150.00	350.00	900.00	2200.
	1834 Pos. A	—	—	—	Proof	3500.
	1834 Pos. B	Inc. Ab.	150.00	350.00	900.00	2200.
	1835 Pos. A	.225	175.00	400.00	950.00	2300.
	1835 Pos. B	Inc. Ab.	200.00	450.00	1000.	2800.
	1838 Pos. A	—	225.00	600.00	1650.	3500.
	1838 Pos. B	—	225.00	600.00	1650.	3500.
	1840 Pos. A	.236	275.00	600.00	1650.	3500.
	1840 Pos. B	Inc. Ab.	275.00	625.00	2000.	4000.
	1841 Pos. A	—	500.00	1200.	4000.	6000.
	1843 Pos. A	.735	125.00	275.00	850.00	2000.
	1843 Pos. B	Inc. Ab.	125.00	275.00	850.00	2000.
	1844 Pos. A	.483	150.00	400.00	900.00	2200.
	1844 Pos. B	Inc. Ab.	150.00	400.00	900.00	2200.

Edge inscription inclined to right.

KM#	Date	Mintage	VG	Fine	VF	XF
9.2	1834 Pos. A	Inc. Ab.	150.00	400.00	900.00	2200.
	1834 Pos. B	Inc. Ab.	150.00	425.00	1000.	2500.
	1835 Pos. A	Inc. Ab.	150.00	350.00	900.00	2200.
	1835 Pos. B	Inc. Ab.	175.00	450.00	1000.	2500.
	1838 Pos. A	.300	200.00	450.00	1000.	2600.
	1838 Pos. B	Inc. Ab.	200.00	450.00	1000.	2600.
	1840 Pos. A	Inc. Ab.	150.00	350.00	900.00	2200.
	1840 Pos. B	Inc. Ab.	150.00	350.00	900.00	2200.
	1841 Pos. A	—	275.00	600.00	2200.	3200.
	1843 Pos. A	Inc Ab.	150.00	350.00	900.00	2100.
	1843 Pos. B	Inc. Ab.	150.00	350.00	900.00	2200.
	1844 Pos. A	Inc. Ab.	150.00	350.00	900.00	2200.
	1844 Pos. B	Inc. Ab.	175.00	400.00	1100.	2600.

KM#	Date	Mintage	VG	Fine	VF	XF
10	1848	(restrike)	—	—	—	—
	1849	—	400.00	900.00	2800.	4700.
	1865	—	450.00	1100.	3200.	5200.

NOTE: The above type was not officially released into circulation.

10.0000 g, .835 SILVER, .2685 oz ASW
Obv. French leg: DES BELGES.

KM#	Date	Mintage	Fine	VF	XF	Unc
30.1	1866	1.942	7.00	35.00	250.00	400.00
	1867	3.789	5.00	30.00	200.00	300.00
	1868	2.164	7.00	35.00	225.00	350.00

NOTE: Edge varieties exist.

Rev: W/o cross on crown.

KM#	Date	Mintage	VG	Fine	VF	XF
30.2	1866	Inc. Ab.	15.00	225.00	475.00	850.00
	1867	Inc. Ab.	12.50	190.00	425.00	750.00
	1868	Inc. Ab.	17.50	250.00	500.00	900.00

Obv. Dutch leg: DER BELGEN.
Rev: Cross on crown.

KM#	Date	Mintage	Fine	VF	XF	Unc
31	1887	.150	75.00	300.00	1200.	2000.

NOTE: Edge varieties exist.

50th Anniversary Independence
Rev. French leg: DE BELGIQUE.

KM#	Date	Mintage	Fine	VF	XF	Unc
39	1880	.118	30.00	100.00	275.00	500.00

2-1/2 FRANCS

12.5000 g, .900 SILVER, .3617 oz ASW
Obv. French leg: ROI DES BELGES.

KM#	Date	Mintage	VG	Fine	VF	XF
11	1848	.559	45.00	150.00	225.00	400.00
	1849	2.003	30.00	85.00	200.00	350.00

Larger head.

KM#	Date	Mintage	VG	Fine	VF	XF
12	1848	Inc. Ab.	125.00	350.00	1200.	2000.
	1849	Inc. Ab.	30.00	110.00	250.00	550.00
	1849	—	—	—	Proof	1500.
	1850	.065	175.00	400.00	1200.	1500.
	1865	—	350.00	750.00	2000.	3250.

NOTE: Coins dated 1865 were not released into circulation.

5 FRANCS/5 FRANK

25.0000 g, .900 SILVER, .7234 oz ASW
Incuse lettered edge.

KM#	Date	Mintage	VG	Fine	VF	XF
3.1	1832 Pos. A	.037	60.00	150.00	800.00	1400.
	1832 Pos. B	Inc. Ab.	55.00	135.00	600.00	1000.
	1833 Pos. A	1.126	16.00	30.00	100.00	750.00
	1833 Pos. B	Inc. Ab.	17.50	35.00	110.00	765.00
	1834 Pos. A	.350	45.00	90.00	250.00	800.00
	1834 Pos. B	Inc. Ab.	45.00	90.00	250.00	800.00
	1835 Pos. A	.370	45.00	90.00	250.00	900.00
	1835 Pos. B	Inc. Ab.	45.00	90.00	250.00	900.00
	1838 Pos. A	5,203	450.00	1200.	3000.	8000.
	1838 Pos. B	Inc. Ab.	500.00	1500.	4000.	9000.
	1840	—	500.00	1700.	3400.	6300.
	1841	—	500.00	1700.	3400.	6300.
	1844 Pos. A	.483	60.00	135.00	400.00	850.00
	1844 Pos. B	Inc. Ab.	150.00	800.00	2000.	4000.

Raised lettered edge.

KM#	Date	Mintage	VG	Fine	VF	XF
3.2	1847	.700	20.00	40.00	85.00	400.00
	1848	2.516	12.00	25.00	50.00	250.00
	1849	3.014	10.00	17.50	45.00	225.00

KM#	Date	Mintage	VG	Fine	VF	XF
17	1849	3.909	12.50	17.50	35.00	75.00
	1850 dot above date	5.265	12.50	17.50	40.00	75.00
	1850 w/o dot above date	Inc. Ab.	10.00	15.00	40.00	65.00
	1850	—	—	—	Proof	500.00
	1851/0	3.708	15.00	20.00	40.00	60.00
	1851 dot above date	Inc. Ab.	10.00	17.50	40.00	60.00
	1851 w/o dot above date	Inc. Ab.	10.00	17.50	40.00	60.00
	1852/1	4.605	15.00	25.00	40.00	75.00
	1852	Inc. Ab.	10.00	17.50	40.00	60.00
	1853	2.427	15.00	30.00	40.00	75.00

KM#	Date	Mintage	VG	Fine	VF	XF
17	1858	.018	60.00	150.00	250.00	550.00
	1865/15 broken M in PREMIER					
		.907	15.00	25.00	80.00	120.00
	1865/55	I.A.	15.00	25.00	80.00	120.00
	1865/55 dot after F					
		Inc. Ab.	15.00	25.00	60.00	110.00
	1865	Inc. Ab.	10.00	20.00	40.00	90.00
	1865 dot after F on reverse					
		Inc. Ab.	15.00	30.00	65.00	100.00

Obv: Smaller head, engravers name near rim, below truncation.

KM#	Date	Mintage	Fine	VF	XF	Unc
24	1865	Inc. 1867	100.00	250.00	350.00	650.00
	1866	Inc. 1867	175.00	275.00	425.00	725.00
	1866 dot after F on reverse					
		Inc. 1867	175.00	325.00	525.00	800.00
	1867	3.693	7.50	15.00	35.00	100.00
	1867 dot after F on reverse					
		Inc. Ab.	10.00	50.00	75.00	125.00
	1868 Pos. A					
		6.751	7.00	10.00	35.00	100.00
	1868 Pos. B					
		Inc. Ab.	85.00	135.00	330.00	825.00
	1869	12.658	6.50	8.00	30.00	75.00
	1870	10.486	6.50	8.00	30.00	75.00
	1871	4.783	6.50	8.00	35.00	80.00
	1872	2.045	7.00	10.00	45.00	85.00
	1873 Pos. A					
		22.341	6.50	8.00	25.00	60.00
	1873 Pos. B					
		Inc. Ab.	75.00	375.00	900.00	1600.
	1874	2.400	6.50	8.00	35.00	85.00
	1875	2.981	6.50	8.00	30.00	85.00
	1876	2.160	7.00	9.00	35.00	85.00
	1878	3 known	—	—	Rare	—

Obv: Larger head, engravers name below truncation.

KM#	Date	Mintage	Fine	VF	XF	Unc
25	1865	Inc. Ab.	450.00	900.00	1350.	2500.
	1866	Inc. Ab.	550.00	1150.	1800.	3400.
	1867	Inc. Ab.	400.00	800.00	1100.	2300.
	1868	Inc. Ab.	550.00	1100.	1650.	3100.

10 FRANCS/10 FRANK

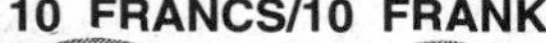

3.1662 g, .900 GOLD, .0916 oz AGW

KM#	Date	Mintage	Fine	VF	XF	Unc
18	1849	.037	500.00	1400.	2500.	3600.
	1850	.063	400.00	1200.	2250.	3200.

NOTE: 54,890 pcs. dated 1849 and 1850 were withdrawn from circulation.

KM#	Date	Mintage	Fine	VF	XF	Unc
A33	1865 (restrike)	—	—	—	—	—
	1867	—	1800.	3200.	6500.	11,000.

20 FRANCS/20 FRANK

6.4516 g, .900 GOLD, .1867 oz AGW

Lettered edge.

KM#	Date	Mintage	Fine	VF	XF	Unc
A23.1	1834	—	950.00	4800.	12,000.	15,000.
	1835	—	1200.	6000.	15,000.	18,500.
	1838	1 known	—	—	—	—
	1841	—	1300.	6500.	16,000.	20,000.

Milled edge.

KM#	Date	Mintage	Fine	VF	XF	Unc
A23.2	1834 (restrike)	—	—	—	—	—
	1835 (restrike)	—	—	—	—	—
	1838 (restrike)	—	—	—	—	—
	1841 (restrike)	—	—	—	—	—

Plain edge.

KM#	Date	Mintage	Fine	VF	XF	Unc
A23.3	1834 (restrike)	—	—	—	—	—
	1835 (restrike)	—	—	—	—	—
	1838 (restrike)	—	—	—	—	—
	1841 (restrike)	—	—	—	—	—

KM#	Date	Mintage	Fine	VF	XF	Unc
23	1862	—	1300.	6500.	16,000.	20,000.
	1864	—	1500.	3000.	5000.	8000.
	1865	1.558	BV	90.00	125.00	175.00

NOTE: Varieties exist.

NOTE: 1864 dated coins were not released for circulation and are considered patterns.

Obv: Heavy coarser beard.

KM#	Date	Mintage	Fine	VF	XF	Unc
32	1866 Pos. A					
		—	1000.	2000.	5000.	8000.
	1866 Pos. B					
		—	900.00	1800.	4000.	6000.
	1866 Pos. B (error) WINNER					
		—	900.00	1800.	4000.	6000.
	1867	1.341	—	BV	85.00	110.00
	1868	1.382	—	BV	85.00	110.00
	1869 Pos. A					
		1.234	—	BV	85.00	110.00
	1869 Pos. B					
		Inc. Ab.	100.00	175.00	250.00	325.00
	1870	3.191	—	BV	85.00	110.00

NOTE: 1866 dated coins were not released for circulation and are considered patterns.

Obv: Finer beard.

KM#	Date	Mintage	Fine	VF	XF	Unc
37	1870 Pos. A					
		Inc. Ab.	—	BV	85.00	110.00
	1870 Pos. B					
		Inc. Ab.	150.00	250.00	400.00	600.00
	1871 long beard					
		Inc. Ab.	BV	80.00	115.00	150.00
	1871	2.259	—	BV	85.00	110.00
	1874	3.046	—	BV	85.00	110.00
	1875 Pos. A					
		4.134	—	BV	85.00	110.00
	1875 Pos. B					
		Inc. Ab.	275.00	600.00	1000.	1500.
	1876 Pos. A					
		2.070	—	BV	85.00	110.00
	1876 Pos. B					
		Inc. Ab.	250.00	400.00	550.00	1000.
	1877 Pos. A					
		5.906	—	BV	85.00	110.00
	1877 Pos. B					
		Inc. Ab.	275.00	600.00	1000.	1500.
	1878 Pos. A					
		2.505	—	BV	85.00	110.00
	1878 Pos. B					
		Inc. Ab.	550.00	1100.	1650.	2200.
	1882	.522	—	BV	85.00	110.00

25 FRANCS/25 FRANK

7.9155 g, .900 GOLD, .2291 oz AGW

KM#	Date	Mintage	Fine	VF	XF	Unc
13.1	1848	*.321	650.00	1500.	2200.	3000.
	1849	**.150	750.00	2000.	4000.	5000.

***NOTE:** 268,411 melted.

****NOTE:** 125,217 melted.

Obv: Larger head.

KM#	Date	Mintage	Fine	VF	XF	Unc
13.2	1850	.074	850.00	2250.	4500.	6000.

NOTE: 61,910 melted.

40 FRANCS/40 FRANK

12.9032 g, .900 GOLD, .3734 oz AGW

Lettered edge.

KM#	Date	Mintage	Fine	VF	XF	Unc
B23.1	1834	—	1500.	7500.	16,750.	23,500.
	1835	—	1500.	7500.	16,750.	23,500.
	1838	—	2000.	8250.	20,000.	30,000.
	1841	—	1600.	8000.	18,500.	26,000.

Medal alignment.

KM#	Date	Mintage	Fine	VF	XF	Unc
B23.2	1834	—	1500.	7500.	16,750.	23,500.

MEDALLIC ISSUES (M)

(5 CENTIMES)

COPPER
25th Anniversary of Independence
Rev. French leg: . . .
DE L'INAUGURATION DU ROI.

KM#	Date	Mintage	Fine	VF	XF	Unc
M1	1856	.214	3.00	7.50	15.00	25.00

Rev. Dutch leg: . . . VAN S'KONINGS.

KM#	Date	Mintage	Fine	VF	XF	Unc
M2	1856	3,000	80.00	200.00	400.00	650.00

BRONZE
Rev. French leg: . . .
DE L'INAUGURATION DU ROI.

KM#	Date	Mintage	Fine	VF	XF	Unc
M3	1856	4,776	55.00	140.00	275.00	450.00

Rev. Dutch leg: . . . VAN S'KONINGS.

KM#	Date	Mintage	Fine	VF	XF	Unc
M4	1856	1,160	130.00	325.00	650.00	1000.

(10 CENTIMES)

COPPER
Marriage of Duke and Duchess of Brabant

KM#	Date	Mintage	Fine	VF	XF	Unc
M5.1	1853 lg.dt.	.104	5.00	20.00	40.00	65.00
M5.2	1853 sm.dt.	I.A.	5.00	20.00	50.00	100.00

(2 FRANCS)

10.0000 g, .835 SILVER, .2685 oz ASW
25th Anniversary of Independence
Rev. French leg: . . .
DE L'INAUGURATION DU ROI.
Coin alignment.

KM#	Date	Mintage	Fine	VF	XF	Unc
M6.1	1856	.012	80.00	200.00	400.00	650.00

Medal alignment.

KM#	Date	Mintage	Fine	VF	XF	Unc
M6.2	1856	Inc. Ab.	90.00	225.00	450.00	750.00

Rev. Dutch leg.: . . . VAN S'KONINGS.

Coin alignment.

KM#	Date	Mintage	Fine	VF	XF	Unc
M7.1	1856	1,898	750.00	1850.	3150.	4650.

Medal alignment.

KM#	Date	Mintage	Fine	VF	XF	Unc
M7.2	1856	Inc. Ab.	800.00	2000.	3650.	5850.

(5 FRANCS)

25.0000 g, .900 SILVER, .7234 oz ASW
Marriage of the Duke and Duchess of Brabant
Rev. date: 21-22 AOUT 1853.

KM#	Date	Mintage	Fine	VF	XF	Unc
M8.1	1853	.032	40.00	100.00	200.00	400.00

Rev. date: 21.22 AOUT 1853.

KM#	Date	Mintage	Fine	VF	XF	Unc
M8.2	1853	Inc. Ab.	40.00	100.00	200.00	400.00

KM#	Date	Mintage	Fine	VF	XF	Unc
M9	1880	6,714	75.00	175.00	250.00	450.00

COPPER

KM#	Date	Mintage	Fine	VF	XF	Unc
M9a	1880	.028	5.00	15.00	30.00	60.00

GOLD

KM#	Date	Mintage	Fine	VF	XF	Unc
M9b	1880	1 pc.	—	—	Unique	—

(40 FRANCS)

12.9000 g, .900 GOLD, .3733 oz AGW
25th Anniversary of Independence
Rev. French leg: . . . DE L'INAUGURATION.

KM#	Date	Mintage	Fine	VF	XF	Unc
M10	1856	449 pcs.	—	6000.	9000.	12,000.

Rev. Dutch leg: . . . VAN S'KONINGS.

KM#	Date	Mintage	Fine	VF	XF	Unc
M12	1856	500 pcs. (restrikes)		1000.	1750.	2000.

NOTE: Forgeries exist w/weight: 16.8 g.

(100 FRANCS)

31.6600 g, .900 GOLD, .9161 oz AGW
Marriage of Duke and Duchess of Brabant
Rev. date: 21-22 AOUT 1853.

KM#	Date	Mintage	Fine	VF	XF	Unc
M11.1	1853	482 pcs.	—	2500.	4000.	6000.

Rev. date: 21.22 AOUT 1853.

KM#	Date	Mintage	Fine	VF	XF	Unc
M11.2	1853	Inc. Ab.	—	2500.	3500.	5500.

NOTE: Examples without raised dot or - between 21 and 22 are restrikes.

PATTERNS (Pn)

(Including off metal strikes)

KM#	Date	Mintage	Identification	Mkt.Val.
Pn1	1832	—	1 Centime, Copper	—
Pn3	1834	—	40 Francs, Bronze, KM#B23.1	300.00
Pn5	1835	—	5 Centimes, Copper	—
Pn6	1835	—	10 Centimes, Copper	—
Pn7	1835	—	20 Francs, Bronze, KM#A23.1	250.00
Pn10	1837	—	1 Centime, Copper	—
Pn11	1837	—	2 Centimes, Copper	—
Pn12	1838	—	1 Centime, Copper	—
Pn13	1838	—	2 Centimes, Copper	—
Pn14	1838	—	5 Centimes, Copper	—
Pn15	1838	—	10 Centimes, Copper	—
Pn16	1838	—	1/4 Franc, Silver	—
Pn20	1840	—	5 Francs, Silver	—
Pn21	1841	—	1 Centime, Copper	—
Pn22	1841	—	10 Centimes, Copper	—
Pn23	1841	—	1/4 Franc, Silver	—
Pn24	1841	—	1/2 Franc, Silver	—
Pn25	1841	—	1 Franc, Silver	—
Pn26	1841	—	2 Francs, Silver	—
Pn27	1841	—	5 Francs, Silver	—

KM#	Date	Mintage	Identification	Mkt.Val.
Pn31	1842	—	5 Francs, Silver	1500.
Pn32	1843	—	1 Franc, Silver	—
Pn33	1847	—	50 Centimes, Silver, KM61, restrike	—
Pn34	1847	—	1/2 Franc, Silver, KM15, restrike	—

KM#	Date	Mintage	Identification	Mkt.Val.
Pn35	1847	—	5 Francs, Gilt Copper	100.00
Pn36	1847	—	5 Francs, Silver	—

KM#	Date	Mintage	Identification	Mkt.Val.
Pn37	1847	—	5 Francs, Gilt Copper	—

KM#	Date	Mintage	Identification	Mkt.Val.
Pn38	18xx	—	5 Francs, Gilt Copper	—

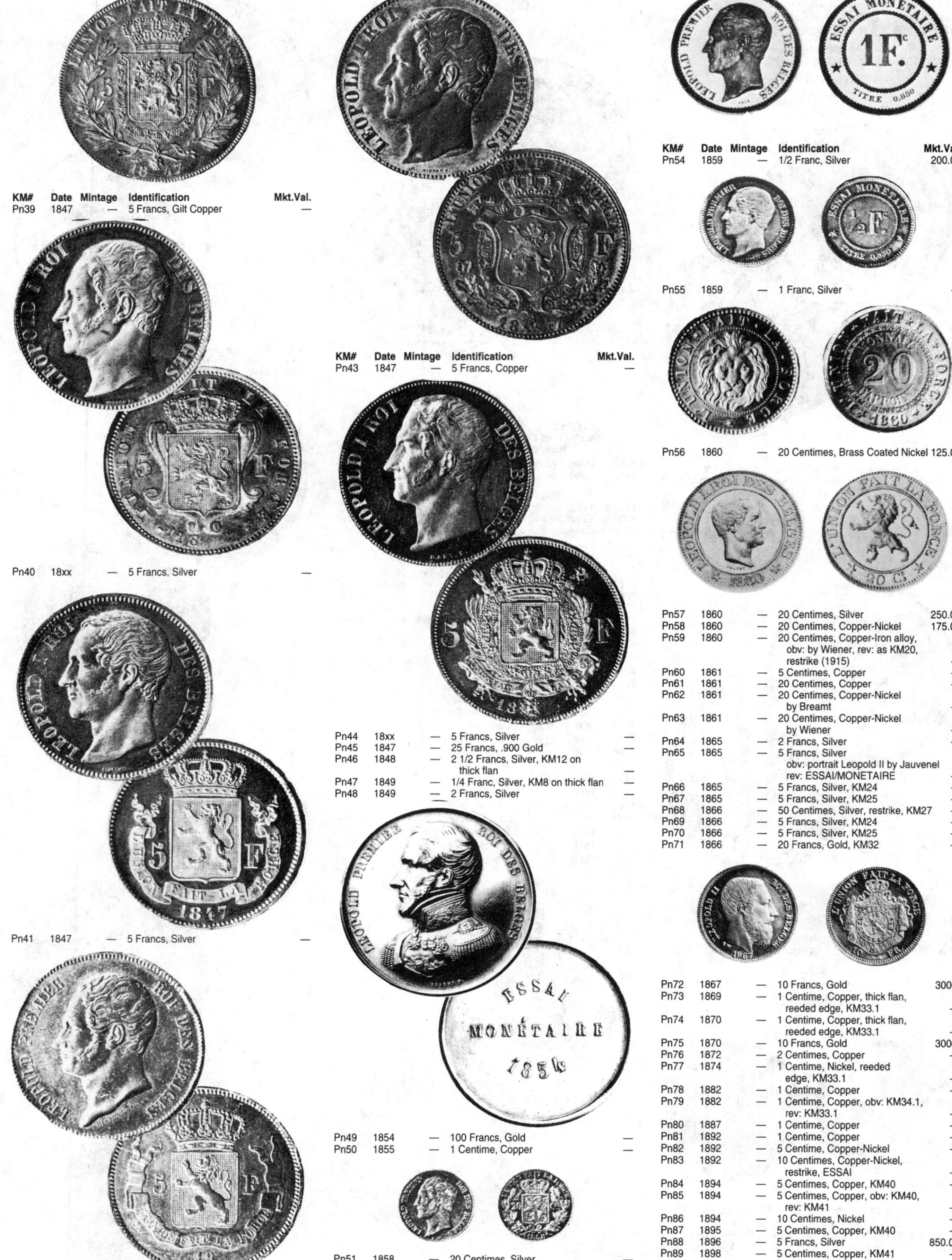

KM#	Date	Mintage	Identification	Mkt.Val.
Pn39	1847	—	5 Francs, Gilt Copper	—
Pn40	18xx	—	5 Francs, Silver	—
Pn41	1847	—	5 Francs, Silver	—
Pn42	18xx	—	5 Francs, Silver	—

KM#	Date	Mintage	Identification	Mkt.Val.
Pn43	1847	—	5 Francs, Copper	—
Pn44	18xx	—	5 Francs, Silver	—
Pn45	1847	—	25 Francs, .900 Gold	—
Pn46	1848	—	2 1/2 Francs, Silver, KM12 on thick flan	—
Pn47	1849	—	1/4 Franc, Silver, KM8 on thick flan	—
Pn48	1849	—	2 Francs, Silver	—
Pn49	1854	—	100 Francs, Gold	—
Pn50	1855	—	1 Centime, Copper	—
Pn51	1858	—	20 Centimes, Silver	—
Pn52	1859	—	2 Centimes, Aluminum	—
Pn53	1859	—	10 Centimes, Nickel clad Copper, ESSAI	100.00

KM#	Date	Mintage	Identification	Mkt.Val.
Pn54	1859	—	1/2 Franc, Silver	200.00
Pn55	1859	—	1 Franc, Silver	—
Pn56	1860	—	20 Centimes, Brass Coated Nickel	125.00
Pn57	1860	—	20 Centimes, Silver	250.00
Pn58	1860	—	20 Centimes, Copper-Nickel	175.00
Pn59	1860	—	20 Centimes, Copper-Iron alloy, obv: by Wiener, rev: as KM20, restrike (1915)	—
Pn60	1861	—	5 Centimes, Copper	—
Pn61	1861	—	20 Centimes, Copper	—
Pn62	1861	—	20 Centimes, Copper-Nickel by Breamt	—
Pn63	1861	—	20 Centimes, Copper-Nickel by Wiener	—
Pn64	1865	—	2 Francs, Silver	—
Pn65	1865	—	5 Francs, Silver obv: portrait Leopold II by Jauvenel rev: ESSAI/MONETAIRE	—
Pn66	1865	—	5 Francs, Silver, KM24	—
Pn67	1865	—	5 Francs, Silver, KM25	—
Pn68	1866	—	50 Centimes, Silver, restrike, KM27	—
Pn69	1866	—	5 Francs, Silver, KM24	—
Pn70	1866	—	5 Francs, Silver, KM25	—
Pn71	1866	—	20 Francs, Gold, KM32	—
Pn72	1867	—	10 Francs, Gold	3000.
Pn73	1869	—	1 Centime, Copper, thick flan, reeded edge, KM33.1	—
Pn74	1870	—	1 Centime, Copper, thick flan, reeded edge, KM33.1	—
Pn75	1870	—	10 Francs, Gold	3000.
Pn76	1872	—	2 Centimes, Copper	—
Pn77	1874	—	1 Centime, Nickel, reeded edge, KM33.1	—
Pn78	1882	—	1 Centime, Copper	—
Pn79	1882	—	1 Centime, Copper, obv: KM34.1, rev: KM33.1	—
Pn80	1887	—	1 Centime, Copper	—
Pn81	1892	—	1 Centime, Copper	—
Pn82	1892	—	5 Centime, Copper-Nickel	—
Pn83	1892	—	10 Centimes, Copper-Nickel, restrike, ESSAI	—
Pn84	1894	—	5 Centimes, Copper, KM40	—
Pn85	1894	—	5 Centimes, Copper, obv: KM40, rev: KM41	—
Pn86	1894	—	10 Centimes, Nickel	—
Pn87	1895	—	5 Centimes, Copper, KM40	—
Pn88	1896	—	5 Francs, Silver	850.00
Pn89	1898	—	5 Centimes, Copper, KM41	—

PIEFORTS (P)

KM#	Date	Mintage	Identification	Mkt.Val.
P1	1849	—	10 Francs, KM18	—

KM#	Date	Mintage	Identification	Mkt.Val.
P2	1859	—	20 Centimes, Silver, piefort	—
P3	1859	—	20 Centimes, Silver, double piefort	—

TRIAL STRIKES (TS)

KM#	Date	Mintage	Identification	Mkt.Val.
TS1	1860	—	20 Centimes, Bronze, rev. uniface	—
TS2	ND(1866)	—	2 Francs, Copper, obv. uniface	—
TS3	1872	—	2 Centimes, Pewter, obv. uniface	—
TS4	1872	—	2 Centimes, Pewter, rev. uniface	—

BELIZE

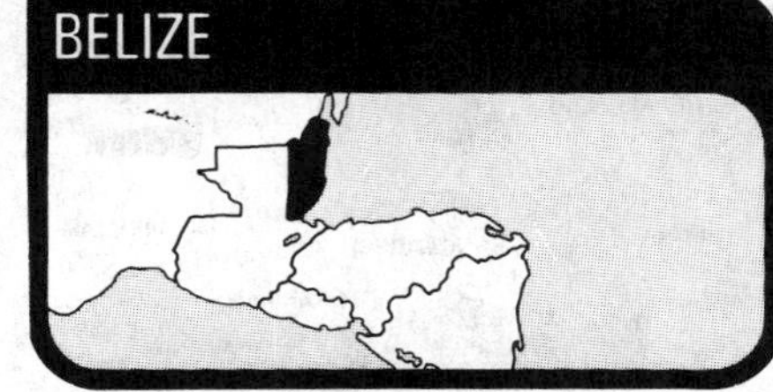

Belize, formerly British Honduras, but now an independent member of the British Commonwealth, is situated in Central America south of Mexico and east and north of Guatemala, with an area of 8,867 sq. mi. (22,960 sq. km.) and a population of 214,061. Capital: Belmopan. Tourism now augments Belize's economy, in addition to sugar, citrus fruits, chicle and hardwoods which are exported.

The area, site of the ancient Mayan civilization, was sighted by Columbus in 1502, and settled by shipwrecked English seamen in 1638. British buccaneers settled the former capital of Belize in the 17th century. Britain claimed administrative right over the area after the emancipation of Central America from Spain. In 1825, Imperial coins were introduced into the colony and were rated against the Spanish dollar and Honduran currency. It was declared a colony subordinate to Jamaica in 1862 and was established as the separate Crown Colony of British Honduras in 1884. In May, 1885 an order in Council authorized coins for the colony, with the first shipment arriving in July. While the Guatemalan peso was originally the standard of value, in 1894 the colony changed to the gold standard, based on the U.S. gold dollar. The anti-British Peoples United Party, which attained power in 1954, won a constitution, effective in 1964 which established self-government under a British appointed governor. British Honduras became Belize on June 1, 1973, following the passage of a surprise bill by the Peoples United Party, but the constitutional relationship with Britain remained unchanged.

In Dec. 1975, the U.N. General Assembly adopted a resolution supporting the right of the people of Belize to self-determination, and asking Britain and Guatemala to renew their negotiations on the future of Belize. Independence was obtained on Sept. 21, 1981.

RULERS

British, until 1981

MINT MARKS

H - Birmingham Mint
No mm - Royal Mint

MONETARY SYSTEM

Circa 1765-1855
6 Shillings 8 Pence (Jamaican) = 8 Reales
1855-1864
1 Dollar = 8 Rials = 4 Shillings (Sterling)
Commencing 1864
100 Cents = 1 Dollar

BRITISH HONDURAS

COUNTERMARKED COINAGE

It is generally believed that the crowned "GR" monogram was placed on certain coins to make them acceptable as trade items with local indigenous peoples. This mark did not affect their currency status, although in light of the Revolutionary War of 1810-1820 it may have been an attempt to localize and keep coins in the colony at a time when the supply of Spanish coins dwindled.

1810-1818

6 SHILLINGS 1 PENNY

.916 SILVER
c/m: Crowned script GR in rectangular indent on Mexico City 8 Reales, KM#109.

KM#	Date	Good	VG	Fine	VF
1.1	ND(1791-1808)	80.00	165.00	250.00	400.00

c/m: Crowned script GR in rectangular indent on Mexico City 8 Reales, KM#110.

KM#	Date	Good	VG	Fine	VF
1.2	ND(1808-1811)	80.00	165.00	250.00	400.00

c/m: Crowned script GR in rectangular indent on Peru (Lima) 8 Reales, KM#97.

KM#	Date	Good	VG	Fine	VF
5	ND(1791-1808)	80.00	165.00	250.00	400.00

c/m: Crowned script GR in oval indent on Mexico City 8 Reales, KM#111.

KM#	Date	Good	VG	Fine	VF
2	ND(1811-1818)	70.00	140.00	200.00	350.00

c/m: Crowned script GR in oval indent on France 5 Francs, C#138.

KM#	Date	Good	VG	Fine	VF
3	ND(L'an 4-11)	100.00	175.00	300.00	500.00

c/m: Incuse crowned script GR on Mexico City 8 Reales, KM#111.

KM#	Date	Good	VG	Fine	VF
4	ND(1811-1818)	75.00	150.00	250.00	400.00

NOTE: KM#4 is considered a local issue. The c/m crowned GR in octagonal indent is considered a modern fabrication. Refer to *"UNUSUAL WORLD COINS"* third edition, Krause Publications.

DECIMAL COINAGE

CENT

BRONZE

KM#	Date	Mintage	Fine	VF	XF	Unc
6	1885	.072	4.50	10.00	25.00	75.00
	1885	—	—	—	Proof	250.00
	1888	.100	3.50	8.50	25.00	85.00
	1888	—	—	—	Proof	275.00
	1889	.050	6.00	15.00	40.00	90.00
	1889	—	—	—	Proof	275.00
	1894	.050	8.00	20.00	50.00	275.00
	1894	*25 pcs.	—	—	Proof	300.00

5 CENTS

1.1620 g, .925 SILVER, .0346 oz ASW

KM#	Date	Mintage	Fine	VF	XF	Unc
7	1894	.128	5.00	15.00	30.00	75.00
	1894	*25 pcs.	—	—	Proof	350.00

10 CENTS

2.3240 g, .925 SILVER, .0691 oz ASW

KM#	Date	Mintage	Fine	VF	XF	Unc
8	1894	.126	6.00	20.00	60.00	150.00
	1894	*25 pcs.	—	—	Proof	450.00

25 CENTS

5.8100 g, .925 SILVER, .1728 oz ASW

KM#	Date	Mintage	Fine	VF	XF	Unc
9	1894	.048	10.00	20.00	65.00	285.00
	1894	*25 pcs.	—	—	Proof	600.00
	1895	.047	15.00	25.00	75.00	300.00
	1897	.040	15.00	25.00	85.00	375.00

NOTE: Later date (1901) exists for this type.

50 CENTS

11.6200 g, .925 SILVER, .3456 oz ASW

KM#	Date	Mintage	Fine	VF	XF	Unc
10	1894	.038	15.00	30.00	90.00	375.00
	1894	*25 pcs.	—	—	Proof	1500.
	1895	.036	15.00	30.00	110.00	400.00
	1897	.020	15.00	40.00	160.00	550.00

NOTE: Later date (1901) exists for this type.

TOKEN ISSUES (Tn)

1/4 RIYAL

BRASS

Obv: Indian head.

KM#	Date	Mintage	Fine	VF	XF	Unc
Tn1	1871	—	175.00	300.00	400.00	—

NOTE: Issued by John Jex.

1-1/2 PENCE

COPPER

Henry Gansz

KM#	Date	Mintage	Fine	VF	XF	Unc
Tn2	1885	—	—	—	550.00	850.00

PROOF SETS (PS)

KM#	Date	Mintage	Identification	Issue Price	Mkt. Val.
PS1	1894(5)	*25	KM6-10	—	3000.

BHUTAN

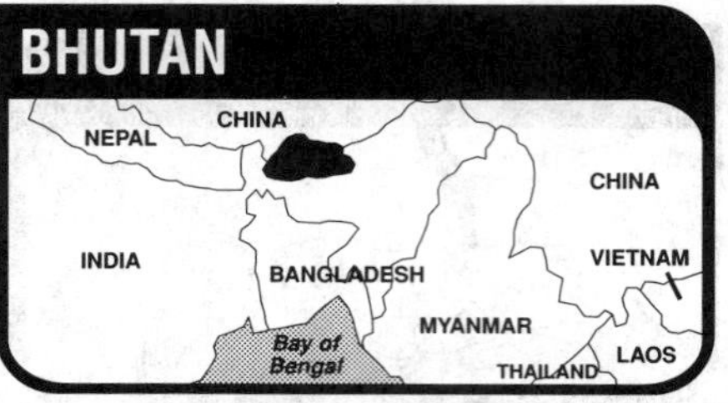

The Kingdom of Bhutan, a landlocked Himalayan country bordered by Tibet and India, has an area of 18,150 sq. mi. (47,000 sq. km.) and a population of 1.8 million. Capital: Thimphu. Virtually the entire population is engaged in agricultural and pastoral activities. Rice, wheat, barley, and yak butter are produced in sufficient quantity to make the country self-sufficient in food. The economy of Bhutan is primitive and many transactions are conducted on a barter basis.

Bhutan's early history is obscure, but is thought to have resembled that of rural medieval Europe. The country was conquered by Tibet, in the 9th century, and a dual temporal and spiritual rule developed which operated until the mid-19th century, when the southern part of the country was occupied by the British and annexed to British India. Bhutan was established as a hereditary monarchy in 1907, and in 1910 agreed to British control of its external affairs. In 1949, India and Bhutan concluded a treaty whereby India assumed Britain's role in subsidizing Bhutan and guiding its foreign affairs. In 1971 Bhutan became a full member of the United Nations.

DEB (1/2) RUPEE

NOTE: Prior to their own issues the coins (1/2 Rupees) of Cooch Behar circulated freely. After the Cooch Behar Mint closed in 1789, Bhutan began to strike copies of the Cooch Behar coins. As time went on these coins were remelted and increasing amounts of debasing alloys were used until a copper or brass issue resulted, sometimes with a slight silver wash.

Period I

C.1790-1820AD

'Ma'

SILVER

KM#	Date	Mintage	Good	VG	Fine	VF
1	ND	—	4.00	6.50	8.50	12.50

'Sa'

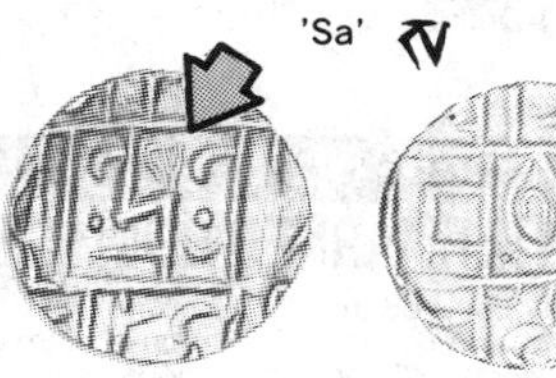

KM#	Date	Mintage	Good	VG	Fine	VF
2	ND	—	4.00	6.50	8.50	12.50

Period II

c.1820-1835AD

"Ma-tam"

'Sa'

SILVER, LEAD alloying

KM#	Date	Mintage	Good	VG	Fine	VF
3	ND	—	3.50	4.50	6.00	8.00

SILVER, COPPER alloying

KM#	Date	Mintage	Good	VG	Fine	VF
4.1	ND	—	3.50	4.50	6.00	8.00

Obv: Dot added.

KM#	Date	Mintage	Good	VG	Fine	VF
4.2	ND	—	3.50	4.50	6.00	8.00

Obv: Small *Sa* added.

KM#	Date	Mintage	Good	VG	Fine	VF
4.3	ND	—	3.50	4.50	6.00	8.00

Obv: Leaf spray.

KM#	Date	Mintage	Good	VG	Fine	VF
5	ND	—	3.50	4.50	6.00	8.00

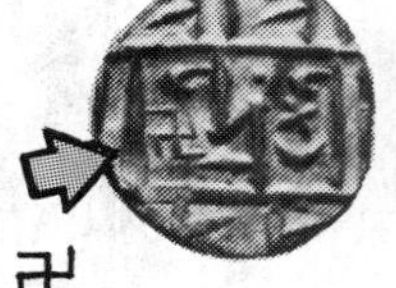

Obv: Swastika.

Rev: Center inscription retrograde.

KM#	Date	Mintage	Good	VG	Fine	VF
6	ND	—	3.50	5.00	7.50	10.00

Period III

1835-1910 AD

"Ma-tam"

'Sa'

COPPER or BRASS

Obv: Small *Sa* at upper right.

KM#	Date	Mintage	Good	VG	Fine	VF
A7	ND	—	1.00	2.25	3.50	5.00

'Sa'

Obv: *Sa* at lower left.

KM#	Date	Mintage	Good	VG	Fine	VF
7.1	ND	—	1.00	1.50	2.25	3.50

Small flan, 1.85g

KM#	Date	Mintage	Good	VG	Fine	VF
7.1a	ND	—	1.00	1.50	2.25	3.50

Obv: Dots added.

KM#	Date	Mintage	Good	VG	Fine	VF
7.2	ND	—	1.00	1.50	2.25	3.50

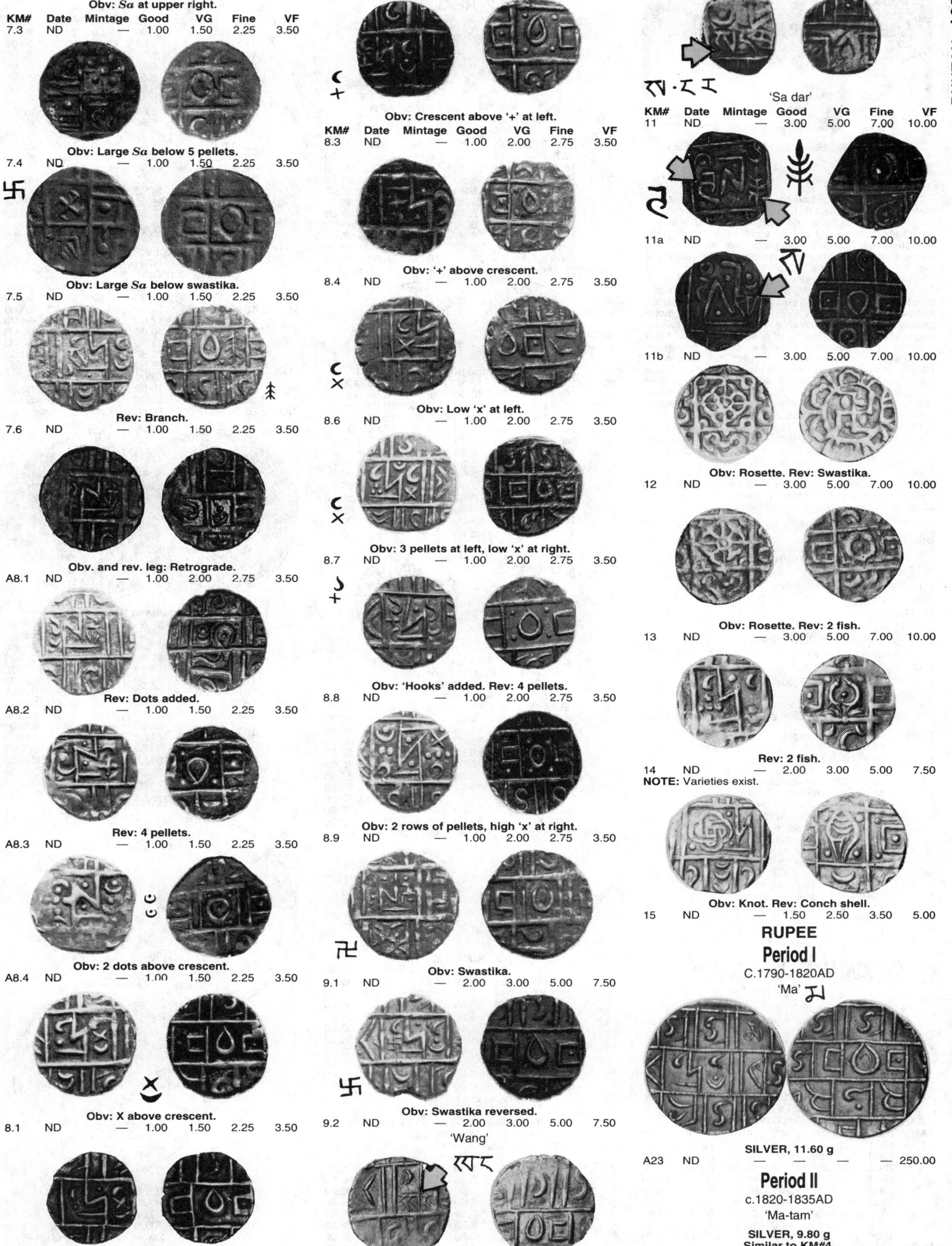

KM#	Description	Date	Mintage	Good	VG	Fine	VF
7.3	Obv: *Sa* at upper right.	ND	—	1.00	1.50	2.25	3.50
7.4	Obv: Large *Sa* below 5 pellets.	ND	—	1.00	1.50	2.25	3.50
7.5	Obv: Large *Sa* below swastika.	ND	—	1.00	1.50	2.25	3.50
7.6	Rev: Branch.	ND	—	1.00	1.50	2.25	3.50
A8.1	Obv. and rev. leg: Retrograde.	ND	—	1.00	2.00	2.75	3.50
A8.2	Rev: Dots added.	ND	—	1.00	1.50	2.25	3.50
A8.3	Rev: 4 pellets.	ND	—	1.00	1.50	2.25	3.50
A8.4	Obv: 2 dots above crescent.	ND	—	1.00	1.50	2.25	3.50
8.1	Obv: X above crescent.	ND	—	1.00	1.50	2.25	3.50
8.2	Obv: 1 or 2 dots in center inscription.	ND	—	.50	1.00	1.75	2.50
8.3	Obv: Crescent above '+' at left.	ND	—	1.00	2.00	2.75	3.50
8.4	Obv: '+' above crescent.	ND	—	1.00	2.00	2.75	3.50
8.6	Obv: Low 'x' at left.	ND	—	1.00	2.00	2.75	3.50
8.7	Obv: 3 pellets at left, low 'x' at right.	ND	—	1.00	2.00	2.75	3.50
8.8	Obv: 'Hooks' added. Rev: 4 pellets.	ND	—	1.00	2.00	2.75	3.50
8.9	Obv: 2 rows of pellets, high 'x' at right.	ND	—	1.00	2.00	2.75	3.50
9.1	Obv: Swastika.	ND	—	2.00	3.00	5.00	7.50
9.2	Obv: Swastika reversed.	ND	—	2.00	3.00	5.00	7.50

'Wang'

KM#	Date	Mintage	Good	VG	Fine	VF
10	ND	—	3.00	5.00	7.00	10.00

'Sa dar'

KM#	Description	Date	Mintage	Good	VG	Fine	VF
11		ND	—	3.00	5.00	7.00	10.00
11a		ND	—	3.00	5.00	7.00	10.00
11b		ND	—	3.00	5.00	7.00	10.00
12	Obv: Rosette. Rev: Swastika.	ND	—	3.00	5.00	7.00	10.00
13	Obv: Rosette. Rev: 2 fish.	ND	—	3.00	5.00	7.00	10.00
14	Rev: 2 fish.	ND	—	2.00	3.00	5.00	7.50

NOTE: Varieties exist.

KM#	Description	Date	Mintage	Good	VG	Fine	VF
15	Obv: Knot. Rev: Conch shell.	ND	—	1.50	2.50	3.50	5.00

RUPEE

Period I

C.1790-1820AD

'Ma'

KM#	Description	Date	Mintage	Good	VG	Fine	VF
A23	SILVER, 11.60 g	ND	—	—	—	—	250.00

Period II

c.1820-1835AD

'Ma-tam'

KM#	Description	Date	Mintage	Good	VG	Fine	VF
B23	SILVER, 9.80 g Similar to KM#4.	ND	—	—	—	—	200.00

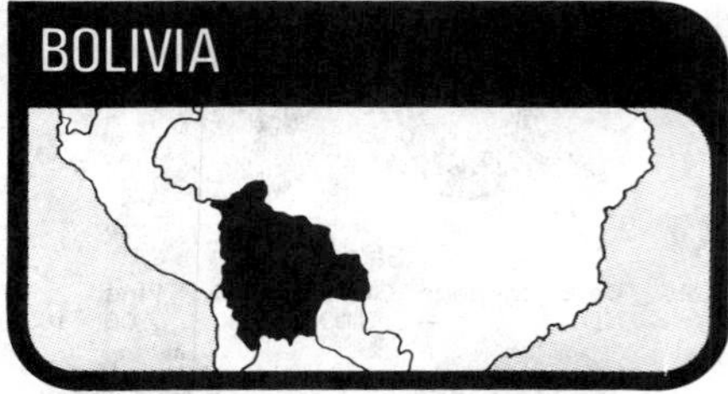

The Republic of Bolivia, a landlocked country in westcentral South America, has an area of 424,165 sq. mi. (1,098,580 sq. km.) and a population of 7.9 million. Its capitals are: La Paz (administrative) and Sucre (constitutional). Principal exports are tin, zinc, antimony, tungsten, petroleum, natural gas, cotton and coffee.

Much of present day Bolivia was first dominated by the Tiahuanaco Culture ca.400 BC. It had in turn been incorporated into the Inca Empire by 1440AD prior to the arrival of the Spanish, in 1535, who reduced the Indian population to virtual slavery. When Joseph Napoleon was placed upon the throne of occupied Spain in 1809, a fervor of revolutionary activity quickened throughout Alto Peru - culminating in the 1809 Proclamation of Liberty. Sixteen bloody years of struggle ensued before the republic, named for the famed liberator Simon Bolivar, was established on August 6, 1825. Since then Bolivia has survived more than 16 constitutions, 78 Presidents, 3 military juntas and over 160 revolutions.

The Imperial City of Potosi, founded by Villaroel in 1546, was established in the midst of what is estimated to have been the world's richest silver mines (having produced in excess of 2 billion dollars worth of silver).

Most pre-decimal coinage of independent Bolivia carries the assayers' initials on the reverse near the rim to the right of the date, in 7 to 8 o'clock position. The mint mark or name appears in the 4 to 5 o'clock area.

RULERS

Spanish until 1825

MINT MARKS

A - Paris
(a) - Paris, privy marks only
CHI - Valcambia
H - Heaton
KN - Kings' Norton
PTA monogram - La Plata (Sucre)
OR monogram - Oruro
PAZ - La Paz
P or PTS monogram - Potosi
So - Santiago

ASSAYERS INITIALS

Letter	Date	Name
F	1815	Francisco Jose de Matos
F	1830,1848-1867	Fortunato Equivar
FE	1867-1890	Fortunato Equivar
J	1803-1812,1814-1832	Juan Palomo y Sierra
J	1813	Jose Antonio de Sierra
J	1853-1862	Joaquin Zemborain
L	1825-26	Leandro Osio
L	1825,1830-1843	Luis de Aguilar
M	1826-1829,1833-1839	Digo Miguel Lopez
M	1848-1855	Manuel Berrios
P	1776-1802	Pedro de Mazondo
P	1795-1824	Pedro Martin de Albizu
R	1839-1847	Rafael Mariano Bustillo
R	1848	Manuel Telesforo Ramires

COLONIAL MILLED COINAGE

1/4 REAL

.8460 g, .896 SILVER, .0243 oz ASW
Mint mark: PTS monogram
Obv: Castle. Rev: Lion.

KM#	Date	Mintage	VG	Fine	VF	XF
82	1801	.017	15.00	35.00	75.00	210.00
	1802	.165	8.00	14.00	25.00	65.00
	1803	.029	10.00	16.00	37.50	85.00
	1804	5,724	20.00	50.00	150.00	315.00
	1805	.011	20.00	50.00	150.00	315.00
	1806	.030	8.00	14.00	28.00	75.00
	1807	.010	12.50	25.00	50.00	130.00
	1808	8,161	8.00	14.00	28.00	75.00
	1809	—	25.00	60.00	175.00	350.00

NOTE: There is a variety of 1802 with base of 2 not struck up and frequently miscataloged as 1809.
NOTE: Earlier dates (1796-1800) exist for this type.

1/2 REAL

1.6921 g, .896 SILVER, .0487 oz ASW
Mint mark: PTS monogram
Carolus IIII

KM#	Date	Mintage	VG	Fine	VF	XF
69	1801 PP	.190	5.00	9.00	20.00	38.00
	1802 PP	.098	5.00	9.00	20.00	38.00
	1803 PJ	.066	5.00	9.00	20.00	38.00
	1804 PJ	.058	5.00	9.00	20.00	38.00
	1805 PJ	.084	5.00	9.00	20.00	38.00
	1806 PJ	.094	5.00	9.00	20.00	38.00
	1807 PJ	.114	5.00	9.00	20.00	38.00
	1808/7 PJ	.239	5.00	9.00	20.00	38.00
	1808 PJ	I.A.	5.00	9.00	20.00	38.00
	1809 PJ	—	25.00	40.00	55.00	100.00

NOTE: Earlier dates (1791-1800) exist for this type.

Ferdinand VII

KM#	Date	Mintage	VG	Fine	VF	XF
90	1814 PJ	—	12.50	20.00	75.00	100.00
	1815 PJ	—	10.00	17.50	70.00	100.00
	1816 PJ	.074	4.00	8.00	35.00	55.00
	1817 PJ	.093	4.00	7.00	18.50	35.00
	1818 PJ	.106	3.50	6.00	17.50	35.00
	1819 PJ	—	3.50	6.00	17.50	35.00
	1820 PJ	—	3.50	6.00	17.50	35.00
	1821 PJ	—	3.50	6.00	17.50	35.00
	1822 PJ	—	3.50	6.00	17.50	35.00
	1823 PJ	—	7.50	15.00	27.50	55.00
	1823 JL	—	3.50	6.00	20.00	50.00
	1824 PJ	—	3.50	6.00	17.50	35.00
	1825 JL	—	3.50	6.00	17.50	35.00

REAL

3.3841 g, .896 SILVER, .0975 oz ASW
Mint mark: PTS monogram
Obv. leg: CAROLUS IIII. . .
Rev: Pillars.

KM#	Date	Mintage	VG	Fine	VF	XF
70	1801 PP	.309	5.50	9.00	17.50	50.00
	1802 PP	.197	5.50	10.00	20.00	62.00
	1803 PP	.143	7.00	11.50	35.00	80.00
	1803 PJ	I.A.	5.50	9.00	18.00	50.00
	1804 PJ	.143	5.50	9.00	17.50	37.50
	1805 PJ	.072	5.50	10.00	20.00	55.00
	1806 PJ	.090	5.50	10.00	20.00	55.00
	1807 PJ	.107	5.50	10.00	20.00	55.00
	1808 PJ	.238	5.50	9.00	18.00	50.00
	1808/9 PJ	I.A.	25.00	45.00	80.00	175.00
	1809 PJ	—	32.00	55.00	110.00	145.00

NOTE: Earlier dates (1791-1800) exist for this type.

Obv. leg: FERDIN. VII. . ., bust.

KM#	Date	Mintage	VG	Fine	VF	XF
87	1813 PJ	—	9.00	15.00	35.00	55.00
	1816 PJ	.038	5.50	9.00	17.50	35.00
	1817 PJ	.046	5.50	9.00	17.50	35.00
	1818 PJ	.056	5.50	9.00	17.50	35.00
	1819 PJ	—	5.50	9.00	17.50	35.00
	1820 PJ	—	5.50	9.00	17.50	35.00
	1821 PJ	—	5.50	9.00	17.50	35.00
	1822 PJ	—	5.50	9.00	17.50	35.00
	1823 PJ	—	5.50	9.00	17.50	35.00
	1824 PJ	—	5.50	9.00	17.50	35.00
	1825 JL	—	5.50	9.00	17.50	35.00

2 REALES

6.7682 g, .896 SILVER, .1950 oz ASW
Mint mark: PTS monogram
Obv. leg: CAROLUS IIII. . ., bust.
Rev: Pillars.

KM#	Date	Mintage	VG	Fine	VF	XF
71	1801 PP	.168	5.50	10.00	28.00	55.00
	1802 PP	.046	5.50	10.00	28.00	55.00
	1803/2 PJ	.048	5.50	10.00	32.00	80.00
	1803 PJ	I.A.	5.50	10.00	28.00	55.00
	1804 PJ	.052	5.50	10.00	28.00	55.00
	1805 PJ	.043	5.50	10.00	28.00	55.00
	1806 PJ	.054	5.50	10.00	28.00	55.00
	1807 PJ	.098	5.50	10.00	28.00	55.00
	1808 PJ	.203	5.50	10.00	28.00	55.00

NOTE: Earlier dates (1791-1800) exist for this type.

Obv. leg: FERDIN VII. . ., bust.

KM#	Date	Mintage	VG	Fine	VF	XF
83	1808 PJ	I.A.	15.00	22.00	55.00	90.00
	1809 PJ	—	5.50	11.50	35.00	55.00
	1813 PJ	—	5.50	11.50	35.00	55.00
	1814 PJ	—	5.50	11.50	35.00	55.00
	1816 PJ	.048	5.50	11.50	35.00	62.00
	1817 PJ	.066	5.50	11.50	35.00	62.00
	1818 PJ	.064	5.50	11.50	35.00	62.00
	1818/7 PJ	—	8.50	18.50	45.00	85.00
	1819 PJ	—	5.50	11.50	35.00	55.00
	1820 PJ	—	5.50	11.50	35.00	62.00
	1821 PJ	—	5.50	11.50	35.00	55.00
	1822 PJ	—	5.50	11.50	35.00	55.00
	1823 PJ	—	5.50	11.50	35.00	55.00
	1824 PJ	—	5.50	11.50	35.00	55.00
	1825 PJ	—	11.50	35.00	68.00	145.00
	1825 J	—	35.00	68.00	210.00	345.00
	1825 JL	—	15.00	22.00	55.00	110.00

4 REALES

13.5365 g, .896 SILVER, .3900 oz ASW
Mint mark: PTS monogram
Obv. leg: CAROLUS IIII. . ., bust.

KM#	Date	Mintage	VG	Fine	VF	XF
72	1801 PP	.090	15.00	25.00	45.00	90.00
	1802 PP	.053	17.50	30.00	50.00	90.00
	1803 PJ	.030	17.50	30.00	50.00	90.00
	1804 PJ	.053	17.50	30.00	50.00	90.00
	1805 PJ	.049	30.00	50.00	75.00	100.00
	1806/5 PJ	.059	23.50	37.50	65.00	100.00
	1806 PJ	I.A.	15.00	25.00	50.00	90.00
	1807 PJ	.101	15.00	25.00	50.00	90.00
	1808 PJ	.102	15.00	25.00	50.00	90.00
	1808/9 PJ	I.A.	15.00	25.00	50.00	90.00
	1809 PJ	—	30.00	50.00	75.00	150.00

NOTE: Earlier dates (1791-1800) exist for this type.

Ferdinand VII

KM#	Date	Mintage	VG	Fine	VF	XF
88	1813 PJ	—	—	Reported, not confirmed		
	1814 PJ	—	—	Reported, not confirmed		
	1815 PJ	—	—	Reported, not confirmed		
	1816 PJ	.031	17.50	30.00	50.00	90.00
	1817 PJ	.033	17.50	30.00	50.00	90.00
	1818 PJ	.034	20.00	35.00	60.00	100.00
	1819 PJ	—	20.00	35.00	60.00	100.00
	1820 PJ	—	20.00	35.00	60.00	100.00
	1821 PJ	—	30.00	50.00	75.00	125.00
	1822 PJ	—	20.00	35.00	60.00	100.00
	1823 PJ	—	17.50	30.00	50.00	90.00
	1824 PJ	—	30.00	50.00	75.00	125.00
	1825 PJ	—	225.00	350.00	475.00	650.00
	1825 J	—	175.00	275.00	375.00	500.00
	1825 JL	—	15.00	25.00	50.00	90.00

8 REALES

27.0730 g, .896 SILVER, .7799 oz ASW
Mint mark: PTS monogram

KM#	Date	Mintage	VG	Fine	VF	XF
73.1	1801 PP	3.965	20.00	35.00	70.00	140.00
	1802 PP	2.083	20.00	35.00	70.00	140.00
	1803 PJ	2.310	20.00	35.00	70.00	140.00
	1804 PJ	3.074	20.00	35.00	70.00	140.00
	1805 PJ	3.199	20.00	35.00	70.00	140.00
	1806/5 PJ					

KM#	Date	Mintage	VG	Fine	VF	XF
73.1		3.101	25.00	45.00	95.00	180.00
	1806 PJ	I.A.	20.00	35.00	70.00	140.00
	1807 PJ	3.588	20.00	35.00	70.00	140.00
	1808 PJ	3.299	20.00	35.00	70.00	140.00

NOTE: Earlier dates (1791-1800) exist for this type.

Rev: Similar to KM#89.

KM#	Date	Mintage	VG	Fine	VF	XF
84	1808 PJ	I.A.	25.00	40.00	70.00	175.00
	1809 PJ	—	25.00	40.00	70.00	135.00
	1813 PJ	—	20.00	30.00	50.00	100.00
	1814/13 PJ	—	22.00	45.00	90.00	185.00
	1814 PJ	—	20.00	35.00	70.00	110.00
	1815 PJ	—	20.00	35.00	70.00	110.00
	1816 PJ	1.877	20.00	35.00	70.00	110.00
	1817 PJ	1.906	20.00	35.00	70.00	110.00
	1818 PJ	1.649	20.00	35.00	70.00	110.00
	1819 PJ	—	20.00	35.00	70.00	110.00
	1820 PJ	—	20.00	35.00	70.00	110.00
	1821 PJ	—	20.00	35.00	70.00	110.00
	1822 PJ	—	20.00	35.00	70.00	110.00
	1823/2 PJ	—	50.00	95.00	175.00	350.00
	1823 PJ	—	20.00	35.00	70.00	110.00
	1823 JP	—	25.00	35.00	75.00	175.00
	1824 PJ	—	40.00	65.00	100.00	200.00
	1824 J	—	200.00	350.00	650.00	1250.
	1825 J	—	75.00	150.00	275.00	550.00
	1825 JL	—	20.00	27.50	40.00	75.00

NOTE: 1825 JL are also struck with coin rotation.

Obv. leg: FERDIN IIV (error). . .

KM#	Date	Mintage	VG	Fine	VF	XF
89	1813 PJ	—	250.00	450.00	750.00	1200.

ESCUDO

3.3841 g, .875 GOLD, .0952 oz AGW
Mint mark: PTS monogram
Obv. leg: CAROL IIII. . ., bust.
Rev: Similar to 2 Escudos, KM#79.

KM#	Date	Mintage	VG	Fine	VF	XF
78	1801 PP	1,363	150.00	200.00	275.00	475.00
	1802 PP	376 pcs.	150.00	200.00	275.00	475.00
	1803 PJ	410 pcs.	150.00	200.00	275.00	600.00
	1804 PJ	476 pcs.	150.00	200.00	275.00	600.00
	1805 PJ	613 pcs.	150.00	200.00	275.00	600.00
	1806 PJ	204 pcs.	150.00	200.00	275.00	600.00
	1807 PJ	1,123	150.00	200.00	275.00	600.00
	1808 PJ	884 pcs.	150.00	200.00	275.00	600.00

NOTE: Earlier dates (1791-1800) exist for this type.

Obv. leg: FERDIN VII. . .

KM#	Date	Mintage	VG	Fine	VF	XF
92	1822 PJ	—	200.00	300.00	450.00	1200.
	1823 PJ	—	250.00	400.00	650.00	1450.
	1824 PJ	—	300.00	500.00	800.00	1750.

2 ESCUDOS

6.7682 g, .875 GOLD, .1904 oz AGW
Mint mark: PTS monogram
Obv. leg: CAROL IIII. . .

KM#	Date	Mintage	VG	Fine	VF	XF
79	1801 PP	545 pcs.	250.00	400.00	525.00	1000.
	1802 PP	273 pcs.	400.00	550.00	700.00	1300.
	1803 PP	273 pcs.	400.00	550.00	700.00	1300.
	1804 PJ	204 pcs.	250.00	400.00	525.00	1050.
	1805 PJ	306 pcs.	325.00	475.00	700.00	1300.
	1806 PJ	476 pcs.	400.00	550.00	800.00	1300.
	1807 PJ	748 pcs.	250.00	350.00	525.00	850.00
	1808 PJ	647 pcs.	325.00	475.00	700.00	1100.

NOTE: Earlier dates (1791-1800) exist for this type.

4 ESCUDOS

13.5365 g, .875 GOLD, .3808 oz AGW
Mint mark: PTS monogram
Obv. leg: CAROL IIII. . ., bust. Rev: Arms.

KM#	Date	Mintage	VG	Fine	VF	XF
80	1801 PP	.013	400.00	525.00	875.00	1900.
	1802 PP	698 pcs.	475.00	600.00	1000.	1650.
	1803 PP	408 pcs.	800.00	1100.	1600.	3200.
	1804 PJ	187 pcs.	950.00	1300.	1750.	3200.
	1804 PP	I.A.	950.00	1300.	1750.	3200.
	1805 PJ	255 pcs.	550.00	725.00	1000.	1800.
	1806 PJ	221 pcs.	400.00	525.00	800.00	1800.
	1807 PJ	527 pcs.	475.00	600.00	875.00	1800.
	1808 PJ	323 pcs.	475.00	600.00	875.00	1800.

NOTE: Earlier dates (1791-1800) exist for this type.

8 ESCUDOS

27.0730 g, .875 GOLD, .7616 oz AGW
Mint mark: PTS monogram
Obv. leg: CAROL IIII. . .

KM#	Date	Mintage	VG	Fine	VF	XF
81	1801 PP	.029	375.00	450.00	675.00	1100.
	1802 PP	.020	375.00	450.00	675.00	1100.
	1803 PJ	.017	375.00	450.00	675.00	1100.
	1804 PJ	.022	375.00	450.00	675.00	1100.
	1805 PJ	.049	375.00	450.00	675.00	1100.
	1806 PJ	.038	375.00	450.00	675.00	1100.
	1807 PJ	.039	375.00	450.00	675.00	1100.
	1808 PJ	.035	375.00	450.00	675.00	1100.

NOTE: Earlier dates (1741-1800) exist for this type.

Obv. leg: FERDIN VII. . ., uniformed bust.

KM#	Date	Mintage	VG	Fine	VF	XF
86	1809 PJ	—	— Reported, not confirmed			

Obv. leg: FERDIN. VII. . .

KM#	Date	Mintage	VG	Fine	VF	XF
91	1817 PJ	—	675.00	900.00	1650.	4800.
	1822 PJ	—	375.00	450.00	675.00	1100.
	1823 PJ	—	500.00	750.00	1250.	3600.
	1824 PJ	—	400.00	550.00	1000.	1800.

REPUBLIC

MONETARY SYSTEM

8 Soles = 1 Peso
16 Soles = 1 Scudo

NOTE: The low quality of steel used for production of dies from the beginning of Republican coinage thru the late 1890s resulted in most series having multiple dies with differences in spacing, dots and even style of letters and numbers. Only major differences or errors will be listed.

1/4 SOL

.8500 g, .667 SILVER, .0182 oz ASW
Obv: Llama in plain field, POTOSI below.
Reeded edge.

KM#	Date	Mintage	VG	Fine	VF	XF
111	1852	—	7.00	15.00	30.00	65.00

NOTE: 3 different die pairs known.

Obv: Branches flank llama.

KM#	Date	Mintage	VG	Fine	VF	XF
117	1853	—	15.00	40.00	75.00	120.00

NOTE: The values above are for holed coins, unholed specimens command a premium of 1-1/2 to 2 times these figures.

1/2 SOL

1.5000 g, .903 SILVER, .0435 oz ASW
Mint mark: PTS monogram
Rev. leg. ends: . . . CONSTITUCI; 6-pointed stars in field.

KM#	Date	Mintage	VG	Fine	VF	XF
93.1	1827 JM	—	2.50	4.00	7.50	28.00
	1828/7 JM	—	3.50	7.50	12.50	35.00

Rev. leg. ends: . . . CONSTITUC.

KM#	Date	Mintage	VG	Fine	VF	XF
93.2	1827 JM	—	4.00	8.50	14.00	40.00
	1828/7 JM	—	3.50	7.50	12.50	35.00
	1828 JM	—	1.50	3.00	5.00	22.50
	1829 JM	—	2.00	3.50	6.00	22.50

1.5000 g, .667 SILVER, .0322 oz ASW
Obv: Six 6-pointed stars in arc above arms.

KM#	Date	Mintage	VG	Fine	VF	XF
93.2a	1830 J	—	2.50	4.00	7.50	27.00
	1830 J (error) inverted N in CONSTITUC.	—	4.00	9.00	20.00	45.00
	1830 JF	—	2.50	4.00	7.00	25.00
	1830 JL	—	1.00	2.00	3.50	18.00
	1830 JL (error) CONSTITU(C/.)	—	2.50	5.00	9.00	35.00

Rev: 5-pointed stars in field.

KM#	Date	Mintage	VG	Fine	VF	XF
93.3	1830 JL	—	6.00	12.00	28.00	55.00

NOTE: Believed to have been struck after 1853.

Obv: W/o denomination, nine 5-pointed stars in arc above arms. Rev: BOLIVAR on truncation.

KM#	Date	Mintage	VG	Fine	VF	XF
118.1	1853 FP	—	2.50	5.00	10.00	28.00
	1853 FP inverted A for V in BOLIVIANA					
		—	3.00	6.00	12.00	35.00
	1854 MJ	—	2.00	3.00	6.00	18.00
	1854 MJ	*	2.50	4.00	7.50	20.00
	1855 MJ	—	2.50	5.00	10.00	28.00
	1856 FJ w/period after CONSTITUCION					
		—	4.00	6.00	12.50	40.00
	1856 FJ	—	3.00	5.00	10.00	30.00
	1856 MJ	—	5.00	6.50	11.50	35.00

***NOTE:** Inverted A for V and inverted V for first A in BOLIVIANA for 1854 MJ.

Obv: Denomination added.

KM#	Date	Mintage	VG	Fine	VF	XF
118.2	1856 FJ	—	3.00	5.50	10.00	22.50
	1857/6 FJ	—	3.50	7.00	11.00	25.00
	1857 FJ	—	1.50	3.50	7.50	20.00
	1857 FJ (error) LIBRE POCA/R LA					
		—	5.00	11.00	25.00	55.00
	1858/7 FJ	—	2.50	5.50	9.50	22.00
	1858 FJ	—	2.50	5.50	10.00	22.50

NOTE: Varieties exist w/and w/o period after CONSTITUCION, and with variance in bust size.

Rev: BOLIVAR below truncation.

KM#	Date	Mintage	VG	Fine	VF	XF
118.3	1859 FJ	—	8.00	12.00	35.00	80.00
	1859 FJ (error) BOLIVRA w/inverted V for A					
		—	12.50	25.00	55.00	125.00

Mint mark: PAZ
Rev: Crude "La Paz style" head.

KM#	Date	Mintage	VG	Fine	VF	XF
127	1855 P	—	8.00	15.00	35.00	70.00
	1856/5 P	—	12.00	20.00	45.00	90.00
	1856 P	—	8.00	15.00	35.00	70.00

Rev: Crude, so-called "ugly head".

KM#	Date	Mintage	VG	Fine	VF	XF
132	1858/7 P	—	10.00	17.50	40.00	80.00
	1858 P	—	8.00	15.00	35.00	70.00
	1859 P	—	—	—	—	—

1.3000 g, .667 SILVER, .0279 oz ASW
Mint mark: PTS monogram
Rev. weight: PESO 25 Gs.

KM#	Date	Mintage	VG	Fine	VF	XF
133.1	1859 FJ	—	5.00	10.00	25.00	45.00

1.3000 g, .903 SILVER, .0377 oz ASW
Rev. weight: 25 G.

KM#	Date	Mintage	VG	Fine	VF	XF
133.2	1859 FJ	—	5.00	7.50	15.00	65.00
	1860 FJ	—	5.00	7.50	15.00	45.00
	1861 FJ	—	5.00	7.50	15.00	45.00
	1861 FJ w/P/T for Potosi monogram					
		—	10.00	15.00	25.00	75.00
	1862 FP	—	5.00	7.50	15.00	60.00
	1863/2 FP	—	5.00	7.50	15.00	50.00
	1863 FP	—	5.00	7.50	15.00	45.00

SOL

3.0000 g, .903 SILVER, .0871 oz ASW
Mint mark: PTS monogram
Obv: Six 6-pointed stars in arc above arms.
Rev: BOLIVAR on truncation.

KM#	Date	Mintage	VG	Fine	VF	XF
94	1827 JM	—	7.00	14.00	35.00	85.00
	1828 JM	—	7.00	14.00	35.00	85.00
	1829 JM	—	5.00	10.00	25.00	65.00

3.0000 g, .667 SILVER, .0643 oz ASW

KM#	Date	Mintage	VG	Fine	VF	XF
94a	1830 J	—	5.00	10.00	20.00	40.00
	1830 JL	—	3.50	5.00	7.50	20.00

2.60-3.60 g, .667 SILVER, .056-.077 oz ASW
Mint mark: Oruro monogram
Obv. leg: . . . SOCABON.

KM#	Date	Mintage	VG	Fine	VF	XF
85.1	1849 JM	—	40.00	60.00	90.00	200.00

Obv. leg: . . . SOCN.

KM#	Date	Mintage	VG	Fine	VF	XF
85.2	1849 JM	—	40.00	60.00	90.00	200.00

NOTE: The prices above are for holed coins, unholed specimens command a substantial premium.

3.0000 g, .667 SILVER, .0643 oz ASW
Obv: W/o denomination, nine 5-pointed stars in arc above arms. Rev: BOLIVAR on truncation.

KM#	Date	Mintage	VG	Fine	VF	XF
119.1	1853 FP	—	7.50	12.50	35.00	70.00
	1853 FP (error) BOLIVLANA					
		—	6.00	12.00	25.00	55.00
	1854 MJ	—	5.00	7.50	15.00	40.00

Obv: Denomination added.

KM#	Date	Mintage	VG	Fine	VF	XF
119.2	1855 MJ	—	4.00	8.00	15.00	35.00
	1856/5 (F/M)J					
		—	5.00	12.00	27.50	55.00
	1856 FJ	—	4.00	8.00	15.00	35.00
	1857/6 FJ	—	6.00	12.00	27.50	55.00
	1857 FJ	—	4.00	8.00	15.00	35.00
	1858/7 FJ	—	6.00	12.00	27.50	55.00
	1858 FJ	—	4.00	8.00	15.00	35.00

Rev: BOLIVAR below truncation.

KM#	Date	Mintage	VG	Fine	VF	XF
119.3	1859 FJ	—	13.50	20.00	45.00	70.00
	1859 FJ (error) A's are inverted V's					
		—	13.50	20.00	45.00	70.00

Mint mark: PAZ
Rev: "Potosi style" laureate head.

KM#	Date	Mintage	VG	Fine	VF	XF
120	1855 P	—	10.00	17.50	35.00	65.00
	1855 F	—	10.00	17.50	35.00	65.00

Rev: Crude "La Paz style" head.

KM#	Date	Mintage	VG	Fine	VF	XF
128	1855 F	—	20.00	50.00	75.00	130.00
	1856 P	—	15.00	25.00	45.00	75.00

NOTE: The prices above are for holed coins. Unholed specimens command a substantial premium.

Rev: Crude, so-called "ugly head".

KM#	Date	Mintage	VG	Fine	VF	XF
131	1857 P	—	15.00	25.00	60.00	90.00
	1858/7 PAZ	—	20.00	30.00	65.00	100.00
	1858 P	—	15.00	25.00	55.00	80.00
	1859/7 P	—	20.00	30.00	70.00	110.00
	1859 P	—	15.00	25.00	50.00	80.00

NOTE: The prices above are for holed coins. Unholed specimens command a substantial premium.

2.5000 g, .667 SILVER, .0536 oz ASW
Mint mark: PTS monogram
Rev. weight: PESO 50 Gs.

KM#	Date	Mintage	VG	Fine	VF	XF
134.1	1859 FJ	—	10.00	15.00	35.00	70.00
	1859 FJ (error) R(E/R)P(U/B)BLICA, all A's are inverted V's					
		—	15.00	25.00	50.00	100.00

2.5000 g, .903 SILVER, .0726 oz ASW
Rev. weight: 50 G or 50 Gs.

KM#	Date	Mintage	VG	Fine	VF	XF
134.2	1860 FJ	—	4.00	7.00	12.00	25.00
	1860 (F/J)J	—	5.00	8.00	18.00	30.00
	1861 FJ	—	4.00	7.00	12.00	25.00
	1862/1 FP	—	5.00	9.00	20.00	40.00
	1862 FJ	—	5.00	9.00	20.00	40.00
	1862 FP	—	4.00	7.00	12.00	25.00
	1863/2 FP	—	5.00	8.00	18.00	30.00
	1863 FP	—	3.50	6.50	10.00	20.00

2 SOLES

6.2000 g, .903 SILVER, .1799 oz ASW
Mint mark: PTS monogram

KM#	Date	Mintage	VG	Fine	VF	XF
95	1827 JM	—	10.00	20.00	40.00	80.00
	1828/7 JM	—	25.00	40.00	65.00	115.00
	1828 JM	—	6.00	10.00	20.00	40.00
	1829 JM	—	12.50	22.00	45.00	90.00

6.2000 g, .667 SILVER, .1324 oz ASW

KM#	Date	Mintage	VG	Fine	VF	XF
95a	1830/27 J	—	20.00	35.00	55.00	90.00
	1830 J	—	6.00	10.00	15.00	32.00
	1830 JF	—	10.00	18.00	27.50	55.00
	1830/20 JL	—	20.00	35.00	55.00	90.00
	1830 JL	—	5.00	7.50	12.50	25.00
	1830 JL (error) CONSTITU (C/I) ION					
		—	17.00	30.00	50.00	85.00
	1831 J	—	—	—	Rare	—

Obv: W/o denomination.

KM#	Date	Mintage	VG	Fine	VF	XF
121.1	1853 FP	—	20.00	35.00	70.00	110.00

Obv: Denomination added.

KM#	Date	Mintage	VG	Fine	VF	XF
121.2	1854 MJ	—	5.00	10.00	32.00	60.00
	1855 MJ	—	5.00	10.00	32.00	60.00
	1856 FJ	—	7.50	12.50	40.00	80.00
	1856/5 MJ	—	7.50	12.50	40.00	80.00
	1857 MJ	—	7.50	12.50	40.00	80.00
	1857 FJ	—	5.00	10.00	32.00	60.00
	1858 FJ	—	7.50	12.50	40.00	80.00

NOTE: Varieties with and without period after CONSTITUTION exist.

Rev: BOLIVAR below truncation.

KM#	Date	Mintage	VG	Fine	VF	XF
121.3	1859/7 FJ	—	15.00	25.00	50.00	100.00
	1859 FJ	—	15.00	25.00	50.00	100.00

Mint mark: PAZ

Rev: Bare head.

KM#	Date	Mintage	VG	Fine	VF	XF
122	1853 J	—	750.00	1000.	1250.	1500.

Rev: "Potosi style" laureate head.

KM#	Date	Mintage	VG	Fine	VF	XF
126	1854 F	—	80.00	150.00	260.00	450.00

Rev: Crude "La Paz style" head.

KM#	Date	Mintage	VG	Fine	VF	XF
129	1855 F	—	250.00	500.00	750.00	1000.
	1856 P	—	150.00	300.00	600.00	900.00

Mint mark: PTS monogram
Rev. weight: PESO 100 Gs.

KM#	Date	Mintage	VG	Fine	VF	XF
135.1	1859/7 FJ	—	15.00	25.00	65.00	125.00
	1859 FJ	—	15.00	25.00	65.00	125.00

4.5000 g, .903 SILVER, .1306 oz ASW
Rev. weight: 100 Gs.

KM#	Date	Mintage	VG	Fine	VF	XF
135.2	1859 FJ	—	—	Reported, not confirmed		
	1860 FJ	—	7.50	12.50	20.00	35.00
	1860 FJ (error) 6 over smaller 6	—	12.00	25.00	50.00	75.00
	1861 FJ	—	7.50	12.50	20.00	35.00
	1862/1 FJ	—	6.00	9.00	15.00	30.00
	1862 FJ	—	7.50	12.50	20.00	35.00
	1862/1 FP	—	5.00	8.00	12.50	25.00
	1862 FP	—	4.50	7.50	12.50	25.00
	1863/2 FP	—	7.50	12.50	20.00	35.00
	1863 FP	—	5.00	8.00	12.50	25.00

4 SOLES

13.5000 g, .903 SILVER, .3918 oz ASW
Mint mark: PTS monogram
Reeded edge w/incuse
lettering: AYACUCHO * SUCRE *1824*.

KM#	Date	Mintage	VG	Fine	VF	XF
96	1827 JM	—	15.00	30.00	70.00	125.00
	1828/7 JM	—	16.50	35.00	80.00	140.00
	1828 JM	—	15.00	30.00	70.00	125.00
	1829 JM	—	15.00	30.00	70.00	125.00

13.5000 g, .667 SILVER, .2895 oz ASW

KM#	Date	Mintage	VG	Fine	VF	XF
96a.1	1830 J	—	4.00	8.00	20.00	40.00
	1830/20 JL	—	5.00	10.00	25.00	50.00
	1830/27 JL	—	4.00	8.00	20.00	40.00
	1830 JL	—	3.50	7.50	12.50	25.00

Additional mintmark on island.

KM#	Date	Mintage	VG	Fine	VF	XF
96a.2	1830 JL	—	4.00	10.00	25.00	50.00
	1830/3 JL	—	7.00	20.00	50.00	110.00

Obv: W/o denomination.

KM#	Date	Mintage	VG	Fine	VF	XF
123.1	1853 FP	—	7.50	12.50	35.00	75.00

Obv: Denomination added.

KM#	Date	Mintage	VG	Fine	VF	XF
123.2	1853 MF	—	5.00	10.00	25.00	45.00
	1854 MF	—	5.00	10.00	25.00	45.00
	1854 MJ	—	5.00	10.00	25.00	45.00
	1855 MJ	—	5.00	10.00	25.00	45.00
	1855 MJ (error) CONSTITUCIN	—	6.00	15.00	35.00	55.00
	1855 FJ	—	8.00	20.00	40.00	60.00
	1856 FJ	—	5.00	10.00	25.00	45.00
	1856/5 MJ	—	5.00	10.00	25.00	45.00
	1856 MJ	—	5.00	10.00	25.00	45.00
	1857 FJ	—	5.00	10.00	25.00	45.00
	1857 FJ (error) V in BOLIVIANA inverted A	—	8.00	20.00	35.00	55.00
	1857/F FJ	—	12.00	35.00	65.00	100.00
	1857 FJ (error) CONSTITUCIO	—	10.00	30.00	60.00	100.00
	1858 FJ	—	8.00	20.00	35.00	55.00

NOTE: Varieties exist with and without period after CONSTITUTION.

Rev: BOLIVAR below truncation.

KM#	Date	Mintage	VG	Fine	VF	XF
123.3	1859 FJ	—	15.00	35.00	70.00	125.00
	1859 FJ (error) A in BOLIVAR inverted V	—	10.00	25.00	50.00	75.00

Mint mark: PAZ

KM#	Date	Mintage	VG	Fine	VF	XF
124	1853 J	—	100.00	200.00	350.00	500.00

Mint mark: PAZ.
Rev: "Potosi style" laureate head.

KM#	Date	Mintage	VG	Fine	VF	XF
125	1853 J	—	15.00	35.00	60.00	120.00
	1854 J	—	—	Reported, not confirmed		
	1854 F	—	15.00	20.00	50.00	110.00
	1855 F	—	10.00	25.00	40.00	95.00

Rev: Crude "La Paz style" head.

KM#	Date	Mintage	VG	Fine	VF	XF
130	1855 F	—	12.50	20.00	35.00	80.00
	1(8/S)56 P(A/P)Z	—	30.00	60.00	90.00	160.00
	1856/5 P/F	—	15.00	25.00	45.00	90.00
	1856 P	—	12.50	20.00	35.00	80.00
	1857/6 P	—	30.00	45.00	65.00	95.00
	1857 P	—	100.00	200.00	300.00	500.00
	1858 P	—	100.00	200.00	300.00	500.00
136	1859 P	—	150.00	225.00	300.00	500.00

13.5000 g, .903 SILVER, .3918 oz ASW
Mint mark: PTS monogram
W/o denomination, only weight indicated as 200 Gs.

KM#	Date	Mintage	VG	Fine	VF	XF
139	1860 FJ	—	75.00	150.00	200.00	400.00

8 SOLES

27.0000 g, .903 SILVER, .7836 oz ASW
Reeded edge,
incuse lettering: AYACUCHO*SUCRE *1824*.

KM#	Date	Mintage	VG	Fine	VF	XF
97	1827 JM	—	15.00	25.00	45.00	75.00
	1827 JM (large alpacas)*	—	20.00	35.00	60.00	100.00
	1828 JM	—	15.00	25.00	45.00	75.00
	1829 JM	—	15.00	25.00	45.00	75.00
	1829 JM V in BOLIVIANA inverted A	—	30.00	50.00	225.00	350.00
	1830/20 JF	—	30.00	50.00	80.00	190.00
	1830 JF	—	15.00	25.00	45.00	75.00
	1830 JF/J	—	35.00	55.00	95.00	125.00
	1830 J	—	25.00	35.00	55.00	100.00
	1830 J V in BOLIVIANA inverted A	—	30.00	50.00	225.00	350.00
	1830 L	—	—	Reported, not confirmed		
	1831 JF	—	20.00	35.00	60.00	125.00
	1831 JL	—	15.00	25.00	45.00	75.00
	1832 JL	—	15.00	25.00	45.00	75.00
	1833 L	—	150.00	225.00	325.00	450.00
	1833 LM	—	15.00	25.00	45.00	75.00
	1834 LM	—	15.00	25.00	45.00	75.00
	1835 LM	—	20.00	30.00	50.00	90.00
	1836/5 LM	—	20.00	30.00	50.00	90.00
	1836/6 LM	—	20.00	30.00	50.00	90.00
	1836 LM	—	15.00	25.00	45.00	75.00
	1837 LM	—	15.00	25.00	45.00	75.00
	1838 LM	—	15.00	25.00	45.00	75.00
	1839 LM	—	15.00	25.00	45.00	75.00
	1839 LR	—	25.00	35.00	55.00	100.00
	1840 (4 over inverted 4) LR	—	30.00	50.00	90.00	220.00
	1840 LR	—	15.00	25.00	45.00	75.00

***NOTE:** Using the alpaca (llama-like animal) at the right as a guide, the overall size from bottom of legs to tip of ears is + /-8.3mm vs + /-7.2mm.

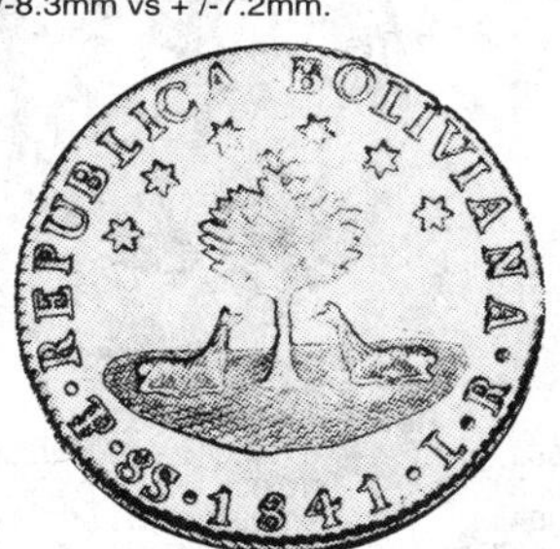

KM#	Date	Mintage	VG	Fine	VF	XF
103	1841 LR	—	15.00	25.00	45.00	75.00
	1841 LR (error: CONSTITUCIN)					
		—	150.00	250.00	350.00	600.00
	1842 LR	—	15.00	25.00	45.00	75.00
	1843/2 LR	—	20.00	35.00	55.00	100.00
	1843 LR	—	17.50	30.00	50.00	80.00
	1844 R	—	17.50	30.00	50.00	80.00
	1845 R	—	15.00	25.00	45.00	75.00
	1846/5 R	—	25.00	45.00	75.00	155.00
	1846 R	—	17.50	30.00	50.00	80.00
	1847 R	—	17.50	30.00	50.00	80.00
	1848 R	—	50.00	100.00	200.00	300.00
	1848 M	—	—	—	Rare	—
	1848 M/R	—	—	—	Rare	—

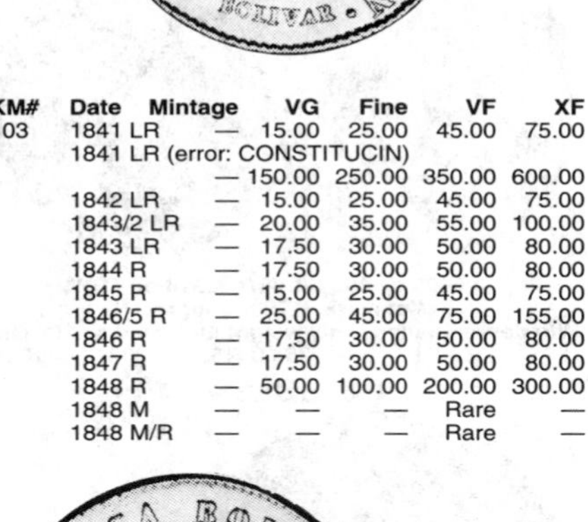

Obv: W/o denomination. Rev: Bare head.

KM#	Date	Mintage	VG	Fine	VF	XF
109	1848 FM lg. dt.					
		—	15.00	22.50	35.00	70.00
	1848 FM sm. dt.					
		—	15.00	22.50	35.00	70.00
	1849 FM	—	12.50	22.50	35.00	70.00
	1850 FM	—	10.00	20.00	32.50	65.00
	1851 FM	—	17.50	25.00	45.00	80.00
	1851 FM	—	10.00	20.00	32.50	65.00
	1851 FR	—	75.00	125.00	175.00	300.00

Rev: Laureate head.

KM#	Date	Mintage	VG	Fine	VF	XF
112.1	1852 FM	—	17.50	25.00	45.00	90.00
	1853 FP	—	40.00	80.00	125.00	200.00
	1854 M	—	40.00	80.00	125.00	200.00
	1856 FJ	—	25.00	45.00	85.00	140.00

Obv: Denomination added.

KM#	Date	Mintage	VG	Fine	VF	XF
112.2	1854 MJ	—	17.50	27.50	50.00	90.00
	1855/4 MJ	—	17.50	25.00	50.00	90.00
	1855 MJ	—	12.50	20.00	35.00	75.00

KM#	Date	Mintage	VG	Fine	VF	XF
137	1859 FJ	—	400.00	600.00	1250.	1750.

20.0000 g, .903 SILVER, .5807 oz ASW
Mint mark: PTS monogram
Rev. weight: Po 400 Gs.

KM#	Date	Mintage	VG	Fine	VF	XF
138.1 (138.3)	1859 FJ	—	1500.	2000.	2800.	—

Rev. weight: PESO/Po 400 Gs.

KM#	Date	Mintage	VG	Fine	VF	XF
138.2	1859 FJ	—	40.00	80.00	160.00	—

Rev. weight: PESO 400 Gs.

KM#	Date	Mintage	VG	Fine	VF	XF
138.3	1859 FJ.	—	15.00	30.00	65.00	145.00
(138.1)	1859 F.J.	—	15.00	30.00	65.00	145.00

Rev. weight: 400 Gs.

KM#	Date	Mintage	VG	Fine	VF	XF
138.4	1859 FJ	—	150.00	250.00	500.00	900.00

Obv: Tree divides 10Ds-20Gs.
Rev. weight: Po 400 Gs.

KM#	Date	Mintage	VG	Fine	VF	XF
138.5	1860 FJ	—	300.00	500.00	1000.	1700.

Rev. weight: 400 Gs.

KM#	Date	Mintage	VG	Fine	VF	XF
138.6	1859 FJ	—	75.00	125.00	200.00	350.00
	1860 FJ	—	10.00	15.00	30.00	65.00
	1861 FJ	—	10.00	15.00	30.00	65.00
	1861 FJ inverted A for V in Bolivar					
		—	15.00	25.00	40.00	85.00
	1862/1 FJ	—	10.00	15.00	30.00	65.00
	1862 FJ	—	10.00	15.00	30.00	65.00
	1862 FP	—	10.00	15.00	30.00	65.00
	1863/2 FP	—	10.00	15.00	35.00	70.00
	1863 FP	—	10.00	15.00	35.00	70.00
	1863 FP (error) REPUBLICA BOLIVANA					
		—	50.00	110.00	250.00	500.00

1/2 SCUDO

1.7000 g, .875 GOLD, .0478 oz AGW

KM#	Date	Mintage	VG	Fine	VF	XF
100	1834 LM	—	—	—	Rare	—
	1838 LM	—	80.00	140.00	210.00	400.00
	1839 LM	—	80.00	130.00	200.00	375.00
	1840 LR	—	80.00	140.00	210.00	400.00

KM#	Date	Mintage	VG	Fine	VF	XF
104	1841 LR/PL	—	65.00	85.00	120.00	200.00
	1841 LR	—	65.00	85.00	120.00	200.00
	1842 LR	—	65.00	85.00	120.00	200.00
	1842 LR (error) "BOLIAR" below bust					
		—	65.00	85.00	120.00	200.00
	1843 LR	—	65.00	85.00	120.00	200.00
	1844 R	—	65.00	85.00	120.00	200.00
	1845 R	—	65.00	85.00	120.00	200.00
	1846 R	—	65.00	85.00	120.00	200.00
	1847 R	—	65.00	85.00	120.00	200.00

KM#	Date	Mintage	Fine	VF	XF	Unc
113	1852/1 FP	—	110.00	185.00	300.00	600.00
	1852 MJ	—	100.00	165.00	250.00	450.00
	1852 FP	—	85.00	140.00	225.00	425.00
	1853 FP	—	85.00	140.00	225.00	425.00
	1854 FP	—	100.00	165.00	250.00	450.00
	1855 MF/FJ	—	85.00	140.00	225.00	425.00
	1855 FP	—	85.00	140.00	225.00	425.00
	1855 M	—	85.00	140.00	225.00	425.00
	1855 MJ	—	85.00	140.00	225.00	425.00
	1855 FS	—	85.00	140.00	225.00	425.00
	1856 FJ	—	85.00	140.00	225.00	425.00
	1856 FS	—	85.00	140.00	225.00	425.00
	1857 FP	—	225.00	385.00	550.00	900.00

1.2500 g, .900 GOLD, .0361 oz AGW

KM#	Date	Mintage	Fine	VF	XF	Unc
140	1868 FE	—	300.00	550.00	650.00	1000.

SCUDO

3.4000 g, .875 GOLD, .0956 oz AGW

KM#	Date	Mintage	VG	Fine	VF	XF
98	1831 JL	—	95.00	130.00	250.00	375.00
	1832 JL	—	95.00	130.00	250.00	350.00
	1833 JL	—	95.00	130.00	250.00	375.00
	1833 LM	—	95.00	130.00	250.00	375.00
	1834 JL	—	75.00	115.00	225.00	350.00
	1834 LM	—	95.00	130.00	250.00	375.00
	1835 LM	—	95.00	130.00	250.00	375.00
	1836 LM	—	95.00	130.00	250.00	375.00
	1837 LM	—	95.00	130.00	250.00	375.00
	1838 LM	—	95.00	130.00	250.00	375.00
	1839 LM	—	95.00	130.00	250.00	375.00
	1840 LR	—	125.00	175.00	325.00	500.00

KM#	Date	Mintage	Fine	VF	XF	Unc
105	1841 LR	—	100.00	150.00	200.00	350.00
	1842 LR	—	100.00	150.00	200.00	350.00
	1846 R	—	100.00	150.00	200.00	350.00

KM#	Date	Mintage	Fine	VF	XF	Unc
114	1852 FP	—	100.00	150.00	225.00	400.00
	1853 FP	—	100.00	150.00	225.00	400.00
	1855 LM/J	—	100.00	150.00	225.00	400.00
	1856 FJ	—	100.00	150.00	225.00	400.00

2.5000 g, .900 GOLD, .0723 oz AGW

KM#	Date	Mintage	Fine	VF	XF	Unc
141	1868 FE	—	200.00	300.00	450.00	775.00

2 SCUDOS

6.8000 g, .875 GOLD, .1913 oz AGW

KM#	Date	Mintage	VG	Fine	VF	XF
101	1834 LM	—	250.00	375.00	600.00	900.00
	1835 JM	—	—	Reported, not confirmed		
	1835 LM	—	225.00	325.00	550.00	800.00
	1839 JM	—	—	Reported, not confirmed		
	1839 LM	—	—	Reported, not confirmed		

KM#	Date	Mintage	VG	Fine	VF	XF
106	1841 LR	—	400.00	550.00	825.00	1350.

4 SCUDOS

13.5000 g, .875 GOLD, .3798 oz AGW

KM#	Date	Mintage	VG	Fine	VF	XF
102	1834 JL	—	650.00	1000.	1650.	3150.
	1834 LM	—	—	—	Rare	—

KM#	Date	Mintage	VG	Fine	VF	XF
107	1841 LR	—	900.00	1500.	2500.	3450.

8 SCUDOS

27.0000 g, .875 GOLD, .7596 oz AGW

KM#	Date	Mintage	VG	Fine	VF	XF
99	1831 JL	—	550.00	675.00	1000.	1750.
	1832 JL	—	550.00	675.00	1000.	1750.
	1833 JL	—	550.00	675.00	1000.	1750.
	1833 LM	—	550.00	675.00	1000.	1750.
	1834 JL	—	550.00	675.00	1000.	1750.
	1834 JM	—	650.00	780.00	1100.	1850.
	1834 LM	—	550.00	675.00	1000.	1750.
	1835 JM	—	550.00	675.00	1000.	1750.
	1835 LM	—	550.00	675.00	1000.	1750.
	1836 LM	—	650.00	780.00	1100.	1850.
	1837 LM	—	500.00	625.00	950.00	1550.
	1838 LM	—	600.00	675.00	1000.	1750.
	1839 LM	—	500.00	625.00	950.00	1550.
	1840 LR	—	500.00	625.00	950.00	1550.

Large bust.

KM#	Date	Mintage	VG	Fine	VF	XF
108.1	1841 LR	—	600.00	700.00	900.00	1500.

KM#	Date	Mintage	VG	Fine	VF	XF
108.2	1841 LR	—	450.00	550.00	650.00	1000.
	1842 LR	—	450.00	550.00	650.00	1000.
	1843 LR	—	450.00	550.00	650.00	1000.
	1844 LR	—	450.00	550.00	650.00	1000.
	1844 R	—	650.00	750.00	1000.	1750.
	1845 R	—	650.00	750.00	1000.	1750.
	1846 R	—	650.00	750.00	1000.	1750.
	1847 R	—	650.00	750.00	1000.	1750.

KM#	Date	Mintage	VG	Fine	VF	XF
110	1851 MF	—	900.00	1500.	2750.	4500.

KM#	Date	Mintage	Fine	VF	XF	Unc
115	1852 FP	—	3500.	6000.	8500.	12,500.

KM#	Date	Mintage	Fine	VF	XF	Unc
116	1852 FP	—	450.00	650.00	1000.	1850.
	1853 FP	—	450.00	650.00	1000.	1850.
	1854 M	—	450.00	650.00	1000.	1750.
	1854 MJ	—	450.00	650.00	1000.	1750.
	1855 LM	—	450.00	650.00	1000.	1750.
	1855 MJ	—	450.00	650.00	1000.	1750.
	1856 FJ/MJ	—	—	—	—	—
	1856 FJ	—	450.00	650.00	1000.	1750.
	1857/6 FJ	—	450.00	650.00	1000.	1750.
	1857 FJ	—	450.00	650.00	1000.	1750.

MELGAREJO COINAGE

1/4 MELGAREJO

5.0000 g, .666 SILVER, .1071 oz ASW

KM#	Date	Mintage	VG	Fine	VF	XF
144	1865	—	8.00	15.00	25.00	90.00

1/2 MELGAREJO

10.0000 g, .666 SILVER, .2141 oz ASW
Obv: Long beards.

KM#	Date	Mintage	VG	Fine	VF	XF
145.1	1865	—	10.00	20.00	30.00	80.00

Obv: Short beards.

KM#	Date	Mintage	VG	Fine	VF	XF
145.2	1865	—	10.00	20.00	30.00	80.00
	1865 (error) MELGREJO	—	20.00	40.00	70.00	120.00
	1865 (error) CATERIA	—	20.00	40.00	70.00	120.00
	1868	—	275.00	400.00	—	—

MELGAREJO

20.0000 g, .666 SILVER, .4282 oz ASW

KM#	Date	Mintage	VG	Fine	VF	XF
146	1865 FP	—	40.00	60.00	90.00	210.00

DECIMAL COINAGE

100 Centecimos = 1 Boliviano

CENTECIMO

COPPER
Mint mark: Potosi
Reeded edge.

KM#	Date	Mintage	VG	Fine	VF	XF
147	1864	.010	50.00	90.00	200.00	300.00

2 CENTECIMOS

COPPER
Mint mark: Potosi
Reeded edge.

KM#	Date	Mintage	VG	Fine	VF	XF
148	1864	.150	75.00	125.00	250.00	500.00

1/20 BOLIVIANO

1.2500 g, .900 SILVER, .0361 oz ASW
Obv. leg: REPUBLICA BOLIVIANA around oval shield above 9 stars. Reeded edge.
Rev. leg: LA UNION ES LA FUERZA around wreath, inscription: 1/20/BOLIVIANO/25GS/9.DSFINO., w/dots below S's.

KM#	Date	Mintage	Fine	VF	XF	Unc
149	1864 FP	—	10.00	17.50	40.00	100.00
	1864 FP (error) 1st N in UNION inverted	—	20.00	50.00	90.00	140.00
	1865/4 FP	—	6.50	15.00	30.00	100.00
	1865 FP	—	5.00	10.00	22.50	70.00

1/10 BOLIVIANO

2.5000 g, .900 SILVER, .0723 oz ASW
Obv. leg: REPUBLICA BOLIVIANA around oval shield above 9 stars.
Rev. leg: LA UNION ES LA FUERZA, inscription: 1/10/BOLIVIANO/50.GS/9.DS FINO., w/dots below S's.

KM#	Date	Mintage	Fine	VF	XF	Unc
150	1864 FP	—	5.00	10.00	20.00	45.00
	1865 FP	—	5.00	10.00	20.00	45.00
	1867 FP	—	22.50	45.00	75.00	125.00

1/5 BOLIVIANO

5.0000 g, .900 SILVER, .1446 oz ASW
Obv: Widely spaced stars.

KM#	Date	Mintage	VG	Fine	VF	XF
151.1	1864 FP	—	5.00	10.00	20.00	45.00
	1864 FP (error) 9.(D/I)s FINO	—	7.00	15.00	30.00	60.00

Obv: Smaller, closely spaced stars.

KM#	Date	Mintage	VG	Fine	VF	XF
151.2	1864 FP	—	5.00	10.00	20.00	45.00
	1865 FP	—	4.00	7.50	15.00	35.00
	1866 FP	—	4.00	7.50	15.00	35.00
	1866/5 FP	—	10.00	20.00	40.00	85.00

BOLIVIANO

25.0000 g, .900 SILVER, .7234 oz ASW
Obv: 9 stars. Rev: I/BOLIVIANO/500 Gs/ 9 Ds FINO inside wide wreath. Raised edge leg: BOLIVIA LIBRE E INDEPENDIENTE 1825.

KM#	Date	Mintage	VG	Fine	VF	XF
152.1	1864 FP (error) inverted P	—	25.00	50.00	90.00	185.00
	1864 FP (error) BOLIVIAN(A/O)	—	350.00	600.00	975.00	1500.
	1864 FP (P/inverted P)	—	18.00	30.00	55.00	125.00
	1864 FP	—	12.00	17.00	30.00	65.00
	1865/1 FP (error) 9. (D/reversed D)	—	15.00	25.00	55.00	100.00
	1865/4 FP	—	15.00	25.00	55.00	100.00
	1865 FP	—	10.00	15.00	30.00	60.00
	1866/5 FP	—	12.00	15.00	30.00	60.00
	1866 FP (F/p)P	—	18.00	30.00	55.00	125.00
	1866 FP	—	10.00	15.00	30.00	60.00
	1866 PF inverted FP	—	150.00	250.00	450.00	800.00
	1867/6 FP	—	13.00	22.00	40.00	80.00
	1867 FP	—	13.00	20.00	35.00	75.00
	1868 FP	—	—	—	Rare	—

NOTE: Some dates medal rotation strikes.

Reduced size: 35mm
Obv: 11 stars.

KM#	Date	Mintage	VG	Fine	VF	XF
152.2	1867/6 FP	—	11.50	17.50	25.00	55.00
(152.3)	1867/6 FE/P	—	10.00	15.00	22.00	50.00

KM#	Date	Mintage	VG	Fine	VF	XF
(152.3)	1867 FE/P	—	11.50	17.50	25.00	55.00
	1867 FE (error) REPUBLICA BOLIVIANO					
		—	300.00	500.00	850.00	1300.
	1867 FE	—	9.00	14.00	20.00	45.00
	1867 FP	—	10.00	16.00	30.00	65.00
	1868/7 FE	.720	11.50	18.00	30.00	65.00
	1868 FE	I.A.	9.00	14.00	20.00	45.00
	1868 FP	—	9.00	14.00	20.00	45.00
	1869 FE	.260	10.00	16.00	30.00	65.00
	1869 FP	—	12.50	20.00	35.00	70.00

NOTE: Some dates medal rotation strikes.

ONZA

32.4000 g, .900 GOLD, .9375 oz AGW

KM#	Date	Mintage	Fine	VF	XF	Unc
142	1868 FE	—	—	—	*Rare	—
	1868 FP	—	—	—	Rare	—

***NOTE:** Stack's Hammel sale 9-82 AU realized $13,000., Pacific Coast Auction Galleries, Long Beach sale 6-86 AU realized $15,500., Superior Parker/Casterline sale 12-89 AU realized $15,400.

MONETARY REFORM

100 Centavos = 1 Boliviana

NOTE: In 1870 the weight of the silver coins was modified by adjusting it to the metric system. 9Ds (Decimos) = .900 fineness.

CENTAVO

COPPER

KM#	Date	Mintage	VG	Fine	VF	XF
162	1878	—	50.00	100.00	200.00	450.00

Obv: Denomination below condor.
Rev: 'LA UNION ES LA FUERZA' in wreath, date below.

KM#	Date	Mintage	VG	Fine	VF	XF
163	1878	—	75.00	190.00	300.00	550.00

Rev: Cornucopia and fasces flank date.

KM#	Date	Mintage	Fine	VF	XF	Unc
167	1883/73 A	.500	5.00	10.00	22.00	50.00
	1883A	Inc. Ab.	3.50	7.50	15.00	35.00

2 CENTAVOS

COPPER

KM#	Date	Mintage	VG	Fine	VF	XF
164	1878	—	30.00	60.00	100.00	250.00

Obv: Denomination 2 cents beneath condor.

KM#	Date	Mintage	VG	Fine	VF	XF
165	1878	—	150.00	300.00	600.00	950.00

Rev: Cornucopia and fasces flank date.

KM#	Date	Mintage	VG	Fine	VF	XF
168	1883A	.250	3.50	7.50	15.00	50.00

5 CENTAVOS

1.2500 g, .900 SILVER, .0361 oz ASW
Obv. leg: REPUBLICA DE BOLIVIA around rectangular shield w/11 stars beneath.
Rev. leg: LA UNION HACE LA FUERZA, inscription: CINCO CS/1G. Y 5CS/9 DS FINO., w/dots below S's.

KM#	Date	Mintage	VG	Fine	VF	XF
156.1	1871/0 ER	—	—	—	Rare	—
	1871 ER	—	30.00	50.00	80.00	120.00
	1871 ER w/o dots in inscription					
		—	20.00	35.00	60.00	100.00
	1871 FP	—	50.00	90.00	170.00	—

1.1500 g, .900 SILVER, .0333 oz ASW
Rev. inscription: CINCO/CENT./9 D.FINO.

KM#	Date	Mintage	VG	Fine	VF	XF
156.2	1871 ER	—	5.00	10.00	25.00	45.00
	1872 ER	—	65.00	100.00	175.00	—
	1872/1 FE	—	10.00	20.00	40.00	80.00
	1872 FE	—	60.00	90.00	165.00	—

Obv: 9 stars at bottom.

KM#	Date	Mintage	VG	Fine	VF	XF
156.3	1872 FE	—	4.00	7.00	15.00	40.00

Obv. leg: REPUBLICA BOLIVIANA around oval shield above 9 stars.
Rev. leg: LA UNION ES LA FUERZA.

KM#	Date	Mintage	VG	Fine	VF	XF
157.1	1872 FE	—	2.00	3.50	6.00	12.50
	1873 FE	—	1.50	2.50	5.00	10.00
	1874 FE	—	2.00	4.00	7.50	15.00
	1875 FE	—	1.50	2.50	5.00	10.00
	1875 FE w/o dot after CENT					
		—	3.00	6.00	10.00	20.00
	1875 FE (error) RE(P/E)(U/P)LICA					
		—	4.00	7.00	15.00	35.00
	1876 FE	—	4.00	7.00	15.00	30.00
	1876 FE (error) F(U/E)ERZA					
		—	3.00	6.00	10.00	20.00
	1877 FE	—	2.00	3.00	6.00	12.00
	1878 FE	—	2.50	3.50	6.00	12.00
	1878 FE V in BOLIVIANA inverted A					
		—	2.50	3.50	7.00	14.00
	1879 FE	—	3.50	5.00	10.00	17.50
	1879 FE V in BOLIVIANA inverted A					
		—	5.00	10.00	17.50	40.00
	1880 FE	—	3.00	6.00	10.00	20.00
	1881 FE	—	2.00	3.50	5.00	12.50
	1882/1 FE	—	4.00	7.00	12.00	30.00
	1882 FE	—	3.75	6.50	10.00	25.00
	1883 FE (error) RE (F/P) UBLICA					
		—	4.00	6.00	15.00	25.00
	1883 FE	—	3.50	4.75	9.00	15.00
	1884 FE	—	4.00	6.00	10.00	20.00
	1884/3 FE	—	4.50	8.50	16.00	35.00

Rev: Bar between CENT and 9 D.FINO.

KM#	Date	Mintage	VG	Fine	VF	XF
157.2	1884 FE	—	—	—	Proof	Rare
	1885 FE	—	3.00	5.00	7.50	17.50
	1886/5 FE	—	3.00	5.00	7.50	17.50
	1886 FE	—	2.75	4.00	6.00	15.00
	1887 FE	—	2.75	4.00	6.00	15.00
	1888 FE	—	4.00	9.00	15.00	40.00
	1889/8 FE	—	7.50	15.00	20.00	27.50
	1889 FE	—	5.00	8.00	11.50	20.00
	1890 CB	—	2.00	5.00	7.50	15.00
	1891/0 CB	—	10.00	20.00	30.00	50.00
	1891 CB	—	3.00	6.50	10.00	17.50
	1893/83 CB	—	2.50	4.00	6.50	15.00
	1893 CB	.070	2.00	3.50	6.00	12.00
	1895 ES/CB	—	10.00	20.00	30.00	50.00
	1895 ES	.020	5.00	15.00	20.00	35.00
	1899 MM	—	2.50	5.00	8.00	16.00
	1900 MM	.050	2.00	4.00	6.00	12.00

COPPER-NICKEL
Rev: Cornucopia and fasces flank star.

KM#	Date	Mintage	Fine	VF	XF	Unc
169.1	1883A	2.200	10.00	20.00	40.00	90.00

NOTE: KM#169.1 was withdrawn from circulation due to confusion with contemporary silver 10 centavos. Eventually most of these Paris Mint pieces were officially hole punched and released back into circulation as KM#169.2.

KM#	Date	Mintage	Fine	VF	XF	Unc
169.2	1883A	Inc. Ab.	3.00	8.00	18.00	40.00

KM#	Date	Mintage	Fine	VF	XF	Unc
171	1892H	2.000	3.00	6.00	18.00	35.00
	1892H	—	—	—	Proof	200.00

NOTE: Medal rotation strike.

KM#	Date	Mintage	Fine	VF	XF	Unc
173.1	1893	2.500	3.50	6.00	12.00	27.50
	1893	—	—	—	Proof	100.00
	1899	2.000	1.00	1.75	4.00	12.00

NOTE: Later dates (1909-1919) exist for this type.

NOTE: Coins dated 1893, 1918 and 1919 medal rotation strike at Heaton Mint.

Rev: Cornucopia and fasces flank date.

KM#	Date	Mintage	Fine	VF	XF	Unc
173.2	1895	2.000	1.00	1.75	4.00	12.00

Rev: Cornucopia and torch flank date.

KM#	Date	Mintage	Fine	VF	XF	Unc
173.3	1897	1.500	1.00	1.75	4.00	12.00

NOTE: Later dates (1902-1909) exist for this type.

10 CENTAVOS

2.5000 g, .900 SILVER, .0723 oz ASW
Obv. leg: REPUBLICA DE BOLIVIA around rectangular shield above 11 stars.
Rev. leg: LA UNION HACE LA FUERZA, inscription: DIEZ CTS/2 GMS Y 5 Ds/9 Ds FINO.,

w/dots below S's in DS.

KM#	Date	Mintage	VG	Fine	VF	XF
153.1	1870 ER	—	2.00	4.00	8.00	15.00
	1870 ER (error) LA UION HACE					
		—	4.00	8.00	15.00	30.00
	1871 ER	—	2.00	4.00	7.00	15.00
	1871 ER A in REPUBLICA inverted V and BOLI(V/L)IA		2.50	5.00	12.00	20.00
	1871 FP	—	4.00	8.00	15.00	30.00
	1871 FP A in REPUBLICA inverted V and BOLI(V/L)IA		3.00	6.00	12.00	25.00

2.3000 g, .900 SILVER, .0666 oz ASW
Rev. inscription: DIEZ/CENT./9 Ds FINO., w/dot below S.

KM#	Date	Mintage	VG	Fine	VF	XF
153.2	1871 ER	—	2.00	5.00	10.00	17.50

Obv: 9 stars at bottom.

KM#	Date	Mintage	VG	Fine	VF	XF
153.3	1871 ER	—	1.50	3.00	6.00	15.00
	1872 FE	—	1.50	3.00	6.00	15.00
	1872 FE (error) V in BOLIVIA inverted A					
		—	—	5.00	9.00	25.00

Obv. leg: REPUBLICA BOLIVIANA around oval shield above 9 stars. Rev. leg: LA UNION ES LA FUERZA around wreath inscription: DIEZ/CENTs/9 Ds FINO.

KM#	Date	Mintage	VG	Fine	VF	XF
158.1	1872 FE	—	2.00	4.00	8.00	15.00
	1873 FE	—	2.00	4.00	8.00	15.00
	1874 FE	—	2.50	5.00	10.00	20.00
	1875 FE	—	3.00	6.00	12.00	25.00

Rev. inscription: DIEZ/CENTs/9D.FINO.

KM#	Date	Mintage	VG	Fine	VF	XF
158.2	1872 FE	—	3.00	6.00	10.00	15.00
	1873 FE	—	1.25	2.25	4.50	9.00
	1874 FE	—	1.25	2.25	4.50	9.00
	1875 FE	—	1.25	2.00	4.00	8.00
	1875 FE (error) LA UNIO ES					
		—	5.00	10.00	18.00	35.00
	1876 FE	—	1.25	2.00	4.00	8.00
	1877 FE	—	1.25	2.00	4.00	8.00
	1878 FE	—	1.50	2.50	5.00	10.00
	1879 FE	—	1.25	2.00	4.00	8.00
	1880 FE	—	1.25	2.25	4.50	9.00
	1881 FE	—	1.25	2.00	4.00	8.00
	1882 FE	—	1.50	2.50	5.00	10.00
	1883/2 FE	—	2.00	3.50	8.00	15.00
	1883 FE (error) (F/E)E					
			2.00	3.50	8.00	15.00
	1883 FE	—	1.50	2.50	5.00	10.00
	1884/3 FE	—	3.00	5.00	10.00	17.50
	1884/3 FE (error) A in REPUBLICA inverted V					
		—	4.00	8.00	15.00	25.00

Obv: Larger oval shield. Rev: Reduced size lettering, bar between CENTS and 9D.

KM#	Date	Mintage	VG	Fine	VF	XF
158.3	1884 FE	—	4.00	7.00	15.00	27.50
	1884 FE	—	—	—	Proof	Rare
	1885 FE	—	1.50	2.50	5.00	10.00
	1886 FE	—	1.25	2.00	4.00	8.00
	1887 FE	—	5.00	8.00	15.00	27.50
	1888 FE	—	5.00	10.00	18.00	35.00
	1889 FE	—	2.50	5.00	10.00	17.50
	1890 FE	—	2.50	5.00	10.00	17.50
	1890 CB 1 over horizontal 1					
		—	7.50	15.00	25.00	45.00
	1890 CB	—	2.50	5.00	10.00	17.50
	1891 CB	—	1.50	3.00	6.00	12.00
	1893 CB	.050	1.50	3.00	6.00	12.00
	1895 ES	.020	4.00	7.00	13.50	20.00
	1899 MM	—	1.50	3.00	6.00	12.00
	1900 MM	.030	2.00	4.00	7.50	15.00

Rev: DIEZ/CENT./9D.FINO

KM#	Date	Mintage	VG	Fine	VF	XF
158.4	1884/3 FE	—	5.00	10.00	20.00	45.00

COPPER-NICKEL
Rev: Cornucopia and fasces flank star.

KM#	Date	Mintage	Fine	VF	XF	Unc
170.1	1883A	.800	14.00	30.00	60.00	130.00

NOTE: KM#170.1 was withdrawn from circulation due to confusion with contemporary silver 20 Centavos. Eventually most of these Paris Mint pieces were officially hole punched and released back into circulation as KM#170.2.

KM#	Date	Mintage	Fine	VF	XF	Unc
170.2	1883A	Inc. Ab.	3.00	6.00	15.00	50.00

KM#	Date	Mintage	Fine	VF	XF	Unc
172	1892H	1.000	2.25	5.50	15.00	45.00
	1892H	—	—	—	Proof	350.00

NOTE: Medal rotation strike.

Rev: W/o privy marks.

KM#	Date	Mintage	Fine	VF	XF	Unc
174.1	1893	1.250	5.00	10.00	15.00	30.00
	1893	—	—	—	Proof	175.00
	1899	3.000	1.00	2.00	4.00	12.00

NOTE: Later dates (1918-1919) exist for this type.
NOTE: Coins dated 1893, 1918 and 1919 medal rotation strike at the Heaton Mint.

Rev: Cornucopia and fasces flank date.

KM#	Date	Mintage	Fine	VF	XF	Unc
174.2	1895	1.000	4.00	8.00	17.50	30.00

Rev: Cornucopia and torch flank date.

KM#	Date	Mintage	Fine	VF	XF	Unc
174.3	1897	2.250	1.00	2.00	4.00	12.00

NOTE: Later dates (1901-1909) exist for this type.

20 CENTAVOS

5.0000 g, .900 SILVER, .1446 oz ASW
Obv: 11 stars at bottom.
Rev. leg: LA UNION HACE LA FUERZA, weight.

KM#	Date	Mintage	VG	Fine	VF	XF
154.1	1870 ER	—	25.00	35.00	60.00	90.00
	1871 ER	—	20.00	30.00	50.00	80.00
	1871 ER (error) LA (UN/LA)ION					
		—	25.00	40.00	65.00	100.00
	1871 FP	—	—	—	—	—

4.6000 g, .900 SILVER, .1331 oz ASW
Obv: 11 stars. Rev: W/o weight.

KM#	Date	Mintage	VG	Fine	VF	XF
154.2	1871 ER	—	12.00	25.00	50.00	100.00
	1871 ER (rev. rotated 90 degrees)					
		—	20.00	40.00	80.00	175.00

Obv: 9 stars at bottom

KM#	Date	Mintage	VG	Fine	VF	XF
154.3	1871 ER	—	8.00	15.00	25.00	45.00
	1872 ER	—	10.00	20.00	35.00	55.00
	1872 FE	—	2.50	5.00	10.00	25.00

Rev. leg: LA UNION ES LA FUERZA.

KM#	Date	Mintage	VG	Fine	VF	XF
159.1	1872 FE	—	30.00	60.00	100.00	200.00
	1873 FE	—	1.50	3.00	6.00	10.00

KM#	Date	Mintage	VG	Fine	VF	XF
159.1	1874 FE	—	4.00	6.00	12.50	20.00
	1875 FE	—	2.25	3.00	5.00	8.00
	1876 FE	—	2.25	3.00	6.00	9.00
	1876 FE (error) UNI(O/N)N					
		—	6.50	9.00	15.00	25.00
	1877 FE	—	2.25	3.00	5.00	8.00
	1878 FE	—	2.25	3.00	5.00	8.00
	1878 FE (error) BOLI(V/inverted V)IANA					
		—	6.50	9.00	20.00	50.00
	1879/8 FE	—	3.00	6.00	12.00	20.00
	1879 FE	—	2.25	3.00	5.00	8.00
	1880 FE (error) REPUB(L/B)ICA					
		—	6.00	12.00	25.00	45.00
	1880 FE	—	2.25	3.00	5.00	8.00
	1881 FE	—	2.25	3.00	5.00	8.00
	1882 FE	—	2.25	3.00	5.00	8.00
	1883 FE	—	2.25	3.00	5.00	8.00
	1883 EF	—	45.00	75.00	125.00	—
	1884/3 FE	—	4.00	6.00	12.50	20.00
	1884 FE (error) VE(I/N)NTE					
		—	7.00	15.00	30.00	50.00
	1884 FE	—	2.25	3.00	5.00	8.00

Reduced size dates and lettering, bar below CENTS.

KM#	Date	Mintage	VG	Fine	VF	XF
159.2	1884 FE	—	—	—	Proof	Rare
	1885 FE	—	2.25	3.00	5.00	8.00
	1886 FE	—	2.25	3.00	6.00	9.00
	1887 FE	—	2.25	3.00	5.00	8.00
	1888 FE	—	2.25	3.00	5.00	8.00
	1889 FE	—	2.25	3.00	5.00	8.00
	1889/8 FE	—	2.50	4.00	6.50	10.00
	1890 FE	—	2.25	3.00	5.00	8.00
	1890/80 CB	—	2.50	4.00	6.50	10.00
	1890 CB	—	2.25	3.00	5.00	8.00
	1891 CB (error) C B/E					
		—	3.00	5.00	8.00	16.00
	1891 CB	—	2.25	3.50	6.00	9.00
	1892 CB	—	2.25	3.50	6.00	9.00
	1893 CB	.500	2.25	3.00	5.00	8.00
	1894 ES (error) E S/B					
		—	3.00	5.00	8.00	16.00
	1894 ES	.490	2.25	4.50	7.00	15.00
	1895 ES	—	2.25	3.50	6.00	9.00
	1896 ES	.100	2.25	3.00	5.00	8.00
	1896 CB	I.A.	6.50	10.00	20.00	30.00
	1897 CB	.170	2.25	3.00	5.00	8.00
	1898 CB	—	10.00	15.00	25.00	35.00
	1899 CB	—	—	—	Rare	—
	1899 MM	—	2.25	3.50	6.00	9.00
	1900 MM	.170	2.25	3.50	6.00	9.00

NOTE: Later dates (1901-1907) exist for this type.
NOTE: The small bar usually found below "S" in "9DS" is missing in 1886-1888 dates.

Daza Commemorative

KM#	Date	Mintage	VG	Fine	VF	XF
166	1879	—	12.50	27.50	35.00	60.00
	1879 (error) A's in DAZA inverted V's					
		—	15.00	30.00	50.00	80.00

50 CENTAVOS

(1/2 Boliviano)

12.5000 g, .900 SILVER, .3617 oz ASW
Rev. leg: 12 GS. 500 MS. 9 DS. FINO.

KM#	Date	Mintage	VG	Fine	VF	XF
161.1	1873 FE	—	7.50	15.00	30.00	65.00

Rev. leg: 12 GMS 500 MMS.

KM#	Date	Mintage	VG	Fine	VF	XF
161.2	1873 FE	—	20.00	30.00	50.00	125.00

Rev: W/o 50 Cents and weight.

KM#	Date	Mintage	VG	Fine	VF	XF
161.3	1879/7 FE	—	50.00	100.00	185.00	350.00
	1879 FE	—	50.00	100.00	165.00	300.00
	1882 FE	—	50.00	100.00	165.00	285.00

11.5000 g, .900 SILVER, .3328 oz ASW
Rev: Reduced size lettering w/weight.

KM#	Date	Mintage	VG	Fine	VF	XF
161.4	1884 FE	—	—	—	Proof	Rare
	1887 FE	—	—	—	Rare	—
	1889 MM	—	—	—	Rare	—
	1891 CB	—	45.00	75.00	150.00	300.00

Rev: Reduced size lettering w/o weight.

KM#	Date	Mintage	VG	Fine	VF	XF
161.5	1891 CB	—	BV	3.50	6.50	12.00
	1892 CB	—	BV	3.50	6.50	12.00
	1893 CB	3.150	BV	3.50	6.50	12.00
	1894/1 CB	2.470	BV	5.00	8.50	25.00
	1894 CB	I.A.	BV	3.50	6.50	12.00
	1894/84 ES	—	BV	6.00	10.00	40.00
	1894 ES	I.A.	BV	4.00	7.00	15.00
	1895/85 ES	—	BV	6.00	10.00	40.00
	1895 ES	3.390	BV	3.50	6.50	12.00
	1896 ES	2.980	BV	3.50	6.50	12.00
	1897 CB	2.300	BV	3.50	6.50	12.00
	1897 ES	—	BV	4.50	7.50	20.00
	1898/7 CB	—	BV	4.00	7.00	15.00
	1898 CB	—	BV	3.50	6.50	12.00
	1899 CB	—	BV	3.50	6.50	12.00
	1899 MM	—	BV	3.50	6.50	12.00
	1899/69 first 9 over inverted 9	—	BV	4.00	7.00	15.00
	1900 MM	3.820	BV	3.50	6.50	12.00
175.1	1900 MM	I.A.	BV	3.50	6.50	12.00

NOTE: Later dates (1901-1908) exist for this type.

KM#	Date	Mintage	VG	Fine	VF	XF
175.2	1900So	.900	BV	6.50	9.50	20.00

BOLIVIANO

25.0000 g, .900 SILVER, .7234 oz ASW
Obv. leg: REPUBLICA DE BOLIVIA around rectangular shield, 11 stars below.
Rev. leg: LA UNION HACE LA FUERZA, large wreath, leg: UN/BOLIVIANO/25G 9D FINO.

KM#	Date	Mintage	VG	Fine	VF	XF
155.1 (155.4)	1870 ER	—	40.00	60.00	120.00	180.00

Rev. leg: UN/BOLIVIANO/25 Gms 9Ds FINO, dot under MS.

KM#	Date	Mintage	VG	Fine	VF	XF
155.2 (155.1)	1870 ER	—	10.00	12.50	20.00	30.00

NOTE: Wide wreaths have 4 leaves at top while normal size wreaths have 2 leaves at top.

Rev: Line and dot under MS and S, normal wreath.

KM#	Date	Mintage	VG	Fine	VF	XF
155.3	1870 ER	—	10.00	17.00	25.00	50.00
(155.2)	1870 ER	—	—	—	Proof	1000.
	1871/0 ER	—	15.00	25.00	35.00	65.00
	1871 ER	—	13.00	20.00	30.00	60.00
	1871 FP	—	13.00	20.00	30.00	60.00

Obv: 9 stars at bottom.

KM#	Date	Mintage	VG	Fine	VF	XF
155.4	1870 ER	—	15.00	25.00	35.00	65.00
(155.3)	1871 ER	—	12.50	17.50	25.00	55.00
	1871 FP	—	12.50	17.50	25.00	55.00
	1871 EF	—	12.50	17.50	25.00	55.00
	1872 FE	—	20.00	30.00	40.00	70.00
	1872 FE (error) REPUB(L/B)ICA	—	20.00	40.00	60.00	100.00

Obv. leg: REPUBLICA BOLIVIANA around oval wreath, 9 stars below.
Rev. leg: LA UNION ES LA FUERZA.

KM#	Date	Mintage	VG	Fine	VF	XF
160.1	1872 FE	—	10.00	15.00	25.00	40.00
	1872 FE (error) ES (L/E)A FUERZA	—	50.00	80.00	160.00	250.00
	1873 FE	—	10.00	15.00	25.00	40.00
	1874 FE	—	10.00	15.00	25.00	40.00
	1875 FE	—	10.00	15.00	25.00	40.00
	1877/5 FE	—	100.00	175.00	250.00	500.00
	1877 FE	—	45.00	65.00	120.00	200.00

Rev. leg: 25 Gs 9Ds FINO, w/line under s's.

KM#	Date	Mintage	VG	Fine	VF	XF
160.2	1879 F.E.	—	60.00	120.00	225.00	375.00

Rev. leg: 25 GMS, horizontal bar between denomination and weight.

KM#	Date	Mintage	VG	Fine	VF	XF
160.3	1884 FE	—	—	—	Proof	Rare
	1887 FE	—	—	—	Rare	—
	1893 CB	—	—	1000.	1500.	2500.

ESSAIS (E)

Standard metals unless otherwise noted

KM#	Date	Mintage	Identification	Mkt.Val.
E1	1883A	—	1 Centavo, KM167	60.00

KM#	Date	Mintage	Identification	Mkt.Val.
E2	1883EG	—	1 Centavo, KM167	70.00
E3	1883A	—	2 Centavos, KM168	50.00
E4	1883EG	—	2 Centavos, KM168	50.00
E5	1883A	—	5 Centavos, KM169	80.00

KM#	Date	Mintage	Identification	Mkt.Val.
E6	1883EG	—	5 Centavos, KM169	90.00
E7	1883A	—	10 Centavos, KM170	85.00

KM#	Date	Mintage	Identification	Mkt.Val.
E8	1883EG	—	10 Centavos, KM170	95.00

PATTERNS (Pn)

(Including off metal strikes)

Mintmark: Potosi monogram

KM#	Date	Mintage	Identification	Mkt.Val.
Pn1	1827 JM	—	4 Soles, Silver, bare head right	6000.
Pn2	1865	—	1/4 Melgarejo, Copper, KM144	30.00

KM#	Date	Mintage	Identification	Mkt.Val.
PnA2	1854 MJ	—	1/2 Sol, brass, 16.77mm, KM118.1	—
Pn3	1865	—	1/2 Melgarejo, Copper, KM145	50.00
Pn4	1865 FP	—	1 Onza, Gold	25,000.

KM#	Date	Mintage	Identification	Mkt.Val.
Pn5	1868 CT	—	1 Boliviano, Silver, reeded edge	—
Pn6	1868 CT	—	1 Boliviano, Silver, plain edge	2150.
PnA7	1868 CT	—	1 Boliviano, w/o E, Copper, reeded edge	700.00
PnB7	1868 CT	—	1 Boliviano, Gold, reeded edge	20,900.
Pn7	1868 FE	—	1/2 Scudo, Silver, KM140	450.00

Pn8	1868 FE	—	1 Onza, Silver	2000.

Mint mark: PAZ

Pn11	1868 CT	—	5 Centavos, Silver	—

Pn12	1868 CT	—	5 Centavos, Silver	250.00
PnA13	1868 CT	—	5 Centavos, Gold	—

Pn13	1868 CT	—	10 Centavos, Silver	200.00
Pn14	1868 CT	—	10 Centavos, Gold	—

Pn15	1868 CT	—	20 Centavos, Copper, plain edge	150.00
Pn16	1868 CT	—	20 Centavos, Silver, reeded edge	200.00

KM#	Date	Mintage	Identification	Mkt.Val.
Pn17	1868 CT	—	Un Boliviano, w/o E, Copper, plain edge	450.00
Pn18	1868 CT	—	Un Boliviano, Copper, reeded edge	450.00
Pn19	1868 CT	—	Un Boliviano, Silver, reeded edge	—
Pn23	1868	—	Un Boliviano, w/E Copper, plain edge	500.00

Pn24	1868	—	Un Boliviano, w/o E, plain edge	500.00
Pn25	1868	—	1 Boliviano, Copper, plain edge	—
Pn26	1868	—	1 Boliviano, w/E Silver, reeded edge	2500.

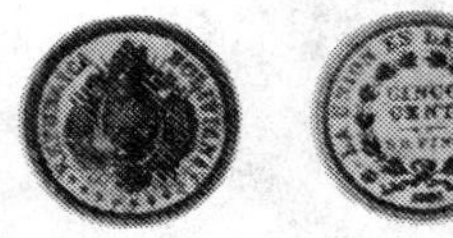

Pn27	1884 F.E.	—	5 Centavos, Silver	150.00

Pn28	1884 F.E.	—	10 Centavos, Silver	250.00

Pn29	1884 F.E.	—	20 Centavos, Silver	350.00

KM#	Date	Mintage	Identification	Mkt.Val.
Pn30	1884 F.E.	—	50 Centavos, Silver	1100.

Pn31	1884 F.E.	—	1 Boliviano, Silver	2200.

Pn32	1887 F.E.	—	1 Escudo, Silver	850.00
PnA33	1887 F.E.	—	1 Escudo, Gold	2500.
PnB33	1887 F.E.	—	Medio Bolivar, Gold	—
PnC33	1887 F.E.	—	UN Bolivar, Gold	—
PnD33	1897 C.B.	—	20 Centavos, Brass, KM159.2	—

Pn33	1900	—	20 Centavos, Silver	675.00
Pn34	1900 MM	—	20 Centavos, Brass	60.00

Pn35	1900 So	—	50 Centavos, .900 Gold, KM175.2	5000.

PIEFORTS (P)

KM#	Date	Mintage	Identification	Issue Price	Mkt. Val.
P1	1855 MJ	—	1 Escudo, Silver	—	250.00

P2	1856 FJ	—	1 Escudo, Silver	—	260.00

KM#	Date	Mintage	Identification	Issue Price	Mkt. Val.
P3	1865 FP	—	1/10 Boliviano, Silver	—	400.00
P4	1868 CT	—	10 Centavos, Silver	—	200.00

KM#	Date	Mintage	Identification	Issue Price	Mkt. Val.
P5	1868 CT	—	20 Centavos, Silver	—	200.00
P6	1868 CT	—	1 Boliviano, Silver	—	2000.

KM#	Date	Mintage	Identification	Issue Price	Mkt. Val.
P7	1868 FE	—	1 Escudo, Silver	—	260.00

KM#	Date	Mintage	Identification	Issue Price	Mkt. Val.
P8	1868 FE	—	1/2 Escudo, Silver	—	260.00

The Federative Republic of Brazil, which comprises half the continent of South America and is the only Latin American country deriving its culture and language from Portugal, has an area of 3,286,488 sq. mi. (8,511,965 sq. km.) and a population of 160.7 million. Capital: Brasilia. The economy of Brazil is as varied and complex as any in the developing world. Agriculture is a mainstay of the economy, while only 4 percent of the area is under cultivation. Known mineral resources are almost unlimited in variety and size of reserves. A large, relatively sophisticated industry ranges from basic steel and chemical production to finished consumer goods. Coffee, cotton, iron ore and cocoa are the chief exports.

Brazil was discovered and claimed for Portugal by Admiral Pedro Alvares Cabral in 1500. Portugal established a settlement in 1532 and proclaimed the area a royal colony in 1549. During the Napoleonic Wars, Dom Joao VI established the seat of Portuguese government in Rio de Janeiro. When he returned to Portugal, his son Dom Pedro I declared Brazil's independence on Sept. 7, 1822, and became emperor of Brazil. The Empire of Brazil was maintained until 1889 when the federal republic was established. The Federative Republic was established in 1946 by terms of a constitution drawn up by a constituent assembly. Following a coup in 1964 the armed forces retained overall control under a dictatorship until civilian government was restored on March 15, 1985. The current constitution was adopted in 1988.

RULERS

Portuguese

Maria I, Widow, 1786-1816
Joao, Prince Regent, 1799-1818
Joao VI, 1818-1822

Brazilean

Pedro I, 1822-1831
Pedro II, 1831-1889

MINT MARKS

(a) - Paris, privy marks only
B - Bahia
C - Cuiaba (Mato Grosso) 1823-1833
G - Goias 1823-1833
M - Minas Gerais 1823-1828
P - Pernambuco
R - Rio de Janeiro
SP - Sao Paulo 1825-1832
W/o mint mark - Lisbon 1715-1805

MONETARY SYSTEM

(Until 1833)

120 Reis = 1 Real
6400 Reis 1 Peca (Dobra = Johannes (Joe)
= 4 Escudos

(1833-1942)

1000 Reis = 1 Milreis

COLONIAL COINAGE

NOTE All coins, unless noted otherwise, have medal rotation.

X (10) REIS

COPPER
Mint: Lisbon, w/o mint mark.
Obv. leg: JOANNES.D.G.P.E. BRASILIAE. . .

KM#	Date	Mintage	VG	Fine	VF	XF
232.1	1802	.612	10.00	15.00	30.00	50.00
232.1	1803	1.167	3.50	7.50	15.00	25.00
	1805	1.248	3.50	7.50	15.00	25.00

Mint mark: B

KM#	Date	Mintage	VG	Fine	VF	XF
232.2	1815	—	3.00	7.50	10.00	30.00
	1816	.413	5.00	10.00	15.00	40.00
	1818	—	3.00	7.50	10.00	30.00

Mint mark: R

KM#	Date	Mintage	VG	Fine	VF	XF
232.3	1805	.400	10.00	15.00	30.00	50.00
	1806	1.136	3.00	8.00	12.00	20.00
	1812	—	—	—	Rare	—
	1814	.066	15.00	30.00	75.00	150.00
	1815	.302	10.00	15.00	30.00	50.00

Mint mark: R
Obv. leg: JOANNES VI.D.G.PORT. . .

KM#	Date	Mintage	VG	Fine	VF	XF
314.1	1818 cross on crown					
		.496	5.00	10.00	17.50	35.00
	1819 cross and star on crown					
		1.440	2.50	5.00	10.00	20.00
	1820 star and cross on crown					
		1.646	2.50	5.00	10.00	20.00
	1821 star and cross on crown					
		2.003	2.50	5.00	10.00	20.00
	1822 cross and crown					
		1.839	2.50	5.00	10.00	20.00

Mint mark: B

KM#	Date	Mintage	VG	Fine	VF	XF
314.2	1821	—	2.50	5.00	10.00	20.00
	1822	—	2.50	5.00	10.00	20.00
	1822/29	—	10.00	20.00	40.00	90.00
	1823	—	2.50	5.00	10.00	18.00

XX (20) REIS

COPPER
Mint: Lisbon, w/o mint mark.
Obv. leg: JOANNES D.G.PORT.ET.BRAS.P. REGENS. . . Rev: Globe.

KM#	Date	Mintage	VG	Fine	VF	XF
233.1	1802	.788	5.00	10.00	15.00	25.00
	1803	1.920	2.50	5.00	10.00	20.00

Mint mark: B

KM#	Date	Mintage	VG	Fine	VF	XF
233.2	1812	—	3.00	6.00	15.00	30.00
	1813	.160	10.00	15.00	20.00	50.00
	1815 cross on crown					
		.448	7.50	12.50	17.50	35.00
	1816	.700	5.00	10.00	15.00	25.00

Mint mark: R

KM#	Date	Mintage	VG	Fine	VF	XF
233.3	1812	.012	10.00	20.00	35.00	75.00
	1813	.717	5.00	10.00	15.00	25.00
	1813/14	—	10.00	20.00	35.00	75.00
	1814	1.164	3.00	6.00	12.50	20.00
	1815 star on crown					
		.302	7.50	14.00	25.00	35.00
	1817	.116	7.50	14.00	25.00	45.00
	1818	.060	8.00	15.00	30.00	60.00

Obv. leg: JOANNES D.G.PORT.BRAS.ET ALG.

KM#	Date	Mintage	VG	Fine	VF	XF
309	1816	.206	5.00	70.00	20.00	45.00

Minted for Goias and Mato Grosso
Obv. leg: JOANNES D.G.P.E. . . . crowned value.
Rev. leg: PECUNIA.TOTUM.CIRCUMIT. . . globe.

KM#	Date	Mintage	VG	Fine	VF	XF
315	1818	—	8.00	16.00	35.00	70.00

Mint mark: R
Obv. leg: JOANNES. VI. D.G.PORT. . .

KM#	Date	Mintage	VG	Fine	VF	XF
316.1	1818 star on crown					
		.174	5.00	10.00	20.00	45.00
	1819 star and cross on crown					
		1.440	3.00	6.00	12.50	25.00
	1820 star and cross on crown					
		4.872	2.50	5.00	10.00	20.00
	1821 star on crown					
		10.828	2.50	5.00	10.00	20.00
	1821 cross on crown					
		—	3.00	6.00	10.00	25.00
	1822 star and cross on crown					
		7.046	2.50	5.00	9.00	17.50

Mint mark: B

KM#	Date	Mintage	VG	Fine	VF	XF
316.2	1820	—	2.50	5.00	10.00	20.00
	1821 cross on crown					
		—	2.50	5.00	10.00	20.00

37-1/2 REIS

COPPER
Mint mark: M
Minted for Minas Gerais
Obv. leg: JOANNES.VI.D.G.PORT.BRAS. . .
Rev. leg: PECUNIA.TOTUM.CIRCUMIT. . .

KM#	Date	Mintage	VG	Fine	VF	XF
317.1	1818	.200	10.00	25.00	50.00	75.00
	1819	—	10.00	25.00	50.00	75.00
	1821	—	10.00	25.00	50.00	75.00

Mint mark: R

KM#	Date	Mintage	VG	Fine	VF	XF
317.2	1818	—	45.00	100.00	200.00	325.00

XL (40) REIS

COPPER
Mint: Lisbon, w/o mint mark.
Obv. leg: JOANNES D.G.P. ET.BRASILAE. . .
Rev: Similar to 10 Reis, KM#232.1.

KM#	Date	Mintage	VG	Fine	VF	XF
234.1	1802	.584	5.00	10.00	20.00	50.00
	1803	1.143	2.50	6.50	12.50	30.00

NOTE: Crown varieties exist for both dates.

Mint mark: B

KM#	Date	Mintage	VG	Fine	VF	XF
234.2	1809	—	7.50	15.00	25.00	50.00
	1810	—	7.50	15.00	25.00	50.00
	1811	—	3.00	7.50	15.00	35.00
	1812 ball on crown					
		—	3.00	7.50	15.00	30.00
	1814	.132	5.00	10.00	20.00	45.00
	1816 cross on crown					
		.286	5.00	10.00	20.00	45.00

Mint mark: R

KM#	Date	Mintage	VG	Fine	VF	XF
234.3	1812	.252	5.00	10.00	17.50	35.00
	1813	.307	5.00	10.00	17.50	35.00
	1815	.131	5.00	10.00	17.50	35.00
	1816	.453	3.50	7.50	12.50	30.00
	1817	.379	6.00	15.00	25.00	50.00

Obv. leg: JOANNES D.G. PORT.BRAS. ET.ALG. . .

KM#	Date	Mintage	VG	Fine	VF	XF
311	1816	—	5.00	10.00	20.00	45.00

Minted for Goias and Mato Grosso
Obv. leg: JOANNES.D.G.P.E. . .
Rev. leg: PECUNIA.TOTUM.CIRCUMIT. . .

KM#	Date	Mintage	VG	Fine	VF	XF
318	1818	—	15.00	40.00	100.00	150.00

Mint mark: R

KM#	Date	Mintage	VG	Fine	VF	XF
319.1	1818 star on crown					
		.687	3.50	7.50	20.00	35.00
	1819	2.50	5.00	10.00	22.00	45.00
	1820 star on crown					
		2.018	2.50	6.50	15.00	25.00
	1821 cross on crown					
		5.307	2.50	6.50	15.00	25.00
	1822	4.583	2.50	6.50	15.00	25.00

Mint mark: B

KM#	Date	Mintage	VG	Fine	VF	XF
319.2	1820	—	3.50	8.50	22.00	35.00
	1821	—	3.50	8.50	22.00	35.00
	1822	—	3.50	8.50	22.00	35.00
	1823	—	3.50	8.50	25.00	50.00

Minted for Goias and Mato Grosso
Obv. leg: JOANNES.VI.D.G.PORT.BRAS.

KM#	Date	Mintage	VG	Fine	VF	XF
340	1820 cross on crown					
		—	5.00	35.00	100.00	150.00
	1821 cross on crown					
		—	5.00	35.00	100.00	150.00
	1822 cross on crown					
		—	5.00	35.00	100.00	150.00

75 REIS

COPPER
Mint mark: M
Minted for Minas Gerais
Obv. leg: JOANNES.VI.D.G.PORT.BRAS. . .
Rev. leg: PECUNIA.TOTUM.CIRCUMIT. . ., arms on globe.

KM#	Date	Mintage	VG	Fine	VF	XF
320	1818	.269	15.00	30.00	75.00	110.00
	1819	—	15.00	30.00	80.00	120.00
	1821	—	15.00	30.00	75.00	110.00

LXXX (80) REIS

2.2400 g, .917 SILVER, .0660 oz ASW
Mint mark: R
Obv. leg: JOANNES.D.G.PORT.P.REGENS. . .

KM#	Date	Mintage	VG	Fine	VF	XF
305	1810	—	—	—	Rare	—
	1814	—	30.00	70.00	150.00	300.00
	1816	—	25.00	50.00	120.00	200.00

COPPER
Similar to 10 Reis, KM#232.2.

KM#	Date	Mintage	VG	Fine	VF	XF
308	1811	.013	10.00	25.00	55.00	150.00
	1812	.013	10.00	25.00	55.00	150.00

Mint mark: B
Minted for Goias and Mato Grosso
Obv. leg: JOANNES D.G.PORT. . . crowned value.
Rev. leg: PECUNIA.TOTUM.CIRCUMIT. . . globe.

KM#	Date	Mintage	VG	Fine	VF	XF
321.1	1818	—	4.00	15.00	25.00	45.00

Mint mark: R

KM#	Date	Mintage	VG	Fine	VF	XF
321.2	1818	—	4.00	15.00	25.00	45.00

2.2400 g, .917 SILVER, .0660 oz ASW
Obv: Crowned 80 within wreath, leg: JOANNES.VI. D.G.PORT. BRAS. . .

KM#	Date	Mintage	VG	Fine	VF	XF
322.1	1818	—	25.00	50.00	90.00	200.00

Mint mark: B

KM#	Date	Mintage	VG	Fine	VF	XF
322.2	1821	.125	15.00	25.00	60.00	120.00

COPPER
Mint mark: R
Minted for Goias and Mato Grosso
Obv. leg: JOANNES.VI.D.G.PORT. . . crowned value. Rev: Arms on globe.

KM#	Date	Mintage	VG	Fine	VF	XF
341	1820	—	10.00	20.00	40.00	95.00

Mint mark: B

KM#	Date	Mintage	VG	Fine	VF	XF
342.1	1820	—	7.50	15.00	25.00	45.00
	1821	—	7.50	15.00	25.00	45.00
	1822/1	—	10.00	20.00	40.00	95.00
	1822	—	7.50	15.00	30.00	60.00
	1823	—	7.50	15.00	30.00	60.00

Mint mark: R

KM#	Date	Mintage	VG	Fine	VF	XF
342.2	1821	.210	5.00	10.00	17.50	35.00
	1822	.617	5.00	10.00	17.50	35.00

160 REIS

4.4800 g, .917 SILVER, .1320 oz ASW
Mint mark: R
Obv. leg: JOANNES.D.G.PORT.P. REGENS. . ., crowned value. Rev: Globe.

KM#	Date	Mintage	VG	Fine	VF	XF
306.1	1810	—	17.50	35.00	80.00	160.00
	1813	—	6.00	10.00	25.00	50.00
	1813R/B	—	8.50	17.50	30.00	50.00
	1815	—	12.50	25.00	35.00	60.00

Medal strike.

KM#	Date	Mintage	VG	Fine	VF	XF
306.3	1810	—	17.00	40.00	80.00	180.00
	1813	—	17.00	40.00	80.00	180.00

Mint mark: B

KM#	Date	Mintage	VG	Fine	VF	XF
306.2	1811	—	—	—	Rare	—
	1812	—	150.00	350.00	700.00	1500.

4.4509 g, .917 SILVER, .1312 oz ASW
Mint mark: R
Obv. leg: JOANNES.VI.D.G.PORT.BRAS. . .

KM#	Date	Mintage	VG	Fine	VF	XF
323.1	1818	—	10.00	25.00	40.00	80.00
	1820	—	—	—	Rare	—

Mint mark: B

KM#	Date	Mintage	VG	Fine	VF	XF
323.2	1821	5,639	40.00	80.00	120.00	150.00

320 REIS

8.9018 g, .917 SILVER, .2623 oz ASW
Mint mark: R
Similar to KM#255.1 but obv. leg: MARIA.I.D.G. . .

KM#	Date	Mintage	VG	Fine	VF	XF
221.3	1802	—	11.00	20.00	27.50	45.00

NOTE: Earlier date (1800) exists for this type.

8.9600 g, .917 SILVER, .2641 oz ASW
Obv. leg: JOANNES.D.G.PORT.P.REGENS. . .

KM#	Date	Mintage	VG	Fine	VF	XF
255.1	1809	—	11.50	22.50	30.00	45.00
	1812	—	9.00	18.00	28.00	40.00
	1813	—	9.00	18.00	28.00	40.00
	1817	—	15.00	30.00	50.00	75.00

Medal strike.

KM#	Date	Mintage	VG	Fine	VF	XF
255.4	1813	—	30.00	50.00	100.00	250.00

Mint mark: B

KM#	Date	Mintage	VG	Fine	VF	XF
255.2	1810	—	17.50	40.00	90.00	160.00
	1816	—	65.00	110.00	200.00	350.00

Mint mark: M

KM#	Date	Mintage	VG	Fine	VF	XF
255.3	1812	—	60.00	130.00	220.00	460.00
	1814	—	75.00	200.00	350.00	750.00
	1816	—	75.00	200.00	350.00	750.00

Obv. leg: JOANNES.VI.D.G.PORT.BRAS. . .

KM#	Date	Mintage	VG	Fine	VF	XF
324.1	1818	—	1500.	2800.	5000.	8000.

Mint mark: R

KM#	Date	Mintage	VG	Fine	VF	XF
324.2	1818	—	11.00	20.00	50.00	100.00
	1819	—	17.50	35.00	60.00	125.00
	1820 star on crown	—	12.00	18.00	35.00	70.00

Mint mark: B

KM#	Date	Mintage	VG	Fine	VF	XF
324.3	1821	—	18.50	37.50	55.00	125.00

640 REIS

17.7600 g, .917 SILVER, .5233 oz ASW
Mint mark: R
Similar to KM#231 but obv. leg: MARIA.I.D.G. PORT. REGINA. . .

KM#	Date	Mintage	VG	Fine	VF	XF
222.2	1802	56.126	15.00	20.00	35.00	60.00

NOTE: Earlier dates (1791-1800) exist for this type.

Mint mark: B
Rev. leg: SUBQ. . .

KM#	Date	Mintage	VG	Fine	VF	XF
231.2	1801	—	18.50	25.00	40.00	65.00
	1802	—	18.50	25.00	40.00	65.00
	1803	—	18.50	25.00	40.00	65.00
	1804	—	18.50	25.00	40.00	65.00
	1805	—	35.00	65.00	120.00	250.00

NOTE: Earlier dates (1799-1800) exist for this type.

17.9200 g, .917 SILVER, .5280 oz ASW
Obv. leg: JOANNES.D.G.PORT.P.REGENS. . .

KM#	Date	Mintage	VG	Fine	VF	XF
237	1806	—	30.00	75.00	150.00	350.00
	1807	—	30.00	75.00	150.00	350.00
	1808/7	—	20.00	35.00	60.00	75.00
	1808	—	16.50	25.00	35.00	70.00
256.1	1809	—	16.50	25.00	35.00	70.00
	1810	—	17.50	27.50	40.00	80.00
	1816	—	—	—	Rare	—

Mint mark: R

KM#	Date	Mintage	VG	Fine	VF	XF
256.2	1809	—	18.50	35.00	45.00	75.00
	1811	—	18.50	35.00	45.00	75.00
	1812	—	25.00	80.00	175.00	350.00
	1813	—	50.00	125.00	250.00	450.00
	1814	—	55.00	150.00	300.00	650.00
	1815	—	55.00	150.00	300.00	650.00
	1816	—	55.00	150.00	300.00	650.00

Mint mark: M

KM#	Date	Mintage	VG	Fine	VF	XF
256.3	1810	—	—	—	Rare	—
	1811	—	50.00	120.00	250.00	500.00
	1812	—	70.00	150.00	275.00	600.00
	1813	—	70.00	150.00	300.00	700.00
	1816	—	70.00	175.00	400.00	1000.

19.3200 g, .917 SILVER, .5693 oz ASW
Obv. leg: JOANNES.VI.

KM#	Date	Mintage	VG	Fine	VF	XF
325.1	1818	—	350.00	1250.	3750.	6000.

Mint mark: R

KM#	Date	Mintage	VG	Fine	VF	XF
325.2	1818	—	17.50	45.00	90.00	180.00
	1819	—	25.00	50.00	100.00	200.00
	1820	—	16.50	25.00	45.00	65.00
	1821	—	16.50	25.00	45.00	65.00
	1822	—	25.00	75.00	250.00	400.00

Mint mark: B

KM#	Date	Mintage	VG	Fine	VF	XF
325.3	1821	—	40.00	75.00	140.00	350.00

960 REIS

26.8900 g, .896 SILVER, .7746 oz ASW
Mint mark: B

KM#	Date	Mintage	VG	Fine	VF	XF
307.1	1810	—	17.50	27.50	40.00	55.00
	1810 small crown	—	—	—	Rare	—
	1810 . . . P.REGENES. . .	—	50.00	80.00	180.00	350.00
	1811	—	25.00	40.00	60.00	100.00
	1812	—	17.50	27.50	40.00	60.00
	1813	—	17.50	27.50	40.00	60.00
	1813 . . . P.REGENES. . .	—	50.00	80.00	150.00	300.00
	1814	—	17.50	27.50	40.00	60.00
	1815	—	17.50	27.50	40.00	60.00
	1816	—	17.50	27.50	40.00	60.00
	1817	—	17.50	27.50	40.00	60.00

Mint mark: M

KM#	Date	Mintage	VG	Fine	VF	XF
307.2	1810	—	—	—	Rare	—
	1816	—	—	—	Rare	—

Mint mark: R

KM#	Date	Mintage	VG	Fine	VF	XF
307.3	1810	—	17.50	27.50	40.00	60.00
	1811	—	17.50	27.50	40.00	60.00
	1812	—	17.50	27.50	40.00	60.00
	1813/2	—	20.00	30.00	50.00	80.00
	1813	—	17.50	27.50	40.00	60.00
	1814	—	17.50	27.50	40.00	60.00
	1815	—	17.50	27.50	40.00	60.00
	1815 . . . STAB.NATA. . .	—	—	—	Rare	—
	1816	—	17.50	27.50	40.00	60.00
	1817	—	17.50	27.50	40.00	60.00
	1818 star on crown	—	17.50	27.50	40.00	60.00

27.0700 g, .903 SILVER, .7859 oz ASW
Obv. leg. ends:. . . BRAS.ET.ALG. P.REGENS.

KM#	Date	Mintage	VG	Fine	VF	XF
313	1816	—	30.00	70.00	150.00	250.00

KM#	Date	Mintage	VG	Fine	VF	XF
326.1	1818	—	17.50	27.50	40.00	60.00
	1819	—	17.50	27.50	40.00	60.00
	1820	—	17.50	27.50	40.00	60.00
	1820 small castle within zero of denomination					
		—	750.00	1350.	1850.	—
	1821	—	17.50	27.50	40.00	60.00
	1822	—	25.00	45.00	85.00	130.00
	Mint mark: B					
326.2	1819	—	—	—	Rare	—
	1820/19	—	—	—	Rare	—
	1820	—	17.50	25.00	35.00	60.00
	1820 . . . BARS.ET. . .					
		—	25.00	40.00	60.00	100.00
	1821/0	—	20.00	35.00	45.00	70.00
	1821	—	17.50	25.00	35.00	60.00
	1822	—	400.00	1000.	2500.	4000.

NOTE: KM#307.1-307.3, 313 and 326.1-326.2 are usually found struck over Spanish Colonial 8 Reales. Specimens of Spanish types with original elements visible command the following approximate premiums: 30% for mint mark, 40% for mint mark and assayer initial and 55% for mint mark, assayer initial and date. Specimens of Spanish Colonial types with original elements visible command the following approximate premiums: 10% for mint mark, 20% for mint mark and assayer initial and 35% for mint mark, assayer initial and date. In addition KM#326.1 and 326.2 are sometimes found struck over early South American Republic Peso and 8 Reales types. Specimens of Republic issues with original elements visible command the following approximate premiums: 25% for mint mark, 50% for mint mark and assayer initial and 100% for mint mark, assayer initial and date.

4000 REIS

8.0600 g, .917 GOLD, .2376 oz AGW
Mint: Bahia - w/o mint mark.
Obv. leg: MARIA I.D.G. . .

KM#	Date	Mintage	Fine	VF	XF	Unc
225.2	1801	3,705	150.00	260.00	400.00	600.00
	1802	7,738	150.00	260.00	400.00	600.00
	1803	7,807	150.00	260.00	400.00	600.00
	1804/2	Inc. Ab.	150.00	260.00	400.00	600.00
	1805/2	Inc. Be.	150.00	260.00	400.00	600.00

Obv. leg: JOANNES.D.G. . ., large crown.
Rev: Dots on either side of date.

KM#	Date	Mintage	Fine	VF	XF	Unc
235.1	1805	.010	125.00	225.00	375.00	500.00
	1806	.012	125.00	225.00	375.00	500.00
	1807	7,725	125.00	225.00	375.00	500.00
	1808	.037	125.00	225.00	375.00	500.00
	1809/8	.019	125.00	225.00	375.00	500.00
	1809	Inc. Ab.	125.00	225.00	375.00	500.00
	1810	.018	125.00	225.00	375.00	500.00

KM#	Date	Mintage	Fine	VF	XF	Unc
235.1	1811	.019	125.00	225.00	375.00	500.00
	1811 flowers at date					
		Inc. Ab.	125.00	225.00	375.00	500.00
	1813	.011	125.00	225.00	375.00	500.00
	1814	9,494	125.00	225.00	375.00	500.00
	1815	—	125.00	225.00	375.00	500.00
	1816	7,522	125.00	225.00	375.00	500.00

Mint: Rio - w/o mint mark.
Obv: Small crown.
Rev: Flower on either side of date.

KM#	Date	Mintage	Fine	VF	XF	Unc
235.2	1808	.128	125.00	225.00	375.00	500.00
	1809/08	.094	125.00	225.00	375.00	500.00
	1809	Inc. Ab.	125.00	225.00	375.00	500.00
	1810/09	.066	125.00	225.00	400.00	500.00
	1810	Inc. Ab.	125.00	225.00	400.00	500.00
	1811/10	.087	125.00	225.00	400.00	500.00
	1811	Inc. Ab.	125.00	225.00	400.00	500.00
	1812	.124	125.00	225.00	400.00	500.00
	181.2	Inc. Ab.	125.00	275.00	400.00	500.00
	1812 PROT (error)					
		Inc. Ab.	150.00	275.00	500.00	700.00
	1813/2	.148	125.00	225.00	400.00	500.00
	1813	Inc. Ab.	125.00	225.00	400.00	500.00
	1814/3	.102	125.00	225.00	400.00	500.00
	1814	Inc. Ab.	125.00	225.00	400.00	500.00
	1815	.083	125.00	225.00	400.00	500.00
	1816	.091	125.00	225.00	400.00	500.00
	1817	.071	125.00	225.00	400.00	500.00
	Obv. leg: PORT.ET.BRAS. (error).					
235.3	1812	Inc. Ab.	150.00	275.00	450.00	600.00

Obv. leg: PORT.BRAS ET ALG.
Rev. leg: PRINCEPS.REGENS. . .

KM#	Date	Mintage	Fine	VF	XF	Unc
312	1816	Inc. Ab.	200.00	650.00	1200.	2000.

Obv: 6-petal flower on either side of date.

KM#	Date	Mintage	Fine	VF	XF	Unc
327.1	1818	.064	140.00	300.00	500.00	700.00
	1819	.049	200.00	400.00	500.00	700.00
	1820	.087	140.00	300.00	500.00	700.00
	1821/0	.035	140.00	300.00	500.00	700.00
	1821	Inc. Ab.	140.00	300.00	500.00	700.00
	1822/0	.054	150.00	320.00	510.00	710.00
	1822/1	Inc. Ab.	150.00	320.00	510.00	710.00
	1822	Inc. Ab.	150.00	320.00	510.00	710.00

Obv: 4-petal flower on either side of date.

KM#	Date	Mintage	Fine	VF	XF	Unc
327.2	1819	Inc. Ab.	150.00	300.00	500.00	700.00

Mint: Bahia - w/o mint mark.
Obv: Date between crosses.

KM#	Date	Mintage	Fine	VF	XF	Unc
327.3	1819	1,864	600.00	1200.	2000.	2500.
	1820	4,374	850.00	1500.	2500.	3000.

6400 REIS

14.3400 g, .917 GOLD, .4228 oz AGW
Mint mark: R
Obv: Bust right w/bejeweled headdress.
Rev: Crowned arms.

KM#	Date	Mintage	Fine	VF	XF	Unc
226.1	1801	.185	250.00	325.00	450.00	650.00
	1802	.168	250.00	325.00	450.00	650.00
	1803	.176	250.00	325.00	450.00	650.00
	1804	.128	250.00	325.00	450.00	650.00
	1805	.109	250.00	325.00	450.00	650.00

NOTE: Earlier dates (1789-1800) exist for this type.

Mint mark: B

KM#	Date	Mintage	Fine	VF	XF	Unc
226.2	1801	.012	260.00	375.00	550.00	700.00
	1802	3,324	260.00	375.00	550.00	700.00
	1803	3,743	260.00	375.00	550.00	700.00
	1804	3,539	260.00	375.00	550.00	700.00

NOTE: Earlier dates (1790-1800) exist for this type.

Mint mark: R
Obv. leg: JOANNES.D.G.PORT.ET.ALG.P.REGENS.

KM#	Date	Mintage	Fine	VF	XF	Unc
236.1	1805	Inc. Ab.	260.00	350.00	500.00	800.00
	1806	.096	260.00	350.00	500.00	800.00
	1807	.059	260.00	350.00	500.00	800.00
	1808/7	.133	260.00	350.00	500.00	800.00
	1808	Inc. Ab.	280.00	350.00	500.00	800.00
	1809/8	.188	280.00	350.00	500.00	800.00
	1809	Inc. Ab.	300.00	350.00	500.00	800.00
	1810/09	.159	300.00	350.00	500.00	800.00
	1810	Inc. Ab.	300.00	400.00	600.00	1000.
	1811/10	.082	350.00	400.00	600.00	1000.
	1811	Inc. Ab.	350.00	400.00	600.00	1000.
	1812	.064	350.00	450.00	600.00	1000.
	1813	.053	350.00	450.00	600.00	1000.
	1814/3	.042	360.00	475.00	750.00	1000.
	1814	Inc. Ab.	360.00	475.00	750.00	1200.
	1815	.040	400.00	450.00	750.00	1200.
	1816	.039	420.00	500.00	1000.	2800.
	1817	.032	450.00	500.00	1000.	3500.
	Obv. leg. ends: . . . PORT.BRAS.ET.ALG.P.REG.					
236.2	1816	Inc. Ab.	2800.	3500.	4500.	6000.

Obv. leg: JOANNES.VI.D.G.PORT.
BRAS.ET.ALG.REX.

KM#	Date	Mintage	Fine	VF	XF	Unc
328	1818	.014	1000.	2000.	2500.	3000.
	1819	9,227	2000.	3000.	4000.	4500.
	1820	3,286	2700.	4000.	5000.	5500.
	1821	2,122	—	—	Unique	—
	1822	599 pcs.	—	—	Rare	—

COUNTERMARKED COINAGE

Shield Countermark

Authorized on April 18, 1809.

The purpose of the shield countermark was to double the value of the earlier Colonial copper coinage and raise the value of the earlier silver coinage. Other Portuguese and Portuguese Colonial coins are known with this countermark. There are basically 8 types of shields that vary in size from 7mmx7mm to 11mmx11mm.

75 = 80 Reis	300 = 320 Reis
150 = 160 Reis	600 = 640 Reis

10 REIS

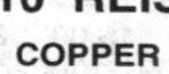

COPPER

c/m: Shield on V (5) Reis, KM#142.5.

KM#	Date	Year	Good	VG	Fine	VF
260	(1809)	1749	2.50	6.00	12.50	25.00

c/m: Shield on V (5) Reis, KM#173.1.

KM#	Date	Year	Good	VG	Fine	VF
261	(1809)	1752	10.00	25.00	70.00	140.00
		1753	2.50	6.50	12.50	25.00
		1768	2.50	6.50	7.50	25.00
		1773	2.50	6.50	7.50	25.00
		1774	2.50	6.50	7.50	25.00

c/m: Shield on V (5) Reis, KM#188.

KM#	Date	Year	Good	VG	Fine	VF
262	(1809)	1762B	2.50	5.00	10.00	20.00
		1763B	2.50	5.00	10.00	20.00
		1764B	2.50	5.00	10.00	20.00
		1766B	2.50	5.00	10.00	20.00
		1767B	2.50	5.00	10.00	20.00
		1768B	2.50	5.00	10.00	20.00
		1769B	2.50	5.00	10.00	20.00

c/m: Shield on V (5) Reis, KM#200.

KM#	Date	Year	Good	VG	Fine	VF
263	(1809)	1778	2.50	5.00	10.00	20.00
		1781	2.50	5.00	10.00	20.00
		1782	2.50	5.00	10.00	20.00
		1784	2.50	5.00	10.00	20.00
		1785	2.50	5.00	10.00	20.00

c/m: Shield on V (5) Reis, w/low flat arch crown, KM#214.1.

KM#	Date	Year	Good	VG	Fine	VF
264.1	(1809)	1786	2.50	5.00	12.50	25.00
		1787	2.50	5.00	12.50	25.00
		1790	2.50	5.00	12.50	25.00
		1791	2.50	5.00	12.50	25.00
		1797	7.50	15.00	25.00	45.00

c/m: Shield on V (5) Reis, w/high full arch crown, KM#214.2.

KM#	Date	Year	Good	VG	Fine	VF
264.2	(1809)	1786	2.50	5.00	12.50	25.00
		1787	2.50	5.00	12.50	25.00
		1790	2.50	5.00	12.50	25.00
		1791	2.50	5.00	12.50	25.00

20 REIS

COPPER

c/m: Shield on X (10) Reis, KM#71.

KM#	Date	Year	Good	VG	Fine	VF
265	(1809)	1694P	10.00	30.00	55.00	90.00
		1696P	10.00	17.50	30.00	55.00
		1697P	7.50	15.00	25.00	50.00
		1699P	7.50	15.00	25.00	50.00

c/m: Shield on X (10) Reis, KM#107.

KM#	Date	Year	Good	VG	Fine	VF
266	(1809)	ND	30.00	45.00	85.00	160.00

c/m: Shield on X (10) Reis, KM#108.

KM#	Date	Year	Good	VG	Fine	VF
267	(1809)	1715	2.50	5.00	12.50	25.00
		1718	2.50	5.00	12.50	25.00
		1719	2.50	5.00	12.50	25.00
		1720	2.50	5.00	12.50	25.00

c/m: Shield on X (10) Reis, KM#142.1.

KM#	Date	Year	Good	VG	Fine	VF
268.1	(1809)	1729B	2.50	5.00	7.50	15.00
		1730B	2.50	5.00	7.50	15.00
		1731B	2.50	5.00	7.50	15.00

c/m: Shield on X (10) Reis, KM#142.2.

KM#	Date	Year	Good	VG	Fine	VF
268.2	(1809)	1729	2.50	5.00	10.00	20.00
		1730	2.50	5.00	10.00	20.00
		1731	2.50	5.00	10.00	20.00
		1732	2.50	5.00	10.00	20.00
		1747	10.00	17.50	25.00	45.00
		1748	20.00	50.00	80.00	150.00

c/m: Shield on X (10) Reis, KM#142.3.

KM#	Date	Year	Good	VG	Fine	VF
268.3	(1809)	1735	2.50	5.00	10.00	20.00
		1736	2.50	5.00	10.00	20.00
		1746	2.50	5.00	10.00	20.00

c/m: Shield on X (10) Reis, KM#142.4.

KM#	Date	Year	Good	VG	Fine	VF
268.4	(1809)	1746	2.50	5.00	10.00	20.00

c/m: Shield on X (10) Reis, KM#142.5.

KM#	Date	Year	Good	VG	Fine	VF
268.5	(1809)	1749	2.50	5.00	10.00	20.00

c/m: Shield on X (10) Reis, KM#165.1.

KM#	Date	Year	Good	VG	Fine	VF
269	(1809)	1751	20.00	40.00	85.00	150.00

c/m: Shield on X (10) Reis, KM#174.1.

KM#	Date	Year	Good	VG	Fine	VF
270	(1809)	1752	4.00	10.00	20.00	35.00
		1753	2.50	5.00	10.00	20.00
		1773	3.00	10.00	20.00	35.00
		1774	2.50	5.00	10.00	20.00
		1775	2.50	5.00	10.00	20.00
		1776	2.50	5.00	10.00	20.00

c/m: Shield on X (10) Reis, KM#174.2.

KM#	Date	Year	Good	VG	Fine	VF
271	(1809)	1762B	2.50	5.00	10.00	20.00

c/m: Shield on X (10) Reis, KM#201.

KM#	Date	Year	Good	VG	Fine	VF
272	(1809)	1778	2.50	5.00	7.50	15.00
		1781	2.50	5.00	7.50	15.00
		1782	2.50	5.00	7.50	15.00
		1784	2.50	5.00	7.50	15.00
		1785	2.50	5.00	7.50	15.00

c/m: Shield on X (10) Reis, w/low flat arch crown, KM#215.1.

KM#	Date	Year	Good	VG	Fine	VF
273.1	(1809)	1786	2.50	5.00	8.50	17.50
		1787	2.50	5.00	8.50	17.50
		1790	2.50	5.00	8.50	17.50
		1796	2.50	5.00	8.50	17.50

c/m: Shield on X (10) Reis, w/high full arch crown, KM#215.2.

KM#	Date	Year	Good	VG	Fine	VF
273.2	(1809)	1786	2.50	5.00	8.50	17.50
		1787	2.50	5.00	8.50	17.50
		1790	2.50	5.00	8.50	17.50

c/m: Shield on X (10) Reis, KM#228.

KM#	Date	Year	Good	VG	Fine	VF
274	(1809)	1799	5.00	10.00	20.00	50.00

40 REIS

COPPER

c/m: Shield on XX (20) Reis, KM#70.

KM#	Date	Year	Good	VG	Fine	VF
275	(1809)	1693P	20.00	35.00	75.00	125.00
		1694P	10.00	20.00	40.00	75.00
		1695P	10.00	15.00	30.00	60.00
		1697P	7.50	12.50	25.00	45.00
		1698P	7.50	12.50	25.00	45.00
		1699P	7.50	12.50	25.00	45.00

c/m: Shield on XX (20) Reis, KM#109.

KM#	Date	Year	Good	VG	Fine	VF
276	(1809)	1715	5.00	7.50	10.00	20.00
		1718	5.00	7.50	10.00	20.00
		1719	5.00	7.50	10.00	20.00
		1729	5.00	7.50	10.00	20.00

c/m: Shield on XX (20) Reis, KM#110.

KM#	Date	Year	Good	VG	Fine	VF
277	(1809)	1722	5.00	7.50	10.00	20.00

c/m: Shield on XX (20) Reis, KM#143.1.

KM#	Date	Year	Good	VG	Fine	VF
278.1	(1809)	1729B	2.50	5.00	8.50	17.50
		1730B	2.50	5.00	8.50	17.50
		1731B	2.50	5.00	10.00	20.00
		1748B	17.00	35.00	85.00	150.00

c/m: Shield on XX (20) Reis, KM#143.2.

KM#	Date	Year	Good	VG	Fine	VF
278.2	(1809)	1729B	2.50	5.00	10.00	22.50
		1730B	2.50	5.00	10.00	22.50
		1731B	2.50	5.00	10.00	22.50

c/m: Shield on XX (20) Reis, KM#143.3.

KM#	Date	Year	Good	VG	Fine	VF
278.3	(1809)	1735	2.50	5.00	7.50	15.00
		1736	2.50	5.00	7.50	15.00

c/m: Shield on XX (20) Reis, KM#143.4.

KM#	Date	Year	Good	VG	Fine	VF
278.4	(1809)	1735	2.50	4.50	7.50	12.50
		1736	2.50	4.50	7.50	12.50
		1746	2.50	4.50	7.50	12.50

c/m: Shield on XX (20) Reis, KM#143.5.

KM#	Date	Year	Good	VG	Fine	VF
278.5	(1809)	1749	2.50	5.00	10.00	22.50

c/m: Shield on XX (20) Reis, KM#166.1.

KM#	Date	Year	Good	VG	Fine	VF
279	(1809)	1751	10.00	25.00	55.00	90.00
		1752	5.00	7.50	15.00	25.00

c/m: 11mm shield on XX (20) Reis, KM#175.1.

KM#	Date	Year	Good	VG	Fine	VF
280.1	(1809)	1752	2.50	5.00	10.00	20.00
		1753	2.50	5.00	10.00	20.00
		1773	2.50	5.00	10.00	20.00
		1774	2.50	5.00	10.00	20.00
		1775	2.50	5.00	10.00	20.00
		1776	2.50	5.00	10.00	20.00

c/m: 8mm shield on XX (20) Reis, KM#175.1.

KM#	Date	Year	Good	VG	Fine	VF
280.2	(1809)	1776	10.00	15.00	25.00	45.00

c/m: Shield on XX (20) Reis, KM#175.2.

KM#	Date	Year	Good	VG	Fine	VF
281	(1809)	1761B	5.00	7.50	12.50	25.00

c/m: Shield on XX (20) Reis, KM#202.

KM#	Date	Year	Good	VG	Fine	VF
282	(1809)	1778	2.50	5.00	8.50	17.50
		1781	2.50	5.00	8.50	17.50
		1782	2.50	5.00	8.50	17.50
		1784	2.50	5.00	8.50	17.50

c/m: Shield on XX (20) Reis w/low flat arch crown, KM#216.1.

KM#	Date	Year	Good	VG	Fine	VF
283.1	(1809)	1786	2.50	5.00	10.00	20.00
		1787	2.50	5.00	10.00	20.00
		1790	2.50	5.00	10.00	20.00
		1796	2.50	5.00	10.00	20.00
		1799	2.50	5.00	10.00	20.00

c/m: Shield on XX (20) Reis w/high full arch crown, KM#216.2.

KM#	Date	Year	Good	VG	Fine	VF
283.2	(1809)	1786	2.50	5.00	10.00	18.00
		1787	2.50	5.00	10.00	18.00
		1790	2.50	5.00	10.00	18.00
		1799	2.50	5.00	10.00	18.00

c/m: Shield on XX (20) Reis, KM#229.

KM#	Date	Year	Good	VG	Fine	VF
284	(1809)	1799	5.00	10.00	20.00	40.00

c/m: Shield on XX (20) Reis, KM#233.1.

KM#	Date	Year	Good	VG	Fine	VF
285	(1809)	1802	2.50	5.00	8.50	17.50
		1803	2.50	5.00	8.50	17.50

80 REIS

COPPER

c/m: Shield on XL (40) Reis, KM#111.

KM#	Date	Year	Good	VG	Fine	VF
286	(1809)	1722	5.00	7.50	12.50	20.00

c/m: Shield on XL (40) Reis, KM#184.1.

KM#	Date	Year	Good	VG	Fine	VF
287	(1809)	1753	2.50	5.00	8.50	17.50
		1760	2.50	5.00	8.50	17.50
		1774	2.50	5.00	8.50	17.50

c/m: Shield on Angola XL Reis, KM#9.

KM#	Date	Year	Good	VG	Fine	VF
301	(1809)	1757	25.00	40.00	60.00	90.00

c/m: Shield on XL (40) Reis, KM#189.

KM#	Date	Year	Good	VG	Fine	VF
288	(1809)	1762B	2.50	5.00	8.50	17.50

c/m: Shield on XL (40) Reis, KM#203.

KM#	Date	Year	Good	VG	Fine	VF
289	(1809)	1778	2.50	5.00	8.50	17.50
		1781	2.50	5.00	8.50	17.50
		1784	2.50	5.00	8.50	17.50

c/m: 11mm shield on XL (40) Reis w/low flat arch crown, KM#217.1.

KM#	Date	Year	Good	VG	Fine	VF
290.1	(1809)	1786	5.00	7.50	10.00	20.00
		1790	5.00	7.50	10.00	25.00
		1791	10.00	15.00	25.00	35.00
		1796	5.00	10.00	20.00	35.00

c/m: 8mm shield on XL (40) Reis w/low flat arch crown, KM#217.1.

KM#	Date	Year	Good	VG	Fine	VF
209.3	(1809)	1796	10.00	15.00	25.00	45.00

c/m: 11mm shield on XL (40) Reis w/high full arch crown, KM#217.2.

KM#	Date	Year	Good	VG	Fine	VF
290.2	(1809)	1786	5.00	7.50	10.00	20.00
		1787	5.00	7.50	10.00	20.00
		1790	5.00	7.50	10.00	20.00
		1791	5.00	7.50	10.00	20.00

c/m: 8mm shield on XL (40) Reis w/high full arch crown, KM#217.2.

KM#	Date	Year	Good	VG	Fine	VF
290.4	(1809)	1787	10.00	15.00	25.00	50.00

c/m: Shield on XL (40) Reis, KM#230.

KM#	Date	Year	Good	VG	Fine	VF
291	(1809)	1799	10.00	17.50	35.00	75.00

c/m: Shield on XL (40) Reis, KM#234.1.

KM#	Date	Year	Good	VG	Fine	VF
292	(1809)	1802	5.00	7.50	10.00	20.00
		1803	5.00	7.50	10.00	20.00

2.2600 g, .917 SILVER, .0666 oz ASW
c/m: Shield on 75 Reis, KM#176.1.

KM#	Date	Year	Good	VG	Fine	VF
293	(1809)	1752B	50.00	150.00	650.00	1000.
		1753B	7.00	30.00	125.00	200.00
		1754B	7.00	30.00	125.00	200.00

c/m: Shield on 75 Reis, KM#176.2.

KM#	Date	Year	Good	VG	Fine	VF
294	(1809)	1754R	20.00	45.00	75.00	200.00
		1755R	20.00	45.00	75.00	200.00
		1760R	27.00	60.00	150.00	400.00

160 REIS

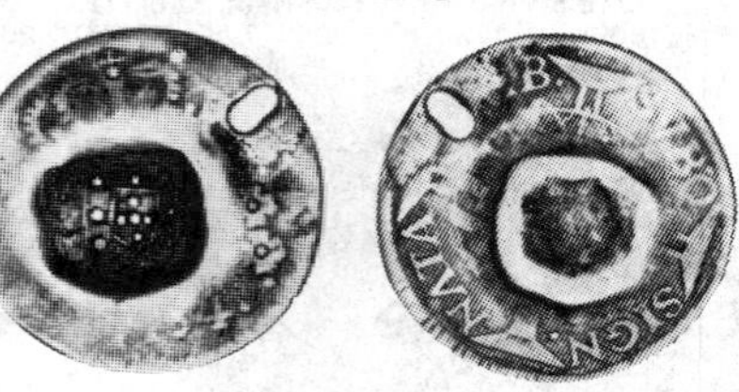

4.5200 g, .917 SILVER, .1332 oz ASW
c/m: Shield on 150 Reis, KM#177.

KM#	Date	Year	Good	VG	Fine	VF
295	(1809)	1752B	9.00	60.00	250.00	1200.
		1753B	9.00	45.00	75.00	200.00
		1754B	9.00	45.00	75.00	200.00
		1756B	70.00	150.00	400.00	1500.
		1768B	—	—	Rare	—

c/m: Shield on 150 Reis, KM#185.

KM#	Date	Year	Good	VG	Fine	VF
296	(1809)	1754R	9.00	30.00	70.00	125.00
		1754 R ATAN NGIS				
			10.00	40.00	80.00	130.00
		1755R	9.00	18.00	40.00	80.00
		1758R	9.00	18.00	40.00	80.00
		1760R	40.00	85.00	150.00	300.00
		1771R	30.00	75.00	100.00	200.00

320 REIS

9.0500 g, .917 SILVER, .2668 oz ASW
c/m: Shield on 300 Reis, KM#178.

KM#	Date	Year	Good	VG	Fine	VF
297	(1809)	1752B	25.00	45.00	85.00	160.00
		1753B	19.00	35.00	65.00	120.00
		1754B	19.00	35.00	65.00	120.00
		1756B	25.00	45.00	85.00	200.00
		1757B	25.00	50.00	90.00	240.00
		1768B	—	—	Rare	—

c/m: Shield on 300 Reis, KM#186.

KM#	Date	Year	Good	VG	Fine	VF
298	(1809)	1754R	12.50	30.00	45.00	85.00
		1755R	12.50	30.00	45.00	85.00
		1756R	12.50	30.00	45.00	85.00
		1757R	12.50	30.00	45.00	85.00
		1758R	12.50	30.00	45.00	85.00
		1764R	12.50	30.00	45.00	85.00
		1771R	15.00	35.00	50.00	90.00

640 REIS

18.1100 g, .917 SILVER, .5339 oz ASW
c/m: Shield on 600 Reis, KM#179.

KM#	Date	Year	Good	VG	Fine	VF
299	(1809)	1752B	100.00	350.00	500.00	800.00
		1754B	30.00	60.00	105.00	350.00
		1756B	30.00	60.00	105.00	300.00
		1757B	35.00	65.00	110.00	200.00
		1758B	30.00	60.00	100.00	150.00
		1760B	50.00	200.00	350.00	680.00
		1768B	—	—	Rare	—

c/m: Shield on 600 Reis, KM#187.

KM#	Date	Year	Good	VG	Fine	VF
300	(1809)	1754R	25.00	45.00	90.00	140.00
		1755R	30.00	50.00	100.00	150.00
		1756R	30.00	50.00	100.00	150.00
		1758R	30.00	50.00	100.00	150.00
		1760R	80.00	150.00	250.00	550.00
		1764R	25.00	30.00	50.00	75.00
		1765R	65.00	95.00	140.00	320.00
		1770R	40.00	60.00	120.00	220.00
		1771R	30.00	50.00	100.00	200.00
		1774R	30.00	50.00	100.00	200.00

REGIONAL COINAGE

MATO GROSSO

A large state in the center of Brazil. One of the issuers of the counterstamps of the 1808 law. The name of the province appears below the arms on the obverse.

COUNTERSTAMPED COINAGE

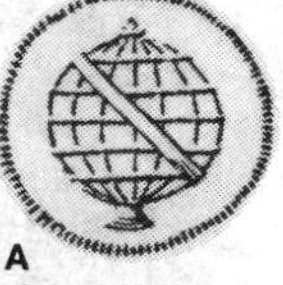

TYPE A
Authorized November 4, 1818
c/s: Crowned shield above MATO GROSSO.
Rev. c/s: Banded globe.

NOTE: The c/s having the crown made up of close large pearls is considered a counterfeit.

960 REIS

SILVER
c/s: Type A on Argentina 8 Reales, KM#5.

KM#	Date	Year	VG	Fine	VF	XF
330	ND	(1813-15)	3000.	5000.	7000.	—

c/s: Type A on Bolivia 8 Reales, KM#73.

KM#	Date	Year	VG	Fine	VF	XF
331.1	ND	(1791-1808)	2000.	4000.	—	—

c/s: Type A on Bolivia 8 Reales, KM#84.

KM#	Date	Year	VG	Fine	VF	XF
331.2	ND	(1808-18)	2000.	4000.	—	—

CUIABA

Cuiaba is the present capital of the Mato Grosso state. In 1820 this city name appeared as "CUYABA" or "C" on a counterstamp appearing on Spanish-American 8 Reales coins. This is the rarest Brazilian counterstamp.

COUNTERSTAMPED COINAGE

Type B
Authorized 1820
Obv. c/s: Crowned shield above CUYABA.
Rev. c/s: Banded globe.

960 REIS

SILVER
c/s: On Spanish Colonial 8 Reales.

KM#	Date	Year	VG	Fine	VF	XF
345	ND	(1808)	3000.	5000.	7000.	—

General C/S Issue

TYPE C
Authorized in January, 1821.
Obv. c/s: Crowned 960/C (C. or .C. or C) within branches. Rev. c/s: Shield on globe.

c/s: Type C on Argentina 8 Reales, KM#5.

KM#	Date	Year	VG	Fine	VF	XF
351.1	ND	(1813)	550.00	950.00	1650.	2700.

c/s: Type C on Argentina 8 Reales, KM#14.

KM#	Date	Year	VG	Fine	VF	XF
351.2	ND	(1815)	550.00	950.00	1650.	2700.

c/s: Type C on Bolivia 8 Reales, KM#73.

KM#	Date	Year	VG	Fine	VF	XF
350	ND	(1791-1808)	450.00	850.00	1500.	2500.

c/s: Type C on Bolivia 8 Reales, KM#84.

KM#	Date	Year	VG	Fine	VF	XF
352	ND	(1808-18)	300.00	550.00	800.00	1600.

c/s: Type C on Chile 8 Reales KM#80.

KM#	Date	Year	VG	Fine	VF	XF
A353	ND	(1812-1817)	450.00	850.00	1500.	2500.

c/s: Type C on Peru 8 Reales, KM#97.

KM#	Date	Year	VG	Fine	VF	XF
353	ND	(1791-1808)	550.00	950.00	1650.	2700.

MINAS GERAIS

Minas Gerais is a state in eastern Brazil. In September of 1808 an edict was issued for the authorization of various counterstamps to be used on the many circulating Spanish 8 reales in the country. The Minas Gerais counterstamp was issued both with and w/o the M on the reverse. The silver value was 750 to 800 Reis per coin but they were marked and passed at 960 Reis giving the government a nice profit.

COUNTERSTAMPED COINAGE

Authorized Sept. 1, 1808
until 1810
Obv. c/s: Crowned shield in branches/960.
Rev. c/s: Banded globe with cross.

960 REIS

SILVER
c/s: On Bolivia 8 Reales, KM#55.

KM#	Date	Year	Mintage	Fine	VF	XF
240	ND	(1773-89)	—	550.00	1000.	1500.

c/s: On Bolivia 8 Reales, KM#64.

KM#	Date	Year	Mintage	Fine	VF	XF
241	ND	(1789-91)	—	450.00	650.00	1200.

c/s: On Bolivia 8 Reales, KM#73.

KM#	Date	Year	Mintage	Fine	VF	XF
242	ND (1791-1808)		—	80.00	170.00	300.00

c/s: On Chile 8 Reales, KM#51.

KM#	Date	Year	Mintage	Fine	VF	XF
243	ND (1791-1808)		—	350.00	550.00	800.00

c/s: On Guatemala 8 Reales.

KM#	Date	Year	Mintage	Fine	VF	XF
244	ND	—	—	—	Rare	—

c/s: On Mexico City 8 Reales, KM#105.

KM#	Date	Year	Mintage	Fine	VF	XF
245	ND	(1760-72)	—	—	Rare	—

c/s: On Mexico City 8 Reales, KM#106.

KM#	Date	Year	Mintage	Fine	VF	XF
246	ND	(1772-89)	—	650.00	1000.	1500.

c/s: On Mexico City 8 Reales, KM#107.

KM#	Date	Year	Mintage	Fine	VF	XF
247	ND	(1789-90)	—	400.00	600.00	1100.

c/s: On Mexico City 8 Reales, KM#108.

KM#	Date	Year	Mintage	Fine	VF	XF
A248	ND	(1790)	—	1500.	2000.	—

c/s: On Mexico City 8 Reales, KM#109.

KM#	Date	Year	Mintage	Fine	VF	XF
248	ND (1791-1808)		—	400.00	600.00	1150.

c/s: On Peru 8 Reales, KM#78.

KM#	Date	Year	Mintage	Fine	VF	XF
249	ND	(1772-89)	—	450.00	650.00	1200.

c/s: On Peru 8 Reales, KM#87.

KM#	Date	Year	Mintage	Fine	VF	XF
250	ND	(1789-91)	—	100.00	200.00	350.00

c/s: On Peru 8 Reales, KM#97.

KM#	Date	Year	Mintage	Fine	VF	XF
251	ND (1791-1808)		—	80.00	170.00	300.00

c/s: On Spanish 8 Reales.

KM#	Date	Year	Mintage	Fine	VF	XF
252	ND	—	—	—	Rare	—

UNITED KINGDOM

Copper Coinage

The imperial copper coins of Brazil (1823-1833) Were struck to several different standards simultaneously, each intended for a different part of the empire. The following table shows the standards used at each mint:

Weights of Imperial Brazilian copper coins in oitavos:

MINT MARK DENOMINATION (REIS)

	MARK	10	20	40	80	37½	75
Rio De Janeiro	R	1	2	4	8	—	—
Bahia	B	1	2	4	8	—	—
Goias	G	—	1	2	4	—	4
Cuiaba	C	—	1	2	4	—	—
Minas Gerais	M	—	—	—	—	2	—
Sao Paulo	SP	—	—	—	5⅓	—	—

NOTE: 1 Oitavo = 3.586 g,; 8 Oitavos = 1 Onza (28.68 g); thus 5-1/3 Oitavos plus 1 Escropalo) is precisely 2/3 Onza (ounce).

Lightweight Coins: Many coppers are found as much as 15 percent or more below the official weights, and even heavy specimens are occasionally observed. Most of the above coins were counterfeited, as their face value exceeded the cost of the metal and minting. Though usually crude and carelessly engraved, some counterfeits are of decent workmanship, and entirely undistinguishable from government issues. Brazilian collectors generally accept these contemporary counterfeits as collectable, due to their historical value. Before Pedro I began his regular coinage, colonial coppers were revalued with a special countermark, probably in 1822.

Imperial Countermarks

These countermarks consist of a crowned 20, 40 or 80 within a wreath in a circle and opposite a shield in a circle is used.

20 REIS

COPPER

c/m: Crowned 20 in sprays on various Colonial X (10) Reis.

KM#	Date	Year	Good	VG	Fine	VF
355	Various	—	900.00	1500.	2500.	3500.

NOTE: Many authorities consider all known examples of KM#355 to be counterfeit.

40 REIS

COPPER

c/m: Crowned 40 on various X(10) Reis.

KM#	Date	Year	Good	VG	Fine	VF
358	Various	—	750.00	1250.	2000.	3000.

c/m: Crowned 40 in sprays on various Colonial

XX (20) Reis.

KM#	Date	Year	Good	VG	Fine	VF
356	Various	—	700.00	1150.	1750.	2500.

NOTE: Three of 8 known dies are believed counterfeit.

80 REIS

COPPER
c/m: 80 on Colonial XX (20) Reis.

KM#	Date	Year	Good	VG	Fine	VF
354	Various	—	1250.	2250.	3500.	5000.

c/m: Crowned 80 in sprays on various Colonial XL (40) Reis.

KM#	Date	Year	Good	VG	Fine	VF
357	Various	—	1500.	2500.	4000.	6000.

NOTE: One of 11 known dies are believed counterfeit.

c/m: Crowned 80 on 75 Reis.

KM#	Date	Year	Good	VG	Fine	VF
359	Various	—	—	—	Rare	—

Regular Coinage

CAUTION: Prices are for specimens without any countermark. Countermarked pieces follow these listings.

10 REIS

COPPER
Mint mark: R

KM#	Date	Mintage	Good	VG	Fine	VF
371.1	1824	.235	3.00	7.50	15.00	25.00
	Mint mark: B					
371.2	1827	.104	5.00	10.00	17.50	30.00
	1828	.728	2.50	5.00	12.50	20.00

20 REIS

COPPER
Mint mark: R
PEDRO I
Weight: 2 oitavos, 7.17 g

KM#	Date	Mintage	Good	VG	Fine	VF
360.1	1822	—	Counterfeit		—	—
	1823 cross on crown					
		1.700	2.00	3.00	5.00	12.50
	1824	4.956	2.00	3.00	5.00	12.50
	1824 BRSA					
		I.A.	7.00	10.00	20.00	60.00
	1825	9.054	2.00	3.00	5.00	12.50
	1826	4.419	2.00	3.00	5.00	12.50
	1827	4.648	2.00	3.00	5.00	12.50
	1828	4.474	2.00	3.00	5.00	12.50
	1829	6.806	2.00	3.00	5.00	12.50
	1830	—	2.00	3.00	5.00	12.50
	1831	—	Counterfeit		—	—
	Mint mark: B					
360.2	1825	.582	3.00	5.00	7.50	15.00
	1827	.044	5.00	7.50	10.00	25.00
	1828	.585	3.00	5.00	7.50	15.00
	1830	.316	3.00	5.00	7.50	15.00

Mint mark: C
PEDRO I
Reduced weight: 1 oitavo = 3.59 g

KM#	Date	Mintage	Good	VG	Fine	VF
375.1	1825	—	15.00	30.00	80.00	150.00
	Mint mark: G					
375.2	1829	—	Counterfeit		—	—

Mint mark: R
PEDRO II
Reduced weight: 2 oitavos = 7.17 g

KM#	Date	Mintage	Good	VG	Fine	VF
380	1832	.014	35.00	75.00	150.00	250.00

37-1/2 REIS

COPPER
Mint mark: M
PEDRO I
Weight: 2 oitavos = 7.17 g

KM#	Date	Mintage	Good	VG	Fine	VF
362	1823	—	15.00	30.00	50.00	90.00
	1824	—	10.00	22.00	40.00	80.00
	1825	—	10.00	22.00	40.00	80.00
	1826	—	10.00	22.00	40.00	80.00
	1827	—	10.00	22.00	40.00	80.00
	1828	—	10.00	22.00	40.00	80.00

40 REIS

COPPER
Mint mark: R
PEDRO I
Weight: 4 oitavos = 14.34 g

KM#	Date	Mintage	VG	Fine	VF	XF
363.1	1823	.920	5.00	7.50	15.00	25.00
	1824	9.170	2.50	5.00	7.50	20.00
	1825	6.774	2.50	5.00	7.50	20.00
	1826 cross on crown					
		10.507	2.50	5.00	7.50	20.00
	1826 PETRUST					
		Inc. Ab.	15.00	30.00	50.00	90.00
	1827	17.892	2.50	5.00	10.00	20.00
	1828	15.570	2.50	5.00	10.00	20.00
	1829	8.924	2.50	5.00	10.00	20.00
	1830	—	2.50	5.00	10.00	20.00
	1831/0	—	5.00	7.50	15.00	35.00
	1831	—	2.50	5.00	10.00	20.00
	Mint mark: B					
363.2	1824	.230	5.00	7.50	15.00	30.00
	1825	Inc. Ab	5.00	7.50	15.00	30.00
	1827	.161	5.00	7.50	15.00	30.00
	1828	.051	7.50	12.50	20.00	50.00
	1829	2.052	2.50	5.00	10.00	25.00
	1830	1.032	2.50	5.00	10.00	25.00

NOTE: Most known examples of 1828R, 1829R, and 1830R are counterfeit!

Mint mark: C
PEDRO I
Reduced weight: 2 oitavos = 7.17 g

KM#	Date	Mintage	Good	VG	Fine	VF
364.1	1823	—	7.50	15.00	20.00	35.00
	1824	—	5.00	10.00	15.00	30.00
	1825	—	5.00	10.00	15.00	30.00
	1826	—	5.00	10.00	15.00	30.00
	1827	—	5.00	10.00	15.00	30.00
	1828	—	5.00	10.00	15.00	30.00
	1829	—	5.00	10.00	15.00	30.00
	1830	—	5.00	10.00	15.00	30.00
	1831	—	7.50	15.00	20.00	35.00
	Mint mark: G					
364.2	1823	—	7.50	12.50	25.00	50.00
	1825	—	5.00	7.50	15.00	30.00
	1826	—	7.50	12.50	25.00	50.00
	1827	—	5.00	7.50	15.00	30.00
	1828	—	5.00	7.50	15.00	30.00
	1829	—	5.00	7.50	15.00	30.00
	1830	—	5.00	7.50	15.00	30.00

NOTE: 1823C is considered a counterfeit by many authorities.

Mint mark: R
PEDRO II
Weight: 4 oitavos = 14.34 g

KM#	Date	Mintage	VG	Fine	VF	XF
378	1831	—	Counterfeit issue			—
	1832	.816	2.50	5.00	10.00	20.00

NOTE: 1833R exists as a pattern.

Mint mark: G
PEDRO II
Reduced weight: 2 oitavos = 7.17 g

KM#	Date	Mintage	Good	VG	Fine	VF
381.1	1832 Petrus II					
		—	5.00	10.00	25.00	50.00
	1832 Petrus 2.o					
		—	7.50	15.00	35.00	75.00
	Mint mark: C					
381.2	1833	—	5.00	10.00	20.00	45.00

75 REIS

COPPER
Mint mark: G
PEDRO I
Weight: 4 oitavos = 14.34 g

KM#	Date	Mintage	Good	VG	Fine	VF
365	1823	—	20.00	40.00	85.00	175.00

80 REIS

COPPER
Mint mark: R
PEDRO I
Weight: 8 oitavos = 28.69 g

KM#	Date	Mintage	VG	Fine	VF	XF
366.1	1823	.100	10.00	15.00	25.00	50.00
	1824	.825	7.50	10.00	15.00	30.00
	1825	1.027	7.50	10.00	15.00	30.00
	1826	10.507	2.50	5.00	10.00	25.00
	1827	17.892	2.50	5.00	10.00	25.00
	1828	26.524	2.50	5.00	10.00	25.00
	1829	20.180	2.50	5.00	10.00	25.00
	1830	—	2.50	5.00	10.00	25.00
	1831	—	2.50	5.00	10.00	25.00

Mint mark: B

KM#	Date	Mintage	VG	Fine	VF	XF
366.2	1824	.879	5.00	8.00	15.00	30.00
	1825	Inc. Ab.	5.00	8.00	15.00	30.00
	1826	.695	5.00	8.00	15.00	30.00
	1827	.352	5.00	10.00	17.50	40.00
	1828	2.539	3.50	7.00	15.00	30.00
	1829	3.993	3.50	7.00	15.00	30.00
	1830	.359	5.00	8.50	16.50	35.00
	1831	—	10.00	20.00	60.00	120.00

NOTE: Coins with P mint mark are all counterfeit. Counterfeits of the 1831 B are common.

Mint mark: SP
PEDRO I
Weight: 5 1/3 oitavos = 19.13 g

KM#	Date	Mintage	Good	VG	Fine	VF
376	1825	—	10.00	17.50	35.00	75.00
	1828	—	5.00	8.50	16.50	35.00
	1829	—	7.50	12.50	20.00	45.00

NOTE: Many varieties of the Sao Paulo coins exist.

Mint mark: C
PEDRO I
Weight: 4 oitavos = 14.34 g

KM#	Date	Mintage	Good	VG	Fine	VF
377.1	1826	—	5.00	7.50	15.00	35.00
	1827	—	15.00	25.00	40.00	90.00
	1828	—	7.50	10.00	20.00	45.00
	1830	—	10.00	30.00	60.00	100.00

Mint mark: G

KM#	Date	Mintage	Good	VG	Fine	VF
377.2	1826	—	7.50	12.50	17.50	40.00
	1828	—	7.50	12.50	17.50	40.00
	1829	—	7.50	12.50	17.50	40.00
	1830	—	7.50	12.50	17.50	40.00
	1831	—	10.00	15.00	25.00	65.00

NOTE: Coins dated 1826G are believed to be counterfeit.

Rev: Arms w/o stars.

KM#	Date	Mintage	Good	VG	Fine	VF
377.3	1828	—	30.00	50.00	70.00	100.00

Mint mark: R
PEDRO II
Weight: 8 oitavos = 28.69 g
Rev: Similar to KM#366.1.

KM#	Date	Mintage	VG	Fine	VF	XF
379	1831	—	5.00	7.50	15.00	35.00
	1832 cross above crown					
		6.119	2.50	5.00	12.50	25.00
	1833	—	— Reported, not confirmed			

Mint mark: SP
PEDRO II
Weight: 5 1/3 oitavos = 19.13 g

KM#	Date	Mintage	Good	VG	Fine	VF
382	1832	—	30.00	70.00	120.00	200.00

NOTE: The 1832SP is considered a counterfeit by many authorities.

Mint mark: G
PEDRO II
Weight: 4 oitavos = 14.34 g

KM#	Date	Mintage	Good	VG	Fine	VF
383	1832	—	5.00	7.50	15.00	30.00
	1833	—	5.00	7.50	15.00	30.00
	1833 Petrus I (error)					
		—	50.00	90.00	150.00	225.00

REGIONAL COUNTERMARKS

NOTE: Due to variations in value from one part of the country to another, copper coins tended to flow to areas where their buying power was greatest. To prevent the outflow, some districts ordered coinage countermarked and reduced in value. There is speculation that silver coins were also ordered to be countermarked, but no documentation is available to substantiate this claim. The following issues are recognized as genuine. Prices are for countermarks on common coins of each variety. Countermarked rare dates bring a premium.

CEARA

Ceara is a state in northeastern Brazil. Due to coin shortages a law was passed October 3, 1833 that copper coins would be countermarked and pass for 1/2 of their face value. In November of 1834 legislation was passed to stop the star countermarks.

Coins of 10, 20, 40, and 80 Reis were countermarked CEARA in a 5-pointed star to indicate a 50 percent reduction in value (to 5, 10, 20, and 40 Reis).

5 REIS

COPPER
c/m: Star on 10 Reis.

KM#	Date	Year	Good	VG	Fine	VF
395	ND (1834)	—	—	—	Rare	—

10 REIS

COPPER
c/m: Star on various 20 Reis.

KM#	Date	Good	VG	Fine	VF
396	ND (1834) —	7.50	10.00	12.50	25.00

20 REIS

COPPER
c/m: Star on various 40 Reis.

KM#	Date	Good	VG	Fine	VF
397	ND (1834) —	10.00	12.50	17.50	35.00

40 REIS

COPPER
c/m: Star on various 80 Reis.

KM#	Date	Good	VG	Fine	VF
398	ND (1834) —	12.50	15.00	20.00	45.00

NOTE: A few silver coins bearing this c/m are considered trial pieces and are rare. Many imitations of this c/m exist on various silver coins and are listed in "Unusual World Coins."

MARANHAO

Maranhao is a state in northeastern Brazil. Coin shortages caused 2 issues of countermarked coins. The first was to make the coins pass for 1/4 their face value. These had M and the new value in Roman numerals. Trial impressions of unadopted designs using M and the new value in Arabic numerals are also known. The second issue was to make the coins pass for 1/2 the face value. These were countermarked with an M. These too were soon recalled.

FIRST SERIES (1834)
Obv: M and denomination in Roman numerals within a rectangle.

5 REIS

COPPER
c/m: M/V on various 20 Reis.

KM#	Date	Year	Good	VG	Fine	VF
401	ND	(1834)	12.00	15.00	25.00	40.00

10 REIS

COPPER
c/m: M/X on various 40 Reis.

KM#	Date	Year	Good	VG	Fine	VF
402	ND	(1834)	10.00	12.50	22.50	35.00

20 REIS

COPPER
c/m: M/XX on various 80 Reis.

KM#	Date	Year	Good	VG	Fine	VF
403	ND	(1834)	10.00	12.50	25.00	50.00

SECOND SERIES (1835)
Large M on reverse of coin.

10 REIS

COPPER
c/m: M on various 20 Reis.

KM#	Date	Year	Good	VG	Fine	VF
404	ND	(1835)	7.50	10.00	20.00	30.00

20 REIS

COPPER
c/m: M on various 40 Reis.

KM#	Date	Year	Good	VG	Fine	VF
405	ND	(1835)	7.50	10.00	20.00	30.00

40 REIS

COPPER
c/m: M on various 80 Reis.

KM#	Date	Year	Good	VG	Fine	VF
406	ND	(1835)	20.00	35.00	75.00	100.00

NOTE: Second series countermarks are found struck

over coins which already have the first series countermark. They are worth about 50 percent more than ordinary second series coins.

PARA

Para is a state in northern Brazil. Two series of countermarks were issued from this state. On January 14, 1835 Governor Malcher authorized a law for the countermarking of the recently withdrawn Mato Grosso coppers to 1/4 of their previous value. On March 6, 1835 Governor Vinagre authorized the countermarking of coppers at 1/2 their face value. Although heavily counterfeited because of their crudeness these coins stayed in circulation until 1868 and even later.

Crude Arabic 10, 20, or 40 countermarked on obverse of coins weighing 2, 4, and 8 oitavos, respectively. The numerals are quite crude and styles vary and are easily distinguished from the general countermarks. Examples of the Para marks are:

10 20 40

10 REIS

COPPER

c/m: 10 on various Colonial XX (20) Reis.

KM#	Date	Year	Good	VG	Fine	VF
407	ND	(1835)	5.00	7.50	10.00	20.00

c/m: 10 on Imperial 20 Reis, R or B mints.

KM#	Date	Year	Good	VG	Fine	VF
408	ND	(1835)	5.00	7.50	10.00	20.00

c/m: 10 on Imperial 40 Reis, C or G mints, KM#364.1 and KM#364.2.

KM#	Date	Year	Good	VG	Fine	VF
409	ND	(1835)	7.50	10.00	15.00	35.00

20 REIS

COPPER

c/m: 20 on Colonial XL (40) Reis.

KM#	Date	Year	Good	VG	Fine	VF
410	ND	(1835)	5.00	7.50	12.50	30.00

c/m: 20 on Imperial 40 Reis, R or B mints.

KM#	Date	Year	Good	VG	Fine	VF
411	ND	(1835)	5.00	7.50	12.50	30.00

c/m: 20 on Imperial 80 Reis, C or G mints, KM#377.1 and KM#377.2.

KM#	Date	Year	Good	VG	Fine	VF
412	ND	(1835)	7.50	12.50	20.00	40.00

40 REIS

COPPER

c/m: 40 on Colonial LXXX (80) Reis.

KM#	Date	Year	Good	VG	Fine	VF
413	ND	(1835)	10.00	15.00	20.00	35.00

c/m: 40 on Imperial 80 Reis, R or B mints.

KM#	Date	Year	Good	VG	Fine	VF
414	ND	(1835)	7.50	12.50	17.50	25.00

REPUBLIC OF PIRATINI

As a result of a revolt in 1835 in the southern Brazilian state of Rio Grande do Sol the "Republic of Piratini" was briefly established and all coins then circulating in the province were countermarked with the arms of the new republic. This series is probably the most counterfeited of all of the elaborate countermarks.

1835-1845

Two hands grasping a sword with Liberty cap on point within oval. Similar countermarks with either the date 1835 or PIRATINI at the bottom or date divided are considered to be fantasies.

20 REIS

COPPER

c/m: On various 20 Reis.

KM#	Date	Year	VG	Fine	VF	XF
A415	ND	—	45.00	90.00	150.00	225.00

40 REIS

COPPER

c/m: On various 40 Reis.

KM#	Date	Year	VG	Fine	VF	XF
B415	ND	—	45.00	90.00	150.00	225.00

80 REIS

COPPER

c/m: On various 80 Reis.

KM#	Date	Year	VG	Fine	VF	XF
C415	ND	—	45.00	90.00	150.00	225.00

320 REIS

SILVER

c/m: On 320 Reis, KM#374.

KM#	Date	Year	VG	Fine	VF	XF
E415	ND(1825R)	—	450.00	700.00	1150.	1750.

640 REIS

SILVER

c/m: On 640 Reis, KM#367.

KM#	Date	Year	VG	Fine	VF	XF
F415	ND(1825R)	—	—	—	Rare	—

960 REIS

SILVER

c/m: On Columbia-Cundinamarca 8 Reales, KM#6.

KM#	Date	Year	VG	Fine	VF	XF
G415	ND(1821)	—	—	—	Rare	—

c/m: On Spain 8 Reales, C#93.

KM#	Date	Year	VG	Fine	VF	XF
H415	ND(1809 IG)	—	—	—	Rare	—

c/m: On Brazil 960 Reis, KM#368.1.

KM#	Date	Year	VG	Fine	VF	XF
I415	ND(1826R)	—	—	—	Rare	—

ICO

Ico is a city in the state of Ceara in northeastern Brazil. It was the center of a revolutionary movement from 1829-1832. Various copper and silver coins countermarked ICO, YCO, JGO and IGO are all considered counterfeit, countermarked after the suppression of the revolt. They have little value, but are collected as curiosities. Average value, about $4.00.

NOTE: In addition to local countermarks, over 280 private countermarks are known. A list of these is given by Kurt Prober, in his "Catalogo das Moedas Brasileiras".

NATIONAL COUNTERMARKS

In order to prevent chaotic conditions resulting from local and private countermarking, the government passed law #54 of 6 October 1835 ordering all coppers countermarked according to the following standards:

2 Oitavos = 7.18 g = 10 Reis
4 Oitavos = 14.34 g = 20 Reis
8 Oitavos = 28.69 g = 40 Reis

The countermarks consist of neat numerals within a circle, having a plain or shaded field. These countermarks were applied to various Brazilian coinage from 1799 to 1833. In addition, wrong countermarks are occasionally found, as well as various Portuguese, Angolan,

San Tome, Mozambiquean and pre-1799 Brazilian coins.

10 REIS

COPPER

Mint: Lisbon - w/o mint mark.
c/m: 10 on XX (20) Reis, KM#229.

KM#	Date	Year	Good	VG	Fine	VF
416	ND(1835)	1799	6.00	10.00	20.00	40.00

c/m: 10 on XX (20) Reis, KM#233.1.

KM#	Date	Year	Good	VG	Fine	VF
417.1	ND(1835)	1802	2.75	5.50	12.00	20.00
		1803	2.75	5.50	12.00	20.00
		1805	2.75	5.50	12.00	20.00

Mint mark: B

KM#	Date	Year	Good	VG	Fine	VF
417.2	ND(1835)	1812	3.50	6.50	12.50	20.00
		1813	2.75	5.50	8.00	18.00
		1815	2.75	5.50	8.00	18.00
		1816	2.75	5.50	8.00	18.00

Mint mark: R

KM#	Date	Year	Good	VG	Fine	VF
417.3	ND(1835)	1812	3.50	7.00	14.00	28.00
		1813	3.50	7.00	14.00	28.00
		1814	3.50	7.00	14.00	28.00
		1815	3.50	7.00	14.00	28.00

c/m: 10 on XX (20) Reis, KM#309.

KM#	Date	Year	Good	VG	Fine	VF
418	ND(1835)	1816	3.50	7.00	14.00	28.00
		1817	3.50	7.00	14.00	28.00
		1818	5.00	10.00	18.00	35.00

c/m: 10 on XL (40) Reis, KM#318.

KM#	Date	Year	Good	VG	Fine	VF
419	ND(1835)	1818	15.00	20.00	30.00	45.00

c/m: 10 on XX (20) Reis, KM#316.1.

KM#	Date	Year	Good	VG	Fine	VF
420.1	ND(1835)	1818	2.75	5.50	8.00	18.00
		1819	2.75	5.50	8.00	18.00
		1820	2.75	5.50	8.00	18.00
		1821	2.75	5.50	8.00	18.00
		1822	2.75	5.50	8.00	18.00

Mint mark: B

KM#	Date	Year	Good	VG	Fine	VF
420.2	ND(1835)	1820	3.50	6.50	12.50	20.00
		1821	3.50	6.50	12.50	20.00

Mint mark: M
c/m: 10 on 37-1/2 Reis, KM#317.1.

KM#	Date	Year	Good	VG	Fine	VF
421.1	ND(1835)	1818	3.00	9.00	16.00	25.00
		1819	3.00	9.00	16.00	25.00
		1819 medal strike	3.50	12.00	20.00	28.00
		1821	3.00	9.00	16.00	25.00
		1821 medal strike	3.00	9.00	16.00	25.00

Mint mark: R

KM#	Date	Year	Good	VG	Fine	VF
421.2	ND(1835)	1818	12.50	30.00	50.00	110.00

Mint: Lisbon - w/o mint mark.
c/m: 10 on XL (40) Reis, KM#340.

KM#	Date	Year	Good	VG	Fine	VF
422	ND(1835)	1820	25.00	75.00	100.00	150.00

Mint mark: R
c/m: 10 on 20 Reis, Pedro I, KM#360.1.

KM#	Date	Year	Good	VG	Fine	VF
423.1	ND(1835)	1823	2.50	4.50	7.50	15.00
		1824	2.50	4.50	7.50	15.00
		1825	2.50	4.50	7.50	15.00
		1826	2.50	4.50	7.50	15.00
		1827	2.50	4.50	7.50	15.00
		1828	2.50	4.50	7.50	15.00
		1829	2.50	4.50	7.50	15.00
		1830	2.50	4.50	7.50	15.00

Mint mark: B
c/m: 10 on 20 Reis of Pedro I, KM#360.2.

KM#	Date	Year	Good	VG	Fine	VF
423.2	ND(1835)	1825	3.00	5.00	9.00	17.50
		1827	3.00	5.00	9.00	17.50
		1828	3.00	5.00	9.00	17.50
		1830	3.00	5.00	9.00	17.50

Mint mark: C
c/m: 10 on 20 Reis of Pedro I, KM#375.1.

KM#	Date	Year	Good	VG	Fine	VF
424.1	ND(1835)	1825	50.00	100.00	150.00	240.00

Mint mark: G

KM#	Date	Year	Good	VG	Fine	VF
424.2	ND(1835)	1827	20.00	32.50	50.00	100.00

NOTE: The above two pieces were not supposed to have been countermarked, as they only weigh one oitavo-3.59 g.

Mint mark: R
c/m: 10 on 20 Reis of Pedro II, KM#380.

KM#	Date	Year	Good	VG	Fine	VF
425	ND(1835)	1832	30.00	70.00	120.00	200.00

Mint mark: M
c/m: 10 on 37-1/2 Reis of Pedro I.

KM#	Date	Year	Good	VG	Fine	VF
426	ND(1835)	1823	7.50	20.00	40.00	75.00
		1824	7.50	20.00	40.00	75.00
		1825	7.50	20.00	40.00	75.00
		1826	7.50	20.00	40.00	75.00
		1827	7.50	20.00	40.00	75.00
		1828	7.50	20.00	40.00	75.00

Mint mark: C
c/m: 10 on 40 Reis of Pedro I, KM#364.1.

KM#	Date	Year	Good	VG	Fine	VF
427.1	ND(1835)	1823	4.50	7.50	12.50	20.00
		1824	2.50	5.00	7.50	15.00
		1825	2.50	5.00	7.50	15.00
		1826	2.50	5.00	7.50	15.00
		1827	2.50	5.00	7.50	15.00
		1828	2.50	5.00	7.50	15.00
		1829	2.50	5.00	7.50	15.00
		1830	2.50	5.00	7.50	15.00
		1831	2.50	5.00	7.50	15.00

Mint mark: G
c/m: 10 on 40 Reis of Pedro I, KM#364.2.

KM#	Date	Year	Good	VG	Fine	VF
427.2	ND(1835)	1823	5.00	7.50	15.00	30.00
		1825	5.00	7.50	15.00	30.00
		1826	5.00	7.50	15.00	30.00
		1827	2.50	5.00	12.50	20.00
		1828	2.50	5.00	12.50	20.00
		1829	2.50	5.00	12.50	20.00
		1830	2.50	5.00	12.50	20.00

c/m: 10 on 40 Reis of Pedro II, KM#381.1.

KM#	Date	Year	Good	VG	Fine	VF
428.1	ND(1835)	1832 PETRUS II	3.00	7.50	12.50	20.00
		1832 Petrus 2.o	3.00	7.50	12.50	20.00

Mint mark: C

KM#	Date	Year	Good	VG	Fine	VF
428.2	ND(1835)	1833	5.00	7.50	15.00	35.00

c/m: 10 on Mozambique 40 Reis, KM#19.

KM#	Date	Year	Good	VG	Fine	VF
429	ND(1835)	1819	5.00	10.00	15.00	30.00
		1820	5.00	10.00	15.00	30.00
		1821	5.00	10.00	15.00	30.00
		1821	5.00	10.00	17.50	45.00
		1822	5.00	10.00	17.50	45.00
		1825	5.00	10.00	17.50	45.00

20 REIS

COPPER

Mint: Lisbon - w/o mint mark.
c/m: 20 on XL (40) Reis, KM#230.

KM#	Date	Year	Good	VG	Fine	VF
430	ND(1835)	1799	5.00	8.00	14.00	25.00

c/m: 20 on XL (40) Reis, KM#234.1.

KM#	Date	Year	Good	VG	Fine	VF
431.1	ND(1835)	1802	2.50	3.50	6.00	12.00
		1803	2.50	3.50	6.00	12.00

Mint mark: B

KM#	Date	Year	Good	VG	Fine	VF
431.2	ND(1835)	1809	3.00	6.00	12.00	25.00
		1810	3.00	6.00	12.00	25.00
		1811	2.50	4.50	9.00	18.00
		1812	2.50	4.50	9.00	18.00
		1814	2.50	3.50	6.00	12.00
		1816	2.50	3.50	6.00	12.00

Mint mark: R

KM#	Date	Year	Good	VG	Fine	VF
431.3	ND(1835)	1812	2.50	5.50	12.00	25.00
		1813	2.50	5.50	12.00	25.00
		1815	2.50	5.50	12.00	25.00

c/m: 20 on XL (40) Reis, KM#311.

KM#	Date	Year	Good	VG	Fine	VF
432	ND(1835)	1816	2.50	5.50	12.00	25.00
		1817	2.50	5.50	12.00	25.00

c/m: 20 on XL (40) Reis, KM#319.1.

KM#	Date	Year	Good	VG	Fine	VF
433.1	ND(1835)	1818	2.50	4.50	9.00	18.00
		1819	2.50	4.50	9.00	18.00
		1820	2.50	4.50	9.00	18.00
		1821	2.50	4.50	9.00	18.00
		1822	2.50	4.50	9.00	18.00

Mint mark: B

KM#	Date	Year	Good	VG	Fine	VF
433.2	ND(1835)	1820	3.00	6.00	12.00	25.00
		1821	3.00	6.00	12.00	25.00
		1822	3.00	6.00	12.00	25.00
		1823	5.00	8.00	15.00	30.00

Mint mark: M
c/m: 20 on 75 Reis, KM#320.

KM#	Date	Year	Good	VG	Fine	VF
434	ND(1835)	1818	7.50	15.00	30.00	65.00
		1819	7.50	15.00	30.00	65.00
		1819 medal strike	7.50	15.00	30.00	60.00
		1821	7.50	15.00	30.00	60.00

Mint: Lisbon - w/o mint mark.
c/m: 20 on LXXX (80) Reis, KM#341.

KM#	Date	Year	Good	VG	Fine	VF
435	ND(1835)	1820	7.50	15.00	25.00	50.00

Mint mark: R
c/m: 20 on 40 Reis of Pedro I, KM#363.1.

KM#	Date	Year	Good	VG	Fine	VF
436.1	ND(1835)	1823	2.50	5.00	7.50	15.00
		1824	2.50	5.00	7.50	15.00
		1825	2.50	5.00	7.50	15.00
		1826	2.50	5.00	7.50	15.00
		1827	2.50	5.00	7.50	15.00
		1828	2.50	5.00	7.50	15.00
		1829	2.50	5.00	7.50	15.00
		1830	2.50	5.00	7.50	15.00
		1831	2.50	5.00	7.50	15.00

Mint mark: B

KM#	Date	Year	Good	VG	Fine	VF
436.2	ND(1835)	1824	2.50	5.00	8.00	16.00
		1825	2.50	5.00	8.00	16.00
		1827	2.50	5.00	8.00	16.00
		1828	2.50	5.00	8.00	16.00
		1829	2.50	5.00	8.00	16.00
		1830	2.50	5.00	8.00	16.00

Mint mark: R
c/m: 20 on 40 Reis of Pedro II, KM#378.

KM#	Date	Year	Good	VG	Fine	VF
437	ND(1835)	1831	2.50	5.00	7.50	15.00
		1832	2.50	5.00	7.50	15.00

Mint mark: G
c/m: 20 on 75 Reis of Pedro I, KM#365.

KM#	Date	Year	Good	VG	Fine	VF
438	ND(1835)	1823	10.00	25.00	40.00	75.00

Mint mark: C
c/m: 20 on 80 Reis of Pedro I, KM#377.1.

KM#	Date	Year	Good	VG	Fine	VF
439.1	ND(1835)	1826	5.00	7.50	10.00	15.00
		1827	7.50	10.00	15.00	35.00
		1828	5.00	7.50	10.00	17.50
		1830	5.00	7.50	10.00	17.50

Mint mark: G

KM#	Date	Year	Good	VG	Fine	VF
439.2	ND(1835)	1826	3.50	5.00	7.50	20.00
		1828	3.50	5.00	7.50	15.00
		1829	3.50	5.00	7.50	15.00
		1830	3.50	5.00	7.50	15.00
		1831	7.50	12.50	20.00	50.00

c/m: 20 on 80 Reis of Pedro II, KM#383.

KM#	Date	Year	Good	VG	Fine	VF
440	ND(1835)	1832	3.50	5.00	7.50	15.00
		1833	3.50	5.00	7.50	15.00
		1833 Petrus I	10.00	25.00	50.00	100.00

c/m: 20 on Mozambique 80 Reis, KM#20.

KM#	Date	Year	Good	VG	Fine	VF
441	ND(1835)	1819	7.50	15.00	25.00	50.00
		1820	7.50	15.00	25.00	50.00

40 REIS

COPPER

Mint mark: R
c/m: 40 on LXXX (80) Reis, KM#308.

KM#	Date	Year	Good	VG	Fine	VF
442	ND(1835)	1811	4.50	9.00	15.00	30.00
		1812	4.50	9.00	15.00	30.00

Mint mark: B
c/m: 40 on LXXX (80) Reis, KM#342.1.

KM#	Date	Year	Good	VG	Fine	VF
443.1	ND(1835)	1820	2.50	5.00	10.00	20.00
		1821	2.50	5.00	10.00	20.00
		1822	2.50	5.00	10.00	20.00
		1823	2.50	5.50	11.50	25.00

Mint mark: R

KM#	Date	Year	Good	VG	Fine	VF
443.2	ND(1835)	1821	2.50	5.50	11.50	25.00
		1822	2.50	5.50	11.50	25.00

c/m: 40 on 80 Reis of Pedro I, KM#366.1.

KM#	Date	Year	Good	VG	Fine	VF
444.1	ND(1835)	1823	5.00	7.50	10.00	20.00
		1824	2.50	5.00	7.50	12.50
		1825	2.50	5.00	7.50	12.50

KM#	Date	Year	Good	VG	Fine	VF
444.1		1826	2.50	5.00	7.50	12.50
		1827	2.50	5.00	7.50	12.50
		1828	2.50	5.00	7.50	12.50
		1829	2.50	5.00	7.50	12.50
		1830	2.50	5.00	7.50	12.50
		1831	2.50	5.00	7.50	12.50

Mint mark: B

KM#	Date	Year	Good	VG	Fine	VF
444.2	ND(1835)	1824	2.50	5.00	7.50	12.50
		1825	2.50	5.00	7.50	12.50
		1826	2.50	5.00	7.50	12.50
		1827	2.50	5.00	7.50	12.50
		1828	2.50	5.00	7.50	12.50
		1829	2.50	5.00	7.50	12.50
		1830	2.50	5.00	7.50	12.50
		1831	3.50	7.50	12.50	25.00

Mint mark: SP
c/m: 40 on 80 Reis of Pedro I, KM#376.

KM#	Date	Year	Good	VG	Fine	VF
445	ND(1835)	1825	7.50	12.50	17.50	35.00
		1828	7.50	12.50	17.50	35.00
		1829	7.50	12.50	17.50	35.00

Mint mark: R
c/m: 40 on 80 Reis of Pedro II, KM#379.

KM#	Date	Year	Good	VG	Fine	VF
446	ND(1835)	1831	7.50	12.50	20.00	30.00
		1832	5.00	7.50	10.00	20.00

Mint mark: SP
c/m: 40 on 80 Reis of Pedro II, KM#382.

KM#	Date	Year	Good	VG	Fine	VF
447	ND(1835)	1832	40.00	75.00	125.00	180.00

EMPIRE

80 REIS

2.2400 g, .917 SILVER, .0660 oz ASW
Mint mark: R
Obv. leg: PETRUS I D.G. . . around value in floral circle. Rev: Crowned arms in branches.

KM#	Date	Mintage	Fine	VF	XF	Unc
372	1824	—	200.00	450.00	1100.	2000.
	1826	—	200.00	450.00	1200.	2250.

Obv. leg: PETRUS II D.G. . .

KM#	Date	Mintage	Fine	VF	XF	Unc
388	1833	418 pcs.	180.00	300.00	750.00	1500.

160 REIS

4.4800 g, .917 SILVER, .1320 oz ASW
Mint mark: R
Obv. leg: PETRUS I D.G. . .

KM#	Date	Mintage	Fine	VF	XF	Unc
373	1824	—	200.00	400.00	850.00	2000.
	1826	—	200.00	400.00	850.00	2000.

Obv. leg: PETRUS II D.G. . .

KM#	Date	Mintage	Fine	VF	XF	Unc
389	1833	492 pcs.	300.00	600.00	1350.	2500.

320 REIS

8.9600 g, .917 SILVER, .2640 oz ASW
Mint mark: R
Obv. leg: PETRUS I D.G. . .

KM#	Date	Mintage	Fine	VF	XF	Unc
374	1824	642 pcs.	—	—	Rare	—
	1825 cross above crown					
		.018	20.00	40.00	90.00	175.00
	1826	—	800.00	1450.	2250.	—
	1827	—	—	—	Unique	—
	1830	4,190	—	—	Rare	—

Obv. leg: PETRUS II D.G. . .

KM#	Date	Mintage	Fine	VF	XF	Unc
390	1833	22 pcs.	—	—	Rare	—

640 REIS

17.9200 g, .917 SILVER, .5280 oz ASW
Mint mark: R
Obv. leg: PETRUS I D.G. . .

KM#	Date	Mintage	Fine	VF	XF	Unc
367	1823		Counterfeit		—	—
	1824/3	.080	10.00	25.00	50.00	85.00
	1824	Inc. Ab.	10.00	25.00	50.00	85.00
	1825	.353	10.00	25.00	50.00	85.00
	1826	9,472	500.00	1000.	2550.	3850.
	1827	Inc. Ab.	600.00	1250.	2800.	4000.

Obv. leg: PETRUS II D.G. . .

KM#	Date	Mintage	Fine	VF	XF	Unc
384	1832	118 pcs.	—	—	Rare	—
	1833	5 pcs.	—	—	Rare	—

960 REIS

26.8900 g, .896 SILVER, .7746 oz ASW
Mint mark: R

KM#	Date	Mintage	Fine	VF	XF	Unc
368.1	1823 SIGNO above crown					
		.395	12.50	25.00	45.00	85.00
	1823 IGNO above crown					
		Inc. Ab.	150.00	350.00	650.00	1000.
	1824	.600	12.50	25.00	45.00	85.00
	1825 small 960					
		.600	12.50	25.00	50.00	90.00
	1825 large 960					
		Inc. Ab.	50.00	160.00	400.00	600.00
	1826 cross above crown					
		.500	12.50	25.00	50.00	90.00
	1827	.018	1450.	2750.	4500.	—
	1828	—	Counterfeit		—	—

Mint mark: B

KM#	Date	Mintage	Fine	VF	XF	Unc
368.2	1824	—	40.00	80.00	140.00	200.00
	1825	—	40.00	80.00	140.00	200.00
	1826	—	200.00	450.00	1000.	1750.

NOTE: KM#368 is occasionally found struck over Spanish Colonial 8 Reales. Specimens having the original elements visible command a premium. Discernable mint mark, assayer initial and date all factor into premium values. See note below Colonial 960 Reis, KM#326.2 for additional information.

Mint mark: R

KM#	Date	Mintage	Fine	VF	XF	Unc
385	1832	3,039	450.00	850.00	1750.	3000.
	1833	Inc. Ab.	850.00	1750.	3500.	6000.
	1834	154 pcs.	2000.	4500.	8500.	14,500.

4000 REIS

8.2000 g, .917 GOLD, .2417 oz AGW
Mint mark: R

KM#	Date	Mintage	Fine	VF	XF	Unc
369.1	1823	.021	250.00	450.00	650.00	1200.
	1824	.038	250.00	450.00	650.00	1200.
	1825	.020	250.00	450.00	650.00	1400.
	1826	9,142	350.00	650.00	1450.	2000.
	1827/6	7,771	3000.	6000.	12,000.	—
	1827	Inc. Ab.	3000.	6000.	12,000.	—

Mint mark: B

KM#	Date	Mintage	Fine	VF	XF	Unc
369.2	1825	—	1200.	2500.	6000.	12,500.
	1826	—	1500.	3000.	7000.	15,000.
	1828	—	3000.	5000.	—	—

Mint mark: R

KM#	Date	Mintage	Fine	VF	XF	Unc
386.1	1832	64 pcs.	—	—	*Rare	—
	1833/2					
		257 pcs.	4500.	7500.	12,500.	—

***NOTE:** Spink America Norweb sale 3-97 unc. realized $14,300.

Obv: AZEVEDO below bust.

KM#	Date	Mintage	Fine	VF	XF	Unc
386.2	1832	5 known	—	—	Rare	—

6400 REIS

14.3400 g, .917 GOLD, .4228 oz AGW
Mint mark: R
Pedro I Coronation

KM#	Date	Mintage	Fine	VF	XF	Unc
361	1822	64 pcs.	—	—	*Rare	—

***NOTE:** Spink London sale No. 52, 6-86 near XF realized $87,000. Spink America Norweb sale 3-97 choice VF realized $82,500.

KM#	Date	Mintage	Fine	VF	XF	Unc
370.1	1823	931 pcs.	1200.	4500.	6000.	9000.
	1824	235 pcs.	2000.	5000.	8000.	12,500.
	1825	776 pcs.	1500.	4500.	6500.	11,500.
	1827	637 pcs.	1500.	4500.	6500.	11,500.
	1828	650 pcs.	1500.	4500.	6500.	11,500.
	1830	—	—	—	Unique	—

Mint mark: B

KM#	Date	Mintage	Fine	VF	XF	Unc
370.2	1825	—	3000.	5500.	9000.	13,500.
	1826	—	3000.	5500.	9000.	13,500.
	1828	423 pcs.	3000.	5500.	9000.	13,500.

Mint mark: R

KM#	Date	Mintage	Fine	VF	XF	Unc
387.1	1832	.030	450.00	850.00	1650.	2500.
	1833	.011	450.00	850.00	1650.	2500.

Obv: AZEVEDO below bust.

KM#	Date	Mintage	Fine	VF	XF	Unc
387.2	1832	4,101	500.00	1500.	3000.	4500.

MONETARY REFORM

10 REIS

BRONZE
Obv: CL below bust.

KM#	Date	Mintage	Fine	VF	XF	Unc
473	1868	89.604	.50	2.00	4.00	7.00
	1869	Inc. Ab.	.50	2.00	4.00	7.00
	1870	—	.50	2.00	6.00	18.00

20 REIS

BRONZE
Obv: CL below bust.

KM#	Date	Mintage	Fine	VF	XF	Unc
474	1868	90.360	1.50	2.25	4.00	7.00
	1869	Inc. Ab.	1.50	2.25	4.00	7.00
	1870	—	1.75	3.50	7.50	20.00

NOTE: Varieties exist on 1869 dated coins.

40 REIS

BRONZE
Obv: ESRC below bust.

KM#	Date	Mintage	Fine	VF	XF	Unc
479	1873	3.750	1.00	2.50	15.00	65.00
	1874	.890	1.00	2.50	15.00	65.00
	1875	1.208	1.00	2.50	15.00	65.00
	1876	.549	1.00	4.00	25.00	125.00
	1877	.465	1.00	3.00	15.00	70.00
	1878	1.223	1.00	2.50	15.00	70.00
	1879	2.771	1.00	2.50	15.00	70.00
	1880	1.569	1.00	2.50	15.00	70.00

50 REIS

COPPER-NICKEL

KM#	Date	Mintage	Fine	VF	XF	Unc
482	1886	.590	1.00	2.00	7.00	17.50
	1887	Inc. Ab.	1.00	2.50	7.00	20.00
	1888	.153	1.00	2.50	7.00	35.00

100 REIS

2.2400 g, .917 SILVER, .0660 oz ASW
Obv: Value in floral circle.
Rev: Crowned arms in branches.

KM#	Date	Mintage	Fine	VF	XF	Unc
452	1834	7,709	20.00	45.00	85.00	150.00
	1835	Inc. Ab.	20.00	45.00	85.00	150.00
	1836	5,592	400.00	700.00	1200.	2750.
	1837	9,562	20.00	45.00	85.00	150.00
	1840	910 pcs.	100.00	175.00	275.00	600.00
	1844	—	—	—	Rare	—
	1846	4,699	20.00	45.00	85.00	140.00
	1847/4	682 pcs.	100.00	180.00	250.00	450.00
	1848	486 pcs.	300.00	500.00	800.00	1750.

COPPER-NICKEL

KM#	Date	Mintage	Fine	VF	XF	Unc
477	1871	4.000	.50	1.25	3.00	50.00
	1872	100 pcs.	600.00	900.00	1800.	3000.

KM#	Date	Mintage	Fine	VF	XF	Unc
477	1874	—	.75	2.50	20.00	80.00
	1875	—	5.00	30.00	150.00	600.00
	1876	—	2.50	20.00	135.00	600.00
	1877	—	.75	2.50	20.00	80.00
	1878	—	1.00	3.00	30.00	200.00
	1879	—	1.00	2.50	20.00	80.00
	1880	—	1.50	5.00	100.00	500.00
	1881	—	.75	2.50	15.00	70.00
	1882	—	.75	2.50	15.00	70.00
	1883	2,700	.75	2.50	15.00	70.00
	1884	—	.75	2.50	15.00	70.00
	1885	—	.75	2.50	15.00	70.00

KM#	Date	Mintage	Fine	VF	XF	Unc
483	1886	.877	.75	2.00	10.00	70.00
	1887	—	.75	2.00	10.00	70.00
	1888	1.696	.75	2.00	10.00	70.00
	1889	.862	.75	2.00	10.00	70.00

200 REIS

4.4800 g, .917 SILVER, .1320 oz ASW

KM#	Date	Mintage	Fine	VF	XF	Unc
455	1835	4,894	20.00	50.00	100.00	300.00
	1837	5,007	20.00	50.00	100.00	300.00
	1840	624 pcs.	125.00	300.00	500.00	800.00
	1844	893 pcs.	100.00	200.00	300.00	500.00
	1846	406 pcs.	150.00	300.00	450.00	500.00
	1847	2,936	25.00	60.00	125.00	300.00
	1848/7	501 pcs.	250.00	450.00	850.00	1200.
	1848	Inc. Ab.	250.00	450.00	850.00	1200.

2.5500 g, .917 SILVER, .0752 oz ASW

KM#	Date	Mintage	Fine	VF	XF	Unc
469	1854	.037	6.00	10.00	30.00	100.00
	1855	.228	3.00	6.00	10.00	25.00
	1856/5	.103	3.00	6.00	10.00	25.00
	1856	Inc. Ab.	3.00	6.00	10.00	25.00
	1857	.128	3.00	6.00	10.00	25.00
	1858	.245	3.00	6.00	10.00	25.00
	1859	.152	3.00	6.00	10.00	25.00
	1860	.028	3.00	6.00	10.00	25.00
	1861	—	4.00	10.00	30.00	100.00
	1862	—	3.00	6.00	10.00	25.00
	1863	—	3.00	5.00	10.00	25.00
	1864	—	3.00	6.00	10.00	25.00
	1865/4	—	—	—	—	—
	1865	—	3.00	6.00	10.00	25.00
	1866	—	3.00	6.00	10.00	25.00
	1867	—	3.00	6.00	10.00	25.00

2.5000 g, .835 SILVER, .0671 oz ASW
Obv: Globe and cross flank date.
Rev: Caduceus and scales flank denomination.

KM#	Date	Mintage	Fine	VF	XF	Unc
471	1867	—	2.50	5.00	10.00	25.00
	1868	—	2.50	5.00	10.00	25.00
	1869	—	5.00	12.50	25.00	50.00

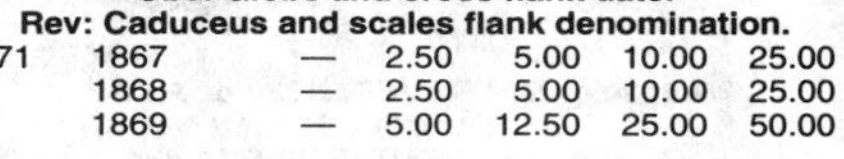

COPPER-NICKEL

KM#	Date	Mintage	Fine	VF	XF	Unc
478	1871	3.650	.50	1.50	12.00	60.00
	1874	—	1.00	2.50	15.00	90.00

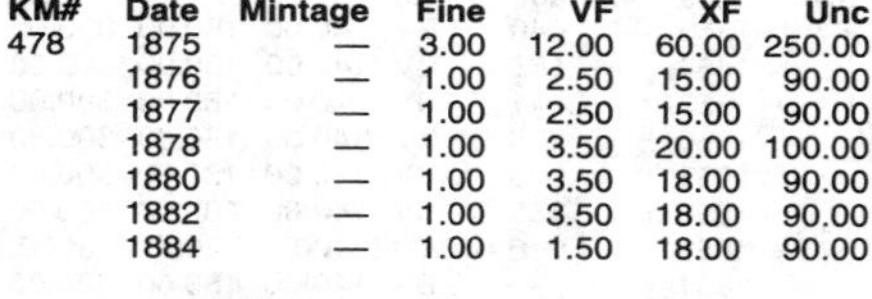

KM#	Date	Mintage	Fine	VF	XF	Unc
478	1875	—	3.00	12.00	60.00	250.00
	1876	—	1.00	2.50	15.00	90.00
	1877	—	1.00	2.50	15.00	90.00
	1878	—	1.00	3.50	20.00	100.00
	1880	—	1.00	3.50	18.00	90.00
	1882	—	1.00	3.50	18.00	90.00
	1884	—	1.00	1.50	18.00	90.00

KM#	Date	Mintage	Fine	VF	XF	Unc
484	1886	.177	4.50	25.00	100.00	300.00
	1887	—	1.00	2.50	15.00	70.00
	1888	.967	1.00	2.50	15.00	70.00
	1889	.511	1.50	3.00	16.00	75.00

400 REIS

8.9600 g, .917 SILVER, .2640 oz ASW
Obv: Value in floral circle.
Rev: Crowned arms in branches.

KM#	Date	Mintage	Fine	VF	XF	Unc
453	1834	6,197	50.00	100.00	175.00	325.00
	1835	Inc. Ab.	50.00	100.00	175.00	325.00
	1837	7,837	50.00	100.00	175.00	325.00
	1840	—	100.00	300.00	700.00	1200.
	1841	—	200.00	600.00	1000.	1800.
	1843	161 pcs.	400.00	850.00	1600.	2500.
	1844	649 pcs.	100.00	300.00	600.00	1100.
	1845	179 pcs.	250.00	650.00	1200.	2250.
	1847/0	878 pcs.	100.00	275.00	500.00	1000.
	1847	Inc. Ab.	100.00	275.00	500.00	1000.
	1848	510 pcs.	200.00	600.00	1000.	1800.

500 REIS

6.3750 g, .917 SILVER, .1880 oz ASW

KM#	Date	Mintage	Fine	VF	XF	Unc
458	1848	—	—	—	Rare	—
	1849	.026	25.00	50.00	80.00	200.00
	1850	.067	7.50	10.00	18.00	50.00
	1851	.095	7.50	10.00	18.00	50.00
	1852	.167	7.50	10.00	18.00	50.00

KM#	Date	Mintage	Fine	VF	XF	Unc
464	1853	.241	5.00	8.50	10.00	35.00
	1854	.317	5.00	8.50	10.00	35.00
	1855	.212	5.00	8.50	10.00	35.00
	1856	.223	5.00	8.50	10.00	35.00
	1857	.265	5.00	7.50	10.00	35.00
	1858	.791	5.00	7.50	10.00	35.00
	1859	.152	5.00	7.50	10.00	35.00
	1860/50	*.108	5.00	7.50	10.00	50.00
	1860	Inc. Ab.	5.00	7.50	10.00	35.00
	1861	—	5.00	7.50	10.00	35.00
	1862	—	5.00	7.50	10.00	35.00
	1863	—	5.00	7.50	10.00	35.00
	1864	—	5.00	7.50	10.00	35.00
	1865	—	5.00	7.50	10.00	35.00
	1866	—	5.00	7.50	10.00	35.00
	1867	—	5.00	7.50	10.00	35.00

***NOTE:** The 1860 mintage figure includes only first six month's production.

6.2500 g, .835 SILVER, .1678 oz ASW
Obv: CL below truncation, globe and cross flank date. Rev: Caduceus and scales flank denomination.

KM#	Date	Mintage	Fine	VF	XF	Unc
472	1867	—	5.00	7.50	10.00	35.00
	1868	—	5.00	7.50	10.00	35.00

6.3750 g, .917 SILVER, .1879 oz ASW
Obv: W/o CL. Rev. leg: DECRETO DE 1870.

KM#	Date	Mintage	Fine	VF	XF	Unc
480	1876	.076	4.50	10.00	20.00	50.00
	1886	5,283	50.00	100.00	150.00	350.00
	1887	768 pcs.	180.00	250.00	400.00	600.00
	1888	.333	4.50	7.00	10.00	35.00
	1889	.278	4.50	7.00	10.00	35.00

800 REIS

17.9300 g, .917 SILVER, .5283 oz ASW

KM#	Date	Mintage	Fine	VF	XF	Unc
456	1835	1,698	300.00	600.00	1000.	2350.
	1838	497 pcs.	500.00	900.00	1200.	2500.
	1840	145 pcs.	600.00	1000.	2000.	4000.
	1843	127 pcs.	2500.	4500.	7000.	10,000.
	1844	628 pcs.	500.00	850.00	1150.	2400.
	1846	672 pcs.	500.00	850.00	1150.	2400.

1000 REIS

12.7500 g, .917 SILVER, .3757 oz ASW

KM#	Date	Mintage	Fine	VF	XF	Unc
459	1849	965 pcs.	200.00	400.00	600.00	1800.
	1850	.169	6.00	8.00	20.00	60.00
	1851	.099	6.00	8.00	20.00	65.00
	1852	.196	6.00	8.00	20.00	60.00

KM#	Date	Mintage	Fine	VF	XF	Unc
465	1853	.266	6.00	8.00	20.00	40.00
	1854	.228	6.00	8.00	20.00	40.00
	1855	.312	6.00	8.00	20.00	40.00
	1856	.426	6.00	8.00	20.00	40.00
	1857	.512	6.00	8.00	20.00	40.00
	1858	.430	6.00	8.00	20.00	40.00
	1859	.996	6.00	8.00	20.00	40.00
	1860/50	.387	8.00	12.00	30.00	60.00
	1860	Inc. Ab.	6.00	8.00	20.00	40.00
	1861	—	6.00	8.00	20.00	40.00
	1862	—	6.00	8.00	20.00	40.00
	1863	—	6.00	8.00	20.00	40.00
	1864	—	6.00	8.00	20.00	40.00
	1865	—	6.00	8.00	20.00	40.00
	1866	—	6.00	8.00	20.00	40.00

12.5000 g, .900 SILVER, .3617 oz ASW
Obv: LUSTER F below truncation, globe and cross flank date.
Rev: Caduceus and scales flank denomination.

KM#	Date	Mintage	Fine	VF	XF	Unc
476	1869	—	15.00	25.00	50.00	85.00

12.7500 g, .917 SILVER, .3759 oz ASW
Obv: W/o LUSTER F. Rev. leg: DECRETO DE 1870.

KM#	Date	Mintage	Fine	VF	XF	Unc
481	1876	.194	7.50	12.50	20.00	60.00
	1877	.012	15.00	20.00	35.00	100.00
	1878	.047	12.50	17.50	30.00	90.00
	1879	.035	12.50	17.50	30.00	85.00
	1880	.020	12.50	17.50	30.00	90.00
	1881	.020	20.00	40.00	75.00	140.00
	1882	.018	25.00	45.00	85.00	175.00
	1883	.031	12.50	17.50	30.00	80.00
	1884	.022	20.00	35.00	65.00	150.00
	1885	.011	30.00	40.00	75.00	175.00
	1886	.048	8.50	17.50	35.00	100.00
	1887	9,875	35.00	60.00	85.00	175.00
	1888	.100	7.50	12.50	20.00	65.00
	1889	.089	50.00	70.00	100.00	200.00

1200 REIS

26.8900 g, .917 SILVER, .7924 oz ASW

KM#	Date	Mintage	Fine	VF	XF	Unc
454	1834	891 pcs.	75.00	200.00	350.00	600.00
	1835	.010	75.00	175.00	325.00	600.00
	1837	6,304	75.00	175.00	325.00	600.00
	1839	186 pcs.	2000.	3500.	6000.	9000.
	1840/37	633 pcs.	200.00	400.00	650.00	1500.
	1840	Inc. Ab.	200.00	350.00	550.00	850.00
	1843	1,803	100.00	250.00	500.00	1150.
	1845	292 pcs.	350.00	650.00	1000.	2000.
	1846	1,898	200.00	450.00	800.00	1800.
	1847	.010	75.00	175.00	350.00	750.00

NOTE: The above type dated 1841 and 1842 are counterfeit.

2000 REIS

25.5000 g, .917 SILVER, .7514 oz ASW

KM#	Date	Mintage	Fine	VF	XF	Unc
462	1851	.256	10.00	15.00	30.00	100.00
	1852	.277	10.00	15.00	30.00	100.00

KM#	Date	Mintage	Fine	VF	XF	Unc
466	1853	.145	10.00	20.00	35.00	80.00
	1854	.086	20.00	30.00	60.00	125.00
	1855	.300	10.00	20.00	35.00	100.00
	1856	.229	10.00	20.00	35.00	80.00
	1857	.105	20.00	30.00	50.00	80.00
	1858	.022	35.00	65.00	100.00	200.00
	1859	.041	200.00	400.00	650.00	1150.
	1863	—	10.00	20.00	35.00	80.00
	1864	—	35.00	65.00	100.00	300.00
	1865	—	20.00	30.00	50.00	80.00
	1866	—	200.00	400.00	650.00	1150.
	1867	—	200.00	400.00	650.00	1150.

25.0000 g, .900 SILVER, .7234 oz ASW
Obv: LUSTER F below truncation, globe and cross flank date.
Rev: Caduceus and scales flank denomination.

KM#	Date	Mintage	Fine	VF	XF	Unc
475	1868	—	20.00	30.00	80.00	200.00
	1869	—	15.00	20.00	50.00	150.00

25.5000 g, .917 SILVER, .7515 oz ASW

KM#	Date	Mintage	Fine	VF	XF	Unc
475a	1875	—	15.00	25.00	50.00	150.00
	1876	—	75.00	125.00	250.00	500.00

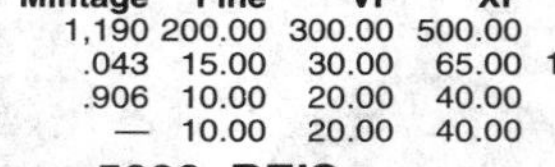

Obv: W/o LUSTER F. Rev. leg: DECRETO DE 1870.

KM#	Date	Mintage	Fine	VF	XF	Unc
485	1886	1,190	200.00	300.00	500.00	1150.
	1887	.043	15.00	30.00	65.00	125.00
	1888	.906	10.00	20.00	40.00	65.00
	1889	—	10.00	20.00	40.00	65.00

5000 REIS

4.4824 g, .917 GOLD, .1321 oz AGW

KM#	Date	Mintage	Fine	VF	XF	Unc
470	1854	.021	75.00	100.00	125.00	200.00
	1855	.047	90.00	120.00	150.00	250.00
	1856	.027	75.00	100.00	125.00	200.00
	1857	4,631	800.00	1200.	2000.	2500.
	1858	1,146	2000.	4000.	7000.	12,000.
	1859	493 pcs.	3000.	5000.	8000.	—

10,000 REIS

14.3400 g, .917 GOLD, .4228 oz AGW

KM#	Date	Mintage	Fine	VF	XF	Unc
451	1833	7,304	200.00	500.00	700.00	1000.
	1834	5,617	200.00	500.00	700.00	1000.
	1835	.013	200.00	500.00	700.00	1000.
	1836	.011	300.00	550.00	750.00	1150.
	1838	482 pcs.	650.00	1250.	2500.	4000.
	1839	567 pcs.	650.00	1250.	2500.	4000.
	1840	4,462	200.00	700.00	1450.	2200.

Obv: Military bust.

KM#	Date	Mintage	Fine	VF	XF	Unc
457	1841	3,454	700.00	1500.	3500.	7000.
	1842	1,146	700.00	1500.	3500.	7000.
	1843	544 pcs.	2000.	3500.	6500.	10,000.
	1844	1,989	700.00	1500.	3500.	7000.
	1845	3,834	700.00	1500.	3500.	7000.
	1847	.026	450.00	900.00	2000.	4000.
	1848	4,567	500.00	1000.	2500.	5000.

8.9648 g, .917 GOLD, .2643 oz AGW
Reduced size, 26mm.

KM#	Date	Mintage	Fine	VF	XF	Unc
460	1849	1,678	350.00	850.00	1250.	2200.
	1850	7,359	150.00	250.00	350.00	500.00
	1851	.011	150.00	250.00	350.00	500.00

KM#	Date	Mintage	Fine	VF	XF	Unc
467	1853	.040	BV	140.00	180.00	300.00
	1854	.163	BV	140.00	180.00	300.00
	1855	.041	BV	140.00	180.00	300.00
	1856	.208	BV	140.00	180.00	300.00
	1857	.098	BV	140.00	180.00	300.00
	1858	.055	BV	140.00	180.00	300.00
	1859	.016	400.00	1000.	2000.	3000.
	1861	—	BV	140.00	180.00	300.00
	1863	—	400.00	1000.	2000.	3000.
	1865	—	BV	140.00	180.00	300.00
	1866	—	BV	140.00	180.00	300.00
	1867	—	BV	140.00	180.00	300.00
	1871	—	BV	160.00	300.00	400.00
	1872	—	BV	160.00	300.00	400.00
	1873	—	BV	160.00	300.00	400.00
	1874	—	BV	160.00	300.00	400.00
	1875	—	BV	160.00	300.00	400.00
	1876	.020	BV	160.00	300.00	400.00
	1877	3,441	BV	200.00	320.00	420.00
	1878	.010	BV	150.00	320.00	420.00
	1879	6,431	BV	150.00	320.00	420.00
	1880	9,806	BV	200.00	350.00	500.00
	1882	4,671	BV	220.00	350.00	500.00
	1883	.010	BV	240.00	350.00	500.00
	1884	.011	BV	240.00	350.00	500.00
	1885	7,955	100.00	300.00	400.00	600.00
	1886	3,782	BV	300.00	400.00	600.00
	1887	1,180	150.00	450.00	700.00	1200.
	1888	5,359	BV	350.00	500.00	800.00
	1889	—	100.00	400.00	600.00	900.00

20,000 REIS

17.9296 g, .917 GOLD, .5286 oz AGW

KM#	Date	Mintage	Fine	VF	XF	Unc
461	1849	6,464	275.00	500.00	700.00	900.00
	1850	.042	240.00	300.00	450.00	650.00
	1851	.303	240.00	300.00	450.00	650.00

KM#	Date	Mintage	Fine	VF	XF	Unc
463	1851	Inc. Ab.	230.00	270.00	350.00	600.00
	1852	.186	230.00	270.00	350.00	600.00

Obv: Larger bust.

KM#	Date	Mintage	Fine	VF	XF	Unc
468	1853	.246	BV	260.00	300.00	550.00
	1854	.026	BV	320.00	450.00	650.00
	1855	.048	BV	260.00	300.00	550.00
	1856	.262	BV	260.00	300.00	550.00
	1857/6	.315	BV	260.00	300.00	550.00
	1857	Inc. Ab.	BV	260.00	300.00	550.00
	1858	.032	BV	260.00	300.00	550.00
	1859	.047	BV	260.00	300.00	550.00
	1860	—	BV	275.00	400.00	750.00
	1861	—	BV	275.00	400.00	750.00
	1862	—	—	—	*Rare	—
	1863	—	425.00	500.00	700.00	1000.
	1864	—	300.00	500.00	700.00	1000.
	1865	—	BV	275.00	400.00	700.00
	1867	—	BV	275.00	400.00	700.00
	1889	—	BV	275.00	400.00	700.00

***NOTE:** Spink America Norweb sale 3-97 VF realized $11,000.

REPUBLIC

20 REIS

BRONZE

KM#	Date	Mintage	Fine	VF	XF	Unc
490	1889	.630	1.00	5.00	10.00	20.00
	1893	.250	1.00	5.00	10.00	20.00
	1894	Inc. Ab.	1.00	5.00	10.00	25.00
	1895	2.118	1.00	2.00	5.00	10.00
	1896	.490	5.00	20.00	40.00	100.00
	1897	.273	1.00	5.00	10.00	20.00
	1898	.300	3.00	8.00	18.00	40.00
	1899	1.065	3.00	8.00	18.00	40.00
	1900	1.718	1.00	5.00	10.00	20.00

NOTE: Later dates (1901-1912) exist for this type.

40 REIS

BRONZE
Rev: FC above star.

KM#	Date	Mintage	Fine	VF	XF	Unc
491	1889	1.781	.50	1.00	2.00	15.00
	1893	1.085	1.50	3.00	5.00	22.50
	1894	.770	1.50	3.00	5.00	22.50
	1895	Inc. Ab.	2.00	3.50	6.00	25.00
	1896	.191	10.00	40.00	80.00	300.00
	1897	1.236	.75	2.00	3.50	17.50
	1898	.300	10.00	20.00	40.00	80.00
	1900	2.115	.75	2.50	4.50	20.00

NOTE: Later dates (1901-1912) exist for this type.

100 REIS

COPPER-NICKEL

KM#	Date	Mintage	Fine	VF	XF	Unc
492	1889	7.686	.75	3.00	8.50	30.00
	1893	3.589	1.00	3.00	8.50	30.00
	1894	1.881	1.00	3.00	8.50	30.00
	1895	2.308	1.00	3.00	8.50	30.00
	1896	3.390	1.00	3.00	8.50	30.00
	1897	2.875	3.00	6.50	12.00	40.00
	1898	3.685	3.00	6.50	12.00	40.00
	1899	2.990	3.00	6.50	12.00	40.00
	1900	.539	15.00	40.00	200.00	—

200 REIS

COPPER-NICKEL

KM#	Date	Mintage	Fine	VF	XF	Unc
493	1889	4.829	1.50	3.00	10.00	65.00
	1893	2.586	2.00	4.50	12.50	65.00
	1894	1.562	2.00	4.50	12.50	65.00
	1895	1.633	2.00	4.50	12.50	75.00
	1896	2.850	2.50	5.00	15.00	75.00
	1897	2.405	2.50	5.50	17.50	75.00
	1898	3.925	2.50	5.00	15.00	75.00
	1899	2.724	3.00	6.00	20.00	75.00
	1900	.330	15.00	50.00	220.00	—

400 REIS

5.1000 g, .917 SILVER, .1503 oz ASW
400th Anniversary of Discovery
Reeded edge.

KM#	Date	Mintage	Fine	VF	XF	Unc
499	1900	.055	10.00	25.00	40.00	80.00

500 REIS

6.3750 g, .917 SILVER, .1879 oz ASW
Obv: FC below bust. Reeded edge.

KM#	Date	Mintage	Fine	VF	XF	Unc
494	1889	4.541	3.50	12.50	25.00	45.00

1000 REIS

12.7500 g, .917 SILVER, .3758 oz ASW

KM#	Date	Mintage	Fine	VF	XF	Unc
495	1889	.296	12.00	20.00	40.00	80.00

400th Anniversary of Discovery

KM#	Date	Mintage	Fine	VF	XF	Unc
500	1900	.033	40.00	65.00	80.00	120.00

2000 REIS

25.5000 g, .917 SILVER, .7515 oz ASW

KM#	Date	Mintage	Fine	VF	XF	Unc
498	1891	.040	500.00	1200.	2500.	4000.
	1896	.010	500.00	1200.	2500.	4000.
	1897	.160	200.00	500.00	800.00	2000.

400th Anniversary of Discovery

KM#	Date	Mintage	Fine	VF	XF	Unc
501	1900	.020	60.00	100.00	200.00	300.00

4000 REIS

51.0000 g, .917 SILVER, 1.5030 oz ASW
400th Anniversary of Discovery
Obv: Star w/16 rays.

KM#	Date	Mintage	Fine	VF	XF	Unc
502.1	1900	6,850	125.00	300.00	500.00	700.00

Obv: Star w/20 rays.

KM#	Date	Mintage	Fine	VF	XF	Unc
502.2	1900	Inc. Ab.	125.00	300.00	500.00	700.00

10,000 REIS

8.9645 g, .917 GOLD, .2643 oz AGW

KM#	Date	Mintage	Fine	VF	XF	Unc
496	1889	7,302	150.00	250.00	600.00	1000.
	1892	2,289	—	—	Rare	—
	1893	—	150.00	250.00	600.00	1000.
	1895	306 pcs.	150.00	250.00	700.00	1100.
	1896	383 pcs.	—	—	Rare	—
	1897	421 pcs.	150.00	250.00	600.00	1000.
	1898	216 pcs.	250.00	500.00	1500.	2000.
	1899	238 pcs.	150.00	250.00	700.00	1100.

NOTE: Later dates (1901-1922) exist for this type.

20,000 REIS

17.9290 g, .917 GOLD, .5286 oz AGW

KM#	Date	Mintage	Fine	VF	XF	Unc
497	1889	.091	BV	300.00	550.00	1000.
	1892	7,738	—	—	Rare	—
	1893	4,303	BV	300.00	550.00	1000.
	1894	4,267	BV	300.00	550.00	1000.
	1895	4,811	BV	300.00	550.00	1000.
	1896	7,043	BV	300.00	550.00	1000.
	1897	.011	BV	300.00	550.00	1000.
	1898	.014	BV	300.00	550.00	1000.
	1899	9,558	BV	300.00	550.00	1000.
	1900	7,551	BV	300.00	550.00	1000.

NOTE: Later dates (1901-1922) exist for this type.

PATTERNS (Pn)

(Including off metal strikes)

KM#	Date	Mintage	Identification	Mkt.Val.
Pn8	1809	—	960 Reis, Silver	3000.
Pn9	1809M	—	960 Reis, Silver	2800.
Pn10	1809P	—	960 Reis, Silver	2800.
Pn11	1809	—	960 Reis, Silver Gilt	2000.

KM#	Date	Mintage	Identification	Mkt.Val.
Pn12	1809	—	960 Reis, Copper	1350.
Pn13	1809	—	960 Reis, Copper Gilt	1350.
Pn14	1809	—	960 Reis, Lead	600.00
Pn15	1810	—	960 Reis, Copper	1750.

KM#	Date	Mintage	Identification	Mkt.Val.
Pn16	1811	—	20 Reis, Copper, globe rev.	350.00
Pn17	1811	—	20 Reis, Copper, crowned arms rev.	350.00
Pn18	1818	—	4000 Reis, Copper	Unique
Pn19	1818	—	6400 Reis, Copper	Unique
Pn20	1822	—	6400 Reis, Copper	Rare
Pn21	1823	—	640 Reis, Silver	Rare
Pn22	1823	—	960 Reis, Nickel	—
Pn23	1823	—	4000 Reis, Copper	400.00
Pn24	1823	—	4000 Reis, Silver	800.00
Pn25	1823	—	6400 Reis, Silver	Rare
Pn26	1826	—	6400 Reis, Copper	Rare
Pn27	1827	—	40 Reis, Copper	250.00

KM#	Date	Mintage	Identification	Mkt.Val.
Pn28	1827	—	80 Reis, Copper	725.00
Pn29	1827	—	960 Reis, Nickel	1200.
Pn30	1827	—	6400 Reis, Copper	Rare

KM#	Date	Mintage	Identification	Mkt.Val.
Pn31	1828	—	6400 Reis, Copper, broad planchet	2350.

KM#	Date	Mintage	Identification	Mkt.Val.
Pn32	1830	—	40 Reis, Copper, crowned monogram	1450.

KM#	Date	Mintage	Identification	Mkt.Val.
Pn33	1830	—	40 Reis, Copper, crowned P	1500.
Pn34	1830	—	320 Reis, Silver	750.00
Pn35	1830	—	4000 Reis, Copper	500.00
Pn36	1830	—	6400 Reis, Copper	800.00
Pn37	1830	—	6400 Reis, Gold	Unique

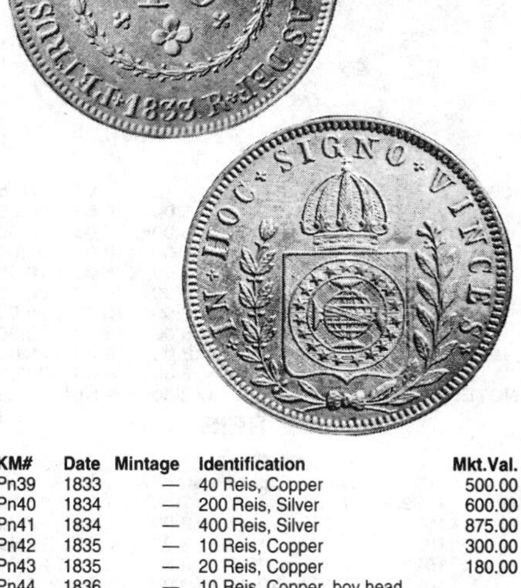

KM#	Date	Mintage	Identification	Mkt.Val.
Pn39	1833	—	40 Reis, Copper	500.00
Pn40	1834	—	200 Reis, Silver	600.00
Pn41	1834	—	400 Reis, Silver	875.00
Pn42	1835	—	10 Reis, Copper	300.00
Pn43	1835	—	20 Reis, Copper	180.00
Pn44	1836	—	10 Reis, Copper, boy head of Peter II	180.00
Pn45	1836	—	200 Reis, Silver	375.00
Pn46	1836	—	400 Reis, Silver	600.00
Pn47	1836	—	800 Reis, Silver	1500.
Pn48	1836	—	1200 Reis, Silver	900.00
Pn49	1837	—	400 Reis, Copper	300.00
Pn50	1838	—	10 Reis, Copper, boy head of Peter II	180.00

KM#	Date	Mintage	Identification	Mkt.Val.
Pn51	1838	—	10 Reis, Copper	175.00
Pn52	1838	—	20 Reis, Copper, boy head of Peter II	200.00

KM#	Date	Mintage	Identification	Mkt.Val.
Pn53	1838	—	20 Reis, Copper	225.00
Pn54	1838	—	200 Reis, Silver	375.00
Pn55	1838	—	1200 Reis, Silver	900.00
Pn56	1839	—	400 Reis, Bronze	450.00
Pn57	1839	—	400 Reis, Silver	600.00
Pn58	1840	—	10,000 Reis, Copper, monogram on rev.	400.00

KM#	Date	Mintage	Identification	Mkt.Val.
Pn59	1840	—	10,000 Reis, Silver, monogram on rev.	Rare
Pn60	1840	—	10,000 Reis, Gold, monogram on rev.	Rare

KM#	Date	Mintage	Identification	Mkt.Val.
Pn61	1840	—	10,000 Reis, Copper, arms on rev.	175.00
Pn62	1840	—	10,000 Reis, Silver, arms on rev.	Rare
Pn63	1840	—	10,000 Reis, Gold, arms on rev.	Rare
Pn64	1841	—	100 Reis, Silver	900.00
Pn65	1841	—	200 Reis, Silver	600.00
Pn66	1841	—	800 Reis, Silver	1500.

KM#	Date	Mintage	Identification	Mkt.Val.
Pn67	1841	—	1200 Reis, Silver	900.00
Pn68	1842	—	10 Reis, Copper	250.00
Pn69	1842	—	20 Reis, Copper	200.00
Pn70	1842	—	1200 Reis, Silver	900.00
Pn71	1844	—	1200 Reis, Silver	900.00
Pn72	1845	—	800 Reis, Silver	1500.
Pn73	1847	—	800 Reis, Silver	1500.
Pn74	1848	—	10 Reis	250.00
Pn75	1848	—	200 Reis, Copper	600.00
Pn76	1848	—	200 Reis, Copper	600.00
Pn77	1848	—	800 Reis, Silver	1500.
Pn78	1848	—	1200 Reis, Silver	900.00
Pn79	1849	—	100 Reis, Silver	750.00
Pn80	1849	—	200 Reis, Silver	600.00
Pn81	1849	—	400 Reis, Silver	900.00
Pn82	1849	—	1200 Reis, Silver	900.00
Pn83	1849	—	2000 Reis, Silver	1250.
Pn84	1850	—	2000 Reis, Silver	1250.
Pn85	1855	—	1000 Reis, Silver	350.00
Pn86	1855	—	20,000 Reis, Gold	2500.
Pn87	1859	—	2000 Reis	500.00

KM#	Date	Mintage	Identification	Mkt.Val.
Pn88	1860	—	20 Reis, Copper	165.00
Pn89	1860	—	1000 Reis, Copper	125.00

KM#	Date	Mintage	Identification	Mkt.Val.
Pn90	1861	—	20 Reis, Copper	150.00
Pn91	1861	—	200 Reis, Nickel-Silver	100.00

KM#	Date	Mintage	Identification	Mkt.Val.
Pn92	1862	—	20 Reis, Copper	100.00
Pn93	1862	—	40 Reis, Copper	100.00
Pn94	1862	—	40 Reis, Nickel	100.00
Pn95	1862	—	1000 Reis, Nickel	125.00
Pn96	1862	—	2000 Reis, Copper, 2$000 on rev.	600.00
Pn97	1862	—	2000 Reis, Copper 2,000 on rev.	600.00
Pn98	1862	—	2000 Reis, Silver 2$000 on rev.	1500.
Pn99	1862	—	2000 Reis, Silver 2000 on rev.	1500.
Pn100	1863	—	10 Reis, Copper	150.00
Pn101	1863	—	10 Reis, Copper w/o legend	150.00
Pn102	1863	—	10 Reis, Silver, w/raised border	165.00
Pn103	1863	—	10 Reis, Silver w/o raised border	165.00

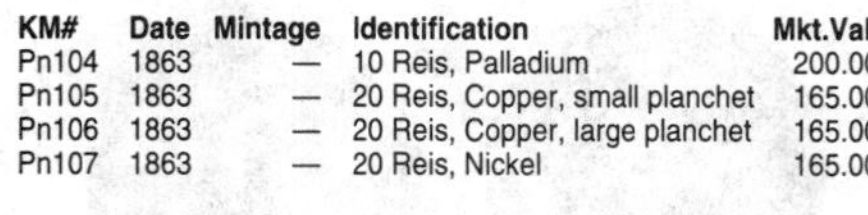

KM#	Date	Mintage	Identification	Mkt.Val.
Pn104	1863	—	10 Reis, Palladium	200.00
Pn105	1863	—	20 Reis, Copper, small planchet	165.00
Pn106	1863	—	20 Reis, Copper, large planchet	165.00
Pn107	1863	—	20 Reis, Nickel	165.00

KM#	Date	Mintage	Identification	Mkt.Val.
Pn108	1863	—	40 Reis, Copper, small date	165.00
Pn109	1863	—	40 Reis, Copper Gilt, large date	165.00
Pn110	1863	—	40 Reis, Nickel	140.00
Pn111	1863	—	2000 Reis, Copper 2$000 on rev.	1000.

KM#	Date	Mintage	Identification	Mkt.Val.
Pn112	1863	—	2000 Reis, Copper 2000 on rev.	1000.
Pn113	1863	—	2000 Reis, Silver 2$000 on rev.	2550.

KM#	Date	Mintage	Identification	Mkt.Val.
Pn114	1863	—	2000 Reis, Silver 2000 on rev.	2550.
Pn115	1864	—	10 Reis, Copper	80.00
Pn116	1864	—	10 Reis, Silver	80.00
Pn117	1864	—	10 Reis	80.00
Pn118	1864	—	20 Reis, Bronze	175.00
Pn119	1864	—	20 Reis, Silver	200.00
Pn120	1865	—	10 Reis, Silver	125.00
Pn121	1865	—	40 Reis, Copper	125.00
Pn122	1865	—	40 Reis, Nickel	125.00
Pn123	1865	—	40 Reis, Silver	150.00

KM#	Date	Mintage	Identification	Mkt.Val.
Pn124	1865	—	100 Reis, Copper	200.00
Pn125	1865	—	100 Reis, Nickel	225.00

KM#	Date	Mintage	Identification	Mkt.Val.
PnA126	1865	—	100 Reis, Silvered Copper	125.00
Pn126	1865	—	100 Reis, Silver	100.00
Pn127	1865	—	1000 Reis, Silver	300.00
Pn128	1866	—	10 Reis, Copper	200.00
Pn129	1866	—	40 Reis, Copper	275.00
Pn130	1867	—	500 Reis, Silver	400.00
Pn131	1867	—	1000 Reis, Silver	400.00

KM#	Date	Mintage	Identification	Mkt.Val.
Pn132	1867	—	20,000 Reis, Wood	400.00

KM#	Date	Mintage	Identification	Mkt.Val.
Pn133	1869	—	10 Reis, Nickel	125.00
Pn134	1869	—	10 Reis, Nickel Gilt	150.00

KM#	Date	Mintage	Identification	Mkt.Val.
Pn135	1869	—	20 Reis, Nickel	150.00
Pn136	1869	—	20 Reis, Nickel Gilt	150.00
Pn137	1869	—	1000 Reis, Copper	250.00
Pn138	1870	—	200 Reis, Silver	375.00
Pn139	1870	—	500 Reis, Silver	600.00
Pn140	1870	—	1000 Reis, Silver	600.00
Pn141	1870	—	2000 Reis, Wood	600.00
Pn142	1870	—	2000 Reis, Silver	800.00
Pn143	1871	—	50 Reis, Nickel	3500.
Pn144	1871	—	100 Reis, Copper	280.00
Pn145	1871	—	100 Reis, Bronze	150.00

KM#	Date	Mintage	Identification	Mkt.Val.
Pn146	1871	—	100 Reis, Nickel	280.00
Pn147	1871	—	200 Reis, Copper	200.00
Pn148	1872	—	10 Reis, Copper	500.00
Pn149	1872	—	100 Reis, Bronze	200.00
Pn150	1875	—	2000 Reis, Silver	1200.
Pn151	1876	—	100 Reis, Wood	325.00
Pn152	1876	—	500 Reis, Wood	350.00

KM#	Date	Mintage	Identification	Mkt.Val.
PnA153	1876	—	2000 Reis, Wood	375.00
Pn153	1881	—	100 Reis, Zinc	180.00
Pn154	1884	—	20 Reis, Silver	300.00
Pn155	1884	—	10,000 Reis, Wood	375.00
Pn156	1885	—	1000 Reis, Wood	375.00
Pn157	1886	—	50 Reis, Wood	300.00
Pn158	1886	—	100 Reis, Wood	300.00
Pn159	1886	—	100 Reis, Zinc	250.00

Pn160	1886	—	200 Reis, Wood	200.00
Pn161	1886	—	500 Reis, Wood	450.00
Pn162	1886	—	1000 Reis, Wood	600.00
Pn163	1886	—	2000 Reis, Wood	600.00

Pn164	1887	—	500 Reis, Wood	800.00

Pn165	1887	—	1000 Reis, Wood	500.00
Pn166	1887	—	2000 Reis, Wood	500.00

KM#	Date	Mintage	Identification	Mkt.Val.
Pn167	1888	—	100 Reis, Copper	280.00
Pn168	1888	—	100 Reis, Nickel	280.00
Pn169	1888	—	200 Reis	280.00
Pn170	1888	—	5000 Reis, Silver, small planchet	200.00

Pn171	1889	—	40 Reis, Copper, value in center on rev.	350.00

Pn172	1889	—	40 Reis, Copper, value at bottom on rev.	150.00
Pn173	1889	—	200 Reis, Nickel	150.00
Pn174	1891	—	2000 Reis, Copper	4500.
Pn175	1893	—	40 Reis, Nickel	250.00
Pn176	1893	—	40 Reis, Silver	350.00
Pn177	1899	—	200 Reis, Nickel	400.00

Pn178	1899	—	400 Reis, Nickel	400.00

TRIAL STRIKES (TS)

TS3	1831	—	6400 Reis, Copper, uniface, obv.	Rare

GOLD BARS

Cuiaba

c/s: "CUYABA" below crown in branches.

Known dates: 1821, 1822.

Goias

Illustration reduced. Actual size: 112x18mm.

c/m: GOIAS: in an incuse rectangle.

Known dates: 1801, 1813, 1814, 1817, 1819, 1820, 1821, 1822, 1823.

NOTE: Earlier date (1790) exists for this type.

Mato Grosso

Illustration reduced. Actual size: 83x17mm.

c/s: MATO GROSSO above crown in branches.

Known dates: 1811, 1812, 1813, 1815, 1816, 1817, 1818, 1819, 1820.

NOTE: Earlier dates (1784-1800) exist for this type.

Rio Das Mortes

Illustration reduced. Actual size: 64x16mm.

c/s: RIO DAS M. below crowned arms in branches.

Known dates: 1804, 1817, 1818.

NOTE: Earlier dates (1796-1800) exist for this type.

Sabara

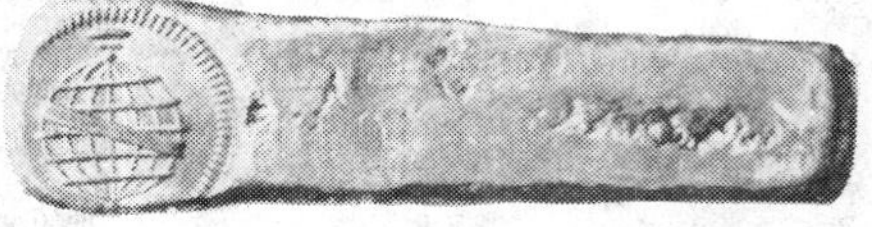

Illustration reduced. Actual size: Top - 78x20mm, Bottom - 66x13mm.

c/s: SABARA or V.DO SABARA below or V.DO-SAB above crowned arms.

Known dates: 1801, 1804, 1805, 1806, 1807, 1808, 1809, 1810, 1811, 1812, 1813, 1814, 1815, 1816, 1817, 1818, 1819, 1828, 1832, 1833.

NOTE: Earlier dates (1778-1796) exist for this type.

Serro Frio

Both illustrations reduced. Actual size: Top - 80x17mm, Bottom - 55x12mm.

c/s: "S.-F." above or "SERRO FRIO" below crowned arms and AAB monogram in beaded circle.

Known dates: 1809, 1810, 1811, 1812, 1813, 1814, 1816, 1818, 1820, 1829, 1830, 1831, 1832.

Vila Rica

Illustration reduced. Actual size: 107x17mm.
c/s: Crowned arms or crowned arms with V.-R. above and c/m: script VCR monogram.

Known dates: 1802, 1804, 1807, 1808, 1809, 1810, 1811, 1812, 1813, 1814, 1815, 1816, 1817, 1818, 1828.
NOTE: Earlier dates (1786-1799) exist for this type.

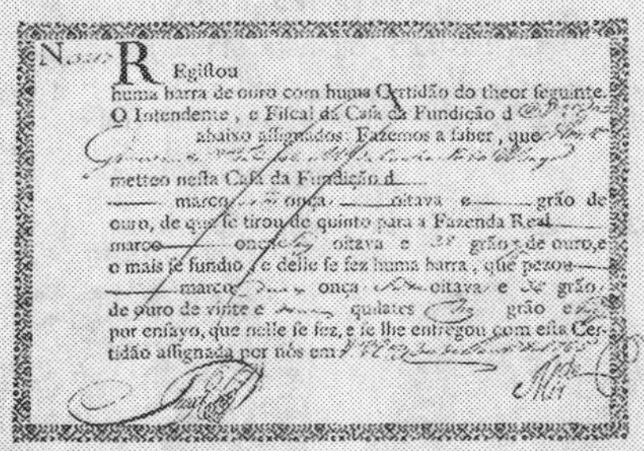

N.º R Egiſtou huma barra de ouro com huma Certidão do theor ſeguinte. O Intendente, e Fiſcal da Caſa da Fundição d abaixo aſſignados: Fazemos a ſaber, que metteo neſta Caſa da Fundição d marco onça oitava e grão de ouro, de que ſe tirou de quinto para a Fazenda Real marco onça oitava e grão, e de ouro, e mais ſe fundio, e delle ſe fez huma barra, que pezou marco onça oitava e grão de ouro de vinte e quilates grão e por enſayo, que nelle ſe fez, e ſe lhe entregou com eſta Certidão aſſignada por nós em

A receipt for a gold bar.

Listings For

BRITISH GUIANA: refer to Guyana

BRITISH HONDURAS: refer to Belize

BRITISH NORTH BORNEO: refer to Malaysia

BRITISH VIRGIN IS.

The Colony of the Virgin Islands, a British colony situated in the Caribbean Sea northeast of Puerto Rico and west of the Leeward Islands, has an area of 59 sq. mi. (155 sq. km.) and a population of 13,000. Capital: Road Town. The principal islands of the 36-island group are Tortola, Virgin Gorda, Anegada, and Jost Van Dyke. The chief industries are fishing and stock raising. Fish, livestock and bananas are exported.

The Virgin Islands were discovered by Columbus in 1493, and named by him, Las Virgienes, in honor of St. Ursula and her companions. The British Virgin Islands were formerly part of the administration of the Leeward Islands but received a separate administration as a Crown Colony in 1950. A new constitution promulgated in 1967 provided for a ministerial form of government headed by the Governor.

The Government of the British Virgin Islands issued the first official coinage in its history on June 30, 1973, in honor of 300 years of constitutional government in the islands. U.S. coins and currency continue to be the primary medium of exchange, though the coinage of the British Virgin Islands is legal tender.

TORTOLA

Tortola, which has an area of about 24 sq. mi. (62 sq. km.), is the largest of thirty-six islands which comprise the British Virgin Islands. It was settled by the Dutch in 1648 and was occupied by the British in 1666. They have held it ever since.

MONETARY SYSTEM
8 Shillings, 3 Pence = 11 Bits = 8 Reales

COUNTERMARKED COINAGE

Tortola

Type I: TORTOLA in odd shaped rectangle.

NOTE: Market valuations listed for "TORTOLA" c/m issues are just for the "TORTOLA" c/m and do not take into consideration any other c/m that may be encountered on the same piece.

1-1/2 PENCE

Black Dog

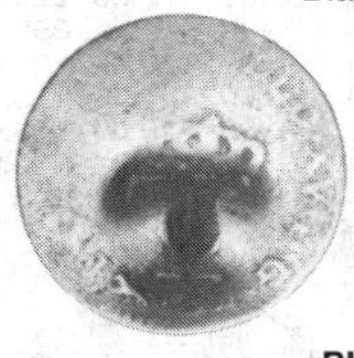

BILLON
c/m: Incuse 'T' on French and French Guiana, Colony of Cayenne 2 Sous.

KM#	Date	Year	Good	VG	Fine	VF
3	ND	(1801)	22.50	40.00	70.00	125.00

9 PENCE or 1 BIT

SILVER
c/m: Type I on 1/2 cut of Spanish or Spanish Colonial 2 Reales.

KM#	Date	Year	Good	VG	Fine	VF
4	ND	(1801)	40.00	90.00	180.00	250.00

SHILLING

SILVER
c/m: Type I on 1/8 cut of Spanish or Spanish Colonial 8 Reales.

KM#	Date	Year	Good	VG	Fine	VF
5	ND	(1801)	70.00	125.00	200.00	275.00

2 SHILLINGS

SILVER
c/m: Type I on 1/4 cut of Spanish or Spanish Colonial 8 Reales.

KM#	Date	Year	Good	VG	Fine	VF
6	ND	(1801)	75.00	150.00	250.00	300.00

4 SHILLINGS, 1-1/2 PENCE

SILVER
c/m: Type I on 1/2 cut of Spanish or Spanish Colonial 8 Reales.

KM#	Date	Year	Good	VG	Fine	VF
7	ND	(1801)	100.00	200.00	350.00	700.00

Type II: TORTOLA in rectangle

SHILLING

SILVER
c/m: Type II on 1/8 cut of Spanish or Spanish Colonial 8 Reales.

KM#	Date	Year	Good	VG	Fine	VF
8	ND	(1801-05)	100.00	200.00	320.00	450.00

2 SHILLINGS

SILVER
c/m: Type II on 1/4 cut of Spanish or Spanish Colonial 8 Reales.

KM#	Date	Year	Good	VG	Fine	VF
9	ND	(1801-05)	40.00	80.00	150.00	275.00

4 SHILLINGS, 1-1/2 PENCE

SILVER
c/m: Type II on 1/2 cut of Spanish or Spanish Colonial 8 Reales.

KM#	Date	Year	Good	VG	Fine	VF
10	ND	(1801-05)	50.00	100.00	200.00	370.00

PRIVATE COUNTERMARKED ISSUES

Hodge Plantation

"Black Dog"

c/m: Small 3mm incuse 'H' in square indent on French and French Guiana, Colony of Cayenne 2 Sous.

KM#	Date	Year	VG	Fine	VF	XF
11	ND	(1792-1811)	12.50	25.00	40.00	75.00

c/m: Large 5mm incuse 'H' in square indent on French and French Guiana, Colony of Cayenne 2 Sous.

KM#	Date	Year	Good	VG	Fine	VF
12	ND	(1792-1811)	12.00	22.50	37.50	70.00

Tirtila

Type III: TIRTILA

Type IV: TIRTILA w/inverted V for A.

NOTE: Market valuations listed for TIRTOLA c/m issues are just for the TIRTOLA c/m and do not take into consideration any other c/m that may be encountered on the same piece. Multiple c/m issues tend to have a higher market value.

9 PENCE or 1 BIT

SILVER
c/m: Type III on 1/2 cut of Spanish or Spanish Colonial 2 Reales.

KM#	Date	Year	Good	VG	Fine	VF
13	ND	(1805-24)	125.00	185.00	280.00	450.00

c/m: Type IV on 1/2 cut of Spanish or Spanish Colonial 2 Reales.

KM#	Date	Year	Good	VG	Fine	VF
14	ND	(1805-24)	150.00	225.00	350.00	560.00

SHILLING

SILVER
c/m: Type III on 1/8 cut of Spanish or Spanish Colonial 8 Reales.

KM#	Date	Year	Good	VG	Fine	VF
15	ND	(1805-24)	125.00	185.00	280.00	450.00

c/m: Type IV on 1/8 cut of Spanish or Spanish Colonial 8 Reales.

KM#	Date	Year	Good	VG	Fine	VF
16	ND	(1805-24)	125.00	185.00	280.00	450.00

2 SHILLINGS

SILVER
c/m: Type III on 1/4 cut of Spanish or Spanish Colonial 8 Reales.

KM#	Date	Year	Good	VG	Fine	VF
17	ND	(1805-24)	85.00	120.00	190.00	300.00

c/m: Type IV on 1/4 cut of Spanish or Spanish Colonial 8 Reales.

KM#	Date	Year	Good	VG	Fine	VF
18	ND	(1805-24)	85.00	120.00	190.00	300.00

4 SHILLINGS, 1-1/2 PENCE

SILVER
c/m: Type III on 1/2 cut of Spanish or Spanish Colonial 8 Reales.

KM#	Date	Year	Good	VG	Fine	VF
19	ND	(1805-24)	125.00	175.00	250.00	400.00

c/m: Type IV on 1/2 cut of Spanish or Spanish Colonial 8 Reales.

KM#	Date	Year	Good	VG	Fine	VF
20	ND	(1805-24)	125.00	175.00	250.00	400.00

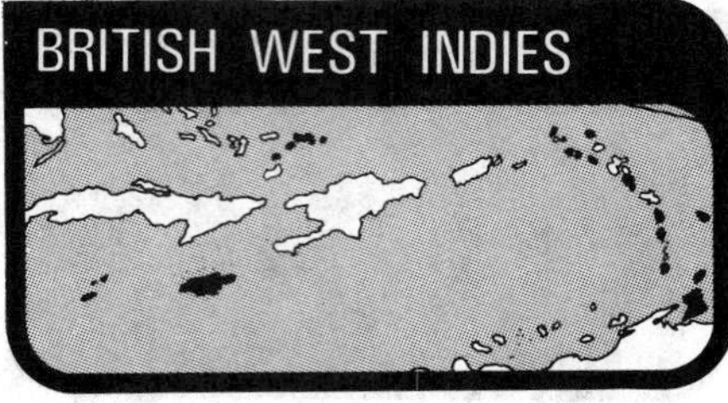

The 'Anchor Coins' catalogued under this heading do not bear a particular place identification. They were issued for use in various British colonies in both the New World and the Orient. Coins of this type dated 1820 are traditionally assigned to Mauritius and other holdings in the Indian Ocean. Those of 1822 were initially struck for Mauritius but after the introduction of sterling as the denomination of public accounts in Mauritius, they found their widest circulation in Canada and colonies in the Caribbean Sea. In Jamaica they were limited to military transactions only. In the Leeward Islands they were used on all the islands except the Virgin Islands, Windward Islands, Barbados, Tobago and Trinidad.

RULERS

British

ANCHOR COINAGE

1/16 DOLLAR

.892 SILVER

KM#	Date	Mintage	Fine	VF	XF	Unc
1	1820	.162	12.50	30.00	60.00	165.00
	1820	—	—	—	Proof	350.00
	1822/1	.142	15.00	35.00	65.00	185.00
	1822	Inc. Ab.	7.50	15.00	30.00	125.00
	1822	—	—	—	Proof	350.00

1/8 DOLLAR

.892 SILVER

KM#	Date	Mintage	Fine	VF	XF	Unc
2	1820	.120	15.00	35.00	75.00	225.00
	1820	—	—	—	Proof	350.00
	1822/0	.142	12.50	30.00	60.00	200.00
	1822/1	Inc. Ab.	10.00	20.00	45.00	175.00
	1822	Inc. Ab.	7.50	18.00	40.00	165.00
	1822	—	—	—	Proof	350.00

1/4 DOLLAR

.892 SILVER

KM#	Date	Mintage	Fine	VF	XF	Unc
3	1820	.100	30.00	50.00	100.00	275.00
	1820	—	—	—	Proof	400.00
	1822/1	.071	10.00	20.00	45.00	225.00
	1822	Inc. Ab.	7.50	18.00	40.00	200.00
	1822	—	—	—	Proof	400.00

1/2 DOLLAR

.892 SILVER

KM#	Date	Mintage	Fine	VF	XF	Unc
4	1821	—	—	—	Proof	Unique
	1822/1	.089	100.00	200.00	500.00	750.00
	1822	Inc. Ab.	85.00	175.00	300.00	600.00
	1822	—	—	—	Proof	800.00

PATTERNS (Pn)

(Including off metal strikes)

KM#	Date	Mintage	Identification	Mkt.Val.
Pn1	1820	—	1/16 Dollar, Silver, as KM1 but George III in legend, 17-18mm	Rare
Pn2	1820	—	1/8 Dollar, Silver, as KM2 but George III in legend, 21-22mm	Rare
Pn3	1820	—	1/4 Dollar, Silver, as KM3 but George III in legend, 27-28mm	Rare

KM#	Date	Mintage	Identification	Mkt.Val.
Pn4	1823	—	1/100 Dollar, Copper	1850.

KM#	Date	Mintage	Identification	Mkt.Val.
Pn5	1823	—	1/50 Dollar, Copper	2350.

NOTE: KM#Pn4 and Pn5 were intended for Sierra Leone and other colonies. Records show that 5 tons were struck but were remelted in 1825. Restrikes with Hibernia 1823 were reportedly produced by the Royal Mint ca. 1890.

BRUNEI

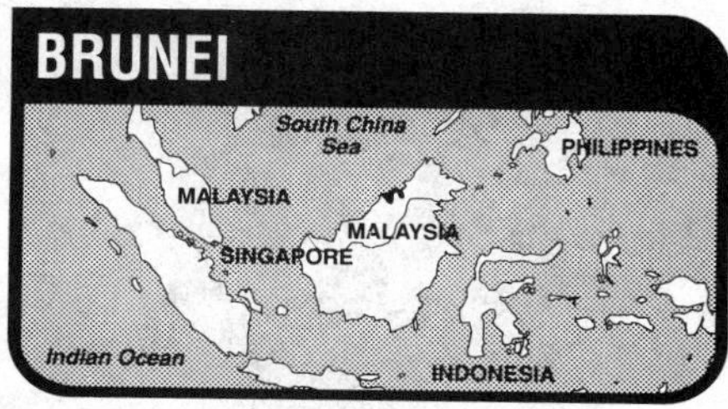

Negara Brunei Darussalam (State of Brunei), an independent sultanate on the northwest coast of the island of Borneo, has an area of 2,226 sq. mi. (5,765 sq. km.) and a population of 292,266. Capital: Bandar Seri Begawan. Crude oil and rubber are exported.

Magellan was the first European to visit Brunei in 1521. It was a powerful state, ruling over northern Borneo and adjacent islands from the 16th to the 19th century. Brunei became a British protectorate in 1888 and a British dependency in 1905. The Constitution of 1959 restored control over internal affairs to the sultan, while delegating responsibility for defense and foreign affairs to Britain. On January 1, 1984 it became independent.

TITLES

Negri Brunei

RULERS

Sultan Muhammad Tajuddin, 1795-1804
Sultan Muhammad Jamalul Alam I, 1804
Sultan Muhammad Tajuddin, 1804-1807
Sultan Muhammad Kanzul Alam, 1807-1826
Sultan Muhammad Alam, 1826-1828
Sultan Omar Ali Saifuddin II, 1828-1852
Sultan Abdul Mumin, 1852-1885
Sultan Hashim Jelal, 1885-1906

MONETARY SYSTEM

100 Cents = 1 Straits Dollar
100 Sen = 1 Dollar

1/2 PITIS

TIN, 24mm

KM#	Date	Mintage	Good	VG	Fine	VF
1	AH1285	—	20.00	30.00	50.00	90.00

PITIS

TIN
Obv: Flag at top to right.

KM#	Date	Mintage	Good	VG	Fine	VF
2.1	AH1285	—	15.00	25.00	40.00	65.00

Obv: Flag at top to left.

KM#	Date	Mintage	Good	VG	Fine	VF
2.2	AH1285	—	15.00	25.00	40.00	65.00

CENT

COPPER

KM#	Date	Mintage	Fine	VF	XF	Unc
3	AH1304	1.000	8.00	16.00	45.00	125.00
	1304	—	—	—	Proof	450.00

BULGARIA

The Republic of Bulgaria, formerly the Peoples Republic of Bulgaria, a Balkan country on the Black Sea in southeastern Europe, has an area of 42,855 sq. mi. (110,910 sq. km.) and a population of 8.8 million. Capital: Sofia. Agriculture remains a key component of the economy but industrialization, particularly heavy industry, has been emphasized since the late 1940s. Machinery, tobacco and cigarettes, wines and spirits, clothing and metals are the chief exports.

The area now occupied by Bulgaria was conquered by the Bulgars, an Asiatic tribe, in the 7th century. Bulgarian kingdoms continued to exist on the Bulgarian peninsula until it came under Turkish rule in 1395. In 1878, after nearly 500 years of Turkish rule, Bulgaria was made a principality under Turkish suzerainty. Union seven years later with Eastern Rumelia created a Balkan state with borders approximating those of present-day Bulgaria. A Bulgarian kingdom, fully independent of Turkey, was proclaimed Sept. 22, 1908. During WWI Bulgaria had been aligned with Germany. After the Armistice certain land concessions were given to Greece and Romania. In 1934 King Boris III suspended all political parties and established a dictatorial monarchy. In 1938 the military began rearming through the aide of the Anglo-French loan. As WW II developed, Bulgaria again supported the Germans but protected their Jewish community. Boris died mysteriously in 1943 and Simeon II became King at the age of six. The country was then ruled by a pro-Nazi regency until it was liberated by Soviet forces in 1944.

The monarchy was abolished and Simeon was ousted by plebiscite in 1946 and Bulgaria became a Peoples Republic on the Soviet pattern. After democratic reforms in 1989 the name was changed to the Republic of Bulgaria.

RULERS

Alexander I, as Prince, 1879-1886
Ferdinand I, as Prince, 1887-1908

MINT MARKS

KB - Kormoczbanya

MONETARY SYSTEM

100 Stotinki = 1 Lev

2 STOTINKI

BRONZE
Rev: HEATON below wreath.

KM#	Date	Mintage	Fine	VF	XF	Unc
1	1881	5.000	3.00	6.00	12.00	35.00
	1881	—	—	—	Proof	90.00

2-1/2 STOTINKI

COPPER-NICKEL

KM#	Date	Mintage	Fine	VF	XF	Unc
8	1888	11.647	2.00	6.00	12.00	35.00
	1888	—	—	—	Proof	85.00

5 STOTINKI

BRONZE
Rev: HEATON below ribbon bow.

KM#	Date	Mintage	Fine	VF	XF	Unc
2	1881	10.000	2.00	5.00	12.00	40.00
	1881	—	—	—	Proof	120.00

COPPER-NICKEL

KM#	Date	Mintage	Fine	VF	XF	Unc
9	1888	14.000	1.00	2.50	9.00	25.00
	1888	—	—	—	Proof	70.00

10 STOTINKI

BRONZE
Rev: HEATON below ribbon bow.

KM#	Date	Mintage	Fine	VF	XF	Unc
3	1881	15.000	1.50	3.50	7.00	35.00
	1881	—	—	—	Proof	80.00

COPPER-NICKEL

KM#	Date	Mintage	Fine	VF	XF	Unc
10	1888	10.000	1.00	2.50	8.50	20.00

20 STOTINKI

COPPER-NICKEL

KM#	Date	Mintage	Fine	VF	XF	Unc
11	1888	5.000	2.00	6.00	14.00	30.00
	1888	—	—	—	Proof	80.00

50 STOTINKI

2.5000 g, .835 SILVER, .0671 oz ASW

KM#	Date	Mintage	Fine	VF	XF	Unc
6	1883	3.000	1.50	2.50	6.00	20.00

KM#	Date	Mintage	Fine	VF	XF	Unc
12	1891KB	2.000	1.50	2.50	8.00	25.00

LEV

5.0000 g, .835 SILVER, .1342 oz ASW

KM#	Date	Mintage	Fine	VF	XF	Unc
4	1882	4.500	2.00	5.00	12.00	30.00

KM#	Date	Mintage	Fine	VF	XF	Unc
13	1891KB	4.000	2.00	6.00	15.00	35.00

KM#	Date	Mintage	Fine	VF	XF	Unc
16	1894KB	1.000	2.50	7.00	18.00	40.00

2 LEVA

10.0000 g, .835 SILVER, .2685 oz ASW

KM#	Date	Mintage	Fine	VF	XF	Unc
5	1882	2.000	3.00	7.00	16.00	50.00

KM#	Date	Mintage	Fine	VF	XF	Unc
14	1891KB	1.500	3.00	7.50	18.00	55.00

KM#	Date	Mintage	Fine	VF	XF	Unc
17	1894KB	1.000	3.50	9.00	20.00	60.00
	1894KB	—	—	—	Proof	320.00

5 LEVA

25.0000 g, .900 SILVER, .7234 oz ASW

KM#	Date	Mintage	Fine	VF	XF	Unc
7	1884	.512	10.00	20.00	55.00	165.00
	1885	1.426	8.00	14.00	45.00	135.00

KM#	Date	Mintage	Fine	VF	XF	Unc
15	1892KB	1.001	8.00	12.50	28.00	125.00
	1892KB	—	—	—	Proof	1200.

Obv. leg. rearranged.

KM#	Date	Mintage	Fine	VF	XF	Unc
18	1894KB	1.800	6.00	12.00	25.00	115.00
	1894KB	—	—	—	Proof	1200.

10 LEVA

3.2258 g, .900 GOLD, .0933 oz AGW

KM#	Date	Mintage	Fine	VF	XF	Unc
19	1894KB	.075	45.00	70.00	115.00	245.00
	1894KB	—	—	—	Proof	2000.

20 LEVA

6.4516 g, .900 GOLD, .1867 oz AGW

KM#	Date	Mintage	Fine	VF	XF	Unc
20	1894KB	.100	80.00	100.00	160.00	325.00
	1894KB	—	—	—	Proof	4500.

100 LEVA

32.2580 g, .900 GOLD, .9334 oz AGW

KM#	Date	Mintage	Fine	VF	XF	Unc
21	1894KB	2,500	450.00	650.00	1150.	2350.

KINGDOM
ESSAIS (E)

KM#	Date	Mintage	Identification	Mkt.Val.
E1	1880 O.M.	—	10 Santim, Copper	175.00

KM#	Date	Mintage	Identification	Mkt.Val.
E3	1887 A.B.	—	10 Santim, Copper	200.00
E4	1887 A.D.	—	10 Stotinki, Copper	—

PATTERNS (Pn)

(Including off metal strikes)

KM#	Date	Mintage	Identification	Mkt.Val.
Pn1	1887 A.B.	8	10 Santim, Copper	—
Pn2	1887 A.D.	—	10 Stotinki, Copper	—
PnA3	1888	—	10 Stotinki, Nickel-Alloy, plain edge	—
		—	thick planchet	—
Pn3	1889	—	10 Stotinki, Copper, broad flan	—

PIEFORTS (P)

KM#	Date	Mintage	Identification	Mkt.Val.
P1	1888	—	5 Stotinki, Nickel alloy	—
P2	1888	—	10 Stotinki, Nickel alloy	—

Listings For

BURMA: refer to Myanmar

CAMBODIA

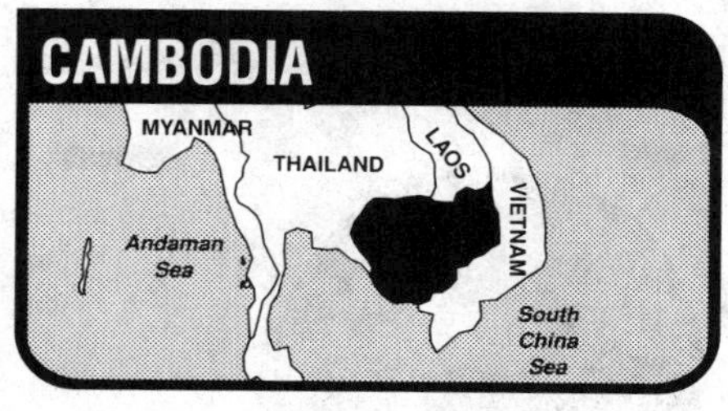

The State of Cambodia, formerly Democratic Kampuchea and the Khmer Republic, a land of paddy fields and forest-clad hills located on the Indo-Chinese peninsula, fronting on the Gulf of Thailand, has an area of 70,238 sq. mi. (181,040 sq. km.) and a population of 10.6 million. Capital: Phnom Penh. Agriculture is the basis of the economy, with rice the chief crop. Native industries include cattle breeding, weaving and rice milling. Rubber, cattle, corn, and timber are exported.

The region was the nucleus of the Khmer empire which flourished from the 5th to the 12th century and attained an excellence in art and architecture still evident in the magnificent ruins at Angkor. The Khmer empire once ruled over much of Southeast Asia, but began to decline in the 13th century as the Thai and Vietnamese invaded the region and attached its territories. At the request of the Cambodian king, a French protectorate attached to Cochin-China was established over the country in 1863, saving it from dissolution, and in 1885, Cambodia was included in the French Union of Indo-China.

RULERS

Kings of Cambodia

Norodom I, 1835-1904

MONETARY SYSTEM

(Until 1860)

2 Att = 1 Pe (Pey)
4 Pe = 1 Fuang (Fuong)
8 Fuang = 1 Tical
4 Salong = 1 Tical

(Commencing 1860)

100 Centimes = 1 Franc

KINGDOM
ATT

COPPER, 1.40-2.50 g, uniface
Similar to 1 Pe, KM#2.

KM#	Date	Year	VG	Fine	VF	XF
1.1	CS1208	(1847)	4.00	6.50	12.00	25.00

KM#	Date	Year	VG	Fine	VF	XF
1.2	CS1208	(1847)	—	—	—	—

PE

COPPER, 4.00-4.60 g, uniface
W/or w/o silver wash

KM#	Date	Year	VG	Fine	VF	XF
2	CS1208	(1847)	9.00	15.00	27.50	55.00

COPPER or BILLON 0.20-0.90 g, uniface

KM#	Date	VG	Fine	VF	XF
3	ND	6.00	8.50	12.50	27.50

Cocoa bean.

KM#	Date	VG	Fine	VF	XF
4	ND	6.00	9.00	15.00	30.00

Crab

KM#	Date	VG	Fine	VF	XF
5	ND	9.00	15.00	27.50	50.00

2 PE
(1/2 Fuang)

COPPER or BILLON 1.00-2.00 g, uniface
Rooster left.

KM#	Date	Year	VG	Fine	VF	XF
7	ND		3.00	4.50	8.00	20.00

Peacock

KM#	Date	VG	Fine	VF	XF
9	ND	5.00	8.00	15.00	35.00

'Chi' above bird.

KM#	Date	VG	Fine	VF	XF
11	ND	3.00	6.00	10.00	15.00

NOTE: Some specimens show light silver wash.

Cobra

KM#	Date	VG	Fine	VF	XF
13	ND	4.00	7.00	12.00	22.50

Pond Lily

KM#	Date	VG	Fine	VF	XF
14	ND	4.00	7.00	12.00	22.50

Goat

KM#	Date	VG	Fine	VF	XF
15	ND	5.50	8.00	12.50	27.50

Horse

KM#	Date	VG	Fine	VF	XF
17	ND	5.50	8.00	12.50	27.50

Uniface
Similar to 1 Pe, KM#5.

KM#	Date	VG	Fine	VF	XF
19	ND	10.00	15.00	27.50	55.00

Chinze

KM#	Date	VG	Fine	VF	XF
21	ND	10.00	15.00	27.50	55.00

Elephant

KM#	Date	VG	Fine	VF	XF
23	ND	10.00	15.00	27.50	55.00

Garuda bird.
Rev: Leg. in Cambodian script. Hand struck.

KM#	Date	VG	Fine	VF	XF
25	ND	5.00	8.00	15.00	35.00

Obv: Similar to KM#25 but w/o border around Garuda bird. Machine struck.

KM#	Date	VG	Fine	VF	XF
26	ND	3.00	6.00	10.00	15.00

SILVER, 1.85 g, 14.5mm
Uniface

Similar to KM25, but w/o snake in hand.

KM#	Date	Year	VG	Fine	VF	XF
28	ND	—	—	—	—	300.00

BRASS or COPPER, 23mm
Obv: Similar to KM26, but 3 line legend on rev.

KM#	Date	Year	VG	Fine	VF	XF
30	ND		50.00	100.00	125.00	175.00

FUANG

SILVER or BILLON, 2.70-3.00 g, uniface

KM#	Date	VG	Fine	VF	XF
27	ND	4.00	6.50	12.00	25.00

Uniface
Hippogriff walking to right.
Similar to 2 Pe, KM#21.

KM#	Date	VG	Fine	VF	XF
29	ND	10.00	15.00	27.50	55.00

NOTE: KM#'s 1 through 29 above were struck between 1650 and 1850. All are believed to have been struck at Battambang except KM#25 which is thought to have been made at Siem Reap.

1/8 TICAL

(1 Fuang)

COPPER, SILVER or
BILLON, 1.50-1.75 g, 11-16mm
Uniface, w/Hamza Bird

KM#	Date	Year	VG	Fine	VF	XF
32.1	ND	(1847)	4.50	7.00	12.50	27.50

W/o small circle at left.

KM#	Date	Year	VG	Fine	VF	XF
32.2	ND	(1847)	—	—	—	—

NOTE: Varieties exist.

SILVER, 14mm
Machine struck

KM#	Date	Year	Fine	VF	XF	Unc
33	ND	(1847)	85.00	125.00	225.00	350.00

NOTE: Modern counterfeits exist in copper, silver and gold.

1/4 TICAL

(1 Salong)

SILVER, 3.20 g, 20mm

KM#	Date	Year	Fine	VF	XF	Unc
34	CS1208	(1847)	200.00	350.00	550.00	800.00

3.60 g, 22mm

KM#	Date	Year	Fine	VF	XF	Unc
35	CS1208	(1847)	150.00	250.00	400.00	550.00

KM#	Date	Year	Fine	VF	XF	Unc
39	CS1209	(1848)	—	—	—	—

TICAL

SILVER, 15.258 g, 30mm, thick flan

KM#	Date	Year	Fine	VF	XF	Unc
36	CS1208	(1847)	50.00	100.00	200.00	500.00

14.209 g, 35mm, thin flan

KM#	Date	Year	Fine	VF	XF	Unc
37	CS1208	(1847)	35.00	75.00	150.00	350.00

NOTE: Various local merchant c/m's in Chinese or other scripts are known to exist for KM36-37.

4 TICAL

SILVER, 60.50 g

KM#	Date	Year	Fine	VF	XF	Unc
38	CS1209	(1848)	—	—	Rare	—

MILLED COINAGE

The 1860 dated coins were struck in Belgium in 1875, engraved by C. Wurden whose name appears below the bust.

RESTRIKES

In 1899 after the death of the Queen Mother of Cambodia, all of the 1860 series coins except the 1 Piastre, were restruck with the original dies. These dies were rusty and dirty from long storage and these restrike coins have a grainy appearance to them.

CINQ (5) CENTIMES

BRONZE

KM#	Date	Mintage	Fine	VF	XF	Unc
42.1	1860	11.467	5.00	12.00	35.00	75.00
	1860	—	—	—	Proof	90.00
42.2	1860	(restrike)	—	10.00	30.00	65.00

DIX (10) CENTIMES

BRONZE

KM#	Date	Mintage	Fine	VF	XF	Unc
43.1	1860	10.267	6.00	15.00	40.00	90.00
	1860	—	—	—	Proof	175.00
43.2	1860	(restrike)	—	12.00	35.00	75.00

Local manufacture. Rev: W/error CENTINES

KM#	Date	Mintage	Fine	VF	XF	Unc
43.3	1860	—	15.00	40.00	75.00	150.00

25 CENTIMES

1.2500 g, .900 SILVER, .0361 oz ASW

KM#	Date	Mintage	Fine	VF	XF	Unc
44.1	1860	—	10.00	30.00	100.00	250.00
	1860	—	—	—	Proof	500.00

Reduced weight

KM#	Date	Mintage	Fine	VF	XF	Unc
44.2	1860	(restrike)	—	15.00	30.00	75.00

50 CENTIMES

2.5000 g, .900 SILVER, .0723 oz ASW

KM#	Date	Mintage	Fine	VF	XF	Unc
45.1	1860	—	20.00	60.00	125.00	300.00
	1860	—	—	—	Proof	600.00

Reduced weight, 1.70 g

KM#	Date	Mintage	Fine	VF	XF	Unc
45.2	1860	(restrike)	—	20.00	40.00	100.00

UN (1) FRANC

5.0000 g, .900 SILVER, .1446 oz ASW

KM#	Date	Mintage	Fine	VF	XF	Unc
46.1	1860	—	25.00	70.00	175.00	400.00
	1860	—	—	—	Proof	700.00

Reduced weight, 3.50 g

KM#	Date	Mintage	Fine	VF	XF	Unc
46.2	1860	(restrike)	—	35.00	60.00	125.00

DEUX (2) FRANCS

10.0000 g, .900 SILVER, .2893 oz ASW

KM#	Date	Mintage	Fine	VF	XF	Unc
47.1	1860	—	45.00	125.00	250.00	500.00
	1860	—	—	—	Proof	850.00

Reduced weight, 8.00 g

KM#	Date	Mintage	Fine	VF	XF	Unc
47.2	1860	(restrike)	—	45.00	75.00	225.00

QUATRE (4) FRANCS

20.0000 g, .900 SILVER, .5786 oz ASW

KM#	Date	Mintage	Fine	VF	XF	Unc
48.1	1860	—	75.00	200.00	350.00	650.00
	1860	—	—	—	Proof	1600.

Reduced weight, 15.60 g

KM#	Date	Mintage	Fine	VF	XF	Unc
48.2	1860	(restrike)	—	60.00	120.00	350.00

PIASTRE/PESO/YUAN/5 FRANCS

27.0000 g, .900 SILVER, .7812 oz ASW

KM#	Date	Mintage	Fine	VF	XF	Unc
49	1860	—	300.00	600.00	1250.	2600.
	1860	—	—	—	Proof	3200.

ESSAIS (E)

KM#	Date	Mintage	Identification	Issue Price	Mkt. Val.
E1	1860	—	5 Centimes, large bust, E left of truncation	—	125.00
E2	1860	—	10 Centimes, small bust, ESSAI below truncation	—	150.00
E2a	1860	—	10 Centimes, Silver	—	250.00
EA3 (E2b)	1860	—	10 Centimes, large bust, E left of truncation	—	125.00
E3	1860	—	25 Centimes	—	200.00
E4	1860	—	50 Centimes	—	250.00
E5	1860	—	1 Franc	—	350.00
E6	1860	—	2 Francs	—	450.00
E7	1860	—	4 Francs, w/E	—	1000.
E8	1860	—	1 Piastre	—	5000.

PATTERNS (Pn)

(Including off metal strikes)

KM#	Date	Mintage	Identification	Mkt.Val.
Pn1	CS1208(1846)	—	3 Ticals, white metal	5000.
Pn2	CS1208(1846)	—	3 Ticals, white metal	5000.
Pn3	1860	—	5 Centimes, Gold, KM42	—

KM#	Date	Mintage	Identification	Mkt.Val.
Pn4	1860	—	(10 Centimes), Gold, plain edge	Rare
Pn5	1860	—	10 Centimes, Gold, KM43	—
Pn6	1860	—	25 Centimes, Gold, KM44	—
Pn7	1860	—	50 Centimes, Gold, KM45	—
Pn8	1860	—	1 Franc, Gold, KM46	—
Pn9	1860	—	2 Francs, Gold, KM47	—
Pn10	1860	—	4 Francs, Gold, KM48	2250.
Pn11	1860	—	1 Piastre, Gold, KM49	—
Pn12	1860	—	1 Piastre, Silvered white metal, KM49	1000.
Pn13	1860	—	1 Piastre, Copper, reeded edge, KM49	650.00
Pn14	1860	—	1 Piastre, Copper, plain edge, KM49	650.00

PIEFORTS (P)

(Double thickness)

Standard metals etc.

KM#	Date	Mintage	Identification	Issue Price	Mkt. Val.
P1	1860	—	5 Centimes	—	300.00
P2	1860	—	10 Centimes	—	400.00
P3	1860	—	20 Centimes	—	500.00
P4	1860	—	50 Centimes	—	600.00
P5	1860	—	1 Franc	—	700.00
P6	1860	—	2 Francs	—	800.00
P7	1860	—	4 Francs	—	1500.
P8	1860	—	1 Piastre	—	6000.

FRENCH PROTECTORATE

(1863)

TOKEN ISSUES (Tn)

Pnom-Pehn Merchants Issue

CENTIME

BRASS
Round, center hole.

KM#	Date	Mintage	Fine	VF	XF	Unc
Tn1	ND(1897)	—	45.00	85.00	175.00	—
		W/o center hole				
Tn2	ND(1897)	—	50.00	90.00	200.00	—
		Square center hole				
Tn3	ND(1897)	—	60.00	100.00	150.00	275.00

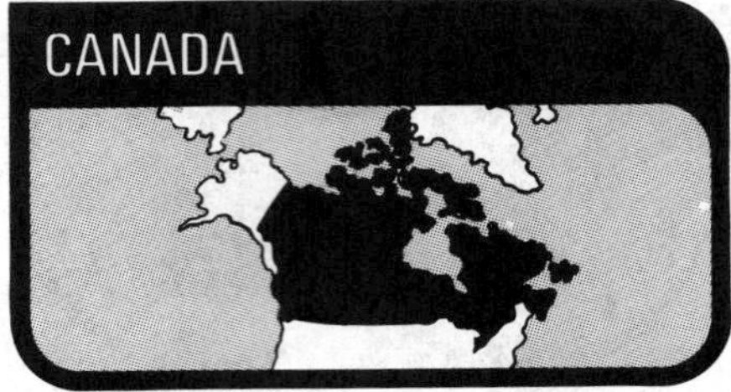

Jacques Cartier, a French explorer, took possession of Canada for France in 1534, and for more than a century the history of Canada was that of a French colony. Samuel de Champlain helped to establish the first permanent French colony in North America, in 1604 at Port Royal, Acadia - now Annapolis Royal, Nova Scotia. Four years later he founded the settlement of Quebec.

The British settled along the coast to the south while the French, motivated by a grand design, pushed into the interior. France's plan for a great American empire was to occupy the Mississippi heartland of the country, and from there to press in upon the narrow strip of English coastal settlements from the rear. Inevitably, armed conflict erupted between the French and the British, as a consequence of which Britain acquired Hudson Bay, Newfoundland, and Nova Scotia from the French in 1713. British control of the rest of New France was secured in 1763, largely because of James Wolfe's great victory over Montcalm near Quebec in 1759.

After the American Revolution, Canada became a refuge for great numbers of American loyalists, most of whom settled in Ontario, thereby creating an English majority west of the Ottawa River. This ethnic imbalance contravened the effectiveness of the prevailing French type of government, and in 1791 the Constitutional Act was passed by the British Parliament, dividing Canada at the Ottawa River into two parts, each with its own government: Upper Canada, chiefly English and consisting of the southern section of what is now Ontario; and Lower Canada, chiefly French and consisting principally of the southern section of Quebec. Subsequent revolt by dissidents in both sections caused the British government to pass the Union Act, July 23, 1840, which united Lower and Upper Canada (as Canada East and Canada West) to form the Province of Canada, with one council and one assembly in which the two sections had equal numbers.

The union of the two provinces did not encourage political stability; the equal strength of the French and British made the task of government all but impossible. A further change was made with the passage of the British North America Act, which took effect on July 1, 1867, and established Canada as the first federal union in the British Empire. Four provinces entered the union at first: Canada West as Ontario, Canada East as Quebec, Nova Scotia and New Brunswick. The Hudsons Bay Company's territories were acquired in 1869 out of which were formed the provinces of Manitoba in 1870 and Saskatchewan and Alberta later in 1905. British Columbia joined in 1871 and Prince Edward Island in 1873. Canada took over the Arctic Archipelago in 1895. In 1949 Newfoundland came into the confederation. Canada is a member of the Commonwealth of Nations. The Queen of England is Chief of State.

RULERS

British

MONETARY SYSTEM

2 Sous = 1 Penny (Pence)
12 Pence = 1 Shilling
5 Shillings = 1 Dollar
(Commencing 1858)
100 Cents = 1 Dollar

LOWER CANADA

The Colonial coinages of Canada began with the copper deniers, billon marques and half-marques, and silver sols issued under the French regime. Of these, only the 5 and 15 sols of 1670, the 9 deniers of 1721 and 1722, and the marques and half-marques of 1738-60 saw actual circulation.

Unfortunately for local commerce, gold and silver coins passed out of the colonies faster than they could be brought in. France, and to a lesser extent Great Britain, endeavored to supply their colonies with coin, but mercantilism operated to see that coined money was exported. After 1800 local merchants began to import and issue halfpenny and penny coppers, particularly the basic halfpenny token, to alleviate the shortage of copper coin. When these were issued in such quantities as to discredit them in the public mind, the banks stepped in and replaced the private issues with bank tokens. Semi-regal tokens, which had most of the characteristics of coins were issued by the authorities in some colonies.

The first Bank Tokens (1835-37) appeared because the banks refused to accept the trashy pieces in circulation except by weight. In 1835 the Bank of Montreal issued half-penny coppers of good weight on which the value was inscribed incorrectly as SOUS, rather than SOU. The bank received permission from the government to strike its coppers in 1836 and added its name to the reverse inscription. The denomination error was not corrected because the people had come to regard it as a mark of authenticity. The Bank of Montreal Sous were struck in Birmingham.

An interesting variety of this token known as the 'Rebellion Sou' was issued in 1837 by the Banque du Peuple. It received its name when an accountant who favored the cause of the rebels of 1837 surreptitiously caused a small star and liberty cap to be added to the design.

TOKEN ISSUES (Tn)

'Bouquet Sous'

UN (1) SOU

COPPER
Rev: BANK TOKEN, MONTREAL.

KM#	Date	Mintage	Fine	VF	XF	Unc
Tn1	ND(1835)	—	3.00	6.50	15.00	75.00

Rev: BANK OF MONTREAL TOKEN.

KM#	Date	Mintage	Fine	VF	XF	Unc
Tn2	ND(1836)	—	3.00	6.50	25.00	110.00

Rev: Star - BANK DU PEUPLE - Liberty cap.

KM#	Date	Mintage	Fine	VF	XF	Unc
Tn3	ND(1837)	—	5.50	12.50	30.00	90.00

Rev: W/o star and liberty cap.

KM#	Date	Mintage	Fine	VF	XF	Unc
Tn4	ND(1838)	—	4.00	12.00	25.00	80.00
		BRASS				
Tn4a	ND(1838)	—	5.00	15.00	30.00	95.00

COPPER
Rev: TOKEN/MONTREAL.

KM#	Date	Mintage	Fine	VF	XF	Unc
Tn5	ND(1837-8)	—	2.00	5.00	12.00	50.00

NOTE: Many varieties of Tn#5 exist. All are inscribed TOKEN-MONTREAL, and were privately struck during the period 1837-38.

QUEBEC TOKEN ISSUES (Tn)

The Bouquet Sous of 1835-37 were followed by the Quebec Habitant tokens of 1837, the Bank of Montreal tokens of 1842-45, and the Quebec Bank tokens of 1852.

The Habitant tokens were so named because they show on obverse a Canadian habitant in traditional winter garb. For years the habitant was popularly identified with the rebel and politician Louis Joseph Papineau and the tokens known as 'Papineaus,' but there is no valid reason for the association. The Habitants were struck by Boulton & Watt in denominations of penny and halfpenny.

After Upper and Lower Canada were united as the Province of Canada, the Bank of Montreal was granted the right to coin copper and ordered the 'Side View' tokens bearing a side view of the bank in 1837-38 which were rejected, being returned to the Mint of Cotterill, Hill & Co. of Walsall, England. It later issued in 1842-45, a series of tokens bearing a front view of the bank, and commonly known as the 'Front View' tokens. The tokens were struck by Boulton & Watt in denominations of penny and halfpenny.

In 1852 the Quebec Bank was granted the authority to coin copper because of a severe shortage of copper coin in the province, and issued an exceptionally attractive Colonial issue with the habitant obverse and reverse depicting the arms of the city of Quebec. They were struck by Ralph Heaton & Sons in denominations of penny and halfpenny.

UN (1) SOU-1/2 PENNY

COPPER
Obv. leg: PROVINCE DU BAS CANADA.
Rev: CITY BANK on ribbon.

KM#	Date	Mintage	Fine	VF	XF	Unc
Tn1	1837	.240	2.00	4.50	11.50	50.00
	1837	—	—	—	Proof	400.00

Rev: QUEBEC BANK on ribbon.

Tn2	1837	.240	2.00	4.50	11.50	50.00
	1837	—	—	—	Proof	1100.

Rev: BANQUE DU PEUPLE on ribbon.

Tn3	1837	.240	3.75	9.00	18.00	60.00
	1837	—	—	—	Proof	1100.

Rev: BANK OF MONTREAL on ribbon.

Tn4	1837	.480	3.75	9.00	16.50	60.00
	1837	—	—	—	Proof	350.00

Obv: Side view of bank, leg: BANK OF MONTREAL.
Rev: BANK OF MONTREAL on ribbon.

Tn10	1838	*.240	150.00	250.00	350.00	600.00
	1839	*.240	150.00	250.00	350.00	600.00

***NOTE:** The above issues were not officially released.

Obv. leg: PROVINCE OF CANADA-BANK OF MONTREAL.

Tn13	1842	.480	4.50	6.50	12.75	55.00
	1844	1.440	2.50	3.75	7.25	40.00
	1844	—	—	—	Proof	600.00
	1845	2 Known		—	Rare	—

NOTE: 3 varieties of trees exist for 1842 and 1844 tokens.

Obv. leg: PROVINCE DU CANADA.
Rev. leg: QUEBEC BANK TOKEN.

Tn15	1852	—	2.50	4.50	10.00	50.00

BRONZE

Tn15a	1852	—	—	—	Proof	400.00

DEUX (2) SOUS - PENNY

COPPER
Obv. leg: PROVINCE DU BAS CANADA.
Rev: CITY BANK on ribbon.

KM#	Date	Mintage	Fine	VF	XF	Unc
Tn5	1837	.120	2.50	6.00	12.00	60.00

Rev: QUEBEC BANK on ribbon.

Tn6	1837	.120	2.50	6.00	12.00	60.00

Rev: BANQUE DU PEUPLE on ribbon.

Tn7	1837	.120	7.25	18.00	26.00	85.00

Rev: BANK OF MONTREAL on ribbon.

Tn8	1837	.240	4.50	11.50	18.50	75.00

Obv: Side view of bank, leg: BANK OF MONTREAL. Rev: BANK OF MONTREAL on ribbon.

Tn11	1838	*.120	300.00	500.00	800.00	1500.
	1839	*.120	300.00	500.00	800.00	1500.

Rev: BANQUE DU PEUPLE on ribbon.

KM#	Date	Mintage	Fine	VF	XF	Unc
Tn12	1839	*—	1500.	2200.	3500.	—

NOTE: KM#Tn11 and Tn12 were not officially released.

Obv. leg: PROVINCE OF CANADA-BANK OF MONTREAL. Rev: CITY BANK on ribbon.

Tn9	1837	—	55.00	75.00	125.00	200.00
	1837	—	—	—	Proof	500.00

NOTE: The authenticity of the above issue is doubtful.

Rev: BANK OF MONTREAL on ribbon.

Tn14	1842	.240	2.75	5.50	12.75	75.00

Obv. leg: PROVINCE DU CANADA.
Rev. leg: QUEBEC BANK TOKEN.

KM#	Date	Mintage	Fine	VF	XF	Unc
Tn16	1852	—	3.00	7.50	15.00	90.00
			BRONZE			
Tn16a	1852	—	—	—	Proof	1500.

UPPER CANADA

PROVINCE OF UPPER CANADA TOKENS (Tn)

1/2 PENNY

COPPER

KM#	Date	Mintage	Fine	VF	XF	Unc
Tn1	1832	—	12.00	25.00	55.00	145.00

BANK OF UPPER CANADA TOKENS (Tn)

In 1849, rioting mobs, angered by the passage of the French Rebellion Losses bill, burned the Parliament Buildings at Montreal. The capital was then transferred to Toronto and the Bank of Upper Canada was granted the right to coin copper. Penny and halfpenny tokens struck by Ralph Heaton and Sons were issued during the period of 1850-57. Because of their design, these attractive tokens are frequently called the 'St. George' tokens. The initials R K & CO on obverse are those of Rowe, Kentish & Co., London, the agents through whom the token orders were placed for Ralph Heaton, Birmingham Mint.

1/2 PENNY

COPPER

KM#	Date	Mintage	Fine	VF	XF	Unc
Tn2	1850	1.500	2.00	5.00	10.00	75.00
	1850	—	—	—	Proof	400.00
	1852	1.500	2.00	5.00	10.00	50.00
	1854	1.500	2.00	5.00	10.00	40.00
	1854 crosslet 4					
		Inc. Ab.	15.00	30.00	50.00	120.00
	1857	3.000	1.75	4.00	10.00	50.00
			BRONZE			
Tn2a	1857	—	—	—	Proof	350.00

PENNY

COPPER

KM#	Date	Mintage	Fine	VF	XF	Unc
Tn3	1850	.750	3.00	7.00	12.50	60.00
	1850 dot between cornucopias					
		Inc. Ab.	5.00	15.00	30.00	100.00
	1852	*.750	3.00	7.00	12.50	50.00
	1852	—	—	—	Proof	400.00
	1854	.750	3.00	5.00	10.00	45.00
	1854 crosslet 4					
		Inc. Ab.	7.00	15.00	30.00	100.00
	1857	1.500	3.00	5.00	10.00	40.00

NOTE: 4 varieties exist in '2' of 1852.

BRONZE

KM#	Date	Mintage	Fine	VF	XF	Unc
3a	1854	—	—	—	Proof	350.00
	1857	—	—	—	Proof	350.00

MAGDALEN ISLANDS

A group of 13 islands in the Gulf of St. Lawrence north of Prince Edward Island and west of Newfoundland. The island was awarded to Sir Isaac Coffin after the American Revolution. In an effort to exercise his authority on his property Coffin had 1 penny tokens made at Birmingham, England in 1815. The British government felt this was overstepping his authority and revoked his grant of the island. Today it is a part of the province of Quebec.

TOKEN ISSUES (Tn)

PENNY

COPPER

KM#	Date	Mintage	Fine	VF	XF	Unc
Tn1	1815	—	65.00	175.00	325.00	900.00

NOTE: Issued by Sir Isaac Coffin while the islands were under the administration of Newfoundland. In 1825 the islands were transferred under the administration of Lower Canada (Quebec).

PRINCE EDWARD ISLAND

An island in the Gulf of St. Lawrence off the coast of New Brunswick and Nova Scotia. In 1813, due to a coin shortage, Governor Smith authorized the perforation of Spanish-American dollars. The centre was to pass for 1 shilling, the balance of the coin 5 shillings. They circulated until 1824 despite wide spread counterfeiting.

SHILLING

(ca.1813)

.903 SILVER
c/m: Sunburst on center plug of Spanish or Spanish Colonial 8 Reales.

KM#	Date	Mintage	Good	VG	Fine	VF
1	ND	1,000	500.00	1000.	1500.	2500.

5 SHILLINGS

(ca.1813)

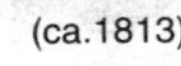

.903 SILVER
c/m: Sunburst on holed Mexico City 8 Reales, KM#109.

KM#	Date	Mintage	Good	VG	Fine	VF
2	ND(1791-1808)					
		Inc. Ab.	300.00	600.00	1200.	1800.
			c/m: Sunburst on holed Lima 8 Reales, C#96.			
3	ND(1808-11)					
		1,000	400.00	800.00	1400.	2000.

CANADA

The history of Canadian coinage parallels that of the United States in many respects, although in several aspects it also contrasts quite sharply. Canadian coins are widely collected in the U.S., particularly in the northern tier of states, where at times the issues of our northern neighbors have been encountered in substantial circulating quantities.

This is a most logical situation, as when the dollar was established as the monetary unit of Canada, in 1857 it was given the same intrinsic value as the U.S. dollar. Through the years the Canadian dollar has traded on an approximate par with the U.S. dollar, although from time to time one or the other units has traded at a slight premium.

The first Canadian decimal coins were issued in 1858 — 1, 5, 10 and 20 cents — in the name of the Province of Canada (Upper and Lower Canada, or the provinces of Ontario and Quebec as we know them today). The first truly Canadian coinage was offered in 1870 — 5, 10, 25 and 50 cents — following the confederation of these provinces with Nova Scotia and New Brunswick in 1867. Both of the latter had offered their own distinctive coinages in the early 1860s.

Prince Edward Island also offered a single issue of a one cent coin in 1871, prior to its 1873 entry into the confederation. A coinage of Newfoundland was also initiated during this period, in 1865, which continued through 1947, with the British dependency moving into the confederation in 1949.

In contrast to the .900 fine standard of American silver coins, Canada's coinage was originally launched with a .925 fine silver content, and as a result slightly smaller coin sizes. In 1920 the standard was reduced to .800 fine, remaining there until mid-1967 when it was lowered to .500 fine, then abandoned in favor of pure nickel a year later. Another contrast with U.S. coinage was evident in the issue of the large cent from 1858 to 1920, when a small cent of similar size, content and weight to the U.S. cent was introduced.

When Canada's dominion coin issue of 1870 was introduced, the 1858 provincial issue of a decimal 20 cent piece was abandoned in favor of a quasi-decimal 25 cent piece. This move was made, in part, because of the confusion between the 20 cent piece and the U.S. 25 cent piece, which also circulated in Canada, forecasting the similar fate which would befall the U.S. 20 cent piece a few years later. Although tentative steps aimed at the creation of a dollar coin were instituted in 1911, it was not until 1935, the year the issue of silver dollars was halted in the U.S., that Canada launched the issue of a silver dollar.

The first dollar was a commemorative of the silver jubilee of the reign of George V, while the other George V dollar coin (1936) utilized dies which had been prepared at the Royal Mint in London in anticipation of the 1911 dollar which did not materialize. From the beginning, Canada's dollar series has been frequently employed as a vehicle for the commemoration of national events. In addition, a 1951 nickel commemorated the 200th anniversary of the isolation of nickel, of which Canada is the world's leading producer, while the entire 1967 series commemorates the centennial of Canadian confederation.

In the early years, Canada's coins were struck in England at London's Royal Mint or at the Heaton Mint in Birmingham. Issues struck at the Royal Mint do not bear a mint mark, but those produced by Heaton carry an "H". All Canadian coins have been struck since January 2, 1908, at the Royal Canadian Mints at Ottawa and recently at Winnipeg except for some 1968 pure nickel dimes struck at the U.S. Mint in Philadelphia, and do not bear mint marks. Ottawa's mint mark (C) does not appear on some 20th century Newfoundland issues, however, as it does on English type sovereigns struck there from 1908 through 1918.

Canadian coins are graded on MS (Mint State) standards similar to those used for the U.S. series. The points of greatest wear are generally found on the obverses in the bands of the crowns, the sprays of laurel around the head and in the hairlines above or over the ear. The susceptibility of these varying points to wear has decreed that Canadian coins are almost exclusively graded accordingly, with little concentration on the reverses, unless they are abnormally worn or weakly struck.

LARGE CENTS

BRONZE, 3.24 g

KM#	Date	Mintage	VG-8	F-12	VF-20	XF-40	MS-60	MS-63
1	1858	421,000	35.00	45.00	60.00	90.00	215.00	600.00
	1859/8 wide 9	I.A.	22.00	29.00	40.00	60.00	145.00	275.00
	1859 narrow 9	9,579,000	1.50	2.00	3.00	5.00	22.00	140.00
	1859 double punched narrow 9 Type I	I.A.	175.00	250.00	350.00	540.00	1150.	2000.
	1859 double punched narrow 9 Type II	I.A.	32.00	42.00	60.00	85.00	220.00	400.00

KM#	Date	Mintage	VG-8	F-12	VF-20	XF-40	MS-60	MS-63
7	1876H	4,000,000	1.50	2.50	4.00	7.00	40.00	180.00
	1881H	2,000,000	2.50	3.50	5.00	10.00	50.00	200.00
	1882H	4,000,000	1.50	2.50	3.00	6.00	30.00	140.00
	1884	2,500,000	2.00	3.00	4.00	7.50	40.00	160.00
	1886	1,500,000	3.25	4.50	7.00	11.50	60.00	220.00
	1887	1,500,000	2.50	3.25	5.00	8.00	40.00	170.00
	1888	4,000,000	1.50	2.00	3.00	5.00	30.00	100.00
	1890H	1,000,000	4.00	6.50	11.50	20.00	100.00	300.00
	1891 lg. date	1,452,000	4.50	7.00	11.00	18.50	90.00	300.00
	1891 S.D.L.L.	I.A.	40.00	60.00	85.00	115.00	300.00	750.00
	1891 S.D.S.L.	I.A.	30.00	45.00	60.00	90.00	200.00	550.00
	1892	1,200,000	3.00	4.50	6.00	10.00	40.00	130.00
	1893	2,000,000	2.00	2.50	4.00	8.00	30.00	100.00
	1894	1,000,000	5.50	8.00	13.00	20.00	85.00	215.00
	1895	1,200,000	3.00	5.00	7.00	10.00	50.00	160.00
	1896	2,000,000	1.75	2.75	3.50	5.50	30.00	100.00
	1897	1,500,000	2.00	3.50	5.00	6.00	30.00	110.00
	1898H	1,000,000	4.00	6.00	8.00	11.00	55.00	200.00
	1899	2,400,000	1.50	2.25	3.00	5.00	30.00	100.00
	1900	1,000,000	5.00	8.00	12.00	20.00	65.00	190.00
	1900H	2,600,000	1.50	2.25	3.50	5.00	22.00	70.00

NOTE: Later date (1901) exists for this type.

FIVE CENTS

Round 0's

Oval 0's

1.1620 g, .925 SILVER, .0346 oz ASW

KM#	Date	Mintage	VG-8	F-12	VF-20	XF-40	MS-60	MS-63
2	1858 sm. date	1,500,000	10.00	15.00	25.00	40.00	225.00	425.00
	1858 lg. date over sm. date	Inc. Ab.	100.00	150.00	250.00	375.00	1000.	2250.
	1870 flat rim	2,800,000	9.00	15.00	25.00	45.00	200.00	450.00
	1870 wire rim	Inc. Ab.	9.00	15.00	25.00	45.00	200.00	450.00
	1871	1,400,000	9.00	15.00	25.00	45.00	200.00	500.00
	1872H	2,000,000	6.00	12.00	25.00	40.00	225.00	600.00
	1874H plain 4	800,000	12.50	27.00	55.00	100.00	325.00	875.00
	1874H crosslet 4	Inc. Ab.	10.00	20.00	40.00	65.00	350.00	750.00
	1875H lg. date	1,000,000	125.00	175.00	325.00	575.00	2200.	4250.
	1875H sm. date	Inc. Ab.	80.00	150.00	250.00	450.00	1400.	3250.
	1880H	3,000,000	4.00	7.50	16.00	35.00	200.00	500.00
	1881H	1,500,000	4.25	9.00	17.50	35.00	200.00	600.00
	1882H	1,000,000	5.00	10.00	18.00	40.00	225.00	650.00
	1883H	600,000	11.50	25.00	60.00	125.00	650.00	1750.
	1884	200,000	75.00	125.00	225.00	475.00	2200.	6000.
	1885 sm. 5	1,000,000	7.50	14.00	35.00	70.00	400.00	1100.
	1885 lg. 5	Inc. Ab.	8.25	15.50	35.00	80.00	425.00	1200.
	1885 lg. 5 over sm. 5	Inc. Ab.	35.00	70.00	150.00	400.00	1950.	2750.
	1886 sm. 6	1,700,000	4.50	9.00	17.50	35.00	250.00	700.00
	1886 lg. 6	Inc. Ab.	7.00	10.00	20.00	45.00	300.00	750.00
	1887	500,000	12.50	25.00	45.00	85.00	300.00	675.00
	1888	1,000,000	3.50	6.00	14.00	25.00	140.00	350.00
	1889	1,200,000	13.50	28.00	60.00	100.00	350.00	1000.
	1890H	1,000,000	4.50	8.00	18.00	35.00	165.00	400.00
	1891	1,800,000	3.00	5.00	10.00	16.00	125.00	285.00
	1892	860,000	4.50	8.00	16.00	35.00	200.00	550.00
	1893	1,700,000	3.00	5.00	10.00	18.00	150.00	350.00
	1894	500,000	9.50	20.00	40.00	80.00	285.00	850.00
	1896	1,500,000	3.50	7.00	12.00	25.00	150.00	325.00
	1897	1,319,283	3.75	6.50	12.00	25.00	125.00	265.00
	1898	580,717	8.00	15.00	30.00	50.00	180.00	500.00
	1899	3,000,000	2.75	4.00	7.50	18.00	85.00	250.00
	1900 oval 0's	1,800,000	3.00	4.50	8.00	18.00	90.00	265.00
	1900 round 0's	Inc. Ab.	13.00	25.00	45.00	90.00	250.00	750.00

NOTE: Later date (1901) exists for this type.

TEN CENTS

2.3240 g, .925 SILVER, .0691 oz ASW

KM#	Date	Mintage	VG-8	F-12	VF-20	XF-40	MS-60	MS-63
3	1858/5	Inc. Below	325.00	500.00	875.00	1350.	3100.	—
	1858	1,250,000	13.50	24.00	45.00	80.00	275.00	700.00
	1870 narrow 0	1,600,000	12.00	25.00	50.00	90.00	285.00	725.00
	1870 wide 0	Inc. Ab.	17.00	30.00	60.00	110.00	350.00	800.00
	1871	800,000	15.00	30.00	70.00	125.00	325.00	1200.
	1871H	1,870,000	18.00	32.50	70.00	125.00	450.00	1000.
	1872H	1,000,000	70.00	125.00	225.00	425.00	1300.	2750.
	1874H	600,000	8.00	15.00	30.00	70.00	275.00	750.00
	1875H	1,000,000	175.00	325.00	575.00	1150.	4050.	7500.
	1880H	1,500,000	7.00	12.00	25.00	55.00	250.00	700.00
	1881H	950,000	8.50	18.00	40.00	90.00	275.00	700.00
	1882H	1,000,000	8.50	18.00	35.00	75.00	300.00	800.00
	1883H	300,000	25.00	60.00	125.00	250.00	800.00	1800.
	1884	150,000	140.00	300.00	575.00	1300.	5150.	10,000.
	1885	400,000	22.00	50.00	125.00	275.00	1500.	3250.
	1886 sm. 6	800,000	12.00	22.00	50.00	110.00	550.00	1500.
	1886 lg. 6	Inc. Ab.	15.00	27.50	60.00	140.00	500.00	1200.
	1887	350,000	23.00	55.00	125.00	275.00	1150.	2750.
	1888	500,000	6.75	13.00	30.00	60.00	250.00	600.00
	1889	600,000	400.00	725.00	1450.	2900.	8750.	14,000.
	1890H	450,000	11.50	20.00	45.00	90.00	325.00	750.00
	1891 21 leaves	800,000	12.00	22.00	50.00	110.00	375.00	825.00
	1891 22 leaves	Inc. Ab.	12.00	22.00	50.00	110.00	375.00	825.00
	1892/1	520,000	115.00	185.00	325.00	525.00	—	—
	1892	Inc. Ab.	9.50	20.00	37.50	75.00	350.00	800.00
	1893 flat top 3	500,000	14.00	32.00	70.00	130.00	475.00	1300.
	1893 rd. top 3	Inc. Ab.	425.00	875.00	1700.	2900.	6950.	13,000.
	1894	500,000	13.00	25.00	55.00	110.00	350.00	1000.
	1896	650,000	7.00	12.00	25.00	55.00	250.00	550.00
	1898	720,000	7.00	14.00	30.00	60.00	275.00	600.00
	1899 sm. 9's	1,200,000	6.75	10.50	25.00	55.00	210.00	575.00
	1899 lg. 9's	Inc. Ab.	10.00	20.00	35.00	90.00	325.00	850.00
	1900	1,100,000	6.75	10.50	25.00	50.00	150.00	390.00

NOTE: Later date (1901) exists for this type.

TWENTY CENTS

4.6480 g, .925 SILVER, .1382 oz ASW

KM#	Date	Mintage	VG-8	F-12	VF-20	XF-40	MS-60	MS-63
4	1858	750,000	40.00	60.00	90.00	170.00	725.00	1850.

TWENTY-FIVE CENTS

5.8100 g, .925 SILVER, .1728 oz ASW

KM#	Date	Mintage	VG-8	F-12	VF-20	XF-40	MS-60	MS-63
5	1870	900,000	11.00	20.00	45.00	100.00	600.00	1350.
	1871	400,000	14.00	25.00	65.00	170.00	700.00	1850.
	1871H	748,000	16.00	27.50	80.00	200.00	700.00	1500.
	1872H	2,240,000	6.00	9.00	25.00	75.00	350.00	975.00
	1874H	1,600,000	7.00	10.00	27.00	80.00	375.00	975.00
	1875H	1,000,000	225.00	450.00	1200.	2200.	8250.	14,000.
	1880H narrow 0	400,000	30.00	60.00	165.00	360.00	900.00	2250.
	1880H wide 0	Inc. Ab.	95.00	175.00	350.00	775.00	1850.	4000.
	1880H wide/narrow 0	Inc. Ab.	90.00	165.00	350.00	650.00	—	—
	1881H	820,000	12.00	25.00	55.00	140.00	800.00	1400.
	1882H	600,000	13.00	27.00	65.00	170.00	800.00	1600.
	1883H	960,000	10.00	18.00	45.00	120.00	600.00	1450.
	1885	192,000	75.00	150.00	325.00	825.00	3000.	6000.
	1886/3	540,000	12.00	25.00	65.00	190.00	950.00	2200.
	1886	Inc. Ab.	10.00	20.00	60.00	175.00	800.00	1950.
	1887	100,000	75.00	150.00	325.00	825.00	3000.	6000.
	1888	400,000	10.00	20.00	50.00	130.00	550.00	1400.
	1889	66,324	95.00	175.00	350.00	825.00	3600.	6750.
	1890H	200,000	15.00	27.00	70.00	175.00	950.00	2250.
	1891	120,000	45.00	90.00	190.00	410.00	1200.	2500.
	1892	510,000	9.00	16.00	45.00	130.00	550.00	1600.
	1893	100,000	75.00	125.00	275.00	540.00	1500.	3000.
	1894	220,000	15.00	28.00	70.00	180.00	700.00	1600.
	1899	415,580	6.00	9.75	27.00	80.00	450.00	1000.
	1900	1,320,000	6.00	9.75	27.00	80.00	350.00	975.00

NOTE: Later date (1901) exists for this type.

FIFTY CENTS

11.6200 g, .925 SILVER, .3456 oz ASW

KM#	Date	Mintage	VG-8	F-12	VF-20	XF-40	MS-60	MS-63
6	1870	450,000	550.00	975.00	1800.	3250.	13,000.	21,000.
	1870 LCW	Inc. Ab.	40.00	70.00	160.00	355.00	3250.	10,000.
	1871	200,000	45.00	100.00	220.00	500.00	4000.	10,500.
	1871H	45,000	90.00	180.00	425.00	925.00	6500.	11,000.
	1872H	80,000	40.00	70.00	170.00	350.00	3600.	10,250.
	1872H inverted A for V in VICTORIA	Inc. Ab.	95.00	180.00	425.00	925.00	6500.	11,000.
	1881H	150,000	40.00	80.00	175.00	375.00	4000.	10,500.
	1888	60,000	110.00	220.00	490.00	975.00	5400.	11,000.
	1890H	20,000	700.00	1200.	2000.	3500.	11,000.	20,000.
	1892	151,000	45.00	90.00	225.00	450.00	6000.	10,500.
	1894	29,036	245.00	410.00	920.00	1900.	8100.	15,000.
	1898	100,000	45.00	100.00	225.00	450.00	4500.	10,500.
	1899	50,000	95.00	200.00	435.00	1100.	7100.	12,000.
	1900	118,000	40.00	60.00	160.00	350.00	4000.	10,500.

NOTE: Later date (1901) exists for this type.

NEWFOUNDLAND

LARGE CENTS

BRONZE

KM#	Date	Mintage	VG-8	F-12	VF-20	XF-40	MS-60	MS-63
1	1865	240,000	2.00	3.00	6.00	14.50	120.00	325.00
	1872H	200,000	2.00	3.00	6.00	14.50	65.00	180.00
	1872H	—	—	—	—	—	Proof	800.00
	1873	200,025	2.50	4.50	10.00	25.00	225.00	750.00
	1873	—	—	—	—	—	Proof	800.00
	1876H	200,000	2.00	3.00	6.00	16.00	160.00	450.00
	1876H	—	—	—	—	—	Proof	600.00
	1880 round O, even date	400,000	2.00	3.00	6.00	14.50	100.00	300.00
	1880 round O, low O	Inc. Ab.	2.25	4.00	9.00	25.00	150.00	450.00
	1880 oval 0	Inc. Ab.	85.00	130.00	180.00	325.00	850.00	1400.
	1885	40,000	16.50	27.00	55.00	115.00	500.00	1250.
	1888	50,000	15.00	25.00	45.00	100.00	500.00	1300.
	1890	200,000	2.00	3.00	5.50	14.50	140.00	450.00
	1894	200,000	2.00	3.00	5.50	14.50	120.00	350.00
	1896	200,000	2.00	3.00	5.50	14.50	120.00	350.00

FIVE CENTS

1.1782 g, .925 SILVER, .0350 oz ASW

KM#	Date	Mintage	VG-8	F-12	VF-20	XF-40	MS-60	MS-63
2	1865	80,000	20.00	32.50	60.00	125.00	775.00	1500.
	1870	40,000	35.00	50.00	90.00	175.00	1100.	2000.
	1870	—	—	—	—	—	Proof	3900.
	1872H	40,000	22.00	32.00	60.00	140.00	600.00	1400.
	1873	44,260	45.00	70.00	145.00	335.00	1975.	2850.
	1873H	Inc. Ab.	710.00	1100.	1875.	3300.	8200.	12,500.
	1876H	20,000	75.00	110.00	200.00	350.00	1450.	2750.
	1880	40,000	22.00	40.00	80.00	150.00	1000.	1850.
	1881	40,000	15.00	30.00	45.00	120.00	900.00	1850.
	1882H	60,000	15.00	27.00	40.00	100.00	800.00	1500.
	1882H	—	—	—	—	—	Proof	2800.
	1885	16,000	90.00	150.00	250.00	525.00	2000.	4500.
	1888	40,000	20.00	30.00	50.00	140.00	800.00	1600.
	1890	160,000	6.00	12.00	30.00	70.00	600.00	1500.
	1890	—	—	—	—	—	Proof	2100.
	1894	160,000	6.50	12.50	30.00	75.00	600.00	1500.
	1896	400,000	4.00	8.00	20.00	45.00	575.00	1350.

TEN CENTS

2.3564 g, .925 SILVER, .0701 oz ASW

KM#	Date	Mintage	VG-8	F-12	VF-20	XF-40	MS-60	MS-63
3	1865	80,000	13.50	22.00	55.00	160.00	1100.	2250.
	1865 plain edge	—	—	—	—	—	Proof	5500.
	1870	30,000	120.00	190.00	335.00	750.00	2500.	5000.
	1872H	40,000	13.50	20.00	50.00	135.00	800.00	1700.
	1873 flat 3	23,614	15.00	35.00	90.00	225.00	1675.	2900.
	1873 round 3	Inc. Ab.	15.00	35.00	90.00	225.00	1675.	2900.
	1876H	10,000	20.00	35.00	75.00	250.00	1800.	2950.
	1880/70	10,000	22.00	45.00	100.00	275.00	2000.	2950.
	1882H	20,000	12.50	30.00	70.00	150.00	1400.	2200.
	1882H	—	—	—	—	—	Proof	3400.
	1885	8,000	50.00	100.00	210.00	485.00	2100.	4250.
	1888	30,000	11.50	27.50	70.00	225.00	1400.	2500.
	1890	100,000	5.50	11.50	20.00	75.00	700.00	1550.
	1890	—	—	—	—	—	Proof	3200.
	1894	100,000	5.50	11.50	20.00	75.00	700.00	1550.
	1894	—	—	—	—	—	Proof	1750.
	1896	230,000	5.00	10.00	20.00	75.00	600.00	1500.

TWENTY CENTS

4.7127 g, .925 SILVER, .1401 oz ASW

KM#	Date	Mintage	VG-8	F-12	VF-20	XF-40	MS-60	MS-63
4	1865	100,000	11.00	16.00	45.00	125.00	950.00	2000.
	1865 plain edge	—	—	—	—	—	Proof	4500.
	1870	50,000	12.00	20.00	60.00	140.00	1250.	2500.
	1872H	90,000	7.00	14.00	30.00	90.00	750.00	1800.
	1873	45,797	9.00	18.00	60.00	160.00	1500.	3000.
	1876H	50,000	10.00	16.00	50.00	175.00	1350.	2700.
	1880/70	30,000	15.00	25.00	65.00	160.00	1350.	3000.
	1881	60,000	5.00	12.00	35.00	90.00	900.00	1900.
	1882H	100,000	5.00	12.00	27.50	80.00	900.00	1900.
	1882H	—	—	—	—	—	Proof	3700.
	1885	40,000	8.00	12.50	40.00	120.00	1300.	2600.
	1888	75,000	5.00	10.00	32.00	100.00	900.00	2200.
	1890	100,000	4.00	7.00	22.00	70.00	625.00	1600.
	1890	—	—	—	—	—	Proof	2750.
	1894	100,000	4.00	7.00	22.00	60.00	650.00	1700.
	1896 small 96	125,000	3.00	6.00	20.00	70.00	700.00	1800.
	1896 large 96	Inc. Ab.	4.00	10.00	22.00	90.00	725.00	1900.
	1899 small 99	125,000	10.00	25.00	45.00	125.00	850.00	2200.
	1899 large 99	Inc. Ab.	3.25	6.50	18.00	65.00	700.00	1900.
	1900	125,000	3.00	5.00	15.00	55.00	700.00	1900.

FIFTY CENTS

11.7818 g, .925 SILVER, .3504 oz ASW

KM#	Date	Mintage	VG-8	F-12	VF-20	XF-40	MS-60	MS-63
6	1870	50,000	12.00	15.00	45.00	200.00	1400.	3600.
	1870 plain edge	—	—	—	—	—	Proof	6500.
	1872H	48,000	10.00	15.00	40.00	150.00	1250.	3600.
	1873	37,675	28.00	60.00	150.00	570.00	4350.	6000.
	1874	80,000	20.00	30.00	80.00	350.00	2500.	5000.
	1876H	28,000	18.00	30.00	80.00	275.00	2250.	5250.
	1880	24,000	18.00	30.00	80.00	300.00	2250.	5250.
	1881	50,000	10.00	20.00	70.00	225.00	2250.	5250.
	1882H	100,000	8.00	12.50	40.00	150.00	1600.	3600.
	1882H	—	—	—	—	—	Proof	5500.
	1885	40,000	12.00	20.00	70.00	250.00	2250.	5500.
	1888	20,000	15.00	30.00	80.00	300.00	2200.	5200.
	1894	40,000	5.00	12.00	50.00	175.00	2000.	3800.
	1896	60,000	4.00	7.00	26.00	130.00	1400.	3600.
	1898	76,607	5.00	8.00	35.00	140.00	1700.	3600.
	1899 wide 9's	150,000	5.00	8.00	28.00	125.00	1500.	3600.
	1899 narrow 9's	Inc. Ab.	5.00	8.00	28.00	125.00	1500.	3600.
	1900	150,000	5.00	8.00	28.00	125.00	1500.	3600.

TWO DOLLARS

3.3284 g, .917 GOLD, .0981 oz AGW

KM#	Date	Mintage	F-12	VF-20	XF-40	AU-50	MS-60	MS-63
5	1865	10,000	150.00	200.00	275.00	600.00	1450.	5700.
	1865 plain edge	about 10 known		—	—	—	Proof	10,000.
	1870	10,000	175.00	225.00	325.00	650.00	1450.	6700.
	1870 plain edge	—	—	—	—	—	Proof	10,000.
	1872	6,050	200.00	285.00	385.00	750.00	2500.	10,300.
	1880	2,500	1000.	1300.	1600.	2300.	4650.	16,500.
	1880	—	—	—	—	—	Proof	18,500.
	1881	10,000	120.00	165.00	225.00	350.00	1550.	7200.
	1882H	25,000	110.00	155.00	210.00	250.00	475.00	1550.
	1882H	—	—	—	—	—	Proof	6000.
	1885	10,000	120.00	165.00	235.00	350.00	580.00	2850.
	1888	25,000	110.00	155.00	210.00	250.00	475.00	1550.

NEW BRUNSWICK

HALF PENNY TOKEN

COPPER

KM#	Date	Mintage	VG-8	F-12	VF-20	XF-40	MS-60	MS-63
1	1843	480,000	3.00	6.00	11.50	30.00	100.00	265.00
	1843	—	—	—	—	—	Proof	750.00

KM#	Date	Mintage	VG-8	F-12	VF-20	XF-40	MS-60	MS-63
3	1854	864,000	3.00	6.00	11.50	30.00	100.00	265.00

BRONZE

KM#	Date	Mintage	VG-8	F-12	VF-20	XF-40	MS-60	MS-63
3a	1854	—	—	—	—	—	Proof	400.00

ONE PENNY TOKEN

COPPER

KM#	Date	Mintage	VG-8	F-12	VF-20	XF-40	MS-60	MS-63
2	1843	480,000	3.75	7.50	15.00	37.50	165.00	325.00
	1843	—	—	—	—	—	Proof	800.00

KM#	Date	Mintage	VG-8	F-12	VF-20	XF-40	MS-60	MS-63
4	1854	432,000	3.75	7.50	15.00	40.00	175.00	350.00

DECIMAL COINAGE
HALF CENT

BRONZE

KM#	Date	Mintage	VG-8	F-12	VF-20	XF-40	MS-60	MS-63
5	1861	222,800	65.00	100.00	150.00	200.00	490.00	1450.
	1861	—	—	—	—	—	Proof	2200.

ONE CENT

BRONZE

KM#	Date	Mintage	VG-8	F-12	VF-20	XF-40	MS-60	MS-63
6	1861	1,000,000	2.00	4.00	6.00	11.00	90.00	245.00
	1861	—	—	—	—	—	Proof	450.00
	1864 short 6	1,000,000	2.00	4.00	6.00	11.00	90.00	245.00
	1864 long 6	Inc. Ab.	2.00	4.00	6.00	11.00	90.00	245.00

FIVE CENTS

1.1620 g, .925 SILVER, .0346 oz ASW

KM#	Date	Mintage	VG-8	F-12	VF-20	XF-40	MS-60	MS-63
7	1862	100,000	35.00	65.00	125.00	245.00	1225.	3200.
	1862	—	—	—	—	—	Proof	3500.
	1864 small 6	100,000	35.00	65.00	125.00	245.00	1225.	3200.
	1864 large 6	Inc. Ab.	35.00	65.00	125.00	245.00	1225.	3200.

TEN CENTS

2.3240 g, .925 SILVER, .0691 oz ASW

KM#	Date	Mintage	VG-8	F-12	VF-20	XF-40	MS-60	MS-63
8	1862	150,000	35.00	65.00	125.00	245.00	975.00	2550.
	1862 recut 2	Inc. Ab.	35.00	65.00	140.00	250.00	1100.	2600.
	1862	—	—	—	—	—	Proof	2850.
	1864	100,000	35.00	65.00	125.00	245.00	1000.	2550.

TWENTY CENTS

4.6480 g, .925 SILVER, .1382 oz ASW

KM#	Date	Mintage	VG-8	F-12	VF-20	XF-40	MS-60	MS-63
9	1862	150,000	16.00	26.00	65.00	155.00	825.00	2550.
	1862	—	—	—	—	—	Proof	2850.
	1864	150,000	16.00	26.00	65.00	155.00	825.00	2550.

NOVA SCOTIA
STERLING COINAGE
HALF PENNY TOKEN

COPPER

KM#	Date	Mintage	VG-8	F-12	VF-20	XF-40	MS-60	MS-63
1	1823	400,000	3.00	5.00	8.00	20.00	75.00	150.00
	1823 w/o hyphen	Inc. Ab.	5.00	10.00	20.00	35.00	170.00	350.00
	1824	118,636	3.00	5.00	12.50	25.00	150.00	225.00
	1832	800,000	3.00	5.00	7.50	15.00	60.00	150.00
1a	1382(error)	—	150.00	300.00	1650.	—	—	—
	1832/1382	—	500.00	700.00	—	—	—	—
	1832 (imitation)	—	3.00	6.00	9.50	34.00	50.00	100.00

KM#	Date	Mintage	VG-8	F-12	VF-20	XF-40	MS-60	MS-63
3	1840 small 0	300,000	3.50	5.00	10.00	22.00	115.00	165.00
	1840 medium 0	Inc. Ab.	2.50	4.00	7.50	15.00	95.00	125.00
	1840 large 0	Inc. Ab.	4.00	6.00	12.50	27.50	125.00	185.00
	1843	300,000	3.00	5.00	9.00	20.00	85.00	160.00

KM#	Date	Mintage	VG-8	F-12	VF-20	XF-40	MS-60	MS-63
5	1856 w/o LCW	720,000	2.00	4.00	7.50	15.00	70.00	175.00
	1856 w/o LCW	—	—	—	—	—	Proof	600.00
	1856 w/o LCW, inverted A for V in PROVINCE				—	—	Proof	600.00
	BRONZE							
5a	1856 w/LCW	—	—	—	—	—	Proof	600.00

ONE PENNY TOKEN

COPPER

KM#	Date	Mintage	VG-8	F-12	VF-20	XF-40	MS-60	MS-63
2	1824	217,776	3.00	6.00	10.00	25.00	100.00	250.00
	1832	200,000	3.00	6.00	10.00	22.50	80.00	230.00
2a	1832 (imitation)	—	3.75	7.50	22.50	42.50	—	—

KM#	Date	Mintage	VG-8	F-12	VF-20	XF-40	MS-60	MS-63
4	1840	150,000	2.50	5.00	7.50	20.00	100.00	175.00
	1843/0	150,000	12.00	20.00	40.00	80.00	150.00	—
	1843	Inc. Ab.	3.00	6.00	10.00	22.50	110.00	200.00

KM#	Date	Mintage	VG-8	F-12	VF-20	XF-40	MS-60	MS-63
6	1856 w/o LCW	360,000	2.50	5.00	8.50	19.00	110.00	135.00
	1856 w/LCW	Inc. Ab.	2.50	5.00	7.00	15.00	85.00	115.00
	BRONZE							
6a	1856	—	—	—	—	—	Proof	400.00

DECIMAL COINAGE
HALF CENT

BRONZE

KM#	Date	Mintage	VG-8	F-12	VF-20	XF-40	MS-60	MS-63
7	1861	400,000	3.00	5.00	8.00	12.00	60.00	160.00
	1864	400,000	3.00	5.00	8.00	12.00	55.00	155.00
	1864	—	—	—	—	—	Proof	300.00

ONE CENT

BRONZE

KM#	Date	Mintage	VG-8	F-12	VF-20	XF-40	MS-60	MS-63
8	1861	800,000	2.00	3.00	5.00	10.00	70.00	185.00
	1862	(Est.) 100,000	15.00	22.50	40.00	90.00	300.00	625.00
	1864	800,000	2.00	3.00	5.00	10.00	70.00	185.00

NOTE: The Royal Mint Report records mintage of 1,000,000 for 1862 which is considered incorrect.

PRINCE EDWARD ISLAND
ONE CENT

BRONZE

KM#	Date	Mintage	VG-8	F-12	VF-20	XF-40	MS-60	MS-63
4	1871	2,000,000	1.75	2.50	4.50	10.50	75.00	185.00
	1871	—	—	—	—	—	Proof	2000.

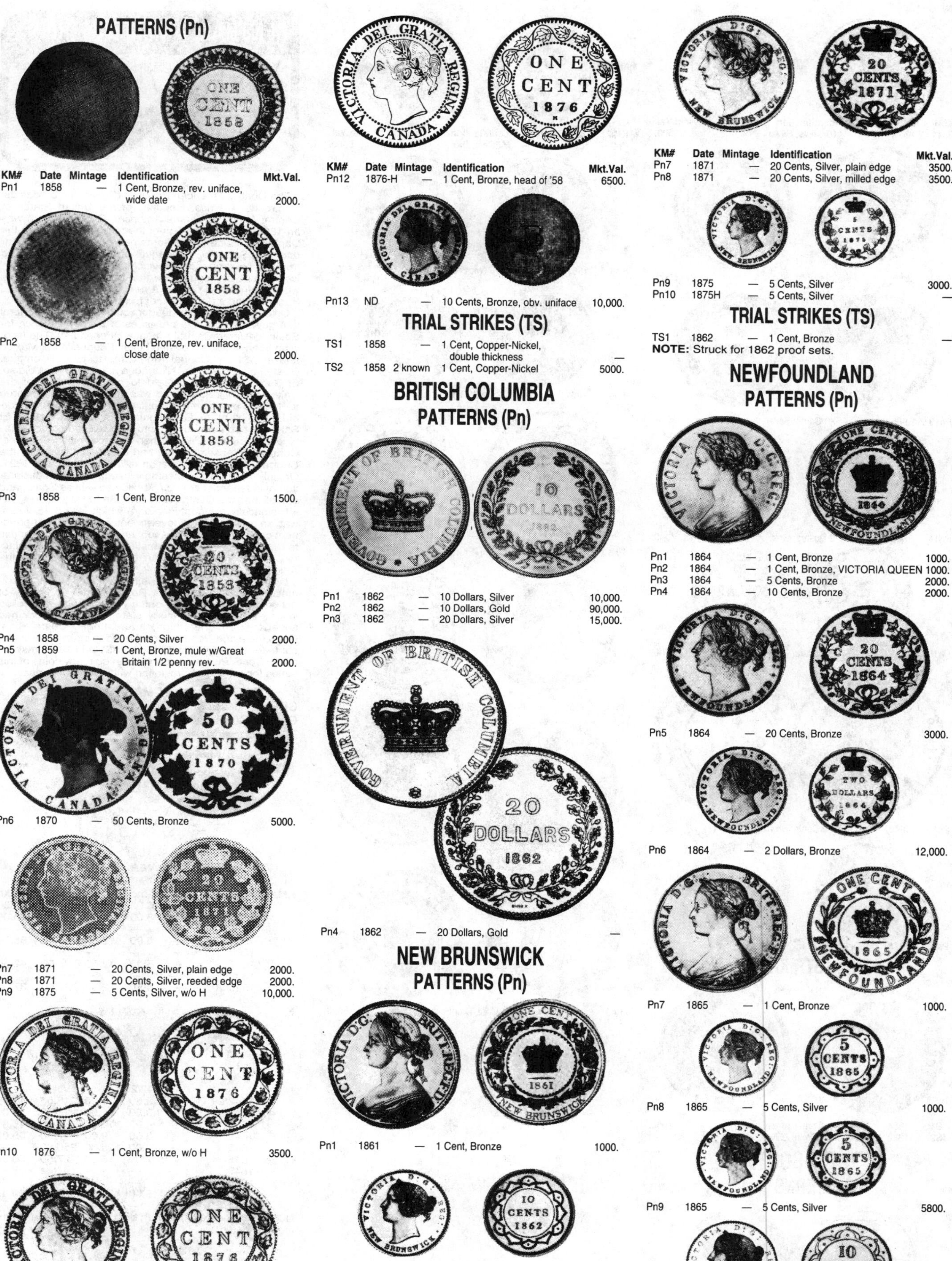

PATTERNS (Pn)

KM#	Date	Mintage	Identification	Mkt.Val.
Pn1	1858	—	1 Cent, Bronze, rev. uniface, wide date	2000.
Pn2	1858	—	1 Cent, Bronze, rev. uniface, close date	2000.
Pn3	1858	—	1 Cent, Bronze	1500.
Pn4	1858	—	20 Cents, Silver	2000.
Pn5	1859	—	1 Cent, Bronze, mule w/Great Britain 1/2 penny rev.	2000.
Pn6	1870	—	50 Cents, Bronze	5000.
Pn7	1871	—	20 Cents, Silver, plain edge	2000.
Pn8	1871	—	20 Cents, Silver, reeded edge	2000.
Pn9	1875	—	5 Cents, Silver, w/o H	10,000.
Pn10	1876	—	1 Cent, Bronze, w/o H	3500.
Pn11	1876-H	—	1 Cent, Copper-Nickel	5000.
Pn12	1876-H	—	1 Cent, Bronze, head of '58	6500.
Pn13	ND	—	10 Cents, Bronze, obv. uniface	10,000.

TRIAL STRIKES (TS)

KM#	Date	Mintage	Identification	Mkt.Val.
TS1	1858	—	1 Cent, Copper-Nickel, double thickness	—
TS2	1858	2 known	1 Cent, Copper-Nickel	5000.

BRITISH COLUMBIA

PATTERNS (Pn)

KM#	Date	Mintage	Identification	Mkt.Val.
Pn1	1862	—	10 Dollars, Silver	10,000.
Pn2	1862	—	10 Dollars, Gold	90,000.
Pn3	1862	—	20 Dollars, Silver	15,000.
Pn4	1862	—	20 Dollars, Gold	—

NEW BRUNSWICK

PATTERNS (Pn)

KM#	Date	Mintage	Identification	Mkt.Val.
Pn1	1861	—	1 Cent, Bronze	1000.
Pn2	1862	—	10 Cents, Silver	3500.
Pn3	1862	—	20 Cents, Silver, WYON on obv.	—
Pn4	1870	—	5 Cents, Silver	3500.
Pn5	1870	—	10 Cents, Silver	3500.
Pn6	1871	—	10 Cents, Silver	3500.
Pn7	1871	—	20 Cents, Silver, plain edge	3500.
Pn8	1871	—	20 Cents, Silver, milled edge	3500.
Pn9	1875	—	5 Cents, Silver	3000.
Pn10	1875H	—	5 Cents, Silver	—

TRIAL STRIKES (TS)

KM#	Date	Mintage	Identification	Mkt.Val.
TS1	1862	—	1 Cent, Bronze	—

NOTE: Struck for 1862 proof sets.

NEWFOUNDLAND

PATTERNS (Pn)

KM#	Date	Mintage	Identification	Mkt.Val.
Pn1	1864	—	1 Cent, Bronze	1000.
Pn2	1864	—	1 Cent, Bronze, VICTORIA QUEEN	1000.
Pn3	1864	—	5 Cents, Bronze	2000.
Pn4	1864	—	10 Cents, Bronze	2000.
Pn5	1864	—	20 Cents, Bronze	3000.
Pn6	1864	—	2 Dollars, Bronze	12,000.
Pn7	1865	—	1 Cent, Bronze	1000.
Pn8	1865	—	5 Cents, Silver	1000.
Pn9	1865	—	5 Cents, Silver	5800.
Pn10	1865	—	10 Cents, Silver	2000.

KM#	Date	Mintage	Identification	Mkt.Val.
Pn11	1865	—	10 Cents, Silver	10,500.
Pn12	1865	—	20 Cents, Silver	3000.
Pn13	1865	—	20 Cents, Silver	3000.
Pn14	1865	—	2 Dollars, Gold	7000.
Pn15	1865	—	2 Dollars, Gold	7000.
Pn16	1870	—	50 Cents, Bronze	5000.
Pn17	1870	—	2 Dollars, Gold	7000.

TRIAL STRIKES (TS)

KM#	Date	Mintage	Identification	Mkt.Val.
TS1	1864	—	1 Cent, Bronze	1000.
TS2	1882	—	50 Cents, Silver, w/o H	—

NOVA SCOTIA
PATTERNS (Pn)

KM#	Date	Mintage	Identification	Mkt.Val.
Pn1	186x	—	1/2 Cent, Bronze	5000.

KM#	Date	Mintage	Identification	Mkt.Val.
Pn2	1861	—	1/2 Cent, Bronze	5000.

KM#	Date	Mintage	Identification	Mkt.Val.
Pn3	1861	—	1/2 Cent, Bronze	5000.

KM#	Date	Mintage	Identification	Mkt.Val.
Pn4	1861	—	1/2 Cent, Bronze	5000.

KM#	Date	Mintage	Identification	Mkt.Val.
Pn6	1861	—	1 Cent, Bronze	5000.

KM#	Date	Mintage	Identification	Mkt.Val.
Pn7	1861	—	1 Cent, Bronze	5000.

KM#	Date	Mintage	Identification	Mkt.Val.
Pn8	1861	—	1 Cent, Bronze	5000.

KM#	Date	Mintage	Identification	Mkt.Val.
Pn9	1861	—	1 Cent, Bronze	5000.

CENTRAL AMERICAN REP

The Central American Republic (Provincias Unidas del Centro de America, Republic of the United States of Central America, Central American Confederation) was an 1823-39 confederation of the former provinces of the Captaincy General of Guatemala - Guatemala, Honduras, El Salvador, Nicaragua and Costa Rica - formed from the southernmost provinces of the short-lived Mexican empire of Augustin de Iturbide. The confederation, which included all Central America between Mexico and Panama, had a population of fewer than 1.5 million.

On Sept. 15, 1821, the leaders of the Captaincy General that governed the five provinces of Central America for Spain, declared Central America independent. The following year, Iturbide crowned himself Augustin I of Mexico and invited the Central Americans to join his empire. Guatemala, Honduras, Nicaragua and Costa Rica did so. El Salvador, which desired to become a part of the United States, refused and was invaded and conquered for Mexico by Vicente Filisola, the military governor Iturbide had sent to Guatemala. But almost before El Salvador had been forced into the Mexican empire, Iturbide was ousted. Filisola then reconvened the National Constituent Assembly that had been established by the Central American declaration of independence of 1821. On July 1, 1823, the Assembly issued a second declaration of independence, from Mexico as well as Spain, and established the Central American Republic.

Historically the confederation, which lasted 15 years, was an anomaly for a government: it had neither permanent capital, army nor treasury and was all but powerless to raise funds. Its writen constitution, was as unsatisfactory as the first constitution of the United States, the Articles of Confederation.

Divided by geography as well as religious and class animosity the citizens of the Republic had no sense of nationhood. By 1827 the entire Republic was embroiled in civil war. By 1839 every state but El Salvador had seceded from the union; interestingly, Costa Rica, Guatemala and Honduras continued to strike coins in the confederation style - until 1850, 1851 and 1861, respectively. Costa Rica then countermarked many coins of this series for continued circulation within its boundaries.

MINT MARKS

CR - San Jose, Costa Rica
G, NG - Guatemala
T - Tegucigalpa, Honduras

MONETARY SYSTEM

16 Reales = 1 Escudo

1/4 REAL

.8500 g, .903 SILVER, .0246 oz ASW
Mint mark: G

KM#	Date	Mintage	Fine	VF	XF	Unc
1	1824	—	10.00	20.00	40.00	90.00
	1826	—	6.00	12.50	25.00	60.00
	1828	—	—	—	Rare	—
	1831	—	6.00	12.50	30.00	65.00
	1833	—	—	—	Rare	—
	1837	—	5.00	12.50	28.00	42.50
	1838	—	—	—	Rare	—
	1840/30	—	4.50	12.50	27.50	37.50
	1841	—	—	—	Rare	—

1842/29

KM#	Date	Mintage	Fine	VF	XF	Unc
	1842/29	—	3.50	9.00	18.50	40.00
	1842/37	—	3.50	9.00	17.50	35.00
	1843	—	4.00	12.00	20.00	45.00
	1844	—	3.50	9.00	17.50	35.00
	1845	—	70.00	125.00	250.00	—
	1846	—	7.00	15.00	27.50	50.00
	1847	—	—	—	Rare	—
	1848	—	—	—	Rare	—
	1850	—	15.00	35.00	60.00	120.00
	1851	—	—	—	Rare	—

NOTE: 1846 date exists with both coin and medal alignment.

Mint mark: CR

KM#	Date	Mintage	Fine	VF	XF	Unc
23	1845	—	60.00	130.00	225.00	500.00

1/2 REAL

1.6900 g., .903 SILVER, .0490 oz ASW
Mint mark: NG

KM#	Date	Mintage	Fine	VF	XF	Unc
2	1824 M	—	13.50	30.00	70.00	225.00

Mint mark: T
Similar to KM#20.

KM#	Date	Mintage	VG	Fine	VF	XF
18	1830 F	3 known	—	—	Rare	—
	1831 F	—	— Reported, not confirmed			

Mint mark: CR

KM#	Date	Mintage	VG	Fine	VF	XF
20	1831 E	—	6.00	16.50	35.00	60.00
	1831 F	—	4.50	12.50	25.00	42.50
	1843 M	—	3.00	7.50	20.00	45.00
	1845 B	—	15.00	35.00	75.00	150.00

1.6900 g, .750 SILVER, .0407 oz ASW

KM#	Date	Mintage	VG	Fine	VF	XF
20a	1846 JB CRESCA	—	6.00	15.00	30.00	60.00
	1846 JB CREZCA	—	20.00	45.00	85.00	180.00
	1847 JB CRESCA	—	20.00	45.00	80.00	170.00
	1847 JB CREZCA	—	5.00	13.50	30.00	60.00
	1848 JB	—	3.00	8.50	22.50	47.50
	1849 JB	—	15.00	35.00	75.00	150.00

REAL

3.3800 g, .903 SILVER, .0981 oz ASW
Mint mark: NG

KM#	Date	Mintage	Fine	VF	XF	Unc
3	1824 M	—	13.50	32.50	55.00	175.00
	1828 M	—	45.00	115.00	200.00	—

Mint mark: T
Obv. leg: REP. DEL CENT. DE AMER.
Rev. leg: LIB. CRESC. FEC.

KM#	Date	Mintage	Fine	VF	XF	Unc
19.1	1824 NR	3 known	—	—	Rare	—

KM#	Date	Mintage	Fine	VF	XF	Unc
19.2	1825 M	1 known	—	—	Rare	—
	1830 F	—	10.00	25.00	55.00	300.00
	1831 F	—	— Reported, not confirmed			

Mint mark: CR

KM#	Date	Mintage	VG	Fine	VF	XF
21	1831 E	—	12.50	25.00	65.00	130.00
	1831 F	—	9.00	20.00	50.00	100.00

3.3800 g, .750 SILVER, .0815 oz ASW

KM#	Date	Mintage	VG	Fine	VF	XF
21a	1848 JB	—	27.50	60.00	125.00	225.00
	1849 JB	—	13.50	30.00	50.00	110.00

2 REALES

6.7700 g, .903 SILVER, .1965 oz ASW
Mint mark: T
Obv. leg: REP.D.CENT.D.AMER.
Rev. leg: LIB.CRESC.FEC.

KM#	Date	Mintage	Good	VG	Fine	VF
10	1825 JD	2 known	—	—	Rare	—
	1825 NR	—	65.00	110.00	250.00	400.00

Obv. leg: REPUBLICA DE CENTRO AMERIC.
Rev. leg: LIBRE CRESCA FECUNDO.

KM#	Date	Mintage	VG	Fine	VF	XF
9.1	1825 M	—	—	—	Rare	—

Obv. leg: REPUBLICA DEL CENTRO AMER.
Rev. leg: LIBRE CRESCA FECUND.

KM#	Date	Mintage	VG	Fine	VF	XF
9.2	1825 M	—	—	—	Rare	—

Obv. leg: REPUBLICA DEL CENTRO DE AMER.
Rev. leg: LIBRE CRESCA FECUNDO.

KM#	Date	Mintage	VG	Fine	VF	XF
9.3	1831 F	—	4.50	9.00	20.00	35.00
	1832 F	—	12.50	25.00	45.00	100.00

6.5000 g, .750 SILVER, .1567 oz ASW
Mint mark: CR

KM#	Date	Mintage	VG	Fine	VF	XF
24	1849 JB	*4-5 known	150.00	300.00	600.00	900.00

8 REALES

27.0700 g, .903 SILVER, .7859 oz ASW
Mint mark: NG

KM#	Date	Mintage	Fine	VF	XF	Unc
4	1824 M	—	25.00	50.00	125.00	750.00
4	1825 M	—	25.00	50.00	125.00	750.00
	1826/5 M	—	30.00	60.00	150.00	750.00
	1826 M	—	25.00	50.00	125.00	750.00
	1827 M	—	25.00	60.00	150.00	750.00
	1828 M	—	25.00	70.00	175.00	750.00
	1829 M	—	25.00	50.00	125.00	750.00
	1830 M rev. of 1830	—	250.00	500.00	900.00	—
	1830 M rev. of 1831, 2 crossed marks below 8	—	300.00	600.00	1000.	—
	1831 M	—	400.00	750.00	1200.	—
	1834 M	—	120.00	200.00	350.00	800.00
	1835 M coin	—	25.00	50.00	125.00	750.00
	1835 M medal		25.00	50.00	125.00	750.00
	1836 M	—	25.00	50.00	125.00	750.00
	1836 BA	—	25.00	60.00	150.00	750.00
	1837 BA	—	25.00	50.00	125.00	750.00
	1838 BA	—	— Reported, not confirmed			
	1839/7 MA/BA	—	60.00	100.00	250.00	750.00
	1840/37 MA/BA	—	25.00	65.00	150.00	750.00
	1840/39 MA	—	25.00	50.00	125.00	750.00
	1840 MA	—	25.00	50.00	125.00	750.00
	1841/37 MA/BA	—	125.00	250.00	500.00	900.00
	1841 MA	—	100.00	200.00	400.00	850.00
	1842/37 MA/BA	—	25.00	60.00	150.00	750.00
	1842/0 MA	—	25.00	60.00	150.00	750.00
	1842 MA	—	25.00	50.00	125.00	750.00
	1846 MA	—	75.00	150.00	400.00	950.00
	1846/2 AE/MA w/CREZCA over CRESCA	—	40.00	75.00	200.00	750.00
	1846 A	—	25.00	65.00	150.00	750.00
	1847 A	—	40.00	75.00	200.00	750.00

Mint mark: CR

KM#	Date	Mintage	Fine	VF	XF	Unc
22	1831 E	—	2000.	4000.	7500.	15,000.
	1831 F	—	400.00	1000.	2500.	—

1/2 ESCUDO

1.6875 g, .875 GOLD, .0474 oz AGW
Mint mark: NG

KM#	Date	Mintage	VG	Fine	VF	XF
5	1824 M	—	35.00	55.00	100.00	200.00
	1825/4 M	—	40.00	60.00	115.00	180.00
	1825 M	—	30.00	45.00	85.00	150.00
	1826 M	—	40.00	60.00	115.00	180.00
	1843 M	—	70.00	120.00	225.00	325.00

Mint mark: CR
Provisional Issue

KM#	Date	Mintage	VG	Fine	VF	XF
11	1825 MU	2-4 known	—	—	Rare	—

KM#	Date	Mintage	VG	Fine	VF	XF
13.1	1828 F	4,435	75.00	125.00	200.00	350.00
	1843 M	593	90.00	180.00	360.00	600.00
	1846 JB	.013	30.00	50.00	80.00	140.00
	1847 JB	.023	30.00	50.00	80.00	140.00
	1848 JB	.014	30.00	50.00	80.00	140.00
	1849 JB	I.A.	90.00	180.00	350.00	550.00

Mint mark: CR w/inverted C.

KM#	Date	Mintage	VG	Fine	VF	XF
13.2	1847 JB	I.A.	30.00	50.00	80.00	140.00
	1848 JB	I.A.	30.00	50.00	80.00	140.00

ESCUDO

3.3750 g, .875 GOLD, .0949 oz AGW
Mint mark: NG

KM#	Date	Mintage	VG	Fine	VF	XF
6	1824 M	—	100.00	300.00	750.00	1200.
	1825 M	—	70.00	175.00	350.00	800.00

Mint mark: CR

KM#	Date	Mintage	VG	Fine	VF	XF
14	1828 F	—	—	—	Rare	—
	1833 E	.010	40.00	100.00	150.00	250.00
	1833 F	Inc. Ab.	— Reported, not confirmed			

KM#	Date	Mintage	VG	Fine	VF	XF
14	1844 M	6,353	40.00	100.00	150.00	250.00
	1845 JB	8,672	40.00	150.00	250.00	375.00
	1846 JB	2,722	40.00	100.00	175.00	260.00
	1847 JB	3,510	40.00	100.00	175.00	260.00
	1848 JB	.010	40.00	80.00	150.00	225.00
	1849 JB	.013	40.00	90.00	150.00	225.00
	1850 JB	—	—	Reported, not confirmed		

2 ESCUDOS

6.7500 g, .875 GOLD, .1899 oz AGW
Mint mark: NG

KM#	Date	Mintage	VG	Fine	VF	XF
12	1825 M	—	90.00	180.00	320.00	450.00
	1826 M	—	90.00	180.00	320.00	450.00
	1827 M	—	90.00	180.00	320.00	450.00
	1828 M	—	90.00	180.00	320.00	450.00
	1830 M	—	90.00	250.00	400.00	550.00
	1834 M	—	90.00	375.00	750.00	1000.
	1835 M	—	90.00	190.00	320.00	450.00
	1836 M	—	100.00	200.00	400.00	500.00
	1837 BA	—	100.00	200.00	425.00	750.00
	1840 MA	—	—	—	Rare	—
	1842 MA	—	100.00	200.00	400.00	725.00
	1844 B	—	100.00	200.00	425.00	750.00
	1846 A	—	100.00	200.00	400.00	550.00
	1847 A	—	100.00	200.00	400.00	625.00

Mint mark: CR

KM#	Date	Mintage	VG	Fine	VF	XF
15	1828 F	2,750	90.00	190.00	350.00	700.00
	1835 F	5,452	80.00	170.00	275.00	550.00
	1843 M	4,482	90.00	190.00	350.00	700.00
	1846 JB	—	—	Reported, not confirmed		
	1850 JB	7,432	BV	125.00	200.00	400.00

4 ESCUDOS

13.5000 g, .875 GOLD, .3798 oz AGW
Mint mark: NG

KM#	Date	Mintage	VG	Fine	VF	XF
7	1824 M	—	700.00	1450.	2500.	4500.
	1825 M	—	950.	1700.	2800.	4800.
	1826 M	—	—	Reported, not confirmed		

Mint mark: CR

KM#	Date	Mintage	VG	Fine	VF	XF
16	1828 F	3,048	400.00	600.00	1150.	2750.
	1835 F	697 pcs.	275.00	500.00	1000.	2500.
	1837 E	.011	275.00	525.00	1100.	2750.
	1837 F	Inc. Ab.	—	—	Rare	—
	1849 JB	441 pcs.	1200.	2000.	3750.	6000.

8 ESCUDOS

27.0000 g, .875 GOLD, .7596 oz AGW
Mint mark: NG

KM#	Date	Mintage	VG	Fine	VF	XF
8	1824 M	—	1000.	2000.	4000.	7500.
	1825 M	—	1500.	3500.	7000.	12,000.

NOTE: Stack's Hammel sale 9-82 Unc 1824 M realized $27,000.

Mint mark: CR

KM#	Date	Mintage	VG	Fine	VF	XF
17	1828 F	5,302	500.00	1000.	2000.	3200.
	1833 F	4,459	500.00	1000.	2000.	3200.
	1837 E	2,028	950.00	1550.	3250.	5500.
	1837 F	Inc. Ab.	1200.	2100.	4000.	6500.

NOTE: Stack's Hammel sale 9-82 AU 1828 F realized $9500.

Listings For

CEYLON: refer to Sri (Shri) Lanka

CHILE

The Republic of Chile, a ribbon-like country on the Pacific coast of southern South America, has an area of 292,135 sq. mi. (756,950 sq. km.) and a population of 14.2 million. Capital: Santiago. Historically, the economic base of Chile has been the rich mineral deposits of its northern provinces. Copper has accounted for more than 75 percent of Chile's export earnings in recent years. Other important mineral exports are iron ore, iodine and nitrate of soda. Fresh fruits and vegetables, as well as wine are increasingly significant in inter-hemispheric trade.

Diego de Almargo was the first Spaniard to attempt to wrest Chile from the Incas and Araucanian tribes in 1536. He failed, and was followed by Pedro de Valdivia, a favorite of Pizarro, who founded Santiago in 1541. When the Napoleonic Wars involved Spain, leaving the constituent parts of the Spanish Empire to their own devices, Chilean patriots formed a national government and proclaimed the country's independence, Sept. 18, 1810. Independence however, was not secured until Feb. 12, 1818, after a bitter struggle led by Bernardo O'Higgins and San Martin. Despite a long steady history of monetary devaluation - reflected in declining weight and fineness in its currency, Chile developed a strong democracy. This was displaced when rampant inflation characterized chaotic and subsequently repressive governments in the mid to late 20th century.

RULERS

Spanish until 1818

MINT MARKS

So - Santiago

MINTMASTERS INITIALS

Letter	Date	Name
AJ	1800-1801	Agustin de Infante y Prado and Jose Maria de Bobadilla
D		Domingo Eizaguirre
F		Francisco Rodriguez Brochero
FJ,JF	1803-1817	Francisco Rodriguez Brochero & Jose Maria de Bobadilla

MONETARY SYSTEM

16 Reales = 1 Escudo

COLONIAL MILLED COINAGE

1/4 REAL

.8460 g, .896 SILVER, .0243 oz ASW
Mint mark: So

KM#	Date	Mintage	VG	Fine	VF	XF
63	1801	.057	10.00	15.00	32.00	65.00
	1802	.056	10.00	15.00	32.00	65.00
	1803	.054	10.00	15.00	32.00	65.00
	1804	.056	10.00	15.00	32.00	65.00
	1805	.056	10.00	15.00	32.00	65.00
	1806/5	.054	10.00	15.00	32.00	65.00
	1806	Inc. Ab.	10.00	15.00	32.00	65.00
	1807	.057	10.00	15.00	32.00	65.00
	1808	.057	10.00	15.00	32.00	65.00

NOTE: Earlier dates (1796-1800) exist for this type.

Obv: Lion. Rev: Castle.

KM#	Date	Mintage	VG	Fine	VF	XF
73	1809	.054	15.00	25.00	50.00	100.00
	1810	.054	10.00	15.00	32.00	65.00
	1811	.054	10.00	15.00	32.00	65.00
	1812	.071	10.00	15.00	32.00	65.00
	1813	.063	10.00	15.00	32.00	65.00
	1814	.067	10.00	15.00	32.00	65.00
	1815	.054	10.00	15.00	32.00	65.00
	1816/5	.082	10.00	15.00	32.00	65.00
	1816	Inc.Ab.	10.00	15.00	32.00	65.00
	1817	—	10.00	15.00	32.00	65.00
	1818/6	.403	15.00	20.00	40.00	80.00
	1818	Inc. Ab.	15.00	20.00	40.00	80.00

NOTE: 1817 and 1818 dated coins struck under the Republic.

1/2 REAL

1.6921 g, .896 SILVER, .0487 oz ASW
Obv. leg: CAROLUS IIII. . ., bust of Charles IV.
Rev: Similar to KM#64.

KM#	Date	Mintage	VG	Fine	VF	XF
57	1801 AJ	.059	8.00	12.00	22.00	55.00
	1801 AI (broken J)	Inc. Ab.	8.00	12.00	22.00	55.00
	1802 JJ	.078	8.00	12.00	22.00	55.00
	1803 FJ	.036	20.00	40.00	75.00	150.00
	1804/3 FJ	.058	10.00	15.00	30.00	70.00
	1804 FJ	I.A.	8.00	12.00	22.00	70.00
	1805 FJ	.028	12.00	20.00	40.00	80.00
	1806 FJ	.059	8.00	12.00	22.00	55.00
	1807 FJ	.040	8.00	12.00	22.00	55.00
	1808/7 FJ	.058	10.00	15.00	30.00	60.00
	1808 FJ	I.A.	8.00	12.00	22.00	55.00

NOTE: Earlier dates (1792-1800) exist for this type.

Obv. leg: FERDIN VII, bust of Charles IV.

KM#	Date	Mintage	VG	Fine	VF	XF
64	1808 FJ	I.A.	5.00	10.00	20.00	60.00
	1809/8 FJ	.051	7.50	15.00	30.00	70.00
	1809 FJ	I.A.	6.50	12.00	22.00	55.00
	1810 FJ	.050	6.50	12.00	22.00	55.00
	1811 FJ	.018	6.50	12.00	22.00	55.00
	1812 FJ	.125	6.50	12.00	22.00	55.00
	1813 FJ	.218	6.50	12.00	22.00	55.00
	1814 FJ	.077	6.00	10.00	20.00	50.00
	1815 FJ	.099	6.00	10.00	20.00	50.00
	1816 FJ	.119	6.00	10.00	20.00	50.00
	1817 FJ	—	6.50	12.00	25.00	65.00
	1817 FD	—	35.00	60.00	120.00	250.00
	1817 FI	—	—	Reported, not confirmed		

REAL

3.3841 g, .896 SILVER, .0975 oz ASW
Obv. leg: CAROLUS IIII. . ., bust of Charles IV.
Rev: Similar to KM#65.

KM#	Date	Mintage	VG	Fine	VF	XF
58	1801 AJ	.053	6.00	12.00	22.50	60.00
	1801 AI (broken J)	Inc. Ab.	6.00	12.00	22.50	60.00
	1802 JJ	.081	6.00	11.50	20.00	55.00
	1801 AI (broken J)	Inc. Ab.	6.00	12.00	22.50	60.00
	1803 FJ	.018	100.00	200.00	—	—
	1804 FJ	.035	6.00	11.50	20.00	55.00
	1804 FJ/JJ	I.A.	9.00	22.00	35.00	100.00
	1805 FJ	.019	6.50	15.00	27.50	70.00
	1806 FJ	.038	6.50	15.00	35.00	90.00
	1807/6 FJ	.023	9.00	22.00	35.00	100.00
	1807 FJ	I.A.	6.50	15.00	35.00	80.00
	1808/7 FJ	.034	—	—	—	—
	1808 FJ	I.A.	6.50	15.00	27.50	70.00

NOTE: Earlier dates (1792-1800) exist for this type.

Obv. leg: FERDIN. VII. . ., bust of Charles IV.

KM#	Date	Mintage	VG	Fine	VF	XF
65	1808 FJ	I.A.	20.00	40.00	75.00	150.00
	1809/8 FJ	.029	7.50	15.00	25.00	70.00
	1809 FJ	I.A.	7.50	15.00	25.00	70.00
	1810 FJ	.079	7.50	15.00	25.00	70.00
	1811 FJ	.020	10.00	20.00	40.00	90.00
	1812/1 FJ	.043	12.00	22.50	50.00	100.00
	1812 FJ	I.A.	7.50	15.00	25.00	70.00
	1813 FJ	.213	7.50	15.00	25.00	70.00
	1814 FJ	.054	7.50	15.00	25.00	70.00
	1815 FJ	.041	7.50	15.00	25.00	70.00
	1816 FJ	.123	7.50	15.00	25.00	70.00
	1817 FJ	—	7.50	15.00	25.00	70.00

2 REALES

6.7682 g, .896 SILVER, .1950 oz ASW
Obv. leg: CAROLUS IIII. . ., bust of Charles IV.

KM#	Date	Mintage	VG	Fine	VF	XF
59	1801 AJ	.039	10.00	22.50	50.00	100.00
	1802 JJ	.028	10.00	22.50	50.00	100.00
	1803 FJ	.025	10.00	22.50	50.00	100.00
	1803 FJ/JJ	I.A.	12.00	25.00	60.00	120.00
	1804 FJ	.028	10.00	22.50	50.00	100.00
	1804 FJ/inverted mm	Inc. Ab.	12.00	25.00	60.00	120.00
	1805 FJ	.024	10.00	22.50	50.00	100.00

KM#	Date	Mintage	VG	Fine	VF	XF
59	1806/5 FJ	.066	12.00	25.00	60.00	120.00
	1806 FJ inverted mm					
		Inc. Ab.	12.00	25.00	60.00	120.00
	1806 FJ	I.A.	10.00	22.50	50.00	100.00
	1807 FJ	.042	10.00	22.50	50.00	100.00
	1808 FJ	.054	10.00	22.50	50.00	100.00

NOTE: Earlier dates (1792-1800) exist for this type.

Obv. leg: FERDIN. VII. . ., bust of Charles IV.

KM#	Date	Mintage	VG	Fine	VF	XF
66	1808 FJ	I.A.	20.00	40.00	80.00	160.00
	1809 FJ	.041	20.00	40.00	80.00	160.00

Obv. leg: FERDIN. VII. . ., imaginary laureate military bust.

KM#	Date	Mintage	VG	Fine	VF	XF
74	1810 FJ	.045	20.00	35.00	75.00	200.00
	1810 FJ inverted A for V in VII					
		Inc. Ab.	35.00	70.00	—	—
	1811 FJ	.027	25.00	50.00	100.00	250.00

Obv. leg: FERDIN. VII. . ., bust of Ferdinand.

KM#	Date	Mintage	VG	Fine	VF	XF
79	1812 FJ	.069	12.00	20.00	40.00	80.00
	1813 FJ	.136	10.00	18.00	35.00	70.00
	1813 FJ/inverted mm					
		Inc. Ab.	12.00	20.00	40.00	80.00
	1814 FJ	4,000	80.00	150.00	250.00	—
	1815 FJ	.024	15.00	30.00	65.00	130.00
	1816 FJ	.067	10.00	18.00	35.00	70.00
	1817 FJ	—	12.00	20.00	40.00	80.00

4 REALES

13.5365 g, .896 SILVER, .3900 oz ASW
Obv. leg: CAROLUS IIII. . ., bust of Charles IV.

KM#	Date	Mintage	VG	Fine	VF	XF
60	1801 AJ	2,000	135.00	245.00	360.00	—
	1802 JJ	.018	60.00	120.00	190.00	—
	1803 FJ	9,000	75.00	165.00	250.00	—
	1804/3 FJ					
		6,000	65.00	120.00	190.00	—
	1804 FJ	I.A.	35.00	65.00	115.00	225.00
	1805 FJ	9,000	70.00	100.00	190.00	325.00
	1806 FJ	.020	30.00	45.00	95.00	200.00
	1807 FJ	.048	30.00	45.00	95.00	200.00
	1808/7 FJ	.025	35.00	65.00	115.00	225.00
	1808 FJ	I.A.	45.00	80.00	130.00	285.00

NOTE: Earlier dates (1792-1800) exist for this type.

Obv. leg: FERDIN. VII. . ., bust of Charles IV.

KM#	Date	Mintage	VG	Fine	VF	XF
67	1808/7 FJ inverted J					
		Inc. Ab.	30.00	50.00	90.00	225.00
	1808 FJ	I.A.	30.00	50.00	90.00	225.00
	1808 FJ/inverted J					
		Inc. Ab.	30.00	50.00	90.00	225.00
	1809 FJ	.015	115.00	170.00	280.00	480.00
	1810 FJ	.010	45.00	70.00	115.00	250.00
	1811 FJ	6,000	45.00	85.00	125.00	275.00
	1811 FJ/inverted J					
		Inc. Ab.	65.00	90.00	125.00	275.00
	1812 FJ	.027	30.00	45.00	85.00	200.00
	1813 FJ	.034	30.00	45.00	75.00	180.00
	1813 FJ/inverted J					
		Inc. Ab.	30.00	45.00	75.00	180.00
	1815 FJ	.010	90.00	170.00	400.00	750.00

8 REALES

27.0730 g, .896 SILVER, .7799 oz ASW
Obv. leg: CAROLUS IIII. . ., bust of Charles IIII.

KM#	Date	Mintage	VG	Fine	VF	XF
51	1801 AJ	.185	65.00	100.00	200.00	350.00
	1802/1 JJ/AJ					
		—	100.00	175.00	280.00	550.00
	1802 JJ	.160	65.00	100.00	200.00	350.00
	1803/2 FJ/JJ					
		.111	65.00	120.00	240.00	450.00
	1803 FJ	I.A.	160.00	280.00	475.00	725.00
	1804/3 FJ	.129	100.00	175.00	280.00	550.00
	1804 FJ	I.A.	65.00	100.00	200.00	400.00
	1805 FJ	.159	65.00	100.00	200.00	400.00
	1806/5 FJ	.155	160.00	280.00	400.00	625.00
	1806 FJ	I.A.	160.00	280.00	400.00	625.00
	1807 FJ	.094	160.00	280.00	400.00	675.00
	1808 FJ	.134	125.00	200.00	320.00	625.00

NOTE: Earlier dates (1791-1800) exist for this type.

Obv. leg: FERDIN. VII. . ., imaginary military bust.

KM#	Date	Mintage	VG	Fine	VF	XF
68	1808 FJ	I.A.	350.00	650.00	1750.	4000.
	1809 FJ	.123	100.00	200.00	500.00	1000.

Obv. leg: FERDIN. VII. . ., imaginary laureate military bust.

KM#	Date	Mintage	VG	Fine	VF	XF
75	1810 FJ	.126	100.00	200.00	400.00	700.00
	1811 FJ	.097	100.00	200.00	400.00	700.00

Obv. leg: FERDIN. VII. . ., bust of Ferdinand.

KM#	Date	Mintage	VG	Fine	VF	XF
80	1812 FJ	.307	70.00	100.00	150.00	300.00
	1813 FJ	.415	70.00	100.00	150.00	300.00
	1814 FJ	.368	70.00	100.00	150.00	300.00
	1815 FJ	.388	70.00	100.00	150.00	300.00
	1816 FJ	.386	70.00	100.00	150.00	300.00
	1816/6 FJ	I.A.	85.00	160.00	250.00	450.00
	1817 FJ	*.132	750.00	1350.	2250.	3500.

ESCUDO

3.3841 g, .875 GOLD, .0952 oz AGW
Obv. leg: CAROL IIII. . ., bust of Charles IV.
Rev: Arms, order chain.

KM#	Date	Mintage	VG	Fine	VF	XF
61	1801 AJ	1,088	125.00	200.00	450.00	900.00
	1802 JJ					
		748 pcs.	200.00	400.00	650.00	1150.
	1803 FJ/JJ					
		1,156	250.00	450.00	850.00	1500.
	1803 FJ					
		Inc. Ab.	175.00	265.00	450.00	900.00
	1804 FJ	1,428	175.00	265.00	450.00	900.00
	1805 FJ/JJ					
		816 pcs.	200.00	350.00	700.00	1250.
	1805 FJ					
		Inc. Ab.	175.00	265.00	450.00	900.00
	1806 FJ					
		544 pcs.	200.00	400.00	650.00	1150.
	1807 FJ					
		544 pcs.	200.00	400.00	650.00	1150.
	1808 FJ	2,448	125.00	200.00	350.00	700.00

NOTE: Earlier dates (1792-1800) exist for this type.

Obv. leg: FERDIN, VII. . ., imaginary military bust. Rev: Arms.

KM#	Date	Mintage	VG	Fine	VF	XF
69	1808	3,986	—	—	Rare	—
	1809	5,026	—	—	Rare	—

Obv. leg: FERDIN. VII.D.G. . ., bust of Charles IV.

KM#	Date	Mintage	VG	Fine	VF	XF
76	1810 FJ					
		816 pcs.	125.00	300.00	450.00	900.00
	1811 FJ					

KM#	Date	Mintage	VG	Fine	VF	XF
76		680 pcs.	125.00	300.00	450.00	900.00
	1812/1 FJ	952 pcs.	150.00	350.00	550.00	1100.
	1812 FJ	Inc. Ab.	125.00	300.00	450.00	750.00
	1813 FJ	4,556	95.00	145.00	200.00	450.00
	1814 FJ	1,152	125.00	300.00	450.00	900.00
	1815 FJ	816 pcs.	125.00	300.00	450.00	900.00
	1816 FJ	408 pcs.	175.00	350.00	500.00	1000.
	1817 FJ	.022	95.00	145.00	200.00	450.00
	1817 JF	I.A.	100.00	200.00	275.00	525.00

NOTE: An additional 17,860 pcs. were struck between 1818-1823; the actual date on the coin is unknown.

2 ESCUDOS

6.7682 g, .875 GOLD, .1904 oz AGW
Obv. leg: CAROL IIII. . ., bust of Charles III.
Rev: Arms.

KM#	Date	Mintage	VG	Fine	VF	XF
53	1801 AJ	680 pcs.	400.00	800.00	1450.	2250.
	1802 JJ	374 pcs.	525.00	900.00	1550.	2500.
	1803 FJ	578 pcs.	400.00	800.00	1450.	2250.
	1804 FJ	544 pcs.	400.00	800.00	1450.	2250.
	1805 FJ	646 pcs.	400.00	800.00	1450.	2250.
	1806 FJ	306 pcs.	525.00	900.00	1650.	2700.
	1807 FJ	340 pcs.	525.00	900.00	1650.	2700.
	1808/7 FJ	1,020	400.00	800.00	1450.	2250.
	1808 FJ	Inc. Ab.	400.00	800.00	1450.	2250.
	1810 FJ	510 pcs.	400.00	800.00	1450.	2250.
	1811 FJ	340 pcs.	400.00	800.00	1450.	2250.
	1812 FJ	476 pcs.	350.00	600.00	1150.	1850.
	1813 FJ	2,958	350.00	550.00	900.00	1600.

NOTE: Earlier dates (1791-1800) exist for this type.

Obv. leg: FERDIN.VII. . ., bust of Charles III.

KM#	Date	Mintage	VG	Fine	VF	XF
70	1810 FJ	Inc. Ab.	250.00	400.00	750.00	1400.
	1811 FJ	Inc. Ab.	300.00	500.00	900.00	1650.

Obv. leg: FERDIN. VII. . ., bust of Charles IV.

KM#	Date	Mintage	VG	Fine	VF	XF
81	1813 FJ	—	350.00	600.00	1000.	1850.
	1814 FJ	682 pcs.	250.00	400.00	700.00	1350.
	1815 FJ	408 pcs.	325.00	500.00	900.00	1650.
	1816 FJ	608 pcs.	325.00	500.00	900.00	1650.
	1817 FJ	168 pcs.	450.00	850.00	1600.	2600.

NOTE: An additional 19,876 pcs. were struck between 1818-1823; the actual dates of these coins are unknown.

4 ESCUDOS

13.5365 g, .875 GOLD, .3808 oz AGW
Obv. leg: CAROL IIII. . ., bust of Charles IV.
Rev: Arms.

KM#	Date	Mintage	VG	Fine	VF	XF
62	1801 AJ	340 pcs.	500.00	750.00	1100.	1750.
	1802 JJ	374 pcs.	500.00	750.00	1100.	1750.
	1803 FJ	476 pcs.	500.00	750.00	1100.	1750.
	1804 FJ	255 pcs.	575.00	850.00	1250.	2000.
	1805 FJ	323 pcs.	575.00	850.00	1250.	2000.
	1806 FJ	204 pcs.	575.00	850.00	1250.	2000.
	1807 FJ	187 pcs.	600.00	900.00	1500.	2250.
	1808/7 FJ	1,207	550.00	800.00	1200.	2000.
	1808 FJ	I.A.	500.00	750.00	1000.	1650.

NOTE: Earlier dates (1792-1800) exist for this type.

Obv. leg: FERDIN. VII. . ., bust of Ferdinand.
Rev: Arms.

KM#	Date	Mintage	VG	Fine	VF	XF
71	1808 FJ	I.A.	—	—	Rare	—
	1809 FJ	I.A.	—	—	Rare	—

Obv. leg: FERDIN. VII. . ., bust of Charles IV.

KM#	Date	Mintage	VG	Fine	VF	XF
77	1810 FJ	272 pcs.	425.00	700.00	1250.	2000.
	1811 FJ	170 pcs.	750.00	1250.	1850.	3000.
	1812 FJ	254 pcs.	425.00	700.00	1250.	2000.
	1813 FJ	1,462	375.00	650.00	1150.	1850.
	1814 FJ	340 pcs.	425.00	700.00	1250.	2000.
	1815 FJ	290 pcs.	425.00	700.00	1250.	2000.
	1816 FJ	100 pcs.	650.00	1000.	1500.	2250.
	1817 FJ	68 pcs.	1000.	1600.	2250.	3000.

NOTE: An additional 6,560 pcs. were struck between 1818-1823; the actual date on the coin is unknown.

8 ESCUDOS

27.0730 g, .875 GOLD, .7616 oz AGW
Obv. leg: CAROL IIII. . ., bust of Charles III.

KM#	Date	Mintage	VG	Fine	VF	XF
54	1801 AJ	.046	375.00	525.00	650.00	900.00
	1802 JJ	.049	375.00	525.00	650.00	900.00
	1803/2 FJ/JJ	.044	375.00	600.00	750.00	1100.
	1803 FJ	I.A.	375.00	525.00	650.00	900.00
	1804 FJ	.040	375.00	525.00	650.00	900.00
	1805 FJ	.044	375.00	525.00	650.00	900.00
	1806/5 FJ	.040	375.00	525.00	650.00	900.00
	1806 FJ	I.A.	375.00	525.00	650.00	900.00
	1806 JF	I.A.	400.00	700.00	850.00	1250.
	1807 FJ	.039	375.00	650.00	725.00	1100.
	1807 JF	I.A.	375.00	650.00	725.00	1100.
	1808 FJ	.039	375.00	525.00	650.00	900.00

NOTE: Earlier dates (1791-1800) exist for this type.

Obv. leg: FERDIN. VII. . ., imaginary military bust.

KM#	Date	Mintage	VG	Fine	VF	XF
72	1808 FJ	I.A.	700.00	1200.	1500.	2750.
	1809 FJ	.041	400.00	650.00	1000.	1650.
	1810 FJ	.055	400.00	650.00	1000.	1650.
	1810 FJ inverted mint mark	Inc. Ab.	700.00	1200.	1500.	2750.
	1811 FJ	.044	400.00	650.00	1000.	1650.

Obv. leg: FERDIN. VII. . ., bust of Charles IV.

KM#	Date	Mintage	VG	Fine	VF	XF
78	1811 FJ	—	900.00	1500.	2400.	4500.
	1812 FJ	.048	375.00	525.00	650.00	900.00
	1813/2 FT	.037	375.00	525.00	650.00	900.00
	1813 FJ	I.A.	375.00	525.00	650.00	900.00
	1814 FJ	.029	375.00	525.00	650.00	900.00
	1815 FJ	.039	375.00	525.00	650.00	900.00
	1816 FJ	.030	375.00	400.00	500.00	900.00
	1817/6 FJ	.011	375.00	425.00	500.00	900.00
	1817/7/8 FJ	I.A.	400.00	800.00	1500.	2500.
	1817 FJ	I.A.	375.00	425.00	500.00	900.00

ROYALIST COINAGE

CHILOE

An island off the southwest coast of Chile. The island was the last outpost of the Spanish in their effort to deny Chilean independence. Antonio Quintanilla had coins cast to show that the empire of Ferdinand VII of Spain still exerted some authority in the New World.

COUNTERMARKED COINAGE

(Issued by Antonio Quintanilla)

8 REALES

CAST SILVER
c/m: Chi-loe on sand cast copy of Peru-Lima 8 Reales.

KM#	Date	Mintage	Good	VG	Fine	VF
1	1818	—	900.00	1500.	2500.	4500.

NOTE: The authenticity of these pieces has been questioned by leading authorities.

c/m: Chi-loe on sand cast copy of Bolivia-Potosi 8 Reales.

KM#	Date	Mintage	Good	VG	Fine	VF
2	1822	—	900.00	1500.	2500.	4500.
	1825	—	900.00	1500.	2500.	4500.

PROVISIONAL REPUBLICAN COINAGE

VALDIVIA

Emergency coinage issued by Don Antonio Adriazola by order of the Governor during a shortage of coin with which to pay the local garrison.

REAL

BILLON

KM#	Date	Mintage	VG	Fine	VF	XF
1.1	1822	—	125.00	200.00	300.00	—

c/m: APDLVA monogram.

KM#	Date	Mintage	VG	Fine	VF	XF
1.2	1822	—	125.00	200.00	300.00	—

2 REALES

BILLON

KM#	Date	Mintage	VG	Fine	VF	XF
2.1	1822	—	100.00	185.00	275.00	—

c/m: APDLVA monogram.

KM#	Date	Mintage	VG	Fine	VF	XF
2.2	1822	—	100.00	185.00	275.00	—

8 REALES

BILLON

KM#	Date	Mintage	VG	Fine	VF	XF
3.1	1822	—	300.00	450.00	700.00	—

c/m: APDLVA monogram.

KM#	Date	Mintage	VG	Fine	VF	XF
3.2	1822	—	300.00	450.00	700.00	—

REPUBLIC

MONETARY SYSTEM

8 Reales = 1 Peso

16 Reales = 1 Escudo

UN QUART (1/4) REAL

.900 SILVER

KM#	Date	Mintage	VG	Fine	VF	XF
89	1832/1	.054	13.50	25.00	50.00	100.00
	1832	Inc. Ab.	13.50	25.00	50.00	100.00
	1833	.082	13.50	25.00	50.00	100.00
	1834	.134	100.00	200.00	300.00	500.00

1/2 REAL

.900 SILVER

KM#	Date	Mintage	VG	Fine	VF	XF
90	1833 I	.014	12.00	20.00	40.00	80.00
	1834/3 I	.022	15.00	25.00	45.00	90.00
	1834 I	Inc. Ab.	12.00	20.00	40.00	80.00

NOTE: 1834 dated coins are medal rotation strikes.

Rev. leg: POR LA RAZ. Y LA FUER.

KM#	Date	Mintage	VG	Fine	VF	XF
98.1	1838 IJ	.015	15.00	32.00	50.00	90.00
	1840 IJ	.014	13.50	28.50	47.50	85.00

Rev. leg: POR LA RAZON Y LA FUERZA.

KM#	Date	Mintage	VG	Fine	VF	XF
98.3	1841 IJ	.016	15.00	32.00	50.00	90.00
	1842 IJ	.027	12.00	30.00	45.00	80.00

KM#	Date	Mintage	VG	Fine	VF	XF
98.2	1844 IJ RAZON V (Y) LA	—	3.00	7.50	15.00	25.00
	1845 IJ	—	3.00	7.50	15.00	25.00
	1846/5 IJ	—	5.00	10.00	20.00	30.00
	1846 IJ	—	3.00	7.50	15.00	25.00
	1847 IJ	—	3.00	7.50	15.00	25.00
	1848 JM	—	75.00	150.00	225.00	—
	1849 ML	—	3.00	7.50	15.00	25.00
	1851 LA	—	4.25	9.00	18.50	30.00

UN (1) REAL

3.2000 g, .900 SILVER, .0925 oz ASW

KM#	Date	Mintage	VG	Fine	VF	XF
91	1834 IJ	.016	7.50	15.00	35.00	75.00

Obv: Large plumes, large shield, pointed sprays.

KM#	Date	Mintage	VG	Fine	VF	XF
94.1	1838 IJ	.012	10.00	20.00	40.00	85.00
	1840 IJ	6,800	10.00	20.00	35.00	75.00

Obv: Small shield, blunt sprays w/berries.

KM#	Date	Mintage	VG	Fine	VF	XF
94.3	1841 IJ	7,928	10.00	20.00	35.00	75.00

Obv: Small shield, blunt sprays w/o berries. Reeded edge.

KM#	Date	Mintage	VG	Fine	VF	XF
94.4	1842 IJ	4,768	10.00	20.00	35.00	75.00

KM#	Date	Mintage	VG	Fine	VF	XF
94.2	1843 IJ	—	3.50	7.00	12.00	25.00
	1844 IJ	—	3.50	7.00	12.00	25.00
	1845 IJ	—	3.50	7.00	12.00	25.00
	1846 IJ	—	3.50	7.00	12.00	25.00
	1847 IJ	—	15.00	30.00	50.00	80.00
	1848/7/6 JM	—	6.00	12.00	20.00	40.00
	1848/7 JM	—	5.00	10.00	15.00	30.00
	1848 JM	—	3.50	7.00	12.00	25.00
	1849 ML	—	10.00	20.00	35.00	60.00
	1850/9 LA/ML	—	5.00	10.00	15.00	30.00
	1850 LA	—	3.50	7.00	12.00	25.00

DOS (2) REALES

.900 SILVER

KM#	Date	Mintage	VG	Fine	VF	XF
92	1834 IJ	3,740	20.00	35.00	65.00	120.00

24.5mm

KM#	Date	Mintage	VG	Fine	VF	XF
100.1	1843 IJ	—	5.00	10.00	20.00	40.00

23-23.5mm

KM#	Date	Mintage	VG	Fine	VF	XF
100.2	1843 IJ	—	5.00	10.00	20.00	40.00
	1844 IJ	—	3.00	6.00	10.00	20.00
	1845/3 IJ	—	16.00	30.00	40.00	—
	1845/4 IJ	—	16.00	30.00	40.00	—
	1845 IJ	—	3.00	6.00	10.00	20.00
	1846/5 IJ	—	12.00	30.00	40.00	—
	1846/6 IJ	—	12.00	30.00	40.00	—
	1846 IJ	—	3.00	6.00	10.00	20.00
	1847 IJ	—	3.00	6.00	10.00	20.00
	1848/7 JM	—	2.50	5.00	8.00	15.00
	1848 JM	—	2.50	5.00	8.00	15.00
	1849 ML	—	5.00	10.00	15.00	27.50
	1850/49 LA/ML	—	10.00	20.00	35.00	50.00
	1850 LA	—	8.00	12.50	18.00	30.00
	1850 LA/ML	—	8.00	12.50	18.00	30.00
	1851 LA	—	10.00	20.00	35.00	50.00
	1851 LA (error) GHILE	—	10.00	20.00	35.00	50.00
	1852 LA	—	10.00	20.00	35.00	50.00

UN (1) PESO

.900 SILVER
Rev: Y above pillar.

KM#	Date	Mintage	VG	Fine	VF	XF
82.1	1817	—	125.00	210.00	650.00	1500.

Rev: Y to left of pillar.

KM#	Date	Mintage	VG	Fine	VF	XF
82.2	1817 FJ	—	40.00	85.00	150.00	300.00
	1817 FD	—	55.00	120.00	275.00	500.00
	1818/7 FD	.371	65.00	135.00	300.00	550.00
	1818 FD	I.A.	65.00	135.00	300.00	550.00
	1819/8 FD	.236	65.00	135.00	300.00	550.00
	1819 FD	I.A.	60.00	125.00	275.00	500.00
	1820 FD	.116	45.00	95.00	200.00	350.00
	1821 FD	.126	100.00	200.00	450.00	750.00
	1822 FI	.148	40.00	85.00	175.00	350.00
	1823 FI	.045	60.00	125.00	250.00	475.00
	1824 I	.011	200.00	350.00	800.00	1400.
	1825 I	3,400	150.00	300.00	750.00	1350.
	1826 I	6,111	—	—	Rare	—
	1830 I	6,868	200.00	400.00	950.00	1700.
	1831 I	.051	65.00	135.00	275.00	500.00
	1832 I	.040	55.00	110.00	250.00	475.00
	1833 I	.088	40.00	85.00	175.00	350.00
	1834 I	.043	80.00	180.00	375.00	650.00
	1834 IJ	Inc. Ab.	120.00	250.00	500.00	900.00

Coquimbo Mint
Rev: Similar to KM#82.2.

KM#	Date	Mintage	VG	Fine	VF	XF
88	1828TH	—	—	—	—	15,000.

8 REALES

27.0700 g, .900 SILVER, .7853 oz ASW, 39mm

KM#	Date	Mintage	VG	Fine	VF	XF
96.1	1837 IJ	5,404	—	—	Rare	—
	1839 IJ	.205	45.00	75.00	125.00	350.00
	1840 IJ	4,556	850.00	1250.	1600.	2750.

Rev: Similar to KM#96.1 but w/larger leg.
Reduced size, 38.5mm, same weight and fineness

KM#	Date	Mintage	VG	Fine	VF	XF
96.2	1848 JM	—	40.00	75.00	125.00	300.00
	1849 ML	—	50.00	90.00	150.00	360.00

ESCUDO

3.4000 g, .875 GOLD, .0956 oz AGW
Obv: Sun above mountains in wreath.
Rev: Crossed flags behind pillar in wreath, date below.

KM#	Date	Mintage	VG	Fine	VF	XF
85	1824 I	3,400	95.00	135.00	170.00	350.00
	1825 I	2,920	95.00	135.00	170.00	350.00
	1826 I	4,280	95.00	135.00	170.00	350.00
	1827 I	408 pcs.	150.00	240.00	300.00	500.00
	1828 I	4,488	95.00	135.00	170.00	350.00
	1830 I	3,328	95.00	135.00	170.00	350.00
	1832 I	2,338	95.00	135.00	170.00	350.00
	1833/0 I	2,620	130.00	200.00	250.00	450.00
	1833 I	Inc. Ab.	115.00	180.00	225.00	400.00
	1834 I	10,614	115.00	180.00	225.00	400.00

Obv: Plumed and supported arms, date below.
Rev: Hand on book below sun rays.

KM#	Date	Mintage	VG	Fine	VF	XF
99	1838 IJ	6,122	125.00	175.00	215.00	375.00

Rev: Liberty standing, column at left, fasces and cornucopia at right.

KM#	Date	Mintage	VG	Fine	VF	XF
101.1	1839 IJ	4,946	100.00	135.00	175.00	250.00
	1840 IJ	4,312	100.00	135.00	175.00	250.00
	1841 IJ	3,992	100.00	135.00	175.00	250.00
	1842 IJ	5,076	100.00	135.00	175.00	250.00
	1843 IJ	4,632	100.00	135.00	175.00	250.00
	1844 IJ	—	100.00	135.00	175.00	250.00
	1845 IJ	—	100.00	135.00	175.00	250.00

Rev: Liberty standing scene rendered on smaller scale.

KM#	Date	Mintage	VG	Fine	VF	XF
101.2	1846 IJ	—	150.00	200.00	350.00	550.00
	1847 IJ	—	125.00	175.00	225.00	375.00
	1848 JM	—	100.00	135.00	200.00	350.00
	1849 ML	—	100.00	135.00	200.00	350.00
	1850 LA	—	100.00	135.00	200.00	350.00
	1851 LA	—	125.00	175.00	225.00	375.00

2 ESCUDOS

6.8000 g, .875 GOLD, .1913 oz AGW

KM#	Date	Mintage	VG	Fine	VF	XF
86	1824 I	1,700	150.00	200.00	350.00	500.00
	1825 I	1,460	150.00	200.00	350.00	500.00
	1826 I	1,936	150.00	200.00	350.00	500.00
	1827 I	204 pcs.	200.00	300.00	400.00	650.00
	1832 I	493 pcs.	200.00	300.00	400.00	650.00
	1833 I	224 pcs.	150.00	200.00	350.00	550.00
	1834 IJ	4,648	120.00	175.00	300.00	500.00

KM#	Date	Mintage	VG	Fine	VF	XF
97	1837 IJ	331 pcs.	200.00	255.00	400.00	600.00
	1838 IJ	3,449	150.00	200.00	250.00	450.00

KM#	Date	Mintage	VG	Fine	VF	XF
102.1	1839 IJ	3,064	225.00	275.00	425.00	550.00
	1840 IJ	2,396	225.00	275.00	425.00	550.00
	1841 IJ	2,552	180.00	235.00	375.00	500.00
	1842 IJ	2,986	180.00	235.00	375.00	500.00
	1843 IJ	2,464	180.00	235.00	375.00	500.00
	1844 IJ	—	180.00	235.00	375.00	500.00
	1845 IJ	—	180.00	235.00	375.00	500.00

Rev: Liberty standing scene rendered on smaller scale.

KM#	Date	Mintage	VG	Fine	VF	XF
102.2	1846 IJ	—	150.00	225.00	300.00	375.00
	1847 IJ	—	150.00	225.00	300.00	375.00
	1848 JM	—	150.00	225.00	300.00	375.00
	1849 ML	—	150.00	225.00	300.00	375.00
	1850 LA	—	150.00	225.00	300.00	375.00
	1851 LA	—	150.00	225.00	300.00	375.00

4 ESCUDOS

13.5000 g, .875 GOLD, .3798 oz AGW

KM#	Date	Mintage	VG	Fine	VF	XF
87	1824 FD	1,530	325.00	450.00	700.00	1350.

KM#	Date	Mintage	VG	Fine	VF	XF
87	1825 I	986 pcs.	350.00	550.00	900.00	1600.
	1826 I	1,326	325.00	450.00	700.00	1350.
	1833 I	321 pcs.	375.00	600.00	950.00	1750.
	1834 IJ	2,564	325.00	450.00	700.00	1350.

KM#	Date	Mintage	VG	Fine	VF	XF
95	1836 IJ	1,389	275.00	375.00	575.00	950.00
	1837 IJ	321 pcs.	375.00	600.00	950.00	1750.

KM#	Date	Mintage	VG	Fine	VF	XF
103	1839 IJ	—	1200.	2000.	3500.	—
	1840 IJ	108 pcs.	—	—	Rare	—
	1841 IJ	100 pcs.	—	—	Rare	—

8 ESCUDOS

27.0000 g, .875 GOLD, .7596 oz AGW

KM#	Date	Mintage	VG	Fine	VF	XF
84	1818 FD Constit	.029	BV	350.00	400.00	850.00
	1818 FD Constitu	Inc. Ab.	BV	375.00	500.00	950.00
	1819 FD	.037	BV	350.00	400.00	850.00
	1820 FD	.035	BV	350.00	400.00	850.00
	1821 FD	.016	BV	350.00	400.00	850.00
	1822 FI	.031	BV	350.00	400.00	850.00
	1823 FI	.019	BV	350.00	400.00	850.00
	1824 I	.010	BV	350.00	400.00	850.00
	1825 I	8,483	BV	350.00	400.00	800.00
	1826 I	7,607	BV	350.00	400.00	800.00
	1827 I	2,176	BV	350.00	400.00	800.00
	1828/7 I	4,250	400.00	700.00	1200.	2500.
	1828 I	Inc. Ab.	BV	350.00	400.00	850.00
	1829 I	—	BV	350.00	400.00	800.00
	1830 I	3,068	BV	350.00	400.00	800.00
	1831 I	1,745	BV	375.00	500.00	900.00
	1832/1 I	.011	BV	350.00	400.00	800.00
	1832 I	Inc. Ab.	BV	350.00	400.00	800.00
	1833/2 I	.025	BV	500.00	800.00	1400.
	1833 I	Inc. Ab.	BV	350.00	400.00	800.00
	1834 IJ	.031	BV	350.00	400.00	750.00

KM#	Date	Mintage	VG	Fine	VF	XF
93	1835 IJ	.028	BV	350.00	450.00	900.00
	1836 IJ	.027	BV	350.00	450.00	900.00
	1837 IJ	.017	BV	350.00	450.00	900.00
	1838 IJ	.033	BV	350.00	450.00	900.00

NOTE: KM#93 has been rarely encountered struck over KM#84.

Reeded edge

KM#	Date	Mintage	VG	Fine	VF	XF
104.1	1839 IJ	.027	BV	350.00	400.00	700.00
	1840 IJ	.025	BV	350.00	400.00	700.00
	1841 IJ	.025	BV	350.00	400.00	700.00
	1842 IJ	.027	BV	350.00	400.00	700.00
	1843/2 IJ	.027	BV	400.00	500.00	800.00
	1843 IJ	Inc. Ab.	BV	350.00	400.00	700.00

Lettered edge

KM#	Date	Mintage	VG	Fine	VF	XF
104.2	1843 IJ	—	BV	400.00	550.00	850.00
	1844 IJ	—	BV	400.00	550.00	850.00
	1845 IJ	—	BV	400.00	550.00	850.00

KM#	Date	Mintage	VG	Fine	VF	XF
105	1846 IJ	—	BV	350.00	400.00	675.00
	1847 IJ	—	BV	350.00	400.00	675.00
	1848/7 JM	—	BV	350.00	400.00	675.00
	1848 JM	—	BV	350.00	400.00	675.00
	1849 ML	—	BV	350.00	400.00	675.00
	1850 LA	—	BV	350.00	400.00	675.00
	1851 LA	—	BV	350.00	400.00	675.00

NOTE: For KM#104.2 and 105 edge lettering includes month of issue.

COUNTERMARKED COINAGE

On March 29, 1833, the government ordered the legal circulation of the Argentinian 8 Reales struck at Potosi. The coins struck at Potosi must have the countermark of the coat of arms of Chile and the abbreviation of the place where the countermark was applied.

CHILOE

1 REAL

SILVER

c/m: Mountains/CHIL on Argentina 1 Real, KM#2.

KM#	Date	Year	Good	VG	Fine	VF
A106	ND	(1815)	—	1250.	—	—

NOTE: Sold Bank Leu #51, Bostonian Collection 10-90.

8 REALES

SILVER

c/m: Mountains/CHIL on Argentina 8 Reales, KM#5.

KM#	Date	Year	Good	VG	Fine	VF
106.1	ND	(1813)	—	—	Rare	—

c/m: Mountains/CHIL on Argentina 8 Reales, KM#14.

KM#	Date	Year	Good	VG	Fine	VF
106.2	ND	(1815)	—	—	Rare	—

CONCEPCION

8 REALES

SILVER

c/m: Mountains/CON on Argentina 8 Reales, KM#5.

KM#	Date	Year	Good	VG	Fine	VF
107.1	ND	(1813)	—	—	Rare	—

c/m: Mountains/CON on Argentina 8 Reales, KM#14.

KM#	Date	Year	Good	VG	Fine	VF
107.2	ND	(1815)	—	—	Rare	—

SANTIAGO

2 REALES

SILVER

c/m: Mountains/SAN on Argentina 2 Reales.

KM#	Date	Year	Good	VG	Fine	VF
A108	ND	—	—	—	Rare	—

4 REALES

SILVER

c/m: Mountains/SAN on Argentina 4 Reales, KM#4

KM#	Date	Year	Good	VG	Fine	VF
B108	ND	(1815)	—	—	—	9500.

NOTE: Offered by D.A. Perry in World Coin News 9-97.

8 REALES

SILVER

c/m: Mountains/SAN on Argentina 8 Reales, KM#5.

108.1 ND (1813) Reported, not confirmed

c/m: Mountains/SAN on Argentina 8 Reales, KM#14.

108.2 ND (1815) Reported, not confirmed

SERENA

4 REALES

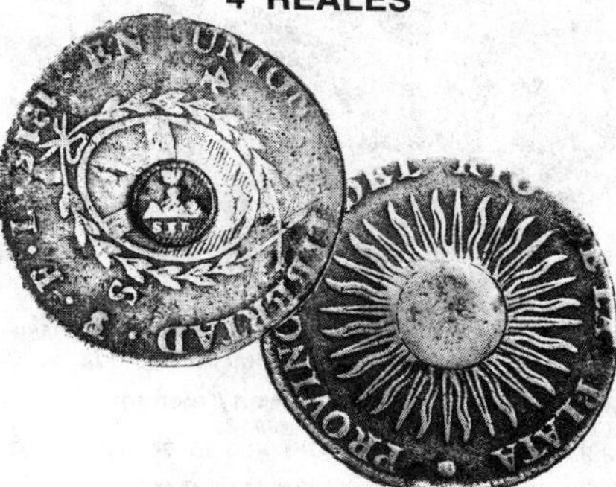

SILVER

c/m: Mountains/SER on Argentina 4 Soles, KM#13.

KM#	Date	Year	Good	VG	Fine	VF
113	ND	(1813)	—	3500.	—	—

NOTE: Sold Bank Leu #51, Bostonian Collection 10-90.

8 REALES

SILVER
c/m: Mountains/SER on Argentina 8 Reales, KM#5.

KM#	Date	Year	Good	VG	Fine	VF
109.1	ND	(1813)	175.00	300.00	475.00	750.00

c/m: Mountains/SER on Argentina 8 Reales, KM#15.

KM#	Date	Year	Good	VG	Fine	VF
109.2	ND	(1815)	175.00	300.00	475.00	750.00

VALDIVIA

4 REALES

SILVER
c/m: Mountains/VALD on Argentina 4 Reales, KM#4.

KM#	Date	Year	Good	VG	Fine	VF
110	ND	(1813)	225.00	400.00	700.00	1200.
	ND	(1815)	225.00	400.00	700.00	1200.

8 REALES

SILVER
c/m: Mountains/VALD on Argentina 8 Reales, KM#5.

KM#	Date	Year	Good	VG	Fine	VF
111.1	ND	(1813)	225.00	400.00	700.00	1200.

c/m: Mountains/VALD on Argentina 8 Reales, KM#14.

KM#	Date	Year	Good	VG	Fine	VF
111.2	ND	(1815)	225.00	400.00	700.00	1200.

VALPARAISO

8 REALES

SILVER
c/m: Mountains/VALP on Argentina 8 Reales, KM#5.

KM#	Date	Year	Good	VG	Fine	VF
112.1	ND	(1813)	225.00	400.00	700.00	1200.

c/m: Mountains/VALP on Argentina 8 Reales, KM#14.

KM#	Date	Year	Good	VG	Fine	VF
112.2	ND	(1815)	225.00	400.00	700.00	1200.

DECIMAL COINAGE

10 Centavos = 1 Decimo
10 Decimos = 1 Peso
10 Pesos = 1 Condor

MEDIO (1/2) CENTAVO

COPPER
Plain edge.

KM#	Date	Mintage	VG	Fine	VF	XF
114	1835	2.000	1.00	2.00	3.50	20.00
	1835	Inc. Ab.	—	—	Proof	—

Obv: Flat star, stars flank date.
Rev: Dot below stems.

KM#	Date	Mintage	VG	Fine	VF	XF
117	1851	1.620	2.00	4.00	6.00	25.00

Obv: Raised star, dots flank date.
Rev: Diamond below stems.

KM#	Date	Mintage	VG	Fine	VF	XF
118	1851	2.200	1.00	2.00	4.00	20.00

KM#	Date	Mintage	VG	Fine	VF	XF
126	1853	2.667	1.00	2.00	4.00	20.00
	1853	—	—	—	Proof	—

COPPER-NICKEL

KM#	Date	Mintage	VG	Fine	VF	XF
148	1871	.133	2.00	4.50	9.00	17.50
	1872/1	.506	2.00	4.50	9.00	17.50
	1872	Inc. Ab.	3.50	6.00	12.00	22.50
	1873	1.265	2.00	4.50	9.00	17.50

COPPER

KM#	Date	Mintage	VG	Fine	VF	XF
148a	1883/73	.714	1.50	3.00	5.00	12.00
	1883	Inc. Ab.	1.00	2.00	3.50	10.00
	1884	.104	1.50	3.00	6.00	15.00
	1885	.132	1.00	2.00	3.50	10.00
	1886	.469	1.00	2.00	3.50	10.00
	1888/78	.294	1.25	2.50	5.00	12.00
	1888	Inc. Ab.	1.50	3.00	6.00	15.00
	1890/70	.070	2.00	4.00	7.00	16.00
	1890/73	I.A.	2.50	5.00	8.50	18.00
	1890	Inc. Ab.	3.25	6.00	10.00	22.50
	1893/88	.071	2.50	5.00	8.50	18.00
	1893	Inc. Ab.	2.00	4.00	6.00	14.50
	1894	.251	1.00	2.00	3.50	10.00

UN (1) CENTAVO

COPPER, 3.3mm, thick flan, 18.01 g

KM#	Date	Mintage	VG	Fine	VF	XF
115	1835	2.000	2.00	4.00	8.00	22.50
	1835	—	—	—	Proof	130.00

2.4mm, thin flan, 13.35 g

KM#	Date	Mintage	VG	Fine	VF	XF
116	1835	Inc. Ab.	2.00	4.00	8.00	22.50

Obv: Flat star, stars flank date.
Rev: W/o diamond below wreath.

KM#	Date	Mintage	VG	Fine	VF	XF
119	1851	2.430	2.50	5.00	12.50	30.00

Obv: Raised star, dots flank date.
Rev: Diamond below wreath.

KM#	Date	Mintage	VG	Fine	VF	XF
120	1851	3.300	3.00	8.00	17.50	45.00

Rev: Different sprays.

KM#	Date	Mintage	VG	Fine	VF	XF
127	1853	2.667	2.00	5.00	15.00	35.00
	1853	—	—	—	Proof	150.00

NOTE: The 1853 coins were struck with coin and medal rotation.

COPPER-NICKEL

KM#	Date	Mintage	VG	Fine	VF	XF
146	1870/60	—	—	—	—	—
	1871	1.687	1.50	3.00	5.50	12.00
	1872/1	.690	2.50	4.50	7.50	20.00
	1872	Inc. Ab.	2.00	4.00	6.00	17.50
	1873/1	.779	10.00	20.00	35.00	50.00
	1873/2	Inc. Ab.	10.00	20.00	35.00	50.00
	1873	Inc. Ab.	2.00	4.00	6.00	17.50
	1874/1	.263	3.50	6.00	10.00	25.00
	1874	Inc. Ab.	3.00	5.00	7.50	19.00
	1875/1	.113	3.50	6.50	8.50	22.00
	1875	Inc. Ab.	3.00	5.00	8.00	20.00
	1876	.022	12.00	20.00	35.00	60.00
	1877	.016	15.00	30.00	50.00	75.00

COPPER

KM#	Date	Mintage	VG	Fine	VF	XF
146a	1878/1	—	2.25	3.50	7.00	15.00
	1878	.177	2.00	4.00	7.00	25.00
	1879	.793	1.50	3.00	5.50	15.00
	1880/70	.478	2.00	4.00	6.00	20.00
	1880/79	I.A.	2.00	4.00	6.00	20.00
	1880	Inc. Ab.	1.50	3.00	5.50	15.00
	1881	.318	1.75	3.25	6.00	16.00
	1882	.492	1.50	3.00	5.50	15.00
	1883	.274	2.00	4.00	6.00	20.00
	1884/3	.171	2.25	4.50	7.50	25.00
	1884	Inc. Ab.	2.00	4.00	6.00	20.00
	1885	.205	1.50	3.00	5.50	15.00
	1886	.510	1.50	3.00	5.50	15.00
	1887/4	.231	1.75	3.50	7.00	18.00
	1887	Inc. Ab.	1.50	3.00	5.50	15.00
	1888	.141	2.00	4.00	6.00	20.00
	1890	.047	4.25	8.50	15.00	28.00
	1891/81	.099	15.00	30.00	50.00	80.00
	1891	Inc. Ab.	2.50	5.00	10.00	25.00
	1893	.115	1.50	3.00	5.50	15.00
	1894	.244	1.00	2.00	4.00	8.00
	1895	.449	1.00	2.00	3.50	7.00
	1895 1 over inverted 1	Inc. Ab.	4.50	9.00	16.00	30.00
	1896	.139	1.25	2.50	4.00	8.00
	1898	1.605	.50	1.00	2.00	5.00

NOTE: Varieties exist.

DOS (2) CENTAVOS

COPPER-NICKEL

KM#	Date	Mintage	Fine	VF	XF	Unc
147	1870/60	—	5.00	9.00	18.00	35.00
	1871	.639	3.50	7.50	15.00	30.00
	1872/1	.207	3.50	7.50	15.00	30.00
	1872	Inc. Ab.	12.00	20.00	30.00	60.00
	1873	.461	3.50	7.50	15.00	30.00
	1874	.263	5.00	9.00	18.00	35.00
	1875	.294	5.00	9.00	18.00	35.00
	1876	.108	12.00	20.00	30.00	60.00
	1877	.021	15.00	35.00	50.00	120.00
		COPPER				
147a	1878/6	.112	—	—	—	—
	1878	Inc. Ab.	5.00	9.00	15.00	45.00
	1879	.479	2.50	6.00	10.00	30.00
	1880/70	—	3.00	7.00	12.00	35.00
	1880	.278	2.50	6.00	10.00	30.00
	1881	.172	3.00	7.00	12.00	35.00
	1882	.361	2.50	6.00	10.00	30.00
	1883/73	.405	3.00	7.00	12.00	35.00
	1883	Inc. Ab.	2.00	5.00	8.00	25.00
	1884	.182	2.50	6.00	10.00	30.00
	1885	.146	2.50	6.00	10.00	30.00
	1886	.494	2.00	5.00	8.00	25.00
	1887	.106	2.50	6.00	10.00	30.00
	1888	.186	3.00	7.00	12.00	35.00
	1890	.155	5.00	9.00	15.00	40.00
	1891/8	.089	—	—	—	—
	1891	Inc. Ab.	8.00	20.00	30.00	60.00
	1893/1	.141	2.50	6.00	10.00	30.00
	1893	Inc. Ab.	2.50	6.00	10.00	30.00
	1894	.190	3.00	7.00	12.00	35.00

DOS I MEDIO (2-1/2) CENTAVOS

COPPER

KM#	Date	Mintage	Fine	VF	XF	Unc
150	1886	.381	2.50	6.00	18.00	45.00
	1887/6	.500	5.00	10.00	25.00	65.00
	1887	Inc. Ab.	2.75	7.00	18.00	45.00
	1895/85	.366	3.00	8.00	20.00	50.00
	1895	Inc. Ab.	2.50	6.00	18.00	45.00
	1896/86	.172	3.00	8.00	20.00	50.00
	1896	Inc. Ab.	2.75	7.00	18.00	50.00
	1898/86	2.177	3.00	8.00	20.00	50.00
	1898/88	I.A.	3.00	8.00	20.00	50.00
	1898/5	Inc. Ab.	3.00	8.00	20.00	50.00
	1898/87	I.A.	3.00	8.00	20.00	50.00
	1898	Inc. Ab.	2.50	6.00	18.00	45.00

MEDIO (1/2) DECIMO

1.2500 g, .900 SILVER, .0361 oz ASW
Reeded edge.

KM#	Date	Mintage	VG	Fine	VF	XF
121	1851	.233	100.00	200.00	300.00	450.00
	1853	Inc. Ab.	3.00	5.00	9.00	20.00
	1854	.122	20.00	35.00	55.00	80.00
	1855/3	1.257	—	—	—	—
	1855/4	Inc. Ab.	3.50	6.00	12.00	25.00
	1855	Inc. Ab.	3.00	5.00	9.00	20.00
	1856/5	.767	4.00	7.00	15.00	30.00
	1856	Inc. Ab.	3.50	6.00	12.00	25.00
	1857	1.655	3.00	5.00	9.00	20.00
	1858	.318	3.50	6.00	12.00	25.00
	1859/8	.041	3.00	5.00	10.00	22.00
	1859	Inc. Ab.	20.00	35.00	55.00	90.00

1.1500 g, .900 SILVER, .0332 oz ASW

KM#	Date	Mintage	VG	Fine	VF	XF
121a	1860/59	.372	10.00	20.00	27.50	55.00
	1860	Inc. Ab.	7.00	15.00	22.00	50.00
	1861	.338	5.00	10.00	18.00	45.00
	1862	4,400	—	—	Rare	—

KM#	Date	Mintage	VG	Fine	VF	XF
137.1	1865	.040	17.50	30.00	45.00	90.00
	1866	.082	10.00	20.00	32.50	50.00

1.2500 g, .835 SILVER, .0336 oz ASW

KM#	Date	Mintage	VG	Fine	VF	XF
137.2	1867	.028	4.00	8.00	20.00	35.00
	1868	.181	2.00	4.00	6.00	12.50
	1869	.293	1.50	3.00	4.75	9.50
	1870/69	.540	1.25	2.50	4.00	8.00
	1870	Inc. Ab.	1.25	2.00	3.25	6.50
	1871/0	.171	1.50	3.00	5.00	10.00
	1871	Inc. Ab.	3.00	5.00	7.50	15.00
	1872	.286	2.00	4.00	7.00	12.50
	1873/2	.170	5.00	10.00	30.00	50.00
	1873/9	Inc. Ab.	5.00	10.00	30.00	50.00
	1873	Inc. Ab.	3.00	5.00	7.50	15.00
	1874/3	.588	3.00	7.00	15.00	20.00
	1874	Inc. Ab.	2.00	4.00	7.00	12.50
	1875/2	.097	3.00	7.00	12.00	20.00
	1875/3	I.A.	3.00	7.00	12.00	20.00
	1875/4	I.A.	3.00	7.00	12.00	20.00
	1875	Inc. Ab.	5.00	8.00	12.50	25.00
	1876	.082	3.00	7.00	12.00	16.00
	1877	.327	2.00	6.00	9.00	14.00
	1878	.306	2.00	6.50	10.00	15.00
	1880	.194	3.00	7.00	12.00	16.00
	1881	.264	3.00	7.00	12.00	16.00

1.2500 g, .500 SILVER, .0200 oz ASW
Obv. leg: 0.5 added.

KM#	Date	Mintage	Fine	VF	XF	Unc
137.3	1879	.916	2.00	3.00	6.00	20.00
	1880	1.205	1.50	3.00	5.00	15.00
	1881	1.687	1.50	3.00	5.00	15.00
	1882	.235	2.50	5.00	8.00	20.00
	1883/2	—	3.00	6.00	12.00	25.00
	1883	.117	3.75	7.50	12.50	25.00
	1884	.664	2.50	3.50	6.50	20.00
	1885/2	.489	2.50	3.50	6.50	20.00
	1885/3	I.A.	2.00	3.00	5.50	18.00
	1885/4/3	—	2.50	5.00	8.00	20.00
	1885/4	I.A.	2.00	3.00	5.50	18.00
	1885	Inc. Ab.	3.00	6.00	12.00	25.00
	1887	3.081	1.50	3.00	5.00	15.00
	1888/7	2.448	2.50	3.50	6.50	20.00
	1888	Inc. Ab.	1.50	3.00	5.00	15.00
	1892/72	1.684	2.50	3.50	7.50	20.00
	1892/82	I.A.	2.50	3.50	6.50	20.00
	1892/82/72 Inc. Ab.		3.50	6.50	12.50	35.00
	1892/88	I.A.	2.50	4.00	7.00	20.00
	1892	Inc. Ab.	3.50	6.50	12.50	35.00
	1893/73	.850	3.50	6.00	12.00	30.00
	1893/78	I.A.	3.50	6.00	12.00	30.00
	1893/8/7	I.A.	3.50	6.00	12.00	30.00
	1893/83	I.A.	3.50	6.00	12.00	30.00
	1893/2	I.A.	2.00	4.00	6.00	20.00
	1893	Inc. Ab.	1.50	3.00	5.00	15.00
	1894/73	.784	2.00	4.50	7.50	18.00
	1894/83	Inc. Ab.	2.00	4.50	7.50	18.00
	1894/84	I.A.	2.00	4.50	7.50	18.00
	1894/3	Inc. Ab.	2.00	4.50	7.50	18.00
	1894	Inc. Ab.	3.50	6.00	12.00	30.00

NOTE: Varieties exist.

Mule. Obv: KM#137.2. Rev: KM#137.3.

KM#	Date	Mintage	Fine	VF	XF	Unc
149	1884	—	—	—	20.00	50.00

CINCO (5) CENTAVOS

1.0000 g, .835 SILVER, .0268 oz ASW
Obv: O. ROTY on stone below condor.
Rev: Hammer and sickle.

KM#	Date	Mintage	Fine	VF	XF	Unc
155.1	1896 large 6	.888	3.00	6.00	10.00	20.00
	1896 small 6	Inc. Ab.	3.00	6.00	10.00	20.00
	1899 2nd 9 inverted 6	Inc. Ab.	—	—	—	—

1.0000 g, .500 SILVER, .0160 oz ASW
Obv: 0.5 below condor.

KM#	Date	Mintage	Fine	VF	XF	Unc
155.2	1899	1.794	2.00	3.00	5.00	15.00

NOTE: Later dates (1901-1909) exist for this type.
NOTE: Varieties exist w/0.5, 0.5. or 05. below condor.

UN (1) DECIMO

2.5000 g, .900 SILVER, .0723 oz ASW

KM#	Date	Mintage	VG	Fine	VF	XF
124	1852	.211	2.50	5.00	15.00	50.00
	1853	Inc. Ab.	2.50	5.00	15.00	50.00
	1855	.585	2.50	5.00	15.00	50.00
	1856/5	.580	2.50	5.00	15.00	50.00
	1856	Inc. Ab.	2.50	5.00	12.00	35.00
	1857	1.481	2.50	5.00	12.00	35.00
	1858	.540	2.50	5.00	15.00	50.00
	1859	.020	40.00	65.00	100.00	—
	1860/59	—	5.00	10.00	30.00	60.00
		2.3000 g, .900 SILVER, .0665 oz ASW				
124a	1860/50	.382	6.00	12.50	22.00	55.00
	1860	Inc. Ab.	2.50	6.00	12.50	30.00
	1861	.236	2.50	6.00	12.50	30.00
	1862	.095	3.00	7.00	15.00	40.00

KM#	Date	Mintage	VG	Fine	VF	XF
136.1	1864 thick flan	.096	5.50	10.00	22.00	40.00
	1864 thin flan	Inc. Ab.	—	—	—	—
	1865/4	.222	6.00	9.00	15.00	30.00
	1865/inverted 5	Inc. Ab.	6.00	9.00	15.00	30.00
	1865	Inc. Ab.	6.00	9.00	15.00	30.00
	1866	.096	5.50	10.00	22.00	40.00

2.5000 g, .835 SILVER, .0671 oz ASW

KM#	Date	Mintage	VG	Fine	VF	XF
136.2	1867	.020	7.00	12.00	20.00	40.00
	1868	.207	2.00	3.00	5.00	10.00
	1869/8	.245	—	—	—	—
	1869	Inc. Ab.	2.00	3.00	5.00	10.00
	1870/60	.192	3.00	4.00	7.00	15.00
	1870	Inc. Ab.	2.50	3.50	6.00	12.00
	1871	.091	2.50	3.50	6.00	12.00
	1872/1	.288	—	—	—	—
	1872	Inc. Ab.	2.00	3.00	5.00	10.00
	1873/2	.305	—	—	—	—
	1873/9	I.A.	—	—	—	—
	1873	Inc. Ab.	2.00	3.00	5.00	10.00
	1874/64	.271	—	—	—	—
	1874	Inc.Ab.	2.00	3.00	5.00	10.00
	1875/4	.050	3.00	5.00	9.00	16.50
	1875	Inc. Ab.	5.00	10.00	20.00	40.00
	1876	.100	2.25	3.25	5.50	11.00
	1877	.096	2.25	3.25	5.50	11.00
	1878	.512	2.00	3.00	5.00	10.00
	1880/70	.243	—	—	—	—
	1880	Inc. Ab.	2.00	3.00	5.00	10.00

2.5000 g, .500 SILVER, .0401 oz ASW
Obv. leg: 0.5 added.

KM#	Date	Mintage	Fine	VF	XF	Unc
136.3	1879/8	1.268	1.25	2.25	3.50	8.00
	1879	Inc. Ab.	1.00	2.00	3.00	7.50
	1880/70	.705	1.50	3.00	5.00	10.00
	1880	Inc. Ab.	1.00	2.00	5.00	10.00
	1881	2.186	1.00	2.00	5.00	10.00
	1882	.233	1.00	2.00	5.00	10.00
	1882/2	I.A.	2.00	5.00	10.00	15.00
	1883	.178	1.00	2.00	5.00	10.00
	1884/2	.319	5.00	10.00	17.00	25.00
	1884	Inc. Ab.	1.00	2.00	5.00	10.00
	1885	.116	6.00	12.00	18.00	25.00
	1887/6	1.514	1.25	2.25	3.50	8.00
	1887 R/B in Republica	Inc. Ab.	1.25	2.25	3.50	8.00
	1887	Inc. Ab.	1.00	2.00	3.00	7.50
	1891	—	—	—	Rare	—
	1892/82	.994	1.00	2.00	5.00	10.00
	1892/0	Inc. Ab.	3.00	6.00	12.00	20.00

KM#	Date	Mintage	Fine	VF	XF	Unc
136.3	1892	Inc. Ab.	1.00	2.00	3.00	7.50
	1893/83	.516	1.25	2.25	3.50	8.00
	1893/inverted 3	Inc. Ab.	3.50	5.50	10.00	18.00
	1893	Inc. Ab.	1.00	2.00	3.00	7.50
	1894/84	.826	1.00	2.00	3.00	7.50
	1894/3	I.A.	1.00	2.00	3.00	7.50
	1894/3 E/R in REPUBLICA	Inc. Ab.	1.25	2.25	3.50	8.00
	1894	Inc. Ab.	1.00	2.00	3.00	7.50

NOTE: 1 in 10 pieces dated 1887 has R/B in REPUBLICA.

2.0000 g, .500 SILVER, .0321 oz ASW

KM#	Date	Mintage	Fine	VF	XF	Unc
136.3a	1891/81	.264	35.00	80.00	160.00	300.00
	1891	I.A.	35.00	80.00	160.00	300.00

DIEZ (10) CENTAVOS

2.0000 g, .835 SILVER, .0536 oz ASW
Obv: O. ROTY on stone below condor.
Rev: Hammer and sickle.

KM#	Date	Mintage	Fine	VF	XF	Unc
156.1	1896	2.561	2.00	3.50	7.00	16.50

2.0000 g, .500 SILVER, .0321 oz ASW
Obv: 0.5 below condor.

KM#	Date	Mintage	Fine	VF	XF	Unc
156.2	1899	2.013	2.00	3.50	7.00	16.50
	1900	.104	20.00	35.00	50.00	85.00

NOTE: Later dates (1901-1907) exist for this type.
NOTE: Varieties exist for dated coins w/0.5, 0,5, 0.5. or 0.5/9 below condor.

VEINTE (20) CENTAVOS

5.0000 g, .900 SILVER, .1446 oz ASW
Reeded edge.

KM#	Date	Mintage	VG	Fine	VF	XF
125	1852	.077	10.00	15.00	20.00	38.00
	1853	.906	5.00	6.50	11.00	22.50
	1854	.417	5.00	6.50	11.00	22.50
	1855	.325	5.00	6.50	12.00	25.00
	1856/5	.396	6.00	8.00	12.50	25.00
	1856	Inc. Ab.	5.00	6.50	11.00	22.50
	1857	.748	5.00	6.50	11.00	22.50
	1858	.532	7.50	10.00	15.00	28.00
	1859/8	.120	15.00	25.00	50.00	80.00
	1859	Inc. Ab.	50.00	75.00	—	—

4.6000 g, .900 SILVER, .1331 oz ASW

KM#	Date	Mintage	VG	Fine	VF	XF
125a	1860/50	.388	—	—	—	—
	1860/59	I.A.	3.00	6.00	10.00	20.00
	1860	Inc. Ab.	3.00	6.00	10.00	20.00
	1861/51	1.471	5.00	7.00	10.00	25.00
	1861/58	I.A.	5.00	7.00	10.00	25.00
	1861/91	I.A.	5.00	7.00	10.00	22.50
	1861	Inc. Ab.	5.00	7.00	10.00	22.50
	1862/52	.324	5.00	7.00	10.00	25.00
	1862	Inc. Ab.	5.00	7.00	10.00	22.50

KM#	Date	Mintage	VG	Fine	VF	XF
135	1863	.160	5.00	7.50	11.50	22.50
	1864	.226	4.50	6.00	10.00	17.00
	1865	1.505	2.00	3.00	5.00	9.00
	1866	4.298	2.00	3.00	5.00	9.00
	1867	Inc. Be.	10.00	15.00	25.00	42.00

5.0000 g, .835 SILVER, .1343 oz ASW
Obv: Smaller sprays.

KM#	Date	Mintage	VG	Fine	VF	XF
138.1	1867	.286	4.50	6.00	8.00	14.00
	1868	.197	2.00	3.50	5.00	8.00
	1869/8	.163	3.00	5.00	7.00	12.00
	1869	Inc. Ab.	2.00	3.50	5.00	8.00
	1870/60	.992	3.00	5.00	7.00	10.00
	1870	Inc. Ab.	2.00	3.50	5.00	8.00
	1871	1.144	2.00	3.50	5.00	8.00

KM#	Date	Mintage	VG	Fine	VF	XF
138.1	1872/0	1.979	—	—	—	—
	1872	Inc. Ab.	2.00	3.50	5.00	8.00
	1873/2	.846	—	—	—	—
	1873	Inc. Ab.	2.00	3.50	5.00	8.00
	1874 wide date	1.256	2.00	3.50	5.00	8.00
	1874 narrow date	Inc. Ab.	2.00	3.50	5.00	8.00
	1875	.120	5.00	7.50	15.00	28.00
	1876 lg. stars	.749	2.75	4.50	6.00	9.00
	1876 sm. stars	Inc.Ab.	2.75	4.50	6.00	9.00
	1877	.549	2.75	4.50	6.00	9.00
	1878	2.639	2.75	4.50	6.00	9.00
	1879	9,645	60.00	100.00	175.00	250.00

NOTE: Varieties exist.

5.0000 g, .500 SILVER, .0803 oz ASW
Obv. leg: 0.5 added, w/o dash below S in CENTS.

KM#	Date	Mintage	VG	Fine	VF	XF
138.2	1879	5.073	2.50	4.00	6.00	10.00
	1880/70	6.846	2.75	4.50	7.00	12.00
	1880/79	I.A.	2.75	4.50	7.00	12.00
	1880	Inc. Ab.	2.50	4.00	6.00	10.00
	1881	6.408	2.50	4.00	6.00	10.00
	1882	—	2.50	4.00	6.00	10.00
	1893	1.397	2.50	4.00	6.00	10.00

4.0000 g, .500 SILVER, .0643 oz ASW
Obv: Dash below S in CENTS.

KM#	Date	Mintage	VG	Fine	VF	XF
138.2a	1890	—	—	—	—	—
	1891/81	2.953	—	—	—	—
	1891	Inc. Ab.	3.00	6.00	15.00	25.00

4.6000 g, .200 SILVER, .0296 oz ASW
Obv. leg: 0.2 added.

KM#	Date	Mintage	VG	Fine	VF	XF
138.3	1891/81	.787	10.00	15.00	20.00	50.00
	1891	Inc. Ab.	10.00	15.00	20.00	50.00

NOTE: Varieties exist for 1891/81 with 0.2 and 0.2/5.

5.0000 g, .500 SILVER, .0803 oz ASW
Obv: Dash below S in CENTS, leg: 0.5.

KM#	Date	Mintage	VG	Fine	VF	XF
138.4	1891	—	3.00	5.00	9.00	16.00
	1892/82	3.719	2.75	4.50	7.00	12.50
	1892	Inc. Ab.	2.50	4.00	6.00	11.50
	1893	Inc. Ab.	2.50	4.00	6.00	11.50

4.0000 g, .835 SILVER, .1073 oz ASW
Obv: O. ROTY below condor.
Rev: Hammer and sickle.

KM#	Date	Mintage	VG	Fine	VF	XF
151.1	1895	.146	12.50	20.00	30.00	70.00

4.0000 g, .500 SILVER, .0643 oz ASW
Obv: 0.5 below condor.

KM#	Date	Mintage	Fine	VF	XF	Unc
151.2	1899/69	4.343	—	—	—	—
	1899/7	I.A.	—	—	—	—
	1899/8	I.A.	—	—	—	—
	1899	Inc. Ab.	1.00	2.00	3.00	7.50
	1899/sideways 9	Inc. Ab.	—	—	—	—
	1900/899	.334	60.00	80.00	—	—
	1900	Inc. Ab.	30.00	40.00	80.00	150.00

NOTE: Later dates (1906-1907) exist for this type.
NOTE: Varieties with 0.5 or 0.5. exist.

50 CENTAVOS

12.5000 g, .900 SILVER, .3617 oz ASW
Reeded edge.

KM#	Date	Mintage	VG	Fine	VF	XF
128	1853	.769	7.50	10.00	20.00	65.00
	1854	.551	7.50	10.00	20.00	65.00
	1855	1.354	7.50	10.00	20.00	65.00
	1856/5	.606	12.00	20.00	35.00	90.00
	1856	Inc. Ab.	7.50	10.00	20.00	65.00
	1856 1/inverted 1	Inc. Ab.	12.00	20.00	40.00	100.00
	1858	.245	14.00	22.00	45.00	110.00

KM#	Date	Mintage	VG	Fine	VF	XF
128	1859	.489	10.00	15.00	30.00	80.00
	1860/59	.020	—	—	Rare	—
	1860	Inc. Ab.	250.00	350.00	450.00	600.00
	1862/52	.123	25.00	40.00	75.00	180.00
	1862	Inc. Ab.	20.00	30.00	60.00	150.00

Obv: Large sprays. Rev: Eagle w/shield.

KM#	Date	Mintage	VG	Fine	VF	XF
134	1862	Inc. Ab.	22.00	30.00	45.00	90.00
	1863/2	.080	13.00	22.00	32.00	55.00
	1863	Inc. Ab.	12.00	20.00	30.00	50.00
	1864/3	.068	12.00	20.00	30.00	50.00
	1864	Inc. Ab.	12.00	20.00	30.00	50.00
	1865/4	.287	7.00	12.00	20.00	32.50
	1865	Inc. Ab.	6.50	11.00	18.00	30.00
	1866/5	.200	6.50	11.00	18.00	30.00
	1866	Inc. Ab.	9.00	13.00	22.00	35.00
	1867	.047	35.00	60.00	90.00	150.00

Obv: Smaller sprays.

KM#	Date	Mintage	VG	Fine	VF	XF
139	1867	Inc. Ab.	15.00	22.00	30.00	50.00
	1868	.147	7.00	9.00	11.00	20.00
	1870/60	.271	10.00	15.00	22.00	40.00
	1870/68	I.A.	10.00	15.00	22.00	40.00
	1870	Inc. Ab.	5.50	7.00	9.00	15.00
	1872/0	.104	7.00	9.00	11.00	20.00
	1872	Inc. Ab.	7.00	9.00	11.00	20.00

UN (1) PESO

25.0000 g, .900 SILVER, .7234 oz ASW
Reeded edge.

KM#	Date	Mintage	VG	Fine	VF	XF
129	1853	.394	15.00	25.00	45.00	80.00
	1854	.567	15.00	25.00	45.00	80.00
	1855	.683	15.00	25.00	45.00	80.00
	1856/5	.406	24.00	38.00	62.00	150.00
	1856	Inc. Ab.	— Reported, not confirmed			
	1858	.051	22.50	40.00	70.00	125.00
	1859/8	.330	18.50	28.50	50.00	90.00
	1859	Inc. Ab.	15.00	25.00	45.00	80.00
	1862	.103	45.00	90.00	200.00	340.00

1.5235 g, .900 GOLD, .0441 oz AGW
Crude style.

KM#	Date	Mintage	Fine	VF	XF	Unc
133	1860	.156	30.00	45.00	75.00	110.00
	1861	.176	30.00	45.00	75.00	110.00
	1862	.011	40.00	60.00	80.00	125.00
	1863	.055	30.00	45.00	75.00	110.00
	1864	.029	40.00	60.00	80.00	125.00

Fine style.

KM#	Date	Mintage	Fine	VF	XF	Unc
140	1867	949 pcs.	75.00	100.00	250.00	400.00
	1873	.016	40.00	60.00	80.00	125.00

25.0000 g, .900 SILVER, .7234 oz ASW
Obv. value: 1 PESO. Rev: Eagle w/shield.

KM#	Date	Mintage	Fine	VF	XF	Unc
141	1867	Inc. Be.	600.00	1500.	2500.	6000.

Obv. value: UN PESO

KM#	Date	Mintage	Fine	VF	XF	Unc
142.1	1867	.220	20.00	40.00	60.00	200.00
	1868	1.037	8.00	12.00	30.00	150.00
	1869	.467	10.00	15.00	30.00	150.00
	1870/69	.556	10.00	15.00	30.00	80.00
	1870	Inc. Ab.	10.00	15.00	30.00	75.00
	1871	.795	25.00	45.00	60.00	200.00
	1872	Inc. Ab.	10.00	17.50	30.00	75.00
	1873/2	.323	20.00	35.00	65.00	100.00
	1873	Inc. Ab.	8.00	12.00	20.00	60.00
	1874	1.204	8.00	12.00	20.00	60.00
	1875	2.128	8.00	12.00	20.00	60.00
	1876	1.508	8.00	12.00	20.00	60.00
	1877	1.930	8.00	12.00	20.00	60.00
	1878	.950	8.00	12.00	20.00	60.00
	1879	.780	8.00	12.00	20.00	60.00
	1880	.693	8.00	12.00	20.00	60.00
	1881	1.420	8.00	12.00	20.00	60.00
	1882/1	1.648	10.00	15.00	25.00	75.00
	1882	Inc. Ab.	8.00	12.00	20.00	60.00
	1883/2	1.397	—	—	—	—
	1883 round top 3	Inc. Ab.	8.00	12.00	20.00	70.00
	1884	1.812	8.00	12.00	20.00	60.00
	1885/3	.528	12.50	20.00	40.00	115.00
	1885	Inc. Ab.	10.00	15.00	30.00	95.00
	1886	.966	10.00	15.00	25.00	70.00
	1887	.023	350.00	750.00	1100.	1650.
	1889	.241	20.00	35.00	55.00	160.00
	1890/80	.109	25.00	45.00	65.00	190.00
	1890/89	I.A.	25.00	45.00	65.00	190.00
	1890	Inc. Ab.	20.00	35.00	55.00	160.00
	1891	.109	50.00	100.00	200.00	400.00

Flat top 3, medal alignment.

KM#	Date	Mintage	Fine	VF	XF	Unc
142.2	1883(1925)	.712	—	150.00	300.00	465.00

Flat top 3, coin alignment.

KM#	Date	Mintage	Fine	VF	XF	Unc
142.3	1883(1926)	.149	—	150.00	300.00	465.00

NOTE: Above issue minted in 1925-6 and most coins were melted down in 1927.

20.0000 g, .835 SILVER, .5369 oz ASW

KM#	Date	Mintage	Fine	VF	XF	Unc
152.1	1895/4	6.086	15.00	25.00	40.00	70.00
	1895	Inc. Ab.	8.00	12.50	16.50	40.00
	1896	1.556	10.00	15.00	28.00	55.00
	1897	.037	25.00	40.00	55.00	90.00

DOS (2) PESOS

3.0506 g, .900 GOLD, .0882 oz AGW
Fine style.

KM#	Date	Mintage	Fine	VF	XF	Unc
132	1856	—	120.00	250.00	350.00	—
	1857	.207	BV	50.00	75.00	125.00
	1858/7	.056	BV	65.00	100.00	150.00
	1858	Inc. Ab.	BV	50.00	75.00	125.00
	1859	.097	BV	50.00	75.00	125.00
	1860	.078	BV	50.00	75.00	125.00
	1862	.010	BV	50.00	75.00	125.00
	1865	—	120.00	250.00	350.00	—

Modified arms.

KM#	Date	Mintage	Fine	VF	XF	Unc
143	1867	841 pcs.	175.00	350.00	600.00	950.00
	1873	.054	BV	50.00	75.00	100.00
	1874	.061	BV	50.00	75.00	100.00
	1875	.037	45.00	60.00	80.00	120.00

CINCO (5) PESOS

7.6265 g, .900 GOLD, .2207 oz AGW
Crude style.

KM#	Date	Mintage	Fine	VF	XF	Unc
122	1851	3,735	BV	135.00	160.00	250.00
	1852	.020	BV	125.00	150.00	225.00
	1853	5,987	BV	135.00	160.00	250.00

Fine style.

KM#	Date	Mintage	Fine	VF	XF	Unc
130	1854	953 pcs.	—	—	Rare	—
	1855	7,609	BV	135.00	160.00	250.00
	1856/5	4,753	125.00	225.00	300.00	400.00
	1856	Inc. Ab.	BV	135.00	160.00	250.00
	1857/6	.025	BV	150.00	200.00	300.00
	1857	Inc. Ab.	BV	125.00	150.00	225.00
	1858	.011	BV	125.00	150.00	225.00
	1859/8	.066	BV	125.00	150.00	225.00
	1859	Inc. Ab.	BV	125.00	150.00	225.00
	1862	6,738	BV	135.00	160.00	250.00
	1865	5,110	BV	135.00	160.00	250.00
	1866/5	6,249	BV	150.00	200.00	300.00
	1866	Inc. Ab.	BV	135.00	160.00	250.00
	1867	.010	BV	125.00	150.00	225.00

Modified arms.

KM#	Date	Mintage	Fine	VF	XF	Unc
144	1867	Inc. Ab.	—	—	Rare	—
	1868	4,065	BV	135.00	160.00	250.00
	1869	5,913	BV	135.00	160.00	250.00
	1870	.013	BV	125.00	150.00	225.00
	1872	.023	BV	125.00	150.00	225.00
	1873	.050	BV	125.00	150.00	225.00

2.9955 g, .917 GOLD, .0883 oz AGW

KM#	Date	Mintage	Fine	VF	XF	Unc
153	1895	3.002	BV	50.00	60.00	90.00
	1896	.024	BV	85.00	175.00	275.00

KM#	Date	Mintage	Fine	VF	XF	Unc
159	1897	—	—	—	Rare	—
	1898	.426	BV	55.00	85.00	100.00
	1900	1.265	60.00	100.00	120.00	150.00

NOTE: Later date (1911) exists for this type.

DIEZ (10) PESOS

15.2530 g, .900 GOLD, .4414 oz AGW
Crude style.

KM#	Date	Mintage	Fine	VF	XF	Unc
123	1851	.050	BV	225.00	275.00	350.00
	1852	.135	BV	225.00	275.00	350.00
	1853	.206	BV	225.00	250.00	300.00

Fine style.

KM#	Date	Mintage	Fine	VF	XF	Unc
131	1854	.195	BV	225.00	275.00	350.00
	1855	.061	BV	225.00	275.00	350.00
	1856	.066	BV	225.00	275.00	350.00
	1857	.020	BV	225.00	275.00	350.00
	1858/7	.052	BV	225.00	275.00	350.00
	1858	Inc. Ab.	BV	225.00	275.00	350.00
	1859	.281	BV	225.00	275.00	350.00
	1860	.031	BV	225.00	275.00	350.00
	1861	.015	BV	225.00	275.00	350.00
	1862	.021	BV	225.00	275.00	350.00
	1863/2	.025	BV	225.00	275.00	350.00
	1863	Inc. Ab.	BV	225.00	275.00	350.00
	1864	.026	BV	225.00	275.00	350.00
	1865	.045	BV	225.00	275.00	350.00
	1866	.066	BV	225.00	275.00	350.00
	1867/6	.121	BV	225.00	275.00	350.00
	1867	Inc. Ab.	BV	225.00	275.00	350.00

Obv: Modified arms.

KM#	Date	Mintage	Fine	VF	XF	Unc
145	1867	Inc. Ab.	BV	225.00	275.00	350.00
	1868	.054	BV	225.00	275.00	350.00
	1869	.036	BV	225.00	275.00	350.00
	1870	.076	BV	225.00	275.00	350.00
	1871	.041	BV	225.00	275.00	350.00
	1872	.235	BV	225.00	275.00	350.00
	1873	.112	BV	225.00	275.00	350.00
	1874	1,277	BV	235.00	285.00	375.00
	1876	2,106	BV	235.00	285.00	375.00
	1877	8,208	BV	235.00	285.00	375.00
	1878	7,983	BV	235.00	285.00	375.00
	1879	9,805	BV	235.00	285.00	375.00
	1880	.011	BV	225.00	275.00	350.00
	1881	.013	BV	225.00	275.00	350.00
	1882	.014	BV	225.00	275.00	350.00
	1883	8,381	BV	235.00	285.00	375.00
	1884	9,888	BV	235.00	285.00	375.00
	1885	7,758	BV	235.00	285.00	375.00
	1886	3,721	BV	235.00	285.00	375.00
	1887	5,236	BV	235.00	285.00	375.00
	1888	4,217	BV	235.00	285.00	375.00
	1889	4,650	BV	235.00	285.00	375.00

KM#	Date	Mintage	Fine	VF	XF	Unc
145	1890	2,344	BV	235.00	285.00	375.00
	1892	1,192	BV	235.00	285.00	375.00

5.9910 g, .917 GOLD, .1766 oz AGW

KM#	Date	Mintage	Fine	VF	XF	Unc
154	1895	.808	—	BV	100.00	160.00

KM#	Date	Mintage	Fine	VF	XF	Unc
157	1896	1.163	—	BV	100.00	125.00
	1898	.276	—	BV	100.00	150.00
	1900	—	—	Reported, not confirmed		

NOTE: Later date (1901) exists for this type.

VEINTE (20) PESOS

11.9821 g, .917 GOLD, .3532 oz AGW

KM#	Date	Mintage	Fine	VF	XF	Unc
158	1896	.149	—	BV	185.00	250.00

NOTE: Later dates (1906-1917) exist for this type.

PATTERNS (Pn)

(Including off metal strikes)

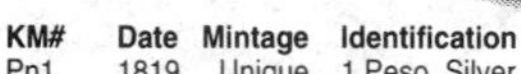

KM#	Date	Mintage	Identification	Mkt.Val.
Pn1	1819	Unique	1 Peso, Silver	9000.

KM#	Date	Mintage	Identification	Mkt.Val.
PnA2	ND	—	8 Escudos, Copper, similar to KM84	175.00
Pn2	1828	—	1/2 Real, Silver, Coquimbo Mint	—

KM#	Date	Mintage	Identification	Mkt.Val.
PnA3	ND	—	8 Reales, Copper	550.00

KM#	Date	Mintage	Identification	Mkt.Val.
Pn3	ND	—	4 Escudos	—
Pn4	1836 I.J.	—	8 Escudos, Copper, Santiago Mint	275.00
Pn5	1836 I.J.	—	8 Escudos, Copper-Gilt, Santiago Mint	350.00

KM#	Date	Mintage	Identification	Mkt.Val.
Pn6	1836 I.J.	—	8 Escudos, Silver, Santiago Mint	450.00

KM#	Date	Mintage	Identification	Mkt.Val.
Pn7	(1842)R.N.	—	8 Escudos, Copper, Santiago Mint	—

KM#	Date	Mintage	Identification	Mkt.Val.
Pn8	ND	—	8 Escudos, Copper, Paris Mint	—

KM#	Date	Mintage	Identification	Mkt.Val.
Pn9	1851	—	1 Peso, Copper, plain edge, Paris Mint, Essai, obv. bust, rev. legend	350.00
Pn10	1851	—	5 Pesos, Copper, obv. bust, rev. legend	400.00
Pn11	1867	—	20 Centavos, Copper, KM138	400.00
Pn12	1867	—	50 Centavos, Copper, KM139	500.00
Pn13	1868	—	1/2 Decimo, Copper, KM137.2	200.00
Pn14	1868	—	1 Decimo, Copper, KM136.2	200.00
Pn15	1868	—	1 Peso, Copper, KM141	1750.
Pn16	1868	—	1 Peso, Copper, KM140	200.00
Pn17	1868	—	1 Peso, Gold-Plated Copper, KM140	250.00
Pn18	1868	—	2 Pesos, Copper, KM143	200.00
Pn19	1868	—	2 Pesos, Gold-Plated Copper, KM143	400.00
Pn20	1868	—	5 Pesos, Copper, KM144	400.00
Pn21	1868	—	5 Pesos, Gold-Plated Copper, KM145	400.00
Pn22	1868	—	10 Pesos, Copper, KM145	500.00
Pn23	1868	—	10 Pesos, Gold-Plated Copper, KM145	500.00

KM#	Date	Mintage	Identification	Mkt.Val.
PnA24	1878//1876	—	10 Pesos, Copper, obv: Arms, Rev: Liberty	—
Pn24	1894	6 known	1 Peso, Silver, Essai, KM152.1, Santiago Mint	1500.

Pn25	1895	—	5 Pesos	—

PIEFORTS (P)

P1	1835	—	1/2 Centavo, KM114	150.00
P2	1851	—	1 Centavo	300.00

TRIAL STRIKES (TS)

TS1	1824	—	4 Escudos, Pewter, uniface, obverse KM#87	275.00
TS2	1851	—	20 Centavos, Copper, plain edge, obv. bust, rev. legend	175.00
TS3	1851	—	5 Peso, Copper	—

NECESSITY COINAGE

COPIAPO

Revolution of 1859

Issued by Don Pedro Leon Gallo.

50 CENTAVOS

SILVER, uniface
Star in relief, small shield pointing down.

KM#	Date	Mintage	VG	Fine	VF	XF
1.1	ND	—	25.00	35.00	50.00	70.00

Star in relief, wide body shield pointing down.

1.2	ND	—	25.00	35.00	50.00	70.00

Star flat, small shield pointing down.

1.3	ND	—	25.00	35.00	50.00	70.00

Star flat, wide shield pointing down.

1.4	ND	—	25.00	35.00	50.00	70.00

PESO

SILVER, uniface

2.1	ND	—	20.00	30.00	40.00	50.00

Inverted shield.

KM#	Date	Mintage	VG	Fine	VF	XF
2.2	ND	—	20.00	30.00	40.00	50.00

Similar to 50 Centavos, KM#1.

2.3 (2.2)	ND	—	20.00	30.00	40.00	50.00

NOTE: Denomination appears as either "1.P" or "I.P". Other varieties exist.

Blockade of Puerto de Caldera

Issued during the War of 1865 with Spain.

50 CENTAVOS

SILVER
Obv: COPIAPO-CHILE around shield. Rev: Date.

3	1865	6 known	—	—	350.00	500.00

NOTE: All known 50 Centavos are restrikes made from original dies circa 1909 by Medina.

PESO

SILVER, 36.5mm

4	1865(restrike)	—	—	25.00	50.00	75.00

COPPER, 32mm

4a	1865*	—	850.00	1350.	2000.	—

***NOTE:** Possibly a pattern.

SAN BERNARDO de MAYPO

1/4 REAL

COPPER
Obv: Mountains (volcano in center) in circle.
Rev: View of Canal de San Bernardo.

1	1821	—	150.00	300.00	500.00	800.00

NOTE: Struck to pay canal workers.

TARAPACA

Tarapaca is the northernmost province of Chile. It was annexed to Chile from Peru in 1885 after a war between those two countries, in which Chile was the victor. In that same year the Liberal Party came to power in Chile, instituting reforms. In response to these reforms the Conservative Party rebelled and formed a provisional government, and within a few years defeated the Liberals.

REVOLUTIONARY COINAGE

Struck at Iquique by the revolutionary Junta.

PESO

25.0000 g, .620 SILVER, .4983 oz ASW, 37.5mm
Rev. leg: 25 GRs/620 FINO.

KM#	Date	Mintage	Fine	VF	XF	Unc
1	1891	—	250.00	500.00	1000.	1750.

COPPER

2	1891*	—	—	880.00	—	—

BRASS

3	1891*	—	—	700.00	—	—

***NOTE:** KM#2 and KM#3 are possible patterns.

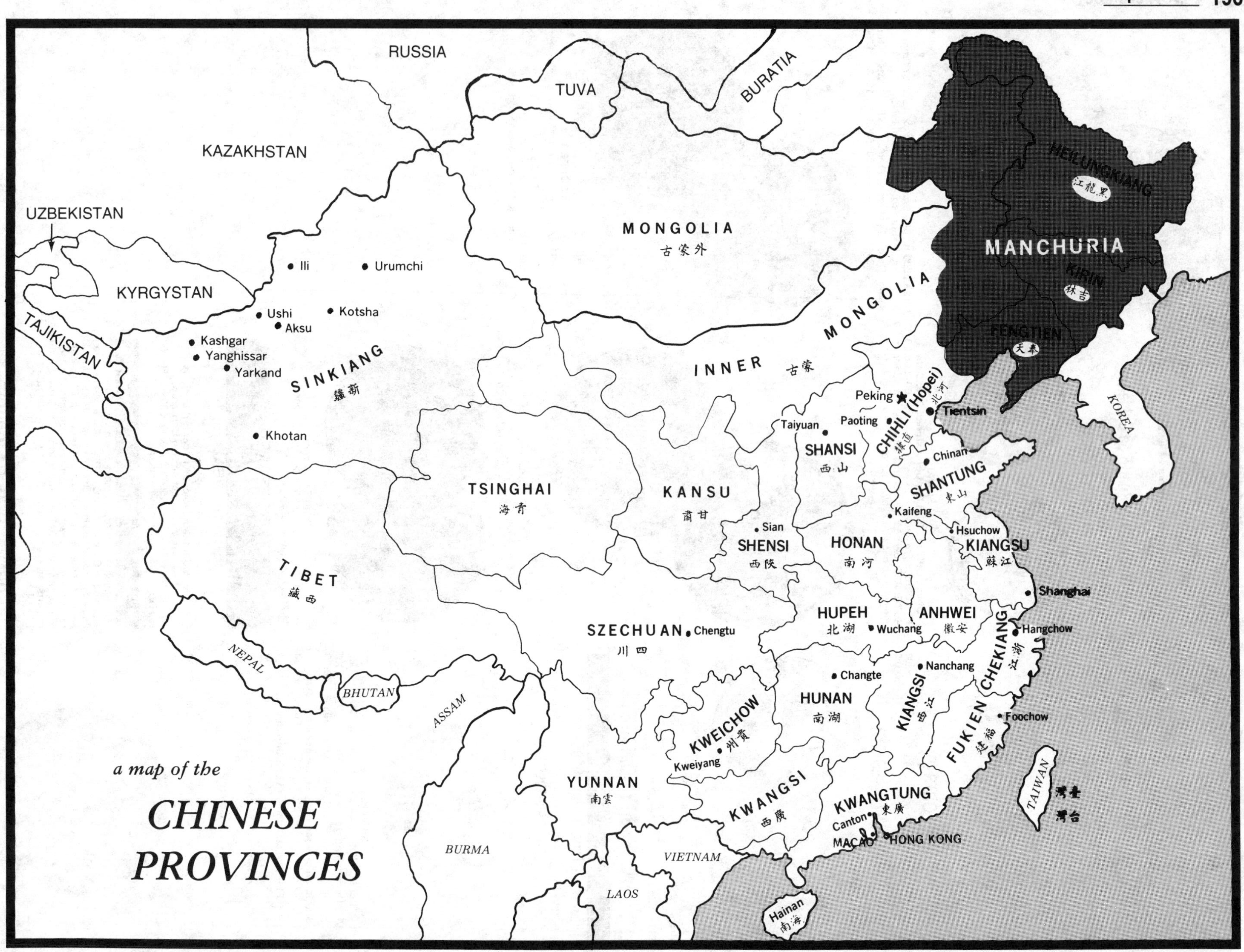

a map of the

CHINESE PROVINCES

CHINA

Before 1912, China was ruled by an imperial government. The republican administration which replaced it was itself supplanted on the Chinese mainland by a communist government in 1949, but it has remained in control of Taiwan and other offshore islands in the China Sea with a land area of approximately 14,000 square miles and a population of more than 14 million. The People's Republic of China administers some 3.7 million square miles and an estimated 1.19 billion people. This communist government, officially established on October 1, 1949, was admitted to the United Nations, replacing its nationalist predecessor, the Republic of China, in 1971.

Cast coins in base metals were used in China many centuries before the Christian era, but locally struck coinages of the western type in gold, silver, copper and other metals did not appear until 1888. In spite of the relatively short time that modern coins have been in use, the number of varieties is exceptionally large.

Both Nationalist and Communist China, as well as the pre-revolutionary Imperial government and numerous provincial or other agencies, including some foreign-administered agencies and governments, have issued coins in China. Most of these have been in dollar (yuan) or dollar-fraction denominations, based on the internationally used dollar system, but coins in tael denominations were issued in the 1920's and earlier. The striking of coins nearly ceased in the late 1930's through the 1940's due to the war effort and a period of uncontrollable inflation while vast amounts of paper currency were issued by the Nationalist, Communist and Japanese occupation institutions.

EMPERORS

OBVERSE TYPES

NOTE: Obverse Type B, *Chung-pao* and Type C *Yuan-pao* were normally used for multiple-cash issues.

JEN TSUNG 仁 宗
1796-1820

Type A

Reign title: Chia-ch'ing 嘉 慶

Chia-ch'ing T'ung-pao 嘉 慶 通 寶

HSUAN TSUNG 宣 宗
1821-1851

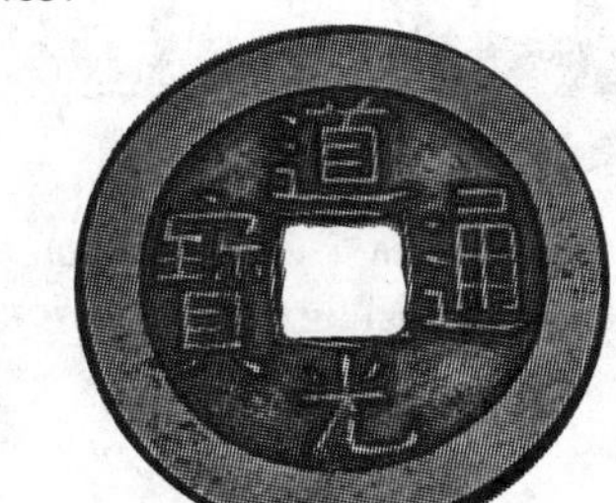

Type A

Reign title: Tao-kuang 道 光

Tao-kuang T'ung-pao 道 光 通 寶

WEN TSUNG 文 宗
1851-1861

Type A

Reign title: Hsien-feng 咸 豐

Hsien-feng T'ung-pao 咸 豐 通 寶

Type B-1

Hsien-feng Chung-pao 咸 豐 重 寶

Type B-2

Left character *Pao* in another style, called *"Chen" Pao*.

Hsien-feng Chung-pao 咸 豐 重 寶

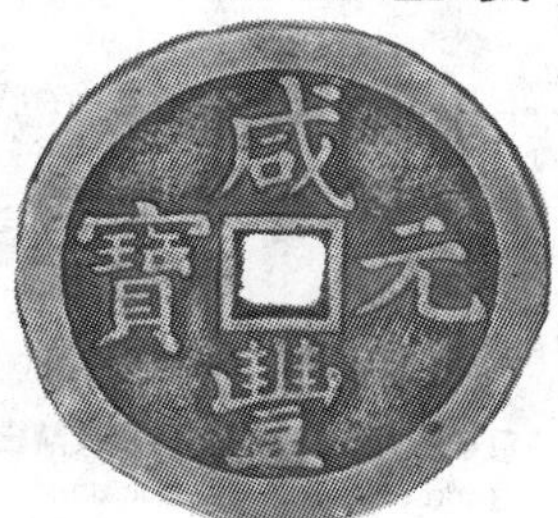

Type C

Hsien-feng Yuan-pao 咸 豐 元 寶

MU TSUNG 穆 宗
1861

Type A-1

1st reign title: Ch'i-hsiang 祺 祥

Ch'i-hsiang T'ung-pao 祺 祥 通 寶

Type B-1

Ch'i-hsiang Chung-pao 祺 祥 重 寶

MU TSUNG 穆 宗
1862-1875

Type A-2

2nd reign title: T'ung-chih 同 治

T'ung-chih T'ung-pao 同 治 通 寶

Type B-2

T'ung-chih Chung-pao 同 治 重 寶

TE TSUNG 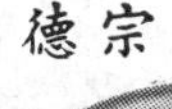 德 宗
1875-1908

Type A

Reign title: Kuang-hsu 光 緒

Kuang-hsu T'ung-pao 光 緒 通 寶

Type B

Kuang-hsu Chung-pao 光 緒 重 寶

Type C

Kuang-hsu Yuan-pao 光 緒 元 寶

NOTE: For other legend types refer to Rebel Issues listed after Yunnan-Szechuan.

PROVINCIAL NAMES

(and other source indicators)

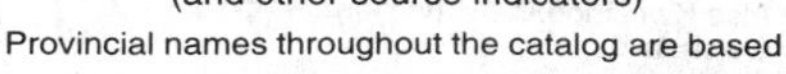

Provincial names throughout the catalog are based on

the Wade-Giles transliteration of the Chinese word. Current spellings, known as the "Pinyin" form, are widely adopted by the printed media. Example: Sinkiang = Xinjiang.

	Single Character (1)	Full Names (Right to left reading)
ANHWEI Also An-hwi, Anhui, now Anhui (Wan)	皖	徽安
CHEKIANG Also Cheh-kiang, now Zhejiang (Che)	浙	江浙
CHIHLI Also Hopei (after 1928)(Chih) now Hebei	直	隸直
CH'ING DYNASTY Also Tsing Dynasty, now Qing Dynasty		清大
CHING-KIANG Also Tsing-kiang now Qingjiang (Huai)	淮	江清
FENGTIEN Also Fung-tien, Fun-tien, Shengching, Manchurian Provinces, now Liaoning (Feng)	奉	天奉
FUKIEN Also Foo-kien, F.K., now Fujian (Min)	閩	建福
HEILUNGKIANG Also Hei Lung Kiang, now Heilongjiang (Hei)	黑	江龍黑
HONAN Also Ho-nan, now Henan (Yu)	豫	南河
HOPEH Also Chihli, Hopei, now Hebei (Chi)	冀	北河
HUNAN Also Hu-nan, now Hunan (Hsiang)	湘	南湖
HUPEH Also Hupei, Hu-peh, now Hubei (O)	鄂	北湖
HU PU (Board of Revenue) Also Hu Poo, Hoo Poo (Hu)	戶	部戶
KANSU Now Gansu (Kan)	甘	肅甘
KIANGNAN Also Kiang Nan Now Jiangnan (Ning)	寧	南江
KIANGSI Also Kiang-si, Kiang-see, now Jiangxi (Kan)	贛	西江
KIANGSI (Alternate) (Kan)	贑	贑
KIANGSU Also Kiang-soo, now Jiangsu (Su)	蘇	蘇江
KIRIN Also Chi-lin Now Jilin (Chi)	吉	林吉
KWANGSI, KWANGSEA Also Kwang-si, now Guangxi (Kuei)	桂	西廣
KWANGTUNG Also Kwang-tung, now Guangdong (Yueh)	粵	東廣
KWEICHOW Also Kweichou, now Guizhou (Ch'ien)	黔	州貴
PEIYANG MINT (Tientsin) Also Pei-uang, Pei Yang		洋北
SHANSI Now Shanxi (Shan) or (Chin)	山	西山
SHENSI Also Shen-si, now Shaanxi (Shan)	陝	西陝
SHANTUNG, SHAN-TUNG Also Shang-tung, (Tung)	東	東山
now Shandong (Lu)	魯	
SIKANG		
SINKIANG (Chinese Turkestan) Also Sin-kiang, Hsin kiang Sungarei, now Xinjiang (Hsin)	新	疆新
SZECHUAN Also Szechwan, Szechuen, Now Sichuan	川 (Ch'uan) or (Shu) 蜀	川四
TAIWAN Also Tai-wan, now Taiwan (Tai)	臺	灣臺
TAIWAN (Alternate) (Tai)		灣台
YUNNAN Also Yun-nan, now Yunnan (Yun)	雲	南雲
YUNNAN (Alternate) (Tien)	滇	南雲
TUNG SAN SHENG Manchuria		省三東
YUNNAN-SZECHUAN		滇川

GOVERNMENTAL NAMES
(and other source indicators)

	Full Names (Right to left reading)
CHITUNG (Japanese puppet)	府政東冀
CHINESE SOVIET REPUBLIC	國和共埃維蘇華中
MANCHOUKUO (Japanese puppet)	國洲滿大
MENGCHIANG (Japanese puppet) (2)	行銀疆蒙
PEOPLES REPUBLIC OF CHINA (Communist) (3)	中華人民共和國
REPUBLIC OF CHINA (Nationalist)	國民華中
NORTH CHINA (Japanese puppet)	行銀備準合聯國中

(1) Single-character designators for provincial or regional mints are used primarily on copper coins of the Tai Ching Ti Kuo series.
(2) Vertical readings predominate.
(3) Reads left to right.
(4) For lists of mints in Sinkiang, see that section.

ADDITIONAL CHARACTERS

The additional characters illustrated and defined below are found on the reverse of cast bronze cash coins, usually above the square center hole. In the period covered by this catalog the following mints produced cash coins with these additional marks: Board of Revenue and Board of Works in Peking, Kweichow, Aksu and Ili in Sinkiang, Shantung, Szechuan, and all three mints listed in Yunnan.

一	I,Yi	士	Shih i	心	Hsin
二	Erh	合	Ho	宇	Yu
三	San	工	Kung	宙	Chou
四	Szu	主	Chu	來	Lai
五	Wu	川	Ch'uan	往	Wang
六	Liu	之	Chih	金	Chin
七	Ch'i	正	Cheng	村	Ts'un
八	Pa	又	Yu	日	Jih
九	Chiu	山	Shan	列	Lieh
十	Shih	大	Ta	仁	Jen
主	Chu	中	Chung	丰	Feng
上	Shang	順	Shun	云	Yun
	Shou	手		—	

MINT MARK IDENTIFIER

There are more than 30 different mints covered in the following text. For ease in identification the more common varieties are illustrated with the Manchu legend.

Boo-Ciowan (Peking) BOARD OF REVENUE

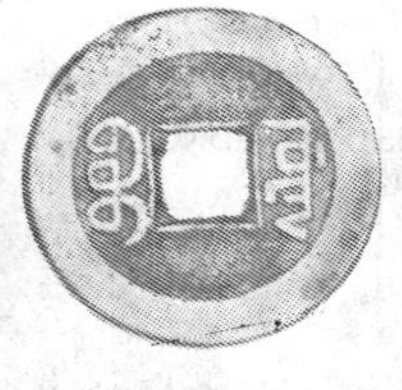

Boo Yuwan (Peking) BOARD OF PUBLIC WORKS

Boo Hu Hu Mint ANHWEI

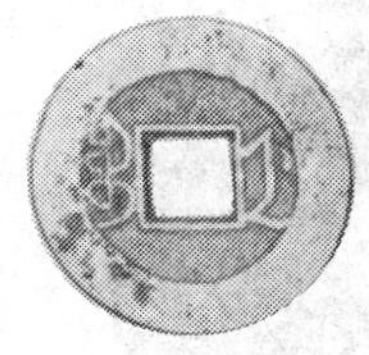

Boo Je Che Mint Hangchow CHEKIANG

Boo Ji Chihli Mint Paoting CHIHLI

Boo Gi
Chi Mint
Chichow
CHIHLI
(Through Hsien-Feng era)

Boo Jiyen
Ching Mint
Tientsin
CHIHLI

Boo Fung
FENGTIEN

Boo Fu
Fu Mint
Fuchou
FUKIEN

Boo Ho
Ho Mint
K'aifeng
HONAN

Boo Nan
Nan Mint
Ch'ang-sha
HUNAN

Boo De
Teh Mint
Chengte
CHIHLI

Boo U
Wu Mint
Wuch'ang
HUPEH

Boo Gung
Kungchang
KANSU

Nanchang
KIANGSI

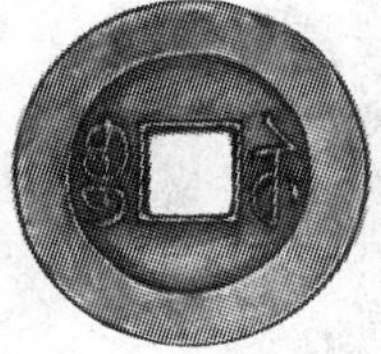

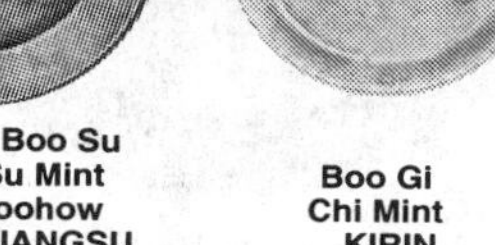

Boo Su
Su Mint
Soohow
KIANGSU

Boo Gi
Chi Mint
KIRIN
(Kuang-hsu era)

Boo Gui
Kuelin
KWANGSI

Boo Guwang
Canton
KWANGTUNG

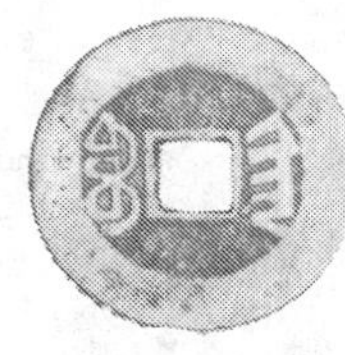

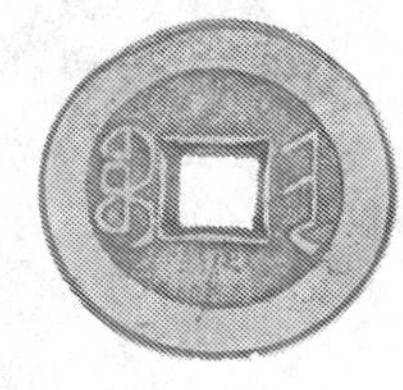

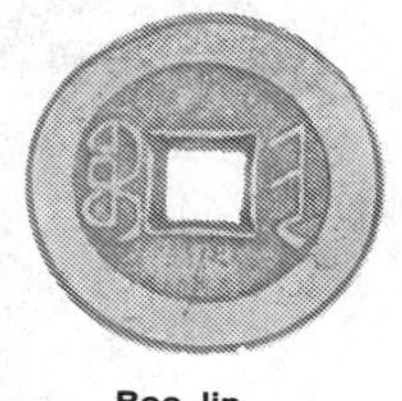

Boo Giyan
Kweiyang
KWEICHOW

Boo Jin
Taiyuan
SHANSI

Boo Ji
Chinan
SHANTUNG

Boo Cuwan
Chengtu
SZECHUAN

Boo San
Shan Mint
Sian
SHENSI

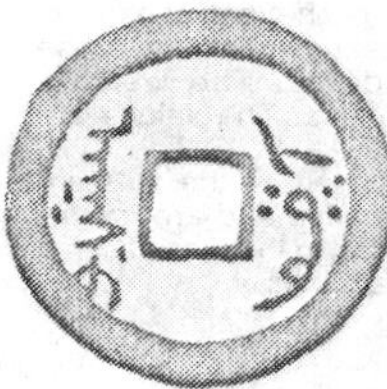

Aksu (Hocheng)
SINKIANG

Ili (Hweiyuan)
SINKIANG

Kotsha (Kuche)
SINKIANG

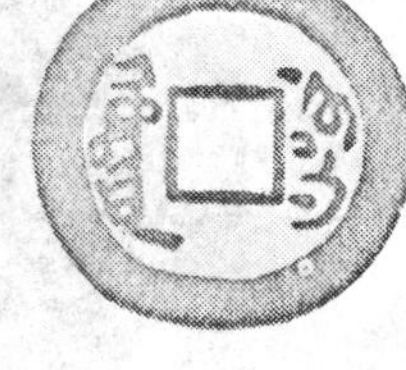

Kashgar (Shufu)
SINKIANG

Khotan (Hotien)
SINKIANG

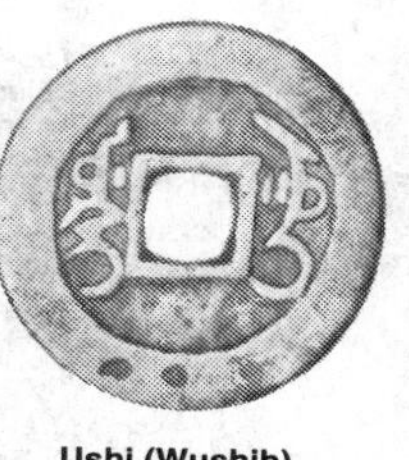

Urumchi (Tihwa)
SINKIANG

Ushi (Wushih)
SINKIANG

Yarkand (Soche)
SINKIANG

Tai Mint
TAIWAN

Boo Yon
Yun Mint
Yunnanfu
YUNNAN

Boo Dong
Tung Mint
Tungch'uan
YUNNAN

Taku (Dagu) Mint
TIENTSIN

Chou Mint
Location uncertain
(Refer to Yunnan)

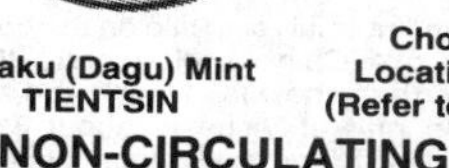

NON-CIRCULATING ISSUES

Along with regular circulation coinage produced by the various mints certain cash types were cast in various sizes with the emperor's reign title on the obverse but with various characters and/or symbols not found in our mint identifiers. This listing is not complete but it will benefit the collector as an aid to proper identification.

PALACE ISSUES

(Palace Cash)

Usually 1-6 mace in weight, made of 60% copper and 40% zinc. Made for distribution in the palace during new year. Usually given to eunuchs and guards. Recipients hanged them under lamps - "lamp 'hanging' money."

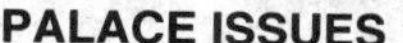

Rev. leg: ***T'ien-hsia T'ai-p'ing***
"Peace under Heaven."

The market value is about $60.00-100.00 in VF condition.

Obv: Chia-ch'ing

Tao-kuang
Hsien-feng
Kuang-hsu

Rev: ***I-t'ung T'ien-hsia***

"Unify the whole country".

The market value is about $50.00-70.00 in VF condition.

Obv: Hsien-feng

BIRTHDAY CASH

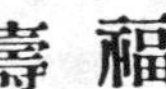

These issues have the normal reign title on the obverse but the reverse has two Chinese characters 'Fu' in normal or seal script (happiness), at right and 'Shou' (birthday) at left. The market value is about $60.00-100.00 in F/VF condition. Some are palace issues, but most are made by private sources as good luck amulets.

Hsien-feng

T'ung-chih

Kuang-hsu

AMULETS

Eight Trigrams

Hsien-feng

The eight trigrams (Pa Kua) of the Book of Changes (I Ching). This book, one of the Five Classics, consists of a set of sixty-four figures known as "trigrams". The trigram is composed of combinations of pairs of eight trigrams each of which represents some power in nature, either active or passive, such as fire, water, thunder, earth, etc. These trigrams are said to have been invented 2000 years and more B.C. by the legendary monarch Fu Hsi, who copied them from the back of a tortoise. Attached to each hexagram are explanatory notes and expository comments. The notes are said to have been written by the Chou King Wen Wang and the comments by Confucius. The notes are made in symbolic language which only mystics could understand, but the comments are written in plain language. These comments have lifted the Book of Changes from a primitive book of divination and oracles to an ethical and philosophical importance. The market value is about $30.00-40.00 in VF condition. Many cash coins have been privately decorated with engraved designs on the rims, in the fields, or both, to convert them to amulets.

MULTIPLE CASH

The size and weight of multiple cash coins cannot be used to determine the correct denomination as these were issued on various standards. The weights decreased considerably in later years. The values are given in various manners.

Additional character(s) handstamped on the rims are occasionally encountered in this series and are merely private marks, but the characters cast in the rims of some Fukien and Shensi multiple cash are official.

4 CASH

Ili Mint, Sinkiang

5 CASH

Board of Public Works Mint, Peking

8 CASH

Tihwa Mint, Sinkiang

10 CASH

Normal Ten
Board of Public Works Mint, Peking

Official Ten
Board of Revenue Mint, Peking

Fukien Mint

20 CASH

Fukien Mint

30 CASH

Kiangsu Mint

40 CASH

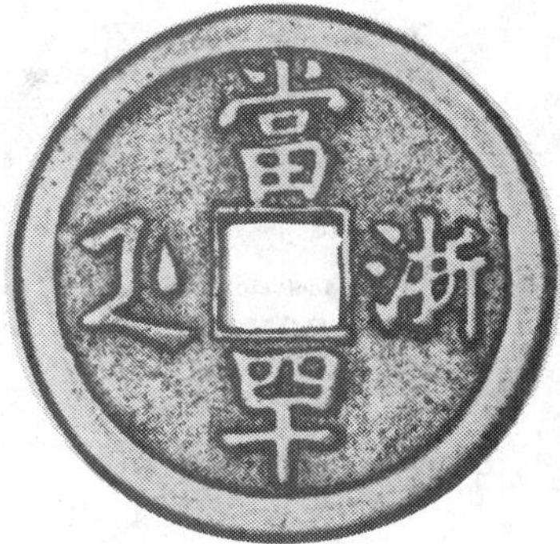

Chekiang Mint

50 CASH

Fukien Mint
(Weighing) 2 Tael 5 Mace (on rim)

Fukien Mint

100 CASH

Board of Revenue Mint, Peking

500 CASH

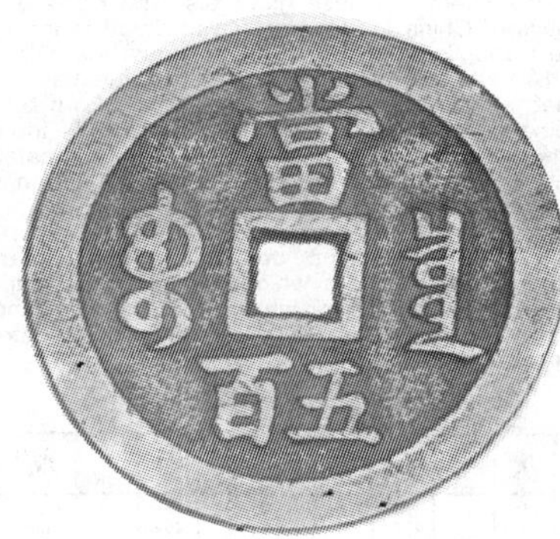

Board of Revenue Mint, Peking

1000 CASH

Board of Revenue Mint, Peking

DENOMINATION VARIETIES

The denominations for multiple cash may appear in at least three methods. The 50 Cash of Fukien previously illustrated has the 5 above and the 10 below the center hole. The 50 Cash of Kwangsi has the denomination written horizontally below the center hole while the 50 cash of Chekiang has the denomination written vertically below the center hole.

50 CASH

Kwangsi Mint

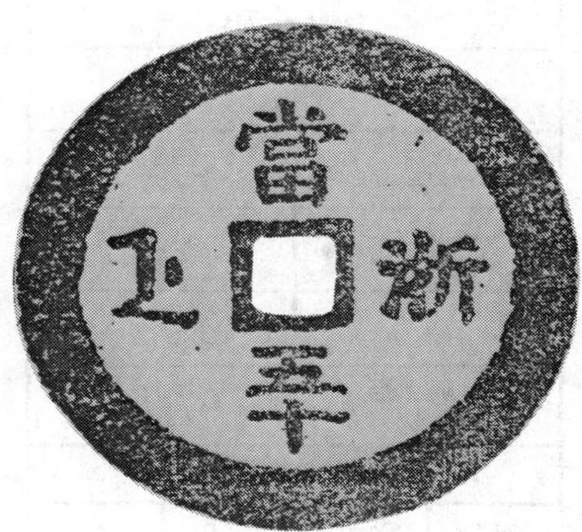

Chekiang Mint

NUMERALS

NUMBER	CONVENTIONAL		FORMAL		COMMERCIAL
1	一	元	壹	弌	〡
2	二		弍	貳	〢
3	三		叁	弎	〣
4	四		肆		〤
5	五		伍		〥
6	六		陸		〦
7	七		柒		〧
8	八		捌		〨
9	九		玖		〩
10	十		拾	什	十
20	十 二 or 廿		拾貳		〢十
25	五 十 二 or 五廿		伍拾貳		〢十〥
30	十 三 or 卅		拾叁		〣十
100	百 一		佰壹		〡百
1,000	千 一		仟壹		〡千
10,000	萬 一		萬壹		〡万
100,000	萬 十	億 一 (old)	萬拾	億 壹	十万
1,000,000	萬百一	億 一 (new)	萬佰壹		〡百万

NOTE: This table has been adapted from *Chinese Bank Notes* by Ward Smith and Brian Matravers.

MONETARY UNITS

Dollar Amounts		
DOLLAR *(Yuan)*	元 or 員	圓 or 圜
HALF DOLLAR *(Pan Yuan)*	圓 半	元中
50¢ *(Chiao/Hao)*	角伍	毫伍
10¢ *(Chiao/Hao)*	角壹	毫壹
1¢ *(Fen/Hsien)*	分壹	仙壹

Copper and Cash Coin Amounts			
COPPER *(Mei)*	枚	CASH *(Wen)*	文

Tael Amounts	
1 TAEL *(Liang)*	兩
HALF TAEL *(Pan Liang)*	兩半
5 MACE *(Wu Ch'ien)*	錢伍
1 MACE *(I Ch'ien)*	錢壹
1 CANDEREEN *(I Fen)*	分壹

Common Prefixes			
COPPER *(T'ung)*	銅	GOLD *(Chin)*	金
SILVER *(Yin)*	銀	Ku Ping *(Tael)**	平庫

NOTE: This table has been adapted from *Chinese Bank Notes* by Ward Smith and Brian Matravers.

MONETARY SYSTEM

Cash Coin System

800-1600 Cash = 1 Tael
400 Sinkiang 'red' cash = 1 Tael

In theory, 1000 cash were equal to a tael of silver, but in actuality the rate varied from time to time and place to place.

Dollar System

10 Cash (Wen, Ch'ien) = 1 Cent (Fen, Hsien)
10 Cents = 1 Chiao (Hao)
100 Cents = 1 Dollar (Yuan)
1 Dollar = 0.72 Tael

Imperial silver coins normally bore no denomination, but were inscribed with their weights as follows:

1 Dollar = 7 Mace and 2 Candareens
50 Cents = 3 Mace and 6 Candareens
20 Cents = 1 Mace and 4.4 Candareens
10 Cents = 7.2 Candareens
5 Cents = 3.6 Candareens

NOTE: *Candareen* is spelled *Candarin* and misspelled as *Caindarin* on Kirin Province Imperial coinage.

Tael System

10 Li = 1 Fen (Candareen)
10 Fen (Candareen) = 1 Ch'ien (Mace)
10 Ch'ien (Mace) = 1 Liang (Tael)

DATING

Yuan: (first)
Chung Hua Min Kuo (Republic of China)
Nien (year)

Most struck Chinese coins are dated by year within a given period, such as the regnal eras or the republican periods. A 1907 issue, for example, would be dated in the 33rd year of the Kuang Hsu era (1875 + 33 - 1 = 1907) or a 1926 issue is dated in the 15th year of the Republic (1912 + 15 - 1 = 1926). The mathematical discrepancy in both instances is accounted for by the fact that the first year is included in the elapsed time. Modern Chinese Communist coins are dated in western numerals using the western calendar, but earlier issues use conventional Chinese numerals. The coins of the Republic of China (Taiwan) are also dated in the year of the Republic, which is added to equal the calendar year. Still another method is a 60-year, repeating cycle, outlined in the table below. The date is shown by the combination of two characters, the first from the top row and the second from the column at left. In this catalog, when a cyclical date is used, the abbreviation CD appears before the AD date.

Dates not in parentheses are those which appear on the coins. For undated coins, dates appearing in parentheses are the years in which the coin was actually minted. Undated coins for which the year of minting is unknown are listed with ND (No Date) in the date or year column.

CYCLICAL DATES

	庚	辛	壬	癸	甲	乙	丙	丁	戊	己
戌	1850 1910		1862 1922		1874 1934		1886 1946		1838 1898	
亥		1851 1911		1863 1923		1875 1935		1887 1947		1839 1899
子	1840 1900		1852 1912		1864 1924		1876 1936		1888 1948	
丑		1841 1901		1853 1913		1865 1925		1877 1937		1889 1949
寅	1830 1890		1842 1902		1854 1914		1866 1926		1878 1938	
卯		1831 1891		1843 1903		1855 1915		1867 1927		1879 1939
辰	1880 1940		1832 1892		1844 1904		1856 1916		1868 1928	
巳		1881 1941		1833 1893		1845 1905		1857 1917		1869 1929
午	1870 1930		1882 1942		1834 1894		1846 1906		1858 1918	
未		1871 1931		1883 1943		1835 1895		1847 1907		1859 1919
申	1860 1920		1872 1932		1884 1944		1836 1896		1848 1908	
酉		1861 1921		1873 1933		1885 1945		1837 1897		1849 1909

NOTE: This table has been adapted from *Chinese Bank Notes* by Ward Smith and Brian Matravers.

GRADING

Chinese coins should not be graded entirely by western standards. In addition to Fine, Very Fine, Extremely Fine (XF), and Uncirculated, the type of strike should be considered weak, medium or sharp strike. China had no rigid minting rules as we know them. For instance, Kirin (Jilin) and Sinkiang (Xinjiang) Provinces used some dies made of iron - hence, they wore out rapidly. Some communist army issues were apparently struck by crude hand methods on soft dies (it is hard to find two coins of the same die!). In general, especially for some minor coins, dies were used until they were worn well beyond western standards. Subsequently, one could have an uncirculated coin struck from worn dies with little of the design or letters still visible, but still uncirculated! All prices quoted are for well-struck (sharp struck), well-centered specimens. Most silver coins can be found from very fine to uncirculated. Some copper coins are difficult to find except in poorer grades.

REFERENCES

The following references have been used for this section:

K Edward Kann - Illustrated Catalog of Chinese Coins.

Hsu - T.K. Hsu - Illustrated Catalog of Chinese Coins, 1981 edition.

W - A.M. Tracey Woodward - The Minted Ten-Cash Coins of China.

DATING

Yuan: (first)
Chung Hua Min Kuo (Republic of China)
Nien (year)

NOTE: The die struck 10 and 20 Cash coins are often found silver plated. This was not done at the mint. They were apparently plated to be passed to the unwary as silver coins.

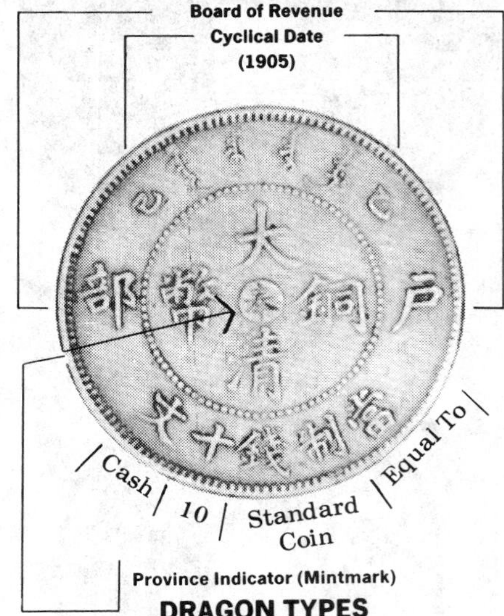

Province Indicator (Mintmark)

DRAGON TYPES

(Chinese Imperial Coins)

(1900)
Made in Kiangnan Province

Coin
Province Indicator (Mintmark)
Central leg: *Kuang Hsu Yuan Pao*
Coin of Kuang Hsu

DRAGON TYPES

(Chinese Imperial Coins)

Side View Dragon-left (Silver Coins)

First used by the Kwangtung Mint in 1889. This was the standard (though not the only) dragon used on silver coins. Normally there is no circle around the dragon. Note the fireball beneath the dragon's chin. Normally there are seven flames on the fireball.

SYCEE (INGOTS)

Prior to 1889 the general coinage issued by the Chinese government was the copper-alloy cash coin. Despite occasional shortlived experiments with silver and gold coinage, and disregarding paper money which tended to be unreliable, the government expected the people to get by solely with cash coins. This system worked well for individuals making purchases for themselves, but was unsatisfactory for trade and large business transactions, since a dollar's worth of cash coins weighed about four pounds. As a result, a private currency consisting of silver ingots, usually stamped by the firm which made them, came into use. These were the sycee ingots.

It is not known when these ingots first came into use. Some sources date them to the Yuan (Mongol) dynasty but they are certainly much older. Examples are known from as far back as the Han dynasty (206 BC - 220 AD) but prior to the Sung era (960 - 1280AD) they were used mainly for hoarding wealth. The development of commerce by the Sung dynasty, however, required the use of silver or gold to pay for large purchases. By the Mongol period (1280-1368) silver ingots and paper money had become the dominant currencies, especially for trade. The western explorers who traveled to China during this period (such as Marco Polo) mention both paper money and sycee but not a single one refers to cash coins.

During the Ming dynasty (1368-1644) trade fell off and the use of silver decreased. But toward the end of that dynasty, Dutch and British ships began a new China trade and sycee once again became common. During the 19th and early 20th centuries, the trade in sycee became enormous. Most of the sycee around today are from this period. In 1935 the Chinese government and in 1939 Sinkiang banned the use of sycee and it soon disappeared.

The word sycee (pronounced "sigh - see") is a western corruption of the Chinese word hsi-szu ("fine silk") or hsi yin ("fine silver") and is first known to have appeared in the English language in the late 1600's. By the early 1700's the word appeared regularly in the records of the British East India Company. Westerners also called these ingots "boat money" or "shoe money" owing to the fact that the most common type of ingot resembles a Chinese shoe. The Chinese, however, called the ingots by a variety of names, the most common of which were yuan pao, wen - yin (fine silver) and yin-ting (silver ingot).

The ingots were cast in molds (giving them their characteristic shapes) and while the metal was still semi-liquid, the inscription was impressed. It was due to this procedure that the sides of some sycee are higher than the center. The manufacturers were usually silver firms, often referred to as lu fang's, and after the sycee was finished it was occasionally tested and marked by the kung ku (public assayer).

Sycee were not circulated as we understand it. One didn't usually carry a sycee to market and spend it. Usually the ingots were used as a means of carrying a large amount of money on trips (as we would carry $100 bills instead of $5 bills) or for storing wealth. Large transactions between merchants or banks were paid by means of crates of sycee - each containing 60 fifty tael ingots.

Sycee are known in a variety of shapes the most common of which are the shoe or boat shaped, drum shaped, and loaf shaped (rectangular or hourglass-shaped, with a generally flat surface). Other shapes include one that resembles a double headed axe (this is the oldest type known), one that is square and flat, and others that are "fancy" (in the form of fish, butterflies, leaves, etc.).

Sycee have no denominations as they were simply ingots that passed by weight. Most are in more or less standard weights, however, the most common being 1, 5, 10 and 50 taels. Other weights known include 1/10, 1/5, 1/4, 1/3, 1/2, 2/3, 72/100 (this is the weight of a dollar), 3/4, 2, 3, 4, 6, 7, 8 and 25 taels. Most of the pieces weighing less than 5 taels were used as gifts or souvenirs.

The actual weight of any given value of sycee varied considerably due to the fact that the tael was not a single weight but a general term for a wide range of local weight standards. The weight of the tael varied depending upon location and type of tael in question. For example in one town, the weight of a tael of rice, of silver and of stones may each be different. In addition, the fineness of silver also varied depending upon location and type of tael in question. It was not true, as westerners often wrote, that sycee were made of pure silver. For most purposes, a weight of 37 grams may be used for the tael.

Weights and Current Market Value of Sycee (Weights are approximate)

1/2 tael	17-19 grams	26.00
72/100 tael	25-27 grams	36.00
1 tael	35-38 grams	46.00
2 taels	70-75 grams	70.00
3 taels	100-140 grams	85.00
5 taels	175-190 grams	110.00
7 taels	240-260 grams	125.00
10 taels	350-380 grams	250.00
25 taels	895-925 grams	3500.
50 taels	1790-1850 grams	2000.
50 taels, square	1790-1850 grams	1600.

REFERENCE

Catalog reference Sch.#: *Chinese Currency* by Fredrik Schjoth c. 1965 by Virgil Hancock, published by Krause Publications, Iola, Wisconsin, U.S.A.

JEN TSUNG

1796-1820

Reign title: ***Chia-ch'ing***

Chia-ch'ing T'ung-pao

CASH

CAST BRASS, 21-26mm
Obv. leg: ***Chia-ch'ing T'ung-pao.***

Sch.#—

KM#	Date	Good	VG	Fine	VF
440.1 (C1-2)	ND(1796-1820)	.20	.35	.50	.75

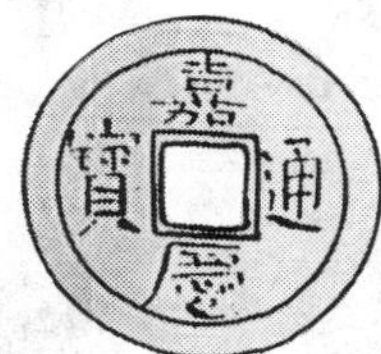

Rev: Dot at upper left.

Sch.#1489

440.2 (C1-2.2)	ND(1796-1820)	2.00	3.50	5.00	7.00

Rev: Dot below.

Sch.#—

440.3 (C1-2.3)	ND(1796-1820)	2.00	3.50	5.00	7.00

28-30mm

441 (C1-2.1)	ND(1796-1820)	10.00	17.50	25.00	35.00

Rev: Manchu ***Boo-yuwan***

Sch.#1490

442.1 (C2-2)	ND(1796-1820)	.20	.30	.50	.75

Rev: Dot above.

Sch.#1489

442.2 (C2-2.1)	ND(1796-1820)	2.00	3.00	5.00	7.50

Rev: Dot below.

Sch.#1491

442.3 (C2-2.2)	ND(1796-1820)	2.00	3.00	5.00	7.50

Rev: Manchu ***Boo-an*** **(An-hwei).**

Sch.#—

KM#	Date	Good	VG	Fine	VF
444	ND (1796-1820)	—	—	Rare	—

NOTE: Not to be confused with similar coins from the Changsha Mint in Hunan Province. The Changsha Mint coins have an extra dot or vertical stroke to the left of the mint mark at right of the center hole.

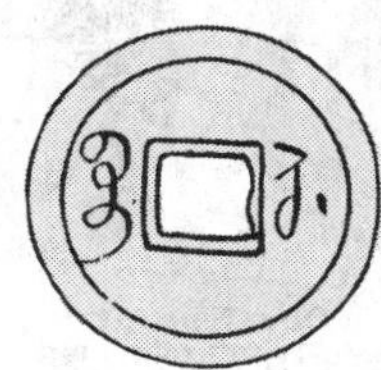

Rev: Manchu ***Boo-su*** **(Kiangsu).**

Sch.#1492

446 (C16-2)	ND(1796-1820)	.85	1.35	2.00	3.00

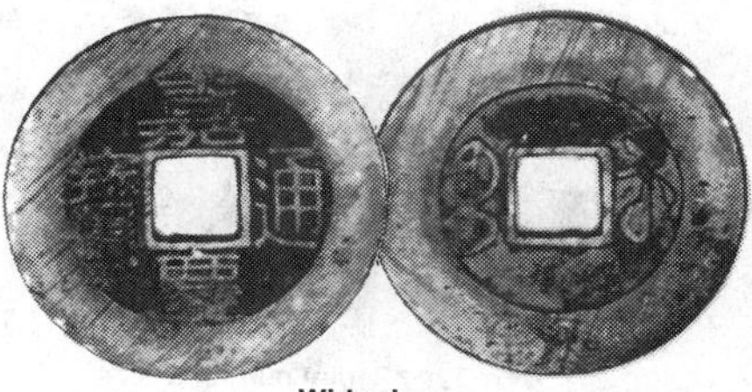

Wide rims.

Sch.#—

447s (C16-2.1)	ND(1796-1820)	35.00	60.00	85.00	120.00

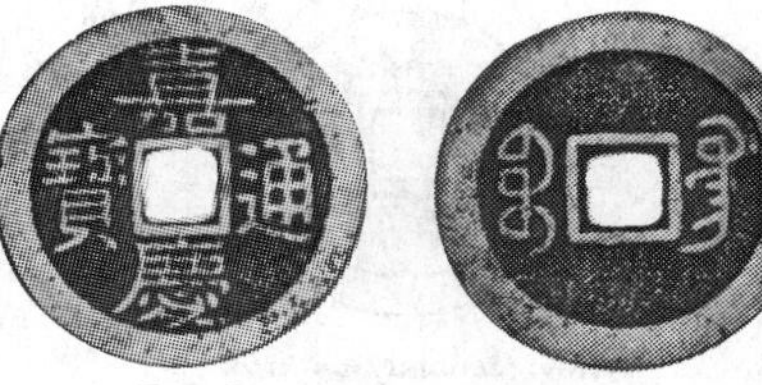

Rev: Boo-guwang (Kwangtung).

Sch.#1493

449 (C19-2)	ND(1796-1820)	.85	1.35	2.00	3.00

CAST IRON

Sch.#—

449a (C19-2a)	ND(1796-1820)	—	—	Rare	—

CAST BRASS
Rev: Manchu ***Boo-nan*** **(Hunan).**

Sch.#1494

451 (C12-2)	ND(1796-1820)	1.50	2.50	3.50	5.00

Obv: Type A.
Rev: Manchu ***Boo-yon*** **(Yun, Yunnan).**

Sch.#1495

453.1 (C26-2)	ND(1796-1820)	.40	.70	1.00	1.50

Rev: Dot at upper right.

Sch.#1496

453.2	ND(1796-1820)	1.25	2.00	2.75	4.00

Rev: Crescent above.

Sch.#1497

KM#	Date	Good	VG	Fine	VF
453.3	ND(1796-1820)	1.75	3.00	4.25	6.00

(C26-2.1)

Obv: Type A-1.
Rev: Type 1 mint mark,
Manchu, *Boo-dung* (T'ung, Tat'ung) Shansi.

Sch.#1498
455 ND(1796-1820) 1.75 3.00 4.25 6.00
(C27-1)

Rev: Type 2 mint mark.

Sch.#—
456 ND(1796-1820) 10.00 17.50 25.00 35.00
(C27-1.1)

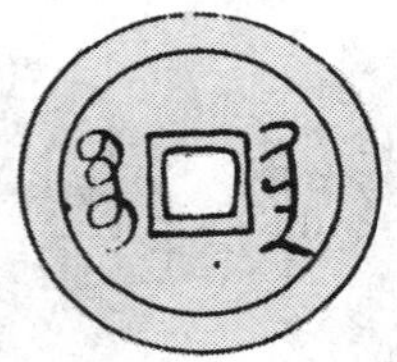

Rev: Manchu *Boo-kian*
(Chien, Kwelyang) Kwekhow.

Sch.#1499
458.1 ND(1796-1820) 1.25 2.00 2.75 4.00
(C20-2)

Rev: Dot above.

Sch.#—
458.2 ND(1796-1820) 1.50 2.50 3.50 5.00
(C20-2.1)

Rev: Character *Erh* (two) above.

Sch.#—
460 ND(1796-1820) 7.50 12.50 17.50 25.00
(C20.2-2)

Rev: Wide Manchu *Boo-fu* (Fukien).

Sch.#1500
462 ND(1796-1820) .85 1.35 2.00 3.00
(C10-2)

Rev: Thin Manchu at right.

Sch.#—
463 ND(1796-1820) 1.75 3.00 4.25 6.00
(C10-2.1)

Rev: Different Manchu at right.

Sch.#—

KM#	Date	Good	VG	Fine	VF
464	ND(1796-1820)	1.50	2.50	3.50	5.00

(C10-2.2)

25-26mm
Obv: Type A.
Rev: Manchu *Boo-c'y* (Chi, Chihli).

Sch.#1501
465 ND (1796-1820) .85 1.35 2.00 3.00
(C5-2)

31mm

Sch.#—
466 ND(1796-1820) 60.00 100.00 140.00 200.00
(C5-2.1)

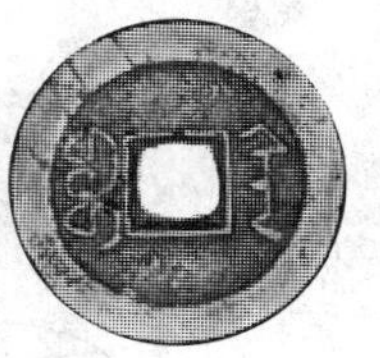

Obv: Type A.

Sch.#1502
468 ND(1796-1820) 2.25 3.75 5.50 8.00
(C23-2)

Rev: Large mint mark and normal rims,

Sch.#1503
470.1 ND (1796-1820) .50 .90 1.35 2.00
(C4-2)

Rev: Dot at bottom.

470.2 ND (1796-1820) 3.50 6.00 8.50 12.00
(C4-2.2)

CAST IRON

Sch.#—
470a ND (1796-1820) — — Rare —
(C4-2.1a)

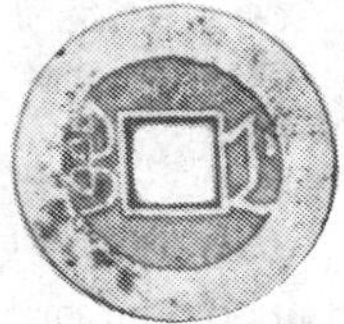

Rev: Small mint mark and wide rims.

Sch.#—
471 ND (1796-1820) .50 .90 1.35 2.00
(C4-2.1)

Sch.#1504
474.1 ND(1796-1820) 1.75 3.00 4.25 6.00
(C13-2)

Rev: Circle above.

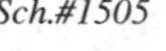

Sch.#1505

KM#	Date	Good	VG	Fine	VF
474.2	ND(1796-1820)	4.00	6.50	9.00	12.00

(C13-2a)

Rev: Crescent above, dot below.

Sch.#1506
474.3 ND(1796-1820) 4.00 7.00 10.00 15.00
(C13-2.1)

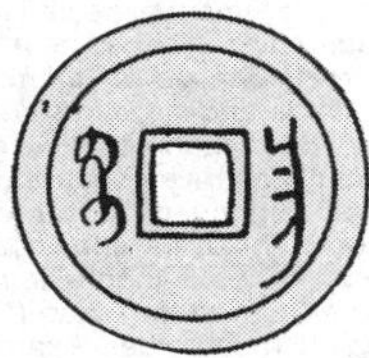

Rev: Manchu *Boo-cang* (Chang, Nanchang).

Sch.#1507
476.1 ND(1796-1820) .50 .90 1.35 2.00
(C15-2)

Rev: Dot in upper left corner.

Sch.#1508 var.
476.2 ND(1796-1820) 3.00 5.00 7.00 10.00
(C15-2.1)

Sch.#1509
478 ND(1796-1820) .75 1.00 1.75 3.00
(C18-2)

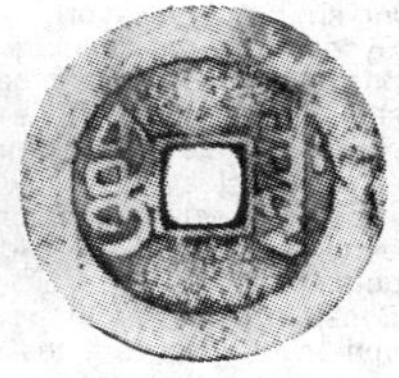

Sch.#1510
Rev: Manchu *Boo-cuwan (Szechuan)*.
480 ND(1796-1820) 1.00 1.75 3.00 4.00
(C24-2)

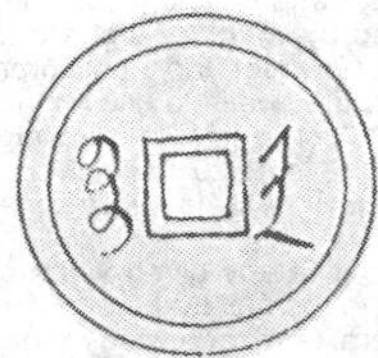

Rev: Manchu *Boo-jin* (Chin, Shansi).

Sch.#1511
482 ND(1796-1820) 1.25 2.00 2.75 4.00
(C21-2)

GENERAL ISSUE

EMPIRE

Peking Hu Pu Mint

(Board of Revenue)

CASH

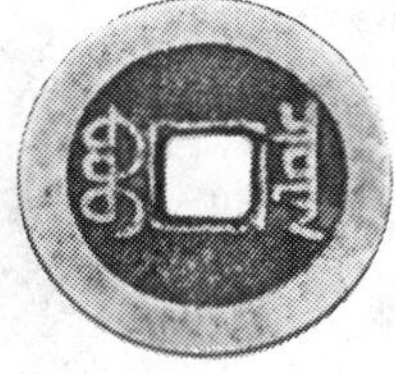

CAST BRASS, 20-26mm

Obv. leg: *Tao-kuang T'ung-pao.*

Sch.#1512

C#	Date	Emperor	Good	VG	Fine	VF
1-3	ND(1821-51)	Tao-kuang	.20	.30	.40	.75

28-30mm

C#	Date	Emperor	Good	VG	Fine	VF
1-3.1	ND(1821-51)	Tao-kuang	10.00	14.00	18.00	24.00

Rev: Dot above.

Sch.#1513

C#	Date	Emperor	Good	VG	Fine	VF
1-3.2	ND(1821-51)	Tao-kuang	1.75	3.00	4.50	8.00

Rev: Dot below.

C#	Date	Emperor	Good	VG	Fine	VF
1-3.3	ND(1821-51)	Tao-kuang	1.75	3.00	4.50	8.00

Obv. leg: *Hsien-feng T'ung-pao.*

Sch.#1534

C#	Date	Emperor	Good	VG	Fine	VF
1-4	ND(1851-61)	Hsien-feng	.60	1.00	2.50	4.00

CAST IRON

C#	Date	Emperor	Good	VG	Fine	VF
1-4a	ND(1851-61)	Hsien-feng	7.50	10.00	15.00	30.00

Obv: Type B-2.

C#	Date	Emperor	Good	VG	Fine	VF
1-4.2a	ND(1851-61)	Hsien-feng	—	—	—	—

CAST ZINC

C#	Date	Emperor	Good	VG	Fine	VF
1-4b	ND(1851-61)	Hsien-feng	—	—	Rare	—

CAST BRASS

Obv. leg: *Ch'i-hsiang T'ung-pao.*

C#	Date	Emperor	Good	VG	Fine	VF
1-12	ND(1861)	Ch'i-hsiang	—	—	Rare	—

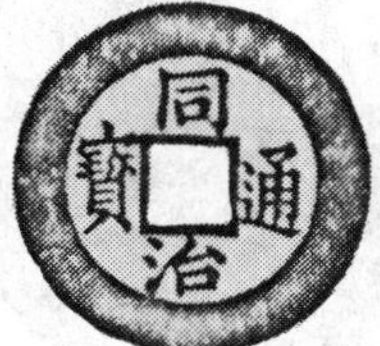
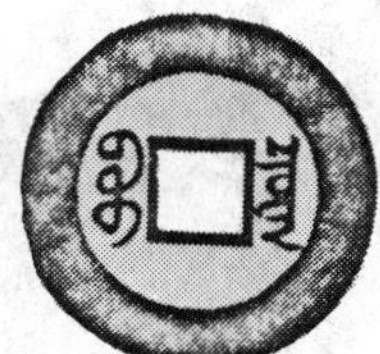

Obv. leg: *T'ung-chih T'ung-pao.*

C#	Date	Emperor	Good	VG	Fine	VF
1-14	ND(1862-74)	T'ung-chih	3.50	5.50	8.50	15.00

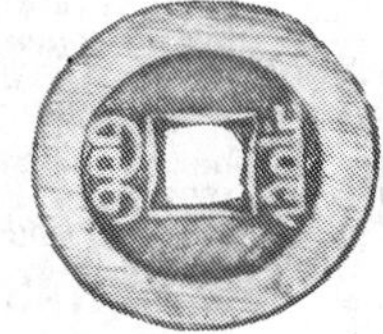

Obv. leg: *Kuang-hsu T'ung-pao.*

C#	Date	Emperor	Good	VG	Fine	VF
1-16	ND(1875-1908)	Kuang-hsu	1.50	2.00	2.75	4.00

NOTE: Crude cast, red copper strikes, see Sinkiang General coinage.

Rev: Dot below.

C#	Date	Emperor	Good	VG	Fine	VF
1-16.8	ND(1899-1901)	Kuang-hsu	1.75	3.00	4.00	6.00

Rev: Dot above.

C#	Date	Emperor	Good	VG	Fine	VF
1-16.9	ND(1899-1901)	Kuang-hsu	1.75	3.00	4.00	6.00

Thousand Character Classic Series

Rev: *Chih* above.

Sch.#1578?

C#	Date	Emperor	Good	VG	Fine	VF
1-16.1	ND(1875-1908)	Kuang-hsu	6.00	9.00	13.50	20.00

Rev: *Chou* above.

C#	Date	Emperor	Good	VG	Fine	VF
1-16.2	ND(1875-1908)	Kuang-hsu	6.00	9.00	13.50	20.00

Rev: *Jih* above.

C#	Date	Emperor	Good	VG	Fine	VF
1-16.3	ND(1875-1908)	Kuang-hsu	6.00	9.00	13.50	20.00

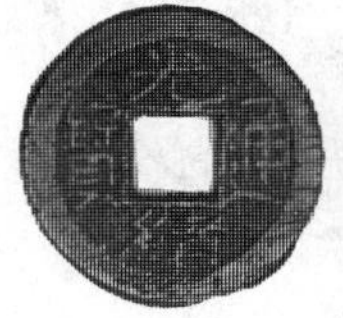

Rev: *Lai* above.

C#	Date	Emperor	Good	VG	Fine	VF
1-16.4	ND(1875-1908)	Kuang-hsu	7.00	12.00	16.50	25.00

Rev: *Lieh* above.

C#	Date	Emperor	Good	VG	Fine	VF
1-16.5	ND(1875-1908)	Kuang-hsu	6.00	9.00	13.50	20.00

Rev: *Wang* above.

C#	Date	Emperor	Good	VG	Fine	VF
1-16.6	ND(1875-1908)	Kuang-hsu	7.00	12.00	16.50	25.00

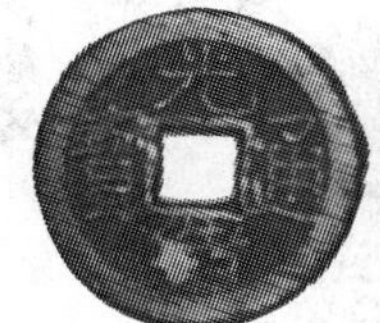

Rev: *Yu* above.

C#	Date	Emperor	Good	VG	Fine	VF
1-16.7	ND(1875-1908)	Kuang-hsu	7.00	12.00	16.50	25.00

Rev: *Shou* above.

C#	Date	Emperor	Good	VG	Fine	VF
1-16.10	ND(1875-1908)	Kuang-hsu	7.00	12.00	16.50	25.00

5 CASH

CAST BRASS

Obv. leg: *Hsien-feng Chung-pao.*

C#	Date	Emperor	Good	VG	Fine	VF
1-5	ND(1851-61)	Hsien-feng	—	—	Rare	—

10 CASH

CAST BRASS, 36-39mm

Obv: Type B-1.

Obv. leg: *Hsien-feng Chung-pao.*

C#	Date	Emperor	Good	VG	Fine	VF
1-6	ND(1851-61)	Hsien-feng	4.00	5.00	7.00	9.00

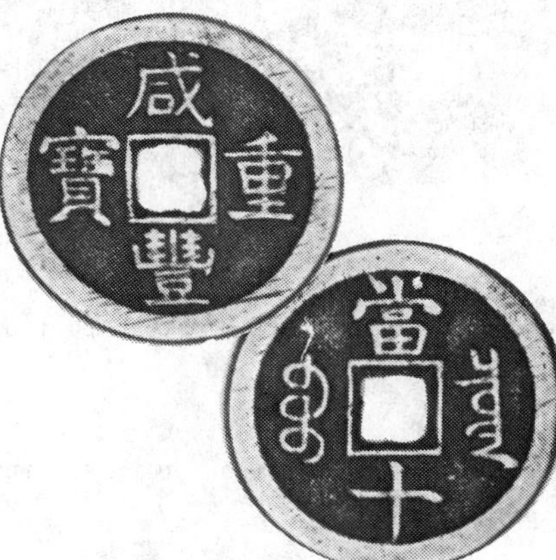

29-35mm

C#	Date	Emperor	Good	VG	Fine	VF
1-6.1	ND(1851-61)	Hsien-feng	3.00	5.00	6.00	8.00

CAST IRON, 37-39mm

C#	Date	Emperor	Good	VG	Fine	VF
1-6a	ND(1851-61)	Hsien-feng	10.00	15.00	25.00	40.00

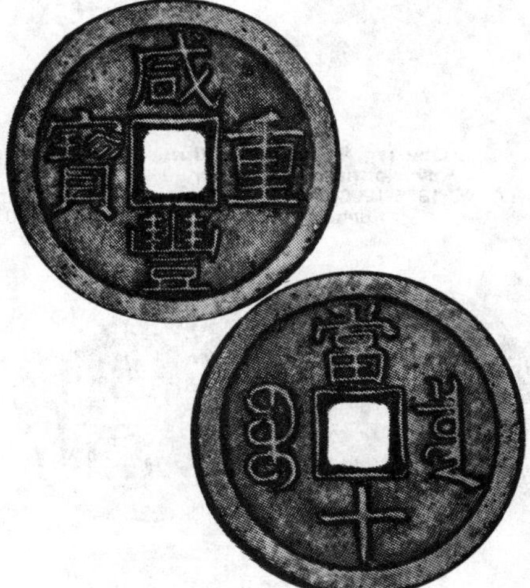

35-36mm

Obv: Type B-2.

C#	Date	Emperor	Good	VG	Fine	VF
1-6.2a	ND(1851-61)	Hsien-feng	75.00	125.00	175.00	225.00

NOTE: Varieties exist.

CAST BRASS, 35mm
Obv: Type B-1.

C#	Date	Emperor	Good	VG	Fine	VF
1-13	ND(1861)	Ch'i-hsiang	400.00	500.00	650.00	800.00

28-33mm
Obv. leg: *T'ung-chih Chung-pao.*

C#	Date	Emperor	Good	VG	Fine	VF
1-15	ND(1862-74)	T'ung-chih	1.50	3.00	5.50	10.00

23-27mm

C#	Date	Emperor	Good	VG	Fine	VF
1-15.1	ND(1862-74)	T'ung-chih	1.50	3.00	5.50	8.00

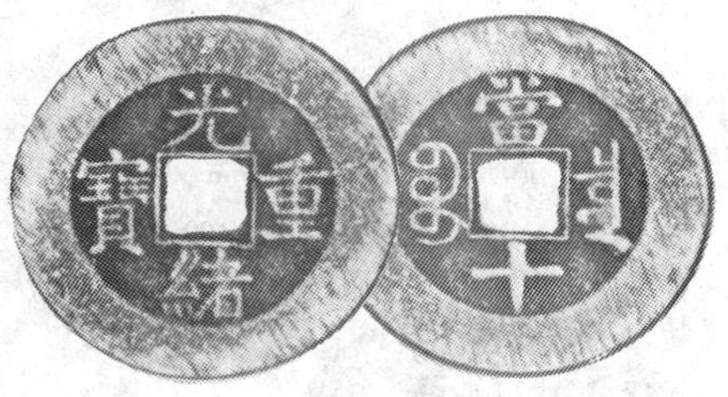

Obv. leg: *Kuang-hsu Chung-pao.*
Rev: Normal character for 10 below.

C#	Date	Emperor	Good	VG	Fine	VF
1-17	ND(1875-1908)	Kuang-hsu	3.00	5.00	8.00	10.00

28mm
Rev: Official character for 10 below.

C#	Date	Emperor	Good	VG	Fine	VF
1-18	ND(1875-1908)	Kuang-hsu	4.50	7.50	10.00	15.00

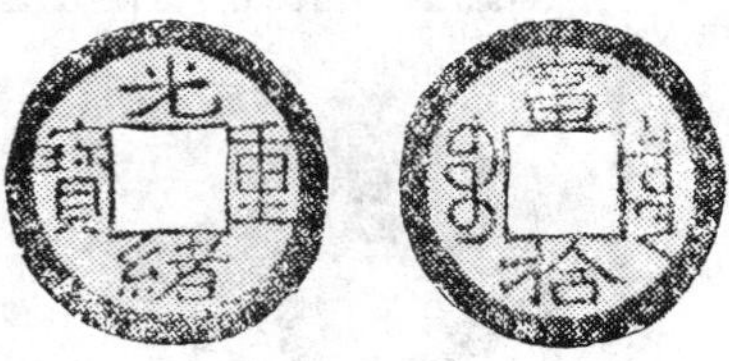

22mm

C#	Date	Emperor	Good	VG	Fine	VF
1-18.1	ND(1875-1908)	Kuang-hsu	6.00	9.00	15.00	20.00

50 CASH

CAST BRASS, 54-58mm
Obv. leg: *Hsien-feng Chung-pao.*

C#	Date	Emperor	Good	VG	Fine	VF
1-7	ND(1851-61)	Hsien-feng	12.50	20.00	30.00	45.00

40-48mm

C#	Date	Emperor	Good	VG	Fine	VF
1-7.1	ND(1851-61)	Hsien-feng	10.00	15.00	25.00	40.00

Rev: Dot upper right, crescent upper left.

C#	Date	Emperor	Good	VG	Fine	VF
1-7.2	ND(1851-61)	Hsien-feng	15.00	30.00	60.00	100.00

NOTE: This is one of a series of coins from this mint marked with a dot and crescent to indicate that they were issued by Ching Hui, the Hereditary Prince of K'o Ch'in.

CAST IRON

C#	Date	Emperor	Good	VG	Fine	VF
1.7a	ND(1851-61)	Hsien-feng	—	—	Rare	—

100 CASH

CAST BRASS
Obv. leg: *Hsien-feng Yuan-pao.*

C#	Date	Emperor	Good	VG	Fine	VF
1-8	ND(1851-61)	Hsien-feng	7.50	12.00	17.50	35.00

Rev: Dot and crescent similar to 50 Cash, C#1-7.2.

C#	Date	Emperor	Good	VG	Fine	VF
1-8.1	ND(1851-61)	Hsien-feng	60.00	100.00	125.00	200.00

CAST IRON

C#	Date	Emperor	Good	VG	Fine	VF
1.8a	ND(1851-61)	Hsien-feng	—	—	Rare	—

200 CASH

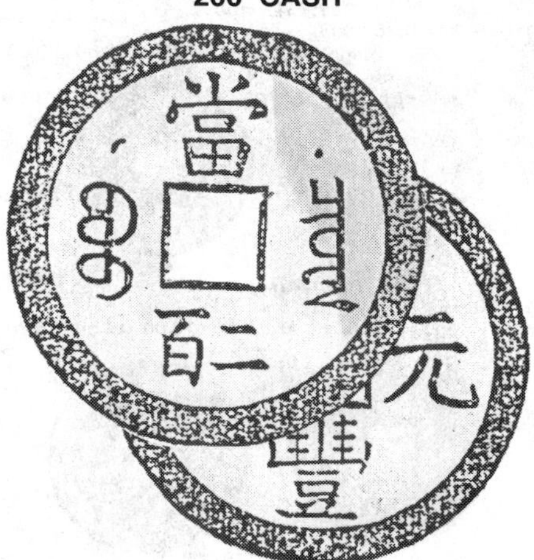

CAST BRASS
Obv. leg: *Hsien-feng Yuan-pao.*

Rev: Dot and crescent similar to 50 Cash, C#1-7.2.

C#	Date	Emperor	Good	VG	Fine	VF
1-9	ND(1851-61)	Hsien-feng	125.00	175.00	225.00	300.00

500 CASH

CAST COPPER, 46mm
Obv. leg: *Hsien-feng Yuan-pao.*

C#	Date	Emperor	Good	VG	Fine	VF
1-10	ND(1851-61)	Hsien-feng	20.00	35.00	60.00	90.00

CAST BRASS

C#	Date	Emperor	Good	VG	Fine	VF
1-10a	ND (1851-61)	Hsien-feng	17.50	30.00	50.00	75.00

CAST BRASS, 56-58mm

C#	Date	Emperor	Good	VG	Fine	VF
1-10.1	ND(1851-61)	Hsien-feng	25.00	35.00	55.00	85.00

Rev: Dot and crescent similar to 50 Cash, C#1-7.2.

C#	Date	Emperor	Good	VG	Fine	VF
1-10.2	ND(1851-61)	Hsien-feng	25.00	50.00	70.00	120.00

1000 CASH

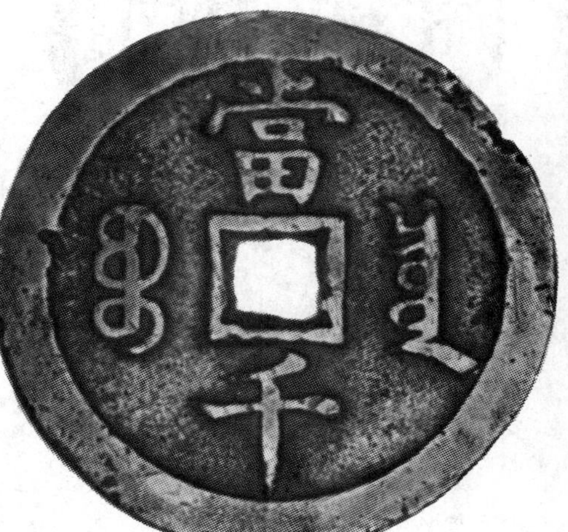

CAST BRASS, 63-64mm
Obv. leg: *Hsien-feng Yuan-pao.*

C#	Date	Emperor	Good	VG	Fine	VF
1-11	ND(1851-61)	Hsien-feng	40.00	70.00	125.00	200.00

Rev: Dot and crescent similar to 50 Cash, C#1-7.2.

C#	Date	Emperor	Good	VG	Fine	VF
1-11.1	ND(1851-61)	Hsien-feng	100.00	150.00	200.00	300.00

FANTASY ISSUES

NOTE: Coins of this mint in denominations of 6, 9, 20, 30, 90, 300, 400, 600, 700, 800, 900, 4000 and 5000 Cash are considered fantasy issues.

Peking Kung Pu Mint

(Board of Public Works)

CASH

Obv. leg: *Tao-kuang T'ung-pao.*

C#	Date	Emperor	Good	VG	Fine	VF
2-3	ND(1821-51)	Tao-kuang	.30	.40	.60	1.00

Rev: Dot above.

C#	Date	Emperor	Good	VG	Fine	VF
2-3.1	ND(1821-51)	Tao-kuang	2.50	4.00	6.00	7.50

Rev: Dot below.

C#	Date	Emperor	Good	VG	Fine	VF
2-3.2	ND(1821-51)	Tao-kuang	2.50	4.00	6.00	7.50

Obv. leg: *Hsien-feng T'ung-pao.*
Wide borders, 27mm.

C#	Date	Emperor	Good	VG	Fine	VF
2-4	ND(1851-61)	Hsien-feng	3.00	5.00	9.00	14.00

20-24mm

C#	Date	Emperor	Good	VG	Fine	VF
2-4.1	ND(1851-61)	Hsien-feng	1.00	1.50	3.00	4.00

CAST IRON

C#	Date	Emperor	Good	VG	Fine	VF
2-4a	ND(1851-61)	Hsien-feng	30.00	50.00	65.00	80.00

CAST ZINC

C#	Date	Emperor	Good	VG	Fine	VF
2-4b	ND(1851-61)	Hsien-feng	—	—	Rare	—

CAST BRASS
Obv. leg: *Ch'i-hsiang T'ung-pao.*

C#	Date	Emperor	Good	VG	Fine	VF
2-11	ND(1861)	Ch'i-hsiang	375.00	650.00	1100.	1800.

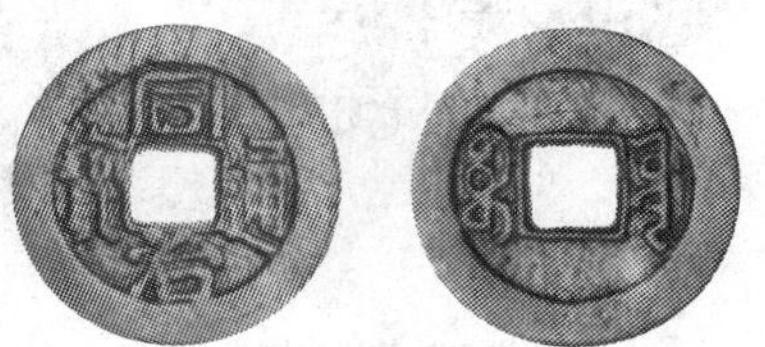

Obv. leg: *T'ung-chih T'ung-pao.*

C#	Date	Emperor	Good	VG	Fine	VF
2-13	ND(1862-74)	T'ung-chih	30.00	60.00	90.00	120.00

Obv. leg: *Kuang-hsu T'ung-pao.*

C#	Date	Emperor	Good	VG	Fine	VF
2-15	ND(1875-1908)	Kuang-hsu	1.50	3.00	6.00	7.00

NOTE: Crude cast copper strikes, see Sinkiang General Coinage.

Thousand Character Classic Series

Rev: *Chou* above.

C#	Date	Emperor	Good	VG	Fine	VF
2-15.1	ND(1899-1901)	Kuang-hsu	6.00	10.00	15.00	20.00

Rev: *Lai* above.

C#	Date	Emperor	Good	VG	Fine	VF
2-15.2	ND(1899-1901)	Kuang-hsu	6.00	10.00	15.00	20.00

Rev: *Lieh* above.

C#	Date	Emperor	Good	VG	Fine	VF
2-15.3	ND(1899-1901)	Kuang-hsu	6.00	10.00	15.00	20.00

Rev: *Yu* above.

C#	Date	Emperor	Good	VG	Fine	VF
2-15.4	ND(1899-1901)	Kuang-hsu	6.00	10.00	15.00	20.00

Rev: *Jih* above.

C#	Date	Emperor	Good	VG	Fine	VF
2-15.5	ND(1899-1901)	Kuang-hsu	6.00	10.00	15.00	20.00

Rev: *Wang* above.

C#	Date	Emperor	Good	VG	Fine	VF
2-15.6	ND(1899-1901)	Kuang-hsu	6.00	10.00	15.00	20.00

Rev: *Jih* above, dot below.

C#	Date	Emperor	Good	VG	Fine	VF
2-15.7	ND(1899-1901)	Kuang-hsu	6.00	10.00	15.00	20.00

5 CASH

CAST BRASS, 28-32mm
Obv. leg: *Hsien-feng Chung-pao.*

C#	Date	Emperor	Good	VG	Fine	VF
2-5	ND(1851-61)	Hsien-feng	10.00	12.50	17.50	35.00

23-26mm

C#	Date	Emperor	Good	VG	Fine	VF
2-5.1	ND(1851-61)	Hsien-feng	10.00	20.00	30.00	50.00

CAST IRON

C#	Date	Emperor	Good	VG	Fine	VF
2-5a	ND(1851-61)	Hsien-feng	—	—	—	—

CAST BRASS
Obv. leg: *Kuang-hsu Chung-pao.*

C#	Date	Emperor	Good	VG	Fine	VF
2-16	ND(1875-1908)	Kuang-hsu	200.00	350.00	500.00	700.00

10 CASH

CAST BRASS, 33-38mm
Obv: Type B-1.
Obv. leg: *Hsien-feng Chung-pao.*

C#	Date	Emperor	Good	VG	Fine	VF
2-6	ND(1851-61)	Hsien-feng	2.50	5.00	8.00	18.00

29-31mm

C#	Date	Emperor	Good	VG	Fine	VF
2-6.1	ND(1851-61)	Hsien-feng	2.50	5.00	8.00	18.00

CAST IRON
Obv: Type B-2.

C#	Date	Emperor	Good	VG	Fine	VF
2-6a	ND(1851-61)	Hsien-feng	—	—	Rare	—

CAST BRASS

Obv. leg: *Ch'i-hsiang Chung-pao.*

C#	Date	Emperor	Good	VG	Fine	VF
2-12	ND(1861)	Ch'i-hsiang	400.00	550.00	625.00	900.00

Obv. leg: *T'ung-chih Chung-pao.*

C#	Date	Emperor	Good	VG	Fine	VF
2-14	ND(1862-74)	T'ung-chih	4.50	7.50	12.00	25.00

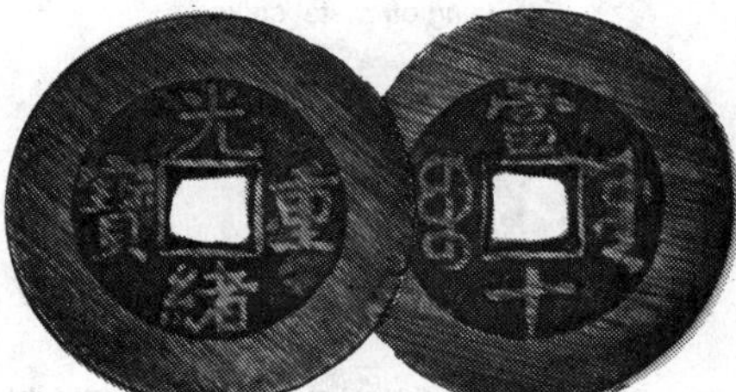

Obv. leg: *Kuang-hsu T'ung-pao.*
Rev: Normal *Shih* (10) below.

C#	Date	Emperor	Good	VG	Fine	VF
2-17	ND(1875-1908)	Kuang-hsu	4.50	7.50	10.00	25.00

Rev: Official *Shih* (10) below.

C#	Date	Emperor	Good	VG	Fine	VF
2-18	ND(1875-1908)	Kuang-hsu	6.00	10.00	15.00	35.00

50 CASH

CAST BRASS, 51-57mm
Obv. leg: *Hsien-feng Chung-pao.*

C#	Date	Emperor	Good	VG	Fine	VF
2-7	ND(1851-61)	Hsien-feng	15.00	20.00	30.00	65.00

42-45mm

C#	Date	Emperor	Good	VG	Fine	VF
2-7.1	ND(1851-61)	Hsien-feng	10.00	15.00	25.00	50.00

100 CASH

CAST BRASS
Obv. leg: *Hsien-feng Yuan-pao.*

C#	Date	Emperor	Good	VG	Fine	VF
2-8	ND(1851-61)	Hsien-feng	13.50	18.00	22.50	50.00

500 CASH

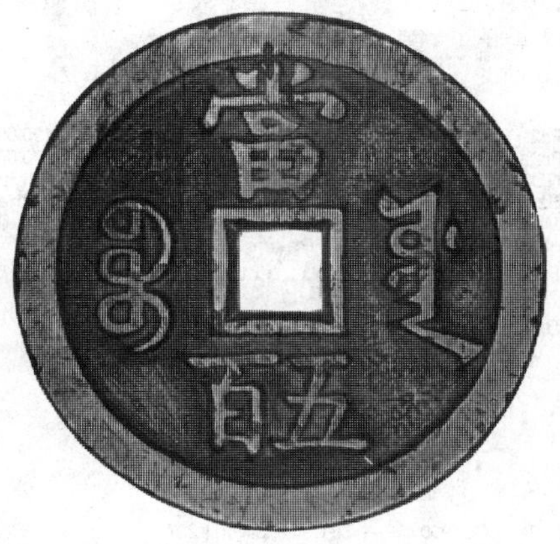

CAST BRASS

Obv. leg: *Hsien-feng Yuan-pao.*

C#	Date	Emperor	Good	VG	Fine	VF
2-9	ND(1851-61)	Hsien-feng	30.00	50.00	75.00	130.00

CAST COPPER

C#	Date	Emperor	Good	VG	Fine	VF
2-9.1	ND(1851-61)	Hsien-feng	60.00	100.00	175.00	250.00

1000 CASH

CAST BRASS

Obv. leg: *Hsien-feng Yuan-pao.*

C#	Date	Emperor	Good	VG	Fine	VF
2-10	ND(1851-61)	Hsien-feng	100.00	150.00	200.00	280.00

FANTASY ISSUES

NOTE: Coins of this mint in denominations of 6, 9, 30, 80 and 90 Cash are considered fantasy issues.

PATTERNS (Pn)

Board of Revenue

(Including off metal strikes)

KM#	Date	Mintage	Identification	Mkt.Val.
Pn1	ND(1899)	—	1 Cash, Brass, Hsu2	Rare

Board of Works

KM#	Date	Mintage	Identification	Mkt.Val.
PnA2	ND(1851-1861)	—	100 Cash, Brass, C1-8	—

KM#	Date	Mintage	Identification	Mkt.Val.
PnB2	ND(1896)	—	4 Cash, Brass, 2-2-1	

KM#	Date	Mintage	Identification	Mkt.Val.
Pn2	ND(1897)	—	1 Cash, Brass, Hsu3	100.00
Pn2a	ND(1897)	—	1 Cash, Brass, w/o hole, Hsu3a	200.00

NOTE: Struck in New Jersey as samples for the mint in Szechuan. The dies apparently were not used as the Manchu on reverse reads *Pao Yuan* indicating the Board of Works mint located in Peking.

Peking Issues

DOLLAR SERIES

KM#	Date	Mintage	Identification	Mkt.Val.
Pn24	CD1900	—	5 Cents, Silver, K237	1500.
Pn25	CD1900	—	10 Cents, Silver, K236	1500.

KM#	Date	Mintage	Identification	Mkt.Val.
Pn26	CD1900	—	20 Cents, Silver, K235	1500.

KM#	Date	Mintage	Identification	Mkt.Val.
Pn27	CD1900	—	50 Cents, Silver, K234	2500.

KM#	Date	Mintage	Identification	Mkt.Val.
Pn28	CD1900	—	1 Dollar, Silver, K233	4000.

NOTE: There are two theories concerning the origin of the Peking coins. One asserts that a few sets of all five denominations were minted during 1900 at the mint erected in Peking the previous year, with equipment partly from the Hangchow, Chekiang, Mint, and partly from Germany. The second theory alleges that some 10 and 20 cent pieces may have been minted in 1900, but that the rest of the set was restruck sometime later by private parties using original dies looted from the mint during the Boxer uprising. The 10 Cash pieces struck in copper and brass are considered fantasies.

TRIAL STRIKES (TS)

KM#	Date	Mintage	Identification	Mkt.Val.
TS1	ND(1897)	—	1 Cash, Brass, obv. KM-Pn2	125.00
TS2	ND(1897)	—	1 Cash, Brass, rev. KM-Pn2	125.00

Rebel Coinage

CASH

CAST COPPER or BRASS, uniface

Obv: *Chin Lung T'ung Pao*

KM#	Date	Emperor	Good	VG	Fine	VF
1	ND(1832)	—	—	—	Rare	—

NOTE: Issued by Chao Chin Lung.

T'AI P'ING REBELLION

A radical political and religious upheaval that lasted from 1850 to 1864. It ravaged 17 provinces and took an estimated 20,000,000 lives. The rebellion began under the leadership of Hung Hsiu-ch'uan (1814-64), a disappointed civil service examination candidate who believed himself to be the son of God, the younger brother of Jesus Christ, sent to reform China.

Their slogan - to share property in common - attracted many famine-stricken peasants, workers, and miners, as did their propaganda against the foreign Manchu rulers of China. Under the Taipings, the Chinese language was simplified, and equality between men and women was decreed. All property was to be held in common, and equal distribution of the land according to a form of communism was planned. Both the Chinese Communists and the Chinese Nationalists trace their origin to the Taipings.

CASH

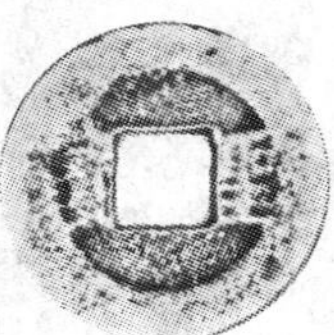

CAST COPPER or BRASS

Obv: *T'ai P'ing T'ien Kuo*

(top-bottom-right-left).

Rev: *Sheng Pao* (right-left). 24-25mm.

C#	Date	Good	VG	Fine	VF
38-8	ND(1853-64)	15.00	25.00	35.00	60.00
	31-35mm				
38-7	ND(1853-64)	20.00	35.00	50.00	75.00
	42-45mm				
38-6	ND(1853-64)	25.00	45.00	70.00	100.00

Rev: *Sheng Pao* (top-bottom).

24-26mm. Narrow rims.

Sch.#1605

C#	Date	Good	VG	Fine	VF
38-5	ND(1853-64)	10.00	25.00	35.00	50.00
	28mm. Wide rims.				
38-5.1	ND(1853-64)	10.00	13.00	20.00	35.00
	31-33mm. Narrow rims.				
38-4	ND(1853-64)	20.00	35.00	50.00	75.00

35mm. Wide rims.

C#	Date	Good	VG	Fine	VF
38-4.1	ND(1853-64)	22.50	40.00	60.00	90.00
	IRON				
38-4.1a	ND(1853-64)	—	—	1000.	—
	BRONZE				
	38-42mm. Narrow rims.				
38-3	ND(1853-64)	60.00	100.00	150.00	220.00
	47-48mm. Wide rims.				
38-3.1	ND(1853-64)	85.00	150.00	225.00	350.00

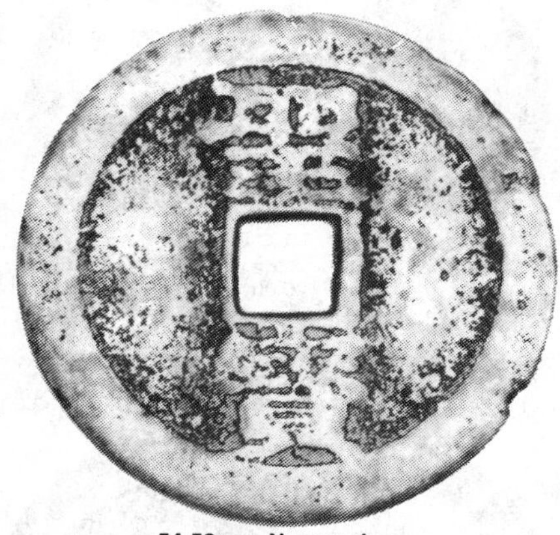

54-56mm. Narrow rims.

C#	Date	Good	VG	Fine	VF
38-2	ND(1853-64)	150.00	250.00	400.00	650.00

Obv: ***T'ai P'ing Sheng Pao.***
Rev: ***T'ien Kuo.***

Sch.#1604

38-12	ND(1853-64)	15.00	20.00	30.00	60.00

Obv: ***T'ien Kuo T'ai P'ing.***
Rev: ***Sheng Pao.***

38-14	ND(1853-64)	20.00	30.00	40.00	65.00

Obv: ***T'ien Kuo Sheng Pao.***
Rev: ***T'ai P'ing.***

38-13	ND(1853-64)	10.00	15.00	25.00	45.00

Obv: ***T'ien Kuo.*** **Rev:** ***Sheng Pao.***

Sch.#1608

38-11	ND(1853-64)	30.00	40.00	50.00	75.00

38mm. Large characters.

38-10	ND(1853-64)	20.00	35.00	50.00	75.00

36mm. Small characters.

38-10.1	ND(1853-64)	50.00	70.00	90.00	120.00

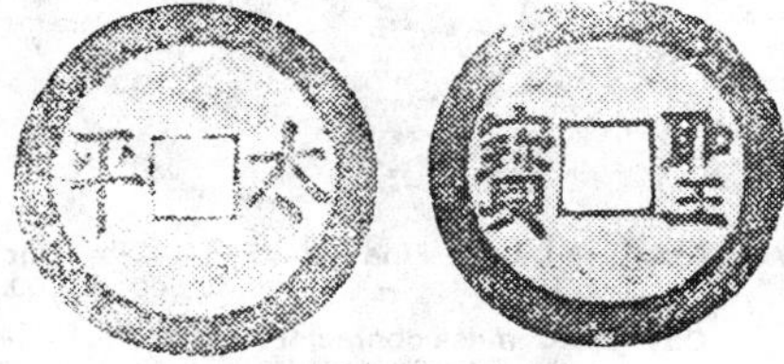

Obv: ***T'ai P'ing.*** **Rev:** ***Sheng Pao.***

38-15	ND(1853-64)	20.00	35.00	50.00	75.00

Obv: ***P'ing Ching Sheng Pao.***
Rev: ***Yu Lin Chun*** **(Royal Guard).**

C#	Date	Good	VG	Fine	VF
39-9	ND(1857)	45.00	75.00	120.00	200.00

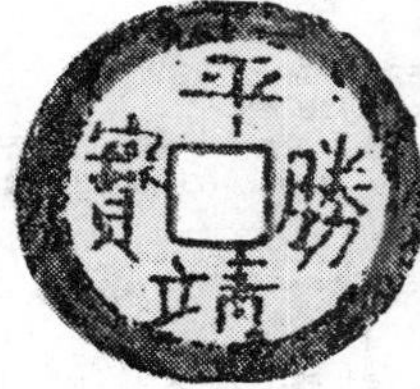

Rev: ***Ch'ien Ying.***

39-10	ND(1857)	35.00	60.00	100.00	160.00

Rev: ***Ch'ang Sheng Chun.***

39-11	ND(1857)	35.00	60.00	100.00	160.00

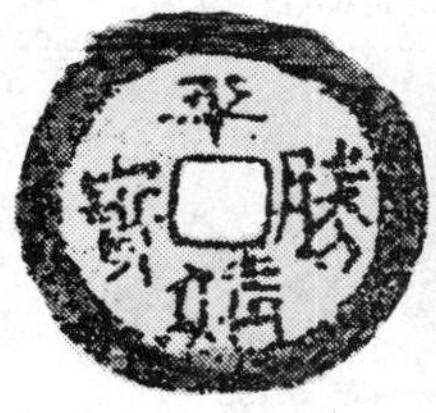

Rev: ***Chung Ying.***

39-12	ND(1857)	35.00	60.00	100.00	160.00

Rev: ***Hou Ying.***

39-13	ND(1857)	35.00	60.00	100.00	160.00

Rev: ***Tso Ying.***

39-14	ND(1857)	35.00	60.00	100.00	160.00

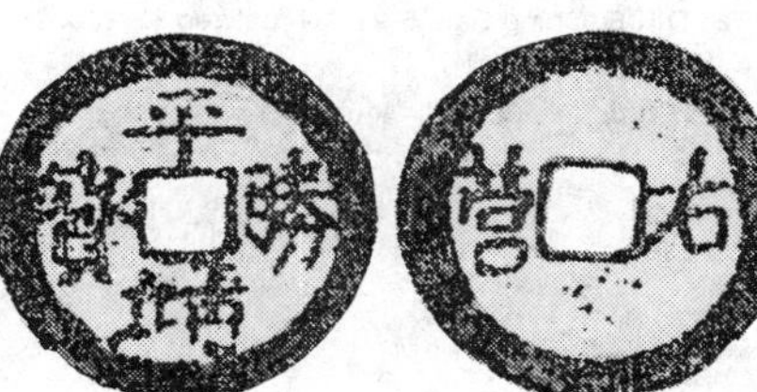

Rev: ***Yu Ying.***

39-15	ND(1857)	35.00	60.00	100.00	160.00

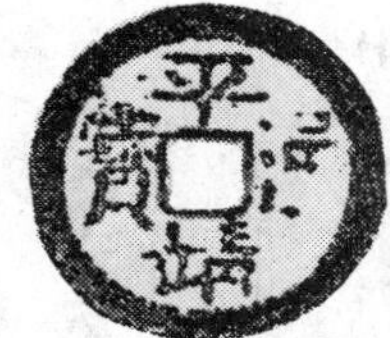

Obv: ***P'ing Ching T'ung Pao.***
Rev: ***Chung*** **in seal script.**

C#	Date	Good	VG	Fine	VF
39-16	ND(1857)	35.00	60.00	100.00	160.00

NOTE: There are numerous other Cash coins issued by Taiping supporters and military units.

1/4 TAEL

SILVER

Obv: ***T'ien Kuo.*** **Rev:** ***Sheng Pao.***

KM#	Date	Mintage	VG	Fine	VF	XF
2	ND(1853-64)	5 known	—	—	—	2750.

1/2 TAEL

SILVER

Obv: ***T'ien Kuo.*** **Rev:** ***Sheng Pao.***

3	ND(1853-64)	14 known	—	—	—	2250.

5 TAELS

GOLD

4	ND(1853-64)	1 known	—	—	—	—

NOTE: For additional listings of Rebel Coins, refer to Sinkiang (Xinjiang) Province.

SMALL SWORD SOCIETY

A Triad group located on the outskirts of Shanghai led by Liu Li-ch'uan. Driven out by the foreign community Shanghai volunteers in 1854.

CASH

COPPER

Obv: ***T'ai P'ing T'ung Pao.***
Rev: Crescent above and ***Ming*** **below.**

C#	Date	Good	VG	Fine	VF
39-1	ND(1853-54)	35.00	50.00	85.00	125.00

Rev: Dot above and crescent below.

39-2	ND(1853-54)	35.00	50.00	85.00	125.00

Rev: ***Wen*** **above.**

39-3	ND(1853-54)	35.00	50.00	85.00	125.00

Rev: ***Wen*** **at right.**

39-4	ND(1853-54)	35.00	50.00	85.00	125.00

HEAVEN AND EARTH SOCIETY

A Triad group located in Chekiang Province of which

little is known.

CASH

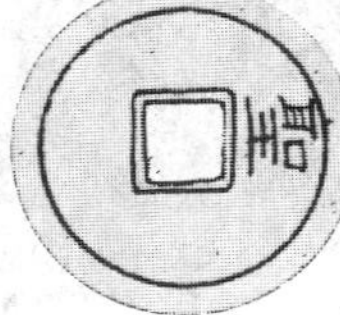

COPPER
Obv: *Huang Ti T'ung Pao.*
Rev: *Sheng* at right (sideways).

C#	Date	Good	VG	Fine	VF
39-5	ND(1853-54)	35.00	50.00	85.00	125.00

Obv: *Huang Ti T'ung Pao.*
Rev: *Che Pao.*

C#	Date	Good	VG	Fine	VF
39-6	ND(1853-54)	35.00	75.00	115.00	150.00

Obv: *K'ai Yuan T'ung Pao.* Rev: *Wu.*

C#	Date	Good	VG	Fine	VF
39-7	ND(1853-54)	35.00	50.00	85.00	125.00

Obv: *T'ien Ch'ao T'ung Pao.* Rev: *Yung.*

C#	Date	Good	VG	Fine	VF
39-8	ND(1853-54)	35.00	50.00	85.00	125.00

PROVINCIAL COINAGE

ANHWEI PROVINCE

Anhui

A province located in eastern China. Made a separate province during the Manchu dynasty in the 17th century. Principally agricultural with some mining of coal and iron ore. Spanish-American 8 Reales saw wide circulation in this province until the end of World War I. The provincial mint at Anking began operations in 1897, closed in 1899, and later reopened in 1902. The primary production of the mint was Cash coins but included a series of silver coinage.

EMPIRE

CAST BRASS
Obv: Type A.

C#	Date	Emperor	Good	VG	Fine	VF
—	ND(1820-51)	Tao-kuang	—	—	Rare	—

NOTE: Not to be confused with similar coins from the Changsha Mint in Hunan Province. The Changsha Mint coins have an extra dot or vertical stroke to the left of the mint mark at right of the center hole.

MILLED COINAGE

5 CENTS

1.3300 g, .820 SILVER, .0351 oz ASW

Y#	Date	Mintage	Fine	VF	XF	Unc
41	ND(1897)	—	40.00	75.00	130.00	250.00

Y#	Year	Date	Fine	VF	XF	Unc
41.1	25	(1899)	35.00	60.00	100.00	200.00

10 CENTS

2.6500 g, .820 SILVER, .0699 oz ASW
Obv: Rosettes divide leg.

Y#	Date	Mintage	Fine	VF	XF	Unc
42	ND(1897)	—	12.00	30.00	65.00	135.00

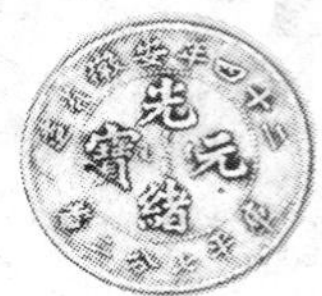

Obv: W/o rosettes dividing leg.

Y#	Year	Date	Fine	VF	XF	Unc
42.1	24	(1898)	10.00	25.00	50.00	120.00

Obv: Rosettes divide leg.

Y#	Year	Date	Fine	VF	XF	Unc
42.2	24	(1898)	10.00	25.00	50.00	120.00

Obv: A S T C in field.

Y#	Year	Date	Fine	VF	XF	Unc
42.3	24	(1898)	10.00	25.00	50.00	135.00

Obv. leg: 6 characters at top.

Y#	Date	Mintage	Fine	VF	XF	Unc
42.4	CD1898	—	15.00	30.00	70.00	150.00

20 CENTS

5.3000 g, .820 SILVER, .1397 oz ASW
Rev: Large dragon and small English leg.

Y#	Date	Mintage	Fine	VF	XF	Unc
43	ND(1897)	—	20.00	40.00	80.00	185.00

Rev: Smaller dragon and larger English leg.

Y#	Date	Mintage	Fine	VF	XF	Unc
43.1	ND(1897)	—	20.00	40.00	80.00	185.00
43.2	23(1897)	2 known	—	—	—	—

NOTE: D.K.E. Ching Sale 6-91 AU realized $2,200.

Y#	Year	Date	Fine	VF	XF	Unc
43.3	24	(1898)	20.00	40.00	80.00	200.00

Obv: A S T C in field.

Y#	Year	Date	Fine	VF	XF	Unc
43.4	24	(1898)	20.00	40.00	80.00	200.00

50 CENTS

13.5000 g, .860 SILVER, .3733 oz ASW
Obv: A S T C in field.

Y#	Year	Date	Fine	VF	XF	Unc
44.1	24	(1898)	100.00	185.00	300.00	850.00

Y#	Year	Date	Fine	VF	XF	Unc
44.2 (Y44)	24	(1898)	100.00	185.00	275.00	650.00

NOTE: Struck from reworked dies. Usually ASTC is faintly discernable.

DOLLAR

27.1000 g, .900 SILVER, .7842 oz ASW

Y#	Date	Mintage	Fine	VF	XF	Unc
45	ND(1897)	—	200.00	300.00	500.00	1500.

Y#	Year	Date	Fine	VF	XF	Unc
45.1	23	(1897)	—	—	17,500.	25,000.

Obv: Tall Chinese character '4' in date.
Rev: Similar to Y#45.

Y#	Year	Date	Fine	VF	XF	Unc
45.2	24	(1898)	125.00	200.00	500.00	1400.

Obv: Short Chinese character '4' in date. Rev: Similar to Y#45.

Y#	Year	Date	Fine	VF	XF	Unc
45.5	24	(1898)	125.00	200.00	500.00	1400.

Obv: Tall Chinese character '4' in date, A S T C in field. Rev: Similar to Y#45.

Y#	Year	Date	Fine	VF	XF	Unc
45.3	24	(1898)	100.00	200.00	400.00	1200.

26.90 g
Obv. leg: 6 characters at top.
Rev: Similar to Y#45.1

Y#	Date	Mintage	Fine	VF	XF	Unc
45.4	CD1898	—	200.00	300.00	500.00	1600.

PATTERNS (Pn)

(Including off metal strikes)

KM#	Date	Mintage	Identification	Mkt.Val.
Pn1	Yr.23 (1897)	—	1 Dollar, Silver plated Bronze, Y45.1	18,500.
Pn2	Yr.24 (1898)	—	50 Cents, Brass, Y44	1000.

CHEKIANG PROVINCE

Zhejiang

A province located along the east coast of China. Although the smallest of the Chinese mainland provinces, it is one of the most densely populated. Mostly agricultural with iron and coal mining and some fishing. A small mint opened in 1897. This was replaced by a larger mint which operated briefly 1898-99. Other mints opened in 1903 and 1905. These were merged with the Fukien Mint in 1906-07.

EMPIRE

CASH

Obv: Type A.
Rev: Large mint mark. 23-25mm.

C#	Date	Emperor	Good	VG	Fine	VF
4-3	ND(1820-51)	Tao-kuang	.35	.60	.75	1.50

Rev: Small mint mark. 21-23mm.

C#	Date	Emperor	Good	VG	Fine	VF
4-3.1	ND(1820-51)	Tao-kuang	.35	.75	1.00	2.00

21-25mm
Obv: Type A.

C#	Date	Emperor	Good	VG	Fine	VF
4-3.5	ND(1851-61)	Hsien-feng	1.00	2.00	3.00	6.00

16-20mm

C#	Date	Emperor	Good	VG	Fine	VF
4-3.6	ND(1851-61)	Hsien-feng	1.00	2.00	3.00	6.00

CAST IRON

C#	Date	Emperor	Good	VG	Fine	VF
4-3.6a	ND(1851-61)	Hsien-feng	6.50	12.50	25.00	55.00

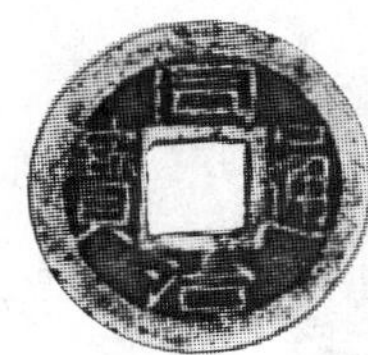
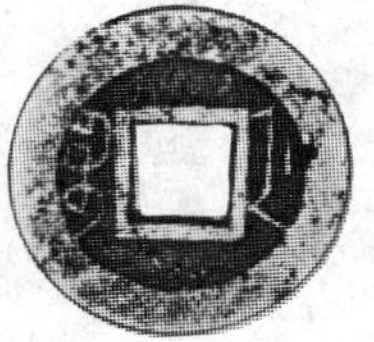

CAST BRASS
Obv: Type A-2.

C#	Date	Emperor	Good	VG	Fine	VF
4-17	ND(1862-74)	T'ung-chih	1.25	2.50	4.00	8.00

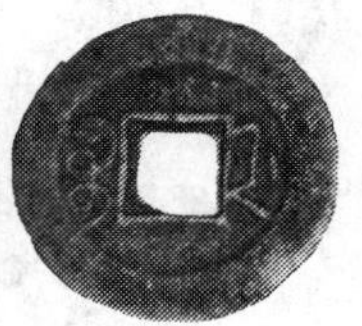

Obv: Type A.
Rev: Mint mark as C#4-2.

C#	Date	Emperor	Good	VG	Fine	VF
4-19	ND(1875-1908)	Kuang-hsu	3.00	4.50	6.50	12.00

Rev: More angular mint mark.

C#	Date	Emperor	Good	VG	Fine	VF
4-19.1	ND(1875-1908)	Kuang-hsu	2.00	3.00	4.00	6.00

CAST ZINC

C#	Date	Emperor	Good	VG	Fine	VF
4-19a	ND(1875-1908)	Kuang-hsu	—	—	Rare	—

10 CASH

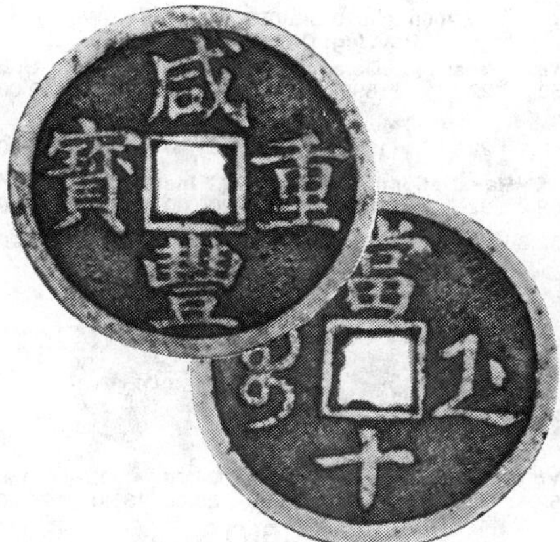

CAST BRASS
Obv: Type B-1.
Rev: Manchu mint mark to right as above. Denomination at bottom in Chinese.

C#	Date	Emperor	Good	VG	Fine	VF
4-4	ND(1851-61)	Hsien-feng	3.00	4.50	6.00	10.00

IRON, 36mm

C#	Date	Emperor	Good	VG	Fine	VF
4-4a	ND(1851-61)	Hsien-feng	—	—	—	—

CAST BRASS
Rev: Chinese character '10' at top.

C#	Date	Emperor	Good	VG	Fine	VF
4-9	ND(1851-61)	Hsien-feng	—	—	Rare	—

Rev: Manchu mint mark left and Chinese mint mark right. Denomination at bottom.

C#	Date	Emperor	Good	VG	Fine	VF
4-11	ND(1851-61)	Hsien-feng	50.00	85.00	140.00	200.00
4-18	ND(1862-74)	T'ung-chih	—	—	Rare	—

Obv: Type A.

C#	Date	Emperor	Good	VG	Fine	VF
4-20	ND(1875-1908)	Kuang-hsu	—	—	Rare	—

20 CASH

CAST BRASS
Obv: Type B-1.

C#	Date	Emperor	Good	VG	Fine	VF
4-5	ND(1851-61)	Hsien-feng	60.00	120.00	200.00	275.00

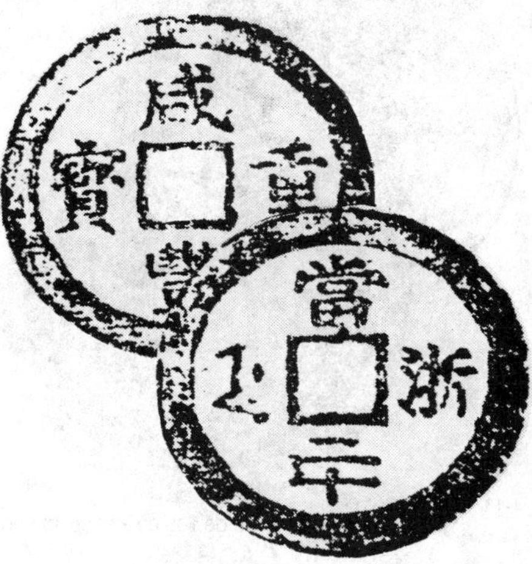

C#	Date	Emperor	Good	VG	Fine	VF
4-12	ND(1851-61)	Hsien-feng	60.00	120.00	200.00	275.00

30 CASH

CAST BRASS
Obv: Type B-1.
Rev: Similar to 10 Cash, C#4-4.

C#	Date	Emperor	Good	VG	Fine	VF
4-6	ND(1851-61)	Hsien-feng	80.00	150.00	250.00	350.00

Rev: Similar to 40 Cash, C#4-14.

C#	Date	Emperor	Good	VG	Fine	VF
4-13	ND(1851-61)	Hsien-feng	80.00	150.00	250.00	350.00

40 CASH

CAST BRASS
Obv: Type B-1.

C#	Date	Emperor	Good	VG	Fine	VF
4-7	ND(1851-61)	Hsien-feng	90.00	165.00	275.00	400.00

C#	Date	Emperor	Good	VG	Fine	VF
4-14	ND(1851-61)	Hsien-feng	90.00	165.00	275.00	400.00

50 CASH

CAST BRASS
Obv: Type B-1.
Rev: Similar to 10 Cash, C#4-4.

C#	Date	Emperor	Good	VG	Fine	VF
4-8	ND(1851-61)	Hsien-feng	100.00	200.00	350.00	500.00

Rev: Similar to 40 Cash, C#4-14.

C#	Date	Emperor	Good	VG	Fine	VF
4-15	ND(1851-61)	Hsien-feng	80.00	150.00	250.00	350.00

100 CASH

CAST BRASS
Obv: Type B-1.

C#	Date	Emperor	Good	VG	Fine	VF
4-10	ND(1851-61)	Hsien-feng	100.00	165.00	275.00	400.00

Rev: Similar to 40 Cash, C#4-14.

C#	Date	Emperor	Good	VG	Fine	VF
4-16	ND(1851-61)	Hsien-feng	100.00	165.00	275.00	400.00

FANTASY ISSUES

NOTE: Coins of this mint in denominations of 400 Cash are considered fantasy issues.

MILLED COINAGE

CASH

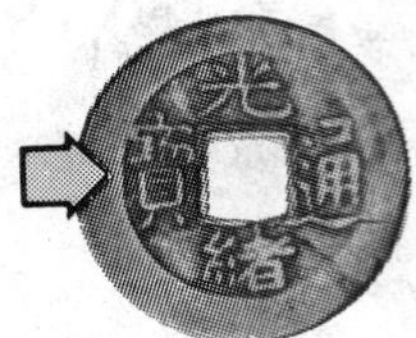

BRASS, struck
Obv: Type A, large *Pao* at left.

Hsu#	Date	Mintage	VG	Fine	VF	XF
151	ND(1887)	—	35.00	50.00	65.00	80.00

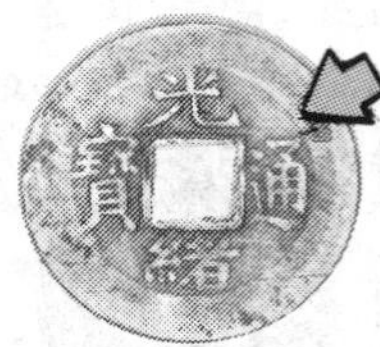
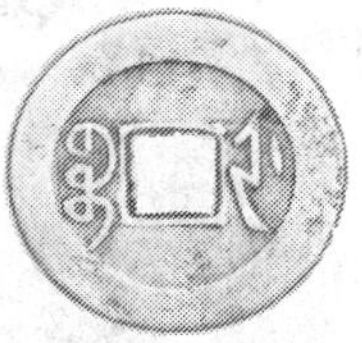

Obv: Top part of *T'ung* shaped like a triangle.

Hsu#	Date	Mintage	VG	Fine	VF	XF
151.1	ND(1897-98)	—	35.00	50.00	60.00	70.00

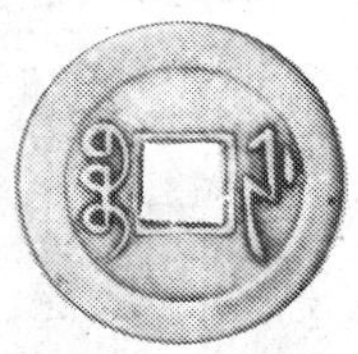

Obv: Top part of *T'ung* shaped like a box.

Hsu#	Date	Mintage	VG	Fine	VF	XF
151.2	ND(1897-98)	—	35.00	50.00	60.00	80.00

5 CENTS

1.3500 g, .820 SILVER, .0356 oz ASW
Rev. leg: CHEH-KIANG. . .,
3.2 CANDAREENS.

Y#	Date	Mintage	Fine	VF	XF	Unc
51	ND(1898-99)	—	15.00	25.00	40.00	100.00

10 CENTS

2.7000 g, .820 SILVER, .0712 oz ASW
Rev. leg: CHEH-KIANG. . .

Y#	Year	Date	Fine	VF	XF	Unc
52	22	(1896)	100.00	250.00	400.00	600.00
	Rev. leg: N's retrograde.					
52.1	22	(1896)	100.00	250.00	400.00	600.00
	Rev: Denomination reads 2.7 instead of 7.2.					
52.2	22	(1896)	75.00	200.00	350.00	500.00
52.3	23	(1897)	100.00	250.00	450.00	600.00

Y#	Date	Mintage	Fine	VF	XF	Unc
52.4	ND(1898-99)	—	15.00	25.00	35.00	75.00

20 CENTS

5.4000 g, .820 SILVER, .1424 oz ASW
Rev: 6 rows of scales on dragon.

Y#	Year	Date	Fine	VF	XF	Unc
53	22	(1896)	100.00	300.00	450.00	650.00
	Rev. leg: Letter E retrograde in CHEH-KIANG.					
53.1	22	(1896)	100.00	300.00	450.00	650.00
	Rev. leg: Additional cross-strokes in letter H in CHEH-KIANG. 8 rows of scales on dragon.					
53.2	22	(1896)	100.00	300.00	450.00	650.00
	Rev. leg: W/o hyphen in CHEH KIANG.					
53.3	22	(1896)	100.00	300.00	450.00	650.00
	Rev. leg: Dot in CHEH.KIANG.					
53.4	22	(1896)	100.00	300.00	450.00	650.00

Rev: Rosettes made of 7 dots dividing leg.

Y#	Year	Date	Fine	VF	XF	Unc
53.5	23	(1897)	125.00	300.00	450.00	700.00
	Rev: Rosettes replaced by a cross; leg: MACE misspelled NACE.					
53.6	23	(1897)	125.00	300.00	450.00	700.00

Rev. leg: CHEH-KIANG. . .

Y#	Date	Mintage	Fine	VF	XF	Unc
53.7	ND(1898-99)	—	15.00	30.00	50.00	150.00

50 CENTS

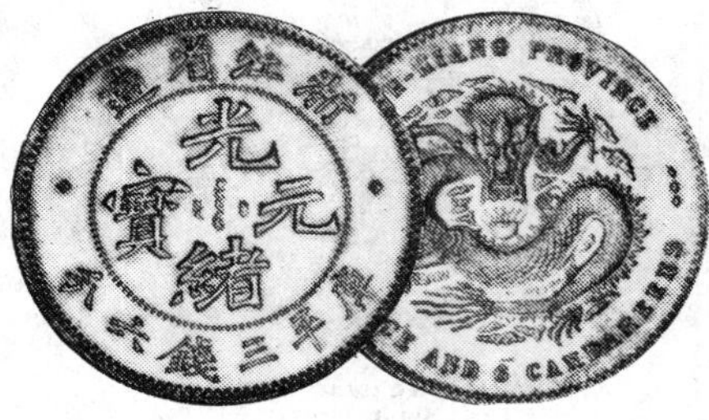

13.5000 g, .860 SILVER, .3733 oz ASW
Rev. leg: CHEH-KIANG. . .

Y#	Date	Mintage	Fine	VF	XF	Unc
54	ND(1898-99)	—	175.00	350.00	650.00	1200.

DOLLAR

27.5000 g, .900 SILVER, .7958 oz ASW
Rev. leg: CHEH-KIANG. . .

Y#	Date	Mintage	Fine	VF	XF	Unc
56	Yr.23 (1897)	—	—	—	Rare	—

NOTE: Superior Goodman Sale 6-91 AU realized $46,200.

Y#	Date	Mintage	Fine	VF	XF	Unc
55	ND(1898-99)	—	—	—	9900.	13,500.

PATTERNS (Pn)

(Including off metal strikes)

KM#	Date	Mintage	Identification	Mkt.Val.
Pn1	ND(1866)	—	1 Cash, Tung Chih	350.00

KM#	Date	Mintage	Identification	Mkt.Val.
Pn2	Yr.23 (1897)	—	5 Cents, Silver	1200.
Pn3	Yr.23 (1897)	—	5 Cents, Brass	500.00

CHIHLI PROVINCE

Hebei, Hopei

A province located in northeastern China which contains the eastern end of the Great Wall. An important producer of coal and some iron ore. In 1928 the provincial name was changed from Chihli to Hopei. The Paoting mint was established in 1745 and only produced cast cash coins.

A mint for struck cash was established in 1888 and the mint for the Peiyang silver coinage was added in 1896. This was destroyed during the Boxer Rebellion. A replacement mint was built in 1902 for the provincial coinage and merged with the Tientsin (Tianjin) Central mint in 1910.

EMPIRE

Included here are coins inscribed PEI YANG. These were produced by the mint in the Peiyang Arsenal in Tianjin.For coins inscribed PEKING, see General Issues.

Chengde Mint

(Jehol)

CASH

CAST BRASS
Obv: Type A.

C#	Date	Emperor	Good	VG	Fine	VF
6-1	ND(1851-61)	Hsien-feng	45.00	65.00	75.00	110.00

CAST IRON

C#	Date	Emperor	Good	VG	Fine	VF
6-1a	ND(1851-61)	Hsien-feng	20.00	30.00	50.00	

5 CASH

CAST BRASS

C#	Date	Emperor	Good	VG	Fine	VF
6-2	ND(1851-61)	Hsien-feng	50.00	80.00	125.00	200.00

CAST IRON

C#	Date	Emperor	Good	VG	Fine	VF
6-2a	ND(1851-61)	Hsien-feng	20.00	30.00	50.00	90.00

10 CASH

CAST BRASS
Obv: Type B-1.

C#	Date	Emperor	Good	VG	Fine	VF
6-3	ND(1851-61)	Hsien-feng	30.00	40.00	75.00	100.00

CAST IRON

C#	Date	Emperor	Good	VG	Fine	VF
6-3a	ND(1851-61)	Hsien-feng	30.00	40.00	90.00	150.00

50 CASH

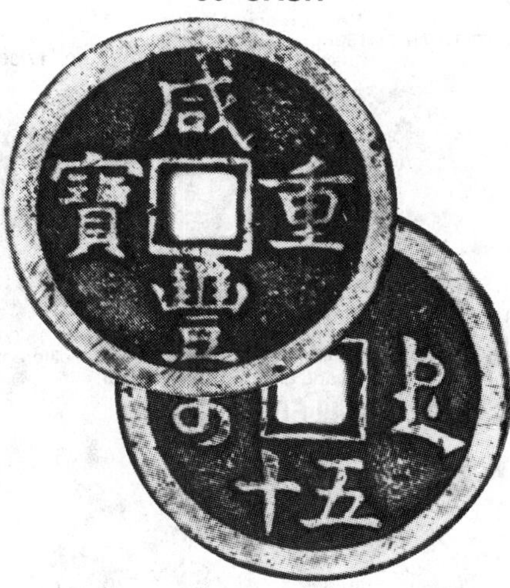

CAST BRASS
Obv: Type B-1.

C#	Date	Emperor	Good	VG	Fine	VF
6-4	ND(1851-61)	Hsien-feng	13.50	20.00	30.00	45.00

100 CASH

CAST BRASS

C#	Date	Emperor	Good	VG	Fine	VF
6-5	ND(1851-61)	Hsien-feng	30.00	50.00	75.00	125.00

FANTASY ISSUES

NOTE: Coins of this mint in denominations of 500 and 1000 Cash are considered fantasy issues.

Chichow Mint

5 CASH

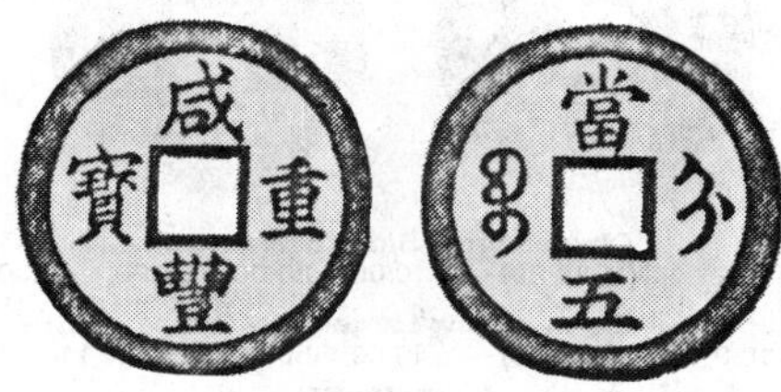

CAST BRASS
Obv: Type B-1.

C#	Date	Emperor	Good	VG	Fine	VF
7-1	ND(1851-61)	Hsien-feng	27.50	45.00	75.00	125.00

CAST IRON

C#	Date	Emperor	Good	VG	Fine	VF
7-1a	ND(1851-61)	Hsien-feng	30.00	50.00	85.00	140.00

10 CASH

CAST BRASS
Large size, 35mm.

C#	Date	Emperor	Good	VG	Fine	VF
7-2	ND(1851-61)	Hsien-feng	22.50	37.50	60.00	100.00

Small size, 27mm.

C#	Date	Emperor	Good	VG	Fine	VF
7-2.1	ND(1851-61)	Hsien-feng	20.00	32.50	55.00	80.00

CAST IRON

C#	Date	Emperor	Good	VG	Fine	VF
7-2a	ND(1851-61)	Hsien-feng	27.50	45.00	75.00	125.00

50 CASH

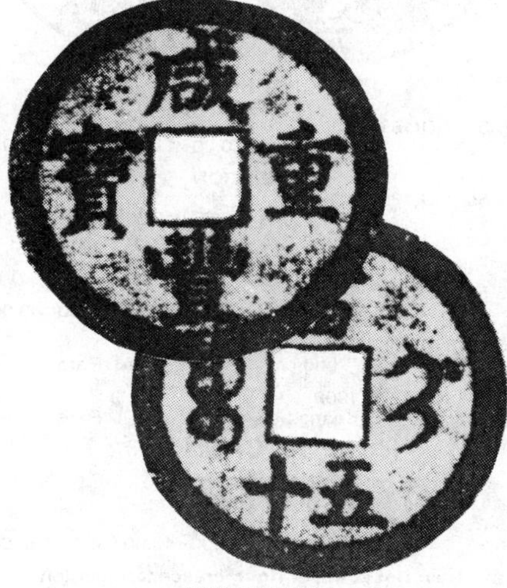

CAST BRASS

C#	Date	Emperor	Good	VG	Fine	VF
7-3	ND(1851-61)	Hsien-feng	20.00	32.50	55.00	100.00

100 CASH

CAST BRASS

C#	Date	Emperor	Good	VG	Fine	VF
7-4	ND(1851-61)	Hsien-feng	25.00	40.00	65.00	135.00

NOTE: This mint mark was later transferred to the Kirin Mint; the Chichow Mint operated through the reign of Hsien Feng.

Paoting Mint

CASH

Obv: Type A.

C#	Date	Emperor	Good	VG	Fine	VF
5-3	ND(1820-51)	Tao-kuang	.60	.90	1.50	2.50

Rev: Dot below.

C#	Date	Emperor	Good	VG	Fine	VF
5-3.1	ND(1820-51)	Tao-kuang	2.50	3.50	6.00	10.00

Obv: Type A.

C#	Date	Emperor	Good	VG	Fine	VF
5-4	ND(1851-61)	Hsien-feng	2.00	3.50	6.00	10.00

CAST IRON

C#	Date	Emperor	Good	VG	Fine	VF
5-4a	ND(1851-61)	Hsien-feng	11.50	18.50	30.00	55.00

CAST BRASS
Obv: Type A-2.

C#	Date	Emperor	Good	VG	Fine	VF
5-8	ND(1862-74)	T'ung-chih	3.50	6.00	10.00	16.50

Obv: Type A.

Sch.#1572

C#	Date	Emperor	Good	VG	Fine	VF
5-10	ND(1875-1908)	Kuang-hsu	3.50	6.00	10.00	16.50

Rev: Dot above.

Sch.#1568

C#	Date	Emperor	Good	VG	Fine	VF
5-10.1	ND(1875-1908)	Kuang-hsu	4.50	7.50	12.50	25.00

Rev: Crescent above.

C#	Date	Emperor	Good	VG	Fine	VF
5-10.2	ND(1875-1908)	Kuang-hsu	4.50	7.50	12.00	20.00

NOTE: The crescent is known in various positions above the center hole.

Rev: Circle above.

C#	Date	Emperor	Good	VG	Fine	VF
5-10.3	ND(1875-1908)	Kuang-hsu	4.50	7.50	12.50	25.00

Rev: Dot below.

C#	Date	Emperor	Good	VG	Fine	VF
5-10.4	ND(1875-1908)	Kuang-hsu	3.50	6.00	10.00	16.00

Rev: Circle below.

C#	Date	Emperor	Good	VG	Fine	VF
5-10.5	ND(1875-1908)	Kuang-hsu	4.50	7.50	12.00	20.00

Rev: Dash above.

C#	Date	Emperor	Good	VG	Fine	VF
5-10.6	ND(1875-1908)	Kuang-hsu	4.50	7.50	12.00	20.00

Rev: Dash below.

C#	Date	Emperor	Good	VG	Fine	VF
5-10.7	ND(1875-1908)	Kuang-hsu	4.50	7.50	12.00	20.00

10 CASH

CAST BRASS
Obv: Type B-1.

C#	Date	Emperor	Good	VG	Fine	VF
5-5	ND(1851-61)	Hsien-feng	10.00	17.50	30.00	50.00

CAST IRON

C#	Date	Emperor	Good	VG	Fine	VF
5-5a	ND(1851-61)	Hsien-feng	30.00	45.00	75.00	125.00

CAST BRASS
Rev: Dot above.

C#	Date	Emperor	Good	VG	Fine	VF
5-5.1	ND(1851-61)	Hsien-feng	13.50	21.50	37.50	60.00
5-9	ND(1862-74)	T'ung-chih	—	—	Rare	—
5-11	ND(1875-1908)	Kuang-hsu	—	—	Rare	—

50 CASH

CAST BRASS
Obv: Type B-1.

C#	Date	Emperor	Good	VG	Fine	VF
5-6	ND(1851-61)	Hsien-feng	25.00	40.00	65.00	130.00

Rev: Dot at upper right; crescent upper left.

C#	Date	Emperor	Good	VG	Fine	VF
5-6.1	ND(1851-61)	Hsien-feng	27.50	45.00	75.00	140.00

100 CASH

CAST BRASS
Obv: Type C.

C#	Date	Emperor	Good	VG	Fine	VF
5-7	ND(1851-61)	Hsien-feng	25.00	40.00	65.00	130.00

1000 CASH

CAST BRASS

C#	Date	Emperor	Good	VG	Fine	VF
A5-7	ND(1851-61)	Hsien-feng	Reported, not confirmed			

Peiyang Arsenal Mint

(Tientsin)

CASH

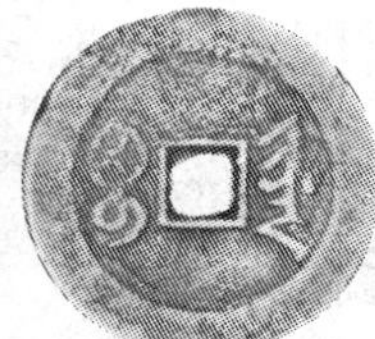

CAST BRASS
Obv: Type A.

C#	Date	Emperor	Good	VG	Fine	VF
8-1	ND(1875-1908)	Kuang-hsu	2.50	4.50	7.50	12.00

Rev: Dot above.

C#	Date	Emperor	Good	VG	Fine	VF
8-1.1	ND(1875-1908)	Kuang-hsu	2.75	4.50	7.50	15.00

Rev: Dot below.

C#	Date	Emperor	Good	VG	Fine	VF
8-1.2	ND(1875-1908)	Kuang-hsu	2.00	3.50	6.00	10.00

Rev: 2 dots below.

C#	Date	Emperor	Good	VG	Fine	VF
8-1.3	ND(1875-1908)	Kuang-hsu	3.50	5.50	9.00	15.00

Rev: Circle above.

C#	Date	Emperor	Good	VG	Fine	VF
8-1.4	ND(1875-1908)	Kuang-hsu	3.50	5.50	9.00	18.00

Rev: Circle below.

C#	Date	Emperor	Good	VG	Fine	VF
8-1.5	ND(1875-1908)	Kuang-hsu	3.50	5.50	9.00	18.00

Rev: Crescent above.

C#	Date	Emperor	Good	VG	Fine	VF
8-1.6	ND(1875-1908)	Kuang-hsu	3.50	5.50	9.00	18.00

Rev: Crescent below.

C#	Date	Emperor	Good	VG	Fine	VF
8-1.7	ND(1875-1908)	Kuang-hsu	2.00	3.75	7.50	17.00

Rev: Dash below.

C#	Date	Emperor	Good	VG	Fine	VF
8-1.8	ND(1875-1908)	Kuang-hsu	2.00	3.75	7.50	15.00

NOTE: Varieties exist with dots and crescents in different corners on reverse and also with incuse dots.

MILLED COINAGE

CASH

BRASS
Obv: Type A.
Obv: Small characters. Rev: Large characters.

Hsu#	Date	Mintage	VG	Fine	VF	XF
410	ND(1888-89)	—	40.00	50.00	75.00	120.00

Obv: Large characters. Rev: Small characters.

Hsu#	Date	Mintage	VG	Fine	VF	XF
410.1	ND(1888-89)	—	40.00	50.00	75.00	120.00

Obv: and rev: Small characters.

Hsu#	Date	Mintage	VG	Fine	VF	XF
410.2	ND(1888-89)	—	10.00	20.00	30.00	45.00

Obv: and rev: Large characters.

Hsu#	Date	Mintage	VG	Fine	VF	XF
410.3	ND(1888-89)	—	40.00	50.00	75.00	110.00

5 CENTS

1.3200 g, .820 SILVER, .0348 oz ASW

Y#	Date	Mintage	Fine	VF	XF	Unc
61	Yr.22 (1896)	7,000	200.00	250.00	300.00	650.00

Obv. leg: *TAI TSING. . .*

Y#	Date	Mintage	Fine	VF	XF	Unc
61.1	Yr.23 (1897)	Inc. Ab.	25.00	50.00	85.00	225.00

Rev: Redesigned dragon.

Y#	Date	Mintage	Fine	VF	XF	Unc
61.2 (61.1)	Yr.23 (1897)	.039	20.00	35.00	55.00	120.00
	Yr.24 (1898)	.231	18.00	30.00	40.00	100.00

Y#	Date	Mintage	Fine	VF	XF	Unc
69	Yr.25 (1899)	.097	20.00	50.00	75.00	125.00
	Yr.26 (1900)	—	125.00	250.00	500.00	1000.

10 CENTS

2.6500 g, .820 SILVER, .0699 oz ASW

Y#	Date	Mintage	Fine	VF	XF	Unc
62	Yr.22 (1896)	5,000	100.00	150.00	250.00	600.00

Obv. leg: *TAI TSING. . .*

Y#	Date	Mintage	Fine	VF	XF	Unc
62.1	Yr.23 (1897)	.148	15.00	30.00	50.00	120.00
	Yr.24 (1898)	.614	12.00	25.00	40.00	120.00
70	Yr.25 (1899)	.153	20.00	50.00	75.00	150.00

20 CENTS

5.3000 g, .820 SILVER, .1397 oz ASW

Y#	Date	Mintage	Fine	VF	XF	Unc
63.1	Yr.22 (1896)	.012	100.00	225.00	400.00	750.00

Obv. leg: *TAI TSING. . .*

Y#	Date	Mintage	Fine	VF	XF	Unc
63.2	Yr.23 (1897)	.147	16.50	30.00	45.00	120.00
	Yr.24 (1898)	.350	15.00	25.00	40.00	100.00

Y#	Date	Mintage	Fine	VF	XF	Unc
71	Yr.25 (1899)	.152	25.00	50.00	100.00	300.00
	Yr.26 (1900)	—	500.00	650.00	900.00	1500.

50 CENTS

13.3000 g, .860 SILVER, .3678 oz ASW

Y#	Date	Mintage	Fine	VF	XF	Unc
64	Yr.22 (1896)	2,500	400.00	800.00	1500.	3000.

Obv. leg: *TAI TSING. . .*
Rev: Dragon w/beady eyes.

Y#	Date	Mintage	Fine	VF	XF	Unc
64.1	Yr.23 (1897)	.021	30.00	65.00	150.00	300.00
	Yr.24 (1898)	I.A.	30.00	65.00	150.00	300.00

Rev: Dragon w/eyelids.

Y#	Date	Mintage	Fine	VF	XF	Unc
64.2	Yr.24 (1898)	.176	20.00	50.00	90.00	240.00

Y#	Date	Mintage	Fine	VF	XF	Unc
72	Yr.25 (1899)	.056	75.00	140.00	225.00	400.00

DOLLAR

26.7000 g, .900 SILVER, .7727 oz ASW

Y#	Date	Mintage	Fine	VF	XF	Unc
65	Yr.22 (1896)	3,000	1000.	2000.	4000.	8000.

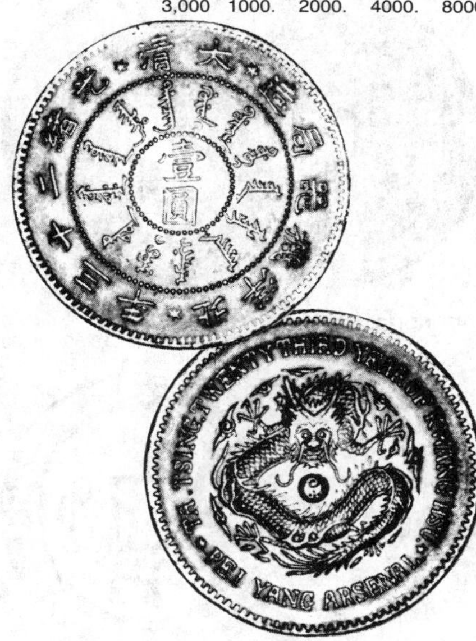

Rev: Dragon w/beady eyes.

Y#	Date	Mintage	Fine	VF	XF	Unc
65.1	Yr.23 (1897)	1.120	60.00	150.00	400.00	1000.

Rev: Dragon w/eyelids.

Y#	Date	Mintage	Fine	VF	XF	Unc
65.2	Yr.24 (1898)	2.806	60.00	150.00	400.00	1000.

Obv: Similar to Y#73.2.

Y#	Date	Mintage	Fine	VF	XF	Unc
73	Yr.25 (1899)	1.566	25.00	40.00	75.00	450.00
	Yr.26 (1900)	—	40.00	75.00	125.00	750.00

NOTE: Later date (Yr.29 (1903) exists for this type.

Taku Mint

(Imperial Naval Yard) Taku was a military installation that guarded the harbor of Tienstein. It had a strong fortress and a large garrison. The Taku fort was leveled during the Boxer Rebellion.

CASH

CAST BRASS
Obv: Type A. Rev: Type 2 mint mark.

C#	Date	Emperor	Good	VG	Fine	VF
3-1.1	ND(1875-1908)	Kuang-hsu	120.00	180.00	275.00	400.00

Obv: Type A. Rev: Type 2 mint mark.

C#	Date	Emperor	Good	VG	Fine	VF
3-1.2	ND(1875-1908)	Kuang-hsu	25.00	40.00	60.00	90.00

PATTERNS (Pn)

(Including off metal strikes)

 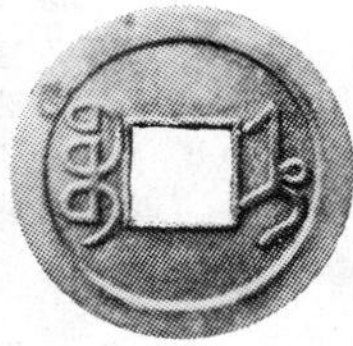

KM#	Date	Mintage	Identification	Mkt.Val.
Pn1	ND	—	Cash, Brass	—

NOTE: Mint mark *Pao Ting* produced at the Birmingham Mint, England.

KM#	Date	Mintage	Identification	Mkt.Val.
Pn2	ND	—	Cash, Copper	650.00

NOTE: Mint mark *Ku* for Taku Mint. Produced at the Imperial Naval Ship Yard.

KM#	Date	Mintage	Identification	Mkt.Val.
Pn3	ND	—	1 Tael, Copper	700.00
Pn4	ND	—	10 Taels, Brass	—
Pn5	Yr.25 (1899)	—	5 Cents, Copper, Y69	—

CHINGKIANG

For coins of Chingkiang refer to listings under Kiangsu.

FENGTIEN PROVINCE

(Fungtien)

Liaoning

The southernmost province of the Three Eastern Provinces was known by a variety of names including Fengtien, Shengching, and Liaoning. The modern Mukden (Fengtien Province) Mint operated from 1897 to 1931.

EMPIRE

CASH

CAST BRASS
Obv: Type A.

C#	Date	Emperor	Good	VG	Fine	VF
9-1	ND(1875-1908)	Kuang-hsu	20.00	30.00	50.00	—

MILLED COINAGE

5 CENTS

SILVER, 1.20 g

Y#	Year	Date	Fine	VF	XF	Unc
83	25	(1899)	20.00	50.00	80.00	200.00

10 CENTS

SILVER

Y#	Year	Date	Fine	VF	XF	Unc
84	24	(1898)	20.00	50.00	80.00	200.00

20 CENTS

SILVER, 5.20 g
Rev: 4 rows of scales on dragon. Clockwise spiral on pearl.

Y#	Year	Date	Fine	VF	XF	Unc
85	24	(1898)	15.00	30.00	55.00	160.00

Rev: 5 rows of scales on dragon. Counter-clockwise spiral on pearl.

Y#	Year	Date	Fine	VF	XF	Unc
85.1	24	(1898)	15.00	30.00	55.00	160.00

50 CENTS

SILVER, 13.10 g

Y#	Year	Date	Fine	VF	XF	Unc
86	Yr.(sic)	(1897)*	—	—	Rare	—
	Yr.24	(1898)	100.00	150.00	250.00	500.00
	Yr.25	(1899)	200.00	350.00	500.00	800.00

***NOTE:** (error) year 32 should read year 23 (1897). Workmanship on this coin is inferior to that on the succeeding years.

DOLLAR

26.4000 g, .850 SILVER, .7215 oz ASW

Y#	Year	Date	Fine	VF	XF	Unc
87	24	(1898)	125.00	250.00	400.00	750.00
	25	(1899)	300.00	450.00	650.00	1000.

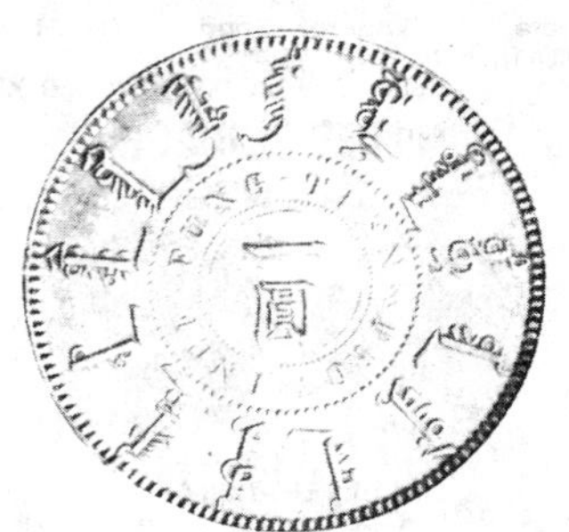

Obv: 2 center Chinese characters within double circle, 1 of dots around 1 solid.

Y#	Year	Date	Fine	VF	XF	Unc
87.1	25	(1899)	250.00	400.00	600.00	900.00

FUKIEN PROVINCE

Fujian

A province located on the southeastern coast of China, including the island of Taiwan until it became its own separate province in 1885. Although known mainly as an agricultural area, forestry and some mining, particularly iron ore and coal, are also important to the economy. The Foochow Mint operated throughout the Manchu dynasty. The Viceroy's or City mint was opened in 1896 for struck coinage. Two other mints were established in 1905, the Mamoi Arsenal Mint which struck the Custom-House issues until it closed in 1906, and the West Mint which later became the main Fukien (Fujian) Mint. It closed between 1914 and 1920. Various subsidiary mints were in operation from 1924 to 1925.

EMPIRE

Fuchow Mint

CASH

C#	Date	Emperor	Good	VG	Fine	VF
10-3	ND(1821-51)	Tao-kuang	1.00	2.50	3.00	4.50

Rev: Line right of mint mark. 26mm.

C#	Date	Emperor	Good	VG	Fine	VF
10-4	ND(1851-61)	Hsien-feng	2.00	3.00	4.00	10.00

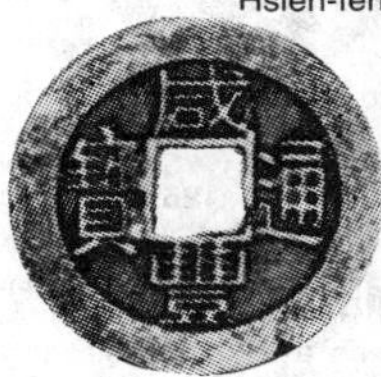
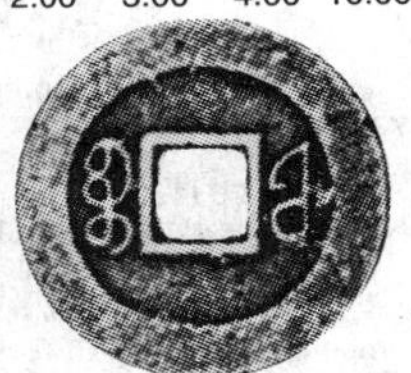

Rev: Dot right of mint mark. 22-24mm.

C#	Date	Emperor	Good	VG	Fine	VF
10-4.1	ND(1851-61)	Hsien-feng	2.50	3.50	5.50	12.50

CAST IRON

C#	Date	Emperor	Good	VG	Fine	VF
10-4a.1	ND(1851-61)	Hsien-feng	15.00	27.00	37.50	60.00

Larger size. Wide rims.

C#	Date	Emperor	Good	VG	Fine	VF
10-4a.2	ND(1851-61)	Hsien-feng	20.00	35.00	50.00	75.00

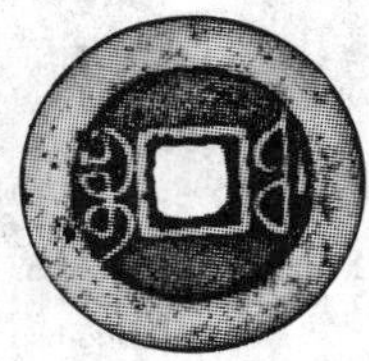

CAST BRASS
Obv: Type A-2.

Sch.#1557

C#	Date	Emperor	Good	VG	Fine	VF
10-22	ND(1862-74)	T'ung-chih	1.25	2.50	4.00	6.00

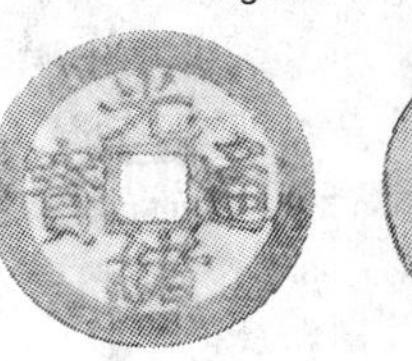

Obv: Type A.

Sch.#1581

C#	Date	Emperor	Good	VG	Fine	VF
10-25	ND(1875-1908)	Kuang-hsu	1.00	2.00	4.00	6.00

Rev: Dot at top of hole.

C#	Date	Emperor	Good	VG	Fine	VF
10-25.1	ND(1875-1908)	Kuang-hsu	2.50	4.00	6.50	10.00

Rev: Inverted.

C#	Date	Emperor	Good	VG	Fine	VF
10-25.2	ND(1875-1908)	Kuang-hsu	—	—	—	—

5 CASH

BRASS, 31mm
Rev: Weight on the rim similar to 20 Cash, C#10-12.

C#	Date	Emperor	Good	VG	Fine	VF
10-5	ND(1851-61)	Hsien-feng	40.00	70.00	110.00	150.00

Rev: *5 Wen* at top.

C#	Date	Emperor	Good	VG	Fine	VF
10-5.1	ND(1854)	Hsien-feng	—	—	—	—

10 CASH

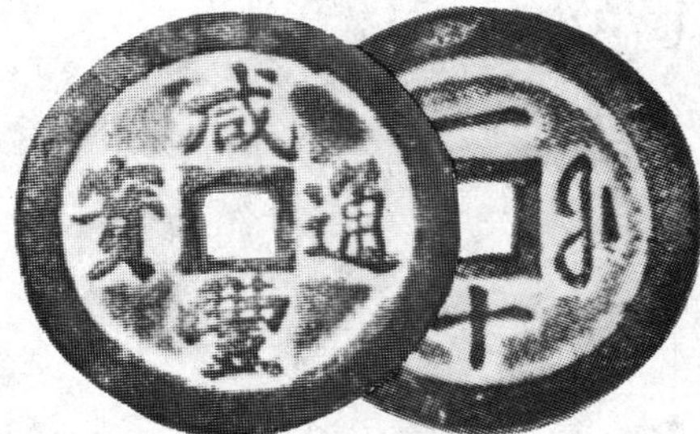

CAST BRASS, 35-40mm.
Obv: Type A.

C#	Date	Emperor	Good	VG	Fine	VF
10-6	ND(1851-61)	Hsien-feng	4.00	8.00	17.00	30.00

Rev: Characters *Ta Ching* appear at upper left and right.

C#	Date	Emperor	Good	VG	Fine	VF
10-6.1	ND(1851-61)	Hsien-feng	—	—	Rare	—

Obv: Type B-1.

C#	Date	Emperor	Good	VG	Fine	VF
10-7	ND(1851-61)	Hsien-feng	8.50	15.00	18.50	35.00

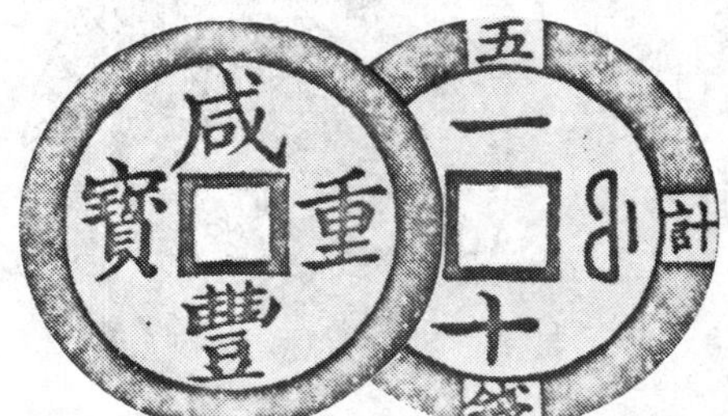

Rev: 4 characters appearing on rim.

C#	Date	Emperor	Good	VG	Fine	VF
10-8	ND(1851-61)	Hsien-feng	12.50	20.00	30.00	100.00

CAST IRON

C#	Date	Emperor	Good	VG	Fine	VF
10-8a	ND(1851-61)	Hsien-feng	—	—	Rare	—

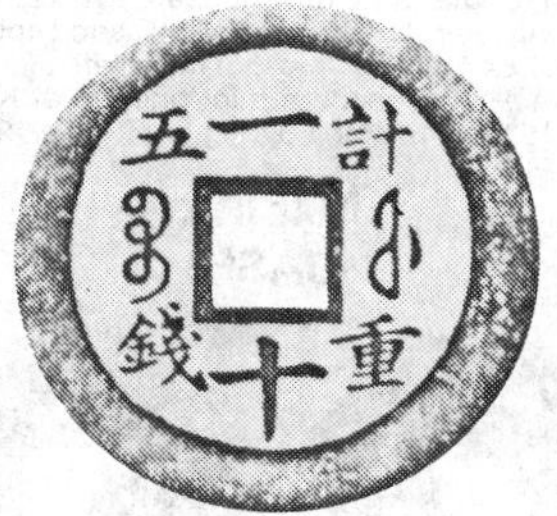

CAST BRASS

C#	Date	Emperor	Good	VG	Fine	VF
10-9	ND(1851-61)	Hsien-feng	70.00	110.00	150.00	275.00

42mm
Rev. leg: 4 characters at top, 4 different characters at bottom. Mint mark (at right) has a crescent at right instead of a dot.

C#	Date	Emperor	Good	VG	Fine	VF
10-9.1	ND(1851-61)	Hsien-feng	—	—	Rare	—

35mm
Rev: Chinese mint mark at right, Manchu mint mark at left.

C#	Date	Emperor	Good	VG	Fine	VF
10-9.2	ND(1851-61)	Hsien-feng	—	—	Rare	—
10-23	ND(1862-74)	T'ung-chih	—	—	Rare	—
10-26	ND(1875-1908)	Kuang-hsu	—	—	Rare	—

NOTE: C#10-9.2, 10-23 and 10-26 are unofficial issues.

20 CASH

CAST BRASS, 45-46mm
Obv: Type A.

C#	Date	Emperor	Good	VG	Fine	VF
10-10	ND(1851-61)	Hsien-feng	5.50	10.00	16.50	40.00

CAST IRON

C#	Date	Emperor	Good	VG	Fine	VF
10-10a	ND(1851-61)	Hsien-feng	Reported, not confirmed			

CAST BRASS, 44mm
Obv: Type B-1. Rev: Similar to C10-10.

Sch.#1591

C#	Date	Emperor	Good	VG	Fine	VF
10-11	ND(1851-61)	Hsien-feng	13.50	22.50	30.00	55.00

Rev: 4 characters appearing on rim.

C#	Date	Emperor	Good	VG	Fine	VF
10-12	ND(1851-61)	Hsien-feng	30.00	50.00	75.00	170.00

CAST IRON

C#	Date	Emperor	Good	VG	Fine	VF
10-12a	ND(1851-61)	Hsien-feng	Reported, not confirmed			

CAST COPPER, 46mm

Rev: 8 characters in the field.

C#	Date	Emperor	Good	VG	Fine	VF
10-13	ND(1851-61)	Hsien-feng	100.00	175.00	250.00	350.00

CAST IRON

C#	Date	Emperor	Good	VG	Fine	VF
10-13a	ND(1851-61)	Hsien-feng	—	—	—	—

50 CASH

CAST COPPER, 55-57mm
Obv: Type A. Rev: 4 characters.

C#	Date	Emperor	Good	VG	Fine	VF
10-14	ND(1851-61)	Hsien-feng	15.00	25.00	30.00	60.00

65mm
Rev: Mint mark w/long vertical stroke at right instead of dot.

C#	Date	Emperor	Good	VG	Fine	VF
10-14.1	ND(1851-61)	Hsien-feng	—	—	Rare	—

55mm
Obv: Type B-1. Rev: 4 characters.

C#	Date	Emperor	Good	VG	Fine	VF
10-15	ND(1851-61)	Hsien-feng	25.00	40.00	55.00	100.00

Rev: 4 characters appearing on rim.

C#	Date	Emperor	Good	VG	Fine	VF
10-16	ND(1851-61)	Hsien-feng	50.00	85.00	150.00	250.00

Rev: 8 characters in field.

C#	Date	Emperor	Good	VG	Fine	VF
10-17	ND(1851-61)	Hsien-feng	175.00	300.00	425.00	550.00

100 CASH

CAST COPPER, 70mm
Obv: Type A. Rev: 4 characters.

C#	Date	Emperor	Good	VG	Fine	VF
10-18	ND(1851-61)	Hsien-feng	35.00	50.00	75.00	125.00

74mm
Rev: Mint mark w/long vertical stroke at right instead of dot.

C#	Date	Emperor	Good	VG	Fine	VF
10-18.1	ND(1851-61)	Hsien-feng	—	—	Rare	—

CAST ZINC
Rev: 4 characters.

C#	Date	Emperor	Good	VG	Fine	VF
10-18a	ND(1851-61)	Hsien-feng	—	—	Rare	—

NOTE: Composition of this coin is reportedly a mixture of zinc, lead and tin. The coin is blue-gray in color and has a large mint mark, written differently from any of the above.

CAST COPPER
Obv: Type B-1. Rev: 4 characters.

C#	Date	Emperor	Good	VG	Fine	VF
10-19	ND(1851-61)	Hsien-feng	25.00	40.00	55.00	90.00

72mm
Rev: 4 characters appearing on rim and small characters in field.

C#	Date	Emperor	Good	VG	Fine	VF
10-20	ND(1851-61)	Hsien-feng	75.00	125.00	175.00	250.00

78mm
Rev: Larger characters in field.

C#	Date	Emperor	Good	VG	Fine	VF
10-20.1	ND(1851-61)	Hsien-feng	35.00	50.00	75.00	125.00

Rev: 8 characters in field.

C#	Date	Emperor	Good	VG	Fine	VF
10-21	ND(1851-61)	Hsien-feng	Reported, not confirmed			

FANTASY ISSUES

NOTE: 30, 40, 500 and 1000 Cash pieces are reported for this mint, but their existence is doubtful and any encountered would most likely be considered fantasies.

MILLED COINAGE

5 CENTS

1.3500 g, .820 SILVER, .0356 oz ASW
Obv. leg: 5 characters at top.
Rev: Side-view dragon-left.

Y#	Date	Mintage	Fine	VF	XF	Unc
102	ND(1896-1903)		8.00	14.00	25.00	60.00

10 CENTS

2.7000 g, .820 SILVER, .0712 oz ASW
Obv. leg: 5 characters at top.
Rev: Rosette at either side of side-view dragon-left.

Y#	Date	Mintage	Fine	VF	XF	Unc
103	ND(1896-1903)	13.425	5.00	9.00	17.50	35.00

Rev: Dot at either side of side-view dragon-left.

Y#	Date	Mintage	Fine	VF	XF	Unc
103.1	ND(1896-1903)	Inc. Ab.	8.00	15.00	30.00	60.00

20 CENTS

5.4000 g, .820 SILVER, .1424 oz ASW
Obv. leg: 5 characters at top.
Rev: Dot at either side of side-view dragon-left.

Y#	Date	Mintage	Fine	VF	XF	Unc
104	ND(1896-1903)	31.772	3.00	6.00	12.50	30.00

Rev: Rosette at either side of side-view dragon-left.

Y#	Date	Mintage	Fine	VF	XF	Unc
104.1	ND(1898-1903)	Inc. Ab.	3.00	6.00	12.50	30.00

DOLLAR

SILVER, 25.70 g
Obv. leg: 4 characters at top "Changchow Soldier's Pay".

Kann#	Date	Mintage	VG	Fine	VF	XF
6	ND(ca.1844)	—	1800.	2500.	3000.	4500.

27.20 g
Obv: Lower character written in different style.

Kann#	Date	Mintage	VG	Fine	VF	XF
5	ND(ca.1844)	—	3000.	4000.	5000.	7500.

26.20 g
Obv. and rev: 2 rosettes.
Obv. leg: 2 characters at top "Soldier's Pay".

Kann#	Date	Mintage	VG	Fine	VF	XF
7	ND(ca.1844)	—	350.00	700.00	1200.	2500.

Obv: 2 rosettes and 2 five-petalled flowers.

Kann#	Date	Mintage	VG	Fine	VF	XF
7c	ND(ca.1844)	—	850.00	1250.	1500.	3000.

Kann #5-7 above were issued by military authorities at the city of Changchow. Though Kann dates these pieces in the 1860's they were already circulating in the 1840's.

27.00 g

Y#	Date	Mintage	Fine	VF	XF	Unc
105	ND(ca.1899)	—	—	—	Rare	—

PATTERNS (Pn)

(Including off metal strikes)

KM#	Date	Mintage	Identification	Mkt.Val.
Pn1	ND(1898-1908)	—	10 Cents, Copper, Y103	—
Pn2	ND(1896-1908)	—	20 Cents, Copper, Y104	—

HONAN PROVINCE

Henan

A province in east-central China. As well as being one of the most densely populated provinces it is also one of the most important agriculturally. It is the area of earliest settlement in China and has housed the capital during various dynasties. The Kaifeng Mint issued coins from its opening in 1647 through most of the rulers of the Manchu dynasty. In 1905 a modern mint opened at Kaifeng but closed in 1914. A mint in Loyang opened in 1924.

EMPIRE

CASH

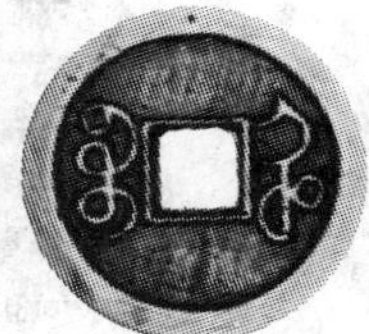

CAST BRASS
Obv: Type A. Rev: Type 1.

C#	Date	Emperor	Good	VG	Fine	VF
11-1	ND(1851-61)	Hsien-feng	20.00	30.00	40.00	60.00
	Rev: Crescent above.					
11-1.1	ND(1851-61)	Hsien-feng	20.00	30.00	40.00	60.00
	Rev: Circle above.					
11-1.2	ND(1851-61)	Hsien-feng	20.00	30.00	40.00	60.00
	CAST IRON					
11-1a	ND(1851-61)	Hsien-feng	12.50	20.00	30.00	60.00
	CAST BRASS Obv: Type A.					
11-9	ND(1875-1908)	Kuang-hsu	4.00	8.00	10.00	12.00

Rev: Circle above.

C#	Date	Emperor	Good	VG	Fine	VF
11-9.1	ND(1875-1908)	Kuang-hsu	5.00	9.00	13.50	35.00

Rev: Circle below.

C#	Date	Emperor	Good	VG	Fine	VF
11-9.2	ND(1875-1908)	Kuang-hsu	5.00	9.00	13.50	25.00

Rev: Crescent above.

C#	Date	Emperor	Good	VG	Fine	VF
11-9.3	ND(1875-1908)	Kuang-hsu	5.00	9.00	13.50	25.00

Rev: Crescent below.

C#	Date	Emperor	Good	VG	Fine	VF
11-9.4	ND(1875-1908)	Kuang-hsu	5.00	9.00	13.50	25.00

Sch.#1571

Rev: Crescent above, dot below.

C#	Date	Emperor	Good	VG	Fine	VF
11-9.5	ND(1875-1908)	Kuang-hsu	5.00	9.00	13.50	25.00

Rev: Dot above.

C#	Date	Emperor	Good	VG	Fine	VF
11-9.6	ND(1875-1908)	Kuang-hsu	5.00	9.00	13.50	20.00

Rev: Dot below.

C#	Date	Emperor	Good	VG	Fine	VF
11-9.7	ND(1875-1908)	Kuang-hsu	5.00	9.00	13.50	20.00

Rev: Dot at upper left.

C#	Date	Emperor	Good	VG	Fine	VF
11-9.8	ND(1875-1908)	Kuang-hsu	5.00	9.00	13.50	20.00

NOTE: Crescent and dot varieties exist for this type.

CAST ZINC

C#	Date	Emperor	Good	VG	Fine	VF
3-1.1a	ND(1875-1908)	Kuang-hsu	—	—	Rare	—

10 CASH

CAST BRASS
Obv: Type B-1.

C#	Date	Emperor	Good	VG	Fine	VF
11-2	ND(1851-61)	Hsien-feng	6.00	12.00	20.00	40.00

50 CASH

CAST BRASS
Obv: Type B-1.

C#	Date	Emperor	Good	VG	Fine	VF
11-5	ND(1851-61)	Hsien-feng	8.00	15.00	25.00	50.00

100 CASH

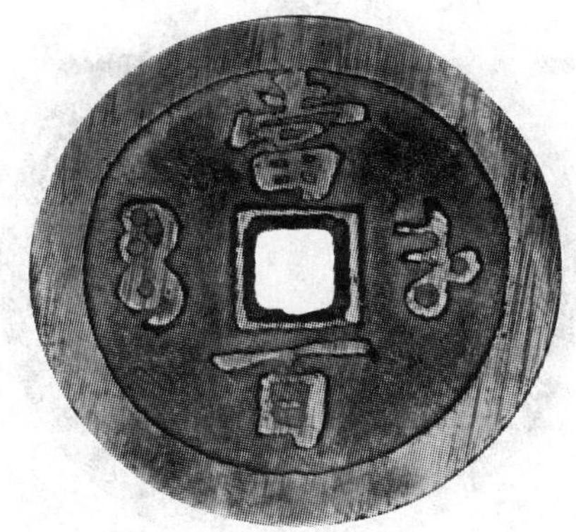

CAST BRASS
Obv: Type C.

C#	Date	Emperor	Good	VG	Fine	VF
11-6	ND(1851-61)	Hsien-feng	10.00	20.00	30.00	60.00

500 CASH

CAST BRASS
Obv: Type C.

C#	Date	Emperor	Good	VG	Fine	VF
11-7	ND(1851-61)	Hsien-feng	75.00	150.00	220.00	300.00

1000 CASH

CAST BRASS
Obv: Type C.

C#	Date	Emperor	Good	VG	Fine	VF
11-8	ND(1851-61)	Hsien-feng	200.00	300.00	400.00	500.00

FANTASY ISSUES

Coins of this mint in denominations of 20 (C#11-3), 30 (C#11-4), 40 and 70 cash are considered fantasy issues.

HUNAN PROVINCE

A province in south-central China. Mining of coal, antimony, tungsten and tin is important as well as raising varied agricultural products. The Changsha Mint produced Cash coins from early in the Manchu dynasty. Its facility for struck coinage opened in 1897, and two further copper mints were added in 1905. All three mints were closed down in 1907, but one mint was reopened at a later date and produced vast quantities of republican copper coinage until 1926.

EMPIRE

Changsha Mint

CASH

Obv: Type A.

Sch.#1532

C#	Date	Emperor	Good	VG	Fine	VF
12-3	ND(1821-50)	Tao-kuang	2.00	4.00	6.50	10.00

Obv: Type A.

Sch.#1543

C#	Date	Emperor	Good	VG	Fine	VF
12-4	ND(1851-61)	Hsien-feng	2.00	4.00	6.50	10.00

Obv: Type A-2.

C#	Date	Emperor	Good	VG	Fine	VF
12-5	ND(1862-74)	T'ung-chih	6.00	12.50	18.50	25.00

Obv: Type A.

C#	Date	Emperor	Good	VG	Fine	VF
12-7	ND(1875-1908)	Kuang-hsu	7.50	15.00	21.50	30.00

10 CASH

CAST BRASS

C#	Date	Emperor	Good	VG	Fine	VF
12-6	ND(1862-74)	T'ung-chih	—	—	Rare	—
12-8	ND(1875-1908)	Kuang-hsu	—	—	Rare	—

MILLED COINAGE

NOTE: 2, 5 and 20 Cash Tai Ching Ti Kuo type patterns are reported, not confirmed.

5 CENTS

1.3000 g, .820 SILVER, .0343 oz ASW
Similar to 20 Cents, Y#116.

Y#	Date	Mintage	Fine	VF	XF	Unc
—	ND(1897)	—	—	—	Rare	—

10 CENTS

2.5000 g, .820 SILVER, .0659 oz ASW
Obv: 2 rosettes at both sides.

Y#	Date	Mintage	Fine	VF	XF	Unc
115	ND(1897)	—	7.00	15.00	25.00	100.00

Obv: 1 rosette at both sides.

Y#	Date	Mintage	Fine	VF	XF	Unc
115.1	ND(1897)	—	14.00	25.00	45.00	120.00
	CD1898	—	17.50	35.00	60.00	150.00
	CD1899	—	22.50	45.00	75.00	175.00

20 CENTS

5.3000 g, .820 SILVER, .1397 oz ASW

Y#	Date	Mintage	Fine	VF	XF	Unc
116	ND(1897)	—	35.00	75.00	125.00	250.00

PATTERNS (Pn)

(Including off metal strikes)

KM#	Date	Mintage	Identification	Mkt.Val.
Pn1	ND(1897)	—	10 Cents, Antimony, Y115	—

KM#	Date	Mintage	Identification	Mkt.Val.
Pn2	ND(1897)	—	50 Cents, Silver	7500.

KM#	Date	Mintage	Identification	Mkt.Val.
Pn3	ND(1897)	—	1 Dollar, Silver	25,000.

NOTE: The dollar and half dollar above were produced at the Heaton Mint, Birmingham, England as trials before sending the dies and machinery to China. About 6 pieces of each denomination exist.

HUPEH PROVINCE

Hubei

A province located in east-central China. Hilly, with some lakes and swamps, it has rich coal and iron deposits plus a varied agricultural program. The Wuchang Mint had been active from early in the Manchu dynasty and its modern equipment began operations in 1895. It probably closed in 1929.

EMPIRE

CASH

Obv: Type A.

C#	Date	Emperor	Good	VG	Fine	VF
13-3	ND(1821-50)	Tao-kuang	1.00	2.00	3.00	5.00

Obv: Type A.

C#	Date	Emperor	Good	VG	Fine	VF
13-4	ND(1851-61)	Hsien-feng	3.00	6.00	7.50	10.00

Obv: Type A-2.

C#	Date	Emperor	Good	VG	Fine	VF
13-9	ND(1862-74)	T'ung-chih	3.50	7.50	11.50	16.50

Obv: Type A.

C#	Date	Emperor	Good	VG	Fine	VF
13-11	ND(1875-1908)	Kuang-hsu	12.00	20.00	30.00	45.00

5 CASH

CAST BRASS
Obv: Type B-1.

C#	Date	Emperor	Good	VG	Fine	VF
13-5	ND(1851-61)	Hsien-Feng	40.00	70.00	100.00	130.00

10 CASH

CAST BRASS
Obv: Type B-1.

C#	Date	Emperor	Good	VG	Fine	VF
13-6	ND(1851-61)	Hsien-feng	6.00	12.50	25.00	60.00

Rev: Crescent in upper right corner.

C#	Date	Emperor	Good	VG	Fine	VF
13-6.1	ND(1851-61)	Hsien-feng	10.00	20.00	30.00	60.00

Obv: Type B.

C#	Date	Emperor	Good	VG	Fine	VF
13-10	ND(1862-74)	T'ung-chih	—	—	Rare	—

Obv: Type B.

C#	Date	Emperor	Good	VG	Fine	VF
13-12	ND(1875-1908)	Kuang-hsu	—	—	Rare	—

50 CASH

CAST BRASS
Obv: Type B.
Obv: and rev: Large characters.

C#	Date	Emperor	Good	VG	Fine	VF
13-7	ND(1851-61)	Hsien-feng	10.00	20.00	35.00	60.00

Rev: Crescent in upper right corner.

C#	Date	Emperor	Good	VG	Fine	VF
13-7.1	ND(1851-61)	Hsien-feng	52.50	85.00	110.00	175.00

100 CASH

CAST BRASS
Obv: Type C.

C#	Date	Emperor	Good	VG	Fine	VF
13-8	ND(1851-61)	Hsien-feng	10.00	20.00	30.00	70.00

Rev: Crescent in upper right corner.

C#	Date	Emperor	Good	VG	Fine	VF
13-8.1	ND(1851-61)	Hsien-feng	35.00	55.00	75.00	110.00

Chingchow Mint

CASH

CAST BRASS
Obv: Type A.

C#	Date	Emperor	Good	VG	Fine	VF
13-11.1	ND(1875-1908)	Kuang-hsu	12.00	15.00	22.50	30.00

NOTE: The reverse mint mark spells "Ching" in Manchu. Attribution of this mint mark to Chingchow is uncertain. Certain authorities claim the Taku (Dagu) Mint in Tientsin to have struck this coin.

MILLED COINAGE

CASH

BRASS, struck
Obv: Small characters, 22.5mm.

Hsu#	Date	Mintage	VG	Fine	VF	XF
181	ND(1898)	—	22.50	40.00	50.00	85.00

Mule. Obv: Hsu#181. Rev: Hsu#182.

Hsu#	Date	Mintage	VG	Fine	VF	XF
A182	ND(1898)	—	—	—	—	—

Obv: Larger characters, 20.5mm.

Hsu#	Date	Mintage	VG	Fine	VF	XF
182	ND(1898)	—	17.50	25.00	35.00	55.00

5 CENTS

1.3500 g, .820 SILVER, .0356 oz ASW

Y#	Date	Mintage	Fine	VF	XF	Unc
123	ND(1895-1905)	4.278	50.00	100.00	150.00	250.00

10 CENTS

2.7000 g, .820 SILVER, .0712 oz ASW
Rev: Character at either side of dragon *Pen Sheng* indicating coin was for provincial use.

Y#	Date	Mintage	Fine	VF	XF	Unc
124	ND(1894)	—	300.00	700.00	1300.	2000.

Rev: W/o characters beside dragon.
2 varieties of edge milling.

Y#	Date	Mintage	Fine	VF	XF	Unc
124.1	ND(1895-1907)		2.00	4.00	7.50	20.00

20 CENTS

5.3000 g, .820 SILVER, .1397 oz ASW
Rev: Character at either side of dragon *Pen Sheng* indicating coin was for provincial use.

Y#	Date	Mintage	Fine	VF	XF	Unc
125	ND(1894)	—	1500.	3500.	4000.	5000.

Rev: W/o characters beside dragon.

Y#	Date	Mintage	Fine	VF	XF	Unc
125.1	ND(1895-1907)		5.00	10.00	15.00	30.00

50 CENTS

13.5000 g, .860 SILVER, .3733 oz ASW

Y#	Date	Mintage	Fine	VF	XF	Unc
126	ND(1895-1905)		35.00	65.00	120.00	250.00

DOLLAR

26.7000 g, .900 SILVER, .7727 oz ASW
Obv: Similar to Y#127.1.
Rev: Characters *Pen Sheng* at either side of dragon indicating coin was for provincial use.

Y#	Date	Mintage	Fine	VF	XF	Unc
127	ND(1894)	—	7500.	10,000.	15,000.	25,000.

Rev: W/o *Pen Sheng* at either side of dragon.

Y#	Date	Mintage	Fine	VF	XF	Unc
127.1	ND(1895-1907)	19.935	20.00	30.00	50.00	250.00

PATTERNS (Pn)

(Including off metal strikes)

KM#	Date	Mintage	Identification	Mkt.Val.
Pn1	ND(1895-1907)	—	5 Cents, Copper, Y123	—
Pn2	ND(1895-1907)	—	10 Cents, Copper, Y124.1	—
Pn3	ND(1895-1907)	—	20 Cents, Copper, Y125.1	—
Pn4	ND(1895-1905)	—	50 Cents, Copper, Y126	—
Pn5	ND(1895-1907)	—	1 Dollar, Copper, Y127.1	350.00

KANSU PROVINCE

Gansu

A province located in north-central China with a contrast of mountains and sandy plains. The west end of the Great Wall with its branches lies in Kansu (Gansu). Kansu (Gansu) was the eastern end of the "Silk, Road" that led to central and western Asia. Two mints issued Cash coins. It has been reported, but not confirmed, that the Lanchow Mint operated as late as 1949.

EMPIRE

CASH

CAST BRASS
Obv: Type A.

C#	Date	Emperor	Good	VG	Fine	VF
14-1	ND(1851-61)	Hsien-feng	15.00	30.00	45.00	67.50
14-8	ND(1862-74)	T'ung-chih	8.00	16.00	25.00	35.00

5 CASH

CAST BRASS
Obv: Type B-1.

C#	Date	Emperor	Good	VG	Fine	VF
14-2	ND(1851-61)	Hsien-feng	20.00	30.00	50.00	75.00

Rev: Large Manchu.

C#	Date	Emperor	Good	VG	Fine	VF
14-2.1	ND(1851-61)	Hsien-feng	30.00	50.00	75.00	95.00

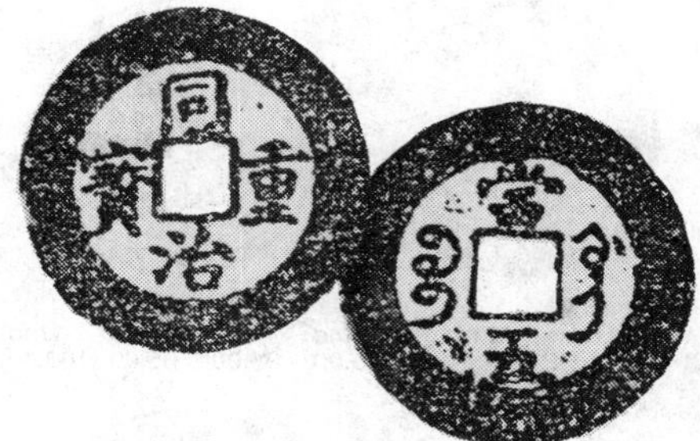

Obv: Type B.

C#	Date	Emperor	Good	VG	Fine	VF
14-9	ND(1862-74)	T'ung-chih	30.00	40.00	60.00	100.00

10 CASH

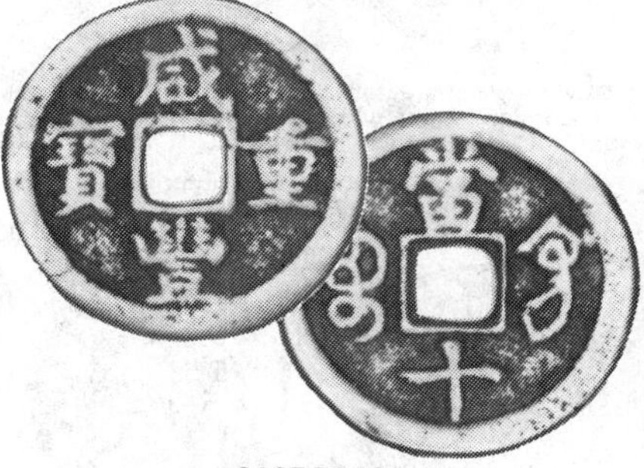

CAST BRASS
Obv: Type B.

C#	Date	Emperor	Good	VG	Fine	VF
14-3	ND(1851-61)	Hsien-feng	7.00	10.00	20.00	35.00

Obv: Type B.

C#	Date	Emperor	Good	VG	Fine	VF
14-10	ND(1862-74)	T'ung-chih	20.00	35.00	45.00	55.00

50 CASH

CAST BRASS, 48mm.
Obv: Type B-1.

C#	Date	Emperor	Good	VG	Fine	VF
14-4	ND(1851-61)	Hsien-feng	35.00	65.00	80.00	150.00

43mm

C#	Date	Emperor	Good	VG	Fine	VF
14-4.1	ND(1851-61)	Hsien-feng	40.00	62.50	90.00	165.00

100 CASH

CAST BRASS
Obv: Type C.

C#	Date	Emperor	Good	VG	Fine	VF
14-5	ND(1851-61)	Hsien-feng	20.00	25.00	35.00	50.00

500 CASH

CAST BRASS
Obv: Type C.

C#	Date	Emperor	Good	VG	Fine	VF
14-6	ND(1851-61)	Hsien-feng	80.00	110.00	150.00	250.00

1000 CASH

CAST BRASS
Obv: Type C.
Illustration reduced, actual size 66mm.

C#	Date	Emperor	Good	VG	Fine	VF
14-7	ND(1851-61)	Hsien-feng	165.00	250.00	350.00	600.00

KIANGNAN

A district in eastern China made up of Anhwei (Anhui) and Kiangsu (Jiangsu) provinces. In 1667 the province of Kiangnan was divided into the present provinces of Anhwei (Anhui) and Kiangsu (Jiangsu). In 1723 Nanking, formerly the capital of Kiangnan, was made the capital of Liang-Chiang Chiang (an administrative area consisting of Anhwei (Anhui), Kiangsu (Jiangsu), and Kiangsi (Jiangxi) provinces).

Always highly regarded because of location, agriculture and manufacturing, Kiangnan has frequently been sought after by contending forces.

The Nanking Mint had been active during imperial times. Modern minting facilities began operations in 1897. A second mint was planned for the Kiangnan Arsenal in Shanghai in 1905. Mints for copper coins also operated in Chingkiang (Qingjiang) in central Kiangsu and at Soochow which is further south. A silver mint was planned for Shanghai in 1921. The Nanking Mint, the most important of the group, burned down in 1929. The Nationalist Government Central Mint was completed in Shanghai in 1930 and opened in 1933.

EMPIRE

MILLED COINAGE

CASH

COPPER
Obv: Type A

Hsu#	Date	Mintage	VG	Fine	VF	XF
261	ND(1898)	—	15.00	25.00	35.00	75.00

NOTE: This coin has been erroneously attributed to Ningpo in Chekiang (Zhejang) and to Changchow in Fukien (Fujian). The coin was minted at Nanking from dies produced by the Heaton Mint.

Obv: Smaller characters.
Rev: Mint mark written differently.

Y#	Date	Mintage	VG	Fine	VF	XF
—	ND	—	90.00	135.00	200.00	325.00

5 CENTS

1.3000 g, .820 SILVER, .0343 oz ASW
Rev: Circled dragon.

Y#	Date	Mintage	Fine	VF	XF	Unc
141	ND(1898)	.100	20.00	30.00	80.00	180.00

Y#	Date	Mintage	Fine	VF	XF	Unc
141	ND(1898)	—	—	—	Proof	700.00

Rev: W/o circle around dragon.

Y#	Date	Mintage	Fine	VF	XF	Unc
141a	ND(1898)	I.A.	10.00	15.00	30.00	50.00
	CD1899	3,812	50.00	100.00	150.00	300.00
	CD1900	.618	10.00	15.00	30.00	50.00

NOTE: Later date (CD1901) exists for this type.

10 CENTS

2.6000 g, .820 SILVER, .0686 oz ASW
Rev: Circled dragon.

Y#	Date	Mintage	Fine	VF	XF	Unc
142	ND(1898)	8.000	12.00	25.00	50.00	150.00
	ND(1898)	—	—	—	Proof	700.00

Y#	Date	Mintage	Fine	VF	XF	Unc
142.1	CD1898	I.A.	7.00	15.00	25.00	45.00

Rev: W/o circle around dragon w/small rosettes at sides.

Y#	Date	Mintage	Fine	VF	XF	Unc
142a	CD1898	I.A.	3.50	7.00	15.00	30.00

Rev: Large rosettes at sides of dragons.

Y#	Date	Mintage	Fine	VF	XF	Unc
142a.1	CD1898	I.A.	3.50	7.00	15.00	30.00

Obv: Large characters in center, small characters in outer ring.

Y#	Date	Mintage	Fine	VF	XF	Unc
142a.2	CD1899	10.784	2.25	4.50	9.00	30.00

Obv: Small characters in center, large characters in outer ring.

Y#	Date	Mintage	Fine	VF	XF	Unc
142a.3	CD1899	I.A.	2.25	4.50	9.00	30.00

Y#	Date	Mintage	Fine	VF	XF	Unc
142a.4	CD1900	5.460	2.50	5.00	10.00	35.00

20 CENTS

5.3000 g, .820 SILVER, .1397 oz ASW
Obv: Rosettes at 2 and 10 o'clock.
Rev: Circle around dragon.

Y#	Date	Mintage	Fine	VF	XF	Unc
143	ND(1898)	7.000	17.50	40.00	70.00	180.00

Y#	Date	Mintage	Fine	VF	XF	Unc
143.1	CD1898	I.A.	15.00	35.00	65.00	100.00

Obv: Large characters in outer ring. Rev: Large English letters, w/o circle around dragon.

Y#	Date	Mintage	Fine	VF	XF	Unc
143a	CD1898	I.A.	3.75	7.50	15.00	35.00

Obv: Small characters in outer ring.
Rev: Small English letters.

Y#	Date	Mintage	Fine	VF	XF	Unc
143a.1	CD1898	I.A.	3.75	7.50	15.00	35.00

Rev: Old type dragon w/long face, flanked by short rosettes.

Y#	Date	Mintage	Fine	VF	XF	Unc
143a.2	CD1899	11.096	3.50	7.50	15.00	35.00

Rev: New type dragon w/shorter face and larger forehead, flanked by long rosettes.

Y#	Date	Mintage	Fine	VF	XF	Unc
143a.3	CD1899	I.A.	5.00	10.00	25.00	60.00

Rev: Old type dragon w/long face, flanked by long rosettes.

Y#	Date	Mintage	Fine	VF	XF	Unc
143a.4	CD1900	5.796	5.00	10.00	25.00	60.00

Rev: New type dragon w/shorter face and larger forehead.

Y#	Date	Mintage	Fine	VF	XF	Unc
143a.5	CD1900	I.A.	10.00	25.00	50.00	100.00

50 CENTS

13.2000 g, .860 SILVER, .3650 oz ASW
Rev: Circled dragon

Y#	Date	Mintage	Fine	VF	XF	Unc
144	ND(1898)	.100	175.00	325.00	500.00	1200.
	ND(1898)	—	—	—	Proof	2500.

Rev: W/o circle around dragon.

Y#	Date	Mintage	Fine	VF	XF	Unc
144a	CD1899	155 pcs.	—	1000.	2000.	3500.
	CD1900	—	500.00	1000.	1750.	3000.

DOLLAR

27.0000 g, .900 SILVER, .7814 oz ASW
Rev: Circled dragon. Normal edge reeding.

Y#	Date	Mintage	Fine	VF	XF	Unc
145	ND(1898)	1.603	200.00	400.00	800.00	1500.

Ornamented edge

Y#	Date	Mintage	Fine	VF	XF	Unc
145.1	ND(1898)	I.A.	125.00	175.00	300.00	800.00

Rev: W/o circle around old style dragon.

Y#	Date	Mintage	Fine	VF	XF	Unc
145a.1	CD1898	I.A.	25.00	75.00	150.00	600.00

Similar to Y#145a.1 but w/smaller letters.

Y#	Date	Mintage	Fine	VF	XF	Unc
145a.2	CD1898	I. A.	100.00	175.00	300.00	800.00
	CD1899	2.039	30.00	75.00	150.00	600.00

Obv: Chinese date characters *Wu Shu* reversed.

Y#	Date	Mintage	Fine	VF	XF	Unc
145a.18	CD1898	I.A.	1500.	2750.	—	—

Rev: Redesigned dragon w/shorter face and larger forehead, similar to 1900.

Y#	Date	Mintage	Fine	VF	XF	Unc
145a.3	CD1899	I. A.	100.00	150.00	250.00	750.00

Rev: Large scales on dragon.
26.7 g

Y#	Date	Mintage	Fine	VF	XF	Unc
145a.4	CD1900	2.531	30.00	75.00	150.00	600.00

Rev: Small scales on dragon.

Y#	Date	Mintage	Fine	VF	XF	Unc
145a.20	CD1900	I.A.	22.50	50.00	125.00	600.00

PATTERNS (Pn)

(Including off metal strikes)

KM#	Date	Mintage	Identification	Mkt.Val.
Pn1	ND(1898)	—	1 Dollar, Silver, plain edge, Y145	5500.
Pn2	ND(1898)	—	1 Dollar, Copper, Y145	1200.

KIANGSI PROVINCE

Jiangxi, Kiangsee

A province located in southeastern China. Mostly hilly with some mountains on the borders that produce coal and tungsten. Some of China's finest porcelain comes from this province. Kiangsi was visited by Marco Polo. A mint was opened in Nanchang in 1729, closed in 1733, reopened in 1736 and operated with reasonable continuity from that time. Modern machinery was introduced in 1901 although it only produced copper coins. The mint closed amidst internal problems in the 1920's.

EMPIRE

CASH

Obv: Type A.

C#	Date	Emperor	Good	VG	Fine	VF
15-3	ND(1821-51)	Tao-kuang	.50	.85	1.50	2.00

CAST ZINC

C#	Date	Emperor	Good	VG	Fine	VF
15-3a	ND(1821-51)	Tao-kuang	—	—	Rare	—

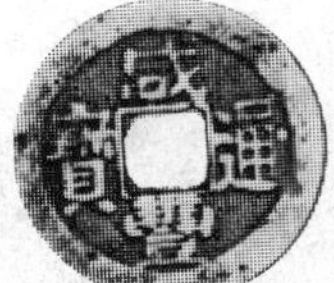

CAST BRASS
Obv: Type A.

C#	Date	Emperor	Good	VG	Fine	VF
15-4	ND(1851-61)	Hsien-feng	1.00	2.00	3.00	4.00

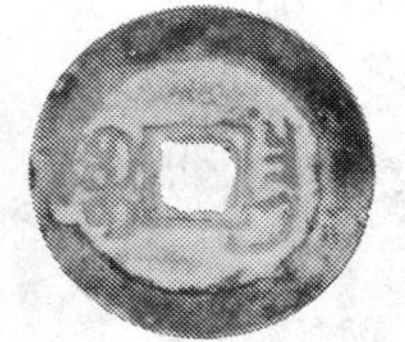

Obv: Type A.

C#	Date	Emperor	Good	VG	Fine	VF
15-7	ND(1862-74)	T'ung-chih	1.20	3.00	4.00	5.00

Obv: Type A. Rev: Type 1 mint mark.

C#	Date	Emperor	Good	VG	Fine	VF
15-9	ND(1875-1908)	Kuang-hsu	4.50	6.50	12.00	15.00

10 CASH

CAST BRASS
Obv: Type B-1.

C#	Date	Emperor	Good	VG	Fine	VF
15-5	ND(1851-61)	Hsien-feng	3.00	6.00	10.00	30.00

Obv: Type B.

C#	Date	Emperor	Good	VG	Fine	VF
15-8	ND(1862-74)	T'ung-chih	—	—	Rare	—

Obv: Type B.

C#	Date	Emperor	Good	VG	Fine	VF
15-10	ND(1875-1908)	Kuang-hsu	—	—	Rare	—

50 CASH

CAST COPPER
Obv: Type B-1.

C#	Date	Emperor	Good	VG	Fine	VF
15.6	ND(1851-61)	Hsien-feng	8.00	16.00	30.00	60.00

CAST BRASS

C#	Date	Emperor	Good	VG	Fine	VF
15-6.1	ND(1851-61)	Hsien-feng	6.00	12.00	18.00	35.00

MILLED COINAGE

Horizontal rosette

Vertical rosette

10 CASH

COPPER
Obv: Vertical rosette at center.
Rev: Province name spelled KIANG-SEE.

Y#	Date	Mintage	VG	Fine	VF	XF
149	ND	—	3.25	8.00	12.50	22.50

Obv: Horizontal rosette at center.

Y#	Date	Mintage	VG	Fine	VF	XF
149.1	ND	—	3.25	8.00	12.50	22.50

Obv: Different Manchu word at right.
Rev: Circled dragon.

Y#	Date	Mintage	VG	Fine	VF	XF
149.2	ND	—	—	—	Rare	—

NOTE: May be a pattern.

Obv: Manchu reading *Pao Yuan*.
Rev: Province name spelled KIANG-SI; 2 stars at either side of dragon.

Y#	Date	Mintage	Fine	VF	XF	Unc
150	ND	—	6.00	11.00	17.50	35.00

Obv: Manchu reading *Pao Ch'ang* at center and Chinese reading *Ku P'ing* at 3 and 9 o'clock.

Y#	Date	Mintage	Fine	VF	XF	Unc
150.1	ND	—	3.00	6.00	12.00	25.00

Obv: Manchu reading *Pao Ch'ang* at 3 and 9 o'clock, horizontal rosette in center.

Y#	Date	Mintage	Fine	VF	XF	Unc
150.2	ND	—	1.00	2.00	5.00	20.00

BRASS

Y#	Date	Mintage	Fine	VF	XF	Unc
150.2a	ND	—	5.00	10.00	20.00	40.00

COPPER
Obv: Vertical rosette in center.

Y#	Date	Mintage	Fine	VF	XF	Unc
150.3	ND	—	1.00	2.00	5.00	20.00

Obv: Horizontal rosette. Rev: 1 star at either

side of dragon, large English lettering.

Y#	Date	Mintage	Fine	VF	XF	Unc
150.4	ND	—	1.00	2.00	5.00	20.00

BRASS

150.4a	ND	—	5.00	9.00	17.50	35.00

COPPER
Obv: Vertical rosette.

150.5	ND	—	1.00	2.00	5.00	20.00

Rev: Smaller English lettering, 1 star at either side of dragon.

150.6	ND	—	1.00	2.00	5.00	20.00

Obv: Small rosette center.
Rev: 1 star at either side of dragon.

150.7	ND	—	6.00	11.00	17.50	35.00

Rev: 3 stars at either side of dragon.

150.8	ND	—	12.00	20.00	30.00	60.00

Obv: Manchu *Pao Ch'ang* at 3 and 9 o'clock.
Rev: Province name spelled KIANG-SI; front view dragon, mountain below pearl.

Y#	Date	Mintage	VG	Fine	VF	XF
152	ND	—	2.50	4.00	6.00	12.00

Obv: Horizontal rosette in center and Manchu *Pao Ch'ang* at 3 and 9 o'clock.

152.1	ND	—	2.50	4.00	6.00	12.00

Obv: Horizontal rosette in center and Manchu *Pao Ch'ang* at 3 and 9 o'clock, small character '10'.

152.2	ND	—	5.00	12.00	17.50	27.50

Obv: Horizontal rosette in center and Manchu *Pao Ch'ang* at 3 and 9 o'clock, large character '10'.

Rev: W/o mountain below dragon.

Y#	Date	Mintage	VG	Fine	VF	XF
152.3	ND	—	3.50	8.00	12.00	17.50

Obv: Vertical rosette in center.

152.7	ND	—	—	—	—	—

Obv: Horizontal rosette in center, small character '10'.

152.4	ND	—	3.50	8.00	12.00	17.50

Obv: Manchu *Pao Ch'ang* in center, Chinese *K'u P'ing* at 3 and 9 o'clock. Rev: W/o mountain below pearl, dragon's body repositioned.

152.5	ND	—	3.50	8.00	12.00	17.50

Rev: Mountain below dragon.

152.6	ND	—	3.25	7.50	11.00	16.00

Rev. leg: KIANG-SEE PROVINCE above front view dragon.

153	ND	—	2.00	4.50	7.00	11.00

Obv: Manchu *Pao Ch'ang* at center and Chinese *K'u P'ing* at 3 and 9 o'clock.

153.1	ND	—	.80	2.00	3.50	7.00

Obv: Small Manchu *Pao Ch'ang* at 3 and 9 o'clock, small horizontal rosette in center.

153.2	ND	—	.80	2.00	3.50	7.00

Obv: Small vertical rosette in center.

153.3	ND	—	2.00	5.00	10.00	17.50

NOTE: All 4 varieties of Y#153 are found with and without a swirl on the pearl below dragon's mouth.

Rev. leg: KIANG-SI above flying dragon.

154	ND	—	40.00	60.00	80.00	100.00

KIANGSU/KIANGSOO PROVINCE

Jiangsu

A province located on the east coast of China. One of the smallest and most densely populated of all Chinese provinces. A mint opened in Soochow in 1667, but closed shortly after in 1670. A new mint opened in 1734 for producing cast coins and had continuous operation until about 1870. Modern equipment was introduced in 1898 and a second mint was opened in 1904. Both mints closed down production in 1906. Taels were produced in Shanghai by local silversmiths as early as 1856. These saw limited circulation in the immediate area.

EMPIRE

Kiangsu Mint

CASH

Obv: Type A.
Narrow rims.

Sch.#1515

C#	Date	Emperor	Good	VG	Fine	VF
16-3	ND(1821-51)	Tao-kuang	.50	1.00	2.00	4.00

Medium rims.

16-3.1	ND(1821-51)	Tao-kuang	.50	1.00	2.00	4.00

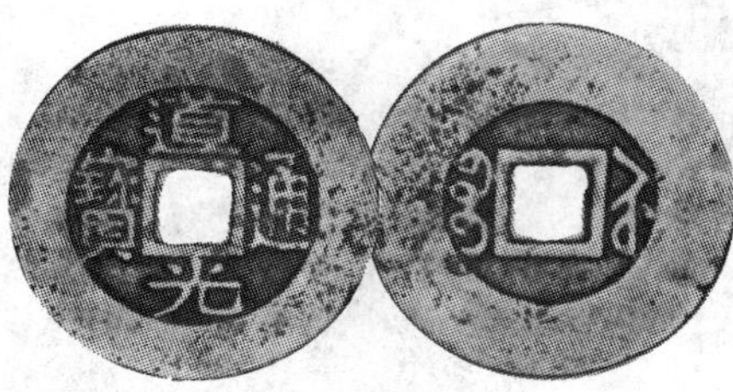

Wide rims.

16-3.2	ND(1821-51)	Tao-kuang	30.00	50.00	70.00	110.00

Narrow rims.

Sch.#1536

16-4	ND(1851-61)	Hsien-feng	1.00	2.00	3.00	4.50

Medium rims.

16-4.1	ND(1851-61)	Hsien-feng	1.00	2.00	3.00	4.50

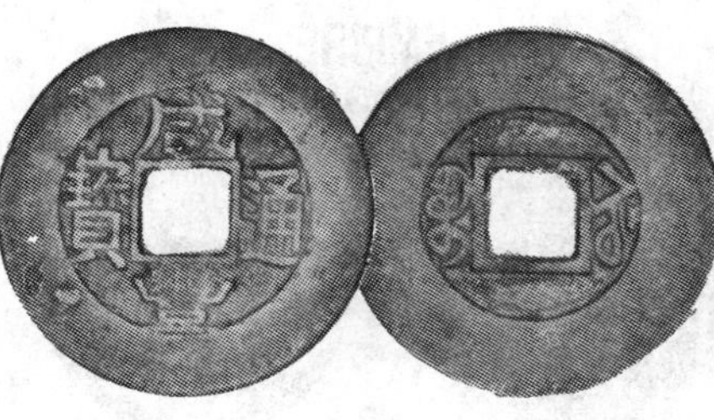

Wide rims.

16-4.2	ND(1851-61)	Hsien-feng	—	—	Rare	—

Rev: Crescent above.

Sch.#1536

16-4.3	ND(1851-61)	Hsien-feng	4.25	8.50	17.50	35.00

Sch.#1556

C#	Date	Emperor	Good	VG	Fine	VF
16-11	ND(1862-74)	T'ung-chih	2.75	5.50	9.00	15.00

Obv: Type A.

C#	Date	Emperor	Good	VG	Fine	VF
16-12	ND(1875-1908)	Kuang-hsu	2.25	4.50	8.00	13.00

Rev: Circle above.

C#	Date	Emperor	Good	VG	Fine	VF
16-12.1	ND(1875-1908)	Kuang-hsu	3.00	6.00	10.00	16.00

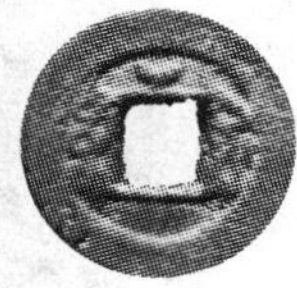

Rev: Crescent above.

C#	Date	Emperor	Good	VG	Fine	VF
16-12.2	ND(1875-1908)	Kuang-hsu	3.00	6.00	10.00	16.00

5 CASH

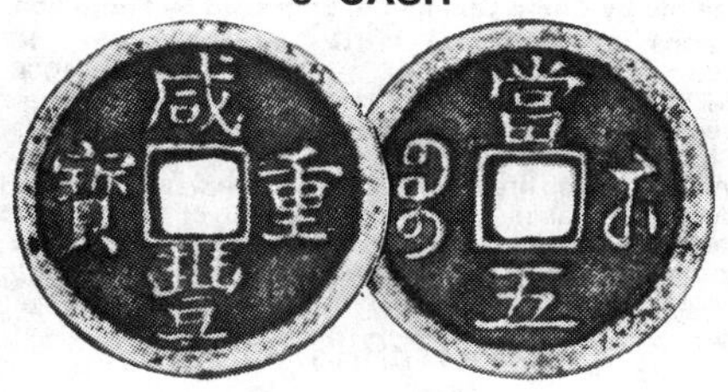

CAST BRASS
Obv: Type B-1.

C#	Date	Emperor	Good	VG	Fine	VF
16-5	ND(1851-61)	Hsien-feng	30.00	45.00	65.00	100.00

CAST IRON

C#	Date	Emperor	Good	VG	Fine	VF
16-5a	ND(1851-61)	Hsien-feng	40.00	55.00	80.00	120.00

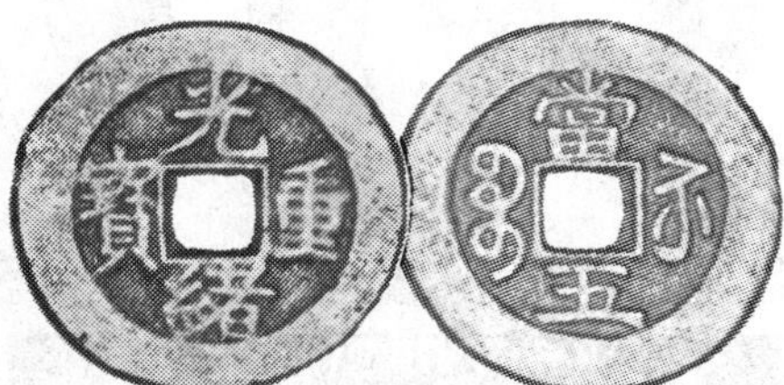

CAST BRASS
Obv: Type B.

C#	Date	Emperor	Good	VG	Fine	VF
16-13	ND(1875-1908)	Kuang-hsu	30.00	40.00	50.00	75.00

10 CASH

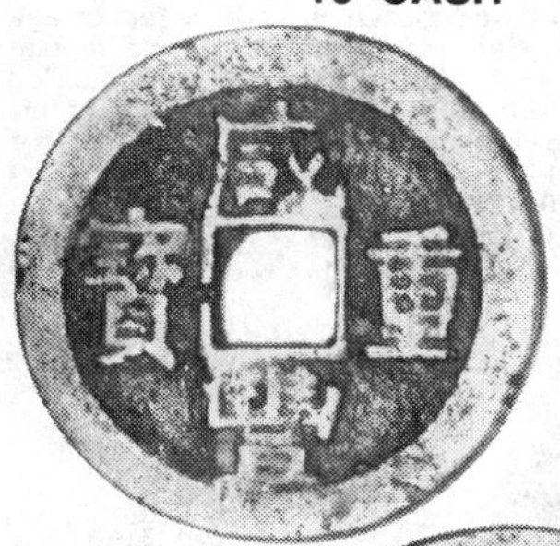

CAST BRASS, 36-40mm

Obv: Type B-1.

C#	Date	Emperor	Good	VG	Fine	VF
16-6	ND(1851-61)	Hsien-feng	5.00	7.50	15.00	25.00

30-34mm

Sch.#1594

C#	Date	Emperor	Good	VG	Fine	VF
16-6.1	ND(1851-61)	Hsien-feng	5.00	7.50	10.00	20.00

CAST IRON

C#	Date	Emperor	Good	VG	Fine	VF
16-6a	ND(1851-61)	Hsien-feng	27.50	50.00	75.00	100.00

CAST BRASS
Obv: Type B.

C#	Date	Emperor	Good	VG	Fine	VF
16-14	ND(1875-1908)	Kuang-hsu	—	—	Rare	—

20 CASH

CAST BRASS, 39mm
Obv: Type B-1.

C#	Date	Emperor	Good	VG	Fine	VF
16-7	ND(1851-61)	Hsien-feng	35.00	55.00	75.00	100.00

30 CASH

CAST BRASS, 46mm
Obv: Type B-1.

C#	Date	Emperor	Good	VG	Fine	VF
16-8	ND(1851-61)	Hsien-feng	85.00	120.00	150.00	200.00

Rev: Crescent in upper left and right corners; dot in lower left and right corners.

C#	Date	Emperor	Good	VG	Fine	VF
16-8.1	ND(1851-61)	Hsien-feng	250.00	350.00	500.00	750.00

50 CASH

CAST COPPER, 50mm
Obv: Type B-1. Rev: Small characters.

C#	Date	Emperor	Good	VG	Fine	VF
16-9.1	ND(1851-61)	Hsien-feng	8.00	22.00	35.00	60.00

CAST BRASS, 55mm
Rev: Large characters.

C#	Date	Emperor	Good	VG	Fine	VF
16-9.2	ND(1851-61)	Hsien-feng	8.00	22.00	35.00	60.00

100 CASH

CAST BRASS
Obv: Type C.
Obv. and rev: Small characters.

C#	Date	Emperor	Good	VG	Fine	VF
16-10	ND(1851-61)	Hsien-feng	10.00	25.00	35.00	85.00

Obv. and rev: Large characters.

Sch.#1589

C#	Date	Emperor	Good	VG	Fine	VF
16-10.1	ND(1851-61)	Hsien-feng	10.00	25.00	35.00	85.00

MILLED COINAGE

CASH

BRASS
Obv: Type A.

Hsu#	Date	Mintage	Fine	VF	XF	Unc
85	ND ca.1890	—	35.00	55.00	90.00	120.00

10 CASH

BRASS

Y#	Date	Mintage	Fine	VF	XF	Unc
—	ND(1898)	—	—	—	Rare	—

Shanghai Coinage

An important port city in Kiangsu (Jiangsu) province. Although there was no mint in Shanghai prior to the 1930's a number of coins were minted for Shanghai by silversmiths.

5 CH'IEN

SILVER, 18.40 g
Issued by Wang Yung-sheng. Engraved by Wan Ch'uan. Similar to K#902.

Kann#	Year	Date	VG	Fine	VF	XF
908	6	(1856)	—	—	600.00	900.00

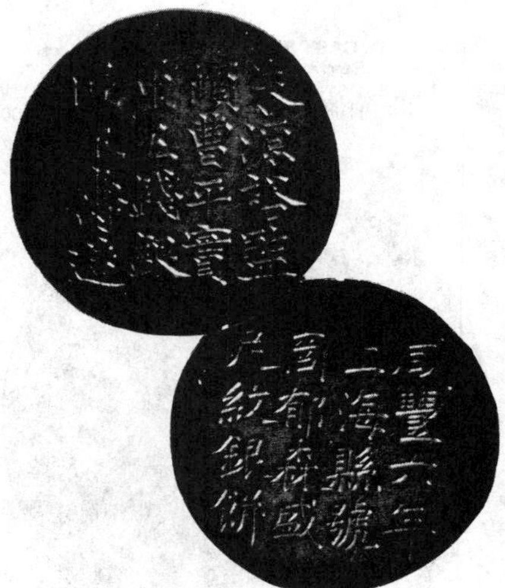

Issued by Yu Shen-sheng. Engraved by Wang Shou.

Kann#	Year	Date	VG	Fine	VF	XF
907	6	(1856)	—	—	500.00	800.00

Issued by Ching Cheng-chi. Engraved by Wan Ch'uan.

Kann#	Year	Date	VG	Fine	VF	XF
910	6	(1856)	—	—	500.00	800.00

LIANG (TAEL)

SILVER, 36.70 g
Issued by Wang Yung-sheng. Engraved by Wan Ch'uan.

Kann#	Year	Date	VG	Fine	VF	XF
900	6	(1856)	—	—	800.00	1300.

Issued by Yu Sen-sheng. Engraved by P'ing Cheng.

Kann#	Year	Date	VG	Fine	VF	XF
902	6	(1856)	—	—	700.00	1000.

Issued by Yu Sen-sheng. Engraved by Feng-nien.

Kann#	Year	Date	VG	Fine	VF	XF
901	6	(1856)	—	—	700.00	1000.

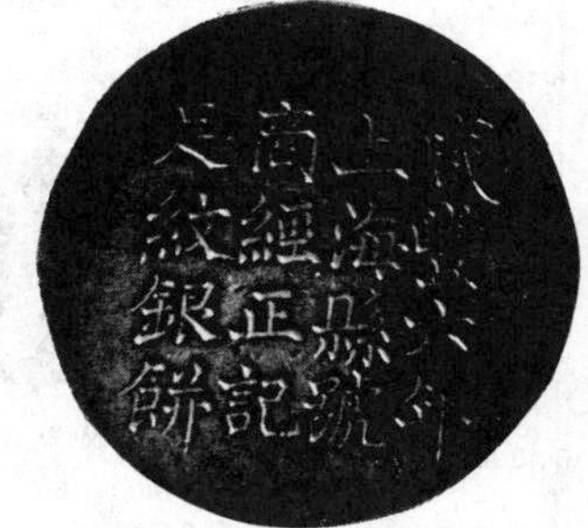

Issued by Ching Cheng-chi. Engraved by Feng-nien.

Kann#	Year	Date	VG	Fine	VF	XF
903	6	(1856)	—	—	700.00	1000.

K#900-910 above are known as "Silversmith" Taels because each bears the name of a silver smelting firm in Shanghai. The engravers' names are all given names; their surnames are unknown. The coins were authorized by the Taotai (a government official) of Shanghai to facilitate foreign trade and to replace the vanishing Mexican 8 Reales which had become very scarce due to hoarding Counterfeits exist.

PATTERNS (Pn)

(Including off metal strikes)

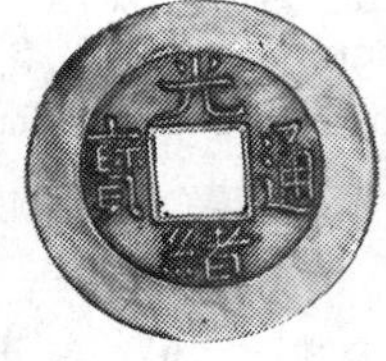

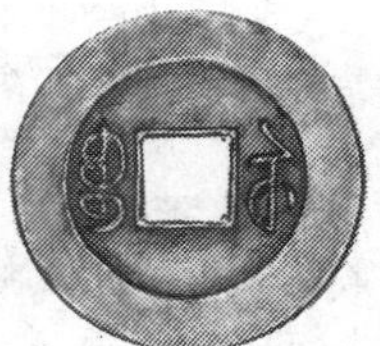

KM#	Date	Mintage	Identification	Mkt.Val.
Pn1	ND ca.1890	—	1 Cash, Brass, Hsu 85.1	Rare

KIRIN PROVINCE

Jilin

A province of northeast China that was formed in 1945. Before that it was one of the three original provinces of Manchuria. Besides growing corn, wheat and tobacco, there is also coal mining. An arsenal in Kirin (Jilin) opened in 1881 and was chosen as a source for coinage attempts. In 1884 Tael trials were struck and regular coinage began in 1895. Modern equipment was installed in a new mint in Kirin (Jilin) in 1901. The issues of this mint were very prolific and many varieties exist due to the use of hand cut dies for the earlier issues. The mint burned down in 1911.

EMPIRE

CASH

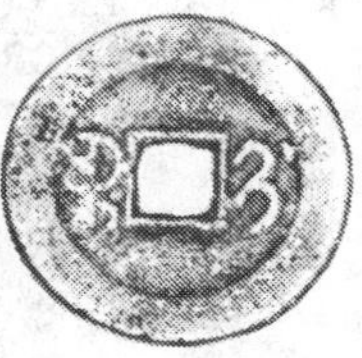

CAST BRASS
Obv: Type A.

C#	Date	Emperor	Good	VG	Fine	VF
17-1	(1875-1908)	Kuang-hsu	15.00	25.00	35.00	50.00

NOTE: This coin is sometimes erroneously attributed to Chichou (Chichow) in Chihli (Hebei) province, which used this mint mark in the Hsien-feng and earlier reigns.

10 CASH

CAST BRASS
Obv: Type C.

C#	Date	Emperor	Good	VG	Fine	VF
17-2	(1875-1908)					
		Kuang-hsu	—	—	Rare	—

MILLED COINAGE

NOTE: Errors in the English legends are very common in the Kirin coinage. It has been estimated there are over 2500 die varieties of Kirin (Jilin) silver coins and more than 1000 varieties of copper 10 Cash. Listed here are basic types and major varieties only.

CASH

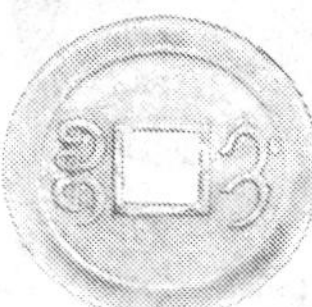

BRASS, struck
Obv: Type A.

Hsu#	Date	Mintage	Fine	VF	XF	Unc
481	ND	—	30.00	50.00	75.00	100.00

NOTE: This coin is sometimes erroneously attributed to Chichou (Chichow) in Chihli (Hebei) province, which used this mint mark in the Hsien-feng and earlier reigns. Many varieties exist.

2 CASH

COPPER

Y#	Date	Mintage	VG	Fine	VF	XF
175	ND	—	80.00	120.00	160.00	250.00

10 CASH(ES)

COPPER

174	ND	—	—	—	Rare	—

5 CENTS

SILVER, 1.27 g
Obv: Flower vase center.
Rev: Cross before and after weight:
CANDARINS .36.

Y#	Date	Mintage	Fine	VF	XF	Unc
179	ND	—	10.00	25.00	45.00	85.00

Rev: W/o crosses flanking weight.

Y#	Date	Mintage	Fine	VF	XF	Unc
179.1	ND	—	5.00	10.00	20.00	50.00
Kann#394						
	CD1899	—	6.50	12.50	25.00	60.00
Kann#416						
	CD1900	—	10.00	20.00	30.00	75.00

NOTE: Later dates (CD1906-1908) exist for this type.

Obv: Yin-yang in center.

Y#	Date	Mintage	Fine	VF	XF	Unc
179a	CD1900	—	7.50	15.00	30.00	60.00

NOTE: Later dates (CD1901-1905) exist for this type.

10 CENTS

SILVER, 2.55 g
Obv: Small flower vase center.
Rev: Cross before and after weight:
CANDARINS .76.

180	ND	—	5.50	11.50	22.50	65.00

Obv: Large flower vase center.
Rev: W/o crosses flanking weight.

Kann#393						
180.1	CD1899	—	6.50	12.50	25.00	60.00
Kann#416						
	CD1900	—	6.50	12.50	25.00	60.00
	ND	—	5.50	11.50	22.50	50.00

NOTE: Later dates (CD1906-1907) exist for this type.

Obv: Yin-yang in center.

180a	CD1900	—	7.50	15.00	30.00	75.00

NOTE: Later dates (CD1901-1905) exist for this type.

20 CENTS

SILVER, 5.10 g
Obv: Flower vase center.

181	CD1899	—	6.50	12.50	25.00	50.00
	CD1900	—	7.50	15.00	30.00	60.00
	ND	—	7.50	15.00	30.00	60.00

NOTE: Later dates (CD1906-1908) exist for this type.

Obv: Yin-yang in center.

181a	CD1900	—	7.50	15.00	30.00	60.00

NOTE: Later dates (CD1901-1905) exist for this type.

50 CENTS

SILVER, 13.10 g
Obv: Flower vase center w/rosette at either side.
Rev: W/o crosses flanking weight.

182	ND	—	15.00	25.00	50.00	150.00

Obv: Rosette at either side. Rev: Crosses before and after weight: *3 CANDARENS 6.*

182.1	ND	—	15.00	25.00	50.00	150.00

Obv: W/o rosettes. Rev: W/o crosses flanking weight.

182.2	ND	—	—	—	—	—

Y#	Date	Mintage	Fine	VF	XF	Unc
182.3	CD1899	—	25.00	45.00	80.00	200.00
	CD1900	—	20.00	35.00	60.00	150.00

NOTE: Later dates (CD1906-1908) exist for this type.

Obv: Figure-8 yin-yang in center.

182a	CD1900	—	20.00	35.00	60.00	150.00

DOLLAR

SILVER, 26.10 g
Obv: Flower vase center.
Rev: Small rosettes before and after weight
7 CANDARINS 2 or 7 CAINDARINS 2.

183	CD1899	—	60.00	100.00	250.00	500.00
	CD1900	—	60.00	100.00	300.00	600.00
	ND	—	60.00	100.00	250.00	500.00

NOTE: Later dates (CD1906-1908) exist for this type.

Obv: Large rosettes.
Rev: W/o rosettes flanking weight.

183.1	ND	—	750.00	1350.	2500.	4500.

Obv: Small rosettes. Rev: Small rosettes before and after weight 7 CANDARINS 2.

Y#	Date	Mintage	Fine	VF	XF	Unc
183.3	ND	—	100.00	135.00	175.00	500.00

Obv: Small leaves out of left of basket. Rev: Similar to Y#183.2.

Y#	Date	Mintage	Fine	VF	XF	Unc
183.4	ND	—	60.00	100.00	150.00	400.00

Obv: Figure '8' Yin-yang in center.

Y#	Date	Mintage	Fine	VF	XF	Unc
183a	CD1900	—	100.00	200.00	350.00	850.00

TAEL SERIES

CH'IEN (MACE)

SILVER, 3.60 g
Rev: Numeral 1 in simple Chinese.

Kann#	Year	Date	Fine	VF	XF	Unc
919	10	(1885)	—	—	500.00	750.00

Rev: Different, more complicated character for 1.

Kann#	Year	Date	Fine	VF	XF	Unc
920	10	(1885)	—	—	400.00	650.00

3 CH'IEN

SILVER, 10.80 g
Vertical edge reeding.

Kann#	Year	Date	Fine	VF	XF	Unc
918	10	(1884)	—	—	500.00	750.00

Diagonal edge reeding.

Kann#	Year	Date	Fine	VF	XF	Unc
918b	10	(1885)	—	—	500.00	750.00

5 CH'IEN

(1/2 Tael)

SILVER, 17.80 g

Kann#	Year	Date	Fine	VF	XF	Unc
917	10	(1885)	—	—	850.00	1500.

7 CH'IEN

SILVER, 25.40 g

Kann#	Year	Date	Fine	VF	XF	Unc
916	10	(1885)	—	—	3500.	5000.

TAEL

SILVER, 35.50 g

Kann#	Year	Date	Fine	VF	XF	Unc
915	10	(1885)	—	—	Rare	—

NOTE: Superior Goodman sale 6-91 AU realized $35,200.

PATTERNS (Pn)

(Including off metal strikes)

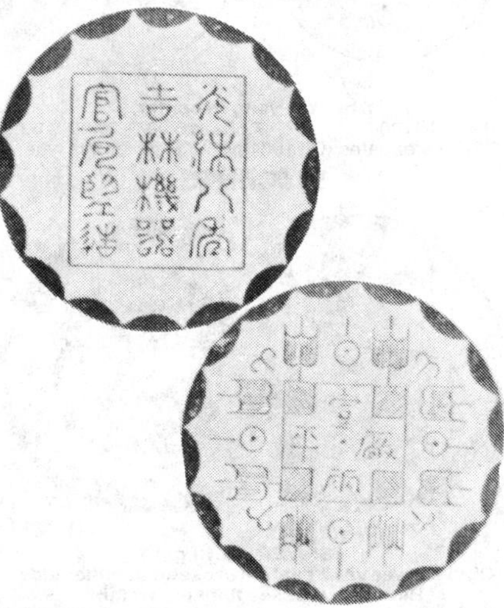

KM#	Date	Mintage	Identification	Mkt.Val.
Pn1	Yr.8 (1882)	—	1 Tael, Silver, K914	—
Pn2	Yr.8 (1882)	—	1 Tael, Copper, K914x	—
Pn3	Yr.10 (1884)	—	1 Ch'ien, White metal, K920	—
Pn4	Yr.10 (1884)	—	3 Ch'ien, White metal, K918	—
Pn5	Yr.10 (1884)	—	3 Ch'ien, Brass, K918	1500.
Pn6	Yr.10 (1884)	—	5 Ch'ien, White metal, K917	—
Pn7	Yr.10 (1884)	—	7 Ch'ien, White metal, K916	—
Pn8	Yr.10 (1884)	—	1 Tael, White metal, K915	—

KWANGSI/KWANGSEA

Guangxi

A hilly region in southeast China with many forests. Large amounts of rice are grown adjacent to the many rivers. A mint opened in Kweilin in 1667, closed in 1670, reopened in 1679, closed again in 1681. It reopened in the mid-1700's and was a rather prolific issuer of Cash coins. In 1905 the government allowed modern mints to be established in Kwangsi (Guangxi) at Nanning (1905) and Kweilin (1905). The Nanning Mint began operation in 1919 and closed in 1923. In 1920 a new mint was opened at Wuchow and operated sporadically until 1929. In 1938 part of the Shanghai Central Mint was moved to Kweilin where it operated until at least 1945 and perhaps as late as 1949.

EMPIRE

CASH

Obv: Type A.

C#	Date	Emperor	Good	VG	Fine	VF
18-3	ND(1821-51)	Kuang-hsu	.50	1.00	1.75	3.00

Rev: Dot below left.

C#	Date	Emperor	Good	VG	Fine	VF
18-3.1	ND(1821-51)	Tao-kuang	.60	1.00	2.00	3.00

Obv: Type A.

C#	Date	Emperor	Good	VG	Fine	VF
18-4	ND(1851-61)	Hsien-feng	1.00	2.00	3.00	5.00

Obv: Type A-2.
Rev: Large Manchu words.

C#	Date	Emperor	Good	VG	Fine	VF
18-7	ND(1862-74)	T'ung-chih	2.50	3.50	6.50	9.00

Rev: Small Manchu words.

C#	Date	Emperor	Good	VG	Fine	VF
18-7.1	ND(1862-74)	T'ung-chih	2.50	3.50	6.50	9.00

Rev: Circle above.

Sch.#1566

C#	Date	Emperor	Good	VG	Fine	VF
18-7.2	ND(1862-74)	T'ung-chih	5.50	8.50	13.50	25.00

Obv: Type A.

C#	Date	Emperor	Good	VG	Fine	VF
18-9	ND(1875-1908)	Kuang-hsu	5.50	8.50	13.50	25.00

10 CASH

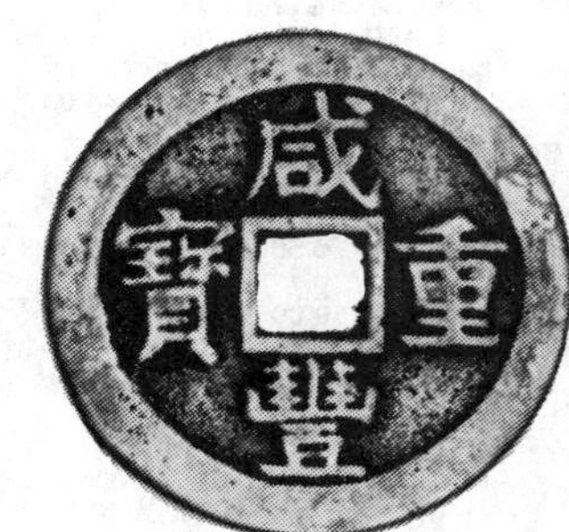

CAST BRASS
Obv: Type B-1.

C#	Date	Emperor	Good	VG	Fine	VF
18-5	ND(1851-61)	Hsien-feng	3.00	7.00	9.00	15.00

Obv: Type B-2.

C#	Date	Emperor	Good	VG	Fine	VF
18-8	ND(1862-74)	T'ung-chih	—	—	Rare	—

Obv: Type B.

C#	Date	Emperor	Good	VG	Fine	VF
18-10	ND(1875-1908)	Kuang-hsu	—	—	Rare	—

50 CASH

CAST BRASS
Obv: Type B-1.

C#	Date	Emperor	Good	VG	Fine	VF
18-6	ND(1851-61)	Hsien-feng	40.00	60.00	80.00	165.00

KWANGTUNG PROVINCE

Guangdong

A province located on the southeast coast of China. Kwangtung (Guangdong) lies mostly in the tropics and has both mountains and plains. Its coastline is nearly 800 miles long and provides many good harbors. Because of the location of Guangzhou (Canton) in the province, Kwangtung (Guangdong) was the first to be visited by seaborne foreign traders. Hong Kong was ceded to Great Britain after the First Opium War in 1841. Kowloon was later ceded to Britain in 1860 and the New Territories (100 year lease) in 1898 and Macao to Portugal in 1887, Kwangchowwan was leased to France in 1898 (a property was restored in 1946). A modern mint opened Guangzhou (Canton) in 1889 with Edward Wyon as superintendent. The mint was a large issuer of coins until it closed in 1931. The Nationalists reopened the mint briefly in 1949, striking a few silver dollars, before abandoning the mainland for their retreat to Taiwan.

The large island of Hainan was split off from Kwangtung (Guangdong) Province in 1988 and established as a separate province.

Hong Kong was returned to China by Britain on July 1, 1997 and established as a special administrative region, retaining its own coinage. Macao returns to China a few weeks before the end of 1999.

EMPIRE

CASH

CAST BRASS
Obv: Type A.

Sch.#1522

C#	Date	Emperor	Good	VG	Fine	VF
19-3	ND(1821-51)	Tao-kuang	.25	.50	1.00	2.00

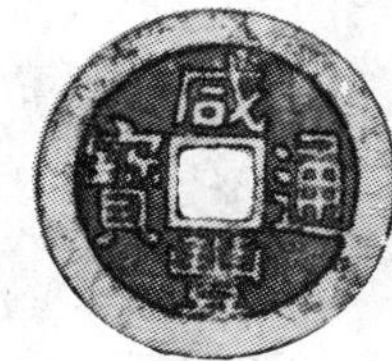

Obv: Type A.

Sch.#1542

C#	Date	Emperor	Good	VG	Fine	VF
19-4	ND(1851-61)	Hsien-feng	1.50	2.50	3.50	5.00

Obv: Type A-2.

C#	Date	Emperor	Good	VG	Fine	VF
19-5	ND(1862-74)	T'ung-chih	2.00	3.00	4.00	6.00

Obv: Type A.

C#	Date	Emperor	Good	VG	Fine	VF
19-7	ND(1875-1908)	Kuang-hsu	12.00	22.00	32.00	45.00

10 CASH

CAST BRASS
Obv: Type B-2.

C#	Date	Emperor	Good	VG	Fine	VF
19-6	ND(1862-74)	T'ung-chih	—	—	Rare	—

Obv: Type B.

C#	Date	Emperor	Good	VG	Fine	VF
19-8	ND(1875-1908)	Kuang-hsu	—	—	Rare	—

MILLED COINAGE

CASH

BRASS, struck
Obv: Type A.

Y#	Date	Mintage	Fine	VF	XF	Unc
189	ND(1889)	—	.25	.45	.85	3.00
	ND(1889)	—	—	—	Proof	275.00

Obv: *Kuang* in a different style.

Y#	Date	Mintage	Fine	VF	XF	Unc
189.1	ND(1889)	—	20.00	25.00	40.00	75.00

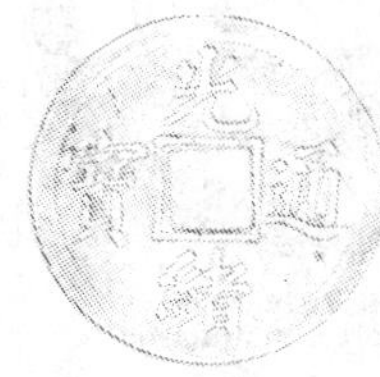
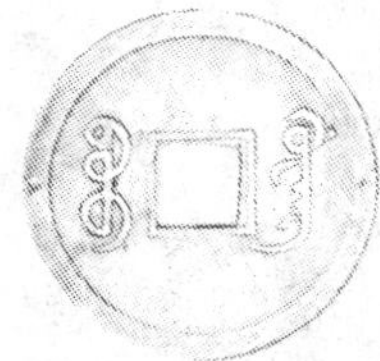

Y#	Date	Mintage	Fine	VF	XF	Unc
190	ND(1890-1908)	1059.253	—	1.00	3.00	15.00

CENT (10 CASH)

COPPER
Obv. leg: 6 characters at bottom. Rev: ONE CENT.

Y#	Date	Mintage	Fine	VF	XF	Unc
192	ND(1900-06)		.75	1.50	3.00	20.00

Mule. Obv: Y#192. Rev: Chihli 10 Cash Y#67.

Y#	Date	Mintage	Fine	VF	XF	Unc
A192	ND	—	25.00	35.00	50.00	125.00

Obv. leg: 7 characters at bottom. Rev: TEN CASH.

Y#	Date	Mintage	Fine	VF	XF	Unc
193	ND(1900-06)		1.00	2.00	4.00	20.00

NOTE: Varieties in lettering exist.

Mule: Obv. Y#192. Rev: Y#193.

Y#	Date	Mintage	Fine	VF	XF	Unc
A193	ND	—	20.00	28.50	40.00	100.00

Mule. Obv: Y#193. Rev: Y#192.

Y#	Date	Mintage	Fine	VF	XF	Unc
B193	ND	—	20.00	28.50	40.00	100.00

W#	Date	Mintage	VG	Fine	VF	XF
896	—	—	65.00	100.00	150.00	225.00

5 CENTS

1.3000 g, .820 SILVER, .0343 oz ASW
Obv: 3.65 CANDAREENS.
Rev. leg: Chinese characters around dragon.

Y#	Date	Mintage	Fine	VF	XF	Unc
194	ND(1889)	—	150.00	400.00	600.00	1000.

Obv: 3.6 CANDAREENS.

Y#	Date	Mintage	Fine	VF	XF	Unc
194.1	ND(1889)	—	275.00	700.00	1000.	1500.

Rev: English legend around dragon.

Y#	Date	Mintage	Fine	VF	XF	Unc
199	ND(1890-1905)	—	3.50	6.00	10.00	30.00

10 CENTS

2.7000 g, .820 SILVER, .0712 oz ASW
Obv: 7 3/10 CANDAREENS.

Y#	Date	Mintage	Fine	VF	XF	Unc
195	ND(1889)	—	100.00	175.00	275.00	500.00
	ND(1889)	—	—	—	Proof	—

Obv: 7.2 CANDAREENS.

Y#	Date	Mintage	Fine	VF	XF	Unc
195.1	ND(1889)	—	2000.	3000.	4500.	—

Rev: English legends around dragon.

Y#	Date	Mintage	Fine	VF	XF	Unc
200	ND(1890-1908)	—	2.00	4.00	6.00	15.00

20 CENTS

5.3000 g, .820 SILVER, .1397 oz ASW
Obv: 1 MACE AND 4 3/5 CANDAREENS.

Y#	Date	Mintage	Fine	VF	XF	Unc
196	ND(1889)	—	125.00	225.00	375.00	600.00
	ND(1889)	—	—	—	Proof	—

Obv: 1 MACE AND 4.4 CANDAREENS.

Y#	Date	Mintage	Fine	VF	XF	Unc
196.1	ND(1889)	—	2500.	3500.	5000.	—

Rev: English legends around dragon.

Y#	Date	Mintage	Fine	VF	XF	Unc
201	ND(1890-1908)	—	1.50	2.50	3.50	10.00
	ND(1890-1908)	10 known	—	—	Proof	400.00

50 CENTS

13.8000 g, .860 SILVER, .3816 oz ASW
Obv: 3 MACE AND 6-1/2 CANDAREENS.

Y#	Date	Mintage	Fine	VF	XF	Unc
197	ND(1889)	—	325.00	625.00	900.00	1600.

Obv: 3 MACE AND 6 CANDAREENS.

Y#	Date	Mintage	Fine	VF	XF	Unc
197.1	ND(1889)	—	—	6500.	10,000.	15,000.

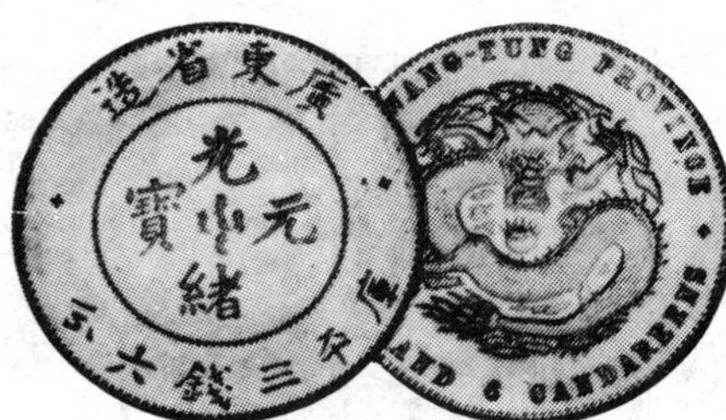

13.5000 g, .860 SILVER, .3733 oz ASW
Rev: English legends around dragon.

Y#	Date	Mintage	Fine	VF	XF	Unc
202	ND(1890-1905)	—	20.00	40.00	75.00	250.00
	ND(1890-1905)	—	—	—	Proof	650.00

DOLLAR

27.4000 g, .900 SILVER, .7929 oz ASW
Obv: 7 MACE AND 3 CANDAREENS.

Y#	Date	Mintage	Fine	VF	XF	Unc
198	ND(1889)	—	1250.	1750.	2500.	4800.
	ND(1889)	—	—	—	Proof	10,000.

Obv: 7 MACE AND 2 CANDAREENS.

Y#	Date	Mintage	Fine	VF	XF	Unc
198.1	ND(1889)	—	—	—	—	35,000.

NOTE: Considered a pattern.

27.0000 g, .900 SILVER, .7814 oz ASW
Rev: English legends around dragon.

Y#	Date	Mintage	Fine	VF	XF	Unc
203	ND(1890-1908)	—	15.00	25.00	50.00	350.00
	ND(1890-1908)	—	—	—	Proof	1000.

PATTERNS (Pn)

(Including off metal strikes)

KM#	Date	Mintage	Identification	Mkt.Val.
Pn1	ND	—	5 Cash, Brass	—

KM#	Date	Mintage	Identification	Mkt.Val.
Pn3	ND	—	10 Cash, Brass	1200.

KM#	Date	Mintage	Identification	Mkt.Val.
Pn5	ND	—	1 Tael, Silver, K932	*Rare

***NOTE:** Superior Goodman sale 6-91 proof realized, $41,800.

KM#	Date	Mintage	Identification	Mkt.Val.
Pn6	ND	—	1 Tael, White metal, K932y	—
Pn7	ND(1889)	—	10 Cents, Copper, Y195	3500.
Pn8	ND(1889)	—	20 Cents, Copper, Y196	5500.
Pn9	ND(1889)	—	50 Cents, Copper, Y197	7500.
Pn10	ND(1889)	—	50 Cents, Copper, Y197.1	7500.
Pn11	ND(1889)	—	1 Dollar, Copper, Y198.1	12,500.
Pn12	ND(1890-1905)	—	5 Cents, Copper, Y199	—
Pn13	ND(1890-1900)	—	10 Cents, Copper, Y200	—
Pn14	ND(1890-1900)	—	10 Cents, Brass, Y200	—
Pn15	ND(1890-1908)	—	20 Cents, Copper, Y201	—
Pn16	ND(1890-1908)	—	20 Cents, Brass, Y201	—
Pn17	ND(1890-1905)	—	50 Cents, Copper, Y202	—
Pn18	ND(1890-1908)	—	1 Dollar, Copper, Y203	—

SPECIMEN SETS (SS)

KM#	Date	Mintage	Identification	Issue Price	Mkt. Val.
SS1	1889(10)	—	Y189,195-198 (2 each)	—	—
SS2	1890(?)	—	Y189-190,199-203	—	2000.

KWEICHOW PROVINCE

Guizhou

A province located in southern China. It is basically a plateau region that is somewhat remote from the general traffic of China. The Kweichow Mint opened in 1730 and produced Cash coins until the end of the reign of Kuang Hsu. The Republic issues for this province are enigmatic as to their origin, as a mint supposedly did not exist in Kweichow (Guizhou) at this time.

EMPIRE

CASH

Obv: Type A.

Sch.#1527

C#	Date	Emperor	Good	VG	Fine	VF
20-3	ND(1821-50)	Tao-kuang	2.00	3.00	4.00	6.00

Rev: Crescent above.

Sch.#1529

C#	Date	Emperor	Good	VG	Fine	VF
20-3.1	ND(1821-50)	Tao-kuang	3.50	6.00	9.00	13.50

Rev: Circle above.

Sch.#1528

C#	Date	Emperor	Good	VG	Fine	VF
20-3.2	ND(1821-50)	Tao-kuang	3.50	6.00	9.00	18.00

Rev: Dot inside circle above.

20-3.3	ND(1821-50)	Tao-kuang	2.50	5.00	6.50	9.00

Rev: Dot above.

20-3.4	ND(1821-50)	Tao-kuang	2.50	5.00	6.50	9.00

Rev: "X"above.

Sch.#1530

20-3.5	ND(1821-50)	Tao-kuang	5.50	8.50	13.50	20.00

Rev: A triangle above.

20-3.6	ND(1821-50)	Tao-kuang	5.50	8.50	13.50	20.00

Rev: Character *Yi* (one) above.

Sch.#1531

20-3.7	ND(1821-50)	Tao-kuang	5.50	8.50	13.50	20.00

Rev: Character *Ta* (large) above.

20-3.8	ND(1821-50)	Tao-kuang	5.50	8.50	13.50	20.00

NOTE: This coin and C#20-3.14 are difficult to distinguish.

Rev: Crescent below.

20-3.9	ND(1821-50)	Tao-kuang	3.50	6.00	9.00	13.50

Rev: "X" below.

20-3.10	ND(1821-50)	Tao-kuang	5.50	50	13.50	25.00

Rev: Dot below.

20-3.11	ND(1821-50)	Tao-kuang	3.00	5.50	8.00	11.50

Rev: Inverted triangle below.

20-3.12	ND(1821-50)	Tao-kuang	5.50	8.50	13.50	20.00

Rev: *Yi* (one) below.

20-3.13	ND(1821-50)	Tao-kuang	5.50	8.50	13.50	20.00

Rev: *Liu* (six) above.

20-3.14	ND(1821-50)	Tao-kuang	5.50	8.50	13.50	20.00

NOTE: This coin and C#20-3.8 are difficult to distinguish.

Rev: *Ch'i* (seven) below.

C#	Date	Emperor	Good	VG	Fine	VF
20-3.15	ND(1821-50)	Tao-kuang	5.50	8.50	13.50	20.00

Obv: Type A.

20-4	ND(1851-61)	Hsien-feng	1.50	2.50	4.00	6.00

Rev: Dot above.

20-4.1	ND(1851-61)	Hsien-feng	2.50	4.00	5.00	7.00

Rev: 2 vertical lines above.

20-4.2	ND(1851-61)	Hsien-feng	5.50	8.50	13.50	25.00

Rev: 3 vertical lines above.

20-4.3	ND(1851-61)	Hsien-feng	5.50	8.50	13.50	25.00

Rev: "X" above.

20-4.4	ND(1851-61)	Hsien-feng	5.50	8.50	13.50	25.00

Rev: Character *Ch'i* (seven) above.

20-4.5	ND(1851-61)	Hsien-feng	5.50	8.50	13.50	25.00

Rev: Character *Shih* (ten) above.

20-4.6	ND(1851-61)	Hsien-feng	5.50	8.50	13.50	25.00

Rev: Character *Wen* (unit) lying on its side above.

20-4.7	ND(1851-61)	Hsien-feng	5.50	8.50	13.50	25.00

Rev: Character *Shih* above and crescent below.

20-4.8	ND(1851-61)	Hsien-feng	5.50	8.50	13.50	25.00

Obv: Type A-2.

20-7	ND(1862-74)	T'ung-chih	—	—	Rare	—

Obv: Type A.

20-9	ND(1875-1908)	Kuang-hsu	4.00	7.50	10.00	14.00

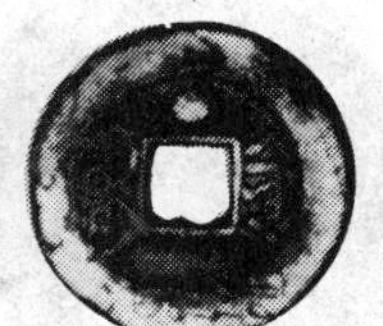

Rev: Dot above.

20-9.1	ND(1875-1908)	Kuang-hsu	5.00	9.00	12.50	17.50

Rev: Character *Kung* above.

20-9.2	ND(1875-1905)	Kuang-hsu	8.50	11.50	16.50	25.00

10 CASH

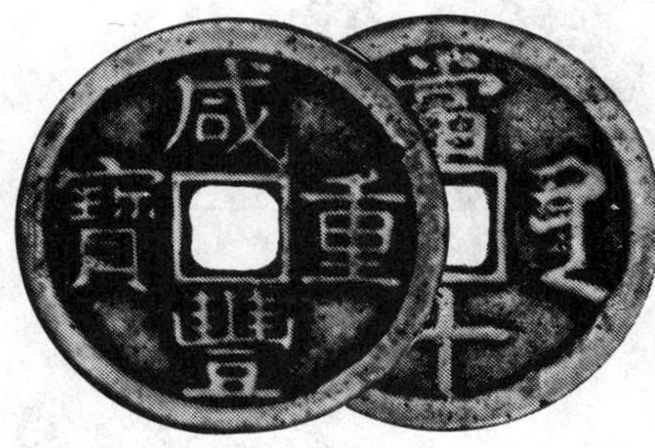

CAST BRASS, 38mm
Obv: Type B-1.

C#	Date	Emperor	Good	VG	Fine	VF
20-5	ND(1851-61)	Hsien-feng	18.00	25.00	35.00	60.00

25mm

20-5.1	ND(1851-61)	Hsien-feng	35.00	55.00	75.00	100.00

Obv: Type B-2.

20-8	ND(1862-74)	T'ung-chih	—	—	Rare	—

Obv: Type B.

20-10	ND(1875-1908)	Kuang-hsu	—	—	Rare	—

50 CASH

CAST BRASS
Obv: Type B-1.

20-6	ND(1851-61)	Hsien-feng	60.00	85.00	110.00	165.00

MILLED COINAGE

50 CENTS

SILVER

Kann#	Year	Date	VG	Fine	VF	XF
10	14	(1888)	—	—	Rare	—

DOLLAR

SILVER, 24.80 g

9	14	(1888)	—	—	*Rare	—

***NOTE:** Superior Goodman Sale 6-91 Choice XF realized $46,200.

Kann#	Year	Date	VG	Fine	VF	XF
11	14	(1888)	—	—	Rare	—

22.60 g

Kann#	Year	Date	VG	Fine	VF	XF
12	16	(1890)	—	—	Rare	—

Kann#	Year	Date	VG	Fine	VF	XF
13	16	(1890)	—	—	Rare	—

NOTE: The Kweichow (Guizhou) coins above, obviously copied from contemporary Japanese coins, are still a mystery. Even as late as the 1920's Kweichow (Guizhou) was a very primitive area. It is highly unlikely that the coins were made there in the 1880's and 1890's. It is possible that they were minted elsewhere, possibly in one of the central coastal provinces.

MANCHURIAN PROVINCES

For coins of Manchuria refer to listings under Fengtien (Liaoning).

PEI YANG

For coins of Pei Yang refer to listings under Chihli (Hebei).

SHANSI PROVINCE

Shanxi

A province located in northeastern China that has some of the richest coal deposits in the world. Parts of the Great Wall cross the province. Extensive agriculture of early China started here. Cited as a "model province" in the new Chinese Republic. Intermittently active mints from 1645. The modern mint was established in 1919. It operated until the mid-1920's and closed because of the public's resistance against the coins that were being produced.

EMPIRE

CASH

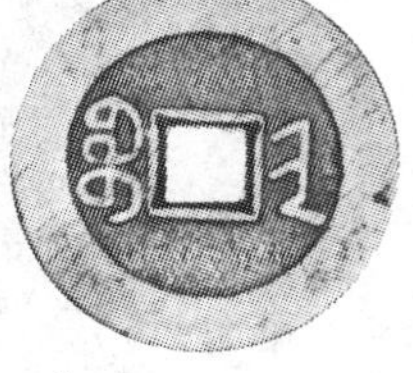

Obv: Type A.

C#	Date	Emperor	Good	VG	Fine	VF
21-3	ND(1821-50)	Tao-kuang	1.25	2.50	3.00	6.00

Obv: Type A.

C#	Date	Emperor	Good	VG	Fine	VF
21-4	ND(1851-61)	Hsien-feng	18.50	27.50	37.50	45.00

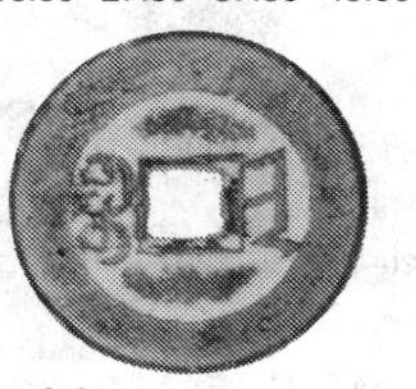

Obv: Type A-2.

C#	Date	Emperor	Good	VG	Fine	VF
21-6	ND(1862-74)	T'ung-chih	8.50	17.50	25.00	40.00

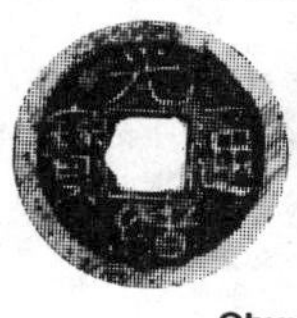

Obv: Type A.

C#	Date	Emperor	Good	VG	Fine	VF
21-8	ND(1875-1908)	Kuang-hsu	6.50	11.50	17.50	35.00

10 CASH

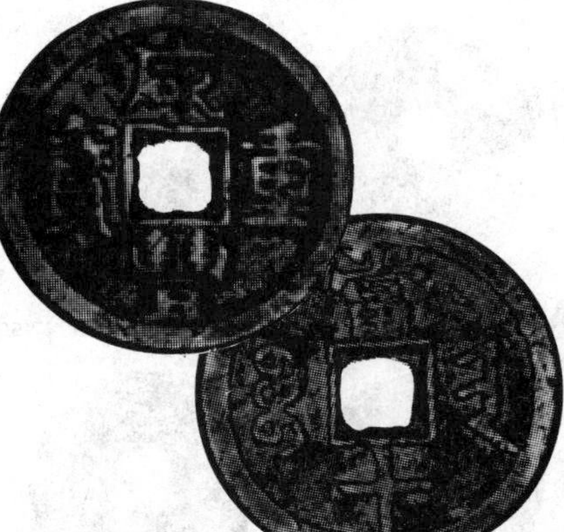

CAST BRASS
Obv: Type B-1.

C#	Date	Emperor	Good	VG	Fine	VF
21-5	ND(1851-61)	Hsien-feng	12.00	20.00	27.50	50.00

Obv: Type B-2.

C#	Date	Emperor	Good	VG	Fine	VF
21-7	ND(1862-74)	T'ung-chih	—	—	Rare	—

PATTERNS (Pn)

(Including off metal strikes)

KM#	Date	Mintage	Identification	Mkt.Val.
Pn1	Yr.16 (1890)	—	1 Tael, Silver, K922	Rare

NOTE: The authenticity of K922 was questioned by Kann and other authorities. However, 2 specimens were sold in the Superior Goodman sale 6-91; an AU plain edge realized $19,250. and an XF milled edge realized $11,000.

SHANTUNG PROVINCE

Shandong

A province located on the northeastern coast of China. Confucius was born in this province. Parts of the province were leased to Great Britain and to Germany. Farming, fishing and mining are the chief occupations. A mint was opened at Tsinan in 1647 and was an intermittent producer for the empire. A modern mint was opened at Tsinan in 1905, but closed in 1906. Patterns were prepared between 1926-1933 in anticipation of a new coinage, but none were struck for circulation.

EMPIRE

CASH

Mint: Chinan
Obv: Type A.

Sch.#1547

C#	Date	Emperor	Good	VG	Fine	VF
22-2	ND(1851-61)	Hsien-feng	16.50	30.00	45.00	60.00

Obv: Type A-2.

C#	Date	Emperor	Good	VG	Fine	VF
22-5	ND(1862-74)	T'ung-chih	10.00	18.50	27.50	40.00

Obv: Type A. Rev: Type 1 mint mark.

C#	Date	Emperor	Good	VG	Fine	VF
22-6	ND(1875-1908)	Kuang-hsu	10.00	18.50	27.50	40.00

Mint: Chefoo (now Yantai)
Obv: Type A.

C#	Date	Emperor	Good	VG	Fine	VF
27-6	ND(1875-1908)	Kuang-hsu	4.00	6.50	9.00	15.00

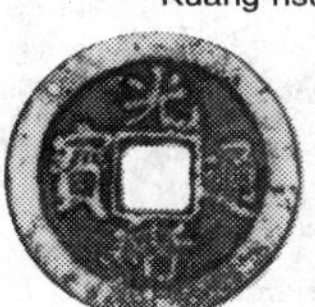

Rev: Character *Chin* above.

C#	Date	Emperor	Good	VG	Fine	VF
27-6.1	ND(1875-1908)	Kuang-hsu	5.00	7.50	10.00	15.00

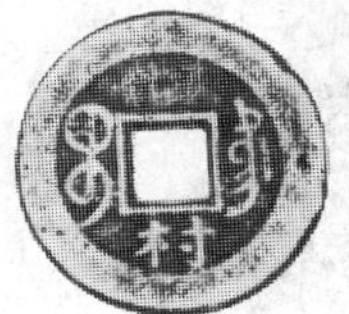

Rev: Character *Ts'un* below.

C#	Date	Emperor	Good	VG	Fine	VF
27-6.2	ND(1875-1908)	Kuang-hsu	5.00	7.50	10.00	15.00

NOTE: C#27 coins were previously listed in Yunnan Province, however some authorities do not attribute these coins to the Chefoo Mint.

PATTERNS (Pn)

(Including off metal strikes)

KM#	Date	Mintage	Identification	Mkt.Val.
Pn1	(1851-61)	—	10 Cash, Cast Brass, C22-7	—
Pn2	(1851-61)	—	50 Cash, Cast Brass, C22-3	—
Pn3	(1851-61)	—	100 Cash, Cast Brass, C22-4	—

KM#	Date	Mintage	Identification	Mkt.Val.
Pn4	Yr.16 (1890)	—	5 Mace, Silver, K924	—
Pn5	Yr.16 (1890)	—	5 Mace, Copper, K924x	—

KM#	Date	Mintage	Identification	Mkt.Val.
Pn6	Yr.16 (1890)	—	1 Tael, Silver, K923	Unique

NOTE: Superior Goodman sale 6-91 VF realized $45,100.

KM#	Date	Mintage	Identification	Mkt.Val.
Pn7	ND	—	1 Cash, Copper	Rare

SHENSI PROVINCE

Shaanxi

A province located in central China that is a rich agricultural area. A very important province in the early development of China. An active imperial mint was located at Sian (Xi'an).

EMPIRE

CASH

Obv: Type A.

Sch.#1520

C#	Date	Emperor	Good	VG	Fine	VF
23-3	ND(1821-50)	Tao-kuang	2.50	5.00	7.50	12.50

Obv: Type A.

Sch.#1550

C#	Date	Emperor	Good	VG	Fine	VF
23-4	ND(1851-61)	Hsien-feng	4.00	7.00	12.00	20.00

CAST IRON

C#	Date	Emperor	Good	VG	Fine	VF
23-4a	ND(1851-61)	Hsien-feng	10.00	20.00	40.00	—

CAST BRASS
Obv: Type A-2.

C#	Date	Emperor	Good	VG	Fine	VF
23-11	ND(1862-74)	T'ung-chih	—	—	Rare	—

Obv: Type A.

C#	Date	Emperor	Good	VG	Fine	VF
23-13	ND(1875-1908)	Kuang-hsu	20.00	35.00	50.00	75.00

10 CASH

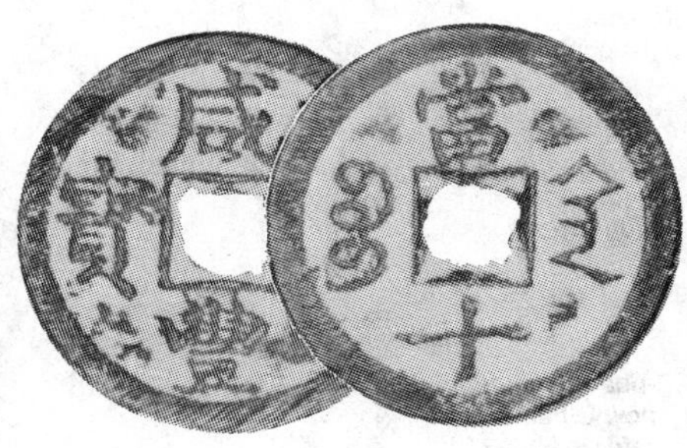

CAST BRASS, 43mm
Obv: Type B-1.

C#	Date	Emperor	Good	VG	Fine	VF
23-5	ND(1851-61)	Hsien-feng	10.00	15.00	25.00	45.00

36mm

C#	Date	Emperor	Good	VG	Fine	VF
23-5.1	ND(1851-61)	Hsien-feng	6.00	10.00	15.00	28.00

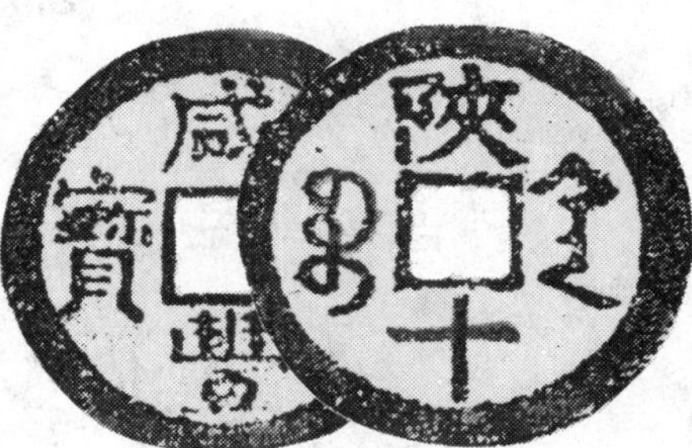

Rev: Character *Shan* (for Shensi) above center hole.

C#	Date	Emperor	Good	VG	Fine	VF
23-6	ND(1851-61)	Hsien-feng	40.00	65.00	90.00	125.00

Obv: Type B-2.

C#	Date	Emperor	Good	VG	Fine	VF
23-12	ND(1862-74)	T'ung-chih	—	—	Rare	—

Obv: Type B.

C#	Date	Emperor	Good	VG	Fine	VF
23-14	ND(1875-1908)	Kuang-hsu	—	—	Rare	—

50 CASH

CAST BRASS
Obv: Type B-1.

C#	Date	Emperor	Good	VG	Fine	VF
23-7	ND(1851-61)	Hsien-feng	10.00	20.00.	35.00	70.00

100 CASH

CAST BRASS, 57-58mm
Obv: Type C.

C#	Date	Emperor	Good	VG	Fine	VF
23-8.1	ND(1851-61)	Hsien-feng	35.00	55.00	75.00	125.00

48-49mm

C#	Date	Emperor	Good	VG	Fine	VF
23-8.2	ND(1851-61)	Hsien-feng	10.00	17.50	25.00	45.00

500 CASH

CAST BRASS
Obv: Type C.

C#	Date	Emperor	Good	VG	Fine	VF
23-9	ND(1851-61)	Hsien-feng	75.00	110.00	150.00	200.00

Rev: Character *Kuan* (official) cast on rim.

C#	Date	Emperor	Good	VG	Fine	VF
23-9.1	ND(1851-61)	Hsien-feng	125.00	175.00	250.00	350.00

1000 CASH

CAST BRASS
Obv: Type C.

C#	Date	Emperor	Good	VG	Fine	VF
23-10	ND(1851-61)	Hsien-feng	110.00	165.00	225.00	300.00

CAST COPPER

C#	Date	Emperor	Good	VG	Fine	VF
23-10a	ND(1851-61)	Hsien-feng	120.00	175.00	250.00	350.00

CAST BRASS
Rev: Character *Kuan* cast on rim.
Illustration reduced, actual size 74mm.

C#	Date	Emperor	Good	VG	Fine	VF
23-10.1	ND(1851-61)	Hsien-feng	150.00	220.00	300.00	400.00

PATTERNS (Pn)

(Including off metal strikes)

KM#	Date	Mintage	Identification	Mkt.Val.
Pn1	(1898)	—	5 Cents, Silver, K159	2600.
Pn2	(1898)	—	10 Cents, Silver, K158	—

KM#	Date	Mintage	Identification	Mkt.Val.
Pn3	(1898)	—	20 Cents, Silver, K157	3000.

KM#	Date	Mintage	Identification	Mkt.Val.
Pn4	(1898)	—	50 Cents, Silver, K156	6000.

KM#	Date	Mintage	Identification	Mkt.Val.
Pn5	(1898)	—	1 Dollar, Silver, K155	35,000.

NOTE: The Shensi (Shaanxi) patterns above were made at the Heaton Mint, Birmingham, England as samples to be sent, along with the dies and machinery, to Shensi (Shaanxi). The machinery never reached the province, having been diverted instead to the Hupeh Mint. Beware of forgeries.

SINKIANG PROVINCE

Hsinkiang, Xinjiang
"New Dominion"

An autonomous region in western China, often referred to as Chinese Turkestan. High mountains surround 2000 ft. tableland on three sides with a large desert in center of this province. Many salt lakes, mining and some farming and oil. Inhabited by early man and was referred to as the "Silk Route" to the West. Sinkiang (Xinjiang) has been historically under the control of many factions, including Genghis Khan. It became a province in 1884. China has made claim to Sinkiang (Xinjiang) for many, many years. This rule has been more nominal than actual. Sinkiang (Xinjiang) had eight imperial mints, only three of which were in operation toward the end of the reign of Kuang Hsu. Only two mints operated during the early years of the republic. In 1949, due to a drastic coin shortage and lack of confidence in the inflated paper money, it was planned to mint some dollars in Sinkiang (Xinjiang). These did not see much circulation, however, due to the defeat of the nationalists, though they have recently appeared in considerable numbers in today's market.

PATTERNS

NOTE: A number of previously listed cast coins of Sinkiang Province are now known to be patterns - "mother" cash or "seed" cash for which no circulating issues are known. The following coins are, therefore, no longer listed. Most were probably manufactured in Beijing. They are generally made of brass rather than the purer copper usual to Sinkiang. The following coins are, therefore, no longer listed here: Craig #30-9, 30-11a, 30-12a, 30-14, 30-15a, 30-16, 30-17, 28-4.1, 28-8a, 28-9a, 28-9c, 28-10, 31-1a, 31-1v, 31-2, 32-4, 32-5, 33-12, 33-21, 34-2, 34-3, 35-5a and 35-6.

MONETARY SYSTEM

2 Pul = 1 Cash
2 Cash = 5 Li
4 Cash = 10 Li = 1 Fen
25 Cash = 10 Fen = 1 Miscal = 1 Ch'ien, Mace, Tanga
10 Miscals (Mace) = 1 Liang (Tael or Sar)
20 Miscals (Tangas) = 1 Tilla

MINT NAME
LOCAL MINT NAMES AND MARKS

MINT	CHINESE	TURKI	MANCHU
Aksu	城阿	اقصو	
Ili now Yining (Gulja)	犁伊 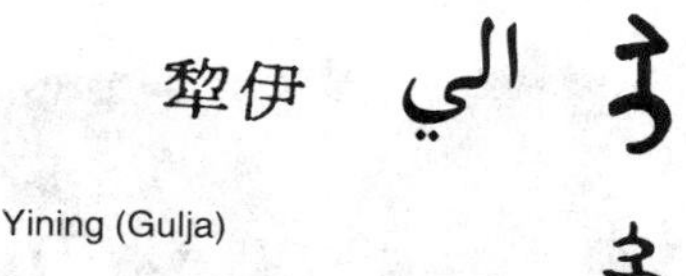	الي	
Kashgar now Kashi	什喀	كشقر	
Khotan now Hotan	闐和	خوتن	
Kotsha (Kuche)		كوتشر	
Kuche now Kuqa	車庫	كوچا	
Ti-hua now Dihua, refer to Urumchi	化廸		
Urumchi now Urumqi	化廸	ارومجي	
Ushi now Wushi (Uqturpan)	什烏	اوش	
Yangihissar now Yengisar	沙吉英		
Yarkand now Shache (Yarkant)	羌爾葉	يارقند	

GENERAL COINAGE
EMPIRE
CASH

CAST COPPER
Rev: *Boo Chiowan* (Manchu for Pao Chuan-Board of Revenue).

KM#	Date	Emperor	Good	VG	Fine	VF
10	ND(1875-1908)	Kuang-hsu	1.50	3.50	6.00	9.50

NOTE: For previously listed KM#11 and #12 refer to Kuche Mint listings.

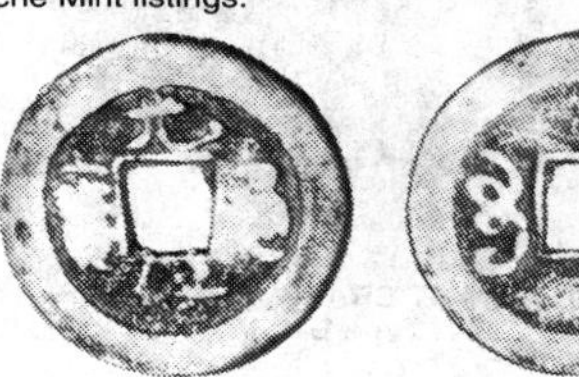

Rev: Similar to KM#11.

KM#	Date	Emperor	Good	VG	Fine	VF
12	ND(1875-1908)	Kuang-hsu	1.50	3.50	6.00	9.50

Rev: *Boo Chaun* or *Yaun* (illiterate Manchu).

KM#	Date	Emperor	Good	VG	Fine	VF
13	ND(1875-1908)	Kuang-hsu	1.50	3.50	6.00	9.50

Rev: *Boo Choan* (illiterate Manchu).

KM#	Date	Emperor	Good	VG	Fine	VF
14	ND(1875-1908)	Kuang-hsu	1.50	3.00	5.00	8.50

NOTE: The five one-cash varieties listed above could be confused with Beijing issues C1-16 or C2-15, but they are much more crudely cast, and are made of red copper rather than brass. See Landon Ross, 1986, Numismatics International Bulletin 20(3) for a more detailed review.

10 CASH

NOTE: For previously listed KM#3,5,8 and 9 refer to Tihwa Mint listings and for previously listed KM#6,7.1 and 7.2 refer to Kucha Mint listings.

CAST COPPER
Rev: *Pao Yuan?* w/A (for Aksu) above.

KM#	Date	Emperor	
15	ND(1875-1908)	Kuang-hsu	Reported, not confirmed

HAMMERED COINAGE
1/2 MISCAL
(5 Fen)

SILVER, 1.45 g
Obv. leg: *On Gumush*.
Rev. leg: *Besh Fen* (5 Fen), w/o mint name.

Y#	Date	Mintage	VG	Fine	VF	XF
A7.1	ND	—	7.00	12.00	18.00	25.00
	AH1294	—	7.00	12.00	18.00	25.00
	1295	—	7.00	12.00	18.00	25.00

Obv: *Chu*. Rev. Turki leg: *Besh Fen*.

Y#	Date	Mintage	VG	Fine	VF	XF
A7.2	AH1295	—	32.50	55.00	90.00	150.00

Obv. leg: Turki. Rev. leg: Manchu.

Y#	Date	Mintage	VG	Fine	VF	XF
A7.3	ND	—	—	—	Rare	—

MILLED COINAGE

Fen and Li Series

FEN, 5 LI

COPPER
Obv: Large dots in circle, dentilated rims.

Y#	Date	Mintage	Good	VG	Fine	VF
1	ND	—	150.00	200.00	350.00	550.00

NOTE: Two varieties are reported.

Obv: Small dots in circle, dotted rims.

Y#	Date	Mintage	Fine	VF	XF	Unc
1a	ND	(modern copy)		—	25.00	35.00

NOTE: The legend on this coin states that it is valued at 1 Fen 5 Li of silver (about 15 Cash). The coin is the size of a normal 10 Cash piece of Sinkiang (Xinjiang), but these pieces are usually larger than those of the other provinces. For this reason, it is assumed the coin was overvalued to benefit the government.

2 FEN, 5 LI

COPPER

Y#	Date	Mintage	Good	VG	Fine	VF
A1	ND	—	—	—	Rare	—

NOTE: This denomination was recalled shortly after issue and the dies re-engraved 1 Fen and 5 Li to produce Y#1. Do not confuse poorly re-engraved Chinese numeral *2* examples of Y#1 for Y#A1. Note the difference in spacing of the Chinese characters below the rosettes between Y#1 and Y#A1.

Y#	Date	Mintage	Good	VG	Fine	VF
B1	ND	—	—	—	Rare	—

NOTE: Status unknown.

Cash Series

MISCAL (MACE)

SILVER
Obv. leg: *Tsu Yin I Ch'ien*
(Pure silver 1 Mace)

Kann#	Date	Mintage	VG	Fine	VF	XF
1000	ND	—	150.00	250.00	425.00	800.00

NOTE: Kann #1000 was minted at the Arsenal of Lanchowfu in Kansu (Gansu) by order of General Tso Tsung-tang when he was campaigning against Yakub Beg's Sinkian (Xinjiang) armies. It was struck circa 1876.

3.50 g
Obv. outer leg: Turki w/o dot in center.
Rev: W/o Turki leg.

Y#	Date	Mintage	VG	Fine	VF	XF
3	ND	—	75.00	125.00	200.00	325.00

Obv. outer leg: Turki w/ dot in center.
Rev: W/o Turki leg.

Y#	Date	Mintage	VG	Fine	VF	XF
3.1	ND	—	75.00	125.00	200.00	325.00

Obv: W/o outer Turki leg. Rev. leg: Turki.

Y#	Date	Mintage	VG	Fine	VF	XF
3.2	ND	—	325.00	550.00	900.00	1500.

Obv. & rev: W/o outer Turki leg.

Y#	Date	Mintage	VG	Fine	VF	XF
3.3	ND	—	90.00	150.00	250.00	400.00

Rev. leg: SUNGAREI above dragon, 1 MACE below.

Y#	Date	Mintage	VG	Fine	VF	XF
10	ND	—	110.00	225.00	400.00	650.00

2 MISCALS (2 MACE)

SILVER, 7.20 g
Obv. outer leg: Turki. Rev: W/o Turki leg.

Y#	Date	Mintage	VG	Fine	VF	XF
4	ND	—	50.00	75.00	150.00	400.00

Obv. outer leg: Continuous Turki.
Rev: W/o Turki leg.

Y#	Date	Mintage	VG	Fine	VF	XF
4.1	ND	—	100.00	150.00	250.00	325.00

Obv: W/o outer Turki leg. Rev. leg: Turki.

Y#	Date	Mintage	VG	Fine	VF	XF
4.2	ND	—	150.00	250.00	400.00	650.00

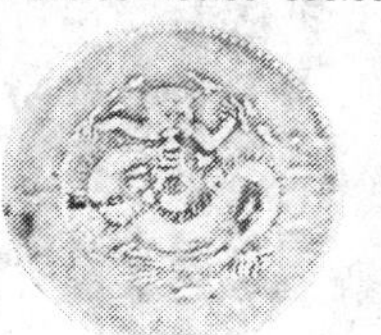

Rev: Redesigned dragon w/o Turki legends.

Y#	Date	Mintage	VG	Fine	VF	XF
4.3	ND	—	150.00	250.00	400.00	650.00

Obv. outer leg: Turki.
Rev: Circled dragon w/o Turki leg.

Y#	Date	Mintage	VG	Fine	VF	XF
4.4	ND	—	—	—	Rare	—

Rev. leg: SUNGAREI above dragon, 2 MACE below.

Y#	Date	Mintage	VG	Fine	VF	XF
11	ND	—	200.00	425.00	850.00	1350.

4 MISCALS (4 MACE)

SILVER, 14.20 g

Y#	Date	Mintage	VG	Fine	VF	XF
5	ND	—	80.00	125.00	200.00	400.00

5 MISCALS (5 MACE)

SILVER, 17.90 g
Obv: W/o dot or rosette in center.
Rev: Uncircled dragon.

Y#	Date	Mintage	VG	Fine	VF	XF
6	ND	—	15.00	25.00	60.00	175.00

Rev: Circled dragon, w/o rosettes.

Y#	Date	Mintage	VG	Fine	VF	XF
6.1	ND	—	15.00	25.00	50.00	90.00

Rev: Large rosettes at sides of dragon.

Y#	Date	Mintage	VG	Fine	VF	XF
6.2	ND	—	15.00	25.00	50.00	90.00

Obv: Dot in center. Rev: W/o rosettes, circled dragon.

Y#	Date	Mintage	VG	Fine	VF	XF
6.3	ND	—	15.00	25.00	50.00	90.00

Obv: Cross in center.

Y#	Date	Mintage	VG	Fine	VF	XF
6.4	ND	—	15.00	25.00	50.00	90.00

Obv: Large rosette in center, middle of which is depressed.

Y#	Date	Mintage	VG	Fine	VF	XF
6.5	ND	—	15.00	25.00	50.00	90.00

Obv: 8-petalled rosette in center, middle of which is raised. Rev: Small rosettes at sides of dragon.

Y#	Date	Mintage	VG	Fine	VF	XF
6.6	ND	—	15.00	25.00	50.00	90.00

Rev: Bat above uncircled dragon's head.

Y#	Date	Mintage	VG	Fine	VF	XF
6.7	ND	—	175.00	300.00	450.00	700.00

Rev: Turki leg. around uncircled dragon.

Y#	Date	Mintage	VG	Fine	VF	XF
6.8	ND	—	400.00	600.00	—	—

Rev. leg: SUNGAREI above uncircled dragon, 5 MACE below.

Y#	Date	Mintage	VG	Fine	VF	XF
6.9	ND	—	—	—	Rare	—

NOTE: Some authorities consider this coin a fantasy.

Rev: W/o SUNGAREI w/4 bats and many clouds around dragon.

Y#	Date	Mintage	VG	Fine	VF	XF
6.10	ND	—	—	—	Rare	—

Obv: Turki leg. rotated.
Rev: Bat above dragon's head.

Y#	Date	Mintage	VG	Fine	VF	XF
6.11	ND	—	—	—	Rare	—

SAR (TAEL)

SILVER, 35.50 g
Obv: W/o outer Turki leg. Rev: W/o Turki leg.,

rosettes at sides of uncircled dragon.

Y#	Date	Mintage	VG	Fine	VF	XF
7	ND	—	25.00	40.00	60.00	140.00

Rev: Turki leg. around circled dragon, w/o rosettes.

Y#	Date	Mintage	VG	Fine	VF	XF
7.1	ND	—	40.00	65.00	100.00	300.00

Rev: Turki leg. around uncircled dragon.

Y#	Date	Mintage	VG	Fine	VF	XF
7.2	ND	—	500.00	850.00	1250.	1600.

Obv: Outer Turki leg., rosette in center.
Rev: W/o Turki leg., w/rosettes at sides of uncircled dragon.

Y#	Date	Mintage	VG	Fine	VF	XF
7.3	ND	—	35.00	50.00	70.00	150.00

GOLD MISCAL (MACE)

GOLD, 3.90 g
Rev: Turki leg. around uncircled dragon.

Y#	Date	Mintage	Fine	VF	XF	Unc
8	ND	—	600.00	1000.	1400.	2000.

Rev: Turki leg. at left differs.

Y#	Date	Mintage	Fine	VF	XF	Unc
8.2	ND	—	700.00	1200.	1750.	2500.

Rev: W/o Turki leg. around uncircled dragon.

Y#	Date	Mintage	Fine	VF	XF	Unc
8.1	ND	—	1150.	1900.	2800.	4000.

Obv: Turki leg. in outer circle.

Y#	Date	Mintage	Fine	VF	XF	Unc
8.3	ND	—	875.00	1450.	2100.	3000.

GOLD 2 MISCALS

GOLD, 7.80 g
Obv: Narrow spaced Chinese "2".
Rev: Turki leg. around uncircled dragon.

Y#	Date	Mintage	Fine	VF	XF	Unc
9	ND	—	750.00	1350.	2000.	2800.

Obv: Wide spaced Chinese "2".
Rev: Redesigned dragon.

Y#	Date	Mintage	Fine	VF	XF	Unc
9.1	ND	—	750.00	1350.	2000.	2800.

Similar to 2 Miscals (Silver) Y#11.

Kann#	Date	Mintage	Fine	VF	XF	Unc
1505	ND	—	—	Reported, not confirmed		

PATTERNS (Pn)

(Including off metal strikes)

KM#	Date	Mintage	Identification	Mkt.Val.
Pn1	ND	—	1 Mace, Copper, SUNGAREI, Y10	1600.
Pn2	ND	—	2 Mace, Silver, SUNGAREI, Y11	3000.
Pn3	ND	—	2 Mace, Copper, SUNGAREI	1200.

KM#	Date	Mintage	Identification	Mkt.Val.
Pn4	ND	—	4 Mace, Silver, SUNGAREI	8000.
Pn5	ND	—	4 Mace, Brass, SUNGAREI	1250.
Pn6	ND	—	5 Mace, Silver, w/o bats around large dragon	—

KM#	Date	Mintage	Identification	Mkt.Val.
Pn7	ND	—	7 Mace 2 Candareens, Silver, SUNGAREI, Y12	Rare

LOCAL COINAGE

Aksu Mint

EMPIRE

CASH

CAST COPPER

Obv: Type A.
Rev: Character *Chiu* (nine) above.

C#	Date	Emperor	Good	VG	Fine	VF
30-5	ND(1796-1820)	Chia-ch'ing	1.75	4.25	8.00	10.00

Obv: Type A.

C#	Date	Emperor	Good	VG	Fine	VF
30-6	ND(1821-50)	Tao-kuang	1.00	2.00	3.50	6.00

Obv: Type A-1.
Rev: Character *Chiu* (nine) above.

C#	Date	Emperor	Good	VG	Fine	VF
30-4	ND(1883)	Ch'ien-lung	13.50	18.50	25.00	35.00

NOTE: Cast as a commemorative of the establishment of Hsinchiang (Xinjiang) Province (1884).

5 CASH

CAST COPPER
Obv: Type A.
Rev: Characters *Pa Nien* (= year 8 = 1828) above.

C#	Date	Emperor	Good	VG	Fine	VF
30-7	Yr.8 (1828)	Tao-kuang	1.50	3.00	6.00	10.00

C#	Date	Emperor	Good	VG	Fine	VF
30-10	ND(1851-61)	Hsien-feng	6.00	12.00	22.50	35.00

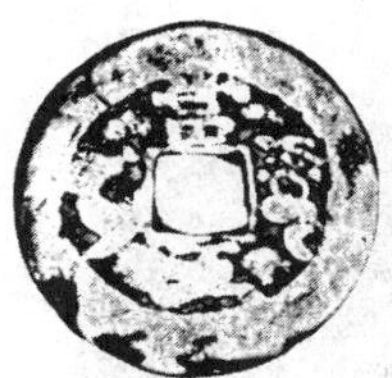

C#	Date	Emperor	Good	VG	Fine	VF
30-A15	ND(1862-74)	T'ung-chih	75.00	95.00	120.00	150.00

10 CASH

CAST COPPER
Obv: Type A.
Rev: Characters *Pa Nien*
(= year 8 = 1828) above.

C#	Date	Emperor	Good	VG	Fine	VF
30-8	Yr.8 (1828)	Tao-kuang	1.00	1.75	2.75	5.50

NOTE: C#30-7 and 30-8 are commemoratives marking the supression of a revolt in Sinkiang in 1828. Numerous counterfeits, presumably contemporary, have recently come on the market. Many of these modern counterfeits have coin alignment. Refer to page 28 of Ch'en Hung-hsi's 1987 *Hsinchiang Hung Ch'ien Chiako Mulu* for illustrations.

25 mm
Obv: Type A.

C#	Date	Emperor	Good	VG	Fine	VF
30-11	ND(1851-61)	Hsien-feng	3.00	5.00	8.00	15.00

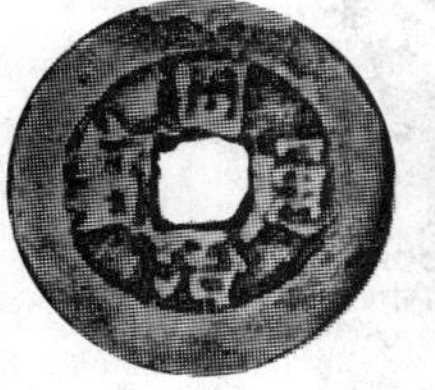

Obv: Type A.

C#	Date	Emperor	Good	VG	Fine	VF
30-15	ND(1862-74)	T'ung-chih	3.00	5.00	8.00	15.00

Rev: Character *A* (for Aksu) above center hole, *Aksu* in Turki at right, in Manchu at left.

C#	Date	Emperor	Good	VG	Fine	VF
30-18	ND(1875-1908)	Kuang-hsu	1.50	2.50	4.00	8.00

Rev: *Aksu* in Manchu at right, in Turki at left.

C#	Date	Emperor	Good	VG	Fine	VF
30-18.1	ND(1875-1908)	Kuang-hsu	7.50	12.50	19.00	35.00

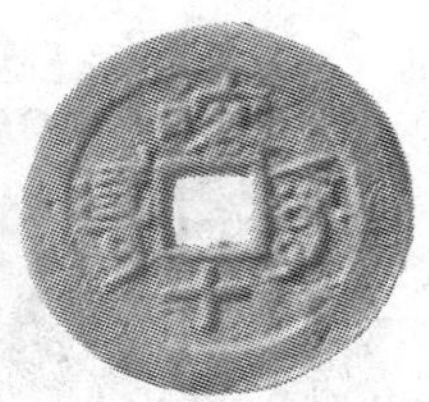

Rev: Character *K'a* (for Kashgar) above.

C#	Date	Emperor	Good	VG	Fine	VF
30-19	ND(1886-1908)	Kuang-hsu	2.00	4.50	6.50	13.50

NOTE: Cast in the Aksu Mint for the Kashgar Mint, beginning in 1886 during the reign of Kuang-Hsu.

50 CASH

CAST BRASS, 36-37mm
Obv: Type B-1.

C#	Date	Emperor	Good	VG	Fine	VF
30-12	ND(1851-61)	Hsien-feng	100.00	150.00	200.00	300.00

100 CASH

CAST COPPER, 44-45mm
Obv: Type C.

C#	Date	Emperor	Good	VG	Fine	VF
30-13	ND(1851-61)	Hsien-feng	140.00	200.00	275.00	400.00

40-41mm

C#	Date	Emperor	Good	VG	Fine	VF
30-13.1	ND(1851-61)	Hsien-feng	30.00	55.00	85.00	150.00

Hammered Coinage

1/2 MISCAL (5 FEN)

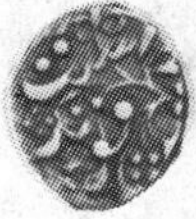

SILVER, 1.45 g
Obv. and rev: Turki script.

Y#	Date	Emperor	VG	Fine	VF	XF
A7.4	ND	—	27.50	45.00	75.00	125.00
	AH1296	—	27.50	45.00	75.00	125.00

Obv: Large Chinese *Kuang* above square w/Turki leg. below. Rev: Turki leg.

Y#	Date	Emperor	VG	Fine	VF	XF
A7.5	AH1296	Kuang-hsu	55.00	90.00	150.00	250.00
	1297	—	11.50	18.50	30.00	50.00
	1298/1297 (mule)	Kuang-hsu	11.50	18.50	30.00	50.00
	1298	Kuang-hsu	11.50	18.50	30.00	50.00

Milled Coinage

MISCAL (MACE)

SILVER, 3.50 g
Similar to 3 Miscals, Y#14.

Y#	Date	Mintage	VG	Fine	VF	XF
A13	AH1310	—	275.00	450.00	750.00	1250.

2 MISCALS (2 MACE)

SILVER, 7.20 g
Similar to 3 Miscals, Y#14.

Y#	Date	Mintage	VG	Fine	VF	XF
13	AH1310	—	40.00	80.00	150.00	225.00
	1311	—	30.00	60.00	100.00	165.00

3 MISCALS (3 MACE)

SILVER, 10.50 g

Y#	Date	Mintage	VG	Fine	VF	XF
14	AH1310	—	40.00	80.00	140.00	225.00
	1311	—	32.50	65.00	110.00	200.00
	1312	—	32.50	65.00	110.00	200.00

5 MISCALS (5 MACE)

SILVER, 17.50 g

Y#	Date	Mintage	VG	Fine	VF	XF
15	AH1310	—	55.00	110.00	190.00	325.00
	1311	—	50.00	100.00	165.00	275.00
	1312	—	40.00	80.00	150.00	250.00

PATTERNS (Pn)

(Including off metal strikes)

KM#	Date	Mintage	Identification	Mkt.Val.
Pn1	ND(1851-61)		1 Cash, Cast Brass,	

KM#	Date	Mintage	Identification	Mkt.Val.
Pn1			Hsien Feng, C30-9	350.00
Pn2	ND(1851-61)		10 Cash, Cast Brass, Hsien Feng, C30-11a	350.00
Pn3	ND(1851-61)		50 Cash, Cast Brass, 54mm, Hsien Feng, C30-12a	350.00
Pn4	ND(1861)		1 Cash, Ch'i Hsiang	500.00
Pn5	ND(1862-74)		1 Cash, Cast Brass, T'ung Chih, C30-14	350.00
Pn6	ND(1862-74)		10 Cash, Cast Brass, T'ung Chih, C30-15a	350.00
Pn7	ND(1875-1908)		1 Cash, Cast Brass, Kuang Hsu, C30-16	350.00
Pn8	ND(1875-1908)		10 Cash, Cast Brass, Kuang Hsu, C30-17	350.00

Ili Mint

(Huiyuan, Kuldja, Kuldsha, Kwlja)

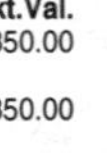

EMPIRE

CASH

CAST COPPER

C#	Date	Emperor	Good	VG	Fine	VF
28-2	ND(1796-1820)	Chia-ch'ing	15.00	30.00	55.00	100.00

Rev: Vertical line below.

C#	Date	Emperor	Good	VG	Fine	VF
28-2.1	ND(1796-1820)	Chia-ch'ing	30.00	50.00	85.00	125.00

Rev: Vertical line above.

C#	Date	Emperor	Good	VG	Fine	VF
28-2.2	ND(1796-1820)	Chia-ch'ing	30.00	50.00	85.00	125.00

Obv: Type A.

C#	Date	Emperor	Good	VG	Fine	VF
28-3	ND(1821-50)	Tao-kuang	25.00	35.00	50.00	85.00

Rev: Dot above.

C#	Date	Emperor	Good	VG	Fine	VF
28-3.1	ND(1821-50)	Tao-kuang	30.00	50.00	85.00	125.00

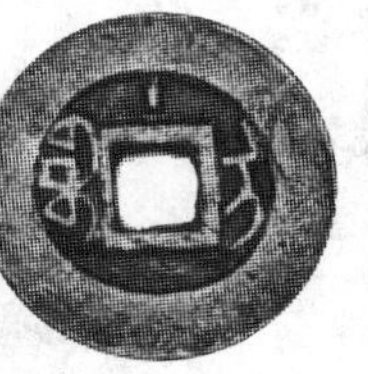

Rev: Vertical line above.

C#	Date	Emperor	Good	VG	Fine	VF
28-3.2	ND(1821-50)	Tao-kuang	30.00	50.00	85.00	125.00

Rev: Character *Shih* (10) above.

C#	Date	Emperor	Good	VG	Fine	VF
28-3.3	ND(1821-50)	Tao-kuang	60.00	75.00	110.00	150.00

Rev: Short vertical lines above and below.

C#	Date	Emperor	Good	VG	Fine	VF
28-3.4	ND(1821-50)	Tao-kuang	35.00	55.00	95.00	140.00

CAST BRASS
Obv: Type A.
Narrow rims.

C#	Date	Emperor	Good	VG	Fine	VF
28-4	ND(1851-61)	Hsien-feng	40.00	80.00	125.00	250.00

4 CASH

CAST COPPER, 33mm
Obv: Type B-2.

C#	Date	Emperor	Good	VG	Fine	VF
28-5	ND(1851-61)	Hsien-feng	22.50	30.00	42.50	90.00

C#	Date	Emperor	Good	VG	Fine	VF
28-9	ND(1862-74)	T'ung-chih	90.00	150.00	200.00	350.00

10 CASH

CAST COPPER, 35mm
Obv: Type B-2.

C#	Date	Emperor	Good	VG	Fine	VF
28-6	ND(1851-61)	Hsien-feng	125.00	200.00	350.00	500.00

50 CASH

CAST COPPER

C#	Date	Emperor	Good	VG	Fine	VF
28-7	ND(1851-61)	Hsien-feng	100.00	150.00	220.00	300.00

100 CASH

CAST COPPER
Obv: Type C.

C#	Date	Emperor	Good	VG	Fine	VF
28-8	ND(1851-61)	Hsien-feng	20.00	30.00	45.00	70.00

NOTE: Numerous counterfeits of C28-8, presumably contemporary, have recently come on the market. Refer to page 39 of Ch'en Hung-hsi's 1987 *Hsinchiang Hung Ch'ien Chiako Mulu* for illustrations. The characters for *Feng* and *Pao* on the obverse are greatly abbreviated, and the bottom horizontal line of the box at the bottom of *Tang* at the top on the reverse is merged with the upper hole frame line.

CAST BRASS

C#	Date	Emperor	Good	VG	Fine	VF
28-8a	ND(1851-61)	Hsien-feng	35.00	55.00	75.00	100.00

500 CASH

CAST COPPER or BRASS

C#	Date	Emperor	Good	VG	Fine	VF
28-11	ND(1851-61)	Hsien-feng	250.00	325.00	400.00	500.00

PATTERNS (Pn)

(Including off metal strikes)

KM#	Date	Mintage	Identification	Mkt.Val.
Pn1	ND(1851-61)		1 Cash, Cast Brass, Hsien Feng, wide rims, C28-4.1.	600.00

KM#	Date	Mintage	Identification	Mkt.Val.
Pn2	ND(1862-74)		1 Cash, Cast Brass, T'ung Chih, C28-8a	500.00

KM#	Date	Mintage	Identification	Mkt.Val.
Pn3	ND(1862-74)		10 Cash, Cast Brass, T'ung Chih, C28-9a	600.00

KM#	Date	Mintage	Identification	Mkt.Val.
Pn4	ND(1875-1908)		1 Cash, Cast Brass, Kuang Hsu, C28-9c	500.00
Pn5	ND(1875-1908)		10 Cash, Cast Brass, Kuang Hsu, C28-10	600.00

Kashgar (Shufu) now Kashi Mint

EMPIRE

CASH

10 CASH

CAST COPPER
Obv: Type A.

C#	Date	Emperor	Good	VG	Fine	VF
32-2	ND(1851-61)	Hsien-feng	12.00	17.50	35.00	55.00

Obv: Type A.
Rev: *Kashgar* in Turki at left; in Manchu at right, *K'a* (Kashgar) above.

C#	Date	Emperor	Good	VG	Fine	VF
32-6	ND(1875-1908)	Kuang-hsu	5.00	9.50	15.00	25.00

Rev: *Kashgar Pao* (right-left).

C#	Date	Emperor	Good	VG	Fine	VF
32-6.1	ND(1875-1908)	Kuang-hsu	5.00	9.50	15.00	25.00

50 CASH

CAST COPPER

C#	Date	Emperor	Good	VG	Fine	VF
32-3	ND(1851-61)	Hsien-feng	135.00	225.00	350.00	500.00

32mm
Obv: Type B-2.
Rev. leg: Stylized Turki mintname.

C#	Date	Emperor	Good	VG	Fine	VF
32-3.1	ND(1851-61)	Hsien-feng	90.00	150.00	250.00	350.00

100 CASH

CAST COPPER, 35mm
Obv: Type B-2.
Rev. leg: Stylized Turki mintname.

C#	Date	Emperor	Good	VG	Fine	VF
32-4	ND(1851-61)	Hsien-feng	100.00	160.00	265.00	375.00

Hammered Coinage

1/2 MISCAL (5 FEN)

SILVER, 1.45 g
Obv. leg: Manchu, Chinese and Manchu w/outer border of S's at rim w/o square in center.
Rev: Turki leg.

Y#	Date	Emperor	VG	Fine	VF	XF
A7.6	ND	—	15.00	25.00	40.00	65.00
	AH(12)95	—	15.00	25.00	40.00	65.00

Obv. & rev: Square in center.
Rev. leg: Manchu, Chinese official "5" above Turki.

Y#	Date	Emperor	VG	Fine	VF	XF
A7.7	ND	Kuang-hsu	15.00	25.00	40.00	65.00
	AH(12)95	Kuang-hsu	15.00	25.00	40.00	65.00

Similar to Y#A7.7, but w/normal "5" above.

Y#	Date	Emperor	VG	Fine	VF	XF
A7.23	ND	Kuang-hsu	15.00	25.00	40.00	65.00

Obv: *Kuang* in unusual script, dot in central square.

Y#	Date	Emperor	VG	Fine	VF	XF
A7.24	ND	Kuang-hsu	15.00	25.00	40.00	65.00

Y#	Date	Emperor	VG	Fine	VF	XF
A7.19	ND	Kuang-hsu	—	—	Rare	—

NOTE: Believed to be degenerate copy of Y#A7.7 by certain authority.

Obv. & rev: W/o square in center.
Obv. leg: Turki. Rev. leg: Chinese for 5 Fen.

Y#	Date	Emperor	VG	Fine	VF	XF
A7.8	AH1313	—	100.00	175.00	300.00	500.00

Y#	Date	Emperor	VG	Fine	VF	XF
A7.9	ND	—	100.00	175.00	300.00	500.00

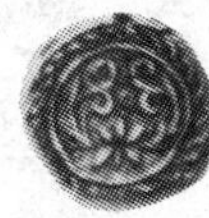

Obv: Arabesque, wreath and flower replaces Turki leg. Rev. leg: Chinese for 5 Fen.

Y#	Date	Emperor	VG	Fine	VF	XF
A7.10	ND	—	100.00	175.00	300.00	500.00

Obv. Turki leg: *Besh Fen*.
Rev. Turki leg: *Darb Kashgar*.

Y#	Date	Emperor	VG	Fine	VF	XF
A7.20	ND	Kuang-hsu	9.00	15.00	25.00	40.00

MISCAL (MACE)

SILVER, 2.90 g
Rev. leg: In Chinese, Turki and Manchu.

Y#	Date	Emperor	VG	Fine	VF	XF
B7	AH1292	Kuang-hsu	250.00	400.00	700.00	1200.
	1295	Kuang-hsu	250.00	400.00	700.00	1200.

Milled Coinage

MISCAL (MACE)

SILVER, 3.50 g
Obv: 6 characters. Rev: Wreath around Turki leg.

Y#	Date	Mintage	VG	Fine	VF	XF
16	ND	—	50.00	75.00	150.00	250.00
	AH1309	—	50.00	75.00	150.00	250.00
	1310	—	50.00	75.00	150.00	250.00
	1311	—	50.00	75.00	150.00	250.00

Obv: Like Y#A16. Rev: Like Y#16.

Y#	Date	Mintage	VG	Fine	VF	XF
D16	AH1310	—	150.00	250.00	400.00	650.00

Obv: 4 characters. Rev: W/o wreath.

Y#	Date	Mintage	VG	Fine	VF	XF
A16	ND	—	90.00	150.00	250.00	400.00
	AH1310	—	90.00	150.00	250.00	400.00

2 MISCALS (2 MACE)

SILVER, 7.20 g

Y#	Date	Mintage	VG	Fine	VF	XF
17	ND	—	60.00	100.00	175.00	300.00
	AH1310	—	16.50	27.50	45.00	75.00
	1311	—	12.00	20.00	30.00	50.00
	1312	—	10.00	14.00	30.00	65.00
	1313	—	17.50	30.00	45.00	75.00

Obv: Chinese characters *K'a Shih* at right.

Y#	Date	Mintage	VG	Fine	VF	XF
17a	AH1311(error)	—	—	—	—	—
	1312	—	12.50	22.50	32.50	50.00
	1313	—	12.50	22.50	32.50	50.00
	1314	—	12.50	22.50	32.50	50.00
	1315	—	12.50	22.50	32.50	50.00
	1317	—	12.50	22.50	32.50	50.00

NOTE: Later dates (AH1319-1320) exist for this type.

3 MISCALS

SILVER, 10.50 g

Y#	Date	Mintage	VG	Fine	VF	XF
A18	AH1307	—	1250.	2250.	3750.	5500.

NOTE: Struck at Tihua (Wulumuqi).

Y#	Date	Mintage	VG	Fine	VF	XF
18	ND	—	—	—	Rare	—
	AH1310	—	15.00	25.00	40.00	65.00
	1311	—	17.50	30.00	45.00	75.00
	1312	—	20.00	35.00	55.00	100.00

Obv: Chinese characters *K'a Shih* to right.

Y#	Date	Mintage	VG	Fine	VF	XF
18a	AH1311 (error)	—	—	—	Rare	—
	1313	—	10.00	20.00	32.50	65.00
	1314	—	10.00	20.00	32.50	65.00
	1315	—	10.00	20.00	32.50	65.00
	1316	—	10.00	20.00	32.50	65.00
	1317	—	10.00	20.00	32.50	65.00

NOTE: Later dates (AH1319-1320) exist for this type.

5 MISCALS

SILVER, 17.20 g
Obv. leg. in Turki, Chinese and Manchu.

Kann#	Date	Mintage	VG	Fine	VF	XF
1040	AH1307	—	1250.	2000.	3500.	5000.

NOTE: Struck at Tihua (Wulumuqi).

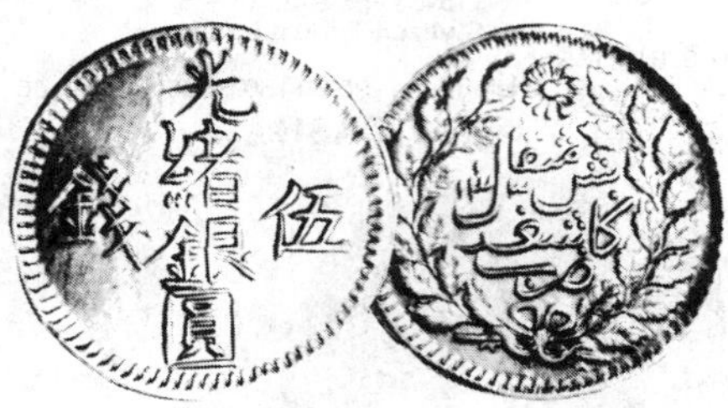

Y#	Date	Mintage	VG	Fine	VF	XF
19	AH1310	—	17.50	30.00	55.00	100.00
	1311	—	10.00	20.00	35.00	70.00
	1312	—	15.00	27.50	45.00	90.00
	1313	—	15.00	27.50	45.00	90.00
	1315	—	15.00	27.50	45.00	90.00

Obv: Chinese characters *K'a Shih* at right.

Y#	Date	Mintage	VG	Fine	VF	XF
19a	AH1311(error)	—	—	—	Rare	—
	1313	—	17.50	25.00	40.00	70.00
	1314	—	17.50	25.00	40.00	70.00
	1315	—	17.50	25.00	40.00	70.00
	1316	—	17.50	25.00	40.00	70.00
	1317	—	17.50	25.00	40.00	70.00

NOTE: Later dates (AH1319-1320) exist for this type.

PATTERNS (Pn)

(Including off metal strikes)

KM#	Date	Mintage	Identification	Mkt.Val.
Pn1	ND(1851-61)	—	1 Cash, Hsien Feng	350.00
Pn2	ND(1851-61)	—	500 Cash, Hsien Feng	500.00

REBEL COINAGE

Yakub Beg

Most of these coins were struck at Kashgar (Kashi) in the name of the Ottoman Sultan Abdul Aziz by the rebel Yakub Beg, who controlled much of Sinkiang (Xinjiang) between 1865 and 1877.

In the name of Abdul Aziz

FALUS

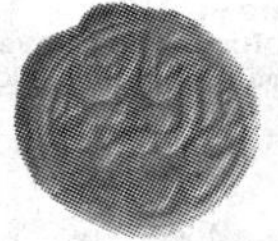

COPPER
Obv. and rev: Date.

C#	Date	Good	VG	Fine	VF
37.4	AH1290	20.00	32.50	40.00	50.00
	1292	20.00	32.50	40.00	50.00

Obv: Date.

C#	Date	Good	VG	Fine	VF
37.5	AH1291	20.00	32.50	40.00	50.00
	1293	20.00	32.50	40.00	50.00
	1294	20.00	32.50	40.00	50.00

Rev: Date.

C#	Date	Good	VG	Fine	VF
37.6	AH1292	20.00	32.50	40.00	50.00

Obv. and rev: W/o date.

C#	Date	Good	VG	Fine	VF
37.7	ND	15.00	21.50	30.00	40.00

1/2 MISCAL (MACE)

SILVER

C#	Date	VG	Fine	VF	XF
37-1.1	AH1290/91	9.00	15.00	25.00	40.00
	1291	9.00	15.00	25.00	40.00
	1291/92	9.00	15.00	25.00	40.00
	1292	9.00	15.00	25.00	40.00
	1293	9.00	15.00	25.00	40.00
	1294	9.00	15.00	25.00	40.00
	ND	9.00	15.00	25.00	40.00

Legends arranged differently.

C#	Date	VG	Fine	VF	XF
37-1.2	AH1291	9.00	15.00	25.00	40.00
	1292	9.00	15.00	25.00	40.00
	1292/93	9.00	15.00	25.00	40.00
	1293	9.00	15.00	25.00	40.00
	1293/94	9.00	15.00	25.00	40.00
	1294	9.00	15.00	25.00	40.00
	ND	9.00	15.00	25.00	40.00

TILLA

GOLD, 4.50 g
Rev. leg: *Zarb Mahrusah Kashgar*.

C#	Date	VG	Fine	VF	XF
37-2.1	AH1290	125.00	250.00	425.00	700.00

3.70 g
Rev. leg: *Zarb Dar us-Sultanat Kashgar*.

C#	Date	VG	Fine	VF	XF
37-2.2	AH1291/1290 (mule)	140.00	280.00	475.00	800.00
	1291	110.00	220.00	360.00	600.00

Obv. leg. within dotted border within circles.
Rev. leg. within circle.

C#	Date	VG	Fine	VF	XF
37-2.3	AH1291	110.00	220.00	360.00	600.00

Rev. leg. within segmented circles.

C#	Date	VG	Fine	VF	XF
37-2.4	AH1291	110.00	220.00	360.00	600.00

Obv. leg. within dotted border within circles w/loop.
Rev. leg. within dotted border within circles.

C#	Date	VG	Fine	VF	XF
37-2.5	AH1292	125.00	250.00	425.00	700.00

Obv. leg. within segmented circles w/loop.
Rev. leg. within segmented circles.

C#	Date	VG	Fine	VF	XF
37-2.6	AH1292	90.00	180.00	300.00	500.00
	1293	125.00	250.00	425.00	700.00
	1294	125.00	250.00	425.00	700.00
	1295	125.00	250.00	425.00	700.00

In the name of Abdulhamid II

C#	Date	VG	Fine	VF	XF
37-3	AH12xx	—	—	—	—

Khotan (Hotien) now Hotan Mint

Hammered Coinage

1/2 MISCAL

SILVER, 1.45 g
Rev: *Kho-tan* in Arabic. Retrograde and inverted Chinese '5'.

Y#	Date	Mintage	VG	Fine	VF	XF
A7.11	ND		27.50	45.00	72.50	120.00

Rev: *Zarb Khotan* in Arabic.

Y#	Date	Mintage	VG	Fine	VF	XF
A7.12	ND		27.50	45.00	72.50	120.00

PATTERNS (Pn)

(Including off metal strikes)

KM#	Date	Mintage	Identification	Mkt.Val.
Pn1	ND(1851-61)	—	100 Cash, Copper, Hsien Feng, C31-1v	750.00
Pn2	ND(1851-61)	—	500 Cash, Copper, Hsien Feng, C31-1a	900.00
Pn3	ND(1851-61)	—	1000 Cash, Copper, Hsien Feng, C31-2	2350.

REBEL COINAGE

Ghazi Rashid

AH1279-84/1862-67AD

A rebel in Sinkiang (Xinjiang) about whom little is known. He was in power from 1862 until his death in 1867.

TENGA

SILVER

C#	Date	VG	Fine	VF	XF
36-5	AH1283	100.00	165.00	250.00	350.00

Kuche (Kucha) Mint

Kuche is about 140 miles east and a little north of Aksu and has sometimes been confused with Kulja (Kuldja).

EMPIRE

CASH

CAST COPPER
Rev: Characters *Boo Yuan* left and right, *K'u* above.

C#	Date	Emperor	Good	VG	Fine	VF
33-20	ND(1862-74)	T'ung-chih	7.50	14.00	22.00	32.50

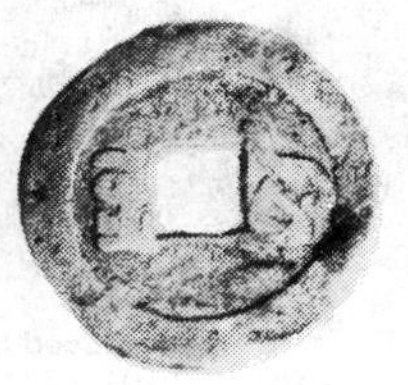

C#	Date	Emperor	Good	VG	Fine	VF
33-23	ND(1875-1908)	Kuang-Hsu	6.00	8.00	12.00	20.00

Rev: Similar to General Coinage KM#10 but entire reverse is in inverted mirror image.

KM#	Date	Emperor	Good	VG	Fine	VF
11	ND(1875-1908)	Kuang-hsu	3.50	6.00	9.00	13.50

5 CASH

CAST COPPER
Obv: Type A.

C#	Date	Emperor	Good	VG	Fine	VF
33-8	ND(1851-61)	Hsien-feng	50.00	75.00	100.00	175.00

Obv: Type A-2.

C#	Date	Emperor	Good	VG	Fine	VF
33-22	ND(1862-74)	T'ung-chih	135.00	225.00	350.00	500.00

10 CASH

CAST COPPER
Rev: Character *K'u* (Kuche) above.

C#	Date	Emperor	Good	VG	Fine	VF
33-6	ND(1821-50)	Tao-kuang	2.50	4.00	10.00	18.00

NOTE: This coin was struck during a later reign beginning in 1875.

Obv: Type A.

C#	Date	Emperor	Good	VG	Fine	VF
33-9	ND(1851-61)	Hsien-feng	2.00	3.00	9.00	16.00

Obv: Type A-2.

C#	Date	Emperor	Good	VG	Fine	VF
33-13	ND(1862-74)	T'ung-chih	1.50	3.00	9.00	16.00

Rev: Character *K'u* (Kuche) above.

C#	Date	Emperor	Good	VG	Fine	VF
33-14	ND(1862-74)	T'ung-chih	4.00	6.00	12.00	20.00

Obv: Type A.

C#	Date	Emperor	Good	VG	Fine	VF
33-16	ND(1875-1908)	Kuang-hsu	10.00	20.00	30.00	50.00

Rev: Characters *Chiu Nien* (year 9 = 1883) above.

C#	Date	Emperor	Good	VG	Fine	VF
33-17	ND(1883)	Kuang-hsu	10.00	17.50	25.50	45.00

NOTE: Cast as a commemorative of the 1884 establishment of Hsinchiang (Xinjiang) as a province.

Rev: Character *K'u* above.

C#	Date	Emperor	Good	VG	Fine	VF
33-18	ND(1875-1908)	Kuang-hsu	7.50	12.00	17.50	35.00

Rev: Semi-circle at lower right.

C#	Date	Emperor	Good	VG	Fine	VF
33-18.1	ND(1875-1908)	Kuang-hsu	7.50	13.50	22.50	35.00

C#	Date	Emperor	Good	VG	Fine	VF
33-19	ND(1875-1908)	Kuang-hsu	2.00	3.00	10.00	18.00

NOTE: Other varieties are reported for T'ung Chih and

Kuang Hsu reigns.

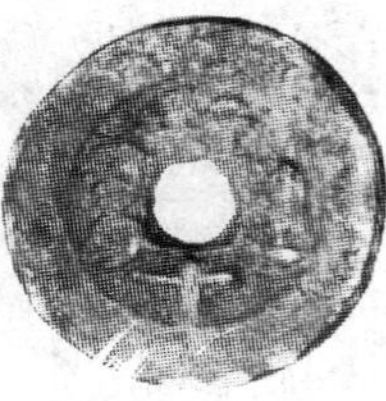

Rev: *Pao Ku* w/*Hsin* (new) above.

KM#	Date	Emperor	Good	VG	Fine	VF
3	ND(1886)					
(C33-7)		Tao-kuang	5.50	9.00	15.00	25.00

NOTE: Cast by the Kucha Mint for the Tihwa (Urumqi) or Bao Xin (Hsin), Mint.

Rev: *Pao Ku* w/*Hsin* (new) above.

KM#	Date	Emperor	Good	VG	Fine	VF
5	ND(1886)					
		T'ung-chih	5.50	9.00	15.00	25.00

NOTE: Cast by the Kucha Mint for the Tihwa (Urumqi) or Bao Xin, Mint.

Obv: Type A
Rev: *Pao Ku* w/*K'a* (for Kuche) above.

KM#	Date	Emperor	Good	VG	Fine	VF
6	ND(1886)					
		Kuang-hsu	5.50	8.00	14.00	22.50

NOTE: Cast by the Kucha Mint for the Kashgar Mint.
NOTE: KM#3 and 5-6 were cast in the reign of Kuang Hsu (1875-1908), beginning in 1886.

Rev: *Pao Ku* w/*K'u* (for Kuche) above.

KM#	Date	Emperor	Good	VG	Fine	VF
7.1	ND(1875-1908)					
		Kuang-hsu	1.50	3.00	5.00	10.00

Rev: *Pao* (for Kuche) at left reversed.

KM#	Date	Emperor	Good	VG	Fine	VF
7.2	ND(1875-1908)					
		Kuang-hsu	7.50	13.50	22.50	35.00

50 CASH

CAST COPPER

C#	Date	Emperor	Good	VG	Fine	VF
33-10	ND(1851-61)					
		Hsien-feng	100.00	150.00	250.00	400.00

100 CASH

CAST COPPER, 49mm

C#	Date	Emperor	Good	VG	Fine	VF
33-11	ND(1851-61)					
		Hsien-feng	100.00	125.00	150.00	225.00

Reduced size, 34mm

C#	Date	Emperor	Good	VG	Fine	VF
33-11a	ND(1851-61)					
		Hsien-feng	60.00	75.00	90.00	125.00

Hammered Coinage

1/2 MISCAL (5 FEN)

SILVER, 1.45 g

Y#	Date	Emperor	VG	Fine	VF	XF
A7.2	ND(AH1294)					
		Kuang-hsu	5.50	9.00	15.00	25.00
	(AH1295) yr.4					
		Kuang-hsu	16.50	27.50	45.00	75.00
	AH1295					
		Kuang-hsu	5.50	9.00	15.00	25.00

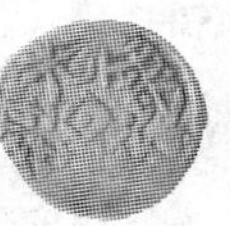

Y#	Date	Emperor	VG	Fine	VF	XF
A7.13	ND (1877)					
		Kuang-hsu	—	—	Rare	—

PATTERNS (Pn)

(Including off metal strikes)

KM#	Date	Mintage	Identification	Mkt.Val.
Pn1	ND(1851-61)	—	1 Cash, Hsien Feng	350.00
Pn2	ND(1851-61)	—	500 Cash, Cast Copper, Hsien Feng, C33-21	500.00
Pn3	ND(1851-61)	—	1000 Cash, Cast Copper, Hsien Feng, C33-12	500.00

Urumchi (Urumqi) Mint

Tihwa, *Ti-hua,* (Dihua)

EMPIRE

8 CASH

CAST COPPER
Obv: Type B-1.

C#	Date	Emperor	Good	VG	Fine	VF
29-1	ND(1851-61)					
		Hsien-feng	21.50	35.00	50.00	75.00

10 CASH

CAST COPPER, 33mm
Obv: Type B-1.

C#	Date	Emperor	Good	VG	Fine	VF
29-2	ND(1851-61)					
		Hsien-feng	20.00	35.00	50.00	75.00

27mm

C#	Date	Emperor	Good	VG	Fine	VF
29-2.1	ND(1851-61)					
		Hsien-feng	8.50	15.00	25.00	40.00

Rev: *Pao Hsin* w/*Hsin* (new, but here standing for the Tihwa (now Urumqi) Mint) above.

KM#	Date	Emperor	Good	VG	Fine	VF
8	ND(1875-1908)					
		Kuang-hsu	3.50	5.00	7.50	15.00

Rev: *Pao Hsin* (for Tihwa Mint) w/ *Hsin* (new) above.

KM#	Date	Emperor	Good	VG	Fine	VF
9	ND(1875-1908)					
		Kuang-hsu	3.00	4.50	7.00	15.00

50 CASH

CAST COPPER

C#	Date	Emperor	Good	VG	Fine	VF
29-3	ND(1851-61)					
		Hsien-feng	Reported, not confirmed			

80 CASH

CAST BRASS, 50mm
Obv: Type C.

C#	Date	Emperor	Good	VG	Fine	VF
29-5	ND(1851-61)	Hsien-feng	275.00	500.00	850.00	1350.

NOTE: Smaller 40mm examples are considered to be counterfeits.

100 CASH

CAST COPPER

C#	Date	Emperor	Good	VG	Fine	VF
29-4	ND(1851-61)	Hsien-feng	—	—	Rare	—

Ushi (Wushih) now Wushi/or Urumqi Mint
EMPIRE
PATTERNS (Pn)

(Including off metal strikes)

KM#	Date	Mintage	Identification	Mkt.Val.
Pn1	ND(1851-61)	—	1 Cash, Hsien Feng	350.00

KM#	Date	Mintage	Identification	Mkt.Val.
Pn2	ND(1851-61)	—	100 Cash, Hsien Feng, C34-2	350.00
Pn3	ND(1851-61)	—	500 Cash, Hsien Feng, C34-3	500.00

Yanghissar (Han-cheng) Mint now Yengisar Mint
EMPIRE
1/2 MISCAL

SILVER, 1.45 g

Y#	Date	Mintage	VG	Fine	VF	XF
A7.14	ND(1875-1908)		55.00	90.00	150.00	250.00

PATTERNS (Pn)

(Including off metal strikes)

KM#	Date	Mintage	Identification	Mkt.Val.
Pn1	ND(1851-61)	—	1 Cash, Hsien Feng	400.00
Pn2	ND(1851-61)	—	100 Cash, Hsien Feng	500.00
Pn3	ND(1851-61)	—	500 Cash, Hsien Feng	600.00
Pn4	ND(1851-61)	—	1000 Cash, Hsien Feng	600.00

Yarkand (Soche) Mint now Shache (Yarkant) Mint
EMPIRE
10 CASH

CAST COPPER, 25mm

C#	Date	Emperor	Good	VG	Fine	VF
35-3	ND(1851-61)	Hsien-feng	4.00	7.00	10.00	16.00

Obv: Type A-2.

C#	Date	Emperor	Good	VG	Fine	VF
35-7	ND(1862-74)	T'ung-chih	4.00	7.00	10.00	16.00

50 CASH

CAST BRASS, 37mm
Obv: Type B-1.

C#	Date	Emperor	Good	VG	Fine	VF
35-4	ND(1851-61)	Hsien-feng	80.00	135.00	175.00	250.00

32mm

C#	Date	Emperor	Good	VG	Fine	VF
35-4.1	ND(1851-61)	Hsien-feng	65.00	115.00	140.00	200.00

100 CASH

CAST COPPER, 50-56mm
Obv: Type C.

C#	Date	Emperor	Good	VG	Fine	VF
35-5.1	ND(1851-61)	Hsien-feng	85.00	125.00	200.00	400.00

45mm

C#	Date	Emperor	Good	VG	Fine	VF
35-5.2	ND(1851-61)	Hsien-feng	85.00	125.00	200.00	400.00

Hammered Coinage
1/2 MISCAL

SILVER, 1.45 g
Rev: Turki and Chinese leg.

Y#	Date	Mintage	VG	Fine	VF	XF
A7.15	ND		20.00	35.00	60.00	100.00

Rev: Date at left.

Y#	Date	Mintage	VG	Fine	VF	XF
A7.16	AH1295	—	45.00	75.00	120.00	200.00

Rev: Date at right.

Y#	Date	Mintage	VG	Fine	VF	XF
A7.17	AH1295	—	55.00	90.00	150.00	250.00

Rev: Turki, Chinese and Manchu leg.

Y#	Date	Mintage	VG	Fine	VF	XF
A7.18	ND		15.00	25.00	40.00	65.00

TRIBAL COINAGE

In the outset of the Ch'ing Dynasty the Zhungar (Tzungar or Sungar) tribes in the northern sector of Sinkiang were very powerful.

In 1700, the 39th year of Emperor K'ang-hsi, Khan Tsewang Arabtan went on a successful expedition to the south conquering Yarkand Khanate. He ordered them to produce the "pul" coppers with his name Tsewang.

After Tsewang's death, his succeeding son Khardan Chirin ordered the minting of new "pul" coppers exchange one new "pul" for two old "pul" of his father.

In 1757, the 22nd year of the Emperor Ch'ien-lung the

campaign against the Zhungar Tribes was initiated and Imperial forces finally gained control of the area in the early 1760's.

Ghazi Rashid

A rebel in Sinkiang (Xinjiang) about whom little is known. He was in power from 1862 until his death in 1867.

CASH

COPPER
Small legends

C#	Date	Mint	Good	VG	Fine	VF
36-1	AH1280	Kuche	10.00	15.00	25.00	40.00

NOTE: Exists w/coin or medal rotation.

Large legends

C#	Date	Mint	Good	VG	Fine	VF
36-2	AH1280	Kuche	10.00	15.00	25.00	40.00

NOTE: The date of C#36-1 and 36-2 is found at the top of the reverse. These coins are usually undated or with the date illegible. Even in clearly dated specimens, which are worth a substantial premium, the "0" never seems to be detectable.

C#	Date	Mint	Good	VG	Fine	VF
36-3	—	Aksu	—	—	Rare	—

PATTERNS (Pn)

(Including off metal strikes)

KM#	Date	Mintage	Identification	Mkt.Val.
Pn1	ND(1851-61)	—	1 Cash, Hsien Feng	350.00
Pn2	ND(1851-61)	—	500 Cash, Cast Copper, Hsien Feng, C35-5a	500.00
Pn3	ND(1851-61)	—	1000 Cash, Cast Copper, Hsien Feng, C35-6	500.00
Pn4	ND(1861)	—	1 Cash, Ch'i Hsiang	500.00

KM#	Date	Mintage	Identification	Mkt.Val.
Pn5	ND(1875-1908)	—	1 Cash, Cast Copper, Kuang Hsu, C35-8	—

SZECHUAN PROVINCE

Sichuan

A province located in south-central China. The largest of the traditional Chinese provinces, Szechuan (Sichuan) is a plateau region watered by many rivers. These rivers carry much trading traffic. Agriculture or mining are the occupational choices of most of the populace. In World War II the national capital was moved to Chungking in Szechuan (Sichuan). Chengtu was an active imperial mint that opened in 1732 and was in practically continuous operation until the advent of modern equipment. Modern minting was introduced in the province when Chengtu began milled coinage in 1898. A mint was authorized for Chungking in 1905 but it did not begin operations until 1913. The Chengtu Mint was looted by soldiers in 1925. The last republic issues from Szechuan (Sichuan) were dated 1932.

The machinery for the first Szechuan (Sichuan) Mint was produced in New Jersey and the dies were engraved in Philadelphia. The mint was opened in 1898, but closed within a few months and did not reopen until 1901. There is no doubt now that Y#234-238 (K#145-149) were the first issues of this mint, contrary to the Kann listings.

EMPIRE

CASH

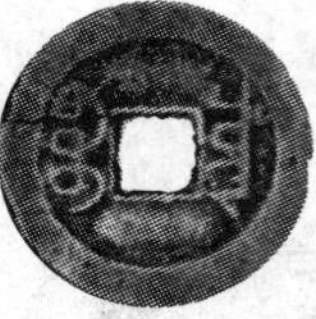

COPPER
Obv: Type A.

C#	Date	Emperor	Good	VG	Fine	VF
24-3	ND(1821-50)	Tao-kuang	1.00	1.75	2.50	4.00

C#	Date	Emperor	Good	VG	Fine	VF
24-4	ND(1851-61)	Hsien-feng	4.50	7.50	11.50	18.00

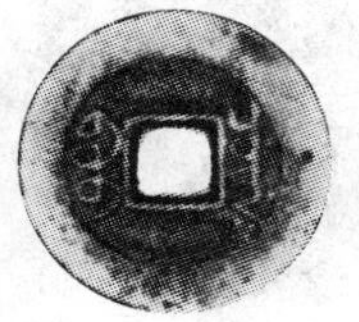

C#	Date	Emperor	Good	VG	Fine	VF
Reduced size.						
24-4a	ND(1851-61)	Hsien-feng	1.50	3.00	4.00	5.00
Rev: Character *Shih* (ten) above.						
24-4.1	ND(1851-61)	Hsien-feng	5.00	8.00	12.50	20.00
Rev: Character *Wen* above.						
24-4.2	ND(1851-61)	Hsien-feng	5.00	8.00	12.50	20.00
Rev: Character *Kung* (work) above.						
24-4.3	ND(1851-61)	Hsien-feng	5.00	8.00	12.50	20.00
Rev: Character *Erh* (two) above.						
24-4.4	ND(1851-61)	Hsien-feng	5.00	8.00	12.50	20.00
Rev: Circle above.						
24-4.5	ND(1851-61)	Hsien-feng	5.00	8.00	12.50	20.00
Rev: Crescent standing on end above.						
24-4.6	ND(1851-61)	Hsien-feng	5.00	8.00	12.50	20.00
Rev: 2 horizontal and 1 vertical lines above.						
24-4.7	ND(1851-61)	Hsien-feng	5.00	8.00	12.50	20.00
Rev: 2 figures above, possibly 15.						
24-4.8	ND(1851-61)	Hsien-feng	5.00	8.00	12.50	20.00
Rev: Crescent below.						
24-4.9	ND(1851-61)	Hsien-feng	5.00	8.00	12.50	20.00
Obv: Type A-2.						
24-8	ND(1862-74)	T'ung-chih	5.00	8.00	12.50	20.00

Rev: Character *Shih* (ten) above and dot below.

C#	Date	Emperor	Good	VG	Fine	VF
24-8.1	ND(1862-74)	T'ung-chih	5.00	8.00	12.50	20.00

Rev: Character *Shih* above and crescent on end below.

C#	Date	Emperor	Good	VG	Fine	VF
24-8.2	ND(1862-74)	T'ung-chih	5.00	8.00	12.50	20.00

C#	Date	Emperor	Good	VG	Fine	VF
Rev: Character *Shih* above and *San* below.						
24-8.3	ND(1862-74)	T'ung-chih	5.00	8.00	12.50	20.00
Rev: Character *Shih* above and *Lin* below.						
24-8.4	ND(1862-74)	T'ung-chih	5.00	8.00	12.50	20.00
Rev: Character *Wen* above and *Yi.* below.						
24-8.5	ND(1862-74)	T'ung-chih	5.00	8.00	12.50	20.00
Rev: Character *Wen* above and *Ch'i* below.						
24-8.6	ND(1862-74)	T'ung-chih	5.00	8.00	12.50	20.00
Rev: Character *Wen* above and *Ch'uan* below.						
24-8.7	ND(1862-74)	T'ung-chih	5.00	8.00	12.50	20.00

NOTE: Refer to "Additional Characters" chart in the introduction to China.

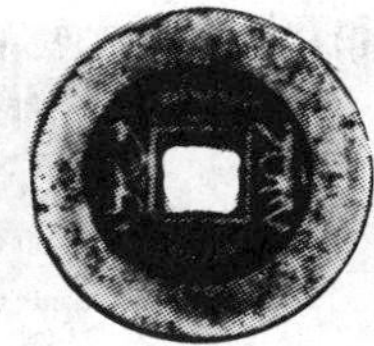

Obv: Type A.

C#	Date	Emperor	Good	VG	Fine	VF
24-9	ND(1875-1908)	Kuang-hsu	4.50	7.50	11.50	22.50

10 CASH

CAST BRASS
Obv: Type B-1.
Rev: Type I mint mark.

C#	Date	Emperor	Good	VG	Fine	VF
24-5	ND(1851-61)	Hsien-feng	15.00	25.00	35.00	60.00

C#	Date	Emperor	Good	VG	Fine	VF
Rev: Type II mint mark.						
24-5.1	ND(1851-61)	Hsien-feng	35.00	45.00	60.00	85.00
Rev: Type I mint mark.						
24-10	ND(1875-1908)	Kuang-hsu	—	—	Rare	—

50 CASH

CAST BRASS
Obv: Type B-1.
Rev: Type II mint mark.

C#	Date	Emperor	Good	VG	Fine	VF
24-6	ND(1851-61)	Hsien-feng	55.00	75.00	100.00	135.00

100 CASH

CAST BRASS
Obv: Type C.
Rev: Type II mint mark.

C#	Date	Emperor	Good	VG	Fine	VF
24-7	ND(1851-61)	Hsien-feng	70.00	90.00	120.00	165.00

MILLED COINAGE

5 CENTS

1.3000 g, .820 SILVER, .0343 oz ASW

Y#	Date	Mintage	Fine	VF	XF	Unc
234	ND(1898; 1901-08)	.671	12.00	17.50	30.00	80.00

20 CENTS

5.3000 g, .820 SILVER, .1397 oz ASW
Rev: 5 flames on pearl.

Y#	Date	Mintage	Fine	VF	XF	Unc
236	ND(1898; 1901-08)	.897	10.00	20.00	40.00	100.00

Rev: 6 flames on pearl.

Y#	Date	Mintage	Fine	VF	XF	Unc
236.1	ND(1898; 1901-08)	Inc. Ab.	10.00	20.00	40.00	100.00

Rev: 7 flames on pearl.

Y#	Date	Mintage	Fine	VF	XF	Unc
236.2	ND(1898; 1901-08)	Inc. Ab.	10.00	20.00	40.00	100.00

50 CENTS

13.2000 g, .860 SILVER, .3650 oz ASW
Rev: Dragon w/narrow face, small cross at either side, large fireball.

Y#	Date	Mintage	Fine	VF	XF	Unc
237	ND(1898; 1901-08)	.474	22.00	40.00	100.00	300.00

DOLLAR

26.8000 g, .900 SILVER, .7756 oz ASW
Rev: Dragon w/narrow face and large fireball, small cross at either side of dragon.

Y#	Date	Mintage	Fine	VF	XF	Unc
238	ND(1898; 1901-08)	6.487	20.00	30.00	75.00	500.00

PATTERNS (Pn)

(Including off metal strikes)

For previously listed KM-Pn1 and Pn2 refer to Standard General Issues - pattern listings.

KM#	Date	Mintage	Identification	Mkt.Val.
Pn4	ND(1896)	—	30 Cash, Copper, front view dragon, Y233.1	Rare
Pn5	ND(1896)	—	30 Cash, Brass	Rare
Pn6	ND	—	30 Cash, Copper, flying dragon, Y232.2	Rare
Pn7	ND(1896)	—	30 Cash, Brass	Rare
Pn8	ND(1898)	—	5 Cents, Brass, Y234	350.00
Pn9	ND(1898)	—	10 Cents, Brass, Y235	350.00
Pn10	ND(1898)	—	20 Cents, Silver, K142	1500.
Pn11	ND(1898)	—	20 Cents, Brass, Y236	—
Pn12	ND(1898)	—	50 Cents, Silver, K141	3500.
Pn13	ND(1898)	—	50 Cents, Brass, Y237	550.00

KM#	Date	Mintage	Identification	Mkt.Val.
Pn14	ND(1898)	—	1 Dollar, Silver, K140	10,000.
Pn15	ND(1898)	—	1 Dollar, Brass, Y238	850.00

PIEFORT (P)

KM#	Date	Mintage	Identification	Mkt.Val.
P1	ND(1898)	—	5 Cents, White metal, Y234	350.00

TAIWAN

For historical information refer to introductory paragraph of the Republic of China following the Peoples Republic of China listings.

Chinese migration to Taiwan began as early as the sixth century. The Dutch established a base on the island in 1624 and held it until 1661, when they were driven out by supporters of the Ming dynasty who used it as a base for their unsuccessful attempt to displace the ruling Manchu dynasty of mainland China. After being occupied by Manchu forces in 1683, Taiwan remained under the suzerainty of China until its cession to Japan in 1895. The island was part of the province of Fukien (Fujian) until established as a separate province in the period 1885-1895. (It took 10 years to complete the conversion to a full-fledged province.)

EMPIRE

CASH

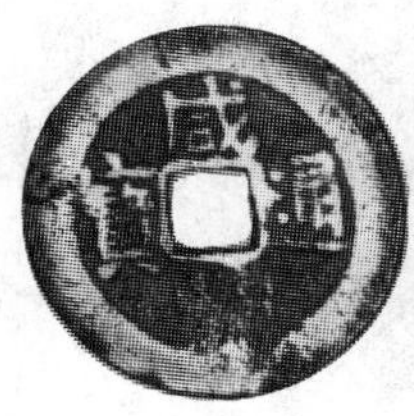

CAST BRASS
Obv: Type A.

C#	Date	Emperor	Good	VG	Fine	VF
25-6	ND(1851-61)	Hsien-feng	60.00	70.00	80.00	100.00

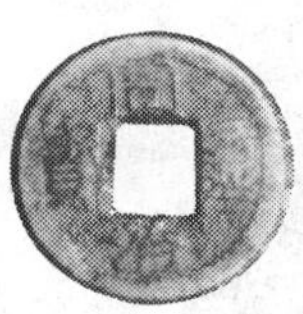
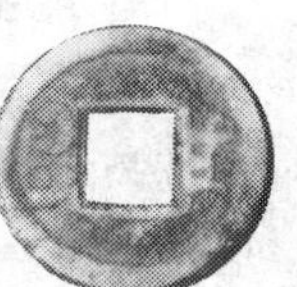

C#	Date	Emperor	Good	VG	Fine	VF
25-9	ND(1862-74)	Tung-chih	—	60.00	90.00	—

MILLED COINAGE

Made in Taiwan 臺灣製局

Made in Tai Province 臺省製造

5 CENTS

1.3000 g, .820 SILVER, .0343 oz ASW
Similar to 10 Cents, Y#247.

Y#	Date	Mintage	Fine	VF	XF	Unc
246	ND(1893-94)		200.00	350.00	500.00	1000.

10 CENTS

2.7000 g, .820 SILVER, .0712 oz ASW
Obv: 4 Chinese characters above meaning: *Made in Taiwan;* large characters in outside circle; small characters inside.

Y#	Date	Mintage	Fine	VF	XF	Unc
247	ND(1893-94)		80.00	175.00	400.00	600.00

Obv: Smaller characters in outside circle, larger characters inside circle.

Y#	Date	Mintage	Fine	VF	XF	Unc
247.1	ND(1893-94)		75.00	175.00	400.00	600.00

Obv: 4 Chinese characters above meaning: *Made in Tai Province.*

Y#	Date	Mintage	Fine	VF	XF	Unc
247.2	ND(1893-94)		100.00	200.00	400.00	750.00

20 CENTS

5.4000 g, .820 SILVER, .1424 oz ASW
Obv: 4 Chinese characters above, meaning *Made in Taiwan.*

Y#	Date	Mintage	Fine	VF	XF	Unc
248	ND(1894)	—	—	—	Rare	—

Obv: 4 Chinese characters above, meaning: *Made in Tai Province.*

Y#	Date	Mintage	Fine	VF	XF	Unc
248.1	ND(1894)	—	—	—	Rare	—

NOTE: These coins were minted at an arsenal in Taiwan.

DOLLAR

"Old Man"

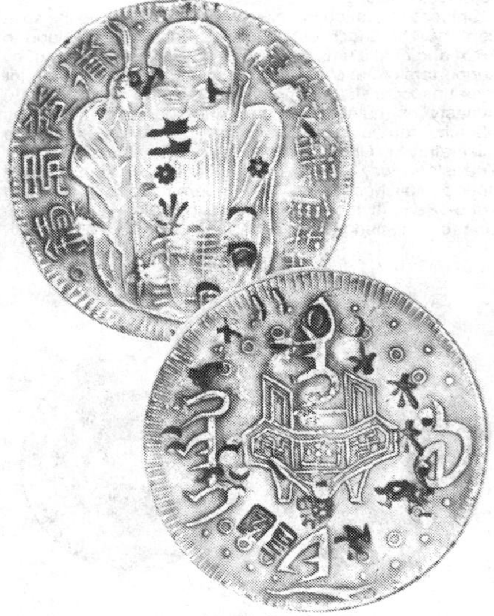

SILVER, 26.80 g

C#	Date	Mintage	VG	Fine	VF	XF
25-3	ND(1837-1845)		350.00	600.00	1200.	2500.

NOTE: C#25-3 normally comes w/2 chops at lower left on the reverse. Many varieties exist.

"Soldier's Pay"

25.00 g
Obv: Chinese *Chia Yi Hsien Tsao*.

Kann#	Year	Date	VG	Fine	VF	XF
3	1	(1862)	1800.	3000.	4500.	6500.

NOTE: Market valuations for the dollar coins above are for specimens with a few light chops. For unchopped specimens, add 10 percent and for heavily chopped specimens deduct 20 percent.

Rev: Crossed lotus flowers.

C#	Date	Mintage	VG	Fine	VF	XF
25-4	ND(1853)	—	300.00	600.00	1200.	3500.

NOTE: C#25-4 normally comes w/2 chops (one being a Chinese numeral *six*) on the reverse.

25.30 g
Rev: Crossed brushes.

C#	Date	Mintage	VG	Fine	VF	XF
25-5	ND(1862)	—	300.00	700.00	1500.	3700.

NOTE: The market values shown for C#25-3/25-5 are for coins which have been lightly chopmarked. Attribution of C#25-4 and C#25-5 to Taiwan is not fully accepted. Other sources attribute these coins to Chihli (Hebei) Province.

YUNNAN PROVINCE

A province located in south China bordering Burma, Laos and Vietnam. It is very mountainous with many lakes. Yunnan was the home of various active imperial mints. A modern mint was established at Kunming in 1905 and the first struck copper coins were issued in 1906 and the first struck silver coins in 1908. General Tang Chi-Yao issued coins in gold, silver and copper with his portrait in 1919. The last Republican coins were struck here in 1949.

EMPIRE

Yunnanfu Mint

CASH

Obv: Type A.

C#	Date	Emperor	Good	VG	Fine	VF
26-3	ND(1821-50)	Tao-kuang	.25	.50	.75	1.25
Rev: Crescent above.						
26-3.1	ND(1821-50)	Tao-kuang	2.50	3.50	5.00	7.50
Rev: Horizontal line above.						
26-3.2	ND(1821-50)	Tao-kuang	1.50	2.00	4.00	6.00

Obv: Type A.

C#	Date	Emperor	Good	VG	Fine	VF
26-4	ND(1851-61)	Hsien-feng	.50	1.00	1.50	2.50
Rev: Crescent above.						
26-4.1	ND(1851-61)	Hsien-feng	5.00	7.50	10.00	15.00
Rev: Crescent below.						
26-4.2	ND(1851-61)	Hsien-feng	5.00	7.50	10.00	15.00

Rev: Crescent standing on end above.

C#	Date	Emperor	Good	VG	Fine	VF
26-4.3	ND(1851-61)	Hsien-feng	5.00	7.50	10.00	15.00

C#	Date	Emperor	Good	VG	Fine	VF
Rev: Dot within crescent above (Pregnant Moon).						
26-4.4	ND(1851-61)	Hsien-feng	5.00	7.50	10.00	15.00
Rev: Circle above.						
26-4.5	ND(1851-61)	Hsien-feng	5.00	7.50	10.00	15.00
Rev: Circle below.						
26-4.6	ND(1851-61)	Hsien-feng	5.00	7.50	10.00	15.00
Rev: Dot within circle above.						
26-4.7	ND(1851-61)	Hsien-feng	5.00	7.50	10.00	15.00
Rev: Dot within circle below.						
26-4.8	ND(1851-61)	Hsien-feng	5.00	7.50	10.00	15.00
Rev: An X above the center.						
26-4.9	ND(1851-61)	Hsien-feng	5.00	7.50	10.00	15.00
Rev: Character *Ho* above and circle below.						
26-4.10	ND(1851-61)	Hsien-feng	5.00	7.50	10.00	15.00
Rev: Character *Ho* above and dot within circle below.						
26-4.11	ND(1851-61)	Hsien-feng	5.00	7.50	10.00	15.00
Rev: Character *Kung* above.						
26-4.12	ND(1851-61)	Hsien-feng	5.00	7.50	10.00	15.00
Rev: Character *Yi* (one) above.						
26-4.13	ND(1851-61)	Hsien-feng	5.00	7.50	10.00	15.00
Rev: Character *Erh* (two) above.						
26-4.14	ND(1851-61)	Hsien-feng	Reported, not confirmed			
Rev: Character *San* (three) above.						
26-4.15	ND(1851-61)	Hsien-feng	5.00	7.50	10.00	15.00
Rev: Character *Szu* (four) above.						
26-4.16	ND(1851-61)	Hsien-feng	5.00	7.50	10.00	15.00
Rev: Character above probably meaning "five".						
26-4.17	ND(1851-61)	Hsien-feng	5.00	7.50	10.00	15.00
Rev: Character *Shih* (ten) above and a crescent below.						
26-4.18	ND(1851-61)	Hsien-feng	5.00	7.50	10.00	15.00

C#	Date	Emperor	Good	VG	Fine	VF
Rev: Character *Chin* above and dot in circle below.						
26-4.19	ND(1851-61)	Hsien-feng	5.00	7.50	10.00	15.00

C#	Date	Emperor	Good	VG	Fine	VF
Rev: Manchu words above.						
26-4.20	ND(1851-61)	Hsien-feng	5.00	7.50	10.00	15.00

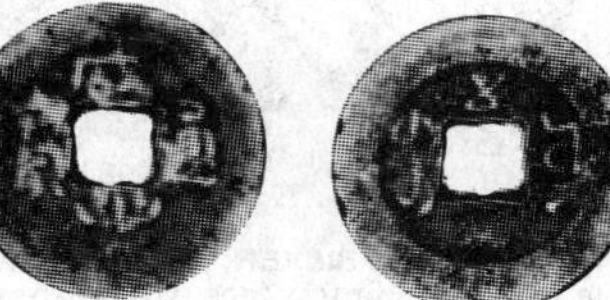

C#	Date	Emperor	Good	VG	Fine	VF
Rev: X above hole in center.						
26-4.21	ND(1851-61)	Hsien-feng	5.00	7.50	10.00	15.00

Rev: *Yuan* above and inverted crescent below hole.

C#	Date	Emperor	Good	VG	Fine	VF
26-4.22	ND(1851-61)	Hsien-feng	5.00	7.50	10.00	15.00

Obv: Type A-2.

26-7 ND(1862-74) T'ung-chih 1.50 3.00 4.00 6.00

NOTE: Varieties w/wide and narrow rims exist.

Rev: Circle above.

26-7.1 ND(1862-74) T'ung-chih 5.00 7.50 10.00 15.00

Rev: Dot within circle above.

26-7.2 ND(1862-74) T'ung-chih 5.00 7.50 10.00 15.00

Rev: Dot within crescent above.

26-7.3 ND(1862-74) T'ung-chih 5.00 7.50 10.00 15.00

Rev: Crescent below.

26-7.4 ND(1862-74) T'ung-chih 5.00 7.50 10.00 15.00

Rev: Vertical line above.

26-7.5 ND(1862-74) T'ung-chih 5.00 7.50 10.00 15.00

Rev: Vertical line below.

26-7.6 ND(1862-74) T'ung-chih 5.00 7.50 10.00 15.00

Rev: Character *Kung* above center.

26-7.7 ND(1862-74) T'ung-chih 5.00 7.50 10.00 15.00

Rev: Character *Ho* above.

26-7.8 ND(1862-74) T'ung-chih 5.00 7.50 10.00 15.00

Rev: Character *Ta* above.

26-7.9 ND(1862-74) T'ung-chih 5.00 7.50 10.00 15.00

Rev: Character *Shan* above.

26-7.10 ND(1862-74) T'ung-chih 5.00 7.50 10.00 15.00

Rev: Character *Ch'uan* below.

26-7.11 ND(1862-74) T'ung-chih 5.00 7.50 10.00 15.00

Rev: Character *Yi* (one) above.

26-7.12 ND(1862-74) T'ung-chih 5.00 7.50 10.00 15.00

Rev: Character *Wu* (five) inverted below.

26-7.13 ND(1862-74) T'ung-chih 5.00 7.50 10.00 15.00

Rev: Character *Liu* (six) above.

26-7.14 ND(1862-74) T'ung-chih 5.00 7.50 10.00 15.00

Rev: Characters *Liu* (six) above, but sideways.

26-7.15 ND(1862-74) T'ung-chih 5.00 7.50 10.00 15.00

Rev: Character *Pa* (eight) above.

26-7.16 ND(1862-74) T'ung-chih 5.00 7.50 10.00 15.00

Rev: Character *Shih* (ten) above.

26-7.17 ND(1862-74) T'ung-chih 5.00 7.50 10.00 15.00

Rev: Character *Shih* (ten) above, crescent below.

26-7.18 ND(1862-74) T'ung-chih 5.00 7.50 10.00 15.00

Rev: Characters *Shih Yi* (eleven) above.

26-7.19 ND(1862-74) T'ung-chih 5.00 7.50 10.00 15.00

Rev: Characters *Shih* (ten) above and *Yi* (one) below.

C#	Date	Emperor	Good	VG	Fine	VF
26-7.20	ND(1862-74)	T'ung-chih	5.00	7.50	10.00	15.00

Rev: Characters *Shih* (ten) above *San* (three) below.

26-7.21 ND(1862-74) T'ung-chih 5.00 7.50 10.00 15.00

Rev: Character *Jen* above.

26-7.22 ND(1862-74) T'ung-chih 5.00 7.50 10.00 15.00

Rev: Inverted crescent above.

26-7.23 ND(1862-74) T'ung-chih 5.00 7.50 10.00 15.00

26-9 ND(1875-1908) Kuang-hsu 2.00 4.00 6.50 9.00

Rev: Character *Kung* above.

26-9.1 ND(1875-1908) Kuang-hsu 2.00 5.00 7.50 10.00

Rev: Character *Ssu* (four) above.

26-9.2 ND(1875-1908) Kuang-hsu 2.50 5.00 7.50 10.00

Rev: Character *Chin* above.

26-9.3 ND(1875-1908) Kuang-hsu 2.50 5.00 7.50 10.00

Rev: Crescent above, dot below.

26-9.4 ND(1875-1908) Kuang-hsu 2.50 5.00 7.50 12.00

Rev: Dot above hole.

26-9.5 ND(1875-1908) Kuang-hsu 2.50 5.00 7.50 12.00

10 CASH

CAST BRASS, 37-39mm
Obv: Type B-1.

C#	Date	Emperor	Good	VG	Fine	VF
26-5	ND(1851-61)	Hsien-feng	2.00	5.00	7.00	15.00

Rev: Dot at upper left.

26-5.1 ND(1851-61) Hsien-feng — — — —

37mm

26-8 ND(1862-74) T'ung-chih 30.00 40.00 45.00 60.00

35mm

26-8.1 ND(1862-74) T'ung-chih 30.00 40.00 45.00 60.00

26-10 ND(1875-1908) Kuang-hsu — — Rare —

50 CASH

CAST BRASS

26-6 ND(1851-61) Hsien-feng 50.00 60.00 70.00 90.00

Tungch'uan Mint

CASH

Obv: Type A.
Rev: Type 1 mint mark.

27-2 ND(1821-50) Tao-kuang .50 1.00 1.50 2.50

Rev: Type 3 mint mark.

27-2.1 ND(1821-50) Tao-kuang .50 1.00 1.50 2.50

Obv: Type A.

27-3 ND(1851-61) Hsien-feng 2.00 4.00 5.00 7.00

Rev: Character *Cheng* above.

27-3.1 ND(1851-61) Hsien-feng 5.00 7.50 10.00 15.00

Obv: Type A-2.

27-5 ND(1862-74) T'ung-chih 5.00 9.00 12.00 18.00

Rev: Character *Cheng* above and crescent below.

C#	Date	Emperor	Good	VG	Fine	VF
27-5.1	ND(1862-74)	T'ung-chih	5.00	7.50	10.00	15.00

Rev: Character *Cheng* above, dot below.

C#	Date	Emperor	Good	VG	Fine	VF
27-5.2	ND(1862-74)	T'ung-chih	5.00	7.50	10.00	15.00

NOTE: Previously listed C#27-6, 27-6.1 and 27-6.2 are now listed under the Chefoo (Yantai) Mint, Shantung (Shandong) Province.

10 CASH

BRASS
Obv: Type B-1.

C#	Date	Emperor	Good	VG	Fine	VF
27-4	ND(1851-61)	Hsien-feng	5.00	9.00	16.00	30.00

Uncertain Mint

州

The following coins bear a Manchu mint mark, different from Fukien (Fujian) which reads, 'FU', though previously attributed to Fukien (Fujian), they are now believed to have been produced at the Chou (district, city or department) Mint while awaiting actual location information. They are not regarded as being produced in Yunnan.

CASH

CAST BRASS
Obv: Type A-2.
Rev: Crescent above.

KM#	Date	Emperor	Good	VG	Fine	VF
1	ND(1851-61)	Hsien-feng	10.00	15.00	20.00	25.00

Rev: Circle above.

KM#	Date	Emperor	Good	VG	Fine	VF
2	ND(1851-61)	Hsien-feng	10.00	15.00	20.00	25.00

Obv: Type A-2.
Rev: W/o characters above or below center hole.

KM#	Date	Emperor	Good	VG	Fine	VF
10	ND(1862-74)	T'ung-chih	10.00	15.00	20.00	25.00

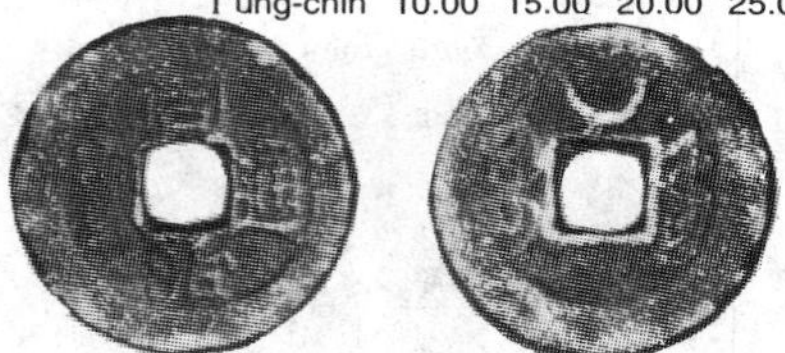

Rev: Crescent above.

KM#	Date	Emperor	Good	VG	Fine	VF
11	ND(1862-74)	T'ung-chih	10.00	15.00	20.00	25.00

Rev: Vertical line above.

KM#	Date	Emperor	Good	VG	Fine	VF
12	ND(1862-74)	T'ung-chih	25.00	30.00	35.00	40.00

Rev: Vertical line below.

KM#	Date	Emperor	Good	VG	Fine	VF
13	ND(1862-74)	T'ung-chih	25.00	30.00	35.00	40.00

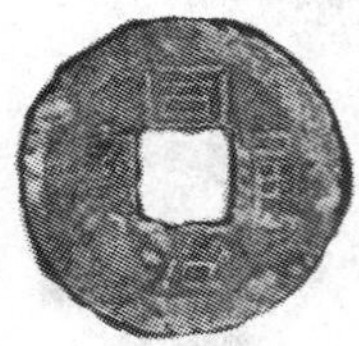 

Rev: Dot above.

KM#	Date	Emperor	Good	VG	Fine	VF
14	ND(1862-74)	T'ung-chih	25.00	30.00	35.00	40.00

Rev: Dot below.

KM#	Date	Emperor	Good	VG	Fine	VF
15	ND(1862-74)	T'ung-chih	25.00	30.00	35.00	40.00

Rev: With "X" above.

KM#	Date	Emperor	Good	VG	Fine	VF
16	ND(1862-74)	T'ung-chih	25.00	30.00	35.00	40.00

Rev: Character *Cheng* above.

KM#	Date	Emperor	Good	VG	Fine	VF
21	ND(1862-74)	T'ung-chih	25.00	30.00	35.00	40.00

Rev: Character *Cheng* above and circle below.

KM#	Date	Emperor	Good	VG	Fine	VF
22	ND(1862-74)	T'ung-chih	25.00	30.00	35.00	40.00

Rev: Character *Chih* above.

KM#	Date	Emperor	Good	VG	Fine	VF
23	ND(1862-74)	T'ung-chih	25.00	30.00	35.00	40.00

Rev: Character *Chu* above.

KM#	Date	Emperor	Good	VG	Fine	VF
25	ND(1862-74)	T'ung-chih	25.00	30.00	35.00	40.00

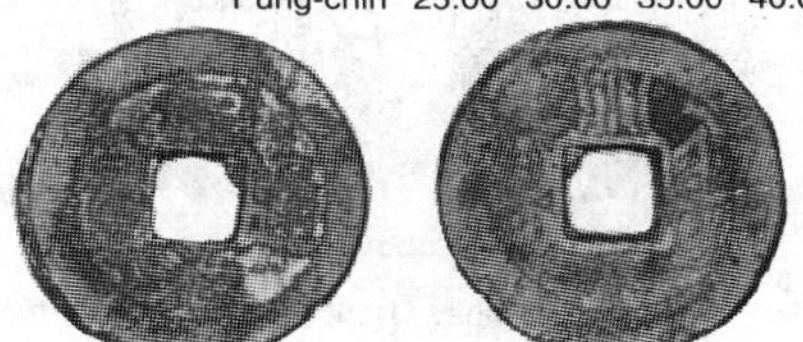

Rev: Character *Ch'uan* above.

KM#	Date	Emperor	Good	VG	Fine	VF
27	ND(1862-74)	T'ung-chih	25.00	30.00	35.00	40.00

Rev: Character *Chung* above.

KM#	Date	Emperor	Good	VG	Fine	VF
29	ND(1862-74)	T'ung-chih	25.00	30.00	35.00	40.00

Rev: Character *Feng* above.

KM#	Date	Emperor	Good	VG	Fine	VF
31	ND(1862-74)	T'ung-chih	25.00	30.00	35.00	40.00

Rev: Character *Ho* above.

KM#	Date	Emperor	Good	VG	Fine	VF
33	ND(1862-74)	T'ung-chih	25.00	30.00	35.00	40.00

Rev: Character *Jen* above.

KM#	Date	Emperor	Good	VG	Fine	VF
35	ND(1862-74)	T'ung-chih	25.00	30.00	35.00	40.00

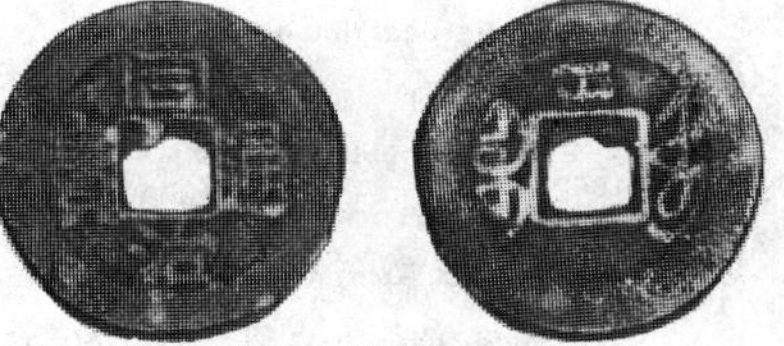

Rev: Character *Kung* above.

KM#	Date	Emperor	Good	VG	Fine	VF
37	ND(1862-74)	T'ung-chih	25.00	30.00	35.00	40.00

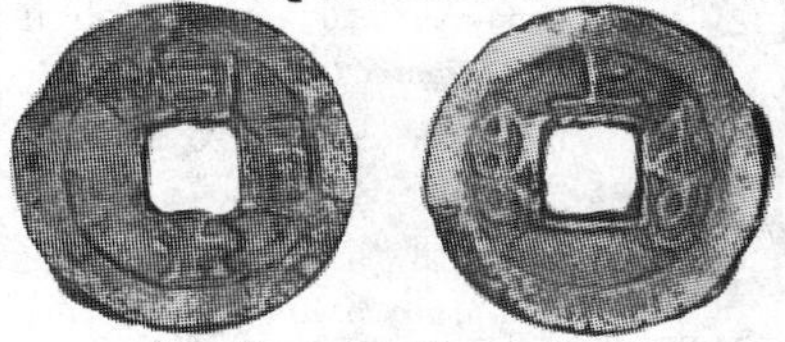

Rev: Character *Shang* above.

KM#	Date	Emperor	Good	VG	Fine	VF
39	ND(1862-74)	T'ung-chih	25.00	30.00	35.00	40.00

Rev: Character *Shun* above.

KM#	Date	Emperor	Good	VG	Fine	VF
41	ND(1862-74)	T'ung-chih	25.00	30.00	35.00	40.00

Rev: Character *Hsin* above.

KM#	Date	Emperor	Good	VG	Fine	VF
43	ND(1862-74)	T'ung-chih	25.00	30.00	35.00	40.00

Rev: Character *Ta* above.

KM#	Date	Emperor	Good	VG	Fine	VF
45	ND(1862-74)	T'ung-chih	25.00	30.00	35.00	40.00

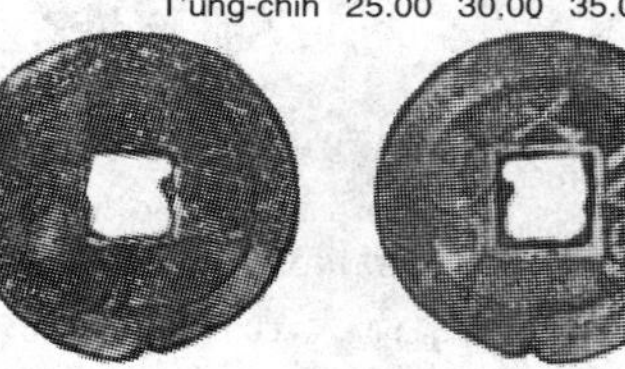

Rev: Character *Yu* above.

KM#	Date	Emperor	Good	VG	Fine	VF
47	ND(1862-74)	T'ung-chih	25.00	30.00	35.00	40.00

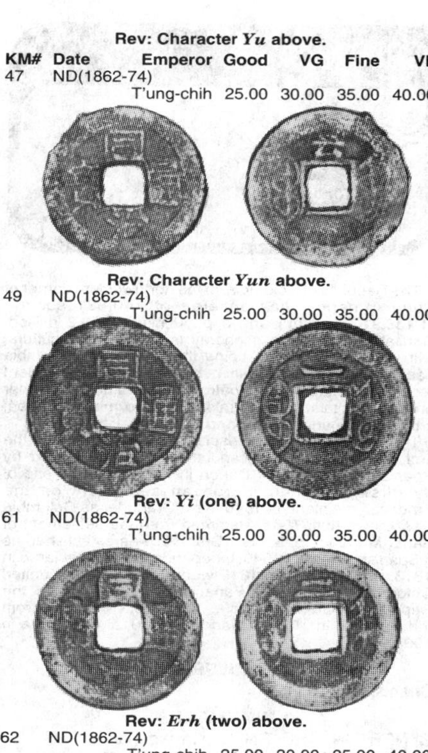

Rev: Character *Yun* above.

KM#	Date	Emperor	Good	VG	Fine	VF
49	ND(1862-74)	T'ung-chih	25.00	30.00	35.00	40.00

Rev: *Yi* (one) above.

KM#	Date	Emperor	Good	VG	Fine	VF
61	ND(1862-74)	T'ung-chih	25.00	30.00	35.00	40.00

Rev: *Erh* (two) above.

KM#	Date	Emperor	Good	VG	Fine	VF
62	ND(1862-74)	T'ung-chih	25.00	30.00	35.00	40.00

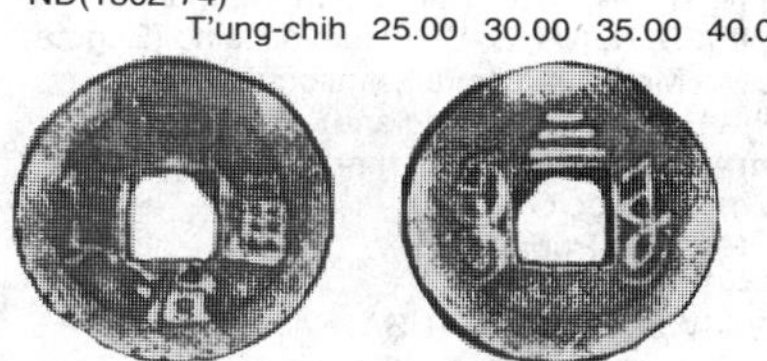

Rev: *San* (three) above.

KM#	Date	Emperor	Good	VG	Fine	VF
63	ND(1862-74)	T'ung-chih	25.00	30.00	35.00	40.00

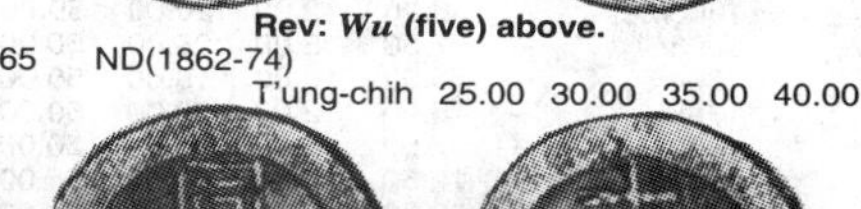

Rev: *Wu* (five) above.

KM#	Date	Emperor	Good	VG	Fine	VF
65	ND(1862-74)	T'ung-chih	25.00	30.00	35.00	40.00

Rev: Character *Shih* (ten) above.

KM#	Date	Emperor	Good	VG	Fine	VF
70	ND(1862-74)	T'ung-chih	25.00	30.00	35.00	40.00

NOTE: Other varieties probably exist. Refer to "Additional Characters" chart in the introduction.

FOREIGN ENCLAVES

The Age of Exploration brought European traders to China as early as the 16th century. By 1560, the Portuguese were firmly in control of Macao. British, French and Dutch traders soon followed, and in 1784 the first clipper ship of the United States arrived.

Commerce, however, was severely limited by the refusal of the Chinese ruling class to treat the representative of foreign powers as equals. By the end of the 18th century, only the port of Canton (Guangzhou) had been opened to European merchants, who were forbidden to enter Canton (Guangzhou) proper or travel inland.

The need for raw materials and expanded markets created by the Industrial Revolution brought increased pressure on China to open its doors to foreign traders. Actual military operations between 1839 and 1860, followed in the main by the threat of further attack by the western nations, procured from China extensive trade concessions. Among the more notable were the cession of Hong Kong to Great Britain, and the establishment of foreign enclaves at Kiau Chau (Germany), Kwangchowwan (France), Kuantung (Russia), Shanghai and elsewhere that were virtually sovereign enclaves within the Chinese Empire.

Military defeats, territorial and trade concessions, and the interference by Christian missionaries in local Chinese governments and customs created mass antagonism toward foreigners, and increased the activities of secret societies who became dedicated to ousting the foreigner from China. Chief among the xenophobic organizations was the I Ho Ch'uan "Righteous Harmony Fists", a society known as the 'Boxers' because its members practiced ritual shadow-boxing to make themselves invulnerable to bullets. In the autumn of 1899, they began to murder Chinese Christians and foreigners. The Empress Dowager Tz's Hsi abetted their work by procrastination and allowing many foreigners in China to be killed. The resulting 'Boxer Uprising' was a fiasco, albeit a bloody one.

Slaughtering Christians and foreigners as they moved north, the Boxers entered Peking (Beijing) in June 1900. There they beseiged some 1,000 foreigners and 3,000 Chinese Christians in the Legation Quarter until a seven-nation expeditionary force drove them off 55 days later. Although the nations had not declared war on China, they exacted additional concessions and heavy indemnities from the Manchu government. The United States, one of the principal recipients of the Boxer indemnities, later returned a major portion to China for educational development. Another portion was used to establish a fund to assist Chinese students in American schools.

HONG KONG

The free port of Hong Kong, a commercial center and entrepot, is located 90 miles (145 km.) southeast of Canton (Guangzhou). It was controlled by Great Britain until July 1, 1997. For historical background and coin listings, refer to Hong Kong.

KIAU CHAU

Kiau Chau (Kiao Chau, Kiaochow, Kiautscho, now Jiaozhou), a former German trading enclave, including the port of Tsingtao (Qingdao), was located on the Shantung (Shandong) Peninsula of eastern China. Following the murder of two missionaries in Shantung in 1897, Germany occupied Kiaochow Bay, and during subsequent negotiations with the Chinese government obtained a 99 year lease on 177 sq. mi. of land. The enclave was established as a free port in 1899, and a customs house set up to collect tariffs on goods moving to and from the Chinese interior. The Japanese took seige to the port on Aug. 27, 1914 as their first action in World War I to deprive German sea marauders of their east Asian supply and refitting base. Aided by the British forces, the siege ended Nov. 7. Japan retained possession until 1922, when it was restored to China by the Washington Conference on China and naval armaments. It fell again to Japan in 1938, but not before the Chinese had destroyed its manufacturing facilities. It is presently a part of the Peoples Republic of China. The major city is Tsingtao (Qingdao) and is noted for its beer.

KWANGCHOWWAN

Kwangchowwan (Kuang-Chou Wan), a French commercial center including Fort Bayard (Chan-Chiang) and free port, was located on the Luichow (Leizhou) Peninsula which projects southward from China toward the island of Hainan. France acquired a 99-year lease to the 309 sq. mi. (800 sq. km.) enclave, with full territorial jurisdiction, in 1898. It was occupied by Japan during 1943-1945 in accordance with the Vichy-Tokyo agreement of 1941 which gave control of French Indochina to Japan. Upon relinquishment of all French claims in 1946, it became the Chinese municipality of Chankiang (Zhanjiang). In 1949 it was incorporated in the Peoples Republic of China. There are no known coins issued specifically for Kwangchowwan.

KWANTUNG

Kwantung (Kuan-tung), a name applied in the late 19th century to the southern tip of the Liaotung peninsula which projects southward into the Gulf of Chihli from present Liaoning province. The British captured Lushun on the southeast tip of the peninsula in 1860 and renamed it Port Arthur. In 1898, Russia forced a 25-year lease to the 925 sq. mi. enclave from the Ch'ing dynasty, but lost it to Japan as a result of the Russo-Japanese War of 1904-05. Japan controlled the area until defeated in World War II. From 1945 to 1955, Port Arthur was under joint RussianChinese administration, following which it passed to Chinese control. During the Russian occupation, Russian copper and silver coins circulated in the area. Under the Japanese, demonetized silver yen counterstamped *Gin* also circulated. The main city of Kwantung, on which construction was started by the Russians and completed by the Japanese, was Dalny in Russian, Dairen in Japanese, and Ta-lien (Dalian) in Chinese. **NOTE:** Kwantung should not be confused with Kwangtung (Guangdong), a coastal province in Southern China.

MACAO

Macao, the oldest European settlement in the Far East, is 35 miles (56 km.) southwest of Hong Kong. It is to be returned to China in late 1999. For historical background and coin listings, refer to Macao.

SHANGHAI

The port of Shanghai was opened to foreign trade in 1842 as demanded by the foreign victors in the Opium War, and quickly grew to become the most important port in China. Several countries acquired control over certain sections of the city, and beginning in 1854 organized themselves into what was to become the International Settlement. This confederation remained virtually autonomous until occupied by the Japanese in December 1941; the Japanese occupied the surrounding area of Shanghai in 1937. A number of different tokens and encased postage stamps were issued for use in Shanghai.

PATTERNS (Pn)

Shanghai Tael Series

The 1867 Tael and 2 Mace coins of 'Shanghai Tael' were minted at the Hong Kong mint as proposed trade coins for China. The Chinese expressed no interest in any form of struck coinage and the scheme was dropped.

KM#	Date	Mintage	Identification	Mkt.Val.
Pn1	1867	—	2 Mace, Silver, K913	Rare

NOTE: Superior Goodman sale 5-95 brilliant proof realized, $39,100.

KM#	Date	Mintage	Identification	Mkt.Val.
Pn2	1867	—	1 Liang, Silver, w/o rays from ring, K911a	Rare

NOTE: Superior Goodman sale 5-95 choice brilliant proof realized, $80,500.

KM#	Date	Mintage	Identification	Mkt.Val.
Pn3	1867	—	1 Liang, Silver, w/rays from ring, K912	Rare

NOTE: Superior Goodman sale 5-95 proof realized, $60,375.

Kwan Ping (Customs Tael) Series

Until recently these coins were a mystery, attributed by some to Taiwan and by others to Korea. Both attributions were wrong. It is now believed that they were struck at the Hong Kong mint as possible alternatives to the Hong Kong 'Shanghai Tael' patterns. The dies were presented to the Royal Mint, London in 1888 from the estate of the former Director of the Hong Kong mint.

KM#	Date	Mintage	Identification	Mkt.Val.
Pn1	C.1868	—	5 Fen, Silver, K926-III	3500.

KM#	Date	Mintage	Identification	Mkt.Val.
Pn2	C.1868	—	1 Ch'ien, Silver, K926-II	6000.

KM#	Date	Mintage	Identification	Mkt.Val.
Pn3	C.1868	—	2 Ch'ien, Silver, K926-I	8000.

KM#	Date	Mintage	Identification	Mkt.Val.
Pn4	C.1868	—	5 Ch'ien, Silver, K926	10,000.

KM#	Date	Mintage	Identification	Mkt.Val.
Pn5	C.1868	—	1 Liang, Silver, K925	*Rare

***NOTE:** Superior Goodman sale 6-91 proof realized $50,600.

TAIWAN

The island of Taiwan (Formosa) had been a part of the Chinese empire since the 17th century. In 1895, however, the island was ceded to Japan following the Sino-Japanese War. Japan held the island until 1945 when it was returned to China.

Prior to 1895, Chinese cash coins and dragon silver coins were issued for the island (see Taiwan Province), but under the Japanese no coins were minted specifically for Taiwan. Demonetized Japanese silver yen coins, counterstamped *Gin* were placed in circulation there following the occupation.

COLOMBIA

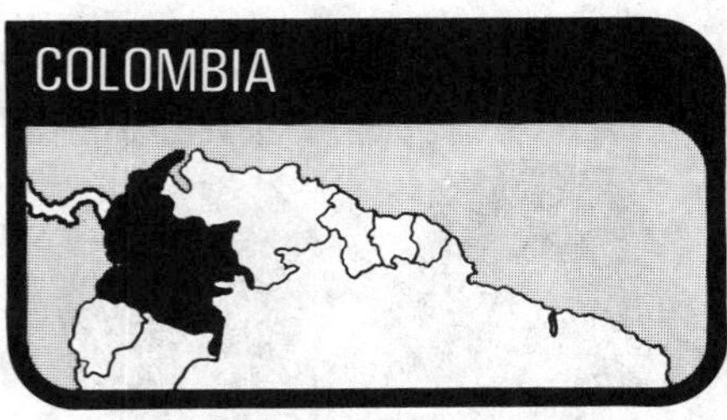

The Republic of Colombia, in the northwestern corner of South America, has an area of 440,831 sq. mi. (1,138,910 sq. km.) and a population of 36.2 million. Capital: Bogota. The economy is primarily agricultural with a mild, rich coffee being the chief crop. Colombia has the world's largest platinum deposits and important reserves of coal, iron ore, petroleum and limestone; other precious metals and emeralds are also mined. Coffee, crude oil, bananas, sugar and emeralds are exported.

The northern coast of present Colombia was one of the first parts of the American continent to be visited by Spanish navigators. At Darien in Panama is the site of the first permanent European settlement on the American mainland in 1510. New Granada, as Colombia was known until 1861, stemmed from the settlement of Santa Marta in 1525. New Granada was established as a Spanish colony in 1549. Independence was declared in 1813, and secured in 1819 when Simon Bolivar united Colombia, Venezuela, Panama and Ecuador as the Republic of Gran Colombia. Venezuela withdrew from the Republic in 1829; Ecuador in 1830; and Panama in 1903.

RULERS

Spanish, until 1819

MINT MARKS

C, NER, NR, NRE, RN, S - Cartagena
B, F, FS, N, NR, S, SF - Nuevo Reino (Bogota)
A, M - Medellin (capital), Antioquia (state)
(H) - Heaton (Birm. England)
(m) - Medellin, w/o mint mark
(Mo) - Mexico City
P, PN, Pn - Popayan
(P) - Philadelphia
(W) - Waterbury, CT (USA, Scoville mint)
caduceus - Bogota
floral spray - Popayan

COLONIAL MILLED COINAGE

1/4 REAL

.8462 g, .896 SILVER, .0243 oz ASW
Mint mark: NR
Obv: Castle. Rev: Lion.

KM#	Date	Mintage	VG	Fine	VF	XF
63	1801	—	5.00	10.00	15.00	50.00
	1802	—	10.00	20.00	35.00	70.00
	1803/2	—	6.00	12.00	20.00	50.00
	1803	—	7.50	15.00	25.00	50.00
	1804	—	5.00	10.00	15.00	50.00
	1805	—	6.00	12.00	20.00	50.00
	1806	—	7.50	15.00	25.00	50.00
	1807	—	12.50	25.00	40.00	65.00
	1808/6	—	20.00	40.00	65.00	110.00
	1808	—	5.00	10.00	15.00	50.00

NOTE: Earlier dates (1796-1800) exist for this type.

KM#	Date	Mintage	VG	Fine	VF	XF
67.1	1809	—	17.50	35.00	55.00	75.00
	1810/09/01	—	10.00	20.00	32.50	60.00
	1810/09	—	10.00	18.50	30.00	55.00
	1810/1	—	10.00	18.50	30.00	55.00
	1810	—	7.50	15.00	25.00	45.00
	1811	—	12.50	25.00	45.00	65.00
	1812	—	7.50	15.00	30.00	50.00
	1813	—	12.50	25.00	45.00	70.00
	1814	—	5.00	10.00	20.00	35.00
	1815	—	10.00	20.00	40.00	65.00
	1816	—	6.00	12.00	25.00	40.00
	1817	—	5.00	10.00	15.00	30.00
	1818/7	—	6.00	13.50	20.00	40.00
	1818	—	5.00	10.00	15.00	35.00
	1819	—	25.00	45.00	65.00	85.00

Mint mark: PN
Similar to KM#63.

KM#	Date	Mintage	VG	Fine	VF	XF
67.2	1816	—	9.00	18.50	37.50	85.00
	1822	—	— Reported, not confirmed			

1/2 REAL

1.6925 g, .896 SILVER, .0487 oz ASW
Mint mark: NR

Obv. leg: FERND. VII. . ., bust of Charles IV.

KM#	Date	Mintage	VG	Fine	VF	XF
69.1	1810 JJ	—	32.50	55.00	80.00	140.00
	1812 JF(error)	—	50.00	100.00	150.00	—
	1816 FJ	—	32.50	55.00	80.00	140.00
	1818 FJ	—	32.50	55.00	80.00	140.00
	1819 FJ	—	32.50	55.00	80.00	140.00

Mint mark: P

KM#	Date	Mintage	VG	Fine	VF	XF
69.2	1810 JF	—	12.00	25.00	60.00	125.00
	1816 FJ	—	27.50	50.00	85.00	150.00
	1819 MF	—	10.00	15.00	50.00	90.00

REAL

3.3834 g, .896 SILVER, .0974 oz ASW
Mint mark: NR
Obv: Bust of Charles IV.

KM#	Date	Mintage	VG	Fine	VF	XF
58	1801/797 JJ	—	10.00	25.00	75.00	—
	1801 JJ	—	6.00	12.50	60.00	125.00
	1802 JJ	—	6.00	12.50	60.00	125.00
	1804 JJ	—	12.50	25.00	65.00	125.00

NOTE: Earlier dates (1792-1800) exist for this type.

Obv. leg: FERDND VII. . ., bust of Charles IV.

KM#	Date	Mintage	VG	Fine	VF	XF
68.1	1809 FJ	—	—	Reported, not confirmed		
	1810 JF	—	5.50	13.50	35.00	80.00
	1810 JJ	—	15.00	30.00	65.00	125.00
	1812 FJ	—	6.50	15.00	40.00	85.00
	1812/4 JF	—	10.00	20.00	55.00	100.00
	1812 JF	—	7.50	20.00	40.00	85.00
	1816 FJ	—	5.50	13.50	35.00	80.00
	1817 FJ	—	6.50	15.00	40.00	85.00
	1818 FJ	—	7.50	17.50	60.00	100.00
	1819 FJ	—	7.50	17.50	40.00	85.00
	1819 FJ (inverted J)	—	6.00	15.00	40.00	85.00
	1819 J	—	6.00	15.00	40.00	85.00
	1820 FJ	—	25.00	50.00	90.00	150.00
	1821 FJ	—	30.00	55.00	100.00	175.00

Mint mark: P

KM#	Date	Mintage	VG	Fine	VF	XF
68.2	1810 JF	—	18.00	35.00	90.00	170.00
	1813 JF	—	30.00	55.00	130.00	225.00
	1820 FM	—	18.00	35.00	90.00	170.00
	1822 FM	—	—	Reported, not confirmed		

2 REALES

6.7680 g, .896 SILVER, .1949 oz ASW
Mint mark: NR
Obv. leg: FERDND VII. . ., bust of Charles IV.

KM#	Date	Mintage	VG	Fine	VF	XF
70.1	1811 JF	—	16.50	35.00	75.00	125.00
	1816 FJ	—	16.50	35.00	75.00	125.00
	1816 JJ/FJ	—	16.50	35.00	75.00	125.00
	1817 FJ	—	16.50	35.00	75.00	125.00
	1818/7 FJ	—	45.00	85.00	150.00	225.00
	1818 FJ	—	25.00	55.00	125.00	200.00
	1819/8 FJ	—	25.00	55.00	125.00	200.00
	1819 FJ	—	25.00	55.00	125.00	200.00

Mint mark: P

KM#	Date	Mintage	VG	Fine	VF	XF
70.2	1810 JF	—	12.00	20.00	40.00	100.00
	1811/0 JF	—	32.50	50.00	70.00	140.00
	1811 JF	—	22.50	40.00	55.00	120.00
	1813 JF	—	22.50	40.00	55.00	120.00
	1814/3 JF	—	75.00	150.00	250.00	500.00
	1814 JF	—	50.00	100.00	200.00	400.00
	1818 MF	—	22.50	40.00	55.00	120.00
	1819 MF	—	12.00	20.00	40.00	100.00
	1820/10 MF	—	35.00	85.00	150.00	300.00
	1820 MF	—	20.00	35.00	50.00	110.00
	1820 FM	—	20.00	35.00	50.00	110.00

Obv. leg: FERDND. 7.D.G.ET. CONST.

KM#	Date	Mintage	VG	Fine	VF	XF
74	1822 O	—	45.00	90.00	175.00	275.00

NOTE: The P mint mark on this coin has been traditionally attributed to Popayan, but arguments are currently being put forth that the P may stand for Pasto, making this the first coin of Ecuador.

8 REALES

27.0730 g, .896 SILVER, .7799 oz ASW
Mint mark: P
Obv. leg: FERDND VII. . ., bust of Charles IV.

KM#	Date	Mintage	VG	Fine	VF	XF
71	1810 JF	—	1000.	2000.	4250.	9500.
	1811 JF	—	1000.	2000.	4250.	9500.
	1812 JF	—	1000.	2000.	4000.	9000.
	1813/2 JF	—	1000.	2000.	4000.	9000.
	1813 JF	—	1000.	2000.	4000.	9000.
	1813 F	—	—	—	Rare	—
	1814/3 JF	—	450.00	800.00	1600.	3500.
	1814 JF	—	500.00	900.00	1800.	3750.
	1815 JF	—	—	—	Rare	—
	1816 F	—	1200.	2200.	4500.	10,500.
	1820 FM	—	—	—	Rare	—
	1820 MF	—	—	—	Rare	—

ESCUDO

3.3841 g, .875 GOLD, .0952 oz AGW
Mint mark: NR
Obv: Bust of Charles IV.

KM#	Date	Mintage	VG	Fine	VF	XF
56.1	1801 JJ	—	75.00	125.00	185.00	275.00
	1802/1 JJ	—	75.00	125.00	185.00	275.00
	1802 JJ	—	50.00	100.00	150.00	225.00
	1803 JJ	—	50.00	100.00	150.00	225.00
	1804/3 JJ	—	80.00	125.00	200.00	275.00
	1804 JJ	—	50.00	100.00	150.00	225.00
	1805 JJ	—	50.00	100.00	150.00	225.00
	1806 JJ	—	75.00	125.00	185.00	275.00
	1807 JJ	—	100.00	150.00	225.00	325.00
	1808 JJ	—	50.00	100.00	150.00	225.00

NOTE: Earlier dates (1791-1800) exist for this type.

Mint mark: P

KM#	Date	Mintage	VG	Fine	VF	XF
56.2	1801 JF	—	60.00	85.00	125.00	185.00
	1802 JF	—	60.00	85.00	125.00	185.00
	1803 JF	—	75.00	125.00	285.00	275.00
	1804 JF	—	75.00	125.00	285.00	275.00
	1804 JT	—	100.00	150.00	225.00	350.00
	1805 JT	—	75.00	125.00	285.00	275.00
	1805 JF	—	100.00	150.00	225.00	350.00
	1806 JT	—	75.00	125.00	285.00	275.00
	1806 JF	—	75.00	125.00	185.00	275.00
	1807 JF	—	75.00	125.00	185.00	275.00
	1808 JF	—	75.00	125.00	185.00	275.00

NOTE: Earlier dates (1792-1800) exist for this type.

Mint mark: NR
Obv. leg: FERDND VII. . ., bust of Charles IV.
Rev: Arms, order chain.

KM#	Date	Mintage	VG	Fine	VF	XF
64.1	1808 JF	—	100.00	150.00	225.00	400.00
	1809 JF	—	80.00	125.00	175.00	300.00
	1810 JF	—	50.00	100.00	175.00	275.00
	1811 JJ	—	100.00	150.00	225.00	400.00
	1811 JF	—	125.00	200.00	300.00	500.00
	1812 JF	—	50.00	100.00	150.00	200.00
	1813 JF	—	50.00	100.00	150.00	175.00
	1814 JF	—	50.00	100.00	150.00	175.00
	1815 JF	—	50.00	100.00	150.00	175.00
	1816 JF	—	50.00	100.00	150.00	175.00
	1817 JF	—	50.00	100.00	150.00	175.00
	1818 JF	—	50.00	100.00	150.00	175.00
	1819 JF	—	50.00	100.00	150.00	175.00
	1820 JF	—	80.00	125.00	175.00	275.00

Mint mark: P

KM#	Date	Mintage	VG	Fine	VF	XF
64.2	1808 JF	—	65.00	100.00	150.00	225.00
	1809 JF	—	65.00	100.00	150.00	225.00
	1810 JF	—	65.00	100.00	150.00	225.00
	1812 JF	—	65.00	100.00	150.00	225.00
	1813 JF	—	65.00	100.00	150.00	225.00
	1814 JF	—	65.00	100.00	150.00	225.00
	1816 FM	—	65.00	100.00	150.00	225.00
	1816 FR	—	65.00	100.00	150.00	225.00
	1816 F	—	65.00	100.00	150.00	225.00
	1817 FM	—	65.00	100.00	150.00	225.00
	1818 FM	—	65.00	100.00	150.00	225.00
	1819 FM	—	65.00	100.00	150.00	225.00

2 ESCUDOS

6.7682 g, .875 GOLD, .1904 oz AGW
Mint mark: NR
Obv: Bust right. Rev: Crowned arms, Order chain.

KM#	Date	Mintage	VG	Fine	VF	XF
60.1	1801 JJ	—	125.00	200.00	275.00	350.00
	1803 JJ	—	175.00	225.00	300.00	375.00
	1804 JJ	—	200.00	275.00	325.00	450.00
	1805 JJ	—	100.00	150.00	225.00	300.00
	1806 JJ	—	325.00	400.00	500.00	725.00
	1807 JJ	—	100.00	150.00	225.00	300.00
	1808 JJ	—	125.00	200.00	275.00	350.00

NOTE: Earlier dates (1792-1800) exist for this type.

Mint mark: P

KM#	Date	Mintage	VG	Fine	VF	XF
60.2	1802 JF	—	100.00	150.00	225.00	300.00
	1804 JF	—	125.00	200.00	275.00	350.00
	1804 SF	—	200.00	275.00	350.00	500.00
	1805 JT	—	325.00	425.00	525.00	850.00

NOTE: Earlier dates (1793-1799) exist for this type.

Mint mark: NR
Obv. leg: FERDND VII. . ., bust of Charles IV.
Rev: Arms, Order chain.

KM#	Date	Mintage	VG	Fine	VF	XF
65.1	1808 JF	—	200.00	275.00	350.00	525.00
	1809 JJ	—	125.00	200.00	275.00	450.00
	1810 JF	—	225.00	300.00	400.00	650.00
	1811 JF	—	200.00	275.00	350.00	550.00

Mint mark: P

KM#	Date	Mintage	VG	Fine	VF	XF
65.2	1817 FM	—	225.00	300.00	400.00	650.00
	1818 FM	—	225.00	300.00	400.00	650.00
	1819 FM	—	225.00	300.00	400.00	650.00

4 ESCUDOS

13.5365 g, .875 GOLD, .3808 oz AGW
Mint mark: NR
Obv. leg: CAROL IIII. . ., bust of Charles IV.

KM#	Date	Mintage	VG	Fine	VF	XF
61.1	1801 JJ	—	225.00	450.00	550.00	1100.
	1803 JJ	—	225.00	450.00	550.00	1100.
	1804 JJ	—	225.00	450.00	650.00	1300.
	1805 JJ	—	225.00	450.00	600.00	1250.
	1806 JJ	—	225.00	450.00	600.00	1250.
	1807 JJ	—	350.00	650.00	1000.	1650.

NOTE: Earlier dates (1792-1799) exist for this type.

Mint mark: P
Obv. leg: CAROL IIII. . ., bust of Charles IV.
Rev: Crowned arms in Order chain.

KM#	Date	Mintage	VG	Fine	VF	XF
61.2	1801 JF	—	300.00	550.00	650.00	1375.
	1802 JF	—	250.00	500.00	625.00	1300.
	1807 SF	—	550.00	1100.	1500.	2000.
	1808 JF	—	650.00	1300.	1800.	2600.

NOTE: Earlier dates (1792-1798) exist for this type.

Mint mark: NR
Obv. leg: FERDND VII. . ., bust of Charles IV.
Rev: Arms, Order chain.

KM#	Date	Mintage	VG	Fine	VF	XF
72	1818 JF	—	300.00	550.00	750.00	1550.
	1819 JF	—	300.00	550.00	750.00	1550.

8 ESCUDOS

27.0730 g, .875 GOLD, .7616 oz AGW
Mint mark: NR
Obv. leg: CAROL IIII. . ., bust of Charles IV.
Rev: Crowned arms, Order chain.

KM#	Date	Mintage	VG	Fine	VF	XF
62.1	1801/0 JJ	—	325.00	425.00	625.00	875.00
	1801 JJ	—	325.00	425.00	625.00	875.00
	1802/1 JJ	—	325.00	425.00	625.00	875.00
	1802 JJ	—	325.00	425.00	625.00	875.00
	1803/2 JJ	—	325.00	425.00	625.00	875.00
	1803 JJ	—	325.00	425.00	625.00	875.00
	1804/3 JJ	—	325.00	425.00	625.00	875.00
	1804 JJ	—	325.00	425.00	625.00	875.00
	1805 JJ	—	325.00	425.00	625.00	875.00
	1806 JJ	—	325.00	425.00	625.00	875.00
	1807 JJ	—	325.00	425.00	625.00	875.00
	1808 JJ	—	325.00	425.00	625.00	875.00
	1808 JF	—	2000.	3500.	6000.	8500.

NOTE: Earlier dates (1792-1800) exist for this type.

Mint mark: P

KM#	Date	Mintage	VG	Fine	VF	XF
62.2	1801 JF	—	325.00	425.00	625.00	875.00
	1802 JF	—	325.00	425.00	625.00	875.00
	1803 JF	—	325.00	425.00	625.00	875.00
	1804 JT	—	1500.	2500.	3500.	4500.
	1804 JF	—	325.00	425.00	625.00	875.00
	1805 JF	—	750.00	1500.	2000.	3000.
	1805 JT	—	500.00	800.00	1200.	2000.
	1806 JF	—	325.00	425.00	625.00	875.00
	1807 JF	—	325.00	425.00	625.00	875.00
	1808 JF	—	350.00	450.00	650.00	925.00

NOTE: Earlier dates (1791-1800) exist for this type.

Mint mark: NR
Obv. leg: FERDND. VII. . ., bust of Charles IV.

KM#	Date	Mintage	VG	Fine	VF	XF
66.1	1808 JJ	—	600.00	1000.	1400.	2000.
	1808 JF/JJ	—	650.00	1200.	1750.	2250.
	1808 JF	—	650.00	1200.	1750.	2250.
	1809 JF	—	325.00	425.00	600.00	850.00
	1810 JF	—	325.00	425.00	600.00	850.00
	1811/0 JF	—	325.00	425.00	600.00	850.00
	1811 JF	—	325.00	425.00	600.00	850.00
	1812 JF	—	325.00	425.00	600.00	850.00
	1813/2 JF	—	325.00	425.00	800.00	1300.
	1813 JF	—	325.00	425.00	600.00	850.00
	1814/3 JF	—	325.00	425.00	600.00	850.00
	1814 JF	—	325.00	425.00	600.00	850.00
	1815/4 JF	—	325.00	425.00	600.00	850.00
	1815 JF	—	325.00	425.00	600.00	850.00
	1816 JF	—	325.00	425.00	600.00	850.00
	1817 JF	—	325.00	425.00	600.00	850.00
	1818 JF	—	325.00	425.00	600.00	850.00
	1819 JF	—	325.00	425.00	600.00	850.00
	1820 JF	—	325.00	425.00	600.00	850.00

Mint mark: P

KM#	Date	Mintage	VG	Fine	VF	XF
66.2	1808 JF	—	325.00	425.00	600.00	850.00
	1809/8 JF	—	325.00	425.00	600.00	850.00
	1809 JF	—	325.00	425.00	600.00	850.00
	1810/09 JF	—	325.00	425.00	600.00	850.00
	1810 JF	—	325.00	425.00	600.00	850.00
	1811/0 JF	—	325.00	425.00	600.00	850.00
	1811 JF	—	325.00	425.00	600.00	850.00
	1812 JF	—	325.00	425.00	600.00	850.00
	1813 JF	—	325.00	425.00	600.00	850.00
	1814 JF	—	325.00	425.00	600.00	850.00
	1815 JF	—	325.00	425.00	600.00	850.00
	1816 FM	—	450.00	700.00	1000.	1500.
	1816 JF	—	900.00	1500.	2000.	3000.
	1816 F	—	600.00	1000.	1300.	1800.
	1817 FM	—	325.00	425.00	600.00	850.00
	1818 FM	—	325.00	425.00	600.00	850.00
	1819 FM	—	325.00	425.00	600.00	850.00

Mint mark: Pn

KM#	Date	Mintage	VG	Fine	VF	XF
66.3	1814 FR	—	550.00	900.00	1500.	2000.
	1815 FR	—	2250.	4500.	6500.	—
	1816 FR	—	450.00	700.00	1000.	1550.
	1820 FM	—	450.00	700.00	1000.	1550.

POPAYAN

MEDIO (1/2) REAL

COPPER
Obv: P/ANO/1813. Rev: Value.

KM#	Date	Mintage	VG	Fine	VF	XF
1	1813	5 known	200.00	300.00	500.00	750.00

2 REALES

COPPER
Obv: NUEVO REYNO DE GRANADA, ANO/1813
Rev: PROVINCIA DE POPAYAN, value.

KM#	Date	Mintage	Fine	VF	XF	Unc
2	1813	—	32.50	55.00	85.00	120.00

8 REALES

COPPER

KM#	Date	Mintage	VG	Fine	VF	XF
3	1813	—	60.00	100.00	175.00	300.00

SANTA MARTA

A city, on the Caribbean shore of the Caribbean Sea, founded in 1525, is the oldest in Colombia. Santa Marta was one of several areas in Colombia that remained under Spanish rule longer. Beseiged by Republican forces, Royalists made a necessity coinage that reflects certain design elements of Spanish Imperial issues.

1/4 REAL

COPPER

KM#	Date	Mintage	Good	VG	Fine	VF
2	1813	—	15.00	30.00	60.00	90.00

KM#	Date	Mintage	VG	Fine	VF	XF
2	1813	—	10.00	20.00	40.00	85.00
	1821	—	— Reported, not confirmed			

NOTE: Varieties exist.

1/2 REAL

COPPER

KM#	Date	Mintage	Good	VG	Fine	VF
1	ND (1812-13)	—	45.00	80.00	175.00	280.00

KM#	Date	Mintage	Good	VG	Fine	VF
3	1813	—	—	—	Rare	—

2 REALES

SILVER

KM#	Date	Mintage	Good	VG	Fine	VF
5	1820	—	180.00	350.00	500.00	700.00

COUNTERMARKED COINAGE

8 REALES

27.0700 g, .903 SILVER, .7859 oz ASW
c/m: S.M. and VPB monogram on Mexico KM#110.

KM#	Date	Mintage	Good	VG	Fine	VF
6	1809 TH	—	350.00	500.00	750.00	1100.

REPUBLICAN COINAGE

CARTAGENA

This port city on Colombia's northern coast was very important for the Spanish colonies and was heavily fortified to ward off British and French privateers. Cartagena was the first major city in Colombia to declare independence from Spain - November 11, 1811. In 1815, after a four month siege, it fell to the Royalists. In the interim the besieged Republicans struck coins for local use. All these coins are crude in die-work, planchets and striking.

1/2 REAL

NOTE: Most examples of KM#1 and KM#2 are poorly struck. Fully struck-up pieces are worth about 20-25% more, while pieces with non-struck areas are generally worth a percent less equivalent to the area of poor striking.

COPPER

KM#	Date	Mintage	Good	VG	Fine	VF
2	1812	—	7.50	13.50	25.00	42.50
	1813	—	8.00	16.50	30.00	47.50
	ND	—	5.00	9.00	15.00	32.50

DOS (2) REALES

COPPER

KM#	Date	Mintage	Good	VG	Fine	VF
1	1811	—	10.00	22.50	45.00	80.00
	1812	—	10.00	22.50	45.00	80.00
	1813	—	10.00	22.50	45.00	80.00

KM#	Date	Mintage	Good	VG	Fine	VF
1	1814	—	7.50	17.50	35.00	60.00
	ND	—	5.00	10.00	25.00	45.00

CUNDINAMARCA STATE

This province in central Colombia, with Bogota as its capital, was the first to declare independence - July 16, 1813. Spain regained control in 1816 and held on until 1819. After the battle of Boyaca, the province was again free. Coins made before and after the Spanish re-occupation, (1814-16) and 1819-23--when the Gran Colombia plan was put into effect--bear the provincial designation. Imperial Spanish types were struck during the Spanish re-occupation.

1/4 REAL

.7000 g, .583 SILVER, .0131 oz ASW

KM#	Date	Mintage	Good	VG	Fine	VF
2	1814	—	18.50	32.50	57.50	100.00
	1815	—	22.00	37.50	65.00	115.00

1/2 REAL

SILVER
Obv: Indian head. Rev: Pomegranate.

KM#	Date	Mintage	Good	VG	Fine	VF
3	1814 JF	—	35.00	75.00	150.00	275.00

REAL

2.5000 g, .583 SILVER, .0468 oz ASW

KM#	Date	Mintage	Good	VG	Fine	VF
1	1813 JF	—	16.50	37.50	57.50	90.00
	1814 JF	—	16.50	37.50	65.00	100.00
	1815 JF	—	20.00	42.50	75.00	130.00
	1816 JF	—	18.50	40.00	70.00	100.00

2 REALES

4.9000 g, .583 SILVER, .0918 oz ASW

KM#	Date	Mintage	Good	VG	Fine	VF
4	1815 JF	—	13.50	27.50	42.50	87.50
	1816/5 JF	—	15.00	30.00	50.00	100.00
	1816 JF	—	13.50	27.50	45.00	90.00

PROVINCIAL COINAGE

REPUBLIC OF COLOMBIA

1820-1823

Cundinamarca Province

1/2 REAL

1.3000 g, .666 SILVER, .0278 oz ASW

KM#	Date	Mintage	Good	VG	Fine	VF
8	1821 Ba JF	—	9.00	22.50	55.00	115.00

REAL

2.7800 g, .666 SILVER, .0595 oz ASW

KM#	Date	Mintage	Good	VG	Fine	VF
9	1821 Ba JF	—	7.50	17.50	35.00	75.00

2 REALES

4.9800 g, .666 SILVER, .1066 oz ASW

KM#	Date	Mintage	Good	VG	Fine	VF
5	1820 JF	—	32.50	75.00	150.00	325.00
	1820 Ba JF	—	—	—	Rare	—
	1821 Ba JF	—	5.50	13.50	30.00	70.00
	1821 JF	—	27.50	65.00	150.00	300.00
	1823 JF	—	85.00	160.00	275.00	400.00

8 REALES

23.0000 g, .666 SILVER, .4924 oz ASW

KM#	Date	Mintage	Good	VG	Fine	VF
6	1820 JF	—	10.00	30.00	50.00	110.00
	1820 Ba JF	—	50.00	75.00	125.00	250.00
	1821 JF	—	10.00	25.00	45.00	100.00
	1821 Ba JF	—	10.00	30.00	50.00	110.00

Mule. Obv: KM#6. Rev: Similar to Nueva Granada, KM#78.

KM#	Date	Mintage	Good	VG	Fine	VF
7	1820 JF	—	1000.	1500.	2000.	2500.

NATIONAL COINAGE

MINT MARKS

A - Antioquia
AM - Bogota
B, BA, BOGOTA - Santa Fe de Bogota
H - Birmingham - Heaton & Sons
M - Medellin
P, PN, POPAYAN - Popayan

UNITED PROVINCES OF NUEVA GRANADA

PROVISIONAL ISSUE

1819-1822

1/4 REAL

.7000 g, .666 SILVER, .0149 oz ASW
Obv: Liberty cap. Rev: Pomegranate.

KM#	Date	Mintage	Good	VG	Fine	VF
79.1	1820	—	11.50	22.00	40.00	60.00
	1821	—	20.00	42.50	85.00	125.00

Mint mark: BA

KM#	Date	Mintage	Good	VG	Fine	VF
79.2	1821	—	13.50	27.50	60.00	120.00

Mint mark: Pn

KM#	Date	Mintage	Good	VG	Fine	VF
79.3	1822	—	—	—	Rare	—

REAL

3.1500 g, .666 SILVER, .0674 oz ASW
Obv. leg: LIBERTAD AMERICANA around Indian head.
Rev. leg: NUEVA GRANADA around pomegranate.

KM#	Date	Mintage	Good	VG	Fine	VF
75	1819 JF	—	22.50	47.50	100.00	200.00

2 REALES

5.9000 g, .666 SILVER, .1263 oz ASW

KM#	Date	Mintage	Good	VG	Fine	VF
76	1819 JF	—	20.00	40.00	120.00	250.00

Rev: Pomegranate divides value.

KM#	Date	Mintage	Good	VG	Fine	VF
77	1819 JF	—	22.50	50.00	75.00	135.00
	1820 JF	—	32.50	65.00	115.00	185.00

8 REALES

23.0000 g, .666 SILVER, .4924 oz ASW

KM#	Date	Mintage	Good	VG	Fine	VF
78	1819 JF	—	25.00	45.00	90.00	175.00
	1819/20 JF	—	30.00	50.00	100.00	200.00
	1820 JF	—	25.00	45.00	90.00	175.00

COUNTERSTAMPED COINAGE

8 REALES

SILVER
c/s: Pomegranate on Cundinamarca
8 Reales, KM#6.

KM#	Date	Mintage	Good	VG	Fine	VF
73	ND (1820 JF)	—	50.00	85.00	150.00	250.00
	ND (1821 JF)	—	50.00	85.00	150.00	250.00
	ND (1821 Ba JF)	—	50.00	85.00	150.00	250.00

REPUBLIC OF COLOMBIA

1821-1837

1/4 REAL

.7000 g, .666 SILVER, .0149 oz ASW
Mint mark: B
Rev: Mint mark and initials below 1/4.

KM#	Date	Mintage	Good	VG	Fine	VF
85.1	1826 TR	—	30.00	50.00	70.00	100.00

NOTE: Contemporary counterfeits of the above type with initials RS are reported for 1825-27.

Rev: Mint mark above 1/4, initials.

KM#	Date	Mintage	Good	VG	Fine	VF
85.2	1826 RS	—	10.00	17.50	30.00	45.00
	1827 RS	—	5.00	8.50	12.00	25.00
	1828 RS	—	5.00	8.50	12.00	25.00
	1829 RS	—	4.00	7.50	10.00	22.50
	1833 RS	—	25.00	50.00	100.00	150.00
	1834 RS	—	4.00	7.50	10.00	22.50
	1835 RS	—	25.00	50.00	100.00	165.00
	1836 RS	—	5.00	8.50	11.50	25.00

Mint mark: P

KM#	Date	Mintage	Good	VG	Fine	VF
85.3	1826 RU	—	5.00	10.00	18.00	30.00
	1832 RU	—	—	—	Rare	—
	1833 RU	—	8.50	15.00	25.00	40.00
	1834 RU	—	5.00	8.50	13.50	25.00
	1836 RU	—	7.00	12.50	20.00	35.00

1/2 REAL

1.5500 g, .666 SILVER, .0331 oz ASW
Mint mark: BA
Obv: Fasces between crossed cornucopias.
Rev: Value in wreath.

KM#	Date	Mintage	Good	VG	Fine	VF
88.1	1833 RS	—	8.50	15.00	28.00	57.50
	1834 RS	—	8.00	13.50	25.00	50.00
	1835 RS	—	10.00	17.50	30.00	60.00

Mint mark: PN

KM#	Date	Mintage	Good	VG	Fine	VF
88.2	1834 RU	—	9.00	16.50	27.50	52.50
	1835 RU	—	—	—	Rare	—
	1836 RU	—	8.50	15.00	25.00	42.50

REAL

3.1000 g, .666 SILVER, .0663 oz ASW
Mint mark: BA or B

KM#	Date	Mintage	Good	VG	Fine	VF
87.1	1827 B RR	—	22.50	50.00	100.00	200.00
	1827 RR	—	3.50	7.50	12.00	22.00
	1828 RR	—	4.50	10.00	17.50	30.00
	1828 RS	—	3.50	7.50	12.50	22.00
	1829 RS	—	200.00	350.00	—	—
	1833/29 RS	—	5.00	12.00	22.00	45.00
	1833 RS	—	3.00	6.00	10.00	20.00
	1834 RS	—	20.00	40.00	70.00	—
	1835 RS	—	2.50	5.25	9.00	17.50
	1836 RS	—	2.50	5.25	9.00	15.00

Mint mark: PN

KM#	Date	Mintage	Good	VG	Fine	VF
87.2	1827 RU	—	—	—	Rare	—
	1828/7 RU	—	6.00	10.00	17.50	30.00
	1828 MF	—	3.00	6.50	12.00	22.00
	1828 RU	—	3.00	6.50	12.00	22.00
	1828 RU/MF	—	—	—	—	—
	1829 MF	—	3.00	6.50	12.00	22.00
	1829 RU	—	3.00	6.50	12.00	22.00
	1830 RU	—	2.00	5.00	9.00	17.50
	1831 RU	—	2.00	5.00	9.00	17.50
	1832 RU	—	3.00	6.50	12.00	22.00
	1833 RU	—	3.00	6.50	12.00	22.00
	1834 RU	—	7.00	13.50	25.00	35.00
	1835 RU	—	— Reported, not confirmed			

8 REALES

27.0200 g, .835 SILVER, .7253 oz ASW

KM#	Date	Mintage	Good	VG	Fine	VF
89	1834 RS	—	25.00	55.00	150.00	300.00
	1835/4 RS	—	18.50	40.00	80.00	175.00
	1835 RS	—	22.50	50.00	135.00	275.00
	1836 RS	—	18.50	40.00	80.00	175.00

PESO

1.6875 g., .875 GOLD, .0474 oz AGW
Mint: Bogota

KM#	Date	Mintage	Good	VG	Fine	VF
80	1821 JF	—	100.00	200.00	350.00	500.00

NOTE: Authenticity currently under study.

KM#	Date	Mintage	VG	Fine	VF	XF
84	1825 JF	—	55.00	60.00	80.00	125.00
	1826 JF	—	55.00	60.00	80.00	125.00
	1826/5 JF	—	55.00	60.00	80.00	125.00
	1826 JR	—	55.00	60.00	80.00	125.00
	1826 PJ	—	55.00	60.00	80.00	125.00
	1827 JF	—	55.00	60.00	80.00	125.00
	1827 RR	—	55.00	60.00	80.00	125.00
	1829/7 PJ	—	55.00	60.00	80.00	125.00
	1829 JF	—	55.00	60.00	80.00	125.00
	1829 RS	—	55.00	60.00	80.00	125.00
	1830 RS	—	55.00	60.00	80.00	125.00
	1833 RS	—	— Reported, not confirmed			
	1834 RS	—	55.00	60.00	80.00	125.00
	1835 RS	—	55.00	60.00	80.00	125.00
	1836 RS	—	55.00	60.00	80.00	125.00

ESCUDO

3.3841 g, .875 GOLD, .0952 oz AGW
Mint: Bogota

KM#	Date	Mintage	VG	Fine	VF	XF
81.1	1822 MF	—	— Reported, not confirmed			
	1823 JF	—	100.00	125.00	225.00	350.00
	1824 JF	—	— Reported, not confirmed			
	1825 JF	—	75.00	100.00	200.00	300.00
	1826 JF	—	— Reported, not confirmed			
	1832 PR	—	— Reported, not confirmed			
	1832 EM	—	— Reported, not confirmed			

NOTE: An 1821 dated piece is known and considered to be a contemporary counterfeit.

Mint: Popayan

KM#	Date	Mintage	VG	Fine	VF	XF
81.2	1823 FM	—	55.00	65.00	115.00	175.00
	1824 FM	—	55.00	65.00	100.00	150.00
	1825 FM	—	55.00	65.00	100.00	150.00
	1826/5 FM	—	— Reported, not confirmed			
	1826 FM	—	55.00	65.00	100.00	150.00

KM#	Date	Mintage	VG	Fine	VF	XF
81.2	1826 RU	—	—	Reported, not confirmed		
	1827 FM	—	55.00	65.00	100.00	150.00
	1827 RU/FM	—	—	Reported, not confirmed		
	1827 RU	—	55.00	65.00	115.00	175.00
	1828 RU	—	55.00	65.00	115.00	175.00
	1829 RU	—	55.00	65.00	100.00	150.00
	1830 RU	—	55.00	65.00	100.00	150.00
	1831/21 RM	—	65.00	75.00	125.00	200.00
	1831 RU	—	65.00	75.00	125.00	200.00
	1832 RU	—	55.00	65.00	100.00	150.00
	1833/2 RU	—	55.00	65.00	115.00	175.00
	1834 RU	—	55.00	65.00	115.00	175.00
	1835 RU	—	—	Reported, not confirmed		
	1836/4 RU	—	55.00	65.00	115.00	175.00
	1836 RU	—	55.00	65.00	115.00	175.00

2 ESCUDOS

6.7682 g, .875 GOLD, .1904 oz AGW
Mint: Bogota

KM#	Date	Mintage	VG	Fine	VF	XF
83	1823 JF	—	150.00	250.00	400.00	600.00
	1824 JF	—	135.00	235.00	375.00	550.00
	1825 JF	—	135.00	235.00	375.00	550.00
	1826 JF	—	135.00	235.00	375.00	550.00
	1829 JF	—	150.00	250.00	400.00	600.00
	1829 PJ	—	150.00	250.00	400.00	600.00
	1829 RS	—	125.00	225.00	350.00	500.00
	1836 RS	—	125.00	225.00	350.00	500.00

4 ESCUDOS

13.5365 g, .875 GOLD, .3808 oz AGW
Mint: Bogota

KM#	Date	Mintage	VG	Fine	VF	XF
86	1826 JF	—	1550.	2150.	3650.	—

8 ESCUDOS

27.0730 g, .875 GOLD, .7616 oz AGW
Mint: Bogota

KM#	Date	Mintage	VG	Fine	VF	XF
82.1	1822 JF	—	400.00	600.00	850.00	1350.
	1823 JF	—	375.00	425.00	625.00	850.00
	1824/3 JF	—	375.00	425.00	625.00	850.00
	1824 JF	—	375.00	425.00	625.00	850.00
	1825 JF	—	375.00	425.00	625.00	850.00
	1826 JF	—	375.00	425.00	625.00	850.00
	1827 JF	—	375.00	450.00	675.00	950.00
	1827 RR	—	400.00	550.00	800.00	1250.
	1828 RR	—	400.00	550.00	800.00	1250.
	1828 RS	—	375.00	425.00	625.00	850.00
	1829 RS	—	375.00	425.00	625.00	850.00
	1830 RS	—	375.00	425.00	625.00	850.00
	1831 RS	—	375.00	425.00	625.00	850.00
	1832 RS	—	375.00	425.00	625.00	850.00
	1833 RS	—	375.00	425.00	625.00	850.00
	1834 RS	—	375.00	425.00	625.00	850.00
	1835 RS	—	375.00	425.00	625.00	850.00
	1836 RS	—	375.00	425.00	625.00	850.00

Mint: Popayan

KM#	Date	Mintage	VG	Fine	VF	XF
82.2	1822 FM	—	400.00	600.00	850.00	1350.
	1823 FM	—	375.00	425.00	625.00	900.00
	1824 FM	—	375.00	425.00	625.00	850.00
	1825 FM	—	375.00	425.00	625.00	850.00
	1826 FM	—	375.00	425.00	625.00	850.00
	1827 FM	—	375.00	425.00	625.00	900.00
	1827 UR	—	400.00	500.00	750.00	1150.
	1828 FM	—	375.00	425.00	625.00	900.00
	1829 FM	—	400.00	550.00	750.00	1150.
	1829 UR	—	375.00	425.00	625.00	850.00
	1830 FW M inverted					
		—	400.00	600.00	1000.	1500.
	1830 FM	—	400.00	600.00	1000.	1500.
	1830 UR	—	375.00	425.00	625.00	850.00
	1831 UR	—	400.00	600.00	1000.	1500.
	1832/1 UR	—	375.00	425.00	625.00	850.00
	1832 UR	—	375.00	425.00	625.00	850.00
	1833/22 UR	—	425.00	650.00	1250.	2000.
	1833 UR	—	375.00	425.00	625.00	850.00
	1834/3 UR	—	500.00	850.00	1650.	2500.
	1834 UR	—	425.00	650.00	1250.	2000.
	1835 UR	—	375.00	425.00	625.00	850.00
	1836 UR	—	375.00	425.00	625.00	850.00
	1838 UR	—	—	—	Rare	—

REPUBLIC OF NUEVA GRANADA

1837-1859

1/4 REAL

.6800 g, .666 SILVER, .0145 oz ASW
Mint: Bogota

KM#	Date	Mintage	Good	VG	Fine	VF
90.1	1837	—	5.00	10.00	15.00	30.00
	1838	—	6.00	11.00	17.50	35.00
	1839	—	4.00	8.00	12.50	25.00
	1840	—	5.00	10.00	15.00	30.00
	1841	—	4.00	8.00	12.50	25.00
	1842	—	5.00	10.00	15.00	30.00
	1843	—	3.75	8.00	12.50	25.00
	1844	—	3.75	8.00	12.50	25.00
	1845	—	4.50	10.00	15.00	30.00
	1846	—	2.50	5.00	11.00	17.50
	1847	—	3.00	6.50	12.50	22.00
	1848	—	18.00	30.00	55.00	115.00

Mint: Popayan

KM#	Date	Mintage	Good	VG	Fine	VF
90.2	1838	—	8.50	17.50	28.00	45.00
	1841	—	3.50	7.25	12.50	22.00
	1842	—	3.50	7.25	12.50	22.00
	1843	—	3.50	7.25	12.50	22.00
	1844	—	5.00	10.00	17.50	32.50
	1845	—	5.00	10.00	17.50	32.50
	1846	—	3.00	7.00	11.00	20.00

1/2 REAL

1.2600 g, .666 SILVER, .0269 oz ASW
Mint: Bogota

KM#	Date	Mintage	Good	VG	Fine	VF
96.1	1838 RS	—	—	—	Rare	—
	1839 RS	—	3.50	7.00	10.00	20.00
	1840/39 RS	—	4.00	8.50	15.00	27.50
	1840 RS	—	3.50	7.50	12.50	25.00
	1841 RS	—	—	Reported, not confirmed		
	1842 RS	—	3.50	7.50	12.50	25.00
	1843 RS	—	4.00	8.50	15.00	27.50
	1844 RS	—	3.50	7.50	12.50	25.00
	1845 RS	—	2.25	5.50	10.00	20.00
	1846 RS	—	2.50	6.00	12.00	22.50
	1847/6 RS	—	2.50	5.50	10.00	20.00
	1847 RS	—	2.00	4.50	7.50	17.50

Mint: Popayan

KM#	Date	Mintage	Good	VG	Fine	VF
96.2	1838 RU	—	3.00	7.50	12.00	22.50
	1839 RU	—	2.75	6.50	11.00	20.00
	1840 RU	—	5.50	12.00	17.50	32.50
	1841 RU	—	5.50	12.00	17.50	32.50
	1841 VU	—	12.50	17.50	40.00	80.00
	1842 UM	—	5.50	12.00	17.50	35.00
	1843 UM	—	7.50	13.00	22.00	45.00
	1844 UE	—	3.00	7.50	13.50	25.00
	1844 UM	—	—	—	Rare	—
	1845 UE	—	4.50	11.00	17.50	35.00
	1846/5 UE	—	4.50	10.00	15.00	30.00
	1846 UE	—	1.75	4.00	9.00	17.50
	1846 UM	—	2.50	5.00	11.00	20.00
	1848 UE	—	18.00	32.50	47.50	85.00
	1848 UE star over last 8 in date					
		—	—	—	Rare	—

REAL

2.7000 g, .666 SILVER, .0578 oz ASW
Mint: Bogota

KM#	Date	Mintage	Good	VG	Fine	VF
91.1	1837 RS	—	2.00	4.50	9.00	16.50
	1838 RS	—	2.00	4.50	8.00	15.00
	1839 RS	—	2.25	5.00	11.00	18.50
	1840/30 RS					
		—	4.50	10.00	18.00	30.00
	1840/39 RS					
		—	4.50	10.00	18.00	30.00
	1841 RS	—	—	Reported, not confirmed		
	1842 RS	—	—	Reported, not confirmed		
	1843 RS	—	3.00	7.00	13.50	20.00
	1844 RS	—	3.00	7.00	13.50	20.00
	1845 RS	—	2.25	5.00	12.00	18.50
	1846 RS	—	4.00	9.00	16.50	27.50
	1847	—	6.00	13.50	25.00	50.00

Mint: Popayan

KM#	Date	Mintage	Good	VG	Fine	VF
91.2	1839 RU	—	3.75	8.50	15.00	25.00
	1840 RU	—	6.00	12.00	18.00	35.00
	1841 VU/RU					
		—	6.00	12.00	18.00	35.00
	1841 VU	—	—	Reported, not confirmed		
	1844 UM	—	3.75	8.50	14.00	20.00
	1845 UM	—	4.00	9.00	15.00	25.00
	1846/4 UM	—	4.00	9.00	15.00	25.00
	1846 UM	—	5.00	11.50	17.50	32.50

2 REALES

5.5000 g, .666 SILVER, .1177 oz ASW
Mint: Bogota

KM#	Date	Mintage	Good	VG	Fine	VF
97.1	1839 RS	—	—	—	Rare	—
	1840 RS	—	2.75	5.00	11.50	25.00
	1841/0 RS	—	13.50	35.00	65.00	125.00
	1841 RS	—	13.50	35.00	65.00	125.00
	1842 RS	—	—	Reported, not confirmed		
	1843 RS	—	2.75	5.00	11.50	25.00
	1844/3 RS	—	3.50	8.00	17.50	40.00
	1844 RS	—	3.00	7.00	15.00	35.00
	1845 RS	—	4.50	11.00	25.00	50.00
	1846/5 RS	—	13.50	35.00	60.00	100.00

Mint: Popayan

KM#	Date	Mintage	Good	VG	Fine	VF
97.2	1840 RU	—	9.00	20.00	35.00	65.00
	1841 VU	—	7.00	15.00	27.50	50.00
	1842/0/1 UM					
		—	17.50	37.50	80.00	150.00
	1842 VU	—	16.00	35.00	75.00	155.00
	1842 UM	—	7.00	15.00	27.50	55.00
	1843/2 UM	—	13.50	30.00	45.00	85.00
	1843 UM	—	15.00	32.50	65.00	120.00
	1844 UM	—	9.00	22.00	35.00	55.00
	1846 UM	—	—	—	Rare	—
	1849 UM	—	—	—	Rare	—

8 REALES

SILVER

KM#	Date	Mintage	VG	Fine	VF	XF
92	1837 RS	—	75.00	200.00	425.00	850.00
	1838 RS	1 known	—	—	Rare	—

KM#	Date	Mintage	Good	VG	Fine	VF
98	1839 RS	—	6.00	13.50	30.00	60.00
	1840 RS	—	6.50	15.00	35.00	70.00
	1841 RS	—	7.50	17.50	40.00	80.00
	1842 RS	—	7.50	17.50	40.00	80.00
	1843 RS	—	6.50	15.00	35.00	70.00
	1844 RS	—	7.50	17.50	40.00	80.00
	1845 RS	—	7.50	17.50	40.00	80.00
	1846/4 RS	—	10.00	20.00	45.00	90.00
	1846/5 RS	—	10.00	20.00	45.00	90.00
	1846 RS	—	7.50	17.50	40.00	80.00

PESO

1.6875 g, .875 GOLD, .0474 oz AGW
Mint: Bogota

KM#	Date	Mintage	VG	Fine	VF	XF
93	1837 RS	—	40.00	60.00	90.00	150.00
	1838 RS	—	60.00	90.00	135.00	225.00
	1839 RS	—	60.00	90.00	135.00	225.00
	1840/39 RS	—	50.00	80.00	120.00	200.00
	1840 RS	—	45.00	70.00	100.00	175.00
	1841 RS	—	— Reported, not confirmed			
	1842 RS	—	40.00	60.00	90.00	150.00
	1844 RS	—	45.00	70.00	100.00	175.00
	1846/3	—	— Reported, not confirmed			
	1846 RS	—	40.00	60.00	90.00	150.00

2 PESOS

3.3750 g, .900 GOLD, .0976 oz AGW
Mint: Popayan

KM#	Date	Mintage	VG	Fine	VF	XF
95	1838 RU	—	55.00	80.00	120.00	200.00
	1842 VU	—	55.00	80.00	160.00	275.00
	1843 UM	—	55.00	80.00	120.00	200.00
	1843 VU	—	55.00	80.00	160.00	275.00
	1844 UM	—	55.00	80.00	130.00	225.00
	1845 UM	—	55.00	80.00	120.00	200.00
	1845 UE	—	55.00	80.00	160.00	275.00
	1846 UE	—	55.00	80.00	120.00	200.00
	1846 UM	—	55.00	80.00	120.00	200.00

3.2258 g, .900 GOLD, .0933 oz AGW

Mint: Bogota

KM#	Date	Mintage	VG	Fine	VF	XF
99	1848	—	— Reported, not confirmed			
	1849	—	400.00	650.00	950.00	1550.
	1851	—	600.00	1200.	1800.	2700.

DIEZ I SEIS (16) PESOS

27.0000 g, .900 GOLD, .7813 oz AGW
Mint: Bogota

KM#	Date	Mintage	VG	Fine	VF	XF
94.1	1837 RS	—	350.00	400.00	500.00	650.00
	1838/7 RS	—	375.00	425.00	550.00	750.00
	1838 RS	—	350.00	400.00	500.00	650.00
	1839/8 RS	—	375.00	425.00	550.00	750.00
	1839 RS	—	350.00	400.00	500.00	650.00
	1840 RS	—	350.00	400.00	500.00	650.00
	1841 RS	—	350.00	400.00	500.00	650.00
	1842 RS	—	350.00	400.00	500.00	650.00
	1843 RS	—	350.00	400.00	500.00	650.00
	1844 RS	—	350.00	400.00	500.00	650.00
	1845 RS	—	350.00	400.00	500.00	650.00
	1846 RS	—	350.00	400.00	500.00	650.00
	1847 RS	—	350.00	400.00	500.00	650.00
	1848 RS	—	425.00	525.00	650.00	900.00
	1849 RS	—	475.00	625.00	950.00	1350.

Mint: Popayan

KM#	Date	Mintage	VG	Fine	VF	XF
94.2	1837 RU	—	350.00	400.00	500.00	650.00
	1838 RU	—	350.00	400.00	500.00	650.00
	1839 RU	—	350.00	400.00	500.00	650.00
	1840 RU	—	350.00	400.00	600.00	1200.
	1841/0 RU	—	450.00	—	—	—
	1841 RU	—	425.00	650.00	—	—
	1841 VU	—	350.00	400.00	500.00	650.00
	1842 VU	—	350.00	400.00	500.00	650.00
	1842 UM	—	350.00	400.00	500.00	650.00
	1843 UM	—	350.00	400.00	500.00	650.00
	1844 UM	—	350.00	400.00	500.00	650.00
	1845 UM	—	350.00	400.00	500.00	650.00
	1846 UM	—	350.00	400.00	500.00	650.00
	1846 UE	—	350.00	400.00	600.00	1200.
	1846 UR	—	425.00	650.00	950.00	—

25.8064 g, .900 GOLD, .7468 oz AGW
Mint: Bogota

KM#	Date	Mintage	VG	Fine	VF	XF
100	1848	—	600.00	1200.	2000.	3500.
	1849	—	600.00	1200.	2000.	3500.
	1850	—	600.00	1200.	2000.	3500.
	1851	—	700.00	1500.	2500.	4000.
	1852	—	600.00	1200.	2000.	3500.
	1853	—	600.00	1200.	2000.	3500.

FIRST DECIMAL COINAGE

MONETARY SYSTEM

10 Decimos de Real = 1 Real (1847-53)
10 Reales = 1 Peso (1847-53)
10 Decimos = 1 Peso (1853-72)

1/2 DECIMO DE REAL

(1/20 Real)

COPPER

KM#	Date	Mintage	Fine	VF	XF	Unc
101	1847	—	3.00	7.00	22.50	50.00
	1847	—	—	—	Proof	85.00
	1848	—	7.50	18.50	50.00	85.00

DECIMO DE REAL

(1/10 Real)

COPPER
Plain edge.

KM#	Date	Mintage	Fine	VF	XF	Unc
102	1847	—	3.00	7.50	22.50	50.00
	1847	—	—	—	Proof	125.00
	1848	—	12.50	25.00	65.00	90.00

1/4 REAL

.9000 g, .900 SILVER, .0260 oz ASW
Mint: Bogota

KM#	Date	Mintage	VG	Fine	VF	XF
108.1	1850	—	8.50	15.00	30.00	60.00
	1851	—	4.00	8.50	17.50	45.00
	1852	—	—	—	Rare	—

Mint: Popayan
Plain edge.

KM#	Date	Mintage	VG	Fine	VF	XF
108.2	1849	—	3.00	7.00	15.00	35.00
	1850	—	2.50	6.50	15.00	35.00
	1851	—	3.50	8.00	17.50	50.00
	1852	—	3.50	8.00	17.50	50.00
	1853	—	3.00	7.00	15.00	35.00
	1854	—	— Reported, not confirmed			
	1855	—	5.50	9.00	20.00	50.00
	1856	—	8.00	15.00	25.00	55.00
	1858	—	15.00	27.50	47.50	100.00

Mint: Bogota
Obv: Similar to KM#108.2. Rev: Caduceus at each side of '1/4' instead of 3 stars below.

KM#	Date	Mintage	VG	Fine	VF	XF
113	1852	—	13.50	35.00	75.00	165.00
	1858	—	—	—	Rare	—

MEDIO (1/2) REAL

1.4000 g, .900 SILVER, .0405 oz ASW
Mint: Bogota

KM#	Date	Mintage	VG	Fine	VF	XF
110	1850	5.000	9.00	18.00	30.00	70.00
	1851	2.500	5.50	12.00	20.00	50.00
	1852/1	—	5.50	11.00	18.00	50.00
	1852	2.500	5.00	10.00	16.50	40.00
	1853	2.500	4.50	8.50	15.00	35.00
	1854	—	— Reported, not confirmed			

MEDIO (1/2) DECIMO

1.5000 g, .900 SILVER, .0434 oz ASW
Mint: Bogota

KM#	Date	Mintage	VG	Fine	VF	XF
114	1853	—	6.00	12.50	21.50	35.00
	1854	—	7.50	16.50	25.00	42.50
	1855	—	6.00	13.00	22.00	37.50
	1856	—	6.00	12.00	22.50	37.50
	1857	—	7.50	16.50	23.50	40.00
	1858/4	—	6.50	12.50	22.00	35.00
	1858	—	8.00	16.50	24.00	40.00

UN (1) REAL

2.7000 g, .900 SILVER, .0781 oz ASW
Mint: Bogota
Reeded edge.

KM#	Date	Mintage	VG	Fine	VF	XF
103	1847	—	5.00	10.00	17.50	30.00

2.5000 g, .900 SILVER, .0723 oz ASW

KM#	Date	Mintage	VG	Fine	VF	XF
112	1851	—	4.00	8.50	18.50	40.00
	1852	—	2.50	5.50	10.00	17.50
	1853	—	2.75	6.00	15.50	38.00

UN (1) DECIMO

2.5000 g, .900 SILVER, .0723 oz ASW
Mint: Bogota

KM#	Date	Mintage	VG	Fine	VF	XF
115	1853	—	4.00	7.50	12.50	30.00
	1854	—	2.75	4.50	8.00	22.00
	1855/4/3	—	10.00	16.50	30.00	—
	1855/4	—	5.00	9.50	15.00	32.50
	1855	—	2.75	4.50	8.00	22.00
	1856	—	2.25	4.00	7.50	20.00
	1857	—	3.50	6.50	10.00	27.50
	1858/6	—	7.00	12.00	20.00	—
	1858/7	—	3.75	5.50	9.00	30.00
	1858	—	3.50	6.50	10.00	27.50

DOS (2) REALES

5.0000 g, .900 SILVER, .1447 oz ASW
Mint: Bogota
Obv: Date above shield.

KM#	Date	Mintage	VG	Fine	VF	XF
104	1847	—	—	—	Rare	—

NOTE: Probably a pattern.

Obv: Date below shield

KM#	Date	Mintage	VG	Fine	VF	XF
105	1847	—	5.00	10.00	25.00	50.00
	1848	—	3.50	6.50	15.00	35.00
	1849	—	3.50	6.50	15.00	35.00

KM#	Date	Mintage	VG	Fine	VF	XF
109	1849	—	—	—	Rare	—
	1850	—	3.50	7.00	15.00	37.50
	1851	—	3.50	7.00	15.00	37.50
	1852	—	6.00	10.00	25.00	65.00
	1853	—	6.50	11.00	27.50	67.50

DOS (2) DECIMOS

5.0000 g, .900 SILVER, .1447 oz ASW
Mint: Bogota

KM#	Date	Mintage	VG	Fine	VF	XF
117	1854/3	—	7.50	20.00	60.00	150.00
	1854	—	6.00	12.00	27.50	65.00
	1855/3	—	4.50	9.00	35.00	75.00
	1855	—	3.50	7.50	16.50	30.00
	1856/5	—	5.50	12.00	38.00	75.00
	1857	—	4.00	9.00	22.00	47.50
	1858/7	—	18.50	42.50	80.00	165.00

OCHO (8) REALES

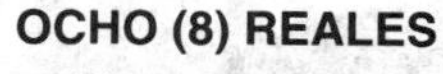

20.0000 g, .900 SILVER, .5787 oz ASW
Mint: Bogota

KM#	Date	Mintage	VG	Fine	VF	XF
106	1847	—	30.00	70.00	120.00	250.00

DIEZ (10) REALES

25.0000 g, .900 SILVER, .7234 oz ASW

KM#	Date	Mintage	VG	Fine	VF	XF
107	1847	—	25.00	45.00	70.00	200.00
	1848	—	20.00	35.00	60.00	175.00
	1849/8	—	30.00	60.00	120.00	260.00
	1849	—	25.00	50.00	90.00	225.00

NOTE: Struck at Bogota and Popayan without mint marks.

Mint: Bogota

KM#	Date	Mintage	VG	Fine	VF	XF
111	1850	—	25.00	50.00	100.00	200.00
	1851	—	25.00	50.00	100.00	200.00

PESO

25.0000 g, .900 SILVER, .7234 oz ASW

KM#	Date	Mintage	VG	Fine	VF	XF
118	1855/1	—	18.00	37.50	75.00	125.00
	1855	—	15.00	30.00	45.00	65.00
	1856/5	—	12.50	25.00	40.00	60.00
	1856	—	17.50	32.50	50.00	70.00
	1857/6	—	15.00	30.00	45.00	65.00
	1857	—	12.50	25.00	40.00	60.00
	1858/7	—	15.00	30.00	45.00	65.00
	1858	—	12.50	25.00	40.00	60.00
	1859/6	—	18.00	35.00	65.00	115.00

1.6875 g, .875 GOLD, .0474 oz AGW
Similar to 2 Pesos, KM#121.

KM#	Date	Mintage	VG	Fine	VF	XF
119	1856	—	65.00	150.00	300.00	500.00
	1857	—	— Reported, not confirmed			
	1858	—	65.00	150.00	300.00	500.00

2 PESOS

3.2258 g, .900 GOLD, .0933 oz AGW
Mint mark: P
Rev: Value in wreath.

KM#	Date	Mintage	VG	Fine	VF	XF
121	1857	—	60.00	100.00	175.00	300.00
	1858/48	—	— Reported, not confirmed			
	1858	—	60.00	100.00	175.00	300.00

5 PESOS

8.0648 g, .900 GOLD, .2333 oz AGW
Mint mark: B

KM#	Date	Mintage	VG	Fine	VF	XF
120.1	1849	—	—	— Unique		—
	1856	—	— Reported, not confirmed			
	1857	—	175.00	400.00	850.00	1350.

Rev: PESOS in small letters.

KM#	Date	Mintage	VG	Fine	VF	XF
120.2	1858	—	200.00	500.00	1000.	1750.

10 PESOS

16.4000 g, .900 GOLD, .4745 oz AGW
Mint: Bogota

KM#	Date	Mintage	VG	Fine	VF	XF
116.1	1853	—	450.00	800.00	1450.	1850.
	1854	—	350.00	650.00	1250.	1500.
	1855	—	350.00	650.00	1250.	1500.
	1856	—	350.00	650.00	1250.	1500.
	1857	—	350.00	650.00	1250.	1500.

Mint: Popayan

KM#	Date	Mintage	VG	Fine	VF	XF
116.2	1853	—	250.00	400.00	600.00	1000.
	1856	—	450.00	800.00	1450.	1850.
	1857	—	—	—	800.00	1250.

16.1290 g, .900 GOLD, .4667 oz AGW
Mint: Bogota
Rev. leg: DIEZ PESOS

KM#	Date	Mintage	VG	Fine	VF	XF
122.1	1857	—	275.00	500.00	850.00	1250.
	1858/7	—	300.00	550.00	900.00	1350.
	1858	—	300.00	550.00	900.00	1350.

Mint: Popayan

KM#	Date	Mintage	VG	Fine	VF	XF
122.2	1853	—	— Reported, not confirmed			
	1856	—	— Reported, not confirmed			
	1857	—	225.00	325.00	500.00	900.00
	1858	—	225.00	325.00	500.00	900.00

PATTERNS (Pn)

(Including off metal strikes)

KM#	Date	Mintage	Identification	Mkt.Val.
Pn1	1842	—	1 Centavo, Copper	350.00

KM#	Date	Mintage	Identification	Mkt.Val.
Pn2	1847	—	1/2 Decimo De Real, Bronzed Copper, KM101	135.00

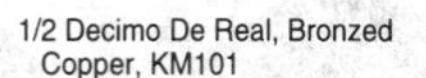

KM#	Date	Mintage	Identification	Mkt.Val.
Pn3	1847	—	1 Decimo De Real, Bronzed Copper, KM102	165.00

KM#	Date	Mintage	Identification	Mkt.Val.
Pn4	1847	—	8 Reales, Copper, KM115	300.00
Pn5	1847	—	1 Peso, Copper	300.00
Pn6	1847	—	16 Pesos, Copper, KM100	400.00
Pn7	1848/7	—	2 Reales, .900 Silver, Bogota, KM109	500.00

KM#	Date	Mintage	Identification	Mkt.Val.
Pn8	1848	—	1/2 Real, .900 Silver, Popayan	1350.
Pn9	1848	—	1/2 Real, .900 Silver, Bogota, piefort, KM109	350.00
Pn10	1848	—	1 Real, Silver, Bogota, KM112	450.00

KM#	Date	Mintage	Identification	Mkt.Val.
Pn11	1848	—	1 Real, .900 Silver, Popayan	1100.

KM#	Date	Mintage	Identification	Mkt.Val.
Pn12	1848	—	2 Reales, .900 Silver, Popayan	1450.
Pn13	1848	—	8 Reales, Silver, Bogota, KM115	1750.

KM#	Date	Mintage	Identification	Mkt.Val.
Pn14	1848	—	8 Reales, .900 Silver, Popayan	3550.

KM#	Date	Mintage	Identification	Mkt.Val.
Pn15	1848	—	2 Pesos, .900 Gold, Popayan	4500.

KM#	Date	Mintage	Identification	Mkt.Val.
Pn16	1848	—	4 Pesos, .900 Gold, Popayan	7750.

KM#	Date	Mintage	Identification	Mkt.Val.
Pn17	1848	—	8 Pesos, .900 Gold, Popayan	19,800.

KM#	Date	Mintage	Identification	Mkt.Val.
Pn18	1848	—	16 Pesos, .900 Gold, Popayan	25,300.
Pn19	1848	—	16 Pesos, Silver, KM100	—
Pn20	1849	—	8 Reales, Bronze	500.00

KM#	Date	Mintage	Identification	Mkt.Val.
Pn21	1849	—	8 Reales, Silver	1750.
Pn22	1849	—	1 Peso, Silver 3.2258 g	550.00
Pn23	1849	—	1 Peso, Silver 6.4516 g	650.00
Pn24	1849	—	1 Peso, Silver 12.9032 g	900.00

KM#	Date	Mintage	Identification	Mkt.Val.
Pn25	1849	—	10 Pesos, Silver, Popayan	4500.
Pn26	1858	—	1 Peso, Silver	700.00

KM#	Date	Mintage	Identification	Mkt.Val.
Pn27	1858	—	20 Pesos, Bronze	800.00
Pn28	1858	—	20 Pesos, Silver	1600.

GRANADINE CONFEDERATION

1859-1862

MONETARY SYSTEM

10 Reales = 1 Peso
10 Decimos = 1 Peso

1/4 REAL

.9000 g, .666 SILVER, .0192 oz ASW
Mint: Popayan
Rev: 3 stars.

KM#	Date	Mintage	Good	VG	Fine	VF
123	1859	—	3.00	7.00	15.00	32.50
	1860	—	2.50	6.00	13.50	27.50
	1861	—	2.50	6.00	13.50	27.50
	1862/1	—	—	—	—	—
	1862	—	4.00	9.00	17.50	37.50

1/4 DECIMO

.9000 g, .666 SILVER, .0192 oz ASW
Mint: Bogota
Rev: Caducei flanking fraction.

KM#	Date	Mintage	Good	VG	Fine	VF
131	1860	—	8.00	18.50	40.00	65.00

Rev: 9 stars below fraction.

KM#	Date	Mintage	Good	VG	Fine	VF
132.1	1861	—	3.50	7.50	12.50	27.50
	1862	—	4.50	9.00	15.00	40.00

Mint: Popayan

KM#	Date	Mintage	Good	VG	Fine	VF
132.2	1860	—	12.50	27.50	55.00	125.00

1/2 REAL

1.2500 g, .900 SILVER, .0362 oz ASW
Mint: Popayan

KM#	Date	Mintage	Good	VG	Fine	VF
133	1862	—	5.50	11.50	25.00	55.00
	1862/48	—	6.50	12.50	27.50	60.00

MEDIO (1/2) DECIMO

1.2500 g, .900 SILVER, .0362 oz ASW
Mint: Bogota

KM#	Date	Mintage	VG	Fine	VF	XF
124	1859	—	7.00	17.50	30.00	75.00
	1860/59	—	8.00	20.00	35.00	80.00
	1860	—	6.00	14.00	25.00	55.00
	1861	—	7.00	17.50	30.00	75.00

UN (1) DECIMO

2.5000 g, .900 SILVER, .0723 oz ASW

KM#	Date	Mintage	VG	Fine	VF	XF
125	1859	—	4.00	9.00	20.00	37.50
	1860	—	7.50	20.00	32.50	75.00

DOS (2) REALES

5.0000 g, .900 SILVER, .1447 oz ASW
Mint: Popayan

KM#	Date	Mintage	VG	Fine	VF	XF
134	1862/48/47	—	6.00	15.00	27.50	62.50
	1862/48	—	5.50	13.50	25.00	60.00
	1862/49	—	4.50	10.00	22.50	55.00
	1862/52	—	25.00	45.00	85.00	130.00
	1862	—	7.00	15.00	27.50	60.00

NOTE: These are struck from reworked dies of KM#109.

PESO

25.0000 g, .900 SILVER, .7234 oz ASW
Mint: Bogota

KM#	Date	Mintage	VG	Fine	VF	XF
126	1859	—	15.00	25.00	50.00	100.00
	1860	—	15.00	25.00	50.00	100.00
	1861	—	25.00	50.00	100.00	200.00

1.6129 g, .900 GOLD, .0466 oz AGW
Mint mark: M

KM#	Date	Mintage	VG	Fine	VF	XF
135	1862	2 known	—	—	Rare	—

2 PESOS

3.2258 g, .900 GOLD, .0933 oz AGW
Mint mark: P

KM#	Date	Mintage	VG	Fine	VF	XF
127	1859	—	75.00	150.00	300.00	550.00
	1860	—	125.00	250.00	550.00	1000.

5 PESOS

8.0645 g, .900 GOLD, .2333 oz AGW
Mint mark: P

KM#	Date	Mintage	VG	Fine	VF	XF
128	1859	—	—	—	—	4750.

Mint mark: M

KM#	Date	Mintage	VG	Fine	VF	XF
136	1862	—	—	—	—	5750.

DIEZ (10) PESOS

16.1290 g, .900 GOLD, .4667 oz AGW
Mint: Bogota

KM#	Date	Mintage	VG	Fine	VF	XF
129.1	1859	3,481	250.00	350.00	600.00	1000.
	1860	9,687	225.00	300.00	500.00	900.00
	1861	834 pcs.	275.00	450.00	750.00	1200.

Mint: Popayan

KM#	Date	Mintage	VG	Fine	VF	XF
129.2	1858	—	225.00	300.00	500.00	900.00
	1859/58	—	250.00	350.00	600.00	1000.
	1859	—	225.00	300.00	500.00	900.00
	1860	—	250.00	350.00	600.00	1000.
	1861	—	275.00	400.00	700.00	1100.
	1862	—	250.00	350.00	600.00	1000.

VEINTE (20) PESOS

32.2580 g, .900 GOLD, .9335 oz AGW
Mint: Bogota

KM#	Date	Mintage	VG	Fine	VF	XF
130	1859	2,002	900.00	1750.	3000.	5000.

ESTADOS UNIDOS DE NUEVA GRANADA

1861-1862

UN (1) DECIMO

2.5000 g, .900 SILVER, .0723 oz ASW
Mint: Bogota

KM#	Date	Mintage	VG	Fine	VF	XF
137	1861	—	25.00	60.00	130.00	250.00

PESO

25.0000 g, .900 SILVER, .7234 oz ASW
Mint: Bogota

KM#	Date	Mintage	VG	Fine	VF	XF
138	1861	—	125.00	250.00	400.00	700.00

ESTADOS UNIDOS DE COLOMBIA

1862-1886

1/4 DECIMO

.8500 g, .900 SILVER, .0245 oz ASW
Mint: Bogota

KM#	Date	Mintage	VG	Fine	VF	XF
143.1	1863	.048	3.00	6.00	11.00	25.00
	1864	.435	2.00	5.00	9.50	20.00
	1865	.206	2.00	5.00	10.00	22.00
	1866	.267	2.00	5.00	10.00	22.00
	1867	.208	2.00	5.00	10.00	22.00

.8500 g, .666 SILVER, .0182 oz ASW

KM#	Date	Mintage	VG	Fine	VF	XF
143.1a	1868	.023	—	—	Rare	—
	1869	.183	5.00	10.00	16.50	32.50
	1870	.092	6.00	12.00	18.00	35.00
	1871	.413	4.50	10.00	16.50	32.50
	1873	Inc.KM169	—	—	Rare	—
	1881	Inc.KM169	8.50	17.50	25.00	55.00

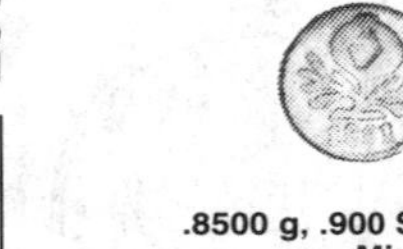

.8500 g, .900 SILVER, .0245 oz ASW
Mint: Popayan

KM#	Date	Mintage	VG	Fine	VF	XF
143.2	1863	—	4.50	8.00	13.50	30.00
	1864	.504	4.00	7.50	12.50	28.00
	1865/3	—	10.00	18.00	27.50	50.00
	1865	.291	4.50	10.00	18.50	35.00
	1866	.157	6.00	13.50	25.00	45.00
	1867	.055	6.00	13.50	25.00	45.00

.8500 g, .666 SILVER, .0182 oz ASW

KM#	Date	Mintage	VG	Fine	VF	XF
143.2a	1868	—	8.50	17.50	27.50	52.50
	1869	—	6.00	14.00	20.00	45.00
	1870	—	6.50	15.00	25.00	47.50
	1871	.155	6.00	14.00	20.00	45.00
	1872/1	.041	9.00	18.00	32.50	55.00
	1872	Inc. Ab.	5.00	10.00	17.50	38.50
	1873/2	—	9.00	18.00	30.00	55.00
	1873	—	5.00	10.00	17.50	38.50
	1874	—	6.50	16.50	27.50	52.00
	1875	—	6.00	14.50	27.50	50.00
	1876	—	7.00	16.00	27.50	50.00
	1877	.025	6.50	16.50	27.50	50.00
	1878	.025	9.00	18.50	32.50	55.00
	1879	—	6.00	14.00	22.50	47.50
	1880	—	7.00	16.00	27.50	55.00
	1881	—	7.00	16.00	27.50	55.00
	1883	—	— Reported, not confirmed			
	1888	—	—	—	Rare	—

NOTE: Date varieties exist for 1880 and 1881.

Mint: Medellin

KM#	Date	Mintage	VG	Fine	VF	XF
143.3	1874	—	8.00	18.00	30.00	60.00

MEDIO (1/2) DECIMO

1.2500 g, .900 SILVER, .0362 oz ASW
Mint: Bogota

KM#	Date	Mintage	VG	Fine	VF	XF
144	1863	.028	10.00	20.00	40.00	85.00
	1864	Inc. Ab.	12.00	25.00	50.00	100.00
	1865	.029	15.00	30.00	65.00	150.00

1.2500 g, .666 SILVER, .0268 oz ASW

KM#	Date	Mintage	VG	Fine	VF	XF
144a	1867 reverse .666/.900	.363	10.00	18.50	40.00	85.00

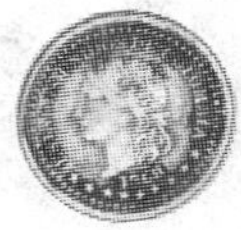

KM#	Date	Mintage	VG	Fine	VF	XF
150.1	1868	Inc. KM144a	4.50	12.50	26.50	40.00
	1869	.173	—	—	Rare	—
	1870	.140	12.00	22.50	35.00	60.00
	1871	.100	13.50	25.00	40.00	65.00

Mint: Medellin

KM#	Date	Mintage	VG	Fine	VF	XF
150.2	1868	.062	8.00	16.00	35.00	50.00
	1869	.026	10.00	22.50	47.50	85.00
	1870	—	— Reported, not confirmed			
	1873	.014	8.00	16.00	40.00	60.00
	1874	—	8.00	16.00	40.00	75.00

Mint: Popayan

KM#	Date	Mintage	VG	Fine	VF	XF
150.3	1868 PN	—	25.00	45.00	85.00	—
	1869	—	6.50	15.00	30.00	50.00
	1870	.382	6.50	15.00	30.00	50.00
	1874	—	6.50	15.00	30.00	50.00
	1875	.573	6.50	15.00	30.00	50.00
	1876	—	7.50	20.00	40.00	75.00
	1878	—	—	—	Rare	—

1.2500 g, .835 SILVER, .0336 oz ASW
Mint: Medellin

KM#	Date	Mintage	VG	Fine	VF	XF
150.2a	1870	Inc. Ab.	7.50	17.50	35.00	55.00
	1871	.061	4.50	10.00	22.50	37.50
	1872/1	Inc. Ab.	6.50	13.50	35.00	55.00
	1872 small head, .835/.666	—	6.50	13.50	35.00	55.00
	1873 AB below large head	—	7.50	15.00	32.50	52.50
	1874/61	—	8.50	13.50	35.00	60.00
	1874	—	5.25	11.50	24.00	37.50

Mint: Popayan

KM#	Date	Mintage	VG	Fine	VF	XF
150.3a	1872 reverse w/0.835/0.666	Inc. Ab.	5.00	12.00	25.00	50.00
	1875/65	—	10.00	25.00	40.00	85.00
	1875	Inc. Ab.	8.50	20.00	37.50	65.00

UN (1) DECIMO

2.5000 g, .900 SILVER, .0723 oz ASW
Mint: Bogota

KM#	Date	Mintage	VG	Fine	VF	XF
145.1	1863	.096	5.00	11.50	22.00	45.00
	1864	.039	6.00	13.00	26.00	55.00
	1866	.112	5.00	11.00	18.00	40.00

Mint: Popayan

KM#	Date	Mintage	VG	Fine	VF	XF
145.2	1863//1848	—	7.00	15.00	30.00	60.00
	1864//1848	.028	7.00	15.00	28.50	57.50
	1864	—	18.50	37.50	55.00	115.00

NOTE: The overdates appear to have been struck from re-cut dies of Un Real, 1848 Popayan, Pn7 w/stars over 1848 on obverse and 1863 or 1864 on reverse.

2.5000 g, .835 SILVER, .0671 oz ASW
Mint: Bogota

KM#	Date	Mintage	VG	Fine	VF	XF
145.1a	1866	.606	5.00	12.00	20.00	45.00

Mint: Popayan

KM#	Date	Mintage	VG	Fine	VF	XF
145.2a	1866	.034	12.50	27.50	52.50	115.00

NOTE: Some, or all, appear to have been struck from re-cut dies of Un Real, 1848 Popayan, Pn7 w/stars over 1848 on obverse and 1866 on reverse.

Mint: Bogota

KM#	Date	Mintage	VG	Fine	VF	XF
151.1	1868	.146	4.00	9.00	22.50	50.00
	1869	.082	3.00	8.00	18.50	45.00
	1870	—	—	—	Rare	—
	1871	.144	2.50	6.50	15.00	37.50
	1872	.133	2.50	6.50	15.00	37.50

Mint: Medellin
Obv: AB below bust.

KM#	Date	Mintage	VG	Fine	VF	XF
151.2	1874/3	—	18.50	45.00	85.00	175.00

DOS (2) REALES

5.0000 g, .835 SILVER, .1342 oz ASW
Mint: Popayan

KM#	Date	Mintage	VG	Fine	VF	XF
162	1880	3,000	60.00	120.00	225.00	365.00

NOTE: Apparently struck from heavily re-cut dies of Dos Decimos, 1854-1858.

DOS (2) DECIMOS

5.0000 g, .900 SILVER, .1447 oz ASW
Mint: Bogota

KM#	Date	Mintage	VG	Fine	VF	XF
149	1865	—	35.00	80.00	135.00	200.00

5.0000 g, .835 SILVER, .1342 oz ASW

KM#	Date	Mintage	VG	Fine	VF	XF
149a.1	1866	—	4.50	12.00	25.00	55.00
	1867	—	3.50	9.00	17.50	40.00

Mint: Popayan

KM#	Date	Mintage	VG	Fine	VF	XF
149a.2	1867 reverse 0.835/0.900	—	6.50	15.00	30.00	70.00
149b	1867 (error) reverse 0.666	—	11.50	25.00	50.00	90.00
	1867 reverse 0.835/0.666	—	16.50	37.50	75.00	120.00

Mint: Bogota

KM#	Date	Mintage	VG	Fine	VF	XF
155.1	1872	.024	18.50	37.50	65.00	120.00

Mint: Medellin

KM#	Date	Mintage	VG	Fine	VF	XF
155.2	1870	.015	6.75	14.50	27.50	46.50
	1871	.036	13.50	30.00	57.50	100.00
	1872	.045	4.00	9.50	20.00	37.50

NOTE: Each date of KM#155.2 has slightly different head, with 2 varieties for 1872. Legend spacings also vary.

Obv: Similar to 5 Decimos, KM#153.4.
Rev: Inverted fineness.

KM#	Date	Mintage	VG	Fine	VF	XF
159	1873	800 pcs.	—	—	Rare	—

Obv: Large head. Rev: Arms.

KM#	Date	Mintage	VG	Fine	VF	XF
160	1874	—	1.25	3.50	11.50	32.50

MEDIO (1/2) PESO

12.5000 g, .835/.900 SILVER, .3356 oz ASW
Mint: Medellin
Edge: DIOS LEI LIBERTAD.

KM#	Date	Mintage	VG	Fine	VF	XF
152	1868	—	—	—	Rare	—

CINCO (5) DECIMOS

12.5000 g, .835 SILVER, .3356 oz ASW
Mint: Bogota
Edge: DIOS LEI LIBERTAD.

KM#	Date	Mintage	VG	Fine	VF	XF
153.1	1868	9,161	35.00	60.00	130.00	225.00
	1869	.187	7.50	16.50	42.50	90.00
	1870	.206	7.50	16.50	42.50	85.00
	1871	.273	8.50	20.00	50.00	115.00

Mint: Medellin

KM#	Date	Mintage	VG	Fine	VF	XF
153.2	1868	5 known	—	—	Rare	—
	1869	1,054	275.00	500.00	750.00	1000.

KM#	Date	Mintage	VG	Fine	VF	XF
153.3	1872	.030	18.50	40.00	75.00	135.00
	1873	.090	9.00	22.50	40.00	85.00

Obv: Small round head. Rev: Small arms, fineness faces in.

KM#	Date	Mintage	VG	Fine	VF	XF
153.4	1873	Inc. Ab.	35.00	75.00	150.00	250.00
	1874	.185	7.00	15.00	35.00	75.00
	1875/4	.197	7.00	15.00	35.00	75.00

Rev: Fineness faces out.
Lettered edge.

KM#	Date	Mintage	VG	Fine	VF	XF
153.5	1875	Inc. Ab.	6.50	12.50	30.00	60.00
	1876/5	—	12.50	25.00	45.00	100.00
	1876	—	6.50	12.50	32.50	70.00
	1877	2 known	—	—	Rare	—

NOTE: Varieties exist.

Mint: Popayan
Edge: DIOS LEI LIBERTAD.

KM#	Date	Mintage	Good	VG	Fine	VF
153.6	1869	1 known	—	—	Rare	—
	1870/9	7,774	—	Reported, not confirmed		
	1870	Inc. Ab.	55.00	115.00	185.00	300.00
	1871	—	57.50	125.00	220.00	400.00
	1873/69	7,743	—	—	Rare	—
	1873	Inc. Ab.	45.00	100.00	175.00	250.00
	1874	.011	125.00	275.00	450.00	750.00
	1878	3,158	85.00	175.00	300.00	500.00
	1880	2 known	—	—	Rare	—

NOTE: 1874 dated coins w/0,835/0,900 overprint are known.

Mint: Medellin
Obv: Large head. Rev: Large arms.
Edge: DIOS LEI LIBERTAD.

KM#	Date	Mintage	VG	Fine	VF	XF
161.1	1877/4	.168	9.00	18.00	45.00	110.00
	1878/4	.318	6.25	17.50	35.00	65.00
	1878/4 lg.8	I.A.	—	—	Rare	—
	1879/4 pointed tail 9	.379	5.50	15.00	27.50	55.00
	1879/4 ball tailed 9	Inc. Ab.	8.00	22.00	40.00	75.00
	1880/74	.411	22.50	55.00	115.00	225.00
	1880	Inc. Ab.	3.50	7.50	15.00	35.00
	1881	.379	4.50	10.00	20.00	40.00
	1882	—	2.75	6.50	12.50	30.00
	1883	1.096	2.75	6.50	12.50	30.00
	1884/3	1.429	40.00	80.00	135.00	225.00
	1884	Inc. Ab.	2.75	6.50	12.50	30.00
	1885	—	3.25	7.00	12.50	30.00

NOTE: Date varieties exist.

Edge: DIOS PATRIA LIBERTAD.

KM#	Date	Mintage	VG	Fine	VF	XF
161.1a	1886	—	22.50	55.00	100.00	200.00
	1886 round top 3 in fineness	—	—	—	Rare	—

Obv: 8-pointed stars, different head.
Edge: DIOS LEI LIBERTAD.

KM#	Date	Mintage	VG	Fine	VF	XF
161.2	1880	2 known	—	—	Rare	—
	1882	—	—	—	Rare	—
	1883	—	—	—	Rare	—

12.2000 g, .500/.835 SILVER

KM#	Date	Mintage	VG	Fine	VF	XF
161.2a	1886/4	—	65.00	140.00	250.00	400.00
	1886/6	—	—	—	Rare	—

Edge: DIOS PATRIA LIBERTAD.

KM#	Date	Mintage	VG	Fine	VF	XF
161.2b	1886	—	45.00	125.00	225.00	330.00

NOTE: First A in PATRIA is inverted V.

Rev: 4 stars.

KM#	Date	Mintage	VG	Fine	VF	XF
161.2c	1886	—	100.00	200.00	350.00	500.00

Obv: Different head. Rev: 3 stars, 1 dot, leg: LEV.

KM#	Date	Mintage	VG	Fine	VF	XF
161.2d	1886	—	—	—	Rare	—

NOTE: The above coins always show traces of 0.835 under 0.500.

Obv: Square Liberty head
Edge: DIOS LEI LIBERTAD.

KM#	Date	Mintage	VG	Fine	VF	XF
161.3	1881	Inc. KM161.1	50.00	85.00	140.00	200.00

12.5000 g, .500 SILVER, .2009 oz ASW
Obv: Modified head w/curl on top, 5-pointed stars.
Rev: 2 stars and 2 dots, leg: LEV.
Edge: DIOS LIE LIBERTAD.

KM#	Date	Mintage	VG	Fine	VF	XF
164.1	1886	—	—	—	Rare	—

Rev: W/o stars or dots, leg: LEI.

KM#	Date	Mintage	VG	Fine	VF	XF
164.2	1886	—	—	—	Rare	—

.500/.835 SILVER
Rev: W/o stars or dots, leg: LEI.

KM#	Date	Mintage	VG	Fine	VF	XF
164.3	1886	1 known	—	—	Rare	—

PESO

25.0000 g, .900 SILVER, .7234 oz ASW
Mint: Bogota

KM#	Date	Mintage	VG	Fine	VF	XF
139.1	1862	.055	12.50	35.00	60.00	115.00
	1863	.018	10.00	30.00	55.00	100.00
	1864	.104	9.00	25.00	50.00	90.00
	1865	.122	9.00	25.00	50.00	90.00
	1866	.091	9.00	25.00	50.00	90.00
	1867	.044	12.50	35.00	60.00	115.00
	1868	.017	12.50	35.00	60.00	115.00

Mint: Popayan

KM#	Date	Mintage	VG	Fine	VF	XF
139.2	1863	—	200.00	500.00	700.00	1000.

1.6129 g, .900 GOLD, .0466 oz AGW
Mint: Medellin
Obv. leg: ESTADOS UNIDOS DE COLOMBIA.

KM#	Date	Mintage	VG	Fine	VF	XF
146.1	1863	.011	100.00	200.00	300.00	500.00

Obv. leg: COLOMBIA.

KM#	Date	Mintage	VG	Fine	VF	XF
146.2	1864	1,072	500.00	850.00	1250.	1650.

25.0000 g, .900 SILVER, .7234 oz ASW
Mint: Bogota

KM#	Date	Mintage	VG	Fine	VF	XF
154.1	1868	—	300.00	500.00	800.00	1200.
	1869	—	—	—	Rare	—
	1870	.046	55.00	100.00	165.00	300.00
	1871	.040	42.50	85.00	150.00	275.00

Mint: Medellin

KM#	Date	Mintage	VG	Fine	VF	XF
154.2	1869	3,598	65.00	135.00	200.00	400.00
	1870/69	.048	75.00	150.00	225.00	450.00
	1870	Inc. Ab.	50.00	100.00	165.00	300.00
	1871	.055	40.00	75.00	135.00	265.00

1.6129 g, .900 GOLD, .0466 oz AGW
Rev: Arms.

KM#	Date	Mintage	VG	Fine	VF	XF
156	1872/1	.062	45.00	75.00	115.00	175.00
	1872	Inc. Ab.	30.00	60.00	90.00	125.00
	1873	.018	45.00	75.00	115.00	175.00

Rev: Condor

KM#	Date	Mintage	VG	Fine	VF	XF
157.1	1872	Inc. Ab.	30.00	45.00	65.00	100.00
	1873/2	—	50.00	90.00	150.00	250.00
	1873	—	50.00	90.00	150.00	250.00

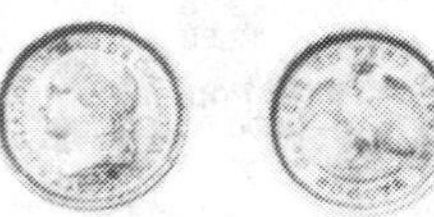

Mint: Bogota

KM#	Date	Mintage	VG	Fine	VF	XF
157.2	1871	—	60.00	120.00	200.00	400.00
	1872	—	30.00	50.00	75.00	115.00
	1873	3,374	30.00	50.00	75.00	115.00
	1874	.014	30.00	50.00	80.00	125.00
	1875	7,002	30.00	50.00	80.00	125.00
	1878	—	75.00	150.00	250.00	350.00

NOTE: The 1871 date is more commonly encountered as a counterfeit than an authentic striking.

2 PESOS

3.2258 g, .900 GOLD, .0933 oz AGW
Mint mark: M

KM#	Date	Mintage	VG	Fine	VF	XF
147	1863	2,996	150.00	280.00	450.00	700.00

Mint: Medellin

KM#	Date	Mintage	VG	Fine	VF	XF
A154	1871	.066	55.00	65.00	80.00	125.00
	1872	.030	65.00	80.00	120.00	175.00
	1876	—	80.00	100.00	140.00	200.00

3.2258 g, .666 GOLD, .0690 oz AGW

KM#	Date	Mintage	VG	Fine	VF	XF
A154a	1885/74	—	—	—	Rare	—

5 PESOS

8.0645 g, .900 GOLD, .2333 oz AGW
Mint: Medellin
Obv. leg: ESTADOS UNIDOS DE COLOMBIA.

KM#	Date	Mintage	VG	Fine	VF	XF
140	1862	—	— Reported, not confirmed			
	1863	.029	1500.	2500.	4000.	5500.

Mule. Obv. of KM#140. Rev. of KM#48.

KM#	Date	Mintage	VG	Fine	VF	XF
A148	1864	—	—	—	Unique	—

Obv. leg: COLOMBIA above.

KM#	Date	Mintage	VG	Fine	VF	XF
148	1864	8,035	2000.	3000.	4500.	6000.

8.0645 g, .666 GOLD, .1728 oz AGW

KM#	Date	Mintage	VG	Fine	VF	XF
163	1885/inverted 5	—	800.00	1350.	1750.	2850.
	1885/74	—	800.00	1350.	1750.	2850.

10 PESOS

16.1290 g, .900 GOLD, .4667 oz AGW
Mint: Bogota

KM#	Date	Mintage	VG	Fine	VF	XF
141.1	1862	.011	250.00	450.00	750.00	1200.
	1863	.017	250.00	450.00	750.00	1150.
	1864	—	600.00	1000.	2000.	3000.
	1866	—	1000.	2000.	3500.	5000.

Mint: Medellin

KM#	Date	Mintage	VG	Fine	VF	XF
141.2	1863	—	— Reported, not confirmed			
	1864	—	300.00	475.00	775.00	1250.
	1867	.014	250.00	350.00	600.00	900.00
	1868	.018	225.00	325.00	500.00	800.00
	1869	.018	225.00	325.00	500.00	800.00
	1870	7,786	250.00	350.00	600.00	900.00
	1871	6,018	250.00	350.00	600.00	900.00
	1872	.014	— Reported, not confirmed			

NOTE: Varieties exist.

Obv: Small date, inverted LEI 0.900.
Rev: Small Phrygian cap.

KM#	Date	Mintage	VG	Fine	VF	XF
141.4	1873	8,623	250.00	375.00	650.00	1000.
	1874	—	250.00	350.00	625.00	950.00
	1875	—	225.00	325.00	550.00	850.00
	1876/5	—	225.00	325.00	550.00	850.00
	1876	—	225.00	325.00	550.00	850.00

NOTE: Varieties exist.

16.1290 g, .666 GOLD, .3453 oz AGW

KM#	Date	Mintage	VG	Fine	VF	XF
141.2a	1886/74	—	—	—	Rare	—

16.1290 g, .900 GOLD, .4667 oz AGW
Mint: Popayan

KM#	Date	Mintage	VG	Fine	VF	XF
141.3	1863	—	250.00	375.00	650.00	900.00
	1864	.010	225.00	325.00	450.00	750.00
	1865	8,727	250.00	375.00	650.00	900.00
	1866	.013	225.00	325.00	450.00	750.00
	1867	—	300.00	400.00	700.00	1000.
	1869	—	300.00	400.00	700.00	1000.
	1870	—	600.00	1000.	2000.	3000.
	1871	2,617	— Reported, not confirmed			
	1874	—	— Reported, not confirmed			

20 PESOS

32.2580 g, .900 GOLD, .9335 oz AGW
Mint: Bogota

KM#	Date	Mintage	VG	Fine	VF	XF
142.1	1862	—	450.00	575.00	1000.	1850.
	1863	—	450.00	575.00	1000.	1850.
	1867	—	700.00	1200.	2000.	3250.
	1868	—	500.00	650.00	1250.	2150.
	1869	—	500.00	650.00	1250.	2150.
	1870	.017	500.00	650.00	1250.	2150.
	1871	1,641	550.00	800.00	1600.	2750.
	1872	1,471	500.00	650.00	1250.	2150.
	1873	2,731	500.00	650.00	1250.	2150.
	1874	1,656	500.00	650.00	1250.	2150.
	1875	1,696	500.00	650.00	1250.	2150.
	1876	2,299	700.00	1200.	2000.	3250.
	1877	—	900.00	1500.	2750.	4500.

1868

1869

Mint: Medellin

NOTE: On 1868, arrows in shield on reverse point between zeros in 0.900. On 1869, arrows point at zeros in 0.900.

KM#	Date	Mintage	VG	Fine	VF	XF
142.2	1863	—	—	Reported, not confirmed		
	1867	—	2000.	3500.	6000.	9500.
	1868	7,984	450.00	550.00	1000.	1500.
	1869/8	7,313	475.00	600.00	1200.	1850.
	1869	Inc. Ab.	450.00	550.00	1000.	1500.
	1870	.012	—	Reported, not confirmed		
	1871	5,996	650.00	1100.	2250.	3800.
	1872	.017	450.00	550.00	1000.	1600.

Mint: Popayan

KM#	Date	Mintage	VG	Fine	VF	XF
142.3	1862	—	—	Reported, not confirmed		
	1863	—	475.00	600.00	1100.	1700.
	1868	—	475.00	600.00	1100.	1700.
	1869	—	475.00	600.00	1100.	1700.
	1870	8,247	475.00	550.00	1000.	1600.
	1871	5,885	475.00	600.00	1100.	1700.
	1872	—	475.00	600.00	1100.	1700.
	1873	—	475.00	600.00	1100.	1700.
	1874/3	5,352	475.00	600.00	1100.	1700.
	1874	Inc. Ab.	475.00	600.00	1100.	1700.
	1875	5,240	475.00	600.00	1100.	1700.
	1877	1,219	900.00	1500.	2750.	5000.
	1878	2,873	500.00	650.00	1400.	2250.

Mint: Medellin
Modified design

KM#	Date	Mintage	VG	Fine	VF	XF
158	1873	—	1000.	2000.	4000.	6500.

MODERN DECIMAL SYSTEM

100 Centavos = 1 Peso

1-1/4 CENTAVOS

COPPER-NICKEL
Mint: Bogota
Plain edge.

KM#	Date	Mintage	Fine	VF	XF	Unc
173	1874	2.400	1.00	2.00	4.50	15.00
	1874	—	—	—	Proof	Rare

NOTE: Proof-like, or specimen strikes are sometimes mistaken for Proofs.

2-1/2 CENTAVOS

.9000 g, .666 SILVER, .0192 oz ASW

KM#	Date	Mintage	VG	Fine	VF	XF
169	1872	.328	2.75	5.50	9.00	15.00
	1873	.302	2.00	4.50	8.00	14.00
	1874	.075	3.00	6.00	10.00	22.50
	1875	.056	2.50	5.00	8.50	15.00
	1876	.071	3.25	7.00	15.00	27.00
	1877	.078	2.50	5.00	8.50	15.00
	1878	.347	2.00	3.25	4.75	10.00
	1879	.402	2.00	3.25	4.75	10.00
	1880	.123	2.00	3.25	4.75	10.00
	1881	.123	2.00	3.25	4.75	10.00

NOTE: Date varieties exist.

COPPER-NICKEL, 14-14.5mm

KM#	Date	Mintage	Fine	VF	XF	Unc
179	1881(W)	24.000	.10	.25	.75	4.50

18mm

KM#	Date	Mintage	Fine	VF	XF	Unc
180	1881(H)	4.000	.65	1.75	3.50	15.00

COPPER
Reeded edge

KM#	Date	Mintage	Fine	VF	XF	Unc
181	1885(B)	—	1.00	3.50	8.50	35.00

NOTE: Many die varieties exist.

COPPER-NICKEL
Plain edge, 15mm.

KM#	Date	Mintage	Fine	VF	XF	Unc
182	1886(H)	12.000	.35	1.00	3.00	8.00

CINCO (5) CENTAVOS

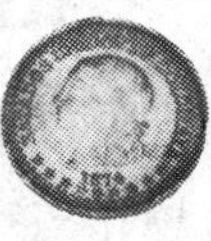

1.2500 g, .666 SILVER, .0268 oz ASW
Mint: Bogota

KM#	Date	Mintage	VG	Fine	VF	XF
170	1872	—	3.50	10.00	17.50	32.50
	1873	.089	3.00	6.75	12.50	23.50
	1874	.276	2.00	4.00	9.00	18.50

1.2300 g, .835 SILVER, .0330 oz ASW
Mint: Medellin

KM#	Date	Mintage	VG	Fine	VF	XF
174	1874	—	25.00	50.00	100.00	150.00

1.2500 g, .666 SILVER, .0268 oz ASW
Mint: Bogota

KM#	Date	Mintage	VG	Fine	VF	XF
174a.1	1875	.077	1.50	3.00	5.00	15.00
	1876	.019	3.50	9.00	16.00	27.50
	1877	.094	2.00	5.00	8.50	18.00
	1878	.190	1.00	2.75	5.00	15.00
	1879/8	.177	1.00	2.75	5.00	15.00
	1879	Inc. Ab.	1.00	2.75	5.00	15.00
	1880	.044	2.50	7.50	16.00	30.00
	1881	.219	2.50	7.50	15.00	28.00
	1882/1	—	2.50	7.50	15.00	28.00
	1882	—	1.25	3.00	5.00	15.00
	1883	.412	1.25	3.00	5.00	15.00
	1884	.220	2.50	5.50	8.50	18.50
	1885	—	1.50	3.50	6.50	15.00

Mint: Medellin

KM#	Date	Mintage	VG	Fine	VF	XF
174a.2	1875	—	22.00	45.00	70.00	135.00

10 CENTAVOS

2.5000 g, .835 SILVER, .0671 oz ASW
Mint: Bogota

KM#	Date	Mintage	VG	Fine	VF	XF
171	1872	Inc. Ab.	4.00	9.00	22.50	47.50
	1873	.043	2.75	7.00	20.00	40.00
	1874	Inc. Be.	2.50	5.00	12.00	17.50

KM#	Date	Mintage	VG	Fine	VF	XF
175.1	1874	.179	1.00	2.50	3.50	8.50
	1875	.265	1.00	2.50	3.50	8.50
	1878	.419	1.50	3.00	6.00	15.00
	1879	Inc. Ab.	1.00	2.50	3.50	8.50
	1880/79	.134	5.00	12.00	17.50	30.00
	1880	Inc. Ab.	4.00	10.00	17.50	30.00
	1881	.020	1.50	3.00	4.00	10.00
	1882	—	2.50	4.00	6.00	15.00
	1882(0.835/0.500)	—	2.50	4.00	6.00	15.00
	1883	.202	1.00	2.50	3.50	8.50
	1884/3	—	3.00	9.00	15.00	27.50
	1884	—	1.00	2.50	3.50	8.50
	1885	—	6.00	15.00	20.00	37.50

Mint: Medellin

KM#	Date	Mintage	VG	Fine	VF	XF
175.2	1885(0.835)	—	9.00	15.00	27.50	50.00
	1885(0.835/0.500)	—	12.50	20.00	35.00	70.00

2.5000 g, .500 SILVER, .0402 oz ASW

KM#	Date	Mintage	VG	Fine	VF	XF
175.2a	1885(0.500)	—	10.00	17.50	32.50	70.00
	1885(0.500/0.835)	—	13.50	22.50	35.00	75.00
	1886	—	18.50	32.50	50.00	100.00

20 CENTAVOS

5.0000 g, .835 SILVER, .1342 oz ASW
Mint: Medellin
Obv: Large head. Rev. leg: GRAM 5.

KM#	Date	Mintage	VG	Fine	VF	XF
176.1	1874	—	8.50	20.00	45.00	95.00

Rev. leg: GRAMOS 5.

KM#	Date	Mintage	VG	Fine	VF	XF
176.2	1874	—	32.50	50.00	85.00	150.00
	1882/74	—	16.50	28.50	40.00	70.00

Mint: Bogota
Obv: Small head. Rev. leg: GRAMOS 5.

KM#	Date	Mintage	VG	Fine	VF	XF
176.3	1884/3	—	15.00	32.50	60.00	110.00
	1884	—	13.50	30.00	55.00	100.00

Mint: Medellin
Obv: Small head. Rev. leg: GRAM 5.

KM#	Date	Mintage	VG	Fine	VF	XF
178.1	1875	—	7.50	12.50	20.00	35.00
	1876	—	2.00	3.75	8.00	20.00
	1877	—	4.50	10.00	17.50	30.00
	1882	—	3.00	6.50	11.50	25.00

NOTE: Size of stars varies.

Obv: Small head, tiny B in O of ESTADOS.

KM#	Date	Mintage	VG	Fine	VF	XF
178.2	1875	—	10.00	18.00	26.50	40.00
	1876/5	—	9.00	16.00	25.00	40.00
	1876	—	8.00	14.00	23.00	37.50

Obv: Small head. Rev. leg: GRAMOS 5

KM#	Date	Mintage	VG	Fine	VF	XF
178.3	1882/1	—	2.50	5.50	10.00	15.00
	1882	—	2.00	3.50	7.50	13.50
	1884	—	2.50	5.00	10.00	15.00
	1885/4	—	20.00	42.50	85.00	140.00
	1885	—	13.50	30.00	52.50	95.00
	1885/4 (0.835/0.500)	—	18.50	45.00	70.00	120.00
	1885(0.835/0.500)	—	17.50	35.00	65.00	110.00

5.0000 g, .500 SILVER, .0804 oz ASW

KM#	Date	Mintage	VG	Fine	VF	XF
178.3a	1886(0.500)	—	35.00	75.00	135.00	220.00
	1886(0.500/0.835)	—	35.00	75.00	135.00	220.00

50 CENTAVOS

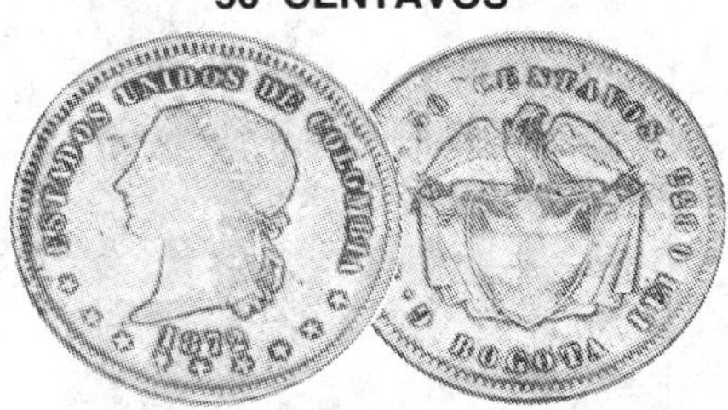

12.5000 g, .835 SILVER, .3356 oz ASW
Mint: Bogota
Rev: '50' in numerals
Obv. and rev: Small letters.
Edge: DIOS LEI LIBERTAD.

KM#	Date	Mintage	VG	Fine	VF	XF
172.1	1872	.027	12.50	35.00	65.00	125.00
	1873	.101	7.00	17.50	35.00	75.00

Obv. and rev: Large letters.

KM#	Date	Mintage	VG	Fine	VF	XF
172.2	1874	.280	5.00	12.00	22.00	50.00
	1875	—	—	—	Rare	—

NOTE: Varieties exist.

Rev: CINCUENTA for denomination.

KM#	Date	Mintage	VG	Fine	VF	XF
177.1	1874	Inc. Ab.	3.00	7.50	15.00	25.00
	1875	.621	2.50	7.00	13.00	22.50
	1876	.259	3.75	10.00	20.00	45.00
	1877/6	.133	6.00	15.00	27.50	55.00
	1877	Inc. Ab.	3.75	9.50	20.00	40.00
	1878	.264	3.75	9.50	20.00	40.00
	1879	.307	3.00	8.00	14.00	25.00
	1880	1.249	2.50	6.00	12.00	20.00
	1881	1.086	2.50	6.00	12.00	20.00
	1882/1	—	—	—	Rare	—
	1882	—	2.50	7.00	13.00	22.50
	1883	.221	2.50	7.50	14.00	25.00
	1884	.993	2.50	6.00	12.00	20.00
	1885	—	8.50	20.00	40.00	80.00

Mint: Popayan

KM#	Date	Mintage	VG	Fine	VF	XF
177.2	1880	—	150.00	265.00	450.00	800.00

12.5000 g, .500 SILVER, .2009 oz ASW
Mint: Bogota

KM#	Date	Mintage	VG	Fine	VF	XF
177a.1	1885	—	3.00	7.50	15.00	30.00
	1886/76	—	—	—	Rare	—
	1886/5	—	—	—	Rare	—
	1886	—	5.00	15.00	25.00	45.00

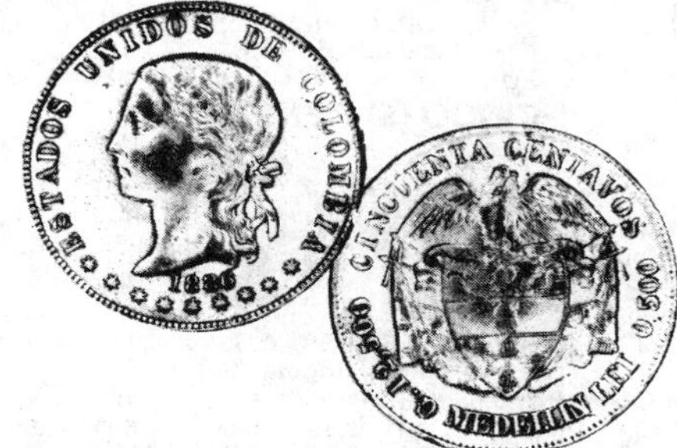

Mint: Medellin
Edge: DIOS LEI LIBERTAD.

KM#	Date	Mintage	VG	Fine	VF	XF
177a.2	1886	—	125.00	250.00	500.00	700.00

Edge: DIOS PATRIA LIBERTAD.

KM#	Date	Mintage	VG	Fine	VF	XF
177a.3	1886	—	65.00	135.00	275.00	600.00

Obv: KM#161. Rev: KM#177a.2.

KM#	Date	Mintage	VG	Fine	VF	XF
A183	1886	—	—	—	Rare	—

ANTIOQUIA

PATTERNS (Pn)

(Including off metal strikes)

KM#	Date	Mintage	Identification	Mkt.Val.
Pn1	1890	—	2 Centavos, Copper	85.00

BOLIVAR

PATTERNS (Pn)

(Including off metal strikes)

KM#	Date	Mintage	Identification	Mkt.Val.
Pn1	1890	—	2 Centavos, Copper	70.00

BOYACA

PATTERNS (Pn)

(Including off metal strikes)

KM#	Date	Mintage	Identification	Mkt.Val.
Pn1	1890	—	2 Centavos, Copper	65.00

CAUCA

PATTERNS (Pn)

(Including off metal strikes)

KM#	Date	Mintage	Identification	Mkt.Val.
Pn1	1890	—	2 Centavos, Copper	65.00

CUNDINAMARCA

PATTERNS (Pn)

(Including off metal strikes)

KM#	Date	Mintage	Identification	Mkt.Val.
Pn1	1890	—	2 Centavos, Copper	70.00

MAGDALENA

PATTERNS (Pn)

(Including off metal strikes)

KM#	Date	Mintage	Identification	Mkt.Val.
Pn1	1890	—	2 Centavos, Copper	250.00

SANTANDER

PATTERNS (Pn)

(Including off metal strikes)

KM#	Date	Mintage	Identification	Mkt.Val.
Pn1	1890	—	2 Centavos, Copper	70.00

TOLIMA

PATTERNS (Pn)

(Including off metal strikes)

KM#	Date	Mintage	Identification	Mkt.Val.
Pn1	1890	—	2 Centavos, Copper	65.00

REPUBLIC

2-1/2 CENTAVOS

COPPER-NICKEL

KM#	Date	Mintage	Fine	VF	XF	Unc
190	1900(W)	—	—	—	Rare	—

NOTE: Later date (1902) exists for this type.

CINCO (5) CENTAVOS

COPPER-NICKEL
Rev: Large top 5.
Plain edge.

KM#	Date	Mintage	Fine	VF	XF	Unc
183.1	1886(W)	1.000	.25	.75	2.00	6.00

Rev: Small top 5.

KM#	Date	Mintage	Fine	VF	XF	Unc
183.2	1886(W)	—	.25	.75	2.00	6.00
	1886(W)	—	—	—	Proof	165.00
	1888(W)	—	.25	.75	2.00	6.00

KM#	Date	Mintage	Fine	VF	XF	Unc
184	1886/5(W)					
	1886(W)	Inc. Ab.	.30	.85	2.75	7.50

NOTE: Later date (1902) exists for this type.

DIEZ (10) CENTAVOS

2.5000 g, .666 SILVER, .0536 oz ASW

KM#	Date	Mintage	Fine	VF	XF	Unc
188	1897 (Brussels)	2.642	.75	1.50	3.50	10.00

VEINTE (20) CENTAVOS

5.0000 g, .666 SILVER, .1072 oz ASW

KM#	Date	Mintage	Fine	VF	XF	Unc
189	1897 (Brussels)	1.441	1.25	2.50	5.00	15.00

CINCO (5) DECIMOS

12.5000 g, .500 SILVER, .2009 oz ASW
Obv: So-called Greek profile.
Edge: DIOS PATRIA LIBERTAD.

KM#	Date	Mintage	VG	Fine	VF	XF
165	1887	.084	35.00	70.00	150.00	300.00
	1888	—	50.00	100.00	250.00	500.00

Obv: Large head.
Edge: DIOS LEI LIBERTAD.

KM#	Date	Mintage	VG	Fine	VF	XF
166	1888	—	30.00	60.00	125.00	250.00
	1889	—	—	—	Rare	—

Obv: Long-necked Liberty head.

KM#	Date	Mintage	VG	Fine	VF	XF
167	1888	—	—	—	Rare	—

12.5000 g, .835 SILVER, .3356 oz ASW
Edge: DIOS PATRIA LIBERTAD.
Obv: Large head. Rev: 2 stars and 2 dots.

KM#	Date	Mintage	VG	Fine	VF	XF
168	1889	—	—	—	Rare	—

50 CENTAVOS

12.5000 g, .500 SILVER, .2009 oz ASW
Mint: Bogota
Edge: DIOS LEI LIBERTAD.

KM#	Date	Mintage	Fine	VF	XF	Unc
185	1887	1.764	6.00	13.50	32.50	85.00
	1888	—	—	—	Rare	—

Similar to KM#186.1a.

KM#	Date	Mintage	Fine	VF	XF	Unc
186.1	1888	—	32.50	85.00	175.00	350.00

12.5000 g, .835 SILVER, .3356 oz ASW
Edge: DIOS LEI LIBERTAD.

KM#	Date	Mintage	Fine	VF	XF	Unc
186.1a	1889	.130	13.50	30.00	55.00	100.00
	1898	—	12.00	25.00	47.50	90.00
	1899	—	55.00	125.00	250.00	525.00

30.4mm
400th Anniversary of Columbus' Discovery of America
Obv: Tip of cap points to left side of A in REPUBLICA.

KM#	Date	Mintage	Fine	VF	XF	Unc
187.1	1892	4.826	7.50	15.00	32.50	100.00

Reduced size, 29.6mm.
Obv: Tip of cap points to right side of A in REPUBLICA.

KM#	Date	Mintage	Fine	VF	XF	Unc
187.2	1892	Inc. Ab.	5.00	10.00	23.50	90.00
	1892	3 known	—	—	Proof	1750.

PATTERNS (Pn)

(Including off metal strikes)

KM#	Date	Mintage	Identification	Mkt.Val.
Pn1	1871	—	5 Decimos, .835 Silver, small Liberty head	—
Pn2	1871	—	5 Decimos, Copper, LEI .835	—
PnA3	1871	—	2 Pesos, Copper	—
PnB3	1872	—	2 Pesos, Copper	—

KM#	Date	Mintage	Identification	Mkt.Val.
Pn3	1872	—	20 Pesos, Gold, ESSAI on obv. and rev.	12,500.
PnA4	1873	—	1/2 Decimo, Silver	—

KM#	Date	Mintage	Identification	Mkt.Val.
Pn4	1873	—	2 Decimos, Silver, ESSAI	350.00
Pn5	1873	—	50 Centavos, .835 Silver, small Liberty head, ESSAI, A.B.	—
Pn6	1873	—	50 Centavos, Copper, LEI .835	—
Pn7	1873	—	5 Decimos, Silver	3000.
PnA8	1873	—	1 Peso, Silver, Obv: Bust by Barre w/o legend or date	—
PnB8	1873	—	1 Peso, Silver, Obv: Bust by Wyon, plain edge	—
Pn8	1873	—	10 Pesos, Copper, Medellin	400.00

KM#	Date	Mintage	Identification	Mkt.Val.
Pn9	1873	—	10 Pesos, Gold	—

KM#	Date	Mintage	Identification	Mkt.Val.
Pn10	1873	—	10 Pesos, Gold, ESSAI on obv. and rev.	7150.

KM#	Date	Mintage	Identification	Mkt.Val.
Pn11	1873	—	20 Pesos, Gold, ESSAI on obv. and rev.	8500.
Pn12	1873	—	20 Pesos, Copper	800.00

KM#	Date	Mintage	Identification	Mkt.Val.
Pn13	1873	—	20 Pesos, Silver	1400.
PnA14	1874	—	1-1/4 Centavo, Copper	—
Pn14	1874	—	50 Centavos, Silver plated Copper, small Liberty head	—
Pn15	1874	—	50 Centavos, .835 Silver, small Liberty head	2750.
Pn16	1875	—	50 Centavos, .835 Silver, small Liberty head	—

KM#	Date	Mintage	Identification	Mkt.Val.
PnA17	1881	—	2-1/2 Centavos, Aluminum, KM179	200.00
Pn17	1881	—	2-1/2 Centavos, Copper	200.00
Pn18	1881	—	2-1/2 Centavos, Copper-Nickel, KM179	200.00
Pn19	1881	—	2-1/2 Centavos, Silver, KM179	1000.
PnA20	1881	—	2-1/2 Centavos, Copper, flat base on cap	250.00
PnB20	1881	—	2-1/2 Centavos, Copper-Nickel, flat base on cap	250.00
PnC20	1881	—	2-1/2 Centavos, Silver, flat base on cap	1250.
PnD20	1881	—	2-1/2 Centavos, Copper, slanted base on cap	300.00
PnE20	1881	—	2-1/2 Centavos, Copper-Nickel, slanted base on cap	300.00
PnF20	1881	—	2-1/2 Centavos, Silver, slanted base on cap	1500.
Pn20	1881	—	5 Centavos, Copper-Nickel	250.00
PnA21	1881	—	5 Centavos, Copper-Nickel, different bust similar to 5 Centavos, Copper-Nickel, KM184	—
Pn21	1886	—	1 Centavo, Copper,	—
PnA22	1886	—	2-1/2 Centavos, Copper-Nickel	—
PnB22	1886	—	5 Centavos, Copper-Nickel, KM183	—
Pn22	1891	1	50 Centavos, Copper	—
Pn23	1891	—	50 Centavos, .835 Silver, small bust and condor	—
Pn24	1891	2	50 Centavos, .835 Silver	—

KM#	Date	Mintage	Identification	Mkt.Val.
Pn26	1900	—	5 Centavos, Copper-Nickel	275.00
Pn27	1900	—	10 Centavos, Copper-Nickel	175.00
Pn28	1900	—	10 Centavos, Copper-Nickel, Rev: ESSAI MONETAIRE	100.00
Pn29	1900	—	10 Centavos, Copper-Nickel, quartefoil on rev.	100.00
Pn30	1900	—	10 Centavos, Silver, reeded edge	—
Pn31	1900	—	20 Centavos, Silver, reeded edge	—
Pn32	1900	—	50 Centavos, .835 Silver, plain edge	—
Pn33	1900	—	50 Centavos, .835 Silver, reeded edge	—

PIEFORTS (P)

KM#	Date	Mintage	Identification	Mkt.Val.
P1	1848	—	1/2 Real, Bogota, .900 Silver, KM110	—
P2	1848	—	1 Real, Popayan, .900 Silver, KM112	—

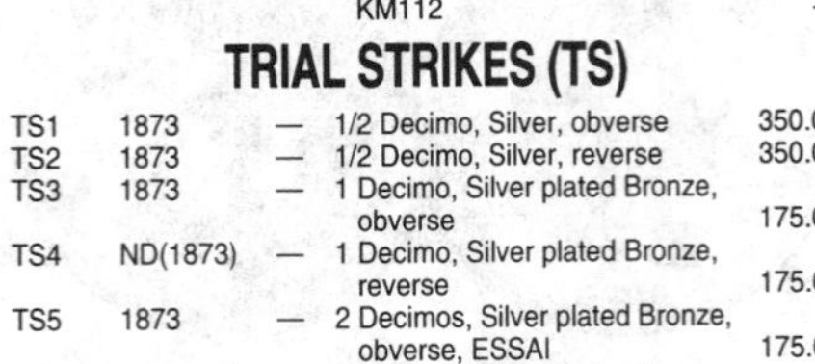

TRIAL STRIKES (TS)

KM#	Date	Mintage	Identification	Mkt.Val.
TS1	1873	—	1/2 Decimo, Silver, obverse	350.00
TS2	1873	—	1/2 Decimo, Silver, reverse	350.00
TS3	1873	—	1 Decimo, Silver plated Bronze, obverse	175.00
TS4	ND(1873)	—	1 Decimo, Silver plated Bronze, reverse	175.00
TS5	1873	—	2 Decimos, Silver plated Bronze, obverse, ESSAI	175.00
TS6	ND(1873)	—	2 Decimos, Silver plated Bronze, reverse, ESSAI	175.00

KM#	Date	Mintage	Identification	Mkt.Val.
TS7	1873	—	1 Peso, Silver, obverse, ESSAI	600.00

KM#	Date	Mintage	Identification	Mkt.Val.
TS8	ND(1873)	—	1 Peso, Silver, reverse, ESSAI	600.00

KM#	Date	Mintage	Identification	Mkt.Val.
TS9	1873	—	10 Pesos, Gold plated Bronze, obverse, ESSAI	400.00

KM#	Date	Mintage	Identification	Mkt.Val.
TS10	ND(1873)	—	10 Pesos, Gold plated Bronze, reverse, ESSAI	400.00

KM#	Date	Mintage	Identification	Mkt.Val.
TS11	1873	—	20 Pesos, Gold plated Bronze, obverse, ESSAI	450.00
TS12	ND(1873)	—	20 Pesos, Gold plated Bronze, obverse, ESSAI	450.00
TS13	ND(1886)	1	50 Centavos, Lead, reverse	—

Listings For

CRETE: Refer to Greece.

COMOROS

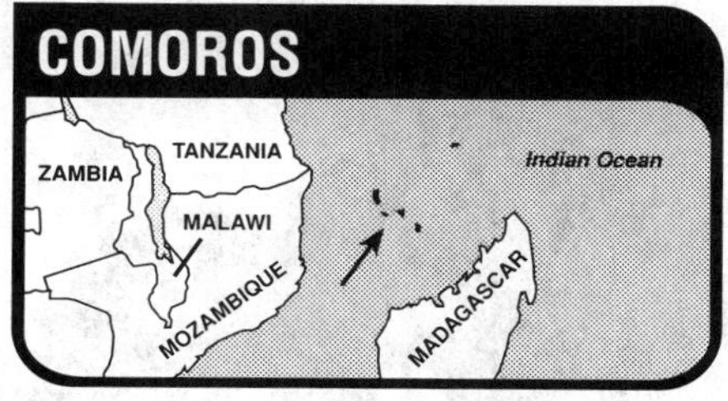

The Federal Islamic Republic of the Comoros, a volcanic archipelago located in the Mozambique Channel of the Indian Ocean 300 miles (483 km.) northwest of Madagascar, has an area of 719 sq. mi. (2,171 sq. km.) and a population of 549,338. Capital: Moroni. The economy of the islands is based on agriculture. There are practically no mineral resources. Vanilla, essence for perfumes, copra, and sisal are exported.

Ancient Phoenician traders were probably the first visitors to the Comoro Islands, but the first detailed knowledge of the area was gathered by Arab sailors. Arab dominion and culture were firmly established when the Portuguese, Dutch, and French arrived in the 16th century. In 1843 a Malagasy ruler ceded the island of Mayotte to France; the other three principal islands of the archipelago-Anjouan, Moheli, and Grand Comore came under French protection in 1886. The islands were joined administratively with Madagascar in 1912. The Comoros became partially autonomous, with the status of a French overseas territory, in 1946, and achieved complete internal autonomy in 1961. On Dec. 31, 1975, after 133 years of French association, the Comoro Islands became the independent Republic of the Comoros.

Mayotte retained the option of determining its future ties and in 1976 voted to remain French. Its present status is that of a French Territorial Collectivity. French currency now circulates there.

TITLES

Daulat Anjazanchiyah

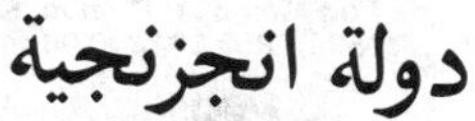

RULERS

Said Ali ibn Said Amr, regnant, 1890
French, 1886-1975

MINT MARKS

(a) - Paris, privy marks only
A - Paris

MONETARY SYSTEM

100 Centimes = 1 Franc

ANJOUAN SULTANATE

5 CENTIMES

BRONZE PRIVY MARK
Rev. privy mark: Fasces

KM#	Date	Mintage	Fine	VF	XF	Unc
1.1	AH1308A	.100	6.50	12.00	20.00	65.00
	Rev. privy mark: Torch					
1.2	AH1308A	.200	6.50	12.00	20.00	65.00

10 CENTIMES

BRONZE PRIVY MARK
Rev. privy mark: Fasces

KM#	Date	Mintage	Fine	VF	XF	Unc
2.1	AH1308A	.050	10.00	16.00	30.00	75.00
	Rev. privy mark: Torch					
2.2	AH1308A	.100	10.00	18.00	35.00	80.00

5 FRANCS

.900 SILVER

KM#	Date	Mintage	Fine	VF	XF	Unc
3	AH1308A	2,050	300.00	450.00	675.00	1350.

COSTA RICA

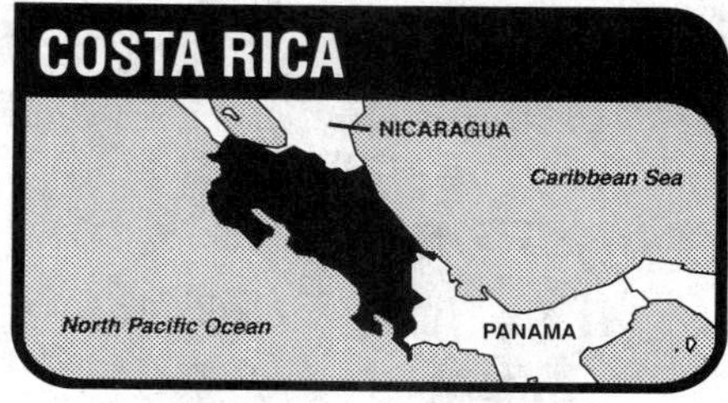

The Republic of Costa Rica, located in southern Central America between Nicaragua and Panama, has an area of 19,730 sq. mi. (51,100 sq. km.) and a population of 3.4 million. Capital: San Jose. Agriculture predominates; tourism and coffee, bananas, beef and sugar contribute heavily to the country's export earnings.

Costa Rica was discovered by Christopher Columbus in 1502, during his last voyage to the New World, and was a colony of Spain from 1522 until independence in 1821. Columbus named the territory Nueva Cartago; the name Costa Rica wasn't generally applied until 1540. Bartholomew Columbus attempted the first settlement but was driven off by Indian attacks and the country wasn't pacified until 1530. After centuries as part of the Spanish Captaincy-General of Guatemala, Costa Rica was absorbed into the Mexican Empire of Augustin de Iturbide from 1821-1823. From 1823 to 1848, it was a constituent state of the Central American Republic (q.v.). Established as a republic in 1848, Costa Rica adopted democratic reforms in the 1870's and 80's. Today, Costa Rica remains a model of orderly democracy in Latin America, although, like most of the hemisphere - its economy is in stress.

NOTE: Also see Central American Republic.

MINT MARKS

CR - San Jose 1825-1947
HEATON - Heaton, Birmingham, England, 1889-93
BIRMm - Heaton, Birmingham, England, 1889-93

ASSAYERS INITIALS

MM - 1842
JB - 1847-1864
GW - Guillermo Witting, 1850-1890

MONETARY SYSTEM

8 Reales = 1 Peso
16 Pesos = 8 Escudos = 1 Onza

REAL SERIES

1/2 REAL

.903 SILVER
Mint: San Jose
Obv: Radiant 6-pointed star in circle above branches. Rev: Tobacco plant and value in circle, date below.

KM#	Date	Mintage	VG	Fine	VF	XF
32	1842 MM	—	25.00	40.00	80.00	165.00

NOTE: Holed examples are valued at about 40% of the above figures.

REAL

.903 SILVER
Mint: San Jose

KM#	Date	Mintage	VG	Fine	VF	XF
65	1847 JB	—	5.75	10.00	15.00	35.00
	1847 JB (error) backwards B	—	6.50	12.00	17.50	37.50

.750 SILVER

KM#	Date	Mintage	VG	Fine	VF	XF
66	1849 JB	—	3.00	6.50	10.00	27.50
	1850 JB	—	3.75	8.00	15.00	35.00

1/2 ESCUDO

1.6000 g, .875 GOLD, .0450 oz AGW
Mint: San Jose

KM#	Date	Mintage	VG	Fine	VF	XF
97	1850 JB	3,388	38.50	65.00	100.00	150.00
	1851 JB	6,565	38.50	65.00	100.00	150.00
	1853 JB	8,491	38.50	65.00	100.00	150.00

KM#	Date	Mintage	VG	Fine	VF	XF
97	1854 JB	4,663	38.50	65.00	100.00	150.00
	1855 JB	8,822	38.50	65.00	100.00	150.00
	1855 GW	I.A.	38.50	65.00	100.00	150.00
	1864 JB	9,018	38.50	65.00	100.00	150.00

ESCUDO

3.1000 g, .875 GOLD, .0872 oz AGW
Mint: San Jose
Rev: Denomination .1-E.

33.1	1842 MM	.010	300.00	600.00	1200.	2000.

Rev: Denomination 1.-E.

33.2	1842 MM	I.A.	350.00	800.00	1500.	2250.

98	1850 JB	6,167	55.00	100.00	150.00	265.00
	1851 JB	4,388	55.00	100.00	150.00	265.00
	1853 JB	2,979	65.00	150.00	250.00	500.00
	1855 JB	4,095	60.00	125.00	200.00	350.00

2 ESCUDOS

6.3000 g, .875 GOLD, .1772 oz AGW
Mint: San Jose

99	1850 JB	3,641	100.00	150.00	200.00	400.00
	1854 JB	I.A.	100.00	150.00	200.00	400.00
	1854 GW	I.A.	100.00	150.00	200.00	400.00
	1855 JB	.060	100.00	125.00	175.00	400.00
	1855 GW	I.A.	100.00	150.00	200.00	400.00
	1858 GW	.017	100.00	125.00	175.00	400.00
	1862 GW	5,896	110.00	200.00	325.00	550.00
	1863 GW	5,632	110.00	200.00	325.00	550.00

1/2 ONZA

12.6000 g, .875 GOLD, .3545 oz AGW
Mint: San Jose

100	1850 JB	.018	200.00	300.00	400.00	800.00
	1850 JB	—	—	—	Proof	4200.

COUNTERMARKED COINAGE

1841-1842

Type I
c/m: Radiant 6-pointed star in 7mm circle.
NOTE: An additional plug was cut from each coin to 'pay for the work'. Market valuations are for holed coins.

1/2 REAL

SILVER
c/m: Type I on Mexico 1/2 Real, KM#72.

KM#	Date	Year	Good	VG	Fine	VF
1	ND	(1792-1808)	150.00	200.00	350.00	—

REAL

SILVER
c/m: Type I on Mexico 1 Real, KM#77.

KM#	Date	Year	Good	VG	Fine	VF
4	ND	(1760-1771)	150.00	200.00	350.00	—

2 REALES

SILVER

KM#	Date	Year	Good	VG	Fine	VF
	c/m: Type I on Bolivia (Potosi) 2 Reales, KM#53.					
7	ND	(1773-89)	15.00	30.00	60.00	90.00
	c/m: Type I on Guatemala 2 Reales, KM#34.1.					
8	ND	(1772-76)	15.00	30.00	60.00	90.00
	c/m: Type I on Mexico 2 Reales, KM#91.					
12	ND	(1800)	15.00	30.00	60.00	90.00
	c/m: Type I on Mexico 2 Reales, KM#92.					
9	ND	(1809-12)	15.00	30.00	60.00	90.00
	c/m: Type I on Mexico 2 Reales, KM#372.8.					
10	ND	(1825-41)	15.00	30.00	60.00	90.00

c/m: Type I on Peru 2 Reales, KM#141.1.

11	ND	(1825-40)	15.00	30.00	60.00	90.00

c/m: Type I on Peru 2 Reales, KM#95.

13	ND	(1791-1808)	15.00	30.00	60.00	90.00

4 REALES

SILVER
c/m: Type I on Bolivia (Potosi) 4 Reales, KM#54.

14	ND	(1773-89)	150.00	275.00	425.00	1000.

c/m: Type I on Bolivia (Potosi) 4 Reales, KM#72.

KM#	Date	Year	Good	VG	Fine	VF
15	ND	(1791-1808)	150.00	275.00	425.00	1000.

c/m: Type I on Guatemala, 4 Reales, KM#35.1.

16	ND	(1772-76)	750.00	1250.	2500.	—

8 REALES

SILVER
c/m: Type I on Mexico 8 Reales, KM#106.

19	ND	(1772-89)	150.00	275.00	425.00	950.00

c/m: Type I on Mexico 8 Reales, KM#376.

20	ND	(1824)	200.00	300.00	450.00	1000.

	c/m: Type I on Mexico 8 Reales, KM#377.					
21	ND	(1824-41)	150.00	250.00	400.00	900.00
	c/m: Type I on Peru 8 Reales, KM#78.					
22	ND	(1772-89)	150.00	275.00	425.00	950.00

c/m: Type I on Peru 8 Reales, KM#142.1.

23	ND	(1825-28)	150.00	250.00	400.00	900.00

c/m: Type I on Peru 8 Reales, KM#142.3.

KM#	Date	Year	Good	VG	Fine	VF
24	ND	(1828-40)	150.00	250.00	400.00	900.00

c/m: Type I on North Peru 8 Reales, KM#155.

25	ND	(1836-39)	150.00	275.00	425.00	950.00

c/m: Type I on Spanish 8 Reales, C#136.

26	ND	(1809-30)	150.00	275.00	425.00	950.00

c/m: Type I on Mexico 8 Reales, KM#111.

27	ND	(1812-22)	—	—	—	2500.

1841-1842

Type II
c/m: Radiant 6-pointed star in 4mm circle.

2 ESCUDOS

GOLD
c/m: Type II on Central American Republic 2 Escudos, KM#15.

28	ND	(1825-37)	—	—	Rare	—

4 ESCUDOS

GOLD
c/m: Type II on Central American Republic 4 Escudos, KM#16.

29	ND	(1828-37)	—	—	Rare	—

COUNTERSTAMPED COINAGE

1845

Type III

Obv. c/s: COSTA RICA and 2 R. around female head.
Rev. c/s: HABILITADA POR EL GOB. around tree.

2 REALES

SILVER
c/s: Type III on Spanish (Seville) 2 Reales.

KM#	Date	Year	Good	VG	Fine	VF
35	ND	(1732)	20.00	35.00	60.00	100.00

c/s: Type III on Spanish (Madrid) 2 Reales, C#38.

36	ND	(1772-88)	8.50	15.00	27.50	50.00

NOTE: The coin illustrated above also has the lattice c/m of the Province of Trinidad (Cuba) and would command a premium.

c/s: Type III on Spanish (Madrid) 2 Reales, C#69.

37	ND	(1788-1808)	8.50	15.00	27.50	50.00

c/s: Type III on Spanish (Seville) 2 Reales, C#69.

38	ND	(1793-1808)	8.50	15.00	27.50	50.00

c/s: Type III on Spanish 2 Reales, C#89.

39	ND	(1811-13)	15.00	25.00	40.00	65.00

c/s: Type III on Spanish 4 Reales, C#90.

40	ND	(1808-13)	10.00	15.00	35.00	60.00

c/s: Type III on Spanish (Madrid) 2 Reales, C#134.

41	ND	(1814-33)	10.00	17.50	30.00	55.00

c/s: Type III on Spanish (Seville) 2 Reales, C#134.

42	ND	(1815-33)	10.00	17.50	30.00	55.00

c/s: Type III on Spanish 4 Reales, C#135.

43	ND	(1811-33)	25.00	50.00	95.00	150.00

c/s: Type III on Trinidad, Cuba c/s on Spanish (Seville) 2 Reales, KM#12.

44	ND	(1793-1808)	14.00	18.00	32.50	55.00

NOTE: The coin illustrated above also has the lattice c/m of the Province of Trinidad and would command a premium.

1846

Type IV
Obv. c/s: REPUB. DE CENT. DE AMER. 1846 around sun above mountains in a 14mm circle.
Rev. c/s: HABILITADA EN COSTA RICA J.B. . . around tree, 1-R.

REAL

SILVER
c/s: Type IV on Spanish American 'cob' 1 Real.

KM#	Date	Good	VG	Fine	VF
47	1846	12.50	25.00	40.00	75.00

4 REALES

SILVER
c/s: Type IV with additional c/m 4 in square on Guatemala 'cob' 4 Reales, KM#5.

KM#	Date	Year	Good	VG	Fine	VF
50	1846	—	250.00	400.00	600.00	800.00

c/s: Type IV with additional c/m 4 in square on United States Capped Bust 50 Cents, C#32.

51.1	1846	(1809)	1250.	2750.	5000.	8000.

c/s: Type IV with additional c/m 4 in square on United States Capped Bust 50 Cents, C#32a.

51.2	1846	(1837)	850.00	1750.	3250.	5000.

c/s: Type IV with additional c/m 4 in square on United States Seated Liberty 50 cents.

52	1846	(1843)	850.00	1750.	3250.	5000.

1846

Type V
Obv. c/s: REPUB. DE CENT. DE AMER. 1846 around sun above mountains in a 14mm circle.
Rev. c/s: HABILITADA EN COSTA RICA J-B around tree, 2-R.

2 REALES

SILVER
c/s: Type V on Bolivia (Potosi) 'cob' 2 Reales, KM#29.

KM#	Date	Year	Good	VG	Fine	VF
54	1846	(1700-46)	20.00	35.00	65.00	100.00

c/s: Type V on Peru (Lima) 'cob' 2 Reales, KM#30.

KM#	Date	Year	Good	VG	Fine	VF
55	1846	(1700-46)	20.00	35.00	65.00	100.00

c/s: Type V on Guatemula 2 Reales proclamation medal.

KM#	Date	Year	Good	VG	Fine	VF
56	1846	(1808)	150.00	350.00	550.00	900.00

8 REALES

SILVER
c/s: Type V with additional c/m 8 in circle on Bolivia (Potosi) 'cob' 8 Reales, KM#31.

KM#	Date	Year	Good	VG	Fine	VF
58	1846	(1700-46)	400.00	550.00	800.00	1000.

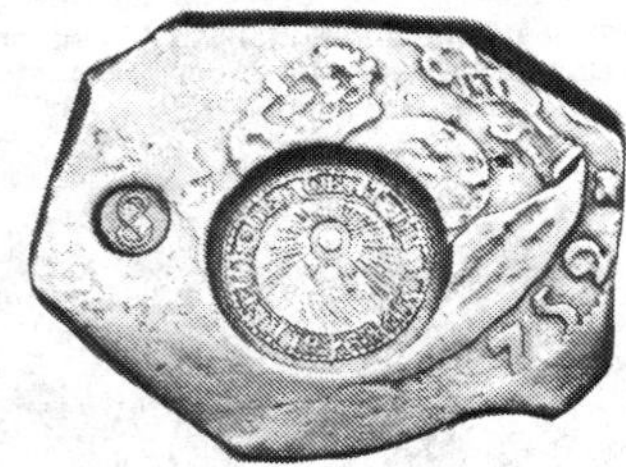

c/s: Type V on Guatemala 'cob' 8 Reales, KM#12.

KM#	Date	Year	Good	VG	Fine	VF
59	1846	(1747-53)	400.00	550.00	800.00	1000.

c/s: Type V on Peru (Lima) 'cob' 8 Reales of Charles II.

KM#	Date	Year	Good	VG	Fine	VF
60	1846	(1665-1700)	400.00	550.00	800.00	1000.

c/s: Type V on Peru (Lima) 'cob' 8 Reales, KM#34.

KM#	Date	Year	Good	VG	Fine	VF
61	1846	(1700-46)	400.00	550.00	800.00	1000.

c/s: Type V on Mexico City 'cob' 8 Reales, KM#48.

KM#	Date	Year	Good	VG	Fine	VF
62	1846	(1733-34)	400.00	550.00	800.00	1000.

COUNTERMARKED COINAGE

1849-1857

Type VI
c/m: HABILITADA POR EL GOBIERNO around lion in 5mm circle.

Local Series

1/2 REAL

SILVER
c/m: Type VI on Central American Republic 1/2 Real, KM#20.

KM#	Date	Year	Good	VG	Fine	VF
67	(1849)	1831 E	5.00	9.00	15.00	22.00
		1831 F	5.00	9.00	15.00	22.00
		1843 M	4.00	6.00	11.00	20.00
		1845 B	4.00	6.00	11.00	20.00

c/m: Type VI on Central American Republic 1/2 Real, KM#20a.

KM#	Date	Year	Good	VG	Fine	VF
68	(1849)	1846 JB 'CRESCA'	3.50	5.00	10.00	17.50
		1846 JB 'CREZCA'	3.50	5.00	10.00	17.50
		1847 JB 'CRESCA'	3.50	5.00	10.00	17.50
		1847 JB 'CREZCA'	3.50	5.00	10.00	17.50
		1848 JB	3.50	5.00	10.00	17.50
		1849 JB	3.50	7.00	12.00	22.00

c/m: Type VI on Costa Rica 1/2 Real, KM#32.

KM#	Date	Year	Good	VG	Fine	VF
69	(1849)	1842 MM	12.00	17.50	32.50	55.00

NOTE: Values listed for KM#67-69 are for unholed pieces, holed examples are worth substantially less.

REAL

SILVER

c/m: Type VI on Central American Republic 1 Real, KM#21.

KM#	Date	Year	Good	VG	Fine	VF
72	(1849)	1831	7.50	12.50	27.50	47.50
	(1849)	1831 F	6.00	9.50	25.00	42.50
	(1849)	1848 JB	9.00	18.00	32.50	50.00

c/m: Type VI on Central American Republic 1 Real, KM#21a.

KM#	Date	Year	Good	VG	Fine	VF
72a	(1849)	1848 JB	9.00	18.00	30.00	50.00
		1849 JB	5.50	10.00	25.00	42.50

c/m: Type VI on Costa Rica 1 Real, KM#65.

KM#	Date	Year	Good	VG	Fine	VF
73	(1849)	1847 JB	13.50	25.00	42.50	65.00
		1847 JB (error) backwards B	15.00	30.00	55.00	75.00

c/m: Type VI on Costa Rica 1 Real, KM#66.

KM#	Date	Year	Good	VG	Fine	VF
74	(1849)	1849 JB	13.50	25.00	42.50	70.00
		1850 JB	14.00	30.00	47.50	72.50

NOTE: Values listed for KM#72-74 are for unholed pieces, holed examples are worth substantially less.

2 REALES

SILVER
c/m: Type VI on Central American Republic 2 Reales, KM#24.

KM#	Date	Year	Good	VG	Fine	VF
77	(1849)	1849 JB	4.75	10.00	18.50	32.50

NOTE: Values listed for KM#77 are for unholed pieces, holed examples are worth substantially less.

4 REALES

NOTE: Half dollar size coins with Type VI c/m are modern fabrications. Refer to listings in *UNUSUAL WORLD COINS*, 3rd edition, Krause Publications 1992.

8 REALES

NOTE: Crown size coins with Type VI c/m are modern fabrications. Refer to listings in *UNUSUAL WORLD COINS*, 3rd edition, Krause Publications, 1992.

1/2 ESCUDO

GOLD
Mint mark: CR
c/m: Type VI on Central American Republic 1/2 Escudo, KM#13.

KM#	Date	Year	VG	Fine	VF	XF
80	(1857)	1828 F	50.00	100.00	150.00	225.00
		1843 M	50.00	100.00	150.00	225.00
		1846 JB	40.00	80.00	125.00	200.00
		1847 JB	40.00	80.00	125.00	200.00
		1848 JB	40.00	80.00	125.00	200.00
		1849 JB	50.00	100.00	150.00	225.00

Mint mark: NG
c/m: Type VI on Central American Republic 1/2 Escudo, KM#5.

KM#	Date	Year	VG	Fine	VF	XF
81	(1857)	1825 M	—	—	—	—

ESCUDO

GOLD
Mint mark: CR
c/m: Type VI on Central American Republic 1 Escudo, KM#14.

KM#	Date	Year	VG	Fine	VF	XF
84	(1857)	1833 E	90.00	175.00	275.00	375.00
		1833 F	90.00	175.00	275.00	375.00
		1844 M	55.00	125.00	225.00	325.00
		1845 JB	90.00	175.00	275.00	375.00
		1846 JB	65.00	125.00	225.00	325.00
		1847 JB	65.00	125.00	225.00	325.00
		1848 JB	65.00	125.00	225.00	325.00
		1849 JB	65.00	125.00	225.00	325.00

English Series

REAL

SILVER

c/m: Type VI on Great Britain 6 Pence, KM#665.

KM#	Date	Year	Good	VG	Fine	VF
87	(1857)	1816-20	7.50	11.00	17.50	30.00

c/m: Type VI on Great Britain 6 Pence, KM#698.

KM#	Date	Year	Good	VG	Fine	VF
88	(1857)	1826-29	8.50	17.50	32.50	55.00

c/m: Type VI on Great Britain 6 Pence, KM#712.

KM#	Date	Year	Good	VG	Fine	VF
89	(1857)	1831,34-37	7.50	13.50	27.50	45.00

c/m: Type VI on Great Britain 6 Pence, KM#733.

KM#	Date	Year	Good	VG	Fine	VF
90	(1857)	1838-46,48-49	6.00	10.00	17.50	30.00

2 REALES

SILVER

c/m: Type VI on Great Britain Shilling, KM#666.

KM#	Date	Year	Good	VG	Fine	VF
93	(1857)	1816-20	7.50	12.50	22.50	37.50

c/m: Type VI on Great Britain Shilling, KM#734.

KM#	Date	Year	Good	VG	Fine	VF
94	(1857)	1838-46,49	6.50	12.00	20.00	35.00

Peso Series

1/16 PESO

1.4600 g, .903 SILVER, .0423 oz ASW
Reeded edge.

KM#	Date	Mintage	VG	Fine	VF	XF
101	1850 JB	—	7.50	17.50	35.00	70.00
	1855/0 JB	—	10.00	22.50	42.00	85.00
	1855 JB	—	6.00	15.00	30.00	65.00
	1862 JB	—	—	—	Rare	—
	1862 GW	—	27.50	45.00	75.00	165.00

1/8 PESO

2.9500 g, .903 SILVER, .0856 oz ASW

KM#	Date	Mintage	VG	Fine	VF	XF
102	1850 JB	—	6.00	13.50	22.50	50.00
	1853 JB	—	7.50	16.50	37.50	75.00
	1855 JB	—	5.00	12.50	22.50	50.00

1/4 PESO

6.4000 g, .903 SILVER, .1858 oz ASW

KM#	Date	Mintage	VG	Fine	VF	XF
103	1850 JB	—	4.50	10.00	20.00	50.00
	1853 JB	—	8.00	18.00	37.50	70.00
	1855 JB	—	12.50	27.50	50.00	80.00

DECIMAL COINAGE

100 Centavos = 1 Peso (1864-1896)

1/4 CENTAVO

COPPER-NICKEL
Plain edge.

KM#	Date	Mintage	VG	Fine	VF	XF
108	ND(1865)	.020	32.50	55.00	90.00	160.00

CENTAVO

COPPER-NICKEL

KM#	Date	Mintage	VG	Fine	VF	XF
109	1865	.033	3.75	10.00	22.50	40.00
	1866	.039	6.00	13.50	27.50	55.00
	1867	.044	7.00	17.50	32.50	65.00
	1868	.020	3.00	8.00	13.50	25.00

KM#	Date	Mintage	Fine	VF	XF	Unc
120	1874	.032	2.25	4.00	8.00	15.00

5 CENTAVOS

1.2680 g, .750 SILVER, .0305 oz ASW
Reeded edge.

KM#	Date	Mintage	VG	Fine	VF	XF
110	1865 GW	.233	2.50	6.00	15.00	30.00
	1869 GW	—	3.50	10.00	25.00	50.00
	1870 GW	.027	10.00	25.00	55.00	100.00
	1871 GW	.328	6.00	15.00	40.00	75.00
	1872 GW	I.A.	7.00	16.50	45.00	90.00
	1875/1 GW	I.A.	2.00	5.50	13.50	30.00
	1875 GW	I.A.	2.00	5.00	12.00	28.00

KM#	Date	Mintage	Fine	VF	XF	Unc
125	1885 GW	.180	1.50	3.50	8.00	22.00
	1886/5 GW	.251	2.75	6.50	12.50	35.00
	1887 GW	.491	1.25	3.00	7.50	20.00

Mint mark: HEATON BIRMM

KM#	Date	Mintage	Fine	VF	XF	Unc
128	1889	.520	.65	1.75	4.00	15.00
	1889	—	—	—	Proof	150.00
	1890	.431	.65	1.75	4.00	15.00
	1892	.280	.75	2.00	4.50	18.00

10 CENTAVOS

2.5360 g, .750 SILVER, .0611 oz ASW

KM#	Date	Mintage	VG	Fine	VF	XF
111	1865 GW	.185	3.50	8.00	17.50	40.00
	1868 GW	.010	50.00	95.00	185.00	—
	1870 GW	.048	15.00	30.00	60.00	120.00
	1872 GW	.018	45.00	85.00	160.00	—

KM#	Date	Mintage	VG	Fine	VF	XF
121	1875 GW	.286	2.25	5.50	12.50	30.00

2.5000 g, .750 SILVER, .0602 oz ASW
Obv: CB below shield.

KM#	Date	Mintage	Fine	VF	XF	Unc
126	1886 GW	.120	2.75	6.00	14.00	38.00
	1887 GW	.245	2.50	4.50	12.00	30.00

Mint mark: HEATON BIRMM

KM#	Date	Mintage	Fine	VF	XF	Unc
129	1889	.260	1.00	2.50	4.50	15.00
	1889	—	—	—	Proof	200.00
	1890	.215	1.00	2.75	5.00	18.00
	1892	.140	1.25	3.00	6.50	20.00

25 CENTAVOS

6.2500 g, .750 SILVER, .1507 oz ASW
Rev: Small 25Cs.

KM#	Date	Mintage	VG	Fine	VF	XF
105	1864 GW	.223	5.50	17.50	55.00	125.00

Rev: Large 25Cs.

KM#	Date	Mintage	VG	Fine	VF	XF
106	1864 GW	I.A.	13.50	28.50	85.00	190.00
	1865 GW	.042	5.00	12.50	25.00	80.00
	1875 GW	.121	3.25	8.50	18.00	55.00

Rev: GW 9Ds

KM#	Date	Mintage	Fine	VF	XF	Unc
127.1	1886 GW	.100	4.50	8.50	17.50	45.00
	1887 GW	.200	5.50	11.50	22.50	55.00

Obv: CB below shield. Rev: 9Ds GW

KM#	Date	Mintage	Fine	VF	XF	Unc
127.2	1886 GW	I.A.	6.50	14.00	25.00	65.00
	1887 GW	I.A.	3.00	7.50	18.50	47.50

Mint mark: HEATON BIRMM.

KM#	Date	Mintage	Fine	VF	XF	Unc
130	1889/8	.410	1.50	3.75	7.50	20.00
	1889/93	I.A.	1.50	4.00	8.50	22.00
	1889/99	I.A.	1.50	4.50	9.50	28.00
	1889	Inc. Ab.	1.50	3.75	7.50	20.00
	1889	—	—	—	Proof	250.00
	1890/80	.395	1.50	4.50	9.00	28.00
	1890	Inc. Ab.	1.50	3.75	7.50	20.00

KM#	Date	Mintage	Fine	VF	XF	Unc
130	1892	.440	1.50	3.75	7.50	20.00
	1893	.670	1.25	2.50	5.00	18.00

50 CENTAVOS

12.5000 g, .750 SILVER, .3014 oz ASW

KM#	Date	Mintage	Good	VG	Fine	VF
112	1865 GW	.029	5.00	15.00	40.00	100.00
	1866/5 GW	.117	6.00	16.50	45.00	110.00
	1866 GW	I.A.	7.50	18.50	55.00	125.00
	1867 GW	5,168	45.00	85.00	220.00	375.00
	1870 GW	6,267	75.00	150.00	325.00	—
	1872 GW	I.A.	100.00	225.00	—	—
	1875 GW	.069	4.50	13.50	37.50	90.00

KM#	Date	Mintage	Fine	VF	XF	Unc
124	1880 GW	.389	5.75	12.50	25.00	75.00
	1885 GW	.152	6.00	13.50	22.50	70.00
	1886 GW	.097	6.50	14.50	30.00	80.00
	1887 GW	.208	6.50	14.50	27.50	75.00
	1889 GW*	.205	—	—	Rare	—
	1890/80 GW inverted N in CENTAVOS					
		.058	5.25	11.50	22.00	60.00
	1890 GW	I.A.	5.25	11.50	22.00	60.00

***NOTE:** Not released for circulation.

PESO

1.5253 g, .875 GOLD, .0429 oz AGW

KM#	Date	Mintage	VG	Fine	VF	XF
107.1	1864 GW	6,383	35.00	70.00	100.00	135.00
	1866 GW	.035	27.50	55.00	85.00	115.00
	1868 GW	—	45.00	85.00	120.00	160.00

Rev: Large UN in center of wreath.

KM#	Date	Mintage	VG	Fine	VF	XF
107.2	1866 GW	I.A.	27.50	55.00	85.00	115.00

Rev: Smaller UN, fineness omitted.

KM#	Date	Mintage	VG	Fine	VF	XF
107.3	1866 GW	I.A.	27.50	55.00	85.00	115.00

Design modified

KM#	Date	Mintage	VG	Fine	VF	XF
116	1871 GW	.011	28.50	52.50	80.00	115.00
	1872 GW	.037	28.50	52.50	80.00	115.00

2 PESOS

2.9355 g, .875 GOLD, .0825 oz AGW

KM#	Date	Mintage	VG	Fine	VF	XF
113	1866 GW	.013	45.00	70.00	115.00	150.00
	1867 GW	—	60.00	100.00	155.00	200.00
	1868 GW	—	45.00	70.00	115.00	150.00

Design modified (19mm)

KM#	Date	Mintage	VG	Fine	VF	XF
122	1876 GW	2,161	—	—	Rare	—

5 PESOS

7.3387 g, .875 GOLD, 22mm, .2064 oz AGW

KM#	Date	Mintage	VG	Fine	VF	XF
114	1867 GW	.039	100.00	125.00	165.00	250.00
	1868 GW	6,752	100.00	125.00	165.00	250.00
	1869 GW	.011	100.00	125.00	165.00	250.00
	1870 GW	.015	100.00	125.00	165.00	250.00

21mm

KM#	Date	Mintage	VG	Fine	VF	XF
117	1873 GW	5,167	165.00	300.00	650.00	1000.
	1875 GW	I.A.	165.00	300.00	650.00	1000.

8.0645 g, .900 GOLD, .2333 oz AGW

KM#	Date	Mintage	VG	Fine	VF	XF
118	1873 GW	I.A.	1750.	2250.	2750.	3250.

10 PESOS

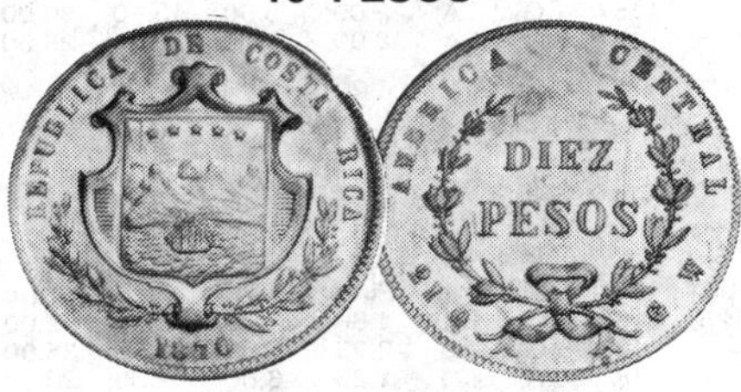

14.6774 g, .875 GOLD, .4129 oz AGW

KM#	Date	Mintage	VG	Fine	VF	XF
115	1870 GW	.020	225.00	275.00	350.00	500.00
	1871 GW	.030	250.00	325.00	400.00	600.00
	1872 GW	4,555	250.00	350.00	425.00	650.00

Design modified

KM#	Date	Mintage	VG	Fine	VF	XF
123	1876 GW	3,389	500.00	1000.	1500.	2000.

20 PESOS

32.2580 g, .900 GOLD, .9334 oz AGW

KM#	Date	Mintage	Fine	VF	XF	Unc
119	1873 GW	—	—	—	*Rare	—

***NOTE:** Stack's Hammel sale 9-82 AU realized $16,000., Pacific Coast Auction Galleries, Long Beach sale 6-86 AU realized $17,000, Superior Galleries Casterline sale 5-89 XF realized $16,500.

COUNTERSTAMPED COINAGE

Necessity issue undertaken in 1889 (and 1890) consequent to supply, by Heaton Mint of underweight 50 centavo coinage of the general type of the Heaton-made 5, 10 & 25 centavos of 1889-93. The host coins were particularly available, due to the adoption by Colombia of a .500 fine debasement of its silver coinage under President Nunez in 1886. This led to runaway inflation, rampant printing press money and hoarding of good (.835-.902 fine) silver. The Colombian peso declined in value to about 1 Centavo of the old silver and gold currency.

1889

Type VII
Obv. c/s: COSTA RICA above national arms.
Rev: HABILITADA POR EL GOBIERNO around lion/CR in 7mm circle.

50 CENTAVOS

SILVER

c/s: Type VII on Colombia (Bogota) Cinco Decimos, KM#153.1.

KM#	Date	Year	Good	VG	Fine	VF
136	(1889)	1868	37.50	75.00	150.00	300.00
		1870	25.00	50.00	100.00	200.00

c/s: Type VII on Colombia (Bogota) 50 Centavos, KM#172.1.

KM#	Date	Year	Good	VG	Fine	VF
133.1	(1889)	1872	20.00	35.00	75.00	100.00
		1873	15.00	25.00	50.00	75.00

c/s: Type VII on Colombia (Bogota) 50 Centavos, KM#172.2.

KM#	Date	Year	Good	VG	Fine	VF
133.2	(1889)	1874	12.00	20.00	40.00	60.00

c/s: Type VII on Colombia (Bogota) Cincuenta Centavos, KM#177.1.

KM#	Date	Year	Good	VG	Fine	VF
134	(1889)	1874	17.50	30.00	45.00	70.00
		1875	17.50	30.00	45.00	70.00
		1876	17.50	30.00	45.00	70.00
		1877	17.50	30.00	45.00	70.00
		1878	17.50	30.00	45.00	70.00
		1879	15.00	25.00	40.00	65.00
		1880	15.00	25.00	40.00	65.00
		1881	15.00	25.00	40.00	65.00
		1882	15.00	25.00	40.00	65.00
		1883	15.00	25.00	40.00	65.00
		1884	15.00	25.00	40.00	65.00
		1885	30.00	50.00	80.00	125.00

c/s: Type VII on Colombia (Medellin) Cinco Decimos, KM#161.1.

KM#	Date	Year	Good	VG	Fine	VF
135.1	(1889)	1874	20.00	35.00	50.00	75.00
		1875	20.00	35.00	50.00	75.00
		1876	20.00	35.00	50.00	75.00

c/s: Type VII on Colombia (Medellin) Cinco Decimos, KM#153.4.

KM#	Date	Year	Good	VG	Fine	VF
135.3	(1889)	1874	25.00	40.00	60.00	90.00

c/s: Type VII on Colombia (Medellin) Cinco Decimos, KM#153.5.

KM#	Date	Year	Good	VG	Fine	VF
135.4	(1889)	1875	25.00	40.00	60.00	90.00

c/s: Type VII on Colombia (Medellin) Cinco Decimos, KM#153.6.

KM#	Date	Year	Good	VG	Fine	VF
135.2	(1889)	1877/4	20.00	35.00	50.00	75.00
		1878/4	20.00	35.00	50.00	75.00
		1879/4	20.00	35.00	50.00	75.00
		1880	20.00	35.00	50.00	75.00
		1881	17.50	30.00	45.00	65.00
		1882	17.50	30.00	45.00	65.00
		1883	17.50	30.00	45.00	65.00
		1884	15.00	25.00	40.00	60.00
		1885	15.00	25.00	40.00	60.00
		1886	45.00	75.00	100.00	150.00

MONETARY REFORM

100 Centimos = 1 Colon

DOS (2) COLONES

1.5560 g, .900 GOLD, .0450 oz AGW
Christopher Columbus

KM#	Date	Mintage	Fine	VF	XF	Unc
139	1897	500 pcs.	—	—	Proof	750.00
	1900	.045	30.00	35.00	45.00	55.00

NOTE: Later dates (1915-1928) exist for this type.

CINCO (5) COLONES

3.8900 g, .900 GOLD, .1125 oz AGW
Christopher Columbus

KM#	Date	Mintage	Fine	VF	XF	Unc
142	1899	.100	BV	60.00	75.00	115.00
	1900	.100	BV	60.00	75.00	115.00

DIEZ (10) COLONES

7.7800 g, .900 GOLD, .2251 oz AGW
Christopher Columbus

KM#	Date	Mintage	Fine	VF	XF	Unc
140	1897	.060	BV	115.00	125.00	175.00
	1899	.050	BV	115.00	125.00	175.00
	1900	.140	BV	115.00	125.00	175.00

VEINTE (20) COLONES

15.5600 g, .900 GOLD, .4502 oz AGW
Christopher Columbus

KM#	Date	Mintage	Fine	VF	XF	Unc
141	1897	.020	BV	225.00	275.00	400.00
	1899	.025	BV	225.00	275.00	400.00
	1900	5,000	BV	250.00	375.00	675.00

ESSAIS (E)

KM#	Date	Mintage	Identification	Mkt.Val.
E1	1872	—	5 Centavos, Nickel	325.00

KM#	Date	Mintage	Identification	Mkt.Val.
E2	1872	—	10 Centavos, Nickel	350.00

PATTERNS (Pn)

(Including off metal strikes)

KM#	Date	Mintage	Identification	Mkt.Val.
Pn1	1850	—	1/2 Peso, White metal	—

KM#	Date	Mintage	Identification	Mkt.Val.
PnA2	1850	—	1 Peso, White metal	—
Pn2	1850	—	1 Onza, Gold	—
Pn3	1889	—	50 Centavos, Silver	2500.
Pn4	1892	—	1 Centavo, Copper-Nickel	300.00
Pn5	1892	—	1 Centavo, Copper	—
Pn6	1892	—	1 Centavo, Copper, obv: arms. Rev: value and wreath	—

PIEFORTS (P)

KM#	Date	Mintage	Identification	Mkt.Val.
P1	1892	—	1 Centavo, Copper, Pn6	—
P2	1892	—	1 Centavo, Nickel, Pn4	—
P3	1892	—	Un Centavo, Bronze	—
P4	1892	—	Un Centavo, Nickel	—

Listings For

CRETE: refer to Greece

CROATIA

The Republic of Croatia, (Hrvatska) bordered on the west by the Adriatic Sea and the northeast by Hungary, has an area of 21,829 sq. mi. (56,538 sq. km.) and a population of 4.7 million. Capital: Zagreb.

The country was attached to the Kingdom of Hungary until Dec. 1, 1918, when it joined with the Serbs and Slovenes to form the Kingdom of the Serbs, Croats and Slovenes, which changed its name to the Kingdom of Yugoslavia on Oct. 3, 1929. On April 6, 1941, Hitler, angered by the coup d'etat that overthrew the pro-Nazi regime of regent Prince Paul, sent the Nazi armies crashing across the Yugoslav borders from Germany, Hungary, Romania and Bulgaria. Within a week the army of the Balkan Kingdom was prostrate and broken. Yugoslavia was dismembered to reward Hitler's Balkan allies. Croatia, reconstituted as a nominal kingdom, was given to the administration of an Italian princeling, who wisely decided to remain in Italy. By 1947 it was again totally part of the 6 Yugoslav Socialist Republics.

Croatia proclaimed their independence from Yugoslavia on Oct. 8, 1991.

PATTERNS (Pn)

(Including off metal strikes)

KM#	Date	Mintage	Identification	Mkt.Val.
Pn1	1848	—	1 Forint, Silver, 9.50 g, obv: portrait right, rev: star and crescent	Rare
Pn2	1848	—	2 Forint, reported not confirmed	—
Pn3	1849	46 pcs.	1 Kreuzer, Copper, obv: crowned triune arms, rev: Star/ JEDEN/KRIZAR/date	Rare
Pn4	1849	—	20 Kreuzer, Silver	—

NOTE: Issued in Zagreb by Governor Jelacic in 1849. Destroyed by decree of Franz Joseph.

ZARA

(Zadar)

Zara, a port and fortress in Dalmatia, Croatia, was occupied by the French during the period of 1807-13. While the French defenders of the city were under siege in 1813, they issued a silver emergency coinage.

FRENCH SIEGE COINAGE

4 FRANCS - 60 CENTIMES

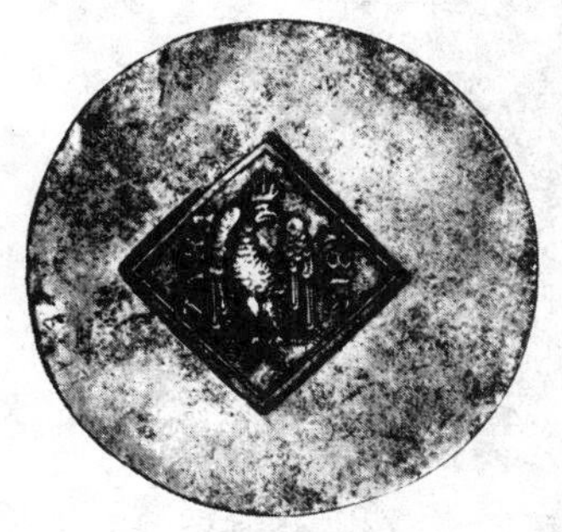

SILVER, 30.59 g

KM#	Date	Mintage	VG	Fine	VF	XF
1	1813	—	400.00	600.00	800.00	1200.

9 FRANCS - 20 CENTIMES

SILVER, 61.12 g

KM#	Date	Mintage	VG	Fine	VF	XF
2	1813	—	500.00	750.00	1000.	1500.

18 FRANCS - 40 CENTIMES

SILVER, 122.38 g
Obv: Large stamp.

KM#	Date	Mintage	VG	Fine	VF	XF
3	1813	—	750.00	1500.	2750.	5000.

Obv: Small stamp.

KM#	Date	Mintage	VG	Fine	VF	XF
4	1813	—	800.00	1600.	2850.	5500.

CUBA

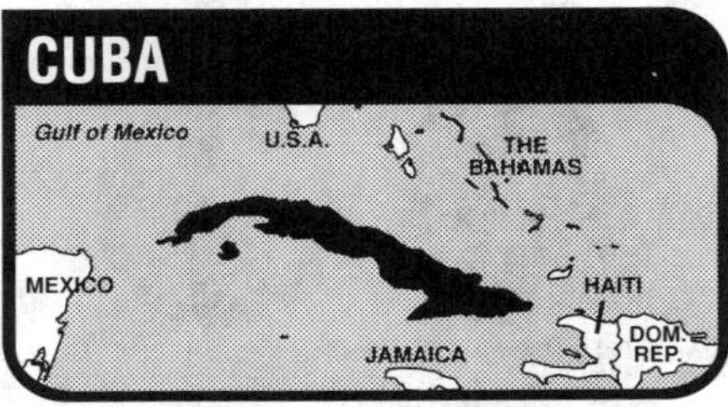

The Republic of Cuba, situated at the northern edge of the Caribbean Sea about 90 miles (145 km.) south of Florida, has an area of 42,804 sq. mi. (110,860 sq. km.) and a population of 10.9 million. Capital: Havana. The Cuban economy is based on the cultivation and refining of sugar, which provides 80 percent of export earnings.

Discovered by Columbus in 1492 and settled by Diego Velasquez in the early 1500s, Cuba remained a Spanish possession until 1898, except for a brief British occupancy of Havana in 1762-63. Cuban attempts to gain freedom were crushed, even while Spain was granting independence to its other American possessions. Ten years of warfare, 1868-78, between Spanish troops and Cuban rebels exacted guarantees of rights which were never implemented. The final revolt, begun in 1895, evoked American sympathy, and with the aid of U.S. troops independence was proclaimed on May 20, 1902. Fulgencio Batista seized the government in 1952 and established a dictatorship. Opposition to Batista, led by Fidel Castro, drove him into exile on Jan. 1, 1959. A communist-type, 25-member collective leadership headed by Castro was inaugurated in March, 1962.

RULERS

Spanish, until 1898

MINT MARKS

Key - Havana, 1977-

MONETARY SYSTEM

100 Centavos = 1 Peso

COUNTERMARKED COINAGE

The loss of the Spanish Colonial mints in the new world caused a severe shortage of coinage in Cuba. Clandestine traders introduced the silver inflationary "reales de vellow" of Spain. The ratio was 2 1/2 New Reales to 1 Old Colonial Real. They were accepted easily by the Cuban public, ignorant of the devaluation in Spain where the silver "Peso" was now divided into 20 Reales.

In 1827 the Spanish governor of Cuba banned their importation. Various exchange rates were used until March 22, 1841 when a Royal Order decreed all will be recalled, counted and recorded with receipts issued and devalued with a countermark in the provinces Trinidad, Santiago de Cuba and Puerto Principe. Fifty punches were prepared.

2 REALES

.903 SILVER

KM#	Date	Good	VG	Fine	VF
	c/m: Lattice on Spanish (Madrid) 2 Reales, C#38.1.				
1.1	ND(1772-88)	12.50	22.50	35.00	50.00
	c/m: Lattice on Spanish (Seville) 2 Reales, C#38.2.				
1.2	ND(1773-88)	12.50	22.50	35.00	50.00
	c/m: Lattice on Spanish (Madrid) 2 Reales, C#69.1.				
2	ND(1788-1808)	10.00	20.00	30.00	45.00
	c/m: Lattice on Spanish (Seville) 2 Reales, C#69.2.				
3	ND(1788-1808)	10.00	20.00	30.00	45.00
	c/m: Lattice on Spanish (Catalonia) 2 Reales, C#134.1.				
4.1	ND(1811-14)	13.50	27.00	40.00	60.00
	c/m: Lattice on Spanish (Cadiz) 2 Reales, C#134.2.				
4.2	ND(1810-12)	13.50	27.00	40.00	60.00

KM#	Date	Good	VG	Fine	VF
	c/m: Lattice on Spanish (Madrid) 2 Reales, C#134.3.				
5	ND(1814-33)	10.00	20.00	30.00	45.00

KM#	Date	Good	VG	Fine	VF
	c/m: Lattice on Spanish (Seville) 2 Reales, C#134.4.				
6	ND(1815-33)	10.00	20.00	30.00	45.00
	c/m: Lattice on Spanish (Madrid) 2 Reales, C#134a.3.				
9	ND(1812-14)	10.00	20.00	30.00	45.00

4 REALES

KM#	Date	Good	VG	Fine	VF
	c/m: Lattice on Spanish (Madrid) 4 Reales, C#90.				
7	ND(1808-13)	10.00	20.00	30.00	45.00
	c/m: Lattice on Spanish (Seville) 4 Reales, C#90.2.				
8	ND(1810-12)	10.00	20.00	30.00	45.00

KM#	Date	Good	VG	Fine	VF
	c/m: Lattice on Spanish (Madrid) 4 Reales, C#137.6.				
10	ND(1822-23)	10.00	20.00	30.00	45.00
	c/m: Lattice on Spanish (Valencia) 4 Reales, C#137.1.				
11	ND(1823)	13.50	27.00	40.00	60.00
	c/m: Lattice on Spanish (Madrid) Proclamation medal of Charles IV.				
12	ND(1789)	—	—	—	—

REPUBLIC

PESO

22.5500 g, .900 SILVER, .6526 oz ASW

KM#	Date	Mintage	Fine	VF	XF	Unc
8	1898	1,000	300.00	750.00	1750.	3500.
	1898	—	—	—	Proof	4500.

COUNTERMARKED COINAGE

1872-77 REVOLUTIONARY FUND

It is thought that these c/m were most likely used 1872-1877 by the Cuban revolutionary troops as a fund raising device. Commonly encountered on Mexican coins.

KEY COUNTERMARK VARIETIES

A - Short & thick

B - Long & thin

Values for these pieces vary according to the rarity of the date and type of coin on which the c/m is found. Prices listed here are for the most common host coins.

REAL SERIES

2 REALES

.903 SILVER
c/m: Key on Mexican 2 Reales, KM#374.

KM#	Date	Year	Good	VG	Fine	VF
R1	ND	1825-70	15.00	25.00	40.00	60.00

4 REALES

.903 SILVER
c/m: Key on Mexican 4 Reales, KM#375.

KM#	Date	Year	Good	VG	Fine	VF
R2	ND	1827-70	20.00	30.00	45.00	70.00

8 REALES

.903 SILVER
c/m: Key on Mexican 8 Reales, KM#377.

KM#	Date	Year	Good	VG	Fine	VF
R3	ND	1824-77	30.00	45.00	65.00	100.00

DECIMAL SERIES

25 CENTAVOS

.903 SILVER
c/m: Key on Mexican 25 Centavos, KM#406.

KM#	Date	Year	Good	VG	Fine	VF
R4.1	ND	1869-77	15.00	20.00	30.00	55.00

c/m: Key on United States Liberty Seated Quarters with arrows at date and rays on reverse.

KM#	Date	Year	Good	VG	Fine	VF
R4.2	ND	1853	65.00	125.00	185.00	275.00

c/m: Key on United States Liberty Seated Quarters plain date without rays on reverse.

KM#	Date	Year	Good	VG	Fine	VF
R4.3	ND	1858	65.00	125.00	185.00	275.00

c/m: Key on United States Capped Bust Quarters.

KM#	Date	Year	Good	VG	Fine	VF
R4.4	ND	1835	65.00	125.00	185.00	275.00

50 CENTAVOS

.903 SILVER
c/m: Key on Mexican 50 Centavos, KM#407.

KM#	Date	Year	Good	VG	Fine	VF
R5.1	ND	1869-77	20.00	30.00	40.00	60.00

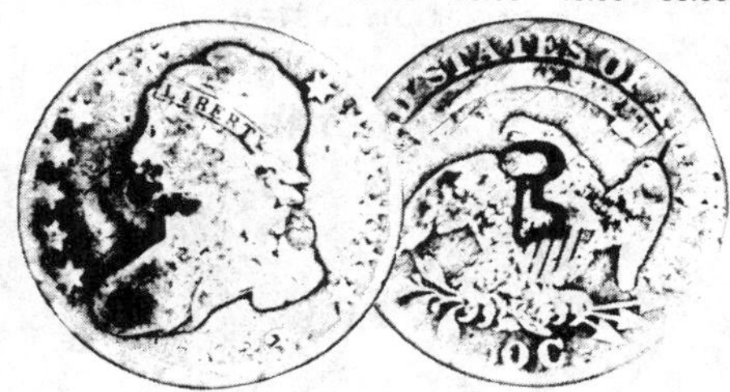

c/m: Key on U.S. Bust Half Dollar, C#32.

KM#	Date	Year	Good	VG	Fine	VF
R5.2	ND	1833	550.00	—	—	—

PESO

.903 SILVER
c/m: Key on Mexican Peso, KM#388.

KM#	Date	Year	Good	VG	Fine	VF
R6	ND	1866-67	40.00	75.00	125.00	225.00

c/m: Key on Mexican Peso, KM#408.

KM#	Date	Year	Good	VG	Fine	VF
R7	ND	1869-77	30.00	55.00	80.00	125.00

MEDALLIC ISSUES (M)

SOUVENIR PESO

22.5500 g, .900 SILVER, .6525 oz ASW
Rev: PAT. 97 on truncation, date widely spaced.

KM#	Date	Mintage	Fine	VF	XF	Unc
M1	1897	828 pcs.	175.00	400.00	900.00	2500.
	1897	—	—	—	Proof	4000.
		BRONZE				
M1a	1897	—	—	—	—	—

22.5500 g, .900 SILVER, .6525 oz ASW
Rev: Date closely spaced, star below 97 baseline.

KM#	Date	Mintage	Fine	VF	XF	Unc
M2	1897	4,286	30.00	50.00	75.00	250.00
		BRONZE				
M2a	1897	—	—	—	750.00	1200.

22.5500 g, .900 SILVER, .6525 oz ASW
Rev: Date closely spaced, star above 97 baseline.

KM#	Date	Mintage	Fine	VF	XF	Unc
M3	1897	4,856	30.00	50.00	75.00	250.00
		BRONZE				
M3a	1897	—	—	—	750.00	1200.

PATTERNS (Pn)

(Including off metal strikes)

KM#	Date	Mintage	Identification	Mkt.Val.
Pn1	1870 PCT	10	5 Centavos, Silver	Rare
Pn1a	1870 PCT	40	5 Centavos, Copper	200.00

KM#	Date	Mintage	Identification	Mkt.Val.
Pn2	1870 PCT	10	10 Centavos, Silver	4000.
Pn2a	1870 PCT	40	10 Centavos, Copper	225.00

KM#	Date	Mintage	Identification	Mkt.Val.
Pn3	1870 PCT	10	20 Centavos, Silver	4500.
Pn3a	1870 PCT	40	20 Centavos, Copper	250.00

KM#	Date	Mintage	Identification	Mkt.Val.
Pn4	1870 PCT	10	1/2 Peso, Silver	Rare
Pn4a	1870 PCT	40	1/2 Peso, Copper	1500.

KM#	Date	Mintage	Identification	Mkt.Val.
Pn5	1870 PCT	10	1 Peso, Silver	6500.
Pn5a	1870 PCT	40	1 Peso, Copper	2250.

KM#	Date	Mintage	Identification	Mkt.Val.
Pn9	1898	—	20 Centavos, Silver	850.00
Pn-A10	1898	—	1 Peso, Copper, KM8	5000.

PIEFORTS (P)

KM#	Date	Mintage	Identification	Mkt.Val.
P1	1870 PCT	—	1 Peso, Silver	7500.
P2	1870 PCT	—	1 Peso, Copper	3750.

Listings For

CURACAO: refer to Netherlands Antilles
DAHOMEY: refer to Benin

CYPRUS

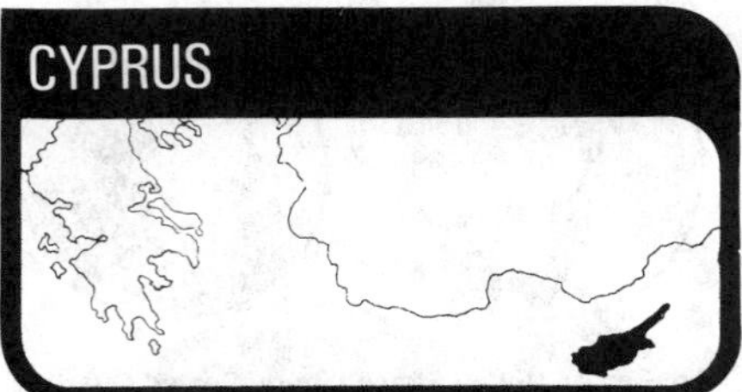

The Republic of Cyprus, a member of the British Commonwealth, lies in the eastern Mediterranean Sea 44 miles (71 km.) south of Turkey and 60 miles (97 km.) west of Syria. It is the third largest island in the Mediterranean Sea, having an area of 3,572 sq. mi. (9,251 sq. km.) and a population of 736,636. Capital: Nicosia. Agriculture, light manufacturing and tourism are the chief industries. Citrus fruit, potatoes, footwear and clothing are exported

The importance of Cyprus dates from the Bronze Age when it was desired as a principal source of copper (from which the island derived its name) and as a strategic trading center. It was during this period that large numbers of Greeks settled on the island and gave it the predominantly Greek character. Its role as an international marketplace made it a prime disseminator of the then prevalent cultures, a role that still influences the civilization of Western man. Because of its fortuitous position and influential role, Cyprus was conquered by a succession of empires: the Assyrian, Egyptian, Persian, Macedonian, Ptolemaic, Roman and Byzantine. It was taken from Isaac Comnenus by Richard the Lion-Heart in 1191, sold to the Templar Knights and for the following 7 centuries was ruled by the Franks, the Venetians and the Ottomans. During the Ottoman period Cyprus acquired its Turkish community (18% of its population). In 1878 the island fell into British hands and was made a crown colony of Britain in 1925.

RULERS

British, until 1960

MINT MARKS

no mint mark - Royal Mint, London, England
H - Birmingham, England

MONETARY SYSTEM

9 Piastres = 1 Shilling
20 Shillings = 1 Pound

1/4 PIASTRE

BRONZE, 21.8mm

KM#	Date	Mintage	Fine	VF	XF	Unc
1.1	1879	.150	5.00	15.00	30.00	100.00
	1879	—	—	—	Proof	850.00
	1880	.072	10.00	25.00	50.00	120.00
	1880	—	—	—	Proof	375.00
	1881	.072	10.00	25.00	50.00	120.00
	1881	—	—	—	Proof	350.00
	1881H	.108	5.50	16.00	40.00	110.00
	1881H	—	—	—	Proof	300.00
	1882H	.036	15.00	30.00	90.00	165.00
	1884	.072	10.00	25.00	65.00	160.00
	1885	.036	20.00	50.00	125.00	200.00
	1887	.060	12.50	32.50	80.00	150.00
	1887	—	—	—	Proof	360.00
	1895	.072	12.00	30.00	80.00	150.00
	1898	.072	12.00	30.00	80.00	150.00
	Reduced size, 21mm					
1.2	1900	.036	15.00	30.00	75.00	175.00
	1900	—	—	—	Proof	600.00

NOTE: Later date (1901) exists for this type.

1/2 PIASTRE

BRONZE

KM#	Date	Mintage	Fine	VF	XF	Unc
2	1879	.250	7.50	15.00	45.00	165.00
	1879	—	—	—	Proof	850.00
	1881	.054	15.00	25.00	80.00	250.00
	1881	—	—	—	Proof	500.00
	1881H	.072	10.00	20.00	55.00	140.00
	1881H	—	—	—	Proof	325.00
	1882H	.054	10.00	20.00	60.00	180.00
2	1882H	—	—	—	Proof	325.00
	1884	.036	20.00	50.00	120.00	275.00
	1884	—	—	—	Proof	325.00
	1885	.054	15.00	30.00	90.00	260.00
	1886	.122	7.50	15.00	45.00	165.00
	1887	.060	10.00	20.00	70.00	200.00
	1887	—	—	—	Proof	325.00
	1889	.054	15.00	35.00	125.00	380.00
	1890	.180	20.00	50.00	100.00	300.00
	1890	—	—	—	Proof	400.00
	1891	.108	27.50	75.00	150.00	300.00
	1896	.036	35.00	110.00	200.00	450.00
	1900	.036	35.00	110.00	200.00	450.00
	1900	—	—	—	Proof	700.00

PIASTRE

BRONZE
Rev: Thin '1'

KM#	Date	Mintage	Fine	VF	XF	Unc
3.1	1879	.250	8.00	25.00	50.00	150.00
	1879	—	—	—	Proof	950.00
	1881	.036	15.00	35.00	150.00	325.00
	1881	—	—	—	Proof	600.00
	1881H	.036	15.00	35.00	150.00	500.00
	1881H	—	—	—	Proof	650.00

Rev: Thick '1'

KM#	Date	Mintage	Fine	VF	XF	Unc
3.2	1881	Inc. Ab.	—	—	Proof	1000.
	1881H	Inc. Ab.	10.00	35.00	120.00	500.00
	1881H	—	—	—	Proof	900.00
	1882H	.018	135.00	225.00	450.00	1250.
	1882H	—	—	—	Proof	2000.
	1884	.018	135.00	225.00	450.00	1250.
	1884	—	—	—	Proof	1800.
	1885	.054	25.00	70.00	115.00	275.00
	1885	—	—	—	Proof	1220.
	1886	.227	10.00	30.00	85.00	175.00
	1887	.045	10.00	32.50	100.00	200.00
	1889	.027	30.00	90.00	250.00	500.00
	1890	.090	20.00	70.00	150.00	350.00
	1891	.054	25.00	80.00	200.00	400.00
	1891	—	—	—	Proof	780.00
	1895	.054	25.00	80.00	200.00	400.00
	1896	.054	25.00	80.00	200.00	400.00
	1900	.027	35.00	100.00	250.00	500.00
	1900	—	—	—	Proof	1900.

TRIAL STRIKES (TS)

KM#	Date	Mintage	Identification	Mkt.Val.
TS1	1879	—	1 Piastre, obv. uniface	2000.

PROOF SETS (PS)

KM#	Date	Mintage	Identification	Issue Price	Mkt. Val.
PS1	1879(3)	—	KM1.1,2,3.1	—	3000.
PS2	1881(3)	—	KM1.1,2,3.1	—	1800.
PS3	1900(3)	—	KM1.2,2,3.2	—	3500.

DANISH WEST INDIES

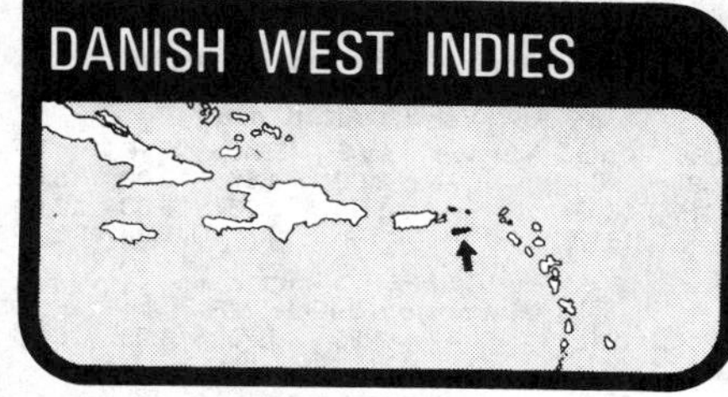

The Danish West Indies (now the U.S. organized unincorporated territory of the Virgin Islands of the United States) consisted of the islands of St. Thomas, St. John, St. Croix, and 62 islets in the Caribbean Sea roughly 40 miles (64 km.) east of Puerto Rico. The islands have a combined area of 133 sq. mi. (352 sq. km.) and a population of *106,000. Capital: Charlotte Amalie. Tourism is the principal industry. Watch movements, costume jewelry, pharmaceuticals, and rum are exported.

The Virgin Islands were discovered by Columbus in 1493, during his second voyage to America. During the 17th century, individual islands, actually the peaks of a submerged mountain range, were held by Spain, Holland, England, France and Denmark. These islands were also the favorite resorts of the buccaneers operating in the Caribbean and the coastal waters of eastern North America. Control of most of the 100-island group finally passed to Denmark, with England securing the easterly remainder. The Danish islands had their own coinage from the early 18th century, based on but unequal to, Denmark's homeland system. In the late 18th and early 19th centuries, Danish minor copper and silver coinage augmented the islands currency. The Danish islands were purchased by the United States in 1917 for $25 million, mainly to forestall their acquisition by Germany and because they command the Anegada Passage into the Caribbean Sea, a strategic point on the defense perimeter of the Panama Canal.

RULERS

Danish, until 1917

MINT MARKS

Three mints were used for coinage of the eighteenth century.

(a) - Altona - tall, widely spaced crown
(c) - Copenhagen - symetrical crown
(h) - Copenhagen - heart
(o) - Altona - orb

MINTMASTERS INITIALS

MONETARY SYSTEM

(Until 1849)

96 Skilling = 1 Daler

II SKILLING

1.2180 g, .250 SILVER, .0098 oz ASW
Obv: Crowned arms. Rev: Value and date.

KM#	Date	Mintage	VG	Fine	VF	XF
13	1816	.096	8.50	15.00	27.50	65.00
	1837 flat top 3	.493	6.50	12.00	25.00	50.00
	1837 round top 3	Inc. Ab.	10.00	17.50	30.00	55.00
18	1847	.244	6.50	12.00	25.00	50.00

KM#	Date	Mintage	VG	Fine	VF	XF
19	1848	.958	6.00	10.00	18.50	40.00

X SKILLING

2.4360 g, .625 SILVER, .0489 oz ASW

KM#	Date	Mintage	VG	Fine	VF	XF
14	1816	*.080	8.50	20.00	45.00	75.00

KM#	Date	Mintage	VG	Fine	VF	XF
16	1840	.103	7.50	16.50	30.00	60.00
	1845	.097	6.50	15.00	27.50	50.00
	1845	—	—	—	Proof	—
	1847	.109	8.50	18.50	32.50	55.00

Incuse edge.

KM#	Date	Mintage	VG	Fine	VF	XF
20.1	1848	.389	7.50	17.50	32.50	65.00
	1848	—	—	—	Proof	—

Plain edge.

KM#	Date	Mintage	VG	Fine	VF	XF
20.2	1848(1856)	.085	8.50	20.00	35.00	70.00

XX SKILLING

4.8720 g, .625 SILVER, .0979 oz ASW
Obv: Crowned arms. Rev: Value and date.

KM#	Date	Mintage	VG	Fine	VF	XF
15	1816	*.020	13.50	32.50	85.00	165.00

KM#	Date	Mintage	VG	Fine	VF	XF
17	1840	*.050	11.50	27.50	70.00	135.00
	1845	*.055	11.50	27.50	70.00	135.00
	1847	*.050	11.50	27.50	70.00	135.00

Incuse edge.

KM#	Date	Mintage	VG	Fine	VF	XF
21.1	1848	.071	11.50	27.50	70.00	135.00
	1848	—	—	—	Proof	350.00

Plain edge.

KM#	Date	Mintage	VG	Fine	VF	XF
21.2	1848(1856)	.040	18.50	35.00	90.00	175.00

COUNTERMARKED COINAGE

1850

The only countermark authorized for the Danish West Indies was the crowned F R VII monogram, which was used to countermark a quantity of U.S. 25 cent and 50 cent coins between March and June 1850. A total face value of $1,140. in U.S. coins was imported for use during that time, including 1 cent, 5 cent and 10 cent coins which were not countermarked.

COUNTERFEITS: This series has been counterfeited extensively. A common counterfeit countermark lacks the small cross on top of the crown and small shallow striking of c/m especially in beads of crown. Other more deceptive countermarks also have been detected. Extreme care should be taken in ensuring the authenticity of these pieces.

MONETARY SYSTEM

(1849-1903)

100 Cents = 1 Rigsdater

U. S. SERIES

25 CENTS

SILVER
c/m: Crowned FRVII on U.S.A. Liberty Seated 25 Cent.

KM#	Date	Year	Good	VG	Fine	VF
26	ND	1849	—	—	—	4000.

NOTE: 1849 host, 10 known.

50 CENTS

SILVER
c/m: Crowned FRVII on U.S.A. Liberty Seated 50 Cent.

KM#	Date	Year	Good	VG	Fine	VF
27	ND	1848	—	—	—	6000.
	ND	1849	—	—	—	6000.
	ND	1850	—	—	—	5000.

NOTE: 1848 host, 4-5 known; 1849 host, 4-5 known; 1850 host, 6 known.

DECIMAL COINAGE

CENT

BRONZE

KM#	Date	Mintage	VG	Fine	VF	XF
63	1859(o)	.216	1.50	3.50	8.00	17.50
	1859(o)	10 pcs.	—	—	P/L	250.00
	1860(o)	.250	2.00	4.00	9.00	30.00

KM#	Date	Mintage	VG	Fine	VF	XF
68	1868(c)	.240	1.50	3.50	8.00	17.50
	1868(c)	—	—	—	P/L	—
	1878(h)	.020	3.00	7.50	15.00	35.00
	1879(h)	.040	135.00	225.00	300.00	550.00
	1883(h)	.210	1.75	5.00	12.00	25.00

3 CENTS

1.0440 g, .625 SILVER, .0210 oz ASW

KM#	Date	Mintage	VG	Fine	VF	XF
64	1859(o)	.291	2.75	6.00	14.00	35.00
	1859(o)	10 pcs.	—	—	P/L	300.00

5 CENTS

1.7400 g, .625 SILVER, .0349 oz ASW

KM#	Date	Mintage	VG	Fine	VF	XF
65	1859(c)	.150	2.00	4.50	12.00	30.00
	1859(c)	10 pcs.	—	—	P/L	300.00

KM#	Date	Mintage	VG	Fine	VF	XF
69	1878(h)	.500	5.00	15.00	25.00	60.00
	1878(h)	—	—	—	P/L	400.00
	1879(h)	Inc. Ab.	5.00	15.00	30.00	75.00
	1879(h)	—	—	—	P/L	325.00

10 CENTS

3.4850 g, .625 SILVER, .0699 oz ASW

KM#	Date	Mintage	VG	Fine	VF	XF
66	1859(c)	.250	2.75	5.50	15.00	35.00
	1859(c)	10 pcs.	—	—	P/L	300.00
	1862(c)	.140	5.00	10.00	16.50	40.00
	1862(c)	—	—	—	P/L	325.00

KM#	Date	Mintage	VG	Fine	VF	XF
70	1878(h)	.080	6.50	14.50	30.00	60.00
	1878(h)	—	—	—	P/L	300.00
	1879(h)	.120	11.50	22.50	50.00	85.00
	1879(h)	—	—	—	P/L	400.00

20 CENTS

6.9610 g, .625 SILVER, .1399 oz ASW

KM#	Date	Mintage	VG	Fine	VF	XF
67	1859(c)	.430	7.50	16.50	27.50	58.00
	1859(c)	10 pcs.	—	—	P/L	450.00
	1862(c)	.560	7.50	16.50	27.50	58.00
	1862(c)	—	—	—	P/L	400.00

KM#	Date	Mintage	VG	Fine	VF	XF
71	1878(h)	.200	13.50	22.50	42.50	100.00
	1878(h)	—	—	—	P/L	500.00
	1879(h)	.300	40.00	100.00	200.00	325.00

PROOFLIKE SETS (PL)

KM#	Date	Mintage	Identification	Issue Price	Mkt. Val.
PL1	1859(5)	10	KM63-67	—	Rare
PL2	1862(2)	—	—	—	Rare
PL3	1878	—	—	—	Rare

Listings For

DANZIG: refer to Poland

DENMARK

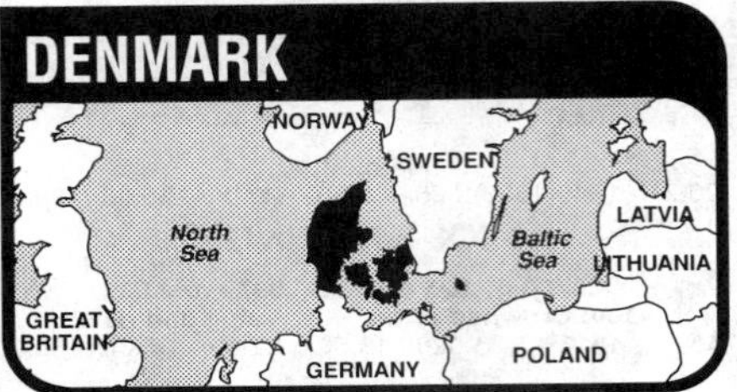

The Kingdom of Denmark, a constitutional monarchy located at the mouth of the Baltic Sea, has an area of 16,639 sq. mi. (43,070 sq. km.) and a population of 5.2 million. Capital: Copenhagen. Most of the country is arable. Agriculture, which employs the majority of the people, is conducted by small farmers served by cooperatives. The largest industries are food processing, iron and metal, and fishing. Machinery, meats (chiefly bacon), dairy products and chemicals are exported.

Denmark, a great power during the Viking period of the 9th-11th centuries, conducted raids on western Europe and England, and in the 11th century united England, Denmark and Norway under the rule of King Canute. Despite a struggle between the crown and the nobility (13th-14th centuries) which forced the King to grant a written constitution, Queen Margaret (1387-1412) succeeded in uniting Denmark, Norway, Sweden, Finland and Greenland under the Danish crown, placing all of Scandinavia under the rule of Denmark. An unwise alliance with Napoleon contributed to the dismembering of the empire and fostered a liberal movement which succeeded in making Denmark a constitutional monarchy in 1849.

The present decimal system of coinage was introduced in 1874.

RULERS

Christian VII, 1766-1808
Frederik VI, 1808-1839
Christian VIII, 1839-1848
Frederik VII, 1848-1863
Christian IX, 1863-1906

MINT MARKS

(a) - Altona (1842 issues), apple
(c) - Copenhagen, crown
(h) - Copenhagen, heart
(o) - Altona, orb
KM - Copenhagen

NOTE: (ch) - crossed hammers - Kongsberg.

MINTMASTERS INITIALS

Altona

Letter	Date	Name
MF	1786-1816	Michael Flor
CB	1817-1819	Cajus Branth
FF, IFF	1819-1856	Johan Friedrich Freund
TA	1848-1851	Theodor Andersen
FA	1856-1863	Hans Frederik Alsing

Copenhagen

Letter	Date	Name
HIAB	1797-1810	Hans Jacob Arnold Branth
none	1810-1821	Ole Varberg
CFG	1821-1831	Conrad Frederik Gerlach
VS, WS	1835-1861	Georg Wilhelm Svendsen
RH	1861-1869	Rasmus Hinnerup
CS	1869-1893	Diderik Christian Andreas Svendsen
*P,VBP	1893-1918	Vilhelm Buchard Poulsen

MONEYERS INITIALS

Altona

Letter	Date	Name
FA	1825-1855	Hans Frederik Alsing
FK	1841-1863	Frederik Christopher Krohn
HL	1848-1851	Carl Heinrich Lorenz
PP	1852-1863	Peter Petersen

Copenhagen

Letter	Date	Name
D I ADLER FE	1808	Daniel Jensen Adzer
PG	1798-1807	Peter Leonard Gianelli
IC, ICF	1810-1841	Johannes Conradsen
M	1813	Christian Andreas Muller
CC	1836	Christen Christensen
FK	1841-1873	Frederik Christopher Krohn
HC	1873-1901	Harald Conradsen

MONETARY SYSTEM

(Until 1813)

4 Penning = 1 Huid = 1/4 Skilling
6 Penning = 1 Sosling = 1/2 Skilling
16 Skillings = 1 Mark
64 Skilling Danske = 4 Mark = 1 Krone
96 Skilling Danske = 6 Mark = 1 Daler Specie
12 Mark = 1 Ducat

SKILLING

.9230 g, .138 SILVER, .0041 oz ASW
Mint: Altona. Mintmasters initials: MF.
Obv: Crowned FR VI monogram.
Rev: Value, DANSK, date.

KM#	Date	Mintage	VG	Fine	VF	XF
662	1808	—	2.00	4.50	10.00	16.00
(C104)	1809	—	1.50	2.75	6.00	12.00
	1810	—	—	—	Unique	—

COPPER, 15mm
Mintmasters initials: MF.

KM#	Date	Mintage	VG	Fine	VF	XF
671 (C87.1)	1812	—	1.25	1.75	3.25	5.75

2 SKILLING

1.5000 g, .250 SILVER, .0121 oz ASW
Mint: Copenhagen. Mintmasters initials: HIAB.

KM#	Date	Mintage	VG	Fine	VF	XF
660.1 (C53.1)	1801	—	1.25	2.50	5.50	12.00

Mint: Altona. Mintmasters initials: MF.

KM#	Date	Mintage	VG	Fine	VF	XF
660.2	1801	—	2.25	4.00	7.50	17.50
(C53.2)	1805	—	1.75	3.25	6.50	15.00

COPPER
Obv: Truncation in a curved line.

KM#	Date	Mintage	VG	Fine	VF	XF
663	1809	—	1.25	2.50	6.50	13.50
(C88a)	1810	—	1.25	2.50	6.00	12.50

Obv: Truncation in a broken curved line.

KM#	Date	Mintage	VG	Fine	VF	XF
670	1810	—	1.50	3.00	6.50	13.50
(C88b)	1811	—	1.75	3.50	8.00	16.00

3 SKILLING

COPPER

KM#	Date	Mintage	VG	Fine	VF	XF
672 (C89)	1812	—	1.50	3.00	6.50	12.50

4 SKILLING

2.5980 g, .250 SILVER, .0209 oz ASW
Mint: Altona. Mintmasters initials: MF.

KM#	Date	Mintage	VG	Fine	VF	XF
661 (C56)	1807	—	3.00	5.50	10.00	20.00

12 SKILLING

COPPER
Struck over 1 Skilling, KM#616.

KM#	Date	Mintage	VG	Fine	VF	XF
673 (C90)	1812	—	5.50	12.50	25.00	55.00

1/6 RIGSDALER

5.0490 g, .406 SILVER, .0659 oz ASW
Mint: Altona. Mintmasters initials: MF.
Offering for Fatherland

KM#	Date	Mintage	VG	Fine	VF	XF
664 (C105)	1808	—	6.00	12.50	20.00	37.50

NOTE: Varieties exist.

DALER

(Specie)

28.8930 g, .875 SILVER, .8128 oz ASW
Mintmasters initials: MF. Moneyers initial: B.
Obv: Head of Christian VII right.
Rev: Crowned oval arms.

Dav.#1313

KM#	Date	Mintage	VG	Fine	VF	XF
651.1 (C82.1)	1801	—	235.00	300.00	430.00	—

NOTE: Earlier dates (1795-1799) exist for this type.

TRADE COINAGE

DUCAT SPECIE

3.4900 g, .979 GOLD, .1098 oz AGW
Rev: 5-line leg. in square tablet.

KM#	Date	Mintage	Fine	VF	XF	Unc
650 (C85.2)	1802	—	275.00	625.00	775.00	1000.

NOTE: Earlier dates (1791-1794) exist for this type.

MONETARY REFORM

(Commencing 1813)

96 Rigsbank Skilling = 1 Rigs(bank)daler
30 Schilling Courant = 1 Rigs(bank)daler
2 Rigsbankdaler = 1 Rigsdaler Specie
2 Rigsbankdaler = 1 Specie(daler)
5 Species(daler) = 1 D'Or

1/5 RIGSBANKSKILLING

COPPER
Mint: Altona. Mintmasters initials: FF.

KM#	Date	Mintage	VG	Fine	VF	XF
723 (C118)	1842	—	4.00	8.00	16.00	30.00

Rev. denomination: 1/5 R.B.S.

KM#	Date	Mintage	VG	Fine	VF	XF
724 (C118a)	1842	—	1.25	3.00	6.00	10.00

1/2 RIGSBANKSKILLING

COPPER

KM#	Date	Mintage	VG	Fine	VF	XF
715 (C100)	1838	—	1.25	2.25	6.00	10.00

Mint: Copenhagen. Mintmasters initials: VS.

KM#	Date	Mintage	VG	Fine	VF	XF
725 (C119)	1842	—	2.00	4.00	8.00	20.00

Mintmasters initials: VS.

KM#	Date	Mintage	VG	Fine	VF	XF
753 (C131)	1852	—	1.75	3.00	6.50	14.00

1/2 RIGSMONTSKILLING

BRONZE

KM#	Date	Mintage	VG	Fine	VF	XF
767 (C134)	1857(o)	—	1.00	1.75	3.25	7.00
	1857(c)	—	—	—	—	250.00

KM#	Date	Mintage	VG	Fine	VF	XF
776	1868	—	1.00	2.00	4.00	8.00

RIGSBANKSKILLING

COPPER

KM#	Date	Mintage	VG	Fine	VF	XF
680 (C93)	1813	—	1.00	1.75	5.00	12.00

Obv: Crowned oval arms.
Rev: Value and date.

KM#	Date	Mintage	VG	Fine	VF	XF
688 (C101)	1818	—	1.25	2.50	7.50	18.00

Mintmasters initials: FF.

KM#	Date	Mintage	VG	Fine	VF	XF
726.1 (C120.1)	1842(o)	—	1.75	4.00	8.50	22.00

Mintmasters initials: VS.

KM#	Date	Mintage	VG	Fine	VF	XF
726.2 (C120.2)	1842(c)	—	1.75	4.00	8.50	22.00

Mint: Copenhagen. Mintmasters initials: VS.
Obv: Large bust.

KM#	Date	Mintage	VG	Fine	VF	XF
754 (C132)	1852	—	3.00	6.50	16.00	35.00

NOTE: KM#755 formerly listed here, is now recognized as a pattern, PnD55.

Obv: Medium bust.

KM#	Date	Mintage	VG	Fine	VF	XF
756 (C132b)	1853	—	1.75	3.75	7.25	16.00

RIGSMONTSKILLING

BRONZE

KM#	Date	Mintage	VG	Fine	VF	XF
763 (C135)	1856(o)	—	1.00	2.00	5.00	10.00
	1856(c)	—	—	—	—	175.00
	1860(o)	—	1.00	2.00	4.00	10.00
	1863(c)	—	1.25	2.25	5.00	10.00

KM#	Date	Mintage	VG	Fine	VF	XF
774	1867	—	.75	1.50	3.25	7.25
	1869	—	1.00	2.00	4.50	10.00
	1870	—	1.25	3.00	7.00	13.50
	1871	—	1.75	3.75	8.50	17.50
	1872	—	1.00	1.75	4.00	8.00

2 RIGSBANKSKILLING

COPPER

KM#	Date	Mintage	VG	Fine	VF	XF
689 (C102)	1818	—	4.00	9.00	18.00	45.00
				18.00	45.00	

1.1120 g, .208 SILVER, .0074 oz ASW
Mint: Altona. Mintmasters initials: IFF.

KM#	Date	Mintage	VG	Fine	VF	XF
710 (C106)	1836	.152	2.00	5.00	7.50	12.50

COPPER
Mint: Copenhagen. Mintmasters initials: VS.

KM#	Date	Mintage	VG	Fine	VF	XF
728 (C121)	1842	—	15.00	35.00	75.00	155.00

3 RIGSBANKSKILLING

1.5190 g, .229 SILVER, .0112 oz ASW
Mint: Altona. Mintmasters initials: IFF.

KM#	Date	Mintage	VG	Fine	VF	XF
711 (C107)	1836	.130	5.00	12.50	27.50	55.00

Mintmasters initials: FF.

KM#	Date	Mintage	VG	Fine	VF	XF
729 (C122)	1842	—	1.50	3.25	8.50	22.00

Rev. denomination: 3 R.B.S.

KM#	Date	Mintage	VG	Fine	VF	XF
730 (C122a)	1842	—	1.50	3.00	8.00	20.00

4 RIGSBANKSKILLING

1.8560 g, .250 SILVER, .0149 oz ASW
Mint: Altona. Mintmasters initials: IFF.

KM#	Date	Mintage	VG	Fine	VF	XF
712 (C108)	1836	.073	6.00	15.00	30.00	60.00

Mint: Copenhagen.
For use in Schleswig-Holstein
Rev: 1-1/4 SCH.

KM#	Date	Mintage	VG	Fine	VF	XF
721.1 (C123.1)	1841(h)	—	1.75	3.50	8.50	20.00

Mintmasters initials: VS.

KM#	Date	Mintage	VG	Fine	VF	XF
721.2 (C123.2)	1842(c)	—	1.50	3.25	6.50	17.50

Mint: Altona. Mintmasters initials: FF.

KM#	Date	Mintage	VG	Fine	VF	XF
721.3 (C123.3)	1842(o)	—	—	—	Rare	—

4 RIGSMONTSKILLING

1.8560 g, .250 SILVER, .0149 oz ASW
Mint: Altona. Mintmasters initials: FF.

KM#	Date	Mintage	VG	Fine	VF	XF
758.1	1854(o)	—	1.75	3.50	11.50	30.00
(C136.1)	1854(o)	—	—	—	Proof	Rare

Mint: Copenhagen. Mintmasters initials: VS.

KM#	Date	Mintage	VG	Fine	VF	XF
758.2 (C136.2)	1856(c)	—	1.00	2.00	6.00	15.00

Mint: Copenhagen. Mintmasters initials: RH.

KM#	Date	Mintage	VG	Fine	VF	XF
775.1	1867	—	1.75	3.75	9.00	20.00
	1867	—	—	—	Proof	Rare

Mintmasters initials: CS.

KM#	Date	Mintage	VG	Fine	VF	XF
775.2	1869	—	2.00	4.50	10.00	22.00
	1870	—	1.75	4.00	9.00	20.00
	1871	—	1.75	3.50	8.00	15.00
	1872	—	2.25	5.00	10.00	22.00
	1873	—	3.00	6.00	12.00	24.00
	1874	—	6.50	15.00	35.00	65.00

8 RIGSBANKSKILLING

2.8090 g, .375 SILVER, .0339 oz ASW
Mint: Altona. Mintmasters initials: FF.
For use in Schleswig-Holstein
Rev: 2-1/2 SCHILL.COUR.

KM#	Date	Mintage	VG	Fine	VF	XF
737 (C124)	1843	—	10.00	20.00	45.00	90.00

NOTE: For 8 Reichsbank Schillinge dated 1816-1819 see Schleswig-Holstein in Denmark listings.

16 RIGSBANKSKILLING

4.2140 g, .500 SILVER, .0677 oz ASW
Mint: Copenhagen. Mintmasters initials: VS.
For use in Schleswig-Holstein
Rev: 5 SCHILL.COURANT.

KM#	Date	Mintage	VG	Fine	VF	XF
733	1842	—	14.00	28.00	50.00	100.00
(C125)	1844	—	150.00	275.00	—	—

16 RIGSMONTSKILLING

3.8980 g, .500 SILVER, .0626 oz ASW
Mint: Copenhagen. Mintmasters initials: VS.

KM#	Date	Mintage	VG	Fine	VF	XF
765	1856(c)	—	1.50	3.25	7.75	17.50
(C137)	1857(c)	—	2.00	4.00	9.00	18.00
	1858(c)	—	2.25	5.00	12.00	24.00

32 RIGSBANKSKILLING

6.1290 g, .687 SILVER, .1354 oz ASW
Mint: Altona. Mintmasters initials: CB.

KM#	Date	Mintage	VG	Fine	VF	XF
690.1 (C109.1)	1818	—	—	—	Rare	—

Mintmasters initials: IFF

KM#	Date	Mintage	VG	Fine	VF	XF
690.2 (C109.2)	1820	—	20.00	45.00	85.00	175.00

Mint: Altona. Mintmasters initials: FF.
For use in Schleswig-Holstein
Rev: 10 SCHILL.COURANT.

KM#	Date	Mintage	VG	Fine	VF	XF
734	1842	—	15.00	27.50	45.00	90.00
(C126)	1843	—	17.50	30.00	50.00	100.00
	1843 FF/FK	—	60.00	110.00	175.00	250.00

1/2 RIGSDALER

7.2240 g, .875 SILVER, .2032 oz ASW
Mintmasters initials: VS.

KM#	Date	Mintage	VG	Fine	VF	XF
759	1854(c)	—	8.00	20.00	32.50	50.00
(C138)	1855(c)	—	7.00	17.50	30.00	45.00

RIGSBANKDALER

14.4470 g, .875 SILVER, .4064 oz ASW
Mint: Copenhagen. Moneyers initial: M.

KM#	Date	Mintage	VG	Fine	VF	XF
683.1 (C110.1)	1813	—	45.00	80.00	145.00	240.00

Moneyers initials: IC.

KM#	Date	Mintage	VG	Fine	VF	XF
683.2 (C110.2)	1813	—	25.00	30.00	60.00	100.00

Moneyers initials: IC. Mintmasters initials: MF.

KM#	Date	Mintage	VG	Fine	VF	XF
683.3 (C110.3)	1813	—	30.00	45.00	85.00	155.00

Moneyers initials: IC. Mintmasters initials: CB.

KM#	Date	Mintage	VG	Fine	VF	XF
683.4 (C110.4)	1818	—	30.00	37.50	65.00	125.00

Moneyers initials: IC. Mintmasters initials: FF.

KM#	Date	Mintage	VG	Fine	VF	XF
683.5 (C110.5)	1819	—	35.00	45.00	85.00	155.00

Mint: Altona. Mintmasters initials: FF.

Obv: Small head.

KM#	Date	Mintage	VG	Fine	VF	XF
696.1 (C110a.1)	1826	—	35.00	80.00	130.00	210.00
	1827	—	40.00	95.00	145.00	225.00
	1828	—	35.00	80.00	140.00	220.00
	1833	—	30.00	70.00	130.00	210.00

Mint: Copenhagen

KM#	Date	Mintage	VG	Fine	VF	XF
696.2 (C110a.2)	1833 KM	—	55.00	100.00	160.00	260.00
	1834 KM	—	55.00	100.00	160.00	260.00

Mint: Altona. Mintmasters initials: FF.
Obv: Large head.

KM#	Date	Mintage	VG	Fine	VF	XF
706.1 (C110b.1)	1833	—	40.00	80.00	145.00	225.00
	1834	—	75.00	140.00	220.00	320.00
	1835	—	75.00	140.00	220.00	320.00
	1836	—	40.00	90.00	155.00	240.00
	1839	—	40.00	85.00	145.00	225.00

Mint: Copenhagen

KM#	Date	Mintage	VG	Fine	VF	XF
706.2 (C110b.2)	1834 KM	—	55.00	100.00	160.00	260.00

Mintmasters initials: WS.

KM#	Date	Mintage	VG	Fine	VF	XF
706.3 (C110b.3)	1835	—	100.00	180.00	275.00	365.00
	1838	—	30.00	60.00	110.00	210.00

Mint: Copenhagen. Mintmasters initials: VS.
For use in Schleswig-Holstein.
Rev: 30 SCHILL.COURANT.

KM#	Date	Mintage	VG	Fine	VF	XF
735.1 (C127.1)	1842(c)	—	15.00	32.00	50.00	90.00
	1843(c)	—	20.00	45.00	60.00	100.00
	1843(c)	—	—	—	Proof	Rare
	1846(c)	—	17.00	40.00	60.00	100.00
	1847(c)	—	12.50	30.00	50.00	90.00
	1847(c)	—	—	—	Proof	Rare
	1848(c)	—	12.50	30.00	50.00	90.00

Mint: Altona. Mintmasters initials: FF.

KM#	Date	Mintage	VG	Fine	VF	XF
735.2 (C127.2)	1844(o)	—	20.00	40.00	65.00	115.00
	1845(o)	—	16.00	37.50	60.00	100.00
	1847(o)	—	17.00	35.00	55.00	95.00

Mint: Copenhagen. Mintmasters initials: VS.

KM#	Date	Mintage	VG	Fine	VF	XF
743	1849	—	40.00	90.00	160.00	320.00
(C139)	1851	—	35.00	70.00	140.00	275.00

RIGSDALER

14.4470 g, .875 SILVER, .4064 oz ASW
Mint: Copenhagen. Mintmasters initials: VS.

KM#	Date	Mintage	VG	Fine	VF	XF
760.1	1854(c)	—	10.00	18.00	35.00	55.00

KM#	Date	Mintage	VG	Fine	VF	XF
(C140.1)						
	1855(c)	—	15.00	27.50	50.00	75.00

Mint: Altona. Mintmasters initials: FF.

KM#	Date	Mintage	VG	Fine	VF	XF
760.2 (C140.2)	1855(o)	—	12.50	22.50	40.00	60.00

DALER

(Species)

28.8930 g, .875 SILVER, .8128 oz ASW
Mint: Altona. Mintmasters initials: IFF.
Obv: Head of Frederik VI right.

KM#	Date	Mintage	VG	Fine	VF	XF
693 (C111)	1819	—	200.00	500.00	900.00	1550.

Mint: Altona. Mintmasters initials: FF.

KM#	Date	Mintage	VG	Fine	VF	XF
695.1 (C112.1)	1820	—	30.00	55.00	100.00	145.00
	1822	—	30.00	55.00	100.00	145.00
	1824	—	30.00	55.00	100.00	145.00
	1825	—	30.00	55.00	80.00	130.00
	1826	—	30.00	55.00	100.00	145.00
	1827	—	40.00	75.00	110.00	160.00
	1828	—	27.00	55.00	90.00	130.00
	1829	—	30.00	55.00	100.00	145.00
	1833	—	30.00	55.00	100.00	145.00
	1834	—	30.00	55.00	90.00	130.00
	1835	—	30.00	55.00	100.00	145.00
	1838	—	27.00	50.00	80.00	125.00
	1839	—	27.00	50.00	80.00	125.00

Mint: Copenhagen. Mintmasters initials: CFG.

KM#	Date	Mintage	VG	Fine	VF	XF
695.2 (C112.2)	1820	—	40.00	70.00	130.00	180.00
	1822	—	40.00	70.00	130.00	180.00
	1824	—	30.00	55.00	100.00	145.00
	1825	—	30.00	55.00	100.00	145.00
695.3 (C112.3)	1833KM	—	35.00	65.00	130.00	180.00
	1834KM	—	40.00	70.00	130.00	180.00

Mintmasters initials: WS.

KM#	Date	Mintage	VG	Fine	VF	XF
695.4 (C112.4)	1835	—	30.00	55.00	100.00	145.00
	1837	—	30.00	55.00	100.00	145.00
	1838	—	27.00	50.00	80.00	125.00
	1838 SW (error)	—	—	—	—	—
	1839	—	27.00	55.00	80.00	125.00

Mint: Altona. Mintmasters initials: FF.
Obv. leg: CHRISTIANUS. . . small letters.

KM#	Date	Mintage	VG	Fine	VF	XF
720.1 (C128.1)	1840	—	25.00	60.00	100.00	160.00
	1844(o)	—	30.00	70.00	110.00	180.00
	1845(o)	—	25.00	50.00	85.00	155.00
	1847(o)	—	25.00	55.00	100.00	160.00

Mint: Copenhagen

KM#	Date	Mintage	VG	Fine	VF	XF
720.2 (C128.2)	1840(h)	—	25.00	60.00	100.00	160.00
	1841(h)	—	55.00	155.00	195.00	300.00

Mintmasters initials: VS.

KM#	Date	Mintage	VG	Fine	VF	XF
720.3 (C128.3)	1843(h)	—	100.00	200.00	300.00	425.00
	1843(c)	—	30.00	70.00	110.00	180.00
	1845(h)	—	125.00	250.00	375.00	—
	1845(c)	—	25.00	55.00	85.00	155.00
	1846(c)	—	25.00	55.00	85.00	155.00

Mintmasters initials: VS.
Obv. leg: CHRISTIANVS. . . large letters.

KM#	Date	Mintage	VG	Fine	VF	XF
741 (C128a)	1846(c)	—	40.00	60.00	100.00	180.00
	1847(c)	—	40.00	60.00	100.00	180.00
	1848	—	40.00	65.00	115.00	180.00

Mintmasters initials: VS.
Christian VIII Death
And Accession of Frederik VII

KM#	Date	Mintage	VG	Fine	VF	XF
742 (C141)	1848	.047	50.00	100.00	170.00	275.00

Mintmasters initials: VS.

KM#	Date	Mintage	VG	Fine	VF	XF
744.1 (C142.1)	1849(c)	—	35.00	60.00	120.00	235.00
	1853(c)	—	40.00	65.00	130.00	245.00
	1854(c)	—	90.00	140.00	210.00	325.00

Mint: Altona. Mintmasters initials: FF.

KM#	Date	Mintage	VG	Fine	VF	XF
744.2 (C124.2)	1851(o)	—	200.00	350.00	—	—
	1853(o)	—	40.00	75.00	145.00	250.00

2 DALER

(Rigs)

28.8930 g, .875 SILVER, .8128 oz ASW
Mint: Altona. Mintmasters initials: FF.

KM#	Date	Mintage	VG	Fine	VF	XF
761.1 (C143.1)	1854(o)	—	30.00	50.00	90.00	155.00
	1855(o)	—	30.00	55.00	100.00	165.00
	1856(o)	—	—	—	Rare	—

Mint: Copenhagen. Mintmasters initials: VS.

KM#	Date	Mintage	VG	Fine	VF	XF
761.2 (C143.2)	1854(c)	—	32.50	55.00	100.00	165.00
	1855(c)	—	30.00	50.00	90.00	160.00

Mintmasters initials: RH.

KM#	Date	Mintage	VG	Fine	VF	XF
761.3 (C143.3)	1863(c)	.360	37.50	70.00	140.00	225.00

Mintmasters initials: RH.
Frederik VII Death
and Accession of Christian IX

KM#	Date	Mintage	VG	Fine	VF	XF
770	1863	.101	50.00	100.00	160.00	250.00

Mintmasters initials: RH.

KM#	Date	Mintage	VG	Fine	VF	XF
772.1	1864	.237	55.00	110.00	180.00	320.00
	1868	.261	60.00	125.00	190.00	350.00

Mintmasters initials: CS.

KM#	Date	Mintage	VG	Fine	VF	XF
772.2	1871	.586	65.00	140.00	210.00	380.00
	1872	.149	65.00	140.00	210.00	380.00

CHR(ISTIANS) D'OR

6.6420 g, .896 GOLD, .1913 oz AGW
Mint: Altona. Mintmasters initials: FF.

KM#	Date	Mintage	VG	Fine	VF	XF
730	1843(o)	.038	250.00	525.00	900.00	1450.
(C129)	1844(o)	I.A.	250.00	550.00	975.00	1550.
	1845(o)	I.A.	250.00	550.00	975.00	1550.
	1847(o)	I.A.	250.00	550.00	975.00	1550.

Mint: Copenhagen. Mintmasters initials: CS.

KM#	Date	Mintage	VG	Fine	VF	XF
778	1869	539 pcs.	500.00	1125.	1800.	2600.

FR(EDERIKS) D'OR

6.6420 g, .896 GOLD, .1913 oz AGW
Mint: Altona. Mintmasters initials: IFF.

KM#	Date	Mintage	VG	Fine	VF	XF
698 (C113)	1827	—	500.00	1000.	3000.	4000.

Mintmasters initials: FF.

KM#	Date	Mintage	VG	Fine	VF	XF
699 (C114)	1828	.021	400.00	900.00	1500.	2750.

Mintmasters initials: FF.

KM#	Date	Mintage	VG	Fine	VF	XF
701	1829	7,625	300.00	600.00	1500.	2000.
(C114a)	1830	.012	—	—	Rare	—
	1831	—	300.00	600.00	1500.	2000.
	1833	—	300.00	600.00	1500.	2000.
	1834	—	450.00	750.00	1850.	2500.
	1835	—	300.00	600.00	1500.	2000.
	1837	—	300.00	600.00	1500.	2000.
	1838	—	300.00	600.00	1500.	2000.

Mintmasters initials: FF.

KM#	Date	Mintage	VG	Fine	VF	XF
757 (C144)	1853	678 pcs.	500.00	1100.	1600.	3500.

2 FR(EDERIKS) D'OR

13.2840 g, .896 GOLD, .3827 oz AGW
Mint: Altona. Mintmasters initials: IFF.

KM#	Date	Mintage	VG	Fine	VF	XF
697	1826	—	—	—	Unique	—
(C115)	1827	—	500.00	1000.	2000.	3000.

Mintmasters initials: FF.

KM#	Date	Mintage	VG	Fine	VF	XF
700	1828	.168	350.00	800.00	1700.	2450.
(C116)	1829	.096	375.00	850.00	1800.	2600.
	1830	.105	350.00	800.00	1750.	2500.
	1833	—	350.00	800.00	1750.	2500.
	1834	—	375.00	850.00	1800.	2600.
	1835	—	400.00	875.00	1850.	2650.
	1836	—	—	—	Rare	—

Mintmasters initials: FF.

KM#	Date	Mintage	VG	Fine	VF	XF
713.1 (C117.1)	1836	—	350.00	850.00	1800.	2600.
	1837	—	325.00	800.00	1700.	2350.
	1838	—	325.00	800.00	1700.	2350.
	1839	—	325.00	800.00	1900.	2600.

Mint: Copenhagen. Mintmasters initials: WS.

KM#	Date	Mintage	VG	Fine	VF	XF
713.2 (C117.2)	1838	—	650.00	1300.	2300.	3250.

Mint: Copenhagen. Mintmasters initials: VS.

KM#	Date	Mintage	VG	Fine	VF	XF
750.1 (C145.1)	1850 KF(c)	*	300.00	700.00	1700.	2550.

Mint: Altona. Mintmasters initials: FF.

KM#	Date	Mintage	VG	Fine	VF	XF
750.2 (C145.2)	1851(o)	1.205	325.00	750.00	1800.	2675.
	1852(o)	I.A.	325.00	750.00	1800.	2675.
	1853(o)	I.A.	300.00	700.00	1700.	2550.
	1854(o)	I.A.	325.00	750.00	1800.	2675.
	1855(o)	I.A.	325.00	750.00	1800.	2675.

Mintmasters initials: FA.

KM#	Date	Mintage	VG	Fine	VF	XF
750.3 (C145.3)	1856(o)	I.A.	325.00	800.00	1900.	2700.
	1857(o)	I.A.	300.00	700.00	1700.	2550.
	1859(o)	I.A.	300.00	700.00	1700.	2550.

Mint: Copenhagen. Mintmasters initials: RH.

KM#	Date	Mintage	VG	Fine	VF	XF
750.4 (C145.4)	1863(c)	*	475.00	950.00	2000.	3000.

*Total mintage 1850VS and 1863RH .031.

2 CHR(ISTIANS) D'OR

13.2840 g, .896 GOLD, .3827 oz AGW
Mint: Copenhagen

KM#	Date	Mintage	VG	Fine	VF	XF
722.1 (C130.1)	1841(h)	*	350.00	700.00	2100.	3500.

Mint: Altona. Mintmasters initials: FF.

KM#	Date	Mintage	VG	Fine	VF	XF
722.2 (C130.2)	1842(o)	**	250.00	575.00	1900.	3100.
	1844(o)	**	375.00	675.00	2100.	3300.

Mint: Copenhagen. Mintmasters initials: VS.

KM#	Date	Mintage	VG	Fine	VF	XF
722.3 (C130.3)	1844(c)	*	325.00	650.00	2000.	3200.
	1845(o)	**	250.00	575.00	1900.	3100.
	1847(o)	**	225.00	550.00	1850.	3000.

*Total mintage 1841(h) and 1844(c) 9,222 pcs.
**Total mintage 1842-47(o) .551.

Mint: Copenhagen. Mintmasters initials: RH.

KM#	Date	Mintage	VG	Fine	VF	XF
773.1	1866	.042	500.00	1200.	3000.	4000.
	1867	Inc. Ab.	—	—	Rare	—

Mintmasters initials: CS.

KM#	Date	Mintage	VG	Fine	VF	XF
773.2	1869	Inc. Ab.	500.00	1200.	3000.	4000.
	1870	Inc. Ab.	—	—	Rare	—

DECIMAL COINAGE

100 Ore = 1 Krone

ORE

BRONZE
Mintmasters initials: CS.

KM#	Date	Mintage	Fine	VF	XF	Unc
792.1	1874(h)	5.540	4.00	8.00	20.00	45.00
	1875(h)	2.361	4.50	9.00	22.00	55.00
	1876(h)	1.483	230.00	350.00	500.00	825.00
	1878(h)	1.016	30.00	50.00	100.00	285.00
	1879(h)	1.491	18.00	35.00	80.00	240.00
	1880(h)	1.989	6.00	15.00	30.00	65.00
	1881(h)	.260	350.00	550.00	750.00	1250.
	1882(h)	1.782	6.00	14.00	25.00	60.00
	1883(h)	2.989	3.00	6.00	15.00	35.00
	1886(h)	.997	30.00	50.00	70.00	135.00
	1887(h)	3.007	6.00	13.50	22.50	55.00
	1888(h)	1.505	7.00	15.00	30.00	60.00
	1889(h)	2.999	2.50	5.00	12.00	32.00
	1891(h)	4.488	1.50	3.00	5.50	22.00
	1892(h)	.492	50.00	100.00	200.00	325.00

Mintmasters initials: VBP.

KM#	Date	Mintage	Fine	VF	XF	Unc
792.2	1894(h)	4.982	1.00	2.50	4.50	16.00
	1897/4(h)	2.988	2.00	3.50	7.50	22.00
	1897(h)	I.A.	2.00	3.50	7.50	22.00
	1899/7(h)	5.012	.75	1.25	4.00	14.50
	1899(h)	I.A.	.75	1.25	3.75	12.50

NOTE: Later dates (1902-1904) exist for this type.

2 ORE

BRONZE

Mintmasters initial: CS.

KM#	Date	Mintage	Fine	VF	XF	Unc
793.1	1874(h)	8.828	1.50	3.50	7.50	25.00
	1875(h)	2.817	3.00	8.00	25.00	65.00
	1876(h)	.231	60.00	120.00	200.00	425.00
	1880(h)	1.012	10.00	20.00	45.00	100.00
	1881(h)	1.484	7.00	15.00	28.00	70.00
	1883(h)	1.990	3.00	6.00	15.00	45.00
	1886(h)	1.493	5.00	10.00	20.00	50.00
	1887(h)	I.A.	35.00	65.00	120.00	285.00
	1889/7(h)	1.993	3.50	5.50	12.50	40.00
	1889(h)	I.A.	3.50	5.50	12.50	40.00
	1891(h)	1.903	2.50	4.00	8.00	25.00
	1892(h)	.573	20.00	40.00	70.00	165.00

Mintmasters initials: VBP.

KM#	Date	Mintage	Fine	VF	XF	Unc
793.2	1894(h)	2.486	1.50	3.00	6.00	20.00
	1897/4(h)	2.479	2.00	3.25	6.50	20.00
	1897(h)	I.A.	1.50	2.75	5.00	18.00
	1899/7(h)	2.504	1.25	2.50	5.00	18.00
	1899(h)	I.A.	1.25	2.50	5.00	18.00

NOTE: Later dates (1902-1906) exist for this type.

5 ORE

BRONZE

Mintmasters initials: CS.

KM#	Date	Mintage	Fine	VF	XF	Unc
794.1	1874(h)	2.762	4.00	7.00	30.00	100.00
	1875(h)	.207	20.00	40.00	100.00	225.00
	1882(h)	.076	18.00	30.00	80.00	220.00
	1884(h)	.321	8.00	18.00	50.00	200.00
	1890(h)	.598	40.00	80.00	175.00	350.00
	1891(h)	.787	8.00	16.00	45.00	165.00

Mintmasters initials: VBP.

KM#	Date	Mintage	Fine	VF	XF	Unc
794.2	1894(h)	.595	6.50	14.00	40.00	150.00
	1898(h)	.397	12.00	22.50	60.00	160.00
	1899(h)	.601	6.00	12.50	30.00	130.00

NOTE: Later dates (1902-1906) exist for this type.

10 ORE

1.4500 g, .400 SILVER, .0186 oz ASW

Mintmasters initials: CS.

KM#	Date	Mintage	Fine	VF	XF	Unc
795.1	1874(h)	8.975	5.00	10.00	25.00	100.00
	1875(h)	1.387	7.00	15.00	35.00	120.00
	1882(h)	1.057	25.00	40.00	75.00	135.00
	1884(h)	1.019	25.00	45.00	85.00	145.00
	1886(h)	.508	45.00	80.00	130.00	200.00
	1888(h)	.306	65.00	100.00	145.00	220.00
	1889(h)	1.030	7.00	15.00	30.00	60.00
	1891(h)	1.507	5.00	10.00	20.00	45.00

1.4500 g, .400 SILVER, .0186 oz ASW

Mintmasters initials: VBP.

KM#	Date	Mintage	Fine	VF	XF	Unc
795.2	1894(h)	1.521	5.00	10.00	20.00	45.00
	1897(h)	2.044	3.00	6.00	12.00	25.00
	1899(h)	2.050	3.00	6.00	12.00	25.00

NOTE: Later dates (1903-1905) exist for this type.

25 ORE

2.4200 g, .600 SILVER, .0467 oz ASW

Mintmasters initials: CS.

KM#	Date	Mintage	Fine	VF	XF	Unc
796.1	1874(h)	8.139	6.00	18.00	35.00	90.00
	1891(h)	1.214	8.00	20.00	32.00	75.00

Mintmasters initials: VBP.

KM#	Date	Mintage	Fine	VF	XF	Unc
796.2	1894(h)	1.206	6.00	18.00	30.00	65.00
	1900/800(h)	1.206	5.00	15.00	25.00	55.00
	1900(h)	I.A.	4.50	14.00	22.00	50.00

NOTE: Later dates (1904-1905) exist for this type.

KRONE

7.5000 g, .800 SILVER, .1929 oz ASW

Mintmasters initials: CS.

KM#	Date	Mintage	Fine	VF	XF	Unc
797.1	1875(h)	4.040	5.00	25.00	65.00	175.00
	1876(h)	1.284	12.00	35.00	85.00	250.00
	1892(h)	.701	12.00	25.00	40.00	70.00

Mintmasters initials: VBP.

KM#	Date	Mintage	Fine	VF	XF	Unc
797.2	1898(h)	.201	35.00	55.00	80.00	130.00

2 KRONER

15.0000 g, .800 SILVER, .3858 oz ASW

Mintmasters initials: CS.

KM#	Date	Mintage	Fine	VF	XF	Unc
798.1	1875(h)	3.396	8.00	22.00	65.00	160.00
	1876(h)	1.381	8.00	22.00	65.00	160.00

Mintmasters initials: VBP.

KM#	Date	Mintage	Fine	VF	XF	Unc
798.2	1897(h)	.151	50.00	80.00	120.00	200.00
	1899(h)	.152	40.00	70.00	100.00	175.00

Mintmasters initials: CS.

25th Anniversary of Reign

KM#	Date	Mintage	Fine	VF	XF	Unc
799	1888(h)	.101	12.50	22.00	32.00	60.00

Mintmasters initials: CS.

Golden Wedding Anniversary

KM#	Date	Mintage	Fine	VF	XF	Unc
800	1892(h)	.101	12.50	22.00	32.00	60.00

10 KRONER

4.4803 g, .900 GOLD, .1296 oz AGW

Mintmasters initials: CS.

KM#	Date	Mintage	Fine	VF	XF	Unc
790.1	1873(h)	.369	80.00	110.00	145.00	225.00
	1874(h)	I.A.	80.00	125.00	170.00	260.00
	1877(h)	.098	80.00	150.00	185.00	275.00
	1877(h)	—	—	—	Proof	1750.
	1890(h)	.151	80.00	115.00	140.00	210.00

Mintmasters initials: VBP.

KM#	Date	Mintage	Fine	VF	XF	Unc
790.2	1898(h)	.100	80.00	120.00	150.00	220.00
	1900(h)	.204	80.00	110.00	120.00	180.00

20 KRONER

8.9606 g, .900 GOLD, .2592 oz AGW

Mintmasters initials: CS.

KM#	Date	Mintage	Fine	VF	XF	Unc
791.1	1873(h)	1.153	110.00	135.00	150.00	200.00
	1874(h)	I.A.	475.00	950.00	1350.	1800.
	1876(h)	.351	110.00	135.00	150.00	200.00
	1877(h)	I.A.	110.00	135.00	175.00	225.00
	1890(h)	.102	110.00	135.00	150.00	200.00
	1890(h)	—	—	—	Proof	2000.

Mintmasters initials: VBP.

KM#	Date	Mintage	Fine	VF	XF	Unc
791.2	1900(h)	.100	110.00	130.00	140.00	200.00
	1900(h)	—	—	—	Proof	2000.

MEDALLIC ISSUES (M)

The Medallic Issues are similar to circulation coinage except they are without a denomination.

(2 KRONER)

GOLD

Golden Wedding Anniversary

KM#	Date	Mintage	Fine	VF	XF	Unc
MA1	1892	2 pcs.	—	—	—	15,000.

TOKEN ISSUES (Tn)

2 SKILLING

1.5000 g, .250 SILVER, .0121 oz ASW

KM#	Date	Mintage	VG	Fine	VF	XF
Tn4 (685)	1815	—	1.25	2.50	6.00	14.00

3 SKILLING

COPPER

KM#	Date	Mintage	VG	Fine	VF	XF
Tn5 (686)	1815	—	1.50	3.50	12.50	28.00

4 SKILLING

COPPER

KM#	Date	Mintage	VG	Fine	VF	XF
Tn6 (687)	1815	—	2.50	5.00	15.00	35.00

6 SKILLING

COPPER

KM#	Date	Mintage	VG	Fine	VF	XF
Tn1 (681)	1813	—	2.50	6.00	18.00	38.00

12 SKILLING

COPPER

KM#	Date	Mintage	VG	Fine	VF	XF
Tn2 (682)	1813	—	2.50	6.50	20.00	40.00

16 SKILLING

COPPER

KM#	Date	Mintage	VG	Fine	VF	XF
Tn3 (684)	1814	—	3.50	7.50	22.00	55.00

PATTERNS (Pn)

(Including off metal strikes)

KM#	Date	Mintage	Identification	Mkt.Val.
Pn48	1809	—	1 Skilling, Copper	—
PnA49	1810	—	2 Skilling, Silver, KM670	—
PnB49	1811	—	2 Skilling, Silver, KM670	—

KM#	Date	Mintage	Identification	Mkt.Val.
Pn49	1811	—	3 Skilling, Copper	—
PnA50	1811	—	3 Skilling, Pewter	—
PnB50	1811	—	3 Skilling, Silver	—
PnC50	1812	—	1 Skilling, Silver, KM671	—
PnD50	1812	—	3 Skilling, Silver, KM672	—
Pn50	1812	—	4 Skilling, Copper	Rare
PnA51	1812	—	6 Skilling, Copper uniface rev. Pn51	—

KM#	Date	Mintage	Identification	Mkt.Val.
Pn51	1812	—	6 Skilling, Copper	—
PnA52	1812	—	6 Skilling, Silver	—
PnB52	1812	—	12 Skilling, Pewter, KM673	—
PnC52	1813	—	1 Rigsbankskilling, Silver, KM680	—

KM#	Date	Mintage	Identification	Mkt.Val.
Pn52	1818	—	2 Rigsbankskilling, Copper	800.00
PnA53	1822	—	1 Rigsdaler species, bimetallic, Copper center, Pewter ring, mint: Altona	—
PnB53	1822	—	1 Rigsdaler species, Pewter, mint: Altona	—
PnC53	1824	—	1 Rigsdaler species, Copper, mint: Copenhagen	—
PnD53	1825	—	2 Frederik d'or, Pewter, mint: Altona	—
PnE53	1826	—	1 Rigsdaler species, Pewter, mint: Copenhagen	—
PnF53	1827	—	1 Frederik d'or, Silver	—

KM#	Date	Mintage	Identification	Mkt.Val.
Pn53	1833	—	1/4 Rigsbankdaler, Silver	1000.
PnA54	1835	—	1 Frederik d'or, Silver, mint: Altona	—
PnB54	1835	—	2 Frederik d'or, Pewter, mint: Altona	—
PnC54	1836	—	2 Frederik d'or, Pewter mint: Altona	—
PnD54	1840	—	1 Rigsdaler species, Pewter, mint: Copenhagen	—
PnE54	1842	—	1/5 Rigsbankskilling, Gold plated Silver	—
Pn54	1842	—	1 Rigsbankskilling, Copper	Rare
PnA55	1842	—	32 Rigsbankskilling, Copper, mint: Altona	—
PnB55	1842	—	2 Christian d'or, Silver	—
PnC55	1843	—	1 Christian d'or, Copper, rev. only, mint: Copenhagen	—
PnD55	1852	—	1 Rigsbankskilling, Copper, KM754	—
Pn55	1854	—	1/2 Rigsmontskilling, Copper	Rare

KM#	Date	Mintage	Identification	Mkt.Val.
Pn56	1854	—	1 Rigsmontskilling, Copper	Rare
Pn57	1854VS	—	16 Rigsmontskilling, Silver	Rare
Pn58	1856	—	1 Skilling	—
Pn59	1857	—	1/2 Skilling	—

KM#	Date	Mintage	Identification	Mkt.Val.
Pn60	1857	—	2 Rigsdaler, Silver	Rare
Pn61	1857	—	2 Rigsdaler, Copper	Rare
PnA63	1875	—	1 Krone, no HC on neck, Proof	—

PROVAS (Pr)

These modern Provas carry an incuse 'PROVE' stamp as well as a Roman numeral. The Roman numeral signifies experimental metallurgical alloys as follows:

ALUMINUM-BRONZE

I = 70% Copper, 26% Zinc, 4% Nickel
II = 65% Copper, 30% Zinc, 5% Nickel

KM#	Date	Mintage	Identification	Mkt.Val.
Pr1	1900	—	10 Kroner, Aluminum-Bronze, I	2450.

KM#	Date	Mintage	Identification	Mkt.Val.
Pr2	1900	—	20 Kroner, Aluminum-Bronze, II	1450.

TRIAL STRIKES (TS)

KM#	Date	Mintage	Identification	Mkt.Val.
TS1	ND(1839)	—	Daler Specie uniface obv. Fredericus VI	200.00

KM#	Date	Mintage	Identification	Mkt.Val.
TS2	ND(1839)	—	Daler Specie uniface rev. crowned arms, wildmen at sides	200.00

HOLSTEIN-NORBURG

NOTE: For previously listed issues refer to German States.

HOLSTEIN-PLOEN

NOTE: For previously listed issues refer to German States.

SCHLESWIG-HOLSTEIN

NOTE: For previously listed issues refer to German States.

DJIBOUTI

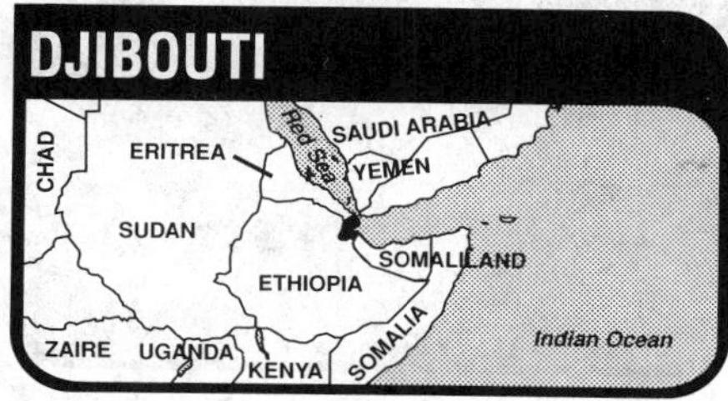

The Republic of Djibouti (formerly French Somaliland and the French Overseas Territory of Afars and Issas), located in northeast Africa at the Bab el Mandeb Strait connecting the Suez Canal and the Red Sea with the Gulf of Aden and the Indian Ocean, has an area of 8,950 sq. mi. (22,000 sq. km.) and a population of 421,320. Capital: Djibouti. The tiny nation has less than one sq. mi. of arable land, and no natural resources except salt, sand, and camels. The commercial activities of the transshipment port of Djibouti and the Addis Abada-Djibouti railroad are the basis of the economy. Salt, fish and hides are exported.

French interest in former French Somaliland began in 1839 with concessions obtained by a French naval lieutenant from the provincial sultans. French Somaliland was made a protectorate in 1884 and its boundaries were delimited by the Franco-British and Ethiopian accords of 1887 and 1897. It became a colony in 1896 and a territory within the French Union in 1946. In 1958 it voted to join the new French Community as an overseas territory, and reaffirmed that choice by a referendum in March, 1967. Its name was changed from French Somaliland to the French Territory of Afars and Issas on July 5, 1967.

The French Tricolor, which had flown over the strategically important territory for 115 years, was lowered for the last time on June 27, 1977, when French Afars and Issas became Africa's 49th independent state, under the name of the Republic of Djibouti.

Djibouti, a seaport and capital city of the Republic of Djibouti (and formerly of French Somaliland and French Afars and Issas) is located on the east coast of Africa at the southernmost entrance to the Red Sea. The capital was moved from Obok to Djibouti in 1892 and established as the transshipment point for Ethiopia's foreign trade via the Franco-Ethiopian railway linking Djibouti and Addis Ababa.

RULERS

French, until 1977

COUNTERMARKED COINAGE

RUPEE-TALER (RYAL) COINAGE SERIES

'Abd Latif Ma'a al-Fazah bi Jibuti

Coins privately countermarked (c/m) around 1900 with 12 scalloped square with Arabic inscription. Sometimes coins have additional c/m's on the coin showing silver fineness.

1/2 RUPEE SIZE

.917 SILVER
c/m: On India 1/2 Rupee, KM#491

KM#	Date	VG	Fine	VF	XF
1	ND(1877-1900)	55.00	90.00	175.00	350.00

RUPEE SIZE

SILVER, dump
c/m: On Murshidabad Rupee, KM#99.

KM#	Date	VG	Fine	VF	XF
2.6	ND(r.y.19)	120.00	200.00	350.00	—

.917 SILVER
c/m: On India Rupee, KM#450.

KM#	Date	VG	Fine	VF	XF
2.1	ND(1835,40)	35.00	65.00	125.00	250.00

c/m: On India Rupee, KM#457.

KM#	Date	VG	Fine	VF	XF
2.2	ND(1840)	35.00	65.00	125.00	250.00

c/m: On India Rupee, KM#458.

KM#	Date	VG	Fine	VF	XF
2.3	ND(1840)	35.00	65.00	125.00	250.00

c/m: On India Rupee, KM#473.

KM#	Date	VG	Fine	VF	XF
2.4	ND(1862-1901)	35.00	65.00	125.00	250.00

RYAL SIZE (TALER)

.833 SILVER
c/m: On Austria M.T. Thaler, KM#T1.

KM#	Date	VG	Fine	VF	XF
3.1	ND(1780)	50.00	85.00	150.00	300.00

c/m: With additional Arabic *"830"*.

KM#	Date	VG	Fine	VF	XF
3.2	ND(1780)	65.00	120.00	200.00	425.00

DOMINICA

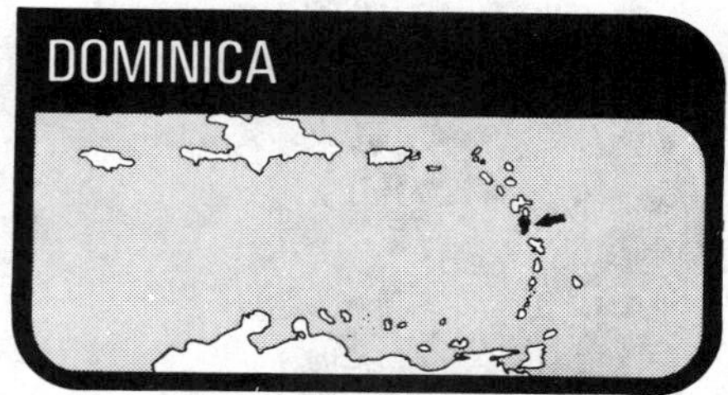

The Commonwealth of Dominica, situated in the Lesser Antilles midway between Guadeloupe to the north and Martinique to the south, has an area of 290 sq. mi. (750 sq. km.) and a population of 82,608. Capital: Roseau. Agriculture is the chief economic activity of the mountainous island. Bananas are the chief export.

Columbus discovered and named the island on Nov. 3, 1493. Spain neglected it and it was finally colonized by the French in 1632. The British drove the French from the island in 1756. Thereafter it changed hands between the French and British a dozen or more times before becoming permanently British in 1805. Around 1761, pierced or mutilated silver from Martinique was used on the island. A council in 1798 acknowledged and established value for these mutilated coins and ordered other cut and countermarked to be made in Dominica. These remained in use until 1862, when they were demonitized and sterling became the standard.

RULERS

British, until 1978

MONETARY SYSTEM

(From 1798 until 1813)
11 Bits = 8 Shillings 3 Pence = 1 Dollar
(Commencing 1813)
16 Bits = 12 Shillings = 1 Dollar (Spanish)
100 Cents = 10 Shillings = 1 Dollar (Dominican)

ISSUES OF 1813

3 BITS

SILVER
c/m: Crowned 3 on 1/2 of 23mm center plug cut from Spanish or Spanish Colonial 8 Reales.

KM#	Date	Good	VG	Fine	VF
4	ND(1813)	100.00	200.00	320.00	525.00

4 BITS

SILVER
c/m: Crowned '4' on center ring segment of Spanish or Spanish Colonial 8 Reales.

KM#	Date	Good	VG	Fine	VF
5	ND(1813)	200.00	400.00	850.00	1500.

6 BITS

SILVER
c/m: Crowned "6" on obv. or rev. of center plug cut from Spanish or Spanish Colonial 8 Reales.

KM#	Date	Good	VG	Fine	VF
6	ND(1813)	35.00	60.00	125.00	275.00

12 BITS

SILVER
c/m: Crowned 12 on holed Peru - Lima 8 Reales, KM#97.

KM#	Date	Year	Good	VG	Fine	VF
7	ND(1813) (1791-1808)		—	—	Rare	—

NOTE: Modern copies are common.

16 BITS

SILVER
c/m: Crowned "16" on obv. of holed Mexico City 8 Reales, KM#107.

KM#	Date	Year	Good	VG	Fine	VF
8.1	ND(1813)	(1789-90)	600.00	1250.	4000.	7500.

c/m: Crowned "16" on obv. and rev. of Mexico City 8 Reales, KM#108.

KM#	Date	Year	Good	VG	Fine	VF
8.2	ND(1813)	(1790)	600.00	1250.	4000.	7000.

c/m: Crowned "16" on obv. and rev. of holed Mexico City 8 Reales, KM#109.

KM#	Date	Year	Good	VG	Fine	VF
8.3	ND(1813)	(1791-1808)	500.00	1150.	3500.	7000.

ISSUES OF 1816

2 BITS

SILVER
Holed Spanish or Spanish Colonial 2 Reales.

KM#	Date	Good	VG	Fine	VF
9	ND(1816)	100.00	180.00	225.00	350.00

2 SHILLINGS - 6 PENCE

SILVER
c/m: '2.6' on 1/4 segment of Spanish or Spanish Colonial 8 Reales.

KM#	Date	Good	VG	Fine	VF
10	ND(1816-18)	150.00	275.00	400.00	700.00

DOMINICAN REPUBLIC

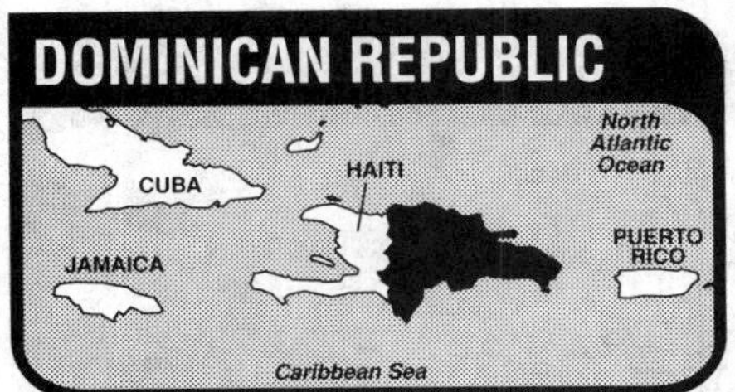

The Dominican Republic, which occupies the eastern two-thirds of the island of Hispaniola, has an area of 18,704 sq. mi. (48,734 sq. km.) and a population of 7.9 million. Capital: Santo Domingo. The largely agricultural economy produces sugar, coffee, tobacco and cocoa. Tourism and casino gaming are also a rising source of revenue.

Columbus discovered Hispaniola in 1492, and named it La Isla Espanola - 'the Spanish Island'. Santo Domingo, the oldest white settlement in the Western Hemisphere, was the base from which Spain conducted its exploration of the New World. Later, French buccaneers settled the western third of Hispaniola, naming the colony St. Dominique, which in 1697, was ceded to France by Spain. In 1804, following a bloody revolt by former slaves, the French colony became the Republic of Haiti - 'mountainous country'. The Spanish called their part of Hispaniola Santo Domingo. In 1822, the Haitians conquered the entire island and held it until 1844, when Juan Pablo Duarte, the national hero of the Dominican Republic, drove them out of Santo Domingo and established an independent Dominican Republic. The republic returned voluntarily to Spanish dominion from 1861 to 1865, after being rejected by France, Britain and the United States. Independence was reclaimed in 1866.

MINT MARKS

A - Paris
(a) - Berlin
(c) - Stylized maple leaf, Royal Canadian Mint
H - Heaton, Birmingham, England
Mo - Mexico
(o) - CHI in oval - Valcambi, Chiasso, Italy
(t) - Tower, Tower Mint, London

RULERS

Spanish, until 1822, 1861-1865
Haiti, 1822-1844

MONETARY SYSTEM

16 Reales = 1 Escudo

SANTO DOMINGO

1/4 REAL

NOTE: Coin previously listed here has been moved to Venezuela, Province of Maracaibo.

COPPER

KM#	Date	Mintage	Good	VG	Fine	VF
2	ND	—	12.50	22.50	37.50	55.00

NOTE: Several varieties exist of fraction and letter arrangement on reverse and crowned F.7 on obverse. Planchet sizes and weights vary, but values given are for well struck specimens which carry the full design.

2/4 REAL

NOTE: Coin previously listed here has been moved to Venezuela, Province of Maracaibo.

REAL

SILVER

KM#	Date	Mintage	Good	VG	Fine	VF
4.1	ND	—	200.00	300.00	450.00	700.00

Rev: Castles and lions reversed in shield.

KM#	Date	Mintage	Good	VG	Fine	VF
4.2	ND	—	200.00	300.00	450.00	700.00

2 REALES

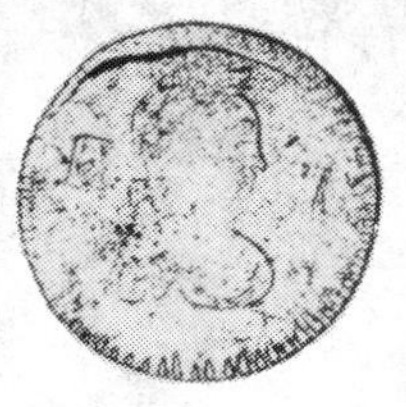

SILVER

KM#	Date	Mintage	Good	VG	Fine	VF
5	ND	—	400.00	600.00	900.00	1350.

COUNTERMARKED COINAGE

ca.1820

REAL

.903 SILVER
c/m: Crowned F.7o on Mexico 1 Real, KM#75.

KM#	Date	Good	VG	Fine	VF
8	ND(1732-47)	40.00	65.00	100.00	175.00

8 REALES

.903 SILVER
c/m: Crowned F.7o on Mexico 8 Reales, KM#109.

11	ND(1791-1808)	900.00	1200.	—	—

DOMINICAN REPUBLIC

MONETARY SYSTEM
8 Reales = 1 Peso

1/4 REAL

BRONZE

KM#	Date	Mintage	Fine	VF	XF	Unc
1	1844	1.600	6.00	13.50	37.50	—

BRASS

2	1844	—	3.75	8.50	22.50	75.00
	1848 plain 4	—	3.75	8.50	22.50	75.00
	1848 crosslet 4	—	3.75	8.50	22.50	75.00

NOTE: Many varieties exist.

DECIMAL COINAGE

100 Centavos = 1 Peso

CENTAVO

BRASS

KM#	Date	Mintage	Fine	VF	XF	Unc
3	1877	1.000	.50	1.50	2.75	7.00

1-1/4 CENTAVOS

COPPER-NICKEL

6	1882	.400	7.00	13.50	32.50	80.00
	1888A	.500	2.50	5.00	12.50	40.00
	1888A	—	—	—	Proof	300.00

2-1/2 CENTAVOS

COPPER-NICKEL

4	1877	.021	17.50	25.00	47.50	100.00

Obv: Small book on shield.

7.1	1882	—	4.50	10.00	27.50	70.00

Obv: Large book w/thin cross on shield, small date.

7.2	1888A	.950	1.25	3.00	7.50	42.50
	1888A	—	—	—	Proof	275.00

Obv: Large book w/thick cross, large date.

7.3	1888A	8.000	.75	2.00	6.00	40.00
	1888A	—	—	—	Proof	275.00
	1888HH	4.000	.75	2.00	6.00	40.00
	1888HH	—	—	—	Proof	325.00

NOTE: Star on reverse is flanked by H's.

5 CENTAVOS

COPPER-NICKEL

5	1877	.130	10.00	20.00	32.50	75.00

MONETARY REFORM

100 Centesimos = 1 Franco

5 CENTESIMOS

BRONZE

8	1891A	.400	1.75	5.00	16.50	50.00
	1891A	—	—	—	Proof	—

10 CENTESIMOS

BRONZE

KM#	Date	Mintage	Fine	VF	XF	Unc
9	1891A	.300	2.00	6.00	22.00	60.00
	1891A	—	—	—	Proof	—

50 CENTESIMOS

2.5000 g, .835 SILVER, 0671 oz ASW

10	1891A	.150	5.00	13.50	32.50	100.00
	1891A	—	—	—	Proof	—

FRANCO

5.000 g, .835 SILVER, .1342 oz ASW

11	1891A	.125	11.50	18.50	40.00	150.00
	1891A	—	—	—	Proof	—

5 FRANCOS

25.0000 g, .900 SILVER, .7234 oz ASW

12	1891A	.150	45.00	90.00	165.00	750.00
	1891A	—	—	—	Proof	—

MONETARY REFORM

100 Centavos = 1 Peso

10 CENTAVOS

2.5000 g, .350 SILVER, .0281 oz ASW

13	1897A	.764	2.50	10.00	25.00	135.00

20 CENTAVOS

5.0000 g, .350 SILVER, .0563 oz ASW

14	1897A	1.395	1.75	7.50	22.50	125.00

1/2 PESO

12.5000 g, .350 SILVER, .1407 oz ASW

KM#	Date	Mintage	Fine	VF	XF	Unc
15	1897A	.917	4.00	15.00	40.00	300.00

PESO

25.0000 g, .350 SILVER, .2813 oz ASW

KM#	Date	Mintage	Fine	VF	XF	Unc
16	1897A	1.455	25.00	65.00	175.00	850.00

ESSAIS (E)

KM#	Date	Mintage	Identification	Mkt.Val.
E1	1874	—	2 Centavos, Bronze, E (for Essai)	100.00

KM#	Date	Mintage	Identification	Mkt.Val.
E2	1877	—	1 Centavo, Bronze, LIBERTAT, E below spray (Unc & Proof)	Unc 70.00
E3	1877	—	1 Centavo, Gilt-Bronze	—
E4	1877	—	1 Centavo, Nickel	—

KM#	Date	Mintage	Identification	Mkt.Val.
E5	1877	—	2 Centavos, Bronze, LIBERTAT, E below spray (Unc & Proof)	Unc 70.00
E6	1877	—	2 Centavos, Gilt-Bronze, LIBERTAT, E below spray	70.00
E7	1877	—	2 Centavos, Nickel	—

KM#	Date	Mintage	Identification	Mkt.Val.
E8	1878	—	1 Centavo, Bronze, LIBERTAD, E below spray (Unc & Proof)	Unc 60.00
E9	1878	—	1 Centavo, Nickel	—

KM#	Date	Mintage	Identification	Mkt.Val.
E10	1878	—	1 Centavo, Bronze, LIBERTAD, E below spray, wreath rev. (Unc & Proof)	Unc 60.00
E11	1878	—	1 Centavo, Nickel	—

KM#	Date	Mintage	Identification	Mkt.Val.
E12	1878	—	2 Centavos, Bronze, LIBERTAD, E below spray (Unc & Proof)	Unc 60.00

KM#	Date	Mintage	Identification	Mkt.Val.
E13	1878	—	2 Centavos, Nickel	—
E14	1878	—	2 Centavos, Bronze, LIBERTAD, E below spray, wreath rev. (Unc & Proof)	Unc 60.00
E15	1878	—	2 Centavos, Nickel	—
E16	1887	—	1-1/4 Centavos, Copper-Nickel, KM6	300.00
E17	1887	—	2-1/2 Centavos, Copper-Nickel, KM7	300.00

PATTERNS (Pn)

(Including off metal strikes)

KM#	Date	Mintage	Identification	Mkt.Val.
Pn1	1855	3 known	10 Reales, .835 Silver	15,000.
Pn2	1855	1 known	10 Reales, Copper	10,000.

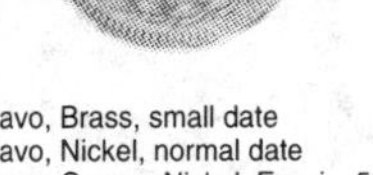

KM#	Date	Mintage	Identification	Mkt.Val.
Pn3	1877	1 known	1 Centavo, Brass, small date	Rare
Pn4	1877	2 known	1 Centavo, Nickel, normal date	Rare
Pn5	1892	—	1 Centavo, Copper-Nickel, Essai	500.00

EAST AFRICA

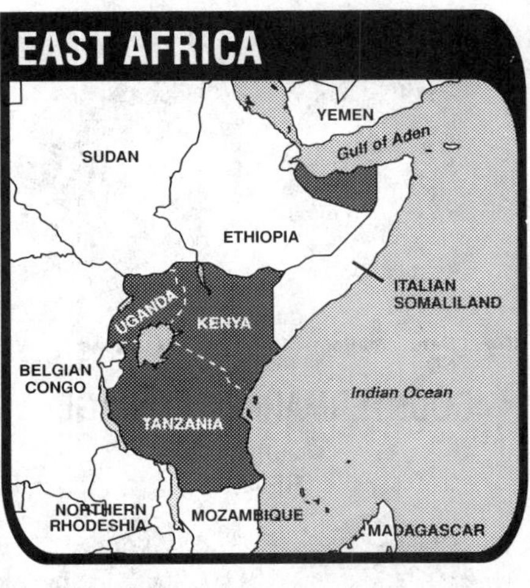

East Africa was an administrative grouping of five separate British territories: Kenya, Tanganyika (now part of Tanzania), the Sultanate of Zanzibar and Pemba (now part of Tanzania), Uganda and British Somaliland (now part of Somalia). See individual entries for specific statistics and history.

The common interest of Kenya, Tanzania and Uganda invited cooperation in economic matters and consideration of political union. The territorial governors, organized as the East Africa High Commission, met periodically to administer such common activities as taxation, industrial development and education. The authority of the Commission did not infringe upon the constitution and internal autonomy of the individual colonies. A common coinage and banknotes, which were also legal tender in Aden, were provided for use of the member colonies by the East Africa Currency Board. The coinage through 1919 had the legend "East Africa and Uganda Protectorate". From 1920 on, the legend has read, "East Africa".

The East African coinage includes two denominations of 1936 which bear the style and titles of Edward VIII.

NOTE: For later coinage see Kenya, Tanzania and Uganda.

RULERS

British

MINT MARKS

A - Ackroyd & Best, Morley
I - Bombay Mint
H - Heaton Mint, Birmingham, England
K,KN - King's Norton Mint, Birmingham, England
SA - Pretoria Mint, South Africa
no mint mark - Royal Mint, London

EAST AFRICA PROTECTORATE

MONETARY SYSTEM

64 Pice = 1 Rupee

PICE

BRONZE

KM#	Date	Mintage	Fine	VF	XF	Unc
1	1897	.640	6.00	12.50	30.00	85.00
	1897	—	—	—	Proof	200.00
	1898	6.400	4.00	10.00	25.00	75.00
	1898	—	—	—	Proof	200.00
	1899	3.200	4.00	10.00	25.00	75.00
	1899	—	—	—	Proof	200.00

PATTERNS (Pn)

(Including off metal strikes)

KM#	Date	Mintage	Identification	Mkt.Val.
Pn1	1897	—	1 Pice, Silver, KM1	500.00
Pn2	1897	—	1 Pice, Gold, KM1	2500.
Pn3	1898	—	1 Pice, Silver, KM1	500.00
Pn4	1899	—	1 Pice, Silver, KM1	500.00
Pn5	1899	—	1 Pice, Gold, KM1	2500.

ECUADOR

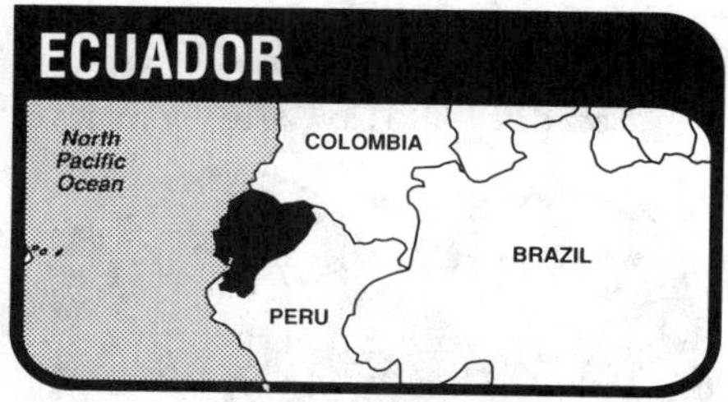

The Republic of Ecuador, located astride the equator on the Pacific Coast of South America, has an area of 105,037 sq. mi. (283,560 sq. km.) and a population of 10.9 million. Capital: Quito. Agriculture is the mainstay of the economy but there are appreciable deposits of minerals and petroleum. It is one of the world's largest exporters of bananas and balsa wood. Coffee, cacao, sugar and petroleum are also valuable exports.

Ecuador was first sighted in 1526 by Francisco Pizarro. Conquest was undertaken by Sebastian de Benalcazar, who founded Quito in 1534. Ecuador was part of the Viceroyalty of New Granada through the 16th and 17th centuries. After previous attempts to attain independence were crushed, Antonio Sucre, the able lieutenant of Bolivar, secured Ecuador's freedom in the Battle of Pinchincha, May 24, 1822. It then joined Venezuela and Colombia in a confederation known as Gran Colombia, and became an independent republic when it left the confederacy in 1830.

MINT MARKS

BIRMm - Birmingham
D - Denver
H - Heaton, Birmingham
HEATON - Heaton, Birmingham
HEATON BIRMINGHAM
HF - LeLocle (Swiss)
LIMA - Lima
Mo - Mexico
PHILA.U.S.A. - Philadelphia
PHILADELPHIA - Philadelphia
QUITO - Quito
SANTIAGO - Chile

ASSAYERS INITIALS

FP - Feliciano Paredes
GJ Guillermo Jameson
MV - Miguel Vergara
ST - Santiago Taylor

MONETARY SYSTEM

16 Reales = 1 Escudo

COUNTERMARKED COINAGE

1831

M.D.Q. - Moneda de Quito

1/4 REAL

SILVER
c/m: MDQ monogram on Colombia (Nueva Granada) 1/4 Real, KM#79.1.

KM#	Date	Mintage	Good	VG	Fine	VF
1	ND(1820)	—	—	—	Rare	—
	ND(1821)	—	—	—	Rare	—

c/m: MDQ monogram on Colombia (Nueva Granada) 1/4 Real, KM#79.2.

KM#	Date	Mintage	Good	VG	Fine	VF
2	ND(1821 Ba)	—	—	—	Rare	—

1/2 REAL

SILVER
c/m: MDQ monogram on Colombia (Cundinamarca) 1/2 Real, KM#8.

KM#	Date	Mintage	Good	VG	Fine	VF
3	ND(1821)	—	—	—	Rare	—

REAL

SILVER
c/m: MDQ monogram on Colombia (Nueva Granada) Real, KM#75.

KM#	Date	Mintage	Good	VG	Fine	VF
4	ND(1819 JF)	—	—	—	Rare	—

c/m: MDQ monogram on Colombia (Cundinamarca) Real, KM#9.

KM#	Date	Mintage	Good	VG	Fine	VF
5	ND(1821)	—	—	—	Rare	—

2 REALES

SILVER
c/m: MDQ on Colombia, 2 Reales, KM#4.

KM#	Date	Mintage	VG	Fine	VF	XF
A6	ND(1815 JF)	—	—	—	Rare	—

c/m: MDQ monogram on Colombia (Nueva Granada) 2 Reales, KM#76.

KM#	Date	Mintage	Good	VG	Fine	VF
6	ND(1819 JF)	—	—	—	Rare	—

c/m: MDQ monogram on Colombia (Nueva Granada) 2 Reales, KM#77.

KM#	Date	Mintage	Good	VG	Fine	VF
7	ND(1819 JF)	—	—	—	Rare	—
	ND(1820 JF)	—	—	—	Rare	—

c/m: MDQ monogram on Colombia (Cundinamarca) 2 Reales, KM#5.

KM#	Date	Mintage	Good	VG	Fine	VF
8	ND(1820 JF)	—	—	—	Rare	—
	ND(1820 Ba JF)	—	—	—	Rare	—
	ND(1821 Ba JF)	—	150.00	250.00	350.00	500.00
	ND(1821 JF)	—	100.00	150.00	—	—
	ND(1823 JF)	—	—	—	Rare	—

8 REALES

SILVER
c/m: MDQ monogram on Colombia (Nueva Granada) 8 Reales, KM#78.

KM#	Date	Mintage	Good	VG	Fine	VF
9	ND(1819 JF)	—	—	—	Rare	—
	ND(1820/19 JF)	—	—	—	Rare	—
	ND(1820 JF)	—	—	—	Rare	—

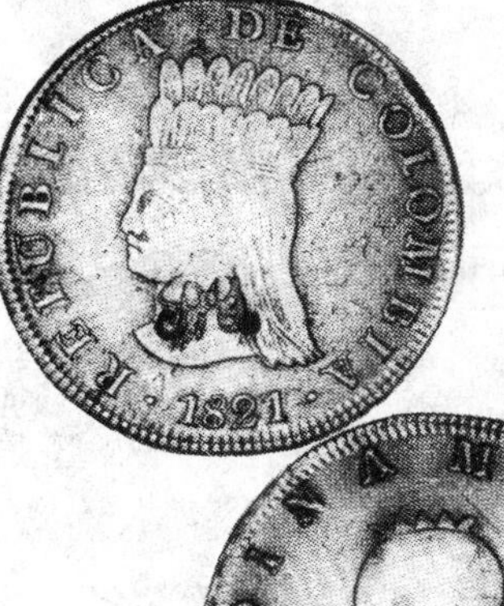

c/m: MDQ monogram on Colombia (Cundinamarca) 8 Reales, KM#6.

KM#	Date	Mintage	Good	VG	Fine	VF
10	ND(1820 JF)	—	—	—	Rare	—
	ND(1820 Ba JF)	—	—	—	Rare	—
	ND(1821 JF)	—	150.00	200.00	325.00	800.00
	ND(1821 Ba JF)	—	200.00	350.00	600.00	1250.

c/m: MDQ monogram on Colombia (Cundinamarca) 8 Reales, KM#7.

KM#	Date	Mintage	Good	VG	Fine	VF
11	ND(1820 JF)	—	—	—	Rare	—

REGULAR COINAGE

UN QUARTO (1/4) REAL

.333 SILVER, 0.72-.83 g
Rev: Fortress and 2 eliptical lines.

KM#	Date	Mintage	VG	Fine	VF	XF
25	1842 MV	—	350.00	600.00	900.00	1750.

14mm. Rev: Fortress on hill w/bird above.

KM#	Date	Mintage	VG	Fine	VF	XF
26	1842 MV-S	—	125.00	275.00	450.00	700.00
	1843 MV	—	85.00	175.00	275.00	400.00
	1843 MV-A	—	50.00	120.00	225.00	350.00

NOTE: The A and S above are found on the hill below the fortress.

.667 SILVER

KM#	Date	Mintage	VG	Fine	VF	XF
36	1849 GJ	—	10.00	20.00	45.00	75.00
	1850 GJ	—	40.00	80.00	150.00	250.00
	1851 GJ	—	10.00	20.00	45.00	75.00
	1852 GJ	—	10.00	20.00	45.00	75.00
	1855 GJ	—	12.00	25.00	50.00	85.00
	1856 GJ	—	12.00	25.00	50.00	85.00
	1862 GJ	—	425.00	750.00	1150.	2200.

1/2 REAL

.667 SILVER, 1.30 g
Obv. leg: EL ECUADOR EN COLOMBIA, MoR (Medio Real).

KM#	Date	Mintage	VG	Fine	VF	XF
12.1	1833 GJ	—	100.00	175.00	300.00	500.00
	1835 GJ	—	— Reported, not confirmed			

Rev: Denomination 1/2 R.

KM#	Date	Mintage	VG	Fine	VF	XF
12.2	1833 GJ	—	175.00	300.00	550.00	—
	1835 GJ	—	—	—	Rare	—

Obv. leg: REPUBLICA DEL ECUADOR.

KM#	Date	Mintage	VG	Fine	VF	XF
22	1838 ST	—	30.00	60.00	120.00	250.00
	1840 MV	—	35.00	65.00	135.00	285.00
	1840 WV W is inverted M	—	40.00	90.00	150.00	300.00
	1843	—	— Reported, not confirmed			

1.55-1.85 g, 15-17mm

KM#	Date	Mintage	VG	Fine	VF	XF
35	1848 GJ	—	7.50	15.00	30.00	60.00
	1849 GJ	—	10.00	20.00	40.00	80.00

REAL

.667 SILVER, 3.00-3.40 g
Obv. leg: EL ECUADOR EN COLOMBIA.

KM#	Date	Mintage	VG	Fine	VF	XF
13	1833 GJ	—	15.00	35.00	70.00	145.00
	1834 GJ	—	15.00	30.00	60.00	100.00
	1835 GJ	—	17.50	45.00	85.00	175.00

3.40-3.92 g

Obv. leg: REPUBLICA DEL ECUADOR.

KM#	Date	Mintage	VG	Fine	VF	XF
17	1836 GJ	—	35.00	75.00	150.00	250.00
	1836 FP	—	37.50	80.00	165.00	275.00
	1837 FP	—	300.00	500.00	850.00	—
	1838 ST	—	15.00	40.00	85.00	175.00
	1838 MV	—	45.00	120.00	225.00	400.00
	1839 MV	—	13.50	32.50	75.00	165.00
	1840 MV	—	13.50	32.50	75.00	165.00
	1841 MV	—	500.00	800.00	1600.	—

Obv. and rev. legends transposed.

KM#	Date	Mintage	VG	Fine	VF	XF
20	1837 FP	—	200.00	350.00	550.00	800.00
	1838 ST	—	120.00	250.00	400.00	650.00

2 REALES

.667 SILVER, 5.17-5.60 g, 25-27mm
Obv. leg: EL ECUADOR EN COLOMBIA.

KM#	Date	Mintage	VG	Fine	VF	XF
14	1833 GJ	—	250.00	450.00	700.00	1000.
	1834 GJ	—	17.50	35.00	75.00	175.00
	1835 GJ	—	16.50	30.00	70.00	165.00
	1836 GJ	—	100.00	200.00	350.00	500.00

5.80-6.10 g
Obv. leg: REPUBLICA DEL ECUADOR

KM#	Date	Mintage	VG	Fine	VF	XF
18	1836 GJ	—	13.50	25.00	45.00	120.00
	1836 FP	—	15.00	32.50	55.00	140.00
	1837 FP	—	400.00	650.00	—	—
	1838 ST	—	20.00	40.00	80.00	200.00
	1838 MV	—	13.50	25.00	45.00	120.00
	1839/8 MV	—	30.00	50.00	—	—
	1839 MV	—	17.50	35.00	60.00	150.00
	1839 MV A is inverted V in LA					
		—	30.00	55.00	95.00	225.00
	1840 MV	—	17.50	35.00	60.00	150.00
	1840 MV V is inverted A					
		—	30.00	55.00	100.00	250.00
	1841 MV	—	30.00	55.00	95.00	225.00

Obv. and rev. legends transposed.

KM#	Date	Mintage	VG	Fine	VF	XF
21	1837 FP	—	30.00	60.00	120.00	270.00
	1838 ST	—	200.00	300.00	450.00	650.00

5.50-6.05 g

KM#	Date	Mintage	VG	Fine	VF	XF
33	1847 GJ	—	12.50	25.00	50.00	150.00
	1848/7 GJ	—	12.50	25.00	65.00	200.00
	1849 GJ	—	15.00	27.50	65.00	185.00
	1850 GJ	—	12.50	25.00	50.00	150.00
	1851 GJ	—	12.50	25.00	50.00	150.00
	1852 GJ	—	12.50	25.00	50.00	150.00

Obv: 2 R flanking arms.
Rev: Liberty head w/long hair.

KM#	Date	Mintage	VG	Fine	VF	XF
38	1857 GJ	—	—	—	Rare	—
	1862 GJ	—	—	—	Rare	—

***NOTE:** Ponterio C.I.C.F. sale #86 4-97 AU-58 realized $24,000.

6.7600 g, .666 SILVER, .1447 oz ASW
Rev: Liberty head w/short hair.

KM#	Date	Mintage	VG	Fine	VF	XF
40	1862 GJ	—	—	—	*Rare	—

***NOTE:** Ponterio C.I.C.F. sale #86 4-97 MS-62 realized $8,000.

4 REALES

.667 SILVER, 12.30-12.75 g

KM#	Date	Mintage	VG	Fine	VF	XF
24	1841 MV	—	15.00	35.00	85.00	370.00
	1841 MV V is inverted A					
		—	25.00	50.00	100.00	400.00
	1842 MV	—	15.00	32.50	75.00	350.00
	1843 MV	—	15.00	32.50	75.00	350.00

12.30 g

KM#	Date	Mintage	VG	Fine	VF	XF
27	1844 MV-A	—	225.00	425.00	750.00	1800.

NOTE: The A above is found on the breast of the condor.

11.70 g

KM#	Date	Mintage	VG	Fine	VF	XF
29	1845 MV-A	—	225.00	425.00	800.00	1850.

NOTE: The A above is found on the breast of the condor.

13.35 g

KM#	Date	Mintage	VG	Fine	VF	XF
37	1855 GJ	—	20.00	50.00	165.00	400.00
	1857 GJ	—	15.00	40.00	80.00	225.00

13.4300 g, .666 SILVER, .2876 oz ASW

KM#	Date	Mintage	VG	Fine	VF	XF
37a	1862 GJ	—	2000.	4000.	7000.	11,500.

KM#	Date	Mintage	VG	Fine	VF	XF
41	1862	—	75.00	150.00	350.00	750.00

8 REALES

25.0000 g, .900 SILVER, .7234 oz ASW

KM#	Date	Mintage	VG	Fine	VF	XF
32	1846 GJ	—	750.00	1250.	2250.	4750.

5 FRANCOS

25.0000 g, .900 SILVER, .7234 oz ASW

KM#	Date	Mintage	VG	Fine	VF	XF
39	1858 GJ	—	125.00	250.00	350.00	750.00

ESCUDO

3.3000 g, .875 GOLD, .0928 oz AGW

KM#	Date	Mintage	VG	Fine	VF	XF
15	1828	—	—	—	—	—
	1833 GJ	—	175.00	425.00	850.00	1450.
	1834 GJ	—	100.00	275.00	400.00	550.00
	1835 GJ	—	200.00	450.00	900.00	1500.
	1845 GJ	—	—	—	—	—

NOTE: The 1828 dated coins are considered contemporary counterfeits. The 1845 dated coins are suspicious.

DOUBLE ESCUDO

6.7666 g, .875 GOLD, .1903 oz AGW

KM#	Date	Mintage	VG	Fine	VF	XF
16	1833 GJ	—	—	—	Rare	—
	1834 GJ	—	550.00	900.00	1400.	—
	1835 GJ	—	250.00	450.00	750.00	1600.
	1835 FP					
		3 known	—	—	Rare	—

4 ESCUDOS

13.5000 g, .875 GOLD, .3798 oz AGW

KM#	Date	Mintage	VG	Fine	VF	XF
19	1836 FP-A	—	250.00	375.00	600.00	1000.
	1837 FP-A	—	250.00	375.00	650.00	1150.
	1838 FP-A	—	700.00	1350.	2200.	3650.
	1838 ST-A					
		3 to 4 pcs. known		2500.	4000.	—
	1838 MV-A	—	425.00	900.00	1450.	2500.
	1839 MV-A	—	350.00	650.00	1100.	1750.
	1841 MV-A					
		2 known	—	—	6000.	—

NOTE: Engravers initial A in front drape of bust.

8 ESCUDOS

27.0640 g, .875 GOLD, .7614 oz AGW

KM#	Date	Mintage	VG	Fine	VF	XF
23.1	1838 ST-A	—	650.00	1250.	1850.	3250.
	1838 MV-A	—	850.00	2200.	3500.	5000.
	1839 MV-A	—	550.00	1000.	1750.	3000.
	1840 MV-A	—	450.00	750.00	1600.	2500.
	1841 MV-A	—	400.00	700.00	1500.	2250.

NOTE: Engravers initial A in front drape of bust.

Reduced size.

KM#	Date	Mintage	VG	Fine	VF	XF
23.2	1841 MV-S	—	750.00	2000.	3000.	4000.
	1842 MV-S	—	450.00	750.00	1550.	2500.
	1843 MV-S	—	450.00	750.00	1600.	2600.

NOTE: Engravers initial S sideways in back drape of bust.

KM#	Date	Mintage	VG	Fine	VF	XF
28	1844 MV	—	—	—	*Rare	—
	1845 MV	—	—	—	Rare	—

***NOTE:** Stack's Hammel sale 9-82 VF/G 1844 MV realized $32,000.

Obv: Flagpoles extend below arms.

KM#	Date	Mintage	VG	Fine	VF	XF
30	1845 MV	—	3000.	4500.	5750.	8500.

Obv: W/o flagpoles below arms.

KM#	Date	Mintage	VG	Fine	VF	XF
31	1845 MV	—	2500.	4000.	5500.	8500.

KM#	Date	Mintage	VG	Fine	VF	XF
34.1	1847 GJ	—	—	2250.	3250.	5000.
	1848 GJ	—	—	2500.	3500.	5500.
	1849/7 GJ	—	—	—	*Rare	—
	1849 GJ	—	—	Reported, not confirmed		
	1850 GJ	—	—	1800.	3000.	5000.
	1852/0 GJ	—	—	1200.	2000.	2500.
	1854 GJ	—	—	1500.	2250.	3500.
	1855/2 GJ	—	—	1000.	1750.	2150.
	1855 GJ	—	—	1500.	2150.	3250.

***NOTE:** Smith & Daughter sale No.2 9-96 choice AU realized $23,000.

Rev: Larger bust w/different hairstyle.

KM#	Date	Mintage	VG	Fine	VF	XF
34.2	1856 GJ	—	—	1500.	2250.	3500.

DECIMAL COINAGE

10 Centavos = 1 Decimo
10 Decimos = 1 Sucre
25 Sucres = 1 Condor

MEDIO (1/2) CENTAVO

COPPER-NICKEL
Mint mark: HEATON BIRMINGHAM

KM#	Date	Mintage	Fine	VF	XF	Unc
47	1884	.600	10.00	15.00	27.50	50.00
	1884	—	—	—	Proof	200.00
	1886	.400	—	Reported, not confirmed		

COPPER

KM#	Date	Mintage	Fine	VF	XF	Unc
54	1890H	2.000	8.00	15.00	30.00	60.00
		—	—	—	Proof	210.00

UN (1) CENTAVO

COPPER

KM#	Date	Mintage	Fine	VF	XF	Unc
45	1872HEATON		12.50	20.00	50.00	100.00
	1872HEATON		—	—	Proof	225.00
	1890H	2.000	6.00	12.00	25.00	75.00
	1890H	—	—	—	Proof	210.00

COPPER-NICKEL
Mint mark: HEATON BIRMINGHAM

KM#	Date	Mintage	Fine	VF	XF	Unc
48	1884	.500	7.50	20.00	45.00	100.00
	1884	—	—	—	Proof	210.00
	1886	1.000	5.00	12.50	25.00	55.00

DOS (2) CENTAVOS

COPPER
Mint mark: HEATON

KM#	Date	Mintage	Fine	VF	XF	Unc
46	1872	—	18.00	35.00	70.00	150.00
	1872	—	—	—	Proof	250.00

MEDIO (1/2) DECIMO

COPPER-NICKEL
Mint mark: HEATON. BIRMINGHAM.

KM#	Date	Mintage	Fine	VF	XF	Unc
49	1884	.600	8.50	17.50	35.00	75.00
	1884	—	—	—	Proof	200.00
	1886	.600	7.50	16.50	32.50	70.00
	1886	—	—	—	Proof	250.00

1.2500 g, .900 SILVER, .0361 oz ASW
Mint mark: LIMA

KM#	Date	Mintage	Fine	VF	XF	Unc
55.1	1893 TF rev: "G.1.250"					
		1.718	1.00	1.75	3.50	8.00
	1893 TF rev: "G.1:250"					
		Inc. Ab.	1.00	1.75	3.50	8.00
	1894/3 TF	.243	3.00	5.00	10.00	30.00
	1897 JF	.800	2.00	3.50	6.50	18.00
	1899/87 JF					
		.560	3.00	5.00	15.00	45.00
	1899 JF	I.A.	1.50	3.00	7.00	15.00
	1899 JF (error) obv: ECUADO.R					
		Inc. Ab.	1.50	3.00	10.00	25.00

NOTE: Later dates (1902-1912) exist for this type.

UN (1) DECIMO

2.5000 g, .900 SILVER, .0723 oz ASW
Mint mark: HEATON/BIRMINGHAM
Rev: LEI in legend.

KM#	Date	Mintage	VG	Fine	VF	XF
50.1	1884	.050	4.00	9.00	25.00	80.00
	1884	—	—	—	Proof	350.00
	1889	.100	2.00	5.00	18.00	40.00
	1890	.150	2.00	5.00	18.00	40.00
	1890	—	—	—	Proof	150.00

Mint mark: SANTIAGO-CHILE

KM#	Date	Mintage	VG	Fine	VF	XF
50.2	1889/789 DT					
		1.000	6.00	10.00	25.00	65.00
	1889 DT	I.A.	2.00	4.00	8.00	20.00

Mint mark: LIMA
Rev. leg: W/o LEY.

KM#	Date	Mintage	VG	Fine	VF	XF
50.3	1892 TF	.350	2.00	3.00	10.00	22.50
	1893 TF	.848	.75	1.75	3.00	7.00
	1894 TF	.206	.75	2.00	4.00	12.00
	1899/4 JF/TF					
		.220	2.00	3.00	8.00	20.00
	1899 JF	I.A.	3.00	6.00	15.00	42.50
	1900 F	—	—	—	—	—
	1900 JF/TF rev: w/JR below fasces					
		.480	2.00	3.50	7.00	17.50
	1900 JF	I.A.	1.00	2.50	5.00	10.00
	1900 JF rev: w/o JR below fasces					
		Inc. Ab.	2.00	3.00	6.00	12.50

NOTE: Later dates (1902-1912) exist for this type.

DOS (2) DECIMOS

5.0000 g, .900 SILVER, .1446 oz ASW
Mint mark: HEATON/BIRMINGHAM
Rev: LEI in legend.

KM#	Date	Mintage	VG	Fine	VF	XF
51.1	1884	.025	6.00	12.00	25.00	45.00
	1884	—	—	—	Proof	550.00
	1889	.050	6.00	12.00	27.50	50.00
	1890	.075	4.00	7.50	12.50	37.50
	1890	—	—	—	Proof	200.00

Mint mark: SANTIAGO-CHILE

KM#	Date	Mintage	VG	Fine	VF	XF
51.2	1889 DT	1.000	2.00	4.50	9.00	20.00
	1891 DT	.230	4.00	7.50	12.50	27.50

Mint mark: LIMA. or LIMA
Rev. leg: W/o LEY.

KM#	Date	Mintage	VG	Fine	VF	XF
51.3	1889 TF	.075	4.00	7.50	12.50	30.00
	1891/89 TF					
		.025	7.00	15.00	28.00	45.00
	1892/89 TF					
		1.138	2.00	4.00	7.50	18.00
	1892 TF	I.A.	6.00	12.00	25.00	40.00
	1893/89 TF					
		.390	2.50	6.00	10.00	25.00
	1894/89 TF					
		.409	2.00	5.00	8.00	20.00
	1895/89 TF					
		.160	3.00	5.00	8.00	20.00
	1895 TF	—	—	—	Proof	Rare
	1896/89 TF					
		.109	3.50	7.00	15.00	35.00

NOTE: Later dates (1912-1915) exist for this type.

Mint mark: PHILADELPHIA

KM#	Date	Mintage	VG	Fine	VF	XF
51.4	1895 TF	5.000	1.50	3.00	4.00	6.50
	1895 TF	—	—	—	Proof	500.00

NOTE: Later dates (1914-1916) exist for this type.

MEDIO (1/2) SUCRE

12.5000 g, .900 SILVER, .3617 oz ASW
Mint mark: HEATON/BIRMINGHAM

KM#	Date	Mintage	VG	Fine	VF	XF
52	1884	.020	25.00	40.00	75.00	250.00
	1884	—	—	—	Proof	2500.

UN (1) SUCRE

25.0000 g, .900 SILVER, .7234 oz ASW
Mint mark: HEATON/BIRMINGHAM

KM#	Date	Mintage	VG	Fine	VF	XF
53.1	1884	.250	6.50	12.50	22.00	45.00
	1884	—	—	—	Proof	2000.
	1888	.100	10.00	20.00	35.00	85.00
	1889	.150	6.50	12.50	22.00	45.00
	1890	.012	30.00	55.00	125.00	300.00
	1892	.060	20.00	35.00	65.00	150.00
	1895	.102	10.00	20.00	32.00	65.00

Mint mark: SANTIAGO-CHILE

KM#	Date	Mintage	VG	Fine	VF	XF
53.2	1888 DT	.373	6.50	12.50	25.00	55.00
	1889 DT	.327	6.50	12.50	25.00	55.00

Mint mark: LIMA

KM#	Date	Mintage	VG	Fine	VF	XF
53.3	1890 TF	.287	6.50	12.50	17.50	35.00
	1891 TF	.143	6.50	12.50	17.50	35.00
	1892 TF	.058	15.00	30.00	55.00	120.00
	1895 TF	.174	6.50	12.50	17.50	35.00
	1896 TF	.148	12.00	25.00	45.00	100.00
	1896 F	Inc. Ab.	10.00	20.00	40.00	90.00
	1897 JF	.462	6.50	12.50	17.50	35.00

DIEZ (10) SUCRES

8.1360 g, .900 GOLD, .2354 oz AGW
Mint mark: BIRMINGHAM

KM#	Date	Mintage	Fine	VF	XF	Unc
56	1899 JM	.050	100.00	125.00	150.00	285.00
	1900 JM	.050	100.00	125.00	150.00	285.00

PATTERNS (Pn)

(Including off metal strikes)

KM#	Date	Mintage	Identification	Mkt.Val.
PnA1	1832	—	2 Reales, Copper, KM14	—
PnE1	1833 GJ	—	1 Escudo, Silver, KM15, reeded edge, thick planchet	Unique
PnF1	1835 GJ	—	1 Escudo, Silver, KM15, plain edge, 1.92 g	1450.

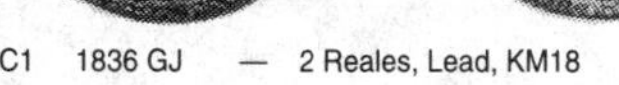

KM#	Date	Mintage	Identification	Mkt.Val.
PnC1	1836 GJ	—	2 Reales, Lead, KM18	300.00

KM#	Date	Mintage	Identification	Mkt.Val.
PnB1	1862 GJ	—	2 Reales, Silver	12,000.

KM#	Date	Mintage	Identification	Mkt.Val.
PnD1	1862	—	4 Reales	—

Pn1	1862	—	8 Reales, Silver, plain edge	Rare
Pn2	1862	—	8 Reales, Silver, reeded edge	Rare

Pn3	1862 GJ	—	50 Francos, .900 Gold	Unique

PROOF SETS (PS)

KM#	Date	Mintage	Identification	Issue Price	Mkt. Val.
PS1	1884(8)	—	KM50.1, 51.1, 52, 53.1 (2 of each)	—	Unique

GALAPAGOS ISLANDS

The Galapagos Islands, a territory of Ecuador situated in the Pacific Ocean 650 miles west of Ecuador, have an area of 3,028 sq. mi. (7,842 sq. km.) and a population of 3,100. Capital: San Cristobal, on the island of that name. The archipelago of more than 60 islands scattered over 23,000 sq. mi. of the Pacific was discovered by the Spaniards early in the 16th century, and became part of Ecuador in 1832. The islands are notable for their unique plant and animal life, including 15 species of giant tortoise which are the longest-lived animals on earth, with life spans of more than 200 years.

COUNTERMARKED COINAGE

c/m: Script RA on 1/2 Decimo, KM#55.

c/m: Script RA on 1 Decimo, KM#50.
c/m: Script RA on 2 Decimos, KM#51.
c/m: Script RA on 1/2 Sucre, KM#52.
c/m: Script RA on Un Sucre, KM#53.

Until recently the script RA countermarks, believed to be initials of a well-known merchant, Rogelio Alvarado, were attributed to the Galapagos Islands. The coins were said to have been used to pay prisoners in a penal colony. Without documentation, these pieces must be considered suspect.

EGYPT

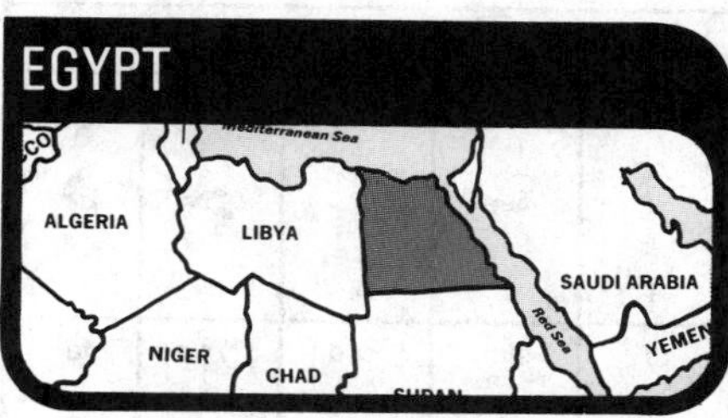

The Arab Republic of Egypt, located on the northeastern corner of Africa, has an area of 385,229 sq. mi. (1,1001,450 sq. km.) and a population of 62.4 million. Capital: Cairo. Although Egypt is an almost rainless expanse of desert, its economy is predominantly agricultural. Cotton, rice and petroleum are exported. Other main sources of income are revenues from the Suez Canal, remittances of Egyptian workers abroad and tourism.

Egyptian history dates back to about 3000 B.C. when the empire was established by uniting the upper and lower kingdoms. Following its 'Golden Age' (16th to 13th centuries B.C.), Egypt was conquered by Persia (525 B.C.) and Alexander the Great (332 B.C.). The Ptolemies, descended from one of Alexander's generals, ruled until the suicide of Cleopatra (30 B.C.) when Egypt became the private domain of the Roman emperor, and subsequently part of the Byzantine world. Various Muslim dynasties ruled Egypt from 641 on, including Ayyubid Sultans to 1250 and Mamluks to 1517, when it was conquered by the Ottoman Turks, interrupted by the occupation of Napoleon (1798-1801). A semi-independent dynasty was founded by Muhammad Ali in 1805 which lasted until 1952. Turkish rule became increasingly casual, permitting Great Britain to inject its influence by purchasing shares in the Suez Canal. British troops occupied Egypt in 1882, becoming the de facto rulers. On Dec. 14, 1914, Egypt was made a protectorate of Britain. British occupation ended on Feb. 28, 1922, when Egypt became a sovereign, independent kingdom. The monarchy was abolished and a republic proclaimed on July 23, 1952.

On Feb. 1, 1958, Egypt and Syria formed the United Arab Republic. Yemen joined on March 8 in an association known as the United Arab States. Syria withdrew from the United Arab Republic on Sept. 29, 1961, and on Dec. 26 Egypt dissolved its ties with Yemen in the United Arab States. On Sept. 2, 1971, Egypt finally shed the name United Arab Republic in favor of the Arab Republic of Egypt.

RULERS

Ottoman, until 1882

Local Viceroys

Muhammad Ali, 1805-1848
Ibrahim Pasha, 1848
Abbas I Pasha, 1848-1854
Sa'id Pasha, 1854-1863

Local Khedives

Isma'il Pasha, 1863-1879
Mohammed Tewfik Pasha, 1879-
British, 1882-1922

Local Khedives

Mohammed Tewfik Pasha, 1882-
Abbas II Hilmi, 1892-1914

MONETARY SYSTEM

40 Paras = 1 Qirsh (Piastre)
(1885-1916)

MINT MARKS

Egyptian coins issued prior to the advent of the British Protectorate series of Sultan Hussein Kamil introduced in 1916 were very similar to Turkish coins of the same period. They can best be distinguished by the presence of the Arabic word *Misr* (Egypt) on the reverse, which generally appears immediately above the Muslim accession date of the ruler, which is presented in Arabic numerals. Each coin is individually dated according to the regnal years.

BP - Budapest, Hungary
H - Birmingham, England
KN - King's Norton, England

ENGRAVER

W - Emil Weigand, Berlin

INITIAL LETTERS, NUMERALS

Alif	ba	ha	ha	dal
ا	ب	ح	حـ	د
i	ii	iii	iv	v
ra	sin	sad	(?) sm	ta
ر	س	ص	صم	ط
vi	vii	viii	ix	x
tha	'ain	(hamza)	kaf	mim
ظ	ع	ء	ق	م
xi	xii	xiii	xiv	xv
noon	noon w/o dot	ha	(?) ra	ah
ن	ں	ھ	ر	اح
xvi	xvii	xviii	xix	xx
es	ba	bkr	ha	raa
اس	با	بكر	حا	را
xxi	xxii	xxiii	xxiv	xxv
ragib	sma	msi	'aa	gha
راغب	سلا	صسے	عا	غا
xxvi	xxvii	xxviii	xxvix	xxx
'ab	'abd	'ad	'an	md
عب	عبد	عد	عن	مد
xxxi	xxxii	xxxiii	xxxiv	xxxv
mr	mk	mdm	mha	ha
مر	مط	مصر	مها	ده
xxxvi	xxxvii	xxxviii	xxxix	xl
ya	42a	md6	6md	6mdm
يا	١٣٤	مد٦	٦مد	٦مصر
xli	xlii	xliii	xliv	xlv

REGNAL YEAR IDENTIFICATION

4
Duriba fi

Misr Accession Date

DENOMINATIONS

Para *Qirsh*

NOTE: The unit of value on coins of this period is generally presented on the obverse immediately below the toughra, as shown in the illustrations above.

TITLES

المصرية

al-Mamlaka *al-Misriya*
(The Kingdom of Egypt)

OTTOMAN COINAGE

SELIM III

AH1203-1212, 1216-1222/
1789-1798, 1801-1807AD
R.Y. 1-12, 13-21

Toughra Types

First Second

First Toughra inscribed: *Han Selim bin-Mustafa al-Muzaffer Dai'ma.*
Second Toughra inscribed: *Selim Han bin-Mustafa al-Muzaffer Dai'ma.*

FIRST TOUGHRA SERIES

Heavy coinage based on a Piastre weighing approximately 19.20 g with first Toughra.

SECOND TOUGHRA SERIES

Light coinage based on a Piastre weighing approximately 12.80 g with second Toughra.

AKCE

BILLON, 0.15 g
Accession Date: AH1203

KM#	Year	Mintage	Good	VG	Fine	VF
133	15	—	— Reported, not confirmed			
	16	—	— Reported, not confirmed			

NOTE: Earlier dates (Yr. 1-11) reported for this type.

PARA

BILLON, 0.35 g
Accession Date: AH1203

KM#	Year	Mintage	Good	VG	Fine	VF
134	15	—	3.00	4.50	6.50	10.00
	16	—	3.00	4.50	6.50	10.00
	17	—	3.00	6.00	10.00	20.00
	18	—	3.00	6.00	10.00	20.00
	19	—	3.00	6.00	10.00	25.00
	20	—	3.00	6.00	10.00	35.00
	21	—	5.00	10.00	20.00	50.00
	22	—	—	—	—	—
	23	—	—	—	—	—

NOTE: Earlier dates (Yr. 1-12) exist for this type.

5 PARA

BILLON, 1.60 g
Accession Date: AH1203

KM#	Year	Mintage	Good	VG	Fine	VF
135	16	—	50.00	100.00	150.00	250.00

NOTE: Earlier date (Yr. 12) exists for this type.

10 PARA

BILLON, 2.45 g
Accession Date: AH1203

KM#	Year	Mintage	Good	VG	Fine	VF
136	16	—	300.00	600.00	1000.	1400.

20 PARA

BILLON, 27.5-29mm, 6.90 g
Accession Date: AH1203
Similar to 5 Para, KM#135.

KM#	Year	Mintage	Good	VG	Fine	VF
137	15	—	150.00	200.00	300.00	500.00
	16	—	120.00	180.00	250.00	400.00

QIRSH

(40 Para)

BILLON, 12.80 g
Accession Date: AH1203

KM#	Year	Mintage	Good	VG	Fine	VF
138	16	—	30.00	50.00	90.00	180.00

RUBIYA

(1/4 Zeri Mahbub)

GOLD, 16mm, 0.50-0.90 g
Accession Date: AH1203

KM#	Year	Mintage	Good	VG	Fine	VF
139	21	—	—	—	—	—
	ND	—	60.00	100.00	180.00	250.00

NOTE: Earlier date (Yr.3) exists for this type.

1/2 ZERI MAHBUB

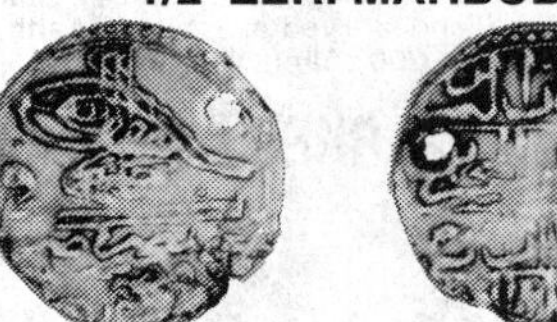

GOLD, 0.95-1.30 g
Accession Date: AH1203

KM#	Year	Mintage	VG	Fine	VF	XF
140	20	—	50.00	100.00	200.00	400.00
	21	—	50.00	100.00	200.00	400.00

NOTE: Earlier dates (Yr.2, 4) exist for this type.

ZERI MAHBUB

GOLD, 2.50-2.60 g
Accession Date: AH1203

KM#	Year	Mintage	VG	Fine	VF	XF
141	15	—	75.00	125.00	200.00	265.00
	16	—	75.00	125.00	200.00	265.00
	*'aleph-sin'	—	75.00	125.00	200.00	265.00
	*'sad'	—	75.00	125.00	200.00	265.00

***NOTE:** Initial letters.

NOTE: Earlier date (Yr.1) exists for this type.

2 ZERI MAHBUB

GOLD, 3.76-5.00 g
Accession Date: AH1203

KM#	Year	Mintage	VG	Fine	VF	XF
142	21	—	200.00	300.00	500.00	900.00
	*'aleph-sin'	—	200.00	300.00	500.00	900.00

***NOTE:** Initial letters.

OTTOMAN COINAGE

MUSTAFA IV

AH1222-1223/1807-1808AD

PARA

BILLON, 13-14mm, 0.20-0.40 g
Accession Date: AH1222
Obv: Toughra. Rev: Mintname above date.

KM#	Year	Mintage	Good	VG	Fine	VF
155	1	—	10.00	20.00	35.00	60.00

20 PARA

BILLON
Accession Date: AH1222

KM#	Year	Mintage	VG	Fine	VF	XF
156	1	—	500.00	800.00	1300.	2000.

QIRSH

(40 Para)

BILLON, 10.65 g
Accession Date: AH1222

KM#	Year	Mintage	VG	Fine	VF	XF
157	1	—	550.00	1000.	1800.	3100.

1/2 ZERI MAHBUB

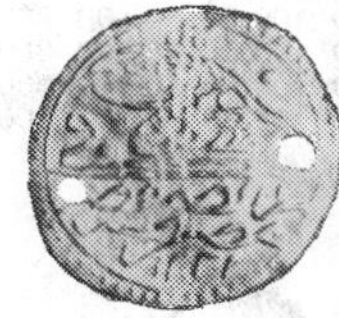

GOLD, 20mm, 1.65 g
Accession Date: AH1222

KM#	Year	Mintage	VG	Fine	VF	XF
158	1	—	350.00	500.00	800.00	1200.

ZERI MAHBUB

GOLD, 2.30 g
Accession Date: AH1222

KM#	Year	Mintage	VG	Fine	VF	XF
159	1	—	275.00	400.00	700.00	1000.

2 ZERI MAHBUB

GOLD, 32mm, 4.70 g
Accession Date: AH1222

KM#	Year	Mintage	VG	Fine	VF	XF
160	1	—	400.00	600.00	900.00	1500.

MAHMUD II

AH1223-1255/1808-1839AD

ASPER

BRASS, uniface
Accession Date: AH1223

KM#	Year	Mintage	Good	VG	Fine	VF
—	—	—	50.00	80.00	110.00	150.00

NOTE: The precise status of this piece is undetermined.

AKCHEH

BILLON, 11-12mm, 0.10-0.13 g
Accession Date: AH1223

KM#	Year	Mintage	Good	VG	Fine	VF
A161	16	—	1.00	2.00	3.00	10.00
	17	—	1.00	2.00	3.00	10.00
	18	—	1.00	2.00	3.00	10.00
	19	—	1.00	2.00	3.00	10.00
	20	—	1.00	2.00	3.00	10.00
	21	—	1.00	2.00	3.00	10.00

PARA

BILLON, 12-15mm, 0.15-0.28 g
Accession Date: AH1223

KM#	Year	Mintage	Good	VG	Fine	VF
161	1	—	.75	1.50	4.00	8.50
	2	—	.75	1.50	4.00	8.50
	3	—	.75	1.50	4.00	8.50
	4	—	.75	1.50	4.00	.8.50
	5	—	.75	1.50	4.00	8.50
	6	—	.75	1.50	4.00	8.50
	7	—	.75	1.50	4.00	8.50
	8	—	.75	1.50	4.00	8.50
	9	—	.75	1.50	4.00	8.50
	10	—	.75	1.50	4.00	8.50
	11	—	.75	1.50	4.00	8.50
	12	—	.75	1.50	4.00	8.50
	13	—	.75	1.50	4.00	8.50
	14	—	.75	1.50	4.00	8.50
	15	—	.75	1.50	4.00	8.50
	16	—	.75	1.50	4.00	8.50
	17	—	1.00	3.00	10.00	15.00
	18	—	1.00	3.00	10.00	15.00
	19	—	2.00	4.00	15.00	20.00
	20	—	—	—	—	—
	21	—	Reported, not confirmed			
	25	—	—	—	—	—

COPPER

KM#	Year	Mintage	Good	VG	Fine	VF
162	28	—	8.00	20.00	45.00	100.00
	29	—	8.00	20.00	45.00	100.00

15mm

KM#	Year	Mintage	Good	VG	Fine	VF
163	29	—	8.00	20.00	45.00	100.00

NOTE: KM#163 does not bear any denomination.

15-17mm

KM#	Year	Mintage	Good	VG	Fine	VF
164	29	—	8.00	20.00	45.00	100.00
	30	—	8.00	20.00	45.00	100.00
	31	—	8.00	20.00	45.00	100.00
	32	—	8.00	20.00	45.00	100.00

5 PARA

BILLON, 15-16mm., 0.50-0.70 g
Accession Date: AH1223

KM#	Year	Mintage	Good	VG	Fine	VF
165	5	—	15.00	20.00	40.00	80.00
	6	—	15.00	20.00	40.00	80.00
	7	—	15.00	20.00	40.00	80.00
	8	—	15.00	20.00	40.00	80.00
	9	—	10.00	15.00	35.00	65.00
	10	—	10.00	15.00	35.00	65.00
	11	—	10.00	15.00	35.00	65.00
	12	—	10.00	15.00	35.00	65.00
	13	—	10.00	15.00	35.00	65.00
	14	—	10.00	15.00	35.00	65.00
	15	—	10.00	15.00	35.00	65.00
	16	—	10.00	15.00	35.00	65.00
	17	—	10.00	15.00	35.00	65.00
	18	—	10.00	15.00	35.00	65.00
	19	—	10.00	15.00	35.00	65.00
	20	—	10.00	15.00	35.00	65.00
	21	—	10.00	15.00	35.00	65.00

Obv. and rev: Beaded circle around toughra and legend.

KM#	Year	Mintage	Good	VG	Fine	VF
A166	18	—	35.00	60.00	120.00	200.00

14mm., 0.40 g
Obv: Rose added to right of toughra.

KM#	Year	Mintage	Good	VG	Fine	VF
166	21	—	7.00	20.00	40.00	80.00
	22	—	5.00	15.00	30.00	60.00
	23	—	5.00	15.00	30.00	60.00
	24	—	5.00	15.00	30.00	60.00
	25	—	5.00	15.00	30.00	60.00
	26	—	7.00	20.00	40.00	80.00
	27	—	45.00	70.00	120.00	185.00
	28	—	45.00	70.00	120.00	185.00

COPPER, 22-24mm, 6.14-7.41 g

Floral designs in wreath.

KM#	Year	Mintage	Good	VG	Fine	VF
167	28	—	5.00	10.00	20.00	40.00
	29	—	5.00	10.00	20.00	40.00

W/o wreath and denomination.

KM#	Year	Mintage	Good	VG	Fine	VF
168.1	29	—	15.00	25.00	40.00	75.00

Rev: Larger legend.

KM#	Year	Mintage	Good	VG	Fine	VF
168.2	29	—	15.00	25.00	40.00	75.00

Obv: Denomination added below toughra.

KM#	Year	Mintage	Good	VG	Fine	VF
169	29	—	2.00	5.00	10.00	20.00
	30	—	2.00	5.00	10.00	20.00
	31	—	2.00	5.00	10.00	20.00
	32	—	3.00	7.00	15.00	25.00

10 PARA

BILLON, 17-18mm., 0.90-1.40 g
Accession Date: AH1223
Plain dotted borders.

KM#	Year	Mintage	Good	VG	Fine	VF
170.1	8	—	20.00	40.00	80.00	150.00
	9	—	10.00	20.00	50.00	90.00
	10	—	10.00	20.00	50.00	90.00
	11	—	10.00	20.00	50.00	90.00
	12	—	10.00	20.00	50.00	90.00
	15	—	10.00	20.00	50.00	90.00
	—	—	—	—	Rare	—

NOTE: Border varieties exist.

Ornate borders.

KM#	Year	Mintage	Good	VG	Fine	VF
170.2	18	—	5.00	15.00	35.00	65.00
	19	—	5.00	15.00	35.00	65.00
	20	—	5.00	15.00	35.00	65.00
	21	—	5.00	15.00	35.00	65.00

0.75-0.78 g
Wavy borders.

KM#	Year	Mintage	Good	VG	Fine	VF
171	21	—	6.00	15.00	25.00	50.00
	22	—	5.00	12.50	20.00	40.00
	23	—	5.00	12.50	20.00	40.00
	24	—	5.00	12.50	20.00	40.00
	25	—	5.00	12.50	20.00	40.00
	26	—	13.50	30.00	75.00	150.00
	27	—	25.00	55.00	120.00	200.00

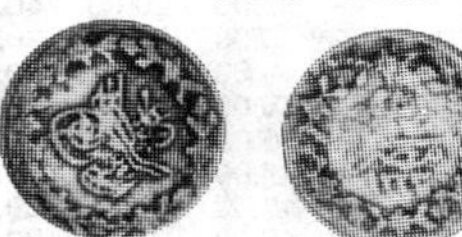

Obv: *Adli* right of toughra.
Wreath borders, 12mm, 0.30 g

KM#	Year	Mintage	Good	VG	Fine	VF
172	28	—	30.00	60.00	135.00	275.00
	29	—	25.00	45.00	95.00	185.00

NOTE: Varieties exist.

.833 SILVER, 14mm, 0.35 g

Obv: Denomination below toughra.

KM#	Year	Mintage	VG	Fine	VF	XF
173	29	—	50.00	100.00	180.00	300.00
	30	—	50.00	100.00	180.00	300.00
	31	—	50.00	100.00	180.00	300.00
	32	—	50.00	100.00	180.00	300.00

20 PARA

BILLON, 22-24mm, 2.40-3.80 g
Accession Date: AH1223
Rev: Date.

KM#	Year	Mintage	Good	VG	Fine	VF
174	1	—	65.00	115.00	200.00	300.00
	5	—	45.00	65.00	100.00	150.00
	6	—	45.00	65.00	100.00	150.00
	7	—	45.00	65.00	100.00	150.00
	8	—	45.00	65.00	100.00	150.00
	9	—	45.00	65.00	100.00	150.00
	10	—	45.00	65.00	100.00	150.00
	11	—	45.00	65.00	100.00	150.00

Obv: Mintname and date below toughra.

KM#	Year	Mintage	Good	VG	Fine	VF
175	5	—	50.00	100.00	200.00	400.00

21mm, 1.38-1.62 g

KM#	Year	Mintage	Good	VG	Fine	VF
176	21	—	20.00	35.00	60.00	100.00
	22	—	20.00	35.00	60.00	100.00
	23	—	20.00	35.00	60.00	100.00
	24	—	20.00	35.00	60.00	100.00
	25	—	20.00	35.00	60.00	100.00
	26	—	40.00	80.00	150.00	250.00
	27	—	40.00	65.00	100.00	150.00

15mm, 0.58-0.62 g
Obv: *Adli* right of toughra.

KM#	Year	Mintage	Good	VG	Fine	VF
177	28	—	12.00	25.00	70.00	120.00
	29	—	12.00	25.00	70.00	120.00

NOTE: Varieties exist.

.833 SILVER, 15-16mm, 0.68-0.70 g
Obv: Denomination below toughra.

KM#	Year	Mintage	VG	Fine	VF	XF
178	29	—	20.00	40.00	80.00	160.00
	30	—	20.00	40.00	80.00	160.00
	31	—	20.00	40.00	80.00	160.00
	32	—	20.00	40.00	80.00	160.00

QIRSH

BILLON, 29-31mm, 9.20 g
Accession Date: AH1223

KM#	Year	Mintage	Good	VG	Fine	VF
179.1	1	—	25.00	50.00	100.00	150.00

BILLON, 7.00 g

KM#	Year	Mintage	Good	VG	Fine	VF
179.2	3	—	15.00	40.00	50.00	100.00
	5	—	15.00	40.00	50.00	100.00
	6	—	12.50	30.00	45.00	80.00
	7	—	12.50	30.00	45.00	80.00
	8	—	15.00	35.00	50.00	90.00

NOTE: Varieties exist.

Obv: Flower right of toughra.

KM#	Year	Mintage	Good	VG	Fine	VF
179.3	7	—	—	—	Rare	—

Obv: Mintname and date below toughra.

KM#	Year	Mintage	Good	VG	Fine	VF
180	5	—	40.00	70.00	140.00	250.00

(Yeni Kurus)

2.67-3.15 g
Wavy borders, 26-27mm.

KM#	Year	Mintage	Good	VG	Fine	VF
181	21	—	10.00	20.00	45.00	75.00
	22	—	10.00	20.00	45.00	75.00
	23	—	10.00	20.00	45.00	75.00
	24	—	10.00	20.00	45.00	75.00
	25	—	10.00	20.00	45.00	75.00
	26	—	10.00	20.00	45.00	75.00
	27	—	15.00	25.00	50.00	100.00

NOTE: For coins w/accession date 1213H, 1223H, and regnal year 13, see Danfur.

19mm, 1.00-1.31 g
Obv: *Adli* right of toughra.
Wreath borders

KM#	Year	Mintage	Good	VG	Fine	VF
182	28	—	15.00	20.00	45.00	65.00
	29	—	15.00	20.00	45.00	65.00

NOTE: Varieties exist.

.833 SILVER, 19-20mm, 1.40 g
Obv: Denomination below toughra.

KM#	Year	Mintage	VG	Fine	VF	XF
183	29	—	15.00	45.00	75.00	125.00

KM#	Year	Mintage	VG	Fine	VF	XF
183	30	—	15.00	45.00	75.00	125.00
	31	—	15.00	45.00	75.00	125.00
	32	—	15.00	45.00	75.00	125.00

5 QIRSH

.833 SILVER, 24-26mm, 7.00 g
Accession Date: AH1223

KM#	Year	Mintage	VG	Fine	VF	XF
184	29	—	100.00	200.00	600.00	900.00
	30	—	200.00	300.00	600.00	900.00
	31	—	200.00	300.00	600.00	900.00

10 QIRSH

.833 SILVER, 30mm, 13.75-14.00 g
Accession Date: AH1223

KM#	Year	Mintage	VG	Fine	VF	XF
185	29	—	—	—	6500.	7500.

20 QIRSH

.833 SILVER, 37mm, 27.15-28.06 g
Accession Date: AH1223

KM#	Year	Mintage	VG	Fine	VF	XF
186	29	—	400.00	700.00	1000.	1450.
	30	—	425.00	750.00	1250.	1650.
	31	—	350.00	650.00	900.00	1350.
	32	—	550.00	900.00	1400.	1900.

GOLD COINAGE

NOTE: The following listings are incomplete, and any information about additional dates, years and types would be appreciated.

PRE-REFORM COINAGE

Prior to AH1251 (1834AD)

The basic unit was the 'Mahbub' or 'Zer Mahbub' (Zer = Gold), which weighed approximately 2.35 g from AH1223 until 1247 (Yr. 15), when it was reduced to about 1.6 g. Fractional denominations were Halves (Nisfiya) and Quarters (Rubiya). The value of the Mahbub in terms of silver Piastres fluctuated according to the relative value of gold and silver, and the price of debased Egyptian silver coin.

1/4 MAHBUB

(Rubiya)

.875 GOLD, 13-14mm, 0.35-0.60 g
Accession Date: AH1223
Plain borders of dots
Rev. leg: *Azze Nasruhu Duribe Fi. . .*

KM#	Year	Mintage	VG	Fine	VF	XF
189	—	—	150.00	225.00	300.00	450.00

KM#	Year	Mintage	VG	Fine	VF	XF
190	7	—	40.00	60.00	85.00	110.00
	8	—	40.00	60.00	85.00	110.00
	9	—	40.00	60.00	85.00	110.00
	10	—	40.00	60.00	85.00	110.00
	11	—	40.00	60.00	85.00	110.00
	12	—	40.00	60.00	85.00	110.00
	13	—	40.00	60.00	85.00	110.00
	14	—	40.00	60.00	85.00	110.00

12-13mm, 0.35-0.40 g
Plain borders of dots.

KM#	Year	Mintage	VG	Fine	VF	XF
191	15	—	25.00	40.00	60.00	85.00
	16	—	17.50	27.50	45.00	65.00
	17	—	25.00	40.00	60.00	85.00
	18	—	17.50	27.50	45.00	65.00
	19	—	20.00	35.00	55.00	80.00
	20	—	20.00	35.00	55.00	80.00
	21	—	20.00	35.00	55.00	80.00

(Saadiya)

Ornamental borders

KM#	Year	Mintage	VG	Fine	VF	XF
192	19	—	30.00	50.00	65.00	75.00
	20	—	40.00	65.00	90.00	115.00
	21	—	60.00	90.00	115.00	140.00

(Coyrek Rumi)

Vine-like borders

KM#	Year	Mintage	VG	Fine	VF	XF
193	21	—	25.00	35.00	50.00	100.00
	22	—	25.00	35.00	50.00	100.00
	23	—	25.00	35.00	50.00	100.00
	24	—	25.00	35.00	50.00	100.00
	25	—	25.00	35.00	50.00	100.00
	26	—	20.00	30.00	40.00	90.00
	27	—	30.00	40.00	70.00	150.00
	28	—	100.00	175.00	275.00	375.00

Different design and w/o year.

KM#	Year	Mintage	VG	Fine	VF	XF
201	—	—	—	—	—	—

1/2 ZERI MAHBUB

(Nisfiya)

.875 GOLD, 19-20mm, 1.15-1.20 g
Accession Date: AH1223

KM#	Year	Mintage	VG	Fine	VF	XF
194	1	—	85.00	140.00	350.00	650.00
	5	—	85.00	140.00	350.00	650.00
	8	—	85.00	140.00	350.00	650.00

(Khayriya)

.875 GOLD, 16mm, 0.70-0.80 g

KM#	Year	Mintage	VG	Fine	VF	XF
195	21	—	20.00	30.00	75.00	150.00
	22	—	20.00	30.00	60.00	125.00
	23	—	20.00	30.00	60.00	125.00
	24	—	20.00	30.00	60.00	125.00
	25	—	20.00	30.00	60.00	125.00
	26	—	20.00	30.00	75.00	150.00
	27	—	30.00	40.00	100.00	200.00
	28	—	40.00	50.00	125.00	250.00

ZERI MAHBUB

(Altin)

.875 GOLD, 23-26mm, 2.19-2.38 g, crude flan
Accession Date: AH1223

KM#	Year	Mintage	VG	Fine	VF	XF
197	1	—	90.00	175.00	350.00	600.00
	1 dot right of toughra					
		—	—	—	—	—
	2	—	100.00	200.00	400.00	750.00
	3	—	90.00	175.00	350.00	600.00
	5	—	90.00	175.00	350.00	600.00
	7	—	150.00	250.00	425.00	800.00
	8	—	150.00	250.00	425.00	800.00
	10 dot next to toughra					
		—	150.00	250.00	425.00	800.00
	10 rose branch next to toughra					
		—	180.00	300.00	425.00	800.00
	11	—	90.00	175.00	350.00	600.00
	12 rose branch right of toughra					
		—	—	—	—	—
	13	—	150.00	250.00	350.00	600.00
	14	—	90.00	175.00	350.00	600.00

23mm, 2.35 g, thicker & well-shaped flan

KM#	Year	Mintage	VG	Fine	VF	XF
198	15	—	120.00	220.00	425.00	1000.

W/o *Azza Nashruhu.*

KM#	Year	Mintage	VG	Fine	VF	XF
199	5	—	100.00	200.00	375.00	700.00

2 ZERI MAHBUB

.875 GOLD, 28mm, 3.25-3.60 g
Accession Date: AH1223

KM#	Year	Mintage	VG	Fine	VF	XF
200	5	—	300.00	500.00	850.00	1750.

NOTE: The above piece may be a medal or token.

TEK RUMI

GOLD, 23mm, 2.35 g
Accession Date: AH1223
Similar to 1/4 Mahbub, KM#193.

KM#	Year	Mintage	VG	Fine	VF	XF
202	11	—	—	—	Rare	—

CHIFTE RUMI

GOLD, 28mm, 3.60 g
Accession Date: AH1223
Similar to 1/4 Mahbub, KM#193.

KM#	Year	Mintage	VG	Fine	VF	XF
203	5	—	—	—	Rare	—

NOUSF or 1/2 MISRIYA

(10 Qirsh)

.875 GOLD, 0.70-0.75 g
Accession Date: AH1223

KM#	Year	Mintage	VG	Fine	VF	XF
213	28	—	30.00	50.00	125.00	200.00
	29	—	30.00	50.00	125.00	200.00

REFORMED COINAGE

AH1251-1326/1834-1908AD

5 QIRSH

(Rubiya, or 1/4 Misriya)

.875 GOLD, 0.30-0.35 g
Accession Date: AH1223

KM#	Year	Mintage	VG	Fine	VF	XF
210	28	—	85.00	140.00	215.00	325.00
	29	—	60.00	100.00	150.00	250.00

0.42 g
Obv: W/o value below toughra.

KM#	Year	Mintage	VG	Fine	VF	XF
211	29	—	60.00	100.00	150.00	250.00

Obv: Denomination added below toughra.

KM#	Year	Mintage	VG	Fine	VF	XF
212	29	—	65.00	100.00	150.00	200.00
	30	—	65.00	100.00	150.00	200.00
	31	—	65.00	100.00	150.00	200.00
	32	—	65.00	100.00	150.00	200.00

10 QIRSH

(Nousf or 1/2 Misriya)

.875 GOLD, 15mm, 0.85 g
Obv: Denomination beneath toughra.

KM#	Year	Mintage	VG	Fine	VF	XF
214	29	—	65.00	100.00	200.00	350.00
	30	—	65.00	100.00	200.00	350.00
	32	—	65.00	100.00	200.00	350.00

20 QIRSH

(Misriya)

.875 GOLD, 18mm, 1.70 g
Accession Date: AH1223

KM#	Year	Mintage	VG	Fine	VF	XF
215	29	—	60.00	100.00	150.00	300.00
	30	—	60.00	100.00	150.00	300.00
	31	—	60.00	100.00	150.00	300.00
	32	—	60.00	100.00	150.00	300.00

Obv. and rev: 4 roses around edge.

KM#	Year	Mintage	VG	Fine	VF	XF
216	32	—	75.00	125.00	200.00	400.00

100 QIRSH

(1 Pound)

.875 GOLD, 22mm, 8.40 g
Accession Date: AH1223

KM#	Year	Mintage	VG	Fine	VF	XF
217	30	—	750.00	1000.	2000.	3000.
	31	—	750.00	1000.	2000.	3000.

ABDUL MEJID

AH1255-1277/1839-1861AD

PARA

COPPER, 16mm, 1.20 g
Accession Date: AH1255

KM#	Year	Mintage	Good	VG	Fine	VF
220	1	—	12.00	30.00	75.00	150.00
	2	—	10.00	20.00	50.00	100.00
	4	—	10.00	20.00	50.00	100.00
	5	—	10.00	20.00	50.00	100.00
	6	—	10.00	20.00	50.00	100.00
	7	—	—	—	Unique	—
	Common date		—	—	Unc	400.00

15mm

KM#	Year	Mintage	Good	VG	Fine	VF
221	8	—	—	—	Rare	—

5 PARA

COPPER, 21mm, 6.40 g
Accession Date: AH1255

KM#	Year	Mintage	Good	VG	Fine	VF
222	1	—	1.00	2.00	5.00	12.50
	2	—	1.00	2.00	5.00	12.50
	3	—	1.00	2.00	5.00	12.50
	4	—	1.00	2.00	5.00	12.50
	5	—	1.00	2.00	5.00	12.50
	6	—	1.00	2.00	5.00	12.50

NOTE: Varieties of size of toughra exist.

KM#	Year	Mintage	Good	VG	Fine	VF
223	6	—	2.00	3.00	7.50	17.00
	7	—	1.00	2.00	5.00	16.00
	8	—	4.50	8.50	15.00	27.50

Similar to KM#224.2.

KM#	Year	Mintage	Good	VG	Fine	VF
224.1	8	—	4.00	10.00	20.00	35.00

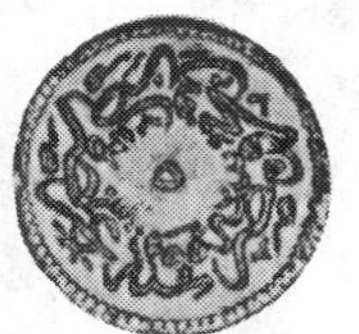

KM#	Year	Mintage	Good	VG	Fine	VF
224.2	10	—	Reported, not confirmed			
	12	—	Reported, not confirmed			
	13	—	2.00	5.00	12.50	25.00
	14	—	1.00	2.50	10.00	20.00
	15	—	1.00	2.00	7.50	15.00
	16	—	1.00	2.00	7.50	15.00
	Common date		—	—	Unc	45.00

10 PARA

.833 SILVER, 15mm, 0.37 g
Accession Date: AH1255

KM#	Year	Mintage	VG	Fine	VF	XF
225	1	—	15.00	30.00	60.00	90.00
	2	—	15.00	30.00	60.00	75.00
	3	—	12.50	25.00	50.00	75.00
	4	—	12.50	25.00	50.00	75.00
	5	—	12.50	25.00	50.00	75.00
	6	—	12.50	25.00	50.00	75.00
	7	—	12.50	25.00	50.00	75.00
	8	—	12.50	25.00	50.00	75.00
	9	—	12.50	25.00	50.00	75.00
	10	—	15.00	30.00	60.00	90.00
	11	—	15.00	30.00	60.00	90.00
	12	—	15.00	30.00	60.00	90.00
	13	—	30.00	60.00	120.00	180.00
	14	—	15.00	30.00	60.00	90.00
	15	—	15.00	30.00	60.00	90.00
	18	—	17.50	35.00	65.00	100.00
	19	—	17.50	35.00	65.00	100.00
	20	—	17.50	35.00	65.00	100.00
	21	—	— Reported, not confirmed			
	22	—	17.50	35.00	65.00	100.00
	23	—	15.00	30.00	60.00	90.00

COPPER, 29mm, 12.90 g

KM#	Year	Mintage	Good	VG	Fine	VF
226	15	—	4.50	8.00	15.00	45.00
	16	—	6.00	15.00	22.00	60.00

NOTE: Varieties of size of toughra exist.

20 PARA

.833 SILVER, 16mm, 0.68 g
Accession Date: AH1255

KM#	Year	Mintage	VG	Fine	VF	XF
227	1	—	15.00	30.00	50.00	75.00
	2	—	15.00	30.00	50.00	75.00
	3	—	15.00	30.00	50.00	75.00
	4/3	—	17.50	35.00	60.00	90.00
	4	—	15.00	30.00	50.00	75.00
	5	—	15.00	30.00	50.00	75.00
	6	—	15.00	30.00	50.00	75.00
	7	—	15.00	30.00	50.00	75.00
	8	—	15.00	30.00	50.00	75.00
	9	—	15.00	30.00	50.00	75.00
	10	—	15.00	30.00	50.00	75.00
	11	—	17.50	35.00	60.00	90.00
	12	—	17.50	35.00	60.00	90.00

KM#	Year	Mintage	VG	Fine	VF	XF
227	13	—	17.50	35.00	60.00	90.00
	14	—	17.50	35.00	60.00	90.00
	15	—	17.50	35.00	60.00	90.00
	18/6	—	20.00	40.00	70.00	110.00
	18	—	20.00	40.00	70.00	110.00
	19	—	30.00	60.00	90.00	150.00
	20	—	20.00	40.00	70.00	110.00
	21	—	20.00	40.00	70.00	110.00
	22	—	20.00	40.00	70.00	110.00
	23	—	17.50	35.00	60.00	90.00
	Common date		—	—	Unc	150.00

QIRSH

.833 SILVER, 19mm, 1.42 g
Accession Date: AH1255

KM#	Year	Mintage	VG	Fine	VF	XF
228	1	—	15.00	30.00	50.00	85.00
	2	—	15.00	30.00	50.00	85.00
	3	—	15.00	30.00	50.00	85.00
	4	—	17.50	35.00	60.00	100.00
	5	—	15.00	30.00	50.00	85.00
	6	—	15.00	30.00	50.00	85.00
	7	—	17.50	35.00	60.00	100.00
	8/7	—	17.50	35.00	60.00	100.00
	8	—	17.50	35.00	60.00	100.00
	9	—	17.50	35.00	60.00	100.00
	10	—	17.50	35.00	60.00	100.00
	11	—	17.50	35.00	60.00	100.00
	12	—	17.50	35.00	60.00	100.00
	13	—	17.50	35.00	60.00	100.00
	14	—	17.50	35.00	60.00	100.00
	15	—	17.50	35.00	60.00	100.00
	16	—	17.50	35.00	60.00	100.00
	17	—	22.50	45.00	75.00	125.00
	18	—	22.50	45.00	75.00	125.00
	19	—	22.50	45.00	75.00	125.00
	20	—	22.50	45.00	75.00	125.00
	21	—	— Reported, not confirmed			
	22	—	22.50	45.00	75.00	125.00
	23	—	17.50	35.00	65.00	110.00
	Common date		—	—	Unc	150.00

5 QIRSH

.833 SILVER, 25-26mm, 6.80-7.00 g
Accession Date: AH1255

KM#	Year	Mintage	VG	Fine	VF	XF
229	1	—	150.00	250.00	500.00	800.00
	2	—	150.00	250.00	500.00	800.00
	3	—	150.00	250.00	500.00	800.00
	4	—	150.00	250.00	500.00	800.00
	5	—	150.00	250.00	500.00	800.00
	6	—	150.00	250.00	500.00	800.00
	16	—	200.00	300.00	750.00	1250.
	23	—	— Reported, not confirmed			

.875 GOLD, 0.427 g

KM#	Year	Mintage	VG	Fine	VF	XF
230	1	—	17.50	30.00	45.00	85.00
	2	—	17.50	30.00	45.00	85.00
	3	—	17.50	30.00	45.00	85.00
	4	—	17.50	30.00	45.00	85.00
	5	—	17.50	30.00	45.00	85.00
	6	—	17.50	30.00	45.00	85.00
	7	—	17.50	30.00	45.00	85.00
	8	—	17.50	30.00	45.00	85.00
	9	—	17.50	30.00	45.00	85.00
	10	—	17.50	30.00	45.00	85.00
	11	—	17.50	30.00	45.00	85.00
	12	—	17.50	30.00	45.00	85.00
	13	—	22.50	37.50	60.00	125.00
	14	—	17.50	30.00	45.00	85.00
	15	—	17.50	30.00	45.00	85.00
	16	—	17.50	30.00	45.00	85.00
	18	—	17.50	30.00	45.00	85.00
	19	—	17.50	30.00	45.00	85.00
	20	—	17.50	30.00	45.00	85.00
	22	—	17.50	30.00	45.00	85.00
	23	—	17.50	30.00	45.00	85.00

10 QIRSH

.833 SILVER, 29-30mm, 13.60-14.00 g
Accession Date: AH1255

KM#	Year	Mintage	VG	Fine	VF	XF
231	1	—	200.00	350.00	800.00	1500.
	2	—	175.00	350.00	800.00	1500.
	3	—	175.00	350.00	800.00	1500.
	4	—	175.00	350.00	800.00	1500.
	5	—	200.00	350.00	800.00	1500.
	6	—	240.00	400.00	900.00	1800.
	10	—	—	Reported, not confirmed		
	16	—	—	Reported, not confirmed		
	Common date		—	—	Unc	2000.

NOTE: Oblique or vertical milled edges.

.875 GOLD, 15mm, 0.840 g

KM#	Year	Mintage	VG	Fine	VF	XF
231a	1	—	—	—	—	—

20 QIRSH

.833 SILVER, 36-38mm, 27.70-28.00 g
Accession Date: AH1255

KM#	Year	Mintage	VG	Fine	VF	XF
232	1	—	350.00	600.00	1100.	1500.
	2	—	325.00	575.00	1100.	1500.
	3	—	375.00	650.00	1250.	1750.
	4	—	325.00	575.00	1100.	1500.
	Common date		—	—	Unc	3400.

.875 GOLD, 1.71 g

KM#	Year	Mintage	VG	Fine	VF	XF
233	1	—	400.00	650.00	1000.	1750.

50 QIRSH

(1/2 Pound)

.875 GOLD, 4.274 g
Accession Date: AH1255
Beaded border.

KM#	Year	Mintage	VG	Fine	VF	XF
234.1	1	550 pcs.	200.00	300.00	600.00	800.00
	2	—	100.00	150.00	300.00	500.00
	3	—	100.00	125.00	250.00	400.00
	4	—	75.00	100.00	200.00	300.00
	5	—	75.00	100.00	200.00	300.00

Toothed border.

KM#	Year	Mintage	VG	Fine	VF	XF
234.2	6	—	75.00	125.00	250.00	400.00
	7	—	75.00	150.00	300.00	500.00
	8	—	75.00	150.00	300.00	500.00
234.2	11	—	75.00	150.00	300.00	500.00
	15	—	40.00	75.00	150.00	250.00
	16	—	75.00	100.00	200.00	350.00

100 QIRSH

(1 Pound)

8.5440 g, .875 GOLD, .2404 oz AGW
Accession Date: AH1255
Beaded border.

KM#	Year	Mintage	VG	Fine	VF	XF
235.1	1	—	BV	200.00	300.00	500.00
	2	—	BV	150.00	250.00	475.00
	3	—	BV	125.00	225.00	450.00
	4	—	BV	115.00	200.00	400.00
	5	—	BV	115.00	200.00	400.00

NOTE: For crude copy of regnal year 2 see Sudan Y#3.

Toothed border.

KM#	Year	Mintage	VG	Fine	VF	XF
235.2	6	—	BV	115.00	125.00	275.00
	7	—	BV	125.00	150.00	350.00
	8	—	BV	125.00	150.00	350.00
	9	—	135.00	200.00	240.00	500.00
	10	—	135.00	200.00	240.00	500.00
	11	—	BV	125.00	150.00	350.00
	12	—	BV	125.00	150.00	350.00
	13	—	BV	125.00	150.00	350.00
	14	—	BV	125.00	150.00	350.00
	15	—	BV	115.00	125.00	250.00
	16	—	BV	115.00	135.00	275.00
	17	—	BV	125.00	150.00	350.00
	18	—	—	Reported, not confirmed		

ABDUL AZIZ

AH1277-1293/1861-1876AD

4 PARA

BRONZE, 22mm, 2.26 g
Accession Date: AH1277

KM#	Year	Mintage	Fine	VF	XF	Unc
240	4	—	3.50	7.50	15.00	30.00

10 PARA

BRONZE, 30mm, 6.10-6.60 g
Accession Date: AH1277
Obv: W/o flower at right of toughra.

KM#	Year	Mintage	Fine	VF	XF	Unc
241	4	—	1.00	2.50	10.00	25.00
	5	—	1.00	2.50	10.00	25.00
	6	—	2.00	3.50	12.00	35.00
	7	—	2.00	3.50	12.00	40.00
	9	—	1.00	2.50	10.00	25.00
	10	—	2.00	3.50	12.00	35.00

COPPER, 5.80 g
Obv: Flower added at right of toughra.

KM#	Year	Mintage	Fine	VF	XF	Unc
242	8	.204	400.00	700.00	1550.	—
	9	—	300.00	600.00	1400.	—
	11	200 pcs.	—	—	—	5000.

.833 SILVER, 16mm, 0.29-0.33 g

KM#	Year	Mintage	Fine	VF	XF	Unc
243	2	—	20.00	40.00	70.00	160.00
	3	—	15.00	25.00	50.00	125.00
	4	—	15.00	25.00	50.00	125.00
	5	—	20.00	35.00	60.00	150.00
	6	—	10.00	20.00	35.00	75.00
	7	—	7.50	15.00	30.00	60.00
	8	—	6.00	12.50	25.00	40.00
	9	—	6.00	12.50	25.00	50.00

.900 SILVER, 0.30-0.33 g

KM#	Year	Mintage	Fine	VF	XF	Unc
243a	10	—	5.00	10.00	22.00	45.00
	11	—	5.00	10.00	22.00	45.00
	12	—	10.00	15.00	32.00	65.00
	13	—	10.00	15.00	32.00	65.00
	14	—	12.00	20.00	45.00	100.00
	15	—	18.00	32.00	65.00	140.00
	16	—	15.00	30.00	60.00	120.00

20 PARA

BRONZE, 29.5-32mm, 12.10-12.70 g
Accession Date: AH1277
Obv: W/o flower at right of toughra.

KM#	Year	Mintage	Fine	VF	XF	Unc
244	3	—	2.50	6.00	20.00	50.00
	4	—	2.50	6.00	20.00	50.00
	5	—	1.50	4.00	15.00	35.00
	6	—	1.50	4.00	15.00	35.00
	7	—	—	—	Rare	—
	8	—	2.00	5.00	17.50	45.00
	9	—	1.00	3.00	12.00	35.00
	10	—	2.00	5.00	17.50	45.00

29mm, 12.50 g
Similar, but crude & thick, (struck at Cairo).

KM#	Year	Mintage	Fine	VF	XF	Unc
245	7	1.190	200.00	300.00	600.00	1250.

COPPER, 12.50 g
Obv: Flower at right of toughra.

KM#	Year	Mintage	Fine	VF	XF	Unc
246	7	—	—	—	Rare	—
	8	2.395	15.00	30.00	65.00	180.00
	9	3.089	10.00	25.00	55.00	140.00
	10	.966	12.00	30.00	80.00	150.00
	11	200 pcs.	—	—	Rare	2500.

.833 SILVER, 15-16mm, 0.65-0.70 g

KM#	Year	Mintage	Fine	VF	XF	Unc
247	1	—	50.00	100.00	175.00	350.00
	2	—	25.00	50.00	100.00	175.00
	3	—	12.50	25.00	50.00	125.00
	4	—	10.00	20.00	45.00	100.00
	5	—	12.50	30.00	60.00	125.00

KM#	Year	Mintage	Fine	VF	XF	Unc
247	6	—	10.00	20.00	45.00	100.00
	7	—	7.50	15.00	35.00	85.00
	8	—	6.00	12.00	20.00	50.00
	9	—	6.00	12.00	20.00	50.00

.900 SILVER, 0.65-0.70 g

KM#	Year	Mintage	Fine	VF	XF	Unc
247a	10	—	6.00	12.00	25.00	50.00
	11	—	6.00	12.00	25.00	50.00
	12	—	6.00	12.00	25.00	50.00
	13	—	10.00	20.00	40.00	80.00
	14	—	10.00	20.00	40.00	80.00
	15	—	20.00	40.00	80.00	150.00
	16	—	— Reported, not confirmed			

40 PARA

(1 Qirsh)

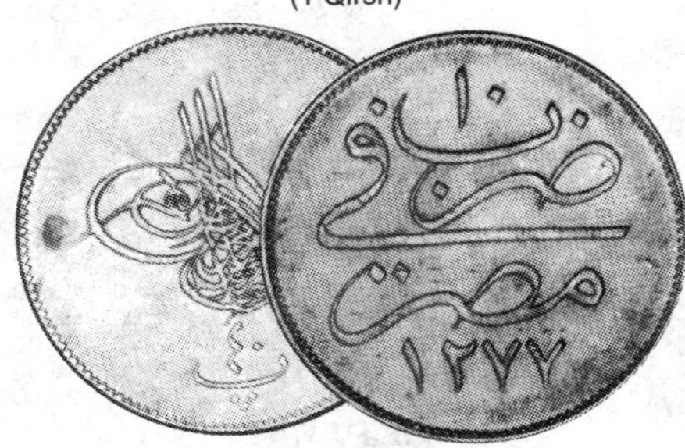

BRONZE, 37mm, 25.63 g
Accession Date: AH1277

KM#	Year	Mintage	Fine	VF	XF	Unc
248	10	—	3.00	10.00	30.00	100.00

NOTE: Exists w/large or small toughra.

COPPER, 36mm, 24.00 g
Obv: Flower added at right of toughra.

KM#	Year	Mintage	Fine	VF	XF	Unc
249	9	125 pcs.	—	—	—	5000.
	10	.150	600.00	900.00	1700.	3000.
	11	200 pcs.	—	—	—	5000.

NOTE: An example of year 10 struck in gold is reported, not confirmed.

QIRSH

.833 SILVER, 18mm, 1.18-1.25 g
Accession Date: AH1277

KM#	Year	Mintage	Fine	VF	XF	Unc
250	1	—	30.00	50.00	100.00	250.00
	2	—	20.00	35.00	75.00	150.00
	3	—	15.00	25.00	50.00	100.00
	4	—	15.00	25.00	50.00	100.00
	5	—	20.00	35.00	75.00	150.00
	6	—	12.50	25.00	45.00	90.00
	7	—	10.00	20.00	40.00	80.00
	8	—	5.00	10.00	20.00	50.00
	9	—	5.00	10.00	20.00	50.00

.900 SILVER, 1.18-1.23 g

KM#	Year	Mintage	Fine	VF	XF	Unc
250a	10	—	5.00	10.00	20.00	60.00
	11/10	—	6.00	12.00	25.00	65.00
	11	—	5.00	10.00	20.00	50.00
	12	—	5.00	10.00	20.00	50.00
	13	—	7.50	15.00	35.00	75.00
	14	—	7.50	15.00	35.00	75.00
	15	—	5.00	10.00	20.00	50.00
	16	—	5.00	10.00	20.00	50.00

Mule. Obv: KM#250a. Rev: KM#270.
Accession Date: AH1293

KM#	Year	Mintage	Fine	VF	XF	Unc
A270	1	—	—	—	Rare	—

2-1/2 QIRSH

3.1500 g, .833 SILVER, .0844 oz ASW
20mm
Accession Date: AH1277

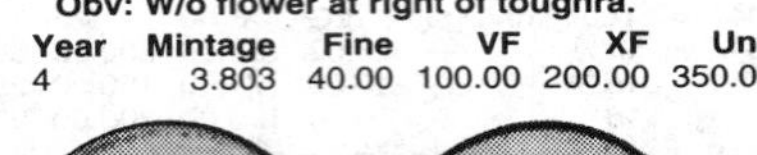

Obv: W/o flower at right of toughra.

KM#	Year	Mintage	Fine	VF	XF	Unc
251	4	3.803	40.00	100.00	200.00	350.00

3.5000 g, .833 SILVER, .0938 oz ASW
22mm
Obv: Flower at right of toughra.

KM#	Year	Mintage	Fine	VF	XF	Unc
252	8	—	185.00	350.00	650.00	1000.
	9	—	185.00	350.00	650.00	1000.

3.6000 g, .900 SILVER, .1013 oz ASW

KM#	Year	Mintage	Fine	VF	XF	Unc
252a	10	—	225.00	450.00	750.00	1100.
	11	—	275.00	550.00	1000.	1800.
	12	—	400.00	750.00	1500.	2750.
	13	—	400.00	750.00	1500.	2750.
	15	—	600.00	1000.	1800.	3000.

5 QIRSH

6.2000 g, .833 SILVER, .1661 oz ASW
Accession Date: AH1277
Obv: W/o flower at right of toughra.
25-26mm

KM#	Year	Mintage	Fine	VF	XF	Unc
253.1	4	4.108	40.00	100.00	185.00	375.00

Rev: Regnal year retrograde.

KM#	Year	Mintage	Fine	VF	XF	Unc
253.2	4	Inc. Ab.	60.00	150.00	285.00	550.00

6.60-7.00 g
Obv: Flower at right of toughra.

KM#	Year	Mintage	Fine	VF	XF	Unc
254	1	—	250.00	550.00	900.00	1400.
	2	—	200.00	450.00	850.00	1200.
	3	—	200.00	450.00	850.00	1200.
	4	—	200.00	450.00	850.00	1400.
	5	—	250.00	600.00	950.00	2000.
	6	—	250.00	600.00	950.00	2000.
	7	—	250.00	600.00	950.00	2000.
	8	—	200.00	450.00	875.00	1250.
	9	—	200.00	450.00	875.00	1250.
	10	—	250.00	600.00	950.00	2000.

.900 SILVER, 6.60-7.00 g

KM#	Year	Mintage	Fine	VF	XF	Unc
254a	10	—	200.00	450.00	850.00	1250.
	11	—	300.00	600.00	950.00	1800.
	12	—	400.00	700.00	1350.	3000.
	13	—	400.00	700.00	1350.	3000.
	15	—	400.00	700.00	1350.	3000.

0.4272 g, .875 GOLD, .0120 oz AGW

KM#	Year	Mintage	VG	Fine	VF	XF
255	3	—	20.00	30.00	40.00	65.00
255	4	—	20.00	30.00	40.00	65.00
	5	—	20.00	30.00	40.00	65.00
	6	—	20.00	30.00	40.00	65.00
	7	—	20.00	30.00	40.00	65.00
	8	—	20.00	30.00	40.00	65.00
	9	—	20.00	30.00	40.00	65.00
	10	—	20.00	30.00	40.00	65.00
	11	—	20.00	30.00	40.00	65.00
	12	—	20.00	30.00	40.00	65.00
	13	—	20.00	30.00	40.00	65.00
	14	—	20.00	30.00	40.00	65.00
	15	—	20.00	30.00	40.00	65.00

10 QIRSH

14.0000 g, .900 SILVER, .4051 oz ASW
Accession Date: AH1277
Obv: Flower at right of toughra.

KM#	Year	Mintage	VG	Fine	VF	XF
256	2	—	250.00	400.00	650.00	1400.
	3	—	250.00	400.00	650.00	1400.
	4	—	250.00	400.00	650.00	1400.

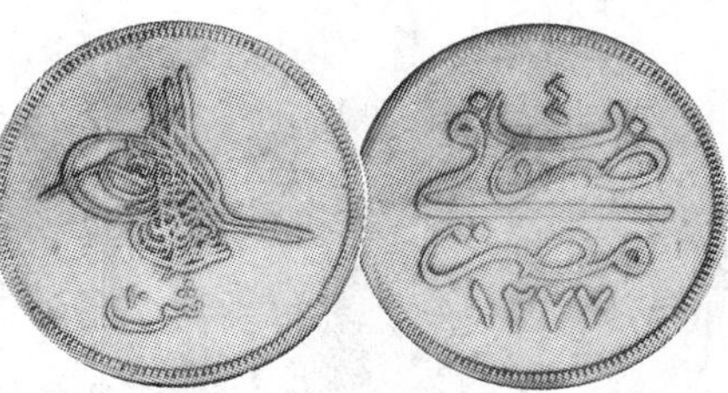

12.5000 g, .833 SILVER, .3617 oz ASW
Obv: W/o flower at right of toughra.

KM#	Year	Mintage	Fine	VF	XF	Unc
257	4	3.803	60.00	120.00	220.00	500.00

14.0000 g, .900 SILVER, .4051 oz ASW
Similar to KM#256.

KM#	Year	Mintage	VG	Fine	VF	XF
258	10	—	400.00	800.00	1400.	3000.
	11	—	—	—	Unc	7500.

0.8554 g, .875 GOLD, .0240 oz AGW

KM#	Year	Mintage	Fine	VF	XF	Unc
259	10	—	50.00	75.00	90.00	115.00
	11	—	50.00	75.00	90.00	115.00
	12	—	50.00	75.00	90.00	115.00
	14	—	50.00	75.00	90.00	115.00

20 QIRSH

28.0000 g, .833 SILVER, .7500 oz ASW
Accession Date: AH1277
Obv: Flower right of toughra.

KM#	Year	Mintage	VG	Fine	VF	XF
260	1	—	350.00	550.00	1250.	1750.
	2	—	375.00	600.00	1500.	2000.

28.0000 g, .900 SILVER, .8103 oz ASW

KM#	Year	Mintage	VG	Fine	VF	XF
260a	11	—	—	—	Unc	12,500.

25 QIRSH

(1/4 Pound)

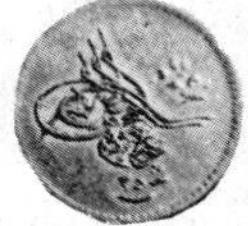

2.1360 g, .875 GOLD, .0601 oz AGW

Accession Date: AH1277

KM#	Year	Mintage	VG	Fine	VF	XF
261	8	—	35.00	50.00	75.00	150.00
	9	—	35.00	50.00	75.00	150.00
	10	—	35.00	50.00	75.00	150.00
	11	—	35.00	50.00	75.00	150.00
	12	—	35.00	50.00	75.00	150.00
	13	—	50.00	75.00	125.00	200.00
	14	—	50.00	75.00	125.00	200.00
	15	—	50.00	75.00	125.00	200.00

50 QIRSH

(1/2 Pound)

4.2740 g, .875 GOLD, .1202 oz AGW
Accession Date: AH1277

262	11	—	100.00	150.00	350.00	500.00
	12	—	80.00	115.00	220.00	325.00
	13	—	100.00	135.00	300.00	450.00
	14	—	80.00	115.00	220.00	325.00
	15	—	80.00	115.00	220.00	325.00
	16	—	80.00	115.00	220.00	325.00

100 QIRSH

(1 Pound)

8.5440 g, .875 GOLD, .2404 oz AGW
Accession Date: AH1277
Obv: Flower at right of toughra.

263	1	—	—	Reported, not confirmed		
	2	—	150.00	175.00	225.00	300.00
	3	—	—	Reported, not confirmed		
	4	—	BV	120.00	155.00	225.00
	5	—	BV	120.00	155.00	225.00
	6	—	BV	120.00	155.00	225.00
	7	—	BV	120.00	155.00	225.00
	8	—	BV	120.00	155.00	225.00
	9	—	BV	120.00	155.00	225.00
	10	—	BV	120.00	155.00	225.00
	11	—	BV	120.00	155.00	225.00
	12	—	BV	120.00	155.00	225.00
	13	—	BV	120.00	155.00	225.00
	14	—	150.00	200.00	265.00	350.00
	15	—	BV	120.00	155.00	225.00
	16	—	150.00	200.00	265.00	350.00

Obv: W/o flower at right of toughra.

264	4	.020	150.00	300.00	600.00	1000.

500 QIRSH

(5 Pounds)

42.7200 g, .875 GOLD, 1.2018 oz AGW
Accession Date: AH1277

KM#	Year	Mintage	Fine	VF	XF	Unc
265	8	118 pcs.	3500.	7500.	12,500.	17,500.
	9	Inc. Ab.	3000.	6000.	10,000.	15,000.
	11	200 pcs.	3000.	6000.	10,000.*	15,000.
	15	56 pcs.	3000.	6000.	10,000.	15,000.

***NOTE:** Spink Zurich Auction 31 6-89 AU realized $13,400.

MURAD V

AH1293/1876AD

QIRSH

.900 SILVER, 18mm, 1.20 g
Accession Date: AH1293
Obv: Toughra of Murad V.

270	1	—	100.00	150.00	300.00	500.00

50 QIRSH

(1/2 Egyptian Pound)

4.2740 g, .875 GOLD, .1202 oz AGW
Accession Date: AH1293
Obv: Toughra of Murad V.

KM#	Year	Mintage	VG	Fine	VF	XF
271	1	—	400.00	650.00	1000.	1500.

100 QIRSH

(1 Egyptian Pound)

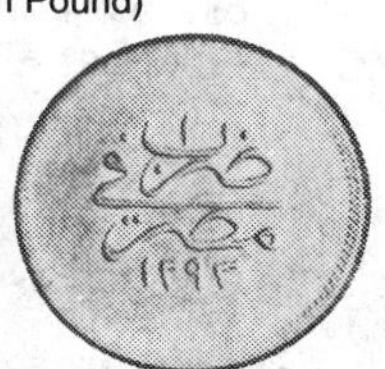

8.5440 g, .875 GOLD, .2402 oz AGW
Accession Date: AH1293
Obv: Toughra of Murad V.

272	1	—	250.00	750.00	1250.	1750.

ABDUL HAMID II

AH1293-1327/1876-1909AD

1/40 QIRSH

BRONZE
Accession Date: AH1293

KM#	Year	Mintage	Fine	VF	XF	Unc
287	10	1.669	.50	1.50	5.00	15.00
	12	2.476	.50	1.50	4.00	15.00
	18	—	40.00	60.00	100.00	160.00
	19	—	.75	1.50	5.00	15.00
	20	—	5.00	10.00	20.00	40.00
	24	1.601	.75	1.50	5.00	15.00

NOTE: Later dates (Yr.26-35) exist for this type.

1/20 QIRSH

BRONZE
Accession Date: AH1293

288	10	4.105	.50	1.50	4.00	12.00
	12	4.457	.50	1.50	4.00	12.00
	18	—	10.00	20.00	30.00	75.00
	19	—	2.50	5.00	10.00	20.00
	20	—	8.00	15.00	30.00	75.00
	21	—	2.00	3.50	10.00	20.00
	24	.801	1.00	3.00	5.00	15.00

NOTE: Later dates (Yr.26-35) exist for this type.

1/10 QIRSH

COPPER-NICKEL
Accession Date: AH1293

KM#	Year	Mintage	Fine	VF	XF	Unc
289	10	2.307	.50	1.00	4.00	12.50
	12	3.435	.50	1.00	4.00	12.50
	18	—	6.00	12.00	30.00	75.00
	19	—	.50	1.00	5.00	15.00
	20	—	.50	1.00	5.00	15.00
	21	—	.50	1.00	5.00	15.00
	22	—	4.00	10.00	20.00	60.00
	23	—	.50	1.00	6.00	17.50
	24	1.005	.50	1.00	4.00	12.50
	25	2.000	.50	1.00	5.00	15.00
	Common date		—	—	Proof	100.00

NOTE: Later dates (Yr.27-35) exist for this type.

2/10 QIRSH

COPPER-NICKEL
Accession Date: AH1293

290	10	3.201	1.00	3.00	6.00	20.00
	12	2.009	1.00	3.00	6.00	20.00
	20	—	8.00	15.00	30.00	75.00
	21	.500	2.00	6.00	12.00	40.00
	24	.500	1.00	3.00	6.00	20.00
	25	.250	3.00	5.00	10.00	35.00

NOTE: Later dates (Yr.27-35) exist for this type.

10 PARA

.833 SILVER
Accession Date: AH1293

275	1	—	75.00	100.00	160.00	325.00
	2	—	80.00	120.00	180.00	430.00
	3	—	75.00	100.00	160.00	325.00
	4	—	—	Reported, not confirmed		
	5	—	—	Reported, not confirmed		

20 PARA

0.5500 g, .833 SILVER, .0147 oz ASW
Accession Date: AH1293

276	1	—	75.00	135.00	175.00	425.00
	2	—	70.00	125.00	140.00	400.00
	3	—	75.00	135.00	175.00	425.00
	4	—	—	Reported, not confirmed		
	5	—	—	—	750.00	1000.

5/10 QIRSH

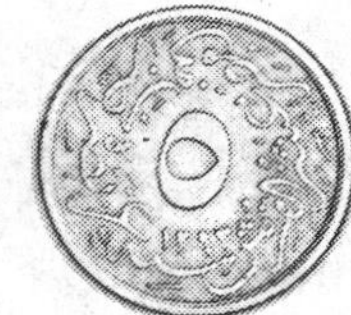

COPPER-NICKEL
Accession Date: AH1293

291	10	7.003	2.00	4.00	12.50	40.00
	11	10.005	.50	2.00	6.00	20.00
	13	5.003	.50	2.00	6.00	20.00
	20	1.002	3.00	10.00	20.00	60.00
	21	3.404	.65	2.50	7.50	25.00
	23	1.000	2.50	5.00	12.50	40.00
	24	3.605	.45	2.00	6.00	20.00
	25	1.998	.45	2.00	6.00	20.00
	Common date		—	—	Proof	145.00

NOTE: Later dates (Yr.27-33) exist for this type.

QIRSH

.833 SILVER
Accession Date: AH1293

277	1	—	3.00	10.00	20.00	65.00
	2	—	3.00	10.00	18.00	55.00
	3	—	2.50	8.00	15.00	45.00
	4	—	3.00	10.00	18.00	55.00
	5	—	4.00	12.00	20.00	65.00

1.4000 g, .833 SILVER, .0375 oz ASW

KM#	Year	Mintage	Fine	VF	XF	Unc
292	10 W	8.192	1.00	3.00	7.50	20.00
	17 W	.546	1.00	4.00	10.00	30.00
	Common date		—	—	Proof	135.00

NOTE: Later dates (Yr.27-33) exist for this type.

COPPER-NICKEL

299	22	.200	10.00	25.00	45.00	100.00
	23	1.500	2.00	6.00	20.00	50.00
	25	.751	3.00	8.00	30.00	60.00

NOTE: Later dates (Yr.27-33) exist for this type.

2 QIRSH

2.8000 g, .833 SILVER, .0750 oz ASW
Accession Date: AH1293
Obv: Flower to right of toughra.

293	10 W	4.011	1.00	3.00	7.50	30.00
	11 W	.989	2.00	5.00	12.50	35.00
	17 W	.540	2.00	5.00	12.50	35.00
	19 W	—	—	Reported, not confirmed		
	20 W	1.113	2.00	5.00	12.50	40.00
	24 W	.500	2.00	5.00	12.50	50.00
	Common date		—	—	Proof	145.00

NOTE: Later dates (Yr.27-33) exist for this type.

2-1/2 QIRSH

3.4600 g, .833 SILVER, .0927 oz ASW
Accession Date: AH1293

278	6	2 pcs.	—	—	—	4500.

5 QIRSH

6.9200 g, .833 SILVER, .1854 oz ASW
Accession Date: AH1293
Obv: Flower at right of toughra.

279	2	—	700.00	1200.	1800.	—
	6	2 pcs.	—	—	—	4000.

7.0000 g, .833 SILVER, .1875 oz ASW

294	10 W	4.195	3.00	7.50	15.00	50.00
	11 W	Inc. Ab.	4.00	10.00	25.00	75.00
	15 W	.600	8.00	20.00	40.00	125.00
	16 W	1.205	5.00	12.50	25.00	75.00
	17 W	.872	6.00	15.00	30.00	100.00
	19 W	—	—	Reported, not confirmed		
	20 W	.464	10.00	25.00	50.00	125.00
	21 W	.633	5.00	12.50	20.00	60.00
	22 W	1.118	5.00	12.50	20.00	60.00
	24 W	1.050	5.00	12.50	20.00	60.00
	Common date		—	—	Proof	285.00

NOTE: Later dates (Yr.27-33) exist for this type.

0.4200 g, .875 GOLD, .0118 oz AGW
Obv: Flower at right of toughra.

KM#	Year	Mintage	VG	Fine	VF	XF
280	1	—	—	Reported, not confirmed		
	2	—	100.00	200.00	400.00	800.00
	3	—	40.00	65.00	75.00	100.00
	4	—	—	Reported, not confirmed		
	5	—	100.00	150.00	200.00	250.00
	6	—	150.00	250.00	400.00	650.00
	7	—	40.00	65.00	75.00	100.00
	22	—	100.00	150.00	200.00	300.00

Obv: *Al-Ghazi* at right of toughra.

KM#	Year	Mintage	VG	Fine	VF	XF
298	7	—	—	Reported, not confirmed		
	15	—	100.00	200.00	350.00	600.00
	16	—	20.00	45.00	70.00	90.00
	18	—	15.00	25.00	40.00	65.00
	24	—	25.00	50.00	100.00	150.00

NOTE: Later dates (Yr.26-34) exist for this type.

Rev: Leg. in wreath.

A299	15	—	100.00	200.00	350.00	600.00

10 QIRSH

14.0000 g, .833 SILVER, .3749 oz ASW
Accession Date: AH1293
Obv: Flower at right of toughra.

KM#	Year	Mintage	Fine	VF	XF	Unc
281	6	2 pcs.	—	—	—	6000.

295	10 W	4.030	5.00	10.00	35.00	100.00
	11 W	Inc. Ab.	8.00	15.00	40.00	100.00
	15 W	.300	15.00	30.00	65.00	150.00
	15 W	—	—	—	Proof	450.00
	16 W	.602	8.00	15.00	45.00	125.00
	17 W	.380	10.00	20.00	55.00	150.00
	20 W	.340	15.00	30.00	55.00	150.00
	21 W	.420	10.00	20.00	45.00	125.00
	22 W	.600	10.00	20.00	45.00	125.00
	24 W	.500	10.00	20.00	45.00	125.00
	Common date		—	—	Proof	435.00

NOTE: Later dates (Yr.27-33) exist for this type.

0.8544 g, .875 GOLD, .0240 oz AGW
Obv: Flower at right of toughra.

KM#	Year	Mintage	VG	Fine	VF	XF
A282	4	—	300.00	500.00	900.00	1500.

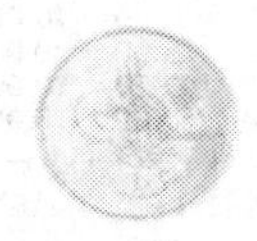 

Obv: *Al-Ghazi* at right of toughra.

282	5	—	—	Reported, not confirmed		
	7	—	—	Reported, not confirmed		
	8	—	—	Reported, not confirmed		
	17	—	20.00	40.00	75.00	120.00
	18	—	25.00	50.00	80.00	125.00
	23	—	35.00	55.00	90.00	145.00

NOTE: Later date (Yr.34) exists for this type.

20 QIRSH

27.5700 g, .833 SILVER, .7385 oz ASW
Accession Date: AH1293

KM#	Year	Mintage	VG	Fine	VF	XF
283	1	—	550.00	900.00	1500.	2000.
	5	—	650.00	1750.	2500.	3500.
	6	2 pcs.	—	—	—	12,500.

28.0000 g, .833 SILVER, .7499 oz ASW

KM#	Year	Mintage	Fine	VF	XF	Unc
296	10 W	.874	12.00	25.00	70.00	375.00
	11 W	.126	15.00	40.00	100.00	425.00
	15 W	.029	17.50	50.00	150.00	500.00
	16 W	.055	15.00	40.00	100.00	425.00
	17 W	.054	17.50	50.00	150.00	500.00
	17 W	—	—	—	Proof	800.00
	20 W	.172	12.00	40.00	100.00	425.00
	21 W	.158	12.00	30.00	85.00	400.00
	22 W	.287	12.00	30.00	85.00	400.00
	24 W	.500	12.00	30.00	85.00	400.00
	Common date		—	—	Proof	825.00

NOTE: Later dates (Yr.27-33) exist for this type.

25 QIRSH

2.1360 g, .875 GOLD, .0601 oz AGW
Accession Date: AH1293
Obv: Flower right of toughra.

A284	2	—	—	Reported, not confirmed		
	6	2 pcs.	—	—	—	7500.

50 QIRSH

(1/2 Pound)

4.2720 g, .875 GOLD, .1202 oz AGW
Accession Date: AH1293

KM#	Year	Mintage	VG	Fine	VF	XF
284	2	—	—	Reported, not confirmed		
	3	—	—	Reported, not confirmed		
	6	2 pcs.	—	—	—	8000.

NOTE: Previously reported year 1 examples are those of Murad V.

100 QIRSH

(1 Pound)

8.5440 g, .875 GOLD, .2404 oz AGW
Accession Date: AH1293
Obv: Toughra of Abdul Hamid II.

KM#	Year	Mintage	Fine	VF	XF	Unc
285	1	—	400.00	800.00	1350.	2250.
	3	—	—	Reported, not confirmed		
	4	—	400.00	800.00	1350.	2250.
	5	—	—	Reported, not confirmed		
	6	4 pcs.	—	—	—	8200.
	7	—	—	Reported, not confirmed		
	8	—	—	—	Rare	—

8.5000 g, .875 GOLD, .2391 oz AGW
Floral border.

KM#	Year	Mintage	Fine	VF	XF	Unc
297	12	.052	120.00	160.00	190.00	280.00

500 QIRSH

(5 Pounds)

42.7400 g, .875 GOLD, 1.2024 oz AGW
Accession Date: AH1293

KM#	Year	Mintage	Fine	VF	XF	Unc
286	1	—	1250.	3000.	4750.	7500.
	6	**5 pcs.	2500.	5500.	9750.	*14,500.

***NOTE:** Spinks & Son Zurich Auction 18 2-86 superb Unc. realized $14,520.

****NOTE:** Although the mint report documents only 5 pieces, perhaps 10 pieces are thought to exist.

TOKEN ISSUES (Tn)

The following token issues were struck for firms participating in the construction of the Suez Canal, and were used as currency by the company employees. All are multisided and appear round if the edge isn't examined.

Ch. & A. Bazin

20 CENTIMES

COPPER, 15mm, 16 sides

KM#	Date	Mintage	VG	Fine	VF	XF
Tn1	1865	—	50.00	75.00	120.00	185.00

50 CENTIMES

COPPER, 18 sides

KM#	Date	Mintage	VG	Fine	VF	XF
Tn2	1865	—	125.00	150.00	185.00	285.00

FRANC

COPPER, 25.5mm, 24 sides

KM#	Date	Mintage	VG	Fine	VF	XF
Tn3	1865	—	125.00	150.00	185.00	285.00

5 FRANCS

COPPER, 29 sides

KM#	Date	Mintage	VG	Fine	VF	XF
Tn4	1865	—	250.00	350.00	500.00	750.00

Borel Lavalley et Cie

20 CENTIMES

BRASS, 18mm, 20 sides

KM#	Date	Mintage	VG	Fine	VF	XF
Tn5	1865	—	40.00	65.00	90.00	165.00

50 CENTIMES

BRASS, 24 sides

KM#	Date	Mintage	VG	Fine	VF	XF
Tn6	1865	—	35.00	60.00	85.00	150.00

FRANC

BRASS, 24 sides

KM#	Date	Mintage	VG	Fine	VF	XF
Tn7	1865	—	65.00	100.00	145.00	225.00

5 FRANCS

BRASS

KM#	Date	Mintage	VG	Fine	VF	XF
Tn8	1865	—	—	—	Rare	—

NOTE: The only known example of KM#Tn8 was illustrated in Wayte Raymond's "Coins of the World" nineteenth century issues and is not to be confused with the modern fantasies encountered in today's market.

Societe Cooperative du Canal de Suez

5 CENTIMES

ALUMINUM, 17.5mm
Similar to 1 Franc, Tn11 but octagonal.

KM#	Date	Mintage	Fine	VF	XF	Unc
Tn13	1892	—	—	—	—	—

10 CENTIMES

ALUMINUM, 20.5mm
Similar to 1 Franc, Tn11 but octagonal.

KM#	Date	Mintage	Fine	VF	XF	Unc
Tn9	1892	—	100.00	175.00	250.00	425.00

50 CENTIMES

ALUMINUM, 24.5mm
Similar to 1 Franc, Tn11 but octagonal.

KM#	Date	Mintage	Fine	VF	XF	Unc
Tn10	1892	—	125.00	200.00	275.00	475.00

FRANC

ALUMINUM

KM#	Date	Mintage	Fine	VF	XF	Unc
Tn11	1892	1 known	—	—	900.00	—

2 FRANCS

ALUMINUM, 26mm
Similar to 1 Franc, Tn11.

KM#	Date	Mintage	Fine	VF	XF	Unc
Tn12	1892	—	150.00	250.00	350.00	525.00

5 FRANCS

ALUMINUM, 32mm
Similar to 1 Franc, Tn11.

KM#	Date	Mintage	Fine	VF	XF	Unc
Tn14	1892	—	—	—	—	—

PATTERNS (Pn)

(Including off metal strikes)

KM#	Date	Mintage	Identification	Mkt.Val.
Pn2	AH1277,yr.4	—	4 Para, Bronze, ESSAI	300.00
Pn3	AH1277,yr.10	—	40 Para, Bronze, ESSAI	400.00
Pn4	AH1277,yr.4	—	25 Qirsh, .875 Gold, plain edge, w/o flower	Rare
Pn5	AH1277,yr.4	—	50 Qirsh, .875 Gold, plain edge, w/o flower.	Rare

KM#	Date	Mintage	Identification	Mkt.Val.
Pn5a	AH1277,yr.4	—	50 Qirsh, Bronze, reeded edge, w/o flower, ESSAI.	575.00
Pn6	AH1277,yr.4	—	100 Qirsh, .875 Gold, plain edge, w/o flower	Rare
Pn7	AH1277,yr.4	—	200 Qirsh, .875 Gold, plain edge, w/o flower	Rare
Pn8	AH1277,yr.4	—	400 Qirsh, .875 Gold, plain edge, w/o flower.	Rare
Pn9	1860	—	20 Paras, Copper	—
Pn10	AH1277,yr.10	—	80 Para, Copper	2500.

KM#	Date	Mintage	Identification	Mkt.Val.
Pn11	AH1277,yr.10	—	80 Para Bronze, struck on France, 10 Centimes, Y21.3	

KM#	Date	Mintage	Identification	Mkt.Val.
Pn12	AH1279	—	20 Para, Said Pasha	400.00
Pn13	AH1293,yr.9	—	1/40 Qirsh, Bronze	1000.
Pn14	AH1293,yr.9	—	1/20 Qirsh, Bronze	1000.
Pn15	AH1293,yr.9	—	1/10 Qirsh, Nickel	1500.
Pn16	AH1293,yr.9	—	2/10 Qirsh, Nickel	1500.
Pn17	AH1293,yr.9	—	5/10 Qirsh, Nickel	1500.
Pn18	AH1293,yr.9	—	1 Qirsh, Nickel	1500.
Pn19	AH1293,yr.9	—	2 Qirsh, Silver	1500.
Pn20	AH1293,yr.9	—	5 Qirsh, Silver	1500.
Pn21	AH1293,yr.9	—	10 Qirsh, Silver	2500.

KM#	Date	Mintage	Identification	Mkt.Val.
Pn22	AH1293,yr.9	—	20 Qirsh, Silver	2500.
Pn23	AH1293,yr.11	—	100 Qirsh, Copper	475.00
Pn24	AH1293,yr.15	—	5 Qirsh, Gold	750.00
Pn25	AH1293,yr.19	—	1/40 Girsh, Silver, KM287	500.00

PIEFORTS (P)

KM#	Date	Mintage	Identification	Mkt.Val.
P1	AH1277,yr.10	—	80 Para, Nickel, 16.8 g, 3mm thick	400.00

EL SALVADOR

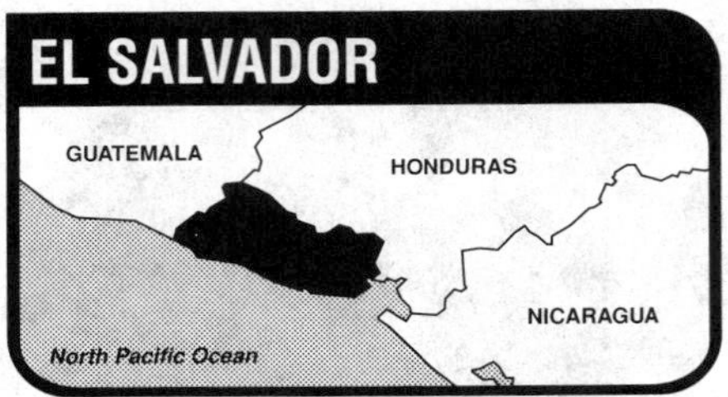

The Republic of El Salvador, a Central American country bordered by Guatemala, Honduras and the Pacific Ocean, has an area of 8,124 sq. mi. (21,040 sq. km.) and a population of 5.9 million. Capital: San Salvador. This most intensely cultivated of Latin America countries produces coffee (the major crop), sugar and balsam for export. Gold, silver and other metals are largely unexploited.

The first Spanish attempt to subjugate the area was undertaken in 1523 by Pedro de Alvarado, Cortes' lieutenant. He was forced to retreat by Indian forces, but returned in 1525 and succeeded in bringing the region under control of the Captaincy General of Guatemala. In 1821, El Salvador and the other Central American provinces jointly declared independence from Spain. In 1823, the Republic of Central America was formed by the five Central American states. When this federation dissolved in 1839, El Salvador became an independent republic.

Clashes with Honduras occurred over a period of several years. A military coup in 1979 overthrew the Romero government but the ruling military-civilian junta failed to quell the civil war. Leftist insurgents, armed by Cuba and Nicaragua, control about 25% of the country. The U.S. supported the right wing government with military aid.

In the May 1984 presidential election, voters elected Christian Democrat Jose Napoleon Duarte.

A twelve-year civil war ended in 1992 with the signing of a United Nations-sponsored Peace Accord. Free elections, with full participation of all political parties, were held in 1994 and early 1997. Armando Calderon-Sol was elected president in 1994 for a 5-year term.

MINT MARKS

C.A.M. - Central American Mint, San Salvador
H - Heaton Mint, Birmingham
S - San Francisco
Mo - Mexico

PROVISIONAL COINAGE

MONETARY SYSTEM

16 Reales = 1 Escudo

1/4 REAL

.903 SILVER
Obv: Volcano between S.-S., date below.
Rev: Column w/liberty cap on top between 1/4-1/4.

KM#	Date	Mintage	Good	VG	Fine	VF
1	1828 (3 known)		—	—	Rare	—

1/2 REAL

.903 SILVER
Obv. leg: POR LA LIVERTAD DEL SAL, star above volcano within branches.
Rev. leg: MONEDA PROVISIONAL, halo above column within branches.

KM#	Date	Mintage	Good	VG	Fine	VF
14	1833	—	100.00	200.00	350.00	500.00

Obv. leg: POR LA LIBERTAD DEL SAL.
S - volcano - S above water within circle.
Rev: Liberty cap over 1. - column - 1/2 over water.

KM#	Date	Mintage	Good	VG	Fine	VF
21.1	1835	—	100.00	175.00	275.00	400.00

Obv. leg: POR LA LIBERTAD DEL SAL,
S - volcano - S above water within circle.

KM#	Date	Mintage	Good	VG	Fine	VF
21.2	1835	—	110.00	200.00	300.00	425.00
	1835 retrograde 2 in 1/2	—	120.00	225.00	325.00	450.00

Obv. leg: POR LA LIBERTAD DEL SALVA,
star above S - volcano - S above water.
Rev. leg: MONEDA PROVISIONAL,
Liberty cap over column: 1 - column - M

KM#	Date	Mintage	Good	VG	Fine	VF
21.3	1835	—	90.00	175.00	250.00	375.00

REAL

.903 SILVER
Obv. leg: ESTADO DEL SALVADOR,
star above volcano within branches.
Rev. leg: MONEDA PROVISIONAL IND*, star in wreath above 1. - column - R. within branches.

KM#	Date	Mintage	Good	VG	Fine	VF
17	1833	—	75.00	150.00	250.00	350.00

Obv. leg: POR LA LIVERTAD DEL SALVADOR.
Rev: 1. - (thin) column - R. within branches.

KM#	Date	Mintage	Good	VG	Fine	VF
18.1	1833	—	50.00	100.00	175.00	275.00

Obv: Similar to KM#18.1.
Rev: 1. - (thick) column - R. within branches.

KM#	Date	Mintage	Good	VG	Fine	VF
18.2	1833	—	50.00	100.00	175.00	275.00

Obv. leg: POR LA LIVERTAD DEL SALVADOR*
Rev: Similar to KM#18.2.

KM#	Date	Mintage	Good	VG	Fine	VF
18.3	1833	—	50.00	100.00	175.00	275.00

Obv: Star above volcano above water in 1/2 circle of stars.

KM#	Date	Mintage	Good	VG	Fine	VF
18.4	1833	—	75.00	150.00	250.00	350.00

Obv. leg: POR LA LIVERTAD DE SAL,
volcano within branches.
Rev. leg: MONEDA PROVISIONAL IND,
column within branches.

KM#	Date	Mintage	Good	VG	Fine	VF
18.5	1834	—	75.00	150.00	250.00	350.00

Obv. leg: POR LA LIVERTAD DEL SAL,
star above S. - volcano - S. within circle.
Rev. leg: MONEDA PROVISIONAL, Liberty cap above I. - column - R., water below within circle.

KM#	Date	Mintage	Good	VG	Fine	VF
18.6	1835	—	50.00	115.00	175.00	275.00

Obv. leg: POR LA LIVERTAD DEL SAL.

KM#	Date	Mintage	Good	VG	Fine	VF
18.7	1835 NA	—	75.00	150.00	250.00	350.00
	ND	—	—	—	—	—

Obv. leg: POR LA LIBERTAD DEL SAL, star above S - volcano - S above water within circle.

KM#	Date	Mintage	Good	VG	Fine	VF
18.8	1835	—	50.00	115.00	175.00	275.00

NOTE: Varieties also exist with 2 or 3 dots after SAL.

Obv. leg: POR LA LIBERTAD DEL SAL,

star above S - volcano - S above water
within circle of dots.

KM#	Date	Mintage	Good	VG	Fine	VF
18.9	1835	—	50.00	115.00	175.00	275.00

Obv. leg: POR LA LIBERTAD DEL SA:

18.10	1835	—	50.00	115.00	200.00	300.00

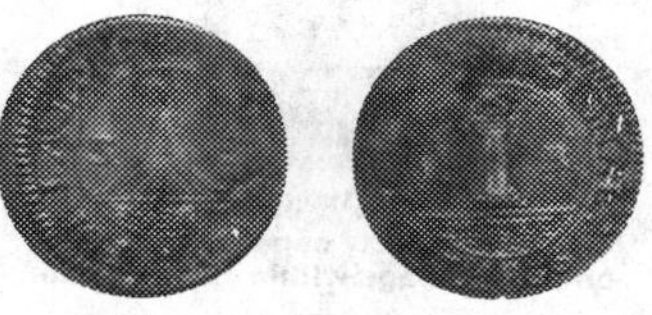

Obv. leg: POR LA LIBERTAD DE SALV.

18.11	1835	—	50.00	115.00	175.00	275.00

2 REALES

.903 SILVER
Obv. leg: POR LA LIVERTAD. SALV,
Liberty cap above 2. column - R. above water.
Rev. leg: MONEDA PROVISIONAL, volcano.

4	1828 FP	—	30.00	55.00	100.00	165.00

Obv: Inner circle added.

5.1	1828 FP	—	30.00	55.00	100.00	165.00
	1828 F	—	35.00	65.00	125.00	200.00

Obv. leg: POR LA LIBERTAD. SALB.

5.2	1828 FP	—	30.00	55.00	100.00	165.00

Obv. leg: POR LA LIBERTAD SALVAD.
Rev. leg: MONEDA PROBISIONAL.

5.3	1829 RL	—	35.00	75.00	150.00	200.00

Obv. leg: POR LA LIBERTAD SALVAD.

5.4	1829 RL	—	35.00	65.00	125.00	175.00

Obv. leg: POR LA LIBERTAD SALVADOR.

5.5	1829	—	35.00	65.00	125.00	175.00

Obv. leg: POR LA LIBERTAD DEL SALVADR,
star above S - volcano - S. above water.
Rev: Liberty cap above 2 - column - R.

11.1	1832	—	35.00	65.00	125.00	175.00

Obv. leg: POR LA LIBERTAD DEL SALVADOR
Rev: Liberty cap above 2 - column - R between
sprays within dotted circle.

11.2	1832 RL	—	35.00	65.00	125.00	175.00

Rev: 2 - column - R within solid circle.

KM#	Date	Mintage	Good	VG	Fine	VF
11.3	1832 RL	—	35.00	65.00	125.00	175.00

Obv. leg: POR LA LIBERTAD SALVADOR,
w/o waves beneath volcano.

11.15	1829 RL	—	40.00	80.00	150.00	200.00

Obv. leg: POR LA LIBERTAD SALVADOR,
w/o waves beneath volcano, denomination
flanks volcano.

11.16	1832	—	40.00	80.00	150.00	200.00

Obv. leg: POR LA LIBERTAD SALVADORE

11.4	1832	—	35.00	65.00	125.00	175.00

Obv. leg: POR LA LIBERTAD DEL SALVADO

11.5	1832 RL	—	35.00	65.00	125.00	175.00

Obv. leg: POR LA LIVERTAD DEL SALV,
star above retrograde S - volcano - S above
water. Rev: Liberty cap above 2. - column -
R within branches.

11.6	1833	—	35.00	65.00	125.00	175.00
	1834/3T	—	40.00	80.00	150.00	200.00

Obv: Regular S' recut above retrograde S'.

11.7	1834/3	—	40.00	80.00	150.00	200.00

Obv. leg: POR LA LIBERTAD DEL SALVA,
star above S - volcano - S above water.

KM#	Date	Mintage	Good	VG	Fine	VF
11.8	1833 RL	—	35.00	65.00	125.00	175.00

NOTE: Varieties exist with 2 or 3 dots after SALVA.

Obv. leg: POR LA LIBERTAD DEL SALVAD

11.9	1833/2 RL	—	40.00	80.00	150.00	200.00
	1833 RL	—	35.00	65.00	125.00	175.00

Obv. leg: POR LA LIBERTAD DEL SALV

11.10	1833 L	—	35.00	65.00	125.00	175.00

Obv. leg: LIBERTAD SALVO DORENO

11.11	1833	—	35.00	65.00	125.00	175.00

Obv. leg: POR LA LIBERTAD DEL SALVADOR.

11.12	1833 RL	—	35.00	65.00	125.00	175.00

Obv. leg: POR LA LIVERTAD DEL SALV.
Rev. leg: MONEDA PROVISIONAL
with retrograde "S".

11.13	1834	—	40.00	75.00	135.00	200.00

Obv. leg: POR LA LIBERTAD DEL SALV.
Rev. leg: MONEDA PROVISIONAL
with retrograde "N".

11.14	1834	1 known	300.00	485.00	—	—

NOTE: The one known example of this variety grades G/VG.

4 REALES

.903 SILVER
Obv. leg: POR LA LIBERTAD SALV,
Liberty cap above column between retrograde R. - 4.

KM#	Date	Mintage	Good	VG	Fine	VF
8.1	1828 F	—	1000.	2000.	3000.	5000.

Obv. leg: POR LA LIBERTAD DEL SALV,
corrected 4. - R.
Rev. leg: MONEDA PROVISIONAL.

KM#	Date	Mintage	Good	VG	Fine	VF
8.2	1828 F	—	1250.	2250.	3250.	5500.

COUNTERMARKED COINAGE

2 REALES

SILVER
c/m: SAP monogram on 2 Reales, KM#5.

KM#	Date	Mintage	Good	VG	Fine	VF
24.1	ND(1828) FP	—	—	—	—	—
	ND(1829) RL	—	—	—	—	—

c/m: SAP monogram on 2 Reales, KM#11.6.

KM#	Date	Mintage	Good	VG	Fine	VF
26	ND(1833-34)	—	50.00	100.00	200.00	300.00

c/m: SAP monogram on Central American
Republic 2 Reales, KM#9.

KM#	Date	Mintage	Good	VG	Fine	VF
25	ND(1831) F	—	100.00	200.00	400.00	600.00

NOTE: This countermark, appearing to be a SAP monogram has previously been attributed to El Salvador, and also to various Caribbean islands. Inclusion here for reference only.

REPUBLIC

COUNTERMARKED COINAGE

1830

Type I
Volcano, 'S' on either side, '1830' below, in rectangle.

4 REALES

SILVER
c/m: Type I on Mexico 4 Reales, KM#97.

KM#	Date	Year	Mintage	Good	VG	Fine
27	1830	(1772-89)	—	—	Rare	—

1839

Type II
Volcano, '1839' below, in rectangle.
Exists with normal 3 and retrograde 3 in date.

1/2 REAL

SILVER
c/m: Type II on Chile 1/2 Real, KM#90.

KM#	Date	Year	Mintage	Good	VG	Fine
30	1839	(1833-4)	—	—	Rare	—

REAL

SILVER
c/m: Type II on Peru 1 Real, KM#145.1.

KM#	Date	Year	Mintage	Good	VG	Fine
33	1839	(1826-36)	—	—	Rare	—

2 REALES

SILVER
c/m: Type II on Peru (Lima) 2 Reales, KM#141.1.

KM#	Date	Year	Mintage	Good	VG	Fine
36	1839	(1825-36)	—	100.00	200.00	300.00

c/m: Type II on South Peru 2 Reales, KM#169.1.

KM#	Date	Year	Mintage	Good	VG	Fine
37	1839	(1837)	—	—	Rare	—

8 REALES

SILVER
c/m: Type II on South Peru 8 Reales, KM#170.2.

KM#	Date	Year	Mintage	Good	VG	Fine
40	1839	(1837-39)	—	—	Rare	—

TYPE III-A
Plain Liberty cap above shield on draped flags within 10mm circle.

TYPE III-B
Radiant Liberty cap above shield on draped flags within 12mm circle.

TYPE III-C
Liberty cap above shield within branches in 12mm circle.

NOTE: Other countermark varieties are known to exist.

SPANISH 'REAL' SERIES

1/2 REAL

SILVER
c/m: Type III on Guatemala 1/2 Real, KM#2.

KM#	Date	Year	Good	VG	Fine	VF
43	ND	—	35.00	50.00	70.00	100.00

REAL

SILVER
c/m: Type III on Bolivia (Potosi) 'cob' 1 Real, KM#42.

KM#	Date	Year	Good	VG	Fine	VF
46	ND	—	17.50	25.00	42.50	65.00

c/m: Type III on Bolivia (Potosi) 1 Real, KM#52.

KM#	Date	Year	Good	VG	Fine	VF
47	ND	(1773-89)	15.00	20.00	30.00	50.00

c/m: Type III on Chile 1 Real, KM#65.

KM#	Date	Year	Good	VG	Fine	VF
48	ND	(1808-17)	17.50	25.00	40.00	60.00

c/m: Type III on Colombia 1 Real, KM#91.1.

KM#	Date	Year	Good	VG	Fine	VF
49	ND	(1837-46)	17.50	25.00	40.00	60.00

c/m: Type III on Mexico Charles and Johanna 1 Real, KM#9.

KM#	Date	Year	Good	VG	Fine	VF
50	ND	(1536-72)	20.00	30.00	45.00	75.00

c/m: Type III on Mexico City Philip II Real, KM#27.

KM#	Date	Year	Good	VG	Fine	VF
51	ND	(1556-98)	20.00	30.00	45.00	75.00

c/m: Type III on Mexico 1 Real, KM#81.

KM#	Date	Year	Good	VG	Fine	VF
A53	ND	(1801-08)	15.00	22.50	35.00	50.00

c/m: Type III on Mexico 1 Real, KM#82.

KM#	Date	Year	Good	VG	Fine	VF
B53	ND	(1809-14)	15.00	22.50	35.00	50.00

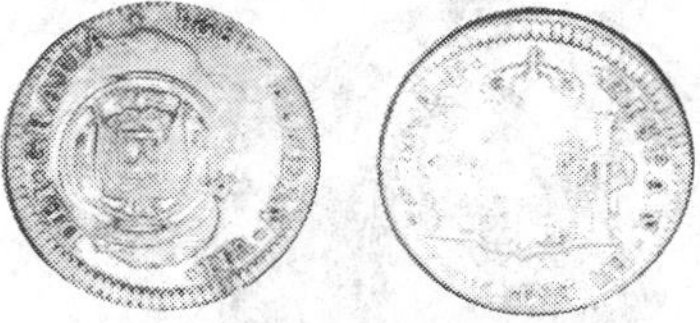

c/m: Type III on Peru 1 Real, KM#114.

53	ND	(1839)	15.00	22.50	35.00	50.00

c/m: Type III on Spain 1 Real, C#37.

52	ND	(1772-88)	15.00	22.50	35.00	50.00

2 REALES

SILVER

c/m: Type III on Bolivia (Potosi) 2 Reales, KM#53.

55	ND	(1773-89)	20.00	30.00	45.00	75.00

c/m: Type III on Colombia 2 Reales, KM#97.

56	ND	(1837-46)	22.50	35.00	50.00	85.00

c/m: Type III on Guatemala 2 Reales, KM#34.2.

54	ND	(1787 M)	35.00	60.00	85.00	150.00

c/m: Type III on Mexico 2 Reales, KM#86.

57	ND	(1747-60)	22.50	35.00	50.00	85.00

c/m: Type III on Mexico 2 Reales, KM#89.

58	ND	(1789-90)	20.00	30.00	45.00	75.00

c/m: Type III on Mexico 2 Reales, KM#90.

59	ND	(1790)	25.00	37.50	55.00	90.00

c/m: Type III on Mexico 2 Reales, KM#91.

60	ND	(1792-1808)	20.00	30.00	45.00	75.00

c/m: Type III on Mexico 2 Reales, KM#93.

61	ND	(1812-21)	20.00	30.00	45.00	75.00

c/m: Type III on Mexico Iturbide 2 Reales, KM#303.

65	ND	(1823 JM)	50.00	100.00	175.00	300.00

c/m: Type III on Peru 2 Reales, KM#53.

62	ND	(1752-59)	20.00	30.00	45.00	75.00

c/m: Type III on Peru (Lima) 2 Reales, KM#95.

63	ND	(1791-1808)	15.00	22.50	35.00	50.00

c/m: Type III on Spanish 2 Reales, C#134.

KM#	Date	Year	Good	VG	Fine	VF
64	ND	(1810-33)	17.50	25.00	40.00	60.00

4 REALES

SILVER

c/m: Type III on Guatemala 4 Reales, KM#76.1.

67	ND	(1747-53)	—	—	Rare	—

c/m: Type III on Mexico Sombrerte 4 Reales, KM#175.

68	ND	(1812)	—	—	Rare	—

8 REALES

SILVER

c/m: Type III on Chile 8 Reales, KM#31.

71	ND	(1773-89)	—	—	Rare	—

c/m: Type III on Peru 8 Reales, KM#A64.2.

72	ND	(1765)	—	—	Rare	—

ENGLISH 'STERLING' SERIES

6 PENCE

.925 SILVER

c/m: Type III on Great Britain 6 Pence, KM#394.

74	ND	(1816-20)	22.00	30.00	42.50	55.00

c/m: Type III on Great Britain 6 Pence, KM#425.

75	ND	(1831-37)	22.00	30.00	42.50	55.00

SHILLING

.925 SILVER

c/m: Type III on Great Britain Shilling, KM#395.

78	ND	(1816-20)	25.00	32.50	45.00	60.00

c/m: Type III on Great Britain Shilling, KM#409.

79	ND	(1823-25)	25.00	32.50	45.00	60.00

c/m: Type III on Great Britain Shilling, KM#414.

80	ND	(1825-29)	25.00	32.50	45.00	60.00

REVALIDATED GUATEMALA SERIES

Type IV
R in beaded 5mm circle.

1/2 REAL

SILVER

c/m: Type IV on Guatemala 1/2 Real, KM#131.

KM#	Date	Year	Good	VG	Fine	VF
83	ND	(1859-61)	100.00	150.00	200.00	300.00

c/m: Type IV on Guatemala 1/2 Real, KM#138.

84	ND	(1862-65)	60.00	100.00	150.00	275.00

REAL

SILVER

c/m: Type IV on Colombia 1 Real, KM#87.

87 ND (1827-36) — Reported, not confirmed

c/m: Type IV on Guatemala 1 Real, KM#132.

88	ND	(1859-60)	15.00	22.00	30.00	42.50

c/m: Type IV on Guatemala 1 Real, KM#137.

89	ND	(1862-65)	15.00	22.00	30.00	42.50

2 REALES

SILVER

c/m: Type IV on Guatemala 2 Reales, KM#133.

91	ND	(1859)	200.00	300.00	450.00	—

c/m: Type IV on Guatemala 2 Reales, KM#134.

92	ND	(1860-61)	17.50	25.00	32.50	45.00

c/m: Type IV on Guatemala 2 Reales, KM#139.

93	ND	(1861-65)	17.50	25.00	32.50	45.00

4 REALES

SILVER

c/m: Type IV on Guatemala 4 Reales, KM#136.

96	ND	(1860-61)	75.00	150.00	225.00	350.00

8 REALES

SILVER
c/m: Type IV on Guatemala 1 Peso, KM#178.

KM#	Date	Year	Good	VG	Fine	VF
99	ND	(1859)	—	—	Rare	—

NOTE: Two copper coins of Brazil have also been reported with the Type IV c/m. A 20 Reis dated 1827 and an 80 Reis of the 1820's c/m: '40'. These copper pieces are not genuine.

TYPE V
Zig-Zag Test Mark

2 REALES

SILVER
c/m: Type V on EL Salvador 2 Reales, KM#11.

101	ND	(1833)	60.00	85.00	125.00	175.00

c/m: Type V on Guatemala 2 Reales, KM#82, (Peru 2 Reales).

102	ND	(1825-40)	60.00	85.00	125.00	175.00

c/m: Type V on Peru 2 Reales, KM#141.1.

103	ND	(1825-40)	60.00	85.00	125.00	175.00

4 REALES

c/m: Type V on Guatemala 4 Reales, KM#92 (Bolivia 4 Soles).

104	ND	(1827-30)	60.00	85.00	125.00	175.00

DECIMAL COINAGE

100 Centavos = 1 Peso

CENTAVO

COPPER-NICKEL

KM#	Date	Mintage	Fine	VF	XF	Unc
106	1889H	1.500	1.00	3.00	5.00	15.00
	1889H	—	—	—	Proof	150.00

NOTE: Later date (1913) exists for this type.

COPPER

KM#	Date	Mintage	Fine	VF	XF	Unc
108	1892/1	.182	45.00	80.00	120.00	225.00
	1892	Inc. Ab.	25.00	45.00	65.00	100.00
	1892	10 pcs.	—	—	Proof	750.00
	1893	—	200.00	300.00	400.00	700.00

3 CENTAVOS

COPPER-NICKEL

107	1889H	.333	1.50	4.50	9.00	25.00
	1889H	—	—	—	Proof	200.00

NOTE: Later dates (1913) exists for this type.

5 CENTAVOS

1.2500 g, .835 SILVER, .0336 oz ASW

109	1892CAM	.080	6.00	12.50	25.00	50.00
	1892CAM	—	—	—	Proof	500.00
	1893CAM	I.A.	6.00	12.50	25.00	50.00

10 CENTAVOS

2.5000 g, .835 SILVER, .0671 oz ASW

110	1892CAM	.012	25.00	50.00	80.00	200.00
	1892CAM	—	—	—	Proof	500.00

20 CENTAVOS

5.0000 g, .835 SILVER, .1342 oz ASW

111	1892CAM	.146	10.00	25.00	50.00	125.00
	1892CAM	—	—	—	Proof	350.00
	1893CAM	—	— Reported, not confirmed			

50 CENTAVOS

12.5000 g, .900 SILVER, .3617 oz ASW

112	1892CAM	.043	20.00	50.00	150.00	400.00
	1892CAM	—	—	—	Proof	750.00

113	1892CAM	.340	10.00	20.00	50.00	200.00
	1893CAM	I.A.	10.00	20.00	50.00	175.00
	1894CAM	I.A.	14.00	27.50	75.00	300.00

UN (1) PESO

25.0000 g, .900 SILVER, .7234 oz ASW

KM#	Date	Mintage	Fine	VF	XF	Unc
114	1892CAM	.041	40.00	85.00	150.00	700.00
	1892CAM	—	—	—	Proof	2000.

115.1	1892CAM	.950	20.00	40.00	75.00	250.00
	1893/2 CAM					
		Inc. Ab.	10.00	22.50	37.50	100.00
	1893CAM	I.A.	6.50	12.00	20.00	80.00
	1894CAM	I.A.	6.50	12.00	20.00	100.00
	1895CAM	I.A.	6.50	12.00	20.00	150.00
	1896CAM	I.A.	75.00	150.00	400.00	—

NOTE: Later dates (1904-1914) exist for this type.
NOTE: Struck in San Salvador and European mints.

2-1/2 PESOS

4.0323 g, .900 GOLD, .1167 oz AGW

116	1892CAM					
		597 pcs.	225.00	450.00	650.00	1400.
	1892CAM	—	—	—	Proof	1750.

5 PESOS

8.0645 g, .900 GOLD, .2334 oz AGW

117	1892CAM					
		558 pcs.	300.00	600.00	900.	1950.
	1892CAM	—	—	—	Proof	3000.

10 PESOS

16.1290 g, .900 GOLD, .4667 oz AGW

KM#	Date	Mintage	Fine	VF	XF	Unc
118	1892CAM	321 pcs.	500.00	800.00	1400.	3500.
	1892CAM	—	—	—	Proof	3750.

20 PESOS

32.2580 g, .900 GOLD, .9334 oz AGW

KM#	Date	Mintage	Fine	VF	XF	Unc
119	1892CAM	200 pcs.	1000.	1500.	2500.	6500.
	1892CAM	—	—	—	Proof	8000.

MEDALLIC ISSUES (M)

Vice-Royalty of New Spain

(REAL)

SILVER
Obv. leg: FERNANDO • VII • REY • DE • ESP • IN DIAS • *
Rev. leg: PROCLAMADO • EN • S • SALVADOR • DE • G •

KM#	Date	Mintage	VF	XF	Unc
M2	1808	30.00	55.00	90.00	175.00

(2 REALES)

SILVER
Obv. leg: A FERNANDO * VII * ANO * I * DE SU REINA *
Rev. leg: PROCLAMADO EN LA • N • C • DES • SALVADOR • EN GUATEM *

KM#	Date	Mintage	VF	XF	Unc
M3	1808	30.00	55.00	95.00	180.00

Obv. leg: A FERNANDO * VII * ANO * I * DE SU REYN *
Rev. leg: PROCLAMADO EN LA • N • C • DES • SALVADOR • EN GUATEM *

KM#	Date	Mintage	VF	XF	Unc
M4	1808	35.00	60.00	100.00	185.00

Santa Ana la Grande

(REAL)

SILVER
Ferdinand VII

KM#	Date	Mintage	Fine	VF	XF	Unc
M1	1808	—	35.00	60.00	100.00	185.00

NOTE: Struck for Ferdinand VII as the new King of Spain while he was under Napoleonic French guard.

ESSAIS (E)

KM#	Date	Mintage	Identification	Mkt.Val.
E1	1892	—	1 Centavo, Copper, Obv: arms. Rev: Value in wreath. ESSAI/DE/MONNAIE.	—

PATTERNS (Pn)

(Including off metal strikes)

KM#	Date	Mintage	Identification	Mkt.Val.
Pn1	1861	—	25 Centavos, Brass	600.00

NOTE: Well worn examples of Pn1 exist and are valued accordingly. A VG piece sold in 1997 for $130.00.

KM#	Date	Mintage	Identification	Mkt.Val.
Pn2	1861	—	1 Peso, Bronze	100.00
Pn3	1861	—	1 Peso, Silver	2000.
Pn4	1892	—	1 Centavo, White metal, KM108	600.00
Pn5	1892	—	1 Centavo, Copper, date within wreath	—
Pn6	1892	—	1 Peso, Silver plated copper, KM114	—
Pn7	1892 CAM	—	2-1/2 Pesos, .900 Gold, KM16	—
Pn8	1892 CAM	—	5 Pesos, Copper, KM117	650.00
Pn9	1892 CAM	—	10 Pesos, Copper, KM118	750.00
Pn10	1892 CAM	—	20 Pesos, Gilt Bronze, KM119	1100.

KM#	Date	Mintage	Identification	Mkt.Val.
Pn11	1893	—	25 Centavos, Silver	650.00
Pn12	1894	—	50 Centavos, Copper, KM113	750.00
Pn13	1894	—	1 Peso, Copper, KM115.1	650.00
Pn14	1895	—	1 Peso, Copper, KM115.1	650.00

PIEFORTS (P)

KM#	Date	Mintage	Identification	Mkt.Val.
P1	1862	—	25 Centavos, Brass	Rare

PROOF SETS (PS)

KM#	Date	Mintage	Identification	Issue Price	Mkt. Val.
PS1	1889H(2)	—	KM106-107	—	350.00
PS2	1892(10)	—	KM108-112,114,116-119	—	16,000.

ERITREA

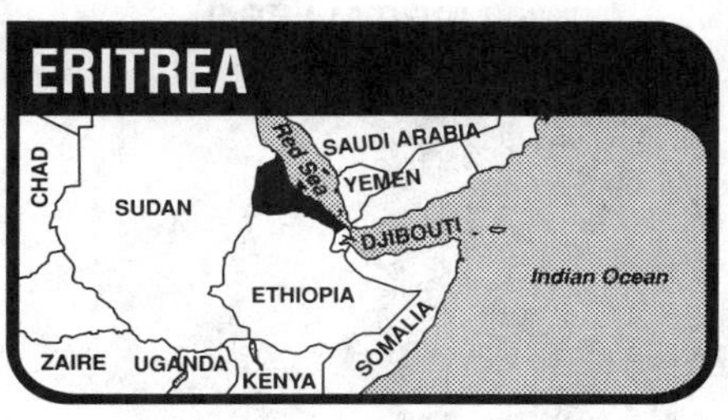

The State of Eritrea, a former Ethiopian province fronting on the Red Sea, has an area of 45,300 sq. mi. (117,600 sq. km.) and a population of 3.6 million. It was an Italian colony from 1889 until its incorporation into Italian East Africa in 1936. It was under the British Military Administration from 1941 to Sept. 15, 1952, when the United Nations designated it an autonomous unit within the federation of Ethiopia and Eritrea. On Nov. 14, 1962, it was annexed with Ethiopia. In 1991 the Eritrean Peoples Liberation Front extended its control over the entire territory of Eritrea. Following 2 years of provisional government, Eritrea held a referendum on independence in May 1993. Overwhelming popular approval led to the proclamation of an independent Republic of Eritrea on May 24.

RULERS

Umberto I, 1889-1900
Vittorio Emanuele III, 1900-1945

MINT MARKS

M - Milan
PM - Pobjoy
R - Rome

MONETARY SYSTEM

100 Centesimi = 1 Lira
5 Lire = 1 Tallero

COLONIAL COINAGE

50 CENTESIMI

2.5000 g, .835 SILVER, .0671 oz ASW

KM#	Date	Mintage	Fine	VF	XF	Unc
1	1890M	1.800	22.50	45.00	90.00	175.00

LIRA

5.0000 g, .835 SILVER, .1342 oz ASW

KM#	Date	Mintage	Fine	VF	XF	Unc
2	1890R	.598	20.00	40.00	95.00	235.00
	1891R	2.401	20.00	40.00	80.00	200.00
	1896R	1.500	40.00	75.00	150.00	550.00

2 LIRE

10.0000 g, .835 SILVER, .2685 oz ASW

KM#	Date	Mintage	Fine	VF	XF	Unc
3	1890R	1.000	30.00	60.00	125.00	335.00
	1896R	.750	35.00	70.00	145.00	400.00

5 LIRE/TALLERO

28.1250 g, .800 SILVER, .7235 oz ASW

KM#	Date	Mintage	Fine	VF	XF	Unc
4	1891	.196	75.00	165.00	400.00	1200.
	1896	.200	90.00	185.00	425.00	1350.

ETHIOPIA

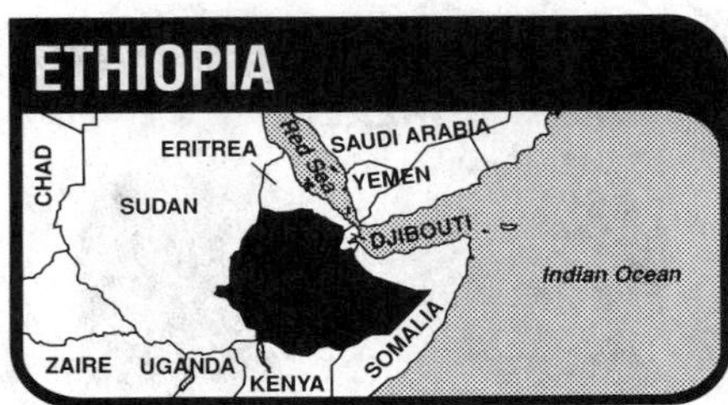

The People's Federal Republic of Ethiopia (formerly the Peoples Democratic Republic and the Empire of Ethiopia), Africa's oldest independent nation, faces the Red Sea in East-Central Africa. The country has an area of 424,214 sq. mi. (1,004,390 sq. km.) and a population of 56 million people who are divided among 40 tribes that speak some 270 languages and dialects. Capital: Addis Ababa. The economy is predominantly agricultural and pastoral. Gold and platinum are mined and petroleum fields are being developed. Coffee, oilseeds, hides and cereals are exported.

Legend claims that Menelik I, the son born to Solomon, King of Israel, by the Queen of Sheba, settled in Axum in North Ethiopia to establish the dynasty which reigned with only brief interruptions until 1974. Modern Ethiopian history began with the reign of Emperor Menelik II (1889-1913) under whose guidance the country emerged from medieval isolation. Progress continued throughout the reigns of Menelik's daughter, Empress Zauditu, and her successor Emperor Haile Selassie I who was coronated in 1930. Ethiopia was invaded by Italy in 1935, and together with Italian Somaliland and Eritrea became part of Italian East Africa. Liberated by British and Ethiopian troops in 1941, Ethiopia reinstated Haile Selassie I to the throne. The 225th consecutive Solomonic ruler was deposed by a military committee on Sept 12, 1974. In July 1976 Ethiopia's military provisional government referred to the country as Socialist Ethiopia. After establishing a new regime in 1991, Ethiopia became a federated state and is now the Federal Republic of Ethiopia. Following 2 years of provisional government, the province of Eritrea held a referendum on independence in May 1993 leading to the proclamation of its independence on May 24.

No coins, patterns or presentation pieces are known bearing Emperor Lij Yasu's likeness or titles. Coins of Menelik II were struck during this period with dates frozen.

RULERS

Menelik II, 1889-1913

MINT MARKS

A - Paris
(a) - Paris, privy marks only

Coinage of Menelik II, 1889-1913

NOTE: The first national issue coinage, dated 1887 and 1888 E.E., carried a cornucopia, A, and fasces on the reverse. Subsequent dates have a torch substituted for the fasces, the A being dropped. All issues bearing these marks were struck at the Paris Mint. Coins without mint marks were struck in Addis Ababa.

MONETARY SYSTEM

(Until about 1903)

40 Besa = 20 Gersh = 1 Birr

DATING

Ethiopian coinage is dated by the Ethiopian Era calendar (E.E.) which commenced 7 years and 8 months after the advent of A.D. dating.

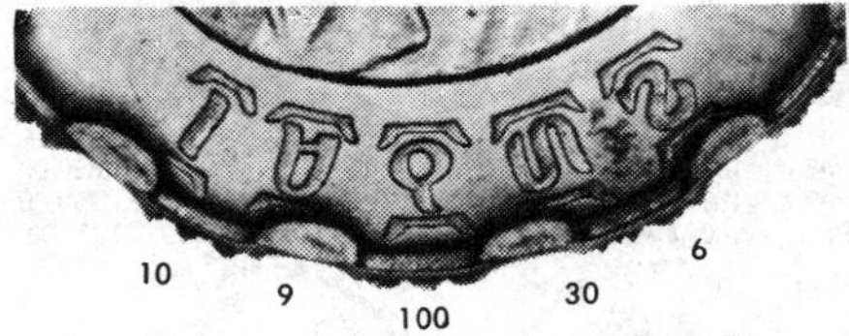

EXAMPLE

1900 (10 and 9 = 19 x 100)
36 (Add 30 and 6)
1936 E.E.
8 (Add)
1943/4 AD

KINGDOM OF ABYSSINIA

MAHALEKI

SILVER, 15mm, 1.04 g
Obv: Crown. Rev: Date, denomination, and Ethiopian script.

KM#	Date	Mintage	Fine	VF	XF	Unc
1	EE1885 (1892/93)	—	85.00	145.00	250.00	350.00

NOTE: The above issue has been reported to be the last issue of the Harrar Mint following the capture of that city in 1887 by Menelik's forces.

MONETARY REFORM

1/100 BIRR

(Matonya)

COPPER

KM#	Date	Mintage	Fine	VF	XF	Unc
9	EE1889A (1897)	.500	4.00	8.00	15.00	45.00

1/4 GERSH

(Ya Gersh Rub)

COPPER, 26mm

KM#	Date	Mintage	Fine	VF	XF	Unc
6	EE1888A (1896)	200 pcs.	350.00	700.00	1150.	2000.

1/2 GERSH

(Ya Gersh Alad)

COPPER

KM#	Date	Mintage	Fine	VF	XF	Unc
7	EE1888A (1896)	200 pcs.	250.00	400.00	700.00	1250.

1/32 BIRR

(Ya Birr 32nd)

First Issue

COPPER or BRASS
Enlargement (below lion)

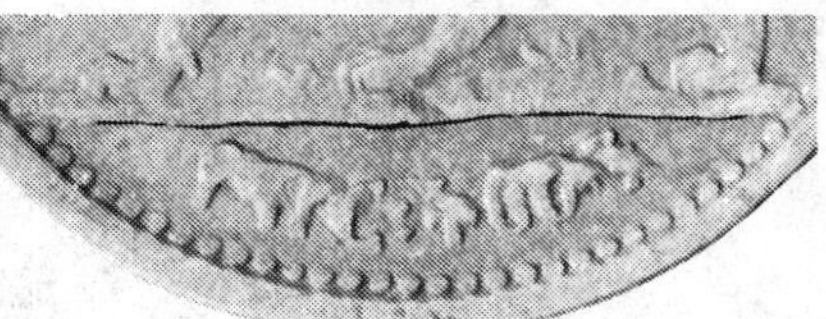

Defaced, with plain and rough edge.

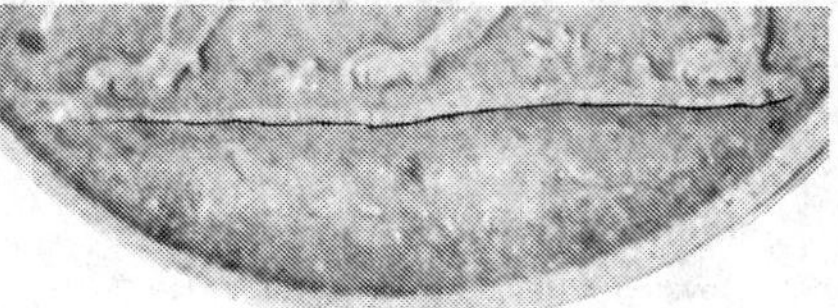

Obliterated, plain and reeded edge.

KM#	Date	Fine	VF	XF	Unc
10	EE1889 (1897)	3.50	7.50	15.00	50.00

NOTE: This issue was struck from dies intended for a silver 1/8 Birr of the die series that included KM#13, 14 and 15. These are found with the denomination partially to almost totally effaced from beneath the lion.

Second Issue

Enlargement (below lion)

KM#	Date	Mintage	Fine	VF	XF	Unc
11	EE1889 (1897)					
		3.353	4.00	10.00	20.00	60.00

NOTE: Struck at the Addis Ababa Mint in 1922, 1931 and 1933 from newly prepared dies having corrected denominations.

GERSH

(1/20 Birr)

COPPER

KM#	Date	Mintage	Fine	VF	XF	Unc
8	EE1888A (1896)					
		200 pcs.	275.00	450.00	700.00	1250.

1.4038 g, .835 SILVER, .0377 oz ASW
Rev: Lion's left foreleg raised.

KM#	Date	Mintage	Fine	VF	XF	Unc
12	EE1889A (1897)					
		1.000	6.00	12.00	20.00	40.00
	1891A (1898)					
		4.000	4.00	6.50	12.00	22.00

NOTE: Later date (EE1895) exists for this type.

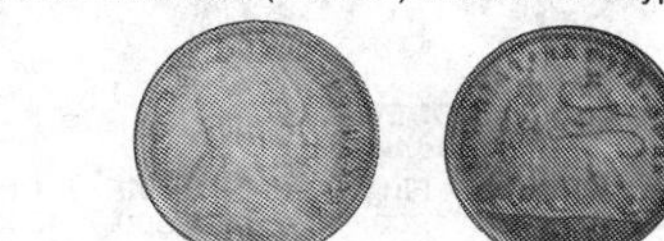

Rev: Lion's right foreleg raised.

KM#	Date	Mintage	Fine	VF	XF	Unc
13	EE1889 (1897)					
		—	60.00	100.00	165.00	375.00

1/8 BIRR

(Ya Birr Tamun/of Birr Eighth)

3.5094 g, .835 SILVER, .0942 oz ASW
Rev: Lion's left foreleg raised.

KM#	Date	Mintage	Fine	VF	XF	Unc
2	EE1887A (1894)					
		.025	15.00	30.00	65.00	225.00
	1888A (1896)					
		200 pcs.	200.00	300.00	500.00	850.00

1/4 BIRR

(Ya Birr Rub/of Birr Fourth)

7.0188 g, .835 SILVER, .1884 oz ASW
Rev: Lion's left foreleg raised.

KM#	Date	Mintage	Fine	VF	XF	Unc
3	EE1887A (1894)					
		.015	10.00	20.00	40.00	125.00
	1888A (1896)					
		200 pcs.	150.00	250.00	400.00	750.00
	1889A (1897)					
		.400	5.00	10.00	25.00	100.00

NOTE: Later date (EE1895) exists for this type.

Rev: Lion's right foreleg raised.

KM#	Date	Mintage	Fine	VF	XF	Unc
14	EE1889 (1897)					
		—	25.00	45.00	75.00	250.00

1/2 BIRR

(Ya Birr Alad/of Birr Half)

14.0375 g, .835 SILVER, .3768 oz ASW
Rev: Lion's left foreleg raised.

KM#	Date	Mintage	Fine	VF	XF	Unc
4	EE1887A (1894)					
		.010	12.00	25.00	45.00	150.00
	1888A (1896)					
		200 pcs.	175.00	275.00	450.00	900.00
	1889A (1897)					
		*.420	10.00	17.50	35.00	135.00

***NOTE:** Struck between 1897 and 1925.

Rev: Lion's right foreleg raised.

KM#	Date	Mintage	Fine	VF	XF	Unc
15	EE1889 (1897)					
		—	60.00	100.00	175.00	400.00

BIRR

28.0750 g, .835 SILVER, .7537 oz ASW
Rev: Lion's left foreleg raised.

KM#	Date	Mintage	Fine	VF	XF	Unc
5	EE1887A (1894)					
		.020	20.00	40.00	100.00	325.00
	1887A (1894)					
		—	—	—	Proof	450.00
	1888A (1896)					
		200 pcs.	—	—	—	—
	1889A (1897)					
		.418	15.00	30.00	85.00	250.00

Rev: Lion's right foreleg raised.

KM#	Date	Mintage	Fine	VF	XF	Unc
19	EE1892 (1899)					
		.401	15.00	30.00	90.00	265.00
	1892 (1899)					
		—	—	—	Proof	450.00
		—	—		Matte Proof	400.00

NOTE: Later date (EE1895) exists for this type.

1/4 WERK

(Ya Werk Rub/of Werk Fourth)

1.7500 g, .900 GOLD, 16mm, .0506 oz AGW

KM#	Date	Mintage	Fine	VF	XF	Unc
16	EE1889 (1897)					
		—	50.00	100.00	180.00	285.00

1/2 WERK

(Ya Werk Alad/of Werk Half)

3.5000 g, .900 GOLD, .1012 oz AGW

KM#	Date	Mintage	Fine	VF	XF	Unc
17	EE1889 (1897)					
		—	100.00	165.00	245.00	385.00

WERK

7.0000 g, .900 GOLD, .2025 oz AGW

KM#	Date	Mintage	Fine	VF	XF	Unc
18	EE1889 (1897)					
		—	120.00	185.00	265.00	425.00

NOTE: KM#16-18 vary considerably in weight due to disparities in planchet thicknesses.

PATTERNS (Pn)

(Including off metal strikes)

KM#	Date	Mintage	Identification	Mkt.Val.
Pn1	EE1889(1897)	—	1 Gersh, Gold, KM13	2250.
Pn2	EE1889(1897)	—	1/4 Birr, Gold, 6.75 g, reeded edge, KM14	2500.
Pn3	EE1889(1897)	—	1/4 Birr, Gold, 14.50 g, plain edge, KM14	3500.
Pn4	EE1889(1897)	—	1/2 Birr, Gold, KM15	2000.

KM#	Date	Mintage	Identification	Mkt.Val.
Pn5	EE1889(1897)	—	1 Birr, Gold	6000.

TRIAL STRIKES (TS)

KM#	Date	Mintage	Identification	Mkt.Val.
TS1	EE1887(1894)	—	1 Birr, Copper, obv. KM5 (matte proof)	70.00
TS2	ND(EE1887)	—	1 Birr, Copper, rev. KM5 (matte proof)	70.00
TS3	EE1889(1897)	—	1/4 Werk, Gold, obv. KM16, plain edge (proof)	—
TS4	ND(EE1889)	—	1/4 Werk, Gold, rev. KM16, plain edge (proof)	—
TS5	EE1889(1897)	—	1/2 Werk, Gold, obv. KM17, reeded edge (proof)	—
TS6	ND(EE1889)	—	1/2 Werk, Gold, rev. KM17, reeded edge (proof)	—
TS7	EE1889(1897)	—	1 Werk, Gold, obv. KM18, reeded edge (proof)	—
TS8	ND(EE1889)	—	1 Werk, Gold, rev. KM18, plain edge (proof)	—

PROOF SETS (PS)

KM#	Date	Mintage	Identification	Issue Price	Mkt. Val.
PS1	1894(4)	—	KM2-5	—	2500.

ERITREA

For coins previously listed here refer to Eritrea.

HARAR

Harar, a province and city located in eastern Ethiopia, was founded by Arab immigrants from Yemen in the 7th century. The sultanate conquered Ethiopia in the mid-16th century, and was in turn conquered by Egypt in 1875 and by Ethiopia in 1887.

TITLES

الهرر

al-Harar

RULERS

Ahmad II,
AH1209-1236/AD1794-1821

'Abd al-Rahman,
AH1236-1240/AD1821-1825

'Abd al-Karim,
AH1240-1250/AD1825-1834

Abu Baker II,
AH1250-1268/AD1834-1852

Muhammad II,
AH1272-1292/AD1856-1875

'Abdallah,
AH1303-1304/AD1885-1887

MONETARY SYSTEM

Not known; 22 Mahallak were said to be equal to one Ashrafi. In the late 18th and the 19th century the Ashrafi in Harar was a fictitious medium used in accounts, which varied in value against the Maria Theresa Dollar, In the 1st half of the 19th century, 3 Ashrafi were thought to be one Maria Theresa Dollar.

The brass coins are of various sizes, but were probably all called 'Mahallak'. The denominations of the billon and silver are unknown.

BRASS COINAGE

MAHALLAK

Anonymous, without name of ruler.

COPPER-BRASS, 7-10mm, 0.13-0.26 g

KM#	Date	Mintage	Good	VG	Fine	VF
4	AH1222	—	10.00	15.00	25.00	40.00
	1226	—	10.00	15.00	25.00	40.00
	1227	—	10.00	15.00	25.00	40.00

NOTE: Other dates reported to exist.

BRASS, 5-7mm, 0.10-0.20 g

KM#	Date	Mintage	Good	VG	Fine	VF
5	ND	—	4.00	7.50	12.50	22.00

NOTE: Believed to be an issue of 'Abd al-Karim.

Anonymous

About 10-11mm, 0.40-0.65 g

KM#	Date	Mintage	Good	VG	Fine	VF
6	AH1257	—	8.00	15.00	25.00	40.00
	1258	—	8.00	15.00	25.00	40.00

In the name of Muhammad II.

COPPER-BRASS, 9-11mm, 0.19-0.25 g
Obv: ***Sultan Muhammad bin Ali.***
Rev: ***Al-Sultan abd-al Shakur and date.***

KM#	Date	Mintage	Good	VG	Fine	VF
7	AH1274	—	6.00	12.00	20.00	30.00

10-12mm, 0.35-0.48 g
Obv: ***Sultan Muhammad bin Ali and date.*** **Rev:** ***City of al Harar.***

KM#	Date	Mintage	Good	VG	Fine	VF
8	AH1279	—	7.00	14.00	22.00	35.00

10-14mm, 0.35-0.70 g
Obv: ***Sultan Muhammad bin Ali.***
Rev: ***Struck at Harar and date.***

KM#	Date	Mintage	Good	VG	Fine	VF
9	AH1284	—	3.00	6.00	12.00	20.00

Anonymous. in name of 'THE WEAK SLAVE'

15-19mm, 0.85-1.55 g

KM#	Date	Mintage	Good	VG	Fine	VF
11	AH1303	—	3.00	6.00	11.00	17.00
	1305	—	5.00	10.00	17.50	25.00

NOTE: Varieties exist.

SILVER COINAGE

In the name of Muhammad II

9.5-10mm, 0.05-0.12 g

KM#	Date	Mintage	Good	VG	Fine	VF
10	AH1288	—	35.00	65.00	110.00	185.00

FINLAND

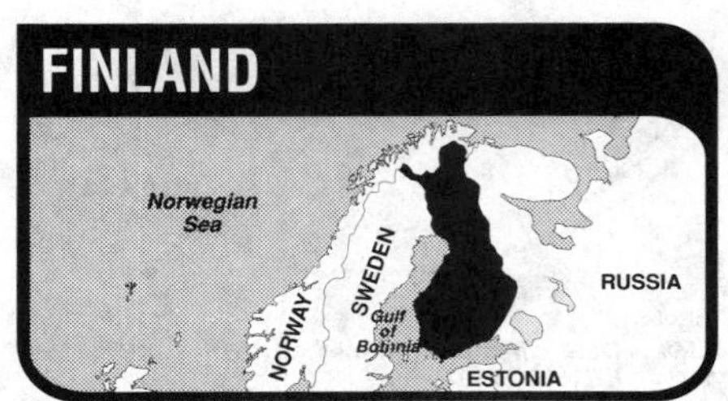

The Republic of Finland, the second most northerly state of the European continent, has an area of 130,559 sq. mi.(338,127 sq. km.) and a population of 5.1 million. Capital: Helsinki. Lumbering, shipbuilding, metal and woodworking are the leading industries. Paper, timber, woodpulp, plywood and metal products are exported.

The Finns, who probably originated in the Volga region of Russia, took Finland from the Lapps late in the 7th century. They were conquered in the 12th century by Eric IX of Sweden, and brought into contact with Western Christendom. In 1809, Sweden was conquered by Alexander I of Russia, and the peace terms gave Finland to Russia which became a grand duchy within the Russian Empire until Dec. 6, 1917, when, shortly after the Bolshevik revolution it declared its independence. After a brief but bitter civil war between the Russian sympathizers and Finnish nationalists in which the Whites (nationalists) were victorious, a new constitution was adopted, and on Dec. 6, 1917 Finland was established as a republic. In 1939 Soviet troops invaded Finland over disputed territorial concessions which were later granted in the peace treaty of 1940. When the Germans invaded Russia, Finland became involved and in the Armistice of 1944 lost the Petsamo area to the Soviets.

RULERS

Alexander II, 1855-1881
Alexander III, 1881-1894
Nicholas II, 1894-1917

MONETARY SYSTEM

100 Pennia = 1 Markka

MINT MARKS

No mm - Helsinki

MINTMASTERS INITIALS

Letter	Date	Name
L	1885-1912	Johan Conrad Lihr
S	1864-1885	Aug. F. Soldan

GRAND DUCHY

PENNI

COPPER
Dotted border

KM#	Date	Mintage	Fine	VF	XF	Unc
1.1	1864	.030	1200.	1750.	2500.	4000.
	1865	.515	15.00	25.00	50.00	120.00
	1866/5	3.673	25.00	40.00	85.00	175.00
	1866	Inc. Ab.	8.00	12.00	25.00	50.00
	1867	3.843	7.00	12.00	25.00	50.00
	1869	1.575	15.00	20.00	35.00	70.00
	1870	.500	40.00	60.00	120.00	180.00
	1871	1.500	7.00	12.00	25.00	50.00

Dentilated border

KM#	Date	Mintage	Fine	VF	XF	Unc
1.2	1872	1.000	12.00	20.00	40.00	75.00
	1873	2.000	5.00	8.00	20.00	40.00
	1874	1.450	5.00	8.00	20.00	50.00
	1875	1.550	5.00	8.00	17.00	50.00
	1876	2.005	5.00	8.00	17.00	40.00

KM#	Date	Mintage	Fine	VF	XF	Unc
10	1881	.600	7.00	12.00	20.00	60.00
	1882	.100	30.00	50.00	95.00	145.00
	1883	3.900	1.00	3.00	6.00	20.00
	1884	.404	30.00	60.00	110.00	165.00
	1888	2.290	1.00	3.00	5.00	15.00
	1891	1.008	2.00	5.00	15.00	30.00
	1892	1.510	1.00	3.00	7.00	15.00
	1893	2.290	.75	1.50	4.00	10.00
	1893 dot after date					
		Inc. Ab.	.75	1.50	4.00	10.00
	1894	1.810	.75	1.50	4.00	10.00
13	1895	.880	3.00	5.00	10.00	25.00
	1898	1.430	.75	1.25	3.00	10.00
	1899	1.540	.75	1.25	3.00	7.50
	1900	3.550	.50	1.00	2.00	4.00

NOTE: Later dates (1901-1916) exist for this type.

5 PENNIA

COPPER
Dotted border

KM#	Date	Mintage	Fine	VF	XF	Unc
4.1	1865	.480	6.00	20.00	40.00	130.00
	1866	2.490	1.00	5.00	15.00	70.00
	1867	1.660	2.00	6.00	18.00	80.00
	1870	.300	5.00	15.00	50.00	150.00

NOTE: Varieties exist.

Dentilated border

KM#	Date	Mintage	Fine	VF	XF	Unc
4.2	1872	.500	3.00	10.00	30.00	125.00
	1873	1.000	1.00	5.00	15.00	80.00
	1875	1.000	1.00	5.00	15.00	80.00

NOTE: Varieties exist.

KM#	Date	Mintage	Fine	VF	XF	Unc
11	1888	.600	2.00	7.00	15.00	80.00
	1889	1.070	1.00	5.00	10.00	75.00
	1892	.330	3.00	7.00	20.00	125.00

KM#	Date	Mintage	Fine	VF	XF	Unc
15	1896	.410	2.00	8.00	25.00	80.00
	1897	.590	1.00	5.00	15.00	75.00
	1898	1.150	1.00	5.00	15.00	60.00
	1899	.860	1.00	5.00	15.00	60.00

NOTE: Later dates (1901-1917) exist for this type.

10 PENNIA

COPPER
Dotted border

KM#	Date	Mintage	Fine	VF	XF	Unc
5.1	1865	.250	3.00	12.00	60.00	175.00
	1866/5	.850	5.00	17.00	50.00	175.00
	1866	Inc. Ab.	2.00	8.00	40.00	150.00
	1867	1.440	2.00	7.00	40.00	130.00

Dentilated border

KM#	Date	Mintage	Fine	VF	XF	Unc
5.2	1875	.100	40.00	70.00	150.00	500.00
	1876	.300	3.00	10.00	50.00	175.00

NOTE: Varieties exist.

KM#	Date	Mintage	Fine	VF	XF	Unc
12	1889	.100	10.00	25.00	70.00	350.00
	1890	.106	8.00	25.00	70.00	350.00
	1891	.295	5.00	12.00	35.00	125.00
14	1895	.210	3.00	10.00	50.00	150.00
	1896	.294	3.00	10.00	30.00	125.00
	1897	.502	1.50	5.00	20.00	100.00
	1898	.040	25.00	45.00	125.00	350.00
	1899	.440	1.25	5.00	20.00	100.00
	1900	.524	1.25	5.00	20.00	100.00

NOTE: Later dates (1905-1917) exist for this type.

25 PENNIA

1.2747 g, .750 SILVER, .0307 oz ASW
Dotted border

KM#	Date	Mintage	Fine	VF	XF	Unc
6.1	1865S	.705	10.00	25.00	50.00	150.00
	1866S	.810	7.00	15.00	40.00	120.00
	1867S	.400	250.00	350.00	700.00	2000.
	1868S	.136	125.00	200.00	450.00	1000.
	1869S	.264	25.00	40.00	80.00	250.00
	1871S	.150	40.00	70.00	150.00	400.00

Dentilated border.

KM#	Date	Mintage	Fine	VF	XF	Unc
6.2	1872S	.400	6.00	15.00	40.00	125.00
	1873S	.800	3.00	10.00	30.00	75.00
	1875S	.810	3.00	10.00	30.00	75.00
	1876S	1,200	1000.	1500.	2500.	4000.
	1889L	.404	3.00	8.00	20.00	70.00
	1890L	.800	1.50	3.00	10.00	50.00
	1891L	.280	2.50	6.00	15.00	65.00
	1894L	.820	1.50	3.00	10.00	50.00
	1897L	.450	1.50	3.00	12.00	50.00
	1898L	.444	1.50	3.00	10.00	40.00
	1898L/inverted L	Inc. Ab.	15.00	25.00	40.00	125.00
	1899L	.312	1.50	3.00	15.00	65.00

NOTE: Later dates (1901-1917) exist for this type.

50 PENNIA

2.5494 g, .750 SILVER, .0615 oz ASW
Dotted border

KM#	Date	Mintage	Fine	VF	XF	Unc
2.1	1864S	.104	5.00	20.00	75.00	300.00
	1865S	1.184	3.50	10.00	50.00	150.00
	1866S	.363	10.00	25.00	100.00	300.00
	1868S	.140	50.00	100.00	300.00	750.00
	1869S	.144	15.00	30.00	80.00	350.00
	1869S slanted 9	Inc. Ab.	15.00	30.00	100.00	400.00
	1871S	.320	3.00	8.00	30.00	150.00

Dentilated border.

KM#	Date	Mintage	Fine	VF	XF	Unc
2.2	1872S	*.200	3.00	10.00	40.00	200.00
	1874S	.402	2.50	8.00	30.00	150.00
	1876S	600 pcs.	3500.	5000.	6000.	8000.
	1889L	.312	2.50	5.00	25.00	120.00
	1890L	.693	1.00	2.50	15.00	50.00
	1891L	.282	1.00	3.00	15.00	75.00
	1892L	.344	1.00	2.50	12.00	70.00
	1893L	.400	1.00	2.50	12.00	70.00

NOTE: Later dates (1907-1917) exist for this type.

MARKKA

5.1828 g, .868 SILVER, .1446 oz ASW
Dotted border.

KM#	Date	Mintage	Fine	VF	XF	Unc
3.1	1864S	.075	25.00	40.00	100.00	250.00
	1865S	1.673	2.50	5.00	20.00	85.00
	1866S	1.990	2.50	5.00	20.00	75.00
	1867S	.852	10.00	20.00	50.00	250.00
	1870S	5 known	—	—	Rare	—

Dentilated border.

KM#	Date	Mintage	Fine	VF	XF	Unc
3.2	1872S	.538	4.00	10.00	35.00	150.00
	1874S	1.002	2.50	6.00	15.00	65.00
	1890L	.841	2.50	6.00	15.00	70.00
	1892L	.484	2.50	6.00	15.00	80.00
	1893L	.254	3.00	7.50	25.00	100.00

NOTE: Later dates (1907-1915) exist for this type.

2 MARKKAA

10.3657 g, .868 SILVER, .2893 oz ASW
Dotted border

KM#	Date	Mintage	Fine	VF	XF	Unc
7.1	1865S	.203	5.00	10.00	30.00	150.00
	1866/5S	.820	10.00	25.00	60.00	250.00
	1866S	Inc. Ab.	10.00	25.00	55.00	220.00
	1867S	6 known	—	—	*	—
	1870S	.500	5.00	10.00	30.00	150.00

***NOTE:** Helsingin Numismaattinen Yhdistys Auction 3-1990 VF-EF realized $45,500.

Dentilated border.

KM#	Date	Mintage	Fine	VF	XF	Unc
7.2	1872S	.250	5.00	10.00	30.00	150.00
	1874S	.502	5.00	10.00	30.00	120.00

NOTE: Later dates (1905-1908) exist for this type.

10 MARKKAA

Obv: Wide eagle.
3.2258 g, .900 GOLD, .0933 oz AGW
Regal Issues

KM#	Date	Mintage	Fine	VF	XF	Unc
8.1	1878S	.254	60.00	80.00	100.00	125.00
8.2	1879/0S	.200	150.00	300.00	700.00	1200.
	1879S	Inc. Ab.	60.00	80.00	100.00	125.00
	1881S	.100	80.00	100.00	115.00	150.00
	1882S	.386	60.00	80.00	100.00	125.00

NOTE: Later dates (1904-1913) exist for this type.

20 MARKKAA

6.4516 g, .900 GOLD, .1867 oz AGW
Regal Issues
Similar to 10 Markkaa, KM#8.1.
Obv: Narrow eagle.

KM#	Date	Mintage	Fine	VF	XF	Unc
9.1	1878S	*.235	150.00	175.00	200.00	250.00

Obv: Wide eagle.

KM#	Date	Mintage	Fine	VF	XF	Unc
9.2	1879S	.300	100.00	110.00	120.00	150.00
	1880S	.090	450.00	550.00	650.00	750.00
	1891L	.091	110.00	125.00	175.00	200.00

NOTE: Later dates (1903-1913) exist for this type.

PATTERNS (Pn)

(Including off metal strikes)

KM#	Date	Mintage	Identification	Mkt.Val.
Pn1	1863	—	1 Penni, Copper	Rare
Pn2	1863	—	5 Pennia, Copper	Rare
Pn3	1863	—	10 Pennia, Copper	Rare
Pn4	1863	—	20 Pennia, Copper	Rare
Pn5	1863	—	1 Markka, Tin	Unique
Pn6	1866	—	20 Pennia, Silver	Rare
Pn7	1867	—	10 Pennia, Gold	Unique
Pn8	1867	8 pcs.	2 Markkaa, Silver. obv. KM7.1	Rare
Pn9	1870	5 pcs.	1 Markka, Silver, obv. KM3.1	Rare
Pn10	1890	—	10 Pennia, Copper-Nickel	Unique

TRIAL STRIKES (TS)

KM#	Date	Mintage	Identification	Mkt.Val.
TS1	1866	—	2 Pennia, Copper, w/pearls	4500.
TS2	1866	—	2 Pennia, Copper, w/o pearls	Rare
TS3	1866	—	20 Pennia, Silver, w/pearls	Rare
TS-A4	1867	—	10 Pennia, Gold	Unique
TS4	1867	—	2 Markkaa, Tin	Rare
TS5	1870	—	1 Markka, Tin	Rare

Listings For

FORMOSA: refer to China, Republic of (Taiwan)

FRANCE

The French Republic, largest of the West European nations, has an area of 210,026 sq. mi. (547,030 sq. km.) and a population of 58.1 million. Capital: Paris. Agriculture, mining and manufacturing are the most important elements of France's diversified economy. Textiles and clothing, iron and steel products, machinery and transportation equipment, agricultural products and wine are exported.

France, the Gaul of ancient times, emerged from the Renaissance as a modern centralized national state which reached its zenith during the reign of Louis XIV (1643-1715) when it became an absolute monarchy and the foremost power in Europe. Although his reign marks the golden age of French culture, the domestic abuses and extravagance of Louis XIV plunged France into a series of costly wars. This, along with a system of special privileges granted the nobility and other favored groups, weakened the monarchy and brought France to bankruptcy.This laid the way for the French Revolution of 1789-94 that shook Europe and affected the whole world.

The monarchy was abolished and the First Republic formed in 1793. The new government fell in 1799 to a coup led by Napoleon Bonaparte who, after declaring himself First Consul for life, had himself proclaimed Emperor of France and King of Italy. Napoleon's military victories made him master of much of Europe, but his disastrous Russian campaign of 1812 initiated a series of defeats that led to his abdication in 1814 and exile to the island of Elba. The monarchy was briefly restored under Louis XVIII. Napoleon returned to France in March 1815, but his efforts to regain power were totally crushed at the battle of Waterloo. He was exiled to the island of St. Helena where he died in 1821.

The monarchy under Louis XVIII was again restored in 1815, but the ultrareactionary regime of Charles X (1824-30) was overthrown by a liberal revolution and Louis Philippe of Orleans replaced him as monarch. The monarchy was ousted by the Revolution of 1848 and the Second Republic proclaimed. Louis Napoleon Bonaparte (nephew of Napoleon I) was elected president of the Second Republic. He was proclaimed emperor in 1852. As Napoleon III, he gave France two decades of prosperity under a stable, autocratic regime, but led it to defeat in the Franco-Prussian War of 1870, after which the third Republic was established.

RULERS

Consulate, 1799-1803, L'an 8-11
Napoleon as Consul, 1799-1804
Napoleon I as Emperor, 1804-1814
(first restoration)
Louis XVIII, 1814-1815
Napoleon I, 1815
(second restoration)
Louis XVIII, 1815-1824
Charles X, 1824-1830
Louis Philippe, 1830-1848
Second Republic, 1848-1852
Napoleon III, 1852-1870
Government of National Defense, 1870-1871
Third Republic, 1871-1940

MINT MARKS AND PRIVY MARKS

In addition to the date and mint mark which are customary on western civilization coinage, most coins manufactured by the French Mints contain two small 'Marques et Differents' as the French call them. These privy marks represent the men responsible for the dies which struck the coins. One privy mark is for the Engraver General (since 1880 the title is Chief Engraver). The other privy mark is the signature of the Mint Director of each mint. Since 1880 this privy mark has represented the office rather than the personage of the Mint Director, and a standard privy mark has been used (cornucopia).

For most dates these privy marks are unimportant minor features. During some issue dates, however, the marks changed. To be even more accurate sometimes the marks changed when the date didn't, even though it should have. These coins can be attributed to the proper mintage report only by considering the privy marks. Previous references have by and large ignored these privy marks. It is entirely possible that unattributed varieties may exist for any privy mark transition. All transition years which may have two varieties of privy marks have the known attribution indicated after the date (if it has been confirmed).

ENGRAVER GENERAL'S PRIVY MARKS

Engraver Generals' privy marks may appear on coins of other mints which are dated as follows:

Mark	Date	Name
	AN XI-1816	Tiolier (in script)
	AN 13-1815	T (in script)
	1817-1824	T (in script) on 1/4 Fr. only
	1816-1824	Horse's head on other Louis XVIII coins
	1824-1830	T (in script)
	1830-1842	Star
	1843-1855	Dog's head (d)
	1855-1879	Anchor (a)
	1879	Anchor w/bar
	1880-1896	Fasces
	1896-1926	Torch

MINT DIRECTOR'S PRIVY MARKS

Some modern coins struck from dies produced at the Paris Mint have the 'A' mint mark. In the absence of a mint mark, the cornucopia privy mark serves to attribute a coin to Paris design.

A - PARIS

Cock
L'AN 6-1821

Anchor
1822-1842

Prow of ship (p)
1843-1845

Hand (ha)
1845-1860

Bee (b)
1860-1879

(Commune), Trident (tr)
1871

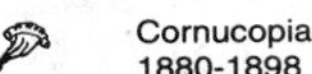
Cornucopia
1880-1898

None (n)
1897-1920

B - DIEPPE

B - ROUEN

Vase
L'AN 5-7

Sheep
L'AN 12-1844

Hand
1845-1846

Pick & Shovel
1853-1857

BB - STRASBOURG

Sheaf
L'AN 5-1825

Beaver (ba)
1826-1834

Bee (be)
1834-1860

Cross (c)
1860-1870

BD - PAU

CC, CL - GENOA

Prow of ship
1805, 1813-1814

CH - CHALONS

D - LYON

Monogram
L'AN 8-XI

Bee (b)
L'AN XI-1823

Mark	Date	Name
	Ark (a) 1823-1839	
	Tower (to) 1839-1842	
	Lion 1848-1857	

G - GENEVE

Cat L'AN 7-12

Fish L'AN 12

H - La ROCHELLE

Monogram L'AN 11-1817

Lyre 1817-1824

Trident 1824-1837

I - LIMOGES

Horizontal clasped hands L'AN XI-1822

Vertical clasped hands 1823-1837

K - BORDEAUX

Oil lamp L'AN 4-13

Fish L'AN 13-1809

Leaf 1809-1857

Pick & Hammer 1861-1868

Anchor 1870

M w/star 1870-1871

Cross 1870-1878

L - BAYONNE

Lion's head L'AN 4-AN XI

Tulip L'AN XI-1828

M - TOULOUSE

Hammer L'AN 14-1811

Monogram 1811-1837

Q - PERPIGNAN

Grapes L'AN 4-1837

R - LONDON

Fleur-de-lis 1815

R - SAINT ANDRE

T - NANTES

Anchor L'AN 4-1818

Key 1818-1820

Mark	Date	Name
	Olive branch 1826-1835	

U - TURIN

Heart L'AN 11-1814

W - LILLE

Caduceus L'AN 4-1840

Retort 1840-1846

Lamp 1853-1857

Monogram - MARSEILLE

Monogram 1809-1823

Palm tree 1824-1838

Shell 1853-1857

Flag - (u) UTRECHT

Fish 1811-1814

Crowned R - (R) ROME

Wolf 1811-1814

LOUIS D'OR

MONETARY SYSTEM

(Commencing 1794)

10 Centimes = 1 Decime
10 Decimes = 1 Franc

UN (1) CENTIME

BRONZE
Mint mark: A
Second Republic

KM#	Date	Mintage	Fine	VF	XF	Unc
754	1848	8.615	2.00	5.00	10.00	22.00
	1849	8.664	2.00	5.00	10.00	22.00
	1850	2.721	6.00	12.00	30.00	60.00
	1851	2.712	4.00	8.00	25.00	45.00

Second Empire

KM#	Date	Mintage	Fine	VF	XF	Unc
775.1	1853	4.076	2.00	5.00	9.00	15.00
	1854	2.750	4.00	7.00	15.00	28.00
	1855(d)	6.034	3.00	5.00	12.00	25.00
	1855(a)	I.A.	6.00	15.00	35.00	60.00
	1855(a)	—	—	—	Proof	400.00
	1856	2.878	4.00	10.00	23.00	40.00
	1857	2.000	5.00	12.00	27.00	50.00
		Mint mark: B				
775.2	1853	.824	5.00	12.00	22.00	35.00
	1854	1.709	10.00	20.00	40.00	75.00
	1855(d)	1.971	10.00	20.00	40.00	75.00
	1855(a)	I.A.	12.00	25.00	50.00	90.00
	1856	4.373	2.00	5.00	9.00	15.00
	1857	3.000	3.00	7.00	20.00	40.00
		Mint mark: BB				
775.3	1853	2.558	3.00	5.00	12.00	25.00
	1854	1.447	4.00	7.00	15.00	28.00
	1855(d)	.248	15.00	30.00	75.00	150.00
	1855(a)	I.A.	15.00	30.00	75.00	150.00
	1856	1.874	10.00	15.00	30.00	55.00
	1857	—	—	—	Rare	—
		Mint mark: D				
775.4	1853	.964	3.00	6.00	18.00	30.00
	1854	1.546	8.00	16.00	35.00	60.00
	1855(d)	2.466	6.00	15.00	30.00	50.00
	1855(a)	I.A.	10.00	25.00	50.00	100.00
	1856	.880	15.00	40.00	80.00	175.00
	1857	1.000	12.00	28.00	55.00	90.00

NOTE: The 1853 dated coins exist with large and small D mint mark.

Mint mark: K

KM#	Date	Mintage	Fine	VF	XF	Unc
775.5	1853	.405	8.00	18.00	45.00	75.00
	1854	1.150	6.00	14.00	35.00	65.00
	1855(d)	I.A.	7.00	15.00	45.00	75.00
	1855(a)	1.455	10.00	20.00	50.00	95.00
	1856	2.062	4.00	8.00	20.00	45.00
	1857	1.000	8.00	18.00	40.00	65.00
		Mint mark: MA				
775.6	1853	.225	20.00	35.00	60.00	125.00
	1854	1.976	3.00	6.00	15.00	35.00
	1855(d)	2.839	15.00	25.00	65.00	150.00
	1855(a)	I.A.	3.00	7.00	15.00	35.00
	1856	.305	12.00	30.00	65.00	150.00
	1857	1.500	3.00	10.00	20.00	45.00
		Mint mark: W				
775.7	1853	1.634	2.00	5.00	12.00	25.00
	1854	1.399	— Reported, not confirmed			
	1855(d)	3.102	2.00	5.00	12.00	20.00
	1855(a)	I.A.	5.00	15.00	30.00	55.00
	1856	2.707	3.00	8.00	20.00	35.00
	1857	2.500	3.00	10.00	22.00	40.00

Mint mark: A

KM#	Date	Mintage	Fine	VF	XF	Unc
795.1	1861	7.398	.50	2.00	5.00	10.00
	1862	15.561	.50	1.00	3.00	6.00
	1870	1.000	5.00	18.00	30.00	60.00
		Mint mark: BB				
795.2	1861	3.012	1.00	3.00	9.00	15.00
	1862	4.493	1.00	3.00	9.00	15.00
		Mint mark: K				
795.3	1861	1.999	2.00	5.00	10.00	20.00
	1862	7.431	.50	1.00	3.00	6.50

Mint mark: A
Third Republic

KM#	Date	Mintage	Fine	VF	XF	Unc
826.1	1872	1.250	2.00	5.00	9.00	15.00
	1874	1.000	2.00	5.00	9.00	15.00
	1875	1.000	2.00	5.00	9.00	15.00
	1877	1.000	2.00	5.00	9.00	15.00
	1878	1.500	1.50	3.00	7.00	12.00
	1879(ab)	.800	2.00	6.00	11.00	16.00
	1882	.419	3.00	9.00	16.00	30.00
	1884	.400	4.00	10.00	18.00	35.00
	1885	.400	3.00	9.00	16.00	30.00
	1886	.400	3.00	9.00	16.00	30.00
	1887	.400	3.00	9.00	16.00	30.00
	1888	.400	3.00	9.00	16.00	30.00
	1889	.400	3.00	9.00	16.00	30.00
	1890	.400	3.00	9.00	16.00	30.00
	1891	1.400	.75	4.00	8.00	12.00
	1892	.800	1.00	5.00	10.00	18.00
	1893	.300	3.00	9.00	16.00	30.00
	1894	.500	2.00	7.00	14.00	22.00
	1895	3.000	1.50	2.50	5.00	10.00
	1896(f)	3.000	1.50	2.50	5.00	10.00
	1897	2.000	2.00	3.00	6.00	12.00
		Mint mark: K				
826.2	1872	.750	3.00	9.00	16.00	30.00
	1875	2.000	2.00	5.00	9.00	15.00
	1878	.289	10.00	20.00	45.00	80.00

Mint: Paris - w/o mint mark.

KM#	Date	Mintage	Fine	VF	XF	Unc
840	1898	.250	3.00	8.00	15.00	25.00
	1898	—	—	—	Proof	300.00
	1899	1.500	1.00	2.00	4.00	12.00
	1900	.221	15.00	30.00	55.00	100.00
	1900	—	—	—	Proof	325.00

NOTE: Later dates (1901-1920) exist for this type.
NOTE: No privy marks on KM#840 of any date.

DEUX (2) CENTIMES

Small D Large D

BRONZE
Mint mark: A
Second Empire

KM#	Date	Mintage	Fine	VF	XF	Unc
776.1	1853	.610	4.00	10.00	18.00	30.00
	1854	3.118	.75	2.00	6.00	18.00
	1855(d)	5.417	.25	2.00	6.00	12.00
	1855(a)	I.A.	.25	2.00	6.00	12.00
	1856	1.738	1.00	3.00	7.00	15.00
	1857	1.250	1.50	5.00	10.00	20.00

Mint mark: B

KM#	Date	Mintage	Fine	VF	XF	Unc
776.2	1853	.539	5.00	12.00	20.00	35.00
	1854	1.995	1.00	3.00	7.00	15.00
	1855(d)	1.754	1.50	4.00	8.00	15.00
	1855(a)	I.A.	1.50	4.00	8.00	15.00
	1856	4.324	.25	2.00	6.00	12.00
	1857	2.000	1.50	5.00	15.00	25.00

Mint mark: BB

KM#	Date	Mintage	Fine	VF	XF	Unc
776.3	1853	.168	6.00	15.00	35.00	100.00
	1854	2.003	1.00	3.00	7.00	15.00
	1855(d)	2.135	1.00	3.00	7.00	15.00
	1855(a)	I.A.	2.00	5.00	9.00	18.00
	1856	1.282	1.00	3.00	6.00	12.00

Mint mark: D

KM#	Date	Mintage	Fine	VF	XF	Unc
776.4	1853 sm.D	—	10.00	25.00	40.00	90.00
	1853 lg.D	—	13.00	35.00	55.00	110.00
	1854 small D	2.524	7.00	12.00	25.00	50.00
	1854 lg.D	I.A.	10.00	15.00	30.00	60.00
	1855(d) small D	2.554	4.00	10.00	18.00	30.00
	1855(d) large D	Inc. Ab.	10.00	20.00	35.00	100.00
	1855(a) small D	Inc. Ab.	6.00	12.00	25.00	60.00
	1855(a) large D	Inc. Ab.	1.00	3.00	8.00	15.00
	1856	.774	—	—	—	—
	1857 small D	1.000	10.00	20.00	50.00	125.00
	1857 lg.D	I.A.	6.00	10.00	25.00	50.00

Mint mark: K

KM#	Date	Mintage	Fine	VF	XF	Unc
776.5	1853	.117	10.00	25.00	45.00	100.00
	1854	1.545	1.50	4.00	8.00	20.00
	1855(d)	1.068	2.50	6.00	15.00	30.00
	1855(a)	I.A.	2.00	5.00	12.00	25.00
	1856	2.281	1.00	3.00	7.00	15.00
	1857	.750	6.00	12.00	25.00	60.00

Mint mark: MA

KM#	Date	Mintage	Fine	VF	XF	Unc
776.6	1853	.163	6.00	16.00	35.00	100.00
	1854	1.312	3.00	8.00	16.00	25.00
	1855(d)	2.438	2.00	6.00	16.00	25.00
	1855(a)	I.A.	4.00	10.00	20.00	35.00
	1856	2.781	1.00	3.00	7.00	15.00
	1857	1.250	7.00	14.00	28.00	65.00

Mint mark: W

KM#	Date	Mintage	Fine	VF	XF	Unc
776.7	1853	.070	20.00	40.00	100.00	135.00
	1854	3.402	1.00	3.00	7.00	15.00
	1855(d)	.939	3.00	7.00	14.00	25.00
	1856	2.581	1.00	3.00	7.00	15.00
	1857	2.250	1.00	3.00	7.00	15.00

Mint mark: A
Obv: Bust points to 1 in date.

KM#	Date	Mintage	Fine	VF	XF	Unc
796.1	1861	4.054	.50	1.50	3.00	7.00

Mint mark: BB

KM#	Date	Mintage	Fine	VF	XF	Unc
796.2	1861	2.440	.75	3.00	6.00	14.00

Mint mark: K

KM#	Date	Mintage	Fine	VF	XF	Unc
796.3	1861	3.291	.75	2.50	5.00	8.00

Mint mark: A
Obv: Recut die (r), bust points to 8 in date.

KM#	Date	Mintage	Fine	VF	XF	Unc
796.4	1861(r)	I.A.	1.00	3.00	5.00	10.00
	1862	7.515	.50	1.50	3.00	5.00

Mint mark: BB

KM#	Date	Mintage	Fine	VF	XF	Unc
796.5	1861(r)	I.A.	1.00	3.00	5.00	10.00
	1862	2.807	1.50	3.50	6.00	12.00

Mint mark: K

KM#	Date	Mintage	Fine	VF	XF	Unc
796.6	1861(r)	I.A.	.25	2.00	4.00	10.00
	1862	13.692	.10	1.50	3.00	5.00

Mint mark: A
Third Republic

KM#	Date	Mintage	Fine	VF	XF	Unc
827.1	1877	.500	3.00	6.00	10.00	18.00
	1878	.750	2.00	4.00	8.00	15.00
	1879(ab)	.600	2.00	4.00	8.00	15.00
	1882	.290	4.00	8.00	18.00	35.00
	1883	.500	3.00	6.00	10.00	18.00
	1884	.300	4.00	8.00	15.00	25.00
	1885	.300	4.00	8.00	15.00	25.00
	1886	.300	4.00	8.00	15.00	25.00
	1887	.300	4.00	8.00	15.00	25.00
	1888	.400	3.00	6.00	12.00	18.00
	1889	.600	2.00	4.00	8.00	15.00
	1890	.300	4.00	8.00	15.00	25.00
	1891	.300	4.00	8.00	15.00	25.00
	1892	.500	3.00	6.00	10.00	18.00
	1893	.250	8.00	15.00	35.00	50.00
	1894	.150	10.00	20.00	40.00	70.00
	1895	1.000	1.00	3.00	5.00	10.00
	1896(f)	1.000	1.00	3.00	5.00	10.00
	1897	1.250	.75	2.00	4.00	8.00

Mint mark: K

KM#	Date	Mintage	Fine	VF	XF	Unc
827.2	1878	.363	3.00	8.00	16.00	25.00

Mint: Paris - w/o mint mark.

KM#	Date	Mintage	Fine	VF	XF	Unc
841	1898	.125	4.00	10.00	15.00	25.00
	1898		—	—	Proof	300.00
	1899	.750	2.00	5.00	10.00	20.00
	1900	.101	40.00	75.00	150.00	200.00
	1900	—	—	—	Proof	325.00

NOTE: Later dates (1901-1920) exist for this type.
NOTE: No privy marks appeared on KM#841 of any date.

CINQ (5) CENTIMES

COPPER
Mint mark: BB

KM#	Date	Mintage	Good	VG	Fine	VF
689	1808	—	20.00	40.00	100.00	225.00

BRONZE
Mint mark: A
Second Empire

KM#	Date	Mintage	Fine	VF	XF	Unc
777.1	1853	13.928	2.00	5.00	16.00	30.00
	1854	28.767	2.00	5.00	14.00	28.00
	1855(d)	26.932	1.00	4.00	12.00	25.00
	1855(a)	I.A.	3.00	6.00	15.00	35.00
	1856	25.799	1.00	4.00	12.00	25.00
	1857	5.729	8.00	18.00	35.00	50.00

Mint mark: B

KM#	Date	Mintage	Fine	VF	XF	Unc
777.2	1853	4.424	4.00	10.00	25.00	45.00
	1854	16.354	2.00	5.00	16.00	30.00
	1855(d)	18.290	2.00	5.00	16.00	30.00
	1855(a)	I.A.	3.00	6.00	18.00	35.00
	1856	14.813	2.00	5.00	16.00	30.00
	1857	1.843	20.00	35.00	100.00	175.00

Mint mark: BB

KM#	Date	Mintage	Fine	VF	XF	Unc
777.3	1853	4.148	4.00	10.00	25.00	45.00
	1854	20.380	2.00	5.00	16.00	30.00
	1855(d)	17.108	2.00	5.00	16.00	30.00
	1855(a)	I.A.	2.00	5.00	16.00	30.00
	1856	10.372	2.00	5.00	14.00	28.00
	1857	1.662	25.00	40.00	125.00	200.00

Mint mark: D

KM#	Date	Mintage	Fine	VF	XF	Unc
777.4	1853	5.013	3.00	6.00	18.00	35.00
	1854	18.597	2.00	5.00	16.00	30.00
	1855(d) small D	14.250	10.00	20.00	45.00	90.00
	1855(d) large D	Inc. Ab.	10.00	20.00	45.00	90.00
	1855(a) small D	Inc. Ab.	3.00	6.00	18.00	35.00
	1855(a) large D	Inc. Ab.	3.00	6.00	18.00	35.00
	1856 small D	7.669	2.00	6.00	15.00	30.00
	1856 large D	Inc Ab.	2.00	6.00	15.00	30.00
	1857 small D	1.531	25.00	40.00	125.00	200.00
	1857 large D	Inc. Ab.	25.00	40.00	125.00	200.00

Mint mark: K

KM#	Date	Mintage	Fine	VF	XF	Unc
777.5	1853	1.652	8.00	18.00	35.00	50.00
	1854	13.608	2.00	5.00	16.00	30.00
	1855(d)	15.761	10.00	20.00	40.00	75.00
	1855(a)	I.A.	3.00	6.00	18.00	35.00
	1856	14.775	2.00	5.00	16.00	30.00
	1857	2.417	12.00	25.00	50.00	90.00

Mint mark: MA

KM#	Date	Mintage	Fine	VF	XF	Unc
777.6	1853	1.654	8.00	18.00	35.00	50.00
	1854	14.835	2.00	5.00	16.00	30.00
	1855(d)	15.417	10.00	20.00	50.00	100.00
	1855(a)	I.A.	2.00	5.00	14.00	28.00
	1856	16.997	2.00	5.00	16.00	30.00
	1857	4.188	10.00	20.00	45.00	90.00

Mint mark: W

KM#	Date	Mintage	Fine	VF	XF	Unc
777.7	1853	5.398	4.00	10.00	25.00	50.00
	1854	14.957	2.00	5.00	15.00	30.00
	1855(d)	17.473	2.00	5.00	15.00	30.00
	1855(a)	I.A.	2.00	5.00	15.00	30.00
	1856	15.472	2.00	5.00	15.00	30.00
	1857	1.842	25.00	40.00	125.00	200.00

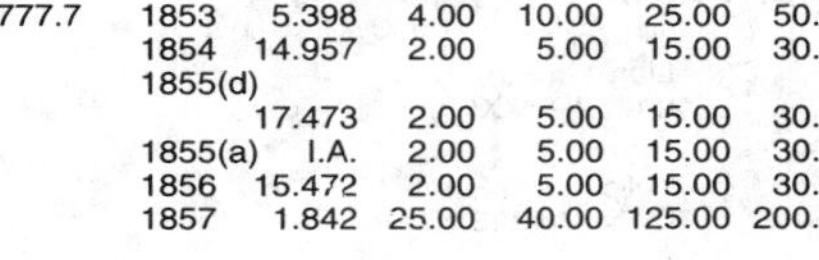

Mint mark: A

KM#	Date	Mintage	Fine	VF	XF	Unc
797.1	1861	6.857	5.00	12.00	25.00	60.00
	1862	5.300	5.00	12.00	25.00	60.00
	1863	12.128	3.00	6.00	20.00	45.00
	1864	3.053	7.00	20.00	40.00	75.00
	1865	2.619	10.00	25.00	50.00	90.00

Mint mark: BB

KM#	Date	Mintage	Fine	VF	XF	Unc
797.2	1861	7.124	4.00	10.00	20.00	50.00
	1862	8.584	4.00	10.00	20.00	50.00
	1863	2.323	20.00	40.00	75.00	100.00
	1864	6.110	5.00	12.00	25.00	60.00
	1865	7.226	4.00	10.00	20.00	50.00

Mint mark: K

KM#	Date	Mintage	Fine	VF	XF	Unc
797.3	1861	6.582	5.00	12.00	25.00	60.00
	1862	7.065	4.00	10.00	20.00	50.00
	1863	9.437	3.00	8.00	18.00	40.00
	1864	5.831	5.00	12.00	25.00	60.00

Mint mark: A
Third Republic

KM#	Date	Mintage	Fine	VF	XF	Unc
821.1	1871	2.238	3.00	8.00	18.00	40.00
	1872	4.263	2.00	5.00	10.00	20.00
	1873	1.492	4.00	10.00	20.00	50.00
	1874	1.730	4.00	10.00	20.00	50.00
	1875	1.193	4.00	10.00	20.00	50.00
	1876	2.481	2.00	5.00	12.00	25.00
	1877	.766	10.00	25.00	40.00	100.00
	1878	.300	25.00	50.00	100.00	175.00
	1879(a)	1.955	2.00	5.00	10.00	20.00
	1879 anchor w/bar	Inc. Ab.	30.00	50.00	125.00	200.00
	1880	1.172	4.00	10.00	20.00	50.00
	1881	2.502	2.00	5.00	10.00	20.00
	1882	1.600	3.00	8.00	18.00	40.00
	1883	2.400	2.00	5.00	10.00	20.00
	1884	1.680	3.00	8.00	18.00	40.00
	1885	2.000	2.00	5.00	10.00	20.00
	1886	1.680	3.00	8.00	18.00	40.00
	1887	1.008	4.00	10.00	20.00	50.00
	1888	1.660	2.00	5.00	12.00	25.00
	1889	1.660	2.00	5.00	12.00	25.00
	1890	1.680	2.00	5.00	12.00	25.00
	1891	1.600	2.00	5.00	12.00	25.00
	1892	1.600	2.00	5.00	12.00	25.00
	1893	1.600	2.00	5.00	12.00	25.00
	1894	2.240	1.50	4.00	8.00	18.00
	1896(f)	6.695	1.00	2.00	5.00	12.00
	1896(t)	I.A.	40.00	85.00	200.00	400.00
	1897	12.600	1.00	2.00	5.00	12.00
	1898	1.200	4.00	10.00	20.00	50.00

Mint mark: K

KM#	Date	Mintage	Fine	VF	XF	Unc
821.2	1871	.016	100.00	200.00	300.00	500.00
	1872	4.064	2.00	5.00	10.00	20.00
	1873	1.997	4.00	10.00	20.00	50.00
	1874	1.326	5.00	12.00	22.00	55.00
	1875	.760	10.00	25.00	40.00	100.00
	1876	1.597	5.00	12.00	22.00	55.00
	1877	1.193	6.00	15.00	25.00	65.00
	1878	.166	40.00	85.00	175.00	325.00

Mint: Paris - w/o mint mark.

KM#	Date	Mintage	Fine	VF	XF	Unc
842	1898	7.900	1.00	3.00	8.00	18.00
	1898	—	—	—	Proof	350.00
	1899	7.400	1.00	3.00	8.00	18.00
	1900	7.400	1.00	3.00	8.00	18.00
	1900	—	—	—	Proof	350.00

NOTE: Later dates (1901-1921) exist for this type.

DIX (10) CENTIMES

BILLON
Mint mark: A

KM#	Date	Mintage	Fine	VF	XF	Unc
676.1	1807	—	150.00	250.00	500.00	—
	1808	6.269	2.00	10.00	50.00	125.00
	1809	7.529	2.00	10.00	50.00	125.00
	1810	—	—	—	Unique	—

Mint mark: B

KM#	Date	Mintage	Fine	VF	XF	Unc
676.2	1808	.163	25.00	60.00	125.00	300.00
	1809	.831	6.00	20.00	60.00	150.00
	1810	1.231	5.00	18.00	55.00	135.00

Mint mark: BB

KM#	Date	Mintage	Fine	VF	XF	Unc
676.3	1808	1.425	3.00	15.00	40.00	100.00
	1809	.695	6.00	20.00	60.00	150.00
	1810	—	—	—	Unique	—

Mint mark: H

KM#	Date	Mintage	Fine	VF	XF	Unc
676.4	1808	.129	20.00	40.00	150.00	350.00
	1809	.631	7.00	15.00	40.00	125.00
	1810	.673	7.00	15.00	40.00	125.00

Mint mark: I

KM#	Date	Mintage	Fine	VF	XF	Unc
676.5	1808	1.062	4.00	10.00	25.00	90.00
	1809	3.473	3.00	7.00	20.00	75.00
	1810	3.066	3.00	7.00	20.00	75.00

Mint mark: M

KM#	Date	Mintage	Fine	VF	XF	Unc
676.6	1808	.860	7.00	15.00	40.00	125.00
	1809	1.070	4.00	10.00	25.00	90.00

Mint mark: Q

KM#	Date	Mintage	Fine	VF	XF	Unc
676.7	1808	—	—	—	Rare	—
	1809	.555	8.00	25.00	55.00	150.00
	1810	.130	25.00	60.00	125.00	250.00

Mint mark: T

KM#	Date	Mintage	Fine	VF	XF	Unc
676.8	1808	.054	40.00	100.00	200.00	500.00
	1809	.134	25.00	50.00	100.00	200.00
	1810	.103	35.00	75.00	150.00	350.00

Mint mark: W

KM#	Date	Mintage	Fine	VF	XF	Unc
676.9	1808	1.576	4.00	10.00	25.00	90.00
	1809	1.160	4.00	10.00	25.00	90.00

Mint mark: A
Second Empire

KM#	Date	Mintage	Fine	VF	XF	Unc
771.1	1852	.577	18.00	30.00	85.00	190.00
	1853	12.256	2.00	5.00	18.00	50.00
	1854	13.327	2.00	5.00	18.00	50.00
	1855(d)	14.816	2.00	5.00	18.00	45.00
	1855(a)	I.A.	3.00	6.00	20.00	60.00
	1856	19.149	1.50	4.00	15.00	30.00
	1857	3.096	5.00	10.00	25.00	75.00

Mint mark: B

KM#	Date	Mintage	Fine	VF	XF	Unc
771.2	1853	3.546	3.00	7.00	20.00	50.00
	1854	8.065	3.00	9.00	25.00	50.00
	1855(d)	9.960	3.00	10.00	30.00	75.00
	1855(a)	I.A.	2.00	6.00	18.00	45.00
	1856	11.637	2.00	6.00	18.00	45.00
	1857	1.620	15.00	30.00	85.00	200.00

Mint mark: BB

KM#	Date	Mintage	Fine	VF	XF	Unc
771.3	1853	4.582	3.00	7.00	20.00	50.00
	1854	8.433	2.00	6.00	18.00	45.00
	1855(d)	11.953	2.00	6.00	18.00	45.00
	1855(a)	I.A.	1.50	5.00	15.00	40.00
	1856	7.781	2.00	6.00	18.00	45.00
	1857	1.685	15.00	30.00	85.00	200.00

Mint mark: D

KM#	Date	Mintage	Fine	VF	XF	Unc
771.4	1853	3.709	3.00	7.00	20.00	50.00
	1854	8.487	2.00	6.00	18.00	45.00
	1855(d)	12.099	5.00	10.00	30.00	100.00
	1855(a)	I.A.	3.00	8.00	25.00	75.00
	1856	5.118	3.00	8.00	25.00	75.00

Mint mark: K

KM#	Date	Mintage	Fine	VF	XF	Unc
771.5	1853	1.203	5.00	18.00	50.00	135.00
	1854	7.083	10.00	20.00	40.00	90.00
	1855(d)	11.797	5.00	10.00	30.00	100.00
	1855(a)	I.A.	2.00	7.00	20.00	60.00
	1856	8.871	2.00	7.00	18.00	50.00
	1857	1.179	20.00	40.00	100.00	220.00

Mint mark: MA

KM#	Date	Mintage	Fine	VF	XF	Unc
771.6	1853	.889	15.00	30.00	60.00	135.00
	1854	7.995	3.00	7.00	20.00	50.00
	1855(d)	11.309	5.00	10.00	30.00	100.00
	1855(a)	I.A.	2.00	7.00	18.00	50.00
	1856	10.937	1.50	5.00	15.00	40.00
	1857	2.052	20.00	40.00	80.00	190.00

Mint mark: W

KM#	Date	Mintage	Fine	VF	XF	Unc
771.7	1853	3.107	2.00	8.00	20.00	60.00
	1854	8.242	2.00	7.00	18.00	50.00
	1855(d)	9.837	4.00	10.00	25.00	65.00
	1855(a)	I.A.	2.00	7.00	18.00	50.00
	1856	11.402	1.50	5.00	15.00	40.00
	1857	1.858	10.00	20.00	60.00	125.00

Mint mark: A

KM#	Date	Mintage	Fine	VF	XF	Unc
798.1	1861	3.638	4.00	12.00	30.00	75.00
	1862	4.736	3.00	10.00	28.00	65.00
	1863	4.873	3.00	10.00	28.00	65.00
	1864	1.556	20.00	50.00	150.00	300.00
	1865	1.608	8.00	20.00	40.00	90.00

Mint mark: BB

KM#	Date	Mintage	Fine	VF	XF	Unc
798.2	1861	4.625	3.00	10.00	28.00	65.00
	1862	4.702	3.00	10.00	28.00	65.00
	1863	1.340	6.00	15.00	35.00	80.00
	1864	3.053	5.00	12.00	30.00	70.00
	1865	4.797	3.00	10.00	28.00	65.00

Mint mark: K

KM#	Date	Mintage	Fine	VF	XF	Unc
798.3	1861	4.363	3.00	10.00	28.00	65.00
	1862	5.244	2.00	10.00	25.00	60.00
	1863	4.521	3.00	10.00	28.00	65.00
	1864	3.075	4.00	12.00	30.00	75.00

Mint mark: A
Third Republic

KM#	Date	Mintage	Fine	VF	XF	Unc
815.1	1870	.889	3.00	10.00	28.00	65.00
	1871	1.840	2.00	8.00	20.00	45.00
	1872	4.399	1.00	4.00	8.00	25.00
	1873	2.096	1.50	5.00	10.00	30.00
	1874	1.194	2.50	7.00	20.00	45.00
	1875	1.434	30.00	65.00	175.00	300.00
	1876	.458	8.00	25.00	50.00	90.00
	1877	.392	12.00	35.00	65.00	135.00
	1878	.150	15.00	40.00	75.00	160.00
	1879	.823	4.00	12.00	28.00	55.00
	1880	1.414	2.00	6.00	18.00	40.00
	1881	.749	4.00	12.00	28.00	55.00
	1882	1.100	2.00	8.00	20.00	45.00
	1883	.700	6.00	20.00	40.00	80.00
	1884	1.060	2.00	8.00	20.00	45.00
	1885	.900	2.50	7.00	20.00	45.00
	1886	1.060	2.00	8.00	20.00	45.00
	1887	.874	2.50	7.00	20.00	45.00
	1888	1.050	2.00	8.00	20.00	45.00
	1889	1.010	2.00	8.00	20.00	45.00
	1890	1.060	2.00	8.00	20.00	45.00
	1891	1.000	2.00	8.00	20.00	45.00
	1892	1.020	2.00	8.00	20.00	45.00
	1893	1.120	2.00	8.00	20.00	45.00
	1894	.800	2.50	10.00	25.00	50.00
	1895	.600	3.00	8.00	28.00	55.00
	1896(f)	I.A.	1.00	3.00	8.00	30.00
	1896(t)	I.A.	30.00	75.00	250.00	400.00
	1897	7.250	.50	3.00	6.00	15.00
	1898	1.400	2.00	6.00	18.00	40.00

Mint mark: K

KM#	Date	Mintage	Fine	VF	XF	Unc
815.2	1871	.027	75.00	175.00	300.00	650.00
	1872	4.359	1.00	4.00	8.00	25.00
	1873	2.001	2.00	6.00	18.00	40.00
	1874	1.337	6.00	20.00	40.00	80.00
	1875	.430	6.00	20.00	40.00	80.00
	1876	.601	5.00	18.00	35.00	75.00
	1877	.403	6.00	20.00	40.00	80.00
	1878	.100	40.00	100.00	175.00	300.00

BRONZE
Mint: Paris - w/o mint mark.

KM#	Date	Mintage	Fine	VF	XF	Unc
843	1898	4.000	1.00	3.00	8.00	20.00
	1898	—	—	Matte Proof		450.00
	1899	4.000	1.00	3.00	8.00	20.00
	1900(n)	5.000	1.00	3.00	8.00	20.00
	1900(n)	—	—	—	Proof	400.00

NOTE: Later dates (1901-1921) exist for this type.

VINGT (20) CENTIMES

1.0000 g, .900 SILVER, .0289 oz ASW
Mint mark: A
Second Republic

KM#	Date	Mintage	Fine	VF	XF	Unc
758.1	1849	4,877	125.00	250.00	450.00	700.00
	1850	6.157	3.00	10.00	18.00	45.00
	1851	3.309	5.00	15.00	25.00	55.00

Mint mark: BB

KM#	Date	Mintage	Fine	VF	XF	Unc
758.2	1850	.048	40.00	75.00	200.00	450.00

Mint mark: K

KM#	Date	Mintage	Fine	VF	XF	Unc
758.3	1850	.344	20.00	35.00	85.00	210.00

Mint mark: A
Second Empire - Napoleon III

KM#	Date	Mintage	Fine	VF	XF	Unc
778.1	1853 small head					

KM#	Date	Mintage	Fine	VF	XF	Unc
778.1		.680	10.00	20.00	50.00	100.00
	1853 large head	Inc. Ab.	100.00	200.00	400.00	700.00
	1854	1.683	5.00	12.00	25.00	60.00
	1855(d)	.362	10.00	25.00	45.00	100.00
	1856	.603	8.00	17.50	40.00	80.00
	1857	.840	6.00	15.00	35.00	70.00
	1858	.704	10.00	20.00	40.00	80.00
	1859	3.620	3.00	10.00	20.00	45.00
	1860/50	6.536	6.00	15.00	40.00	85.00
	1860(h)	I.A.	3.00	6.00	15.00	35.00
	1862	.054	75.00	175.00	300.00	600.00

Mint mark: BB

KM#	Date	Mintage	Fine	VF	XF	Unc
778.2	1856	.013	125.00	275.00	450.00	800.00
	1860(b)	2.986	5.00	12.00	25.00	80.00
	1863	.398	20.00	45.00	90.00	200.00

Mint mark: D

KM#	Date	Mintage	Fine	VF	XF	Unc
778.3	1856	.396	12.50	25.00	50.00	125.00

1.0000 g, .835 SILVER, .0268 oz ASW
Mint mark: A

KM#	Date	Mintage	Fine	VF	XF	Unc
805.1	1864	.268	10.00	25.00	75.00	175.00
	1865	—	— Reported, not confirmed			
	1866	1.460	5.00	10.00	30.00	65.00

Mint mark: BB

KM#	Date	Mintage	Fine	VF	XF	Unc
805.2	1864	.112	15.00	30.00	75.00	175.00
	1866	.843	7.00	15.00	35.00	75.00

Mint mark: K

KM#	Date	Mintage	Fine	VF	XF	Unc
805.3	1864	.058	30.00	60.00	150.00	260.00
	1866	.413	10.00	25.00	55.00	150.00

Mint mark: A

KM#	Date	Mintage	Fine	VF	XF	Unc
808.1	1867	5.611	2.00	4.00	10.00	20.00
	1868	.353	7.00	15.00	35.00	90.00

Mint mark: BB

KM#	Date	Mintage	Fine	VF	XF	Unc
808.2	1867	3.114	2.50	5.00	12.00	25.00
	1868	.200	15.00	30.00	65.00	115.00
	1869	Inc. Ab.	—	—	—	—

Mint mark: K

KM#	Date	Mintage	Fine	VF	XF	Unc
808.3	1867	.091	20.00	50.00	125.00	250.00

1.0000 g, .900 SILVER, 15mm, .0289 oz ASW
Mint mark: A

KM#	Date	Mintage	Fine	VF	XF	Unc
828.1	1878	30 pcs.	—	—	1400.	2000.

16mm

KM#	Date	Mintage	Fine	VF	XF	Unc
828.2	1889	100 pcs.	—	—	900.00	1100.

NOTE: Considered an Essai.

25 CENTIMES

1.2500 g, .900 SILVER, .0362 oz ASW
Mint mark: A

KM#	Date	Mintage	Fine	VF	XF	Unc
755.1	1845	Inc. Ab.	5.00	10.00	25.00	85.00
	1846	1.748	4.00	8.00	18.00	55.00
	1847	3.000	3.00	6.00	15.00	45.00
	1848	.142	5.00	10.00	25.00	85.00

Mint mark: B

KM#	Date	Mintage	Fine	VF	XF	Unc
755.2	1845	Inc. Ab.	3.00	6.00	12.50	45.00

Mint mark: BB

KM#	Date	Mintage	Fine	VF	XF	Unc
755.3	1845	Inc. Ab.	5.00	10.00	35.00	125.00
	1846	7,922	20.00	40.00	100.00	250.00
	1847	9,939	20.00	40.00	100.00	250.00
	1848	5,886	25.00	75.00	150.00	300.00

Mint mark: K

KM#	Date	Mintage	Fine	VF	XF	Unc
755.4	1845	Inc. Ab.	15.00	30.00	70.00	200.00
	1846	.012	20.00	40.00	100.00	275.00
	1847	3,905	30.00	75.00	200.00	350.00

Mint mark: W

KM#	Date	Mintage	Fine	VF	XF	Unc
755.5	1845	Inc. Ab.	5.00	10.00	25.00	85.00
	1846	.039	5.00	10.00	35.00	125.00

50 CENTIMES

2.5000 g, .900 SILVER, .0723 oz ASW
Mint mark: A

KM#	Date	Mintage	Fine	VF	XF	Unc
768.1	1845	.494	10.00	20.00	40.00	90.00
	1846	3.165	7.50	15.00	30.00	80.00
	1847	3.437	7.50	15.00	30.00	80.00
	1848	.218	10.00	20.00	40.00	90.00

Mint mark: B

KM#	Date	Mintage	Fine	VF	XF	Unc
768.2	1845	Inc. C198.2	7.50	15.00	30.00	75.00
	1846	1.000	7.50	15.00	30.00	75.00

Mint mark: BB

KM#	Date	Mintage	Fine	VF	XF	Unc
768.3	1845	Inc. KM741.3	12.00	25.00	50.00	135.00
	1846	.017	12.00	25.00	50.00	135.00
	1847	.044	10.00	20.00	40.00	100.00
	1848	.018	12.00	25.00	50.00	135.00

Mint mark: K

KM#	Date	Mintage	Fine	VF	XF	Unc
768.4	1845	Inc. KM741.7	35.00	70.00	150.00	300.00
	1846	.022	10.00	20.00	45.00	125.00
	1847	8,915	25.00	50.00	110.00	250.00

Mint mark: W

KM#	Date	Mintage	Fine	VF	XF	Unc
768.5	1845	Inc. KM741.13	7.00	15.00	30.00	90.00
	1846	.070	10.00	25.00	40.00	100.00

Mint mark: A
Second Republic

KM#	Date	Mintage	Fine	VF	XF	Unc
769.1	1849	2,655	150.00	300.00	600.00	1000.
	1850	2.165	8.00	18.00	40.00	150.00
	1851	.850	15.00	35.00	100.00	175.00
	1851	—	—	—	Proof	800.00

Mint mark: BB

KM#	Date	Mintage	Fine	VF	XF	Unc
769.2	1850	.040	40.00	110.00	250.00	450.00

Mint mark: K

KM#	Date	Mintage	Fine	VF	XF	Unc
769.3	1850	.031	60.00	125.00	275.00	600.00

Mint mark: A
President Louis-Napoleon

KM#	Date	Mintage	Fine	VF	XF	Unc
793	1852	1.010	25.00	60.00	150.00	325.00

Second Empire

KM#	Date	Mintage	Fine	VF	XF	Unc
794.1	1853	.154	35.00	90.00	200.00	450.00
	1854	1.080	15.00	30.00	75.00	175.00
	1855	.400	25.00	60.00	125.00	250.00
	1856	1.436	15.00	30.00	75.00	175.00
	1857	1.632	15.00	30.00	75.00	175.00
	1858	5.559	8.00	18.00	40.00	125.00
	1859	3.880	9.00	20.00	45.00	135.00
	1860(h)	2.657	10.00	22.00	50.00	150.00
	1862	1.549	15.00	30.00	75.00	175.00

Mint mark: BB

KM#	Date	Mintage	Fine	VF	XF	Unc
794.2	1856	1.196	15.00	30.00	75.00	175.00
	1859	1.112	15.00	30.00	75.00	175.00
	1860	1.555	15.00	30.00	75.00	175.00
	1861	.355	30.00	80.00	175.00	400.00
	1862	1.007	20.00	50.00	125.00	250.00
	1863	.137	45.00	120.00	250.00	500.00

Mint mark: D

KM#	Date	Mintage	Fine	VF	XF	Unc
794.3	1856	1.246	15.00	30.00	75.00	175.00

2.5000 g, .835 SILVER, .0671 oz ASW
Mint mark: A

KM#	Date	Mintage	Fine	VF	XF	Unc
814.1	1864	7.598	5.00	10.00	20.00	60.00
	1865	7.398	5.00	10.00	20.00	60.00
	1866	5.921	6.00	12.00	25.00	75.00
	1867	14.528	3.00	6.00	15.00	40.00
	1868	2.789	8.00	18.00	40.00	100.00

Mint mark: BB

KM#	Date	Mintage	Fine	VF	XF	Unc
814.2	1864	4.626	6.00	12.00	25.00	75.00
	1865	5.175	6.00	12.00	25.00	75.00
	1866	5.256	6.00	12.00	25.00	75.00
	1867	9.992	5.00	10.00	20.00	60.00
	1868	Inc. Be.	40.00	100.00	200.00	400.00
	1869	1.800	30.00	75.00	150.00	250.00

Mint mark: K

KM#	Date	Mintage	Fine	VF	XF	Unc
814.3	1864	1.828	15.00	35.00	75.00	150.00
	1865	4.901	6.00	12.00	25.00	75.00
	1866	3.500	8.00	16.00	35.00	100.00
	1867	4.692	6.00	12.00	25.00	75.00

Mint mark: A
Third Republic

KM#	Date	Mintage	Fine	VF	XF	Unc
834.1	1871	.236	15.00	40.00	100.00	225.00
	1872	4.243	4.00	10.00	25.00	60.00
	1873	.926	10.00	25.00	60.00	125.00
	1874	1.228	8.00	15.00	35.00	80.00
	1878	30 pcs.	—	—	Proof	2250.
	1881	5.391	2.00	4.00	15.00	40.00
	1882	2.320	3.00	6.00	20.00	50.00
	1886	.309	15.00	40.00	100.00	225.00
	1887	1.866	6.00	12.00	25.00	65.00
	1888	4.517	1.50	3.00	15.00	40.00
	1889	100 pcs.	—	—	Proof	2200.
	1894	3.600	1.50	3.00	15.00	40.00
	1895	7.200	1.50	3.00	10.00	25.00

Mint mark: K

KM#	Date	Mintage	Fine	VF	XF	Unc
834.2	1871	.723	8.00	15.00	40.00	85.00
	1872	1.643	7.00	14.00	30.00	70.00
	1873	.166	100.00	250.00	450.00	800.00

Mint: Paris - w/o mint mark.

KM#	Date	Mintage	Fine	VF	XF	Unc
854	1897	.088	30.00	75.00	125.00	200.00
	1897	—	—	—	Proof	300.00
	1898	30.000	1.00	2.00	10.00	20.00
	1898	—	—	—	Proof	300.00
	1899	18.000	1.50	3.00	8.00	25.00
	1900	9.195	3.00	6.00	15.00	40.00
	1900	—	—	—	Proof	300.00

NOTE: Later dates (1901-1920) exist for this type.

UN (1) DECIME

STRASBOURG PROVISIONAL ISSUES

BRONZE
Mint mark: BB

KM#	Date	Mintage	VG	Fine	VF	XF
700	1814	.544	7.50	15.00	45.00	125.00
	1814 DECIME.	Inc. Ab.	15.00	35.00	90.00	225.00
	1814.	I.A.	10.00	20.00	50.00	145.00
	1814. DECIME.	Inc. Ab.	10.00	20.00	40.00	140.00
	1815	Inc. Ab.	12.50	25.00	55.00	150.00
	1815. DECIME.	Inc. Ab.	15.00	30.00	65.00	175.00

KM#	Date	Mintage	VG	Fine	VF	XF
701	1814	1.208	15.00	30.00	60.00	150.00
	1814. DECIME.	Inc. Ab.	15.00	30.00	60.00	150.00
	1815	I.A.	7.50	15.00	30.00	125.00
	1815. DECIME.	Inc. Ab.	10.00	20.00	40.00	140.00

QUART (1/4) FRANC

1.2500 g, .900 SILVER, .0362 oz ASW

Mint mark: A
Obv. leg: BONAPARTE PR. CONSUL.

KM#	Date	Mintage	VG	Fine	VF	XF
653.1	AN12	.171	15.00	27.50	65.00	110.00
	Mint mark: BB					
653.2	AN12	1,565	60.00	120.00	300.00	550.00
	Mint mark: D					
653.3	AN12	—	60.00	120.00	300.00	550.00
	Mint mark: I					
653.4	AN12	.041	22.50	45.00	110.00	225.00
	Mint mark: L					
653.5	AN12	.019	30.00	60.00	150.00	275.00
	Mint mark: M					
653.6	AN12	.039	17.50	32.50	80.00	200.00
	Mint mark: MA					
653.7	AN12	9,080	30.00	60.00	150.00	300.00
	Mint mark: Q					
653.8	AN12	.028	25.00	50.00	90.00	250.00
	Mint mark: T					
653.9	AN12	.010	30.00	60.00	150.00	300.00
	Common date					Unc. 275.00

Mint mark: A
Obv. leg: NAPOLEON EMPEREUR.

KM#	Date	Mintage	VG	Fine	VF	XF
654.1	AN12	.019	25.00	45.00	85.00	225.00
	AN13	.128	12.50	25.00	45.00	115.00
	AN14	—	—Reported, not confirmed			
	Mint mark: BB					
654.2	AN13	2,194	60.00	115.00	235.00	480.00
	Mint mark: D					
654.3	AN12	5,156	45.00	100.00	175.00	400.00
	Mint mark: H					
654.4	AN12	.012	30.00	60.00	145.00	350.00
	AN13/12	—	45.00	90.00	225.00	460.00
	AN13	2,744	45.00	90.00	225.00	460.00
	Mint mark: I					
654.5	AN12	.032	20.00	40.00	85.00	225.00
	AN13	.118	15.00	30.00	75.00	175.00
	Mint mark: K					
654.6	AN12	8,122	30.00	60.00	145.00	350.00
	AN13	.018	25.00	45.00	100.00	225.00
	AN14	1,757	70.00	140.00	290.00	650.00
	Mint mark: L					
654.7	AN13	.025	25.00	45.00	85.00	280.00
	AN14	—	70.00	135.00	280.00	575.00
	Mint mark: M					
654.8	AN12	.016	25.00	45.00	115.00	280.00
	AN13	.039	20.00	40.00	80.00	225.00
	Mint mark: MA					
654.9	AN13	8,114	30.00	60.00	145.00	350.00
	Mint mark: T					
654.10	AN12	3,606	60.00	115.00	200.00	425.00
	AN13	6,801	35.00	70.00	140.00	280.00
	Mint mark: U					
654.11	AN13	.014	60.00	115.00	280.00	575.00
	AN14	100 pcs.	400.00	600.00	1000.	2000.
	Common date					Unc. 325.00

KM#	Date	Mintage	VG	Fine	VF	XF
	Mint mark: A					
670.1	1806	.031	25.00	50.00	90.00	200.00
	1807	—	—	—	—	—
	Mint mark: I					
670.2	1806	4,583	35.00	70.00	140.00	280.00
	1807	8,356	30.00	60.00	115.00	225.00
	Mint mark: K					
670.3	1806	4,359	35.00	70.00	140.00	280.00
	1807	5,538	35.00	70.00	140.00	280.00
	Mint mark: L					
670.4	1806	.018	25.00	50.00	90.00	225.00
	1807	7,618	30.00	75.00	115.00	250.00
	Mint mark: M					
670.5	1807	1,626	85.00	1750.	300.00	700.00
	Mint mark: Q					
670.6	1806	8,948	30.00	60.00	115.00	225.00
	1807	9,713	30.00	60.00	115.00	225.00
	Mint mark: U					
670.7	1806	1,361	85.00	175.00	300.00	700.00
	1807	.013	30.00	50.00	90.00	225.00

Mint mark: A
Negro head.

KM#	Date	Mintage	VG	Fine	VF	XF
677	1807	.041	45.00	100.00	250.00	425.00

Laureate head.

KM#	Date	Mintage	VG	Fine	VF	XF
678.1	1807	.017	45.00	100.00	225.00	400.00
	1808	—	50.00	125.00	250.00	650.00
	Mint mark: I					
678.2	1808	1,466	60.00	150.00	300.00	750.00
	Mint mark: L					
678.3	1808	4,393	50.00	100.00	225.00	400.00

Mint mark: A

KM#	Date	Mintage	VG	Fine	VF	XF
690	1809	.034	30.00	75.00	125.00	250.00

Mint mark: A

KM#	Date	Mintage	Fine	VF	XF	Unc
714.1	1817	.100	10.00	25.00	75.00	200.00
	1818	.028	20.00	50.00	100.00	300.00
	1819	.011	25.00	60.00	150.00	400.00
	1820	.012	25.00	60.00	150.00	400.00
	1821	.022	20.00	50.00	100.00	325.00
	1822	.036	20.00	50.00	100.00	250.00
	1823	.044	20.00	50.00	100.00	250.00
	1824	.083	15.00	30.00	75.00	175.00
	Mint mark: B					
714.2	1617	.021	22.50	50.00	100.00	300.00
	1818	.016	25.00	60.00	110.00	350.00
	1819	.015	25.00	60.00	110.00	350.00
	1822	.030	22.50	50.00	100.00	325.00
	1823	.013	25.00	60.00	150.00	400.00
	1824	.018	22.50	55.00	110.00	350.00
	Mint mark: BB					
714.3	1817	3,772	35.00	90.00	250.00	500.00
	Mint mark: D					
714.4	1817	.012	25.00	50.00	100.00	300.00
	Mint mark: I					
714.5	1817	.016	30.00	60.00	90.00	275.00
	1823	1,870	75.00	150.00	250.00	600.00
	Mint mark: L					
714.6	1817	.014	25.00	50.00	100.00	300.00
	1823	.012	25.00	50.00	100.00	300.00
	1824	.031	20.00	40.00	100.00	300.00
	Mint mark: M					
714.7	1817	4,314	35.00	90.00	250.00	500.00
	1823	3,994	40.00	100.00	260.00	525.00
	1824	7,774	35.00	75.00	175.00	425.00
	Mint mark: MA					
714.8	1817	2,132	60.00	125.00	225.00	500.00
	Mint mark: Q					
714.9	1817	.013	25.00	60.00	150.00	400.00
	1823	.011	25.00	60.00	150.00	400.00
	Mint mark: T					
714.10	1817	7,606	35.00	75.00	175.00	500.00
	Mint mark: W					
714.11	1817	.014	25.00	60.00	150.00	400.00
	1818	3,294	40.00	100.00	260.00	550.00
	1819	3,170	40.00	100.00	260.00	550.00
	1820	5,894	35.00	75.00	145.00	475.00
	1822	4,486	40.00	100.00	175.00	525.00
	1823	.016	25.00	50.00	120.00	350.00
	1824	.011	25.00	60.00	150.00	400.00

Mint mark: A

KM#	Date	Mintage	Fine	VF	XF	Unc
722.1	1825	9,448	35.00	75.00	150.00	350.00
	1826	.083	15.00	30.00	75.00	175.00
	1827	.322	6.00	15.00	60.00	100.00
	1828	.446	6.00	15.00	60.00	100.00
	1829	.154	7.00	17.50	65.00	150.00
	1830	.659	6.00	15.00	40.00	100.00
	1830 reeded edge					
		Inc.Ab.	60.00	125.00	225.00	425.00
	Mint mark: B					
722.2	1826	.023	20.00	35.00	75.00	200.00
	1827	.017	20.00	35.00	75.00	200.00
	1828	.023	20.00	35.00	75.00	200.00
	1829	.032	15.00	25.00	50.00	175.00
	Mint mark: BB					
722.3	1827	1,567	60.00	175.00	300.00	550.00
	1827	1,567	60.00	175.00	300.00	550.00
	1829	.014	25.00	60.00	150.00	300.00
	Mint mark: D					
722.4	1826	.013	25.00	60.00	150.00	300.00
	1827	7,820	35.00	75.00	175.00	350.00
	1828	.013	25.00	60.00	150.00	300.00
	1829	.052	15.00	25.00	50.00	175.00
	Mint mark: H					
722.5	1828	.016	20.00	35.00	75.00	225.00
	Mint mark: I					
722.6	1827	828	—	—	—	—
	1828	2,226	45.00	125.00	250.00	385.00
	1829	.010	20.00	50.00	100.00	275.00
	Mint mark: K					
722.7	1829	.027	20.00	35.00	75.00	200.00
	1830	.021	20.00	35.00	75.00	200.00
	Mint mark: L					
722.8	1826	.011	20.00	50.00	100.00	275.00
	1827	7,582	35.00	85.00	175.00	300.00
	1828	.015	20.00	35.00	75.00	225.00
	1829	6,486	35.00	85.00	175.00	300.00
	1830	.015	20.00	35.00	75.00	225.00
	Mint mark: M					
722.9	1826	4,861	40.00	100.00	175.00	350.00
	1827	4,292	40.00	100.00	175.00	350.00
	1828	.048	15.00	30.00	65.00	200.00
	1829	.014	20.00	35.00	75.00	225.00
	Mint mark: Q					
722.10	1826	7,534	35.00	85.00	175.00	320.00
	1828	.013	20.00	35.00	75.00	225.00
	Mint mark: T					
722.11	1826	1,753	—	—	—	—
	1828	6,316	25.00	75.00	175.00	320.00
	1829	6,481	25.00	75.00	175.00	320.00
	Mint mark: W					
722.12	1826	.015	20.00	35.00	75.00	225.00
	1827	.022	20.00	35.00	75.00	200.00
	1828	.047	15.00	30.00	65.00	200.00
	1829	.108	10.00	20.00	50.00	125.00
	1830	.074	15.00	25.00	60.00	150.00

Mint mark: A

KM#	Date	Mintage	Fine	VF	XF	Unc
740.1	1831	.075	15.00	25.00	60.00	175.00
	1832	.286	7.00	15.00	30.00	80.00
	1833	.155	8.00	18.00	35.00	90.00
	1834	.770	4.00	10.00	20.00	55.00
	1835	.801	4.00	10.00	20.00	55.00
	1836	.898	4.00	7.00	17.50	42.50
	1837	.830	4.00	7.00	17.50	42.50
	1838	.922	4.00	7.00	17.50	42.50
	1839	1.180	4.00	7.00	17.50	42.50
	1840	1.246	4.00	7.00	17.50	42.50
	1841	1.303	4.00	7.00	17.50	42.50
	1842	.647	4.00	7.00	17.50	42.50
	1843	.478	4.00	7.00	17.50	42.50
	1844	.816	4.00	7.00	17.50	42.50
	1845	.396	4.00	7.00	17.50	42.50
	Mint mark: B					
740.2	1831	.052	6.00	12.00	27.50	75.00
	1832	.135	5.00	10.00	20.00	55.00
	1833	.080	5.00	10.00	20.00	65.00
	1834	.070	5.00	10.00	20.00	65.00
	1835 3 known		—	500.00	—	—
	1835 (error): PRANCAIS					
		Inc. Ab.	—	—	400.00	—
	1836	8,413	20.00	40.00	100.00	200.00
	1837	.094	5.00	10.00	20.00	55.00
	1838	.049	10.00	20.00	40.00	90.00
	1839	.053	10.00	20.00	40.00	90.00
	1840/30					
		1 known	—	750.00	—	—
	1840	.053	10.00	20.00	40.00	90.00
	1841	.289	4.00	8.00	20.00	55.00
	1842	.642	4.00	8.00	17.50	50.00
	1843	.762	4.00	8.00	17.50	50.00
	1844	.018	10.00	20.00	40.00	90.00
	1845	4.603	3.00	6.00	17.50	50.00
	Mint mark: BB					
740.3	1831	3,629	30.00	65.00	125.00	250.00
	1832	.011	15.00	30.00	60.00	150.00
	1833	7,890	20.00	40.00	100.00	200.00

KM#	Date	Mintage	Fine	VF	XF	Unc
740.3	1834	6,063	20.00	40.00	100.00	200.00
	1835	.010	10.00	20.00	40.00	100.00
	1836	.011	10.00	20.00	40.00	100.00
	1837	9,762	20.00	40.00	100.00	200.00
	1838	6,561	20.00	40.00	100.00	225.00
	1839	.013	10.00	20.00	45.00	110.00
	1844	.036	10.00	20.00	40.00	90.00
	1845	.051	10.00	20.00	40.00	90.00
Mint mark: D						
740.4	1831	.034	10.00	20.00	40.00	90.00
	1832	.141	6.00	12.00	28.00	75.00
	1833	.016	15.00	30.00	60.00	150.00
	1834	.030	6.00	12.00	27.50	75.00
	1835	.028	6.00	12.00	27.50	75.00
	1837	8,352	20.00	40.00	100.00	225.00
	1838	6,199	20.00	40.00	100.00	225.00
	1839	5,163	25.00	50.00	125.00	250.00
	1840	.015	15.00	30.00	60.00	150.00
Mint mark: H						
740.5	1831	.026	10.00	20.00	50.00	115.00
	1832	.040	10.00	20.00	40.00	90.00
	1833	.014	15.00	30.00	60.00	150.00
	1834	.046	10.00	20.00	40.00	90.00
	1835	9,989	20.00	40.00	100.00	225.00
Mint mark: I						
740.6	1831	967 pcs.	—	—	—	—
	1832	.034	10.00	20.00	50.00	115.00
	1833	.024	10.00	20.00	50.00	115.00
	1834	.040	6.00	12.00	27.50	75.00
	1835	.044	6.00	12.00	27.50	75.00
Mint mark: K						
740.7	1831	.036	6.00	12.00	27.50	75.00
	1832	.020	6.00	12.00	27.50	75.00
	1833	.022	6.00	12.00	27.50	75.00
	1834	.036	6.00	12.00	27.50	75.00
	1835	.041	6.00	12.00	27.50	75.00
	1836	9,500	20.00	40.00	100.00	200.00
	1837	.011	15.00	30.00	60.00	150.00
	1838	.016	15.00	30.00	60.00	150.00
	1839	.016	15.00	30.00	60.00	150.00
	1840	.030	10.00	20.00	40.00	90.00
	1841	.092	8.00	15.00	35.00	80.00
	1842	.023	10.00	20.00	50.00	115.00
	1843	.027	10.00	20.00	50.00	115.00
	1844	.023	10.00	20.00	50.00	115.00
	1845	.016	12.00	25.00	60.00	125.00
Mint mark: L						
740.8	1831	6,182	20.00	40.00	100.00	225.00
	1832	.022	10.00	20.00	50.00	115.00
	1833	8,927	20.00	40.00	100.00	225.00
	1834	8,789	20.00	40.00	100.00	225.00
Mint mark: M						
740.9	1831	6,831	20.00	40.00	100.00	225.00
	1832	.035	6.00	12.00	27.50	75.00
	1833	.017	15.00	30.00	60.00	150.00
	1834	8,218	20.00	40.00	100.00	225.00
	1835	.011	15.00	30.00	60.00	150.00
Mint mark: MA						
740.10	1832	1 known	—	—	Rare	—
	1833	3,452	—	—	—	—
Mint mark: Q						
740.11	1831	.011	15.00	30.00	60.00	150.00
	1832	.018	12.00	25.00	50.00	125.00
	1834	.014	15.00	30.00	60.00	150.00
Mint mark: T						
740.12	1832	8,486	20.00	40.00	100.00	225.00
	1833	.018	12.00	25.00	50.00	125.00
	1834	.034	7.00	15.00	30.00	80.00
Mint mark: W						
740.13	1831	.160	5.00	10.00	20.00	50.00
	1832	.218	5.00	10.00	20.00	60.00
	1833	.141	5.00	10.00	20.00	60.00
	1834	.404	4.00	8.00	18.00	45.00
	1835	.133	5.00	10.00	20.00	55.00
	1836	.089	6.00	12.00	30.00	70.00
	1837	.168	5.00	10.00	20.00	55.00
	1838/3	.100	—	—	—	—
	1838	Inc. Ab.	5.00	10.00	20.00	55.00
	1839	.114	5.00	10.00	20.00	55.00
	1840	.042	10.00	20.00	40.00	90.00
	1841	.168	5.00	10.00	20.00	55.00
	1842	.091	5.00	10.00	20.00	55.00
	1843	.073	5.00	10.00	20.00	55.00
	1844	.367	4.00	8.00	17.50	50.00
	1845	.330	4.00	8.00	17.50	50.00

DEMI (1/2) FRANC

2.5000 g, .900 SILVER, .0723 oz ASW

Mint mark: A

Obv. leg: BONAPARTE PREMIER CONSUL.

KM#	Date	Mintage	VG	Fine	VF	XF
648.1	ANXI	.031	20.00	50.00	150.00	275.00
	AN12	.280	10.00	20.00	50.00	200.00
Mint mark: BB						
648.2	AN12	2,125	75.00	150.00	325.00	650.00
Mint mark: D						
648.3	AN12	.015	25.00	60.00	175.00	300.00
Mint mark: G						
648.4	AN12	7,407	75.00	175.00	350.00	750.00
Mint mark: H						
648.5	AN12	1,988	100.00	175.00	350.00	800.00
Mint mark: I						
648.6	AN12	.416	9.00	18.00	40.00	150.00
Mint mark: K						
648.7	AN12	.012	30.00	70.00	200.00	375.00
Mint mark: L						
648.8	AN12	.067	10.00	25.00	65.00	200.00
Mint mark: M						
648.9	AN12	.136	10.00	20.00	50.00	200.00
Mint mark: MA						
648.10	AN12	.026	20.00	50.00	125.00	250.00
Mint mark: Q						
648.11	AN12	.054	15.00	40.00	100.00	225.00
Mint mark: T						
648.12	AN12	.017	25.00	50.00	175.00	300.00
Mint mark: U						
648.13	AN12	3,150	80.00	200.00	400.00	850.00
	Common date					Unc. 350.00

Mint mark: A

Obv. leg: NAPOLEON EMPEREUR.

KM#	Date	Mintage	VG	Fine	VF	XF
655.1	AN12	.039	12.00	25.00	60.00	250.00
	AN13	.427	9.00	18.00	40.00	150.00
	AN14	.020	25.00	50.00	125.00	350.00
Mint mark: BB						
655.2	AN12	1,825	50.00	125.00	275.00	500.00
	AN13	895 pcs.	100.00	275.00	450.00	1000.
Mint mark: D						
655.3	AN13	2,402	35.00	70.00	150.00	350.00
Mint mark: G						
655.4	AN13	1,181	—	—	Rare	—
Mint mark: H						
655.5	AN12	7,286	25.00	60.00	125.00	300.00
	AN13	5,036	30.00	75.00	150.00	350.00
Mint mark: I						
655.6	AN12	.022	20.00	50.00	100.00	225.00
	AN13	.206	12.00	22.00	50.00	200.00
Mint mark: K						
655.7	AN12	.019	20.00	50.00	100.00	250.00
	AN13	.037	18.00	40.00	80.00	200.00
	AN14	1,757	—	—	Rare	—
Mint mark: L						
655.8	AN13	.046	15.00	30.00	65.00	180.00
	AN14	3,889	50.00	100.00	225.00	500.00
Mint mark: M						
655.9	AN12	.099	12.00	25.00	60.00	175.00
	AN13	.212	10.00	20.00	50.00	150.00
Mint mark: MA						
655.10	AN13	6,103	30.00	75.00	150.00	350.00
Mint mark: Q						
655.11	AN13	.034	18.00	40.00	80.00	200.00
Mint mark: T						
655.12	AN12	3,735	35.00	70.00	150.00	350.00
	AN13	6,140	30.00	70.00	140.00	300.00
Mint mark: U						
655.13	AN13	1,662	50.00	90.00	200.00	400.00
	AN14	—	100.00	200.00	400.00	800.00
	Common date					Unc. 350.00
Mint mark: A						
671.1	1806	.156	12.00	25.00	60.00	175.00
Mint mark: I						
671.2	1806	7,027	30.00	75.00	150.00	350.00
	1807	3,848	40.00	90.00	175.00	400.00
Mint mark: K						
671.3	1806	1,673	50.00	100.00	200.00	450.00
	1807	2,983	40.00	90.00	175.00	400.00
Mint mark: L						
671.4	1806	.042	15.00	30.00	75.00	200.00
	1807/6	.017	20.00	40.00	100.00	225.00
	1807	Inc. Ab.	20.00	40.00	100.00	250.00
Mint mark: M						
671.5	1807	1,791	—Reported, not confirmed			
Mint mark: Q						
671.6	1806	.015	20.00	40.00	100.00	250.00
	1807	.014	20.00	40.00	100.00	250.00
Mint mark: U						
671.7	1806	9,592	30.00	75.00	150.00	350.00

KM#	Date	Mintage	VG	Fine	VF	XF
671.7	1807	4,448	40.00	90.00	175.00	400.00
	Common date					Unc. 325.00
Mint mark: A						
Negro head.						
679	1807	.058	75.00	175.00	375.00	800.00
Laureate head.						
680.1	1807	.046	60.00	125.00	250.00	500.00
	1808	6.606	5.00	10.00	20.00	75.00
Mint mark: B						
680.2	1808	.559	8.00	15.00	30.00	100.00
Mint mark: BB						
680.3	1808	1.596	5.00	10.00	25.00	75.00
Mint mark: D						
680.4	1808	.871	6.00	12.00	30.00	90.00
Mint mark: H						
680.5	1808	.336	8.00	18.00	45.00	100.00
Mint mark: I						
680.6	1808	.298	10.00	20.00	40.00	100.00
Mint mark: K						
680.7	1808	.363	8.00	18.00	45.00	100.00
Mint mark: L						
680.8	1808	3,394	50.00	100.00	200.00	375.00
Mint mark: M						
680.9	1808	.054	20.00	50.00	100.00	200.00
Mint mark: MA						
680.10	1808	.028	30.00	60.00	125.00	250.00
Mint mark: Q						
680.11	1808	.289	10.00	20.00	40.00	100.00
Mint mark: T						
680.12	1808	.128	12.00	25.00	50.00	125.00
Mint mark: U						
680.13	1808	3,339	50.00	100.00	200.00	375.00
Mint mark: W						
680.14	1808	1.069	5.00	10.00	25.00	75.00
	Common date					Unc. 200.00
Mint mark: A						
691.1	1809	1.680	5.00	10.00	20.00	75.00
	1810	1.362	5.00	10.00	20.00	75.00
	1811	1.860	5.00	10.00	20.00	75.00
	1812	1.720	5.00	10.00	20.00	75.00
	1813	.627	8.00	15.00	30.00	85.00
	1814	.107	10.00	20.00	50.00	100.00
Mint mark: B						
691.2	1809	.014	15.00	30.00	90.00	225.00
	1810	.285	8.00	15.00	35.00	100.00
	1811	.252	8.00	15.00	35.00	100.00
	1812	.192	9.00	18.00	40.00	115.00
Mint mark: BB						
691.3	1810	.011	20.00	40.00	100.00	250.00
	1811	.037	10.00	22.00	55.00	140.00
Mint mark: CL						
691.4	1813	8,385	50.00	100.00	225.00	550.00
Mint mark: D						
691.5	1809	.043	10.00	20.00	45.00	125.00
	1810	.071	9.00	18.00	40.00	115.00
	1811	.221	8.00	15.00	35.00	100.00
	1812	.155	8.00	15.00	35.00	100.00
	1813	.110	8.00	18.00	45.00	125.00
Mint mark: H						
691.6	1810	3,563	40.00	80.00	175.00	350.00
	1811	.120	8.00	15.00	35.00	100.00
	1812	.270	6.00	12.00	30.00	90.00
	1813	.138	8.00	15.00	35.00	100.00
Mint mark: I						
691.7	1811	.134	8.00	15.00	35.00	100.00
	1812	.137	8.00	15.00	35.00	100.00
	1813	.097	9.00	18.00	40.00	115.00
Mint mark: K						
691.8	1809	.043	10.00	20.00	45.00	125.00
	1810	.041	10.00	20.00	45.00	125.00

KM#	Date	Mintage	VG	Fine	VF	XF
691.8	1811	.016	15.00	30.00	75.00	175.00
	1812	.034	12.00	25.00	60.00	150.00
	1813	.058	10.00	20.00	50.00	125.00
	Mint mark: L					
691.9	1810	.055	10.00	22.00	50.00	125.00
	1810(Tr)	I.A.	—Reported, not confirmed			
	1811	.095	8.00	17.50	40.00	100.00
	1812	.052	10.00	20.00	50.00	125.00
	1813	.044	10.00	22.00	55.00	140.00
	Mint mark: M					
691.10	1809	.021	12.00	25.00	65.00	160.00
	1810	.033	12.00	25.00	60.00	150.00
	1811	.049	10.00	22.00	55.00	140.00
	1812	.105	8.00	17.50	40.00	110.00
	1813	.159	7.00	15.00	35.00	100.00
	1814	.036	40.00	75.00	150.00	350.00
	Mint mark: MA					
691.11	1809	3,176	40.00	75.00	150.00	400.00
	1810	.011	20.00	40.00	100.00	300.00
	1811	.069	10.00	20.00	50.00	125.00
	1812	.052	10.00	20.00	50.00	125.00
	1813	.070	8.00	17.50	45.00	120.00
	Mint mark: Q					
691.12	1809	.070	10.00	22.00	50.00	125.00
	1811	.126	7.50	15.00	35.00	100.00
	1812	.106	8.00	17.50	40.00	110.00
	1813	.044	10.00	22.00	50.00	140.00
	1814	—	—Reported, not confirmed			
	Mint mark: T					
691.13	1811	.114	8.00	17.50	40.00	100.00
	1812	.081	7.00	15.00	45.00	120.00
	1813	.053	10.00	20.00	50.00	125.00
	Mint mark: U					
691.14	1809	5,853	30.00	65.00	125.00	300.00
	1811	.039	12.00	25.00	60.00	150.00
	Mint mark: W					
691.15	1809	.314	6.00	12.00	30.00	100.00
	1810	.240	7.00	14.00	32.00	110.00
	1811	.246	7.00	14.00	32.00	110.00
	1812	.337	6.00	12.00	30.00	100.00
	1813	.058	10.00	20.00	50.00	125.00
	Mint mark: Flag					
691.16	1812	5,084	50.00	100.00	225.00	500.00
	1813	6,894	50.00	100.00	225.00	500.00
	Common date					Unc. 275.00

KM#	Date	Mintage	VG	Fine	VF	XF
	Mint mark: A					
708.1	1816	.261	8.00	16.00	40.00	125.00
	1817	.236	8.00	16.00	40.00	125.00
	1818	.050	10.00	20.00	55.00	140.00
	1819	.047	10.00	22.00	55.00	140.00
	1820	.043	10.00	22.00	55.00	140.00
	1821	.082	8.00	17.50	45.00	125.00
	1822	.584	6.00	12.00	35.00	90.00
	1823	.500	6.00	12.00	35.00	90.00
	1824	.613	6.00	12.00	35.00	90.00
	Mint mark: B					
708.2	1816	.019	15.00	30.00	60.00	150.00
	1817	8,759	20.00	40.00	80.00	200.00
	1818	7,803	20.00	40.00	80.00	200.00
	1822	.034	12.00	25.00	55.00	140.00
	1823	.018	15.00	30.00	60.00	150.00
	1824	.042	10.00	22.00	55.00	140.00
	Mint mark: D					
708.3	1824	.018	15.00	30.00	60.00	150.00
	Mint mark: H					
708.4	1817	.086	8.00	17.50	40.00	110.00
	1818	.014	16.00	35.00	70.00	165.00
	1819	2,463	30.00	60.00	125.00	250.00
	1822	1,332	35.00	75.00	125.00	300.00
	1823	3,558	25.00	50.00	110.00	250.00
	1824	.020	15.00	30.00	60.00	150.00
	Mint mark: I					
708.5	1816	2,692	30.00	60.00	125.00	250.00
	1823	3,113	25.00	50.00	110.00	250.00
	1824	.011	16.00	35.00	70.00	165.00
	Mint mark: K					
708.6	1817	.213	8.00	16.00	40.00	125.00
	1820	7,794	20.00	40.00	80.00	200.00
	1823	8,136	20.00	40.00	80.00	200.00
	1824	.053	10.00	20.00	55.00	140.00
	Mint mark: L					
708.7	1816	3,273	25.00	50.00	110.00	250.00
	1817	8,767	20.00	40.00	80.00	200.00
	1818	2,816	30.00	60.00	125.00	250.00
	1823	.036	12.00	25.00	55.00	140.00
	1824	.056	12.00	25.00	60.00	150.00
	Mint mark: M					
708.8	1816	4,682	20.00	40.00	90.00	225.00
	1823	8,632	20.00	40.00	80.00	200.00
	1824	.011	16.00	35.00	70.00	165.00
	Mint mark: Q					

KM#	Date	Mintage	VG	Fine	VF	XF
708.9	1816	.012	16.00	35.00	70.00	165.00
	1819	4,488	20.00	40.00	90.00	250.00
	1820	.017	15.00	30.00	60.00	150.00
	1823	.101	9.00	18.00	45.00	135.00
	1824	.170	8.00	16.00	40.00	125.00
	Mint mark: T					
708.10	1816	5,964	20.00	40.00	90.00	225.00
	1819	1,741	35.00	65.00	150.00	300.00
	Mint mark: W					
708.11	1816	8,728	20.00	40.00	80.00	200.00
	1817	.025	12.00	25.00	60.00	150.00
	1818	7,811	15.00	30.00	70.00	175.00
	1819	5,166	20.00	40.00	90.00	250.00
	1821	.037	12.00	25.00	55.00	140.00
	1822	.015	12.00	25.00	60.00	150.00
	1823	.070	8.00	17.50	45.00	125.00
	1824	.102	9.00	18.00	45.00	135.00
	Common date					Unc. 250.00

KM#	Date	Mintage	VG	Fine	VF	XF
	Mint mark: A					
723.1	1825	.011	30.00	60.00	125.00	250.00
	1826	.361	6.00	12.00	35.00	90.00
	1827	.786	4.00	10.00	25.00	75.00
	1828	.508	6.00	12.00	27.00	80.00
	1829	.538	4.00	10.00	25.00	75.00
	1830	.377	5.00	12.00	30.00	80.00
	Mint mark: B					
723.2	1826	6,019	20.00	45.00	90.00	225.00
	1827	.019	12.00	25.00	55.00	140.00
	1828	.056	10.00	20.00	40.00	115.00
	1829	.116	6.00	12.00	35.00	100.00
	Mint mark: BB					
723.3	1826	.011	15.00	30.00	60.00	150.00
	1827	2,476	30.00	60.00	120.00	250.00
	1828	.023	10.00	20.00	45.00	125.00
	1829	.022	10.00	20.00	45.00	125.00
	Mint mark: D					
723.4	1826	.020	12.00	25.00	50.00	125.00
	1827	5,629	25.00	50.00	100.00	200.00
	1828	.083	7.50	15.00	35.00	100.00
	1829	.028	10.00	20.00	45.00	120.00
	Mint mark: H					
723.5	1826	.023	10.00	20.00	45.00	120.00
	1827	.014	15.00	30.00	60.00	150.00
	1828	.026	10.00	20.00	45.00	120.00
	1829	.058	7.50	15.00	35.00	100.00
	Mint mark: I					
723.6	1826	1,435	25.00	60.00	140.00	280.00
	1827	1,520	25.00	60.00	140.00	280.00
	1828	2,526	25.00	60.00	140.00	280.00
	1829	.015	12.00	25.00	50.00	125.00
	Mint mark: K					
723.7	1826	.017	12.00	25.00	50.00	125.00
	1827	9,597	22.00	45.00	80.00	200.00
	1828	.027	10.00	20.00	45.00	125.00
	1829	.037	8.00	17.50	40.00	110.00
	1830	.022	10.00	20.00	45.00	125.00
	Mint mark: L					
723.8	1826	.036	8.00	17.50	40.00	100.00
	1827	.031	8.00	17.50	40.00	110.00
	1828	.027	10.00	20.00	45.00	120.00
	1829	.016	14.00	30.00	55.00	130.00
	1830	.018	12.00	25.00	50.00	125.00
	Mint mark: M					
723.9	1826	9,192	20.00	40.00	75.00	200.00
	1827	7,288	22.00	45.00	85.00	225.00
	1828	.072	7.50	15.00	35.00	100.00
	1829	.016	12.00	25.00	50.00	125.00
	1830	7,826	22.00	45.00	85.00	225.00
	Mint mark: MA					
723.10	1829	.032	10.00	22.00	50.00	125.00
	Mint mark: Q					
723.11	1826	.063	7.50	15.00	35.00	100.00
	1827	.011	15.00	30.00	60.00	150.00
	1828	.030	8.00	17.50	40.00	110.00
	1829	.019	10.00	20.00	50.00	125.00
	Mint mark: T					
723.12	1827	8,815	20.00	40.00	75.00	200.00
	1828	.018	12.00	25.00	50.00	125.00
	1829	3,609	25.00	50.00	100.00	250.00
	Mint mark: W					
723.13	1826	.038	8.00	17.50	40.00	100.00
	1827	.030	8.00	17.50	40.00	100.00
	1828	.170	6.00	12.00	30.00	90.00
	1829	.126	6.00	12.00	30.00	90.00
	1830	.131	6.00	12.00	30.00	90.00
	Common date					Unc. 265.00

Mint mark: A

KM#	Date	Mintage	Fine	VF	XF	Unc
741.1	1831	.110	7.50	15.00	35.00	100.00
	1832	.345	6.00	12.00	30.00	90.00
	1833	.272	6.00	12.00	30.00	90.00
	1834	.419	6.00	12.00	30.00	90.00
	1835	.831	6.00	12.00	30.00	75.00
	1836	.432	6.00	12.00	30.00	90.00
	1837	.137	7.50	15.00	35.00	100.00
	1838	.385	6.00	12.00	30.00	90.00
	1839	.636	6.00	12.00	30.00	90.00
	1840	1.107	5.00	10.00	25.00	90.00
	1841	1.119	5.00	10.00	25.00	90.00
	1842	.338	7.50	15.00	35.00	100.00
	1843	.152	8.00	16.00	40.00	115.00
	1844	.196	7.50	15.00	35.00	100.00
	1845	.494	7.50	15.00	35.00	90.00
	Mint mark: B					
741.2	1831	.136	7.50	15.00	35.00	100.00
	1832	.256	6.00	12.00	30.00	100.00
	1833	.093	7.50	15.00	35.00	110.00
	1834	.086	9.00	17.50	35.00	110.00
	1835	.054	10.00	20.00	45.00	125.00
	1836	.043	10.00	20.00	45.00	125.00
	1837	.158	7.50	15.00	35.00	110.00
	1838	.084	9.00	17.50	35.00	110.00
	1839	.116	9.00	17.50	35.00	110.00
	1840	.117	9.00	17.50	35.00	110.00
	1841	.831	6.00	12.00	30.00	90.00
	1842	.250	7.50	15.00	35.00	95.00
	1843	.213	7.50	15.00	35.00	95.00
	1844	.046	10.00	20.00	45.00	125.00
	1845	2.501	5.00	10.00	25.00	75.00
	Mint mark: BB					
741.3	1831	2,767	30.00	60.00	120.00	250.00
	1832	.010	15.00	30.00	60.00	150.00
	1833	.029	10.00	20.00	45.00	125.00
	1834	.020	10.00	20.00	45.00	125.00
	1835	5,346	22.00	45.00	85.00	225.00
	1836	.022	10.00	20.00	45.00	125.00
	1837	5,952	22.00	45.00	85.00	225.00
	1838	5,820	22.00	45.00	85.00	225.00
	1839	6,896	20.00	40.00	75.00	200.00
	1840	770 pcs.	—	—	—	—
	1841	.010	15.00	30.00	60.00	150.00
	1842	.308	7.50	15.00	30.00	90.00
	1844	.025	10.00	20.00	45.00	125.00
	1845	.044	10.00	20.00	45.00	125.00
	Mint mark: D					
741.4	1831	.016	10.00	20.00	45.00	125.00
	1832	.206	7.50	15.00	30.00	90.00
	1833	.032	10.00	20.00	45.00	125.00
	1834	.064	9.00	18.00	35.00	110.00
	1835	.015	15.00	30.00	60.00	150.00
	1836	8,706	20.00	40.00	75.00	200.00
	1837	7,556	20.00	40.00	75.00	200.00
	1838	2,432	25.00	50.00	100.00	250.00
	1840	.019	10.00	20.00	45.00	125.00
	Mint mark: H					
741.5	1831	.018	10.00	20.00	45.00	125.00
	1832	.077	9.00	18.00	35.00	110.00
	1833	.043	10.00	20.00	45.00	125.00
	1834	.086	9.00	18.00	35.00	110.00
	Mint mark: I					
741.6	1831	.013	15.00	30.00	60.00	150.00
	1832	.026	10.00	20.00	45.00	125.00
	1833	.049	8.00	18.00	35.00	100.00
	1834	.025	10.00	20.00	45.00	125.00
	1835	.045	8.00	18.00	35.00	100.00
	Mint mark: K					
741.7	1831	.035	10.00	20.00	45.00	125.00
	1832	.040	8.00	18.00	35.00	100.00
	1833	.029	10.00	20.00	45.00	125.00
	1834	.069	8.00	18.00	35.00	100.00
	1835	.050	8.00	18.00	35.00	100.00
	1836	.015	15.00	30.00	60.00	150.00
	1837	.026	10.00	20.00	45.00	125.00
	1838	.017	12.00	25.00	50.00	135.00
	1839	.018	12.00	25.00	50.00	135.00
	1840	.043	8.00	18.00	35.00	100.00
	1841	.026	10.00	20.00	45.00	125.00
	1842	.035	8.00	18.00	35.00	100.00
	1843	.034	8.00	18.00	35.00	100.00
	1844	.023	10.00	20.00	45.00	125.00
	1845	.022	10.00	20.00	45.00	125.00
	Mint mark: L					
741.8	1831	4,723	22.00	45.00	85.00	225.00
	1832	.034	8.00	18.00	35.00	100.00
	1833	.016	12.00	25.00	50.00	135.00
	1834	.010	15.00	30.00	60.00	150.00
	Mint mark: M					
741.9	1831	8,289	20.00	40.00	75.00	200.00
	1832	.092	9.00	18.00	35.00	110.00
	1833	.026	10.00	20.00	45.00	125.00
	1834	.019	10.00	20.00	45.00	125.00
	1835	.023	10.00	20.00	45.00	125.00
	1836	6,173	22.00	45.00	85.00	225.00

Mint mark: MA

KM#	Date	Mintage	Fine	VF	XF	Unc
741.10	1831	—	400.00	—	—	—
	1832	.052	8.00	18.00	35.00	100.00
	1834	—	—	—	—	—
	1835	.029	10.00	20.00	45.00	125.00

Mint mark: Q

KM#	Date	Mintage	Fine	VF	XF	Unc
741.11	1831	.012	15.00	30.00	60.00	150.00
	1832	.021	10.00	20.00	45.00	125.00
	1833	.055	8.00	18.00	35.00	100.00
	1834	1,824	200.00	400.00	—	—

Mint mark: T

KM#	Date	Mintage	Fine	VF	XF	Unc
741.12	1831	5,573	22.00	45.00	85.00	225.00
	1832	.033	8.00	18.00	35.00	100.00
	1833	.014	15.00	30.00	60.00	150.00
	1834	.055	8.00	18.00	35.00	100.00

Mint mark: W

KM#	Date	Mintage	Fine	VF	XF	Unc
741.13	1831	.125	8.00	15.00	35.00	100.00
	1832	.427	6.00	12.00	25.00	90.00
	1833	.151	8.00	15.00	35.00	100.00
	1834	.683	6.00	12.00	25.00	90.00
	1835	.183	8.00	15.00	35.00	100.00
	1836	.087	8.00	15.00	35.00	100.00
	1837	.267	7.00	14.00	30.00	95.00
	1838	.132	8.00	15.00	35.00	100.00
	1839	.119	8.00	15.00	35.00	100.00
	1840	.079	9.00	18.00	40.00	110.00
	1841	.234	7.00	14.00	30.00	95.00
	1842	.215	7.00	14.00	30.00	95.00
	1843	.233	7.00	14.00	30.00	95.00
	1844	.408	6.00	12.00	25.00	90.00
	1845	.525	6.00	12.00	25.00	75.00

FRANC

5.0000 g, .900 SILVER, .1446 oz ASW
Mint mark: A
Obv. leg: BONAPARTE PREMIER CONSUL.

KM#	Date	Mintage	VG	Fine	VF	XF
649.1	ANXI	.232	20.00	50.00	125.00	275.00
	AN12	1.311	15.00	30.00	90.00	215.00
	Mint mark: BB					
649.2	AN12	5,737	100.00	200.00	400.00	800.00
	Mint mark: D					
649.3	ANXI	.012	75.00	150.00	350.00	650.00
	AN12	.053	35.00	60.00	150.00	350.00
	Mint mark: G					
649.4	ANXI	.013	100.00	200.00	400.00	900.00
	AN12	7,397	125.00	280.00	500.00	1000.
	Mint mark: H					
649.5	AN12	.057	35.00	60.00	150.00	350.00
	Mint mark: I					
649.6	AN12	.279	20.00	45.00	100.00	250.00
	Mint mark: K					
649.7	AN12	.102	30.00	55.00	125.00	300.00
	Mint mark: L					
649.8	ANXI	.022	40.00	75.00	200.00	500.00
	AN12	.125	25.00	50.00	115.00	275.00
	Mint mark: M					
649.9	AN12	.285	20.00	45.00	100.00	250.00
	Mint mark: MA					
649.10	ANXI	.012	45.00	90.00	250.00	600.00
	AN12	.141	25.00	50.00	115.00	275.00
	Mint mark: Q					
649.11	ANXI	.034	40.00	75.00	200.00	500.00
	AN12	.140	25.00	50.00	115.00	275.00
	Mint mark: T					
649.12	AN12	.046	35.00	60.00	150.00	350.00
	Mint mark: U					
649.13	AN12	5,580	75.00	150.00	350.00	650.00
	Mint mark: W					
649.14	ANXI	5,756	75.00	150.00	350.00	650.00
	AN12	.028	40.00	75.00	200.00	500.00
	Common date				Unc.	800.00

Mint mark: A
Obv. leg: NAPOLEON EMPEREUR.

KM#	Date	Mintage	VG	Fine	VF	XF
656.1	AN12	.326	20.00	40.00	100.00	225.00
	AN13	2.454	15.00	30.00	85.00	200.00
	AN14	.298	25.00	50.00	110.00	275.00
	Mint mark: B					
656.2	AN12	.030	30.00	60.00	135.00	300.00
	AN13	2,906	65.00	125.00	275.00	600.00
	Mint mark: BB					
656.3	AN13	3,410	65.00	125.00	275.00	600.00
	AN14	491 pcs.	325.00	750.00	1250.	2000.
	Mint mark: D					
656.4	AN12	3,968	65.00	125.00	275.00	600.00
	AN13	.010	40.00	75.00	175.00	350.00
	AN14	2,450	65.00	125.00	275.00	650.00
	Mint mark: G					
656.5	AN13	.011	125.00	250.00	550.00	1250.
	Mint mark: H					
656.6	AN12	4,398	65.00	125.00	275.00	600.00
	AN13	.043	30.00	60.00	135.00	300.00
	AN14	7,164	65.00	125.00	275.00	600.00
	Mint mark: I					
656.7	AN12	.043	30.00	60.00	135.00	300.00
	AN13	.390	20.00	40.00	100.00	225.00
	AN14	2,847	100.00	200.00	400.00	800.00
	Mint mark: K					
656.8	AN12	.024	35.00	65.00	150.00	350.00
	AN13	.061	30.00	60.00	135.00	300.00
	AN14	1,526	100.00	200.00	400.00	900.00
	Mint mark: L					
656.9	AN12	4,253	65.00	125.00	275.00	600.00
	AN13	.073	30.00	60.00	135.00	300.00
	AN14	4,107	65.00	125.00	275.00	600.00
	Mint mark: M					
656.10	AN12	.300	20.00	40.00	100.00	225.00
	AN13	.651	15.00	30.00	70.00	200.00
	AN14	1,096	100.00	200.00	400.00	900.00
	Mint mark: MA					
656.11	AN12	5,582	65.00	125.00	275.00	600.00
	AN13	.028	35.00	65.00	150.00	350.00
	AN14	6,910	65.00	125.00	275.00	600.00
	Mint mark: Q					
656.12	AN12	.025	35.00	65.00	150.00	350.00
	AN13	.117	25.00	50.00	125.00	275.00
	Mint mark: T					
656.13	AN12	3,462	65.00	125.00	275.00	700.00
	AN13	.013	40.00	75.00	175.00	350.00
	Mint mark: U					
656.14	AN12	1,166	100.00	200.00	400.00	900.00
	AN13	.015	60.00	120.00	250.00	650.00
	AN14	4,667		3 known	1000.	—
	Mint mark: W					
656.15	AN13	.017	40.00	75.00	175.00	350.00
	AN14	4,667	75.00	150.00	300.00	700.00
	Common date				Unc.	1000.

Mint mark: A

KM#	Date	Mintage	VG	Fine	VF	XF
672.1	1806	.828	20.00	40.00	100.00	225.00
	Mint mark: B					
672.2	1807	3,465	65.00	125.00	275.00	600.00
	Mint mark: H					
672.3	1806	8,472	55.00	100.00	225.00	500.00
	1807	4,728	60.00	110.00	240.00	525.00
	Mint mark: I					
672.4	1806	.034	35.00	65.00	150.00	350.00
	1807	.011	50.00	100.00	200.00	450.00
	Mint mark: K					
672.5	1806	3,173	75.00	150.00	400.00	800.00
	1807	2,362	75.00	150.00	400.00	800.00
	Mint mark: L					
672.6	1806	.253	25.00	50.00	125.00	275.00
	1807	.177	25.00	50.00	125.00	275.00
	Mint mark: M					
672.7	1806	1,066	100.00	200.00	400.00	900.00
	1807	.023	35.00	65.00	150.00	350.00
	Mint mark: MA					
672.8	1806	1,010	100.00	200.00	400.00	900.00
	1807	1,493	100.00	200.00	400.00	900.00
	Mint mark: Q					
672.9	1806	.016	40.00	75.00	175.00	350.00
	1807	9,659	50.00	100.00	225.00	450.00
	Mint mark: U					
672.10	1806	.015	40.00	75.00	175.00	350.00
	1807	.011	50.00	100.00	225.00	450.00
	Mint mark: W					
672.11	1806	.028	35.00	65.00	150.00	350.00
	1807	.015	40.00	75.00	175.00	350.00
	Common date				Unc.	800.00

Mint mark: A

Negro head.

KM#	Date	Mintage	VG	Fine	VF	XF
681	1807	.100	150.00	350.00	750.00	1800.

Laureate head.

KM#	Date	Mintage	VG	Fine	VF	XF
682.1	1807	.050	100.00	200.00	350.00	900.00
	1808	4.599	6.00	12.00	55.00	175.00
	Mint mark: B					
682.2	1808	.765	10.00	20.00	65.00	175.00
	Mint mark: BB					
682.3	1808	2.126	8.00	16.00	55.00	150.00
	Mint mark: D					
682.4	1808	.752	10.00	20.00	65.00	175.00
	Mint mark: H					
682.5	1808	.316	12.00	25.00	75.00	200.00
	Mint mark: I					
682.6	1808	.256	12.00	25.00	75.00	200.00
	Mint mark: K					
682.7	1808	.228	12.00	25.00	75.00	200.00
	Mint mark: L					
682.8	1808	.016	40.00	80.00	150.00	325.00
	Mint mark: M					
682.9	1808	.130	20.00	40.00	80.00	200.00
	Mint mark: MA					
682.10	1808	.029	35.00	75.00	135.00	300.00
	Mint mark: Q					
682.11	1808	.064	30.00	65.00	125.00	275.00
	Mint mark: T					
682.12	1808	.106	20.00	40.00	80.00	200.00
	Mint mark: U					
682.13	1808	.013	50.00	125.00	300.00	550.00
	Mint mark: W					
682.14	1808	2.422	8.00	16.00	55.00	150.00
	Common date				Unc.	500.00

Mint mark: A

KM#	Date	Mintage	VG	Fine	VF	XF
692.1	1809	.980	8.00	16.00	55.00	150.00
	1810	1.676	8.00	16.00	55.00	150.00
	1811	1.347	8.00	16.00	55.00	150.00
	1812	.563	10.00	20.00	45.00	140.00
	1813	.446	10.00	20.00	45.00	140.00
	1814	.042	35.00	75.00	135.00	300.00
	Mint mark: B					
692.2	1809	.202	10.00	20.00	50.00	150.00
	1810	.167	12.00	22.50	60.00	160.00
	1811	.253	10.00	20.00	50.00	150.00
	1812	.118	12.00	25.00	65.00	175.00
	1813	.061	15.00	30.00	75.00	200.00
	Mint mark: BB					
692.3	1810	4,336	50.00	100.00	175.00	375.00
	1811	.012	40.00	80.00	150.00	325.00
	1812	5,571	50.00	100.00	175.00	375.00
	Mint mark: CL					
692.4	1813	7,229	100.00	200.00	350.00	800.00
	Mint mark: D					
692.5	1809	.047	30.00	65.00	125.00	275.00
	1810	.039	30.00	65.00	125.00	275.00
	1811	.242	10.00	20.00	50.00	150.00
	1812	.147	12.00	22.50	65.00	170.00
	1813	.078	15.00	30.00	75.00	200.00
	Mint mark: H					
692.6	1809	.034	30.00	65.00	125.00	275.00
	1810	.016	35.00	75.00	150.00	325.00
	1811	.105	12.00	25.00	65.00	175.00
	1812	.165	10.00	22.00	60.00	160.00
	1813	.096	15.00	30.00	75.00	200.00
	Mint mark: I					
692.7	1810	.018	40.00	80.00	150.00	325.00
	1811	.085	15.00	30.00	75.00	200.00
	1812	.091	15.00	30.00	75.00	200.00
	1813	.076	15.00	30.00	75.00	200.00
	Mint mark: K					
692.8	1809	.074	15.00	30.00	75.00	200.00
	1810	.093	15.00	30.00	75.00	200.00
	1811	.048	20.00	40.00	85.00	225.00
	1812	.041	20.00	40.00	85.00	225.00
	1813	.068	15.00	30.00	75.00	200.00

Mint mark: L

KM#	Date	Mintage	VG	Fine	VF	XF
692.9	1809	.028	30.00	65.00	125.00	275.00
	1810	.047	30.00	65.00	125.00	275.00
	1810(Tr)	I.A.	—	—	Unique	—
	1811	.188	10.00	22.00	60.00	160.00
	1812	.047	20.00	40.00	85.00	225.00
	1813	.033	20.00	40.00	85.00	225.00

Mint mark: M

KM#	Date	Mintage	VG	Fine	VF	XF
692.10	1809	8,855	50.00	100.00	175.00	375.00
	1810	.035	30.00	65.00	125.00	275.00
	1811	.081	15.00	30.00	75.00	200.00
	1812	.125	12.00	25.00	65.00	175.00
	1813	.181	12.00	25.00	65.00	175.00
	1814	.029	40.00	80.00	150.00	325.00

Mint mark: MA

KM#	Date	Mintage	VG	Fine	VF	XF
692.11	1809	.020	40.00	80.00	150.00	325.00
	1810	.028	30.00	65.00	125.00	275.00
	1811	.044	25.00	60.00	110.00	250.00
	1812	.036	25.00	60.00	110.00	250.00
	1813	.044	25.00	60.00	110.00	250.00

Mint mark: Q

KM#	Date	Mintage	VG	Fine	VF	XF
692.12	1809	.163	12.00	25.00	65.00	175.00
	1810	.073	15.00	30.00	75.00	200.00
	1811	.161	12.00	25.00	65.00	175.00
	1812	.034	30.00	65.00	125.00	275.00
	1813	.075	15.00	30.00	75.00	200.00

Mint mark: R

KM#	Date	Mintage	VG	Fine	VF	XF
692.13	1812	.012	75.00	150.00	350.00	700.00
	1813	779 pcs.	250.00	500.00	900.00	1350.

Mint mark: T

KM#	Date	Mintage	VG	Fine	VF	XF
692.14	1811	.042	25.00	60.00	110.00	250.00
	1812	.041	25.00	60.00	110.00	250.00
	1813	.020	40.00	80.00	150.00	325.00

Mint mark: U

KM#	Date	Mintage	VG	Fine	VF	XF
692.15	1809	5,549	60.00	125.00	250.00	500.00
	1810	10,200	50.00	100.00	225.00	400.00
	1812	.021	45.00	90.00	200.00	350.00
	1813	6,065	100.00	200.00	350.00	800.00

Mint mark: W

KM#	Date	Mintage	VG	Fine	VF	XF
692.16	1809	.196	12.00	25.00	65.00	175.00
	1810	.187	12.00	25.00	65.00	175.00
	1811	.265	12.00	25.00	65.00	175.00
	1812	.143	12.00	25.00	65.00	175.00
	1813	.093	15.00	30.00	75.00	200.00

Mint mark: Flag

KM#	Date	Mintage	VG	Fine	VF	XF
692.17	1812	.012	100.00	200.00	400.00	800.00
	1813	.069	75.00	150.00	300.00	650.00
	Common date					Unc. 450.00

Mint mark: A

KM#	Date	Mintage	VG	Fine	VF	XF
709.1	1816	.253	10.00	20.00	65.00	150.00
	1817	.178	12.00	25.00	75.00	175.00
	1818	.060	15.00	30.00	85.00	200.00
	1819	.027	18.00	35.00	90.00	215.00
	1820	.028	18.00	35.00	90.00	215.00
	1821	.100	12.00	25.00	75.00	175.00
	1822	.635	6.00	12.00	45.00	125.00
	1823	.360	7.50	15.00	50.00	125.00
	1824	.417	6.00	12.00	45.00	125.00

Mint mark: B

KM#	Date	Mintage	VG	Fine	VF	XF
709.2	1816	.016	20.00	40.00	100.00	250.00
	1817	.031	18.00	35.00	90.00	215.00
	1818	3,866	25.00	60.00	150.00	375.00
	1819	.010	20.00	40.00	100.00	250.00
	1820	.016	20.00	40.00	100.00	250.00
	1822	.031	18.00	35.00	90.00	215.00
	1823	7,577	20.00	50.00	125.00	300.00
	1824	.066	12.00	25.00	75.00	175.00

Mint mark: D

KM#	Date	Mintage	VG	Fine	VF	XF
709.3	1817	5,362	22.00	45.00	125.00	275.00
	1823	3,485	25.00	60.00	150.00	375.00
	1824	.030	18.00	35.00	90.00	215.00

Mint mark: H

KM#	Date	Mintage	VG	Fine	VF	XF
709.4	1817	.048	12.00	25.00	75.00	175.00
	1818	8,477	20.00	50.00	115.00	280.00
	1819	8,141	20.00	50.00	115.00	280.00
	1820	6,709	22.00	50.00	115.00	280.00
	1821	5,083	22.00	50.00	115.00	280.00
	1822	.016	20.00	40.00	100.00	250.00
	1823	.014	20.00	40.00	100.00	250.00
	1824	.033	18.00	35.00	90.00	215.00

Mint mark: I

KM#	Date	Mintage	VG	Fine	VF	XF
709.5	1816	5,041	22.00	50.00	125.00	300.00
	1823	5,273	22.00	50.00	125.00	300.00
	1824	.033	18.00	35.00	90.00	215.00

Mint mark: K

KM#	Date	Mintage	VG	Fine	VF	XF
709.6	1817	.307	10.00	20.00	65.00	150.00
	1820	.020	20.00	40.00	100.00	250.00
	1823	5,173	22.00	50.00	125.00	300.00
	1824	.123	10.00	20.00	65.00	150.00

Mint mark: L

KM#	Date	Mintage	VG	Fine	VF	XF
709.7	1816	5,770	22.00	50.00	125.00	300.00
	1817	5,059	22.00	50.00	125.00	300.00
	1818	1,450	40.00	85.00	200.00	400.00
	1823	.036	18.00	35.00	90.00	215.00
	1824	.054	12.00	25.00	75.00	175.00

Mint mark: M

KM#	Date	Mintage	VG	Fine	VF	XF
709.8	1816	.070	12.00	25.00	75.00	175.00
	1817	.021	20.00	40.00	100.00	250.00
	1823	.036	18.00	35.00	90.00	215.00
	1824	.059	12.00	25.00	75.00	175.00

Mint mark: MA

KM#	Date	Mintage	VG	Fine	VF	XF
709.9	1824	7,209	20.00	50.00	125.00	285.00

Mint mark: Q

KM#	Date	Mintage	VG	Fine	VF	XF
709.10	1816	.025	20.00	40.00	100.00	250.00
	1817	5,045	22.00	50.00	125.00	300.00
	1819	.013	20.00	40.00	100.00	250.00
	1820	.022	18.00	35.00	90.00	215.00
	1821	4,942	25.00	60.00	150.00	375.00
	1822	3,838	25.00	60.00	150.00	375.00
	1823	.033	18.00	35.00	90.00	215.00
	1824	.052	12.00	25.00	75.00	175.00

Mint mark: T

KM#	Date	Mintage	VG	Fine	VF	XF
709.11	1816	2,240	35.00	75.00	175.00	400.00
	1818	1,728	45.00	100.00	275.00	500.00
	1819	4,094	25.00	60.00	150.00	375.00

Mint mark: W

KM#	Date	Mintage	VG	Fine	VF	XF
709.12	1816	.015	20.00	40.00	100.00	250.00
	1817	.019	20.00	40.00	100.00	250.00
	1818	.016	20.00	40.00	100.00	250.00
	1819	.024	20.00	40.00	100.00	250.00
	1820	.013	25.00	50.00	125.00	275.00
	1821	.200	10.00	20.00	65.00	150.00
	1822	.061	12.00	25.00	75.00	175.00
	1823	.277	10.00	20.00	65.00	150.00
	1824	.388	10.00	20.00	65.00	150.00
	Common date					Unc. 450.00

Mint mark: A

KM#	Date	Mintage	VG	Fine	VF	XF
724.1	1825	.335	10.00	20.00	55.00	150.00
	1826	.326	10.00	20.00	55.00	150.00
	1827	.431	10.00	20.00	55.00	150.00
	1828	.517	10.00	20.00	55.00	150.00
	1829	.290	10.00	20.00	55.00	150.00
	1830	.234	10.00	20.00	55.00	150.00
	1830 reeded edge	—	100.00	200.00	400.00	950.00

Mint mark: B

KM#	Date	Mintage	VG	Fine	VF	XF
724.2	1825	.017	20.00	40.00	80.00	175.00
	1826	.020	20.00	40.00	80.00	175.00
	1827	.096	15.00	30.00	70.00	175.00
	1828	.070	15.00	30.00	70.00	160.00
	1829	.124	10.00	20.00	45.00	140.00
	1830	.075	12.00	25.00	70.00	160.00

Mint mark: BB

KM#	Date	Mintage	VG	Fine	VF	XF
724.3	1825	9,256	30.00	60.00	125.00	300.00
	1826	.012	25.00	50.00	100.00	250.00
	1827	.013	25.00	50.00	100.00	250.00
	1828	.024	20.00	40.00	80.00	200.00
	1829	.021	20.00	40.00	80.00	200.00

Mint mark: D

KM#	Date	Mintage	VG	Fine	VF	XF
724.4	1825	.040	15.00	30.00	70.00	170.00
	1826	.028	20.00	40.00	80.00	200.00
	1827	.036	15.00	30.00	70.00	170.00
	1828	.076	12.00	25.00	65.00	150.00
	1829	.031	20.00	40.00	80.00	200.00

Mint mark: H

KM#	Date	Mintage	VG	Fine	VF	XF
724.5	1825	.023	20.00	40.00	80.00	200.00
	1826	.028	20.00	40.00	80.00	200.00
	1827	5,444	35.00	70.00	150.00	350.00
	1828	.027	20.00	40.00	80.00	200.00
	1829	.051	12.00	25.00	65.00	150.00

Mint mark: I

KM#	Date	Mintage	VG	Fine	VF	XF
724.6	1825	6,663	35.00	70.00	150.00	350.00
	1826	4,206	35.00	70.00	150.00	350.00
	1827	6,850	35.00	70.00	150.00	350.00
	1828	5,236	35.00	70.00	150.00	350.00
	1829	.020	20.00	40.00	80.00	200.00
	1830	1,025	60.00	125.00	250.00	500.00

Mint mark: K

KM#	Date	Mintage	VG	Fine	VF	XF
724.7	1825	.024	20.00	40.00	80.00	200.00
	1826	.038	20.00	40.00	80.00	200.00
	1827	.044	18.00	35.00	75.00	185.00
	1828	.132	8.00	17.50	55.00	140.00
	1829	.050	15.00	30.00	70.00	170.00
	1830	.021	20.00	40.00	80.00	200.00

Mint mark: L

KM#	Date	Mintage	VG	Fine	VF	XF
724.8	1825	3,830	35.00	70.00	150.00	350.00
	1826	.028	20.00	40.00	80.00	200.00
	1827	.047	18.00	35.00	75.00	185.00
	1828	.044	18.00	35.00	75.00	185.00
	1829	.033	20.00	40.00	80.00	200.00
	1830	.013	22.00	38.00	75.00	185.00

Mint mark: M

KM#	Date	Mintage	VG	Fine	VF	XF
724.9	1825	6,069	35.00	70.00	150.00	350.00
	1826	.031	20.00	40.00	80.00	200.00
	1827	.024	20.00	40.00	80.00	200.00
	1828	.072	12.00	25.00	65.00	150.00
	1829	.046	18.00	35.00	75.00	185.00
	1830	.021	20.00	40.00	80.00	200.00

Mint mark: MA

KM#	Date	Mintage	VG	Fine	VF	XF
724.10	1829	.066	12.00	25.00	65.00	160.00

Mint mark: Q

KM#	Date	Mintage	VG	Fine	VF	XF
724.11	1825	5,653	35.00	70.00	150.00	350.00
	1826	.025	20.00	40.00	80.00	200.00
	1827	.020	20.00	40.00	80.00	200.00
	1828	.018	20.00	40.00	80.00	200.00
	1829	.013	22.00	45.00	90.00	225.00

Mint mark: T

KM#	Date	Mintage	VG	Fine	VF	XF
724.12	1826	5,930	35.00	70.00	150.00	350.00
	1827	.014	22.00	45.00	90.00	225.00
	1828	.036	20.00	40.00	80.00	200.00
	1829	.014	22.00	45.00	90.00	225.00
	1830	8,871	30.00	60.00	135.00	300.00

Mint mark: W

KM#	Date	Mintage	VG	Fine	VF	XF
724.13	1825	.078	12.00	25.00	65.00	150.00
	1826	.130	8.00	17.50	55.00	140.00
	1827	.519	6.00	12.00	40.00	120.00
	1828	.418	6.00	12.00	45.00	120.00
	1829	.149	8.00	17.50	55.00	140.00
	1830	.078	12.00	25.00	65.00	150.00
	Common date					Unc. 375.00

KM#	Date	Mintage	VG	Fine	VF	XF
Mint mark: A						
742.1	1831	.202	30.00	85.00	200.00	450.00
Mint mark: B						
742.2	1831	.400	25.00	65.00	175.00	400.00
Mint mark: BB						
742.3	1831	.018	60.00	150.00	300.00	600.00
Mint mark: D						
742.4	1831	.127	40.00	110.00	225.00	450.00
Mint mark: H						
742.5	1831	.027	50.00	125.00	275.00	500.00
Mint mark: I						
742.6	1831	.021	50.00	125.00	275.00	500.00
Mint mark: K						
742.7	1831	.053	40.00	115.00	250.00	475.00
Mint mark: L						
742.8	1831	2,406	100.00	250.00	425.00	850.00
Mint mark: M						
724.9	1831	.038	45.00	125.00	250.00	475.00
Mint mark: Q						
742.10	1831	.018	60.00	150.00	300.00	600.00
Mint mark: T						
742.11	1831	.043	40.00	115.00	250.00	475.00
Mint mark: W						
742.12	1831	.453	30.00	75.00	175.00	400.00

Mint mark: A
Laureate head

KM#	Date	Mintage	Fine	VF	XF	Unc
748.1	1832	.379	10.00	35.00	75.00	225.00
	1833	.114	12.00	40.00	90.00	275.00
	1834	.330	10.00	35.00	75.00	200.00
	1835	.483	10.00	35.00	75.00	200.00
	1836	.138	15.00	40.00	85.00	150.00
	1837	.241	12.00	35.00	75.00	200.00
	1838	.183	15.00	40.00	85.00	150.00
	1839	.243	12.00	35.00	75.00	225.00
	1840	.481	10.00	35.00	75.00	250.00
	1841	.623	10.00	35.00	75.00	225.00
	1842	.130	15.00	40.00	85.00	150.00
	1843	.074	18.00	40.00	80.00	200.00
	1844	.072	18.00	40.00	80.00	200.00
	1845	.215	15.00	40.00	85.00	150.00
	1846	1.225	8.00	18.00	40.00	125.00
	1847	2.401	8.00	18.00	40.00	125.00
	1848	.228	15.00	40.00	85.00	150.00

Mint mark: B

KM#	Date	Mintage	Fine	VF	XF	Unc
748.2	1832	.197	15.00	45.00	90.00	185.00
	1833	.098	12.00	35.00	70.00	185.00
	1834	.146	10.00	25.00	50.00	185.00

KM#	Date	Mintage	Fine	VF	XF	Unc
748.2	1835	.103	12.00	30.00	60.00	185.00
	1836	.093	12.00	35.00	70.00	185.00
	1837	.212	12.00	30.00	60.00	185.00
	1838	.145	12.00	30.00	60.00	185.00
	1839	.184	12.00	30.00	60.00	185.00
	1840	.148	10.00	25.00	50.00	185.00
	1841	.663	8.00	18.00	40.00	175.00
	1842	.158	12.00	30.00	60.00	185.00
	1843	.130	12.00	30.00	60.00	185.00
	1844	.045	15.00	45.00	90.00	185.00
	1845	.882	8.00	18.00	40.00	175.00
	1846	.818	8.00	18.00	40.00	175.00

Mint mark: BB

KM#	Date	Mintage	Fine	VF	XF	Unc
748.3	1832	.042	15.00	45.00	90.00	185.00
	1833	.079	15.00	45.00	90.00	185.00
	1834	.068	15.00	45.00	90.00	185.00
	1835	.046	15.00	45.00	90.00	185.00
	1836	.050	15.00	45.00	90.00	185.00
	1837	.013	20.00	50.00	100.00	200.00
	1838	.024	15.00	40.00	80.00	175.00
	1839	.043	15.00	45.00	90.00	185.00
	1840	.017	20.00	50.00	100.00	200.00
	1841	.053	15.00	45.00	90.00	185.00
	1842	.244	12.00	30.00	60.00	175.00
	1843	.072	15.00	45.00	90.00	185.00
	1844	.076	15.00	45.00	90.00	185.00
	1845	.083	15.00	45.00	90.00	185.00
	1846	.024	15.00	40.00	80.00	175.00
	1847	.068	15.00	45.00	90.00	185.00
	1848	.021	25.00	60.00	125.00	250.00

Mint mark: D

KM#	Date	Mintage	Fine	VF	XF	Unc
748.4	1832	.127	10.00	25.00	50.00	160.00
	1833	.024	15.00	40.00	80.00	175.00
	1834	.059	15.00	45.00	95.00	210.00
	1835	.052	15.00	45.00	95.00	210.00
	1836	.019	25.00	60.00	125.00	250.00
	1837	2,531	40.00	100.00	200.00	500.00
	1838	.012	20.00	50.00	95.00	210.00
	1839	.011	20.00	50.00	95.00	210.00
	1840	7,130	40.00	80.00	175.00	350.00

Mint mark: H

KM#	Date	Mintage	Fine	VF	XF	Unc
748.5	1832	.080	15.00	45.00	95.00	210.00
	1833	.026	15.00	45.00	95.00	210.00
	1834	.079	15.00	45.00	95.00	210.00
	1835	.017	20.00	50.00	110.00	225.00

Mint mark: I

KM#	Date	Mintage	Fine	VF	XF	Unc
748.6	1832	.037	15.00	45.00	95.00	210.00
	1833	.034	15.00	45.00	95.00	210.00
	1834	.045	15.00	45.00	95.00	210.00
	1835	.048	15.00	45.00	95.00	210.00

Mint mark: K

KM#	Date	Mintage	Fine	VF	XF	Unc
748.7	1832	.035	15.00	45.00	90.00	190.00
	1833	.030	15.00	45.00	90.00	190.00
	1834	.070	15.00	45.00	90.00	190.00
	1835	.058	15.00	45.00	90.00	190.00
	1836	.040	15.00	40.00	80.00	185.00
	1837	.034	20.00	50.00	100.00	225.00
	1838	.017	20.00	50.00	100.00	225.00
	1839	.048	15.00	45.00	90.00	185.00
	1840	.048	15.00	45.00	90.00	185.00
	1841	.042	15.00	45.00	90.00	185.00
	1842	.032	15.00	45.00	90.00	185.00
	1843	.039	15.00	45.00	90.00	185.00
	1844	.023	15.00	45.00	90.00	185.00
	1845	.023	15.00	45.00	90.00	185.00
	1846	.023	15.00	45.00	90.00	185.00
	1847	*6,787	—	500.00	—	—

***NOTE:** One piece known.

Mint mark: L

KM#	Date	Mintage	Fine	VF	XF	Unc
748.8	1832	.031	15.00	45.00	90.00	200.00
	1833	.018	20.00	50.00	100.00	225.00
	1834	.012	20.00	50.00	100.00	225.00
	1835	3,647	80.00	180.00	350.00	—

Mint mark: M

KM#	Date	Mintage	Fine	VF	XF	Unc
748.9	1832	.051	15.00	45.00	90.00	175.00
	1833	.049	15.00	45.00	90.00	175.00
	1834	.037	15.00	45.00	90.00	175.00
	1835	.025	18.00	45.00	90.00	175.00

Mint mark: MA

KM#	Date	Mintage	Fine	VF	XF	Unc
748.10	1832	.078	15.00	45.00	90.00	200.00
	1833	.057	15.00	45.00	90.00	200.00
	1834	.018	20.00	50.00	100.00	225.00
	1835	.012	20.00	50.00	100.00	225.00
	1837	—	—	—	Rare	—
	1838	.020	20.00	50.00	100.00	225.00

Mint mark: Q

KM#	Date	Mintage	Fine	VF	XF	Unc
748.11	1832	—	—	—	Rare	—
	1833	.019	25.00	65.00	125.00	250.00
	1834	.057	15.00	45.00	90.00	200.00

Mint mark: T

KM#	Date	Mintage	Fine	VF	XF	Unc
748.12	1832	.034	20.00	50.00	100.00	225.00
	1833	.031	15.00	50.00	100.00	225.00
	1834	.102	12.00	30.00	60.00	175.00
	1835	.051	15.00	45.00	90.00	200.00

Mint mark: W

KM#	Date	Mintage	Fine	VF	XF	Unc
748.13	1832	.155	12.00	30.00	60.00	175.00
	1833	.213	12.00	30.00	60.00	175.00
	1834	.608	8.00	18.00	40.00	150.00
	1835	.206	12.00	30.00	60.00	175.00
	1836	.049	15.00	45.00	90.00	200.00
	1837	.266	12.00	30.00	60.00	175.00
	1838	.162	12.00	30.00	60.00	175.00
	1839	.120	12.00	30.00	60.00	175.00

KM#	Date	Mintage	Fine	VF	XF	Unc
748.13	1840	.079	15.00	45.00	85.00	190.00
	1841	.321	12.00	30.00	55.00	165.00
	1842	.195	12.00	30.00	55.00	165.00
	1843	.271	12.00	30.00	55.00	165.00
	1844	.381	10.00	25.00	50.00	160.00
	1845	.478	10.00	25.00	50.00	160.00
	1846	.074	15.00	45.00	90.00	200.00

Mint mark: A
Second Republic

KM#	Date	Mintage	Fine	VF	XF	Unc
759.1	1849	1.289	20.00	45.00	90.00	200.00
	1850	1.041	25.00	60.00	115.00	225.00
	1851	.638	40.00	100.00	175.00	300.00

Mint mark: BB

KM#	Date	Mintage	Fine	VF	XF	Unc
759.2	1849	.015	100.00	250.00	600.00	1000.
	1850	.213	60.00	150.00	300.00	600.00

Mint mark: K

KM#	Date	Mintage	Fine	VF	XF	Unc
759.3	1849	.019	100.00	250.00	600.00	1000.
	1850	.035	75.00	200.00	375.00	700.00

Mint mark: A
President Louis-Napoleon

KM#	Date	Mintage	Fine	VF	XF	Unc
772	1852	1.015	45.00	80.00	185.00	385.00
	1852	—	—	—	Proof	1350.

Second Empire - Napoleon III

KM#	Date	Mintage	Fine	VF	XF	Unc
779.1	1853 lg. head	.183	150.00	400.00	700.00	1200.
	1853 lg. head		—	—	Proof	625.00
	1853 sm. head	Inc. Ab.	60.00	125.00	300.00	600.00
	1854	.764	25.00	50.00	150.00	350.00
	1855(d)	.757	35.00	90.00	175.00	300.00
	1855(a)	I.A.	75.00	150.00	225.00	500.00
	1856	1.196	20.00	50.00	125.00	250.00
	1857	1.681	20.00	40.00	100.00	250.00
	1858	5.607	10.00	25.00	75.00	200.00
	1859	3.830	15.00	35.00	90.00	225.00
	1860(h)	2.740	15.00	35.00	90.00	225.00
	1860(b)	I.A.	15.00	35.00	90.00	225.00
	1861	2.012	100.00	200.00	450.00	700.00
	1863	.019	325.00	600.00	900.00	1300.
	1864	.022	— Reported, not confirmed			

Mint mark: BB

KM#	Date	Mintage	Fine	VF	XF	Unc
779.2	1856	1.635	20.00	50.00	125.00	250.00
	1859	1.333	20.00	50.00	125.00	250.00
	1860	I.A.	20.00	50.00	125.00	250.00
	1861	.218	100.00	250.00	500.00	850.00
	1862	1.124	80.00	200.00	400.00	800.00
	1863	.054	125.00	300.00	650.00	900.00

Mint mark: D

KM#	Date	Mintage	Fine	VF	XF	Unc
779.3	1856	1.227	20.00	50.00	725.00	250.00

5.0000 g, .835 SILVER, .1342 oz ASW
Mint mark: A
Laureate head.

KM#	Date	Mintage	Fine	VF	XF	Unc
806.1	1866	14.638	5.00	12.00	25.00	75.00
	1867	12.131	5.00	12.00	25.00	75.00
	1868	14.942	5.00	12.00	25.00	75.00
	1869	2.935	10.00	25.00	75.00	150.00
	1870	.788	—	—	—	—

Mint mark: BB

KM#	Date	Mintage	Fine	VF	XF	Unc
806.2	1866	7.204	6.00	15.00	30.00	90.00
	1867	7.295	6.00	15.00	30.00	90.00
	1868	10.230	5.00	12.00	25.00	75.00
	1869	3.094	10.00	25.00	75.00	150.00
	1870	1.992	15.00	40.00	90.00	200.00

Mint mark: K

KM#	Date	Mintage	Fine	VF	XF	Unc
806.3	1866	1.402	15.00	40.00	90.00	200.00
	1867	6.092	5.00	15.00	35.00	90.00
	1868	.022	150.00	300.00	425.00	1000.

Mint mark: A
Third Republic

KM#	Date	Mintage	Fine	VF	XF	Unc
822.1	1871 small A	2.980	4.00	8.00	25.00	75.00
	1871 large A	Inc. Ab.	3.00	6.00	20.00	60.00
	1872 small A	10.129	2.00	4.00	15.00	50.00
	1872 large A	Inc. Ab.	10.00	25.00	50.00	100.00
	1878	30 pcs.	—	—	Proof	3200.
	1881	2.010	4.00	8.00	25.00	75.00
	1887	3.292	4.00	8.00	25.00	75.00
	1888	3.244	4.00	8.00	25.00	75.00
	1889	100 pcs.	—	—	Proof	2300.
	1894	1.600	4.00	8.00	25.00	75.00
	1895	3.200	4.00	8.00	25.00	75.00

Mint mark: K

KM#	Date	Mintage	Fine	VF	XF	Unc
822.2	1871 small K	1.252	4.00	8.00	25.00	75.00
	1871 large K	Inc. Ab.	3.00	6.00	20.00	60.00
	1872 large K	5.779	15.00	35.00	65.00	150.00
	1872 small K	Inc. Ab.	4.00	8.00	25.00	75.00
	1873	.019	150.00	350.00	700.00	1200.

Mint: Paris - w/o mint mark.

KM#	Date	Mintage	Fine	VF	XF	Unc
844.1	1898	15.000	2.00	3.00	6.00	30.00
	1898		—	—	Proof	400.00
	1899	11.000	2.00	4.00	8.00	35.00
	1900	.099	125.00	225.00	450.00	850.00
	1900	—	—	—	Proof	425.00

NOTE: Later dates (1901-1920) exist for this type.

2 FRANCS

10.0000 g, .900 SILVER, .2893 oz ASW
Mint mark: A
Obv. leg: BONAPARTE PREMIER CONSUL.

KM#	Date	Mintage	VG	Fine	VF	XF
657.1	AN12	.187	40.00	65.00	175.00	500.00
	AN12	—	—	—	Proof	2500.

Mint mark: BB

KM#	Date	Mintage	VG	Fine	VF	XF
657.2	AN12	1,965	200.00	350.00	600.00	1200.

Mint mark: D

KM#	Date	Mintage	VG	Fine	VF	XF
657.3	AN12	2,672	—Reported, not confirmed			

Mint mark: G

KM#	Date	Mintage	VG	Fine	VF	XF
657.4	AN12	2,859	100.00	250.00	400.00	900.00

Mint mark: H

KM#	Date	Mintage	VG	Fine	VF	XF
657.5	AN12	.012	50.00	115.00	250.00	650.00

Mint mark: I

KM#	Date	Mintage	VG	Fine	VF	XF
657.6	AN12	.102	40.00	90.00	200.00	500.00

Mint mark: K

KM#	Date	Mintage	VG	Fine	VF	XF
657.7	AN12	.026	45.00	100.00	225.00	450.00

Mint mark: L

KM#	Date	Mintage	VG	Fine	VF	XF
657.8	AN12	.015	50.00	115.00	250.00	650.00

Mint mark: M

KM#	Date	Mintage	VG	Fine	VF	XF
657.9	AN12	.066	40.00	90.00	200.00	500.00

Mint mark: MA

KM#	Date	Mintage	VG	Fine	VF	XF
657.10	AN12	6,804	60.00	125.00	275.00	700.00

Mint mark: Q

KM#	Date	Mintage	VG	Fine	VF	XF
657.11	AN12	.021	45.00	100.00	225.00	500.00

Mint mark: T

KM#	Date	Mintage	VG	Fine	VF	XF
657.12	AN12	4,484	—Reported, not confirmed			

KM#	Date	Mintage	VG	Fine	VF	XF
Mint mark: U						
657.13	AN12	—	—	—	Unique	—
Mint mark: W						
657.14	AN12	5,850	65.00	135.00	300.00	775.00
Mint mark: A						
Obv. leg: NAPOLEON EMPEREUR.						
658.1	AN12	.060	100.00	250.00	400.00	900.00
	AN13/2	.742	30.00	65.00	150.00	475.00
	AN13	I.A.	30.00	60.00	125.00	450.00
	AN14	.232	35.00	70.00	150.00	475.00
	1806	.169	35.00	70.00	150.00	475.00
Mint mark: B						
658.2	AN12	.014	45.00	115.00	225.00	500.00
	1807	563	—Reported, not confirmed			
Mint mark: BB						
658.3	AN12	1,798	—	—	—	—
	AN13	4,341	150.00	—	—	—
	1806	1,477	—Reported, not confirmed			
Mint mark: D						
658.4	AN13	2,560	—Reported, not confirmed			
	AN14	204	—Reported, not confirmed			
	1806	530	—Reported, not confirmed			
Mint mark: G						
658.5	AN13	.013	200.00	350.00	600.00	1200.
Mint mark: H						
658.6	AN12	2,800	—Reported, not confirmed			
	AN13	3,727	65.00	150.00	300.00	775.00
	AN14	1,063	200.00	350.00	600.00	1200.
Mint mark: I						
658.7	AN12	3,561	—Reported, not confirmed			
	AN13/2	.124	20.00	40.00	150.00	450.00
	AN13	I.A.	35.00	70.00	175.00	500.00
	AN14	6,299	150.00	350.00	750.00	—
	1806	.021	45.00	115.00	225.00	450.00
	1807	.082	35.00	70.00	150.00	450.00
Mint mark: K						
658.8	AN12	.010	45.00	115.00	225.00	450.00
	AN13	.036	100.00	250.00	400.00	900.00
	AN14	1,210	—	—	Rare	—
	1806	754	—Reported, not confirmed			
	1807	3,665	200.00	460.00	750.00	1300.
Mint mark: L						
658.9	AN12	1,247	200.00	350.00	600.00	1200.
	AN13	.022	100.00	250.00	400.00	900.00
	AN14	5,183	75.00	200.00	500.00	—
	1806	.072	35.00	70.00	150.00	450.00
	1807	.054	30.00	65.00	160.00	400.00
Mint mark: M						
658.10	AN12	.016	40.00	100.00	200.00	500.00
	AN13	.334	35.00	70.00	150.00	450.00
	1807	8,878	65.00	150.00	300.00	775.00
Mint mark: MA						
658.11	AN12	5,249	—Reported, not confirmed			
	AN13	.011	45.00	115.00	225.00	450.00
	AN14	—	200.00	400.00	800.00	—
	1806	2,289	—Reported, not confirmed			
Mint mark: Q						
658.12	AN13	.052	35.00	70.00	150.00	450.00
	1806	.042	45.00	115.00	225.00	450.00
	1807	.033	45.00	115.00	225.00	450.00
Mint mark: T						
658.13	AN12	1,444	200.00	350.00	600.00	1200.
	AN13	4,600	65.00	150.00	300.00	775.00
Mint mark: U						
658.14	AN13	7,221	200.00	400.00	750.00	1300.
	AN14	—	200.00	400.00	800.00	—
	1806	.010	125.00	300.00	600.00	1200.
	1807	.010	125.00	300.00	600.00	1200.
Mint mark: W						
658.15	AN13	.011	45.00	115.00	225.00	450.00
	AN14	—	200.00	400.00	750.00	1300.
	1806	.010	65.00	150.00	300.00	775.00
	1807	4,114	200.00	400.00	750.00	1300.

Mint mark: A

KM#	Date	Mintage	VG	Fine	VF	XF
Negro head.						
683	1807	—	300.00	650.00	1200.	3750.
Laureate head.						
684.1	1807	.019	175.00	325.00	750.00	1850.
	1808	1.100	30.00	60.00	150.00	400.00
Mint mark: B						
684.2	1808	.161	40.00	80.00	175.00	450.00
Mint mark: I						
684.3	1808	.106	45.00	90.00	175.00	400.00
Mint mark: K						
684.4	1808	.038	55.00	90.00	200.00	450.00
Mint mark: L						
684.5	1808	.019	65.00	110.00	235.00	500.00
Mint mark: M						
684.6	1808	.028	55.00	90.00	200.00	450.00
Mint mark: MA						
684.7	1808	7,676	70.00	125.00	250.00	550.00
Mint mark: Q						
684.8	1808	4,965	75.00	140.00	300.00	600.00
Mint mark: U						
684.9	1808	2,297	150.00	300.00	550.00	1200.
Mint mark: W						
684.10	1808	.040	55.00	90.00	200.00	450.00
	Common date					Unc. 650.00
Mint mark: A						
693.1	1809	.469	18.00	35.00	100.00	300.00
	1810	.771	16.00	32.00	90.00	275.00
	1811	2.509	14.00	32.00	75.00	250.00
	1812	.308	18.00	35.00	100.00	300.00
	1813	.442	18.00	35.00	100.00	300.00
	1814	.095	32.00	70.00	150.00	350.00
Mint mark: B						
693.2	1809	.136	27.50	55.00	125.00	300.00
	1810	.072	32.50	70.00	150.00	350.00
	1811	.290	18.00	35.00	100.00	300.00
	1812	.057	32.50	70.00	150.00	350.00
	1813	.031	32.50	75.00	175.00	450.00
Mint mark: BB						
693.3	1810	1,389	—Reported, not confirmed			
	1811	.012	35.00	90.00	200.00	500.00
	1812	2,835	—Reported, not confirmed			
Mint mark: CL						
693.4	1813	906	400.00	800.00	1500.	3250.
Mint mark: D						
693.5	1810	.018	35.00	90.00	200.00	450.00
	1811	.037	32.50	75.00	175.00	425.00
	1812	.061	32.50	70.00	150.00	350.00
	1813	.033	32.50	75.00	175.00	425.00
Mint mark: H						
693.6	1809	4,534	75.00	150.00	250.00	600.00
	1810	5,710	75.00	150.00	250.00	575.00
	1811	.044	32.00	70.00	150.00	350.00
	1812	.081	32.00	70.00	150.00	350.00
	1813	.080	32.00	70.00	150.00	350.00
Mint mark: I						
693.7	1810	.029	32.00	75.00	175.00	425.00
	1811	.137	27.50	55.00	125.00	300.00
	1812	.209	18.00	35.00	100.00	300.00
	1813	.098	32.00	70.00	150.00	335.00
Mint mark: K						
693.8	1809	3,451	100.00	225.00	350.00	725.00
	1810	3,518	100.00	225.00	350.00	725.00
	1811	.028	32.00	75.00	175.00	425.00
	1812	.021	32.00	75.00	175.00	425.00
	1813	.027	32.00	75.00	175.00	425.00
Mint mark: L						
693.9	1809	.027	32.00	75.00	175.00	425.00
	1810	.032	32.00	75.00	175.00	425.00
	1811	.099	32.00	70.00	150.00	350.00
	1812	.042	32.00	70.00	150.00	350.00
	1813	.033	32.00	75.00	175.00	425.00
Mint mark: M						
693.10	1810	.011	50.00	100.00	225.00	425.00

KM#	Date	Mintage	VG	Fine	VF	XF
693.10	1811	.124	20.00	40.00	100.00	300.00
	1812	.145	20.00	40.00	100.00	300.00
	1813	.221	30.00	60.00	125.00	300.00
	1814	.046	35.00	75.00	150.00	350.00
Mint mark: MA						
693.11	1809	.027	32.00	75.00	175.00	425.00
	1810	8,843	45.00	90.00	225.00	500.00
	1811	.039	32.00	70.00	150.00	350.00
	1812	.016	35.00	90.00	200.00	450.00
	1813	.018	35.00	90.00	200.00	450.00
Mint mark: Q						
693.12	1809	.020	45.00	75.00	175.00	425.00
	1810	4,857	75.00	150.00	250.00	600.00
	1811	.075	32.00	70.00	150.00	350.00
	1812	.086	32.00	70.00	150.00	350.00
	1813	.253	18.00	35.00	100.00	300.00
	1814	.016	45.00	90.00	225.00	500.00
Mint mark: T						
693.13	1811	.035	32.00	75.00	175.00	425.00
	1812	.019	35.00	90.00	200.00	500.00
	1813	.011	18.00	35.00	100.00	300.00
Mint mark: U						
693.14	1809	3,149	100.00	200.00	400.00	850.00
	1810	3,077	100.00	200.00	400.00	850.00
	1811	3,893	100.00	200.00	400.00	850.00
Mint mark: W						
693.15	1809	.062	32.00	70.00	150.00	350.00
	1810	.048	32.00	70.00	150.00	350.00
	1811	.118	27.00	60.00	125.00	300.00
	1812	.108	27.00	60.00	125.00	300.00
	1813	.088	32.00	70.00	150.00	350.00
Mint mark: Flag						
164.16	1812	9,493	150.00	300.00	600.00	1350.
	1813/2	.041	—	—	—	—
	1813	Inc. Ab.	100.00	200.00	400.00	900.00
	Common date					Unc. 600.00
Mint mark: A						
703	1815	6,783	175.00	350.00	700.00	1500.
	1815	—	—	—	Proof	3500.
Mint mark: A						
710.1	1816	.061	25.00	55.00	150.00	375.00
	1817	.214	20.00	40.00	100.00	350.00
	1818	.013	35.00	75.00	185.00	475.00
	1819	2,334	50.00	100.00	225.00	525.00
	1820	.053	25.00	55.00	150.00	375.00
	1821	.139	22.00	45.00	125.00	350.00
	1822	.421	20.00	40.00	100.00	300.00
	1823	.268	20.00	40.00	100.00	250.00
	1824	.284	20.00	40.00	100.00	250.00
Mint mark: B						
710.2	1816	4,398	40.00	85.00	250.00	500.00
	1817	.015	35.00	75.00	175.00	450.00
	1818	3,039	45.00	90.00	225.00	500.00
	1819	.012	35.00	75.00	175.00	450.00
	1822	.030	30.00	65.00	150.00	400.00
	1824	.071	25.00	50.00	145.00	375.00
Mint mark: D						
710.3	1820	2,282	—	—	—	—
	1822	2,181	50.00	100.00	250.00	500.00
	1823	7,251	40.00	85.00	250.00	500.00
	1824	.108	22.00	45.00	120.00	350.00
Mint mark: H						
710.4	1816	7,037	40.00	85.00	250.00	500.00
	1817	.037	30.00	65.00	150.00	400.00
	1818	8,530	40.00	85.00	250.00	500.00
	1819	5,309	40.00	85.00	250.00	500.00
	1820	2,801	—	—	—	—
	1821	2,897	45.00	90.00	225.00	500.00
	1822	9,806	40.00	85.00	250.00	500.00
	1823	.020	30.00	65.00	150.00	400.00
	1824	.027	30.00	65.00	150.00	400.00
Mint mark: I						
710.5	1816	3,956	45.00	90.00	225.00	500.00
	1823	.010	40.00	85.00	250.00	500.00
	1824	.053	25.00	55.00	150.00	375.00
Mint mark: K						
710.6	1817	.213	20.00	40.00	100.00	250.00

KM#	Date	Mintage	VG	Fine	VF	XF
710.6	1820	.011	40.00	85.00	250.00	500.00
	1823	2,545	—	—	—	—
	1824	.038	30.00	65.00	150.00	400.00
	Mint mark: L					
710.7	1816	1,068	—	—	—	—
	1817	3,026	—	—	—	—
	1818	444 pcs.	—	—	—	—
	1823	.027	30.00	65.00	150.00	400.00
	1824	.048	25.00	55.00	150.00	375.00
	Mint mark: M					
710.8	1816	1,699	—	—	—	—
	1817	.030	30.00	65.00	150.00	400.00
	1822	1,496	—	—	—	—
	1823	.094	25.00	55.00	150.00	375.00
	1824	.132	22.00	45.00	125.00	350.00
	Mint mark: MA					
710.9	1824	7,455	40.00	85.00	250.00	500.00
	Mint mark: Q					
710.10	1816	.013	35.00	75.00	175.00	450.00
	1817	.047	25.00	55.00	150.00	400.00
	1818	.052	25.00	55.00	150.00	400.00
	1819	.064	25.00	55.00	150.00	400.00
	1820	.047	25.00	55.00	150.00	400.00
	1821	.028	30.00	65.00	150.00	400.00
	1822	.011	40.00	85.00	250.00	500.00
	1823	3,399	50.00	100.00	250.00	500.00
	1824	.053	25.00	55.00	150.00	375.00
	Mint mark: T					
710.11	1817	1,456	—	—	—	—
	Mint mark: W					
710.12	1817	8,504	40.00	85.00	250.00	500.00
	1818	3,208	—	—	—	—
	1821	.022	30.00	65.00	150.00	400.00
	1822	.102	22.00	45.00	125.00	350.00
	1823	.265	20.00	30.00	75.00	225.00
	1824	.460	20.00	30.00	75.00	225.00
	Common date					Unc. 700.00

KM#	Date	Mintage	VG	Fine	VF	XF
	Mint mark: A					
725.1	1825	.034	30.00	60.00	150.00	400.00
	1826	.122	25.00	50.00	125.00	350.00
	1827	.268	20.00	45.00	100.00	325.00
	1828	.235	20.00	45.00	100.00	325.00
	1829	.145	25.00	50.00	150.00	400.00
	1830	.044	30.00	60.00	150.00	400.00
	1830 reeded edge	Inc. Ab.	150.00	300.00	600.00	1400.
	Mint mark: B					
725.2	1825	.017	35.00	70.00	175.00	400.00
	1826	.024	35.00	70.00	175.00	400.00
	1827	.138	25.00	50.00	125.00	350.00
	1828	.059	30.00	60.00	150.00	400.00
	1829	.102	25.00	50.00	125.00	250.00
	1830	.064	30.00	60.00	150.00	400.00
	Mint mark: BB					
725.3	1825	5,856	40.00	80.00	200.00	500.00
	1826	.019	35.00	70.00	175.00	400.00
	1827	.019	35.00	70.00	175.00	400.00
	1828	.025	35.00	70.00	175.00	400.00
	1829	.018	35.00	70.00	175.00	400.00
	Mint mark: D					
725.4	1825	.027	35.00	70.00	175.00	400.00
	1826	.072	30.00	60.00	150.00	400.00
	1827	.116	25.00	50.00	125.00	250.00
	1828	.108	25.00	50.00	125.00	250.00
	1829	.096	30.00	60.00	150.00	400.00
	Mint mark: H					
725.5	1825	3,215	—	—	—	—
	1826	.019	35.00	70.00	175.00	400.00
	1827	.019	35.00	70.00	175.00	400.00
	1828	.016	35.00	70.00	175.00	400.00
	1829	.049	30.00	60.00	150.00	400.00
	Mint mark: I					
725.6	1825	6,239	40.00	80.00	200.00	500.00
	1826	.032	30.00	60.00	150.00	400.00
	1827	.022	35.00	70.00	175.00	400.00
	1828	4,863	45.00	100.00	200.00	500.00
	1829	.016	35.00	70.00	175.00	400.00
	1830	5,635	45.00	100.00	200.00	500.00
	Mint mark: K					
725.7	1825	.011	35.00	70.00	175.00	400.00
	1826	.011	35.00	70.00	175.00	400.00
	1827	.033	30.00	60.00	150.00	400.00
	1828	.081	30.00	60.00	150.00	400.00
	1829	.033	30.00	60.00	150.00	400.00
	1830	.014	35.00	70.00	175.00	400.00
	Mint mark: L					
725.8	1825	4,397	45.00	100.00	200.00	500.00
	1826	.025	30.00	60.00	150.00	400.00

KM#	Date	Mintage	VG	Fine	VF	XF
725.8	1827	.052	30.00	60.00	150.00	400.00
	1828	.046	30.00	60.00	150.00	400.00
	1829	.021	35.00	70.00	175.00	400.00
	1830	.013	35.00	60.00	150.00	400.00
	Mint mark: M					
725.9	1825	6,770	40.00	80.00	200.00	500.00
	1826	.040	30.00	60.00	150.00	400.00
	1827	.031	30.00	60.00	150.00	400.00
	1828	.120	25.00	50.00	125.00	250.00
	1829	.049	30.00	60.00	150.00	400.00
	1830	.016	35.00	70.00	175.00	400.00
	Mint mark: MA					
725.10	1829	.041	30.00	60.00	150.00	400.00
	Mint mark: Q					
725.11	1825	4,956	50.00	100.00	200.00	500.00
	1826	.021	40.00	60.00	150.00	400.00
	1827	.014	50.00	70.00	175.00	400.00
	1828	.024	50.00	70.00	175.00	400.00
	1829	.011	50.00	70.00	175.00	400.00
	1830	6,688	60.00	125.00	200.00	500.00
	Mint mark: T					
725.12	1826	9,189	45.00	100.00	200.00	500.00
	1827	.043	30.00	60.00	150.00	400.00
	1828	.031	30.00	60.00	150.00	400.00
	1829	.050	30.00	60.00	150.00	400.00
	1830	.012	35.00	70.00	175.00	400.00
	Mint mark: W					
725.13	1825	.015	35.00	70.00	175.00	400.00
	1826	.155	25.00	50.00	125.00	250.00
	1827	.481	15.00	35.00	90.00	275.00
	1828	.358	15.00	35.00	90.00	275.00
	1829	.105	25.00	50.00	125.00	400.00
	1830	.109	25.00	50.00	125.00	400.00
	Common date					Unc. 750.00

Mint mark: A

KM#	Date	Mintage	Fine	VF	XF	Unc
743.1	1831	.010	45.00	100.00	275.00	600.00
	1832	.688	18.00	45.00	125.00	400.00
	1833	.194	22.00	60.00	135.00	450.00
	1834	.493	18.00	45.00	100.00	300.00
	1835	.452	18.00	45.00	125.00	400.00
	1836	.112	22.00	60.00	135.00	450.00
	1837	.104	22.00	60.00	135.00	450.00
	1838	.093	22.00	60.00	135.00	450.00
	1839	.036	40.00	85.00	200.00	500.00
	1840	.042	40.00	85.00	200.00	500.00
	1841	.068	40.00	85.00	200.00	500.00
	1842	.017	45.00	100.00	275.00	600.00
	1843	.068	40.00	85.00	200.00	500.00
	1844	.030	40.00	85.00	200.00	500.00
	1845(p)	.019	20.00	50.00	125.00	400.00
	1845(ha)	I.A.	20.00	50.00	125.00	400.00
	1846	.305	18.00	45.00	100.00	300.00
	1847	.784	18.00	45.00	125.00	400.00
	1848	.098	22.00	55.00	135.00	450.00
	Mint mark: B					
743.2	1831	.049	40.00	85.00	200.00	500.00
	1832	.384	18.00	45.00	90.00	300.00
	1833	.105	25.00	50.00	125.00	400.00
	1834	.296	18.00	45.00	90.00	300.00
	1835	.066	40.00	85.00	200.00	500.00
	1836	.113	25.00	50.00	125.00	400.00
	1837	.256	18.00	45.00	90.00	300.00
	1838	.156	20.00	50.00	100.00	300.00
	1839	.102	25.00	50.00	125.00	400.00
	1840	.121	25.00	50.00	125.00	400.00
	1841	.022	20.00	50.00	125.00	400.00
	1842	.147	20.00	50.00	100.00	300.00
	1843	.067	40.00	85.00	200.00	500.00
	1844	.013	45.00	100.00	275.00	600.00
	1845	.155	20.00	50.00	100.00	300.00
	1846	.046	40.00	85.00	200.00	500.00
	Mint mark: BB					
743.3	1832	.055	40.00	85.00	200.00	500.00
	1833	.074	40.00	85.00	200.00	500.00
	1834(ba)	.077	40.00	85.00	200.00	500.00
	1834(be)	I.A.	40.00	85.00	200.00	500.00
	1835	.038	40.00	85.00	200.00	500.00
	1836	.073	40.00	85.00	200.00	500.00
	1837	.022	20.00	50.00	125.00	400.00
	1838	.082	40.00	85.00	200.00	500.00
	1839	.047	40.00	85.00	200.00	500.00
	1840	.064	40.00	85.00	200.00	500.00
	1841	.061	40.00	85.00	200.00	500.00
	1842	.026	20.00	50.00	125.00	400.00
	1843	.059	40.00	85.00	200.00	500.00
	1844	.086	40.00	85.00	200.00	500.00
	1845	.076	40.00	85.00	200.00	500.00
	1846	.044	40.00	85.00	200.00	500.00
	1847	.060	40.00	85.00	200.00	500.00
	1848	.027	20.00	50.00	125.00	400.00

Mint mark: D

KM#	Date	Mintage	Fine	VF	XF	Unc
743.4	1832	.239	20.00	50.00	100.00	300.00
	1833	.098	40.00	85.00	200.00	500.00
	1834	.098	40.00	85.00	200.00	500.00
	1835	.040	40.00	85.00	200.00	500.00
	1836	5,519	55.00	125.00	300.00	800.00
	1837	6,306	55.00	125.00	300.00	800.00
	1838	3,478	—	—	—	—
	1839(a)	7,299	50.00	110.00	300.00	750.00
	1839(t)	I.A.	50.00	110.00	300.00	750.00
	1840	.010	45.00	100.00	275.00	600.00
	1848	.012	45.00	100.00	275.00	600.00
	Mint mark: H					
743.5	1832	.186	25.00	50.00	125.00	400.00
	1833	.022	20.00	50.00	125.00	400.00
	1834	.072	40.00	85.00	200.00	500.00
	1835	.023	20.00	50.00	125.00	400.00
	Mint mark: I					
743.6	1831	.038	40.00	85.00	200.00	500.00
	1832	.034	40.00	85.00	200.00	500.00
	1833	.034	40.00	85.00	200.00	500.00
	1834	.048	40.00	85.00	200.00	500.00
	1835	.048	40.00	85.00	200.00	500.00
	Mint mark: K					
743.7	1832	.076	40.00	85.00	200.00	500.00
	1833	.023	20.00	50.00	125.00	400.00
	1834	.057	40.00	85.00	200.00	500.00
	1835	.042	40.00	85.00	200.00	500.00
	1836	.020	40.00	100.00	350.00	700.00
	1837	.036	40.00	85.00	200.00	500.00
	1838	.019	40.00	100.00	350.00	700.00
	1839	.031	40.00	85.00	200.00	500.00
	1840	.039	40.00	85.00	200.00	500.00
	1841	.029	40.00	85.00	200.00	500.00
	1842	.033	40.00	85.00	200.00	500.00
	1843	.037	40.00	85.00	200.00	500.00
	1844	.031	40.00	85.00	200.00	500.00
	1845	.018	40.00	100.00	350.00	700.00
	1846	.018	40.00	100.00	350.00	700.00
	1847	6,504	55.00	125.00	300.00	800.00
	Mint mark: L					
743.8	1832	.024	20.00	50.00	125.00	400.00
	1833	.014	45.00	100.00	275.00	600.00
	1834	.015	45.00	100.00	275.00	600.00
	1835	2,669	—	—	—	—
	Mint mark: M					
743.9	1832	.069	40.00	85.00	200.00	500.00
	1833	.050	40.00	85.00	200.00	500.00
	1834	.078	40.00	85.00	200.00	500.00
	1835	.041	40.00	85.00	200.00	500.00
	1836	6,733	55.00	125.00	300.00	800.00
	Mint mark: MA					
743.10	1832	.064	45.00	85.00	200.00	500.00
	1833	.021	45.00	100.00	275.00	600.00
	1834	.019	45.00	100.00	275.00	600.00
	1835	.015	45.00	100.00	275.00	600.00
	1837	—	250.00	600.00	1200.	—
	1838	.025	20.00	50.00	125.00	400.00
	Mint mark: Q					
743.11	1832	.022	45.00	100.00	275.00	600.00
	1833	.037	40.00	85.00	200.00	500.00
	1834	.069	40.00	85.00	200.00	500.00
	Mint mark: T					
743.12	1832	.104	25.00	50.00	125.00	400.00
	1833	.028	40.00	85.00	200.00	500.00
	1834	.104	25.00	50.00	125.00	400.00
	1835	.017	45.00	100.00	275.00	600.00
	Mint mark: W					
743.13	1831	.033	40.00	85.00	200.00	500.00
	1832	.427	18.00	45.00	100.00	300.00
	1833	.168	25.00	50.00	125.00	400.00
	1834	.583	18.00	45.00	100.00	300.00
	1835	.147	25.00	50.00	125.00	400.00
	1836	.060	40.00	85.00	200.00	500.00
	1837	.230	25.00	50.00	125.00	400.00
	1838	.170	25.00	50.00	125.00	400.00
	1839	.105	25.00	50.00	125.00	400.00
	1840(c)	.063	40.00	85.00	200.00	500.00
	1840(r)	I.A.	40.00	85.00	200.00	500.00
	1841	.290	25.00	50.00	125.00	400.00
	1842	.190	25.00	50.00	125.00	400.00
	1843	.296	22.00	45.00	120.00	400.00
	1844	.290	22.00	45.00	120.00	400.00
	1845	.353	22.00	45.00	120.00	400.00
	1846	.049	40.00	85.00	200.00	500.00

Mint mark: A
Second Republic

KM#	Date	Mintage	Fine	VF	XF	Unc
760.1	1849	.665	100.00	275.00	650.00	1250.
	1850	.857	85.00	250.00	600.00	1150.
	1851	.351	110.00	300.00	700.00	1500.
	Mint mark: BB					
760.2	1849	.014	250.00	500.00	1000.	2000.
	1850	.202	160.00	350.00	850.00	1600.

Mint mark: K

KM#	Date	Mintage	Fine	VF	XF	Unc
760.3	1849	.017	250.00	500.00	1000.	2000.
	1850	9,914	275.00	650.00	1500.	—

Mint mark: A
Second Empire

KM#	Date	Mintage	Fine	VF	XF	Unc
780.1	1853	.049	350.00	600.00	1200.	3000.
	1854	.215	250.00	500.00	1000.	2000.
	1854	—	—	—	Proof	—
	1855(d)	.082	300.00	550.00	1150.	2500.
	1856	.241	200.00	500.00	1000.	2000.
	1857	.389	200.00	450.00	800.00	1800.
	1858	1,288	600.00	1000.	1750.	3750.
	1858	Inc. Ab.	—	—	Proof	4000.
	1859	894 pcs.	800.00	1350.	2250.	5000.

Mint mark: BB

KM#	Date	Mintage	Fine	VF	XF	Unc
780.2	1856 lg. BB	.693	200.00	400.00	900.00	1500.
	1856 sm. BB	I.A.	200.00	400.00	900.00	1500.

NOTE: Date varieties exist.

Mint mark: D

KM#	Date	Mintage	Fine	VF	XF	Unc
780.3	1856	.289	200.00	400.00	1000.	2000.

10.0000 g, .835 SILVER, .2684 oz ASW
Mint mark: A

KM#	Date	Mintage	Fine	VF	XF	Unc
807.1	1866	3.226	10.00	25.00	75.00	150.00
	1867	3.695	10.00	25.00	75.00	150.00
	1868	3.762	10.00	25.00	75.00	150.00
	1869	1.104	20.00	40.00	90.00	225.00
	1870	3.187	10.00	25.00	75.00	150.00

Mint mark: BB

KM#	Date	Mintage	Fine	VF	XF	Unc
807.2	1866	3.090	10.00	25.00	75.00	150.00
	1867	3.471	10.00	25.00	75.00	150.00
	1868	.733	30.00	75.00	175.00	400.00
	1869	.367	35.00	90.00	200.00	500.00
	1870	1.001	—	—	—	—

Mint mark: K

KM#	Date	Mintage	Fine	VF	XF	Unc
807.3	1866	.437	50.00	125.00	250.00	600.00
	1867	1.744	15.00	40.00	100.00	250.00
	1868	.087	—	—	—	—

Mint mark: A
Third Republic

KM#	Date	Mintage	Fine	VF	XF	Unc
816.1	1870	.239	50.00	125.00	350.00	700.00

Mint mark: K

KM#	Date	Mintage	Fine	VF	XF	Unc
816.2	1870(a)	.560	50.00	125.00	300.00	600.00
	1870(s)	I.A.	50.00	125.00	300.00	625.00
	1871	1.256	40.00	100.00	225.00	500.00

10.0000 g, .835 SILVER, .2684 oz ASW
Mint mark: A

KM#	Date	Mintage	Fine	VF	XF	Unc
817.1	1870 lg.A	1.324	8.00	18.00	50.00	150.00
	1870 sm.a	Inc. Ab.	10.00	20.00	60.00	175.00
	1871 lg.A	4.757	7.00	15.00	40.00	100.00
	1871 sm.a	Inc. Ab.	7.00	15.00	40.00	100.00
	1872	2.306	7.00	15.00	40.00	100.00
	1873	.528	30.00	75.00	175.00	400.00

KM#	Date	Mintage	Fine	VF	XF	Unc
817.1	1878	30 pcs.	—	—	Proof	6000.
	1881	1.014	10.00	30.00	75.00	150.00
	1887	2.343	7.00	15.00	40.00	100.00
	1888	.131	65.00	150.00	300.00	650.00
	1889	100 pcs.	—	—	Proof	4750.
	1894	.300	15.00	40.00	100.00	250.00
	1895	.600	12.00	30.00	75.00	175.00

Mint mark: K

KM#	Date	Mintage	Fine	VF	XF	Unc
817.2	1871 lg. K	1.215	15.00	40.00	100.00	250.00
	1871 sm. k	I.A.	12.00	30.00	75.00	175.00
	1872	1.467	12.00	30.00	75.00	175.00

Mint: Paris - w/o mint mark.

KM#	Date	Mintage	Fine	VF	XF	Unc
845.1	1898	5.000	3.00	5.00	20.00	45.00
	1898	—	—	—	Proof	425.00
	1899	3.500	4.00	7.00	25.00	50.00
	1900	.500	30.00	80.00	200.00	450.00
	1900	—	—	—	Proof	400.00

NOTE: Later dates (1901-1920) exist for this type.

5 FRANCS

25.0000 g, .900 SILVER, .7234 oz ASW
Mint mark: A

Dav.#1337

KM#	Date	Mintage	VG	Fine	VF	XF
639.1	L'AN 10	.561	35.00	75.00	175.00	550.00
	L'AN 11	1.558	25.00	60.00	150.00	450.00

NOTE: Earlier dates (L'AN 4-9) exist for this type.

Mint mark: G

KM#	Date	Mintage	VG	Fine	VF	XF
639.4	L'AN 10	4,447	125.00	300.00	600.00	2200.

NOTE: Earlier date (L'AN 9) exists for this type.

Mint mark: K

KM#	Date	Mintage	VG	Fine	VF	XF
639.5	L'AN 10	.060	40.00	100.00	250.00	700.00
	L'AN 11	.029	60.00	125.00	350.00	1250.

NOTE: Earlier dates (L'AN 5-9) exist for this type.

Mint mark: L

KM#	Date	Mintage	VG	Fine	VF	XF
639.6	L'AN 10	.165	35.00	90.00	225.00	550.00
	L'AN 11	.170	35.00	90.00	225.00	550.00

NOTE: Earlier dates (L'AN 5-9) exist for this type.

Mint mark: MA

KM#	Date	Mintage	VG	Fine	VF	XF
639.7	L'AN 10	.039	50.00	125.00	300.00	1150.
	L'AN 11	.160	35.00	90.00	225.00	550.00

NOTE: Earlier date (L'AN 9) exists for this type.

Mint mark: Q

KM#	Date	Mintage	VG	Fine	VF	XF
639.8	L'AN 10	.134	35.00	90.00	225.00	550.00
	L'AN 11	.360	30.00	80.00	200.00	500.00

NOTE: Earlier dates (L'AN 5-9) exist for this type.

Mint mark: T

KM#	Date	Mintage	VG	Fine	VF	XF
639.9	L'AN 10	5,232	—Reported, not confirmed			
	L'AN 11	9,950	70.00	165.00	400.00	1350.

NOTE: Earlier dates (L'AN 5-9) exist for this type.

Mint mark: A
Obv. leg: BONAPARTE PREMIER CONSUL.

KM#	Date	Mintage	VG	Fine	VF	XF
650.1	ANXI	3.878	20.00	50.00	150.00	300.00
	ANXI w/o dots flanking privy mark	Inc. Ab.	150.00	300.00	700.00	—

Mint mark: D

KM#	Date	Mintage	VG	Fine	VF	XF
650.2	ANXI	5,547	100.00	200.00	500.00	900.00

Mint mark: K

KM#	Date	Mintage	VG	Fine	VF	XF
650.3	ANXI	.031	50.00	125.00	300.00	800.00

Mint mark: L

KM#	Date	Mintage	VG	Fine	VF	XF
650.4	ANXI	.119	35.00	90.00	225.00	550.00

Mint mark: MA

KM#	Date	Mintage	VG	Fine	VF	XF
650.5	ANXI	.206	30.00	80.00	200.00	500.00

Mint mark: Q

KM#	Date	Mintage	VG	Fine	VF	XF
650.6	ANXI	.309	30.00	80.00	200.00	450.00

Mint mark: T

KM#	Date	Mintage	VG	Fine	VF	XF
650.7	ANXI	.018	75.00	200.00	400.00	650.00

KM#	Date	Mintage	VG	Fine	VF	XF
	Mint mark: A					
659.1	AN12	3.454	20.00	40.00	125.00	300.00
	Mint mark: B					
659.2	AN12	.035	50.00	125.00	300.00	800.00
	Mint mark: BB					
659.3	AN12	.018	75.00	200.00	400.00	650.00
	Mint mark: D					
659.4	AN12	.116	35.00	90.00	225.00	550.00
	Mint mark: G					
659.5	AN12	.014	200.00	500.00	1000.	3000.
	Mint mark: H					
659.6	AN12	.070	50.00	125.00	300.00	800.00
	Mint mark: I					
659.7	AN12	.422	30.00	80.00	200.00	350.00
	Mint mark: K					
659.8	AN12	.462	40.00	80.00	200.00	350.00
	Mint mark: L					
659.9	AN12	.311	40.00	80.00	200.00	350.00
	Mint mark: M					
659.10	AN12	1.199	30.00	70.00	175.00	300.00
	Mint mark: MA					
659.11	AN12	.148	35.00	90.00	225.00	550.00
	Mint mark: Q					
659.12	AN12	.578	40.00	80.00	200.00	350.00
	Mint mark: T					
659.13	AN12	.113	35.00	90.00	225.00	550.00
	Mint mark: U					
659.14	AN12	9,953	150.00	350.00	1000.	2200.
	Mint mark: W					
659.15	AN12	.028	50.00	125.00	300.00	700.00

KM#	Date	Mintage	VG	Fine	VF	XF
	Mint mark: A					
	Obv. leg: NAPOLEON EMPEREUR.					
660.1	AN12	.767	40.00	125.00	300.00	500.00
	Mint mark: B					
660.2	AN12	.010	60.00	150.00	400.00	800.00
	Mint mark: D					
660.3	AN12	.014	50.00	125.00	300.00	600.00
	Mint mark: H					
660.4	AN12	.015	50.00	125.00	300.00	600.00
	Mint mark: I					
660.5	AN12	.090	40.00	100.00	200.00	500.00
	Mint mark: K					
660.6	AN12	.071	40.00	100.00	200.00	500.00
	Mint mark: L					
660.7	AN12	.016	50.00	125.00	300.00	600.00
	Mint mark: M					
660.8	AN12	.427	40.00	100.00	200.00	500.00
	Mint mark: MA					
660.9	AN12	2,030	—Reported, not confirmed			
	Mint mark: Q					
660.10	AN12	.055	40.00	100.00	200.00	500.00
	Mint mark: T					
660.11	AN12	.011	100.00	200.00	400.00	800.00
	Mint mark: W					
660.12	AN12	4,366	120.00	250.00	500.00	1800.

KM#	Date	Mintage	VG	Fine	VF	XF
	Mint mark: A					
	Obv: Monogram below bust.					
662.1	AN13	5.121	20.00	40.00	100.00	295.00
	AN14	1.855	25.00	50.00	135.00	365.00
	Mint mark: B					
662.2	AN13	4,901	60.00	150.00	400.00	800.00
	Mint mark: BB					
662.3	AN13	7,510	—	—	—	—
	AN14	.831	—	—	—	—
	Mint mark: D					
662.4	AN13	.024	40.00	100.00	200.00	500.00
	AN14	3,890	100.00	250.00	500.00	1500.
	Mint mark: G					
662.5	AN13	6,487	200.00	400.00	1000.	2500.
	Mint mark: H					
662.6	AN13	.035	40.00	100.00	200.00	500.00
	AN14	3,780	100.00	250.00	500.00	1150.
	Mint mark: I					
662.7	AN13	.333	40.00	100.00	200.00	500.00
	AN14	.012	—	—	—	—
	Mint mark: K					
662.8	AN13	.161	50.00	125.00	300.00	600.00
	AN14	2,113	200.00	400.00	700.00	2000.
	Mint mark: L					
662.9	AN13	.207	40.00	110.00	275.00	475.00
	AN14	.015	50.00	125.00	300.00	600.00
	Mint mark: M					
662.10	AN13	1.547	30.00	60.00	125.00	300.00
	AN14	.040	40.00	100.00	200.00	500.00
	Mint mark: MA					
662.11	AN13	.064	40.00	100.00	200.00	450.00
	Mint mark: Q					
662.12	AN13	.245	35.00	75.00	175.00	375.00
	Mint mark: T					
662.13	AN13	.025	40.00	100.00	200.00	500.00
	AN14	632	—Reported, not confirmed			
	Mint mark: U					
662.14	AN13	.021	100.00	200.00	400.00	800.00
	AN14	.014	125.00	250.00	550.00	1150.
	Mint mark: W					
662.15	AN13	.034	40.00	100.00	200.00	500.00
	AN14	.014	50.00	125.00	300.00	600.00

KM#	Date	Mintage	VG	Fine	VF	XF
	Mint mark: A					
673.1	1806	.826	35.00	75.00	150.00	350.00
	Mint mark: B					
673.2	1806	.025	40.00	100.00	200.00	500.00
	1807	.044	40.00	100.00	200.00	500.00
	Mint mark: BB					
673.3	1806	.660	35.00	75.00	150.00	350.00
	1807	1,296	—	—	—	—
	Mint mark: D					
673.4	1806	2,771	—	—	—	—
	1807	2,423	—	—	—	—
	Mint mark: H					
673.5	1806	.028	—Reported, not confirmed			
	1807	4,847	100.00	250.00	500.00	1300.
	Mint mark: I					
673.6	1806	.239	35.00	70.00	150.00	325.00
	1807	.091	35.00	80.00	175.00	400.00
	Mint mark: K					
673.7	1806	.029	40.00	100.00	200.00	500.00
	1807	.010	60.00	175.00	350.00	800.00
	Mint mark: L					
673.8	1806	.551	35.00	75.00	150.00	350.00
	1807	.375	35.00	70.00	150.00	325.00
	Mint mark: M					
673.9	1806	.022	40.00	100.00	200.00	500.00
	1807	.101	35.00	80.00	175.00	400.00
	Mint mark: Q					
673.10	1806	.078	35.00	70.00	150.00	350.00
	1807	.025	40.00	100.00	200.00	500.00
	Mint mark: T					
673.11	1806	706 pcs.	—Reported, not confirmed			
	1807	449 pcs.	—	—	Rare	—
	Mint mark: U					
673.12	1806	.031	100.00	200.00	400.00	800.00
	1807	.030	125.00	250.00	500.00	1400.
	Mint mark: W					
673.13	1806	.032	40.00	100.00	200.00	500.00
	1807	.029	40.00	100.00	200.00	500.00
	Mint mark: A					
	Obv: Similar to KM#662.1.					
	Rev: Similar to KM#686.1.					
685	1807	.049	300.00	650.00	1200.	2500.

KM#	Date	Mintage	VG	Fine	VF	XF
	Rev. leg: REPUBLIQUE FRANCAISE.					
686.1	1807	.041	350.00	700.00	1300.	2000.
	1807	—	—	—	Proof	5000.
	1808	6.462	20.00	35.00	55.00	120.00
	Mint mark: B					
686.2	1808	1.542	22.00	40.00	65.00	135.00
	Mint mark: BB					
686.3	1808	.068	35.00	70.00	150.00	325.00
	Mint mark: D					
686.4	1808	.065	35.00	70.00	150.00	325.00
	Mint mark: H					
686.5	1808	7,204	—Reported, not confirmed			
	Mint mark: I					
686.6	1808	.107	35.00	70.00	150.00	300.00
	Mint mark: K					
686.7	1808	.054	35.00	70.00	150.00	325.00
	Mint mark: L					
686.8	1808	.144	35.00	70.00	125.00	275.00
	Mint mark: M					
686.9	1808	.351	25.00	40.00	65.00	150.00
	Mint mark: MA					
686.10	1808	2,681	100.00	225.00	450.00	900.00
	Mint mark: Q					
686.11	1808	.012	55.00	95.00	200.00	500.00
	Mint mark: T					
686.12	1808	2,682	—Reported, not confirmed			
	Mint mark: U					
686.13	1808	.014	75.00	200.00	400.00	750.00
	Mint mark: W					
686.14	1808	.550	25.00	40.00	65.00	150.00
	Common date					Unc. 400.00

KM#	Date	Mintage	VG	Fine	VF	XF
	Mint mark: A					
	Rev. leg: EMPIRE FRANCAIS.					
694.1	1809	3.254	15.00	25.00	50.00	125.00
	1810	8.797	12.50	20.00	45.00	110.00
	1811	31.050	12.50	17.50	35.00	90.00
	1812	9.311	12.50	20.00	45.00	110.00
	1813	9.757	12.50	20.00	45.00	110.00
	1814	1.329	20.00	35.00	85.00	175.00
	Mint mark: B					
694.2	1809	3.036	15.00	25.00	50.00	125.00
	1810	.632	25.00	40.00	65.00	150.00
	1811	3.772	15.00	25.00	50.00	125.00
	1812	3.039	15.00	25.00	50.00	125.00

KM#	Date	Mintage	VG	Fine	VF	XF
694.2	1813	.728	25.00	40.00	65.00	150.00
	1814	.020	35.00	75.00	125.00	250.00
	Mint mark: BB					
694.3	1809	2,856	—Reported, not confirmed			
	1810	.028	30.00	60.00	100.00	225.00
	1811	.327	25.00	40.00	65.00	150.00
	1812	.139	30.00	50.00	120.00	200.00
	1813	.025	35.00	75.00	135.00	275.00
	1814	5,382	—Reported, not confirmed			
	Mint mark: CL					
694.4	1813	.014	300.00	500.00	900.00	2500.
	1814	1,191	1500.	2500.	4500.	6500.
	Mint mark: D					
694.5	1809	.011	35.00	75.00	150.00	325.00
	1810	.043	30.00	60.00	100.00	225.00
	1811	1.568	20.00	35.00	85.00	175.00
	1812	2.295	15.00	30.00	50.00	125.00
	1813	.917	20.00	35.00	85.00	175.00
	Mint mark: H					
694.6	1809	9,006	50.00	125.00	250.00	475.00
	1811	1.029	20.00	35.00	85.00	175.00
	1812	1.824	20.00	35.00	85.00	175.00
	1813	1.795	20.00	35.00	85.00	175.00
	1814	.169	30.00	50.00	125.00	200.00
	Mint mark: I					
694.7	1809	.065	30.00	60.00	100.00	225.00
	1810	.026	35.00	75.00	135.00	275.00
	1811	1.830	20.00	35.00	85.00	175.00
	1812	2.672	15.00	30.00	60.00	125.00
	1813	2.555	20.00	35.00	85.00	175.00
	1814	.027	35.00	75.00	135.00	275.00
	Mint mark: K					
694.8	1809	.105	30.00	50.00	125.00	200.00
	1810	.120	30.00	50.00	125.00	200.00
	1811	1.081	20.00	35.00	85.00	175.00
	1812	1.664	20.00	35.00	85.00	175.00
	1813	1.281	20.00	35.00	85.00	175.00
	Mint mark: L					
694.9	1809	.217	30.00	50.00	120.00	200.00
	1810 mint mark at right					
		.185	30.00	50.00	120.00	200.00
	1810 mint mark at left					
		Inc. Ab.	35.00	75.00	135.00	275.00
	1811	1.123	20.00	35.00	85.00	175.00
	1812	.936	20.00	35.00	85.00	175.00
	1813	1.161	20.00	35.00	85.00	175.00
	Mint mark: M					
694.10	1809	.034	30.00	60.00	100.00	225.00
	1810	.072	30.00	60.00	100.00	225.00
	1811	1.101	20.00	35.00	85.00	175.00
	1812	1.617	20.00	35.00	85.00	175.00
	1813	2.213	20.00	35.00	85.00	175.00
	1814	.369	25.00	45.00	90.00	200.00
	Mint mark: MA					
694.10	1809	.012	35.00	75.00	150.00	325.00
	1810	.012	35.00	75.00	150.00	325.00
	1811	.671	25.00	40.00	90.00	200.00
	1812	.612	25.00	40.00	90.00	200.00
	1813	.834	25.00	40.00	90.00	200.00
	1814	.016	40.00	85.00	200.00	300.00
	Mint mark: Q					
694.12	1810	.118	30.00	50.00	125.00	200.00
	1811	1.213	20.00	35.00	85.00	175.00
	1812	1.460	20.00	35.00	85.00	175.00
	1813	1.826	20.00	35.00	85.00	175.00
	1814	.367	25.00	45.00	100.00	190.00
	Mint mark: R					
694.13	1812R/cr					
		.049	100.00	250.00	550.00	1100.
	1813R/cr					
		.017	175.00	400.00	850.00	2000.
	Mint mark: T					
694.14	1809	2,218	—Reported, not confirmed			
	1811	.724	20.00	35.00	85.00	175.00
	1812	.926	20.00	35.00	85.00	175.00
	1813	.564	20.00	35.00	85.00	175.00
	1814	8,745	55.00	125.00	275.00	500.00
	Mint mark: U					
694.15	1809	.016	100.00	200.00	450.00	900.00
	1810	.014	100.00	250.00	500.00	1000.
	1811	.169	30.00	60.00	100.00	225.00
	1812/1	—	75.00	150.00	250.00	500.00
	1812	.105	30.00	60.00	100.00	225.00
	1813	.060	35.00	75.00	150.00	325.00
	Mint mark: W					
694.16	1809	1.221	20.00	35.00	85.00	175.00
	1810	.297	30.00	50.00	120.00	200.00
	1811	3.290	15.00	30.00	60.00	125.00
	1812	4.342	15.00	30.00	60.00	125.00
	1813	1.824	20.00	35.00	85.00	175.00
	1814	.033	35.00	75.00	150.00	325.00
	Mint mark: Flag					
694.17	1812	.055	150.00	300.00	650.00	1300.
	1813	.362	125.00	250.00	500.00	1000.
	Common date					Unc. 300.00

Mint mark: A
First Restoration

KM#	Date	Mintage	VG	Fine	VF	XF
702.1	1814	1.466	20.00	45.00	100.00	250.00
	1814					
		4 known	—	—	Proof	2750.
	1815	.413	25.00	50.00	125.00	275.00
	Mint mark: B					
702.2	1814	.634	25.00	50.00	125.00	275.00
	1815	.254	30.00	65.00	150.00	350.00
	Mint mark: BB					
702.3	1814	4,913	75.00	175.00	400.00	900.00
	1815	1,551	100.00	225.00	500.00	1200.
	Mint mark: D					
702.4	1814	.082	35.00	75.00	175.00	400.00
	1815	7,482	65.00	150.00	325.00	700.00
	Mint mark: H					
702.5	1814	.046	40.00	85.00	200.00	500.00
	1815	.034	40.00	85.00	200.00	500.00
	Mint mark: I					
702.6	1814	1.554	20.00	45.00	100.00	250.00
	1815	1.739	20.00	45.00	100.00	250.00
	Mint mark: K					
702.7	1814	.355	30.00	60.00	120.00	350.00
	1815	.108	30.00	60.00	120.00	350.00
	Mint mark: L					
702.8	1814	1.902	20.00	45.00	100.00	250.00
	1815	1.130	20.00	45.00	100.00	250.00
	Mint mark: M					
702.9	1814	2.377	20.00	45.00	100.00	250.00
	1815	1.406	20.00	45.00	100.00	250.00
	Mint mark: MA					
702.10	1814	.099	35.00	75.00	135.00	300.00
	1815	7,461	75.00	175.00	400.00	900.00
	Mint mark: Q					
702.11	1814	1.182	20.00	45.00	100.00	250.00
	1815/4	.925	30.00	50.00	75.00	200.00
	1815	Inc. Ab.	20.00	45.00	100.00	250.00
	Mint mark: T					
702.12	1814	5,235	75.00	175.00	400.00	850.00
	1815	8,006	—Reported, not confirmed			
	Mint mark: W					
702.13	1814	.104	35.00	75.00	135.00	300.00
	1815	.114	35.00	75.00	135.00	300.00
	Common date					Unc. 600.00

Mint mark: A

"The Hundred Days"

KM#	Date	Mintage	VG	Fine	VF	XF
704.1	1815	.473	80.00	165.00	300.00	700.00
	Mint mark: B					
704.2	1815	.093	100.00	200.00	350.00	1000.
	Mint mark: BB					
704.3	1815	3,723	250.00	600.00	1200.	2200.
	Mint mark: I					
704.4	1815	.596	65.00	125.00	250.00	550.00
	Mint mark: L					
704.5	1815	.097	90.00	200.00	350.00	1000.
	Mint mark: M					
704.6	1815	.080	100.00	225.00	375.00	1250.
	Mint mark: Q					
704.7	1815	.021	120.00	280.00	550.00	1500.
	Mint mark: W					
704.8	1815	.021	120.00	280.00	550.00	1500.

Mint mark: A
Second Restoration

KM#	Date	Mintage	VG	Fine	VF	XF
711.1	1816	3.210	12.00	20.00	45.00	150.00
	1817	3.778	12.00	20.00	45.00	150.00
	1818	.086	20.00	40.00	75.00	225.00
	1819	.658	17.50	30.00	65.00	175.00
	1820	3.226	12.00	20.00	45.00	150.00
	1821	9.526	12.00	20.00	40.00	135.00
	1822	13.453	12.00	20.00	40.00	125.00
	1823	6.536	12.00	20.00	40.00	125.00
	1824	9.066	12.00	20.00	40.00	125.00
	Mint mark: B					
711.2	1816	.922	18.00	30.00	65.00	175.00
	1817	1.580	15.00	25.00	55.00	150.00
	1818	2.190	12.00	20.00	45.00	150.00
	1819	3.437	12.00	20.00	45.00	150.00
	1820	.210	20.00	45.00	100.00	225.00
	1821	.123	30.00	55.00	125.00	250.00
	1822	.897	12.00	20.00	45.00	150.00
	1823	.393	20.00	45.00	100.00	225.00
	1824	1.246	15.00	25.00	55.00	150.00
	Mint mark: BB					
711.3	1816	8,115	40.00	75.00	150.00	475.00
	1817	3,510	55.00	110.00	200.00	550.00
	1818	1,119	55.00	110.00	200.00	550.00
	1819	2,469	55.00	110.00	200.00	550.00
	1820	1,976	55.00	110.00	200.00	550.00
	1821	1,527	60.00	120.00	240.00	700.00
	1823	3,712	55.00	110.00	200.00	550.00
	Mint mark: D					
711.4	1816	6,446	35.00	65.00	125.00	400.00
	1817	3,605	35.00	65.00	125.00	450.00
	1820	.017	—	45.00	75.00	300.00
	1823	.994	12.00	20.00	45.00	150.00
	1824	2.448	12.00	20.00	45.00	150.00
	1824 inverted D					
		Inc. Ab.	—	—	Rare	—
	Mint mark: H					
711.5	1816	6,575	35.00	80.00	165.00	550.00
	1817	.110	22.00	45.00	85.00	250.00
	1818	.012	55.00	110.00	220.00	500.00
	1819	.033	35.00	65.00	120.00	325.00
	1820	.018	40.00	85.00	165.00	375.00
	1821	.018	55.00	110.00	220.00	450.00
	1822	.077	27.50	60.00	100.00	275.00
	1823	.329	20.00	40.00	75.00	200.00
	1824	.771	12.00	20.00	45.00	150.00
	Mint mark: I					
711.6	1816	.306	20.00	40.00	75.00	200.00
	1817	4,204	45.00	65.00	115.00	400.00
	1818	1,568	55.00	110.00	285.00	575.00
	1819	1,104	55.00	110.00	285.00	575.00
	1820	639	140.00	250.00	400.00	800.00
	1821	6,320	50.00	85.00	145.00	440.00
	1822	8,712	45.00	70.00	145.00	440.00
	1823	.269	20.00	40.00	75.00	200.00
	1824	1.039	12.00	20.00	45.00	150.00

KM#	Date	Mintage	VG	Fine	VF	XF
Mint mark: K						
711.7	1816	.034	25.00	55.00	90.00	250.00
	1817	.386	20.00	40.00	75.00	200.00
	1818	.017	—	65.00	135.00	300.00
	1820	.018	25.00	65.00	135.00	300.00
	1822	.393	20.00	40.00	75.00	200.00
	1823	.800	12.00	20.00	45.00	150.00
	1824	1.010	12.00	20.00	45.00	150.00
Mint mark: L						
711.8	1816	1.001	12.00	20.00	45.00	150.00
	1817	.377	20.00	40.00	75.00	200.00
	1818	.010	35.00	75.00	150.00	250.00
	1823	.898	12.00	20.00	45.00	150.00
	1824	1.068	12.00	20.00	45.00	150.00
Mint mark: M						
711.9	1816	.651	12.00	20.00	45.00	150.00
	1817	.188	20.00	40.00	75.00	225.00
	1818	2,920	40.00	80.00	175.00	350.00
	1823	.958	12.00	20.00	45.00	150.00
	1824	1.589	12.00	20.00	40.00	125.00
Mint mark: MA						
711.10	1816	.018	35.00	75.00	150.00	350.00
	1817	.010	40.00	80.00	165.00	375.00
	1818	7,805	50.00	100.00	200.00	500.00
	1819	1,186	60.00	120.00	250.00	600.00
	1820	440 pcs.	100.00	200.00	350.00	750.00
	1821	198	150.00	250.00	500.00	900.00
	1823	3,847	55.00	110.00	225.00	550.00
	1824	1.422	12.00	20.00	45.00	150.00
Mint mark: Q						
711.11	1816	.591	18.00	30.00	65.00	175.00
	1817	.105	20.00	40.00	75.00	225.00
	1819	1,618	60.00	120.00	250.00	600.00
	1820	2,770	55.00	110.00	225.00	550.00
	1821	5,626	50.00	100.00	200.00	500.00
	1822	.020	35.00	75.00	150.00	350.00
	1823	.715	12.00	20.00	45.00	150.00
	1824	1.006	12.00	20.00	45.00	150.00
Mint mark: T						
711.12	1816	.011	40.00	80.00	165.00	325.00
	1817	.025	35.00	70.00	135.00	300.00
	1818	.024	35.00	70.00	135.00	300.00
	1819	.020	35.00	70.00	135.00	300.00
	1820	.011	40.00	80.00	165.00	325.00
Mint mark: W						
711.13	1816	.072	25.00	55.00	90.00	250.00
	1817	.438	18.00	30.00	65.00	175.00
	1818	.066	25.00	55.00	90.00	250.00
	1819	.034	30.00	65.00	125.00	275.00
	1820	.106	20.00	40.00	75.00	225.00
	1821	3.674	12.00	20.00	45.00	150.00
	1822	4.839	12.00	20.00	45.00	150.00
	1823	4.168	12.00	20.00	45.00	150.00
	1824	9.807	10.00	15.00	35.00	100.00
	Common date					Unc. 400.00

Mint mark: A
Obv: Type I. Rev: Similar to KM#711.

KM#	Date	Mintage	VG	Fine	VF	XF
720.1	1824	.408	60.00	125.00	275.00	800.00
	1825	2.492	10.00	15.00	35.00	90.00
	1826	7.171	10.00	15.00	35.00	90.00
Mint mark: B						
720.2	1825	.113	20.00	50.00	75.00	150.00
	1826	.595	15.00	35.00	60.00	125.00
Mint mark: BB						
720.3	1825	.157	20.00	50.00	75.00	150.00
	1826	.411	15.00	35.00	60.00	125.00
Mint mark: D						
720.4	1825	.185	20.00	50.00	75.00	150.00
	1826	1.437	10.00	15.00	35.00	90.00
Mint mark: H						
720.5	1825	.157	20.00	50.00	75.00	150.00
	1826	.573	15.00	35.00	60.00	125.00
Mint mark: I						
720.6	1825	.155	20.00	50.00	75.00	150.00
	1826	.536	15.00	35.00	60.00	125.00
Mint mark: K						
720.7	1825	.326	15.00	35.00	60.00	115.00
	1826	.429	15.00	35.00	60.00	115.00
Mint mark: L						
720.8	1825	.227	15.00	35.00	60.00	125.00
	1826	.720	10.00	15.00	35.00	90.00
Mint mark: M						
720.9	1825	.154	20.00	50.00	75.00	150.00
	1826	.670	10.00	15.00	35.00	90.00
Mint mark: MA						
720.10	1825	.176	20.00	50.00	75.00	150.00
	1826	1.072	10.00	15.00	35.00	90.00
Mint mark: Q						
720.11	1825	.163	20.00	50.00	75.00	150.00
	1826	.346	15.00	35.00	60.00	125.00
Mint mark: T						
720.12	1826	.203	15.00	35.00	60.00	125.00
Mint mark: W						
720.13	1825	1.104	10.00	15.00	35.00	90.00
	1826	3.583	10.00	15.00	35.00	90.00

Edge inscription in relief.

KM#	Date	Mintage	VG	Fine	VF	XF
727	1827A	Inc. KM720.1	75.00	125.00	250.00	500.00
	1830A	Inc. KM720.1	75.00	125.00	250.00	500.00

Mint mark: A
Obv: Type II.

KM#	Date	Mintage	VG	Fine	VF	XF
728.1	1827	6.822	10.00	25.00	50.00	100.00
	1828	8.803	10.00	25.00	50.00	100.00
	1829	4.827	10.00	25.00	50.00	100.00
	1830	6.333	10.00	25.00	50.00	100.00
Mint mark: B						
728.2	1827	2.792	10.00	25.00	50.00	100.00
	1828	1.898	10.00	25.00	50.00	100.00
	1829	2.834	10.00	25.00	50.00	100.00
	1830	2.910	10.00	25.00	50.00	100.00
Mint mark: BB						
728.3	1827	.393	20.00	45.00	75.00	125.00
	1828	.699	20.00	45.00	75.00	125.00
	1829	.548	20.00	45.00	75.00	125.00
	1830	.112	20.00	45.00	90.00	150.00
Mint mark: D						
728.4	1827	1.651	10.00	25.00	50.00	100.00
	1828	2.743	10.00	25.00	50.00	100.00
	1829	1.608	10.00	25.00	50.00	100.00
	1830	.631	15.00	35.00	65.00	125.00
Mint mark: H						
728.5	1827	.419	20.00	45.00	75.00	125.00
	1828	.490	20.00	45.00	75.00	125.00
	1829	1.155	10.00	25.00	50.00	100.00
	1830	.574	20.00	45.00	75.00	125.00
Mint mark: I						
728.6	1827	.335	20.00	45.00	75.00	125.00
	1828	.124	20.00	45.00	90.00	150.00
	1829	.475	20.00	45.00	75.00	125.00
	1830	.067	35.00	80.00	150.00	300.00
Mint mark: K						
728.7	1827	1.147	10.00	25.00	50.00	100.00
	1828	1.632	10.00	25.00	50.00	100.00
	1829	1.011	10.00	25.00	50.00	100.00
	1830	.713	15.00	25.00	45.00	125.00
Mint mark: L						
728.8	1827	1.144	10.00	25.00	50.00	100.00
	1828	1.083	10.00	25.00	50.00	100.00
	1829	.857	10.00	25.00	50.00	100.00
	1830	.399	20.00	45.00	75.00	125.00
Mint mark: M						
728.9	1827	.806	10.00	25.00	50.00	100.00
	1828	1.818	10.00	25.00	50.00	100.00
	1829	.873	10.00	25.00	50.00	100.00
	1830	.496	20.00	45.00	75.00	125.00
Mint mark: MA						
728.10	1827	1.531	10.00	25.00	50.00	100.00
	1828	1.201	10.00	25.00	50.00	100.00
	1829	1.258	10.00	25.00	50.00	100.00
	1830	1.803	10.00	25.00	50.00	100.00
Mint mark: Q						
728.11	1827	.484	20.00	45.00	75.00	125.00
	1828	.394	20.00	45.00	75.00	125.00
	1829	.360	20.00	45.00	75.00	125.00
	1830	.151	20.00	45.00	90.00	150.00
Mint mark: T						
728.12	1827	.865	10.00	25.00	50.00	100.00
	1828	.933	10.00	25.00	50.00	100.00
	1829	.888	10.00	25.00	50.00	100.00
	1830	.137	20.00	35.00	55.00	125.00
	Common date					Unc. 350.00
Mint mark: W						
728.13	1827	11.525	15.00	25.00	45.00	125.00
	1828	9.610	15.00	25.00	45.00	125.00
	1829	3.235	15.00	25.00	45.00	125.00
	1830	4.134	15.00	25.00	45.00	125.00

Mint mark: A
Incused edge lettering.
Obv. leg: LOUIS PHILIPPE I ROI. . .

KM#	Date	Mintage	VG	Fine	VF	XF
735.1	1830	2.421	12.00	25.00	50.00	175.00
	1831	11.785	10.00	20.00	35.00	90.00
Mint mark: B						
735.2	1830	1.025	15.00	35.00	75.00	150.00
	1831	7.889	10.00	20.00	35.00	90.00
Mint mark: BB						
735.3	1830	5,125	75.00	175.00	300.00	600.00
	1831	.983	15.00	35.00	75.00	150.00
Mint mark: D						
735.4	1830	.368	20.00	40.00	80.00	175.00
	1831	3.460	12.00	25.00	50.00	175.00
Mint mark: H						
735.5	1830	.030	35.00	75.00	175.00	375.00
	1831	.843	15.00	35.00	75.00	150.00
Mint mark: I						
735.6	1830	.028	35.00	75.00	175.00	375.00
	1831	.502	20.00	40.00	80.00	175.00
Mint mark: K						
735.7	1830	.123	25.00	50.00	100.00	200.00
	1831	1.523	15.00	35.00	75.00	175.00
Mint mark: L						
735.8	1830	8,931	40.00	100.00	200.00	400.00
	1831	.430	20.00	40.00	80.00	175.00
Mint mark: M						
735.9	1830	.050	35.00	75.00	125.00	275.00
	1831	1.337	15.00	35.00	75.00	175.00
Mint mark: MA						
735.10	1830	.065	35.00	75.00	125.00	275.00
	1831	2.062	12.00	25.00	50.00	175.00
Mint mark: Q						
735.11	1830	.012	40.00	80.00	175.00	375.00
	1831	.357	20.00	40.00	80.00	175.00
Mint mark: T						
735.12	1830	.125	25.00	50.00	100.00	200.00
	1831	1.261	15.00	35.00	75.00	175.00
Mint mark: W						
735.13	1830	1.020	15.00	35.00	75.00	175.00
	1831	8.226	12.00	20.00	35.00	85.00
	Common date					Unc. 400.00

Mint mark: A
Raised edge lettering.

KM#	Date	Mintage	VG	Fine	VF	XF
736.1	1830	Inc. Ab.	15.00	45.00	90.00	275.00
	1831	Inc. Ab.	15.00	45.00	90.00	275.00
Mint mark: B						
736.2	1831	Inc. Ab.	75.00	125.00	250.00	—

Mint mark: W

KM#	Date	Mintage	VG	Fine	VF	XF
736.3	1830	1 known	—	—	—	—
	1831	Inc. Ab.	15.00	45.00	75.00	275.00

Mint mark: A
Incused edge lettering.
Obv. leg: LOUIS PHILIPPE ROI. . .

KM#	Date	Mintage	VG	Fine	VF	XF
737.1	1830	Inc. Ab.	40.00	90.00	250.00	500.00

Mint mark: B

KM#	Date	Mintage	VG	Fine	VF	XF
737.2	1830	Inc. Ab.	50.00	125.00	300.00	600.00

Mint mark: D

KM#	Date	Mintage	VG	Fine	VF	XF
737.3	1830	Inc. Ab.	75.00	175.00	450.00	800.00

Mint mark: W

KM#	Date	Mintage	VG	Fine	VF	XF
737.4	1830	Inc. Ab.	50.00	125.00	300.00	600.00

Mint mark: A
Raised edge lettering.

KM#	Date	Mintage	VG	Fine	VF	XF
738	1830	Inc. Ab.	100.00	225.00	450.00	900.00

Mint mark: A
Incused edge lettering.

KM#	Date	Mintage	VG	Fine	VF	XF
744.1	1831	Inc. Ab.	40.00	100.00	225.00	450.00

Mint mark: B

KM#	Date	Mintage	VG	Fine	VF	XF
744.2	1831	Inc. Ab.	40.00	100.00	225.00	450.00

Mint mark: BB

KM#	Date	Mintage	VG	Fine	VF	XF
744.3	1831	Inc. Ab.	20.00	40.00	100.00	300.00

Mint mark: D

KM#	Date	Mintage	VG	Fine	VF	XF
744.4	1831	Inc. Ab.	25.00	50.00	125.00	350.00

Mint mark: I

KM#	Date	Mintage	VG	Fine	VF	XF
744.5	1831	Inc. Ab.	25.00	50.00	125.00	350.00

Mint mark: K

KM#	Date	Mintage	VG	Fine	VF	XF
744.6	1831	Inc. Ab.	25.00	50.00	125.00	350.00

Mint mark: M

KM#	Date	Mintage	VG	Fine	VF	XF
744.7	1831	Inc. Ab.	20.00	40.00	100.00	300.00

Mint mark: MA

KM#	Date	Mintage	VG	Fine	VF	XF
744.8	1831	Inc. Ab.	25.00	50.00	125.00	350.00

Mint mark: Q

KM#	Date	Mintage	VG	Fine	VF	XF
744.9	1831	Inc. Ab.	25.00	50.00	125.00	350.00

Mint mark: A
Raised edge lettering.

KM#	Date	Mintage	VG	Fine	VF	XF
745.1	1831	Inc. Ab.	12.00	20.00	50.00	125.00

Mint mark: B

KM#	Date	Mintage	VG	Fine	VF	XF
745.2	1831	Inc. Ab.	12.00	20.00	50.00	125.00

Mint mark: BB

KM#	Date	Mintage	VG	Fine	VF	XF
745.3	1831	Inc. Ab.	20.00	45.00	90.00	175.00

Mint mark: D

KM#	Date	Mintage	VG	Fine	VF	XF
745.4	1831	Inc. Ab.	12.00	20.00	50.00	125.00

Mint mark: H

KM#	Date	Mintage	VG	Fine	VF	XF
745.5	1831	Inc. Ab.	20.00	45.00	90.00	175.00

Mint mark: I

KM#	Date	Mintage	VG	Fine	VF	XF
745.6	1831	Inc. Ab.	20.00	45.00	90.00	175.00

Mint mark: K

KM#	Date	Mintage	VG	Fine	VF	XF
745.7	1831	Inc. Ab.	20.00	45.00	90.00	175.00

Mint mark: L

KM#	Date	Mintage	VG	Fine	VF	XF
745.8	1831	Inc. Ab.	25.00	50.00	125.00	275.00

Mint mark: M

KM#	Date	Mintage	VG	Fine	VF	XF
745.9	1831	Inc. Ab.	20.00	45.00	90.00	175.00

Mint mark: MA

KM#	Date	Mintage	VG	Fine	VF	XF
745.10	1831	Inc. Ab.	20.00	45.00	90.00	175.00

Mint mark: Q

KM#	Date	Mintage	VG	Fine	VF	XF
745.11	1831	Inc. Ab.	20.00	45.00	90.00	175.00

Mint mark: T

KM#	Date	Mintage	VG	Fine	VF	XF
745.12	1831	Inc. Ab.	20.00	45.00	90.00	175.00

Mint mark: W

KM#	Date	Mintage	VG	Fine	VF	XF
745.13	1831	Inc. Ab.	12.00	20.00	50.00	125.00

Mint mark: A
Rev: Mint marks at edge outside wreath.

KM#	Date	Mintage	Fine	VF	XF	Unc
749.1	1832	7.800	9.00	25.00	50.00	185.00
	1833	8.211	9.00	25.00	50.00	185.00
	1834	11.307	9.00	25.00	50.00	185.00
	1835	5.807	9.00	25.00	50.00	185.00
	1836	1.940	9.00	25.00	50.00	185.00
	1837	6.884	9.00	25.00	50.00	185.00
	1838	4.805	9.00	25.00	50.00	185.00
	1839	5.071	9.00	25.00	50.00	185.00
	1840	4.769	9.00	25.00	50.00	185.00
	1841	1.005	9.00	25.00	50.00	150.00
	1842	.755	15.00	50.00	85.00	265.00
	1843	1.838	9.00	25.00	50.00	185.00
	1844	1.971	9.00	25.00	50.00	185.00
	1845(p)	3.096	9.00	25.00	50.00	185.00
	1845(ha)	I.A.	9.00	25.00	50.00	185.00
	1846	5.434	9.00	25.00	50.00	185.00
	1847	12.578	9.00	25.00	50.00	185.00
	1848	3.196	9.00	25.00	50.00	185.00
	1848	—	—	—	Proof	1500.

Mint mark: B

KM#	Date	Mintage	Fine	VF	XF	Unc
749.2	1832	2.852	9.00	25.00	50.00	185.00
	1833	3.791	9.00	25.00	50.00	185.00
	1834	4.453	9.00	25.00	50.00	185.00
	1835	2.793	9.00	25.00	50.00	185.00
	1836	2.631	9.00	25.00	50.00	185.00
	1837	6.075	9.00	25.00	50.00	185.00
	1838	4.002	9.00	25.00	50.00	185.00
	1839	3.467	9.00	25.00	50.00	185.00
	1840	3.337	9.00	25.00	50.00	185.00
	1841	1.652	9.00	25.00	50.00	185.00
	1842	3.489	9.00	25.00	50.00	185.00
	1843	2.472	9.00	25.00	50.00	185.00
	1844	.361	15.00	50.00	85.00	250.00

Mint mark: BB

KM#	Date	Mintage	Fine	VF	XF	Unc
749.3	1832	1.725	9.00	25.00	50.00	185.00
	1833	1.799	9.00	25.00	50.00	185.00
	1834(b)	1.621	9.00	25.00	50.00	185.00
	1834 bee	I.A.	15.00	25.00	50.00	185.00
	1835	1.286	9.00	25.00	50.00	185.00
	1836	1.188	9.00	25.00	50.00	185.00
	1837	.600	15.00	50.00	85.00	250.00
	1838	1.535	9.00	25.00	50.00	185.00
	1839	1.064	9.00	25.00	50.00	185.00
	1840	1.186	9.00	25.00	50.00	185.00
	1841	2.082	9.00	25.00	50.00	185.00
	1842	2.471	9.00	25.00	50.00	185.00
	1843	1.422	9.00	25.00	50.00	185.00
	1844	1.890	9.00	25.00	50.00	185.00
	1845	2.041	9.00	25.00	50.00	185.00
	1846	.840	12.00	30.00	65.00	200.00
	1847	1.577	9.00	25.00	50.00	185.00
	1848	.935	12.00	30.00	65.00	200.00

Mint mark: D

KM#	Date	Mintage	Fine	VF	XF	Unc
749.4	1832	3.007	9.00	25.00	50.00	185.00
	1833	1.487	9.00	25.00	50.00	185.00
	1834	2.119	9.00	25.00	50.00	185.00
	1835	1.084	9.00	25.00	50.00	185.00
	1836	.200	20.00	50.00	125.00	300.00
	1837	.093	40.00	125.00	250.00	500.00
	1838	.149	20.00	50.00	125.00	300.00
	1839(a)	.519	15.00	30.00	60.00	250.00
	1839(t)	I.A.	15.00	30.00	60.00	250.00
	1840	.070	60.00	150.00	275.00	600.00

Mint mark: H

KM#	Date	Mintage	Fine	VF	XF	Unc
749.5	1832	.900	9.00	25.00	50.00	185.00
	1833/2	.844	15.00	30.00	60.00	250.00
	1833	Inc. Ab.	9.00	25.00	50.00	185.00
	1834	2.184	9.00	25.00	50.00	185.00
	1835	.467	15.00	30.00	60.00	250.00

Mint mark: I

KM#	Date	Mintage	Fine	VF	XF	Unc
749.6	1832	.703	9.00	25.00	50.00	185.00
	1833	1.014	9.00	25.00	50.00	185.00
	1834	1.933	9.00	25.00	50.00	185.00
	1835	.598	15.00	30.00	60.00	250.00

Mint mark: K

KM#	Date	Mintage	Fine	VF	XF	Unc
749.7	1832	.602	15.00	30.00	60.00	250.00
	1833	.749	9.00	25.00	50.00	185.00
	1834	2.157	9.00	25.00	50.00	185.00
	1835	.928	9.00	25.00	50.00	185.00
	1836	.296	20.00	50.00	125.00	300.00
	1837	.813	9.00	25.00	50.00	185.00
	1838	.450	15.00	30.00	60.00	250.00
	1839	.897	9.00	25.00	50.00	185.00
	1840	1.186	9.00	25.00	50.00	185.00
	1841	.995	9.00	25.00	50.00	185.00
	1842	1.026	9.00	25.00	50.00	185.00
	1843	.794	9.00	25.00	50.00	185.00
	1844	.398	15.00	30.00	60.00	250.00
	1845	.537	15.00	30.00	60.00	250.00
	1846	.511	15.00	30.00	60.00	250.00
	1847	.167	20.00	50.00	125.00	300.00
	1848	.166	20.00	50.00	125.00	300.00

Mint mark: L

KM#	Date	Mintage	Fine	VF	XF	Unc
749.8	1832	.567	20.00	50.00	125.00	300.00
	1833	.378	20.00	50.00	125.00	300.00
	1834	.359	20.00	50.00	125.00	300.00
	1835	.064	50.00	125.00	250.00	600.00

Mint mark: M

KM#	Date	Mintage	Fine	VF	XF	Unc
749.9	1832	.729	20.00	50.00	125.00	300.00
	1833	.669	20.00	50.00	125.00	300.00
	1834	.889	20.00	50.00	125.00	300.00
	1835	.412	20.00	50.00	125.00	300.00
	1836	.072	50.00	125.00	250.00	600.00

Mint mark: MA

KM#	Date	Mintage	Fine	VF	XF	Unc
749.10	1832	1.184	9.00	50.00	125.00	300.00
	1833	.872	15.00	50.00	125.00	300.00
	1834	.489	15.00	30.00	60.00	250.00
	1835	.373	15.00	30.00	60.00	250.00
	1836	.362	15.00	30.00	60.00	250.00
	1837	.724	9.00	25.00	50.00	185.00
	1838	2.116	9.00	25.00	50.00	185.00
	1839	.020	100.00	175.00	375.00	800.00

Mint mark: Q

KM#	Date	Mintage	Fine	VF	XF	Unc
749.11	1832	.716	9.00	25.00	50.00	185.00
	1833	.663	9.00	25.00	50.00	185.00
	1834	.982	9.00	25.00	50.00	185.00

Mint mark: T

KM#	Date	Mintage	Fine	VF	XF	Unc
749.12	1832	1.592	9.00	25.00	50.00	185.00
	1833	1.437	9.00	25.00	50.00	185.00
	1834	2.119	9.00	25.00	50.00	185.00
	1835	.294	20.00	35.00	60.00	250.00

Mint mark: W

KM#	Date	Mintage	Fine	VF	XF	Unc
749.13	1832	4.483	9.00	25.00	50.00	170.00
	1833	9.270	9.00	25.00	50.00	170.00
	1834	11.733	9.00	25.00	50.00	170.00
	1835	5.016	9.00	25.00	50.00	170.00
	1836	1.614	9.00	25.00	50.00	170.00
	1837	6.652	9.00	25.00	50.00	170.00
	1838	4.190	9.00	25.00	50.00	170.00
	1839	3.269	9.00	25.00	50.00	170.00
	1840(c)	1.714	9.00	25.00	50.00	170.00
	1840(r)	I.A.	15.00	30.00	60.00	250.00
	1841	8.926	9.00	25.00	50.00	170.00
	1842	5.436	9.00	25.00	50.00	170.00
	1843	7.846	9.00	25.00	50.00	170.00
	1844	8.775	9.00	25.00	50.00	170.00
	1845	11.107	9.00	25.00	50.00	170.00
	1846	1.658	9.00	25.00	50.00	170.00

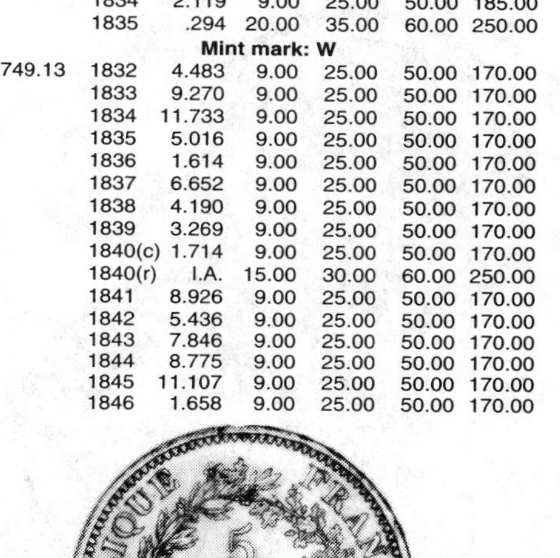

Mint mark: A
Second Republic

KM#	Date	Mintage	Fine	VF	XF	Unc
756.1	1848	16.648	10.00	20.00	75.00	200.00
	1848 plain edge		—	—	Proof	5000.
	1849	29.338	8.00	15.00	65.00	150.00
	Mint mark: BB					
756.2	1848	2.300	15.00	40.00	125.00	275.00
	1849	2.594	15.00	40.00	125.00	275.00
	Mint mark: D					
756.3	1848	.136	100.00	200.00	400.00	900.00
	1849	9,711	300.00	650.00	1500.	3500.
	Mint mark: K					
756.4	1848	.428	45.00	125.00	275.00	550.00
	1849	.471	45.00	125.00	275.00	550.00

Mint mark: A

KM#	Date	Mintage	Fine	VF	XF	Unc
761.1	1849	7.437	20.00	40.00	125.00	300.00
	1850	14.619	15.00	35.00	100.00	225.00
	1851	13.223	15.00	35.00	100.00	225.00
	Mint mark: BB					
761.2	1849	.916	35.00	80.00	200.00	500.00
	1850	1.169	30.00	70.00	175.00	450.00
	Mint mark: K					
761.3	1850	.332	100.00	200.00	400.00	750.00

Mint mark: A

KM#	Date	Mintage	Fine	VF	XF	Unc
773.1	1852	16.117	12.50	35.00	100.00	350.00
	1852 sign. J.J.Barre					
		Inc. Ab.	350.00	600.00	1000.	1750.
	1852	—	—	—	Proof	5000.
	Mint mark: BB					
773.2	1852	.041	350.00	650.00	1250.	3000.

Mint mark: A
Second Empire

KM#	Date	Mintage	Fine	VF	XF	Unc
782.1	1854	.011	250.00	500.00	700.00	2000.
	1855	4.075	35.00	85.00	175.00	600.00
	1856	4.683	35.00	85.00	175.00	600.00
	1856	—	—	—	Proof	1250.
	1857	.093	250.00	500.00	800.00	2500.
	1858	.027	275.00	550.00	900.00	2600.
	1859	3,365	400.00	1200.	2000.	3500.
	Mint mark: BB					
782.2	1855	.786	50.00	150.00	275.00	1000.
	1856	2.223	40.00	125.00	275.00	800.00
	Mint mark: D					
782.3	1855	—	60.00	150.00	300.00	1000.
	1856	2.249	40.00	110.00	200.00	800.00

1.6129 g, .900 GOLD, .0467 oz AGW
Mint mark: A
Bare head, 14.4mm.

KM#	Date	Mintage	Fine	VF	XF	Unc
783	1854	3.562	35.00	65.00	100.00	275.00
	1854 plain edge					
		Inc. Ab.	50.00	100.00	150.00	300.00
	1855	.938	65.00	110.00	200.00	400.00

16.7mm.

KM#	Date	Mintage	Fine	VF	XF	Unc
787.1	1856	2.960	30.00	40.00	65.00	175.00
	1857	3.479	30.00	40.00	65.00	175.00
	1858	2.983	30.00	40.00	65.00	175.00
	1859	5.660	30.00	40.00	65.00	175.00
	1860	4.798	30.00	40.00	65.00	175.00
	Mint mark: BB					
787.2	1858	—	65.00	125.00	200.00	450.00
	1859	2.279	30.00	40.00	65.00	175.00
	1860	2.022	30.00	40.00	65.00	175.00

25.0000 g, .900 SILVER, .7234 oz ASW
Mint mark: A

KM#	Date	Mintage	Fine	VF	XF	Unc
799.1	1861	.022	225.00	450.00	800.00	2000.
799.1	1861	—	—	—	Proof	7000.
	1862	.021	225.00	450.00	800.00	2000.
	1863	.022	225.00	450.00	800.00	2000.
	1864	.032	225.00	450.00	800.00	2000.
	1865	.025	225.00	450.00	800.00	2000.
	1866	.038	225.00	450.00	800.00	2000.
	1867	6.586	10.00	20.00	90.00	275.00
	1868	6.634	10.00	20.00	90.00	275.00
	1869	2.056	15.00	30.00	125.00	325.00
	1870	6.620	10.00	20.00	90.00	275.00
	Mint mark: BB					
799.2	1865	.073	225.00	450.00	800.00	2000.
	1867	4.224	10.00	20.00	65.00	200.00
	1868	12.090	8.00	15.00	50.00	175.00
	1869	9.597	8.00	15.00	50.00	175.00
	1870	2.055	12.00	30.00	90.00	275.00

1.6129 g, .900 GOLD, .0467 oz AGW
Mint mark: A
Laureate head

KM#	Date	Mintage	Fine	VF	XF	Unc
803.1	1862	1.101	30.00	35.00	65.00	175.00
	1863	1.591	30.00	35.00	65.00	175.00
	1864	2.240	30.00	35.00	65.00	175.00
	1865	.824	30.00	35.00	65.00	175.00
	1866	1.949	30.00	35.00	65.00	175.00
	1867	1.006	30.00	35.00	65.00	175.00
	1868	1.864	30.00	35.00	65.00	175.00
	Mint mark: BB					
803.2	1862	.882	30.00	35.00	65.00	175.00
	1863	1.104	30.00	35.00	65.00	175.00
	1864	1.000	30.00	35.00	65.00	175.00
	1865	.828	30.00	35.00	65.00	175.00
	1866	1.388	30.00	35.00	65.00	175.00
	1867	1.504	30.00	35.00	65.00	175.00
	1868	.439	30.00	35.00	70.00	200.00
	1869	.288	30.00	35.00	75.00	225.00

25.0000 g, .900 SILVER, .7234 oz ASW
Mint mark: A
Obv: E.A.OUDINE F. below truncation.

KM#	Date	Mintage	Fine	VF	XF	Unc
818.1	1870(a)	.064	50.00	125.00	450.00	850.00
	Mint mark: K					
818.2	1870(a)	.544	60.00	150.00	550.00	1000.
	1870 M/star					
		I.A.	50.00	125.00	450.00	800.00
	1871 M/star					
		.630	45.00	110.00	400.00	700.00
	Obv: A.E.OUDINE F. (error) below truncation.					
818.3	1870 M/star					
		Inc. Ab.	300.00	650.00	1200.	1800.
	Obv: E.A.OUDIИE F. (error) below truncation.					
818.4	1870 M/star					
		Inc. Ab.	— Reported, not confirmed			

Mint mark: A
Third Republic

KM#	Date	Mintage	Fine	VF	XF	Unc
819	1870	1.185	30.00	125.00	250.00	500.00

Obv: Similar to KM#823.

KM#	Date	Mintage	Fine	VF	XF	Unc
820.1	1870	.261	45.00	125.00	275.00	600.00
	1871	.238	50.00	150.00	300.00	700.00
	1872	.057	45.00	125.00	275.00	600.00
	1873	27.077	7.00	9.00	12.00	25.00
	1874	7.999	8.00	10.00	25.00	60.00
	1875	13.339	8.00	10.00	18.00	50.00
	1876	8.800	8.00	10.00	25.00	60.00
	1877	2.632	12.00	20.00	40.00	90.00
	1878	1,154	600.00	1200.	2000.	4000.
	1878	30 pcs.	—	—	Proof	6200.
	1889C	20 pcs.	—	—	Proof	6750.

NOTE: Varieties of mint mark size exist for 1875 dated coins.

Mint mark: K

KM#	Date	Mintage	Fine	VF	XF	Unc
820.2	1871	.075	100.00	250.00	500.00	900.00
	1872	.021	300.00	500.00	850.00	2000.
	1873	3.853	8.00	11.00	25.00	60.00
	1874	4.000	8.00	11.00	25.00	60.00
	1875	1.661	15.00	30.00	50.00	150.00
	1876	1.732	15.00	30.00	50.00	150.00
	1877	.661	20.00	35.00	75.00	250.00
	1878	.263	40.00	100.00	200.00	450.00

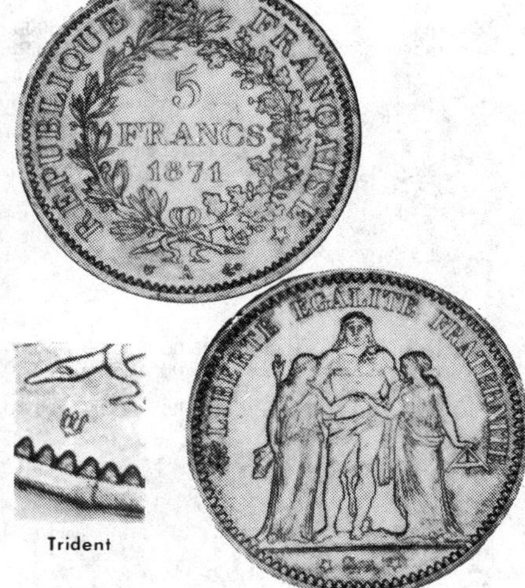

Trident

Mint mark: A
Edge inscription: DIEU PROTEGE LA FRANCE.
Trident symbol-issued by Commune.

KM#	Date	Mintage	Fine	VF	XF	Unc
823	1871	.075	200.00	350.00	675.00	1850.

Edge inscription: TRAVAIL-GARANTIE-NATIONALE.

KM#	Date	Mintage	Fine	VF	XF	Unc
824	1871	.010	—	—	—	—

1.6129 g, .900 GOLD, .0467 oz AGW

KM#	Date	Mintage	Fine	VF	XF	Unc
829	1878	30 pcs.	—	—	Proof	5750.
	1889	40 pcs.	—	—	Proof	5750.

10 FRANCS

3.2258 g, .900 GOLD, .0933 oz AGW
Mint mark: A

KM#	Date	Mintage	Fine	VF	XF	Unc
770	1850	.592	55.00	100.00	200.00	600.00
	1850	—	—	—	Proof	4000.
	1851	3.115	BV	65.00	150.00	450.00
	1851	—	—	—	Proof	4000.

Bare head, 17.2mm

KM#	Date	Mintage	Fine	VF	XF	Unc
784.1	1854	3.900	BV	75.00	200.00	450.00
	1855	6.117	BV	65.00	150.00	350.00

Plain edge

KM#	Date	Mintage	Fine	VF	XF	Unc
784.2	1854	Inc. Ab.	60.00	125.00	300.00	500.00
	1854	—	—	—	Proof	1250.

19mm

KM#	Date	Mintage	Fine	VF	XF	Unc
784.3	1855	6.117	BV	55.00	75.00	175.00
	1856	10.778	BV	55.00	75.00	175.00
	1857	14.498	BV	55.00	75.00	175.00
	1858	7.534	BV	55.00	75.00	175.00
	1859	10.111	BV	55.00	75.00	175.00
	1860	6.000	BV	55.00	75.00	175.00

Mint mark: BB

KM#	Date	Mintage	Fine	VF	XF	Unc
784.4	1855	32,188	BV	100.00	150.00	500.00
	1858	.677	BV	55.00	75.00	200.00
	1859	2,279	BV	55.00	75.00	175.00
	1860	3.104	BV	55.00	75.00	175.00

Mint mark: A
Laureate head

KM#	Date	Mintage	Fine	VF	XF	Unc
800.1	1861	.363	BV	75.00	125.00	250.00
	1862	2.844	BV	55.00	75.00	175.00
	1863	2.346	BV	55.00	75.00	175.00
	1864	3.339	BV	55.00	75.00	175.00
	1865	1.673	BV	55.00	75.00	175.00
	1866	3.720	BV	55.00	75.00	175.00
	1867	1.205	BV	55.00	75.00	175.00
	1868	3.416	BV	55.00	75.00	175.00

Mint mark: BB

KM#	Date	Mintage	Fine	VF	XF	Unc
800.2	1861	.044	75.00	100.00	150.00	300.00
	1862	1.462	BV	55.00	75.00	175.00
	1863	1.905	BV	55.00	75.00	175.00
	1864	1.449	BV	55.00	75.00	175.00
	1865	1.576	BV	55.00	75.00	175.00
	1866	2.776	BV	55.00	75.00	175.00
	1867	2.346	BV	55.00	75.00	175.00
	1868	1.117	BV	55.00	75.00	175.00
	1869	.109	50.00	75.00	125.00	175.00

Mint mark: A

KM#	Date	Mintage	Fine	VF	XF	Unc
830	1878	30 pcs.	—	—	Proof	8000.
	1889	100 pcs.	—	—	Proof	8000.
	1895	.214	BV	55.00	65.00	200.00
	1896	.585	BV	55.00	65.00	150.00
	1899	1.600	BV	55.00	65.00	150.00
846	1899	.699	BV	55.00	70.00	125.00
	1899	—	—	Matte	Proof	1200.
	1900	1.570	BV	55.00	60.00	100.00
	1900	—	—	—	Proof	1000.

NOTE: Later dates (1901-1914) exist for this type.

20 FRANCS

6.4516 g, .900 GOLD, .1867 oz AGW
Mint mark: A
Bare head

KM#	Date	Mintage	Fine	VF	XF	Unc
651	ANXI	.058	150.00	225.00	450.00	1400.
	AN12	.988	125.00	150.00	300.00	900.00
	AN12	—	—	—	Proof	5500.

Obv. leg: NAPOLEON EMPEREUR.

KM#	Date	Mintage	Fine	VF	XF	Unc
661	AN12	.428	125.00	150.00	350.00	1000.

Redesigned head.

KM#	Date	Mintage	Fine	VF	XF	Unc
663.1	AN13	.519	100.00	125.00	275.00	850.00
	AN14	.148	125.00	150.00	350.00	900.00

Mint mark: I

KM#	Date	Mintage	Fine	VF	XF	Unc
663.2	AN13	—	—	—	—	—
	AN14	1,646	750.00	1250.	2500.	3500.

Mint mark: Q

KM#	Date	Mintage	Fine	VF	XF	Unc
663.3	AN13	522 pcs.	1000.	1500.	3000.	4000.
	AN14	2,710	375.00	625.00	1250.	2250.

Mint mark: T

KM#	Date	Mintage	Fine	VF	XF	Unc
663.4	AN13	918 pcs.	875.00	1400.	2750.	3750.

Mint mark: U

KM#	Date	Mintage	Fine	VF	XF	Unc
663.5	AN14	1,755	500.00	800.00	1500.	2500.

Mint mark: W

KM#	Date	Mintage	Fine	VF	XF	Unc
663.6	AN14	—	—	—	—	—

Mint mark: A

KM#	Date	Mintage	Fine	VF	XF	Unc
674.1	1806	.964	100.00	125.00	225.00	600.00
	1807	.826	100.00	125.00	225.00	600.00

Mint mark: I

KM#	Date	Mintage	Fine	VF	XF	Unc
674.2	1806	8,143	200.00	400.00	800.00	1500.

Mint mark: M

KM#	Date	Mintage	Fine	VF	XF	Unc
674.3	1807	5,296	225.00	450.00	850.00	1500.

Mint mark: Q

KM#	Date	Mintage	Fine	VF	XF	Unc
674.4	1806	3,973	300.00	600.00	1000.	1750.

Mint mark: U

KM#	Date	Mintage	Fine	VF	XF	Unc
674.5	1806	.017	150.00	300.00	600.00	1250.
	1807	2,557	400.00	800.00	1250.	2000.

Mint mark: W

KM#	Date	Mintage	Fine	VF	XF	Unc
674.6	1806	4,242	200.00	400.00	800.00	1500.
	1807	5,181	200.00	400.00	850.00	1500.

Mint mark: A
Laureate head

KM#	Date	Mintage	Fine	VF	XF	Unc
687.1	1807	I.A.	100.00	125.00	175.00	500.00
	1808	1.450	100.00	125.00	175.00	500.00

Mint mark: K

KM#	Date	Mintage	Fine	VF	XF	Unc
687.2	1808	281 pcs.	—	—	Rare	—

Mint mark: M

KM#	Date	Mintage	Fine	VF	XF	Unc
687.3	1808	.022	150.00	250.00	500.00	900.00

Mint mark: Q

KM#	Date	Mintage	Fine	VF	XF	Unc
687.4	1808	646 pcs.	—	—	Rare	—

Mint mark: U

KM#	Date	Mintage	Fine	VF	XF	Unc
687.5	1808	1,505	375.00	625.00	1250.	1750.

Mint mark: W

KM#	Date	Mintage	Fine	VF	XF	Unc
687.6	1808	8,489	200.00	350.00	750.00	1250.

Mint mark: A

KM#	Date	Mintage	Fine	VF	XF	Unc
695.1	1809	.688	100.00	125.00	200.00	550.00
	1810	1.936	100.00	125.00	150.00	400.00
	1811	3.705	100.00	125.00	150.00	400.00
	1812	3.072	100.00	125.00	150.00	400.00
	1813	2.798	100.00	125.00	150.00	400.00
	1814	.328	100.00	125.00	225.00	600.00

Mint mark: CL

KM#	Date	Mintage	Fine	VF	XF	Unc
695.2	1813	4,380	500.00	1000.	2000.	4000.
	1814	887 pcs.	750.00	1500.	3000.	6000.

Mint mark: H

KM#	Date	Mintage	Fine	VF	XF	Unc
695.3	1809	501 pcs.	750.00	1500.	3000.	4500.
	1810	2,454	500.00	1000.	2000.	3000.
	1811	1,278	625.00	1250.	2500.	5000.
		Mint mark: K				
695.4	1809	3,614	250.00	500.00	1000.	1500.
	1810	.015	225.00	450.00	900.00	1750.
	1811	.011	225.00	450.00	900.00	1750.
	1812	2,650	375.00	750.00	1500.	3000.
	1813	869 pcs.	600.00	1200.	2250.	4500.
		Mint mark: L				
695.5	1809	2,383	325.00	650.00	1250.	2500.
	1812	.018	125.00	175.00	300.00	800.00
	1813	.019	125.00	175.00	300.00	800.00
		Mint mark: M				
695.6	1809	5,007	225.00	450.00	900.00	1750.
	1810	1,983	300.00	600.00	1200.	2500.
	1811	4,971	250.00	400.00	850.00	1750.
	1812	6,498	175.00	300.00	650.00	1400.
		Mint mark: Q				
695.7	1810	2,343	450.00	875.00	1750.	3500.
	1812	5,470	250.00	500.00	1000.	2000.
	1813	.013	175.00	350.00	700.00	1400.
	1814	3,289	300.00	600.00	1200.	2400.
		Mint mark: R				
695.8	1812(c)	.014	250.00	500.00	750.00	2000.
	1813	5,532	300.00	600.00	1000.	2500.
		Mint mark: U				
695.9	1809	3,400	375.00	750.00	1500.	3000.
	1810	5,891	225.00	450.00	900.00	2000.
	1811	.020	150.00	250.00	450.00	1100.
	1812	7,339	175.00	300.00	550.00	1500.
	1813	925 pcs.	750.00	1500.	3000.	4500.
		Mint mark: W				
695.10	1809	.017	125.00	200.00	400.00	1000.
	1810	.223	100.00	125.00	175.00	550.00
	1811	.328	100.00	125.00	175.00	550.00
	1812	.346	100.00	125.00	175.00	550.00
	1813	.104	100.00	125.00	175.00	600.00
	1814	.016	125.00	200.00	350.00	900.00
		Mint mark: Flag				
695.11	1813	.090	150.00	250.00	350.00	1100.
		Mint mark: A The Hundred Days				
705.1	1815	.436	120.00	200.00	300.00	750.00
		Mint mark: L				
705.2	1815	.018	150.00	200.00	400.00	1000.
		Mint mark: W				
705.3	1815	9,369	200.00	350.00	700.00	1500.

KM#	Date	Mintage	Fine	VF	XF	Unc
		Mint mark: A Engraver: Tiolier				
706.1	1814	2.684	100.00	125.00	150.00	375.00
	1815	2.113	100.00	125.00	150.00	375.00
		Mint mark: B				
706.2	1815	1,539	300.00	600.00	1200.	1500.
		Mint mark: K				
706.3	1814	.063	100.00	150.00	200.00	600.00
	1815	.030	100.00	150.00	200.00	600.00
		Mint mark: L				
706.4	1814	.045	100.00	150.00	200.00	600.00
	1815	.034	100.00	150.00	200.00	600.00
		Mint mark: Q				
706.5	1814	.029	125.00	175.00	250.00	700.00
	1815	.039	100.00	150.00	200.00	600.00
		Mint mark: W				
706.6	1814	.060	100.00	150.00	200.00	600.00
	1815	.088	100.00	150.00	200.00	600.00

KM#	Date	Mintage	Fine	VF	XF	Unc
		Mint mark: R Engraver: T. Wyon, Jr.				
707	1815	.872	100.00	125.00	175.00	450.00

KM#	Date	Mintage	Fine	VF	XF	Unc
		Mint mark: A				
712.1	1816	.522	100.00	125.00	150.00	325.00
	1817	2.135	100.00	125.00	150.00	325.00
	1818	2.681	100.00	125.00	150.00	325.00
	1819	2.350	100.00	125.00	150.00	325.00
	1820	1.317	100.00	125.00	150.00	325.00
	1821	.012	125.00	200.00	300.00	650.00
	1822	.213	100.00	125.00	150.00	325.00
	1823	.012	125.00	200.00	300.00	600.00
	1824	1.510	100.00	125.00	150.00	325.00
		Mint mark: B				
712.2	1816	.022	—	—	—	—
		Mint mark: H				
712.3	1822	1,253	500.00	850.00	1100.	1850.
		Mint mark: K				
712.4	1816	4,947	—	—	—	—
	1817	4,803	175.00	275.00	475.00	900.00
		Mint mark: L				
712.5	1816	.022	—	—	—	—
	1817	.036	125.00	200.00	300.00	650.00
	1818	5,394	150.00	225.00	350.00	850.00
		Mint mark: MA				
712.6	1824	2,001	625.00	1250.	1500.	1750.
		Mint mark: Q				
712.7	1816	.016	100.00	150.00	225.00	550.00
	1817	.097	100.00	125.00	200.00	500.00
	1818	.025	100.00	150.00	200.00	500.00
	1819	.034	100.00	125.00	225.00	550.00
	1820	.060	100.00	125.00	225.00	550.00
	1824	.012	100.00	150.00	275.00	650.00
		Mint mark: T				
712.8	1818	.016	100.00	125.00	200.00	550.00
	1819	8,734	100.00	150.00	250.00	625.00
	1820	5,749	100.00	150.00	250.00	625.00
		Mint mark: W				
712.9	1816	.054	100.00	125.00	200.00	600.00
	1817	.156	100.00	125.00	150.00	500.00
	1818	1.315	100.00	125.00	150.00	500.00
	1819	.219	100.00	125.00	150.00	500.00
	1820	.044	100.00	125.00	200.00	600.00
	1821	8,446	100.00	150.00	250.00	650.00
	1822	.020	100.00	125.00	200.00	600.00
	1823	7,655	100.00	150.00	250.00	650.00
	1824	.253	100.00	125.00	150.00	500.00

KM#	Date	Mintage	Fine	VF	XF	Unc
		Mint mark: A				
726.1	1825	.664	100.00	125.00	200.00	900.00
	1826	.035	150.00	225.00	375.00	1400.
	1827	.154	100.00	150.00	250.00	1200.
	1828	.279	100.00	150.00	250.00	900.00
	1829	7,783	150.00	250.00	425.00	1500.
	1830	.431	100.00	150.00	250.00	950.00
		Mint mark: Q				
726.2	1826	4,574	500.00	1000.	1250.	2250.
		Mint mark: T				
726.3	1828	3,175	500.00	1000.	1250.	2250.
		Mint mark: W				
726.4	1825	.062	125.00	200.00	350.00	1200.
	1826	6,436	200.00	275.00	450.00	1400.
	1827	3,431	225.00	350.00	550.00	1600.
	1828	.015	150.00	250.00	350.00	1200.
	1829	5,946	200.00	275.00	450.00	1400.
	1830	.015	150.00	250.00	350.00	1200.

KM#	Date	Mintage	Fine	VF	XF	Unc
		Mint mark: A Incuse edge lettering.				
739.1	1830	.018	125.00	200.00	300.00	1200.
	1831	2.162	100.00	125.00	150.00	1000.
		Mint mark: B				
739.2	1831	.088	150.00	300.00	550.00	1500.
		Mint mark: W				
739.3	1831	.107	110.00	150.00	200.00	1200.
		Mint mark: A Raised edge lettering.				
746.1	1831	Inc. Ab.	110.00	150.00	200.00	800.00
		Mint mark: B				
746.2	1831	—	125.00	175.00	250.00	950.00
		Mint mark: T				
746.3	1831	—	500.00	800.00	1250.	2000.
		Mint mark: W				
746.4	1831	Inc. Ab.	110.00	150.00	250.00	1500.

KM#	Date	Mintage	Fine	VF	XF	Unc
		Mint mark: A				
750.1	1832	6,360	175.00	350.00	700.00	1500.
	1832	—	—	—	Proof	5500.
	1833	.207	100.00	125.00	175.00	900.00
	1834	.744	100.00	125.00	175.00	600.00
	1835	.097	100.00	125.00	175.00	850.00
	1836	.139	100.00	125.00	175.00	850.00
	1837	.034	100.00	150.00	200.00	900.00
	1838	.173	100.00	125.00	175.00	850.00
	1839	1.012	100.00	125.00	150.00	600.00
	1840	2.045	100.00	125.00	150.00	600.00
	1841	.610	100.00	125.00	175.00	600.00
	1842	.071	125.00	150.00	200.00	900.00
	1843	.106	100.00	125.00	175.00	900.00
	1844	.103	100.00	125.00	175.00	900.00
	1845	939 pcs.	625.00	1250.	1800.	3200.
	1846	.103	100.00	125.00	175.00	900.00
	1847	.385	100.00	125.00	175.00	600.00
	1848	.442	100.00	125.00	150.00	600.00
		Mint mark: B				
750.2	1832	.015	100.00	150.00	200.00	900.00
	1833	.155	100.00	125.00	175.00	900.00
	1834	.077	100.00	125.00	175.00	900.00
	1835	.026	100.00	150.00	225.00	900.00
		Mint mark: L				
750.3	1834	.021	100.00	150.00	200.00	900.00
	1835	856 pcs.	625.00	1250.	2000.	3200.
		Mint mark: T				
750.4	1832	868 pcs.	750.00	1500.	2250.	3250.
		Mint mark: W				
750.5	1832	.027	100.00	150.00	200.00	850.00
	1833	.032	100.00	150.00	200.00	850.00
	1834	.041	100.00	150.00	200.00	850.00
	1835	.030	100.00	150.00	200.00	850.00
	1836	.010	100.00	150.00	225.00	850.00
	1837	.011	100.00	150.00	225.00	850.00
	1838	.012	100.00	150.00	225.00	850.00
	1839	.022	100.00	125.00	200.00	850.00
	1840	4,550	150.00	300.00	425.00	1350.
	1841	8,524	125.00	275.00	400.00	1200.
	1842	.022	100.00	125.00	200.00	850.00
	1843	.035	100.00	125.00	200.00	850.00
	1844	.034	100.00	125.00	200.00	850.00
	1845	5,018	125.00	250.00	375.00	1200.
	1846	1,408	375.00	750.00	1250.	2500.

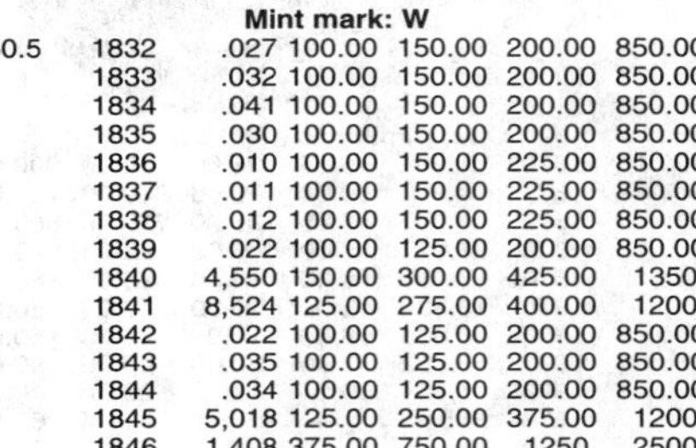

KM#	Date	Mintage	Fine	VF	XF	Unc
		Mint mark: A				
757	1848	1.543	100.00	125.00	175.00	500.00
	1848	—	—	—	Proof	5000.
	1849	1.303	100.00	125.00	175.00	500.00

KM#	Date	Mintage	Fine	VF	XF	Unc
762	1849	.053	100.00	125.00	200.00	750.00
	1850	3.964	BV	100.00	125.00	450.00
	1850	—	—	—	Proof	4500.
	1851	12.704	BV	100.00	125.00	400.00

KM#	Date	Mintage	Fine	VF	XF	Unc
774	1852	10.494	BV	100.00	125.00	550.00
	1852	—	—	—	Proof	4500.

KM#	Date	Mintage	Fine	VF	XF	Unc
781.1	1853	5.729	BV	100.00	115.00	175.00
	1853	—	—	—	Proof	4500.
	1854	23.486	BV	100.00	115.00	175.00
	1854	—	—	—	Proof	3750.
	1855(d)	16.595	BV	100.00	115.00	175.00
	1855(a)	I.A.	BV	100.00	115.00	175.00
	1856	17.303	BV	100.00	115.00	175.00
	1857	19.193	BV	100.00	115.00	175.00
	1858	16.861	BV	100.00	115.00	175.00
	1859	20.295	BV	100.00	115.00	175.00
	1860	10.220	BV	100.00	115.00	175.00

Mint mark: BB

KM#	Date	Mintage	Fine	VF	XF	Unc
781.2	1855	1.760	BV	100.00	125.00	200.00
	1856	1.125	BV	100.00	125.00	200.00
	1858	2.017	BV	100.00	125.00	200.00
	1859	5.871	BV	100.00	115.00	175.00
	1860	5.727	BV	100.00	115.00	175.00

Mint mark: D

KM#	Date	Mintage	Fine	VF	XF	Unc
781.3	1855	.045	100.00	125.00	200.00	450.00

Mint mark: A

KM#	Date	Mintage	Fine	VF	XF	Unc
801.1	1861	2.607	BV	100.00	110.00	175.00
	1861	—	—	—	Proof	5000.
	1862	4.826	BV	100.00	110.00	175.00
	1863	3.920	BV	100.00	110.00	175.00
	1864	7.059	BV	100.00	110.00	175.00
	1865	2.951	BV	100.00	110.00	175.00
	1866	6.992	BV	100.00	110.00	175.00
	1867	2.923	BV	100.00	110.00	175.00
	1868	9.281	BV	100.00	110.00	175.00
	1869	4.046	BV	100.00	110.00	175.00
	1870	.865	BV	100.00	110.00	200.00

Mint mark: BB

KM#	Date	Mintage	Fine	VF	XF	Unc
801.2	1861	1.423	BV	100.00	110.00	175.00
	1862	2.907	BV	100.00	110.00	175.00
	1863	4.753	BV	100.00	110.00	175.00
	1864	3.323	BV	100.00	110.00	175.00
	1865	3.088	BV	100.00	110.00	175.00
	1866	6.979	BV	100.00	110.00	175.00
	1867	4.516	BV	100.00	110.00	175.00
	1868	4.829	BV	100.00	110.00	175.00
	1869	7.317	BV	100.00	110.00	175.00
	1870	1.853	BV	100.00	110.00	200.00

Mint mark: A

KM#	Date	Mintage	Fine	VF	XF	Unc
825	1871	2.508	BV	100.00	110.00	175.00
	1874	1.216	BV	100.00	110.00	125.00
	1875	11.746	BV	100.00	110.00	125.00
	1876	8.825	BV	100.00	110.00	125.00
	1877	12.759	BV	100.00	110.00	125.00
	1878	9.189	BV	100.00	110.00	125.00
	1878	30 pcs.	—	—	Proof	7000.
	1879	1.038	BV	100.00	110.00	125.00
	1886	.985	BV	100.00	110.00	125.00
	1887	1.231	BV	100.00	110.00	125.00
	1887	—	—	—	Proof	5000.
	1888	.028	100.00	125.00	175.00	300.00
	1889	.873	BV	100.00	110.00	125.00
	1889	100 pcs.	—	—	Proof	6000.
	1890	1.030	BV	100.00	110.00	125.00
	1891	.871	BV	100.00	110.00	125.00
	1892	.226	BV	100.00	110.00	125.00
	1893	2.517	BV	100.00	110.00	125.00
	1894	.491	BV	100.00	110.00	125.00
	1895	5.293	BV	100.00	110.00	125.00
	1897	11.069	BV	100.00	110.00	125.00
	1898	8.866	BV	100.00	110.00	125.00

Edge inscription: DIEU PROTEGE LA FRANCE.

KM#	Date	Mintage	Fine	VF	XF	Unc
847	1899	1.500	BV	100.00	110.00	125.00
	1900	.615	BV	100.00	110.00	150.00
	1900	Inc. Ab.	—	—	Proof	2000.

NOTE: Later dates (1901-1906) exist for this type.

40 FRANCS

12.9039 g, .900 GOLD, .3734 oz AGW
Mint mark: A

KM#	Date	Mintage	Fine	VF	XF	Unc
652	ANXI	.226	200.00	225.00	325.00	1500.
	AN12	.253	200.00	225.00	325.00	1500.

KM#	Date	Mintage	Fine	VF	XF	Unc
664.1	AN13	.252	200.00	225.00	325.00	1200.
	AN13	—	—	—	Proof	15,000.
	AN14	.121	200.00	225.00	325.00	1200.

Mint mark: U

KM#	Date	Mintage	Fine	VF	XF	Unc
664.2	AN14	—	—	—	Rare	—

Mint mark: W

KM#	Date	Mintage	Fine	VF	XF	Unc
664.3	AN14	—	—	—	Rare	—

Mint mark: A

KM#	Date	Mintage	Fine	VF	XF	Unc
675.1	1806	.196	200.00	225.00	400.00	1000.
	1807	.017	200.00	400.00	800.00	1600.

Mint mark: CL

KM#	Date	Mintage	Fine	VF	XF	Unc
675.2	1806	—	—	—	Rare	—

Mint mark: I

KM#	Date	Mintage	Fine	VF	XF	Unc
675.3	1806	7,103	250.00	500.00	1250.	2500.
	1807	1,859	350.00	750.00	2000.	3500.

Mint mark: M

KM#	Date	Mintage	Fine	VF	XF	Unc
675.4	1806	—	—	—	—	—
	1807	4,994	300.00	600.00	1250.	3000.

Mint mark: U

KM#	Date	Mintage	Fine	VF	XF	Unc
675.5	1806	.059	200.00	275.00	500.00	1400.
	1807	619 pcs.	1000.	2000.	3500.	—

Mint mark: W

KM#	Date	Mintage	Fine	VF	XF	Unc
675.6	1806	4,336	300.00	650.00	1250.	3000.
	1807	6,043	300.00	650.00	1250.	3000.

Mint mark: A
Laureate head

KM#	Date	Mintage	Fine	VF	XF	Unc
688.1	1807	*.253	200.00	225.00	350.00	1000.
	1808	.044	200.00	225.00	350.00	1000.

Mint mark: H

KM#	Date	Mintage	Fine	VF	XF	Unc
688.2	1808	.012	225.00	450.00	900.00	2250.

Mint mark: M

KM#	Date	Mintage	Fine	VF	XF	Unc
688.3	1808	4,226	300.00	500.00	1000.	2750.

Mint mark: U

KM#	Date	Mintage	Fine	VF	XF	Unc
688.4	1808	346 pcs.	—	—	Rare	—

Mint mark: W

KM#	Date	Mintage	Fine	VF	XF	Unc
688.5	1808	6.356	225.00	450.00	950.00	2750.

Mint mark: A

KM#	Date	Mintage	Fine	VF	XF	Unc
696.1	1809	.013	225.00	375.00	700.00	1800.
	1809	—	—	—	Proof	10,000.
	1811	1.262	200.00	225.00	300.00	750.00
	1812	.693	200.00	225.00	325.00	1100.
	1813	.045	200.00	300.00	600.00	1500.
	1813	—	—	—	Proof	9000.

Mint mark: CL

KM#	Date	Mintage	Fine	VF	XF	Unc
696.2	1813	3,070	500.00	1000.	2000.	3500.

Mint mark: K

KM#	Date	Mintage	Fine	VF	XF	Unc
696.3	1810	886 pcs.	650.00	1250.	2500.	4000.
	1811	6,333	300.00	625.00	1250.	2500.

Mint mark: M

KM#	Date	Mintage	Fine	VF	XF	Unc
696.4	1809	1,402	500.00	1000.	1750.	3250.

Mint mark: U

KM#	Date	Mintage	Fine	VF	XF	Unc
696.5	1809	—	—	—	Rare	—

Mint mark: W

KM#	Date	Mintage	Fine	VF	XF	Unc
696.6	1809	5,925	300.00	600.00	1200.	2400.
	1810	.057	200.00	250.00	450.00	1500.
	1812	.014	200.00	275.00	550.00	1700.

Mint mark: A

KM#	Date	Mintage	Fine	VF	XF	Unc
713.1	1816	.041	200.00	300.00	600.00	900.00
	1817	.090	200.00	300.00	500.00	850.00
	1818	.011	200.00	350.00	750.00	1250.
	1820	5,480	250.00	500.00	1000.	2250.
	1822	373 pcs.	—	—	Rare	—
	1823	161 pcs.	—	—	Rare	—
	1824	.015	200.00	275.00	450.00	900.00

Mint mark: B

KM#	Date	Mintage	Fine	VF	XF	Unc
713.2	1816	767 pcs.	1000.	2000.	3500.	5000.

Mint mark: H

KM#	Date	Mintage	Fine	VF	XF	Unc
713.3	1822	611 pcs.	1000.	2000.	3500.	5000.

Mint mark: L

KM#	Date	Mintage	Fine	VF	XF	Unc
713.4	1816	2,923	375.00	675.00	1000.	2750.
	1817	377 pcs.	—	—	Rare	—

Mint mark: Q

KM#	Date	Mintage	Fine	VF	XF	Unc
713.5	1816	.011	200.00	300.00	450.00	1250.

Mint mark: W

KM#	Date	Mintage	Fine	VF	XF	Unc
713.6	1816	3,210	200.00	300.00	600.00	1200.
	1818	.353	200.00	225.00	300.00	700.00
	1819	4,610	200.00	300.00	600.00	1200.

Mint mark: A

KM#	Date	Mintage	Fine	VF	XF	Unc
721.1	1824	.050	225.00	275.00	450.00	1900.
	1826	62 pcs.	—	—	Rare	—
	1827	106 pcs.	—	—	Rare	—
	1828	.052	225.00	275.00	450.00	1900.
	1829	.021	225.00	300.00	500.00	1900.
	1830	.354	200.00	250.00	300.00	1650.

Mint mark: MA

KM#	Date	Mintage	Fine	VF	XF	Unc
721.2	1830	1,026	—	—	Rare	—

Mint mark: A

KM#	Date	Mintage	Fine	VF	XF	Unc
747.1	1831	.063	200.00	250.00	500.00	1200.
	1832	.022	200.00	275.00	500.00	1200.
	1832	—	—	—	Proof	9000.
	1833	.221	200.00	250.00	450.00	1200.
	1834	.303	200.00	225.00	400.00	1000.
	1835	.036	200.00	275.00	500.00	1200.
	1836	.053	200.00	275.00	500.00	1200.
	1837	.028	200.00	275.00	500.00	1200.
	1838	.031	200.00	275.00	500.00	1200.
	1839	23 pcs.	—	—	Rare	—

Mint mark: B

KM#	Date	Mintage	Fine	VF	XF	Unc
747.2	1832	3,947	300.00	450.00	900.00	2200.
	1833	1,392	450.00	900.00	1750.	3500.

Mint mark: L

KM#	Date	Mintage	Fine	VF	XF	Unc
747.3	1834	.012	225.00	325.00	600.00	1800.
	1835	856 pcs.	600.00	1200.	2000.	4000.

50 FRANCS

16.1290 g, .900 GOLD, .4667 oz AGW
Mint mark: A
Bare head

KM#	Date	Mintage	Fine	VF	XF	Unc
785.1	1855	.152	250.00	275.00	300.00	500.00
	1856	.097	250.00	275.00	350.00	500.00
	1857	.320	250.00	275.00	300.00	500.00
	1858	.085	250.00	275.00	350.00	500.00
	1859	.034	250.00	275.00	350.00	500.00

Mint mark: BB

KM#	Date	Mintage	Fine	VF	XF	Unc
785.2	1855	3,051	250.00	350.00	600.00	1000.
	1856	3,803	250.00	375.00	600.00	1000.
	1858	9,135	250.00	350.00	550.00	1000.
	1859	.032	250.00	275.00	400.00	600.00
	1860	.029	—	—	—	—

Mint mark: A
Laureate head

KM#	Date	Mintage	Fine	VF	XF	Unc
804.1	1862	.024	250.00	275.00	375.00	600.00
	1862	—	—	—	Proof	7500.
	1864	.029	250.00	275.00	375.00	600.00
	1865	3,740	250.00	400.00	600.00	950.00
	1866	.039	250.00	275.00	375.00	600.00
	1867	2,000	250.00	400.00	600.00	950.00
	1868	.016	250.00	275.00	375.00	650.00

Mint mark: BB

KM#	Date	Mintage	Fine	VF	XF	Unc
804.2	1862	7,310	250.00	300.00	400.00	750.00
	1863	8,251	250.00	300.00	400.00	750.00
	1866	.017	250.00	275.00	375.00	650.00
	1867	.020	250.00	275.00	375.00	650.00
	1868	1,795	350.00	450.00	650.00	1250.

Mint mark: A

KM#	Date	Mintage	Fine	VF	XF	Unc
831	1878	5,294	350.00	700.00	1200.	2000.
	1887	301 pcs.	550.00	1250.	2250.	3500.
	1889	100 pcs.	—	—	Proof	6500.
	1896	800 pcs.	450.00	900.00	1800.	3000.
	1900	200 pcs.	650.00	1500.	2500.	4500.

NOTE: Later date (1904) exists for this tupe.

100 FRANCS

32.2581 g, .900 GOLD, .9335 oz AGW
Mint mark: A

KM#	Date	Mintage	Fine	VF	XF	Unc
786.1	1855	.051	450.00	500.00	550.00	850.00
	1856	.057	450.00	500.00	550.00	850.00
	1857	.103	450.00	500.00	550.00	850.00
	1858	.092	450.00	500.00	550.00	850.00
	1859	.022	450.00	500.00	550.00	900.00

Mint mark: BB

KM#	Date	Mintage	Fine	VF	XF	Unc
786.2	1855	4,173	450.00	500.00	600.00	1150.
	1856	876 pcs.	600.00	1000.	1500.	3000.
786.2	1858	1,928	475.00	525.00	625.00	1300.
	1859	9,305	450.00	500.00	550.00	1100.
	1860	5,405	450.00	500.00	600.00	1150.

Mint mark: A

KM#	Date	Mintage	Fine	VF	XF	Unc
802.1	1861	—	—	—	Proof	8000.
	1862	6,650	450.00	550.00	750.00	1200.
	1864	5,536	450.00	550.00	750.00	1200.
	1865	1,517	475.00	600.00	1000.	1800.
	1866	9,041	450.00	550.00	700.00	1100.
	1867	4,309	450.00	550.00	750.00	1200.
	1868	2,315	450.00	550.00	1000.	1800.
	1869	.029	450.00	500.00	700.00	1100.
	1870	.010	3000.	6000.	12,000.	20,000.

Mint mark: BB

KM#	Date	Mintage	Fine	VF	XF	Unc
802.2	1862	3,078	450.00	600.00	800.00	1400.
	1863	3,745	450.00	600.00	800.00	1400.
	1864	1,333	475.00	600.00	850.00	1800.
	1866	3,075	450.00	600.00	850.00	1600.
	1867	2,807	450.00	600.00	850.00	1600.
	1868	789 pcs.	525.00	800.00	1200.	2000.
	1869	.014	450.00	550.00	750.00	1100.

Mint mark: A
Edge inscription: DIEU PROTEGE LA FRANCE.

KM#	Date	Mintage	Fine	VF	XF	Unc
832	1878	.013	450.00	475.00	550.00	750.00
	1878	30 pcs.	—	—	Proof	16,000.
	1879	.039	450.00	475.00	550.00	725.00
	1881	.022	450.00	475.00	550.00	725.00
	1882	.037	450.00	475.00	550.00	725.00
	1885	2,894	450.00	650.00	850.00	1250.
	1886	.039	450.00	475.00	550.00	750.00
	1887	234 pcs.	750.00	1750.	3500.	7500.
	1889	100 pcs.	—	—	Proof	13,000.
	1894	143 pcs.	1250.	2750.	5500.	10,000.
	1896	400 pcs.	500.00	1000.	2500.	6000.
	1899	.010	450.00	475.00	550.00	750.00
	1900	.020	450.00	475.00	550.00	750.00

NOTE: Later dates (1901-1906) exist for this type.

ESSAIS (E)

KM#	Date	Mintage	Identification	Mkt.Val.
E5	ND(1815-24)	—	No denomination, bust of Louis XVIII left, rev: crowned arms in crossed branches above ESSAI	—

KM#	Date	Mintage	Identification	Mkt.Val.
E6	ND(1815-24)	—	No denomination, uniformed bust of Louis XVIII left	—

KM#	Date	Mintage	Identification	Mkt.Val.
E7	1816	—	1/4 Franc, Napoleon II left, rev: denomination within wreath, date below	—

KM#	Date	Mintage	Identification	Mkt.Val.
E-A8	1816	—	5 Centimes, Napoleon II left, rev: denomination within wreath, date below	—

KM#	Date	Mintage	Identification	Mkt.Val.
E8	1821A	—	10 Centimes, bust of Louis XVIII left, rev: denomination above date	165.00

KM#	Date	Mintage	Identification	Mkt.Val.
E9	1824A	—	20 Francs, bust of Louis XVIII right, rev: crowned arms in branches above date, KM726.1	—

KM#	Date	Mintage	Identification	Mkt.Val.
E10	ND(ca.1840)	—	1 Decime, laureate bust of Louis Philippe left, rev: denomination in wreath, ESSAI below	150.00

KM#	Date	Mintage	Identification	Mkt.Val.
E11	1847	—	2 Centimes, laureate bust of Louis Philippe left, rev: crown above branches, denomination and date below	120.00

KM#	Date	Mintage	Identification	Mkt.Val.
E12	1848	—	5 Centimes, Liberty standing w/shield and Liberty cap on pole, rev: denomination and ESSAI within wreath	135.00

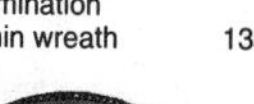

KM#	Date	Mintage	Identification	Mkt.Val.
E13	1848	—	20 Francs, Gold	—

KM#	Date	Mintage	Identification	Mkt.Val.
E14	1848A	—	20 Francs, Gold	4000.

KM#	Date	Mintage	Identification	Mkt.Val.
E15	1851	—	5 Centimes, Bronze, crowned tablet divides CINQ-CENT, rev: ESSAI/DE BRONZE/1851	—

KM#	Date	Mintage	Identification	Mkt.Val.
E16	1851	—	10 Centimes, Bronze	—

KM#	Date	Mintage	Identification	Mkt.Val.
E17	1851	—	1 Decime, Bronze, crowned tablet divides UN-DE	—
E18	1852(a)	—	10 Centimes, KM771	200.00

KM#	Date	Mintage	Identification	Mkt.Val.
E19	1854	—	100 Francs, Napoleon III, ESSAI and date below, rev: eagle on crowned and mantled shield	—

KM#	Date	Mintage	Identification	Mkt.Val.
E20	ND(1855)	—	10 Centimes, Nickel, 10 CENTS in inner circle, rev: ESSAI/DE/MONNAIES/EN/NICKEL	—

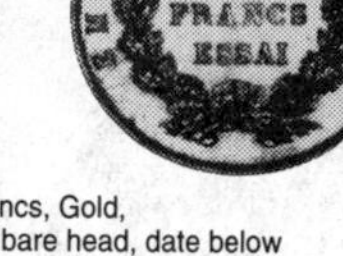

KM#	Date	Mintage	Identification	Mkt.Val.
E-A21	1855	—	10 Francs, Gold, obv: bare head, date below rev: denom. in wreath	1250.

KM#	Date	Mintage	Identification	Mkt.Val.
E-B21	ND(1860)	—	1 Franc, obv: bare head left, rev: crowned and mantled arms, ESSAI below	750.00
E21	1860(a)	—	1 Franc, KM779	400.00
E22	1861(a)	—	2 Centimes, KM796	150.00
E23	1861(a)	—	5 Centimes, KM777	200.00
E24	1861(a)	—	5 Francs, KM799	1500.

KM#	Date	Mintage	Identification	Mkt.Val.
E25	1861	—	20 Francs, Gold	—
E26	1864(a)	—	20 Centimes, KM805	200.00
E27	1866(a)	—	1 Franc, KM806	300.00
E28	1866(a)	—	2 Francs, KM807	600.00

KM#	Date	Mintage	Identification	Mkt.Val.
E29	1867	—	5 Dollars/25 Francs, Gold	6000.
E30	1867	—	10 Florins/25 Francs, Gold	6000.
E33	1878(a)	—	50 Francs, KM831	5000.
E34	1878(a)	—	100 Francs, KM832	6000.

KM#	Date	Mintage	Identification	Mkt.Val.
E35	1881A	—	10 Centimes, Nickel, 12-sided, Liberty left, date below, rev: denomination in wreath	—

KM#	Date	Mintage	Identification	Mkt.Val.
E36	1881A	—	25 Centimes, Nickel, laureate bust right, date below, rev: denomination and mint mark in wreath, ESSAI below	—

KM#	Date	Mintage	Identification	Mkt.Val.
E37	1887A	—	20 Centimes, Nickel, laureate bust right, date below, rev: denomination incircle, legend around, ESSAI below	—
E-A38	1898	—	10 Centimes, KM843	125.00

MEDALLIC ISSUES

"Mint Visit"

(5 CENTIMES)

BRONZE
Mint: Lille
Emperor and Empress to the Bourse.

KM#	Date	Mintage	Fine	VF	XF	Unc
M23	1853(w)	2,000	12.00	20.00	40.00	125.00
		SILVER				
M23a	1853(w)	—	40.00	80.00	150.00	250.00
		GOLD				
M23b	1853(w)	—	350.00	500.00	900.00	1800.

(10 CENTIMES)

BRONZE
Mint: Lille
Emperor and Empress to the Bourse.

KM#	Date	Mintage	Fine	VF	XF	Unc
M24	1853(w)	1,000	15.00	25.00	50.00	125.00
		SILVER				
M24a	1853(w)	100 pcs.	50.00	100.00	150.00	250.00
		GOLD				
M24b	1853(w)	2 pcs.	—	—	Rare	—

BRONZE
Monument of Napoleon I Erected

KM#	Date	Mintage	Fine	VF	XF	Unc
M25	1854(w)	—	25.00	50.00	100.00	265.00
		SILVER				
M25a	1854(w)	—	75.00	150.00	250.00	425.00
		GOLD				
M25b	1854(w)	—	400.00	800.00	1200.	2100.

BRONZE
Mint: Paris
Napoleon III to the Mint

KM#	Date	Mintage	Fine	VF	XF	Unc
M26	1854(a)	—	20.00	40.00	65.00	125.00
		SILVER				
M26a	1854(a)	—	50.00	250.00	150.00	250.00
		GOLD				
M26b	1854(a)	—	400.00	700.00	1200.	2000.

(2 FRANCS)

PEWTER
Mint: Paris
Prince Charles of Baden Visit
Obv: 2 shields of arms in branches.
Rev: 6-line legend.

KM#	Date	Mintage	VF	XF	Unc
M1	1806	—	50.00	100.00	200.00
		BRONZE			
M1a	1806	—	50.00	125.00	250.00
		10.0000 g, .900 SILVER, .2893 oz ASW			
M1b	1806	—	200.00	300.00	625.00

BRONZE
Prince Ludwig of Bavaria Visit
Obv: Uniformed bust of Max. Josef right.
Rev: 6-line legend.

KM#	Date	Mintage	VF	XF	Unc
M2	1806	—	50.00	125.00	250.00
		10.0000 g, .900 SILVER, .2893 oz ASW			
M2a	1806	—	150.00	300.00	600.00

BRONZE
King of Saxony Visit

KM#	Date	Mintage	VF	XF	Unc
M3	1809	—	50.00	125.00	265.00
		10.0000 g, .900 SILVER, .2893 oz ASW			
M3a	1809	—	100.00	250.00	525.00
		GOLD			
M3b	1809	—	750.00	1500.	2400.

BRONZE
King of Wurttemberg Visit

KM#	Date	Mintage	VF	XF	Unc
M4	1809	—	50.00	115.00	250.00
		10.0000 g, .900 SILVER, .2893 oz ASW			
M4a	1809	—	100.00	250.00	500.00
		GOLD			
M4b	1809	—	750.00	1600.	2800.

BRONZE
King of Wurttemberg Visit

KM#	Date	Mintage	VF	XF	Unc
M5	1809	—	50.00	100.00	200.00
		10.0000 g, .900 SILVER, .2893 oz ASW			
M5a	1809	—	100.00	250.00	500.00

BRONZE
King and Queen of Bavaria Visit

KM#	Date	Mintage	VF	XF	Unc
M6	1810	—	50.00	100.00	200.00
		10.0000 g, .900 SILVER, .2893 oz ASW			
M6a	1810	—	150.00	250.00	500.00
		GOLD			
M6b	1810	—	1000.	1750.	3500.

BRONZE
Duke and Duchess de Berry Visit

KM#	Date	Mintage	VF	XF	Unc
M7	1817	—	50.00	100.00	215.00
		10.0000 g, .900 SILVER, .2893 oz ASW			
M7a	1817	—	200.00	400.00	850.00
		PEWTER			
M7b	1817	—	40.00	100.00	235.00

BRONZE
Prince and Princess of Denmark Visit
Obv: Crowned shields of arms.
Rev: 7-line legend.

KM#	Date	Mintage	VF	XF	Unc
M8	1822	—	50.00	100.00	200.00
		10.0000 g, .900 SILVER, .2893 oz ASW			
M8a	1822	—	200.00	300.00	600.00

(5 FRANCS)

PEWTER
Mint: Paris
Napoleon as First Consul Visit

KM#	Date	Mintage	VF	XF	Unc
M9	1803(AN XI) (restrike)		50.00	125.00	250.00
		25.0000 g, .900 SILVER, 36.5mm, .7234 oz ASW			
M9a	1803(AN XI)	—	750.00	1500.	2100.
	1803(AN XI) (restrike)		100.00	200.00	400.00
		GOLD, 36.5mm			
M9b	1803(AN XI)	—	—	Unique	—
	1803(AN XI) (restrike)		—	Unique	—

BRONZE
Mint: Lille
Duke de Berry Visit
Obv: Uniformed bust of Louis XVIII.
Rev: 6-line legend.

KM#	Date	Mintage	VF	XF	Unc
M10	1814	—	75.00	150.00	285.00
		25.0000 g, .900 SILVER, .7234 oz ASW			
M10a	1814	—	350.00	600.00	950.00

NOTE: Exist w/smooth and engraved edges.

BRONZE
Mint: Marseille
Comte D'Artois Visit
Obv: Uniformed bust of Louis XVIII.
Rev: 6-line legend.

KM#	Date	Mintage	VF	XF	Unc
M11	1814	—	50.00	100.00	225.00
		25.0000 g, .900 SILVER, .7234 oz ASW			
M11a	1814	60 pcs.	250.00	350.00	750.00
		GOLD			
M11b	1814	1 pc.	—	Unique	—

PEWTER
Mint: Paris
Duchess D'Angouleme Visit

KM#	Date	Mintage	VF	XF	Unc
M12	1817	—	50.00	100.00	250.00

BRONZE

KM#	Date	Mintage	VF	XF	Unc
M12a	1817	—	50.00	100.00	200.00

GILT BRONZE

KM#	Date	Mintage	VF	XF	Unc
M12b	1817	—	75.00	150.00	250.00

25.0000 g, .900 SILVER, .7234 oz ASW

KM#	Date	Mintage	VF	XF	Unc
M12c	1817	—	250.00	400.00	750.00

GOLD

KM#	Date	Mintage	VF	XF	Unc
M12d	1817	—	1500.	2000.	3000.

PEWTER
Mint: La Rochelle
Duke D'Angouleme Visit

KM#	Date	Mintage	VF	XF	Unc
M13	1817	—	75.00	150.00	275.00

25.0000 g, .900 SILVER, .7234 oz ASW

KM#	Date	Mintage	VF	XF	Unc
M13a	1817	—	300.00	450.00	750.00

BRONZE
Mint: Paris
Duke and Duchess de Berry Visit

KM#	Date	Mintage	VF	XF	Unc
M14	1817	—	50.00	100.00	200.00

25.0000 g, .900 SILVER, .7234 oz ASW

KM#	Date	Mintage	VF	XF	Unc
M14a	1817	—	300.00	450.00	750.00

25.0000 g, .900 SILVER, .7234 oz ASW
Count of Corvetto Visit

KM#	Date	Mintage	VF	XF	Unc
M25	1817	—	350.00	450.00	750.00

PEWTER
Charles Philippe (later Charles X) Visit

KM#	Date	Mintage	VF	XF	Unc
M15	1818	—	50.00	115.00	275.00

BRONZE

KM#	Date	Mintage	VF	XF	Unc
M15a	1818	—	75.00	160.00	275.00

25.0000 g, .900 SILVER, .7234 oz ASW

KM#	Date	Mintage	VF	XF	Unc
M15b	1818	—	400.00	600.00	1100.

Minister Secretary of Finance Visit

KM#	Date	Mintage	VF	XF	Unc
M26	1820	—	350.00	500.00	800.00

BRONZE
Prince of Salerno and Duchess de Berry Visit
Obv: Head of Charles X left.
Rev: 8-line legend.

KM#	Date	Mintage	VF	XF	Unc
M16	1825	—	50.00	125.00	250.00

25.0000 g, .900 SILVER, .7234 oz ASW

KM#	Date	Mintage	VF	XF	Unc
M16a	1825	—	400.00	600.00	900.00

BRONZE
Mint: Lille
Visit of the King
Obv: Head of Charles X left.
Rev: 7-line legend.

KM#	Date	Mintage	VF	XF	Unc
M17	1827	—	50.00	125.00	250.00

25.0000 g, .900 SILVER, .7234 oz ASW

KM#	Date	Mintage	VF	XF	Unc
M17a	1827	—	300.00	500.00	750.00

BRONZE
Mint: Paris
Duke de Bordeaux (later Pretender Henri V) Visit
Obv: Crowned arms in branches.
Rev: 7-line legend.

KM#	Date	Mintage	VF	XF	Unc
M18	1828	50 pcs.	100.00	200.00	400.00

25.0000 g, .900 SILVER, .7234 oz ASW

KM#	Date	Mintage	VF	XF	Unc
M18a	1828	50 pcs.	300.00	500.00	1000.

GOLD

KM#	Date	Mintage	VF	XF	Unc
M18b	1828	5 pcs.	2000.	3000.	5500.

BRONZE
King and Queen of the 2 Sicilies.
Obv: Crowned shields of arms in branches.
Rev: 7-line legend.

KM#	Date	Mintage	VF	XF	Unc
M19	1830	200 pcs.	50.00	100.00	200.00

SILVERED BRONZE

KM#	Date	Mintage	VF	XF	Unc
M19a	1830	—	75.00	150.00	250.00

25.0000 g, .900 SILVER, .7234 oz ASW

KM#	Date	Mintage	VF	XF	Unc
M19b	1830	197 pcs.	300.00	500.00	750.00

GOLD

KM#	Date	Mintage	VF	XF	Unc
M19c	1830	13 pcs.	1500.	2000.	3500.

PEWTER
Mint: Rouen
Visit of the King

KM#	Date	Mintage	VF	XF	Unc
M20	1831	—	50.00	100.00	200.00
		BRONZE			
M20a	1831	50 pcs.	75.00	150.00	250.00
		25.0000 g, .900 SILVER, .7234 oz ASW			
M20b	1831	—	150.00	300.00	400.00
		GOLD			
M20c	1831	—	—	Rare	—

BRONZE
Mint: Paris
Prince of Salerno Visit
Obv: Laureate head of Louis Philippe right.
Rev: 7-line legend.

KM#	Date	Mintage	VF	XF	Unc
M21	1846	50 pcs.	75.00	150.00	250.00
		25.0000 g, .900 SILVER, .7234 oz ASW			
M21a	1846	12 pcs.	300.00	500.00	900.00

BRONZE
Ibrahim Pasha Visit
Obv: Laureate head of Louis Philippe right.
Rev: 6-line legend.

KM#	Date	Mintage	VF	XF	Unc
M22	1846	20 pcs.	125.00	200.00	400.00
		25.0000 g, .900 SILVER, .7234 oz ASW			
M22a	1846	4 pcs.	—	1000.	2000.

PATTERNS (Pn)

(Including off metal strikes)

KM#	Date	Mintage	Identification	Mkt.Val.
Pn20	1808BB	1 known	5 Centimes, Billon	Rare

KM#	Date	Mintage	Identification	Mkt.Val.
Pn21	1815A	—	5 Francs, Napoleon right	—

KM#	Date	Mintage	Identification	Mkt.Val.
Pn22	1815A	—	5 Francs, Bronze, Louis XVIII left	—

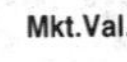

KM#	Date	Mintage	Identification	Mkt.Val.
Pn23	1815A	—	5 Francs, Silver, Louis XVIII left, date below	—

KM#	Date	Mintage	Identification	Mkt.Val.
Pn24	1815A	—	5 Francs, Bronze, rev: legend within chain	—

KM#	Date	Mintage	Identification	Mkt.Val.
Pn25	1815	—	5 Francs, Bronze, uniformed bust of Louis XVIII, rev: ornately draped arms, date below	—

KM#	Date	Mintage	Identification	Mkt.Val.
Pn26	1815	—	5 Francs, Silver, head of Louis XVIII left, rev: crowned shield divides 5 F within branches	—

KM#	Date	Mintage	Identification	Mkt.Val.
Pn27	1815A	—	5 Francs, crowned bust of Louis XVIII, rev: date within branches	—

KM#	Date	Mintage	Identification	Mkt.Val.
Pn28	1815A	—	5 Francs, Silver, rev: date above crowned arms in branches, legend around	—

KM#	Date	Mintage	Identification	Mkt.Val.
Pn29	1815	—	5 Francs, laureate head of Louis XVIII left, rev: crowned and mantled arms, order chains around, date below	—

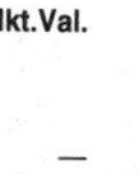

KM#	Date	Mintage	Identification	Mkt.Val.
Pn30	1815	—	5 Francs, Tin, plain head of Louis XVIII left, date below, rev: crowned round arms above denomination	—

KM#	Date	Mintage	Identification	Mkt.Val.
Pn31	1815A	—	5 Francs, Bronze, uniformed bust of Louis XVIII left, rev: crowned arms above crossed branches, date	—

KM#	Date	Mintage	Identification	Mkt.Val.
Pn32	1824A	—	5 Francs, bust of Charles X left, rev: crowned arms divide 5 F above branches, date below	—

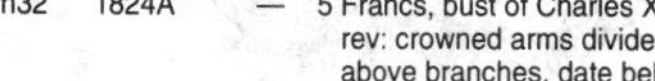

KM#	Date	Mintage	Identification	Mkt.Val.
Pn33	1830A	—	5 Francs, Gold, Galle	5000.

KM#	Date	Mintage	Identification	Mkt.Val.
Pn-A34	1831A	—	5 Francs, Pewter	175.00

KM#	Date	Mintage	Identification	Mkt.Val.
Pn-B34	1831A	—	100 Francs, Pewter	150.00

KM#	Date	Mintage	Identification	Mkt.Val.
Pn34	1838	—	10 Centimes, LP monogram, rev: denomination above date in branches	135.00

KM#	Date	Mintage	Identification	Mkt.Val.
Pn35	1840	—	1 Franc, bust of Louis Philippe right, rev: denomination and date in wreath	—
Pn36	1847	—	5 Centimes, Louis Philippe left in inner circle, rev: crowned tablet divides 5-C, crossed swords behind	85.00

KM#	Date	Mintage	Identification	Mkt.Val.
Pn37	1847	—	5 Centimes, Silver, rev: crowned tablet divides CINQ CENT	70.00
Pn38	1847	—	1 Decime, Silver, Louis Philippe left in inner circle, date below, rev: crowned tablet divides UN-Dms, crossed swords behind	120.00

KM#	Date	Mintage	Identification	Mkt.Val.
Pn39	1847	—	10 Centimes, Silver, Louis Philippe left in circle, rev: crowned tablet divides 10-Cmes	100.00

KM#	Date	Mintage	Identification	Mkt.Val.
Pn40	1848	—	10 Centimes, crowned laureate Liberty bust left, heart necklace, rev: 10 CENTIMES and date within wreath, legend around at top	100.00

KM#	Date	Mintage	Identification	Mkt.Val.
Pn41	1848	—	10 Centimes, Liberty left wearing crown of cherubs, rev: 10 C and date within small circle, legend around, wreath	—

KM#	Date	Mintage	Identification	Mkt.Val.
Pn42	1848	—	10 Centimes, laureate bust of Liberty left w/hair in back, rev: 10 CENTIMES and date within wreath, legend at top	85.00
Pn43	1848	—	10 Centimes, laureate bust of Liberty left w/hair to front, rev: 10 CENTIMES and date within wreath, legend at top	85.00
Pn44	1848	—	10 Centimes, Liberty left, rays behind, rev: small letters and date	65.00

KM#	Date	Mintage	Identification	Mkt.Val.
Pn45	1848	—	10 Centimes, similar to Pn44 but larger letters	65.00

KM#	Date	Mintage	Identification	Mkt.Val.
Pn46	1848	—	10 Centimes, Liberty left w/scarf over hair, rev: similar to Pn45	75.00

KM#	Date	Mintage	Identification	Mkt.Val.
Pn-A47	1848	—	10 Centimes, Billon, obv: laureate bust left, rev: denom. in wreath, date below	85.00

KM#	Date	Mintage	Identification	Mkt.Val.
Pn-B47	1848	—	10 Centimes, Billon, obv: laureate bust left, rev: denom. date in wreath	75.00

KM#	Date	Mintage	Identification	Mkt.Val.
Pn-CA7	1848	—	10 Centimes, Billon, obv: laureate bust, left rev: denom. in triangle	65.00

KM#	Date	Mintage	Identification	Mkt.Val.
Pn47	1848	—	5 Francs, Liberty left wearing helmet, rev: 5 FRANCS, date within wreath, legend at top	125.00

KM#	Date	Mintage	Identification	Mkt.Val.
Pn48	1848	—	5 Francs, Liberty left w/crown of cherubs, rev: 5-F, date in small circle, within wreath, legend around spaced	125.00
Pn49	1848	—	5 Francs, Liberty left w/hair knot tied w/ribbon, rev: 5 FRANCS, date within wreath, legend around spaced	—

KM#	Date	Mintage	Identification	Mkt.Val.
Pn50	1848	—	5 Francs, Liberty left wearing band w/24 FEVRIER 1848, rev: similar to Pn30	—

KM#	Date	Mintage	Identification	Mkt.Val.
Pn51	1848	—	5 Francs, Liberty left w/long flowing hair, rev: 5 FRANCS, date in flower rectangle, LIBERTE, EGALITE and FRATERNITE in individual flower cartouche	125.00

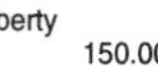

KM#	Date	Mintage	Identification	Mkt.Val.
Pn52	1848A	—	5 Francs, laureate bust of Liberty left, rev: similar to Pn50	150.00

KM#	Date	Mintage	Identification	Mkt.Val.
Pn53	1848	—	5 Francs, Liberty left w/wheat branches and spears in hair, rev: 5 FRANCS within wreath, legend around, date below	250.00

KM#	Date	Mintage	Identification	Mkt.Val.
Pn54	1848	—	5 Francs, Liberty left w/long hair, triangle symbol behind head, rev: similar to Pn52	—

KM#	Date	Mintage	Identification	Mkt.Val.
Pn55	1848	—	5 Francs, crowned laureate bust of Liberty left, hearts around neck, rev: similar to Pn47	120.00

KM#	Date	Mintage	Identification	Mkt.Val.
Pn56	1848	—	5 Francs, White metal, facing Liberty, rev: similar to Pn54	—

KM#	Date	Mintage	Identification	Mkt.Val.
Pn57	1848	—	5 Francs, Liberty left w/hair to front, rev: similar to Pn53	—

KM#	Date	Mintage	Identification	Mkt.Val.
Pn58	1848	—	5 Francs, laureate Liberty bust left w/short hair, rev: similar to Pn57	145.00

KM#	Date	Mintage	Identification	Mkt.Val.
Pn59	1848	—	5 Francs, facing Liberty, band in hair, hair flowing over shoulders to front, rev: similar to Pn55 but w/o legend	—

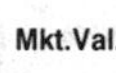

KM#	Date	Mintage	Identification	Mkt.Val.
Pn60	1848	—	5 Francs, similar to Pn58, rev: similar to Pn59	165.00

KM#	Date	Mintage	Identification	Mkt.Val.
Pn61	1848	—	5 Francs, laureate bust w/short hair left, beads around neck, rev: branches in field around 5 FRANCS and date	—

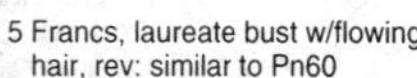

KM#	Date	Mintage	Identification	Mkt.Val.
Pn62	1848	—	5 Francs, laureate bust w/flowing hair, rev: similar to Pn60	—

KM#	Date	Mintage	Identification	Mkt.Val.
Pn63	1848	—	5 Francs, similar to Pn62 but 1 symbol added below bust	—

KM#	Date	Mintage	Identification	Mkt.Val.
Pn64	1848	—	5 Francs, similar to Pn62 but 3 symbols added below bust	—
Pn65	1848	—	5 Francs, laureate bust left w/hair tied w/bow, symbol above, rev: similar to Pn64 but wreath closer to bottom	—

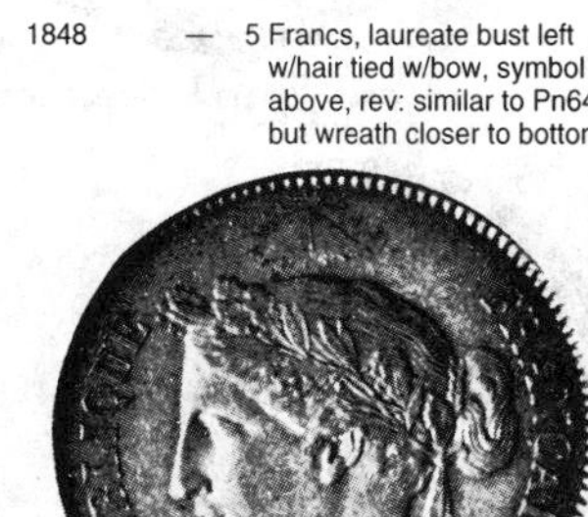

KM#	Date	Mintage	Identification	Mkt.Val.
Pn66	1848	—	5 Francs, similar to Pn65 but larger wreath, date below	—

KM#	Date	Mintage	Identification	Mkt.Val.
Pn67	1848	—	5 Francs, crowned laureate bust left w/long hair, rev: similar to Pn65	125.00

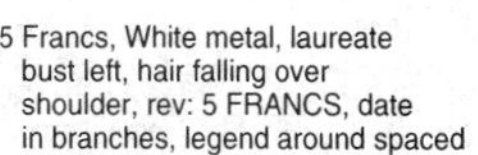

KM#	Date	Mintage	Identification	Mkt.Val.
Pn68	1848	—	5 Francs, White metal, laureate bust left, hair falling over shoulder, rev: 5 FRANCS, date in branches, legend around spaced	—

KM#	Date	Mintage	Identification	Mkt.Val.
Pn69	1848	—	5 Francs, laureate bust w/long hair left, 3 symbols around, rev: 5 FRANCS, date in wreath	—
Pn70	1848	—	5 Francs, White metal, laureate bust w/long hair showing at both sides, 2 symbols at front and back, rev: similar to Pn56	—
Pn71	1848A	—	5 Francs, White metal, laureate bust w/hair hanging on shoulder, rev: outer legend spaced	—

KM#	Date	Mintage	Identification	Mkt.Val.
Pn72	1848	—	5 Francs, bust left w/wide band in hair, rev: similar to Pn68 but symbol below crossed branches	200.00
Pn73	1848	—	5 Francs, White metal, VG3063	—
Pn74	1848	—	5 Francs, White metal, VG3064	—

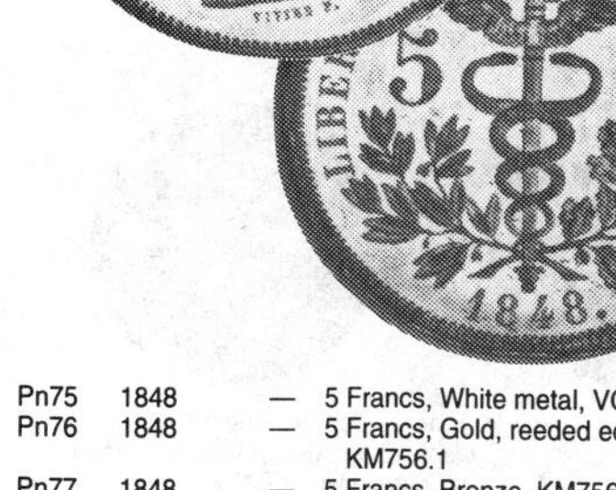

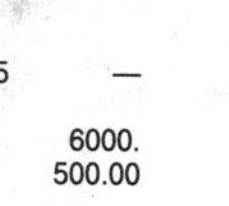

KM#	Date	Mintage	Identification	Mkt.Val.
Pn75	1848	—	5 Francs, White metal, VG3095	—
Pn76	1848	—	5 Francs, Gold, reeded edge, KM756.1	6000.
Pn77	1848	—	5 Francs, Bronze, KM756.1	500.00

KM#	Date	Mintage	Identification	Mkt.Val.
Pn78	1848	—	5 Francs, laureate bust left, rev: 5-F divided by fasces, date below	—

KM#	Date	Mintage	Identification	Mkt.Val.
Pn79	ND(1848)	—	20 Francs, Bronze-gilt, facing laureate bust, rev: legend in 4 lines in oak and laurel wreath	135.00

KM#	Date	Mintage	Identification	Mkt.Val.
Pn80	1848	—	20 Francs, bust wearing helmet left, rev: 20 FRANCS, date in wreath	—

KM#	Date	Mintage	Identification	Mkt.Val.
Pn81	1848	—	20 Francs, laureate bust right	—

KM#	Date	Mintage	Identification	Mkt.Val.
Pn82	1848	—	20 Francs	2750.

KM#	Date	Mintage	Identification	Mkt.Val.
Pn83	1849	—	20 Centimes, laureate bust left	—

KM#	Date	Mintage	Identification	Mkt.Val.
Pn84	1849	—	5 Francs, laureate bust left	—
Pn85	1849	—	5 Francs, Bronze, KM756.1	500.00
Pn86	1852	—	5 Francs, Louis Napoleon Bonaparte	—

KM#	Date	Mintage	Identification	Mkt.Val.
Pn87	1853	—	1 Centime, rev: eagle	—
Pn88	1853A	—	20 Centimes, Silver, large head, KM778.1	375.00
Pn89	1853A	—	20 Centimes, Silver, large head, plain edge, KM778.1	325.00

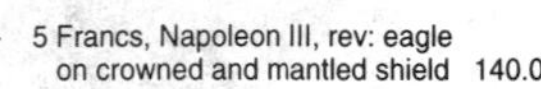

KM#	Date	Mintage	Identification	Mkt.Val.
Pn90	1853	—	5 Francs, Napoleon III, rev: eagle on crowned and mantled shield	140.00

KM#	Date	Mintage	Identification	Mkt.Val.
Pn91	1856	—	2 Francs, Napoleon III left, obv: eagle on round, crowned and mantled arms	—

KM#	Date	Mintage	Identification	Mkt.Val.
Pn92	1857	—	10 Centimes, Napoleon III left in inner circle, rev: eagle in circle	—

KM#	Date	Mintage	Identification	Mkt.Val.
Pn93	1867	—	25 Francs/10 Florins, Gold, Napoleon III left w/o legend, rev: denominations in inner circle, legend around, date below	—

KM#	Date	Mintage	Identification	Mkt.Val.
Pn94	1870	—	5 Francs, laureate bust of Napoleon III left, rev: crowned and mantled round eagle arms	—
Pn96	18xx	—	Nickel, laureate bust left, rev: 12gr/31mm	—

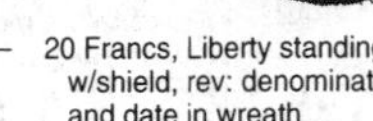

KM#	Date	Mintage	Identification	Mkt.Val.
Pn98	1887	—	20 Francs, Liberty standing w/shield, rev: denomination and date in wreath	—

KM#	Date	Mintage	Identification	Mkt.Val.
Pn99	1898	75 pcs.	5 Francs, Silver	Rare
Pn100	1899	—	10 Francs, Gold	2400.
Pn101	1899	—	20 Francs, Gold	2850.

PIEFORTS (P) WITH ESSAI (PE)

(Double thickness)

Standard metals unless otherwise noted

KM#	Date	Mintage	Identification	Mkt.Val.
P150	1848	—	20 Francs, laureate bust right, rev: 20 FRANCS, date in wreath	—

KM#	Date	Mintage	Identification	Mkt.Val.
P151	1848	—	20 Francs, facing laureate bust w/long flowing hair, copper	100.00
PE200	1888	—	5 Centimes, Aluminum, KM821	125.00
PE201	1888	—	10 Centimes, Aluminum, KM815	150.00
P250	1899	—	20 Francs, KM847	Rare

PRETENDER COINAGE (PT) W/ESSAI (PTE)

Napoleon II

1815-1816

CENTIME

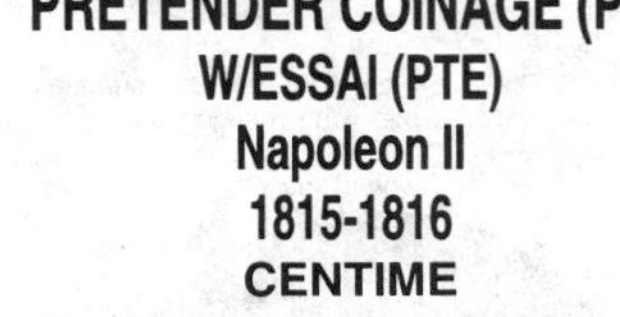

BRONZE, 2.85 g

KM#	Date	Fine	VF	XF	Unc
PTE6	1816	15.00	25.00	40.00	80.00

3 CENTIMES

BRONZE, 7.07 g

KM#	Date	Fine	VF	XF	Unc
PTE7	1816	20.00	30.00	50.00	90.00

5 CENTIMES

BRONZE, 10.67 g

KM#	Date	Fine	VF	XF	Unc
PTE8	1816	27.50	45.00	75.00	135.00

10 CENTIMES

BRONZE, 13.90 g

KM#	Date	Fine	VF	XF	Unc
PTE9	1816	35.00	60.00	100.00	150.00

1/4 FRANC

KM#	Date	Fine	VF	XF	Unc
SILVER, 1.24 g					
PTE10	1816	45.00	75.00	120.00	225.00
BRONZE					
PTE10a	1816	18.00	30.00	50.00	85.00

1/2 FRANC

KM#	Date	Fine	VF	XF	Unc
SILVER, 2.35 g					
PTE11	1816	45.00	75.00	125.00	225.00
BRONZE					
PTE11a	1816	27.50	45.00	75.00	125.00

FRANC

KM#	Date	Fine	VF	XF	Unc
SILVER					
PTE12	1816	72.00	120.00	200.00	425.00
BRONZE					
PTE12a	1816	35.00	60.00	100.00	150.00

2 FRANCS

KM#	Date	Fine	VF	XF	Unc
SILVER					
PTE13	1816	120.00	200.00	350.00	750.00
BRONZE					
PTE13a	1816	35.00	60.00	100.00	200.00
WHITE METAL					
PTE13b	1816	20.00	35.00	60.00	120.00

5 FRANCS

KM#	Date	Fine	VF	XF	Unc
SILVER, 21.17 g					
PTE14	1816	275.00	550.00	950.00	1600.
BRONZE					
PTE14a	1816	60.00	125.00	250.00	500.00
GOLD					
PTE14b	1816	—	2000.	3000.	4400.

NOTE: Unofficial pieces (patterns?) struck during the reign of Napoleon III, possibly to give continuity to the dynasty.

20 FRANCS

LEAD

KM#	Date	Fine	VF	XF	Unc
PTE48	1815	—	—	300.00	500.00

Henry V
1832-1873

2-1/2 CENTIMES

KM#	Date	Fine	VF	XF	Unc
BRONZE					
PTE49	ND	—	150.00	250.00	425.00
LEAD					
PTE49a	ND	—	125.00	225.00	400.00

5 CENTIMES

SILVER
Obv: Small uniformed bust left.

KM#	Date	Fine	VF	XF	Unc
PT15	1832	35.00	75.00	200.00	375.00

Obv: Head right.

KM#	Date	Fine	VF	XF	Unc
PT16	1832	35.00	75.00	200.00	450.00

Reduced size

KM#	Date	Fine	VF	XF	Unc
PT17	1832	35.00	75.00	165.00	300.00

10 CENTIMES

SILVER
Obv: Small uniformed bust left.

KM#	Date	Fine	VF	XF	Unc
PT18	1832	40.00	75.00	200.00	425.00

Obv: Larger uniformed bust left.

KM#	Date	Fine	VF	XF	Unc
PT19	1832	40.00	75.00	200.00	425.00

Obv: Head left.

KM#	Date	Fine	VF	XF	Unc
PT20	1832	40.00	75.00	200.00	425.00

Reduced size

KM#	Date	Fine	VF	XF	Unc
PT21	1832	55.00	100.00	225.00	475.00

1/4 FRANC

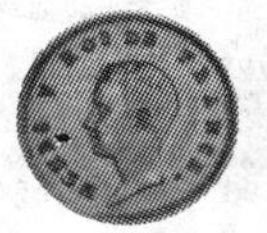

KM#	Date	Fine	VF	XF	Unc
SILVER, plain edge					
PT22	1832	60.00	100.00	175.00	350.00
	1833	75.00	120.00	200.00	400.00
BRONZE					
PT22a	1833	15.00	25.00	50.00	100.00
SILVER, 3.93 g Piedfort					
PTP22b	1833	80.00	135.00	225.00	500.00
GILT BRONZE Piedfort					
PTP22c	1833	35.00	60.00	100.00	200.00

1/2 FRANC

KM#	Date	Fine	VF	XF	Unc
SILVER					
PT23	1832	35.00	65.00	120.00	250.00
	1833	35.00	65.00	120.00	250.00
BRONZE					
PT23a	1833	25.00	40.00	65.00	125.00
Obv: Uniformed bust left, child's head.					
PT24	1833	35.00	60.00	100.00	200.00
Obv: Small uniformed bust left.					
PT25	1833	35.00	60.00	100.00	200.00

KM#	Date	Fine	VF	XF	Unc
PT26	1858A	75.00	125.00	200.00	400.00

FRANC

SILVER
Obv: Large bust.

KM#	Date	Fine	VF	XF	Unc
PT27	1831	20.00	35.00	75.00	175.00

Obv: Small bust, 4.40 g.
Plain edge.

KM#	Date	Fine	VF	XF	Unc
PT28.1	1831	20.00	35.00	75.00	250.00
		Reeded edge.			
PT28.2	1831	20.00	35.00	75.00	180.00
	1832	20.00	35.00	75.00	180.00
		GOLD **Obv: Small bust.** **Piedfort, reeded edge.**			
PTP28.1a	1832	500.00	600.00	800.00	1300.
		BRONZE			
PTP28.1b	1832	50.00	75.00	150.00	275.00
		Piedfort, plain edge, 8.98 g.			
PTP28.1c	1832	—	—	170.00	400.00
		SILVER **Piedfort, 8.50 g.**			
PTP28.1d	1832	75.00	120.00	200.00	500.00
		Piedfort, plain edge, 12.00 g.			
PTP28.1e	1832	—	—	350.00	650.00
		T.W.I. below bust, plain edge.			
P29	1832	25.00	40.00	80.00	300.00

2 FRANCS

KM#	Date	Fine	VF	XF	Unc
		SILVER			
PTE30	ND	80.00	150.00	250.00	400.00
		BRONZE or GILT BRASS			
PTE30a	ND	35.00	65.00	125.00	175.00

KM#	Date	Fine	VF	XF	Unc
		SILVER **Reeded edge.**			
PT31.1	1831	100.00	200.00	300.00	500.00
	1832	100.00	150.00	250.00	450.00
	1833	100.00	200.00	300.00	500.00
		Lettered edge.			
PT31.2	1833	150.00	250.00	300.00	700.00
		GOLD **Lettered edge.**			
PTP31.3a	1832	—	—	550.00	1000.
		BRONZE **Plain edge.**			
PT31.3b	1833	25.00	65.00	125.00	175.00
		SILVER **Piedfort.**			
PTP31.3c	1832	—	—	300.00	850.00
		SILVER **Double piedfort.**			
PTP31.3d	1832	—	—	600.00	1600.

KM#	Date	Fine	VF	XF	Unc
		SILVER, 34.64 g **Double piedfort.**			
PTP50	1833	—	—	600.00	1500.

5 FRANCS

KM#	Date	Fine	VF	XF	Unc
		SILVER			
PT32	1830	175.00	250.00	350.00	750.00
		BRONZE			
PT32a	1830	30.00	80.00	150.00	250.00
		PEWTER			
PT32b	1830	30.00	50.00	100.00	200.00
		BRONZE, 17.19 g **Obv: Head left.** **Rev: Crowned arms in wreath; date below.**			
PT33	1831	50.00	75.00	150.00	300.00
		PEWTER			
PT33a	1831	35.00	60.00	100.00	200.00

KM#	Date	Fine	VF	XF	Unc
		SILVER, 24.96 g			
PT35	1831	125.00	200.00	325.00	600.00
	1832	150.00	225.00	350.00	625.00
		GOLD			
PT35a	1832	—	—	1250.	2000.
		SILVER, 58.79 g **Piedfort (double thickness) - plain edge.**			
PTP35c	1832	300.00	500.00	800.00	2000.
		109.46 g **Double piedfort (quadruple thickness).**			
PTP35d	1832	400.00	600.00	1250.	3500.
		Quadruple piedfort (octuple thickness).			
PTP35e	1832	—	—	—	5000.
		BRONZE			
PT35b	1831	35.00	75.00	125.00	200.00
		Piedfort, 33.32 g			
PTP35f	1832	—	100.00	175.00	425.00

KM#	Date	Fine	VF	XF	Unc
		BRONZE **Visit of Henry V to England**			
PT36	1843	—	—	250.00	500.00
		SILVER			
PT36a	1843	—	—	600.00	1000.
		GOLD **Visit of Henry V to England**			
PT36b	1843	—	—	1600.	2300.

KM#	Date	Fine	VF	XF	Unc
		SILVER **Plain edge.**			
PTE37.1	1871	250.00	350.00	600.00	1200.
		25.17 g **Reeded edge.**			
PTE37.2	1871	200.00	300.00	600.00	1200.
		24.87 g **Lettered edge.**			
PTE37.3	1871	—	—	1350.	2700.
		BRONZE			
PTE37.2a	1871	50.00	90.00	175.00	400.00
		GOLD **Reeded edge.**			
PTE37.2b	1871	—	—	1600.	2500.

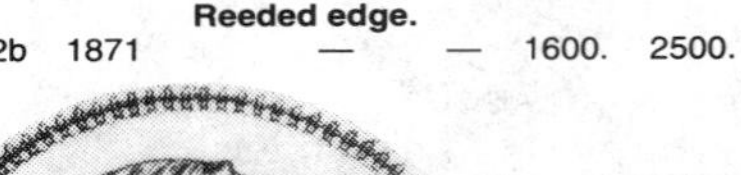

KM#	Date	Fine	VF	XF	Unc
		SILVER, 23.63 g **Plain edge.**			
PT38	1873	—	—	1000.	2000.

BRONZE

KM#	Date	Fine	VF	XF	Unc
PT38a	1873	—	—	300.00	600.00

SILVER, 47.54 g
Piedfort (double thickness).

KM#	Date	Fine	VF	XF	Unc
PT38b	1873	—	—	1900.	3750.

Napoleon IV

10 CENTIMES

BRONZE, 9.61 g

KM#	Date	Fine	VF	XF	Unc
PT39	1874	—	50.00	75.00	125.00

20 CENTIMES

SILVER
Obv: Head left.
Rev: Crown above value and date.

KM#	Date	Fine	VF	XF	Unc
PTE40	1874	—	40.00	80.00	150.00

50 CENTIMES

SILVER
Obv: Head left.
Rev: Crown above value and date.

KM#	Date	Fine	VF	XF	Unc
PTE41	1874	—	40.00	80.00	150.00

FRANC

SILVER

KM#	Date	Fine	VF	XF	Unc
PTE42	1874	—	75.00	150.00	250.00

2 FRANCS

SILVER

KM#	Date	Fine	VF	XF	Unc
PTE43	1874	—	150.00	300.00	500.00

5 FRANCS

SILVER, 25.62 g
Plain edge.

KM#	Date	Fine	VF	XF	Unc
PTE45.1	1870	—	750.00	1500.	2000.

Reeded edge, 26.07 g

KM#	Date	Fine	VF	XF	Unc
PTE45.2	1874	—	600.00	900.00	1250.

Piedfort, 49.38 g

KM#	Date	Fine	VF	XF	Unc
PTP45.2a	1874	—	800.00	1600.	2750.

TRIAL STRIKES (TS)

KM#	Date	Mintage	Identification	Mkt.Val.
TS2	1853	—	5 Francs, Napoleon III left	—
TS3	ND(1855)	—	5 Francs, Napoleon III left, obv.	—
TS4	1855	—	5 Francs, rev: crowned and mantled round arms	—
TS5	ND(1855)	—	5 Francs, Gold, obv: Napoleon III III right	—
TS6	1855	—	5 Francs, Gold, rev: denomination and date in wreath	—
TS7	ND(1855)	—	10 Francs, obv: Napoleon III right	—
TS8	1855A	—	10 Francs, rev. denomination and date in wreath	—
TS9	ND(1855)	—	20 Francs, obv: Napoleon III right	—
TS10	1855A	—	20 Francs, rev: denomination and date in wreath	—
TS11	ND(1855)	—	50 Francs, obv: Napoleon III right	—
TS12	1855	—	50 Francs, rev: eagle on shield of crowned, mantled arms	—
TS13	ND(1855)	—	100 Francs, obv. Napoleon III right	—
TS14	1855	—	100 Francs, rev: eagle on shield on crowned and mantled arms	—
TS15	ND(1856)	—	2 Francs, obv: Napoleon III left	—

KM#	Date	Mintage	Identification	Mkt.Val.
TS16	1856A	—	2 Francs, rev: denomination and date in wreath	—

KM#	Date	Mintage	Identification	Mkt.Val.
TS17	1862	10	5 Francs, Gilt Bronze, obv.	—
TS18	1862	10	5 Francs, Gilt Bronze, rev.	—
TS19	1862	10	10 Francs, Gilt Bronze, obv.	—
TS20	1862	10	10 Francs, Gilt Bronze, rev.	—
TS21	1862	10	20 Francs, Gilt Bronze, obv.	—
TS22	1862	10	20 Francs, Gilt Bronze. rev.	—
TS23	1862	10	50 Francs, Gilt Bronze, obv.	—
TS24	1862	10	50 Francs, Gilt Bronze, rev.	—

KM#	Date	Mintage	Identification	Mkt.Val.
TS25	1862	10	100 Francs, Gilt Bronze, obv.	400.00

KM#	Date	Mintage	Identification	Mkt.Val.
TS26	1862	10	100 Francs, Gilt Bronze, rev.	400.00

KM#	Date	Mintage	Identification	Mkt.Val.
TS27	1889	—	5 Francs, White Metal, obv.	325.00

KM#	Date	Mintage	Identification	Mkt.Val.
TS28	1889C	—	5 Francs, White Metal, rev.	325.00

ANTWERP

ANVERS

Antwerp, a town in Belgium, grew from a tiny walled marquisate under Godfrey of Bouillon, one of the leaders of the First Crusade in the 11th century, to the chief port and commercial center of 15th-century western Europe. Not only was it an acknowledged leader in trade and commerce, but also in the arts. The following centuries carried as much tragedy as triumph. Antwerp was plundered by Spain and its Protestant citizens murdered during the religious troubles of the 16th century. It served as the chief military harbor of Napoleon during the fall of the First Empire. It was the scene of the most famous siege of World War I, and was repeatedly battered by V-bombs during World War II. The French-auspice Antwerp coins of 1814-15 were a necessity money issued while Antwerp, under General Carnot, was besieged by the Allies.

SIEGE COINAGE

The following coins were minted from captured cannons by the French while besieged in Antwerp, Belgium. Some have an *N* for Napoleon while others have a double *L* monogram for King Louis XVIII of France.

ENGRAVERS INITIALS

JLGN - Jean-Louis Gagnepain
R - Ransonnet
V - Van Goor
W - Wolschot Foundry

5 CENTIMES

18 g, BRONZE, 29-32mm
Obv: N in wreath.

KM#	Date	Mintage	VG	Fine	VF	XF
1	1814	180 pcs.	100.00	200.00	400.00	800.00
		SILVER				
1a	1814	—	—	—	Rare	—
		12-15 g, BRONZE, 29-30mm				
2.1	1814	—	16.00	35.00	65.00	160.00

KM#	Date	Mintage	VG	Fine	VF	XF
		Obv: V above ribbon.				
2.2	1814	.011	14.00	32.00	55.00	135.00
		SILVER				
2.2a	1814	—	—	—	350.00	600.00

KM#	Date	Mintage	VG	Fine	VF	XF
		Obv: V below ribbon bow.				
2.3	1814	2,800	25.00	50.00	90.00	180.00
		Obv: JLGN on ribbon.				
2.4	1814	.017	14.00	32.00	55.00	135.00
		Obv. Type I: Narrow LL monogram.				
3.1	1814	.010	— Reported. not confirmed			

Obv: V below ribbon bow.

KM#	Date	Mintage	VG	Fine	VF	XF
3.2	1814	—	22.00	45.00	85.00	175.00

Obv: JLGN on ribbon.

KM#	Date	Mintage	VG	Fine	VF	XF
3.3	1814	.031	— Reported, not confirmed			

Obv. Type II: Wide LL monogram, JLGN on ribbon.

KM#	Date	Mintage	VG	Fine	VF	XF
4.1	1814	—	16.00	35.00	70.00	165.00

SILVER

KM#	Date	Mintage	VG	Fine	VF	XF
4.1a	1814	—	—	—	600.00	1000.

BRONZE
Obv: V below ribbon.

KM#	Date	Mintage	VG	Fine	VF	XF
4.2	1814	—	— Reported, not confirmed			

10 CENTIMES

BRONZE
Obv: JEAN LOUIS//GAGNEPAIN on ribbon.

KM#	Date	Mintage	VG	Fine	VF	XF
5.1	1814	.018	22.00	45.00	90.00	200.00

SILVER

KM#	Date	Mintage	VG	Fine	VF	XF
5.1a	1814	—	—	—	Rare	—

BRONZE
Obv: W/o initials or name on ribbon.

KM#	Date	Mintage	VG	Fine	VF	XF
5.2	1814	7,500	25.00	60.00	130.00	265.00

Obv: R below ribbon bow.

KM#	Date	Mintage	VG	Fine	VF	XF
5.3	1814	.066	15.00	35.00	60.00	125.00

Obv: W above ribbon bow.

KM#	Date	Mintage	VG	Fine	VF	XF
5.4	1814	.029	16.00	38.00	65.00	140.00

Obv. Type I: Narrow LL monogram.

KM#	Date	Mintage	VG	Fine	VF	XF
6.1	1814	—	— Reported, not confirmed			

Obv: JEAN LOUIS//GAGNEPAIN on ribbon.

KM#	Date	Mintage	VG	Fine	VF	XF
6.2	1814	.035	20.00	50.00	75.00	175.00

Obv. Type II: Wide LL monogram, JEAN LOUIS GAGNEPAIN on ribbon.

KM#	Date	Mintage	VG	Fine	VF	XF
7.1	1814	.020	22.00	55.00	85.00	200.00

Obv: R below ribbon bow.

KM#	Date	Mintage	VG	Fine	VF	XF
7.2	1814	.053	18.00	45.00	65.00	160.00

SILVER

KM#	Date	Mintage	VG	Fine	VF	XF
7.2a	1814	—	—	—	550.00	900.00

Listings For

FRENCH COCHIN CHINA: refer to Vietnam

FRENCH COLONIES

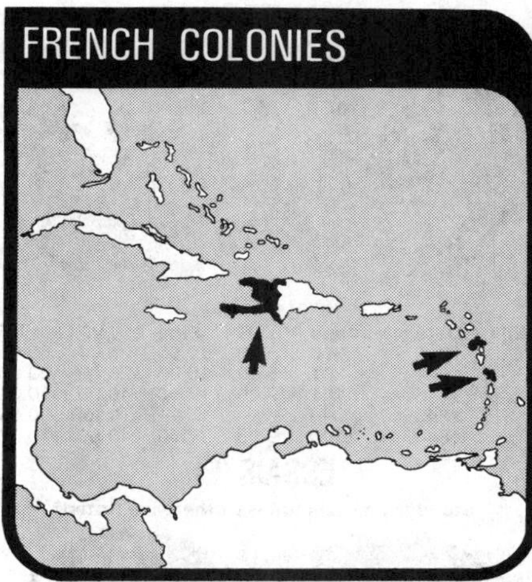

The coins catalogued under this heading were not issued for use in any particular colony but were intended for general use in the West Indies, particularly Martinique, Guadeloupe, and Saint-Dominique (western Hispaniola) until it attained independence as Haiti in 1804.

RULERS

French

MINT MARKS

A Paris
H - LaRochelle

MONETARY SYSTEM

100 Centimes = 1 Franc

5 CENTIMES

BRONZE
Mint mark: A

KM#	Date	Mintage	VG	Fine	VF	XF
10.1	1825	.607	2.50	6.00	15.00	40.00
	1828	.501	3.00	7.50	18.00	45.00
	1829	.299	5.00	10.00	30.00	65.00
	1830	.402	4.50	9.00	22.00	55.00

Mint mark: H

KM#	Date	Mintage	VG	Fine	VF	XF
10.2	1827	.600	2.50	6.00	15.00	40.00

Mint mark: A

KM#	Date	Mintage	VG	Fine	VF	XF
12	1839	.600	2.50	6.00	20.00	50.00
	1839	—	—	—	Proof	400.00
	1841	.602	2.50	6.00	20.00	50.00
	1843	.202	7.50	15.00	35.00	75.00
	1844	.201	7.50	15.00	38.00	80.00

10 CENTIMES

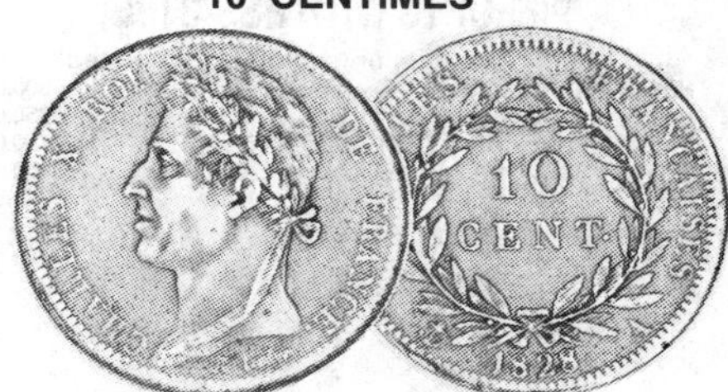

BRONZE
Mint mark: A

KM#	Date	Mintage	VG	Fine	VF	XF
11.1	1825	.301	5.00	10.00	25.00	60.00
	1828	.253	7.50	15.00	30.00	65.00
	1829	.152	9.00	17.50	40.00	90.00

Mint mark: H

KM#	Date	Mintage	VG	Fine	VF	XF
11.2	1827	.300	5.00	10.00	25.00	60.00

Mint mark: A

KM#	Date	Mintage	VG	Fine	VF	XF
13	1839	.300	5.00	10.00	25.00	60.00
	1841	.301	5.00	10.00	25.00	60.00
	1843	.101	9.00	17.50	40.00	110.00
	1843	—	—	—	Proof	500.00
	1844	.100	9.00	17.50	40.00	110.00

ESSAIS (E)

Standard metals unless otherwise noted.

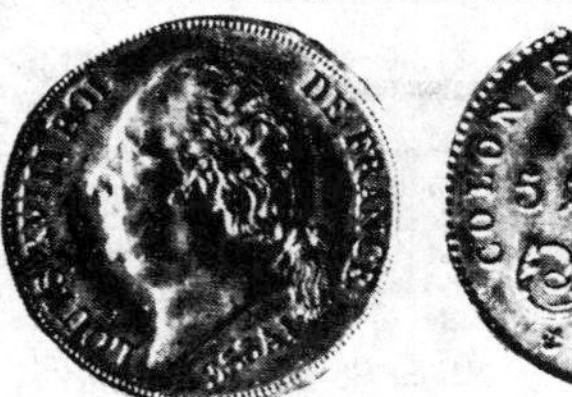

KM#	Date	Mintage	Identification	Mkt.Val.
E3	1824A	—	5 Centimes, Bronze	125.00
E4	1824A	—	5 Centimes, Silver	275.00

KM#	Date	Mintage	Identification	Mkt.Val.
E5	1824A	—	10 Centimes, Bronze	150.00
E6	1824A	—	10 Centimes, Silver	325.00

KM#	Date	Mintage	Identification	Mkt.Val.
E7	1839A	—	5 Centimes	325.00
E8	1839A	—	10 Centimes	375.00

KM#	Date	Mintage	Identification	Mkt.Val.
E9	ND	—	1 Decime	200.00

PIEFORTS (P)

PIEFORTS WITH ESSAI (PE)

Standard metals unless otherwise noted.

KM#	Date	Mintage	Identification	Mkt.Val.
PE1	1824A	—	5 Centimes, Silver	600.00
PE2	1824A	—	5 Centimes, Bronze	250.00
PE3	1824A	—	10 Centimes, Silver	750.00
PE4	1824A	—	10 Centimes, Bronze	350.00
PE5	1839A	—	10 Centimes, Bronze	325.00

FRENCH GUIANA

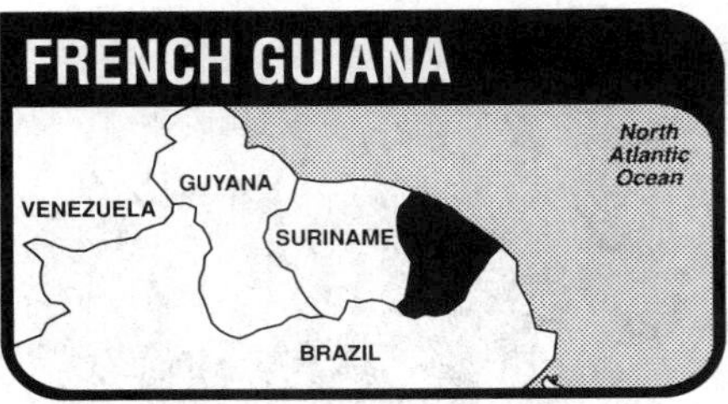

The French Overseas Department of Guiana, located on the northeast coast of South America, bordered by Surinam and Brazil, has an area of 33,399 sq. mi. (91,000 sq. km.) and a population of 145,270. Capital: Cayenne. Placer gold mining and shrimp processing are the chief industries. Shrimp, lumber, gold, cocoa, and bananas are exported.

The coast of Guiana was sighted by Columbus in 1498 and explored by Amerigo Vespucci in 1499. The French established the first successful trading stations and settlements, and placed the area under direct control of the French Crown in 1674. Portuguese and British forces occupied French Guiana for five years during the Napoleonic Wars. Devil's Island, the notorious penal colony in French Guiana where Capt. Alfred Dreyfus was imprisoned, was established in 1852 - and finally closed in 1947. When France adopted a new constitution in 1946, French Guiana voted to remain within the French Union as an Overseas Department. It now hosts some of the French and Common Market space and satellite stations.

In the late eighteenth century, a series of 2 sous coins was struck for the colony. It is probable that contemporary imitations of these issues, many emanating from Birmingham, England, outnumber the originals. These, both genuine and bogus, host coins for many West Indies counterstamps. As an Overseas Department, Guiana now uses the coins of metropolitan France, however, the franc used in the former colony was always distinct in value from that of the homeland as well as that used in the islands of the French West Indies.

RULERS

French

MINT MARKS

A - Paris

MONETARY SYSTEM

(until 1794)

4 Liards = 1 Sol (Sou)
20 Sols (Sous) = Livre

(Commencing 1794)

100 Centimes = 10 Decimes = 1 Franc

COLONY OF CAYENNE

2 SOUS

BILLON
Mint mark: A

KM#	Date	Mintage	VG	Fine	VF	XF
3	1816	—	40.00	80.00	175.00	350.00

PIEFORTS (P)

KM#	Date	Mintage	Identification	Mkt.Val.
P2	1816A	*3-4	2 Sous, Tin, 5.40 g, KM3	500.00

FRENCH GUIANA

10 CENTIMES

BILLON, 2.50 g
Mint mark: A

KM#	Date	Mintage	VG	Fine	VF	XF
1	1818	2.000	9.00	18.00	40.00	90.00

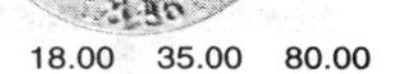

KM#	Date	Mintage	VG	Fine	VF	XF
2	1846	1.400	9.00	18.00	35.00	80.00

PIEFORTS (P)

KM#	Date	Mintage	Identification	Mkt.Val.
P1	ND(1817-18)A		10 Centimes, Tin, 4.95 g	350.00
P2	ND	—	10 Centimes, White Metal	350.00

REPUBLIC

This republic was formed by citizens in a region of French Guiana called Counani, south of Cayenne. It was in an area that was, at that time, in dispute between Brazil and France. The republic lasted approximately one year and was presided over by a man named Cros. Final boundary definition was not accomplished until this century.

ESSAIS (E)

KM#	Date	Mintage	Identification	Mkt.Val.
E1	1887	—	10 Centimes, Bronze, "E" below value	250.00

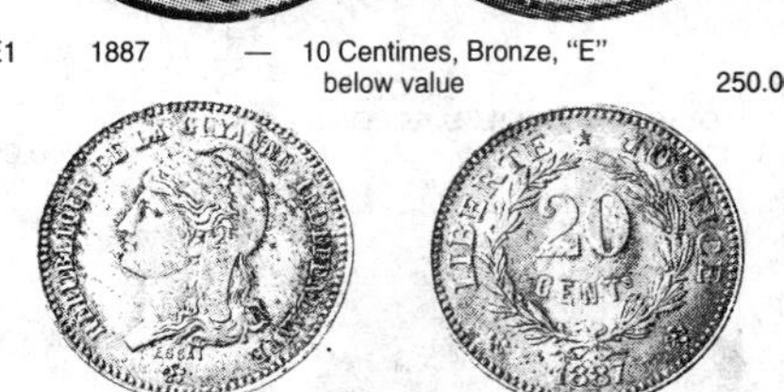

KM#	Date	Mintage	Identification	Mkt.Val.
E2	1887	—	20 Centimes, Copper-Nickel-Zinc, 4.92 g	300.00

KM#	Date	Mintage	Identification	Mkt.Val.
E3	1887	—	5 Francs, .900 Silver, 25.0 g	3000.
E4	1887	—	5 Francs, White Metal	750.00

KM#	Date	Mintage	Identification	Mkt.Val.
E5	1889	—	10 Centimes, Bronze, "E" below bust	525.00

FRENCH INDO-CHINA

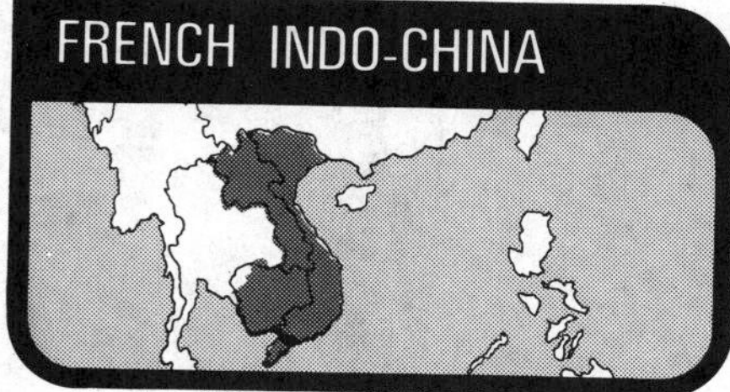

French Indo-China, made up of the protectorates of Annam, Tonkin, Cambodia and Laos and the colony of Cochin-China was located on the Indo-Chinese peninsula of Southeast Asia. The colony had an area of 286,194 sq. mi. (741,242 sq. km.). and a population of 30 million. Principal cities: Saigon, Haiphong, Vientiane, Pnom-Penh and Hanoi.

The forebears of the modern Indo-Chinese peoples originated in the Yellow River Valley of northern China, from whence they were driven into the Indo-Chinese peninsula by the Han Chinese. The Chinese followed southward in the second century B.C., conquering the peninsula and ruling it until 938, leaving a lingering heritage of Chinese learning and culture. Indo-Chinese independence was basically maintained until the arrival of the French in the mid-19th century who established control over all of Vietnam, Laos and Cambodia. Activities directed toward obtaining self-determination accelerated during the Japanese occupation of World War II. The dependencies were changed from colonies to territories within the French Union in 1946, and all the inhabitants were made French citizens.

In Aug. of 1945, an uprising erupted involving the French and Vietnamese Nationalists, culminated in the French military disaster at Dien Bien Phu (May, 1954) and the subsequent Geneva Conference that brought an end to French colonial rule in Indo-China.

For later coinage see Kampuchea, Laos and Vietnam.

RULERS

French, until 1954

MINT MARKS

A - Paris
(a) - Paris, privy marks only
B - Beaumont-le-Roger
C - Castlesarrasin
H - Heaton, Birmingham
(p) - Thunderbolt - Poissy
S - San Francisco, U.S.A.
None - Osaka, Japan
None - Hanoi, Tonkin

MONETARY SYSTEM

5 Sapeques = 1 Cent
100 Cents = 1 Piastre

SAPEQUE

BRONZE
Mint mark: A

KM#	Date	Mintage	Fine	VF	XF	Unc
6	1887	5.000	1.50	4.00	15.00	40.00
	1888	5.000	3.00	7.00	20.00	50.00
	1889	100 pcs.	—	—	Proof	500.00
	1892	1.636	60.00	150.00	275.00	450.00
	1893	.864	40.00	100.00	200.00	350.00
	1894	2.500	6.00	15.00	35.00	100.00
	1897	2.829	6.00	15.00	35.00	100.00
	1898	2.171	50.00	125.00	225.00	350.00
	1899	5.000	2.50	7.50	15.00	50.00
	1900	2.657	7.50	20.00	45.00	125.00
	1900	100 pcs.	—	—	Proof	500.00

NOTE: Later dates (1901-1902) exist for this type.

CENT

BRONZE
Mint mark: A

KM#	Date	Mintage	Fine	VF	XF	Unc
1	1885	3.673	1.25	4.00	10.00	30.00
	1885	—	—	—	Proof	400.00
	1886	1.883	2.00	6.00	20.00	65.00
	1887	2.362	1.50	5.00	15.00	40.00
	1888	2.564	1.50	5.00	15.00	40.00
	1889	1.573	2.00	6.00	20.00	55.00
	1889	100 pcs.	—	—	Proof	725.00
	1892	2.648	1.50	4.00	20.00	50.00
	1893	1.852	6.00	15.00	40.00	125.00
	1894	.465	10.00	17.50	45.00	150.00

Rev. leg: UN CENTIEME DE PIASTRE

KM#	Date	Mintage	Fine	VF	XF	Unc
7	1895	.290	30.00	60.00	175.00	375.00

KM#	Date	Mintage	Fine	VF	XF	Unc
8	1896	5.690	2.00	3.00	7.50	25.00
	1897	11.055	1.00	2.00	5.00	20.00
	1898	5.000	5.00	7.50	25.00	60.00
	1899	8.000	1.00	2.00	4.00	20.00
	1900	3.000	3.00	5.00	10.00	40.00
	1900	100 pcs.	—	—	Proof	1250.

NOTE: Later dates (1901-1906) exist for this type.

10 CENTS

2.7210 g, .900 SILVER, .0787 oz ASW
Mint mark: A
Rev. leg: TITRE 0.900. POIDS 2.721

KM#	Date	Mintage	Fine	VF	XF	Unc
2	1885	2.040	5.00	10.00	30.00	100.00
	1885	—	—	—	Proof	675.00
	1888	1.000	5.00	10.00	40.00	150.00
	1889	100 pcs.	—		Proof	875.00
	1892	.200	40.00	75.00	125.00	300.00
	1893	.600	15.00	25.00	65.00	165.00
	1894	.500	20.00	40.00	85.00	200.00
	1895	.600	20.00	40.00	75.00	175.00

2.7000 g, .900 SILVER, .0781 oz ASW
Rev. leg: TITRE 0.900. POIDS 2 GR. 7

KM#	Date	Mintage	Fine	VF	XF	Unc
2a	1895	.300	225.00	350.00	500.00	1000.
	1896 fasces	.650	30.00	75.00	125.00	250.00
	1896 torch	Inc. Ab.	60.00	100.00	175.00	450.00
	1897	.900	20.00	60.00	100.00	175.00

2.7000 g, .835 SILVER, .0725 oz ASW
Rev. leg: TITRE 0,835. POIDS 2 GR. 7

KM#	Date	Mintage	Fine	VF	XF	Unc
9	1898	.500	60.00	120.00	250.00	625.00
	1899	4.100	4.00	10.00	30.00	100.00
	1900	3.600	4.00	10.00	30.00	100.00
	1900	100 pcs.	—	—	Proof	1850.

NOTE: Later dates (1901-1919) exist for this type.

20 CENTS

5.4430 g, .900 SILVER, .1575 oz ASW
Mint mark: A
Rev. leg: TITRE 0.900. POIDS 5.443

KM#	Date	Mintage	Fine	VF	XF	Unc
3	1885	1.280	10.00	30.00	75.00	225.00
	1885	—	—	—	Proof	850.00
	1887	.250	40.00	100.00	175.00	375.00
	1887	—	—	—	Proof	500.00
	1889	100 pcs.	—	—	Proof	1100.
	1892	.200	50.00	100.00	225.00	500.00
	1893	.200	35.00	100.00	200.00	400.00
	1894	.250	30.00	70.00	150.00	400.00
	1895	.300	25.00	55.00	100.00	275.00

5.4000 g, .900 SILVER, .1562 oz ASW
Rev. leg: TITRE 0.900. POIDS 5 GR. 4

KM#	Date	Mintage	Fine	VF	XF	Unc
3a	1895	.250	50.00	100.00	250.00	700.00
	1896 torch	.300	60.00	125.00	400.00	850.00
	1896 fasces	I.A.	50.00	100.00	350.00	750.00
	1897	.300	50.00	100.00	350.00	700.00

5.4000 g, .835 SILVER, .1450 oz ASW

KM#	Date	Mintage	Fine	VF	XF	Unc
10	1898	.250	50.00	120.00	275.00	550.00
	1899	2.050	7.50	20.00	50.00	200.00
	1900	1.750	10.00	35.00	100.00	275.00
	1900	100 pcs.	—	—	Proof	2450.

NOTE: Later dates (1901-1916) exist for this type.

50 CENTS

13.6070 g, .900 SILVER, .3937 oz ASW
Mint mark: A
Rev. leg: TITRE 0.900. POIDS 13.607 GR.

KM#	Date	Mintage	Fine	VF	XF	Unc
4	1885	.040	100.00	175.00	400.00	1000.
	1885	—	—	—	Proof	2500.
	1889	100 pcs.	—	—	Proof	3350.
	1894	.100	35.00	100.00	300.00	675.00
	1895	.100	45.00	125.00	350.00	700.00

13.5000 g, .900 SILVER, .3906 oz ASW
Rev. leg: TITRE 0.900. POIDS 13 GR. 5

KM#	Date	Mintage	Fine	VF	XF	Unc
4a.1	1896	.110	35.00	85.00	250.00	600.00
	1900	—	—	—	—	—
	1900	100 pcs.	—	—	Proof	6150.

PIASTRE

27.2150 g, .900 SILVER, .7875 oz ASW
Mint mark: A
Rev. leg: TITRE 0.900 POIDS 27.215 GR.

KM#	Date	Mintage	Fine	VF	XF	Unc
5	1885	.800	25.00	50.00	150.00	450.00
	1885	—	—	—	Proof	6150.
	1886	3.216	10.00	20.00	65.00	225.00
	1886	—	—	—	Proof	3700.
	1887	3.076	10.00	20.00	65.00	225.00
	1888	.948	20.00	40.00	100.00	350.00
	1889	1.240	15.00	25.00	75.00	300.00
	1889	100 pcs.	—	—	Proof	5750.
	1890	6,108	2000.	3000.	5000.	—
	1893	.795	25.00	50.00	110.00	400.00

KM#	Date	Mintage	Fine	VF	XF	Unc
5	1894	1.308	15.00	25.00	75.00	285.00
	1895	1.782	10.00	20.00	65.00	250.00

27.0000 g, .900 SILVER, .7812 oz ASW
Rev. leg: TITRE 0.900. POIDS 27 GR.

KM#	Date	Mintage	Fine	VF	XF	Unc
5a.1	1895	3.798	8.00	12.50	22.50	135.00
	1896	11.858	8.00	10.00	17.50	100.00
	1897	2.511	8.00	12.50	22.50	150.00
	1898	4.304	8.00	12.50	22.50	125.00
	1899	4.681	8.00	12.50	22.50	125.00
	1900	13.319	8.00	10.00	17.50	100.00
	1900	100 pcs.	—	—	Proof	7250.

NOTE: Later dates (1901-1928) exist for this type.

ESSAIS (E)

Standard metals unless otherwise noted

KM#	Date	Mintage	Identification	Mkt.Val.
E1	1887(a)	—	1 Sapeque, Copper-Nickel, w/o mm, 16 sided, KM6	175.00
E2	1895	—	1 Cent, Copper-Nickel, KM7	—
E3	1896A	—	1 Cent, w/ESSAI	80.00
E4	1896	—	1 Cent, Tin	1000.
E5	1896	—	1 Cent, Zinc, w/o mint mark, ESSAI on rev., KM4	—
E6	1897A	—	1 Cent, Copper-Nickel, w/o Essai, Y3	150.00

PIEFORTS (P)

KM#	Date	Mintage	Identification	Mkt.Val.
P1	1896	—	1 Cent, Bronze, BRONZE ESSAI on edge, KM8	245.00

PROOF SETS (PS)

KM#	Date	Mintage	Identification	Issue Price	Mkt. Val.
PS1	1889(6)	100	KM1-6	—	12,300.
PS2	1900(6)	100	KM4a.1-5a.1,6,8-10	—	19,450.

NOTE: The Superior Irving Goodman sale 5-95 offered many well matched choice proof pieces. The values given here and in the individual listings above are reflective of the prices realized in this sale. Less attractive proofs may be valued at as little as 1/2 to 1/3 of these figures.

FRENCH WEST AFRICA

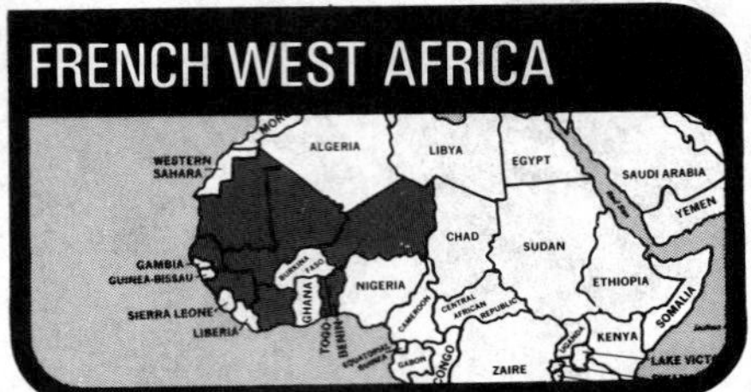

French West Africa (Afrique Occidentale Francaise), a former federation of French colonial territories on the northwest coast of Africa, had an area of 1,831,079 sq. mi. (4,742,495 sq. km.) and a population of about 17.4 million. Capital: Dakar. The constituent territories were Mauritania, Senegal, Dahomey, French Sudan, Ivory Coast, Upper Volta, Niger, French Guinea, and later on the mandated area of Togo. Peanuts, palm kernels, cacao, coffee and bananas were exported.

Prior to the mid-19th century, France, as the other European states, maintained establishments on the west coast of Africa for the purpose of trading in slaves and gum, but made no serious attempt at colonization. From 1854 onward, the coastal settlements were gradually extended into the interior until, by the opening of the 20th century, acquisition ended and organization and development began. French West Africa was formed in 1895 by grouping the several colonies under one administration (at Dakar) while retaining a large measure of autonomy to each of the constituent territories. The inhabitants of French West Africa were made French citizens in 1946. With the exception of French Guinea, all of the colonies voted in 1958 to become autonomous members of the new French Community. French Guinea voted to become the fully independent Republic of Guinea. The present-day independent states are members of the "Union Monetaire Ouest-Africaine".

For later coinage see West African States.

RULERS

French

MONETARY SYSTEM

100 Centimes = 1 Franc
5 Francs = 1 Unit

TOKEN ISSUES (Tn)

(GABON, MIDDLE CONGO, EQUATORIAL AFRICA)

In 1883, Savorgnan de Brazza replaced existing paper currencies with a series of eight metal tokens. The five lower denominations, cut from sheet zinc, marked with an "F", lacked denominations but were identifiable to value by the shape in which they were cut. The three high values were struck on brass planchets. This issue was made legal tender in 1887 and circulated until September 19, 1888, the day of the fire at the station at Franceville. Rather than scrap all the damaged tokens, the zinc pieces were countermarked with an additional "P". A new issue of the regular zinc tokens was made in 1893.

0.10 FRANC

ZINC, Uniface
Countermarked F

KM#	Date	Good	VG	Fine	VF
Tn1	ND (1883,93)	15.00	25.00	45.00	85.00
	Additional mark P				
Tn9	ND (1888)	25.00	40.00	75.00	135.00

0.20 FRANC

ZINC, Uniface
Countermarked F

KM#	Date	Good	VG	Fine	VF
Tn2	ND (1883,93)	15.00	25.00	45.00	90.00
	Additional mark P				
Tn10	ND (1888)	25.00	40.00	75.00	140.00

0.50 FRANC

ZINC Uniface
Countermarked F

KM#	Date	Good	VG	Fine	VF
Tn3	ND (1883,93)	15.00	25.00	45.00	85.00
	Additional mark P				
Tn11	ND (1888)	25.00	40.00	75.00	140.00

FRANC

ZINC, Uniface
Countermarked F

KM#	Date	Good	VG	Fine	VF
Tn4	ND (1883,93)	18.00	30.00	50.00	95.00

Additional mark P

KM#	Date	Good	VG	Fine	VF
Tn12	ND (1888)	35.00	55.00	85.00	165.00

1.50 FRANCS

ZINC, Uniface
Countermarked F

KM#	Date	Good	VG	Fine	VF
Tn5	ND (1883,93)	20.00	35.00	65.00	110.00

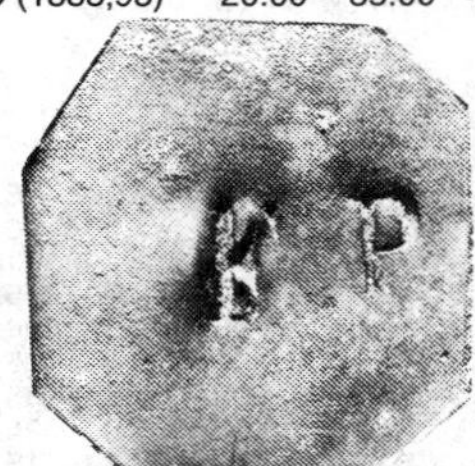

Additional mark P

KM#	Date	Good	VG	Fine	VF
Tn13	ND (1888)	35.00	60.00	90.00	180.00

1 UNIT

(5 Francs)

BRASS
Similar to Tn7.

KM#	Date	Mintage	Fine	VF	XF	Unc
Tn6	1883	—	55.00	85.00	225.00	350.00

5 UNITS

(25 Francs)

BRASS

KM#	Date	Mintage	Fine	VF	XF	Unc
Tn7	1883	—	75.00	125.00	300.00	425.00

10 UNITS

(50 Francs)

BRASS
Similar to Tn7.

KM#	Date	Mintage	Fine	VF	XF	Unc
Tn8	1883	—	100.00	150.00	350.00	500.00

GEORGIA

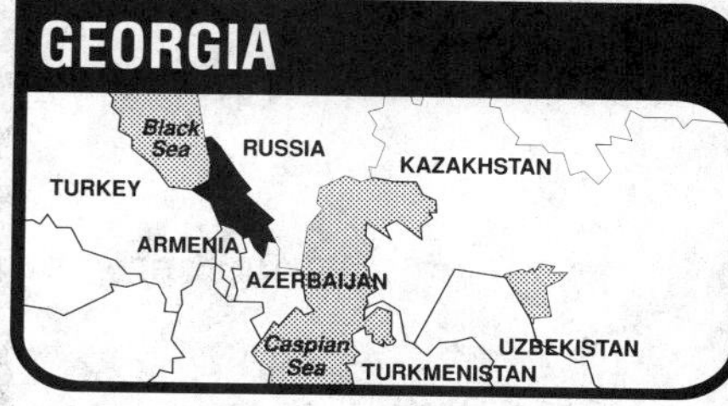

Georgia (formerly the Georgian Social Democratic Republic under the U.S.S.R.), is bounded by the Black Sea to the west and by Turkey, Armenia and Azerbaijan. It occupies the western part of Transcaucasia covering an area of 26,900 sq. mi. (69,700 sq. km.) and a population of 5.7 million. Capitol: Tbilisi. Hydroelectricity, minerals, forestry and agriculture are the chief industries.

The Georgian dynasty first emerged after the Macedonian victory over the Achaemenid Persian empire in the 4th century B.C. Roman "friendship" was imposed in 65 B.C. after Pompey's victory over Mithradates. The Georgians embraced Christianity in the 4th century A.D. During the next three centuries Georgia was involved in the ongoing conflicts between the Byzantine and Persian empires. The latter developed control until Georgia regained its independence in 450-503 A.D. but then it reverted to a Persian province in 533 A.D., then restored as a kingdom by the Byzantines in 562 A.D. It was established as an Arab emirate in the 8th century. The Seljuk Turks invaded but the crusades thwarted their interests. Over the following centuries, Turkish and Persian rivalries along with civil strife divided the area under the two influences.

Through significant contributions of Georgian kings (King David the Builder 1089-1124 and King Tamara 1136-1224), Georgia reached its peak of political, economic, and military development from the XI - to the XIII century. During these centuries the significant architectural and literary masterpieces that had won international recognition were created. Georgia had also regained territories that had been invaded by Islamic countries.

Czarist Russian interests increased and a treaty of alliance was signed on July 24, 1773 whereby Russia guaranteed Georgian independence and it acknowledged Russian suzerainty. Persia invaded again in 1795 leaving Tiflis in ruins. Russia slowly took over annexing piece by piece and soon developed total domination. After the Russian Revolution the Georgians, Armenians, and Azerbaijanis formed the short-lived Transcaucasian Federal Republic on Sept. 20, 1917 which broke up into three independent republics on May 26, 1918. A Germano-Georgian treaty was signed on May 28, 1918, followed by a Turko-Georgian peace treaty on June 4. The end of WW I and the collapse of the central powers allowed free elections.

On May 20, 1920, Soviet Russia concluded a peace treaty, recognizing its independence, but later invaded on Feb. 11, 1921 and a soviet republic was proclaimed. On March 12, 1922 Stalin included Georgia in a newly formed Transcaucasian Soviet Federated Socialist Republic. On Dec. 5, 1936 the T.S.F.S.R. was dissolved and Georgia became a direct member of the U.S.S.R. The collapse of the U.S.S.R. allowed full transition to independence and on April 9, 1991 a unanimous vote declared the republic an independent state based on its original treaty of independence of May, 1918.

RUSSIAN ISSUES

Struck under the authority of Alexander I (1801-25) and Nicholas I (1825-55) of Russia at the Tiflis (Tbilisi) Mint.

MINTMASTERS INITIALS

Letter	Date	Name
TT3	1804-1806	Peter Zaitsev
AK	1806-1824	Alexei Karpinski
AT	1810-1831	Alexander Trifonov
BK	1831-1833	Vasili Kleimenov

MONETARY SYSTEM

5 Dinars = 1 Puli
2 Puli = 1 Kopek
4 Puli = 1 Bisti
50 Bisti = 1 Abaze

DATING

The dates are shown in a quantitive manner ex. 1000 plus 800 plus 10 plus 9 = 1819.

NOTE: The fine style 1 and 2 Abaze coins of 1828 are patterns, struck at St. Petersburg.

PULI
(1/2 Kopek)

COPPER

KM#	Date	Mintage	VG	Fine	VF	XF
70	1804	4,000	—	—	Rare	—
	1805	Inc. Ab.	50.00	100.00	175.00	275.00
	1806	.015	50.00	100.00	175.00	275.00

2 PULI
(Kopek)

COPPER

KM#	Date	Mintage	VG	Fine	VF	XF
71	1804	3,000	—	—	Rare	—
	1805	Inc. Ab.	60.00	120.00	200.00	325.00
	1806	.034	30.00	60.00	100.00	150.00
	1808	.012	30.00	60.00	100.00	150.00
	1810	.050	30.00	60.00	100.00	150.00

BISTI
(2 Kopeks)

COPPER

KM#	Date	Mintage	VG	Fine	VF	XF
72	1804	1,000	—	—	Rare	—
	1805	Inc. Ab.	65.00	125.00	175.00	275.00
	1806	.025	20.00	40.00	80.00	150.00
	1808	.020	20.00	40.00	80.00	150.00
	1810	.315	20.00	40.00	80.00	150.00

1/2 ABAZI
(10 Kopeks)

.917 SILVER

KM#	Date	Mintage	VG	Fine	VF	XF
73	1804 ПЗ	5,000	35.00	75.00	150.00	300.00
	1805 ПЗ	I.A.	25.00	50.00	100.00	200.00
	1806 AK	1,070	—	—	Rare	—
	1807 AK	80 pcs.	—	—	Rare	—
	1810 AT	398 pcs.	—	—	Rare	—
	1813 AT	2,000	—	—	Rare	—
	1820 AT	4,000	30.00	60.00	110.00	225.00
	1821 AT	I.A.	25.00	50.00	100.00	200.00
	1822 AK	1,000	25.00	50.00	100.00	200.00
	1823 AK	4,000	25.00	50.00	100.00	200.00
	1824 AK	4,000	25.00	50.00	100.00	200.00
	1826 AT	5,000	25.00	50.00	100.00	200.00
	1827 AT	7,000	25.00	50.00	100.00	200.00
	1828 AT	.016	20.00	30.00	60.00	100.00
	1831 AT	—	25.00	50.00	100.00	225.00
	1832 BK	—	25.00	50.00	100.00	200.00
	1833 BK	—	25.00	50.00	95.00	200.00

ABAZI
(20 Kopeks)

SILVER, 19mm

KM#	Date	Mintage	VG	Fine	VF	XF
74	1804 ПЗ	—	35.00	75.00	150.00	300.00
	1805 ПЗ	.019	20.00	30.00	45.00	65.00
	1806 ПЗ	.023	20.00	30.00	50.00	80.00
	1806 AK	I.A.	20.00	30.00	45.00	65.00
	1807 AK	9,000	20.00	30.00	45.00	65.00
	1808 AK	.014	20.00	30.00	45.00	65.00
	1809 AK	.017	20.00	30.00	45.00	65.00
	1810 AT	4,000	25.00	50.00	75.00	110.00
	1811 AT	1,000	—	—	Rare	—
	1812 AT	9,000	20.00	30.00	50.00	80.00
	1813 AT	7,000	20.00	30.00	50.00	80.00
	1814 AT	3,000	20.00	30.00	45.00	65.00
	1815 AT	3,000	25.00	40.00	60.00	90.00
	1816 AT	.012	20.00	30.00	45.00	65.00
	1818 AT	8,000	20.00	30.00	45.00	65.00
	1819 AT	.010	20.00	30.00	45.00	65.00
	1820 AT	.012	20.00	30.00	45.00	65.00
	1821 AT	.014	20.00	30.00	45.00	65.00
	1822 AT	5,000	25.00	40.00	60.00	90.00

KM#	Date	Mintage	VG	Fine	VF	XF
74	1822 AK	I.A.	20.00	30.00	45.00	65.00
	1823 AK	5,000	20.00	30.00	45.00	65.00
	1824 AK	5,000	20.00	30.00	45.00	65.00
	1826 AT	5,000	20.00	30.00	45.00	65.00
	1828 AT	—	—	—	Rare	—
	1830 AT	—	20.00	30.00	45.00	65.00
	1831 AT	—	20.00	30.00	45.00	65.00

2 ABAZI
(40 Kopeks)

.917 SILVER, 23mm

KM#	Date	Mintage	VG	Fine	VF	XF
75	1804 ПЗ	.033	35.00	75.00	150.00	300.00
	1805 ПЗ	I.A.	20.00	30.00	50.00	80.00
	1806 AK	.042	20.00	30.00	50.00	80.00
	1807 AK	.071	20.00	30.00	50.00	80.00
	1807 AT	I.A.	30.00	60.00	90.00	150.00
	1808 AK	.065	20.00	30.00	50.00	80.00
	1809 AK	.086	20.00	30.00	50.00	80.00
	1810 AK	.020	25.00	35.00	55.00	85.00
	1811 AT	.005	25.00	40.00	60.00	90.00
	1812 AT	.059	20.00	30.00	50.00	80.00
	1813 AT	.048	20.00	30.00	50.00	80.00
	1814 AT	.020	20.00	30.00	50.00	80.00
	1815 AT	.021	20.00	30.00	50.00	80.00
	1816 AT	.079	20.00	30.00	50.00	80.00
	1818 AT	.085	20.00	30.00	50.00	80.00
	1819 AT	.105	20.00	30.00	50.00	80.00
	1820 AT	.112	20.00	30.00	50.00	80.00
	1821 AT	.075	20.00	30.00	50.00	80.00
	1822 AT	.024	25.00	45.00	65.00	100.00
	1822 AK	I.A.	20.00	30.00	50.00	80.00
	1823 AK	.039	20.00	30.00	50.00	80.00
	1824 AK	.032	20.00	30.00	50.00	80.00
	1826 AT	.075	20.00	30.00	50.00	80.00
	1827 AT	.172	20.00	30.00	50.00	80.00
	1828 AT	.126	20.00	30.00	50.00	80.00
	1829 AT	.213	18.00	25.00	40.00	60.00
	1830 AT	.273	18.00	25.00	40.00	60.00
	1831 AT	.338	18.00	25.00	40.00	60.00
	1831 BK	I.A.	18.00	25.00	40.00	60.00
	1832 BK	.210	18.00	25.00	40.00	60.00
	1833 BK	.114	20.00	30.00	50.00	80.00

ESSAIS (E)

Standard metals unless otherwise noted

KM#	Date	Mintage	Identification	Mkt.Val.
E1	1828	—	1 Abazi, KM74	—
E2	1828	—	2 Abazi, KM75	—

PATTERNS (Pn)

(Including off metal strikes)

KM#	Date	Mintage	Identification	Mkt.Val.
Pn1	1804	—	1 Abazi, Silver, 20 (Kopeks) KM74	—

1 Aachen
2 Anhalt-Bernburg
3 Anhalt-Dessau
4 Baden
5 Bavaria
6 Berg
7 Birkenfeld
8 Brandenburg-Ansbach Bayreuth
9 Brunswick-Luneburg & Wolfenbuttel
10 Cleve
11 Coesfeld
12 Corvey
13 East Friesland
14 Eichstadt
15 Erfurt
16 Freising
17 Friedberg
18 Fulda
19 Furstenberg
20 Halle
21 Hannover
22 Hesse-Cassel
23 Hesse-Darmstadt
24 Hildesheim
25 Hohenzollern
26 Jever
27 Julich
28 Knyphausen
29 Lauenburg
30 Lippe-Detmold
31 Mainz
32 Mansfeld
33 Mecklenburg-Schwerin
34 Mecklenburg-Strelitz
35 Muhlhausen
36 Munster
37 Nassau
38 Oldenburg
39 Osnabruck
40 Paderborn
41 Passau
42 Prussia
43 Pyrmont
44 Reuss-Greiz
45 Reuss-Schleiz
46 Rhein-Pfalz
47 Saxe-Altenburg
48 Saxe-Coburg-Gotha
49 Saxe-Meiningen
50 Saxe-Weimar-Eisenach
51 Saxony
52 Schaumberg-Hessen & Lippe
53 Schleswig-Holstein
54 Schwarzburg-Rudolstadt
55 Schwarzburg Sonderhausen
56 Stolberg-Wernigerode
57 Trier
58 Wallmoden-Pyrmont
59 Wallmoden-Gimborn
60 Wurttemberg
61 Wurzburg

GERMAN STATES

Although the origin of the German Empire can be traced to the Treaty of Verdun that ceded Charlemagne's lands east of the Rhine to German Prince Louis, it was for centuries little more than a geographic expression, consisting of hundreds of effectively autonomous big and little states. Nominally the states owed their allegiance to the Holy Roman Emperor, who was also a German king, but as the Emperors exhibited less and less concern for Germany the actual power devolved on the lords of the individual states. The fragmentation of the empire climaxed with the tragic denouement of the Thirty Years War, 1618-48, which devastated much of Germany, destroyed its agriculture and medieval commercial eminence and ended the attempt of the Hapsburgs to unify Germany. Deprived of administrative capacity by a lack of resources, the imperial authority became utterly powerless. At this time Germany contained an estimated 1,800 individual states, some with a population of as little as 300. The German Empire of recent history (the creation of Bismarck) was formed on April 14, 1871, when the king of Prussia became German Emperor William I. The new empire comprised 4 kingdoms, 6 grand duchies, 12 duchies and principalities, 3 free cities and the nonautonomous province of Alsace-Lorraine. The states had the right to issue gold and silver coins of higher value than 1 Mark; coins of 1 Mark and under were general issues of the empire.

MINT MARKS

A - Berlin, 1750-date
A - Clausthal (Hannover) 1833-1849
B - Bayreuth, Franconia (Prussia) 1796-1804
B - Breslau (Prussia, Silesia) 1750-1826
B - Brunswick (Brunswick) 1850-1860
B - Brunswick (Westphalia) 1809-1813
B - Dresden (Saxony) 1861-1872
B - Hannover (Brunswick) 1860-1871
B - Hannover (East Friesland) 1823-1825
B - Hannover (Germany) 1872-1878
B - Hannover (Hannover) 1821-1866
B - Hannover (Prussia) 1866-1873
B - Regensburg (Regensburg) 1809
B.H. Frankfurt (Free City of Frankfurt) 1808
B (rosette) H - Regensburg (Rhenish Confederation) 1802-1812
C - Cassel (Westphalia) 1810-1813
C - Clausthal (Brunswick)
C - Clausthal (Hannover) 1813-1834
C - Clausthal (Westphalia) 1810-1811
C - Dresden (Saxony) 1779-1804
C - Frankfurt (Germany) 1866-1879
D - Aurich (East Friesland under Prussia) 1750-1806
D - Dusseldorf, Rhineland (Prussia) 1816-1848
D - Munich (Germany) 1872-date
E - Dresden (Germany) 1872-1887
E - Muldenhutte (Germany) 1887-1953
F - Dresden (Saxony) 1845-1858
F - Magdeburg (Prussia) 1750-1806
F - Cassel (Hesse-Cassel) 1803-1807
F - Stuttgart (Germany) 1872-date
G - Dresden (Saxony) 1833-1844, 1850-1854
G - Glatz (Prussian Silesia) 1807-1809
G - Karlsruhe (Germany) 1872-date
G - Stettin In Pomerania (Prussia) 1750-1806
GN-BW - Bamberg (Bamberg)
H - Darmstadt (Germany) 1872-1882
H - Dresden (Saxony) 1804-1812
H.K. - Rostock (Rostock) 1862-1864
I - Hamburg (Germany)
J - Hamburg (Germany) 1873-date
J - Paris (Westphalia) 1808-1809
M.C. - Brunswick (Brunswick) 1813-14, 1820
P.R. - Dusseldorf (Julich-Berg) 1783-1804
S - Dresden (Saxony) 1813-1832
S - Hannover (Hannover) 1839-1844

MONETARY SYSTEM

Until 1871 the Mark (Marck) was a measure of weight.

North German States until 1837

2 Heller = 1 Pfennig
8 Pfennige = 1 Mariengroschen
12 Pfennige = 1 Groschen
24 Groschen = 1 Thaler
2 Gulden = 1-1/3 Reichsthaler
1 Speciesthaler (before 1753)
1 Convention Thaler (after 1753)

North German States after 1837

12 Pfennige = 1 Groschen
30 Groschen = 1 Thaler
1 Vereinsthaler (after 1857)

South German States until 1837

8 Heller = 4 Pfennige = 1 Kreuzer
24 Kreuzer Landmunze = 20 Kreuzer Convention Munze
120 Convention Kreuzer = 2 Convention Gulden = 1 Convention Thaler

South German States after 1837

8 Heller = 4 Pfennige = 1 Kreuzer

German States 1857-1871

As a result of the Monetary Convention of 1857, all the German States adopted a Vereinsthaler of uniform weight being 1/30 fine pound silver. They did continue to use their regional minor coin units to divide the Vereinsthaler for small change purposes.

After the German unification in 1871 when the old Thaler system was abandoned in favor of the Mark system (100 Pfennig = 1 Mark) the Vereinsthaler continued to circulate as a legal tender 3 Mark coin, and the double Thaler as a 6 Mark coin until 1908. In 1908 the Vereinsthalers were officially demonetized and the Thaler coinage was replaced by the new 3 Mark coin which had the same specifications as the old Vereinsthaler. The double Thaler coinage was not replaced as there was no great demand for a 6 Mark coin. Until the 1930's the German public continued to refer to the 3 Mark piece as a "Thaler".

Commencing 1871
100 Pfennig = 1 Mark

ANHALT-BERNBURG

Located in north-central Germany. Appeared as part of the patrimony of Albrecht the Bear of Brandenburg in 1170. Bracteates were first made in the 12th century. It was originally in the inheritance of Heinrich the Fat in 1252 and became extinct in 1468. The division of 1603, among the sons of Joachim Ernst, revitalized Anhalt-Bernburg. Bernburg passed to Dessau after the death of Alexander Carl in 1863.

RULERS

Alexius Friedrich Christian, 1796-1834
Alexander Carl, 1834-1863

MINTMASTERS INITIALS

Letter	Date	Name
HS	1795-1821	Hans Schluter
Z	1821-1848	Johann Carl Ludwig Zincken

PFENNIG

COPPER

KM#	Date	Mintage	Fine	VF	XF	Unc
74	1807	—	9.00	15.00	35.00	75.00

Rev. leg: SCHEIDE MUNTZ

KM#	Date	Mintage	Fine	VF	XF	Unc
76	1808	—	10.00	20.00	45.00	90.00

Rev. leg: SCHEIDEMUNZE, value: PFENNIG.

KM#	Date	Mintage	Fine	VF	XF	Unc
77.1	1822	—	7.00	12.00	25.00	60.00
	1823	—	7.00	12.00	25.00	60.00
	1827	—	7.00	12.00	25.00	60.00

Rev. leg: SCHEIDEMUNZE HZL ANHALT, value: PFENNING.

KM#	Date	Mintage	Fine	VF	XF	Unc
77.2	1831 Z	—	8.00	12.50	25.00	60.00

4 PFENNIG

COPPER

KM#	Date	Mintage	Fine	VF	XF	Unc
78.1	1822	—	8.00	16.50	40.00	85.00
	1823	—	8.00	16.50	40.00	85.00

Rev. value: 4 PFENNINGE

KM#	Date	Mintage	Fine	VF	XF	Unc
78.2	1831 Z	—	9.00	17.50	45.00	90.00

1/48 THALER

.9700 g, .250 SILVER, .0077 oz ASW
Obv: Crowned arms in branches. Rev: Value.

KM#	Date	Mintage	Fine	VF	XF	Unc
75	1807	—	10.00	20.00	48.00	100.00

1/24 THALER

1.9800 g, .350 SILVER, .0234 oz ASW
Rev. leg: HANH BERNB . . .

KM#	Date	Mintage	Fine	VF	XF	Unc
79	1822	—	7.50	15.00	30.00	65.00
	1823	—	7.50	15.00	30.00	65.00
	1827	—	7.50	15.00	30.00	65.00

Rev. leg: HZL. ANHALT. . .

KM#	Date	Mintage	Fine	VF	XF	Unc
81	1831 Z	—	7.50	15.00	30.00	75.00

1/6 THALER

5.3400 g, .520 SILVER, .0892 oz ASW

KM#	Date	Mintage	Fine	VF	XF	Unc
85	1856A	.060	15.00	30.00	50.00	100.00

KM#	Date	Mintage	Fine	VF	XF	Unc
87	1861A	.062	10.00	20.00	40.00	80.00
	1862A	.060	10.00	20.00	40.00	80.00

2/3 THALER

14.0300 g, .833 SILVER, .3757 oz ASW
Rev. leg: HERZOG ZU ANHALT. . .

KM#	Date	Mintage	Fine	VF	XF	Unc
72	1806 HS	—	35.00	75.00	125.00	185.00
	1808 HS	—	50.00	100.00	150.00	220.00
	1809 HS	—	35.00	75.00	125.00	185.00

THALER

(Convention)

28.0600 g, .833 SILVER, .7515 oz ASW

KM#	Date	Mintage	Fine	VF	XF	Unc
73	1806 HS	—	250.00	500.00	1200.	3500.
	1809 HS	—	400.00	800.00	2000.	5000.

(Mining)

22.2700 g, .750 SILVER, .5370 oz ASW

KM#	Date	Mintage	Fine	VF	XF	Unc
82	1834	.015	35.00	75.00	175.00	400.00

KM#	Date	Mintage	Fine	VF	XF	Unc
84	1846A	.010	25.00	45.00	85.00	175.00
	1852A	.010	25.00	45.00	85.00	175.00
	1855A	.020	20.00	35.00	65.00	160.00

(Vereins)

18.5200 g, .900 SILVER, .5358 oz ASW

KM#	Date	Mintage	Fine	VF	XF	Unc
86	1859A	.024	40.00	65.00	150.00	325.00

(Mining)

KM#	Date	Mintage	Fine	VF	XF	Unc
88	1861A	.010	25.00	45.00	85.00	175.00
	1862A	.020	20.00	35.00	65.00	160.00

2 THALER

(3-1/2 Gulden)

37.1200 g, .900 SILVER, 1.0741 oz ASW

KM#	Date	Mintage	Fine	VF	XF	Unc
83	1840A	3,600	350.00	500.00	800.00	1750.
	1845A	7,200	300.00	450.00	700.00	1650.
	1855A	5,000	300.00	450.00	700.00	1650.

TRADE COINAGE

DUCAT

3.5000 g, .986 GOLD, .1109 oz AGW
Obv. leg: EX AURO ANHALTINO.
Rev. leg: ALEXIUS FRIED CHRIST. . .

KM#	Date	Mintage	Fine	VF	XF	Unc
80	1825 Z	116 pcs.	850.00	1400.	2400.	3500.

JOINT COINAGE

UNDER ALEXANDER CARL
FOR ANHALT-COTHEN
AND ANHALT-DESSAU

PFENNIG

COPPER
Rev. leg: 288 EINEN THALER.

KM#	Date	Mintage	Fine	VF	XF	Unc
91	1839	.589	3.00	6.00	15.00	65.00
	1840	.654	3.00	6.00	15.00	65.00

KM#	Date	Mintage	Fine	VF	XF	Unc
96	1856A	.360	2.00	4.00	8.00	35.00
	1862A	.360	2.00	4.00	8.00	35.00
	1864A	.300	2.00	4.00	8.00	35.00
	1867B	.180	2.00	4.00	8.00	35.00

3 PFENNIGE

COPPER

KM#	Date	Mintage	Fine	VF	XF	Unc
92	1839	.386	3.00	6.00	15.00	65.00
	1840	.292	3.00	6.00	15.00	65.00

KM#	Date	Mintage	Fine	VF	XF	Unc
98	1861A	.240	2.50	5.00	12.50	50.00
	1864A	.200	2.50	5.00	12.50	50.00
	1867B	.240	2.50	5.00	12.50	50.00

6 PFENNIGE

.8100 g, .375 SILVER, .0097 oz ASW

KM#	Date	Mintage	Fine	VF	XF	Unc
94	1840	.322	3.00	6.00	20.00	85.00

GROSCHEN

1.6200 g, .375 SILVER, .0195 oz ASW
Obv: Crowned shield. Rev. leg: 24 EINEN THALER.

KM#	Date	Mintage	Fine	VF	XF	Unc
93	1839	.319	2.00	4.50	12.00	48.00
	1840	Inc. Ab.	2.00	4.50	12.00	48.00

SILBERGROSCHEN

2.1900 g, .222 SILVER, .0156 oz ASW

KM#	Date	Mintage	Fine	VF	XF	Unc
95	1851A	.176	2.00	4.50	12.50	50.00
	1852A	.197	2.00	4.50	12.50	50.00
	1855A	.303	2.00	4.50	12.50	50.00
	1859A	.150	2.00	4.50	12.50	50.00
	1862A	.300	2.00	4.50	12.50	50.00

2-1/2 SILBERGROSCHEN

3.2400 g, .375 SILVER, .0390 oz ASW

KM#	Date	Mintage	Fine	VF	XF	Unc
97	1856A	.120	2.50	5.50	15.00	70.00
	1859A	.060	2.50	5.50	15.00	70.00
	1861A	.120	2.50	5.50	15.00	70.00
	1862A	.240	2.50	5.50	15.00	70.00
	1864A	.120	2.50	5.50	15.00	70.00

ANHALT-COTHEN

Cothen has a checkered history after the patrimony of Heinrich the Fat in 1252. It was often ruled with other segments of the House of Anhalt. Founded as a separate line in 1603, became extinct in 1665 and passed to Plotzkau which changed the name to Cothen. It passed to Dessau after the death of Heinrich in 1847.

RULERS

Heinrich, 1830-1847

2 THALER

(3-1/2 Gulden)

37.1200 g, .900 SILVER, 1.0743 oz ASW

KM#	Date	Mintage	Fine	VF	XF	Unc
39	1840A	3,100	400.00	850.00	2750.	6000.

ANHALT-DESSAU

Dessau was part of the 1252 division that included Zerbst and Cothen. In 1396 Zerbst divided into Zerbst and Dessau. In 1508 Zerbst was absorbed into Dessau. Dessau was given to the eldest son of Joachim Ernst in the division of 1603. As other lines became extinct, they fell to Dessau, which united all branches in 1863.

RULERS

Leopold Friedrich Franz, 1751-1817
Leopold Friedrich, 1817-1871
Friedrich I, 1871-1904

VI EINEN (1/6) THALER

5.3400 g, .520 SILVER, .0892 oz ASW

KM#	Date	Mintage	Fine	VF	XF	Unc
19	1865A	.120	12.50	25.00	50.00	150.00

EIN (1) THALER

(Vereins)

18.5200 g, .900 SILVER, .5359 oz ASW
Leopold Friedrich

KM#	Date	Mintage	Fine	VF	XF	Unc
14	1858A	.027	30.00	60.00	125.00	350.00

Separation of Anhalt Duchies - 1603
Reunion of Anhalt Duchies - 1863

KM#	Date	Mintage	Fine	VF	XF	Unc
15	1863A	.050	30.00	60.00	100.00	200.00

KM#	Date	Mintage	Fine	VF	XF	Unc
20	1866A	.031	30.00	60.00	120.00	275.00
	1869A	.032	30.00	60.00	100.00	250.00

2 THALER

(3-1/2 Gulden)

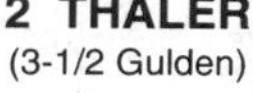

37.1200 g, .900 SILVER, 1.0741 oz ASW
Leopold Friedrich

KM#	Date	Mintage	Fine	VF	XF	Unc
13	1839A	4,700	250.00	500.00	800.00	1500.
	1843A	4,700	250.00	500.00	800.00	1500.
	1846A	4,700	250.00	500.00	800.00	1500.

MONETARY REFORM

2 MARK

11.1110 g, .900 SILVER, .3215 oz ASW
Friedrich I

KM#	Date	Mintage	Fine	VF	XF	Unc
22	1876A	.200	100.00	200.00	600.00	1150.

25th Year of Reign of Friedrich I

KM#	Date	Mintage	Fine	VF	XF	Unc
23	1896A	.050	175.00	350.00	575.00	900.00
	1896A	—	—	—	Proof	1000.

5 MARK

27.7770 g, .900 SILVER, .8038 oz ASW
25th Year of Reign of Friedrich I

KM#	Date	Mintage	Fine	VF	XF	Unc
24	1896A	.010	500.00	800.00	1500.	2000.
	1896A	—	—	—	Proof	2500.

10 MARK

3.9820 g, .900 GOLD, .1152 oz AGW
Friedrich I

KM#	Date	Mintage	Fine	VF	XF	Unc
25	1896A	.020	450.00	750.00	1000.	1500.
	1896A	200 pcs.	—	—	Proof	1600.

NOTE: Later date (1901) exists for this type.

20 MARK

7.9650 g, .900 GOLD, .2304 oz AGW
Friedrich I

KM#	Date	Mintage	Fine	VF	XF	Unc
21	1875A	.025	450.00	800.00	1200.	1700.
	1875A	—	—	—	Proof	3500.

KM#	Date	Mintage	Fine	VF	XF	Unc
26	1896A	.015	450.00	750.00	1100.	1500.
	1896A	200 pcs.	—	—	Proof	2000.

NOTE: Later date (1901) exists for this type.

AUGSBURG

FREE CITY

Founded as a Roman colony in the reign of Augustus it was declared a Free City in 1276. The mint rights were granted in 1521 but the first coins are dated somewhat earlier. Augsburg was given to Bavaria in 1806.

HELLER

COPPER
Obv: Crowned arms. Rev: Value, date.

KM#	Date	Mintage	VG	Fine	VF	XF
188	1801	—	2.00	5.00	10.00	25.00

NOTE: Earlier dates (1780-1798) exist for this type.

Obv: State arms in oval shield.
Rev: Value and date.

KM#	Date	Mintage	Fine	VF	XF	Unc
190	1801	—	2.00	4.00	15.00	50.00
	1803	—	2.00	4.00	15.00	50.00
	1804	—	2.00	4.00	15.00	50.00
	1805	—	2.00	4.00	15.00	50.00

PFENNING

COPPER
Obv: Arms in shield.
Rev. inscription: STADTMYNZ.

KM#	Date	Mintage	VG	Fine	VF	XF
189	1801	—	3.00	6.00	12.00	30.00
	1802	—	3.00	6.00	12.00	30.00
	1803	—	3.00	6.00	12.00	30.00

NOTE: Earlier dates (1780-1800) exist for this type.

KM#	Date	Mintage	Fine	VF	XF	Unc
191	1803	—	2.50	5.00	15.00	50.00
	1804	—	2.50	5.00	15.00	50.00
	1805	—	2.50	5.00	15.00	50.00

Obv: Different arms.
Rev. inscription: STADT MUNZ.

KM#	Date	Mintage	Fine	VF	XF	Unc
192	1801	—	2.50	5.00	15.00	50.00
	1803	—	2.00	4.00	10.00	50.00
	1804	—	2.00	4.00	10.00	50.00
	1805	—	2.00	4.00	10.00	50.00

BADEN

Located in southwest Germany. The ruling house of Baden began in 1112. Various branches developed and religious wars between the branches were settled in1648. The branches unified under Baden-Durlach after the extinction of the Baden-Baden line in 1771. The last ruler abdicated at the end of World War I. The first coins were issued in the late 1300s.

BADEN LINE

RULERS

Extinct to Baden-Durlach

DURLACH LINE

RULERS

Karl Friedrich,
Margrave in all Baden, 1771-1803
As Elector, 1803-1806
As Grand Duke, 1806-1811
Karl Ludwig Friedrich, 1811-1818
Ludwig I, 1818-1830
Leopold I, 1830-1852
Ludwig II, 1852-1856, Insane and deposed
Friedrich I as Prince Regent, 1852-1856
As Grand Duke, 1856-1907

MINTMASTERS INITIALS

Letter	Date	Name
B	1778-1808	Johann Martin Buckle
B,HB	1790-1812	Johann Heinrich Boltschauser, die-cutter and mint warden
CS,S	1761-1811	Ernst Christoph Steinhauser, mint warden
FE	1802	Franz Eberle, mint warden

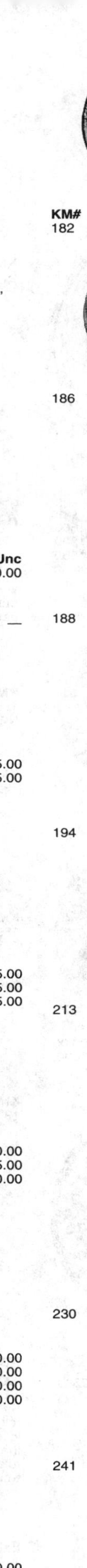

UNITED BADEN LINE

1/4 KREUZER

COPPER

KM#	Date	Mintage	Fine	VF	XF	Unc
132	1802	.024	15.00	25.00	150.00	300.00

Obv: Crowned shield. Rev: Value, date within wreath.

KM#	Date	Mintage	Fine	VF	XF	Unc
153	1810	—	—	—	Rare	—

KM#	Date	Mintage	Fine	VF	XF	Unc
181	1821	—	3.00	8.00	20.00	65.00
	1824	.128	3.00	8.00	20.00	65.00

1/2 KREUZER

COPPER

KM#	Date	Mintage	Fine	VF	XF	Unc
133	1803	.027	8.00	15.00	40.00	225.00
	1804	.104	8.00	15.00	25.00	175.00
	1805	.157	8.00	15.00	25.00	175.00

KM#	Date	Mintage	Fine	VF	XF	Unc
139	1809	.877	3.00	7.00	15.00	100.00
	1810	.129	3.00	7.00	15.00	125.00
	1812	.105	3.00	7.00	15.00	100.00

Obv: Crowned draped arms. Rev: Similar to KM#165.

KM#	Date	Mintage	Fine	VF	XF	Unc
164	1814	.078	3.00	7.00	20.00	100.00
	1815	.062	3.00	7.00	20.00	100.00
	1816	.039	3.00	7.00	20.00	100.00
	1817	.102	3.00	7.00	20.00	100.00

Obv: Smaller crowned draped arms.

KM#	Date	Mintage	Fine	VF	XF	Unc
165	1814	Inc. Ab.	3.00	7.00	15.00	80.00

Rev. value: 1/2 KREU/ZER

KM#	Date	Mintage	Fine	VF	XF	Unc
171	1817	—	3.00	7.00	15.00	80.00

KM#	Date	Mintage	Fine	VF	XF	Unc
182	1821	.127	3.00	7.00	15.00	70.00

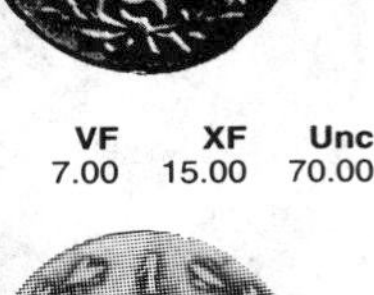

KM#	Date	Mintage	Fine	VF	XF	Unc
186	1822	.109	3.00	7.00	12.00	65.00
	1823	.035	3.00	7.00	15.00	110.00
	1824	.066	3.00	7.00	15.00	80.00
	1825	.053	3.00	7.00	15.00	90.00
	1826	.191	3.00	7.00	12.00	60.00

Ludwig I

KM#	Date	Mintage	Fine	VF	XF	Unc
188	1828	.137	3.00	7.00	15.00	75.00
	1829	.204	3.00	7.00	15.00	75.00
	1830	Inc. Ab.	3.00	7.00	15.00	75.00

Leopold I

Obv: D on truncation.

KM#	Date	Mintage	Fine	VF	XF	Unc
194	1830	.024	3.00	7.00	15.00	85.00
	1834	.076	3.00	7.00	12.00	60.00
	1835	.028	3.00	7.00	15.00	90.00

KM#	Date	Mintage	Fine	VF	XF	Unc
213	1842	.101	1.00	4.00	10.00	55.00
	1844	.052	1.00	4.00	10.00	65.00
	1845	.074	1.00	4.00	10.00	60.00
	1846	.090	1.00	4.00	10.00	60.00
	1847	.256	1.00	4.00	10.00	50.00
	1848	.089	1.00	4.00	10.00	60.00
	1849	.102	1.00	4.00	10.00	55.00
	1850	.074	1.00	4.00	10.00	60.00
	1851/0	.087	1.00	4.00	10.00	65.00
	1851	Inc. Ab.	1.00	4.00	10.00	60.00
	1852	.227	1.00	4.00	10.00	50.00

Friedrich I

KM#	Date	Mintage	Fine	VF	XF	Unc
230	1856	.195	1.00	4.00	10.00	45.00

KM#	Date	Mintage	Fine	VF	XF	Unc
241	1859	.219	1.00	2.00	10.00	35.00
	1860	.120	1.00	2.00	10.00	45.00
	1861	.109	1.00	2.00	10.00	45.00
	1862	.117	1.00	2.00	10.00	45.00
	1863	.298	1.00	2.00	10.00	35.00
	1864	.094	2.00	4.00	12.00	50.00
	1865	.349	1.00	2.00	10.00	35.00
	1866	.239	1.00	2.00	10.00	35.00
	1867	—	1.00	2.00	10.00	35.00
	1870	.038	5.00	10.00	25.00	125.00
	1871	—	1.75	6.00	15.00	35.00

EIN (1) KREUZER

COPPER

KM#	Date	Mintage	Fine	VF	XF	Unc
134	1803	.146	10.00	20.00	35.00	200.00
	1805	.096	10.00	20.00	35.00	200.00
	1806	—	—	—	Rare	—

KM#	Date	Mintage	Fine	VF	XF	Unc
141	1807	.096	6.00	14.00	30.00	125.00
	1808	1.704	3.00	7.00	15.00	65.00

KM#	Date	Mintage	Fine	VF	XF	Unc
147	1809	1.263	3.00	7.00	10.00	75.00
	1810	.639	3.00	7.00	10.00	75.00
	1811	.125	3.00	7.00	10.00	75.00
	1812	.285	3.00	10.00	50.00	125.00

Obv: Leg., crowned arms. Rev. value: 1 KREUZ/ER, date.

KM#	Date	Mintage	Fine	VF	XF	Unc
157	1813	—	3.00	6.00	15.00	100.00

Rev. value: 1/KREUZER/1813 within circle of dots.

KM#	Date	Mintage	Fine	VF	XF	Unc
158	1813	.320	3.00	6.00	15.00	100.00

KM#	Date	Mintage	Fine	VF	XF	Unc
159	1813	—	3.00	6.00	15.00	100.00

KM#	Date	Mintage	Fine	VF	XF	Unc
160	1813	—	3.00	6.00	15.00	100.00

Obv: Date between dots.

KM#	Date	Mintage	Fine	VF	XF	Unc
166.1	1814	.489	3.00	6.00	15.00	100.00

Obv: Date between stars.

KM#	Date	Mintage	Fine	VF	XF	Unc
166.2	1814	Inc. Ab.	3.00	7.00	10.00	65.00
	1815	.490	3.00	7.00	10.00	65.00
	1816	.464	3.00	7.00	10.00	65.00
	1817	.327	3.00	7.00	10.00	65.00

Obv: Date between crosses.

KM#	Date	Mintage	Fine	VF	XF	Unc
166.3	1815	—	3.00	7.00	10.00	65.00

Rev. value: 1 KREU=/ZER

KM#	Date	Mintage	Fine	VF	XF	Unc
167	1814	—	3.00	7.00	10.00	65.00
	1815	.490	3.00	7.00	10.00	65.00
	1816	.464	3.00	7.00	10.00	65.00
	1817	Inc. Ab.	3.00	7.00	10.00	65.00
	1820	—	3.00	7.00	10.00	65.00

KM#	Date	Mintage	Fine	VF	XF	Unc
183	1821	.055	3.00	7.00	10.00	65.00
	1822	.197	3.00	7.00	10.00	65.00
	1823	.205	3.00	7.00	10.00	65.00
	1824	.253	3.00	7.00	10.00	65.00
	1825	.335	3.00	7.00	10.00	65.00
	1826	—	3.00	7.00	10.00	65.00

Ludwig I

KM#	Date	Mintage	Fine	VF	XF	Unc
189	1827	.515	2.00	7.00	10.00	50.00
	1827 D	Inc. Ab.	2.00	7.00	10.00	50.00
	1828	1.206	2.00	7.00	10.00	50.00
	1828 D	Inc. Ab.	2.00	7.00	10.00	50.00
	1829	.603	2.00	7.00	10.00	50.00
	1829 D	Inc. Ab.	2.00	7.00	10.00	50.00
	1830	.149	2.00	7.00	10.00	50.00
	1830 D	Inc. Ab.	2.00	7.00	10.00	50.00

Leopold I

Obv. leg: Period after BADEN.

KM#	Date	Mintage	Fine	VF	XF	Unc
197.1	1831	.227	1.00	4.00	10.00	50.00

Obv. leg: W/o period after BADEN.

KM#	Date	Mintage	Fine	VF	XF	Unc
197.2	1831	Inc. Ab.	1.00	3.00	6.00	40.00
	1832	.172	1.00	3.00	6.00	40.00
	1833	.181	1.00	3.00	6.00	40.00
	1834	.250	1.00	3.00	6.00	40.00
	1835	.294	1.00	3.00	6.00	40.00
	1836	.163	1.00	3.00	6.00	40.00
	1837	—	1.00	3.00	6.00	40.00

Obv: W/o D on truncation.

KM#	Date	Mintage	Fine	VF	XF	Unc
203	1836	.321	1.00	3.00	6.00	40.00
	1837	Inc. Ab.	1.00	3.00	6.00	40.00
	1838	.642	1.00	3.00	6.00	40.00
	1839	.254	1.00	3.00	6.00	40.00
	1840	.573	1.00	3.00	6.00	40.00
	1841	.423	1.00	3.00	6.00	40.00
	1842	.865	1.00	3.00	6.00	40.00
	1843	.527	1.00	3.00	6.00	40.00
	1844	.663	1.00	3.00	6.00	40.00
	1845	1.442	1.00	3.00	6.00	40.00

Erection of Carl Friedrich's Statue

KM#	Date	Mintage	Fine	VF	XF	Unc
216	1844	.054	15.00	25.00	50.00	125.00

Obv: W/o period after Baden.

KM#	Date	Mintage	Fine	VF	XF	Unc
218.1	1845	Inc. Ab.	1.00	3.00	7.00	40.00
	1846	.452	1.00	3.00	7.00	40.00

Obv: Period after Baden.

KM#	Date	Mintage	Fine	VF	XF	Unc
218.2	1847	.639	1.00	3.00	7.00	40.00
	1848	.232	1.00	3.00	7.00	40.00
	1849	.872	1.00	3.00	7.00	40.00
	1850	.238	1.00	3.00	7.00	40.00
	1851	1.208	1.00	3.00	7.00	40.00
	1852	.821	1.00	3.00	7.00	40.00

Friedrich I

Titles as Prince Regent

KM#	Date	Mintage	Fine	VF	XF	Unc
231	1856	.707	20.00	35.00	65.00	140.00

Titles as Grand Duke

KM#	Date	Mintage	Fine	VF	XF	Unc
232	1856	.660	2.00	4.00	10.00	40.00

Birth of Heir

KM#	Date	Mintage	Fine	VF	XF	Unc
238	1857	.012	3.00	6.00	15.00	60.00

KM#	Date	Mintage	Fine	VF	XF	Unc
242	1859	.898	1.00	2.00	6.00	25.00
	1860	.655	1.00	2.00	6.00	25.00
	1861	.726	1.00	2.00	6.00	25.00
	1862	.623	1.00	2.00	6.00	25.00
	1863	.765	1.00	2.00	6.00	25.00
	1864	.724	1.00	2.00	6.00	25.00
	1865	.778	1.00	2.00	6.00	25.00
	1866	.732	1.00	2.00	6.00	25.00
	1867	.698	1.00	2.00	6.00	25.00
	1868	.885	1.00	2.00	6.00	25.00
	1869	.858	1.00	2.00	6.00	25.00
	1870	.918	1.00	2.00	6.00	25.00
	1871	—	1.00	2.00	6.00	25.00

Leopold Memorial

KM#	Date	Mintage	Fine	VF	XF	Unc
244	1861	—	18.00	30.00	50.00	75.00

50th Anniversary Baden's Constitution

KM#	Date	Mintage	Fine	VF	XF	Unc
250	1868	.025	18.00	30.00	50.00	75.00

Church at Seckenheim

KM#	Date	Mintage	Fine	VF	XF	Unc
251	1869	1,000	45.00	75.00	125.00	200.00

Victory in War with France

KM#	Date	Mintage	Fine	VF	XF	Unc
252	1871	—	2.00	4.00	8.00	25.00

Obv: SCHEIDE MUNZE below shield.

KM#	Date	Mintage	Fine	VF	XF	Unc
253	1871	—	32.50	45.00	60.00	80.00

Buehl Commemorating Victory Over France

KM#	Date	Mintage	Fine	VF	XF	Unc
254	1871	—	45.00	75.00	125.00	200.00

Karlsruhe Commemorating Victory Over France

Obv: Arms. Rev: Legend.

KM#	Date	Mintage	Fine	VF	XF	Unc
255	1871	.076	18.00	30.00	45.00	75.00

Offenburg Commemorating Victory Over France

KM#	Date	Mintage	Fine	VF	XF	Unc
256	1871	2,100	35.00	60.00	90.00	150.00

DREI (3) KREUZER

1.4230 g, .313 SILVER, .0143 oz ASW

KM#	Date	Mintage	Fine	VF	XF	Unc
135	1803	.189	10.00	35.00	125.00	350.00
	1805	.445	10.00	25.00	75.00	200.00
	1806	.126	10.00	25.00	100.00	300.00

Obv: Lion in shield faces left.

KM#	Date	Mintage	Fine	VF	XF	Unc
144	1808	.410	10.00	25.00	100.00	300.00

Obv: Lion in shield faces right.

KM#	Date	Mintage	Fine	VF	XF	Unc
148.1	1809	.208	8.00	20.00	65.00	300.00
	1810	.262	8.00	20.00	65.00	300.00
	1811	.316	8.00	20.00	65.00	300.00
	1812	.734	2.00	6.00	15.00	65.00
	1813	.273	2.00	6.00	15.00	65.00

Rev: Z backwards in KREUZER

KM#	Date	Mintage	Fine	VF	XF	Unc
148.2 (155.2)	1812	Inc. Ab.	7.50	18.50	50.00	125.00

1.2470 g, .313 SILVER, .0125 oz ASW
Rev. value: 3 KREUTZER within branches

KM#	Date	Mintage	Fine	VF	XF	Unc
161	1813	—	2.00	7.00	15.00	65.00
	1814	.280	2.00	7.00	15.00	65.00
	1815	.214	2.00	7.00	15.00	65.00
	1816	.243	2.00	7.00	15.00	65.00

Rev. value: 3 KREU=/ZER.

KM#	Date	Mintage	Fine	VF	XF	Unc
172	1817	.371	2.00	7.00	15.00	65.00
	1818	.593	2.00	7.00	15.00	65.00
	1819	.815	2.00	7.00	15.00	65.00
	1820	Inc. Ab.	2.00	7.00	15.00	65.00

Obv: Larger shield, w/o drape.

KM#	Date	Mintage	Fine	VF	XF	Unc
178	1820	Inc. Ab.	2.00	7.00	15.00	65.00
	1821	.065	2.00	7.00	15.00	65.00
	1824	.096	2.00	7.00	15.00	65.00
	1825	.073	2.00	7.00	15.00	65.00

1.1400 g, .375 SILVER, .0134 oz ASW
Rev. value: DREI KREUZER

KM#	Date	Mintage	Fine	VF	XF	Unc
191	1829	1.277	2.00	7.00	10.00	40.00
	1830	1.009	2.00	7.00	10.00	40.00

Rev. value: 3 KREUZER

KM#	Date	Mintage	Fine	VF	XF	Unc
199	1832	.729	2.00	7.00	10.00	50.00
	1833	.846	2.00	7.00	10.00	50.00
	1834	.549	2.00	7.00	10.00	50.00
	1835	.476	1.00	4.00	10.00	50.00
	1836	.723	1.00	4.00	10.00	50.00
	1837	—	1.00	4.00	10.00	50.00

1.2990 g, .333 SILVER, .0139 oz ASW

KM#	Date	Mintage	Fine	VF	XF	Unc
211	1841	.328	1.00	4.00	10.00	40.00
	1842	.420	1.00	4.00	10.00	40.00
	1843	.168	1.00	4.00	10.00	40.00
	1844	.361	1.00	4.00	10.00	40.00
	1845	.385	1.00	4.00	10.00	40.00
	1846	.219	1.00	4.00	10.00	40.00
	1847	.392	1.00	4.00	10.00	40.00
	1848	.195	1.00	4.00	10.00	40.00
	1849	.397	1.00	4.00	10.00	40.00
	1850	.212	1.00	4.00	10.00	40.00
	1851	.196	1.00	4.00	10.00	40.00
	1852	.192	1.00	4.00	10.00	40.00
(226)	1853	—	3.00	8.00	15.00	60.00
	1854	—	3.00	8.00	15.00	60.00
	1855	—	3.00	8.00	15.00	60.00
	1856	—	3.00	8.00	15.00	60.00

1.2320 g, .350 SILVER, .0138 oz ASW
Obv: SCHEIDE/MUNZE below arms.

KM#	Date	Mintage	Fine	VF	XF	Unc
246	1866	.240	1.00	3.00	7.00	40.00
	1867	.389	1.00	3.00	7.00	40.00
	1868	.315	1.00	3.00	7.00	40.00
246	1869	.285	1.00	3.00	7.00	40.00
	1870	.259	1.00	3.00	7.00	40.00
	1871	—	1.00	3.00	7.00	40.00

6 KREUZER

2.3530 g, .375 SILVER, .0283 oz ASW

KM#	Date	Mintage	Fine	VF	XF	Unc
137	1804	.055	15.00	50.00	150.00	400.00

KM#	Date	Mintage	Fine	VF	XF	Unc
138	1804	Inc. Ab.	15.00	40.00	125.00	300.00
	1805	.461	15.00	40.00	125.00	300.00

Obv: Lion in arms facing left.

KM#	Date	Mintage	Fine	VF	XF	Unc
140	1806	.131	7.00	20.00	60.00	250.00
	1807	.371	7.00	20.00	60.00	250.00
	1808	1.118	6.00	15.00	45.00	200.00

Obv: Lion in arms facing right, leg: G.H.BADEN. . .

KM#	Date	Mintage	Fine	VF	XF	Unc
149 (156)	1809	.539	10.00	25.00	75.00	200.00
	1812	.339	5.00	10.00	35.00	125.00
	1813	.559	5.00	10.00	35.00	125.00

Obv. leg: G B BADEN. . .

KM#	Date	Mintage	Fine	VF	XF	Unc
162	1813	Inc. Ab.	5.00	10.00	45.00	100.00

2.2270 g, .375 SILVER, .0268 oz ASW
Rev. value: 6 KREUT=/ZER within olive branches.

KM#	Date	Mintage	Fine	VF	XF	Unc
168	1814	.115	5.00	10.00	50.00	125.00
	1815	.244	5.00	10.00	50.00	125.00
	1816	1.603	5.00	10.00	50.00	125.00
	1817	.563	5.00	10.00	50.00	125.00

Rev. value: 6 KREU=/ZER within olive branches.

KM#	Date	Mintage	Fine	VF	XF	Unc
170	1816	Inc. Ab.	4.00	10.00	25.00	75.00
	1817	Inc. Ab.	4.00	10.00	25.00	75.00
	1818	.112	4.00	10.00	25.00	75.00

Ludwig I

KM#	Date	Mintage	Fine	VF	XF	Unc
173	1819	.390	5.00	15.00	40.00	150.00

Obv: Larger head right, hair combed forward.
Rev: Crowned shield

KM#	Date	Mintage	Fine	VF	XF	Unc
179	1820	.095	5.00	15.00	40.00	150.00

Rev: Crowned shield within branches.

KM#	Date	Mintage	Fine	VF	XF	Unc
180	1820	Inc. Ab.	5.00	15.00	30.00	125.00
	1821	.186	5.00	15.00	30.00	125.00

Leopold I
Obv: D on truncation.

KM#	Date	Mintage	Fine	VF	XF	Unc
198.1	1831	.862	3.00	7.00	15.00	75.00
	1832	.929	3.00	7.00	15.00	75.00
	1833	1.003	3.00	7.00	15.00	75.00
	1834	.898	3.00	7.00	15.00	75.00
	1835	1.025	3.00	7.00	15.00	75.00
	1836	.917	3.00	7.00	15.00	75.00

Obv: W/o D on truncation.

KM#	Date	Mintage	Fine	VF	XF	Unc
198.2	1835	Inc. Ab.	3.00	8.00	20.00	125.00
	1837	.415	3.00	8.00	20.00	125.00

2.5980 g, .333 SILVER, .0278 oz ASW

KM#	Date	Mintage	Fine	VF	XF	Unc
210	1840	1.317	3.00	5.00	10.00	50.00
	1841	.168	3.00	5.00	10.00	50.00
	1842	.612	3.00	5.00	10.00	50.00
	1843	.615	3.00	5.00	10.00	50.00
	1844	.757	3.00	5.00	10.00	50.00
	1845	.262	3.00	5.00	10.00	50.00
	1846	.368	3.00	5.00	10.00	50.00
	1847	.857	3.00	5.00	10.00	50.00
	1848	.377	3.00	5.00	10.00	50.00
	1849	.371	3.00	5.00	10.00	50.00
	1850	.200	3.00	5.00	10.00	50.00
(228)	1855	—	5.00	10.00	25.00	100.00
	1856	—	5.00	10.00	25.00	100.00

ZEHN (10) KREUZER

3.8980 g, .500 SILVER, .0626 oz ASW
Carl Friedrich

KM#	Date	Mintage	Fine	VF	XF	Unc
145	1808	.068	50.00	175.00	250.00	450.00

Obv: Bust w/short hair.

KM#	Date	Mintage	Fine	VF	XF	Unc
150	1809	Inc. Ab.	15.00	25.00	75.00	250.00

2.7840 g, .500 SILVER, .0447 oz ASW
Ludwig I

KM#	Date	Mintage	Fine	VF	XF	Unc
192	1829	.527	5.00	10.00	30.00	125.00
	1830	.510	5.00	10.00	30.00	125.00

20 KREUZER

6.6820 g, .583 SILVER, .1252 oz ASW
Obv: Carl Friedrich w/long hair. Rev: Lion in shield facing left.

KM#	Date	Mintage	Fine	VF	XF	Unc
142	1807 B	.015	65.00	140.00	275.00	600.00

Rev: Lion in shield facing right.

KM#	Date	Mintage	Fine	VF	XF	Unc
146	1808	—	45.00	100.00	180.00	350.00
	1808 B	—	60.00	150.00	250.00	500.00

Obv: Bust w/short hair.

KM#	Date	Mintage	Fine	VF	XF	Unc
151	1809	—	50.00	100.00	200.00	350.00
	1810	.170	20.00	50.00	100.00	225.00

1/2 GULDEN

5.3030 g, .900 SILVER, .1534 oz ASW
Leopold I

KM#	Date	Mintage	Fine	VF	XF	Unc
209	1838	1.044	12.50	30.00	45.00	125.00
	1839	.500	15.00	35.00	60.00	140.00
	1840	.511	15.00	35.00	60.00	140.00
	1841	.417	15.00	35.00	60.00	140.00
	1842	.362	15.00	35.00	60.00	140.00
	1843	.469	15.00	35.00	60.00	140.00
	1844	.274	15.00	35.00	60.00	140.00
	1845	.322	15.00	35.00	60.00	140.00
	1846	.118	15.00	35.00	60.00	140.00

Obv: W/o D on truncation, larger head.

KM#	Date	Mintage	Fine	VF	XF	Unc
221	1846	Inc. Ab.	15.00	45.00	75.00	180.00
	1847	.537	12.50	40.00	65.00	150.00
	1848	.332	12.50	40.00	65.00	150.00
	1849	.069	15.00	45.00	75.00	180.00
	1850	—	15.00	45.00	75.00	180.00
	1851	.122	15.00	45.00	75.00	180.00
	1852	.026	15.00	45.00	75.00	180.00

Obv: Head of Friedrich I right.

KM#	Date	Mintage	Fine	VF	XF	Unc
233	1856	—	15.00	45.00	75.00	180.00

Obv: VOIGT below head.

KM#	Date	Mintage	Fine	VF	XF	Unc
234	1856	.150	25.00	50.00	100.00	250.00
	1860	.342	25.00	50.00	100.00	250.00

5.2910 g, .900 SILVER, .0850 oz ASW

KM#	Date	Mintage	Fine	VF	XF	Unc
243	1860	Inc. Ab.	25.00	50.00	75.00	200.00
	1861	.264	25.00	50.00	75.00	200.00
	1862	.233	25.00	50.00	75.00	200.00
	1863	.227	25.00	50.00	75.00	200.00
	1864	.117	25.00	50.00	75.00	200.00
	1865	.184	25.00	50.00	75.00	200.00

KM#	Date	Mintage	Fine	VF	XF	Unc
248	1867	.155	25.00	50.00	75.00	200.00
	1868	.070	25.00	50.00	75.00	200.00
	1869	.073	25.00	50.00	75.00	200.00

EIN (1) GULDEN

12.7270 g, .750 SILVER, .3069 oz ASW
Obv: Ludwig I w/short hair.

KM#	Date	Mintage	Fine	VF	XF	Unc
184	1821	.090	150.00	300.00	600.00	1000.
	1822	.045	150.00	300.00	600.00	1000.
	1823	.039	150.00	300.00	600.00	1000.
	1824	.050	150.00	300.00	600.00	1000.
	1825	.022	150.00	300.00	600.00	1000.

Obv: Ludwig I w/curly hair.

KM#	Date	Mintage	Fine	VF	XF	Unc
187	1826	.094	700.00	1200.	1800.	3000.

10.6060 g, .900 SILVER, .3069 oz ASW
Obv: Leopold I w/o period after BADEN.

KM#	Date	Mintage	Fine	VF	XF	Unc
207	1837	.629	25.00	50.00	100.00	250.00
	1838	.210	25.00	50.00	100.00	250.00
	1839	.485	25.00	50.00	100.00	250.00
	1840	.468	25.00	50.00	100.00	250.00
	1841	.387	25.00	50.00	100.00	250.00

Obv: Period after BADEN.

KM#	Date	Mintage	Fine	VF	XF	Unc
214	1842	.390	25.00	50.00	100.00	250.00
	1843	.444	25.00	50.00	100.00	250.00
	1844	.585	25.00	50.00	100.00	250.00
	1845	.439	25.00	50.00	100.00	250.00

KM#	Date	Mintage	Fine	VF	XF	Unc
219	1845	Inc. Ab.	25.00	50.00	100.00	250.00
	1846	—	25.00	50.00	100.00	250.00
	1847	.397	25.00	50.00	100.00	250.00
	1848	.116	25.00	50.00	100.00	250.00
	1849	.021	25.00	50.00	100.00	250.00
	1850	8,652	25.00	50.00	100.00	250.00
	1851	.089	25.00	50.00	100.00	250.00
	1852	.033	75.00	125.00	200.00	300.00

Blessing on the Baden Mines

KM#	Date	Mintage	Fine	VF	XF	Unc
224	1852	Inc. Ab.	75.00	125.00	200.00	300.00

10.5820 g, .900 SILVER, .3062 oz ASW
Obv. leg: FRIEDRICH PRINZ. . .

KM#	Date	Mintage	Fine	VF	XF	Unc
235	1856	.149	100.00	225.00	375.00	675.00

Obv. leg: FRIEDRICH GROSHERZOG. . .
Rev: Similar to KM#235.

KM#	Date	Mintage	Fine	VF	XF	Unc
236	1856	.342	50.00	75.00	100.00	250.00
	1859	.195	50.00	75.00	100.00	250.00
	1860	.044	50.00	75.00	100.00	250.00

Mint Visit

KM#	Date	Mintage	Fine	VF	XF	Unc
239	1857	776 pcs.	225.00	375.00	500.00	900.00

First Shooting Festival at Mannheim

KM#	Date	Mintage	Fine	VF	XF	Unc
247	1863	.012	60.00	90.00	125.00	200.00

Second Shooting Festival at Karlsruhe

KM#	Date	Mintage	Fine	VF	XF	Unc
249	1867	.014	45.00	90.00	175.00	250.00

ZWEI (2) GULDEN

25.4540 g, .750 SILVER, .6138 oz ASW
Ludwig I

KM#	Date	Mintage	Fine	VF	XF	Unc
185	1821	.030	150.00	250.00	500.00	1500.
	1822	.020	150.00	250.00	500.00	1500.
	1823	7,040	150.00	250.00	500.00	1500.
	1824	.017	150.00	250.00	500.00	1500.
	1825	6.642	150.00	250.00	500.00	1500.

21.2100 g, .900 SILVER, .6138 oz ASW
Leopold I

KM#	Date	Mintage	Fine	VF	XF	Unc
222	1846	.592	50.00	75.00	150.00	400.00
	1847	.232	50.00	75.00	150.00	400.00
	1848	.273	50.00	75.00	150.00	400.00
	1849	.041	50.00	100.00	200.00	500.00
	1850	.140	50.00	75.00	150.00	400.00
	1851	.124	50.00	75.00	150.00	400.00
	1852	.142	50.00	75.00	150.00	400.00

Friedrich I
Rev: Similar to KM#222.

KM#	Date	Mintage	Fine	VF	XF	Unc
237	1856	.084	125.00	250.00	400.00	750.00

5 GULDEN

3.4390 g, .903 GOLD, .0998 oz AGW
Ludwig I

KM#	Date	Mintage	Fine	VF	XF	Unc
176.1	1819 PH	3,000	500.00	1000.	1500.	2000.

Obv: W/o engravers initials below head.

KM#	Date	Mintage	Fine	VF	XF	Unc
176.2	1819	695 pcs.	650.00	1000.	1500.	2000.
	1821	465 pcs.	675.00	1125.	1750.	2400.
	1822	1,718	525.00	875.00	1500.	2000.
	1823	1,854	525.00	875.00	1500.	2000.
	1824	2,763	450.00	750.00	1350.	1750.
	1825	1,508	525.00	875.00	1500.	2000.
	1826	887 pcs.	600.00	1000.	1650.	2250.

Obv: Curly hair.

KM#	Date	Mintage	Fine	VF	XF	Unc
190	1827	2,877	450.00	850.00	2250.	3000.
	1828	2,317	450.00	850.00	2250.	3000.

10 GULDEN

6.8780 g, .903 GOLD, .1997 oz AGW
Ludwig I

KM#	Date	Mintage	Fine	VF	XF	Unc
177.1	1819 PH	4,332	950.00	1500.	2000.	3250.

Obv: W/o engravers initials below head.

KM#	Date	Mintage	Fine	VF	XF	Unc
177.2	1821	812 pcs.	1150.	1800.	2500.	3750.
	1823	373 pcs.	1250.	2000.	2750.	4000.
	1824	328 pcs.	1400.	2200.	3000.	4250.
	1825	Inc. Ab.	1400.	2200.	3000.	4250.

EIN (1) THALER

28.0600 g, .833 SILVER, .7515 oz ASW
Carl Friedrich

KM#	Date	Mintage	Fine	VF	XF	Unc
136	1803 FE HB	675 pcs.	500.00	900.00	1750.	4000.

KM#	Date	Mintage	Fine	VF	XF	Unc
152	1809 B E	6,219	300.00	550.00	1100.	2200.
	1810 B	2,815	250.00	450.00	900.00	2000.
	1811 B E	3,885	225.00	400.00	850.00	1800.

(Krone)

29.5160 g, .871 SILVER, .8266 oz ASW

KM#	Date	Mintage	Fine	VF	XF	Unc
163	1813 D	—	150.00	275.00	600.00	1200.
	1814 D	.036	150.00	275.00	600.00	1200.

Rev: W/o mintmasters initial.

KM#	Date	Mintage	Fine	VF	XF	Unc
169	1814	Inc. Ab.	150.00	225.00	475.00	1000.
	1815	.038	125.00	185.00	375.00	800.00
	1816	.036	100.00	165.00	325.00	700.00
	1817	.052	100.00	165.00	325.00	700.00
	1818	.039	100.00	165.00	365.00	800.00
	1819	—	125.00	200.00	500.00	1200.

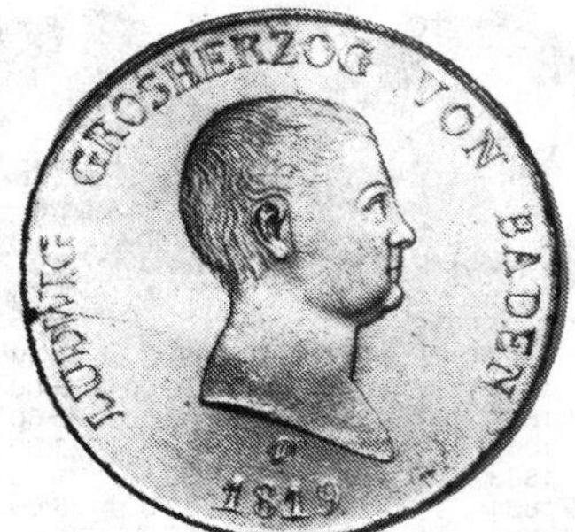

Ludwig I

Obv: WD monogram below bust.

KM#	Date	Mintage	Fine	VF	XF	Unc
175.1	1819	—	175.00	325.00	800.00	1750.

Obv: DOELL on truncation.

KM#	Date	Mintage	Fine	VF	XF	Unc
175.2	1819	—	150.00	325.00	700.00	1500.
	1820	.038	150.00	350.00	800.00	1600.
	1821	.019	150.00	375.00	875.00	1800.

18.1480 g, .875 SILVER, .5105 oz ASW

KM#	Date	Mintage	Fine	VF	XF	Unc
193	1829	.168	50.00	100.00	175.00	400.00
	1830	.101	50.00	100.00	175.00	400.00

Leopold

Obv. leg: W/o dot after BADEN.

KM#	Date	Mintage	Fine	VF	XF	Unc
195.1	1830	.238	85.00	175.00	250.00	650.00
	1831	.168	85.00	115.00	200.00	450.00
	1832	.176	85.00	115.00	200.00	450.00
	1832 star	I.A.	85.00	125.00	200.00	475.00

Obv. leg: Dot after BADEN.

KM#	Date	Mintage	Fine	VF	XF	Unc
195.2	1832 star	I.A.	85.00	125.00	200.00	475.00
	1833 star	.115	85.00	125.00	200.00	475.00
	1833	Inc. ab.	75.00	100.00	200.00	450.00
	1834	.036	75.00	100.00	200.00	450.00
	1835	.075	75.00	100.00	200.00	450.00
	1836 lg.6	.085	85.00	135.00	200.00	475.00
	1837	—	75.00	100.00	200.00	450.00

Rev. leg: Hyphen between KRONEN-THALER.

KM#	Date	Mintage	Fine	VF	XF	Unc
195.3	1834	Inc. Ab.	75.00	100.00	200.00	450.00
	1836	Inc. Ab.	100.00	125.00	225.00	700.00

Mint Visit

KM#	Date	Mintage	Fine	VF	XF	Unc
200	1832	—	600.00	850.00	1100.	2000.

Blessings on the Baden Mines

KM#	Date	Mintage	Fine	VF	XF	Unc
202	1834	6,517	200.00	300.00	500.00	1300.

KM#	Date	Mintage	Fine	VF	XF	Unc
204	1836	8,250	175.00	250.00	500.00	1150.

Mule. Obv: KM#195.2 rev. Rev: KM#204.

KM#	Date	Mintage	Fine	VF	XF	Unc
205	1836	—	—	—	Rare	—

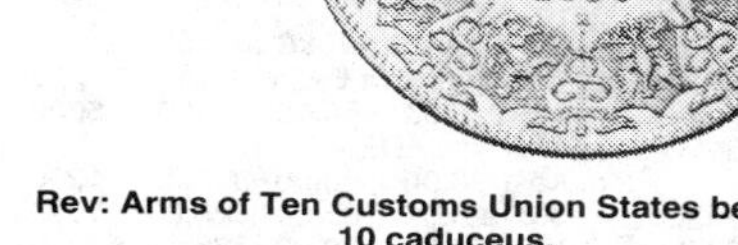

Rev: Arms of Ten Customs Union States between 10 caduceus.

KM#	Date	Mintage	Fine	VF	XF	Unc
206	1836	.018	65.00	90.00	150.00	300.00

(Vereins)

18.5190 g, .900 SILVER, .5359 oz ASW

Friedrich I

KM#	Date	Mintage	Fine	VF	XF	Unc
240	1857	.019	50.00	80.00	150.00	350.00
	1858	.232	35.00	65.00	125.00	225.00
	1859	.289	35.00	65.00	125.00	225.00
	1860	.174	35.00	65.00	125.00	225.00
	1861	.358	35.00	65.00	125.00	225.00
	1862	.400	35.00	65.00	125.00	225.00
	1863	.326	35.00	65.00	125.00	225.00
	1864	.322	35.00	65.00	125.00	225.00
	1865	.265	35.00	65.00	125.00	225.00

KM#	Date	Mintage	Fine	VF	XF	Unc
245	1865	Inc. Ab.	35.00	65.00	135.00	275.00
	1866	.149	35.00	65.00	135.00	275.00
	1867	.096	35.00	65.00	135.00	275.00
	1868	.102	35.00	65.00	135.00	275.00
	1869	.062	35.00	65.00	135.00	275.00
	1870	.022	35.00	65.00	135.00	275.00
	1871	—	35.00	65.00	135.00	275.00

2 THALER

(3-1/2 Gulden)

37.1200 g, .900 SILVER, 1.0743 oz ASW

Leopold I

KM#	Date	Mintage	Fine	VF	XF	Unc
212	1841	.231	125.00	175.00	400.00	1000.
	1842	.033	150.00	200.00	550.00	1150.
	1843	.035	150.00	200.00	600.00	1250.

Monument of Carl Friedrich

KM#	Date	Mintage	Fine	VF	XF	Unc
217.1	1844	4,323	125.00	200.00	350.00	750.00

Plain edge.

KM#	Date	Mintage	Fine	VF	XF	Unc
217.2	1844	—	—	—	Rare	—

KM#	Date	Mintage	Fine	VF	XF	Unc
220	1845	.057	150.00	200.00	425.00	800.00
	1846	1,130	300.00	400.00	900.00	1500.
	1847	.031	150.00	200.00	400.00	700.00
	1852	.060	135.00	185.00	350.00	625.00

Friedrich I
Obv: BALBACH below truncation.

KM#	Date	Mintage	Fine	VF	XF	Unc
225	1852	9 pcs.	—	—	Rare	—
	1854	.085	450.00	800.00	2000.	4000.

Obv: Modified head, w/o engravers name below truncation.

KM#	Date	Mintage	Fine	VF	XF	Unc
229	1855	2 pcs.	—	—	Rare	—

FUNF (5) THALER

(500 Kreuzer)

5.7320 g, .903 GOLD, .1664 oz AGW
Ludwig I

KM#	Date	Mintage	Fine	VF	XF	Unc
196	1830	1,788	800.00	1250.	2000.	2500.

MONETARY REFORM

2 MARK

11.1110 g, .900 SILVER, .3215 oz ASW
Friedrich I

KM#	Date	Mintage	Fine	VF	XF	Unc
265	1876G	1.739	35.00	100.00	800.00	1600.
	1877G	.764	35.00	100.00	700.00	1800.
	1880G	.074	60.00	160.00	900.00	2000.
	1883G	.045	65.00	160.00	750.00	2000.
	1888G	.075	70.00	140.00	1000.	2000.

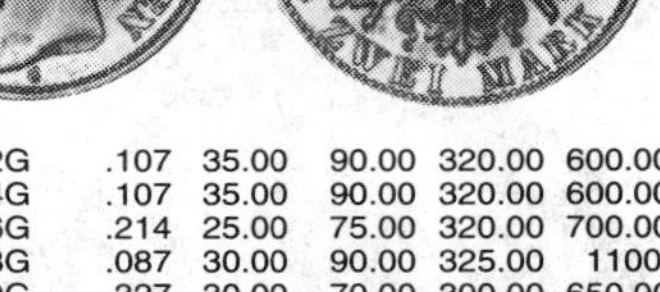

KM#	Date	Mintage	Fine	VF	XF	Unc
269	1892G	.107	35.00	90.00	320.00	600.00
	1894G	.107	35.00	90.00	320.00	600.00
	1896G	.214	25.00	75.00	320.00	700.00
	1898G	.087	30.00	90.00	325.00	1100.
	1899G	.327	30.00	70.00	300.00	650.00
	1900G	.222	25.00	75.00	300.00	600.00

NOTE: Later dates (1901-1902) exist for this type.

5 MARK

27.7770 g, .900 SILVER, .8038 oz ASW
Friedrich I

KM#	Date	Mintage	Fine	VF	XF	Unc
263.1	1875G	.314	35.00	70.00	800.00	3250.
	1876G	.473	35.00	70.00	950.00	2750.
	1888G	.030	300.00	625.00	1650.	4500.

Obv.leg: Inverted V for 'A' of BADEN.

KM#	Date	Mintage	Fine	VF	XF	Unc
263.2	1875G	Inc. Ab.	35.00	70.00	700.00	2400.
	1876G	Inc. Ab.	35.00	70.00	1000.	2500.
	1888G	Inc. Ab.	45.00	100.00	650.00	2000.
	Common date		—	—	Proof	4500.

1.9910 g, .900 GOLD, .0576 oz AGW

KM#	Date	Mintage	Fine	VF	XF	Unc
266	1877G	.345	150.00	250.00	400.00	600.00
	1877G	—	—	—	Proof	1500.

27.7770 g, .900 SILVER, .8038 oz ASW

KM#	Date	Mintage	Fine	VF	XF	Unc
268	1891G inverted V for 'A' in BADEN					
		.043	225.00	450.00	1500.	6000.
	1891G normal 'A' in BADEN					
		Inc. Ab.	30.00	90.00	375.00	1250.
	1893G	.043	25.00	65.00	325.00	1000.
	1894G	.061	25.00	60.00	225.00	950.00
	1895G	.073	25.00	60.00	250.00	950.00
	1898G	.131	25.00	60.00	250.00	1000.
	1899G	.061	27.50	70.00	375.00	750.00
	1900G	.128	27.50	70.00	375.00	900.00
	Common date		—	—	Proof	900.00

NOTE: Later dates (1901-1902) exist for this type.

10 MARK

3.9820 g, .900 GOLD, .1152 oz AGW
Friedrich I
Rev: Type I.

KM#	Date	Mintage	Fine	VF	XF	Unc
260	1872G	.273	65.00	125.00	200.00	325.00
	1873G	.466	65.00	125.00	200.00	325.00
	1873G	—	—	—	Proof	1750.

Rev: Type II.

KM#	Date	Mintage	Fine	VF	XF	Unc
264	1875G	.339	75.00	150.00	200.00	325.00
	1876G	1.396	65.00	125.00	225.00	350.00
	1877G	.159	65.00	125.00	200.00	325.00
	1878G	.236	65.00	125.00	200.00	325.00
	1879G	.098	100.00	200.00	275.00	400.00
	1880G	1,169	6000.	10,000.	15,000.	30,000.
	1881G	.196	75.00	150.00	250.00	375.00
	1888G	.122	65.00	125.00	200.00	325.00
	Common date		—	—	Proof	1300.

Rev: Type III.

KM#	Date	Mintage	Fine	VF	XF	Unc
267	1890G	.073	125.00	225.00	325.00	500.00
	1891G	.110	125.00	175.00	250.00	350.00
	1893G	.183	125.00	175.00	250.00	325.00
	1896G	.052	125.00	200.00	300.00	450.00
	1897G	.070	125.00	225.00	275.00	400.00
	1898G	.256	115.00	165.00	250.00	325.00
	1900G	.031	150.00	400.00	500.00	800.00
	Common date		—	—	Proof	1300.

NOTE: Later date (1901) exists for this type.

20 MARK

7.9650 g, .900 GOLD, .2304 oz AGW
Friedrich I
Rev: Type I.

KM#	Date	Mintage	Fine	VF	XF	Unc
261	1872G	.398	125.00	150.00	225.00	325.00
	1873G	.517	125.00	160.00	300.00	350.00
	Common date		—	—	Proof	2250.

Rev: Type II.

KM#	Date	Mintage	Fine	VF	XF	Unc
262	1874G	.155	225.00	400.00	600.00	900.00
	1874G	—	—	—	Proof	3000.

Rev: Type III.

KM#	Date	Mintage	Fine	VF	XF	Unc
270	1894G sm. 4					
		.400	135.00	160.00	250.00	400.00
	1894G lg.4	.400	135.00	160.00	250.00	400.00
	1895G	.100	135.00	225.00	300.00	450.00
	Common date		—	—	Proof	1300.

TRADE COINAGE

DUCAT

3.6600 g, .938 GOLD, .1103 oz AGW
Carl Friedrich

KM#	Date	Mintage	Fine	VF	XF	Unc
143	1807	1,022	—	1500.	2500.	4000.

Leopold

KM#	Date	Mintage	Fine	VF	XF	Unc
201	1832	6,631	—	1000.	1500.	2000.
	1833	2,496	—	1100.	1600.	2100.
	1834	1,992	—	1150.	1650.	2200.
	1835	2,470	—	1100.	1600.	2100.
	1836	1,777	—	1150.	1650.	2200.

Obv: W/o designers initial or star below head.

KM#	Date	Mintage	Fine	VF	XF	Unc
208	1837	1,467	—	1125.	1650.	2200.
	1838	2,095	—	1125.	1650.	2200.
	1839	2,448	—	1100.	1600.	2100.
	1840	2,044	—	1125.	1650.	2200.
	1841	2,145	—	1125.	1650.	2200.
	1842	2,130	—	1125.	1650.	2200.

KM#	Date	Mintage	Fine	VF	XF	Unc
215	1843	1,350	—	1300.	1700.	2200.
	1844	850 pcs.	—	1500.	2000.	2500.
	1845	2,097	—	1200.	1600.	2000.
	1846	1,950	—	1200.	1600.	2000.

Obv: Larger head.

KM#	Date	Mintage	Fine	VF	XF	Unc
223.1	1847	1,870	—	1200.	1600.	2100.
	1848	1,590	—	1200.	1600.	2100.
	1849	1,420	—	1200.	1600.	2100.
	1850	1,390	—	1200.	1600.	2100.
	1851	1,280	—	1200.	1600.	2100.
	1852	1,450	—	1350.	1750.	2250.

Obv: Star below head.

KM#	Date	Mintage	Fine	VF	XF	Unc
223.2	1852	Inc. Ab.	—	1350.	1750.	2250.

NOTE: Posthumous issue.

Friedrich I

KM#	Date	Mintage	Fine	VF	XF	Unc
227	1854	1,820	—	1500.	3000.	4000.

MEDALLIC ISSUES (M)

(KREUZER)

COPPER
Recovery of Grand Duchess Sophie

KM#	Date	Mintage	Fine	VF	XF	Unc
M1	1832	—	25.00	50.00	65.00	100.00

Evangelical Church at Eppingen

KM#	Date	Mintage	Fine	VF	XF	Unc
M2	1879	—	20.00	40.00	60.00	100.00

Evangelical Church at Feudenheim

KM#	Date	Mintage	Fine	VF	XF	Unc
M3	1889	—	20.00	40.00	60.00	100.00

PATTERNS (Pn)

(Including off metal strikes)

KM#	Date	Mintage	Identification	Mkt.Val.
Pn21	ND(1805)	—	1 Ducat, Silver, KM143	—
Pn22	ND(1805)	—	1 Ducat, Copper, KM143	—

KM#	Date	Mintage	Identification	Mkt.Val.
Pn23	1808A	4 pcs. known	5 Frank, Silver	
Pn24	1839	—	6 Kreuzer, .333 Billon, KM210	—
Pn25	1842	—	1 Kreuzer, Gold, KM203	—
Pn26	1842	—	1 Kreuzer, Silver, KM203	—
Pn27	1844	—	1 Kreuzer, Gold, KM203	—
Pn28	1844	—	1 Kreuzer, Silver, KM203	—
Pn29	1844	—	1 Kreuzer, Nickel, KM203	—
Pn30	1874G	—	5 Mark, Silver, KM263.1	—

KM#	Date	Mintage	Identification	Mkt.Val.
Pn31	1875G	—	10 Mark, Copper, KM264	—

TRIAL STRIKES (TS)

KM#	Date	Mintage	Identification	Mkt.Val.
TS1	ND(1860)	—	1/4 Gulden, Pewter, obv.	—

KM#	Date	Mintage	Identification	Mkt.Val.
TS2	1860	—	1/4 Gulden, Pewter, rev.	—

BAMBERG

Bishopric in northern Bavaria. The see was founded in 1007 and the first coinage appeared soon after. The bishops were made princes of the empire in the mid-1200s. It was annexed to Bavaria in 1802.

RULERS

Christoph Franz, Freiherr von Buseck, Bishop, 1795-1802
Georg Karl, von Fechenbach, 1802-1803

TRADE COINAGE

DUCAT

3.5000 g, .986 GOLD, .1109 oz AGW
Union of Bamberg with Bavaria

KM#	Date	Mintage	Fine	VF	XF	Unc
154	1802	—	400.00	800.00	1350.	1900.

PATTERNS (Pn)

(Including off metal strikes)

KM#	Date	Mintage	Identification	Mkt.Val.
Pn11	1802	—	1 Ducat, Silver, KM154	—

BAVARIA

Located in south Germany. In 1180 the Duchy of Bavaria was given to the Count of Wittelsbach by the emperor. He is the ancestor of all who ruled in Bavaria until 1918. Primogeniture was proclaimed in 1506 and in 1623 the dukes of Bavaria were given the electoral right. Bavaria, which had been divided for the various heirs, was reunited in 1799. The title of king was granted to Bavaria in 1805.

RULERS

Maximilian IV, Josef as Elector, 1799-1805
Maximilian IV,
As King Maximilian I, Josef, 1806-1825
Ludwig I, 1825-1848
Maximilian II, 1848-1864
Ludwig II, 1864-1886
Otto, 1886-1913
Prince Regent Luitpold, 1886-1912

MINT MARKS

M-Munich

HELLER

COPPER
Obv: Shield and date in diamond.
Rev. value: 1/HEL/LER in diamond.

KM#	Date	Mintage	Fine	VF	XF	Unc
305	1801	—	8.00	15.00	30.00	65.00
	1802	—	8.00	15.00	30.00	65.00
	1803	—	8.00	15.00	30.00	65.00
	1804	—	8.00	15.00	30.00	65.00
	1805	—	8.00	15.00	30.00	65.00

NOTE: Earlier dates (1799-1800) exist for this type.

Plain edge.

KM#	Date	Mintage	Fine	VF	XF	Unc
340	1806	—	3.00	5.00	10.00	35.00
	1807	—	3.00	5.00	10.00	35.00
	1808	—	3.00	5.00	10.00	35.00
	1809	—	3.00	5.00	10.00	35.00
	1810	—	3.00	5.00	10.00	35.00
	1811	—	3.00	5.00	10.00	35.00
	1812	—	3.00	5.00	10.00	35.00
	1813	—	3.00	5.00	10.00	35.00
	1814	—	3.00	5.00	10.00	35.00
	1815	—	3.00	5.00	10.00	35.00
	1816	—	3.00	5.00	10.00	35.00
	1817	—	3.00	5.00	10.00	35.00
	1818	—	3.00	5.00	10.00	35.00
	1819	—	3.00	5.00	10.00	35.00
	1820	—	3.00	5.00	10.00	35.00
	1821	—	3.00	5.00	10.00	35.00
	1822	—	3.00	5.00	10.00	35.00
	1823	—	3.00	5.00	10.00	35.00
	1824	—	3.00	5.00	10.00	35.00
	1825	—	3.00	5.00	10.00	35.00
	1828	—	3.00	5.00	10.00	35.00
	1829	—	3.00	5.00	10.00	35.00

Reeded edge.

KM#	Date	Mintage	Fine	VF	XF	Unc
383	1830	—	3.00	5.00	10.00	35.00
	1831	—	3.00	5.00	10.00	35.00
	1832	—	3.00	5.00	10.00	35.00
	1833	—	3.00	5.00	10.00	35.00
	1834	—	3.00	5.00	10.00	35.00
	1835	—	3.00	5.00	10.00	35.00

KM#	Date	Mintage	Fine	VF	XF	Unc
419	1839	.256	1.00	2.00	5.00	25.00
	1840	.169	1.00	2.00	5.00	25.00
	1841	—	1.00	2.00	5.00	25.00
	1842	—	1.00	2.00	5.00	25.00
	1843	—	1.00	2.00	5.00	25.00
	1844	.190	1.00	2.00	5.00	25.00
	1845	.434	1.00	2.00	5.00	25.00
	1846	—	1.00	2.00	5.00	25.00
	1847	.074	1.00	2.00	5.00	25.00
	1848	.514	1.00	2.00	5.00	25.00
(449)	1849	.346	1.00	2.00	5.00	20.00
	1850	.306	1.00	2.00	5.00	20.00
	1851	.437	1.00	2.00	5.00	20.00
	1852	.206	1.00	2.00	5.00	20.00
	1853	.279	1.00	2.00	5.00	20.00
	1854	.193	1.00	2.00	5.00	20.00
	1855	.132	1.00	2.00	5.00	20.00
	1856	.034	1.00	2.00	5.00	20.00

PFENNIG

COPPER
Obv: Bavaria shield in ornamental cartouche.
Rev: Value above date.

KM#	Date	Mintage	Fine	VF	XF	Unc
306	1801	—	4.00	12.00	24.00	50.00
	1802	—	4.00	12.00	24.00	50.00
	1803	—	4.00	12.00	24.00	50.00
	1804	—	4.00	12.00	24.00	50.00
	1805	—	4.00	12.00	24.00	50.00

NOTE: Earlier dates (1799-1800) exist for this type.

Plain edge.

KM#	Date	Mintage	Fine	VF	XF	Unc
341	1806	—	1.00	3.00	7.00	25.00
	1807	—	1.00	3.00	7.00	25.00
	1808	—	1.00	3.00	7.00	25.00
	1809	—	1.00	3.00	7.00	25.00
	1810	—	1.00	3.00	7.00	25.00
	1811	—	1.00	3.00	7.00	25.00
	1812	—	1.00	3.00	7.00	25.00
	1813	—	1.00	3.00	7.00	25.00
	1814	—	1.00	3.00	7.00	25.00
	1815	—	1.00	3.00	7.00	25.00
	1816	—	1.00	3.00	7.00	25.00
	1817	—	1.00	3.00	7.00	25.00
	1818	—	1.00	3.00	7.00	25.00
	1819	—	1.00	3.00	7.00	25.00
	1820	—	1.00	3.00	7.00	25.00
	1821	—	1.00	3.00	7.00	25.00
	1822	—	1.00	3.00	7.00	25.00
	1823	—	1.00	3.00	7.00	25.00
	1824	—	1.00	3.00	7.00	25.00
	1825	—	1.00	3.00	7.00	25.00
	1828	—	1.00	3.00	7.00	20.00
	1829	—	1.00	3.00	7.00	20.00

Reeded edge.

KM#	Date	Mintage	Fine	VF	XF	Unc
384	1830	—	1.00	3.00	7.00	20.00
	1831	—	1.00	3.00	7.00	20.00
	1832	—	1.00	3.00	7.00	20.00
	1833	—	1.00	3.00	7.00	20.00
	1834	—	1.00	3.00	7.00	20.00
	1835	—	1.00	3.00	7.00	20.00

KM#	Date	Mintage	Fine	VF	XF	Unc
420	1839	.801	1.00	2.00	5.00	15.00
	1840	.732	1.00	2.00	5.00	15.00
	1841	.970	1.00	2.00	5.00	15.00
	1842	.817	1.00	2.00	5.00	15.00
	1843	.892	1.00	2.00	5.00	15.00
	1844	.645	1.00	2.00	5.00	15.00
	1845	1.037	1.00	2.00	5.00	15.00
	1846	1.487	1.00	2.00	5.00	15.00
	1847	1.808	1.00	2.00	5.00	15.00
	1848	1.815	1.00	2.00	5.00	15.00
(450)	1849	2.120	1.00	2.00	5.00	15.00
	1850	2.494	1.00	2.00	5.00	15.00
	1851	2.162	1.00	2.00	5.00	15.00
	1852	2.634	1.00	2.00	5.00	15.00
	1853	1.950	1.00	2.00	5.00	15.00
	1854	1.842	1.00	2.00	5.00	15.00
	1855	1.576	1.00	2.00	5.00	15.00
	1856	1.530	1.00	2.00	5.00	15.00

KM#	Date	Mintage	Fine	VF	XF	Unc
471	1858	—	1.00	2.00	5.00	15.00
	1859	—	1.00	2.00	5.00	15.00
	1860	—	1.00	2.00	5.00	15.00
	1861	—	1.00	2.00	5.00	15.00
	1862	—	1.00	2.00	5.00	15.00
	1863	2.284	1.00	2.00	5.00	15.00
	1864	2.304	1.00	2.00	5.00	15.00
(486)	1865	1.401	1.00	2.00	5.00	15.00
	1866	1.485	1.00	2.00	5.00	15.00
	1867	1.633	1.00	2.00	5.00	15.00
	1868	1.394	1.00	2.00	5.00	15.00
	1869	1.474	1.00	2.00	5.00	15.00
	1870	1.608	1.00	2.00	5.00	15.00
	1871	1.534	1.00	2.00	5.00	15.00

2 PFENNIG

COPPER

KM#	Date	Mintage	Fine	VF	XF	Unc
307	1801	—	5.00	15.00	30.00	65.00
	1802	—	5.00	15.00	30.00	65.00
	1803	—	5.00	15.00	30.00	65.00
	1804	—	5.00	15.00	30.00	65.00
	1805	—	5.00	15.00	30.00	65.00

NOTE: Earlier dates (1799-1800) exist for this type.

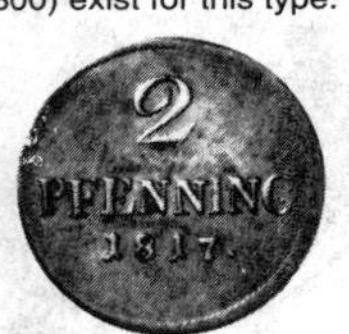

Plain edge.

KM#	Date	Mintage	Fine	VF	XF	Unc
342	1806	—	1.00	3.00	7.00	30.00
	1807	—	1.00	3.00	7.00	30.00
	1808	—	1.00	3.00	7.00	30.00
	1809	—	1.00	3.00	7.00	30.00
	1810	—	1.00	3.00	7.00	30.00
	1811	—	1.00	3.00	7.00	30.00
	1812	—	1.00	3.00	7.00	30.00
	1813	—	1.00	3.00	7.00	30.00
	1814	—	1.00	3.00	7.00	30.00
	1815	—	1.00	3.00	7.00	30.00
	1816	—	1.00	3.00	7.00	30.00
	1817	—	1.00	3.00	7.00	30.00
	1818	—	1.00	3.00	7.00	30.00
	1819	—	1.00	3.00	7.00	30.00
	1820	—	1.00	3.00	7.00	30.00
	1821	—	1.00	3.00	7.00	30.00
	1822	—	1.00	3.00	7.00	30.00
	1823	—	1.00	3.00	7.00	30.00
	1824	—	1.00	3.00	7.00	30.00
	1825	—	1.00	3.00	7.00	30.00
	1828	—	1.00	3.00	7.00	30.00
	1829	—	1.00	3.00	7.00	30.00

Reeded edge.

KM#	Date	Mintage	Fine	VF	XF	Unc
385	1830	—	1.00	3.00	7.00	30.00
	1831	—	1.00	3.00	7.00	30.00
	1832	—	1.00	3.00	7.00	30.00
	1833	—	1.00	3.00	7.00	30.00
	1834	—	1.00	3.00	7.00	30.00
	1835	—	1.00	3.00	7.00	30.00

KM#	Date	Mintage	Fine	VF	XF	Unc
421	1839	.320	1.00	3.00	7.00	25.00
	1840	.320	1.00	3.00	7.00	25.00
	1841	.442	1.00	3.00	7.00	25.00
	1842	.353	1.00	3.00	7.00	25.00
	1843	.203	1.00	3.00	7.00	25.00
	1844	.226	1.00	3.00	7.00	25.00
	1845	.242	1.00	3.00	7.00	25.00
	1846	.232	1.00	3.00	7.00	25.00
	1847	.663	1.00	3.00	7.00	25.00
	1848	.776	1.00	3.00	7.00	25.00
(451)	1849	.454	1.00	3.00	7.00	25.00
	1850	1.477	1.00	3.00	7.00	25.00

KM#	Date	Mintage	Fine	VF	XF	Unc
472	1858	—	1.00	2.00	4.00	20.00
	1859	—	1.00	2.00	4.00	20.00
	1860	—	1.00	2.00	4.00	20.00
	1861	—	1.00	2.00	4.00	20.00
	1862	—	1.00	2.00	4.00	20.00
	1863	.228	1.00	2.00	4.00	20.00
(478)	1864	.589	1.00	2.00	4.00	20.00
	1865	.358	1.00	2.00	4.00	20.00
	1866	.234	1.00	2.00	4.00	20.00
	1867	.481	1.00	2.00	4.00	20.00
	1868	.208	1.00	2.00	4.00	20.00
	1869	.466	1.00	2.00	4.00	20.00
	1870	.476	1.00	2.00	4.00	20.00
	1871	.466	1.00	2.00	4.00	20.00

1/2 KREUZER

COPPER

KM#	Date	Mintage	Fine	VF	XF	Unc
463	1851	.796	1.00	3.00	5.00	25.00
	1852	.981	1.00	3.00	5.00	25.00
	1853	.797	1.00	3.00	5.00	25.00
	1854	.528	1.00	3.00	5.00	25.00
	1855	.641	1.00	3.00	5.00	25.00
	1856	.462	1.00	3.00	5.00	25.00

KREUZER

.7700 g, .187 SILVER, .0046 oz ASW
Obv: Head right, MAX. IOS.
Rev: Crowned shield within palm branches.

KM#	Date	Mintage	Fine	VF	XF	Unc
308	1802	—	8.00	20.00	40.00	100.00
	1803	—	8.00	20.00	40.00	100.00

NOTE: Earlier dates (1799-1800) exist for this type.

KM#	Date	Mintage	Fine	VF	XF	Unc
317	1801	—	5.00	10.00	30.00	80.00
	1802	—	5.00	10.00	30.00	80.00

Obv. leg: MAX. IOS. H.I.B.C.
Rev: W/o numeric value.

KM#	Date	Mintage	Fine	VF	XF	Unc
315	1801	—	5.00	10.00	30.00	80.00
	1802	—	5.00	10.00	30.00	80.00
	1803	—	5.00	10.00	30.00	80.00
	1806/0	—	5.50	11.00	32.50	90.00

NOTE: Earlier date (1800) exists for this type.

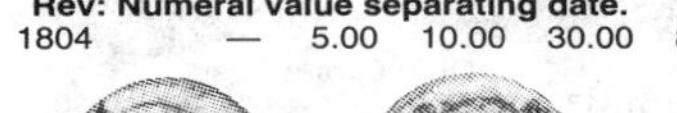

Rev: Numeral value separating date.

KM#	Date	Mintage	Fine	VF	XF	Unc
329	1804	—	5.00	10.00	30.00	80.00

Obv. leg: MAX. IOS. C.Z.P.B.
Rev: LAND MUNZ, oval arms separating value.

KM#	Date	Mintage	Fine	VF	XF	Unc
330	1804	—	5.00	10.00	30.00	80.00
	1805	—	5.00	10.00	30.00	80.00

COPPER

KM#	Date	Mintage	Fine	VF	XF	Unc
343	1806	.145	25.00	50.00	125.00	250.00

NOTE: Minted for use in Tyrol, then occupied by Bavaria.

.7700 g, .187 SILVER, .0046 oz ASW

KM#	Date	Mintage	Fine	VF	XF	Unc
344	1806	—	3.00	5.00	10.00	65.00
	1807	—	3.00	5.00	10.00	65.00
	1808	—	3.00	5.00	10.00	65.00

KM#	Date	Mintage	Fine	VF	XF	Unc
344	1809	—	3.00	5.00	10.00	65.00
	1810	—	3.00	5.00	10.00	65.00
	1811	—	3.00	5.00	10.00	65.00
	1812	—	3.00	5.00	10.00	65.00
	1813	—	3.00	5.00	10.00	65.00
	1814	—	3.00	5.00	10.00	65.00
	1815	—	3.00	5.00	10.00	65.00
	1816	—	3.00	5.00	10.00	65.00
	1817	—	3.00	5.00	10.00	65.00
	1818	—	3.00	5.00	10.00	65.00
	1819	—	3.00	5.00	10.00	65.00
	1820	—	3.00	5.00	10.00	65.00
	1821	—	3.00	5.00	10.00	65.00
	1822	—	3.00	5.00	10.00	65.00
	1823	—	3.00	5.00	10.00	65.00
	1824	—	3.00	5.00	10.00	65.00
	1825	—	3.00	5.00	10.00	65.00

Obv. leg: LUDWIG KOENIG. . .

KM#	Date	Mintage	Fine	VF	XF	Unc
376	1827	—	3.00	5.00	10.00	75.00
	1828	—	3.00	5.00	10.00	75.00
	1829	—	3.00	5.00	10.00	75.00
	1830	—	3.00	5.00	10.00	75.00

Obv. leg: LUDWIG I KOENIG. . .

KM#	Date	Mintage	Fine	VF	XF	Unc
390	1830	—	3.00	5.00	10.00	60.00
	1831	—	3.00	5.00	10.00	60.00
	1832	—	3.00	5.00	10.00	60.00
	1833	—	3.00	5.00	10.00	60.00
	1834	—	3.00	5.00	10.00	60.00
	1835	—	3.00	5.00	10.00	60.00

.8400 g, .166 SILVER, .0044 oz ASW

KM#	Date	Mintage	Fine	VF	XF	Unc
422	1839	1.474	1.00	2.00	5.00	20.00
	1840	1.769	1.00	2.00	5.00	20.00
	1841	1.591	1.00	2.00	5.00	20.00
	1842	1.855	1.00	2.00	5.00	20.00
	1843	1.373	1.00	2.00	5.00	20.00
	1844	1.324	1.00	2.00	5.00	20.00
	1845	1.660	1.00	2.00	5.00	20.00
	1846	1.849	1.00	2.00	5.00	20.00
	1847	1.519	1.00	2.00	5.00	20.00
	1848	1.746	1.00	2.00	5.00	20.00
(452)	1849	1.971	1.00	2.00	5.00	20.00
	1850	3.135	1.00	2.00	5.00	20.00
	1851	2.084	1.00	2.00	5.00	20.00
	1852	1.915	1.00	2.00	5.00	20.00
	1853	1.528	1.00	2.00	5.00	20.00
	1854	1.650	1.00	2.00	5.00	20.00
	1855	1.510	1.00	2.00	5.00	20.00
	1856	1.335	1.00	2.00	5.00	20.00

KM#	Date	Mintage	Fine	VF	XF	Unc
473	1858	2.400	1.00	2.50	4.50	10.00
	1859	—	1.00	2.50	4.50	10.00
	1860	.231	1.00	2.50	4.50	10.00
	1861	3.276	1.00	2.50	4.50	10.00
	1862	3.358	1.00	2.50	4.50	10.00
	1863	3.356	1.00	2.50	4.50	10.00
	1864	3.293	1.00	2.50	4.50	10.00

KM#	Date	Mintage	Fine	VF	XF	Unc
487	1865	1.837	1.00	2.50	4.50	10.00
	1866	2.542	1.00	2.50	4.50	10.00
	1867	2.305	1.00	2.50	4.50	10.00
	1868	2.526	1.00	2.50	4.50	10.00
	1869	2.774	1.00	2.50	4.50	10.00
	1870	2.199	1.00	2.50	4.50	10.00
	1871	2.634	1.00	2.50	4.50	10.00

3 KREUZER

(1 Groschen)

1.3500 g, .333 SILVER, .0144 oz ASW
Obv: Head right, leg: MAX. IOS. P. B.
Rev: Crowned oval arms separating value.

KM#	Date	Mintage	Fine	VF	XF	Unc
309	1801	—	10.00	25.00	60.00	125.00
	1802	—	10.00	25.00	60.00	125.00

NOTE: Earlier dates (1799-1800) exist for this type.

Obv. leg: MAX. IOS. H.I.B.C. &

KM#	Date	Mintage	Fine	VF	XF	Unc
322	1803	—	10.00	25.00	60.00	125.00
	1804	—	10.00	25.00	60.00	125.00

Obv. leg: MAX. IOS. C.Z.P.B.

KM#	Date	Mintage	Fine	VF	XF	Unc
331	1804	—	10.00	25.00	60.00	125.00
	1805	—	10.00	25.00	60.00	125.00

Obv: Head right. Rev: Shield w/crown above crossed scepter and sword.

KM#	Date	Mintage	Fine	VF	XF	Unc
352	1807	—	8.00	20.00	60.00	125.00
	1808	—	8.00	20.00	60.00	125.00
	1809	—	8.00	20.00	60.00	125.00
	1810	—	8.00	20.00	60.00	125.00
	1811	—	8.00	20.00	60.00	125.00
	1812	—	8.00	20.00	60.00	125.00
	1813	—	8.00	20.00	60.00	125.00
	1814	—	8.00	20.00	60.00	125.00
	1815	—	8.00	20.00	60.00	125.00
	1816	—	8.00	20.00	60.00	125.00
	1817	—	8.00	20.00	60.00	125.00
	1818	—	8.00	20.00	60.00	125.00
	1819	—	8.00	20.00	60.00	125.00
	1820	—	8.00	20.00	60.00	125.00
	1821	—	8.00	20.00	60.00	125.00
	1822	—	8.00	20.00	60.00	125.00
	1823	—	8.00	20.00	60.00	125.00
	1824	—	8.00	20.00	60.00	125.00
	1825	—	8.00	20.00	60.00	125.00

1.3000 g, .333 SILVER, .0139 oz ASW
Obv. leg: LUDWIG KOENIG. . .

KM#	Date	Mintage	Fine	VF	XF	Unc
377	1827	—	8.00	20.00	60.00	125.00
	1828	—	8.00	20.00	60.00	125.00
	1829	—	8.00	20.00	60.00	125.00
	1830	—	8.00	20.00	60.00	125.00

Obv. leg: LUDWIG I KOENIG. . .

KM#	Date	Mintage	Fine	VF	XF	Unc
391	1830	—	5.00	10.00	25.00	75.00
	1831	—	5.00	10.00	25.00	75.00
	1832	—	5.00	10.00	25.00	75.00
	1833	—	5.00	10.00	25.00	75.00
	1834	—	5.00	10.00	25.00	75.00
	1835	—	5.00	10.00	25.00	75.00
	1836	—	5.00	10.00	25.00	75.00

KM#	Date	Mintage	Fine	VF	XF	Unc
423	1839	.456	2.00	5.00	7.00	25.00
	1840	.235	2.00	5.00	7.00	30.00
	1841	.337	2.00	5.00	7.00	30.00
	1842	.370	2.00	5.00	7.00	30.00
	1843	.337	2.00	5.00	7.00	30.00
	1844	.269	2.00	5.00	7.00	30.00
	1845	.361	2.00	5.00	7.00	30.00
	1846	.463	2.00	5.00	7.00	30.00
	1847	.563	2.00	5.00	7.00	30.00
	1848	.447	2.00	5.00	7.00	30.00
(453)	1849	.373	2.00	5.00	7.00	30.00
	1850	.615	2.00	5.00	7.00	30.00
	1851	.582	2.00	5.00	7.00	30.00
	1852	.282	2.00	5.00	7.00	30.00
	1853	.280	2.00	5.00	7.00	30.00
	1854	.388	2.00	5.00	7.00	30.00
	1855	.285	2.00	5.00	7.00	30.00
	1856	.091	2.00	5.00	7.00	30.00

1.2300 g, .350 SILVER, .0138 oz ASW

KM#	Date	Mintage	Fine	VF	XF	Unc
488	1865	.832	2.00	5.00	7.00	30.00
	1866	.566	2.00	5.00	7.00	30.00
	1867	.099	2.00	5.00	7.00	30.00
	1868	.065	2.00	5.00	7.00	30.00

6 KREUZER

2.7000 g, .333 SILVER, .0289 oz ASW
Obv: Head right, leg: MAX. IOS. P.B.
Rev: Crowned arms, date below.

KM#	Date	Mintage	Fine	VF	XF	Unc
310	1802	—	20.00	50.00	90.00	225.00
	1803	—	20.00	50.00	90.00	225.00

NOTE: Earlier dates (1799-1800) exist for this type.

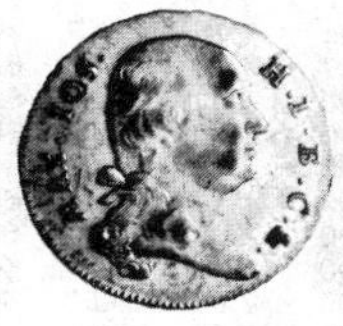

Obv. leg: MAX. IOS. H.I.B.C. &

KM#	Date	Mintage	Fine	VF	XF	Unc
318	1801	—	10.00	20.00	40.00	125.00
	1803	—	10.00	20.00	40.00	125.00
	1804	—	10.00	20.00	40.00	125.00

Obv. leg: MAX. IOS. C.Z.P.B.

KM#	Date	Mintage	Fine	VF	XF	Unc
332	1804	—	20.00	40.00	80.00	200.00
	1805	—	20.00	40.00	80.00	200.00

Obv: Head right.
Rev: Crowned arms w/shield divided.

KM#	Date	Mintage	Fine	VF	XF	Unc
345	1806	—	25.00	50.00	100.00	250.00

KM#	Date	Mintage	Fine	VF	XF	Unc
346	1806	—	5.00	20.00	50.00	125.00
	1807	—	5.00	20.00	50.00	125.00
	1808	—	5.00	20.00	50.00	125.00
	1809	—	5.00	20.00	50.00	125.00
	1810	—	5.00	20.00	50.00	125.00
	1811	—	5.00	20.00	50.00	125.00
	1812	—	5.00	20.00	50.00	125.00
	1813	—	5.00	20.00	50.00	125.00
	1814	—	5.00	20.00	50.00	125.00
	1815	—	5.00	20.00	50.00	125.00
	1816	—	5.00	20.00	50.00	125.00
	1817	—	5.00	20.00	50.00	125.00
	1818	—	5.00	20.00	50.00	125.00
	1819	—	5.00	20.00	50.00	125.00
	1820	—	5.00	20.00	50.00	125.00
	1821/0	—	5.00	20.00	50.00	125.00
	1821	—	5.00	20.00	50.00	125.00
	1822	—	5.00	20.00	50.00	125.00
	1823	—	5.00	20.00	50.00	125.00
	1824	—	5.00	20.00	50.00	125.00
	1825	—	5.00	20.00	50.00	125.00

2.6000 g, .333 SILVER, .0278 oz ASW
Obv. leg: LUDWIG KOENIG. . .

KM#	Date	Mintage	Fine	VF	XF	Unc
378	1827	—	5.00	25.00	65.00	125.00
	1828	—	5.00	25.00	65.00	125.00
	1829	—	5.00	25.00	65.00	125.00

Obv. leg: LUDWIG I KOENIG. . .

KM#	Date	Mintage	Fine	VF	XF	Unc
392	1830	—	5.00	15.00	50.00	100.00
	1831	—	5.00	15.00	50.00	100.00
	1832	—	5.00	15.00	50.00	100.00
	1833	—	5.00	15.00	50.00	100.00
	1834	—	5.00	15.00	50.00	100.00
	1835	—	5.00	15.00	50.00	100.00

KM#	Date	Mintage	Fine	VF	XF	Unc
424	1839	.800	4.00	7.00	20.00	60.00
	1840	—	4.00	7.00	20.00	60.00
	1841	—	4.00	7.00	20.00	60.00
	1842	—	4.00	7.00	20.00	60.00
	1843	—	4.00	7.00	20.00	60.00
	1844	—	4.00	7.00	20.00	60.00
	1845	—	4.00	7.00	20.00	60.00
	1846	—	4.00	7.00	20.00	60.00
	1847	—	4.00	7.00	20.00	60.00
	1848	—	4.00	7.00	20.00	60.00
(454)	1849	—	4.00	7.00	20.00	60.00
	1850	—	4.00	7.00	20.00	60.00
	1851	—	4.00	7.00	20.00	60.00
	1852	—	4.00	7.00	20.00	60.00
	1853	—	4.00	7.00	20.00	60.00
	1854	—	4.00	7.00	20.00	60.00
	1855	—	4.00	7.00	20.00	60.00
	1856	—	4.00	7.00	20.00	60.00

2.4600 g, .350 SILVER, .0276 oz ASW
Obv. leg: SCHEIDE MUNZE added.

KM#	Date	Mintage	Fine	VF	XF	Unc
491	1866	.087	7.50	15.00	50.00	175.00
	1867	.024	10.00	25.00	75.00	200.00

10 KREUZER

3.9000 g, .500 SILVER, .0626 oz ASW
Obv: Maximillian IV Josef right in wreath.
Rev: Crowned 3-fold oval arms.

KM#	Date	Mintage	Fine	VF	XF	Unc
316	1801	—	35.00	75.00	150.00	300.00

NOTE: Earlier date (1800) exists for this type.

Rev. leg: POPOLO

KM#	Date	Mintage	Fine	VF	XF	Unc
319	1801	—	40.00	60.00	150.00	375.00

20 KREUZER

6.6800 g, .583 SILVER, .1252 oz ASW
Obv: Maximillian IV Josef right within wreath.
Rev: Crowned arms within crossed branches, date and value below.

KM#	Date	Mintage	Fine	VF	XF	Unc
311	1801	—	55.00	90.00	150.00	275.00
	1802	—	75.00	130.00	225.00	400.00
	1803	—	55.00	90.00	150.00	275.00

NOTE: Earlier dates (1799-1800) exist for this type.

KM#	Date	Mintage	Fine	VF	XF	Unc
333	1804	—	55.00	100.00	200.00	475.00
	1805	—	55.00	100.00	200.00	475.00

KM#	Date	Mintage	Fine	VF	XF	Unc
347	1806	—	25.00	60.00	125.00	225.00
	1807	—	25.00	60.00	125.00	225.00
	1808	—	25.00	60.00	125.00	225.00
	1809	—	25.00	60.00	125.00	225.00
	1810	—	25.00	60.00	125.00	225.00
	1811	—	25.00	60.00	125.00	225.00
	1812	—	25.00	60.00	125.00	225.00
	1813	—	25.00	60.00	125.00	225.00
	1814	—	25.00	60.00	125.00	225.00
	1815	—	25.00	60.00	125.00	225.00
	1816	—	25.00	60.00	125.00	225.00
	1817	—	25.00	60.00	125.00	225.00
	1818	—	25.00	60.00	125.00	225.00
	1819	—	25.00	60.00	125.00	225.00
	1820	—	25.00	60.00	125.00	225.00
	1821	—	25.00	60.00	125.00	225.00
	1822	—	25.00	60.00	125.00	225.00
	1823	—	25.00	60.00	125.00	225.00

KM#	Date	Mintage	Fine	VF	XF	Unc
347	1824	—	25.00	60.00	125.00	225.00
	1825	—	25.00	60.00	125.00	225.00

1/2 GULDEN

5.3000 g, .900 SILVER, .1533 oz ASW
Ludwig I

KM#	Date	Mintage	Fine	VF	XF	Unc
417	1838	1.750	15.00	25.00	50.00	100.00
	1839	.474	15.00	25.00	50.00	100.00
	1840	.233	15.00	25.00	50.00	125.00
	1841	.243	15.00	25.00	50.00	125.00
	1842	.508	15.00	25.00	50.00	100.00
	1843	.337	15.00	25.00	50.00	125.00
	1844	1.452	15.00	25.00	50.00	100.00
	1845	1.869	15.00	25.00	50.00	100.00
	1846	1.181	15.00	25.00	50.00	100.00
	1847	.241	15.00	25.00	50.00	125.00
	1848	.407	15.00	25.00	50.00	125.00

Maximillian II

KM#	Date	Mintage	Fine	VF	XF	Unc
444	1848	Inc. Ab.	20.00	30.00	50.00	125.00
	1849	.218	20.00	30.00	50.00	125.00
	1850	.189	20.00	30.00	50.00	125.00
	1851	.171	20.00	30.00	50.00	125.00
	1852	.120	20.00	30.00	50.00	125.00
	1853	.206	20.00	30.00	50.00	125.00
	1854	.146	20.00	30.00	50.00	125.00
	1855	.060	20.00	30.00	50.00	100.00
	1856	.074	20.00	30.00	50.00	100.00
	1857	.020	25.00	40.00	65.00	150.00
	1858	.183	20.00	30.00	50.00	100.00
	1859	.405	20.00	30.00	50.00	100.00
	1860	.292	20.00	30.00	50.00	100.00
	1861	.254	20.00	30.00	50.00	100.00
	1862	.141	20.00	30.00	50.00	100.00
	1863	.190	20.00	30.00	50.00	100.00
	1864	.160	20.00	30.00	50.00	100.00

Obv: Ludwig II w/part in hair.

KM#	Date	Mintage	Fine	VF	XF	Unc
479	1864	Inc. Ab.	40.00	75.00	125.00	250.00
	1865	.227	35.00	60.00	100.00	200.00
	1866	.101	40.00	75.00	125.00	250.00

Obv: W/o part in hair.

KM#	Date	Mintage	Fine	VF	XF	Unc
492	1866	Inc. Ab.	40.00	75.00	125.00	250.00
	1867	.100	35.00	60.00	100.00	200.00
	1868	.121	35.00	75.00	100.00	200.00
	1869	.133	35.00	75.00	100.00	200.00
	1870	.111	35.00	75.00	100.00	200.00
	1871	.051	40.00	75.00	125.00	225.00

GULDEN

10.6000 g, .900 SILVER, .3067 oz ASW

Ludwig I

KM#	Date	Mintage	Fine	VF	XF	Unc
414	1837	2.057	15.00	25.00	75.00	125.00
	1838	2.045	15.00	25.00	75.00	125.00
	1839	2.320	15.00	25.00	75.00	125.00
	1840	3.591	15.00	25.00	75.00	125.00
	1841	4.362	15.00	25.00	75.00	125.00
	1842	1.449	15.00	25.00	75.00	125.00
	1843	4.832	15.00	25.00	75.00	125.00
	1844	3.491	15.00	25.00	75.00	125.00
	1845	1.115	15.00	25.00	75.00	125.00
	1846	.686	15.00	25.00	85.00	150.00
	1847	.387	15.00	25.00	85.00	150.00
	1848	.437	15.00	25.00	85.00	150.00

Maximillian I

KM#	Date	Mintage	Fine	VF	XF	Unc
445	1848	Inc. Ab.	20.00	40.00	75.00	125.00
	1849	.366	20.00	40.00	75.00	125.00
	1850	.343	20.00	40.00	75.00	125.00
	1851	.224	20.00	40.00	75.00	125.00
	1852	.453	20.00	40.00	75.00	125.00
	1853	.257	20.00	40.00	75.00	125.00
	1854	.513	20.00	40.00	75.00	125.00
	1855	1.076	20.00	40.00	75.00	125.00
	1856	.455	20.00	40.00	75.00	125.00
	1857	.032	25.00	60.00	100.00	150.00
	1858	.144	25.00	60.00	100.00	150.00
	1859	.529	25.00	60.00	100.00	150.00
	1860	.452	25.00	60.00	100.00	150.00
	1861	.358	25.00	60.00	100.00	150.00
	1862	.266	25.00	60.00	100.00	150.00
	1863	.234	25.00	60.00	100.00	150.00
	1864	.414	25.00	60.00	100.00	150.00

Obv: Ludwig II w/part in hair.

KM#	Date	Mintage	Fine	VF	XF	Unc
480	1864	Inc. Ab.	50.00	100.00	150.00	250.00
	1865	.167	50.00	100.00	150.00	250.00
	1866	.122	50.00	100.00	150.00	250.00

Obv: W/o part in hair.

KM#	Date	Mintage	Fine	VF	XF	Unc
493	1866	Inc. Ab.	50.00	100.00	150.00	250.00
	1867	.086	50.00	100.00	150.00	250.00
	1868	.122	50.00	100.00	150.00	250.00
	1869	.122	50.00	100.00	150.00	250.00
	1870	.072	50.00	100.00	150.00	250.00
	1871	.035	60.00	120.00	175.00	275.00

ZWEY (2) GULDEN

21.2100 g, .900 SILVER, .6138 oz ASW
Obv. leg: LUDWIG I KOENIG V. BAYERN.

KM#	Date	Mintage	Fine	VF	XF	Unc
438	1845	.883	30.00	50.00	125.00	275.00
	1846	1.523	30.00	50.00	125.00	275.00
	1847	1.491	30.00	50.00	125.00	275.00
	1848	.950	30.00	50.00	125.00	275.00

Obv. leg: MAXIMILIAN II KOENIG V. BAYERN.
Rev: Similar to KM#438.

KM#	Date	Mintage	Fine	VF	XF	Unc
446	1848	Inc. Ab.	27.50	50.00	120.00	250.00
	1849	.741	27.50	50.00	120.00	250.00
	1850	.915	27.50	50.00	120.00	250.00
	1851	1.157	27.50	50.00	120.00	250.00
	1852	1.356	27.50	50.00	120.00	250.00
	1853	.634	27.50	50.00	120.00	250.00
	1854	.430	27.50	50.00	120.00	250.00
	1855	.585	30.00	60.00	150.00	300.00
	1856	.510	30.00	60.00	150.00	300.00

Restoration of Madonna Column in Munich

KM#	Date	Mintage	Fine	VF	XF	Unc
465	1855	1.000	20.00	30.00	50.00	125.00

1/2 THALER

14.0300 g, .833 SILVER, .3757 oz ASW
Similar to 1 Thaler, KM#313.

KM#	Date	Mintage	Fine	VF	XF	Unc
312	1801	—	175.00	350.00	750.00	1500.
	1802	—	175.00	350.00	750.00	1500.
	1803	—	175.00	350.00	750.00	1500.

NOTE: Earlier dates (1799-1800) exist for this type.

KM#	Date	Mintage	Fine	VF	XF	Unc
323	1803	—	100.00	200.00	450.00	850.00
	1804	—	100.00	200.00	450.00	850.00
	1805	—	100.00	200.00	450.00	850.00

(School Prize w/o Denomination)

KM#	Date	Mintage	Fine	VF	XF	Unc
324	ND (1799-1805)	—	75.00	165.00	300.00	600.00

KM#	Date	Mintage	Fine	VF	XF	Unc
348	ND (1806-08)	*1,500	100.00	250.00	400.00	750.00

Obv: Script letters.

KM#	Date	Mintage	Fine	VF	XF	Unc
353	ND (1807-08)	—	100.00	200.00	400.00	800.00

Obv: Block or normal letters.

KM#	Date	Mintage	Fine	VF	XF	Unc
357	ND (1808-37)	.025	95.00	200.00	300.00	625.00

THALER

28.0000 g, .833 SILVER, .7500 oz ASW
Maximillian IV Josef

KM#	Date	Mintage	Fine	VF	XF	Unc
313	1801	—	100.00	175.00	400.00	900.00
	1802	—	120.00	200.00	475.00	1000.

NOTE: Earlier dates (1799-1800) exist for this type.

Obv. leg: D.G. MAXIM. IOSEPH

KM#	Date	Mintage	Fine	VF	XF	Unc
320.1	1802	—	1000.	1500.	3500.	5000.

Obv. leg: D.G. MAX. IOSEPH

KM#	Date	Mintage	Fine	VF	XF	Unc
320.2	1802	—	650.00	1250.	1750.	3000.
	1803	—	650.00	1250.	1750.	3000.

Obv: Uniformed bust right, leg: MAXIMILIAN. . .

KM#	Date	Mintage	Fine	VF	XF	Unc
321	1802	—	350.00	700.00	1500.	3000.

KM#	Date	Mintage	Fine	VF	XF	Unc
325	1803	—	125.00	200.00	450.00	1000.

Rev. leg: GOTT UND DAS - VATERLAND.

KM#	Date	Mintage	Fine	VF	XF	Unc
326	1803	—	175.00	400.00	1000.	2200.
	1804	—	175.00	400.00	1000.	2200.
	1805	—	175.00	400.00	1000.	2200.

Rev. leg: FUR GOTT UND - VATERLAND.

KM#	Date	Mintage	Fine	VF	XF	Unc
334	1804	—	1500.	3000.	4000.	6000.
	1805	—	125.00	200.00	450.00	1000.

KM#	Date	Mintage	Fine	VF	XF	Unc
349	1806	—	100.00	250.00	600.00	1750.

Rev: Crowned lions facing outward.

KM#	Date	Mintage	Fine	VF	XF	Unc
350	1806	—	200.00	400.00	1000.	2000.

Obv: Bust w/pigtail.

KM#	Date	Mintage	Fine	VF	XF	Unc
354	1807	.100	1500.	3000.	5000.	7500.

KM#	Date	Mintage	Fine	VF	XF	Unc
355	1807	Inc. Ab.	75.00	150.00	250.00	700.00
	1808	.055	75.00	150.00	250.00	700.00
	1809	8,932	85.00	150.00	275.00	750.00
	1810	6,721	90.00	160.00	300.00	900.00
	1811	.011	90.00	160.00	300.00	900.00
	1812	8,432	90.00	160.00	300.00	900.00
	1813	5,888	90.00	160.00	300.00	900.00
	1814	4,579	90.00	160.00	300.00	900.00
	1815	6,913	90.00	160.00	300.00	900.00
	1816	.011	90.00	160.00	300.00	900.00
	1817	4,638	90.00	160.00	300.00	900.00
	1818	—	90.00	160.00	300.00	900.00
	1819	—	90.00	160.00	300.00	900.00
	1820	3,974	90.00	160.00	300.00	900.00
	1821	3,826	90.00	160.00	300.00	900.00
	1822	—	90.00	160.00	300.00	900.00

(Krone)

29.3400 g, .868 SILVER, .8188 oz ASW

KM#	Date	Mintage	Fine	VF	XF	Unc
358.1	1809	.063	40.00	75.00	175.00	325.00
	1810	.924	40.00	75.00	175.00	325.00
	1811	.196	40.00	75.00	200.00	425.00
	1812	.618	40.00	75.00	125.00	325.00
	1813	.656	40.00	75.00	125.00	325.00
	1814	.975	40.00	75.00	125.00	325.00
	1815	.769	40.00	75.00	125.00	325.00
	1816	2.453	40.00	75.00	125.00	325.00
	1817	.399	40.00	75.00	125.00	325.00
	1818	.119	40.00	100.00	200.00	425.00
	1819	.292	40.00	100.00	200.00	425.00
	1820	.132	40.00	100.00	200.00	425.00
	1821	.260	40.00	75.00	185.00	350.00
	1822	.052	40.00	100.00	200.00	425.00
	1823	.016	40.00	100.00	200.00	425.00
	1824	.031	40.00	100.00	200.00	425.00
	1825	.081	40.00	75.00	185.00	350.00

Obv. leg: JOEPHUS (Error).

KM#	Date	Mintage	Fine	VF	XF	Unc
358.2	1813	Inc. Ab.	100.00	225.00	625.00	1250.

(Convention)

28.0600 g, .833 SILVER, .7515 oz ASW
Granting of Bavarian Constitution

KM#	Date	Mintage	Fine	VF	XF	Unc
361	1818	.040	30.00	60.00	100.00	175.00

Rev: Similar to KM#355.

KM#	Date	Mintage	Fine	VF	XF	Unc
367	1822	.051	100.00	200.00	450.00	1000.
	1823	.047	150.00	350.00	750.00	1800.
	1824	3,907	100.00	225.00	500.00	1200.
	1825	1,932	100.00	200.00	450.00	1000.

Coronation of Ludwig I

KM#	Date	Mintage	Fine	VF	XF	Unc
370	1825	—	150.00	200.00	300.00	500.00

Death of Reichenbach and Fraunhofer
Obv: Similar to KM#370.

KM#	Date	Mintage	Fine	VF	XF	Unc
371	1826	—	150.00	200.00	275.00	450.00

Removal of University From Landshut to Munich
Obv: Similar to KM#370.

KM#	Date	Mintage	Fine	VF	XF	Unc
372	1826	—	150.00	200.00	275.00	450.00

(Krone)

29.5400 g, .871 SILVER, .8272 oz ASW

KM#	Date	Mintage	Fine	VF	XF	Unc
373	1826	.051	100.00	150.00	250.00	500.00
	1827	.066	130.00	200.00	300.00	750.00
	1828	.079	100.00	150.00	300.00	500.00
	1829	.094	130.00	200.00	300.00	750.00

(Convention)

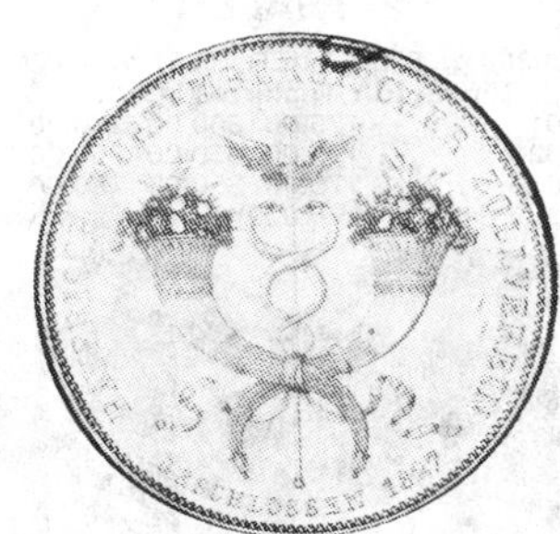

28.0600 g, .833 SILVER, .7515 oz ASW
Bavaria-Wurttemberg Customs Treaty Signing
Obv: Similar to KM#370.

KM#	Date	Mintage	Fine	VF	XF	Unc
379	1827	—	150.00	200.00	275.00	500.00

Founding of Order of Ludwig
Obv: Similar to KM#370.

KM#	Date	Mintage	Fine	VF	XF	Unc
380	1827	—	150.00	200.00	275.00	500.00

Founding of Theresien Order
Obv: Similar to KM#370.

KM#	Date	Mintage	Fine	VF	XF	Unc
381	1827	—	150.00	200.00	275.00	500.00

Blessings of Heaven On Royal Family

KM#	Date	Mintage	Fine	VF	XF	Unc
386	1828	—	100.00	125.00	175.00	375.00

Constitution Monument Dedication

KM#	Date	Mintage	Fine	VF	XF	Unc
387	1828	—	150.00	200.00	275.00	450.00

Commercial Treaty Between Bavaria, Prussia, Hesse and Wurttemberg

KM#	Date	Mintage	Fine	VF	XF	Unc
389	1829	—	150.00	200.00	275.00	500.00

Loyalty of Bavarians to Royal Family

KM#	Date	Mintage	Fine	VF	XF	Unc
393	1830	—	150.00	200.00	250.00	450.00

(Krone)

29.5400 g, .871 SILVER, .8272 oz ASW

KM#	Date	Mintage	Fine	VF	XF	Unc
394	1830	.061	75.00	150.00	300.00	650.00
	1831	.064	75.00	150.00	300.00	650.00
	1832	.070	75.00	150.00	300.00	650.00
	1833	.040	75.00	200.00	400.00	900.00
	1834	.017	90.00	150.00	300.00	650.00
	1835	7,502	100.00	200.00	400.00	900.00
	1836	7,816	100.00	150.00	300.00	650.00
	1837	.212	75.00	150.00	300.00	600.00

(Convention)

28.0600 g, .833 SILVER, .7515 oz ASW
Opening of the Legislature

KM#	Date	Mintage	Fine	VF	XF	Unc
401	1831	—	150.00	225.00	450.00	650.00

Prince Otto of Bavaria First King of Greece

KM#	Date	Mintage	Fine	VF	XF	Unc
402	1832	—	150.00	200.00	250.00	500.00

Formation of Customs Union With Prussia, Saxony, Hesse and Thuringia

KM#	Date	Mintage	Fine	VF	XF	Unc
403	1833	—	150.00	200.00	250.00	500.00

Monument For Bavarians Who Fell In Russia

KM#	Date	Mintage	Fine	VF	XF	Unc
404	1833	—	150.00	200.00	250.00	500.00

Provincial Legislature

KM#	Date	Mintage	Fine	VF	XF	Unc
405	1834	—	150.00	200.00	275.00	500.00

Erection of Monument at Oberwittelsbach

KM#	Date	Mintage	Fine	VF	XF	Unc
406	1834	—	150.00	200.00	300.00	550.00

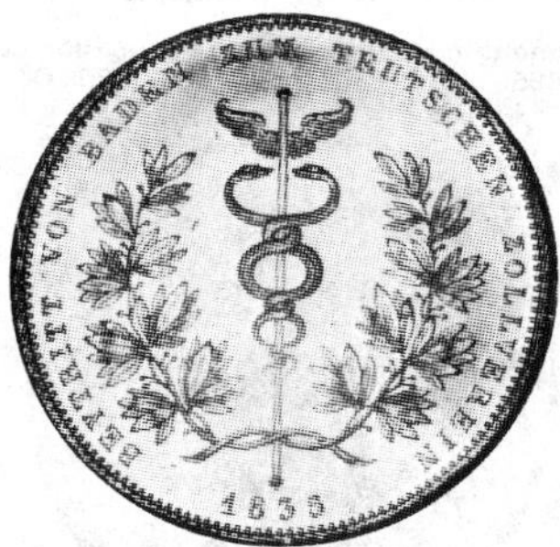

Entry of Baden to German Customs Union

KM#	Date	Mintage	Fine	VF	XF	Unc
407	1835	—	150.00	200.00	250.00	550.00

Establishment of Bavarian Mortgage Bank

KM#	Date	Mintage	Fine	VF	XF	Unc
408	1835	—	150.00	225.00	300.00	575.00

Monument for King Otto Leaving His Mother

KM#	Date	Mintage	Fine	VF	XF	Unc
409	1835	—	150.00	200.00	250.00	450.00

Construction of First Steam Railway

KM#	Date	Mintage	Fine	VF	XF	Unc
410	1835	—	150.00	200.00	275.00	500.00

Monument in Munich to King Maximilian Josef

KM#	Date	Mintage	Fine	VF	XF	Unc
411.1	1835	—	150.00	200.00	300.00	500.00

Rev: Sceptre not beyond shoulder.

KM#	Date	Mintage	Fine	VF	XF	Unc
411.2	1835	—	175.00	300.00	450.00	750.00

School Given To Benedictine Order

KM#	Date	Mintage	Fine	VF	XF	Unc
412	1835	—	150.00	225.00	350.00	550.00

Erection of Otto Chapel at Kiefersfelden

KM#	Date	Mintage	Fine	VF	XF	Unc
413	1836	—	150.00	200.00	275.00	500.00

Order of St. Michael as Order of Merit

KM#	Date	Mintage	Fine	VF	XF	Unc
415	1837	—	150.00	200.00	300.00	575.00

(Vereins)

18.5200 g, .900 SILVER, .5360 oz ASW
Maximillian II

KM#	Date	Mintage	Fine	VF	XF	Unc
468	1857	1.560	20.00	40.00	80.00	150.00
	1858	2.283	20.00	40.00	80.00	150.00
	1859	2.661	20.00	40.00	80.00	150.00
	1860	2.471	20.00	40.00	80.00	150.00
	1861	2.682	20.00	40.00	80.00	150.00
	1862	2.587	20.00	40.00	80.00	150.00
	1863	2.587	20.00	40.00	80.00	150.00
	1864	1.458	20.00	40.00	80.00	150.00

Obv: Ludwig II w/part in hair.

KM#	Date	Mintage	Fine	VF	XF	Unc
481	1864	Inc. Ab.	60.00	135.00	250.00	500.00
	1865	1.144	35.00	75.00	150.00	400.00
	1866	1.075	40.00	80.00	175.00	450.00

Obv: W/o part in hair. Rev: Arms.

KM#	Date	Mintage	Fine	VF	XF	Unc
494.1	1866	Inc. Ab.	35.00	50.00	150.00	175.00
	1867	.595	35.00	55.00	160.00	190.00
	1868	.312	35.00	60.00	160.00	325.00
	1869	.277	35.00	75.00	180.00	375.00
	1870	.264	35.00	60.00	160.00	325.00
	1871	.718	35.00	55.00	150.00	300.00

Rev: New arabesques below arms.

KM#	Date	Mintage	Fine	VF	XF	Unc
494.2	1871	—	300.00	600.00	1100.	1800.

Obv: J. REIS below truncation.

KM#	Date	Mintage	Fine	VF	XF	Unc
495	1871	Inc. Ab.	125.00	250.00	400.00	600.00

KM#	Date	Mintage	Fine	VF	XF	Unc
489	ND(1865)	.110	20.00	35.00	75.00	115.00
	1866	Inc. Ab.	20.00	35.00	60.00	100.00
	1867	Inc. Ab.	20.00	35.00	60.00	100.00
	1868	Inc. Ab.	20.00	35.00	60.00	100.00
	1869	Inc. Ab.	20.00	35.00	60.00	100.00
	1870	Inc. Ab.	20.00	35.00	60.00	100.00
	1871	Inc. Ab.	20.00	35.00	60.00	100.00

German Victory In Franco-Prussian War

KM#	Date	Mintage	Fine	VF	XF	Unc
496	1871	.150	30.00	45.00	70.00	130.00
	1871	—	—	—	Proof	375.00

ZWEI (2) THALER

(3-1/2 Gulden)

37.1200 g, .900 SILVER, 1.0743 oz ASW
Monetary Union of Six South German States
Ludwig I

KM#	Date	Mintage	Fine	VF	XF	Unc
416	1837	—	150.00	200.00	275.00	450.00

Reapportionment of Bavaria
Obv: Similar to KM#416.

KM#	Date	Mintage	Fine	VF	XF	Unc
418	1838	—	150.00	300.00	450.00	750.00

Maximilian I, Elector of Bavaria
Obv: Similar to KM#416.

KM#	Date	Mintage	Fine	VF	XF	Unc
425	1839	—	150.00	200.00	375.00	575.00

Obv: Similar to KM#416.

KM#	Date	Mintage	Fine	VF	XF	Unc
426	1839	.113	150.00	250.00	500.00	1400.
	1840	.193	125.00	200.00	400.00	1200.
	1841	.450	150.00	250.00	500.00	1400.

Albrecht Durer
Obv: Similar to KM#416.

KM#	Date	Mintage	Fine	VF	XF	Unc
427	1840	—	150.00	200.00	300.00	550.00

Jean Paul Friedrich Richter
Obv: Similar to KM#416.

KM#	Date	Mintage	Fine	VF	XF	Unc
429	1841	—	150.00	200.00	300.00	550.00

Walhalla Commemorative
Obv: Similar to KM#416.

KM#	Date	Mintage	Fine	VF	XF	Unc
430	1842	—	150.00	200.00	250.00	450.00

Marriage of Crown Prince of Bavaria and Marie, Royal Princess of Prussia
Obv: Similar to KM#416.

KM#	Date	Mintage	Fine	VF	XF	Unc
431.1	1842	—	150.00	200.00	250.00	450.00

Obv: 1 OCTB. 1842 (Error date).

KM#	Date	Mintage	Fine	VF	XF	Unc
431.2	1842	—	150.00	200.00	250.00	450.00

Obv: Similar to KM#416.

KM#	Date	Mintage	Fine	VF	XF	Unc
432	1842	.085	100.00	250.00	450.00	1200.
	1843	.277	100.00	150.00	250.00	700.00
	1844	.122	100.00	175.00	300.00	800.00
	1845	.167	100.00	175.00	300.00	800.00
	1846	.132	100.00	225.00	400.00	1000.
	1847	.012	100.00	225.00	400.00	1000.
	1848	.192	100.00	150.00	250.00	700.00

100th Anniversary Academy of Erlangen
Obv: Similar to KM#416.

KM#	Date	Mintage	Fine	VF	XF	Unc
434	1843	—	150.00	200.00	300.00	550.00

Completion of the General's Hall in Munich
Obv: Similar to KM#416.

KM#	Date	Mintage	Fine	VF	XF	Unc
437	1844	—	150.00	200.00	325.00	600.00

Chancellor Baron von Kreittmayr
Obv: Similar to KM#416.

KM#	Date	Mintage	Fine	VF	XF	Unc
439	1845	—	200.00	325.00	550.00	1000.

Birth of 2 Grandsons
Obv: Similar to KM#416.

KM#	Date	Mintage	Fine	VF	XF	Unc
440	1845	—	150.00	275.00	400.00	650.00

Completion of Canal Between Danube and Main Rivers
Obv: Similar to KM#416.

KM#	Date	Mintage	Fine	VF	XF	Unc
441	1846	—	200.00	325.00	450.00	725.00

Bishop Julius Echter von Mespelbrunn
Obv: Similar to KM#416.

KM#	Date	Mintage	Fine	VF	XF	Unc
442	1847	—	200.00	400.00	600.00	1300.

Abdication of Ludwig I for Maximilian
Obv: Similar to KM#416.

KM#	Date	Mintage	Fine	VF	XF	Unc
443	1848	—	400.00	900.00	1600.	3200.

New Constitution
Maximillian II
Edge: VEREINSMUNZE

KM#	Date	Mintage	Fine	VF	XF	Unc
447.1	1848	—	175.00	225.00	400.00	700.00

Edge: CONVENTION-VOM

KM#	Date	Mintage	Fine	VF	XF	Unc
447.2	1848	—	175.00	325.00	500.00	775.00

Edge: DREY EIN HALB GULDEN

KM#	Date	Mintage	Fine	VF	XF	Unc
447.3	1848	—	225.00	425.00	700.00	1100.

NOTE: Restrike post 1857.

Johann Christoph von Gluck
Obv: Similar to KM#447.1. Edge: VEREINSMUNZE.

KM#	Date	Mintage	Fine	VF	XF	Unc
448.1	1848	—	500.00	750.00	1500.	3000.

Edge: DREY EIN HALB GULDEN

KM#	Date	Mintage	Fine	VF	XF	Unc
448.2	1848	—	500.00	750.00	1500.	3000.

NOTE: Restrike post 1857.

Orlando Di Lasso
Obv: Similar to KM#447.1. Edge: VEREINSMUNZE.

KM#	Date	Mintage	Fine	VF	XF	Unc
455.1	1849	—	700.00	1250.	1750.	3500.

Edge: DREY EIN HALB GULDEN

KM#	Date	Mintage	Fine	VF	XF	Unc
455.2	1849	—	700.00	1250.	1750.	3500.

NOTE: Restrike post 1857.

KM#	Date	Mintage	Fine	VF	XF	Unc
456	1849	—	125.00	250.00	500.00	1200.
	1850	—	100.00	200.00	400.00	900.00
	1851	—	100.00	175.00	350.00	700.00
	1852	—	100.00	200.00	400.00	900.00
	1853	—	100.00	175.00	350.00	700.00
	1854	—	100.00	150.00	250.00	550.00
	1855	.417	100.00	150.00	250.00	550.00
	1856	.142	100.00	150.00	250.00	550.00

Exhibition of German Products in Crystal Palace
Obv: Similar to KM#447.1. Edge: VEREINS MUNZE.

KM#	Date	Mintage	Fine	VF	XF	Unc
464.1	1854	—	175.00	250.00	350.00	550.00

Edge: CONVENTION-VOM

KM#	Date	Mintage	Fine	VF	XF	Unc
464.2	1854	—	175.00	250.00	350.00	550.00

Erection of Monument to King Maximilian II
Obv: Similar to KM#447.1.

KM#	Date	Mintage	Fine	VF	XF	Unc
467	1856	1,152	300.00	425.00	750.00	1400.

(Vereins)

37.0400 g, .900 SILVER, 1.0717 oz ASW
Obv: Similar to KM#447.1.

KM#	Date	Mintage	Fine	VF	XF	Unc
474	1859	.028	350.00	700.00	1350.	2700.
	1860	.069	200.00	375.00	600.00	1250.

Obv: Different hair style.

KM#	Date	Mintage	Fine	VF	XF	Unc
475	1861	.029	300.00	450.00	800.00	1600.
	1862	8,727	400.00	550.00	1000.	2000.
	1863	.011	350.00	500.00	800.00	1800.
	1864	8,201	350.00	550.00	1000.	2000.

Ludwig II

KM#	Date	Mintage	Fine	VF	XF	Unc
490	1865	2,490	2750.	4500.	6000.	8500.
	1867	1,760	3750.	6500.	8500.	14,000.
	1869	—	3750.	6500.	8500.	14,000.

1/2 KRONE

5.0000 g, .900 GOLD, .1446 oz AGW
Maximillian II

KM#	Date	Mintage	Fine	VF	XF	Unc
469	1857	1,749	—	2500.	4000.	7000.
	1858	1,020	—	3000.	4500.	7500.
	1859	1,200	—	3000.	4500.	7500.
	1860	—	—	—	8000.	12,000.
	1861	32 pcs.	—	—	8000.	12,000.
	1863	—	—	—	8000.	12,000.
	1863	—	—	—	Proof	*
	1864	—	—	—	8000.	12,000.

***NOTE:** Stack's Hammel sale 9/82 Proof realized $13,000.

Ludwig II

KM#	Date	Mintage	Fine	VF	XF	Unc
482	1864	—	—	—	Rare	—
	1865	—	—	—	Rare	—
	1866	—	—	—	Rare	—
	1867	12 pcs.	—	—	Rare	—
	1868	—	—	—	Rare	—
	1869	—	—	—	Rare	—
	1869	—	—	—	Proof	*

***NOTE:** Stack's Hammel sale 9/82 Proof realized $17,000.

KRONE

10.0000 g, .900 GOLD, .2892 oz AGW
Maximillian II

KM#	Date	Mintage	Fine	VF	XF	Unc
470	1857	771 pcs.	—	5000.	8000.	12,000.
	1858	753 pcs.	—	5000.	8000.	12,000.
	1859	200 pcs.	—	6000.	10,000.	15,000.
	1860	45 pcs.	—	—	12,000.	18,000.
	1861	65 pcs.	—	—	12,000.	18,000.
	1863	—	—	—	12,000.	18,000.
	1864	—	—	—	12,000.	18,000.

Ludwig II

KM#	Date	Mintage	Fine	VF	XF	Unc
483	1864	—	—	—	Rare	—
	1865	—	—	—	Rare	—
	1865	12 pcs.	—	—	Proof	*
	1866	—	—	—	Rare	—
	1867	12 pcs.	—	—	Rare	—
	1868	—	—	—	Rare	—
	1869	—	—	—	Rare	—

***NOTE:** Stack's Hammel sale 9/82 Proof realized $29,000.

MONETARY REFORM

2 MARK

11.1110 g, .900 SILVER, .3215 oz ASW
Ludwig II

KM#	Date	Mintage	Fine	VF	XF	Unc
505	1876D	5.370	35.00	70.00	225.00	550.00
	1877D	1.512	35.00	70.00	250.00	700.00
	1880D	.169	75.00	150.00	600.00	1200.
	1883D	.104	60.00	150.00	325.00	800.00

Otto

KM#	Date	Mintage	Fine	VF	XF	Unc
507	1888D	.172	150.00	300.00	700.00	1200.

Obv: Closed curl.

KM#	Date	Mintage	Fine	VF	XF	Unc
511.1	1891D	.246	12.00	32.50	90.00	240.00
	1893D	.246	20.00	37.50	90.00	200.00
	1896D	.492	12.00	25.00	55.00	150.00
	1898D	.201	50.00	100.00	225.00	500.00
	1899D	.753	12.00	25.00	50.00	140.00
	1900D	.722	12.00	25.00	45.00	125.00

NOTE: Later dates (1901-1913) exist for this type.

Obv: Open curl.

KM#	Date	Mintage	Fine	VF	XF	Unc
511.2	1891D	Inc. Ab.	—	—	—	—
	1893D	Inc. Ab.	—	—	—	—
	1896D	Inc. Ab.	—	—	—	—
	1898D	Inc. Ab.	—	—	—	—
	1899D	Inc. Ab.	—	—	—	—

5 MARK

27.7770 g, .900 SILVER, .8038 oz ASW
Ludwig II

KM#	Date	Mintage	Fine	VF	XF	Unc
502	1874D	.085	40.00	70.00	350.00	800.00
	1875D	.657	40.00	70.00	325.00	700.00
	1876D	1.130	35.00	60.00	250.00	600.00

1.9910 g, .900 GOLD, .0576 oz AGW

KM#	Date	Mintage	Fine	VF	XF	Unc
506	1877D	.635	125.00	200.00	275.00	400.00
	1877D	—	—	—	Proof	1500.
	1878D	.128	350.00	800.00	1000.	1400.

27.7770 g, .900 SILVER, .8038 oz ASW
Otto

KM#	Date	Mintage	Fine	VF	XF	Unc
508	1888D	.069	250.00	400.00	950.00	1650.
	1888D	—	—	—	Proof	3750.

Obv: Closed curl.

KM#	Date	Mintage	Fine	VF	XF	Unc
512.1	1891D	.098	17.50	35.00	100.00	300.00
	1893D	.098	25.00	50.00	120.00	300.00
	1894D	.141	17.50	35.00	120.00	300.00
	1895D	.141	22.50	45.00	110.00	300.00
	1896D	.028	55.00	125.00	600.00	1000.
	1898D	.303	15.00	30.00	65.00	175.00
	1899D	.141	25.00	50.00	90.00	225.00
	1900D	.295	15.00	30.00	80.00	200.00
	Common date		—	—	Proof	900.00

NOTE: Later dates (1901-1913) exist for this type.

Obv: Open curl.

KM#	Date	Mintage	Fine	VF	XF	Unc
512.2	1898D	Inc. Ab.	15.00	30.00	70.00	180.00

NOTE: Later dates (1901-1913) exist for this type.

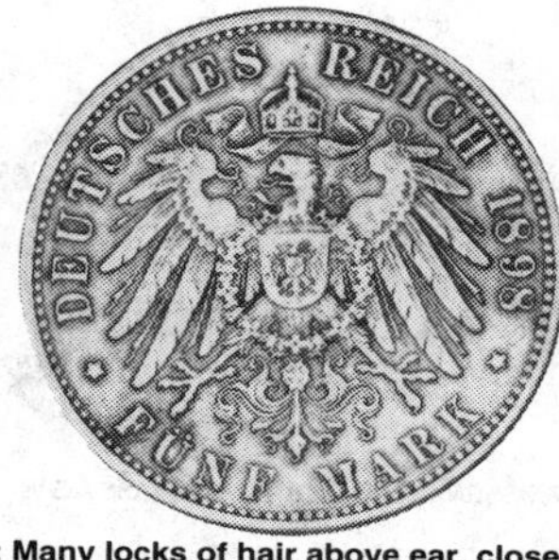

Obv: Many locks of hair above ear, closed curl.

KM#	Date	Mintage	Fine	VF	XF	Unc
512.3	1891D	Inc. Ab.	17.50	25.00	100.00	300.00
	1893D	Inc. Ab.	25.00	50.00	120.00	300.00
	1894D	Inc. Ab.	17.50	35.00	120.00	300.00
	1898D	Inc. Ab.	15.00	30.00	60.00	185.00
	1899D	Inc. Ab.	25.00	50.00	90.00	225.00

NOTE: Later date (1913) exists for this type.

Obv: Large lock of hair above ear, closed curl.

KM#	Date	Mintage	Fine	VF	XF	Unc
512.4	1895D	Inc. Ab.	22.50	45.00	110.00	300.00
	1896D	Inc. Ab.	55.00	125.00	600.00	1000.
	1898D	Inc. Ab.	15.00	30.00	60.00	185.00
	1899D	Inc. Ab.	25.00	50.00	90.00	225.00
	1900D	Inc. Ab.	15.00	30.00	80.00	200.00

NOTE: Later dates (1901-1913) exist for this type.

10 MARK

3.9820 g, .900 GOLD, .1152 oz AGW
Ludwig II
Obv: J. REIS below truncation. Rev: Type I.

KM#	Date	Mintage	Fine	VF	XF	Unc
500	1872D	.626	65.00	125.00	175.00	350.00
	1872D	—	—	—	Proof	1600.
	1873D	1.198	65.00	125.00	175.00	300.00
	1873D	—	—	—	Proof	1600.

Rev: Type II.

KM#	Date	Mintage	Fine	VF	XF	Unc
503	1874D	.407	65.00	120.00	160.00	250.00
	1874D	—	—	—	Proof	1300.
	1875D	.816	65.00	120.00	160.00	250.00
	1876D	.684	65.00	120.00	160.00	250.00
	1877D	.283	65.00	120.00	160.00	250.00
	1878D	.638	65.00	120.00	160.00	250.00
	1879D	.224	65.00	120.00	160.00	250.00
	1880D	.299	65.00	120.00	160.00	250.00
	1881D	.157	65.00	120.00	160.00	250.00
	1881D	—	—	—	Proof	1300.

Otto
Obv. leg: . . . VON BAYERN. Rev: Type II.

KM#	Date	Mintage	Fine	VF	XF	Unc
509	1888D	.281	100.00	200.00	275.00	450.00
	1888D	—	—	—	Proof	1300.

Rev: Type III.

KM#	Date	Mintage	Fine	VF	XF	Unc
510	1890D	.420	65.00	130.00	150.00	200.00
	1893D	.422	65.00	130.00	150.00	200.00
	1896D	.281	65.00	120.00	170.00	225.00
	1898D	.589	65.00	130.00	150.00	200.00
	1900D	.141	125.00	150.00	225.00	300.00
	1900D	—	—	—	Proof	700.00

Obv. leg: . . . V. BAYERN

KM#	Date	Mintage	Fine	VF	XF	Unc
514	1900D	Inc. Ab.	65.00	140.00	225.00	325.00
	Common date		—	—	Proof	800.00

NOTE: Later dates (1901-1912) exist for this type.

20 MARK

7.9650 g, .900 GOLD, .2304 oz AGW
Ludwig II
Rev: Type I.

KM#	Date	Mintage	Fine	VF	XF	Unc
501	1872D	1.556	125.00	150.00	250.00	500.00
	1872D	—	—	—	Proof	1600.
	1873D	2.770	125.00	150.00	250.00	400.00
	1873D	—	—	—	Proof	1600.

Rev: Type II.

KM#	Date	Mintage	Fine	VF	XF	Unc
504	1874D	.615	125.00	150.00	200.00	300.00
	1875D	—	725.00	1400.	2000.	2500.
	1875D	—	—	—	Proof	1500.
	1876D	.454	125.00	150.00	200.00	350.00
	1878D	.050	300.00	625.00	850.00	1400.
	1878D	—	—	—	Proof	1500.

Otto
Rev: Type III.

KM#	Date	Mintage	Fine	VF	XF	Unc
513	1895D	.501	125.00	140.00	160.00	250.00
	1895D	—	—	—	Proof	800.00
	1900D	.501	125.00	140.00	160.00	250.00

NOTE: Later dates (1905-1913) exist for this type.

TRADE COINAGE

DUCAT

3.4900 g, .937 GOLD, .1051 oz AGW
Obv. leg: D.G. MAX. IOS. . .

KM#	Date	Mintage	Fine	VF	XF	Unc
314.1	1801	—	750.00	1250.	2250.	2850.
	1802	—	1000.	1500.	2500.	3100.

NOTE: Earlier dates (1799-1800) exist for this type.

Obv. leg: D.G. MAXIM. IOSEPH

KM#	Date	Mintage	Fine	VF	XF	Unc
314.2	1801	—	1000.	1500.	2500.	3000.
	1802	—	1000.	1500.	2500.	3000.
	1803	—	1250.	1750.	2750.	3250.

NOTE: Earlier dates (1799-1800) exist for this type.

Obv. leg: MAXIMILIAN IOSEPH. . .

KM#	Date	Mintage	Fine	VF	XF	Unc
335	1804	—	1750.	2250.	3000.	3750.
	1805	—	1250.	1750.	2500.	3250.

KM#	Date	Mintage	Fine	VF	XF	Unc
351	1806	3,937	1750.	2250.	3250.	4250.

KM#	Date	Mintage	Fine	VF	XF	Unc
356	1807	2,260	650.00	1125.	1750.	2500.
	1808	1,465	500.00	1050.	1600.	2250.
	1809	3,263	750.00	1250.	2000.	2750.
	1810	3,124	850.00	1350.	2250.	3000.
	1811	—	600.00	1100.	1750.	2500.
	1812	—	850.00	1350.	2250.	3000.
	1813	—	600.00	1100.	1750.	2500.
	1814	—	600.00	1100.	1750.	2500.
	1815	—	750.00	1250.	2000.	2750.
	1816	—	600.00	1000.	1600.	2250.
	1817	—	600.00	1100.	1750.	2500.
	1818	—	600.00	1100.	1750.	2500.
	1819	—	750.00	1250.	2000.	2750.
	1820	—	600.00	1100.	1750.	2500.
	1821	—	500.00	1050.	1600.	2250.
	1822	—	600.00	1100.	1750.	2500.

Obv. leg: BAEIRN. . .

KM#	Date	Mintage	Fine	VF	XF	Unc
362	1821	—	1250.	1950.	3000.	4200.
	1822	—	750.00	1250.	1850.	2650.

Rev. leg: EX AURO DANUBII above river god.

KM#	Date	Mintage	Fine	VF	XF	Unc
363	1821	—	2250.	3250.	4250.	5500.

Rev. leg: EX AURO OENI above river god.

KM#	Date	Mintage	Fine	VF	XF	Unc
364	1821	—	2500.	3500.	5500.	8500.

Isar - Gold Ducat

KM#	Date	Mintage	Fine	VF	XF	Unc
365	1821	—	1750.	2750.	5000.	7750.

Rhine - Gold Ducat

KM#	Date	Mintage	Fine	VF	XF	Unc
366	1821	—	1000.	1750.	3500.	4750.

Obv: Older head.

KM#	Date	Mintage	Fine	VF	XF	Unc
368	1823	4,400	600.00	1000.	1600.	2250.
	1824	.019	750.00	1250.	2000.	2750.
	1825	3,000	600.00	1100.	1650.	2300.

Ludwig I

KM#	Date	Mintage	Fine	VF	XF	Unc
375	1826	696 pcs.	1250.	1850.	2375.	2850.
	1827	4,200	1750.	2500.	3250.	3850.
	1828	3,090	1750.	2000.	2500.	3000.

Obv. leg: LUDWIG I

KM#	Date	Mintage	Fine	VF	XF	Unc
388.1	1828	1,351	800.00	1300.	1800.	2350.
	1829	1,143	600.00	1000.	1500.	2100.
	1830	1,731	600.00	1000.	1500.	2100.
	1831	3,907	1000.	1500.	2100.	2600.
	1832	1,884	600.00	1000.	1500.	2100.
	1833	1,230	1000.	1500.	2100.	2600.
	1834	1,711	1200.	1800.	2600.	3250.

Struck in collared dies.

KM#	Date	Mintage	Fine	VF	XF	Unc
388.2	1835	2,048	600.00	1000.	1500.	2100.

KM#	Date	Mintage	Fine	VF	XF	Unc
428	1840	5,000	600.00	1000.	1500.	2100.
	1841	2,309	650.00	1150.	1800.	2350.
	1842	810 pcs.	650.00	1150.	1800.	2350.
	1843	2,358	650.00	1150.	1800.	2350.
	1844	4,259	850.00	1500.	2350.	3150.
	1845	2,470	600.00	1000.	1500.	2100.
	1846	3,642	650.00	1150.	1800.	2350.
	1847	5,122	600.00	1000.	1500.	2100.
	1848	1,470	600.00	1000.	1500.	2100.

Rev. leg: EX AURO DANUBII above river god.

KM#	Date	Mintage	Fine	VF	XF	Unc
395.1	1830	—	1500.	3000.	4500.	6250.

Rev: Inverted "C" in date.

KM#	Date	Mintage	Fine	VF	XF	Unc
395.2	1830	—	1500.	3250.	4750.	6500.

Obv. leg: LUDWIG I. . .

KM#	Date	Mintage	Fine	VF	XF	Unc
396	1830	—	1500.	3000.	4500.	6250.

Inn - Gold Ducat

KM#	Date	Mintage	Fine	VF	XF	Unc
397	1830	—	1500.	3000.	4500.	6250.

Isar - Gold Ducat

KM#	Date	Mintage	Fine	VF	XF	Unc
398	1830	—	1750.	3600.	5350.	7500.

Rhine - Gold Ducat

KM#	Date	Mintage	Fine	VF	XF	Unc
399	1830	—	1000.	2500.	4000.	5750.

Obv. leg: LUDWIG I. . .

KM#	Date	Mintage	Fine	VF	XF	Unc
400	1830	—	1000.	2500.	4000.	5750.

Rhine - Gold Ducat

KM#	Date	Mintage	Fine	VF	XF	Unc
433	1842	—	500.00	1250.	2250.	3250.
	1846	—	400.00	1000.	2000.	3000.

Maximilian II

Obv. leg: . . . KOENIG V BAYERN

KM#	Date	Mintage	Fine	VF	XF	Unc
457	1849	1,470	750.00	1250.	1750.	2250.
	1850	1,519	500.00	1000.	1250.	1750.
	1851	3,815	400.00	600.00	900.00	1200.
	1852	4,396	400.00	600.00	900.00	1200.
	1853	5,603	400.00	600.00	900.00	1200.
	1854	5,707	400.00	600.00	900.00	1200.
	1855	1,540	500.00	1000.	1250.	1750.
	1856	3,782	400.00	600.00	900.00	1200.
		Obv. leg: . . . BAVARIAE REX				
461	1850	100 pcs.	1750.	2250.	3500.	5250.
		Rev. leg: . . . BERGBAU BEI GOLDKRONACH.				
466	1855	—	12,500.	17,500.	25,000.	35,000.

Rhine - Gold Ducat

KM#	Date	Mintage	Fine	VF	XF	Unc
462	1850	—	500.00	1000.	1700.	2000.
	1851	—	550.00	1200.	2000.	2250.
	1852	—	500.00	1000.	1700.	2000.
	1853	—	500.00	1000.	1700.	2000.
	1854	—	425.00	900.00	1500.	1800.
	1855	—	600.00	1400.	2500.	3000.
	1856	—	425.00	900.00	1500.	1800.
		Reduced size				
477	1863	—	1500.	2500.	4000.	4950.

PATTERNS (Pn)

(Including off metal strikes)

KM#	Date	Mintage	Identification	Mkt.Val.
Pn2	1818	—	1 Thaler, Silver	—
Pn3	1818	—	1 Thaler, Gold	—

KM#	Date	Mintage	Identification	Mkt.Val.
Pn4	1827	—	1 Thaler, KM381	—

KM#	Date	Mintage	Identification	Mkt.Val.
Pn5	1832	—	1 Thaler, KM402	—

KM#	Date	Mintage	Identification	Mkt.Val.
Pn9	1871D	—	20 Mark, Tin, like KM501	—
Pn10	1874D	—	5 Mark, Lead. Obv: KM502. Rev: Value within wreath.	1000.
Pn11	1876D	—	2 Mark, Silver, slightly larger eagle, KM505	—
Pn12	1877D	—	5 Mark, Silver, KM502	—
Pn13	1877D	—	5 Mark, Silver, KM506	—

TRIAL STRIKES (TS)

KM#	Date	Mintage	Identification	Mkt.Val.
TS1	1826	—	1 Thaler, Pewter, rev. KM371	—

KM#	Date	Mintage	Identification	Mkt.Val.
TS2	1826	—	1 Thaler, Pewter, rev. KM372	—

KM#	Date	Mintage	Identification	Mkt.Val.
TS3	1827	—	1 Thaler, Pewter, rev. KM380	—

KM#	Date	Mintage	Identification	Mkt.Val.
TS4	1827	—	1 Thaler, Pewter, rev. KM381	—

KM#	Date	Mintage	Identification	Mkt.Val.
TS5	1831	—	1 Thaler, Pewter, rev. KM401	—

KM#	Date	Mintage	Identification	Mkt.Val.
TS6	1835	—	1 Thaler, Pewter, rev. KM412	—
TS7	1842	—	2 Thaler, Pewter, rev. KM430	—

KM#	Date	Mintage	Identification	Mkt.Val.
TS8	1842	—	2 Thaler, Pewter, rev. KM431.1	—

KM#	Date	Mintage	Identification	Mkt.Val.
TS9	1843	—	2 Gulden, Pewter, rev. KM438	—

KM#	Date	Mintage	Identification	Mkt.Val.
TS10	ND	—	1 Thaler, Silver	—
TS11	1855	—	1 Ducat, Gold	—
TS12	ND	—	1 Thaler, Copper	—

KM#	Date	Mintage	Identification	Mkt.Val.
TS13	1863	—	6 Kreuzer, Copper	—
TS14	ND(1865)	—	1 Thaler, Gold	—

BERG

Located in western Germany. The first Count of Berg took his title in 1101 and the first coins appeared c. 1135. Not until 1380, did a duke rule in Berg. In 1801 Berg was absorbed by France but in 1806, along with Cleves and Julich, became the Grand Duchy of Berg. It was transferred to Westphalia in 1808 and given to Prussia in 1815.

RULERS

Maximilian IV, Joseph (of Bavaria) 1799-1806

Joachim Murat, 1806-1808

MINTMASTERS INITIALS

Letter	Date	Name
PR,R.,.R.	1783-1804	Peter Rudesheim
TS,S,S.,T:s,Sr	1805-1818	Theodor Stockmar

1/2 STUBER

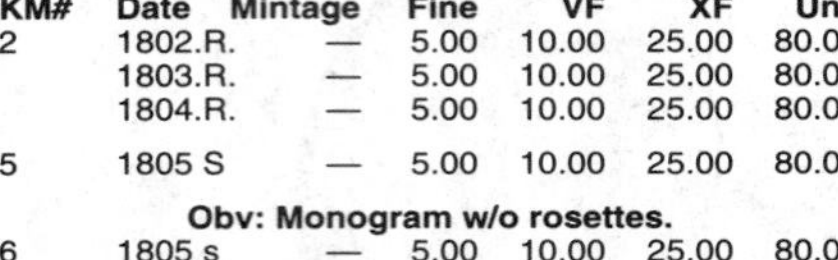

COPPER

KM#	Date	Mintage	Fine	VF	XF	Unc
2	1802.R.	—	5.00	10.00	25.00	80.00
	1803.R.	—	5.00	10.00	25.00	80.00
	1804.R.	—	5.00	10.00	25.00	80.00
5	1805 S	—	5.00	10.00	25.00	80.00

Obv: Monogram w/o rosettes.

KM#	Date	Mintage	Fine	VF	XF	Unc
6	1805 s	—	5.00	10.00	25.00	80.00

3 STUBER

1.8500 g, .220 SILVER, .0130 oz ASW

KM#	Date	Mintage	Fine	VF	XF	Unc
1	1801.R.	—	6.00	12.00	30.00	90.00
	1802.R.	—	6.00	12.00	30.00	90.00
	1803.R.	—	6.00	12.00	30.00	90.00
	1804.R.	—	6.00	12.00	30.00	90.00
	1805.R.	—	6.00	12.00	30.00	90.00
	1806.R.	—	6.00	12.00	30.00	90.00

KM#	Date	Mintage	Fine	VF	XF	Unc
7	1805 S	—	8.00	16.00	35.00	100.00
	1805 T.S.	—	8.00	16.00	35.00	100.00
	1806 S	—	8.00	16.00	35.00	100.00

Obv: Royal crown.

KM#	Date	Mintage	Fine	VF	XF	Unc
9	1806 S	—	10.00	20.00	50.00	135.00

KM#	Date	Mintage	Fine	VF	XF	Unc
10	1806 S	—	7.00	14.00	32.00	95.00
	1806 Sr	—	7.00	14.00	32.00	95.00
	1807 S	—	7.00	14.00	32.00	95.00
	1807 Sr	—	7.00	14.00	32.00	95.00

NOTE: KM#1, 9 and 10 were restruck officially in 1808-09 for circulation and were equal to 10 Centimes.

1/2 THALER

(Reichs)

9.7440 g, .750 SILVER, .2349 oz ASW
Maximillian IV Joseph

KM#	Date	Mintage	Fine	VF	XF	Unc
4	1803 R	—	150.00	300.00	650.00	1500.
	1804 R	—	150.00	300.00	650.00	1500.

THALER

(Reichs)

19.4880 g, .750 SILVER, .4690 oz ASW
Maximillian IV Joseph

KM#	Date	Mintage	Fine	VF	XF	Unc
3	1802 PR	—	225.00	450.00	850.00	2000.
	1803 PR	—	250.00	500.00	900.00	2250.
	1804 PR	—	275.00	550.00	950.00	2500.
	1805 PR	—	300.00	600.00	1000.	2750.

Obv: T. S. below larger head.

KM#	Date	Mintage	Fine	VF	XF	Unc
8	1805 TS	9,396	350.00	550.00	1000.	2500.
	1806 TS	7,044	400.00	600.00	1200.	2750.

Joachim

KM#	Date	Mintage	Fine	VF	XF	Unc
11	1806 TS	8,356	450.00	650.00	1300.	2750.

(Cassa)

17.3230 g, .751 SILVER, .4177 oz ASW

KM#	Date	Mintage	Fine	VF	XF	Unc
12	1807 TS	784 pcs.	1000.	2000.	3000.	5000.

Obv: Similar to KM#12.

KM#	Date	Mintage	Fine	VF	XF	Unc
13	1807 TS	I.A.	1500.	2500.	5000.	10,000.

BIBERACH

Located in Wurttemberg 22 miles to the southwest of Ulm, Biberach became a free imperial city in 1312. The city came under the control of Baden in 1803 and then of Wurttemberg in 1806.

DUCAT

3.5000 g, .986 GOLD, .1109 oz AGW

Peace of Luneville
Obv: City god kneeling at altar, eye of God w/rays above.
Rev: 9-line inscription w/Roman numeral date.

KM#	Date	Mintage	VG	Fine	VF	XF
20	1801	—	—	850.00	1500.	2250.

PATTERNS (Pn)

(Including off metal strikes)

KM#	Date	Mintage	Identification	Mkt.Val.
Pn3	1801	—	1 Ducat, Copper, KM20	150.00
Pn4	1801	—	1 Ducat, Silver, KM20	180.00

BIRKENFELD

Located in southwest Germany. For most of the time prior to 1801, Birkenfeld was in the possession of the Counts Palatine. It was a part of France from 1801-1814, Prussia from 1814-1817 and was made a principality in 1817 and given to the Duke of Oldenburg.

RULERS

Paul Friedrich August (of Oldenburg), 1829-1853

Nikolaus Friedrich Peter (of Oldenburg), 1853-1900

MINT MARKS

B - Hannover

PFENNIG

SILVER, uniface
Schussel-type: Small arms of Pfalz-Veldenz (rampant lion left) on larger arms of Sponheim (checkerboard), SP above.

KM#	Date	Mintage	VG	Fine	VF	XF
1	ND	—	30.00	60.00	95.00	150.00

COPPER

KM#	Date	Mintage	Fine	VF	XF	Unc
6	1848	.158	45.00	80.00	125.00	175.00

KM#	Date	Mintage	Fine	VF	XF	Unc
20	1859B	.072	25.00	60.00	90.00	140.00

2 PFENNIGE

COPPER

KM#	Date	Mintage	Fine	VF	XF	Unc
7	1848	.117	15.00	35.00	65.00	150.00

KM#	Date	Mintage	Fine	VF	XF	Unc
15	1858B	.072	15.00	35.00	60.00	120.00

3 PFENNIGE

COPPER

KM#	Date	Mintage	Fine	VF	XF	Unc
8	1848	.121	17.00	37.50	75.00	150.00

Obv: Crowned NFP monogram.

KM#	Date	Mintage	Fine	VF	XF	Unc
16	1858B	.072	17.00	37.50	75.00	150.00

ALBUS

SILVER
Obv: Small shield of 3-fold arms on larger shield of Sponheim arms. Rev: I/ALB in center, MONETA.NOVA.ARGENT BIRK in legend.

KM#	Date	Mintage	VG	Fine	VF	XF
2	ND	—	45.00	75.00	110.00	175.00

1/2 SILBER GROSCHEN

1.0900 g, .220 SILVER, .0077 oz ASW

KM#	Date	Mintage	Fine	VF	XF	Unc
17	1858B	.060	40.00	80.00	120.00	275.00

SILBER GROSCHEN

2.1900 g, .220 SILVER, .0154 oz ASW
Obv: Crowned arms. Rev: Value.

KM#	Date	Mintage	Fine	VF	XF	Unc
9	1848	.063	35.00	70.00	110.00	225.00

Obv: Different arms.

KM#	Date	Mintage	Fine	VF	XF	Unc
18	1858B	.060	35.00	70.00	110.00	225.00

2-1/2 SILBER GROSCHEN

(1/12 Thaler)

3.2200 g, .375 SILVER, .0388 oz ASW
Obv: Crowned arms. Rev: Value.

KM#	Date	Mintage	Fine	VF	XF	Unc
10	1848	.023	35.00	70.00	110.00	225.00

Obv: Different arms.

KM#	Date	Mintage	Fine	VF	XF	Unc
19	1858B	.036	35.00	70.00	110.00	225.00

BRANDENBURG-ANSBACH-BAYREUTH

Held by Prussia from 1791 to 1805 and then given to Bavaria.

RULERS

Friedrich Wilhelm III of Prussia, 1797-1805

PFENNIG

.2600 g, .111 SILVER, .0009 oz ASW
Obv: Crowned FWR monogram. Rev: Value.

KM#	Date	Mintage				
17	1801B	.616	3.00	7.00	15.00	40.00
	1803B	.984	3.00	7.00	15.00	40.00

NOTE: Earlier date (1799) exists for this type.

KREUZER

.7200 g, .163 SILVER, .0037 oz ASW

KM#	Date	Mintage				
18	1802B	.324	3.00	7.00	20.00	50.00
	1803B	.533	3.00	7.00	20.00	50.00
	1804B	1.243	3.00	7.00	20.00	50.00

3 KREUZER

1.0500 g, .336 SILVER, .0113 oz ASW

KM#	Date	Mintage				
15	1801B	1.335	7.00	15.00	30.00	100.00
	1802B	1.330	7.00	15.00	30.00	100.00

NOTE: Earlier dates (1798-1800) exist for this type.

6 KREUZER

2.4400 g, .375 SILVER, .0294 oz ASW

KM#	Date	Mintage	Fine	VF	XF	Unc
16	1801B	.340	10.00	20.00	60.00	125.00
	1802B	.249	10.00	20.00	60.00	125.00

NOTE: Earlier dates (1798-1800) exist for this type.

TRADE COINAGE

DUCAT

3.5000 g, .986 GOLD, .1109 oz AGW

KM#	Date	Mintage	Fine	VF	XF	Unc
19	1803B	—	—	—	Rare	—

BREMEN

Located in northwest Germany. The city was founded c. 787 but was nominally under control of the archbishops until 1646 when it became a Free Imperial City. Bremen was granted the mint right in 1369 and there was practically continuous coinage until 1907.

FREE CITY

MINTMASTERS INITIALS

Letter	Date	Name
B	1844-1868	Th. W. Bruel, in Hannover
OHK	1761-1805	Otto Heinrich Knorre

SCHWAREN

COPPER

KM#	Date	Mintage	Fine	VF	XF	Unc
241	1859	.069	2.00	5.00	10.00	30.00

2-1/2 SCHWAREN

COPPER
Rev: D.B. in exergue.

KM#	Date	Mintage	Fine	VF	XF	Unc
220	1802	.196	5.00	10.00	20.00	50.00

NOTE: Earlier date (1797) exists for this type.

KM#	Date	Mintage	Fine	VF	XF	Unc
225	1820	.183	5.00	10.00	20.00	50.00

KM#	Date	Mintage	Fine	VF	XF	Unc
234	1841	.131	7.50	15.00	30.00	70.00
	1853	.177	2.50	5.00	10.00	30.00
	1861	.072	2.50	5.00	10.00	30.00
	1866	.162	2.50	5.00	10.00	30.00
235	1841	Inc. Ab.	—	—	—	—

1/2 GROTE

COPPER

KM#	Date	Mintage	Fine	VF	XF	Unc
236	1841	Inc.KM234	9.00	18.00	40.00	135.00

GROTEN

.7700 g, .281 SILVER, .0069 oz ASW

KM#	Date	Mintage	Fine	VF	XF	Unc
230	1840	.262	3.00	6.00	12.00	40.00

6 GROTE/ 1/12 THALER

1.9440 g, .740 SILVER, .0462 oz ASW

KM#	Date	Mintage	Fine	VF	XF	Unc
231	1840	.079	7.00	16.50	35.00	90.00

2.9200 g, .494 SILVER, .0463 oz ASW

KM#	Date	Mintage	Fine	VF	XF	Unc
240	1857	.311	4.00	8.00	18.00	50.00

KM#	Date	Mintage	Fine	VF	XF	Unc
245	1861	.127	4.50	9.00	20.00	60.00

12 GROTE

(= 1/6 Thaler)

3.8890 g, .740 SILVER, .0925 oz ASW

KM#	Date	Mintage	Fine	VF	XF	Unc
232	1840	.193	7.00	12.00	30.00	100.00
	1841	.112	7.00	12.00	30.00	110.00
	1845	.063	7.00	12.00	35.00	140.00
	1846	.056	7.00	12.00	35.00	140.00

Obv: Crowned cornered arms.

KM#	Date	Mintage	Fine	VF	XF	Unc
242	1859	.450	4.00	8.00	20.00	75.00
	1860	.150	5.00	10.00	25.00	85.00

36 GROTE

(=1/2 Thaler)

8.7700 g, .986 SILVER, .2780 oz ASW

KM#	Date	Mintage	Fine	VF	XF	Unc
233	1840	.170	20.00	40.00	75.00	165.00
	1841	.044	25.00	50.00	90.00	185.00
	1845	.084	20.00	40.00	80.00	175.00
	1846	.085	20.00	40.00	80.00	175.00
	1859	.121	20.00	40.00	80.00	175.00

KM#	Date	Mintage	Fine	VF	XF	Unc
243	1859	.050	30.00	60.00	100.00	200.00
	1864	.100	20.00	40.00	75.00	165.00

EIN (1) THALER

(Vereins)

17.5390 g, .986 SILVER, .5560 oz ASW
50th Anniversary - Liberation of Germany

KM#	Date	Mintage	Fine	VF	XF	Unc
246	1863	.020	35.00	55.00	100.00	185.00

2nd German Shooting Festival

KM#	Date	Mintage	Fine	VF	XF	Unc
248	1865 B	.050	30.00	50.00	95.00	165.00

Victory Over France

KM#	Date	Mintage	Fine	VF	XF	Unc
249	1871 B	.061	30.00	50.00	90.00	160.00

MEDALLIC ISSUES (M)

THALER

17.5390 g, .986 SILVER, .5560 oz ASW
Opening of New Business Exchange

KM#	Date	Mintage	Fine	VF	XF	Unc
M1	1864 B	5,000	60.00	100.00	175.00	265.00

PATTERNS (Pn)

(Including off metal strikes)

KM#	Date	Mintage	Identification	Mkt.Val.
Pn38	1802	—	2-1/2 Schwaren, Silver, KM220	200.00
Pn39	1840	—	1 Groten, Gold, KM230	475.00

BRUNSWICK-LUNEBURG-CALENBERG-HANNOVER

Located in north-central Germany. The first duke began his rule in 1235. The first coinage appeared c. 1175. There was considerable shuffling of territory until 1692 when Ernst August became the elector of Hannover. George Ludwig became George I of England in 1714. There was separate coinage for Luneburg until during the reign of George III. The name was changed to Hannover in 1814.

RULERS

George III, (King of Great Britain), 1760-1814

After 1814 see Kingdom of Hannover

BRUNSWICK MINTS AND MINTMASTERS

Clausthal Mint

Letter	Date	Name
A	1833-1849	Vacant Mintmastership
C	1751-1753,1790-1792,1800-1802	Commission
GM,GFM	1802-1807	Georg Friedrich Michaelis
IWL	1807-1819	Johann Wilhelm Lunde
WAJA	1821-1838	Wilhelm August Julius Albert

Hannover Mint

Letter	Date	Name
C	1800-1806	Commission

PFENNING

COPPER
Obv: Wildman holding staff. Rev: Value and date.

KM#	Date	Mintage	Fine	VF	XF	Unc
330.4	1804 GFM	—	10.00	20.00	40.00	80.00

NOTE: Earlier dates (1760-1796) exist for this type.

Obv: Crowned GR monogram.
Rev: Denomination: PFENN

KM#	Date	Mintage	Fine	VF	XF	Unc
360	1801 .C.	—	4.00	7.00	10.00	40.00
	1802 .C.	—	4.00	7.00	10.00	40.00
	1802 GFM	—	4.00	7.00	10.00	40.00
	1803 GFM	—	4.00	7.00	10.00	40.00
	1804 GFM	—	4.00	7.00	10.00	40.00
	1806 GFM	—	4.00	7.00	10.00	40.00

NOTE: Earlier dates (1768-1800) exist for this type.

Obv: Mint mark under monogram

KM#	Date	Mintage	Fine	VF	XF	Unc
360.2	1814 H	—	4.00	7.00	10.00	40.00
	1814 C	—	4.00	7.00	10.00	40.00

Mint mark on rev.

KM#	Date	Mintage	Fine	VF	XF	Unc
360.3	1814 C	—	4.00	7.00	10.00	40.00
	1817 C	—	4.00	7.00	10.00	40.00
	1818 C	—	4.00	7.00	10.00	40.00
	1819 C	—	4.00	7.00	10.00	40.00
	1820 C	—	4.00	7.00	10.00	40.00

Obv: Saint Andrew w/cross. Rev: Value and date.

KM#	Date	Mintage	Fine	VF	XF	Unc
380	1801 C	—	4.00	7.00	14.00	45.00
	1802 C	—	4.00	7.00	14.00	45.00

NOTE: Earlier dates (1780-1793) exist for this type.

2 PFENNING

COPPER

KM#	Date	Mintage	Fine	VF	XF	Unc
402	1801 .C.	—	5.00	9.00	22.00	70.00
	1802 GFM	—	5.00	9.00	22.00	70.00
	1803 GFM	—	5.00	9.00	22.00	70.00
	1804 GFM	—	5.00	9.00	22.00	70.00
	1807 GFM	—	5.00	9.00	22.00	70.00

NOTE: Earlier dates (1794-1800) exist for this type.

4 PFENNING

BILLON

Obv: Crowned GR monogram. Rev: Value, date.

KM#	Date	Mintage	Fine	VF	XF	Unc
344	1802 .C.	—	10.00	20.00	40.00	75.00
	1804 GFM	—	10.00	20.00	40.00	75.00

NOTE: Earlier dates (1762-1799) exist for this type.

MARIENGROSCHEN

BILLON
Obv: Crowned GR monogram.
Rev: Value, date.

KM#	Date	Mintage	Fine	VF	XF	Unc
345	1802 .C.	—	5.00	12.00	25.00	50.00
	1803 GFM	—	5.00	12.00	25.00	50.00
	1804 GFM	—	5.00	12.00	25.00	50.00

NOTE: Earlier dates (1762-1799) exist for this type.

24 MARIENGROSCHEN

SILVER
Obv: Crowned arms above 2/3 in. oval.
Rev: Value above date.

KM#	Date	Mintage	Fine	VF	XF	Unc
341	1801 PLM	—	30.00	50.00	85.00	185.00

NOTE: Earlier dates (1761-1800) exist for this type.

12 EINEN (1/12) THALER

(2 Groschen)

SILVER

KM#	Date	Mintage	Fine	VF	XF	Unc
336	1801 PLM	—	4.00	10.00	20.00	65.00
	1801 EC	—	4.00	10.00	20.00	65.00
	1801 .C.	8,780	4.00	10.00	20.00	65.00
	1801 GFM	—	4.00	10.00	20.00	65.00
	1802 .C.	—	4.00	10.00	20.00	65.00
	1802 GFM	—	4.00	10.00	20.00	65.00
	1803 GFM	—	4.00	10.00	20.00	65.00
	1804 GFM	—	4.00	10.00	20.00	65.00
	1805 GFM	—	4.00	10.00	20.00	65.00
	1806 GFM	—	4.00	10.00	20.00	65.00
	1807 GFM	—	4.00	10.00	20.00	65.00

NOTE: Earlier dates (1760-1800) exist for this type.

1/6 THALER

SILVER
George III
W/o French arms or titles.

KM#	Date	Mintage	Fine	VF	XF	Unc
415	1802 C.	—	20.00	30.00	60.00	175.00
	1802 GFM	—	20.00	30.00	60.00	175.00
	1803 GFM	—	20.00	30.00	60.00	175.00
	1804/3 GFM	—	37.50	65.00	120.00	250.00
	1804 GFM	—	—	—	—	—

KM#	Date	Mintage	Fine	VF	XF	Unc
419	1804 GFM	—	15.00	25.00	75.00	200.00

KM#	Date	Mintage	Fine	VF	XF	Unc
420	1804 GFM	—	15.00	25.00	75.00	200.00

KM#	Date	Mintage	Fine	VF	XF	Unc
423	1807 GM	—	15.00	20.00	40.00	125.00

1/3 THALER

SILVER
George III

KM#	Date	Mintage	Fine	VF	XF	Unc
417	1803 GFM	—	30.00	50.00	115.00	260.00
	1804 GFM	—	30.00	50.00	115.00	260.00

KM#	Date	Mintage	Fine	VF	XF	Unc
421	1804 GFM	—	40.00	65.00	135.00	285.00

1/2 THALER

(Cassen)

SILVER
George III
Rev. value: CASSEN GELD

KM#	Date	Mintage	Fine	VF	XF	Unc
410	1801 C	372 pcs.	—	—	Rare	—

Rev. value: CASSEN=GELD

KM#	Date	Mintage	Fine	VF	XF	Unc
411	1801 C	—	80.00	160.00	275.00	450.00

2/3 THALER

SILVER
George III

KM#	Date	Mintage	Fine	VF	XF	Unc
412	1801 .C.	—	30.00	55.00	125.00	265.00
	1802 .C.	—	30.00	55.00	125.00	265.00

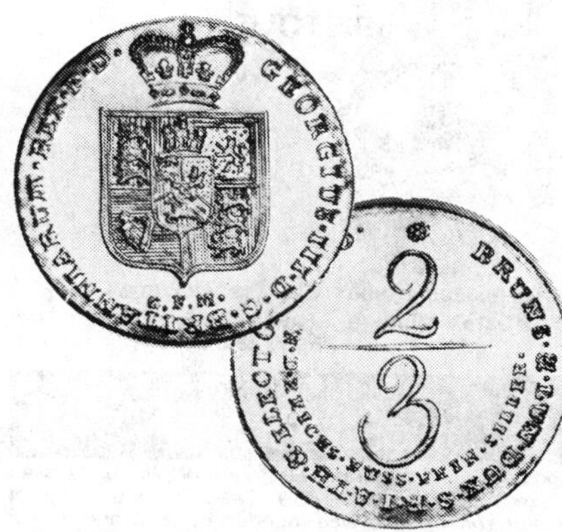

KM#	Date	Mintage	Fine	VF	XF	Unc
413	1801 .C.	—	30.00	50.00	110.00	245.00
	1802	—	30.00	50.00	110.00	245.00
	1802 .C.	—	30.00	50.00	110.00	245.00
	1802 GFM	—	30.00	50.00	110.00	245.00
	1803 GFM	—	30.00	50.00	110.00	245.00
	1804 GFM	—	30.00	50.00	110.00	245.00
	1805 GFM	—	30.00	50.00	110.00	245.00

KM#	Date	Mintage	Fine	VF	XF	Unc
422	1805 GFM	—	30.00	50.00	110.00	245.00
	1806 GFM	—	30.00	50.00	110.00	245.00
	1807 GFM	—	30.00	50.00	110.00	245.00

THALER

(Cassengeld)

SILVER
George III

KM#	Date	Mintage	Fine	VF	XF	Unc
414	1801 C	126 pcs.	400.00	750.00	1250.	2000.

TRADE COINAGE

DUCAT

3.5000 g, .986 GOLD, .1109 oz AGW
Obv: Large modified arms.
Rev. leg: EX AURO . . . above horse.

KM#	Date	Mintage	Fine	VF	XF	Unc
416	1802 .C.	—	350.00	525.00	900.00	1400.
	1802 GFM	—	400.00	600.00	1000.	1600.
	1804 GFM	—	300.00	525.00	800.00	1200.

PISTOLE

6.6500 g, .900 GOLD, .1924 oz AGW

KM#	Date	Mintage	Fine	VF	XF	Unc
418	1803 C	—	350.00	650.00	1100.	2000.

BRUNSWICK-WOLFENBUTTEL

Located in north-central Germany. Wolfenbuttel was annexed to Brunswick in 1257. The Wolfenbuttel line of the Brunswick house was founded in 1318 and was a fairly constant line until 1884 when Prussia installed a government that lasted until 1913. Brunswick was given to the Kaiser's son-in-law, who was the previous duke's grandson in 1913 and he was forced to abdicate in 1918.

RULERS

Karl Wilhelm Ferdinand, 1780-1806
Friedrich Wilhelm, 1806-1815
Karl II (under regency of George III of Great Britain), 1815-1820
Karl II (under regency of George IV of Great Britain), 1820-1823
Karl II, 1823-1830
Wilhelm, 1831-1884
Prussian rule, 1884-1913

MINTMASTERS INITIALS

Letter	Date	Name
B,LB	1844-1866	Theodor Wilhelm Bruel, in Hannover
B	1850-1859	Johann W. Chr. Brumleu, in Brunswick
CvC	1820-1850	Cramer von Clausbruch, in Brunswick
FR	1814-1820	Friedrich Ritter, in Brunswick
K	1776-1802	Christian Friedrich Krull, die-cutter in Brunswick
MC	1779-1806,1820	Munz - Commission at Brunswick

PFENNIG

COPPER
Obv: Horse left.

KM#	Date	Mintage	Fine	VF	XF	Unc
995	1801 MC	—	3.00	8.00	15.00	50.00
	1802 MC	—	3.00	8.00	15.00	40.00
	1803 MC	—	3.00	8.00	15.00	50.00
	1804 MC	—	3.00	8.00	15.00	50.00
	1805 MC	—	3.00	8.00	15.00	50.00
	1806 MC	—	3.00	8.00	15.00	50.00

NOTE: Earlier dates (1780-1800) exist for this type.

Obv: M.C. below horse.

KM#	Date	Mintage	Fine	VF	XF	Unc
1050.1	1813 MC	—	2.00	3.50	6.00	50.00
	1814 MC	—	2.00	3.50	6.00	50.00

Obv: F.R. below horse.

KM#	Date	Mintage	Fine	VF	XF	Unc
1050.2	1814 FR	—	1.00	2.00	5.00	40.00
	1815 FR	—	1.00	2.00	5.00	40.00

Obv: F.R. below horse, leg: GEORG P.R.T.N.

KM#	Date	Mintage	Fine	VF	XF	Unc
1068	1816 FR	—	3.00	6.00	10.00	60.00
	1818 FR	—	3.00	6.00	10.00	60.00

KM#	Date	Mintage	Fine	VF	XF	Unc
1069	1816 FR	—	2.00	3.50	6.00	50.00
	1817 FR	—	2.00	3.50	6.00	50.00
	1818 FR	—	2.00	3.50	6.00	50.00
	1819 FR	—	2.00	3.50	6.00	50.00
	1820 FR	—	2.00	3.50	6.00	50.00

Obv. leg: FRIEDRICH WILHELM. . .

KM#	Date	Mintage	Fine	VF	XF	Unc
1075	1818	—	15.00	30.00	60.00	140.00

Obv. leg: GEORG D.G.

KM#	Date	Mintage	Fine	VF	XF	Unc
1076	1818 FR	—	2.50	4.50	8.00	50.00

Obv. leg: GEORG T.N. . . begins at upper left.

KM#	Date	Mintage	Fine	VF	XF	Unc
1077	1818 FR	—	2.50	4.50	8.00	50.00
	1819 FR	—	2.50	4.50	8.00	50.00
	1820 FR	—	2.50	4.50	8.00	50.00

Obv. leg: GEORG T.N. begins at lower left.

KM#	Date	Mintage	Fine	VF	XF	Unc
1078	1819 FR	—	2.50	4.50	8.00	50.00

Obv: W/o F.R., leg: GEORG IV. R.TVT. . .
Rev: MC below date.

KM#	Date	Mintage	Fine	VF	XF	Unc
1079	1819 MC	—	2.50	4.50	8.00	50.00
	1820 MC	—	2.50	4.50	8.00	50.00

Obv. leg: GEORGE IV D.G.R.TVT. . .

KM#	Date	Mintage	Fine	VF	XF	Unc
1085	1820 MC	—	2.50	4.50	8.00	50.00
	1822 MC	—	2.50	4.50	8.00	50.00
	1823 MC	—	2.50	4.50	8.00	50.00

Obv. leg: GEORGE IV D.G.R.T.N. . . ET.L.

KM#	Date	Mintage	Fine	VF	XF	Unc
1094	1822 CvC	—	2.50	4.50	8.00	50.00
	1823 CvC	—	2.50	4.50	8.00	50.00

Obv. leg. ends: . . . BR. U.LUEN.

KM#	Date	Mintage	Fine	VF	XF	Unc
1098	1823 CvC	—	1.00	2.00	3.00	40.00
	1824 CvC	—	1.00	2.00	3.00	40.00
	1825 CvC	—	1.00	2.00	3.00	40.00
	1826 CvC	—	1.00	2.00	3.00	40.00
	1828 CvC	—	1.00	2.00	3.00	40.00
	1829/8 CvC	—	3.00	6.00	12.50	50.00
	1829 CvC	—	1.00	2.00	3.00	40.00
	1830 CvC	—	1.00	2.00	3.00	40.00

Obv. leg. ends: . . . BR.U.L.

KM#	Date	Mintage	Fine	VF	XF	Unc
1107	1824 Cvc	—	1.00	2.00	3.00	40.00

Obv. leg. ends: . . . BR. U. LUEN.
Rev. value: PFENNIG.

KM#	Date	Mintage	Fine	VF	XF	Unc
1120	1831 CvC	—	1.00	3.00	5.00	40.00
	1832 CvC	—	1.00	3.00	5.00	40.00
	1833 CvC	—	1.00	3.00	5.00	40.00
	1834 CvC	—	1.00	3.00	5.00	40.00

Rev. value: PFENNIG.

KM#	Date	Mintage	Fine	VF	XF	Unc
1127	1834 CvC	—	1.00	3.00	5.00	40.00

KM#	Date	Mintage	Fine	VF	XF	Unc
1142	1851 B	—	1.00	2.00	5.00	35.00
	1852 B	.270	1.00	2.00	5.00	35.00
	1853 B	.139	1.00	2.00	5.00	35.00
	1855 B	.079	1.00	2.00	5.00	35.00
	1856 B	.514	1.00	2.00	5.00	35.00

Rev: W/o B below date.

KM#	Date	Mintage	Fine	VF	XF	Unc
1148	1854	.126	3.00	5.00	10.00	90.00
	1856	Inc.Ab.	3.00	5.00	10.00	90.00

Obv. leg: HERZOGTH.BRAUNSCHWEIG.

KM#	Date	Mintage	Fine	VF	XF	Unc
1154	1859	.103	1.00	2.00	3.50	25.00
	1860	.307	1.00	2.00	3.50	25.00

2 PFENNIGE

COPPER

KM#	Date	Mintage	Fine	VF	XF	Unc
1056	1814 FR	—	3.00	5.00	14.00	50.00
	1815 FR	—	3.00	5.00	14.00	50.00

Obv: W/o F.R. below monogram.

KM#	Date	Mintage	Fine	VF	XF	Unc
1064	1815	—	3.50	6.00	15.00	50.00

Rev: M.C. below date.

KM#	Date	Mintage	Fine	VF	XF	Unc
1086	1820 MC	—	2.50	4.00	10.00	45.00

Rev: C.v.C. below date.

KM#	Date	Mintage	Fine	VF	XF	Unc
1099	1823 CvC	—	3.00	5.00	14.00	50.00

KM#	Date	Mintage	Fine	VF	XF	Unc
1108	1824 CvC	—	2.50	4.00	10.00	45.00
	1826 CvC	—	2.50	4.00	10.00	45.00
	1827 CvC	—	2.50	4.00	10.00	45.00
	1828 CvC	—	2.50	4.00	10.00	45.00
	1829 CvC	—	2.50	4.00	10.00	45.00
	1830 CvC	—	2.50	4.00	10.00	45.00

Obv. leg: WILHELM. . .

KM#	Date	Mintage	Fine	VF	XF	Unc
1123	1832 CvC	—	6.00	12.00	25.00	65.00
	1833 CvC	—	6.00	12.00	25.00	65.00
	1834 CvC	—	6.00	12.00	25.00	65.00

Rev. value: PFENNIG.

KM#	Date	Mintage	Fine	VF	XF	Unc
1128	1834 CvC	—	10.00	20.00	35.00	125.00

KM#	Date	Mintage	Fine	VF	XF	Unc
1143	1851 B	—	1.50	3.00	6.00	35.00
	1852 B	.135	1.50	3.00	6.00	35.00
	1853 B	.124	1.50	3.00	6.00	35.00
	1854 B	.063	1.50	3.00	6.00	35.00
	1855 B	.189	1.50	3.00	6.00	35.00
	1855	—	—	—	—	—
	1856 B	.253	1.50	3.00	6.00	35.00

KM#	Date	Mintage	Fine	VF	XF	Unc
1155	1859	.062	1.00	2.00	4.00	32.00
	1860	.147	1.00	2.00	4.00	32.00

4 PFENNIGE

BILLON
Obv: Horse. Rev: Value

KM#	Date	Mintage	Fine	VF	XF	Unc
997	1801 MC	—	5.00	12.00	25.00	50.00
	1802 MC	—	5.00	12.00	25.00	50.00
	1803 MC	—	5.00	12.00	25.00	50.00
	1804 MC	—	5.00	12.00	25.00	50.00

NOTE: Earlier dates (1780-1800) exist for this type.

1.2300 g, .187 SILVER, .0073 oz ASW
Obv: Prancing horse left, 'F.R.' below, leg. ends: BRIETL. Rev: Value.

KM#	Date	Mintage	Fine	VF	XF	Unc
1087	1820 FR	.035	6.00	18.00	45.00	175.00

Obv: W/o F.R. Rev: C.V.C. below date.

KM#	Date	Mintage	Fine	VF	XF	Unc
1100	1823 CvC	.063	3.00	10.00	25.00	90.00

6 PFENNIGE

BILLON
Obv: Horse. Rev: Value.

KM#	Date	Mintage	Fine	VF	XF	Unc
1019	1802 MC	—	5.00	15.00	30.00	60.00
	1804 MC	—	5.00	15.00	30.00	60.00

NOTE: Earlier dates (1784-1800) exist for this type.

1.3900 g, .250 SILVER, .0111 oz ASW
Obv: M.C. below horse.

KM#	Date	Mintage	Fine	VF	XF	Unc
1057	1814 MC	—	3.00	6.00	15.00	50.00

Obv: B. instead of BR in legend.

KM#	Date	Mintage	Fine	VF	XF	Unc
1058	1814 MC	—	3.00	6.00	15.00	50.00

Obv: F.R. below mound.

KM#	Date	Mintage	Fine	VF	XF	Unc
1059	1814 FR	—	3.00	7.00	20.00	60.00
	1815 FR	.133	3.00	7.00	20.00	60.00

BILLON
Obv. leg: GEORG T.N. CAROLI D. BR.

KM#	Date	Mintage	Fine	VF	XF	Unc
1070	1816 FR	.036	5.00	10.00	25.00	100.00
	1819 FR	.030	5.00	10.00	25.00	100.00

Obv. leg: GEORG IV. . . Rev: C.V.C. below date.

KM#	Date	Mintage	Fine	VF	XF	Unc
1101	1823 CvC	.060	3.00	7.00	20.00	80.00

Obv. leg. ends: . . . BR U L.

KM#	Date	Mintage	Fine	VF	XF	Unc
1116	1828 CvC	—	3.00	7.00	15.00	50.00

1/2 GROSCHEN

(1/60 Thaler)
(Vereins)

1.0900 g, .220 SILVER, .0077 oz ASW

KM#	Date	Mintage	Fine	VF	XF	Unc
1151	1858	.576	2.00	4.00	8.00	35.00
	1859	.131	2.50	5.00	10.00	40.00
	1860	.313	2.00	4.00	8.00	35.00

MARIENGROSCHEN

BILLON
Obv: Horse left. Rev: Value, date.

KM#	Date	Mintage	Fine	VF	XF	Unc
1031	1802 MC	—	5.00	15.00	30.00	60.00
	1803 MC	—	5.00	15.00	30.00	60.00
	1804 MC	—	5.00	15.00	30.00	60.00
	1805 MC	—	5.00	15.00	30.00	60.00
	1806 MC	—	5.00	15.00	30.00	60.00

NOTE: Earlier dates (1788-1800) exist for this type.

GROSCHEN

SILVER

KM#	Date	Mintage	VG	Fine	VF	XF
1137	1847 CVC	—	400.00	750.00	1250.	2000.

(1/30 Thaler)
(Vereins)

2.1900 g, .220 SILVER, .0154 oz ASW

KM#	Date	Mintage	Fine	VF	XF	Unc
1150	1857	.039	5.00	10.00	20.00	50.00
	1858	.713	3.00	6.00	12.00	40.00
	1859	.594	3.00	6.00	12.00	40.00
	1860	.095	4.00	8.00	16.00	45.00

2 MARIENGROSCHEN

BILLON

KM#	Date	Mintage	Fine	VF	XF	Unc
1045	1804 M.C.	—	5.00	10.00	20.00	50.00

4 GUTE GROSCHEN

5.3500 g, .521 SILVER, .0896 oz ASW

KM#	Date	Mintage	Fine	VF	XF	Unc
1135	1840 CvC	.060	20.00	40.00	75.00	225.00

8 GUTE GROSCHEN

SILVER

KM#	Date	Mintage	Fine	VF	XF	Unc
1026	1801 MC	—	15.00	35.00	80.00	200.00
	1803 MC	—	15.00	35.00	80.00	200.00
	1804 MC	—	15.00	35.00	80.00	200.00
	1805 MC	—	15.00	35.00	80.00	200.00

NOTE: Earlier dates (1786-1799) exist for this type.

16 GUTE GROSCHEN

SILVER
Obv: Arms. Rev: Value.

KM#	Date	Mintage	Fine	VF	XF	Unc
1020	1801 MC	—	18.00	40.00	100.00	220.00
	1802 MC	—	18.00	40.00	100.00	220.00
	1803 MC	—	18.00	40.00	100.00	220.00
	1804 MC	—	18.00	40.00	100.00	220.00
	1805 MC	—	18.00	40.00	100.00	220.00

NOTE: Earlier dates (1784-1799) exist for this type.

24 MARIENGROSCHEN

(= 2/3 Thaler)

SILVER

KM#	Date	Mintage	Fine	VF	XF	Unc
1034	1801 MC	—	25.00	60.00	140.00	325.00
	1802 MC	—	25.00	60.00	140.00	325.00
	1803 MC	—	25.00	60.00	140.00	325.00
	1804 MC	—	25.00	60.00	140.00	325.00
	1805 MC	—	25.00	60.00	140.00	325.00
	1806 MC	—	25.00	60.00	140.00	325.00

NOTE: Earlier dates (1789-1800) exist for this type.

13.0800 g, .993 SILVER, .4176 oz ASW
Obv. leg: FRIDERICVS. . .

KM#	Date	Mintage	Fine	VF	XF	Unc
1060	1814 FR	—	100.00	175.00	300.00	525.00
	1815 FR	.036	100.00	175.00	300.00	525.00

KM#	Date	Mintage	Fine	VF	XF	Unc
1065	1815 FR	—	90.00	150.00	250.00	450.00
	1816 FR	.027	90.00	150.00	250.00	450.00
	1817 FR	.019	90.00	150.00	250.00	450.00
	1818 FR	.017	90.00	150.00	250.00	450.00

Obv. leg: REX BRITANNIAR.

KM#	Date	Mintage	Fine	VF	XF	Unc
1088	1820 MC	.024	100.00	180.00	300.00	550.00

Rev: CvC below date.

KM#	Date	Mintage	Fine	VF	XF	Unc
1091	1821 CvC	.029	85.00	145.00	250.00	450.00
	1823 CvC	.030	85.00	145.00	250.00	450.00

Obv. leg: ZU BRAUNS.

KM#	Date	Mintage	Fine	VF	XF	Unc
1102	1823 CvC	—	85.00	145.00	275.00	500.00
	1824 CvC	—	85.00	145.00	275.00	500.00
	1825 CvC	—	85.00	145.00	275.00	500.00
	1826 CvC	.040	85.00	145.00	275.00	500.00
	1828 CvC	—	85.00	145.00	275.00	500.00
	1829 CvC	.034	85.00	145.00	275.00	500.00

Obv. leg: ZU BRAUNSCHW.

KM#	Date	Mintage	Fine	VF	XF	Unc
1109	1824 CvC	.032	50.00	100.00	150.00	250.00
	1825 CvC	.032	50.00	100.00	150.00	250.00
	1826 CvC	—	50.00	100.00	150.00	250.00
	1828 CvC	—	50.00	100.00	150.00	250.00
	1829 CvC	—	50.00	100.00	150.00	250.00

KM#	Date	Mintage	Fine	VF	XF	Unc
1124	1832 CvC	.032	40.00	80.00	125.00	225.00
	1833 CvC	.027	40.00	80.00	125.00	225.00
	1834 CvC	.030	40.00	80.00	125.00	225.00

24 EINEN (1/24) THALER

BILLON

Obv: Horse. Rev: Value.

999	1802 MC	—	5.00	15.00	30.00	60.00

NOTE: Earlier dates (1780-1798) exist for this type.

1.9400 g, .375 SILVER, .0233 oz ASW

Rev: F.R. below date.

1061	1814 FR	—	3.00	6.00	10.00	50.00
	1815 FR	.066	3.00	6.00	10.00	50.00

Obv. leg: GEORG T.N.CAROLI D.BR:. Rev: Value.

1080	1819 FR	.058	4.00	10.00	40.00	150.00

Obv. leg: GEORG IV. Rev: Value, M.C. below date.

1089	1820 MC	—	3.00	7.00	15.00	60.00

Rev: C.v.C. below date.

1103	1823 CvC	—	3.00	7.00	20.00	80.00

Obv. leg: BRAUNSCHW. U. LUEN.

1112	1825 CvC	—	5.00	15.00	25.00	100.00

1/12 THALER

BILLON

Similar to KM#1051.3.

1000	1801 MC	—	5.00	12.00	25.00	50.00
	1802 MC	—	5.00	12.00	25.00	50.00
	1803 MC	—	5.00	12.00	25.00	50.00
	1804 MC	—	5.00	12.00	25.00	50.00
	1805 MC	—	5.00	12.00	25.00	50.00
	1806 MC	—	5.00	12.00	25.00	50.00

NOTE: Earlier dates (1780-1800) exist for this type.

3.3400 g, .437 SILVER, .0469 oz ASW

Obv: Prancing horse left, MC below. Rev: Value.

1051.1	1813 MC	—	4.00	8.00	15.00	60.00
	1814 MC	—	4.00	8.00	15.00	60.00

Obv: FR below horse.

1051.2	1815 FR	—	3.00	5.00	10.00	50.00

Obv: W/o initials below horse. Rev: FR below date.

1051.3	1815 FR	—	3.00	5.00	10.00	50.00

BILLON

Obv. leg: GEORG D.

KM#	Date	Mintage	Fine	VF	XF	Unc
1071	1816 FR	—	3.00	8.00	20.00	80.00
	1817 FR	—	3.00	8.00	20.00	80.00
	1818 FR	—	3.00	8.00	20.00	80.00
	1819 FR	—	3.00	8.00	20.00	80.00

Obv. leg: GEORG IV.

1090	1820 MC	—	3.00	7.00	15.00	60.00

Rev: CvC below date.

1092	1821 CvC	—	3.00	5.00	10.00	60.00
	1822 CvC	—	3.00	5.00	10.00	60.00
	1823 CvC	—	3.00	5.00	10.00	60.00

Obv. leg: BRAUNSCHW. U. LUEN.

1104	1823 CvC	—	3.00	5.00	10.00	60.00
	1824 CvC	—	3.00	5.00	10.00	60.00
	1825 CvC	—	3.00	5.00	10.00	60.00
	1826 CvC	—	3.00	5.00	10.00	60.00
	1827 CvC	—	3.00	5.00	10.00	60.00
	1828 CvC	—	3.00	5.00	10.00	60.00
	1829 CvC	—	3.00	5.00	10.00	60.00
	1830 CvC	—	3.00	5.00	10.00	60.00

Obv. leg: BRAUNSCHW. U.L.

1105	1823 CvC	—	7.50	15.00	30.00	125.00
	1824 CvC	—	7.50	15.00	30.00	125.00
	1825 CvC	—	7.50	15.00	30.00	125.00
	1826 CvC	—	7.50	15.00	30.00	125.00

Obv. leg: BRAUNS. U. LUEN.

1106	1823 CvC	—	3.00	5.00	10.00	60.00
	1824 CvC	—	3.00	5.00	10.00	60.00
	1828 CvC	—	3.00	5.00	10.00	60.00
	1829 CvC	—	3.00	5.00	10.00	60.00

1/6 THALER

SILVER

1001	1801 MC	—	6.00	15.00	30.00	90.00
	1802 MC	—	6.00	15.00	30.00	90.00
	1803 MC	—	6.00	15.00	30.00	90.00
	1804 MC	—	6.00	15.00	30.00	90.00

NOTE: Earlier dates (1780-1799) exist for this type.

5.2000 g, .563 SILVER, .0941 oz ASW

Obv: Prancing horse left, M.C. below.

KM#	Date	Mintage	Fine	VF	XF	Unc
1052	1813 MC	—	7.50	15.00	40.00	125.00
	1814 MC	—	7.50	15.00	40.00	125.00

THALER

SILVER

Obv: Small arms. Rev: Value, date.

1030	1801 MC	—	—	—	Rare	—

NOTE: Earlier dates (1787-1796) exist for this coin.

28.0600 g, .833 SILVER, .7516 oz ASW

1093	1821 CvC	1,480	1000.	2000.	3500.	5500.

(Convention)

22.2700 g, .750 SILVER, .5371 oz ASW

Wilhelm

Obv: FRITZ.F. at truncation.

1129	1837 CvC	2,788	75.00	150.00	400.00	900.00
	1838 CvC	.033	50.00	100.00	300.00	600.00

Obv: Smaller head.

1130	1839 CvC	.041	35.00	70.00	200.00	500.00

Obv: Smaller head, w/o name at truncation.

1131	1839 CvC	I.A.	25.00	50.00	150.00	400.00
	1840 CvC	.086	25.00	50.00	150.00	400.00
	1841 CvC	.304	20.00	40.00	125.00	350.00
	1842 CvC	.117	20.00	40.00	125.00	350.00
	1848 CvC	.011	30.00	60.00	200.00	550.00
	1850 CvC	5,671	35.00	80.00	250.00	700.00

Obv. leg. ends: . . . U.L.
Rev: Similar to KM#1129.

KM#	Date	Mintage	Fine	VF	XF	Unc
1144	1851 B	5,742	50.00	135.00	325.00	850.00

Obv. leg. ends: . . . LUN.

KM#	Date	Mintage	Fine	VF	XF	Unc
1146	1853 B	.024	35.00	125.00	285.00	750.00
	1854 B	.097	25.00	45.00	160.00	425.00
	1855 B	.010	40.00	135.00	315.00	825.00

(Vereins)

18.5200 g, .900 SILVER, .5360 oz ASW

KM#	Date	Mintage	Fine	VF	XF	Unc
1152	1858 B	.049	30.00	55.00	125.00	250.00
	1859 B	.030	35.00	65.00	150.00	330.00
	1865 B	.020	30.00	55.00	125.00	250.00
	1866 B	.010	25.00	45.00	110.00	215.00
	1867 B	.010	30.00	55.00	125.00	250.00
	1870 B	.107	30.00	55.00	125.00	250.00
	1871 B	.048	25.00	45.00	110.00	215.00

2 THALER

(3-1/2 Gulden)

37.1200 g, .900 SILVER, 1.0743 oz ASW
Wilhelm

KM#	Date	Mintage	Fine	VF	XF	Unc
1136	1842 CvC	.052	100.00	200.00	500.00	1200.
	1843 CvC	.068	100.00	200.00	500.00	1200.
	1844 CvC	.015	125.00	275.00	650.00	1600.
	1845 CvC	.011	125.00	275.00	650.00	1600.
	1846 CvC	.015	125.00	275.00	650.00	1600.
	1847 CvC	.015	125.00	240.00	550.00	1400.
	1848 CvC	.011	125.00	240.00	550.00	1400.
	1849 CvC	.013	125.00	275.00	650.00	1600.
	1850 CvC	.077	125.00	275.00	650.00	1600.

KM#	Date	Mintage	Fine	VF	XF	Unc
1140	1850	—	—	—	—	—
	1850 B	Inc.Ab.	100.00	150.00	400.00	850.00
	1851 B	.010	125.00	200.00	625.00	1250.
	1852 B	.011	125.00	200.00	625.00	1250.
	1854 B	.253	90.00	125.00	150.00	400.00
	1855 B	.620	90.00	125.00	150.00	400.00

25th Anniversary of Reign

KM#	Date	Mintage	Fine	VF	XF	Unc
1149	1856 B	.017	90.00	125.00	175.00	300.00

2 1/2 THALER

3.3200 g, .900 GOLD, .0961 oz AGW
Similar to KM#1072.

KM#	Date	Mintage	Fine	VF	XF	Unc
1032	1801 MC	—	375.00	750.00	1350.	2000.
	1802 MC	—	300.00	625.00	1150.	1750.
	1806 MC	—	300.00	625.00	1150.	2000.

NOTE: Earlier dates (1788-1800) exist for this type.

Obv: Crowned many quartered arms w/garlands.
Rev: Value, F.R. below.

KM#	Date	Mintage	Fine	VF	XF	Unc
1066	1815 FR	—	600.00	1000.	1650.	2500.

KM#	Date	Mintage	Fine	VF	XF	Unc
1072	1816 FR	—	575.00	800.00	1125.	1750.
	1818 FR	—	825.00	1150.	1350.	2000.
	1819 FR	—	700.00	950.00	1250.	1750.

KM#	Date	Mintage	Fine	VF	XF	Unc
1095	1822 CvC	—	550.00	900.00	1500.	2000.

Rev: W/o legend around border.

KM#	Date	Mintage	Fine	VF	XF	Unc
1113	1825 CvC	—	350.00	500.00	875.00	1500.
	1828 CvC	—	425.00	625.00	1000.	1650.

Karl II

KM#	Date	Mintage	Fine	VF	XF	Unc
1117	1829 CvC	—	400.00	600.00	900.00	1500.

KM#	Date	Mintage	Fine	VF	XF	Unc
1125	1832 CvC	—	450.00	650.00	1000.	1500.

Wilhelm

KM#	Date	Mintage	Fine	VF	XF	Unc
1145	1851 B	4,138	350.00	500.00	750.00	1100.

5 THALER

6.6500 g, .900 GOLD, .1924 oz AGW
Obv: Similar to KM#1110. Rev: Similar to KM#1062.

KM#	Date	Mintage	Fine	VF	XF	Unc
1025	1801 MC	—	575.00	875.00	1250.	2000.
	1802 MC	—	425.00	625.00	1000.	1800.
	1803 MC	—	—	—	Rare	—
	1804 MC	—	575.00	875.00	1250.	2000.
	1805 MC	—	500.00	750.00	1150.	1850.
	1806 MC	—	500.00	750.00	1150.	1850.

NOTE: Earlier dates (1785-1800) exist for this type.

Obv. leg: FRIDERICVS. . .

KM#	Date	Mintage	Fine	VF	XF	Unc
1081	1814 FR	—	—	—	—	—

KM#	Date	Mintage	Fine	VF	XF	Unc
1062	1814 FR	—	600.00	925.00	1350.	2000.
	1815 FR	—	525.00	800.00	1200.	1850.

Rev. leg. ends: . . . BR. ET LVN.

KM#	Date	Mintage	Fine	VF	XF	Unc
1073	1816 FR	—	675.00	1000.	1650.	2250.
	1817 FR	—	575.00	875.00	1500.	2150.
	1818 FR	—	675.00	1000.	1650.	2250.
	1819 FR	—	675.00	1000.	1650.	2250.
1096	1822 CvC	—	675.00	1000.	1650.	2250.
	1823 CvC	—	850.00	1250.	1850.	2750.

KM#	Date	Mintage	Fine	VF	XF	Unc
1110	1824 CvC	—	425.00	625.00	950.00	1500.
	1825 CvC	—	445.00	675.00	1000.	1650.
	1828 CvC	—	445.00	675.00	1000.	1650.
	1830 CvC	—	500.00	775.00	1150.	1750.

KM#	Date	Mintage	Fine	VF	XF	Unc
1126	1832 CvC	—	525.00	800.00	1250.	1850.
	1834 CvC	—	575.00	900.00	1500.	2150.

10 THALER

13.3000 g, .900 GOLD, .3848 oz AGW
Similar to KM#1054.

KM#	Date	Mintage	Fine	VF	XF	Unc
1041	1801 MC	—	675.00	1150.	2000.	3000.
	1804 MC	—	750.00	1250.	2000.	3000.
	1805 MC	—	550.00	875.00	1500.	2500.
	1806 MC	—	750.00	1250.	1850.	2750.

NOTE: Earlier dates (1794-1800) exist for this type.

KM#	Date	Mintage	Fine	VF	XF	Unc
1054	1813 MC	—	750.00	1250.	1850.	2750.
	1814 MC	—	675.00	1150.	1750.	2350.
1055	1814 FR	—	750.00	1250.	1850.	3000.

KM#	Date	Mintage	Fine	VF	XF	Unc
1074	1817 FR	—	675.00	1150.	1750.	2500.
	1818 FR	—	550.00	875.00	1500.	2500.
	1819 FR	—	675.00	1150.	1750.	2500.
1097	1822 CvC	—	750.00	1250.	1850.	3000.

KM#	Date	Mintage	Fine	VF	XF	Unc
1111	1824 CvC	—	750.00	1250.	1850.	2750.
	1825 CvC	—	600.00	1000.	1650.	2500.
	1829 CvC	—	825.00	1350.	2000.	2750.
	1830 CvC	—	750.00	1250.	1850.	2500.

Karl II

KM#	Date	Mintage	Fine	VF	XF	Unc
1115	1827 CvC	—	900.00	1500.	2500.	3750.
	1828 CvC	—	900.00	1500.	2500.	3750.
	1829 CvC	—	825.00	1350.	2000.	3000.
	1829 CvC	—	—	—	Proof	5500.

KM#	Date	Mintage	Fine	VF	XF	Unc
1121	1831 CvC	—	750.00	1250.	1850.	2500.

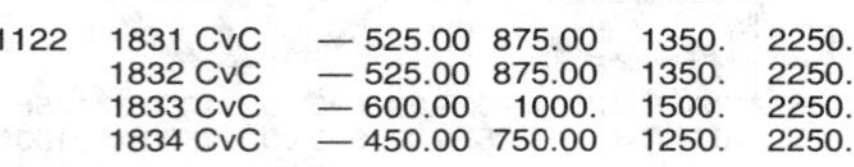

KM#	Date	Mintage	Fine	VF	XF	Unc
1122	1831 CvC	—	525.00	875.00	1350.	2250.
	1832 CvC	—	525.00	875.00	1350.	2250.
	1833 CvC	—	600.00	1000.	1500.	2250.
	1834 CvC	—	450.00	750.00	1250.	2250.

Wilhelm
Obv. leg. ends: . . . U.L.

KM#	Date	Mintage	Fine	VF	XF	Unc
1141	1850 B	9,763	975.00	1650.	2150.	2750.

Obv. leg. ends: . . . LUN.

KM#	Date	Mintage	Fine	VF	XF	Unc
1147	1853 B	.150	400.00	650.00	1000.	2000.
	1854 B	.163	400.00	650.00	1000.	2000.
	1855 B	.020	750.00	1250.	1750.	2500.
	1856 B	.057	400.00	650.00	1000.	2000.
	1857 B	.054	400.00	650.00	1100.	2250.

KRONE

11.1110 g, .900 GOLD, .3215 oz AGW
Wilhelm

KM#	Date	Mintage	Fine	VF	XF	Unc
1153	1858 B	.032	500.00	900.00	1350.	2350.
	1859 B	.013	600.00	1100.	1750.	2750.

MONETARY REFORM

20 MARK

7.9650 g, .900 GOLD, .2304 oz AGW
Wilhelm
Rev: Type II.

KM#	Date	Mintage	Fine	VF	XF	Unc
1160	1875A	.100	250.00	500.00	1000.	1500.
	1876A	—	—	—	—	3600.

TRADE COINAGE

DUCAT

3.5000 g, .986 GOLD, .1109 oz AGW
Similar to KM#1067.

KM#	Date	Mintage	Fine	VF	XF	Unc
1023	1801 MC	—	450.00	750.00	1250.	1600.

NOTE: Earlier dates (1784-1800) exist for this type.

Obv: Crowned many quartered arms w/garlands.
Rev: Value, EX AVRO HERCINIA.

KM#	Date	Mintage	Fine	VF	XF	Unc
1063	1814 HC	376 pcs.	575.00	1000.	1750.	2350.

KM#	Date	Mintage	Fine	VF	XF	Unc
1067	1815 FR	220 pcs.	725.00	1250.	2000.	2750.
1114	1825 CvC	530 pcs.	750.00	1250.	2100.	2850.

PATTERNS (Pn)

(Including off metal strikes)

KM#	Date	Mintage	Identification	Mkt.Val.
Pn44	1813	—	5 Thaler	—

KM#	Date	Mintage	Identification	Mkt.Val.
Pn45	1814	—	4 Pfenning	1450.

KM#	Date	Mintage	Identification	Mkt.Val.
Pn46	1827	—	10 Thaler, Copper	—
Pn47	1827	—	10 Thaler, Silver	—
Pn48	1827	—	10 Thaler, uniface	—

KM#	Date	Mintage	Identification	Mkt.Val.
Pn49	1837	—	1 Thaler	Rare
Pn50	1846	—	1 Pfennig	—

KM#	Date	Mintage	Identification	Mkt.Val.
Pn51	1849	—	2 Thaler	—

KM#	Date	Mintage	Identification	Mkt.Val.
Pn52	1850	—	2 Thaler	—
Pn53	1857 B	—	1 Krone, .900 Gold, KM1153	3000.

EAST FRIESLAND

A county located on the North Sea coast between the Ems and Weser Rivers in North Germany. The count was raised to rank of prince in 1654. At the death of the last prince in 1744, East Friesland passed to Prussia. From 1815 to 1866 East Friesland was part of Hannover until Hannover was absorbed by Prussia in 1866.

RULERS

Friedrich Wilhelm III (of Prussia), 1797-1807

George IV (of Hannover and Great Britain), 1815-1820

MINT MARKS

A - Berlin
B - Breslau
D - Aurich
F - Magdeburg
Star - Dresden

MONETARY SYSTEM

Witte = 4 Hohlpfennig = 1/3 Schilling = 1/20 Schaf = 1/10 Stuber
Ciffert = 6 Witten
Stuber = 10 Witten = 1/30 Reichstaler
Schaf = 20 Witten = 2 Stuber
Flindrich = 3 Stuber
Schilling = 6 Stuber
288 Pfennige = 54 Stuber = 36 Mariengroschen = 1 Reichsthaler

1/4 STUBER

COPPER

Obv: Crowned FW monogram. Rev: Value, date.

KM#	Date	Mintage	Fine	VF	XF	Unc
272	1802A	1.296	5.00	15.00	30.00	60.00
	1803A	Inc. Ab.	5.00	15.00	30.00	60.00
	1804A	.216	5.00	15.00	30.00	60.00

NOTE: Earlier date (1799) exists for this type.

KM#	Date	Mintage	Fine	VF	XF	Unc
290	1823	.710	5.00	12.00	25.00	70.00
	1824	Inc. Ab.	5.00	12.00	25.00	70.00
	1825	Inc. Ab.	5.00	12.00	25.00	70.00

STUBER

BILLON

KM#	Date	Mintage	Fine	VF	XF	Unc
280	1804A	.378	20.00	32.50	55.00	100.00

KM#	Date	Mintage	Fine	VF	XF	Unc
291	1823B	.161	12.00	20.00	45.00	85.00

2 STUBER

BILLON

Obv: Bust. Rev: Value.

KM#	Date	Mintage	Fine	VF	XF	Unc
281	1804A	.216	25.00	50.00	100.00	220.00

Obv: Crowned monogram GR. Rev: Value.

KM#	Date	Mintage	Fine	VF	XF	Unc
292	1823B	.081	15.00	30.00	70.00	125.00

ERFURT

A city in central Germany. It was a mint for the archbishops of Mainz in the 11th, 12th and 13th centuries. It also served as an Imperial Mint in the 12th century. Independence was granted in 1255 and the mint right was obtained in 1341 and 1354. Erfurt was occupied by Swedish force from 1631 until 1648, during the Thirty Years War. A local coinage was produced until 1802 when Erfurt fell to Prussia.

RULERS

Friedrich Carl Josef, Freiherr von und zu Erthal, Archbishop, 1774-1802

MINTMASTERS INITIALS

Letter	Date	Name
C	1779-1804	Julianus Eberhard Volkmar Claus, Mint director
S	1801-1802	Johann Blasius Siegling, Mint director

6 PFENNIG

BILLON

Obv: Wheel in crowned shield. Rev: Value.

KM#	Date	Mintage	Fine	VF	XF	Unc
122	1801 S	—	10.00	20.00	55.00	120.00

GROSCHEN

(1/24 Taler)

BILLON

KM#	Date	Mintage	Fine	VF	XF	Unc
123	1801 S	—	8.00	16.00	45.00	100.00

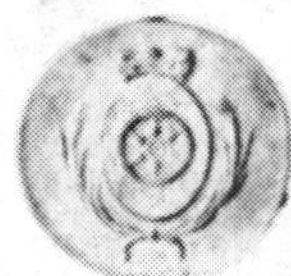

Obv: Shield within branches.

KM#	Date	Mintage	Fine	VF	XF	Unc
124	1802 S	—	8.00	16.00	45.00	100.00

PATTERNS (Pn)

KM#	Date	Mintage	Identification	Mkt.Val.
Pn8	1801	—	6 Pfennig, Copper, KM122	150.00

FRANKFURT am MAIN

A free city in west-central Germany, founded as a Roman settlement in the 1st century and for several centuries the site of the election of the Holy Roman Emperors. It housed the Imperial Mint from early times and obtained the mint right in 1428 with almost continuous coinage until 1866. Frankfurt am Main was merged into the Confederation of the Rhine in 1806 and was made the Grand Duchy of Frankfurt in 1810. The Congress of Vienna restored its freedom in 1815 but when the city sided with the Austrians in the Austro-Prussian War, victorious Prussia absorbed it in 1866.

RULERS

Carl Theodor v. Dalberg, 1810-15

MINT MARKS

F = Frankfurt

MINTMASTERS INITIALS

Frankfurt Mint

Letter	Date	Name
G.B., I.G.B.	1790-1825	Johann Georg Bunsen
S.T.	1836-1837	Samuel Tomschutz
Z	1843-1856	Johann Philipp Zollman

WARDENS INITIALS

Frankfurt Mint

Letter	Date	Name
GH	1798-1816	Georg Hille

ENGRAVERS INITIALS

Frankfurt Mint

Letter	Date	Name
A.V. NORDHEIM	1857-1866	

Wiesbaden Mint

Letter	Date	Name
ZOLLMANN	1818-1843	Johann Philipp Zollman

In some instances old dies were used later with initials beyond the date range of the man that held the position.

HELLER

COPPER

KM#	Date	Mintage	Fine	VF	XF	Unc
300.1	1814 G.B.	.332	12.00	30.00	60.00	175.00

W/o mintmaster's initials.

KM#	Date	Mintage	Fine	VF	XF	Unc
300.2	1814	Inc. Ab.	25.00	50.00	100.00	250.00

Mint mark: F

KM#	Date	Mintage	Fine	VF	XF	Unc
301	1814 GB	I.A.	2.00	4.00	8.00	45.00
	1815 GB	.166	2.00	4.00	8.00	45.00
	1816 GB	—	2.00	4.00	8.00	45.00
	1817 GB	—	2.00	4.00	8.00	45.00
	1818 GB	—	2.00	4.00	8.00	45.00
	1819 GB	—	2.00	4.00	8.00	45.00
	1820 GB	—	2.00	4.00	8.00	45.00
	1821 GB	—	2.00	4.00	8.00	45.00
	1822 GB	—	2.00	4.00	8.00	45.00
	1824 GB	—	2.00	4.00	8.00	45.00
	1825 GB	—	2.00	4.00	8.00	45.00
	1836 ST	.120	4.00	8.00	16.00	65.00
	1837 ST	.144	4.00	8.00	16.00	65.00

NOTE: Varieties exist.

KM#	Date	Mintage	Fine	VF	XF	Unc
311	1838	—	4.00	8.00	16.00	65.00

KM#	Date	Mintage	Fine	VF	XF	Unc
327	1841	.173	2.00	4.00	8.00	45.00
	1842	.328	2.00	4.00	8.00	45.00
	1843	—	2.00	4.00	8.00	45.00
	1844	.162	2.00	4.00	8.00	45.00
	1845	.169	2.00	4.00	8.00	45.00
	1846	.205	2.00	4.00	8.00	45.00
	1847	.453	2.00	4.00	8.00	45.00
	1849	.396	2.00	4.00	8.00	45.00
	1850	.669	2.00	4.00	8.00	45.00
	1851	.275	2.00	4.00	8.00	45.00
	1852	.325	2.00	4.00	8.00	45.00

Obv. leg: FREIE STADT.

KM#	Date	Mintage	Fine	VF	XF	Unc
332	1843	.038	20.00	35.00	65.00	175.00

KM#	Date	Mintage	Fine	VF	XF	Unc
351	1853	.411	2.00	4.00	6.00	25.00
	1854	.271	2.00	4.00	6.00	25.00
	1855	.430	2.00	4.00	6.00	25.00
	1856	.484	2.00	4.00	6.00	25.00
	1857	.723	2.00	4.00	6.00	25.00
	1858	.377	2.00	4.00	6.00	25.00

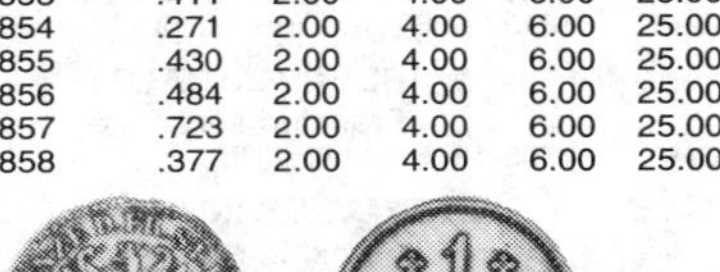

KM#	Date	Mintage	Fine	VF	XF	Unc
356	1859	.377	2.00	4.00	6.00	25.00
	1860	.353	2.00	4.00	6.00	25.00
	1861	.378	2.00	4.00	6.00	25.00
	1862	.391	2.00	4.00	6.00	25.00
	1863	.370	2.00	4.00	6.00	25.00
	1864	.390	2.00	4.00	6.00	25.00
	1865	.384	2.00	4.00	6.00	25.00

PFENNIG

COPPER

Mint mark: F

Obv: Displayed eagle. Rev: Value, date.

KM#	Date	Mintage	Fine	VF	XF	Unc
268	1801 GB	—	2.00	4.00	10.00	35.00
	1802 GB	—	2.00	4.00	10.00	35.00
	1803 PB	—	2.00	4.00	10.00	35.00
	1803 GB	—	2.00	4.00	10.00	35.00
	1804 GB	—	2.00	4.00	10.00	35.00
	1805 GB	—	2.00	4.00	10.00	35.00
	1806 GB	—	2.00	4.00	10.00	35.00

NOTE: Varieties exist.

NOTE: Earlier dates (1786-1800) exist for this type.

KREUZER

(Convention)

BILLON

KM#	Date	Mintage	VG	Fine	VF	XF
295	1803 GB GH	—	5.00	15.00	30.00	65.00
	1804 GB GH	—	5.00	15.00	30.00	65.00
	1805 GB GH	—	5.00	15.00	30.00	65.00

NOTE: Varieties exist w/dots, rosettes, stars and roses at sides of 1.

Obv: Rosette below date.

KM#	Date	Mintage	VG	Fine	VF	XF
298	1805 GB GH	—	5.00	15.00	30.00	65.00

.8350 g, .167 SILVER, .0044 oz ASW

KM#	Date	Mintage	Fine	VF	XF	Unc
312	1838	.078	2.00	4.00	10.00	30.00
	1841	.123	2.00	4.00	10.00	25.00
	1842	.402	2.00	4.00	10.00	25.00
	1843	.169	2.00	4.00	10.00	25.00
	1844	.215	2.00	4.00	10.00	25.00
	1845	.205	2.00	4.00	10.00	25.00
	1846	.101	2.00	4.00	10.00	25.00
	1847	.553	2.00	4.00	10.00	25.00
	1848	.482	2.00	4.00	10.00	25.00
	1849	.627	2.00	4.00	10.00	25.00
	1850	.612	2.00	4.00	10.00	25.00
	1851	.543	2.00	4.00	10.00	25.00
	1852	.889	2.00	4.00	10.00	25.00
	1853	.526	2.00	4.00	10.00	25.00
	1854	.589	2.00	4.00	10.00	25.00
	1855	.677	2.00	4.00	10.00	25.00
	1856	1.227	2.00	4.00	10.00	25.00
	1857	.774	2.00	4.00	10.00	25.00

KM#	Date	Mintage	Fine	VF	XF	Unc
317	ND (1839)	—	1.00	3.00	10.00	30.00

NOTE: Varieties exist.

Obv: Eagle w/long body.

KM#	Date	Mintage	Fine	VF	XF	Unc
357	1859	.358	2.00	4.00	10.00	27.50
	1860	.640	2.00	4.00	10.00	27.50
	1861	.313	2.00	4.00	10.00	27.50
	1862	—	25.00	52.50	80.00	125.00

Obv: Eagle w/heart-shaped body.

KM#	Date	Mintage	Fine	VF	XF	Unc
367	1862	.645	2.00	4.00	8.00	20.00
	1863	.611	2.00	4.00	8.00	20.00
	1864	.344	2.00	4.00	8.00	20.00
	1865	.366	2.00	4.00	8.00	20.00
	1866	.151	2.00	5.00	10.00	25.00

3 KREUZER

1.2990 g, .333 SILVER, .0139 oz ASW

KM#	Date	Mintage	Fine	VF	XF	Unc
313	1838	.080	3.00	7.00	18.00	40.00
	1841	.085	3.00	7.00	18.00	40.00
	1842	.109	3.00	7.00	18.00	40.00
	1843	.089	3.00	7.00	18.00	40.00
	1846	.154	3.00	7.00	18.00	40.00

KM#	Date	Mintage	Fine	VF	XF	Unc
334	1846	Inc. Ab.	2.00	5.00	12.50	35.00
	1848	.038	2.00	5.00	12.50	35.00
	1849	.950	2.00	5.00	12.50	40.00
	1850	.182	2.00	5.00	12.50	35.00
	1851	.158	2.00	5.00	12.50	35.00
	1852	.129	2.00	5.00	12.50	35.00
	1853	.069	2.00	5.00	12.50	35.00
	1854	.154	2.00	5.00	12.50	35.00
	1855	.148	2.00	5.00	12.50	35.00
	1856	.084	2.00	5.00	12.50	35.00

1.2900 g, .350 SILVER, .0145 oz ASW

KM#	Date	Mintage	Fine	VF	XF	Unc
373	1866	.096	5.00	10.00	20.00	60.00

6 KREUZER

2.5980 g, .333 SILVER, .0277 oz ASW

KM#	Date	Mintage	Fine	VF	XF	Unc
314	1838	.110	2.00	6.00	15.00	60.00
	1841	.123	2.00	6.00	15.00	60.00
	1842	.161	2.00	6.00	15.00	60.00
	1843	.260	2.00	6.00	15.00	60.00
	1844	.370	2.00	6.00	15.00	60.00
	1845	.105	2.00	6.00	15.00	60.00
	1846	.211	2.00	6.00	15.00	60.00

.333 SILVER

KM#	Date	Mintage	Fine	VF	XF	Unc
335	1846	Inc. Ab.	2.00	6.00	15.00	50.00
	1848	.291	2.00	6.00	15.00	50.00
	1849	.171	2.00	6.00	15.00	50.00
	1850	.152	2.00	6.00	15.00	50.00
	1851	.159	2.00	6.00	15.00	50.00
	1852	.221	2.00	6.00	15.00	50.00
	1853	.106	2.00	6.00	15.00	50.00
	1855	.181	2.00	6.00	15.00	50.00
	1856	.166	2.00	6.00	15.00	50.00

KM#	Date	Mintage	Fine	VF	XF	Unc
350	1852	Inc. Ab.	3.50	10.00	25.00	65.00
	1853	Inc. Ab.	3.50	10.00	25.00	65.00
	1854	.212	3.50	10.00	25.00	65.00
	1856	Inc. Ab.	3.50	10.00	25.00	65.00

2.4630 g, .350 SILVER, .0276 oz ASW

KM#	Date	Mintage	Fine	VF	XF	Unc
374	1866	.038	5.00	10.00	20.00	70.00

1/2 GULDEN

5.3030 g, .900 SILVER, .1533 oz ASW

KM#	Date	Mintage	Fine	VF	XF	Unc
315	1838	.120	25.00	40.00	90.00	200.00
	1838	—	—	—	Proof	225.00
	1840	.391	15.00	30.00	70.00	150.00
	1841	.161	25.00	40.00	90.00	200.00

KM#	Date	Mintage	Fine	VF	XF	Unc
330	1842	.075	25.00	40.00	90.00	200.00
	1843	.056	25.00	40.00	90.00	200.00
	1844	.049	25.00	40.00	90.00	200.00
	1845	.072	25.00	40.00	90.00	200.00
	1846	.047	25.00	40.00	90.00	200.00
	1847	.051	25.00	40.00	90.00	200.00
	1849	.055	25.00	40.00	90.00	200.00

5.2910 g, .900 SILVER, .1533 oz ASW

KM#	Date	Mintage	Fine	VF	XF	Unc
368	1862	.014	100.00	200.00	350.00	700.00

GULDEN

10.6060 g, .900 SILVER, .3067 oz ASW

KM#	Date	Mintage	Fine	VF	XF	Unc
316	1838	.120	35.00	75.00	145.00	250.00
	1838	—	—	—	Proof	200.00
	1840	.391	35.00	75.00	145.00	250.00
	1841	.161	35.00	75.00	145.00	250.00

Obv: Eagle w/large arabesques.

KM#	Date	Mintage	Fine	VF	XF	Unc
331	1842	.123	22.00	45.00	90.00	200.00
	1843	.172	22.00	45.00	90.00	200.00
	1844	.122	22.00	45.00	90.00	200.00
	1845	.101	22.00	45.00	90.00	200.00
	1846	.120	22.00	45.00	90.00	200.00
	1847	.121	22.00	45.00	90.00	200.00
	1848	.078	22.00	45.00	90.00	225.00
	1849	.090	22.00	45.00	90.00	225.00
	1850	.030	30.00	60.00	120.00	250.00
	1851	.064	30.00	60.00	120.00	250.00
	1852	.064	30.00	60.00	120.00	250.00
	1853	.029	30.00	60.00	120.00	250.00
	1854	.034	30.00	60.00	120.00	250.00
	1855	.038	30.00	60.00	120.00	250.00

10.5820 g, .900 SILVER, .3069 oz ASW
Obv: Eagle w/small arabesques.

KM#	Date	Mintage	Fine	VF	XF	Unc
358	1859	.059	30.00	60.00	135.00	275.00
	1861	.211	20.00	40.00	80.00	165.00

Obv: Eagle w/o arabesques.

KM#	Date	Mintage	Fine	VF	XF	Unc
369	1862	.011	100.00	200.00	400.00	800.00
	1863	.056	45.00	90.00	165.00	300.00

ZWEY (2) GULDEN

21.1100 g, .900 SILVER, .6138 oz ASW

KM#	Date	Mintage	Fine	VF	XF	Unc
333	1845	.114	50.00	80.00	140.00	290.00
	1846	.281	50.00	80.00	140.00	290.00
	1847	.215	50.00	80.00	140.00	290.00
	1848	.147	50.00	80.00	140.00	290.00
	1849	.023	90.00	140.00	240.00	500.00
	1850	.031	100.00	175.00	325.00	600.00
	1851	.032	70.00	90.00	190.00	400.00
	1852	.026	85.00	125.00	225.00	450.00
	1853	.056	70.00	90.00	190.00	400.00
	1854	6,028	100.00	150.00	250.00	500.00
	1856	.036	70.00	90.00	190.00	400.00

Constitutional Convention, May 1, 1848

KM#	Date	Mintage	Fine	VF	XF	Unc
336	1848	—	—	—	Rare	—

Constitutional Convention, May 18, 1848

KM#	Date	Mintage	Fine	VF	XF	Unc
337	1848	8,600	50.00	100.00	160.00	240.00

NOTE: Coins were struck in anticipation of the Constitutional Convention scheduled to take place May 1, 1848. When the convention was delayed until May 18, 1848 the coins were recalled and the dies were altered to reflect this new date.

Archduke Johann of Austria elected as Vicar

KM#	Date	Mintage	Fine	VF	XF	Unc
338	1848	.036	30.00	60.00	120.00	200.00
	1848	—	—	—	Proof	250.00

Archduke Johann of Austria elected as Vicar

KM#	Date	Mintage	Fine	VF	XF	Unc
339	1848	—	2000.	3500.	5000.	7500.

Opening of German Parliament
Mule. Obv: KM#337. Rev: KM#333.

KM#	Date	Mintage	Fine	VF	XF	Unc
340	1848	—	2000.	3500.	5000.	7500.

Friedrich Wilhelm IV of Prussia elected as Emperor of Germany

KM#	Date	Mintage	Fine	VF	XF	Unc
341.1	1849	200 pcs.	2000.	3500.	5000.	7500.

Plain edge.

KM#	Date	Mintage	Fine	VF	XF	Unc
341.2	1849 (1890)	(restrike)		—	—	—

Mule. Obv: Similar to KM#333.

KM#	Date	Mintage	Fine	VF	XF	Unc
342	1849	—	—	—	—	8300.

Centenary of Goethe's Birth

KM#	Date	Mintage	Fine	VF	XF	Unc
343	1849	8,500	50.00	90.00	120.00	165.00
	1849	—	—	—	Proof	250.00

300th Anniversary of Religious Peace

KM#	Date	Mintage	Fine	VF	XF	Unc
353	1855	.032	40.00	60.00	90.00	140.00

EIN (1) THALER

(Vereins)

18.5200 g, .900 SILVER, .5360 oz ASW

KM#	Date	Mintage	Fine	VF	XF	Unc
354	1857	1,350	125.00	250.00	550.00	1200.

Obv: House roofs visible around tower at left.

KM#	Date	Mintage	Fine	VF	XF	Unc
355	1857	—	150.00	300.00	600.00	1200.
	1858	.012	50.00	100.00	200.00	400.00

(Gedenk)

Schiller Centennial

KM#	Date	Mintage	Fine	VF	XF	Unc
359	1859	.025	30.00	55.00	75.00	150.00
	1859	—	—	—	Proof	175.00

(Vereins)

KM#	Date	Mintage	Fine	VF	XF	Unc
360	1859	.283	25.00	45.00	70.00	140.00
	1860	1.700	20.00	40.00	60.00	120.00

Obv: Different hair-knot.

KM#	Date	Mintage	Fine	VF	XF	Unc
366	1861	.016	150.00	300.00	600.00	1200.

Obv: Different dress.

KM#	Date	Mintage	Fine	VF	XF	Unc
370	1862	.312	20.00	40.00	60.00	125.00
	1863	.021	25.00	50.00	100.00	200.00
	1864	.105	20.00	40.00	60.00	125.00
	1865	.207	20.00	40.00	60.00	125.00

(Gedenk)

German Shooting Festival
Obv: Similar to KM#359.

KM#	Date	Mintage	Fine	VF	XF	Unc
371	1862	.044	25.00	50.00	70.00	120.00
	1862	—	—	—	Proof	225.00

Assembly of Princes

KM#	Date	Mintage	Fine	VF	XF	Unc
372	1863	.020	50.00	80.00	140.00	225.00
	1863	—	—	—	Proof	250.00

ZWEI (2) THALER

(3-1/2 Gulden)

37.1000 g, .900 SILVER, 1.0743 oz ASW
New Mint Opening in 1840

KM#	Date	Mintage	Fine	VF	XF	Unc
325	1840	649 pcs.	425.00	750.00	1250.	2800.

KM#	Date	Mintage	Fine	VF	XF	Unc
326	1840	Inc. KM329	75.00	150.00	265.00	550.00
	1841	Inc. KM329	60.00	130.00	200.00	400.00
	1842	Inc. KM329	—	—	Rare	—
	1843	Inc. KM329	75.00	150.00	275.00	575.00
	1844	Inc. KM329	75.00	150.00	275.00	575.00

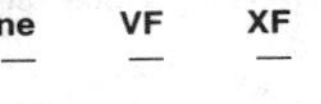

Mule. Obv: KM#326. Rev: Obv. of KM#329.

KM#	Date	Mintage	Fine	VF	XF	Unc
328	ND(1838)	—	—	—	—	7500.

Rev: Value.

KM#	Date	Mintage	Fine	VF	XF	Unc
329	1841	.121	60.00	110.00	200.00	400.00
	1841	—	—	—	Proof	450.00
	1842	.287	60.00	110.00	200.00	400.00
	1843	.123	60.00	110.00	200.00	400.00
	1844	.196	60.00	110.00	200.00	400.00
	1845	.036	75.00	125.00	250.00	550.00
	1846	.072	65.00	115.00	225.00	450.00
	1847	.071	65.00	115.00	225.00	450.00
	1851	8,354	100.00	175.00	300.00	600.00
	1854	.107	60.00	110.00	200.00	400.00
	1855	.072	65.00	115.00	225.00	450.00

37.0400 g, .900 SILVER, 1.0717 oz ASW

KM#	Date	Mintage	Fine	VF	XF	Unc
365	1860	.341	40.00	65.00	100.00	180.00
	1861	1.787	40.00	65.00	100.00	180.00
	1862	.344	40.00	65.00	100.00	180.00
	1866	.637	40.00	65.00	100.00	180.00

TRADE COINAGE

DUCAT

3.5000 g, .986 GOLD, .1109 oz AGW
300th Anniversary of the Reformation

302	1817	—	75.00	125.00	200.00	400.00

352	1853	1,121	300.00	500.00	950.00	1500.
	1856	665 pcs.	325.00	550.00	1000.	1600.

2 DUCAT

7.0000 g, .986 GOLD, .2219 oz AGW
300th Anniversary of Reformation

303 (M18)	1817	—	100.00	200.00	400.00	600.00

PATTERNS (Pn)

(Including off metal strikes)

KM#	Date	Mintage	Identification	Mkt.Val.
Pn48	1817	—	1 Heller, Silver, KM301	150.00
Pn49	1817	—	1 Ducat, Silver, KM302, Reformation	60.00
Pn50	1817	—	2 Ducat, Silver, KM303, Reformation	100.00
Pn51	1837	—	1 Heller, Silver, KM310	150.00
Pn52	1838	—	1 Heller, Silver, KM310	150.00
Pn53	1839	—	1/2 Gulden	—
Pn54	1839	—	1 Gulden, KM316	—
Pn55	1848	—	2 Gulden, Gold, KM333	—
Pn56	1849	—	2 Gulden, Gold, KM341.1	—
Pn57	1852	—	1 Heller, Copper, KM351	—
Pn58	1852	—	6 Kreuzer, Silver, KM350	—

TOKEN ISSUES (Tn)

Jewish Pfennigs

JUDEN PFENNIGE =
'Jew Pennies'

THELER

COPPER

KM#	Date	Mintage	Fine	VF	XF	Unc
Tn1	1807	—	3.00	6.00	12.00	40.00

ATRIBUO

COPPER

Tn2	1809	—	2.00	5.00	10.00	35.00

1/4 HALBAG

COPPER

Tn3	1818	—	3.00	6.00	12.00	40.00

HELLER

COPPER
Obv: Griffin. Rev: Value.

Tn4	1819	—	5.00	12.50	20.00	50.00

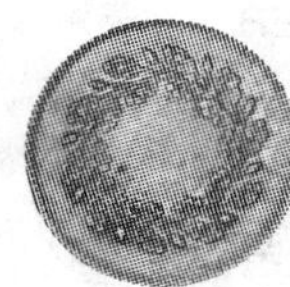

KM#	Date	Mintage	Fine	VF	XF	Unc
Tn10	1820	—	2.00	4.00	8.00	25.00

Rev: W/o asterisks on sides of "1".

Tn11	1820	—	2.00	4.00	8.00	25.00

Tn12	1821	—	2.00	4.00	8.00	25.00

PFENNIG

COPPER

Tn5	1819	—	1.50	3.00	6.00	25.00

Tn6	1819	—	1.50	3.00	6.00	25.00

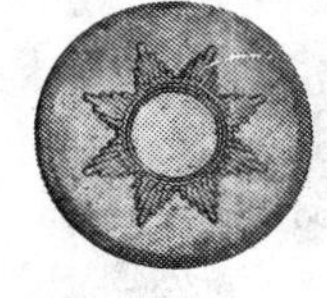

Tn7	1819	—	1.50	3.00	6.00	25.00

Obv: Lion.

Tn8	1819	—	3.00	6.00	12.00	35.00

Obv: Rose branch.

Tn9	1819	—	5.00	12.50	20.00	50.00

Tn13	1822	—	2.00	4.00	8.00	25.00

1/4 ROPELL

COPPER

Tn15	1816	—	—	—	—	—

FRIEDBERG

IMPERIAL CITY

The fortified town of Friedberg, located in Hesse about 14 miles north of Frankfurt am Main, dates from Roman times. It attained free status in 1211 and was the site of an imperial mint until the mid-13th century. In 1349 Friedberg passed to the countship of Schwarzburg, losing its free status shortly thereafter. Local nobles began electing one among themselves to the office of burgrave-for-life. The burgraves obtained the mint right in 1541 and recognized only the emperor as overlord. In 1802 Friedberg passed in fief to Hesse-Darmstadt and was mediatized in 1818.

RULERS

Johann Maria Rudolph von Waldbott-Bassenheim, 1777-1805
Clemens August von Westphalen, 1805-1818

MINTMASTERS INITIALS

Letter	Date	Name
GB(F)GH	1790-1833	Johann Georg Bunsen, in Frankfurt
	1798-1816	Georg Hille, warden in Frankfurt

EIN (1) THALER

(Convention)

SILVER
Obv: Titles of Francis II.

KM#	Date	Mintage	Fine	VF	XF	Unc
75	1804 GB(F)GH	—	200.00	350.00	750.00	1500.

NOTE: Legend varieties exist.

FAMILY ARMS:

FURSTENBERG

A noble family with holdings in Baden and Wurttemberg. The lord of Furstenberg assumed the title of Count in the 13th century which was raised to the rank of Prince in 1664. The Furstenberg possessions were mediatized in 1806.

FURSTENBERG-STUHLINGEN

RULERS

Karl Joachim, 1796-1804
Carl Egon, 1804-1854

MINT MARKS

G - Gunzburg

MINTMASTERS INITIALS

Letter	Date	Name
CH	1784-1808	Christian Heugelin, warden in Stuttgart
ILW,W	1798-1845	Johann Ludwig Wagner, die-cutter in Stuttgart

EIN (1) KREUZER

COPPER

KM#	Date	Mintage	Fine	VF	XF	Unc
35	1804 W.	.040	30.00	70.00	150.00	275.00

3 KREUZER

1.4200 g, .312 SILVER, .0142 oz ASW

36	1804 W.	.012	65.00	135.00	265.00	465.00

6 KREUZER

2.3500 g, .375 SILVER, .0283 oz ASW

KM#	Date	Mintage	Fine	VF	XF	Unc
37	1804 W.	6,720	75.00	155.00	285.00	525.00

10 KREUZER

3.8900 g, .500 SILVER, .0625 oz ASW

KM#	Date	Mintage	Fine	VF	XF	Unc
38	1804 W.	6,075	100.00	175.00	300.00	550.00

20 KREUZER

6.6800 g, .583 SILVER, .1252 oz ASW
Obv: Bust right, leg. ends: PRINC. IN FURSTENBERG.
Rev: Crowned arms.

KM#	Date	Mintage	Fine	VF	XF	Unc
39	1804 W.	3,011	150.00	250.00	425.00	750.00

Obv. leg. ends: PRINC FURSTENBERG.

KM#	Date	Mintage	Fine	VF	XF	Unc
40	1804	Inc. Ab.	135.00	225.00	375.00	650.00

EIN (1) THALER

(Convention)

28.0600 g, .833 SILVER, .7515 oz ASW
Karl Joachim

KM#	Date	Mintage	Fine	VF	XF	Unc
41	1804 ILW//CH	388 pcs.	600.00	1200.	2000.	4000.

FURTHER AUSTRIA

(Vorderoesterreich)

Name given to imperial lands in South Swabia in the 18th century. In 1805 it was divided by Baden and Bavaria.

RULERS

Franz II (Austria), 1792-1805

MINT MARKS

A - Wien
F - Hall
G - Baia Mare (Nagybanya)
H - Gunzburg

HELLER

COPPER

KM#	Date	Mintage	Fine	VF	XF	Unc
21	1801H	—	6.00	12.00	25.00	125.00
	1803H	—	6.00	12.00	25.00	125.00

NOTE: Varieties exist w/ and w/o period after date.
NOTE: Earlier dates (1793-1799) exist for this type.

1/4 KREUTZER

COPPER, 1.40 g
Reduced weight, 1.40 g. Rev: Smaller lettering.

KM#	Date	Mintage	Fine	VF	XF	Unc
25	1801H	—	—	—	Rare	—
	1802H	—	10.00	25.00	50.00	125.00
	1803H	—	7.50	22.50	45.00	100.00

1/2 KREUTZER

COPPER, 2.80 g

KM#	Date	Mintage	Fine	VF	XF	Unc
26	1801H	—	—	—	Rare	—
	1802H	—	20.00	85.00	125.00	185.00
	1803H	—	10.00	25.00	45.00	90.00
	1804H	—	—	—	Rare	—
31	1805H	—	—	—	Rare	—

EIN (1) KREUTZER

COPPER, 5.70 g
Obv. leg: D.G.R.I.S. . .

KM#	Date	Mintage	Fine	VF	XF	Unc
27	1801H	—	4.00	12.00	25.00	50.00
	1802H	—	4.00	12.00	25.00	50.00
	1803H	—	4.00	12.00	25.00	50.00
	1804H	—	4.00	12.00	25.00	50.00

Obv. leg: D.G.ROM.ET. . .

KM#	Date	Mintage	Fine	VF	XF	Unc
30	1804H	—	—	—	Rare	—
	1805H	—	4.50	12.50	28.00	55.00

3 KREUTZER

1.4100 g, .312 SILVER, .0141 oz ASW

KM#	Date	Mintage	Fine	VF	XF	Unc
28	1802A	—	—	—	Rare	—
	1802G	—	—	—	Rare	—
	1802H	—	—	—	Rare	—
	1803H	—	—	—	Rare	—
	1804H	—	—	—	Rare	—
	1805H	—	—	—	Rare	—

6 KREUTZER

2.3500 g, .375 SILVER, .0283 oz ASW

KM#	Date	Mintage	Fine	VF	XF	Unc
29	1802A	—	—	—	Rare	—
	1802G	—	—	—	Rare	—
	1802H	—	4.50	12.50	30.00	65.00
	1803H	—	4.50	12.50	30.00	65.00
	1804H	—	4.50	12.50	30.00	65.00
	1805A	—	4.50	12.50	30.00	65.00
	1805H	—	4.50	12.50	30.00	65.00

HAMBURG

The city of Hamburg is located on the Elbe River about 75 miles from the North Sea. It was founded by Charlemagne in the 9th century. In 1241 it joined Lubeck to form the Hanseatic League. The mint right was leased to the citizens in 1292, however the first local hohlpfennings had been struck almost 50 years earlier. In 1510 Hamburg was formally made a Free City, though in fact it had been free for about 250 years. It was occupied by the French during the Napoleonic period. In 1866 it joined the North German Confederation and became a part of the German Empire in 1871. The Hamburg coinage is almost continuous up to the time of World War I.

MINTMASTERS INITIALS

Letter	Date	Name
CAIG, CAJG		
29	1813	C.A.J. Ginquembre, French director of mint
HSK	1805-1842	Hans Schierven Knoph
OHK	1761-1805	Otto Heinrich Knorre

CITY ARMS

A triple-turreted gate

DREILING

(3 Pfennig - 1/4 Schilling - 1/128 Thaler)

.5100 g, .187 SILVER, .0030 oz ASW
Obv: Castle w/O.H.K. below.
Rev: 'I' between rosettes.

KM#	Date	Mintage	Fine	VF	XF	Unc
220	1803 OHK	.355	2.00	4.00	10.00	30.00

NOTE: Earlier dates (1783-1800) exist for this type.

Obv: Castle w/H.S.K. below.

KM#	Date	Mintage	Fine	VF	XF	Unc
235	1807 HSK	.384	1.00	3.00	6.00	25.00
	1809 HSK	.768	1.00	3.00	6.00	25.00

Rev: 'I' between dots.

KM#	Date	Mintage	Fine	VF	XF	Unc
250	1823 HSK	.021	1.00	3.00	6.00	25.00
	1832 HSK	.036	1.00	3.00	6.00	25.00
	1833 HSK	.303	1.00	3.00	6.00	25.00
	1836 HSK	.293	1.00	3.00	6.00	25.00
	1839 HSK	.299	1.00	3.00	6.00	25.00

Obv: Redesigned castle. Rev: 'I' between rosettes.

KM#	Date	Mintage	Fine	VF	XF	Unc
260	1841 HSK	.554	1.00	3.00	6.00	25.00

Obv: W/o initials below castle.
Rev: 'I' between 5-pointed stars.

KM#	Date	Mintage	Fine	VF	XF	Unc
264	1846	.574	1.00	3.00	6.00	25.00

Rev: 'I' between 6-pointed stars.

KM#	Date	Mintage	Fine	VF	XF	Unc
270	1851	.578	1.00	3.00	6.00	25.00

Beaded borders.

KM#	Date	Mintage	Fine	VF	XF	Unc
275	1855A	.320	1.00	2.50	5.00	25.00
	1855	2.613	1.00	2.00	4.00	25.00

SECHSLING

(6 Pfennig - 1/2 Schilling - 1/64 Thaler)

.7600 g, .250 SILVER, .0061 oz ASW
Obv: Castle w/O.H.K. below.
Rev: 'I' between rosettes.

KM#	Date	Mintage	Fine	VF	XF	Unc
213	1803 OHK	.182	1.00	3.00	6.00	40.00

NOTE: Earlier dates (1778-1800) exist for this type.

Obv: Small castle w/H.S.K. below.

KM#	Date	Mintage	Fine	VF	XF	Unc
236.1	1807 HSK	.096	2.00	4.00	8.00	50.00
	1809 HSK	.192	1.00	3.00	6.00	40.00
	1817 HSK	.048	2.00	4.00	8.00	50.00

Obv: Large castle.

KM#	Date	Mintage	Fine	VF	XF	Unc
236.2	1823 HSK	.030	2.00	4.00	8.00	50.00
	1833 HSK	.135	1.00	3.00	6.00	40.00
	1836 HSK	.155	1.00	3.00	6.00	40.00
	1839 HSK	.354	1.00	3.00	6.00	40.00

Rev: 'I' between dots.

KM#	Date	Mintage	Fine	VF	XF	Unc
255	1832 HSK	.066	2.00	4.00	8.00	45.00

Obv: Redesigned castle. Rev: 'I' between rosettes.

KM#	Date	Mintage	Fine	VF	XF	Unc
261	1841 HSK	.293	1.00	3.00	6.00	40.00

Obv: W/o initials below castle.
Rev: 'I' between 5-pointed stars.

KM#	Date	Mintage	Fine	VF	XF	Unc
265	1846	.480	1.00	3.00	6.00	30.00

Rev: 'I' between 6-pointed stars.

KM#	Date	Mintage	Fine	VF	XF	Unc
271	1851	.480	1.00	3.00	6.00	30.00

Beaded borders.

KM#	Date	Mintage	Fine	VF	XF	Unc
276	1855A	.098	2.00	4.00	8.00	35.00
	1855	1.841	1.00	3.00	6.00	30.00

SCHILLING

(12 Pfennig - 1/32 Thaler)

1.0800 g, .375 SILVER, .0130 oz ASW
Obv: Castle w/H.S.K. below.

KM#	Date	Mintage	Fine	VF	XF	Unc
246	1817 HSK	.019	2.00	6.00	10.00	60.00
	1818 HSK	.029	2.00	6.00	10.00	60.00
	1819 HSK	.149	2.00	6.00	10.00	60.00

Rev. leg: HAMB. COVR., 'I' between dots.

KM#	Date	Mintage	Fine	VF	XF	Unc
251.1	1823 HSK	.138	1.00	3.00	6.00	35.00
	1828 HSK	.142	1.00	3.00	6.00	35.00
	1832 HSK	.142	1.00	3.00	6.00	35.00

Rev: 'I' between rosettes.

KM#	Date	Mintage	Fine	VF	XF	Unc
251.2	1837 HSK	.153	1.00	3.00	6.00	35.00
	1840 HSK	.144	1.00	3.00	6.00	35.00

Obv: Redesigned castle.

KM#	Date	Mintage	Fine	VF	XF	Unc
262	1841 HSK	.149	1.00	3.00	6.00	35.00

Rev: 'I' between 5-pointed stars.

KM#	Date	Mintage	Fine	VF	XF	Unc
266	1846	.240	1.00	3.00	6.00	35.00

Rev: 'I' between 6-pointed stars.

KM#	Date	Mintage	Fine	VF	XF	Unc
272	1851	.240	1.00	3.00	6.00	35.00

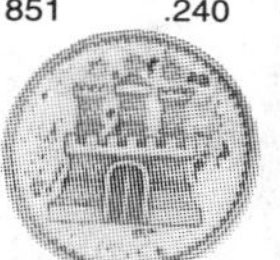

Beaded borders.

KM#	Date	Mintage	Fine	VF	XF	Unc
277	1855A	.112	1.00	2.00	5.00	25.00
	1855	1.841	1.00	2.00	5.00	25.00

32 SCHILLING

18.3200 g, .750 SILVER, .4417 oz ASW

KM#	Date	Mintage	Fine	VF	XF	Unc
238	1808 HSK	.210	40.00	80.00	130.00	325.00

14.1700 g, .968 SILVER, .4410 oz ASW

KM#	Date	Mintage	Fine	VF	XF	Unc
241	1809 HSK	.390	30.00	60.00	115.00	265.00

KM#	Date	Mintage	Fine	VF	XF	Unc
242	1809 CAIG	3.058	25.00	50.00	90.00	245.00

MONETARY REFORM

2 MARK

11.1110 g, .900 SILVER, .3215 oz ASW

KM#	Date	Mintage	Fine	VF	XF	Unc
290	1876J	3.962	20.00	45.00	250.00	450.00
	1877J	.500	25.00	50.00	275.00	550.00
	1878J	.350	25.00	50.00	325.00	625.00
	1880J	.099	40.00	100.00	350.00	750.00
	1883J	.060	40.00	100.00	350.00	675.00
	1888J	.100	30.00	60.00	300.00	575.00
294	1892J	.141	15.00	25.00	75.00	325.00
	1893J	.146	15.00	25.00	75.00	275.00
	1896J	.286	15.00	20.00	50.00	175.00
	1898J	.118	25.00	60.00	160.00	400.00
	1899J	.286	15.00	20.00	60.00	175.00
	1900J	.577	12.50	25.00	60.00	175.00
	Common date		—	—	Proof	275.00

NOTE: Later dates (1901-1914) exist for this type.

5 MARK

27.7770 g, .900 SILVER, .8038 oz ASW
Rev: Type I.

KM#	Date	Mintage	Fine	VF	XF	Unc
287	1875J	.286	30.00	75.00	400.00	1250.
	1876J	.930	30.00	50.00	350.00	1000.
	1888J	.040	50.00	150.00	400.00	1250.

1.9910 g, .900 GOLD, .0576 oz AGW

KM#	Date	Mintage	Fine	VF	XF	Unc
291	1877J	.441	125.00	200.00	275.00	450.00
	1877J	—	—	—	Proof	Rare

27.7770 g, .900 SILVER, .8038 oz ASW
Rev: Type II.

KM#	Date	Mintage	Fine	VF	XF	Unc
293	1891J	.059	20.00	65.00	135.00	450.00
	1893J	.055	20.00	50.00	135.00	400.00
	1894J	.082	20.00	50.00	135.00	350.00
	1895J	.082	25.00	50.00	135.00	350.00
	1896J	.016	100.00	250.00	600.00	1200.
	1898J	.176	20.00	50.00	135.00	350.00
	1899J	.082	20.00	50.00	135.00	350.00
	1900J	.172	17.50	40.00	95.00	300.00
	Common date		—	—	Proof	1500.

NOTE: Later dates (1901-1913) exist for this type.

10 MARK

3.9820 g, .900 GOLD, .1152 oz AGW
Rev: Type I.

KM#	Date	Mintage	Fine	VF	XF	Unc
285	1873B	.025	600.00	900.00	1400.	2500.
	1873B	—	—	—	Proof	Rare

Rev: Type II.

KM#	Date	Mintage	Fine	VF	XF	Unc
286	1874B	.050	400.00	650.00	1000.	1400.

KM#	Date	Mintage	Fine	VF	XF	Unc
288	1875J	.608	65.00	110.00	160.00	250.00
	1875J	—	—	—	Proof	1000.
	1876J	6,321	700.00	1000.	1500.	1900.
	1877J	.221	65.00	110.00	160.00	250.00
	1878J	.316	65.00	110.00	160.00	250.00
	1879J	.255	65.00	110.00	160.00	250.00
	1880J	.139	65.00	110.00	160.00	250.00
	1888J	.163	65.00	110.00	160.00	250.00

KM#	Date	Mintage	Fine	VF	XF	Unc
292	1890J	.245	65.00	110.00	160.00	250.00
	1893J	.246	65.00	110.00	160.00	250.00
	1896J	.164	65.00	110.00	160.00	250.00
	1898J	.344	65.00	110.00	160.00	225.00
	1900J	.082	65.00	110.00	160.00	250.00

NOTE: Later dates (1901-1913) exist for this type.

20 MARK

7.9650 g, .900 GOLD, .2304 oz AGW
Rev: Type II.

KM#	Date	Mintage	Fine	VF	XF	Unc
289	1875J	.313	115.00	165.00	200.00	300.00
	1876J	1.723	115.00	135.00	150.00	225.00
	1877J	1.324	115.00	135.00	150.00	225.00
	1878J	2.008	115.00	135.00	150.00	225.00
	1879J	.104	250.00	425.00	750.00	1250.
	1880J	.120	115.00	150.00	275.00	400.00
	1881J	500 pcs.	15,000.	20,000.	25,000.	30,000.
	1883J	.125	115.00	140.00	180.00	350.00
	1884J	.639	115.00	140.00	180.00	350.00
	1887J	.251	115.00	140.00	180.00	350.00
	1889J	.014	500.00	1000.	1250.	1750.

Rev: Type III.

KM#	Date	Mintage	Fine	VF	XF	Unc
295	1893J	.815	115.00	135.00	160.00	225.00
	1894J	.501	115.00	135.00	160.00	225.00
	1895J	.501	115.00	135.00	160.00	225.00
	1897J	.500	115.00	135.00	160.00	225.00
	1899J	1.002	115.00	135.00	160.00	225.00
	1900J	.501	115.00	135.00	160.00	225.00

NOTE: Later dates (1908-1913) exist for this type.

TRADE COINAGE

DUCAT

3.4900 g, .979 GOLD, .1099 oz AGW
Obv: Titles of Franz II.

KM#	Date	Mintage	Fine	VF	XF	Unc
227.1	1801	7,236	375.00	625.00	1150.	1500.
	1802	9,199	375.00	625.00	1150.	1500.
	1803	6,365	375.00	625.00	1150.	1500.
	1804	7,284	375.00	625.00	1150.	1500.
	1805	9,466	375.00	625.00	1150.	1500.

NOTE: Earlier dates (1793-1800) exist for this type.

KM#	Date	Mintage	Fine	VF	XF	Unc
227.2	1806	7,521	375.00	625.00	1150.	1500.

KM#	Date	Mintage	Fine	VF	XF	Unc
237	1807	6,000	375.00	625.00	1150.	1650.

KM#	Date	Mintage	Fine	VF	XF	Unc
239	1808	7,500	350.00	575.00	950.00	1450.
	1809	7,500	300.00	500.00	875.00	1400.
	1810	7,407	300.00	500.00	875.00	1400.

KM#	Date	Mintage	Fine	VF	XF	Unc
245	1811	.011	300.00	500.00	875.00	1250.
	1815	9,965	300.00	500.00	875.00	1250.
	1817	5,000	325.00	550.00	975.00	1350.
	1818	7,000	325.00	550.00	975.00	1350.
	1819	8,901	300.00	500.00	875.00	1250.
	1820	7,000	300.00	500.00	875.00	1250.
	1821	9,900	300.00	500.00	875.00	1250.
	1822	.013	300.00	500.00	875.00	1250.
	1823	8,700	300.00	500.00	875.00	1250.
	1824	6,970	300.00	500.00	875.00	1250.
	1825	.010	300.00	500.00	875.00	1250.
	1826	.012	300.00	500.00	875.00	1250.
	1827	.011	300.00	500.00	875.00	1250.
	1828	8,601	300.00	500.00	875.00	1250.
	1829	9,606	300.00	500.00	875.00	1250.
245	1830	.012	300.00	500.00	875.00	1250.
	1831	9,200	300.00	500.00	875.00	1250.
	1832	9,500	300.00	500.00	875.00	1250.
	1833	9,440	300.00	500.00	875.00	1250.
	1834	.010	250.00	400.00	750.00	1000.

KM#	Date	Mintage	Fine	VF	XF	Unc
256	1835	.010	250.00	425.00	750.00	1150.
	1836	8,067	250.00	425.00	750.00	1150.
	1837	8,156	250.00	425.00	750.00	1150.
	1838	9,000	250.00	425.00	750.00	1150.
	1839	9,045	250.00	425.00	750.00	1150.
	1840	9,882	250.00	425.00	750.00	1150.
	1841	.010	250.00	425.00	750.00	1150.
	1842	.012	225.00	375.00	625.00	1000.

Struck in a collar.

KM#	Date	Mintage	Fine	VF	XF	Unc
263	1843	.012	225.00	375.00	625.00	1000.
	1844	9,768	250.00	425.00	750.00	1150.
	1845	.012	200.00	325.00	550.00	875.00
	1846	.011	200.00	325.00	550.00	875.00
	1847	.010	200.00	325.00	550.00	875.00
	1848	.013	200.00	325.00	550.00	875.00
	1849	.010	200.00	325.00	550.00	875.00
	1850	.011	200.00	325.00	550.00	875.00

Obv: Knights shield redesigned.

KM#	Date	Mintage	Fine	VF	XF	Unc
273	1851	8,497	225.00	375.00	750.00	1000.
	1852	9,476	225.00	375.00	750.00	1000.
	1853	.010	225.00	375.00	750.00	1000.

Rev. leg. ends:. . . 979 MILLES

KM#	Date	Mintage	Fine	VF	XF	Unc
274	1854	.012	175.00	250.00	400.00	750.00
	1855	.011	175.00	250.00	400.00	750.00
	1856	.011	175.00	250.00	400.00	750.00
	1857	.012	175.00	250.00	400.00	750.00
	1858	.010	175.00	250.00	400.00	750.00
	1859	.014	175.00	250.00	400.00	750.00
	1860	.015	175.00	250.00	400.00	750.00
	1861	.015	175.00	250.00	400.00	750.00
	1862	.017	150.00	200.00	350.00	700.00
	1863	.020	150.00	200.00	350.00	700.00
	1864	.024	150.00	200.00	350.00	700.00
	1865	.017	150.00	200.00	350.00	700.00
	1866	.024	150.00	200.00	350.00	700.00
	1867	.026	150.00	200.00	350.00	700.00

Rev: Mint mark B below shell.

KM#	Date	Mintage	Fine	VF	XF	Unc
280	1868B	.025	135.00	175.00	300.00	600.00
	1869B	.026	135.00	175.00	300.00	600.00
	1870B	.030	135.00	175.00	300.00	600.00
	1871B	.030	135.00	175.00	300.00	600.00
	1872B	.030	135.00	175.00	300.00	600.00

2 DUCAT

6.9800 g, .979 GOLD, .2197 oz AGW
Obv. leg: FRANCISVS II D.G.ROM.IMP. . .

KM#	Date	Mintage	Fine	VF	XF	Unc
228.1	1801	1,273	650.00	1250.	1750.	2350.
	1802	1,256	650.00	1250.	1750.	2350.
	1803	837 pcs.	650.00	1350.	2350.	3000.
	1804	—	650.00	1300.	2000.	2500.
	1805	Inc. KM227.1	650.00	1250.	1750.	2350.

NOTE: Earlier dates (1793-1800) exist for this type.

Obv. leg: . . . D.G.R.IMP. . .

KM#	Date	Mintage	Fine	VF	XF	Unc
228.2	1804	1,072	650.00	1250.	1750.	2350.
	1806	1,201	650.00	1250.	1750.	2350.

KM#	Date	Mintage	Fine	VF	XF	Unc
240	1808	1,250	500.00	1000.	1500.	2000.
	1809	1,250	500.00	1000.	1500.	2000.
	1810	1,050	500.00	1000.	1500.	2000.

5 DUCAT

(1/2 Portugaloser)

17.5000 g, .986 GOLD, .5548 oz AGW

KM#	Date	Mintage	Fine	VF	XF	Unc
234	1801	—	—	700.00	1000.	1500.

PATTERNS (Pn)

(Including off metal strikes)

KM#	Date	Mintage	Identification	Mkt.Val.
Pn15	1826 HSK	—	1 Schilling, Gold, KM251.1	400.00
Pn16	1836 HSK	—	1 Sechsling, Gold, KM236	175.00
Pn17	1877J	—	10 Mark, Silver, plain edge, KM288	—
Pn18	1877J	—	10 Mark, Copper	—
Pn19	1882J	—	20 Mark, Silver, plain edge, KM289	—

HANNOVER

KINGDOM

A state located in northwest Germany which became Hannover when Ernst August of Brunswick-Luneburg chose the title of Elector of Hannover after his capital city. During the Napoleonic wars it was first occupied by Prussia and then incorporated into the Kingdom of Westphalia. In 1814 it was raised to the status of a Kingdom. Hannover was absorbed by Prussia in 1866.

RULERS

George III, 1760-1820
Georg IV, 1820-1830
Wilhelm IV, 1830-1837
Ernst August, 1837-1851
Georg V, 1851-1866

MINT MARKS

A - Clausthal, 1832-1849
B - Hannover, 1866-1878
C - Clausthal, 1814-1833

MINTMASTERS INITIALS

Letter	Date	Name
B	1817-1838	Ludwig August Bruel
B	1844-1868	Theodor Wilhelm Bruel
CHH,H	1802-1817	Christian Heinrich Haase
LAB,LB	1817-1838	Ludwig August Bruel
S	1839-1844	Carl Schulter

PFENNIG

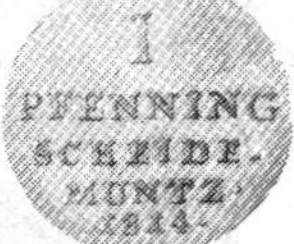

COPPER

Obv: H below crowned GR monogram.

KM#	Date	Mintage	Fine	VF	XF	Unc
103.1	1814 H	—	4.00	8.00	22.00	65.00

Obv: C below crowned monogram.

KM#	Date	Mintage	Fine	VF	XF	Unc
103.2	1814C	—	5.00	10.00	25.00	75.00

KM#	Date	Mintage	Fine	VF	XF	Unc
104	1814C	—	2.50	5.00	15.00	45.00
	1817C	—	2.50	5.00	15.00	45.00
	1818C	—	2.50	5.00	15.00	45.00
	1819C	—	2.50	5.00	15.00	45.00
	1820C	—	2.50	5.00	15.00	45.00

KM#	Date	Mintage	Fine	VF	XF	Unc
125.1	1821C	—	3.50	6.00	18.00	50.00
	1822C	—	2.00	4.00	10.00	30.00
	1823C	—	2.00	4.00	10.00	30.00
	1824C	—	2.00	4.00	10.00	30.00
	1825C	—	2.00	4.00	10.00	30.00
	1826C	—	2.00	4.00	10.00	30.00
	1827 w/o mint mark	—	2.00	4.00	10.00	30.00
	1827C	—	2.00	4.00	10.00	30.00
	1828C	—	2.00	4.00	10.00	30.00
	1829C	—	2.00	4.00	10.00	30.00
	1830C	—	2.00	4.00	10.00	30.00

Rev: B below value.

KM#	Date	Mintage	Fine	VF	XF	Unc
125.2	1826 B	—	2.00	4.00	10.00	30.00
	1828 B	—	2.00	4.00	10.00	30.00
	1829 B	—	2.00	4.00	10.00	30.00
	1830 B	—	2.00	4.00	10.00	30.00

Obv: Date below crowned WR monogram. Rev: A below value.

KM#	Date	Mintage	Fine	VF	XF	Unc
150.1	1832A	—	2.00	4.00	10.00	30.00
	1833A	—	2.00	4.00	10.00	30.00
	1834A	—	2.00	4.00	10.00	30.00

Rev: B below value.

KM#	Date	Mintage	Fine	VF	XF	Unc
150.2	1832 B	—	2.00	4.00	10.00	32.00
	1833 B	—	2.00	4.00	10.00	32.00
	1834 B	—	2.00	4.00	10.00	32.00
	1835 B	—	2.00	4.00	10.00	32.00

Rev: C below value.

KM#	Date	Mintage	Fine	VF	XF	Unc
150.3	1831/30C	—	2.00	4.50	12.00	35.00
	1831C	—	2.00	4.00	10.00	30.00
	1832C	—	2.00	4.00	10.00	30.00
	1833C	—	2.00	4.00	10.00	30.00

Obv: IV below WR monogram.

KM#	Date	Mintage	Fine	VF	XF	Unc
156	1834A	—	6.00	12.00	30.00	100.00

Obv: Crowned shield w/prancing horse. Rev: A below value.

KM#	Date	Mintage	Fine	VF	XF	Unc
166.1	1835A	—	2.00	4.00	10.00	30.00
	1836A	—	2.00	4.00	10.00	30.00
	1837A	—	2.00	4.00	10.00	30.00

Rev: B below value.

KM#	Date	Mintage	Fine	VF	XF	Unc
166.2	1835 B	—	2.00	4.00	10.00	30.00
	1836 B	—	2.00	4.00	10.00	30.00
	1837 B	—	2.00	4.00	10.00	30.00

Obv: Crowned EAR monogram. Rev: A below value.

KM#	Date	Mintage	Fine	VF	XF	Unc
173.1	1837A	—	2.00	4.00	10.00	30.00
	1838A	—	2.00	4.00	10.00	30.00
	1839A	—	2.00	4.00	10.00	30.00
	1840A	—	2.00	4.00	10.00	30.00
	1841A	—	2.00	4.00	10.00	30.00
	1842A	—	2.00	4.00	10.00	30.00
	1843A	—	2.00	4.00	10.00	30.00
	1844A	—	2.00	4.00	10.00	30.00
	1845A	—	2.00	4.00	10.00	30.00
	1846A	—	2.00	4.00	10.00	30.00

Rev: B below value.

KM#	Date	Mintage	Fine	VF	XF	Unc
173.2	1838 B	—	3.00	7.00	20.00	75.00

Rev: S below value.

KM#	Date	Mintage	Fine	VF	XF	Unc
173.3	1839 S	—	3.00	7.00	20.00	75.00
	1841 S	—	3.00	7.00	20.00	75.00
	1842 S	—	3.00	7.00	20.00	75.00

Obv: Date below monogram. Rev: SCHEIDEMUNZE below value, B mint mark.

KM#	Date	Mintage	Fine	VF	XF	Unc
176	1838 B	—	20.00	40.00	75.00	150.00

Rev: B below value.

KM#	Date	Mintage	Fine	VF	XF	Unc
201.1	1845 B	—	1.50	3.00	7.00	25.00
	1846 B	—	1.50	3.00	7.00	25.00
	1847 B	—	1.50	3.00	7.00	25.00
	1848 B	—	1.50	3.00	7.00	25.00
	1849 B	—	1.50	3.00	7.00	25.00
	1850 B	—	1.50	3.00	7.00	25.00
	1851 B	—	1.50	3.00	7.00	25.00

Rev: A below value.

KM#	Date	Mintage	Fine	VF	XF	Unc
201.2	1846A	—	1.50	3.00	7.00	25.00
	1847A	—	1.50	3.00	7.00	25.00
	1848A	—	1.50	3.00	7.00	25.00
	1849A	—	1.50	3.00	7.00	25.00

Obv: V below monogram.

KM#	Date	Mintage	Fine	VF	XF	Unc
216	1852 B	—	15.00	30.00	60.00	125.00

KM#	Date	Mintage	Fine	VF	XF	Unc
221	1853 B	—	2.00	4.00	10.00	30.00
	1854 B	—	2.00	4.00	10.00	30.00
	1855 B	—	2.00	4.00	10.00	30.00
	1856 B	—	2.00	4.00	10.00	30.00

KM#	Date	Mintage	Fine	VF	XF	Unc
233	1858 B	—	1.50	3.00	7.00	25.00
	1859 B	—	1.50	3.00	7.00	25.00
	1860 B	—	1.50	3.00	7.00	25.00
	1861 B	—	1.50	3.00	7.00	25.00
	1862 B	—	1.50	3.00	7.00	25.00
	1863 B	2.324	1.50	3.00	7.00	25.00
	1864 B	—	1.50	3.00	7.00	25.00

2 PFENNIG

COPPER

Obv: Crowned GR monogram, date below. Rev: Value.

KM#	Date	Mintage	Fine	VF	XF	Unc
115	1817C	—	5.00	10.00	25.00	100.00
	1818C	—	5.00	10.00	25.00	100.00

KM#	Date	Mintage	Fine	VF	XF	Unc
126.1	1821C	—	3.00	6.00	18.00	55.00
	1822C	—	3.00	6.00	18.00	55.00
	1823C	—	3.00	6.00	18.00	55.00
	1824C	—	3.00	6.00	18.00	55.00
	1825C	—	3.00	6.00	18.00	55.00

KM#	Date	Mintage	Fine	VF	XF	Unc
126.1	1826C	—	3.00	6.00	18.00	55.00
	1827C	—	3.00	6.00	18.00	55.00
	1828C	—	3.00	6.00	18.00	55.00
	1829C	—	3.00	6.00	18.00	55.00
	1830C	—	3.00	6.00	18.00	55.00

Rev: B below value.

KM#	Date	Mintage	Fine	VF	XF	Unc
126.2	1826 B	.154	3.00	7.00	20.00	70.00

Obv: Crowned WR monogram above date. Rev: C below value.

KM#	Date	Mintage	Fine	VF	XF	Unc
147.1	1831C	—	3.50	9.00	25.00	85.00
	1833C	—	3.50	9.00	25.00	85.00
	1834C	—	3.50	9.00	25.00	85.00

Rev: A below value.

KM#	Date	Mintage	Fine	VF	XF	Unc
147.2	1834A	—	4.00	10.00	25.00	85.00

Obv: IV below monogram. Rev: Date.

KM#	Date	Mintage	Fine	VF	XF	Unc
157	1834A	—	4.00	10.00	25.00	85.00

Obv: Crowned shield w/prancing horse.

KM#	Date	Mintage	Fine	VF	XF	Unc
167.1	1835A	—	3.00	7.00	20.00	70.00
	1836A	—	3.00	7.00	20.00	70.00
	1837A	—	3.00	7.00	20.00	70.00

Pearl border

KM#	Date	Mintage	Fine	VF	XF	Unc
167.2	1837A	—	15.00	30.00	60.00	200.00

Obv: Crowned EAR monogram. Rev: Value, A below date.

KM#	Date	Mintage	Fine	VF	XF	Unc
174.1	1837A	—	2.00	4.00	12.00	45.00
	1838A	—	2.00	4.00	12.00	45.00
	1839A	—	2.00	4.00	12.00	45.00
	1840A	—	2.00	4.00	12.00	45.00
	1841A	—	2.00	4.00	12.00	45.00
	1842A	—	2.00	4.00	12.00	45.00
	1843A	—	2.00	4.00	12.00	45.00
	1844A	—	2.00	4.00	12.00	45.00
	1845A	—	2.00	4.00	12.00	45.00
	1846A	—	2.00	4.00	12.00	45.00

Rev: S below date.

KM#	Date	Mintage	Fine	VF	XF	Unc
174.2	1842 S	—	3.00	6.00	18.00	65.00
	1844 S	—	3.00	6.00	18.00	65.00

Rev: B below date, struck in a ring.

KM#	Date	Mintage	Fine	VF	XF	Unc
202.1	1845 B	—	1.50	3.00	10.00	32.00
	1846 B	—	1.50	3.00	10.00	32.00
	1847 B	—	1.50	3.00	10.00	32.00
	1848 B	—	1.50	3.00	10.00	32.00
	1849 B	—	1.50	3.00	10.00	32.00
	1850 B	—	1.50	3.00	10.00	32.00
	1851 B	—	1.50	3.00	10.00	32.00

Rev: A below date.

KM#	Date	Mintage	Fine	VF	XF	Unc
202.2	1846A	—	1.50	3.00	10.00	32.00
	1847A	—	1.50	3.00	10.00	32.00
	1848A	—	1.50	3.00	10.00	32.00
	1849A	—	1.50	3.00	10.00	32.00

Rev: B below date.

KM#	Date	Mintage	Fine	VF	XF	Unc
217	1852 B	—	1.25	2.50	8.00	30.00
	1853 B	—	1.25	2.50	8.00	30.00
	1854 B	—	1.25	2.50	8.00	30.00
	1855 B	—	1.25	2.50	8.00	30.00
	1856 B	—	1.25	2.50	8.00	30.00

KM#	Date	Mintage	Fine	VF	XF	Unc
234	1858 B	—	1.25	2.50	7.00	28.00
	1859 B	—	1.25	2.50	7.00	28.00
	1860 B	—	1.25	2.50	7.00	28.00
	1861 B	—	1.25	2.50	7.00	28.00
	1862 B	—	1.25	2.50	7.00	28.00
	1863 B	.607	1.25	2.50	7.00	28.00
	1864 B	—	1.25	2.50	7.00	28.00

4 PFENNIG

(1/2 Mariengroschen)

1.2300 g, .187 SILVER, .0073 oz ASW
Obv. C below crowned GR monogram.
Rev. leg: NACH DEM REICHS FUSS

KM#	Date	Mintage	Fine	VF	XF	Unc
105.1	1814C	—	20.00	40.00	100.00	250.00
	1815C	—	20.00	40.00	100.00	250.00

Obv: H below monogram.

KM#	Date	Mintage	Fine	VF	XF	Unc
105.2	1815 H	—	15.00	30.00	80.00	225.00
	1816 H	—	15.00	30.00	80.00	225.00

Obv. leg: CONVENT MUNZE

KM#	Date	Mintage	Fine	VF	XF	Unc
112	1816 H	.071	10.00	20.00	50.00	125.00
	1817 H	Inc. Ab.	10.00	20.00	50.00	125.00

Obv: IV below monogram,
leg: CONVENTIONS MUNZE.

KM#	Date	Mintage	Fine	VF	XF	Unc
135	1822 B	—	6.00	12.00	25.00	65.00
	1826 B	—	6.00	12.00	25.00	65.00
	1828 B	—	6.00	12.00	25.00	65.00
	1830 B	—	6.00	12.00	25.00	65.00

COPPER
Obv: Date below monogram.
Rev: C below SCHEIDEMUNZE.

KM#	Date	Mintage	Fine	VF	XF	Unc
143	1827C	—	50.00	90.00	150.00	350.00

KM#	Date	Mintage	Fine	VF	XF	Unc
148	1831C	—	50.00	85.00	140.00	325.00

.9200 g, .218 SILVER, .0064 oz ASW
Rev: B below date.

KM#	Date	Mintage	Fine	VF	XF	Unc
168	1835 B	—	2.00	4.00	12.00	35.00
	1836 B	—	2.00	4.00	12.00	35.00
	1837 B	—	2.00	4.00	12.00	35.00
177.1	1838 B	—	2.00	4.00	10.00	32.00

Rev: S below date.

KM#	Date	Mintage	Fine	VF	XF	Unc
177.2	1840 S	—	2.00	4.00	10.00	32.00
	1841 S	—	2.00	4.00	10.00	32.00
	1842 S	—	2.00	4.00	10.00	32.00

6 PFENNIG

1.3900 g, .218 SILVER, .0097 oz ASW
Obv: Crowned shield w/prancing horse.
Rev: S below value.

KM#	Date	Mintage	Fine	VF	XF	Unc
198.1	1843 S	—	3.00	7.00	18.00	55.00
	1844 S	—	3.00	7.00	18.00	55.00

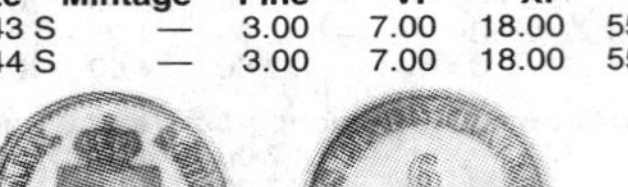

Obv: B below shield.

KM#	Date	Mintage	Fine	VF	XF	Unc
198.2	1844 B	—	3.00	7.00	16.00	45.00
	1845 B	—	3.00	7.00	16.00	45.00
	1846 B	—	3.00	7.00	16.00	45.00

KM#	Date	Mintage	Fine	VF	XF	Unc
205	1846 B	—	2.00	3.50	9.00	30.00
	1847 B	—	2.00	3.50	9.00	30.00
	1848 B	—	2.00	3.50	9.00	30.00
	1849 B	—	2.00	3.50	9.00	30.00
	1850 B	—	2.00	3.50	9.00	30.00
	1851 B	—	2.00	3.50	9.00	30.00

KM#	Date	Mintage	Fine	VF	XF	Unc
218	1852 B	—	2.00	3.50	9.00	32.00
	1853 B	—	2.00	3.50	9.00	32.00
	1854 B	—	2.00	3.50	9.00	32.00
	1855 B	—	2.00	3.50	9.00	32.00

1/2 GROSCHEN

1.0900 g, .220 SILVER, .0077 oz ASW

KM#	Date	Mintage	Fine	VF	XF	Unc
235	1858 B	—	2.00	3.50	7.50	28.00
	1859 B	—	2.00	3.50	7.50	28.00
	1861 B	—	2.00	3.50	7.50	28.00
	1862 B	—	2.00	3.50	7.50	28.00
	1863 B	.047	2.00	3.50	7.50	28.00
	1864 B	—	2.00	3.50	7.50	28.00
	1865 B	—	2.00	3.50	7.50	28.00

MARIENGROSCHEN

(1/36 Thaler)

1.4800 g, .312 SILVER, .0148 oz ASW
Obv: C below crowned GR monogram.
Rev: Value, leg: NACH DEM REICHFUSS.

KM#	Date	Mintage	Fine	VF	XF	Unc
106	1814C	—	15.00	35.00	85.00	200.00

Rev: H below date.

KM#	Date	Mintage	Fine	VF	XF	Unc
113	1816 H	.443	5.00	10.00	28.00	85.00
	1817 H	Inc. Ab.	5.00	10.00	28.00	85.00
	1818 H	Inc. Ab.	5.00	10.00	28.00	85.00

GROSCHEN

2.1900 g, .220 SILVER, .0154 oz ASW

KM#	Date	Mintage	Fine	VF	XF	Unc
236	1858 B	—	2.00	3.50	7.50	28.00
	1859 B	—	2.00	3.50	7.50	28.00
	1860 B	—	2.00	3.50	7.50	28.00
	1861 B	—	2.00	3.50	7.50	28.00
	1862 B	—	2.00	3.50	7.50	28.00
	1863 B	.069	2.00	3.50	7.50	28.00
	1864 B	—	2.00	3.50	7.50	28.00
	1865 B	—	2.00	3.50	7.50	28.00
	1866 B	.076	2.00	3.50	7.50	28.00

3 MARIENGROSCHEN

3.3400 g, .437 SILVER, .0469 oz ASW
Obv. leg: CONVENTIONSMUNZE.
Rev: C.H.H. below ledge.

KM#	Date	Mintage	Fine	VF	XF	Unc
114.1	1816 CHH	—	6.00	15.00	40.00	100.00
	1817 CHH	—	6.00	15.00	40.00	100.00
	1818 CHH	12.000	6.00	15.00	40.00	100.00

Rev: .L.A.B. below ledge.

KM#	Date	Mintage	Fine	VF	XF	Unc
114.2	1819 LAB	—	6.00	15.00	40.00	100.00
	1820 LAB	I.A.	6.00	15.00	40.00	100.00

Rev: L.B. below ledge.

KM#	Date	Mintage	Fine	VF	XF	Unc
114.3	1819 LB	I.A.	6.00	15.00	40.00	100.00
	1820 LB	—	6.00	15.00	40.00	100.00

KM#	Date	Mintage	Fine	VF	XF	Unc
120	1820 LB	—	6.00	15.00	40.00	100.00
	1821 LB	I.A.	6.00	15.00	40.00	100.00

16 GUTE GROSCHEN

11.7700 g, .993 SILVER, .3758 oz ASW
Obv: Prancing horse w/M on ledge,
leg: GEORGIUS.III.D.G.BRITAN.&.HANNOV.REX.

KM#	Date	Mintage	Fine	VF	XF	Unc
121.1	1820	—	150.00	250.00	375.00	850.00

Obv. leg: GEORGIUS.III.D.G.BRITANNIARUM.

KM#	Date	Mintage	Fine	VF	XF	Unc
121.2	1820	—	125.00	200.00	325.00	750.00

Obv: Prancing horse, M on ledge
XX.EINE.F.MARK. below,
leg: GEORGIUS.IV.D.G.BRITAN.& HANNOV.REX.
Rev: Value, CONVENTIONS-MUNZE. below.

KM#	Date	Mintage	Fine	VF	XF	Unc
122	1820	—	30.00	60.00	120.00	185.00

Obv: XX.E.F. MARK below ledge.
Rev. leg: CONV-MUNZE FEIN SILBER.

KM#	Date	Mintage	Fine	VF	XF	Unc
123	1820	—	30.00	55.00	100.00	175.00

Obv: XX.EINE.F.MARK. below ledge.

KM#	Date	Mintage	Fine	VF	XF	Unc
124	1820	—	25.00	45.00	80.00	145.00

Obv: XX.E.F.MARK. below ledge.
Rev: FEIN SILB.

KM#	Date	Mintage	Fine	VF	XF	Unc
127	1821	—	25.00	45.00	75.00	135.00

Rev: CONV MUNZE FEIN SILB around bottom.

KM#	Date	Mintage	Fine	VF	XF	Unc
128	1821	—	30.00	60.00	125.00	200.00

NOTE: 7 obverse legend varieties exist.

Rev: FEINES SILB below GROSCHEN.

KM#	Date	Mintage	Fine	VF	XF	Unc
136	1822	—	30.00	60.00	125.00	200.00

NOTE: 2 obverse legend varieties exist.

KM#	Date	Mintage	Fine	VF	XF	Unc
137	1822	—	30.00	55.00	100.00	175.00

NOTE: 2 obverse legend varieties exist.

KM#	Date	Mintage	Fine	VF	XF	Unc
138	1822	—	20.00	30.00	65.00	140.00
	1823	—	20.00	30.00	65.00	140.00
	1824	—	20.00	30.00	65.00	140.00
	1825	—	20.00	30.00	65.00	140.00
	1826	—	20.00	30.00	65.00	140.00
	1827	—	20.00	30.00	65.00	140.00
	1828	—	20.00	30.00	65.00	140.00
	1829	—	20.00	30.00	65.00	140.00
	1830	—	20.00	30.00	65.00	140.00

NOTE: 2 obverse legend varieties exist for 1822, 1823 and 1825.

KM#	Date	Mintage	Fine	VF	XF	Unc
145.1	1830	—	20.00	30.00	65.00	140.00

KM#	Date	Mintage	Fine	VF	XF	Unc
145.2	1831	—	20.00	30.00	65.00	140.00
	1832	—	20.00	30.00	65.00	140.00
	1832A	—	20.00	30.00	65.00	140.00

Obv: W/'L' on ledge.

KM#	Date	Mintage	Fine	VF	XF	Unc
145.3	1832A	—	20.00	30.00	65.00	140.00
	1833A	—	20.00	30.00	65.00	140.00
	1834A	—	20.00	30.00	65.00	140.00

Obv: W/'M' on ledge.

KM#	Date	Mintage	Fine	VF	XF	Unc
145.4	1832A	—	20.00	30.00	65.00	140.00

Obv: W/'W' on ledge.

KM#	Date	Mintage	Fine	VF	XF	Unc
145.5	1834A	—	20.00	30.00	65.00	140.00

1/24 THALER

1.9400 g, .312 SILVER, .0194 oz ASW
Obv: Date below prancing horse.
Rev. value, leg: NACH DEM REICHFUSS.

KM#	Date	Mintage	Fine	VF	XF	Unc
107	1814C	—	7.00	15.00	40.00	150.00

KM#	Date	Mintage	Fine	VF	XF	Unc
116	1817 H	.946	5.00	10.00	30.00	120.00
	1818	—	5.00	10.00	30.00	120.00

Obv: IV below monogram.

KM#	Date	Mintage	Fine	VF	XF	Unc
141	1826 B	.139	4.00	7.00	15.00	60.00
	1827 B	.328	4.00	7.00	15.00	60.00
	1828 B	.904	4.00	7.00	15.00	60.00

Rev: B below date.

KM#	Date	Mintage	Fine	VF	XF	Unc
158.1	1834 B	—	3.00	6.00	12.50	50.00
	1834 .B.	—	—	—	—	—
	1835 B	—	3.00	6.00	12.50	50.00
	1836 B	—	3.00	6.00	12.50	50.00
	1837 B	—	3.00	6.00	12.50	50.00

Rev: A below date.

KM#	Date	Mintage	Fine	VF	XF	Unc
158.2	1835A	—	4.50	9.00	20.00	70.00
	1836A	—	4.50	9.00	20.00	70.00

Rev: B below date.

KM#	Date	Mintage	Fine	VF	XF	Unc
178.1	1838 B	—	2.50	6.00	12.00	40.00

Rev: S below date.

KM#	Date	Mintage	Fine	VF	XF	Unc
178.2	1839 S	—	2.50	6.00	12.00	40.00
	1841 S	—	2.50	6.00	12.00	40.00
	1842 S	—	2.50	6.00	12.00	40.00

Rev: A below date.

KM#	Date	Mintage	Fine	VF	XF	Unc
178.3	1839A	—	2.50	6.00	12.50	50.00
	1840A	—	2.50	6.00	12.50	50.00
	1841A	—	2.50	6.00	12.50	50.00
	1842A	—	2.50	6.00	12.50	50.00
	1843A	—	2.50	6.00	12.50	50.00
	1844A	—	2.50	6.00	12.50	50.00
	1845A	—	2.50	6.00	12.50	50.00
	1846A	—	2.50	6.00	12.50	50.00

Obv: B below prancing horse. Rev: Value, SCHEIDEMUNZE.

KM#	Date	Mintage	Fine	VF	XF	Unc
203	1845 B	—	2.50	6.00	12.50	50.00
	1846 B	—	2.50	6.00	12.50	50.00

Obv. leg: NEC ASPERA TERRENT.

KM#	Date	Mintage	Fine	VF	XF	Unc
227	1854 B	—	2.50	6.00	12.00	40.00
	1855 B	—	2.50	6.00	12.00	40.00
	1856 B	—	2.50	6.00	12.00	40.00

1/12 THALER

(3 Mariengroschen)

3.2400 g, .437 SILVER, .0455 oz ASW
Obv: Prancing horse, S on ledge.
Rev: Value, leg: NACH DEM REICHS FUSS.

KM#	Date	Mintage	Fine	VF	XF	Unc
108	1814C	—	7.00	18.00	55.00	150.00
	1815C	—	7.00	18.00	55.00	150.00
	1816C	—	7.00	18.00	55.00	150.00

KM#	Date	Mintage	Fine	VF	XF	Unc
139	1822 LB	1.908	5.00	15.00	40.00	100.00
	1823 L.B.	1.900	5.00	15.00	40.00	100.00
	1823 LB	I.A.	5.00	15.00	40.00	100.00
	1824 LB	.502	5.00	15.00	40.00	100.00

2.6700 g, .520 SILVER, .0446 oz ASW
Obv: B below head.

KM#	Date	Mintage	Fine	VF	XF	Unc
159	1834 B	—	5.00	15.00	40.00	100.00
	1835 B	—	5.00	15.00	40.00	100.00
	1836 B	—	5.00	15.00	40.00	100.00
	1837 B	—	5.00	15.00	40.00	100.00

Obv: Ernst August, B below head.

KM#	Date	Mintage	Fine	VF	XF	Unc
179.1	1838 B	—	5.00	15.00	40.00	100.00

Obv: S below head.

KM#	Date	Mintage	Fine	VF	XF	Unc
179.2	1839 S	—	5.00	15.00	40.00	100.00
	1840 S	—	5.00	15.00	40.00	100.00

KM#	Date	Mintage	Fine	VF	XF	Unc
194.1	1841 S	—	4.00	10.00	25.00	70.00
	1842 S	—	4.00	10.00	25.00	70.00
	1843 S	—	4.00	10.00	25.00	70.00
	1844 S	—	4.00	10.00	25.00	70.00

Obv: B below head.

KM#	Date	Mintage	Fine	VF	XF	Unc
194.2	1844 B	—	3.50	8.00	20.00	60.00
	1845 B	—	3.50	8.00	20.00	60.00
	1846 B	—	3.50	8.00	20.00	60.00
	1847 B	—	3.50	8.00	20.00	60.00

Obv: Larger head.

KM#	Date	Mintage	Fine	VF	XF	Unc
206	1848 B	—	3.50	7.50	15.00	45.00
	1849 B	—	3.50	7.50	15.00	45.00
	1850 B	—	3.50	7.50	15.00	45.00
	1851 B	—	3.50	7.50	15.00	45.00

Obv: BREHMER F at truncation.

KM#	Date	Mintage	Fine	VF	XF	Unc
219	1852 B	—	3.50	7.50	15.00	45.00
	1853 B	—	3.50	7.50	15.00	45.00

3.2200 g, .375 SILVER, .0388 oz ASW
Obv: W/o name at truncation.
Rev. value: SCHEIDEMUNZE.

KM#	Date	Mintage	Fine	VF	XF	Unc
237	1859 B	—	5.00	15.00	45.00	120.00
	1860 B	—	5.00	15.00	45.00	120.00
	1862 B	—	5.00	15.00	45.00	120.00

1/6 THALER

5.8500 g, .500 SILVER, .0940 oz ASW
Obv: B below ledge.

KM#	Date	Mintage	Fine	VF	XF	Unc
129	1821 B	.150	15.00	30.00	75.00	225.00

5.3500 g, .520 SILVER, .0895 oz ASW

KM#	Date	Mintage	Fine	VF	XF	Unc
160	1834	.360	20.00	40.00	85.00	250.00
	Obv: S below larger head. Rev: Crowned arms on cartouche.					
190	1840 S	.457	20.00	40.00	85.00	250.00
	Rev: Shield w/square corners.					
195	1841 S	Inc. Ab.	20.00	40.00	85.00	250.00

KM#	Date	Mintage	Fine	VF	XF	Unc
199	1844 B	Inc. Ab.	20.00	40.00	85.00	250.00
	1845 B	Inc. Ab.	20.00	40.00	85.00	250.00
	1847 B	Inc. Ab.	20.00	40.00	85.00	250.00

5.3400 g, .520 SILVER, .0893 oz ASW

KM#	Date	Mintage	Fine	VF	XF	Unc
238	1859 B	—	12.00	20.00	35.00	85.00
	1860 B	—	12.00	20.00	35.00	85.00
	1862 B	—	12.00	20.00	35.00	85.00
	1863 B	.087	12.00	20.00	35.00	85.00
	1866 B	5,904	30.00	50.00	90.00	165.00

2/3 THALER

13.0800 g, .993 SILVER, .4176 oz ASW

KM#	Date	Mintage	Fine	VF	XF	Unc
100.1	1813C	—	45.00	100.00	150.00	250.00
	1814C	—	45.00	100.00	150.00	250.00
	Obv: M below truncation.					
100.2	1814	—	50.00	110.00	175.00	275.00

KM#	Date	Mintage	Fine	VF	XF	Unc
140	1822C	—	40.00	80.00	125.00	250.00
	1823C	—	40.00	80.00	125.00	250.00
	1824C	—	40.00	80.00	125.00	250.00
	1825C	—	40.00	80.00	125.00	250.00
	1826C	—	40.00	80.00	125.00	250.00
	1827C	—	40.00	80.00	125.00	250.00
	1828C	—	40.00	80.00	125.00	250.00
	1829C	—	40.00	80.00	125.00	250.00

NOTE: Several varieties exist.

17.3200 g, .750 SILVER, .4177 oz ASW
Rev. value: 18 STUCK EINE MARK FEIN.

KM#	Date	Mintage	Fine	VF	XF	Unc
142	1826 B	—	55.00	125.00	250.00	450.00
	1827 B	—	55.00	125.00	250.00	450.00
	1828 B	—	55.00	125.00	250.00	450.00

13.0800 g, .993 SILVER, .4176 oz ASW
Obv: Ribbon inscribed
HONI SOIT QUI MAL Y PENSE.

KM#	Date	Mintage	Fine	VF	XF	Unc
151	1832	—	37.50	80.00	135.00	250.00
	1833	—	37.50	80.00	135.00	250.00

Rev: Similar to KM#151.

KM#	Date	Mintage	Fine	VF	XF	Unc
154	1833A	.050	150.00	265.00	450.00	750.00

KM#	Date	Mintage	Fine	VF	XF	Unc
161.1	1834A	Inc. Ab.	135.00	250.00	385.00	650.00

Obv. and rev: Raised edge and circle of dots around legend. Struck in collar.

KM#	Date	Mintage	Fine	VF	XF	Unc
161.2	1834A	Inc. Ab.	—	—	—	—

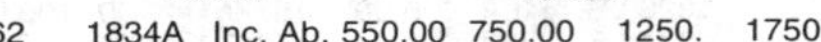

KM#	Date	Mintage	Fine	VF	XF	Unc
162	1834A	Inc. Ab.	550.00	750.00	1250.	1750.

Rev: AUSBEUTE DER GRUBE

KM#	Date	Mintage	Fine	VF	XF	Unc
163	1834A	Inc. Ab.	1350.	2000.	3000.	4500.

Obv: Different head right, A below.

KM#	Date	Mintage	Fine	VF	XF	Unc
180	1838A	—	50.00	110.00	250.00	375.00
	1839A	—	50.00	110.00	250.00	375.00

THALER

23.5400 g, .993 SILVER, .7516 oz ASW
Silver Mines of Clausthal
Rev: Large date.

KM#	Date	Mintage	Fine	VF	XF	Unc
146.1	1830	—	400.00	650.00	1150.	2250.

Rev: Flat topped 3 in small date.

KM#	Date	Mintage	Fine	VF	XF	Unc
146.2	1830	—	400.00	650.00	1150.	2250.

22.2700 g, .750 SILVER, .5370 oz ASW

KM#	Date	Mintage	Fine	VF	XF	Unc
164	1834 B	.044	40.00	115.00	350.00	1000.

16.8200 g, .993 SILVER, .5370 oz ASW

KM#	Date	Mintage	Fine	VF	XF	Unc
165	1834A	—	45.00	100.00	325.00	850.00
	1835A	—	45.00	90.00	250.00	700.00

Wilhelm IV

KM#	Date	Mintage	Fine	VF	XF	Unc
169	1835A	—	70.00	100.00	375.00	900.00
	1836A	—	30.00	50.00	150.00	450.00
	1837A	—	30.00	50.00	150.00	450.00

22.2700 g, .750 SILVER, .5370 oz ASW

KM#	Date	Mintage	Fine	VF	XF	Unc
172	1836 B	—	70.00	100.00	300.00	800.00

16.8200 g, .993 SILVER, .5370 oz ASW
Ernst August V

KM#	Date	Mintage	Fine	VF	XF	Unc
181	1838A	—	35.00	75.00	185.00	500.00
	1839A	—	35.00	75.00	185.00	500.00

KM#	Date	Mintage	Fine	VF	XF	Unc
182	1838A	—	35.00	75.00	185.00	500.00
	1839A	—	35.00	75.00	185.00	500.00
	1840A	—	45.00	90.00	225.00	600.00

King's Visit to Clausthal Mint

KM#	Date	Mintage	Fine	VF	XF	Unc
184	1839A	—	150.00	250.00	450.00	700.00

Obv: Similar to KM#182.

KM#	Date	Mintage	Fine	VF	XF	Unc
191	1840A	—	—	—	Rare	—

KM#	Date	Mintage	Fine	VF	XF	Unc
192	1840A	—	40.00	70.00	175.00	450.00
	1841A	—	40.00	70.00	175.00	450.00

Obv: S below truncation.

KM#	Date	Mintage	Fine	VF	XF	Unc
193	1840 S	—	75.00	150.00	500.00	1300.

Obv: BRANDT F. at truncation.

KM#	Date	Mintage	Fine	VF	XF	Unc
196	1841 S	—	40.00	80.00	200.00	625.00

Obv: A below head.

KM#	Date	Mintage	Fine	VF	XF	Unc
197.1	1842A	.620	20.00	40.00	135.00	325.00
	1843A	.638	22.00	50.00	175.00	400.00
	1844A	.622	22.00	50.00	175.00	400.00
	1845A	.656	22.00	50.00	175.00	400.00
	1846A	.650	22.00	50.00	175.00	400.00
	1847A	.625	20.00	40.00	135.00	325.00
	1848A	.661	20.00	40.00	135.00	325.00
	1849A	.357	22.00	50.00	175.00	400.00

Obv: B below head.

KM#	Date	Mintage	Fine	VF	XF	Unc
197.2	1844 B	—	45.00	85.00	200.00	550.00
	1845 B	—	25.00	50.00	135.00	350.00
	1846 B	—	45.00	85.00	200.00	550.00
	1847 B	—	50.00	90.00	250.00	600.00

Wedding of Crown Prince Georg of Hannover and Duchess Marie of Sachsen-Altenburg

KM#	Date	Mintage	Fine	VF	XF	Unc
207	1843 S	1,010	175.00	350.00	600.00	1000.

Obv: BREHMER F. at truncation.

KM#	Date	Mintage	Fine	VF	XF	Unc
208	1848 B	—	22.00	50.00	150.00	400.00
	1849 B	—	22.00	50.00	150.00	400.00

Rev: HARZ SEGEN above crown.

KM#	Date	Mintage	Fine	VF	XF	Unc
209.1	1849 B	—	50.00	125.00	300.00	850.00

Rev: BERGSEGEN DES HARZES above crown.

KM#	Date	Mintage	Fine	VF	XF	Unc
209.2	1850 B	.712	22.00	50.00	100.00	250.00
	1851 B	.453	22.00	50.00	100.00	250.00

KM#	Date	Mintage	Fine	VF	XF	Unc
220	1852 B	.170	22.00	50.00	100.00	250.00
	1853 B	.180	22.00	50.00	100.00	250.00

KM#	Date	Mintage	Fine	VF	XF	Unc
220	1854/3 B	—	—	—	—	—
	1854 B	.951	22.00	50.00	100.00	250.00
	1855 B	.974	22.00	50.00	100.00	250.00
	1856 B	.077	22.00	50.00	100.00	250.00

18.5200 g, .900 SILVER, .5360 oz ASW

KM#	Date	Mintage	Fine	VF	XF	Unc
230	1857 B	.274	20.00	40.00	70.00	140.00
	1858 B	.432	20.00	40.00	70.00	140.00
	1859 B	.554	20.00	40.00	65.00	120.00
	1860 B	.790	20.00	40.00	65.00	120.00
	1861 B	.736	20.00	40.00	65.00	120.00
	1862 B	.133	20.00	40.00	65.00	120.00
	1863 B	.233	20.00	40.00	65.00	120.00
	1864 B	.158	20.00	40.00	65.00	120.00
	1865 B	—	20.00	35.00	55.00	120.00
	1866 B	.159	20.00	35.00	50.00	100.00

50th Anniversary - Battle of Waterloo

KM#	Date	Mintage	Fine	VF	XF	Unc
241	1865 B	.015	30.00	50.00	90.00	175.00

NOTE: This coin was given to veterans of the battle in pension payments.

50th Anniversary Union East Friesia and Hannover

KM#	Date	Mintage	Fine	VF	XF	Unc
242	1865 B	1,000	175.00	300.00	500.00	850.00
	1865 B	—	—	—	Proof	900.00

Frisian Oath Commemorative

KM#	Date	Mintage	Fine	VF	XF	Unc
243	1865 B	2,000	125.00	250.00	400.00	650.00

2 THALER

(3-1/2 Gulden)

37.1200 g, .900 SILVER, 1.0742 oz ASW

KM#	Date	Mintage	Fine	VF	XF	Unc
229	1854 B	.102	100.00	150.00	200.00	350.00
	1855 B	.842	90.00	125.00	175.00	325.00

37.0400 g, .900 SILVER, 1.0719 oz ASW

KM#	Date	Mintage	Fine	VF	XF	Unc
240	1862 B	.133	100.00	150.00	200.00	350.00
	1866 B	.038	90.00	125.00	175.00	325.00

2-1/2 THALER

3.3400 g, .903 GOLD, .0970 oz AGW

KM#	Date	Mintage	Fine	VF	XF	Unc
109	1814 CHH	—	325.00	500.00	750.00	1150.

KM#	Date	Mintage	Fine	VF	XF	Unc
130	1821 B	—	225.00	450.00	675.00	1100.
	1827 B	—	225.00	450.00	675.00	1100.
	1830 B	—	225.00	450.00	675.00	1100.

KM#	Date	Mintage	Fine	VF	XF	Unc
152	1832 B	—	200.00	400.00	600.00	1000.
	1833 B	—	200.00	400.00	600.00	1000.
	1835 B	—	200.00	400.00	600.00	1000.

3.3200 g, .896 GOLD, .0956 oz AGW

KM#	Date	Mintage	Fine	VF	XF	Unc
152a	1836 B	—	150.00	300.00	550.00	900.00
	1837 B	—	150.00	300.00	550.00	900.00

KM#	Date	Mintage	Fine	VF	XF	Unc
185.1	1839 S	—	225.00	400.00	600.00	1000.
	1840 S	—	225.00	400.00	600.00	1000.
	1843 S	—	225.00	400.00	600.00	1000.

KM#	Date	Mintage	Fine	VF	XF	Unc
185.2	1845 B	—	225.00	400.00	600.00	1000.
	1846 B	—	225.00	400.00	600.00	1000.
	1847 B	—	225.00	400.00	600.00	1000.
	1848 B	—	225.00	400.00	600.00	1000.

KM#	Date	Mintage	Fine	VF	XF	Unc
215	1850 B	—	200.00	300.00	500.00	900.00

Obv: BREHMER F. at truncation, B below.

KM#	Date	Mintage	Fine	VF	XF	Unc
223	1853 B	—	250.00	500.00	1000.	1500.
	1855 B	—	175.00	350.00	700.00	1000.

5 THALER

6.6500 g, .896 GOLD, .1916 oz AGW

KM#	Date	Mintage	Fine	VF	XF	Unc
101	1813 TW	—	200.00	300.00	750.00	1500.
	1814 TW	—	200.00	300.00	750.00	1500.
	1815 TW	—	250.00	400.00	875.00	1750.

6.6800 g, .903 GOLD, .1940 oz AGW

KM#	Date	Mintage	Fine	VF	XF	Unc
110	1814C	—	825.00	1200.	2000.	3250.
	1815C	—	—	—	Rare	—

KM#	Date	Mintage	Fine	VF	XF	Unc
131	1821C	185 pcs.	1500.	2000.	3000.	7500.

KM#	Date	Mintage	Fine	VF	XF	Unc
132	1821 B	—	250.00	450.00	700.00	1000.
	1825 B	—	250.00	450.00	700.00	1000.
	1828 B	—	250.00	450.00	700.00	1000.
	1829 B	—	250.00	450.00	700.00	1000.
	1830 B	—	250.00	450.00	700.00	1000.

6.6500 g, .896 GOLD, .1916 oz AGW

KM#	Date	Mintage	Fine	VF	XF	Unc
170	1835 B	—	350.00	500.00	750.00	1500.

KM#	Date	Mintage	Fine	VF	XF	Unc
186	1839 S	—	400.00	700.00	1000.	1800.

Obv: B below head.

KM#	Date	Mintage	Fine	VF	XF	Unc
204	1845 B	—	300.00	500.00	800.00	1350.
	1846 B	—	375.00	650.00	1000.	1600.
	1848 B	—	375.00	650.00	1000.	1600.

KM#	Date	Mintage	Fine	VF	XF	Unc
210	1849 B	—	300.00	500.00	750.00	1350.
	1851 B	—	300.00	500.00	750.00	1350.

Rev. leg: HARZ GOLD added.

KM#	Date	Mintage	Fine	VF	XF	Unc
211	1849 B	—	350.00	550.00	800.00	1400.
	1850 B	—	300.00	500.00	750.00	1300.

Obv: BREHMER F. at truncation, B below.

KM#	Date	Mintage	Fine	VF	XF	Unc
224	1853 B	—	300.00	500.00	750.00	1200.
	1855 B	—	300.00	500.00	750.00	1200.
	1856 B	—	400.00	800.00	1000.	2000.

Rev. leg: HARZ GOLD added.

KM#	Date	Mintage	Fine	VF	XF	Unc
225	1853 B	—	500.00	875.00	1200.	2250.
	1856 B	—	550.00	1150.	1500.	2650.

10 THALER

13.3600 g, .903 GOLD, .3879 oz AGW

KM#	Date	Mintage	Fine	VF	XF	Unc
102	1813 CHH	—	1000.	1500.	2000.	3250.
	1814 CHH	—	750.00	1100.	1500.	2500.

KM#	Date	Mintage	Fine	VF	XF	Unc
133	1821 B	—	600.00	1000.	1500.	2200.
	1822 B	—	475.00	800.00	1300.	1800.
	1823 B	—	475.00	800.00	1300.	1800.
	1824 B	—	475.00	800.00	1300.	1800.
	1825 B	—	325.00	550.00	1100.	1600.
	1827 B	—	325.00	550.00	1100.	1600.
	1828 B	—	325.00	550.00	1100.	1600.
	1829 B	—	325.00	550.00	1100.	1600.
	1830 B	—	325.00	550.00	1100.	1600.

KM#	Date	Mintage	Fine	VF	XF	Unc
153	1832	—	550.00	900.00	1250.	2500.

KM#	Date	Mintage	Fine	VF	XF	Unc
155	1833	—	550.00	900.00	1250.	2500.

13.3000 g, .896 GOLD, .3832 oz AGW
Obv: B below head.

KM#	Date	Mintage	Fine	VF	XF	Unc
171	1835 B	—	675.00	1150.	1900.	2650.
	1836 B	—	650.00	1125.	1875.	2600.
	1837 B	—	550.00	900.00	1500.	2250.

KM#	Date	Mintage	Fine	VF	XF	Unc
175	1837 B	—	—	—	10,000.	15,000.
	1838 B	—	500.00	900.00	1500.	2250.

Obv: S below head.

KM#	Date	Mintage	Fine	VF	XF	Unc
187	1839 S	—	400.00	600.00	1200.	2000.

Obv: BRANDT F. on truncation.

KM#	Date	Mintage	Fine	VF	XF	Unc
200.1	1844 S	—	600.00	1000.	1500.	2250.

Obv: B below head.

KM#	Date	Mintage	Fine	VF	XF	Unc
200.2	1844 B	—	600.00	1000.	1500.	2500.

Obv: W/o markings on truncation,
leg. ends: . . . V. HANNOVER.

KM#	Date	Mintage	Fine	VF	XF	Unc
200.3	1846 B	—	400.00	800.00	1200.	2000.
	1847 B	—	400.00	800.00	1200.	2000.
	1848 B	—	300.00	600.00	900.00	1500.

Obv. leg. ends: . . . VON HANNOVER

KM#	Date	Mintage	Fine	VF	XF	Unc
212	1849 B	—	500.00	1000.	1500.	2250.
	1850 B	—	350.00	600.00	1000.	1500.
	1851 B	—	500.00	1000.	1500.	2250.

KM#	Date	Mintage	Fine	VF	XF	Unc
226	1853 B	—	450.00	750.00	1250.	1750.
	1854 B	—	300.00	500.00	900.00	1250.
	1855 B	—	450.00	750.00	1250.	1750.
	1856 B	—	500.00	900.00	1500.	2150.

TRADE COINAGE

DUCAT

3.5000 g, .986 GOLD, .1109 oz AGW

KM#	Date	Mintage	Fine	VF	XF	Unc
111	1815C	—	525.00	875.00	1400.	2000.
	1818C	—	600.00	1000.	1650.	2250.
134	1821C	252 pcs.	975.00	1650.	2400.	3250.
	1824C	749 pcs.	900.00	1500.	2250.	3000.
	1827C	1,300	825.00	1400.	2000.	2750.

KM#	Date	Mintage	Fine	VF	XF	Unc
149	1831C	1,550	750.00	1250.	1900.	2500.

1/2 KRONE

5.5500 g, .900 GOLD, .1606 oz AGW

KM#	Date	Mintage	Fine	VF	XF	Unc
231	1857 B	4,105	300.00	600.00	1000.	1500.
	1858 B	116 pcs.	900.00	1500.	2000.	3000.
	1859 B	790 pcs.	400.00	800.00	1200.	1750.
	1862 B	96 pcs.	1500.	2000.	2500.	5000.
	1864 B	.013	300.00	600.00	1000.	1500.
	1866 B	2,909	300.00	600.00	850.00	1500.

KRONE

11.1100 g, .900 GOLD, .3215 oz AGW

KM#	Date	Mintage	Fine	VF	XF	Unc
232	1857 B	.145	350.00	500.00	900.00	1500.
	1858 B	.047	450.00	800.00	1200.	1800.
	1859 B	.020	500.00	850.00	1300.	1900.
	1860 B	.015	550.00	1000.	1500.	2250.
	1861 B	780 pcs.	1000.	1500.	2000.	3000.
	1862 B	.020	525.00	875.00	1400.	1900.
	1863 B	.126	350.00	500.00	900.00	1500.
	1864 B	.014	450.00	800.00	1100.	1700.
	1866 B	.383	350.00	500.00	900.00	1500.

MEDALLIC ISSUES (M)

THALER

SILVER
Shooting Festival

KM#	Date	Mintage	VF	XF	Unc
M1	1872	6,317	65.00	120.00	185.00

PATTERNS (Pn)

(Including off metal strikes)

KM#	Date	Mintage	Identification	Mkt.Val.
Pn3	1813 T.W.	—	2/3 Thaler, Silver	850.00

KM#	Date	Mintage	Identification	Mkt.Val.
Pn4	1813	—	5 Thaler, Gold, plain edge, KM101	1500.

KM#	Date	Mintage	Identification	Mkt.Val.
Pn5	1834A	—	16 Gute Groschen, Silver, plain edge, KM122	—
Pn6	1834.B	—	1/24 Thaler, Billon, KM158.1	—
Pn7	1834A	—	2/3 Thaler, .993 Silver, KM161.2	1150.
Pn8	1840A	—	1 Thaler, Silver, KM191	30,000.

HESSE-CASSEL

(Hessen-Kassel)

The Hesse principalities were located for the most part north of the Main River, bounded by Westphalia on the west, the Brunswick duchies on the north, the Saxon duchies on the east and Rhine Palatinate and the bishoprics of Mainz and Fulda on the south. The rule of the landgraves of Hesse began in the second half of the 13th century, the dignity of Prince of the Empire being acquired in 1292. In 1567 the patrimony was divided by four surviving sons, only those of Cassel and Darmstadt surviving for more than a generation. In Hesse-Cassel the landgrave was raised to the rank of elector in 1803. The electorate formed part of the Kingdom of Westphalia from 1806 to 1813. In 1866 In 1866 Hesse-Cassel fell to Prussia.

RULERS

Wilhelm IX, 1785-1803
Wilhelm I, As Elector, 1803-1821
Wilhelm II, 1821-1847
Friedrich Wilhelm, 1847-1866

MINT MARKS

C - Cassel
(.L.) - Lippoldsberg

MINTMASTERS INITIALS

Letter	Date	Name
CP	1820-1861	Christoph Pfeuffer, die-cutter
D.F., F.	1774-1831	Dietrich Flalda
FH	1786-1821	Friedrich Heenwagen
H	1775-1820	Carl Ludwig Holzemer, die-cutter
K	1804-1833	Wilhelm Korner

ARMS

Hessian lion rampant left.

HELLER

COPPER
Similar to KM#553 but 19mm.

KM#	Date	Mintage	Fine	VF	XF	Unc
543	1801	—	2.50	4.50	12.50	65.00
	1802	—	2.50	4.50	12.50	65.00
	1803	—	2.50	4.50	12.50	65.00

NOTE: Earlier dates (1791-1800) exist for this type.

KM#	Date	Mintage	Fine	VF	XF	Unc
553	1803	—	3.00	6.00	18.00	80.00
	1805	—	3.00	6.00	18.00	80.00
	1806	—	3.00	6.00	18.00	80.00
	1814	—	3.00	6.00	18.00	80.00

Obv: Crowned WK monogram w/1 ring at base of W.

KM#	Date	Mintage	Fine	VF	XF	Unc
565	1817	—	2.50	5.00	15.00	70.00
	1818	—	2.50	5.00	15.00	70.00
	1819	—	2.50	5.00	15.00	70.00
	1820	—	2.50	5.00	15.00	70.00
575	1822	—	2.00	4.00	10.00	45.00
	1823	—	2.00	4.00	10.00	45.00
	1824	—	2.00	4.00	10.00	45.00
	1825	—	2.00	4.00	10.00	45.00
	1827	—	2.00	4.00	10.00	45.00
	1828	—	5.00	10.00	30.00	90.00

Obv: Crowned WK monogram w/2 rings at base of W.

KM#	Date	Mintage	Fine	VF	XF	Unc
576	1822	—	2.00	4.00	8.00	42.00
	1825	—	2.00	4.00	8.00	42.00
	1827	—	2.00	4.00	8.00	42.00
	1828	—	2.00	4.00	8.00	42.00
	1829	—	2.00	4.00	8.00	42.00
	1831	—	2.00	4.00	8.00	42.00

Obv. leg: KURHESSEN, crowned arms.
Rev. value: SCHEIDE MUNZE.

KM#	Date	Mintage	Fine	VF	XF	Unc
602	1842	.037	6.00	12.00	30.00	110.00

Obv. leg: 360 EINEN THALER.

KM#	Date	Mintage	Fine	VF	XF	Unc
605	1843	—	1.00	2.00	6.00	35.00
	1845	—	1.00	2.00	6.00	35.00
	1847	—	1.00	2.00	6.00	35.00

KM#	Date	Mintage	Fine	VF	XF	Unc
613	1849	—	1.00	2.00	4.00	30.00
	1852	—	1.00	2.00	4.00	30.00
	1854	—	1.00	2.00	4.00	30.00
	1856	—	1.00	2.00	4.00	30.00
	1858	—	1.00	2.00	4.00	30.00
	1859	—	1.00	2.00	4.00	30.00
	1860	—	1.00	2.00	4.00	30.00
	1861	—	1.00	2.00	4.00	30.00
	1862	—	1.00	2.00	4.00	30.00
	1863	—	1.00	2.00	4.00	30.00
	1864	—	1.00	2.00	4.00	30.00
	1865	—	1.00	2.00	4.00	30.00
	1866	—	1.00	2.00	4.00	30.00

2 HELLER

COPPER

KM#	Date	Mintage	Fine	VF	XF	Unc
561	1814	—	5.00	10.00	22.00	100.00

Obv: Crowned WK monogram w/1 ring at base of W.

KM#	Date	Mintage	Fine	VF	XF	Unc
564	1816	—	3.00	7.00	18.00	75.00
	1818	—	3.00	7.00	18.00	75.00
	1820	—	3.00	7.00	18.00	75.00
585	1831	—	2.00	4.50	12.50	50.00

Obv: Crowned WK monogram w/2 rings at base of W.

KM#	Date	Mintage	Fine	VF	XF	Unc
589	1833	—	2.00	4.50	12.50	50.00

KM#	Date	Mintage	Fine	VF	XF	Unc
606	1843	—	2.00	4.50	12.50	45.00

3 HELLER

COPPER

KM#	Date	Mintage	Fine	VF	XF	Unc
607	1843	—	2.00	4.00	10.00	40.00
	1844	—	2.00	4.00	10.00	40.00
	1845	—	2.00	4.00	10.00	40.00
	1846	—	2.00	4.00	10.00	40.00

KM#	Date	Mintage	Fine	VF	XF	Unc
612	1848	—	1.50	3.00	7.00	32.00
	1849	—	1.50	3.00	7.00	32.00
	1850	—	1.50	3.00	7.00	32.00
	1851	—	1.50	3.00	7.00	32.00
	1852	—	1.50	3.00	7.00	32.00
	1853	—	1.50	3.00	7.00	32.00
	1854	—	1.50	3.00	7.00	32.00
	1856	—	1.50	3.00	7.00	32.00
	1858	—	1.50	3.00	7.00	32.00
	1859	—	1.50	3.00	7.00	32.00
	1860	—	1.50	3.00	7.00	32.00
	1861	—	1.50	3.00	7.00	32.00
	1862	—	1.50	3.00	7.00	32.00
	1863	—	1.50	3.00	7.00	32.00
	1864	—	1.50	3.00	7.00	32.00
	1865	—	1.50	3.00	7.00	32.00
	1866	—	1.50	3.00	7.00	32.00

4 HELLER

COPPER
Obv: Crowned WK monogram w/1 loop at base of W.

KM#	Date	Mintage	Fine	VF	XF	Unc
562	1815	—	3.00	8.00	25.00	125.00
	1816	—	3.00	8.00	25.00	125.00
	1817	—	3.00	8.00	25.00	125.00
	1818	—	3.00	8.00	25.00	125.00
	1819	—	3.00	8.00	25.00	125.00
	1820	—	3.00	8.00	25.00	125.00
	1821	—	3.00	8.00	25.00	125.00

Obv: Crowned WK monogram w/2 loops at base of W.

KM#	Date	Mintage	Fine	VF	XF	Unc
571	1821	—	2.00	5.00	15.00	85.00

KM#	Date	Mintage	Fine	VF	XF	Unc
571	1822	—	2.00	5.00	15.00	85.00
	1824	—	2.00	5.00	15.00	85.00
	1826	—	2.00	5.00	15.00	85.00
	1827	—	2.00	5.00	15.00	85.00
	1828	—	2.00	5.00	15.00	85.00
	1829	—	2.00	5.00	15.00	85.00
	1830	—	2.00	5.00	15.00	85.00
	1831	—	2.00	5.00	15.00	85.00

1/2 SILBER GROSCHEN

.9700 g, .250 SILVER, .0077 oz ASW
Obv: Crowned arms.
Rev. value: SILBER GROSCHEN.

KM#	Date	Mintage	Fine	VF	XF	Unc
603	1842	1.491	2.00	5.00	15.00	75.00

SILBER GROSCHEN

1.5600 g, .312 SILVER, .0156 oz ASW

KM#	Date	Mintage	Fine	VF	XF	Unc
601	1841	5.925	1.00	3.00	8.00	60.00
	1845	.062	2.00	4.00	10.00	65.00
	1847	.456	2.00	4.00	10.00	65.00

KM#	Date	Mintage	Fine	VF	XF	Unc
615	1851	.262	1.00	3.00	7.00	35.00
	1852	.147	1.00	3.00	7.00	35.00
	1853	.125	1.00	3.00	7.00	35.00
	1854	.098	1.00	3.00	7.00	35.00
	1855	.054	1.00	3.00	7.00	35.00
	1856	.234	1.00	3.00	7.00	35.00
	1857	.119	1.00	3.00	7.00	35.00
	1858	.058	1.00	3.00	7.00	35.00
	1859	.235	1.00	3.00	7.00	35.00
	1860	.156	1.00	3.00	7.00	35.00
	1861	.165	1.00	3.00	7.00	35.00
	1862	—	1.00	3.00	7.00	35.00
	1863	—	1.00	3.00	7.00	35.00
	1864	.122	1.00	3.00	7.00	35.00
	1865	.192	1.00	3.00	7.00	35.00
	1866	.182	1.00	3.00	7.00	35.00

2 SILBER GROSCHEN

2.6000 g, .375 SILVER, .0313 oz ASW

KM#	Date	Mintage	Fine	VF	XF	Unc
604	1842	2.414	12.00	25.00	65.00	150.00

2-1/2 SILBER GROSCHEN

3.2500 g, .375 SILVER, .0391 oz ASW

KM#	Date	Mintage	Fine	VF	XF	Unc
620	1852 CP	.034	3.00	7.00	20.00	80.00
	1853 CP	.049	3.00	7.00	20.00	80.00
	1856 CP	.039	3.00	7.00	20.00	80.00
	1859 CP	.069	3.00	7.00	20.00	80.00
	1860 CP	.042	3.00	7.00	20.00	80.00
	1861 CP	.034	3.00	7.00	20.00	80.00
	1862 CP	.031	3.00	7.00	20.00	80.00
	1865 CP	.023	3.00	7.00	20.00	80.00

24 EINEN (1/24) THALER

BILLON
Obv: Rampant lion left. Rev: Value, date below.

KM#	Date	Mintage	Fine	VF	XF	Unc
529	1801	—	7.00	15.00	35.00	100.00
	1802	—	7.00	15.00	35.00	100.00

NOTE: Earlier dates (1786-1800) exist for this type.

KM#	Date	Mintage	Fine	VF	XF	Unc
554.1	1803 F	.526	7.00	15.00	35.00	100.00
	1804 F	—	7.00	15.00	35.00	100.00
	1805 F	—	7.00	15.00	35.00	100.00
	1806 F	—	7.00	15.00	35.00	100.00
	1807 F	.997	7.00	15.00	35.00	100.00

Obv: Rampant lion left.
Rev: Value, w/o mint mark below date.

KM#	Date	Mintage	Fine	VF	XF	Unc
554.2	1814	—	6.00	12.00	30.00	100.00
	1815	—	6.00	12.00	30.00	100.00
	1816	—	6.00	12.00	30.00	100.00
	1817	—	6.00	12.00	30.00	100.00
	1818	—	6.00	12.00	30.00	100.00
	1819	—	6.00	12.00	30.00	100.00
	1820	—	6.00	12.00	30.00	100.00
	1821	—	6.00	12.00	30.00	100.00
577	1822	—	17.50	35.00	70.00	165.00

VI EINEN (1/6) THALER

SILVER

KM#	Date	Mintage	Fine	VF	XF	Unc
546	1801 F	—	10.00	20.00	40.00	150.00
	1802 F	—	10.00	20.00	40.00	150.00

NOTE: Earlier dates (1798-1800) exist for this type.

.625 SILVER
Obv: Crowned arms within laurel branches.
Rev: Value.

KM#	Date	Mintage	Fine	VF	XF	Unc
555	1803 F	—	12.00	25.00	55.00	185.00

KM#	Date	Mintage	Fine	VF	XF	Unc
556	1803 F	—	10.00	20.00	45.00	165.00
	1804 F	—	10.00	20.00	45.00	165.00
	1805 F	—	10.00	20.00	45.00	165.00
	1806 F	—	10.00	20.00	45.00	165.00
	1807 F	.040	10.00	20.00	45.00	165.00

Obv: Lion in oval shield. Rev: Value, date.

KM#	Date	Mintage	Fine	VF	XF	Unc
572	1821	.038	18.00	35.00	125.00	300.00
	1822	.056	15.00	30.00	100.00	250.00

5.3200 g, .500 SILVER, .0855 oz ASW
Obv. leg: . . . KURF S.L.V. HESSEN. . .

KM#	Date	Mintage	Fine	VF	XF	Unc
579.1	1823	.182	10.00	20.00	40.00	150.00
	1824	.276	10.00	20.00	40.00	150.00
	1825	.306	10.00	20.00	40.00	150.00
	1826	.147	10.00	20.00	40.00	150.00
	1827	.280	10.00	20.00	40.00	150.00
	1828	.395	10.00	20.00	40.00	150.00
	1829	.590	10.00	20.00	40.00	150.00
	1830	.524	10.00	20.00	40.00	150.00
	1831	.201	10.00	20.00	40.00	150.00

Obv. leg: . . .KURF. V. HESSEN. . .

KM#	Date	Mintage	Fine	VF	XF	Unc
579.2	1831	.022	75.00	140.00	250.00	475.00

Rev: THAELR (error)

KM#	Date	Mintage	Fine	VF	XF	Unc
579.3	1828	—	50.00	115.00	200.00	350.00

Obv. leg. ends: . . . KURPR.U.MITREG.

KM#	Date	Mintage	Fine	VF	XF	Unc
590	1833	.046	5.00	15.00	35.00	165.00
	1834	.599	5.00	10.00	25.00	85.00
	1835	.810	5.00	10.00	25.00	85.00

KM#	Date	Mintage	Fine	VF	XF	Unc
590	1836	.528	5.00	10.00	25.00	85.00
	1837	.624	5.00	10.00	25.00	85.00
	1838	.558	5.00	10.00	25.00	85.00
	1839	.228	5.00	10.00	25.00	100.00
	1840	6,000	5.00	20.00	50.00	225.00
	1841	.192	5.00	10.00	20.00	100.00
	1842	1.404	5.00	10.00	20.00	85.00
	1843	—	5.00	10.00	25.00	100.00
	1844	6,132	5.00	20.00	50.00	225.00
	1845	.095	5.00	10.00	25.00	120.00
	1846	.045	5.00	15.00	35.00	165.00

Obv. leg. ends: . . . KURPR.=MITREG

KM#	Date	Mintage	Fine	VF	XF	Unc
609	1846	Inc.Ab.	75.00	145.00	250.00	475.00
	1847	.103	65.00	125.00	225.00	400.00

5.3500 g, .520 SILVER, .0894 oz ASW
Obv: C.P. at truncation.

KM#	Date	Mintage	Fine	VF	XF	Unc
616	1851 CP	.030	10.00	20.00	40.00	175.00
	1852 CP	.033	10.00	20.00	40.00	175.00
	1854 CP	.013	10.00	20.00	40.00	175.00
	1855 CP	.022	10.00	20.00	40.00	175.00
	1856 CP	—	15.00	30.00	60.00	250.00

1/3 THALER

8.5000 g, .625 SILVER, .1708 oz ASW

KM#	Date	Mintage	Fine	VF	XF	Unc
578	1822	.105	10.00	40.00	75.00	265.00
	1823	.125	10.00	40.00	75.00	265.00
	1824	.099	10.00	40.00	75.00	265.00
	1825	.162	10.00	40.00	75.00	265.00
	1826	.280	10.00	40.00	75.00	265.00
	1827	.278	10.00	40.00	75.00	265.00
	1828	—	10.00	40.00	75.00	265.00
	1829	.219	10.00	40.00	75.00	265.00

1/2 THALER

11.1200 g, .750 SILVER, .2681 oz ASW

KM#	Date	Mintage	Fine	VF	XF	Unc
567	1819	—	25.00	50.00	120.00	350.00
	1820	—	25.00	50.00	120.00	350.00

THALER

SILVER
Obv: Small bust right.
Rev: Crowned oval arms w/griffon supporters.

KM#	Date	Mintage	Fine	VF	XF	Unc
552	1802 FH	—	—	—	Rare	—

KM#	Date	Mintage	Fine	VF	XF	Unc
560	1813 K	—	600.00	1500.	3000.	4500.

NOTE: Possibly a pattern.

22.2700 g, .750 SILVER, .5371 oz ASW
Obv. leg: KURF. SOUV.

KM#	Date	Mintage	Fine	VF	XF	Unc
568	1819	—	60.00	100.00	425.00	1000.
	1820	—	75.00	140.00	575.00	1200.

Obv. leg: SOUV.LANDGR.Z.HESSEN.

KM#	Date	Mintage	Fine	VF	XF	Unc
573.1	1821	2,385	85.00	200.00	700.00	1500.
	1822	3,456	100.00	260.00	900.00	1900.

Obv: W/o period after HESSEN.

KM#	Date	Mintage	Fine	VF	XF	Unc
573.2	1821	Inc. Ab.	85.00	200.00	700.00	1500.

KM#	Date	Mintage	Fine	VF	XF	Unc
587	1832	.020	22.00	50.00	150.00	450.00
	1833	.017	22.00	50.00	150.00	450.00
	1834	.037	22.00	50.00	150.00	450.00
	1835	.014	22.00	50.00	150.00	450.00
	1836	.040	25.00	55.00	175.00	575.00
	1837	.026	25.00	50.00	175.00	450.00
	1838	4,041	40.00	70.00	200.00	800.00
	1839	2,574	25.00	50.00	150.00	450.00
	1841	.025	22.00	50.00	150.00	450.00
	1842	.031	25.00	55.00	175.00	575.00

Obv: C.PFEUFFER F. at truncation.

KM#	Date	Mintage	Fine	VF	XF	Unc
617	1851	3,963	75.00	150.00	500.00	1500.
	1854	7,338	60.00	100.00	325.00	1250.
	1855	.028	35.00	65.00	275.00	800.00

18.5200 g, .900 SILVER, .5360 oz ASW
Obv: W/C.P. at truncation.

KM#	Date	Mintage	Fine	VF	XF	Unc
621.1	1858 CP	.062	25.00	55.00	150.00	500.00
	1859 CP	.037	25.00	55.00	150.00	500.00
	1860 CP	.031	25.00	55.00	150.00	500.00
	1862 CP	.032	25.00	55.00	150.00	500.00
	1864 CP	.032	25.00	55.00	150.00	500.00
	1865 CP	.031	25.00	55.00	150.00	500.00

Obv: W/o C.P. at truncation.

KM#	Date	Mintage	Fine	VF	XF	Unc
621.2	1858	Inc. Ab.	25.00	55.00	150.00	500.00
	1859	Inc. Ab.	25.00	55.00	150.00	500.00
	1860	Inc. Ab.	25.00	60.00	150.00	500.00
	1861	.032	25.00	60.00	150.00	500.00
	1862	—	25.00	60.00	150.00	500.00
	1863	.032	25.00	60.00	150.00	500.00
	1864	Inc. Ab.	25.00	55.00	150.00	500.00
	1865	Inc. Ab.	25.00	55.00	150.00	500.00

2 THALER

(Reichs)

(3-1/2 Gulden)

37.1200 g, .900 SILVER, 1.0742 oz ASW

KM#	Date	Mintage	Fine	VF	XF	Unc
600	1840	.019	90.00	150.00	375.00	1200.
	1841	.019	100.00	175.00	425.00	1350.
	1842	.019	100.00	175.00	425.00	1350.
	1843	.018	115.00	185.00	460.00	1425.
	1844	.059	130.00	200.00	500.00	1600.
	1845	—	130.00	200.00	500.00	1600.

Obv: Larger letters.

KM#	Date	Mintage	Fine	VF	XF	Unc
608	1844	Inc. Ab.	90.00	150.00	375.00	1200.
	1845	—	130.00	210.00	500.00	1600.

Obv. leg: KURPRINZ-MITREGENT.

KM#	Date	Mintage	Fine	VF	XF	Unc
610	1847	.010	400.00	750.00	1700.	3800.

Obv: CP on truncation.

KM#	Date	Mintage	Fine	VF	XF	Unc
618	1851 CP	3,996	150.00	300.00	500.00	1100.
	1854 CP	.141	100.00	150.00	325.00	800.00
	1855 CP	.357	85.00	125.00	275.00	600.00

5 THALER

6.6500 g, .900 GOLD, .1924 oz AGW
Obv: Bust right. Rev: Similar to KM#557.

KM#	Date	Mintage	Fine	VF	XF	Unc
545	1801 F	—	300.00	650.00	1000.	1750.

NOTE: Earlier dates (1791-1800) exist for this type.

KM#	Date	Mintage	Fine	VF	XF	Unc
557	1803 F	1,659	700.00	1400.	2500.	3750.
	1805 F	1,941	650.00	1250.	2250.	3250.
	1806 F	875 pcs.	900.00	1750.	3000.	4750.

KM#	Date	Mintage	Fine	VF	XF	Unc
563	1815	2,226	900.00	1500.	2500.	3750.

Obv. leg: WILHELMUS I.ELECT.HASS.

KM#	Date	Mintage	Fine	VF	XF	Unc
566	1817	2,352	900.00	1500.	2500.	3750.
	1819	1,548	1050.	1750.	3000.	4750.

Obv. leg: WILHELM I KURF. . .

KM#	Date	Mintage	Fine	VF	XF	Unc
570	1820	534 pcs.	1000.	1850.	3500.	5250.

Obv. leg: . . . KURF.S.L. Z. HESSEN. . .

KM#	Date	Mintage	Fine	VF	XF	Unc
574.1	1821	1,142	500.00	1200.	2250.	4500.
	1823	1,140	500.00	1200.	2250.	4500.

Obv. leg: . . . KURF.S.L.V.HESSEN. . .

KM#	Date	Mintage	Fine	VF	XF	Unc
574.2	1823	518 pcs.	750.00	1500.	2500.	4500.
	1825	409 pcs.	750.00	1500.	2500.	4500.
	1828	952 pcs.	675.00	1250.	2250.	4000.
	1829	502 pcs.	750.00	1500.	2500.	4500.

KM#	Date	Mintage	Fine	VF	XF	Unc
591	1834	1,025	500.00	875.00	1500.	2000.
	1836	2,002	500.00	875.00	1500.	2000.
	1837	256 pcs.	575.00	1000.	1750.	2250.
	1839	1,996	500.00	875.00	1500.	2000.
	1840	.017	425.00	750.00	1250.	1750.
	1841	.016	425.00	750.00	1250.	1750.
	1842	6,909	425.00	750.00	1250.	1750.
	1843	1,657	500.00	875.00	1500.	2000.
	1844	1,495	500.00	875.00	1500.	2000.
	1845	1,364	500.00	875.00	1500.	2000.

Obv. leg. ends: . . . KURPR.-MITREG.

KM#	Date	Mintage	Fine	VF	XF	Unc
611	1847	1,438	750.00	1250.	2000.	3000.

Obv: CP on truncation.

KM#	Date	Mintage	Fine	VF	XF	Unc
619	1851 CP	596 pcs.	800.00	1300.	2000.	3500.

10 THALER

13.3000 g, .900 GOLD, .3848 oz AGW

KM#	Date	Mintage	Fine	VF	XF	Unc
594	1838	126 pcs.	1400.	2000.	3000.	4000.
	1840	Inc. KM591	1000.	1500.	2500.	3500.
	1841	Inc. KM591	1000.	1500.	2500.	3500.

PATTERNS (Pn)

(Including off metal strikes)

KM#	Date	Mintage	Identification	Mkt.Val.
Pn31	1814	3 pcs.	5 Thaler, .900 Gold	—
Pn32	1842	—	2 Heller, Copper	—
Pn33	1842	—	3 Heller, Copper	—

OBER-HESSEN

1/4 KREUZER

COPPER

Obv: Arms, leg: HESSEN CASSEL. Rev: Value.

KM#	Date	Mintage	Fine	VF	XF	Unc
550	1801	—	5.00	7.00	15.00	75.00
	1802	—	5.00	7.00	15.00	75.00

Obv: Crowned arms. Rev: Value within rosettes.

KM#	Date	Mintage	Fine	VF	XF	Unc
580	1824	—	2.00	4.00	10.00	50.00
	1825	—	2.00	4.00	10.00	50.00
	1827	—	2.00	4.00	10.00	50.00
	1829	—	2.00	4.00	10.00	50.00
	1830	—	2.00	4.00	10.00	50.00

Similar to KM#580.

KM#	Date	Mintage	Fine	VF	XF	Unc
592	1834	—	2.00	4.00	10.00	50.00
	1835	—	2.00	4.00	10.00	50.00

1/2 KREUZER

COPPER

Obv: Arms, HESSEN CASSEL. Rev: Value.

KM#	Date	Mintage	Fine	VF	XF	Unc
551	1801	—	3.00	6.00	18.00	80.00
	1802	—	3.00	6.00	18.00	80.00
	1803	—	3.00	6.00	18.00	80.00

Obv: Elector's cap above arms. Rev: Value.

KM#	Date	Mintage	Fine	VF	XF	Unc
558	1803 F	—	3.00	7.00	18.00	80.00
	1804 F	—	3.00	7.00	18.00	80.00

KM#	Date	Mintage	Fine	VF	XF	Unc
581	1824	—	2.00	5.00	12.00	60.00
	1825	—	2.00	5.00	12.00	60.00
	1826	—	2.00	5.00	12.00	60.00
	1827	—	2.00	5.00	12.00	60.00
	1828	—	2.00	5.00	12.00	60.00
	1829	—	2.00	5.00	12.00	60.00
	1830	—	2.00	5.00	12.00	60.00

Similar to KM#581.

KM#	Date	Mintage	Fine	VF	XF	Unc
593	1834	—	2.00	5.00	12.00	60.00

KREUZER

COPPER

Obv: Crowned arms. Rev: Value within rosettes.

KM#	Date	Mintage	Fine	VF	XF	Unc
582	1825	—	2.50	8.00	25.00	110.00
	1828	—	2.50	8.00	25.00	110.00
	1829	—	2.50	8.00	25.00	110.00

Similar to KM#582.

KM#	Date	Mintage	Fine	VF	XF	Unc
588	1832	—	2.50	8.00	25.00	110.00
	1833	—	2.50	8.00	25.00	110.00
	1835	—	2.50	8.00	25.00	110.00

6 KREUZER

BILLON

Obv: Crowned arms. Rev: Value within rosettes.

KM#	Date	Mintage	Fine	VF	XF	Unc
583	1826	—	6.00	12.00	42.00	165.00
	1827	—	6.00	12.00	42.00	165.00
	1828	—	6.00	12.00	42.00	165.00

Rev: W/o rosettes.

KM#	Date	Mintage	Fine	VF	XF	Unc
586	1831	—	3.50	8.00	28.00	125.00
	1832	—	3.50	8.00	28.00	125.00
	1833	—	3.50	8.00	28.00	125.00
	1834	—	3.50	8.00	28.00	125.00

PATTERNS (Pn)

(Including off metal strikes)

KM#	Date	Mintage	Identification	Mkt.Val.
Pn2	1821	—	1 Thaler, Silver	—
Pn3	1835	—	1/2 Kreuzer, Copper, KM593	—

HESSE-DARMSTADT

A state located in southwest Germany founded in 1567. The Landgrave was elevated to the status of Grand Duke in 1806. In 1815 the Congress of Vienna awarded Hesse-Darmstadt the cities of Mainz and Worms which were relinquished along with the newly acquired Hesse-Homburg, to the Prussians in 1866. It became part of the German Empire in 1871.

RULERS

Ludwig X, 1790-1806
As Grand Duke Ludwig I, 1806-1830
Ludwig II, 1830-1848
Ludwig III, 1848-1877
Ludwig IV, 1877-1892
Ernst Ludwig, 1892-1918

MINTMASTERS INITIALS

Letter	Date	Name
HR	1817-	Hector Roessler
RF	1772-1809	Remigius Fehr

HELLER

COPPER

Obv: Crowned pointed arms, G.H.-K.M. Rev: Value.

KM#	Date	Mintage	Fine	VF	XF	Unc
291	1824	—	1.00	2.00	7.00	40.00

KM#	Date	Mintage	Fine	VF	XF	Unc
302	1837	—	1.00	2.00	7.00	35.00
	1840	—	1.00	2.00	7.00	35.00
	1841	—	1.00	2.00	7.00	35.00
	1842	.103	1.00	2.00	7.00	35.00
	1843	.175	1.00	2.00	7.00	35.00
	1844	.241	1.00	2.00	7.00	35.00
	1845	—	1.00	2.00	7.00	35.00
	1846	—	1.00	2.00	7.00	35.00
	1847	—	1.00	2.00	7.00	35.00

Obv: Crowned square arms.

KM#	Date	Mintage	Fine	VF	XF	Unc
322	1847	—	1.00	2.00	5.00	35.00

KM#	Date	Mintage	Fine	VF	XF	Unc
323	1848	—	1.00	2.00	5.00	35.00
	1849	—	1.00	2.00	5.00	35.00
	1850	—	1.00	2.00	5.00	35.00
	1851	—	1.00	2.00	5.00	35.00
	1852	—	1.00	2.00	5.00	35.00
	1853	—	1.00	2.00	5.00	35.00
	1854	—	1.00	2.00	5.00	35.00
	1855	—	1.00	2.00	5.00	35.00

PFENNIG

COPPER

KM#	Date	Mintage	Fine	VF	XF	Unc
251	1801	—	2.00	4.00	8.00	40.00
	1802	—	2.00	4.00	8.00	40.00
	1803	—	2.00	4.00	8.00	40.00
	1804	—	2.00	4.00	8.00	40.00
	1805	—	2.00	4.00	8.00	40.00
	1806 RF	—	2.00	4.00	8.00	40.00

NOTE: Earlier dates (1797-1800) exist for this type.

.333 SILVER

KM#	Date	Mintage	Fine	VF	XF	Unc
280	1811	—	2.00	4.00	8.00	40.00
	1819	—	2.00	4.00	8.00	40.00

Obv: GH-KM.

KM#	Date	Mintage	Fine	VF	XF	Unc
283	1819	—	2.00	5.00	9.00	40.00

KM#	Date	Mintage	Fine	VF	XF	Unc
337	1857	.140	1.00	2.00	3.00	30.00
	1858	.202	1.00	2.00	3.00	30.00
	1859	.257	1.00	2.00	3.00	30.00
	1860	.268	1.00	2.00	3.00	30.00
	1861	.311	1.00	2.00	3.00	30.00
	1862	.324	1.00	2.00	3.00	30.00
	1863	.190	1.00	2.00	3.00	30.00
	1864	—	1.00	2.00	3.00	30.00
	1865	.279	1.00	2.00	3.00	30.00
	1866	.317	1.00	2.00	3.00	30.00
	1867	.296	1.00	2.00	3.00	30.00
	1868	.332	1.00	2.00	3.00	30.00
	1869	.322	1.00	2.00	3.00	30.00
	1870	.526	1.00	2.00	3.00	30.00
	1871	.322	1.00	2.00	3.00	30.00
	1872	.338	1.00	2.00	3.00	30.00

1/4 STUBER

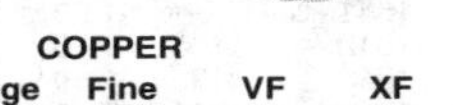

COPPER

KM#	Date	Mintage	Fine	VF	XF	Unc
258	1805 RF	—	4.00	8.00	25.00	70.00

1/2 STUBER

COPPER
Obv: Crowned LLX monogram. Rev: Value.

KM#	Date	Mintage	Fine	VF	XF	Unc
259	1805	—	5.00	10.00	30.00	90.00

1/4 KREUZER

COPPER

KM#	Date	Mintage	Fine	VF	XF	Unc
272	1809	—	3.00	6.00	20.00	85.00
	1816	—	3.00	6.00	20.00	85.00

Obv. leg: G.H.-S.M.

KM#	Date	Mintage	Fine	VF	XF	Unc
273	1809	—	3.00	6.00	20.00	85.00
	1816	—	3.00	6.00	20.00	85.00
	1817	—	3.00	6.00	20.00	85.00

1/2 KREUZER

COPPER

KM#	Date	Mintage	Fine	VF	XF	Unc
274	1809	—	2.00	4.00	12.00	60.00
	1817	—	2.00	4.00	12.00	60.00

Obv. leg: G.H.-S.M.

KM#	Date	Mintage	Fine	VF	XF	Unc
281	1817	—	2.00	4.00	15.00	70.00

KREUZER

.7700 g, .187 SILVER, .0046 oz ASW
Obv: Lion divides H.D. Rev: LAND MUNZE, value.

KM#	Date	Mintage	Fine	VF	XF	Unc
257	1801	—	1.00	3.00	7.00	50.00
	1802	—	1.00	3.00	7.00	50.00
	1803	—	1.00	3.00	7.00	50.00
	1804	—	1.00	3.00	7.00	50.00
	1805	—	1.00	3.00	7.00	50.00

Obv: Crowned lion between H.D.
Rev: Value, LAND MUNZ.

KM#	Date	Mintage	Fine	VF	XF	Unc
260	1806	—	1.00	3.00	7.00	50.00

Obv: Crowned lion w/sword between H.D.

KM#	Date	Mintage	Fine	VF	XF	Unc
261	1806	—	1.00	3.00	8.00	65.00

Obv: Crowned lion between H.D.-L.M. Rev: Value.

KM#	Date	Mintage	Fine	VF	XF	Unc
262	1806	—	1.00	4.00	20.00	110.00
	1807	—	1.00	4.00	20.00	110.00

Obv: Crowned lion w/sword between H.D.-L.M.

KM#	Date	Mintage	Fine	VF	XF	Unc
263	1807	—	1.00	3.00	8.00	65.00

Obv: Crowned lion w/sword between G.H.-L.M.
Rev: Value, LAND MUNZ.

KM#	Date	Mintage	Fine	VF	XF	Unc
264	1807	—	1.00	3.00	8.00	65.00
	1808	—	1.00	3.00	8.00	65.00
	1809	—	1.00	3.00	8.00	65.00

Obv: Crowned arms between G.H.-L.M.

KM#	Date	Mintage	Fine	VF	XF	Unc
275	1809	—	1.00	4.00	8.00	60.00
	1810	—	1.00	4.00	8.00	60.00
	1817	—	1.00	4.00	8.00	60.00

Obv: Crowned arms between G.H.-S.M.

KM#	Date	Mintage	Fine	VF	XF	Unc
284	1819	—	1.00	4.00	8.00	60.00

KM#	Date	Mintage	Fine	VF	XF	Unc
299	1834	—	1.00	3.00	6.00	40.00
	1835	—	1.00	3.00	6.00	40.00
	1836	—	1.00	3.00	6.00	40.00
	1837	—	1.00	3.00	6.00	40.00
	1838	—	1.00	3.00	6.00	40.00

.8300 g, .166 SILVER, .0044 oz ASW

KM#	Date	Mintage	Fine	VF	XF	Unc
303	1837	—	1.00	3.00	6.00	40.00
	1838	—	1.00	3.00	6.00	40.00
	1839	—	1.00	3.00	6.00	40.00
	1840	—	1.00	3.00	6.00	40.00
	1841	—	1.00	3.00	6.00	40.00
	1842	.438	1.00	3.00	6.00	40.00

KM#	Date	Mintage	Fine	VF	XF	Unc
316	1843	.129	1.00	3.00	6.00	40.00
	1844	—	1.00	3.00	6.00	40.00
	1845	.516	1.00	3.00	6.00	40.00
	1847	—	1.00	3.00	6.00	40.00

KM#	Date	Mintage	Fine	VF	XF	Unc
324	1848	.546	1.00	3.00	6.00	40.00
	1849	—	1.00	3.00	6.00	40.00
	1850	—	1.00	3.00	6.00	40.00
	1852	—	1.00	3.00	6.00	40.00
	1854	.236	1.00	3.00	6.00	40.00
	1855	.162	1.00	3.00	6.00	40.00
	1856	.334	1.00	3.00	6.00	40.00

KM#	Date	Mintage	Fine	VF	XF	Unc
339	1858	.271	1.00	3.00	6.00	25.00
	1859	.147	1.00	3.00	6.00	25.00
	1860	.268	1.00	3.00	6.00	25.00
	1861	.207	1.00	3.00	6.00	25.00
	1862	.211	1.00	3.00	6.00	25.00
	1863	.190	1.00	3.00	6.00	25.00
	1864	.376	1.00	3.00	6.00	25.00
	1865	.181	1.00	3.00	6.00	25.00
	1866	.247	1.00	3.00	6.00	25.00
	1867	.273	1.00	3.00	6.00	25.00
	1868	.199	1.00	3.00	6.00	25.00
	1869	.249	1.00	3.00	6.00	25.00
	1870	.349	1.00	3.00	6.00	25.00
	1871	.366	1.00	3.00	6.00	25.00
	1872	.128	1.00	3.00	6.00	25.00

3 KREUZER

1.3900 g, .281 SILVER, .0125 oz ASW
Obv: Lion divides H.D.
Rev: LAND MUNZE, value.

KM#	Date	Mintage	Fine	VF	XF	Unc
256	1801	—	4.00	8.00	30.00	125.00
	1802	—	4.00	8.00	30.00	125.00
	1803	—	4.00	8.00	30.00	125.00
	1804	—	4.00	8.00	30.00	125.00
	1805	—	4.00	8.00	30.00	125.00

NOTE: Earlier date (1800) exists for this type.

Obv: Crowned arms G.H.-L.M.
Rev. value: III KREUZER.

KM#	Date	Mintage	Fine	VF	XF	Unc
269	1808	—	4.00	8.00	30.00	125.00
	1809	—	4.00	8.00	30.00	125.00
	1810	—	4.00	8.00	30.00	125.00

Rev. value: 3 KREUZER

KM#	Date	Mintage	Fine	VF	XF	Unc
282	1817	—	4.00	8.00	30.00	125.00
285	1819	—	3.00	7.00	15.00	75.00
	1822	—	3.00	7.00	15.00	75.00

Obv: Crowned arms, GR HERZOGTH.
Rev: Value, SCHEIDEMUNZE.

KM#	Date	Mintage	Fine	VF	XF	Unc
295	1833	—	5.00	10.00	20.00	80.00

KM#	Date	Mintage	Fine	VF	XF	Unc
296	1833	—	2.00	6.00	12.00	70.00
	1834	—	2.00	6.00	12.00	70.00
	1835	—	2.00	6.00	12.00	70.00
	1836	—	2.00	6.00	12.00	70.00

KM#	Date	Mintage	Fine	VF	XF	Unc
305	1838	—	2.00	4.00	8.00	55.00
	1839	—	2.00	4.00	8.00	55.00
	1840	—	2.00	4.00	8.00	55.00
	1841	—	2.00	4.00	8.00	55.00
	1842	.280	2.00	4.00	8.00	55.00

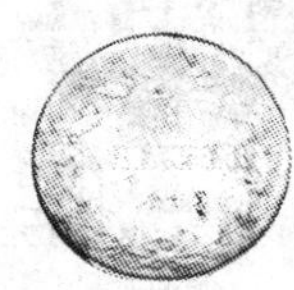

Obv. leg: GROSHERZOGTHUM HESSEN.

KM#	Date	Mintage	Fine	VF	XF	Unc
317	1843	.288	1.00	3.00	6.00	45.00
	1844	—	1.00	3.00	6.00	45.00
	1845	.245	1.00	3.00	6.00	45.00
	1846	—	1.00	3.00	6.00	45.00
	1847	—	1.00	3.00	6.00	45.00

KM#	Date	Mintage	Fine	VF	XF	Unc
325	1848	.082	1.00	3.00	6.00	40.00
	1850	—	1.00	3.00	6.00	40.00
	1851	—	1.00	3.00	6.00	40.00
	1852	—	1.00	3.00	6.00	40.00
	1853	—	1.00	3.00	6.00	40.00
	1854	.076	1.00	3.00	6.00	40.00
	1855	.148	1.00	3.00	6.00	40.00
	1856	.062	1.00	3.00	6.00	40.00

1.2300 g, .250 SILVER, .0138 oz ASW

KM#	Date	Mintage	Fine	VF	XF	Unc
345	1864	.095	1.00	3.00	6.00	40.00
	1865	.087	1.00	3.00	6.00	40.00
	1866	.090	1.00	3.00	6.00	40.00
	1867	.077	1.00	3.00	6.00	40.00

5 KREUZER

(Convention)

2.2300 g, .437 SILVER, .0313 oz ASW
Obv: Crowned L. Rev: Value.

KM#	Date	Mintage	Fine	VF	XF	Unc
265	1807	—	15.00	30.00	90.00	325.00

Obv: Curled edges on L

KM#	Date	Mintage	Fine	VF	XF	Unc
266	1807	—	15.00	35.00	100.00	350.00

Obv: L at truncation. Rev: R.IUSTIRT F. below arms.

KM#	Date	Mintage	Fine	VF	XF	Unc
270	1808	—	18.00	40.00	120.00	400.00

6 KREUZER

2.4300 g, .343 SILVER, .0267 oz ASW

KM#	Date	Mintage	Fine	VF	XF	Unc
286	1819	—	6.00	12.00	35.00	150.00
	1820	—	6.00	12.00	35.00	150.00

KM#	Date	Mintage	Fine	VF	XF	Unc
290	1821	—	3.00	6.00	15.00	60.00
	1824	—	3.00	6.00	15.00	60.00
	1826	—	3.00	6.00	15.00	60.00
	1827	—	3.00	6.00	15.00	60.00
	1828	—	3.00	6.00	15.00	60.00
	1833	—	3.00	6.00	15.00	60.00

KM#	Date	Mintage	Fine	VF	XF	Unc
297	1833	—	3.00	6.00	15.00	60.00
	1834	—	3.00	6.00	15.00	60.00
	1835	—	3.00	6.00	15.00	60.00
	1836	—	3.00	6.00	15.00	60.00
	1837	—	3.00	6.00	15.00	60.00

2.4600 g, .350 SILVER, .0276 oz ASW

KM#	Date	Mintage	Fine	VF	XF	Unc
306	1838	—	2.50	5.00	12.50	50.00
	1839	—	2.50	5.00	12.50	50.00
	1840	—	2.50	5.00	12.50	50.00
	1841	—	2.50	5.00	12.50	50.00
	1842	.816	2.50	5.00	12.50	50.00

KM#	Date	Mintage	Fine	VF	XF	Unc
318	1843	.775	2.50	5.00	15.00	60.00
	1844	.331	2.50	5.00	15.00	60.00
	1845	.235	2.50	5.00	15.00	60.00
	1846	.897	2.50	5.00	15.00	60.00
	1847	—	2.50	5.00	15.00	60.00
326	1848	.243	2.00	5.00	15.00	60.00
	1850	—	2.00	5.00	15.00	60.00
	1851	—	2.00	5.00	15.00	60.00
	1852	—	2.00	5.00	15.00	60.00
	1853	—	2.00	5.00	15.00	60.00
	1854	.033	2.00	5.00	15.00	60.00
	1855	.072	2.00	5.00	15.00	60.00
	1856	.044	2.00	5.00	15.00	60.00

KM#	Date	Mintage	Fine	VF	XF	Unc
346	1864	.052	2.00	5.00	15.00	65.00
	1865	.039	2.00	5.00	15.00	65.00
	1866	.043	2.00	5.00	15.00	65.00
	1867	.060	2.00	5.00	15.00	65.00

10 KREUZER

(Convention)

3.9000 g, .500 SILVER, .0626 oz ASW

KM#	Date	Mintage	Fine	VF	XF	Unc
271	1808 RF	—	15.00	35.00	200.00	350.00

20 KREUZER

(Convention)

6.6800 g, .583 SILVER, .1252 oz ASW
Obv: Head right, FRISCH F. at truncation.
Rev: Crowned arms dividing date, R.F. below.

KM#	Date	Mintage	Fine	VF	XF	Unc
267	1807 RF	—	20.00	50.00	225.00	575.00

Obv. leg: LUDEWIG. . .

KM#	Date	Mintage	Fine	VF	XF	Unc
268	1807 RF	—	20.00	50.00	200.00	500.00
	1808 RF	—	20.00	50.00	200.00	500.00
	1809 RF	—	20.00	50.00	200.00	500.00

Obv. leg: LUDWIG. . .

KM#	Date	Mintage	Fine	VF	XF	Unc
276	1809 RF	—	20.00	50.00	200.00	500.00

1/2 GULDEN

5.3000 g, .900 SILVER, .1533 oz ASW
Obv: VOIGHT below head.

KM#	Date	Mintage	Fine	VF	XF	Unc
307	1838	1.080	15.00	30.00	65.00	200.00
	1839	Inc. Ab.	15.00	30.00	65.00	200.00
	1840	Inc. Ab.	15.00	30.00	65.00	200.00
	1841	Inc. Ab.	15.00	30.00	65.00	200.00
	1843	.151	15.00	30.00	65.00	200.00
	1844	.081	20.00	40.00	75.00	250.00
	1845	.167	15.00	30.00	65.00	200.00
	1846	.033	20.00	40.00	85.00	300.00

Obv: VOIGHT below head.

KM#	Date	Mintage	Fine	VF	XF	Unc
336	1855	.047	30.00	60.00	150.00	400.00

GULDEN

(2/3 Thaler)

10.6000 g, .900 SILVER, .3067 oz ASW
Obv: Small head left. Rev: Value within wreath.

KM#	Date	Mintage	Fine	VF	XF	Unc
304	1837	1.122	25.00	40.00	85.00	225.00

KM#	Date	Mintage	Fine	VF	XF	Unc
308	1838	Inc. Ab.	30.00	50.00	100.00	275.00

Obv: VOIGT below head.

KM#	Date	Mintage	Fine	VF	XF	Unc
309	1839	Inc. Ab.	20.00	40.00	75.00	200.00
	1840	Inc. Ab.	20.00	40.00	75.00	200.00
	1841	Inc. Ab.	20.00	40.00	75.00	200.00
	1842	.605	20.00	40.00	75.00	200.00
	1843	.314	20.00	40.00	75.00	200.00
	1844	.191	20.00	40.00	75.00	200.00
	1845	.176	20.00	40.00	75.00	200.00
	1846	.144	20.00	40.00	75.00	200.00
	1847	.251	20.00	40.00	75.00	200.00

Visit of Crown Prince of Russia
Obv: VOIGHT below head.

KM#	Date	Mintage	Fine	VF	XF	Unc
319	1843	—	125.00	250.00	400.00	850.00

Public Freedom Through German Parliament

KM#	Date	Mintage	Fine	VF	XF	Unc
327	1848	—	125.00	175.00	275.00	600.00

10.5800 g, .900 SILVER, .3061 oz ASW
Obv: VOIGHT below head.

KM#	Date	Mintage	Fine	VF	XF	Unc
328	1848	.090	40.00	75.00	200.00	400.00
	1854	.044	40.00	75.00	200.00	400.00
	1855	.090	40.00	75.00	200.00	400.00
	1856	.153	20.00	40.00	125.00	300.00

ZWEY (2) GULDEN

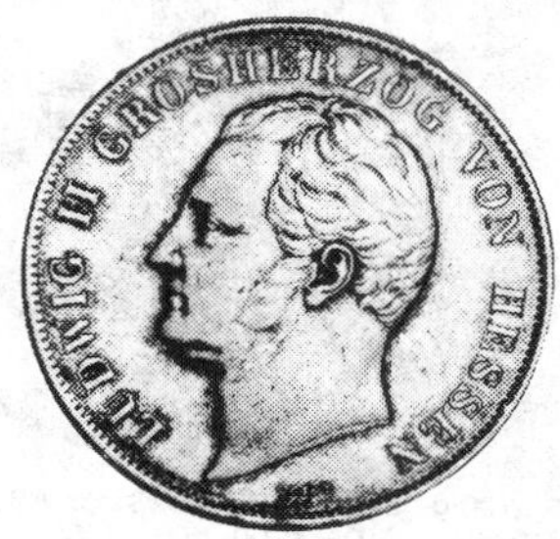

21.2100 g, .900 SILVER, .6138 oz ASW
Obv: VOIGHT below head.

KM#	Date	Mintage	Fine	VF	XF	Unc
321	1845	.044	50.00	100.00	225.00	550.00
	1846	.270	45.00	100.00	210.00	500.00
	1847	.030	55.00	115.00	275.00	700.00

Obv: VOIGHT below head.

KM#	Date	Mintage	Fine	VF	XF	Unc
329	1848	.252	70.00	150.00	350.00	900.00
	1849	Inc. Ab.	70.00	150.00	350.00	900.00
	1853	Inc. Ab.	50.00	100.00	270.00	650.00
	1854	.127	40.00	80.00	215.00	500.00
	1855	.149	40.00	80.00	215.00	500.00
	1856	.064	40.00	80.00	215.00	500.00

EIN (1) THALER

28.0600 g, .833 SILVER, .7516 oz ASW

KM#	Date	Mintage	Fine	VF	XF	Unc
277	1809 L	—	200.00	350.00	700.00	1600.

(Krone)

29.5100 g, .871 SILVER, .8264 oz ASW

KM#	Date	Mintage	Fine	VF	XF	Unc
287	1819 HR	.019	275.00	400.00	850.00	1800.

KM#	Date	Mintage	Fine	VF	XF	Unc
292	1825 HR	.171	100.00	165.00	350.00	950.00

Obv: VOIGHT below head.

KM#	Date	Mintage	Fine	VF	XF	Unc
298	1833 HR	.124	75.00	150.00	300.00	800.00
	1835 HR	.558	100.00	175.00	375.00	1100.
	1836 HR	I.A.	75.00	150.00	300.00	800.00
	1837 HR	I.A.	100.00	175.00	375.00	1100.

(Vereins)

18.5200 g, .900 SILVER, .5360 oz ASW

KM#	Date	Mintage	Fine	VF	XF	Unc
338	1857	.091	25.00	60.00	150.00	350.00
	1858	.537	25.00	60.00	150.00	300.00
	1859	.594	25.00	60.00	150.00	300.00
	1860	.608	25.00	60.00	150.00	300.00
	1861	.414	25.00	60.00	150.00	300.00
	1862	.242	25.00	60.00	150.00	300.00
	1863	.215	25.00	60.00	150.00	300.00
	1864	.073	25.00	65.00	175.00	350.00
	1865	.078	25.00	65.00	175.00	350.00
	1866	.059	25.00	65.00	175.00	350.00
	1867	.024	25.00	65.00	175.00	350.00
	1868	.048	25.00	65.00	185.00	425.00
	1869	.034	25.00	65.00	185.00	425.00
	1870	.039	25.00	65.00	175.00	350.00
	1871	.033	35.00	70.00	175.00	350.00

2 THALER

(3-1/2 Gulden)

37.1200 g, .900 SILVER, 1.0742 oz ASW

KM#	Date	Mintage	Fine	VF	XF	Unc
310	1839	.024	100.00	175.00	350.00	800.00
	1840	.368	85.00	140.00	275.00	600.00
	1841	.688	75.00	125.00	200.00	525.00
	1842	.286	90.00	150.00	315.00	700.00

Obv: Similar to KM#310.

KM#	Date	Mintage	Fine	VF	XF	Unc
320	1844	.377	90.00	150.00	300.00	700.00

Rev: Similar to KM#320.

KM#	Date	Mintage	Fine	VF	XF	Unc
335	1854	.043	300.00	500.00	1000.	2200.

5 GULDEN

3.4250 g, .904 GOLD, .0995 oz AGW
Obv: Head left, C.V. below.
Rev: Crowned draped arms,
value 5G, leg: AUS HESS. RHEINGOLD.

KM#	Date	Mintage	Fine	VF	XF	Unc
300	1835 CV-HR	60 pcs.	2000.	4000.	7500.	12,500.

KM#	Date	Mintage	Fine	VF	XF	Unc
301	1835 CV-HR	.022	700.00	1500.	2000.	3250.
	1840 CV-HR	I.A.	300.00	500.00	800.00	1550.
	1841 CV-HR	I.A.	300.00	500.00	850.00	1650.
	1842 CV-HR	I.A.	300.00	500.00	850.00	1650.

10 GULDEN

6.8500 g, .904 GOLD, .1991 oz AGW

KM#	Date	Mintage	Fine	VF	XF	Unc
293	1826 HR	1,700	600.00	1500.	2500.	4000.
	1827 HR	1,705	600.00	1500.	2500.	3500.

KM#	Date	Mintage	Fine	VF	XF	Unc
315	1840 CV-HR	.017	300.00	750.00	1250.	2000.
	1841 CV-HR	I.A.	300.00	750.00	1250.	2000.
	1842 CV-HR	I.A.	300.00	750.00	1250.	2000.

MONETARY REFORM

2 MARK

11.1110 g, .900 SILVER, .3215 oz ASW

KM#	Date	Mintage	Fine	VF	XF	Unc
355	1876H	.202	125.00	300.00	2100.	4200.
	1877H	.338	125.00	325.00	2250.	4500.

KM#	Date	Mintage	Fine	VF	XF	Unc
359	1888A	.022	450.00	1250.	2000.	3500.
	1888A	500 pcs.	—	—	Proof	5200.

Rev: Type III.

KM#	Date	Mintage	Fine	VF	XF	Unc
363	1891A	.063	275.00	625.00	1000.	2250.
	1891A	—	—	—	Proof	2750.

KM#	Date	Mintage	Fine	VF	XF	Unc
368	1895A	.054	150.00	300.00	600.00	1000.
	1896A	8,950	300.00	600.00	900.00	1400.
	1896A	200 pcs.	—	—	Proof	2000.
	1898A	.034	175.00	325.00	650.00	1100.
	1898A	360 pcs.	—	—	Proof	1500.
	1899A	.054	175.00	325.00	650.00	1100.
	1899A	128 pcs.	—	—	Proof	1600.
	1900A	8,950	350.00	625.00	950.00	1500.
	1900A	200 pcs.	—	—	Proof	2100.

5 MARK

27.7770 g, .900 SILVER, .8038 oz ASW
Rev: Type II.

KM#	Date	Mintage	Fine	VF	XF	Unc
353	1875H	.148	45.00	125.00	1700.	4200.
	1876H	.290	45.00	125.00	1500.	3500.

1.9910 g, .900 GOLD, .0576 oz AGW

KM#	Date	Mintage	Fine	VF	XF	Unc
356	1877H	.103	175.00	400.00	700.00	1200.
	1877H	—	—	—	Proof	Rare

Rev: Type II.

KM#	Date	Mintage	Fine	VF	XF	Unc
357	1877H	.079	300.00	600.00	800.00	1200.
	1877H	—	—	—	Proof	2000.

27.7770 g, .900 SILVER, .8038 oz ASW
Rev: Type II.

KM#	Date	Mintage	Fine	VF	XF	Unc
360	1888A	8,940	425.00	1200.	2250.	4000.
	1888A	400 pcs.	—	—	Proof	4000.

Rev: Type III.

KM#	Date	Mintage	Fine	VF	XF	Unc
364	1891A	.025	225.00	400.00	1500.	3000.
	1891A	—	—	—	Proof	4000.

KM#	Date	Mintage	Fine	VF	XF	Unc
369	1895A	.039	90.00	200.00	750.00	1750.
	1895A	200 pcs.	—	—	Proof	2000.
	1898A	.037	90.00	200.00	750.00	1750.
	1898A	240 pcs.	—	—	Proof	2000.
	1899A	.018	110.00	225.00	800.00	2000.
	1899A	176 pcs.	—	—	Proof	2200.
	1900A	.018	200.00	350.00	1000.	2500.
	1900A	150 pcs.	—	—	Proof	2500.

10 MARK

3.9820 g, .900 GOLD, .1152 oz AGW

KM#	Date	Mintage	Fine	VF	XF	Unc
350	1872H	.030	120.00	175.00	425.00	700.00
	1872H	—	—	—	Proof	Rare
	1873H	.432	110.00	150.00	325.00	600.00
	1873H	—	—	—	Proof	Rare

Rev: Type II.

KM#	Date	Mintage	Fine	VF	XF	Unc
354	1875H	.191	100.00	170.00	250.00	400.00
	1876H	.513	120.00	150.00	225.00	350.00
	1877H	.094	140.00	180.00	300.00	500.00

KM#	Date	Mintage	Fine	VF	XF	Unc
358	1878H	.132	140.00	275.00	425.00	750.00
	1878H	—	—	—	Proof	2000.
	1879H	.056	200.00	300.00	600.00	1000.
	1879H	—	—	—	Proof	2000.
	1880H	.109	220.00	325.00	625.00	1100.
	1880H	—	—	—	Proof	2000.
361	1888A	.036	220.00	325.00	625.00	1000.
	1888A	500 pcs.	—	—	Proof	2750.

Edge: Vines and stars.

KM#	Date	Mintage	Fine	VF	XF	Unc
362	1890A	.054	275.00	400.00	750.00	1100.

Rev: Type III.

KM#	Date	Mintage	Fine	VF	XF	Unc
366	1893A	.054	275.00	400.00	750.00	1100.
	1893A	450 pcs.	—	—	Proof	2700.

KM#	Date	Mintage	Fine	VF	XF	Unc
370	1896A	.036	200.00	450.00	800.00	1200.
	1896A	230 pcs.	—	—	Proof	2250.
	1898A	.075	175.00	325.00	600.00	1000.
	1898A	500 pcs.	—	—	Proof	2250.

20 MARK

7.9650 g, .900 GOLD, .2304 oz AGW
Rev: Type I.

KM#	Date	Mintage	Fine	VF	XF	Unc
351	1872H	.183	125.00	225.00	400.00	650.00
	1872H	—	—	—	Proof	Rare
	1873H	.521	120.00	175.00	350.00	600.00

Rev: Type II.

KM#	Date	Mintage	Fine	VF	XF	Unc
352	1874H	.134	175.00	300.00	700.00	1000.

KM#	Date	Mintage	Fine	VF	XF	Unc
365	1892A	.025	500.00	750.00	1100.	1800.
	1892A	—	—	—	Proof	4500.

Rev: Type III.

KM#	Date	Mintage	Fine	VF	XF	Unc
367	1893A	.025	500.00	750.00	1000.	1400.
	1893A	—	—	—	Proof	2500.

KM#	Date	Mintage	Fine	VF	XF	Unc
371	1896A	.015	300.00	500.00	900.00	1500.
	1896A	230 pcs.	—	—	Proof	1500.
	1897A	.045	125.00	175.00	350.00	650.00
	1897A	400 pcs.	—	—	Proof	1300.
	1898A	.070	125.00	175.00	350.00	550.00
	1898A	500 pcs.	—	—	Proof	1300.
	1899A	.040	125.00	175.00	400.00	750.00
	1899A	600 pcs.	—	—	Proof	1300.
	1900A	.040	125.00	175.00	350.00	600.00
	1900A	500 pcs.	—	—	Proof	1300.

NOTE: Later dates (1901-1903) exist for this type.

MEDALLIC ISSUES (M)
(6 KREUZER)

BILLON
Visit of Princes Ludwig and Heinrich to Darmstadt Mint

KM#	Date	Mintage	Fine	VF	XF	Unc
M7	ND(1848)	—	—	350.00	500.00	750.00

Visit of Prince Wilhelm and Princess Anna to Darmstadt Mint

KM#	Date	Mintage	Fine	VF	XF	Unc
M8	1859	—	—	350.00	500.00	750.00

HESSE-HOMBURG

Hesse-Homburg located in southwest Germany was created from part of Hesse-Darmstadt in 1596 and was mediatized to Darmstadt 1801-1815. In 1815 it was restored to independence and added the Lordships of Meisenheim and Kreuznach. The Homburg line became extinct in 1866, passed to Darmstadt and was almost immediately annexed to Prussia.

RULERS

Friedrich V Ludwig, 1751-1820
Friedrich VI Josef, 1820-1829
Ludwig Wilhelm, 1829-1839
Philipp August, 1839-1846
Gustav Adolph, 1846-1848
Ferdinand Heinrich, 1848-1866

MINTMASTERS INITIALS

Letter	Date	Name
RS	1817-1845	Rudolph Stadelmann, die-cutter in Darmstadt and Homburg
C.SCHNITZSPAHN	d.1877	Christian Schnitzspahn, chief die-cutter and medalleur in Darmstadt
C.VOIGT, VOIGT	1829-?	Carl F. Voigt, chief die-cutter and medalleur in Munich

KREUZER

.8300 g, .166 SILVER, .0044 oz ASW

KM#	Date	Mintage	Fine	VF	XF	Unc
13	1840	.048	30.00	60.00	100.00	250.00

3 KREUZER

1.3800 g, .281 SILVER, .0124 oz ASW

KM#	Date	Mintage	Fine	VF	XF	Unc
14	1840	.015	50.00	125.00	250.00	600.00

SILVER
Obv: Hessian lion in shield, leg: LANDGRAFTHUM HESSEN. Rev: 3/KREUZER/date in oak wreath.

KM#	Date	Mintage	Fine	VF	XF	Unc
19	1856	—	—	—	—	—

6 KREUZER

2.4300 g, .343 SILVER, .0267 oz ASW

KM#	Date	Mintage	Fine	VF	XF	Unc
15	1840	.057	30.00	75.00	150.00	350.00

1/2 GULDEN

5.3000 g, .900 SILVER, .1533 oz ASW

KM#	Date	Mintage	Fine	VF	XF	Unc
11	1838 VOIGT	.011	75.00	150.00	225.00	375.00
	1839	—	—	—	Proof	475.00

Obv: RS at truncation.

KM#	Date	Mintage	Fine	VF	XF	Unc
16	1840 RS	.010	60.00	120.00	200.00	400.00
	1841 RS	6,560	60.00	120.00	200.00	400.00
	1843 RS	6,900	60.00	120.00	200.00	400.00
	1844 RS	.018	60.00	120.00	200.00	400.00
	1845	Inc. Ab.	60.00	120.00	200.00	400.00
	1846 RS	4,300	60.00	120.00	200.00	400.00

GULDEN

10.6000 g, .900 SILVER, .3067 oz ASW

KM#	Date	Mintage	Fine	VF	XF	Unc
12	1838 VOIGT	.011	60.00	140.00	300.00	725.00
	1839	—	—	—	Proof	875.00

KM#	Date	Mintage	Fine	VF	XF	Unc
17	1841 RS	.014	60.00	140.00	300.00	700.00
	1843 RS	6,800	60.00	140.00	300.00	700.00
	1844 RS	.014	60.00	140.00	300.00	700.00
	1845 RS	8,100	60.00	140.00	300.00	700.00
	1846 RS	8,100	60.00	140.00	300.00	700.00

ZWEY (2) GULDEN

21.2100 g, .900 SILVER, .6317 oz ASW

KM#	Date	Mintage	Fine	VF	XF	Unc
18	1846 C.VOIGT	.011	300.00	600.00	1200.	3000.

EIN (1) THALER
(Vereins)

18.5200 g, .900 SILVER, .5358 oz ASW

KM#	Date	Mintage	Fine	VF	XF	Unc
20	1858	5,000	50.00	100.00	200.00	500.00
	1859	6,579	50.00	100.00	200.00	500.00
	1860	6,593	50.00	100.00	200.00	500.00
	1861	6,588	50.00	100.00	200.00	500.00
	1862	6,592	50.00	100.00	200.00	500.00
	1863	6,575	50.00	100.00	200.00	500.00

HOHENLOHE

This south German family traces its ancestry to the 900's. In 1209 the house divided but one of the lines became extinct in 1390. Thereafter were numerous divisions with the last major one being in 1600.

MINT MARKS

S - Schwabach

MINTMASTERS INITIALS

Letter	Date	Name
D	1800-1806	Anton Paul Dallinger, die-cutter in Nuremberg
ICE	1803	Johann Christoph Eberhardt, in Wertheim

HOHENLOHE-KIRCHBERG

This principality was located in southern Germany. The Kirchberg line was founded in 1701. The count was raised to the rank of prince of the empire in 1764 and the last prince died in 1819.

RULERS

Christian Friedrich Karl, 1767-1806

1/2 THALER
(Convention)

SILVER

KM#	Date	Mintage	Fine	VF	XF	Unc
15	1804 D	—	250.00	450.00	800.00	1450.

HOHENLOHE-NEUENSTEIN-OEHRINGEN

This principality was located in southern Germany. The Neuenstein-Oehringen line was founded in 1610 and the first prince of the empire from this line was proclaimed in 1764. The line became extinct in 1805 and the lands passed to Ingelfingen.

RULERS

Ludwig Friedrich Karl, 1765-1805

10 KREUZER

(Convention)

SILVER

KM#	Date	Mintage	VG	Fine	VF	XF
70	1803 IC-E	—	20.00	40.00	100.00	250.00

TRADE COINAGE

DUCAT

3.5000 g, .986 GOLD, .1109 oz AGW
81st Birthday - L.F. Karl

KM#	Date	Mintage	Fine	VF	XF	Unc
71	1804 D	—	750.00	1750.	3000.	5000.

2 DUCAT

7.0000 g, .986 GOLD, .2219 oz AGW
81st Birthday L.F. Karl
Obv: Bust right. Rev: Crowned arms.

KM#	Date	Mintage	Fine	VF	XF	Unc
72	1804 D	—	1000.	2000.	3750.	6750.

PATTERNS (Pn)

(Including off metal strikes)

KM#	Date	Mintage	Identification	Mkt.Val.
Pn1	1804 D	—	1 Ducat, Silver, 81st Birthday	150.00

HOHENZOLLERN-HECHINGEN

Located in southern Germany, the Hechingen line was founded in 1576. The family received the mint right in 1471 and the counts were raised to the rank of prince of the empire in 1623. As a result of the 1848 revolutions the prince abdicated in favor of Prussia in 1849.

RULERS

Hermann Friedrich Otto, 1798 - 1810
Friedrich Hermann Otto, 1810 - 1838
Friedrich Wilhelm Constantin, 1838-1849

MINTMASTERS INITIALS

Letter	Date	Name
CH, ICH	1783-1808	Johann Christian Heuglin
C.VOIGT	1829-1873	Carl Friedrich Voigt, medalist in Munich
ILW, W	1798-1845	Johann Ludwig Wagner, die-cutter

ARMS

Hohenzollern: Quartered silver and black.
Office of hereditary chamberlain to the emperor: Crossed sceptres.

3 KREUZER

1.2900 g, .333 SILVER, .0138 oz ASW
Obv: Crowned arms. Rev: Value within wreath.

KM#	Date	Mintage	Fine	VF	XF	Unc
47	1845	.030	10.00	25.00	50.00	160.00
47	1846	.030	10.00	25.00	50.00	160.00
	1847	8,000	15.00	30.00	60.00	200.00

6 KREUZER

2.5900 g, .333 SILVER, .0277 oz ASW
Obv: Crowned arms. Rev: Value within wreath.

KM#	Date	Mintage	Fine	VF	XF	Unc
45	1841	.024	15.00	35.00	60.00	175.00
	1842	.026	15.00	35.00	60.00	175.00
	1845	.025	15.00	35.00	60.00	175.00
	1846	.025	15.00	35.00	60.00	175.00
	1847	.026	15.00	35.00	60.00	175.00

1/2 GULDEN

5.3000 g, .900 SILVER, .1533 oz ASW

KM#	Date	Mintage	Fine	VF	XF	Unc
40	1839	.015	35.00	75.00	150.00	300.00
	1841	6,000	35.00	75.00	150.00	325.00
	1842	5,540	35.00	75.00	150.00	325.00
	1843	6,000	35.00	75.00	150.00	325.00
	1844	6,000	35.00	75.00	150.00	325.00
	1845	6,000	35.00	75.00	150.00	325.00
	1846	6,000	35.00	75.00	150.00	325.00
	1847	6,000	35.00	75.00	150.00	325.00

GULDEN

10.6000 g, .900 SILVER, .3067 oz ASW

KM#	Date	Mintage	Fine	VF	XF	Unc
41	1839	.015	50.00	125.00	200.00	450.00
	1841	6,000	50.00	125.00	200.00	500.00
	1842	6,000	50.00	125.00	200.00	500.00
	1843	8,280	50.00	125.00	200.00	500.00
	1844	6,000	50.00	125.00	200.00	500.00
	1845	5,465	50.00	125.00	200.00	500.00
	1846	5,718	50.00	125.00	200.00	500.00
	1847	6,324	50.00	125.00	200.00	500.00

ZWEY (2) GULDEN

21.2100 g, .900 SILVER, .6138 oz ASW

KM#	Date	Mintage	Fine	VF	XF	Unc
48	1846	4,300	175.00	450.00	1000.	1500.
	1847	4,300	175.00	450.00	800.00	1400.

EIN (1) THALER

28.0600 g, .833 SILVER, .7516 oz ASW

KM#	Date	Mintage	Fine	VF	XF	Unc
35	1804 W-CH	2,000	400.00	800.00	1400.	3000.

Obv: ILH below shoulder.

KM#	Date	Mintage	Fine	VF	XF	Unc
36	1804 ILH-CH	—	400.00	800.00	1400.	3000.

2 THALER

(3-1/2 Gulden)

37.1200 g, .900 SILVER, 1.0742 oz ASW

KM#	Date	Mintage	Fine	VF	XF	Unc
46	1844	2,346	400.00	800.00	1600.	2800.
	1845	1,000	425.00	925.00	1800.	3200.
	1846	570 pcs.	500.00	1000.	2000.	3600.

HOHENZOLLERN-SIGMARINGEN

Located in southern Germany, the Sigmaringen line was founded in 1576. The counts obtained the mint right in 1471 amd were raised to the rank of Prince of the Empire in 1623. As a result of the 1848 revolutions the princes abdicated in favor of Prussia in 1849.

RULERS

Anton Aloys, 1785-1831
Carl, 1831-1848
Carl Anton, 1848-1849

MINTMASTERS INITIALS

Letter	Date	Name
D	1828-1848	Carl Wilhelm Doell, in Karlsruhe
BALBACH	1848-1856	Othemar Balbach, medalist in Karlsruhe

ARMS

Hohenzollern - quartered black and silver
Sigmaringen - stag left

EIN (1) KREUZER

COPPER
Obv: Crowned arms. Rev. value: EIN KREUZER.

KM#	Date	Mintage	Fine	VF	XF	Unc
21	1842	.180	3.00	8.00	25.00	100.00
	1846	.055	4.00	9.00	30.00	120.00

.6200 g, .250 SILVER, .0049 oz ASW
Rev. value: 1 KREUZER.

KM#	Date	Mintage	Fine	VF	XF	Unc
22	1842	.120	3.00	8.00	25.00	100.00
	1846	.060	4.00	9.00	30.00	120.00

3 KREUZER

1.2900 g, .333 SILVER, .0138 oz ASW

KM#	Date	Mintage	Fine	VF	XF	Unc
17	1839	.052	6.00	12.00	35.00	145.00
	1841	.068	6.00	12.00	35.00	145.00
	1842	.072	6.00	12.00	35.00	145.00
	1844	.170	6.00	12.00	35.00	145.00
	1845	.126	6.00	12.00	35.00	145.00
	1846	.126	6.00	12.00	35.00	145.00
	1847	.060	6.00	12.00	35.00	145.00

6 KREUZER

2.5900 g, .333 SILVER, .0277 oz ASW
Obv: Crowned arms. Rev: Value within wreath.

KM#	Date	Mintage	Fine	VF	XF	Unc
18	1839	.075	7.00	15.00	45.00	160.00
	1840	.075	7.00	15.00	45.00	160.00
	1841	.075	7.00	15.00	45.00	160.00
	1842	.074	7.00	15.00	45.00	160.00
	1844	.140	7.00	15.00	45.00	160.00
	1845	.208	7.00	15.00	45.00	160.00
	1846	.208	7.00	15.00	45.00	160.00
	1847	—	7.00	15.00	45.00	160.00

1/2 GULDEN

5.3000 g, .900 SILVER, .1533 oz ASW

KM#	Date	Mintage	Fine	VF	XF	Unc
15	1838	.012	50.00	75.00	135.00	225.00
	1839	.012	50.00	75.00	135.00	225.00
	1840	.012	50.00	75.00	135.00	225.00
	1841	.012	50.00	75.00	135.00	225.00
	1842	.012	50.00	75.00	135.00	225.00
	1843	.012	50.00	75.00	135.00	225.00
	1844	.012	50.00	75.00	135.00	225.00
	1845	.012	50.00	75.00	135.00	225.00
	1846	.012	50.00	75.00	135.00	225.00
	1847	3,068	70.00	110.00	150.00	300.00
	1848	—	50.00	75.00	135.00	225.00

GULDEN

10.6000 g, .900 SILVER, .3067 oz ASW
Obv: Head left, D below. Rev: Value within wreath.

KM#	Date	Mintage	Fine	VF	XF	Unc
16.1	1838 D	—	65.00	125.00	200.00	350.00

Obv: DOELL below head.

KM#	Date	Mintage	Fine	VF	XF	Unc
16.2	1838	.018	65.00	120.00	200.00	350.00
	1839	.012	65.00	120.00	200.00	350.00
	1840	.012	65.00	120.00	200.00	350.00
	1841	.012	65.00	120.00	200.00	350.00
	1842	.012	65.00	120.00	200.00	350.00
	1843	.012	65.00	120.00	200.00	350.00
	1844	.012	65.00	120.00	200.00	350.00
	1845	.012	65.00	120.00	200.00	350.00
	1846	.012	65.00	120.00	200.00	350.00
	1847	.012	65.00	120.00	200.00	350.00
	1848	3,068	90.00	150.00	250.00	425.00

Obv: BALBACH below head

KM#	Date	Mintage	Fine	VF	XF	Unc
25	1849	5,000	150.00	250.00	450.00	675.00

ZWEI (2) GULDEN

21.2100 g, .900 SILVER, .6138 oz ASW

KM#	Date	Mintage	Fine	VF	XF	Unc
24	1845 D	9,206	125.00	250.00	650.00	1200.
	1846 D	9,206	125.00	250.00	650.00	1200.
	1847 D	9,206	125.00	250.00	650.00	1200.
	1848 D	6,905	125.00	250.00	700.00	1300.

Obv: BALBACH below bust.

KM#	Date	Mintage	Fine	VF	XF	Unc
26	1849	1,213	325.00	600.00	900.00	1800.

2 THALER

(3-1/2 Gulden)

37.1200 g, .900 SILVER, 1.0742 oz ASW

KM#	Date	Mintage	Fine	VF	XF	Unc
20	1841	2,857	325.00	600.00	1200.	2400.
	1842	2,857	325.00	600.00	1200.	2400.
	1843	2,877	325.00	600.00	1200.	2400.

Obv: Similar to KM#20.

KM#	Date	Mintage	Fine	VF	XF	Unc
23	1844	3,300	325.00	600.00	1100.	2000.
	1846	6,600	300.00	550.00	1100.	2200.
	1847	2,000	350.00	650.00	1200.	2200.

PIEFORTS (P)

KM#	Date	Mintage	Identification	Mkt.Val.
P1	1840	3	1 Gulden, Silver, KM16.2	—

HOHENZOLLERN (under Prussia)

In 1849, Prussia obtained the Hohenzollern lands due to the 1848 revolutions and political unrest. One series of coins was issued by Prussia for their Hohenzollern holdings.

RULERS

Friedrich Wilhelm IV (of Prussia), 1849-1861

KREUZER

COPPER

KM#	Date	Mintage	Fine	VF	XF	Unc
1	1852A	.030	15.00	30.00	60.00	100.00

3 KREUZER

1.2900 g, .333 SILVER, .0138 oz ASW

KM#	Date	Mintage	Fine	VF	XF	Unc
2	1852A	.022	15.00	30.00	75.00	150.00
	1852A	—	—	—	Proof	150.00

6 KREUZER

2.5900 g, .333 SILVER, .0277 oz ASW

KM#	Date	Mintage	Fine	VF	XF	Unc
3	1852A	.027	20.00	40.00	100.00	200.00
	1852A	—	—	—	Proof	200.00

1/2 GULDEN

5.3000 g, .900 SILVER, .1537 oz ASW

KM#	Date	Mintage	Fine	VF	XF	Unc
4	1852A	.053	65.00	100.00	150.00	225.00

GULDEN

10.6000 g, .900 SILVER, .3067 oz ASW

KM#	Date	Mintage	Fine	VF	XF	Unc
5	1852A	.050	65.00	100.00	150.00	275.00
	1852A	—	—	—	Proof	350.00

Listings For

HOLSTEIN: refer to Denmark
HOLSTEIN-GOTTORP: refer to Denmark

ISENBURG

The lands of the counts of Isenburg lay on both sides of the Main River to the east of Frankfurt. The dynasty traces its lineage back to the 10th century and began issuing coins in the mid-13th century. The county underwent many divisions in the Middle Ages, but by the early 17th century only one dominant branch was producing coins. This was Isenburg-Birstein, divided once again into Isenburg-Offenbach-Birstein and Isenburg-Budingen in 1635. The latter was further divided into four branches in 1673/1687 and two of the substrata became extinct in 1725 and 1780 respectively. Isenburg-Offenbach-Birstein was raised to the rank of prince in 1744 and all other branches had to relinquish their sovereignty to his descendant in 1806. The latter lost his sole leadership in 1813 because he sided with Napoleon and the lands of Isenburg-Offenbach-Birstein were mediatized to Hesse-Darmstadt in 1815. The subdivisions of Isenburg-Budigen did not issue a regular coinage, but struck the series of the quasi-official snipe hellers during the 19th century.

RULERS

Wolfgang Ernst II, 1754-1803
Karl I, 1803-1820
Wolfgang Ernst III, 1820-1866
Karl II, 1866-

Isenburg-Budingen

Ernst Kasimir II, 1775-1801
Ernst Kasimir III, 1801-1848
Adolf II (in Wachtersbach), 1805-1847
Ernst Kasimir IV, 1848-1861
Bruno, 1861-1906

6 KREUZER

BILLON

KM#	Date	Mintage	Fine	VF	XF	Unc
46	1811	1,000	50.00	100.00	225.00	425.00

12 KREUZER

(Kipper)

SILVER
Obv: J. LAROQUE F. at truncation.

KM#	Date	Mintage	Fine	VF	XF	Unc
47	1811	500 pcs.	65.00	135.00	275.00	475.00

EIN (1) THALER

(Reichs)

SILVER

KM#	Date	Mintage	Fine	VF	XF	Unc
48	1811	100 pcs.	600.00	1200.	2500.	4500.

TRADE COINAGE

DUCAT

3.5000 g, .986 GOLD, .1109 oz AGW

KM#	Date	Mintage	Fine	VF	XF	Unc
49	1811	—	—	—	—	—

2 DUCAT

7.0000 g, .986 GOLD, .2218 oz AGW

KM#	Date	Mintage	Fine	VF	XF	Unc
50	1811	—	1500.	3000.	6000.	10,000.

NOTE: Struck w/1 Ducat dies, KM#49.

MEDALLIC ISSUES

(HELLER)

(Snipe Heller)

COPPER
Obv: In laurel wreath, ECGJ in script monogram.
Rev: Snipe standing left in grass.

KM#	Date	Mintage	VG	Fine	VF	XF
M1	ND(1824)	—	10.00	20.00	40.00	60.00

Obv: ECGY monogram. Rev: W/o grass.

KM#	Date	Mintage	VG	Fine	VF	XF
M2	ND(1828)	—	10.00	20.00	40.00	60.00

Obv: ECFzY monogram. Rev: Snipe on mound.

KM#	Date	Mintage	VG	Fine	VF	XF
M3	ND(1840)	—	10.00	20.00	40.00	60.00

Struck at Frankfurt am Main

Obv: AJ script monogram in laurel wreath.

KM#	Date	Mintage	VG	Fine	VF	XF
M4	ND(1847)	—	10.00	20.00	40.00	60.00

Obv: BFzY in laurel wreath.

KM#	Date	Mintage	VG	Fine	VF	XF
M5	ND(1861)	—	10.00	20.00	40.00	60.00
	ND(1861)	—	—	—	Proof	100.00

Obv: WFzY monogram.
Rev: Snipe standing right in grass.

KM#	Date	Mintage	VG	Fine	VF	XF
M6	ND	—	15.00	30.00	60.00	85.00
	ND	—	—	—	Proof	140.00

PATTERNS (Pn)

(Including off metal strikes)

KM#	Date	Mintage	Identification	Mkt.Val.
Pn1	ND	—	1 Heller, Silver, KM58	—
Pn2	1805	—	1 Pfennig, Silver, KM45	—
Pn3	1811	—	12 Kreuzer, Copper, KM47	—
Pn4	1811	—	1 Thaler, Copper, KM48	—

KM#	Date	Mintage	Identification	Mkt.Val.
Pn5	1811	—	1 Ducat, Silver, KM49	200.00
Pn6	1811	—	2 Ducat, Silver, KM50	300.00

PIEFORTS (P)

KM#	Date	Mintage	Identification	Mkt.Val.
P1	1811	—	1 Thaler, Silver, KM48	*Rare

***NOTE:** Munzhandlung Moller Auction 10 10-92 XF+/VF realized $50,600.

KNYPHAUSEN

The district of Knyphausen was located in northwestern Germany in East Friesland. Local nobility ruled from the 14th century until 1623 when it was sold to Oldenburg. It became autonomous in 1653 and was acquired through marriage to the Bentinck family in 1733. Coins were struck c. 1800. It was claimed by both Anhalt and Oldenburg and the arms of Knyphausen appear on coins of both places.

RULERS

Wilhelm Gustav Friedrich, 1774-1835

9 GROTE

(1/8 Thaler)

SILVER
Obv: Arms.
Rev: Crowned double-headed eagle dividing value.

KM#	Date	Mintage	Fine	VF	XF	Unc
5 (C2)	1807	—	350.00	650.00	1400.	2000.

KM#	Date	Mintage	Fine	VF	XF	Unc
6 (C1)	1807	.016	145.00	285.00	550.00	825.00

PATTERNS (Pn)

(Including off metal strikes)

KM#	Date	Mintage	Identification	Mkt.Val.
Pn1	1806	10 pcs.	2-1/2 Thaler, Gold	—
Pn2	1806	—	5 Thaler, Gold	—
Pn3	1806	—	10 Thaler, Gold	—

LAUENBURG

The line of rulers of this Saxon duchy became extinct in 1689 and passed to Brunswick-Luneburg-Celle, then to Brunswick-Luneburg-Calenberg-Hannover in 1705. After the Napoleonic Wars, Lauenburg went to Prussia in 1813, to Denmark in 1814, and was regained by Prussia as part of the latter's annexation of Holstein in 1864. The Brunswick duches struck special coins for Lauenburg. See Saxe-Lauenburg for coinage prior to 1689.

RULERS

Georg III von Brunswick-Luneburg-Calenberg-Hannover, 1760-1818

Frederick VI (of Denmark), 1816-1839

MINTMASTERS INITIALS

Letter	Date	Name
FF	1830	Johann Friedrich Freund

2/3 THALER

17.3200 g, .750 SILVER, .4177 oz ASW

KM#	Date	Mintage	Fine	VF	XF	Unc
25 (C1)	1830 FF	—	150.00	300.00	550.00	900.00

LEININGEN-DAGSBURG-HARTENBURG

Established from an early division of Leiningen in 1317 and further divided in 1541, Leiningen-Dagsburg-Hartenburg was located some 30 miles west-southwest of Mannheim. The count was raised to the rank of prince in 1779 and was the only member of his line to issue any coins. His possessions were taken by France in 1801.

RULERS

Karl Friedrich Wilhelm, 1756-1807

PFENNIG

BILLON
Obv: Eagles below crown within branches.
Rev: Value.

KM#	Date	Mintage	Fine	VF	XF	Unc
7	1805	—	35.00	75.00	165.00	300.00

2 PFENNIG

BILLON
Obv: Crowned arms. Rev: Value, branch below.

KM#	Date	Mintage	Fine	VF	XF	Unc
8	1805	—	50.00	100.00	220.00	400.00

3 KREUZER

BILLON
Obv: Crowned arms within branches.
Rev: Value, branch below.

KM#	Date	Mintage	Fine	VF	XF	Unc
5	1804	—	40.00	90.00	220.00	400.00

KM#	Date	Mintage	Fine	VF	XF	Unc
9	1805	—	35.00	75.00	185.00	350.00

6 KREUZER

BILLON
Obv: Crowned arms within branches.
Rev: Value, branch below.

KM#	Date	Mintage	Fine	VF	XF	Unc
6	1804	—	50.00	125.00	325.00	600.00

KM#	Date	Mintage	Fine	VF	XF	Unc
10	1805	—	40.00	90.00	220.00	400.00

LIPPE-DETMOLD

The Counts of Lippe ruled over a small state in northwestern Germany. In 1528/9 they became counts; in 1720 they were raised to the rank of princes, but did not use the title until 1789. Another branch of the family ruled the even smaller Schaumburg-Lippe. Lippe joined North German Confederation in 1866, and became part of the German Empire in 1871. When the insane Prince Alexander succeeded to the throne in 1895, the main branch reached an end, and a ten-year testamentary dispute between the Biesterfeld and the Schaumburg-Lippe lines followed - a Wilhelmine cause celebre. The Biesterfeld line gained the principality in 1905, but abdicated in 1918. In 1947 Lippe was absorbed by the German Land of North Rhine-Westphalia.

RULERS

Friedrich Wilhelm Leopold
Alone, 1789-1802

Paul Alexander Leopold II
under Regency of Pauline of Anhalt-Bernburg, 1802-1820
As Independent Prince, 1820-1851

Paul Friedrich Emil Leopold III, 1851-1875

Woldemar, 1875 - 1895

Alexander, 1895 - 1905

MINT MARKS

A - Berlin, 1843-1918
ST - Strickling (Blomberg), 1820-1840
T - Trebbe (Lemgo), 1812-1820

MINTMASTERS INITIALS

Letter	Date	Name
ST	1820-40	Strickling of Blomberg
T	1812-20	Trebbe of Lemgo
	1789-1803	Balthasar Reinhard
	1803	Siegmann

HELLER

COPPER

KM#	Date	Mintage	Fine	VF	XF	Unc
225	1802 T	.166	9.00	15.00	30.00	65.00
	1802	Inc. Ab.	2.00	5.00	15.00	55.00
	1809 T	.108	2.00	5.00	15.00	55.00
	1812 T	—	2.00	5.00	15.00	55.00
	1814 T	—	2.00	5.00	15.00	55.00
	1816 T	—	2.00	5.00	15.00	55.00
	1816	—	2.00	5.00	15.00	55.00

Obv: Blooming rose. Rev. value: I HELLER, date.

KM#	Date	Mintage	Fine	VF	XF	Unc
241	1821ST	—	2.00	4.00	10.00	40.00
	1822ST	—	2.00	4.00	10.00	40.00
	1825ST	—	2.00	4.00	10.00	40.00
	1826ST	—	2.00	4.00	10.00	40.00
	1828ST	—	2.00	4.00	10.00	40.00
	1835ST	—	2.00	4.00	10.00	40.00
	1836ST	—	2.00	4.00	10.00	40.00
	1840ST	—	2.00	4.00	10.00	40.00

Rev. value: 1 HELLER, date.

KM#	Date	Mintage	Fine	VF	XF	Unc
244	1826 ST	—	2.00	4.00	10.00	40.00

PFENNING

COPPER

KM#	Date	Mintage	Fine	VF	XF	Unc
226	1802	.120	5.00	10.00	30.00	100.00

Rev: T below date.

KM#	Date	Mintage	Fine	VF	XF	Unc
235	1818 T	—	4.00	8.00	20.00	90.00

Rev: W/o T.

KM#	Date	Mintage	Fine	VF	XF	Unc
236	1818	—	4.00	8.00	20.00	90.00

Rev: ST below date.

KM#	Date	Mintage	Fine	VF	XF	Unc
240	1820 ST	—	3.00	7.00	15.00	60.00
	1821 ST	—	3.00	7.00	15.00	60.00
	1824 ST	—	3.00	7.00	15.00	60.00
	1825 ST	—	3.00	7.00	15.00	60.00

Rev. value: PFENNING

KM#	Date	Mintage	Fine	VF	XF	Unc
242	1821 ST	—	—	—	—	—
	1824 ST	—	3.00	7.00	20.00	85.00

KM#	Date	Mintage	Fine	VF	XF	Unc
245	1828 ST	—	2.00	5.00	15.00	60.00
	1829 ST	—	2.00	5.00	15.00	60.00
	1830 ST	—	2.00	5.00	15.00	60.00
	1836 ST	—	2.00	5.00	15.00	60.00
	1840 ST	—	2.00	5.00	15.00	60.00

KM#	Date	Mintage	Fine	VF	XF	Unc
251	1847 A	.972	1.00	3.00	7.00	40.00

KM#	Date	Mintage	Fine	VF	XF	Unc
260	1851 A	1.080	1.00	3.00	7.00	35.00
	1858 A	.900	1.00	3.00	7.00	35.00

1-1/2 PFENNING

(1/192 Thaler)

COPPER

KM#	Date	Mintage	Fine	VF	XF	Unc
243	1821 T	—	3.00	6.00	18.00	65.00
	1823 T	—	3.00	6.00	18.00	65.00
	1824 T	—	3.00	6.00	18.00	65.00
	1825 T	—	3.00	6.00	18.00	65.00

2 PFENNING

COPPER
Obv: Blooming rose.
Rev: Value, rosette below date.

KM#	Date	Mintage	Fine	VF	XF	Unc
227	1802	.127	6.00	12.00	35.00	120.00

3 PFENNINGE

COPPER
Obv: Crowned shield w/blooming rose. Rev: Value.

KM#	Date	Mintage	Fine	VF	XF	Unc
252	1847A	1.020	2.00	5.00	15.00	60.00

KM#	Date	Mintage	Fine	VF	XF	Unc
261	1858A	.060	3.00	7.00	20.00	75.00

1/2 SILBER GROSCHEN

.9700 g, .250 SILVER, .0077 oz ASW
Obv: Head right. Rev: Value.

KM#	Date	Mintage	Fine	VF	XF	Unc
253	1847A	.321	6.00	12.00	35.00	100.00

MARIENGROSCHEN

BILLON

Obv: Arms. Rev: Value and date.

KM#	Date	Mintage	VG	Fine	VF	XF
228	1802	—	3.00	6.00	18.00	45.00
	1803	—	3.00	6.00	18.00	45.00

KM#	Date	Mintage	VG	Fine	VF	XF
229	1804	—	3.00	6.00	18.00	45.00

SILBER GROSCHEN

1.5500 g, .312 SILVER, .0155 oz ASW

KM#	Date	Mintage	Fine	VF	XF	Unc
254	1847A	.750	5.00	10.00	25.00	60.00

2.1900 g, .220 SILVER, .0154 oz ASW

KM#	Date	Mintage	Fine	VF	XF	Unc
265	1860A	.432	6.00	12.00	30.00	75.00

2-1/2 SILBER GROSCHEN

3.2400 g, .375 SILVER, .0390 oz ASW

Obv: Head right. Rev: Value.

KM#	Date	Mintage	Fine	VF	XF	Unc
255	1847A	.363	5.00	10.00	25.00	85.00

3.2200 g, .375 SILVER, .0388 oz ASW

KM#	Date	Mintage	Fine	VF	XF	Unc
266	1860A	.120	5.00	10.00	25.00	85.00

EIN (1) THALER

18.5200 g, .900 SILVER, .5360 oz ASW

KM#	Date	Mintage	Fine	VF	XF	Unc
267	1860A	.026	40.00	75.00	150.00	300.00
	1866A	.018	45.00	80.00	165.00	325.00

2 THALER

(3-1/2 Gulden)

37.1200 g, .900 SILVER, 1.0742 oz ASW

KM#	Date	Mintage	Fine	VF	XF	Unc
250	1843A	.017	200.00	400.00	750.00	1500.

LOWENSTEIN-WERTHEIM-ROCHEFORT

Rochefort was the Catholic branch of Lowenstein-Wertheim, established in 1635. From 1622 until about 1650, coinage for Lowenstein-Wertheim-Rochefort was struck at the mint of Cugnon in Luxembourg. The ruler was made Prince of the Empire in 1711. All lands in his possession were mediatized in 1806.

RULERS

Dominik Constantin, 1789-1806

MINT

Cugnon Mint in Luxembourg

PFENNING

COPPER

KM#	Date	Mintage	VG	Fine	VF	XF
100	1801	—	6.00	12.00	40.00	185.00
	1802	—	6.00	12.00	40.00	185.00

NOTE: Earlier date (1800) exists for this type.

LOWENSTEIN-WERTHEIM-VIRNEBURG & ROCHEFORT

JOINT COINAGE

PFENNING

COPPER

KM#	Date	Mintage	VG	Fine	VF	XF
28	1802	—	3.00	6.00	12.00	50.00
	1804	—	3.00	6.00	12.00	50.00

Obv: Spade shield

KM#	Date	Mintage	VG	Fine	VF	XF
30	1804	—	3.00	5.00	10.00	40.00

Obv: (error) L.M. above shield.

KM#	Date	Mintage	VG	Fine	VF	XF
31	1804	—	7.00	15.00	40.00	100.00

BILLON, uniface

Eagle above 3 roses, value: 1 PF above.

KM#	Date	Mintage	VG	Fine	VF	XF
25	1801	—	5.00	10.00	25.00	65.00
(C138)	1802	—	5.00	10.00	25.00	65.00
	1803	—	5.00	10.00	25.00	65.00
	1804	—	5.00	10.00	25.00	65.00

NOTE: Earlier dates (1798-1800) exist for this type.

Tear shaped arms.

KM#	Date	Mintage	VG	Fine	VF	XF
29	1802	—	6.00	12.00	30.00	70.00

KREUZER

BILLON

KM#	Date	Mintage	VG	Fine	VF	XF
26	1801	—	4.00	9.00	20.00	60.00
	1802	—	4.00	9.00	20.00	60.00
	1803	—	4.00	9.00	20.00	60.00
	1804	—	4.00	9.00	20.00	60.00
	1805	—	4.00	9.00	20.00	60.00
	1806	—	4.00	9.00	20.00	60.00

NOTE: Varieties exist.

NOTE: Earlier date (1800) exists for this type.

3 KREUZER

BILLON

Obv: Arms. Rev: Value

KM#	Date	Mintage	Fine	VF	XF	Unc
27.1	1801	—	8.00	16.00	45.00	150.00

NOTE: Earlier date (1800) exists for this type.

KM#	Date	Mintage	Fine	VF	XF	Unc
27.2	1802	—	8.00	16.00	45.00	150.00
	1803	—	8.00	16.00	45.00	150.00

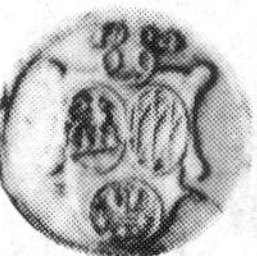

KM#	Date	Mintage	Fine	VF	XF	Unc
27.3	1804	—	8.00	14.00	40.00	130.00
	1805	—	8.00	14.00	40.00	130.00

NOTE: Earlier date (1800) exists for this type.

SILVER

KM#	Date	Mintage	Fine	VF	XF	Unc
32	1805	—	—	—	225.00	—

LUBECK

FREE CITY

Lubeck became a free city of the empire in 1188 and from c. 1190 into the 13th century an imperial mint existed in the town. It was granted the mint right in 1188, 1226 and 1340, but actually began its first civic coinage c. 1350. Occupied by the French during the Napoleonic Wars, it was restored as a free city in 1813 and became part of the German Empire in 1871.

MINTMASTERS INITIALS

Letter	Date	Name
HDF	1773-1801	Hermann David Friederichsen

TRADE COINAGE

DUCAT

3.5000 g, .986 GOLD, .1109 oz AGW

KM#	Date	Mintage	Fine	VF	XF	Unc
205	1801 HDF	—	400.00	750.00	1250.	1650.

MECKLENBURG-SCHWERIN

The duchy of Mecklenburg was located along the Baltic coast between Holstein and Pomerania. Schwerin was annexed to Mecklenburg in 1357. During the Thirty Years' War, the dukes of Mecklenburg sided with the Protestant forces against the emperor. Albrecht von Wallenstein, the imperialist general, ousted the Mecklenburg dukes from their territories in 1628. They were restored to their lands in 1632. In 1658 the Mecklenburg dynasty was divided into two lines. No coinage was produced for Mecklenburg-Schwerin from 1708 until 1750. The 1815 Congress of Vienna elevated the duchy to the status of grand duchy and it became a part of the German Empire in 1871 until 1918 when the last grand duke abdicated.

RULERS

Friedrich Franz I, 1785-1837
Paul Friedrich, 1837-1842
Friedrich Franz II, 1842-1883
Friedrich Franz III, 1883-1897
Friedrich Franz IV, 1897-1918

MINT MARKS

A - Berlin
B - Hannover

PFENNIG

COPPER

KM#	Date	Mintage	Fine	VF	XF	Unc
280	1831	.514	3.00	6.00	12.00	45.00

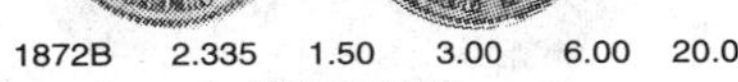

KM#	Date	Mintage	Fine	VF	XF	Unc
315	1872B	2.335	1.50	3.00	6.00	20.00

2 PFENNIG

COPPER

KM#	Date	Mintage	Fine	VF	XF	Unc
281	1831	.257	3.00	6.00	12.00	60.00

KM#	Date	Mintage	Fine	VF	XF	Unc
316	1872B	1.155	2.00	4.00	8.00	30.00

3 PFENNIG

(1 Dreiling)

.5000 g, .187 SILVER, .0030 oz ASW
Rev. leg ends: . . . MECK.SCHWERIN:SCHEID

KM#	Date	Mintage	Fine	VF	XF	Unc
240	1801	.204	3.50	6.50	14.00	65.00
	1803	.117	3.50	6.50	14.00	65.00
	1804	.113	3.50	6.50	14.00	65.00
	1805	.414	3.50	6.50	14.00	65.00
	1810	.117	3.50	6.50	14.00	65.00
	1811	.273	3.50	6.50	14.00	65.00
	1813	—	3.50	6.50	15.00	80.00
	1814	.060	3.50	6.50	15.00	80.00
	1815	.081	3.50	6.50	15.00	80.00

BILLON
Obv: Crowned FF monogram.
Rev: Value.

KM#	Date	Mintage	Fine	VF	XF	Unc
251	1816	.199	3.00	6.00	15.00	70.00
	1817	.083	3.00	6.00	15.00	80.00
	1818	.077	3.00	6.00	15.00	80.00
	1819	.251	3.00	6.00	15.00	70.00

Rev. value: I DREILING, date.

KM#	Date	Mintage	Fine	VF	XF	Unc
255	1819	.596	2.50	5.00	10.00	45.00
	1820	.845	2.50	5.00	10.00	45.00
	1821	.516	2.50	5.00	10.00	45.00
	1822	1.021	2.50	5.00	10.00	45.00
	1824	.235	2.50	5.00	10.00	45.00

.4500 g, .125 SILVER, .0018 oz ASW

KM#	Date	Mintage	Fine	VF	XF	Unc
267	1828	.684	2.00	4.00	8.00	40.00
	1829	.207	2.00	4.00	8.00	40.00
	1830	.793	2.00	4.00	8.00	40.00

KM#	Date	Mintage	Fine	VF	XF	Unc
282	1831	.064	3.00	6.00	12.00	60.00
	1832	.308	3.00	5.00	8.00	40.00
	1833	.048	4.00	8.00	20.00	70.00
	1836	.452	3.00	5.00	8.00	40.00

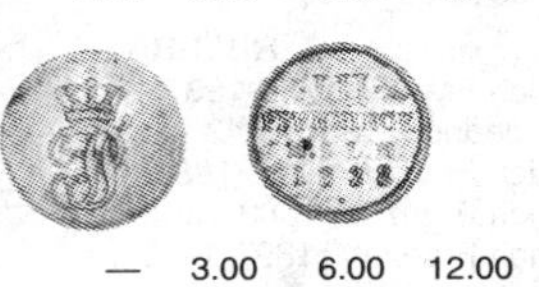

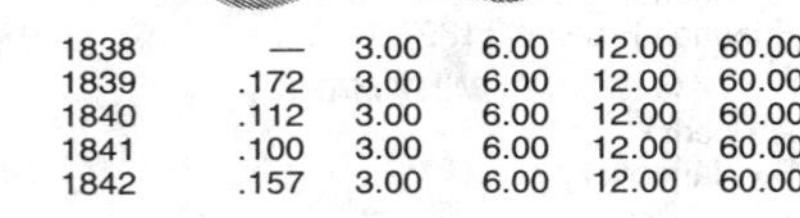

KM#	Date	Mintage	Fine	VF	XF	Unc
285	1838	—	3.00	6.00	12.00	60.00
	1839	.172	3.00	6.00	12.00	60.00
	1840	.112	3.00	6.00	12.00	60.00
	1841	.100	3.00	6.00	12.00	60.00
	1842	.157	3.00	6.00	12.00	60.00

KM#	Date	Mintage	Fine	VF	XF	Unc
297	1842	.203	3.00	5.00	10.00	55.00
	1843	.230	3.00	5.00	10.00	55.00
	1844	.125	3.00	5.00	10.00	55.00
	1845	.170	3.00	5.00	10.00	55.00
	1846	.077	3.00	6.00	14.00	65.00

COPPER

KM#	Date	Mintage	Fine	VF	XF	Unc
299	1843	.089	2.50	5.00	10.00	45.00
	1845	.151	2.50	5.00	10.00	45.00
	1846	.073	2.50	5.00	10.00	45.00
	1848	—	2.50	5.00	10.00	45.00

KM#	Date	Mintage	Fine	VF	XF	Unc
310	1852A	—	2.00	3.50	7.00	32.00
	1853A	—	2.00	3.50	7.00	32.00
	1854A	—	2.00	3.50	7.00	32.00
	1855A	1.135	2.00	3.50	7.00	32.00
	1858A	—	2.00	3.50	7.00	32.00
	1859A	—	2.00	3.50	7.00	32.00
	1860A	—	2.00	3.50	7.00	32.00
	1861A	—	2.00	3.50	7.00	32.00
	1863A	—	2.00	3.50	7.00	32.00
	1864A	1.076	2.00	3.50	7.00	32.00

5 PFENNIG

COPPER

KM#	Date	Mintage	Fine	VF	XF	Unc
317	1872B	.459	7.00	15.00	35.00	75.00

6 PFENNIG

.7600 g, .250 SILVER, .0061 oz ASW

KM#	Date	Mintage	Fine	VF	XF	Unc
241	1801	.080	4.00	7.00	20.00	65.00
	1802	.141	4.00	7.00	20.00	65.00
	1803	.060	4.00	7.00	20.00	65.00
	1804	.062	4.00	7.00	20.00	65.00
	1805	.321	4.00	7.00	20.00	65.00
	1809	.084	4.00	7.00	20.00	65.00
	1810	.081	4.00	7.00	20.00	65.00
	1811	.222	4.00	7.00	20.00	65.00
	1813	.254	4.00	7.00	20.00	65.00
	1815	.199	4.00	7.00	20.00	65.00

Obv: Crowned FF monogram. Rev: Value 6 PFEN.

KM#	Date	Mintage	Fine	VF	XF	Unc
252	1816	.255	4.00	7.00	20.00	65.00
	1817	.300	4.00	7.00	20.00	65.00

.9000 g, .125 SILVER, .0036 oz ASW
W/o legends.

KM#	Date	Mintage	Fine	VF	XF	Unc
283	1831	.128	4.00	8.00	22.00	75.00

SECHSLING

.7600 g, .250 SILVER, .0061 oz ASW

KM#	Date	Mintage	Fine	VF	XF	Unc
260	1820	.150	3.00	6.00	12.00	60.00
	1821	.249	3.00	6.00	12.00	60.00
	1822	.272	3.00	6.00	12.00	60.00
	1823	.320	3.00	6.00	12.00	60.00
	1824	.419	3.00	6.00	12.00	60.00

.9000 g, .125 SILVER, .0036 oz ASW

KM#	Date	Mintage	Fine	VF	XF	Unc
268	1828	—	3.00	6.00	12.00	60.00
	1829	.190	3.00	6.00	12.00	60.00

SCHILLING

1.0800 g, .375 SILVER, .0130 oz ASW
Obv: Crowned FF monogram. Rev. value: 1/SCHILLING/COURANT/MECKLENB/
1.0800 g, .375 SILVER, .0130 oz ASW

KM#	Date	Mintage	Fine	VF	XF	Unc
220	1801	1.301	4.00	8.00	20.00	65.00
	1802	2.431	4.00	8.00	20.00	65.00
	1803	2.348	4.00	8.00	20.00	65.00
	1804	2.603	4.00	8.00	20.00	65.00
	1805	2.501	4.00	8.00	20.00	65.00
	1806	1.766	4.00	8.00	20.00	65.00
	1807	.585	4.00	8.00	20.00	65.00
	1808	.243	4.00	8.00	20.00	65.00
	1809	.342	4.00	8.00	20.00	65.00
	1810	.250	4.00	8.00	20.00	65.00

NOTE: Earlier dates (1785-1800) exist for this type.

Rev: Value.

KM#	Date	Mintage	Fine	VF	XF	Unc
253	1817	.031	10.00	20.00	50.00	250.00

1.1100 g, .312 SILVER, .0111 oz ASW
Obv. leg: GR. HZ. U.M.S.

KM#	Date	Mintage	Fine	VF	XF	Unc
263	1826	.159	3.00	7.00	20.00	80.00
	1827	.342	3.00	7.00	20.00	80.00

Obv. leg: GR. HERZOG V. Rev: Value, legend.

KM#	Date	Mintage	Fine	VF	XF	Unc
273	1829	.054	5.00	10.00	25.00	90.00
	1830	.501	3.00	6.00	12.00	55.00
	1831	.528	3.00	6.00	12.00	55.00
	1832	.119	3.00	7.00	15.00	75.00
	1833	.091	3.00	7.00	15.00	75.00
	1834	.118	3.00	7.00	15.00	75.00
	1835	.109	3.00	7.00	15.00	75.00
	1836	.163	3.00	7.00	15.00	75.00
	1837	.082	3.00	7.00	15.00	75.00

Obv: Crowned PF monogram

KM#	Date	Mintage	Fine	VF	XF	Unc
286	1838	.021	5.00	10.00	25.00	115.00
	1839	.125	4.00	7.00	15.00	65.00
	1840	.052	4.00	7.00	15.00	75.00
	1841	.046	4.00	7.00	15.00	75.00
	1842	.030	5.00	10.00	25.00	100.00

BILLON

KM#	Date	Mintage	Fine	VF	XF	Unc
298	1842	.108	3.00	6.00	12.00	50.00
	1843	.139	3.00	6.00	12.00	50.00
	1844	.116	3.00	6.00	12.00	50.00
	1845	.246	3.00	6.00	12.00	50.00
	1846	.154	3.00	6.00	12.00	50.00

4 SCHILLING

3.0600 g, .562 SILVER, .0553 oz ASW

KM#	Date	Mintage	Fine	VF	XF	Unc
221	1809	1,408	50.00	90.00	150.00	500.00

NOTE: Earlier date (1785) exists for this type.

3.3000 g, .437 SILVER, .0464 oz ASW

KM#	Date	Mintage	Fine	VF	XF	Unc
264	1826	.621	10.00	15.00	35.00	130.00

3.0600 g, .500 SILVER, .0492 oz ASW
Obv: Head left, leg: GR. HERZOG. . .

KM#	Date	Mintage	Fine	VF	XF	Unc
269	1828	.070	15.00	25.00	50.00	185.00

Obv. leg: GROSSHERZOG. . .

KM#	Date	Mintage	Fine	VF	XF	Unc
274	1829	.200	10.00	15.00	35.00	120.00
	1830	1.793	10.00	15.00	35.00	120.00
	1831	.476	10.00	15.00	35.00	120.00
	1832	.121	10.00	15.00	35.00	120.00
	1833	.049	10.00	20.00	40.00	135.00

Obv: Crowned arms within 2 crossed branches.

KM#	Date	Mintage	Fine	VF	XF	Unc
287	1838	.015	10.00	20.00	45.00	145.00
	1839	.039	10.00	20.00	40.00	135.00

8 SCHILLING

6.6000 g, .437 SILVER, .0927 oz ASW

KM#	Date	Mintage	Fine	VF	XF	Unc
266	1827	.025	22.00	45.00	135.00	300.00

1/48 THALER

1.3000 g, .208 SILVER, .0086 oz ASW

KM#	Date	Mintage	Fine	VF	XF	Unc
301	1848	—	4.00	8.00	20.00	75.00

KM#	Date	Mintage	Fine	VF	XF	Unc
311	1852A	—	3.00	6.00	15.00	65.00
	1853A	—	3.00	6.00	15.00	65.00
	1855A	2.819	3.00	6.00	15.00	65.00
	1858A	—	3.00	6.00	15.00	65.00
	1860A	—	3.00	6.00	15.00	65.00
	1861A	—	3.00	6.00	15.00	65.00
	1862A	—	3.00	6.00	15.00	65.00
	1863A	—	3.00	6.00	15.00	65.00
	1864A	—	3.00	6.00	15.00	65.00
	1866A	2.034	3.00	6.00	15.00	65.00

1/12 THALER

2.4400 g, .500 SILVER, .0392 oz ASW

KM#	Date	Mintage	Fine	VF	XF	Unc
302	1848	2.047	6.00	12.00	35.00	90.00

NOTE: Varieties exist.

1/6 THALER

5.3500 g, .520 SILVER, .0894 oz ASW

KM#	Date	Mintage	Fine	VF	XF	Unc
303	1848A	.137	10.00	25.00	75.00	125.00

2/3 THALER

17.3200 g, .750 SILVER, .4177 oz ASW

KM#	Date	Mintage	Fine	VF	XF	Unc
225	1801	.169	30.00	70.00	120.00	260.00
	1808	.655	30.00	70.00	120.00	260.00
	1810	.338	30.00	70.00	120.00	260.00

NOTE: Earlier dates (1789-1800) exist for this type.

KM#	Date	Mintage	Fine	VF	XF	Unc
250	1813	9,918	75.00	125.00	250.00	450.00

Obv. leg: . . . G.G. HERZOG. . .
Rev: Date below value.

KM#	Date	Mintage	Fine	VF	XF	Unc
254	1817	6,783	275.00	450.00	800.00	1250.

Obv: leg: . . . G.G. GR. HERZ. . .

KM#	Date	Mintage	Fine	VF	XF	Unc
261	1825	.035	85.00	175.00	325.00	625.00

Obv. leg. ends: . . . SCHW.

KM#	Date	Mintage	Fine	VF	XF	Unc
262	1825	.043	100.00	175.00	300.00	600.00
	1826	—	100.00	175.00	300.00	600.00

Obv. leg. ends: . . . SCHWERIN.

KM#	Date	Mintage	Fine	VF	XF	Unc
265	1826	.103	100.00	175.00	300.00	600.00

KM#	Date	Mintage	Fine	VF	XF	Unc
270	1828	.057	100.00	175.00	300.00	600.00
275	1829	—	—	—	Rare	—

13.1700 g, .986 SILVER, .4175 oz ASW

KM#	Date	Mintage	Fine	VF	XF	Unc
288	1839	.291	30.00	70.00	125.00	250.00
	1840	.856	25.00	50.00	100.00	200.00
	1841	.118	35.00	75.00	150.00	300.00

KM#	Date	Mintage	Fine	VF	XF	Unc
300	1845	1,563	375.00	550.00	825.00	1250.

EIN (1) THALER

22.2700 g, .750 SILVER, .5370 oz ASW

KM#	Date	Mintage	Fine	VF	XF	Unc
304 (C111)	1848A	.528	30.00	60.00	120.00	225.00

18.5200 g, .900 SILVER, .5360 oz ASW

KM#	Date	Mintage	Fine	VF	XF	Unc
310 (C112)	1864A	.100	30.00	65.00	150.00	285.00

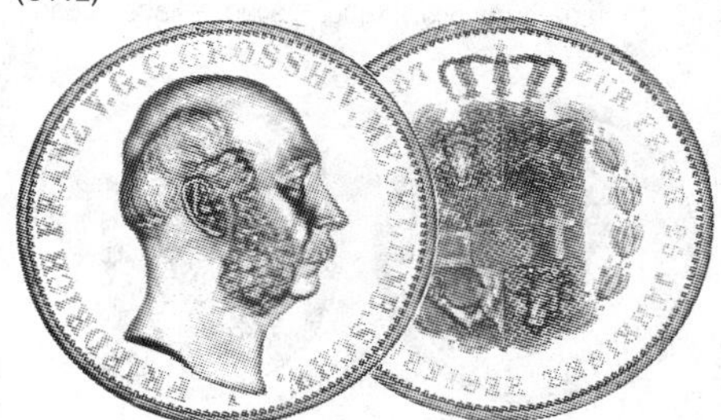

25th Anniversary of Reign

KM#	Date	Mintage	Fine	VF	XF	Unc
311 (C113)	1867A	.010	35.00	75.00	175.00	325.00

ZWEI EIN HALB (2-1/2) THALER

3.3300 g, .896 GOLD, .0959 oz AGW

KM#	Date	Mintage	Fine	VF	XF	Unc
284	1831	7,755	375.00	750.00	1250.	2500.
(C90)	1833	124 pcs.	600.00	1000.	1750.	2500.
	1835	195 pcs.	600.00	1000.	1750.	2500.

KM#	Date	Mintage	Fine	VF	XF	Unc
295 (C98)	1840	2,910	300.00	500.00	750.00	1100.

FUNF (5) THALER

6.6600 g, .896 GOLD, .1919 oz AGW

KM#	Date	Mintage	Fine	VF	XF	Unc
271	1828	1,753	600.00	1200.	1800.	3000.
(C92)	1831	3,878	600.00	1200.	1800.	3000.
	1832	3,334	600.00	1200.	1800.	3000.
	1833	125 pcs.	1000.	1200.	3000.	4000.
	1835	100 pcs.	1000.	1200.	3000.	4000.

KM#	Date	Mintage	Fine	VF	XF	Unc
296 (C99)	1840	1,454	650.00	1250.	1750.	3000.

ZEHN (10) THALER

13.3200 g, .896 GOLD, .3837 oz AGW

KM#	Date	Mintage	Fine	VF	XF	Unc
272	1828	876 pcs.	1250.	2500.	3750.	5000.
(C93)	1831	1,938	1000.	2000.	3250.	4250.
	1832	1,667	1000.	2000.	3250.	4250.
	1833	128 pcs.	1500.	3000.	4500.	6000.

KM#	Date	Mintage	Fine	VF	XF	Unc
289 (C100)	1839	.092	500.00	1100.	1500.	2000.

MONETARY REFORM

ZWEI (2) MARK

11.1110 g, .900 SILVER, .3215 OZ ASW

KM#	Date	Mintage	Fine	VF	XF	Unc
320	1876A	.300	100.00	250.00	750.00	1750.
(Y89)	1876A	—	—	—	Proof	2000.

10 MARK

3.9820 g, .900 GOLD, .1152 oz AGW
Rev: Type I.

KM#	Date	Mintage	Fine	VF	XF	Unc
318	1872A	.016	700.00	1000.	1500.	2750.
(Y90)	1872A	100 pcs.	—	—	Proof	Rare

Rev: Type II.

KM#	Date	Mintage	Fine	VF	XF	Unc
321	1878A	.050	300.00	500.00	700.00	1000.
(Y90a)	1878A	—	—	—	Proof	2500.

KM#	Date	Mintage	Fine	VF	XF	Unc
325	1890A	.100	150.00	300.00	500.00	900.00
(Y92)	1890A	—	—	—	Proof	1800.

20 MARK

7.9650 g, .900 GOLD, .2304 oz AGW
Rev: Type I.

KM#	Date	Mintage	Fine	VF	XF	Unc
319	1872A	.069	375.00	650.00	1000.	1750.
(Y91)	1872A	—	—	—	Proof	Rare

PATTERNS (Pn)

(Including off metal strikes)

KM#	Date	Mintage	Identification	Mkt.Val.
Pn24	1828	5-6 pcs.	5 Thaler, Gold, KM271	10,000.
Pn25	1830	—	2 Thaler, .875 Gold	6000.

MECKLENBURG-STRELITZ

The duchy of Mecklenburg was located along the Baltic Coast between Holstein and Pomerania. The Strelitz line was founded in 1658 when the Mecklenburg line was divided into two lines. The 1815 Congress of Vienna elevated the duchy to the status of grand duchy. It became a part of the German Empire in 1871 until 1918 when the last grand duke died.

RULERS

Karl II, 1794-1816
Georg, 1816-1860
Friedrich Wilhelm, 1860-1904

MINTMASTERS INITIALS

Letter	Date	Name
FN	1832-1849	Franz Anton Nubell
IHL	1725-1759 1813	Johann Heinrich Lowe in Berlin
IHL	1813	Johann Heinrich Lowe in Berlin

PFENNIG

COPPER
Obv: Crowned G. Rev: Value.

KM#	Date	Mintage	Fine	VF	XF	Unc
81	1838	.060	6.00	12.00	35.00	145.00

KM#	Date	Mintage	Fine	VF	XF	Unc
101	1872	.626	2.00	4.00	9.00	35.00

1-1/2 PFENNIG

COPPER

KM#	Date	Mintage	Fine	VF	XF	Unc
82	1838	.039	6.00	12.00	35.00	145.00

2 PFENNIG

COPPER

KM#	Date	Mintage	Fine	VF	XF	Unc
102	1872 B	.203	2.50	5.00	12.00	40.00

3 PFENNIG

COPPER

KM#	Date	Mintage	Fine	VF	XF	Unc
80	1832 FN	.466	3.00	6.00	18.00	45.00
	1843	.195	3.00	6.00	18.00	45.00
	1845/3	.193	3.00	6.00	18.00	45.00
	1845	Inc.Ab.	3.00	6.00	18.00	45.00
	1847	.204	3.00	6.00	18.00	45.00

KM#	Date	Mintage	Fine	VF	XF	Unc
90	1855A	.305	3.00	6.00	18.00	45.00
	1859A	.192	3.00	6.00	18.00	45.00

KM#	Date	Mintage	Fine	VF	XF	Unc
95	1862A	.192	2.50	5.00	14.00	40.00
	1864A	.192	2.50	5.00	14.00	40.00

5 PFENNIG

COPPER

KM#	Date	Mintage	Fine	VF	XF	Unc
103	1872 B	.118	3.00	6.00	15.00	42.00

4 SCHILLINGE

3.2500 g, .375 SILVER, .0392 oz ASW

KM#	Date	Mintage	Fine	VF	XF	Unc
85	1846	.166	5.00	15.00	35.00	110.00

KM#	Date	Mintage	Fine	VF	XF	Unc
(C44)	1847	.273	5.00	15.00	35.00	110.00
	1849	.031	5.00	15.00	35.00	110.00

1/48 THALER

1.3000 g, .208 SILVER, .0086 oz ASW

KM#	Date	Mintage	Fine	VF	XF	Unc
83	1838	.180	3.00	6.00	15.00	60.00
	1841	.138	4.00	7.00	20.00	65.00
	1845	.097	4.00	7.00	20.00	65.00
	1847	.231	3.00	6.00	15.00	60.00

KM#	Date	Mintage	Fine	VF	XF	Unc
91	1855A	.270	2.00	4.00	12.00	40.00
	1859A	.240	2.00	4.00	12.00	40.00

KM#	Date	Mintage	Fine	VF	XF	Unc
96	1862A	.240	2.00	4.00	12.00	40.00
	1864A	.240	2.00	4.00	12.00	40.00

EIN (1) THALER

18.5200 g, .900 SILVER, .5360 oz ASW

KM#	Date	Mintage	Fine	VF	XF	Unc
100	1870A	.050	35.00	55.00	120.00	225.00

MONETARY REFORM

ZWEI (2) MARK

11.1110 g, .900 SILVER, .3215 oz ASW

KM#	Date	Mintage	Fine	VF	XF	Unc
108	1877A	.100	125.00	250.00	1400.	2750.
(Y100)	1877A	—	—	—	Proof	3000.

10 MARK

3.9820 g, .900 GOLD, .1152 oz AGW
Rev: Type I.

KM#	Date	Mintage	Fine	VF	XF	Unc
104	1873A	1,500	3500.	5000.	6500.	7500.
(Y101)	1873A	—	—	—	Proof	13,000.

KM#	Date	Mintage	Fine	VF	XF	Unc
106	1874A	3,000	2000.	4000.	5000.	7000.
(Y101a)	1880A	4,000	1500.	3250.	4000.	5000.

20 MARK

7.9650 g, .900 GOLD, .2304 oz AGW

KM#	Date	Mintage	Fine	VF	XF	Unc
105	1873A	6,750	1500.	2750.	4000.	6500.
(Y102)						

Rev: Type II.

KM#	Date	Mintage	Fine	VF	XF	Unc
107	1874A	6,000	1500.	2750.	4000.	6500.
(Y102a)						

MUNSTER

BISHOPRIC

A Bishopric, located in Westphalia, was established c. 802. The first Munster coinage was struck c. 1228. In 1802 the bishopric was secularized and divided. From 1806-1810 most of Munster belonged to Berg, from 1810-1814 to France and from 1814 onward, to Prussia.

During the 16th and 17th centuries treasury tokens, mostly counterstamped with the arms or initials of the current treasurer were issued. These were replaced in the middle of the 17th century by Cathedral coins, showing St. Paul with a sword. They last appeared at the end of the 18th century.

RULERS

Maximilian Franz of Austria, 1784-1801
Sede Vacante, 1801
Anton Victor of Prussia, 1801-1802

1/24 THALER

(Reichs)

BILLON
Obv: Value. Rev: Date.

KM#	Date	Mintage	Fine	VF	XF	Unc
210	1801	—	20.00	40.00	80.00	125.00

1/3 THALER

(Reichs)

SILVER

KM#	Date	Mintage	Fine	VF	XF	Unc
211	1801	—	90.00	140.00	200.00	350.00

2/3 THALER

(Reichs)

SILVER

KM#	Date	Mintage	Fine	VF	XF	Unc
212	1801	—	150.00	250.00	400.00	650.00

EIN (1) THALER

(Species)

SILVER

KM#	Date	Mintage	Fine	VF	XF	Unc
213	1801	200 pcs.	750.00	1200.	2200.	4500.

NASSAU

The duchy of Nassau, located on both sides of the River Lahn in the Middle Rhineland was established in 1158. The lands were frequently divided and combined. The first coins were struck c. 1260. The Weilburg line was founded in 1355 and the Usingen line in 1642. In 1806 they united under a common administration. The Usingen line became extinct in 1816 leaving a fully united duchy under the Weilburg rulers. The house ended with the ouster of the duke in 1866 by Prussia.

JOINT COINAGE

Nassau-Weilburg & Nassau-Usingen

RULERS

Friedrich August, 1803-1816
Friedrich Wilhelm, 1788-1816

MINTMASTERS INITIALS

Letter	Date	Name
CT	—	Christian Teichmann

1/4 KREUZER

COPPER
Obv: Crowned arms, leg: HERZOGL NASS.
Rev: L below date.

C#	Date	Mintage	Fine	VF	XF	Unc
1	1808	.449	2.50	5.50	12.00	55.00

C#	Date	Mintage	Fine	VF	XF	Unc
1a	1808	Inc. Ab.	1.50	3.50	7.00	45.00
	1809	—	1.50	3.50	7.00	45.00
	1810	—	1.50	3.50	7.00	45.00
	1811	—	1.50	3.50	7.00	45.00
	1812	1.470	1.50	3.50	7.00	45.00
	1813	.280	1.50	3.50	7.00	45.00
	1814	.278	1.50	3.50	7.00	45.00

NOTE: Several varieties exist.

1/2 KREUZER

COPPER

C#	Date	Mintage	Fine	VF	XF	Unc
2	1813	.445	2.00	4.00	10.00	65.00

KREUZER

COPPER

C#	Date	Mintage	Fine	VF	XF	Unc
3	1808	.799	15.00	40.00	85.00	275.00
	1809	—	2.00	4.00	8.00	50.00

Rev: L below wreath.

C#	Date	Mintage	Fine	VF	XF	Unc
3a	1808	Inc. Ab.	15.00	40.00	85.00	275.00

Obv. leg: HERZ:

C#	Date	Mintage	Fine	VF	XF	Unc
3b	1809	—	5.00	10.00	25.00	100.00
	1810	—	3.00	5.00	15.00	50.00
	1813	.131	3.00	5.00	15.00	50.00

3 KREUZER

(1 Groschen)

1.3800 g, .281 SILVER, .0124 oz ASW
Obv. leg: HERZ.NASS.SCHEIDE.M.
Rev: Value and date.

C#	Date	Mintage	Fine	VF	XF	Unc
4a	1809	.010	10.00	25.00	80.00	200.00

Obv. leg: HERZ.NASSAU.SCHEIDEMUNZ.

C#	Date	Mintage	Fine	VF	XF	Unc
4	1810.	.750	7.00	20.00	40.00	125.00
	1811	—	10.00	30.00	60.00	150.00

Obv. leg: HERZ.NASSAU.SCHEIDE.M.

C#	Date	Mintage	Fine	VF	XF	Unc
4b	1811	.270	7.00	15.00	25.00	125.00
	1812	.480	5.00	10.00	20.00	100.00
	1813	.506	5.00	10.00	20.00	90.00
	1814	.844	2.50	5.00	10.00	40.00
	1815	.675	2.50	5.00	10.00	40.00
	1816	.091	2.50	5.00	10.00	40.00
	1817	.259	2.50	5.00	10.00	40.00
	1818	.675	2.50	5.00	10.00	40.00
	1819	.928	2.50	5.00	10.00	40.00

Obv. legend: HERZ.NASS.SCH.M.

C#	Date	Mintage	Fine	VF	XF	Unc
4c	1810	—	10.00	30.00	60.00	150.00

5 KREUZER

2.2200 g, .437 SILVER, .0311 oz ASW

Obv. leg: HERZ.NASSAU. . .

C#	Date	Mintage	Fine	VF	XF	Unc
5	1808	4,000	150.00	300.00	600.00	1000.
	1809	—	10.00	20.00	50.00	125.00

Obv. leg: HERZOGL.NASS. . .

C#	Date	Mintage	Fine	VF	XF	Unc
5a	1808	Inc. Ab.	10.00	20.00	50.00	140.00

Obv. leg: HERZ.NASSAUISCHE.
Rev: Value, L below.

C#	Date	Mintage	Fine	VF	XF	Unc
5b	1808	—	10.00	20.00	50.00	140.00
	1809	—	10.00	20.00	50.00	140.00

10 KREUZER

3.8900 g, .500 SILVER, .0625 oz ASW
Obv. leg: HERZ. NASSAUISCHE CONVENTIONS MUNZ. Rev: L below value.

C#	Date	Mintage	Fine	VF	XF	Unc
6	1809	—	200.00	400.00	750.00	1250.

Obv. leg: HERZ.NASSAU.CONVENT.MUNZ.

C#	Date	Mintage	Fine	VF	XF	Unc
6a	1809	—	20.00	45.00	90.00	150.00

Obv. leg: HERZ.NASSAUISCHE. . .

C#	Date	Mintage	Fine	VF	XF	Unc
6b	1809	—	20.00	45.00	90.00	150.00

Obv. leg: HERZ.NASSAU. Rev: W/o L.

C#	Date	Mintage	Fine	VF	XF	Unc
6c	1809	—	20.00	45.00	90.00	150.00

20 KREUZER

6.6800 g, .583 SILVER, .1252 oz ASW
Obv. leg: HERZ. NASSAUISCHE CONVENTIONS MUNZ.

C#	Date	Mintage	Fine	VF	XF	Unc
7	1809	—	100.00	200.00	400.00	750.00

Obv. leg: HERZ. NASSAUISCHE CONVENT. MUNZ.

C#	Date	Mintage	Fine	VF	XF	Unc
7a	1809	—	20.00	40.00	60.00	125.00

Rev: Wreath w/o bow, running horse below.

C#	Date	Mintage	Fine	VF	XF	Unc
7b	1809	—	20.00	40.00	60.00	125.00

Rev: 60 between rosettes

C#	Date	Mintage	Fine	VF	XF	Unc
7c	1809	—	20.00	40.00	60.00	125.00

Obv. leg: . . . CONVENTIONS. Rev: Value within branches.

C#	Date	Mintage	Fine	VF	XF	Unc
7d	1809	—	20.00	40.00	60.00	125.00

Obv. leg: . . . CONVENT. Rev: L below wreath.

C#	Date	Mintage	Fine	VF	XF	Unc
7e	1809	—	20.00	40.00	60.00	125.00

Rev: W/o bow on wreath, prancing horse below.

C#	Date	Mintage	Fine	VF	XF	Unc
7f	1809	—	20.00	40.00	60.00	125.00

Obv. leg: HERZ:NASS:CONV:MUNZ:

C#	Date	Mintage	Fine	VF	XF	Unc
7g	1809	—	20.00	40.00	60.00	125.00

TRADE COINAGE

DUCAT

3.5000 g, .986 GOLD, .1109 oz AGW

C#	Date	Mintage	Fine	VF	XF	Unc
8	1809	3,543	500.00	1000.	1600.	3000.

SEPARATE COINAGE

Nassau-Usingen

RULERS

Friedrich August, 1803-1816

10 KREUZER

3.8900 g, .500 SILVER, .0625 oz ASW

C#	Date	Mintage	Fine	VF	XF	Unc
9.1	1809	—	200.00	375.00	700.00	1200.

Obv: L at truncation.

C#	Date	Mintage	Fine	VF	XF	Unc
9.2	1809 L	—	200.00	375.00	700.00	1200.

20 KREUZER

6.6800 g, .583 SILVER, .1252 oz ASW
Obv: Head right, L at truncation.
Rev: Crowned arms.

C#	Date	Mintage	Fine	VF	XF	Unc
10	1809 L	—	20.00	45.00	90.00	250.00

C#	Date	Mintage	Fine	VF	XF	Unc
10a	1809 L	—	20.00	45.00	90.00	250.00

1/2 THALER

(Convention)

14.0300 g, .833 SILVER, .3757 oz ASW

C#	Date	Mintage	Fine	VF	XF	Unc
11	1809 L	—	50.00	110.00	200.00	500.00

EIN (1) THALER

(Convention)

28.0600 g, .833 SILVER, .7515 oz ASW
Obv: Head right, L at truncation.
Rev: Similar to C#12c.

C#	Date	Mintage	Fine	VF	XF	Unc
12	1809 L	—	350.00	550.00	1200.	2500.

Rev: Date dividing C.T.

C#	Date	Mintage	Fine	VF	XF	Unc
12c	1810 CT	—	200.00	350.00	800.00	1600.
	1811 CT	—	200.00	275.00	600.00	1200.
	1812 CT	—	200.00	300.00	725.00	1500.
	1813 CT	.042	200.00	300.00	725.00	1500.
	1815 CT	—	200.00	300.00	725.00	1500.

MEDALLIC ISSUES (THALER)

28.0600 g, .833 SILVER, .7515 oz ASW
Patriot Nicolaus Fischer
Obv: Similar to 1 Thaler, C#12c.

C#	Date	Mintage	Fine	VF	XF	Unc
M1 (C12a)	1812	—	—	—	7000.	10,000.

Nassau-Weilburg

RULERS

Friedrich Wilhelm II, 1788-1816

10 KREUZER

3.8900 g, .500 SILVER, .0625 oz ASW

C#	Date	Mintage	Fine	VF	XF	Unc
30	1809	—	25.00	50.00	150.00	250.00

Obv: L at truncation.

C#	Date	Mintage	Fine	VF	XF	Unc
30a	1809	—	25.00	50.00	150.00	250.00

20 KREUZER

6.6800 g, .583 SILVER, .1252 oz ASW

C#	Date	Mintage	Fine	VF	XF	Unc
31	1809	—	25.00	50.00	150.00	250.00
	1810	—	25.00	50.00	150.00	250.00

1/2 THALER

(Convention)

14.0300 g, .833 SILVER, .3757 oz ASW
Obv: L on truncation.

C#	Date	Mintage	Fine	VF	XF	Unc
32	1809 L	—	80.00	160.00	250.00	350.00

EIN (1) THALER

(Convention)

28.0600 g, .833 SILVER, .7515 oz ASW
Obv: L on truncation.

C#	Date	Mintage	Fine	VF	XF	Unc
33	1809 L	—	450.00	850.00	1700.	3400.

Rev: Arms between laurel and palm branches.

C#	Date	Mintage	Fine	VF	XF	Unc
33a	1809 L	—	450.00	850.00	1700.	3400.

Obv: L on truncation.
Rev: Date dividing C.T.

C#	Date	Mintage	Fine	VF	XF	Unc
33b	1810 CT	—	175.00	375.00	900.00	1900.
	1811 CT	—	175.00	275.00	700.00	1500.
	1812 CT	—	175.00	375.00	900.00	1900.

Obv: Long bust.

C#	Date	Mintage	Fine	VF	XF	Unc
33d	1811 CT	—	175.00	275.00	700.00	1500.

C#	Date	Mintage	Fine	VF	XF	Unc
33c	1813 CT	.042	275.00	450.00	1000.	2000.
	1815 CT	—	300.00	560.00	1150.	2400.

United Nassau

RULERS

Duke Wilhelm, 1816-1839
Duke Adolph, 1839-1866

MINTMASTERS INITIALS

Letter	Date	Name
CT	1816-1825	Christian Teichmann

HELLER

COPPER
Obv: Crowned arms. Rev: Value.

C#	Date	Mintage	Fine	VF	XF	Unc
51	1842	.182	2.00	4.00	8.00	35.00

PFENNIG

COPPER

C#	Date	Mintage	Fine	VF	XF	Unc
52	1859	.220	2.00	4.00	8.00	35.00
	1860	.580	2.00	4.00	8.00	35.00
	1862	.490	2.00	4.00	8.00	35.00

1/4 KREUZER

COPPER

C#	Date	Mintage	Fine	VF	XF	Unc
35	1817.	.433	1.00	2.00	4.00	20.00
	1818.	.894	1.00	2.00	4.00	20.00
	1819.	4.932	1.00	2.00	4.00	20.00

Rev: W/o period after date.

C#	Date	Mintage	Fine	VF	XF	Unc
35a	1817	Inc. Ab.	1.00	2.00	4.00	20.00
	1818	—	1.00	2.00	4.00	20.00
	1819	Inc. Ab.	1.00	2.00	4.00	20.00
	1822	4.210	1.00	2.00	4.00	20.00

NOTE: Several varieties exist.

EIN (1) KREUZER

COPPER, 22-24mm
Obv: Crowned spade-shaped arms.
Rev: Value in wreath.

C#	Date	Mintage	Fine	VF	XF	Unc
36	1817	.203	1.00	3.00	6.00	30.00
	1818	.084	1.00	3.00	6.00	30.00

.5300 g, .229 SILVER, .0039 oz ASW
Rev: W/o wreath.

C#	Date	Mintage	Fine	VF	XF	Unc
38	1817	.079	1.00	3.00	6.00	30.00
	1823	.545	1.00	3.00	6.00	30.00
	1824	.564	1.00	3.00	6.00	30.00
	1828	—	1.00	3.00	6.00	30.00

COPPER, 22-24mm

C#	Date	Mintage	Fine	VF	XF	Unc
37	1830	.265	1.00	3.00	6.00	30.00
	1832	.517	1.00	3.00	6.00	30.00
	1834	.326	1.00	3.00	6.00	30.00
	1836	.200	1.00	3.00	6.00	30.00
	1838	.269	1.00	3.00	6.00	30.00

.5300 g, .229 SILVER, .0039 oz ASW

C#	Date	Mintage	Fine	VF	XF	Unc
39	1832	.144	1.00	3.00	6.00	30.00
	1833	1.037	1.00	3.00	6.00	30.00
	1835	.408	1.00	3.00	6.00	30.00

COPPER

C#	Date	Mintage	Fine	VF	XF	Unc
53	1842	.480	1.00	3.00	6.00	30.00
	1844	.188	1.00	3.00	6.00	30.00
	1848	.249	1.00	3.00	6.00	30.00
	1854	.274	1.00	3.00	6.00	30.00
	1855	—	1.00	3.00	6.00	30.00
	1856	.357	1.00	3.00	6.00	30.00

C#	Date	Mintage	Fine	VF	XF	Unc
54	1859	.836	1.00	3.00	6.00	30.00
	1860	.610	1.00	3.00	6.00	30.00
	1861	.556	1.00	3.00	6.00	30.00
	1862	.610	1.00	3.00	6.00	30.00
	1863	.576	1.00	3.00	6.00	30.00

.5300 g, .229 SILVER, .0039 oz ASW

C#	Date	Mintage	Fine	VF	XF	Unc
55	1861	.664	1.00	3.00	6.00	30.00

3 KREUZER

1.3800 g, .281 SILVER, .0124 oz ASW
Obv: Crowned spade-shaped arms, NASSAU.
Rev: Value.

C#	Date	Mintage	Fine	VF	XF	Unc
40	1817	.259	2.50	5.00	10.00	40.00
	1818	.675	2.50	5.00	10.00	40.00
	1819	.928	2.50	5.00	10.00	40.00

C#	Date	Mintage	Fine	VF	XF	Unc
40a	1822	.671	2.50	5.00	10.00	40.00
	1823	.671	2.50	5.00	10.00	40.00
	1824	—	2.50	5.00	10.00	40.00
	1825	.192	2.50	5.00	10.00	40.00
	1826	.352	2.50	5.00	10.00	40.00
	1827	.308	2.50	5.00	10.00	40.00
	1828	.308	2.50	5.00	10.00	40.00

1.2900 g, .281 SILVER, .0116 oz ASW

C#	Date	Mintage	Fine	VF	XF	Unc
41	1831	.509	2.50	5.00	10.00	40.00
	1832	.388	2.50	5.00	10.00	40.00
	1833	.042	2.50	5.00	10.00	40.00
	1834	.292	2.50	5.00	10.00	40.00
	1836	.340	2.50	5.00	10.00	40.00

1.2900 g, .333 SILVER, .0138 oz ASW

C#	Date	Mintage	Fine	VF	XF	Unc
56	1839	—	—	—	Rare	—
	1841	—	60.00	100.00	150.00	225.00
	1842	.112	2.00	4.00	8.00	35.00
	1844	.056	2.00	4.00	8.00	35.00
	1845	—	2.00	4.00	8.00	35.00
	1847	.210	2.00	4.00	8.00	35.00
	1848	.541	2.00	4.00	8.00	35.00
	1853	.091	2.00	4.00	8.00	35.00
	1855	.179	2.00	4.00	8.00	35.00

6 KREUZER

2.2200 g, .375 SILVER, .0267 oz ASW
Obv: Crowned square arms, leg: NASSAUISCHE.
Rev: Value in wreath.

C#	Date	Mintage	Fine	VF	XF	Unc
42	1817	.109	3.00	6.00	12.00	40.00
	1818	.263	3.00	6.00	12.00	40.00
	1819	.378	3.00	6.00	12.00	40.00

Obv. leg: NASSAU.

C#	Date	Mintage	Fine	VF	XF	Unc
42a	1822	.306	3.00	6.00	12.00	40.00
	1823	.306	3.00	6.00	12.00	40.00
	1824	.083	4.00	8.00	15.00	50.00
	1825	.176	3.00	6.00	12.00	40.00
	1826	.314	3.00	6.00	12.00	40.00
	1827	.302	3.00	6.00	12.00	40.00
	1828	.303	3.00	6.00	12.00	40.00

C#	Date	Mintage	Fine	VF	XF	Unc
43	1831	1.100	3.00	6.00	12.00	40.00
	1832	.377	3.00	6.00	12.00	40.00
	1833	.641	3.00	6.00	12.00	40.00
	1834	.565	3.00	6.00	12.00	40.00
	1835	.832	3.00	6.00	12.00	40.00
	1836	.452	3.00	6.00	12.00	40.00
	1837	.314	3.00	6.00	12.00	40.00

2.5900 g, .333 SILVER, .0277 oz ASW

C#	Date	Mintage	Fine	VF	XF	Unc
43a	1838	.201	3.00	6.00	12.00	40.00
	1839	.109	3.00	6.00	12.00	40.00

C#	Date	Mintage	Fine	VF	XF	Unc
57	1840	.094	4.00	8.00	15.00	50.00
	1841	.321	3.00	6.00	12.00	40.00
	1844	.073	4.00	8.00	15.00	50.00
	1846	—	3.00	6.00	12.00	40.00
	1847	—	3.00	6.00	12.00	40.00
	1848	.198	3.00	6.00	12.00	40.00
	1855	.190	3.00	6.00	12.00	40.00

1/2 GULDEN

5.3000 g, .900 SILVER, .1533 oz ASW

C#	Date	Mintage	Fine	VF	XF	Unc
44	1838	.108	20.00	40.00	75.00	150.00
	1839	.108	20.00	40.00	75.00	150.00

C#	Date	Mintage	Fine	VF	XF	Unc
58	1840	.095	20.00	40.00	75.00	150.00
	1841	.125	20.00	40.00	75.00	150.00
	1842	.031	20.00	40.00	75.00	150.00
	1843	.104	20.00	40.00	75.00	150.00
	1844	.117	20.00	40.00	75.00	150.00
	1845	.072	20.00	40.00	75.00	150.00

Obv: Head left.

C#	Date	Mintage	Fine	VF	XF	Unc
59	1856	.313	20.00	40.00	75.00	150.00
	1860	.104	20.00	40.00	75.00	150.00

GULDEN

10.6000 g, .900 SILVER, .3067 oz ASW

C#	Date	Mintage	Fine	VF	XF	Unc
45	1838	.190	25.00	50.00	100.00	250.00
	1839	.108	25.00	50.00	100.00	250.00

Obv: ZOLLMANN on truncation.

C#	Date	Mintage	Fine	VF	XF	Unc
60	1840	.117	25.00	50.00	100.00	175.00
	1841	.124	25.00	50.00	100.00	175.00
	1842	.020	25.00	50.00	100.00	175.00
	1843	.236	25.00	50.00	100.00	175.00
	1844	.093	25.00	50.00	100.00	175.00
	1845	.138	25.00	50.00	100.00	175.00
	1846	.048	25.00	50.00	100.00	175.00
	1847	.231	25.00	50.00	100.00	175.00
	1855	.188	25.00	50.00	100.00	175.00

C#	Date	Mintage	Fine	VF	XF	Unc
61	1855	Inc. Ab.	25.00	50.00	100.00	200.00
	1856	.040	25.00	50.00	100.00	200.00

ZWEI (2) GULDEN

21.2100 g, .900 SILVER, .6138 oz ASW
Obv: ZOLLMANN on truncation.

C#	Date	Mintage	Fine	VF	XF	Unc
65	1846	.177	50.00	125.00	300.00	800.00
	1847	.088	60.00	150.00	350.00	875.00

EIN (1) THALER

(Krone)

29.5300 g, .871 SILVER, .8270 oz ASW
Obv: Head right, L below. Rev: Crowned draped arms, date below dividing C.T.

C#	Date	Mintage	Fine	VF	XF	Unc
46	1816 CT	—	—	—	Rare	—

C#	Date	Mintage	Fine	VF	XF	Unc
47	1817 CT-L	.013	250.00	500.00	1200.	2500.

Obv: Similar to C#49 w/P.Z. on truncation.

C#	Date	Mintage	Fine	VF	XF	Unc
48	1818 CT	4,500	250.00	500.00	1200.	2400.
	1825 CT	2,000	300.00	600.00	1400.	2800.

Obv: ZOLLMANN. F on truncation.

C#	Date	Mintage	Fine	VF	XF	Unc
49	1831	9,385	200.00	350.00	500.00	1400.
	1832	567 pcs.	125.00	225.00	350.00	800.00
	1833	—	125.00	225.00	350.00	800.00
	1836	—	125.00	225.00	350.00	800.00
	1837	2,683	125.00	225.00	350.00	800.00

Visit of Duke to the Mint
Obv: Similar to C#49.

C#	Date	Mintage	Fine	VF	XF	Unc
49a	1831	Inc. Ab.	500.00	900.00	1600.	2400.

(Vereins)

18.5200 g, .900 SILVER, .5360 oz ASW
Obv: Z on truncation.

C#	Date	Mintage	Fine	VF	XF	Unc
62	1859 Z	.050	45.00	80.00	175.00	400.00
	1860 Z	.030	45.00	80.00	175.00	400.00

Obv: F. KORN on truncation.

C#	Date	Mintage	Fine	VF	XF	Unc
62a	1863	.145	45.00	80.00	200.00	500.00

Visit of Duke to Mint

C#	Date	Mintage	Fine	VF	XF	Unc
63	1861	3 pcs.	—	—	Proof 12,000.	

25th Anniversary of Reign

C#	Date	Mintage	Fine	VF	XF	Unc
64	1864	6,162	35.00	55.00	115.00	190.00

ZWEI (2) THALER

(3-1/2 Gulden)

37.1200 g, .900 SILVER, 1.0742 oz ASW
Obv: Similar to C#67a, ZOLLMANN on truncation.

C#	Date	Mintage	Fine	VF	XF	Unc
66	1840	.056	250.00	450.00	1000.	2000.

C#	Date	Mintage	Fine	VF	XF	Unc
67a	1844	.021	175.00	300.00	650.00	1400.
	1847	—	—	—	Rare	—

Obv: Truncation bare.

C#	Date	Mintage	Fine	VF	XF	Unc
67	1844	Inc. Ab.	175.00	300.00	650.00	1400.
	1854	.072	175.00	300.00	600.00	1250.

37.0400 g, .900 SILVER, 1.0719 oz ASW

Obv: C ZOLLMANN on truncation.

C#	Date	Mintage	Fine	VF	XF	Unc
68	1860	.130	125.00	225.00	400.00	1000.

TRADE COINAGE

DUCAT

3.5000 g, .986 GOLD, .1109 oz AGW
Obv: Head right. Rev: Crowned draped arms.

KM#	Date	Mintage	Fine	VF	XF	Unc
50	1818 CT	501 pcs.	650.00	1150.	2150.	4000.

PATTERNS (Pn)

(Including off metal strikes)

KM#	Date	Mintage	Identification	Mkt.Val.
Pn1	1839	—	3 Kreuzer, C56	—

NURNBERG

Nurnberg, in Franconia, was made a Free City in 1219. In that same year an Imperial mint was established there and continued throughout the rest of the century. The mint right was obtained in 1376 and again in 1422. City coins were struck from ca. 1390 to 1806 when the city was made part of Bavaria.

MINTMASTERS INITIALS

Letter	Date	Name
IER	1806-1807	Johann Egydius Rosch

City Arms

Divided vertically, eagle (or half eagle) on left, six diagonal bars downward to right on right side.

KM#	Date	Mintage	Fine	VF	XF	Unc
397	1806	—	3.00	7.00	15.00	40.00

NOTE: Earlier date (1799) exists for this type.

Oval state shield w/garland draped above urn, value below date.

KM#	Date	Mintage	Fine	VF	XF	Unc
406	1806	—	3.00	7.00	16.00	42.00

Oval state shield, garland w/loop above value and date.

KM#	Date	Mintage	Fine	VF	XF	Unc
407	1806	—	3.00	8.00	17.00	45.00

Garland hanging from urn on pedestal above state shield, value and date below.

KM#	Date	Mintage	Fine	VF	XF	Unc
408	1806	—	3.00	7.00	16.00	42.00
	1807	—	5.00	10.00	30.00	90.00

State shield in front of altar, value and date below.

KM#	Date	Mintage	Fine	VF	XF	Unc
409	1806	—	3.00	7.00	15.00	40.00
(C11a)	1807	—	3.00	7.00	15.00	40.00

BILLON
Obv: Pyramid w/city arms, date below.
Rev: City view.

KM#	Date	Mintage	VG	Fine	VF	XF
410	1806 IER	—	2.50	4.00	9.00	25.00

Rev: Rose bush.

KM#	Date	Mintage	VG	Fine	VF	XF
411	1806	—	2.25	3.00	7.50	25.00

Obv: Spade arms w/mural crown and garlands.

KM#	Date	Mintage	VG	Fine	VF	XF
412	1806	—	4.50	9.00	18.00	40.00
	1807	—	4.50	9.00	18.00	40.00

Obv: Pyramid w/city arms, date below.
Rev: City view.

KM#	Date	Mintage	VG	Fine	VF	XF
419	1807 IER	—	4.00	8.00	16.00	35.00

3 KREUZER

BILLON
Obv: Crowned shield w/garland.
Rev: Value within wreath, date below.

KM#	Date	Mintage	Fine	VF	XF	Unc
413	1806	—	5.00	10.00	25.00	75.00

Rev. leg: NURNB: SCHEIDE MUNZ.

KM#	Date	Mintage	Fine	VF	XF	Unc
414	1806	—	5.00	10.00	20.00	60.00
	1807	—	5.00	10.00	20.00	60.00

6 KREUZER

BILLON

KM#	Date	Mintage	Fine	VF	XF	Unc
415	1806	—	5.00	10.00	25.00	75.00
	1807	—	5.00	10.00	25.00	75.00

TRADE COINAGE

DUCAT

3.5000 g, .986 GOLD, .1109 oz AGW

KM#	Date	Mintage	Fine	VF	XF	Unc
416	1806 KR	—	200.00	400.00	650.00	1000.

Obv: 2 figures before altar w/crucifix.
Rev: 2 figures standing beside Christ.

KM#	Date	Mintage	Fine	VF	XF	Unc
404	ND	—	—	—	—	—

2 DUCAT

7.0000 g, .986 GOLD, .2219 oz AGW
Obv: City view. Rev: Lamb w/flag.

KM#	Date	Mintage	Fine	VF	XF	Unc
417 (C90)	1806 KR	—	450.00	1000.	1900.	3200.

3 DUCAT

10.5000 g, .986 GOLD, .3329 oz AGW
Obv: City view. Rev: Lamb w/flag.

KM#	Date	Mintage	Fine	VF	XF	Unc
418	1806 KR	—	1000.	2100.	3600.	6000.

OLDENBURG

The county of Oldenburg was situated on the North Sea coast, to the east of the principality of East Friesland. It was originally part of the old duchy of Saxony and the first recorded lord ruled from the beginning of the 11th century. The first count was named in 1091 and had already acquired the county of Delmenhorst prior to that time. The first identifiable Oldenburg coinage was struck in the first half of the 13th century. Oldenburg was divided into Oldenburg and Delmenhorst in 1270, but the two lines were reunited by marriage five generations later. Through another marriage to the heiress of the duchy of Schleswig and county of Holstein, the royal house of Denmark descended through the Oldenburg line beginning in 1448, while a junior branch continued as counts of Oldenburg. The lordship of Jever was added to the county's domains in 1575. In 1667, the last count died without a direct heir and Oldenburg reverted to Denmark until 1773. In the following year, Oldenburg was given to the bishop of Lubeck, of the Holstein-Gottorp line, and raised to the status of a duchy. Oldenburg was occupied several times during the Napoleonic Wars and became a grand duchy in 1829. In 1817, Oldenburg acquired the principality of Birkenfeld from Prussia and struck coins in denominations used there. World War I spelled the end of temporal power for the grand duke in 1918, but the title has continued up to the present time. Grand Duke Anton Gunther was born in 1923.

RULERS

Peter Friedrich Wilhelm, 1785-1823
Peter Friedrich Ludwig, as Administrator 1785-1823, as Duke, 1823-1829
Paul Friedrich August, 1829-1853
Nicolaus Friedrich Peter, 1853-1900
Friedrich August, 1900-1918

MINTMASTERS INITIALS

Letter	Date	Name
B	1817-1838	Ludwig August Bruel, in Hannover
B	1844-1868	Theodor Wilhelm Bruel, in Hannover
S	1839-1844	Karl Schluter, in Hannover
	1622-1637	Mintmaster

ARMS

Oldenburg: Two bars on field.
Delmenhorst: Cross with pointed bottom bar.
Jever: Lion rampant to left.

NOTE: Coins struck for lordship of Jever are listed under the latter.

SCHWAREN

COPPER

KM#	Date	Mintage	Fine	VF	XF	Unc
174	1846	.126	2.50	5.00	12.00	48.00

Rev: B below date.

KM#	Date	Mintage	Fine	VF	XF	Unc
185	1852 B	.144	2.50	5.00	12.00	48.00

KM#	Date	Mintage	Fine	VF	XF	Unc
188	1854 B	.072	2.00	4.00	10.00	45.00
	1856 B	.180	2.00	4.00	10.00	45.00

KM#	Date	Mintage	Fine	VF	XF	Unc
190	1858 B	1.084	1.00	3.00	8.00	38.00
	1859 B	.108	1.00	3.00	8.00	38.00
	1860 B	.288	1.00	3.00	8.00	38.00
	1862 B	.180	1.00	3.00	8.00	38.00
	1864 B	.180	1.00	3.00	8.00	38.00
	1865 B	.108	1.00	3.00	8.00	38.00
	1866 B	.144	1.00	3.00	8.00	38.00
	1869 B	.180	1.00	3.00	8.00	38.00

3 SCHWAREN

(3 Pfennig)

COPPER

KM#	Date	Mintage	Fine	VF	XF	Unc
191	1858 B	.372	1.00	3.00	8.00	38.00
	1859 B	.432	1.00	3.00	8.00	38.00
	1860 B	.060	2.00	4.00	10.00	45.00
	1862 B	.012	2.00	4.00	10.00	45.00
	1864 B	.060	2.00	4.00	10.00	45.00
	1865 B	.060	2.00	4.00	10.00	45.00
	1866 B	.036	2.00	4.00	10.00	45.00
	1869 B	.096	2.00	4.00	10.00	45.00

1/4 GROTEN

(1 Pfennig)

COPPER

KM#	Date	Mintage	Fine	VF	XF	Unc
175	1846	.090	3.00	6.00	18.00	55.00

1/2 GROTEN

COPPER

KM#	Date	Mintage	Fine	VF	XF	Unc
150	1802	.078	4.00	8.00	25.00	75.00
	1816	.149	3.00	7.00	20.00	65.00

KM#	Date	Mintage	Fine	VF	XF	Unc
165	1831	.072	4.00	8.00	25.00	75.00
	1835	.075	4.00	8.00	25.00	75.00

KM#	Date	Mintage	Fine	VF	XF	Unc
170	1840	.122	3.00	6.00	18.00	55.00

KM#	Date	Mintage	Fine	VF	XF	Unc
176	1846	.088	3.00	6.00	18.00	55.00

KM#	Date	Mintage	Fine	VF	XF	Unc
186	1853 B	.072	2.00	4.00	10.00	45.00
	1856 B	.072	2.00	4.00	10.00	45.00

GROTEN

.9700 g, .208 SILVER, .0064 oz ASW
Obv: Crowned arms w/garland, N.D.C.F.

KM#	Date	Mintage	Fine	VF	XF	Unc
160	1817	.391	6.00	12.00	35.00	100.00

.9200 g, .218 SILVER, .0064 oz ASW
Obv. leg: SCHEIDE-M.

KM#	Date	Mintage	Fine	VF	XF	Unc
166	1836 B	.361	4.00	8.00	25.00	85.00

KM#	Date	Mintage	Fine	VF	XF	Unc
179	1849 B	.043	4.00	7.00	20.00	65.00
	1850 B	.081	3.00	6.00	18.00	55.00

KM#	Date	Mintage	Fine	VF	XF	Unc
187	1853 B	.057	3.00	6.00	18.00	55.00
	1856 B	.072	3.00	6.00	18.00	55.00
	1857 B	.027	3.00	6.00	18.00	55.00

2 GROTE

(1/36 Thaler - 18 Witten)

1.3900 g, .291 SILVER, .0130 oz ASW
Obv. leg: N.D.C.F.

KM#	Date	Mintage	Fine	VF	XF	Unc
155	1815	1.080	7.00	15.00	45.00	150.00

3 GROTE

(1/24 Thaler)

1.9400 g, .312 SILVER, .0194 oz ASW

KM#	Date	Mintage	Fine	VF	XF	Unc
171	1840 S	.486	4.00	8.00	25.00	85.00

KM#	Date	Mintage	Fine	VF	XF	Unc
189	1856 B	.156	4.00	8.00	25.00	85.00

4 GROTE

(1/18 Thaler)

2.3900 g, .340 SILVER, .0261 oz ASW
Obv: Crowned arms w/garlands, N.D.C.F.
Rev: Value.

KM#	Date	Mintage	Fine	VF	XF	Unc
156	1816	.393	5.00	10.00	30.00	120.00
	1818	.126	5.00	10.00	30.00	120.00

KM#	Date	Mintage	Fine	VF	XF	Unc
172	1840 S	.380	4.00	8.00	25.00	90.00

6 GROTE

(1/12 Thaler)

3.5700 g, .340 SILVER, .0390 oz ASW

KM#	Date	Mintage	Fine	VF	XF	Unc
157	1816	.309	6.00	12.00	35.00	140.00
	1818	.060	7.00	15.00	45.00	165.00

12 GROTE

(1/6 Thaler)

4.8700 g, .520 SILVER, .0783 oz ASW

KM#	Date	Mintage	VG	Fine	VF	XF
158	1816	.036	7.00	15.00	45.00	165.00
	1818	.066	7.00	15.00	45.00	165.00

1/2 GROSCHEN

1.0900 g, .220 SILVER, .0077 oz ASW

KM#	Date	Mintage	Fine	VF	XF	Unc
192	1858 B	1.020	2.00	4.00	12.00	40.00
	1864 B	.060	3.00	6.00	18.00	50.00
	1865 B	.048	3.00	6.00	18.00	50.00
	1866 B	.168	2.50	5.00	15.00	45.00
	1869 B	.120	2.50	5.00	15.00	45.00

GROSCHEN

2.1900 g, .220 SILVER, .0154 oz ASW

KM#	Date	Mintage	Fine	VF	XF	Unc
193	1858 B	.720	3.50	7.00	20.00	65.00

KM#	Date	Mintage	Fine	VF	XF	Unc
194	1858 B	1.080	3.50	7.00	20.00	60.00
	1864 B	.030	3.50	7.00	20.00	65.00
	1865 B	.030	3.50	7.00	20.00	65.00
	1866 B	.120	3.50	7.00	20.00	65.00
	1869 B	.090	3.50	7.00	20.00	65.00

2-1/2 GROSCHEN

(1/12 Thaler)

3.2200 g, .375 SILVER, .0388 oz ASW

KM#	Date	Mintage	Fine	VF	XF	Unc
195	1858 B	.600	4.00	8.00	25.00	80.00

1/6 THALER

5.3500 g, .520 SILVER, .0894 oz ASW

KM#	Date	Mintage	Fine	VF	XF	Unc
177	1846 B	.164	25.00	50.00	100.00	225.00

1/3 THALER

7.7900 g, .625 SILVER, .1565 oz ASW

KM#	Date	Mintage	Fine	VF	XF	Unc
159	1816	.018	60.00	120.00	350.00	550.00
	1818	.033	50.00	100.00	300.00	500.00

EIN (1) THALER

22.2700 g, .750 SILVER, .5370 oz ASW

KM#	Date	Mintage	Fine	VF	XF	Unc
178 (C52)	1846 B	.042	75.00	125.00	500.00	1250.

18.5200 g, .900 SILVER, .5360 oz ASW

KM#	Date	Mintage	Fine	VF	XF	Unc
196 (C63)	1858 B	.017	70.00	140.00	250.00	450.00
	1860 B	.047	60.00	120.00	200.00	400.00
	1866 B	.072	50.00	100.00	175.00	350.00

2 THALER

(3-1/2 Gulden)

37.1200 g, .900 SILVER, 1.0742 oz ASW

KM#	Date	Mintage	Fine	VF	XF	Unc
173	1840	.010	700.00	1250.	2500.	4750.
(C53)	1840	—	—	—	Proof	4500.

MONETARY REFORM

2 MARK

11.1110 g, .900 SILVER, .3215 oz ASW

KM#	Date	Mintage	Fine	VF	XF	Unc
201	1891A	.100	125.00	250.00	400.00	650.00
(Y108)	1891A	—	—	—	Proof	700.00
202	1900A	.050	100.00	200.00	450.00	850.00
(Y109)	1900A	—	—	—	Proof	950.00

NOTE: Later date (1901) exists for this type.

5 MARK

27.7770 g, .900 SILVER, .8038 oz ASW

KM#	Date	Mintage	Fine	VF	XF	Unc
203	1900A	.020	225.00	500.00	1500.	2500.
(Y110)	1900A	—	—	—	Proof	3250.

NOTE: Later date (1901) exists for this type.

10 MARK

3.9820 g, .900 GOLD, .1152 oz AGW

KM#	Date	Mintage	Fine	VF	XF	Unc
200	1874B	.015	750.00	1250.	2000.	3750.
(Y107)	1874B	—	—	—	Proof	Rare

PATTERNS (Pn)

(Including off metal strikes)

KM#	Date	Mintage	Identification	Mkt.Val.
Pn1	1816	—	6 Grote, Gold, KM157	—
Pn2	1816	—	1/3 Thaler, Gold, KM159	—

OSNABRUCK

The city of Osnabruck is located northeast of Munster. Although the city owed its original growth to the bishopric it achieved considerable independence from the bishops and joined the Hanseatic League. It had its own local coinage from the early 16th century until 1805. It was absorbed by Hannover in 1803.

CITY

HELLER

COPPER
Obv: Wheel. Rev: Value, date below.

C#	Date	Mintage	Fine	VF	XF	Unc
1a	1801	—	4.00	8.00	20.00	75.00

NOTE: Earlier dates (1791-1795) exist for this type.

1-1/2 PFENNING

COPPER

C#	Date	Mintage	Fine	VF	XF	Unc
5	1805	—	4.00	8.00	20.00	75.00

NOTE: Earlier dates (1791-1795) exist for this type.

2 PFENNING

COPPER
Similar to 3 Pfennig, C#11.

C#	Date	Mintage	Fine	VF	XF	Unc
7	1801	—	5.00	9.00	25.00	100.00
	1802	—	5.00	9.00	25.00	100.00
	1803	—	5.00	9.00	25.00	100.00
	1804	—	5.00	9.00	25.00	100.00
	1805	—	5.00	9.00	25.00	100.00

NOTE: Earlier dates (1791-1800) exist for this type.

3 PFENNING

COPPER

C#	Date	Mintage	Fine	VF	XF	Unc
11	1805	—	7.50	15.00	40.00	125.00

PFALZ

(Rhenish Palatinate, Rheinpfalz)

The Counts Palatine originally administered and exercized judicial functions over the imperial household of the Holy Roman Emperor, based at the center of Charlemagne's empire, Aachen. They gradually acquired territories in the middle Rhine. From 1214 onwards the position was hereditary in the Wittelsbach family, who also controlled Bavaria. For a time the electoral dignity alternated between the Bavarian and Palatinate branches of the Wittelsbach family, until the Golden Bull in 1356 settled it upon the Palatinate branch. The electoral dignity was taken away from the Palatinate during the Thirty Years War, when the Protestant Frederick V rebelled against the Emperor Ferdinand II and was declared king of Bohemia ("the Winter King"). In the Peace of Westphalia, the electoral dignity was conferred upon Bavaria, but an eighth electoral position was created for the Palatinate. The conversion of the electors to Roman Catholicism led to the expulsion of Huguenots and other Protestants from their territories, many of whom made their way to America, founding New Paltz, New York. In the course of the later seventeenth and eighteenth centuries, the various branches of the Palatinate were left without any legitimate heirs, so that Karl Theodor was able to combine the thrones of Julich-Berg, the Palatinate, and Bavaria after the War of the Bavarian Succession.

Karl Theodor was a great Maecenas, whose orchestra at Mannheim was one of the greatest in Europe. He was a patron of Mozart, who wrote *Idomeneo* for the opera house in Munich, and of the chemist Benjamin Thompson, later Count Rumford, who fled Massachusetts when the American Revolution broke out and sought refuge in Bavaria.

The Palatinate was administered as part of Bavaria from 1777, and did not mint any separate coins after 1802. The territories which composed the Palatinate were scattered over central Germany, and now form part of the West German states of Bavaria, Baden, Hesse, and Rheinland-Pfalz. The chief industry is bulk chemicals, from the great BASF factory at Ludwigshafen.

In 1753 Bavaria and Austria concluded a monetary convention, reducing the fineness of the thaler to the point that 20 gulden could be coined from a Mark of fine silver. The most important result was that henceforth the gulden, rather than being worth 2/3 of a thaler, was henceforth worth half a thaler. This Convention standard was soon afterwards adopted by most of the states of southwest Germany, including the Palatinate.

The Electors Palatine and the Saxon Elector acted as Vicars of the Empire after the death of a Holy Roman Emperor and before a new one was elected; the Elector Palatine in the areas of Franconian and Suevic law, the Saxon Elector in the areas where Saxon law applied. Both principalities issued coins commemorating the vicariates. Thus the Elector Palatine Karl Theodor acted as Vicar of the Empire in 1790, after the death of Josef II, and again in 1792, after the early death of Leopold II, and issued coins in those two years. These coins are analogous to the "Sede Vacante" coins of ecclesiastical principalities.

Rhein Pfalz

RULERS

Maximilian Joseph,
Elector of Pfalz-Bayern,
1799-1805

1/2 KREUZER

COPPER
Obv: Crowned shield w/lion, dividing RP.
Rev: Value and date within wreath.

KM#	Date	Mintage	Fine	VF	XF	Unc
185 (C1)	1802	—	7.00	15.00	40.00	135.00

KREUZER

COPPER
Obv: Crowned shield w/lion, dividing RP.
Rev: Value and date within wreath.

KM#	Date	Mintage	Fine	VF	XF	Unc
186 (C2)	1802	—	8.00	16.00	45.00	160.00

EIN (1) THALER

(Convention)

SILVER
Obv: Head right.
Rev: Crowned shield within branches.

KM#	Date	Mintage	Fine	VF	XF	Unc
187 (C3)	1802	—	2500.	4000.	6500.	10,000.

POMERANIA

A duchy on the Baltic Sea, near modern day Poland, was founded in the late 11th century. After many divisions, Pomerania was annexed to Sweden in 1637. Brandenburg-Prussia had an interest in the area and slowly acquired bits until in 1815 all of Pomerania belonged to Prussia. The arms of Pomerania appear on coins of Brandenburg-Prussia from the 17th century onward.

RULERS

Gustav IV Adolf of Sweden, 1792-1809

3 PFENNINGE

COPPER
Obv: Griffin left w/sceptor, K.S.P.L.M. above.
Rev: Value above date.

KM#	Date	Mintage	VG	Fine	VF	XF
29	1806	.384	4.00	8.00	15.00	35.00
	1808	.258	4.00	8.00	15.00	35.00

NOTE: Earlier date (1792) exists for this type.

Obv. leg: "K. SCHWED. POM. LANDES M".

KM#	Date	Mintage	VG	Fine	VF	XF
30	1806	—	—	—	Rare	—

Obv. leg: "K.S.P. LANDESM".

KM#	Date	Mintage	VG	Fine	VF	XF
31	1808	—	—	—	Rare	—

PRUSSIA

The Kingdom of Prussia, located in north central Germany, came into being in 1701. The ruler received the title of King in Prussia in exchange for his support during the War of the Spanish Succession. During the Napoleonic Wars, Prussia allied itself with Saxony. When they were defeated in 1806 they were forced to cede a large portion of their territory. In 1813 the French were expelled and their territories were returned to them plus additional territories. After defeating Denmark and Austria, in 1864 and 1866 they acquired more territory. Prussia was the pivotal state of unification of Germany in 1871 and their King was proclaimed emperor of all Germany. World War I brought an end to the Empire and the Kingdom of Prussia in 1918.

RULERS

Friedrich Wilhelm III, 1797-1840
Friedrich Wilhelm IV, 1840-1861
Wilhelm I, 1861-1888
Friedrich III, March 1888-June 1888
Wilhelm II, 1888-1918

MINT MARKS

A - Berlin = Prussia, East Friesland, East Prussia, Posen
B - Bayreuth = Brandenburg-Ansbach-Bayreuth
B - Breslau = Silesia, Posen, South Prussia
C - = Cleve
D - Aurich = East Friesland, Prussia
E - Konigsberg = East Prussia
F - Magdeburg
G - Stettin
G - Schwerin, Plon-Rethwisch Mint, 1763 only
S - Schwabach = Brandenburg-Ansbach-Bayreuth
Star - Dresden

PFENNIG

COPPER
Mint mark: A

KM#	Date	Mintage	VG	Fine	VF	XF
	1801A	—	2.00	4.00	12.00	50.00
372	1801A	—	2.00	4.00	12.00	50.00
	1804A	—	2.00	4.00	12.00	50.00
	1806A	—	2.00	4.00	12.00	50.00

NOTE: Earlier date (1799) exists for this type.

BILLON

Obv: Crowned FRW monogram.

KM#	Date	Mintage	VG	Fine	VF	XF
373	1801A	—	2.00	4.00	12.00	50.00
	1802A	—	2.00	4.00	12.00	50.00
	1803A	—	2.00	4.00	12.00	50.00
	1804A	—	2.00	4.00	12.00	50.00

NOTE: Earlier date (1799) exists for this type.

Obv: Smaller W in crowned FRW monogram.

KM#	Date	Mintage	VG	Fine	VF	XF
383	1804A	—	4.00	8.00	25.00	75.00
	1806A	—	4.00	8.00	25.00	75.00

COPPER
Brandenburg Provincial Issue

KM#	Date	Mintage	Fine	VF	XF	Unc
390	1810	—	2.50	5.00	15.00	55.00
	1811	—	2.50	5.00	15.00	55.00
	1814	—	2.50	5.00	15.00	55.00
	1816	—	2.50	5.00	15.00	55.00
405	1821A	—	1.50	3.50	7.00	35.00
	1821B	—	1.50	3.50	7.00	35.00
	1821D	—	1.50	3.50	7.00	35.00
	1822A	—	1.50	3.50	7.00	35.00
	1822B	—	1.50	3.50	7.00	35.00
	1822D	—	1.50	3.50	7.00	35.00
	1823D	—	1.50	3.50	7.00	35.00
	1824D	—	1.50	3.50	7.00	35.00
	1825A	—	1.50	3.50	7.00	35.00
	1825D	—	1.50	3.50	7.00	35.00
	1826A	—	1.50	3.50	7.00	35.00
	1826C	—	1.00	3.50	7.00	35.00
	1826D	—	1.50	3.50	7.00	35.00
	1827A	—	1.50	3.50	7.00	35.00
	1827D	—	1.50	3.50	7.00	35.00
	1828A	—	1.50	3.50	7.00	35.00
	1828D	—	1.50	3.50	7.00	35.00
	1829D	—	1.50	3.50	7.00	35.00
	1830D	—	1.50	3.50	7.00	35.00
	1831D	—	1.50	3.50	7.00	35.00
	1832A	—	1.50	3.50	7.00	35.00
	1832D	—	1.50	3.50	7.00	35.00
	1833A	—	1.50	3.50	7.00	35.00
	1833D	—	1.50	3.50	7.00	35.00
	1834D	—	1.50	3.50	7.00	35.00
	1835A	—	1.50	3.50	7.00	35.00
	1835D	—	1.50	3.50	7.00	35.00
	1836A	—	1.50	3.50	7.00	35.00
	1836D	—	1.50	3.50	7.00	35.00
	1837A	—	1.50	3.50	7.00	35.00
	1837D	—	1.50	3.50	7.00	35.00
	1838A	—	1.50	3.50	7.00	35.00
	1838D	—	1.50	3.50	7.00	35.00
	1839A	—	1.50	3.50	7.00	35.00
	1839D	—	1.50	3.50	7.00	35.00
	1840A	—	1.50	3.50	7.00	35.00
	1840D	—	1.50	3.50	7.00	35.00
430	1841A	—	.75	1.50	5.00	32.00
	1841D	—	.75	1.50	5.00	32.00
	1842A	—	.75	1.50	5.00	32.00
	1842D	—	.75	1.50	5.00	32.00
447	1843A	—	.75	1.50	5.00	32.00
	1844A	—	.75	1.50	5.00	32.00
	1844D	—	.75	1.50	5.00	32.00
	1845A	—	.75	1.50	5.00	32.00
	1845D	—	.75	1.50	5.00	32.00
451	1846A	—	.75	1.50	5.00	32.00
	1846D	—	.75	1.50	5.00	32.00
	1847A	—	.75	1.50	5.00	32.00
	1847D	—	.75	1.50	5.00	32.00
	1848A	—	.75	1.50	5.00	32.00
	1848D	—	.75	1.50	5.00	32.00
	1849A	—	.75	1.50	5.00	32.00
	1850A	—	.75	1.50	5.00	32.00
	1851A	—	.75	1.50	5.00	32.00
	1852A	—	.75	1.50	5.00	32.00
	1853A	—	.75	1.50	5.00	32.00

KM#	Date	Mintage	Fine	VF	XF	Unc
451	1854A	—	.75	1.50	5.00	32.00
	1855A	—	.75	1.50	5.00	32.00
	1856A	—	.75	1.50	5.00	32.00
	1857A	—	.75	1.50	5.00	32.00
	1858A	—	.75	1.50	5.00	32.00
	1859A	—	.75	1.50	5.00	32.00
	1860A	—	.75	1.50	5.00	32.00
480	1861A	—	.50	1.00	2.50	20.00
	1862A	—	.50	1.00	2.50	20.00
	1863A	—	.50	1.00	2.50	20.00
	1864A	—	.50	1.00	2.50	20.00
	1865A	—	.50	1.00	2.50	20.00
	1866A	—	.50	1.00	2.50	20.00
	1867A	—	.50	1.00	2.50	20.00
	1867B	—	.50	1.00	2.50	20.00
	1867C	—	.50	1.00	2.50	20.00
	1868A	—	.50	1.00	2.50	20.00
	1868B	—	.50	1.00	2.50	20.00
	1868C	—	.50	1.00	2.50	20.00
	1869A	—	.50	1.00	2.50	20.00
	1869B	—	.50	1.00	2.50	20.00
	1870A	—	.50	1.00	2.50	20.00
	1870B	—	.50	1.00	2.50	20.00
	1870C	—	.50	1.00	2.50	20.00
	1871A	—	.50	1.00	2.50	20.00
	1871B	—	.50	1.00	2.50	20.00
	1871C	—	.50	1.00	2.50	20.00
	1872A	—	.50	1.00	2.50	20.00
	1872B	—	.50	1.00	2.50	20.00
	1872C	—	.50	1.00	2.50	20.00
	1873A	—	.50	1.00	2.50	20.00
	1873B	—	.50	1.00	2.50	20.00
	1873C	—	.50	1.00	2.50	20.00

2 PFENNIG

COPPER
Mint mark: A
Brandenburg Provincial Issue

KM#	Date	Mintage	Fine	VF	XF	Unc
391	1810	—	2.50	5.00	15.00	55.00
	1814	—	2.50	5.00	15.00	55.00
	1816	—	2.50	5.00	15.00	55.00

KM#	Date	Mintage	Fine	VF	XF	Unc
406	1821A	—	2.00	4.00	8.00	40.00
	1821B	—	2.00	4.00	8.00	40.00
	1822A	—	2.00	4.00	8.00	40.00
	1822B	—	2.00	4.00	8.00	40.00
	1823D	—	2.00	4.00	8.00	40.00
	1824D	—	2.00	4.00	8.00	40.00
	1825A	—	2.00	4.00	8.00	40.00
	1825D	—	2.00	4.00	8.00	40.00
	1826A	—	2.00	4.00	8.00	40.00
	1826D	—	2.00	4.00	8.00	40.00
	1827A	—	2.00	4.00	8.00	40.00
	1827D	—	2.00	4.00	8.00	40.00
	1828A	—	2.00	4.00	8.00	40.00
	1828D	—	2.00	4.00	8.00	40.00
	1829D	—	2.00	4.00	8.00	40.00
	1830A	—	2.00	4.00	8.00	40.00
	1830D	—	2.00	4.00	8.00	40.00
	1831D	—	2.00	4.00	8.00	40.00
	1832A	—	2.00	4.00	8.00	40.00
	1832D	—	2.00	4.00	8.00	40.00
	1833A	—	2.00	4.00	8.00	40.00
	1833D	—	2.00	4.00	8.00	40.00
	1834D	—	2.00	4.00	8.00	40.00
	1835A	—	2.00	4.00	8.00	40.00
	1835D	—	2.00	4.00	8.00	40.00
	1836A	—	2.00	4.00	8.00	40.00
	1836D	—	2.00	4.00	8.00	40.00
	1837A	—	2.00	4.00	8.00	40.00
	1837D	—	2.00	4.00	8.00	40.00
	1838A	—	2.00	4.00	8.00	40.00
	1838D	—	2.00	4.00	8.00	40.00
	1839A	—	2.00	4.00	8.00	40.00
	1839D	—	2.00	4.00	8.00	40.00
	1840A	—	2.00	4.00	8.00	40.00

KM#	Date	Mintage	Fine	VF	XF	Unc
431	1841A	—	1.00	2.00	5.00	35.00
	1841D	—	1.00	2.00	5.00	35.00
	1842A	—	1.00	2.00	5.00	35.00
	1842D	—	1.00	2.00	5.00	35.00

KM#	Date	Mintage	Fine	VF	XF	Unc
448	1843A	—	1.00	2.00	5.00	35.00
	1844A	—	1.00	2.00	5.00	35.00
	1844D	—	1.00	2.00	5.00	35.00
	1845A	—	1.00	2.00	5.00	35.00
	1845D	—	1.00	2.00	5.00	35.00

KM#	Date	Mintage	Fine	VF	XF	Unc
452	1846A	—	.75	1.50	4.00	32.00
	1846D	—	.75	1.50	4.00	32.00
	1847A	—	.75	1.50	4.00	32.00
	1847D	—	.75	1.50	4.00	32.00
	1848A	—	.75	1.50	4.00	32.00
	1848D	—	.75	1.50	4.00	32.00
	1849A	—	.75	1.50	4.00	32.00
	1850A	—	.75	1.50	4.00	32.00
	1851A	—	.75	1.50	4.00	32.00
	1852A	—	.75	1.50	4.00	32.00
	1853A	—	.75	1.50	4.00	32.00
	1854A	—	.75	1.50	4.00	32.00
	1855A	—	.75	1.50	4.00	32.00
	1856A	—	.75	1.50	4.00	32.00
	1857A	—	.75	1.50	4.00	32.00
	1858A	—	.75	1.50	4.00	32.00
	1859A	—	.75	1.50	4.00	32.00
	1860A	—	.75	1.50	4.00	32.00

KM#	Date	Mintage	Fine	VF	XF	Unc
481	1861A	—	.50	1.25	2.50	20.00
	1862A	—	.50	1.25	2.50	20.00
	1863A	—	.50	1.25	2.50	20.00
	1864A	—	.50	1.25	2.50	20.00
	1865A	—	.50	1.25	2.50	20.00
	1866A	—	.50	1.25	2.50	20.00
	1867A	—	.50	1.25	2.50	20.00
	1867B	—	.50	1.25	2.50	20.00
	1867C	—	.50	1.25	2.50	20.00
	1868A	—	.50	1.25	2.50	20.00
	1868B	—	.50	1.25	2.50	20.00
	1868C	—	.50	1.25	2.50	20.00
	1869A	—	.50	1.25	2.50	20.00
	1869B	—	.50	1.25	2.50	20.00
	1870A	—	.50	1.25	2.50	20.00
	1870B	—	.50	1.25	2.50	20.00
	1871A	—	.50	1.25	2.50	20.00
	1871B	—	.50	1.25	2.50	20.00
	1871C	—	.50	1.25	2.50	20.00
	1872C	—	.50	1.25	2.50	20.00
	1873B	—	.50	1.25	2.50	20.00
	1873C	—	.50	1.25	2.50	20.00

3 PFENNIG

.7000 g, .250 SILVER, .0056 oz ASW

KM#	Date	Mintage	VG	Fine	VF	XF
374	1801A	—	2.00	4.00	12.00	50.00
	1801A	—	2.00	4.00	12.00	50.00
	1802A	—	2.00	4.00	12.00	50.00
	1803A	—	2.00	4.00	12.00	50.00
	1804A	—	2.00	4.00	12.00	50.00
	1806A	—	2.00	4.00	12.00	50.00

NOTE: Earlier date (1799) exists for this type.

Obv: Smaller crown.

KM#	Date	Mintage	VG	Fine	VF	XF
384	1804	—	4.00	8.00	25.00	55.00
	1806	—	— Reported, not confirmed			

COPPER

KM#	Date	Mintage	Fine	VF	XF	Unc
407	1821A	—	2.00	4.00	9.00	45.00
	1821B	—	2.00	4.00	9.00	45.00
	1822A	—	2.00	4.00	9.00	45.00
	1822B	—	2.00	4.00	9.00	45.00
	1823A	—	— Reported, not confirmed			
	1823D	—	2.00	4.00	9.00	45.00
	1824A	—	— Reported, not confirmed			
	1824D	—	2.00	4.00	9.00	45.00
	1825A	—	2.00	4.00	9.00	45.00
	1825D	—	2.00	4.00	9.00	45.00
	1826A	—	2.00	4.00	9.00	45.00
	1826D	—	2.00	4.00	9.00	45.00
	1827A	—	2.00	4.00	9.00	45.00
	1827D	—	2.00	4.00	9.00	45.00
	1828A	—	2.00	4.00	9.00	45.00
	1828D	—	2.00	4.00	9.00	45.00
	1829A	—	2.00	4.00	9.00	45.00
	1829D	—	2.00	4.00	9.00	45.00
	1830A	—	2.00	4.00	9.00	45.00
	1830D	—	2.00	4.00	9.00	45.00
	1831A	—	2.00	4.00	9.00	45.00
	1831D	—	2.00	4.00	9.00	45.00
	1832A	—	2.00	4.00	9.00	45.00
	1832D	—	2.00	4.00	9.00	45.00
	1833A	—	2.00	4.00	9.00	45.00
	1833D	—	2.00	4.00	9.00	45.00
	1834D	—	2.00	4.00	9.00	45.00
	1835A	—	2.00	4.00	9.00	45.00
	1835D	—	2.00	4.00	9.00	45.00
	1836A	—	2.00	4.00	9.00	45.00
	1836D	—	2.00	4.00	9.00	45.00
	1837A	—	2.00	4.00	9.00	45.00
	1837D	—	2.00	4.00	9.00	45.00
	1838A	—	2.00	4.00	9.00	45.00
	1838D	—	2.00	4.00	9.00	45.00
	1839A	—	2.00	4.00	9.00	45.00
	1839D	—	2.00	4.00	9.00	45.00
	1840A	—	2.00	4.00	9.00	45.00
	1840D	—	2.00	4.00	9.00	45.00

KM#	Date	Mintage	Fine	VF	XF	Unc
432	1841A	—	1.50	3.00	6.00	38.00
	1841D	—	1.50	3.00	6.00	38.00
	1842A	—	1.50	3.00	6.00	38.00
	1842D	—	1.50	3.00	6.00	38.00

KM#	Date	Mintage	Fine	VF	XF	Unc
449	1843A	—	1.50	3.00	6.00	38.00
	1843D	—	1.50	3.00	6.00	38.00
	1844A	—	1.50	3.00	6.00	38.00
	1844D	—	1.50	3.00	6.00	38.00
	1845A	—	1.50	3.00	6.00	38.00

Struck in collared dies.

KM#	Date	Mintage	Fine	VF	XF	Unc
453	1846A	—	1.00	2.00	5.00	32.00
	1846D	—	1.00	2.00	5.00	32.00
453	1847A	—	1.00	2.00	5.00	32.00
	1847D	—	1.00	2.00	5.00	32.00
	1848A	—	1.00	2.00	5.00	32.00
	1848D	—	1.00	2.00	5.00	32.00
	1849A	—	1.00	2.00	5.00	32.00
	1850A	—	1.00	2.00	5.00	32.00
	1851A	—	1.00	2.00	5.00	32.00
	1852A	—	1.00	2.00	5.00	32.00
	1853A	—	1.00	2.00	5.00	32.00
	1854A	—	1.00	2.00	5.00	32.00
	1855A	—	1.00	2.00	5.00	32.00
	1856A	—	1.00	2.00	5.00	32.00
	1857A	—	1.00	2.00	5.00	32.00
	1858A	—	1.00	2.00	5.00	32.00
	1859A	—	1.00	2.00	5.00	32.00
	1860A	—	1.00	2.00	5.00	32.00

Mule. Rev: Reuss-Schleiz 3 PFENNIGE.

KM#	Date	Mintage	Fine	VF	XF	Unc
460	1850A	—	15.00	40.00	75.00	150.00

KM#	Date	Mintage	Fine	VF	XF	Unc
482	1861A	—	.75	1.50	3.00	20.00
	1862A	—	.75	1.50	3.00	20.00
	1863A	—	.75	1.50	3.00	20.00
	1864A	—	.75	1.50	3.00	20.00
	1865A	—	.75	1.50	3.00	20.00
	1866A	—	.75	1.50	3.00	20.00
	1867A	—	.75	1.50	3.00	20.00
	1867B	—	.75	1.50	3.00	20.00
	1867C	—	.75	1.50	3.00	20.00
	1868A	—	.75	1.50	3.00	20.00
	1868B	—	.75	1.50	3.00	20.00
	1868C	—	.75	1.50	3.00	20.00
	1869A	—	.75	1.50	3.00	20.00
	1869B	—	.75	1.50	3.00	20.00
	1869C	—	.75	1.50	3.00	20.00
	1870A	—	.75	1.50	3.00	20.00
	1870B	—	.75	1.50	3.00	20.00
	1870C	—	.75	1.50	3.00	20.00
	1871A	—	.75	1.50	3.00	20.00
	1871B	—	.75	1.50	3.00	20.00
	1871C	—	.75	1.50	3.00	20.00
	1872A	—	.75	1.50	3.00	20.00
	1872B	—	.75	1.50	3.00	20.00
	1872C	—	.75	1.50	3.00	20.00
	1873A	—	.75	1.50	3.00	20.00
	1873B	—	.75	1.50	3.00	20.00
	1873C	—	.75	1.50	3.00	20.00

4 PFENNIG

COPPER

Similar to KM#412.

KM#	Date	Mintage	Fine	VF	XF	Unc
408	1821A	—	3.50	7.00	22.00	60.00
	1821B	—	3.50	7.00	22.00	60.00
	1822A	—	3.50	7.00	22.00	60.00
	1822B	—	3.50	7.00	22.00	60.00
	1825A	—	3.50	7.00	22.00	60.00
	1825B	—	3.50	7.00	22.00	60.00
	1826A	—	3.50	7.00	22.00	60.00
	1827A	—	3.50	7.00	22.00	60.00
	1829A	—	3.50	7.00	22.00	60.00
	1830A	—	3.50	7.00	22.00	60.00
	1832A	—	3.50	7.00	22.00	60.00
	1834A	—	— Reported, not confirmed			
	1836A	—	3.50	7.00	22.00	60.00
	1837A	—	3.50	7.00	22.00	60.00
	1838A	—	3.50	7.00	22.00	60.00
	1839A	—	3.50	7.00	22.00	60.00
	1840A	—	3.50	7.00	22.00	60.00

KM#	Date	Mintage	Fine	VF	XF	Unc
412	1823D	—	3.50	7.00	22.00	60.00
	1824D	—	3.50	7.00	22.00	60.00
	1825D	—	3.50	7.00	22.00	60.00
	1826D	—	3.50	7.00	22.00	60.00
	1828D	—	3.50	7.00	22.00	60.00
	1829D	—	3.50	7.00	22.00	60.00
	1831D	—	3.50	7.00	22.00	60.00
412	1832D	—	3.50	7.00	22.00	60.00
	1833D	—	3.50	7.00	22.00	60.00
	1834D	—	3.50	7.00	22.00	60.00
	1836D	—	3.50	7.00	22.00	60.00
	1837D	—	3.50	7.00	22.00	60.00
	1838D	—	3.50	7.00	22.00	60.00
	1839D	—	3.50	7.00	22.00	60.00
	1840D	—	— Reported, not confirmed			

KM#	Date	Mintage	Fine	VF	XF	Unc
433	1841A	—	3.00	6.00	18.00	50.00
	1841D	—	3.00	6.00	18.00	50.00
	1842A	—	3.00	6.00	18.00	50.00
	1842D	—	3.00	6.00	18.00	50.00

KM#	Date	Mintage	Fine	VF	XF	Unc
450	1843A	—	3.00	6.00	18.00	50.00
	1844A	—	3.00	6.00	18.00	50.00
	1844D	—	3.00	6.00	18.00	50.00
	1845A	—	3.00	6.00	18.00	50.00

Struck in collared dies.

KM#	Date	Mintage	Fine	VF	XF	Unc
454	1846A	—	3.00	6.00	18.00	50.00
	1846D	—	3.00	6.00	18.00	50.00
	1847A	—	3.00	6.00	18.00	50.00
	1847D	—	3.00	6.00	18.00	50.00
	1848A	—	3.00	6.00	18.00	50.00
	1848D	—	3.00	6.00	18.00	50.00
	1849A	—	— Reported, not confirmed			
	1850A	—	3.00	6.00	18.00	50.00
	1851A	—	3.00	6.00	18.00	50.00
	1852A	—	3.00	6.00	18.00	50.00
	1853A	—	3.00	6.00	18.00	50.00
	1854A	—	3.00	6.00	18.00	50.00
	1855A	—	3.00	6.00	18.00	50.00
	1856A	—	3.00	6.00	18.00	50.00
	1857A	—	3.00	6.00	18.00	50.00
	1858A	—	3.00	6.00	18.00	50.00
	1860A	—	3.00	6.00	18.00	50.00

KM#	Date	Mintage	Fine	VF	XF	Unc
483	1861A	—	2.00	4.00	10.00	40.00
	1862A	—	2.00	4.00	10.00	40.00
	1863A	—	2.00	4.00	10.00	40.00
	1864A	—	2.00	4.00	10.00	40.00
	1865A	—	2.00	4.00	10.00	40.00
	1866A	—	2.00	4.00	10.00	40.00
	1867A	—	2.00	4.00	10.00	40.00
	1867C	—	2.00	4.00	10.00	40.00
	1868A	—	2.00	4.00	10.00	40.00
	1868C	—	2.00	4.00	10.00	40.00
	1869A	—	2.00	4.00	10.00	40.00
	1870A	—	2.00	4.00	10.00	40.00
	1871A	—	2.00	4.00	10.00	40.00
	1871C	—	2.00	4.00	10.00	40.00

1/2 SILBER GROSCHEN

1.0900 g, .222 SILVER, .0077 oz ASW

KM#	Date	Mintage	Fine	VF	XF	Unc
409	1821A	—	3.00	6.00	15.00	50.00
	1822A	—	3.00	6.00	15.00	50.00

KM#	Date	Mintage	Fine	VF	XF	Unc
409	1823A	—	3.00	6.00	15.00	50.00
	1824A	—	3.00	6.00	15.00	50.00
	1824D	—	3.00	6.00	15.00	50.00
	1825A	—	3.00	6.00	15.00	50.00
	1825D	—	3.00	6.00	15.00	50.00
	1826A	—	3.00	6.00	15.00	50.00
	1826D	—	3.00	6.00	15.00	50.00
	1827A	—	3.00	6.00	15.00	50.00
	1828A	—	3.00	6.00	15.00	50.00
	1828D	—	3.00	6.00	15.00	50.00
	1829A	—	3.00	6.00	15.00	50.00
	1830A	—	3.00	6.00	15.00	50.00
	1831A	—	3.00	6.00	15.00	50.00
	1832A	—	3.00	6.00	15.00	50.00
	1833A	—	3.00	6.00	15.00	50.00
	1834A	—	3.00	6.00	15.00	50.00
	1835A	—	3.00	6.00	15.00	50.00
	1836A	—	3.00	6.00	15.00	50.00
	1837A	—	3.00	6.00	15.00	50.00
	1838A	—	3.00	6.00	15.00	50.00
	1839A	—	3.00	6.00	15.00	50.00
	1840A	—	3.00	6.00	15.00	50.00

Mint mark: A

KM#	Date	Mintage	Fine	VF	XF	Unc
434	1841	—	2.50	5.00	12.00	45.00
	1842	—	2.50	5.00	12.00	45.00
	1843	—	2.50	5.00	12.00	45.00
	1844	—	2.50	5.00	12.00	45.00
	1845	—	2.50	5.00	12.00	45.00
	1846	—	2.50	5.00	12.00	45.00
	1847	—	2.50	5.00	12.00	45.00
	1848	—	2.50	5.00	12.00	45.00
	1849	—	2.50	5.00	12.00	45.00
	1850	—	2.50	5.00	12.00	45.00
	1851	—	2.50	5.00	12.00	45.00
	1852	—	2.50	5.00	12.00	45.00

Obv: Older head.

KM#	Date	Mintage	Fine	VF	XF	Unc
461	1853	—	4.00	8.00	20.00	65.00
	1854	—	4.00	8.00	20.00	65.00
	1855	—	4.00	8.00	20.00	65.00
	1856	—	4.00	8.00	20.00	65.00
	1857	—	— Reported, not confirmed			
	1858	—	4.00	8.00	20.00	65.00
	1859	—	— Reported, not confirmed			
	1860	—	4.00	8.00	20.00	65.00

KM#	Date	Mintage	Fine	VF	XF	Unc
484	1861A	—	1.00	2.00	5.00	22.00
	1862A	—	1.00	2.00	5.00	22.00
	1863A	—	1.00	2.00	5.00	22.00
	1864A	—	1.00	2.00	5.00	22.00
	1865A	—	1.00	2.00	5.00	22.00
	1866A	—	1.00	2.00	5.00	22.00
	1866B	—	1.00	2.00	5.00	22.00
	1867A	—	1.00	2.00	5.00	22.00
	1867B	—	1.00	2.00	5.00	22.00
	1867C	—	1.25	2.50	5.00	22.00
	1868A	—	1.00	2.00	5.00	22.00
	1868B	—	1.00	2.00	5.00	22.00
	1868C	—	1.25	2.50	5.00	22.00
	1869A	—	1.00	2.00	5.00	22.00
	1869B	—	1.00	2.00	5.00	22.00
	1870A	—	1.00	2.00	5.00	22.00
	1870B	—	1.00	2.00	5.00	22.00
	1871A	—	1.00	2.00	5.00	22.00
	1871B	—	1.00	2.00	5.00	22.00
	1872A	—	1.00	2.00	5.00	22.00
	1872B	—	1.00	2.00	5.00	22.00
	1872C	—	1.25	2.50	5.00	22.00
	1873B	—	1.00	2.00	5.00	22.00

GROSCHEN

(Silber)

2.1900 g, .222 SILVER, .0156 oz ASW

KM#	Date	Mintage	Fine	VF	XF	Unc
410	1821A	—	3.00	6.00	15.00	50.00
	1821D	—	3.00	6.00	15.00	50.00
	1822A	—	3.00	6.00	15.00	50.00
	1822D	—	3.00	6.00	15.00	50.00
	1823A	—	3.00	6.00	15.00	50.00
	1823D	—	3.00	6.00	15.00	50.00
	1824A	—	3.00	6.00	15.00	50.00

KM#	Date	Mintage	Fine	VF	XF	Unc
410	1824D	—	3.00	6.00	15.00	50.00
	1825A	—	3.00	6.00	15.00	50.00
	1825D	—	3.00	6.00	15.00	50.00
	1826A	—	3.00	6.00	15.00	50.00
	1826D	—	3.00	6.00	15.00	50.00
	1827A	—	3.00	6.00	15.00	50.00
	1827D	—	3.00	6.00	15.00	50.00
	1828A	—	3.00	6.00	15.00	50.00
	1828D	—	3.00	6.00	15.00	50.00
	1829A	—	3.00	6.00	15.00	50.00
	1830A	—	3.00	6.00	15.00	50.00
	1830D	—	3.00	6.00	15.00	50.00
	1831A	—	3.00	6.00	15.00	50.00
	1832A	—	3.00	6.00	15.00	50.00
	1832D	—	3.00	6.00	15.00	50.00
	1833A	—	3.00	6.00	15.00	50.00
	1833D	—	3.00	6.00	15.00	50.00
	1834A	—	3.00	6.00	15.00	50.00
	1834D	—	3.00	6.00	15.00	50.00
	1835A	—	3.00	6.00	15.00	50.00
	1836A	—	3.00	6.00	15.00	50.00
	1837A	—	3.00	6.00	15.00	50.00
	1837D	—	3.00	6.00	15.00	50.00
	1838A	—	3.00	6.00	15.00	50.00
	1839A	—	3.00	6.00	15.00	50.00
	1839D	—	3.00	6.00	15.00	50.00
	1840A	—	3.00	6.00	15.00	50.00
	1840D	—	3.00	6.00	15.00	50.00

KM#	Date	Mintage	Fine	VF	XF	Unc
435	1841A	—	2.00	4.00	10.00	40.00
	1841D	—	2.00	4.00	10.00	40.00
	1842A	—	2.00	4.00	10.00	40.00
	1842D	—	2.00	4.00	10.00	40.00
	1843A	—	2.00	4.00	10.00	40.00
	1843D	—	2.00	4.00	10.00	40.00
	1844A	—	2.00	4.00	10.00	40.00
	1844D	—	2.00	4.00	10.00	40.00
	1845A	—	2.00	4.00	10.00	40.00
	1845D	—	2.00	4.00	10.00	40.00
	1846A	—	2.00	4.00	10.00	40.00
	1847A	—	2.00	4.00	10.00	40.00
	1847D	—	2.00	4.00	10.00	40.00
	1848A	—	2.00	4.00	10.00	40.00
	1848D	—	2.00	4.00	10.00	40.00
	1849A	—	2.00	4.00	10.00	40.00
	1850A	—	2.00	4.00	10.00	40.00
	1851A	—	2.00	4.00	10.00	40.00
	1852A	—	2.00	4.00	10.00	40.00

Obv: Older head.

KM#	Date	Mintage	Fine	VF	XF	Unc
462	1853A	—	2.00	4.00	10.00	40.00
	1854A	—	2.00	4.00	10.00	40.00
	1855A	—	2.00	4.00	10.00	40.00
	1856A	—	2.00	4.00	10.00	40.00
	1857A	—	2.00	4.00	10.00	40.00
	1858A	—	2.00	4.00	10.00	40.00
	1859A	—	2.00	4.00	10.00	40.00
	1860A	—	2.00	4.00	10.00	40.00

KM#	Date	Mintage	Fine	VF	XF	Unc
485	1861A	—	1.00	2.00	5.00	30.00
	1862A	—	1.00	2.00	5.00	30.00
	1863A	—	1.00	2.00	5.00	30.00
	1864A	—	1.00	2.00	5.00	30.00
	1865A	—	1.00	2.00	5.00	30.00
	1866A	—	1.00	2.00	5.00	30.00
	1866B	—	1.00	2.00	5.00	30.00
	1867A	—	1.00	2.00	5.00	30.00
	1867B	—	1.00	2.00	5.00	30.00
	1867C	—	1.00	2.00	5.00	30.00
	1868A	—	1.00	2.00	5.00	30.00
	1868B	—	1.00	2.00	5.00	30.00
	1868C	—	1.00	2.00	5.00	30.00
	1869A	—	1.00	2.00	5.00	30.00
	1869B	—	1.00	2.00	5.00	30.00
	1869C	—	1.00	2.00	5.00	30.00
	1870A	—	1.00	2.00	5.00	30.00
	1870B	—	1.00	2.00	5.00	30.00
	1870C	—	1.00	2.00	5.00	30.00
	1871A	—	1.00	2.00	5.00	30.00
	1871B	—	1.00	2.00	5.00	30.00
	1871C	—	1.00	2.00	5.00	30.00
	1872A	—	1.00	2.00	5.00	30.00
	1872B	—	1.00	2.00	5.00	30.00
	1872C	—	1.00	2.00	5.00	30.00
	1873A	—	1.00	2.00	5.00	30.00
	1873B	—	1.00	2.00	5.00	30.00
	1873C	—	1.00	2.00	5.00	30.00

2-1/2 SILBER GROSCHEN

3.2400 g, .375 SILVER, .0390 oz ASW
Mint mark: A

KM#	Date	Mintage	Fine	VF	XF	Unc
444	1842A	—	3.00	6.00	15.00	55.00
	1843A	—	3.00	6.00	15.00	55.00
	1844A	—	3.00	6.00	15.00	55.00
	1848A	—	3.00	6.00	15.00	55.00
	1849A	—	3.00	6.00	15.00	55.00
	1850A	—	3.00	6.00	15.00	55.00
	1851A	—	3.00	6.00	15.00	55.00
	1852A	—	3.00	6.00	15.00	55.00

KM#	Date	Mintage	Fine	VF	XF	Unc
463	1853A	—	3.00	6.00	15.00	55.00
	1854A	—	3.00	6.00	15.00	55.00
	1855A	—	3.00	6.00	15.00	55.00
	1856A	—	3.00	6.00	15.00	55.00
	1857A	—	3.00	6.00	15.00	55.00
	1858A	—	3.00	6.00	15.00	55.00
	1859A	—	3.00	6.00	15.00	55.00
	1860A	—	3.00	6.00	15.00	55.00

KM#	Date	Mintage	Fine	VF	XF	Unc
486	1861A	—	2.00	4.00	10.00	40.00
	1862A	—	2.00	4.00	10.00	40.00
	1863A	—	2.00	4.00	10.00	40.00
	1864A	—	2.00	4.00	10.00	40.00
	1865A	—	2.00	4.00	10.00	40.00
	1866A	—	2.00	4.00	10.00	40.00
	1867A	—	2.00	4.00	10.00	40.00
	1867C	—	2.00	4.00	10.00	40.00
	1868A	—	2.00	4.00	10.00	40.00
	1868C	—	2.00	4.00	10.00	40.00
	1869A	—	2.00	4.00	10.00	40.00
	1869B	—	2.00	4.00	10.00	40.00
	1869C	—	2.00	4.00	10.00	40.00
	1870A	—	2.00	4.00	10.00	40.00
	1870B	—	2.00	4.00	10.00	40.00
	1870C	—	2.00	4.00	10.00	40.00
	1871A	—	2.00	4.00	10.00	40.00
	1871B	—	2.00	4.00	10.00	40.00
	1871C	—	2.00	4.00	10.00	40.00
	1872A	—	2.00	4.00	10.00	40.00
	1872B	—	2.00	4.00	10.00	40.00
	1872C	—	2.00	4.00	10.00	40.00
	1873A	—	2.00	4.00	10.00	40.00
	1873B	—	2.00	4.00	10.00	40.00
	1873C	—	2.00	4.00	10.00	40.00

4 GROSCHEN

5.3450 g, .521 SILVER, .0895 oz ASW

KM#	Date	Mintage	Fine	VF	XF	Unc
	1801A	—	10.00	20.00	70.00	185.00
370	1801A	—	10.00	20.00	70.00	185.00
	1802A	—	10.00	20.00	70.00	185.00
	1802B	—	10.00	20.00	70.00	185.00
	1803A	—	10.00	20.00	70.00	185.00
	1803B	—	10.00	20.00	70.00	185.00
	1804A	—	10.00	20.00	70.00	185.00
	1804B	—	10.00	20.00	70.00	185.00
	1805A	—	10.00	20.00	70.00	185.00
	1805B	—	10.00	20.00	70.00	185.00
	1806A	—	12.00	25.00	100.00	225.00
	1807A	—	12.00	25.00	100.00	225.00
	1808A	—	12.00	25.00	100.00	225.00
	1808G	—	12.00	25.00	100.00	225.00
	1809A	—	12.00	25.00	100.00	225.00
	1809G	—	12.00	25.00	100.00	225.00

NOTE: Earlier dates (1798-1800) exist for this type.

KM#	Date	Mintage	Fine	VF	XF	Unc
394	1816A	11.652	12.00	25.00	100.00	250.00
	1817A	14.484	12.00	25.00	100.00	250.00
	1818A	—	12.00	25.00	100.00	250.00
	1818D	—	25.00	50.00	175.00	300.00

1/6 THALER

5.3450 g, .521 SILVER, .0895 oz ASW

KM#	Date	Mintage	Fine	VF	XF	Unc
385	1809A	—	10.00	20.00	75.00	200.00
	1810A	—	10.00	20.00	75.00	200.00
	1811A	—	10.00	20.00	75.00	200.00
	1812A	—	10.00	20.00	75.00	200.00
	1812B	—	10.00	20.00	75.00	200.00
	1813A	—	10.00	20.00	75.00	200.00
	1813B	—	10.00	20.00	75.00	200.00
	1814A	—	10.00	20.00	75.00	200.00
	1814B	—	10.00	20.00	75.00	200.00
	1815A	—	10.00	20.00	75.00	200.00
	1815B	—	10.00	20.00	75.00	200.00
	1816A	—	10.00	20.00	75.00	200.00
	1816B	—	10.00	20.00	75.00	200.00
	1817B	—	10.00	20.00	75.00	200.00
	1817D	—	15.00	30.00	100.00	225.00
	1818D	—	15.00	30.00	100.00	225.00

KM#	Date	Mintage	Fine	VF	XF	Unc
411	1822A	3.264	4.00	10.00	40.00	100.00
	1823A	8.550	4.00	10.00	40.00	100.00
	1823D	.066	7.00	15.00	50.00	150.00
	1824A	3.504	4.00	10.00	40.00	100.00
	1825A	4.662	4.00	10.00	40.00	100.00
	1826A	3.300	4.00	10.00	40.00	100.00
	1826D	.636	4.00	10.00	45.00	125.00
	1827A	.972	4.00	10.00	40.00	100.00
	1827D	.924	4.00	10.00	45.00	125.00
	1828D	—	4.00	10.00	45.00	125.00
	1835A	.060	7.00	15.00	50.00	150.00
	1835D	—	4.00	10.00	45.00	125.00
	1837A	.042	7.00	15.00	50.00	150.00
	1838A	.048	7.00	15.00	50.00	150.00
	1839A	.576	4.00	10.00	40.00	100.00
	1840A	.954	4.00	10.00	40.00	100.00
	1840D	.762	4.00	10.00	45.00	125.00

KM#	Date	Mintage	Fine	VF	XF	Unc
436.1	1841A	.786	4.00	10.00	45.00	125.00
	1841D	.678	4.00	10.00	45.00	125.00
	1842A	3.046	4.00	10.00	45.00	125.00
	1842D	.576	4.00	10.00	45.00	125.00
	1843D	.426	4.00	10.00	45.00	125.00
	1844D	.270	4.00	10.00	45.00	125.00
	1845D	.096	5.00	15.00	50.00	150.00

Rev: Different crown above shield.

KM#	Date	Mintage	Fine	VF	XF	Unc
436.2	1843A	1.566	4.00	10.00	45.00	125.00
(436.3)	1844A	.948	4.00	10.00	45.00	125.00
	1845A	.312	4.00	10.00	45.00	125.00
	1846A	.270	4.00	10.00	45.00	125.00
	1847A	.240	4.00	10.00	45.00	125.00
	1848A	.912	4.00	10.00	45.00	125.00
	1849A	2.556	4.00	10.00	45.00	125.00
	1850A	.078	5.00	15.00	50.00	150.00
	1851A	—	4.00	10.00	45.00	125.00
	1852A	.372	4.00	10.00	45.00	125.00

Obv: Older head.

KM#	Date	Mintage	Fine	VF	XF	Unc
464	1853A	.216	15.00	30.00	90.00	250.00
	1854A	.116	15.00	30.00	90.00	250.00
	1855A	.030	15.00	30.00	90.00	250.00
	1856A	.051	15.00	30.00	90.00	250.00

Rev: Crowned eagle w/sceptre and orb.

KM#	Date	Mintage	Fine	VF	XF	Unc
473	1858	.096	15.00	30.00	90.00	250.00
	1859	.032	15.00	30.00	90.00	250.00
	1860	.128	15.00	30.00	90.00	250.00

KM#	Date	Mintage	Fine	VF	XF	Unc
487	1861	.249	10.00	20.00	75.00	200.00
	1862	1.180	10.00	20.00	75.00	200.00
	1863	.413	10.00	20.00	75.00	200.00
	1864	.441	10.00	20.00	75.00	200.00

Rev: Eagle w/larger head.

KM#	Date	Mintage	Fine	VF	XF	Unc
495	1865	.194	15.00	30.00	90.00	250.00
	1867	.148	15.00	30.00	90.00	250.00
	1868	.128	15.00	30.00	90.00	250.00

1/3 THALER

8.3520 g, .666 SILVER, .1788 oz ASW

KM#	Date	Mintage	Fine	VF	XF	Unc
	1801A	—	15.00	30.00	80.00	275.00
380	1801A	—	15.00	30.00	80.00	275.00
	1802A	—	15.00	30.00	80.00	275.00
	1804A	—	15.00	30.00	80.00	275.00
	1807A	—	15.00	30.00	80.00	275.00
	1809G	—	25.00	50.00	175.00	400.00

NOTE: Earlier date (1800) exists for this type.

KM#	Date	Mintage	Fine	VF	XF	Unc
386	1809A	—	65.00	125.00	300.00	500.00
	1809G	—	50.00	100.00	250.00	450.00

2/3 THALER

(Gulden)

17.3230 g, .750 SILVER, .4177 oz ASW

KM#	Date	Mintage	VG	Fine	VF	XF
363	1801	—	25.00	50.00	90.00	225.00

NOTE: Earlier dates (1796-1797) exist for this type.

Mint mark: A

Similar to KM#363, leg. ends: VON PREUSSEN.

KM#	Date	Mintage	Fine	VF	XF	Unc
392	1810	—	60.00	125.00	250.00	400.00

THALER

(Reichs)

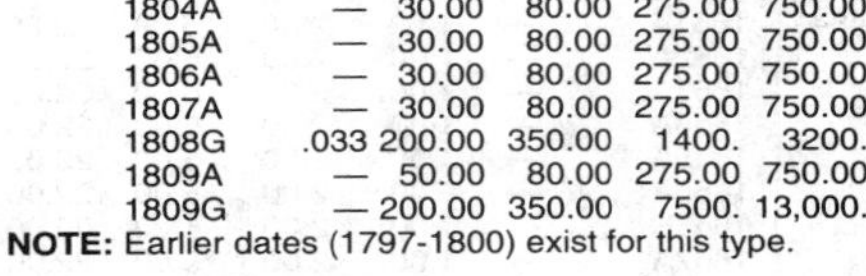

22.2720 g, .750 SILVER, .5371 oz ASW

Mint mark: A

KM#	Date	Mintage	Fine	VF	XF	Unc
368	1801A	—	30.00	80.00	200.00	700.00
	1801B	—	35.00	120.00	300.00	800.00
	1801A	—	30.00	80.00	200.00	700.00
	1802A	—	30.00	80.00	200.00	700.00
	1802B	—	35.00	120.00	300.00	800.00
	1803A	—	30.00	80.00	200.00	700.00
	1803A PRUSSEN(error)	—	—	—	—	—
	1803B	—	40.00	180.00	400.00	1000.
	1804A	—	30.00	80.00	275.00	750.00
	1805A	—	30.00	80.00	275.00	750.00
	1806A	—	30.00	80.00	275.00	750.00
	1807A	—	30.00	80.00	275.00	750.00
	1808G	.033	200.00	350.00	1400.	3200.
	1809A	—	50.00	80.00	275.00	750.00
	1809G	—	200.00	350.00	7500.	13,000.

NOTE: Earlier dates (1797-1800) exist for this type.

KM#	Date	Mintage	Fine	VF	XF	Unc
387	1809A	—	25.00	50.00	175.00	500.00
	1810A	—	25.00	50.00	175.00	500.00
	1810A (error) THAELR	—	—	—	—	—
	1811A	—	25.00	50.00	175.00	600.00
	1812A	—	25.00	50.00	175.00	600.00
	1812B	—	35.00	75.00	300.00	800.00
	1813A	—	25.00	50.00	150.00	325.00

KM#	Date	Mintage	Fine	VF	XF	Unc
387	1813B	—	35.00	75.00	300.00	800.00
	1814A	—	25.00	50.00	125.00	275.00
	1814A (error) WILHELM	—	—	—	—	—
	1815A	—	25.00	50.00	150.00	325.00
	1815B	—	50.00	100.00	400.00	1000.
	1816A	—	25.00	50.00	150.00	325.00
	1816B	—	35.00	75.00	300.00	800.00

Visit of Friedrich Wilhelm IV to Berlin Mint

KM#	Date	Mintage	Fine	VF	XF	Unc
393	1812A	—	1500.	3000.	6000.	10,000.

Obv. leg: FR. WILH. . .

KM#	Date	Mintage	Fine	VF	XF	Unc
395	1816A	—	200.00	375.00	1400.	4000.
	1817A	—	250.00	550.00	1900.	4800.

Obv. leg: FRIEDR. WILHELM. . .

KM#	Date	Mintage	Fine	VF	XF	Unc
396	1816A	—	30.00	100.00	300.00	800.00
	1817A	—	30.00	50.00	160.00	400.00
	1818A	—	30.00	50.00	160.00	400.00
	1818D	—	30.00	60.00	275.00	750.00
	1819A	—	30.00	50.00	160.00	600.00
	1819D	—	30.00	60.00	275.00	750.00
	1820A	—	30.00	50.00	160.00	600.00
	1820D	—	30.00	60.00	275.00	750.00
	1821A	—	30.00	50.00	160.00	600.00
	1821D	—	—	—	Rare	—
	1822A	—	30.00	100.00	300.00	800.00
	1822D	—	30.00	65.00	300.00	850.00

KM#	Date	Mintage	Fine	VF	XF	Unc
413	1823A	.761	25.00	50.00	120.00	400.00
	1823D	.013	75.00	125.00	500.00	1200.
	1824A	1.144	25.00	50.00	120.00	400.00
	1824D	.016	40.00	100.00	300.00	850.00
	1825A	.405	25.00	50.00	120.00	400.00
	1825D	.036	50.00	120.00	350.00	950.00
	1826A	.687	25.00	50.00	120.00	400.00

Rev: Arms of different design.

KM#	Date	Mintage	Fine	VF	XF	Unc
418	1827A	.078	65.00	150.00	500.00	1200.
418	1828A	1.578	30.00	60.00	185.00	500.00
	1828D	.012	75.00	200.00	650.00	1500.

Mint mark: A
Obv: Older head.

KM#	Date	Mintage	Fine	VF	XF	Unc
419	1828A	1.578	—	—	Rare	—
	1829A	4.002	20.00	50.00	90.00	200.00
	1829	.277	30.00	50.00	225.00	650.00
	1830A	6.888	20.00	50.00	90.00	200.00
	1830	.651	30.00	50.00	175.00	550.00
	1831A	4.595	20.00	50.00	90.00	200.00
	1831	.045	30.00	50.00	175.00	550.00
	1832A	.267	25.00	50.00	100.00	300.00
	1832	.029	30.00	60.00	225.00	700.00
	1833A	.448	25.00	50.00	100.00	300.00
	1833	.019	30.00	60.00	225.00	700.00
	1834A	1.299	20.00	50.00	90.00	200.00
	1834	.021	30.00	60.00	225.00	700.00
	1835A	.449	25.00	50.00	100.00	300.00
	1835A	—	—	—	Proof	600.00
	1835	.016	30.00	60.00	225.00	700.00
	1836A	.526	25.00	50.00	100.00	300.00
	1836	.021	30.00	60.00	225.00	700.00
	1837A	.466	25.00	50.00	100.00	300.00
	1837	.015	30.00	60.00	225.00	700.00
	1838A	.314	25.00	50.00	100.00	300.00
	1838	.025	30.00	60.00	225.00	700.00
	1839A	.247	25.00	50.00	100.00	300.00
	1839	.012	30.00	60.00	225.00	700.00
	1840A	1.630	20.00	50.00	90.00	200.00
	1840	.011	30.00	60.00	225.00	700.00
	Common date		—	—	Proof	—

(Mining)

KM#	Date	Mintage	Fine	VF	XF	Unc
417	1826A	.050	35.00	80.00	200.00	600.00
	1827A	.050	35.00	80.00	200.00	600.00
	1828A	.050	35.00	80.00	200.00	600.00

Obv: Older head.

KM#	Date	Mintage	Fine	VF	XF	Unc
420	1829A	.050	25.00	60.00	110.00	250.00
	1830A	.050	25.00	60.00	110.00	250.00
	1831A	.050	25.00	60.00	110.00	250.00
	1832A	.050	25.00	60.00	110.00	325.00
	1833A	.050	25.00	60.00	110.00	325.00
	1834A	.050	25.00	60.00	110.00	300.00
	1835A	.050	25.00	60.00	110.00	325.00
	1836A	.050	25.00	60.00	110.00	325.00
	1837A	.050	25.00	60.00	110.00	325.00
	1838A	.050	25.00	60.00	110.00	325.00
	1839A	.050	25.00	60.00	110.00	325.00
	1840A	.050	25.00	60.00	100.00	225.00

KM#	Date	Mintage	Fine	VF	XF	Unc
437	1841A	2.280	35.00	85.00	275.00	800.00

(Reichs)

KM#	Date	Mintage	Fine	VF	XF	Unc
445	1842A	.518	30.00	60.00	160.00	400.00
	1843A	.600	25.00	50.00	100.00	250.00
	1844A	.918	25.00	50.00	100.00	250.00
	1845A	.720	25.00	50.00	100.00	250.00
	1846A	1.115	25.00	50.00	100.00	250.00
	1847A	1.283	25.00	50.00	100.00	250.00
	1848A	3.743	25.00	50.00	100.00	250.00
	1849A	.892	25.00	50.00	100.00	250.00
	1850A	.350	25.00	50.00	100.00	250.00
	1851A	.731	30.00	60.00	160.00	400.00
	1852A	.329	30.00	60.00	160.00	400.00
	Common date		—	—	Proof	—

Obv: Older head.

KM#	Date	Mintage	Fine	VF	XF	Unc
465	1853A	.300	30.00	60.00	125.00	250.00
	1854A	3.500	25.00	50.00	100.00	225.00
	1855A	7.300	25.00	50.00	100.00	225.00
	1856A	.940	25.00	50.00	100.00	225.00

(Mining)

KM#	Date	Mintage	Fine	VF	XF	Unc
438	1841A	.050	50.00	110.00	300.00	950.00

Obv: Larger head. Rev: Dot after THALER.

KM#	Date	Mintage	Fine	VF	XF	Unc
446	1842A	.050	30.00	65.00	150.00	350.00
	1843A	.050	30.00	65.00	150.00	350.00
	1844A	.050	30.00	65.00	150.00	350.00
	1845A	.050	30.00	65.00	150.00	350.00
	1846A	.050	30.00	65.00	150.00	350.00

Rev: W/o dot after THALER.

KM#	Date	Mintage	Fine	VF	XF	Unc
455	1847A	.050	30.00	65.00	150.00	350.00
	1848A	.050	30.00	65.00	150.00	350.00
	1849A	.050	30.00	65.00	150.00	350.00
	1850A	.050	30.00	65.00	150.00	350.00
	1851A	.050	30.00	65.00	150.00	350.00
	1852A	.050	30.00	65.00	150.00	350.00

Obv: Older head.

KM#	Date	Mintage	Fine	VF	XF	Unc
466	1853A	.050	30.00	65.00	150.00	350.00
	1854A	.050	30.00	65.00	150.00	350.00
	1855A	.050	30.00	65.00	150.00	350.00
	1856A	.050	30.00	65.00	150.00	350.00
	Common date		—	—	Proof	—

(Vereins)

18.5200 g, .900 SILVER, .5360 oz ASW

KM#	Date	Mintage	Fine	VF	XF	Unc
471	1857A	.836	20.00	30.00	60.00	200.00
	1858A	1.120	20.00	30.00	60.00	200.00
	1859A	17.600	17.50	25.00	50.00	150.00
	1860A	17.429	17.50	25.00	50.00	150.00
	1861A	.010	40.00	80.00	125.00	250.00
	1861A	—	—	—	Proof	250.00

(Mining)

Obv: Similar to KM#471.

KM#	Date	Mintage	Fine	VF	XF	Unc
472	1857A	.047	30.00	65.00	150.00	350.00
	1858A	.095	30.00	65.00	150.00	350.00
	1859A	.094	30.00	65.00	150.00	350.00
	1860A	.298	30.00	65.00	150.00	350.00
	Common date		—	—	Proof	—

(Vereins)

Coronation of Wilhelm and Augusta

KM#	Date	Mintage	Fine	VF	XF	Unc
488	1861A	1.000	17.50	25.00	40.00	75.00
	1861A	—	—	—	Proof	—

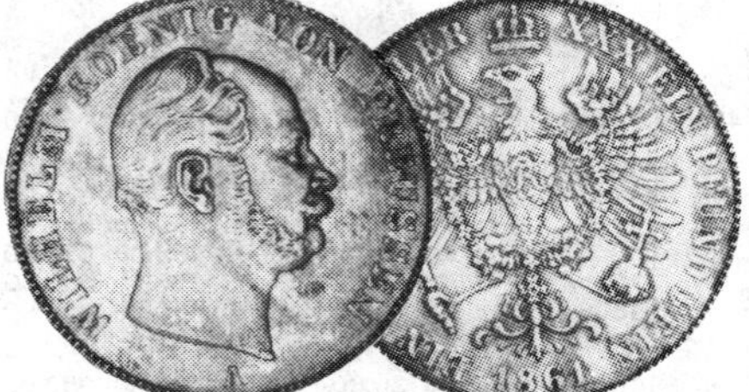

Obv: Similar to KM#494. Rev: Similar to KM#471.

KM#	Date	Mintage	Fine	VF	XF	Unc
489	1861A	13.716	20.00	35.00	65.00	150.00
	1862A	6.057	20.00	35.00	75.00	160.00
	1863A	1.668	20.00	45.00	90.00	200.00

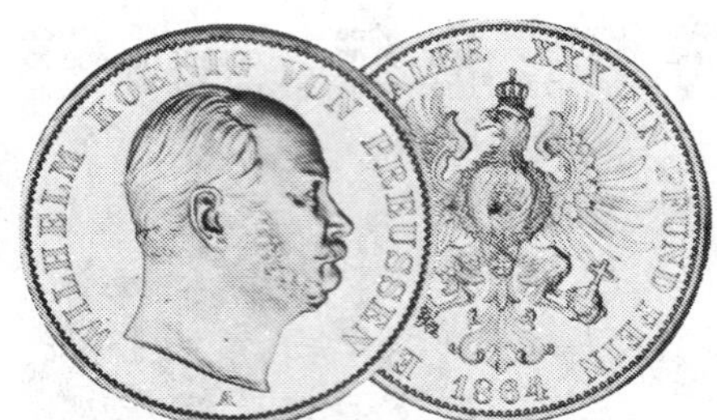

KM#	Date	Mintage	Fine	VF	XF	Unc
494	1864A	1.379	25.00	35.00	75.00	160.00
	1865A	2.584	20.00	35.00	65.00	150.00
	1866A	24.409	20.00	35.00	65.00	150.00
	1866B	.034	25.00	55.00	150.00	350.00
	1867A	31.390	20.00	35.00	65.00	150.00
	1867B	.593	25.00	55.00	150.00	350.00
	1867C	.179	35.00	100.00	250.00	600.00
	1868A	6.286	20.00	35.00	65.00	150.00
	1868B	.048	30.00	75.00	175.00	450.00
	1868C	5,139	75.00	165.00	600.00	1250.
	1869A	3.630	20.00	35.00	65.00	150.00
	1869B	.370	30.00	75.00	175.00	450.00
	1869C	.044	50.00	125.00	300.00	700.00
	1870A	3.140	20.00	35.00	65.00	150.00
	1870B	.611	25.00	55.00	150.00	350.00
	1870C	.190	35.00	100.00	250.00	600.00
	1871A	7.600	20.00	35.00	65.00	150.00
	1871B	.245	25.00	55.00	150.00	350.00
	1871C	.028	50.00	125.00	300.00	700.00
	Common date		—	—	Proof	—

(Mining)

KM#	Date	Mintage	Fine	VF	XF	Unc
490	1861A	.070	35.00	55.00	100.00	300.00
	1862A	.145	30.00	50.00	90.00	250.00

(Vereins)

Victory over Austria

KM#	Date	Mintage	Fine	VF	XF	Unc
497	1866A	.500	30.00	55.00	80.00	125.00

Victory over France

KM#	Date	Mintage	Fine	VF	XF	Unc
500	1871A	.880	17.50	25.00	40.00	75.00
	1871A	—	—	—	Proof	150.00

2 THALER

(3-1/2 Gulden)

37.1190 g, .900 SILVER, 1.0742 oz ASW

KM#	Date	Mintage	Fine	VF	XF	Unc
425	1839A	.172	100.00	150.00	300.00	800.00
	1840A	.789	75.00	125.00	225.00	600.00
439	1841A	—	—	—	Rare	—

KM#	Date	Mintage	Fine	VF	XF	Unc
440.1	1841A	4.307	55.00	85.00	185.00	400.00
	1842A	1.249	55.00	85.00	200.00	475.00

Rev: Different crown above shield.

KM#	Date	Mintage	Fine	VF	XF	Unc
440.2	1843A	.193	55.00	85.00	200.00	475.00
	1844A	1.069	55.00	85.00	200.00	475.00
	1845A	.961	55.00	85.00	200.00	475.00
	1846A	1.472	55.00	85.00	200.00	475.00
	1847A	.232	—	—	Rare	—
	1848A	4,147	—	—	Rare	—
	1850A	.221	55.00	85.00	200.00	475.00
	1851A	.379	55.00	85.00	200.00	475.00

KM#	Date	Mintage	Fine	VF	XF	Unc
467	1853A	2,500	200.00	450.00	1200.	2000.
	1854A	.147	90.00	125.00	275.00	500.00
	1855A	.100	75.00	110.00	225.00	425.00
	1856A	.627	60.00	90.00	160.00	375.00

37.0370 g, .900 SILVER, 1.0718 oz ASW
Obv: Similar to KM#467.

KM#	Date	Mintage	Fine	VF	XF	Unc
474	1858A	.017	200.00	375.00	1000.	1600.
	1859A	.174	150.00	300.00	750.00	1325.

Rev: Similar to KM#474.

KM#	Date	Mintage	Fine	VF	XF	Unc
491	1861A	9,490	500.00	1000.	1800.	3200.
	1862A	.058	250.00	460.00	1200.	2000.
	1863A	337 pcs.	—	—	Rare	—
	1863A	—	—	—	Proof	3000.

KM#	Date	Mintage	Fine	VF	XF	Unc
496	1865A	.023	175.00	350.00	1000.	1500.
	1866A	5,110	225.00	425.00	1100.	2000.
	1866C	.226	150.00	260.00	425.00	800.00
	1867A	1,195	250.00	550.00	1500.	3200.
	1867C	1.049	100.00	200.00	350.00	700.00
	1868A	1,584	250.00	550.00	1500.	3200.
	1869A	1,901	250.00	550.00	1500.	3200.
	1870A	3,155	250.00	550.00	1500.	3200.
	1871A	1,134	235.00	350.00	1100.	1750.
	Common date		—	—	Proof	1800.

1/2 KRONE

5.5550 g, .900 GOLD, .1607 oz AGW

KM#	Date	Mintage	Fine	VF	XF	Unc
475	1858A	2,036	800.00	1500.	2000.	3250.

KM#	Date	Mintage	Fine	VF	XF	Unc
493	1862A	6,365	500.00	900.00	1250.	2000.
	1863A	3,642	500.00	900.00	1250.	2000.
	1864A	4,840	500.00	900.00	1250.	2000.
	1866A	.014	500.00	900.00	1250.	2000.
	1867A	5,711	500.00	900.00	1250.	2000.
	1868A	.092	400.00	800.00	1200.	1600.
	1868B	3,718	800.00	1500.	2000.	3750.
	1869A	—	800.00	1500.	2000.	3200.

KRONE

11.1110 g, .916 GOLD, .3272 oz AGW

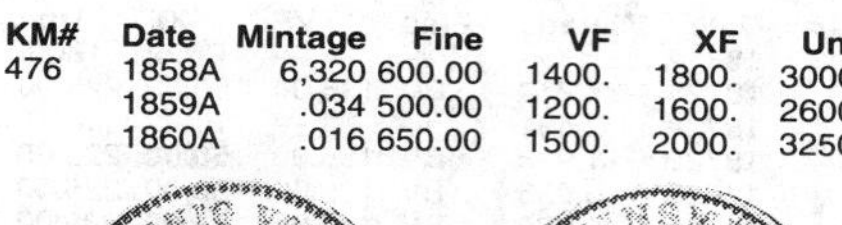

KM#	Date	Mintage	Fine	VF	XF	Unc
476	1858A	6,320	600.00	1400.	1800.	3000.
	1859A	.034	500.00	1200.	1600.	2600.
	1860A	.016	650.00	1500.	2000.	3250.

KM#	Date	Mintage	Fine	VF	XF	Unc
492	1861A	2,488	650.00	1200.	1700.	3000.
	1862A	5,558	650.00	1200.	1700.	3000.
	1863A	2,653	650.00	1200.	1700.	3000.
	1864A	792 pcs.	800.00	1400.	2000.	3250.
	1866A	720 pcs.	800.00	1400.	2000.	3250.
	1867A	4,087	400.00	800.00	1200.	2000.
	1867A	—	—	—	Proof	2500.
	1867B	.015	500.00	1200.	1700.	3000.
	1868A	.097	400.00	800.00	1200.	2000.
	1868B	.040	500.00	1200.	1700.	3000.
	1869A	—	1000.	1400.	2000.	3600.
	1870A	1,764	800.00	1400.	2000.	3250.

MONETARY REFORM

2 MARK

11.1110 g, .900 SILVER, .3215 oz ASW

KM#	Date	Mintage	Fine	VF	XF	Unc
506	1876A	13.368	10.00	35.00	200.00	425.00
	1876B	3.985	10.00	35.00	225.00	475.00
	1876C	5.233	10.00	35.00	275.00	500.00
	1877A	3.634	10.00	35.00	225.00	475.00
	1877B	1.301	15.00	50.00	320.00	625.00
	1877C	1.307	15.00	50.00	320.00	625.00
	1879A	.029	100.00	200.00	800.00	1900.
	1880A	.665	25.00	75.00	550.00	1200.
	1883A	.164	35.00	115.00	400.00	800.00
	1884A	.140	40.00	140.00	450.00	1000.

KM#	Date	Mintage	Fine	VF	XF	Unc
510	1888A	.500	12.50	20.00	40.00	75.00
	1888A	—	—	—	Proof	500.00

KM#	Date	Mintage	Fine	VF	XF	Unc
511	1888A	.141	100.00	250.00	400.00	600.00
	1888A	—	—	—	Proof	750.00

KM#	Date	Mintage	Fine	VF	XF	Unc
522	1891A	.544	10.00	20.00	40.00	150.00
	1891A	—	—	—	Proof	500.00
	1892A	.182	100.00	200.00	400.00	800.00
	1892A	—	—	—	Proof	2500.
	1893A	.948	10.00	20.00	40.00	140.00
	1896A	1.772	10.00	20.00	40.00	140.00
	1898	1.045	12.50	30.00	60.00	175.00
	1899	2.351	10.00	20.00	40.00	140.00
	1900	2.582	10.00	17.50	40.00	125.00

NOTE: Later dates (1901-1912) exist for this type.

5 MARK

27.7770 g, .900 SILVER, .8038 oz ASW

KM#	Date	Mintage	Fine	VF	XF	Unc
503	1874A	.838	17.50	45.00	275.00	575.00
	1875A	.853	17.50	50.00	350.00	1000.
	1875B	.919	17.50	45.00	350.00	1000.
	1876A	2.041	15.00	40.00	225.00	525.00
	1876B	2.098	15.00	40.00	200.00	475.00
	1876C	.812	17.50	45.00	225.00	1000.
	Common date		—	—	Proof	1750.

1.9910 g, .900 GOLD, .0576 oz AGW

KM#	Date	Mintage	Fine	VF	XF	Unc
507	1877A	1.217	100.00	150.00	200.00	300.00
	1877A	—	—	—	Proof	1300.
	1877B	.517	100.00	150.00	200.00	350.00
	1877B	—	—	—	Proof	1100.
	1877C	.688	100.00	150.00	200.00	325.00
	1878A	.502	100.00	150.00	200.00	350.00
	1878A	—	—	—	Proof	1300.

27.7770 g, .900 SILVER, .8038 oz ASW
Mint mark: A

KM#	Date	Mintage	Fine	VF	XF	Unc
512	1888A	.200	40.00	75.00	125.00	175.00
	1888A	—	—	—	Proof	500.00

Rev: Type II.

KM#	Date	Mintage	Fine	VF	XF	Unc
513	1888A	.056	175.00	425.00	800.00	1100.
	1888A	—	—	—	Proof	1750.
523	1891A	.130	15.00	35.00	130.00	625.00
	1892A	.224	15.00	35.00	130.00	625.00
	1893A	.215	15.00	35.00	150.00	525.00
	1894A	.440	15.00	40.00	110.00	525.00
	1895A	.831	15.00	40.00	130.00	525.00
	1896A	.046	95.00	175.00	750.00	1800.
	1898A	1.134	15.00	30.00	100.00	450.00
	1899A	.525	15.00	35.00	140.00	450.00
	1900A	1.080	15.00	30.00	140.00	325.00

NOTE: Later dates (1901-1908) exist for this type.

10 MARK

3.9820 g, .900 GOLD, .1152 oz AGW

KM#	Date	Mintage	Fine	VF	XF	Unc
502	1872A	3.123	60.00	95.00	120.00	200.00
	1872A	—	—	—	Proof	1600.
	1872B	1.418	60.00	95.00	120.00	275.00
	1872C	1.747	60.00	95.00	120.00	275.00
	1873A	3.016	60.00	95.00	120.00	200.00
	1873A	—	—	—	Proof	1600.
	1873B	2.273	60.00	95.00	120.00	275.00
	1873C	2.295	60.00	95.00	120.00	275.00

Rev: Type II.

KM#	Date	Mintage	Fine	VF	XF	Unc
504	1874A	.833	60.00	95.00	120.00	250.00
	1874A	—	—	—	Proof	1100.
	1874B	1.028	60.00	95.00	120.00	300.00
	1874C	.321	60.00	95.00	120.00	250.00
	1874C	—	—	—	Proof	1300.
	1875A	2.430	60.00	95.00	120.00	250.00
	1875B	.456	60.00	95.00	120.00	300.00
	1875C	1.532	60.00	95.00	120.00	250.00
	1876B	2,800	1000.	1600.	2200.	3000.
	1876B	—	—	—	Proof	10,000.
	1876C	.027	500.00	1200.	1500.	2500.
	1877A	.851	60.00	95.00	120.00	250.00
	1877B	.247	60.00	95.00	120.00	350.00
	1877C	.328	60.00	95.00	120.00	300.00
	1878A	1.126	60.00	95.00	120.00	250.00
	1878B	.015	—	—	Rare	—
	1878C	.516	60.00	95.00	120.00	300.00
	1879A	1.012	60.00	95.00	120.00	200.00
	1879	—	—	—	Proof	550.00
	1879C	.282	60.00	95.00	120.00	250.00
	1880A	1.762	60.00	95.00	120.00	200.00
	1882A	8,382	1500.	3300.	4500.	7000.
	1883A	.013	1200.	1800.	2200.	3000.
	1883A	—	—	—	Proof	10,000.
	1886A	.014	1500.	2200.	3200.	5000.
	1888A	.189	—	95.00	120.00	250.00
	1888A	—	—	—	Proof	1300.

KM#	Date	Mintage	Fine	VF	XF	Unc
514	1888A	.876	60.00	95.00	120.00	175.00
	1888A	—	—	—	Proof	600.00

Rev: Type II.

KM#	Date	Mintage	Fine	VF	XF	Unc
517	1889A	.024	1400.	2000.	2500.	3500.
	1889A	—	—	—	Proof	6000.

Rev: Type III.

KM#	Date	Mintage	Fine	VF	XF	Unc
520	1890A	1.512	55.00	95.00	120.00	200.00
	1890A	—	—	- -	Proof	500.00
	1892A	.035	400.00	700.00	1000.	1500.
	1893A	1.591	55.00	95.00	120.00	200.00
	1894A	.018	600.00	1200.	1500.	2000.
	1895A	.029	400.00	750.00	1350.	1900.
	1896A	1.081	55.00	95.00	120.00	200.00
	1897A	.114	55.00	125.00	250.00	400.00
	1898A	2.280	55.00	95.00	120.00	200.00
	1899A	.300	55.00	90.00	165.00	225.00
	1900A	.742	55.00	95.00	120.00	200.00
	1900A	—	—	—	Proof	500.00

NOTE: Later dates (1901-1912) exist for this type.

20 MARK

7.9650 g, .900 GOLD, .2304 oz AGW

KM#	Date	Mintage	Fine	VF	XF	Unc
501	1871A	.502	BV	135.00	150.00	300.00
501	1871A	—	—	—	Proof	1800.
	1872A	7.717	BV	135.00	150.00	225.00
	1872A	2,491	—	—	Proof	1800.
	1872B	1.918	BV	135.00	150.00	225.00
	1872C	3.056	BV	135.00	150.00	225.00
	1873A	9.063	BV	135.00	150.00	225.00
	1873A	—	—	—	Proof	1800.
	1873B	3.441	BV	135.00	150.00	225.00
	1873C	5.228	BV	135.00	150.00	225.00
	1873C	—	—	—	Proof	1800.

Rev: Type II.

KM#	Date	Mintage	Fine	VF	XF	Unc
505	1874A	.762	BV	115.00	140.00	200.00
	1874A	—	—	—	Proof	1300.
	1874B	.824	BV	115.00	150.00	225.00
	1874C	.088	115.00	135.00	165.00	250.00
	1875A	4.203	BV	115.00	140.00	200.00
	1875B	*1,500	165.00	400.00	650.00	1200.
	1876A	2.673	BV	115.00	140.00	200.00
	1876C	.423	135.00	275.00	400.00	550.00
	1877A	1.250	BV	115.00	140.00	200.00
	1877B	.501	BV	125.00	200.00	350.00
	1877C	6,384	1000.	1650.	2200.	2750.
	1878A	2.175	BV	115.00	140.00	200.00
	1878C	.082	120.00	250.00	400.00	600.00
	1879A	1.023	BV	115.00	140.00	200.00
	1881A	.428	BV	115.00	140.00	200.00
	1882A	.655	BV	115.00	140.00	200.00
	1882A	—	—	—	Proof	1300.
	1883A	4.283	BV	115.00	140.00	200.00
	1884A	.224	BV	115.00	140.00	200.00
	1885A	.407	BV	115.00	140.00	200.00
	1886A	.176	BV	115.00	140.00	200.00
	1887A	5.645	BV	115.00	140.00	200.00
	1887A	—	—	—	Proof	1300.
	1888A	.534	BV	115.00	140.00	200.00
	1888A	—	—	—	Proof	1300.

KM#	Date	Mintage	Fine	VF	XF	Unc
515	1888A	5.364	100.00	120.00	150.00	200.00
	1888A	—	—	—	Proof	700.00

KM#	Date	Mintage	Fine	VF	XF	Unc
516	1888A	.756	BV	115.00	135.00	225.00
	1888A	—	—	—	Proof	1000.
	1889A	9.642	BV	115.00	135.00	175.00
	1889A	—	—	—	Proof	1000.

Rev: Type III.

KM#	Date	Mintage	Fine	VF	XF	Unc
521	1890A	3.695	BV	115.00	125.00	150.00
	1891A	2.752	BV	115.00	125.00	150.00
	1891A	—	—	—	Proof	600.00
	1892A	1.815	BV	115.00	125.00	150.00
	1893A	3.172	BV	115.00	125.00	150.00
	1894A	5.815	BV	115.00	125.00	150.00
	1895A	4.135	BV	115.00	125.00	150.00
	1896A	4.239	BV	115.00	125.00	150.00
	1896A	—	—	—	Proof	600.00
	1897A	5.394	BV	115.00	125.00	150.00
	1898A	6.542	BV	115.00	125.00	150.00
	1899A	5.873	BV	115.00	125.00	150.00
	1899A	—	—	—	Proof	600.00
	1900A	5.163	BV	115.00	125.00	145.00

NOTE: Later dates (1901-1913) exist for this type.

TRADE COINAGE

1/2 FREDERICK D'OR

3.3410 g, .903 GOLD, .0970 oz AGW
Obv: L at truncation.

KM#	Date	Mintage	Fine	VF	XF	Unc
382	1802A	—	275.00	350.00	800.00	1500.
	1803A	—	550.00	800.00	1200.	2000.
	1804A	—	300.00	500.00	900.00	1625.
382	1806A	—	275.00	400.00	800.00	1500.
	1814A	—	300.00	500.00	900.00	1625.
	1816A	—	350.00	600.00	1000.	1750.

KM#	Date	Mintage	Fine	VF	XF	Unc
397	1817A	—	300.00	500.00	700.00	1250.

KM#	Date	Mintage	Fine	VF	XF	Unc
414	1825A	—	300.00	500.00	750.00	1000.
	1827A	—	375.00	650.00	875.00	1125.
	1828A	—	600.00	1000.	1250.	1500.
	1829A	—	500.00	875.00	1125.	1375.
	1830A	—	350.00	625.00	875.00	1125.
	1831A	—	350.00	625.00	875.00	1125.
	1832A	—	350.00	625.00	875.00	1125.
	1833A	—	350.00	625.00	875.00	1125.
	1834A	—	350.00	625.00	875.00	1125.
	1838A	—	350.00	625.00	875.00	1125.
	1839A	—	400.00	750.00	1000.	1250.
	1840A	—	500.00	875.00	1125.	1375.

KM#	Date	Mintage	Fine	VF	XF	Unc
441	1841A	—	300.00	500.00	750.00	1000.
	1842A	—	300.00	500.00	750.00	1000.
	1843A	—	400.00	750.00	1000.	1250.
	1844A	—	400.00	750.00	1000.	1250.
	1845A	—	400.00	750.00	1000.	1250.
	1846A	—	400.00	750.00	1000.	1250.
	1849A	—	400.00	750.00	1000.	1250.

KM#	Date	Mintage	Fine	VF	XF	Unc
468	1853A	—	400.00	750.00	1000.	1250.

FREDERICK D'OR

6.6820 g, .903 GOLD, .1940 oz AGW

KM#	Date	Mintage	Fine	VF	XF	Unc
371	1801A	—	400.00	600.00	950.00	1400.
	1801B	—	450.00	600.00	950.00	1400.
	1802A	—	450.00	600.00	950.00	1400.
	1802B	—	450.00	600.00	950.00	1400.
	1803A	—	400.00	475.00	800.00	1200.
	1803B	—	550.00	800.00	1200.	1800.
	1804A	—	450.00	600.00	950.00	1400.
	1804B	—	550.00	800.00	1200.	1800.
	1805A	—	350.00	525.00	950.00	1200.
	1805B	—	550.00	800.00	1200.	1800.
	1806A	—	350.00	525.00	950.00	1200.
	1807A	—	350.00	525.00	950.00	1200.
	1808A	—	550.00	800.00	1200.	1600.
	1809A	—	350.00	475.00	800.00	1200.
	1810A	—	450.00	600.00	950.00	1400.
	1811A	—	450.00	600.00	950.00	1400.
	1812A	—	350.00	475.00	800.00	1200.
	1813A	—	400.00	525.00	875.00	1300.
	1816A	—	450.00	600.00	950.00	1400.

NOTE: Earlier dates (1798-1800) exist for this type.

KM#	Date	Mintage	Fine	VF	XF	Unc
398	1817A	—	500.00	800.00	1200.	1800.
	1818A	—	400.00	550.00	1000.	1500.
	1819A	—	650.00	1000.	1500.	2000.
	1822A	—	400.00	550.00	1000.	1500.

KM#	Date	Mintage	Fine	VF	XF	Unc
415	1825A	—	300.00	400.00	800.00	1250.
	1827A	—	400.00	600.00	1000.	1500.
	1828A	—	300.00	550.00	800.00	1400.
	1829A	—	400.00	550.00	1000.	1500.
	1830A	—	400.00	550.00	1000.	1500.
	1831A	—	300.00	550.00	900.00	1400.
	1832A	—	300.00	550.00	900.00	1400.
	1833A	—	300.00	550.00	900.00	1400.
	1834A	—	300.00	550.00	1000.	1500.
	1836A	—	300.00	550.00	1000.	1500.
	1837A	—	300.00	550.00	800.00	1400.
	1838A	—	300.00	550.00	800.00	1500.
	1839A	—	300.00	550.00	800.00	1400.
	1840A	—	300.00	550.00	800.00	1250.

KM#	Date	Mintage	Fine	VF	XF	Unc
442	1841A	—	300.00	550.00	800.00	1250.
	1842A	—	300.00	550.00	800.00	1250.
	1843A	—	300.00	550.00	800.00	1400.
	1844A	—	300.00	550.00	800.00	1250.
	1845A	—	300.00	550.00	800.00	1250.
	1846A	—	300.00	550.00	800.00	1250.
	1847A	—	300.00	550.00	800.00	1400.
	1848A	—	300.00	550.00	800.00	1250.
	1849A	—	300.00	550.00	800.00	1250.
	1850A	—	300.00	550.00	800.00	1400.
	1851A	—	300.00	550.00	800.00	1500.
	1852A	—	300.00	550.00	800.00	1400.

KM#	Date	Mintage	Fine	VF	XF	Unc
469	1853A	—	300.00	550.00	800.00	1250.
	1854A	—	300.00	550.00	800.00	1250.
	1855A	—	300.00	550.00	800.00	1250.

2 FREDERICK D'OR

13.3630 g, .903 GOLD, .3880 oz AGW
Obv: L at truncation.

KM#	Date	Mintage	Fine	VF	XF	Unc
381	1801A	—	700.00	975.00	1800.	2600.
	1802A	—	800.00	1250.	2200.	3000.
	1806A	—	800.00	1250.	2200.	3000.
	1811A	—	700.00	975.00	1800.	2600.
	1813A	—	725.00	1000.	2000.	2800.
	1814A	—	800.00	1250.	2200.	3000.

NOTE: Earlier date (1800) exists for this type.

KM#	Date	Mintage	Fine	VF	XF	Unc
416	1825A	—	800.00	1200.	1600.	2000.
	1826A	—	700.00	1100.	1500.	1800.
	1827A	—	600.00	1000.	1400.	1600.
	1828A	—	600.00	1000.	1400.	1600.
	1829A	—	700.00	1100.	1500.	1800.
	1830A	—	550.00	900.00	1300.	1500.
	1831A	—	550.00	900.00	1300.	1500.
	1832A	—	700.00	1100.	1500.	1800.
	1836A	—	800.00	1200.	1600.	2000.
	1837A	—	550.00	900.00	1300.	1500.
	1838A	—	600.00	1000.	1400.	1600.
	1839A	—	500.00	800.00	1200.	1400.
	1840A	—	500.00	800.00	1200.	1400.

KM#	Date	Mintage	Fine	VF	XF	Unc
443	1841A	—	500.00	800.00	1200.	1500.
	1842A	—	500.00	800.00	1200.	1500.
	1843A	—	600.00	1250.	1750.	2000.
	1844A	—	800.00	1500.	2000.	2250.
	1845A	—	800.00	1500.	2000.	2250.
	1846A	—	500.00	800.00	1200.	1500.
	1848A	—	500.00	800.00	1200.	1500.
	1849A	—	500.00	800.00	1200.	1500.
	1852A	—	500.00	800.00	1200.	1500.

KM#	Date	Mintage	Fine	VF	XF	Unc
470	1853A	—	500.00	800.00	1200.	2000.
	1854A	—	500.00	800.00	1200.	2000.
	1855A	—	750.00	1500.	2000.	2500.

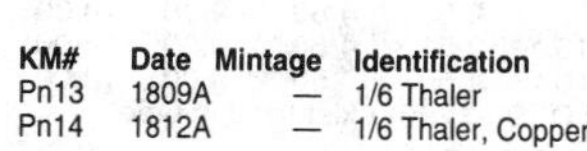

KM#	Date	Mintage	Identification	Mkt.Val.
Pn13	1809A	—	1/6 Thaler	—
Pn14	1812A	—	1/6 Thaler, Copper	—

KM#	Date	Mintage	Identification	Mkt.Val.
Pn15	1817	—	1/6 Thaler	—

KM#	Date	Mintage	Identification	Mkt.Val.
Pn16	1819A	—	1 Thaler	—

KM#	Date	Mintage	Identification	Mkt.Val.
Pn17	1823	—	1 Thaler	—
Pn18	1833	—	2 Pfenninge, Copper, KM406	70.00

KM#	Date	Mintage	Identification	Mkt.Val.
Pn19	1873A	—	5 Mark, Silver, plain edge	—
Pn20	1873A	—	5 Mark, Copper, plain edge	—

KM#	Date	Mintage	Identification	Mkt.Val.
Pn21	1875A	—	2 Mark, Silver, reeded edge	—
Pn22	1875A	—	2 Mark, Copper, plain edge	—
Pn23	1878	—	20 Mark, Silver or Silvered, KM505.1	—

KM#	Date	Mintage	Identification	Mkt.Val.
Pn24	1879A	—	5 Mark, Silver	—
Pn25	1888	—	5 Mark, Tin	—
Pn26	1888A	—	10 Mark, Silver, weak edge, KM517	—
PnA27	1890A	—	10 Mark, Copper, 2.03g	—
PnB27	1890A	—	20 Mark, Copper, 4.13g edge: GOTT MIT UNS	—
Pn27	1900	—	20 Mark, Silver, KM521.1	—

TRIAL STRIKES (TS)

TS1	ND(1888)	—	5 Mark	—

PYRMONT

A county southwest of Hannover, established c. 1160, Pyrmont's first coins were struck in the 13th century. In 1625, it was incorporated with Waldeck. Occasional issues of special coins for Pyrmont were struck in the 18th and 19th centuries.

RULERS

Georg, Prince, 1805-1812

MINTMASTERS INITIALS

Letter	Date	Name
FW	1807-1829	Friedrich Welle

24 EINEN (1/24) THALER

1.9900 g, .368 SILVER, .0235 oz ASW
Obv: Crowned and mantled 2 shields of arms.
Rev: Value above date.

C#	Date	Mintage	VG	Fine	VF	XF
6	1806 FW	—	50.00	100.00	200.00	450.00
	1807 FW	—	50.00	100.00	200.00	450.00

EIN (1) THALER

(Convention)

28.0600 g, .833 SILVER, .7515 oz ASW

C#	Date	Mintage	Fine	VF	XF	Unc
7	1811 FW	—	850.00	1500.	3250.	6000.

REGENSBURG

(Ratisbon)

MINTMASTERS INITIALS

Letter	Date	Name
B,BF,G.C.B.	1773-1803	Georg Christoph Busch
GZ,Z	1791-1802	Johann Leonhard Zollner
K, Kornlein	1773-1802	Johann Nikolaus Kornlein

FREE CITY

RULERS

Holy Roman, until 1802

ARMS

2 crossed keys

HELLER

(Kipper)

COPPER

COPPER, uniface
Crossed keys.

KM#	Date	Mintage	VG	Fine	VF	XF
470	1801	—	2.50	4.50	9.00	18.00
(C2)	1802	.192	2.50	4.50	9.00	18.00
	1803	.104	2.50	4.50	9.00	18.00

NOTE: Earlier dates (1794-1799) exist for this type.

EIN (1) THALER

SILVER

KM#	Date	Mintage	Fine	VF	XF	Unc
475	1801 Z	—	1000.	2000.	2800.	4800.
(C57)	1802 Z	—	1000.	2000.	2800.	4800.

TRADE COINAGE

DUCAT

3.5000 g, .986 GOLD, .1109 oz AGW
Obv: Titles of Franz II.

KM#	Date	Mintage	VG	Fine	VF	XF
467	ND(1792-1803) GCB					
(C103)		—	150.00	350.00	650.00	1000.

REUSS

The Reuss family, whose lands were located in Thuringia, was founded c. 1035. By the end of the 12th century, the custom of naming all males in the ruling house Heinrich had been established. The Elder Line modified this strange practice in the late 17th century to numbering all males from 1 to 100, then beginning over again. The Younger Line, meanwhile, decided to start the numbering of Heinrichs with the first male born in each century. Greiz was founded in 1303. Upper and Lower Greiz lines were founded in 1535 and the territories were divided until 1768. In 1778 the ruler was made a prince of the Holy Roman Empire. The principality endured until 1918.

MINT MARKS

A - Berlin

B - Hannover

MINTMASTERS INITIALS

Letter	Date	Name
DF, DOELL	(d. 1835)	Johann Veit Doll, die-cutter
FA	1785-1790	Facius, die-cutter
	1790-1835	in Eisenach
L	1803-1833	Georg Christoph Lowel, in Saalfeld
S, ST	1785-1790	Johann Leonhard Stockmar, die-cutter
	1790-1835	in Eisenach

REUSS-EBERSDORF

The Reuss family, whose lands were located in Thuringia, was founded c. 1035. The Ebersdorf line was founded in 1671 from the Lobenstein branch. The county became a principality in 1806. They inherited Lobenstein in 1824 and were forced to abdicate in 1849 and Lobenstein-Ebersdorf went to Schleiz.

RULERS

Heinrich LI, 1779-1822

Heinrich LXXII, 1822-1849

PFENNIG

COPPER
Obv: Crowned shield w/hound head. Rev: Value.

KM#	Date	Mintage	Fine	VF	XF	Unc
25	1812	.035	5.00	10.00	20.00	90.00

2 PFENNIG

COPPER
Obv: Crowned shield w/hound head. Rev: Value.

KM#	Date	Mintage	Fine	VF	XF	Unc
26	1812	.029	5.00	10.00	25.00	100.00

3 PFENNIG

COPPER
Obv: Crowned shield w/hound head. Rev: Value.

KM#	Date	Mintage	Fine	VF	XF	Unc
27	1812	.018	5.00	15.00	60.00	150.00

4 PFENNIG

COPPER
Obv: Crowned shield w/hound head. Rev: Value.

KM#	Date	Mintage	Fine	VF	XF	Unc
28	1812	.023	7.00	15.00	30.00	100.00

6 PFENNIG

.9500 g, .250 SILVER, .0076 oz ASW

KM#	Date	Mintage	Fine	VF	XF	Unc
29	1812	7,376	7.00	15.00	30.00	100.00

8 PFENNIG

1.3000 g, .250 SILVER, .0104 oz ASW

KM#	Date	Mintage	Fine	VF	XF	Unc
30	1812	.011	10.00	20.00	40.00	150.00

GROSCHEN

1.7600 g, .368 SILVER, .0208 oz ASW

KM#	Date	Mintage	Fine	VF	XF	Unc
31	1812	8,962	7.00	20.00	35.00	125.00
	1814	.087	7.00	20.00	35.00	125.00

EIN (1) THALER

(Species)

28.0600 g, .833 SILVER, .7515 oz ASW

KM#	Date	Mintage	Fine	VF	XF	Unc
32	1812 L	1,575	350.00	700.00	1400.	3000.

REUSS-LOBENSTEIN

The Reuss family, whose lands were located in Thuringia, was founded ca. 1035. The Lobenstein line was founded in 1635. The county became a principality in 1790. In 1824 Lobenstein was given to Ebersdorf.

RULERS

Heinrich XXXV, 1782-1805
Heinrich LIV, 1805-1824

3 PFENNIG

BILLON

KM#	Date	Mintage	Fine	VF	XF	Unc
		Obv: Crowned lion.				
15	1804	.110	6.00	12.00	25.00	65.00
		Different ruler.				
17	1807	.054	6.00	12.00	25.00	65.00
		Obv: Uncrowned lion.				
18	1807	Inc. Ab.	6.00	12.00	25.00	65.00

1/48 THALER

.9700 g, .250 SILVER, .0077 oz ASW
Obv: Crowned lion. Rev: Value.

KM#	Date	Mintage	Fine	VF	XF	Unc
16	1805	.033	8.00	16.00	35.00	80.00

REUSS-LOBENSTEIN-EBERSDORF

This line was formed by the merger between Ebersdorf and Lobenstein in 1824. The prince abdicated during political troubles in 1848 and the lands went to Schleiz in 1849.

RULERS

Heinrich LXXII (as Prince of Reuss-Ebersdorf) 1822-1824
(as Prince of Reuss-Lobenstein-Ebersdorf), 1824-1849

PFENNIG

COPPER

KM#	Date	Mintage	Fine	VF	XF	Unc
1	1841A	.316	5.00	10.00	20.00	50.00
	1844A	.381	5.00	10.00	20.00	50.00

3 PFENNIG

COPPER

KM#	Date	Mintage	Fine	VF	XF	Unc
2	1841A	.107	6.00	12.00	25.00	60.00
	1844A	.180	6.00	12.00	25.00	60.00

1/2 SILBER GROSCHEN

1.0900 g, .222 SILVER, .0077 oz ASW
Obv: Crowned shield w/crowned lion. Rev: Value.

KM#	Date	Mintage	Fine	VF	XF	Unc
3	1841A	.070	7.00	15.00	30.00	70.00

SILBER GROSCHEN

2.1900 g, .222 SILVER, .0156 oz ASW
Obv: Crowned shield w/crowned lion. Rev: Value.

KM#	Date	Mintage	Fine	VF	XF	Unc
4	1841A	.059	7.00	15.00	30.00	70.00
	1844A	.087	7.00	15.00	30.00	70.00

2 THALER

(3-1/2 Gulden)

37.1200 g, .900 SILVER, 1.0742 oz ASW

KM#	Date	Mintage	Fine	VF	XF	Unc
5	1840A	2,750	225.00	450.00	800.00	1800.
	1847A	5,500	200.00	400.00	750.00	1700.

25th Anniversary of Reign
Obv: Similar to KM#5.

KM#	Date	Mintage	Fine	VF	XF	Unc
6	1847A	500 pcs.	400.00	700.00	1500.	2850.

REUSS-OBERGREIZ

The other branch of the division of 1535, Obergreiz went through a number of consolidations and further divisions. Upon the extinction of the Ruess-Untergreiz line in 1768, the latter passed to Reuss-Obergreiz and this line continued on into the 20th century, obtaining the rank of count back in 1673 and that of prince in 1778.

RULERS

Heinrich XIII, 1800-1817
Heinrich XIX, 1817-1836
Heinrich XX, 1836-1859
Heinrich XXII, 1859-1902

HELLER

COPPER
Obv: Crowned lion on crowned oval shield.
Rev: Value.

KM#	Date	Mintage	Fine	VF	XF	Unc
100	1812	.045	4.00	8.00	20.00	65.00
	1815	.045	4.00	8.00	20.00	65.00
	1817	.040	4.00	8.00	20.00	65.00
	1819	.048	4.00	8.00	20.00	65.00

PFENNIG

COPPER

KM#	Date	Mintage	Fine	VF	XF	Unc
92	1806	.187	3.00	6.00	15.00	60.00
	1808	.273	3.00	6.00	15.00	60.00
		Obv: Crowned lion on crowned oval shield.				
95	1808	—	3.00	6.00	15.00	60.00
	1810	.443	3.00	6.00	15.00	60.00
	1812	—	3.00	6.00	15.00	60.00
	1813	—	3.00	6.00	15.00	60.00
	1814	—	3.00	6.00	15.00	60.00
	1815	—	3.00	6.00	15.00	60.00
	1816	—	3.00	6.00	15.00	60.00

KM#	Date	Mintage	Fine	VF	XF	Unc
102	1817	—	2.50	5.00	15.00	55.00
	1819	—	2.50	5.00	12.00	55.00
	1820	—	2.50	5.00	12.00	55.00
	1821	—	2.50	5.00	12.00	55.00
	1822	—	2.50	5.00	12.00	55.00
	1823	—	2.50	5.00	12.00	55.00
	1824	—	2.50	5.00	12.00	55.00
	1825	—	2.50	5.00	12.00	55.00
	1826	—	2.50	5.00	12.00	55.00
	1827	—	2.50	5.00	12.00	55.00
	1828	—	2.50	5.00	12.00	55.00
	1829	—	2.50	5.00	12.00	55.00
	1830	—	2.50	5.00	12.00	55.00
	1831L	—	2.50	5.00	12.00	55.00
	1832L	—	2.50	5.00	12.00	55.00

Obv: King's crown.

KM#	Date	Mintage	Fine	VF	XF	Unc
115	1864 A	.360	1.50	3.00	7.00	40.00

Obv: Prince's crown.

KM#	Date	Mintage	Fine	VF	XF	Unc
117	1868 A	.360	1.50	3.00	7.00	35.00

3 PFENNIG

COPPER

KM#	Date	Mintage	Fine	VF	XF	Unc
90	1805	.092	3.00	6.00	15.00	60.00
	1806	—	3.00	6.00	15.00	60.00
	1808	.256	3.00	6.00	15.00	60.00
	1810	.415	3.00	6.00	15.00	60.00

KM#	Date	Mintage	Fine	VF	XF	Unc
90	1812	.296	3.00	6.00	15.00	60.00
	1813	—	3.00	6.00	15.00	60.00
	1814	—	3.00	6.00	15.00	60.00
	1815	—	3.00	6.00	15.00	60.00
	1816	—	3.00	6.00	15.00	60.00

KM#	Date	Mintage	Fine	VF	XF	Unc
103	1817	.144	2.50	5.00	12.00	55.00
	1819	—	2.50	5.00	12.00	55.00
	1820	—	2.50	5.00	12.00	55.00
	1821	—	2.50	5.00	12.00	55.00
	1822	—	2.50	5.00	12.00	55.00
	1823	—	2.50	5.00	12.00	55.00
	1824	—	2.50	5.00	12.00	55.00
	1825	—	2.50	5.00	12.00	55.00
	1826	—	2.50	5.00	12.00	55.00
	1827	—	2.50	5.00	12.00	55.00
	1828	—	2.50	5.00	12.00	55.00
	1829	—	2.50	5.00	12.00	55.00
	1830	—	2.50	5.00	12.00	55.00
	1831L	—	2.50	5.00	12.00	55.00
	1832L	—	2.50	5.00	12.00	55.00
	1833 L	—	2.50	5.00	12.00	55.00

NOTE: Varieties exist.

Obv: King's crown.

KM#	Date	Mintage	Fine	VF	XF	Unc
116	1864 A	.360	2.00	4.00	8.00	35.00

Obv: Prince's crown.

KM#	Date	Mintage	Fine	VF	XF	Unc
118	1868 A	.240	2.00	4.00	8.00	35.00

GROSCHEN

1.7600 g, .368 SILVER, .0208 oz ASW

KM#	Date	Mintage	Fine	VF	XF	Unc
91	1805	.251	2.50	5.00	12.00	50.00
	1812	.110	2.50	5.00	12.00	50.00

2.1900 g, .220 SILVER, .0154 oz ASW

KM#	Date	Mintage	Fine	VF	XF	Unc
119	1868 A	.090	3.00	6.00	15.00	65.00

1/6 THALER

5.3600 g, .541 SILVER, .0932 oz ASW

KM#	Date	Mintage	Fine	VF	XF	Unc
96	1808 L	9,006	75.00	150.00	300.00	500.00

1/3 THALER

7.0100 g, .833 SILVER, .1877 oz ASW

KM#	Date	Mintage	Fine	VF	XF	Unc
97	1809 L	1,500	150.00	350.00	650.00	1200.

THALER

28.0600 g, .833 SILVER, .7515 oz ASW
Obv. leg: D.G. HENR. XIII . . .

KM#	Date	Mintage	Fine	VF	XF	Unc
93	1806 DOELL-L	345 pcs.	750.00	1400.	3200.	7500.
	1807 DOELL-L	200 pcs.	750.00	1400.	3200.	7500.

Obv. leg: V.G.G. HEINRICH . . .
Rev: Similar to KM#93.

KM#	Date	Mintage	Fine	VF	XF	Unc
94	1807 DF-L	300 pcs.	1000.	1600.	3500.	7500.
	1812 DF-L	2,275	900.00	1500.	2750.	6500.

KM#	Date	Mintage	Fine	VF	XF	Unc
101	1812 DF-L	I.A.	350.00	700.00	1250.	3000.

18.5200 g, .900 SILVER, .5360 oz ASW

KM#	Date	Mintage	Fine	VF	XF	Unc
110	1858A	9,500	60.00	100.00	200.00	450.00

KM#	Date	Mintage	Fine	VF	XF	Unc
120	1868A	7,100	60.00	100.00	200.00	450.00

2 THALER

(3-1/2 Gulden)

37.1200 g, .900 SILVER, 1.0742 oz ASW

KM#	Date	Mintage	Fine	VF	XF	Unc
105	1841A	2,400	200.00	375.00	750.00	1500.
	1844A	2,400	200.00	375.00	750.00	1500.
	1848A	2,400	200.00	375.00	750.00	1500.
	1851A	2,400	200.00	375.00	750.00	1500.

MONETARY REFORM

2 MARK

11.1110 g, .900 SILVER, .3215 oz ASW
Rev: Type II.

KM#	Date	Mintage	Fine	VF	XF	Unc
126	1877B	.020	150.00	300.00	1500.	2750.
	1877B	—	—	—	Proof	3250.

Rev: Type III.

KM#	Date	Mintage	Fine	VF	XF	Unc
127	1892A	.010	125.00	325.00	650.00	950.00
	1892A	—	—	—	Proof	1250.

KM#	Date	Mintage	Fine	VF	XF	Unc
128	1899A	.010	100.00	200.00	400.00	550.00
	1899A	120 pcs.	—	—	Proof	650.00

NOTE: Later date (1901) exists for this type.

20 MARK

7.9650 g, .900 GOLD, .2304 oz AGW
Rev: Type II.

KM#	Date	Mintage	Fine	VF	XF	Unc
125	1875B	1,510	6000.	9000.	12,500.	17,500.
	1875B	—	—	—	Proof	25,000.

REUSS-SCHLEIZ

Originally part of the holdings of Reuss-Gera, Schleiz was ruled separately on and off during the first half of the 16th century. When the Gera line died out in 1550, Schleiz passed to Obergreiz. Schleiz was reintegrated into a new line of Gera and a separate countship at Schleiz was founded in 1635, only to last one generation. At its extinction in 1666, Schleiz passed to Reuss-Saalburg which thereafter took the name of Reuss-Schleiz.

RULERS

Heinrich XLII, 1784-1818
Heinrich LXII, 1818-1854
Heinrich LXVII, 1854-1867
Heinrich XIV, 1867-1913

1/2 PFENNIG

(1 Heller)

COPPER

KM#	Date	Mintage	Fine	VF	XF	Unc
56	1841A	—	15.00	30.00	60.00	175.00

PFENNIG

COPPER

KM#	Date	Mintage	Fine	VF	XF	Unc
57	1841A	.751	4.00	7.00	20.00	75.00
	1847A	1.138	4.00	7.00	20.00	75.00

KM#	Date	Mintage	Fine	VF	XF	Unc
65	1850A	.540	2.00	4.00	8.00	40.00

KM#	Date	Mintage	Fine	VF	XF	Unc
69	1855A	.362	2.00	4.00	8.00	40.00
	1858A	.360	2.00	4.00	8.00	40.00
	1862A	.202	2.00	4.00	8.00	40.00
	1864A	.540	2.00	4.00	8.00	40.00

KM#	Date	Mintage	Fine	VF	XF	Unc
75	1868A	.360	2.00	4.00	8.00	40.00

3 PFENNIG

COPPER
Obv: Oval crowned shield w/crowned lion.
Rev: Value.

KM#	Date	Mintage	Fine	VF	XF	Unc
50	1815	.076	5.00	10.00	20.00	75.00
	1816	Inc. Ab.	5.00	10.00	20.00	75.00

KM#	Date	Mintage	Fine	VF	XF	Unc
58	1841A	.250	4.00	8.00	15.00	55.00
	1844A	.379	3.00	6.00	12.50	50.00

KM#	Date	Mintage	Fine	VF	XF	Unc
66	1850A	.311	3.00	6.00	12.50	50.00

KM#	Date	Mintage	Fine	VF	XF	Unc
70	1855A	.242	3.00	6.00	12.50	50.00
	1858A	.360	3.00	6.00	12.50	50.00
	1862A	.125	3.00	6.00	12.50	50.00
	1864A	.240	3.00	6.00	12.50	50.00

KM#	Date	Mintage	Fine	VF	XF	Unc
76	1868A	.120	3.00	6.00	12.50	50.00

SILBER GROSCHEN

1.7600 g, .368 SILVER, .0208 oz ASW
Obv: Oval crowned arms, crowned lion w/1 tail.
Rev: Value.

KM#	Date	Mintage	Fine	VF	XF	Unc
51	1815	—	5.00	10.00	20.00	125.00

Obv: Uncrowned lion w/1 tail.

KM#	Date	Mintage	Fine	VF	XF	Unc
52	1816S	.033	5.00	10.00	20.00	125.00

Obv: Crowned lion w/2 tails.

KM#	Date	Mintage	Fine	VF	XF	Unc
53	1816S	Inc. Ab.	5.00	10.00	20.00	125.00

2.1900 g, .222 SILVER, .0156 oz ASW

KM#	Date	Mintage	Fine	VF	XF	Unc
59	1841A	.064	4.00	8.00	15.00	90.00
	1844A	.092	4.00	8.00	15.00	90.00
	1846A	.062	4.00	8.00	15.00	90.00

Obv. leg: JUNGERER LINIE

KM#	Date	Mintage	Fine	VF	XF	Unc
67	1850A	.062	4.00	8.00	15.00	100.00

KM#	Date	Mintage	Fine	VF	XF	Unc
71	1855A	.031	5.00	10.00	20.00	125.00

2 SILBER GROSCHEN

3.1100 g, .312 SILVER, .0311 oz ASW
Obv: Crowned shield w/crowned lion. Rev: Value.

KM#	Date	Mintage	Fine	VF	XF	Unc
68	1850A	.064	5.00	10.00	20.00	125.00

KM#	Date	Mintage	Fine	VF	XF	Unc
72	1855A	.031	10.00	20.00	40.00	150.00

THALER

(Vereins)

18.5200 g, .900 SILVER, .5360 oz ASW

KM#	Date	Mintage	Fine	VF	XF	Unc
73	1858A	10,000	45.00	75.00	140.00	350.00
	1862A	10,000	45.00	75.00	140.00	350.00

Rev: Similar to KM#73.

KM#	Date	Mintage	Fine	VF	XF	Unc
77	1868A	.014	40.00	65.00	125.00	325.00

2 THALER

(3-1/2 Gulden)

37.1200 g, .900 SILVER, 1.0742 oz ASW

KM#	Date	Mintage	Fine	VF	XF	Unc
55	1840A	2,650	250.00	400.00	800.00	1500.
	1844A	3,000	250.00	400.00	800.00	1500.
	1846A	2,650	250.00	400.00	800.00	1500.
	1853A	2,700	250.00	400.00	800.00	1500.
	1854A	2,700	225.00	450.00	1000.	1600.

25th Anniversary of Reign
Obv: Similar to KM#55.

KM#	Date	Mintage	Fine	VF	XF	Unc
60	1843A	500 pcs.	350.00	700.00	1500.	3000.

MONETARY REFORM

2 MARK

11.1110 g, .900 SILVER, .3215 oz ASW

KM#	Date	Mintage	Fine	VF	XF	Unc
82	1884A	.100	150.00	300.00	850.00	1500.
	1884A	—	—	—	Proof	2500.

10 MARK

3.9820 g, .900 GOLD, .1152 oz AGW

81	1882A	4,800	1250.	2500.	4000.	5000.
	1882A	200 pcs.	—	—	Proof	10,000.

20 MARK

7.9650 g, .900 GOLD, .2304 oz AGW

80	1881A	.012	1000.	1500.	2500.	3250.
	1881A	500 pcs.	—	—	Proof	6000.

RHENISH CONFEDERATION

Issues for Carl von Dahlberg,
1804-1817

MINTMASTERS INITIALS

Letter	Date	Name
B,CB	1773-1811	Christoph Busch, Regensburg
BH	1790-1825	Johann Georg Bunsen, mintmaster in Frankfurt
	1798-1816	Johann Georg Hille, mintwarden in Frankfurt

HELLER

COPPER
Obv. leg: FURST PRIM SCHEIDE MUNZ.

C#	Date	Mintage	Fine	VF	XF	Unc
1	1808 BH	.033	10.00	30.00	70.00	150.00
	1810 BH	—	10.00	30.00	70.00	150.00
	1812 BH	—	10.00	30.00	70.00	150.00

Obv. leg: GROSH FRANKF SCHEIDE MUNZ.

2	1810 BH	—	10.00	30.00	70.00	150.00
	1812 BH	—	10.00	30.00	70.00	150.00

KREUZER

BILLON
Obv. leg: SCHEID.MUNZ.

3.1	1808 BH	—	8.00	25.00	50.00	150.00
	1809 BH	—	8.00	25.00	50.00	150.00
	1810 BH	—	8.00	25.00	50.00	150.00

Obv. leg: SCHEIDMUNZ.

3.2	1809 BH	—	8.00	25.00	60.00	150.00

1/2 THALER

(Convention)

.833 SILVER

C#	Date	Mintage	Fine	VF	XF	Unc
5	1809 B	—	65.00	100.00	175.00	300.00

EIN (1) THALER

(Convention)

28.0600 g, .833 SILVER, .7516 oz ASW

4	1808 BH	—	175.00	375.00	650.00	1200.

6	1809 B	—	150.00	325.00	1100.	2500.

C#	Date	Mintage	Fine	VF	XF	Unc
7	1809 CB	—	150.00	325.00	800.00	2200.

TRADE COINAGE

DUCAT

3.5000 g, .986 GOLD, .1109 oz AGW

8	1809 BH	—	500.00	1000.	1750.	2750.

ROSTOCK

A city, near the Baltic Sea in Mecklenburg, has a history from the 12th century. The first municipal charter dates from 1218. In 1325 Rostock obtained the mint right and not long after, joined the Hanseatic League. The city coinage extends to 1864.

MINTMASTERS INITIALS

Letter	Date	Name
AIB	1805	Andreas Joachim Brand
AS	1815-1824	Adam Schiller
BS	1843-1859	Benjamin Steinhorst
FL	1796-1802	Friedrich Lautersack
HK	1862-1864	Heinrich Kehr

PFENNIG

COPPER
Obv: Griffin shield within ring. Rev: Value.

C#	Date	Mintage	Fine	VF	XF	Unc
2a	1801 FL	—	5.00	10.00	25.00	70.00
	1802 FL	—	5.00	10.00	25.00	70.00

NOTE: Earlier dates (1796-1800) exist for this type.

Obv. leg: ROSTOCKER begins at 8 o'clock.

4	1802 FL	—	5.00	10.00	25.00	70.00
	1805 AIB	—	5.00	10.00	25.00	70.00

Obv: W/o circle between griffin and legend.

4a	1815 AS	—	4.00	8.00	20.00	70.00
	1824 AS	—	4.00	8.00	20.00	60.00

5	1848 BS	—	4.00	8.00	20.00	70.00

3 PFENNIG

COPPER

10	1815 AS	—	4.00	8.00	22.00	75.00
	1824 AS	—	4.00	8.00	22.00	75.00
10a	1843 BS	.192	4.00	8.00	22.00	75.00

C#	Date	Mintage	Fine	VF	XF	Unc
11	1855 BS	—	4.00	8.00	22.00	75.00

C#	Date	Mintage	Fine	VF	XF	Unc
12	1859 BS	—	4.00	8.00	22.00	75.00

C#	Date	Mintage	Fine	VF	XF	Unc
12a	1862 HK	—	4.00	8.00	22.00	75.00
	1864 HK	—	4.00	8.00	22.00	75.00

SAXE-ALTENBURG

A duchy, located in Thuringia in northwest Germany. It came into being in 1826 when Saxe-Gotha-Altenburg became extinct. The duke of Saxe-Hildburghausen ceded Hildburghausen to Meiningen in exchange for Saxe- Altenburg. The last duke abdicated in 1918.

RULERS

Joseph, 1834-1848
Georg, 1848-1853
Ernst I, 1853-1908
Ernst II, 1908-1918

MINTMASTERS INITIALS

B - Gustav Julius Buschick
F - Gustav Theodor Fischer
G - Johann Georg Grohmann

PFENNIG

COPPER

Obv: Crowned arms. Rev: Value.

C#	Date	Mintage	Fine	VF	XF	Unc
1	1841 G	.220	1.50	3.00	6.00	40.00

Obv: Crowned heart shaped arms.

C#	Date	Mintage	Fine	VF	XF	Unc
2	1843 G	.089	2.00	4.00	8.00	45.00

Rev: F below date.

C#	Date	Mintage	Fine	VF	XF	Unc
11	1852 F	.120	1.50	3.00	6.00	40.00

Rev: F below date.

C#	Date	Mintage	Fine	VF	XF	Unc
14	1856 F	.041	2.00	4.00	8.00	45.00
	1858 F	.129	1.50	3.00	6.00	40.00

Rev: W/o initial.

C#	Date	Mintage	Fine	VF	XF	Unc
14a	1857	—	1.50	3.00	6.00	40.00

Rev: B below date.

C#	Date	Mintage	Fine	VF	XF	Unc
14b	1861 B	.163	1.50	3.00	6.00	40.00
	1863 B	.302	1.50	3.00	6.00	40.00
	1865 B	.150	1.50	3.00	6.00	40.00

2 PFENNIG

COPPER

Obv: Crowned arms. Rev: Value.

C#	Date	Mintage	Fine	VF	XF	Unc
3	1841 G	.150	2.00	4.00	8.00	45.00

Obv: Crowned heart shaped arms.

C#	Date	Mintage	Fine	VF	XF	Unc
4	1843 G	.046	2.50	5.00	10.00	50.00

C#	Date	Mintage	Fine	VF	XF	Unc
12	1852 F	.060	2.50	5.00	10.00	50.00
15	1856 F	.029	2.50	5.00	10.00	50.00

5 PFENNIG

(1/2 Neugroschen)

1.0600 g, .229 SILVER, .0078 oz ASW

Obv: Crowned arms. Rev: Value.

C#	Date	Mintage	Fine	VF	XF	Unc
5	1841 G	.097	4.00	8.00	20.00	75.00
	1842 G	.130	4.00	8.00	20.00	75.00

10 PFENNIG

(1 Neugroschen)

2.1200 g, .229 SILVER, .0156 oz ASW

Obv: Crowned arms. Rev: Value.

C#	Date	Mintage	Fine	VF	XF	Unc
6	1841 G	.146	4.00	8.00	20.00	75.00
	1842 G	.065	4.00	8.00	20.00	75.00

20 PFENNIG

(2 Neugroschen)

3.1100 g, .312 SILVER, .0311 oz ASW

C#	Date	Mintage	Fine	VF	XF	Unc
7	ND	—	5.00	10.00	20.00	60.00
7a	1841 G	.231	6.00	12.00	25.00	80.00

1/6 THALER

5.3450 g, .520 SILVER, .0894 oz ASW

C#	Date	Mintage	Fine	VF	XF	Unc
8	1841 G	.060	10.00	25.00	100.00	250.00
	1842 G	.060	10.00	25.00	100.00	250.00

THALER

22.2720 g, .750 SILVER, .5371 oz ASW

C#	Date	Mintage	Fine	VF	XF	Unc
9	1841 G	.020	75.00	150.00	325.00	1000.

(Vereins)

18.5200 g, .900 SILVER, .5360 oz ASW

C#	Date	Mintage	Fine	VF	XF	Unc
16	1858 F	.032	40.00	75.00	150.00	325.00
	1858 F	—	—	—	Proof	450.00
	1864 B	.022	30.00	60.00	125.00	300.00
	1869 B	.023	30.00	60.00	125.00	300.00

2 THALER

(3-1/2 Gulden)

37.1190 g, .900 SILVER, 1.0742 oz ASW

C#	Date	Mintage	Fine	VF	XF	Unc
10	1841 G	9,400	200.00	375.00	800.00	1600.
	1842 G	4,700	250.00	500.00	1000.	2000.
	1843 G	4,700	225.00	450.00	900.00	1900.
	1847 F	9,400	200.00	375.00	850.00	1800.

Rev: Similar to 1 Thaler, C#16.

C#	Date	Mintage	Fine	VF	XF	Unc
13	1852 F	9,400	250.00	450.00	900.00	1900.

MONETARY REFORM

20 MARK

7.9650 g, .900 GOLD, .2304 oz AGW

Y#	Date	Mintage	Fine	VF	XF	Unc
146	1887A	.015	800.00	1000.	1500.	2000.
	1887A	—	—	—	Proof	3750.

SAXE-COBURG-GOTHA

Located in northwest Germany, Saxe-Coburg-Gotha was created for the duke of Saxe-Coburg-Saalfeld after the dispersal of Saalfeld and the acquisition of Gotha in 1826. The last duke abdicated in 1918.

RULERS

Ernst I, 1826-1844
Ernst II, 1844-1893
Alfred, 1893-1900
Karl Eduard, 1900-1918

MINTMASTERS INITIALS

Letter	Date	Name
B	1860-1887	Gustav Julius Buschick
EK	1828-38	Ernst Kleinsteuber
F	1845-60	Gustav Theodor Fischer
G	1826-28	Graupner
G	1838-44	Johann Georg Grohmann
ST	1826-1828	Strebel

PFENNIG

COPPER

C#	Date	Mintage	Fine	VF	XF	Unc
83	1833	—	2.00	4.00	8.00	50.00

C#	Date	Mintage	Fine	VF	XF	Unc
83	1834	—	2.00	4.00	8.00	50.00
	1835	—	2.00	4.00	8.00	50.00
	1836	—	2.00	4.00	8.00	50.00
	1837	—	2.00	4.00	8.00	50.00

Obv: Crowned arms within branches.

C#	Date	Mintage	Fine	VF	XF	Unc
100	1841 G	.333	2.00	4.00	8.00	50.00

Obv: F above crowned arms.

C#	Date	Mintage	Fine	VF	XF	Unc
109	1847 F	.207	1.50	3.00	6.00	50.00
	1851 F	.059	1.50	3.00	6.00	50.00
	1852 F	.201	1.50	3.00	6.00	50.00
	1856 F	.600	1.50	3.00	6.00	50.00

Obv: B above arms.

C#	Date	Mintage	Fine	VF	XF	Unc
109a	1865 B	.150	1.50	3.00	6.00	50.00

C#	Date	Mintage	Fine	VF	XF	Unc
109b	1868 B	.200	1.50	3.00	6.00	50.00
	1870 B	.096	1.50	3.00	6.00	50.00

1-1/2 PFENNIG

COPPER

C#	Date	Mintage	Fine	VF	XF	Unc
84	1834	—	2.00	4.00	8.00	50.00
	1835	—	2.00	4.00	8.00	50.00

2 PFENNIG

COPPER

C#	Date	Mintage	Fine	VF	XF	Unc
85	1834	—	2.00	4.00	8.00	50.00
	1835	—	2.00	4.00	8.00	50.00

C#	Date	Mintage	Fine	VF	XF	Unc
101	1841 G	.333	2.00	4.00	8.00	50.00

Obv: F and date below bow.

C#	Date	Mintage	Fine	VF	XF	Unc
110	1847 F	.130	1.50	3.00	6.00	50.00
	1851 F	.125	1.50	3.00	6.00	50.00
	1852 F	.146	1.50	3.00	6.00	50.00
	1856 F	.600	1.50	3.00	6.00	50.00

Obv: B and date below bow.

C#	Date	Mintage	Fine	VF	XF	Unc
110a	1868 B	.136	1.50	3.00	6.00	50.00
	1870 B	.118	1.50	3.00	6.00	50.00

3 PFENNIG

COPPER

C#	Date	Mintage	Fine	VF	XF	Unc
86	1834	—	4.00	8.00	17.50	65.00

KREUZER

.7900 g, .125 SILVER, .0031 oz ASW
Obv: ST below crowned E. Rev: Value in script.

C#	Date	Mintage	Fine	VF	XF	Unc
86.5	1827 ST	—	5.00	12.00	30.00	120.00

C#	Date	Mintage	Fine	VF	XF	Unc
87	1827 ST	—	5.00	12.00	30.00	120.00
	1828 ST	—	5.00	12.00	30.00	120.00

Obv: EK below crowned E.

C#	Date	Mintage	Fine	VF	XF	Unc
87a	1829 EK	—	5.00	12.00	30.00	120.00
	1830 EK	—	5.00	12.00	30.00	120.00

Rev: KREUZER along bottom rim.

C#	Date	Mintage	Fine	VF	XF	Unc
88	1831	—	2.00	6.00	10.00	60.00
	1832	—	2.00	6.00	10.00	60.00
	1833	—	2.00	6.00	10.00	60.00
	1834	—	2.00	6.00	10.00	60.00
	1836	—	2.00	6.00	10.00	60.00
	1837	—	2.00	6.00	10.00	60.00

3 KREUZER

1.5000 g, .243 SILVER, .0117 oz ASW
Obv: Crowned E within branches, ST below.
Rev: Value in script.

C#	Date	Mintage	Fine	VF	XF	Unc
89.5	1827 ST	—	10.00	30.00	50.00	200.00

C#	Date	Mintage	Fine	VF	XF	Unc
90	1827 ST	—	8.00	20.00	40.00	175.00
	1828 ST	—	8.00	20.00	40.00	175.00
	1829 S	—	8.00	20.00	40.00	175.00
	1829 ST	—	8.00	20.00	40.00	175.00

Obv: EK below crowned E.

C#	Date	Mintage	Fine	VF	XF	Unc
90a	1828 EK	—	8.00	20.00	40.00	175.00
	1830 EK	—	8.00	20.00	40.00	175.00
	1831 EK	—	8.00	20.00	40.00	175.00

C#	Date	Mintage	Fine	VF	XF	Unc
91	1831	—	2.00	5.00	15.00	80.00
	1832	—	2.00	5.00	15.00	80.00
	1833	—	2.00	5.00	15.00	80.00
	1834	—	2.00	5.00	15.00	80.00
	1835	—	2.00	5.00	15.00	80.00
	1836	—	2.00	5.00	15.00	80.00
	1837	—	2.00	5.00	15.00	80.00

Obv: Crowned arms. Rev: Value within branches.

C#	Date	Mintage	Fine	VF	XF	Unc
101.3	1838	.358	2.00	5.00	15.00	80.00

6 KREUZER

2.7300 g, .305 SILVER, .0267 oz ASW

C#	Date	Mintage	Fine	VF	XF	Unc
92	1827 G	—	7.00	15.00	50.00	150.00
	1827 ST	—	7.00	15.00	50.00	150.00
	1828 ST	—	7.00	15.00	50.00	150.00
	1828 EK	—	7.00	15.00	50.00	150.00
	1829 EK	—	7.00	15.00	50.00	150.00
	1830 EK	—	7.00	15.00	50.00	150.00

C#	Date	Mintage	Fine	VF	XF	Unc
93	1831	—	3.00	5.00	20.00	100.00
	1832	—	3.00	5.00	20.00	100.00
	1833	—	3.00	5.00	20.00	100.00
	1834	—	3.00	5.00	20.00	100.00
	1835	—	3.00	5.00	20.00	100.00
	1836	—	3.00	5.00	20.00	100.00
	1837	—	3.00	5.00	20.00	100.00

C#	Date	Mintage	Fine	VF	XF	Unc
101.6	1838	.209	3.00	5.00	20.00	100.00

10 KREUZER

3.8900 g, .500 SILVER, .0625 oz ASW
Similar to C#94b.

C#	Date	Mintage	Fine	VF	XF	Unc
94	1831	—	20.00	35.00	70.00	250.00
	1832	—	20.00	35.00	70.00	250.00
	1833	—	20.00	35.00	70.00	250.00
	1834	—	20.00	35.00	70.00	250.00

C#	Date	Mintage	Fine	VF	XF	Unc
94b	1835	—	15.00	30.00	60.00	200.00
	1836	—	15.00	30.00	60.00	200.00
	1837	—	15.00	30.00	60.00	200.00

20 KREUZER

6.6800 g, .583 SILVER, .1252 oz ASW
Obv. leg: . . . COBURG & GOTHA . . .
crowned arms. Rev: ST below value.

C#	Date	Mintage	Fine	VF	XF	Unc
95	1827 ST	—	20.00	50.00	125.00	300.00

Obv. leg: . . . COBURG UND GOTHA . . .

C#	Date	Mintage	Fine	VF	XF	Unc
95a	1827 ST	—	20.00	50.00	125.00	300.00
	1828 ST	—	20.00	50.00	125.00	300.00

Rev: E.K. below branches.

C#	Date	Mintage	Fine	VF	XF	Unc
95b	1828 EK	—	20.00	50.00	125.00	300.00
	1830 EK	—	20.00	50.00	125.00	300.00

Similar to C#96a.

C#	Date	Mintage	Fine	VF	XF	Unc
96	1831	—	20.00	50.00	125.00	300.00
	1834	—	20.00	50.00	125.00	300.00

Obv. leg. ends: . . . SACHSEN COBURG-GOTHA

C#	Date	Mintage	Fine	VF	XF	Unc
96a	1835	—	15.00	35.00	60.00	200.00
	1836	—	15.00	35.00	60.00	200.00

1/2 GROSCHEN

1.0600 g, .229 SILVER, .0078 oz ASW

C#	Date	Mintage	Fine	VF	XF	Unc
102	1841 G	.247	5.00	10.00	35.00	125.00
	1844 G	.065	5.00	10.00	35.00	125.00

C#	Date	Mintage	Fine	VF	XF	Unc
111	1851 F	.032	2.00	4.00	8.00	50.00
	1855 F	.130	2.00	4.00	8.00	50.00
	1858 F	.060	2.00	4.00	8.00	50.00

Obv: B below arms.

C#	Date	Mintage	Fine	VF	XF	Unc
114	1868 B	.032	2.00	4.00	8.00	50.00
	1870 B	.052	2.00	4.00	8.00	50.00

GROSCHEN

1.9800 g, .368 SILVER, .0234 oz ASW

C#	Date	Mintage	Fine	VF	XF	Unc
89	1837	—	5.00	10.00	30.00	125.00

2.1200 g, .229 SILVER, .0156 oz ASW

C#	Date	Mintage	Fine	VF	XF	Unc
103	1841 G	.355	8.00	15.00	40.00	175.00

C#	Date	Mintage	Fine	VF	XF	Unc
112	1847 F	.130	2.00	4.00	8.00	50.00
	1851 F	.049	2.00	4.00	8.00	50.00
	1855 F	.130	2.00	4.00	8.00	50.00
	1858 F	.033	2.00	4.00	8.00	50.00

C#	Date	Mintage	Fine	VF	XF	Unc
115	1865 B	.070	2.00	4.00	8.00	50.00
	1868 B	.031	2.00	4.00	8.00	50.00
	1870 B	.030	2.00	4.00	8.00	50.00

2 GROSCHEN

3.1100 g, .312 SILVER, .0311 oz ASW
Obv: Crowned arms within branches. Rev: Value.

C#	Date	Mintage	Fine	VF	XF	Unc
104	1841 G	.214	8.00	20.00	40.00	150.00
	1844 G	.032	8.00	20.00	40.00	150.00

C#	Date	Mintage	Fine	VF	XF	Unc
113	1847 F	.097	6.00	12.00	25.00	75.00
	1851 F	.032	6.00	12.00	25.00	75.00
	1855 F	.081	6.00	12.00	25.00	75.00
	1858 F	.055	6.00	12.00	25.00	75.00

3.2200 g, .300 SILVER, .0310 oz ASW

C#	Date	Mintage	Fine	VF	XF	Unc
116	1865 B	.070	5.00	10.00	20.00	65.00
	1868 B	.030	5.00	10.00	20.00	65.00
	1870 B	.031	5.00	10.00	20.00	65.00

1/6 THALER

5.3450 g, .521 SILVER, .0895 oz ASW

C#	Date	Mintage	Fine	VF	XF	Unc
105	1841 G	.048	15.00	40.00	75.00	225.00
	1842 G	.048	15.00	40.00	75.00	225.00
	1843 G	.048	15.00	40.00	75.00	225.00

Obv: Different head.

C#	Date	Mintage	Fine	VF	XF	Unc
117	1845 F	.123	15.00	35.00	75.00	225.00

C#	Date	Mintage	Fine	VF	XF	Unc
117a	1848 F	.130	10.00	30.00	60.00	200.00

Obv: Head w/beard.

C#	Date	Mintage	Fine	VF	XF	Unc
117b	1852 F	.048	15.00	35.00	75.00	225.00
	1855 F	.060	15.00	35.00	75.00	225.00

5.3400 g, .520 SILVER, .0892 oz ASW

C#	Date	Mintage	Fine	VF	XF	Unc
118	1864 B	.060	10.00	30.00	60.00	200.00

25th Anniversary of Reign

C#	Date	Mintage	Fine	VF	XF	Unc
119	1869 B	.012	10.00	30.00	50.00	150.00

1/2 THALER

(Convention)
(1 Gulden)

14.0300 g, .833 SILVER, .3757 oz ASW

C#	Date	Mintage	Fine	VF	XF	Unc
97	1830 EK	—	65.00	135.00	300.00	650.00
	1831	—	65.00	135.00	300.00	650.00
	1832	—	65.00	135.00	300.00	650.00
	1834	—	65.00	135.00	300.00	650.00
	1835 HF	—	65.00	135.00	300.00	650.00
97a	1834 HF	—	65.00	135.00	300.00	650.00

EIN (1) THALER

(Krone)

29.3800 g, .871 SILVER, .8228 oz ASW

C#	Date	Mintage	Fine	VF	XF	Unc
98	1827	—	350.00	700.00	1000.	2000.

(Convention)

28.0600 g, .833 SILVER, .7514 oz ASW

C#	Date	Mintage	Fine	VF	XF	Unc
99	1828	31 pcs.	—	—	Rare	—
	1828	—	—	—	Proof 10,000.	

C#	Date	Mintage	Fine	VF	XF	Unc
99a	1829 E-K	1,095	400.00	800.00	1500.	2750.

Rev: W/o mintmasters initials.

C#	Date	Mintage	Fine	VF	XF	Unc
99b	1832	304 pcs.	—	—	Rare	—
	1833	Inc. Ab.	—	—	Rare	—
99c	1835	—	800.00	1700.	3000.	5000.

22.2700 g, .750 SILVER, .5371 oz ASW
Rev: Crowned draped arms within wreath.

C#	Date	Mintage	Fine	VF	XF	Unc
106	1841 G	.016	75.00	150.00	400.00	1000.
	1842 G	.016	75.00	150.00	400.00	1000.

C#	Date	Mintage	Fine	VF	XF	Unc
120	1846 F	.032	75.00	150.00	400.00	1000.

C#	Date	Mintage	Fine	VF	XF	Unc
120a	1848 F	.016	75.00	150.00	400.00	1000.

C#	Date	Mintage	Fine	VF	XF	Unc
120b	1851 F	8,000	75.00	150.00	400.00	1000.
	1852 F	8,000	75.00	150.00	400.00	1000.

(Vereins)

18.5200 g, .900 SILVER, .5360 oz ASW

C#	Date	Mintage	Fine	VF	XF	Unc
121	1862 B	.040	45.00	90.00	200.00	450.00
	1864 B	.040	45.00	90.00	200.00	450.00
	1870 B	.022	60.00	100.00	225.00	500.00

25th Anniversary of Reign

C#	Date	Mintage	Fine	VF	XF	Unc
122	1869 B	6,000	45.00	85.00	150.00	300.00

2 THALER

(3-1/2 Gulden)

37.1200 g, .900 SILVER, 1.0743 oz ASW

C#	Date	Mintage	Fine	VF	XF	Unc
107	1841 G	.011	250.00	500.00	1000.	2200.
	1842 G	5,350	300.00	600.00	1100.	2400.
	1843 G	5,350	300.00	600.00	1100.	2400.

Rev: Similar to C#123a.

C#	Date	Mintage	Fine	VF	XF	Unc
123	1847 F	.011	350.00	625.00	1400.	2800.

C#	Date	Mintage	Fine	VF	XF	Unc
123a	1854 F	.016	225.00	425.00	1000.	2000.

MONETARY REFORM

2 MARK

11.1110 g, .900 SILVER, .3215 oz ASW

Y#	Date	Mintage	Fine	VF	XF	Unc
149	1895A	.015	250.00	650.00	900.00	1250.

5 MARK

27.7770 g, .900 SILVER, .8038 oz ASW

Y#	Date	Mintage	Fine	VF	XF	Unc
150	1895A	4,000	750.00	1500.	2000.	3000.
	1895A	—	—	—	Proof	3250.

20 MARK

7.9650 g, .900 GOLD, .2304 oz AGW
Rev: Type I.

Y#	Date	Mintage	Fine	VF	XF	Unc
148	1872E	1,000	7000.	11,000.	15,000.	19,000.
	1872E	—	—	—	Proof	Rare

Y#	Date	Mintage	Fine	VF	XF	Unc
148a	1886A	.020	500.00	900.00	1400.	1800.
	1886A	—	—	—	Proof	3750.

Y#	Date	Mintage	Fine	VF	XF	Unc
151	1895A	.010	500.00	1200.	2000.	2750.
	1895A	225 pcs.	—	—	Proof	4500.

TRADE COINAGE

DUCAT

3.5000 g, .986 GOLD, .1109 oz AGW

C#	Date	Mintage	Fine	VF	XF	Unc
108	1831 E-K	600 pcs.	900.00	2000.	3250.	4250.

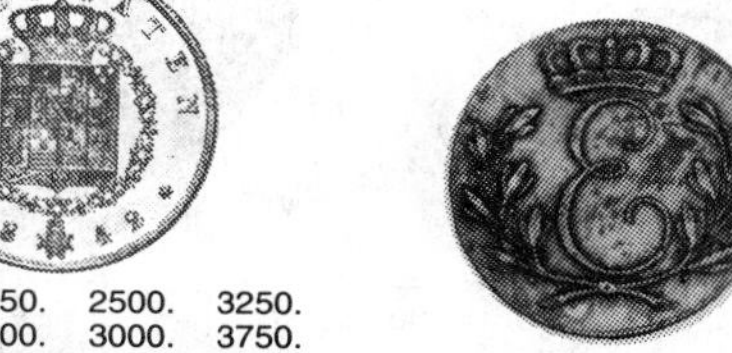

C#	Date	Mintage	Fine	VF	XF	Unc
108a	1836	1,600	600.00	1250.	2500.	3250.
	1842	508 pcs.	600.00	1500.	3000.	3750.

SAXE-COBURG-SAALFELD

A duchy, located in northwest Germany, was founded in 1680 as Saxe-Saalfeld. They obtained Coburg in 1735. In 1826, Saalfeld was given to Meiningen and the ruler became the first duke of Saxe-Coburg-Gotha.

RULERS

Franz, 1800-1806
Ernst I, 1806-1826

MINTMASTERS INITIALS

Letter	Date	Name
L	1803-1816	Georg Christoph Loewel
S	1816-1826	Laurentius Theodor Sommer, warden

HELLER

COPPER

C#	Date	Mintage	Fine	VF	XF	Unc
63	1808	—	2.00	4.00	10.00	50.00
	1809	.112	2.00	4.00	10.00	50.00
	1810	.071	2.00	4.00	10.00	50.00
	1814	.050	2.00	4.00	10.00	50.00
	1815	Inc. Ab.	2.00	4.00	10.00	50.00
	1817	—	2.00	4.00	10.00	50.00
	1818	—	2.00	4.00	10.00	50.00
	1819	—	2.00	4.00	10.00	50.00
	1824	—	2.00	4.00	10.00	50.00
	1826	—	2.00	4.00	10.00	50.00

C#	Date	Mintage	Fine	VF	XF	Unc
68	1809	—	3.00	5.00	10.00	50.00

PFENNIG

COPPER

C#	Date	Mintage	Fine	VF	XF	Unc
47	1804	—	1.50	3.00	6.00	50.00
	1805	—	1.50	3.00	6.00	50.00
	1808	.083	1.50	3.00	6.00	50.00
	1809	.055	1.50	3.00	6.00	50.00
	1814	.043	1.50	3.00	6.00	50.00
	1815	Inc. Ab.	1.50	3.00	6.00	50.00
47	1817	—	1.50	3.00	6.00	50.00
	1819	—	1.50	3.00	6.00	50.00
	1820	—	1.50	3.00	6.00	50.00
	1821	—	1.50	3.00	6.00	50.00
	1822	—	1.50	3.00	6.00	50.00
	1823	—	1.50	3.00	6.00	50.00
	1824	—	1.50	3.00	6.00	50.00
	1826	—	1.50	3.00	6.00	50.00

Rev: W/o rosettes on sides of 'I'.

C#	Date	Mintage	Fine	VF	XF	Unc
47a	1805	—	1.50	3.00	6.00	50.00

BILLON

C#	Date	Mintage	Fine	VF	XF	Unc
56	1805	—	1.50	3.00	6.00	50.00
73	1808	.962	4.00	7.00	15.00	70.00

COPPER

C#	Date	Mintage	Fine	VF	XF	Unc
69	1809	—	3.00	5.00	10.00	60.00

2 PFENNIG

COPPER

C#	Date	Mintage	Fine	VF	XF	Unc
70	1810	.124	3.00	10.00	20.00	60.00
	1817	—	3.00	10.00	20.00	60.00
	1818	—	3.00	10.00	20.00	60.00

Rev: W/o rosettes on sides of 2.

C#	Date	Mintage	Fine	VF	XF	Unc
70a	1810	Inc. Ab.	3.00	10.00	20.00	60.00

3 PFENNIG

.7900 g, .125 SILVER, .0031 oz ASW

C#	Date	Mintage	Fine	VF	XF	Unc
49	1804	—	3.00	7.00	15.00	50.00
	1805	—	3.00	7.00	15.00	50.00
	1806	—	3.00	7.00	15.00	50.00

COPPER
Obv: Arms on crowned cartouche w/festoons.

C#	Date	Mintage	Fine	VF	XF	Unc
48	1806	—	3.00	5.00	10.00	45.00

Rev. value: III PFENNIG

C#	Date	Mintage	Fine	VF	XF	Unc
65	1807	—	4.00	8.00	20.00	60.00
	1808	.063	4.00	8.00	20.00	60.00

C#	Date	Mintage	Fine	VF	XF	Unc
65a	1821	—	2.00	6.00	15.00	50.00
	1822	—	2.00	6.00	15.00	50.00
	1823	—	2.00	6.00	15.00	50.00
	1824	—	2.00	6.00	15.00	50.00
	1825	—	2.00	6.00	15.00	50.00
	1826	—	2.00	6.00	15.00	50.00

4 PFENNIG

COPPER

C#	Date	Mintage	Fine	VF	XF	Unc
71	1809	.027	4.00	8.00	20.00	75.00
	1810	8,106	4.00	8.00	20.00	75.00
	1818	—	4.00	8.00	20.00	75.00
	1820	—	4.00	8.00	20.00	75.00

6 PFENNIG

1.2900 g, .229 SILVER, .0094 oz ASW

C#	Date	Mintage	Fine	VF	XF	Unc
66	1808	.047	5.00	10.00	25.00	75.00
	1810	—	5.00	10.00	25.00	75.00
	1818 S	—	5.00	10.00	25.00	75.00
	1820 S	—	5.00	10.00	25.00	75.00

KREUZER

.7900 g, .125 SILVER, .0031 oz ASW

C#	Date	Mintage	Fine	VF	XF	Unc
57	1805	—	5.00	10.00	20.00	75.00

Obv: Crowned E within 2 crossed branches.
Rev: Value, leg: H.S.C.

C#	Date	Mintage	Fine	VF	XF	Unc
74	1808	.068	4.00	8.00	16.00	60.00
	1812	.018	4.00	8.00	16.00	60.00
	1813	.018	4.00	8.00	16.00	60.00
	1815	.021	4.00	8.00	16.00	60.00
	1817	—	4.00	8.00	16.00	60.00
	1818	—	4.00	8.00	16.00	60.00
	1820	—	4.00	8.00	16.00	60.00

Rev. leg: H.S.C.S.

C#	Date	Mintage	Fine	VF	XF	Unc
74a	1824 S	—	3.00	7.00	14.00	60.00
	1825 S	—	3.00	7.00	14.00	60.00
	1826 S	—	3.00	7.00	14.00	60.00

3 KREUZER

1.5000 g, .243 SILVER, .0117 oz ASW
Obv: Crowned oval arms. Rev: Value.

C#	Date	Mintage	Fine	VF	XF	Unc
58	1804	—	4.00	8.00	16.00	60.00

Obv: Pointed arms.

C#	Date	Mintage	Fine	VF	XF	Unc
58a	1805	—	4.00	8.00	16.00	60.00

Rev. leg: H.S. COBURG. L.M.

C#	Date	Mintage	Fine	VF	XF	Unc
59	1805	—	4.00	8.00	16.00	65.00

Rev. leg: H.S. COBURG LAND. M.

C#	Date	Mintage	Fine	VF	XF	Unc
59a	1805	—	4.00	8.00	16.00	65.00

Obv: Crowned E within, L below crossed branches.
Rev: Value, leg: H.S.C.

C#	Date	Mintage	Fine	VF	XF	Unc
75b	1808	—	4.00	8.00	16.00	65.00
75	1808 L	.137	4.00	8.00	16.00	65.00
	1810 L	.151	4.00	8.00	16.00	65.00
	1812 L	.196	4.00	8.00	16.00	65.00
	1813 L	.143	4.00	8.00	16.00	65.00
	1814 L	.116	4.00	8.00	16.00	65.00
	1815 L	.026	4.00	8.00	16.00	65.00

Obv: S below crossed branches.

C#	Date	Mintage	Fine	VF	XF	Unc
75c	1816 S	—	4.00	8.00	16.00	65.00
	1817 S	—	4.00	8.00	16.00	65.00
	1818 S	—	4.00	8.00	16.00	65.00
	1819 S	—	4.00	8.00	16.00	65.00
	1820 S	—	4.00	8.00	16.00	65.00

Rev. leg: H.S.C.S.

C#	Date	Mintage	Fine	VF	XF	Unc
75a	1821 S	—	5.00	10.00	20.00	70.00
	1822 S	—	5.00	10.00	20.00	70.00
	1823 S	—	5.00	10.00	20.00	70.00
	1824 S	—	5.00	10.00	20.00	70.00
	1825 S	—	5.00	10.00	20.00	70.00
	1826 S	—	5.00	10.00	20.00	70.00

Obv: G below crossed branches.

C#	Date	Mintage	Fine	VF	XF	Unc
75d	1826 G	—	5.00	10.00	20.00	70.00

6 KREUZER

2.7200 g, .305 SILVER, .0266 oz ASW
Obv: Crowned shield. Rev: Value.

C#	Date	Mintage	Fine	VF	XF	Unc
60	1804	—	4.00	8.00	20.00	100.00
	1805	—	4.00	8.00	20.00	100.00

Rev. leg: H.S. COBURG. LAND. M.

C#	Date	Mintage	Fine	VF	XF	Unc
61	1805	—	4.00	8.00	20.00	100.00

Obv: Crowned E within, L below crossed branches.
Rev. leg: H.S.C.

C#	Date	Mintage	Fine	VF	XF	Unc
76	1808 L	.075	4.00	8.00	16.00	65.00
	1810 L	.056	4.00	8.00	16.00	65.00
	1812 L	.089	4.00	8.00	16.00	65.00
	1813 L	.042	4.00	8.00	16.00	65.00
	1814 L	.050	4.00	8.00	16.00	65.00
	1815 L	.011	4.00	8.00	16.00	65.00

Obv: S below crossed branches.

C#	Date	Mintage	Fine	VF	XF	Unc
76b	1816 S	—	4.00	8.00	16.00	65.00
	1817 S	—	4.00	8.00	16.00	65.00
	1818 S	—	4.00	8.00	16.00	65.00
	1819 S	—	4.00	8.00	16.00	65.00
	1820 S	—	4.00	8.00	16.00	65.00

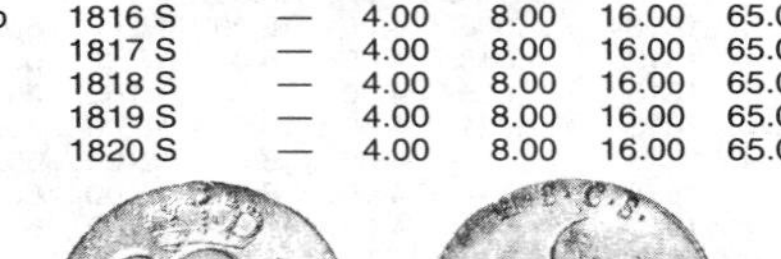

Rev. leg: H.S.C.S.

C#	Date	Mintage	Fine	VF	XF	Unc
76a	1821 S	—	5.00	10.00	25.00	100.00
	1822 S	—	5.00	10.00	25.00	100.00
	1823 S	—	5.00	10.00	25.00	100.00
	1824 S	—	5.00	10.00	25.00	100.00
	1825 S	—	5.00	10.00	25.00	100.00
	1826 S	—	5.00	10.00	25.00	100.00

10 KREUZER

3.8900 g, .500 SILVER, .0625 oz ASW
Obv. leg: . . . SACHS. SOUV . . ., crowned arms.
Rev: Value within bound branches.

C#	Date	Mintage	Fine	VF	XF	Unc
77	1820 S	—	25.00	50.00	150.00	350.00

Obv. leg: . . . SACHS. COBURG.

C#	Date	Mintage	Fine	VF	XF	Unc
77a	1824 S	—	50.00	75.00	175.00	400.00

20 KREUZER

6.6800 g, .583 SILVER, .1252 oz ASW

C#	Date	Mintage	Fine	VF	XF	Unc
79	1807 L	—	25.00	65.00	150.00	400.00

Rev: Date below wreath.

C#	Date	Mintage	Fine	VF	XF	Unc
79a	1807	—	30.00	75.00	175.00	450.00

C#	Date	Mintage	Fine	VF	XF	Unc
80	1812 L	.030	15.00	50.00	125.00	375.00
	1813 L	.046	15.00	50.00	125.00	375.00
	1819 S	—	15.00	50.00	125.00	375.00
	1820 S	—	15.00	50.00	125.00	375.00

C#	Date	Mintage	Fine	VF	XF	Unc
80a	1823 S	—	15.00	50.00	125.00	375.00
	1824 S	—	15.00	50.00	125.00	375.00
	1825 S	—	15.00	50.00	125.00	375.00
	1826 S	—	15.00	50.00	125.00	375.00

GROSCHEN

1.9800 g, .368 SILVER, .0234 oz ASW

C#	Date	Mintage	Fine	VF	XF	Unc
67	1808	.026	2.00	4.00	10.00	60.00
	1810	—	2.00	4.00	10.00	60.00
	1818 S	—	2.00	4.00	10.00	60.00

48 EINEN (1/48) THALER

.9700 g, .250 SILVER, .0077 oz ASW

C#	Date	Mintage	Fine	VF	XF	Unc
52	1804	—	7.00	15.00	30.00	125.00

C#	Date	Mintage	Fine	VF	XF	Unc
52a	1804	—	—	—	Rare	—
	1805	—	6.00	12.00	25.00	125.00
	1806	—	—	—	Rare	—

24 EINEN (1/24) THALER

1.9800 g, .368 SILVER, .0234 oz ASW

C#	Date	Mintage	Fine	VF	XF	Unc
54	1805	—	6.00	15.00	35.00	100.00

EIN (1) THALER

(Convention)

28.0600 g, .833 SILVER, .7516 oz ASW

C#	Date	Mintage	Fine	VF	XF	Unc
62	1805 L	600 pcs.	300.00	600.00	1000.	2000.

C#	Date	Mintage	Fine	VF	XF	Unc
81	1817	—	150.00	300.00	600.00	1200.

Edge: EIN SPECIESTHALER

C#	Date	Mintage	Fine	VF	XF	Unc
81a	1817	—	150.00	300.00	700.00	1500.

(Krone)

29.3800 g, .871 SILVER, .8228 oz ASW

C#	Date	Mintage	Fine	VF	XF	Unc
82	1825	—	1000.	2000.	3500.	6000.
	1825	—	—	—	—	Proof 12,000.

SAXE-HILDBURGHAUSEN

Saxe-Hildburghausen was founded from the division of Saxe-Gotha, by the sixth son of Ernst the Pious. In 1826, the last duke assigned Hildburghausen to Saxe-Meiningen in exchange for Altenburg.

RULERS

Joseph Prince Regent, 1780-1787
Friedrich I, 1780-1826

HELLER

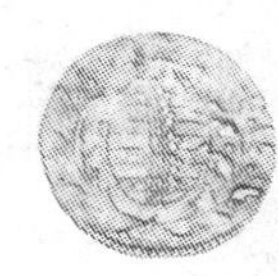

COPPER

KM#	Date	Mintage	Fine	VF	XF	Unc
130	1804	—	3.00	5.00	15.00	50.00
	1805	—	3.00	5.00	15.00	50.00
	1806	—	3.00	5.00	15.00	50.00

KM#	Date	Mintage	Fine	VF	XF	Unc
133	1808	—	1.50	4.00	8.00	40.00
	1809	—	1.50	4.00	8.00	40.00
	1811	—	1.50	4.00	8.00	40.00
	1812	—	1.50	4.00	8.00	40.00
	1816	—	1.50	4.00	8.00	40.00
	1817	—	1.50	4.00	8.00	40.00
	1818	—	1.50	4.00	8.00	40.00

KM#	Date	Mintage	Fine	VF	XF	Unc
140	1820	—	1.50	4.00	8.00	40.00
	1821	—	1.50	4.00	8.00	40.00
	1822	—	1.50	4.00	8.00	40.00
	1823	—	1.50	4.00	8.00	40.00
	1824	—	1.50	4.00	8.00	40.00
	1825	—	1.50	4.00	8.00	40.00

PFENNIG

COPPER

KM#	Date	Mintage	Fine	VF	XF	Unc
142	1823	—	3.00	5.00	15.00	50.00
	1825	—	3.00	5.00	15.00	50.00
	1826	—	3.00	5.00	15.00	50.00

Obv: Crowned rectangular arms.

KM#	Date	Mintage	Fine	VF	XF	Unc
149	1826	—	5.00	10.00	25.00	80.00

1/8 KREUZER

COPPER

Obv: Crowned F within crossed branches.
Rev. leg: KREUZER LANDMUNZE, value.

KM#	Date	Mintage	Fine	VF	XF	Unc
146	1825	—	3.00	5.00	15.00	60.00

1/4 KREUZER

COPPER

KM#	Date	Mintage	Fine	VF	XF	Unc
147	1825	—	4.00	8.00	16.00	60.00

Obv: Crowned heart shaped arms, H.S.H.H.

KM#	Date	Mintage	Fine	VF	XF	Unc
148	1825	—	4.00	8.00	16.00	60.00

1/2 KREUZER

COPPER

Obv: Crowned arms. Rev: Value in script.

KM#	Date	Mintage	Fine	VF	XF	Unc
134	1809	—	5.00	10.00	20.00	70.00
	1809	—	5.00	10.00	20.00	70.00

Obv: Crowned heart-shaped arms, leg: HERZ.Z.S.
Rev: Value

KM#	Date	Mintage	Fine	VF	XF	Unc
143	1823	—	5.00	10.00	25.00	80.00

Obv. leg: HERZOGTHUM

KM#	Date	Mintage	Fine	VF	XF	Unc
144	1823	—	5.00	10.00	25.00	80.00

Rev: Value, leg: KREUZER LANDMUNZE.

KM#	Date	Mintage	Fine	VF	XF	Unc
145	1823	—	6.00	12.00	30.00	90.00

KREUZER

BILLON

KM#	Date	Mintage	Fine	VF	XF	Unc
131	1804	—	7.00	15.00	35.00	125.00
	1805	—	7.00	15.00	35.00	125.00

Obv: Crowned oval arms within branches.
Rev: Value.

KM#	Date	Mintage	Fine	VF	XF	Unc
132	1806	—	6.00	15.00	30.00	100.00
	1811	—	6.00	15.00	30.00	100.00

3 KREUZER

BILLON

Obv: Crowned F within wreath.
Rev: Value within ring.

KM#	Date	Mintage	Fine	VF	XF	Unc
135	1808	—	4.50	9.00	25.00	100.00
	1810	—	4.50	9.00	25.00	100.00
	1811	—	4.50	9.00	25.00	100.00
	1812	—	4.50	9.00	25.00	100.00
	1815	—	4.50	9.00	25.00	100.00
	1816	—	4.50	9.00	25.00	100.00
	1817	—	4.50	9.00	25.00	100.00
	1818	—	4.50	9.00	25.00	100.00
	1820	—	4.50	9.00	25.00	100.00

6 KREUZER

BILLON

KM#	Date	Mintage	Fine	VF	XF	Unc
136	1805	—	6.50	15.00	35.00	125.00
	1808	—	6.50	15.00	35.00	125.00
	1811	—	6.50	15.00	35.00	125.00
	1812	—	6.50	15.00	35.00	125.00
	1815	—	6.50	15.00	35.00	125.00
	1816	—	6.50	15.00	35.00	125.00
	1817	—	6.50	15.00	35.00	125.00
	1818	—	6.50	15.00	35.00	125.00

Obv: Crowned F within crossed branches.
Rev: Value.

KM#	Date	Mintage	Fine	VF	XF	Unc
141	1820	—	6.50	12.50	30.00	110.00
	1821	—	6.50	12.50	30.00	110.00
	1823	—	6.50	12.50	30.00	110.00
	1824	—	6.50	12.50	30.00	110.00
	1825	—	6.50	12.50	30.00	110.00

SAXE-MEININGEN

(Sachsen-Meiningen)

The duchy of Saxe-Meiningen was located in Thuringia, sandwiched between Saxe-Weimar-Eisenach on the west and north and the enclave of Schmalkalden belonging to Hesse-Cassel on the east. It was founded upon the division of the Ernestine line in Saxe-Gotha in 1680. In 1735, due to an exchange of some territory, the duchy became known as Saxe-Coburg-Meiningen. In 1826, Saxe-Coburg-Gotha assigned Saalfeld to Saxe-Meiningen. The duchy came under the strong influence of Prussia from 1866, when Bernhard II was forced to abdicate because of his support of Austria. The monarchy ended with the defeat of Germany in 1918.

RULERS

Georg I, 1782-1803
Bernhard Erich Freund, under Regency of Louise Eleonore, 1803-1821
Bernhard II, 1821-1866
Georg II, 1866-1914
Bernhard III, 1914-1918

MINTMASTERS INITIALS

Letter	Date	Name
F.HELFRICHT	d.1892	Ferdinand Helfricht, die-cutter and chief medailleur
K	1835-1837	Georg Krell, warden then mintmaster
L	1803-1833	Georg Christoph Loewel
VOIGT		J.C. Voigt, die-cutter and medailleur

HELLER

COPPER

Obv: Crowned heart-shaped arms, leg: H.
Rev: Value.

KM#	Date	Mintage	Fine	VF	XF	Unc
106	1814	—	2.00	4.00	8.00	60.00

Obv. leg: HERZ.

KM#	Date	Mintage	Fine	VF	XF	Unc
107	1814	—	2.00	4.00	8.00	60.00

PFENNIG

COPPER

Obv. leg: HERZ.

KM#	Date	Mintage	Fine	VF	XF	Unc
109	1818	.090	3.00	7.00	15.00	75.00

KM#	Date	Mintage	Fine	VF	XF	Unc
135	1832	.275	2.00	4.00	8.00	50.00
	1833	.093	2.00	4.00	8.00	50.00
	1835	.034	2.00	4.00	8.00	50.00

Obv: Crowned arms within branches.

KM#	Date	Mintage	Fine	VF	XF	Unc
143	1839	.079	2.00	4.00	8.00	50.00
	1842	.132	2.00	4.00	8.00	50.00

KM#	Date	Mintage	Fine	VF	XF	Unc
170	1860	.240	1.50	3.00	6.00	50.00
	1862	.243	1.50	3.00	6.00	50.00
	1863	.240	1.50	3.00	6.00	50.00
	1865	.240	1.50	3.00	6.00	50.00
	1866	.480	1.50	3.00	6.00	50.00

KM#	Date	Mintage	Fine	VF	XF	Unc
173	1867	.240	1.50	3.00	6.00	50.00
	1868	.480	1.50	3.00	6.00	50.00

2 PFENNIG

COPPER

KM#	Date	Mintage	Fine	VF	XF	Unc
136	1832	.202	1.50	3.00	6.00	50.00
	1833	.101	1.50	3.00	6.00	50.00
	1835	.036	1.50	3.00	6.00	50.00

KM#	Date	Mintage	Fine	VF	XF	Unc
144	1839	.075	1.50	3.00	6.00	50.00
	1842	.184	1.50	3.00	6.00	50.00

KM#	Date	Mintage	Fine	VF	XF	Unc
171	1860	.361	1.50	3.00	6.00	50.00
	1862	.357	1.50	3.00	6.00	50.00
	1863	.120	1.50	3.00	6.00	50.00
	1864	.480	1.50	3.00	6.00	50.00
	1865	.240	1.50	3.00	6.00	50.00
	1866	.480	1.50	3.00	6.00	50.00

KM#	Date	Mintage	Fine	VF	XF	Unc
174	1867	.480	1.50	3.00	6.00	50.00
	1868	.240	1.50	3.00	6.00	50.00
	1869	.240	1.50	3.00	6.00	50.00
	1870	.720	1.50	3.00	6.00	50.00

1/8 KREUZER

COPPER

KM#	Date	Mintage	Fine	VF	XF	Unc
118	1828	—	2.50	5.00	10.00	50.00

1/4 KREUZER

COPPER

Obv: Crowned heart shaped arms, leg: HERZ.
Rev: Value.

KM#	Date	Mintage	Fine	VF	XF	Unc
100	1812	—	2.50	5.00	10.00	50.00
	1814	—	2.50	5.00	10.00	50.00
	1818	.066	2.50	5.00	10.00	50.00

Obv: Crowned heart shaped arms, leg. HERZ.
Rev. leg: LANDMUNZE, value.

KM#	Date	Mintage	Fine	VF	XF	Unc
115	1823	—	4.00	8.00	15.00	60.00

KM#	Date	Mintage	Fine	VF	XF	Unc
119	1828	—	1.50	3.00	6.00	50.00
	1829	.168	1.50	3.00	6.00	40.00
	1830	.161	1.50	3.00	6.00	40.00
	1831	.321	1.50	3.00	6.00	40.00
	1832	.063	1.50	3.00	6.00	40.00

NOTE: Many varieties in legend size exist.

Obv: Legend below crowned arms.

KM#	Date	Mintage	Fine	VF	XF	Unc
120	1828	—	1.50	3.00	6.00	40.00

Obv. leg: MEINIGEN

KM#	Date	Mintage	Fine	VF	XF	Unc
125	1829	Inc. Ab.	1.50	3.00	6.00	40.00

Rev. value: KREUZER.

KM#	Date	Mintage	Fine	VF	XF	Unc
161	1854	.240	1.50	3.00	6.00	40.00

1/2 KREUZER

COPPER

KM#	Date	Mintage	Fine	VF	XF	Unc
101	1812	—	2.50	5.00	10.00	50.00
	1814	—	2.50	5.00	10.00	50.00
	1818	.102	2.50	5.00	10.00	50.00

KM#	Date	Mintage	Fine	VF	XF	Unc
121	1828	—	2.00	4.00	8.00	45.00
	1831	—	2.00	4.00	8.00	45.00

KM#	Date	Mintage	Fine	VF	XF	Unc
126	1829	.121	1.50	3.00	6.00	40.00
	1830 L	.144	1.50	3.00	6.00	40.00
	1831 L	.341	1.50	3.00	6.00	40.00
	1832 L	.045	1.50	3.00	6.00	40.00

KM#	Date	Mintage	Fine	VF	XF	Unc
162	1854	.240	1.50	3.00	6.00	40.00

KREUZER

(Convention)

.7300 g, .166 SILVER, .0038 oz ASW
Obv: Crowned draped arms, H.S.C.M. Rev: Value.

KM#	Date	Mintage	Fine	VF	XF	Unc
96	1808	—	2.50	5.00	10.00	60.00

Obv: Drape extends beneath crown.

KM#	Date	Mintage	Fine	VF	XF	Unc
102	1812	.307	4.00	8.00	15.00	80.00

COPPER

KM#	Date	Mintage	Fine	VF	XF	Unc
108	1814	—	4.00	8.00	15.00	60.00
	1818	.090	4.00	8.00	15.00	60.00

Obv: Crowned rectangular arms, leg: HERZ.

KM#	Date	Mintage	Fine	VF	XF	Unc
122	1828	—	2.50	5.00	10.00	50.00
	1829	.144	2.50	5.00	10.00	50.00
	1830	.118	2.50	5.00	10.00	50.00

.7300 g, .166 SILVER, .0038 oz ASW
Obv: Crowned arms dividing S.M.

KM#	Date	Mintage	Fine	VF	XF	Unc
123	1828	.211	2.50	5.00	10.00	50.00
	1829	—	2.50	5.00	10.00	50.00
	1829 L	.255	2.50	5.00	10.00	50.00
	1830 L	.092	2.50	5.00	10.00	50.00

COPPER

KM#	Date	Mintage	Fine	VF	XF	Unc
131	1831	.166	2.00	4.00	8.00	40.00
	1832	.032	2.00	4.00	8.00	40.00
	1833	.104	2.00	4.00	8.00	40.00
	1834	.177	2.00	4.00	8.00	40.00
	1835	.035	2.00	4.00	8.00	40.00

.7300 g, .166 SILVER, .0038 oz ASW
Obv: Crowned arms within bound branches, L initial.

KM#	Date	Mintage	Fine	VF	XF	Unc
132	1831 L	.212	2.00	4.00	8.00	50.00
	1832 L	.348	2.00	4.00	8.00	50.00
	1833 L	.272	2.00	4.00	8.00	50.00
	1834 L	.162	2.00	4.00	8.00	50.00

Obv: K mintmasters initial.

KM#	Date	Mintage	Fine	VF	XF	Unc
137	1835 K	.059	2.00	4.00	8.00	50.00
	1836 K	.055	2.00	4.00	8.00	50.00
	1837 K	.049	2.00	4.00	8.00	50.00

.8300 g, .166 SILVER, .0044 oz ASW

KM#	Date	Mintage	Fine	VF	XF	Unc
145	1839	.348	2.00	4.00	8.00	45.00

COPPER
Obv: Crowned arms within branches. Rev: Value.

KM#	Date	Mintage	Fine	VF	XF	Unc
153	1842	.180	2.00	4.00	8.00	40.00

Obv: Six-point star below crowned arms.

KM#	Date	Mintage	Fine	VF	XF	Unc
163	1854	.202	2.00	4.00	8.00	40.00

.8400 g, .165 SILVER, .0044 oz ASW

KM#	Date	Mintage	Fine	VF	XF	Unc
172	1864	.240	2.00	4.00	8.00	45.00
	1866	.240	2.00	4.00	8.00	45.00

3 KREUZER

1.3600 g, .305 SILVER, .0133 oz ASW
Obv: Crowned draped arms.

KM#	Date	Mintage	Fine	VF	XF	Unc
97	1808	—	6.00	10.00	30.00	125.00

Obv: Drape extends beneath crown.

KM#	Date	Mintage	Fine	VF	XF	Unc
103	1812	.263	3.00	6.00	20.00	100.00
	1813	Inc. Ab.	3.00	6.00	20.00	100.00

Obv: Crowned arms dividing S.M. Rev: Value.

KM#	Date	Mintage	Fine	VF	XF	Unc
117	1827	.171	2.00	4.00	8.00	50.00
	1828	.077	2.00	4.00	8.00	50.00
	1829	—	2.00	4.00	8.00	50.00

Obv: L mintmasters initial.

KM#	Date	Mintage	Fine	VF	XF	Unc
127	1829 L	1.263	2.00	4.00	8.00	50.00
	1830 L	.533	2.00	4.00	8.00	50.00

KM#	Date	Mintage	Fine	VF	XF	Unc
133	1831 L	.540	2.00	4.00	8.00	50.00
	1832 L	.918	2.00	4.00	8.00	50.00
	1833 L	1.284	2.00	4.00	8.00	50.00
	1834 L	.187	2.00	4.00	8.00	50.00
	1835 L	—	2.00	4.00	8.00	50.00

KM#	Date	Mintage	Fine	VF	XF	Unc
138	1835 K	.800	2.00	4.00	8.00	50.00
	1836 K	.399	2.00	4.00	8.00	50.00
	1837 K	.246	2.00	4.00	8.00	50.00

1.2900 g, .333 SILVER, .0138 oz ASW
Obv: Crowned arms, leg: HERZOGTHUM.
Rev: Value within branches.

KM#	Date	Mintage	Fine	VF	XF	Unc
150	1840	.207	2.00	4.00	8.00	50.00

6 KREUZER

2.4300 g, .333 SILVER, .0260 oz ASW
Obv. leg: S.COB., crowned, draped arms.
Rev: Value within wreath.

KM#	Date	Mintage	Fine	VF	XF	Unc
98	1808	—	15.00	25.00	50.00	150.00
	1812	—	15.00	25.00	50.00	150.00
	1813	—	15.00	25.00	50.00	150.00

Obv: Drape extends beneath crown.

KM#	Date	Mintage	Fine	VF	XF	Unc
104	1812	.087	10.00	20.00	40.00	150.00
	1813	Inc. Ab.	10.00	20.00	40.00	150.00

2.4400 g, .347 SILVER, .0272 oz ASW

KM#	Date	Mintage	Fine	VF	XF	Unc
116	1826	—	5.00	15.00	25.00	80.00
	1827	.486	5.00	15.00	25.00	80.00
	1828	.179	5.00	15.00	25.00	80.00
	1829	—	5.00	15.00	25.00	80.00

Obv: W/L mintmasters initial.

KM#	Date	Mintage	Fine	VF	XF	Unc
124	1828 L	—	5.00	15.00	25.00	80.00
	1829 L	1.513	5.00	15.00	25.00	80.00
	1830 L	.747	5.00	15.00	25.00	80.00

KM#	Date	Mintage	Fine	VF	XF	Unc
134	1831 L	.684	3.00	5.00	10.00	60.00
	1832 L	.658	3.00	5.00	10.00	60.00
	1833 L	.723	3.00	5.00	10.00	60.00
	1834 L	.409	3.00	5.00	10.00	60.00
	1835 L	—	3.00	5.00	10.00	60.00

Obv: W/K mintmaster initial.

KM#	Date	Mintage	Fine	VF	XF	Unc
139	1835 K	.512	3.00	5.00	10.00	60.00
	1836 K	.432	3.00	5.00	10.00	60.00
	1837 K	.253	3.00	5.00	10.00	60.00

2.5900 g, .333 SILVER, .0277 oz ASW
Obv. leg: HERZOGTHUM, crowned arms.
Rev: Value within branches.

KM#	Date	Mintage	Fine	VF	XF	Unc
151	1840	.097	4.00	7.00	15.00	75.00

20 KREUZER

.583 SILVER

KM#	Date	Mintage	Fine	VF	XF	Unc
105	1812	5 pcs. known		—	Rare	—

1/2 GULDEN

5.3000 g, .900 SILVER, .1533 oz ASW

KM#	Date	Mintage	Fine	VF	XF	Unc
141	1838	.071	20.00	50.00	100.00	250.00
	1839	.045	20.00	50.00	100.00	250.00
	1840	.032	20.00	50.00	100.00	250.00
	1841	.057	20.00	50.00	100.00	250.00

Obv: Different head w/HELFRICHT below.

KM#	Date	Mintage	Fine	VF	XF	Unc
154	1843	.133	20.00	50.00	100.00	225.00
	1846	.106	20.00	50.00	100.00	225.00

KM#	Date	Mintage	Fine	VF	XF	Unc
164	1854	.108	20.00	50.00	100.00	250.00

GULDEN

11.8000 g, .989 SILVER, .3752 oz ASW

KM#	Date	Mintage	Fine	VF	XF	Unc
128	1829	2,000	125.00	200.00	325.00	700.00

12.8300 g, .750 SILVER, .3093 oz ASW

KM#	Date	Mintage	Fine	VF	XF	Unc
130	1830 L	9,118	65.00	125.00	200.00	350.00
	1831 L	5,511	50.00	100.00	150.00	300.00
	1832 L	4,688	50.00	100.00	150.00	300.00
	1833 L	.010	35.00	75.00	120.00	250.00

KM#	Date	Mintage	Fine	VF	XF	Unc
140	1835 K	2,015	75.00	150.00	200.00	400.00
	1836 K	2,028	75.00	150.00	200.00	400.00
	1837 K	2,148	75.00	150.00	200.00	400.00

10.6000 g, .900 SILVER, .3067 oz ASW

KM#	Date	Mintage	Fine	VF	XF	Unc
142	1838	.071	40.00	80.00	160.00	250.00
	1839	.071	40.00	80.00	160.00	250.00
	1840	.032	40.00	80.00	160.00	250.00
	1841	.031	40.00	80.00	160.00	250.00

Obv: HELFRICHT below bust.

KM#	Date	Mintage	Fine	VF	XF	Unc
155	1843	.133	40.00	80.00	160.00	250.00
	1846	.149	40.00	80.00	160.00	250.00

KM#	Date	Mintage	Fine	VF	XF	Unc
165	1854	.108	45.00	90.00	175.00	275.00

2 GULDEN

21.2100 g, .900 SILVER, .6138 oz ASW

KM#	Date	Mintage	Fine	VF	XF	Unc
166	1854	.167	50.00	90.00	185.00	375.00

EIN (1) THALER

(Convention)

28.0600 g, .833 SILVER, .7514 oz ASW
Death of Georg I

KM#	Date	Mintage	Fine	VF	XF	Unc
95	ND(1803)L	—	300.00	600.00	1200.	2000.

18.5200 g, .900 SILVER, .5360 oz ASW
Obv: HELFRICHT on truncation.

KM#	Date	Mintage	Fine	VF	XF	Unc
167	1859	.040	35.00	75.00	135.00	325.00
	1860	.040	35.00	75.00	135.00	325.00
	1861	.040	35.00	75.00	135.00	325.00
	1862	.040	35.00	75.00	135.00	325.00
	1863	.040	35.00	75.00	135.00	325.00
	1866	.040	35.00	75.00	135.00	325.00

Obv: HELFRICHT on truncation.

KM#	Date	Mintage	Fine	VF	XF	Unc
175	1867	6,644	90.00	175.00	450.00	900.00

2 THALER

(3-1/2 Gulden)

37.1200 g, .900 SILVER, 1.0743 oz ASW
Obv: VOIGT below bust.

KM#	Date	Mintage	Fine	VF	XF	Unc
152	1841	.012	300.00	525.00	1400.	2600.

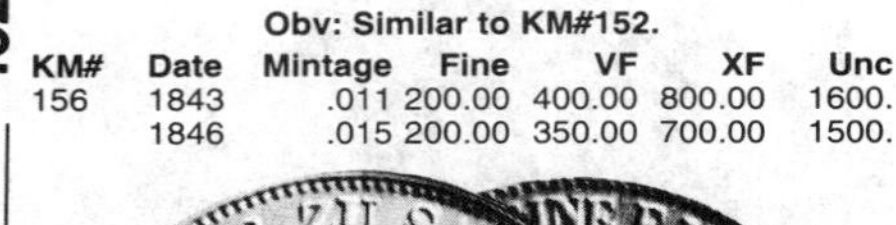

Obv: Similar to KM#152.

KM#	Date	Mintage	Fine	VF	XF	Unc
156	1843	.011	200.00	400.00	800.00	1600.
	1846	.015	200.00	350.00	700.00	1500.

Obv: HELFRICHT below bust.
Rev: Similar to KM#156.

KM#	Date	Mintage	Fine	VF	XF	Unc
160	1853	.014	200.00	350.00	700.00	1500.
	1854	.014	200.00	350.00	700.00	1500.

MONETARY REFORM

10 MARK

3.9820 g, .900 GOLD, .1152 oz AGW

KM#	Date	Mintage	Fine	VF	XF	Unc
190	1890D	2,000	1000.	2000.	2500.	3700.
	1890D	—	—	—	Proof	7000.
	1898D	2,000	800.00	1500.	1850.	2750.
	1898D	—	—	—	Proof	7000.

20 MARK

7.9650 g, .900 GOLD, .2304 oz AGW
Rev: Type I.

KM#	Date	Mintage	Fine	VF	XF	Unc
180	1872D	3,000	3000.	6000.	8000.	12,000.
	1872D	—	—	—	Proof	17,500.

Rev: Type II.

KM#	Date	Mintage	Fine	VF	XF	Unc
185	1882D	3,061	2000.	3500.	4000.	6500.
	1882D	—	—	—	Proof	11,000.

KM#	Date	Mintage	Fine	VF	XF	Unc
186	1889D	4,032	1750.	3000.	4500.	6000.
	1889D	—	—	—	Proof	9000.

Rev: Type III.

KM#	Date	Mintage	Fine	VF	XF	Unc
195	1900D	1,005	1500.	3000.	3500.	5500.
	1900D	—	—	—	Proof	11,000.

NOTE: Later date (1905) exists for this type.

PATTERNS (Pn)

(Including off metal strikes)

KM#	Date	Mintage	Identification	Mkt.Val.
Pn9	ND(1803) L	—	1 Thaler, Copper, KM95	—
Pn10	1881D	—	20 Mark, Copper, plain edge, KM185	—
Pn11	1881D	—	20 Mark, Gold, KM185	Rare
Pn12	1900D	—	2 Mark, Silver, KM196	—
Pn13	1900D	—	5 Mark, Silver	—
Pn14	1900D	—	5 Mark, KM197	—

TRIAL STRIKES (TS)

KM#	Date	Mintage	Identification	Mkt.Val.
TS1	ND	—	20 Mark, Gold, uniface obv.	Rare

SAXE-WEIMAR-EISENACH

Saxe-Weimar-Eisenach was founded in 1644. It was raised to the status of a grand duchy in 1814. The last grand duke abdicated in 1918.

RULERS

Karl August, 1775-1828
Karl Friedrich, 1828-1853
Karl Alexander, 1853-1901

MINTMASTERS INITIALS

Letter	Date	Name
JLST, LS, ST	1785-1790 1793-1835	Johann Leonhard Stockmar, mintmaster

HELLER

COPPER

C#	Date	Mintage	Fine	VF	XF	Unc
55c	1801	—	2.50	5.00	10.00	65.00
	1813	—	2.50	5.00	10.00	65.00

PFENNIG

COPPER
Rev: Value and date; line below date.

C#	Date	Mintage	Fine	VF	XF	Unc
56c	1801	—	3.00	7.00	15.00	60.00
	1803	—	3.00	7.00	15.00	60.00
	1807	.030	3.00	7.00	15.00	60.00

NOTE: Earlier date (1799) exists for this type.

Rev: Value and date; 1's in date reversed, line below date.

C#	Date	Mintage	Fine	VF	XF	Unc
56d	1810	.080	3.00	7.00	15.00	60.00
	1813	—	3.00	7.00	15.00	60.00

Rev: Value and date; line below date.

C#	Date	Mintage	Fine	VF	XF	Unc
61	1821	.100	2.00	4.00	8.00	40.00
	1824	—	2.00	4.00	8.00	40.00
	1826	—	2.00	4.00	8.00	40.00
77	1830	—	2.50	5.00	10.00	50.00

C#	Date	Mintage	Fine	VF	XF	Unc
81	1840A	.760	2.00	4.00	8.00	45.00
	1841A	.760	2.00	4.00	8.00	45.00
	1844A	.361	2.00	4.00	8.00	45.00
	1851A	.360	2.00	4.00	8.00	45.00

Denticled border

C#	Date	Mintage	Fine	VF	XF	Unc
89	1858A	.720	1.50	3.00	6.00	40.00
	1865A	.720	1.50	3.00	6.00	40.00

1-1/2 PFENNIG

COPPER

C#	Date	Mintage	Fine	VF	XF	Unc
57	1807	.034	10.00	20.00	35.00	125.00

NOTE: Earlier date (1799) exists for this type.

C#	Date	Mintage	Fine	VF	XF	Unc
62	1824	—	4.00	8.00	16.00	60.00
78	1830	—	4.00	8.00	16.00	60.00

2 PFENNIG

COPPER

C#	Date	Mintage	Fine	VF	XF	Unc
58c	1803	—	4.00	8.00	20.00	125.00
	1807	.036	3.00	7.00	16.00	80.00

Milled edge

C#	Date	Mintage	Fine	VF	XF	Unc
58d	1803	—	4.00	8.00	20.00	125.00
	1807	.036	3.00	7.00	16.00	80.00

Rev: Similar to C#58c but w/rosette below date.

C#	Date	Mintage	Fine	VF	XF	Unc
58e	1813	—	3.00	7.00	16.00	80.00

Obv: Saxon arms; S.W.E. above.
Rev: Value above date; rosette below date.

C#	Date	Mintage	Fine	VF	XF	Unc
63	1821	.068	2.00	5.00	10.00	60.00
	1826	—	2.00	5.00	10.00	60.00

Rev: Line below date.

C#	Date	Mintage	Fine	VF	XF	Unc
79	1830	—	2.00	5.00	10.00	60.00

Denticled border

C#	Date	Mintage	Fine	VF	XF	Unc
90	1858A	—	1.50	3.00	6.00	25.00
	1865A	—	1.50	3.00	6.00	25.00

3 PFENNIG

COPPER
Leaf edge

C#	Date	Mintage	Fine	VF	XF	Unc
59c	1807	.049	5.00	10.00	25.00	100.00

NOTE: Earlier date (1799) exists for this type.

Reeded edge

C#	Date	Mintage	Fine	VF	XF	Unc
59d	1807	Inc. Ab.	4.00	7.00	17.00	60.00

Rev: Rosette below date.

C#	Date	Mintage	Fine	VF	XF	Unc
59e	1804	—	2.50	5.00	10.00	40.00

Leaf edge

C#	Date	Mintage	Fine	VF	XF	Unc
64	1824	—	2.50	5.00	10.00	40.00

Reeded edge

C#	Date	Mintage	Fine	VF	XF	Unc
64a	1824	—	2.50	5.00	10.00	40.00

C#	Date	Mintage	Fine	VF	XF	Unc
80	1830	—	2.50	5.00	10.00	40.00
	Straight date					
80.1	1830	—	2.50	5.00	10.00	40.00

Obv: Crowned Saxon arms in circular legend.
Rev: Value above date; SCHEIDE MUNZE above.

C#	Date	Mintage	Fine	VF	XF	Unc
82	1840A	—	2.50	5.00	10.00	40.00

4 PFENNIG

COPPER
Obv: Saxon arms; S.W.u.E. above.
Rev: Value above date; w/o line below date.

C#	Date	Mintage	Fine	VF	XF	Unc
60	1810	.146	5.00	10.00	25.00	125.00

Rev: Line below date.

C#	Date	Mintage	Fine	VF	XF	Unc
60a	1810	Inc. Ab.	5.00	10.00	25.00	125.00
	1812	—	5.00	10.00	25.00	125.00

Rev: Rosette below date.

C#	Date	Mintage	Fine	VF	XF	Unc
60b	1813	—	5.00	10.00	25.00	125.00

Reeded edge

C#	Date	Mintage	Fine	VF	XF	Unc
65	1821	.092	4.00	7.00	15.00	100.00
	1826	—	4.00	7.00	15.00	100.00
	Leaf edge					
65a	1821	Inc. Ab.	4.00	7.00	15.00	100.00

1/2 GROSCHEN

1.0900 g, .222 SILVER, .0077 oz ASW
Obv: Crowned arms. Rev: Value.

C#	Date	Mintage	Fine	VF	XF	Unc
85	1840A	2.400	2.00	4.00	8.00	45.00
91	1858A	.300	2.00	4.00	8.00	45.00

GROSCHEN

2.1900 g, .222 SILVER, .0156 oz ASW

C#	Date	Mintage	Fine	VF	XF	Unc
86	1840A	2.408	2.00	4.00	8.00	45.00

C#	Date	Mintage	Fine	VF	XF	Unc
92	1858A	.300	2.00	4.00	8.00	45.00

1/48 THALER

1.0600 g, .229 SILVER, .0078 oz ASW

C#	Date	Mintage	Fine	VF	XF	Unc
67	1801	—	2.00	4.00	10.00	50.00
	1804	—	2.00	4.00	10.00	50.00
	1808	.286	2.00	4.00	10.00	50.00
	1810	.327	2.00	4.00	10.00	50.00
	1813	—	2.00	4.00	10.00	50.00
	1814	—	2.00	4.00	10.00	50.00

NOTE: Earlier dates (1794-1799) exist for this type.

Obv: G.H.S.W.E. above arms.

C#	Date	Mintage	Fine	VF	XF	Unc
68	1815	—	2.00	4.00	10.00	50.00
	Obv: S.W.E. above arms.					
69	1821	.243	3.00	6.00	20.00	80.00
	1824	—	3.00	6.00	20.00	80.00
	1826	—	3.00	6.00	20.00	80.00
	Obv: Saxon arms w/S.W.E. above.					
83	1831	—	3.00	6.00	15.00	70.00
	Rev: Reversed 1's in date.					
83a	1831	—	3.00	6.00	15.00	70.00

1/24 THALER

2.1200 g, .229 SILVER, .0156 oz ASW
Obv: S.W.U.E. above arms. Rev: Value.

C#	Date	Mintage	Fine	VF	XF	Unc
70	1801	—	3.00	7.00	20.00	90.00
	1804	—	3.00	7.00	20.00	90.00
	1808	.199	3.00	7.00	20.00	90.00
	1810	.452	3.00	7.00	20.00	90.00
	1813	—	3.00	7.00	20.00	90.00
	1814 small letters					
		—	3.00	7.00	20.00	90.00

NOTE: Earlier dates (1794-1799) exist for this type.

Obv: G.H.S.W.E. above arms.

C#	Date	Mintage	Fine	VF	XF	Unc
71	1815	—	8.00	15.00	50.00	175.00

Obv: S.W.E. above arms.

C#	Date	Mintage	Fine	VF	XF	Unc
72	1821	.493	5.00	10.00	25.00	90.00
	1824	—	5.00	10.00	25.00	90.00
	1826	—	5.00	10.00	25.00	90.00
	Rev. value: ENIEN					
72a	1821	Inc. Ab.	—	—	—	—
	Rev. value: EINEN					
84	1830	—	3.00	6.00	20.00	80.00

1/2 THALER

(Species)

14.0300 g, .833 SILVER, .3757 oz ASW

C#	Date	Mintage	Fine	VF	XF	Unc
74	1813 LS	—	35.00	75.00	125.00	300.00

EIN (1) THALER

(Convention)

28.0600 g, .833 SILVER, .7514 oz ASW

C#	Date	Mintage	Fine	VF	XF	Unc
75	1813 LS	—	125.00	275.00	600.00	1000.

C#	Date	Mintage	Fine	VF	XF	Unc
76	1815	5,273	250.00	450.00	900.00	2000.

22.2700 g, .750 SILVER, .5370 oz ASW

C#	Date	Mintage	Fine	VF	XF	Unc
87	1841A	.203	40.00	75.00	180.00	475.00

(Vereins)

18.5200 g, .900 SILVER, .5360 oz ASW

C#	Date	Mintage	Fine	VF	XF	Unc
93	1858A	.063	40.00	75.00	140.00	300.00
	1866A	.044	40.00	75.00	140.00	300.00
	1870A	.045	40.00	75.00	140.00	300.00

2 THALER

(3-1/2 Gulden)

37.1200 g, .900 SILVER, 1.0742 oz ASW

C#	Date	Mintage	Fine	VF	XF	Unc
88	1840A	.019	150.00	300.00	600.00	1300.
	1842A	.038	150.00	300.00	600.00	1300.
	1843A	Inc. Ab.	200.00	350.00	700.00	1600.
	1848A	.019	150.00	300.00	600.00	1300.

Rev: Similar to C#88.

C#	Date	Mintage	Fine	VF	XF	Unc
94	1855A	.019	225.00	400.00	900.00	1750.

MONETARY REFORM

2 MARK

11.1110 g, .900 SILVER, .3215 oz ASW
Golden Wedding of Carl Alexander

Y#	Date	Mintage	Fine	VF	XF	Unc
168.1	1892A	.050	75.00	150.00	350.00	550.00

80th Birthday of the Grand Duke

Y#	Date	Mintage	Fine	VF	XF	Unc
168.2	1898A	.100	50.00	125.00	325.00	525.00
	1898A	—	—	—	Proof	650.00

20 MARK

7.9650 g, .900 GOLD, .2304 oz AGW
Golden Wedding of Carl Alexander

Y#	Date	Mintage	Fine	VF	XF	Unc
169	1892A	5,000	600.00	900.00	1250.	2000.
	1892A	—	—	—	Proof	5000.
	1896A	.015	650.00	1250.	1750.	2250.
	1896A	380 pcs.	—	—	Proof	5000.

NOTE: Later date (1901) exists for this type.

SAXONY

Saxony, located in southeast Germany was founded in 850. The first coinage was struck c. 990. It was divided into two lines in 1464. The electoral right was obtained by the elder line in 1547. During the time of the Reformation. Saxony was one of the more powerful states in central Europe. It became a kingdom in 1806. At the Congress of Vienna in 1815, they were forced to cede half its territories to Prussia.

RULERS

Friedrich August III, 1763-1806
as Friedrich August I, 1806-1827
Anton, 1827-1836
Friedrich August II, 1836-1854
Johann, 1854-1873
Albert, 1873-1902

MINT MARKS

L - Leipzig

MINTMASTERS INITIALS

Dresden Mint

Letter	Date	Name
B	1860-1887	Gustav Julius Buschick
C, IC, IEC	1779-1804	Johann Ernst Croll
F	1845-1860	Gustav Theodor Fischer
G	1833-1844	Johann Georg Grohmann
GS, IGS, S	1812-1832	Johann Gotthelf Studer
H, SGH	1804-1813	Samuel Gottlieb Helbig

Arms of Electoral Saxony

2-fold arms divided vertically, 2 crossed swords on left, opened crown curving diagonally from upper left to lower right on right side.

HELLER

COPPER
Obv: Crowned arms. Rev: Value above date.

KM#	Date	Mintage	Fine	VF	XF	Unc
1002.1	1801 C	—	2.50	6.00	15.00	45.00
(C90.1)	1805/705 large H	1.123	2.50	6.00	15.00	45.00
	1805/705 small H	Inc. Ab.	2.50	6.00	15.00	45.00
	1805 H	—	2.50	6.00	15.00	45.00
	1806	7,948	—	—	Rare	—

NOTE: Earlier dates (1778-1799) exist for this type.

Obv: Crowned arms within branches.
Rev: Value, w/o legends.

KM#	Date	Mintage	Fine	VF	XF	Unc
1072	1813 H	.562	4.00	7.00	18.00	60.00
(C157)	1813 S	Inc. Ab.	4.00	7.00	18.00	60.00

NOTE: Varieties exist.

PFENNIG

COPPER
Obv: Crowned arms. Rev: Value above date.

KM#	Date	Mintage	Fine	VF	XF	Unc
1000	1801 C	—	2.50	5.00	10.00	50.00
(C91)	1804/799 C	—	2.50	5.00	10.00	50.00
	1804 C	—	2.50	5.00	10.00	50.00
	1805 H/C	—	2.50	5.00	10.00	50.00
	1805 H	—	2.50	5.00	10.00	50.00
	1806 H/795 C	—	2.50	5.00	10.00	50.00
	1806 H	—	2.50	5.00	10.00	50.00

NOTE: Earlier dates (1772-1800) exist for this type.

Obv: Crowned arms within branches.
Rev: Value, w/o legends, pearl borders both sides.

KM#	Date	Mintage	Fine	VF	XF	Unc
1057	1807 H	.691	3.00	7.00	20.00	75.00
(C158)	1807 H/799 C	—	4.00	8.00	25.00	85.00
	1807/86 H	—	4.00	8.00	25.00	85.00
	1809/89 H	—	4.00	8.00	25.00	85.00

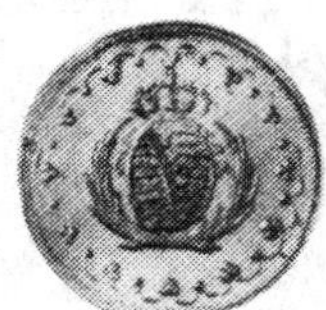

Obv: Trefoil border.

KM#	Date	Mintage	Fine	VF	XF	Unc
1062 (C158a)	1808 H	.014	4.00	8.00	15.00	75.00

KM#	Date	Mintage	Fine	VF	XF	Unc
1070	1811 H	1.267	2.00	4.00	10.00	75.00
(C158b)	1815 S	—	2.00	4.00	10.00	75.00
	1816 S	—	2.00	4.00	10.00	75.00
	1822 S	—	2.00	4.00	10.00	75.00
	1825 S	.230	2.00	4.00	10.00	75.00

KM#	Date	Mintage	Fine	VF	XF	Unc
1132	1831 S	1.154	2.00	4.00	8.00	45.00
(C201)	1832 S	.527	2.00	4.00	8.00	45.00
	1833 G	1.152	2.00	4.00	8.00	45.00

KM#	Date	Mintage	Fine	VF	XF	Unc
1135	1836 G	.226	1.50	3.00	6.00	40.00
(C220)	1837 G	.940	1.50	3.00	6.00	40.00
	1838 G	1.473	1.50	3.00	6.00	40.00

KM#	Date	Mintage	Fine	VF	XF	Unc
1155	1841 G	.492	1.50	3.00	6.00	30.00
(C221)	1842 G	.323	1.50	3.00	6.00	30.00
	1843 G	1.115	1.50	3.00	6.00	30.00
	1846 F	.450	1.50	3.00	6.00	30.00
	1847 F	.546	1.50	3.00	6.00	30.00
	1848 F	1.447	1.50	3.00	6.00	30.00
	1849 F	.783	1.50	3.00	6.00	30.00
	1850 F	.815	1.50	3.00	6.00	30.00
	1851 F	1.556	1.50	3.00	6.00	30.00
	1852 F	.918	1.50	3.00	6.00	30.00
	1853 F	1.164	1.50	3.00	6.00	30.00
	1854 F	.548	1.50	3.00	6.00	30.00

KM#	Date	Mintage	Fine	VF	XF	Unc
1184	1855 F	.657	1.50	3.00	6.00	30.00
(C248)	1856 F	3.457	1.50	3.00	6.00	30.00
	1859 F	2.341	1.50	3.00	6.00	30.00

KM#	Date	Mintage	Fine	VF	XF	Unc
1207 (C248a)	1861 B	.338	1.50	3.00	6.00	30.00

KM#	Date	Mintage	Fine	VF	XF	Unc
1216	1862 B	1.094	1.50	3.00	6.00	30.00
(C250)	1863 B	4.484	1.50	3.00	6.00	30.00
	1865 B	3.877	1.50	3.00	6.00	30.00
	1866 B	1.129	1.50	3.00	6.00	30.00
	1868 B	2.084	1.50	3.00	6.00	30.00
	1871 B	.331	1.50	3.00	6.00	30.00
	1872 B	.591	1.50	3.00	6.00	30.00
	1873 B	.549	1.50	3.00	6.00	30.00

2 PFENNIGE

COPPER, 21mm

KM#	Date	Mintage	Fine	VF	XF	Unc
1156 (C222)	1841 G	1.263	2.00	4.00	8.00	40.00

19.7mm

KM#	Date	Mintage	Fine	VF	XF	Unc
1157	1841 G	Inc. Ab.	1.50	3.00	6.00	40.00
(C222a)	1843 G	.112	1.50	3.00	6.00	40.00
	1846 F	.090	1.50	3.00	6.00	40.00
	1847 F	.401	1.50	3.00	6.00	40.00
	1848 F	.518	1.50	3.00	6.00	40.00
	1849 F	.365	1.50	3.00	6.00	40.00
	1850 F	.647	1.50	3.00	6.00	40.00
	1851 F	.271	1.50	3.00	6.00	40.00
	1852 F	.361	1.50	3.00	6.00	40.00
	1853 F	.576	1.50	3.00	6.00	40.00
	1854 F	.056	2.00	4.00	8.00	45.00

KM#	Date	Mintage	Fine	VF	XF	Unc
1185	1855 F	.536	1.50	3.00	6.00	40.00
(C249)	1856 F	2.182	1.50	3.00	6.00	40.00
	1859 F	1.103	1.50	3.00	6.00	40.00

KM#	Date	Mintage	Fine	VF	XF	Unc
1208	1861 B	.163	2.00	4.00	8.00	45.00
(C249a)						

KM#	Date	Mintage	Fine	VF	XF	Unc
1217	1862 B	.739	1.25	2.50	5.00	30.00
(C251)	1863 B	.456	1.25	2.50	5.00	30.00
	1864 B	3.139	1.25	2.50	5.00	30.00
	1866 B	.551	1.25	2.50	5.00	30.00
	1869 B	2.220	1.25	2.50	5.00	30.00
	1873 B	.262	1.50	3.00	6.00	35.00

3 PFENNIGE

COPPER

KM#	Date	Mintage	Fine	VF	XF	Unc
1037	1801	—	3.00	6.00	18.00	55.00
(C92)	1802 C	—	3.00	6.00	18.00	55.00
	1803 C	2.357	3.00	6.00	18.00	55.00
	1804 SGH	—	3.00	6.00	18.00	55.00
	1804 lg. H	—	3.00	6.00	18.00	55.00
	1804 sm. H	—	3.00	6.00	18.00	55.00
	1806 H	—	3.00	6.00	18.00	55.00

NOTE: Earlier dates (1797-1800) exist for this type.

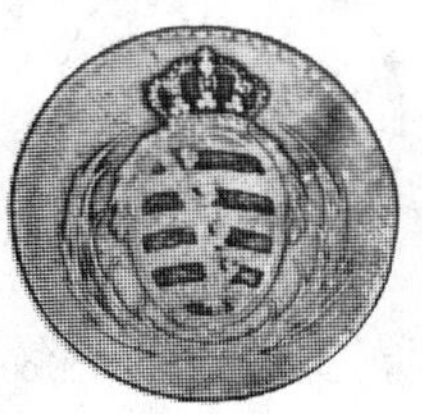

KM#	Date	Mintage	Fine	VF	XF	Unc
1058	1807 H	.317	4.00	8.00	22.00	70.00
(C160)	1808 H	.295	4.00	8.00	22.00	70.00
	1809 H	4,800	15.00	30.00	60.00	125.00
	1811 H	.128	4.00	8.00	22.00	70.00
	1812 H	.096	4.00	8.00	22.00	70.00
	1814 S	.211	4.00	8.00	22.00	70.00
	1815 S	.432	4.00	8.00	22.00	70.00
	1822 S	—	4.00	8.00	22.00	70.00
	1823 S	.019	4.00	8.00	22.00	70.00
	1824 S	.123	4.00	8.00	22.00	70.00

Obv: Crowned arched arms.
Rev. value: 3 PFENNIGE.

KM#	Date	Mintage	Fine	VF	XF	Unc
1100	1825 S	.168	4.00	8.00	22.00	70.00
(C161)	1826 S	.031	5.00	10.00	25.00	80.00
(C202)	1831 S	.077	5.00	10.00	15.00	60.00
	1832 S	.226	3.00	6.00	12.00	50.00
(C202b)						
	1833 G	.069	4.00	8.00	15.00	60.00

Obv. leg: KOEN. SAECHS.

KM#	Date	Mintage	Fine	VF	XF	Unc
1134	1834 G	.500	3.00	6.00	12.00	40.00
(C202a)						

KM#	Date	Mintage	Fine	VF	XF	Unc
1136	1836 G	.039	4.00	8.00	15.00	60.00
(C223)	1837 G	.542	3.00	6.00	12.00	50.00

4 PFENNIGE

COPPER

KM#	Date	Mintage	Fine	VF	XF	Unc
1064	1808 H	1.548	6.00	12.50	30.00	100.00
(C162)	1809/6 H	1.059	6.00	12.50	30.00	100.00
	1809/8 H	I.A.	6.00	12.50	30.00	100.00
	1809 H	Inc. Ab.	6.00	12.50	30.00	100.00
	1810 H	.886	6.00	12.50	30.00	100.00

5 PFENNIGE

COPPER

KM#	Date	Mintage	Fine	VF	XF	Unc
1218	1862 B	2.468	1.50	3.00	6.00	40.00
(C252)	1863 B	.693	1.50	3.00	6.00	40.00
	1864 B	1.090	1.50	3.00	6.00	40.00
	1866 B	.141	1.50	3.00	6.00	40.00
	1867 B	.444	1.50	3.00	6.00	40.00
	1869 B	.860	1.50	3.00	6.00	40.00

8 PFENNIGE

1.2900 g, .250 SILVER, .0103 oz ASW

KM#	Date	Mintage	Fine	VF	XF	Unc
1065	1808 H	2.594	4.00	8.00	20.00	60.00
(C165)	1809 H	4.722	4.00	8.00	20.00	60.00

1/2 NEU-GROSCHEN

(5 Pfennig)

1.0600 g, .229 SILVER, .0078 oz ASW

KM#	Date	Mintage	Fine	VF	XF	Unc
1158	1841 G	2.248	1.50	3.00	5.00	25.00
(C224)	1842 G	2.845	1.50	3.00	5.00	25.00
	1843 G	3.552	1.50	3.00	5.00	25.00
	1844 G	1.354	1.50	3.00	5.00	25.00
	1848 F	.500	1.50	3.00	5.00	25.00
	1849 F	.579	1.50	3.00	5.00	25.00
	1851 F	.506	1.50	3.00	5.00	25.00
	1852 F	.497	1.50	3.00	5.00	25.00
	1853 F	.256	2.00	4.00	6.00	35.00
	1854 F	.107	2.00	4.00	6.00	35.00
(C253)	1855 F	.444	2.00	3.00	5.00	45.00
	1856 F	.713	2.00	3.00	5.00	45.00

NEU-GROSCHEN

(10 Pfennig)

2.1200 g, .229 SILVER, .0156 oz ASW

KM#	Date	Mintage	Fine	VF	XF	Unc
1159	1841 G	4.500	1.50	3.00	6.00	40.00
(C225)	1842 G	2.463	1.50	3.00	6.00	40.00
	1845 F	.457	1.50	3.00	6.00	40.00
	1846 F	1.656	1.50	3.00	6.00	40.00
	1847 F	1.532	1.50	3.00	6.00	40.00
	1848 F	.105	1.50	3.00	6.00	40.00
	1849 F	1.049	1.50	3.00	6.00	40.00

KM#	Date	Mintage	Fine	VF	XF	Unc
(C225)	1850 F	.505	1.50	3.00	6.00	40.00
	1851 F	.676	1.50	3.00	6.00	40.00
	1852 F	.949	1.50	3.00	6.00	40.00
	1853 F	.798	1.50	3.00	6.00	40.00
	1854 F	.443	1.50	3.00	6.00	40.00
(C254)	1855 F	1.106	2.00	3.50	6.00	35.00
	1856 F	1.188	2.00	3.50	6.00	35.00

2.1000 g, .230 SILVER, .0155 oz ASW
Rev: B below value.

KM#	Date	Mintage	Fine	VF	XF	Unc
1209	1861 B	.395	2.50	5.00	7.50	45.00
(C254a)						

KM#	Date	Mintage	Fine	VF	XF	Unc
1219	1863 B	1.514	1.50	3.00	5.00	30.00
(C255)	1865 B	.557	2.00	4.00	6.00	35.00
	1867 B	.296	2.00	4.00	6.00	35.00

KM#	Date	Mintage	Fine	VF	XF	Unc
1221	1867 B	.897	2.00	4.00	8.00	40.00
(C256)	1868 B	.608	2.00	4.00	8.00	40.00
	1870 B	.908	2.00	4.00	8.00	40.00
	1871 B	.293	2.00	4.00	8.00	40.00
	1873 B	.420	2.00	4.00	8.00	40.00

2 NEU-GROSCHEN

(20 Pfennig)

3.1100 g, .312 SILVER, .0311 oz ASW

KM#	Date	Mintage	Fine	VF	XF	Unc
1160	1841 G	3.125	1.50	3.00	6.00	40.00
(C226)	1842 G	1.413	1.50	3.00	6.00	40.00
	1844 G	1.477	1.50	3.00	6.00	40.00
	1846 F	.516	1.50	3.00	6.00	40.00
	1847 F	.425	1.50	3.00	6.00	40.00
	1848 F	1.062	1.50	3.00	6.00	40.00
	1849 F	.656	1.50	3.00	6.00	40.00
	1850 F	.380	1.50	3.00	6.00	40.00
	1851 F	.588	1.50	3.00	6.00	40.00
	1852 F	.974	1.50	3.00	6.00	40.00
	1853 F	.604	1.50	3.00	6.00	40.00
	1854 F	.790	1.50	3.00	6.00	40.00
(C257)	1855 F	.921	2.50	5.00	10.00	60.00
	1856 F	2.207	2.50	5.00	10.00	60.00

3.2200 g, .300 SILVER, .0310 oz ASW

KM#	Date	Mintage	Fine	VF	XF	Unc
1220	1863 B	.557	2.50	5.00	10.00	50.00
(C258)	1864 B	.447	2.50	5.00	10.00	50.00
	1865 B	.371	2.50	5.00	10.00	50.00
	1866 B	.448	2.50	5.00	10.00	50.00

KM#	Date	Mintage	Fine	VF	XF	Unc
1222	1868 B	.419	4.00	8.00	15.00	55.00
(C259)	1869 B	.599	4.00	8.00	15.00	55.00
	1871 B	.245	4.00	8.00	15.00	55.00
	1873 B	.468	4.00	8.00	15.00	55.00

.9700 g, .250 SILVER, .0077 oz ASW
Obv: Crowned shield within crossed laurel branches. Rev: Value, date below.

KM#	Date	Mintage	Fine	VF	XF	Unc
966	1802/799	—	6.00	12.00	25.00	80.00
(C97)	1802 C	—	6.00	12.00	25.00	80.00
	1803 C	—	6.00	12.00	25.00	80.00
	1805/3 H	—	6.00	12.00	25.00	80.00
	1805 H	—	6.00	12.00	25.00	80.00

KM#	Date	Mintage	Fine	VF	XF	Unc
(C97)	1806/97	—	6.00	12.00	25.00	80.00
	1806 H	—	6.00	12.00	25.00	80.00

NOTE: Earlier dates (1764-1799) exist for this type.

KM#	Date	Mintage	Fine	VF	XF	Unc
1048	1806 H	—	4.00	9.00	20.00	75.00
(C163)	1806/797 H	—	6.00	12.00	30.00	100.00
	1807 H	2.990	4.00	9.00	20.00	75.00
	1808 H	1.816	4.00	9.00	20.00	75.00
	1811/01 H	4.242	6.00	12.00	30.00	100.00
	1811 H	Inc. Ab.	4.00	9.00	20.00	75.00
	1812 H	5.382	4.00	9.00	20.00	75.00
	1812 S	Inc. Ab.	4.00	9.00	20.00	75.00
	1813 H	.730	4.00	9.00	20.00	75.00
	1813 S	Inc. Ab.	4.00	9.00	20.00	75.00
	1814 S	2.871	4.00	9.00	20.00	75.00
	1815 S	1.059	4.00	9.00	20.00	75.00

1/24 THALER

1.9800 g, .368 SILVER, .0234 oz ASW
Obv. leg: FRID.AVG. . .

KM#	Date	Mintage	Fine	VF	XF	Unc
968	1801 EDC	—	5.00	12.00	25.00	60.00
(C98)	1802 EDC	—	5.00	12.00	25.00	60.00
	1806 SGH	—	—	—	—	—

NOTE: Earlier dates (1764-1800) exist for this type.

KM#	Date	Mintage	Fine	VF	XF	Unc
1075	1816 IGS	.146	4.00	8.00	20.00	55.00
(C166)	1817 IGS	.252	4.00	8.00	20.00	55.00
	1818 IGS	.166	4.00	8.00	20.00	55.00

Obv. leg: FRIED. . .

KM#	Date	Mintage	Fine	VF	XF	Unc
1082.1	1819 IGS	.337	5.00	10.00	22.00	60.00
(C167)	1820 IGS	.268	5.00	10.00	22.00	60.00
	1821 IGS	.321	5.00	10.00	22.00	60.00
	1822 IGS	.439	5.00	10.00	22.00	60.00

Obv. leg: FRIEDR. . .

KM#	Date	Mintage	Fine	VF	XF	Unc
1082.2	1823 IGS	.368	5.00	10.00	22.00	60.00
(C167a)						

Obv: Crowned arched arms.

KM#	Date	Mintage	Fine	VF	XF	Unc
1094	1824 S	.332	4.00	8.00	20.00	55.00
(C168)	1825 S	.262	4.00	8.00	20.00	55.00
	1826 S	.311	4.00	8.00	20.00	55.00
	1827 S	.067	5.00	10.00	22.00	60.00

Obv: Crowned arched arms within crossed branches.

KM#	Date	Mintage	Fine	VF	XF	Unc
1105	1827 S	.066	7.00	15.00	30.00	90.00
(C203)	1828 S	.100	7.00	15.00	30.00	90.00

3.3400 g, .437 SILVER, .0469 oz ASW
Obv: Crowned large oval arms.
Rev: Value above date.

KM#	Date	Mintage	Fine	VF	XF	Unc
956	1801 EDC	—	5.00	10.00	20.00	70.00
(C100)	1802 EDC	—	5.00	10.00	20.00	70.00

NOTE: Earlier dates (1763-1800) exist for this type.

KM#	Date	Mintage	Fine	VF	XF	Unc
1049.1	1806 SGH	.037	6.00	12.00	25.00	90.00
(C169)	1807 SGH	.038	6.00	12.00	25.00	90.00
	1808 SGH	.140	5.00	10.00	20.00	75.00
	1809 SGH	1.071	5.00	10.00	20.00	75.00
	1810 SGH	.515	5.00	10.00	20.00	75.00
	1811 SGH	—	5.00	10.00	20.00	75.00
	1812 IGS	5.172	5.00	10.00	20.00	75.00
	1812 SGH	I.A.	5.00	10.00	20.00	75.00
	1813 IGS	2.055	5.00	10.00	20.00	75.00
	1813 SGH	I.A.	5.00	10.00	20.00	75.00
	1814 IGS	.063	6.00	12.00	25.00	90.00
	1816 IGS	—	5.00	10.00	20.00	75.00
	1817 IGS	—	5.00	10.00	20.00	75.00
	1818 IGS	—	5.00	10.00	20.00	75.00

Obv. leg. (error): FRID VGVST. . .

KM#	Date	Mintage	Fine	VF	XF	Unc
1049.2	1809 SGH	I.A.	5.00	10.00	20.00	75.00
(C169a)						

Obv. leg: FRIED. . .

KM#	Date	Mintage	Fine	VF	XF	Unc
1083.1	1819 IGS	—	5.00	10.00	20.00	70.00
(C170)	1820 IGS	—	5.00	10.00	20.00	70.00
	1821 IGS	—	5.00	10.00	20.00	70.00
	1822 IGS	—	5.00	10.00	20.00	70.00
	1823 IGS	1.624	5.00	10.00	20.00	70.00

Obv. leg: FRIEDR. . .

KM#	Date	Mintage	Fine	VF	XF	Unc
1083.2	1823 IGS	I.A.	5.00	10.00	20.00	70.00
(C170a)						

Obv: Crowned arched arms.

KM#	Date	Mintage	Fine	VF	XF	Unc
1095	1824 S	2.470	4.00	8.00	18.00	50.00
(C171)	1825 S	1.721	4.00	8.00	18.00	50.00
	1826 S	.763	4.00	8.00	18.00	50.00
	1827 S	.564	4.00	8.00	18.00	50.00

Obv: Crowned arched arms within crossed branches.

KM#	Date	Mintage	Fine	VF	XF	Unc
1106	1827 S	.060	5.00	10.00	20.00	70.00
(C204)	1828 S	.256	4.00	8.00	18.00	50.00

KM#	Date	Mintage	Fine	VF	XF	Unc
1117	1829 S	1.431	4.00	8.00	18.00	50.00
(C204a)						
	1830 S	1.684	4.00	8.00	18.00	50.00
	1831 S	.206	4.00	8.00	18.00	50.00
	1832 S	.882	4.00	8.00	18.00	50.00

KM#	Date	Mintage	Fine	VF	XF	Unc
1137	1836 G	.690	5.00	10.00	20.00	65.00
(C227)						

1/6 THALER

(Reichs)

5.3900 g, .541 SILVER, .0937 oz ASW

KM#	Date	Mintage	Fine	VF	XF	Unc
1045	1803 IEC	—	10.00	20.00	40.00	120.00
(C108)	1804 IEC	—	10.00	20.00	40.00	120.00
	1804 SGH	—	10.00	20.00	40.00	120.00
	1805 SGH	—	10.00	20.00	40.00	120.00
	1806 SGH	—	10.00	20.00	40.00	120.00

KM#	Date	Mintage	Fine	VF	XF	Unc
1050	1806 SGH	.018	15.00	25.00	50.00	150.00
(C172)	1807 SGH	.317	8.00	16.00	35.00	115.00
	1808 SGH	2.421	8.00	16.00	35.00	115.00
	1809 SGH	3.608	8.00	16.00	35.00	115.00
	1810 SGH	2.405	8.00	16.00	35.00	115.00
	1813 SGH	.229	8.00	16.00	35.00	115.00
(C172a)						
	1813 IGS	—	8.00	16.00	35.00	115.00
	1817 IGS	.119	8.00	16.00	35.00	115.00

5.3400 g, .521 SILVER, .0894 oz ASW

KM#	Date	Mintage	Fine	VF	XF	Unc
1101	1825 GS	.068	15.00	30.00	60.00	150.00
(C173)						

Death of King Friedrich August

KM#	Date	Mintage	Fine	VF	XF	Unc
1107	1827 S	.048	7.00	15.00	30.00	60.00
(C174)						

Rev: Crowned arched arms within crossed branches.

KM#	Date	Mintage	Fine	VF	XF	Unc
1108	1827 S	.019	25.00	50.00	100.00	200.00
(C205)	1828 S	.018	25.00	50.00	100.00	200.00

Obv: Older head.

KM#	Date	Mintage	Fine	VF	XF	Unc
1118	1829 S	.124	20.00	40.00	80.00	200.00
(C205a)						

Death of King Anton

KM#	Date	Mintage	Fine	VF	XF	Unc
1138	1836 G	.046	15.00	30.00	60.00	125.00
(C206)						

KM#	Date	Mintage	Fine	VF	XF	Unc
1161	1841 G	.450	6.00	12.00	30.00	90.00
(C228)	1842 G	1.322	6.00	12.00	30.00	90.00
	1843 G	.655	6.00	12.00	30.00	90.00
	1846 F	.601	6.00	12.00	30.00	90.00
	1847 F	.366	6.00	12.00	30.00	90.00
	1848 F	.270	6.00	12.00	30.00	90.00
	1849 F	.449	6.00	12.00	30.00	90.00
	1850 F	.134	6.00	12.00	30.00	90.00

KM#	Date	Mintage	Fine	VF	XF	Unc
1176	1851 F	.228	6.00	12.00	30.00	90.00
(C228a)						
	1852 F	.340	6.00	12.00	30.00	90.00

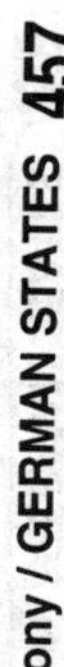

Death of King Friedrich August II
Obv. leg: D.9.AUG. 1854 below head.
Rev: ER SAEETE. . . in sprays.

KM#	Date	Mintage	Fine	VF	XF	Unc
1178 (C229)	1854 F	.521	5.00	10.00	25.00	85.00

KM#	Date	Mintage	Fine	VF	XF	Unc
1186	1855 F	.476	5.00	10.00	25.00	100.00
(C260)	1856 F	1.529	5.00	10.00	25.00	100.00

5.3420 g, .520 SILVER, .0893 oz ASW

KM#	Date	Mintage	Fine	VF	XF	Unc
1205	1860 B	.871	4.00	8.00	17.50	60.00
(C261)	1860 F	.052	6.00	12.50	25.00	100.00
	1861 B	1.099	4.00	8.00	17.50	60.00
	1863 B	.589	4.00	8.00	17.50	60.00
	1864 B	.161	4.00	8.00	17.50	60.00
	1865 B	.683	4.00	8.00	17.50	60.00
	1866/5 B	.475	4.00	8.00	17.50	65.00
	1866 B	Inc. Ab.	4.00	8.00	15.00	60.00
	1869 B	.626	4.00	8.00	15.00	60.00
	1870 B	.280	4.00	8.00	15.00	60.00
	1871 B	.293	4.00	8.00	15.00	60.00

1/3 THALER

(Reichs)

7.0160 g, .833 SILVER, .1880 oz ASW
Obv: Head right.
Rev: Crowned oval arms within crossed branches.

KM#	Date	Mintage	Fine	VF	XF	Unc
1024	1801 IEC	—	20.00	40.00	75.00	150.00
(C113)	1802 IEC	—	20.00	40.00	75.00	150.00

NOTE: Earlier dates (1791-1800) exist for this type.

Rev. leg: VIERZIG EINE FEINE MARK.

KM#	Date	Mintage	Fine	VF	XF	Unc
1051.1	1806 SGH	.027	40.00	80.00	125.00	225.00
(C175)	1808 SGH	.277	20.00	45.00	80.00	160.00
	1809 SGH	.303	20.00	45.00	80.00	160.00
	1810 SGH	.295	20.00	45.00	80.00	160.00
	1811 SGH	.278	20.00	45.00	80.00	160.00
	1812 SGH	.080	30.00	60.00	100.00	175.00
	1815 IGS	5.740	60.00	120.00	200.00	325.00
	1816 IGS	9,049	50.00	100.00	160.00	275.00
	1817 IGS	8,929	50.00	100.00	160.00	275.00

Rev. leg: "FEIN"

KM#	Date	Mintage	Fine	VF	XF	Unc
1051.2 (C175a)	1808	Inc. Ab.	30.00	60.00	90.00	175.00

Rev. leg: "ACHTZIG"

KM#	Date	Mintage	Fine	VF	XF	Unc
1051.3 (C175b)	1808	Inc. Ab.	40.00	85.00	135.00	225.00

KM#	Date	Mintage	Fine	VF	XF	Unc
1079	1818 IGS	.019	40.00	80.00	150.00	250.00
(C176)	1821 IGS	—	40.00	80.00	150.00	250.00

8.2540 g, .708 SILVER, .1880 oz ASW
Obv: Head right. Rev: Crowned arched arms within crossed branches.

KM#	Date	Mintage	Fine	VF	XF	Unc
1109	1827 S	8,700	50.00	100.00	200.00	350.00
(C207)	1828 S	.010	50.00	100.00	200.00	350.00
	1829 S	.021	35.00	70.00	150.00	300.00
	1830 S	.097	35.00	70.00	150.00	300.00

8.3520 g, .667 SILVER, .1790 oz ASW

KM#	Date	Mintage	Fine	VF	XF	Unc
1177	1852 F	.194	15.00	30.00	60.00	125.00
(C230)	1853 F	.403	15.00	30.00	60.00	125.00
	1854 F	1.156	15.00	30.00	60.00	125.00

Death of King Friedrich August II

KM#	Date	Mintage	Fine	VF	XF	Unc
1179 (C231)	1854 F	.029	20.00	40.00	80.00	125.00

Obv: Head left.
Rev: Crowned draped rectangular arms.

KM#	Date	Mintage	Fine	VF	XF	Unc
1191 (C262)	1856 F	.308	25.00	50.00	100.00	175.00

8.3200 g, .667 SILVER, .1784 oz ASW

KM#	Date	Mintage	Fine	VF	XF	Unc
1198	1858 F	.326	20.00	40.00	80.00	150.00
(C263)	1859 F	.617	20.00	40.00	80.00	150.00

KM#	Date	Mintage	Fine	VF	XF	Unc
1206 (C264)	1860 B	.345	17.50	35.00	70.00	125.00

2/3 THALER

(Reichs)

14.0310 g, .833 SILVER, .3760 oz ASW

KM#	Date	Mintage	Fine	VF	XF	Unc
1025	1801 IEC	—	35.00	75.00	150.00	275.00
(C121)	1802 IEC	—	35.00	75.00	150.00	275.00
	1805 SGH	—	35.00	75.00	150.00	275.00
	1806 SGH	—	35.00	75.00	150.00	275.00

NOTE: Earlier dates (1791-1800) exist for this type.

KM#	Date	Mintage	Fine	VF	XF	Unc
1052	1806 SGH	.084	35.00	70.00	140.00	275.00
(C177)	1807 SGH	.075	35.00	70.00	140.00	275.00

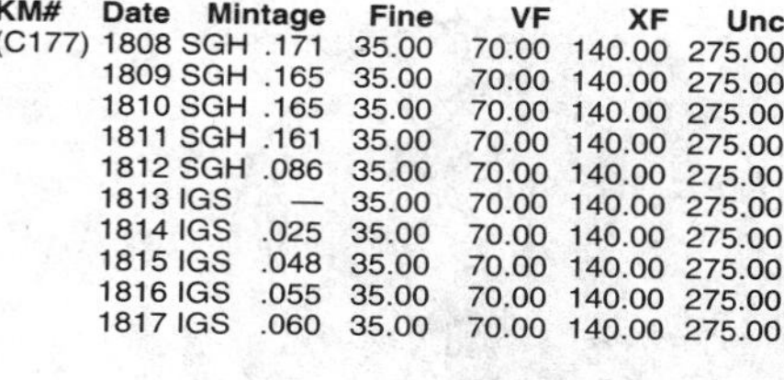

KM#	Date	Mintage	Fine	VF	XF	Unc
(C177)	1808 SGH	.171	35.00	70.00	140.00	275.00
	1809 SGH	.165	35.00	70.00	140.00	275.00
	1810 SGH	.165	35.00	70.00	140.00	275.00
	1811 SGH	.161	35.00	70.00	140.00	275.00
	1812 SGH	.086	35.00	70.00	140.00	275.00
	1813 IGS	—	35.00	70.00	140.00	275.00
	1814 IGS	.025	35.00	70.00	140.00	275.00
	1815 IGS	.048	35.00	70.00	140.00	275.00
	1816 IGS	.055	35.00	70.00	140.00	275.00
	1817 IGS	.060	35.00	70.00	140.00	275.00

KM#	Date	Mintage	Fine	VF	XF	Unc
1090 (C178a)	1822 IGS	.023	60.00	125.00	250.00	450.00

KM#	Date	Mintage	Fine	VF	XF	Unc
1110	1827 S	.011	50.00	100.00	200.00	400.00
(C208)	1828 S	.012	50.00	100.00	200.00	400.00

Obv: Different head right.

KM#	Date	Mintage	Fine	VF	XF	Unc
1119 (C208a)	1829 S	.013	60.00	125.00	250.00	450.00

EIN (1) THALER

(Mining)

28.0630 g, .833 SILVER, .7520 oz ASW
Obv: Head right. Rev: Crowned oval arms, leg: DER SEEGEN DES BERGBAVES.

KM#	Date	Mintage	Fine	VF	XF	Unc
1036 (C136a)	1801 IEC	—	75.00	150.00	300.00	600.00
	1802 IEC	—	75.00	150.00	300.00	600.00
	1803 IEC	—	75.00	150.00	300.00	600.00
	1804 IEC	—	75.00	150.00	300.00	600.00
	1804 SGH	—	75.00	150.00	300.00	600.00
	1805 SGH	—	75.00	150.00	300.00	600.00
	1806 SGH	—	75.00	150.00	300.00	600.00

NOTE: Earlier dates (1794-1800) exist for this type.

(Convention)

Rev. leg: X.EINE.FEINE.MARK, date.

KM#	Date	Mintage	Fine	VF	XF	Unc
1027	1801 IEC	—	35.00	65.00	100.00	300.00
(C135)	1802 IEC	—	35.00	65.00	100.00	300.00
	1803 IEC	—	35.00	65.00	100.00	300.00
	1804 IEC	—	35.00	65.00	100.00	300.00
	1804 SGH	—	35.00	65.00	100.00	300.00
	1805 SGH	—	35.00	65.00	100.00	300.00
	1806 SGH	—	35.00	65.00	100.00	300.00

NOTE: Earlier dates (1791-1800) exist for this type.

KM#	Date	Mintage	Fine	VF	XF	Unc
1053 (C180)	1806 SGH	.663	750.00	1250.	2500.	5000.

Obv: Small bust.

KM#	Date	Mintage	Fine	VF	XF	Unc
1059.1 (C180b)	1807 SGH	.461	35.00	60.00	100.00	225.00
	1808 SGH	1.534	35.00	60.00	100.00	225.00
	1809 SGH	.563	35.00	60.00	100.00	225.00
	1810 SGH	.368	35.00	60.00	100.00	225.00
	1811 SGH	.395	35.00	60.00	100.00	225.00
	1812 SGH	.134	35.00	60.00	100.00	225.00
	1813 IGS	.773	35.00	60.00	100.00	225.00
	1813 IGS (error) ENIE		100.00	130.00	200.00	300.00
	1813 SGH	I.A.	35.00	60.00	100.00	225.00
	1815 IGS	.510	35.00	60.00	150.00	225.00
	1816 IGS	—	35.00	60.00	100.00	225.00
	1817 IGS	—	35.00	60.00	100.00	225.00

Edge inscription: GOTT SEGNE SACHSEN

KM#	Date	Mintage	Fine	VF	XF	Unc
1059.2 (C180a)	1816 IGS	—	50.00	75.00	125.00	250.00

(Mining)

KM#	Date	Mintage	Fine	VF	XF	Unc
1060 (C179)	1807 SGH	—	75.00	175.00	400.00	800.00

KM#	Date	Mintage	Fine	VF	XF	Unc
1061 (C181)	1807 SGH	—	75.00	150.00	400.00	800.00
	1808 SGH	—	75.00	150.00	400.00	800.00
	1809 SGH	—	75.00	150.00	400.00	800.00
	1810 SGH	—	75.00	150.00	400.00	800.00
	1811 SGH	—	75.00	150.00	400.00	800.00
	1812 SGH	—	75.00	150.00	400.00	800.00
	1813 SGH	—	75.00	150.00	400.00	800.00
	1813 IGS	—	40.00	80.00	150.00	300.00
	1815 IGS	—	40.00	80.00	150.00	300.00
	1816 IGS	—	40.00	80.00	150.00	300.00
	1817 IGS	—	200.00	300.00	600.00	1250.

Rev: Legend right to left.

KM#	Date	Mintage	Fine	VF	XF	Unc
1071 (C181a)	1811 SGH	—	75.00	150.00	400.00	800.00
	1813 SGH	—	75.00	150.00	400.00	800.00
	1811 IGS	—	75.00	150.00	400.00	800.00
	1813 IGS	—	75.00	150.00	400.00	800.00
	1815 IGS	—	75.00	150.00	400.00	800.00
	1816 IGS	—	75.00	150.00	400.00	800.00

(Convention)

Prize Thaler - Mining Academy at Freiberg

KM#	Date	Mintage	Fine	VF	XF	Unc
1074 (C182)	1815	—	1000.	1500.	3000.	4500.

KM#	Date	Mintage	Fine	VF	XF	Unc
1076 (C183)	1816 IGS	—	600.00	800.00	1500.	2500.

KM#	Date	Mintage	Fine	VF	XF	Unc
1077 (C184)	1817 IGS	—	35.00	60.00	125.00	250.00
	1818 IGS	—	35.00	60.00	125.00	250.00
	1819 IGS	—	35.00	60.00	125.00	250.00
	1820 IGS	—	35.00	60.00	125.00	250.00
	1821 IGS	—	35.00	60.00	125.00	250.00

(Mining)

Rev. leg: DER SEGEN.

KM#	Date	Mintage	Fine	VF	XF	Unc
1078 (C185)	1817 IGS	—	75.00	150.00	300.00	600.00
	1818 IGS	—	75.00	150.00	300.00	600.00
	1819 IGS	—	75.00	150.00	300.00	600.00
	1820 IGS	—	75.00	150.00	300.00	600.00
	1821 IGS	—	75.00	150.00	300.00	600.00

(Convention)

Obv: Different bust. Rev. leg: W/o DER SEGEN.

KM#	Date	Mintage	Fine	VF	XF	Unc
1091 (C186)	1822 IGS	—	40.00	60.00	150.00	300.00
	1823 IGS	.512	40.00	60.00	150.00	300.00

(Mining)

Obv. leg: W/DER SEGEN added.

KM#	Date	Mintage	Fine	VF	XF	Unc
1092 (C187)	1822 IGS	—	50.00	125.00	350.00	625.00
	1823 IGS	—	50.00	125.00	350.00	625.00

(Convention)

KM#	Date	Mintage	Fine	VF	XF	Unc
1096 (C188)	1824 S	.546	35.00	60.00	125.00	275.00
	1825 S	.546	35.00	60.00	125.00	250.00
	1826 S	.546	35.00	60.00	125.00	250.00
	1827 S	.423	35.00	60.00	125.00	275.00

(Mining)

KM#	Date	Mintage	Fine	VF	XF	Unc
1097 (C189)	1824 S	—	60.00	125.00	225.00	475.00
	1825 S	—	60.00	125.00	225.00	475.00
	1826 S	—	60.00	125.00	225.00	475.00
	1827 S	.018	60.00	125.00	225.00	475.00

KM#	Date	Mintage	Fine	VF	XF	Unc
1098 (C189a)	1824 GS	—	150.00	450.00	1200.	2000.

(Convention)

Death of King Friedrich August

KM#	Date	Mintage	Fine	VF	XF	Unc
1111.1 (C190)	1827 S	.014	60.00	100.00	150.00	250.00

(Mining)

Edge inscription: SEGEN DES BERGBAUS

KM#	Date	Mintage	Fine	VF	XF	Unc
1111.2 (C190a)	1827 S	4,357	75.00	150.00	200.00	400.00

(Convention)

KM#	Date	Mintage	Fine	VF	XF	Unc
1112	1827 S	.107	45.00	80.00	150.00	375.00
(C209)	1828 S	.609	40.00	60.00	125.00	300.00

KM#	Date	Mintage	Fine	VF	XF	Unc
1120 (C209a)	1829 S	.534	30.00	60.00	100.00	200.00
	1830 S	.620	30.00	60.00	100.00	200.00
	1831 S	.697	30.00	60.00	100.00	200.00
	1832 S	.979	30.00	60.00	100.00	200.00
	1833 G	.190	30.00	60.00	100.00	200.00
	1834 G	.486	30.00	60.00	100.00	200.00
	1835 G	.458	30.00	60.00	100.00	200.00
	1836 G	.585	30.00	60.00	100.00	200.00

(Mining)

Rev. leg: SEGEN DES BERGBAUS.

KM#	Date	Mintage	Fine	VF	XF	Unc
1116 (C210)	1828 S	.018	150.00	300.00	750.00	1900.

Obv: Older head.

KM#	Date	Mintage	Fine	VF	XF	Unc
1121 (C210a)	1829 S	.019	65.00	175.00	450.00	1000.
	1830 S	.019	65.00	200.00	500.00	1200.
	1831 S	.019	65.00	175.00	450.00	1000.
	1832 S	.013	65.00	175.00	450.00	1000.
	1833 G	3,000	65.00	200.00	500.00	1200.
	1834 G	5,500	65.00	175.00	450.00	1000.
	1835 G	4,986	65.00	175.00	450.00	1000.
	1836 G	4,836	65.00	200.00	500.00	1200.

(Convention)

Prize Thaler - Mining Academy at Freiberg
Obv: Similar to C#209.

KM#	Date	Mintage	Fine	VF	XF	Unc
1122 (C211)	1829	200 pcs.	1000.	2000.	4000.	6000.

Prize Thaler - Forestry Institute at Tharant

KM#	Date	Mintage	Fine	VF	XF	Unc
1130 (C212)	1830	25 pcs.	—	—	Rare	—

Prize Thaler - Agriculture
Educational Establishment at Tharant
Rev: LANDWIRTSCHAFTL

KM#	Date	Mintage	Fine	VF	XF	Unc
1131 (C213)	1830	25 pcs.	—	—	Rare	—

New Constitution

KM#	Date	Mintage	Fine	VF	XF	Unc
1133 (C214)	1831 S	.014	40.00	80.00	125.00	250.00

Death of King Anton

KM#	Date	Mintage	Fine	VF	XF	Unc
1139 (C215)	1836 G	.012	40.00	80.00	125.00	250.00

(Mining)

Edge inscription: SEGEN DES BERGBAUS

KM#	Date	Mintage	Fine	VF	XF	Unc
1140 (C215a)	1836 G	2,500	100.00	250.00	500.00	1000.

(Convention)

KM#	Date	Mintage	Fine	VF	XF	Unc
1141	1836 G	.034	100.00	200.00	600.00	1200.
(C232)	1837 G	.031	125.00	275.00	700.00	1400.

Obv. legend continuous.

KM#	Date	Mintage	Fine	VF	XF	Unc
1142 (C232a)	1836 G	3,260	450.00	1000.	2200.	4000.
	1837 G	.094	50.00	90.00	225.00	475.00
	1838 G	.139	40.00	75.00	200.00	400.00

(Mining)

Obv. leg: KOENIG. Rev. leg: SEGEN DES, etc.

KM#	Date	Mintage	Fine	VF	XF	Unc
1143	1836 G	3,262	450.00	1000.	2200.	4000.
(C233)	1837 G	5,770	135.00	275.00	700.00	1400.
	1838 G	.036	90.00	175.00	475.00	875.00

(Convention)

22.2720 g, .750 SILVER, .5371 oz ASW
Visit to Dresden Mint
Lettered edge

KM#	Date	Mintage	Fine	VF	XF	Unc
1147.1	1839 G	—	900.00	1800.	3000.	4500.
(C234)						

Plain edge

KM#	Date	Mintage	Fine	VF	XF	Unc
1147.2	1839	—	—	—	Rare	—
(C234a)						

KM#	Date	Mintage	Fine	VF	XF	Unc
1148	1839 G	.643	25.00	50.00	100.00	250.00
(C235)	1840 G	1.406	25.00	50.00	100.00	250.00
	1841 G	2.505	25.00	50.00	100.00	250.00
	1842 G	.974	25.00	50.00	100.00	250.00
	1843 G	1.251	25.00	50.00	100.00	250.00
	1844 G	1.026	25.00	50.00	100.00	250.00
(C235a)						
	1845 F	.973	25.00	50.00	100.00	250.00
	1846 F	.860	25.00	50.00	100.00	250.00
	1847 F	.677	25.00	50.00	100.00	250.00
	1848 F	1.592	25.00	50.00	100.00	250.00
	1849 F	1.368	25.00	50.00	100.00	250.00

KM#	Date	Mintage	Fine	VF	XF	Unc
1175	1850 F	1.074	25.00	50.00	125.00	325.00
(C235b)						
	1851 F	1.351	25.00	50.00	125.00	325.00
	1852 F	1.105	25.00	50.00	125.00	325.00
	1853 F	1.171	25.00	50.00	125.00	325.00
	1854 F	1.075	25.00	50.00	125.00	325.00

(Mining)

Obv: G below head.

KM#	Date	Mintage	Fine	VF	XF	Unc
1162	1841 G	.011	75.00	150.00	450.00	1000.
(C236)	1842 G	.017	75.00	150.00	450.00	1000.
	1843 G	.017	75.00	150.00	450.00	1000.
	1844 G	.011	75.00	150.00	450.00	1000.
(C236b)						
	1845 F	.019	60.00	150.00	300.00	600.00
	1846 F	.022	60.00	150.00	300.00	600.00
	1847 F	.040	60.00	125.00	250.00	500.00
	1848 F	.021	60.00	150.00	300.00	600.00
	1849 F	.038	60.00	150.00	300.00	600.00
(C236a)						
	1850 F	.034	50.00	125.00	250.00	500.00
	1851 F	.033	50.00	100.00	200.00	400.00
	1852 F	.047	50.00	125.00	250.00	500.00
	1853 F	.055	50.00	100.00	200.00	400.00
	1854 F	.037	50.00	100.00	200.00	400.00

Death of King Friedrich August II

KM#	Date	Mintage	Fine	VF	XF	Unc
1180.1	1854 F	.016	30.00	60.00	100.00	200.00
(C237)						

Edge: SEGEN DES BERGBAUS and crossed hammers.

KM#	Date	Mintage	Fine	VF	XF	Unc
1180.2	1854 F	8,829	40.00	75.00	125.00	250.00
(C237a)						

(Convention)

KM#	Date	Mintage	Fine	VF	XF	Unc
1181	1854 F	.525	30.00	60.00	150.00	450.00
(C265)						

(Mining)

Rev: Similar to C#269.

KM#	Date	Mintage	Fine	VF	XF	Unc
1182	1854 F	.027	90.00	175.00	425.00	1000.
(C266)						

(Convention)

Visit to Mint by King Johann

KM#	Date	Mintage	Fine	VF	XF	Unc
1187	1855 F	5,250	35.00	65.00	125.00	300.00
(C267)	1855 F	—	—	—	Proof	400.00

Rev: Similar to C#265.

KM#	Date	Mintage	Fine	VF	XF	Unc
1188	1855 F	.863	25.00	40.00	125.00	300.00
(C268)	1856 F	1.089	25.00	40.00	100.00	250.00

(Mining)

KM#	Date	Mintage	Fine	VF	XF	Unc
1189	1855 F	.056	65.00	125.00	350.00	800.00
(C269)	1856 F	.056	65.00	125.00	350.00	800.00

(Vereins)

18.5200 g, .900 SILVER, .5360 oz ASW

KM#	Date	Mintage	Fine	VF	XF	Unc
1192	1857 F	.969	25.00	45.00	100.00	250.00
(C270)	1858 F	.200	25.00	45.00	100.00	250.00
	1859 F	2.490	20.00	35.00	90.00	225.00

(Mining)

Obv: Similar to C#269.

KM#	Date	Mintage	Fine	VF	XF	Unc
1193	1857 F	.035	75.00	150.00	400.00	800.00
(C271)	1858 F	.034	75.00	150.00	400.00	800.00

Obv. leg: Large letters.
Rev. leg: SEGEN DES BERGBAUS.

KM#	Date	Mintage	Fine	VF	XF	Unc
1199	1858 F	.061	35.00	65.00	135.00	325.00
(C272.1)						
	1859 F	.094	35.00	65.00	135.00	325.00
	1860 B	.298	25.00	50.00	100.00	250.00
	1861 B	.016	40.00	75.00	150.00	350.00

Obv. leg: Small letters.

KM#	Date	Mintage	Fine	VF	XF	Unc
1211	1861 B	.130	75.00	150.00	450.00	1000.
(C272.2)						

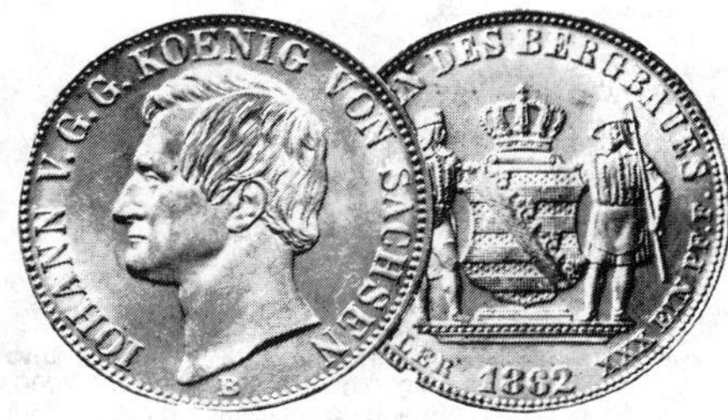

Rev. leg: SEGEN DES BERGBAUES.

KM#	Date	Mintage	Fine	VF	XF	Unc
1212 (C272a)	1861 B	.130	25.00	50.00	70.00	150.00
	1862 B	.145	25.00	50.00	70.00	150.00
	1863 B	.135	25.00	50.00	70.00	150.00
	1864 B	.120	25.00	50.00	70.00	150.00
	1865 B	.221	25.00	50.00	70.00	150.00
	1866 B	.185	25.00	50.00	70.00	150.00
	1867 B	.175	25.00	50.00	70.00	150.00

KM#	Date	Mintage	Fine	VF	XF	Unc
1223 (C272b)	1868 B	.181	25.00	50.00	70.00	150.00
	1869 B	.190	25.00	50.00	70.00	150.00
	1870 B	.236	25.00	50.00	70.00	150.00
	1871 B	.203	25.00	50.00	70.00	150.00

(Vereins)

KM#	Date	Mintage	Fine	VF	XF	Unc
1210	1860 B	2.669	25.00	50.00	90.00	200.00
(C273)	1861 B	1.409	25.00	50.00	90.00	200.00

Obv: KM#1210 obv. Rev: KM1214 rev.

KM#	Date	Mintage	Fine	VF	XF	Unc
1213 (C273a)	1861	.190	—	—	—	—

Obv: Similar to C#273.

KM#	Date	Mintage	Fine	VF	XF	Unc
1214 (C273b)	1861 B	1.070	25.00	50.00	70.00	150.00
	1862 B	2.134	25.00	50.00	70.00	150.00
	1863 B	1.471	25.00	50.00	70.00	150.00
	1864 B	1.904	25.00	50.00	70.00	150.00
	1865 B	1.335	25.00	50.00	70.00	150.00
	1866 B	1.181	25.00	50.00	70.00	150.00
	1867 B	2.020	25.00	50.00	70.00	150.00
	1868 B	1.683	25.00	50.00	70.00	150.00
	1869 B	1.622	25.00	50.00	70.00	150.00
	1870 B	1.693	25.00	50.00	70.00	150.00
	1871 B	1.687	25.00	50.00	70.00	150.00

Victory Over France

KM#	Date	Mintage	Fine	VF	XF	Unc
1230 (C274)	1871 B	.045	35.00	50.00	100.00	200.00

2 THALER

(3-1/2 Gulden)

37.1200 g, .900 SILVER, 1.0742 oz ASW

KM#	Date	Mintage	Fine	VF	XF	Unc
1149	1839 G	.020	90.00	125.00	300.00	600.00
(C238)	1840 G	.068	90.00	125.00	300.00	600.00
	1841 G	.039	90.00	125.00	300.00	600.00
	1842 G	.071	70.00	100.00	250.00	450.00
	1843 G	.059	70.00	100.00	250.00	450.00
(C238a)						
	1847 F	.147	50.00	85.00	185.00	400.00
	1848 F	.078	65.00	125.00	225.00	550.00
	1849 F	.015	65.00	125.00	225.00	550.00
	1850 F	.113	50.00	85.00	185.00	400.00
	1851 F	.246	50.00	85.00	185.00	400.00
	1852 F	.209	50.00	85.00	185.00	400.00
	1853 F	.303	50.00	85.00	185.00	400.00
	1854 F	.886	50.00	85.00	185.00	400.00

Prize Thaler - Mining Academy at Freiberg
Obv: Similar to KM#1149.

KM#	Date	Mintage	Fine	VF	XF	Unc
1163 (C239)	1841 G	200 pcs.	750.00	1500.	3000.	4500.

Prize Thaler - Forest and Agriculture Academy
Obv: Similar to KM#1149.

KM#	Date	Mintage	Fine	VF	XF	Unc
1166 (C240)	1847 F	50 pcs.	3000.	6000.	8500.	12,000.

Death of King Friedrich August II

KM#	Date	Mintage	Fine	VF	XF	Unc
1183	1854 F	6,148	100.00	200.00	300.00	500.00
(C241)	1854 F	—	—	—	Proof	800.00

Rev: Similar to KM#1149.

KM#	Date	Mintage	Fine	VF	XF	Unc
1190	1855 F	.462	50.00	90.00	190.00	350.00
(C275)	1856 F	.091	75.00	110.00	210.00	400.00

Prize Thaler - Mining Academy at Freiberg
Obv: Similar to KM#1190.

KM#	Date	Mintage	Fine	VF	XF	Unc
1194 (C276)	1857 F	100 pcs.	750.00	1500.	3000.	4500.
(C276a)						
	1857 B	206 pcs.	700.00	1400.	2500.	4000.

37.0370 g, .900 SILVER, 1.0718 oz ASW
Obv: Similar to KM#1190.

KM#	Date	Mintage	Fine	VF	XF	Unc
1195	1857 F	.351	50.00	80.00	180.00	365.00
(C277)	1858 F	.454	50.00	80.00	180.00	365.00
	1859 F	.323	50.00	80.00	180.00	365.00

Obv: Similar to KM#1190.
Rev. value: VEREINSTHAELR

KM#	Date	Mintage	Fine	VF	XF	Unc
1200	1858	Inc. Ab.	35.00	90.00	175.00	375.00
(C277a)						

Obv: Similar to KM#1190.

KM#	Date	Mintage	Fine	VF	XF	Unc
1215	1861 B	.730	65.00	100.00	200.00	400.00
(C278)						

Golden Wedding Anniversary

KM#	Date	Mintage	Fine	VF	XF	Unc
1231.1	1872 B	.049	50.00	75.00	125.00	200.00
(C279)						

Plain edge.

KM#	Date	Mintage	Fine	VF	XF	Unc
1231.2	1872 B	Inc. Ab.	100.00	250.00	350.00	500.00
(C279a)						

2-1/2 THALER

3.3410 g, .902 GOLD, .0970 oz AGW

KM#	Date	Mintage	Fine	VF	XF	Unc
1164	1842 G					
(C245)		560 pcs.	300.00	600.00	1000.	2250.
	1845 F	420 pcs.	300.00	600.00	1000.	2250.
	1848 F	2,445	250.00	500.00	1000.	2000.
	1854 F	308 pcs.	400.00	700.00	1200.	2500.

5 THALER

6.6820 g, .902 GOLD, .1940 oz AGW
Obv: Bust right. Rev: Crowned arms.

KM#	Date	Mintage	Fine	VF	XF	Unc
1028	1801 IEC	—	400.00	900.00	1500.	3750.
(C150)	1802 IEC	—	400.00	900.00	1500.	3750.

NOTE: Earlier dates (1791-1800) exist for this type.

KM#	Date	Mintage	Fine	VF	XF	Unc
1047	1805 SGH	—	500.00	1000.	1500.	4000.
(C150a)						
	1806 SGH	—	500.00	1000.	1500.	4000.

KM#	Date	Mintage	Fine	VF	XF	Unc
1054	1806 SGH	.044	500.00	1000.	2000.	5000.
(C195)	1807 SGH	.152	400.00	900.00	1500.	3500.
	1808 SGH	.135	300.00	600.00	1250.	2750.
	1809 SGH	.054	300.00	600.00	1250.	2750.
	1810 SGH	.235	300.00	600.00	1250.	2750.
	1812 SGH	.098	300.00	600.00	1250.	2750.
	1813 SGH	.118	300.00	600.00	1250.	2750.
	1815 IGS	.020	250.00	500.00	1250.	2500.
	1816 IGS	—	400.00	900.00	1500.	3250.
	1817 IGS	—	250.00	500.00	1250.	2500.

Obv: Uniformed bust left.

KM#	Date	Mintage	Fine	VF	XF	Unc
1080	1818 IGS	—	800.00	2000.	4000.	7500.
(C196)						

KM#	Date	Mintage	Fine	VF	XF	Unc
1102	1825 S	.060	250.00	600.00	1500.	3000.
(C197)	1826 S	2,590	400.00	1000.	2000.	4000.
	1827 S	700 pcs.	500.00	1000.	2000.	4000.

KM#	Date	Mintage	Fine	VF	XF	Unc
1113	1827 S	405 pcs.	500.00	1000.	2000.	4000.
(C218)	1828 S	855 pcs.	500.00	1000.	2000.	4000.

Obv: Older head.

KM#	Date	Mintage	Fine	VF	XF	Unc
1123	1829 S	385 pcs.	500.00	1000.	2000.	4000.
(C128a)						
	1830 S	2,800	550.00	1100.	2000.	4250.
	1831 S	245 pcs.	700.00	1500.	3000.	5000.
	1832 S	175 pcs.	700.00	1250.	2500.	4500.
	1834 G	490 pcs.	700.00	1250.	2500.	4500.
	1835 G	380 pcs.	700.00	1250.	2500.	4500.
	1836 G	455 pcs.	700.00	1500.	2500.	5000.

KM#	Date	Mintage	Fine	VF	XF	Unc
1146	1837 G	490 pcs.	400.00	750.00	2000.	3250.
(C243)	1838 G	175 pcs.	500.00	750.00	2000.	3250.
	1839 G	210 pcs.	500.00	850.00	2000.	3500.

KM#	Date	Mintage	Fine	VF	XF	Unc
1165	1842 G	4,455	250.00	400.00	1000.	2000.
(C246)	1845 F	1,483	300.00	500.00	1200.	2250.
	1848 F	1,964	300.00	500.00	1200.	2250.
	1849 F	1,110	300.00	500.00	1200.	2250.
	1853 F	511 pcs.	450.00	800.00	1500.	2500.
	1854 F	4,570	300.00	500.00	1200.	2250.

10 THALER

13.3640 g, .902 GOLD, .3880 oz AGW

KM#	Date	Mintage	Fine	VF	XF	Unc
1029	1801 IEC	—	800.00	2000.	3000.	5000.
(C156)	1802 IEC	—	800.00	2000.	3000.	5000.
	1803 IEC	—	800.00	2000.	3000.	5000.
	1804 IEC	—	600.00	1500.	2750.	4000.
	1804 SGH	—	500.00	1100.	2250.	4000.
	1805 SGH	—	600.00	1500.	2750.	4000.
	1806 SGH	—	500.00	1100.	2250.	4000.

NOTE: Earlier dates (1791-1800) exist for this type.

KM#	Date	Mintage	Fine	VF	XF	Unc
1055	1806 SGH	—	600.00	1250.	2500.	4000.
(C198)	1807 SGH	—	600.00	1250.	2500.	4000.
	1808 SGH	—	500.00	1000.	2000.	4000.
	1809 SGH	—	600.00	1250.	2500.	4000.
	1810 SGH	—	500.00	1000.	2000.	4000.
	1811 SGH	—	500.00	1000.	2000.	3500.
	1812 SGH	—	500.00	1000.	2000.	3500.
	1813 SGH	—	450.00	850.00	1750.	3000.
	1813 IGS	—	500.00	1000.	2000.	3500.
	1815 IGS	—	450.00	850.00	1750.	3000.
	1816 IGS	—	600.00	1250.	2500.	3500.
	1817 IGS	—	450.00	850.00	1750.	3000.

KM#	Date	Mintage	Fine	VF	XF	Unc
1081	1818 IGS	—	2000.	4000.	7500.	9000.
(C199)						

KM#	Date	Mintage	Fine	VF	XF	Unc
1103	1825 S	—	800.00	2000.	4000.	5000.
(C200)	1826 S	—	700.00	1500.	3000.	4000.
	1827 S	9,250	700.00	1500.	3000.	4000.

Obv: Head right. Rev: Crowned arms within crossed branches.

KM#	Date	Mintage	Fine	VF	XF	Unc
1114	1827 S	875 pcs.	1200.	3000.	6000.	7500.
(C219)	1828 S	5,530	800.00	2250.	5000.	6000.

Obv: Older head.

KM#	Date	Mintage	Fine	VF	XF	Unc
1124 (C219a)	1829 S	3,010	800.00	2000.	4000.	5000.
	1830 S	.018	650.00	1600.	3250.	4500.
	1831 S	3,255	1250.	2500.	5000.	7000.
	1832 S	2,625	800.00	2000.	4000.	5000.
	1833 G	—	1250.	2500.	5000.	7000.
	1834 G	3,080	1250.	2500.	5000.	7000.
	1835 G	2,715	1250.	2500.	5000.	7000.
	1836 G	4,655	1250.	2500.	5000.	7000.

Obv: Different head. Rev: Crowned rectangular arms within crossed branches.

KM#	Date	Mintage	Fine	VF	XF	Unc
1144 (C244)	1836 G	1,110	600.00	1250.	2500.	3250.
	1837 G	2,400	600.00	1250.	2500.	3250.
	1838 G	1,750	700.00	1500.	3000.	3750.
	1839 G	1,855	700.00	1500.	3000.	3750.

KM#	Date	Mintage	Fine	VF	XF	Unc
1150 (C247)	1839 G	1,855	800.00	2000.	4000.	5000.
	1845 F	2,100	600.00	1250.	2500.	3250.
	1848 F	4,761	700.00	1500.	3000.	4000.
	1849 F	1,928	700.00	1500.	3000.	4000.
	1853 F	1,038	700.00	1500.	3000.	4000.
	1854 F	1,620	800.00	2000.	4000.	5000.

1/2 KRONE

5.5560 g, .900 GOLD, .1608 oz AGW

KM#	Date	Mintage	Fine	VF	XF	Unc
1196 (C280)	1857 F	4,831	475.00	1000.	2000.	3000.
	1858 F	2,455	475.00	1000.	2000.	3000.
	1862 B	2,177	550.00	1200.	2250.	3000.
	1866 B	1,559	550.00	1200.	2250.	3000.
	1868 B	1,516	550.00	1200.	2500.	3250.
	1870 B	1,740	550.00	1200.	2500.	3250.

KRONE

11.1110 g, .900 GOLD, .3215 oz AGW

KM#	Date	Mintage	Fine	VF	XF	Unc
1197 (C281)	1857 F	3,580	525.00	1350.	2500.	3000.
	1858 F	4,610	525.00	1350.	2500.	3000.
	1859 F	9,040	525.00	1350.	2500.	3000.
	1860 B	5,067	525.00	1350.	2750.	3500.
	1861 B	3,908	525.00	1350.	2500.	3000.
	1862 B	3,229	525.00	1350.	2750.	3500.
	1863 B	3,538	525.00	1350.	2750.	3500.
	1865 B	4,371	525.00	1350.	2500.	3000.
	1867 B	2,155	525.00	1350.	2750.	3500.
	1868 B	5,262	525.00	1350.	2500.	3000.
	1870 B	2,700	525.00	1350.	2500.	3000.
	1871 B	2,140	525.00	1350.	2750.	3500.

MONETARY REFORM

2 MARK

11.1110 g, .900 SILVER, .3215 oz ASW

KM#	Date	Mintage	Fine	VF	XF	Unc
1238 (Y180)	1876E	1.613	30.00	80.00	500.00	1200.
	1877E	.796	30.00	80.00	450.00	1100.
	1877E	—	—	—	Proof	1000.
	1879E	.036	70.00	175.00	700.00	1900.
	1880E	.058	70.00	125.00	550.00	1900.
	1883E	.056	70.00	125.00	550.00	2000.
	1888E	.091	40.00	100.00	450.00	1700.

KM#	Date	Mintage	Fine	VF	XF	Unc
1245 (Y180a)	1891E	.130	25.00	65.00	125.00	300.00
	1893E	.130	25.00	85.00	175.00	325.00
	1895E	.117	30.00	115.00	200.00	375.00
	1896E	.144	25.00	85.00	175.00	350.00
	1898E	.107	25.00	85.00	175.00	400.00
	1899E	.401	15.00	60.00	110.00	225.00
	1900E	.384	15.00	60.00	110.00	200.00

NOTE: Later dates (1901-1902) exist for this type.

5 MARK

27.7770 g, .900 SILVER, .8038 oz ASW

KM#	Date	Mintage	Fine	VF	XF	Unc
1237 (Y181)	1875E	.494	30.00	60.00	750.00	2200.
	1876E	.635	25.00	50.00	650.00	1900.
	1889E	.036	40.00	100.00	750.00	2700.

1.9910 g, .900 GOLD, .0576 oz AGW

KM#	Date	Mintage	Fine	VF	XF	Unc
1239 (Y182)	1877E	.402	100.00	175.00	250.00	400.00
	1877E	—	—	—	Proof	1000.

SILVER

KM#	Date	Mintage	Fine	VF	XF	Unc
1249	1889	—	—	—	2250.	3500.

BRONZE

KM#	Date	Mintage	Fine	VF	XF	Unc
1249a	1889	—	—	—	350.00	550.00

27.7770 g, .900 SILVER, .8038 oz ASW

KM#	Date	Mintage	Fine	VF	XF	Unc
1246 (Y181a)	1891E	.052	30.00	60.00	600.00	1100.
	1893E	.052	30.00	60.00	600.00	1100.
	1894E	.075	30.00	60.00	600.00	1100.
	1895E	.089	30.00	60.00	600.00	1100.
	1898E	.160	25.00	50.00	450.00	800.00
	1899E	.074	25.00	50.00	450.00	900.00
	1900E	.157	25.00	50.00	400.00	800.00

NOTE: Later dates (1901-1902) exist for this type.

10 MARK

3.9820 g, .900 GOLD, .1152 oz AGW
Rev: Type I.

KM#	Date	Mintage	Fine	VF	XF	Unc
1232 (Y178)	1872E	.339	65.00	100.00	150.00	325.00
	1873E	.822	65.00	100.00	150.00	300.00

Rev: Type II.

KM#	Date	Mintage	Fine	VF	XF	Unc
1235 (Y183)	1874E	.048	450.00	750.00	1200.	2500.
	1875E	.528	70.00	100.00	150.00	250.00
	1877E	.201	70.00	100.00	150.00	300.00
	1878E	.225	70.00	100.00	150.00	300.00
	1879E	.182	70.00	100.00	150.00	300.00
	1881E	.240	70.00	100.00	150.00	300.00
	1888E	.149	70.00	100.00	150.00	300.00

Rev: Type III.

KM#	Date	Mintage	Fine	VF	XF	Unc
1247 (Y183a)	1891E	.224	80.00	125.00	150.00	275.00
	1893E	.224	80.00	125.00	150.00	275.00
	1896E	.150	80.00	125.00	150.00	275.00
	1898E	.313	80.00	125.00	150.00	275.00
	1900E	.074	80.00	125.00	150.00	275.00
	1900E	—	—	—	Proof	1500.

NOTE: Later dates (1901-1902) exist for this type.

20 MARK

7.9650 g, .900 GOLD, .2304 oz AGW
Rev: Type I.

KM#	Date	Mintage	Fine	VF	XF	Unc
1233 (Y179.1)	1872E	.890	115.00	130.00	150.00	250.00
	1872E	—	—	—	Proof	Rare

Obv: Large letters in legend.

KM#	Date	Mintage	Fine	VF	XF	Unc
1234 (Y179.2)	1873E	.203	120.00	135.00	160.00	275.00

Rev: Type II.

KM#	Date	Mintage	Fine	VF	XF	Unc
1236	1874E	.153	120.00	135.00	160.00	350.00
(Y184)	1876E	.482	120.00	135.00	160.00	350.00
	1876E	—	—	—	Proof	1800.
	1877E	1,181	9000.	17,000.	25,000.	35,000.
	1878E	1,564	11,000.	22,000.	38,000.	45,000.

Rev: Type III.

KM#	Date	Mintage	Fine	VF	XF	Unc
1248 (Y184a)	1894E	.639	115.00	125.00	150.00	325.00
	1895E	.113	120.00	150.00	225.00	375.00

TRADE COINAGE

3.5000 g, .986 GOLD, .1109 oz AGW

KM#	Date	Mintage	Fine	VF	XF	Unc
1030	1801 IEC	—	300.00	600.00	1250.	3000.
(C145)	1802 IEC	—	200.00	400.00	750.00	2000.
	1803 IEC	—	300.00	600.00	1250.	3000.
	1804 IEC	—	250.00	500.00	1000.	2500.

NOTE: Earlier dates (1791-1800) exist for this type.

KM#	Date	Mintage	Fine	VF	XF	Unc
1046 (C145a)	1804 SGH	—	300.00	700.00	1250.	2500.
	1805 SGH	—	350.00	800.00	1500.	3000.
	1806 SGH	—	300.00	700.00	1250.	2500.

KM#	Date	Mintage	Fine	VF	XF	Unc
1056 (C192)	1806 SGH	3,207	200.00	400.00	1000.	2000.
	1807 SGH	2,660	300.00	800.00	1500.	2500.
	1808 SGH	2,010	300.00	800.00	1500.	2500.
	1809 SGH	1,608	300.00	800.00	1500.	2500.
	1810 SGH	1,072	300.00	800.00	1500.	2500.
	1811 SGH	268 pcs.	350.00	800.00	1750.	3000.
	1812 SGH	67 pcs.	400.00	800.00	1750.	3000.
	1813 SGH	—	300.00	600.00	1500.	2500.

KM#	Date	Mintage	Fine	VF	XF	Unc
1073 (C192a)	1813 IGS	—	300.00	600.00	1500.	2500.
	1814 IGS	134 pcs.	500.00	1000.	2000.	3500.
	1815 IGS	804 pcs.	350.00	800.00	1750.	3000.
	1816 IGS	2,243	300.00	600.00	1300.	2500.
	1817 IGS	1,812	300.00	600.00	1300.	2500.
	1818 IGS	1,466	300.00	600.00	1300.	2500.
	1819 IGS	1,466	300.00	600.00	1300.	2500.
	1820 IGS	2,502	300.00	600.00	1300.	2500.
	1821 IGS	1,948	300.00	600.00	1300.	2500.
	1822 IGS	1,898	300.00	600.00	1300.	2500.

400th Jubilee of Leipzig University
Obv: Bust in coronet and cape right.
Rev. leg: SALVA SIT.

KM#	Date	Mintage	Fine	VF	XF	Unc
1063	1809	—	300.00	600.00	1200.	2000.

Obv: Uniformed bust left, leg: FRIEDR.AUGUST. . .
Rev: Crowned oval arms within crossed branches.

KM#	Date	Mintage	Fine	VF	XF	Unc
1093 (C193)	1823 IGS	1,380	300.00	600.00	1200.	2000.

Obv. leg: FRIEDR.AUG.KOEN. . .

KM#	Date	Mintage	Fine	VF	XF	Unc
1099 (C194)	1824 IGS	2,847	300.00	600.00	1000.	1800.

KM#	Date	Mintage	Fine	VF	XF	Unc
1104 (C194a)	1825 IGS	1,725	300.00	600.00	1200.	2000.
	1826 IGS	2,415	300.00	600.00	1200.	2000.
	1827 IGS	1,639	300.00	600.00	1200.	2000.

KM#	Date	Mintage	Fine	VF	XF	Unc
1115	1827 S	587 pcs.	400.00	900.00	1500.	2500.
(C217)	1828 S	771 pcs.	400.00	900.00	1500.	2500.

KM#	Date	Mintage	Fine	VF	XF	Unc
1125 (C217a)	1829 S	2,070	300.00	600.00	1200.	2000.
	1830 S	1,898	300.00	600.00	1200.	2000.
	1831 S	862 pcs.	400.00	900.00	1500.	2500.
	1832 S	776 pcs.	400.00	900.00	1500.	2500.
	1833 G	2,156	400.00	900.00	1500.	2500.
	1834 G	1,582	400.00	900.00	1500.	2500.
	1835 G	119 pcs.	600.00	1250.	2000.	3000.
	1836 G	804 pcs.	600.00	1250.	2000.	3000.

Obv: Different head.

KM#	Date	Mintage	Fine	VF	XF	Unc
1145	1836 G	100 pcs.	600.00	1250.	2250.	3250.
(C242)	1837 G	168 pcs.	600.00	1250.	2250.	3250.
	1838 G	637 pcs.	400.00	1100.	2250.	3250.

MEDALLIC ISSUES (M)

MINT VISIT

(2 MARK)

SILVER
Muldner Hutte Mint
Visit of King Albert

KM#	Date	Mintage	Fine	VF	XF	Unc
M12	1892	—	—	—	375.00	500.00
	1892	—	—	—	Proof	575.00

PATTERNS (Pn)

(Including off metal strikes)

KM#	Date	Mintage	Identification	Mkt.Val.
Pn59	1800	—	1 Pfennig, Silver, KM1000	85.00
Pn60	1804	—	1 Heller, Gold, KM1002	1200.
Pn61	1804	—	1 Pfennig, Gold, KM1000	—
Pn62	1805	—	1 Pfennig, Gold, KM1000	—
Pn63	1808 H	—	1 Pfennig, Gold, KM1057	—

KM#	Date	Mintage	Identification	Mkt.Val.
Pn64	1808 SGH	—	1 Thaler, Silver	—
Pn65	1813 H	—	1 Heller, Silver, KM1072	125.00

KM#	Date	Mintage	Identification	Mkt.Val.
Pn66	1813 IGS	—	1 Thaler	—
Pn67	1814	—	1 Thaler	—
Pn68	1814 IGS	134	1 Ducat, Gold	4000.
Pn69	1816	—	1/24 Thaler, Gold, KM1075	—

KM#	Date	Mintage	Identification	Mkt.Val.
Pn70	1832 S	—	3 Pfennig, Silver	—

KM#	Date	Mintage	Identification	Mkt.Val.
Pn71	183x G	—	3 Pfennig	—

KM#	Date	Mintage	Identification	Mkt.Val.
Pn72	1857 F	—	5 Pfennig, Copper	—

KM#	Date	Mintage	Identification	Mkt.Val.
Pn73	185x	—	1/6 Thaler	—
Pn74	1873 E	—	10 Mark, Copper. Obv: KM1235. Rev: Plain edge, KM1232.	—
Pn75	1873 E	—	20 Mark, Copper. Obv: KM1233. Rev: Plain edge, KM1236.	—
Pn76	1875 E	—	5 Mark, Zinc, plain edge, KM1237	—
Pn77	1876 E	—	10 Mark, Silver, plain edge, KM1235	—

TRIAL STRIKES (TS)

KM#	Date	Mintage	Identification	Mkt.Val.
TS1	1871	—	1 Thaler, uniface	—

SCHAUMBURG-HESSEN

Located in northwest Germany, Schaumburg-Hessen was founded in 1640 when Schaumburg-Gehmen was divided between Hesse-Cassel and Lippe-Alverdissen. The two became known as Schaumburg-Hessen and Schaumburg-Lippe. Cassel struck coins for its half as late as 1832.

RULERS

Wilhelm (of Hesse-Cassel), 1785-1821

Wilhelm II, (of Hesse-Cassel), 1821-1847

MONETARY SYSTEM

12 Gute Pfennig = 1 Groschen

PFENNIG

(Guter)

COPPER

Obv: Crowned shield separating WL. Rev: Value.

C#	Date	Mintage	Fine	VF	XF	Unc
3	1801	—	5.00	10.00	20.00	60.00
	1802	—	5.00	10.00	20.00	60.00
	1803	—	5.00	10.00	20.00	60.00

NOTE: Earlier dates (1787-1800) exist for this type.

Obv: Elector's cap above arms dividing W.K. Rev: Value, F below.

C#	Date	Mintage	Fine	VF	XF	Unc
4	1804 F	—	6.00	12.00	25.00	70.00
	1805 F	—	6.00	12.00	25.00	70.00
	1806 F	—	6.00	12.00	25.00	70.00
	1807 F	—	6.00	12.00	25.00	70.00
	1814 F	—	6.00	12.00	25.00	70.00

Rev: Rosette below value and date.

C#	Date	Mintage	Fine	VF	XF	Unc
4b	1815	—	7.00	15.00	30.00	80.00

C#	Date	Mintage	Fine	VF	XF	Unc
4a	1816	—	4.00	8.00	16.00	55.00
	1818	—	4.00	8.00	16.00	55.00
	1819	—	4.00	8.00	16.00	55.00
	1820	—	4.00	8.00	16.00	55.00
	1821	—	4.00	8.00	16.00	55.00
5	1824	—	4.00	8.00	16.00	55.00
	1826	—	4.00	8.00	16.00	55.00
	1827	—	4.00	8.00	16.00	55.00
	1828	—	4.00	8.00	16.00	55.00
	1829	—	4.00	8.00	16.00	55.00
	1830	—	4.00	8.00	16.00	55.00
6	1832	—	4.00	8.00	16.00	55.00

SCHAUMBURG-LIPPE

Located in northwest Germany, Schaumburg-Lippe was founded in 1640 when Schaumburg-Gehmen was divided between Hesse-Cassel and Lippe-Alverdissen. The two became known as Schaumburg-Hessen and Schaumburg-Lippe. They were elevated into a county independent of Lippe. Schaumburg-Lippe minted currency into the 20th century. The last prince died in 1911.

RULERS

Georg Wilhelm, 1787-1860

Adolph Georg, 1860-1893

Albrecht Georg, 1893-1911

PFENNIG

(Guter)

COPPER

Obv: Crowned arms. Rev: Value.

C#	Date	Mintage	Fine	VF	XF	Unc
36	1824	—	3.50	7.00	20.00	45.00
	1826	—	3.50	7.00	20.00	45.00

C#	Date	Mintage	Fine	VF	XF	Unc
37	1858A	1.440	2.00	4.00	12.00	35.00

2 PFENNIG

COPPER

C#	Date	Mintage	Fine	VF	XF	Unc
38	1858A	.360	3.00	6.00	18.00	40.00

3 PFENNIG

COPPER

C#	Date	Mintage	Fine	VF	XF	Unc
39	1858A	.360	3.50	7.00	20.00	45.00

4 PFENNIG

COPPER

Obv: Crowned arms, garlands and roses.

Rev: Value.

C#	Date	Mintage	Fine	VF	XF	Unc
30	1802	.288	15.00	30.00	60.00	120.00

.7500 g, .186 SILVER, .0044 oz ASW

Obv: Crowned arms.

C#	Date	Mintage	Fine	VF	XF	Unc
41	1821	.491	7.50	17.50	35.00	65.00

C#	Date	Mintage	Fine	VF	XF	Unc
41a	1828	—	7.50	17.50	35.00	65.00

COPPER

C#	Date	Mintage	Fine	VF	XF	Unc
40	1858A	.180	6.00	12.50	30.00	60.00

1/2 SILBER GROSCHEN

(1/60 Thaler)

1.0900 g, .220 SILVER, .0077 oz ASW

C#	Date	Mintage	Fine	VF	XF	Unc
45	1858A	.120	6.00	12.50	25.00	55.00

MARIENGROSCHEN

1.5500 g, .388 SILVER, .0193 oz ASW

Obv: Crowned arms, garlands and roses.

Rev: Value.

C#	Date	Mintage	Fine	VF	XF	Unc
32	1802	.144	20.00	45.00	75.00	125.00

C#	Date	Mintage	Fine	VF	XF	Unc
42	1821	.143	7.50	17.50	40.00	70.00
	1828	—	7.50	17.50	40.00	70.00

SILBER GROSCHEN

(1/50 Thaler)

2.1900 g, .220 SILVER, .0154 oz ASW

C#	Date	Mintage	Fine	VF	XF	Unc
46	1858A	.210	6.00	12.50	25.00	55.00

2-1/2 SILBER GROSCHEN

(1/12 Thaler)

3.2200 g, .375 SILVER, .0388 oz ASW

C#	Date	Mintage	Fine	VF	XF	Unc
47	1858A	.061	12.50	25.00	60.00	125.00

1/24 THALER

1.9900 g, .368 SILVER, .0235 oz ASW

C#	Date	Mintage	Fine	VF	XF	Unc
43	1821	.195	12.00	25.00	50.00	100.00
	1826	—	12.00	25.00	50.00	100.00

1/2 THALER

14.0310 g, .833 SILVER, .3760 oz ASW

C#	Date	Mintage	Fine	VF	XF	Unc
44	1821	5,400	75.00	150.00	300.00	450.00

THALER

28.0630 g, .833 SILVER, .7520 oz ASW

C#	Date	Mintage	Fine	VF	XF	Unc
34	1802	4,000	175.00	325.00	750.00	1500.

18.5200 g, .900 SILVER, .5360 oz ASW

C#	Date	Mintage	Fine	VF	XF	Unc
48	1860B	8,356	60.00	100.00	250.00	550.00

C#	Date	Mintage	Fine	VF	XF	Unc
51	1865B	7,000	40.00	75.00	175.00	325.00

2 THALER

37.0370 g, .900 SILVER, 1.0718 oz ASW
50th Anniversary of Reign as Prince
Obv: Similar to 1 Thaler, C#48.

C#	Date	Mintage	Fine	VF	XF	Unc
49	1857B	2,000	175.00	275.00	475.00	900.00

10 THALER

13.2840 g, .900 GOLD, .3826 oz AGW

C#	Date	Mintage	Fine	VF	XF	Unc
50	1829 FF					
		874 pcs.	4000.	9500.	18,500.*	25,000.
	1829 w/o FF					
		179 pcs.	4500.	11,500.	22,500.	30,000.

***NOTE:** Stack's Hammel sale 9/82 AU realized $20,000.

MONETARY REFORM

2 MARK

11.1110 g, .900 SILVER, .3215 oz ASW

Y#	Date	Mintage	Fine	VF	XF	Unc
203	1898A	5,000	200.00	400.00	600.00	1000.
	1898A	162 pcs.	—	—	Proof	1250.

NOTE: Later date (1904) exists for this type.

5 MARK

27.7770 g, .900 SILVER, .8038 oz ASW
Similar to Y#203.

Y#	Date	Mintage	Fine	VF	XF	Unc
204	1898A	3,000	350.00	800.00	1150.	1850.
	1898A	90 pcs.	—	—	Proof	3000.

NOTE: Later date (1904) exists for this type.

20 MARK

7.9650 g, .900 GOLD, .2304 oz AGW

Y#	Date	Mintage	Fine	VF	XF	Unc
202	1874B	3,000	2000.	3000.	5000.	8000.
	1874B	—	—	—	Proof	Rare
205	1898A	5,000	600.00	1000.	1500.	2250.
	1898A	250 pcs.	—	—	Proof	4500.

NOTE: Later date (1904) exists for this type.

SCHLESWIG-HOLSTEIN

Schleswig-Holstein is the border area between Denmark and Germany. The duchy of Schleswig was Danish while Holstein was German. The 1773 Treaty of Zarskoje Selo transferred Holstein to the Danes in exchange for Oldenburg. There was a great deal of trouble in the area during the 19th century. Prussia annexed the territory in 1866 After a plebiscite, the area was divided in 1920. North Slesvig went to Denmark and South Schleswig and Holstein went to Germany.

RULERS

Christian VII (of Denmark), 1784-1808
Friedrich VI (of Denmark), 1808-1839
Christian VIII (of Denmark), 1839-1848

ALTONA MINTMASTERS INITIALS

CB - Calus Branth
IFF, FF - Johann Friedrich Freund
MF, M.F, M.F. - Michael Flor
TA - Theodor C.W. Andersen
VS - Georg Vilhelm Svendsen

MONETARY SYSTEM

4 Dreiling = 2 Sechsling = 1 Schilling
60 Schilling = 1 Speciesdaler

N = Nypraeg = Restrike

JOINT COINAGE

2-1/2 SCHILLING

(1/24 Daler Specie)

2.8090 g, .375 SILVER, .0339 oz ASW
Obv: Crowned CR monogram.
Rev: Value above date.

C#	Date	Mintage	Fine	VF	XF	Unc
4	1801 MF	.211	3.00	7.00	20.00	75.00

NOTE: Earlier dates (1787-1800) exist for this type.

C#	Date	Mintage	Fine	VF	XF	Unc
20	1809 MF	.960	10.00	20.00	50.00	175.00
	1812 MF	.528	9.00	18.00	40.00	125.00

5 SCHILLING

(1/12 Daler Specie)

4.2140 g, .500 SILVER, .0677 oz ASW
Obv: Crowned interlaced CR monogram, VII within. Rev: Value.

C#	Date	Mintage	Fine	VF	XF	Unc
5	1801 MF	.103	12.00	25.00	55.00	125.00

NOTE: Earlier dates (1787-1800) exist for this type.

8 SCHILLING

2.8090 g, .375 SILVER, .0339 oz ASW

C#	Date	Mintage	Fine	VF	XF	Unc
21	1816 MF	.056	35.00	100.00	200.00	475.00
	1818 CB	.243	10.00	20.00	45.00	160.00
	1819 IFF	.925	8.00	16.00	40.00	150.00

16 SCHILLING

4.2140 g, .500 SILVER, .0677 oz ASW

C#	Date	Mintage	Fine	VF	XF	Unc
22	1816 MF	.031	35.00	100.00	200.00	475.00
	1818 CB	.125	15.00	40.00	85.00	250.00

Rev: 1/12 SP added.

C#	Date	Mintage	Fine	VF	XF	Unc
22a	1831 IFF	.198	8.00	20.00	50.00	150.00
	1839 IFF	.063	15.00	40.00	85.00	250.00

20 SCHILLING

(1/3 Daler Specie)

9.6310 g, .875 SILVER, .2709 oz ASW

C#	Date	Mintage	Fine	VF	XF	Unc
7	1808 MF	.124	20.00	40.00	80.00	225.00

NOTE: Earlier dates (1787-1799) exist for this type.

40 SCHILLING

(2/3 Daler Specie)

19.2630 g, .875 SILVER, .5419 oz ASW
Similar to 20 Schilling, C#7.

C#	Date	Mintage	Fine	VF	XF	Unc
8	1808 MF	—	85.00	150.00	225.00	500.00

NOTE: Earlier dates (1787-1799) exist for this type.

60 SCHILLING

(Daler Specie)

28.8930 g, .875 SILVER, .8128 oz ASW
Similar to 20 Schilling, C#7.

C#	Date	Mintage	Fine	VF	XF	Unc
9	1801 MF	.312	65.00	125.00	300.00	500.00
	1804 MF	.106	65.00	125.00	300.00	500.00
	1805 MF	—	—	—	Rare	—
	1807 MF	.102	65.00	125.00	300.00	500.00
	1808 MF	1.304	100.00	225.00	600.00	1000.

NOTE: Many die varieties exist.
NOTE: Earlier dates (1787-1800) exist for this type.

PATTERNS (Pn)

(Including off metal strikes)

KM#	Date	Mintage	Identification	Mkt.Val.
Pn10	1801	—	2-1/2 Schilling, Gold, C4	—
Pn11	1805	—	60 Schilling, Tin, C9	—

PROVISIONAL GOVERNMENT

1848-1851

DREILING

COPPER

C#	Date	Mintage	Fine	VF	XF	Unc
23	1850 TA	.200	5.00	10.00	20.00	60.00

SECHSLING

COPPER

C#	Date	Mintage	Fine	VF	XF	Unc
24	1850 TA	.203	5.00	10.00	20.00	60.00
	1851 TA	.163	7.00	15.00	35.00	90.00

SCHWARZBURG-RUDOLSTADT

The Schwarzburg family held territory in central and northern Thuringia. After many divisions, two lines, Sondershausen and Rudolstadt were founded in 1552. The count of Rudolstadt was raised to the rank of prince in 1710. The last prince abdicated in 1918.

RULERS

Ludwig Friedrich II, 1793-1807
Friedrich Gunther, 1807-1867
Albert, 1867-1869
Georg, 1869-1890
Gunther Viktor, 1890-1918

PFENNIG

COPPER
Obv: SCHWARZB/RUD-LM.
Rev: Value, 1 PF in script.

C#	Date	Mintage	Fine	VF	XF	Unc
50	1801	—	4.00	8.00	20.00	65.00
	1802	—	4.00	8.00	20.00	65.00

C#	Date	Mintage	Fine	VF	XF	Unc
63	1825	—	3.50	7.00	18.00	60.00

Obv: Crowned arms. Rev. value: SCHEIDE MUNZE.

C#	Date	Mintage	Fine	VF	XF	Unc
65	1842A	—	2.50	5.50	15.00	45.00

2 PFENNIG

COPPER
Obv: Crowned FG monogram within crossed branches. Rev: Value.

C#	Date	Mintage	Fine	VF	XF	Unc
57	1812	—	4.00	8.00	20.00	70.00

Obv: Crowned arms

C#	Date	Mintage	Fine	VF	XF	Unc
66	1842A	—	3.00	6.00	18.00	50.00

3 PFENNIG

COPPER
Obv. leg: SCHWARZB/RUD-LM.
Rev: Value, 3 PF in script.

C#	Date	Mintage	Fine	VF	XF	Unc
51	1804	—	6.00	12.00	30.00	80.00

Obv: Monogram FG within crossed branches.
Rev: Value.

C#	Date	Mintage	Fine	VF	XF	Unc
58	1813	—	6.00	12.00	30.00	80.00

Obv: Crown above monogram.

C#	Date	Mintage	Fine	VF	XF	Unc
64	1825	—	6.00	12.00	32.00	85.00

Obv: Crowned arms. Rev. leg: SCHEIDEMUNZE.

C#	Date	Mintage	Fine	VF	XF	Unc
67	1842A	—	3.00	6.00	18.00	55.00

4 PFENNIG

COPPER
Obv: Monogram FG within crossed branches.
Rev: Value.

C#	Date	Mintage	Fine	VF	XF	Unc
59	1812	—	6.00	12.00	35.00	90.00
	1813	—	6.00	12.00	35.00	90.00

6 PFENNIG

1.3300 g, .250 SILVER, .0106 oz ASW

C#	Date	Mintage	Fine	VF	XF	Unc
53	1801	—	7.00	15.00	30.00	90.00

NOTE: Earlier date (1800) exists for this type.

C#	Date	Mintage	Fine	VF	XF	Unc
60	1808	—	8.00	16.00	35.00	100.00

Obv: Rosette above & ledge below leg: SCHWARZB/RUD-LM.

C#	Date	Mintage	Fine	VF	XF	Unc
60a	1812	—	7.00	15.00	30.00	90.00
	1813	—	7.00	15.00	30.00	90.00

1/8 KREUZER

COPPER
Obv: Crowned arms within branches. Rev: Value.

C#	Date	Mintage	Fine	VF	XF	Unc
73	1840	.024	4.00	8.00	20.00	50.00
	1855	—	4.00	8.00	20.00	50.00

1/4 KREUZER

COPPER

C#	Date	Mintage	Fine	VF	XF	Unc
74	1840	.972	3.00	6.00	15.00	35.00
	1852	—	3.00	6.00	15.00	35.00
	1853	—	3.00	6.00	15.00	35.00
	1855	—	3.00	6.00	15.00	35.00
	1856	—	3.00	6.00	15.00	35.00

C#	Date	Mintage	Fine	VF	XF	Unc
74a	1857	—	2.50	5.00	12.00	32.00
	1859	—	2.50	5.00	12.00	32.00
	1860	—	2.50	5.00	12.00	32.00
	1861	—	2.50	5.00	12.00	32.00
	1863	—	2.50	5.00	12.00	32.00
	1865	—	2.50	5.00	12.00	32.00
	1866	—	2.50	5.00	12.00	32.00
82	1868	.096	3.00	6.00	15.00	45.00

KREUZER

COPPER

C#	Date	Mintage	Fine	VF	XF	Unc
76	1840	.480	3.00	6.00	15.00	40.00

C#	Date	Mintage	Fine	VF	XF	Unc
76a	1864	—	2.00	4.00	10.00	30.00
	1865	—	2.00	4.00	10.00	30.00
	1866	—	2.00	4.00	10.00	30.00

C#	Date	Mintage	Fine	VF	XF	Unc
83	1868	.037	4.00	8.00	18.00	50.00

3 KREUZER

1.2900 g, .333 SILVER, .0138 oz ASW

C#	Date	Mintage	Fine	VF	XF	Unc
77	1839	.155	5.00	10.00	30.00	100.00
	1840	Inc. Ab.	5.00	10.00	30.00	100.00
	1841	Inc. Ab.	5.00	10.00	30.00	100.00
	1842	Inc. Ab.	5.00	10.00	30.00	100.00
	1846	Inc. Ab.	5.00	10.00	30.00	100.00

1.2300 g, .350 SILVER, .0138 oz ASW
Obv. leg: SCHEIDE MUNZE added.

C#	Date	Mintage	Fine	VF	XF	Unc
77a	1866	.010	10.00	20.00	45.00	135.00

6 KREUZER

2.5900 g, .333 SILVER, .0277 oz ASW

C#	Date	Mintage	Fine	VF	XF	Unc
78	1840	.165	6.00	12.00	35.00	125.00
	1842	Inc. Ab.	6.00	12.00	35.00	125.00
	1846	Inc. Ab.	6.00	12.00	35.00	125.00

2.4600 g, .350 SILVER, .0276 oz ASW
Obv. leg: SCHEIDE MUNZE added.

C#	Date	Mintage	Fine	VF	XF	Unc
78a	1866	.010	12.00	25.00	55.00	165.00

1/2 GROSCHEN

1.0900 g, .222 SILVER, .0077 oz ASW
Obv: Crowned arms. Rev: Value.

C#	Date	Mintage	Fine	VF	XF	Unc
68	1841A	—	4.00	8.00	25.00	100.00

GROSCHEN

BILLON
Obv. leg: SCHWARZB. RUD-LM. Rev: Value.

C#	Date	Mintage	Fine	VF	XF	Unc
61	1803	—	7.00	15.00	45.00	135.00
	1808	—	5.00	10.00	30.00	110.00

Obv: Rosette above, legend below.
Rev: Value w/rosettes.

C#	Date	Mintage	Fine	VF	XF	Unc
61a	1812	—	4.00	8.00	25.00	100.00

2.1900 g, .222 SILVER, .0156 oz ASW
Obv: Crowned arms. Rev: Value.

C#	Date	Mintage	Fine	VF	XF	Unc
69	1841A	—	3.00	7.00	20.00	80.00

1/2 GULDEN

5.3030 g, .900 SILVER, .1535 oz ASW

C#	Date	Mintage	Fine	VF	XF	Unc
79	1841	.157	15.00	30.00	75.00	200.00
	1842	Inc. Ab.	15.00	30.00	75.00	200.00
	1843	Inc. Ab.	15.00	30.00	75.00	200.00
	1846	Inc. Ab.	15.00	30.00	75.00	200.00

GULDEN

10.6060 g, .900 SILVER, .3069 oz ASW
Obv: Similar to 1/2 Gulden, C#79.

C#	Date	Mintage	Fine	VF	XF	Unc
80	1841	.163	25.00	50.00	100.00	250.00
	1842	Inc. Ab.	25.00	50.00	100.00	250.00
	1843	Inc. Ab.	25.00	50.00	100.00	250.00
	1846	Inc. Ab.	25.00	50.00	100.00	250.00

ZWEY (2) GULDEN

21.2110 g, .900 SILVER, .6138 oz ASW
Obv: Similar to 1/2 Gulden, C#79.

C#	Date	Mintage	Fine	VF	XF	Unc
81	1846	500 pcs.	300.00	500.00	1000.	2000.

THALER

(Species)

28.0630 g, .833 SILVER, .7520 oz ASW

C#	Date	Mintage	Fine	VF	XF	Unc
62	1812 L	—	90.00	175.00	300.00	650.00
	1813 L	—	100.00	200.00	350.00	700.00

(Vereins)

18.5200 g, .900 SILVER, .5360 oz ASW

C#	Date	Mintage	Fine	VF	XF	Unc
70	1858	.016	40.00	65.00	130.00	275.00
	1859	6,000	50.00	75.00	150.00	300.00

C#	Date	Mintage	Fine	VF	XF	Unc
70a	1862	.048	40.00	65.00	130.00	275.00
	1863	.017	40.00	65.00	130.00	275.00

C#	Date	Mintage	Fine	VF	XF	Unc
70b	1866	.027	40.00	65.00	130.00	275.00

50th Anniversary of Reign

C#	Date	Mintage	Fine	VF	XF	Unc
71	1864	4,500	65.00	100.00	200.00	350.00
	1864	—	—	—	Proof	600.00

C#	Date	Mintage	Fine	VF	XF	Unc
84	1867	.013	50.00	80.00	175.00	450.00

2 THALER

(3-1/2 Gulden)

37.1200 g, .900 SILVER, 1.0742 oz ASW

C#	Date	Mintage	Fine	VF	XF	Unc
72	1841 A	.010	100.00	200.00	450.00	1000.
	1845 A	5,100	100.00	200.00	450.00	1000.

MONETARY REFORM

2 MARK

11.1110 g, .900 SILVER, .3215 oz ASW

Y#	Date	Mintage	Fine	VF	XF	Unc
207	1898A	.100	125.00	250.00	500.00	600.00
	1898A	375 pcs.	—	—	Proof	900.00

10 MARK

3.9820 g, .900 GOLD, .1152 oz AGW

Y#	Date	Mintage	Fine	VF	XF	Unc
208	1898A	.010	600.00	1100.	1500.	2000.
	1898A	700 pcs.	—	—	Proof	3500.

TRADE COINAGE

DUCAT

3.5000 g, .986 GOLD, .1109 oz AGW

C#	Date	Mintage	Fine	VF	XF	Unc
55	1803	311 pcs.	600.00	1300.	2500.	4000.

PATTERNS (Pn)

(Including off metal strikes)

KM#	Date	Mintage	Identification	Mkt.Val.
Pn1	1803	—	1 Ducat, Copper, C55	—
Pn2	1803	—	1 Ducat, Silver, C55	—

TRIAL STRIKES (TS)

KM#	Date	Mintage	Identification	Mkt.Val.
TS1	1846	—	2 Groschen, rev: C81	225.00

SCHWARZBURG-SONDERSHAUSEN

The Schwarzburg family held territory in central and northern Thuringia. After many divisions, two lines, Sondershausen and Rudolstadt were founded in 1552. The count of Sondershausen was raised to the rank of prince in 1709. The last prince died in 1909 and the lands passed to Rudolstadt.

RULERS

Gunther Friedrich Carl I, 1794-1835

Gunther Friedrich Carl II, 1835-1880
Karl Gunther, 1880-1909

PFENNIG

COPPER

C#	Date	Mintage	Fine	VF	XF	Unc
18	1846A	1.613	1.50	3.00	9.00	35.00
	1858A	.360	2.00	4.00	12.00	40.00

3 PFENNIG

COPPER

C#	Date	Mintage	Fine	VF	XF	Unc
19	1846A	.682	3.00	6.00	18.00	50.00
	1858A	.360	3.00	6.00	18.00	50.00
	1870A	.120	4.00	8.00	22.00	60.00

1/2 SILBER GROSCHEN

1.0900 g, .222 SILVER, .0077 oz ASW

C#	Date	Mintage	Fine	VF	XF	Unc
20	1846A	.657	3.00	6.00	18.00	50.00
	1851A	Inc. Ab.	3.00	6.00	18.00	50.00
	1858A	.180	4.00	8.00	22.00	60.00

SILBER GROSCHEN

2.1900 g, .222 SILVER, .0156 oz ASW

C#	Date	Mintage	Fine	VF	XF	Unc
21	1846A	.584	3.00	6.00	18.00	55.00
	1851A	Inc. Ab.	3.00	6.00	18.00	55.00
	1858A	.150	3.50	7.00	20.00	60.00
	1870A	.120	3.50	7.00	20.00	60.00

THALER

(Vereins)

18.5200 g, .900 SILVER, .5360 oz ASW

C#	Date	Mintage	Fine	VF	XF	Unc
22	1859A	.015	50.00	80.00	160.00	400.00
	1865A	.010	50.00	80.00	160.00	400.00
	1870A	.011	50.00	80.00	160.00	400.00

2 THALER

(3-1/2 Gulden)

37.1200 g, .900 SILVER, 1.0741 oz ASW

C#	Date	Mintage	Fine	VF	XF	Unc
23	1841A	4,300	150.00	250.00	550.00	1200.
	1845A	8,600	100.00	200.00	450.00	1000.
	1854A	8,600	100.00	200.00	450.00	1000.

MONETARY REFORM

2 MARK

11.1110 g, .900 SILVER, .3215 oz ASW

Y#	Date	Mintage	Fine	VF	XF	Unc
209	1896A	.050	100.00	250.00	450.00	600.00
	1896A	190 pcs.	—	—	Proof	850.00

20 MARK

7.9650 g, .900 GOLD, .2304 oz AGW

Y#	Date	Mintage	Fine	VF	XF	Unc
210	1896A	5,000	750.00	1250.	2000.	3000.
	1896A	—	—	—	Proof	5500.

SILESIA

A duchy, located in northeastern Germany, was separated into many segments. They were greatly influenced by Bohemia and Austria. The first coins were struck c. 1169. Special coins for Silesian possessions were struck by Bohemia from 1327. From 1526, when Bohemia and its Silesian possessions fell to Austria, a special series of coins were struck by Austria for the area. After the Prussian invasion in 1740, coins were minted from 1743 through 1797.

RULERS

Friedrich Wilhelm III, 1797-1840

MINT MARKS

A - Berlin
B - Breslau
G - Glatz, 1807-1809
W - Wratislawia (i.e. Breslau)

NOTE: For similar gold coins dated 1787-1805 refer to Prussian listings.

1/2 KREUZER

COPPER
Obv: Crowned FW monogram. Rev: Value.

C#	Date	Mintage	Fine	VF	XF	Unc
53	1806A	—	15.00	30.00	50.00	90.00

KREUZER

BILLON
Obv: Uniformed bust left.
Rev: Crowned arms w/eagle.

C#	Date	Mintage	Fine	VF	XF	Unc
57	1806A	—	17.50	40.00	90.00	200.00
	1808G	—	17.50	40.00	90.00	200.00

Obv: Crowned arms w/eagle within crossed branches. Rev: Value.

C#	Date	Mintage	Fine	VF	XF	Unc
54	1810A	.055	15.00	30.00	60.00	125.00

9 KREUZER

BILLON

C#	Date	Mintage	Fine	VF	XF	Unc
60	1808G	—	55.00	100.00	175.00	300.00

18 KREUZER

.563 SILVER
Obv: Uniformed bust left.
Rev: Crowned eagle w/scepter and orb.

C#	Date	Mintage	Fine	VF	XF	Unc
61	1808G	—	100.00	200.00	375.00	750.00

GROSCHEL

BILLON
Obv: Crowned FWR monogram. Rev: Value.

C#	Date	Mintage	Fine	VF	XF	Unc
56	1805A	—	20.00	40.00	75.00	150.00
	1806A	—	20.00	40.00	75.00	150.00
	1808G	—	20.00	40.00	75.00	150.00
	1809G	—	20.00	40.00	75.00	150.00

NOTE: Earlier date (1797) exists for this type.

STOLBERG

Stolberg, a county located in the Harz mountains of central Germany, had its own coinage from the 11th century.

MINTMASTERS INITIALS

Letter	Date	Name
EHAZ,Z	1792-1807	Ernst Hermann Agathus Ziegler

STOLBERG-ROSSLA

The Rossla line was founded in 1704.

PFENNIG

COPPER
Obv: Stag left before column.
Rev: Value above date.

C#	Date	Mintage	VG	Fine	VF	XF
47	1801 Z	—	6.00	12.00	25.00	45.00

NOTE: Earlier date (1799) exists for this type.

STOLBERG-WERNIGERODE

Stolberg, a county located in the Harz mountains of central Germany, had its own coinage from the 11th century. The lines of Wernigerode and Stolberg were established in 1641. A division of the lands occurred in 1645 but only the Wernigerode branch continued to issue coins after 1800. Although administered by Prussia from 1714, the country retained a certain amount of sovereignty until 1876.

RULERS

Christian Friedrich, 1778-1824
Henrich XII, 1824-1854

TRADE COINAGE

DUCAT

3.5000 g, .986 GOLD, .1109 oz AGW
Golden Wedding Anniversary.

C#	Date	Mintage	Fine	VF	XF	Unc
25	1818	308 pcs.	600.00	1200.	2500.	4500.

Henrich XII

C#	Date	Mintage	Fine	VF	XF	Unc
26	1824	—	450.00	900.00	1800.	3500.

PATTERNS (Pn)

(Including off metal strikes)

KM#	Date	Mintage	Identification	Mkt.Val.
Pn9	1818	—	1 Ducat, Silver, C25	250.00

TEUTONIC ORDER

The Order of Knights was founded during the Third Crusade in 1198. They acquired considerable territory by conquest from the heathen Prussians in the late 13th and early 14th centuries. The seat of the Grand Master moved from Acre to Venice and in 1309 to Marienburg, Prussia. The Teutonic Order began striking coins in the late 13th century. In 1355 permission was granted to strike hellers at Mergentheim. However, the bulk of the Order's coinage until 1525 was schillings and half schoters minted in and for Prussia. In 1809 the Order was suppressed and Mergentheim was annexed to Wurttemberg.

RULERS

Max Franz, 1780-1801
Karl Ludwig, 1801-1804
Anton Victor, 1804-1809

Death of Grand Master Max Franz

C#	Date	Mintage	VG	Fine	VF	XF
—	1801	—	30.00	60.00	120.00	225.00

1/4 THALER

SILVER
Death of Grand Master Max Franz

C#	Date	Mintage	VG	Fine	VF	XF
26	1801	—	60.00	120.00	200.00	400.00

WALDECK

The county of Waldeck was located on the border of Hesse. Their first coinage appeared ca. 1250. Pyrmont was united with Waldeck in 1625 but was ruled separately for a while in the 19th century. They were reunited in 1812. The rulers gained the status of prince in 1712. The administration was turned over to Prussia in 1867 but the princes retained some sovereignty until 1918.

WALDECK-PYRMONT

RULERS

Friedrich Karl August in Waldeck, 1763-1812
Georg (in Pyrmont), 1805-1812 (Refer to Pyrmont for listings in Waldeck-Pyrmont), 1812-1813
Georg Heinrich, 1813-1845
Emma, Regent for Georg Victor, 1845-1852
Georg Victor, 1852-1893
Friedrich, 1893-1918

MINTMASTERS INITIALS

AW - Albert Welle
FW, F*w, W, .W. - Friedrich Welle

PFENNIG

COPPER
Obv: Crowned F monogram. Rev: Value.

C#	Date	Mintage	Fine	VF	XF	Unc
42b	1809 FW	—	6.00	12.00	35.00	120.00
	1810 FW	—	6.00	12.00	35.00	120.00

Obv: Crowned arms.

C#	Date	Mintage	Fine	VF	XF	Unc
43a	1809 FW	—	6.00	12.00	35.00	125.00

Rev. value: 1 PFENNIG.

C#	Date	Mintage	Fine	VF	XF	Unc
43b	1810 FW	—	6.00	12.00	35.00	125.00

Obv: Crowned GH monogram.

C#	Date	Mintage	Fine	VF	XF	Unc
65	1816 FW	—	6.00	12.00	25.00	100.00
	1817 FW	—	6.00	12.00	25.00	100.00

C#	Date	Mintage	Fine	VF	XF	Unc
66	1816 FW	—	6.00	12.00	45.00	135.00
	1817 W	—	6.00	12.00	45.00	135.00

Obv: Crowned Waldeck-Pyrmont arms.

C#	Date	Mintage	Fine	VF	XF	Unc
67	1821 FW	—	5.00	10.00	20.00	80.00

Obv: Arms in beaded border.

C#	Date	Mintage	Fine	VF	XF	Unc
67a	1821 FW	—	5.00	10.00	20.00	80.00

Obv: Crowned draped arms.

C#	Date	Mintage	Fine	VF	XF	Unc
68	1825 FW	—	6.00	12.00	35.00	120.00

C#	Date	Mintage	Fine	VF	XF	Unc
69	1842A	.352	4.00	8.00	16.00	65.00
	1843A	.220	4.00	8.00	16.00	65.00
	1845A	.384	4.00	8.00	16.00	65.00

C#	Date	Mintage	Fine	VF	XF	Unc
85	1855A	.366	3.00	6.00	12.00	45.00
	1855A	—	—	—	Proof	100.00

C#	Date	Mintage	Fine	VF	XF	Unc
85a	1867B	.540	2.00	4.00	8.00	35.00

3 PFENNIG

COPPER
Obv. leg: FURSTL. WALDECK SCH. MUNZ., crowned F monogrm.
Rev. value: III PFENNIGE.

C#	Date	Mintage	Fine	VF	XF	Unc
44a	1809 FW	—	7.00	15.00	45.00	150.00
	1810 FW	—	7.00	15.00	45.00	150.00

NOTE: Earlier date (1781) exists for this type.

Obv: Crowned star arms.

C#	Date	Mintage	Fine	VF	XF	Unc
45	1809 FW	—	7.00	15.00	45.00	155.00

NOTE: Earlier date (1781) exists for this type.

Obv: Arms within pearl circle.

C#	Date	Mintage	Fine	VF	XF	Unc
45a	1810 FW	—	8.00	16.00	50.00	165.00

C#	Date	Mintage	Fine	VF	XF	Unc
70	1819 FW	—	6.00	12.00	35.00	140.00

Rev. value: PFENNIG.

C#	Date	Mintage	Fine	VF	XF	Unc
70b	1819 FW	—	10.00	20.00	60.00	185.00

C#	Date	Mintage	Fine	VF	XF	Unc
70a	1819 FW	—	7.00	15.00	45.00	150.00

C#	Date	Mintage	Fine	VF	XF	Unc
71	1824 FW	—	6.00	12.00	35.00	140.00
	1825 FW	—	6.00	12.00	35.00	140.00

C#	Date	Mintage	Fine	VF	XF	Unc
72	1842A	.247	5.00	10.00	20.00	80.00
	1843A	.114	5.00	10.00	20.00	80.00
	1845A	.249	5.00	10.00	20.00	80.00

C#	Date	Mintage	Fine	VF	XF	Unc
86	1855A	.243	4.00	8.00	16.00	60.00

C#	Date	Mintage	Fine	VF	XF	Unc
86.1	1867B	.420	3.00	6.00	12.00	50.00

1/2 GROSCHEN

COPPER

C#	Date	Mintage	Fine	VF	XF	Unc
46	1809 FW	—	20.00	45.00	90.00	200.00

Obv: Crowned draped arms.

C#	Date	Mintage	Fine	VF	XF	Unc
73	1825 FW	—	20.00	40.00	80.00	175.00

GROSCHEN

(Marien)

1.3900 g, .312 SILVER, .0139 oz ASW

C#	Date	Mintage	Fine	VF	XF	Unc
74	1814 FW	—	12.00	25.00	60.00	185.00
	1820 FW	—	12.00	25.00	60.00	185.00

C#	Date	Mintage	Fine	VF	XF	Unc
74a	1820 FW	—	—	—	Rare	—

Obv: Crowned draped arms.

C#	Date	Mintage	Fine	VF	XF	Unc
74b	1820 FW	—	12.00	25.00	60.00	185.00
	1823 FW	—	12.00	25.00	60.00	185.00

(Silber)

2.1900 g, .222 SILVER, .0156 oz ASW
Obv. leg. ends: . . . WALDECK U.P.

C#	Date	Mintage	Fine	VF	XF	Unc
76	1836 AW	.164	10.00	20.00	45.00	160.00
	1839 AW	.046	10.00	20.00	45.00	160.00

Obv. leg. ends: . . . WALDECK U. PYRMONT

C#	Date	Mintage	Fine	VF	XF	Unc
77	1842A	.310	6.00	12.00	28.00	110.00
	1843A	.191	6.00	12.00	28.00	110.00
	1845A	.182	6.00	12.00	28.00	110.00

Rev: A below value and date.

C#	Date	Mintage	Fine	VF	XF	Unc
87	1855A	.156	7.00	15.00	30.00	125.00

C#	Date	Mintage	Fine	VF	XF	Unc
87a	1867B	.180	6.00	12.00	20.00	90.00

2 MARIENGROSCHEN

2.3900 g, .375 SILVER, .0288 oz ASW

C#	Date	Mintage	Fine	VF	XF	Unc
78	1820 FW	—	8.00	16.00	42.00	160.00
	1822 FW	—	8.00	16.00	42.00	160.00
	1823 FW	—	8.00	16.00	42.00	160.00
	1824 FW	—	8.00	16.00	42.00	160.00
	1825 FW	—	8.00	16.00	42.00	160.00

Rev: A.W. below value.

C#	Date	Mintage	Fine	VF	XF	Unc
78a	1827 AW	—	10.00	20.00	50.00	175.00
	1828 AW	—	10.00	20.00	50.00	175.00

24 EINEN (1/24) THALER

1.9800 g, .368 SILVER, .0234 oz ASW

C#	Date	Mintage	Fine	VF	XF	Unc
75	1818 FW	—	10.00	20.00	45.00	165.00
	1819 FW	—	10.00	20.00	45.00	165.00

1/6 THALER

5.3400 g, .520 SILVER, .0892 oz ASW

C#	Date	Mintage	Fine	VF	XF	Unc
79	1837 AW	.034	22.00	45.00	90.00	225.00

C#	Date	Mintage	Fine	VF	XF	Unc
79a	1843A	.038	20.00	40.00	80.00	200.00
	1845A	.038	20.00	40.00	80.00	200.00

IV EINEN (1/4) THALER

7.0000 g, .620 SILVER, .1395 oz ASW

C#	Date	Mintage	Fine	VF	XF	Unc
53	1810 FW	—	100.00	200.00	375.00	700.00

Rev: Date and value in larger letters.

C#	Date	Mintage	Fine	VF	XF	Unc
53a	1810 FW	—	75.00	150.00	300.00	600.00

Obv. leg. ends: . . . PYRMONT & .

C#	Date	Mintage	Fine	VF	XF	Unc
62	1812 FW	—	600.00	1250.	1750.	2250.

Obv. leg. ends: . . . PYRMONT EC

C#	Date	Mintage	Fine	VF	XF	Unc
62a	1813 FW	—	600.00	1250.	1750.	2250.

3 EINEN (1/3) THALER

8.8000 g, .620 SILVER, .1754 oz ASW

C#	Date	Mintage	Fine	VF	XF	Unc
80	1824 FW	—	55.00	110.00	220.00	375.00

C#	Date	Mintage	Fine	VF	XF	Unc
80a	1824 FW	—	50.00	100.00	200.00	350.00

C#	Date	Mintage	Fine	VF	XF	Unc
81	1824 FW	—	65.00	125.00	275.00	425.00

THALER

28.0600 g, .833 SILVER, .7515 oz ASW
Obv. leg: FRIDERICUS PR. . .

Dav.#922

C#	Date	Mintage	Fine	VF	XF	Unc
59	1810 FW	—	400.00	700.00	1500.	3500.

Obv. leg: FRIDERICUS D.G. PR. . .

C#	Date	Mintage	Fine	VF	XF	Unc
59a	1810 FW	—	600.00	1100.	2500.	5200.

C#	Date	Mintage	Fine	VF	XF	Unc
63	1813 FW	—	600.00	1100.	2500.	5000.

29.5170 g, .868 SILVER, .8237 oz ASW
Similar to C#63.
Edge inscription: KRONEN THALER

C#	Date	Mintage	Fine	VF	XF	Unc
64	1813 FW	—	600.00	1100.	2500.	5000.

Similar to C#63.
Edge inscription: WALDECKISCHER

C#	Date	Mintage	Fine	VF	XF	Unc
64a	1813 FW	—	600.00	1100.	2500.	5000.

Edge: Stars

C#	Date	Mintage	Fine	VF	XF	Unc
64b	1813 FW	—	600.00	1100.	2500.	5000.

29.4500 g, .868 SILVER, .8218 oz ASW

C#	Date	Mintage	Fine	VF	XF	Unc
82	1824 FW	—	200.00	350.00	700.00	1400.

18.5200 g, .900 SILVER, .5358 oz ASW

C#	Date	Mintage	Fine	VF	XF	Unc
88	1859A	.014	40.00	85.00	165.00	325.00
	1867A	.019	40.00	85.00	165.00	325.00

2 THALER

(3-1/2 Gulden)

37.1200 g, .900 SILVER, 1.0742 oz ASW

C#	Date	Mintage	Fine	VF	XF	Unc
83	1842A	4,500	350.00	700.00	1200.	2000.
	1845A	4,500	350.00	700.00	1200.	2000.

Rev: Similar to C#83.

C#	Date	Mintage	Fine	VF	XF	Unc
84	1847A	1,000	650.00	1100.	1900.	3250.

C#	Date	Mintage	Fine	VF	XF	Unc
89	1856A	.011	200.00	400.00	800.00	1600.

WALLMODEN-GIMBORN

The town of Gimborn, located in Westphalia, was purchased from Schwarzenberg in 1782. The following year it was raised to the rank of county. In 1806, Wallmoden-Gimborn was annexed to Berg. In 1815, the land went to Prussia.

RULERS

Johann Ludwig, 1782-1806

1/24 THALER

1.9900 g, .368 SILVER, .0235 oz ASW

C#	Date	Mintage	Fine	VF	XF	Unc
1	1802	—	80.00	225.00	375.00	600.00

1/2 THALER

14.0300 g, .833 SILVER, .3757 oz ASW

C#	Date	Mintage	Fine	VF	XF	Unc
2	1802	—	375.00	525.00	950.00	—

TRADE COINAGE

DUCAT

3.5000 g, .986 GOLD, .1109 oz AGW

C#	Date	Mintage	Fine	VF	XF	Unc
3	1802	400 pcs.	1250.	2500.	4500.	8000.

PATTERNS (Pn)

(Including off metal strikes)

KM#	Date	Mintage	Identification	Mkt.Val.
Pn1	1802	—	1 Ducat, Silver, C3	750.00

WESTPHALIA

A kingdom, located in western Germany, created by Napoleon for his brother. It was comprised of parts of Hesse-Cassel, Brunswick, Hildesheim, Paderborn, Halberstadt, Osnabruck, Minden, etc. In 1813 and 1814, Westphalia was divided and returned to its former owners.

RULERS

Jerome (Hieronymus) Napoleon, 1807-1813

MINT MARKS

B - Brunswick
C,C. - Cassel, mm on rev.
C,C. - Clausthal, mm on obv.
F - Cassel

MINTMASTERS MARKS

C & eagle head - Cassel
J & horse head - Cassel
J & horse head - Paris

MINTMASTERS INITIALS

Letter	Date	Name
F	1783-1831	Dietrich Heinrich Fulda in Cassel

GERMAN STANDARD

PFENNIG

COPPER

C#	Date	Mintage	Fine	VF	XF	Unc
1	1808C	—	7.00	15.00	35.00	100.00

2 PFENNIG

COPPER

Obv: Crowned HN monogram. Rev: Value.

C#	Date	Mintage	Fine	VF	XF	Unc
2	1808C	—	7.00	15.00	35.00	100.00
	1810C	—	7.00	15.00	45.00	120.00

4 PFENNIG

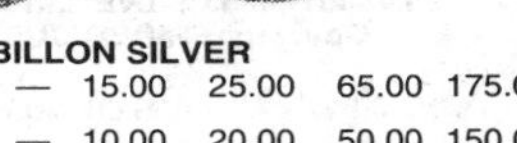

BILLON SILVER

C#	Date	Mintage	Fine	VF	XF	Unc
3	1808C	—	15.00	25.00	65.00	175.00
3a	1809C	—	10.00	20.00	50.00	150.00

MARIENGROSCHEN

BILLON SILVER

C#	Date	Mintage	Fine	VF	XF	Unc
4	1808C	—	10.00	20.00	45.00	135.00
	1810C	—	10.00	20.00	60.00	165.00

24 MARIENGROSCHEN

17.3200 g, .750 SILVER, .4177 oz ASW

C#	Date	Mintage	Fine	VF	XF	Unc
12	1810B	—	60.00	120.00	225.00	375.00

24 EINEN (1/24) THALER

1.9900 g, .368 SILVER, .0235 oz ASW

Obv: Crowned HN monogram w/ribbons. Rev: Value.

C#	Date	Mintage	Fine	VF	XF	Unc
17	1807 F	—	12.00	25.00	50.00	125.00
	1808/7 F	—	10.00	25.00	45.00	125.00
	1808 F	—	10.00	20.00	40.00	100.00
	1809 F	—	15.00	25.00	55.00	140.00

Obv: Crown w/o ribbons.

C#	Date	Mintage	Fine	VF	XF	Unc
17a	1809C	—	10.00	20.00	45.00	150.00

12 EINEN (1/12) THALER

3.3400 g, .437 SILVER, .0469 oz ASW

C#	Date	Mintage	Fine	VF	XF	Unc
5	1808C	—	12.50	25.00	65.00	175.00
	1809C	—	12.50	25.00	65.00	175.00
	1810C	—	12.50	25.00	65.00	175.00

1/6 THALER

(Reichs)

3.1800 g, .994 SILVER, .1016 oz ASW

C#	Date	Mintage	Fine	VF	XF	Unc
6	1808C	—	15.00	30.00	65.00	125.00
	1812C	—	15.00	30.00	65.00	125.00
6a	1810C	—	25.00	65.00	150.00	300.00

5.8500 g, .500 SILVER, .0939 oz ASW

C#	Date	Mintage	Fine	VF	XF	Unc
11	1808B	—	12.50	25.00	55.00	100.00
	1809B	—	12.50	25.00	55.00	100.00
	1810B	—	12.50	25.00	55.00	100.00
	1812B	—	12.50	25.00	55.00	100.00
	1813B	—	12.50	25.00	55.00	100.00

C#	Date	Mintage	Fine	VF	XF	Unc
18	1808 F	—	10.00	20.00	45.00	90.00
	1809 C	—	10.00	20.00	45.00	90.00
	1809 F	—	10.00	20.00	45.00	90.00
	1810 C	—	10.00	20.00	45.00	90.00
	1810 F	—	10.00	20.00	45.00	90.00
	1813 C	—	10.00	20.00	45.00	90.00

2/3 THALER

(Reichs)

13.0800 g, .994 SILVER, .4180 oz ASW

C#	Date	Mintage	Fine	VF	XF	Unc
7	1808C	—	40.00	80.00	150.00	300.00
	1810C	—	40.00	80.00	150.00	300.00

Rev: Similar to C#7.

C#	Date	Mintage	Fine	VF	XF	Unc
7a	1809C	—	75.00	150.00	250.00	400.00
	1810C	—	75.00	125.00	225.00	325.00

C#	Date	Mintage	Fine	VF	XF	Unc
8	1811C	—	50.00	100.00	200.00	400.00

C#	Date	Mintage	Fine	VF	XF	Unc
9	1811C	—	50.00	100.00	150.00	300.00
	1812C	—	60.00	125.00	175.00	350.00
	1813C	—	50.00	100.00	150.00	300.00

THALER

28.0600 g, .833 SILVER, .7515 oz ASW

C#	Date	Mintage	Fine	VF	XF	Unc
19	1810C	5 pcs.	—	—	20,000.	30,000.

C#	Date	Mintage	Fine	VF	XF	Unc
20	1810C	—	100.00	200.00	350.00	850.00
	1811C	—	100.00	200.00	350.00	850.00
	1812C	—	100.00	200.00	350.00	850.00

C#	Date	Mintage	Fine	VF	XF	Unc
20a	1811C	—	100.00	200.00	350.00	850.00
	1812C	—	100.00	200.00	350.00	850.00
	1813C	—	100.00	200.00	350.00	850.00

(Mining)

C#	Date	Mintage	Fine	VF	XF	Unc
10	1811C	—	225.00	450.00	900.00	2250.

Obv: Similar to C#10 but small bust.

C#	Date	Mintage	Fine	VF	XF	Unc
10a	1811C	—	225.00	450.00	900.00	2250.

V (5) THALER

6.6500 g, .900 GOLD, .1924 oz AGW

C#	Date	Mintage	Fine	VF	XF	Unc
13	1810B	—	1000.	2400.	3750.	8500.

Obv: Bust left w/o laurel wreath.

C#	Date	Mintage	Fine	VF	XF	Unc
14	1811B	—	—	—	—	—

C#	Date	Mintage	Fine	VF	XF	Unc
14a	1811B	—	900.00	2000.	4000.	6000.
	1812B	—	800.00	1750.	3500.	5000.
	1813B	—	900.00	2000.	4000.	6000.

X (10) THALER

13.3000 g, .900 GOLD, .3848 oz AGW

C#	Date	Mintage	Fine	VF	XF	Unc
15	1810B	—	1000.	2000.	4000.	6000.

Obv: Bust left, w/o laurel wreath.

C#	Date	Mintage	Fine	VF	XF	Unc
16	1811B	—	—	—	—	—

C#	Date	Mintage	Fine	VF	XF	Unc
16a	1811B	—	725.00	1650.	3000.	5000.
	1812B	—	725.00	1650.	3000.	5000.
	1813B	—	725.00	1650.	2500.	5000.

FRENCH STANDARD

CENTIME

COPPER

C#	Date	Mintage	Fine	VF	XF	Unc
21	1809C	—	2.50	7.50	20.00	50.00
	1812C	—	2.50	7.50	20.00	50.00

2 CENTIMES

COPPER

C#	Date	Mintage	Fine	VF	XF	Unc
22	1808C	—	2.50	5.00	17.50	55.00
	1809C	—	2.50	5.00	17.50	55.00
	1810C	—	2.50	5.00	17.50	55.00
	1812C	—	2.50	5.00	17.50	55.00
22a	1808J	—	25.00	50.00	100.00	225.00

3 CENTIMES

COPPER

C#	Date	Mintage	Fine	VF	XF	Unc
23	1808C	—	2.50	5.00	20.00	55.00
	1809C	—	2.50	5.00	20.00	55.00
	1810C	—	2.50	5.00	20.00	55.00
	1812C	—	2.50	5.00	20.00	55.00
23a	1808J	—	25.00	50.00	100.00	225.00

5 CENTIMES

COPPER

C#	Date	Mintage	Fine	VF	XF	Unc
24	1808C	—	2.50	6.00	25.00	65.00
	1809C	—	2.50	6.00	25.00	65.00
	1812C	—	2.50	6.00	25.00	65.00
24a	1808J	—	30.00	60.00	125.00	325.00
	1809J	—	—	—	Rare	—

10 CENTIMES

1.9700 g, .200 SILVER, .0126 oz ASW

C#	Date	Mintage	Fine	VF	XF	Unc
25	1808C	—	3.00	12.50	35.00	80.00
	1809C	—	3.00	12.50	35.00	80.00
	1810C	—	3.00	12.50	35.00	80.00
	1812C	—	3.00	12.50	35.00	80.00

20 CENTIMES

3.8700 g, .200 SILVER, .0248 oz ASW

C#	Date	Mintage	Fine	VF	XF	Unc
26	1808C	—	4.00	17.50	40.00	110.00
	1810C	—	4.00	17.50	40.00	110.00
	1812C	—	4.00	17.50	40.00	110.00

1/2 FRANK

2.5000 g, .900 SILVER, .0723 oz ASW

C#	Date	Mintage	Fine	VF	XF	Unc
27a	1808J	—	100.00	225.00	450.00	650.00

FRANK

5.0000 g, .900 SILVER, .1447 oz ASW

C#	Date	Mintage	Fine	VF	XF	Unc
28	1808J	—	150.00	325.00	650.00	1150.

2 FRANKEN

10.0000 g, .900 SILVER, .2894 oz ASW

C#	Date	Mintage	Fine	VF	XF	Unc
29	1808J	—	200.00	400.00	750.00	1250.

5 FRANKEN

25.0000 g, .900 SILVER, .7235 oz ASW

C#	Date	Mintage	Fine	VF	XF	Unc
30	1808J	—	500.00	1000.	2000.	3500.
30a	1809J	—	500.00	1000.	2000.	3500.

1.6200 g, .900 GOLD, .0469 oz AGW

C#	Date	Mintage	Fine	VF	XF	Unc
31	1813C	—	225.00	350.00	500.00	1200.

10 FRANKEN

3.2300 g, .900 GOLD, .0936 oz AGW

C#	Date	Mintage	Fine	VF	XF	Unc
32.1	1813C	—	350.00	600.00	900.00	1500.
	Medal alignment.					
32.2	1813C	—	—	—	Proof	Rare

20 FRANKEN

6.4500 g, .900 GOLD, .1868 oz AGW

C#	Date	Mintage	Fine	VF	XF	Unc
	Mintmasters mark: Horses head					
33	1808J	—	225.00	400.00	800.00	1750.
	1809J	—	225.00	400.00	800.00	1750.
	Mintmasters mark: Eagles head					
33a	1808C	.013	225.00	350.00	800.00	1750.
	1809C	9,104	225.00	350.00	800.00	1750.
	1811C	.019	225.00	350.00	800.00	1750.
	1813C	—	500.00	1000.	1500.	4000.
	Mintmasters mark: Horses head					
33b	1809C	—	200.00	300.00	700.00	1800.
	W/o edge inscription (restrikes ca. 1867).					
33c	1813C	—	—	Reported, not confirmed		

40 FRANKEN

12.9000 g, .900 GOLD, .3733 oz AGW

C#	Date	Mintage	Fine	VF	XF	Unc
34	1813C	80 pcs.	3000.	4500.	8000.	12,000.
	W/o edge inscription (restrikes ca. 1867).					
34a	1813C	5,465	—	—	2200.	4000.

PATTERNS (Pn)

(Including off metal strikes)

KM#	Date	Mintage	Identification	Mkt.Val.
Pn1	1808J	—	10 Centimes, Billon, C25a	—
Pn2	1808J	—	20 Centimes, Billon, C26a	—

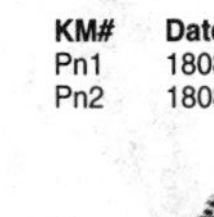

KM#	Date	Mintage	Identification	Mkt.Val.
Pn3	1808C	—	1/2 Frank, Silver, C27	—

KM#	Date	Mintage	Identification	Mkt.Val.
Pn4	18XX	—	2 Franken, Copper, C29	1200.
Pn5	1808S	—	20 Franken, w/o edge inscription	2000.
Pn6	1808C	—	20 Franken, w/o edge inscription	2000.
Pn7	1809C	—	20 Franken, w/o edge inscription	2000.
Pn8	1811C	22	2/3 Thaler, Gold, C8	—

KM#	Date	Mintage	Identification	Mkt.Val.
Pn9	1811C	—	1 Mining Thaler, Copper	—

KM#	Date	Mintage	Identification	Mkt.Val.
Pn10	1812C	—	1 Convention Thaler, Copper	—
Pn11	1813	1 pc.	5 Franken, C31, w/o mint mark	—
Pn12	1813C	—	5 Franken, Copper, C31,	450.00

WISMAR

A seaport on the Baltic, the city of Wismar is said to have obtained municipal rights from Mecklenburg in 1229. It was an important member of the Hanseatic League in the 13th and 14th centuries. Their coinage began at the end of the 13th century and terminated in 1854. They belonged to Sweden from 1648 to 1803. A special plate money was struck by the Swedes in 1715 when the town was under siege. In 1803, Sweden sold Wismar to Mecklenburg-Schwerin. The transaction was confirmed in 1815.

RULERS

Swedish, 1648-1803
Friedrich Franz I, 1785-1837
Paul Friedrich, 1837-1842
Friedrich Franz II, 1842-1883

MINTMASTERS INITIALS

FL - F. Lautersack
FS - Friedrich Schmidt
HM - Joachim Heinrich Meese
ICM - Karl Johann Joachim Mau
IZ - Johann Joachim Zeller
S - Heinrich Schroeder

UNDER MECKLENBURG-SCHWERIN

3 PFENING

COPPER

C#	Date	Mintage	Fine	VF	XF	Unc
3	1824 IZ	—	4.00	8.00	20.00	60.00
	1825 IZ	—	4.00	8.00	20.00	60.00

C#	Date	Mintage	Fine	VF	XF	Unc
3a	1829 HM	—	4.00	8.00	20.00	60.00
	1830 HM	—	4.00	8.00	20.00	60.00

C#	Date	Mintage	Fine	VF	XF	Unc
3b	1835 ICM	—	4.00	8.00	20.00	60.00
3c	1840 FS	—	4.00	8.00	20.00	60.00

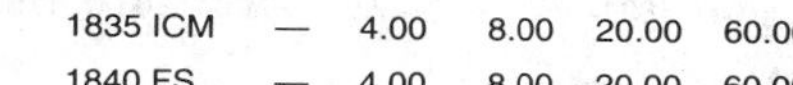

Obv. leg. ends: "MОИETA".

C#	Date	Mintage	Fine	VF	XF	Unc
3d	1840 FS	—	4.00	8.00	20.00	60.00
3e	1845 S	—	4.00	8.00	20.00	60.00

C#	Date	Mintage	Fine	VF	XF	Unc
4	1854 S	—	4.00	8.00	20.00	60.00

WURTTEMBERG

Located in South Germany, between Baden and Bavaria, Wurttemberg obtained the mint right in 1374. In 1495 the rulers became dukes. In 1802 the duke exchanged some of his land on the Rhine with France for territories nearer his capital city. Napoleon elevated the duke to the status of elector in 1803 and made him a king in 1806. The kingdom joined the German Empire in 1871 and endured until the king abdicated in 1918.

RULERS

Friedrich, as Duke Friedrich II, 1797-1803
As Elector Friedrich I, 1803-1806
As King Friedrich I, 1806-1816
Wilhelm I, 1816-1864
Karl I, 1864-1891
Wilhelm II, 1891-1918

MINT MARKS

C, CT - Christophstal Mint
F - Freudenstadt Mint
S - Stuttgart Mint
T - Tubingen Mint

MINTMASTERS INITIALS

Stuttgart Mint

Letter	Date	Name
AD/D	1837-1870	Gottlob August Dietelbach, die-cutter
CH,ICH	1783-1813	Johann Christian Heuglin
ILW,LW,W	1798-1837	Johann Ludwig Wagner, die-cutter
—	(d.1867)	Albert Wagner, die-cutter

Die-cutters of Various Cities

CS,C,Sch F	d.1877	Christian Schnitzspahn, die-cutter
C VOIGT	1838-?	Carl Friedrich Voigt, die-cutter in Berling 1425
PB	d.1850	Peter Bruckman, die-cutter in Heilbronn Augsburg, in Karlsruhe

ARMS

Wurttemberg: 3 stag antlers arranged vertically.
Teck (duchy): Field of lozenges (diamond shapes).
Mompelgart (principality): 2 fish standing on tails.

1/4 KREUZER

COPPER

KM#	Date	Mintage	Fine	VF	XF	Unc
589	1842	.198	3.00	6.50	18.00	50.00
(C158)	1843	.118	3.00	6.50	18.00	50.00
	1852	—	3.00	6.50	18.00	50.00
	1853	—	3.00	6.50	18.00	50.00
	1854	—	3.00	6.50	18.00	50.00
	1855	—	3.00	6.50	18.00	50.00
	1856	—	3.00	6.50	18.00	50.00

KM#	Date	Mintage	Fine	VF	XF	Unc
602	1858	—	3.50	7.00	20.00	55.00
(C159)	1860	—	3.50	7.00	20.00	55.00
	1861	—	3.50	7.00	20.00	55.00
	1862	—	3.50	7.00	20.00	55.00
	1863	—	3.50	7.00	20.00	55.00
	1864	—	3.50	7.00	20.00	55.00

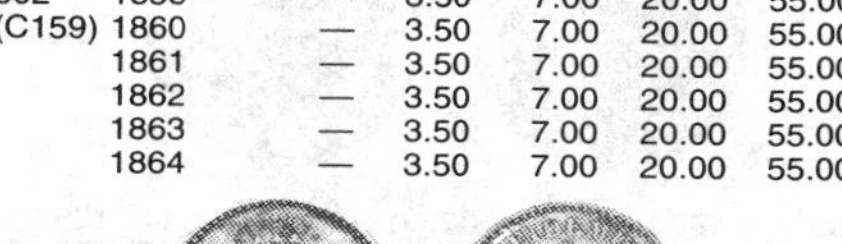

KM#	Date	Mintage	Fine	VF	XF	Unc
610	1865	—	3.00	6.00	14.00	45.00
(203)	1866	—	3.00	6.00	14.00	45.00
	1867	—	3.00	6.00	14.00	45.00
	1868	—	3.00	6.00	14.00	45.00
	1869	—	3.00	6.00	14.00	45.00
	1871	—	3.00	6.00	14.00	45.00
	1872	—	3.00	6.00	14.00	45.00

1/2 KREUZER

BILLON

KM#	Date	Mintage	Fine	VF	XF	Unc
518	1812	—	5.00	10.00	30.00	90.00
(C138)	1813	.470	5.00	10.00	30.00	90.00
	1816	.126	5.00	10.00	30.00	90.00
	ND	—	5.00	10.00	30.00	90.00

Obv: Crowned W.

KM#	Date	Mintage	Fine	VF	XF	Unc
527 (C162)	ND	—	15.00	30.00	65.00	200.00

Obv: Crowned W dividing date.

KM#	Date	Mintage	Fine	VF	XF	Unc
528 (C-A163)	1818	—	10.00	20.00	45.00	135.00

KM#	Date	Mintage	Fine	VF	XF	Unc
547	1824	.840	3.50	7.00	20.00	60.00
(C163)	1828	—	3.50	7.00	20.00	60.00
	1829	.780	3.50	7.00	20.00	60.00
	1831	.620	3.50	7.00	20.00	60.00
	1833	Inc. 1831	3.50	7.00	20.00	60.00
	1834	Inc. 1831	3.50	7.00	20.00	60.00
	1835	Inc. 1831	3.50	7.00	20.00	60.00
	1836	Inc. 1831	3.50	7.00	20.00	60.00
	1837	Inc. 1831	3.50	7.00	20.00	60.00

COPPER

KM#	Date	Mintage	Fine	VF	XF	Unc
585	1840	—	3.00	6.00	14.00	45.00
(C160)	1841	—	3.00	6.00	14.00	45.00
	1842	.452	3.00	6.00	14.00	45.00
	1844	—	3.00	6.00	14.00	45.00
	1845	—	3.00	6.00	14.00	45.00
	1846	—	3.00	6.00	14.00	45.00
	1847	—	3.00	6.00	14.00	45.00
	1848	—	3.00	6.00	14.00	45.00
	1849/7	—	—	—	—	—
	1849	—	3.00	6.00	14.00	45.00
	1850	—	3.00	6.00	14.00	45.00
	1851	—	3.00	6.00	14.00	45.00
	1852	—	3.00	6.00	14.00	45.00
	1853	—	3.00	6.00	14.00	45.00
	1854	—	3.00	6.00	14.00	45.00
	1855	—	3.00	6.00	14.00	45.00
	1856	—	3.00	6.00	14.00	45.00

KM#	Date	Mintage	Fine	VF	XF	Unc
603	1858	—	2.50	5.00	12.00	40.00
(C161)	1859	—	2.50	5.00	12.00	40.00
	1860	—	2.50	5.00	12.00	40.00
	1861	—	2.50	5.00	12.00	40.00
	1862	—	2.50	5.00	12.00	40.00
	1863	—	2.50	5.00	12.00	40.00
	1864	—	2.50	5.00	12.00	40.00

KM#	Date	Mintage	Fine	VF	XF	Unc
611	1865	—	2.50	5.00	12.00	40.00
(C204)	1866	—	2.50	5.00	12.00	40.00
	1867	—	2.50	5.00	12.00	40.00
	1868	—	2.50	5.00	12.00	40.00
	1869	—	2.50	5.00	12.00	40.00
	1870	.147	2.50	5.00	12.00	40.00
	1871	.290	2.50	5.00	12.00	40.00
	1872	.177	2.50	5.00	12.00	40.00

EIN (1) KREUZER

BILLON

Obv: Crowned FII. Rev: Value, branches reach middle of coin.

KM#	Date	Mintage	Fine	VF	XF	Unc
467	1801	—	10.00	20.00	45.00	150.00
(C108a)	1802	—	10.00	20.00	55.00	165.00

NOTE: Earlier dates (1799-1800) exist for this type.

Obv: Legends. Rev: Crowned arms.

KM#	Date	Mintage	Fine	VF	XF	Unc
478 (C122)	1803	—	7.00	15.00	35.00	90.00
	1804	—	7.00	15.00	35.00	90.00

Obv: Crowned F II monogram, w/o leg. Rev: Value above branches.

KM#	Date	Mintage	Fine	VF	XF	Unc
487 (C122a)	1805	—	9.00	18.00	40.00	145.00

Obv: Crowned FR monogram.

KM#	Date	Mintage	Fine	VF	XF	Unc
499 (C139)	1807	—	6.00	12.00	30.00	80.00
	1808	—	6.00	12.00	30.00	80.00
	1809	—	6.00	12.00	30.00	80.00
	1810	—	6.00	12.00	30.00	80.00
	1811	—	6.00	12.00	30.00	80.00
	1812	—	6.00	12.00	30.00	80.00
	1813	.530	6.00	12.00	30.00	80.00
	1814	—	6.00	12.00	30.00	80.00
	1816	.630	6.00	12.00	30.00	80.00

Obv: Crowned W within wreath.

KM#	Date	Mintage	Fine	VF	XF	Unc
529 (C164)	1818	—	10.00	20.00	40.00	125.00

KM#	Date	Mintage	Fine	VF	XF	Unc
548 (C165)	1824 W	.780	5.00	10.00	22.00	60.00
	1825 W	.300	5.00	10.00	22.00	60.00
	1826 W	—	5.00	10.00	22.00	60.00
	1827 W	—	5.00	10.00	22.00	60.00
	1828 W	—	5.00	10.00	22.00	60.00
	1829 W	—	5.00	10.00	22.00	60.00
	1830 W	—	5.00	10.00	22.00	60.00
	1831 W	—	5.00	10.00	22.00	60.00
	1832 W	—	5.00	10.00	22.00	60.00
	1833 W	—	5.00	10.00	22.00	60.00
	1834 W	—	5.00	10.00	22.00	60.00
	1835 W	—	5.00	10.00	22.00	60.00
	1836 W	—	5.00	10.00	22.00	60.00
	1837 W	—	5.00	10.00	22.00	60.00
	1838 W	—	5.00	10.00	22.00	60.00

.6200 g, .250 SILVER, .0049 oz ASW
Obv. leg: WURTTEMBERG, crowned arms. Rev: Value within wreath.

KM#	Date	Mintage	Fine	VF	XF	Unc
576 (C166)	1839	—	6.00	12.00	30.00	80.00
	1840	—	6.00	12.00	30.00	80.00
	1841	—	6.00	12.00	30.00	80.00
	1842	—	6.00	12.00	30.00	80.00

KM#	Date	Mintage	Fine	VF	XF	Unc
590 (C166a)	1842	—	2.00	4.00	10.00	40.00
	1843	—	2.00	4.00	10.00	40.00
	1844	—	2.00	4.00	10.00	40.00
	1845	—	2.00	4.00	10.00	40.00
	1846	—	2.00	4.00	10.00	40.00
	1847	—	2.00	4.00	10.00	40.00
	1848	—	2.00	4.00	10.00	40.00
	1849	—	2.00	4.00	10.00	40.00
	1850	—	2.00	4.00	10.00	40.00
	1851	—	2.00	4.00	10.00	40.00
	1852	—	2.00	4.00	10.00	40.00
	1853	—	2.00	4.00	10.00	40.00
	1854	—	2.00	4.00	10.00	40.00
	1855	—	2.00	4.00	10.00	40.00
	1856/86	—	—	—	—	—
	1856	—	2.00	4.00	10.00	40.00
	1857	—	2.00	4.00	10.00	40.00

.8300 g, .166 SILVER, .0044 oz ASW

KM#	Date	Mintage	Fine	VF	XF	Unc
600 (C166b)	1857	.095	2.00	4.00	8.00	35.00
	1858	.072	2.00	4.00	8.00	35.00
	1859	.050	2.00	4.00	8.00	35.00
	1860	.049	2.00	4.00	8.00	35.00
	1861	.097	2.00	4.00	8.00	35.00
	1862	.056	2.00	4.00	8.00	35.00
	1863	.098	2.00	4.00	8.00	35.00
	1864	.151	2.00	4.00	8.00	35.00

KM#	Date	Mintage	Fine	VF	XF	Unc
612 (C205)	1865/3	.086	2.00	4.00	8.00	35.00
	1865	.086	2.00	4.00	8.00	35.00
	1866	.078	2.00	4.00	8.00	35.00
	1867	.119	2.00	4.00	8.00	35.00
	1868	.119	2.00	4.00	8.00	35.00
	1869	.120	2.00	4.00	8.00	35.00
	1870	.126	2.00	4.00	8.00	35.00
	1871	—	2.00	4.00	8.00	35.00
	1872	.100	2.00	4.00	8.00	35.00
	1873	.080	2.00	4.00	8.00	35.00

3 KREUZER

1.3500 g, .333 SILVER, .0144 oz ASW
Obv: 3 in oval border. Rev: Date divided by W.

KM#	Date	Mintage	Fine	VF	XF	Unc
477 (C110d)	1801	—	15.00	30.00	75.00	165.00
	1802	—	15.00	30.00	75.00	165.00

Obv: F. II. monogram, W below inscription. Rev: Crowned oval arms.

KM#	Date	Mintage	Fine	VF	XF	Unc
479 (C124)	1803	—	15.00	30.00	75.00	165.00

Rev: Crowned rectangular arms.

KM#	Date	Mintage	Fine	VF	XF	Unc
483 (C124a)	1804	—	10.00	20.00	50.00	150.00
	1805	—	10.00	20.00	50.00	150.00
	1806	—	10.00	20.00	50.00	150.00
	1086(error)	—	12.00	25.00	60.00	165.00

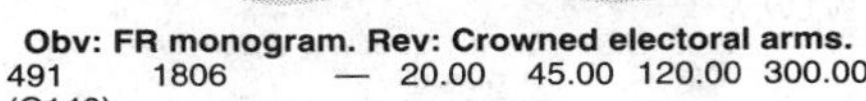

Obv: FR monogram. Rev: Crowned electoral arms.

KM#	Date	Mintage	Fine	VF	XF	Unc
491 (C140)	1806	—	20.00	45.00	120.00	300.00

KM#	Date	Mintage	Fine	VF	XF	Unc
500 (C141)	1807	—	10.00	20.00	50.00	150.00
	1808	—	10.00	20.00	50.00	150.00
	1809	—	10.00	20.00	50.00	150.00
	1810	—	10.00	20.00	50.00	150.00
	1811	—	10.00	20.00	50.00	150.00
	1812	—	10.00	20.00	50.00	150.00
	1813	—	10.00	20.00	50.00	150.00
	1814	.160	10.00	20.00	50.00	150.00

Obv: Crowned W within wreath. Rev: Value.

KM#	Date	Mintage	Fine	VF	XF	Unc
530 (C167)	1818	—	10.00	20.00	45.00	135.00

KM#	Date	Mintage	Fine	VF	XF	Unc
540 (C168)	1823	—	30.00	60.00	150.00	350.00
	1824	—	—	—	—	—

Obv: Date and W below head.

KM#	Date	Mintage	Fine	VF	XF	Unc
541 (C168.1)	1823 W	—	15.00	30.00	65.00	180.00
	1824 W	—	15.00	30.00	65.00	180.00
	1825 W	.380	15.00	30.00	65.00	180.00

KM#	Date	Mintage	Fine	VF	XF	Unc
565 (C168a)	1826	—	7.00	15.00	35.00	125.00
	1827	—	7.00	15.00	35.00	125.00
	1828	—	7.00	15.00	35.00	125.00
	1829	—	7.00	15.00	35.00	125.00
	1830	—	7.00	15.00	35.00	125.00
	1831	—	7.00	15.00	35.00	125.00
	1832	—	7.00	15.00	35.00	125.00
	1834	—	7.00	15.00	35.00	125.00
	1835	—	7.00	15.00	35.00	125.00
	1836	—	7.00	15.00	35.00	125.00
	1837	—	7.00	15.00	35.00	125.00

1.2900 g, .333 SILVER, .0138 oz ASW
Obv. leg: WURTTEMBERG.

KM#	Date	Mintage	Fine	VF	XF	Unc
577 (C169)	1839	—	6.00	12.00	25.00	100.00
	1840	—	6.00	12.00	25.00	100.00
	1841	—	6.00	12.00	25.00	100.00
	1842	—	6.00	12.00	25.00	100.00

KM#	Date	Mintage	Fine	VF	XF	Unc
591 (C169a)	1842	—	2.00	4.00	10.00	40.00
	1843	—	2.00	4.00	10.00	40.00
	1844	—	2.00	4.00	10.00	40.00
	1845	—	2.00	4.00	10.00	40.00
	1846	—	2.00	4.00	10.00	40.00
	1847	—	2.00	4.00	10.00	40.00
	1848	—	2.00	4.00	10.00	40.00
	1849	—	2.00	4.00	10.00	40.00
	1850	—	2.00	4.00	10.00	40.00
	1851	—	2.00	4.00	10.00	40.00
	1852	—	2.00	4.00	10.00	40.00
	1853	—	2.00	4.00	10.00	40.00
	1854	—	2.00	4.00	10.00	40.00
	1855	—	2.00	4.00	10.00	40.00
	1856	—	2.00	4.00	10.00	40.00

6 KREUZER

2.7000 g, .333 SILVER, .0289 oz ASW

KM#	Date	Mintage	Fine	VF	XF	Unc
480 (C126)	1803W	—	15.00	40.00	120.00	250.00
	1804W	—	15.00	40.00	120.00	250.00

Obv: W/o W below monogram.

KM#	Date	Mintage	Fine	VF	XF	Unc
484 (C126a)	1804	—	15.00	40.00	120.00	250.00
	1805	—	15.00	40.00	120.00	250.00

Rev: Electoral arms.

KM#	Date	Mintage	Fine	VF	XF	Unc
492 (C142)	1806	—	15.00	40.00	120.00	250.00

Rev: Crowned arms w/flags in left half of shield.

KM#	Date	Mintage	Fine	VF	XF	Unc
493 (C142a)	1806	—	15.00	40.00	120.00	250.00

Rev: Arms dividing date.

KM#	Date	Mintage	Fine	VF	XF	Unc
494 (C142b)	1806	—	100.00	200.00	350.00	600.00

KM#	Date	Mintage	Fine	VF	XF	Unc
495 (C143)	1806	—	6.00	12.00	32.00	80.00
	1807	—	6.00	12.00	32.00	80.00
	1808	—	6.00	12.00	32.00	80.00
	1809	—	6.00	12.00	32.00	80.00
	1810	—	6.00	12.00	32.00	80.00
	1811	—	6.00	12.00	32.00	80.00
	1812	—	6.00	12.00	32.00	80.00
	1814	—	6.00	12.00	32.00	80.00

Obv: Crowned W within wreath. Rev: Value.

KM#	Date	Mintage	Fine	VF	XF	Unc
524 (C170)	1817	—	10.00	20.00	50.00	150.00
	1818	—	10.00	20.00	50.00	150.00
536 (C170a)	1819	—	10.00	20.00	50.00	150.00
	1821	—	12.00	25.00	60.00	175.00

Obv: Head right, date below. Rev: Crowned circular arms within wreath.

KM#	Date	Mintage	Fine	VF	XF	Unc
542 (C171.1)	1823	—	15.00	30.00	80.00	250.00

Obv: Narrower head.

KM#	Date	Mintage	Fine	VF	XF	Unc
543 (C171.2)	1823	—	12.00	25.00	70.00	225.00

Obv. leg: WILHELM KON. . .

KM#	Date	Mintage	Fine	VF	XF	Unc
544	1823	—	10.00	20.00	60.00	200.00
(C171.3)	1825	—	10.00	20.00	60.00	200.00

Rev: Crowned tapered arms within branches.

KM#	Date	Mintage	Fine	VF	XF	Unc
556	1825	—	10.00	20.00	50.00	175.00
(C171a)	1826	—	10.00	20.00	50.00	175.00
	1827	—	10.00	20.00	50.00	175.00
	1828	—	10.00	20.00	50.00	175.00
	1829	—	10.00	20.00	50.00	175.00
	1830	—	10.00	20.00	50.00	175.00
	1831	—	10.00	20.00	50.00	175.00
	1832	—	10.00	20.00	50.00	175.00
	1833	—	10.00	20.00	50.00	175.00
	1834	—	10.00	20.00	50.00	175.00
	1835	—	10.00	20.00	50.00	175.00
	1836	—	10.00	20.00	50.00	175.00
	1837	—	10.00	20.00	50.00	175.00

2.5900 g, .333 SILVER, .0277 oz ASW

KM#	Date	Mintage	Fine	VF	XF	Unc
572	1838	—	6.00	12.00	28.00	85.00
(C172)	1839	—	6.00	12.00	28.00	85.00
	1840	—	6.00	12.00	28.00	85.00
	1841	—	6.00	12.00	28.00	85.00
	1842	—	6.00	12.00	28.00	85.00

KM#	Date	Mintage	Fine	VF	XF	Unc
592	1842	—	3.00	6.00	18.00	55.00
(C172a)	1843	—	3.00	6.00	18.00	55.00
	1844	—	3.00	6.00	18.00	55.00
	1845	—	3.00	6.00	18.00	55.00
	1846	—	3.00	6.00	18.00	55.00
	1847	—	3.00	6.00	18.00	55.00
	1848	—	3.00	6.00	18.00	55.00
	1849	—	3.00	6.00	18.00	55.00
	1850	—	3.00	6.00	18.00	55.00
	1851	—	3.00	6.00	18.00	55.00
	1852	—	3.00	6.00	18.00	55.00
	1853	—	3.00	6.00	18.00	55.00
	1854	—	3.00	6.00	18.00	55.00
	1855	—	3.00	6.00	18.00	55.00
	1856	—	3.00	6.00	18.00	55.00

10 KREUZER

(Convention)

BILLON

KM#	Date	Mintage	Fine	VF	XF	Unc
488 (C128)	1805 ILW	—	90.00	175.00	325.00	575.00

Rev. leg: AD NORMAN.

KM#	Date	Mintage	Fine	VF	XF	Unc
502	1808 ILW	.025	100.00	200.00	375.00	700.00
(C144)	1809 ILW	.010	110.00	225.00	400.00	750.00

Obv. leg: FRIEDRICH KOENIG. . .
Rev. leg: NACH DEM.

KM#	Date	Mintage	Fine	VF	XF	Unc
519 (C145)	1812 ILW	.026	100.00	200.00	375.00	700.00

Obv. leg: FRID. KOENIG. . .

KM#	Date	Mintage	Fine	VF	XF	Unc
520 (C145.1)	1812 ILW	—	100.00	200.00	375.00	700.00

KM#	Date	Mintage	Fine	VF	XF	Unc
531 (C173)	1818 W	.152	80.00	150.00	300.00	600.00

KM#	Date	Mintage	Fine	VF	XF	Unc
545 (C174)	1823	.011	110.00	225.00	400.00	750.00

12 KREUZER

3.9000 g, .500 SILVER, .0627 oz ASW

KM#	Date	Mintage	Fine	VF	XF	Unc
549 (C175)	1824 W	.045	30.00	70.00	175.00	350.00

KM#	Date	Mintage	Fine	VF	XF	Unc
557 (C175a)	1825 W	.025	35.00	85.00	200.00	400.00

20 KREUZER

(Convention)

6.6800 g, .583 SILVER, .1251 oz ASW
Obv: Bust left, leg: . . . ELECTOR.
Rev: Crowned oval arms.

KM#	Date	Mintage	Fine	VF	XF	Unc
489 (C130)	1805 ILW	—	75.00	150.00	325.00	650.00

Obv. leg. ends: . . . WURTTEMB.

KM#	Date	Mintage	Fine	VF	XF	Unc
501	1807 ILW	—	40.00	80.00	160.00	350.00
(C146)	1808 ILW	—	40.00	80.00	160.00	350.00
	1809 ILW	—	40.00	80.00	160.00	350.00
	1810 ILW	—	40.00	80.00	160.00	350.00

KM#	Date	Mintage	Fine	VF	XF	Unc
510	1810 ILW	—	50.00	100.00	200.00	425.00
(C147)	1812 ILW	—	50.00	100.00	200.00	425.00

Obv: Larger head.

KM#	Date	Mintage	Fine	VF	XF	Unc
511 (C147a)	1810 ILW	—	50.00	100.00	200.00	425.00

KM#	Date	Mintage	Fine	VF	XF	Unc
521 (C148)	1812 ILW	.105	40.00	80.00	160.00	350.00

KM#	Date	Mintage	Fine	VF	XF	Unc
532 (C176)	1818 W	.180	50.00	100.00	225.00	450.00

KM#	Date	Mintage	Fine	VF	XF	Unc
546 (C177)	1823 W	.033	50.00	100.00	225.00	450.00

24 KREUZER

6.6800 g, .583 SILVER, .1251 oz ASW

KM#	Date	Mintage	Fine	VF	XF	Unc
550	1824 W	—	50.00	100.00	225.00	375.00
(C178)	1825 W	—	50.00	100.00	225.00	375.00
	1825	—	50.00	100.00	225.00	375.00

1/2 GULDEN

5.2900 g, .900 SILVER, .1530 oz ASW
Obv: VOIGT below head.

KM#	Date	Mintage	Fine	VF	XF	Unc
573	1838	.824	15.00	50.00	100.00	200.00
(C179)	1839	.464	80.00	175.00	500.00	900.00
	1840	.516	15.00	35.00	75.00	150.00
	1841	.412	15.00	35.00	75.00	150.00
	1844	.154	100.00	200.00	400.00	800.00
	1845	.280	15.00	35.00	75.00	150.00
	1846	.338	15.00	35.00	75.00	150.00
	1847	.682	15.00	35.00	70.00	140.00
	1848	.498	15.00	35.00	70.00	140.00
	1849	.312	15.00	35.00	75.00	150.00
	1850	.286	15.00	35.00	75.00	150.00

KM#	Date	Mintage	Fine	VF	XF	Unc
(C179)	1852	.228	15.00	35.00	75.00	150.00
	1853	.192	15.00	35.00	75.00	150.00
	1854	.140	15.00	35.00	75.00	150.00
	1855	.112	15.00	35.00	75.00	150.00
	1856	.108	15.00	35.00	75.00	150.00
	1858	—	15.00	35.00	75.00	150.00

Obv: W/o VOIGT below head.

KM#	Date	Mintage	Fine	VF	XF	Unc
604	1858	.219	15.00	90.00	150.00	250.00
(C179a)	1859	.072	15.00	90.00	150.00	250.00
	1860	.299	15.00	40.00	80.00	160.00
	1861	.693	15.00	40.00	80.00	160.00
	1862	.149	15.00	50.00	100.00	200.00
	1863	—	15.00	50.00	100.00	200.00
	1864	.161	15.00	37.50	75.00	140.00

Obv: Head right w/C.S. on truncation.

KM#	Date	Mintage	Fine	VF	XF	Unc
613	1865 CS	.166	15.00	50.00	100.00	250.00
(C206)	1866 CS	.276	15.00	50.00	100.00	250.00
	1867 CS	.071	15.00	50.00	100.00	250.00
	1868 CS	.105	15.00	50.00	100.00	250.00

Obv: W/o C.S. on truncation.

KM#	Date	Mintage	Fine	VF	XF	Unc
616	1868	Inc. Ab.	15.00	50.00	100.00	200.00
(C206a)	1869	.072	15.00	50.00	100.00	200.00
	1870	.044	15.00	60.00	100.00	200.00
	1871	.041	15.00	60.00	100.00	200.00

GULDEN

12.7200 g, .750 SILVER, .3067 oz ASW

KM#	Date	Mintage	Fine	VF	XF	Unc
551 (C180)	1824 W	.021	80.00	175.00	500.00	900.00

KM#	Date	Mintage	Fine	VF	XF	Unc
552 (C180a)	1824	—	—	—	Rare	—

KM#	Date	Mintage	Fine	VF	XF	Unc
558 (C181)	1825 W	—	150.00	300.00	600.00	1000.

10.6000 g, .900 SILVER, .3067 oz ASW
Obv: VOIGT below head.

KM#	Date	Mintage	Fine	VF	XF	Unc
574	1838	.712	15.00	50.00	100.00	200.00
(C182)	1839	.365	15.00	50.00	100.00	200.00
	1840	2.561	15.00	50.00	100.00	200.00
	1841	—	25.00	100.00	200.00	400.00
	1842	2.493	15.00	50.00	100.00	200.00
	1843	1.983	15.00	50.00	100.00	200.00

KM#	Date	Mintage	Fine	VF	XF	Unc
(C182)	1844	.379	15.00	50.00	100.00	200.00
	1845	.044	15.00	50.00	100.00	200.00
	1846	.042	15.00	50.00	100.00	200.00
	1847	.056	15.00	50.00	100.00	200.00
	1848/6	.058	17.50	60.00	125.00	250.00
	1848	Inc. Ab.	15.00	50.00	100.00	200.00
	1849	.129	15.00	50.00	100.00	200.00
	1850	.114	15.00	50.00	100.00	200.00
	1851	.096	15.00	50.00	100.00	200.00
	1852	.032	15.00	50.00	100.00	200.00
	1853	.235	15.00	50.00	100.00	200.00
	1854	.090	15.00	50.00	100.00	200.00
	1855	.223	15.00	50.00	100.00	200.00
	1856	—	15.00	50.00	100.00	200.00

Obv: A.D. below head.

KM#	Date	Mintage	Fine	VF	XF	Unc
575	1837 AD	.443	25.00	100.00	150.00	300.00
(C182a)	1838 AD	I.A.	25.00	100.00	150.00	300.00

Obv: W/o VOIGT below head.

KM#	Date	Mintage	Fine	VF	XF	Unc
578	1839	—	15.00	35.00	75.00	150.00
(C182b)	1840	—	15.00	35.00	75.00	150.00
	1841	—	25.00	75.00	125.00	250.00
597 (C182c)	1848	Inc. Ab.	25.00	75.00	125.00	250.00

25th Anniversary of Reign

KM#	Date	Mintage	Fine	VF	XF	Unc
588 (C183)	1841	—	20.00	35.00	60.00	100.00

Visit of King to New Mint

KM#	Date	Mintage	Fine	VF	XF	Unc
593 (C184)	1844	—	650.00	1250.	2000.	3000.

NOTE: Restrikes exist.

Visit of Queen to Mint

KM#	Date	Mintage	Fine	VF	XF	Unc
594 (C185)	1845	17 pcs.	—	—	Rare	—

2 GULDEN

25.4500 gm., .750 SILVER, .6138 oz ASW

KM#	Date	Mintage	Fine	VF	XF	Unc
553 (C187)	1824 W	.015	200.00	350.00	900.00	1800.

Obv: Larger head right.
Rev. leg. ends: SC.

KM#	Date	Mintage	Fine	VF	XF	Unc
554 (C187a)	1824 ILW	Inc. Ab.	—	—	Rare	—

Obv: WAGNER F at truncation, leg: . . . WURTTEMB.
Rev: Crowned pointed arms within branches.

KM#	Date	Mintage	Fine	VF	XF	Unc
559 (C188)	1825 W	9,934	300.00	500.00	1200.	2600.

Obv: W/o name at bottom.

KM#	Date	Mintage	Fine	VF	XF	Unc
560 (C188a)	1825 W	Inc. Ab.	—	—	Rare	—

21.2100 g, .900 SILVER, .6138 oz ASW

KM#	Date	Mintage	Fine	VF	XF	Unc
595	1845	.562	45.00	75.00	150.00	350.00
(C189)	1846	.621	45.00	75.00	150.00	350.00
	1847	1.160	45.00	75.00	150.00	350.00
	1848	.336	45.00	75.00	150.00	350.00
	1849	.486	45.00	75.00	150.00	350.00
	1850	.280	45.00	75.00	150.00	350.00
	1851	.140	45.00	75.00	150.00	350.00
	1852	.225	45.00	75.00	150.00	350.00
	1853	.175	45.00	75.00	150.00	350.00
	1854	.074	45.00	75.00	150.00	350.00
	1855	.133	45.00	75.00	150.00	350.00
	1856	.267	45.00	75.00	150.00	350.00

5 GULDEN

3.4250 g, .904 GOLD, .0997 oz AGW

KM#	Date	Mintage	Fine	VF	XF	Unc
562	1824 W	2,282	500.00	1100.	1800.	2500.
(C198a)	1835 W	1,443	600.00	1400.	2200.	3000.

KM#	Date	Mintage	Fine	VF	XF	Unc
563 (C198)	1825 W	5,956	350.00	650.00	1000.	1800.

KM#	Date	Mintage	Fine	VF	XF	Unc
579 (C198b)	1839 W	822 pcs.	800.00	1600.	2500.	3250.

10 GULDEN

6.8500 g, .904 GOLD, .1990 oz AGW

KM#	Date	Mintage	Fine	VF	XF	Unc
555 (C199)	1824 W	1,896	900.00	1800.	2500.	4000.
	1825 W	1,240	900.00	1800.	2500.	4000.

Visit of King to Mint

KM#	Date	Mintage	Fine	VF	XF	Unc
564 (C200)	1825 W	8 pcs.	—	—	—	15,000.

1/2 THALER

14.0300 g, .833 SILVER, .3759 oz ASW

KM#	Date	Mintage	Fine	VF	XF	Unc
490 (C132)	1805 ILW	—	350.00	750.00	1500.	2250.

THALER

(Convention)

28.0600 g, .833 SILVER, .7515 oz ASW

KM#	Date	Mintage	Fine	VF	XF	Unc
481 (C134)	1803	—	750.00	1200.	2500.	4500.

Obv. leg: . . . WURT. S.R.I.AR.VEXILL.ET ELECT.

KM#	Date	Mintage	Fine	VF	XF	Unc
496 (C149)	1806	—	—	—	Rare	—

Obv. leg. ends: . . . WURTEMBERGIAE.

KM#	Date	Mintage	Fine	VF	XF	Unc
497 (C149a)	1806	—	—	—	Rare	—

Obv: I.L. WAGNER F. below bust.
Rev: Leg. w/larger letters.

KM#	Date	Mintage	Fine	VF	XF	Unc
498 (C149b)	1806	—	—	—	Rare	—

KM#	Date	Mintage	Fine	VF	XF	Unc
504 (C150)	1809	—	—	—	Rare	—

Obv: I.L.W. below bust,
leg. ends: . . . WURTTEMBERGIAE.

KM#	Date	Mintage	Fine	VF	XF	Unc
505 (C150a)	1809 ILW	—	—	—	Rare	—

(Kronen)

29.4900 g, .868 SILVER, .8230 oz ASW
Obv: Military bust; leg:. . . .D.G.REX . . .
Rev: Crowned arms between lion and stag.

KM#	Date	Mintage	Fine	VF	XF	Unc
512 (C151)	1810 ILW	—	—	—	Rare	—

Obv: Bust; leg: FRIDERICH I KOENIG . . .

KM#	Date	Mintage	Fine	VF	XF	Unc
513 (C152)	1810 ILW	—	—	—	Rare	—

Obv: Large head.

KM#	Date	Mintage	Fine	VF	XF	Unc
514 (C-A153)	1810 ILW	—	300.00	800.00	2000.	4500.

Obv: Small head, w/o period before legend.

KM#	Date	Mintage	Fine	VF	XF	Unc
515 (C153)	1810 ILW	—	300.00	800.00	1750.	4000.

KM#	Date	Mintage	Fine	VF	XF	Unc
517 (C153a)	1811 ILW	2,000	400.00	800.00	2000.	4500.

KM#	Date	Mintage	Fine	VF	XF	Unc
522 (C154)	1812 ILW	.015	300.00	600.00	1200.	2500.

(Convention)

28.0600 g, .833 SILVER, .7515 oz ASW
Obv: Head left, WAGNER F below.

Rev: Value within wreath.

KM#	Date	Mintage	Fine	VF	XF	Unc
525 (C190)	1817	—	—	—	Rare	—

KM#	Date	Mintage	Fine	VF	XF	Unc
533 (C190a)	1818	—	500.00	1000.	2000.	4500.

(Kronen)

29.4900 g, .868 SILVER, .8230 oz ASW

KM#	Date	Mintage	Fine	VF	XF	Unc
526 (C191)	1817	.044	400.00	600.00	1500.	3000.

KM#	Date	Mintage	Fine	VF	XF	Unc
534	1818	Inc. Ab.	300.00	550.00	1200.	2500.
(C191a)	1818/7	I.A.	—	—	—	—

KM#	Date	Mintage	Fine	VF	XF	Unc
561	1825	.226	85.00	135.00	300.00	600.00
(C192)	1826	—	100.00	150.00	375.00	800.00
	1827	—	100.00	150.00	375.00	800.00
	1828	—	100.00	150.00	375.00	800.00
	1829	—	100.00	150.00	375.00	800.00
	1830 W below bust	6,695	100.00	150.00	375.00	800.00
	1831	9,074	100.00	150.00	375.00	800.00
	1832 W below bust	—	100.00	150.00	375.00	800.00
	1833	—	100.00	150.00	375.00	800.00

NOTE: Varieties exist.

Obv: W below truncation.

KM#	Date	Mintage	Fine	VF	XF	Unc
571	1834 W	—	100.00	150.00	375.00	800.00
(C192a)	1835 W	—	100.00	150.00	375.00	800.00
	1837 W	.170	85.00	135.00	300.00	600.00

Free Trade

KM#	Date	Mintage	Fine	VF	XF	Unc
570	1833 W	—	75.00	125.00	225.00	450.00
(C193)	1833 LW	—	—	—	—	—

(Vereins)

18.5200 g, .900 SILVER, .5360 oz ASW

KM#	Date	Mintage	Fine	VF	XF	Unc
601	1857	.452	25.00	55.00	135.00	275.00
(C186)	1858	.644	25.00	55.00	135.00	275.00
	1859	1.333	25.00	55.00	135.00	275.00
	1860	.645	25.00	55.00	135.00	275.00
	1861	.754	25.00	55.00	135.00	275.00
	1862	.648	25.00	55.00	135.00	275.00
	1863	.621	25.00	55.00	135.00	275.00
	1864	.533	25.00	55.00	135.00	275.00

Obv: C. SCHNITZSPAHN F on truncation.

KM#	Date	Mintage	Fine	VF	XF	Unc
614 (C207)	1865	.276	125.00	225.00	650.00	1500.

Rev: Antlers extend into leg.

KM#	Date	Mintage	Fine	VF	XF	Unc
615	1865	Inc. Ab.	40.00	75.00	200.00	475.00
(C207a)	1866	.346	40.00	75.00	200.00	475.00
	1867	.165	40.00	75.00	200.00	475.00
617	1868	.078	45.00	90.00	220.00	525.00
(C207b)	1869	.031	50.00	100.00	240.00	550.00
	1870	.044	50.00	100.00	240.00	550.00

Victorious Conclusion of Franco-Prussian War
Rev: C.SCH.F at 7 o'clock.

KM#	Date	Mintage	Fine	VF	XF	Unc
620	1871	.114	25.00	45.00	85.00	150.00
(C208)	1871	—	—	—	Proof	—

2 THALER

(3-1/2 Gulden)

37.1200 g, .900 SILVER, 1.0742 oz ASW

KM#	Date	Mintage	Fine	VF	XF	Unc
586	1840	.162	125.00	225.00	450.00	1000.
(C194)	1842	.051	175.00	300.00	600.00	1200.
	1843	.245	125.00	225.00	450.00	1000.
	1854	.168	125.00	225.00	450.00	1000.
	1855	Inc.Ab.	125.00	225.00	450.00	1000.

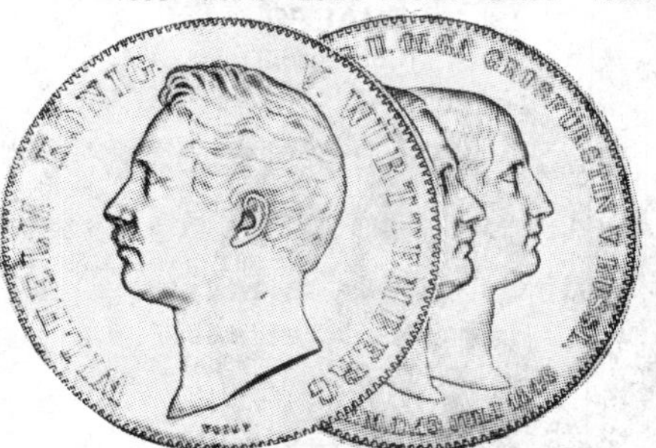

Marriage of Crown Prince Karl to Olga, Grand Duchess of Russia

KM#	Date	Mintage	Fine	VF	XF	Unc
596 (C195)	1846	5,808	100.00	200.00	375.00	750.00

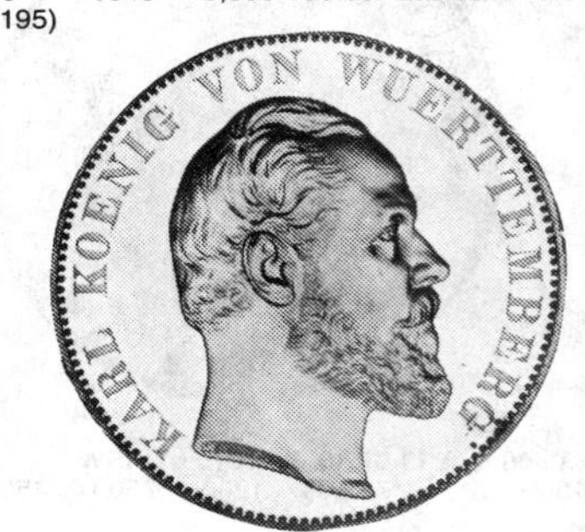

37.0400 g, .900 SILVER, 1.0717 oz ASW
Restoration of Ulm Cathedral

KM#	Date	Mintage	Fine	VF	XF	Unc
618 (C209)	1869	—	125.00	200.00	425.00	800.00
	1871	4,031	100.00	200.00	400.00	600.00

MONETARY REFORM

2 MARK

11.1110 g, .900 SILVER, .3215 oz ASW

KM#	Date	Mintage	Fine	VF	XF	Unc
626 (Y215)	1876F	1.550	30.00	75.00	525.00	1400.
	1877F	1.107	30.00	125.00	600.00	1700.
	1880F	.129	60.00	175.00	700.00	2300.
	1883F	.074	60.00	150.00	675.00	2000.
	1888F	.123	30.00	120.00	575.00	1600.
	1888F	—	—	—	Proof	1600.

11.1110 g, .900 SILVER, .3215 oz ASW

KM#	Date	Mintage	Fine	VF	XF	Unc
631 (Y220)	1892F	.177	16.00	45.00	95.00	200.00
	1893F	.174	16.00	45.00	75.00	175.00
	1896F	.351	12.00	28.00	50.00	125.00
	1898F	.144	20.00	45.00	90.00	195.00
	1899F	.538	9.00	19.00	35.00	125.00
	1900F	.516	8.00	16.00	40.00	100.00
	Common date		—	—	Proof	175.00

NOTE: Later dates (1901-1914) exist for this type.

5 MARK

27.7770 g, .900 SILVER, .8038 oz ASW

KM#	Date	Mintage	Fine	VF	XF	Unc
623 (Y216)	1874F	.113	30.00	60.00	900.00	2400.
	1875F	.318	30.00	60.00	900.00	2000.
	1876F	.897	30.00	60.00	600.00	1700.
	1888F	.049	40.00	100.00	900.00	2100.

1.9910 g, .900 GOLD, .0576 oz AGW

KM#	Date	Mintage	Fine	VF	XF	Unc
627 (Y217)	1877F	.488	100.00	200.00	250.00	425.00
	1877F	—	—	—	Proof	1300.
	1878F	.050	325.00	650.00	1250.	2000.

27.7770 g, .900 SILVER, .8038 oz ASW

KM#	Date	Mintage	Fine	VF	XF	Unc
632 (Y222)	1892F	.069	20.00	70.00	200.00	400.00
	1893F	.071	20.00	70.00	200.00	400.00
	1894F	.020	150.00	400.00	1250.	2000.
	1895F	.201	20.00	40.00	175.00	350.00
	1898F	.216	15.00	30.00	175.00	350.00
	1899F	.112	15.00	30.00	175.00	350.00
	1900F	.211	15.00	30.00	85.00	275.00
	Common date		—	—	Proof	300.00

NOTE: Later dates (1901-1913) exist for this type.

10 MARK

3.9820 g, .900 GOLD, .1152 oz AGW
Rev: Type I.

KM#	Date	Mintage	Fine	VF	XF	Unc
621 (Y218)	1872F	.271	65.00	100.00	200.00	300.00
	1872F	—	—	—	Proof	1300.
	1873F	.675	65.00	100.00	200.00	300.00
	1873F	—	—	—	Proof	1300.

Rev: Type II.

KM#	Date	Mintage	Fine	VF	XF	Unc
624 (Y218a)	1874F	.205	65.00	120.00	170.00	300.00
	1875F	.532	65.00	120.00	150.00	250.00
	1876F	.933	65.00	120.00	160.00	300.00
	1876F	—	—	—	Proof	1300.
	1877F	.271	65.00	120.00	170.00	300.00
	1878F	.337	65.00	120.00	160.00	300.00
	1879F	.211	65.00	120.00	160.00	275.00
	1880F	.245	65.00	120.00	170.00	300.00
	1881F	.079	75.00	150.00	200.00	325.00
	1888F	.200	65.00	120.00	160.00	275.00
	1888F	—	—	—	Proof	1300.

Rev: Type III.

KM#	Date	Mintage	Fine	VF	XF	Unc
630 (Y218b)	1890F	.220	90.00	130.00	190.00	275.00
	1891F	.080	100.00	150.00	225.00	400.00
633 (Y223)	1893F	.300	65.00	100.00	165.00	225.00
	1896F	.200	65.00	100.00	165.00	225.00
	1898F	.420	65.00	100.00	165.00	225.00
	1900F	.090	80.00	125.00	175.00	225.00

NOTE: Later dates (1901-1913) exist for this type.

20 MARK

7.9650 g, .900 GOLD, .2304 oz AGW
Rev: Type I.

KM#	Date	Mintage	Fine	VF	XF	Unc
622 (Y219)	1872F	.662	115.00	135.00	180.00	425.00
	1872F	—	—	—	Proof	1900.
	1873F	1.357	115.00	135.00	180.00	425.00
	1873F	—	—	—	Proof	1900.

Rev: Type II.

KM#	Date	Mintage	Fine	VF	XF	Unc
625 (Y219a)	1874F	.322	115.00	135.00	200.00	450.00
	1876F	.359	115.00	135.00	200.00	450.00

Rev: Type III.

KM#	Date	Mintage	Fine	VF	XF	Unc
634 (Y224)	1894F	.501	100.00	120.00	145.00	250.00
	1897F	.400	100.00	120.00	145.00	250.00
	1897F	—	—	—	Proof	700.00
	1898F	.106	100.00	120.00	145.00	275.00
	1900F	.500	100.00	120.00	145.00	250.00
	1900F	—	—	—	Proof	700.00

NOTE: Later dates (1905-1914) exist for this type.

TRADE COINAGE

DUCAT

3.5000 g, .986 GOLD, .1109 oz AGW
Visit of Duke to Mint
Obv: Bust right. Rev: IN HOCHST. . . within wreath.

KM#	Date	Mintage	Fine	VF	XF	Unc
482 (C136)	1803 ILW	—	—	—	Rare	—

Rev. leg: DEN 9. IAN 1804 added.

KM#	Date	Mintage	Fine	VF	XF	Unc
485 (C136a)	1804 ILW	—	—	—	Rare	—

Rev: Crowned circular arms within branches.

KM#	Date	Mintage	Fine	VF	XF	Unc
486 (C137)	1804 ILW	—	500.00	1000.	2000.	3500.

KM#	Date	Mintage	Fine	VF	XF	Unc
503 (C155)	1808 CH	—	500.00	1000.	2000.	3500.

KM#	Date	Mintage	Fine	VF	XF	Unc
523 (C156)	1813 ILW	—	600.00	1250.	2500.	4000.

KM#	Date	Mintage	Fine	VF	XF	Unc
535 (C196)	1818 W	—	600.00	1250.	2500.	3500.

KM#	Date	Mintage	Fine	VF	XF	Unc
587 (C197)	1840 AD	.081	175.00	350.00	525.00	850.00
	1841	.232	—	—	—	—
	1841/0 AD	I.A.	150.00	300.00	425.00	750.00
	1841 AD	I.A.	150.00	300.00	425.00	750.00
	1842 AD	.025	175.00	350.00	525.00	850.00
	1848 AD	.062	175.00	350.00	525.00	850.00

FREDERICK D'OR = 1 KAROLIN

6.6500 g, .900 GOLD, .1924 oz AGW

KM#	Date	Mintage	Fine	VF	XF	Unc
516 (C157)	1810 ILW	—	1500.	3000.	6000.	9000.

MEDALLIC ISSUES (M)

4 DUCAT

14.0000 g, .986 GOLD, .4438 oz AGW
25th Anniversary of Reign

KM#	Date	Mintage	Fine	VF	XF	Unc
M1 (C201)	1841	6,236	600.00	1200.	1700.	2800.

Visit of King Wilhelm to Mint

KM#	Date	Mintage	Fine	VF	XF	Unc
M2 (C202)	1844	17 pcs.	—	—	8500.	12,500.

PATTERNS (Pn)

(Including off metal strikes)

KM#	Date	Mintage	Identification	Mkt.Val.
Pn27	1804 ILW	—	1 Ducat, Silver, C136a	—
Pn28	1804 CH	—	1 Ducat, Silver, C137	—
Pn29	1808 CH	—	1 Ducat, Silver, C155	—
Pn30	1823	—	1 Gulden, Silver	2000.

KM#	Date	Mintage	Identification	Mkt.Val.
Pn31	1823	—	2 Gulden, Silver	3000.
Pn32	1824	—	2 Gulden	—
Pn33	1824	—	10 Gulden, Tin	—
Pn34	1825	—	10 Gulden, Tin	—
Pn35	1825W	—	10 Gulden, Silver, C200	800.00

KM#	Date	Mintage	Identification	Mkt.Val.
Pn36	1833	—	1 Thaler, Silver	—
Pn37	1837	—	1 Gulden, Silver	
Pn38	1846	—	2 Thaler, Gold, C195, marriage of Crown Prince	—
Pn41	ND(1894)	—	3 Mark, Silver plated copper	—

TRIAL STRIKES (TS)

KM#	Date	Mintage	Identification	Mkt.Val.
TS1	1861	—	1 Thaler, Aluminum, uniface	—
TS2	1862	—	1 Thaler, Aluminum, uniface	—

WURZBURG

BISHOPRIC

The Bishopric, located in Franconia, was established in 741. The mint right was obtained in the 11th century. The first coins were struck c. 1040. In 1441 the bishops were confirmed as dukes. In 1802 the area was secularized and granted to Bavaria. It was made a grand duchy in 1806 but the 1815 Congress of Vienna returned it to Bavaria.

RULERS

Georg Karl, Freiherr von Fechenbach, Bishop, 1795-1802
Ferdinand, Grand Duke, 1806-1814

MINT MARKS

F - Furth
N - Nurnberg
Wurzburg

MONETARY SYSTEM

3 Drier (Kortling) = 1 Shillinger
7 Shillinger = 15 Kreuzer
28 Shillinger = 1 Guter Gulden
44-4/5 Shillinger = 1 Convention Thaler

VIERTEL (1/4) KREUZER

COPPER

KM#	Date	Mintage	Fine	VF	XF	Unc
476 (C151)	1811	—	6.00	12.00	40.00	150.00

1/2 KREUZER

COPPER

KM#	Date	Mintage	Fine	VF	XF	Unc
475	1810	—	5.00	10.00	40.00	150.00
(C152)	1811	—	5.00	10.00	40.00	150.00

KREUZER

SILVER
Obv: Crowned arms, dividing G.W.L.M. above.
Rev: Value.

KM#	Date	Mintage	Fine	VF	XF	Unc
468 (C153)	1808	—	5.00	10.00	35.00	140.00

Obv: W/o legend.

KM#	Date	Mintage	Fine	VF	XF	Unc
469 (C153a)	1808	—	4.00	8.00	25.00	135.00

Rev: G.W.L.M., value.

KM#	Date	Mintage	Fine	VF	XF	Unc
470 (C153b)	1808	—	4.50	9.00	32.00	140.00

3 KREUZER

BILLON, 21mm

KM#	Date	Mintage	Fine	VF	XF	Unc
465	1807	—	4.00	8.00	30.00	125.00
(C154)	1808	—	4.00	8.00	30.00	125.00
	1809	—	4.00	8.00	30.00	125.00

6 KREUZER

SILVER
Obv: Large crown.

KM#	Date	Mintage	Fine	VF	XF	Unc
466	1807	—	10.00	20.00	60.00	185.00
(C155)	1808	—	10.00	20.00	60.00	185.00

Obv: Small crown.

KM#	Date	Mintage	Fine	VF	XF	Unc
471 (C155a)	1809	—	10.00	20.00	60.00	185.00

TRADE COINAGE

GOLDGULDEN

3.2500 g, .770 GOLD, .0805 oz AGW
Obv: Head of Ferdinand right.
Rev: Palm tree, arms, value and date.

KM#	Date	Mintage	Fine	VF	XF	Unc
467	1807	—	1000.	1800.	2800.	3500.
(C159)	1809	—	1000.	1800.	2800.	3500.

KM#	Date	Mintage	Fine	VF	XF	Unc
477 (C160)	1812R	—	1000.	1800.	2800.	3500.

Rev: Crowned battle flag; value and date.

KM#	Date	Mintage	Fine	VF	XF	Unc
478 (C161)	1813R	—	4000.	7000.	10,000.	12,500.

KM#	Date	Mintage	Fine	VF	XF	Unc
479 (C162)	1814R	—	3000.	5000.	8000.	10,000.

MEDALLIC ISSUES (M)

(GOLDGULDEN)

3.2500 g, .770 GOLD, .0805 oz AGW
Obv: Head of Maximilian Joseph right.
Rev: Palm above Wurzburg coat-of-arms, value and date, w/full inscription.

KM#	Date	Mintage	VG	Fine	VF	XF
M7	1803	—	—	—	Rare	—
	Rev: Palm above Wurzburg coat-of-arms and S.P.-Q.W., abbreviated inscription.					
M8	1803	—	—	1500.	2500.	3500.
	Obv: Head of Maximilian Joseph left. Rev: City view of Wurzburg.					
M9	1815	—	—	1250.	2000.	3000.
	Rev: Coat-of-arms, value.					
M10	1817	—	—	1250.	2000.	3000.
M11	ND(1817)	—	—	1250.	2000.	3000.
	Obv: Head of Ludwig left. Rev: 6-line inscription.					
M12	1826	65 pcs.	—	—	Rare	—
	Rev: View of Wurzburg, value and date.					
M13	ND(1827)	—	—	1250.	2000.	3000.
	Roman I follows king's name.					
M14	ND(ca.1835)	—	—	1250.	2000.	3000.
	Rev: City view of Wurzburg.					
M15	ND(ca.1843)	—	—	1500.	2500.	3500.

Rev: Arms in sprays.

KM#	Date	Mintage	VG	Fine	VF	XF
	Slant reeded edge.					
M16	ND(ca.1843)	—	—	1500.	2500.	3500.
	Straight reeded edge.					
M17	ND(ca.1843)	—	—	2000.	3500.	5000.
	Obv: Head of Ludwig right. Rev: City view of Wurzburg.					
M18	ND	300 pcs.	—	1250.	2000.	3000.
	Rev: Arms in sprays, value GOLD GULDEN.					
M19	ND	Inc. Ab.	—	1250.	2000.	3000.
	Rev. value: GOLDGULDEN.					
M20	ND	Inc. Ab.	—	1250.	2250.	3500.
	Obv: Head of Maximilian right, leg:. . . KOENIG.					
M21	ND(1850)	215 pcs.	—	1250.	2000.	3000.
	Obv. leg:. . . REX.					
M22	ND(1850)	Inc. Ab.	—	1250.	2250.	3500.
	Obv. leg:. . . KOENIG. Rev: City view of Wurzburg.					
M23	ND(1850)	Inc. Ab.	—	1250.	2000.	3000.
	Obv. leg:. . . REX.					
M24	ND(1850)	Inc. Ab.	—	1250.	2250.	3500.
	Obv: Head of Ludwig II right. Reeded edge.					
M25	ND(1864)	350 pcs.	—	1250.	2000.	3000.
	Plain edge.					
M26	ND(1864)	Inc. Ab.	—	1250.	2250.	3500.
	Rev: Wurzburg coat-of-arms.					
M27	ND(1864)	350 pcs.	—	1250.	2000.	3000.
	Rev: City view of Wurzburg, St. Kilian and value.					
M28	ND	Inc. Ab.	—	1250.	2000.	3000.
	Obv: Ludwig III. Rev: St. Kilian and value.					

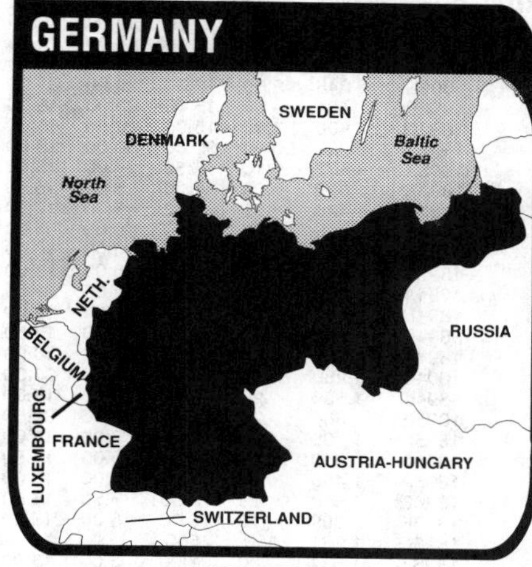

1871-1918

Germany, a nation of north-central Europe which from 1871 to 1945 was, successively, an empire, a republic and a totalitarian state, attained its territorial peak as an empire when it comprised a 208,780 sq. mi. (540,740 sq. km.) homeland and an overseas colonial empire.

As the power of the Roman Empire waned, several warlike tribes residing in northern Germany moved south and west, invading France, Belgium, England, Italy and Spain. In 800 A.D. the Frankish king Charlemagne, who ruled most of France and Germany, was crowned Emperor of the Holy Roman Empire, a loose federation of an estimated 1,800 German States that lasted until 1806. Modern Germany was formed from the eastern part of Charlemagne's empire.

After 1812, the German States were reduced to a federation of 32, of which Prussia was the strongest. In 1871, Prussian chancellor Otto von Bismarck united the German states into an empire ruled by William I, the Prussian king. The empire initiated a colonial endeavor and became one of the world's greatest powers. Germany disintegrated as a result of World War I.

RULERS

Wilhelm I, 1871-1888
Friedrich III, 1888
Wilhelm II, 1888-1918

MINT MARKS

A - Berlin
B - Hannover (1866-1878)
C - Frankfurt (1866-1879)
D - Munich
E - Dresden (1872-1887)
E - Muldenhutten (1887-1953)
F - Stuttgart
G - Karlsruhe
H - Darmstadt (1872-1882)
J - Hamburg

MONETARY SYSTEM

(Until 1923)

100 Pfennig = 1 Mark

PFENNIG

COPPER

KM#	Date	Mintage	Fine	VF	XF	Unc
1	1873A	.184	125.00	250.00	450.00	1000.
	1873B	.095	225.00	525.00	850.00	1450.
	1873D	.052	200.00	500.00	750.00	1250.
	1874A	26.760	.75	2.50	15.00	40.00
	1874B	8.743	2.00	9.00	20.00	65.00
	1874C	15.744	2.00	9.00	20.00	65.00
	1874D	7.074	5.00	15.00	25.00	65.00
	1874E	4.522	10.00	15.00	35.00	90.00
	1874F	3.985	2.50	7.50	17.50	65.00
	1874G	4.768	7.50	30.00	50.00	100.00
	1874H	2.013	30.00	55.00	100.00	300.00
	1875A	64.669	.75	1.50	7.50	20.00
	1875B	27.618	1.00	2.50	15.00	40.00
	1875C	22.654	1.00	2.50	15.00	40.00
	1875D	13.342	1.00	2.50	10.00	30.00
	1875E	7.779	5.00	15.00	30.00	60.00
	1875F	15.271	1.00	3.00	12.50	35.00
	1875G	12.021	5.00	10.00	20.00	60.00
	1875H	3.516	30.00	60.00	90.00	200.00
	1875J	7.242	2.50	8.00	20.00	50.00
	1876A	34.542	.75	1.50	6.50	20.00
	1876B	5.995	3.00	5.00	10.00	32.00
	1876C	11.044	3.00	5.00	10.00	32.00
	1876D	12.651	3.00	5.00	10.00	32.00
	1876E	6.532	2.50	7.50	20.00	50.00
	1876F	11.404	3.00	6.00	10.00	32.00
1	1876G	3.331	7.50	20.00	35.00	70.00
	1876H	2.998	20.00	40.00	85.00	160.00
	1876J	1.165	50.00	100.00	275.00	475.00
	1877A	.472	70.00	165.00	475.00	800.00
	1877B	.088	350.00	650.00	1400.	2150.
	1885A	5.448	1.50	6.00	15.00	30.00
	1885E	.430	35.00	60.00	100.00	200.00
	1885G	1.100	20.00	50.00	80.00	125.00
	1885J	1.696	10.00	20.00	40.00	65.00
	1886A	14.114	1.00	2.50	10.00	25.00
	1886D	2.873	1.00	2.50	12.50	40.00
	1886E	2.060	3.00	6.00	20.00	65.00
	1886F	1.726	2.50	5.00	17.50	45.00
	1886G	.814	25.00	90.00	130.00	225.00
	1886J	1.593	7.50	15.00	30.00	50.00
	1887A	15.923	1.00	1.50	10.00	25.00
	1887D	5.177	2.50	4.00	10.00	25.00
	1887E	2.315	3.00	6.00	20.00	50.00
	1887E dot after PFENNIG.					
		25 pcs.	—	—	7000.	10,000.
	1887F	6.345	2.50	5.00	15.00	35.00
	1887G	1.888	3.00	7.50	20.00	40.00
	1887J	2.082	1.50	3.00	10.00	25.00
	1888A	19.936	.75	1.50	6.50	17.50
	1888D	3.277	6.00	9.00	12.50	40.00
	1888E	1.310	5.00	10.00	20.00	40.00
	1888F	.584	20.00	30.00	95.00	150.00
	1888G	1.385	5.00	10.00	20.00	45.00
	1888J	2.803	2.50	5.00	10.00	40.00
	1889A	20.750	1.00	2.50	10.00	30.00
	1889D	8.454	2.00	3.00	15.00	30.00
	1889E	4.330	1.00	2.50	12.50	25.00
	1889F	5.010	1.00	2.50	12.50	30.00
	1889G	3.411	1.50	3.00	10.00	25.00
	1889J	3.308	1.50	3.00	10.00	25.00
	Common date		—	—	Proof	200.00
10	1890A	17.295	.50	1.50	3.50	10.00
	1890D	7.030	1.00	2.50	5.00	12.50
	1890E	3.730	.50	2.00	6.50	12.50
	1890F	4.189	.50	2.00	6.50	15.00
	1890G	3.050	1.50	3.00	6.50	15.00
	1890J	2.247	1.50	3.00	6.50	15.00
	1891A	12.040	1.50	3.00	5.00	10.00
	1891D	.876	10.00	25.00	75.00	115.00
	1891E	.528	20.00	40.00	75.00	115.00
	1891F	1.263	5.00	10.00	20.00	45.00
	1891G	.360	40.00	75.00	145.00	240.00
	1891J	1.837	7.50	25.00	75.00	135.00
	1892A	22.341	.25	.50	1.50	20.00
	1892D	6.139	2.00	4.00	9.00	40.00
	1892E	3.195	2.00	4.00	9.00	35.00
	1892F	5.013	1.00	2.00	5.00	30.00
	1892G	2.689	1.50	2.50	6.00	30.00
	1892J	3.980	.50	1.50	4.00	20.00
	1893A	18.966	.25	.50	2.00	12.00
	1893D	7.027	.25	1.00	4.00	20.00
	1893E	1.218	10.00	20.00	30.00	60.00
	1893F	1.460	1.00	2.00	6.00	30.00
	1893G	.700	12.50	25.00	35.00	70.00
	1893J	1.825	.50	5.00	15.00	30.00
	1894A	17.592	.25	.50	2.00	7.50
	1894D	5.530	.25	1.00	4.00	12.50
	1894E	5.040	.50	1.50	5.00	15.00
	1894F	4.206	.20	1.00	4.00	15.00
	1894G	2.351	.50	1.50	5.00	10.00
	1894J	2.619	.50	2.00	6.00	12.50
	1895A	20.152	.25	1.00	2.50	8.50
	1895D	1.496	10.00	25.00	35.00	70.00
	1895E	1.191	5.00	10.00	25.00	35.00
	1895F	4.366	.25	2.50	6.50	12.50
	1895G	3.051	1.00	3.00	7.50	15.00
	1895J	3.839	2.00	4.00	10.00	20.00
	1896A	27.094	.10	.25	1.50	6.50
	1896D	7.025	.10	.25	1.50	6.50
	1896E	3.725	.25	2.50	5.00	10.00
	1896F	3.450	.10	.20	1.50	6.50
	1896G	3.028	.25	4.00	7.50	10.00
	1897A	8.534	.25	1.00	3.50	8.50
	1897D	2.600	1.00	2.50	6.00	10.00
	1897E	1.294	3.50	7.50	15.00	35.00
	1897F	2.390	2.50	6.50	20.00	50.00
	1897G	1.122	10.00	20.00	35.00	75.00
	1897J	4.941	1.00	2.00	5.00	10.00
	1898A	18.564	.10	.25	1.50	6.50
	1898D	4.430	.25	2.00	5.00	15.00
	1898E	2.432	.50	5.00	10.00	20.00
	1898F	4.193	.20	1.00	2.50	7.50
	1898G	1.951	.25	5.00	15.00	30.00
	1898J	3.231	.25	2.50	5.00	10.00
	1899A	22.009	.10	.25	2.00	6.00
	1899D	4.590	.10	.25	2.00	6.00
	1899E	3.725	.25	2.50	5.00	12.50
	1899F	4.300	.10	.20	1.50	5.50
	1899G	2.550	.20	1.50	5.00	15.00
	1899J	2.416	.20	1.00	4.00	10.00
	1900A	51.804	.10	.25	1.50	5.50
	1900D	14.635	.10	.25	1.50	5.50
	1900E	7.887	.20	1.00	3.50	8.50
	1900F	10.312	.10	.50	1.50	6.00
	1900G	6.138	.20	1.00	3.50	8.50
	1900J	9.917	.20	1.00	3.50	8.50
	Common date		—	—	Proof	70.00

NOTE: Later dates (1901-1916) exist for this type.

2 PFENNIG

COPPER

KM#	Date	Mintage	Fine	VF	XF	Unc
2	1873A	.877	2.50	7.50	35.00	185.00
	1873B	.290	25.00	60.00	120.00	275.00
	1873C	.161	30.00	70.00	145.00	325.00
	1873D	2.358	5.00	25.00	65.00	225.00
	1873F	.022	125.00	275.00	675.00	1450.
	1873G	.118	75.00	200.00	350.00	550.00
	1874A	37.360	.50	2.50	12.50	50.00
	1874B	10.310	1.50	7.50	17.50	55.00
	1874C	17.474	1.00	5.00	15.00	55.00
	1874D	2.943	3.50	15.00	30.00	125.00
	1874E	5.090	2.50	12.50	30.00	125.00
	1874F	6.405	1.00	7.50	25.00	125.00
	1874G	6.128	1.00	7.50	25.00	185.00
	1874H	2.706	10.00	20.00	60.00	165.00
	1875A	28.963	.50	2.50	12.50	50.00
	1875B	15.844	1.00	3.50	20.00	55.00
	1875C	35.541	.50	1.00	25.00	65.00
	1875D	11.160	.50	1.00	45.00	150.00
	1875E	7.872	1.00	1.50	30.00	125.00
	1875F	9.827	.50	1.00	30.00	125.00
	1875G	11.903	.50	1.00	30.00	125.00
	1875H	3.309	3.50	7.50	30.00	125.00
	1875J	14.210	.50	1.00	20.00	75.00
	1876A	18.906	.50	1.00	12.50	50.00
	1876B	7.097	.50	1.00	15.00	50.00
	1876C	12.280	.50	1.00	15.00	50.00
	1876D	10.296	.50	1.00	15.00	50.00
	1876E	4.988	1.00	1.50	15.00	50.00
	1876F	7.207	.50	1.50	15.00	50.00
	1876G	3.502	1.00	2.50	15.00	50.00
	1876H	3.630	1.00	3.00	20.00	60.00
	1876J	1.995	4.00	7.50	17.50	60.00
	1877A	9.827	.50	1.00	15.00	50.00
	1877B	.060	150.00	300.00	600.00	—
	Common date		—	—	Proof	220.00

5 PFENNIG

COPPER-NICKEL

KM#	Date	Mintage	Fine	VF	XF	Unc
3	1874A	10.003	.25	1.00	12.50	90.00
	1874B	5.054	.50	2.50	15.00	120.00
	1874C	3.707	.50	2.50	15.00	120.00
	1874D	2.447	.50	2.50	15.00	120.00
	1874E	5.465	.50	2.50	15.00	135.00
	1874F	3.562	1.50	4.00	17.50	135.00
	1874G	2.721	1.50	4.00	17.50	140.00
	1875A	30.844	.25	1.00	12.50	65.00
	1875B	11.658	.50	2.50	14.00	90.00
	1875C	18.082	.50	2.50	14.00	90.00
	1875D	12.380	.50	2.50	14.00	90.00
	1875E	6.745	.50	2.50	14.00	90.00
	1875F	9.758	.50	2.50	14.00	90.00
	1875G	10.220	.50	2.50	14.00	90.00
	1875H	.703	20.00	45.00	75.00	175.00
	1875J	9.781	.50	2.50	14.00	90.00
	1876A	22.342	.25	1.00	12.50	65.00
	1876B	8.925	.50	2.50	14.00	75.00
	1876C	8.680	.50	2.50	14.00	75.00
	1876D	14.467	.50	2.50	14.00	75.00
	1876E	6.899	.50	2.50	14.00	75.00
	1876F	6.826	.50	2.50	14.00	75.00
	1876G	6.942	.50	2.50	15.00	135.00
	1876H	3.027	3.00	6.00	25.00	175.00
	1876J	11.920	.50	1.00	11.50	50.00
	1888A	7.366	.25	1.00	11.50	45.00
	1888/855D	1.967	3.00	6.00	25.00	65.00
	1888/78D	I.A.	3.00	6.00	25.00	65.00
	1888D	Inc. Ab.	2.50	5.00	20.00	55.00
	1888E	1.016	3.00	4.00	17.50	50.00
	1888F	1.412	1.00	2.00	11.50	40.00
	1888G	.853	6.00	8.00	22.50	60.00
	1888J	1.130	6.00	8.00	22.50	60.00
	1889A	10.804	.25	1.00	10.00	35.00
	1889D	2.816	1.00	2.50	11.50	45.00
	1889E	1.492	2.00	3.50	12.50	50.00
	1889F	2.010	1.00	2.50	11.50	45.00
	1889G	1.221	2.00	4.00	15.00	50.00
	1889J	1.636	2.50	5.00	17.50	55.00
	Common date		—	—	Proof	225.00
11	1890A	4.548	.10	.50	4.00	12.50
	1890D	2.813	.25	1.00	5.00	15.00
	1890E	1.318	.25	1.00	6.00	17.50
	1890F	1.068	.25	1.00	5.00	15.00
	1890G	.948	.25	1.00	6.00	17.50
	1890J	1.629	.20	1.00	5.00	15.00
	1891A	6.313	.10	.50	4.00	12.50
	1891E	.173	12.50	35.00	50.00	80.00
	1891F	.942	.25	1.00	5.00	15.00
	1891G	.271	5.00	17.50	30.00	55.00
	1892A	2.279	.10	1.00	4.00	12.50
	1892D	.920	.25	1.00	5.00	15.00
	1892E	.346	2.50	12.50	20.00	35.00
	1892F	.464	4.00	15.00	25.00	45.00
	1892G	.800	3.00	15.00	22.50	35.00
	1892J	.093	50.00	90.00	150.00	225.00
	1893A	8.572	.10	.50	4.00	15.00
	1893D	1.892	.25	1.00	5.00	16.50
	1893E	1.149	.25	1.00	6.00	17.50
	1893F	1.546	.15	1.00	5.00	15.00
	1893G	.422	4.00	15.00	20.00	40.00
	1893J	1.544	.20	1.00	5.00	15.00
	1894A	10.830	.10	.50	4.00	12.50
	1894D	2.812	.25	1.00	5.00	15.00
	1894E	.802	.25	1.50	6.00	17.50
	1894F	.300	1.00	4.00	10.00	30.00
	1894G	.280	1.00	5.00	12.50	35.00
	1894J	1.634	.20	1.00	5.00	15.00
	1895E	.686	.25	2.50	7.50	22.50
	1895F	1.705	.15	1.50	5.00	15.00
	1895G	.940	.25	2.00	6.00	17.50
	1896A	1.459	.25	1.00	5.00	15.00
	1896E	.658	.25	2.50	7.50	17.50
	1896F	2.009	.10	1.00	5.00	15.00
	1896G	1.221	1500.	2500.	—	—
	1896J	1.634	.20	1.00	5.00	15.00
	1897A	9.390	.10	.50	3.00	11.50
	1897D	2.812	.25	1.00	3.00	11.50
	1897E	.833	.25	2.00	5.00	15.00
	1897/797G	I.A.	1.00	4.00	10.00	30.00
	1897G	Inc. Ab.	.10	1.00	4.50	15.00
	1898A	10.836	.10	.30	2.25	10.00
	1898D	2.812	.10	.50	2.25	11.50
	1898E	1.492	.10	.50	2.75	14.00
	1898F	2.007	.10	.50	2.75	14.00
	1898G	1.220	.10	.50	2.25	17.50
	1898J	1.635	.20	1.00	2.25	12.00
	1899A	10.884	.10	.30	2.00	11.50
	1899D	2.812	.10	.50	2.75	14.00
	1899E	1.488	.10	.50	3.00	17.50
	1899F	2.006	.10	.50	2.75	14.00
	1899G	1.222	.10	.50	2.25	12.00
	1899J	1.634	.10	.50	2.25	12.00
	1900A	18.941	.10	.30	2.00	10.00
	1900D	4.254	.10	.50	2.25	12.00
	1900E	2.236	.10	.50	2.75	14.00
	1900F	3.209	.10	.25	2.25	12.00
	1900G	2.136	.10	.50	2.25	12.00
	1900J	2.859	.10	.50	2.25	12.00
	Common date		—	—	Proof	80.00

NOTE: Later dates (1901-1915) exist for this type.

10 PFENNIG

COPPER-NICKEL

KM#	Date	Mintage	Fine	VF	XF	Unc
4	1873A	.931	4.00	8.00	22.50	110.00
	1873B	.333	17.50	25.00	90.00	225.00
	1873C	.522	15.00	20.00	70.00	200.00
	1873D	.472	5.00	10.00	40.00	185.00
	1873F	.476	25.00	35.00	70.00	200.00
	1873G	.519	15.00	20.00	70.00	200.00
	1873H	.044	125.00	250.00	500.00	950.00
	1874A	7.664	.25	2.00	15.00	75.00
	1874B	2.669	2.50	5.00	17.50	90.00
	1874C	12.029	.25	2.00	15.00	70.00
	1874D	3.586	8.00	17.50	65.00	150.00
	1874E	3.157	8.00	17.50	40.00	125.00
	1874F	7.309	1.00	2.50	15.00	75.00
	1874G	5.552	1.00	2.50	15.00	80.00
	1874H	3.323	12.50	20.00	40.00	150.00
	1875A	15.523	.25	2.00	12.50	70.00
	1875B	4.120	1.00	2.50	15.00	75.00
	1875C	8.304	1.00	2.50	15.00	70.00
	1875D	13.365	1.00	2.50	15.00	70.00
	1875E	9.833	1.00	2.50	15.00	70.00
	1875F	7.975	1.00	2.50	15.00	70.00
	1875G	5.390	2.50	5.00	17.50	75.00
	1875H	4.268	12.50	20.00	40.00	100.00
	1875J	9.407	1.00	2.50	15.00	70.00
	1876A	34.175	.25	2.00	12.50	45.00
	1876B	10.120	1.00	2.50	14.00	50.00
	1876C	13.214	.25	2.00	12.50	45.00
	1876D	16.787	.25	2.00	12.50	45.00
	1876E	6.161	1.00	2.50	14.00	50.00
	1876F	7.034	1.00	2.50	14.00	50.00
	1876G	6.222	1.00	2.50	14.00	50.00
	1876H	3.227	17.50	30.00	40.00	75.00
	1876J	11.315	1.00	2.50	14.00	45.00
	1888A	8.519	1.00	2.50	16.00	50.00
	1888D	2.493	.50	2.50	14.00	40.00
	1888E	1.268	1.00	7.50	20.00	55.00
	1888F	1.340	1.00	7.50	20.00	55.00
	1888G	1.081	1.00	7.50	20.00	50.00
	1888J	1.436	.50	2.50	14.00	45.00
	1889A	11.542	.25	2.00	12.00	35.00
	1889D	2.813	.50	2.00	12.00	40.00
	1889E	1.493	.50	2.50	14.00	40.00
	1889F	2.432	.50	2.50	14.00	40.00
	1889G	1.223	.50	5.00	20.00	50.00
	1889J	1.638	.50	2.50	14.00	40.00
	Common date		—	—	Proof	350.00

COPPER-NICKEL

KM#	Date	Mintage	Fine	VF	XF	Unc
12	1890A	6.878	.10	.25	6.00	18.00
	1890F	.784	.25	1.50	8.00	25.00
	1890G	.976	.25	2.00	8.00	25.00
	1890J	1.637	.25	1.00	8.00	25.00
	1891A	4.239	.10	.25	3.00	15.00
	1891D	2.812	.10	.30	4.00	16.00
	1891E	1.489	.20	1.00	4.00	16.00
	1891F	1.226	.25	2.50	5.00	20.00
	1891G	.247	7.00	20.00	40.00	70.00
	1892A	2.413	.15	.50	4.00	18.00
	1892D	2.812	.15	.50	4.00	18.00
	1892E	.870	.25	2.50	5.00	20.00
	1892F	.663	.25	2.50	5.00	20.00
	1892G	.300	6.00	15.00	30.00	65.00
	1892J	—	2150.	3600.	—	—
	1893A	8.435	.10	.25	2.25	10.00
	1893E	.362	.50	6.00	12.50	35.00
	1893F	1.345	.15	.50	3.00	16.00
	1893G	.921	.25	1.50	5.00	16.00
	1893J	1.636	.20	1.00	5.00	16.00
	1894E	.260	7.50	25.00	40.00	65.00
	1896A	4.996	.10	1.00	2.25	10.00
	1896D	2.812	.20	1.00	4.00	12.00
	1896E	1.495	.20	1.00	4.00	15.00
	1896F	2.009	.15	1.00	4.00	15.00
	1896G	.200	6.00	15.00	25.00	40.00
	1896J	1.632	.10	.30	4.00	15.00
	1897A	5.842	.10	.25	2.25	10.00
	1897G	1.020	.25	1.50	4.00	15.00
	1898A	10.833	.10	.25	2.00	9.00
	1898D	2.814	.10	.25	3.00	12.00
	1898E	.805	.20	.50	3.00	14.00
	1898F	2.007	.15	.50	2.25	14.00
	1898G	.480	.50	3.00	6.00	22.50
	1898J	1.635	.10	.30	2.25	14.00
	1899A	10.838	.10	.25	2.00	9.00
	1899D	3.813	.10	.25	3.00	12.00
	1899E	2.175	.10	.30	3.00	14.00
	1899F	2.008	.10	.25	3.00	12.00
	1899G	1.382	.10	.25	3.00	12.00
	1899J	1.635	.10	.25	3.00	12.00
	1900A	34.559	.10	.25	1.75	8.00
	1900D	8.694	.10	.25	1.75	12.00
	1900E	4.490	.10	.30	2.00	12.00
	1900F	5.933	.10	.25	1.75	12.00
	1900G	4.239	.10	.25	2.00	14.00
	1900J	5.720	.10	.25	1.75	14.00
	Common date		—	—	Proof	95.00

NOTE: Later dates (1901-1916) exist for this type.

20 PFENNIG

1.1110 g, .900 SILVER, .0321 oz ASW

KM#	Date	Mintage	Fine	VF	XF	Unc
5	1873A	2.159	5.00	12.50	25.00	110.00
	1873B	.664	17.50	40.00	100.00	220.00
	1873C	.904	17.50	25.00	50.00	135.00
	1873D	1.201	8.00	12.50	30.00	110.00
	1873E	100 pcs.	1000.	1400.	1800.	3000.
	1873F	.450	17.50	30.00	90.00	200.00
	1873G	.763	12.50	25.00	70.00	165.00
	1873H	.054	150.00	350.00	750.00	1500.
	1874A	8.830	6.00	10.00	17.50	65.00
	1874B	9.222	6.00	10.00	17.50	75.00
	1874C	1.303	10.00	15.00	25.00	100.00
	1874D	10.087	7.50	10.00	17.50	75.00
	1874E	2.281	7.50	15.00	25.00	90.00
	1874F	7.222	6.50	10.00	17.50	75.00
	1874G	3.281	8.00	12.50	20.00	75.00
	1874H	1.842	12.50	17.50	25.00	100.00
	1875A	9.034	5.00	8.00	15.00	50.00
	1875B	2.768	8.00	12.50	25.00	60.00
	1875C	5.938	5.00	9.00	25.00	60.00
	1875D	15.032	5.00	8.00	15.00	50.00
	1875E	1.486	17.50	27.50	60.00	125.00
	1875F	7.668	6.00	9.00	15.00	60.00
	1875G	3.940	8.00	12.50	25.00	75.00
	1875H	1.340	17.50	27.50	37.50	120.00
	1875J	3.502	10.00	15.00	22.50	60.00
	1876A	6.959	6.00	10.00	15.00	45.00
	1876B	5.089	6.00	10.00	15.00	55.00
	1876C	5.911	6.00	10.00	15.00	70.00
	1876D	14.152	5.00	9.00	14.00	50.00
	1876E	11.648	7.50	12.50	20.00	90.00
	1876F	13.635	5.00	9.00	14.00	65.00
	1876G	7.820	5.00	9.00	14.00	65.00
	1876H	1.433	17.50	35.00	60.00	145.00
	1876J	10.272	6.00	10.00	17.50	45.00
	1877F	.700	125.00	250.00	400.00	650.00
	Common date		—	—	Proof	350.00

COPPER-NICKEL

KM#	Date	Mintage	Fine	VF	XF	Unc
9.1	1887A	2.712	7.50	20.00	30.00	55.00
	1887D	.704	7.50	25.00	35.00	80.00

KM#	Date	Mintage	Fine	VF	XF	Unc
9.1	1887E	.373	15.00	35.00	50.00	125.00
	1887F	.503	15.00	30.00	45.00	90.00
	1887G	.306	15.00	30.00	50.00	200.00
	1887J	.408	15.00	30.00	50.00	125.00
	1888A	5.426	6.50	18.50	27.50	50.00
	1888/7D	1.406	12.00	27.50	40.00	85.00
	1888D	Inc. Ab.	10.00	25.00	35.00	75.00
	1888E	.744	10.00	25.00	35.00	100.00
	1888F	1.005	10.00	25.00	35.00	90.00
	1888G	.611	10.00	25.00	40.00	135.00
	1888/7J	.818	25.00	45.00	60.00	125.00
	1888J	Inc. Ab.	10.00	25.00	35.00	75.00
	Common date		—	—	Proof	250.00

Obv: Star below value.

KM#	Date	Mintage	Fine	VF	XF	Unc
9.2	1887E	50 pcs.	—	—	P/L	6000.

NOTE: Struck at the new mint facility at Muldenhutten.

KM#	Date	Mintage	Fine	VF	XF	Unc
13	1890A	2.716	20.00	37.50	65.00	185.00
	1890/80D	.703	20.00	47.50	90.00	200.00
	1890D	Inc. Ab.	20.00	47.50	90.00	200.00
	1890E	.373	22.50	60.00	165.00	345.00
	1890F	.503	20.00	40.00	95.00	275.00
	1890G	.306	22.50	55.00	150.00	345.00
	1890J	.410	20.00	47.50	90.00	345.00
	1892A	2.712	12.50	35.00	55.00	175.00
	1892D	.703	20.00	47.50	65.00	250.00
	1892E	.372	20.00	55.00	100.00	400.00
	1892F	.502	20.00	47.50	90.00	275.00
	1892G	.304	27.50	67.50	180.00	450.00
	1892J	.409	20.00	55.00	165.00	445.00
	Common date		—	—	Proof	325.00

50 PFENNIG

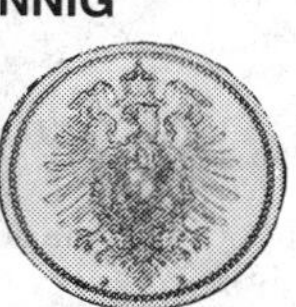

2.7770 g, .900 SILVER, .0803 oz ASW

KM#	Date	Mintage	Fine	VF	XF	Unc
6	1875A	7.095	7.50	15.00	30.00	100.00
	1875B	2.799	8.00	16.00	50.00	125.00
	1875C	2.047	7.50	15.00	30.00	100.00
	1875D	4.668	8.00	16.00	32.50	125.00
	1875E	.353	150.00	325.00	650.00	1800.
	1875F	.874	22.50	50.00	90.00	190.00
	1875G	2.034	15.00	17.50	37.50	155.00
	1875H	.175	150.00	300.00	600.00	1800.
	1875J	2.411	12.50	20.00	50.00	165.00
	1876A	34.475	6.00	12.00	25.00	85.00
	1876B	11.016	6.00	12.00	25.00	90.00
	1876C	10.945	6.00	12.00	25.00	90.00
	1876D	3.641	12.50	25.00	45.00	125.00
	1876E	4.127	12.50	25.00	45.00	125.00
	1876F	4.448	10.00	18.00	40.00	100.00
	1876G	1.797	10.00	18.00	40.00	125.00
	1876H	1.877	12.50	25.00	45.00	155.00
	1876J	3.589	8.00	16.00	35.00	100.00
	1877A	3.249	8.00	16.00	35.00	90.00
	1877B	3.691	10.00	18.00	40.00	100.00
	1877C	2.388	15.00	32.50	45.00	110.00
	1877D	3.004	12.50	20.00	40.00	100.00
	1877E	1.121	22.50	45.00	90.00	190.00
	1877F	1.311	25.00	37.50	70.00	135.00
	1877H	.622	75.00	110.00	185.00	325.00
	1877J	1.526	40.00	65.00	155.00	285.00
	Common date		—	—	Proof	250.00

KM#	Date	Mintage	Fine	VF	XF	Unc
8	1877A	6.746	20.00	40.00	90.00	200.00
	1877B	3.097	22.50	45.00	100.00	250.00
	1877C	2.820	20.00	45.00	100.00	250.00
	1877D	5.315	18.00	35.00	90.00	215.00
	1877E	2.296	20.00	40.00	110.00	255.00
	1877F	2.145	20.00	40.00	110.00	255.00
	1877G	2.061	22.50	50.00	125.00	280.00
	1877H	1.510	30.00	75.00	160.00	315.00
	1877J	1.337	22.50	45.00	110.00	260.00
	1878E	.364	250.00	400.00	600.00	1150.
	Common date		—	—	Proof	450.00

KM#	Date	Mintage	Fine	VF	XF	Unc
15	1896A	.389	100.00	220.00	325.00	475.00
	1898A	.387	100.00	220.00	325.00	475.00
	1900J	.192	100.00	235.00	375.00	550.00
	1900J	—	—	—	Proof	650.00
	Common date		—	—	Proof	525.00

NOTE: Later dates (1901-1903) exist for this type.

MARK

5.5500 g, .900 SILVER, .1606 oz ASW

KM#	Date	Mintage	Fine	VF	XF	Unc
7	1873A	.930	2.50	5.00	45.00	175.00
	1873B	.089	12.50	22.50	100.00	250.00
	1873C	.018	65.00	125.00	275.00	600.00
	1873D	.244	5.00	12.50	80.00	185.00
	1873F	.109	10.00	20.00	80.00	200.00
	1874A	6.310	2.50	6.00	40.00	90.00
	1874B	2.672	6.00	15.00	65.00	185.00
	1874C	.840	6.00	15.00	80.00	200.00
	1874D	7.079	2.50	6.00	30.00	100.00
	1874E	3.240	5.00	20.00	60.00	140.00
	1874F	6.155	2.50	8.00	40.00	125.00
	1874G	4.210	2.50	8.00	40.00	125.00
	1874H	1.893	4.00	15.00	85.00	300.00
	1875A	30.340	2.50	4.00	22.00	100.00
	1875B	7.690	2.50	7.50	50.00	125.00
	1875C	6.209	2.50	7.50	50.00	140.00
	1875D	7.538	2.50	5.00	30.00	100.00
	1875E	4.646	2.50	7.50	50.00	125.00
	1875F	7.074	2.50	4.00	22.00	120.00
	1875G	6.072	2.50	4.00	22.00	100.00
	1875H	2.300	3.50	10.00	65.00	175.00
	1875J	7.728	2.50	7.50	40.00	110.00
	1876A	17.297	2.50	4.00	22.00	90.00
	1876C	4.790	2.50	7.50	45.00	110.00
	1876D	2.956	2.50	7.50	50.00	150.00
	1876F	4.161	2.50	7.50	45.00	100.00
	1876G	2.333	2.50	7.50	40.00	125.00
	1876H	2.481	2.50	7.50	50.00	150.00
	1876J	1.109	2.50	7.50	70.00	180.00
	1877A	.697	4.00	7.50	45.00	165.00
	1877B	.048	200.00	300.00	600.00	1600.
	1878A	1.527	2.50	7.50	55.00	185.00
	1878B	.582	5.00	12.50	85.00	350.00
	1878C	.600	10.00	25.00	125.00	500.00
	1878E	.318	10.00	25.00	160.00	900.00
	1878F	1.039	5.00	12.50	65.00	190.00
	1878G	.525	7.50	20.00	125.00	375.00
	1878J	.895	6.50	18.00	100.00	275.00
	1879A	.156	45.00	90.00	175.00	750.00
	1880A	1.071	5.00	12.50	65.00	225.00
	1880D	.338	5.00	12.50	90.00	375.00
	1880E	.173	12.00	25.00	135.00	525.00
	1880F	.223	12.00	25.00	135.00	575.00
	1880G	.146	50.00	75.00	160.00	750.00
	1880H	.164	25.00	50.00	160.00	750.00
	1880J	.197	10.00	22.50	120.00	750.00
	1881A	6.386	2.50	4.00	25.00	125.00
	1881D	2.040	2.50	4.00	25.00	115.00
	1881E	1.081	5.00	10.00	75.00	175.00
	1881F	1.455	3.00	6.50	45.00	150.00
	1881G	.426	7.50	12.50	80.00	325.00
	1881H	.387	7.50	12.50	80.00	325.00
	1881J	.790	5.00	10.00	65.00	150.00
	1882A	1.474	2.50	8.00	60.00	225.00
	1882G	.459	10.00	25.00	90.00	450.00
	1882H	.109	35.00	80.00	250.00	800.00
	1882J	.098	10.00	30.00	115.00	525.00
	1883A	.809	5.00	10.00	55.00	150.00
	1883D	.208	22.00	50.00	115.00	400.00
	1883E	.112	35.00	80.00	300.00	950.00
	1883F	.148	30.00	75.00	200.00	900.00
	1883G	.091	75.00	150.00	350.00	1250.
	1883J	.121	30.00	75.00	250.00	1100.
	1885A	1.467	2.50	5.00	30.00	120.00
	1885G	.468	5.00	15.00	80.00	325.00
	1885J	.413	7.50	20.00	100.00	260.00
	1886A	1.101	3.00	7.50	40.00	125.00
	1886D	1.445	3.00	7.50	30.00	100.00
	1886E	.764	7.50	15.00	65.00	190.00
	1886F	1.031	2.50	6.00	45.00	155.00
	1886G	.161	15.00	45.00	165.00	335.00
	1886J	.427	7.50	15.00	70.00	200.00
	1887A	3.006	2.50	7.50	30.00	120.00
	Common date		—	—	Proof	250.00
14	1891A	.711	7.50	12.50	22.00	90.00
	1891D	Inc.Be.	350.00	600.00	950.00	1750.
	1892A	.909	5.00	12.50	22.00	90.00
	1892D	.418	5.00	15.00	32.00	120.00
	1892E	.223	10.00	17.50	45.00	185.00

KM#	Date	Mintage	Fine	VF	XF	Unc
14	1892F	.302	5.00	15.00	32.00	145.00
	1892G	.183	12.00	18.00	65.00	185.00
	1892J	.237	14.00	25.00	70.00	150.00
	1893A	1.633	2.50	5.00	12.00	80.00
	1893D	.425	2.50	5.00	32.00	145.00
	1893E	.224	7.50	17.50	45.00	140.00
	1893F	.300	7.50	15.00	32.00	120.00
	1893J	.254	8.00	20.00	50.00	150.00
	1894G	.184	20.00	45.00	100.00	275.00
	1896A	2.160	2.50	5.00	15.00	60.00
	1896D	.562	2.50	6.00	18.00	90.00
	1896E	.297	5.00	15.00	45.00	120.00
	1896F	.401	2.50	6.00	32.00	95.00
	1896G	.243	7.50	20.00	70.00	185.00
	1896J	.326	5.00	15.00	45.00	145.00
	1898A	1.000	5.00	12.50	22.00	95.00
	1899A	1.439	2.50	5.00	15.00	70.00
	1899D	.633	2.50	5.00	18.00	75.00
	1899E	.335	5.00	15.00	28.00	100.00
	1899F	.393	4.00	10.00	22.00	85.00
	1899G	.274	4.00	10.00	28.00	160.00
	1899J	.368	4.00	10.00	28.00	135.00
	1900A	1.625	2.50	5.00	12.00	40.00
	1900/800D	.421	2.50	5.00	12.00	70.00
	1900/801D	.915	2.50	5.00	12.00	70.00
	1900D	Inc. Ab.	2.50	5.00	12.00	70.00
	1900E	.223	10.00	25.00	50.00	150.00
	1900F	.301	7.50	17.50	35.00	100.00
	1900G	.183	12.00	27.00	65.00	185.00
	1900J	.246	10.00	25.00	50.00	150.00
	Common date		—	—	Proof	150.00

NOTE: Later dates (1901-1916) exist for this type.

PATTERNS (Pn)

(Including off metal strikes)

KM#	Date	Mintage	Identification	Mkt.Val.
Pn1	ND	—	1 Pfennig, Copper, w/"PF"	100.00
Pn2	ND	—	1 Pfennig, Copper, w/o "PF"	—

KM#	Date	Mintage	Identification	Mkt.Val.
Pn3	ND	—	2 Pfennig, Copper, plain edge	—
Pn4	1873G	—	2 Pfennig, fine reeding	—
Pn5	1873	—	10 Pfennig, w/o mint mark	—
Pn6	1873A	—	10 Pfennig, fine reeding	250.00
Pn7	1873A	—	10 Pfennig, coarse reeding	250.00
Pn8	1873C	—	10 Pfennig, reeded edge	225.00
Pn8a	1873G	—	10 Pfennig, reeded edge	225.00
PnA9	1873G	—	10 Pfennig, Gold, KM4	—
Pn9	1874G	—	1 Pfennig, reeded edge	—
Pn10	1874A	—	2 Pfennig, coarse reeding	—
Pn10a	1874C	—	2 Pfennig, coarse reeding	150.00
Pn11	1874F	—	2 Pfennig, coarse reeding	—
Pn12	1874G	—	2 Pfennig, fine reeding	—
Pn13	1874F	—	5 Pfennig, reeded edge	—
Pn14	1874	—	10 Pfennig, reeded edge	—
Pn15	1874A	—	10 Pfennig, reeded edge	—
Pn16	1874C	—	10 Pfennig, reeded edge	—
Pn17	1874D	—	10 Pfennig, reeded edge	—
Pn18	1874G	—	10 Pfennig, diagonal reeding	—
Pn19	1875G	—	1 Pfennig, reeded edge	—
Pn20	1875G	—	2 Pfennig, fine reeding	—
Pn21	1875A	—	10 Pfennig, diagonal reeding	—
Pn22	1875G	—	10 Pfennig, fine reeding	—
Pn23	1875J	—	10 Pfennig, reeded edge	—
Pn24	1876G	—	1 Pfennig, reeded edge	—
Pn25	1876G	—	2 Pfennig, fine reeding	—
Pn26	1876A	—	5 Pfennig, reeded edge	—
Pn27	1876A	—	10 Pfennig, reeded edge	75.00
Pn28	1876C	—	10 Pfennig, reeded edge	—
Pn29	1876D	—	10 Pfennig, reeded edge	—
Pn30	1876G	—	10 Pfennig, reeded edge	—
Pn31	1876J	—	10 Pfennig, fine reeding	—

KM#	Date	Mintage	Identification	Mkt.Val.
Pn32	1877A	—	50 Pfennig, Silver	250.00

KM#	Date	Mintage	Identification	Mkt.Val.
Pn33	1877A	—	50 Pfennig, Silver	250.00

KM#	Date	Mintage	Identification	Mkt.Val.
Pn34	1877D	—	1/2 Mark, Silver	950.00
Pn35	1877A	—	1/2 Mark, Silver, diagonal fraction bar	—
Pn36	1877A	—	1/2 Mark, Silver, larger eagle	—
Pn37	1886A	—	20 Pfennig, KM9.1	—
Pn38	1886A	—	20 Pfennig, Silver, scored fields	—

KM#	Date	Mintage	Identification	Mkt.Val.
Pn39	1886A	—	20 Pfennig, Copper-Nickel, scored fields	—
Pn40	1886A	—	20 Pfennig, Silver, stars scored	—

KM#	Date	Mintage	Identification	Mkt.Val.
Pn41	1886A	—	20 Pfennig, Copper-Nickel, stars scored	—
Pn42	1886A	—	20 Pfennig, Silver, stars plain	—
Pn43	1886A	—	20 Pfennig, Copper-Nickel, stars plain	—

KM#	Date	Mintage	Identification	Mkt.Val.
Pn44	1886A	—	20 Pfennig, Silver, eagle plain	250.00
Pn45	1886A	—	20 Pfennig, eagle scored	—
Pn46	1886A	—	20 Pfennig, Silver, eagle looped	—
Pn47	1886A	—	20 Pfennig, Nickel-Silver, eagle looped	—
Pn48	1888A	—	20 Pfennig, eagle scored	—
Pn49	1893A	—	10 Pfennig, reeded edge, KM12	—
Pn50	1898A	—	50 Pfennig, Silver, 24 denticles, plain edge	—
Pn51	1898A	—	50 Pfennig, Silver, reeded edge	—
Pn52	1898A	—	50 Pfennig, Silver, wavy reeding	—
Pn52a	ND	—	50 Pfennig, Silver, reverse uniface	150.00

KM#	Date	Mintage	Identification	Mkt.Val.
Pn57	1900A	—	1/2 Mark, Silver, fine reeded rim	150.00
Pn58	1900A	—	1/2 Mark, Silver, coarse reeded rim	150.00
Pn59	1900A	—	1/2 Mark, .960 Silver, coarse wavy reeded rim	—
Pn60	1900A	—	1/2 Mark, .900 Silver, coarse wavy reeded rim	—
Pn61	1900A	—	1/2 Mark, Silver, flat rims, fine reeding	—
Pn62	1900A	—	1/2 Mark, .585 Silver, large eagle	—
Pn63	1900A	—	1/2 Mark, .750 Silver, large eagle	—
Pn64	1900A	—	1/2 Mark, .900 Silver, large eagle	—
Pn65	1900A	—	1/2 Mark, Silver, deeper fields, weak reeding	—

GIBRALTAR

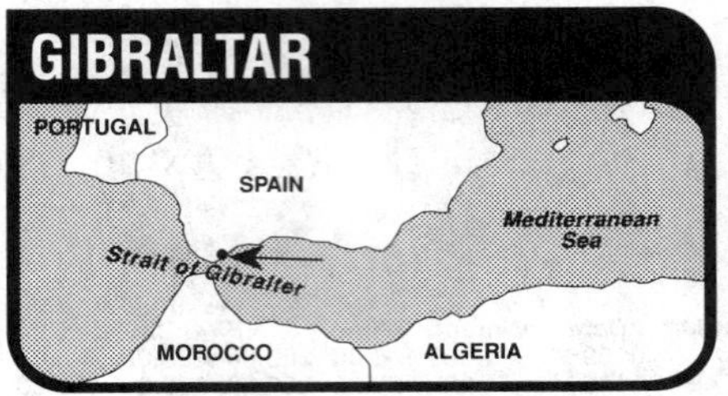

The British Colony of Gibraltar, located at the southernmost point of the Iberian Peninsula, has an area of 2.25 sq. mi. (6.5 sq. km.) and a population of 29,651. Capital (and only town): Gibraltar. Aside from its strategic importance as guardian of the western entrance to the Mediterranean Sea, Gibraltar is also a free port, British naval base, and coaling station.

Gibraltar, rooted in Greek mythology as one of the Pillars of Hercules, has long been a coveted stronghold. Moslems took it from Spain and fortified it in 711. Spain retook it in 1309, lost it again to the Moors in 1333 and retook it in 1462. After 1540 Spain strengthened its defenses and held it until the War of the Spanish Succession when it was captured by a combined British and Dutch force in 1704. Britain held it against the Franco-Spanish attacks of 1704-05 and through the historic 'Great Siege' of 1779-83. Recently Spain has attempted to discourage British occupancy by harassment and economic devices. In 1967, Gibraltar's inhabitants voted 12,138 to 44 to remain under British rule.

Gibraltar's celebrated Barbary Ape, the last monkey to be found in a wild state in Europe, is featured on the colony's first decimal crown, released in 1972.

RULERS

British

MONETARY SYSTEM

24 Quarts (Quartos) = 1 Real

TOKEN ISSUES (Tn)

QUART (QUARTO)

COPPER
Robert Keeling

KM#	Date	Mintage	Fine	VF	XF	Unc
Tn1	1802	—	10.00	25.00	50.00	125.00

KM#	Date	Mintage	Fine	VF	XF	Unc
Tn3.1	1810 large date	—	10.00	17.50	50.00	125.00

KM#	Date	Mintage	Fine	VF	XF	Unc
Tn3.2	1810 small date	—	10.00	17.50	50.00	125.00

Richard Cattons

KM#	Date	Mintage	Fine	VF	XF	Unc
Tn5	1813	—	17.50	30.00	60.00	150.00

James Spittles

KM#	Date	Mintage	Fine	VF	XF	Unc
Tn8	1820	—	10.00	18.50	55.00	135.00

2 QUARTS (QUARTOS)

COPPER
Robert Keeling
Toothed border
Rev: Horizontal and vertical lines in gate.

KM#	Date	Mintage	Fine	VF	XF	Unc
Tn2.1	1802	—	10.00	25.00	50.00	125.00

Plain border
Rev: Horizontal lines in gate.

KM#	Date	Mintage	Fine	VF	XF	Unc
Tn2.2	1802	—	12.00	27.50	55.00	135.00

Rev: Large date 5mm tall.

KM#	Date	Mintage	Fine	VF	XF	Unc
Tn4.1	1810	—	8.00	17.50	50.00	120.00

Rev: Small date 4mm tall.

KM#	Date	Mintage	Fine	VF	XF	Unc
Tn4.2	1810	—	8.00	17.50	50.00	120.00

Richard Cattons

KM#	Date	Mintage	Fine	VF	XF	Unc
Tn6	1813	—	17.50	35.00	75.00	150.00

James Spittles

KM#	Date	Mintage	Fine	VF	XF	Unc
Tn7	1818	—	15.00	30.00	65.00	150.00

KM#	Date	Mintage	Fine	VF	XF	Unc
Tn9	1820	—	10.00	20.00	50.00	120.00

REGULAR ISSUES

1/2 QUART

COPPER

KM#	Date	Mintage	Fine	VF	XF	Unc
1	ND(1841)	—	—	—	Proof	760.00
	1842	.387	4.50	12.50	32.50	80.00
	1861	—	—	—	Proof	800.00

QUART

COPPER

KM#	Date	Mintage	Fine	VF	XF	Unc
2	1841/O	—	—	—	Proof	850.00
	1842/0	.097	9.00	30.00	80.00	160.00
	1842/0	—	—	—	Proof	275.00
	1860	—	—	—	Proof	Rare
	1861	—	—	—	Proof	725.00

2 QUARTS

COPPER

KM#	Date	Mintage	Fine	VF	XF	Unc
3	1841	—	—	—	Proof	Rare
	1842/1	.048	15.00	40.00	90.00	180.00
	1842/1	—	—	—	Proof	325.00
	1860	—	—	—	Proof	Rare
	1861	—	—	—	Proof	820.00

PATTERNS (Pn)

(Including off metal strikes)

KM#	Date	Mintage	Identification	Mkt.Val.
Pn1	1802	3 known	2 Quarts, Copper	3000.
Pn2	1841/0	—	1 Quart, Bronzed Copper, KM2	850.00
Pn3	1842	—	1/2 Quart, Bronzed Copper, KM1	250.00

GOLD COAST

GOLD COAST
Axim
Prince's Town
Takoradi
Commenda
Cape Coast Castle
Cormantin
Dixcove
Shama
Elmina
Mouri
Accra
Christiansborg
Gulf of Guinea

The Gold Coast, a region of Northwest Africa along the Gulf of Guinea, was first visited by Portuguese traders in 1470, and through the 17th century was used by various European powers -England, Denmark, Holland, Germany -as a center for their slave trade. Britain achieved control of the Gold Coast in 1821, and established the colony of Gold Coast in 1874. In 1901 Britain annexed the neighboring Ashanti Kingdom in the same year a northern region known as the Northern Territories became a British protectorate. Part of the former German colony of Togoland was mandated to Britain by the League of Nations and administered as part of the Gold Coast.

The state of Ghana, comprising the Gold Coast and British Togoland, obtained independence on March 6, 1957, becoming the first Negro African colony to do so.

RULERS

British

MONETARY SYSTEM

8 Tackoe = 1 Ackey

1/2 ACKEY

7.0900 g, .925 SILVER, .2108 oz ASW

KM#	Date	Mintage	Fine	VF	XF	Unc
8	1818	*2,170	60.00	135.00	225.00	375.00
	1818	—	—	—	Proof	400.00

ACKEY

14.1300 g, .925 SILVER, .4202 oz ASW

KM#	Date	Mintage	Fine	VF	XF	Unc
9	1818	*1,085	150.00	300.00	450.00	750.00
	1818	—	—	—	Proof	850.00

NOTE: For later issues see British West Africa, in 20th Century edition.

PATTERNS (Pn)

(Including off metal strikes)

KM#	Date	Mintage	Identification	Mkt.Val.
Pn9	1818	—	1/2 Ackey, Silver, 26.5mm flan, umlaut above E in denomination.	1850.
Pn10	1818	—	1/2 Ackey, Bronzed-Copper, KM8	—
Pn11	1818	—	1/2 Ackey, Pewter, KM8	450.00
Pn12	1818	—	1 Ackey, Bronzed-Copper, KM9	—
Pn13	1818	—	1 Ackey, Pewter, KM9	1000.

GREAT BRITAIN

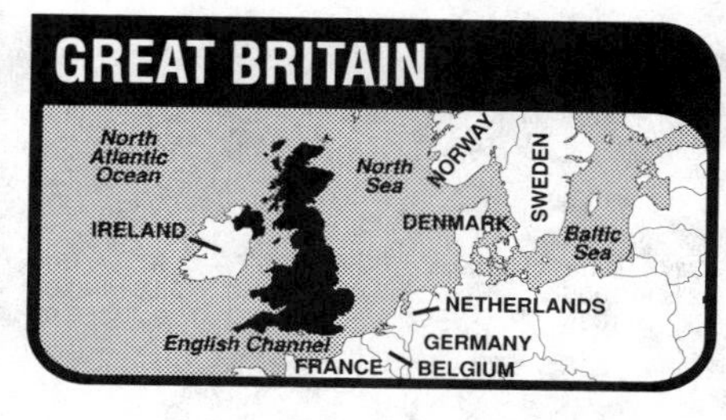

Great Britain, a member of the United Kingdom of Great Britain and Northern Ireland, located off the northwest coast of the European continent, has an area of 94,227 sq. mi. (244,820 sq. km.) and a population of 56.4 million. Capital: London. The economy is based on industrial activity and trading. Machinery, motor vehicles, chemicals, and textile yarns and fabrics are exported.

After the departure of the Romans, who brought Britain into a more active relationship with Europe, it fell prey to invaders from Scandinavia and the Low Countries who drove the original Britons into Scotland and Wales, and established a profusion of kingdoms that finally united in the 11th century under the Danish King Canute. Norman rule, following the conquest of 1066, stimulated the development of those institutions which have since distinguished British life. Henry VIII (1509-47) turned Britain from continental adventuring and faced it to the sea - a decision that made Britain a world power during the reign of Elizabeth I (1558-1603). Strengthened by the Industrial Revolution and the defeat of Napoleon, 19th century Britain turned to the remote parts of the world and established a colonial empire of such extent and prosperity that the world has never seen its like. World Wars I and II sealed the fate of the Empire and relegated Britain to a lesser role in world affairs by draining her resources and inaugurating a world-wide movement toward national self-determination in her former colonies.

RULERS

George III, 1760-1820
George IV, 1820-1830
William IV, 1830-1837
Victoria, 1837-1901

MINT MARKS

Commencing 1874

H - Heaton
KN - King's Norton

MONETARY SYSTEM

(Until 1970)

4 Farthings = 1 Penny
12 Pence = 1 Shilling
2 Shillings = 1 Florin
5 Shillings = 1 Crown
20 Shillings = 1 Pound (Sovereign)
21 Shillings = 1 Guinea

NOTE: Proofs exist for many dates of British coins in the 19th and early 20th centuries and for virtually all coins between 1926 and 1964. Those not specifically listed here are extremely rare.

1/4 FARTHING

COPPER

KM#	Date	Mintage	Fine	VF	XF	Unc
737	1839	3.840	18.00	35.00	75.00	150.00
	1839	—	—	—	Proof	—
	1851	2.215	18.00	35.00	80.00	175.00
	1851	—	—	—	Proof	—
	1852	Inc. Ab.	18.00	35.00	75.00	155.00
	1853	Inc. Ab.	18.00	35.00	80.00	170.00
	1853	—	—	—	Proof	450.00

BRONZED COPPER

KM#	Date	Mintage	Fine	VF	XF	Unc
737a	1852	—	—	—	Proof	600.00
	1853	*10-15	—	—	Proof	450.00
	1868	—	—	—	Proof	450.00

***NOTE:** Although the design of the above series is of the homeland type, the issues were struck for Ceylon.

1/3 FARTHING

COPPER

KM#	Date	Mintage	Fine	VF	XF	Unc
703	1827	—	10.00	17.00	45.00	110.00
	1827	—	—	—	Proof	350.00

KM#	Date	Mintage	Fine	VF	XF	Unc
721	1835	—	7.00	17.00	45.00	110.00
	1835	—	—	—	Proof	350.00

KM#	Date	Mintage	Fine	VF	XF	Unc
743	1844	1.301	25.00	45.00	120.00	250.00
	1844 (error) RE for REG.					
		Inc. Ab.	35.00	60.00	150.00	325.00

BRONZE

KM#	Date	Mintage	Fine	VF	XF	Unc
750	1866	.576	3.50	9.00	18.00	45.00
	1866	—	—	—	Proof	350.00
	1868	.144	3.50	10.00	20.00	45.00
	1868	—	—	—	Proof	300.00
	1876	.162	5.00	10.00	20.00	60.00
	1878	.288	3.50	10.00	20.00	45.00
	1878	—	—	—	Proof	—
	1881	.144	5.00	10.00	20.00	60.00
	1881	—	—	—	Proof	300.00
	1884	.144	3.50	10.00	20.00	50.00
	1885	.288	3.50	9.00	18.00	40.00

***NOTE:** Although the designs of the above types are in the homeland style, the issues were struck for Malta.

1/2 FARTHING

COPPER

Rev: Britannia's head breaks legend.

KM#	Date	Mintage	Fine	VF	XF	Unc
704.1	1828	7.680	10.00	25.00	65.00	180.00
	1828	—	—	—	Proof	350.00
	1830	—	—	—	Proof	350.00

Rev: Britannia's head below legend.

KM#	Date	Mintage	Fine	VF	XF	Unc
704.2	1828	Inc. Ab.	10.00	25.00	65.00	180.00
	1830 large date					
		8.776	10.00	25.00	65.00	170.00
	1830 small date					
		Inc. Ab.	12.00	35.00	85.00	190.00
	1830	—	—	—	Proof	350.00

BRONZED COPPER

KM#	Date	Mintage	Fine	VF	XF	Unc
704.1a	1828	—	—	—	Proof	300.00

COPPER

KM#	Date	Mintage	Fine	VF	XF	Unc
724	1837	1.935	20.00	70.00	200.00	550.00

KM#	Date	Mintage	Fine	VF	XF	Unc
738	1839	2.043	4.00	10.00	25.00	70.00
	1842	—	3.00	7.00	20.00	50.00
	1843	3.441	2.50	6.00	12.00	35.00
	1844	6.451	2.50	5.00	10.00	30.00
	1844 E of REGINA over N					
		Inc. Ab.	8.50	25.00	80.00	200.00
	1847	3.011	3.50	8.00	20.00	70.00
	1851/5851	—	6.00	15.00	35.00	90.00
	1851	—	3.50	10.00	25.00	75.00
	1852	.989	3.50	12.00	30.00	75.00
	1853	.955	6.50	15.00	40.00	100.00
	1853	—	—	—	Proof	300.00
	1854	.677	6.50	15.00	40.00	120.00
	1856 small date					
		.914	8.00	18.00	45.00	130.00
	1856 small date, KRITANNIA					
		Inc. Ab.	—	—	—	—
	1856 large date					
		Inc. Ab.	17.00	40.00	80.00	150.00

***NOTE:** Although the design of the above series is of the homeland type, the issues were originally struck for Ceylon. The issue was made current also in the United Kingdom by proclamation in 1842.

FARTHING

COPPER

KM#	Date	Mintage	Fine	VF	XF	Unc
661	1806	—	2.00	5.00	25.00	65.00
	1806	—	—	—	Proof	225.00
	1807	—	3.00	7.50	35.00	70.00

GILT COPPER

KM#	Date	Mintage	Fine	VF	XF	Unc
661a	1806	—	—	—	Proof	325.00

BRONZED COPPER

KM#	Date	Mintage	Fine	VF	XF	Unc
661b	1806	—	—	—	Proof	225.00

COPPER

KM#	Date	Mintage	Fine	VF	XF	Unc
677	1821	2.688	1.75	4.25	25.00	85.00
	1821	—	—	—	Proof	300.00
	1821. - dot after date					
		Inc. Ab.	1.75	4.25	25.00	85.00
	1822	5.924	1.75	4.25	20.00	70.00
	1822	—	—	—	Proof	300.00
	1823	2.365	2.00	5.00	22.00	75.00
	1823 letter I for 1 in date					
		Inc. Ab.	6.00	15.00	30.00	125.00
	1825	4.300	1.75	4.25	22.00	75.00
	1826	6.666	3.50	7.00	26.00	85.00

KM#	Date	Mintage	Fine	VF	XF	Unc
697	1826	Inc. Ab.	2.50	5.00	30.00	80.00
	1826	—	—	—	Proof	200.00
	1827	2.365	3.00	8.00	30.00	85.00
	1828	2.365	2.50	5.50	30.00	100.00
	1829	1.505	4.00	9.00	35.00	125.00
	1830	2.365	2.50	5.00	30.00	80.00
	1831	—	—	—	Proof	300.00

BRONZED COPPER

KM#	Date	Mintage	Fine	VF	XF	Unc
697a	1826	*150 pcs.	—	—	Proof	185.00

COPPER

KM#	Date	Mintage	Fine	VF	XF	Unc
705	1831	2.688	4.50	10.00	35.00	120.00
	1831	—	—	—	Proof	200.00
	1834	1.935	4.50	10.00	35.00	120.00
	1835	1.720	4.50	10.00	40.00	125.00
	1836	1.290	5.00	12.00	40.00	135.00
	1837	3.011	4.50	10.00	35.00	120.00

KM#	Date	Mintage	Fine	VF	XF	Unc
725	1838	.591	3.00	7.50	20.00	55.00
	1839	4.301	2.75	5.50	16.00	45.00
	1839	—	—	—	Proof	200.00
	1840	3.011	2.75	5.50	17.50	45.00
	1841	1.720	2.75	5.50	17.50	45.00
	1841*	—	—	—	Proof	175.00
	1842	1.290	4.50	14.00	35.00	80.00
	1842 4 over inverted 4					
		—	—	—	Rare	—
	1843	4.086	2.75	5.50	16.00	40.00
	1843 letter I for 1 in date					
		Inc. Ab.	3.50	8.50	32.50	125.00
	1844	.430	27.50	60.00	225.00	475.00
	1845	3.226	3.50	7.00	19.00	50.00
	1846	2.580	4.50	15.00	35.00	85.00
	1847	3.880	3.50	6.00	19.00	45.00
	1848	1.290	3.50	8.00	22.50	50.00

KM#	Date	Mintage	Fine	VF	XF	Unc
725	1849	.645	10.00	30.00	95.00	250.00
	1850/70	.430	10.00	30.00	60.00	175.00
	1850	Inc. Ab.	3.50	6.00	19.00	50.00
	1851	1.935	6.00	15.00	40.00	130.00
	1851 D of DEI/tipped D					
		Inc. Ab.	50.00	150.00	400.00	700.00
	1852	.823	6.00	17.50	40.00	135.00
	1853/2	1.028	75.00	125.00	200.00	350.00
	1853 WW designers initials raised					
		Inc. Ab.	2.50	5.00	17.50	40.00
	1853	—	—	—	Proof	350.00
	1853 WW designers initials incuse					
		Inc. Ab.	7.50	15.00	30.00	55.00
	1853	—	—	—	Proof	350.00
	1854	4.946	2.50	5.00	18.00	50.00
	1855 WW designers initials raised					
		3.441	4.00	15.00	30.00	75.00
	1855 WW designers initials incuse					
		Inc. Ab.	3.50	12.50	27.50	70.00
	1856	1.771	4.25	15.00	35.00	80.00
	1856 R of Victoria over E					
		Inc. Ab.	25.00	60.00	150.00	300.00
	1857	1.075	2.50	5.00	17.50	40.00
	1858	1.720	2.50	5.00	17.50	40.00
	1859	1.290	10.00	20.00	60.00	120.00
	1860/59	—	—	—	—	—
	1860	—	800.00	1500.	3000.	5500.
	1864	—	—	—	Rare	—

NOTE: Proofs dated 1841 were probably restruck at a later date.

BRONZED COPPER

KM#	Date	Mintage	Fine	VF	XF	Unc
725a	1839	*300 pcs.	—	—	Proof	Rare
	1853					
		*10-15 pcs.	—	—	Proof	Rare

BRONZE

Beaded border.

KM#	Date	Mintage	Fine	VF	XF	Unc
747.1	1860	2.867	2.00	4.00	10.00	35.00
	1860	—	—	—	Proof	300.00

Toothed border.

KM#	Date	Mintage	Fine	VF	XF	Unc
747.2	1860	Inc. Ab.	1.00	2.75	8.50	27.50
	1860 toothed/beaded border					
		Inc. Ab.	70.00	150.00	250.00	650.00
	1861	8.602	1.00	2.75	8.50	27.50
	1861	—	—	—	Proof	350.00
	1862 small 8					
		14.336	1.00	2.75	8.50	26.00
	1862 lg.8	I.A.	1.50	3.75	10.00	30.00
	1862	—	—	—	Proof	350.00
	1863	1.434	25.00	50.00	110.00	300.00
	1863	—	—	—	Proof	700.00
	1864	2.509	1.50	4.25	16.00	35.00
	1865/2	4.659	2.00	4.50	12.00	35.00
	1865/3	Inc. Ab.	2.50	5.00	15.00	40.00
	1865 lg.8	I.A.	1.50	2.75	10.00	30.00
	1865 sm.8	I.A.	1.50	2.75	10.00	30.00
	1866	3.584	1.00	2.75	8.00	30.00
	1866	—	—	—	Proof	350.00
	1867	5.018	1.50	3.50	14.00	35.00
	1867	—	—	—	Proof	350.00
	1868	4.851	1.50	3.50	14.00	35.00
	1868	—	—	—	Proof	200.00
	1869	3.226	3.00	7.50	25.00	60.00
	1872	2.150	1.50	3.50	10.00	35.00
	1873	3.226	1.25	2.75	8.00	27.50

Obv: Mature bust.

KM#	Date	Mintage	Fine	VF	XF	Unc
753	1874H	3.584	1.75	4.25	12.00	30.00
	1874H	—	—	—	Proof	200.00
	1874H normal G's over horizontal G's					
		Inc. Ab.	75.00	175.00	300.00	—
	1875 large date, 5 berries					
		.713	9.00	20.00	40.00	120.00
	1875 small date, 5 berries					
		Inc. Ab.	15.00	25.00	50.00	175.00
	1875 small date, 4 berries					
		Inc. Ab.	12.00	22.00	45.00	165.00
	1875H	6.093	1.00	2.00	5.50	17.50
	1875H	—	—	—	Proof	200.00
	1876H	1.075	6.00	15.00	30.00	75.00
	1877	—	—	—	Proof	2500.
	1878	4.009	1.00	2.00	6.00	25.00
	1878	—	—	—	Proof	350.00

KM#	Date	Mintage	Fine	VF	XF	Unc
753	1879	3.977	1.00	2.00	6.00	25.00
	1879 large 9					
		Inc. Ab.	1.50	3.00	8.00	35.00
	1880 3 berries in wreath					
		1.843	3.75	7.50	17.50	55.00
	1880 4 berries in wreath					
		Inc. Ab.	1.25	2.75	12.00	30.00
	1881 3 berries in wreath					
		3.495	1.50	3.00	7.00	25.00
	1881 4 berries in wreath					
		Inc. Ab.	3.50	7.50	20.00	55.00
	1881 shield heraldically colored					
		—	—	—	Proof	800.00
	1881H	1.792	1.75	3.50	9.00	26.00
	1882H	1.792	1.75	3.50	9.00	26.00
	1882H	—	—	—	Proof	400.00
	1883	1.129	2.00	7.50	20.00	45.00
	1883	—	—	—	Proof	400.00
	1884	5.782	.75	1.50	4.25	20.00
	1884	—	—	—	Proof	400.00
	1885	5.442	1.00	2.00	4.25	20.00
	1885	—	—	—	Proof	400.00
	1886	7.708	.75	1.50	4.25	18.00
	1886	—	—	—	Proof	400.00
	1887	1.341	2.00	4.00	9.00	30.00
	1888	1.887	1.50	3.00	6.00	22.50
	1890	2.133	1.50	2.50	5.00	22.00
	1890	—	—	—	Proof	400.00
	1891	4.960	.75	1.50	4.25	20.00
	1891	—	—	—	Proof	350.00
	1892	.887	3.00	7.50	17.00	40.00
	1892	—	—	—	Proof	400.00
	1893	3.904	.75	1.50	4.25	20.00
	1894	2.397	.75	1.50	6.00	22.00
	1895	2.853	10.00	20.00	50.00	120.00
788.1	1895	Inc. Ab.	.50	1.75	3.50	9.50
	1896	3.669	.35	1.75	3.50	9.50
	1896	—	—	—	Proof	300.00
	1897	4.580	.75	2.00	5.00	17.50

Blackened finish

KM#	Date	Mintage	Fine	VF	XF	Unc
788.2	1897	Inc. Ab.	.45	1.75	3.50	12.00
	1898	4.010	.60	1.75	3.50	14.00
	1899	3.865	.35	1.50	3.25	10.00
	1900	5.969	.35	.85	2.75	9.00

NOTE: Later date (1901) exists for this type.

1/2 PENNY

COPPER

KM#	Date	Mintage	Fine	VF	XF	Unc
662	1806 w/o berries					
		—	2.00	5.00	26.00	90.00
	1806 3 berries					
		—	2.00	4.50	25.00	90.00
	1806 w/o berries					
		—	—	—	Proof	250.00
	1806 2 berries					
		—	—	—	Proof	250.00
	1806 3 berries					
		—	—	—	Proof	250.00
	1807	—	2.50	5.50	20.00	100.00

BRONZED COPPER

KM#	Date	Mintage	Fine	VF	XF	Unc
662a	1806	—	—	—	Proof	275.0

COPPER

KM#	Date	Mintage	Fine	VF	XF	Unc
692	1825	.215	8.50	22.00	80.00	150.00
	1825	—	—	—	Proof	275.00
	1826/5	9.032	4.25	10.00	50.00	200.00
	1826	Inc. Ab.	2.75	7.00	35.00	125.00
	1826	—	—	—	Proof	200.00
	1827	5.376	4.25	8.50	45.00	140.00

BRONZED COPPER

KM#	Date	Mintage	Fine	VF	XF	Unc
692a	1826	*150	—	—	Proof	250.00

COPPER

KM#	Date	Mintage	Fine	VF	XF	Unc
706	1831	.806	4.50	9.00	45.00	170.00
	1834	.538	5.00	10.00	50.00	175.00
	1837	.349	4.00	8.00	40.00	155.00

BRONZED COPPER

KM#	Date	Mintage	Fine	VF	XF	Unc
706a	1831	—	—	—	Proof	200.00

COPPER

KM#	Date	Mintage	Fine	VF	XF	Unc
726	1838	.457	2.75	5.25	15.00	85.00
	1841	1.075	2.75	5.25	15.00	85.00
	1843	.968	6.00	15.00	45.00	150.00
	1844	1.075	3.50	8.00	35.00	115.00
	1845	1.075	30.00	70.00	275.00	800.00
	1846	.860	5.00	10.00	30.00	110.00
	1847	.725	6.00	10.00	30.00	110.00
	1848/7	.323	4.25	8.50	25.00	100.00
	1848	Inc. Ab.	4.25	8.50	26.00	110.00
	1851	.215	3.50	7.00	20.00	100.00
	1852	.637	3.50	7.00	20.00	100.00
	1853/2	1.559	6.00	15.00	45.00	150.00
	1853	Inc. Ab.	1.75	3.50	12.00	60.00
	1853	—	—	—	Proof	175.00
	1854	12.257	1.75	3.50	10.00	50.00
	1855	7.456	1.75	3.50	10.00	50.00
	1856	1.942	3.50	7.00	20.00	100.00
	1857	1.183	2.50	5.25	15.00	65.00
	1857 dots on shield					
		Inc. Ab.	2.50	5.25	12.00	60.00
	1858/6	2.473	5.00	12.00	37.50	110.00
	1858/7	Inc. Ab.	2.75	6.00	18.00	70.00
	1858	Inc. Ab.	2.25	5.25	15.00	65.00
	1858 sm.dt.	I.A.	2.00	5.50	18.00	70.00
	1859/8	1.290	4.50	12.00	40.00	115.00
	1859	Inc. Ab.	2.75	6.00	18.00	70.00
	1860	—	200.00	500.00	2350.	4500.
	1860	—	—	—	Proof	5000.

BRONZED COPPER

KM#	Date	Mintage	Fine	VF	XF	Unc
726a	1839 normal alignment					
		*300 pcs.	—	—	Proof	225.00
	1839 coin alignment					
		Inc. Ab.	—	—	Proof	300.00
	1841	—	—	—	Proof	—
	1853					
		*10-15 pcs.	—	—	Proof	Rare

BRONZE
Beaded border

KM#	Date	Mintage	Fine	VF	XF	Unc
748.1	1860	6.630	1.50	4.00	12.50	45.00
	1860	—	—	—	Proof	400.00

Toothed border

KM#	Date	Mintage	Fine	VF	XF	Unc
748.2	1860	Inc. Ab.	1.50	4.00	12.50	45.00
	1860 toothed/beaded border					
		—	—	—	—	—
	1860 w/7 berries in wreath					
		Inc. Ab.	1.50	4.00	12.50	45.00
	1860 w/7 berries in wreath					
		—	—	—	Proof	400.00
	1860 w/7 berries in wreath; rd.top lighthouse					
		Inc. Ab.	4.25	15.00	70.00	225.00
	1860 w/5 berries in wreath					
		Inc. Ab.	2.00	7.25	35.00	70.00
	1860 w/4 berries in wreath					
		Inc. Ab.	1.50	4.00	12.50	45.00
	1860 w/4 berries in wreath; rd.top lighthouse					
		Inc. Ab.	2.25	7.25	40.00	70.00
	1861/81	54.118	—	—	Rare	—
	1861	Inc. Ab.	1.50	4.00	12.00	40.00
	1861	—	—	—	Proof	300.00
	1861 w/5 berries in wreath L.C.W. on rock					
		Inc. Ab.	10.00	25.00	75.00	300.00
	1861 w/4 berries in wreath L.C.W. on rock					
		Inc. Ab.	2.00	3.50	13.50	90.00
	1861 w/4 berries in wreath L.C.W. on rock					
		—	—	—	Proof	550.00
	1861 w/4 berries in wreath					
		Inc. Ab.	2.00	4.00	12.00	40.00
	1861 L.C.W. on rock					
		Inc. Ab.	2.50	7.00	15.00	45.00
	1861 HALF over HALP					
		Inc. Ab.	20.00	60.00	175.00	450.00
	1862 L.C.W. on rock, B to left of lighthouse					
		61.107	50.00	150.00	600.00	1200.
	1862 C to left of lighthouse					
		Inc. Ab.	50.00	150.00	600.00	1200.
	1862 A to left of lighthouse					
748.2		Inc. Ab.	50.00	150.00	600.00	1200.
	1862	—	—	—	Proof	300.00
	1862	Inc. Ab.	1.25	3.50	12.00	50.00
	1862L.C.W.	I.A.	7.00	15.00	40.00	90.00
	1863 sm.3					
		15.949	1.75	5.00	22.00	50.00
	1863 sm.3	—	—	—	Proof	300.00
	1863 lg.3	I.A.	1.75	5.00	22.00	50.00
	1864	.538	3.50	8.00	26.00	85.00
	1865/3	8.064	30.00	85.00	270.00	600.00
	1865	Inc. Ab.	4.00	12.00	35.00	75.00
	1866	2.509	2.50	7.50	25.00	60.00
	1866	—	—	—	Proof	300.00
	1867	2.509	4.00	10.00	35.00	75.00
	1867	—	—	—	Proof	300.00
	1868	3.046	2.50	7.50	27.50	70.00
	1868	—	—	—	Proof	250.00
	1869	3.226	7.50	25.00	80.00	175.00
	1870	4.351	2.50	7.50	22.50	65.00
	1871	1.075	22.50	60.00	150.00	450.00
	1872	4.659	3.00	7.50	21.50	50.00
	1873	3.405	4.50	10.00	26.00	70.00
	1874 w/5 berries in wreath					
		Inc. Ab.	5.00	15.00	55.00	110.00

Obv: Mature bust.

KM#	Date	Mintage	Fine	VF	XF	Unc
754	1874 w/6 berries in wreath; large date					
		1.348	4.50	12.00	50.00	100.00
	1874 w/6 berries in wreath; small date					
		Inc. Ab.	—	12.00	50.00	100.00
	1874 w/4 berries in wreath; large date					
		Inc. Ab.	3.50	15.00	55.00	120.00
	1874H w/6 berries in wreath; small date					
		5.018	3.00	8.00	20.00	50.00
	1874H	—	—	—	Proof	300.00
	1874H w/6 berries in wr.;sm.dt. hvy.plan.					
		—	—	—	—	—
	1875	5.431	1.75	4.50	16.50	45.00
	1875H	1.254	7.00	15.00	35.00	90.00
	1875H	—	—	—	Proof	350.00
	1876H lg.date					
		6.810	3.00	7.50	20.00	60.00
	1876H small date					
		Inc. Ab.	2.00	5.00	17.00	50.00
	1876H sm.dt.	—	—	—	Proof	350.00
	1876H sm.date heavy planchet					
		—	15.00	50.00	150.00	400.00
	1877	5.210	2.00	5.00	17.50	55.00
	1877	—	—	—	Proof	300.00
	1878 small date					
		1.426	8.00	24.00	50.00	200.00
	1878 sm.dt.	—	—	—	Proof	400.00
	1878 lg.date	I.A.	25.00	85.00	275.00	800.00
	1878 lg.date	—	—	—	Proof	850.00
	1879	3.583	1.50	4.00	12.50	40.00
	1880	2.423	2.50	6.50	22.00	50.00
	1880	—	—	—	Proof	400.00
	1881	2.008	2.50	7.50	22.00	50.00
	1881 shield heraldically colored					
		—	—	—	Proof	600.00
	1881 shield heraldically colored, broach on bust					
		2 known	—	—	Proof	1250.
	1881H	1.792	2.50	7.50	20.00	50.00
	1882H	4.480	1.15	4.50	16.50	45.00
	1882H different dies		—	—	Proof	700.00
	1883 rose on front of dress					
		3.001	5.00	10.00	20.00	50.00
	1883 rose on front of dress					
		—	—	—	Proof	400.00
	1883 broach on front of dress					
		Inc. Ab.	3.50	6.00	18.00	50.00
	1884	6.990	1.15	3.00	12.50	45.00
	1884	—	—	—	Proof	350.00
	1885	8.601	1.15	3.00	12.50	45.00
	1885	—	—	—	Proof	350.00
	1886	8.586	1.00	2.75	12.50	45.00
	1886	—	—	—	Proof	175.00
	1887	10.701	1.00	2.75	10.00	35.00
	1888	6.815	1.25	3.25	11.50	40.00
	1889/8	7.748	35.00	60.00	120.00	275.00
	1889/8	2 known	—	—	Proof	—
	1889	Inc. Ab.	1.00	2.75	11.50	40.00
	1890	11.254	1.00	2.75	9.00	35.00
	1890	—	—	—	Proof	400.00
	1891	13.192	1.00	2.75	9.00	35.00
	1891	—	—	—	Proof	400.00
	1892	2.478	1.15	2.75	16.50	40.00
	1892	—	—	—	Proof	400.00
	1893	7.229	.85	2.75	10.00	35.00
	1894	1.768	3.00	7.00	25.00	60.00

KM#	Date	Mintage	Fine	VF	XF	Unc
789	1895	3.032	.75	1.75	5.25	18.00
	1895	—	—	—	Proof	400.00
	1896	9.143	.75	1.50	4.25	15.00
	1896	—	—	—	Proof	400.00
	1897	8.690	.50	1.25	4.50	20.00
	1897 high sea level					
		Inc. Ab.	.60	1.50	4.25	15.00
	1898	8.595	1.00	3.00	7.50	20.00
	1899	12.108	.75	2.00	4.50	15.00
	1900	13.805	.50	1.00	2.75	9.00

NOTE: Later date (1901) exists for this type.

PENNY

COPPER

KM#	Date	Mintage	Fine	VF	XF	Unc
663	1806	—	5.00	10.00	45.00	165.00
	1806	—	—	—	Proof	285.00
	1807	—	6.00	12.00	50.00	180.00
	1808	—	—	—	Unique	—

BRONZED COPPER

KM#	Date	Mintage	Fine	VF	XF	Unc
663a	1806	—	—	—	Proof	300.00

GILT COPPER

KM#	Date	Mintage	Fine	VF	XF	Unc
663b	1806	—	—	—	Proof	500.00

.4713 g, .925 SILVER, .0140 oz ASW

KM#	Date	Mintage	Fine	VF	XF	Unc
668	1817	—	5.00	8.00	15.00	30.00
	1817	.010	—	—	P/L	35.00
	1818	—	5.00	8.00	15.00	30.00
	1818	9,504	—	—	P/L	35.00
	1820	—	5.00	8.00	15.00	30.00
	1820	7,920	—	—	P/L	35.00

KM#	Date	Mintage	Fine	VF	XF	Unc
683	1822	.012	—	—	P/L	35.00
	1823	.013	—	—	P/L	30.00
	1824	9,504	—	—	P/L	35.00
	1825	8,712	—	—	P/L	30.00
	1826	8,712	—	—	P/L	30.00
	1827	7,920	—	—	P/L	30.00
	1828	7,920	—	—	P/L	30.00
	1829	7,920	—	—	P/L	30.00
	1830	7,920	—	—	P/L	30.00

COPPER

KM#	Date	Mintage	Fine	VF	XF	Unc
693	1825	1.075	6.00	20.00	80.00	235.00
	1825	—	—	—	Proof	500.00
	1826	5.914	5.50	18.00	60.00	200.00
	1826	—	—	—	Proof	400.00
	1827	1.452	80.00	250.00	1600.	2500.

BRONZED COPPER

KM#	Date	Mintage	Fine	VF	XF	Unc
693a	1826	—	—	—	Proof	300.00

COPPER

KM#	Date	Mintage	Fine	VF	XF	Unc
707	1831	.806	8.50	35.00	120.00	425.00
	1831 .W.W incuse on truncation					
		Inc. Ab.	10.00	40.00	130.00	460.00
	1831 W.W incuse on truncation					
		Inc. Ab.	12.00	45.00	140.00	500.00
	1834	.323	12.00	50.00	140.00	500.00
	1837	.175	15.00	65.00	150.00	575.00

BRONZED COPPER

KM#	Date	Mintage	Fine	VF	XF	Unc
707a	1831	—	—	—	Proof	400.00

.4713 g, .925 SILVER, .0140 oz ASW

KM#	Date	Mintage	Fine	VF	XF	Unc
708	1831	.010	—	—	P/L	22.50
	1832	8,712	—	—	P/L	22.50
	1833	8,712	—	—	P/L	22.50
	1834	8,712	—	—	P/L	22.50
	1835	8,712	—	—	P/L	22.50
	1836	8,712	—	—	P/L	22.50
	1837	8,712	—	—	P/L	22.50

KM#	Date	Mintage	Fine	VF	XF	Unc
727	1838	8,976	—	—	P/L	15.00
	1839	8,976	—	—	P/L	15.00
	1840	8,976	—	—	P/L	15.00
	1841	7,920	—	—	P/L	15.00
	1842	8,896	—	—	P/L	15.00
	1843	7,920	—	—	P/L	15.00
	1844	7,920	—	—	P/L	15.00
	1845	7,920	—	—	P/L	15.00
	1846	7,920	—	—	P/L	15.00
	1847	7,920	—	—	P/L	15.00
	1848	7,920	—	—	P/L	15.00
	1849	7,920	—	—	P/L	15.00
	1850	7,920	—	—	P/L	15.00
	1851	7,128	—	—	P/L	15.00
	1852	7,920	—	—	P/L	15.00
	1853	7,920	—	—	P/L	15.00
	1854	7,920	—	—	P/L	15.00
	1855	7,920	—	—	P/L	15.00
	1856	7,920	—	—	P/L	15.00
	1857	7,920	—	—	P/L	15.00
	1858	7,920	—	—	P/L	15.00
	1859	7,920	—	—	P/L	15.00
	1860	7,920	—	—	P/L	15.00
	1861	7,920	—	—	P/L	15.00
	1862	7,920	—	—	P/L	15.00
	1863	7,920	—	—	P/L	15.00
	1864	7,920	—	—	P/L	15.00
	1865	7,920	—	—	P/L	15.00
	1866	7,920	—	—	P/L	15.00
	1867	7,920	—	—	P/L	15.00
	1868	7,920	—	—	P/L	15.00
	1869	7,920	—	—	P/L	15.00
	1870	9,002	—	—	P/L	15.00
	1871	9,286	—	—	P/L	15.00
	1872	8,956	—	—	P/L	15.00
	1873	7,932	—	—	P/L	15.00
	1874	8,741	—	—	P/L	15.00
	1875	8,459	—	—	P/L	15.00
	1876	.010	—	—	P/L	15.00
	1877	8,936	—	—	P/L	15.00
	1878	9,903	—	—	P/L	15.00
	1879	.011	—	—	P/L	15.00
	1880	.011	—	—	P/L	15.00
	1881	9,017	—	—	P/L	15.00
	1882	.011	—	—	P/L	15.00
	1883	.012	—	—	P/L	15.00
	1884	.014	—	—	P/L	15.00
	1885	.012	—	—	P/L	15.00
	1886	.016	—	—	P/L	15.00
	1887	.018	—	—	P/L	20.00

COPPER

KM#	Date	Mintage	Fine	VF	XF	Unc
739	1841 REG:	.914	9.00	25.00	90.00	285.00
	1841	—	—	—	Proof	850.00
	1841 w/o colon after REG					
		Inc. Ab.	3.50	10.00	40.00	150.00
	1843 REG:	.484	20.00	80.00	255.00	650.00
	1843 w/o colon after REG					
		Inc. Ab.	25.00	90.00	300.00	700.00
	1844	.215	4.25	8.50	40.00	145.00
	1844	—	—	—	Proof	—
	1845	.323	6.00	15.00	65.00	195.00
	1846 near colon					
		.484	5.25	12.50	50.00	165.00
	1846 far colon					
		Inc. Ab.	5.25	10.00	45.00	145.00
	1847 near colon					
		.430	4.25	10.00	45.00	160.00
	1847 far colon					
		Inc. Ab.	4.25	10.00	45.00	165.00
	1848/6	.161	10.00	25.00	80.00	250.00
	1848/7	Inc. Ab.	5.00	10.00	35.00	145.00
	1848	Inc. Ab.	5.00	10.00	35.00	145.00
	1849	.269	50.00	135.00	450.00	900.00
	1851 far colon					
		.269	5.25	10.00	45.00	165.00
	1851 near colon					
		Inc. Ab.	5.25	12.50	50.00	175.00
	1853 ornamental trident					
		1.021	3.00	10.00	30.00	125.00
	1853	—	—	—	Proof	600.00
	1853 plain trident					
		Inc. Ab.	3.00	10.00	30.00	125.00
	1854/3	6.559	20.00	60.00	120.00	240.00
	1854 ornamental trident					
		Inc. Ab.	2.75	6.00	25.00	85.00
	1854 plain trident					
		Inc. Ab.	2.75	6.00	25.00	85.00
	1855 ornamental trident					
		5.274	2.75	6.00	25.00	85.00
	1855 plain trident					
		Inc. Ab.	2.75	6.00	25.00	85.00
	1856 ornamental trident					
		1.212	25.00	60.00	175.00	450.00
	1856	—	—	—	Proof	1000.
	1856 plain trident					
		Inc. Ab.	30.00	75.00	225.00	550.00
	1857 large date					
		.753	2.75	6.50	30.00	125.00
	1857 small date					
		Inc. Ab.	2.75	6.50	30.00	125.00
	1858/3	Inc. Ab.	8.00	22.00	60.00	175.00
	1858/6	Inc. Ab.	12.00	30.00	100.00	300.00
	1858/7	Inc. Ab.	2.75	6.00	25.00	85.00
	1858 large date					
		Inc. Ab.	2.75	6.00	25.00	85.00
	1858 large date w/o ww					
		Inc. Ab.	2.75	6.00	25.00	85.00
	1858 small date					
		—	2.75	6.00	25.00	85.00
	1858 small date w/o ww					
		Inc. Ab.	3.50	8.00	27.50	120.00
	1859/8	1.075	10.00	22.50	55.00	160.00
	1859	Inc. Ab.	4.00	10.00	45.00	150.00
	1859	—	—	—	Proof	—
	1860/59	.032	125.00	350.00	1000.	1500.

BRONZED COPPER

KM#	Date	Mintage	Fine	VF	XF	Unc
739a	1839	*300 pcs.	—	—	Proof	500.00
	1841	—	—	—	Proof	1000.
	1853					
		*10-15 pcs.	—	—	Proof	700.00

BRONZE
Beaded border.

KM#	Date	Mintage	Fine	VF	XF	Unc
749.1	1860 raised lines on shield					
		5.053	5.00	10.00	45.00	100.00
	1860 raised lines on shield					
		—	—	—	Proof	400.00
	1860 raised lines on shield, extra thick flan					
		—	—	—	Proof	900.00
	1860 incuse lines on shield					

KM#	Date	Mintage	Fine	VF	XF	Unc
749.1		Inc. Ab.	3.00	7.00	35.00	90.00
	1860 incuse lines on shield					
		—	—	—	Proof	800.00

Toothed border.

KM#	Date	Mintage	Fine	VF	XF	Unc
749.2	1860 beaded border/toothed border					
		Inc. Ab.	55.00	145.00	630.00	2700.
	1860 toothed border/beaded border					
		Inc. Ab.	50.00	120.00	550.00	—
	1860 L.C.W. below foot, L.C.WYON on shoulder					
		Inc. Ab.	15.00	45.00	100.00	250.00
	1860 L.C.W. below shield,L.C.WYON below shoulder	I.A.	3.00	7.50	30.00	80.00
	1860 L.C.WYON on shoulder,L.C.W. below shield	I.A.	3.00	7.50	30.00	100.00
	1860 L.C.WYON on shoulder,L.C.W. below shield	—	—	—	Proof	400.00
	1860 w/o obv. sign., 15 leaves					
		Inc. Ab.	4.50	10.00	45.00	100.00
	1860 w/o obv. sign., 16 leaves					
		Inc. Ab.	8.00	20.00	65.00	175.00
	1861 L.C.WYON on trunc.; L.C.W. below shield					
		36.449	2.00	5.25	25.00	75.00
	1861 L.C.WYON on trunc., w/o sign. on rev.					
		Inc. Ab.	3.00	12.00	30.00	80.00
	1861 L.C.WYON below trunc. L.C.W. below shield	I.A.	3.00	10.00	30.00	75.00
	1861 L.C.WYON below trunc., w/o sign. on rev.					
		Inc. Ab.	20.00	45.00	120.00	350.00
	1861 w/o obv. sign., 15 lvs. L.C.W. below shield					
		Inc. Ab.	4.00	12.00	30.00	75.00
	1861 w/o obv. sign., 15 leaves w/o rev. sign.					
		Inc. Ab.	50.00	150.00	300.00	1000.
	1861 w/o obv. sign., 16 lvs. L.C.W. below shield					
		Inc. Ab.	3.00	5.25	27.50	75.00
	1861 w/o obv. sign., 16 lvs. L.C.W. below shield					
		—	—	—	Proof	425.00
	1861/81 w/o obv. sign., 16 lvs. L.C.W. below shield	Inc. Ab.	50.00	150.00	300.00	1000.
	1861 w/o obv. sign., 16 leaves, w/o rev. sign.					
		Inc. Ab.	2.50	8.00	21.00	75.00
	1861 w/o obv. sign., 16 leaves, w/o rev. sign.					
		—	—	—	Proof	375.00
	1862/1662					
		50.534	22.50	75.00	175.00	600.00
	1862	—	—	—	Proof	800.00
	1862 L.C.WYON on shoulder w/o rev. sign.					
		Inc. Ab.	300.00	750.00	1750.	4000.
	1862 w/o sign. on obv.					
		Inc. Ab.	2.00	6.00	19.00	65.00
	1862 date numerals small, from 1/2 Penny Die					
		Inc. Ab.	12.00	30.00	75.00	175.00
	1863	28.063	2.00	6.00	19.00	55.00
	1863	—	—	—	Proof	425.00
	1863 w/small die number 2, 3, or 4 below date					
		Inc. Ab.	100.00	180.00	450.00	1200.
	1863 w/small die number 5 below date					
		Inc. Ab.	—	—	Rare	—
	1864 plain 4 in date					
		3.441	15.00	40.00	170.00	540.00
	1864 crosslet 4 in date					
		Inc. Ab.	20.00	65.00	200.00	625.00
	1865/3	8.602	30.00	90.00	250.00	775.00
	1865	Inc. Ab.	3.50	12.50	35.00	80.00
	1866	9.999	2.50	8.50	27.00	70.00
	1867	5.484	3.50	10.00	40.00	90.00
	1867	—	—	—	Proof	700.00
	1868	1.183	10.00	30.00	120.00	355.00
	1868	—	—	—	Proof	500.00
	1869	2.580	50.00	200.00	500.00	1350.
	1870	5.695	5.00	25.00	120.00	355.00
	1871	1.290	25.00	75.00	250.00	700.00
	1872	8.495	2.75	9.00	25.00	90.00
	1872 rev. upside down					
		Unique	—	—	Proof	—
	1873	8.494	2.75	9.00	25.00	90.00
	1874	5.622	3.00	10.00	35.00	100.00
	1874 16 leaves, small date					
		Inc. Ab.	7.50	17.50	37.50	110.00
	1874H	6.666	3.50	11.00	30.00	100.00
	1874H 16 leaves, large date					
		Inc. Ab.	3.00	7.50	35.00	100.00

Obv: Mature bust.

KM#	Date	Mintage	Fine	VF	XF	Unc
755	1874 17 leaves, thin ribbons					
		Inc. Ab.	3.00	10.00	35.00	100.00
	1874 17 leaves, thin ribbons, small date					
		Inc. Ab.	3.00	10.00	35.00	100.00
	1874 17 leaves, thick ribbons					
		Inc. Ab.	7.50	30.00	100.00	300.00
	1874 17 leaves, thick ribbons, small date					
		Inc. Ab.	3.00	10.00	35.00	100.00
	1874H 17 leaves, thin ribbons					
		Inc. Ab.	4.00	12.00	30.00	75.00
	1874H 17 leaves, thin ribbons, small date					
		Inc. Ab.	4.00	12.00	30.00	75.00
	1874H 17 leaves, thin ribbons, small date					

KM#	Date	Mintage	Fine	VF	XF	Unc
755		—	—	—	Proof	300.00
	1874H 17 leaves, thin ribbons, large date					
		Inc. Ab.	15.00	50.00	250.00	700.00
	1875	10.691	3.00	9.00	22.50	65.00
	1875 small date					
		Inc. Ab.	3.00	9.00	22.50	65.00
	1875 large date					
		Inc. Ab.	3.00	9.00	22.50	65.00
	1875 large date, heavy planchet					
		Unique	—	—	Proof	—
	1875H large date					
		.753	25.00	90.00	250.00	650.00
	1875H large date					
		—	—	—	Proof	800.00
	1876H large date					
		11.075	3.00	8.50	17.50	50.00
	1876H large date					
		Inc. Ab.	—	—	Proof	500.00
	1876H small date					
		Inc. Ab.	3.00	8.50	17.50	50.00
	1877 small date					
		9.625	100.00	300.00	1000.	2000.
	1877 large date					
		Inc. Ab.	3.25	9.50	20.00	55.00
	1877 large date		—	—	Proof	500.00
	1878	2.764	4.50	12.00	30.00	65.00
	1878	—	—	—	Proof	500.00
	1879 large date; raised lines on wreath					
		7.666	15.00	40.00	125.00	250.00
	1879 large date; incuse lines in wreath					
		Inc. Ab.	2.50	8.50	18.00	55.00
	1879 large date; incuse lines in wreath					
		Unique	—	—	Proof	—
	1879 sm.dt.	I.A.	7.50	25.00	100.00	300.00
	1880	3.001	5.00	13.50	35.00	100.00
	1880	—	—	—	Proof	500.00
	1880 rock to left of lighthouse					
		Inc. Ab.	5.00	13.50	35.00	100.00
	1880 obv. 15 leaves as 1881					
		—	—	—	Proof	Rare
	1881	2.302	4.00	12.00	35.00	70.00
	1881	—	—	—	Proof	450.00
	1881 obv. as 1880; shield heraldically colored	I.A.	100.00	300.00	750.00	2250.
	1881 obv. as 1880; shield heraldically colored	I.A.		—	Proof	—
	1881 obv. and rev. as 1880					
		Inc. Ab.	6.00	18.00	50.00	130.00
	1881 shield heraldically colored					
					Proof	1100.
	1881H obv: 15 leaves in wreath					
		3.763	2.50	7.00	22.50	65.00
	1881H obv: 15 leaves in wreath					
		—	—	—	Proof	600.00
	1882H convex shield					
		7.526	2.75	10.00	50.00	100.00
	1882H flat shield					
		Inc. Ab.	2.75	8.00	20.00	65.00
	1882H	—	—	—	Proof	1000.
	1882	Inc. Ab.	75.00	225.00	725.00	1750.
	1883	6.237	2.00	6.50	23.00	70.00
	1883	—	—	—	Proof	450.00
	1884	11.703	1.50	5.00	16.00	55.00
	1884	—	—	—	Proof	500.00
	1885	7.146	1.50	5.00	16.00	55.00
	1885	—	—	—	Proof	500.00
	1886	6.088	1.25	4.25	15.50	50.00
	1886	—	—	—	Proof	700.00
	1887	5.315	1.25	4.50	15.50	50.00
	1888	5.125	1.25	4.50	15.50	50.00
	1889	12.560	1.25	5.00	16.00	55.00
	1889 14 leaves in wreath					
		Inc. Ab.	1.25	5.00	16.00	55.00
	1889 14 leaves in wreath					
		—	—	—	Proof	500.00
	1890	15.331	1.00	4.00	12.00	40.00
	1890	—	—	—	Proof	450.00
	1891	17.886	1.00	4.00	12.00	40.00
	1891	—	—	—	Proof	450.00
	1892	10.502	1.00	4.00	12.00	45.00
	1892	—	—	—	Proof	450.00
	1893	8.162	1.00	4.00	12.00	45.00
	1893	—	—	—	Proof	500.00
	1894	3.883	3.00	8.00	22.00	65.00

.4713 g, .925 SILVER, .0140 oz ASW

KM#	Date	Mintage	Fine	VF	XF	Unc
770	1888	.014	—	—	P/L	15.00
	1889	.014	—	—	P/L	15.00
	1890	.013	—	—	P/L	15.00
	1891	.022	—	—	P/L	15.00
	1892	.016	—	—	P/L	15.00

KM#	Date	Mintage	Fine	VF	XF	Unc
775	1893	.022	—	—	P/L	12.50
	1894	.018	—	—	P/L	12.50
	1895	.017	—	—	P/L	12.50
	1896	.017	—	—	P/L	12.50
	1897	.016	—	—	P/L	12.50
	1898	.017	—	—	P/L	12.50
	1899	.017	—	—	P/L	12.50
	1900	.017	—	—	P/L	12.50

NOTE: Later date (1901) exists for this type.

BRONZE

KM#	Date	Mintage	Fine	VF	XF	Unc
790	1895 P 2mm. from trident					
		5.396	15.00	40.00	120.00	275.00
	1895 P 2mm. from trident					
		Inc. Ab.	—	—	Proof	450.00
	1895 P 1mm. from trident					
		Inc. Ab.	.50	1.75	7.50	30.00
	1895 P 1mm. from trident					
		—	—	—	Proof	350.00
	1896	24.147	.40	1.25	4.50	28.00
	1896	—	—	—	Proof	325.00
	1897 normal sea level					
		20.757	.35	1.00	4.25	22.00
	1897 normal sea level					
		—	—	—	Proof	375.00
	1897 high sea level					
		Inc. Ab.	15.00	40.00	120.00	275.00
	1898	14.297	1.00	3.00	10.00	35.00
	1899	26.441	.40	1.50	5.25	28.00
	1900	31.778	.35	1.00	3.75	17.50

NOTE: Later date (1901) exists for this type.

1-1/2 PENCE

.7069 g, .925 SILVER, .0210 oz ASW

KM#	Date	Mintage	Fine	VF	XF	Unc
719	1834	.800	2.75	6.25	22.00	60.00
	1835/4	.634	12.00	30.00	45.00	150.00
	1835	Inc. Ab.	2.75	6.25	22.00	60.00
	1836	.158	2.75	6.25	22.00	60.00
	1837	.031	12.00	25.00	65.00	175.00

KM#	Date	Mintage	Fine	VF	XF	Unc
728	1838	.539	2.75	6.00	15.50	42.00
	1839	.760	2.50	6.00	15.00	40.00
	1840	.095	6.00	15.00	30.00	70.00
	1841	.158	3.00	7.00	20.00	45.00
	1842	1.869	3.00	7.00	20.00	45.00
	1843/34	.475	8.00	20.00	35.00	90.00
	1843	Inc. Ab.	2.00	5.00	15.00	40.00
	1860	.160	3.50	10.00	35.00	60.00
	1862	.256	3.50	10.00	30.00	55.00
	1870	—	—	—	Proof	900.00

***NOTE:** Although the design of the above series is of the homeland type, the issues were struck for Ceylon and Jamaica.

2 PENCE

.9426 g, .925 SILVER, .0280 oz ASW

KM#	Date	Mintage	Fine	VF	XF	Unc
669	1817	—	6.00	11.00	20.00	45.00
	1817	2,376	—	—	P/L	30.00
	1818	—	6.00	11.00	20.00	45.00
	1818	2,376	—	—	P/L	30.00
	1820	—	6.00	11.00	20.00	45.00
	1820	1,584	—	—	P/L	30.00

KM#	Date	Mintage	Fine	VF	XF	Unc
684	1822	5,940	—	—	P/L	30.00
	1823	3,960	—	—	P/L	35.00
	1824	3,168	—	—	P/L	40.00
	1825	3,960	—	—	P/L	35.00
	1826	3,960	—	—	P/L	35.00
	1827	3,960	—	—	P/L	35.00
	1828	3,960	—	—	P/L	35.00
	1829	3,960	—	—	P/L	35.00
	1830	3,960	—	—	P/L	35.00

KM#	Date	Mintage	Fine	VF	XF	Unc
709	1831	4,752	—	—	P/L	22.50
	1832	3,564	—	—	P/L	22.50
	1833	3,564	—	—	P/L	22.50
	1834	3,564	—	—	P/L	22.50
	1835	3,564	—	—	P/L	22.50
	1836	3,564	—	—	P/L	22.50
	1837	3,564	—	—	P/L	22.50

KM#	Date	Mintage	Fine	VF	XF	Unc
729	1838	*1.045	2.00	4.00	8.00	15.00
	1838	4,488	—	—	P/L	15.00
	1839	4,488	—	—	P/L	15.00
	1840	4,488	—	—	P/L	15.00
	1841	3,960	—	—	P/L	15.00
	1842	4,488	—	—	P/L	15.00
	1843	*.903	2.00	4.00	8.00	15.00
	1843	4,752	—	—	P/L	15.00
	1844	4,752	—	—	P/L	15.00
	1845	4,752	—	—	P/L	15.00
	1846	4,752	—	—	P/L	15.00
	1847	4,752	—	—	P/L	15.00
	1848	*.261	2.00	4.00	8.00	15.00
	1848	4,752	—	—	P/L	15.00
	1849	4,752	—	—	P/L	15.00
	1850	4,752	—	—	P/L	15.00
	1851	4,752	—	—	P/L	15.00
	1852	4,752	—	—	P/L	15.00
	1853	4,752	—	—	P/L	15.00
	1854	4,752	—	—	P/L	15.00
	1855	4,752	—	—	P/L	15.00
	1856	4,752	—	—	P/L	15.00
	1857	4,752	—	—	P/L	15.00
	1858	4,752	—	—	P/L	15.00
	1859	4,752	—	—	P/L	15.00
	1860	4,752	—	—	P/L	15.00
	1861	4,752	—	—	P/L	15.00
	1862	4,752	—	—	P/L	15.00
	1863	4,752	—	—	P/L	15.00
	1864	4,752	—	—	P/L	15.00
	1865	4,752	—	—	P/L	15.00
	1866	4,752	—	—	P/L	15.00
	1867	4,752	—	—	P/L	15.00
	1868	4,752	—	—	P/L	15.00
	1869	4,752	—	—	P/L	15.00
	1870	5,347	—	—	P/L	15.00
	1871	4,753	—	—	P/L	15.00
	1872	4,719	—	—	P/L	15.00
	1873	4,756	—	—	P/L	15.00
	1874	5,578	—	—	P/L	15.00
	1875	5,745	—	—	P/L	15.00
	1876	6,655	—	—	P/L	15.00
	1877	7,189	—	—	P/L	15.00
	1878	6,709	—	—	P/L	15.00
	1879	6,925	—	—	P/L	15.00
	1880	6,247	—	—	P/L	15.00
	1881	6,001	—	—	P/L	15.00
	1882	7,264	—	—	P/L	15.00
	1883	7,232	—	—	P/L	15.00
	1884	6,042	—	—	P/L	15.00
	1885	5,958	—	—	P/L	15.00
	1886	9,167	—	—	P/L	15.00
	1887	8,296	—	—	P/L	20.00

***NOTE:** Struck for use in British Guyana and the West Indies. Other dates included in Maundy sets.

KM#	Date	Mintage	Fine	VF	XF	Unc
771	1888	9,528	—	—	P/L	15.00
	1889	6,727	—	—	P/L	15.00
	1890	8,613	—	—	P/L	15.00
	1891	.010	—	—	P/L	15.00
	1892	.012	—	—	P/L	15.00

KM#	Date	Mintage	Fine	VF	XF	Unc
776	1893	.014	—	—	P/L	12.50
	1894	.012	—	—	P/L	12.50
	1895	.011	—	—	P/L	12.50
	1896	.011	—	—	P/L	12.50
	1897	.011	—	—	P/L	12.50
	1898	.012	—	—	P/L	12.50
	1899	.015	—	—	P/L	12.50
	1900	.011	—	—	P/L	12.50

NOTE: Later date (1901) exists for this type.

3 PENCE

1.4138 g, .925 SILVER, .0420 oz ASW
Obv: George III bust right. Rev: Value.

KM#	Date	Mintage	Fine	VF	XF	Unc
670	1817	—	7.00	15.00	30.00	70.00
	1817	1,584	—	—	P/L	70.00
	1818	—	7.00	15.00	30.00	70.00
	1818	1,584	—	—	P/L	70.00
	1820	—	7.00	15.00	30.00	70.00
	1820	1,320	—	—	P/L	70.00

Obv: Small head.

KM#	Date	Mintage	Fine	VF	XF	Unc
685.1	1822	3,960	—	—	P/L	80.00
	1822	—	—	—	Proof	—

Obv: Large head.

KM#	Date	Mintage	Fine	VF	XF	Unc
685.2	1823	2,640	—	—	P/L	55.00
	1824	2,112	—	—	P/L	65.00
	1825	3,432	—	—	P/L	55.00
	1826	3,432	—	—	P/L	55.00
	1827	3,168	—	—	P/L	55.00
	1828	3,168	—	—	P/L	55.00
	1829	3,168	—	—	P/L	55.00
	1830	3,168	—	—	P/L	55.00

KM#	Date	Mintage	Fine	VF	XF	Unc
710	1831	3,960	—	—	P/L	80.00
	1832	2,904	—	—	P/L	70.00
	1833	2,904	—	—	P/L	70.00
	1834	.400	3.00	8.00	26.00	110.00
	1834	2,904	—	—	P/L	70.00
	1835	.491	3.00	8.00	26.00	110.00
	1835	2,904	—	—	P/L	70.00
	1836	.411	3.00	8.00	25.00	90.00
	1836	2,904	—	—	P/L	70.00
	1837	.430	5.00	12.00	35.00	120.00
	1837	2,904	—	—	P/L	70.00

KM#	Date	Mintage	Fine	VF	XF	Unc
730	1838	1.200	2.50	6.00	30.00	72.00
	1838	4,312	—	—	P/L	40.00
	1839	.570	6.00	12.00	45.00	110.00
	1839	4,356	—	—	P/L	40.00
	1840	.630	2.75	8.00	40.00	80.00
	1840	4,356	—	—	P/L	40.00
	1841	.440	3.50	8.50	45.00	80.00
	1841	2,904	—	—	P/L	45.00
	1842	—	6.00	15.00	50.00	100.00
	1842	4,356	—	—	P/L	45.00
	1843	2.030	2.50	7.50	35.00	75.00
	1843	4,488	—	—	P/L	45.00
	1844	1.050	2.75	9.00	45.00	90.00
	1844	4,488	—	—	P/L	45.00
	1845	1.319	2.50	5.00	20.00	50.00
	1845	4,488	—	—	P/L	45.00
	1846	.052	8.00	20.00	60.00	125.00
	1846	4,488	—	—	P/L	45.00
	1847	4,488	—	—	P/L	45.00
	1848	4,488	—	—	P/L	45.00
	1849	.131	10.00	20.00	50.00	100.00
	1849	4,488	—	—	P/L	45.00
	1850	.955	2.50	5.00	25.00	55.00
	1850	4,488	—	—	P/L	45.00
	1851	.484	3.00	6.00	30.00	60.00
	1851	4,488	—	—	P/L	45.00
	1852	4,488	—	—	P/L	45.00
	1853	.036	10.00	20.00	60.00	150.00
	1853	4,488	—	—	P/L	45.00
	1854	1.472	2.50	5.50	30.00	60.00
	1854	4,488	—	—	P/L	45.00
	1855	.388	3.50	8.50	45.00	80.00
	1855	4,488	—	—	P/L	45.00
	1856	1.018	2.50	8.00	40.00	70.00
	1856	4,488	—	—	P/L	45.00
	1857	1.767	2.75	8.00	40.00	70.00
	1857	4,488	—	—	P/L	45.00
	1858	1.446	2.50	5.50	30.00	60.00
	1858	4,488	—	—	P/L	45.00
	1859	3.584	2.50	5.00	20.00	40.00
	1859	4,488	—	—	P/L	45.00
	1860	3.410	2.50	5.50	26.00	55.00
	1860	4,488	—	—	P/L	45.00
	1861	3.299	2.50	5.00	22.00	40.00
	1861	4,488	—	—	P/L	45.00
	1862	1.161	2.50	5.50	30.00	60.00
	1862	4,488	—	—	P/L	45.00
	1863	.954	4.00	9.00	40.00	75.00
	1863	4,488	—	—	P/L	45.00
	1864	1.335	2.50	5.50	30.00	60.00
	1864	4,488	—	—	P/L	45.00
	1865	1.747	3.00	9.00	40.00	75.00
	1865	4,488	—	—	P/L	45.00
	1866	1.905	2.50	5.50	30.00	65.00
	1866	4,488	—	—	P/L	45.00
	1867	.717	3.00	6.00	40.00	75.00
	1867	4,488	—	—	P/L	45.00
	1868	1.462	2.50	5.00	30.00	65.00
	1868	4,488	—	—	P/L	45.00
	1868 (error) RRITANIAR					
		Inc. Ab.	22.50	55.00	225.00	450.00
	1869	—	50.00	125.00	240.00	500.00
	1869	4,488	—	—	P/L	45.00
	1870	1.288	2.50	4.50	25.00	50.00
	1870	4,488	—	—	P/L	45.00
	1871	1.004	2.50	5.50	26.00	55.00
	1871	4,488	—	—	P/L	45.00
	1872	1.298	1.75	4.25	22.50	45.00
	1872	4,488	—	—	P/L	45.00
	1873	4.060	1.75	4.25	20.00	40.00
	1873	4,488	—	—	P/L	45.00
	1874	4.432	1.75	4.25	20.00	40.00
	1874	4,488	—	—	P/L	45.00
	1875	3.311	1.75	4.25	18.00	35.00
	1875	4,488	—	—	P/L	45.00
	1876	1.839	1.75	4.25	18.00	35.00
	1876	4,488	—	—	P/L	45.00
	1877	2.627	1.75	4.25	18.00	35.00
	1877	4,488	—	—	P/L	45.00
	1878	2.424	1.75	4.25	18.00	35.00
	1878	4,488	—	—	P/L	45.00
	1879	3.145	1.75	4.25	18.00	35.00
	1879	4,488	—	—	P/L	45.00
	1879	—	—	—	Proof	150.00
	1880	1.615	1.50	3.50	18.00	35.00
	1880	4,488	—	—	P/L	45.00
	1881	3.253	1.40	3.25	17.00	35.00
	1881	4,488	—	—	P/L	45.00
	1882	.447	3.00	6.00	30.00	60.00
	1882	4,488	—	—	P/L	45.00
	1883	4.374	1.45	3.50	15.00	30.00
	1883	4,488	—	—	P/L	45.00
	1884	3.327	1.45	3.50	15.00	30.00
	1884	4,488	—	—	P/L	45.00
	1885	5.188	1.45	3.50	15.00	30.00
	1885	4,488	—	—	P/L	45.00
	1886	6.157	1.45	3.50	15.00	30.00
	1886	4,488	—	—	P/L	45.00
	1887	2.785	3.50	8.50	25.00	55.00
	1887	4,488	—	—	P/L	45.00
	1887	—	—	—	Proof	100.00

KM#	Date	Mintage	Fine	VF	XF	Unc
758	1887	Inc. Ab.	1.25	2.25	4.50	15.00
	1887	Inc. Ab.	—	—	Proof	70.00
	1888	.523	3.00	6.00	15.00	30.00
	1888	4,488	—	—	P/L	40.00
	1889	4.591	1.50	2.75	12.50	25.00
	1889	4,488	—	—	P/L	40.00
	1890	4.470	1.50	2.75	12.50	25.00
	1890	4,488	—	—	P/L	40.00
	1891	6.328	1.50	2.75	12.50	25.00
	1891	4,488	—	—	P/L	40.00
	1892	2.583	2.00	3.00	12.50	25.00
	1892	4,488	—	—	P/L	40.00
	1893 open 3					
		3.076	25.00	50.00	120.00	225.00
	1893 closed 3					
		Inc. Ab.	20.00	40.00	100.00	200.00

KM#	Date	Mintage	Fine	VF	XF	Unc
777	1893	Inc. Ab.	1.00	2.00	5.00	25.00
	1893	8,976	—	—	P/L	30.00
	1893	1,312	—	—	Proof	75.00
	1894	1.618	1.00	2.75	8.00	28.00
	1894	8,976	—	—	P/L	30.00
	1895	4.798	.85	2.75	8.00	28.00
	1895	8,976	—	—	P/L	30.00
	1896	4.607	.85	1.75	7.00	20.00
	1896	8,976	—	—	P/L	30.00
	1897	4.550	.85	1.75	5.00	18.00
	1897	8,976	—	—	P/L	30.00
	1898	4.576	.85	1.75	5.00	18.00
	1898	8,976	—	—	P/L	30.00
	1899	6.253	.85	1.75	5.00	18.00
	1899	8,976	—	—	P/L	30.00
	1900	10.661	.85	1.75	4.50	18.00
	1900	8,976	—	—	P/L	30.00

NOTE: Later date (1901) exists for this type.

4 PENCE (GROAT)

1.8851 g, .925 SILVER, .0561 oz ASW
Obv: Old head of George III. Rev: Value.

KM#	Date	Mintage	Fine	VF	XF	Unc
671	1817	—	10.00	22.50	40.00	90.00
	1817	1,386	—	—	P/L	70.00
	1818	—	10.00	22.50	40.00	90.00
	1818	1,188	—	—	P/L	70.00
	1820	—	10.00	22.50	40.00	90.00
	1820	990 pcs.	—	—	P/L	70.00

KM#	Date	Mintage	Fine	VF	XF	Unc
686	1822	—	9.00	15.00	25.00	50.00
	1822	2,970	—	—	P/L	70.00
	1823	—	9.00	15.00	25.00	50.00
	1823	1,980	—	—	P/L	60.00
	1824	—	9.00	15.00	25.00	50.00
	1824	1,584	—	—	P/L	65.00
	1825	—	9.00	15.00	25.00	50.00
	1825	2,376	—	—	P/L	60.00
	1826	—	9.00	15.00	25.00	50.00
	1826	2,376	—	—	P/L	60.00
	1827	—	9.00	15.00	25.00	50.00
	1827	2,772	—	—	P/L	60.00
	1828	—	9.00	15.00	25.00	50.00
	1828	2,772	—	—	P/L	60.00
	1829	—	9.00	15.00	25.00	50.00
	1829	2,772	—	—	P/L	60.00
	1830	—	9.00	15.00	25.00	50.00
	1830	2,772	—	—	P/L	60.00

KM#	Date	Mintage	Fine	VF	XF	Unc
711	1831	—	5.00	12.00	22.50	45.00
	1831	3,564	—	—	P/L	55.00
	1832	—	5.00	12.00	22.50	45.00
	1832	2,574	—	—	P/L	40.00
	1833	—	5.00	12.00	22.50	45.00
	1833	2,574	—	—	P/L	40.00
	1834	—	5.00	12.00	22.50	45.00
	1834	2,574	—	—	P/L	40.00
	1835	—	5.00	12.00	22.50	45.00
	1835	2,574	—	—	P/L	40.00
	1836	—	5.00	12.00	22.50	45.00
	1836	2,574	—	—	P/L	40.00
	1837	—	6.00	12.00	22.50	45.00
	1837	2,574	—	—	P/L	40.00

KM#	Date	Mintage	Fine	VF	XF	Unc
723	1836	4.253	2.25	5.25	17.50	50.00
	1836 reeded edge		—	—	Proof	600.00
	1836 plain edge		—	—	Proof	300.00
	1837	.962	4.00	8.00	20.00	60.00
	1837				Proof	225.00

***NOTE:** Although the design of the above coin is of the homeland type, the issues were primarily used for circulation in British Guiana.

KM#	Date	Mintage	Fine	VF	XF	Unc
731.1	1838	2.150	2.25	5.25	17.50	45.00
	1838/8 second 8 over horizontal 8	Inc. Ab.	6.00	12.50	45.00	100.00
	1839	1.461	3.00	8.00	25.00	60.00
	1840	1.497	2.75	7.00	22.50	50.00
	1841	.345	4.50	13.00	35.00	75.00
	1842/1	.725	6.00	15.00	37.50	90.00
	1842	Inc. Ab.	4.00	8.00	27.50	70.00
	1842	—	—	—	Proof	500.00
	1843	1.818	3.50	8.00	27.50	70.00
	1844	.855	5.00	13.00	35.00	75.00
	1845	.915	3.50	8.00	27.50	60.00
	1846	1.366	3.50	8.00	27.50	60.00
	1847/6	.226	30.00	55.00	120.00	220.00
	1848/6	.713	3.50	10.00	32.50	70.00
	1848/7	Inc. Ab.	3.50	10.00	32.50	70.00
	1848	Inc. Ab.	3.00	7.00	22.50	50.00
	1849/8	.380	6.00	15.00	55.00	125.00
	1849	Inc. Ab.	3.50	10.00	32.50	70.00
	1851	.031	12.50	45.00	130.00	235.00
	1852	—	70.00	135.00	325.00	700.00
	1853	.012	65.00	125.00	300.00	650.00
	1853	—	—	—	Proof	500.00
	1854	1.097	2.75	7.00	22.50	50.00
	1855	.646	4.00	8.00	22.50	50.00
	1857	3-4 known	—	—	Proof	1400.
	1862	—	—	—	Proof	800.00

NOTE: The above issue was produced for circulation in both Great Britain and British Guiana.

Plain edge.

KM#	Date	Mintage	Fine	VF	XF	Unc
731.2	1838	—	—	—	Proof	200.00
	1839	—	—	—	Proof	200.00
	1853	*10-15 pcs.	—	—	Proof	Rare

KM#	Date	Mintage	Fine	VF	XF	Unc
732	1838	4,158	—	—	P/L	17.50
	1839	4,125	—	—	P/L	17.50
	1840	4,125	—	—	P/L	17.50
	1841	2,574	—	—	P/L	20.00
	1842	4,125	—	—	P/L	17.50
	1843	4,158	—	—	P/L	17.50
	1844	4,158	—	—	P/L	17.50
	1845	4,158	—	—	P/L	17.50
	1846	4,158	—	—	P/L	17.50
	1847	4,158	—	—	P/L	17.50
	1848	4,158	—	—	P/L	17.50
	1849	4,158	—	—	P/L	17.50
	1850	4,158	—	—	P/L	17.50
	1851	4,158	—	—	P/L	17.50
	1852	4,158	—	—	P/L	17.50
	1853	4,158	—	—	P/L	17.50
	1854	4,158	—	—	P/L	17.50
	1855	4,158	—	—	P/L	17.50
	1856	4,158	—	—	P/L	17.50
	1857	4,158	—	—	P/L	17.50
	1858	4,158	—	—	P/L	17.50
	1859	4,158	—	—	P/L	17.50
	1860	4,158	—	—	P/L	17.50
	1861	4,158	—	—	P/L	17.50
	1862	4,158	—	—	P/L	17.50
	1863	4,158	—	—	P/L	17.50
	1864	4,158	—	—	P/L	17.50
	1865	4,158	—	—	P/L	17.50
	1866	4,158	—	—	P/L	17.50
	1867	4,158	—	—	P/L	17.50
	1868	4,158	—	—	P/L	17.50
	1869	4,158	—	—	P/L	17.50
	1870	4,569	—	—	P/L	17.50
	1871	4,627	—	—	P/L	17.50
	1872	4,328	—	—	P/L	17.50
	1873	4,162	—	—	P/L	17.50
	1874	5,937	—	—	P/L	17.50
	1875	4,154	—	—	P/L	17.50
	1876	4,862	—	—	P/L	17.50
	1877	4,850	—	—	P/L	17.50
	1878	5,735	—	—	P/L	17.50
	1879	5,202	—	—	P/L	17.50
	1880	5,199	—	—	P/L	17.50
	1881	6,203	—	—	P/L	17.50
	1882	4,146	—	—	P/L	17.50
	1883	5,096	—	—	P/L	17.50
	1884	5,353	—	—	P/L	17.50
	1885	5,791	—	—	P/L	17.50
	1886	6,785	—	—	P/L	17.50
	1887	5,292	—	—	P/L	17.50

KM#	Date	Mintage	Fine	VF	XF	Unc
772	1888	.120	4.00	11.50	25.00	55.00
	1888	—	—	—	Proof	125.00

NOTE: The above piece was exclusively for use in British Guiana and the West Indies.

KM#	Date	Mintage	Fine	VF	XF	Unc
773	1888	9,583	—	—	P/L	20.00
	1889	6,088	—	—	P/L	20.00
	1890	9,087	—	—	P/L	20.00
	1891	.011	—	—	P/L	20.00
	1892	8,524	—	—	P/L	20.00

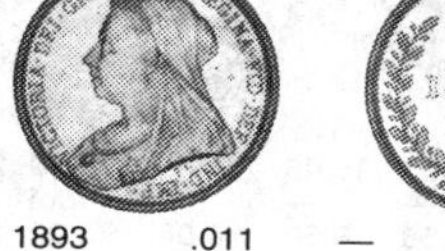

KM#	Date	Mintage	Fine	VF	XF	Unc
778	1893	.011	—	—	P/L	15.00
	1894	9,385	—	—	P/L	15.00
	1896	8,476	—	—	P/L	15.00
	1897	9,388	—	—	P/L	15.00
	1898	9,147	—	—	P/L	15.00
	1899	.014	—	—	P/L	15.00
	1900	9,571	—	—	P/L	15.00

NOTE: Later date (1901) exists for this type.

6 PENCE

2.8276 g, .925 SILVER, .0841 oz ASW

KM#	Date	Mintage	Fine	VF	XF	Unc
665	1816	—	3.50	8.50	25.00	65.00
	1816	—	—	—	Proof	750.00
	1817	10.922	3.50	8.00	25.00	65.00
	1817	—	—	—	Proof	500.00
	1817 plain edge	—	—	—	Proof	500.00
	1818	4.285	8.00	17.50	60.00	140.00
	1818	—	—	—	Proof	700.00
	1819/8	—	6.00	15.00	50.00	140.00
	1819/8	—	—	—	Proof	750.00
	1819	4.712	4.25	9.00	30.00	70.00
	1819	1.489	—	—	Proof	1000.
	1820 inverted 1	1.489	25.00	85.00	275.00	500.00
	1820	Inc. Ab.	4.25	9.00	32.00	85.00
	1820	—	—	—	Proof	—

KM#	Date	Mintage	Fine	VF	XF	Unc
678	1821	.863	8.00	18.00	60.00	200.00
	1821	—	—	—	Proof	500.00
	1821 (error) BBITANNIAR	—	50.00	150.00	500.00	900.00

KM#	Date	Mintage	Fine	VF	XF	Unc
691	1824	.634	8.00	18.00	60.00	185.00
	1824	—	—	—	Proof	750.00
	1825	.483	6.00	14.00	55.00	160.00
	1825	—	—	—	Proof	300.00
	1826	.689	20.00	60.00	220.00	500.00
	1826	—	—	—	Proof	400.00

KM#	Date	Mintage	Fine	VF	XF	Unc
698	1826	Inc. Ab.	5.00	12.00	55.00	145.00
	1826	Inc. Ab.	—	—	Proof	250.00
	1827	.166	20.00	50.00	125.00	300.00
	1828	.016	8.00	25.00	85.00	225.00
	1829	.404	6.00	20.00	75.00	165.00
	1829	—	—	—	Proof	—

KM#	Date	Mintage	Fine	VF	XF	Unc
712	1831	1.340	4.50	17.50	65.00	150.00
	1831	Inc. Ab.	—	—	Proof	250.00
	1831 plain edge	—	—	—	Proof	250.00
	1834	5.892	4.50	15.00	55.00	140.00
	1834	—	—	—	Proof	—
	1834 round-topped 3	Inc. Ab.	—	—	Proof	—
	1835	1.555	6.00	20.00	60.00	145.00
	1835 round-topped 3	Inc. Ab.	—	—	Proof	—
	1836	1.988	11.00	37.50	120.00	240.00
	1836 round-topped 3	Inc. Ab.	—	—	Proof	—
	1837	.507	7.50	22.50	115.00	200.00
	1837	—	—	—	Proof	—

PALLADIUM

KM#	Date	Mintage	Fine	VF	XF	Unc
712a	1831	—	—	—	Proof	—

3.0100 g, .925 SILVER, .0895 oz ASW
Rev: W/o die numbers.

KM#	Date	Mintage	Fine	VF	XF	Unc
733.1	1838	1.608	4.25	12.00	50.00	130.00
	1838	—	—	—	Proof	200.00
	1839	3.311	4.25	12.00	50.00	130.00
	1839	Inc. Ab.	—	—	Proof	300.00
	1840	2.099	5.00	12.50	65.00	140.00
	1841	1.386	5.50	15.00	70.00	145.00
	1842	.602	5.50	15.00	80.00	180.00
	1843	3.160	5.00	12.50	65.00	150.00
	1844	3.976	4.25	12.00	50.00	125.00
	1844 large 44	Inc. Ab.	4.25	15.00	60.00	150.00
	1845	3.714	4.25	12.00	50.00	125.00

KM#	Date	Mintage	Fine	VF	XF	Unc
733.1	1846	4.267	4.25	12.00	50.00	125.00
	1847	—	—	Reported, not confirmed		
	1848/6	.586	22.00	60.00	235.00	525.00
	1848/7	Inc. Ab.	22.00	60.00	235.00	525.00
	1848	Inc. Ab.	22.00	60.00	235.00	525.00
	1849	.210	—	None reported		—
	1850/30	.499	7.50	25.00	90.00	—
	1850	Inc. Ab.	5.50	20.00	75.00	180.00
	1851	2.288	5.50	15.00	50.00	125.00
	1852	.905	5.50	15.00	50.00	135.00
	1853	3.838	4.25	12.00	45.00	120.00
	1853	*40 pcs.	—	—	Proof	450.00
	1854	.840	35.00	95.00	340.00	595.00
	1855	1.129	4.25	12.00	50.00	125.00
	1855	—	—	—	Proof	—
	1856	2.780	4.25	12.00	50.00	125.00
	1857	2.233	4.25	12.00	65.00	140.00
	1858	1.932	4.25	12.00	65.00	140.00
	1858	—	—	—	Proof	600.00
	1859/8	4.689	4.25	15.00	60.00	145.00
	1859	Inc. Ab.	4.25	12.00	50.00	135.00
	1860	1.101	4.25	12.00	60.00	145.00
	1861	.600	—	Reported, not confirmed		
	1862	.990	22.00	45.00	200.00	375.00
	1863	.491	12.00	30.00	135.00	250.00
	1866	5.140	22.50	45.00	75.00	200.00

Rev: W/die numbers.

KM#	Date	Mintage	Fine	VF	XF	Unc
733.2	1864	4.253	4.25	12.00	50.00	125.00
	1865	1.632	5.50	14.00	55.00	135.00
	1866	Inc.Ab.	4.25	12.00	50.00	125.00

Obv: New portrait. Rev: W/die numbers.

KM#	Date	Mintage	Fine	VF	XF	Unc
751.1	1867	1.362	7.00	20.00	70.00	175.00
	1867	—	—	—	Proof	1000.
	1868	1.069	7.00	20.00	70.00	175.00
	1869	.388	7.50	22.50	75.00	200.00
	1869	—	—	—	Proof	1000.
	1870	.480	8.00	20.00	75.00	200.00
	1870	—	—	—	Proof	1000.
	1870 plain edge		—	—	Proof	1000.
	1871	3.663	5.00	12.50	35.00	65.00
	1871	—	—	—	Proof	1000.
	1871 plain edge		—	—	Proof	1000.
	1872	3.382	5.00	12.50	35.00	65.00
	1873	4.595	3.50	10.00	30.00	60.00
	1874	4.226	3.00	9.00	30.00	60.00
	1875	3.257	3.00	9.00	30.00	60.00
	1876	.841	8.00	20.00	65.00	150.00
	1877	4.066	3.50	10.00	30.00	65.00
	1878/7	2.625	25.00	75.00	200.00	400.00
	1878	—	—	—	Proof	1000.
	1878 (error) DRITANNIAR					
		Inc. Ab.	25.00	75.00	350.00	900.00
	1879	3.326	7.00	20.00	70.00	175.00
	1879	—	—	—	Proof	1000.

Rev: W/o die numbers.

KM#	Date	Mintage	Fine	VF	XF	Unc
751.2	1871	Inc. Ab.	8.00	20.00	50.00	125.00
	1877	Inc. Ab.	4.25	11.50	40.00	90.00
	1878	Inc. Ab.	3.50	11.00	40.00	90.00
	1879	Inc. Ab.	4.50	12.00	40.00	90.00
	1880 obverse of 1879					
		3.892	6.00	15.00	50.00	110.00

Obv: New portrait, longer hair waves.

KM#	Date	Mintage	Fine	VF	XF	Unc
757	1880	Inc. Ab.	3.50	10.00	30.00	70.00
	1880	—	—	—	Proof	1000.
	1881	6.239	3.00	8.00	22.00	45.00
	1881	—	—	—	Proof	1000.
	1881 plain edge		—	—	Proof	1000.
	1882	.760	8.00	20.00	60.00	130.00
	1883	4.987	3.25	8.50	22.00	45.00
	1884	3.423	3.25	8.50	22.00	45.00
	1885	4.653	3.25	8.50	22.00	45.00
	1885	—	—	—	Proof	800.00
	1886	2.728	3.25	8.50	22.00	42.00
	1886	—	—	—	Proof	800.00
	1887	3.676	2.75	7.00	22.00	42.00
	1887	—	—	—	Proof	800.00

KM#	Date	Mintage	Fine	VF	XF	Unc
759	1887	Inc.KM757	1.50	3.00	6.00	12.00
	1887	—	—	—	Proof	225.00

KM#	Date	Mintage	Fine	VF	XF	Unc
760	1887	Inc.KM757	2.00	3.50	7.00	15.00
	1887	Inc.KM757	—	—	Proof	225.00
	1888	4.198	2.00	6.00	17.50	40.00
	1888	—	—	—	Proof	1500.
	1889	8.739	2.00	5.00	15.00	40.00
	1890	9.387	2.00	6.00	17.50	40.00
	1890	—	—	—	Proof	700.00
	1891	7.023	2.75	6.00	17.50	40.00
	1892	6.246	2.75	6.00	17.50	40.00
	1893	.341	150.00	300.00	810.00	1800.

KM#	Date	Mintage	Fine	VF	XF	Unc
779	1893	7.010	1.75	4.25	15.00	30.00
	1893	1,312	—	—	Proof	140.00
	1894	3.468	3.50	7.00	17.50	42.00
	1895	7.025	2.50	5.00	15.00	38.00
	1896	6.652	2.50	5.00	15.00	38.00
	1897	5.031	2.50	5.00	12.50	38.00
	1898	5.914	2.50	5.00	12.50	38.00
	1899	7.997	2.50	5.00	15.00	38.00
	1900	8.980	2.50	5.00	12.50	27.50

NOTE: Later date (1901) exists for this type.

SHILLING

5.6552 g, .925 SILVER, .1682 oz ASW

KM#	Date	Mintage	Fine	VF	XF	Unc
666	1816	—	3.50	8.50	30.00	90.00
	1816	—	—	—	Proof	750.00
	1816 plain edge		—	—	Proof	750.00
	1817	23.031	4.25	10.00	35.00	100.00
	1817 plain edge		—	—	Proof	650.00
	1818	1.342	12.50	35.00	75.00	250.00
	1818 (error) GEOR/E					
		Inc. Ab.	—	—	—	—
	1819/8	7.595	9.00	22.00	100.00	300.00
	1819	Inc. Ab.	4.25	10.00	45.00	135.00
	1820	7.975	4.25	10.00	45.00	135.00
	1820	—	—	—	Proof	650.00

KM#	Date	Mintage	Fine	VF	XF	Unc
679	1821	2.463	7.50	15.00	100.00	200.00
	1821	—	—	—	Proof	650.00

KM#	Date	Mintage	Fine	VF	XF	Unc
687	1823	.693	15.00	45.00	130.00	275.00
	1823	—	—	—	Proof	1000.
	1824	4.158	6.50	16.00	75.00	185.00
	1824	—	—	—	Proof	1000.
	1825/3	2.459	6.50	16.00	80.00	225.00
	1825	Inc. Ab.	6.50	16.00	80.00	225.00
	1825	—	—	—	Proof	750.00

KM#	Date	Mintage	Fine	VF	XF	Unc
694	1825	Inc. Ab.	4.25	10.00	75.00	220.00
	1825	—	—	—	Proof	275.00
	1825 plain edge		—	—	Proof	325.00
	1826/2	6.352	—	—	—	—
	1826	Inc.Ab.	4.25	10.00	75.00	220.00
	1826	—	—	—	Proof	275.00
	1827	.574	10.00	30.00	150.00	300.00
	1828	—	10.00	30.00	150.00	300.00
	1829	.879	8.00	25.00	120.00	260.00
	1829	—	—	—	Proof	750.00

KM#	Date	Mintage	Fine	VF	XF	Unc
713	1831 plain edge		—	—	Proof	675.00
	1831 milled edge		—	—	Proof	750.00
	1834	3.223	7.00	20.00	80.00	220.00
	1834	—	—	—	Proof	1200.
	1835	1.449	8.50	30.00	110.00	250.00
	1835	—	—	—	Proof	1200.
	1836	3.568	7.00	20.00	80.00	185.00
	1836	—	—	—	Proof	1400.
	1837	.479	10.00	30.00	125.00	300.00
	1837	—	—	—	Proof	1400.

High relief. W/o die numbers.

KM#	Date	Mintage	Fine	VF	XF	Unc
734.1	1838WW	1.956	7.00	20.00	55.00	160.00
	1838	Inc. Ab.	—	—	Proof	700.00
	1839WW	5.667	7.00	20.00	60.00	165.00
	1839WW	—	—	—	Proof	325.00
	1839	Inc. Ab.	6.50	17.50	50.00	155.00
	1839	Inc. Ab.	—	—	Proof	325.00
	1840	1.639	15.00	50.00	150.00	350.00
	1840	—	—	—	Proof	500.00
	1841	.875	10.00	30.00	95.00	275.00
	1842	2.095	6.50	17.50	50.00	155.00
	1842	—	—	—	Proof	1500.
	1843	1.465	9.00	30.00	85.00	240.00
	1844	4.467	6.50	17.50	50.00	155.00
	1845	4.083	7.00	20.00	70.00	170.00
	1846	4.031	6.50	17.50	65.00	170.00
	1848/6	1.041	25.00	75.00	300.00	425.00
	1849	.645	8.00	20.00	75.00	175.00
	1850/46	.685	175.00	525.00	1600.	3600.
	1850	Inc. Ab.	175.00	525.00	1600.	3600.
	1851	.470	45.00	145.00	550.00	1365.
	1851	—	—	—	Proof	2000.
	1852	1.307	6.50	17.50	50.00	140.00
	1853	4.256	6.50	17.50	45.00	135.00
	1853	—	—	—	Proof	600.00
	1854	.552	40.00	150.00	450.00	1100.
	1855	1.368	6.50	17.50	65.00	165.00
	1856	3.168	6.50	17.50	65.00	165.00
	1857	2.562	6.50	17.50	65.00	165.00
	1858	3.109	6.50	17.50	65.00	165.00
	1858	—	—	—	Proof	1200.
	1859	4.562	6.50	17.50	65.00	165.00
	1860	1.671	8.50	22.50	90.00	200.00
	1861	1.382	8.50	22.50	90.00	200.00
	1862	.954	20.00	70.00	125.00	300.00
	1863	.859	20.00	75.00	190.00	375.00

W/die numbers.

KM#	Date	Mintage	Fine	VF	XF	Unc
734.3	1864	4.519	4.50	15.00	50.00	150.00
	1865	5.619	4.50	15.00	50.00	150.00
	1866	4.990	4.50	15.00	50.00	150.00
	1867	2.166	5.00	17.50	60.00	165.00
	1867 (error) 'BBITANNIAR'					
		—	—	—	—	—
	1867	—	—	—	Proof	1000.
	1867 plain edge		—	—	Proof	—

Low relief, w/die numbers.

KM#	Date	Mintage	Fine	VF	XF	Unc
734.2	1867	—	30.00	80.00	320.00	550.00
	1868	3.330	6.50	18.00	65.00	165.00
	1869	.737	8.00	25.00	85.00	190.00
	1870	1.467	7.00	20.00	80.00	175.00
	1871	4.910	5.50	12.50	45.00	125.00
	1871	—	—	—	Proof	—
	1871 plain edge		—	—	Proof	1000.
	1872	8.898	5.50	12.50	45.00	125.00
	1873	6.590	5.50	12.50	45.00	125.00
	1874	5.504	5.50	12.50	45.00	125.00
	1875	4.354	5.50	12.50	45.00	125.00
	1876	1.057	6.00	15.00	65.00	160.00

KM#	Date	Mintage	Fine	VF	XF	Unc
734.2	1877	2.981	5.00	12.00	40.00	90.00
	1878	3.127	5.00	12.00	40.00	90.00
	1878	—	—	—	Proof	1200.
	1879	3.611	17.00	45.00	150.00	255.00

W/o die numbers.

KM#	Date	Mintage	Fine	VF	XF	Unc
734.4	1879	Inc. Ab.	6.50	17.00	65.00	160.00
	1880	4.843	4.25	9.00	35.00	90.00
	1880	—	—	—	Proof	1000.
	1880 plain edge		—	—	Proof	1200.
	1881	5.255	4.25	9.00	35.00	90.00
	1881	—	—	—	Proof	1200.
	1881 plain edge		—	—	Proof	1500.
	1882	1.612	10.00	27.50	75.00	190.00
	1883	7.281	4.25	8.50	30.00	90.00
	1884	3.924	4.25	8.50	30.00	90.00
	1884	—	—	—	Proof	1000.
	1885	3.337	4.25	8.50	30.00	90.00
	1885	—	—	—	Proof	1000.
	1886	2.087	4.25	8.50	30.00	90.00
	1886	—	—	—	Proof	1000.
	1887	4.034	7.00	19.00	55.00	165.00
	1887	—	—	—	Proof	1000.

Small bust

KM#	Date	Mintage	Fine	VF	XF	Unc
761	1887	Inc. Ab.	2.00	3.00	8.00	25.00
	1887	1,084	—	—	Proof	125.00
	1888/7	4.527	3.50	7.00	30.00	65.00
	1888	Inc. Ab.	3.00	6.00	20.00	55.00
	1889	7.040	35.00	65.00	400.00	800.00
	1889	—	—	—	Proof	2000.

Large bust

KM#	Date	Mintage	Fine	VF	XF	Unc
774	1889	—	2.50	5.50	17.00	60.00
	1889	—	—	—	Proof	150.00
	1890	8.794	3.00	7.50	22.50	65.00
	1891	5.665	3.00	8.00	26.00	75.00
	1891	—	—	—	Proof	1250.
	1892	4.592	3.50	8.00	26.00	120.00

KM#	Date	Mintage	Fine	VF	XF	Unc
780	1893	7.039	2.75	5.50	20.00	45.00
	1893	1,312	—	—	Proof	125.00
	1894	5.953	3.50	7.00	20.00	60.00
	1895	8.800	2.75	6.00	20.00	55.00
	1896	9.265	2.75	6.00	20.00	55.00
	1897	6.270	2.75	6.00	20.00	55.00
	1898	9.769	2.75	6.00	20.00	55.00
	1899	10.965	2.75	6.00	20.00	55.00
	1900	10.938	2.75	6.00	20.00	55.00

NOTE: Later date (1901) exists for this type.

FLORIN - TWO SHILLINGS

11.3104 g, .925 SILVER, .3364 oz ASW

KM#	Date	Mintage	Fine	VF	XF	Unc
745	1848	—	—	—	Proof	3500.
	1848 plain edge		—	—	Proof	1250.
	1849	.414	12.50	30.00	65.00	250.00

Gothic type. Obv. leg: BRIT. . .
W/o die numbers.

KM#	Date	Mintage	Fine	VF	XF	Unc
746.1	1851	1,540	—	—	—	—
	1851	—	25.00	—	Proof	8000.
	1852	1.015	8.50	32.00	90.00	275.00
	1852	—	—	—	Proof	1500.
	1853	3.920	8.75	35.00	100.00	325.00
	1853	—	—	—	Proof	1750.
	1854	.550	350.00	700.00	1500.	2000.
	1855	.831	8.50	32.00	110.00	350.00
	1856	2.202	8.75	35.00	110.00	325.00
	1857	1.671	8.50	32.00	110.00	325.00
	1857	—	—	—	Proof	2000.
	1858	2.239	8.50	32.00	110.00	325.00
	1858	—	—	—	Proof	3000.
	1859	2.568	8.50	32.00	110.00	325.00
	1860	1.475	13.00	40.00	150.00	450.00
	1862	.594	25.00	100.00	400.00	900.00
	1862 plain edge		—	—	Proof	4000.
	1863	.939	35.00	140.00	475.00	1000.
	1863 plain edge		—	—	Proof	3000.

W/die numbers.

KM#	Date	Mintage	Fine	VF	XF	Unc
746.3	1864	1.861	8.00	32.00	110.00	350.00
	1864	—	—	—	Proof	3000.
	1865	1.580	8.50	32.00	110.00	325.00
	1866	.915	8.50	32.00	115.00	400.00
	1867	.424	20.00	60.00	250.00	700.00
	1867 plain edge		—	—	Proof	4000.

Obv. leg: BRITT. . . w/die number.

KM#	Date	Mintage	Fine	VF	XF	Unc
746.2	1868	.870	8.50	32.00	110.00	400.00
	1869	.297	8.50	32.00	95.00	285.00
	1869	—	—	—	Proof	2000.
	1870	1.081	8.50	32.00	110.00	350.00
	1871	3.426	8.50	32.00	110.00	350.00
	1871	—	—	—	Proof	2250.
	1871 plain edge		—	—	Proof	2250.
	1872	7.200	8.00	30.00	90.00	250.00
	1873	5.922	8.00	32.00	90.00	250.00
	1873	—	—	—	Proof	2500.
	1874	1.643	8.50	32.00	95.00	285.00
	1875	1.117	8.50	32.00	95.00	285.00
	1876	.580	8.50	32.00	100.00	320.00
	1877	.682	8.50	32.00	100.00	320.00
	1878	1.787	8.50	32.00	100.00	325.00
	1878	—	—	—	Proof	2750.
	1879	1.512	15.00	50.00	150.00	375.00

W/o die numbers.

KM#	Date	Mintage	Fine	VF	XF	Unc
746.4	1877	Inc. Ab.	25.00	70.00	300.00	650.00
	1878	Inc. Ab.	8.50	32.00	100.00	325.00
	1878	—	—	—	Proof	4500.
	1879	Inc. Ab.	12.50	35.00	125.00	350.00
	1879	—	—	—	Proof	2250.
	1880	2.161	8.00	30.00	85.00	275.00
	1880	—	—	—	Proof	4000.
	1881	2.576	8.00	30.00	85.00	275.00
	1881	—	—	—	Proof	2250.
	1881 plain edge		—	—	Proof	2500.
	1881 (error) MDCCCLXXRI					
		Inc. Ab.	12.00	40.00	120.00	300.00
	1883	3.556	8.00	30.00	90.00	240.00
	1884	1.447	8.00	30.00	90.00	280.00
	1885	1.758	8.00	30.00	80.00	240.00
	1885	—	—	—	Proof	2000.
	1886	.592	8.50	32.00	100.00	300.00
	1886	—	—	—	Proof	2000.
	1887	1.777	10.00	40.00	120.00	375.00
	1887	—	—	—	Proof	2000.

NOTE: Varieties exist.

KM#	Date	Mintage	Fine	VF	XF	Unc
762	1887	Inc. Ab.	3.00	6.00	16.00	40.00
	1887	1,084	—	—	Proof	150.00
	1888	1.548	4.25	8.50	25.00	70.00
	1889	2.974	4.25	8.50	25.00	70.00
	1890	1.685	8.50	30.00	95.00	200.00
	1891	.836	16.50	55.00	165.00	300.00
	1892	.283	17.50	60.00	200.00	400.00
	1892	—	—	—	Proof	1500.

KM#	Date	Mintage	Fine	VF	XF	Unc
781	1893	1.666	4.25	12.50	25.00	70.00
	1893	1,312	—	—	Proof	150.00
	1894	1.953	4.25	12.50	40.00	80.00
	1895	2.183	4.25	12.50	30.00	75.00
	1896	2.944	4.25	12.50	35.00	80.00
	1897	1.700	4.25	12.50	30.00	75.00
	1898	3.061	4.25	12.50	35.00	75.00
	1899	3.970	4.25	12.50	30.00	75.00
	1900	5.529	4.25	12.50	30.00	75.00

NOTE: Later date (1901) exists for this type.

1/2 CROWN

14.1380 g, .925 SILVER, .4205 oz ASW
Obv: Large bust.

KM#	Date	Mintage	Fine	VF	XF	Unc
667	1816	—	12.00	40.00	150.00	450.00
	1816 reeded edge		—	—	Proof	1250.
	1816 plain edge		—	—	Proof	1250.
	1817	8.093	10.00	35.00	130.00	285.00
	1817 reeded edge		—	—	Proof	1250.
	1817 plain edge		—	—	Proof	1250.

Obv: Small head.

KM#	Date	Mintage	Fine	VF	XF	Unc
672	1817	Inc. Ab.	10.00	35.00	130.00	265.00
	1817	—	—	—	Proof	1250.
	1817 plain edge		—	—	Proof	1500.
	1818	2.905	15.00	40.00	150.00	360.00
	1818	—	—	—	Proof	1000.
	1819	4.790	10.00	35.00	135.00	340.00
	1819	—	—	—	Proof	1000.
	1820	2.397	16.50	45.00	165.00	375.00
	1820	—	—	—	Proof	1000.
	1820 plain edge		—	—	Proof	1250.

KM#	Date	Mintage	Fine	VF	XF	Unc
676	1820	Inc. Ab.	12.00	30.00	125.00	285.00
	1820	—	—	—	Proof	900.00
	1820 plain edge		—	—	Proof	1200.
	1821	1.435	15.00	35.00	150.00	300.00
	1821	—	—	—	Proof	800.00
	1823	2.004	225.00	675.00	3250.	5500.

KM#	Date	Mintage	Fine	VF	XF	Unc
688	1823	Inc. Ab.	14.00	35.00	160.00	400.00
	1823	—	—	—	Proof	1250.
	1824	.466	17.50	45.00	190.00	600.00
	1824	—	—	—	Proof	1250.

KM#	Date	Mintage	Fine	VF	XF	Unc
695	1824	—	—	—	Proof	4500.
	1825	2.259	12.00	37.50	135.00	300.00
	1825	—	—	—	Proof	1000.
	1825 plain edge		—	—	Proof	1200.
	1826	2.189	10.00	30.00	115.00	275.00
	1826	—	—	—	Proof	725.00
	1828	.050	17.50	55.00	250.00	600.00
	1829	.508	15.00	55.00	160.00	400.00

KM#	Date	Mintage	Fine	VF	XF	Unc
714.1	1831	—	—	—	Proof	1000.
	1831 plain edge		—	—	Proof	750.00

Obv: Larger, modified bust.

KM#	Date	Mintage	Fine	VF	XF	Unc
714.2	1834 W.W. in caps					
		.993	20.00	60.00	200.00	350.00
	1834	—	—	—	Proof	1500.
	1834 W.W. in script					
		Inc. Ab.	15.00	40.00	135.00	300.00
	1834	—	—	—	Proof	1500.
	1834 plain edge		—	—	Proof	2000.
	1835	.282	25.00	60.00	200.00	400.00
	1836/5	1.589	30.00	65.00	225.00	500.00
	1836	Inc. Ab.	15.00	40.00	135.00	300.00
	1836 plain edge		—	—	Proof	1800.
	1837	.151	25.00	60.00	200.00	400.00

KM#	Date	Mintage	Fine	VF	XF	Unc
740	1839 W.W. in relief					
		—	215.00	750.00	2500.	4000.
	1839 plain edge		—	—	Proof	1100.
	1840 W.W. incuse					
		.386	25.00	75.00	185.00	400.00
	1841	.043	45.00	115.00	470.00	1100.
	1842	.486	15.00	40.00	150.00	350.00
	1843	.455	20.00	70.00	300.00	650.00
	1844	1.999	12.50	35.00	150.00	350.00
	1845/3	2.232	—	—	—	—
	1845	Inc. Ab.	12.50	35.00	130.00	300.00
	1846	1.540	12.50	40.00	140.00	300.00
	1848/6	.367	35.00	110.00	385.00	765.00
	1848	Inc. Ab.	40.00	120.00	400.00	900.00
	1849 large date					
		.261	17.00	55.00	285.00	700.00
	1849 small date					
		Inc. Ab.	17.00	55.00	270.00	685.00
	1850	.485	17.00	50.00	300.00	700.00
	1850	—	—	—	Proof	—
	1851	—	—	—	Proof	—
	1853	—	—	—	Proof	2500.
	1862	—	—	—	Proof	4500.
	1864	—	—	—	Proof	4500.

Obv: Second young head.

KM#	Date	Mintage	Fine	VF	XF	Unc
756	1874	2.189	10.00	25.00	80.00	260.00
	1874	—	—	—	Proof	—
	1874 plain edge		—	—	Proof	—
	1875	1.113	10.00	30.00	90.00	280.00
	1875	—	—	—	Proof	—
	1875 plain edge		—	—	Proof	—
	1876/5	.633	—	200.00	400.00	950.00
	1876	Inc. Ab.	10.00	30.00	90.00	280.00
	1877	.447	10.00	30.00	90.00	275.00
	1878	1.466	10.00	30.00	90.00	275.00
	1878	—	—	—	Proof	—
	1879	.901	12.00	35.00	120.00	320.00
	1879	—	—	—	Proof	—
	1880	1.346	10.00	25.00	80.00	250.00
	1880	—	—	—	Proof	—
	1881	2.301	9.00	25.00	75.00	245.00
	1881	—	—	—	Proof	1500.
	1881 plain edge		—	—	Proof	—
	1882	.808	12.00	32.50	85.00	265.00
	1883	2.983	9.00	27.50	75.00	245.00
	1884	1.569	9.00	27.50	75.00	245.00
	1885	1.628	9.00	27.50	75.00	245.00
	1885	—	—	—	Proof	—
	1886	.892	9.00	27.50	75.00	245.00
	1886	—	—	—	Proof	—
	1887	1.438	10.00	40.00	100.00	265.00
	1887	—	—	—	Proof	—

KM#	Date	Mintage	Fine	VF	XF	Unc
764	1887	Inc. Ab.	4.00	8.00	14.00	45.00
	1887	1,084	—	—	Proof	175.00
	1888	1.429	6.00	12.00	35.00	85.00
	1889	4.812	6.00	12.00	30.00	80.00
	1890	3.228	7.00	14.00	40.00	85.00
	1891	2.285	7.00	14.00	40.00	85.00
	1892	1.711	7.50	15.00	45.00	100.00

KM#	Date	Mintage	Fine	VF	XF	Unc
782	1893	1.793	5.25	13.00	35.00	85.00
	1893	1,312	—	—	Proof	150.00
	1894	1.525	6.00	16.00	45.00	115.00
	1895	1.773	5.25	13.00	35.00	85.00
	1896	2.149	5.25	13.00	35.00	85.00
	1897	1.679	5.25	13.00	35.00	85.00
	1898	1.870	5.25	13.00	35.00	85.00
	1899	2.866	5.25	13.00	35.00	85.00
	1900	4.479	5.25	13.00	35.00	85.00

NOTE: Later date (1901) exists for this type.

DOUBLE FLORIN

22.6207 g, .925 SILVER, .6727 oz ASW

KM#	Date	Mintage	Fine	VF	XF	Unc
763	1887 Roman I					
		.483	10.00	17.50	35.00	85.00
	1887 Roman I					
		1,084	—	—	Proof	950.00
	1887 Arabic 1					
		Inc. Ab.	10.00	17.50	35.00	85.00
	1887 Arabic 1					
		*2,916	—	—	Proof	350.00
	1888	.243	10.00	20.00	45.00	125.00
	1888 2nd I in VICTORIA, inverted 1					
		Inc. Ab.	20.00	35.00	120.00	325.00
	1889	1.185	10.00	17.50	35.00	85.00
	1889 2nd I in VICTORIA, inverted 1					
		Inc. Ab.	20.00	35.00	150.00	500.00
	1890	.782	10.00	20.00	50.00	175.00

CROWN

28.2759 g, .925 SILVER, .8409 oz ASW

KM#	Date	Mintage	Fine	VF	XF	Unc
675	1818 LVIII	.155	25.00	75.00	200.00	600.00
	1818 LIX	I.A.	25.00	75.00	200.00	575.00
	1819/8 LIX	.683	32.50	100.00	350.00	900.00
	1819 LIX	I.A.	25.00	75.00	200.00	600.00
	1819 LX	I.A.	25.00	75.00	200.00	575.00
	1819 plain edge		—	—	Proof	—
	1820/19 LX	—	32.50	100.00	350.00	850.00
	1820 LX	.448	25.00	75.00	200.00	650.00

SECUNDO on edge

KM#	Date	Mintage	Fine	VF	XF	Unc
680.1	1821	.438	30.00	65.00	300.00	850.00
	1821	—	—	—	Proof	2500.
	1822	.125	35.00	80.00	450.00	1200.
	1822	—	—	—	Proof	3000.
	TERTIO on edge					
680.2	1821	—	—	—	Proof	3500.
	1822	—	30.00	65.00	300.00	900.00
	1822	—	—	—	Proof	5000.

699 1826 plain edge
— Reported, not confirmed
1826 SEPTIMO on edge
150 pcs. — — Proof 4000.
1826 LVIII on edge
— — — Proof Rare

715 1831 100 pcs. — — Proof 8000.

KM#	Date	Mintage	Fine	VF	XF	Unc
741	1839	—	—	—	Proof	4500.
	1844	.094	25.00	75.00	450.00	2250.
	1844	—	—	—	Proof	12,000.
	1845	.159	25.00	75.00	450.00	2250.
	1845	—	—	—	Proof	11,000.
	1847	.141	30.00	90.00	600.00	3750.
	1847	—	—	—	Proof	—

744 1847 UN DECIMO on edge
8,000 — — Proof 2500.
Impaired Proof 300.00 475.00 700.00 —
1847 SEPTIMO on edge
— — — Proof 9000.
1847 plain edge — Proof 2400.
Impaired Proof 300.00 575.00 900.00 —
1853 SEPTIMO on edge
460 pcs. — — Proof 7000.
1853 plain edge — — Proof 8000.

KM#	Date	Mintage	Fine	VF	XF	Unc
765	1887	.173	13.50	27.50	45.00	125.00
	1887	1,084	—	—	Proof	400.00
	1888	.132	16.00	35.00	60.00	220.00
	1889	1.807	13.50	27.50	50.00	160.00
	1890	.998	14.50	30.00	55.00	200.00
	1891	.566	16.00	35.00	60.00	210.00
	1892	.451	18.00	40.00	70.00	280.00

KM#	Date	Mintage	Fine	VF	XF	Unc
783	1893LVI	.498	15.00	32.00	95.00	275.00
	1893LVI	1,312	—	—	Proof	650.00
	1893LVII	I.A.	25.00	75.00	185.00	500.00
	1894LVII	.145	15.00	50.00	140.00	350.00
	1894LVIII	I.A.	15.00	35.00	125.00	325.00
	1895LVIII	.253	15.00	35.00	125.00	325.00
	1895LIX	I.A.	15.00	32.00	95.00	300.00
	1896LIX	.318	25.00	50.00	250.00	500.00

KM#	Date	Mintage	Fine	VF	XF	Unc
783	1896LX	I.A.	15.00	32.00	95.00	300.00
	1897LX	.262	15.00	32.00	95.00	300.00
	1897LXI	I.A.	15.00	32.00	95.00	300.00
	1898LXI	.161	30.00	60.00	250.00	400.00
	1898LXII	I.A.	15.00	40.00	125.00	325.00
	1899LXII	.166	15.00	35.00	125.00	325.00
	1899LXIII	I.A.	15.00	35.00	125.00	325.00
	1900LXIII	.353	15.00	32.00	85.00	285.00
	1900LXIV	I.A.	15.00	32.00	85.00	285.00

GUINEA SERIES

1/3 GUINEA

2.7834 g, .917 GOLD, .0820 oz AGW

KM#	Date	Mintage	Fine	VF	XF	Unc
648	1801	—	60.00	90.00	150.00	225.00
	1802	—	60.00	90.00	150.00	225.00
	1803	—	60.00	90.00	150.00	225.00

KM#	Date	Mintage	Fine	VF	XF	Unc
650	1804	—	60.00	90.00	150.00	235.00
	1806	—	60.00	90.00	150.00	235.00
	1808	—	60.00	90.00	150.00	235.00
	1809	—	60.00	90.00	150.00	235.00
	1810	—	60.00	90.00	150.00	235.00
	1811	—	125.00	300.00	800.00	1100.
	1813	—	65.00	130.00	325.00	550.00
	1813	—	—	—	Proof	3000.

1/2 GUINEA

4.1750 g, .917 GOLD, .1230 oz AGW

KM#	Date	Mintage	Fine	VF	XF	Unc
649	1801	—	100.00	125.00	225.00	525.00
	1802	—	100.00	125.00	225.00	525.00
	1803	—	100.00	125.00	225.00	525.00

KM#	Date	Mintage	Fine	VF	XF	Unc
651	1804	—	100.00	125.00	225.00	525.00
	1806	—	100.00	125.00	225.00	525.00
	1808	—	100.00	125.00	225.00	525.00
	1809	—	100.00	125.00	225.00	525.00
	1810	—	100.00	125.00	225.00	525.00
	1811	—	100.00	150.00	325.00	650.00
	1813	—	100.00	125.00	300.00	600.00

GUINEA

8.3500 g, .917 GOLD, .2461 oz AGW

KM#	Date	Mintage	Fine	VF	XF	Unc
664	1813	—	250.00	500.00	850.00	1750.
	1813	—	—	—	Proof	5000.

GOLD SERIES

1/2 SOVEREIGN

MINT MARKS

C - Ottawa, Canada
I - Bombay, India
M - Melbourne, Australia
P - Perth, Australia
S - Sydney, Australia
SA - Pretoria, South Africa

NOTE: 1/2 Sovereigns were struck at various foreign mints. The mint mark on the St. George/dragon type is usually found on the base below the right rear hoof of the horse. On shield type reverse the mint mark is found below the shield. Refer to appropriate country listings elsewhere in this catalog for coins having mint marks.

3.9940 g, .917 GOLD, .1177 oz AGW

KM#	Date	Mintage	Fine	VF	XF	Unc
673	1817	2.080	70.00	150.00	325.00	550.00
	1817	—	—	—	Proof	3500.
	1818/7	1.030	—	—	Rare	—
	1818	Inc. Ab.	75.00	150.00	350.00	650.00
	1818	—	—	—	Proof	5000.
	1820	.035	90.00	175.00	400.00	700.00

KM#	Date	Mintage	Fine	VF	XF	Unc
681	1821	.231	225.00	600.00	1700.	2700.
	1821	—	—	—	Proof	5000.

KM#	Date	Mintage	Fine	VF	XF	Unc
689	1823	.224	100.00	225.00	525.00	800.00
	1823	—	—	—	Proof	5500.
	1824	.592	90.00	200.00	450.00	800.00
	1825	.761	90.00	200.00	450.00	800.00
	1825	—	—	—	Proof	2000.

Obv: Bare head.

KM#	Date	Mintage	Fine	VF	XF	Unc
700	1826	.345	80.00	180.00	450.00	800.00
	1826	—	—	—	Proof	1750.
	1827	.492	85.00	200.00	475.00	1000.
	1828	1.225	80.00	190.00	450.00	900.00

KM#	Date	Mintage	Fine	VF	XF	Unc
716	1831	—	—	—	Proof	2000.

18mm

KM#	Date	Mintage	Fine	VF	XF	Unc
720	1834	.134	115.00	250.00	600.00	1400.

19mm

KM#	Date	Mintage	Fine	VF	XF	Unc
722	1835	.773	95.00	225.00	600.00	1200.
	1836	.147	250.00	500.00	1500.	2400.
	1837	.160	95.00	250.00	550.00	1000.

Rev: W/o die number.

KM#	Date	Mintage	Fine	VF	XF	Unc
735.1	1838	.273	75.00	90.00	225.00	625.00
	1839	1,230	—	—	Proof	3000.
	1841	.509	75.00	90.00	225.00	625.00
	1842	2.223	75.00	90.00	200.00	550.00
	1843	1.252	75.00	90.00	215.00	625.00
	1844	1.127	75.00	90.00	200.00	550.00
	1845	.888	85.00	220.00	450.00	750.00

KM#	Date	Mintage	Fine	VF	XF	Unc
735.1	1846	1.064	75.00	100.00	225.00	625.00
	1847	.983	75.00	90.00	200.00	550.00
	1848	.411	75.00	150.00	275.00	800.00
	1849	.845	75.00	100.00	200.00	550.00
	1850	.180	180.00	275.00	900.00	1625.
	1851	.774	70.00	100.00	225.00	625.00
	1852	1.378	70.00	100.00	200.00	550.00
	1853	2.709	70.00	100.00	200.00	550.00
	1853	—	—	—	Proof	5000.
	1854	1.125	225.00	350.00	650.00	1500.
	1855	1.120	70.00	100.00	200.00	550.00
	1856	2.392	70.00	100.00	200.00	550.00
	1857	.728	70.00	100.00	150.00	450.00
	1858	.856	70.00	100.00	175.00	495.00
	1859	2.204	70.00	90.00	175.00	495.00
	1860	1.132	70.00	90.00	175.00	495.00
	1861	1.131	70.00	100.00	200.00	575.00
	1862	—	350.00	640.00	2700.	6500.
	1863	1.572	70.00	90.00	150.00	450.00
	1880	1.009	60.00	75.00	130.00	325.00
	1883	2.870	60.00	90.00	150.00	325.00
	1884	1.114	60.00	90.00	150.00	325.00
	1885/3	4.469	80.00	110.00	180.00	375.00
	1885	Inc. Ab.	60.00	90.00	100.00	290.00

NOTE: 1854 is much rarer than the mintage figure indicates.

Rev: W/die number.

KM#	Date	Mintage	Fine	VF	XF	Unc
735.2	1863	Inc. Ab.	60.00	85.00	180.00	400.00
	1864	1.758	60.00	85.00	180.00	400.00
	1865	1.835	60.00	85.00	180.00	400.00
	1866	2.059	60.00	85.00	180.00	400.00
	1867	.993	60.00	85.00	180.00	400.00
	1869	1.862	60.00	85.00	200.00	400.00
	1870	.160	60.00	85.00	200.00	400.00
	1871	2.063	60.00	85.00	200.00	400.00
	1871 plain edge		—	—	Proof	4000.
	1872	3.249	60.00	85.00	150.00	400.00
	1873	1.927	60.00	85.00	150.00	400.00
	1874	1.884	60.00	85.00	150.00	400.00
	1875	.516	60.00	85.00	150.00	400.00
	1876	2.785	60.00	85.00	150.00	400.00
	1877	2.197	60.00	75.00	125.00	325.00
	1878	2.082	60.00	75.00	125.00	325.00
	1879	.035	75.00	125.00	215.00	340.00
	1880	Inc. Ab.	60.00	75.00	130.00	325.00

KM#	Date	Mintage	Fine	VF	XF	Unc
766	1887	.872	BV	65.00	100.00	125.00
	1887	797 pcs.	—	—	Proof	500.00
	1890	2.266	BV	65.00	100.00	150.00
	1891	1.079	BV	65.00	100.00	150.00
	1892	13.680	BV	65.00	100.00	150.00
	1893	4.427	BV	65.00	100.00	150.00

KM#	Date	Mintage	Fine	VF	XF	Unc
784	1893	Inc. Ab.	BV	65.00	85.00	115.00
	1893	773 pcs.	—	—	Proof	500.00
	1894	3.795	BV	60.00	75.00	125.00
	1895	2.869	BV	60.00	75.00	125.00
	1896	2.947	BV	60.00	75.00	125.00
	1897	3.568	BV	60.00	75.00	125.00
	1898	2.869	BV	60.00	75.00	125.00
	1899	3.362	BV	60.00	75.00	125.00
	1900	4.307	BV	60.00	75.00	125.00

NOTE: Later date (1901) exists for this type.

SOVEREIGN

MINT MARKS

C - Ottawa, Canada
I - Bombay, India
M - Melbourne, Australia
P - Perth, Australia
S - Sydney, Australia
SA - Pretoria, South Africa

NOTE: Sovereigns were struck at various colonial mints. The mint mark on the St. George/dragon type is usually found on the base below the right rear hoof of the horse. On shield type reverse the mint mark is found below the shield or on the obverse below the truncation. Refer to appropriate country listings elsewhere in this catalog for coins having these mint marks.

7.9881 g, .917 GOLD, .2354 oz AGW

KM#	Date	Mintage	Fine	VF	XF	Unc
674	1817	3.235	150.00	225.00	525.00	1000.
	1817	—	—	—	Proof	8000.
	1818	2.347	150.00	275.00	625.00	1200.
	1819	3,574	—	—	Rare	—
	1820	.932	150.00	225.00	525.00	1000.
	1820	—	—	—	Proof	—

KM#	Date	Mintage	Fine	VF	XF	Unc
682	1821	9.405	150.00	225.00	675.00	1250.
	1821	—	—	—	Proof	4500.
	1822	5.357	160.00	225.00	725.00	1100.
	1823	.617	225.00	500.00	1400.	—
	1824	3.768	175.00	225.00	800.00	1200.
	1825	4.200	225.00	500.00	1200.	3000.

KM#	Date	Mintage	Fine	VF	XF	Unc
696	1825	Inc. Ab.	125.00	225.00	675.00	1200.
	1825	—	—	—	Proof	3500.
	1825 plain edge		—	—	Proof	5000.
	1826	5.724	125.00	200.00	675.00	1100.
	1826	—	—	—	Proof	3500.
	1827	2.267	125.00	225.00	725.00	1200.
	1828 only 6 or 7 known					
		.386	800.00	2500.	6500.	—
	1829	2.445	125.00	225.00	675.00	1200.
	1830	2.388	125.00	225.00	675.00	1200.
	1830	—	—	—	Proof	—
	1830 plain edge		—	—	Proof	10,000.

KM#	Date	Mintage	Fine	VF	XF	Unc
717	1831	.599	150.00	300.00	800.00	1500.
	1831	—	—	—	Proof	5500.
	1832	3.737	125.00	200.00	625.00	1200.
	1833	1.225	125.00	225.00	725.00	1300.
	1835	.723	125.00	225.00	725.00	1300.
	1836	1.714	125.00	225.00	725.00	1300.
	1837	1.173	125.00	225.00	725.00	1300.

Rev: W/o die number.

KM#	Date	Mintage	Fine	VF	XF	Unc
736.1	1838	2.719	BV	160.00	275.00	725.00
	1838	—	—	—	Proof	4000.
	1839	.504	175.00	350.00	1000.	2000.
	1839	—	—	—	Proof	5000.
	1841	.124	1100.	1800.	5500.	—
	1842	4.865	—	BV	275.00	725.00
	1843/2	5.982	500.00	—	—	—
	1843	Inc. Ab.	—	BV	225.00	625.00
	1843 narrow shield					
		Inc. Ab.	4000.	6500.	—	—
	1844	3.000	—	BV	225.00	525.00
	1845	3.801	—	BV	225.00	475.00
	1846	3.803	—	BV	200.00	525.00
	1847	4.667	—	BV	200.00	525.00
	1848	2.247	—	BV	225.00	525.00
	1849	1.755	—	BV	225.00	575.00
	1850	1.402	—	BV	175.00	475.00
	1851	4.014	—	BV	175.00	475.00
	1852	8.053	—	BV	175.00	475.00
	1853	—	—	—	Proof	7200.
	1853 WW raised					
		10.598	—	BV	175.00	475.00
	1853 WW incuse					
		Inc. Ab.	—	BV	175.00	475.00
	1854 WW raised					
		3.590	—	BV	175.00	525.00
	1854 WW incuse					
		Inc. Ab.	—	BV	175.00	525.00
	1855 WW raised				175.00	450.00
		8.448	—	BV	175.00	450.00
	1855 WW incuse					
		Inc. Ab.	—	BV	175.00	450.00
	1856	4.806	—	BV	175.00	450.00
	1856 sm.dt. I.A.		—	BV	175.00	450.00
	1857	4.496	—	BV	175.00	450.00
	1858	.803	BV	125.00	200.00	940.00

KM#	Date	Mintage	Fine	VF	XF	Unc
736.1	1859	1.548	—	BV	175.00	525.00
	1859 sm.dt.	I.A.	—	BV	175.00	525.00
	1860	2.556	—	BV	350.00	700.00
	1861	7.623	—	BV	200.00	450.00
	1862/1	—	—	—	—	—
	1862	7.836	—	BV	175.00	400.00
	1863	5.922	—	BV	150.00	450.00
	1872	13.487	—	BV	150.00	300.00

Rev: Die number below wreath.

KM#	Date	Mintage	Fine	VF	XF	Unc
736.2	1863	Inc. Ab.	—	BV	150.00	400.00
	1864	8.656	—	BV	150.00	400.00
	1865	1.450	—	BV	150.00	400.00
	1866	4.047	—	BV	150.00	400.00
	1868	1.653	—	BV	150.00	400.00
	1869	6.441	—	BV	150.00	400.00
	1869	—	—	—	Proof	4000.
	1870	2.190	—	BV	150.00	400.00
	1871	8.767	—	BV	150.00	275.00
	1872	Inc. Ab.	—	BV	150.00	300.00
	1873	2.368	—	BV	150.00	300.00
	1874	.521	800.00	1800.	—	—

Ansell Variety
Obv: Additional line on lower edge of ribbon.

KM#	Date	Mintage	Fine	VF	XF	Unc
736.3	1859	.168	650.00	1250.	2500.	—

KM#	Date	Mintage	Fine	VF	XF	Unc
752	1871	Inc. Ab.	—	BV	150.00	350.00
	1871	—	—	—	Proof	3500.
	1872	Inc. Ab.	—	BV	120.00	290.00
	1873	Inc. Ab.	—	BV	160.00	350.00
	1874	Inc. Ab.	125.00	150.00	350.00	550.00
	1876	3.319	—	BV	125.00	350.00
	1876	Inc. Ab.	—	—	Proof	6500.
	1878	1.091	—	BV	125.00	350.00
	1879	.020	180.00	450.00	1350.	4000.
	1880	3.650	—	BV	125.00	350.00
	1880 w/o designers initials on rev.					
		—	—	BV	125.00	350.00
	1884	1.770	—	BV	125.00	300.00
	1885	.718	—	BV	125.00	300.00

KM#	Date	Mintage	Fine	VF	XF	Unc
767	1887	1.111	—	BV	110.00	150.00
	1887	797 pcs.	—	—	Proof	750.00
	1888	2.777	—	BV	110.00	150.00
	1889	7.257	—	BV	110.00	165.00
	1890	6.530	—	BV	110.00	165.00
	1891	6.329	—	BV	110.00	165.00
	1892	7.105	—	BV	110.00	165.00

KM#	Date	Mintage	Fine	VF	XF	Unc
785	1893	6.898	—	—	BV	145.00
	1893	773 pcs.	—	—	Proof	900.00
	1894	3.783	—	—	BV	150.00
	1895	2.285	—	—	BV	150.00
	1896	3.334	—	—	BV	150.00
	1898	4.361	—	—	BV	150.00
	1899	7.516	—	—	BV	145.00
	1900	10.847	—	—	BV	145.00

NOTE: Later date (1901) exists for this type.

2 POUNDS

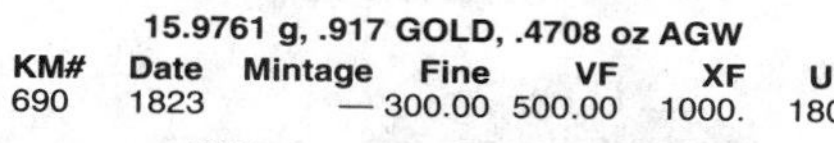

15.9761 g, .917 GOLD, .4708 oz AGW

KM#	Date	Mintage	Fine	VF	XF	Unc
690	1823	—	300.00	500.00	1000.	1800.

KM#	Date	Mintage	Fine	VF	XF	Unc
701	1826	450 pcs.	—	—	Proof	6000.

KM#	Date	Mintage	Fine	VF	XF	Unc
718	1831	225 pcs.	—	—	Proof	7500.

KM#	Date	Mintage	Fine	VF	XF	Unc
768	1887	.091	250.00	300.00	400.00	550.00
	1887	797 pcs.	—	—	Proof	1200.

NOTE: Proof issues with mint mark S below right rear hoof of horse were struck at Sydney, refer to Australia listings.

KM#	Date	Mintage	Fine	VF	XF	Unc
786	1893	.052	250.00	325.00	675.00	900.00
	1893	773 pcs.	—	—	Proof	1750.

NOTE: Proof issues with mint mark S below right rear hoof of horse were struck at Sydney, refer to Australia listings.

5 POUNDS

39.9403 g, .917 GOLD, 1.1773 oz AGW
Lettered Edge

KM#	Date	Mintage	Fine	VF	XF	Unc
702	1826	150 pcs.	—	—	Proof	12,500.

NOTE: Includes lettered edge patterns KM#Pn96.

KM#	Date	Mintage	Fine	VF	XF	Unc
742	1839	400 pcs.	—	—	Proof	28,000.

KM#	Date	Mintage	Fine	VF	XF	Unc
769	1887	.054	625.00	725.00	1000.	1500.
	1887	797 pcs.	—	—	Proof	3250.

NOTE: Proof issues with mint mark S below right rear hoof of horse were struck at Sydney, refer to Australia listings.

KM#	Date	Mintage	Fine	VF	XF	Unc
787	1893	.020	675.00	750.00	1200.	2000.
	1893	773 pcs.	—	—	Proof	3750.

NOTE: Proof issues with mint mark S below right rear hoof of horse were struck at Sydney, refer to Australia listings.

COUNTERMARKED COINAGE

BANK OF ENGLAND

Emergency issue consisting of foreign silver coins, usually Spanish Colonial, having a bust of George III within an oval (1797) or octagonal (1840) frame. Countermarked 8 Reales circulated at 4 Shillings 9 Pence in 1797 and 5 Shillings in 1804. The puncheons used for countermarking foreign coins for this series were available for many years afterward, especially the oval die and apparently a number of foreign coins other than Spanish or Spanish Colonial 8 Reales were countermarked for collectors.

Type II

1804
Head of George III in octagon.

NOTE: Coins other than 8 Reales bearing this countermark are considered spurious by some authorities.

DOLLAR

SILVER

c/m: Type II on Bolivia (Potosi) 8 Reales, KM#73.1.

KM#	Date	Year	VG	Fine	VF	XF
653	ND	(1791-1808)	75.00	125.00	250.00	400.00

c/m: Type II on France 1 Ecu, C#78.

KM#	Date	Year	VG	Fine	VF	XF
654	ND	(1774-92)	—	—	Rare	—

c/m: Type II on Mexico 8 Reales, KM#106.

KM#	Date	Year	VG	Fine	VF	XF
655	ND	(1772-89)	65.00	100.00	200.00	325.00

c/m: Type II on Mexico 8 Reales, KM#109.

KM#	Date	Year	VG	Fine	VF	XF
656	ND	(1791-1808)	65.00	100.00	200.00	325.00

c/m: Type II on Peru (Lima) 8 Reales, KM#78.

KM#	Date	Year	VG	Fine	VF	XF
657	ND	(1772-89)	175.00	345.00	625.00	—

c/m: Type II on Peru (Lima) 8 Reales, KM#97.

KM#	Date	Year	VG	Fine	VF	XF
658	ND	(1791-1808)	175.00	345.00	625.00	—

c/m: Type II on Spanish (Seville) 8 Reales, C#71.

KM#	Date	Year	VG	Fine	VF	XF
659	ND	(1788-1808)	—	—	Rare	—

c/m: Type II on United States 1 Dollar, C#34.

KM#	Date	Year	VG	Fine	VF	XF
660	ND	(1795-98)	—	—	Rare	—

c/m: Type II on United States 1 Dollar, C#34a.

KM#	Date	Year	VG	Fine	VF	XF
660a	ND	(1798-1803)	—	—	Rare	—

COUNTERMARKED COINAGE
ENGLISH TRADESMEN

During the last half of the 18th century and the early years of the 19th century, the gold coinage predominated in Great Britain and the limited issues of silver coins between the years 1758 and 1816 did little to relieve the shortage of smaller denominations. During the 1790's, a partial solution to the problem began to be offered by private tradesmen - through the countermarking of foreign dollars, chiefly Spanish Colonial issues from the Americas, with a punch validating them for local circulation and redemption. The majority of these tradesmen's countermarked issues circulated in Scotland; in England, two cotton mills, two colleries, and a merchant also countermarked foreign silver coins.

4 SHILLINGS 9 PENCE

.903 SILVER

c/m: 4/9 CROMVORD • DERBYSHIRE • on Spanish Colonial 8 Reales.

KM#	Date	Year	Good	VG	Fine	VF
643	ND	(18xx)	—	200.00	300.00	500.00

c/m: 4/9 CROMFORD • DERBYSHIRE • on French Ecu.

KM#	Date	Year	Good	VG	Fine	VF
644	ND	(18xx)	—	—	Rare	—

NOTE: False punches have been used on genuine host coins.

5 SHILLINGS

.903 SILVER

c/m: CBCo in rectangle on Peru 8 Reales KM#87.

KM#	Date	Year	Good	VG	Fine	VF
A645.1	ND	(1790)	—	—	Rare	—

NOTE: Issuer undetermined.

c/m: CBCo in rectangle on Peru 8 Reales KM#97.

KM#	Date	Year	Good	VG	Fine	VF
A645.2	ND	(1792)	—	—	Rare	—

c/m: 5s. CROMFORD • DERBYSHIRE • on Spanish Colonial 8 Reales.

KM#	Date	Year	Good	VG	Fine	VF
B645	ND	(18xx)	—	—	350.00	550.00

c/m: 5/ • DONALD & CO • BIRMINGHAM • on Spanish Colonial 8 Reales.

KM#	Date	Year	Good	VG	Fine	VF
C645	ND	(18xx)	—	—	Rare	—

c/m: 5/PERCY MAIN COLLIERY on Spanish Colonial 8 Reales.

KM#	Date	Year	Good	VG	Fine	VF
D645	ND	(18xx)	—	—	800.00	1100.

TRADE COINAGE
TRADE COINAGE
Britannia Series

Issued to facilitate British trade in the Orient, the reverse design incorporates the denomination in Chinese characters and Malay script.

This issue was struck at the Bombay (B) and Calcutta (C) Mints in India, except for 1925 and 1930 issues which were struck at London. Through error the mint marks did not appear on some early (1895-1900) issues as indicated.

DOLLAR

26.9568 g, .900 SILVER, .7800 oz ASW

KM#	Date	Mintage	Fine	VF	XF	Unc
T5	1895B	3.316	30.00	80.00	125.00	350.00
(T2)	1895B	Inc. Ab.	—	—	Proof	850.00
	1895	Inc. Ab.	40.00	75.00	100.00	300.00
	1895	Inc. Ab.	—	—	Proof	800.00
	1896B	6.136	60.00	90.00	150.00	500.00
	1896B	Inc. Ab.	—	—	Proof	800.00
	1897/6B	21.286	40.00	60.00	100.00	150.00
	1897B	Inc. Ab.	15.00	20.00	25.00	60.00
	1897B	Inc. Ab.	—	—	Proof	800.00
	1897	Inc. Ab.	15.00	20.00	25.00	60.00
	1897	Inc. Ab.	—	—	Proof	800.00
	1898B	21.546	15.00	20.00	25.00	60.00
	1898B	Inc. Ab.	—	—	Proof	800.00
	1898	Inc. Ab.	15.00	20.00	25.00	60.00
	1899B	30.743	15.00	20.00	25.00	60.00
	1899B	Inc. Ab.	—	—	Proof	800.00
	1900/1000B	9.107	40.00	60.00	100.00	200.00
	1900/890B	I.A.	40.00	60.00	100.00	200.00
	1900	—	100.00	175.00	250.00	600.00
	1900B	Inc. Ab.	15.00	20.00	25.00	60.00
	1900B	Inc. Ab.	—	—	Proof	800.00
	1900B (restrike)	25 known	—	—	Proof	1000.
	1900C	.363	90.00	150.00	250.00	500.00

GOLD

KM#	Date	Mintage	Fine	VF	XF	Unc
T5a	1895B (restrike)		—	—	Proof	7500.
(T2a)	1895 (restrike)		—	—	Proof	7500.
	1896B (restrike)		—	—	Proof	7500.
	1897B (restrike)		—	—	Proof	7500.
	1897 (restrike)		—	—	Proof	7500.
	1898B (restrike)		—	—	Proof	7500.
	1899B (restrike)		—	—	Proof	7500.
	1900B (restrike)		—	—	Proof	7500.

PATTERNS (Pn)

(Including off metal strikes)

KM#	Date	Mintage	Identification	Mkt.Val.
Pn66	1804	—	1 Dollar, C.H.K. on truncation	5000.
Pn67	1804	—	1 Dollar, K on truncation	5000.
PnA68	1806	—	1 Farthing, Silver, KM661	—
PnB68	1806	—	1 Farthing, Gold, KM661	—
PnC68	1811	—	5 Shillings 6 Pence, Silver, Britannia	—
PnD68	1811	—	5 Shillings 6 Pence, Copper, Britannia	—
PnE68	1811	—	5 Shillings 6 Pence, Bronzed Copper, Britannia	—
PnF68	1811	—	5 Shillings 6 Pence, Copper gilt, Britannia	—
PnG68	1811	—	5 Shillings 6 Pence, White metal, Britannia	—

KM#	Date	Mintage	Identification	Mkt.Val.
PnH68	1811	—	5 Shillings 6 Pence, Silver, wreath	—
PnJ68	1811	—	5 Shillings 6 Pence, Copper, wreath	—
PnK68	1811	—	5 Shillings 6 Pence, Brass, wreath	—

KM#	Date	Mintage	Identification	Mkt.Val.
Pn68	1813	—	1 Guinea by T.Wyon, Gold, George III, plain edge	10,500.
Pn69	1813	—	1 Guinea by T.Wyon, Gold, George III, reeded edge	Rare
Pn70	1813	—	1 Guinea, Gold, George III, plain edge	Rare
Pn71	1813	—	1 Guinea, Gold, George III, reeded edge	Rare
Pn72	1813	—	1 Guinea, Gold, George III	Rare
PnA73	1816	—	6 Pence, Gold, KM665	—
PnB73	1816	—	1 Schilling, Gold, KM666	—
Pn73	1816	—	1 Guinea, Gold, George III	Rare

KM#	Date	Mintage	Identification	Mkt.Val.
Pn74	1816	—	1 Guinea, Gold, George III	Rare

KM#	Date	Mintage	Identification	Mkt.Val.
Pn75	1816	—	1/2 Sovereign by T.Wyon,, Gold, George III	Rare
Pn76	1816	—	1/2 Sovereign, Gold, George III	Rare

KM#	Date	Mintage	Identification	Mkt.Val.
PnA77	1817	—	1 Crown by Wyon, Silver, George III	—
PnB77	1817	—	1 Crown by Wyon, Silver, George III, plain edge	5000.
PnC77	1817	—	1 Crown, Gold, George III	Rare
PnD77	1817	—	1 Crown, Copper, George III	Rare
PnE77	1817	—	1 Crown, White Metal, George III	Rare
PnF77	1817	—	1 Crown by Pistrucci, Silver, George III, plain edge, obv. leg: . . . GRATIA BRITANNIARUM REX F:D:	Rare
PnG77	1817	—	1 Crown, Silver, George III, obv. leg: . . . GRATIA BRITANNIAR:REX F:D.	Rare
PnH77	1817	—	1 Crown, Silver, George III, obv. leg: . . . D.G.BRITANNIARUM REX F:D	Rare
PnI77	1817	—	1 Crown, Silver, George IIV, rev: INCORRUPTA. .	11,500.

KM#	Date	Mintage	Identification	Mkt.Val.
Pn77	1817	—	1 Crown, .916 Gold, George III	Rare

KM#	Date	Mintage	Identification	Mkt.Val.
PnA78	1818	—	1 Crown by B. Pistrucci, Silver, George III, lettered edge	Rare
PnB78	1818	—	1 Crown by B. Pistrucci, Silver, George III, plain edge	Rare
PnC78	1818	—	1 Crown by B. Pistrucci, White Metal, George III, plain edge	Rare
Pn78	1820	—	6 Pence, Silver, George III	1500.
Pn79	1820	—	1 Shilling, Silver, George III	1500.

KM#	Date	Mintage	Identification	Mkt.Val.
PnB80	ND(1820)	—	1 Crown by T.Webb & G.Mills, Silver, George III, edge	800.00
PnC80	ND(1820)	—	1 Crown, Lead, George III, plain edge	Rare
PnD80	1820	—	1 Crown by Pistrucci, Silver, Obv: George III. Rev: George slaying dragon	Rare
PnE80	1820	—	1 Crown, by Pistrucci, Lead, Obv: George III, Rev: George slaying dragon	Rare

KM#	Date	Mintage	Identification	Mkt.Val.
Pn80	1820	—	1/2 Sovereign, Gold, George III	Rare

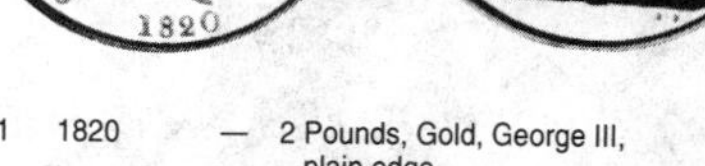

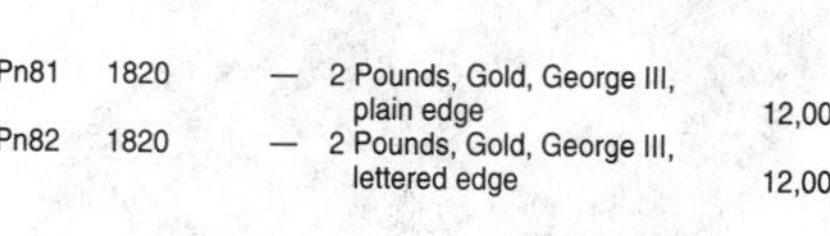

KM#	Date	Mintage	Identification	Mkt.Val.
Pn81	1820	—	2 Pounds, Gold, George III, plain edge	12,000.
Pn82	1820	—	2 Pounds, Gold, George III, lettered edge	12,000.

KM#	Date	Mintage	Identification	Mkt.Val.
Pn83	1820	—	5 Pounds, George III, plain edge	40,000.
Pn84	1820	—	5 Pounds, George III, lettered edge	40,000.
Pn85	1820	—	1/2 Sovereign, Gold, George IV	Rare
PnA86	1821	—	1 Crown, Copper, KM680.1	1100.

KM#	Date	Mintage	Identification	Mkt.Val.
Pn86	1821	—	1/2 Sovereign, Gold, George IV	Rare
PnA87	1823	1 known	1 Crown, White Metal, KM680.1	9500.

KM#	Date	Mintage	Identification	Mkt.Val.
PnB87	1823	—	1/2 Crown, Silver, recut dies, George IV	—
Pn87	1824	—	1 Sovereign, Gold, George IV	Rare
Pn88	1824	—	2 Pounds, Gold, George IV, lettered edge	25,000.
Pn89	1825	—	1/2 Sovereign, Gold, George IV	Rare

KM#	Date	Mintage	Identification	Mkt.Val.
Pn90	1825	—	1 Crown, plain edge	Rare
Pn91	1825	—	2 Pounds, Gold, George IV, plain edge	6000.
Pn92	1825	—	2 Pounds, Gold, George IV, lettered edge	6000.
Pn93	1826	—	2 Pounds, Gold, George IV, plain edge	Rare
Pn94	1826	—	2 Pounds, Gold, George IV, lettered edge	Rare
Pn95	1826	*2 pcs.	5 Pounds, Gold, George IV, plain edge	Rare
Pn96	1826	Inc. KM702	5 Pounds, Gold, George IV, lettered edge	17,000.
PnA97	1829	—	5 Pounds, Gold, George IV, plain edge	nique

***NOTE:** Stack's sale 12-92 BU realized $85,000.

KM#	Date	Mintage	Identification	Mkt.Val.
Pn97	1830	—	1 Sovereign, Gold, William IV, plain edge	Rare

KM#	Date	Mintage	Identification	Mkt.Val.
PnA98	1831	—	1 Crown, Gold, William IV, plain edge	125,000.
Pn98	1831	—	2 Pounds, Gold, William IV, plain edge	Rare
Pn99	1831	—	5 Pounds, Gold, William IV, plain edge	Rare
PnA100	1935	30	1 Crown, Gold, KM842	15,000.

KM#	Date	Mintage	Identification	Mkt.Val.
PnA100	1836	—	4 Pence, Silver, obv. KM723	850.00
PnC100	1836	—	4 Pence, Gold, KM723	4000.
Pn100	1837	—	4 Pence, .925 Silver	450.00
Pn101	1837	—	1 Schilling, Copper, KM713	—
Pn102	1837	—	1 Sovereign, Gold, Victoria	Rare
Pn103	1837	—	1 Sovereign, Gold, Victoria, large head	Rare
Pn104	1837	—	1 Sovereign, Gold, Victoria, wide spaced letter on obv.	Rare

KM#	Date	Mintage	Identification	Mkt.Val.
PnA105	1838	—	3 Pence, Gold, KM730	2500.
Pn105	1838	—	1 Sovereign, Gold, Victoria	Rare
PnA106	1839	300	1/2 Farthing, Bronzed Copper, KM738	Rare
PnB106	1839	—	1 Farthing, Silver, KM725	Rare
Pn106	1839	—	5 Pounds, Gold, Victoria, plain mantle	Rare
Pn107	1839	—	5 Pounds, Gold, Victoria, garter star on mantle	Rare
Pn108	1839	—	5 Pounds, Gold, Victoria, plain edge	Rare
Pn109	1839	—	5 Pounds, Silver, Victoria, lettered edge	—
Pn110	1839	—	5 Pounds, Copper, Victoria	—
PnA111	1841	—	1/2 Penny, Silver, KM726	—
PnB111	1841	—	1 Penny, Silver, KM739	—
PnC111	1843	—	1 Sovereign, Gold, Victoria, KM736	3500.
PnD111	1847	—	1 Crown, Gold, KM741, plain edge	Rare

KM#	Date	Mintage	Identification	Mkt.Val.
Pn111	1848	—	1 Florin, .925 Silver	1000.
PnA112	1848	—	1 Florin, Gold, KM745	10,000.
PnB112	1853	10-15	1/2 Farthing, Bronzed Copper, KM738	Rare
Pn112	1853	—	5 Shillings, Gold, Victoria	Rare

KM#	Date	Mintage	Identification	Mkt.Val.
Pn113	1853	—	1/4 Sovereign, Gold, Victoria	2500.
PnA114	1860	—	1 Penny, Copper, KM749.2, L.C.W. on truncation	300.00
PnB114	1860	—	1 Penny, Silver, KM749.2	2500.
PnC114	1860	—	1 Penny, Gold, KM749.2	Unique
PnD114	1861	—	1 Farthing, Silver, KM747.2	1200.
PnE114	1861	—	1 Farthing, Gold, KM747.2	—
PnF114	1861	—	1/2 Penny, Silver, KM748.2	1250.
PnG114	1861	—	1/2 Penny, Copper-Nickel, KM748.2	650.00
PnH114	1861	—	1/2 Penny, Aluminum-Bronze, KM748.2	750.00
PnJ114	1861	—	1/2 Penny, Gold, KM748.2	Unique
PnK114	1861	—	1/2 Penny, Brass, KM748.2	Unique
PnL114	1861	—	1 Penny, Copper, KM749.2, L.C.WYON below truncation, L.C.W. below shield	375.00
PnM114	1861	—	1 Penny, Silver, KM749.2	3000.
PnN114	1861	—	1 Penny, Gold, KM749.2	Unique
Pn114	1864	—	1 Sovereign, Gold, Victoria	Rare

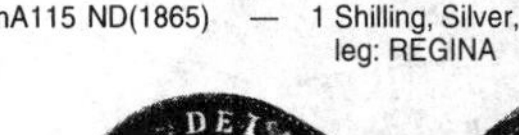

KM#	Date	Mintage	Identification	Mkt.Val.
PnA115	ND(1865)	—	1 Shilling, Silver, Victoria, leg: REGINA	—

KM#	Date	Mintage	Identification	Mkt.Val.
PnB115	ND(1865)	—	1 Shilling, Silver, Victoria, leg: DEI GRATIA	—

KM#	Date	Mintage	Identification	Mkt.Val.
PnC115	1865	—	1/2 Florin, Silver, Victoria	—
PnD115	1865	—	1/2 Florin, Copper, Victoria	—

KM#	Date	Mintage	Identification	Mkt.Val.
PnE115	1865	—	1/2 Florin, Silver, Victoria	—
PnF115	1865	—	1/2 Florin, Copper, Victoria	—

KM#	Date	Mintage	Identification	Mkt.Val.
PnG115	1867	—	1 Franc-10 Pence, Silver, Victoria	—

KM#	Date	Mintage	Identification	Mkt.Val.
PnH115	1867	—	1 Ducat, Gold, Victoria	2500.
PnI115	1868	—	1/4 Farthing, Bronze, KM737	450.00
PnJ115	1868	—	1/4 Farthing, Copper-Nickel, KM737	350.00
PnK115	1868	—	1/3 Farthing, Copper-Nickel, KM750	450.00
PnL115	1868	—	1/3 Farthing, Aluminum, KM750	—
PnM115	1868	—	1/2 Farthing, Bronze, KM738	275.00
PnN115	1868	—	1/2 Farthing, Copper-Nickel, KM738	450.00
PnP115	1868	—	1 Farthing, Copper-Nickel, KM747.2	500.00
PnQ115	1868	—	1/2 Penny, Copper-Nickel, KM748.2	375.00
PnR115	1868	—	1 Penny, Copper-Nickel, KM749.2	600.00

KM#	Date	Mintage	Identification	Mkt.Val.
PnS115	1868	—	Double Florin, Gold, Victoria, plain edge	2250.
Pn115	1868	—	Double Florin, Gold, Victoria, edge grained	2250.
Pn116	1870	—	1 Sovereign, Gold, Victoria	Rare
PnA117	1874	—	1/2 Crown, .917 Gold, KM756	Rare
PnB117	1875	—	1 Penny, Copper-Nickel, KM749.2	1600.
PnC117	1877	—	1 Penny, Copper-Nickel, KM749.2	1750.
Pn117	1880	—	1/2 Sovereign, Gold, Victoria	Rare
PnA118	1880	—	1/2 Sovereign, Silver, Victoria	2150.

KM#	Date	Mintage	Identification	Mkt.Val.
PnB118	1880	1 known	1 Sovereign, Silver, Victoria	4500.
Pn118	1884	—	1/2 Sovereign, Gold, Victoria	Rare

KM#	Date	Mintage	Identification	Mkt.Val.
PnA119	1887	—	1 Penny, Gold	—

KM#	Date	Mintage	Identification	Mkt.Val.
Pn119	1887	—	6 Pence, Silver, Victoria	—
PnB120	1890	—	2 Florin by Wyon, Silver, Victoria	—

PRIVATE PATTERNS (PPn)

KM#	Date	Mintage	Identification	Mkt.Val.
PPn1	1818	—	1 Crown by Pistrucci, Silver, George III, plain edge	9500.
PPn2	1818	—	1 Crown, Gold, George III	Rare
PPn3	1818	—	1 Crown, White Metal, George III	Rare
PPn4	1818	—	1 Crown, Lead, George III	8500.
PPn5	1818	—	1 Crown, Silver, George III, large lettered edge	9500.
PPn6	1818	—	1 Crown, Silver, George III, small lettered edge	9500.
PPn7	1818	—	1 Crown, Silver, George III, incusely inscribed edge	Rare
PPn8	1818	—	1 Crown, Lead, George III, rev: heavy toothed border, incusely inscribed edge	Rare
PPn9	1818	—	1 Crown, Lead, George III, obv. coarse toothed border, rev. plain border, plain edge	Rare
PPn10	1818	—	1 Crown, Silver, George III, finely scribed garter, raised edge lettering, rose stops	9500.
PPn11	1818	—	1 Crown, Silver, George III, raised edge lettering, star stops	9500.
PPn12	1818	—	1 Crown, White Metal, George III	8500.

KM#	Date	Mintage	Identification	Mkt.Val.
PPn13	1820	—	1 Crown by Mills-Whiteaves w/o necktie, Silver, plain edge	8000.
PPn14	1820	—	1 Crown, Gold, plain edge	30,000.

KM#	Date	Mintage	Identification	Mkt.Val.
PPn15	1820	—	1 Crown w/necktie, Silver, plain edge	8000.

KM#	Date	Mintage	Identification	Mkt.Val.
PPn16	1837	150 pcs.	1 Crown by Bonomi & Thomas, silver, plain edge	2500.

NOTE: Numbered T1-T150 on edge.

KM#	Date	Mintage	Identification	Mkt.Val.
PPn17	1837	6 pcs.	1 Crown, Gold, plain edge	8000.
PPn-A18	1837	10 pcs.	1 Crown, Copper, plain edge	1200.
PPn18	1837	10 pcs.	1 Crown, Bronze, plain edge	1200.
PPn19	1837	10 pcs.	1 Crown, Tin, plain edge	800.00
PPn20	1837	10 pcs.	1 Crown, Aluminum, plain edge	800.00
PPn21	1837	—	1 Crown, White metal, plain edge	800.00
PPn22	1837	—	1 Crown, Lead, plain edge	800.00
PPn23	1837	—	1 Crown, Copper, reeded edge	800.00
PPn24	1837	—	1 Crown, White Metal, reeded edge	800.00
PPn25	1837	—	1 Crown, Lead, reeded edge	800.00
PPn26	1837	—	1 Crown, White Metal, w/royal arms rev.	800.00

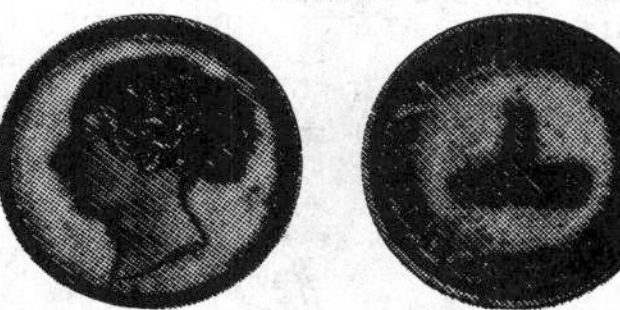

KM#	Date	Mintage	Identification	Mkt.Val.
PPn27	1846	—	1 Cent by Smith, Copper	250.00
PPnA27	1846	—	1 Cent by Smith, Bronzed Copper	200.00

KM#	Date	Mintage	Identification	Mkt.Val.
PPn28	1846	—	1 Centum by Smith, Copper	250.00
PPn-A28	1846	—	1 Centum by Smith, White Metal	200.00

KM#	Date	Mintage	Identification	Mkt.Val.
PPn29	1846	—	2 Cents by Smith, Copper	250.00
PPn-A29	1846	—	2 Cents, Bronzed Copper	200.00
PPn30	1846	(restrike)	2 Cents, White Metal	200.00
PPn31	1846	(restrike)	2 Cents, Silver	600.00
PPn32	1846	(restrike)	2 Cents, Gold	2000.
PPn33	1846	—	5 Cents by Smith, Copper	350.00
PPn34	1846	—	5 Cents, Copper, bronzed	350.00

KM#	Date	Mintage	Identification	Mkt.Val.
PPn35	1846	—	10 Cents by Smith, Copper	550.00
PPn36	1846	—	10 Cents, White Metal, Restrike	550.00
PPn37	1846	—	10 Cents, Copper, Restrike	400.00
PPn38	1846	—	10 Cents, Copper, Bronzed, Restrike	450.00
PPn39	1846	—	10 Cents, Silver, Restrike	1000.

KM#	Date	Mintage	Identification	Mkt.Val.
PPn40	1860	—	1 Farthing, Copper, milled edge	350.00
PPn41	1860	—	1 Farthing, Copper, Bronzed, milled edge	350.00
PPn42	1860	—	1 Farthing, Aluminum, milled edge	300.00
PPn43	1860	—	1 Farthing, Silver, milled edge	500.00
PPn44	1860	—	1 Farthing, Gold, milled edge	2000.
PPn45	1860	—	1 Farthing, Copper, plain edge	350.00
PPn46	1860	—	1 Farthing, Copper, bronzed, plain edge	350.00
PPn47	1860	—	1 Farthing, Aluminum, plain edge	300.00
PPn48	1860	—	1 Farthing, Silver, plain edge	600.00
PPn49	1860	—	1 Farthing, Gold, plain edge	2000.

KM#	Date	Mintage	Identification	Mkt.Val.
PPn50	1860	—	1/2 Penny, Copper, milled edge	400.00
PPn51	1860	—	1/2 Penny, Copper, bronzed, milled edge	400.00
PPn52	1860	—	1/2 Penny, Aluminum, milled edge	300.00
PPn53	1860	—	1/2 Penny, Silver, milled edge	600.00
PPn54	1860	—	1/2 Penny, Gold, milled edge	2200.
PPn55	1860	—	1/2 Penny, Copper, plain edge	400.00
PPn56	1860	—	1/2 Penny, Copper, bronzed, plain edge	400.00
PPn57	1860	—	1/2 Penny, Aluminum, plain edge	300.00
PPn58	1860	—	1/2 Penny, Silver, plain edge	600.00
PPn59	1860	—	1/2 Penny, Gold, plain edge	2200.

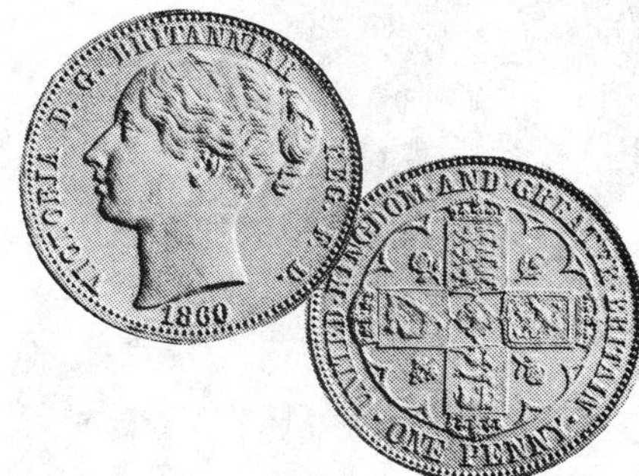

KM#	Date	Mintage	Identification	Mkt.Val.
PPn60	1860	—	1 Penny, Copper, milled edge	450.00
PPn61	1860	—	1 Penny, Copper, bronzed, milled edge	450.00
PPn62	1860	—	1 Penny, Aluminum, milled edge	350.00
PPn63	1860	—	1 Penny, Silver, milled edge	900.00
PPn64	1860	—	1 Penny, Gold, milled edge	3500.
PPn65	1860	—	1 Penny, Copper, plain edge	450.00
PPn66	1860	—	1 Penny, Copper, bronzed, plain edge	450.00
PPn67	1860	—	1 Penny, Aluminum, plain edge	350.00
PPn68	1860	—	1 Penny, Silver, plain edge	900.00
PPn69	1860	—	1 Penny, Gold, plain edge	3500.

KM#	Date	Mintage	Identification	Mkt.Val.
PPn70	1887	—	1 Farthing, Copper, milled edge	350.00
PPn71	1887	—	1 Farthing, Copper, bronzed, milled edge	350.00
PPn72	1887	—	1 Farthing, Aluminum, milled edge	300.00
PPn73	1887	—	1 Farthing, Silver, milled edge	600.00
PPn74	1887	—	1 Farthing, Gold, milled edge	1800.
PPn75	1887	—	1 Farthing, Copper, plain edge	350.00
PPn76	1887	—	1 Farthing, Copper, bronzed, plain edge	350.00
PPn77	1887	—	1 Farthing, Aluminum, plain edge	300.00
PPn78	1887	—	1 Farthing, Silver, plain edge	600.00
PPn79	1887	—	1 Farthing, Gold, plain edge	1800.
PPn80	1887	—	1/2 Penny, Copper, milled edge	400.00
PPn81	1887	—	1/2 Penny, Copper, bronzed, milled edge	400.00
PPn82	1887	—	1/2 Penny, Aluminum, milled edge	300.00
PPn83	1887	—	1/2 Penny, Silver, milled edge	800.00
PPn84	1887	—	1/2 Penny, Gold, milled edge	3000.
PPn85	1887	—	1/2 Penny, Copper, plain edge	400.00
PPn86	1887	—	1/2 Penny, Copper, bronzed, plain edge	400.00
PPn87	1887	—	1/2 Penny, Aluminum, plain edge	300.00
PPn88	1887	—	1/2 Penny, Silver, plain edge	800.00
PPn89	1887	—	1/2 Penny, Gold, plain edge	3000.

KM#	Date	Mintage	Identification	Mkt.Val.
PPn90	1887	—	1 Penny, Copper, milled edge	450.00
PPn91	1887	—	1 Penny, Copper, Bronzed, milled edge	450.00
PPn92	1887	—	1 Penny, Aluminum, milled edge	350.00
PPn93	1887	—	1 Penny, Silver, milled edge	400.00
PPn94	1887	—	1 Penny, Gold, milled edge	3500.
PPn95	1887	—	1 Penny, Copper, plain edge	450.00
PPn96	1887	—	1 Penny, Copper, bronzed, plain edge	450.00
PPn97	1887	—	1 Penny, Aluminum, plain edge	350.00
PPn98	1887	—	1 Penny, Silver, plain edge	900.00
PPn99	1887	—	1 Penny, Gold, plain edge	3500.

KM#	Date	Mintage	Identification	Mkt.Val.
PPn100	1887	64 pcs.	6 Pence by Spink, Silver, plain edge	500.00
PPn101	1887	15 pcs.	6 Pence, Gold	1600.
PPn102	1887	10 pcs.	6 Pence, Copper	350.00
PPn103	1887	20 pcs.	6 Pence, Aluminum	250.00
PPn104	1887	9 pcs.	6 Pence, Tin	250.00

KM#	Date	Mintage	Identification	Mkt.Val.
PPn105	1887	—	1 Crown by Spink, Silver, plain edge w/J.R.T. on truncation.	1750.
PPn106	1887	32 pcs.	1 Crown, Silver w/SPINK & SON on truncation.	1750.
PPn107	1887	—	1 Crown, Silver w/o signature on obv.	1750.

KM#	Date	Mintage	Identification	Mkt.Val.
PPn108	1887	—	1 Crown, Silver, SPINK & SON on bottom rev.	1750.
PPn109	1887	6 pcs.	1 Crown, Gold, plain edge	6000.
PPn110	1887	5 pcs.	1 Crown, Copper, plain edge	1350.
PPn111	1887	10 pcs.	1 Crown, Aluminum, plain edge	1250.
PPn112	1887	—	1 Crown, Pewter, plain edge	1250.
PPn113	1887	—	1 Crown, Lead, plain edge	850.00
PPn114	1887	—	1 Crown, Silver, reeded edge	1700.
PPn115	1887	6 pcs.	1 Crown, Gold, reeded edge	6000.
PPn116	1887	—	1 Crown, Copper, edge inscription: MADE IN BAVARIA.	1300.
PPn117	1887	—	1 Crown, Pewter	1200.
PPn118	1887	—	1 Crown, Aluminum	1200.

TOKEN ISSUES (Tn)

Bank of England

1 SHILLING 6 PENCE

(18 Pence)

.925 SILVER

KM#	Date	Mintage	Fine	VF	XF	Unc
Tn2	1811	—	6.00	16.50	45.00	90.00
	1811	—	—	—	Proof	800.00
	1812	—	6.50	18.00	55.00	110.00
	1812	—	—	—	Proof	800.00

KM#	Date	Mintage	Fine	VF	XF	Unc
Tn3	1812	—	6.00	16.50	45.00	90.00
	1813	—	6.00	16.50	45.00	90.00
	1814	—	6.00	16.50	45.00	90.00
	1815	—	6.00	16.50	45.00	90.00
	1816	—	8.00	20.00	55.00	110.00

3 SHILLINGS

.925 SILVER

KM#	Date	Mintage	Fine	VF	XF	Unc
Tn4	1811	—	10.00	25.00	65.00	150.00
	1811	—	—	—	Proof	1150.
	1812	—	10.00	30.00	70.00	160.00

KM#	Date	Mintage	Fine	VF	XF	Unc
Tn5	1812	—	10.00	25.00	60.00	145.00
	1812	—	—	—	Proof	1150.
	1813	—	10.00	25.00	60.00	145.00
	1814	—	10.00	25.00	60.00	155.00
	1815	—	10.00	25.00	60.00	155.00
	1816	—	125.00	275.00	550.00	1150.

DOLLAR

.903 SILVER
Bank of England

KM#	Date	Mintage	Fine	VF	XF	Unc
Tn1	1804	—	60.00	125.00	350.00	625.00
	1804	—	—	—	Proof	1500.

COPPER

KM#	Date	Mintage	Fine	VF	XF	Unc
Tn1a	1804	—	—	—	Proof	900.00

NOTE: The silver proofs were struck on specially prepared flans while circulation strikes were struck over Spanish and Spanish Colonial 8 Reales.

19TH CENTURY ENGLISH

PENNY

COPPER

SHILLING

SILVER

2 SHILLINGS

SILVER

4 SHILLINGS

SILVER

40 SHILLINGS

GOLD and SILVER

The early 1800's witnessed a severe shortage of both copper and silver. The last issue of shillings and sixpence was in 1787. The turn of the century brought into circulation the countermarked Spanish dollars in two issues, both being heavily counterfeited. The Bank of England introduced its dollar or 5 shillings but the rise in value of silver caused many to be melted down. Private traders' and town tokens appeared in 1811 and 1812 along with regular bank tokens of the Bank of England. Private tokens continued to circulate until 1813 when they were finally forbidden by Act of Parliament. Various denominations were produced, the shilling being the commonest of the silver tokens and the penny of the copper tokens. These can be found listed in *'BRITISH TOKENS AND THEIR VALUES'* by P. Seaby and M. Bussell and *"THE SILVER TOKEN COINAGE, 1811-1812"* by R. Dalton.

MAUNDY SETS (MDS)

These small silver coins are a special ceremonial issue struck each year for use at the traditional ceremony on Maundy Thursday when the reigning monarch (or a representative) distributes them to a selected group of elderly men and women. The amount distributed to each person (in pence) is equal to the present age of the monarch. The issue has consisted of silver 1, 2, 3 and 4 penny pieces since the reign of Charles II.

KM#	Date	Mintage	Identification	Mkt. Val.
MDS63	1817	1,584	KM668-671	*XF* 150.00
MDS64	1818	1,188	KM668-671	*XF* 150.00
MDS65	1820	1,584	KM668-671	*XF* 150.00
MDS66	1822	2,970	KM683,684,685.1,686	*XF* 150.00
MDS67	1822	—	KM683,684,685.1,686	*Proof* 345.00
MDS68	1823	1,980	KM683,684,685.2,686	*XF* 150.00
MDS69	1824	1,584	KM683,684,685.2,686	*XF* 150.00
MDS70	1825	2,376	KM683,684,685.2,686	*XF* 150.00
MDS71	1826	2,376	KM683,684,685.2,686	*XF* 150.00
MDS72	1826	—	KM683,684,685.2,686	*Proof* 345.00
MDS73	1827	2,772	KM683,684,685.2,686	*XF* 150.00
MDS74	1828	2,772	KM683,684,685.2,686	*XF* 150.00
MDS75	1828	—	KM683,684,685.2,686	*Proof* 345.00
MDS76	1829	2,772	KM683,684,685.2,686	*XF* 150.00
MDS77	1830	2,772	KM683,684,685.2,686	*XF* 150.00
MDS78	1831	3,564	KM708-711	*XF* 150.00
MDS79	1831	—	KM708-711	*Proof* 500.00
MDS80	1832	2,574	KM708-711	*XF* 125.00
MDS81	1833	2,574	KM708-711	*XF* 125.00
MDS82	1834	2,574	KM708-711	*XF* 125.00
MDS83	1835	2,574	KM708-711	*XF* 125.00
MDS84	1836	2,574	KM708-711	*XF* 125.00
MDS85	1837	2,574	KM708-711	*XF* 125.00
MDS86	1838	4,158	KM727,729-730,732	100.00
MDS87	1838	—	KM727,729-730,732	200.00
MDS88	1839	4,125	KM727,729-730,732	100.00
MDS89	1839	300	KM727,729-730,732	*Proof* 400.00
MDS90	1840	4,125	KM727,729-730,732	110.00
MDS91	1841	2,574	KM727,729-730,732	110.00
MDS92	1842	4,125	KM727,729-730,732	100.00
MDS93	1843	4,158	KM727,729-730,732	100.00
MDS94	1844	4,158	KM727,729-730,732	100.00
MDS95	1845	4,158	KM727,729-730,732	100.00
MDS96	1846	4,158	KM727,729-730,732	100.00
MDS97	1847	4,158	KM727,729-730,732	100.00
MDS98	1848	4,158	KM727,729-730,732	100.00
MDS99	1849	4,158	KM727,729-730,732	100.00
MDS100	1850	4,158	KM727,729-730,732	100.00
MDS101	1851	4,158	KM727,729-730,732	100.00
MDS102	1852	4,158	KM727,729-730,732	100.00
MDS103	1853	4,158	KM727,729-730,732	100.00
MDS104	1853	—	KM727,729-730,732	*Proof* 750.00
MDS105	1854	4,158	KM727,729-730,732	100.00
MDS106	1855	4,158	KM727,729-730,732	100.00
MDS107	1856	4,158	KM727,729-730,732	100.00
MDS108	1857	4,158	KM727,729-730,732	100.00
MDS109	1858	4,158	KM727,729-730,732	100.00
MDS110	1859	4,158	KM727,729-730,732	100.00
MDS111	1860	4,158	KM727,729-730,732	100.00
MDS112	1861	4,158	KM727,729-730,732	100.00
MDS113	1862	4,158	KM727,729-730,732	100.00
MDS114	1863	4,158	KM727,729-730,732	100.00
MDS115	1864	4,158	KM727,729-730,732	100.00
MDS116	1865	4,158	KM727,729-730,732	100.00
MDS117	1866	4,158	KM727,729-730,732	100.00
MDS118	1867	4,158	KM727,729-730,732	100.00
MDS119	1867	—	KM727,729-730,732	*Proof* 300.00
MDS120	1868	4,158	KM727,729-730,732	100.00
MDS121	1869	4,158	KM727,729-730,732	125.00
MDS122	1870	4,488	KM727,729-730,732	100.00
MDS123	1871	4,488	KM727,729-730,732	100.00
MDS124	1871	—	KM727,729-730,732	*Proof* 300.00
MDS125	1872	4,328	KM727,729-730,732	100.00
MDS126	1873	4,162	KM727,729-730,732	100.00
MDS127	1874	4,488	KM727,729-730,732	100.00
MDS128	1875	4,154	KM727,729-730,732	100.00
MDS129	1876	4,488	KM727,729-730,732	100.00
MDS130	1877	4,488	KM727,729-730,732	100.00
MDS131	1878	4,488	KM727,729-730,732	100.00
MDS132	1878	—	KM727,729-730,732	*Proof* 300.00
MDS133	1879	4,488	KM727,729-730,732	100.00
MDS134	1880	4,488	KM727,729-730,732	100.00
MDS135	1881	4,488	KM727,729-730,732	100.00
MDS136	1881	—	KM727,729-730,732	*Proof* 350.00
MDS137	1882	4,488	KM727,729-730,732	100.00
MDS138	1883	4,488	KM727,729-730,732	100.00
MDS139	1884	4,488	KM727,729-730,732	100.00
MDS140	1885	4,488	KM727,729-730,732	100.00
MDS141	1886	4,488	KM727,729-730,732	100.00
MDS142	1887	4,488	KM727,729-730,732	100.00
MDS143	1888	4,488	KM758,770-771,773	105.00
MDS144	1889	4,488	KM758,770-771,773	105.00
MDS145	1888	—	KM758,770-771,773	*Proof* 200.00
MDS146	1890	4,488	KM758,770-771,773	105.00
MDS147	1891	4,488	KM758,770-771,773	105.00
MDS148	1892	4,488	KM758,770-771,773	105.00
MDS149	1893	8,976	KM775-778	80.00
MDS150	1894	8,976	KM775-778	80.00
MDS151	1895	8,877	KM775-778	80.00
MDS152	1896	8,476	KM775-778	80.00
MDS153	1897	9,388	KM775-778	80.00
MDS154	1898	9,147	KM775-778	80.00
MDS155	1899	8,976	KM775-778	80.00
MDS156	1900	8,976	KM775-778	80.00

PROOF SETS (PS)

KM#	Date	Mintage	Identification	Issue Price	Mkt. Val.
PS1	1821(6)	*2-5	KM677-682	—	Rare
PS2	1826(15)	*150	KM683-686,691,692a 693a,694-695,697a, 699-702	—	35,000.
PS3	1826(11)	Inc. Ab.	KM691,692a-693a,694 696,697a,700-702	—	30,000.
PS4	1831(14)	*225	KM705,706a-707a,709 714,716-718,720, 835	—	26,500.
PS5	1839(15)	300	KM725a-726a,727,729 730,731.2,732-736, 739a,740-742	—	47,000.
PS6	1839/48(16)	Inc. Ab.	KM725a-726a,727,729 730,731.2,732-736, 739a,740-742,745	—	47,000.
PS7	1853(17)	—	KM725a-726a,727,729 730,731.2,732-736, 737a-739a,740a,744, 746	—	35,000.
PS8	1853(16)	Inc. Ab.	KM725a-726a,727,729 730,731.2,732-736, 738a-739a,740a,744, 746	—	33,500.
PS9	1887(11)	797	KM758-759,761-769	—	10,000.
PS10	1887(11)	Inc. Ab.	KM758-762,764-769	—	10,000.
PS11	1887(7)	287	KM758-759,761-765	—	1500.
PS12	1887(7)	Inc. Ab.	KM758-762,764-765	—	1500.
PS13	1893(10)	773	KM777,779,787	—	10,000.
PS14	1893(6)	556	KM777,779-783	—	1800.

The Hellenic (Greek) Republic is situated in southeastern Europe on the southern tip of the Balkan Peninsula. The republic includes many islands, the most important of which are Crete and the Ionian Islands. Greece (including islands) has an area of 50,944 sq. mi. (131,940 sq. km.) and a population of 10.3 million. Capital: Athens. Greece is still largely agricultural. Tobacco, cotton, fruit and wool are exported.

Greece, the Mother of Western civilization, attained the peak of its culture in the 5th century B.C., when it contributed more to government, drama, art and architecture than any other people to this time. Greece fell under Roman domination in the 2nd and 1st centuries B.C., becoming part of the Byzantine Empire until Constantinople fell to the Crusaders in 1202. With the fall of Constantinople to the Turks in 1453, Greece became part of the Ottoman Empire. Independence from Turkey was won with the revolution of 1821-27. In 1833, Greece was established as a monarchy, with sovereignty guaranteed by Britain, France and Russia. After a lengthy power struggle between the monarchist forces and democratic factions, Greece was

RULERS

John Capodistrias, 1828-1831
Othon (Otto of Bavaria), 1832-1862
George I, 1863-1913

MINT MARKS

(a) - Paris, privy marks only
A - Paris
B - Vienna
BB - Strassburg
(c) Aegina (1828-1832), Chain and anchor
H - Heaton, Birmingham
K - Bordeaux
KN - King's Norton
(o) - Athens (1838-1855), Owl
(p) - Poissy - Thunderbolt

MONETARY SYSTEM

Until 1831
100 Lepta = 1 Phoenix
Commencing 1831
100 Lepta = 1 Drachma

KINGDOM

1828-1925

LEPTON

COPPER, 17mm
Obv: Phoenix in solid circle.

KM#	Date	Mintage	Fine	VF	XF	Unc
1	1828	.480	50.00	100.00	250.00	500.00
	1830	.026	60.00	120.00	275.00	600.00

Obv: Phoenix in pearl circle, 17mm.

KM#	Date	Mintage	Fine	VF	XF	Unc
5	1830	.400	50.00	100.00	250.00	500.00

Obv: W/o circle, 16mm.

KM#	Date	Mintage	Fine	VF	XF	Unc
9	1831	.612	50.00	100.00	250.00	500.00

Type 1 — ΒΑΣΙΛΕΙΑ

KM#	Date	Mintage	Fine	VF	XF	Unc
13	1832	2.200	50.00	100.00	250.00	500.00

KM#	Date	Mintage	Fine	VF	XF	Unc
13	1833	Inc. Ab.	20.00	35.00	65.00	110.00
	1834	Inc. Ab.	50.00	100.00	300.00	800.00
	1837	.160	25.00	50.00	150.00	450.00
	1838	.270	25.00	50.00	150.00	450.00
	1839	.150	25.00	50.00	150.00	450.00
	1840	.700	25.00	50.00	150.00	450.00
	1841	.370	25.00	50.00	150.00	450.00
	1842	.120	25.00	50.00	150.00	450.00
	1843	.630	25.00	50.00	150.00	450.00

Type 2 — ΒΑΣΙΛΕΙΟΝ

KM#	Date	Mintage	Fine	VF	XF	Unc
22	1844	.151	30.00	75.00	175.00	475.00
	1845	.160	30.00	75.00	175.00	475.00
	1846	.141	30.00	75.00	175.00	475.00

Obv: Smaller crowned arms.
Rev: Redesigned wreath.

KM#	Date	Mintage	Fine	VF	XF	Unc
26	1847	.273	70.00	120.00	300.00	800.00
	1848	.084	50.00	100.00	200.00	500.00
	1849	.090	50.00	100.00	200.00	500.00

Size reduced to 15mm

KM#	Date	Mintage	Fine	VF	XF	Unc
30	1851	.400	22.00	45.00	100.00	300.00
	1857	.243	22.00	45.00	100.00	300.00

KM#	Date	Mintage	Fine	VF	XF	Unc
40	1869BB	14.976	4.00	10.00	25.00	75.00
	1870BB	Inc. Ab.	10.00	25.00	75.00	150.00

KM#	Date	Mintage	Fine	VF	XF	Unc
52	1878K	7.132	4.00	10.00	25.00	75.00
	1879A	.398	5.00	12.00	50.00	100.00

2 LEPTA

COPPER
Type 1 — ΒΑΣΙΛΕΙΑ

KM#	Date	Mintage	Fine	VF	XF	Unc
14	1832	2.475	35.00	75.00	200.00	450.00
	1833	Inc. Ab.	15.00	30.00	60.00	125.00
	1834	Inc. Ab.	50.00	100.00	250.00	500.00
	1836	.049	100.00	200.00	350.00	750.00
	1837	.222	25.00	50.00	125.00	350.00
	1838	.701	25.00	50.00	125.00	350.00
	1839	.661	25.00	50.00	125.00	350.00
	1840	.520	25.00	50.00	125.00	350.00
	1842	.470	25.00	50.00	125.00	350.00

Type 2 — ΒΑΣΙΛΕΙΟΝ

KM#	Date	Mintage	Fine	VF	XF	Unc
23	1844	.206	45.00	85.00	225.00	475.00
	1845	.242	45.00	85.00	225.00	475.00

Obv: Smaller crowned arms.
Rev: Redesigned wreath.

KM#	Date	Mintage	Fine	VF	XF	Unc
27	1847	.082	50.00	150.00	300.00	750.00
	1848	.258	25.00	50.00	120.00	475.00
	1849	.146	35.00	75.00	200.00	500.00

Size reduced to 17mm.

KM#	Date	Mintage	Fine	VF	XF	Unc
31	1851	.388	20.00	40.00	100.00	250.00
	1857	.544	20.00	40.00	100.00	250.00

KM#	Date	Mintage	Fine	VF	XF	Unc
41	1869BB	7.482	3.00	6.00	18.00	65.00
	1869BB	—	—	—	Proof	220.00

KM#	Date	Mintage	Fine	VF	XF	Unc
53	1878K large anchor					
		3.750	1.50	3.50	12.00	50.00
	1878K small anchor					
		Inc. Ab.	10.00	25.00	40.00	85.00
	1878K	—	—	—	Proof	220.00

5 LEPTA

COPPER, 28mm
Obv: Phoenix in solid circle.

KM#	Date	Mintage	Fine	VF	XF	Unc
2	1828	.400	50.00	100.00	200.00	500.00
	1830	.022	50.00	100.00	250.00	600.00

Obv: Phoenix in pearl circle.

KM#	Date	Mintage	Fine	VF	XF	Unc
6	1830	.150	45.00	90.00	185.00	400.00

Obv: W/o circle.

KM#	Date	Mintage	Fine	VF	XF	Unc
10	1831	.230	45.00	90.00	185.00	400.00

Type 1 — ΒΑΣΙΛΕΙΑ

KM#	Date	Mintage	Fine	VF	XF	Unc
16	1833	2.500	15.00	30.00	70.00	175.00
	1834	Inc. Ab.	50.00	100.00	250.00	750.00
	1836	1,000	400.00	800.00	1500.	3000.
	1837	.116	50.00	100.00	225.00	450.00
	1838/7	1.472	25.00	65.00	150.00	385.00
	1838	Inc. Ab.	25.00	50.00	125.00	350.00
	1839	1.186	25.00	50.00	125.00	350.00
	1840	.417	25.00	50.00	125.00	350.00
	1841	.864	25.00	50.00	125.00	350.00
	1842	.682	25.00	50.00	125.00	350.00

Type 2 — ΒΑΣΙΛΕΙΟΝ

KM#	Date	Mintage	Fine	VF	XF	Unc
24	1844	.089	50.00	100.00	200.00	450.00
	1845	.316	40.00	80.00	150.00	375.00
	1846	.190	40.00	60.00	125.00	350.00

KM#	Date	Mintage	Fine	VF	XF	Unc
28	1847	.270	50.00	100.00	200.00	450.00
	1848	.394	40.00	80.00	150.00	375.00
	1849	.374	40.00	60.00	125.00	350.00

KM#	Date	Mintage	Fine	VF	XF	Unc
32	1851	.620	25.00	50.00	100.00	300.00
	1857	.350	25.00	50.00	100.00	300.00

KM#	Date	Mintage	Fine	VF	XF	Unc
42	1869BB	23.945	2.00	5.00	20.00	70.00
	1870BB	Inc. Ab.	18.00	35.00	90.00	225.00

KM#	Date	Mintage	Fine	VF	XF	Unc
54	1878K	11.528	2.00	6.00	30.00	80.00
	1879A	.470	20.00	50.00	150.00	800.00
	1882A	14.400	3.00	7.00	40.00	120.00

COPPER-NICKEL

KM#	Date	Mintage	Fine	VF	XF	Unc
58	1894A	4.000	2.00	5.00	20.00	50.00
	1895A	4.000	2.00	5.00	20.00	50.00

10 LEPTA

COPPER, 35mm.
Obv: Phoenix in solid circle.

KM#	Date	Mintage	Fine	VF	XF	Unc
3	1828	.450	50.00	100.00	300.00	600.00
	1830	.034	70.00	150.00	400.00	800.00

Obv: Phoenix in pearl circle, 33mm.

KM#	Date	Mintage	Fine	VF	XF	Unc
8	1830	1.200	50.00	100.00	300.00	600.00

NOTE: Varieties exist.

Obv: Phoenix w/o circle.

KM#	Date	Mintage	Fine	VF	XF	Unc
12	1831	1.223	50.00	100.00	200.00	500.00

Set Special Head

KM#	Date	Mintage	Fine	VF	XF	Unc
17	1833	.520	25.00	50.00	100.00	200.00
	1836	.919	40.00	100.00	200.00	500.00
	1837	2.660	40.00	100.00	200.00	500.00
	1838	.918	40.00	100.00	200.00	500.00
	1843	.700	40.00	100.00	200.00	500.00
	1844	1.064	100.00	175.00	400.00	800.00

Set Special Head

KM#	Date	Mintage	Fine	VF	XF	Unc
25	1844	Inc. Ab.	30.00	60.00	200.00	500.00
	1845	.985	30.00	60.00	300.00	600.00
	1846/45	1.275	30.00	60.00	200.00	500.00
	1846	Inc. Ab.	30.00	60.00	200.00	500.00

KM#	Date	Mintage	Fine	VF	XF	Unc
29	1847	.740	50.00	100.00	300.00	750.00
	1848	1.174	40.00	80.00	175.00	450.00
	1849/8 small crown	1.160	40.00	80.00	175.00	450.00
	1849 small crown	Inc. Ab.	40.00	80.00	175.00	450.00
	1849 large crown	Inc. Ab.	200.00	400.00	700.00	1200.
	1850	1.282	40.00	80.00	150.00	350.00
	1851	.587	40.00	80.00	150.00	350.00
	1857	.883	40.00	80.00	150.00	350.00

KM#	Date	Mintage	Fine	VF	XF	Unc
43	1869BB	14.994	3.00	7.00	30.00	80.00
	1869BB	—	—	—	Proof	250.00
	1870BB	Inc. Ab.	15.00	30.00	90.00	250.00

KM#	Date	Mintage	Fine	VF	XF	Unc
55	1878K	7.140	2.00	6.00	28.00	80.00
	1879A	.358	20.00	60.00	175.00	850.00
	1882A	16.000	2.00	6.00	35.00	200.00

COPPER-NICKEL

KM#	Date	Mintage	Fine	VF	XF	Unc
59	1894A	3.000	2.00	5.00	20.00	50.00
	1895A	3.000	2.00	5.00	20.00	50.00

20 LEPTA

COPPER

KM#	Date	Mintage	Fine	VF	XF	Unc
11	1831	2.273	50.00	100.00	300.00	1000.

1.0000 g, .835 SILVER, .0268 oz ASW

KM#	Date	Mintage	Fine	VF	XF	Unc
44	1874A	2.223	3.00	6.00	18.00	40.00
	1874A	—	—	—	Proof	400.00
	1883A	1.000	10.00	25.00	55.00	120.00

COPPER-NICKEL

KM#	Date	Mintage	Fine	VF	XF	Unc
57	1893A	.248	25.00	75.00	150.00	700.00
	1894A	4.752	1.50	3.00	10.00	50.00
	1895A	5.000	1.50	3.00	10.00	50.00

1/4 DRACHMA

1.1190 g, .900 SILVER, .0324 oz ASW
Obv: Young head.

KM#	Date	Mintage	Fine	VF	XF	Unc
18	1833	.780	35.00	65.00	125.00	275.00
	1834A	—	45.00	90.00	175.00	400.00
	1845	—	300.00	500.00	1500.	3000.
	1846	—	400.00	800.00	2000.	4000.

Obv: Old head, 15mm.

KM#	Date	Mintage	Fine	VF	XF	Unc
33	1851	—	300.00	600.00	1250.	3000.
	1855	—	100.00	200.00	500.00	1000.

1/2 DRACHMA

2.2380 g, .900 SILVER, .0648 oz ASW

KM#	Date	Mintage	Fine	VF	XF	Unc
19	1833	.900	25.00	50.00	100.00	225.00
	1834A	—	45.00	90.00	160.00	325.00
	1842(o)	—	250.00	500.00	1200.	2200.
	1843(o)	—	300.00	600.00	1400.	2800.
	1846	—	250.00	500.00	1200.	2200.
	1847	—	300.00	600.00	1400.	2800.

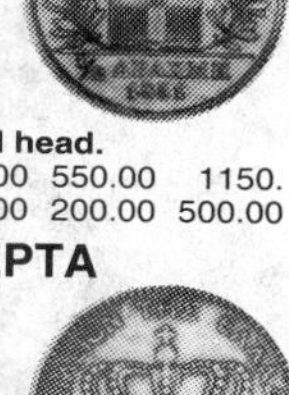

Obv: Old head.

KM#	Date	Mintage	Fine	VF	XF	Unc
34	1851	—	250.00	550.00	1150.	2800.
	1855	—	100.00	200.00	500.00	1000.

50 LEPTA

2.5000 g, .835 SILVER, .0671 oz ASW

KM#	Date	Mintage	Fine	VF	XF	Unc
37	1868A	60 pcs.	—	—	—	6000.
	1874A	4.501	3.00	7.00	20.00	50.00
	1874A	—	—	—	Proof	400.00
	1883A	.600	5.00	12.00	35.00	120.00

PHOENIX

3.8700 g, .943 SILVER, .1173 oz ASW

KM#	Date	Mintage	Fine	VF	XF	Unc
4	1828(Aegina)	.012	250.00	400.00	1000.	2000.

DRACHMA

4.0293 g, .900 SILVER, .1295 oz ASW
Obv: Young head.

KM#	Date	Mintage	Fine	VF	XF	Unc
15	1832	1.125	50.00	100.00	200.00	500.00
	1833	Inc. Ab.	25.00	50.00	100.00	350.00
	1833	—	—	—	Proof	1000.
	1833A	—	50.00	100.00	250.00	600.00
	1833A	—	—	—	Proof	1000.
	1834A	—	150.00	300.00	800.00	1500.
	1845(o)	—	1000.	2000.	4500.	13,500.
	1846	—	200.00	500.00	1000.	2000.
	1847	—	700.00	1500.	3000.	10,000.

Obv: Old head.

KM#	Date	Mintage	Fine	VF	XF	Unc
35	1851	—	350.00	750.00	1500.	3500.

5.0000 g, .835 SILVER, .1342 oz ASW

KM#	Date	Mintage	Fine	VF	XF	Unc
38	1868A	.480	20.00	45.00	100.00	250.00
	1873A	1.802	20.00	40.00	80.00	200.00
	1873A	—	—	—	Proof	500.00
	1874A	2.249	20.00	45.00	120.00	285.00
	1883A	.800	20.00	50.00	300.00	700.00

2 DRACHMAI

10.0000 g, .835 SILVER, .2684 oz ASW

KM#	Date	Mintage	Fine	VF	XF	Unc
39	1868A	.047	50.00	100.00	375.00	900.00
	1873A	.839	40.00	90.00	350.00	800.00
	1873A	—	—	—	Proof	1000.
	1883A	.250	50.00	100.00	425.00	1200.

5 DRACHMAI

22.5000 g, .900 SILVER, .6511 oz ASW

KM#	Date	Mintage	Fine	VF	XF	Unc
20	1833	.378	100.00	200.00	450.00	1200.
	1833	—	—	—	Proof	3000.
	1833A	—	100.00	200.00	450.00	1200.
	1833A	—	—	—	Proof	3000.
	1833(o)	—	1200.	2400.	6000.	10,000.
	1844(o)	—	300.00	700.00	1500.	3500.
	1845	—	3000.	4500.	6500.	12,000.

Obv: Old head. Rev: Similar to KM#20.

KM#	Date	Mintage	Fine	VF	XF	Unc
36	1851	—	500.00	850.00	2500.	6000.
	1851	—	—	—	Proof	—

25.0000 g, .900 SILVER, .7234 oz ASW

KM#	Date	Mintage	Fine	VF	XF	Unc
46	1875A	1.000	25.00	60.00	225.00	600.00
	1875A inverted anchor privy mark	—	150.00	200.00	600.00	2550.
	1875A	—	—	—	Proof	2000.
	1876A	2.092	20.00	50.00	200.00	600.00
	1876A	—	—	—	Proof	2000.

1.6129 g, .900 GOLD, .0467 oz AGW

KM#	Date	Mintage	Fine	VF	XF	Unc
47	1876A	9,294	250.00	450.00	850.00	1750.

10 DRACHMAI

3.2258 g, .900 GOLD, .0933 oz AGW

KM#	Date	Mintage	Fine	VF	XF	Unc
48	1876A	.019	200.00	350.00	575.00	1550.

20 DRACHMAI

5.7760 g, .900 GOLD, .1672 oz AGW

KM#	Date	Mintage	Fine	VF	XF	Unc
21	1833	.018	200.00	450.00	850.00	1750.

6.4516 g, .900 GOLD, .1867 oz AGW

KM#	Date	Mintage	Fine	VF	XF	Unc
49	1876A	.037	125.00	200.00	400.00	850.00
	1876A	1 known	—	—	Proof	*12,000.

***NOTE:** Spink Coin Auctions no. 10 9-80 Brilliant F.D.C. realized $12,000.

KM#	Date	Mintage	Fine	VF	XF	Unc
56	1884A	.550	75.00	100.00	145.00	250.00
	1884A	—	—	—	Proof	3500.

50 DRACHMAI

16.1290 g, .900 GOLD, .4667 oz AGW

KM#	Date	Mintage	Fine	VF	XF	Unc
50	1876A	182 pcs.	2000.	3000.	4000.	8000.

100 DRACHMAI

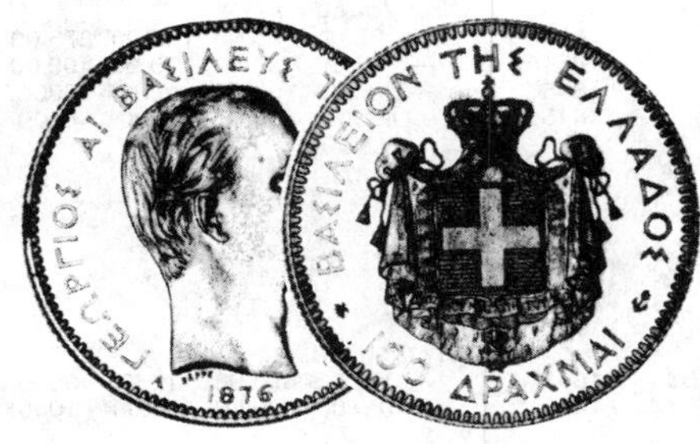

32.2580 g, .900 GOLD, .9335 oz AGW

KM#	Date	Mintage	Fine	VF	XF	Unc
51	1876A	76 pcs.	5000.	8000.	13,000.	20,000.
	1876A	—	—	—	Proof	25,000.

ESSAIS (E)

KM#	Date	Mintage	Identification	Mkt.Val.
E1	1868	4	50 Lepta, Silver, E on obverse	3250.
E2	1868	—	1 Drachma, Silver, E to left of date	1800.

KM#	Date	Mintage	Identification	Mkt.Val.
E3	1868	3	1 Drachma, plain edge, E to left of date	2500.

KM#	Date	Mintage	Identification	Mkt.Val.
E4	1869	—	1 Lepton, Copper, ESSAI	2000.

KM#	Date	Mintage	Identification	Mkt.Val.
E5	1869	—	2 Lepta, Copper, ESSAI	550.00
E6	1869	—	5 Lepta, Copper, ESSAI	700.00

KM#	Date	Mintage	Identification	Mkt.Val.
E7	1869	—	10 Lepta, Copper, ESSAI	1100.

KM#	Date	Mintage	Identification	Mkt.Val.
E8	1869	—	20 Lepta, Silver, E (Essai) below date	3250.

KM#	Date	Mintage	Identification	Mkt.Val.
E9	1869	—	5 Drachmai, Gold, E (Essai)	7500.

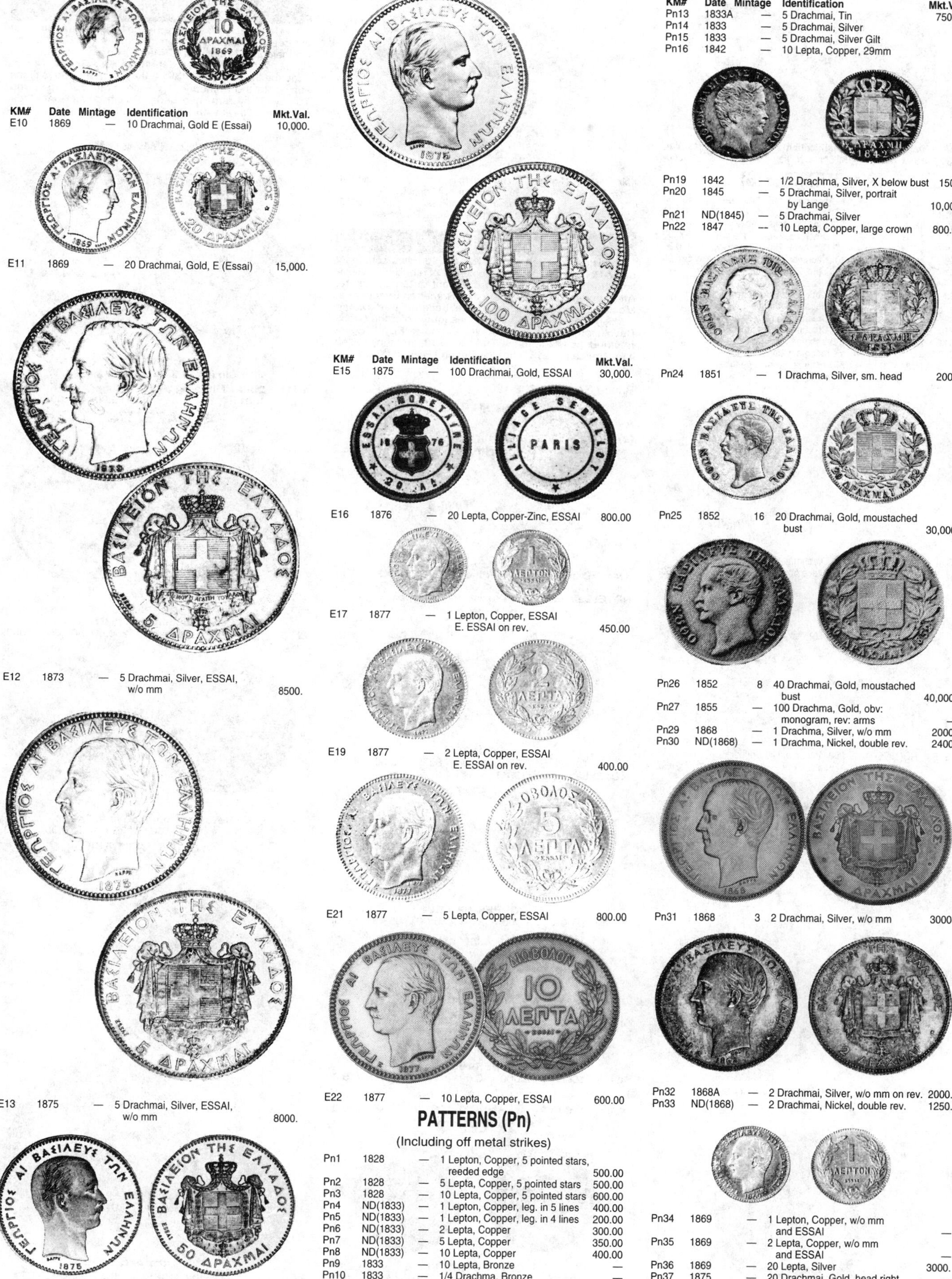

KM#	Date	Mintage	Identification	Mkt.Val.
E10	1869	—	10 Drachmai, Gold E (Essai)	10,000.
E11	1869	—	20 Drachmai, Gold, E (Essai)	15,000.
E12	1873	—	5 Drachmai, Silver, ESSAI, w/o mm	8500.
E13	1875	—	5 Drachmai, Silver, ESSAI, w/o mm	8000.
E14	1875	—	50 Drachmai, Gold, ESSAI	17,500.

KM#	Date	Mintage	Identification	Mkt.Val.
E15	1875	—	100 Drachmai, Gold, ESSAI	30,000.
E16	1876	—	20 Lepta, Copper-Zinc, ESSAI	800.00
E17	1877	—	1 Lepton, Copper, ESSAI E. ESSAI on rev.	450.00
E19	1877	—	2 Lepta, Copper, ESSAI E. ESSAI on rev.	400.00
E21	1877	—	5 Lepta, Copper, ESSAI	800.00
E22	1877	—	10 Lepta, Copper, ESSAI	600.00

PATTERNS (Pn)

(Including off metal strikes)

KM#	Date	Mintage	Identification	Mkt.Val.
Pn1	1828	—	1 Lepton, Copper, 5 pointed stars, reeded edge	500.00
Pn2	1828	—	5 Lepta, Copper, 5 pointed stars	500.00
Pn3	1828	—	10 Lepta, Copper, 5 pointed stars	600.00
Pn4	ND(1833)	—	1 Lepton, Copper, leg. in 5 lines	400.00
Pn5	ND(1833)	—	1 Lepton, Copper, leg. in 4 lines	200.00
Pn6	ND(1833)	—	2 Lepta, Copper	300.00
Pn7	ND(1833)	—	5 Lepta, Copper	350.00
Pn8	ND(1833)	—	10 Lepta, Copper	400.00
Pn9	1833	—	10 Lepta, Bronze	—
Pn10	1833	—	1/4 Drachma, Bronze	—
Pn11	ND(1833)	—	1 Drachma, Copper	500.00
Pn12	ND(1833)	—	5 Drachmai, Copper	800.00

KM#	Date	Mintage	Identification	Mkt.Val.
Pn13	1833A	—	5 Drachmai, Tin	750.00
Pn14	1833	—	5 Drachmai, Silver	—
Pn15	1833	—	5 Drachmai, Silver Gilt	—
Pn16	1842	—	10 Lepta, Copper, 29mm	—
Pn19	1842	—	1/2 Drachma, Silver, X below bust	1500.
Pn20	1845	—	5 Drachmai, Silver, portrait by Lange	10,000.
Pn21	ND(1845)	—	5 Drachmai, Silver	—
Pn22	1847	--	10 Lepta, Copper, large crown	800.00
Pn24	1851	—	1 Drachma, Silver, sm. head	2000.
Pn25	1852	16	20 Drachmai, Gold, moustached bust	30,000.
Pn26	1852	8	40 Drachmai, Gold, moustached bust	40,000.
Pn27	1855	—	100 Drachma, Gold, obv: monogram, rev: arms	—
Pn29	1868	—	1 Drachma, Silver, w/o mm	2000.
Pn30	ND(1868)	—	1 Drachma, Nickel, double rev.	2400.
Pn31	1868	3	2 Drachmai, Silver, w/o mm	3000.
Pn32	1868A	—	2 Drachmai, Silver, w/o mm on rev.	2000.
Pn33	ND(1868)	—	2 Drachmai, Nickel, double rev.	1250.
Pn34	1869	—	1 Lepton, Copper, w/o mm and ESSAI	—
Pn35	1869	—	2 Lepta, Copper, w/o mm and ESSAI	—
Pn36	1869	—	20 Lepta, Silver	3000.
Pn37	1875	—	20 Drachmai, Gold, head right	—
Pn38	1876	—	5 Drachmai, Gold, KM47	—
PnA39	1876	—	100 Drachma, Gold, uniface	—

KM#	Date	Mintage	Identification	Mkt.Val.
Pn39	1889	—	50 Lepta, Nickel	1000.

TRIAL STRIKES (TS)

KM#	Date	Mintage	Identification	Mkt.Val.
TS1	1832	—	1 Drachma, Tin, uniface obv.	400.00
TS2	1832	—	1 Drachma, Tin, uniface rev.	400.00
TS3	1833	—	5 Lepta, Tin, uniface rev.	400.00
TS4	1833	—	1/2 Drachma, Tin, uniface obv.	400.00
TS5	1833	—	1/2 Drachma, Tin, uniface rev.	400.00
TS6	ND(1833)	—	20 Drachmai, Copper, uniface rev.	500.00
TS7	1842	—	10 Lepta, Zinc, 28mm, obv. uniface, octagonal	—
TS8	1842	—	10 Lepta, Zinc, 28mm, rev. uniface, octagonal	—
TS9	1842	—	1/4 Drachma, Silver, obv. uniface	—
TS10	1842	—	1/4 Drachma, Silver, rev. uniface	—
TS11	ND(1845)	—	5 Drachmai, Silver, uniface obv.	3000.
TS12	1851	—	1 Drachma, Copper	600.00
TS13	ND(1873)	—	5 Drachmai, Bronze, uniface rev., ESSAI	3000.

TS14	1875	1	50 Drachmai, Gilt Copper, uniface obv.	2550.

TS15	ND(1875)	1	50 Drachma, Gilt Copper, uniface rev.	2550.

TS16	1875	1	100 Drachmai, Gilt Copper, uniface obv.	2650.

KM#	Date	Mintage	Identification	Mkt.Val.
TS17	ND(1875)	1	100 Drachmai, Gilt Copper, uniface rev. w/Essai	2650.
TS18	ND(1876)	—	20 Drachmai, Copper, uniface rev.	—

CRETE

The island of Crete (Kriti), located 60 miles southeast of the Peloponnesus, was the center of a brilliant civilization that flourished before the advent of Greek culture. After being conquered by the Romans, Byzantines, Moslems and Venetians, Crete became part of the Turkish Empire in 1669. As a consequence of the Greek Revolution of the 1820s, it was ceded to Egypt. Egypt returned the island to the Turks in 1840, and they ceded it to Greece in 1913, after the Second Balkan War.

RULERS

Prince George, 1898-1906

MINT MARKS

A - Paris
(a) - Paris (privy marks only)

LEPTON

BRONZE, 15mm

KM#	Date	Mintage	Fine	VF	XF	Unc
1.1	1900A	.289	3.50	7.50	16.50	45.00

NOTE: Later date (1901) exists for this type.

2 LEPTA

BRONZE

KM#	Date	Mintage	Fine	VF	XF	Unc
2	1900A	.793	3.50	6.50	15.00	42.00

NOTE: Later date (1901) exists for this type.

5 LEPTA

COPPER-NICKEL

KM#	Date	Mintage	Fine	VF	XF	Unc
3	1900A	4.000	2.50	5.00	25.00	100.00

10 LEPTA

COPPER-NICKEL

KM#	Date	Mintage	Fine	VF	XF	Unc
4.1	1900A	2.000	3.00	7.00	28.00	110.00

Medal strike

KM#	Date	Mintage	Fine	VF	XF	Unc
4.2	1900A	—	8.00	20.00	50.00	200.00

20 LEPTA

COPPER-NICKEL

KM#	Date	Mintage	Fine	VF	XF	Unc
5	1900A	1.250	3.50	7.50	35.00	140.00

NOTE: For coins similar to the five listings above, but dated 1893-95, see Greece.

IONIAN ISLANDS

The Ionian Islands, situated in the Ionian Sea to the west of Greece, is the collective name for the islands of Corfu, Cephalonia, Zante, Santa Maura, Ithaca, Cythera and Paxo, with their minor dependencies. Before Britain acquired the islands, 1809-14, they were at various times subject to the authority of Venice, France, Russia and Turkey. They remained under British control until their cession to Greece on March 29, 1864.

(1799-1807)

MONETARY SYSTEM

2 Soldi = 1 Gazetta

GAZETTA

COPPER
Similar to 5 Gazettae, KM#2.

KM#	Date	Mintage	VG	Fine	VF	XF
1	1801	—	75.00	175.00	450.00	900.00

5 GAZETTAE

COPPER
Rev: Denomination in Greek.

KM#	Date	Mintage	VG	Fine	VF	XF
2	1801	—	100.00	250.00	500.00	1000.

Rev: Denomination in Italian.

KM#	Date	Mintage	VG	Fine	VF	XF
3	1801	—	100.00	250.00	500.00	1000.

10 GAZETTAE

COPPER
Obv. leg: ΕΠΤΑΝΗΣΟΣ ΠΟΛΙΤΕΙΑ
Rev: Denomination in Greek.

KM#	Date	Mintage	VG	Fine	VF	XF
4	1801	—	150.00	350.00	750.00	1500.

Obv. leg: ΣΠΤΑΝΗΣΟΣ ΠΟΛΙΤΣΙΑ
Rev: Denomination in Italian.

KM#	Date	Mintage	VG	Fine	VF	XF
5	1801	—	—	—	Rare	—

COUNTERMARKED COINAGE

BRITISH ADMINISTRATION

(1809-1863)

The British military forces under General Campbell were headquartered on the island of Zacynthos (Zante). A shortage of small silver coinage resulted in the countermarking of circulated coins of the Two Sicilies of 10 and 20 Grani denominations and worn Spanish and Spanish Colonial silver 1 and 2 reales coinage.

The Type I countermarks of 1813 were raised numerals 25, 30, 50 and 60 in rectangular indent. These being easily counterfeited lead to the 1814 Type II oval indent with a crudely executed bust of King George III over raised numerals. The Type II countermark was applied to existing Type I countermarked coinage and other coins found in circulation. No single countermarked Type I pieces are known to have survived.

MONETARY SYSTEM

40 Paras = 1 Piastre

220 Paras = 1 Spanish Dollar (8 Reales)

TYPE I

Raised 25, 30, 50 or 60 in rectangular indent.

TYPE II

Portrait of King George III over 25, 30, 50 or 60 in oval indent.

25 PARAS

SILVER
c/m: Type I and II on Naples and Sicily 10 Grani of Charles II.

KM#	Date	Mintage	Good	VG	Fine	VF
18	ND(1814)	—	150.00	250.00	425.00	750.00

c/m: Type II on Spanish or Spanish Colonial 1 Real.

KM#	Date	Mintage	Good	VG	Fine	VF
19	ND(1814)	—	150.00	200.00	325.00	550.00

30 PARAS

SILVER

c/m: Type II on Naples and Sicily 10 Grani.

KM#	Date	Mintage	Good	VG	Fine	VF
20	ND(1814)	—	—	—	Rare	—

c/m: Type II on Spanish or Spanish Colonial 1 Real.

KM#	Date	Mintage	Good	VG	Fine	VF
21	ND(1814)	—	—	—	Rare	—

NOTE: One unusual piece exists with only one countermark on a French coin of Louis XIV. It is considered by some experts to be a contemporary counterfeit, since the authorization for these coins mentions only Spanish and Two Sicilies coinage. However, it may be that the islanders were permitted to present any silver coins in their possession for countermarking.

50 PARAS

SILVER
c/m: Type II on Naples & Sicily 20 Grani of Charles II.

KM#	Date	Mintage	Good	VG	Fine	VF
22.1	ND(1814)	—	150.00	225.00	400.00	700.00

c/m: Type II on Naples & Sicily 20 Grani of Ferdinando IV.

KM#	Date	Mintage	Good	VG	Fine	VF
22.2	ND(1814)	—	150.00	225.00	400.00	700.00

c/m: Type I and II on Spanish or Spanish Colonial 2 Reales.

KM#	Date	Mintage	Good	VG	Fine	VF
23.1	ND(1814)	—	150.00	225.00	400.00	700.00

c/m: Type I and II on worn disc.

KM#	Date	Mintage	Good	VG	Fine	VF
23.2	ND(1814)	—	125.00	200.00	300.00	550.00

60 PARAS

SILVER
c/m: Type II on Naples and Sicily 20 Grani.

KM#	Date	Mintage	Good	VG	Fine	VF
24	ND(1814)	—	275.00	400.00	650.00	1000.

c/m: Type I and II on Spanish 2 Reales of Philip V.

KM#	Date	Mintage	Good	VG	Fine	VF
25	ND(1814)	—	275.00	400.00	650.00	1000.

DECIMAL COINAGE

MONETARY SYSTEM

(Until 1835)

4 Lepta = Obol

100 Oboli = 1 Dollar

(Commencing 1835)

5 Lepta = Obol

100 Oboli = 1 Dollar

LEPTON

COPPER
Obv: Winged lion above date.
Rev: Seated Britannia above 4 (= 1/4 Obol).

KM#	Date	Mintage	Fine	VF	XF	Unc
30	1821	—	100.00	250.00	500.00	1000.

NOTE: Most of these coins are overstruck on Venetian coins by native craftsmen, and are very crude.

KM#	Date	Mintage	Fine	VF	XF	Unc
34	1834.	—	2.00	7.00	20.00	65.00
	1834.	—	—	—	Proof	300.00
	1835.	—	2.00	7.00	20.00	65.00
	1835	—	2.00	7.00	20.00	65.00
	1848.	13.483	3.00	10.00	30.00	75.00
	1848	Inc. Ab.	4.00	12.00	35.00	90.00
	1849.	Inc. Ab.	2.00	7.00	20.00	65.00
	1849	—	—	—	Proof	300.00
	1851.	Inc. Ab.	2.00	7.00	20.00	65.00
	1851.	—	—	—	Proof	300.00
	1853.	1.344	2.00	7.00	20.00	65.00
	1853	—	—	—	Proof	300.00
	1857.	Inc. Ab.	2.00	7.00	20.00	65.00
	1857	Inc. Ab.	2.00	7.00	20.00	65.00
	1862.	Inc. Ab.	2.00	7.00	20.00	65.00
	1862	—	—	—	Proof	300.00

2 LEPTA

COPPER

KM#	Date	Mintage	Fine	VF	XF	Unc
31	1819.	9.462	10.00	25.00	55.00	120.00
	1819	—	—	—	Proof	250.00
	1820.	Inc. Ab.	10.00	25.00	55.00	120.00
	1820	—	—	—	Proof	250.00

OBOL

COPPER

KM#	Date	Mintage	Fine	VF	XF	Unc
32	1819.	8.279	25.00	50.00	85.00	235.00
	1819	—	—	—	Proof	450.00
	1819 medal strike	—	—	—	Proof	500.00

2 OBOLI

COPPER

KM#	Date	Mintage	Fine	VF	XF	Unc
33	1819	4.140	25.00	50.00	100.00	250.00
	1819	—	—	—	Proof	550.00
	1819 medal strike	—	—	—	Proof	600.00

30 LEPTA

1.4100 g, .925 SILVER, .0419 oz ASW

KM#	Date	Mintage	Fine	VF	XF	Unc
35	1834	—	25.00	50.00	75.00	225.00
	1834	—	—	—	Proof	500.00
	1834.	—	25.00	50.00	75.00	250.00
	1848.	.331	65.00	125.00	325.00	750.00
	1849	Inc. Ab.	25.00	50.00	75.00	250.00
	1849	—	—	—	Proof	550.00
	1849.	Inc. Ab.	25.00	50.00	75.00	250.00
	1851	Inc. Ab.	25.00	50.00	75.00	250.00
	1851	—	—	—	Proof	550.00
	1852	Inc. Ab.	25.00	50.00	75.00	250.00
	1852	—	—	—	Proof	550.00
	1857	Inc. Ab.	25.00	50.00	75.00	250.00
	1857.	Inc. Ab.	25.00	50.00	75.00	250.00
	1862	Inc. Ab.	10.00	25.00	60.00	200.00

PATTERNS (Pn)

(Including off metal strikes)

KM#	Date	Mintage	Identification	Mkt.Val.
Pn1	ND	—	Mule. Obv: Ceylon 1 Stiver, C29. Rev: 1 Obol, W on ground line, KM32.	2000.

KM#	Date	Mintage	Identification	Mkt.Val.
Pn2	ND	—	Mule. Obv: Ireland 1 Penny, C12. Rev: 2 Oboli, W WYON on ground line, KM33.	3250.
Pn3	1819	1 known	1 Obol, Silver, KM32	1550.

KM#	Date	Mintage	Identification	Mkt.Val.
Pn4	1819	—	1 Obol, W.W. in exergue	1500.

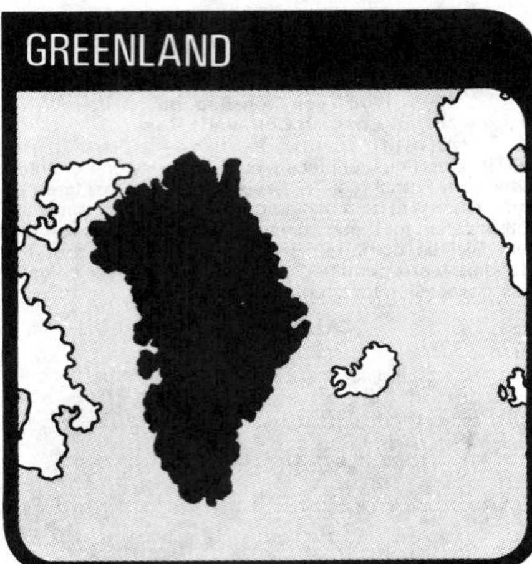

Greenland, an integral part of the Danish realm, is a huge island situated between the North Atlantic Ocean and the Polar Sea, almost entirely within the Arctic Circle. It has an area of 840,000 sq. mi. (2,175,600 sq. km.) and a population of 57,000. Capital: Godthaab. Greenland is the world's only source of natural cryolite, a fluoride of sodium and aluminum important in making aluminum. Fish products and minerals are exported.

Eric the Red discovered Greenland in 982 and established the first settlement in 986. Greenland was a republic until 1261, when the sovereignty of Norway was extended to the island. The original colony was abandoned about 1400 when increasing cold interfered with the breeding of cattle. Successful recolonization was undertaken by Denmark in 1721. In 1921 Denmark extended its claim to include the entire island, and made it a colony of the crown in 1924. The island's colonial status was abolished by amendment to the Danish constitution on June 5, 1953, and Greenland became an integral part of the Kingdom of Denmark. It has been an autonomous state since May 1, 1979.

RULERS

Danish

TOKEN ISSUES (Tn)

Angmagssalik

ORE

ZINC, uniface
Similar to 25 Ore, KM#Tn18.

KM#	Date	Mintage	VG	Fine	VF	XF
Tn15	(1894)	155 pcs.	100.00	175.00	300.00	550.00

5 ORE

ZINC, uniface
Similar to 25 Ore, KM#Tn18.

KM#	Date	Mintage	VG	Fine	VF	XF
Tn16	(1894)	155 pcs.	30.00	60.00	100.00	175.00

10 ORE

ZINC, uniface
Similar to 25 Ore, KM#Tn18.

KM#	Date	Mintage	VG	Fine	VF	XF
Tn17	(1894)	155 pcs.	30.00	60.00	100.00	175.00

25 ORE

ZINC, uniface

KM#	Date	Mintage	VG	Fine	VF	XF
Tn18	(1894)	155 pcs.	30.00	60.00	120.00	185.00

50 ORE

ZINC, uniface

KM#	Date	Mintage	VG	Fine	VF	XF
Tn19	(1894)	*95 pcs.	100.00	165.00	275.00	450.00

W/o hole.

KM#	Date	Mintage	VG	Fine	VF	XF
Tn20	(1894)	*10 pcs.	—	—	—	—

100 ORE

ZINC, uniface

KM#	Date	Mintage	VG	Fine	VF	XF
Tn21	(1894)	205 pcs.	30.00	60.00	125.00	200.00

500 ORE

ZINC, uniface

KM#	Date	Mintage	VG	Fine	VF	XF
Tn23	(1894)	3 pcs.	—	—	Rare	—

Rev: Am.

KM#	Date	Mintage	VG	Fine	VF	XF
Tn24	(1894)	99 pcs.	45.00	90.00	185.00	300.00

GRENADA

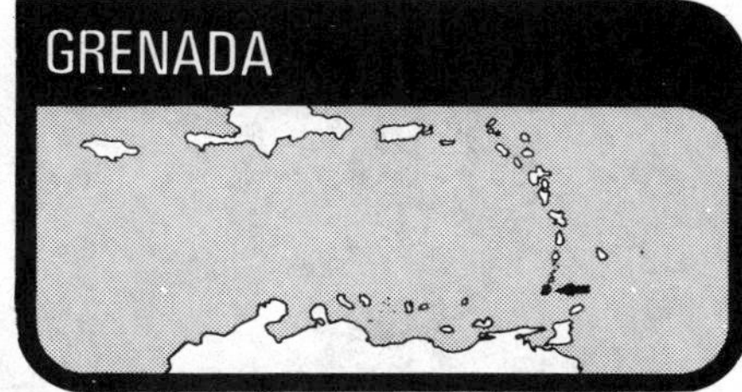

The State of Grenada, located in the Windward Islands of the Caribbean Sea 90 miles (145 km.) north of Trinidad, has (with Carriacou and Petit Martinique) an area of 133 sq. mi. (344 sq. km.) and a population of 94,000. Capital: St. George's. Grenada is the smallest independent nation in the Western Hemisphere. The economy is based on agriculture and tourism. Sugar, coconuts, nutmeg, cocoa and bananas are exported.

Columbus discovered Grenada in 1498 during his third voyage to the Americas. Spain failed to colonize the island, and in 1627 granted it to the British who sold it to the French who colonized it in 1650. Grenada was captured by the British in 1763, retaken by the French in 1779, and finally ceded to the British in 1783. In 1958 Grenada joined the Federation of the West Indies, which was dissolved in 1962. In 1967 it became an internally self-governing British associated state. Full independence was attained on Feb. 4, 1974. Grenada is a member of the Commonwealth of Nations. The prime minister is the Head of Government.

The early coinage of Grenada consists of cut and counterstamped pieces of Spanish or Spanish Colonial Reales, which were valued at 11 Bits. In 1787 8 Reales coins were cut into 11 triangular pieces and counterstamped with an incuse G. Later in 1814 large denomination cut pieces were issued being 1/2, 1/3 or 1/6 cuts and counterstamped with a 'TR', incuse 'G' and a number 6, 4, 2, or 1 indicating the value in bitts.

RULERS

British

MONETARY SYSTEM

1798-1840

12 Bits = 9 Shillings = 1 Dollar

NECESSITY COINAGE

BIT

(9 Pence)

SILVER

c/m: 'TR', 'G', '1' on 1/3 cut of Spanish or Spanish Colonial 2 Reales.

KM#	Date	Mintage	Good	VG	Fine	VF
11	ND(ca.1818)	—	85.00	175.00	300.00	525.00

c/m: 'GS', 'G', '1' on 1/3 cut of Spanish or Spanish Colonial 2 Reales.

KM#	Date	Mintage	Good	VG	Fine	VF
12	ND(ca.1818)	—	165.00	325.00	600.00	1000.

2 BITS

(1 Shilling 6 Pence)

SILVER

c/m: 'TR', 'G', '2' on 1/6 cut of Spanish or Spanish Colonial 8 Reales.

KM#	Date	Mintage	Good	VG	Fine	VF
5	ND(1814)	*9,000	175.00	350.00	650.00	1100.

c/m: 'GS', 'G', '2' on 1/6 cut of Spanish or Spanish Colonial 8 Reales.

KM#	Date	Mintage	Good	VG	Fine	VF
6	ND(1814)	—	600.00	1000.	1750.	2750.

4 BITS

(3 Shillings)

SILVER

c/m: 'TR', 'G', '4' on 1/3 cut of Spanish or Spanish Colonial 8 Reales.

KM#	Date	Mintage	Good	VG	Fine	VF
7	ND(1814)	*9,000	350.00	750.00	1350.	2250.

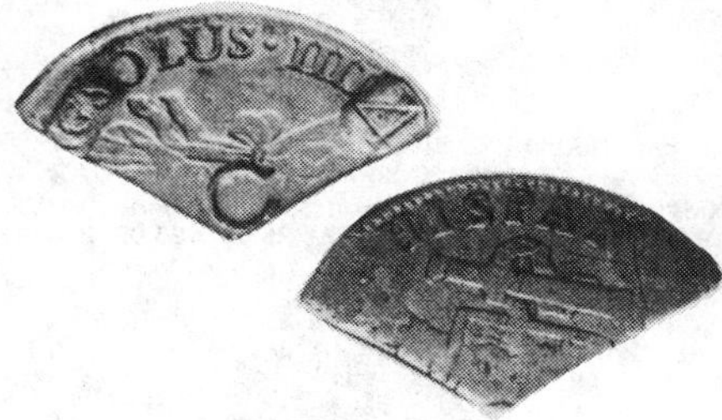

c/m: 'GS', 'G', '4' on 1/3 cut of Spanish or Spanish Colonial 8 Reales.

KM#	Date	Mintage	Good	VG	Fine	VF
8	ND(1814)	—	500.00	900.00	1600.	2650.

6 BITS

(4 Shillings 6 Pence)

SILVER

c/m: 'TR', 'G', '6' on 1/2 cut of Spanish or Spanish Colonial 8 Reales.

KM#	Date	Mintage	Good	VG	Fine	VF
9	ND(1814)	*.012	1000.	2000.	3500.	6000.

c/m: 'GS', 'G', '6' on 1/2 cut of Spanish or Spanish Colonial 8 Reales.

KM#	Date	Mintage	Good	VG	Fine	VF
10	ND(1814)	—	1250.	2250.	4000.	6500.

GUADELOUPE

The French Overseas Department of Guadeloupe, located in the Leeward Islands of the West Indies about 300 miles (493 km.) southeast of Puerto Rico, has an area of 687 sq. mi. (1,780 sq. km.) and a population of 306,000. Actually it is two islands separated by a narrow salt water stream: volcanic Basse-Terre to the west and the flatter limestone formation of Grande-Terre to the east. Capital: Basse-Terre, on the island of that name. The principal industries are agriculture, the distillation of liquors, and tourism. Sugar, bananas, and rum are exported.

Guadeloupe was discovered by Columbus in 1493 and settled in 1635 by two Frenchmen, L'Olive and Duplessis, who took possession in the name of the French Company of the Islands of America. When repeated efforts by private companies to colonize the island failed, it was relinquished to the French crown in 1674, and established as a dependency of Martinique. The British occupied the island on two occasions, 1759-63 and 1810-16, before it passed permanently to France. A colony until 1946 Guadeloupe was then made an overseas territory of the French Union. In 1958 it voted to become an Overseas Department within the new French Community.

The well-known R.F. in garland oval countermark of the French Government is only legitimate if on a French Colonies 12 deniers 1767 C#4. Two other similar but incuse RF countermarks are on cut pieces in the values of 1 and 4 escalins. Contemporary and modern counterfeits are known of both these types.

RULERS

French, until 1759, 1763-1810, 1816-

British, 1759-1763, 1810-1816

MONETARY SYSTEM

3 Deniers = 1 Liard

4 Liards = 1 Sol (Sous)

20 Sols = 1 Livre

6 Livres = 1 Ecu

NOTE: During the British Occupation period the Spanish and Spanish Colonial 8 Reales equalled 10 Livres.

CUT & COUNTERMARKED COINAGE

French Occupation

Until 1810

ESCALIN

SILVER

c/m: 'R.F.' on cut from outside ring of a center cut Spanish or Spanish Colonial 8 Reales.

KM#	Date	Year	Good	VG	Fine	VF
2	ND(1802)	—	200.00	375.00	675.00	1200.

4 E (ESCALINS)

SILVER

c/m: '4E RF' on center plug of Spanish or Spanish Colonial 8 Reales.

KM#	Date	Year	Good	VG	Fine	VF
3	ND(1802)	—	600.00	1200.	2000.	3500.

20 LIVRES

.917 GOLD

c/m: '20 w/small horse's head' on false Brazil 6400 Reis, type of KM#172.2.

KM#	Date	Year	Good	VG	Fine	VF
4.1	ND(1803)	(1751-77)	—	—	4500.	6500.

c/m: '20 w/small horse's head' on false Brazil 6400 Reis, type of KM#199.2.

KM#	Date	Year	Good	VG	Fine	VF
4.2	ND(1803)	(1777-86)	—	—	4500.	6500.

22 LIVRES

GOLD
c/m: '22 w/small bearded human face' on Brazil 6400 Reis, KM#199.2.

KM#	Date	Year	Good	VG	Fine	VF
5	ND(1803)	(1777-86)	—	—	6500.	8500.

NOTE: The previously listed Brazil 6400 Reis with large 'G' in 15 pointed sunburst indent countermark are considered incorrectly attributed and possibly spurious by some authorities. Refer to *"Unusual World Coins"* 3rd edition ca.1992.

British Occupation

1810-1816

10 SOUS

SILVER
c/m: Crowned 'G' on France 6 Sols, C#38.

KM#	Date	Year	Good	VG	Fine	VF
13	ND(1811)	(1726-40)	30.00	50.00	80.00	160.00

c/m: Crowned 'G' on France 6 Sols, C#43.

KM#	Date	Year	Good	VG	Fine	VF
14	ND(1811)	(1743-70)	30.00	50.00	80.00	160.00

c/m: Crowned 'G' on Great Britain 3 Pence, KM#591.

KM#	Date	Year	Good	VG	Fine	VF
12	ND(1811)	(1762-86)	30.00	50.00	80.00	160.00

c/m: Crowned 'G' on Spanish or Spanish Colonial 1/2 Real.

KM#	Date	Year	Good	VG	Fine	VF
11	ND(1811)	—	30.00	50.00	80.00	160.00

20 SOUS

(Livre)

SILVER
c/m: Radiant 'G' on center plug of Spanish or Spanish Colonial 8 Reales.

KM#	Date	Year	Good	VG	Fine	VF
19	ND(1811)	—	35.00	75.00	125.00	250.00

c/m: Crowned 'G' on France 12 Sols, C#39.

KM#	Date	Year	Good	VG	Fine	VF
18	ND(1811)	(1726-32)	40.00	70.00	100.00	185.00

c/m: Crowned 'G' on France 12 Sols, C#44.

KM#	Date	Year	Good	VG	Fine	VF
16	ND(1811)	(1743-70)	40.00	70.00	100.00	185.00

c/m: Crowned 'G' on France 12 Sols, C#75.

KM#	Date	Year	Good	VG	Fine	VF
31	ND(1811)	(1775-89)	40.00	70.00	100.00	185.00

c/m: Crowned 'G' on Great Britain 6 Pence, KM#582.

KM#	Date	Year	Good	VG	Fine	VF
17	ND(1811)	(1743-58)	40.00	70.00	100.00	185.00

c/m: Crowned 'G' on Spanish or Spanish Colonial 1 Real.

KM#	Date	Year	Good	VG	Fine	VF
15	ND(1811)	—	40.00	70.00	100.00	185.00

40 SOUS

(2 Livres)

SILVER
c/m: Crowned 'G' on France 1/3 Ecu, C#30.

KM#	Date	Year	Good	VG	Fine	VF
20	ND(1811)	(1720-23)	45.00	85.00	120.00	200.00

c/m: Crowned 'G' on France 24 Sols, C#40.

KM#	Date	Year	Good	VG	Fine	VF
23	ND(1811)	(1726-37)	45.50	85.00	120.00	200.00

c/m: Crowned 'G' on France 24 Sols, C#45.

KM#	Date	Year	Good	VG	Fine	VF
32	ND(1811)	(1741-70)	50.00	90.00	120.00	200.00

c/m: Crowned 'G' on France 24 Sols, C#45a.

KM#	Date	Year	Good	VG	Fine	VF
33	ND(1811)	(1771-74)	75.00	125.00	150.00	250.00

c/m: Crowned 'G' on France 24 Sols, C#76.

KM#	Date	Year	Good	VG	Fine	VF
21	ND(1811)	(1774-90)	45.00	85.00	120.00	200.00

c/m: Crowned 'G' on Great Britain 1 Shilling, KM#607.

KM#	Date	Year	Good	VG	Fine	VF
22	ND(1811)	(1787)	40.00	80.00	110.00	190.00

2 LIVRES

SILVER
c/m: Crowned 'G' on quarter segment of 9 Livres, KM#24-26, 35-36.

KM#	Date	Year	Good	VG	Fine	VF
34	ND(1811)	—	—	—	—	—

NOTE: No official documentation for the issue of KM34 exists. All known specimens are thought to be modern concoctions. At recent sales examples have sold for as little as $20 and as much as $400.

2 LIVRES 5 SOUS

SILVER
c/m: Crowned 'G' on quarter segment of Spanish or Spanish Colonial 8 Reales.

KM#	Date	Year	Good	VG	Fine	VF
30	ND(1813)	—	300.00	650.00	1250.	2150.

9 LIVRES

SILVER

c/m: Crowned 'G' on obv. and rev. of Mexico 8 Reales, KM#106 w/crenated square hole.

KM#	Date	Year	Good	VG	Fine	VF
24	ND(1811)	(1772-89)	200.00	250.00	350.00	600.00

c/m: Crowned 'G' on obv. and rev. of Mexico 8 Reales, KM#109 w/crenated square hole.

KM#	Date	Year	Good	VG	Fine	VF
25	ND(1811)	(1791-1808)	200.00	250.00	350.00	600.00

c/m: Crowned 'G' on obv. and rev. of Mexico 8 Reales, KM#110 w/crenated square hole.

KM#	Date	Year	Good	VG	Fine	VF
26	ND(1811)	(1808-10)	200.00	250.00	350.00	600.00

c/m: Crowned 'G' on obv. and rev. of Peru (Lima) 8 Reales, KM#97 w/crenated square hole.

KM#	Date	Year	Good	VG	Fine	VF
35	ND(1811)	(1791-1808)	225.00	275.00	375.00	650.00

c/m: Crowned 'G' on obv. and rev. of Peru (Lima) 8 Reales, KM#106.2 w/crenated square hole.

KM#	Date	Year	Good	VG	Fine	VF
36	ND(1811)	(1809-11)	250.00	350.00	650.00	1000.

NOTE: The square plug was used in making 20 Sous, KM#19.

82 LIVRES, 10 SOLS

.917 GOLD

c/m: Crowned 'G' and 82.10 on Brazil 6400 Reis, KM#172.

KM#	Date	Year	Good	VG	Fine	VF
27	ND(1811)	(1751-77)	2150.	3250.	5000.	8500.

c/m: Crowned 'G' and 82.10 on Brazil 6400 Reis, KM#199.

KM#	Date	Year	Good	VG	Fine	VF
28	ND(1811)	(1777-86)	1250.	2000.	3000.	5000.

c/m: Crowned 'G' and 82.10 on Brazil 6400 Reis, KM#226.

KM#	Date	Year	Good	VG	Fine	VF
29	ND(1811)	(1789-1805)	2000.	3000.	4500.	7500.

NOTE: Spurious countermarks on KM#27-29 lack the raised decimal point between "82" and "10".

GUATEMALA

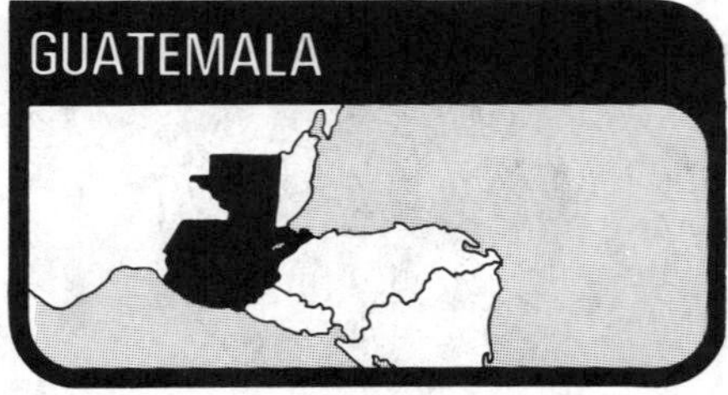

The Republic of Guatemala, the northernmost of the five Central American republics, has an area of 42,042 sq. mi. (108,890 sq. km.) and a population of 10.7 million. Capital: Guatemala City. The economy of Guatemala is heavily dependent on agriculture, however, the country is rich in nickel resources which are being developed. Coffee, cotton and bananas are exported.

Guatemala, once the site of an ancient Mayan civilization, was conquered by Pedro de Alvarado, the resourceful lieutenant of Cortes who undertook the conquest from Mexico. Cruel but strategically skillful, he progressed rapidly along the Pacific coastal lowlands to the highland plain of Quetzaltenango where the decisive battle for Guatemala was fought. After routing the Indian forces, he established the city of Guatemala, 1524. The Spanish Captaincy-General of Guatemala included all Central America but Panama. Guatemala declared its independence of Spain in 1821 and was absorbed into the Mexican empire of Augustin Iturbide, 1822-23. From 1823 to 1839 Guatemala was a constituent state of the Central American Republic. Upon dissolution of that confederation, Guatemala became an independent republic.

RULERS

Spanish until 1821

MINT MARKS

Antigua, the old capital city of Santiago de los Caballeros, including the mint facility, was destroyed by a volcanic eruption and earthquake in 1773. A new mint and capital city was established in Guatemala City. Coin production recommenced in late 1776 using dies with the NG mint mark.

G or G-G - Guatemala until 1776, 1878-1889

H - Heaton, Birmingham

NG - Nueva Guatemala, 1777-1829

ASSAYERS INITIALS

Letter	Date	Name
M	1785-1822	Manuel Eusebio Sanchez

COLONIAL MILLED COINAGE

1/4 REAL

.8460 g, .896 SILVER, .0243 oz ASW
Mint mark: G
Obv: Castle. Rev: Lion.

KM#	Date	Mintage	VG	Fine	VF	XF
59	1801	—	4.00	9.00	20.00	60.00
	1802	—	4.00	9.00	20.00	60.00
	1803	—	4.00	9.00	20.00	60.00
	1804	—	4.00	9.00	20.00	60.00
	1805	—	20.00	40.00	65.00	185.00
	1806	—	10.00	20.00	35.00	90.00
	1807	—	4.00	9.00	20.00	60.00

NOTE: Earlier dates (1796-1800) exist for this type.

KM#	Date	Mintage	VG	Fine	VF	XF
72	1808	—	4.00	9.00	20.00	60.00
	1809	—	4.00	9.00	25.00	65.00
	1810	—	4.00	9.00	20.00	60.00
	1811	—	12.50	25.00	40.00	100.00
	1812	—	20.00	40.00	75.00	200.00
	1813	—	4.00	9.00	20.00	65.00
	1814	—	4.00	9.00	20.00	65.00
	1815	—	4.00	9.00	20.00	65.00
	1816	—	4.00	9.00	20.00	60.00
	1817	—	4.00	9.00	20.00	65.00
	1818	—	4.00	9.00	20.00	65.00
	1819	—	4.00	9.00	20.00	65.00
	1820	—	4.00	9.00	20.00	60.00
	1821	—	3.00	7.00	12.50	45.00
	1822	—	300.00	600.00	1000.	2000.

NOTE: The authenticity of the 1822 1/4 Real has been questioned by leading authorities in Latin American coinage.

1/2 REAL

1.6921 g, .896 SILVER, .0487 oz ASW
Mint mark: NG
Obv: Bust of Charles IV, leg: CAROLUS IIII. . .
Rev: Arms, pillar.

KM#	Date	Mintage	VG	Fine	VF	XF
50	1801 M	—	6.00	12.00	25.00	65.00
	1802 M	—	6.00	12.00	25.00	65.00
	1803 M	—	7.00	15.00	30.00	75.00
	1804 M	—	7.00	15.00	30.00	75.00
	1805 M	—	7.00	15.00	30.00	75.00
	1806 M	—	7.00	15.00	30.00	75.00
	1807 M	—	7.00	15.00	30.00	75.00

NOTE: Earlier dates (1790-1800) exist for this type.

Obv. leg: FERDIND VII. . ., bust of Charles IV.

KM#	Date	Mintage	VG	Fine	VF	XF
60	1808 M	—	15.00	30.00	60.00	125.00
	1809 M	—	4.50	9.00	20.00	40.00
	1810 M	—	5.00	10.00	20.00	45.00

Ferdinand VII

KM#	Date	Mintage	VG	Fine	VF	XF
65	1808 M	—	20.00	40.00	80.00	125.00
	1811 M	—	100.00	—	—	—
	1812 M	—	10.00	18.00	35.00	90.00
	1813 M	—	10.00	18.00	35.00	100.00
	1814 M	—	4.00	7.00	15.00	40.00
	1815 M	—	4.00	7.00	15.00	40.00
	1816 M	—	4.00	7.00	15.00	40.00
	1817 M	—	5.00	10.00	25.00	65.00
	1818 M	—	6.00	12.00	25.00	65.00
	1819 M	—	5.00	10.00	25.00	65.00
	1820 M	—	4.00	7.00	15.00	40.00
	1821 M	—	5.00	12.00	20.00	60.00

REAL

3.3841 g, .896 SILVER, .0975 oz ASW
Mint mark: NG
Obv: Bust of Charles IIII.
Rev: Arms, pillars.

KM#	Date	Mintage	VG	Fine	VF	XF
54	1801 M	—	7.00	15.00	35.00	85.00
	1802/1 M	—	7.00	15.00	35.00	85.00
	1802 M	—	7.00	15.00	35.00	85.00
	1803 M	—	7.00	15.00	35.00	85.00
	1804 M	—	7.00	15.00	35.00	85.00
	1805 M	—	7.00	15.00	35.00	85.00
	1806 M	—	7.00	15.00	35.00	85.00
	1807 M	—	7.00	15.00	35.00	85.00

NOTE: Earlier dates (1791-1800) exist for this type.

Obv. leg: FERDIND VII. . ., bust of Charles IV.

KM#	Date	Mintage	VG	Fine	VF	XF
61	1808 M	—	6.00	10.00	25.00	65.00
	1809 M	—	5.00	9.00	20.00	55.00
	1810 M	—	7.00	15.00	35.00	80.00

Ferdinand VII

KM#	Date	Mintage	VG	Fine	VF	XF
66	1808 M	—	—	—	Rare	—
	1811 M	—	4.00	8.00	18.00	40.00
	1812 M	—	4.00	8.00	18.00	40.00
	1813 M	—	10.00	17.50	35.00	70.00
	1814 M	—	4.00	9.00	20.00	50.00
	1815 M	—	3.00	6.00	15.00	35.00
	1816 M	—	4.00	9.00	20.00	50.00
	1817 M	—	3.00	6.00	15.00	35.00
	1818 M	—	3.00	6.00	12.00	30.00
	1819 M	—	4.00	8.00	18.00	45.00
	1820 M	—	3.00	6.00	12.00	30.00
	1821 M	—	3.00	6.00	12.00	30.00

2 REALES

6.7682 g, .896 SILVER, .1950 oz ASW
Mint mark: NG
Obv: Bust of Charles IIII.
Rev: Arms, pillars.

KM#	Date	Mintage	VG	Fine	VF	XF
51	1801 M	—	4.00	7.00	18.00	55.00
	1802 M	—	6.00	12.00	30.00	65.00
	1803 M	—	12.00	25.00	55.00	120.00
	1804 M	—	4.00	7.00	18.00	55.00
	1805 M	—	4.00	7.00	18.00	55.00
	1806 M	—	18.00	35.00	65.00	145.00
	1807 M	—	18.00	35.00	65.00	145.00

NOTE: Earlier dates (1791-1800) exist for this type.

Obv. leg: FERDIND VII. . ., bust of Charles IV.

KM#	Date	Mintage	VG	Fine	VF	XF
62	1808 M	—	10.00	20.00	45.00	100.00
	1809 M	—	5.00	10.00	28.00	65.00
	1810 M	—	4.00	8.00	22.50	55.00

Ferdinand VII

KM#	Date	Mintage	VG	Fine	VF	XF
67	1808 M	—	20.00	40.00	80.00	170.00
	1811 M	—	12.00	18.00	30.00	65.00
	1812 M	—	5.00	9.00	22.50	55.00
	1813 M	—	12.00	25.00	80.00	170.00
	1814 M	—	12.00	25.00	80.00	170.00
	1815 M	—	5.00	9.00	22.50	55.00
	1816 M	—	6.00	10.00	25.00	65.00
	1817 M	—	5.00	9.00	22.50	55.00
	1818 M	—	5.00	9.00	22.50	55.00
	1819 M	—	5.00	9.00	22.50	55.00
	1820 M	—	5.00	9.00	22.50	55.00
	1821 M	—	4.00	7.00	20.00	50.00

4 REALES

13.5365 g, .896 SILVER, .3900 oz ASW
Mint mark: NG
Charles IIII

KM#	Date	Mintage	VG	Fine	VF	XF
52	1801 M	—	35.00	75.00	150.00	250.00
	1802 M	—	50.00	100.00	175.00	250.00
	1803 M	—	50.00	100.00	175.00	275.00
	1804 M	—	125.00	250.00	400.00	—
	1805 M	—	50.00	100.00	175.00	300.00
	1806/5 M	—	40.00	85.00	165.00	275.00
	1806 M	—	35.00	75.00	150.00	250.00
	1807 M	—	35.00	75.00	125.00	225.00

NOTE: Earlier dates (1790-1800) exist for this type.

Obv. leg: FERDIND VII. . ., bust of Charles IV.

KM#	Date	Mintage	VG	Fine	VF	XF
63	1808 M	—	100.00	200.00	350.00	550.00
	1809 M	—	65.00	125.00	250.00	400.00
	1810 M	—	65.00	125.00	250.00	400.00

Ferdinand VII

KM#	Date	Mintage	VG	Fine	VF	XF
68	1808 M	—	150.00	300.00	500.00	800.00
	1811 M	—	40.00	80.00	175.00	325.00
	1812 M	—	40.00	80.00	175.00	325.00
	1813 M	—	40.00	80.00	175.00	325.00
	1814 M	—	30.00	70.00	120.00	225.00
	1815/4 M	—	40.00	80.00	150.00	275.00
	1815 M	—	30.00	70.00	120.00	225.00
	1816 M	—	40.00	80.00	150.00	250.00
	1817 M	—	40.00	80.00	150.00	250.00
	1818 M	—	30.00	70.00	120.00	225.00
	1819 M	—	30.00	70.00	120.00	225.00
	1820 M	—	45.00	90.00	175.00	365.00
	1821 M	—	30.00	70.00	120.00	225.00

8 REALES

27.0730 g, .896 SILVER, .7799 oz ASW
Mint mark: NG
Obv: Bust of Charles IIII right. Rev: Arms, pillars.
Charles IIII

KM#	Date	Mintage	VG	Fine	VF	XF
53	1801 obv. leg: inverted JJJJ	—	60.00	150.00	225.00	375.00
	1801 obv. leg: IIII	—	55.00	100.00	200.00	350.00
	1802 M	—	60.00	150.00	225.00	375.00
	1803 M	—	55.00	100.00	200.00	350.00
	1804 M	—	55.00	100.00	200.00	350.00
	1805 M	—	55.00	100.00	200.00	350.00
	1806/5 M	—	75.00	200.00	325.00	425.00
	1807 M	—	55.00	100.00	200.00	350.00

NOTE: Earlier dates (1790-1800) exist for this type.

Obv. leg: FERDIND VII. . ., bust of Charles IIII.

KM#	Date	Mintage	VG	Fine	VF	XF
64	1808 M	—	110.00	260.00	450.00	825.00
	1809/8 M	—	85.00	200.00	350.00	675.00
	1809 M	—	75.00	175.00	250.00	600.00
	1810 M	—	75.00	175.00	250.00	525.00

Ferdinand VII

KM#	Date	Mintage	VG	Fine	VF	XF
69	1808 M	—	—	—	*Rare	—
	1811 M	—	100.00	200.00	400.00	750.00
	1812 M	—	25.00	40.00	75.00	150.00
	1813 M	—	25.00	40.00	75.00	150.00
	1814 M	—	25.00	40.00	75.00	150.00
	1815 M	—	25.00	40.00	75.00	150.00
	1816 M	—	25.00	40.00	75.00	150.00
	1817 M	—	25.00	40.00	75.00	150.00
	1818 M	—	25.00	40.00	75.00	150.00
	1819 M	—	25.00	40.00	75.00	150.00
	1820 M	—	25.00	40.00	75.00	150.00
	1821 M	—	25.00	40.00	75.00	150.00

***NOTE:** Superior Dec. 1990 sale choice VF realized $14,300.

ESCUDO

3.3841 g, .875 GOLD, .0952 oz AGW
Mint mark: NG
Charles IIII

KM#	Date	Mintage	VG	Fine	VF	XF
55	1801 M	—	600.00	1200.	1800.	3000.

NOTE: Earlier dates (1794-1797) exist for this type.

Ferdinand VII

KM#	Date	Mintage	VG	Fine	VF	XF
74	1817 M	—	700.00	1500.	2000.	3500.

2 ESCUDOS

6.7682 g, .875 GOLD, .1904 oz AGW
Mint mark: NG
Obv: Bust of Charles IIII.

KM#	Date	Mintage	VG	Fine	VF	XF
56	1801 M	—	1000.	2000.	3500.	6000.

NOTE: Earlier dates (1794-1797) exist for this type.

KM#	Date	Mintage	VG	Fine	VF	XF
70	1808 M	—	600.00	1250.	2000.	3250.
	1811 M	—	—	—	Rare	—
	1817 M	—	300.00	600.00	1000.	1500.

4 ESCUDOS

13.5365 g, .875 GOLD, .3808 oz AGW
Mint mark: NG
Charles IIII

KM#	Date	Mintage	VG	Fine	VF	XF
57	1801 M	—	—	—	Rare	—

NOTE: Earlier dates (1794-1797) exist for this type.

Ferdinand VII

KM#	Date	Mintage	VG	Fine	VF	XF
73	1813 M	—	—	Reported, not confirmed		
	1817 M	—	1000.	2000.	3500.	6000.

8 ESCUDOS

27.0730 g, .875 GOLD, .7616 oz AGW
Mint mark: NG
Charles IIII

KM#	Date	Mintage	VG	Fine	VF	XF
58	1801 M	—	—	3000.	6000.	10,000.

NOTE: Earlier dates (1794-1797) exist for this type.

Ferdinand VII

KM#	Date	Mintage	VG	Fine	VF	XF
71	1808 M	—	—	—	*Rare	—
	1811 M	—	—	6000.	10,000.	17,500.
	1817 M	—	—	2000.	4000.	7000.

***NOTE:** Sotheby's Geneva sale 5-90 VF realized $74,800.

PROVISIONAL COINAGE

(Under Central American Republic)

REAL

.903 SILVER
Mint mark: NG
Obv. leg: ESTADO DE GUATEMALA

KM#	Date	Mintage	VG	Fine	VF	XF
75	1829 M	—	55.00	115.00	225.00	400.00

COUNTERMARKED COINAGE

1838-1841

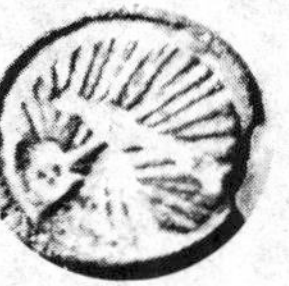

TYPE I
Sun at left behind volcano under long cloud.

2 REALES

SILVER
c/m: Type I on Peru (Lima) 'cob' 2 Reales, KM#16.

KM#	Date	Good	VG	Fine	VF
78	ND(1659-60)	—	—	Rare	—

4 REALES

SILVER
c/m: Type I on Boliva 'cob' 4 Reales, KM#30a.

KM#	Date	Good	VG	Fine	VF
76.3	ND(1729-47)	150.00	225.00	300.00	—

c/m: Type I on Bolivia 'cob' 4 Reales, KM#44.

KM#	Date	Good	VG	Fine	VF
76.4	ND(1760-77)	150.00	225.00	300.00	—

c/m: Type I on 'cob' 4 Reales, KM#11.

KM#	Date	Good	VG	Fine	VF
76.1	ND(1747-53)	225.00	325.00	450.00	—

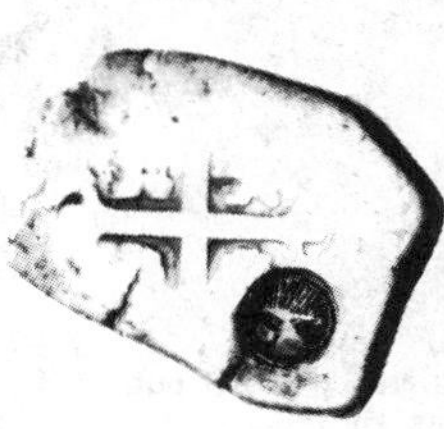

c/m: Type I on Mexico 'cob' 4 Reales, KM#40a.

KM#	Date	Good	VG	Fine	VF
76.5	ND(1729-34)	500.00	700.00	1000.	—

c/m: Type I on Mexico-Sombrerete 4 Reales, KM#175.

KM#	Date	Good	VG	Fine	VF
76.2	ND(1811-12)	500.00	—	—	—

8 REALES

SILVER

c/m: Type I on Bolivia (Potosi) 'Royal' 8 Reales, KM#21.

KM#	Date	Good	VG	Fine	VF
77.10	ND(1621-65)	—	—	—	—

c/m: Type I on Bolivia (Potosi) 'cob' 8 Reales, KM#26.

KM#	Date	Good	VG	Fine	VF
77.15	ND(1679)	—	—	—	—

c/m: Type I on Bolivia (Potosi) 'cob' 8 Reales, KM#31a.

KM#	Date	Good	VG	Fine	VF
77.16	ND(1729)	—	—	—	—

c/m: Type I on Bolivia (Potosi) 'cob' 8 Reales, KM#31a.

KM#	Date	Good	VG	Fine	VF
77.11	ND(1729-47)	225.00	325.00	450.00	—

c/m: Type I on Bolivia (Potosi) 'cob' 8 Reales, KM#40.

KM#	Date	Good	VG	Fine	VF
77.12	ND(1747-60)	225.00	325.00	450.00	—

c/m: Type I on Bolivia (Potosi) 'cob' 8 Reales, KM#45.

KM#	Date	Good	VG	Fine	VF
77.5	ND(1760-73)	225.00	325.00	450.00	—

c/m: Type I on 'cob' 8 Reales, KM#6.

KM#	Date	Good	VG	Fine	VF
77.1	ND(1733-46)	200.00	300.00	400.00	550.00

c/m: Type I on 'cob' 8 Reales, KM#12.

KM#	Date	Good	VG	Fine	VF
77.2	ND(1747-53)	200.00	300.00	400.00	550.00

c/m: Type I on Mexico 'cob' 8 Reales, KM#46.

KM#	Date	Good	VG	Fine	VF
77.6	ND(1668-1701)	225.00	325.00	450.00	—

c/m: Type I on Mexico 'cob' 8 Reales, KM#47a.

KM#	Date	Good	VG	Fine	VF
77.7	ND(1729-33)	225.00	325.00	450.00	—

c/m: Type I on Mexico 'klippe' 8 Reales, KM#48.

KM#	Date	Good	VG	Fine	VF
77.8	ND(1733-34)	225.00	325.00	450.00	—

c/m: Type I on Peru (Lima) 'cob' 8 Reales, KM#24.

KM#	Date	Good	VG	Fine	VF
77.13	ND(1684-1701)	200.00	300.00	400.00	550.00

c/m: Type I on Peru (Lima) 'cob' 8 Reales of Philip V.

KM#	Date	Good	VG	Fine	VF
77.3	ND(1700-46)	200.00	300.00	400.00	550.00

c/m: Type I on Peru 8 Reales, KM#130.

KM#	Date	Good	VG	Fine	VF
77.9	ND(1824)	150.00	220.00	300.00	400.00

c/m: Type I on Peru 8 Reales, KM#142.1.

KM#	Date	Good	VG	Fine	VF
77.14	ND(1825-28)	150.00	220.00	300.00	400.00

c/m: Type I on Peru 8 Reales, KM#142.3.

KM#	Date	Good	VG	Fine	VF
77.4	ND(1828-?)	150.00	220.00	300.00	400.00

Type II
Sun above a row of volcanos in 6.5mm circle.

2 REALES

SILVER

c/m: Type II on Bolivia 2 Soles, KM#95.

KM#	Date	Good	VG	Fine	VF
81	ND(1827-30)	55.00	85.00	110.00	150.00

c/m: Type II on Peru 2 Reales, KM#141.1.

KM#	Date	Good	VG	Fine	VF
82	ND(1825-40)	55.00	85.00	110.00	150.00

4 REALES

SILVER

c/m: Type II on Bolivia (Potosi) 'cob' 4 Reales of Philip II.

KM#	Date	Good	VG	Fine	VF
85.1	ND(1556-98)	125.00	185.00	260.00	350.00

c/m: Type II on Bolivia (Potosi) 'cob' 4 Reales, KM#30.

KM#	Date	Good	VG	Fine	VF
85.4	ND(1712)	—	—	—	—

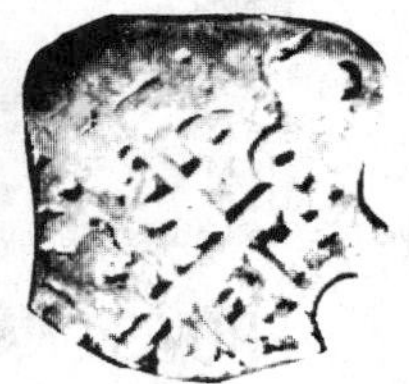

c/m: Type II on Bolivia (Potosi) 'cob' 4 Reales, KM#39.

KM#	Date	Good	VG	Fine	VF
85.5	ND(1746-59)	80.00	125.00	165.00	225.00

c/m: Type II on Bolivia (Potosi) 'cob' 4 Reales, KM#44.

KM#	Date	Good	VG	Fine	VF
85.6	ND(1759-88)	80.00	125.00	165.00	225.00

c/m: Type II on Bolivia 4 Soles, KM#96.

KM#	Date	Good	VG	Fine	VF
92	ND(1827-30)	60.00	110.00	175.00	250.00

c/m: Type II on Guatemala 'cob' 4 Reales, KM#5.

KM#	Date	Good	VG	Fine	VF
87.1	ND(1733-46)	110.00	165.00	225.00	300.00

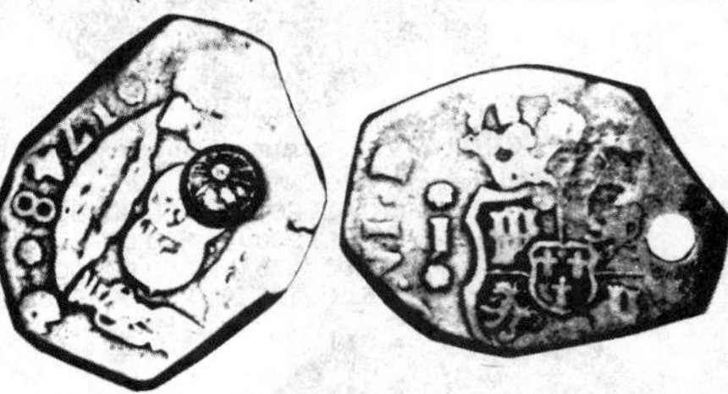

c/m: Type II on Guatemala 'cob' 4 Reales, KM#11.

KM#	Date	Good	VG	Fine	VF
87.2 (88)	ND(1747-53)	110.00	165.00	225.00	300.00

c/m: Type II on Honduras 'cob' 4 Reales, KM#16.1.

KM#	Date	Good	VG	Fine	VF
88	ND(1823-24)	—	—	—	—

c/m: Type II on Mexico 4 Reales of Carlos and Johanna, (late type).

KM#	Date	Good	VG	Fine	VF
89.1	ND	—	—	—	—

c/m: Type II on Mexico 'cob' 4 Reales of Philip II.

KM#	Date	Good	VG	Fine	VF
89.2	ND(1556-98)	125.00	185.00	260.00	350.00

c/m: Type II on Mexico 'klippe' 4 Reales, KM#41.

KM#	Date	Good	VG	Fine	VF
89.5	ND(1733-34)	225.00	300.00	375.00	500.00

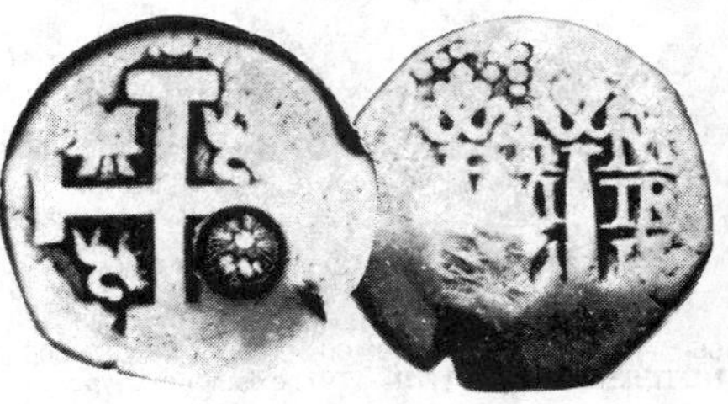

c/m: Type II on Peru (Lima) 'cob' 4 Reales of Charles II.

KM#	Date	Good	VG	Fine	VF
90.1	ND(1665-1700)	80.00	125.00	165.00	225.00

c/m: Type II on Peru (Lima) 'cob' 4 Reales, KM#33.

KM#	Date	Good	VG	Fine	VF
90.2	ND(1700-46)	80.00	125.00	165.00	225.00

c/m: Type II on Peru (Lima) 'Royal' 4 Reales, KM#33.

KM#	Date	Good	VG	Fine	VF
90.3	ND(1700-46)	—	—	—	—

c/m: Type II on Peru (Cuzco) 4 Reales, KM#151.1.

KM#	Date	Good	VG	Fine	VF
91	ND(1835-36)	60.00	110.00	175.00	250.00

8 REALES

SILVER

c/m: Type II on Bolivia (Potosi) 'cob' 8 Reales, KM#5.

KM#	Date	Good	VG	Fine	VF
94.1	ND(1556-98)	80.00	125.00	165.00	225.00

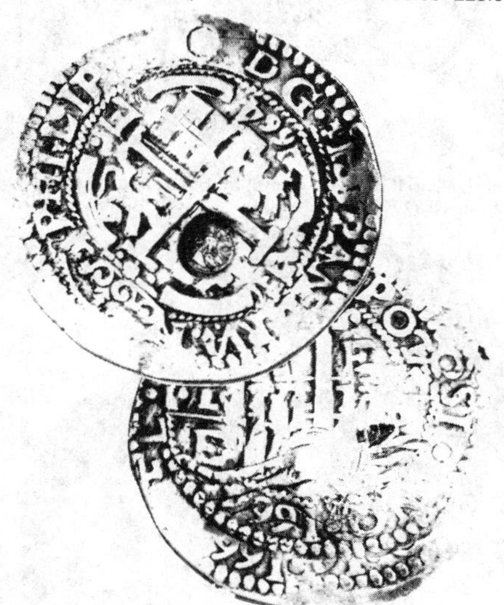

c/m: Type II on Bolivia (Potosi) 'Royal' 8 Reales, KM#5.

KM#	Date	Good	VG	Fine	VF
94.2	ND(1621-65)	750.00	1100.	1500.	2000.

c/m: Type II on Bolivia (Potosi) 'cob' 8 Reales, KM#19.

KM#	Date	Good	VG	Fine	VF
95	ND(1621-65)	80.00	125.00	165.00	225.00

c/m: Type II on Bolivia (Potosi) 'Royal' 8 Reales, KM#26.

KM#	Date	Good	VG	Fine	VF
96.1	ND(1665-1700)	750.00	1100.	1500.	2000.

c/m: Type II on Bolivia (Potosi) 'cob' 8 Reales, KM#26.

KM#	Date	Good	VG	Fine	VF
96.2	ND(1665-1700)	125.00	185.00	250.00	350.00

c/m: Type II on Bolivia (Potosi) 'cob' 8 Reales, KM#31.

KM#	Date	Good	VG	Fine	VF
97.1	ND(1700-46)	110.00	165.00	225.00	300.00

c/m: Type II on Bolivia (Potosi) 'Royal' 8 Reales, KM#31.

KM#	Date	Good	VG	Fine	VF
97.2	ND(1702)	—	—	—	—

c/m: Type II on Bolivia (Potosi) 'cob' 8 Reales, KM#35.

KM#	Date	Good	VG	Fine	VF
98	ND(1725-27)	250.00	450.00	550.00	950.00

c/m: Type II on Bolivia (Potosi) 'cob' 8 Reales, KM#40.

KM#	Date	Good	VG	Fine	VF
99	ND(1746-59)	80.00	125.00	165.00	225.00

c/m: Type II on Bolivia (Potosi) 'cob' 8 Reales, KM#45.

KM#	Date	Good	VG	Fine	VF
100	ND(1759-88)	80.00	125.00	165.00	225.00

c/m: Type II on Bolivia 8 Soles, KM#97.

KM#	Date	Good	VG	Fine	VF
106	ND(1827-40)	50.00	90.00	135.00	200.00

c/m: Type II on Guatemala 'cob' 8 Reales, KM#6.

KM#	Date	Good	VG	Fine	VF
101	ND(1733-46)	125.00	185.00	250.00	350.00

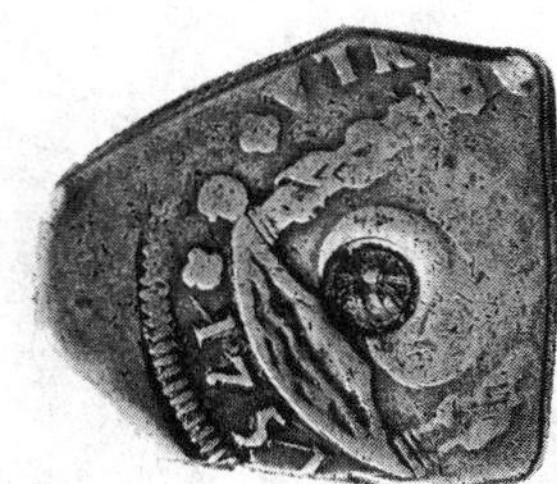

c/m: Type II on Guatemala 'cob' 8 Reales, KM#12.

KM#	Date	Good	VG	Fine	VF
102	ND(1747-53)	110.00	165.00	225.00	300.00

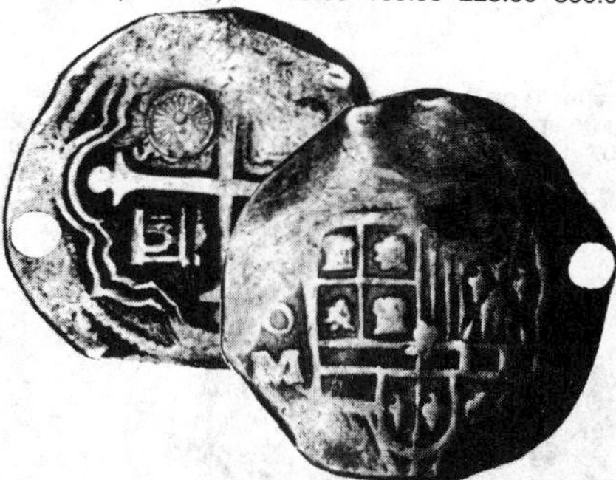

c/m: Type II on Mexico 'cob' 8 Reales, KM#45.

KM#	Date	Good	VG	Fine	VF
104	ND(1621-67)	110.00	165.00	225.00	300.00

c/m: Type II on Mexico 'Royal' 8 Reales, KM#47.

KM#	Date	Good	VG	Fine	VF
105.1	ND(1701-28)	—	—	Rare	—

c/m: Type II on Mexico 'cob' 8 Reales, KM#47a.

KM#	Date	Good	VG	Fine	VF
105.2	ND(1729-33)	85.00	130.00	180.00	240.00

c/m: Type II on Mexico 'Klippe' 8 Reales, KM#48.

KM#	Date	Good	VG	Fine	VF
107	ND(1733-34)	185.00	275.00	375.00	500.00

c/m: Type II on Peru (Lima) 'Royal' 8 Reales of Philip II.

KM#	Date	Good	VG	Fine	VF
108	ND(1555-58)	675.00	1000.	1350.	1800.

c/m: Type II on Peru (Star of Lima) 'cob' 8 Reales of Philip IV, KM#18.

KM#	Date	Good	VG	Fine	VF
109	ND(1659-60)	—	—	Rare	—

c/m: Type II on Peru (Lima) 'cob' 8 Reales, KM#24.

KM#	Date	Good	VG	Fine	VF
110.1	ND(1684-1701)	85.00	130.00	180.00	240.00

c/m: Type II on Peru (Lima) 'Royal' 8 Reales, KM#24.

KM#	Date	Good	VG	Fine	VF
110.2	ND(1684-1701)	550.00	825.00	1125.	1500.

c/m: Type II on Peru (Lima) 'cob' 8 Reales, KM#34.

KM#	Date	Good	VG	Fine	VF
111.1	ND(1701-23)	80.00	125.00	165.00	225.00

c/m: Type II on Peru (Lima) 'cob' 8 Reales, KM#39.

KM#	Date	Good	VG	Fine	VF
111.2	ND(1725-26)	300.00	575.00	800.00	1100.

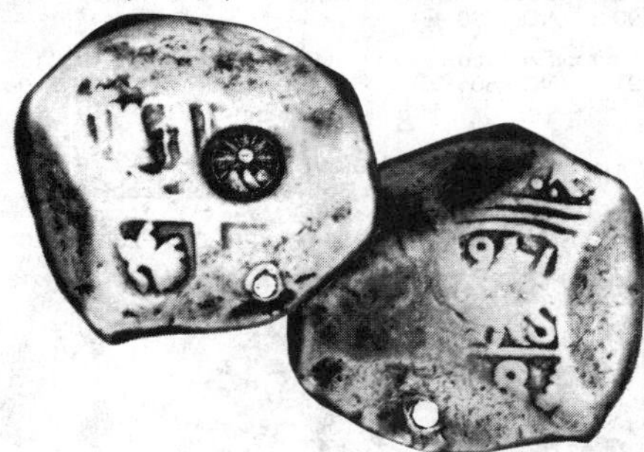

c/m: Type II on Peru (Lima) 'cob' 8 Reales, KM#41.

KM#	Date	Good	VG	Fine	VF
111.3	ND(1727-46)	80.00	125.00	165.00	225.00

c/m: Type II on Peru (Lima) 8 Reales, KM#142.3.

KM#	Date	Good	VG	Fine	VF
111.5	ND(1828-?)	80.00	125.00	165.00	225.00

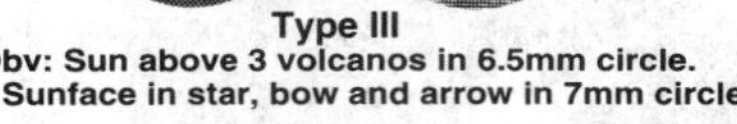

Type III

Obv: Sun above 3 volcanos in 6.5mm circle.
Rev: Sunface in star, bow and arrow in 7mm circle.

8 REALES

SILVER

c/m: Type III on Bolivia 8 Soles, KM#97.

KM#	Date	Good	VG	Fine	VF
112.1	ND(1827-40)	110.00	165.00	225.00	325.00

c/m: Type III on Chile (Santiago) 8 Reales, KM#96.1.

KM#	Date	Good	VG	Fine	VF
112.2	ND(1837-40)	125.00	185.00	250.00	350.00

c/m: Type III on Peru (Lima) 8 Reales, KM#136.

KM#	Date	Good	VG	Fine	VF
120.1	ND(1822-23)	150.00	225.00	300.00	400.00

c/m: Type III on Peru (Lima) 8 Reales, KM#142.1.

KM#	Date	Good	VG	Fine	VF
120.2	ND(1825-28)	45.00	75.00	120.00	175.00

c/m: Type III on Peru (Lima) 8 Reales, KM#142.3.

KM#	Date	Good	VG	Fine	VF
120.3	ND(1828-40)	40.00	65.00	100.00	150.00

c/m: Type III on Peru (Cuzco) 8 Reales, KM#142.2.

KM#	Date	Good	VG	Fine	VF
120.4	ND(1826-36)	45.00	75.00	120.00	175.00

c/m: Type III on Peru (North) 8 Reales, KM#155.

KM#	Date	Good	VG	Fine	VF
120.5	ND(1836-39)	45.00	75.00	120.00	175.00

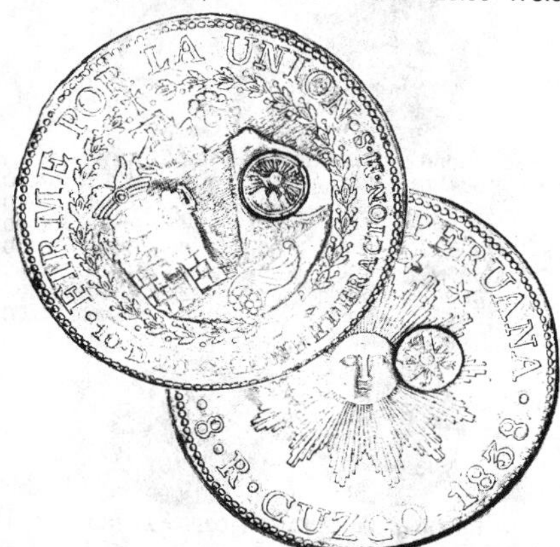

c/s: Type III on Peru (South) 8 Reales, KM#170.4.

KM#	Date	Good	VG	Fine	VF
120.6	ND(1837-39)	375.00	550.00	750.00	1000.

NOTE: Coins dated after 1841 with the Type III c/m are believed to be counterfeit by some authorities.

COUNTERSTAMPED COINAGE

Type IV

NOTE: Similar dies as used for Type III but instead of being applied as individual countermarks they were paired in hinged dies and counterstamped in one application. This was done without respect to the host coins obverse or reverse.

8 REALES

SILVER

c/s: Type IV on Argentina (Potosi) 8 Reales, KM#14.

KM#	Date	Good	VG	Fine	VF
113	ND(1815)	225.00	330.00	450.00	600.00

c/s: Type IV on Bolivia 8 Soles, KM#97.

KM#	Date	Good	VG	Fine	VF
114	ND(1827-40)	45.00	75.00	120.00	175.00

c/s: Type IV on Chile (Santiago) 8 Reales, KM#96.1.

KM#	Date	Good	VG	Fine	VF
115	ND(1837-40)	125.00	185.00	250.00	350.00

c/s: Type IV on Peru (Lima) 8 Reales, KM#136.

KM#	Date	Good	VG	Fine	VF
116	ND(1822-23)	150.00	225.00	300.00	400.00

c/s: Type IV on Peru (Lima) 8 Reales, KM#142.1.

KM#	Date	Good	VG	Fine	VF
117	ND(1825-28)	45.00	75.00	120.00	175.00

c/s: Type IV on Peru (Lima) 8 Reales, KM#142.3.

KM#	Date	Good	VG	Fine	VF
118.1	ND(1828-41)	40.00	65.00	100.00	150.00

c/s: Type IV on Peru (Lima) 8 Reales, KM#142.8.

KM#	Date	Good	VG	Fine	VF
118.2	ND(1828-41)	40.00	65.00	100.00	150.00

c/s: Type IV on Peru (Cuzco) 8 Reales, KM#142.2.

KM#	Date	Good	VG	Fine	VF
119	ND(1826-36)	45.00	75.00	120.00	175.00

c/s: Type IV on Peru (North) 8 Reales, KM#155.

KM#	Date	Good	VG	Fine	VF
121	ND(1836-39)	45.00	75.00	120.00	175.00

NOTE: Coins dated after 1841 with the Type IV c/s are believed to be counterfeit by some authorities.

REPUBLIC

MONETARY SYSTEM

8 Reales = 1 Peso

1/4 REAL

.7600 g, .903 SILVER, .0220 oz ASW

KM#	Date	Mintage	Fine	VF	XF	Unc
130	1859	—	200.00	300.00	500.00	—
	1860	.116	6.00	10.00	20.00	35.00
	1861	—	7.00	12.50	17.50	27.50
	1862	—	6.50	10.00	15.00	25.00
	1863	—	7.00	12.50	17.50	30.00
	1864	—	7.00	12.50	17.50	30.00
	1865	.023	22.50	45.00	75.00	150.00
	1866	.205	5.00	8.50	12.50	22.50
	1867	.169	5.00	8.50	12.50	22.50
	1868	.148	5.00	8.50	12.50	22.50
	1869	.242	5.00	8.50	12.50	22.50

.7700 g, .900 SILVER, .0222 oz ASW
Rev: 0.900 below wreath.

KM#	Date	Mintage	Fine	VF	XF	Unc
146	1872 P	—	2.00	3.50	5.50	9.00
	1873/2 P	.308	5.00	10.00	15.00	25.00
	1873 P	Inc. Ab.	1.00	1.75	3.00	5.00
	1874 P	—	7.50	12.50	20.00	35.00
	1875/3 P	—	1.50	2.50	4.50	15.00
	1875 P	—	1.00	1.75	3.00	12.50
	1876 P	—	10.00	15.00	25.00	40.00
	1878 P	2 known	175.00	250.00	—	—
	1878 F	.680	1.00	1.75	3.00	8.00

NOTE: Varieties exist.

.7700 g, .835 SILVER, .0206 oz ASW
Rev: 0.835 below small wreath.

KM#	Date	Mintage	Fine	VF	XF	Unc
146a.1	1878	Inc.KM146	2.00	3.50	6.50	12.50

Rev: 0.835 below large wreath.

KM#	Date	Mintage	Fine	VF	XF	Unc
146a.2	1878	Inc.KM146	1.50	2.50	4.00	8.00
	1879	.171	1.50	2.50	4.00	8.00

Rev: W/o fineness.

KM#	Date	Mintage	Fine	VF	XF	Unc
146a.3	1878 large G/O	Inc. KM146	2.75	4.50	9.00	15.00
	1878 medium G	Inc. KM146	2.25	3.50	7.50	14.00
	1878 small G	Inc. KM146	2.75	4.50	10.00	17.50
	1879 large G	Inc. KM146a.2	5.50	9.00	15.00	25.00

Obv: Long-rayed sun. Rev: 0.835 added.

KM#	Date	Mintage	Fine	VF	XF	Unc
151	1879					
		Inc. KM146a.2	1.50	2.00	3.00	6.50
	1880	.115	1.00	1.75	3.00	6.50
	1881/79	.073	5.00	10.00	15.00	25.00
	1881	Inc. Ab.	3.00	4.50	8.00	13.50
	1882	—	1.00	1.50	2.50	5.00
	1883	.195	15.00	25.00	40.00	70.00
	1884	.100	1.00	1.50	2.50	5.00
	1885	—	7.50	12.50	20.00	35.00
	1886/5	—	1.50	2.50	4.50	8.00
	1886	—	1.50	2.50	4.50	8.00

Obv: Mountains w/short-rayed sun.

KM#	Date	Mintage	Fine	VF	XF	Unc
156	1887	—	1.50	2.50	4.00	8.00
	1888	—	1.00	1.50	2.25	3.50

NOTE: Varieties exist.

Obv: G below mountains.

KM#	Date	Mintage	Fine	VF	XF	Unc
157	1889	.870	2.00	3.00	5.00	15.00

Rev: 5 stars below wreath.

KM#	Date	Mintage	Fine	VF	XF	Unc
158	1889	Inc.KM157	1.00	1.50	2.50	4.50
	1890	—	1.00	1.50	2.50	4.50
	1891	—	1.50	2.50	4.00	6.50

NOTE: Varieties exist.

Obv: Mountains w/long-rayed sun.

KM#	Date	Mintage	Fine	VF	XF	Unc
159	1892	.512	30.00	65.00	225.00	350.00
	1893/2	.749	2.00	4.00	8.00	15.00
	1893 lg. dt.	I.A.	1.00	1.50	2.00	3.00
	1893 sm. dt.	I.A.	1.00	1.50	2.00	3.00
	1894	—	7.50	12.50	20.00	35.00

Rev: 3 stars below thin wreath.

KM#	Date	Mintage	Fine	VF	XF	Unc
161	1893	Inc.KM159	1.00	1.50	2.00	3.00
	1894	.059	6.50	10.00	15.00	25.00

Rev: 5 stars below full wreath.

KM#	Date	Mintage	Fine	VF	XF	Unc
162	1894	—	.75	1.25	2.25	5.00
	1894H	.800	.50	.75	1.50	2.50
	1894H	—	—	—	Proof	100.00
	1895	1.482	.50	.75	1.25	2.00
	1896	2.071	.50	.75	1.25	2.00
	1897	.989	.50	.75	1.50	2.25
	1898	.384	.50	1.00	1.75	3.00
	1899	.080	1.50	2.50	4.50	8.00

COPPER-NICKEL

KM#	Date	Mintage	Fine	VF	XF	Unc
175	1900H	2.944	.15	.35	1.00	2.50

NOTE: Later date (1901) exists for this type.

MEDIO (1/2) REAL

1.5500 g, .903 SILVER, .0449 oz ASW
Rev: MED: REAL

KM#	Date	Mintage	Fine	VF	XF	Unc
131	1859	—	15.00	30.00	60.00	125.00
	1860 R	.191	6.00	10.00	20.00	50.00
	1861	—	15.00	30.00	60.00	125.00
	1861 R	—	6.00	10.00	20.00	50.00

Obv. leg: RAFAEL CARRERA PTE.
Rev: MED. RL

KM#	Date	Mintage	Fine	VF	XF	Unc
138	1862 R	—	10.00	20.00	40.00	100.00
138	1863/2 R	—	6.00	10.00	20.00	50.00
	1863 R	—	4.50	9.00	15.00	40.00
	1865/3 R	.057	4.50	9.00	15.00	40.00
	1865 R	Inc. Ab.	3.25	6.00	12.00	30.00

Obv. leg: R. CARRERA FUNDADOR

KM#	Date	Mintage	Fine	VF	XF	Unc
143	1867 R	.092	4.00	8.50	15.00	40.00
	1868 R	.102	4.00	8.50	15.00	40.00
	1869	.117	4.00	8.50	15.00	40.00
	1869 R	—	4.25	9.00	17.50	45.00

1.5000 g, .900 SILVER, .0435 oz ASW

KM#	Date	Mintage	Fine	VF	XF	Unc
147	1872 P	—	6.00	11.50	22.50	60.00
	1873 P	.035	7.00	13.50	27.50	65.00

1.5000 g, .835 SILVER, .0402 oz ASW

KM#	Date	Mintage	Fine	VF	XF	Unc
147a.1	1878	—	2.75	4.50	8.50	25.00
	1879	Inc.KM152	3.75	6.50	10.00	28.00

NOTE: Wide and narrow dates exist for 1879. Large and small dates and letters exist for 1878.

Rev: W/o fineness.

KM#	Date	Mintage	Fine	VF	XF	Unc
147a.2	1878 lg. date	—	2.75	4.50	8.50	22.50
	1878 sm. date	—	2.75	4.50	8.50	22.50
	1893	Inc.KM163	5.00	8.50	12.00	30.00

Obv: 1/2 RL.

KM#	Date	Mintage	Fine	VF	XF	Unc
152	1879 D	1.683	2.00	4.00	6.00	10.00
	1879 D.	—	2.50	5.00	8.00	15.00
	1880/79 D					
		2.715	3.00	6.00	9.00	17.50
	1880 D	Inc. Ab.	.75	1.25	2.50	5.00
	1880/70 E	I.A.	—	—	—	—
	1880 E	Inc. Ab.	6.00	10.00	15.00	22.50

NOTE: Varieties exist.

Obv: MEDIO REAL.

KM#	Date	Mintage	Fine	VF	XF	Unc
155.1	1880/770 E					
		Inc. KM152	3.00	4.50	7.50	12.50
	1880/777 E					
		Inc. KM152	3.00	4.50	7.50	12.50
	1880/790 E					
		Inc. KM152	3.00	4.50	7.50	12.50
	1880/79 E					
		Inc. KM152	3.00	4.50	7.50	12.50
	1880 E					
		Inc. KM152	.75	1.50	2.50	4.00
	1881 E	—	.75	2.00	3.00	4.50
	1883/1 E	.046	8.00	12.50	28.00	50.00
	1883 E	Inc. Ab.	4.50	8.50	15.00	22.50

NOTE: Varieties exist.

Rev: Star between fineness and date.

KM#	Date	Mintage	Fine	VF	XF	Unc
155.2	1889/779	.481	1.25	2.25	6.00	12.00
	1889	Inc. Ab.	1.25	2.25	6.00	12.00
	1890/89	—	2.00	4.50	8.50	15.00
	1890	—	1.25	2.25	6.00	12.00

Rev: W/o star between fineness and date.

KM#	Date	Mintage	Fine	VF	XF	Unc
155.3	1892	1 known	—	—	—	—

Rev: W/o fineness, small wreath.

KM#	Date	Mintage	Fine	VF	XF	Unc
163	1893/2	.360	13.50	30.00	70.00	120.00
	1893	Inc. Ab.	12.00	25.00	50.00	90.00

Rev: Large wreath.

KM#	Date	Mintage	Fine	VF	XF	Unc
164	1893 large date, blundered flat top 3					
		Inc. KM163	7.00	15.00	30.00	55.00
	1893 small date, round top 3					
		Inc. KM163	7.00	15.00	30.00	55.00

1.5000 g, .835 SILVER, .0402 oz ASW

KM#	Date	Mintage	Fine	VF	XF	Unc
165	1894	.619	.65	1.25	2.25	4.00
	1894H	.900	.65	1.25	2.00	3.00
	1894H	—	—	—	Proof	100.00
	1895	.819	.65	1.25	2.00	3.00
	1895H	.300	1.25	2.25	3.75	5.50
	1896	1.062	.65	1.25	2.00	3.00
	1897	.528	.65	1.25	2.00	3.00

NOTE: Varieties exist.

1.5500 g, .600 SILVER, .0299 oz ASW

KM#	Date	Mintage	Fine	VF	XF	Unc
170	1899	.486	.75	1.25	2.50	3.50

COPPER-NICKEL

KM#	Date	Mintage	Fine	VF	XF	Unc
176	1900	5.348	.35	.65	1.00	2.50

NOTE: Later date (1901) exists for this type.

UN (1) REAL

3.0000 g, .903 SILVER, .0870 oz ASW
Rev: UN REAL.

KM#	Date	Mintage	Fine	VF	XF	Unc
132	1859	—	60.00	100.00	—	—
	1859/95 R	—	—	—	—	—
	1859 R	—	10.00	18.00	30.00	75.00
	1860 R	.177	5.00	9.00	18.00	40.00

Obv. leg: RAFAEL CARRERA PTE. . . w/FRENER F. below truncation. Rev: UN RL.

KM#	Date	Mintage	Fine	VF	XF	Unc
137.1	1861 R	—	4.00	7.50	15.00	35.00
	1862 R	—	3.00	6.00	12.00	30.00
	1863 R	—	5.00	9.00	18.00	40.00
	1864 R	—	3.00	5.50	11.50	30.00
	1865 R	—	5.50	10.00	20.00	45.00

W/o Frener F below bust.

KM#	Date	Mintage	Fine	VF	XF	Unc
137.2	1865 R	—	3.00	6.00	12.00	30.00

NOTE: Varieties exist.

Obv. leg: R. CARRERA FUNDADOR. . .
Rev: 1 RL.

KM#	Date	Mintage	Fine	VF	XF	Unc
141	1866 R	.385	4.00	9.00	18.00	40.00
	1867 R	.199	4.00	9.00	18.00	40.00

Rev: UN REAL.

KM#	Date	Mintage	Fine	VF	XF	Unc
145	1868 R	.335	4.00	9.00	18.00	40.00
	1868/7 R	—	5.00	10.00	20.00	45.00
	1869 R	.131	4.00	9.00	18.00	40.00

3.1500 g, .900 SILVER, .0911 oz ASW

KM#	Date	Mintage	Fine	VF	XF	Unc
148.1	1872 P	3,816	10.00	22.50	45.00	115.00
	1874 P	—	8.00	16.50	27.50	65.00
	1878 F	.159	9.00	18.00	32.50	75.00

Obv: W/o fineness.

KM#	Date	Mintage	Fine	VF	XF	Unc
148.2	1878	Inc. Ab.	13.50	27.50	50.00	120.00

NOTE: Wide and narrow dates exist.

KM#	Date	Mintage	Fine	VF	XF	Unc
153	1879 D	.037	10.00	22.50	37.50	60.00

3.2500 g, .835 SILVER, .0872 oz ASW

KM#	Date	Mintage	Fine	VF	XF	Unc
153a.1	1883	.046	3.50	6.00	12.00	17.50

Rev: Star between fineness and date.

KM#	Date	Mintage	Fine	VF	XF	Unc
153a.2	1889	.332	1.50	2.75	3.50	6.00
	1890/89	—	2.00	4.50	6.50	12.50
	1890/8	—	2.00	4.50	6.50	12.50
	1890	—	1.50	2.75	3.50	6.00
	1891	—	1.50	2.75	3.50	6.00
	1893	.293	2.00	4.00	5.00	8.00

NOTE: Wide and narrow dates exist on 1893 dated coins.

KM#	Date	Mintage	Fine	VF	XF	Unc
166	1894	.326	2.00	3.00	4.25	6.50
	1894H	.600	2.00	3.00	4.00	5.50
	1894H	—	—	—	Proof	100.00
	1895H	.200	3.00	6.00	9.00	15.00
	1896	.203	2.00	3.00	4.25	6.50
	1897	.701	2.00	3.00	4.00	5.50
	1898	.040	6.50	11.50	20.00	32.50

Rev: W/o fineness.

KM#	Date	Mintage	Fine	VF	XF	Unc
171	1899	—	6.50	10.00	20.00	32.50

3.1500 g, .750 SILVER, .0759 oz ASW

KM#	Date	Mintage	Fine	VF	XF	Unc
172	1899	—	85.00	135.00	250.00	—

3.1000 g, .600 SILVER, .0598 oz ASW

KM#	Date	Mintage	Fine	VF	XF	Unc
173	1899	—	2.00	2.50	5.00	12.50

3.1500 g, .500 SILVER, .0506 oz ASW

KM#	Date	Mintage	Fine	VF	XF	Unc
174	1899/88	—	1.50	3.00	8.00	17.50
	1899	—	1.25	2.75	6.00	12.50
	1900	1.874	1.25	2.75	7.00	15.00

NOTE: Varieties exist.

.500/.550 SILVER

KM#	Date	Mintage	Fine	VF	XF	Unc
174a	1899/8	—	1.50	3.50	9.00	19.00
	1899	—	1.25	3.00	6.50	14.00

COPPER-NICKEL

KM#	Date	Mintage	Fine	VF	XF	Unc
177	1900	4.612	—	.35	.85	1.75

NOTE: Later dates (1901-1912) exist for this type.

DOS (2) REALES

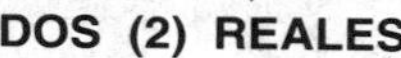

6.3000 g, .903 SILVER, .1829 oz ASW, 27.5mm
Obv. leg: RAFAEL CARRERA PE., thick letters.

KM#	Date	Mintage	VG	Fine	VF	XF
133	1859	—	175.00	275.00	375.00	600.00

NOTE: Often holed; beware of repaired specimens.

6.2000 g, .903 SILVER, .1800 oz ASW, 26mm
Obv: Thin letters.

KM#	Date	Mintage	VG	Fine	VF	XF
134	1860 R	—	2.50	7.50	15.00	45.00
	1861 R	—	3.50	10.00	20.00	50.00

6.1000 g, .903 SILVER, .1770 oz ASW, 24mm
Rev: Narrower shield.

KM#	Date	Mintage	Fine	VF	XF	Unc
139	1862 R	—	6.00	12.00	25.00	50.00
	1863 R	—	6.00	12.00	25.00	50.00
	1864 R	—	6.00	12.00	25.00	50.00
	1865 R	.410	6.00	12.00	25.00	50.00
	1865 R w/o period after date	Inc. Ab.	12.00	25.00	60.00	100.00

NOTE: Wide and narrow dates exist on 1863 dated coins.

Obv. leg: R. CARRERA FUNDADOR. . .

KM#	Date	Mintage	Fine	VF	XF	Unc
142	1866 R	.334	4.00	8.50	16.00	40.00
	1867 R	.293	4.00	8.50	16.00	40.00
	1868 R	.267	4.50	8.50	16.00	40.00
	1869 R	.124	6.50	12.00	20.00	50.00

6.1000 g, .900 SILVER, .1765 oz ASW

KM#	Date	Mintage	Fine	VF	XF	Unc
149	1872 P	—	6.00	12.50	25.00	55.00
	1873 P	.610	3.50	7.50	18.00	40.00

KM#	Date	Mintage	Fine	VF	XF	Unc
154	1879 D	.101	7.50	12.00	18.00	50.00

0.835/0.900 SILVER

KM#	Date	Mintage	Fine	VF	XF	Unc
154a	1881 E	2.975	7.50	10.00	12.50	25.00
	1881 E (error) G/R in GUATEMALA	—	10.00	15.00	20.00	35.00

.835 SILVER

KM#	Date	Mintage	Fine	VF	XF	Unc
154c	1881 E	—	10.00	15.00	20.00	35.00

6.2000 g, .835 SILVER, .1664 oz ASW
Rev: Star between fineness and date.

KM#	Date	Mintage	VG	Fine	VF	XF
154b.1	1892	—	70.00	170.00	280.00	400.00
	1893	1 known	—	—	—	—

Rev: W/o star.

KM#	Date	Mintage	VG	Fine	VF	XF
154b.2	1892	—	70.00	170.00	280.00	400.00

KM#	Date	Mintage	Fine	VF	XF	Unc
167	1894	1.094	2.25	4.50	7.00	12.50
	1894H	.900	2.25	4.50	7.00	12.50
	1894H	—	—	—	Proof	300.00
	1895	2.783	2.25	4.50	7.00	12.50
	1895H	.300	3.75	6.00	9.00	15.00
	1896	.605	2.25	4.50	7.00	12.50

KM#	Date	Mintage	Fine	VF	XF	Unc
167	1897	1.041	2.25	4.50	7.00	12.50
	1898	5.172	1.75	3.25	6.50	12.00
	1899	.040	10.00	17.50	25.00	50.00

CUATRO (4) REALES

0.8459 g, .875 GOLD, .0238 oz AGW

KM#	Date	Mintage	Fine	VF	XF	Unc
135	1860 R	—	20.00	35.00	50.00	90.00
	1861 R	.277	17.50	30.00	40.00	75.00
	1864 R	—	25.00	60.00	100.00	150.00

12.5000 g, .903 SILVER, .3629 oz ASW
Obv. leg: RAFAEL CARRERA PTE. . .

KM#	Date	Mintage	VG	Fine	VF	XF
136	1860 R	4,760	6.50	20.00	35.00	70.00
	1861 R	—	5.00	18.00	30.00	60.00

Rev: Shield narrowed.

KM#	Date	Mintage	Fine	VF	XF	Unc
140	1863 R	—	10.00	20.00	35.00	200.00
	1865/55 R	.082	—	—	—	—
	1865/3 R	I.A.	18.00	30.00	55.00	350.00
	1865 R	Inc. Ab.	10.00	20.00	35.00	200.00

Obv. leg: R. CARRERA FUNDADOR. . .

KM#	Date	Mintage	VG	Fine	VF	XF
144	1867 R	.054	5.00	15.00	20.00	35.00
	1868 R	.036	5.00	15.00	25.00	40.00
	1869 R	—	—	—	Rare	—

12.5000 g, .900 SILVER, .3617 oz ASW

KM#	Date	Mintage	Fine	VF	XF	Unc
150	1873 P	.024	18.50	40.00	100.00	200.00
	1878 D	.010	27.50	60.00	125.00	250.00
	1879 D	7,664	27.50	60.00	125.00	250.00
	1879 P	—	45.00	85.00	145.00	290.00
	1892 R.G.	—	60.00	135.00	275.00	550.00
	1893	—	100.00	225.00	550.00	875.00
	1893 R.G.	—	100.00	225.00	550.00	875.00

12.5000 g, .835 SILVER, .3356 oz ASW

KM#	Date	Mintage	Fine	VF	XF	Unc
160	1892	2,600	275.00	500.00	1000.	2500.

12.5000 g, .900 SILVER, .3617 oz ASW

KM#	Date	Mintage	Fine	VF	XF	Unc
168.1	1894H	.500	6.00	12.50	18.50	32.50
	1894H	—	—	—	Proof	400.00

Obv. and rev: H mint mark.

KM#	Date	Mintage	Fine	VF	XF	Unc
168.2	1894H	Inc. Ab.	80.00	120.00	250.00	500.00

DECIMAL COINAGE

100 Centavos (Centimos) = 1 Peso

CENTAVO

BRONZE

KM#	Date	Mintage	Fine	VF	XF	Unc
196	1871	—	2.00	5.00	10.00	27.50

KM#	Date	Mintage	Fine	VF	XF	Unc
202.1	1881	—	3.50	7.50	12.00	40.00

Die breaks in 1881 have the appearance of 1884.

KM#	Date	Mintage	Fine	VF	XF	Unc
202.2	1881	—	5.00	10.00	15.00	45.00

NOTE: Some specimens overstruck on KM#196.

5 CENTAVOS

1.2500 g, .835 SILVER, .0335 oz ASW

KM#	Date	Mintage	Fine	VF	XF	Unc
203	1881	.118	10.00	25.00	40.00	80.00

10 CENTAVOS

2.5000 g, .835 SILVER, .0671 oz ASW

KM#	Date	Mintage	Fine	VF	XF	Unc
204	1881	.056	16.50	32.50	50.00	115.00

25 CENTIMOS

6.2500 g, .900 SILVER, .1808 oz ASW

KM#	Date	Mintage	Fine	VF	XF	Unc
189	1869 R	.181	6.00	13.50	25.00	70.00
	1870 R	.180	4.50	9.00	20.00	60.00

25 CENTAVOS

6.2500 g, .835 SILVER, .1677 oz ASW

KM#	Date	Mintage	Fine	VF	XF	Unc
205.1	1881 E	5.044	2.50	5.00	18.00	30.00
	1882 E	—	2.50	5.00	18.00	30.00
	1885 E	—	2.50	5.00	18.00	30.00
	1888 E	—	4.00	8.00	22.00	35.00
	1888	—	7.00	15.00	35.00	50.00
	1888 G	—	2.50	5.00	18.00	30.00
	1889 G	.496	2.50	5.00	18.00	30.00
	1889 G medal rotation	Inc. Ab.	—	—	—	—

NOTE: Varieties exist.

Star replaces assayers initial

KM#	Date	Mintage	Fine	VF	XF	Unc
205.2	1889	Inc. Ab.	2.50	5.00	18.00	35.00
	1890	—	3.00	6.00	20.00	35.00
	1891	—	6.00	12.00	25.00	40.00

KM#	Date	Mintage	VG	Fine	VF	XF
206	1882	—	125.00	225.00	325.00	450.00

Rev: W/o star.

KM#	Date	Mintage	Fine	VF	XF	Unc
209.1	1892	—	30.00	50.00	75.00	100.00

Rev: Star between fineness and date.

KM#	Date	Mintage	Fine	VF	XF	Unc
209.2	1890	—	6.00	12.00	22.50	35.00
	1892	—	2.50	5.00	8.00	15.00
	1893	—	2.25	4.50	7.00	12.00

NOTE: Varieties exist.

50 CENTAVOS

12.5000 g., .835 SILVER, .3356 oz ASW

KM#	Date	Mintage	VG	Fine	VF	XF
195	1870 R	.140	5.00	10.00	18.50	50.00

PESO

25.0000 g, .903 SILVER, .7258 oz ASW

KM#	Date	Mintage	VG	Fine	VF	XF
178	1859	—	60.00	175.00	275.00	900.00
	1859 R	—	—	—	Rare	—

1.6917 g, .875 GOLD, .0476 oz AGW

KM#	Date	Mintage	VG	Fine	VF	XF
179	1859 R	—	25.00	35.00	50.00	75.00
	1860 R	.037	25.00	35.00	50.00	75.00

27.0000 g, .903 SILVER, .7839 oz ASW

KM#	Date	Mintage	VG	Fine	VF	XF
182	1862 R	—	15.00	25.00	80.00	125.00
	1863 R	—	12.00	20.00	40.00	80.00
	1864 R	—	6.00	10.00	17.50	37.50
	1864.R	—	6.00	10.00	17.50	37.50
	1865 sm.R	.119	7.00	12.00	20.00	40.00
	1865 lg.R	I.A.	15.00	25.00	80.00	125.00

Rev: L10D.20G

KM#	Date	Mintage	VG	Fine	VF	XF
186.1	1866 R	.109	7.00	12.00	20.00	40.00
	1867 R	.173	6.00	10.00	17.50	37.50
	1868 R	.060	8.00	15.00	25.00	50.00

Rev: W/o 'L' before 10Ds.20Gs.

KM#	Date	Mintage	VG	Fine	VF	XF
186.2	1869	.186	45.00	70.00	125.00	285.00
	1869 R	Inc. Ab.	40.00	60.00	100.00	250.00

25.0000 g, .900 SILVER, .7234 oz ASW
Rev: L0.900

KM#	Date	Mintage	VG	Fine	VF	XF
190.1	1869/99 R	Inc.KM186	10.00	17.50	25.00	75.00
	1869 R	Inc.KM186	6.00	10.00	17.50	37.50
	1870 R	.283	6.00	10.00	15.00	35.00
	1871 R	—	6.00	10.00	15.00	30.00

Rev: W/o 'L' before 0.900.

KM#	Date	Mintage	VG	Fine	VF	XF
190.2	1869 R	Inc.KM186	8.00	15.00	25.00	45.00

Rev: W/o L and 0.900.

KM#	Date	Mintage	VG	Fine	VF	XF
190.3	1869 R	Inc. KM186	30.00	50.00	80.00	120.00
	1869	Inc. KM186	30.00	50.00	80.00	120.00

Rev: Date and fineness at bottom.

KM#	Date	Mintage	Fine	VF	XF	Unc
197.1	1872 P	.014	30.00	60.00	100.00	500.00
	1872 R	—	—	—	Rare	—
	1873 P	.078	20.00	40.00	80.00	300.00
	1873 P (error fineness 0900)	—	30.00	50.00	90.00	250.00

Rev: Quetzal w/short tail.

KM#	Date	Mintage	Fine	VF	XF	Unc
197.2	1873 P	—	30.00	50.00	90.00	250.00

Rev: Date and fineness at top.

KM#	Date	Mintage	VG	Fine	VF	XF
200	1878 D	1,076	300.00	600.00	1200.	2000.
	1879 D	.010	100.00	200.00	300.00	600.00

Rev: Full spray design.

KM#	Date	Mintage	VG	Fine	VF	XF
201	1879 D	Inc. KM200	125.00	250.00	350.00	500.00
	1893 G	—	800.00	—	—	—
	1893 RG	1,119	550.00	1000.	1700.	2750.

Obv: Modified Liberty design.

KM#	Date	Mintage	Fine	VF	XF	Unc
207	1882/1 E	—	—	—	Rare	—
	1888 G	—	350.00	600.00	1100.	2000.
	1889 G	—	350.00	600.00	1100.	2000.

KM#	Date	Mintage	VG	Fine	VF	XF
208	1882 A.E.	—	20.00	30.00	70.00	225.00
	1889 MG	6,794	125.00	200.00	350.00	600.00

KM#	Date	Mintage	Fine	VF	XF	Unc
210	1894	1.696	7.00	12.50	17.50	45.00
	1894H	.875	7.00	12.50	17.50	55.00
	1894H	—	—	—	Proof	800.00
	1895	1.415	7.00	12.50	17.50	50.00
	1895H	.375	8.00	15.00	22.00	75.00
	1895H	—	—	—	Proof	—
	1896/5	1.403	10.00	17.50	25.00	85.00
	1896	Inc. Ab.	7.00	12.50	17.50	50.00
	1897	—	12.00	20.00	30.00	100.00

2 PESOS

3.3834 g, .875 GOLD, .0952 oz AGW

KM#	Date	Mintage	VG	Fine	VF	XF
180	1859 R	—	50.00	65.00	125.00	200.00

4 PESOS

6.7669 g, .875 GOLD, .1904 oz AGW

KM#	Date	Mintage	VG	Fine	VF	XF
181	1861 R	—	175.00	250.00	400.00	550.00
	1862 R	—	175.00	250.00	400.00	550.00

KM#	Date	Mintage	VG	Fine	VF	XF
187	1866 R	561 pcs.	—	—	Rare	—
	1868 R	778 pcs.	250.00	500.00	700.00	950.00
	1869 R	.020	100.00	175.00	250.00	375.00

5 PESOS

8.0645 g, .900 GOLD, .2333 oz AGW

KM#	Date	Mintage	VG	Fine	VF	XF
191	1869 R	.049	110.00	125.00	175.00	250.00

KM#	Date	Mintage	VG	Fine	VF	XF
198	1872 P	—	125.00	200.00	350.00	550.00
	1873 P	—	—	—	Rare	—
	1874 P	—	125.00	200.00	350.00	550.00
	1875 P	—	—	—	Rare	—
	1876 F	—	—	—	Rare	—
	1877 F	—	125.00	200.00	350.00	550.00
	1878 D	—	125.00	200.00	350.00	550.00

8 PESOS

13.5337 g, .875 GOLD, .3807 oz AGW

KM#	Date	Mintage	VG	Fine	VF	XF
184	1864 R	—	300.00	450.00	750.00	1200.

Similar to 4 Pesos, KM#187.

KM#	Date	Mintage	VG	Fine	VF	XF
192	1869 R	—	500.00	650.00	2000.	3000.

10 PESOS

16.1290 g, .900 GOLD, .4667 oz AGW

KM#	Date	Mintage	VG	Fine	VF	XF
193	1869 R	.020	225.00	300.00	450.00	700.00

16 PESOS

27.0296 g, .875 GOLD, .7604 oz AGW

KM#	Date	Mintage	VG	Fine	VF	XF
183	1863 R	—	—	—	3500.	5500.
	1864 R	—	—	—	Rare	—
	1865 R	—	—	—	Rare	—

NOTE: A few AU-Unc specimens of the 1863R were found in a box shook loose from its hiding place during the 1977 Guatemala earthquake.

Reduced size

KM#	Date	Mintage	VG	Fine	VF	XF
185	1865 R	190 pcs.	1000.	2000.	4000.	6000.

KM#	Date	Mintage	VG	Fine	VF	XF
188	1867 R	467 pcs.	850.00	1750.	3500.	5000.
	1869 R	3,465	400.00	600.00	800.00	1500.

20 PESOS

32.2580 g, .900 GOLD, .9334 oz AGW

KM#	Date	Mintage	VG	Fine	VF	XF
194	1869 R	.016	450.00	550.00	700.00	950.00

KM#	Date	Mintage	VG	Fine	VF	XF
199	1877 F	—	1000.	2000.	5000.	8000.
	1878 F	—	1000.	2000.	5000.	8000.

COUNTERSTAMPED COINAGE

By 1894, foreign coins had become so prevalent that on August 10 the government authorized their counterstamping at the mint, with official 1/2 Real dies of 1894, to legitimize their circulation.

(PESO)

.917 SILVER
c/s: On Brazil 2000 Reis, KM#475.

KM#	Date	Year	Mintage	Fine	VF	XF
213	1894	1875	—	—	Rare	—

25.0000 g, .900 SILVER, .7234 oz ASW
c/s: On Chile 8 Reales, KM#96.2.

KM#	Date	Year	Mintage	Fine	VF	XF
214	1894	1848 JM	—	—	Rare	—
	1894	1849 ML	— Reported, not confirmed			

c/s: On Chile Peso, KM#129.

KM#	Date	Year	Fine	VF	XF	
215	1894	1853	550.00	1200.	2000.	—
		1854	350.00	750.00	1250.	—
		1855	350.00	750.00	1250.	—

c/s: On Chile Peso, KM#142.1.

KM#	Date	Year	Mintage	Fine	VF	XF
216	1894	1867	—	125.00	200.00	300.00
		1868	—	125.00	200.00	300.00
		1869	—	50.00	75.00	125.00
		1870/69	—	50.00	75.00	125.00
		1870	—	50.00	75.00	125.00
		1871	—	75.00	125.00	200.00
		1872	—	20.00	30.00	50.00
		1873/2	—	20.00	30.00	50.00
		1873	—	20.00	30.00	50.00
		1874	—	20.00	30.00	50.00
		1875	—	20.00	30.00	50.00
		1876	—	20.00	30.00	50.00
		1877	—	20.00	30.00	50.00
		1878	—	20.00	30.00	50.00
		1879	—	20.00	30.00	50.00
		1880	—	20.00	30.00	50.00
		1881	—	20.00	30.00	50.00
		1882/1	—	20.00	30.00	50.00
		1882	—	20.00	30.00	50.00
		1883	—	20.00	30.00	50.00
		1884	—	20.00	30.00	50.00
		1885/3	—	20.00	30.00	50.00
		1885	—	20.00	30.00	50.00
		1886	—	20.00	30.00	50.00
		1887	—	Reported, not confirmed		
		1889	—	50.00	75.00	125.00
		1890/89	—	150.00	225.00	300.00
		1890	—	150.00	225.00	300.00
		1891	—	Reported, not confirmed		

c/s: Off center on Chile Peso, KM#142.1.

KM#	Date	Year	Mintage	Fine	VF	XF
217	1894	1880	—	—	—	—

.903 SILVER

c/s: On Guatemala Peso, KM#178.

KM#	Date	Year	Mintage	Fine	VF	XF
218	1894	1859	—	Reported, not confirmed		

c/s: On Guatemala Peso, KM#190.1.

KM#	Date	Year	Mintage	Fine	VF	XF
219	1894	1869	—	—	Rare	—

c/s: On Guatemala Peso, KM#208.

KM#	Date	Year	Mintage	Fine	VF	XF
220	1894	1882AE	—	—	Rare	—

c/s: On Guatemala Peso, KM#210.

KM#	Date	Year	Mintage	Fine	VF	XF
221	1894	1894	—	Reported, not confirmed		
		1894 H	—	—	Rare	—

c/s: On Honduras Peso, KM#47.

KM#	Date	Year	Mintage	Fine	VF	XF
222	1894	1882	—	—	Rare	—

c/s: On Honduras Peso, KM#52.

KM#	Date	Year	Mintage	Fine	VF	XF
223	1894	1890	—	850.00	1350.	—
		1891	—	850.00	1350.	—

c/s: On Peru Un Sol, KM#196.

KM#	Date	Year	Mintage	Fine	VF	XF
224	1894	1864 Y.B.	—	15.00	25.00	35.00
		1864 Y.B. Deteano	—	—	Rare	—
		1865 Y.B.	—	50.00	100.00	175.00
		1866 Y.B.	—	20.00	30.00	40.00
		1867 Y.B.	—	20.00	30.00	40.00
		1868 Y.B.	—	20.00	30.00	40.00
		1869 Y.B.	—	20.00	30.00	40.00
		1870 Y.J.	—	20.00	30.00	40.00
		1871 Y.J.	—	20.00	30.00	40.00
		1872 Y.J.	—	20.00	30.00	40.00
		1873 Y.J.	—	50.00	100.00	175.00
		1873 L.D.	—	50.00	100.00	175.00
		1874 Y.J.	—	20.00	30.00	40.00
		1875 Y.J.	—	20.00	30.00	40.00
		1879 Y.J.	—	25.00	45.00	65.00
		1880 Y.J.	—	40.00	60.00	100.00
		1881 B.F.	—	30.00	50.00	75.00
		1882 B.F.	—	40.00	60.00	100.00
		1882 F.N.	—	50.00	100.00	175.00
		1883 F.N.	—	100.00	165.00	250.00
		1884 B.D.	—	40.00	60.00	100.00
		1884 R.D.	—	20.00	30.00	40.00
		1885 R.D.	—	20.00	30.00	40.00
		1885 T.D.	—	20.00	30.00	40.00
		1886 R.D.	—	100.00	165.00	250.00
		1886 T.F.	—	25.00	45.00	65.00

KM#	Date	Year	Mintage	Fine	VF	XF
224		1887 T.F.	—	15.00	22.50	30.00
		1888 T.F.	—	15.00	22.50	30.00
		1889 T.F.	—	15.00	22.50	30.00
		1890/80 T.F.	—	30.00	50.00	75.00
		1890 T.F.	—	15.00	22.50	30.00
		1891 T.F.	—	15.00	22.50	30.00
		1892 T.F.	—	15.00	22.50	30.00
		1893 T.F.	—	15.00	22.50	30.00
		1393 T.F. (error)	—	450.00	600.00	900.00
		1894 T.F.	—	20.00	30.00	40.00

c/s: On Peru 5 Pesetas, KM#201.1.

KM#	Date	Year	Mintage	Fine	VF	XF
225	1894	1880 B.F. w/B below wreath w/o dot	—	80.00	110.00	160.00
		1880 B.F. w/B. below wreath	—	80.00	110.00	160.00

c/s: On Peru 5 Pesetas, KM#201.3.

KM#	Date	Year	Mintage	Fine	VF	XF
226	1894	1881 B	—	Reported, not confirmed		
		1882 LM	—	300.00	500.00	800.00

c/s: On Salvador Peso, KM#115.1.

KM#	Date	Year	Mintage	Fine	VF	XF
227	1894	1892	—	1000.	1400.	2000.
		1893	—	1000.	1400.	2000.
		1894	—	Reported, not confirmed		

PATTERNS (Pn)

(Including off metal strikes)

KM#	Date	Mintage	Identification	Mkt.Val.
Pn1	1854AE	—	8 Reales, Silver, Columbus	18,500.
Pn2	1854AE	—	8 Reales, Copper	6,500.
PnA3	1860R	—	1 Peso, Copper, 1.229 g. Obv: 1/2 Real KM143, Rev: 1 Peso KM179	—

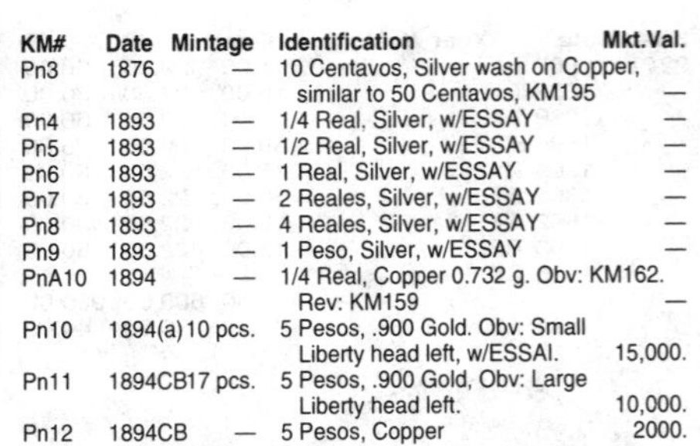

KM#	Date	Mintage	Identification	Mkt.Val.
Pn3	1876	—	10 Centavos, Silver wash on Copper, similar to 50 Centavos, KM195	—
Pn4	1893	—	1/4 Real, Silver, w/ESSAY	—
Pn5	1893	—	1/2 Real, Silver, w/ESSAY	—
Pn6	1893	—	1 Real, Silver, w/ESSAY	—
Pn7	1893	—	2 Reales, Silver, w/ESSAY	—
Pn8	1893	—	4 Reales, Silver, w/ESSAY	—
Pn9	1893	—	1 Peso, Silver, w/ESSAY	—
PnA10	1894	—	1/4 Real, Copper 0.732 g. Obv: KM162. Rev: KM159	—
Pn10	1894(a)	10 pcs.	5 Pesos, .900 Gold. Obv: Small Liberty head left, w/ESSAI.	15,000.
Pn11	1894CB	17 pcs.	5 Pesos, .900 Gold, Obv: Large Liberty head left.	10,000.
Pn12	1894CB	—	5 Pesos, Copper	2000.

KM#	Date	Mintage	Identification	Mkt.Val.
Pn13	1894(a)	10 pcs.	10 Pesos, .900 Gold. Obv: Small Liberty head left, w/ESSAI	20,000.

KM#	Date	Mintage	Identification	Mkt.Val.
Pn14	1894CB	17 pcs.	10 Pesos, .900 Gold. Rev: Large Liberty head left	15,000.

KM#	Date	Mintage	Identification	Mkt.Val.
Pn15	1895CB	*10 pcs.	4 Reales, .900 Silver	2250.

KM#	Date	Mintage	Identification	Mkt.Val.
Pn16	1895H	*10 pcs.	1 Peso, .900 Silver	5000.

PROOF SETS (PS)

KM#	Date	Mintage	Identification	Issue Price	Mkt. Val.
PS1	1894H(6)	—	KM162,165-167,168.1,210	—	1800.
PS2	1895/1896(6)	—	KM162,165-167,210, 4 Reales 1895 Pn9	—	Rare

GUERNSEY

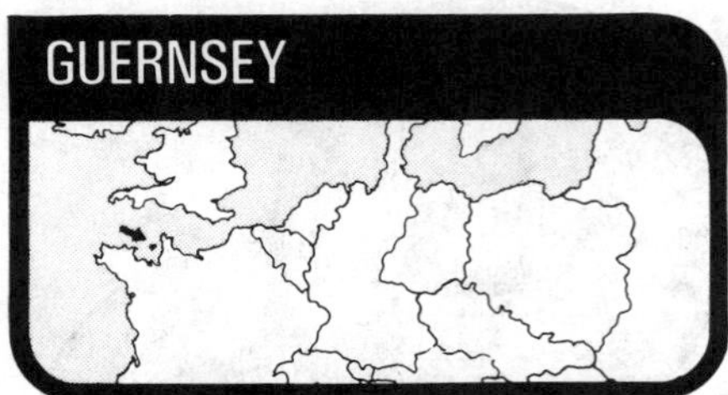

The Bailiwick of Guernsey, a British crown dependency located in the English Channel 30 miles (48 km.) west of Normandy, France, has an area of 30 sq. mi. (194 sq. km.) (including the isles of Alderney, Jethou, Herm, Brechou, and Sark), and a population of 54,000. Capital: St. Peter Port. Agriculture and cattle breeding are the main occupations.

Militant monks from the duchy of Normandy established the first permanent settlements on Guernsey prior to the Norman invasion of England, but the prevalence of prehistoric monuments suggests an earlier occupancy. The island, the only part of the duchy of Normandy belonging to the British crown, has been a possession of Britain since the Norman Conquest of 1066. During the Anglo-French wars, the harbors of Guernsey were employed in the building and outfitting of ships for the English privateers preying on French shipping. Guernsey is administered by its own laws

RULERS

British

MINT MARKS

H - Heaton, Birmingham

MONETARY SYSTEM

8 Doubles = 1 Penny
12 Pence = 1 Shilling
5 Shillings = 1 Crown
20 Shillings = 1 Pound

1 Stem   3 Stems

DOUBLE

KM#	Date	Mintage	Fine	VF	XF	Unc
	COPPER					
1	1830	1.649	1.00	3.00	8.50	25.00
	.1830	Inc. Ab.	5.00	15.00	30.00	45.00
	BRONZED COPPER					
1a	1830	—	—	—	Proof	250.00
	BRONZE					
10	1868/30	.064	1.50	4.50	12.50	30.00
	1868	Inc. Ab.	2.00	6.00	18.00	37.50
	1885H	.056	.50	1.50	4.50	12.50
	1885H	—	—	—	Proof	175.00
	1889H	.112	.30	.85	3.00	7.50
	1889H	—	—	—	Proof	200.00
	1893H	.056	.50	1.50	4.50	12.50
	1899H	.056	.25	.75	3.00	8.50

NOTE: Later dates (1902-1911) exist for this type.

KM#	Date	Mintage	Fine	VF	XF	Unc
	BRONZED COPPER					
10a	1885H	—	—	—	Proof	275.00

2 DOUBLES

KM#	Date	Mintage	Fine	VF	XF	Unc
	COPPER Rev: Leaves w/1 stem.					
4	1858	.056	6.00	18.00	55.00	125.00
	BRONZE Obv: Leaves w/1 stem.					
8	1868	.035	7.50	13.50	35.00	70.00
	1899H	.036	.85	3.00	9.00	18.50

NOTE: Later dates (1902-1911) exist for this type.

KM#	Date	Mintage	Fine	VF	XF	Unc
	BRONZED COPPER					
8a	1885H	—	—	—	Proof	275.00

KM#	Date	Mintage	Fine	VF	XF	Unc
	BRONZE Obv: Leaves w/3 stems.					
9	1868	Inc. KM8	7.50	13.50	35.00	70.00
	1874	.045	4.50	9.00	25.00	50.00
	1885H	.071	1.25	2.75	6.00	12.00
	1885H	—	—	—	Proof	175.00
	1889H	.036	.85	3.00	8.00	15.00
	1889H	—	—	—	Proof	200.00

4 DOUBLES

KM#	Date	Mintage	Fine	VF	XF	Unc
	COPPER					
2	1830	.655	2.25	7.50	30.00	60.00
	1830	—	—	—	Proof	275.00
	1858	.114	3.00	15.00	30.00	60.00

NOTE: A rare mule restrike exists of the St. Helena obv. 1/2 Penny 1821 and rev. of Guernsey 4 Doubles dated 1830. Market valuation $600.00 (VF).

KM#	Date	Mintage	Fine	VF	XF	Unc
	BRONZED COPPER					
2a	1830	—	—	—	Proof	350.00
	BRONZE Obv: Leaves w/3 stems.					
5	1864/54	.213	.85	1.75	9.00	18.50
	1868	.058	2.25	4.00	12.50	25.00
	1874	.069	1.50	3.00	11.50	22.50
	1885H	.070	1.25	2.25	7.50	20.00
	1885H	—	—	—	Proof	175.00
	1889H	.104	.75	1.25	6.00	15.00
	1889H	—	—	—	Proof	200.00
	1893H	.052	1.50	3.00	7.50	20.00

NOTE: Later dates (1902-1911) exist for this type.
NOTE: Varieties exist.

KM#	Date	Mintage	Fine	VF	XF	Unc
	BRONZED COPPER					
5a	1885H	—	—	—	Proof	275.00
	BRONZE Obv: Leaves w/1 stem.					
6	1864	Inc. KM5	1.25	2.25	9.00	18.50

8 DOUBLES

KM#	Date	Mintage	Fine	VF	XF	Unc
	COPPER					
3	1834	.222	4.00	10.00	25.00	75.00
	1834	—	—	—	Proof	350.00
	1858	.111	5.00	12.50	25.00	65.00
	1858	—	—	—	Proof	375.00
	BRONZED COPPER					
3a	1834	—	—	—	Proof	550.00
	BRONZE					
7	1864	.280	1.25	3.00	9.00	27.50
	1864	—	—	—	Proof	175.00
	1868	.060	4.00	9.00	27.50	55.00
	1874	.070	2.25	4.50	9.00	20.00
	1885H	.070	1.50	3.00	9.00	20.00
	1885H	—	—	—	Proof	200.00
	1889H	.222	.75	2.25	6.00	12.50
	1889H	—	—	—	Proof	175.00

KM#	Date	Mintage	Fine	VF	XF	Unc
7	1893H	.118	1.50	3.00	6.00	15.00
	1893H large date and denomination					
		Inc. Ab.	1.50	3.00	6.00	15.00

NOTE: Later dates (1902-1911) exist for this type.

BRONZED COPPER

KM#	Date	Mintage	Fine	VF	XF	Unc
7a	1885H	—	—	—	Proof	325.00

TOKEN ISSUES (Tn)

Bishop de Jersey & Co./ Bank of Guernsey

5 SHILLINGS

.892 SILVER

KM#	Date	Mintage	VG	Fine	VF	XF
Tn1	1809	*7 known	—	—	Rare	—

NOTE: Spink R.J. Ford sale 10-90 good XF realized $19,380.

NOTE: The above issue was struck over Spanish or Spanish Colonial 8 Reales. They were forbidden by the Guernsey legislation to circulate in 1809.

PROOF SETS (PS)

KM#	Date	Mintage	Identification	Issue Price	Mkt. Val.
PS1	1885H(4)	—	KM5,7,8,10	—	725.00
PS2	1885H(4)	—	KM5a,7a,8a,10a	—	1150.

GUYANA (British Guiana)

The Cooperative Republic of Guyana, an independent member of the British Commonwealth situated on the northeast coast of South America, has an area of 83,000 sq. mi. (214,970 sq. km.) and a population of 729,000. Capital: Georgetown. The economy is basically agrarian. Sugar, rice and bauxite are exported.

The original area of Essequibo and Demerary, which included present-day Suriname, French Guiana, and parts of Brazil and Venezuela was sighted by Columbus in 1498. The first European settlement was made late in the 16th century by the Dutch, however, the region was claimed for the British by Sir Walter Raleigh during the reign of Elizabeth I. For the next 150 years, possession alternated between the Dutch and the British, with a short interval of French control. The British exercised de facto control after 1796, although the area, which included the Dutch colonies of Essequibo, Demerary and Berbice, was not ceded to them by the Dutch until 1814. From 1803 to 1831, Essequibo and Demerary were administered separately from Berbice. The three colonies were united in the British Crown Colony of British Guiana in 1831. British Guiana won internal self-government in 1952 and full independence, under the traditional name of Guyana, on May 26, 1966. Guyana became a republic on Feb. 23, 1970. It is a member of the Commonwealth of Nations. The president is the Chief of State. The prime minister is the Head of Government.

RULERS

British, until 1966

MONETARY SYSTEM

(Until 1839)

20 Stiver = 1 Guilder (Gulden)
3 Guilders = 12 Bits = 5 Shillings
= 1 Dollar

(Commencing 1839)

3-1/8 Guilders = 50 Pence

ESSEQUIBO & DEMERARY

NECESSITY COINAGE

1808 EMERGENCY ISSUES

During the time of the countermarked coins of the Bank of England for George III, Spanish or Spanish Colonial 8 Reales were punched to form two new denominations. The plug or center was countermarked 3 Bits while the holed 8 Reales was countermarked 3 Guilders.

3 BITS

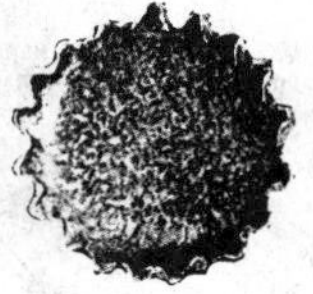

.903 SILVER
c/m: E & D 3 Bt on serrated center plug from 8 Reales.

KM#	Date	Year	VG	Fine	VF	XF
1	ND(1808)	—	950.00	1600.	2650.	3350.

3 GUILDERS

.903 SILVER
c/m: E & D 3 G D in dotted oval on Mexico City. 8 Reales, KM#109.

KM#	Date	Year	VG	Fine	VF	XF
2	ND(1808)	1791	1550.	2550.	4250.	5000.
		1796	1550.	2550.	4250.	5000.
		1803	1550.	2550.	4250.	5000.

COLONIAL COINAGE

1/2 STIVER

COPPER

KM#	Date	Mintage	Fine	VF	XF	Unc
9	1813	.215	5.00	12.50	45.00	100.00
	1813	—	—	—	Proof	350.00

COPPER-GILT

KM#	Date	Mintage	Fine	VF	XF	Unc
9a	1813	—	—	—	Proof	650.00

STIVER

COPPER

KM#	Date	Mintage	Fine	VF	XF	Unc
10	1813	.215	6.50	15.00	50.00	100.00
	1813	—	—	—	Proof	400.00

COPPER-GILT

KM#	Date	Mintage	Fine	VF	XF	Unc
10a	1813	—	—	—	Proof	600.00

1/8 GUILDER

0.9700 g, .816 SILVER, .0255 oz ASW

KM#	Date	Mintage	Fine	VF	XF	Unc
16	1832	.098	6.00	12.00	35.00	75.00
	1832	—	—	—	Proof	250.00
	1835/1	.071	10.00	19.00	37.50	95.00
	1835/3/2	I.A.	15.00	30.00	45.00	100.00
	1835/3	I.A.	10.00	19.00	37.50	95.00
	1835	Inc. Ab.	7.50	17.00	30.00	70.00
	1835 plain edge	—	—		Proof	300.00
	1835 reeded edge	—	—		Proof	400.00

1/4 GUILDER

1.9400 g, .816 SILVER, .0510 oz ASW
Similar to 2 Guilders, KM#7.

KM#	Date	Mintage	Fine	VF	XF	Unc
4	1809	.124	12.50	25.00	65.00	150.00

NOTE: Flan size varies.

KM#	Date	Mintage	Fine	VF	XF	Unc
11	1816	.043	12.50	25.00	65.00	150.00
	1816	—	—	—	Proof	350.00

KM#	Date	Mintage	Fine	VF	XF	Unc
17	1832	.039	12.50	22.50	50.00	150.00
	1833	.097	9.00	17.50	40.00	125.00
	1833	—	—	—	Proof	575.00
	1835/3	.073	9.00	17.50	40.00	125.00
	1835	Inc. Ab.	7.00	12.00	27.50	100.00
	1835 plain edge		—	—	Proof	450.00
	1835 reeded edge		—	—	Proof	500.00

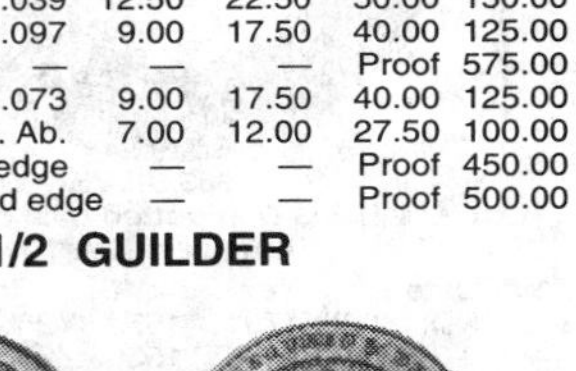

1/2 GUILDER

3.8800 g, .816 SILVER, .1020 oz ASW

KM#	Date	Mintage	Fine	VF	XF	Unc
5	1809	.064	15.00	37.50	110.00	225.00

KM#	Date	Mintage	Fine	VF	XF	Unc
12	1816	.034	13.50	27.50	100.00	200.00
	1816	—	—	—	Proof	350.00

KM#	Date	Mintage	Fine	VF	XF	Unc
18	1832	.087	12.50	25.00	95.00	200.00
	1832	—	—	—	Proof	350.00
	1835/5	.036	13.50	27.50	100.00	210.00
	1835	Inc. Ab.	19.00	27.50	70.00	145.00
	1835 plain edge		—	—	Proof	400.00
	1835 reeded edge		—	—	Proof	500.00

GUILDER

7.7700 g, .816 SILVER, .2040 oz ASW

KM#	Date	Mintage	Fine	VF	XF	Unc
6	1809	.032	18.00	35.00	115.00	335.00

KM#	Date	Mintage	Fine	VF	XF	Unc
13	1816	.034	15.00	30.00	100.00	300.00
	1816	—	—	—	Proof	400.00

KM#	Date	Mintage	Fine	VF	XF	Unc
19	1832	.047	10.00	25.00	60.00	200.00
	1832	—	—	—	Proof	425.00
	1835	.022	15.00	30.00	75.00	250.00
	1835 plain edge		—	—	Proof	550.00
	1835 reeded edge		—	—	Proof	600.00

NOTE: 1832 dated coins exist w/flat and round top 3.

2 GUILDERS

15.5500 g, .816 SILVER, .4079 oz ASW

KM#	Date	Mintage	Fine	VF	XF	Unc
7	1809	.016	75.00	175.00	400.00	2250.

KM#	Date	Mintage	Fine	VF	XF	Unc
14	1816	.015	50.00	125.00	250.00	700.00
	1816	—	—	—	Proof	Rare

KM#	Date	Mintage	Fine	VF	XF	Unc
20	1832	.014	60.00	150.00	400.00	1500.
	1832	—	—	—	Proof	Rare

3 GUILDERS

23.3200 g, .816 SILVER, .6118 oz ASW

KM#	Date	Mintage	Fine	VF	XF	Unc
8	1809	.021	175.00	350.00	700.00	2750.

KM#	Date	Mintage	Fine	VF	XF	Unc
15	1816	.010	150.00	300.00	600.00	1750.
	1816	—	—	—	Proof	Rare

Rev: Similar to 2 Guilders, KM#20.

KM#	Date	Mintage	Fine	VF	XF	Unc
21	1832	7,156	250.00	550.00	1500.	4500.
	1832	—	—	—	Proof	Rare

BRITISH GUIANA

In October, 1835, the minting of currency two pence pieces was approved by the Treasury. These coins, identical to those in the Maundy sets, were circulated in British Guiana with dates of 1838, 1843 and 1848. Groats of the Victorian era and the seated Britannia type were also circulated in this colony. See homeland types in Great Britain.

1/8 GUILDER

0.9700 g, .816 SILVER, .0255 oz ASW

KM#	Date	Mintage	Fine	VF	XF	Unc
22	1836	.180	10.00	20.00	40.00	90.00
	1836	—	—	—	Proof	125.00

1/4 GUILDER

1.9400 g, .816 SILVER, .0509 oz ASW

KM#	Date	Mintage	Fine	VF	XF	Unc
23	1836	.216	15.00	30.00	50.00	125.00
	1836	—	—	—	Proof	225.00

1/2 GUILDER

3.8800 g, .816 SILVER, .1018 oz ASW

KM#	Date	Mintage	Fine	VF	XF	Unc
24	1836	.118	15.00	35.00	70.00	150.00
	1836	—	—	—	Proof	300.00

GUILDER

7.7700 g, .816 SILVER, .2039 oz ASW

KM#	Date	Mintage	Fine	VF	XF	Unc
25	1836	.057	16.50	40.00	95.00	200.00
	1836 plain edge		—	—	Proof	400.00
	1836 reeded edge		—	—	Proof	1250.

BRITISH GUIANA AND WEST INDIES

From 1836 through 1888, regular issue 4 Pence (Groats) as well as general issue strikes of the Maundy type 2 Pence (1838, 1843 & 1848) of Great Britain were circulated in British Guiana and the West Indies. These are listed under Great Britain.

MONETARY SYSTEM

12 Pence = 1 Shilling
4 Shillings 2 Pence = 1 Dollar

4 PENCE

1.8851 g, .925 SILVER, .0560 oz ASW

KM#	Date	Mintage	Fine	VF	XF	Unc
26	1891	.336	1.75	4.50	8.00	35.00
	1894	.120	2.75	6.50	12.50	50.00
	1900	.045	3.25	10.00	20.00	75.00

NOTE: Later date (1901) exists for this type.

PRIVATE TOKEN ISSUES (Tn)

STIVER

COPPER, 33mm
Obv. leg: TRADE & NAVIGATION. Female seated on bale. Rev. leg: PURE COPPER. . . around denomination

KM#	Date	Mintage	Fine	VF	XF	Unc
Tn1	1838	—	4.50	9.00	20.00	45.00

Obv: Branch close to ampersand in legend. Rev: Similar to Tn1.

KM#	Date	Mintage	Fine	VF	XF	Unc
Tn2	1838	—	6.00	12.00	25.00	50.00

Obv: Similar to Tn1. Rev: PURE COPPER. . . around laureate bust.

KM#	Date	Mintage	Fine	VF	XF	Unc
Tn3	1838	—	4.50	9.00	18.00	35.00

HAITI

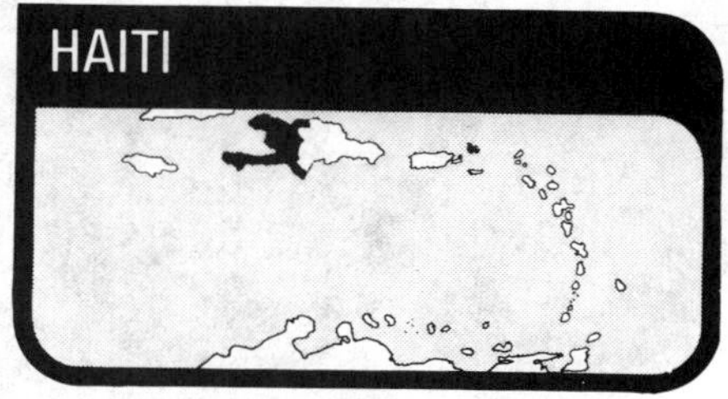

The Republic of Haiti, which occupies the western one-third of the island of Hispaniola in the Caribbean Sea between Puerto Rico and Cuba, has an area of 10,714 sq. mi.(27,750 sq. km.) and a population of 6.5 million. Capital: Port-au-Prince. The economy is based on agriculture; but light manufacturing and tourism are increasingly important. Coffee, bauxite, sugar, essential oils and handicrafts are exported.

Columbus discovered Hispaniola in 1492. Spain colonized the island, making Santo Domingo the base for exploration of the Western Hemisphere. The area that is now Haiti was ceded to France by Spain in 1697. Slaves brought from Africa to work the coffee and sugar cane plantations made it one of the richest colonies of the French Empire. A slave revolt in the 1790's led to the establishment of the Republic of Haiti in 1804, making it the oldest Black republic in the world and the second oldest republic (after the United States) in the Western Hemisphere.

The French language is used on Haitian coins although it is spoken by only about 10" of the populace. A form of Creole is the language of the Haitians.

Two dating systems are used on Haiti's 19th century coins. One is Christian, the other Revolutionary - beginning in 1803 when the French were permanently ousted by a native revolt. Thus, a date of AN30, (i.e., year 30) is equivalent to 1833 A.D. Some coins carry both date forms. In the listings which follow coins dated only in the Revolutionary system are listed by AN years in the date column.

RULERS

French, until 1804
Jacques I (Dessalines), 1804-1806
Henri Christophe (Henri I), 1811-1821
Faustin I (Soulouque), 1849-1858

MINT MARKS

A - Paris
(a) - Paris, privy marks only
HEATON - Birmingham
(w) = Waterbury (Connecticut, USA) (Scoville Mfg. Co.)

MONETARY SYSTEM

12 Deniers = 1 Sol
20 Sols = 1 Livre
100 Centimes = 1 Gourde

HISPANIOLA

TOWN OF LE CAP

(Old Cap Francois)

Port city on the northern coast of Haiti. Under a French edict of July 13, 1781 various Spanish-American and other circulating silver coins were to be counterstamped with a crowned anchor and C for the island. These were made at the capitol and the pieces given values of 1 Escalin and 1/2 Escalin. Copper coins were counterstamped L.C. and S.D.

MONETARY SYSTEM

15 Sols = 1 Escalin (1 Real)

COUNTERMARKED COINAGE

SOL

BRONZE
c/m: L.C. in rectangle on English 1/2 Penny token of 1792.

KM#	Date	Mintage	Good	VG	Fine	VF
5	ND(1802-09)	—	100.00	175.00	275.00	500.00

1/2 ESCALIN

SILVER, 0.93 g
c/m: Crowned C and anchor on Potosi 1/2 Real size cob.

KM#	Date	Mintage	Good	VG	Fine	VF
7.1	ND(1780-1802)		150.00	275.00	400.00	650.00

SILVER, 1.07 g
c/m: Crowned C and anchor on center cut of Potosi, 1 Real size cob.

KM#	Date	Mintage	Good	VG	Fine	VF
7.2	ND(1780-1802)		200.00	375.00	550.00	850.00

SILVER
Ring substituted for crown on anchor.

KM#	Date	Mintage	Good	VG	Fine	VF
6	ND	—	150.00	275.00	400.00	650.00

ESCALIN

SILVER, 2.36 g
c/m: Crowned C and anchor on center cut of Lima or Potosi, 2 Real size cob.

KM#	Date	Mintage	Good	VG	Fine	VF
8.1	ND(1780-1802)		175.00	300.00	450.00	700.00

SILVER, 2.80 g
c/m: Crowned C and anchor on Angola 2 Macutas.

KM#	Date	Mintage	Good	VG	Fine	VF
8.2	ND(1780-1802)		185.00	325.00	500.00	800.00

SILVER
Ring substituted for crown on anchor

KM#	Date	Mintage	Good	VG	Fine	VF
9	ND	—	175.00	300.00	450.00	700.00

FRENCH OCCUPATION COINAGE

SOL

BRONZE
c/m: S:D. in rectangle on French Sol, C#73.

KM#	Date	Mintage	Good	VG	Fine	VF
13	ND(1802-09)	—	90.00	180.00	300.00	525.00

c/m: ND over S:D. on French copper coin.

KM#	Date	Mintage	Good	VG	Fine	VF
14	ND(1802-09)	—	80.00	160.00	275.00	475.00

c/m: Crowned N on English 1/2 Penny, KM#392.

KM#	Date	Mintage	Good	VG	Fine	VF
15	ND(1802-09)	—	90.00	180.00	300.00	525.00

REPUBLICAN COINAGE

RULERS

Toussaint L'Ouverture, 1798-1802

MONETARY SYSTEM

15 Sols (Sous) = 1 Escalin (Real)

DEMY (1/2) ESCALIN

SILVER

KM#	Date	Mintage	VG	Fine	VF	XF
21	ND(1802)	—	125.00	250.00	500.00	750.00

UN (1) ESCALIN

SILVER

KM#	Date	Mintage	VG	Fine	VF	XF
22	ND(1802)	—	100.00	200.00	400.00	600.00

DEUX (2) ESCALIN

SILVER

KM#	Date	Mintage	VG	Fine	VF	XF
23	ND(1802)	—	200.00	300.00	550.00	800.00

PATTERNS (Pn)

(Including off metal strikes)

KM#	Date	Mintage	Identification	Mkt.Val.
Pn1	ND(1802)	—	1 Escalin, Copper plated white metal	Rare
Pn2	ND(1802)	—	2 Escalin, Copper plated white metal	Rare

HAITI

7 SOLS 6 DENIERS

SILVER
Similar to 15 Sols, KM#6.

KM#	Date	Mintage	Good	VG	Fine	VF
3	1807	—	45.00	100.00	225.00	500.00
	1808	—	35.00	60.00	90.00	160.00
	1809	—	27.50	50.00	75.00	140.00

15 SOLS

SILVER

KM#	Date	Mintage	Good	VG	Fine	VF
6	1807	—	20.00	35.00	65.00	125.00
	1808	—	22.00	40.00	85.00	150.00
	1809	—	22.00	40.00	85.00	150.00

30 SOLS

SILVER

KM#	Date	Mintage	Good	VG	Fine	VF
8	1807	2 known	—	—	—	—

NOTE: Christie's Norweb sale 5-85 VF realized $7150. Bank Leu Bostonian sale 10-90 VF realized $4110.

DECIMAL COINAGE

100 Centimes = 1 Gourde

UNE (1) CENTIME

COPPER

KM#	Date	Year	VG	Fine	VF	XF
21	1828	AN 25	6.50	17.50	32.50	50.00
	1829	AN 26	3.75	8.00	17.50	37.50
	1830	AN 27	3.00	7.50	11.50	30.00
	1830	AN 28	16.50	30.00	75.00	150.00
	1830	AN 29	70.00	150.00	250.00	425.00
	1831	AN 28	2.00	4.00	9.00	27.50
	1832	AN 28	20.00	32.50	75.00	150.00
	1832	AN 29	2.00	3.75	9.00	27.50
	1834	AN 31	2.00	4.00	9.00	27.50
	1840	AN 37	2.00	4.00	8.00	25.00
	1841	AN 38	2.50	6.00	10.00	30.00
	1842	AN 39	2.00	3.75	8.00	25.00

NOTE: Die varieties exist and both diework and striking become progressively cruder throughout this series.

22mm

KM#	Date	Year	VG	Fine	VF	XF
24	1846	AN 43	.75	2.25	4.00	10.00

Reduced size, 21mm
Obv: Leaves point inward.
Rev: W/large star after leg.

KM#	Date	Year	VG	Fine	VF	XF
25.1	1846	AN 43	.65	2.00	3.00	7.50

Obv: Leaves point in and out.
Rev: W/o star after leg.

KM#	Date	Year	VG	Fine	VF	XF
25.2	1846	.AN 43	1.00	2.50	4.00	10.00

NOTE: Varieties exist in style of wreath and legend.

Similar to KM#25.2 but stop after legend.

KM#	Date	Year	VG	Fine	VF	XF
30	1849	AN 46	75.00	160.00	275.00	350.00

Similar to KM#25.2 but leg: EMPIRE D'HAITI.

KM#	Date	Year	VG	Fine	VF	XF
33	1850	AN 47	40.00	95.00	180.00	300.00

KM#	Date	Year	VG	Fine	VF	XF
34	1850	—	2.50	5.00	8.00	20.00

BRONZE

KM#	Date	Mintage	Fine	VF	XF	Unc
42	1881	.830	2.00	3.50	5.50	20.00
	1881	—	—	—	Proof	200.00

KM#	Date	Mintage	Fine	VF	XF	Unc
48	1886A	2.500	1.75	3.00	5.00	15.00
	1894A	2.070	1.75	3.00	5.00	20.00
	1895A	5.420	1.75	3.00	5.00	30.00

DEUX (2) CENTIMES

COPPER

KM#	Date	Year	VG	Fine	VF	XF
22	1828	AN 25	12.00	30.00	75.00	150.00
	1828	AN 26	10.00	28.00	65.00	135.00
22	1829	AN 26	2.75	6.00	10.00	28.00
	1830	AN 26	12.50	30.00	65.00	120.00
	1830	AN 27	10.00	28.00	10.00	25.00
	1831	AN 28	2.25	5.00	8.50	20.00
	1840	AN 37	2.25	5.00	8.50	20.00
	1840 backwards 4	AN 37	2.75	6.00	10.00	25.00
	1841	AN 38	2.25	5.00	8.50	20.00
	1841 backwards 4	AN 38	2.75	6.00	10.00	25.00
	1842	AN 39	2.25	5.00	8.50	20.00

NOTE: Die varieties exist and became progressively cruder throughout this series.

26mm

KM#	Date	Year	VG	Fine	VF	XF
26	1846	AN 43	1.25	2.50	4.00	9.00
	1846	AN 43	—	—	Proof	300.00
	1846	AN 43/2	2.00	3.50	5.00	11.00

Reduced size, 24mm
Obv: Leaves point inward.
Rev: W/large star after legend.

KM#	Date	Year	VG	Fine	VF	XF
27.1	1846	AN 43	1.75	3.00	4.50	9.50

Obv: Leaves point in and out.

KM#	Date	Year	VG	Fine	VF	XF
27.2 (27.1)	1846	AN 43	2.25	3.75	4.50	10.00

NOTE: Varieties exist w/o accents on E's, size of star varies.

KM#	Date	Year	VG	Fine	VF	XF
31	1849	AN 46	27.50	42.50	80.00	150.00

Obv. leg: EMPIRE D'HAITI.

KM#	Date	Year	VG	Fine	VF	XF
35	1850	AN 47	40.00	75.00	125.00	250.00

KM#	Date	Mintage	VG	Fine	VF	XF
36	1850	—	1.75	4.75	10.00	20.00

BRONZE

KM#	Date	Mintage	Fine	VF	XF	Unc
43	1881	.830	2.75	4.50	8.00	20.00
	1881	—	—	—	Proof	150.00

KM#	Date	Mintage	Fine	VF	XF	Unc
49	1886A	1.250	1.50	2.50	5.00	35.00
	1894A	3.750	1.50	2.50	5.00	50.00

CINQ (5) CENTIMES

BRONZE

KM#	Date	Mintage	Fine	VF	XF	Unc
39	1863HEATON	1.000	2.00	4.50	9.50	20.00
	1863HEATON	—	—	—	Proof	75.00

COPPER-NICKEL

KM#	Date	Mintage	Fine	VF	XF	Unc
50	1889	.120	15.00	32.50	62.50	115.00

6 CENTIMES

.835 SILVER
Obv: Arms/snake type.

KM#	Date	Year	VG	Fine	VF	XF
10	1813	AN 10	75.00	125.00	200.00	400.00

Rev: Boyer bust.

KM#	Date	Year	VG	Fine	VF	XF
17	1818	AN 15	8.50	18.50	30.00	60.00

COPPER

KM#	Date	Year	VG	Fine	VF	XF
28	1846	AN 43	3.00	6.50	10.00	20.00

KM#	Date	Year	VG	Fine	VF	XF
32	1849	AN 46	20.00	37.50	55.00	100.00

KM#	Date	Year	VG	Fine	VF	XF
37	1850	AN 47	100.00	215.00	375.00	600.00

6-1/4 CENTIMES

COPPER

KM#	Date	Year	VG	Fine	VF	XF
29	1846	AN 43	3.75	8.50	15.00	25.00

KM#	Date	Mintage	VG	Fine	VF	XF
38	1850	—	2.75	5.00	7.50	20.00

DIX (10) CENTIMES

BRONZE
Mint mark: HEATON

KM#	Date	Mintage	Fine	VF	XF	Unc
40	1863	1.000	2.25	4.50	7.50	22.50
	1863	—	—	—	Proof	80.00

2.5000 g, .835 SILVER, .0671 oz ASW

KM#	Date	Mintage	Fine	VF	XF	Unc
44	1881(a)	1.500	1.50	3.00	8.00	25.00
	1881(a)	—	—	—	Proof	450.00
	1882(a)	1.800	1.25	2.25	8.00	25.00
	1882(a)	—	—	—	Proof	400.00
	1886(a)	1.500	2.00	4.00	15.00	40.00
	1886(a)	—	—	—	Proof	550.00
	1887(a)	1.050	1.25	2.25	10.00	30.00
	1887(a)	—	—	—	Proof	350.00
	1890(a)	1.000	1.75	3.50	15.00	40.00
	1890(a)	—	—	—	Proof	550.00
	1894(a)	3.720	1.25	2.25	8.00	25.00
	1894(a)	—	—	—	Proof	400.00

20 CENTIMES

SILVER
Obv: Arms type.

KM#	Date	Year	Good	VG	Fine	VF
11	(1813)	AN 10	18.00	40.00	90.00	160.00
	(1814)	AN XI	3.75	8.00	15.00	30.00
	(1815)	AN 12	6.50	15.00	30.00	60.00
	(1815)	AN 12 (error) 2 in AN 12 upside down	7.50	18.00	35.00	70.00

Rev: Petion type, large head.

KM#	Date	Year	Good	VG	Fine	VF
13	(1817)	AN 14	2.50	6.00	13.50	28.50

NOTE: Varieties exist.

Rev: Petion type, small head.

KM#	Date	Year	Good	VG	Fine	VF
14	(1817)	AN 14	2.50	6.00	13.50	28.50

Rev: Boyer type.

KM#	Date	Year	Good	VG	Fine	VF
19	(1827)	AN 24	4.00	9.00	20.00	40.00
	(1828)	AN 25	9.00	18.00	50.00	100.00
	(1829)	AN 26	20.00	45.00	100.00	200.00

VINGT (20) CENTIMES

BRONZE
Mint mark: HEATON

KM#	Date	Mintage	Fine	VF	XF	Unc
41	1863	1.000	2.00	5.00	9.50	35.00
	1863	—	—	—	Proof	80.00

5.0000 g, .835 SILVER, .1342 oz ASW

KM#	Date	Mintage	Fine	VF	XF	Unc
45	1881(a)	1.250	2.50	4.50	8.00	40.00
	1881(a)	—	—	—	Proof	450.00
	1882(a)	1.250	2.50	4.50	8.00	40.00
	1882(a)	—	—	—	Proof	450.00
	1887(a)	.350	3.00	5.00	10.00	50.00
	1887(a)	—	—	—	Proof	600.00
	1890(a)	.070	4.50	9.00	15.00	75.00
	1890(a)	—	—	—	Proof	800.00
	1894(a)	1.850	2.50	4.50	8.00	50.00
	1894(a)	—	—	—	Proof	450.00
	1895(a)	1.270	2.50	4.50	8.00	50.00
	1895(a)	—	—	—	Proof	450.00

25 CENTIMES

SILVER, 22-25mm
Arms type

KM#	Date	Year	Good	VG	Fine	VF
12.1	(1813)	AN 10	7.50	16.50	30.00	70.00

20-21mm

KM#	Date	Year	Good	VG	Fine	VF
12.2	(1814)	AN XI	3.25	6.50	11.00	22.50
	(1815)	AN 12	2.50	4.00	9.00	18.50
	(1816)	AN 13	3.00	5.00	10.00	20.00

NOTE: The above coins exist w/solid and dotted spear shafts, and other minor die-cutting differences.

Rev: Petion type.

KM#	Date	Year	Good	VG	Fine	VF
15.1	(1817)	AN 14	1.75	3.75	7.50	16.50

KM#	Date	Year	Good	VG	Fine	VF
15.2	(1817)	AN 14P	8.00	16.00	32.50	65.00

NOTE: Varieties exist.

Rev: Boyer type, small head.

KM#	Date	Year	Good	VG	Fine	VF
18.1	(1818)	AN 15	6.00	15.00	32.50	65.00
	(1825)	AN 22	— Reported, not confirmed			
	(1827)	AN 24	1.75	3.75	7.00	15.00
	(1828)	AN 25	2.00	4.00	8.00	16.50
	(1829)	AN 26	3.25	7.50	16.50	37.50
	(1831)	AN 28	2.00	4.50	11.50	27.50
	(1834)	AN 31	2.00	4.50	11.50	27.50

NOTE: Varieties exist.

Rev: Large head.

KM#	Date	Year	Good	VG	Fine	VF
18.2	(1827)	AN 24	5.00	10.00	30.00	65.00

COPPER

KM#	Date	Year	Good	VG	Fine	VF
18.1a	(1828)	AN 25	—	—	—	—

50 CENTIMES

SILVER

KM#	Date	Year	Good	VG	Fine	VF
20	(1827)	AN 24	6.50	17.50	37.50	75.00
	(1828)	AN 25	2.25	5.50	12.00	20.00
	(1829)	AN 26	2.25	6.00	14.00	30.00
	(1830)	AN 27	6.50	17.50	35.00	75.00
	(1831)	AN 28	2.25	5.50	11.00	18.00
	(1832)	AN 29	2.25	6.00	12.00	20.00
	(1833)	AN 30	5.50	13.50	30.00	60.00

COPPER

KM#	Date	Year	Good	VG	Fine	VF
20a	(1828)	AN 25	—	—	—	—

12.5000 g, .835 SILVER, .3356 oz ASW

KM#	Date	Mintage	Fine	VF	XF	Unc
47	1882(a)	.440	3.00	6.00	12.00	60.00
	1882(a)	—	—	—	Proof	600.00
	1883(a)	.400	3.00	6.00	12.00	100.00
	1883(a)	—	—	—	Proof	600.00
	1887(a)	.250	3.00	6.00	12.00	60.00
	1887(a)	—	—	—	Proof	800.00
	1890(a)	.100	4.00	8.00	15.00	100.00
	1890(a)	—	—	—	Proof	1000.
	1895(a)	.900	3.00	6.00	12.00	75.00
	1895(a)	—	—	—	Proof	600.00

100 CENTIMES

SILVER

KM#	Date	Year	VG	Fine	VF	XF
23	(1829)	AN 26	5.00	11.00	20.00	45.00
	(1830)	AN 27	6.00	13.50	25.00	50.00
	(1833)	AN 30	8.75	18.50	35.00	75.00

COPPER

KM#	Date	Year	VG	Fine	VF	XF
23a	(1829)	AN 26	—	—	—	—
	(1830)	AN 27	—	—	—	—

GOURDE

25.0000 g, .900 SILVER, .7234 oz ASW

KM#	Date	Mintage	Fine	VF	XF	Unc
46	1881(a)	.200	20.00	35.00	75.00	300.00
	1881(a)	—	—	—	Proof	2000.
	1882(a)	.500	15.00	25.00	62.50	250.00
	1882(a)	—	—	—	Proof	2000.
	1887(a)	.200	15.00	25.00	62.50	250.00
	1887(a)	—	—	—	Proof	2500.
	1895(a)	.100	20.00	35.00	85.00	350.00
	1895(a)	—	—	—	Proof	3250.

INSURRECTION ISSUE

Issued c. 1889 by General Florvil Hippolyte who became President from 1889-1896.

GOURDE

B.P.1.G. = Bon Pour 1 Gourde

BRONZE, uniface
c/m: B.P.1G/GL.H

KM#	Date	Mintage	Fine	VF	XF	Unc
51	ND(1889)	.100	50.00	125.00	350.00	600.00

NOTE: An 1881 dated 2 Centime with this c/m was reported in the Medina collection.

PATTERNS (Pn)

(Including off metal strikes)

KM#	Date	Mintage	Identification	Mkt.Val.
Pn1	1807	—	1 Centime, Copper, diagonal milling	700.00
Pn2	1807	—	1 Centime, Copper, plain edge	700.00
Pn3	1807	—	1 Centime, Copper, piefort, diagonal milling	800.00
Pn4	1807	—	1 Centime, Silver	1500.

KM#	Date	Mintage	Identification	Mkt.Val.
Pn5	1808	—	7-1/2 Sols, Silver	250.00

KM#	Date	Mintage	Identification	Mkt.Val.
Pn6	1808	—	15 Sols, Copper	600.00
Pn7	1808	—	15 Sols, Silver	400.00

KM#	Date	Mintage	Identification	Mkt.Val.
Pn8	1808	—	30 Sols, Silver	750.00

KM#	Date	Mintage	Identification	Mkt.Val.
Pn13	1812	—	1/2 Crown, Copper, ESSAI, diagonal milling	1000.
Pn14	1812	—	1/2 Crown, Silver, ESSAI, diagonal milling	2000.
Pn15	1812	—	1/2 Crown, Silver, ESSAI, plain edge	—
Pn16	1812	—	1 Crown, Silver, diagonal milling	—

KM#	Date	Mintage	Identification	Mkt.Val.
Pn17	1813	—	1 Crown, Silver	3000.

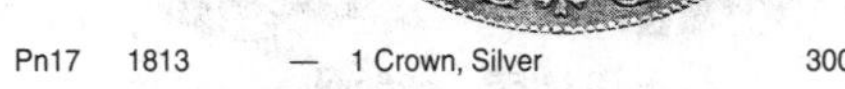

KM#	Date	Mintage	Identification	Mkt.Val.
Pn18	1814	—	1/2 Crown, white metal, diagonal milling	600.00

KM#	Date	Mintage	Identification	Mkt.Val.
Pn19	1814	—	1/2 Crown, Silver, 29mm	1500.
Pn20	1814	—	1/2 Crown, Silver, 33mm	—

KM#	Date	Mintage	Identification	Mkt.Val.
Pn21	1814	—	1 Crown, Silver	3000.
Pn22	1814	—	Base metal (for gold coin) Obv: Crown. Rev: Crowned eagle.	500.00
Pn23	1814	—	Base metal (for gold coin) Obv: Crown. Rev: Crowned eagle.	500.00
Pn24	AN 12(1815)	—	25 Centimes, Copper	—
Pn25	1815	—	1 Crown, Copper, milled edge	3000.
Pn26	1815	—	1 Crown, Silver, milled edge	3000.
Pn27	AN 13(1816)	—	1 Centime, Copper, CENTIME arched	350.00
Pn28	AN 13(1816)	—	1 Centime, Copper, CENTIME straight	350.00
Pn29	AN 13(1816)	—	2 Centimes, Copper	350.00
Pn30	AN 13(1816)	—	2 Centimes, Copper	350.00

KM#	Date	Mintage	Identification	Mkt.Val.
Pn31	1820	—	1 Crown, Aluminum	—
Pn32	1820	—	1 Crown, Copper-Nickel	—
Pn33	1820	—	1 Crown, Copper	Rare
Pn33a	1820	—	1 Crown, Copper, restrike	800.00
Pn34	1820	—	1 Crown, Silver, plain edge	Rare
Pn34a	1820	—	1 Crown, Silver, plain edge, restrike	1000.
Pn35	1820	—	1 Crown, Silver, reeded edge	—

KM#	Date	Mintage	Identification	Mkt.Val.
Pn36	1820	—	1 Crown, White metal, crowned H-LM	—
Pn37	1820	—	1 Crown, Silver, crowned H-LM, restrike	1000.
Pn38	AN 27(1830)	—	100 Centimes, Copper	—

KM#	Date	Mintage	Identification	Mkt.Val.
Pn39	AN 44(1846)	—	100 Centimes, Brass	—
Pn40	AN 44(1846)	—	100 Centimes, Copper	—
Pn41	AN 44(1846)	—	100 Centimes, Silver	—
Pn42	1849	—	100 Centimes, Copper	350.00
Pn43	1849	—	100 Centimes, Silver	350.00
Pn44	1849	—	100 Centimes, Silver	350.00
Pn45	1850	—	6 Centimes, Copper	75.00
Pn46	1850	—	6 Centimes, Copper	75.00
Pn47	1850	—	6 Centimes. Obv: KM#Pn46, Rev: KM#Pn48	100.00
Pn48	1850	—	100 Centimes, Silver	350.00
Pn49	1851	—	100 Centimes, Silvered-Bronze	200.00
Pn50	1852	—	100 Centimes, Silver	—
Pn51	1853	—	10 Centimes, Copper	65.00
Pn52	1853	—	10 Centimes, Silver	—
Pn53	1853	—	1 Gourde, Silver	500.00
Pn54	1854	—	1 Gourde, Silver, ESSAI below bust	1200.
Pn56	1854	—	1 Gourde, Copper	1000.
Pn58	ND(1854)	—	1 Gourde, Copper	—
Pn59	ND(1854)	—	1 Gourde, Bronze	—
Pn60	ND(1854)	—	5 Gourde, Silver, plain edge, small head	1000.
Pn61	ND(1854)	—	5 Gourde, Silver, milled edge, small head	1000.
Pn62	ND(1854)	—	5 Gourde, Bronze, plain edge	1000.
Pn63	ND(1854)	—	5 Gourde, Bronze, milled edge	1000.
Pn64	ND(1854)	—	5 Gourde, Silver, plain edge, large head	1000.
Pn65	ND(1854)	—	5 Gourde, Silver, milled edge, large head	1000.
Pn66	ND(1854)	—	5 Gourde, Silver, thick planchet	1500.
PnA67	1854	—	5 Gourde, Silver	2000.
PnB67	1854	—	5 Gourde, Copper	2000.
Pn67	1854	—	20 Gourdes, Gold	20,000.
Pn68	1854	—	20 Gourdes, Gold, ESSAI	20,000.

KM#	Date	Mintage	Identification	Mkt.Val.
Pn69	1855	—	10 Centimes, Copper	75.00
Pn69a	1855	—	10 Centimes, Brass	—
Pn70	1856	—	1 Piastre, Silver	—
Pn71	1857	—	1 Piastre, Base Silver, milled edge	—
Pn72	1857	—	1 Piastre, Copper, plain edge	—
Pn73	1857	—	1 Piastre, Silver, milled edge	—
Pn74	1858	—	1 Piastre, Silver	—
PnA75	1863 HEATON	—	20 Centimes, Nickel, KM41	—
PnB75	1877 IB CT	—	10 Centimes, Copper-Nickel, Liberty	75.00
PnC75	1877 IB CT	—	10 Centimes, Silver, Liberty	150.00
Pn75	1877 IB CT	—	20 Centimes, Copper, ESSAI	75.00
Pn76	1877 IB CT	—	20 Centimes, Silver, ESSAI	300.00
Pn77	1877 IB	—	20 Centimes, Copper, ESSAI	75.00
Pn78	1877 IB	—	20 Centimes, Silver, ESSAI	300.00
Pn79	1877 IB CT	—	20 Centimes, Nickel	200.00
Pn80	1877 IB CT	—	20 Centimes, Nickel, ESSAI	200.00
Pn81	1877 IB CT	—	20 Centimes, 5.0 g	500.00
Pn82	1877 IB CT	—	20 Centimes, Silver, 5.0 g, ESSAI	500.00
Pn83	1881	—	1 Gourde, Copper	Rare
Pn84	1881	—	1 Gourde, Silver	Rare

KM#	Date	Mintage	Identification	Mkt.Val.
Pn85	1889	—	1 Centime, Copper	50.00

KM#	Date	Mintage	Identification	Mkt.Val.
Pn86	1889	—	2 Centimes, Copper	50.00

PIEFORTS WITH ESSAI (PE)

KM#	Date	Mintage	Identification	Mkt.Val.
PE1	1877 IB CT	—	20 Centimes, Silver, 11.4 g, ESSAI	500.00
PE2	1877 IB CT	—	20 Centimes, Silver, 22.2 g, ESSAI	650.00
PE3	1877 IB	—	20 Centimes, Silver, 11.4 g, ESSAI	500.00

KM#	Date	Mintage	Identification	Mkt.Val.
PE4	1877 IB CT	—	20 Centimes, Silver, 9.8 g, ESSAI	500.00
PE5	1877 IB CT	—	20 Centimes, Silver, 12.2 g, ESSAI	650.00

HONDURAS

The Republic of Honduras, situated in Central America alongside El Salvador, between Nicaragua and Guatemala, has an area of 43,277 sq. mi. (112,090 sq. km.) and a population of 5.3 million. Capital: Tegucigalpa. Agriculture, mining (gold and silver), and logging are the major economic activities, with tourism starting to grow. Bananas, timber and coffee are exported.

The eastern part of Honduras was part of the ancient Mayan Empire; however, the largest Indian community in Honduras was the not too well known Lencas. Honduras was claimed for Spain by Columbus in 1502, during his last voyage to the Americas. The first settlement was made by Cristobal de Olid under orders from Hernando Cortes, then in Mexico. The area, regarded as one of the most promising sources of gold and silver in the New World, was a part of the Captaincy General of Guatemala throughout the colonial period. After declaring its independence from Spain in 1821, Honduras fell under the Mexican empire of Augustin de Iturbide, and then joined the Central American Republic (1823-39). Upon dissolution of that federation, Honduras became an independent republic.

RULERS

Spanish, until 1821
Augustin Iturbide (Emperor of Mexico), 1822-1823

MINT MARKS

A - Paris, 1869-1871
P-Y - Provincia Yoro (?)
T - Tegucigalpa, 1825-1862
T.G. - Yoro
T.L. - Comayagua

NOTE: Extensive die varieties exist for coins struck in Honduras with almost endless date and overdate varieties. Federation style coinage continued to be struck until 1861. (See Central American Republic listings.)

MONETARY SYSTEM

16 Reales = 1 Escudo

COLONIAL COINAGE
Vice-Royalty of New Spain
TRUXILLO
(Trujillo)

2 REALES

SILVER
Ferdinand VII

KM#	Date	Mintage	Fine	VF	XF	Unc
2 (M1)	1808	—	125.00	250.00	425.00	750.00

NOTE: A proclamation issue struck for Ferdinand VII as the new King of Spain while he was under Napoleonic French guard.

8 REALES

SILVER, crude
Obv: Bust of Fernando VII.
Rev: Arms within legends.

KM#	Date	Mintage	Good	VG	Fine	VF
3	1813	—	— Reported, not confirmed			

EMPIRE OF MEXICO
2 REALES

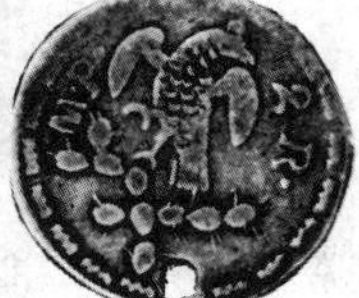

SILVER
Obv: Iturbide. Rev: Eagle on cactus.

KM#	Date	Mintage	Good	VG	Fine	VF
6	1823	—	—	—	Rare	—

PROVISIONAL GOVERNMENT
(1823)

1/2 REAL

SILVER

KM#	Date	Mintage	Good	VG	Fine	VF
9	1823TL	—	—	—	Rare	—

KM#	Date	Mintage	Good	VG	Fine	VF
10	1823	—	—	—	Rare	—

KM#	Date	Mintage	Good	VG	Fine	VF
7.1	1823	—	150.00	250.00	350.00	—
	(18)24	—	125.00	225.00	325.00	—

Rev: Plain fields.

KM#	Date	Mintage	Good	VG	Fine	VF
7.2	(18)24	—	175.00	300.00	425.00	—

REAL

SILVER

KM#	Date	Mintage	Good	VG	Fine	VF
4	(18)23TG	—	40.00	80.00	120.00	200.00

Rev: Lions facing left.

KM#	Date	Mintage	Good	VG	Fine	VF
8.1	(18)23P-Y	—	25.00	55.00	85.00	—

Rev: Lions facing right.

KM#	Date	Mintage	Good	VG	Fine	VF
8.2	(18)24P-Y	—	50.00	100.00	150.00	—
	(18)25P-Y	—	—	—	Rare	—

NOTE: Varieties exist.

2 REALES

SILVER

KM#	Date	Mintage	Good	VG	Fine	VF
5	(18)23TG	—	60.00	120.00	180.00	300.00

KM#	Date	Mintage	Good	VG	Fine	VF
11.1	1823	—	—	—	Rare	—

Rev: Lions and castles reversed.

KM#	Date	Mintage	Good	VG	Fine	VF
11.2	1823	—	—	—	Rare	—

KM#	Date	Mintage	Good	VG	Fine	VF
12.1	1823	3 known	—	—	Rare	—

Rev: Crowned arms.

KM#	Date	Mintage	Good	VG	Fine	VF
12.2	1823	—	—	—	Rare	—

KM#	Date	Mintage	Good	VG	Fine	VF
14	1823	—	—	—	Rare	—

KM#	Date	Mintage	Good	VG	Fine	VF
15.1	(1)823P-Y	—	60.00	120.00	180.00	300.00

Rev: Lions and castles reversed.

KM#	Date	Mintage	Good	VG	Fine	VF
15.2	(1)824P-Y	—	60.00	120.00	180.00	300.00

NOTE: Varieties exist.

4 REALES

SILVER

Rev: Lions facing left.

KM#	Date	Mintage	Good	VG	Fine	VF
16.1	(18)23P-Y	—	100.00	200.00	300.00	500.00

Rev: Lions facing left and castles reversed.

KM#	Date	Mintage	Good	VG	Fine	VF
16.3	(18)23P-Y	—	100.00	200.00	300.00	500.00

Rev: Lions facing right and castles reversed.

KM#	Date	Mintage	Good	VG	Fine	VF
16.2	(18)24P-Y	—	100.00	200.00	300.00	500.00
	(18)24P-Y rev. retrograde 4	—	100.00	200.00	300.00	500.00

STATE OF HONDURAS

1/2 REAL

KM#	Date	Mintage	Good	VG	Fine	VF
	.333 SILVER					
17	1832T F	—	10.00	17.50	35.00	90.00
	1833T F	—	12.50	20.00	40.00	100.00
	1837T F	—	—	Reported, not confirmed		
	.250 SILVER					
17a	1844T F	—	20.00	40.00	80.00	150.00
	1845T G	—	17.50	37.50	70.00	125.00

REAL

KM#	Date	Mintage	Good	VG	Fine	VF
	.333 SILVER					
18	1832T F	—	7.50	13.50	22.50	45.00
	1839T F	—	11.00	20.00	35.00	75.00
	.200 SILVER					
18a	1840T F PROVICIONAL	—	10.00	20.00	35.00	75.00
	1840T F PROVISIONAL	—	—	Reported, not confirmed		
	1844T G CREZCA		6.00	17.50	30.00	60.00
	.172 SILVER					
18b	1845T G FECUNDO	—	7.00	15.00	25.00	45.00
	1845T G FECNDO	—	6.00	13.50	22.50	40.00
	1846T G	—	10.00	20.00	35.00	75.00
	1849T G	—	6.00	12.00	20.00	35.00
	.100 SILVER					
18c	1851T G	—	6.50	13.50	20.00	35.00
	1852T G	—	7.50	17.50	30.00	60.00
	.0400 SILVER					
18d	1853T G	—	15.00	35.00	60.00	150.00

2 REALES

KM#	Date	Mintage	Good	VG	Fine	VF
	.333 SILVER					
19	1832T F	—	4.50	10.00	17.50	30.00
	1833T F	—	5.00	12.00	20.00	35.00
	1839T F	—	6.00	12.50	25.00	50.00

NOTE: Coins dated 1833 struck in copper, with or without silvering, are very common early counterfeits. A common variety contains an error. . . PROVISINAL. . . on obverse.

KM#	Date	Mintage	Good	VG	Fine	VF
	.200 SILVER					
19a	1840T F PROVICIONAL	—	8.50	20.00	35.00	75.00
	1840T F PROVISIONAL	—	7.50	17.50	32.50	65.00
	1842T G CRESCA		6.50	15.00	30.00	60.00
	1842T G CREZCA		6.50	15.00	30.00	60.00
	1844T F	—	5.00	12.50	27.50	55.00
	1844T G CREZCA		4.00	8.50	17.50	27.50
	1845T G	—	4.00	8.00	15.00	25.00
	1846T G	—	—	—	Rare	—
	1847T G	—	6.00	13.50	25.00	37.50
	.172 SILVER					
19b	1848T G CREZCA		4.00	7.50	15.00	25.00
	1848T G CREZUA		4.00	7.50	15.00	25.00
	.100 SILVER					
19c	1851T G	—	6.50	15.00	30.00	60.00
	.0625 SILVER					
19d	1852T G	—	7.00	17.50	35.00	75.00
	.0400 SILVER					
19e	1853T G	—	4.00	9.00	20.00	40.00
	1854T G	—	50.00	100.00	200.00	—
	1855T G	—	—	Reported, not confirmed		
	1857T F	—	60.00	110.00	220.00	—

4 REALES

KM#	Date	Mintage	Good	VG	Fine	VF
	.172 SILVER					
20	1849T G	—	5.00	12.50	20.00	30.00
	1850T G	—	3.50	7.00	12.50	22.50
	.100 SILVER					
20a	1851T G	—	3.00	5.50	10.00	20.00
	.0625 SILVER					
20b	1852T G	—	3.00	5.50	10.00	20.00
	.0400 SILVER					
20c	1853T G	—	3.00	5.50	10.00	20.00
	1854T G	—	3.00	5.50	10.00	20.00
	1855T G HOND		3.00	6.00	12.00	22.00
	1855T G HON		3.25	7.00	15.00	27.50
	COPPER					
20d	1856T G	—	4.50	9.00	18.50	35.00
	1856T F	—	—	—	Rare	—
	1857T F	—	—	—	—	—
	COPPER-LEAD ALLOY					
20e	1857T F	—	6.00	12.00	22.50	45.00
	1857/2T F/G	—	—	—	—	—

8 REALES

KM#	Date	Mintage	Good	VG	Fine	VF
	COPPER					
21	1856T G	—	6.50	12.50	30.00	60.00
	1856T FL	—	—	—	—	—
	COPPER-LEAD ALLOY					
21a	1857T FL	—	4.50	8.00	12.50	25.00
	1858T FL w/HON	—	6.00	12.00	20.00	35.00
	1858T FL w/HOND	—	6.00	12.00	20.00	35.00
	1859T FL w/PROVISIONAL	—	6.50	12.50	25.00	45.00
	1859T FL w/PROVISIONAL and retrograde N's	—	10.00	18.50	30.00	50.00
	1859T FL w/PROVICIONAL (error)	—	10.00	18.50	30.00	50.00
	1860T FL	2 known	—	—	—	—
	1861T FL	—	8.50	15.00	35.00	75.00

PROVISIONAL COINAGE

NOTE: Similar coins, with rosettes instead of dots separating their legends, are patterns or trial strikes of the dies, which were made in England.

PESO

COPPER

Rev: Dots separate legends.

KM#	Date	Mintage	VG	Fine	VF	XF
24	1862T A	—	2.75	7.50	15.00	27.50

2 PESOS

COPPER
Rev: Dots separate legends.

KM#	Date	Mintage	VG	Fine	VF	XF
25	1862T A	—	2.75	7.50	17.50	37.50

4 PESOS

COPPER
Rev: Dots separate legends.

KM#	Date	Mintage	VG	Fine	VF	XF
26	1862T A	—	4.00	12.50	30.00	60.00

8 PESOS

COPPER
Rev: Dots separate legends.

KM#	Date	Mintage	VG	Fine	VF	XF
27	1862T A	—	8.50	25.00	50.00	100.00

REPUBLIC

1/8 REAL

COPPER-NICKEL

KM#	Date	Mintage	Fine	VF	XF	Unc
30	1869A	—	3.50	8.00	12.50	25.00
	1870A	—	3.00	7.00	10.00	17.50

1/4 REAL

COPPER-NICKEL

KM#	Date	Mintage	Fine	VF	XF	Unc
31	1869A	—	1.25	2.75	7.00	14.00
	1870A	—	2.50	5.50	15.00	30.00

1/2 REAL

COPPER-NICKEL

KM#	Date	Mintage	Fine	VF	XF	Unc
32	1869A	—	1.25	3.00	7.00	17.50
	1870A	—	10.00	22.50	40.00	100.00
	1871A	—	—	—	90.00	175.00

REAL

COPPER-NICKEL

KM#	Date	Mintage	Fine	VF	XF	Unc
33	1869A	—	7.50	18.00	32.50	70.00
	1870A	—	5.00	12.00	17.50	40.00

NOTE: Varieties exist.

PESO SERIES

100 Centavos = 1 Peso

1/2 CENTAVO

BRONZE

KM#	Date	Mintage	VG	Fine	VF	XF
45	1881	.171	100.00	200.00	400.00	—
	1883	—	15.00	27.50	42.50	80.00
	1885	.172	12.50	22.50	30.00	50.00
	1886	.097	12.50	22.50	30.00	60.00
	1889	—	15.00	27.50	40.00	70.00
	1891	—	200.00	300.00	500.00	—

UN (1) CENTAVO

BRONZE

KM#	Date	Mintage	VG	Fine	VF	XF
40	1878	.346	50.00	90.00	175.00	300.00
	1879	Inc. Ab.	13.50	27.50	50.00	100.00
	1880	Inc. Ab.	12.00	22.50	45.00	100.00

Plain, reeded, and plain and reeded edges.

KM#	Date	Mintage	VG	Fine	VF	XF
46	1881	.132	5.00	12.50	22.50	45.00
	1884	.024	2.75	7.50	15.00	35.00
	1885	.086	2.50	6.50	12.50	30.00
	1886	.116	3.00	7.50	15.00	30.00
	1889/5	—	6.50	15.00	27.50	50.00
	1889 medal rotation					
		—	6.50	15.00	27.50	50.00
	1890	—	3.00	7.50	15.00	35.00
	1896	.061	5.00	12.50	22.00	40.00
	1897	9,362	—	—	—	—
	1898/88	.054	7.00	18.50	32.50	55.00
	1898	Inc. Ab.	5.00	12.50	22.00	40.00
	1899 small 99					
		.180	5.50	13.50	23.00	42.50
	1899 lg.99	I.A.	5.50	13.50	23.00	42.50
	1900	.029	5.00	12.50	22.00	40.00

NOTE: Later dates (1901-1907) exist for this type.
NOTE: Varieties exist.

Obv: KM#46. Rev: Altered KM#49.

KM#	Date	Mintage	VG	Fine	VF	XF
59	1890	—	10.00	20.00	45.00	100.00
	1893	—	12.50	25.00	40.00	75.00
	1895	.045	10.00	20.00	45.00	100.00
	1900	—	—	Reported, not confirmed		

NOTE: Later dates (1907-1908) exist for this type.
NOTE: Varieties exist.

Mule. Obv: KM#46. Rev: KM#40.

KM#	Date	Mintage	VG	Fine	VF	XF
60	ND	—	125.00	250.00	400.00	600.00

Obv: KM#49. Rev: Altered KM#49.

KM#	Date	Mintage	VG	Fine	VF	XF
61	1890*	—	12.00	25.00	45.00	75.00
	1891*	—	2.00	5.00	10.00	22.50
	1892	—	—	—	Rare	—
	1893/83	—	—	—	—	—
	1893*	—	2.00	5.00	10.00	22.50
	1895	—	10.00	25.00	45.00	75.00

NOTE: Later date (1908) exists for this type.
***NOTE:** These dates found with die-cutting error or broken die that reads REPLBLICA.
NOTE: Varieties exist.

Mule. Obv: KM#59. Rev: KM#40.

KM#	Date	Mintage	VG	Fine	VF	XF
A63	ND(c.1895)	—	—	Reported, not confirmed		

Mule. Obv: KM#35. Rev: KM#40.

KM#	Date	Mintage	VG	Fine	VF	XF
63	1895	—	—	Reported, not confirmed		

5 CENTAVOS

1.2500 g, .835 SILVER, .0336 oz ASW
Obv: Arms. Rev: Tree.

KM#	Date	Mintage	VG	Fine	VF	XF
34	1871	2,056	75.00	165.00	300.00	650.00
	1871	—	—	—	Proof	—

NOTE: The above coin reads "0.900" but is actually 0.835 fine and was not struck until 1879 and 1880.

Obv: Eagle. Rev: Standing Liberty.

KM#	Date	Mintage	VG	Fine	VF	XF
43	1879	—	—	—	Rare	—

KM#	Date	Mintage	VG	Fine	VF	XF
48	1884	—	10.00	22.50	37.50	65.00
	1885	—	12.50	25.00	40.00	75.00
	1886	—	12.50	25.00	40.00	75.00
	1890	—	—	Reported, not confirmed		
	1895	—	—	—	—	—

NOTE: Later date (1902) exists for this type.

KM#	Date	Mintage	VG	Fine	VF	XF
54	1886	—	7.00	15.00	22.00	45.00
	6188 (error)					
	2 known	—	—	—	Rare	—
	1895/85	—	—	—	Rare	—
	1895	—	—	—	Rare	—
	1896/85	.035	3.00	6.00	12.50	20.00
	1896/86	I.A.	3.00	6.00	12.50	20.00
	1896	Inc. Ab.	3.50	7.00	15.00	25.00

NOTE: Varieties exist.

10 CENTAVOS

2.5000 g, .835 SILVER, .0671 oz ASW

KM#	Date	Mintage	VG	Fine	VF	XF
35	1871	.017	20.00	35.00	60.00	100.00

NOTE: The above coin reads "0.900" but is actually 0.835 fine, none struck until 1879-1880.

Obv: Eagle. Rev: Standing Liberty.

KM#	Date	Mintage	VG	Fine	VF	XF
41	1878	—	—	—	Rare	—
	1879	—	—	—	Rare	—

Mule. Obv: KM#41. Rev: KM#35.

KM#	Date	Mintage	VG	Fine	VF	XF
42	1878	—	—	—	Rare	—

KM#	Date	Mintage	VG	Fine	VF	XF
49	1884	—	8.50	22.50	35.00	60.00
	1885	—	7.50	17.50	27.50	50.00
	1886	—	8.50	20.00	30.00	55.00
	1889	—	25.00	50.00	85.00	130.00

KM#	Date	Mintage	VG	Fine	VF	XF
49	1891	—	—	Reported, not confirmed		
	1893*	—	10.00	22.50	37.50	65.00
	1895*	.053	8.00	18.50	40.00	100.00
	1897	.016	—	—	—	—
	1900*	5,300	30.00	60.00	100.00	200.00

***NOTE:** These dates found with die-cutting error or broken die that reads REPLBLICA.

Mule. Obv: KM#35. Rev: KM#49.
P on reverse.

KM#	Date	Mintage	VG	Fine	VF	XF
55.1	1886	—	18.50	35.00	75.00	—
	1895/71	—	—	—	—	—
	1895	—	16.50	30.00	60.00	—
	1 P replaces date.					
55.2	ND	—	30.00	70.00	120.00	—
	Rev: Without P.					
55.3	1895 lg.dt.	—	—	—	—	—
	1895 sm.dt.	—	—	—	—	—

25 CENTAVOS

6.2500 g, .900 SILVER, .1808 oz ASW

KM#	Date	Mintage	VG	Fine	VF	XF
36	1871	.177	2.50	5.50	12.50	35.00

KM#	Date	Mintage	VG	Fine	VF	XF
50	1883	—	2.25	6.00	10.00	18.50
	1884	—	2.00	4.50	9.00	17.50
	1885/4	—	—	—	—	—
	1885	—	2.00	5.00	10.00	18.50
	1886/1	—	2.25	6.00	11.00	20.00
	1887	—	—	Reported, not confirmed		
	1888/7	—	5.00	12.00	22.50	42.50
	1888	—	2.25	5.00	10.00	22.50
	1890/85	—	3.50	7.50	15.00	27.50
	1890/88	—	3.50	7.50	15.00	27.50
	1890/89	—	3.50	7.50	15.00	27.50
	1891/181	—	3.50	7.50	15.00	27.50
	1891/81	—	3.50	7.50	15.00	27.50
	1891	—	3.00	6.75	12.50	25.00
	1892/81	—	2.25	5.00	10.00	20.00
	1892/1	—	2.25	5.00	10.00	20.00
	1893/83	—	2.75	6.00	11.00	22.50
	1893/88	—	2.75	6.00	11.00	22.50
	1895/83	.012	3.50	7.50	15.00	27.50
	1895	Inc. Ab.	2.25	5.00	10.00	21.00
	1896	.274	3.50	7.00	12.50	22.50
	1898	.190	—	Reported, not confirmed		
	1899/88	.030	10.00	20.00	40.00	65.00

NOTE: Varieties exist.

6.2500 g, .835 SILVER, .1678 oz ASW

KM#	Date	Mintage	VG	Fine	VF	XF
50a	1899/88 .835/.900 medal rotation					
		I.A.	6.00	13.50	25.00	40.00
	1899	I.A.	5.00	11.00	17.50	30.00
	1900/800 .835/.900					
		.039	2.75	5.00	11.00	22.50
	1900/891	I.A.	2.75	5.00	11.00	22.50
	1900/1	I.A.	2.75	5.00	11.00	22.50
	1900	Inc. Ab.	2.75	5.00	11.00	22.50

NOTE: Later dates (1901-1913) exist for this type.

50 CENTAVOS

12.5000 g, .900 SILVER, .3617 oz ASW

KM#	Date	Mintage	VG	Fine	VF	XF
37	1871	.040	3.75	10.00	17.50	42.50

KM#	Date	Mintage	VG	Fine	VF	XF
44	1879	—	165.00	350.00	650.00	1250.

KM#	Date	Mintage	VG	Fine	VF	XF
51	1883	—	4.50	10.00	21.50	40.00
	1883P	—	7.00	15.00	27.50	55.00
	1884	—	4.00	9.00	15.00	30.00
	1885 medal rotation					
		—	4.25	9.00	16.50	35.00
	1885 coin rotation					
		—	4.00	10.00	17.50	37.50
	1886/5	—	5.00	12.50	27.50	55.00
	1886	—	5.00	12.50	27.50	52.50
	1887/5	—	7.00	15.00	30.00	60.00
	1887	—	7.00	15.00	30.00	60.00
	1896/86	—	175.00	350.00	650.00	—
	1897	.037	37.50	67.50	110.00	—

NOTE: Later date (1910) exists for this type.

PESO

1.6120 g, .900 GOLD, .0467 oz AGW
Similar to 5 Centavos, KM#34.

KM#	Date	Mintage	Fine	VF	XF	Unc
38	1871	—	—	—	Rare	—

Mule. Obv: KM#38. Rev: KM#56.

KM#	Date	Mintage	Fine	VF	XF	Unc
39	1871	—	325.00	550.00	825.00	1700.

25.0000 g, .900 SILVER, .7234 oz ASW
Rev: Small CENTRO-AMERICA.

KM#	Date	Mintage	VG	Fine	VF	XF
47	1881	.026	20.00	40.00	60.00	120.00
	1882 medal rotation					
		.076	20.00	35.00	50.00	100.00
	1882 coin rotation					
		Inc. Ab.	20.00	35.00	50.00	100.00
	1883	—	20.00	37.50	55.00	110.00

Rev: Large CENTRO-AMERICA.

KM#	Date	Mintage	VG	Fine	VF	XF
52	1883/1	—	50.00	100.00	200.00	400.00
	1884	—	18.00	32.50	50.00	90.00
	1885	—	18.00	30.00	45.00	80.00
	1886	—	18.00	32.50	50.00	90.00
	1887	—	18.00	32.50	50.00	90.00
	1888	—	18.00	30.00	45.00	80.00
	1889/8	—	18.00	30.00	45.00	80.00
	1889	—	18.00	30.00	45.00	80.00
	1890	—	18.00	30.00	45.00	80.00
	1891/88	—	18.00	30.00	45.00	80.00
	1891/89	—	18.00	30.00	45.00	80.00
	1892/0	—	18.00	30.00	45.00	80.00
	1892/1	—	18.00	30.00	45.00	80.00
	1893/1	—	200.00	500.00	950.00	1600.
	1895/0	.080	20.00	35.00	60.00	115.00
	1895	Inc. Ab.	20.00	35.00	60.00	115.00
	1899/87P		400.00	800.00	1500.	—

NOTE: Later dates (1902-1914) exist for this type.

Mule. Obv: KM#47, w/o 25 GMOS above UN PESO.
Rev: KM#52.

KM#	Date	Mintage	VG	Fine	VF	XF
62	1894/82	—	20.00	35.00	60.00	115.00
	1894/2 closed 4					
		—	25.00	40.00	70.00	135.00
	1894/2 open 4					
		—	25.00	40.00	70.00	135.00
	1895/85	I.A.	20.00	35.00	60.00	115.00
	1895/3	I.A.	20.00	35.00	60.00	115.00
	1895/4	I.A.	20.00	35.00	60.00	115.00
	1896/4	.021	30.00	55.00	90.00	—

1.6120 g, .900 GOLD, .0467 oz AGW

KM#	Date	Mintage	Fine	VF	XF	Unc
56	1887	—	—	Reported, not confirmed		
	1888	—	125.00	250.00	375.00	650.00
	1889	—	—	Reported, not confirmed		
	1890	—	—	Reported, not confirmed		
	1895	43 pcs.	125.00	250.00	375.00	650.00
	1896	—	125.00	250.00	375.00	650.00
	1899	—	—	Reported, not confirmed		

NOTE: Later dates (1901-1922) exist for this type.

5 PESOS

8.0645 g, .900 GOLD, .2333 oz AGW

KM#	Date	Mintage	Fine	VF	XF	Unc
53	1883	—	450.00	650.00	1000.	1500.
	1888/3	—	450.00	650.00	1000.	1500.
	1889	—	—	Reported, not confirmed		
	1890	—	600.00	750.00	1100.	1750.
	1895	20 pcs.	600.00	900.00	1350.	2000.
	1896	55 pcs.	600.00	900.00	1350.	2000.
	1897	—	450.00	650.00	1000.	1500.
	1900	—	450.00	650.00	1000.	1500.

NOTE: Later dates (1902-1913) exist for this type.

10 PESOS

16.1290 g, .900 GOLD, .4667 oz AGW

KM#	Date	Mintage	Fine	VF	XF	Unc
58	1889	25 pcs.	5000.	6000.	7500.	10,000.
	1895	10 pcs.	— Reported, not confirmed			

20 PESOS

32.2580 g, .900 GOLD, .9335 oz AGW

KM#	Date	Mintage	Fine	VF	XF	Unc
57	1888	—	3500.	5000.	8000.	15,000.
	1895/88	—	—	—	Rare	—
	1895	—	—	—	Rare	—

NOTE: Later date (1908) exists for this type.

ESSAIS (E)

KM#	Date	Mintage	Identification	Mkt.Val.
E1	1872	—	1/4 Real, Aluminum, plain edge	75.00
E2	1872	—	1/4 Real, Aluminum, reeded edge	75.00

PATTERNS (Pn)

(Including off metal strikes)

NOTE: Rosettes separate legends on Pn1-Pn5a.

KM#	Date	Mintage	Identification	Mkt.Val.
Pn1	1862T A	—	1 Peso, Bronze	—
Pn1a	1862T A	—	1 Peso, Silver	—

KM#	Date	Mintage	Identification	Mkt.Val.
Pn2	1862T A	—	2 Pesos, Bronze	175.00
Pn2a	1862T A	—	2 Pesos, Silver	—

KM#	Date	Mintage	Identification	Mkt.Val.
Pn3	1862T A	—	4 Pesos, Bronze	175.00
Pn3a	1862T A	—	4 Pesos, Silver	3500.

KM#	Date	Mintage	Identification	Mkt.Val.
Pn4	1862T A	—	8 Pesos, Bronze	300.00
Pn4a	1862T A	—	8 Pesos, Silver	—
Pn5	1862T A	—	16 Pesos, Bronze	—
Pn5a	1862T A	—	16 Pesos, Silver	—
Pn6	1869E	—	1/8 Real, Copper-Nickel, KM30	75.00
Pn7	1869E	—	1/4 Real, Copper-Nickel, KM31	75.00
Pn8	1869E	—	1/2 Real, Copper-Nickel, KM32	150.00
Pn9	1869E	—	1 Real, Copper-Nickel, KM33	150.00
Pn9a	1869E	—	1 Real, Copper, KM33	—

KM#	Date	Mintage	Identification	Mkt.Val.
Pn10	1870	—	1 Real, Copper-Nickel, Medina	125.00
Pn10a	1870	—	1 Real, Copper, Medina	—

KM#	Date	Mintage	Identification	Mkt.Val.
Pn11	1870	—	2 Reales, Copper-Nickel, Medina	125.00

KM#	Date	Mintage	Identification	Mkt.Val.
Pn12	1870	—	5 Reales, Copper-Nickel, Medina	225.00
Pn13	1871	—	5 Centavos, Copper, KM34	500.00
Pn14	1871	—	10 Centavos, Copper, KM35	500.00
Pn15	1871	—	25 Centavos, Copper, KM36	500.00
Pn16	1871	—	50 Centavos, Copper, KM37	500.00
Pn16a	1871	—	50 Centavos, Nickel, KM37	—
Pn17	1871	—	5 Pesos, Copper, KM38	R,NC
Pn17a	1871	—	5 Pesos, Gold, KM38	R,NC
PN17b	1871	—	5 Pesos, Silver, 1.61 g, KM38	R,NC
Pn18	1871	—	10 Pesos, Copper	R,NC
Pn18a	1871	—	10 Pesos, Gold	R,NC

NOTE: Preceding 5 & 10 Peso patterns are suspected to be off metal strikes of the 5 & 10 Centavo issues, KM#34-35 respectively. Confirmation would be appreciated.

KM#	Date	Mintage	Identification	Mkt.Val.
Pn20	1878	—	50 Centavos	—
PnA21	1878	—	1 Peso, .900 Silver	Rare
Pn21	1883	—	5 Pesos, Copper, KM53	250.00

TRIAL STRIKES (TS)

KM#	Date	Mintage	Identification	Mkt.Val.
TS1	1869	—	1/4 Real, Aluminum, uniface obv. Pn7	75.00

HONG KONG

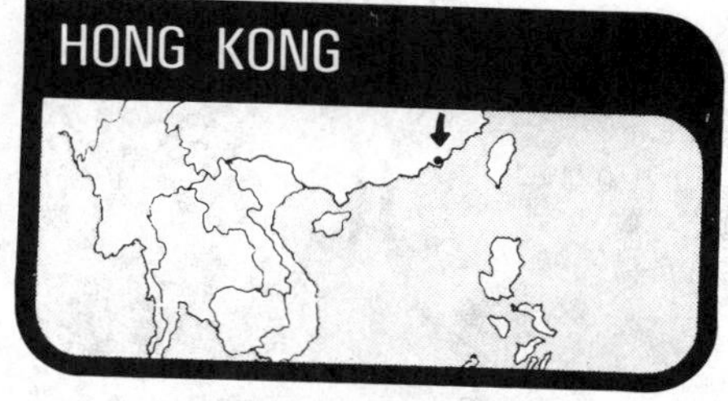

The colony of Hong Kong S.A.R., a former British colony reverted to control of the People's Republic of China on July 1, 1997 as a Special Administrative Region. It is situated at the mouth of the Canton or Pearl River 90 miles (145 km.) southeast of Canton, has an area of 403 sq. mi. (1,040 sq. km.) and an estimated population of 6.3 million. Capital: Victoria. The free port of Hong Kong, the commercial center of the Far East, is a transshipment point for goods destined for China and the countries of the Pacific Rim. Light manufacturing and tourism are important components of the economy.

Long a haven for fishermen-pirates and opium smugglers, the island of Hong Kong was ceded to Britain at the conclusion of the first Opium War, 1839-1842. At the time, the acquisition of a 'barren rock' was ridiculed by both London and English merchants operating in the Far East. The Kowloon Peninsula and Stonecutter's Island were ceded in 1860, and the so-called New Territories, comprising most of the mainland of the colony, were leased to Britain for 99 years in 1898.

The legends on Hong Kong coinage are bilingual: English and Chinese. The rare 1941 cent was dispatched to Hong Kong in several shipments. One fell into Japanese hands while another was melted down by the British and a third was sunk during enemy action.

RULERS

British

MINT MARKS

H - Heaton
KN - King's Norton

MONETARY SYSTEM

10 Mils (Wen, Ch'ien) = 1 Cent (Hsien)
10 Cents = 1 Chiao
100 Cents = 10 Chiao = 1 Dollar (Yuan)

MIL

BRONZE
Obv: Chinese value: ***1 Wen.***

KM#	Date	Mintage	Fine	VF	XF	Unc
1	1863	19.000	7.00	15.00	40.00	150.00
	1863	—	—	—	Proof	400.00
	1864	—	650.00	1000.	2000.	4000.
	1864	—	—	—	Proof	6000.
	1865	40.000	—	—	2150.	4250.

Rev: W/o Hyphen between HONG KONG.

KM#	Date	Mintage	Fine	VF	XF	Unc
2	1865	Inc. Ab.	7.00	15.00	40.00	160.00

Obv: Chinese value: ***1 Ch'ien.***

KM#	Date	Mintage	Fine	VF	XF	Unc
3	1866	20.000	7.00	15.00	45.00	170.00

CENT

BRONZE
Obv: 14 pearls in left arch of crown.

KM#	Date	Mintage	Fine	VF	XF	Unc
4.1	1863	1.000	7.00	15.00	35.00	200.00
	1863	—	—	—	Proof	500.00
	1863 dot on reverse			—	Proof	600.00
	1865/3	1.000	20.00	30.00	60.00	250.00
	1865	Inc. Ab.	6.00	12.00	30.00	185.00
4.1	1865	—	—	—	Proof	550.00
	1866	1.000	5.00	10.00	25.00	170.00
	1866	—	—	—	Proof	550.00
	1875	1.000	5.00	10.00	25.00	170.00
	1875	—	—	—	Proof	550.00
	1876	1.000	5.00	10.00	25.00	170.00
	1876	—	—	—	Proof	550.00
	1877	2.000	6.00	12.00	30.00	185.00
	1877	—	—	—	Proof	750.00

Obv: 15 pearls in left arch of crown.

KM#	Date	Mintage	Fine	VF	XF	Unc
4.2	1877	2.000	6.00	12.00	30.00	185.00
	1877	—	—	—	Proof	550.00
	1879	Inc. Be.	6.00	12.00	30.00	185.00
	1879	—	—	—	Proof	550.00

Obv: 5 pearls in center of crown.

KM#	Date	Mintage	Fine	VF	XF	Unc
4.3	1879	1.000	7.00	16.00	40.00	225.00
	1879	—	—	—	Proof	500.00
	1880	1.000	6.00	12.00	35.00	220.00
	1880	—	—	—	Proof	500.00
	1881	1.000	6.00	12.00	30.00	200.00
	1881	—	—	—	Proof	500.00
	1899	1.000	5.00	10.00	25.00	170.00
	1899	—	—	—	Proof	450.00
	1900H	1.000	3.00	7.50	18.00	100.00
	1900H	—	—	—	Proof	350.00

NOTE: Later date (1901) exists for this type.

5 CENTS

1.3577 g, .800 SILVER, .0349 oz ASW

KM#	Date	Mintage	Fine	VF	XF	Unc
5	1866	1.313	5.00	9.00	28.00	80.00
	1866 milled edge		—	—	Proof	550.00
	1866 plain edge		—	—	Proof	750.00
	1867	Inc. Ab.	6.00	10.00	28.00	80.00
	1867	—	—	—	Proof	450.00
	1868	Inc. Ab.	5.00	7.00	20.00	65.00
	1872/68H	.136	8.00	18.00	45.00	125.00
	1872H Arabic 1	Inc. Ab.	6.00	10.00	28.00	80.00
	1872H Roman I	Inc. Ab.	9.00	20.00	45.00	125.00
	1873/63	.387	6.00	12.50	30.00	90.00
	1873/63H	.256	6.00	10.00	25.00	75.00
	1873H round top 3	Inc. Ab.	6.00	12.50	28.00	85.00
	1873 flat top 3	Inc. Ab.	6.00	12.50	28.00	85.00
	1873	—	—	—	Proof	450.00
	1873 plain edge		—	—	Proof	600.00
	1874H	.280	6.00	15.00	32.00	90.00
	1875H	.280	6.00	12.50	28.00	85.00
	1875H	—	—	—	Proof	500.00
	1876H	.480	6.00	12.50	28.00	85.00
	1877H	.240	6.00	12.50	28.00	85.00
	1879	.288	6.00	12.50	28.00	85.00
	1880H	.300	6.00	12.50	25.00	65.00
	1881/71	.300	6.00	13.50	35.00	90.00
	1881	Inc. Ab.	3.50	9.00	25.00	65.00
	1881	—	—	—	Proof	450.00
	1882H	.600	2.00	4.00	10.00	35.00
	1883	.550	2.00	4.00	10.00	40.00
	1883	—	—	—	Proof	450.00
	1883H	.250	4.00	12.50	25.00	65.00
	1883H	—	—	—	Proof	450.00
	1884	.960	1.50	3.00	6.00	30.00
	1884	—	—	—	Proof	450.00
	1885	3.120	1.00	2.00	5.00	22.00
	1885	—	—	—	Proof	475.00
	1886	2.100	1.00	2.00	5.00	22.00
	1887	2.448	1.00	2.00	5.00	22.00
	1888/78	5.952	1.00	2.00	5.00	22.00
	1888	Inc. Ab.	1.00	2.00	5.00	22.00
	1889	5.169	1.00	2.00	5.00	22.00
	1889	—	—	—	Proof	300.00
	1889H	2.100	1.00	2.00	5.00	22.00
	1890	1.500	1.00	2.00	5.00	22.00
	1890	—	—	—	Proof	300.00
	1890H	5.400	1.00	2.00	5.00	20.00
	1890H	—	—	—	Proof	300.00
	1891	6.900	1.00	2.00	5.00	20.00
	1891H	2.100	1.00	2.00	5.00	20.00
	1892	4.200	1.00	2.00	5.00	20.00
	1892H	1.200	1.50	3.00	6.00	25.00
	1892H	—	—	—	Proof	300.00
	1893	3.000	1.00	2.00	4.50	17.50
	1894	4.600	1.00	2.00	4.50	17.50
	1894	—	—	—	Proof	275.00
	1895	4.000	1.00	2.00	4.50	17.50
	1897	4.000	1.00	2.00	4.50	17.50
	1898	3.500	1.00	2.00	4.50	17.50
	1899	9.377	1.00	2.00	4.00	15.00
	1900	1.623	1.00	2.00	4.00	15.00
	1900H	7.000	1.00	2.00	4.00	15.00

NOTE: Later date (1901) exists for this ype.
NOTE: Coins dated 1866-68 struck at Hong Kong Mint; 1872-1901 at the Royal Mint.

10 CENTS

2.7154 g, .800 SILVER, .0698 oz ASW

KM#	Date	Mintage	Fine	VF	XF	Unc
6.1	1863	.100	10.00	22.00	45.00	150.00
	1863 reeded edge		—	—	Proof	450.00
	1863 plain edge		—	—	Proof	550.00
	1864	.200	250.00	450.00	750.00	1400.
	1864	—	—	—	Proof	1850.
	1865	.550	7.50	16.00	35.00	115.00
	1865	—	—	—	Proof	400.00

Obv: 10 pearls on right arch of crown.

KM#	Date	Mintage	Fine	VF	XF	Unc
6.2	1866	.300	5.00	10.00	25.00	90.00
	1866	—	—	—	Proof	800.00

NOTE: Struck at the Royal Mint.

Obv: 11 pearls on right arch of crown.

KM#	Date	Mintage	Fine	VF	XF	Unc
6.3	1866/5	—	60.00	120.00	200.00	—
	1866	2.479	5.00	10.00	25.00	90.00
	1866	—	—	—	Proof	350.00
	1867	Inc. Ab.	7.50	15.00	35.00	125.00
	1867	—	—	—	Proof	450.00
	1868	Inc. Ab.	4.00	8.00	20.00	60.00
	1869	—	—	—	Proof	650.00
	1872H	.088	10.00	25.00	60.00	275.00
	1872H	—	—	—	Proof	500.00
	1873 round top 3	.197	5.00	10.00	25.00	80.00
	1873	—	—	—	Proof	400.00
	1873 plain edge		—	—	Proof	1200.
	1873H flat top 3	.128	6.50	12.50	32.00	120.00
	1874H	.200	5.00	10.00	25.00	80.00
	1875H	.200	5.00	10.00	30.00	100.00
	1875H	—	—	—	Proof	450.00
	1876H	.480	6.50	12.50	25.00	75.00
	1877H	.240	6.50	12.50	25.00	75.00
	1877H	—	—	—	Proof	450.00
	1879	.288	5.00	10.00	25.00	75.00
	1879	—	—	—	Proof	400.00
	1880H	.300	5.00	10.00	25.00	75.00
	1880H	—	—	—	Proof	400.00
	1881	.300	4.00	8.00	22.00	70.00
	1881	—	—	—	Proof	400.00
	1882H	.500	4.00	8.00	20.00	65.00
	1882H	—	—	—	Proof	500.00
	1883 flat top 3	.550	4.00	8.00	20.00	65.00
	1883	—	—	—	Proof	400.00
	1883H round top 3	.250	5.00	9.00	30.00	80.00
	1883H	—	—	—	Proof	800.00
	1884	.960	2.00	3.50	9.00	40.00
	1884	—	—	—	Proof	250.00
	1885	3.120	1.50	3.00	7.00	35.00
	1885	—	—	—	Proof	700.00
	1886	2.100	1.50	3.00	7.00	35.00
	1886	—	—	—	Proof	250.00
	1887	2.441	1.50	3.00	7.00	35.00
	1887	—	—	—	Proof	350.00
	1888	7.027	1.50	3.00	7.00	35.00
	1888	—	—	—	Proof	250.00
	1889	4.027	1.50	3.00	7.00	35.00
	1889	—	—	—	Proof	250.00
	1889H	2.100	1.50	3.00	7.00	35.00
	1890	1.500	1.50	3.00	9.00	40.00
	1890	—	—	—	Proof	275.00
	1890H	5.400	1.50	3.00	6.00	25.00
	1891	6.150	1.50	3.00	6.00	25.00
	1891H	1.750	1.50	3.00	8.00	38.00
	1892	5.500	1.50	3.00	6.00	25.00
	1892	—	—	—	Proof	250.00
	1892H	1.100	3.00	10.00	15.00	40.00
	1892H	—	—	—	Proof	250.00
	1893	11.250	1.50	3.00	6.00	25.00
	1894	16.750	1.50	3.00	6.00	25.00
	1894	—	—	—	Proof	250.00
	1895	19.000	1.50	3.00	6.00	25.00
	1896	16.500	1.50	3.00	6.00	25.00
	1897	23.500	1.50	3.00	6.00	22.50
	1897H	10.500	1.50	3.00	6.00	22.50
	1897H	—	—	—	Proof	400.00
	1898	29.500	1.50	3.00	6.00	22.50
	1899	33.842	1.00	2.00	3.50	22.50
	1900	7.758	1.00	2.00	3.50	22.50
	1900H	41.500	1.00	2.00	3.50	22.50

NOTE: Coins dated 1866-68 struck at the Hong Kong Mint; 1869-1901 at the Royal Mint.
NOTE: Later date (1901) exists for this type.

20 CENTS

5.4308 g, .800 SILVER, .1397 oz ASW

KM#	Date	Mintage	Fine	VF	XF	Unc
7	1866	.445	12.00	30.00	65.00	335.00
	1866 reeded edge		—	—	Proof	1000.
	1866 plain edge		—	—	Proof	1500.
	1867	Inc. Ab.	16.00	35.00	75.00	400.00
	1867	—	—	—	Proof	1000.
	1868	Inc. Ab.	12.00	30.00	65.00	325.00
	1868	—	—	—	Proof	1000.
	1872/68H	.064	18.00	40.00	80.00	500.00
	1872H	Inc. Ab.	12.00	30.00	65.00	335.00
	1872H	—	—	—	Proof	1600.
	1873	.096	12.00	30.00	70.00	350.00
	1873 plain edge		—	—	Proof	2500.
	1873 reeded edge		—	—	Proof	3450.
	1873H	.064	12.00	30.00	70.00	350.00
	1874H	.070	12.00	30.00	70.00	350.00
	1875H	.070	12.00	30.00	70.00	350.00
	1875H	—	—	—	Proof	1500.
	1876H	.120	10.00	30.00	65.00	350.00
	1877H	.060	12.00	30.00	75.00	375.00
	1879	.020	225.00	500.00	900.00	2000.
	1879	—	—	—	Proof	6325.
	1880H	.025	75.00	125.00	265.00	650.00
	1881	.030	125.00	225.00	500.00	1350.
	1881	—	—	—	Proof	2650.
	1882H	.100	12.00	30.00	65.00	335.00
	1882H	—	—	—	Proof	1600.
	1883	.138	12.00	30.00	65.00	335.00
	1883	—	—	—	Proof	1250.
	1883H	.063	16.00	35.00	75.00	375.00
	1883H	—	—	—	Proof	1250.
	1884	.080	10.00	28.00	60.00	300.00
	1884	—	—	—	Proof	1250.
	1885	.260	10.00	20.00	40.00	225.00
	1885	—	—	—	Proof	1150.
	1886	.175	10.00	20.00	40.00	225.00
	1886	—	—	—	Proof	1150.
	1887	.200	10.00	20.00	40.00	225.00
	1887	—	—	—	Proof	1150.
	1888	.500	8.00	17.50	35.00	200.00
	1888	—	—	—	Proof	1150.
	1889	.440	8.00	17.50	35.00	200.00
	1889	—	—	—	Proof	1150.
	1889H	.175	10.00	20.00	40.00	225.00
	1890	.125	10.00	20.00	40.00	225.00
	1890H	.450	8.00	17.50	35.00	200.00
	1891	.575	8.00	17.50	35.00	200.00
	1891	—	—	—	Proof	2300.
	1891H	.175	10.00	20.00	45.00	240.00
	1892	.450	8.00	17.50	35.00	200.00
	1892	—	—	—	Proof	1725.
	1892H	.100	12.50	22.00	50.00	250.00
	1892H	—	—	—	Proof	1625.
	1893	.750	8.00	16.50	30.00	150.00
	1894	.650	8.00	16.50	30.00	150.00
	1894	—	—	—	Proof	500.00
	1895	.500	8.00	16.50	30.00	150.00
	1896	.250	8.00	16.50	30.00	150.00
	1898	.125	8.00	16.50	30.00	175.00

NOTE: Coins dated 1866-68 struck at the Hong Kong Mint; 1872-98 at the Royal Mint.

1/2 DOLLAR

13.478(-13.58) g, .900 SILVER, .3900 oz ASW

KM#	Date	Mintage	Fine	VF	XF	Unc
8	1866	.059	250.00	450.00	850.00	2400.
	1866 reeded edge		—	—	Proof	5500.
	1866 plain edge		—	—	Proof	*Rare
	1867	Inc. Ab.	300.00	650.00	1450.	4000.
	1867	—	—	—	Proof	**Rare
	1868	—	—	—	Proof	***Rare

NOTE: Struck at the Hong Kong Mint.

***NOTE:** Superior Goodman sale 5-95 choice brilliant proof realized, $14,375.

****NOTE:** Superior Goodman sale 5-95 brilliant proof realized, $16,675.

*****NOTE:** Superior Goodman sale 5-95 choice proof realized, $109,250.

50 CENTS

13.5769 g, .800 SILVER, .3492 oz ASW, 31mm
Obv: W/o mint mark.

KM#	Date	Mintage	Fine	VF	XF	Unc
9.1	1890	.050	25.00	50.00	100.00	600.00
	1890	—	—	—	Proof	1250.
	1891	.150	20.00	40.00	75.00	550.00
	1891	—	—	—	Proof	1450.
	1892	.090	25.00	50.00	100.00	600.00
	1892	—	—	—	Proof	1250.
	1893	.150	20.00	40.00	75.00	550.00
	1894	.130	20.00	40.00	75.00	550.00
	1894	—	—	—	Proof	1200.

32mm
Obv: Mint mark below bust.

KM#	Date	Mintage	Fine	VF	XF	Unc
9.2	1891H	.070	30.00	50.00	90.00	500.00
	1892H	.020	50.00	100.00	200.00	700.00
	1892H	—	—	—	Proof	1500.

DOLLAR

26.9568(-27.25) g, .900 SILVER, .7800 oz ASW

KM#	Date	Mintage	Fine	VF	XF	Unc
10	1866	2.108	165.00	300.00	600.00	1700.
	1866 reeded edge		—	—	Proof	3500.
	1866 plain edge		—	—	Proof	4500.
	1867/6	Inc. Ab.	250.00	450.00	800.00	1850.
	1867	Inc. Ab.	165.00	300.00	600.00	1650.
	1867	—	—	—	Proof	5000.
	1868	Inc. Ab.	165.00	300.00	600.00	1650.
	1868	—	—	—	Proof	4500.

NOTE: Struck at the Hong Kong Mint.

PATTERNS (Pn)

(Including off metal strikes)

OBVERSE TYPES

Type A Type B

Type C Type D

KM#	Date	Mintage	Identification	Mkt.Val.
Pn1	ND	—	1 Cent, Copper, Obv. A, Rev. similar to KM#Pn13. PR#254	1725.
Pn2	ND	—	1 Cent, Copper, Obv. A, Rev. St. George and dragon in center, lion R.M.T.G., and anchors in angles PR#255	—
Pn3	1862	—	1 Cent, Copper, Obv. A, Rev. Wreath around center circle dividing value, HONG KONG at top, date at bottom. PR#256	—
Pn4	1862	—	1 Cent, Copper, Obv. A, Rev: Similar to KM#Pn3 but w/date between lions PR#257	—
Pn5	1862	—	1 Cent, Copper, Obv. A, Rev: Similar to KM#Pn3 but w/T.G. and T.M. at sides. PR#258	—
Pn6	1862	—	1 Cent, Copper, Obv. A, Rev: Similar to KM#Pn24. PR#259	—
Pn7	1862	—	1 Cent, Copper, Obv. A, Rev: Similar to KM#Pn24 but w/date between anchor and lion. PR#260	—
Pn8	1862	—	1 Cent, Copper, Obv. A, Rev: Similar to KM#Pn24 but w/date between crown and dragon. PR#261	2415.
Pn9	1862	—	1 Cent, Copper, Obv. A, Rev: Similar to KM#Pn24 but w/crown in center circle and anchor and lion between date. PR#262	—
Pn10	1862	—	1 Cent, Copper, Obv. A, Rev: Similar to KM#Pn9 but w/date between crown and dragon. PR#263	—

KM#	Date	Mintage	Identification	Mkt.Val.
Pn11	1862	—	1 Cent, Copper. PR#264	—
Pn12	1862	—	1 Cent, Copper, Obv. A, Rev: Center dot value and date in outer circle. PR#265	—

KM#	Date	Mintage	Identification	Mkt.Val.
Pn13	ND	—	1 Cent, Copper. PR#267	1150.
Pn14	1862	—	1 Cent, Copper, Obv. B, Rev: Similar to KM#Pn3. PR#268	—
Pn15	1862	—	1 Cent, Copper, Obv. B, Rev: Similar to KM#Pn4. PR#269	—
Pn16	1862	—	1 Cent, Copper, Obv. B, Rev: Similar to KM#Pn6. PR#270	—
Pn17	1862	—	1 Cent, Copper, Obv. B, Rev: Similar to KM#Pn7. PR#271	—
Pn18	1862	—	1 Cent, Copper, Obv. B, Rev: Similar to KM#Pn11. PR#272	1610.
Pn19	1862	—	1 Cent, Copper, Obv. B, Rev: Similar to KM#Pn12. PR#273	—
Pn20	ND	—	1 Cent, Copper, Obv. C, Rev: Similar to KM#Pn13. PR#275	—

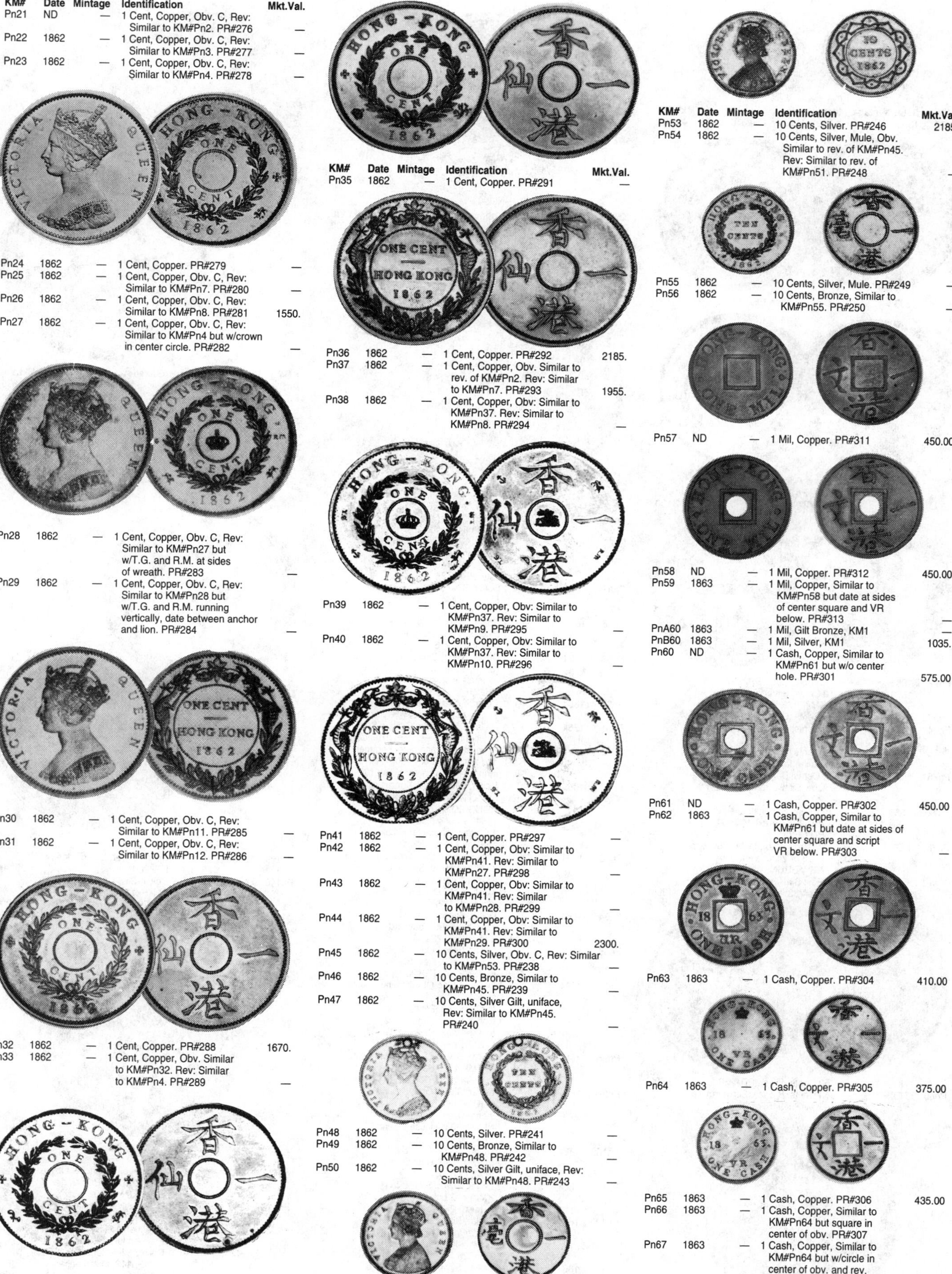

KM#	Date	Mintage	Identification	Mkt.Val.
Pn21	ND	—	1 Cent, Copper, Obv. C, Rev: Similar to KM#Pn2. PR#276	—
Pn22	1862	—	1 Cent, Copper, Obv. C, Rev: Similar to KM#Pn3. PR#277	—
Pn23	1862	—	1 Cent, Copper, Obv. C, Rev: Similar to KM#Pn4. PR#278	—
Pn24	1862	—	1 Cent, Copper. PR#279	—
Pn25	1862	—	1 Cent, Copper, Obv. C, Rev: Similar to KM#Pn7. PR#280	—
Pn26	1862	—	1 Cent, Copper, Obv. C, Rev: Similar to KM#Pn8. PR#281	1550.
Pn27	1862	—	1 Cent, Copper, Obv. C, Rev: Similar to KM#Pn4 but w/crown in center circle. PR#282	—
Pn28	1862	—	1 Cent, Copper, Obv. C, Rev: Similar to KM#Pn27 but w/T.G. and R.M. at sides of wreath. PR#283	—
Pn29	1862	—	1 Cent, Copper, Obv. C, Rev: Similar to KM#Pn28 but w/T.G. and R.M. running vertically, date between anchor and lion. PR#284	—
Pn30	1862	—	1 Cent, Copper, Obv. C, Rev: Similar to KM#Pn11. PR#285	—
Pn31	1862	—	1 Cent, Copper, Obv. C, Rev: Similar to KM#Pn12. PR#286	—
Pn32	1862	—	1 Cent, Copper. PR#288	1670.
Pn33	1862	—	1 Cent, Copper, Obv. Similar to KM#Pn32. Rev: Similar to KM#Pn4. PR#289	—
Pn34	1862	—	1 Cent, Copper, Obv. Similar to KM#Pn32. Rev: Similar to KM#Pn6. PR#290	1725.
Pn35	1862	—	1 Cent, Copper. PR#291	—
Pn36	1862	—	1 Cent, Copper. PR#292	2185.
Pn37	1862	—	1 Cent, Copper, Obv. Similar to rev. of KM#Pn2. Rev: Similar to KM#Pn7. PR#293	1955.
Pn38	1862	—	1 Cent, Copper, Obv: Similar to KM#Pn37. Rev: Similar to KM#Pn8. PR#294	—
Pn39	1862	—	1 Cent, Copper, Obv: Similar to KM#Pn37. Rev: Similar to KM#Pn9. PR#295	—
Pn40	1862	—	1 Cent, Copper, Obv: Similar to KM#Pn37. Rev: Similar to KM#Pn10. PR#296	—
Pn41	1862	—	1 Cent, Copper. PR#297	—
Pn42	1862	—	1 Cent, Copper, Obv: Similar to KM#Pn41. Rev: Similar to KM#Pn27. PR#298	—
Pn43	1862	—	1 Cent, Copper, Obv: Similar to KM#Pn41. Rev: Similar to KM#Pn28. PR#299	—
Pn44	1862	—	1 Cent, Copper, Obv: Similar to KM#Pn41. Rev: Similar to KM#Pn29. PR#300	2300.
Pn45	1862	—	10 Cents, Silver, Obv. C, Rev: Similar to KM#Pn53. PR#238	—
Pn46	1862	—	10 Cents, Bronze, Similar to KM#Pn45. PR#239	—
Pn47	1862	—	10 Cents, Silver Gilt, uniface, Rev: Similar to KM#Pn45. PR#240	—
Pn48	1862	—	10 Cents, Silver. PR#241	—
Pn49	1862	—	10 Cents, Bronze, Similar to KM#Pn48. PR#242	—
Pn50	1862	—	10 Cents, Silver Gilt, uniface, Rev: Similar to KM#Pn48. PR#243	—
Pn51	ND	—	10 Cents, Silver. PR#244	—
Pn52	ND	—	10 Cents, Bronze, Similar to KM#Pn51. PR#245	—
Pn53	1862	—	10 Cents, Silver. PR#246	2185.
Pn54	1862	—	10 Cents, Silver, Mule, Obv. Similar to rev. of KM#Pn45. Rev: Similar to rev. of KM#Pn51. PR#248	—
Pn55	1862	—	10 Cents, Silver, Mule. PR#249	—
Pn56	1862	—	10 Cents, Bronze, Similar to KM#Pn55. PR#250	—
Pn57	ND	—	1 Mil, Copper. PR#311	450.00
Pn58	ND	—	1 Mil, Copper. PR#312	450.00
Pn59	1863	—	1 Mil, Copper, Similar to KM#Pn58 but date at sides of center square and VR below. PR#313	—
PnA60	1863	—	1 Mil, Gilt Bronze, KM1	—
PnB60	1863	—	1 Mil, Silver, KM1	1035.
Pn60	ND	—	1 Cash, Copper, Similar to KM#Pn61 but w/o center hole. PR#301	575.00
Pn61	ND	—	1 Cash, Copper. PR#302	450.00
Pn62	1863	—	1 Cash, Copper, Similar to KM#Pn61 but date at sides of center square and script VR below. PR#303	—
Pn63	1863	—	1 Cash, Copper. PR#304	410.00
Pn64	1863	—	1 Cash, Copper. PR#305	375.00
Pn65	1863	—	1 Cash, Copper. PR#306	435.00
Pn66	1863	—	1 Cash, Copper, Similar to KM#Pn64 but square in center of obv. PR#307	
Pn67	1863	—	1 Cash, Copper, Similar to KM#Pn64 but w/circle in center of obv. and rev. PR#308	410.00
Pn68	1863	—	1 Cash, Copper, Similar to KM#Pn67 but w/round center hole. PR#309	410.00

KM#	Date	Mintage	Identification	Mkt.Val.
Pn69	1863	—	1 Cash, Copper. PR#310	410.00

KM#	Date	Mintage	Identification	Mkt.Val.
Pn70	1863	—	1 Cent, Copper. PR#266	—

KM#	Date	Mintage	Identification	Mkt.Val.
Pn71	1863	—	1 Cent, Copper, Similar to KM#Pn19 but date added. PR#274	1150.
Pn72	1863	—	1 Cent, Copper. PR#287	—
Pn73	1863	—	10 Cents, Silver, Similar to KM#Pn72. PR#247	—
PnA74	1863	—	10 Cents, Copper, KM6.1	—
Pn74	ND	—	10 Cents, Silver Gilt, uniface, Obv. similar to KM#Pn73. PR#251	—
Pn75	1863	—	10 Cents, Silver Gilt, uniface, Rev. Similar to KM#Pn73. PR#252	—
Pn76	ND	—	10 Cents, Bartons metal, uniface Obv. Similar to KM#Pn73. PR#251a	—
Pn77	1863	—	10 Cents, Bartons metal, uniface, Rev. Similar to KM#Pn73. PR#252a	—
Pn78	ND	—	10 Cents, Silver, Mule. Obv. bare head of Victoria left NEW BRUNSWICK below. Rev: Similar to KM#Pn48. PR#253	1200.
Pn79	ND	—	50 Cents, Silver. PR#236	29,900.
Pn80	ND	—	50 Cents, Bronze, Similar to KM#Pn49. PR#237	—

KM#	Date	Mintage	Identification	Mkt.Val.
Pn81	ND	—	1 Dollar, Silver. PR#198	126,500.
Pn82	ND	—	1 Dollar, Bronze, Similar to KM#Pn81. PR#199	—
Pn83	1863	—	1 Dollar, Silver, Similar to KM#Pn84. PR#210	—
Pn84	1863	—	1 Dollar, Silver. PR#211	—
Pn85	1863	—	1 Dollar, Copper, Similar to KM#Pn84. PR#212	—
Pn86	1864	—	1 Dollar, Silver, Obv. C. Rev. Inner circle similar to KM#Pn72 outer border w/archers and dots. PR#213	—
Pn87	1864	—	1 Dollar, Silver, uniface, Rev. Similar to KM#Pn86. PR#214	—
Pn88	1864	—	1 Dollar, Silver, Obv. C. Rev. 4 cruciform shields, branches of oak PR#215	66,125.
Pn89	1864	—	1 Dollar, Silver, Similar to KM#Pn88 but Chinese characters on shields. PR#216	—
Pn90	1864	—	1 Dollar, Silver, uniface, Rev. Similar to KM#Pn89. PR#217	—
Pn91	1864	—	1 Dollar, Silver, Obv. C. Rev. Shields at top, bottom, left, right extending to edge value and date, hammer and retort, anchor, TG and HK monograms in center. PR#218	—
Pn92	1864	—	1 Dollar, Silver, Obv. Portrait of obv. C w/"VICTORIA QUEEN. HONG KONG ONE DOLLAR. 1864" around border. Rev: 4 Chinese characters in circle and oak wreath. PR#219	—
Pn93	1864	—	1 Dollar, Silver, Obv. Similar to KM#Pn92. Rev. Similar to KM#Pn83 but w/"HONG KONG ONE DOLLAR 1864" incuse. PR#220	—
Pn94	1864	—	1 Dollar, Silver, Similar to KM#Pn92 but w/outward arches. PR#221	—
Pn95	1864	—	1 Dollar, Silver, Obv. Similar to KM#Pn92, Rev: Similar to KM#Pn93. PR#222	—
Pn96	1864	—	1 Dollar, Silver, Obv. Similar to KM#Pn92. Rev: Similar to KM#Pn83. PR#223	—
Pn97	1864	—	1 Dollar, Silver, Obv. Similar to KM#Pn92. Rev: Similar to KM#Pn84. PR#224	—
Pn98	1864	—	1 Dollar, Silver, Obv. Similar to KM#Pn92. Rev: Similar to KM#Pn86. PR#225	—
Pn99	1864	—	1 Dollar, Silver, Obv. Similar to KM#Pn92 but legend incuse. Rev. Similar to KM#Pn93 w/incuse legend. PR#226	—
Pn100	1864	—	1 Dollar, Silver, Obv. Similar to KM#Pn99, Rev: Similar to KM#Pn86.	—
Pn101	1864	—	1 Dollar, Silver, Similar to KM#Pn99 but legend in relief. PR#228	—
Pn102	1864	—	1 Dollar, Silver, uniface, Obv. similar to KM#Pn99 but smaller inner circle. PR#229	—
Pn103	1864	—	1 Dollar, Silver, Obv: Similar to KM#Pn102. Rev: Similar to KM#Pn92. PR#230	—
Pn104	1864	—	1 Dollar, Silver, Obv. Similar to KM#Pn88. PR#231	—

KM#	Date	Mintage	Identification	Mkt.Val.
Pn105	1864	—	1 Dollar, Silver. PR#232	71,875.
Pn106	1864	—	1 Dollar, Pewter, Similar to KM#Pn105. PR#233	—
Pn107	1864	—	1 Dollar, Silver, Obv. Similar to KM#Pn104. Rev. Similar to KM#Pn91. PR#234	—
Pn108	1864	—	1 Dollar, Silver, uniface, Rev. similar to KM#Pn91 but w/o devices in angles. PR#235	—
Pn109	1865	—	1 Dollar, Silver. Milled edge. PR#200	25,300.
Pn110	1865	—	1 Dollar, Silver, Similar to KM#Pn109, plain edge. PR#201	29,900.
Pn111	1865	—	1 Dollar, Lead, uniface, Obv. Similar to KM#Pn109, die defaced. PR#202	—
Pn112	1865	—	1 Dollar, Silver, Similar to KM#Pn109 but "TRIAL" in relief behind Queen's head Plain edge. PR#203	—
Pn113	1865	—	1 Dollar, Silver, Similar to KM#Pn112. Milled edge. PR#204	11,500.
Pn114	1865	—	1 Dollar, Copper, Similar to KM#Pn112. Milled edge. PR#205	4370.

KM#	Date	Mintage	Identification	Mkt.Val.
Pn115	1865	—	1 Dollar, Copper, Similar to KM#Pn112. Diagonal milled edge. Obv: w/TRIAL, PR206	—
Pn116	1865	—	1 Dollar, Silver, Obv. C, w/TRIAL incused behind Queen's head. Rev: Similar to KM#Pn109. Milled edge. PR#207	—

KM#	Date	Mintage	Identification	Mkt.Val.
Pn117	1865	—	1 Dollar, Silver. PR#208	10,925.
Pn118	ND (1865)	—	1 Dollar, Silver, Obv. Similar to KM#Pn94. PR#209	—
Pn119	1866	—	5 Cents, Copper, KM5	—
Pn120	1866	—	10 Cents, Copper, KM6.1	485.00
Pn121	1866	—	1 Dollar, Copper, KM10	1725.

KM#	Date	Mintage	Identification	Mkt.Val.
Pn122	1867	—	1 Tael, Silver. PR#314	120,750.
Pn123	1869	—	10 Cents, Copper, KM6.1	1325.
Pn124	1873	—	10 Cents, Copper, KM6.1	—
Pn125	1877	—	1 Cent, Nickel, KM4.2, 15 pearls	—
Pn126	1894	—	10 Cents, Aluminum, c/m: SPECIMEN, KM#6.3	—
Pn127	1897	—	10 Cents, Aluminum, KM6.1, SPECIMEN	—

NOTE: Market values listed in the Pattern section were obtained from the Superior Goorman sale of 5-95.

PIEFORTS (P)

KM#	Date	Mintage	Identification	Mkt.Val.
P1	1886	—	10 Cents, Brass, KM6.3	200.00

PROOF SETS (PS)

KM#	Date	Mintage	Identification	Issue Price	Mkt. Val.
PS1	1866(5)	—	KM5,6.2,7-8,10	—	11,500.
PS2	1873(3)	1 known	KM5,6.3,7	—	7000.
PS3	1885(3)	1 known	KM5,6.3,7	—	5000.

HUNGARY

The Republic of Hungary, located in central Europe, has an area of 35,929 sq. mi. (93,030 sq. km.) and a population of 10.7 million. Capital: Budapest. The economy is based on agriculture, bauxite and a rapidly expanding industrial sector. Machinery, chemicals, iron and steel, and fruits and vegetables are exported.

The ancient kingdom of Hungary, founded by the Magyars in the 9th century, achieved its greatest extension in the mid-14th century when its dominions touched the Baltic, Black and Mediterranean Seas. After suffering repeated Turkish invasions, Hungary accepted Habsburg rule to escape Turkish occupation, regaining independence in 1867 with the Emperor of Austria as king of a dual Austro-Hungarian monarchy.

RULERS

Austrian until 1918

MINT MARKS

A, CA, WI - Vienna (Becs)
B, K, KB - Kremnitz (Kormoczbanya)
BP - Budapest
CH - Pressburg (Pozsony)
CM - Kaschau (Kassa)
(c) - castle - Pressburg
(d) - double trefoil - Pressburg
G, GN, NB - Nagybanya
(g) - GC script monogram - Pressburg
GYF - Karlsburg (Gyulafehervar)
HA - Hall
(L) - ICB monogram - Pressburg
(r) - rampant lion left - Pressburg
S - Schmollnitz (Szomolnok)

MONETARY SYSTEM

Until 1857

2 Poltura = 3 Krajczar
60 Krajczar = 1 Forint (Gulden)
2 Forint = 1 Convention Thaler

1857-1891

100 Krajczar = 1 Forint

1892-1925

100 Filler = 1 Korona

NOTE: Many coins of Hungary through 1948, especially 1925-1945, have been restruck in recent times. These may be identified by a rosette in the vicinity of the mint mark. Restrike mintages for KM#440-449, 451-458, 468-469, 475-477, 480-483, 494, 496-498 are usually about 1000 pieces, later date mintages are not known.

5/10 KRAJCZAR

COPPER
Mint mark: KB

KM#	Date	Mintage	Fine	VF	XF	Unc
468	1882	2.400	2.50	4.00	5.50	9.00
	1882	(restrike)	—	—	Proof	8.00

KRAJCZAR

COPPER
Mint mark: KB

KM#	Date	Mintage	Fine	VF	XF	Unc
441.1	1868	12.530	.50	1.00	2.00	4.50
	1868	(restrike)	—	—	Proof	10.00
	1869	5.070	.50	1.25	3.00	8.50
	1872	—	.50	1.50	3.00	7.50
	1873	—	35.00	65.00	100.00	150.00

Mint mark: GYF

KM#	Date	Mintage	Fine	VF	XF	Unc
441.2	1868	—	—	—	Rare	—

Mint mark: KB

KM#	Date	Mintage	Fine	VF	XF	Unc
458	1878	4.480	12.00	18.00	30.00	45.00
	1879	10.101	3.00	7.50	12.00	17.50
	1881	12.233	3.00	7.50	12.00	17.50
	1882	19.800	5.00	11.00	17.50	27.50
	1883	8.535	9.00	15.00	27.50	35.00
	1885	26.606	1.25	3.50	7.50	12.00
	1886	17.671	2.00	5.50	9.00	15.00
	1887	11.989	2.50	6.00	12.00	18.00
	1888	10.334	3.50	7.00	12.00	18.00

NOTE: Wreath varieties exist for 1878 dated coins.

Mule. Obv: KM#441. Rev: KM#458.

KM#	Date	Mintage	Fine	VF	XF	Unc
459	1878	—	25.00	35.00	60.00	85.00

KM#	Date	Mintage	Fine	VF	XF	Unc
478	1891*	16.272	2.50	5.00	8.00	14.50
	1892	5.871	7.00	15.00	22.50	32.50

***NOTE:** Variations in thickness of planchet exist.

4 KRAJCZAR

COPPER
Mint mark: KB

KM#	Date	Mintage	Fine	VF	XF	Unc
442	1868	3.100	3.00	7.50	15.00	30.00
	1868	(restrike)	—	—	Proof	18.00

NOTE: Wreath varieties exist.

10 KRAJCZAR

3.8900 g, .500 SILVER, .0625 oz ASW

KM#	Date	Mintage	Fine	VF	XF	Unc
421	1837	—	100.00	175.00	300.00	475.00
	1838	—	50.00	90.00	140.00	240.00
	1839	—	4.00	10.00	20.00	35.00
	1840	—	5.00	12.00	24.00	50.00
	1841	—	4.50	10.00	20.00	35.00
	1842	—	4.50	10.00	20.00	35.00
	1843	—	5.00	12.00	24.00	50.00
	1844	—	5.00	9.00	17.50	32.50
	1845	—	5.00	9.00	17.50	32.50
	1846	—	4.00	8.00	15.00	27.00
	1847	—	2.50	4.00	9.00	18.00
	1848	—	2.50	4.00	9.00	18.00

2.0000 g, .500 SILVER, .0321 oz ASW
Mint mark: KB
Obv. leg: . . . AP.KIRALYA.
Rev. leg: VALTO PENZ.

KM#	Date	Mintage	Fine	VF	XF	Unc
440.1	1867	c.1,000	—	—	—	—
	1868	—	15.00	35.00	60.00	120.00
	1868	(restrike)	—	—	Proof	20.00

Mint mark: GYF

KM#	Date	Mintage	Fine	VF	XF	Unc
440.2	1868	—	15.00	35.00	60.00	120.00

1.6600 g, .400 SILVER, .0213 oz ASW
Rev. leg: MAGYAR KIRALYI VALTO PENZ.

KM#	Date	Mintage	Fine	VF	XF	Unc
443.1	1868	3.250	12.00	25.00	40.00	65.00
	1868	(restrike)	—	—	Proof	22.50
	1869	12.747	6.00	22.50	40.00	65.00

Mint mark: GYF

KM#	Date	Mintage	Fine	VF	XF	Unc
443.2	1868	1.012	20.00	40.00	85.00	175.00
	1869	2.747	12.00	25.00	40.00	70.00

NOTE: Varieties exist.

Mint mark: KB
Obv. leg: AP.KIR. Rev. leg: VALTO PENZ.

KM#	Date	Mintage	Fine	VF	XF	Unc
451.1	1870	21.933	3.50	7.50	18.00	35.00
	1870	(restrike)	—	—	Proof	17.50
	1871	(restrike from 1885)		—	Rare	—
	1872	1.154	7.50	15.00	30.00	50.00
	1873	1.066	7.50	15.00	30.00	50.00
	1874	1.324	9.00	18.00	35.00	55.00
	1875	.425	18.00	27.50	55.00	80.00
	1876	.518	10.00	27.50	55.00	80.00
	1877	.460	15.00	32.00	58.00	85.00
	1887	.025	80.00	135.00	190.00	275.00
	1888	.358	9.00	18.00	35.00	65.00
	1889	—	—	Reported, not confirmed		

Mint mark: GYF

KM#	Date	Mintage	Fine	VF	XF	Unc
451.2	1870	3.032	7.50	15.00	30.00	50.00
	1871	3.383	7.50	15.00	30.00	50.00

Mint mark: KB
Mule. Obv: KM#451.1. Rev. KM#440.1.

KM#	Date	Mintage	Fine	VF	XF	Unc
444	1868	—	—	—	Rare	—
	1868	(restrike)	—	—	Proof	20.00

20 KRAJCZAR

SILVER
Mint mark: A
Obv: Ribbons on wreath forward across neck.
Rev: Madonna with child.

KM#	Date	Mintage	Fine	VF	XF	Unc
415.1	1830	—	55.00	110.00	220.00	400.00

Obv: Left ribbon on wreath behind neck.

KM#	Date	Mintage	Fine	VF	XF	Unc
415.2	1830	—	100.00	200.00	350.00	600.00
	1831	—	—	Reported, not confirmed		

Mint mark: B
Obv: Both ribbons on wreath behind neck.

KM#	Date	Mintage	Fine	VF	XF	Unc
415.3	1832	—	40.00	80.00	160.00	325.00
	1833	—	12.50	25.00	50.00	100.00
	1834	—	5.00	10.00	25.00	50.00
	1835	—	10.00	20.00	40.00	80.00

6.6800 g, .583 SILVER, .1252 oz ASW
Obv. leg: FERD. I. Rev. leg: S. MARIA. . .

KM#	Date	Mintage	Fine	VF	XF	Unc
422	1837	—	4.00	7.50	15.00	35.00
	1838	—	4.00	7.50	15.00	35.00
	1839	—	3.50	5.00	7.50	20.00
	1840	—	3.50	5.00	7.50	20.00
	1841	—	3.50	5.00	7.50	20.00
	1842	—	4.00	7.50	15.00	30.00
	1843	—	3.50	5.00	7.50	20.00
	1844	—	3.50	5.00	7.50	20.00
	1845	—	3.50	5.00	7.50	20.00
	1846	—	3.50	5.00	7.50	20.00
	1847	—	3.50	5.00	7.50	20.00
	1848	—	3.50	5.00	7.50	20.00

2.6600 g, .500 SILVER, .0427 oz ASW
Mint mark: KB
Obv. leg: . . . AP.KIRALYA.

Rev. leg: VALTO PENZ.

KM#	Date	Mintage	Fine	VF	XF	Unc
445.1	1868	—	15.00	40.00	70.00	150.00
	1868	(restrike)	—	—	Proof	20.00

Mint mark: GYF

KM#	Date	Mintage	Fine	VF	XF	Unc
445.2	1868	—	35.00	80.00	120.00	170.00

Mint mark: KB
Rev. leg: MAGYAR KIRALYI VALTO PENZ.

KM#	Date	Mintage	Fine	VF	XF	Unc
446.1	1868	3.224	7.50	17.50	32.50	60.00
	1868	(restrike)	—	—	Proof	20.00
	1869	9.487	5.00	14.00	24.00	50.00

Mint mark: GYF

KM#	Date	Mintage	Fine	VF	XF	Unc
446.2	1868	1.039	9.50	20.00	42.00	80.00
	1869	2.299	9.00	17.50	35.00	65.00

NOTE: Varieties exist.

Mint mark: KB
Rev. leg: VALTO PENZ.

KM#	Date	Mintage	Fine	VF	XF	Unc
452.1	1870	4.427	12.50	27.50	65.00	110.00
	1870	(restrike)	—	—	Proof	20.00
	1871	25 pcs. (restrike from 1855)			Proof	—
	1872	1.286	27.50	55.00	110.00	160.00

Mint mark: GYF

KM#	Date	Mintage	Fine	VF	XF	Unc
452.2	1870	7.213	30.00	65.00	110.00	150.00

Mint mark: KB
Mule. Obv: KM#452.1. Rev: KM#445.1.

KM#	Date	Mintage	Fine	VF	XF	Unc
447	1868	—	—	—	Rare	—
	1868	(restrike)	—	—	Proof	20.00

FORINT

12.3457 g, .900 SILVER, .3572 oz ASW
Mint mark: KB

KM#	Date	Mintage	Fine	VF	XF	Unc
449.1	1868	.570	11.00	17.50	35.00	70.00
	1868	(restrike)	—	—	Proof	40.00
	1869	.490	10.00	20.00	27.50	45.00
	1869 plain edge	—	—	—	—	—

Mint mark: GYF

KM#	Date	Mintage	Fine	VF	XF	Unc
449.2	1868	.270	11.00	22.50	30.00	60.00
	1869	.360	7.50	15.00	30.00	45.00

Mint mark: KB

KM#	Date	Mintage	Fine	VF	XF	Unc
453.1	1870	1.250	15.00	32.50	62.50	110.00
	1871	2.440	12.00	25.00	45.00	90.00
	1872	3.456	7.00	15.00	30.00	60.00
	1873	2.338	12.00	25.00	50.00	90.00
	1874	2.082	12.00	25.00	50.00	90.00
	1875	2.074	8.00	16.00	32.50	55.00
	1876	4.136	5.00	8.00	12.50	22.50
	1877	2.241	5.00	8.00	12.50	22.50
	1878	5.717	5.00	8.00	12.50	22.50
	1879	25.756	5.00	8.00	12.50	22.50

Mint mark: GYF

KM#	Date	Mintage	Fine	VF	XF	Unc
453.2	1870	.570	80.00	150.00	225.00	500.00
	1871	.240	300.00	425.00	625.00	1100.

Mint mark: KB
Obv: Larger head and legends.

KM#	Date	Mintage	Fine	VF	XF	Unc
465	1880	3.815	5.00	8.00	12.00	22.50
	1881	15.495	4.50	6.00	9.00	15.00

NOTE: Varieties exist.

KM#	Date	Mintage	Fine	VF	XF	Unc
469	1882	1.897	7.00	12.50	25.00	50.00
	1883	7.041	5.00	8.00	12.50	22.50
	1884	1.722	5.00	10.00	20.00	40.00
	1885	1.672	5.00	10.00	20.00	40.00
	1886	1.566	7.00	12.50	25.00	50.00
	1887	2.022	5.00	10.00	20.00	40.00
	1888	1.841	5.00	10.00	18.00	35.00
	1889	1.974	5.00	10.00	18.00	35.00
	1890	2.022	6.50	12.50	25.00	50.00

NOTE: Variety exists for 1882 date w/larger mint mark.

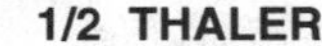

KM#	Date	Mintage	Fine	VF	XF	Unc
475	1890	Inc. Ab.	10.00	20.00	35.00	55.00
	1891	1.470	7.50	15.00	22.50	45.00
	1892	1.607	7.00	15.00	22.50	45.00
	1892	(restrike)	—	—	Proof	25.00

1/2 THALER

14.0300 g, .833 SILVER, .3757 oz ASW
Mint mark: A

KM#	Date	Mintage	Fine	VF	XF	Unc
416	1830	—	100.00	170.00	250.00	400.00

Mint mark: B

KM#	Date	Mintage	Fine	VF	XF	Unc
420	1831	*	125.00	225.00	475.00	725.00
	1833	*	70.00	180.00	320.00	550.00
	1834	—	275.00	450.00	600.00	1000.

NOTE: 1831 and 1833 dated coins are restrikes from 1841.

KM#	Date	Mintage	Fine	VF	XF	Unc
423	1837	—	300.00	550.00	900.00	1250.
	1839	—	450.00	800.00	1350.	1800.

THALER

.833 SILVER
Obv: Head right, ribbons on wreath forward across neck. Rev: Madonna w/child.

KM#	Date	Mintage	Fine	VF	XF	Unc
417.1	1830	—	65.00	140.00	275.00	525.00

Mint mark: B

KM#	Date	Mintage	Fine	VF	XF	Unc
417.2	1830	—	275.00	550.00	900.00	1350.

Obv: Ribbons on wreath behind neck.

KM#	Date	Mintage	Fine	VF	XF	Unc
418	1830	—	—	Reported, not confirmed		
	1831	—	95.00	160.00	400.00	725.00
	1833	—	80.00	120.00	325.00	475.00

NOTE: 1831 and 1833 dated coins are restrikes from 1841.

Obv: Head right, leg: FERD I. D.G. . .

KM#	Date	Mintage	Fine	VF	XF	Unc
424	1837	—	400.00	700.00	1000.	1400.
	1839	—	—	—	Rare	—

WAR OF INDEPENDENCE

1848-1849

EGY (1) KRAJCZAR

COPPER
Mint: Kremnitz

KM#	Date	Mintage	Fine	VF	XF	Unc
430.1	1848	—	2.00	6.00	12.50	25.00

Mint mark: NB

KM#	Date	Mintage	Fine	VF	XF	Unc
430.2	1849	—	20.00	40.00	60.00	100.00

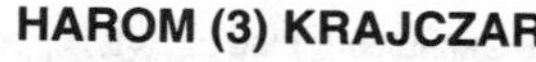

HAROM (3) KRAJCZAR

COPPER
Mint mark: NB

KM#	Date	Mintage	Fine	VF	XF	Unc
434	1849	—	10.00	20.00	40.00	80.00

NOTE: Varieties exist overstruck w/figure of Madonna.

HAT (6) KRAJCZAR

.220 SILVER
Mint mark: NB

KM#	Date	Mintage	Fine	VF	XF	Unc
435	1849	—	5.00	10.00	20.00	35.00

10 KRAJCZAR

3.8900 g, .500 SILVER, .0625 oz ASW
Mint mark: KB
Rev. leg: SZ. MARIA. . .

KM#	Date	Mintage	Fine	VF	XF	Unc
431	1848	—	15.00	30.00	65.00	125.00

20 KRAJCZAR

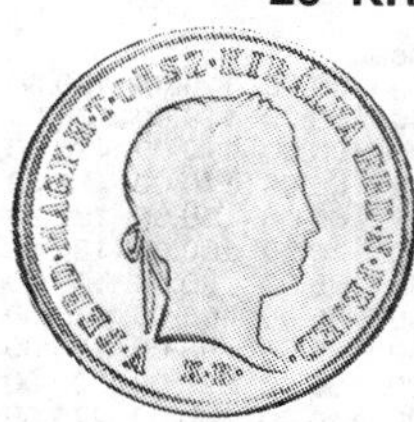

6.6800 g, .583 SILVER, .1252 oz ASW
Mint mark: KB
Rev. leg: SZ. MARIA. . .

KM#	Date	Mintage	Fine	VF	XF	Unc
432	1848	—	2.50	5.00	10.00	25.00

MONETARY REFORM

1892-1925
100 Filler = 1 Korona

FILLER

BRONZE
Mint mark: KB

KM#	Date	Mintage	Fine	VF	XF	Unc
480	1892	8.153	17.50	32.50	60.00	95.00
	1892 (restrike w/rosette)					
		—	—	—	Proof	20.00
	1893	Inc. Ab.	1.75	3.00	5.50	16.00
	1894	8.642	.50	1.00	1.75	6.00
	1895	9.121	.50	1.00	1.75	6.00
	1896	5.397	1.25	3.00	6.00	15.00
	1897	5.157	4.50	7.50	15.00	30.00
	1898	1.419	5.00	10.00	20.00	40.00
	1899	5.066	1.75	3.50	7.00	17.50
	1900	10.461	1.00	2.00	4.00	11.50

NOTE: Later dates (1901-1914) exist for this type.

2 FILLER

BRONZE
Mint mark: KB

KM#	Date	Mintage	Fine	VF	XF	Unc
481	1892	17.176	40.00	60.00	95.00	150.00
	1893	Inc. Ab.	1.75	4.00	6.50	9.00
	1894	39.150	.50	1.00	2.50	5.00
	1895	65.017	.50	1.00	2.50	5.00
	1896	53.716	.50	1.00	2.50	5.00
	1897	37.297	.50	1.00	2.50	5.00
	1898	14.073	2.25	4.50	8.50	12.50
	1899	21.570	2.25	4.50	8.50	12.50
	1900	.584	100.00	150.00	220.00	280.00

NOTE: Later dates (1901-1915) exist for this type.

10 FILLER

NICKEL
Mint mark: KB

KM#	Date	Mintage	Fine	VF	XF	Unc
482	1892	15.753	3.00	6.00	17.50	27.50
	1893	Inc. Ab.	.25	.50	1.50	4.00
	1894	39.463	.25	.50	1.50	4.00
	1895	16.804	.25	.50	1.50	4.00
	1896	—	—	Reported, not confirmed		

NOTE: Later dates (1906-1914) exist for this type.
NOTE: Edge varieties exist.

20 FILLER

NICKEL
Mint mark: KB

KM#	Date	Mintage	Fine	VF	XF	Unc
483	1892	.696	4.50	9.00	15.00	25.00
	1893	27.187	.50	1.25	2.50	6.00
	1894	26.117	.50	1.25	2.50	6.00

NOTE: Later dates (1906-1914) exist for this type.
NOTE: Edge varieties exist.

KORONA

5.0000 g, .835 SILVER, .1342 oz ASW
Mint mark: KB

KM#	Date	Mintage	Fine	VF	XF	Unc
484	1892	.015	4.00	15.00	60.00	200.00
	1893	24.385	BV	3.50	5.00	12.50
	1894	12.077	BV	3.25	4.50	10.00
	1895	18.544	BV	3.25	4.50	10.00
	1896	3.983	3.50	6.00	8.50	13.50

NOTE: Later date (1906) exists for this type.
NOTE: Obverse varieties exist.

Millennium Commemorative

KM#	Date	Mintage	Fine	VF	XF	Unc
487	1896	1.000	2.25	3.25	5.50	15.00
	1896 (restrike)	—	—	Proof	17.50	

NOTE: The above issue has been restruck in proof several times, both with and without edge inscriptions.

5 KORONA

24.0000 g, .900 SILVER, .6944 oz ASW
Mint mark: KB

KM#	Date	Mintage	Fine	VF	XF	Unc
488	1900	3.840	10.00	18.00	40.00	80.00
	1900 (restrike w/rosette)		—	Proof	40.00	
	1900 (restrike w/o rosette)		—	Proof	40.00	

NOTE: Later dates (1906-1909) exist for this type.

10 KORONA

3.3875 g, .900 GOLD, .0980 oz AGW
Mint mark: KB

KM#	Date	Mintage	Fine	VF	XF	Unc
485	1892	1.087	BV	45.00	55.00	65.00
	1892 (restrike)	—	—	Proof	45.00	
	1893	Inc. Ab.	BV	45.00	55.00	65.00
	1894	.986	BV	45.00	55.00	65.00
	1895	—	1500.	2500.	3500.	4500.
	1895 (restrike)	—	—	Proof	50.00	
	1896	.032	60.00	85.00	100.00	125.00
	1897	.259	BV	45.00	55.00	65.00
	1898	.218	BV	45.00	55.00	65.00
	1899	.231	BV	45.00	55.00	65.00
	1900	.228	BV	45.00	55.00	65.00

NOTE: Later dates (1901-1915) exist for this type.

20 KORONA

6.7750 g, .900 GOLD, .1960 oz AGW
Mint mark: KB

KM#	Date	Mintage	Fine	VF	XF	Unc
486	1892	1.779	BV	80.00	90.00	115.00
	1892	(restrike)	—	—	Proof	100.00
	1893	5.089	BV	80.00	90.00	115.00
	1894	2.526	BV	80.00	90.00	115.00
	1895	1.935	BV	80.00	90.00	115.00
	1895	(restrike)	—	—	Proof	100.00
	1896	1.023	BV	80.00	90.00	115.00
	1897	1.819	BV	80.00	90.00	115.00
	1898	1.281	BV	80.00	90.00	115.00
	1899	.712	BV	80.00	90.00	115.00
	1900	.435	BV	80.00	90.00	115.00

NOTE: Later dates (1901-1915) exist for this type.

TRADE COINAGE

DUCAT

3.4900 g, .986 GOLD, .1106 oz AGW
Obv. leg: FRANC I.D.G. . .

KM#	Date	Mintage	Fine	VF	XF	Unc
419	1830	—	175.00	250.00	325.00	500.00
	1832	—	200.00	300.00	400.00	550.00
	1833	—	150.00	225.00	300.00	450.00
	1834	—	150.00	225.00	300.00	450.00
	1835	—	150.00	225.00	300.00	450.00

Obv. leg: FERD. I.D.G. . .

KM#	Date	Mintage	Fine	VF	XF	Unc
425	1837	—	175.00	350.00	500.00	750.00
	1838	—	175.00	350.00	500.00	750.00
	1839	—	150.00	225.00	300.00	500.00
	1840	—	150.00	225.00	300.00	500.00
	1841	—	150.00	225.00	300.00	500.00
	1842	—	150.00	225.00	300.00	500.00
	1843	—	175.00	350.00	450.00	650.00
	1844	—	150.00	225.00	300.00	500.00
	1845	—	175.00	300.00	450.00	650.00
	1846	—	150.00	225.00	300.00	500.00
	1847	—	150.00	225.00	300.00	500.00
	1848	—	150.00	225.00	300.00	500.00

Rev. leg: SZ. MARIA. . .

KM#	Date	Mintage	Fine	VF	XF	Unc
433	1848	—	100.00	175.00	250.00	350.00

Mint mark: KB

KM#	Date	Mintage	Fine	VF	XF	Unc
448.1	1868	.128	100.00	200.00	275.00	400.00
	1869	.090	90.00	150.00	200.00	300.00

Mint mark: GYF

KM#	Date	Mintage	Fine	VF	XF	Unc
448.2	1868	.400	85.00	140.00	200.00	300.00
	1869	.270	90.00	150.00	200.00	300.00

Mint mark: KB

KM#	Date	Mintage	Fine	VF	XF	Unc
457	1870	(restrike)	—	—	Proof	100.00
457	1877	456 pcs.	800.00	1250.	1500.	2000.
	1879	3,651	500.00	900.00	1500.	2000.
	1880	5,075	600.00	1000.	1500.	1750.
	1880	(restrike)	—	—	Proof	—
	1881	*43 pcs.	1250.	2000.	2500.	3000.

4 FORINT/10 FRANCS

3.2258 g, .900 GOLD, .0934 oz AGW
Mint mark: GYF

KM#	Date	Mintage	Fine	VF	XF	Unc
454.1	1870	.049	55.00	70.00	90.00	125.00

Mint mark: KB

KM#	Date	Mintage	Fine	VF	XF	Unc
454.2	1870	.102	55.00	70.00	90.00	125.00
	1870 UP	(restrike)		—	Proof	70.00
	1871	.090	55.00	80.00	100.00	130.00
	1872	.053	55.00	65.00	85.00	125.00
	1873	.013	80.00	115.00	175.00	200.00
	1874	8,228	80.00	115.00	175.00	210.00
	1875	.011	85.00	125.00	175.00	225.00
	1876	.024	55.00	80.00	110.00	130.00
	1877	.024	55.00	75.00	100.00	125.00
	1878	.015	55.00	80.00	110.00	130.00
	1879	.012	55.00	80.00	110.00	130.00

NOTE: Semi official restrikes have the letters UP below the bust.

Older head

KM#	Date	Mintage	Fine	VF	XF	Unc
466	1880	.013	55.00	80.00	110.00	130.00
	1881	.012	55.00	80.00	110.00	130.00
	1882	.013	55.00	80.00	110.00	125.00
	1883	.012	55.00	80.00	110.00	125.00
	1884	.054	55.00	65.00	95.00	125.00
	1885	.064	55.00	70.00	100.00	125.00
	1886	.039	55.00	65.00	80.00	125.00
	1887	.039	55.00	65.00	95.00	125.00
	1888	.049	55.00	65.00	95.00	125.00
	1889	.019	100.00	150.00	225.00	300.00
	1890	Inc.Y19	95.00	140.00	200.00	275.00

Rev: Fiume arms.

KM#	Date	Mintage	Fine	VF	XF	Unc
476.1	1890	.029	200.00	300.00	375.00	500.00
	1891	.032	60.00	75.00	100.00	150.00

Mint: Unknown

KM#	Date	Mintage	Fine	VF	XF	Unc
476.2	1892	20 pcs.	800.00	1100.	1800.	3000.

8 FORINT/20 FRANCS

6.4516 g, .900 GOLD, .1867 oz AGW

KM#	Date	Mintage	Fine	VF	XF	Unc
455.1	1870	.046	BV	110.00	135.00	165.00
	1871	.076	BV	100.00	120.00	140.00
	1872	.273	BV	100.00	120.00	140.00
	1873	.245	BV	100.00	120.00	140.00
	1874	.237	BV	100.00	120.00	160.00
	1875	.261	BV	100.00	120.00	160.00
	1876	.314	BV	100.00	120.00	140.00
	1877	.303	BV	100.00	120.00	140.00
	1878	.308	BV	110.00	130.00	160.00
	1879	.306	BV	100.00	120.00	140.00
	1880	.301	90.00	120.00	150.00	200.00

Mint mark: GYF

KM#	Date	Mintage	Fine	VF	XF	Unc
455.2	1870	.125	BV	100.00	130.00	150.00
	1871	.177	BV	100.00	120.00	140.00

Mint mark: KB
Obv: Larger head.

KM#	Date	Mintage	Fine	VF	XF	Unc
467	1880	Inc. Ab.	BV	100.00	110.00	140.00
	1881	.309	BV	100.00	120.00	140.00
	1882	.304	BV	100.00	120.00	140.00
	1883	.300	BV	100.00	120.00	140.00
	1884	.284	BV	100.00	120.00	140.00
	1885	.267	BV	100.00	120.00	140.00
	1886	.313	BV	100.00	120.00	140.00
	1887	.294	BV	100.00	120.00	140.00
	1888	.296	BV	100.00	120.00	140.00
	1889	.351	BV	100.00	120.00	140.00
	1890	Inc. Be.	BV	100.00	110.00	140.00

Rev: Fiume arms.

KM#	Date	Mintage	Fine	VF	XF	Unc
477	1890	.329	BV	100.00	125.00	175.00
	1891	.378	BV	100.00	130.00	160.00
	1892	.231	BV	120.00	160.00	200.00

MEDALLIC ISSUES (M)

(OBOL)

SILVER, .38 g
Style of Emerich

KM#	Date	Mintage	Fine	VF	XF	Unc
M2	1896	—	—	—	—	—

Klippe

KM#	Date	Mintage	Fine	VF	XF	Unc
M3	1896	—	—	—	—	—

(BRACTEATE)

SILVER, .25 g
Style of Bela III

KM#	Date	Mintage	Fine	VF	XF	Unc
M4	1896	—	—	—	—	—

BRONZE

KM#	Date	Mintage	Fine	VF	XF	Unc
M4a	1896	—	—	—	—	—

(DENAR)

SILVER
Style of Matthias Corvinus

KM#	Date	Mintage	Fine	VF	XF	Unc
M5	1896	—	—	—	—	—

Style of Andreas II

KM#	Date	Mintage	Fine	VF	XF	Unc
M6	1896	—	—	—	—	—

Klippe

KM#	Date	Mintage	Fine	VF	XF	Unc
M7	1896	—	—	—	—	—

Style of St. Stephen

KM#	Date	Mintage	Fine	VF	XF	Unc
M8	1896	—	—	—	—	—

Klippe

KM#	Date	Mintage	Fine	VF	XF	Unc
M9	1896	—	—	—	—	—

(GROSCHEN)

SILVER, 3.41 g
Style of Karl Robert

KM#	Date	Mintage	Fine	VF	XF	Unc
M10	1896	—	—	—	—	—

COPPER

KM#	Date	Mintage	Fine	VF	XF	Unc
M10a	1896	—	—	—	—	—

(5 KORONA)

SILVER
Obv: Franz Joseph. Rev: Arpad horseback.

KM#	Date	Mintage	Fine	VF	XF	Unc
M11	1896KB	—	—	—	—	—
	1896KB-UP	(restrike)		—	—	85.00

Klippe

KM#	Date	Mintage	Fine	VF	XF	Unc
M12	1896KB-UP	(restrike)		—	Proof	125.00

(THALER)

SILVER
Obv: 1/2-length figure right holding sceptre and orb. Rev: Madonna and child above shield.

KM#	Date	Mintage	Fine	VF	XF	Unc
M13	1896KB	—	—	—	Proof	650.00
	1896KB-UP	(restrike)		—	Proof	125.00

GOLD, 30.08 g
Franz Joseph I
Rev: Madonna and child above shield.

KM#	Date	Mintage	Fine	VF	XF	Unc
M13a	1896KB	100 pcs.	—	—	P/L	4500.

SILVER, klippe

KM#	Date	Mintage	Fine	VF	XF	Unc
M14	1896KB	—	—	—	—	—
	1896KB-UP	(restrike)		—	Proof	150.00

(FORINT)

12.3457 g, .900 SILVER, .3572 oz ASW
Reopening of the Joseph II Mine at Schemnitz
Mint mark: KB

KM#	Date	Mintage				
M1	1878	400 pcs.	—	750.00	1250.	2000.

COPPER

M1a	1878	3 pcs.	—	—	Rare	—

BRONZE

M1b	1878	—	— Reported, not confirmed			

GOLD

M1c	1878	3 pcs.	—	—	Rare	—

(GOLDGULDEN)

GOLD, 3.56 g
Style of Karl Robert

M15	1896	100 pcs.	—	—	1350.	2250.

PATTERNS (Pn)

(Including off metal strikes)

KM#	Date	Mintage	Identification	Mkt.Val.
Pn97	1835	—	1/2 Thaler, KM420	—
Pn98	1848	—	3 Kreuzer, w/o mm	—
Pn99	1849Z	46 pcs.	1 Krajczar, Copper, KM430	1400.
Pn100	1849KB	—	1 Krajczar, KM430	—
Pn101	1849KB	—	3 Krajczar, Copper, KM434	—
Pn102	1849	—	6 Kreuzer, Pewter, KM435	—
Pn103	1849	—	20 Kreuzer, Pewter, Ferdinand I	—
Pn104	1849	—	1 Ducat, Pewter	—
Pn105	1857	—	1/4 Florin, Aluminum	—
Pn106	1858	—	3 Kreuzer, Copper	—
Pn107	1858B	—	3 Kreuzer, Lead. Obv: Arms. Rev: 3 in wreath.	—
Pn108	1858E	—	3 Kreuzer, Lead. Obv: Arms. Rev: 3 in wreath.	—
Pn109	1859	—	5 Kreuzer, Aluminum	—
Pn110	1867B	*1,000	10 Krajczar, Silver, 19mm, larger bust, KM440	900.00
Pn111	1867	—	10 Kreuzer, Copper, KM440	—
Pn112	1868GYF	—	4 Krajczar, Copper, KM442	—
Pn113	1868B	—	10 Krajczar, Silver, KM440	—
Pn114	1868GYF	—	10 Krajczar, Silver, KM440	900.00
Pn115	1869	—	20 Krajczar, Copper, KM446	—
Pn116	1878	3	1 Forint, Copper, KM453	250.00
Pn117	1878	—	1 Forint, Gold, KM453	—
Pn118	1882	—	5/10 Krajczar, Aluminum, KM468	—
Pn119	1883KB	—	1 Krajczar, Iron	100.00
Pn120	1889	—	10 Krajczar, Aluminum, KM451, 3 varieties	—
Pn121	1891	—	1 Krajczar, Aluminum. Obv: Bust right. Rev: Crown.	—
Pn122	1892	—	1 Filler, restrike, w/rosette, KM480	—
Pn123	1892	—	1 Krajczar, Brass, KM458	—
Pn124	1892	—	1 Krajczar, Aluminum, KM458	—
Pn125	1896	—	1 Korona, Copper, KM487	360.00

TRIAL STRIKES (TS)

KM#	Date	Mintage	Identification	Mkt.Val.
TS10	1848 w/o mm	-	3 Krajczar, Copper, KM434	—
TS11	1849	—	6 Krajczar, Lead, KM435	—
TS12	1849	—	20 Krajczar, Lead, KM422	—
TS13	1849	—	1 Ducat, Lead, KM425	—
TS14	1867	—	10 Krajczar, Copper, KM440	—
TS15	1868KB	—	4 Krajcar, Silver, KM442	—
TS16	1868KB	—	4 Krajcar, Gold KM442	—
TS17	1868	—	10 Krajczar, Copper, KM440	—
TS18	1868KB	—	20 Krajcar, Aluminum, KM440	—
TS19	1868	—	20 Krajczar, Aluminum, KM445	—
TS20	1869	—	20 Krajczar, Copper, KM446	—
TS21	1870KB	—	4 Forint/10 Francs, Copper, KM454	—
TS22	1870	—	4 Forint/10 Francs, Copper, KM454	—
TS23	1870KB	—	1 Ducat, Lead, KM456	—
TS24	1874KB	—	10 Krajcar, Gold, KM451	—
TS27	1882KB	—	5/10 Krajczar, Aluminum, KM468	—
TS28	1882KB	—	5/10 Krajcar, Nickel, KM468	—
TS29	1883KB	—	1 Krajczar, Nickel, KM458	175.00
TS30	1889	—	10 Krajczar, Aluminum, KM451	—
TS31	1891KB	—	1 Krajczar, thin planchet, KM478	—
TS32	1891KB	—	1 Forint, Aluminum, KM475	—
TS33	1891KB	—	4 Forint/10 Francs, Nickel, KM476	—
TS34	1892KB	—	1 Krajczar, Aluminum, KM478	—
TS35	1892KB	—	1 Krajczar, Brass, KM478	—
TS36	1892KB	—	8 Forint/20 Francs, Nickel, KM477	—
TS37	1894KB	—	2 Filler, Nickel, KM481	—
TS38	1896	—	1 Korona, Lead, KM487	—

ICELAND

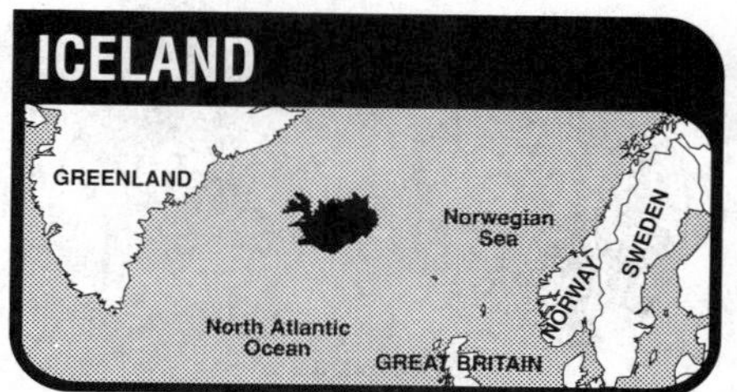

The Republic of Iceland, an island of recent volcanic origin in the North Atlantic east of Greenland and immediately south of the Arctic Circle, has an area of 39,768 sq. mi. (103,000 sq. km.) and a population of 272,064. Capital: Reykjavik. Fishing is the chief industry and accounts for more than 70 percent of the exports.

Iceland was settled by Norwegians in the 9th century and established as an independent republic in 930. The Icelandic assembly called the 'Althing', also established in 930, is the oldest parliament in the world. Iceland came under Norwegian sovereignty in 1262, and passed to Denmark when Norway and Denmark were united under the Danish crown in 1380. In 1918 it was established as a virtually independent kingdom in union with Denmark. On June 17, 1944, while Denmark was still under occupation by troops of the Third Reich, Iceland was established by plebiscite as an independent republic.

TOKEN ISSUES (Tn)

Under the Scandinavian Monetary Convention of 1873, the coinage of Denmark, Norway and Sweden could circulate with validity in Iceland. Despite the various options for exchange, very few coins appear to have made their way to Iceland. As a result, Icelandic merchants resorted to manufacturing their own tokens. While some bare the crudeness of a homemade token, others had been elaborately struck by such well known manufacturers as L. Chr. Lauer of Nurnberg, who most likely had N. Chr. Hansen & Co. Copenhagen as an agent.

Merchants posting inflated token prices alongside legal coinage prices on goods for sale led to the 1901 law which prohibited the manufacture and usage of private coinage, ending the token era which started in the mid 1800's.

NOTE: There are at least four different types of tokens for this time period. Only Type I tokens are cataloged here.

TYPES

I - Tokens with stated values; first in shillings, later in kronur and aurar
II Bread Tokens, used to barter for prearranged quantities of goods or labor
III - Advertising or Address Tokens
IV - Miscellaneous Tokens

OLAFUR ARNASON

Stokkseyri

10 AURAR

BRONZE, 2.2 g
Obv: Merchant's name and shop location in legend, denomination.
Rev: GEGN VORUM (against goods) in wreath.

KM#	Date	Mintage	VG	Fine	VF	XF
Tn1	ND(1900)	—	10.00	22.00	45.00	85.00

25 AURAR

BRONZE, 2.2 g
Similar to KM#Tn1.

KM#	Date	Mintage	VG	Fine	VF	XF
Tn2	ND(1900)	—	7.00	15.00	30.00	75.00

J.R.B. LEFOLII

Eyrarbakka

10 AURAR

BRONZE, 1.6 g
Similar to 100 Aurar, KM#Tn7.

KM#	Date	Mintage	VG	Fine	VF	XF
Tn5	ND(1900)	—	12.00	25.00	50.00	100.00

25 AURAR

BRONZE, 2.3 g
Similar to 100 Aurar, KM#Tn7.

KM#	Date	Mintage	VG	Fine	VF	XF
Tn6	ND(1900)	—	12.00	25.00	50.00	100.00

100 AURAR

BRONZE, 3.3 g
Obv: Merchant's name and shop location in legend, denomination.
Rev: GEGN VORUM (against goods) in wreath.

KM#	Date	Mintage	VG	Fine	VF	XF
Tn7	ND(1900)	—	15.00	30.00	60.00	110.00

C.F. SIEMSEN

Reykjavik

NOTE: Tn8 and Tn9 were also valid at C. F. Siemsen's store on the Faeroe Islands.

4 SKILDINGAR

BRONZE, 1.5 g
Obv: Merchant's initials.
Rev: Denominations, 1 Skilling, 1 Vare (Ware).

KM#	Date	Mintage	VG	Fine	VF	XF
Tn8	ND(1846)	—	40.00	80.00	150.00	250.00

16 SKILDINGAR

BRONZE, 2.5 g
Similar to 4 Skildingar, KM#Tn8.

KM#	Date	Mintage	VG	Fine	VF	XF
Tn9	ND(1846)	—	30.00	60.00	100.00	165.00

P.J. THORSTEINSSON

Bildudal

5 AURAR

BRONZE, 2.2 g
Similar to 10 Aurar, KM#Tn11.

KM#	Date	Mintage	VG	Fine	VF	XF
Tn10	ND(1880)	—	—	—	Rare	—

10 AURAR

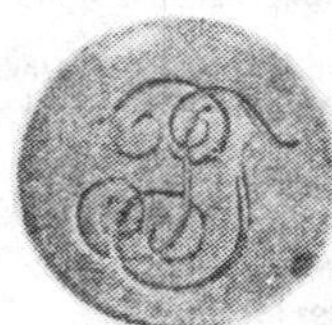

BRONZE, 3.0 g
Obv: PT monogram. Rev: Denomination.

KM#	Date	Mintage	VG	Fine	VF	XF
Tn11	ND(1880)	—	—	—	Rare	—

25 AURAR

BRONZE, 3.7 g
Similar to 10 Aurar, KM#Tn11.

KM#	Date	Mintage	VG	Fine	VF	XF
Tn13	ND(1880)	—	20.00	40.00	80.00	120.00

Obv: PT monogram above 97. Rev: Denomination.

KM#	Date	Mintage	VG	Fine	VF	XF
Tn14	xx97	—	15.00	30.00	60.00	100.00

50 AURAR

BRONZE
Similar to 10 Aurar, KM#Tn11.

KM#	Date	Mintage	VG	Fine	VF	XF
Tn16	ND(1880)	—	20.00	40.00	80.00	120.00

Similar to 25 Aurar, KM#Tn14.

KM#	Date	Mintage	VG	Fine	VF	XF
Tn17	xx97	—	15.00	30.00	60.00	100.00

100 AURAR

BRONZE
Similar to 10 Aurar, KM#Tn11.

KM#	Date	Mintage	VG	Fine	VF	XF
Tn19	ND(1880)	—	—	—	Rare	—

Similar to 25 Aurar, KM#Tn14.

KM#	Date	Mintage	VG	Fine	VF	XF
Tn20	xx97	—	—	—	Rare	—

The Mints of the
MUGHAL EMPERORS

IMPERIAL BOUNDARIES A.D. 1605
IMPERIAL EXPANSION A.D. 1605 - 1707

The Lodi Sultanate of Delhi was conquered by Zahir-uddin Muhammad Babur, a Chagatai Turk descended from Tamerlane, in 1525AD. His son, Nasir-ud-din Muhammad Humayun, lost the new empire in a series of battles with the Bihari Afghan Sher Shah, who founded the shortlived Suri dynasty. Humayun, with the assistance of the Emperor of Persia, recovered his kingdom from Sher Shah's successors in 1555AD. He did not long enjoy the fruits of victory for his fatal fall down his library steps brought his teenage son Jalal-ud-din Muhammad Akbar to the throne in the following year. During Akbar's long reign of a half century, the Mughal Empire was firmly established throughout much of North India. Under Akbar's son and grandson, the emperors Nur-ud-din Muhammad Jahangir and Shihab-ud-din Muhammad Shah Jahan, the state reached its apogee and art, culture and commerce flourished.

One of the major achievements of the Mughal government was the establishment of a universal silver currency, based on the rupee, a coin of 11.6 grams and as close to pure silver content as the metallurgy of the time was capable of attaining. Supplementary coins were the copper dam and gold mohur. The values of these coin denominations were nominally fixed at 40 dams to 1 rupee, and 8 rupees to 1 mohur; however, market forces determined actual exchange rates.

The maximum expansion of the geographical area under direct Mughal rule was achieved during the reign of Aurangzeb Alamgir. By his death in 1707AD, the whole peninsula, with minor exceptions, the whole subcontinent of India owed fealty to the Mughal emperor.

Aurangzeb's wars, lasting decades, upset the stability and prosperity of the kingdom. The internal dissension and rebellion which resulted brought the eclipse of the empire in succeeding reigns. The Mughal monetary system, especially the silver rupee, supplanted most local currencies throughout India. The number of Mughal mints rose sharply and direct central control declined, so that by the time of the emperor Shah Alam II, many nominally Mughal mints served independent states. The common element in all these coinage issues was the presence of the Mughal emperor's name and titles on the obverse. In the following listings no attempt has been made to solve the problem of separating Mughal from Princely State coins by historical criteria: all Mughal-style coins are considered products of the Mughal empire until the death of Muhammad Shah in 1784AD; thereafter all coins are considered Princely State issues unless there is evidence of the mint being under ever-diminishing Imperial control.

EMPERORS

شاه عالم

Shah Alam II,
AH1174-1202/1759-1788AD
and
AH1203-1221/1789-1806AD

محمد اکبر

Muhammad Akbar II,
AH1221-1253/1806-1837AD

سراج الدین محمد بهادر شاه

Bahadur Shah II, Siraj-ud-din Muhammad
AH1253-1273/1837-1858AD

MINTNAMES

Ahmadabad احمد اباد

Akbarabad (Agra) اکبر آباد

Allahabad الله آباد

(Ilahabad)

Gokulgarh گوکل گره

Hardwar (Tirath) هاردوار

Saharanpur سهارنپور

Shahjahanabad (Dehli) شاه جهان آباد

DATING

The Mughal coins were dated both in the Hejira era and in the regnal era of each emperor. The four-digit Hejira year usually was shown on the obverse, with the one or two-digit regnal (jalus) year on the reverse. Since the regnal and calendar years did not coincide, it was common for two different regnal years to appear on the coins produced during any calendar year. The first jalus year of each reign was usually written as a word, *ahd*, rather than as a numeral.

SHAH ALAM II

AH1174-1202/1759-1788AD;
AH1203-1221/1789-1806AD

This ruler was deposed from July, AH1202 to March, AH1203 by the Rohilla rebel Ghulam Qadir Khan. He was restored to the throne of Delhi by the Marathas in March, AH1203/1789.

Except for the Delhi Mint, most of the later coins struck in the name of this Emperor were Princely State issues, and can be found in their appropriate place under the States. Earlier issues come from nearly 100 mints, and it is always a problem to determine in what year coins of a particular mint cease to be Mughal and become State issues.

The following mints, for the most part in the Delhi (Shahjahanabad) area, may be considered the nucleus of Mughal mints during Shah Alam's reign. They were located in provinces governed by Mughal functionaries, whose increasing independence is reflected in the growing eccentricity of coin design.

In some cases the distinctive geometric designs and floral devices found on the coins were true mint marks, representative of a single mint. In other instances the 'mint marks' listed below were temporary privy marks or simply decoration.

Shah Alam II legends were used in some states long after his death, until AH1314/1879AD at Ujjain, for example. This is not the case with true Mughal issues.

NOTICE

Unlike the previous listings by ruler, denomination and mint the following are by ruler, mint and denomination.

Akbarabad Mint

The city and fort of Agra or Akbarabad fell to the Jats of Bharatpur after the battle of Panipat in 1761AD. For issues dated AH1175-1186/1761-1773AD see Indian Princely States, Bharatpur. A succession of governors from 1773AD controlled Agra nominally as officers of the Mughal emperor but actually for themselves and, after 1785, for the Maratha Peshwa.

MUGHAL GOVERNOR ISSUES

Daulat Rao Sindhia
(with John and George Hessing in charge)
AH1213-1218/1799-1803AD

PAISA

COPPER
Rev: JWH.

KM#	Date	Year	Good	VG	Fine	VF
549.1	AH1216	42	12.50	25.00	42.00	60.00
	—	43	12.50	25.00	42.00	60.00
	1218	—	12.50	25.00	42.00	60.00

NOTE: J.W.H. - John William Hessing, Governor of Agra.
NOTE: Earlier date (AH1215) exists for this type.

Rev: Spearhead.

KM#	Date	Year	Good	VG	Fine	VF
549.2	AH1217	(43)	12.50	25.00	42.00	60.00
	1218	—	12.50	25.00	42.00	60.00

Rev: Pistol.

KM#	Date	Year	Good	VG	Fine	VF
550	AH1216	43	6.00	12.00	20.00	32.00
	1217	44	6.00	12.00	20.00	32.00
	1218	44	6.00	12.00	20.00	32.00

Rev: Pistol and fish.

KM#	Date	Year	Good	VG	Fine	VF
551	AH1216	43	5.50	11.00	17.50	25.00
	1217	—	5.50	11.00	17.50	25.00
	1220	—	5.50	11.00	17.50	25.00

RUPEE

SILVER, 11.444 g
Rev: Fish.

KM#	Date	Year	VG	Fine	VF	XF
554	AH1217	44	7.50	15.00	25.00	35.00
	—	45	7.50	15.00	25.00	35.00

NOTE: Earlier dates (Yr.38-43, AH1215) exist for this type.

EAST INDIA COMPANY

From October 18, 1803 (AH1218)

RUPEE

SILVER, 11.444 g
Rev: Fish.

KM#	Date	Year	VG	Fine	VF	XF
560	AH1219	47	10.00	20.00	32.50	45.00
	1220	47	10.00	20.00	32.50	45.00

Gokulgarh Mint

Mint mark: 

Sindhia Governor

RUPEE

SILVER, 11.444 g

KM#	Date	VG	Fine	VF	XF
624	AH1216-1218/46	7.50	15.00	25.00	35.00

NOTE: Earlier dates (AH1202-1215) exist for this type.

Hardwar Mint

A mint of the Mughal governor of Saharanpur.

RUPEE

SILVER, 11.444 g

KM#	Date	Year	VG	Fine	VF	XF
630	AH1219	46	15.00	30.00	42.50	60.00

NOTE: Earlier dates (AH1205/31-1214/41) exist for this type.

Khujista Bunyad Mint

PAISA

COPPER

KM#	Date	Year	Good	VG	Fine	VF
649	AH1219	—	—	—	—	—

MUZAFFARGARH

NOTE: The placing of Muzaffargarh under Khetri has been discontinued as recent research has shown that no rupees had ever been struck there.

Mint marks: 

RUPEE

SILVER, 10.70-11.60 g
Obv. leg: *Sahib Qiran.*

KM#	Date	Year	VG	Fine	VF	XF
2	AH12xx	44	8.50	13.50	20.00	28.50
	12xx	45	8.50	13.50	20.00	28.50
	1218	46	8.50	13.50	20.00	28.50
	12xx	47	8.50	13.50	20.00	28.50

NOTE: Earlier dates (AH1202-121x) exist for this type.

KM#	Date	Year	VG	Fine	VF	XF
3	AH1221	1	22.50	35.00	47.50	65.00
	1222	2	22.50	35.00	47.50	65.00
	1223	3	22.50	35.00	47.50	65.00

Saharanpur Mint

LOCAL GOVERNOR ISSUES

General Perron (for Sindhia)
AH1215-1218/1800-1803

Mint mark:

stylized dagger

PAISA

COPPER
Rev: Additional symbols chakra and hexfoil.

KM#	Date	Year	Good	VG	Fine	VF
673	AH1217	44	4.00	6.50	10.00	15.00
	1218	45	4.00	6.50	10.00	15.00

NOTE: Earlier dates (AH1206-1215) exist for this type.

RUPEE

SILVER, 11.444 g

KM#	Date	Year	VG	Fine	VF	XF
675	AH1216	43	9.00	18.00	30.00	45.00
	1217	44	9.00	18.00	30.00	45.00
	1218/7	43	9.00	18.00	30.00	45.00
	1218	45	9.00	18.00	30.00	45.00

NOTE: Earlier dates (AH1204-1215) exist for this type.

Rev: Circled dot additional symbol.

KM#	Date	Year	VG	Fine	VF	XF
676	AH1216	43	10.00	20.00	35.00	50.00
	1217	44	10.00	20.00	35.00	50.00

EAST INDIA COMPANY

PAISA

COPPER
Rev: St. Stephen's cross.

KM#	Date	Year	Good	VG	Fine	VF
690	AH1218	45	5.00	9.00	13.00	20.00

RUPEE

SILVER, 11.444 g
Rev: St. Stephen's cross.

KM#	Date	Year	VG	Fine	VF	XF
692	AH1218	45	12.50	25.00	42.00	60.00

Rev: Vertical spray.

KM#	Date	Year	VG	Fine	VF	XF
693	AH1217	44	9.00	18.00	30.00	45.00
	1218	45	9.00	18.00	30.00	45.00
	1219	46	9.00	18.00	30.00	45.00

Rev: W/o symbol.

KM#	Date	Year	VG	Fine	VF	XF
694	AH1220	47	9.00	18.00	30.00	45.00
	1220	49	9.00	18.00	30.00	45.00

Shahjahanabad Mint

Mint marks:
(silver and gold)

Obverse:

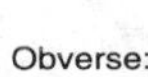

Reverse:

PAISA

COPPER

KM#	Date	Year	Good	VG	Fine	VF
700	AH1219	46	2.00	3.25	5.00	8.50
	1219	47	2.00	3.25	5.00	8.50
	1220	48	2.00	3.25	5.00	8.50

NOTE: Earlier dates (AH1185-1214) exist for this type.

1/4 RUPEE

SILVER, 14mm, 2.861 g
Obv: Additional cinquefoil symbol.

KM#	Date	Year	VG	Fine	VF	XF
704	AH1220	48	14.00	28.00	47.50	65.00

1/2 RUPEE

SILVER, 18mm
Obv: Additional cinquefoil symbol.

KM#	Date	Year	VG	Fine	VF	XF
707	AH1220	47	27.50	45.00	62.50	85.00

RUPEE

NOTE: The size of the Shahjahanabad rupees of Shah Alam II was subject to a wide variance. The early issues tended to be normal size for the hammered coinage (about 22mm). As the power of the emperor waned, the flan size of the Shahjahanabad rupees waxed, reflecting the increasingly ceremonial role of the coinage. The later coins should not be confused with the Nazarana (presentation) coins, which always show a full border design around the legend.

SILVER, 11.444 g
Obv: Additional bush symbol.

KM#	Date	VG	Fine	VF	XF
711	AH1216/44-1218/45				
		10.00	20.00	35.00	50.00

Obv: Additional lion symbol.

KM#	Date	Year	VG	Fine	VF	XF
712	AH1218	46	25.00	50.00	85.00	120.00

Obv: Additional cinquefoil symbol.

KM#	Date	Year	VG	Fine	VF	XF
713	AH1218	46	32.50	65.00	110.00	160.00
	1219	46	32.50	65.00	110.00	160.00

NAZARANA RUPEE

SILVER, 29-36mm, 11.444 g
Obv: Additional bush symbol.

KM#	Date	Year	VG	Fine	VF	XF
718	AH1218	46	55.00	130.00	225.00	175.00

Obv: Additional cinquefoil symbol.

KM#	Date	Year	VG	Fine	VF	XF
B719	AH1218	46	85.00	200.00	325.00	285.00

Obv. and rev. leg: Within wreath of roses, thistles and shamrocks.

KM#	Date	Year	VG	Fine	VF	XF
714	AH1219	47	37.50	85.00	135.00	120.00
	1220	47	37.50	85.00	135.00	120.00
	1220	48	37.50	85.00	135.00	120.00
	1221	48	37.50	85.00	135.00	120.00

Obv: Additional cinquefoil symbol.

KM#	Date	Year	VG	Fine	VF	XF
C719	AH1221	49	45.00	110.00	200.00	150.00

NAZARANA MOHUR

GOLD, 10.70-11.40 g
Obv: Additional bush symbol.

KM#	Date	Year	VG	Fine	VF	XF
721	AH1217	45	300.00	500.00	700.00	1000.
	1218	46	300.00	500.00	700.00	1000.

Obv. and rev. leg: Within wreath of roses, thistles and shamrocks.

KM#	Date	Year	VG	Fine	VF	XF
722	AH1219	47	250.00	400.00	600.00	750.00
	1220	48	250.00	400.00	600.00	750.00
	1221	48	250.00	400.00	600.00	750.00

Surat Mint

The Nawab of Surat continued to issue coins in the name of his nominal Mughal suzerain Shah Alam II until the British took over Surat and its mint in 1800AD (AH1214/5), Shah Alam's 43rd regnal year. These coin types of the Nawab of Surat were replicated by the British East India Company in Surat using privy mark #1 and the frozen regnal year 46 of Shah Alam II, see Bombay Presidency types KM#209.1, 210.1, 211.1, 212.1 and 214.

1/2 RUPEE

SILVER, 5.40-5.80 g
Obv: Privy mark #1.

KM#	Date	Year	VG	Fine	VF	XF
723	AH—	31	5.50	11.00	17.50	25.00

RUPEE

SILVER, 10.70-11.60 g
Obv: Privy mark #1.

KM#	Date	Year	VG	Fine	VF	XF
724	AH—	44	8.00	16.00	28.00	40.00

MUHAMMAD AKBAR II

AH1221-1253/1806-1837AD

Allahabad Mint

RUPEE

SILVER

KM#	Date	Year	Good	VG	Fine	VF
764	(122)1	1	—	—	—	—

Shahjahanabad Mint

The mint of the walled city of Delhi (Shahjahanabad) produced a limited number of coins each year with which the East India Company's resident paid a pension to the Mughal Emperor. KM#777 was struck for this purpose until 1818, when the mint was closed for regular coinage. Thereafter, only a few presentation coins (KM#779.1) were struck annually on the occasion of the king's accession.

PAISA

COPPER

KM#	Date	Year	Good	VG	Fine	VF
770	AH1222	1	2.00	3.25	5.00	8.50
	1222	2	2.00	3.25	5.00	8.50

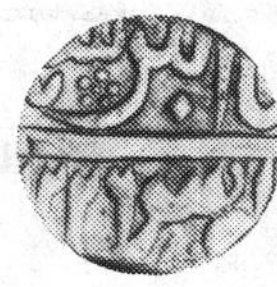

Rev: Letter "S" by regnal year.

KM#	Date	Year	Good	VG	Fine	VF
771	AH1225	4	2.00	3.25	5.00	8.50
	1225	5	2.00	3.25	5.00	8.50
	1226	5	2.00	3.25	5.00	8.50
	1226	6	2.00	3.25	5.00	8.50
	1230	9	2.00	3.25	5.00	8.50
	1231	10	2.00	3.25	5.00	8.50
	1233	12	2.00	3.25	5.00	8.50

1/4 RUPEE

SILVER, 2.861 g

KM#	Date	Year	VG	Fine	VF	XF
773	AH122x	7	12.50	25.00	42.00	60.00

1/2 RUPEE

SILVER, 5.722 g

KM#	Date	Year	VG	Fine	VF	XF
775	AH1221	1	25.00	50.00	85.00	120.00
	1225	4	25.00	50.00	85.00	120.00

RUPEE

SILVER, 11.444 g

KM#	Date	Year	VG	Fine	VF	XF
776	AH1202	1	20.00	40.00	65.00	95.00

Obv: Parasol symbol.

KM#	Date	Year	VG	Fine	VF	XF
777	AH1221	1	20.00	40.00	65.00	95.00
	1222	1	20.00	40.00	65.00	95.00
	1222	2	20.00	40.00	65.00	95.00
	1223	2	20.00	40.00	65.00	95.00
	1223	3	20.00	40.00	65.00	95.00
	1224	3	20.00	40.00	65.00	95.00
	1225	4	20.00	40.00	65.00	95.00
	1226	5	20.00	40.00	65.00	95.00
	1226	6	20.00	40.00	65.00	95.00
	1227	6	20.00	40.00	65.00	95.00
	1227	7	20.00	40.00	65.00	95.00
	1228	7	20.00	40.00	65.00	95.00
	1228	8	20.00	40.00	65.00	95.00
	1229	9	20.00	40.00	65.00	95.00
	12xx	11	20.00	40.00	65.00	95.00

NAZARANA RUPEE

SILVER

KM#	Date	Year	VG	Fine	VF	XF
779.1	AH1223	3	125.00	200.00	325.00	475.00
	1224	3	125.00	200.00	325.00	475.00
	1225	4	125.00	200.00	325.00	475.00
	1226	5	125.00	200.00	325.00	475.00
	1227	7	125.00	200.00	325.00	475.00
	1235	15	125.00	200.00	325.00	475.00
	1236	16	—	—	Rare	—
	1237	17	135.00	225.00	350.00	600.00
	1239	19	135.00	225.00	350.00	600.00
	1240	20	135.00	225.00	350.00	600.00
	1241	21	135.00	225.00	350.00	600.00
	1242	22	135.00	225.00	350.00	600.00
	1248	28	135.00	225.00	350.00	600.00
	1249	29	135.00	225.00	350.00	600.00

SILVER, 11.444 g

KM#	Date	Year	VG	Fine	VF	XF
779.2	AH1251	31	—	—	Rare	—
	1252	32	—	—	Rare	—

MOHUR

GOLD, 10.70-11.40 g

KM#	Date	Year	VG	Fine	VF	XF
781	AH122x	2	200.00	350.00	500.00	700.00
	1223	6	200.00	350.00	500.00	700.00
	122x	6	200.00	350.00	500.00	700.00

NAZARANA MOHUR

GOLD, 10.70-11.40 g

KM#	Date	Year	VG	Fine	VF	XF
783	AH1221	1	—	—	Rare	—
	1234	12	—	—	Rare	—
	1237	17	—	—	Rare	—

SURAJ-UD-DIN MUHAMMAD BAHADUR SHAH II

AH1253-1273/1837-1857AD

Shahjahanabad Mint

NAZARANA RUPEE

SILVER, 11.444 g

KM#	Date	Year	VG	Fine	VF	XF
790	AH1253	1	1000.	1800.	2500.	4200.
	1254	2	1000.	1800.	2500.	4200.
	1255	3	1000.	1800.	2500.	4200.
	1256	4	1000.	1800.	2500.	4200.
	1257	5	1000.	1800.	2500.	4200.
	1258	6	1000.	1800.	2500.	4200.

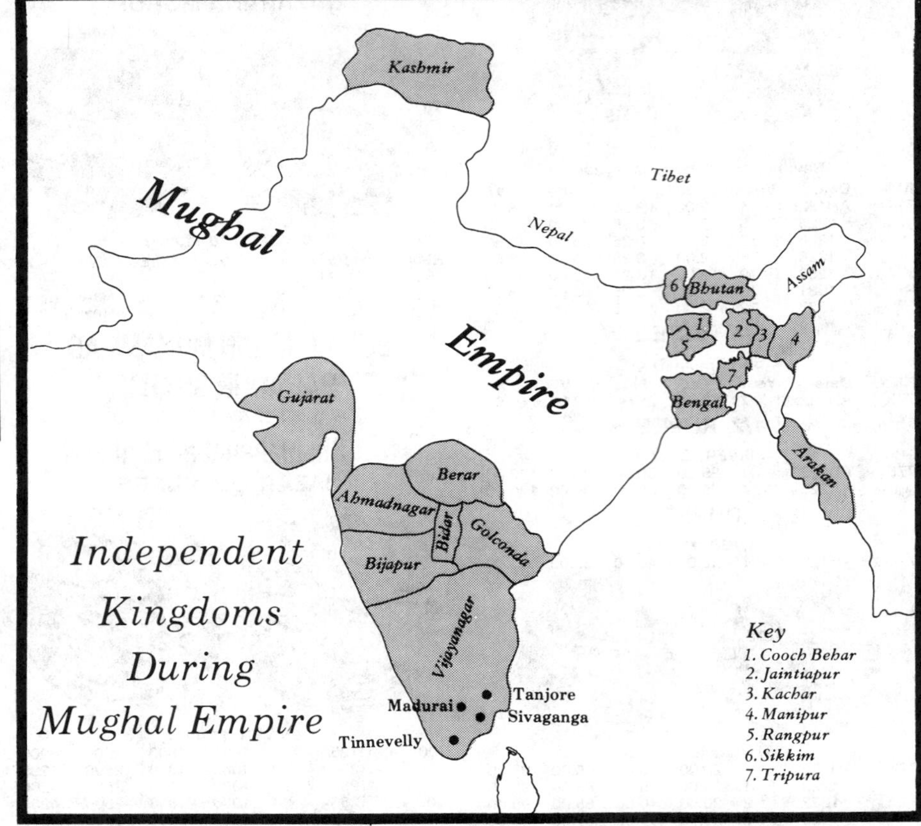

ASSAM

AHOM KINGDOM

It was in the 13th century that a tribal leader called Sukapha, with about 9,000 followers, left their traditional home in the Shan States of Northern Burma, and carved out the Ahom Kingdom in upper Assam.

The Ahom Kingdom gradually increased in power and extent over the following centuries, particularly during the reign of King Suhungmung (1497-1539). This king also took on a Hindu title, Svarga Narayan, which shows the increasing influence of the Brahmins over the court. Although several of the other Hindu states in north-east India started a silver coinage during the 16th century, it was not until the mid-17th century that the Ahoms first struck coin.

From the time of Kusain Shah's invasion of Cooch Behar in 1494AD the Muslims had cast acquisitive eyes towards the valley of the Brahmaputra, but the Ahoms managed to preserve their independence. In 1661 Aurangzeb's governor in Bengal, Mir Jumla, made a determined effort to bring Assam under Mughal rule. Cooch Behar was annexed without difficulty, and in March 1662 Mir Jumla occupied Gargaon, the Ahom capital, without opposition. However, during the rainy season the Muslim forces suffered severely from disease, lack of food and from the occasional attacks from the Ahom forces, who had tactically withdrawn from the capital together with the king. After the end of the monsoon a supply line was opened with Bengal again, but morale in the Muslim army was low, so Mir Jumla was forced to agree to peach terms somewhat less onerous than the Mughals liked to impose on subjugated states. The Ahoms agreed to pay tribute, but the Ahom kingdom remained entirely independent of Mughal control, and never again did a Muslim army venture into upper Assam.

During the eighteenth century the kingdom became weakened with civil war, culminating in the expulsion of Gaurinatha Simha from his capital in 1787 by the Moamarias. The British helped Gaurinatha regain his kingdom in 1794, but otherwise took little interest in the affairs of Assam. The end of the Ahom Kingdom was not due to intervention from Bengal, but from Burma. After initial invasions commencing in 1816, the Burmese conquered the whole of Assam in 1821/2, and seemed bent on expanding their Kingdom even further. The British in Bengal were quick to retaliate and drove the Burmese from Assam in 1824, and from then on Assam became firmly under British control with no further independent coinage.

RULERS

Ruler's names, where present on the coins, usually appear on the obverse (dated) side, starting either at the end of the first line, after *Shri*, or in the second line. Most of the Ahom rulers after the adoption of Hinduism in about 1500AD had both an Ahom and a Hindu name.

HINDU NAME	AHOM NAME
Kamalesvara Simha	**Suklingpha**

কমলেশ্বরসিংহ

SE1717-1733/1795-1811AD

Chandrakanta Simha	**Sudingpha**

চন্দ্রকান্তসিংহ

SE1733-1740/1811-1818AD

Brajanatha Simha

ব্রজনাথসিংহ

SE1740-1741/1818-1819AD

Chandrakanta Simha	**Sudingpha**

চন্দ্রকান্তসিংহ

SE1741-1743/1819-1821AD

Jogesvara Simha

জোগেশ্বরসিংহ

SE1743-1746/1821-1824AD

COINAGE

It is frequently stated that coins were first struck in Assam during the reign of King Suklenmung (1539-1552), but this is merely due to a misreading of the Ahom legend on the coins of King Supungmung (1663-70). The earliest Ahom coins known, therefore, were struck during the reign of King Jayadhvaja Simha (1648-1663).

Although the inscription and general design of these first coins of the Ahom Kingdom were copied from the coins of Cooch Behar, the octagonal shape was entirely Ahom, and according to tradition was chosen because of the belief that the Ahom country was eight sided. Apart from the unique shape, the coins were of similar fabric and weight standard to the Moghul rupee.

The earliest coins had inscriptions in Sanskrit using the Bengali script, but the retreat of the Moghul army under Mir Jumla in 1663 seems to have led to a revival of Ahom nationalism that may account for the fact that most of the coins struck between 1663 and 1696 had inscriptions in the old Ahom script, with invocations to Ahom deities.

Up to this time all the coins, following normal practice in North-East India, were merely dated to the coronation year of the ruler, but Rudra Simha (1696-1714) instituted the practice of dating coins to the year of issue. This ruler was a fervent Hindu, and reinstated Sanskrit inscriptions on the coins. After this the Ahom script was used on a few rare ceremonial issues.

The majority of coins issued were of silver, with binary subdivions down to a fraction of 1/32nd rupee. Cowrie shells were used for small change. Gold coins were struck throughout the period, often using the same dies as were used for the silver coins. A few copper coins were struck during the reign of Brajanatha Simha (1818-19), but these are very rare.

MINTNAMES

Rangpur

CHANDRAKANTA SIMHA

SE1732-39,41,42/1810-17,19,20AD

1/32 RUPEE

SILVER, oval, 0.34-0.36 g

KM#	Date	Year	VG	Fine	VF	XF
245	ND	—	15.00	20.00	26.50	37.50

1/16 RUPEE

SILVER, 7mm, octagonal, 0.67-0.72 g

KM#	Date	Year	VG	Fine	VF	XF
246	ND	—	15.00	20.00	26.50	37.50

1/8 RUPEE

SILVER, 1.34-1.45 g

KM#	Date	Year	VG	Fine	VF	XF
247	ND	—	15.00	20.00	26.50	37.50

1/4 RUPEE

SILVER, 2.68-2.90 g

KM#	Date	Year	VG	Fine	VF	XF
248	SE1741	(1819)	25.00	35.00	45.00	65.00
	1742	(1820)	25.00	35.00	45.00	65.00

1/2 RUPEE

SILVER, 5.35-5.80 g

KM#	Date	Year	VG	Fine	VF	XF
249	ND	—	25.00	35.00	45.00	65.00

RUPEE

SILVER, 10.70-11.60 g

KM#	Date	Year	VG	Fine	VF	XF
250	SE1741	(1819)	30.00	40.00	50.00	75.00
	1742	(1820)	30.00	40.00	50.00	75.00

KM#	Date	Year	VG	Fine	VF	XF
251	SE1742	(1820)	30.00	40.00	50.00	75.00

1/32 MOHUR

GOLD, 0.34-0.36 g

KM#	Date	Year	VG	Fine	VF	XF
252	ND	—	20.00	35.00	50.00	80.00

1/16 MOHUR

GOLD, 0.67-0.72 g

KM#	Date	Year	VG	Fine	VF	XF
253	ND	—	30.00	45.00	70.00	120.00

MOHUR

GOLD, 10.70-11.40 g

KM#	Date	Year	VG	Fine	VF	XF
257	SE1741	(1819)	165.00	210.00	300.00	425.00

BRAJANATHA SIMHA

SE1739-1740/1818-1819AD

PANA

COPPER, 5.60 g

KM#	Date	Year	VG	Fine	VF	XF
258	ND	—	12.50	21.50	35.00	55.00

2 PANA

COPPER, 11.00 g

KM#	Date	Year	VG	Fine	VF	XF
259	SE1739	(1817)	16.50	27.50	45.00	70.00

1/32 RUPEE

SILVER, 6mm, round, 0.34-0.36 g

KM#	Date	Year	VG	Fine	VF	XF
260	ND	—	15.00	20.00	26.50	37.50

1/16 RUPEE

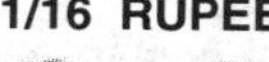

SILVER, 0.67-0.72 g

KM#	Date	Year	VG	Fine	VF	XF
261	ND	—	15.00	20.00	26.50	37.50

1/8 RUPEE

SILVER, 1.34-1.45 g

KM#	Date	Year	VG	Fine	VF	XF
262	ND	—	15.00	20.00	26.50	37.50

1/4 RUPEE

SILVER, 2.68-2.90 g

KM#	Date	Year	VG	Fine	VF	XF
263	SE1739	(1817)	16.50	27.50	40.00	60.00
	1740	(1818)	16.50	27.50	40.00	60.00

1/2 RUPEE

SILVER, 5.35-5.80 g

KM#	Date	Year	VG	Fine	VF	XF
264	ND	7	16.50	27.50	40.00	60.00

RUPEE

SILVER, 10.70-11.60 g

KM#	Date	Year	VG	Fine	VF	XF
265	SE1739	(1817)	18.50	30.00	50.00	75.00
	1740	(1818)	18.50	30.00	50.00	75.00

1/32 MOHUR

GOLD, 0.34-0.36 g

KM#	Date	Year	VG	Fine	VF	XF
266	ND	—	20.00	30.00	50.00	80.00

1/8 MOHUR

GOLD, octagonal, 1.34-1.42 g

KM#	Date	Year	VG	Fine	VF	XF
268	ND	—	35.00	50.00	75.00	125.00

1/4 MOHUR

GOLD, octagonal, 2.68-2.85 g

KM#	Date	Year	VG	Fine	VF	XF
269	SE1739	(1817)	50.00	65.00	85.00	140.00

MOHUR

GOLD, 10.70-11.40 g

KM#	Date	Year	VG	Fine	VF	XF
271	SE1739	(1817)	150.00	185.00	265.00	375.00
	1740	(1818)	150.00	185.00	265.00	375.00

JOGESVARA SIMHA

SE1743/1821AD

1/8 RUPEE

SILVER, 1.34-1.45 g

KM#	Date	Year	VG	Fine	VF	XF
274	ND	—	17.50	25.00	32.50	50.00

1/4 RUPEE

SILVER, octagonal, 2.68-2.90 g

KM#	Date	Year	VG	Fine	VF	XF
275	SE1743	(1821)	20.00	30.00	40.00	60.00

1/2 RUPEE

SILVER, 5.35-5.80 g

KM#	Date	Year	VG	Fine	VF	XF
276	ND	—	30.00	40.00	50.00	80.00

RUPEE

SILVER, 10.70-11.60 g

KM#	Date	Year	VG	Fine	VF	XF
277	SE1743	(1821)	45.00	60.00	75.00	125.00

1/4 MOHUR

GOLD, octagonal, 2.68-2.85 g

KM#	Date	Year	VG	Fine	VF	XF
281	SE1743	(1821)	150.00	185.00	265.00	375.00

COOCH BEHAR

During the 15th century, the area that was to become Cooch Behar was ruled by the powerful Hindu kings of Kamata, who were defeated by Sultan 'Ala al din Husain Shah of Bengal in 1494AD. In 1511AD the kingdom of Cooch Behar was established by Chandan, a chieftain of the Koch tribe.

Chandan was succeeded about 1522 by Visvasimha, who consolidated the kingdom, and set up his capital at the present town of Cooch Behar. It was he who laid the foundations of the prosperity of the area by developing the Tibetan trade routes through Bhutan. Visvasimha is said to have abdicated about 1555AD to become an ascetic, and was succeeded by his son Nara Narayan, under whose reign the state reached the zenith of its power.

From the solid basis set up by his father, Nara Narayan set out, assisted by his brother Sukladhvaja, to extend the borders of his kingdom. Over the next quarter century he proceeded to subdue part of the Assam Valley, Kachar, Manipur, the Khasi and Jaintia Hills and part of Tripura and Sylhet. Nara Narayan was the first king of Cooch Behar to strike coins, and the varied style may indicate that he set up several mints over his empire. The style of one piece is very similar to that of later pieces struck by the Rajas of Jaintiapur, which suggests Jaintiapur as the mint for this variety, but no other varieties have been assigned to specific mints.

After the death of Sukladhvaja, who was a great general, the military strength of the kingdom waned. Nara Narayan quarrelled with Sukladhvaja's son Raghu Deva, and the latter set himself up as ruler of the eastern part of the kingdom in 1581, initially under the suzerainty of his uncle, but after Nara Narayan's death, as full independent ruler.

Nara Narayan's son, Lakshmi Narayan inherited the western part of the kingdom, but no attempt was made to consolidate the conquests made by his father, and Kachar, Tripura and other states reverted to their former fully independent state. Lakshmi Narayan was a weak, peaceloving king, who preferred to declare himself a vassal of the Mughal Emperor in 1596, rather than make any attempt to preserve his independence. In accepting Mughal suzerainty, he gravely offended his subjects, who rose in revolt. The Mughals assisted Lakshmi Narayan quell the rebellion, and in 1603 a treaty was signed under which Lakshmi Narayan agreed never again to strike full rupees and to abandon certain other royal prerogatives. The Eastern Kingdom under Raghu Deva and his son Parikshit refused to bow to Mughal domination in the same way, and in 1612 the Mughals invaded and destroyed their kingdom.

After Lakshmi Narayan's death in 1627, the new ruler Vira Narayan exhibited a certain degree of independence by striking full rupees and retaking the former Eastern Cooch Behar Kingdom from the Mughals. By this time, however, a powerful leader had emerged in Bhutan, and trade was disrupted by wars between Bhutan and Tibet, causing a reduction in the number of coins struck.

The Mughals soon recaptured the eastern territories, but the next ruler, Prana Narayan, was able to reopen trade links with Tibet through Bhutan. In 1661 Prana Narayan was expelled from his capital by the Mughal governor of Bengal, Mir Jumla, and sought refuge in Bhutan. At this time Mir Jumla struck coins in Cooch Behar in the name of the Mughal Emperor Aurangzeb, but while Mir Jumla was stuck in Assam during the monsoon of 1663, Prana Narayan managed to regain control of his kingdom, paying tribute to the Mughal Emperor.

For the next century Cooch Behar was relatively peaceful until there was a dispute over the succession in 1772. After a confusing period during which the Bhutanese installed their own nominated ruler and captured Dhairyendra Narandra, the Chief Minister appealed to the British for assistance. With an eye on the potentially lucrative Tibetan trade, which had increased somewhat in volume since Prithvi Narayan's rise to power in Nepal, the British agreed to support Darendra Narayan, so long as British suzerainty was acknowledged.

Over the following decades the British gradually increased their control over the state. After large numbers of debased silver half, or "Narainy" rupees had been struck, the British decided to close the mint, and after that a few coins only were struck at the coronation of each ruler, although it was only in 1866 that the local coins ceased to be legal tender.

Bhutanese copies: Until the 1780's the Bhutanese used to periodically send surplus silver to the mint in Cooch Behar to strike into coin for local use, as Cooch Behar coins circulated widely in Bhutan. After the Cooch Behar mint was closed in 1788 the Bhutanese established their own mints, striking copies of the 1/2 rupees - initially of fine silver with slight differences in design from the original Cooch Behar coins, but later the silver content reduced until they were of pure copper or brass. For these issues see Bhutan listing.

RULERS

Harendra Narayan, CB273-329/
SE1705-1761/1783-1839AD

Shivendra Narayan, CB329-337/
SE1761-1769/1839-1847AD

Narendra Narayan, CB337-353/
SE1769-1785/1847-1863AD

Nripendra Narayan, CB353-401/
SE1785-1833/1863-1911AD

DATING

The coins are dated in either the Saka era (Saka yr. + 78 = AD year) or the Cooch Behar era (CB yr. + 1510 = AD year) calculated from the year of the founding of the kingdom by Chandan in 1511AD. Some coins have dates in both eras, but as the Saka always refers back to the accession year, and the Cooch Behar year seems to show the actual date of striking, the two years do not necessarily correspond to the same AD year.

Unfortunately the dies for the half rupees were usually rather broader than the flans, so the year is only rarely visible.

HARENDRA NARAYAN

CB273-329/SE1705-1761/1783-1839AD

These names usually cannot be differentiated.

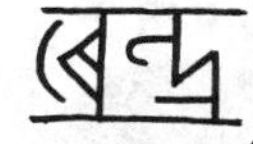

'rendra' center left on obverse

1/2 RUPEE

SILVER, 4.70 g

KM#	Date	Year	VG	Fine	VF	XF
141	ND	—	5.00	8.00	11.00	15.00

PRESENTATION ISSUES

The following 1/2 Rupees and Mohurs are all presentation (nazarana) issues of varying weights. Silver and gold were struck from same dies. They are dated in a local era beginning with the founding of the Koch Kingdom in 1510AD (RE dates).

SHIVENDRA NARAYAN

CB329-337/SE1761-1769/1839-1847AD

NAZARANA 1/2 RUPEE

SILVER, 4.70 g

KM#	Date	Year	VG	Fine	VF	XF
151	ND	—	23.50	37.50	55.00	80.00

NAZARANA MOHUR

GOLD, 21mm, 9.40 g
Similar to Nazarana 1/2 Rupee, KM#151.

KM#	Date	Year	VG	Fine	VF	XF
155	R.Y.39	—	500.00	700.00	1000.	1500.

NARENDRA NARAYAN

CB337-353/SE1769-1785/1847-1863AD

NAZARANA 1/2 RUPEE

SILVER, 4.70 g

KM#	Date	Mintage	VG	Fine	VF	XF
165	ND	1,000	22.50	35.00	50.00	70.00

NAZARANA MOHUR

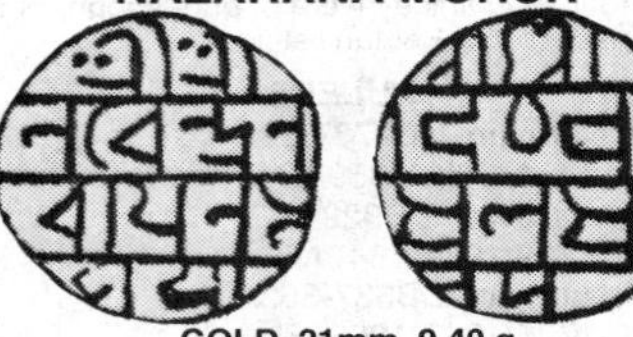

GOLD, 21mm, 9.40 g
Similar to Nazarana 1/2 Rupee, KM#165.

KM#	Date	Year	VG	Fine	VF	XF
170	ND	—	350.00	500.00	700.00	1000.

NRIPENDRA NARAYAN

CB353-401/SE1785-1833/1863-1911AD

NAZARANA 1/2 RUPEE

SILVER, 4.30 g

KM#	Date	Year	Fine	VF	XF	Unc
180	CB354	(1864)	35.00	60.00	85.00	150.00

NAZARANA MOHUR

GOLD, 21mm, 9.40 g
Similar to Nazarana 1/2 Rupee, KM#180.

KM#	Date	Year	Fine	VF	XF	Unc
185	CB354	(1864)	300.00	400.00	550.00	750.00

KACHAR

The Kacharis are probably the original inhabitants of the Assam Valley, and in the 13th century ruled much of the south bank of the Brahmaputra from their capital at Dimapur.

Around 1530 the Ahoms inflicted several crushing defeats on the Kacharis, Dimapur was sacked, and the Kacharis were forced to retreat further south and set up a new capital at Maibong.

Very little is known about this obscure state, and the only time that coins were struck in any quantity was during the late 16th and early 17th centuries. One coin, indeed, proudly announces the conquest of Sylhet, but the military prowess seems to have been short lived, and the small kingdom was only saved from Muslim domination by its isolation and lack of economic worth.

A few coins were struck during the 18th and 19th centuries, but this was probably merely as a demonstration of independence, rather than for any economic reason.

In 1819, the last Kachari ruler, Govind Chandra was ousted by the Manipuri ruler Chaurajit Simha, and during the Burmese occupation of Manipur and Assam, the Manipuris remained in control of Kachar. In 1824, Govind Chandra was restored to his throne by the British, and ruled under British suzerainty. By all accounts his administration was not a success, and in 1832, soon after Govind Chandra had been murdered, the British took over the administration of the State in "compliance with the frequent and earnestly expressed wishes of the people.

The earliest coins of Kachar were clearly copied from the contemporary coins of Cooch Behar, with weight standard also copied from the Bengali standard. The flans are, however, even broader than those of the Cooch Behar coins, making the coins very distinctive.

A number of spectacular gold and silver coins, purporting to come from Kachar, appeared in Calcutta during the 1960's, but as their authenticity has been doubted, they have been omitted from this listing.

RULERS

A list of the Kings of Kachar has been preserved in local traditions, but is rather unreliable. The following list has been compiled from this traditional list, together with names and dates obtained from other sources, but may not be completely accurate.

Krishna Chandra Narayan, SE1712-1735/c.1790-1813AD
Govinda Chandra, SE1735-1741/1814-1819AD
Chaurajit Singh, (of Manipur), SE1741-1745/1819-1823AD
Gambhir Singh, (of Manipur), SE1745-1746/1823-1824AD
Govinda Chandra, SE1746-1752/1824-1830AD

GOVINDA CHANDRA

SE1735-1752/1813-1830AD

RUPEE

SILVER, 25mm, 10.70-11.60 g

KM#	Date	Year	VG	Fine	VF	XF
150	SE1736	(1814)	100.00	150.00	225.00	325.00

MANIPUR

Although the Manipuri traditions preserve a long list of kings which purports to go back to the early years of the Christian era, the first ruler whose existence can be verified from more tangible sources was a Naga called Panheiba, who adopted the Hindu religion and took the name of Gharib Niwaz about 1714AD.

Gharib Niwaz seems to have been a powerful ruler, who was successful in the frequent wars with Burma, and hence raised the country from obscurity. He was murdered in 1750, together with his eldest son, and it was during the reign of the latter's son, Gaura Singh, that the British first came into contact with Manipur. After the death of Gharib Niwaz the Burmese had more success with their incursions into Manipur, and by 1761 there was a danger that the capital would be captured, so the Manipuris appealed to the British for military assistance. This was granted, and in 1762 British troops helped the Manipuris drive out the Burmese, and a treaty of alliance was signed. On this occasion 500 meklee gold rupees were sent to the British as part payment for the expenses of this assistance.

Gaura Singh died in 1764 and from then until 1798 his brother Jai Singh heroically defended his country against the Burmese. In the early years of his reign he suffered many setbacks, but for the last ten years of his reign his position was fairly secure. In 1798 Jai Singh abdicated and died the following year. The next 35 years were to see five of his eight sons on the throne, plotting against each other and enlisting Burmese support for their internecine rivalry. After 1812 the Manipuri King was little more than a puppet in the hands of the Burmese, and when the Kings tried to assert their independence they were ousted to become Kings of Kachar.

In 1824, after the 1st Burma war, the Burmese were finally driven out of Manipur and Gambhir Singh, one of the younger sons of Jai Singh, asked for British assistance to regain control of his kingdom. This was granted, and from 1825 until his death in 1834 Gambhir Singh ruled well and restored an element of prosperity to his kingdom. A British resident was stationed in Manipur, but the king ruled his country independently. The British stayed aloof from several palace intrigues and revolutions, and it was only in 1891, after several British Officials had been killed, that the administration was brought under the control of a British Political Agent.

RULERS

Madhu Chandra, SE1723-1728/1801-1806AD
Chaurajit Singh, SE1728-1734/1806-1812AD
Marjit Singh, under Burmese suzerainty, SE1734-1741/1812-1819AD
Huidromba Subol, SE1741-1742/1819-1820AD
Gambhir Singh, SE1742-1743/1820-1821AD
Jadu Singh, SE1743-1745/1821-1823AD
Raghab Singh, SE1745-1746/1823-1824AD
Bhadra Singh, SE1746-1747/1824-1825AD
Gambhir Singh, restored by the British, SE1747-1756/1825-1834AD
Chandra Kirti, SE1756-1765/1834-1843AD
Nar Singh, SE1765-1771/1843-1849AD
Chandra Kirti, SE1771-1808/1849-1886AD
Sura Chandra Singh, SE1808-1812/1886-1890AD
Kula Chandra Singh, SE1812-1813/1890-1891AD
Chura Chandra, SE1813-1862/1891-1941AD

COINAGE

The only coins struck in quantity for circulation in Manipur were small bell-metal (circa 74 percent copper, 23 percent tin, 3 percent zinc) coins called "sel". According to local tradition these coins were first struck in the 17th century, but this is doubtful, and it seems likely that the sels were first struck in the second half of the 18th century. Unfortunately few of the sels can be attributed to any particular ruler, as they merely bear a Nagari letter deemed auspicious for the particular reign, and it has not been recorded which letter was deemed auspicious for which ruler.

The value of the sel functioned relative to the rupees which also circulated in Manipur for making large purchases, although Government accounts were kept in sel until 1891. Prior to 1838 the sel was valued at about 900 to the rupee, but after that date it fell in value to around 480 to the rupee, although there were occasional fluctuations. About 1878, speculative hoarding of sel forced the value up to 240 to the rupee, but large numbers of sel were struck at this time, and from then until 1891, when the sel were withdrawn from circulation, their value remained fairly stable at about 400 to the rupee.

During the years after 1714AD some square gold and silver coins were struck, but as few have survived, they were probably only struck in small quantities for ceremonial rather than monetary use.

Apart from the coins mentioned above, some larger bell-metal coins have been attributed to Manipur, but the attribution is still somewhat tentative. Also several other gold coins, two with an image of Krishna playing the flute, have been discovered in Calcutta in recent years, but as their authenticity has been queried, they have not been included in the following listing.

DATING

Most of the silver and gold coins of Manipur are dated in the Saka era (Sake date + 78 = AD date), but at least one coin is dated in the Manipuri "Chandrabda" era, which may be converted to the AD year by adding 788 to the Chandrabda date.

MONETARY SYSTEM

(Until 1838AD)
880 to 960 Sel = 1 Rupee
(Commencing 1838AD)
420-480 Sel = 1 Rupee

CHAURAJIT SINGH

SE1725-1734/1803-1812AD

1/4 RUPEE

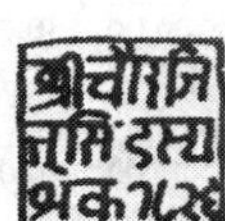

SILVER, 2.68-2.90 g

C#	Date	Year	VG	Fine	VF	XF
55	SE1726	(1804)	42.00	85.00	140.00	200.00
	1729	(1807)	42.00	85.00	140.00	200.00

1/2 RUPEE

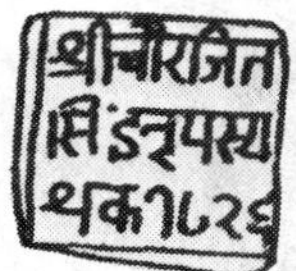
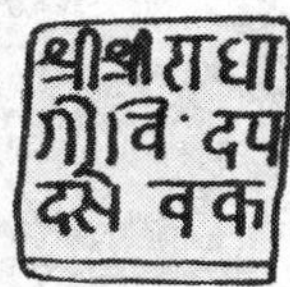

SILVER, 5.35-5.80 g

C#	Date	Year	VG	Fine	VF	XF
56	SE1726	(1804)	50.00	100.00	175.00	250.00

RUPEE

SILVER, 10.70-11.60 g

C#	Date	Year	VG	Fine	VF	XF
57	SE1728	(1806)	90.00	180.00	300.00	450.00
	1729	(1807)	90.00	180.00	300.00	450.00
	1732	(1810)	90.00	180.00	300.00	450.00
	1734	(1812)	60.00	120.00	200.00	300.00

MOHUR

GOLD, 11.20-12.50 g

C#	Date	Year	VG	Fine	VF	XF
61	SE1731	(1809)	225.00	375.00	625.00	875.00

MARJIT SINGH

SE1734-1741/1812-1819AD

RUPEE

SILVER, 11.50 g

C#	Date	Year	VG	Fine	VF	XF
71	SE1736	(1814)	50.00	100.00	175.00	250.00

MOHUR

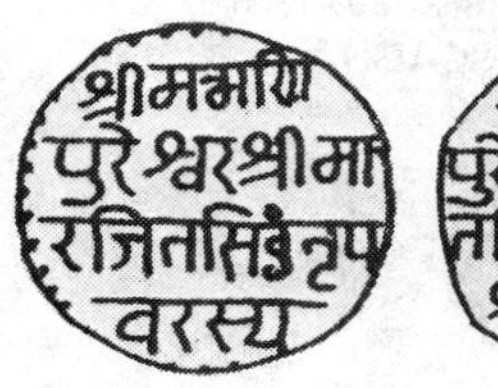
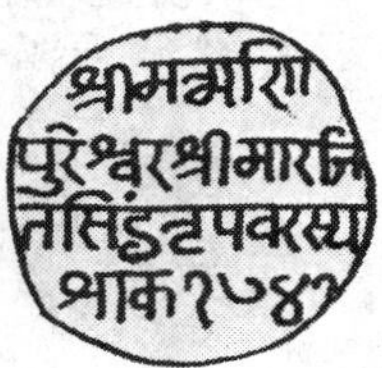

GOLD, 10.70-11.40 g

C#	Date	Year	VG	Fine	VF	XF
75	SE1741	(1819)	375.00	625.00	875.00	1150.

GAMBHIR SINGH

SE1748-1756/1826-1834AD

MOHUR

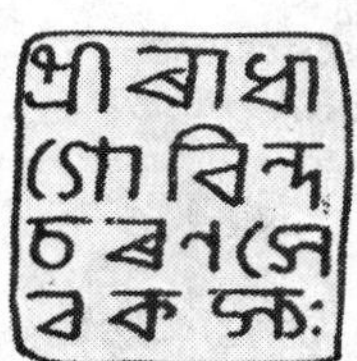
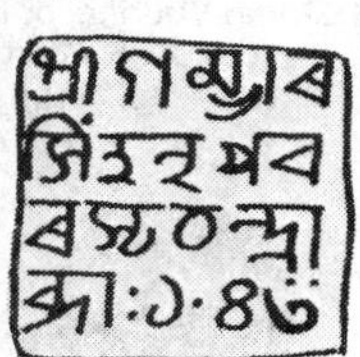

GOLD, 10.70-11.40 g

C#	Date	Year	VG	Fine	VF	XF
85	1043*	(1831)	375.00	625.00	875.00	1150.

***NOTE:** Chandrabdah 1043 (a local date system).

ANONYMOUS ISSUES

These bear a single Bengali character, of uncertain significance, and cannot be assigned to particular rulers. All are uniface.

SEL

BRONZE BELL-METAL, uniface

Sri

C#	Date	Good	VG	Fine	VF
1	ND	3.50	6.00	8.00	10.00

NOTE: Many variations in style exist, 2 varieties are illustrated above.

Ma

C#	Date	Good	VG	Fine	VF
2	ND	5.00	8.00	11.50	15.00

Ra

C#	Date	Good	VG	Fine	VF
3	ND	6.00	10.00	15.00	20.00

(Said to be on issue of Nara Singh, 1843-50)

Ka

C#	Date	Good	VG	Fine	VF
4	ND	6.00	10.00	15.00	20.00

(Struck before 1820)

La

C#	Date	Good	VG	Fine	VF
5	ND	6.00	10.00	15.00	20.00

(Perhaps an issue of Sura Chandra, 1886-90)

Ku

C#	Date	Good	VG	Fine	VF
6	ND	6.00	10.00	15.00	20.00

(Probably an issue of Kula Chandra Singh, 1890-91)

Bha

C#	Date	Good	VG	Fine	VF
7	ND	6.00	10.00	15.00	20.00

L'L

C#	Date	Good	VG	Fine	VF
15	ND	6.00	10.00	15.00	20.00

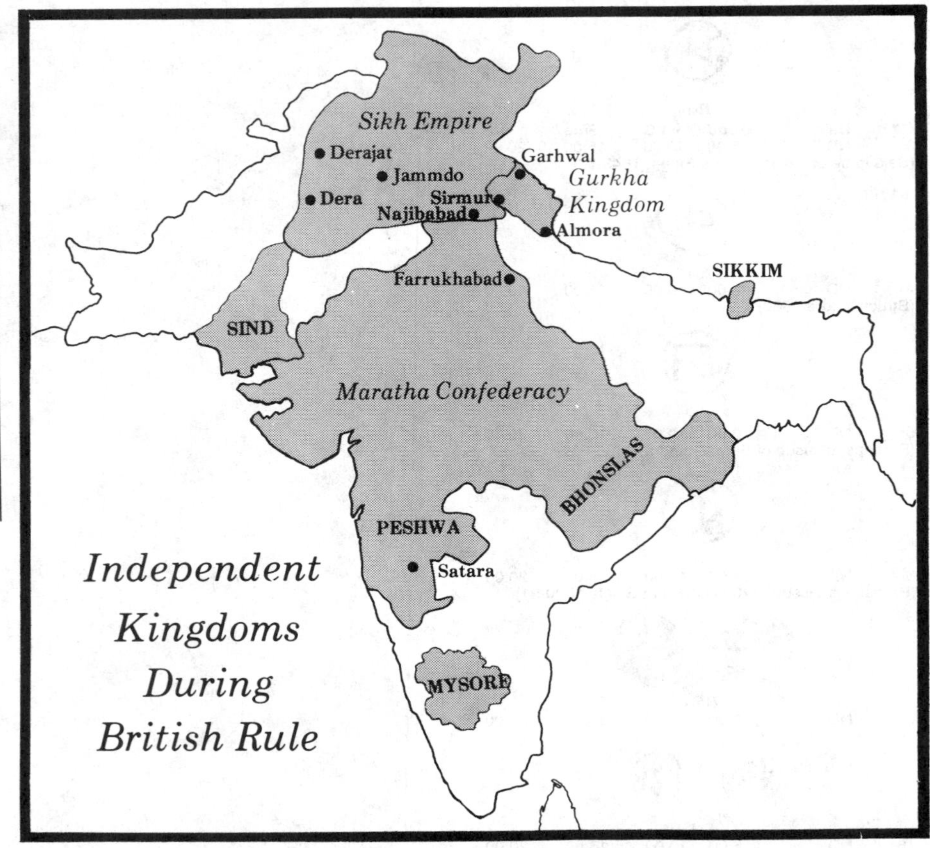

FARRUKHABAD

Farrukhabad, a district in north India, was founded early in the eighteenth century by the Afghan, Mohammed Khan (d.1743), who was governor first of Allahabad and later of Malwa. The subsequent struggles of his sons with Awadh, with the Rohillas and with the Marathas, culminated in Farrukhabad becoming a tributary to Awadh, by which state Farrukhabad was entirely surrounded. In 1801 Farrukhabad was ceded to the British by the Nawab Vizier of Awadh.

For similar coins struck in the name of Ahmad Shah (Durrani) dated AH1174, 1176 refer to Afghanistan, Durrani listings. For later issues with fixed regnal year 45 refer to India-British/Bengal Presidency listings.

MINTNAME

Commencing AH1167

احمدنگر فرخ اباد

Ahmadnagar-Farrukhabad

NOTE: Catalog numbers were in reference to Craig's basic Mughal listings.

AHMADNAGAR - FARRUKHABAD MINT

In the name of Shah Alam II
AH1173-1221/1759-1806AD

FALUS

COPPER

KM#	Date	Year	VG	Fine	VF	XF
20 (C71.5)	AH1219	39	4.50	8.50	13.50	20.00

In the name of Muhammad Akbar II
AH1221-1253/1806-1837AD

1/2 ANNA

COPPER

KM#	Date	Year	VG	Fine	VF	XF
24 (C123.5)	AH1226	6	5.00	10.00	15.00	22.50
	1233	12	4.50	8.50	13.50	20.00

In the name of Shah Alam II
AH1173-1221/1759-1806AD

RUPEE

SILVER, 10.70-11.60 g

KM#	Date	Year	VG	Fine	VF	XF
28	AH1216	39	8.50	13.50	20.00	35.00
(C86.2)	1217	39	8.50	13.50	20.00	35.00
	1218	39	8.50	13.50	20.00	35.00
	1219	39	8.50	13.50	20.00	35.00
	1220	39	8.50	13.50	20.00	35.00
	1224	39	8.50	13.50	20.00	35.00
	1225	39	8.50	13.50	20.00	35.00
	1227	39	8.50	13.50	20.00	35.00
	1228	39	8.50	13.50	20.00	35.00

NOTE: Earlier dates (AH1175-1215) exist for this type.

NAZARANA RUPEE

Issued after cession to the British

SILVER, 10.70-11.60 g

KM#	Date	Year	VG	Fine	VF	XF
30 (C86.2a)	AH1228	39	35.00	65.00	110.00	185.00

GURKHA KINGDOM

GARHWAL

RULERS

Girvan Yuddha, of Nepal
VS1860-1872/1803-1815AD

SRINAGAR MINT

In the names of Shah Alam II and Girvan Yuddha, of Nepal
VS1860-1863/1803-1806AD

TIMASHA

SILVER

C#	Date	Year	VG	Fine	VF	XF
35	VS(18)65	(1808)	6.50	10.00	15.00	22.50
	(18)66	(1809)	6.50	10.00	15.00	22.50
	Date off flan		4.00	6.50	10.00	15.00

In the names of Muhammad Akbar II and Girvan Yuddha, of Nepal
VS1863-1870/1806-1813AD

TIMASHA

SILVER

C#	Date	Year	VG	Fine	VF	XF
36	VS(18)65	(1808)	6.50	10.00	15.00	22.50
	(18)66	(1809)	6.50	10.00	15.00	22.50
	(18)67	(1810)	6.50	10.00	15.00	22.50
	(18)68	(1811)	6.50	10.00	15.00	22.50
	(18)69	(1812)	6.50	10.00	15.00	22.50
	(18)70	(1813)	6.50	10.00	15.00	22.50

In the name of Girvan Yuddha
VS1860-1873/1803-1816AD

PAISA

COPPER

C#	Date	Year	Good	VG	Fine	VF
30	VS1859	(1802)	4.00	6.00	8.00	12.50
	1872	(1815)	3.00	4.50	7.00	10.00
	1873	(1816)	4.00	6.00	8.00	12.50

TIMASHA

SILVER

C#	Date	Year	VG	Fine	VF	XF
37	ND	—	6.50	10.00	15.00	22.50

KUMAON

RULER

Girvan Yuddha, of Nepal
VS1860-1873/1803-1816AD

Almora Mint

PAISA

COPPER

C#	Date	Year	Good	VG	Fine	VF
10	VS(18)66	(1809)	3.00	5.00	8.00	12.50

SIRMUR

RULER

Girvan Yuddha, of Nepal
VS1860-1873/1803-1816AD

NAHAN MINT

1/2 PAISA

COPPER

20	AH1227	(1812)	3.00	5.00	8.00	12.50

PAISA

COPPER

21	AH1227 VS(18)68		4.00	6.00	9.00	13.50

MARATHA CONFEDERACY

The origins of the Marathas are lost in the early history of the remote hill country of the Western Ghats in present-day Maharashtra. By the fifteenth century they had come into occasional prominence for their resistance to Muslim incursions into their homelands. They were a rugged wiry people who, by the seventeenth century, had accomodated themselves to the political realities of their times by becoming feudatories, or mercenaries, to the sultans of Bijapur. It is not clear exactly what happened to suddenly thrust the Marathas into the limelight of Indian history in the seventeenth century. The most likely explanation seems to be that the broad sweep of Aurangzeb's campaigns across the Deccan, his insensitivity towards Hindu sentiment, and the pre-eminence he gave to Islam, all served to politicize a hitherto politically quiescent people. And just as Aurangzeb supplied the occasion, the Marathas found in Sivaji the man.

In the seventeenth century Shahji, the father of Sivaji, was holder of a small fiefdom under the Bijapur sultans. His son, taking advantage of the declining authority of his overlords, seized some of the surrounding territory. Bijapur proved incapable of quelling his insurrection. Drawing encouragement from this experience, Sivaji's forces sacked and plundered the Mughal port of Surat in 1664. From this point until his death in 1680 Sivaji maintained a sort of running guerilla war with Aurangzeb. There were no decisive victories for either side but Sivaji left behind him a cohesive and well organized regional alliance in the Western Deccan, a small isolated kingdom in Tanjore and a few pockets of territory on the west coast.

After Sivaji's death the struggle was renewed as Aurangzeb advanced into the Deccan. It was the years after Aurangzeb's death in 1707 which really saw revival as the Maratha confederacy gained a new cohesiveness and its military successes began to make it look as if the Marathas might even become the new masters of India. The revenues of much of the Deccan now flowed into (finished up in) Maratha pockets. Baji Rao I, the Peshwa, pressed as far north as the gates of Delhi and in 1738 he gained control of Malwa. Parts of Gujarat also were in confederacy hands. Bengal was invaded, Orissa annexed (1751), and the territories of the Nizam of Hyderabad and the Carnatic appeared at risk. It was during this period that some of the great Maratha families gained prominence - the Holkars, the Sindhias, the Gaekwars and the Bhonslas - families who later, as the confederacy began to disintegrate and give way to rivalry, would assert their own regional interests at the expense of the alliance.

The turning point for Maratha fortunes was the battle of Panipat on January 14th 1761. Intending to stop the Afghan, Ahmad Shah Abdali (Durrani), in his tracks, the Marathas assembled the greatest army in their history and placed it under the unified command of the Peshwa of Poona. By nightfall the Peshwa's son and heir, Bhao Sahib, and all the leading chiefs, were dead. Maratha losses were said to have been in excess of a hundred thousand men. The Marathas would still remain a force to be reckoned with, they would again cross the Chambel (1767), and they would still give the Nizam's forces a thrashing (1795), but from 1761 onwards internal dissension grew rife and the Maratha Confederacy would never again exhibit sufficient cohesion to be considered a serious contender for the crown of India.

This powerful alliance of Marathi warriors owed nominal allegiance to the Rajas of Satara (descendents of Shivaji) and drew their unity from the leadership of the Peshwa, the hereditary prime minister of the confederation. In the mid-eighteenth century the Marathas were at the apogee of their influence, having hastened the end of effective Mughal power in the Deccan and western India. They successfully checked the intrusions of the Durranis into north India, although the experience left them so militarily exhausted that the dominance in Hindustan passed to other hands.

The great families of the lieutenants of the Peshwa gradually carved out regional power bases and became progressively less responsive to the authority of their formal superiors. The Maratha power as such was broken in a series of wars with the East India Company, bitterly fought and very close contests which settled the fate of large sections of India. Broadly speaking the Marathas may for convenience sake be listed in two categories, the lines which became extinct through British action and those which accomodated the English after defeat and survived to become Princely States. The latter will be found elsewhere in the catalogue; the non-surviving political units are catalogued below.

BHONSLAS

RULERS

Raghoji II, 1788-1816AD
Raghoji III, 1816-1853AD

MINTS

Cuttack کٹک

Most coins are imitations of Mughal coins of Ahmad Shah (1748-54AD), more or less barbarized. The Bhonslas mints were closed when the state was abolished in 1854.

Cuttack Mint

PAISA

Rev. symbols ۳ and ٯ

"Zareepathka" flag. Additional symbol added after 1825.

COPPER

KM#	Date	Year	Good	VG	Fine	VF
A11	ND	—	2.00	3.00	4.00	7.00

1/16 RUPEE

SILVER, 0.61-0.72 g

KM#	Date	Year	VG	Fine	VF	XF
11	ND	—	7.50	15.00	25.00	35.00

1/8 RUPEE

SILVER, 1.33-1.45 g

12	ND	—	7.50	15.00	25.00	35.00

1/4 RUPEE

SILVER, 2.67-2.90 g

Rev: Flag only.

KM#	Date	Year	VG	Fine	VF	XF
13	ND	—	6.50	13.00	21.00	30.00

Rev: Both symbols.

14	ND	—	6.50	13.00	21.00	30.00

1/2 RUPEE

SILVER, 5.35-5.80 g
Rev: Both symbols.

15	ND	—	7.50	15.00	21.50	35.00

RUPEE

SILVER, 10.70-11.60 g
W/o mint marks. Mintname: Katak
Pseudo regnal year

16	ND	52	12.50	22.50	42.50	55.00
		57	12.50	22.50	42.50	55.00
		512	12.50	22.50	42.50	55.00

Rev: Flag only, pseudo regnal years.

17	ND	5	10.00	20.00	35.00	50.00
		51	10.00	20.00	35.00	50.00
		52	10.00	20.00	35.00	50.00
		511	10.00	20.00	35.00	50.00
		512	10.00	20.00	35.00	50.00
		521	10.00	20.00	35.00	50.00

Rev: Both symbols.

18	ND	5	12.50	25.00	42.00	60.00

NAZARANA RUPEE

SILVER

19	—	22	—	—	—	—

PESHWAS

RULERS

Baji Rao, 1796-1818AD

MINTS

Ahmadabad احمد اباد

Bagalkot بگلکوت

Gulshanabad (Nasik) گلشن آباد

Jalaun جلون

Jhansi بلونت نگر
Mintname: Balwantnagar

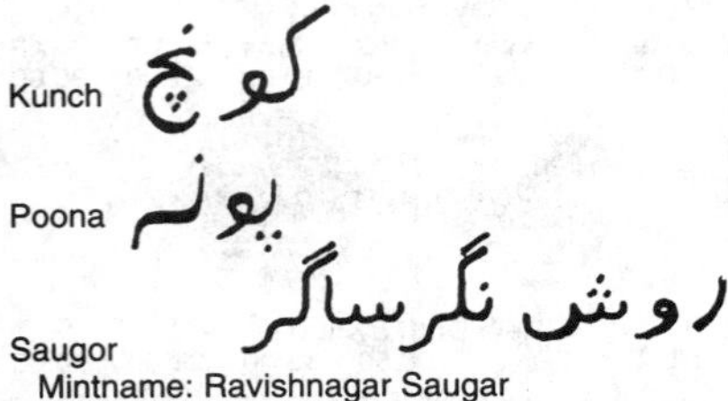

Kunch

Poona

Saugor

Mintname: Ravishnagar Saugar

Ahmadabad Mint

One of Maratha Mints from 1757-1800, it was leased to Baroda from 1800-1804, returned during 1804-1806, released to Baroda in 1806, and ceded to Baroda in 1817 (1232AH). In 1818, it was annexed by the East India Company finally closed in 1835.

MINT MARKS

Obv: Ankus  Ankus w/pennant

Mint symbol on rev. at lower left:

NOTE: Baroda coins of this mint have the Nagari initial of the ruler. British coins have the following mark on rev:

SATARA RAJAS

In the name of Chhatrapati Sivaji

Uncertain Mint

SILVER
Obv: Parasol design.

KM#	Date	Year	Good	VG	Fine	VF
245	AH121(7)	42	—	—	Rare	—

NOTE: Pseudo-Shahjahanabad Maratha issue struck 1801AD.

In the name of Muhammad Akbar II
AH1221-1253/1806-1837AD

PAISA

COPPER

KM#	Date	Year	VG	Fine	VF	XF
53	AH1232	10	3.00	4.00	6.50	9.00

1/2 RUPEE

SILVER, 18mm, 5.35-5.80 g
Mint mark: Ankus.

KM#	Date	Year	VG	Fine	VF	XF
54	AH—	—	6.00	9.00	14.00	20.00

Mint mark: Ankus w/pennant.

KM#	Date	Year	VG	Fine	VF	XF
55	AHxxxx	10	6.00	9.00	14.00	20.00

RUPEE

SILVER, 10.70-11.60 g
Mint mark: Ankus and scissors.

KM#	Date	Year	VG	Fine	VF	XF
56	AH122x	8	12.50	18.50	25.00	35.00
	1230	8	12.50	18.50	25.00	35.00

Mint mark: Ankus.

KM#	Date	Year	VG	Fine	VF	XF
57	AH122x	8	7.50	12.50	18.50	27.50
		9	7.50	12.50	18.50	27.50

Mint mark: Ankus w/pennant.

KM#	Date	Year	VG	Fine	VF	XF
58	AH1231	9	8.50	13.50	20.00	30.00
	1231	10	8.50	13.50	20.00	30.00

Gulshanabad Mint

Nasik

In the name of Shah Alam II
AH1173-1221/1759-1806AD

1/4 RUPEE

SILVER, 2.68-2.90 g

KM#	Date	Year	VG	Fine	VF	XF
107	AH1236	—	10.00	12.50	16.50	21.50

1/2 RUPEE

SILVER, 5.35-5.80 g

KM#	Date	Year	VG	Fine	VF	XF
108	AH1229	—	10.00	16.50	21.50	30.00
	1235	—	10.00	16.50	21.50	30.00

NOTE: Earlier date (AH1207) exists for this type.

RUPEE

SILVER, 10.70-11.60 g

KM#	Date	Year	VG	Fine	VF	XF
109	AH1219	—	12.50	18.50	25.00	35.00
	1227	—	12.50	18.50	25.00	35.00
	1229	—	12.50	18.50	25.00	35.00
	1232	—	12.50	18.50	25.00	35.00
	1234	—	12.50	18.50	25.00	35.00
	1235	—	12.50	18.50	25.00	35.00
	1236	—	12.50	18.50	25.00	35.00
	1251	—	12.50	18.50	25.00	35.00

NOTE: Earlier dates (AH1206-1212) exist for this type.

Jalaun Mint

Obv. symbols: and

Rev: or

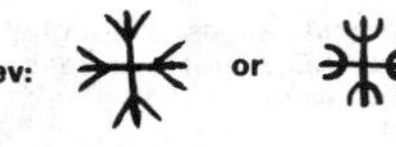

In the name of Shah Alam II
AH1173-1221/1759-1806AD

RUPEE

Mintname: 

Zarb ba Jalaun Hijri

SILVER, 10.70-11.60 g
Crude fabric, narrow flan.

KM#	Date	Year	VG	Fine	VF	XF
124	AH1224	49	12.50	18.50	25.00	35.00
	1222	55	12.50	18.50	25.00	35.00

Mintname: 

Zarb Ku(nch), Kuna(r), Jalaun

Fine fabric, normal flan.

KM#	Date	Year	VG	Fine	VF	XF
125	AH—	49	15.00	21.50	33.50	45.00

Crude fabric, narrow flan.

KM#	Date	Year	VG	Fine	VF	XF
126	AH1222	17	(error)			
			6.50	10.00	15.00	22.50
	1223	17	(error)			
			6.50	10.00	15.00	22.50
	—	21	6.50	10.00	15.00	22.50
	1222	51	6.50	10.00	15.00	22.50
	1222	52	6.50	10.00	15.00	22.50
	1222	53	6.50	10.00	15.00	22.50
	1222	55	6.50	10.00	15.00	22.50
	1222	57	6.50	10.00	15.00	22.50

In the names of Shah Alam II
AH1173-1221/1759-1806AD
and Latif Khan

KM#	Date	Year	VG	Fine	VF	XF
128	AH—	53	30.00	40.00	55.00	75.00

Jhansi Mint

Mint mark: 

on reverse

Mintname: 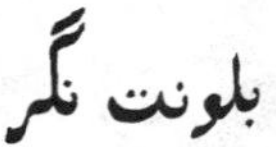

Balwantnagar

In the name of Shah Alam II
AH1173-1221/1759-1806AD

RUPEE

SILVER, 10.70-11.60 g
Obv: 99111 added.

KM#	Date	Year	VG	Fine	VF	XF
144	AH1220	47	10.00	15.00	20.00	27.50
	1221	48	10.00	15.00	20.00	27.50
	1223	50	10.00	15.00	20.00	27.50
	1224	52	10.00	15.00	20.00	27.50
	1234	—	10.00	15.00	20.00	27.50

Rev: Lily.

KM#	Date	Year	VG	Fine	VF	XF
145	AH—	3	11.50	17.50	23.50	33.50
	—	4	11.50	17.50	23.50	33.50
	—	6	11.50	17.50	23.50	33.50

Kunch Mint

Mint marks: 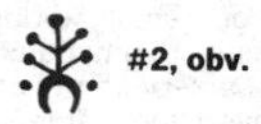

rev. all coins

#1 obv. 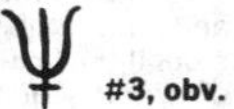 **#2, obv.**

#3, obv.

 **#4, rev.**  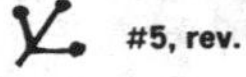 **#5, rev.**

Mintname:

Kunch Hijri

EAST INDIA COMPANY

As administrator of Kunch for Holkar from AH1220-R.Y.47/1805AD.

RUPEE

SILVER, 10.70-11.60 g
Obv: Symbols #1, #2, #3.
Rev: Symbol #4.

KM#	Date	Year	VG	Fine	VF	XF
178	AH1220	47	16.00	22.50	35.00	50.00
	1221	47	16.00	22.50	35.00	50.00

Nasirabad Mint

In the name of Shah Alam "Bahadur Shah" II
AH1173-1221/1759-1806AD

RUPEE

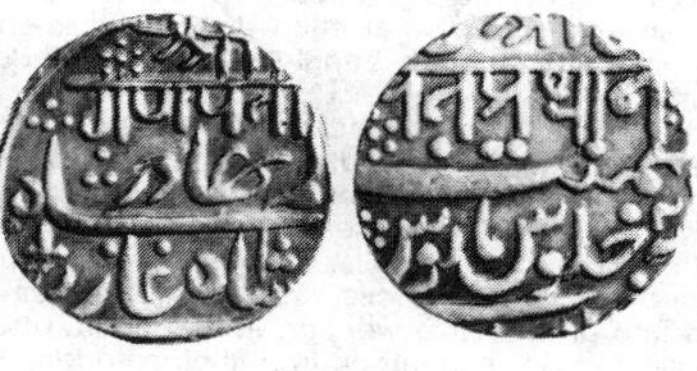

SILVER
Obv. Persian leg: ***Sri Gonapati.***
Rev. Persian leg: ***Sri Pant Pradhan.***

KM#	Date	Year	VG	Fine	VF	XF
195	AH122X	27	—	—	—	—

Poona Mint

"Muhiabad Poona" Mint opened in 1750 and closed between 1834-1835.

In the name of Ali Gauhar, the name of Shah Alam II before his accession

NOTE: On Feb. 10, 1818AD (AH1233, Falsi Era 1128) the British East India Company took over Poona, so all coins of that date or later are British Colonial issues.

Mint marks:

1  Ankus

3  scissors

2  Axe

4  *Sri* in Nagari

1/8 RUPEE

SILVER, 1.34-1.45 g
Rev: Mint mark #1 w/regnal year in Persian numerals.

KM#	Date	Year	VG	Fine	VF	XF
207	—	—	10.00	16.50	21.50	30.00

NOTE: This coin was copied by the local rulers at Alibagh Wai and Wadgaon.

1/4 RUPEE

SILVER, 2.68-2.90 g
Rev: Mint mark #1 w/regnal year in Persian numerals.

KM#	Date	Year	VG	Fine	VF	XF
208	—	—	— Reported, not confirmed			

NOTE: This coin was copied by the local rulers at Alibagh Wai and Wadgaon.

Rev: Mint mark #1 w/Fasli date in Nagari numerals.

KM#	Date	Year	VG	Fine	VF	XF
209	FE1238	(1828)	8.50	13.50	20.00	28.50

Rev: Mint mark: #2.

KM#	Date	Year	VG	Fine	VF	XF
210	FE1242	—	16.00	22.50	35.00	50.00

1/2 RUPEE

SILVER, 5.35-5.80 g
Rev: Mint mark #1 w/regnal year in Persian numerals.

KM#	Date	Year	VG	Fine	VF	XF
211	—	—	13.50	20.00	27.50	37.50

NOTE: This coin was copied by the local rulers at Alibagh Wai and Wadgaon.

Rev: Mint mark #1 w/Fasli date in Nagari numerals.

KM#	Date	Year	VG	Fine	VF	XF
212	FE1233	(1823)	10.00	16.50	21.50	30.00
	1236	(1826)	10.00	16.50	21.50	30.00
	1240	(1830)	10.00	16.50	21.50	30.00

RUPEE

SILVER, 10.70-11.60 g
Ankusi Rupee
Rev: Mint mark #1 w/regnal year in Persian numerals.

KM#	Date	Year	VG	Fine	VF	XF
213	—	11	7.00	11.00	16.50	25.00
	—	12	7.00	11.00	16.50	25.00
	—	15	7.00	11.00	16.50	25.00
	AH1225	—	7.50	12.50	18.50	27.50
	1227	—	7.50	12.50	18.00	27.50
	1229	—	7.50	12.50	18.50	27.50

NOTE: This coin was copied by the local rulers at Alibagh Wai and Wadgaon.

Rev: Mint mark #1, Fasli date in Nagari numerals.

KM#	Date	Year	VG	Fine	VF	XF
214	FE1232	(1822)	6.50	10.00	15.00	22.50
	1233	(1823)	6.50	10.00	15.00	22.50
	1234	(1824)	6.50	10.00	15.00	22.50
	1235	(1825)	6.50	10.00	15.00	22.50
	1236	(1826)	6.50	10.00	15.00	22.50
	1237	(1827)	6.50	10.00	15.00	22.50
	1238	(1828)	6.50	10.00	15.00	22.50
	1239	(1829)	6.50	10.00	15.00	22.50
	1240	(1830)	6.50	10.00	15.00	22.50
	1241	(1831)	6.50	10.00	15.00	22.50
	1242	(1832)	6.50	10.00	15.00	22.50
	1243	(1833)	6.50	10.00	15.00	22.50
	1244	(1834)	6.50	10.00	15.00	22.50

Rev: Mint mark #3, Fasli date in Nagari numerals.

KM#	Date	Year	VG	Fine	VF	XF
217	AH1230	—	10.00	16.50	21.50	30.00
	1231	—	10.00	16.50	21.50	30.00
	1232	—	10.00	16.50	21.50	30.00
	1234	—	10.00	16.50	21.50	30.00
	1236	—	10.00	16.50	21.50	30.00
	1238	—	10.00	16.50	21.50	30.00
	1239	—	10.00	16.50	21.50	30.00
	1240	—	10.00	16.50	21.50	30.00
	1241	—	10.00	16.50	21.50	30.00
	1242	—	10.00	16.50	21.50	30.00
	1243	—	10.00	16.50	21.50	30.00
	1244	—	10.00	16.50	21.50	30.00
	ND	30	11.50	17.50	23.50	33.50

NOTE: Earlier date (AH1207) exists for this type.

Saugor Mint

Mint marks: 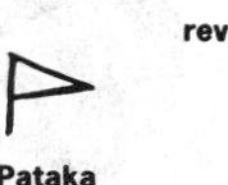 **obv.**

rev.

Pataka
First type

Trisul
First type

Second type

Second type

Mintname: Ravishnagar Sagar

In the name of Shah Alam II
AH1173-1221/1759-1806AD

1/2 PAISA

COPPER, 5.80 g

KM#	Date	Year	Good	VG	Fine	VF
233	—	36	2.00	3.50	6.00	10.00

COPPER

Symbol **on obv.**

KM#	Date	Year	Good	VG	Fine	VF
236	—	55	2.00	3.50	6.00	10.00

NOTE: Earlier date (Yr. 38) exists for this type.

1/2 RUPEE

SILVER, 5.35-5.80 g

KM#	Date	Year	VG	Fine	VF	XF
237	AH—	51	10.00	16.50	21.50	30.00

RUPEE

SILVER, 10.70-11.60 g

KM#	Date	Year	VG	Fine	VF	XF
240	AH1216	42	7.00	11.50	16.50	25.00
	1218	43	7.00	11.50	16.50	25.00
	1218	44	7.00	11.50	16.50	25.00
	1219	44	7.00	11.50	16.50	25.00
	1220	45	7.00	11.50	16.50	25.00
	1222	47	7.00	11.50	16.50	25.00
	122x	48	7.00	11.50	16.50	25.00
	1224	49	7.00	11.50	16.50	25.00

NOTE: Earlier dates (Yr.31-41) exist for this type.

Similar to KM#240 but very crude.

KM#	Date	Year	VG	Fine	VF	XF
241	AH—	52	7.00	11.50	16.50	25.00
	1230	55	7.00	11.50	16.50	25.00

EAST INDIA COMPANY

Local issues post 1818-1819AD

PAISA

COPPER

KM#	Date	Year	Good	VG	Fine	VF
270	FE1230	(1820)	3.50	5.00	7.00	10.00
	1231	(1821)	3.50	5.00	7.00	10.00
	1232	(1822)	3.50	5.00	7.00	10.00
	1233	(1823)	3.50	5.00	7.00	10.00
	1234	(1824)	3.50	5.00	7.00	10.00
	1235	(1825)	3.50	5.00	7.00	10.00
	1237	(1827)	3.50	5.00	7.00	10.00
	1238	(1828)	3.50	5.00	7.00	10.00
	1240	(1830)	3.50	5.00	7.00	10.00

Bagalkot Mint

RUPEE

SILVER, 10.70-11.60 g

KM#	Date	Year	VG	Fine	VF	XF
271	1819	—	25.00	33.50	50.00	70.00

Tanjore

CASH

COPPER, 3.40 g
Obv. leg: *Chatrapati*. Rev. leg: *Sri Siva*.

KM#	Date	Year	VG	Fine	VF	XF
275	ND	—	10.00	14.00	21.50	30.00

Obv. and rev. leg: Similar to KM#275 but retrograde.

KM#	Date	Year	VG	Fine	VF	XF
276	ND	—	10.00	14.00	21.50	30.00

Obv. leg: *Chatrapati*. Rev. leg: *Sri Siva*.

KM#	Date	Year	VG	Fine	VF	XF
277	ND	—	10.00	14.00	21.50	30.00

KM#	Date	Year	VG	Fine	VF	XF
278	ND	—	10.00	14.00	21.50	30.00

Obv. leg: *Chatrapai*. Rev. leg: *Sri Siva*.

KM#	Date	Year	VG	Fine	VF	XF
279	ND	—	10.00	14.00	21.50	30.00

FANAM

GOLD, 0.40 g

KM#	Date	Year	VG	Fine	VF	XF
280	ND	—	7.50	10.00	12.50	15.00

PUDUKKOTTAI

Pudukota

Pudukkottai was founded by Raghunatha Raya Tondaiman in 1686 when he defeated the Pallavaraya chiefs of the area. The family came from Tondaimandalam, a small village near Tirupathi, and belonged to the Kallen (or robber) caste. In the late eighteenth century the Tondaimans aided the British in their struggles against the French in the Carnatic. With British ascendancy, the Pudukkottai rulers were confirmed in their control of the region. This was regularized in 1806 when, subject to a yearly tribute of one elephant, the rajas of Pudukkottai were guaranteed their position. In 1948 the State was merged into the Trichinopoly District.

RULERS

Martanda Bhairava, 1886-1928AD
Rajagopala, 1928-1947AD

DUMP COINAGE

AMMAN CASH

COPPER, 1.30 g
Obv: Goddess Brihadamba. Rev. Telugu: *Vijaya*.

KM#	Date	Mintage	VG	Fine	VF	XF
3	ND	—	.90	1.50	2.50	4.00

HEAVY AMMAN CASH

COPPER, 1.65 g

KM#	Date	Mintage	VG	Fine	VF	XF
4	ND	—	—	—	Rare	—

MILLED COINAGE

AMMAN CASH

COPPER, 1.25 g

KM#	Date	Mintage	Fine	VF	XF	Unc
6	ND(1889)*	5.000	.20	.50	.85	1.50

NOTE: Struck by the Birmingham Mint between 1889-1906. Later contracts were produced by the Calcutta Mint.

ROHILKHAND

The Nawabs of Rohilkhand were Rohillas who traced their origins to Sardar Daud Khan (d. 1749), an Afghan adventurer. Daud Khan's adopted son, Ali Muhammed, annexed a huge tract of land north of the Ganges between Itawa and the Himalayas, and received the Nawab title from the Mughal emperor.

In 1754 this territory was partitioned among his many sons, who thereafter formed a loose confederacy, alternately given to feuding internally and uniting to meet aggression by the Marathas, Awadh, and Imperial forces in turn. By the end of the century Rohilla power had been crushed by the combined forces of Awadh and the British, leaving only Rampur in Rohilla hands under the sovereignty of Nawab Faizullah Khan. In 1801 Rampur was ceded to the East India Company and in 1950 it was absorbed into Uttar Pradesh.

MINT

Mintname: Bareli

BARELI MINT

REVOLT OF 1857

The Mutiny

During the mutiny of 1857-58AD, Khan Bahadur Khan, a descendent of Hafiz Rahmat Khan, declared himself Subahdar of Rohilkhand under the Mughal Emperor Bahadur Shah Zafar. The independent government sat at Bareli, issuing rupees on the Mughal pattern of Shah Alam II, with current Hijri year and a regnal year dating from AH1202/1788AD, the year Rohilla power ended with the death of Ghulam Qadir.

RUPEE

SILVER, 10.70-11.60 g

KM#	Date	Year	VG	Fine	VF	XF
46	AH1274	72	—	—	Rare	—

SIKH EMPIRE

The father of Sikhism, Guru Nanak (1469-1539), was distinguished from almost all others who founded states or empires in India by being a purely religious teacher. Deeply Indian in the basic premises which underlay even those aspects of his theology which differed from the mainstream, he stressed the unity of God and the universal brotherhood of man. He was totally opposed to the divisions of the caste system and his teaching struggled to attain a practical balance between Hinduism and Islam. His message was a message of reconciliation, first with God, then with man. He exhibited no political ambition.

Guru Nanak was succeeded by 9 other gurus of Sikhism. Together they laid the foundations of a religious community in the Punjab which would, much later, transform itself into the Sikh Empire. Gradually this gentle religion of reconciliation became transformed into a formidable, aggressive military power. It was a metamorphosis which was, at least partly, thrust upon the Sikh community by Mughal oppression. The fifth guru of Sikhism, Arjun, was executed in 1606 on the order of Jahangir. His successor, Hargobind, was to spend his years in constant struggle against the Mughals, first against Jahangir and later against Shah Jahan. The ninth guru, Tegh Bahadur, was executed by Aurangzeb for refusing to embrace Islam. The stage had been set for a full confrontation with Mughal authority. It was against such a background that Sikhism's tenth guru, Guru Govind Singh (1675-1708), set about organizing the Sikhs into a military power. He gave new discipline to Sikhism. Its adherents were forbidden wine and tobacco and they were required to conform to the 5 outward signs of allegiance - to keep their hair unshaven and to wear short drawers (kuchcha), a comb (kungha), an iron bangle (kara) and a dagger (kirpan).

With Govind Singh's death the Khalsa, the Sikh brotherhood, emerged as the controlling body of Sikhism and the Granth, the official compilation of Govind Singh's teaching, became the "Bible" of Sikhism. At this point the Sikhs took to the hills. It was here, constantly harassed by Mughal forces, that Sikh militarism was forged into an effective weapon and tempered by fire. Gradually the Sikhs emerged from their safe forts in the hills and made their presence felt in the plains of the Punjab. As Nadir Shah retired from Delhi laden with the prizes of war in 1739, the stragglers of his Persian army were cut down by the Sikhs. Similarly, Ahmad Shah Durrani's first intrusion into India (1747-1748) was made the more lively by Sikh sorties into his rearguard. Gradually the Sikhs became both more confident and more effective, and their quite frequent military reversals served only to strengthen their determination and to deepen their sense of identity. Their first notable success came about 1756 when the Sikhs temporarily occupied Lahore and used the Mughal mint to strike their own rupee bearing the inscription: *Coined by the grace of the Khalsa in the country of Ahmad, conquered by Jessa the Kalal.* But the Sikhs were, as yet, most effective as guerrilla bands operating out of the hill country. On Ahmad Shah's fifth expedition into India (1759-1761) the Sikhs reverted to their well-tried role of forming tight mobile units which could choose both the time and the place of their attacks on the Durrani army. In spite of a serious reverse near Bernala in 1762 at the hands of Ahmad Shah, the Sikhs once again regrouped. In December 1763 they decisively defeated the Durrani governor of Sirhind and occupied the area.

The Sikhs now swept all before them, recapturing Lahore in 1765. The whole tract of land between the Jhelum and the Sutlej was now divided among the Sikh chieftains. At Lahore, and later at Amritsar, the Govind Shahi rupee proclaiming that Guru Govind Singh had received *Deg, Tegh and Fath* (Grace, Power and Victory) from Nanak was struck. The name of the Mughal emperor was pointedly omitted. The Sikhs now subdivided into twelve *misls* "equals", each responsible for its own fate and each conducting its own military adventures into surrounding areas. By 1792 the most prominent chief in the Punjab was Mahan Singh of the Sukerchakia *misl.* His death that same year left the boy destined to become Sikhism's best-known statesman, Ranjit Singh, as his successor. A year later Shah Zaman, King of Kabul, confirmed him as the possessor of Lahore.

For the next forty years Ranjit Singh dominated Sikh affairs. In 1802 he seized Amritsar and followed this by capturing Ludhiana (1806), Multan (1818), Kashmir (1819), Ladakh (1833) and Peshawar (1834). By the time of his death in June 1839 Ranjit was the only leader in India capable of offering a serious challenge to the East India Company.

By a treaty concluded in 1809 with the British, Ranjit had been confirmed as ruler of the tracts he had occupied south of the Sutlej, but the agreement had restricted him from seeking any further expansion to the north or west of the river. In spite of the terms of the treaty, the British remained suspicious of Ranjit's ultimate intentions. His steady policy of expansion frequently left apprehensions in the minds of the British - with whose interests Ranjit's own often clashed - that the Sikhs had secret ambitions against Company controlled territory. But it was to Ranjit's credit that he welded the Sikhs of the Punjab into an effective and unified fighting force, capable of resisting both the Afghans and the Marathas and able to stand up to British pressures. He inherited a loose alliance of fiercely independent chiefs, he left a disciplined and well equipped army of over fifty thousand men. He also left a well consolidated regional empire in the extreme northwest of India, roughly extending over the northern half of present-day Pakistan.

After the death of Ranjit the Sikh empire began to disintegrate as power passed from chief to chief in murderous rivalry. At the same time relationships with the British began to deteriorate. The treaty of 1809 no longer proved able to hold the peace, and the Sikh army attacked the British (1845-1846) only to be badly beaten in a series of confrontations. The Treaty of Lahore which followed this first Anglo-Sikh war reduced the Sikh army to a maximum of twenty thousand men and twelve thousand cavalry. It obliged the Sikhs to cede the Jallandar Doab and Kashmir to the British, and required them to pay an indemnity of fifty thousand pounds and accept a British resident at their court. In 1848 the Sikhs again revolted, and were again crushed. In 1849 the Punjab was annexed and from that time onward they came under British rule.

RULERS

Ranjit Singh,
VS1856-1896/1799-1839AD
Kharak Singh,
VS1896-1897/1839-1840AD
Sher Singh,
VS1897-1900/1840-1843AD
Dulip Singh,
VS1900-1906/1843-1849AD

MINTS

Amritsar (Ambratsar) امبرت سر

Dera ديره

Derajat ديره جات

Kashmir كشمير or ਕਸ਼ ਮੀਰ

Lahore لاهور

Multan ملتان

Nimak (Pind Dadan Khan) نمک

Peshawar پشاور

NOTE: Most coins struck after the accession of Ranjit Singh bear a large leaf on one side, and have Persian or Gurmukhi (Punjabi) legends in the name of Gobind Singh, the tenth and last Guru of the Sikhs, 1675-1708AD. Earlier pieces are similar, but lack the leaf, except the Amritsar Mint where the leaf is present since VS1845.

There is a great variety of coppers, and only representative types are catalogued here; many crude pieces were struck at the official and at unofficial mints, and bear illegible or semi-literate inscriptions. None of the coins bear the name of the Sikh ruler.

AMRITSAR MINT

First Copper Series

Persian legends. Various types.

1/2 PAISA

COPPER

KM#	Date	Year	Good	VG	Fine	VF
3	VS1897	(1840)	3.50	7.00	12.00	18.00

HEAVY PAISA

COPPER, 11.00-12.00 g
Rev: Leaf and date.

KM#	Date	Year	Good	VG	Fine	VF
4	VS1880	(1823)	2.00	3.25	6.00	9.00
(4.1)	1881	(1824)	2.00	3.25	6.00	9.00
	1882	(1825)	2.00	3.25	6.00	9.00

1/4 ANNA

COPPER, 8.00-9.00 g
Obv: Date.
Rev: *Nanak Shahi*, denomination and date.

KM#	Date	Year	Good	VG	Fine	VF
5	VS1896	(1839)	3.00	5.00	9.00	14.00
(4.2)	1897	(1840)	3.00	5.00	9.00	14.00

2 PAISE

COPPER

KM#	Date	Year	Good	VG	Fine	VF
6	VS1880	(1823)	5.00	8.00	15.00	25.00

Second Copper Series

Gurmukhi legends. Obv: Leaf in center.

PAISA

COPPER, 7.00-12.00 g
Obv: Double leaf.

KM#	Date	Year	Good	VG	Fine	VF
7.23	VS1879	(1822)	5.00	10.00	18.00	30.00

Obv: Date in bottom line.

KM#	Date	Year	Good	VG	Fine	VF
7.1	VS1885	(1828)	1.50	3.00	5.00	7.00
	1887	(1830)	2.00	4.00	6.00	9.00

NOTE: Date often off flan on normal strikes.

Similar to KM#7.1 but cruder, undated.

KM#	Date	Year	Good	VG	Fine	VF
7.21 (7a.1)	ND	—	1.00	2.00	4.00	8.00

Obv: Leaf.

KM#	Date	Year	Good	VG	Fine	VF
7.2	VS1885	(1828)	2.00	4.00	7.00	12.00

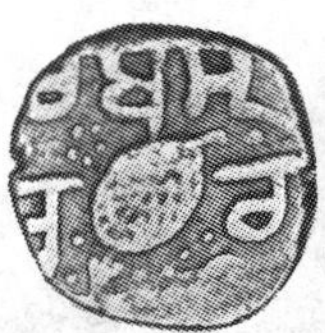

Rev: Banner w/tail end down.

KM#	Date	Year	Good	VG	Fine	VF
7.22 (7a.3)	ND	—	1.75	3.50	7.00	12.00

Rev: Flower.

KM#	Date	Year	Good	VG	Fine	VF
7.3 (7a.5)	ND	—	1.50	3.00	5.00	9.00

Rev: Cross.

KM#	Date	Year	Good	VG	Fine	VF
7.4	VS188x	(18xx)	1.50	3.00	5.00	9.00

Rev: Trident.

KM#	Date	Year	Good	VG	Fine	VF
7.5 (7a.6)	ND	—	1.50	3.00	5.00	9.00

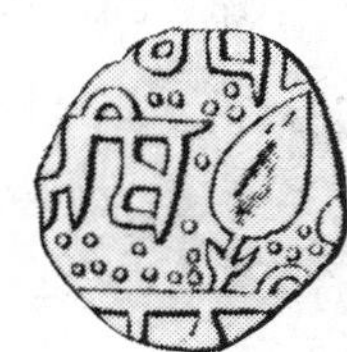

Rev: Katar right.

KM#	Date	Year	Good	VG	Fine	VF
7.6 (7a.7)	ND	—	1.75	3.50	6.00	12.00

NOTE: Variety exists w/Katar facing up.

Rev: Tiger running right.

KM#	Date	Year	Good	VG	Fine	VF
7.7 (7a.9)	ND	—	3.50	8.00	15.00	25.00

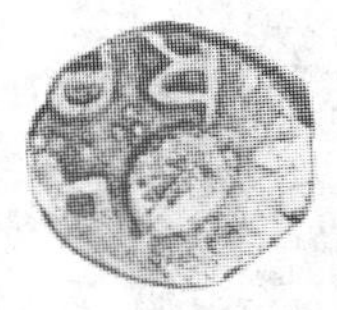

Rev: Leaf spray.

KM#	Date	Year	Good	VG	Fine	VF
7.8 (7a.10)	ND	—	2.25	4.50	7.50	12.50

Rev: Banner w/tail end up.

KM#	Date	Year	Good	VG	Fine	VF
7.9 (7a.4)	ND	—	2.25	4.50	7.50	12.50

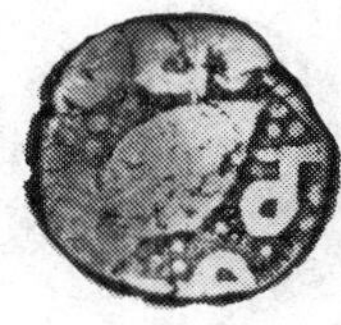

Obv: Cross. Rev: Double line.

KM#	Date	Year	Good	VG	Fine	VF
7.10 (7a.2)	ND	—	1.50	3.00	5.00	9.00

Rev: Katar left.

KM#	Date	Year	Good	VG	Fine	VF
7.11 (7a.8)	ND	—	1.75	3.50	6.00	12.00

Obv: Leaf spray, mintname. Rev: Leaf.

KM#	Date	Year	Good	VG	Fine	VF
7.12	ND	—	3.50	7.00	12.00	20.00

Obv: Leaf spray, mintname. Rev: Quatrefoil.

KM#	Date	Year	Good	VG	Fine	VF
7.13	ND	—	3.50	7.00	12.00	20.00

Obv: Leaf spray, mintname.
Rev: No control mark.

KM#	Date	Year	Good	VG	Fine	VF
7.14	ND	—	3.50	7.00	12.00	20.00

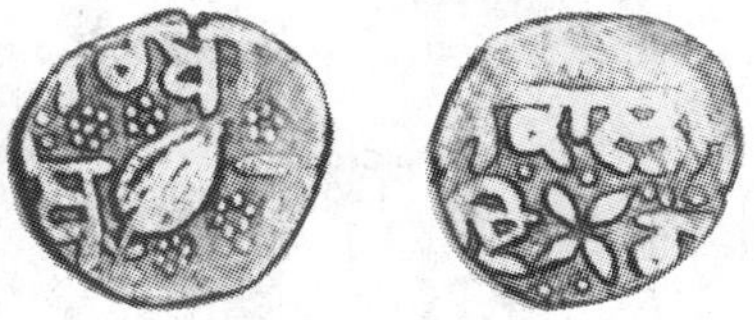

Rev: 4-petal flower.

KM#	Date	Year	Good	VG	Fine	VF
7.15	ND	—	2.00	4.00	7.00	12.00

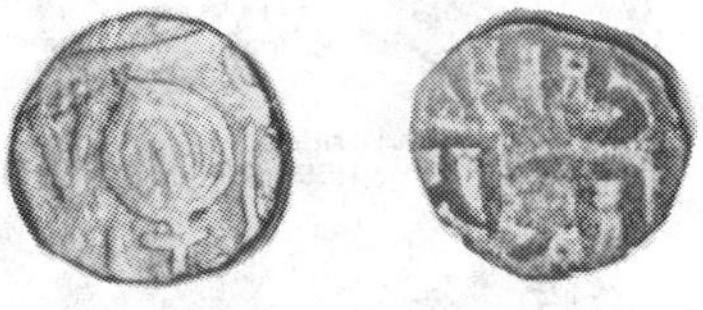

Obv: Leaf facing left.

KM#	Date	Year	Good	VG	Fine	VF
7.16	ND	—	2.00	4.00	7.00	12.00
7.17	ND	—	1.00	3.00	6.00	10.00

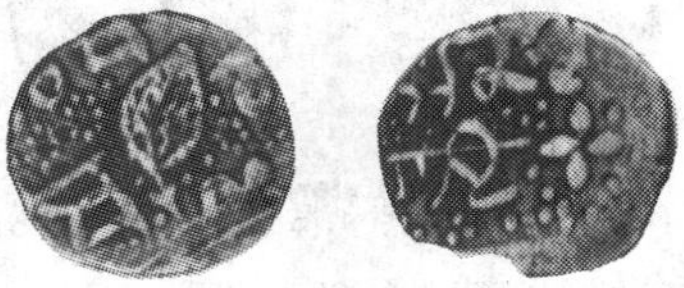

Obv: Leaf facing right.

KM#	Date	Year	Good	VG	Fine	VF
7.18	ND	—	1.00	3.00	6.00	10.00

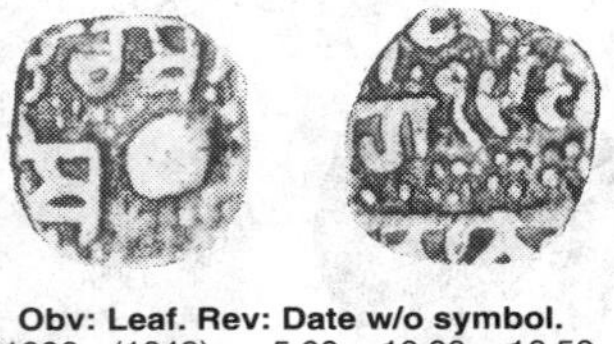

Obv: Leaf. Rev: Date w/o symbol.

KM#	Date	Year	Good	VG	Fine	VF
7.19	VS1906	(1849)	5.00	10.00	16.50	30.00

Obv: Leaf facing left.

KM#	Date	Year	Good	VG	Fine	VF
7.20	ND	—	2.00	4.00	7.00	12.00

Obv: Dotted leaf.

KM#	Date	Year	Good	VG	Fine	VF
7.24	ND	—	3.50	7.00	12.00	20.00

2 PAISE

COPPER, 20.00 g

KM#	Date	Year	Good	VG	Fine	VF
8.1	VS1885	(1819)	13.50	25.00	42.50	60.00

Octagon.

KM#	Date	Year	Good	VG	Fine	VF
8.2	VS—	—	8.00	15.00	25.00	45.00

Diamond shape.

KM#	Date	Year	Good	VG	Fine	VF
8.3	VS1885	(18xx)	7.00	12.00	20.00	35.00
8.4	VS1885	(1828)	5.00	9.00	15.00	25.00

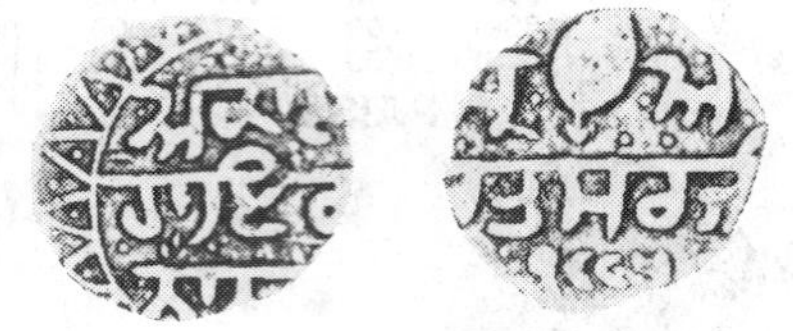

Rev: Cross.

KM#	Date	Year	Good	VG	Fine	VF
8.5	ND	—	5.00	9.00	15.00	25.00

MULTIPLE PAISAS

(Not struck for general circulation)

COPPER, 38.00-40.00 g

KM#	Date	Year	Good	VG	Fine	VF
9.1	VS1885	(1828)	—	—	Rare	—

Rev: Banner.

KM#	Date	Year	Good	VG	Fine	VF
9.2	—	—	—	—	Rare	—

Rev: Cross.

KM#	Date	Year	Good	VG	Fine	VF
9.3	—	—	—	—	Rare	—

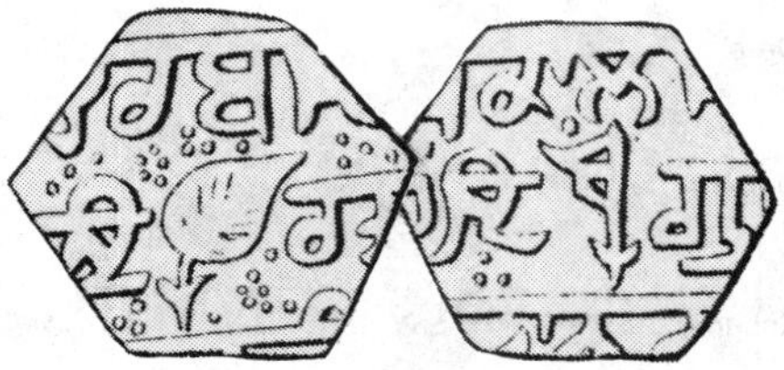

Rev: Banner ?

KM#	Date	Year	Good	VG	Fine	VF
9.4	—	—	—	—	Rare	—

Rev: Trident.

KM#	Date	Year	Good	VG	Fine	VF
9.5	VS188(5)	(1828)	—	—	Rare	—

Third Copper Series

Persian and Gurmukhi legends.

FALUS

COPPER
Obv: *DEVAKI* in Persian.

KM#	Date	Year	Good	VG	Fine	VF
10.1	—	—	6.00	10.00	15.00	25.00
10.2	VS1900	(1843)	2.75	5.00	7.50	12.50
	1901	(1844)	2.75	5.00	7.50	12.50
	ND	—	2.75	5.00	7.50	12.50

KM#	Date	Year	Good	VG	Fine	VF
10.3	—	—	7.00	12.00	20.00	35.00

KM#	Date	Year	Good	VG	Fine	VF
10.4	—	—	7.00	12.00	20.00	35.00

Rev: 4-petal flower.

KM#	Date	Year	Good	VG	Fine	VF
10.5	ND	—	3.00	5.00	8.00	14.00

Silver Series

1/8 RUPEE

SILVER, 1.34-1.45 g
Rev: Dated VS1884.

KM#	Date	Year	VG	Fine	VF	XF
17.1	VS(18)95	(1838)	15.00	25.00	45.00	90.00

Rev: Dated VS1885.

KM#	Date	Year	VG	Fine	VF	XF
17.2	VS(18)95	(1838)	15.00	25.00	45.00	90.00
	(18)99	(1842)	15.00	25.00	45.00	90.00
	1900	(1843)	15.00	25.00	45.00	90.00
	1903	(1846)	15.00	25.00	45.00	90.00

1/4 RUPEE

SILVER, 15mm, 2.68-2.90 g

KM#	Date	Year	VG	Fine	VF	XF
18.1	VS(18)71	(1814)	15.00	25.00	45.00	90.00
	(18)79	(1822)	17.50	30.00	50.00	100.00
	(18)80	(1823)	15.00	25.00	45.00	90.00
	(18)83	(1826)	15.00	25.00	45.00	90.00

Rev: Dated VS1884.

KM#	Date	Year	VG	Fine	VF	XF
18.2	VS(18)85	(1828)	12.00	20.00	40.00	80.00
	(18)86	(1829)	12.00	20.00	40.00	80.00
	(18)89	(1832)	12.00	20.00	40.00	80.00
	(18)92	(1835)	12.00	20.00	40.00	80.00
	(18)95	(1838)	12.00	20.00	40.00	80.00
	(18)97	(1840)	12.00	20.00	40.00	80.00

Rev: Dated VS1885.

KM#	Date	Year	VG	Fine	VF	XF
18.3	VS(18)93	(1836)	12.00	20.00	40.00	80.00
	(18)94	(1837)	12.00	20.00	40.00	80.00
	(18)95	(1838)	12.00	20.00	40.00	80.00
	(18)97	(1840)	12.00	20.00	40.00	80.00
	(18)98	(1841)	12.00	20.00	40.00	80.00
	(18)99	(1842)	12.00	20.00	40.00	80.00
	1900	(1843)	12.00	20.00	40.00	80.00
	1901	(1844)	12.00	20.00	40.00	80.00
	1902	(1845)	12.00	20.00	40.00	80.00
	1903	(1846)	12.00	20.00	40.00	80.00
	1904	(1847)	12.00	20.00	40.00	80.00

1/2 RUPEE

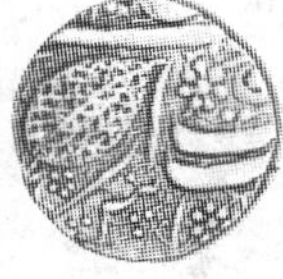

SILVER, 5.30-5.60 g
Rev: Actual date.

KM#	Date	Year	VG	Fine	VF	XF
19.1	VS1871	(1814)	10.00	18.50	35.00	70.00
	1880	(1823)	10.00	18.50	35.00	70.00
	1883	(1826)	10.00	18.50	35.00	70.00

Rev: Dated VS1884.

KM#	Date	Year	VG	Fine	VF	XF
19.2	VS(18)85	(1828)	10.00	18.50	35.00	70.00
	(18)86	(1829)	10.00	18.50	35.00	70.00
	(18)89	(1832)	10.00	18.50	35.00	70.00
	(18)92	(1835)	10.00	18.50	35.00	70.00
	(18)93	(1836)	10.00	18.50	35.00	70.00
	(18)95	(1838)	10.00	18.50	35.00	70.00
	(18)99	(1842)	10.00	18.50	35.00	70.00

Obv: VS date and various symbols.
Rev: Dated VS1885.

KM#	Date	Year	VG	Fine	VF	XF
19.3A	VS(18)93	(1836)	10.00	18.00	35.00	70.00
	(18)94	(1837)	10.00	18.00	35.00	70.00
	(18)95	(1838)	10.00	18.00	35.00	70.00
	(18)96	(1839)	10.00	18.00	35.00	70.00
	(18)97	(1840)	10.00	18.00	35.00	70.00

Obv. leg: Gurmuki *Om*.

KM#	Date	Year	VG	Fine	VF	XF
19.4	VS(18)85/97	—	12.00	20.00	40.00	80.00

Obv: VS date and trident. Rev: Dated VS1885.

KM#	Date	Year	VG	Fine	VF	XF
19.3B	VS(18)98	(1841)	10.00	18.00	35.00	70.00
	(18)99	(1842)	10.00	18.00	35.00	70.00

Obv: VS date and Chhatra (umbrella).
Rev: Dated VS1885.

KM#	Date	Year	VG	Fine	VF	XF
19.3C	VS1900	(1843)	10.00	18.00	35.00	70.00
	1901	(1844)	10.00	18.00	35.00	70.00
	1902	(1845)	10.00	18.00	35.00	70.00

Obv: VS date and Gurmukhi *Sate*.
Rev: Dated VS1885.

KM#	Date	Year	VG	Fine	VF	XF
19.3D	VS1903	(1846)	10.00	18.00	35.00	70.00
	1904	(1847)	10.00	18.00	35.00	70.00
	1905	(1848)	10.00	18.00	35.00	70.00

Obv: Flowers.

KM#	Date	Year	VG	Fine	VF	XF
19.5	VS1902	—	15.00	25.00	45.00	90.00

RUPEE

SILVER, 10.70-11.10 g
Obv: Second legend arrangement.
Rev: Katar.

KM#	Date	Year	VG	Fine	VF	XF
A20.2	VS1859	(1802)	11.50	18.00	30.00	50.00
	1860	(1803)	11.50	18.00	30.00	50.00
	1862	(1805)	11.50	18.00	30.00	50.00
	1863	(1806)	11.50	18.00	30.00	50.00
	1864	(1807)	11.50	18.00	30.00	50.00
	1865	(1808)	11.50	18.00	30.00	50.00

NOTE: Earlier dates (VS1841-1854) exist for this type.

Rev: Mintname and date.

KM#	Date	Year	VG	Fine	VF	XF
20.1	VS1858	(1801)	7.00	11.00	18.00	30.00
	1859	(1802)	7.00	11.00	18.00	30.00
	1860	(1803)	5.50	9.00	15.00	25.00
	1806 error for 1860					
		—	20.00	28.00	40.00	55.00
	1861	(1804)	5.50	9.00	15.00	25.00
	1862	(1805)	5.50	9.00	15.00	25.00
	1863	(1806)	5.50	9.00	15.00	25.00
	1864	(1807)	5.50	9.00	15.00	25.00
	1865	(1808)	5.50	9.00	15.00	25.00
	1866	(1809)	5.50	9.00	15.00	25.00
	1867	(1810)	5.50	9.00	15.00	25.00
	1868	(1811)	5.50	9.00	15.00	25.00
	1869	(1812)	5.50	9.00	15.00	25.00
	1870	(1813)	20.00	35.00	60.00	100.00
	1871	(1814)	15.00	30.00	50.00	80.00
	1872	(1815)	5.50	9.00	15.00	25.00
	1873	(1816)	5.50	9.00	15.00	25.00
	1874	(1817)	5.50	9.00	15.00	25.00
	1875	(1818)	5.50	9.00	15.00	25.00
	1876	(1819)	5.50	9.00	15.00	25.00
	1877	(1820)	5.50	9.00	15.00	25.00
	1878	(1821)	5.50	9.00	15.00	25.00
	1879	(1822)	5.50	9.00	15.00	25.00
(20.7)	1880	(1823)	5.50	9.00	15.00	25.00
	1881	(1824)	5.50	9.00	15.00	25.00
	1882	(1825)	5.50	9.00	15.00	25.00
	1883	(1826)	5.50	9.00	15.00	25.00
	1884	(1827)	5.50	9.00	15.00	25.00
	1885	(1828)	—	—	Rare	—
	1886	(1829)	—	—	Rare	—
	1888	(1831)	—	—	Rare	—
	1889	(1832)	—	—	Rare	—

NOTE: Earlier dates (VS1848-1857) exist for this type.
NOTE: Double lines below dates exist for some 1869, 1870 and 1871 coins and are considered rare. Mint symbols seem to change frequently in the above series.

Rev: "Dar jhang" left of leaf.

KM#	Date	Year	VG	Fine	VF	XF
20.1A	VS1873	(1816)	325.00	500.00	700.00	1000.
	1874	(1817)	250.00	425.00	600.00	850.00

NOTE: Some rare varieties exist with either a trident below the leaf on reverse or a circular symbol.

Obv: 5 dot symbol, sprig at lower left.
Rev: Dotted leaf.

KM#	Date	Year	VG	Fine	VF	XF
20.2A	VS1858	(1801)	13.00	19.00	25.00	35.00

Obv: Double oval. Rev: Dotted leaf.

KM#	Date	Year	VG	Fine	VF	XF
20.2B	VS1858	(1801)	11.50	17.50	23.50	33.50
(20.3)	1859	(1802)	11.50	17.50	23.50	33.50

NOTE: Also exists without special mark on obv.

Obv: Hand. Rev: Dotted leaf.

KM#	Date	Year	VG	Fine	VF	XF
20.2C	VS1859	(1802)	11.50	17.50	23.50	33.50
(20.2)						

Obv: 5-petal flower. Rev: Dotted leaf.

KM#	Date	Year	VG	Fine	VF	XF
20.2D	ND	—	15.00	25.00	40.00	60.00

Obv: Fish at lower left. Rev: Leaf.

KM#	Date	Year	VG	Fine	VF	XF
20.3	VS1861	(1804)	15.00	35.00	40.00	60.00

The "Mora" Rupee
Rev: Branches w/berries.

KM#	Date	Year	VG	Fine	VF	XF
20.4	VS1858	(1801)	17.50	30.00	50.00	80.00
(YB20)	1859	(1802)	17.50	30.00	50.00	80.00
	1860	(1803)	17.50	30.00	50.00	80.00
	1861	(1804)	12.50	18.00	30.00	50.00
	1862	(1805)	12.50	18.00	30.00	50.00
	1863	(1806)	17.50	30.00	50.00	80.00

Rev: Sprig w/2 leaves.

KM#	Date	Year	VG	Fine	VF	XF
20.5	1862	(1805)	17.50	30.00	50.00	80.00
(YD20)	1863	(1806)	15.00	25.00	42.50	70.00

The "Arisi" Rupee
Rev: Symbol said to be mirror.

KM#	Date	Year	VG	Fine	VF	XF
20.6	VS1862	(1805)	17.50	30.00	50.00	80.00
(YC20)	1863	(1806)	15.00	25.00	42.50	70.00

NAZARANA RUPEE

SILVER, 10.42 g
Rev: "Dar jhang" left of leaf.

KM#	Date	Year	VG	Fine	VF	XF
A21.1	VS1873	(1816)	650.00	1100.	1800.	3000.
(20.1a)	1882	(1825)	500.00	900.00	1500.	2300.

RUPEE

SILVER
Nanakshahis
Obv: Partial or full actual dates.
Rev: VS1884 fixed.

KM#	Date	Year	VG	Fine	VF	XF
21.1	VS(18)85	(1828)	5.50	9.00	15.00	25.00
	(18)86	(1829)	5.50	9.00	15.00	25.00
	(18)87	(1830)	5.50	9.00	15.00	25.00
	(18)88	(1831)	5.50	9.00	15.00	25.00
	(18)89	(1832)	5.50	9.00	15.00	25.00
	(18)90	(1833)	5.50	9.00	15.00	25.00
	(18)91	(1834)	5.50	9.00	15.00	25.00
	(18)92	(1835)	5.50	9.00	15.00	25.00
	(18)93	(1836)	5.50	9.00	15.00	25.00
	(18)95	(1838)	5.50	9.00	15.00	25.00

Gobindshahis

KM#	Date	Year	VG	Fine	VF	XF
21.2	VS(18)95	(1838)	—	—	—	—
	(18)96	(1839)	9.00	15.00	25.00	40.00
	(18)97	(1840)	5.50	9.00	15.00	25.00
	(18)98/7	(1841)	10.00	16.50	27.50	45.00
	(18)98	(1841)	5.50	9.00	15.00	25.00
	(18)99	(1842)	5.50	9.00	15.00	25.00
	1900	(1843)	5.50	9.00	15.00	25.00
	1901	(1844)	5.50	9.00	15.00	25.00
	1902	(1845)	5.50	9.00	16.50	25.00
	1903	(1846)	5.50	9.00	15.00	25.00
	1904	(1847)	5.50	9.00	15.00	25.00
	1905	(1848)	8.00	13.50	22.50	37.50

Obv: Partial actual dates.
Rev: VS1885 fixed.

KM#	Date	Year	VG	Fine	VF	XF
22.1	VS(18)93	(1836)	7.50	12.50	20.00	32.50
(22.3)	(18)94	(1837)	7.50	12.50	20.00	32.50
	(18)95	(1838)	5.50	9.00	15.00	25.00
	(18)96	(1839)	5.50	9.00	15.00	25.00
	(18)97	(1840)	5.50	9.00	15.00	25.00
	(18)98	(1841)	5.50	9.00	15.00	25.00
	1903	(1846)	5.50	9.00	15.00	25.00

Rev: Katar.

KM#	Date	Year	VG	Fine	VF	XF
22.2	VS(18)93	(1836)	7.50	12.50	21.50	35.00
	(18)94	(1837)	7.50	12.50	21.50	35.00
	(18)98	(1841)	5.50	9.00	15.00	25.00

Obv. Nagari: *Om.*

KM#	Date	Year	VG	Fine	VF	XF
22.4	VS(18)97	(1840)	8.50	14.00	23.50	40.00

Obv: Trisul (trident).

KM#	Date	Year	VG	Fine	VF	XF
22.5	VS(18)98	(1841)	8.00	13.50	21.50	35.00
	(18)99	(1842)	8.00	13.50	21.50	35.00

Obv: Chhatra (umbrella).

KM#	Date	Year	VG	Fine	VF	XF
22.6	VS(18)99	(1842)	5.50	9.00	15.00	25.00
	1900	(1843)	5.50	9.00	15.00	25.00
	1901	(1844)	5.50	9.00	15.00	25.00

Obv: 3-lobed leaf.
Similar to 1/2 Rupee, KM#19.5.

KM#	Date	Year	VG	Fine	VF	XF
22.7	VS1902	(1845)	18.00	30.00	50.00	80.00

Obv: Pataka (banner).

KM#	Date	Year	VG	Fine	VF	XF
22.8	VS1902	(1845)	7.50	12.00	20.00	35.00
	1903	(1846)	7.50	12.00	20.00	35.00

Obv: Gurmukhi *Sate* beneath chhatra.

KM#	Date	Year	VG	Fine	VF	XF
22.9	VS1903	(1846)	7.50	12.00	20.00	35.00
	1904	(1847)	7.50	12.00	20.00	35.00
	1905	(1848)	7.50	12.00	20.00	35.00

Obv: Lazy W beneath chhatra.

KM#	Date	Year	VG	Fine	VF	XF
22.10	VS1905	(1848)	12.50	20.00	35.00	60.00
	1906	(1849)	25.00	40.00	65.00	110.00

Obv: Nagari *Shiva.*

KM#	Date	Year	VG	Fine	VF	XF
22.11	VS1905	(1848)	12.00	20.00	32.50	55.00

Mule. Obv: Dot cluster. Rev: KM#21.

KM#	Date	Year	VG	Fine	VF	XF
22.12	VS1905	VS1884	15.00	25.00	42.50	70.00

Rev: Dated VS1888.

KM#	Date	Year	VG	Fine	VF	XF
22A (22.14)	VS1904	(1847)	100.00	165.00	275.00	400.00

1/4 MOHUR

GOLD

KM#	Date	Year	VG	Fine	VF	XF
23	VS(18)95	(1838)	—	—	Rare	—
(27)	(18)97	(1840)	—	—	Rare	—

1/2 MOHUR

GOLD

KM#	Date	Year	VG	Fine	VF	XF
24 (A25)	VS1877	(1820)	—	—	Rare	—

MOHUR

GOLD, 10.76 g, 21mm

Obv: 5 dots. Rev: Dotted leaf.

KM#	Date	Year	VG	Fine	VF	XF
25.1 (24.1)	VS1858	(1801)	—	—	Rare	—

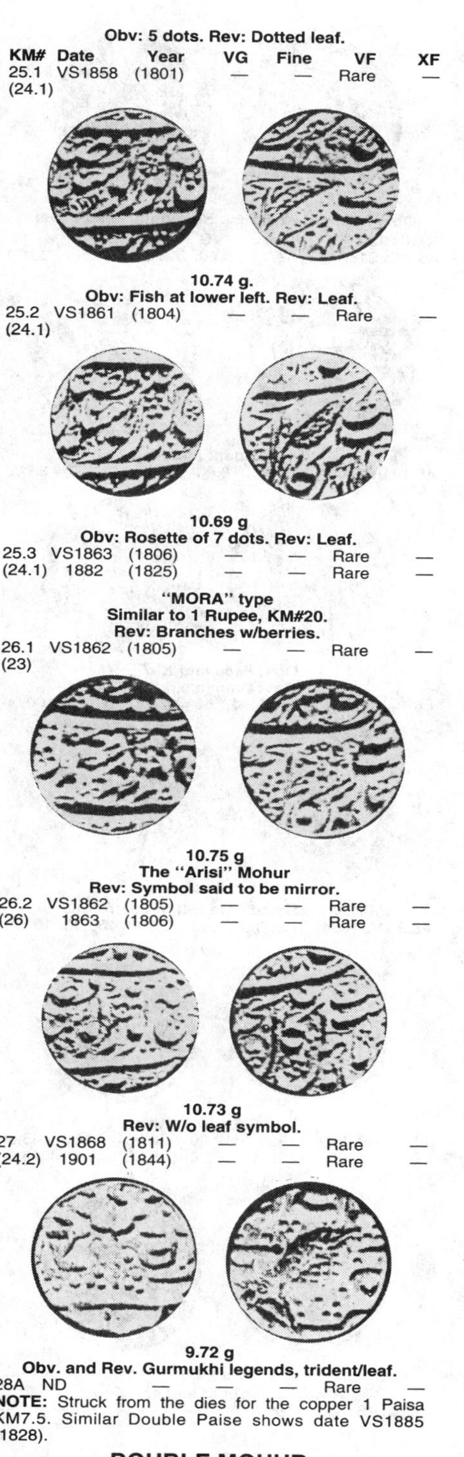

10.74 g.
Obv: Fish at lower left. Rev: Leaf.

KM#	Date	Year	VG	Fine	VF	XF
25.2 (24.1)	VS1861	(1804)	—	—	Rare	—

10.69 g
Obv: Rosette of 7 dots. Rev: Leaf.

KM#	Date	Year	VG	Fine	VF	XF
25.3	VS1863	(1806)	—	—	Rare	—
(24.1)	1882	(1825)	—	—	Rare	—

"MORA" type
Similar to 1 Rupee, KM#20.
Rev: Branches w/berries.

KM#	Date	Year	VG	Fine	VF	XF
26.1 (23)	VS1862	(1805)	—	—	Rare	—

10.75 g
The "Arisi" Mohur
Rev: Symbol said to be mirror.

KM#	Date	Year	VG	Fine	VF	XF
26.2	VS1862	(1805)	—	—	Rare	—
(26)	1863	(1806)	—	—	Rare	—

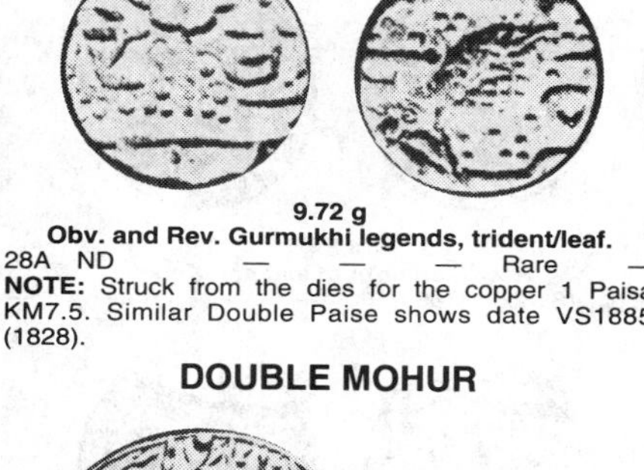

10.73 g
Rev: W/o leaf symbol.

KM#	Date	Year	VG	Fine	VF	XF
27	VS1868	(1811)	—	—	Rare	—
(24.2)	1901	(1844)	—	—	Rare	—

9.72 g
Obv. and Rev. Gurmukhi legends, trident/leaf.

KM#	Date	Year	VG	Fine	VF	XF
28A	ND	—	—	—	Rare	—

NOTE: Struck from the dies for the copper 1 Paisa KM7.5. Similar Double Paise shows date VS1885 (1828).

DOUBLE MOHUR

GOLD, 21.16 g

KM#	Date	Year	VG	Fine	VF	XF
29A	VS1883	(1826)	—	—	Rare	—

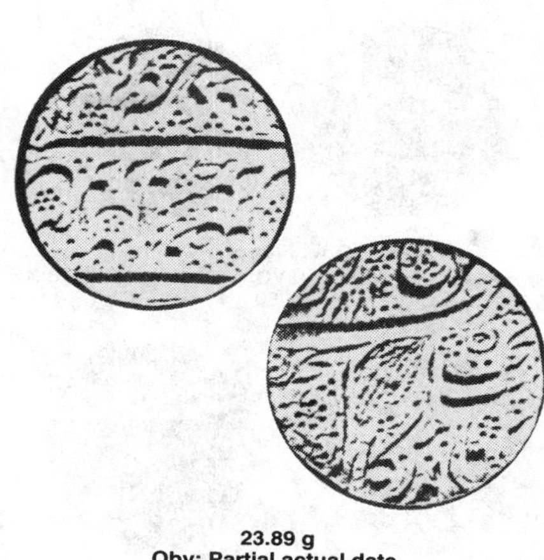

23.89 g
Obv: Partial actual date.
Rev: VS1884 fixed.

KM#	Date	Year	VG	Fine	VF	XF
29B (25)	VS(18)85	(1828)	—	—	Rare	—

KASHMIR MINT

PAISA

COPPER
Gurmukhi and Persian legends.

KM#	Date	Year	Good	VG	Fine	VF
40.1	VS1878	—	6.50	11.50	18.50	30.00

Persian and Gurmukhi legends.

KM#	Date	Year	Good	VG	Fine	VF
40.2	VS188x	—	5.50	9.00	15.00	25.00

KM#	Date	Year	Good	VG	Fine	VF
40.3	VS188x	(18xx)	5.50	9.00	15.00	25.00

Persian legends, sword.

KM#	Date	Year	Good	VG	Fine	VF
41.1	VS1894	(1837)	5.50	9.00	15.00	25.00

Persian legends, rosette.

KM#	Date	Year	Good	VG	Fine	VF
41.2	ND	—	4.50	7.50	12.50	20.00

KM#	Date	Year	Good	VG	Fine	VF
41.3	VS1895	(1838)	5.50	9.00	15.00	25.00

Obv: Nanak Shah. Rev: Rosette.

KM#	Date	Year	Good	VG	Fine	VF
41.4	ND	—	5.50	9.00	15.00	25.00

Banner

KM#	Date	Year	Good	VG	Fine	VF
41.5	ND	VS(1892)	6.50	11.50	18.50	30.00

KM#	Date	Year	Good	VG	Fine	VF
41.6	ND	(VS1897)	4.50	7.50	12.50	20.00

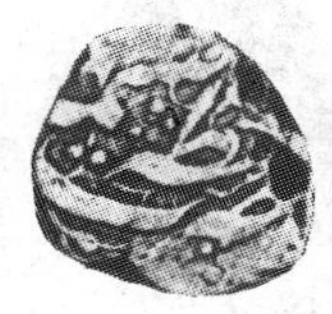

Sikka Nanak Shahi.

KM#	Date	Year	Good	VG	Fine	VF
41.7	ND	—	4.50	7.50	12.50	20.00

KM#	Date	Year	Good	VG	Fine	VF
42	VS189x	(18xx)	5.50	9.00	15.00	25.00

1/4 RUPEE

SILVER, 2.75 g

KM#	Date	Year	VG	Fine	VF	XF
43	VS1898	(1841)	—	—	Rare	—
	ND	—	—	—	—	—

1/2 RUPEE

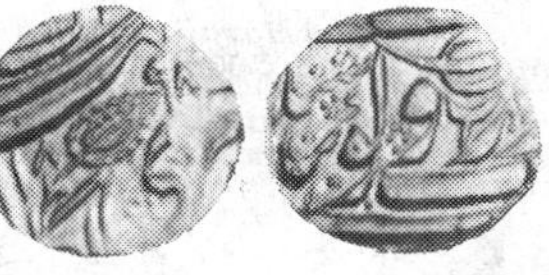

SILVER, 5.50 g

KM#	Date	Year	VG	Fine	VF	XF
44	VS1898	(1841)	20.00	35.00	70.00	100.00
	ND	—	—	—	Rare	—

RUPEE

SILVER, 10.7 g
Obv. and rev: Gurmukhi legends.

KM#	Date	Year	VG	Fine	VF	XF
45	VS1892	(1835)	—	—	Rare	—

7.6 g
Obv: *RAM* in Gurmukhi legend.

KM#	Date	Year	VG	Fine	VF	XF
45a	VS1892	(1835)	—	—	Rare	—

11.00-11.30 g
Obv: Flower spray. Rev: Date to right of leaf.

KM#	Date	Year	VG	Fine	VF	XF
46.1	VS1876	(1819)	6.50	11.50	18.50	30.00

Obv: Flower spray. Rev: Date divided horizontally.

46.2	VS1876	(1819)	6.50	11.50	18.50	30.00

Obv: Flower spray.
Rev: Legend divided vertically, date at top.

46.3	VS1877	(1820)	6.50	11.50	18.50	30.00
	1878	(1821)	6.50	11.50	18.50	30.00

Obv: Gurmukhi *Hara.*

46.4	VS1878	(1821)	6.50	11.50	18.50	30.00
	1879	(1822)	6.50	11.50	18.50	30.00

Obv: Nagari *Om Sri.*

46.5	VS1879	(1822)	8.00	13.50	21.50	35.00

Obv: Nagari *Haraji* or *Hara.*

46.6	VS1879	(1822)	8.00	13.50	21.50	35.00

Rev: Sword across leaf stem,
Sri Ram in Persian.

46.14	VS1880	(1823)	—	—	Rare	—

Obv: Floral symbol, 4-pointed star.

46.7	VS1881	(1824)	6.50	11.50	18.50	30.00

Obv: Banner.

46.8	VS1881	(1824)	6.50	11.50	18.50	30.00
	1882	(1825)	6.50	11.50	18.50	30.00
	1883	(1826)	6.50	11.50	18.50	30.00

Obv: Flower.

KM#	Date	Year	VG	Fine	VF	XF
46.9	VS1883	(1826)	6.50	11.50	18.50	30.00

Obv: Flower, Persian *Kaf.*

46.9A	VS1883	(1826)	6.50	11.00	22.00	30.00

Obv: Persian *Ram* and *Kaf.*

46.10	VS—	—	6.50	11.50	18.50	30.00

Obv: Persian *Kaf.*

46.11	VS1885	(1828)	6.50	11.50	18.50	30.00
	1887	(1830)	8.00	13.50	21.50	35.00

Obv: Persian *Kaf.*
Rev: Cross and letter form "I".

46.12	VS1886	(1829)	8.00	13.50	21.50	35.00

Obv: Sprig and *Kaf.*

46.15	VS1886	(1829)	10.00	16.50	27.50	45.00
	1887	(1830)	10.00	16.50	27.50	45.00

Rev: Letter in field, *Bha.*

46.13	VS1887	(1830)	8.00	13.50	21.50	35.00
	1888	(1831)	8.00	13.50	21.50	35.00

Obv: Sprig and *Kaf.*

46.16	VS1887	(1830)	8.00	13.50	21.50	35.00

Obv: Face and *Kaf.*
Rev: Horizontal line on leaf.

46.17	VS1884	(1827)	8.00	13.50	21.50	35.00

Obv: Star and *Kaf.* Rev: Horizontal line on leaf.

KM#	Date	Year	VG	Fine	VF	XF
46.18	VS1884	(1827)	8.00	13.50	21.50	35.00

Obv: Trident and *Kaf.*

46.19	VS1886	(1829)	8.00	13.50	21.50	35.00

Obv: Face and *Kaf.*
Rev: Date in circle.

48.1	VS1884	(1827)	21.50	35.00	60.00	100.00

Rev: Leaf and date within quatrefoil.

48.2	VS1884	(1827)	21.50	35.00	60.00	100.00

Obv: Date. Rev: Katar.

49	VS1889	(1832)	10.00	16.50	27.50	45.00
	1890	(1833)	10.00	16.50	27.50	45.00

8.5 g
Rev: Lion right of leaf and Katar.

A50	VS1890	(1833)	—	—	Rare	—

11.00-11.30 g
Obv: Sword through circle. Rev: Date at top.

B50	VS1891	(1834)	21.50	35.00	60.00	100.00

8.50 g
Rev: Date divided by leaf, Katar at left.

C50	VS1891	(1834)	15.00	25.00	42.50	70.00

Obv: Sword through circle.

KM#	Date	Year	VG	Fine	VF	XF
50	VS1892	(1835)	8.00	13.50	21.50	35.00
	1893	(1836)	8.00	13.50	21.50	35.00

Rev: Outlined leaf.

KM#	Date	Year	VG	Fine	VF	XF
51	VS1893	(1836)	15.00	25.00	40.00	65.00
	1894	(1837)	15.00	25.00	40.00	65.00
	1895	(1838)	15.00	25.00	40.00	65.00
	1896	(1839)	15.00	25.00	40.00	65.00
	1897	(1840)	15.00	25.00	40.00	65.00
	1898	(1841)	15.00	25.00	40.00	65.00

Obv: Persian letter *Shin* in place of sword.
Rev: Date.

KM#	Date	Year	VG	Fine	VF	XF
52.1	VS1898	(1841)	9.00	15.00	25.00	40.00
	1899	(1842)	9.00	15.00	25.00	40.00

Rev: Date on left side of leaf.

KM#	Date	Year	VG	Fine	VF	XF
52.2	VS1900	(1843)	8.00	13.50	21.50	35.00
	1901	(1844)	8.00	13.50	21.50	35.00
	1902	(1845)	8.00	13.50	21.50	35.00
	1903	(1846)	8.00	13.50	21.50	35.00

LAHORE MINT

Dar-us-Sultanat

PAISA

COPPER

KM#	Date	Year	Good	VG	Fine	VF
60	VS1880	(1823)	4.50	7.50	12.50	20.00
	1881	(1824)	4.50	7.50	12.50	20.00

1/2 RUPEE

SILVER, 18mm, 5.5-5.6 g

KM#	Date	Year	VG	Fine	VF	XF
62	VS1858	(1801)	18.50	30.00	50.00	85.00
	1864	(1807)	18.50	30.00	50.00	85.00
	1889	(1832)	18.50	30.00	50.00	85.00

NOTE: Earlier dates (VS1828-1847) exist for this type.

In the name of Guru Gobind Singh

RUPEE

SILVER, 10.80-11.20 g
Actual VS years.

KM#	Date	Year	VG	Fine	VF	XF
66.1	VS1858	(1801)	8.00	13.50	21.50	35.00
	1859	(1802)	8.00	13.50	21.50	35.00
	1806 (error for 1860)		—	—	—	—
	1860	(1803)	8.00	13.50	21.50	35.00
	1861	(1804)	8.00	13.50	21.50	35.00
	1862	(1805)	8.00	13.50	21.50	35.00
	1863	(1806)	8.00	13.50	21.50	35.00
	1864	(1807)	8.00	13.50	21.50	35.00
	1865	(1808)	8.00	13.50	21.50	35.00
	1866	(1809)	8.00	13.50	21.50	35.00
	1867	(1810)	8.00	13.50	21.50	35.00
	1868	(1811)	8.00	13.50	21.50	35.00
	1869	(1812)	8.00	13.50	21.50	35.00
	1870	(1813)	10.00	20.00	30.00	60.00
	1871	(1814)	8.00	13.50	21.50	35.00
	1872	(1815)	8.00	13.50	21.50	35.00
	1873	(1816)	8.00	13.50	21.50	35.00
	1874	(1817)	8.00	13.50	21.50	35.00
	1875	(1818)	8.00	13.50	21.50	35.00
	1876	(1819)	8.00	13.50	21.50	35.00
	1877	(1820)	8.00	13.50	21.50	35.00
	1878	(1821)	8.00	13.50	21.50	35.00
	1879	(1822)	8.00	13.50	21.50	35.00
	1880	(1823)	8.00	13.50	21.50	35.00
	1881	(1824)	8.00	13.50	21.50	35.00
	1882	(1825)	8.00	13.50	21.50	35.00
	1883	(1826)	8.00	13.50	21.50	35.00
	1884	(1827)	8.00	13.50	21.50	35.00
	1885	(1828)	8.00	13.50	21.50	35.00
	1887	(1830)	8.00	13.50	21.50	35.00

NOTE: Earlier dates (VS1856-1857) exist for this type.

Obv: Actual date. Rev: VS1884.

KM#	Date	Year	VG	Fine	VF	XF
66.2	VS(18)87	(1830)	8.00	13.50	21.50	35.00
	(18)88	(1831)	8.00	13.50	21.50	35.00
	(18)89	(1832)	8.00	13.50	21.50	35.00
	(18)90	(1833)	8.00	13.50	21.50	35.00
	(18)91	(1834)	8.00	13.50	21.50	35.00
	(18)92	(1835)	8.00	13.50	21.50	35.00
	(18)93	(1836)	8.00	13.50	21.50	35.00

Rev: VS1885

KM#	Date	Year	VG	Fine	VF	XF
67	VS(18)94	(1837)	8.00	13.50	21.50	35.00
	(18)95	(1838)	8.00	13.50	21.50	35.00
	(18)96	(1839)	8.00	13.50	21.50	35.00
	(18)97	(1840)	8.00	13.50	21.50	35.00
	1902	(1845)	8.00	13.50	21.50	35.00
	1903	(1846)	8.00	13.50	21.50	35.00

SILVER, 10.80-11.40 g
Rev: Ranjit Singh, Guru Nanak.

KM#	Date	Year	VG	Fine	VF	XF
68.1	VS1885	(1828)	—	—	Rare	—

SILVER, 11.12-11.13 g
Rev: W/banner, fixed year VS1885.

KM#	Date	Year	VG	Fine	VF	XF
68.2	VS(18)93	(1836)	—	—	Rare	—

1/5 MOHUR

GOLD, 2.21 g

KM#	Date	Year	VG	Fine	VF	XF
A87	VS1885/96	(1839)	—	—	Rare	—

MOHUR

GOLD, 10.85 g

KM#	Date	Year	VG	Fine	VF	XF
69	VS1884	(1827)	—	—	Rare	—
	1884/92	(1835)	—	—	Rare	—

MALKARIAN MINT

RUPEE

SILVER, 10.70-11.60 g
Rev: *Sri Akalpur*.

KM#	Date	Year	VG	Fine	VF	XF
72	VS1879	(1822)	100.00	175.00	250.00	350.00
	1880	(1823)	100.00	175.00	250.00	350.00

MULTAN MINT

PAISA

COPPER

KM#	Date	Year	Good	VG	Fine	VF
77	VS1875	(1818)	4.50	7.50	12.50	20.00
	1878	(1821)	4.50	7.50	12.50	20.00

NOTE: Also found with botched or fictitious dates.

DOUBLE PAISA

COPPER

KM#	Date	Year	Good	VG	Fine	VF
78	VS1904	(1847)	21.50	35.00	60.00	100.00

1/2 RUPEE

SILVER

KM#	Date	Year	VG	Fine	VF	XF
81	VS1885	(1828)	18.50	30.00	50.00	85.00

RUPEE

SILVER, 10.70-11.60 g
Obv: Plain. Rev: Leaf.

KM#	Date	Year	VG	Fine	VF	XF
84	VS1875	(1818)	11.00	18.50	30.00	50.00
	1876	(1819)	11.00	18.50	30.00	50.00
	1877	(1820)	11.00	18.50	30.00	50.00
	1878	(1821)	11.00	18.50	30.00	50.00
	1879	(1822)	11.00	18.50	30.00	50.00
	1880	(1823)	11.00	18.50	30.00	50.00

Obv: Trident. Rev: Leaf.

KM#	Date	Year	VG	Fine	VF	XF
85	VS1880	(1823)	10.00	16.50	27.50	45.00
	1881	(1824)	10.00	16.50	27.50	45.00
	1882	(1825)	10.00	16.50	27.50	45.00
	1883	(1826)	10.00	16.50	27.50	45.00
	1884	(1827)	10.00	16.50	27.50	45.00

Obv: Flower. Rev: Leaf.

KM#	Date	Year	VG	Fine	VF	XF
86.1	VS1884	(1827)	8.00	13.50	21.50	35.00
	1885	(1828)	8.00	13.50	21.50	35.00
	1886	(1829)	8.00	13.50	21.50	35.00
	1887	(1830)	8.00	13.50	21.50	35.00
	1888	(1831)	8.00	13.50	21.50	35.00
	1889	(1832)	8.00	13.50	21.50	35.00
	1890	(1833)	8.00	13.50	21.50	35.00
	1891	(1834)	8.00	13.50	21.50	35.00
	1892	(1835)	8.00	13.50	21.50	35.00
	1893	(1836)	8.00	13.50	21.50	35.00
	1894	(1837)	8.00	13.50	21.50	35.00
	1895	(1838)	8.00	13.50	21.50	35.00
	1896	(1839)	8.00	13.50	21.50	35.00
	1897	(1840)	8.00	13.50	21.50	35.00
	1898	(1841)	8.00	13.50	21.50	35.00
	1899	(1842)	8.00	13.50	21.50	35.00
	1900	(1843)	8.00	13.50	21.50	35.00
	1901	(1844)	8.00	13.50	21.50	35.00
	1902	(1845)	8.00	13.50	21.50	35.00
	1903	(1846)	15.00	25.00	50.00	80.00
	1904	(1847)	8.00	13.50	21.50	35.00
	1905	(1848)	8.00	13.50	21.50	35.00

NAZARANA RUPEE

SILVER, 10.70-11.60 g

KM#	Date	Year	VG	Fine	VF	XF
86.2	VS1896	(1839)	55.00	90.00	150.00	250.00

GOLD RUPEE

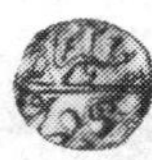

GOLD, 0.57 g

KM#	Date	Year	VG	Fine	VF	XF
87	VS1905	(1848)	17.50	27.50	45.00	75.00

NOTE: Struck by Diwan Mulraj (April 1848 - Jan. 1849/ VS1905).

MOHUR

GOLD, 10.85 g

KM#	Date	Year	VG	Fine	VF	XF
87A	VS1876	(1815)	—	—	Rare	—

NIMAK MINT

(Pind Dadan Khan)

RUPEE

SILVER, 10.70-11.60 g

KM#	Date	Year	VG	Fine	VF	XF
88	VS1904	(1847)	75.00	125.00	200.00	325.00
	1905	(1848)	75.00	125.00	200.00	325.00

Obv: Nagari *Ram Jim*.

KM#	Date	Year	VG	Fine	VF	XF
89	VS1905	(1848)	—	—	Rare	—

PATHANKOT MINT

PAISA

COPPER

KM#	Date	Year	Good	VG	Fine	VF
90 (97)	VS1894	(1837)	10.00	16.50	27.50	45.00

PESHAWAR MINT

Captured by Ranjit Singh in 1832AD.

1/2 RUPEE

SILVER, 4.10-4.25 g

KM#	Date	Year	VG	Fine	VF	XF
97	VS1892	(1835)	—	—	Rare	—

RUPEE

SILVER, 8.50 g
Rev: Plain leaf.

KM#	Date	Year	VG	Fine	VF	XF
98.1	VS1891	(1834)	12.00	20.00	40.00	75.00

Rev: Dotted outline around leaf.

KM#	Date	Year	VG	Fine	VF	XF
98.2	VS1892	(1835)	10.00	16.50	27.50	45.00
	1893	(1836)	10.00	16.50	27.50	45.00
	1894	(1837)	10.00	16.50	27.50	45.00

NOTE: Some specimens with oblique milled edges, dated VS1894 weigh 10.50-11.00 g.

UNCERTAIN MINTS

PAISA

COPPER
Obv: Leaf symbol overstruck on Afghanistan Durrani Falus.

KM#	Date	Year	Good	VG	Fine	VF
A99	ND	—	4.00	6.00	10.00	18.00

Overstrike

KM#	Date	Year	Good	VG	Fine	VF
B99	ND	—	2.00	4.00	8.00	12.00

RUPEE

SILVER, 11.20 g
Obv: Trident. Rev: Lion.
Bearing name of "Sarkar Ahluwalia"

KM#	Date	Year	VG	Fine	VF	XF
99	VS1862	(1805)	85.00	140.00	200.00	300.00

NOTE: Issued by Fateh Singh Ahluwalia.

Rev: *Muzang*.

KM#	Date	Year	VG	Fine	VF	XF
C99	VS1889	(1832)	—	—	Rare	—

NOTE: This coin may have been struck at Gujarat?

TOKEN ISSUES (Tn)

MOHUR

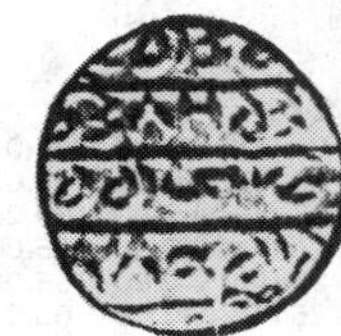

GOLD, 10.74-10.82 g
Obv. and rev: Gurmukhi legends.

KM#	Date	Year	VG	Fine	VF	XF
Tn1 (28B)	ND		—	—	Rare	—

SIKH FEUDATORY STATES

DERA

Sikh Protectorate, 1819-1847AD

Dera is known more fully as Dera Ghazi Khan, as distinguished from Dera Ismail Khan (Derajat).

PAISA

COPPER, 7.00-8.00 g

KM#	Date	Year	Good	VG	Fine	VF
101.1	VS1898	(1841)	3.00	5.50	9.00	15.00

Obv: Gurmukhi legend, date.

KM#	Date	Year	Good	VG	Fine	VF
101.2	VS1898	(1841)	3.00	5.50	9.00	15.00

RUPEE

SILVER, 11.00-11.10 g
Obv: "Ram" in Nagari; actual VS date of issue.
Rev: Dated VS1884 "Dera".

KM#	Date	Year	VG	Fine	VF	XF
102	VS(18)94	1837	100.00	175.00	250.00	350.00
	1884/VS (1)904		—	—	Rare	—
	1884/VS (19)04		—	—	Rare	—

DERAJAT

Sikh Protectorate, 1819-1847AD

Derajat was the region centered about Dera Ismail Khan where the mint was presumably located.

NOTE: There are many varieties of copper coins, only a sample of which are listed below.

PAISA

Obv: Crude lion right.

KM#	Date	Good	VG	Fine	VF
A102 (109)	ND	7.50	12.50	20.00	35.00

Obv: Funny lion right, AH date.

KM#	Date	Good	VG	Fine	VF
B102 (110)	AH1254	—	—	—	—

Obv: Lion left, AH date.

KM#	Date	Good	VG	Fine	VF
C102 (111.1)	AH1246	2.75	4.50	7.50	12.50
	1247	2.75	4.50	7.50	12.50
	1249	2.75	4.50	7.50	12.50
	1254	2.75	4.50	7.50	12.50
	1261	2.75	4.50	7.50	12.50
	1262	2.75	4.50	7.50	12.50
	1265	2.75	4.50	7.50	12.50
	1267	2.75	4.50	7.50	12.50
	1276	2.75	4.50	7.50	12.50

Obv: Lion right, AH date.

KM#	Date	Good	VG	Fine	VF
D102 (111.2)	AH1254	3.50	5.50	9.00	15.00

Obv: Horse, AH date.

KM#	Date	Good	VG	Fine	VF
E102 (111.3)	AH1252	4.50	7.50	12.50	20.00

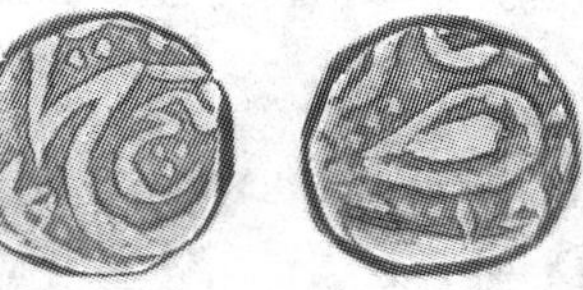

Obv: *Fath*. Rev: Leaf.

KM#	Date	Good	VG	Fine	VF
F102 (112)	—	3.55	5.50	9.00	15.00

Obv: Lion right.

KM#	Date	Good	VG	Fine	VF
G102 (113)	VS1793 (error, for 1893)	3.00	5.00	8.00	13.50

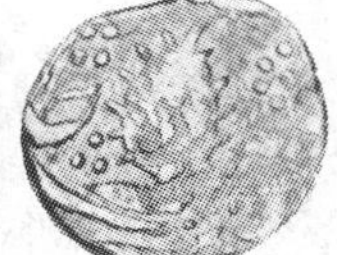

Obv: Leaf and *Gurmukhi*. Rev: *DERAJAT* and fruit.

KM#	Date	Year	Good	VG	Fine	VF
104	ND	—	—	—	—	—

Obv: *Ra'ij*. Mintname: *Derajat*.

KM#	Date	Year	Good	VG	Fine	VF
105	AH1241	—	3.00	5.50	9.00	15.00
	1242	—	3.00	5.50	9.00	15.00

Obv: *Ra'ij*. Rev: *Samadi* monogram.

KM#	Date	Good	VG	Fine	VF
106	AH124x	4.50	7.50	12.50	20.00

Obv: *Sahih*. Rev: Mintname & date.

KM#	Date	Good	VG	Fine	VF
108	AH1252	3.50	6.00	10.00	16.50

Similar to 1 Rupee, KM#120.

KM#	Date	Year	Good	VG	Fine	VF
114	VS1896	—	3.50	6.00	10.00	16.50

RUPEE

SILVER, 10.70-11.60 g
Obv: Date separated by Gurmukhi letter.
Rev: Neat leaf.

KM#	Date	Year	VG	Fine	VF	XF
119	VS1892	(1835)	18.50	30.00	50.00	85.00
	1893	(1836)	18.50	30.00	50.00	85.00
	1894	(1837)	18.50	30.00	50.00	85.00

Obv: Date above Gurmukhi letter.
Rev: Normal leaf.

KM#	Date	Year	VG	Fine	VF	XF
120.1	VS1893	(1835)	18.50	27.00	45.00	75.00
	1894	(1836)	18.50	27.00	45.00	75.00

Rev: Crude leaf.

KM#	Date	Year	VG	Fine	VF	XF
120.2	VS1894	(1837)	18.50	27.00	45.00	75.00
	1895	(1838)	18.50	27.00	45.00	75.00
	1896	(1839)	18.50	27.00	45.00	75.00
	1897	(1840)	18.50	27.00	45.00	75.00
	1898	(1841)	18.50	27.00	45.00	75.00
	1899	(1842)	18.50	27.00	45.00	75.00
	1900	(1843)	18.50	27.00	45.00	75.00
	1901	(1844)	18.50	27.00	45.00	75.00
	1902	(1845)	18.50	27.00	45.00	75.00
	1903	(1846)	18.50	27.00	45.00	75.00
	1904	(1847)	18.50	27.00	45.00	75.00
	1905	(1848)	18.50	27.00	45.00	75.00

NAJIBABAD

Symbols:

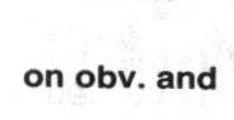

on obv. and on rev.

PAISA

COPPER
Obv: Date.

KM#	Date	Good	VG	Fine	VF
131	Yr.21	4.50	7.50	12.50	20.00
	x4	4.50	7.50	12.50	20.00

SIKKIM

A Kingdom located above northeast India between China, Bhutan and Nepal. In 1890 it became a British protectorate and later in 1949 it became a protectorate of India and in 1975, a state.

The Kingdom of Sikkim covers an area of some 2,800 sq. mi., and is situated on the southern slopes of the Himalayas, sandwiched between India to the south, Tibet to the north, Nepal to the west and Bhutan to the east. On its border with Nepal is the third highest mountain in the world, Kanchenjunga.

The Kingdom was founded in 1642 when Phuntsog Namgyal was proclaimed Chogyal or King. His ancestors had come to the Sikkim area about 150 years earlier from Eastern Tibet and, over the years had gained the confidence and respect of the indigenous inhabitants, the Lapchas. The descendents of Phuntsog Namgyal have ruled Sikkim ever since.

In the latter part of the eighteenth century Sikkim was subject to a number of Gurkha incursions, the impact of which was to place Sikkim on the British side in the Nepal War of 1815-1816. At the conclusion of this campaign Sikkim received certain tracts of land relinquished by Nepal and, in return, was obliged to accept British protection and control.

Initially Sikkim covered an area at least twice as large as it is now, but annexations by neighboring powers reduced its size until in 1835 it reached its present area after the Chogyal "presented" the hills of Darjeeling to the British "out of friendship". In 1861 Sikkim became a protectorate of British India with the British exercising complete control over foreign affairs and defense and the Chogyal being in charge of all other internal matters.

India's independence brought little change to this situation until April 1973 when there was an uprising during which the Chogyal asked for the assistance of the Indian Government. An agreement has now been reached under which the Chogyal's powers are to be greatly reduced and the administration of Sikkim is to be headed by a "chief nomination of the Government of India."

For practically the entire period of its history, Sikkim had no coinage of its own and until the last century, trade was carried out by barter with taxes paid in kind. On the few occasions when inhabitants needed money, Tibetan coins, silver or gold bullion, or later, Indian coins were used. For only three or four years in the 1800's were coins struck in Sikkim, and then they were struck by Nepalese immigrants. Since the beginning of the twentieth century Indian currency has circulated widely and exclusively.

Since the late 18th century the Nepalese have exhibited a strong urge to leave the overcrowded hills of Nepal and seek their fortunes elsewhere. Sikkim, being so close, was an obvious target for settlement and in order to prevent this, the seventh ruler of Sikkim, Tsugphud Namgyal (1793-1864) prohibited the settlement of Nepalese in Sikkim. This ban was effective until the early years of the reign of Thutob Namgyal (1874-1914) when certain powerful landowners realized that it was profitable to allow Nepalese to settle and work the land. Foremost of these were the brothers Kangsa Dewan and Phodong Lama. These two brothers struck a deal with two rich Nepalese traders, the brothers Lachmidas and Chandrabir Pradhan, under which a large tract of land which had recently been confiscated from a Sikkimese nobleman who had been convicted of embezzlement, was made over to the Nepalese brothers. This deal was strongly criticized by the Sikkimese people, but was supported by the British and finally the Kangsa brothers persuaded the Chogyal in 1878 to allow Nepalese settlement in "uninhabited and waste lands of Sikkim". Since then Nepalese immigrants have flooded into Sikkim and now comprise a majority of the population of the country.

It was the Pradhan brothers who were responsible for the Sikkim coinage. Soon after acquiring their lands they obtained licences to mine copper in a number of places, most important of which were Tuk Khani, Bhotan Khani near Rangpo and Pachay Khani. Some of this copper was sold in Nepal and Darjeeling, but some remained unsold, so in 1882 the brothers sought and obtained the permission of the Chogyal to strike copper coins. The minting was done in two places near the mines of Tuk Khani and Pachay Khani. Unfortunately for the Pradhan brothers, the Deputy Commissioner of Darjeeling forbade circulation of the Sikkim coins in the Darjeeling district and this made the coins unpopular among the people. The minting was not profitable and was discontinued in 1885.

The coins themselves are, except for the inscription, exact copies of the Nepalese paisa of Surendra Vira Vikrama Shah. They are very poorly struck and very few specimens have all the details of the design visible. The date is only very rarely legible. Three major types are known, but there is no indication of the mint of origin and die-links exist between the types. The coins are all intended to be the same denomination, one paisa, although the weights of individual specimens vary within the range 6.00 g to 4.00 g around a mean of about 5.20 g.

RULERS

Thutab Namgyel,
VS1931-1968/1874-1911AD

THUTAB NAMGYEL

VS1931-1968/1874-1911AD

PAISA

COPPER, 20-22mm, 4.00-6.00 g
Obv: Leg. in 3 lines within square, date below.
Rev: Leg. in 3 lines within square.

KM#	Date	Year	Good	VG	Fine	VF
1	VS1940	(1883)	10.00	17.50	25.00	35.00
	1941	(1884)	5.00	8.50	12.50	17.50

Obv: Leg. in 4 lines within square, date below.

KM#	Date	Year	Good	VG	Fine	VF
2	VS1941	(1884)	10.00	17.50	25.00	35.00

Obv: Leg. in 3 lines within square, date below, w/*Ti* of *Sikimpati* on third line.

KM#	Date	Year	Good	VG	Fine	VF
3.1	VS1941	(1884)	5.00	8.50	12.50	17.50
	1942	(1885)	5.00	8.50	12.50	17.50

Rev. leg: *Sarkar* spelled incorrectly *Sakar*.

KM#	Date	Year	Good	VG	Fine	VF
3.2	VS1941	(1884)	5.00	8.50	12.50	17.50
	1942	(1885)	5.00	8.50	12.50	17.50

Rev. leg: *Sarkar* spelled incorrectly *Sikar*.

KM#	Date	Year	Good	VG	Fine	VF
3.3	VS1941	(1884)	5.00	8.50	12.50	17.50
	1942	(1885)	5.00	8.50	12.50	17.50

SIND

Sind has an extremely ancient historical record having been successively occupied and governed by the Indus Valley civilization (ca. 1500 BC), Alexander the Great (325BC) Chandragupta Maurya (ca.305BC), Asoka (274-232BC) and others until the first Muslim inroads into Sind after 712AD. For almost the next three hundred years Sind was subject to Arab caliphs, after which it was conquered by Sultan Mahmud of Ghazni who conducted annual raids into India after 1000AD. Even then it remained semi-independent under local dynasties until, under Akbar (who was himself born at Umarkot in Sind), Sind became part of the Mughal empire.

The amirs of Hyderabad and Khairpur came into existence after the Mughal empire had started to disintegrate. Khairpur had been governed by the Kalhoras but in the 1780s they were overthrown by the Talpurs, a Baluchi family. Khairpur State was founded by Mir Sohrab Khan Talpur. In 1813 Khairpur ceased to pay tribute to Afghanistan and, in 1832(1247/48AH), it was recognized by the British as a separate state within Sind. In 1843, when the rest of Sind was annexed by the British in the aftermath of the Anglo-Sikh War, Khairpur remained separate and was only merged into the neighboring territory by its accession in 1947 to Pakistan.

AMIRS of HYDERABAD

Haidarabad Sind Mint

حيدرآباد سند

Mintname: Haidarabad Sind

In the name of Taimur Shah Durrani

RUPEE

SILVER, 10.70-11.60 g

KM#	Date	Year	VG	Fine	VF	XF
17	ND	—	15.00	30.00	50.00	75.00

SIND MINT

سند

RUPEE

SILVER, 10.70-11.60 g
Rev: Sind spelled "Sahind".

KM#	Date	Year	VG	Fine	VF	XF
18	AH1227	—	13.50	25.00	40.00	65.00

NOTE: Several varieties exist w/different symbols on reverse.

KM#	Date	Year	VG	Fine	VF	XF
19	AH1239	—	12.00	20.00	28.00	42.50
	1240	—	12.00	20.00	28.00	42.50
	1241	—	12.00	20.00	28.00	42.50
	1242	—	12.00	20.00	28.00	42.50
	1244	—	12.00	20.00	28.00	42.50
	1245	—	12.00	20.00	28.00	42.50

Rev. mint mark: Star below *Sana*.

KM#	Date	Year	VG	Fine	VF	XF
19.2	ND	—	8.50	14.00	20.00	30.00

Mint mark: Group of 6 dots.

KM#	Date	Year	VG	Fine	VF	XF
19.1	ND	—	8.50	14.00	20.00	30.00

Rev: Star in *S* of *Jalus*.

KM#	Date	Year	VG	Fine	VF	XF
19.3	ND	—	8.50	14.00	20.00	30.00

Rev: Regnal year 8.

KM#	Date	Year	VG	Fine	VF	XF
19.4	ND	8	10.00	16.00	24.00	40.00

7.50-7.80 g

KM#	Date	Year	VG	Fine	VF	XF
20	AH1252	—	8.50	14.00	20.00	30.00
	1255	—	8.50	14.00	20.00	30.00
	1256	—	8.50	14.00	20.00	30.00
	1257	—	8.50	14.00	20.00	30.00

Mint mark: 5-petal flowers.

KM#	Date	Year	VG	Fine	VF	XF
20.1	ND	—	7.50	12.50	18.50	28.00

Mint mark: Cross.

KM#	Date	Year	VG	Fine	VF	XF
20.3	ND	—	8.50	14.00	20.00	30.00

Mint mark: Sprig w/3 berries.

KM#	Date	Year	VG	Fine	VF	XF
20.4	ND	—	8.50	14.00	20.00	30.00

Rev: W/o mark, w/Fath (Victory).

KM#	Date	Year	VG	Fine	VF	XF
21	ND	—	12.00	20.00	28.00	42.50

It is not known to which victory the reference is made.

AMIRS of KHAIRPUR

Formally independent
After AH1248/1832AD

RULERS

Nasir al-Din Muhammad,
AH1239-1260/1823-1843 AD

Bhakhar Mint

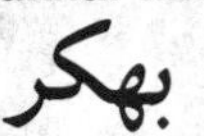

Mintname: Bhakhar, Bakhar, or Bakkar

All Rupees bear 2 mint marks, one on the obverse at the top of the central cartouche, one on the reverse, usually to the upper right of the *J* of *Julus*.

In the name of Mahmud Shah Durrani

RUPEE

SILVER, 11.00-11.50 g
Obv. and rev: W/o mint marks.

C#	Date	Year	VG	Fine	VF	XF
10	AH1240	—	12.50	21.00	30.00	45.00
	1245	—	9.00	15.00	21.50	32.50
	1246	—	9.00	15.00	21.50	32.50
	1252	—	9.00	15.00	21.50	32.50
	1254	—	9.00	15.00	21.50	32.50

Obv. and rev: Star.

C#	Date	Year	VG	Fine	VF	XF
10.1	AH1254	—	9.00	15.00	21.50	32.50
	1255	—	9.00	15.00	21.50	32.50

Obv: Star. Rev: Branch.

C#	Date	Year	VG	Fine	VF	XF
10.2	AH1255	—	9.00	15.00	21.50	32.50

Obv: Branch. Rev: Star.

C#	Date	Year	VG	Fine	VF	XF
10.2a	AH1225 (error) for 1252	—	10.00	16.00	22.50	35.00

Obv. and rev: Ornate crosses.

C#	Date	Year	VG	Fine	VF	XF
10.2b	AH1254	—	12.00	20.00	32.00	50.00

Obv. and rev: Branch.

C#	Date	Year	VG	Fine	VF	XF
10.3	AH1256	—	9.00	15.00	21.50	32.50
	1258	—	9.00	15.00	21.50	32.50

Obv: Pigeon. Rev: Plume.

C#	Date	Year	VG	Fine	VF	XF
10.4	AH1256	—	9.00	15.00	21.50	32.50

Obv: Pigeon. Rev: Peacock.

C#	Date	Year	VG	Fine	VF	XF
10.5	AH1258	—	10.00	17.50	25.00	37.50

Obv: Pigeon. Rev: Leaf.

C#	Date	Year	VG	Fine	VF	XF
10.8	AH1258	—	10.00	17.50	25.00	37.50

Obv: Hare. Rev: Peacock.

C#	Date	Year	VG	Fine	VF	XF
10.6	AH1258	—	10.00	17.50	25.00	37.50

Rev: Date in *S* of *Julus*.

C#	Date	Year	VG	Fine	VF	XF
10.7	AH1259	—	10.00	17.50	25.00	37.50

BRITISH OCCUPATION

From AH1259/1843AD

RUPEE

SILVER

Obv: Hare. Rev: British lion.

C#	Date	Year	VG	Fine	VF	XF
11	AH1259	—	15.00	25.00	35.00	50.00
	1261	—	15.00	25.00	35.00	50.00

Obv. and rev: Floral mint marks of various kinds.

C#	Date	Year	VG	Fine	VF	XF
12	AH1262	—	8.50	14.00	20.00	30.00
	1263	—	8.50	14.00	20.00	30.00
	1264	—	8.50	14.00	20.00	30.00
	1265	—	8.50	14.00	20.00	30.00
	1266	—	8.50	14.00	20.00	30.00
	1267	—	8.50	14.00	20.00	30.00
	1268	—	8.50	14.00	20.00	30.00
	1269	—	8.50	14.00	20.00	30.00

Obv: Hare. Rev: Peacock.

C#	Date	Year	VG	Fine	VF	XF
13	AH1259	—	16.50	23.50	32.50	48.00

LOCAL ISSUES

Shikarpur Mint

Mintname: Shikarpur 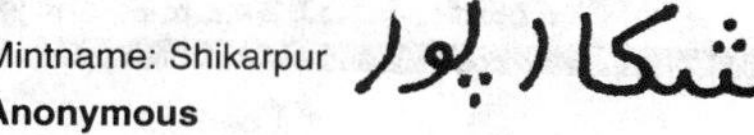

Anonymous

FALUS

COPPER

C#	Date	Year	Good	VG	Fine	VF
30.1	AH1255	—	3.00	5.00	7.50	12.50

Rev: Star at top.

C#	Date	Year	Good	VG	Fine	VF
30.2	AH1255	—	3.00	5.00	7.50	12.50

Tatta Mint

تته

Mintname: Tatta

In the name of Taimur Shah Durrani

RUPEE

SILVER, 10.70-11.60 g

C#	Date	Year	VG	Fine	VF	XF
45	ND	—	8.50	13.50	20.00	30.00

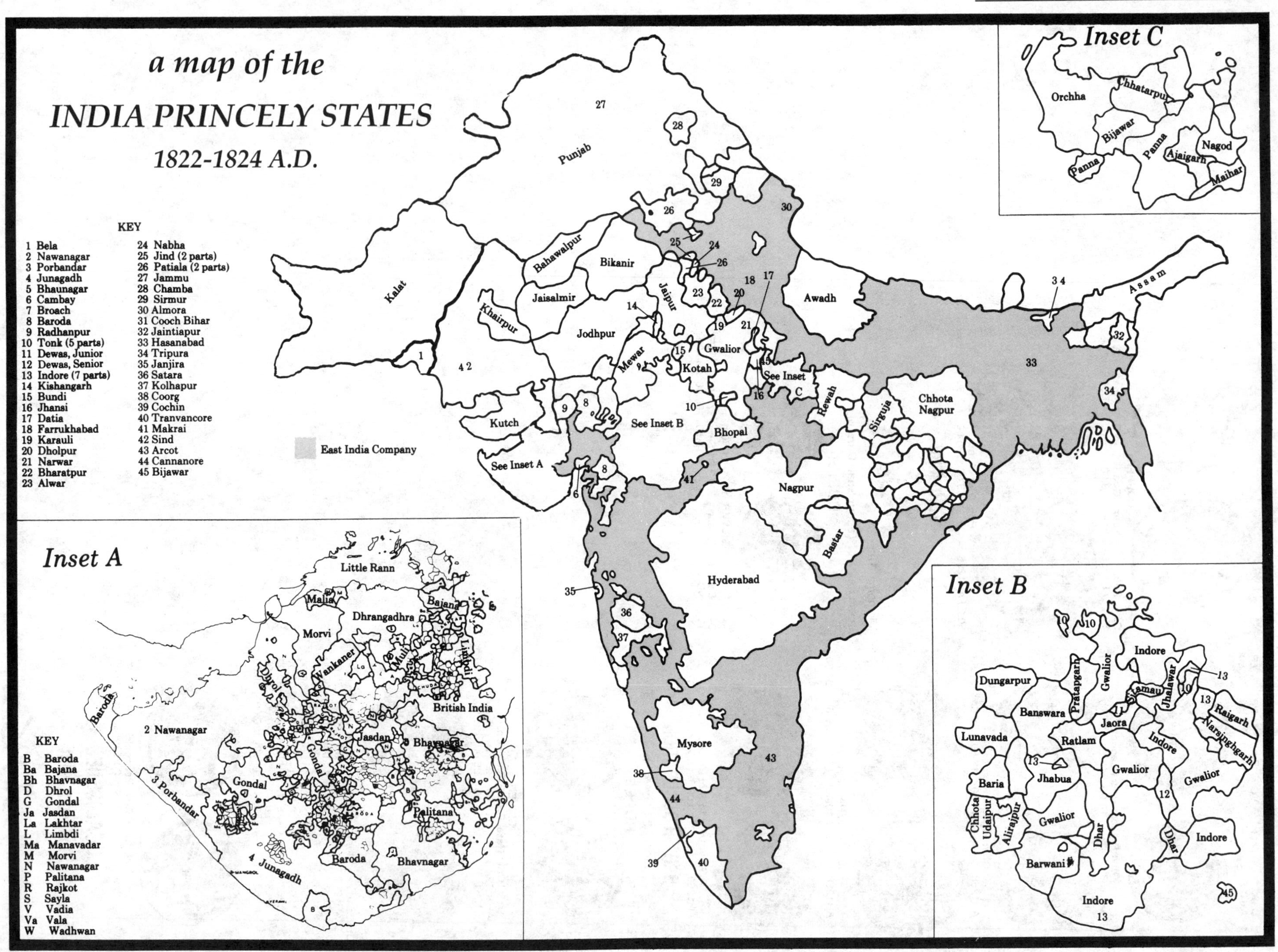
a map of the
INDIA PRINCELY STATES
1822-1824 A.D.
KEY
1 Bela
2 Nawanagar
3 Porbandar
4 Junagadh
5 Bhaunagar
6 Cambay
7 Broach
8 Baroda
9 Radhanpur
10 Tonk (5 parts)
11 Dewas, Junior
12 Dewas, Senior
13 Indore (7 parts)
14 Kishangarh
15 Bundi
16 Jhansi
17 Datia
18 Farrukhabad
19 Karauli
20 Dholpur
21 Narwar
22 Bharatpur
23 Alwar
24 Nabha
25 Jind (2 parts)
26 Patiala (2 parts)
27 Jammu
28 Chamba
29 Sirmur
30 Almora
31 Cooch Bihar
32 Jaintiapur
33 Hasanabad
34 Tripura
35 Janjira
36 Satara
37 Kolhapur
38 Coorg
39 Cochin
40 Tranvancore
41 Makrai
42 Sind
43 Arcot
44 Cannanore
45 Bijawar
East India Company
Punjab
Kalat
Bahawalpur
Bikanir
Jaisalmir
Khairpur
Jodhpur
Jaipur
Mewar
Kotah
Gwalior
Awadh
Assam
Kutch
See Inset A
See Inset B
See Inset C
Bhopal
Rewah
Sirguja
Chhota Nagpur
Nagpur
Bastar
Hyderabad
Mysore
Inset C
Orchha
Chhatarpur
Bijawar
Panna
Ajaigarh
Nagod
Maihar
Inset A
Little Rann
Malia
Bajana
Dhrangadhra
Morvi
Wankaner
Muli
Limbdi
Dhrol
British India
Baroda
2 Nawanagar
Jasdan
Bhavnagar
Gondal
3 Porbandar
Palitana
4 Junagadh
KEY
B Baroda
Ba Bajana
Bh Bhavnagar
D Dhrol
G Gondal
Ja Jasdan
La Lakhtar
L Limbdi
Ma Manavadar
M Morvi
N Nawanagar
P Palitana
R Rajkot
S Sayla
V Vadia
Va Vala
W Wadhwan
Inset B
Indore
Gwalior
Dungarpur
Pratapgarh
Jhalawar
Sitamau
Raigarh
Narsinghgarh
Banswara
Jaora
Lunavada
Ratlam
Baria
Jhabua
Chhota Udaipur
Alirajpur
Dhar
Barwani

INDIAN PRINCELY STATES

MONETARY SYSTEMS

In each state, local rates of exchange prevailed. There was no fixed rate between copper, silver or gold coin but the rates varied in accordance with the values of the metal and by the edict of the local authority.

Within the subcontinent, different regions used distinctive coinage standards. In North India and the Deccan, the silver rupee (11.6 g) and gold mohur (11.0 g) predominated. In Gujarat, the silver kori (4.7 g) and gold kori (6.4 g) were the main currency. In South India the silver fanam (0.7-1.0 g) and gold hun or Pagoda (3.4 g) were current. Copper coins in all parts of India were produced to a myriad of local metrologies with seemingly endless varieties.

NAZARANA ISSUES

Throughout the Indian Princely States listings are Nazarana designations for special full flan strikings of copper, silver and some gold coinage. The purpose of these issues was for presentation to the local monarch to gain favor. For example if one had an audience with one's ruler he would exchange goods, currency notes or the cruder struck circulating coinage for Nazarana pieces which he would present to the ruler as a gift. The borderline between true Nazarana pieces and well struck regular issues is often indistinct. The Nazaranas sometimes circulated alongside the cruder "dump" issues.

PRICING

As the demand for Indian Princely coinage develops, and more dealers handle the material, sale records and price lists enable a firmer basis for pricing most series. For scarcer types adequate sale records are often not available, and prices must be regarded as tentative. Inasmuch as date collectors of Princely States series are few, dates known to be scarce are usually worth little more than common ones. Coins of a dated type which do not show the full date on their flans should be valued at about 70 per cent of the prices indicated.

DATING

Coins are dated in several eras. Arabic and Devanagari numerals are used in conjunction with the Hejira era (AH), the Vikrama Samvat (VS), Saka Samvat (Saka), Fasli era (FE) Mauludi era (AM), and Malabar era (ME), as well as the Christian era (AD).

GRADING

Copper coins are rarely found in high grade, as they were the workhorse of coinage circulation, and were everywhere used for day-to-day transactions. Moreover, they were carelessly struck and even when 'new', can often only be distinguished from VF coins with difficulty, if at all.

Silver coins were often hoarded and not infrequently, turn up in nearly as-struck condition. The silver coins of Hyderabad (dump coins) are common in high grades, and the rupees of some states are scarcer 'used' than 'new'. Great caution must be exercised in determining the value or scarcity of high grade dump coins.

Dump gold was rarely circulated, and usually occurs in high grades, or is found made into jewelry.

TREATY STATES ISSUES

The British Government issued a declaration in 1870 that any Princely State of India could strike coins in its mint or mints with the fineness and weight identical with that prescribed for the Government of India issues with obverse and reverse designs differing from coins already struck or issued in that Princely State with value inscribed in the English language; and that Princely State had to suppress its mint or mints for a period of not less than thirty years.

The States which had coins struck under the authority of this Act were ALWAR, BIKANIR, DEWAS (senior and junior branches) and DHAR.

After the closing of the Indian mints to private coinage in 1893 and the currency difficulties experienced at that period, other Princely States came to agreement with the Government for the substitution of the British for the local rupee, and many of the Princely State mints were closed.

With the one exception of the SAILANA State, which obtained two bronze issues with their own reverse design, all agreements after 1893 with Princely States followed the principle of the Indian Government agreeing to take over all the coins circulating in the State, and giving the Government rupee in exchange at a fixed rate.

All States that were parties to these agreements introduced the Indian Government rupee as the sole legal tender.

ALWAR

State located in Rajputana in northwestern India.

Alwar was founded about 1722 by a Rajput chieftain of the Naruka clan, Rao Pratap Singh of Macheri (1740-1791), a descendant of the family which had ruled Jaipur in the fourteenth century. Alwar was distinguished by being the first of the Princely States to use coins struck at the Calcutta Mint. These, first issued in 1877, were of the same weight and assay as the Imperial Rupee, and carried the bust of Queen Victoria, Empress of India. Alwar State, having allied itself with East India Company interests in their struggles against the Marathas early in the nineteenth century, continued to maintain a good relationship with the British right up to Indian Independence in 1947. In May 1949, Alwar was merged into Rajasthan.

LOCAL RULERS

Bakhtawar Singh,
AH1206-1230/1791-1815AD
Bani Singh,
AH1231-1273/1815-1857AD
Sheodan Singh,
AH1274-1291/1857-1874AD
Mangal Singh,
AH1291-1310/1874-1892

MINT

Rajgarh

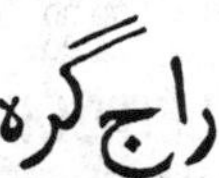

MUGHAL ISSUES

In the name of Muhammad Akbar II
AH1221-1253/1806-1837AD

TAKKA

COPPER, 18.0-18.5 g

KM#	Date	Year	Good	VG	Fine	VF
15	AH—	4	4.00	6.00	10.00	15.00
	—	6	4.00	6.00	10.00	15.00
	—	10	4.00	6.00	10.00	15.00
	—	11	4.00	6.00	10.00	15.00
	—	12	4.00	6.00	10.00	15.00
	—	13	4.00	6.00	10.00	15.00
	—	14	4.00	6.00	10.00	15.00
	—	16	4.00	6.00	10.00	15.00
	122x	17	4.00	6.00	10.00	15.00
	—	20	4.00	6.00	10.00	15.00
	12xx	21	4.00	6.00	10.00	15.00
	—	24	4.00	6.00	10.00	15.00
	—	25	4.00	6.00	10.00	15.00
	—	26	4.00	6.00	10.00	15.00
	—	28	4.00	6.00	10.00	15.00

1/8 RUPEE

SILVER

KM#	Date	Year				
17	AH—	6	—	—	—	—

1/4 RUPEE

SILVER, 13mm, 2.80 g

KM#	Date	Year				
18	ND	22	10.00	15.00	20.00	27.50

1/2 RUPEE

SILVER, 18mm, 5.60 g

KM#	Date	Year	VG	Fine	VF	XF
19	ND	19	8.00	13.50	20.00	28.50
	—	20	8.00	13.50	20.00	28.50
	—	21	8.00	13.50	20.00	28.50
	—	22	8.00	13.50	20.00	28.50

RUPEE

SILVER, 11.20-11.40 g

KM#	Date	Year				
20	AH—	6-31	11.00	17.50	24.00	32.50

NAZARANA RUPEE

SILVER, 11.30 g

KM#	Date	Year				
20a	AH12xx	26	35.00	60.00	85.00	125.00

In the name of Bahadur Shah II
AH1253-1274/1837-1857AD

TAKKA

COPPER, 18.0-18.5 g

KM#	Date	Year	Good	VG	Fine	VF
25	AH—	2	2.50	3.50	5.00	8.00
	—	6	2.50	3.50	5.00	8.00
	—	9	2.50	3.50	5.00	8.00
	—	12	2.50	3.50	5.00	8.00
	—	15	2.50	3.50	5.00	8.00
	—	17	2.50	3.50	5.00	8.00
	—	18	2.50	3.50	5.00	8.00
	—	19	2.50	3.50	5.00	8.00
	—	20	2.50	3.50	5.00	8.00

1/4 RUPEE

SILVER, 16mm, 2.80 g

KM#	Date	Year	VG	Fine	VF	XF
28	AH127x	1x	—	—	—	—
	AH—	20	—	—	Rare	—

1/2 RUPEE

SILVER, 18mm, 5.65 g

KM#	Date	Year	VG	Fine	VF	XF
29	AH—	17	—	—	Rare	—

RUPEE

SILVER, 11.30-11.40 g

KM#	Date	Year				
30	AH—	1	12.50	21.00	28.50	40.00
	1255	2	15.00	25.00	35.00	50.00
	1255	3	15.00	25.00	35.00	50.00
	12xx	4	15.00	25.00	35.00	50.00
	1262	9	15.00	25.00	35.00	[illegible]0.00
	1263	11	15.00	25.00	35.00	50.00
	126x	12	15.00	25.00	35.00	50.00
	1267	13	15.00	25.00	35.00	50.00
	12xx	15	15.00	25.00	35.00	50.00
	—	16	15.00	25.00	35.00	50.00
	(12)73	20	12.50	21.00	28.50	40.00

NAZARANA RUPEE

SILVER, 11.30-11.50 g

KM#	Date	Year				
30a	AH125x	1	37.50	62.50	85.00	125.00
	1261	8	37.50	62.50	85.00	125.00
	1262	9	37.50	62.50	85.00	125.00
	1267	13	37.50	62.50	85.00	125.00

LOCAL ISSUES

In the names of "The Exalted the Queen" (Victoria) and Sheodan Singh
AH1274-1291/1857-1874AD

TAKKA

COPPER, 18.5-19.0 g
Rev. inscription: ***Maharao Rajah Sawai Sheodan Singh Bahadur.***

KM#	Date	Year	Good	VG	Fine	VF
35.1	1859	—	1.50	2.50	3.50	5.00
	1860	3	1.50	2.50	3.50	5.00
	1861	4	1.50	2.50	3.50	5.00

KM#	Date	Year	Good	VG	Fine	VF
35.1	1862	4	1.50	2.50	3.50	5.00
	1864	—	1.50	2.50	3.50	5.00
	1865	9	1.50	2.50	3.50	5.00

Rev. inscription: *Maharaja di-raj Maharao Rajah Shri Sawai Sheodan Singh Bahadur.*

KM#	Date	Year	Good	VG	Fine	VF
35.2	1870	13	1.50	2.50	3.50	5.00
	1871	15	1.50	2.50	3.50	5.00

NAZARANA TAKKA

COPPER, 18.5-19.1 g
Rev. inscription: *Maharao Rajah Sawai Sheodan Singh Bahadur.*

KM#	Date	Year	Good	VG	Fine	VF
35a.1	1865	9	—	—	Rare	—
	1866	9	—	—	Rare	—

Rev. inscription: *Maharaja di-raj Maharao Rajah Shri Sawai Sheodan Singh Bahadur.*

KM#	Date	Year	Good	VG	Fine	VF
35a.2	1871	15	11.50	18.50	25.00	35.00

RUPEE

SILVER, 11.20-11.30 g

KM#	Date	Year	VG	Fine	VF	XF
37	1859	2	12.50	21.50	30.00	40.00
	1860	3	12.50	21.50	30.00	40.00
	1860	4	12.50	21.50	30.00	40.00
	1861	4	12.50	21.50	30.00	40.00
	1863	6	12.50	21.50	30.00	40.00
	1864	7	12.50	21.50	30.00	40.00
	1865	8	15.00	21.50	30.00	40.00
	1865	9	15.00	21.50	30.00	40.00
	—	10	15.00	21.50	30.00	40.00

NAZARANA RUPEE

SILVER, 10.70-11.60 g
Rev. inscription: *Maharao Rajah Sawai Sheodan Singh Bahadur.*

KM#	Date	Year	VG	Fine	VF	XF
37a.1	1859	3	— Reported, not confirmed			
	1865	9	37.50	62.50	85.00	125.00
	1867	10	37.50	62.50	85.00	125.00

Rev. inscription: *Maharaja di-raj Maharao Rajah Shri Sawai Sheodan Singh Bahadur.*

KM#	Date	Year	VG	Fine	VF	XF
37a.2	1870	15	37.50	62.50	85.00	125.00
	(1874)	18	— Reported, not confirmed			

PRESENTATION ISSUES

In the name of Mangal Singh
AH1291-1310/1874-1892AD

Only a few each of KM#40 and 41 were struck at the Rajgarh Mint each year for presentation purposes.

NAZARANA TAKKA

COPPER, 18.5 g
Similar to Nazarana Rupee, KM#41.

KM#	Date	Year	VG	Fine	VF	XF
40	1874	—	8.50	15.00	25.00	40.00
	1891	—	8.50	15.00	25.00	40.00

RUPEE

SILVER, dump, 11.3 g

KM#	Date	Year	VG	Fine	VF	XF
42	—	2	—	—	—	—
	1876	3	—	—	—	—
	1877	4	—	—	—	—

NAZARANA RUPEE

SILVER, 11.30-11.35 g

KM#	Date	Year	VG	Fine	VF	XF
41	1876	3	30.00	50.00	70.00	100.00
	1877	4	30.00	50.00	70.00	100.00
	188x	—	30.00	50.00	70.00	100.00

MILLED COINAGE

RUPEE

11.6600 g, .917 SILVER, .3438 oz ASW

KM#	Date	Mintage	Fine	VF	XF	Unc
45	1788(error)	.200	7.00	12.00	20.00	35.00
	1877	.200	6.00	10.00	17.50	30.00
	1877	—	—	—	Proof	250.00
	1878	.206	7.00	12.00	20.00	35.00
	1880	.196	6.00	10.00	17.50	30.00
	1882	.206	6.00	10.00	17.50	30.00
	1882	—	—	—	Proof	250.00

KM#	Date	Mintage	Fine	VF	XF	Unc
46	1891	.160	6.00	10.00	16.50	27.50
	1891	—	—	—	Proof	250.00

GOLD

KM#	Date	Mintage	Fine	VF	XF	Unc
46a	1891	(restrike)	—	—	Proof	750.00

ASSAM

Refer to Independent Kingdoms during the Mughal Empire.

AWADH

Oudh

Kingdom located in northeastern India. The Nawabs of Awadh traced their origins to Muhammed Amin, a Persian adventurer who had attached himself to the court of Muhammed Shah, the Mughal Emperor, early in the eighteenth century. In 1720 Muhammed Amin was appointed Mughal Subahdar of Awadh, in which capacity he soon exhibited a considerable measure of independence. Until 1819, after Ghazi-ud-din had been encouraged by the Governor-General, Lord Hastings, to accept the title of King, Muhammed Amim's successors were known simply as the Nawabs of Awadh. The British offer, and Ghazi-ud-din's acceptance of it provided a clear indication of just how far Mughal decline had proceeded. The Mughal Emperor was now little more than a pensioner of the East India Company. Yet the coinage of Ghazi-ud-din immediately after 1819 marks also the hesitation he felt in taking so dramatic, and in the eyes of some of the princes of India, so ungrateful a step.

In 1856 Awadh was annexed by the British on the grounds of internal misrule. The king makers were now also seen as the king breakers. In setting aside the royal house of Awadh, the Muslim princes of India were added to that growing list of those who had come to fear the outcome of British hegemony. And it was here, in Awadh, that the Great Revolt of 1857 found its most fertile soil.

In 1877, Awadh along with Agra was placed under one administrator. It was made part of the United Provinces in 1902.

RULERS

Sa'adat Ali,
AH1213-1230/1798-1814AD
Ghazi-ud-Din Haidar, as Nawab,
AH1230-1234/1814-1819AD
as King, AH1234-1243/1819-1827AD
Nasir-ud-Din Haidar,
AH1243-1253/1827-1837AD
Muhammad Ali Shah,
AH1253-1258/1837-1842AD
Amjad Ali Shah,
AH1258-1263/1842-1847AD
Wajid Ali Shah,
AH1263-1272/1847-1856AD
Brijis Qadr,
AH1273-1274/1857-1858AD

MINTS

Allahabad	الله اباد
Asafabad (Bareli)	آصف اباد
Asafnagar	آصف نگر
Awadh	اوده
Banaras	بنارس
Bareli	بريلي
Hathras	هاتهرس
Itawa	اتاوا
Kanauj	قنوج
Kora	كورا
Lucknow	لكهو
Muazzamabad (Gorakhpur)	معظم آباد
Muhammadabad Banaras	محمداباد بنارس
Muradabad	مراد اباد
Najibabad	نجيب اباد
Shahabad	شاه اباد
Tanda	تانده

BARELI MINT

EAST INDIA COMPANY

In the name of Shah Alam II
AH1173-1221/1759-1806AD

RUPEE

SILVER, 10.70-11.60 g
Obv. leg: *Sahib Qirani*, cross.
Rev: Fish, star-shaped flower, Persian letter *Alif*.

KM#	Date	Year	VG	Fine	VF	XF
52.1	AH1216	37	15.00	21.50	31.50	40.00

Rev: Fish, star-shaped flower, Persian letter *He*.

KM#	Date	Year	VG	Fine	VF	XF
52.2	AH1216	37	15.00	21.50	31.50	40.00

Rev: Fish, star-shaped flower, Persian letter *Wa*.

KM#	Date	Year	VG	Fine	VF	XF
52.3	AH1216	37	12.50	17.50	25.00	35.00
	1217	37	12.50	17.50	25.00	35.00
	1218	37	12.50	17.50	25.00	35.00
	1219	37	12.50	17.50	25.00	35.00
	1220	37	12.50	17.50	25.00	35.00

NOTE: The letter *Wa* on East India Company issues was reputedly the initial of the surname of the new settlement officer for Bareli, Henry Wellesley. The earlier issue, with letter *He*, may have been a less majestic initial of his personal name.

LUCKNOW MINT

Mintname: Muhammadabad Banaras

The issues of the Nawab-Wazir in this mintname are distinguished from East India Company issues on the basis of distinctive fabric and fixed regnal year: 26 for Awadh, 17 for East India Company.

In the name of Shah Alam II

AH1173-1221/1759-1806AD

FALUS

COPPER, irregular flan

KM#	Date	Year	Good	VG	Fine	VF
97	AH1217	26	.75	1.50	2.50	4.00
	1218	26	.75	1.50	2.50	4.00
	1219	26	.75	1.50	2.50	4.00
	1222	26	.75	1.50	2.50	4.00
	1224	26	.75	1.50	2.50	4.00
	1227	26	.75	1.50	2.50	4.00
	1229	26	.75	1.50	2.50	4.00
	1230	26	.75	1.50	2.50	4.00
	1231	26	.75	1.50	2.50	4.00
	1232	—	.75	1.50	2.50	4.00
	1233	—	.75	1.50	2.50	4.00
	1234	—	.75	1.50	2.50	4.00

COPPER, round flan

KM#	Date	Year	Good	VG	Fine	VF
98	AH1222	—	1.75	3.00	4.50	7.00
	1223	—	1.75	3.00	4.50	7.00
	1228	26	1.75	3.00	4.50	7.00
	1229	29	1.75	3.00	4.50	7.00
	1233	—	1.75	3.00	4.50	7.00

NOTE: Earlier date (AH1208) exists for this type.

1/8 RUPEE

SILVER, 1.34-1.45 g
Rev: Frozen regnal year, mintmark: Flag and star.

KM#	Date	Year	VG	Fine	VF	XF
100.2	AH1218	26	5.50	8.00	11.50	17.50
	1222	26	5.50	8.00	11.50	17.50
	1226	26	5.50	8.00	11.50	17.50
	1229	26	5.50	8.00	11.50	17.50
	1232	26	5.50	8.00	11.50	17.50
	1233	26	5.50	8.00	11.50	17.50

NOTE: Earlier dates (AH1207-1215) exist for this type.

1/4 RUPEE

SILVER, 2.68-2.90 g
Rev: Frozen regnal year, mintmark: Flag and star.

KM#	Date	Year	VG	Fine	VF	XF
101.2	AH1218	26	5.50	8.00	11.50	17.50
	1225	26	5.50	8.00	11.50	17.50
	1231	26	5.50	8.00	11.50	17.50
	1233	26	5.50	8.00	11.50	17.50

1/2 RUPEE

SILVER, 5.38-5.80 g

KM#	Date	Year	VG	Fine	VF	XF
102.2	AH1223	26	6.00	9.00	13.50	20.00

NOTE: Earlier dates (AH1207-1208) exist for this type.

Obv: W/o AH date.

KM#	Date	Year	VG	Fine	VF	XF
102.3	ND	26	—	—	Rare	—

RUPEE

SILVER, 10.70-11.60 g
Rev: Frozen regnal year, mintmark: Flag and star.

KM#	Date	Year	VG	Fine	VF	XF
103.2	AH1216	26	7.50	12.50	18.50	27.50
	1217	26	7.50	12.50	18.50	27.50
	1218	26	7.50	12.50	18.50	27.50
	1219	26	7.50	12.50	18.50	27.50
	1220	26	7.50	12.50	18.50	27.50
	1221	26	7.00	11.00	16.50	25.00
	1222	26	7.00	11.00	16.50	25.00
	1223	26	7.00	11.00	16.50	25.00
	1224	26	7.00	11.00	16.50	25.00
	1225	26	7.00	11.00	16.50	25.00
	1226	26	7.00	11.00	16.50	25.00
	1227	26	7.00	11.00	16.50	25.00
	1228	26	7.00	11.00	16.50	25.00
	1229	26	7.00	11.00	16.50	25.00
	1230	26	7.00	11.00	16.50	25.00
	1231	26	7.00	11.00	16.50	25.00
	1232	26	7.00	11.00	16.50	25.00
	1233	26	7.00	11.00	16.50	25.00
	1234	26	7.00	11.00	16.50	25.00

NOTE: Earlier dates (AH1201-1215) exist for this type.
NOTE: For similar coins also dated AH1229/R.Y. 26, see KM#386.

Obv: W/o AH date.

KM#	Date	Year	VG	Fine	VF	XF
103.3	ND	26	—	—	Rare	—

NAZARANA RUPEE

SILVER, 10.70-11.60 g, 28mm
Similar to 1 Rupee, KM#103, broad flan.
Rev: Frozen regnal year.

KM#	Date	Year	VG	Fine	VF	XF
104	AH1216	26	32.50	45.00	62.50	85.00

1/2 MOHUR

GOLD, 5.35-5.70 g

Rev: Frozen regnal year.

KM#	Date	Year	VG	Fine	VF	XF
A105	AH1224	26	150.00	250.00	350.00	500.00

MOHUR

GOLD, 10.70-11.40 g
Rev: Frozen regnal year.

KM#	Date	Year	VG	Fine	VF	XF
105	AH1218	26	185.00	225.00	265.00	350.00
	1222	26	185.00	225.00	265.00	350.00
	1229	26	185.00	225.00	265.00	350.00
	1230	26	185.00	225.00	265.00	350.00
	1231	26	185.00	225.00	265.00	350.00

NAJIBABAD MINT

To Awadh in 1774AD(AH1188). For issues before AH1188/R.Y. 15, see Rohilkhand.

In the name of Shah Alam II

AH1173-1221/1759-1806AD

PAISA

Various weight standards

COPPER
Obv: Crescent. Rev: Vertical fish.

KM#	Date	Year	Good	VG	Fine	VF
111	AH1216	43	3.00	4.00	6.00	8.50
	1217	44	3.00	4.00	6.00	8.50
	1218	47	3.00	4.00	6.00	8.50
	1219	—	3.00	4.00	6.00	8.50

NOTE: Earlier dates (AH1198-1215) exist for this type.

Rev: Horizontal fish.

KM#	Date	Year	Good	VG	Fine	VF
113	AH1216	43	5.00	7.00	10.00	15.00
	1217	44	5.00	7.00	10.00	15.00

NOTE: Earlier date (AH1215) exists for this type.

RUPEE

SILVER, 10.70-11.60 g
Obv: W/o horizontal fish.

KM#	Date	Year	VG	Fine	VF	XF
116.11	AHxxxx	47	—	—	—	—

Rev: Persian letter *Mim* written as word; bud, fish.

KM#	Date	Year	VG	Fine	VF	XF
116.7	AH1216	42	12.50	16.50	22.50	32.50

NOTE: Earlier dates (AH1214-15) exist for this type.

Rev: Persian letter *Mim*, Persian word *Ald*, fish, Persian letter *He*.

KM#	Date	Year	VG	Fine	VF	XF
116.8	AH1216	43	12.50	16.50	22.50	32.50

INDEPENDENT KINGS

GHAZI-UD-DIN HAIDAR

King, AH1234-1243/1819-1827AD

In the name of Shah Alam II

AH1173-1221/1759-1806AD

FALUS

COPPER

KM#	Date	Year	Good	VG	Fine	VF
140	AH1234	26	1.50	2.25	2.75	4.00
	1235	26	1.50	2.25	2.75	4.00

1/8 RUPEE

SILVER, 1.34-2.45 g

KM#	Date	Year	VG	Fine	VF	XF
142	AH1234	26	12.50	18.50	25.00	35.00

1/4 RUPEE

SILVER, 2.68-2.90 g

KM#	Date	Year	VG	Fine	VF	XF
144	AH1234	26	12.50	18.50	25.00	35.00

1/2 RUPEE

SILVER

KM#	Date	Year	VG	Fine	VF	XF
145	AH1234	26	17.50	25.00	35.00	50.00

RUPEE

SILVER, 10.70-11.60 g

KM#	Date	Year	VG	Fine	VF	XF
146	AH1234	26	12.50	18.50	25.00	35.00

1/2 MOHUR

GOLD, 5.35-5.70 g

KM#	Date	Year	VG	Fine	VF	XF
148	AH1234	26	110.00	125.00	145.00	165.00

MOHUR

GOLD, 10.70-11.40 g

KM#	Date	Year	VG	Fine	VF	XF
150	AH1234	26	225.00	250.00	285.00	325.00

In his own name

NOTE: Coins dated AH1234 have regnal year 5 for Haidar as Nawab; coins dated AH1235 and later have his regnal year as king AH1235 R.Y. 1.

NOTE: The mintname comes with 2 different epithets:

VARIETY I: AH1234-1235; *Dar ul-Amaret Lakhnau Suba Awadh*

VARIETY II: AH1236-1243 *Dar us-Sultanat Lakhnau Suba Awadh*

FALUS

COPPER
Mintname: Variety I

KM#	Date	Year	Good	VG	Fine	VF
155.1	AH1234	5	1.35	2.75	4.50	7.50
	1235	1	1.00	2.00	3.50	6.00

Mintname: Variety II

KM#	Date	Year	Good	VG	Fine	VF
155.2	AH1236	2	.85	1.75	3.00	5.00
	1237	3	.85	1.75	3.00	5.00
	1238	4	.85	1.75	3.00	5.00
	1239	5	.85	1.75	3.00	5.00

24-25mm

KM#	Date	Year	Good	VG	Fine	VF
155.3	AH1240	6	7.50	12.00	20.00	35.00

NOTE: Struck with 1 Rupee dies.

1/16 RUPEE

(Anna)

SILVER, 0.67-0.72 g

KM#	Date	Year	VG	Fine	VF	XF
157	AH1235	1	15.00	21.50	30.00	40.00

1/8 RUPEE

(2 Annas)

SILVER, 12-14mm, 1.34-1.45 g

KM#	Date	Year	VG	Fine	VF	XF
159	AH1235	1	10.00	15.00	21.50	30.00
	1236	2	10.00	15.00	21.50	30.00
	—	5	10.00	15.00	21.50	30.00

1/4 RUPEE

SILVER, 15-17mm, 2.68-2.90 g

KM#	Date	Year	VG	Fine	VF	XF
161	AH1236	2	7.00	11.00	16.50	25.00
	—	4	7.00	11.00	16.50	25.00
	—	6	7.00	11.00	16.50	25.00
	124x	8	7.00	11.00	16.50	25.00

1/2 RUPEE

SILVER, 5.35-5.80 g

KM#	Date	Year	VG	Fine	VF	XF
163	AH1235	1	15.00	21.50	30.00	40.00
	1236	2	15.00	21.50	30.00	40.00
	1237	3	15.00	21.50	30.00	40.00
	1238	4	10.00	15.00	21.50	30.00
	1239	5	10.00	15.00	21.50	30.00
	1240	6	10.00	15.00	21.50	30.00
	1242	8	10.00	15.00	21.50	30.00

RUPEE

SILVER, 10.70-11.60 g
Mintname: Variety I

KM#	Date	Year	VG	Fine	VF	XF
165.1	AH1234	1	7.50	12.50	18.50	27.50
	1234	5	7.50	12.50	18.50	27.50
	1235	1	7.50	12.50	18.50	27.50

Mintname: Variety II

KM#	Date	Year	VG	Fine	VF	XF
165.2	AH1236	2	7.50	12.50	18.50	27.50
	1237	3	7.50	12.50	18.50	27.50
	1238	4	7.50	12.50	18.50	27.50
	1239	5	7.50	12.50	18.50	27.50
	1240	6	7.50	12.50	18.50	27.50
	1241	7	7.50	12.50	18.50	27.50
	1242	8	7.50	12.50	18.50	27.50
	1243	9	7.50	12.50	18.50	27.50

1/4 ASHRAFI

GOLD, 2.68-2.85 g

KM#	Date	Year	VG	Fine	VF	XF
168	AH1236	—	65.00	85.00	110.00	135.00
	1243	—	65.00	85.00	110.00	135.00

ASHRAFI

GOLD, 10.70-11.40 g
Mintname: Variety I

KM#	Date	Year	VG	Fine	VF	XF
170.1	AH1234	5	250.00	285.00	325.00	425.00

Mintname: Variety II

KM#	Date	Year	VG	Fine	VF	XF
170.2	AH1235	1	250.00	285.00	325.00	425.00
	1236	1	250.00	285.00	325.00	425.00
	1236	2	250.00	285.00	325.00	425.00
	1238	4	250.00	285.00	325.00	425.00
	1239	5	250.00	285.00	325.00	425.00
	1240	6	250.00	285.00	325.00	425.00
	1241	7	250.00	285.00	325.00	425.00
	1242	8	250.00	285.00	325.00	425.00

NASIR-UD-DIN HAIDAR

AH1243-1253/1827-1837AD

In the name of Sulayman Jah

FALUS

COPPER

KM#	Date	Year	Good	VG	Fine	VF
175	AH1243	1	1.25	2.00	3.50	6.00
	1244	1	1.25	2.00	3.50	6.00
	1244	2	1.25	2.00	3.50	6.00

1/8 RUPEE

SILVER, 13mm, 1.34-1.45 g

KM#	Date	Year	VG	Fine	VF	XF
180	AH1244	2	7.00	11.00	16.50	25.00
	1245	3	7.00	11.00	16.50	25.00

1/4 RUPEE

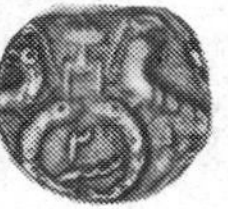

SILVER, 2.68-2.90 g

KM#	Date	Year	VG	Fine	VF	XF
182	AH1244	2	6.50	10.00	15.00	22.50
	1251	8	6.50	10.00	15.00	22.50

1/2 RUPEE

SILVER, 5.35-5.80 g

KM#	Date	Year	VG	Fine	VF	XF
184	AH1243	1	6.00	9.00	13.50	20.00
	1244	2	6.00	9.00	13.50	20.00

RUPEE

SILVER, 10.70-11.60 g

KM#	Date	Year	VG	Fine	VF	XF
186	AH1243	1	7.50	12.50	18.50	27.50
	1244	1	7.50	12.50	18.50	27.50
	1244	2	7.50	12.50	18.50	27.50
	1245	1	7.50	12.50	18.50	27.50
	1245	2	7.00	12.50	18.50	27.50

1/2 ASHRAFI

GOLD

KM#	Date	Year	VG	Fine	VF	XF
189	AH1243	1	—	—	—	—

ASHRAFI

GOLD, 10.70-11.40 g

KM#	Date	Year	VG	Fine	VF	XF
190	AH1243	1	185.00	235.00	300.00	400.00

In the name of Nasir al-Din Haidar

NOTE: This series comes in 2 major varieties, the difference being in the coat of arms and position of regnal years.

Variety I: Katar (knife) above and regnal year between fish.

Variety II: Katar between fish and regnal year now in marginal inscription.

FALUS

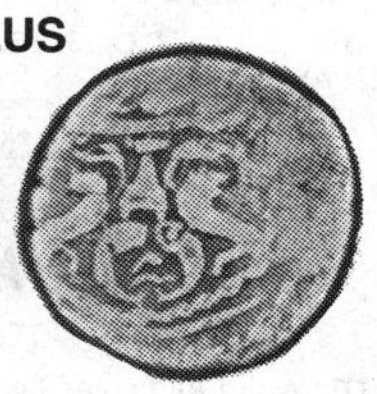

COPPER
Mint mark: Variety I

KM#	Date	Year	Good	VG	Fine	VF
195.1	AH1245	2	2.00	3.50	6.00	10.00
	1245	3	2.00	3.50	6.00	10.00
	1246	3	2.00	3.50	6.00	10.00
	1246	4	2.00	3.50	6.00	10.00
	1247	4	2.00	3.50	6.00	10.00
	1247	5	2.00	3.50	6.00	10.00
	1248	5	2.00	3.50	6.00	10.00
	1249	6	2.00	3.50	6.00	10.00

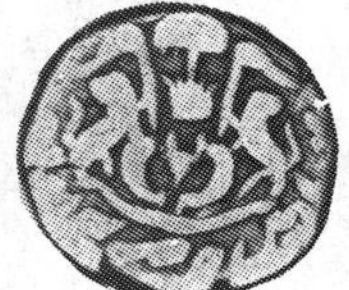

Mint mark: Variety II

KM#	Date	Year	Good	VG	Fine	VF
195.2	AH1249	6	2.00	3.50	6.00	10.00
	1250	7	2.00	3.50	6.00	10.00

1/16 RUPEE

(Anna)

SILVER, 9-13mm, 0.67-0.72 g
Mint mark: Variety II

KM#	Date	Year	VG	Fine	VF	XF
197	AH1250	—	7.00	11.00	16.50	25.00
	1252	—	7.00	11.00	16.50	25.00

1/8 RUPEE

SILVER, 14mm, 1.34-1.45 g
Mint mark: Variety I

KM#	Date	Year	VG	Fine	VF	XF
199.1	AH1246	3	6.50	10.00	15.00	22.50
	1248	5	6.50	10.00	15.00	22.50

Mint mark: Variety II.

KM#	Date	Year	VG	Fine	VF	XF
199.2	AH1250	—	7.00	11.00	16.50	25.00

1/4 RUPEE

SILVER, 2.68-2.90 g
Mint mark: Variety I

KM#	Date	Year	VG	Fine	VF	XF
201.1	AH1245	3	8.50	13.50	20.00	28.50
	124x	4	8.50	13.50	20.00	28.50
	1247	5	8.50	13.50	20.00	28.50
	1248	5	8.50	13.50	20.00	28.50
	—	6	8.50	13.50	20.00	28.50

Mint mark: Variety II

KM#	Date	Year	VG	Fine	VF	XF
201.2	AH1250	—	12.50	18.50	25.00	35.00
	1251	8	12.50	18.50	25.00	35.00

1/2 RUPEE

SILVER, 5.35-5.80 g
Mint mark: Variety I

KM#	Date	Year	VG	Fine	VF	XF
203	AH1243	1	12.50	18.50	25.00	35.00
	1247	5	12.50	18.50	25.00	35.00
	1248	5	12.50	18.50	25.00	35.00
	1248	6	12.50	18.50	25.00	35.00
	1250	7	12.50	18.50	25.00	35.00

RUPEE

SILVER, 10.70-11.60 g
Mint mark: Variety I

KM#	Date	Year	VG	Fine	VF	XF
205.1	AH1245	3	7.50	12.50	18.50	27.50
	1246	3	7.50	12.50	18.50	27.50
	1246	4	7.50	12.50	18.50	27.50
	1247	4	7.50	12.50	18.50	27.50
	1247	5	7.50	12.50	18.50	27.50
	1248	5	7.50	12.50	18.50	27.50
	1248	6	7.50	12.50	18.50	27.50
	1249	6	7.50	12.50	18.50	27.50

Mint mark: Variety II

KM#	Date	Year	VG	Fine	VF	XF
205.2	AH1249	7	7.00	11.50	16.50	25.00
	1250	7	7.00	11.50	16.50	25.00
	1250	8	7.00	11.50	16.50	25.00
	1251	7	7.00	11.50	16.50	25.00
	1251	8	7.00	11.50	16.50	25.00
	1252	7	7.00	11.50	16.50	25.00
	1252	8	7.00	11.50	16.50	25.00

KM#	Date	Year	VG	Fine	VF	XF
205.2	1252	9	7.00	11.50	16.50	25.00
	1253	9	7.00	11.50	16.50	25.00
	1253	10	7.00	11.50	16.50	25.00

Reduced size.

KM#	Date	Year	VG	Fine	VF	XF
205.3	AH1250	7	20.00	31.50	42.50	60.00

NOTE: Struck with 1/4 Rupee dies.

1/2 ASHRAFI

GOLD, 5.35-5.70 g

KM#	Date	Year	VG	Fine	VF	XF
235	AH1251	9	110.00	140.00	180.00	240.00

ASHRAFI

GOLD, 25mm, 10.70-11.40 g
Mint mark: Variety I

KM#	Date	Year	VG	Fine	VF	XF
240	AH1245	3	185.00	235.00	300.00	400.00
	1246	3	185.00	235.00	300.00	400.00
	1252	9	185.00	235.00	300.00	400.00

MUHAMMAD ALI SHAH

AH1253-1258/1837-1842AD

NOTE: Mintname comes in 3 varieties.

VARIETY AIII. *Suba Awadh Dar-as-Sultanat Lakhnau*, on coins dated AH1253/1.

VARIETY III. *Suba Awadh Baitu-s-Sultanat Lakhnau*, on all coins dated through AH1256/Yr. 3.

VARIETY IV. *Mulk Awadh Baitu-s-Sultanat Lakhnau*, on all coins beginning with date AH1256/Yr. 3.

FALUS

COPPER

KM#	Date	Year	Good	VG	Fine	VF
305	AH1253	1	1.25	2.25	3.50	6.00
	1254	2	1.25	2.25	3.50	6.00
	1255	3	1.25	2.25	3.50	6.00

1/8 RUPEE

SILVER, 10mm, 1.34-1.45 g

KM#	Date	Year	VG	Fine	VF	XF
310	AH1253	1	5.50	8.00	12.00	18.50
	1256	(3)	5.50	8.00	12.00	18.50

1/4 RUPEE

SILVER, 2.68-2.90 g

KM#	Date	Year	VG	Fine	VF	XF
312	AH1253	—	5.50	8.00	12.00	18.50
	1254	—	5.50	8.00	12.00	18.50
	1255	—	5.50	8.00	12.00	18.50
	1256	—	5.50	8.00	12.00	18.50

1/2 RUPEE

SILVER, 5.35-5.80 g
Mintname: Variety AIII.

KM#	Date	Year	VG	Fine	VF	XF
313	AH1253	1	—	—	Rare	—

KM#	Date	Year	VG	Fine	VF	XF
	Mintname: Variety III.					
314.1	AH1254	—	5.50	8.00	12.00	18.50
	Mintname: Variety IV.					
314.2	AH1256	3	5.50	8.00	12.00	18.50
	1258	—	5.50	8.00	12.00	18.50

RUPEE

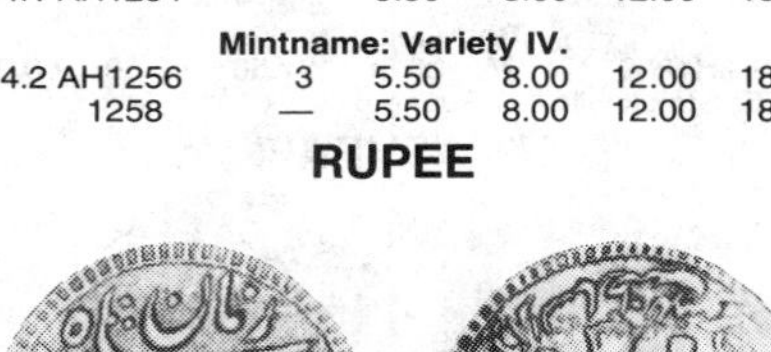

SILVER, 10.70-11.60 g
Mintname: Variety AIII

KM#	Date	Year	VG	Fine	VF	XF
315	AH1253	1	10.00	20.00	35.00	55.00

Mintname: Variety II

KM#	Date	Year	VG	Fine	VF	XF
316.3	AH1253	1	7.50	12.50	18.50	27.50

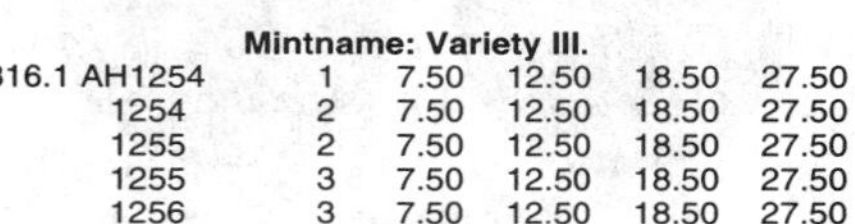

Mintname: Variety III.

KM#	Date	Year	VG	Fine	VF	XF
316.1	AH1254	1	7.50	12.50	18.50	27.50
	1254	2	7.50	12.50	18.50	27.50
	1255	2	7.50	12.50	18.50	27.50
	1255	3	7.50	12.50	18.50	27.50
	1256	3	7.50	12.50	18.50	27.50

Mintname: Variety IV.

KM#	Date	Year	VG	Fine	VF	XF
316.2	AH1254	1	7.50	12.50	18.50	27.50
	1256	3	7.50	12.50	18.50	27.50
	1256	4	7.50	12.50	18.50	27.50
	1257	4	7.50	12.50	18.50	27.50
	1257	5	7.50	12.50	18.50	27.50
	1258	5	7.50	12.50	18.50	27.50

1/2 ASHRAFI

GOLD, 5.35-5.70 g

KM#	Date	Year	VG	Fine	VF	XF
320	AH1253	1	125.00	150.00	185.00	225.00

ASHRAFI

GOLD, 10.70-11.40 g
Mintname: Variety III.

KM#	Date	Year	VG	Fine	VF	XF
322.1	AH1253	1	175.00	225.00	275.00	375.00
	1255	3	175.00	225.00	275.00	375.00
	Mintname: Variety IV.					
322.2	AH1258	—	175.00	225.00	275.00	375.00

AMJAD ALI SHAH

AH1258-1263/1842-1847AD

FALUS

COPPER

KM#	Date	Year	Good	VG	Fine	VF
325	AH1258	1	2.00	3.50	6.00	10.00
	1259	1	2.00	3.50	6.00	10.00
	1259	2	2.00	3.50	6.00	10.00
	1260	2	2.00	3.50	6.00	10.00
	1262	—	2.00	3.50	6.00	10.00
	Finer style, 27mm					
326	AH1258	1	5.00	10.00	15.00	21.50

1/16 RUPEE

SILVER, 0.67-0.72 g

KM#	Date	Year	VG	Fine	VF	XF
328	AH1262	—	6.00	9.00	13.50	20.00

1/8 RUPEE

SILVER, 1.34-1.45 g

KM#	Date	Year	VG	Fine	VF	XF
330	AH1258	—	5.50	8.00	12.00	18.50
	1259	—	5.50	8.00	12.00	18.50
	1262	—	5.50	8.00	12.00	18.50

1/4 RUPEE

SILVER, 2.68-2.90 g

KM#	Date	Year	VG	Fine	VF	XF
332	AH1259	2	5.50	8.50	12.00	18.50
	1260	3	5.50	8.50	12.00	18.50
	1263	—	5.50	8.50	12.00	18.50

1/2 RUPEE

SILVER, 18-20mm, 5.35-5.80 g

KM#	Date	Year	VG	Fine	VF	XF
334	AH1259	2	5.50	8.50	12.00	18.50
	1260	3	5.50	8.50	12.00	18.50
	1261	—	5.50	8.50	12.00	18.50

RUPEE

SILVER, 10.70-11.60 g
Mintname: Variety IV

KM#	Date	Year	VG	Fine	VF	XF
336	AH1258	1	7.50	12.50	18.50	32.50
	1259	1	7.50	12.50	18.50	32.50
	1259	2	7.50	12.50	18.50	32.50
	1260	2	7.50	12.50	18.50	32.50
	1260	3	7.50	12.50	18.50	32.50
	1261	3	7.50	12.50	18.50	32.50
	1261	4	7.50	12.50	18.50	32.50
	1262	4	7.50	12.50	18.50	32.50
	1262	5	7.50	12.50	18.50	32.50
	1263	5	7.50	12.50	18.50	32.50

1/4 ASHRAFI

GOLD, 2.37-2.85 g

KM#	Date	Year	VG	Fine	VF	XF
339	AH1260	—	165.00	240.00	350.00	500.00

1/2 ASHRAFI

GOLD, 5.35-5.70 g

KM#	Date	Year	VG	Fine	VF	XF
340	AH1258	—	125.00	200.00	285.00	400.00
	1259	2	125.00	200.00	285.00	400.00
	1263	—	125.00	200.00	285.00	400.00

ASHRAFI

GOLD, 10.70-11.40 g

KM#	Date	Year	VG	Fine	VF	XF
342	AH1258	—	175.00	225.00	275.00	365.00
	1259	2	175.00	225.00	275.00	365.00
	1261	4	175.00	225.00	275.00	365.00
	1262	5	175.00	225.00	275.00	365.00
	1263	—	175.00	225.00	275.00	365.00

WAJID ALI SHAH

AH1263-1272/1847-1856AD

NOTE: Wajid Alis coins come in 3 varieties, depending on form of mintname:

VARIETY IV: *Mulk Awadh Baitu-s-Sultanat Lakhnau*, AH1263-1267/Yr.4.

VARIETY V: *Mulk Awadh Akhtarnagar*, AH1267/5 reported so far only for Rupees dated 1267/Yr. 5. The same date/year combination is also found in Var. VI.

VARIETY VI: *Baitus-s-Sultanat Lakhnau Mulk Awadh Akhtar-Nagar*, 1267/Yr. 5-1272.

1/8 FALUS

COPPER

KM#	Date	Year	Good	VG	Fine	VF
345	AH1270	7	3.50	6.00	8.00	11.50
	1270	8	3.50	6.00	8.00	11.50
	1271	—	3.00	5.00	7.00	10.00

1/4 FALUS

COPPER

KM#	Date	Year	Good	VG	Fine	VF
347	AH1270	7	3.00	5.00	7.00	10.00

KM#	Date	Year	Good	VG	Fine	VF
347	1270	8	3.50	6.00	8.50	12.00
	1272	9	3.00	5.00	7.00	10.00

1/2 FALUS

COPPER

KM#	Date	Year	Good	VG	Fine	VF
349	AH1269	—	2.75	4.50	6.00	8.50
	1270	7	2.75	4.50	6.00	8.50
	1270	8	2.75	4.50	6.00	8.50
	1271	—	2.75	4.50	6.00	8.50
	1272	—	2.75	4.50	6.00	8.50

FALUS

COPPER
Mintname: Variety IV.

KM#	Date	Year	Good	VG	Fine	VF
351.1	AH—	1	1.50	2.50	3.00	4.50
	1263	—	2.00	3.50	5.00	7.00
	1264	2	2.00	3.50	5.00	7.00

Mintname: Variety V.

KM#	Date	Year	Good	VG	Fine	VF
351.2	AH1267	4	10.00	15.00	25.00	40.00

Mintname: Variety VI.

KM#	Date	Year	Good	VG	Fine	VF
351.3	AH1270	8	2.00	3.50	5.00	7.00
	1270	9	2.00	3.50	5.00	7.00
	1271?	—	2.00	3.50	5.00	7.00
	1272	—	2.00	3.50	5.00	7.00

Rectangular, 14x18mm

KM#	Date	Year	Good	VG	Fine	VF
351.4	AH1271	—	2.00	3.50	5.00	7.00

NOTE: Barbarous versions of KM#351, without legible date or year, are common and worth half of what a legible date specimen commands.

1/16 RUPEE

SILVER, 0.67-0.72 g

KM#	Date	Year	VG	Fine	VF	XF
355	AH126x	—	5.50	8.00	10.00	15.50
	1270	8	5.50	8.00	10.00	15.50
	1270	2(sic)	5.50	8.00	10.00	15.50
	1271	—	5.50	8.00	10.00	15.50
	1272	—	5.50	8.00	10.00	15.50

1/8 RUPEE

SILVER, 1.34-1.45 g
Mintname: Variety IV.

KM#	Date	Year	VG	Fine	VF	XF
357.1	AH1264	1	5.50	8.00	12.50	18.50
	1264	2	5.50	8.00	12.50	18.50
	1265	2	5.50	8.00	12.50	18.50
	1266	—	5.50	8.00	12.50	18.50
	126x	5	5.50	8.00	12.50	18.50
	1268	—	5.50	8.00	12.50	18.50

Mintname: Variety VI.

KM#	Date	Year	VG	Fine	VF	XF
357.2	AH1268	—	5.50	8.00	12.50	18.50
357.2	1269	—	5.50	8.00	12.50	18.50
	1270	8	5.50	8.00	12.50	18.50
	1271	9	5.50	8.00	12.50	18.50

1/4 RUPEE

SILVER, 2.68-2.90 g
Mintname: Variety IV.

KM#	Date	Year	VG	Fine	VF	XF
361.1	AH1263	1	5.50	8.00	12.50	18.50
	1265	—	5.50	8.00	12.50	18.50

Mintname: Variety VI.

KM#	Date	Year	VG	Fine	VF	XF
361.2	AH1267	5	5.50	8.00	12.50	18.50
	1268	—	5.50	8.00	12.50	18.50
	1269	6	5.50	8.00	12.50	18.50
	1271	9	5.50	8.00	12.50	18.50

1/2 RUPEE

SILVER, 5.35-5.80 g
Mintname: Variety IV.

KM#	Date	Year	VG	Fine	VF	XF
363.1	AH1263	2	6.00	9.00	13.50	20.00
	1265	2	6.00	9.00	13.50	20.00
	1266	3	6.00	9.00	13.50	20.00

Mintname: Variety VI.

KM#	Date	Year	VG	Fine	VF	XF
363.2	AH1268	5	6.00	9.00	13.50	20.00
	1269	6	6.00	9.00	13.50	20.00
	1271	8	6.00	9.00	13.50	20.00
	1271	9	6.00	9.00	13.50	20.00

RUPEE

SILVER, 10.70-11.60 g
Mintname: Variety IV.

KM#	Date	Year	VG	Fine	VF	XF
365.1	AH1263	1	7.50	11.00	16.50	25.00
	1264	1	7.50	11.00	16.50	25.00
	1264	2	7.50	11.00	16.50	25.00
	1265	1	7.50	11.00	16.50	25.00
	1265	2	7.50	11.00	16.50	25.00
	1265	3	7.50	11.00	16.50	25.00
	1266	3	7.50	11.00	16.50	25.00
	1266	4	7.50	11.00	16.50	25.00
	1267	3	7.50	11.00	16.50	25.00
	1267	4	7.50	11.00	16.50	25.00
	1268	4	7.50	11.00	16.50	25.00

Mintname: Variety V.

KM#	Date	Year	VG	Fine	VF	XF
365.2	AH1267	5	17.50	25.00	35.00	50.00

Mintname: Variety VI.

KM#	Date	Year	VG	Fine	VF	XF
365.3	AH1267	5	7.00	11.00	16.50	25.00
	1268	5	7.00	11.00	16.50	25.00
	1268	6	7.00	11.00	16.50	25.00
	1269	6	7.00	11.00	16.50	25.00
	1269	2(sic - 2 is a backwards 6)				
			7.00	11.00	16.50	25.00
	1269	7	7.00	11.00	16.50	25.00
	1270	7	7.00	11.00	16.50	25.00
	1270	8	7.00	11.00	16.50	25.00
	1271	8	7.00	11.00	16.50	25.00
	1271	9	7.00	11.00	16.50	25.00
	1272	9	7.00	11.00	16.50	25.00
	1272	10	7.00	11.00	16.50	25.00

1/16 ASHRAFI

GOLD, 10mm, 0.67-0.71 g

KM#	Date	Year	VG	Fine	VF	XF
370	AH1270	—	35.00	45.00	55.00	70.00

1/8 ASHRAFI

GOLD, 1.34-1.42 g

KM#	Date	Year	VG	Fine	VF	XF
372	AH1263-72	1-10	40.00	50.00	60.00	85.00

1/4 ASHRAFI

GOLD, 2.68-2.85 g

KM#	Date	Year	VG	Fine	VF	XF
374	AH1267	5	60.00	75.00	90.00	125.00
	1268	*5	60.00	75.00	90.00	125.00
	1271	—	60.00	75.00	90.00	125.00

1/2 ASHRAFI

GOLD, 5.35-5.70 g
Mintname: Variety IV.

KM#	Date	Year	VG	Fine	VF	XF
376	AH1265	3	110.00	125.00	150.00	185.00
	1266	4	110.00	125.00	150.00	185.00
	1267	4	110.00	125.00	150.00	185.00
	1267	5	110.00	125.00	150.00	185.00

ASHRAFI

GOLD, 10.70-11.40 g
Mintname: Variety IV.

KM#	Date	Year	VG	Fine	VF	XF
378.1	AH1263	1	165.00	200.00	250.00	300.00
	1263	2	165.00	200.00	250.00	300.00
	1264	2	165.00	200.00	250.00	300.00
	1265	2	165.00	200.00	250.00	300.00
	1265	3	165.00	200.00	250.00	300.00
	1266	3	165.00	200.00	250.00	300.00
	1266	4	165.00	200.00	250.00	300.00
	1267	4	165.00	200.00	250.00	300.00
	1268	5	165.00	200.00	250.00	300.00

Mintname: Variety VI.

KM#	Date	Year	VG	Fine	VF	XF
378.3	AH1272	9	165.00	200.00	250.00	300.00

BRIJIS QADR

1857-1858AD

Nawab-Wazir during the Indian Mutiny

NOTE: Fictitious dating in imitation of coinage before AH1234/1819. Identifiable only by style and mintname, *Awadh* at top of reverse, and *Subah* at bottom, dated only AH1229/r.y.26.

FALUS

COPPER

KM#	Date	Year	Good	VG	Fine	VF
380	AH1229	26	12.50	22.50	32.50	50.00

1/8 RUPEE

SILVER, 13-14mm, 1.34-1.45 g

KM#	Date	Year	VG	Fine	VF	XF
382	AH1229	26	50.00	75.00	110.00	150.00

1/4 RUPEE

SILVER, 2.68-2.90 g

KM#	Date	Year	VG	Fine	VF	XF
383	AH1229	26	45.00	70.00	95.00	135.00

1/2 RUPEE

SILVER, 5.35-5.80 g

KM#	Date	Year	VG	Fine	VF	XF
384	AH1229	26	40.00	62.50	85.00	120.00

RUPEE

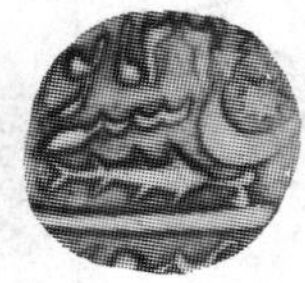

SILVER, 10.70-11.60 g

KM#	Date	Year	VG	Fine	VF	XF
386	AH1229	26	45.00	70.00	100.00	140.00

ASHRAFI

GOLD, 10.70-11.40 g

KM#	Date	Year	VG	Fine	VF	XF
390	AH1229	26	350.00	500.00	700.00	1000.

BAHAWALPUR

The Amirs of Bahawalpur established their independence from Afghan control towards the close of the eighteenth century. In the 1830's the state's independence under British suzerainty became guaranteed by treaty. With the creation of Pakistan in 1947 Bahawalpur, with an area of almost 17,500 square miles, became its premier Princely State. Bahawalpur State, named after its capital, stretched for almost three hundred miles along the left bank of the Sutlej, Panjnad and Indus rivers.

For earlier issues in the names of the Durrani rulers, see Afghanistan.

RULERS

Amirs

Muhammad Bahawal Khan II,
AH1186-1224/1772-1809AD

Sadiq Muhammad Khan II,
AH1224-1241/1809-1825AD

Muhammad Bahawal Khan III,
AH1241-1269/1825-1852AD

Sadiq Muhammad Khan III,
AH1269-1270/1852-1853AD

Fateh Khan,
AH1270-1275/1853-1858AD

Muhammad Bahawal Khan IV,
AH1275-1283/1858-1866AD

Sir Sadiq Muhammad Khan IV,
AH1283-1317/1866-1899AD

Alhaj Muhammad Bahawal Khan V,
AH1317-1325/1899-1907AD

MINTS

Ahmadpur احمد پور

Dar al-Islam دار الاسلام

Bahawalpur بهاولپور

Khanpur خانبور

The mintnames at the bottom of the reverses of Bahawalpur State rupees are often off the flans. In most cases these rupees can be attributed to one of the three mints from other characteristics. Ahmadpur rupees weigh considerably less than those of the other two mints. Bahawalpur and Khanpur rupees can usually be differentiated by the location of their dates and other characteristics, as illustrated below (Y#4 and Y#5).

AHMADPUR MINT

In the name of Mahmud Shah

AH1216-1218/1801-1803AD

RUPEE

SILVER, 10.70-11.60 g

C#	Date	Year	VG	Fine	VF	XF
18	AH1217	48	13.50	20.00	27.50	37.50
	—	49	13.50	20.00	27.50	37.50

Anonymous

Reduced weight, 7.70-7.80 g
Dated on obverse, sometimes also on reverse.

Y#	Date	Year	VG	Fine	VF	XF
3.1	AH1246	—	9.00	18.00	28.00	40.00
	1251	—	9.00	18.00	28.00	40.00
	1252	—	9.00	18.00	28.00	40.00
	1253	—	9.00	18.00	28.00	40.00
	1254	—	9.00	18.00	28.00	40.00
	1256	—	9.00	18.00	28.00	40.00
	1257	—	9.00	18.00	28.00	40.00
	1258	—	9.00	18.00	28.00	40.00
	1259	—	9.00	18.00	28.00	40.00
	1260	—	15.00	30.00	50.00	65.00
	1261	—	9.00	18.00	28.00	40.00
	1262	—	9.00	18.00	28.00	40.00
	1263	—	9.00	18.00	28.00	40.00
	1264	—	9.00	18.00	28.00	40.00
	1265	—	9.00	18.00	28.00	40.00

Obv: Date in oval.

Y#	Date	Year	VG	Fine	VF	XF
3.2 (3.3)	AH1270	—	25.00	37.50	50.00	70.00

7.00-7.60 g
Obv: Date in center.

Y#	Date	Year	VG	Fine	VF	XF
3.3	AH1275	—	12.50	18.50	25.00	35.00
	1276	—	12.50	18.50	25.00	35.00
	1277	—	12.50	18.50	25.00	35.00
	1278	—	12.50	18.50	25.00	35.00
	1279	—	12.50	18.50	25.00	35.00
	1280	—	12.50	18.50	25.00	35.00
	1281	—	12.50	18.50	25.00	35.00
	1282	—	12.50	18.50	25.00	35.00
	1283	—	12.50	18.50	25.00	35.00
	1284	—	12.50	18.50	25.00	35.00

7.90-8.10 g
Dated on obverse and reverse.

Y#	Date	Year	VG	Fine	VF	XF
3.4	AH1285	—	20.00	30.00	45.00	65.00
	1286	—	20.00	30.00	45.00	65.00

BAHAWALPUR MINT

Anonymous

FALUS

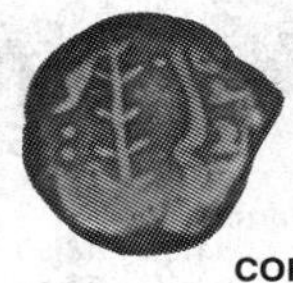

COPPER
Square or round

Y#	Date	Year	Good	VG	Fine	VF
1	AH1225	—	3.00	5.00	7.00	10.00
	1237	13	3.00	5.00	7.00	10.00
	1244	—	3.00	5.00	7.00	10.00
	1248	—	3.00	5.00	7.00	10.00
	1249	—	3.00	5.00	7.00	10.00
	1254	—	3.00	5.00	7.00	10.00
	1259	—	3.00	5.00	7.00	10.00
	1261	—	3.00	5.00	7.00	10.00
	1269	—	3.00	5.00	7.00	10.00
	1270	—	3.00	5.00	7.00	10.00
	1271	—	3.00	5.00	7.00	10.00
	1273	—	3.00	5.00	7.00	10.00
	1276	—	3.00	5.00	7.00	10.00
	1277	—	3.00	5.00	7.00	10.00
	1281	—	3.00	5.00	7.00	10.00

NOTE: Earlier dates (AH1205-1214) exist for this type.

PAISA

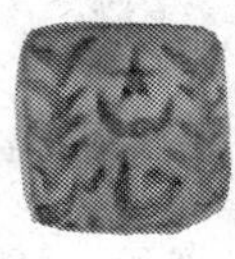

COPPER

Y#	Date	Year	Good	VG	Fine	VF
2.1	AH1301	—	3.50	6.00	8.50	12.00
	1302	—	3.50	6.00	8.50	12.00
	1304	—	3.50	6.00	8.50	12.00
	1311	—	3.50	6.00	8.50	12.00
	1312	—	3.50	6.00	8.50	12.00
	1313	—	3.50	6.00	8.50	12.00
	1315	—	3.50	6.00	8.50	12.00
	1317	—	3.50	6.00	8.50	12.00

NOTE: Later dates (AH1321-1325) exist for this type.

Y#	Date	Year	Good	VG	Fine	VF
2.2	ND	—	4.00	7.50	12.00	20.00

RUPEE

SILVER, 9.80-10.10 g
Obv: Lily, date in center.

Y#	Date	Year	VG	Fine	VF	XF
4.1	AH1254	—	9.00	18.00	28.00	40.00
	1255	—	9.00	18.00	28.00	40.00
	1256	—	9.00	18.00	28.00	40.00
	1258	—	9.00	18.00	28.00	40.00
	1259	—	9.00	18.00	28.00	40.00

10.40-10.50 g
Obv. and rev: Date in rectangle or cinqfoil.

Y#	Date	Year	VG	Fine	VF	XF
4.2	AH1270	—	14.00	28.00	45.00	65.00
	1272	—	14.00	28.00	45.00	65.00
	1273	—	17.50	35.00	60.00	85.00
	1274	—	14.00	28.00	45.00	65.00

10.50-10.70 g
Obv: Date in center.

Y#	Date	Year	VG	Fine	VF	XF
4.3	AH1273	—	9.00	18.00	28.00	40.00
	1274	—	9.00	18.00	28.00	40.00
	1275	—	9.00	18.00	28.00	40.00

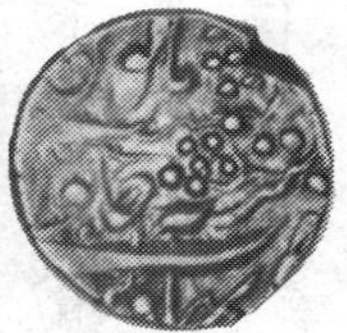

8.50-8.80 g
Obv: Date in center.

Y#	Date	Year	VG	Fine	VF	XF
4.4	AH1278	—	9.00	18.00	28.00	40.00
	1279	—	9.00	18.00	28.00	40.00
	1280	—	9.00	18.00	28.00	40.00
	1281	—	9.00	18.00	28.00	40.00
	1282	—	9.00	18.00	28.00	40.00
	1283	—	9.00	18.00	28.00	40.00
	1283/1	—	9.00	18.00	28.00	40.00
	1283/4	—	9.00	18.00	28.00	40.00

MUHAMMAD BAHAWAL KHAN V

AH1317-1325/1899-1907AD

KHANPUR MINT

Anonymous

RUPEE

SILVER, 9.80-10.10 g
Dated on obverse and reverse.

Y#	Date	Year	VG	Fine	VF	XF
5.1	AH1255	—	15.00	30.00	42.00	60.00
	1256	—	15.00	30.00	42.00	60.00
	1258	—	15.00	30.00	42.00	60.00
	1259	—	15.00	30.00	42.00	60.00
	1260	—	15.00	30.00	42.00	60.00
	1261	—	15.00	30.00	42.00	60.00
	1263	—	15.00	30.00	42.00	60.00
	1264	—	15.00	30.00	42.00	60.00
	1265	—	15.00	30.00	42.00	60.00
	1266	—	15.00	30.00	42.00	60.00
	1267	—	15.00	30.00	42.00	60.00
	1268/7	—	15.00	30.00	42.00	60.00
	1269	—	15.00	30.00	42.00	60.00

8.50-8.80 g
Obv: Date in center.

Y#	Date	Year	VG	Fine	VF	XF
5.2	AH1280	—	10.00	20.00	35.00	50.00
	1281	—	10.00	20.00	35.00	50.00
	1282	—	10.00	20.00	35.00	50.00

 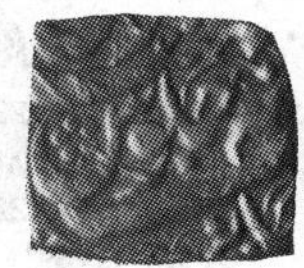

Square

Y#	Date	Year	VG	Fine	VF	XF
5.3	AH1280	—	—	—	—	—

BAJRANGGARH

Bajranggarh was a small state in the district of Gwalior. The mint epithet of Bajranggarh was Jainagar. All the coins, irrespective of when they were minted, were struck in the name of Maharaja Jai Singh and bore similar legends.

RULERS

Jai Singh, 1797-1818AD

PAISA

COPPER

KM#	Date	Year	Good	VG	Fine	VF
2	—	11	4.50	8.00	12.00	17.50
	—	12	4.50	8.00	12.00	17.50

RUPEE

SILVER, 10.70-11.60 g
W/o symbols, thin flan.

KM#	Date	Year	VG	Fine	VF	XF
6	—	12	10.00	20.00	35.00	50.00
	—	13	10.00	25.00	42.00	50.00
	—	15	10.00	20.00	35.00	50.00
	—	16	10.00	20.00	35.00	50.00
	—	17	10.00	20.00	35.00	50.00

Thick flan, 20mm

KM#	Date	Year	VG	Fine	VF	XF
7	—	18	10.00	20.00	35.00	50.00
	—	19	10.00	20.00	35.00	50.00
	—	20	10.00	20.00	35.00	50.00

MOHUR

GOLD, 10.70-11.40 g
Small lettering, w/o symbols.

KM#	Date	Year	VG	Fine	VF	XF
13	—	16	165.00	225.00	350.00	500.00

NOTE: For later issues bearing lotus and bow and arrow symbols (issued by Sindhia) see Gwalior.

BANSWARA

This state in southern Rajputana was founded in 1538 when the state of Dungarpur was divided between 2 sons of the Maharawal, the younger receiving the territory of Banswara with the title also of Maharawal. The rulers of Banswara were Sissodia Rajputs who claimed descent from the powerful Maharanas of Mewar-Udaipur.

Constantly harassed by the Marathas during the 18th Century, Banswara concluded an alliance in 1818 with the British who provided protection from external enemies in exchange for a portion of the state's revenues. In 1935 the state comprised 1,606 square miles with a population of 225,000, a quarter of whom were aboriginal Bhil tribal people.

During most of the 19th Century, Banswara used the "Salim Shahi" coinage of neighboring Pratapgarh State. But around 1870 Maharawal Lakshman Singh, defying a British prohibiting order of that year, introduced a series of crude coins in copper, silver and gold for use within the state. The legends on these coins are in a secret script, said to have been invented by Lakshman Singh himself. The central word in these legends has been tentatively identified as "Samsatraba" (for "Samba Satra", a designation for the Hindu deity Shiva) in the longer form, or "Samba" for the shorter form. All the gold and silver coins, and a few rare copper ones, carry the longer form. The copper coins were made for circulation, but the gold and silver were produced mainly for presentation.

RULERS

Lakshman Singh, 1844-1905AD
Shambhu Singh, 1906-1908AD
British Administration, 1908-1914AD
Pirthi Singh II, 1914-1944AD
Chandravir Singh, 1944-1949AD

LEGENDS

Samba
Samba is a name of Shiva

With *Ba* downwards is a common error of the die cutters.

Samsatraba 
For *Samba Satra*

ANONYMOUS ISSUES

1/4 PAISA

COPPER, 2.40-2.60 g
Obv. and rev: *Samba* in circle, ending downward.

KM#	Date	Year	Good	VG	Fine	VF
1	ND	—	3.00	5.00	8.00	12.50

1/2 PAISA

COPPER, 4.30-5.50 g
Obv. and rev: *Samba* ends upward.

KM#	Date	Year	Good	VG	Fine	VF
3	ND	—	1.75	3.00	6.50	10.00

Obv. and rev: *Samba* ends downward.

KM#	Date	Year	Good	VG	Fine	VF
4	ND	—	1.75	3.00	6.50	10.00

Obv. and rev: *Samba* within leg. ends upwards.

KM#	Date	Year	Good	VG	Fine	VF
5	ND	—	1.00	1.75	4.00	6.50

Obv: *Samba* ends upward.
Rev: *Samba* ends downward.

KM#	Date	Year	Good	VG	Fine	VF
6	ND	—	1.75	3.00	6.50	10.00

PAISA

 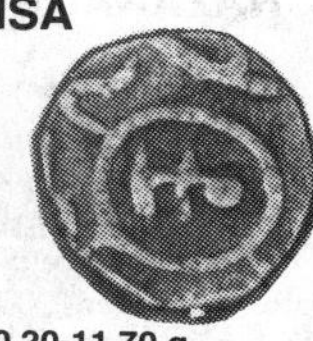

COPPER, 10.20-11.70 g
Obv. and rev: *Samba* ends down, in large circles.

KM#	Date	Year	Good	VG	Fine	VF
7	ND	—	3.00	5.00	8.00	12.50

Obv. and rev: *Samba* within small circle ends downward. Thick flan.

KM#	Date	Year	Good	VG	Fine	VF
8	ND	—	3.00	5.00	8.00	12.00

Obv. and rev: Like KM#8. Broad, thin flan.

KM#	Date	Year	Good	VG	Fine	VF
9	ND	—	4.50	8.00	12.00	17.50

Obv. & rev: *Samba* within leg. ends upward.

KM#	Date	Year	Good	VG	Fine	VF
10	ND	—	1.00	1.75	4.00	6.50

Obv. & rev: *Samba* ends downward.

KM#	Date	Year	Good	VG	Fine	VF
11	ND	—	1.00	1.75	4.00	6.50

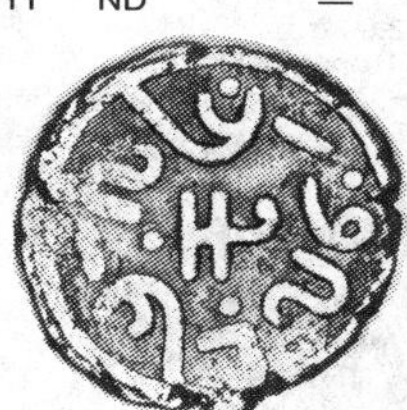 

Obv: *Samba* ends upward.
Rev: *Samba* ends downward.

KM#	Date	Year	Good	VG	Fine	VF
12	ND	—	1.75	3.00	6.50	10.00

Obv: *Samba* within leg. ends downward.
Rev: *Samba* within large circle ends downward.

KM#	Date	Year	Good	VG	Fine	VF
13	ND	—	3.00	5.00	8.00	12.50

Samsatraba Series

Obv. and rev. leg: *Samsatraba* within circle.

KM#	Date	Year	Good	VG	Fine	VF
14	ND	—	3.00	5.00	8.00	12.50

NAZARANA 1/8 RUPEE

SILVER, 1.00 g
Obv. and rev: *Samsatraba*.

KM#	Date	Year	Fine	VF	XF	Unc
20	ND	—	11.00	17.50	23.50	32.50

NAZARANA 1/4 RUPEE

SILVER, 2.00 g
Obv. and rev. leg: *Samsatraba*.

KM#	Date	Year	Fine	VF	XF	Unc
21	ND	—	11.50	18.50	25.00	35.00

NAZARANA 1/2 RUPEE

SILVER, 4.00 g
Obv. and rev. leg: *Samsatraba*.

KM#	Date	Year	Fine	VF	XF	Unc
22	ND	—	12.50	21.50	28.50	40.00

NAZARANA RUPEE

SILVER, 8.00-8.20 g
Thick flan
Obv. and rev. leg: *Samsatraba*.

KM#	Date	Year	VG	Fine	VF	XF
16	ND	—	9.00	15.00	21.50	30.00

Broad thin flan

KM#	Date	Year	Fine	VF	XF	Unc
23	ND	—	6.50	11.00	16.50	25.00

HEAVY RUPEE

SILVER, 12.00 g
Similar to Nazarana Rupee, KM#16.

KM#	Date	Year	Fine	VF	XF	Unc
17	ND	—	—	—	Rare	—

Similar to Nazarana Rupee, KM#23.

KM#	Date	Year	Fine	VF	XF	Unc
24	ND	—	—	—	Rare	—

NAZARANA MOHUR

GOLD, 12.00 g
Thick flan.
Obv. and rev. leg: *Samsatraba*.

KM#	Date	Year	VG	Fine	VF	XF
18	ND	—	150.00	185.00	250.00	350.00

Broad, thin flan.

KM#	Date	Year	Fine	VF	XF	Unc
25	ND	—	135.00	200.00	285.00	375.00

BARODA

Maratha state located in western India. The ruling line was descended from Damaji, a Maratha soldier, who received the title of "Distinguished Swordsman" in 1721 (hence the scimitar on most Baroda coins). The Baroda title "Gaikwara" comes from "gaikwar" or cow herd, Damaji's father's occupation.

The Maratha rulers of Baroda, the Gaekwar family rose to prominence in the mid-eighteenth century by carving out for themselves a dominion from territories which were previously under the control of the Poona Marathas, and to a lesser extent, of the Raja of Jodhpur. Chronic internal disputes regarding the succession to the masnad culminated in the intervention of British troops in support of one candidate, Anand Rao Gaekwar, in 1800. Then, in 1802, an agreement with the East India Company released the Baroda princes from their fear of domination by the Maratha Peshwa of Poona but subordinated them to Company interests. Nevertheless, for almost the next century and a half Baroda maintained a good relationship with the British and continued as a major Princely State right up to 1947, when it acceded to the Indian Union.

RULERS

Gaekwars

Anand Rao,
AH1215-1235/1800-1819AD
Sayaji Rao II,
AH1235-1264/1819-1847AD
Ganpat Rao,
AH1264-1273/1847-1856AD
Khande Rao,
AH1273-1287/1856-1870AD
Malhar Rao,
AH1287-1292/1870-1875AD
Sayaji Rao III,
AH1292-1357/VS1932-1995/1875-1938AD

MINTS

نجيب آباد

Ahmadabad
Amreli
Baroda
Jambusar
Petlad

MINT MARKS

Ahmadabad Mint 

Ankus, Maratha mark.

Nagari letters denoting Baroda ruler:

गा
Ga - Anand Rao's Shah Alam II coins, Ahmadabad Mint (with two verticle stems).

आ
A - Anand Rao's Shah Alam II coins, Petlad Mint.

म
Ma - Manaji Rao's Shah Alam II coins, Baroda Mint.

आ
A - Anand Rao's Muhammad Akbar II coins, Baroda Mint.

गा
Ga-a - Anand Rao's Muhammad Akbar II coins, Ahmadabad Mint (with three verticle stems).

सा
Sa - Sayaji Rao II, Baroda Mint.

सा गा or सा गा
(Sri) Sa Ga - Sayaji Rao II, Amreli Mint.

ग गा
Ga Ga - Ganpat Rao, Amreli Mint.

गा
Ga - Ganpat Rao, Baroda Mint.

श्री ग गा
Sri Ga Ga - Ganpat Rao, Amreli Mint.

खा
Kha - Khande Rao, Muhammad Akbar II coins, Baroda Mint.

ख·गा
Kha Ga - Khande Rao, coins in own name, Baroda Mint.

श्री खगा
Sri Kha Ga - Khande Rao, Amreli Mint.

मा गा
Ma Ga - Malhar Rao.

सा गा
Sa Ga - Sayaji Rao III, Amreli Mint

सा ·गा
Sa Ga - Sayaji Rao III, Baroda Mint.

NOTE: The first 2 marks are found only on the coins of Ahmadabad Mint, and serve to identify it. The remaining 16 marks are used to indicate the ruler under whom the coin was struck; when no mintname is given after the ruler's name in the above list, that shows that the symbol was used at all his mints. Note the various forms of *'G'* and *'Ga'* used above.

AHMADABAD MINT

A Maratha mint from 1757-1800, Ahmadabad was leased to Baroda 1800-1804 and 1806-1817, when it was ceded to Baroda. However, in 1818 it was annexed by the British East India Company.

ANAND RAO

AH1212-1235/1800-1819AD

In the name of Shah Alam II
AH1173-1221/1759-1806AD
Nagari *Ga* and ankus

1/4 RUPEE

SILVER

C#	Date	Year	VG	Fine	VF	XF
17	—	—	7.50	15.00	25.00	35.00

1/2 RUPEE

SILVER, 5.35-5.80 g

C#	Date	Year	VG	Fine	VF	XF
18	—	4x	6.50	13.00	22.00	32.00

RUPEE

SILVER, 10.70-11.60 g

C#	Date	Year	VG	Fine	VF	XF
19	—	3x	5.50	11.00	18.00	28.00
	—	41	5.50	11.00	18.00	28.00
	—	5x	5.50	11.00	18.00	28.00

In the name of Muhammad Akbar II
AH1221-1253/1806-1837AD

Nagari *Ga* and ankus

1/2 RUPEE

SILVER, 5.35-5.80 g

C#	Date	Year	VG	Fine	VF	XF
A28	—	—	6.50	13.00	21.00	30.00

RUPEE

SILVER, 10.70-11.60 g

C#	Date	Year	VG	Fine	VF	XF
28	AH1225	—	5.50	11.00	18.00	28.00
	1227	6	5.50	11.00	18.00	28.00
	—	6	5.50	11.00	18.00	28.00
	1229	7	5.50	11.00	18.00	28.00
	1229	8	5.50	11.00	18.00	28.00
	1231	9	5.50	11.00	18.00	28.00
	1232	10	5.50	11.00	18.00	28.00
	1233	11	5.50	11.00	18.00	28.00

NOTE: The Ahmedabad Mint was acquired by the British in 1818AD (AH1233). Refer to British India, Bombay Presidency KM#257-260.

AMRELI MINT

SAYAJI RAO II

AH1235-1264/1819-1847AD

Nagari *Sa Ga*

1/2 PAISA

COPPER

Similar to 1 Paisa, C#30.

C#	Date	Year	Good	VG	Fine	VF
A29.1	ND	—	2.50	4.50	7.00	10.00

Obv: Katar above scimatar.

C#	Date	Year	Good	VG	Fine	VF
A29.2	AH125x	—	2.50	4.50	7.00	10.00

Obv: Elephant left, flag left.

C#	Date	Year	Good	VG	Fine	VF
A29.3	AH12xx	—	2.50	4.50	7.00	10.00

PAISA

COPPER, 7.00-8.00 g

Obv: Scimitar.

C#	Date	Year	Good	VG	Fine	VF
29.1	AH1253	—	2.50	4.50	7.00	10.00

Obv: Elephant left w/flag right.

C#	Date	Year	Good	VG	Fine	VF
29.2	AH1256	—	3.00	5.50	8.50	11.50

Obv: Elephant and flag left.

C#	Date	Year	Good	VG	Fine	VF
29.3	AH1256	—	2.50	4.50	7.00	10.00

Obv: Katar above scimitar.

C#	Date	Year	Good	VG	Fine	VF
29.4	AH1245	—	2.50	4.50	7.00	10.00
	1256	—	2.50	4.50	7.00	10.00
	1257	—	2.50	4.50	7.00	10.00

Obv: Elephant w/flag right. Rev: Similar to C#29.4.

C#	Date	Year	Good	VG	Fine	VF
29.5	ND	—	5.00	6.50	10.00	15.00

Obv: Scimitar.

C#	Date	Year	Good	VG	Fine	VF
29.6	AH1257	—	2.50	4.50	7.00	10.00

Obv: Crescent.

C#	Date	Year	Good	VG	Fine	VF
29.7	AH1262	—	3.00	5.50	8.50	11.50

Obv: Crescent. Rev: Trident.

C#	Date	Year	Good	VG	Fine	VF
29.8	AH—	—	3.00	5.50	8.50	11.50

Obv: Large *Sa*.

C#	Date	Year	Good	VG	Fine	VF
30.1	ND	—	1.50	2.50	4.00	5.50

C#	Date	Year	Good	VG	Fine	VF
30.2	ND	—	1.50	2.50	4.00	5.50

GANPAT RAO

AH1264-1273/1847-1856AD

Nagari *Ga Ga*

1/2 PAISA

COPPER, 14mm

C#	Date	Year	Good	VG	Fine	VF
A39	AH1266	—	2.50	4.50	6.00	8.50

PAISA

COPPER

Obv: Lotus at left, scimitar at right.

C#	Date	Year	Good	VG	Fine	VF
39.1	ND	—	3.00	5.50	7.00	9.00
	AH1266	3	3.00	5.50	7.00	9.00
	1272	—	3.00	5.50	7.00	9.00

Obv: Scimitar at left, lotus at right.

C#	Date	Year	Good	VG	Fine	VF
39.2	AH1266	—	3.00	5.50	7.00	9.00

KHANDE RAO

AH1273-1287/1856-1870AD

Nagari *Sri Kha Ga*

1/2 PAISA

COPPER

C#	Date	Year	Good	VG	Fine	VF
A1	AH1277	—	—	—	—	—

PAISA

COPPER, 7.00 g

Thin flan

Y#	Date	Year	Good	VG	Fine	VF
1.1	AH1277	—	2.00	3.50	5.50	8.00

Obv: Scimitar at upper left.

Y#	Date	Year	Good	VG	Fine	VF
1.2	AH—	13	2.00	3.50	5.50	8.00

Obv: Scimitar at right.

Y#	Date	Year	Good	VG	Fine	VF
1.3	AH—	—	2.00	3.50	5.50	8.00
1.4	AH1270	—	2.00	3.50	5.50	8.00

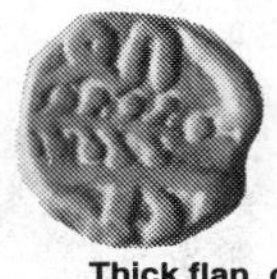

Thick flan, cruder types.

Y#	Date	Year	Good	VG	Fine	VF
1a	ND	—	2.00	3.50	5.50	8.00

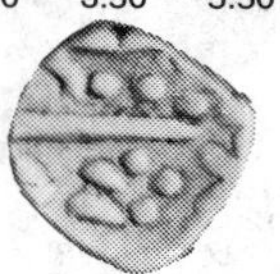

Y#	Date	Year	Good	VG	Fine	VF
1b	ND	—	2.00	3.50	5.50	8.00

1/4 MOHUR

GOLD, 2.80, 15mm

Y#	Date	Year	Good	VG	Fine	VF
B13	AH127x	—	—	—	Rare	—

SAYAJI RAO III

AH1292-1357/1875-1939AD

Nagari *Sa Ga*

1/4 PAISA

COPPER

Y#	Date	Year	Good	VG	Fine	VF
A2	AH1312(retrograde)	—	5.00	8.00	12.00	18.00

1/2 PAISA

COPPER, 16mm

Y#	Date	Year	Good	VG	Fine	VF
2	AH1312	—	1.75	3.25	4.50	6.00

PAISA

COPPER
Obv and rev: Date.

Y#	Date	Year	Good	VG	Fine	VF
3	AH1312(retrograde)	—	3.00	5.00	7.50	10.00
	1313(retrograde)	—	3.00	5.00	7.50	10.00

Rev: English *S* with serifs to left of *Sa Ga* and sword in *S* of *Julus*.

Y#	Date	Year	Good	VG	Fine	VF
3a	ND	—	6.00	10.00	14.00	18.50

Rev: Sunface, sword and English *T* w/serifs in right field.

Y#	Date	Year	Good	VG	Fine	VF
3b	AH1312(retrograde)	—	5.00	8.00	12.00	20.00

NOTE: These coins may have been issued by Sayaji Rao II w/blundered dates.

BARODA MINT

ANAND RAO

AH1215-1235/1800-1819AD

In the name of Muhammad Akbar II
AH1221-1253/1806-1837AD

Nagari *A* and scimitar

1/2 PAISA

COPPER, 14mm

C#	Date	Year	Good	VG	Fine	VF
20	AH1232	11	2.00	3.00	4.00	5.00
	123x	14	2.00	3.00	4.00	5.00

PAISA

COPPER, 9.80 g

C#	Date	Year	Good	VG	Fine	VF
21	AH1226	6	1.25	2.50	3.50	5.00
	1227	7	1.25	2.50	3.50	5.00
	122x	8	1.25	2.50	3.50	5.00
	122x	9	1.25	2.50	3.50	5.00
	1231	11	1.25	2.50	3.50	5.00
	—	13	1.25	2.50	3.50	5.00
	1234	14	1.25	2.50	3.50	5.00
	1236	16	1.25	2.50	3.50	5.00

1/8 RUPEE

SILVER, 1.34-1.45 g

C#	Date	Year	VG	Fine	VF	XF
24	AH122x	—	5.00	7.00	10.00	15.00
	1233	—	5.00	7.00	10.00	15.00
	1234	—	5.00	7.00	10.00	15.00

1/4 RUPEE

SILVER, 2.68-2.90 g

C#	Date	Year	VG	Fine	VF	XF
25	AH1228	—	5.50	8.00	12.50	18.50

1/2 RUPEE

SILVER, 5.35-5.80 g

C#	Date	Year	VG	Fine	VF	XF
26	AH1222	2	6.00	9.00	13.50	20.00
	1226	6	6.00	9.00	13.50	20.00
	1228	8	6.00	9.00	13.50	20.00
	1234	14	6.00	9.00	13.50	20.00

RUPEE

SILVER, 10.70-11.60 g

C#	Date	Year	VG	Fine	VF	XF
27	AH1222	2	7.50	12.50	18.50	27.50
	1224	4	7.50	12.50	18.50	27.50
	1225	5	7.50	12.50	18.50	27.50
	1226	6	7.50	12.50	18.50	27.50
	1227	7	7.50	12.50	18.50	27.50
	1228	8	7.50	12.50	18.50	27.50
	1229	9	7.50	12.50	18.50	27.50
	1232	12	7.50	12.50	18.50	27.50
	1233	13	7.50	12.50	18.50	27.50
	1234	14	7.50	12.50	18.50	27.50

SAYAJI RAO II

AH1235-1264/1819-1847AD

In the name of Muhammad Akbar II
AH1221-1253/1806-1837AD

Nagari *Sa* or *Sa Ga* and other symbols.

1/2 PAISA

COPPER, 14-15mm, 4.30 g
Rev: W/o symbols.

C#	Date	Year	Good	VG	Fine	VF
31.1	AH123x	—	1.25	2.50	4.00	6.00

Rev: Cross.

C#	Date	Year	Good	VG	Fine	VF
31.2	ND	—	1.25	2.50	4.00	6.00
	AH1236	16	2.00	4.00	6.00	10.00

Rev: Sun.

C#	Date	Year	Good	VG	Fine	VF
31.4	ND	—	1.25	2.50	4.00	6.00

Rev: Flag.

C#	Date	Year	Good	VG	Fine	VF
31.5	AH1251	—	2.00	4.00	6.00	10.00

Rev: Shaded ball.

C#	Date	Year	Good	VG	Fine	VF
31.8	AH1260	40	1.25	2.50	4.00	6.00

PAISA

COPPER, 18-24mm, 10.20 g
Rev: W/o symbol.

C#	Date	Year	Good	VG	Fine	VF
33.1	AH1236	16	1.25	2.00	3.00	4.50

Rev: Accented outlined cross.

C#	Date	Year	Good	VG	Fine	VF
33.2	AH1240	20	1.25	2.25	3.50	5.00
	1241	20	1.25	2.25	3.50	5.00

Rev: Simple outlined cross.

C#	Date	Year	Good	VG	Fine	VF
33.3	AH1243	23	1.25	2.25	3.50	5.00
	1244	—	1.25	2.25	3.50	5.00

Accented cross outline

C#	Date	Year	Good	VG	Fine	VF
33.14	AH1243	23	1.25	2.25	3.50	5.00
	1244	—	1.25	2.25	3.50	5.00

In the name of Gaekwar's brother Fateh Singh.

Obv: *Fateh Singh* in Devanagari; Katar left.
Rev: Date.

C#	Date	Year	Good	VG	Fine	VF
33.16	AH1245	—	15.00	25.00	40.00	60.00

NOTE: Fateh Singh was a brother of Maharao Sayaji Rao II.

Rev: Rayed sun.

C#	Date	Year	Good	VG	Fine	VF
33.4	AH124x	23	1.25	2.25	3.50	5.00
	1247	27	1.25	2.25	3.50	5.00

Rev: Person.

C#	Date	Year	Good	VG	Fine	VF
33.13	AH1248	28	1.25	2.25	3.50	5.00
	1249	29	1.25	2.25	3.50	5.00

Rev: Flag.

C#	Date	Year	Good	VG	Fine	VF
33.5	AH12xx	28	1.25	2.25	3.50	5.00
	1249	29	1.25	2.25	3.50	5.00
	12xx	30	1.25	2.25	3.50	5.00
	1250	—	1.25	2.25	3.50	5.00
	1251	—	1.25	2.25	3.50	5.00
	1253	—	1.25	2.25	3.50	5.00

Rev: Upright cross.

C#	Date	Year	Good	VG	Fine	VF
33.6	AH1255	35	1.25	2.25	3.50	5.00

Rev: Tulip

C#	Date	Year	Good	VG	Fine	VF
33.9	AH1253	33	1.25	2.25	3.50	5.00
	1254	—	1.25	2.25	3.50	5.00
	1255	36	1.25	2.25	3.50	5.00

Rev: 4-petal flower.

C#	Date	Year	Good	VG	Fine	VF
33.15	AH1255	35	2.00	3.50	5.00	7.00

Rev: 5-petal flower.

C#	Date	Year	Good	VG	Fine	VF
33.7	AH—	35	1.25	2.25	3.50	5.00
	1255	36	1.25	2.25	3.50	5.00
	1256	36	1.25	2.25	3.50	5.00
	1263	—	1.25	2.25	3.50	5.00

Rev: Shaded ball.

C#	Date	Year	Good	VG	Fine	VF
33.8	AH1260	40	1.00	2.00	3.00	4.00
	1261	41	1.00	2.00	3.00	4.00
	1262	—	1.00	2.00	3.00	4.00
	1263	43	1.00	2.00	3.00	4.00
	126x	44	1.00	2.00	3.00	4.00
	1264	—	1.00	2.00	3.00	4.00

Rev: Hoof

C#	Date	Year	Good	VG	Fine	VF
33.10	AH1260	—	2.50	4.00	7.50	12.00

Rev: Flag and branch.

C#	Date	Year	Good	VG	Fine	VF
33.11	ND	—	2.00	3.50	6.00	10.00

Rev: Flower

C#	Date	Year	Good	VG	Fine	VF
33.12	AH12xx	—	2.00	3.50	6.00	10.00

1/8 RUPEE

SILVER, 11-14mm, 1.34-1.45 g
Rev: Scimitar to left of *Julus*.

C#	Date	Year	VG	Fine	VF	XF
35.1	AH—	17	5.00	7.00	10.00	15.00

Rev: Scimitar above *Julus*.

C#	Date	Year	VG	Fine	VF	XF
35.2	—	26	5.00	7.00	10.00	15.00

Rev: Scimitar to right of *Julus*.

C#	Date	Year	VG	Fine	VF	XF
35.3	AH12xx	—	5.00	7.00	10.00	15.00

1/4 RUPEE

SILVER, 2.68-2.90 g
Rev: Scimitar to left of *Julus*.

C#	Date	Year	VG	Fine	VF	XF
36.1	AH1238	18	5.50	8.00	12.50	18.50

Rev: Scimitar above *Julus*.

C#	Date	Year	VG	Fine	VF	XF
36.2	AH—	24	5.50	8.00	12.50	18.50

Rev: Scimitar to right of *Julus*.

C#	Date	Year	VG	Fine	VF	XF
36.3	AH1249	29	5.50	8.00	12.50	18.50
	1250	29	5.50	8.00	12.50	18.50
36.3	1257	37	5.50	8.00	12.50	18.50
	1262	—	5.50	8.00	12.50	18.50

1/2 RUPEE

SILVER, 5.35-5.80 g
Rev: Scimitar to left of *Julus*.

C#	Date	Year	VG	Fine	VF	XF
37.1	AH1238	18	6.00	9.00	13.50	20.00
	1239	19	6.00	9.00	13.50	20.00
	12xx	20	6.00	9.00	13.50	20.00
	1241	21	6.00	9.00	13.50	20.00
	124x	27	6.00	9.00	13.50	20.00

Rev: Scimitar above *Julus*.

C#	Date	Year	VG	Fine	VF	XF
37.2	AH124x	24	6.00	9.00	13.50	20.00
	124x	26	6.00	9.00	13.50	20.00
	124x	27	6.00	9.00	13.50	20.00

Rev: Scimitar to right of *Julus*.

C#	Date	Year	VG	Fine	VF	XF
37.3	AH1254	33	6.00	9.00	13.50	20.00
	125x	35	6.00	9.00	13.50	20.00
	125x	37	6.00	9.00	13.50	20.00
	125x	38	6.00	9.00	13.50	20.00
	125x	39	6.00	9.00	13.50	20.00
	1260	40	6.00	9.00	13.50	20.00
	126x	42	6.00	9.00	13.50	20.00

RUPEE

SILVER, 10.70-11.60 g
Rev: Scimitar to left of *Julus*.

C#	Date	Year	VG	Fine	VF	XF
38.1	AH1237	17	7.50	12.50	18.50	27.50
	1238	18	7.50	12.50	18.50	27.50
	1239	19	7.50	12.50	18.50	27.50
	1240	19	7.50	12.50	18.50	27.50
	1240	20	7.50	12.50	18.50	27.50
	1241	21	7.50	12.50	18.50	27.50
	1242	22	7.50	12.50	18.50	27.50

Rev: Scimitar above *Julus*.

C#	Date	Year	VG	Fine	VF	XF
38.2	AH1244	24	7.50	12.50	18.50	27.50
	124x	25	7.50	12.50	18.50	27.50
	1248	27	7.50	12.50	18.50	27.50

Rev: Scimitar to right of *Julus*.

C#	Date	Year	VG	Fine	VF	XF
38.3	AH1247	—	7.50	12.50	18.50	27.50
	1249	29	7.50	12.50	18.50	27.50
	1250	30	7.50	12.50	18.50	27.50
	1251	32	7.50	12.50	18.50	27.50
	1253	33	7.50	12.50	18.50	27.50
	1254	33	7.50	12.50	18.50	27.50
	1255	35	7.50	12.50	18.50	27.50
	1256	36	7.50	12.50	18.50	27.50
	1257	37	7.50	12.50	18.50	27.50
	1258	38	7.50	12.50	18.50	27.50
	1259	39	7.50	12.50	18.50	27.50
	1260	40	7.50	12.50	18.50	27.50

GANPAT RAO

AH1264-1273/1847-1856AD

In the name of Muhammad Akbar II
AH1221-1253/1806-1837AD

Nagari *Ga* and scimitar.

1/2 PAISA

COPPER, 15mm, 5.00 g

Obv: Shaded ball in center.

C#	Date	Year	Good	VG	Fine	VF
41	AH1264-1272	—	1.00	2.00	3.00	4.50

PAISA

COPPER, 10.00 g

C#	Date	Year	Good	VG	Fine	VF
42	AH1263	43	2.00	3.00	4.00	5.50
	1264	44	2.00	3.00	4.00	5.50
	1265	45	2.00	3.00	4.00	5.50
	1266	46	2.00	3.00	4.00	5.50
	1272	52	2.00	3.00	4.00	5.50

Obv: Shaded ball in center.

C#	Date	Year	Good	VG	Fine	VF
43	AH1264	4x	2.00	3.00	4.00	5.50
	1266	4x	2.00	3.00	4.00	5.50
	1268	4x	2.00	3.00	4.00	5.50

1/8 RUPEE

SILVER, 11mm, 1.34-1.45 g

C#	Date	Year	VG	Fine	VF	XF
44	AH126x	—	5.50	8.00	10.00	15.00
	1269	—	5.50	8.00	10.00	15.00

1/4 RUPEE

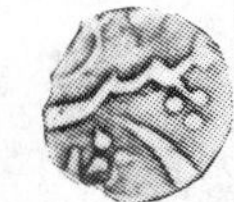

SILVER, 2.68-2.90 g

C#	Date	Year	VG	Fine	VF	XF
45	AH126x	—	5.50	8.00	12.50	18.50
	1272	52	5.50	8.00	12.50	18.50

1/2 RUPEE

SILVER, 5.35-5.80 g

C#	Date	Year	VG	Fine	VF	XF
46	AH126x	43	6.00	9.00	13.50	20.00
	1264	44	6.00	9.00	13.50	20.00
	126x	45	6.00	9.00	13.50	20.00
	1267	46	6.00	9.00	13.50	20.00
	1268	47	6.00	9.00	13.50	20.00
	12xx	49	6.00	9.00	13.50	20.00
	1271	—	6.00	9.00	13.50	20.00
	127x	51	6.00	9.00	13.50	20.00
	1272	52	6.00	9.00	13.50	20.00

RUPEE

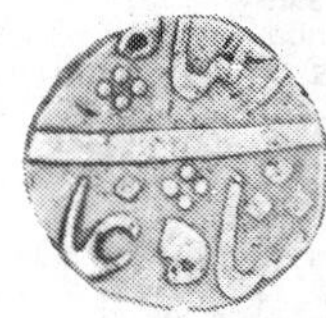

SILVER, 10.70-11.60 g

C#	Date	Year	VG	Fine	VF	XF
47	AH1264	43	7.00	11.00	16.50	25.00
	1265	43	7.00	11.00	16.50	25.00
	1265	44	7.00	11.00	16.50	25.00
	126x	45	7.00	11.00	16.50	25.00
	126x	46	7.00	11.00	16.50	25.00
	1268	47	7.00	11.00	16.50	25.00
	1271	50	7.00	11.00	16.50	25.00
	1272	51	7.00	11.00	16.50	25.00
	1272	52	7.00	11.00	16.50	25.00

KHANDE RAO

AH1273-1287/1856-1870AD

In the name of Muhammad Akbar II
AH1221-1253/1806-1837AD

Nagari *Kha* and scimitar.

1/2 PAISA

COPPER, 15mm, 4.20 g
Rev: Pomegranate.

Y#	Date	Year	Good	VG	Fine	VF
1	ND	—	1.25	2.00	3.00	4.00

PAISA

COPPER, 8.40 g
Rev: Pomegranate.

Y#	Date	Year	Good	VG	Fine	VF
2	AH1273	52	1.50	2.50	3.50	5.00

1/4 RUPEE

SILVER, 2.68-2.90 g

Y#	Date	Year	VG	Fine	VF	XF
3	AH1273	52	5.00	8.00	12.50	18.50
	1278	—	5.00	8.00	12.50	18.50

1/2 RUPEE

SILVER, 5.35-5.80 g

Y#	Date	Year	VG	Fine	VF	XF
4	AH1267	—	5.50	9.00	13.50	20.00
	1272	—	5.50	9.00	13.50	20.00
	127x	52	5.50	9.00	13.50	20.00
	1274	—	5.50	9.00	13.50	20.00
	1275	—	5.50	9.00	13.50	20.00
	1282	—	5.50	9.00	13.50	20.00

RUPEE

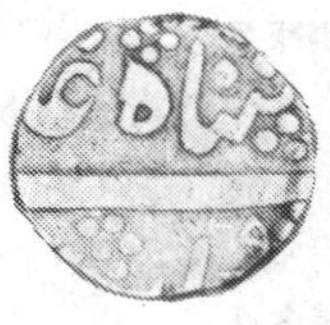 

SILVER, 10.70-11.60 g

Y#	Date	Year	VG	Fine	VF	XF
5	AH1273	5x	6.50	11.00	16.50	25.00
	1274	53	6.50	11.00	16.50	25.00
	1275	—	6.50	11.00	16.50	25.00
	128x	—	6.50	11.00	16.50	25.00

In the name of the Commander of the Sovereign Band (a title of the Gaekwar, ruler of Baroda).

From AH1274 (1857AD)

Nagari *Kha Ga* and scimitar.

1/2 PAISA

COPPER, 3.40 g
Rev: Scimitar.

Y#	Date	Year	Good	VG	Fine	VF
6	AH1275	—	2.00	3.00	4.00	5.50
	1276	—	2.00	3.00	4.00	5.50
	1277	—	3.00	5.00	7.50	12.00

Rev: Scimitar and hoof.

Y#	Date	Year	Good	VG	Fine	VF
6a	AH128x	—	5.00	7.50	10.00	15.00
	1285	—	5.00	7.50	10.00	15.00

PAISA

COPPER, 7.00-8.00 g
Rev: Scimitar.

Y#	Date	Year	Good	VG	Fine	VF
7	AH1274	—	2.00	3.00	4.00	5.50
	1275	—	1.25	2.25	3.25	4.00
	1276	—	1.25	2.25	3.25	4.00
	1277	—	2.00	3.00	4.00	5.50

Rev: Scimitar and hoof.

Y#	Date	Year	Good	VG	Fine	VF
7a	AH1281	—	3.50	4.50	6.00	8.00
	1282	—	3.50	4.50	6.00	8.00
	1283	—	3.50	4.50	6.00	8.00
	1284	—	3.50	4.50	6.00	8.00
	1285	—	3.50	4.50	6.00	8.00

2 PAISA

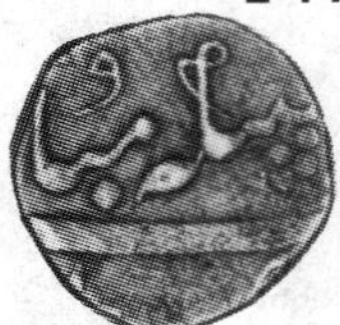 

COPPER, 15.00 g
Rev: Scimitar and hoof.

Y#	Date	Year	Good	VG	Fine	VF
8	AH1281	—	2.50	4.00	5.50	7.50
	1284	—	2.50	4.00	5.50	7.50
	1285	—	2.50	4.00	5.50	7.50

1/8 RUPEE

SILVER, 1.34-1.45 g

Y#	Date	Year	VG	Fine	VF	XF
9	AH1282	—	5.00	7.00	10.00	15.00

1/4 RUPEE

SILVER, 2.68-2.90 g

Y#	Date	Year	VG	Fine	VF	XF
10	AH1274	—	4.50	6.50	9.00	18.50
	1282	—	4.50	6.50	9.00	18.50
	1283	—	4.50	6.50	9.00	18.50
	1286	—	4.50	6.50	9.00	18.50

1/2 RUPEE

SILVER, 5.35-5.80 g

Y#	Date	Year	VG	Fine	VF	XF
11	AH1274	—	6.00	9.00	13.50	20.00
	1275	—	6.00	9.00	13.50	20.00
	1276	—	6.00	9.00	13.50	20.00
	1277	—	6.00	9.00	13.50	20.00
	1278	—	6.00	9.00	13.50	20.00
	1279	—	6.00	9.00	13.50	20.00
	1280	—	6.00	9.00	13.50	20.00
	1282	—	6.00	9.00	13.50	20.00
	1284	—	6.00	9.00	13.50	20.00
	1285	—	6.00	9.00	13.50	20.00
	1286	—	6.00	9.00	13.50	20.00

RUPEE

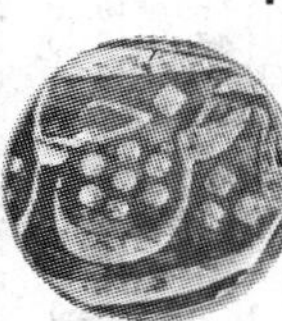 

SILVER, 10.70-11.60 g

Y#	Date	Year	VG	Fine	VF	XF
12	AH1274	—	6.50	10.00	15.00	22.50
	1275	—	6.50	10.00	15.00	22.50
	1276	—	6.50	10.00	15.00	22.50
	1277	—	6.50	10.00	15.00	22.50
	1278	—	6.50	10.00	15.00	22.50
	1280	—	6.50	10.00	15.00	22.50
	1281	—	6.50	10.00	15.00	22.50
	1282	—	6.50	10.00	15.00	22.50
	1283	—	6.50	10.00	15.00	22.50
	1284	—	6.50	10.00	15.00	22.50

Y#	Date	Year	VG	Fine	VF	XF
12	1285	—	6.50	10.00	15.00	22.50
	1286	—	6.50	10.00	15.00	22.50
	1287	—	6.50	10.00	15.00	22.50
	(12)87	—	6.50	10.00	15.00	22.50

NAZARANA 1-1/2 RUPEES

SILVER, 18.10 g

Y#	Date	Year	VG	Fine	VF	XF
A13	AH1275	—	—	—	Rare	—

Milled Coinage

NAZARANA 1/2 RUPEE

SILVER, 5.65 g

Y#	Date	Year	VG	Fine	VF	XF
13	AH1287	—	50.00	85.00	120.00	175.00

NAZARANA RUPEE

SILVER, 11.30 g
Obv. Persian leg: *Kahnde Rao*.

Y#	Date	Year	VG	Fine	VF	XF
14.1	AH1287	—	40.00	70.00	100.00	140.00

Obv. Persian leg: *Khande Rao*.

Y#	Date	Year	VG	Fine	VF	XF
14.2	AH1287	—	60.00	100.00	140.00	200.00

Dump Coinage

MALHAR RAO

AH1287-1292/1870-1875AD

Nagari *Ma Ga* and scimitar.

1/2 PAISA

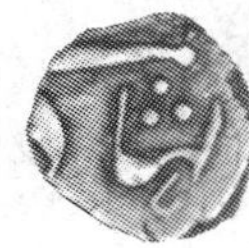 

COPPER, 4.00 g

Y#	Date	Year	Good	VG	Fine	VF
15	AH1288	—	2.00	3.00	4.00	5.50
	1290	—	2.00	3.00	4.00	5.50

PAISA

COPPER, 7.60-8.60 g

Y#	Date	Year	Good	VG	Fine	VF
16	AH1288	—	1.25	2.50	3.50	5.00
	1289	—	1.25	2.50	3.50	5.00
	1290	—	1.25	2.50	3.50	5.00
	ND	—	1.25	2.50	3.50	5.00

2 PAISA

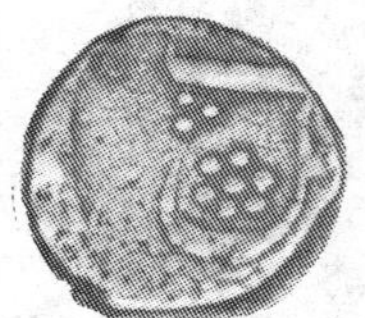

COPPER, 16.10 g

Y#	Date	Year	Good	VG	Fine	VF
17	AH1288	—	2.00	3.00	4.00	5.50
	1289	—	2.00	3.00	4.00	5.50
	1290	—	2.00	3.00	4.00	5.50

NAZARANA 2 PAISA

COPPER

A17	AH1289	—	—	—	Rare	—

1/8 RUPEE

SILVER, 11mm, 1.34-1.45 g

Y#	Date	Year	VG	Fine	VF	XF
18	AH129x	—	4.00	6.00	9.00	13.50

1/4 RUPEE

SILVER, 13mm, 2.68-2.90 g

19	AH1290	—	5.00	7.00	10.00	15.00

1/2 RUPEE

SILVER, 5.35-5.80 g

20	AH1287	—	5.50	8.00	12.50	18.50
	1288	—	5.50	8.00	12.50	18.50
	1289	—	5.50	8.00	12.50	18.50
	1290	—	5.50	8.00	12.50	18.50

RUPEE

SILVER, 10.70-11.60 g

21	AH1287	—	6.00	9.00	13.50	20.00
	1288	—	6.00	9.00	13.50	20.00
	1289	—	6.00	9.00	13.50	20.00
	1290	—	6.00	9.00	13.50	20.00
	—	122	6.00	9.00	13.50	20.00

NAZARANA RUPEE

SILVER, 10.70-11.60 g

21a	AH1288	—	50.00	85.00	120.00	170.00

NAZARANA 2 RUPEES

SILVER, 21.40-23.20 g

Y#	Date	Year	VG	Fine	VF	XF
22	AH1288	—	—	—	Rare	—

NAZARANA 4 RUPEES

SILVER, 44.00 g

22A	AH1288	—	—	—	Rare	—

SAYAJI RAO III

AH1292-1357/VS1932-1995/1875-1938AD

Nagari *Sa Ga* and scimitar.

1/4 PAISA

COPPER

Y#	Date	Year	Good	VG	Fine	VF
A23	VS194x	—	2.50	5.00	8.50	12.50

1/2 PAISA

COPPER

23	VS1937	(1880)	1.50	2.50	4.00	5.50
	1947	(1890)	1.50	2.50	4.00	5.50
	1948	(1891)	1.50	2.50	4.00	5.50

PAISA

COPPER

Y#	Date	Year	Good	VG	Fine	VF
24	VS1937	(1880)	1.50	2.50	4.00	5.50
	1947	(1890)	1.50	2.50	4.00	5.50
	1948/7	(1890)	1.50	2.50	4.00	5.50
	1948	(1891)	1.50	2.50	4.00	5.50

Machine-punched planchets.

24a	VS1949	(1892)	2.00	3.50	5.00	7.00

NOTE: Generally struck off-center.

2 PAISE

COPPER

25	VS1937	(1880)	3.50	5.00	6.50	8.50
	1947	(1890)	3.50	5.00	6.50	8.50
	1948	(1891)	3.50	5.00	6.50	8.50

17.00 g
Machine-punched planchets.

25a	VS1949	(1892)	3.75	5.50	7.50	10.00

NOTE: Generally struck off-center.

1/8 RUPEE

SILVER, 1.34-1.45 g

Y#	Date	Year	VG	Fine	VF	XF
26	AH1294	—	4.00	6.00	9.00	13.50
	1295	—	4.00	6.00	9.00	13.50
	1297	—	4.00	6.00	9.00	13.50
	1299	—	4.00	6.00	9.00	13.50

1/4 RUPEE

SILVER, 13mm, 2.68-2.90 g

27	AH1292	—	5.00	7.00	10.00	15.00
	1299	—	5.00	7.00	10.00	15.00

1/2 RUPEE

SILVER, 5.35-5.80 g

28	AH1292	—	5.50	8.00	12.50	18.50
	1293	—	5.50	8.00	12.50	18.50
	1294	—	5.50	8.00	12.50	18.50
	1295	—	5.50	8.00	12.50	18.50
	1297	—	5.50	8.00	12.50	18.50
	1298	—	5.50	8.00	12.50	18.50
	1299	—	5.50	8.00	12.50	18.50
	1300	—	5.50	8.00	12.50	18.50
	1301	—	5.50	8.00	12.50	18.50
	1302	—	5.50	8.00	12.50	18.50

RUPEE

SILVER, 10.70-11.60 g

29	AH1292	—	6.00	9.00	13.50	20.00

Y#	Date	Year	VG	Fine	VF	XF
29	1293	—	6.00	9.00	13.50	20.00
	1294	—	6.00	9.00	13.50	20.00
	1295	—	6.00	9.00	13.50	20.00
	1298	—	6.00	9.00	13.50	20.00
	1299	—	6.00	9.00	13.50	20.00
	1300	—	6.00	9.00	13.50	20.00
	1301	—	6.00	9.00	13.50	20.00
	1302	—	6.00	9.00	13.50	20.00

Milled Coinage

PAI

COPPER

Obv: Annulets between letters.

Y#	Date	Year	VG	Fine	VF	XF
30.1	VS1944	(1887)	.50	1.00	1.50	2.00

Obv: Pellets between letters.

Y#	Date	Year	VG	Fine	VF	XF
30.1a	VS1944	(1887)	2.50	5.00	8.00	12.00

Obv: W/o annulets.
Thick planchet

Y#	Date	Year	VG	Fine	VF	XF
30.2	VS1944	(1887)	.75	1.50	2.00	2.50
	1945	(1888)	.35	.75	1.00	1.50
	1946	(1889)	.75	1.50	2.00	2.50
	1947	(1890)	.75	1.50	2.00	2.50

Thin planchet. Obv: Large legends.

Y#	Date	Year	VG	Fine	VF	XF
30.2a	VS1948	(1891)	.75	1.50	2.00	2.50
	1949	(1892)	.35	.75	1.00	1.50
	1950/49	(1893)	.75	1.25	1.75	2.25

Obv: Small legends.

Y#	Date	Year	VG	Fine	VF	XF
30.3	VS1950	(1893)	.35	.75	1.00	1.50

PAISA

COPPER

Obv: Inner leg. curved, long hoof.

Y#	Date	Year	VG	Fine	VF	XF
31.1	VS1940	(1883)	1.00	2.00	2.50	3.00
	1941	(1884)	1.00	2.00	2.50	3.00
	1942	(1885)	1.75	2.50	3.75	5.00

Thick planchet, 2mm, 8.00-8.30 g

Obv: Inner leg. straight, short hoof.

Y#	Date	Year	VG	Fine	VF	XF
31.2	VS1941	(1884)	.75	1.50	2.00	2.75
31.2	1942	(1885)	.35	.75	1.25	1.75
	1943	(1886)	.35	.75	1.25	1.75
	1944	(1887)	.35	.75	1.25	1.75
	1945	(1888)	.50	1.00	1.50	2.00
	1946/3	—	—	—	—	—
	1946	(1889)	.50	1.00	1.50	2.00
	1947	(1890)	.35	.75	1.25	1.75
	1948	(1891)	.75	1.50	2.00	2.75

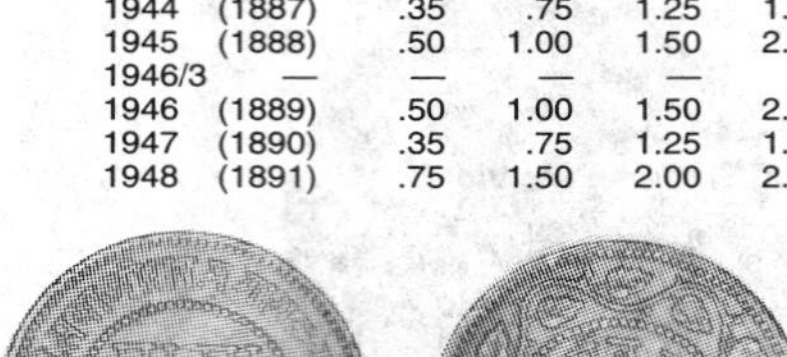

Thin planchet, 1.6mm, 6.50-6.80 g

Obv. & rev: Smaller inner circle.

Y#	Date	Year	VG	Fine	VF	XF
31.2a	AH1948	(1891)	.30	.60	1.00	1.50
	1949	(1892)	.30	.60	1.00	1.50
	1950	(1893)	.30	.60	1.00	1.50

2 PAISA

COPPER

Obv: Inner leg. curved, long hoof.

Rev: Large inner leg. and date.

Y#	Date	Year	VG	Fine	VF	XF
32.1	VS1940	(1883)	2.00	3.50	5.50	9.00
	1941	(1884)	2.00	3.50	5.50	9.00

Thick planchet, 2.9mm, 16.30-16.80 g

Obv: Inner leg. straight, short hoof.

Rev: Small inner leg. and date.

Y#	Date	Year	VG	Fine	VF	XF
32.2	VS1941	(1884)	1.00	2.00	3.00	5.00
	1942	(1885)	1.00	2.00	3.00	5.00
	1943	(1886)	.75	1.50	2.25	3.50
	1944/3	(1887)	.75	1.50	2.25	3.50
	1944	(1887)	.75	1.50	2.25	3.50
	1945/2	(1888)	1.00	2.00	3.00	5.00
	1945	(1888)	.75	1.50	2.25	3.50
	1946	(1889)	1.25	2.50	4.00	7.50
	1947	(1890)	.75	1.50	2.25	3.50
	1948	(1891)	2.50	4.00	6.00	10.00

Thin planchet, 2.4-2.5mm, 12.40-13.30 g

Y#	Date	Year	VG	Fine	VF	XF
32.2a	VS1948	(1891)	.50	1.00	1.50	2.50
	1949/4	(1892)	.50	1.00	1.50	2.50
	1949/8	(1892)	.75	1.50	2.25	3.50
	1949	(1892)	.75	1.50	2.25	3.50
	1950	(1893)	.65	1.25	1.75	3.00

2 ANNAS

SILVER

Y#	Date	Year	Fine	VF	XF	Unc
33	VS1949	(1892)	7.00	11.00	16.50	25.00

Y#	Date	Year	Fine	VF	XF	Unc
33a	VS1951	(1894)	6.50	10.00	15.00	22.50
	1952	(1895)	6.50	10.00	15.00	22.50

4 ANNAS

SILVER

Y#	Date	Year	Fine	VF	XF	Unc
34	VS1949	(1892)	7.00	11.00	16.00	25.00

Y#	Date	Year	Fine	VF	XF	Unc
34a	VS1951	(1894)	6.00	9.00	13.50	20.00
	1952	(1895)	6.00	9.00	13.50	20.00

1/2 RUPEE

SILVER

Y#	Date	Year	Fine	VF	XF	Unc
35	VS1948	(1891)	30.00	40.00	55.00	80.00
	1949	(1892)	30.00	40.00	55.00	80.00

Y#	Date	Year	Fine	VF	XF	Unc
35a	VS1951	(1894)	12.50	18.50	25.00	35.00
	1952	(1895)	12.50	18.50	25.00	35.00

RUPEE

SILVER

Y#	Date	Year	Fine	VF	XF	Unc
36	VS1948	(1891)	13.50	20.00	27.50	37.50
	1949	(1892)	13.50	20.00	27.50	37.50

Y#	Date	Year	Fine	VF	XF	Unc
36a	VS1951	(1894)	11.50	17.50	23.50	32.50
	1952	(1895)	11.50	17.50	23.50	32.50
	1953	(1896)	11.50	17.50	23.50	32.50
	1954	(1897)	11.50	17.50	23.50	32.50
	1955	(1898)	11.50	17.50	23.50	32.50
	1956	(1899)	11.50	17.50	23.50	32.50

1/6 MOHUR

GOLD, 14.5mm, 1.04-1.18 g

Y#	Date	Year	Fine	VF	XF	Unc
A37	VS1943	(1886)	165.00	225.00	275.00	350.00

Y#	Date	Year	Fine	VF	XF	Unc
37	1951	(1894)	165.00	225.00	275.00	350.00
	1953	(1896)	165.00	225.00	275.00	350.00

NOTE: Later date (VS1959) exists for this type.

1/3 MOHUR

GOLD, 16mm, 2.07-2.39 g

Y#	Date	Year	Fine	VF	XF	Unc
A38	VS1942	(1885)	185.00	250.00	325.00	400.00

MOHUR

GOLD, 21mm, 6.20-6.40 g

Y#	Date	Year	Fine	VF	XF	Unc
A39	VS1942	(1885)	265.00	350.00	500.00	750.00

Y#	Date	Year	Fine	VF	XF	Unc
39	VS1945	(1888)	250.00	325.00	450.00	650.00
	1952	(1895)	250.00	325.00	450.00	650.00
	1953	(1896)	250.00	325.00	450.00	650.00

NOTE: Later date (VS1959) exists for this type.

PETLAD MINT

ANAND RAO

AH1215-1235/1800-1819AD

In the name of Shah Alam II

AH1173-1221/1759-1806AD

and Years of Anand Rao

Regnal Years 1-7

Nagari *A*

PAISA

COPPER, 20mm

C#	Date	Year	Good	VG	Fine	VF
10	—	—	2.50	3.50	4.50	7.00

1/2 RUPEE

SILVER

C#	Date	Year	VG	Fine	VF	XF
12	ND	—	—	—	—	—

RUPEE

SILVER, 10.70-11.60 g

C#	Date	Year	VG	Fine	VF	XF
13	—	3	10.00	15.00	21.50	30.00
	—	4	10.00	15.00	21.50	30.00

PATTERNS (Pn)

KM#	Date	Mintage	Identification	Mkt.Val.
Pn1	VS19xx	—	2 Annas, Silver, Y#33a	175.00

KM#	Date	Mintage	Identification	Mkt.Val.
Pn2	VS19xx	—	4 Annas, Silver, Y#34a	200.00

KM#	Date	Mintage	Identification	Mkt.Val.
Pn3	VS19xx	—	1/2 Rupee, Silver, Y#35a	275.00

KM#	Date	Mintage	Identification	Mkt.Val.
Pn4	VS19xx	—	1 Rupee, Silver	400.00
Pn5	VS19xx	—	1 Rupee, White metal	250.00
Pn6	VS1995	—	1/3 Mohur, Silver, Y40	—
Pn7	VS1995	—	1 Mohur, Silver, Y41	—

TRIAL STRIKES (TS)

KM#	Date	Mintage	Identification	Mkt.Val.
TS1	VS1940	—	2 Paisa, Tin, uniface	—

KM#	Date	Mintage	Identification	Mkt.Val.
TS2	VS—	—	2 Paisa, Y32.2	—

BELA

Las Bela, Beylah

State located in Baluchistan.

Of very ancient origins, the later history of Las Bela was intimately associated with that of Kalat to which State it became subject in 1758. Thereafter, however, the Arab chieftains of Las Bela, known as Jams, proved capable of demonstrating a very considerable degree of independence. The State continued up to 1947, at which time it acceded to Pakistan.

RULERS

Mir Jamir Khan,
AH1246-1287/1830-1869AD

Mir Ali Khan III,
AH1287-1294/1869-1877AD

Mir Jamir Khan, restored,
AH1294-1306/1877-1888AD

MIR JAMIR KHAN

AH1246-1287/1830-1869AD

FALUS

COPPER

C#	Date	Year	Good	VG	Fine	VF
5	AH1271	—	10.00	20.00	35.00	60.00
	1276	—	10.00	20.00	35.00	60.00
	1285	—	10.00	20.00	35.00	60.00
	1286	—	10.00	20.00	35.00	60.00

In the name of Mahmud Khan Durani

FALUS

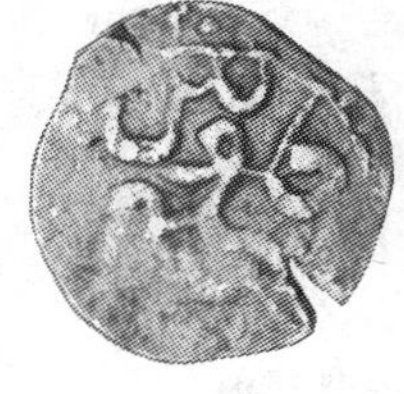

COPPER

C#	Date	Year	Good	VG	Fine	VF
10	ND	—	6.00	12.50	21.50	35.00

BHARATPUR

State located in Rajputana in northwest India.

Bharatpur was founded by Balchand, a Jat chieftain who took advantage of Mughal confusion and weakness after the death of Aurangzeb to seize the area. In 1756 the ruler at that time, Suraj Mal, received the title of Raja. Bharatpur became increasingly associated with Maratha ambitions and, in spite of treaty ties to the East India Company, assisted the Maratha Confederacy in their struggles against the British. This gained them few friends in British circles, but the early attempts by the British to force the submission of Bharatpur fortress proved abortive. In 1826 however, the British took the opportunity offered by a bitter internal feud concerning the succession finally to reduce the stronghold. The rival claimant was exiled to Allahabad and Balwant Singh, then a child of seven, was placed on the throne under the supervision of a British Political Agent. From that time onwards Bharatpur came under British control until it acceded to the Indian Union at Independence.

RULERS

Ranjit Singh,
AH1190-1220/1776-1805AD

Randhir Singh,
AH1220-1239/1805-1823AD

Baldeo Singh,
AH1239-1241/1823-1824AD

Durjan Singh,
AH1241-1242/1825-1826AD

Balwant Singh,
AH1242-1269/1826-1853AD

Jaswant Singh,
AH1269-1311/1853-1893AD/
VS1909-1950

MINTS

بهرت پور

Bharatpur

برج اندرپور

Braj Indrapur

مهاندرپور

Maha Indrapur

BHARATPUR MINT

Mintname: Bharatpur or Braj Indrapur

Mint marks:

In the name of Shah Alam II

AH1173-1221/1759-1806AD

TAKKA

COPPER, 17.50-18.50 g

KM#	Date	Year	Good	VG	Fine	VF
11	AH1216	50	1.25	2.50	4.00	5.50
	—	54	1.25	2.50	4.00	5.50
	—	56	1.25	2.50	4.00	5.50

NOTE: Earlier dates (Yr.4-49) exist for this type.

RUPEE

SILVER, 11.00-11.10 g
Mintname: Braj Indrapur

KM#	Date	Year	VG	Fine	VF	XF
26	AH1216	44	7.00	11.00	16.50	25.00
	1217	45	7.00	11.00	16.50	25.00
	1218	46	7.00	11.00	16.50	25.00
	1219	47	7.00	11.00	16.50	25.00

NOTE: Earlier dates (AH118x-1215) exist for this type.

In the name of Muhammad Akbar II
AH1221-1253/1806-1837AD

TAKKA

COPPER, 17.50-18.50 g

KM#	Date	Year	Good	VG	Fine	VF
101	AH—	20	2.50	4.00	6.50	10.00
	—	22	2.50	4.00	6.50	10.00
	12xx	22	2.50	4.00	6.50	10.00
	1272	48	2.50	4.00	6.50	10.00
	1276	42	2.50	4.00	6.50	10.00
	1279	49	2.50	4.00	6.50	10.00

NOTE: These dates are posthumous.

1/4 RUPEE

SILVER, 15mm, 2.75 g

KM#	Date	Year	VG	Fine	VF	XF
104	AH—	—	10.00	15.00	21.50	30.00

1/2 RUPEE

SILVER, 5.50 g

KM#	Date	Year	VG	Fine	VF	XF
105	AH—	22	8.50	13.50	20.00	28.50
	12xx	34	8.50	13.50	20.00	28.50
	—	35	8.50	13.50	20.00	28.50

RUPEE

SILVER, 11.00-11.10 g
Thick flan.

KM#	Date	Year	VG	Fine	VF	XF
106	AH1221	—	7.00	11.00	16.50	25.00
	1222	2	7.00	11.00	16.50	25.00
	122x	3	7.00	11.00	16.50	25.00
	1224	4	7.00	11.00	16.50	25.00
	1225	4	7.00	11.00	16.50	25.00
	1225	5	7.00	11.00	16.50	25.00
	1226	6	7.00	11.00	16.50	25.00
	1227	7	7.00	11.00	16.50	25.00
	1228	8	7.00	11.00	16.50	25.00
	1229	9	7.00	11.00	16.50	25.00
	1230	10	7.00	11.00	16.50	25.00
	1231	11	7.00	11.00	16.50	25.00
106	1232	12	7.00	11.00	16.50	25.00
	1233	13	7.00	11.00	16.50	25.00
	1234	14	7.00	11.00	16.50	25.00
	xxxx	15	7.00	11.00	16.50	25.00
	1236	16	7.00	11.00	16.50	25.00
	1238	18	7.00	11.00	16.50	25.00
	1239	19	7.00	11.00	16.50	25.00
	12xx	21	7.00	11.00	16.50	25.00
	1243	22	7.00	11.00	16.50	25.00
	1244	23	7.00	11.00	16.50	25.00
	124x	24	7.00	11.00	16.50	25.00
	124x	25	7.00	11.00	16.50	25.00
	12xx	26	7.00	11.00	16.50	25.00
	1247	27	7.00	11.00	16.50	25.00
	1248	28	7.00	11.00	16.50	25.00
	1249	29	7.00	11.00	16.50	25.00
	12xx	30	7.00	11.00	16.50	25.00
	1251	31	7.00	11.00	16.50	25.00
	1252	32	7.00	11.00	16.50	25.00
	1253	34	7.00	11.00	16.50	25.00
	1252	35	7.00	11.00	16.50	25.00
	1254	35	7.00	11.00	16.50	25.00
	12xx	36	7.00	11.00	16.50	25.00
	1256	38	7.00	11.00	16.50	25.00
	12xx	39	7.00	11.00	16.50	25.00
	1270	40	7.00	11.00	16.50	25.00
	1270	41	7.00	11.00	16.50	25.00
	1271	41	7.00	11.00	16.50	25.00
	—	42	7.00	11.00	16.50	25.00
	—	45	7.00	11.00	16.50	25.00
	—	46	7.00	11.00	16.50	25.00
	12xx	47	7.00	11.00	16.50	25.00
	—	48	7.00	11.00	16.50	25.00
	12xx	49	7.00	11.00	16.50	25.00

NOTE: Regnal years 34-48 (AH1253-1278) were posthumous, being struck during the reign of the Mughal emperor Bahadur Shah Zafar.

Thin flan

KM#	Date	Year	VG	Fine	VF	XF
106a	AH1233	13	18.50	26.50	37.50	55.00
	1234	14	18.50	26.50	37.50	55.00
	1235	14	18.50	26.50	37.50	55.00
	1235	15	18.50	26.50	37.50	55.00
	1236	16	18.50	26.50	37.50	55.00
	1236	19	18.50	26.50	37.50	55.00
	1237	17	18.50	26.50	37.50	55.00
	1238	18	18.50	26.50	37.50	55.00

NAZARANA RUPEE

SILVER, 11.00-11.15 g

KM#	Date	Year	VG	Fine	VF	XF
107	AH1233	13	35.00	50.00	70.00	100.00
	1235	15	35.00	50.00	70.00	100.00

MOHUR

GOLD, 10.70-11.40 g

KM#	Date	Year	VG	Fine	VF	XF
110	AH12xx	1	275.00	450.00	650.00	950.00
	12xx	3	275.00	450.00	650.00	950.00
	123x	11	275.00	450.00	650.00	950.00
	12xx	14	275.00	450.00	650.00	950.00
	12xx	15	275.00	450.00	650.00	950.00

In the name of Bahadur Shah II
AH1253-1274/1837-1858AD

Mintname: Braj Indrapur

Mint marks:

Katar  Star 

RUPEE

SILVER, 11.00-11.10 g

KM#	Date	Year	VG	Fine	VF	XF
146	AH127x/VS1911	17	13.50	20.00	27.50	37.50
	127x/VS1912	18	13.50	20.00	27.50	37.50
	1273/VS1913	19	13.50	20.00	27.50	37.50
	-/VS1914	20	13.50	20.00	27.50	37.50

In the names of Queen Victoria

and Jaswant Singh

Mintnames: Bharatpur and Braj Indrapur

Mint marks:

RUPEE

SILVER, 11.00-11.10 g
Rev: Katar at left of star and date.

KM#	Date	Year	VG	Fine	VF	XF
156	VS1910	1858	50.00	70.00	100.00	150.00

Rev: Star at left of katar and date.

KM#	Date	Year	VG	Fine	VF	XF
157	VS1910	1858	40.00	60.00	85.00	120.00

MOHUR

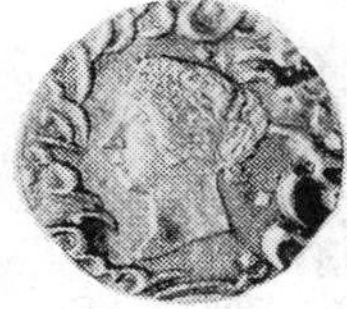

GOLD, 10.70-11.40 g
Rev: Katar at left of star and date.

KM#	Date	Year	VG	Fine	VF	XF
160	VS1910	1858	600.00	1000.	1400.	2000.

With titles of Queen Victoria

RUPEE

SILVER, 11.00-11.10 g

KM#	Date	Year	VG	Fine	VF	XF
166	VS1914	1858	40.00	70.00	85.00	120.00
	1915	1858	40.00	70.00	85.00	120.00
	1916	1859	40.00	70.00	85.00	120.00
	1917	1861	40.00	70.00	85.00	120.00
	1917	1851 (error)	40.00	70.00	85.00	120.00
	1922	1865	40.00	70.00	85.00	120.00

MOHUR

GOLD, 10.70-11.40 g

KM#	Date	Year	VG	Fine	VF	XF
170	VS1915	1858	600.00	1000.	1400.	2000.
	1916	1859	600.00	1000.	1400.	2000.
	1918	1862	600.00	1000.	1400.	2000.
	1919	1862	600.00	1000.	1400.	2000.

NOTE: For similar coins with dagger at left and sword at right of Queen's bust, see Bindraban State.

DIG MINT

In the name of Muhammad Akbar II
AH1221-1253/1806-1837AD

Mintname: Mahe Indrapur

Mint marks:

RUPEE

SILVER, 10.70-11.60 g
Narrow flan

KM#	Date	Year	VG	Fine	VF	XF
126	AH—	1	7.00	11.00	16.50	25.00
	—	3	7.00	11.00	16.50	25.00
	12xx	7	7.00	11.00	16.50	25.00
	1229	9	7.00	11.00	16.50	25.00
	—	10	7.00	11.00	16.50	25.00
	1231	11	7.00	11.00	16.50	25.00
	1232	12	7.00	11.00	16.50	25.00
	123x	13	7.00	11.00	16.50	25.00
	AH1237	18	7.00	11.00	16.50	25.00
	12xx	19	7.00	11.00	16.50	25.00
	12xx	21	7.00	11.00	16.50	25.00
	12xx	24	7.00	11.00	16.50	25.00
	12xx	26	7.00	11.00	16.50	25.00
	1246	27	7.00	11.00	16.50	25.00
	12xx	28	7.00	11.00	16.50	25.00
	12xx	29	7.00	11.00	16.50	25.00
	12xx	31	7.00	11.00	16.50	25.00
	—	32	7.00	11.00	16.50	25.00
	1257	36	7.00	11.00	16.50	25.00
	125x	40	7.00	11.00	16.50	25.00
	1257	41	7.00	11.00	16.50	25.00
	—	42	7.00	11.00	16.50	25.00
	12xx	44	7.00	11.00	16.50	25.00
	—	47	7.00	11.00	16.50	25.00

NOTE: Issues with regnal years 32-47 are posthumous.

Wide flan

KM#	Date	Year	VG	Fine	VF	XF
126a	AH1234	14	22.50	35.00	47.50	65.00
	12xx	15	22.50	35.00	47.50	65.00
	123x	16	22.50	35.00	47.50	65.00
	—	17	22.50	35.00	47.50	65.00

With titles of Queen Victoria

1/4 RUPEE

SILVER, 2.68-2.90 g

KM#	Date	Year	VG	Fine	VF	XF
174	VS1910	1858	70.00	100.00	140.00	200.00

RUPEE

SILVER, 10.70-11.60 g
Rev: Katar at left of star and date.

KM#	Date	Year	VG	Fine	VF	XF
176.1	VS1910	1858	45.00	75.00	110.00	160.00

Rev: Star at left of Katar and date.

KM#	Date	Year	VG	Fine	VF	XF
176.2	VS1910	1858	45.00	75.00	110.00	160.00

KUMBER MINT

In the name of Shah Alam II
AH1173-1221/1759-1806AD

Mintname: Maha Indrapur

Mint marks:

RUPEE

In the name of Muhammad Akbar II
AH1221-1253/1806-1837AD

SILVER, 11.05-11.10 g
Narrow flan

KM#	Date	Year	VG	Fine	VF	XF
116	AH1222	3	7.00	11.00	16.50	25.00
	12xx	5	7.00	11.00	16.50	25.00
	12xx	6	7.00	11.00	16.50	25.00
	12xx	7	7.00	11.00	16.50	25.00
	122x	8	7.00	11.00	16.50	25.00
	1229	9	7.00	11.00	16.50	25.00
	1229	10	7.00	11.00	16.50	25.00
	—	11	7.00	11.00	16.50	25.00
	1233	13	7.00	11.00	16.50	25.00
	12xx	21	7.00	11.00	16.50	25.00
	1243	22	7.00	11.00	16.50	25.00
	12xx	23	7.00	11.00	16.50	25.00
	—	24	7.00	11.00	16.50	25.00
	124x	25	7.00	11.00	16.50	25.00
	124x	26	7.00	11.00	16.50	25.00
	12xx	27	7.00	11.00	16.50	25.00
	1248	28	7.00	11.00	16.50	25.00
	1249	29	7.00	11.00	16.50	25.00
	12xx	46	7.00	11.00	16.50	25.00
	1261	47	7.00	11.00	16.50	25.00
	1262	48	7.00	11.00	16.50	25.00

NOTE: The issues of regnal years 32 and later are posthumous.

Wide flan

KM#	Date	Year	VG	Fine	VF	XF
116a	AH1234	14	20.00	31.50	42.50	60.00
	1235	15	20.00	31.50	42.50	60.00
	1238	16	20.00	31.50	42.50	60.00

UNCERTAIN MINT

Possibly the fortress of Ver (Wair).
Arabic *Wa* = ver?

Mint marks:

In the name of Muhammad Akbar II
AH1221-1253/1806-1837AD

RUPEE

SILVER, 11.05-11.10 g

KM#	Date	Year	VG	Fine	VF	XF
136	AH12xx	3	7.00	11.00	16.50	25.00
	12xx	5	7.00	11.00	16.50	25.00
	12xx	6	7.00	11.00	16.50	25.00
	122x	7	7.00	11.00	16.50	25.00
	12xx	8	7.00	11.00	16.50	25.00
	12xx	9	7.00	11.00	16.50	25.00
136	123x	11	7.00	11.00	16.50	25.00
	123x	12	7.00	11.00	16.50	25.00
	12xx	15	7.00	11.00	16.50	25.00
	1238	16	7.00	11.00	16.50	25.00
	—	19	7.00	11.00	16.50	25.00
	124x	21	7.00	11.00	16.50	25.00
	—	23	7.00	11.00	16.50	25.00
	124x	25	7.00	11.00	16.50	25.00
	12xx	26	7.00	11.00	16.50	25.00
	124x	28	7.00	11.00	16.50	25.00
	—	31	7.00	11.00	16.50	25.00
	1252	32	7.00	11.00	16.50	25.00
	12xx	41	7.00	11.00	16.50	25.00
	1261	47	7.00	11.00	16.50	25.00

BHAUNAGAR

State located in northwest India on the west shore of the Gulf of Cambay.

The Thakurs of Bhaunagar, as the rulers were titled, were Gohel Rajputs. They traced their control of the area back to the thirteenth century. Under the umbrella of British paramountcy, the Thakurs of Bhaunagar were regarded as relatively enlightened rulers. The State was absorbed into Saurashtra in February 1948.

Anonymous Types: Bearing the distinguishing Nagari legend *Bahadur* in addition to the Mughal legends.

MONETARY SYSTEM

2 Trambiyo = 1 Dokda
1-1/2 Dokda = 1 Dhingla

Mughal Issues

In the name of Shah Jahan III

DOKDO

COPPER
Rev: 1825 incuse in panel.

C#	Date	Year	Good	VG	Fine	VF
15b	1825	—	3.00	5.00	8.00	12.00

NOTE: Acutal date of striking unknown.

In the name of Muhammad Akbar II
AH1221-1253/1806-1837AD

DHINGLO

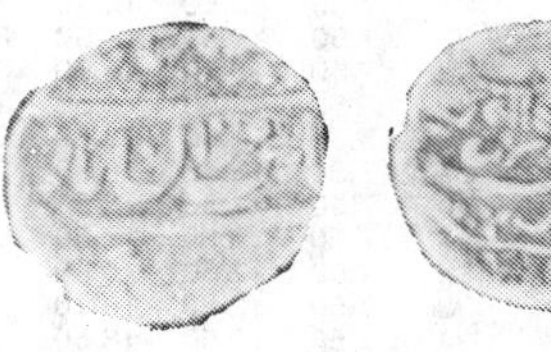

COPPER

C#	Date	Year	Good	VG	Fine	VF
30	ND	—	3.00	5.00	8.00	12.00

BHOPAL

Bhopal was the second largest Muslim state located in central India. It was founded in 1723 by Dost Muhammed Khan, an Afghan adventurer of the Mirazi Khel clan, who was in the service of Aurangzeb. After the Emperor's death in 1707 Dost Muhammed asserted his independence. Early in the following century his successors, threatened by the Marathas and subjected to Pindari raids into their territory, sought to cultivate a good relationship with the British. In 1817, at the time of the Maratha and Pindari War, Bhopal signed a treaty with the British East India Company which placed them squarely under imperial protection and control. After 1897 the British rupee was recognized as the only legal tender.

RULERS

Kudsia Begam,
AH1235-1253/1819-1837AD
Jahangir Muhammad Khan,
AH1253-1261/1837-1844AD
Sikandar Begam,
AH1261-1285/1844-1868AD
Shah Jahan Begam,
AH1285-1319/1868-1901AD

Mint

Bhopal

Mughal Issues

In the name of Muhammad Akbar II
AH1221-1253/1806-1837AD

1/8 RUPEE

SILVER, 12mm, 1.34-1.45 g

C#	Date	Year	VG	Fine	VF	XF
24	AH—	11	7.00	11.00	16.50	25.00
	—	16	7.00	11.00	16.50	25.00
	—	29	7.00	11.00	16.50	25.00

1/4 RUPEE

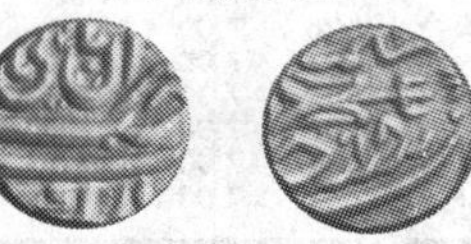

SILVER, 13mm, 2.68-2.90 g

C#	Date	Year	VG	Fine	VF	XF
25	AH—	16	6.50	10.00	15.00	22.50
	—	18	6.50	10.00	15.00	22.50
	—	26	6.50	10.00	15.00	22.50
	—	29	6.50	10.00	15.00	22.50

1/2 RUPEE

SILVER, 15mm, 5.35-5.80 g

C#	Date	Year	VG	Fine	VF	XF
26	AH—	9	7.00	11.00	16.50	25.00
	—	16	7.00	11.00	16.50	25.00
	—	29	7.00	11.00	16.50	25.00

RUPEE

SILVER, 10.70-11.60 g

C#	Date	Year	VG	Fine	VF	XF
27	AH—	1	7.50	12.50	18.50	27.50
	—	4	7.50	12.50	18.50	27.50
	—	5	7.50	12.50	18.50	27.50
	—	6	7.50	12.50	18.50	27.50
	—	7	7.50	12.50	18.50	27.50
	—	8	7.50	12.50	18.50	27.50
	—	9	7.50	12.50	18.50	27.50
	—	10	7.50	12.50	18.50	27.50
	—	11	7.50	12.50	18.50	27.50
	—	12	7.50	12.50	18.50	27.50
	—	13	7.50	12.50	18.50	27.50
	—	14	7.50	12.50	18.50	27.50
	—	15	7.50	12.50	18.50	27.50
	—	16	7.50	12.50	18.50	27.50
	—	17	7.50	12.50	18.50	27.50
	—	18	7.50	12.50	18.50	27.50
	—	19	7.50	12.50	18.50	27.50
	—	20	7.50	12.50	18.50	27.50
	—	21	7.50	12.50	18.50	27.50
	—	22	7.50	12.50	18.50	27.50
	—	23	7.50	12.50	18.50	27.50
	—	25	7.50	12.50	18.50	27.50
	—	26	7.50	12.50	18.50	27.50
	—	27	7.50	12.50	18.50	27.50
	—	30	7.50	12.50	18.50	27.50
	—	31	7.50	12.50	18.50	27.50
	—	32	7.50	12.50	18.50	27.50
	—	33	7.50	12.50	18.50	27.50
	—	34	7.50	12.50	18.50	27.50
	—	35	7.50	12.50	18.50	27.50

Anonymous Issues

PAISA

COPPER, 21-22mm
Obv: *Bhopal*. Rev: Year in circle.

C#	Date	Year	Good	VG	Fine	VF
20	—	25	2.00	3.25	5.00	8.50
	—	29	2.00	3.25	5.00	8.50

Rev: Whisk.

C#	Date	Year	Good	VG	Fine	VF
21	—	28	4.00	6.50	10.00	17.50

UNIFACE PAISA

COPPER
Persian *Bhopal* in circular depressed area.

C#	Date	Year	Good	VG	Fine	VF
20a	ND	—	3.00	5.00	8.00	12.50

Persian *Sikka Bhopal* and date.

C#	Date	Year	Good	VG	Fine	VF
21a	AH1255	—	3.00	5.00	8.00	12.50

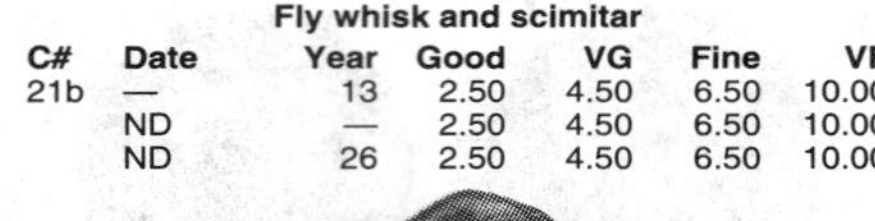

Fly whisk and scimitar

C#	Date	Year	Good	VG	Fine	VF
21b	—	13	2.50	4.50	6.50	10.00
	ND	—	2.50	4.50	6.50	10.00
	ND	26	2.50	4.50	6.50	10.00

Persian *Fateh* and scimitar.

C#	Date	Year	Good	VG	Fine	VF
21c	ND	8	2.50	4.50	6.50	10.00

Persian *Jim* and year

C#	Date	Year	Good	VG	Fine	VF
21d	ND	5	2.00	3.25	5.00	8.50
		10	2.00	3.25	5.00	8.50
		11	2.00	3.25	5.00	8.50
		12	2.00	3.25	5.00	8.50
		47	2.00	3.25	5.00	8.50

Persian *Fateh* w/o scimitar.

C#	Date	Year	Good	VG	Fine	VF
21e	ND	—	—	—	—	—

1/4 ANNA

COPPER, 7.00-8.00 g
Rev: Denomination.

Y#	Date	Year	Good	VG	Fine	VF
1	AH1266	—	1.50	2.25	3.50	6.50
	1269	—	1.50	2.25	3.50	6.50
	1270	—	1.50	2.25	3.50	6.50
	1272	—	1.50	2.25	3.50	6.50
	1273	—	1.50	2.25	3.50	6.50
	1276	—	1.50	2.25	3.50	6.50
	1279	—	1.50	2.25	3.50	6.50
	1282	—	1.50	2.25	3.50	6.50

Rev: Date and denomination.

Y#	Date	Year	Good	VG	Fine	VF
4.1	AH1285	—	1.00	1.75	2.50	4.50

Y#	Date	Year	Good	VG	Fine	VF
4.2	AH1285	—	1.00	1.75	2.50	4.50
	1286	—	1.00	1.75	2.50	4.50
	1287	—	1.00	1.75	2.50	4.50
	1288	—	1.00	1.75	2.50	4.50
	1289	—	1.00	1.75	2.50	4.50
	1292	—	1.00	1.75	2.50	4.50
	1293	—	1.00	1.75	2.50	4.50
	1296	—	1.00	1.75	2.50	4.50
	1299	—	1.00	1.75	2.50	4.50
	1300	—	1.00	1.75	2.50	4.50

NOTE: Coins dated 1286 exist w/o word *Hejira* above date on reverse, and w/split date.

1/2 ANNA

COPPER, 20-21mm
Rev: Denomination.

Y#	Date	Year	Good	VG	Fine	VF
2	AH1276	—	2.00	3.25	5.00	8.50
	1278	—	2.00	3.25	5.00	8.50
	1285	—	2.00	3.25	5.00	8.50

Rev: Date and denomination.

Y#	Date	Year	Good	VG	Fine	VF
5	AH1286	—	2.00	3.25	5.00	8.50
	1289	—	2.00	3.25	5.00	8.50
	1299	—	2.00	3.25	5.00	8.50
	1300	—	2.00	3.25	5.00	8.50

ANNA

COPPER
Rev: Denomination.

Y#	Date	Year	Good	VG	Fine	VF
3	AH1276	—	3.00	5.00	10.00	15.00

27-30mm
Rev: Date and denomination.

Y#	Date	Year	Good	VG	Fine	VF
6	AH1286	—	4.00	6.50	12.50	18.00
	1288	—	4.00	6.50	12.50	18.00
	1289	—	4.00	6.50	12.50	18.00
	1300	—	4.00	6.50	12.50	18.00

1/8 RUPEE

SILVER, 1.34-1.45 g
Obv: *Zarb* above *Bhopal*.

Y#	Date	Year	VG	Fine	VF	XF
7	AH1271	5	4.50	9.00	15.00	22.00
	1275	—	4.50	9.00	15.00	22.00
	1288	7	4.50	9.00	15.00	22.00
	1289	8	4.50	9.00	15.00	22.00
	1291	8	4.50	9.00	15.00	22.00

Obv: *Zarb* below *Bhopal*.

Y#	Date	Year	VG	Fine	VF	XF
11	AH129x	8	4.25	8.50	14.00	20.00
	1294	9	4.25	8.50	14.00	20.00
	1303	15	4.25	8.50	14.00	20.00
	1306	17	4.25	8.50	14.00	20.00

1/4 RUPEE

SILVER, 2.68-2.90 g
Obv: *Zarb* above *Bhopal*.

Y#	Date	Year	VG	Fine	VF	XF
8	AH1275	—	4.25	8.50	14.00	20.00
	1282	2	4.25	8.50	14.00	20.00
	1283	2	4.25	8.50	14.00	20.00
	1284	8	4.25	8.50	14.00	20.00
	1285	8	4.25	8.50	14.00	20.00
	1287	8	4.25	8.50	14.00	20.00
	1288	8	4.25	8.50	14.00	20.00

Obv: *Zarb* below *Bhopal*.

Y#	Date	Year	VG	Fine	VF	XF
12	AH1293	8	3.75	7.50	12.50	18.50
	1294	9	3.75	7.50	12.50	18.50
	1295	10	3.75	7.50	12.50	18.50
	1297	12	3.75	7.50	12.50	18.50
	1301	—	3.75	7.50	12.50	18.50
	1303	15	3.75	7.50	12.50	18.50
	1305	16	3.75	7.50	12.50	18.50

1/2 RUPEE

SILVER, 5.35-5.80 g
Obv: *Zarb* above *Bhopal*.

Y#	Date	Year	VG	Fine	VF	XF
9	AH1275	—	5.00	10.00	17.50	25.00
	1278	—	5.00	10.00	17.50	25.00
	1279	5	5.00	10.00	17.50	25.00
	1280	—	5.00	10.00	17.50	25.00
	1281	—	5.00	10.00	17.50	25.00
	1282	2	5.00	10.00	17.50	25.00
	1283	8	4.50	9.00	15.00	22.00
	1285	5	4.50	9.00	15.00	22.00
	1287	8	4.50	9.00	15.00	22.00
	1288	7	4.50	9.00	15.00	22.00
	1288	8	4.50	9.00	15.00	22.00
	1289	8	4.50	9.00	15.00	22.00
	1291	8	4.50	9.00	15.00	22.00
	1292	8	4.50	9.00	15.00	22.00

Obv: *Zarb* below *Bhopal*.

Y#	Date	Year	VG	Fine	VF	XF
13	AH1294	4	4.25	8.50	14.00	20.00
	1294	9	4.25	8.50	14.00	20.00
	1295	—	4.25	8.50	14.00	20.00
	1296	11	4.25	8.50	14.00	20.00
	1298	13	4.25	8.50	14.00	20.00
	130(2)	14	4.25	8.50	14.00	20.00
	1303	15	4.25	8.50	14.00	20.00
	1306	17	4.25	8.50	14.00	20.00
	130(5)	16	4.25	8.50	14.00	20.00
	1307	19	4.25	8.50	14.00	20.00
	1308	20	4.25	8.50	14.00	20.00
	130x	24	4.25	8.50	14.00	20.00

RUPEE

SILVER, 10.70-11.60 g
Obv: *Zarb* above *Bhopal*.

Y#	Date	Year	VG	Fine	VF	XF
10	AH1271	5	6.00	12.00	20.00	28.00
	1272	—	6.00	12.00	20.00	28.00
	1275	—	6.00	12.00	20.00	28.00
	1276	—	6.00	12.00	20.00	28.00
	1277	—	6.00	12.00	20.00	28.00
	1278	2	6.00	12.00	20.00	28.00
	1279	3	6.00	12.00	20.00	28.00
	1279	4	6.00	12.00	20.00	28.00
	1279	5	6.00	12.00	20.00	28.00
	1280	5	6.00	12.00	20.00	28.00
	1281	8	6.00	12.00	20.00	28.00
	1282	2	6.00	12.00	20.00	28.00
	1282	6	6.00	12.00	20.00	28.00
	1282	8	6.00	12.00	20.00	28.00
	1283	7	6.00	12.00	20.00	28.00
	1283	8	6.00	12.00	20.00	28.00
	1284	8	6.00	12.00	20.00	28.00
	1285	5	6.00	12.00	20.00	28.00
	1285	8	6.00	12.00	20.00	28.00
	1288	7	6.00	12.00	20.00	28.00
	1288	8	6.00	12.00	20.00	28.00
	1289	8	6.00	12.00	20.00	28.00
	1289	9	6.00	12.00	20.00	28.00
	1291	8	6.00	12.00	20.00	28.00
	1292	8	6.00	12.00	20.00	28.00
	1293	8	6.00	12.00	20.00	28.00

Obv: *Zarb* below *Bhopal*.

Y#	Date	Year	VG	Fine	VF	XF
14	AH1293	8	5.00	10.00	17.50	25.00
	1294	8	5.00	10.00	17.50	25.00
	1294	9	5.00	10.00	17.50	25.00
	1295	10	5.00	10.00	17.50	25.00
	1295	11	5.00	10.00	17.50	25.00
	1296	11	5.00	10.00	17.50	25.00
	1297	12	5.00	10.00	17.50	25.00
	1298	9	5.00	10.00	17.50	25.00
	1298	10	5.00	10.00	17.50	25.00
	1298	13	5.00	10.00	17.50	25.00
	1298	15	5.00	10.00	17.50	25.00
	1302	14	5.00	10.00	17.50	25.00
	1304	15	5.00	10.00	17.50	25.00
	1305	16	5.00	10.00	17.50	25.00
	1306	17	5.00	10.00	17.50	25.00
	1308	14	5.00	10.00	17.50	25.00

Anonymous Issues

NAZARANA RUPEE

SILVER, 10.85 g
Obv. and rev: Kalima.

KM#	Date	Year	Fine	VF	XF	Unc
A14	AH1286	2	—	—	200.00	350.00

1-1/2 NAZARANA RUPEES

SILVER, 16.44 g

KM#	Date	Year	Fine	VF	XF	Unc
B14	AH1286	2	—	—	250.00	400.00

2 NAZARANA RUPEES

SILVER, 21.40-23.20 g

KM#	Date	Year	Fine	VF	XF	Unc
C14	AH1286	2	—	—	300.00	500.00

SHAH JAHAN BEGAM

AH1285-1319/1868-1901AD

PIE (or 1/2 Paisa)

COPPER

Y#	Date	Year	Good	VG	Fine	VF
15	AH1305	—	1.50	2.25	3.50	6.50
	1306	—	1.50	2.25	3.50	6.50

1/4 ANNA

COPPER

Y#	Date	Year	Good	VG	Fine	VF
16	AH1302	—	1.00	1.75	2.50	4.50
	1303	—	1.00	1.75	2.50	4.50
	1305	—	1.00	1.75	2.50	4.50
	1306	—	1.00	1.75	2.50	4.50

1/2 ANNA

COPPER

Y#	Date	Year	Good	VG	Fine	VF
17.1	AH1302	—	1.25	2.00	3.00	5.50
	1303	—	1.25	2.00	3.00	5.50
	1304	—	1.25	2.00	3.00	5.50
	1305	—	1.25	2.00	3.00	5.50
	1306	—	1.25	2.00	3.00	5.50

Large flan.

Y#	Date	Year	Good	VG	Fine	VF
17.2	AH1309	—	2.00	3.25	5.00	8.50

ANNA

COPPER

Y#	Date	Year	Good	VG	Fine	VF
18	AH1302	—	2.50	4.50	6.50	10.00
	1303	—	2.50	4.50	6.50	10.00
	1304	—	2.50	4.50	6.50	10.00
	1305	—	2.50	4.50	6.50	10.00
	1306	—	2.50	4.50	6.50	10.00

Struck from 1/2 Anna dies

Y#	Date	Year	Good	VG	Fine	VF
18a	—	—	2.50	4.50	6.50	10.00

NAZARANA ANNA

COPPER, 30.20 g

Y#	Date	Year	Good	VG	Fine	VF
18b	AH1303	—	—	—	Rare	—

BHOPAL FEUDATORY

NARSINGHGARH

The Rajput rulers of this feudatory traced their origins back into the fourteenth century when their ancestors migrated from Malwa through Sind before settling at Narsinghgarh.

PAISA

COPPER

KM#	Date	Year	Good	VG	Fine	VF
1 (Y91)	ND	—	2.50	4.50	6.50	10.00

BIJAWAR

State located in Bundelkhand District in north-central India. The rulers of Bijawar were Bundela Rajputs. They were descended from Maharaja Chhatarsal who, earlier, having ruled a much larger territory, became forebearer to a number of Rajput royal families in the region. As far as the British were concerned, the authority of the rulers of Bijawar stemmed from a mandate issued by the East India Company in 1811 which required, in return, a guarantee of allegiance. In 1866 the ruler became a maharaja.

RULERS

Lakshman Singh, 1833-1847AD
Bhau Pratap Singh, 1847-1900AD

In the name of Shah Alam II

AH1173-1221/1759-1806AD

RUPEE

SILVER, 10.70-11.60 g

KM#	Date	Year	VG	Fine	VF	XF
15	ND	—	12.50	21.00	28.50	40.00

BIKANIR

Bikanir, located in Rajputana was established as a state sometime between 1465 and 1504 by Jodhpur Rathor Rajput named Rao Bikaji. During the period of the Great Mughals Bikanir was intimately linked to Delhi by ties of both loyalty and marriage. Both Akbar and Jahangir contracted marriages with princesses of the Bikanir Rajputs, and the Bikanir nobility rendered outstanding service in the Mughal armies. Bikanir came under British influence in 1817 and after 1947 was incorporated into Rajasthan.

RULERS

Surat Singh,
AH1204-1244/1788-1828AD
Ratan Singh,
AH1244-1268/1828-1851AD
Sardar Singh,
AH1268-1289/1851-1872AD
Dungar Singh,
AH1289-1305/1872-1887AD
Ganga Singhji,
VS1944-1999/1887-1942AD

MINT

Bikanir بيكنير or بيكانير

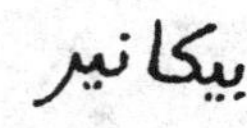

RULER'S SYMBOLS

1. Gaj Singh, AH1159-1202

2. (")

3. Surat Singh, AH1202-1244

4. (")

5. (")

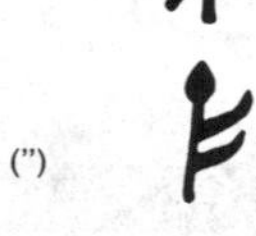

6. Ratan Singh, AH1244-1268 (2 Vars.)

7. Sardar Singh, AH1268-1289

8. Dungar Singh, AH1289-1305

9. Ganga Singh, VS1949-1999

NOTE: The above symbols normally occur in groups on the obverse or reverse of the coins; the various combinations are shown for each series.

Mughal Issues

SURAT SINGH

AH1202-1244/1787-1828AD

Regnal years of Shah Alam II

Years 28-52

RUPEE

SILVER, 10.70-11.60 g
Obv: Mark #1. Rev: Mark #3.

KM#	Date	Year	VG	Fine	VF	XF
17	AH1217	41	7.50	12.50	18.50	27.50
	1217	42	7.50	12.50	18.50	27.50
	1217	43	7.50	12.50	18.50	27.50
	1217	45	7.50	12.50	18.50	27.50
	1227	47	7.50	12.50	18.50	27.50
	1229	45	7.50	12.50	18.50	27.50
	1229	51	7.50	12.50	18.50	27.50
	1229	52	7.50	12.50	18.50	27.50

NOTE: Earlier dates (AH1204-1209) exist for this type.

In the name of Shah Alam II

AH1173-1221/1759-1806AD

RATAN SINGH

AH1244-1268/1828-1851AD

In the name of Alamgir II

AH1167-1173/1754-1759AD

1/2 PAISA

COPPER

KM#	Date	Year	Good	VG	Fine	VF
20	ND	—	—	—	—	—

PAISA

COPPER, 7.4-8 g
Rev: Mark #6.

KM#	Date	Year	Good	VG	Fine	VF
22	ND	25	.75	1.25	2.00	3.00
	—	41	.75	1.25	2.00	3.00

TAKKA

COPPER, 16-17 g
Rev: Mark #6.

KM#	Date	Year	Good	VG	Fine	VF
23	ND	41	.75	1.25	2.00	3.00

NOTE: So called year 21 is debased copy of year 41.

Regnal years of Muhammad Akbar II

Years 21-52

RUPEE

SILVER, 10.70-11.60 g
Obv: Mark #1. Rev: Marks #3 and 6.

KM#	Date	Year	VG	Fine	VF	XF
32	AH1229	25	7.00	11.00	16.50	25.00
	1229	31	7.00	11.00	16.50	25.00
	1229	32	7.00	11.00	16.50	25.00
	1229	41	7.00	11.00	16.50	25.00
	1229	47	7.00	11.00	16.50	25.00

In the name of Shah Alam II

AH1173-1221/1759-1806AD

NAZARANA RUPEE

SILVER, 10.70-11.60 g

KM#	Date	Year	VG	Fine	VF	XF
32a	AH1229	25	25.00	37.50	50.00	70.00

SARDAR SINGH

AH1268-1289/1851-1872AD

In the Name of Alamgir II

AH1167-1173/1754-1759AD

1/2 PAISA

COPPER, 17mm, 7.3-7.6 g

KM#	Date	Year	Good	VG	Fine	VF
34	AH1229	18	2.00	3.00	4.50	6.50

Regnal years of Bahadur Shah II

Years 18-21

RUPEE

SILVER, 10.70-11.60 g
Rev: Marks #1, 4 (or 5), 6, and 7.
Years of Bahadur Shah II

KM#	Date	Year	VG	Fine	VF	XF
37	AH1229	18	6.00	9.00	13.50	20.00
	1229	21	6.00	9.00	13.50	20.00

NAZARANA RUPEE

SILVER, 29mm, 10.70-11.60 g

KM#	Date	Year	VG	Fine	VF	XF
37a	AH1229	21	32.50	45.00	62.50	85.00

Regal Issues

In the Name of Queen Victoria

Beginning 1859AD

Reverse marks from left to right: #6, 7, 2, 5.

All types in this series from KM41 to KM54a carry the frozen years VS1916/1859AD.

PAISA

COPPER, 7.4-7.7 g

KM#	Date	Year	Good	VG	Fine	VF
41	VS1916	1859	.75	1.25	2.00	3.00

1/8 RUPEE

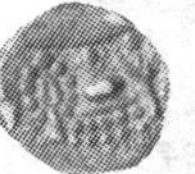

SILVER, 11-12mm, 1.40 g

KM#	Date	Year	VG	Fine	VF	XF
42	VS1916	1859	4.00	6.00	9.00	13.50

1/4 RUPEE

SILVER, 15mm, 2.80 g

KM#	Date	Year	VG	Fine	VF	XF
43	VS1916	1859	5.00	7.00	10.00	15.00

1/2 RUPEE

SILVER, 18mm, 5.60 g

KM#	Date	Year	VG	Fine	VF	XF
44	VS1916	1859	6.00	9.00	12.50	18.50

RUPEE

SILVER, 11.30 g

KM#	Date	Year	VG	Fine	VF	XF
45	VS1916	1859	7.00	11.00	16.50	25.00
	1912 error for 1916		—	—	—	—

NAZARANA RUPEE

SILVER, 30mm, 11.35 g

KM#	Date	Year	VG	Fine	VF	XF
46	VS1916	1859	37.50	52.50	75.00	110.00

Local Issues

SARDAR SINGH

VS1908-1929/1851-1872AD

Reverse marks, left to right: #6, 7, 8, 2, 5.

PAISA

COPPER, 7.5-7.75 g

KM#	Date	Year	Good	VG	Fine	VF
50	VS1916	1859	.75	1.25	2.00	3.00

1/8 RUPEE

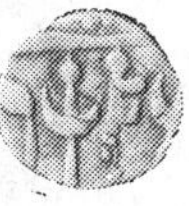

SILVER, 12mm, 1.40 g

KM#	Date	Year	VG	Fine	VF	XF
51	VS1916	1859	4.00	6.00	9.00	13.50

1/4 RUPEE

SILVER, 14mm, 2.80 g

KM#	Date	Year	VG	Fine	VF	XF
52	VS1916	1859	5.00	7.00	10.00	15.00

1/2 RUPEE

SILVER, 17mm, 5.60 g

KM#	Date	Year	VG	Fine	VF	XF
53	VS1916	1859	6.00	9.00	12.50	18.50

RUPEE

SILVER, 11.30-11.35 g

KM#	Date	Year	VG	Fine	VF	XF
54	VS1916	1859	7.00	11.00	16.50	25.00

NAZARANA RUPEE

SILVER, 30mm, 11.35 g

KM#	Date	Year	VG	Fine	VF	XF
54a	VS1916	1859	37.50	52.50	75.00	110.00

GANGA SINGH

VS1944-1999/SE1965-2020/1887-1942AD

Reverse marks, left to right: #6, 7, 9, 8, 2, 5. All dump coins w/frozen date VS1916/1859AD and actual VS date.

PAISA

COPPER, 18mm, 5.6-5.9 g

KM#	Date	Year	Good	VG	Fine	VF
61	VS1946	(1889)	1.75	2.50	3.50	5.00

NAZARANA PAISA

COPPER

KM#	Date	Year	Good	VG	Fine	VF
60	VS1946	(1889)	—	—	Rare	—

1/8 RUPEE

SILVER, 12mm, 1.40 g

KM#	Date	Year	VG	Fine	VF	XF
62	VS1944	(1887)	4.00	6.00	9.00	13.50

1/4 RUPEE

SILVER, 2.80 g

KM#	Date	Year	VG	Fine	VF	XF
63	VS1944	(1887)	5.00	7.00	10.00	15.00

1/2 RUPEE

SILVER, 5.70 g

KM#	Date	Year	VG	Fine	VF	XF
64	VS1944	(1887)	6.00	9.00	12.50	18.00

RUPEE

SILVER, 11.40 g

KM#	Date	Year	VG	Fine	VF	XF
65	VS1944	(1887)	7.00	11.00	16.50	25.00

NAZARANA RUPEE

KM#	Date	Year	VG	Fine	VF	XF
	SILVER, 30mm, 10.70-11.60 g					
65a	VS1944	(1887)	37.50	52.50	75.00	110.00
	SILVER, 22-23mm					
65b	VS1946	(1889)	100.00	150.00	225.00	325.00

Milled Coinage

1/2 PICE

KM#	Date	Mintage	Fine	VF	XF	Unc
	COPPER					
70	1894	.500	5.00	12.00	20.00	35.00
	1894	—	—	—	Proof	100.00
	SILVER					
70a	1894	(restrike)	—	—	Proof	125.00
	GOLD					
70b	1894	(restrike)	—	—	Proof	450.00

1/4 ANNA

KM#	Date	Mintage	Fine	VF	XF	Unc
	COPPER					
71	1895	6.156	4.00	10.00	17.50	30.00
	1895	—	—	—	Proof	125.00
	SILVER					
71a	1895	(restrike)	—	—	Proof	125.00
	GOLD					
71b	1895	(restrike)	—	—	Proof	650.00

RUPEE

SILVER, 11.66 g

KM#	Date	Mintage	Fine	VF	XF	Unc
72	1892	.596	7.50	12.50	18.50	27.50
	1892	—	—	—	Proof	200.00
	1897	.111	20.00	31.50	42.50	60.00
	1897	—	—	—	Proof	200.00

BINDRABAN

This city, the modern Vrindavan, was not a princely state. The area surrounding the city, including the neighboring city of Mathura, was under Jat control in the mid-eighteenth century, although nominally subject to Awadh. After varying fortunes the area passed to the East India Company in 1803-05 (i.e. AH1217-1220; VS18601862). The coins below display symbols of Awadh, Mughals, Delhi and Bhartpur, although it is clear that they were not mints of any of those authorities, especially in the British period.

MINTS AND MINTNAMES

Bindraban	بندرابن
Muminabad	مومن اباد
Shahjahanabad	شاهجهان اباد
Gokul	گوکل
Mathura Islamabad	اسلام اباد

BINDRABAN MINT

MINTNAMES

Muminabad	مومن اباد
Shahjahanabad	شاهجهان اباد

Mughal Issues

In the name of Shah Alam II

AH1173-1221/1759-1806AD

PAISA

COPPER

Mintname: *Muminabad.*

KM#	Date	Year	Good	VG	Fine	VF
5	AH1216	44	1.75	2.50	4.00	7.50

NOTE: Earlier dates (AH1211-1212) exist for this type.

RUPEE

SILVER, 10.70-11.60 g
Rev: Trident and 5 trident figure.

KM#	Date	Year	VG	Fine	VF	XF
10.6	AH1217	45	11.50	17.50	23.50	32.50

Local Issues

In the name of Queen Victoria

1/4 RUPEE

SILVER, 2.68-2.90 g

KM#	Date	Year	VG	Fine	VF	XF
16	VS1915	1858	20.00	35.00	50.00	70.00
	1916	1859	20.00	35.00	50.00	70.00
	1924	1867	20.00	35.00	50.00	70.00

1/2 RUPEE

SILVER, 5.35-5.80 g

KM#	Date	Year	VG	Fine	VF	XF
17	VS1915	1858	22.50	38.50	55.00	80.00
	1916	1859	22.50	38.50	55.00	80.00
	1924	1867	22.50	38.50	55.00	80.00

RUPEE

SILVER, 10.70-11.60 g

KM#	Date	Year	VG	Fine	VF	XF
18	VS1915	1858	30.00	50.00	75.00	110.00
	1916	1859	30.00	50.00	75.00	110.00

Rev: *Fazl Hami-din*

KM#	Date	Year	VG	Fine	VF	XF
19	AD1867	12	35.00	60.00	85.00	120.00

MATHURA MINT

MINTNAME

Islamabad اسلام آباد

In the name of Muhammad Akbar II
AH1221-1253/1806-1837AD

1/2 PAISA

COPPER, 3.00 g
Similar to 1 Paisa, KM#35, but w/royal leg.

KM#	Date	Year	Good	VG	Fine	VF
51	ND	—	2.50	3.50	5.00	7.00

PAISA

COPPER, 6.00 g
Similar to 1/2 Paisa, KM#51.

KM#	Date	Year	Good	VG	Fine	VF
52	ND	—	2.25	3.25	5.00	8.50

BROACH

From very early times Broach, located on the north bank of the Narmada River 30 miles from the Gulf of Cambay, was an important port on the sea route to Europe. It was known as Barakacheva to early Chinese travellers, and as Barygaza to Ptolemy. After the Islamic invasions of India it was incorporated into the Muslim kingdom of Gujerat and remained so until 1572 when it was annexed by Akbar. During the reign of Aurangzeb, Broach first began to experience Maratha incursions. In 1772, it came briefly under British influence before being ceded to Sindhia in 1783. It was returned to the East India Company in 1803 and thereafter remained in British control.

RULERS

To British 1772-1783 and 1803 on
To Gwalior 1783-1803

MINT

Broach

Mint marks:

Cross **(Gwalior and E.I.C.)**

EAST INDIA COMPANY

1/2 RUPEE

SILVER, 5.35-5.80 g
Rev: Cross.

C#	Date	Year	VG	Fine	VF	XF
A36	ND	—	17.50	25.00	35.00	50.00

RUPEE

SILVER, 10.70-11.60 g

C#	Date	Year	VG	Fine	VF	XF
36	AH—	2x	22.50	31.50	42.50	60.00

NOTE: Other coins with cross mint mark were probably also issued under the Sindhias. For other Broach issues see Gwalior.

BUNDI

State in Rajputana in northwest India.

Bundi was founded in 1342 by a Chauhan Rajput, Rao Dewa (Deoraj). Until the Maratha defeat early in the nineteenth century, Bundi was greatly harassed by the forces of Holkar and Sindhia. In 1818 it came under British protection and control and remained so until 1947. In 1948 the State was absorbed into Rajasthan.

RULERS

Ajit Singh, AH1185-1187/
VS1828-1830/1771-1773AD
Bishen Singh, AH1187-1236/
VS1830-1878/1773-1821AD
Ram Singh, AH1236-1306/
VS1878-1946/1824-1889AD
Raghubir Singh
VS1946-1984/1889-1927AD

MINT

Bundi بوندي

Mintname: Bundi

All of the coins of Bundi struck prior to the Mutiny (1857) are in the name of the Mughal emperor and bear the following 2 marks on the reverse, to the left and right of the regnal year, respectively:

On all Mughal issues:

Only on Muhammad Akbar and Muhammad Bahadur issues:

The same symbols appear on the coins of Kotah, but the difference is that the Kotah pieces have the mint name *Kotahurf Nandgaon* and later issues only have *Nandgaon.*

Mughal Issues

In the name of Muhammad Akbar II
AH1221-1253/1806-1837AD

TAKKA

COPPER, 17.50-18.00 g, round
W/leg: *Shah Akbar Bahadur Badshah Ghazi.*

C#	Date	Year	Good	VG	Fine	VF
15	AH—	1	2.50	3.50	4.50	6.00
	—	2	2.50	3.50	4.50	6.00
	—	3	2.50	3.50	4.50	6.00

W/leg: *Sahib Qiran Sani.*

C#	Date	Year	Good	VG	Fine	VF
17	AH—	3	1.25	2.00	3.00	4.50
	—	4	1.25	2.00	3.00	4.50
	—	5	1.25	2.00	3.00	4.50
	—	6	1.25	2.00	3.00	4.50
	—	7	1.25	2.00	3.00	4.50
	—	9	1.25	2.00	3.00	4.50
	—	11	1.25	2.00	3.00	4.50
	—	12	1.25	2.00	3.00	4.50
	—	13	1.25	2.00	3.00	4.50
	—	14	1.25	2.00	3.00	4.50
	—	15	1.50	2.50	3.50	5.00
	—	16	1.50	2.50	3.50	5.00

COPPER, 17.50-18.00 g, square
W/leg: *Sahib Qiran Sani.*

C#	Date	Year	Good	VG	Fine	VF
17a	AH—	4	1.50	2.50	3.50	5.00
	—	5	1.50	2.50	3.50	5.00
	—	6	1.50	2.50	3.50	5.00
	—	11	1.50	2.50	3.50	5.00
	—	14	1.50	2.50	3.50	5.00
	—	24	1.50	2.50	3.50	5.00
	—	25	1.25	2.00	3.00	4.50
	—	26	1.25	2.00	3.00	4.50

1/2 RUPEE

SILVER, 15mm, 5.50 g
W/leg: *Bad Shah Ghazi.*

C#	Date	Year	VG	Fine	VF	XF
25	AH—	1	11.50	17.50	23.50	32.50

RUPEE

SILVER, 11.10-11.15 g
W/leg: *Bad Shah Ghazi.*

C#	Date	Year	VG	Fine	VF	XF
29	AH—	1	10.00	15.00	21.00	30.00
	1222	2	10.00	15.00	21.00	30.00
	—	3	10.00	15.00	21.00	30.00

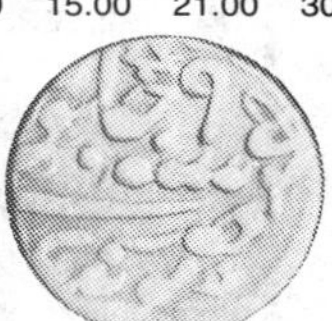

W/leg: *Sahib Qiran Sani.*

C#	Date	Year	VG	Fine	VF	XF
30	AH—	3	8.00	13.50	20.00	28.50
	—	5	8.00	13.50	20.00	28.50
	—	6	8.00	13.50	20.00	28.50
	—	9	8.00	13.50	20.00	28.50
	—	10	8.00	13.50	20.00	28.50
	—	11	8.00	13.50	20.00	28.50
	—	12	8.00	13.50	20.00	28.50
	—	13	8.00	13.50	20.00	28.50
	—	15	8.00	13.50	20.00	28.50
	—	16	8.00	13.50	20.00	28.50
	—	17	8.00	13.50	20.00	28.50
	—	18	8.00	13.50	20.00	28.50
	—	19	8.00	13.50	20.00	28.50
	—	20	8.00	13.50	20.00	28.50
	—	21	8.00	13.50	20.00	28.50
	—	22	8.00	13.50	20.00	28.50
	—	24	8.00	13.50	20.00	28.50
	—	27	8.00	13.50	20.00	28.50
	—	30	8.00	13.50	20.00	28.50
	—	31	8.00	13.50	20.00	28.50
	—	32	8.00	13.50	20.00	28.50
	—	33	8.00	13.50	20.00	28.50

Rev: Additional *Katar* above *Zarb.*

C#	Date	Year	VG	Fine	VF	XF
30a	AH—	20	16.50	27.50	40.00	58.00
	—	21	16.50	27.50	40.00	58.00

NAZARANA RUPEE

SILVER, 11.10 g, square

C#	Date	Year	VG	Fine	VF	XF
31	AH1246	25	10.00	15.00	21.00	30.00

MOHUR

GOLD, 10.70 g

C#	Date	Year	VG	Fine	VF	XF
33	AH—	15	220.00	240.00	265.00	300.00

In the name of Bahadur Shah II
AH1253-1274/1837-1858AD

TAKKA

COPPER, 20mm, 17.60-17.70 g

C#	Date	Year	Good	VG	Fine	VF
35	AH—	9	4.50	6.50	8.50	12.50
	—	11	4.50	6.50	8.50	12.50
	—	14	4.50	6.50	8.50	12.50
	—	19	4.50	6.50	8.50	12.50

RUPEE

SILVER, 19mm, 11.15-11.20 g

C#	Date	Year	VG	Fine	VF	XF
40	AH—	1	8.00	13.50	20.00	28.50
	—	2	8.00	13.50	20.00	28.50
	—	3	8.00	13.50	20.00	28.50
	—	4	8.00	13.50	20.00	28.50
	—	5	8.00	13.50	20.00	28.50
	—	6	8.00	13.50	20.00	28.50
	—	7	8.00	13.50	20.00	28.50
	—	8	8.00	13.50	20.00	28.50

C#	Date	Year	VG	Fine	VF	XF
40	—	9	8.00	13.50	20.00	28.50
	—	10	8.00	13.50	20.00	28.50
	—	12	8.00	13.50	20.00	28.50
	—	13	8.00	13.50	20.00	28.50
	—	14	8.00	13.50	20.00	28.50
	—	15	8.00	13.50	20.00	28.50
	—	16	8.00	13.50	20.00	28.50
	—	18	8.00	13.50	20.00	28.50
	—	19	8.00	13.50	20.00	28.50
	—	21	8.00	13.50	20.00	28.50

NAZARANA RUPEE

SILVER, square

C#	Date	Year	VG	Fine	VF	XF
40a	AH	5	—	—	—	—
	—	19	—	—	—	—

Regal Issues

In the name of Queen Victoria

Obv: AD date. Rev: VS date.

1/2 PAISA

COPPER, 9-11mm, 5.50 g
Obv. leg: VICTORIA QUEEN. Rev: Date.

Y#	Date	Year	Good	VG	Fine	VF
1	VS1924	1867	.75	1.25	2.25	3.50

PAISA

COPPER, 10.60-10.70 g

Y#	Date	Year	Good	VG	Fine	VF
2	VS1915	1858	.35	.65	1.00	1.50
	1924	1867	.25	.50	.85	1.25
	1934	1877	.25	.50	.85	1.25
	1935	1878	.25	.50	.85	1.25
	1936	1879	.25	.50	.85	1.25
	1940	1883	.25	.50	.85	1.25
	1942	1885	.25	.50	.85	1.25
	1943	1886	.25	.50	.85	1.25
	1944	1887	.25	.50	.85	1.25
	1945	1888	.25	.50	.85	1.25
	1946	1889	.25	.50	.85	1.25
	1947	—	.25	.50	.85	1.25
	1955	1898	.25	.50	.85	1.25

TAKKA

COPPER, 17.15-17.65 g

Y#	Date	Year	Good	VG	Fine	VF
3	VS1915	1858	.35	.85	1.25	1.75
	1919	1862	.35	.85	1.25	1.75
	1921	1864	.35	.85	1.25	1.75
	1922	1864	.35	.85	1.25	1.75
	1922	1865	.35	.85	1.25	1.75
	1923	1866	.35	.85	1.25	1.75
	1924	1867	.35	.85	1.25	1.75
	1925	1868	.35	.85	1.25	1.75
	1926	1869	.35	.85	1.25	1.75
	1928	1871	.35	.85	1.25	1.75
	1929	1872	.35	.85	1.25	1.75
	1932	1875	.35	.85	1.25	1.75
	1934	1877	.25	.50	.85	1.25
	1935	1878	.25	.50	.85	1.25
	1936	1879	.25	.50	.85	1.25
	1939	1882	.25	.50	.85	1.25
	1940	1883	.25	.50	.85	1.25
	1942	1885	.25	.50	.85	1.25
	1943	1886	.25	.50	.85	1.25
	1944	1887	.25	.50	.85	1.25
	1945	1888	.25	.50	.85	1.25
	1946	1889	.25	.50	.85	1.25
	1955	1898	.85	1.25	2.00	3.00
	1956	1894	.85	1.25	2.00	3.00
	1956	1898	.85	1.25	2.00	3.00
	1956	1899	1.25	2.25	3.50	5.00
	Date off flan		.65	1.10	1.75	2.50

1/4 RUPEE

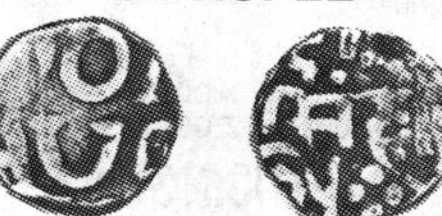

SILVER, 2.80 g

Y#	Date	Year	VG	Fine	VF	XF
4	VS1915	1858	4.00	6.00	9.00	13.50
	1935	1878	4.00	6.00	9.00	13.50
	1936	1879	4.00	6.00	9.00	13.50
	Date off flan		3.00	4.50	6.50	10.00

Y#	Date	Year	VG	Fine	VF	XF
7	VS1944	(1887)	5.00	7.00	10.00	15.00
	1946	(1889)	5.00	7.00	10.00	15.00
	1947	(1890)	4.00	6.00	9.00	13.50
	1953	(1896)	4.00	6.00	9.00	13.50
	1955	(1898)	4.00	6.00	9.00	13.50
	Date off flan		3.00	4.50	6.50	10.00

1/2 RUPEE

SILVER, 5.50-5.60 g

Y#	Date	Year	VG	Fine	VF	XF
5	VS1915	1858	5.00	7.00	10.00	15.00
	1930	1873	5.00	7.00	10.00	15.00
	1933	1876	5.00	7.00	10.00	15.00
	1937	1880	5.00	7.00	10.00	15.00
	1940	1883	5.00	7.00	10.00	15.00
	1941	1884	5.00	7.00	10.00	15.00
	1943	1886	5.00	7.00	10.00	15.00
	Date off flan		3.00	4.50	6.50	10.00

Y#	Date	Year	VG	Fine	VF	XF
8	VS1945	1888	5.50	8.00	12.50	18.50
	1946	(1889)	5.50	8.00	12.50	18.50
	1948	(1891)	5.00	7.00	10.00	15.00
	1949	(1892)	5.00	7.00	10.00	15.00
	1953	(1896)	5.50	8.00	12.50	18.50
	1954	(1897)	5.00	7.00	10.00	15.00
	1955	(1898)	5.50	8.00	12.50	18.50
	Date off flan		3.00	4.50	6.50	10.00

RUPEE

SILVER, 11.00-11.15 g

Y#	Date	Year	VG	Fine	VF	XF
6	VS1915	1858	6.00	9.00	13.50	20.00
	1915	1859	6.00	9.00	13.50	20.00
	1916	1859	6.50	10.00	15.00	22.50
	1916	1860	6.50	10.00	15.00	22.50
	1917	1860	6.00	9.00	13.50	20.00
	1918	1861	6.00	9.00	13.50	20.00
	1919	1862	6.00	9.00	13.50	20.00
	1920	1863	6.00	9.00	13.50	20.00
	1921	1864	6.00	9.00	13.50	20.00
	1922	1865	6.00	9.00	13.50	20.00
	1923	1866	6.00	9.00	13.50	20.00
	1924	1867	6.00	9.00	13.50	20.00
	1925	1868	6.00	9.00	13.50	20.00
	1925 (sic)	1864	6.00	9.00	13.50	20.00
	1926	1869	6.00	9.00	13.50	20.00
	1927	1870	6.00	9.00	13.50	20.00
	1928	1871	6.00	9.00	13.50	20.00
	1929	1872	6.00	9.00	13.50	20.00
	1930	1873	6.00	9.00	13.50	20.00
	1931	1874	6.00	9.00	13.50	20.00
	1932	1875	6.00	9.00	13.50	20.00
	1933	1876	6.00	9.00	13.50	20.00
	1934	1877	6.00	9.00	13.50	20.00
	1935	1878	6.00	9.00	13.50	20.00
	1936	1879	6.00	9.00	13.50	20.00
	1937	1880	6.00	9.00	13.50	20.00
	1938	1881	6.00	9.00	13.50	20.00
	1939	1882	6.00	9.00	13.50	20.00
	1940	1883	6.00	9.00	13.50	20.00
	1941	1884	6.00	9.00	13.50	20.00
	1942	1885	6.00	9.00	13.50	20.00
	1943	1886	6.00	9.00	13.50	20.00
	Date off flan		5.00	7.00	10.00	15.00

Y#	Date	Year	VG	Fine	VF	XF
9	VS1943	(1886)	6.00	9.00	13.50	20.00
	1944	(1887)	6.00	9.00	13.50	20.00
	1945	(1888)	6.00	9.00	13.50	20.00
	1946	(1889)	6.00	9.00	13.50	20.00
	1947	(1890)	6.00	9.00	13.50	20.00
	1948	(1891)	6.00	9.00	13.50	20.00
	1949	(1892)	6.00	9.00	13.50	20.00
	1950	(1893)	6.00	9.00	13.50	20.00
	1951	1894	6.00	9.00	13.50	20.00
	1953	(1894)	6.00	9.00	13.50	20.00
	1954	(1897)	6.00	9.00	13.50	20.00
	1955	(1898)	6.00	9.00	13.50	20.00
	1957	(1900)	6.00	9.00	13.50	20.00
	Date off flan		5.00	7.00	10.00	15.00

NAZARANA RUPEE

SILVER, 10.60-11.00 g, square

Y#	Date	Year	VG	Fine	VF	XF
6a	VS1915	1858	16.00	22.50	31.50	42.50
	1919	1862	16.00	22.50	31.50	42.50
	1925	1868	16.00	22.50	31.50	42.50
	1929	1872	16.00	22.50	31.50	42.50
	1932	1875	16.00	22.50	31.50	42.50
	1934	1877	16.00	22.50	31.50	42.50
	1935	1878	16.00	22.50	31.50	42.50
	1937	1880	16.00	22.50	31.50	42.50

Y#	Date	Year	VG	Fine	VF	XF
9a	VS1943	(1886)	35.00	50.00	70.00	110.00
	1945	(1888)	35.00	50.00	70.00	110.00
	1946	(1889)	35.00	50.00	70.00	110.00
	1947	(1890)	35.00	50.00	70.00	110.00
	1948	(1891)	35.00	50.00	70.00	110.00
	1949	(1892)	35.00	50.00	70.00	110.00
	1950	(1893)	35.00	50.00	70.00	110.00
	1951	(1894)	35.00	50.00	70.00	110.00
	1952	(1895)	35.00	50.00	70.00	110.00
	1953	(1896)	35.00	50.00	70.00	110.00

CAMBAY

Khanbayat

Although of very ancient origins as a port, located at the head of the Gulf of Cambay in West India, Cambay did not come into existence as a separate state until about 1730 after the breakdown of Mughal authority in Delhi. The nawabs of Cambay traced their ancestry to Momin Khan II, the last of the Muslim governors of Gujerat. The State came under British control after two decades of Maratha rule.

RULERS

Hussain Yafar Khan,
AH1257-1297/1841-1880AD

Ja'far Ali Khan,
AH1297-1333/VS1937-1972/1880-1915AD

Mint: Khanbayat 

HUSSAIN YAFAR KHAN

AH1257-1297/1841-1880AD

In the name of Shah Alam II

FALUS

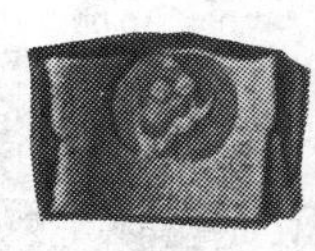

COPPER
Obv. c/m: Persian *Shah* on irregular planchets.

Y#	Date	Year	Good	VG	Fine	VF
A1	ND	—	4.00	5.00	6.50	8.00

RUPEE

SILVER, 10.70-11.60 g

Y#	Date	Year	VG	Fine	VF	XF
1	AH1282	—	8.50	13.50	20.00	28.50
	1294	—	8.50	13.50	20.00	28.50

NOTE: Fractional denominations are reported to exist.

JA'FAR ALI KHAN

AH1297-1333/VS1937-1972/1880-1915AD

In the name of Ja'far Ali Khan

1/8 RUPEE

SILVER, 11mm, 1.34-1.45 g

Y#	Date	Year	VG	Fine	VF	XF
7	AH1313	—	6.50	10.00	15.00	22.50

1/4 RUPEE

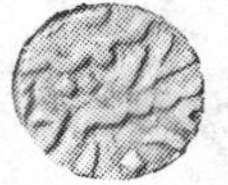

SILVER, 14mm, 2.68-2.90 g

Y#	Date	Year	VG	Fine	VF	XF
8	AH1313	—	7.00	11.00	16.50	25.00

1/2 RUPEE

SILVER, 5.35-5.80 g

Y#	Date	Year	VG	Fine	VF	XF
9	AH1313	17	10.00	15.00	21.50	30.00
	1317	—	10.00	15.00	21.50	30.00

RUPEE

SILVER, 10.70-11.60 g

Y#	Date	Year	VG	Fine	VF	XF
10	AH1311	—	15.00	21.50	30.00	40.00
	1313	17	15.00	21.50	30.00	40.00
	1317	21	15.00	21.50	30.00	40.00

NOTE: Later date (AH1319) exists for this type.

CANNANORE

Cannanore, on the Malabar Coast in southwest India was ruled by the Cherakal Rajas. Late in the eighteenth century it was overrun by Haider Ali, the Muslim ruler of Mysore. Then, in AH1198/1783, Cannanore was captured from Haider Ali's son, Tipu Sultan, by the East India Company. From that time onwards Cannanore was reduced to the status of a British tributary.

RULERS

Ali Rajas, Lord's of the deep,
AH1122-1231/1710-1815AD

1/5 RUPEE

SILVER, 2.14-2.32 g

KM#	Date	Year	VG	Fine	VF	XF
5	AH1220	—	4.00	7.00	10.00	15.00
	1221	—	4.00	7.00	10.00	15.00
	1231	—	4.00	7.00	10.00	15.00
	1241	—	4.00	7.00	10.00	15.00
	1631(error)	—	4.00	7.00	10.00	15.00
	8711(error)	—	4.00	7.00	10.00	15.00

NOTE: Varieties exist.

CHAMBA

The rulers of this mountainous state in north India, the origins of which go back as far as the sixth century, were Rajputs. Although Chamba was sometimes subject to the rulers of Kashmir, and later to the Mughals, even when nominally in subjection the remoteness of the region gave its rulers a considerable degree of autonomy. In 1846 the State came under British protection and in 1948 was merged into Himachal Pradesh.

RULERS

Charhat Singh, 1808-1844AD
Lakar Shah of Basoli, rebel, 1844AD
Sri Singh, 1844-1870AD
Sham Singh, 1870-1904AD

Mint mark: 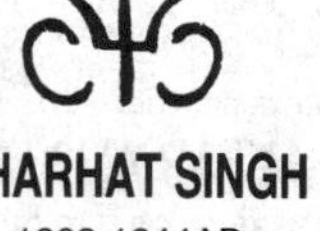

CHARHAT SINGH

1808-1844AD

1/2 PAISA

COPPER

KM#	Date	Year	Good	VG	Fine	VF
2	ND	—	10.00	15.00	22.00	30.00

PAISA

COPPER

KM#	Date	Year	Good	VG	Fine	VF
3	AH—	15	7.00	11.00	16.50	25.00
	—	16	7.00	11.00	16.50	25.00
	—	17	7.00	11.00	16.50	25.00
	ND	—	5.50	8.50	13.50	20.00

LAKAR SHAH of BASOLI

Rebel, 1844AD

PAISA

COPPER, 18-22mm
Obv: W/o trident below leg.

KM#	Date	Year	Good	VG	Fine	VF
6	ND	—	10.00	16.50	25.00	37.50

SRI SINGH

1844-1870AD

PAISA

COPPER
c/m: Trident on 1 Paisa, KM#6.

KM#	Date	Year	Good	VG	Fine	VF
9	ND	—	10.00	20.00	32.50	50.00

Crude, degenerate copy of KM#3.

KM#	Date	Year	Good	VG	Fine	VF
10	ND	—	3.50	5.50	8.00	12.50

NOTE: KM#9 and 10 were also struck during the reign of Sham Singh, 1870-1904AD. They are found struck over KM#3.

CHHOTA UDAIPUR

Formerly one of the non-Aryan-Chota Nagpur states located in Bengal, Chhota Udaipur originated in the late fifteenth century. Its founders were Chauhan Rajputs who, having been expelled from Ajmer, finally re-established themselves in Chhota Udaipur. The rulers were known as Maharawals, and by the nineteenth century became related to the British in India by the usual treaties.

RULERS

Guman Singhji,
SE1744-1773/1822-1851AD
Jitsinghji,
SE1773-1803/VS1908-1938/1851-1881AD
Motisinghji,
VS1938-1952/1881-1905AD

GUMAN SINGHJI

SE1744-1773/1822-1851AD

PAISA

COPPER, 7.40 g

KM#	Date	Year	Good	VG	Fine	VF
10	—	—	4.00	6.00	8.50	11.50

2 PAISA

COPPER, 13.40-14.00 g

KM#	Date	Year	Good	VG	Fine	VF
15.1	SE(1)765	(1843)	3.50	5.50	7.50	10.00
	1767	(1845)	3.50	5.50	7.50	10.00

KM#	Date	Year	Good	VG	Fine	VF
15.2	SE1797	(1875)	3.50	5.50	7.50	10.00

KM#	Date	Year	Good	VG	Fine	VF
15.3	ND	—	3.50	5.50	7.50	10.00

JITSINGHJI

SE1773-1803/VS1908-1938/1851-1881AD

PAISA

COPPER, 22mm, 7.40 g

Y#	Date	Year	Good	VG	Fine	VF
1	SE1787	(1865)	2.50	4.50	6.50	8.50

2 PAISA

COPPER, 13.40-14.00 g

Y#	Date	Year	Good	VG	Fine	VF
2	SE1787	—	5.50	7.00	9.00	12.00

Y#	Date	Year	Good	VG	Fine	VF
3	VS1919	(1862)	7.00	9.00	12.00	16.50
	1924	(1867)	7.00	9.00	12.00	16.50

MOTISINGHJI

VS1938-1952/1881-1905AD

1/2 PAISA

COPPER, 3.60 g

KM#	Date	Year	Good	VG	Fine	VF
A4	VS1948	(1891)	—	—	Rare	—

NOTE: Struck with One Paisa dies.

PAISA

COPPER, 7.40 g

Y#	Date	Year	Good	VG	Fine	VF
4	VS1948	(1891)	6.00	7.50	10.00	13.50

2 PAISA

COPPER, 13.40-14.00 g

Y#	Date	Year	Good	VG	Fine	VF
5	VS1948	(1891)	5.00	6.50	8.50	11.50

CIS - SUTLEJ STATES

The name Cis-Sutlej States was applied to those states in the tract of land south of the Sutlej and to the north of the Delhi territory. Before 1846 the majority of these chieftains were substantially independent, subject only to the general oversight of an agent of the Governor-General. After the first Sikh war (1845-1846) this independence became somewhat circumscribed and in 1849 the Punjab was annexed and the Cis-Sutlej States were merged into the new province of British India. Perhaps surprisingly, most of these States distinguished themselves on the side of the British during the Great Revolt of 1857.

HANSI

RULER

Raja George Thomas

MINT

Sahibabad

RUPEE

SILVER

Obv: Umbrella. Rev: Sunface.

KM#	Date	Year	VG	Fine	VF	XF
1	AH1214	42	—	—	Rare	—

JIND

State located in the southern Punjab and north Haryana states.

The ruling princes belonged to the same Jat family as the maharajas of Patiala. Like them they traced their ancestry back to Baryam, a revenue collector under Babur (1526). The State was founded by Gajpat Singh after he took part in the Sikh uprising against the Afghan governor of Sirhind in 1763. One of Gajpat Singh's daughters became the mother of Ranjit Singh.

RULERS

Bhag Singh, 1786-1819AD
Sangat Singh, 1822-1834AD
Sarup Singh, 1834-1864AD
Raghbir Singh, 1864-1887AD
Ranbir Singh, VS1943/1887AD

RAGHBIR SINGH

1864-1887AD

RUPEE

SILVER, 18mm, 10.70-11.60 g

Rev: Similar to 1 Rupee, KM#1 but finer style.

KM#	Date	Year	VG	Fine	VF	XF
5 (Y1)	AH—	4 (frozen)	20.00	31.50	42.50	60.00

KALSIA

A Sikh state located in the Punjab.

MINT

Chhachrauli

PAISA

COPPER

Obv: Daggar mint mark. Rev: Quatrefoil and sword.

KM#	Date	Year	Good	VG	Fine	VF
32 (610)	AH1216	41 (error)	6.00	10.00	16.00	25.00
	1218	44	6.00	10.00	16.00	25.00

NOTE: Earlier dates (AH1214-1216) exist for this type.

MALER KOTLA

State located in the Punjab in northwest India, founded by the Maler Kotla family who were Sherwani Afghans who had travelled to India from Kabul in 1467 as officials of the Delhi emperors.

Coins are rupees of Ahmad Shah Durrani, and except for the last ruler, contain the chief's initial on the reverse. The chiefs were called Ra'is until 1821, Nawabs thereafter.

For similar issues see Jind, Nabha and Patiala.

RULERS

Amir Khan,
AH1237-1261/1821-1845AD
Sube (Mah bub) Khan,
AH1261-1276/1845-1859AD
Sikandar Ali Khan,
AH1276-1288/1859-1871AD
Ibrahim Ali Khan,
AH1288-1326/1871-1908AD

AMIR KHAN

AH1237-1261/1821-1845AD

Identifying Marks:

On reverse

1/4 RUPEE

SILVER, 2.68-2.90 g

C#	Date	Year	VG	Fine	VF	XF
13	AH—	4 (frozen)	9.00	15.00	21.50	30.00

1/2 RUPEE

SILVER, 16mm, 5.35-5.80 g

C#	Date	Year	VG	Fine	VF	XF
14	AH—	4 (frozen)	9.00	15.00	21.50	30.00

RUPEE

SILVER, 17mm, 10.70-11.60 g

C#	Date	Year	VG	Fine	VF	XF
15	AH—	4 (frozen)	5.50	9.00	13.50	20.00

SUBE (Mahbub) KHAN

AH1261-1276/1845-1859AD

Identifying Marks:

On reverse

1/4 RUPEE

SILVER, 2.68-2.90 g

C#	Date	Year	VG	Fine	VF	XF
18	AH—	4 (frozen)	9.00	15.00	21.50	30.00

1/2 RUPEE

SILVER, 15mm, 5.35-5.80 g

C#	Date	Year	VG	Fine	VF	XF
19	AH—	4 (frozen)	9.00	15.00	21.50	30.00

RUPEE

SILVER, 10.70-11.60 g

C#	Date	Year	VG	Fine	VF	XF
20	ND	—	5.50	9.00	13.50	20.00

SIKANDAR ALI KHAN

AH1276-1288/1859-1871AD

Identifying Marks:

On reverse

1/4 RUPEE

SILVER, 2.68-2.90 g

Y#	Date	Year	VG	Fine	VF	XF
1	ND	—	17.50	25.00	35.00	50.00

1/2 RUPEE

SILVER, 5.35-5.80 g

Y#	Date	Year	VG	Fine	VF	XF
2	ND	—	15.00	21.50	30.00	40.00

RUPEE

SILVER, 10.70-11.60 g

Y#	Date	Year	VG	Fine	VF	XF
3.1	AH1281	—	50.00	60.00	85.00	110.00
	ND	—	7.00	11.00	16.50	25.00

Rev: 11-pointed star w/in *S* of *Falus*.

Y#	Date	Year	VG	Fine	VF	XF
3.2	ND	—	15.00	22.00	30.00	40.00

IBRAHIM ALI KHAN

AH1288-1326/1871-1908AD

Identifying Marks:

On reverse

1/4 RUPEE

SILVER, 2.68-2.90 g

Y#	Date	Year	VG	Fine	VF	XF
4	ND	—	12.50	18.50	25.00	35.00

1/2 RUPEE

SILVER, 16mm, 5.35-5.80 g

Y#	Date	Year	VG	Fine	VF	XF
5	ND	—	11.50	17.50	23.50	32.50

RUPEE

SILVER, 10.70-11.60 g

Y#	Date	Year	VG	Fine	VF	XF
6	ND	—	6.00	9.00	13.50	20.00
	AH1292	—	12.50	15.00	20.00	35.00
	1311	—	12.50	15.00	20.00	35.00

NABHA

State located in the Punjab in northwest India and founded in the 18th century.

The ancestry of these rulers was identical to that of Jind. Until 1845 Nabha's history closely paralleled that of Patiala. At this point, however, the raja sided with the Sikhs. It was left to his son to make amends to the British in 1847.

RULERS

Jaswant Singh,
VS1840-1897/1783-1840AD
Bharpur Singh,
VS1903-1920/1846-1863AD
Hira Singh,
VS1928-1968/1871-1911AD

MINT

سرکار نابهه

Sarkar Nabha

JASWANT SINGH

VS1840-1897/1783-1840AD

Identifying Marks:

On rev. C#20.1-20.3

On rev. C#20.4

In the name of Ahmad Shah Durrani

RUPEE

SILVER, 11.05-11.15 g
Rev: Cross-like symbol below *Sin*.

C#	Date	Year	VG	Fine	VF	XF
20.1	ND	—	12.50	25.00	42.00	60.00

Rev: Star below *Sin*.

C#	Date	Year	VG	Fine	VF	XF
20.2	VS(18)77	(1820)	12.50	25.00	42.00	60.00

Rev: Branch symbol.

C#	Date	Year	VG	Fine	VF	XF
20.3	VS(18)82	(1825)	12.50	25.00	42.00	60.00
	(18)83	(1826)	12.50	25.00	42.00	60.00
	(18)85	(1828)	12.50	25.00	42.00	60.00
	(18)93	(1836)	12.50	25.00	42.00	60.00

In the name of Guru Govind Singh

Rev: Leaf to left of stylized "4."

C#	Date	Year	VG	Fine	VF	XF
20.4	VS1892	(1835)	12.50	25.00	42.00	60.00
	1893	(1836)	12.50	25.00	42.00	60.00
	1895	(1838)	12.50	25.00	42.00	60.00

BHARPUR SINGH

VS1903-1920/1846-1863AD

Identifying Marks:

On reverse

In the name of Guru Govind Singh

RUPEE

SILVER, 11.00-11.10 g
Rev: Leaf to left of stylized '4'; star to right.

Y#	Date	Year	VG	Fine	VF	XF
1.1	VS1907	(1850)	30.00	50.00	70.00	100.00
	1908	(1851)	30.00	50.00	70.00	100.00
	1909	(1852)	30.00	50.00	70.00	100.00
	1911	(1854)	30.00	50.00	70.00	100.00
	1912	(1855)	30.00	50.00	70.00	100.00
	1913	(1856)	30.00	50.00	70.00	100.00
	1916	(1859)	30.00	50.00	70.00	100.00
	1917	(1860)	30.00	50.00	70.00	100.00
	1920	(1863)	30.00	50.00	70.00	100.00

Y#	Date	Year	VG	Fine	VF	XF
1.2	VS1907	(1850)	50.00	100.00	175.00	250.00

NOTE: Struck from Y-A2 mohur dies, possibly for presentation.

MOHUR

GOLD, 9.50-9.60 g

Y#	Date	Year	VG	Fine	VF	XF
A2	VS1907	(1850)	250.00	325.00	400.00	450.00
	1911	(1854)	250.00	325.00	400.00	450.00

HIRA SINGH

VS1927-1968/1870-1911AD

Identifying Marks:

On reverse

RUPEE

SILVER, 10.70-11.60 g
Obv. and rev: Date.
Rev: Katar to left of stylized '4'.

Y#	Date	Year	VG	Fine	VF	XF
2	VS1927	(1870)	18.00	30.00	42.50	60.00
	1928	(1871)	18.00	30.00	42.50	60.00
	1929	(1872)	18.00	30.00	42.50	60.00

PATIALA

State located in the Punjab in northwest India. In the mid-18th century the Raja was given his title and mint right by Ahmad Shah Durrani of Afghanistan, whose coin he copied.

The rulers became Maharajas in 1810AD. The maharaja of Patiala was also recognized as the leader of the Phulkean tribe. Unlike others, Patiala's Sikh rulers had never hesitated to seek British assistance at those times when they felt threatened by their co-religionist neighbors. In 1857 Patiala's forces were immediately made available on the side of the British.

RULERS

Sahib Singh,
AH1196-1229/1781-1813AD
Karm Singh,
AH1229-1261/1813-1845AD
Narindar Singh,
VS1902-1919/1845-1862AD
Mahindar Singh,
VS1919-1933/1862-1876AD
Rajindar Singh,
VS1933-1957/1876-1900AD
Bhupindar Singh,
VS1958-1994/1900-1938AD

MINT

سهرند

Sirhind (Sahrind)

KARM SINGH

AH1229-1261/1813-1845AD

Identifying Marks:

On reverse

1/4 RUPEE

SILVER, 2.80 g

C#	Date	Year	VG	Fine	VF	XF
28	AH—	—	10.00	15.00	21.50	30.00

RUPEE

SILVER, 11.10-11.20 g
Rev: W/o symbols around.

C#	Date	Year	VG	Fine	VF	XF
30.1	AH—	—	11.50	17.50	23.50	32.50

Rev: *Alif* to left of

C#	Date	Year	VG	Fine	VF	XF
30.2	AH—	—	11.50	17.50	23.50	32.50

Rev: Crescent to right of

C#	Date	Year	VG	Fine	VF	XF
30.3	AH—	—	11.50	17.50	23.50	32.50

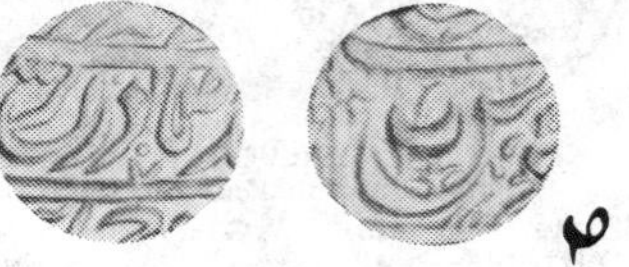

Rev: 3-pointed leaf to right of

C#	Date	Year	VG	Fine	VF	XF
30.4	AH—	—	11.50	17.50	23.50	32.50

Rev: Crescent to right, branch to left of

C#	Date	Year	VG	Fine	VF	XF
30.5	AH—	—	11.50	17.50	23.50	32.50

Rev: Branch to right of

C#	Date	Year	VG	Fine	VF	XF
30.6	AH—	—	11.50	17.50	23.50	32.50

Rev: Branches both sides of

C#	Date	Year	VG	Fine	VF	XF
30.7	AH—	—	11.50	17.50	23.50	32.50

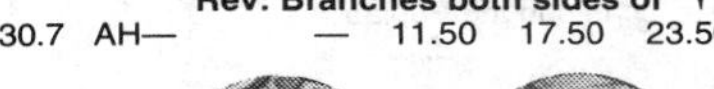

Rev: Scimitar to left of

C#	Date	Year	VG	Fine	VF	XF
31	AH—	—	16.50	23.50	32.50	45.00

NAZARANA RUPEE

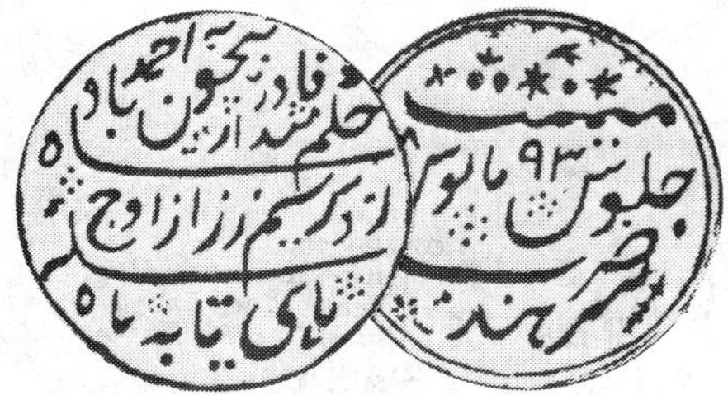

SILVER, 24mm, 11.10-11.20 g

C#	Date	Year	VG	Fine	VF	XF
30a	VS1893	(1836)	—	—	Rare	—
	(18)98	(1841)	—	—	Rare	—

MOHUR

GOLD, 10.50 g
Rev: 3-pointed leaf to right of

35	AH—	—	200.00	250.00	300.00	375.00
	VS(18)96	—	—	—	—	—

NARINDAR SINGH

VS1902-1919/1845-1862AD

Identifying Marks:

On reverse

In the name of Ahmad Shah Durrani

1/4 RUPEE

SILVER, 2.75-2.80 g

Y#	Date	Year	VG	Fine	VF	XF
A1	ND	—	27.50	40.00	52.50	75.00

RUPEE

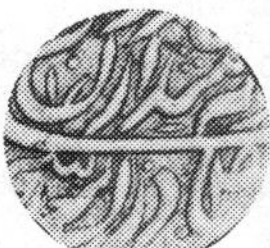 

SILVER, 11.10-11.20 g

1	VS1902	(1845)	15.00	27.50	40.00	55.00

In the name of Guru Govind Singh

w/Sikh leg.

A2	VS1906	—	37.50	52.50	75.00	110.00

MOHUR

GOLD, 17-18mm, 10.50 g

2	VS190x	—	200.00	250.00	300.00	375.00

MAHINDAR SINGH

VS1919-1933/1862-1876AD

Identifying Marks:

On reverse

In the name of Ahmad Shah Durrani

RUPEE

SILVER, 16-17mm, 11.10-11.20 g

Y#	Date	Year	VG	Fine	VF	XF
3	AH—	—	35.00	50.00	70.00	100.00

RAJINDAR SINGH

VS1933-1957/1876-1900AD

Identifying Marks:

On reverse

1/4 RUPEE

SILVER, 13mm, 2.75-2.80 g

4	AH—	—	16.00	22.50	31.50	40.00

1/2 RUPEE

SILVER, 16mm, 5.50-5.60 g

5	AH—	—	16.00	22.50	31.50	40.00

RUPEE

SILVER, 11.10-11.20 g

6	VS(19)42	—	17.50	25.00	35.00	50.00
	(19)43	—	17.50	25.00	35.00	50.00
	(19)44	—	17.50	25.00	35.00	50.00
	(19)45	—	17.50	25.00	35.00	50.00
	(19)46	—	17.50	25.00	35.00	50.00
	(19)47	—	17.50	25.00	35.00	50.00
	(19)48	—	20.00	31.50	42.50	60.00

NAZARANA RUPEE

SILVER, 11.10-11.20 g

6a	AH—	— (frozen)	—	—	Rare	—

1/3 MOHUR

GOLD, 3.50 g
Rev: Katar at left.

7	VS(19)50(1893)	85.00	100.00	125.00	175.00

MOHUR

GOLD, 18mm, 10.50 g

9	ND —	200.00	250.00	300.00	375.00
	VS(19)48(1891)	200.00	250.00	300.00	375.00

DATIA

State located in north-central India, governed by Maharajas.

Datia was founded in 1735 by Bhagwan Das, son of Narsingh Dev of the Orchha royal house. In 1804 the State concluded its first treaty with the East India Company and thereafter came under British protection and control.

RULERS

Parachat,
AH1217-1255/1802-1839AD
Vijaya Bahadur,
AH1255-1274/1839-1857AD
Bhawani Singh,
AH1274-1325/1857-1907AD

MINT

Dalipnagar

Gaja Shahi Series

Struck for more than 100 years, with the AH date on the obverse and the regnal year on the reverse bearing little relationship to each other. These are close copies of Orchha C#24-32 and can only be distinguished by the symbols, which are always different from those of Orchha, except for the Gaja (mace):

Gaja always on reverse

On obverse (Datia Mint Symbol)

On reverse

1/2 PAISA

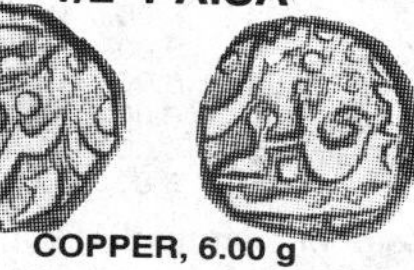

COPPER, 6.00 g

C#	Date	Year	Good	VG	Fine	VF
22	AH—	4x	2.50	3.50	5.00	7.50

NOTE: Later date (AH1320) exists for this type.

PAISA

COPPER, round or squarish, 12.00-13.00 g

23	AH1246	24	2.50	3.25	4.00	5.50
	1248	—	2.50	3.25	4.00	5.50
	1258	—	2.50	3.25	4.00	5.50
	—	39	2.50	3.25	4.00	5.50
	—	40	2.50	3.25	4.00	5.50
	1274	45	2.50	3.25	4.00	5.50
	1278	45	2.50	3.25	4.00	5.50
	1282	4x	2.50	3.25	4.00	5.50
	1283	—	2.50	3.25	4.00	5.50

1/8 RUPEE

SILVER, 1.34-1.45 g

C#	Date	Year	VG	Fine	VF	XF
35	AH—	22	6.00	10.00	14.00	20.00
	—	4x	6.00	10.00	14.00	20.00

1/4 RUPEE

SILVER, 2.68-2.90 g

36	AH1317	23	6.00	12.50	17.50	25.00
	—	36	6.00	12.50	17.50	25.00

1/2 RUPEE

SILVER, 5.35-5.80 g

37	AH1311	19	6.00	12.50	17.50	25.00
	—	23	6.00	12.50	17.50	25.00
	1316	24	6.00	12.50	17.50	25.00
	1317	25	6.00	12.50	17.50	25.00
	—	29	6.00	12.50	17.50	25.00
	—	33	6.00	12.50	17.50	25.00

RUPEE

SILVER, 10.70-11.60 g

38	AH1211	43	6.00	10.00	15.00	22.50
	1214	42	6.00	10.00	15.00	22.50
	1215	23	6.00	10.00	15.00	22.50
	1221	43	6.00	10.00	15.00	22.50

C#	Date	Year	VG	Fine	VF	XF
38	1233	24	6.00	10.00	15.00	22.50
	1233	28	6.00	10.00	15.00	22.50
	1235	14	6.00	10.00	15.00	22.50
	1249	28	6.00	10.00	15.00	22.50
	1250	28	6.00	10.00	15.00	22.50
	1257	48	6.00	10.00	15.00	22.50
	1258	38	6.00	10.00	15.00	22.50
	1262	29	6.00	10.00	15.00	22.50
	1270	36	6.00	10.00	15.00	22.50
	1271	37	6.00	10.00	15.00	22.50
	1272	38	6.00	10.00	15.00	22.50
	1273	39	6.00	10.00	15.00	22.50
	1273	42	6.00	10.00	15.00	22.50
	1274	41	6.00	10.00	15.00	22.50
	1274	44	6.00	10.00	15.00	22.50
	1275	41	6.00	10.00	15.00	22.50
	1277	44	6.00	10.00	15.00	22.50
	1278	45	6.00	10.00	15.00	22.50
	1281	48	6.00	10.00	15.00	22.50
	1282	46	6.00	10.00	15.00	22.50
	1286	46	6.00	10.00	15.00	22.50
	1287	46	6.00	10.00	15.00	22.50
	1311	19	6.00	10.00	15.00	22.50
	1312	24	6.00	10.00	15.00	22.50
	1312	25	6.00	10.00	15.00	22.50
	1312	30	6.00	10.00	15.00	22.50
	1313	24	6.00	10.00	15.00	22.50
	1314	24	6.00	10.00	15.00	22.50
	1314	40	6.00	10.00	15.00	22.50
	1315	23	6.00	10.00	15.00	22.50
	—	35	6.00	10.00	15.00	22.50

In the name of Muhammad Akbar II

RUPEE

SILVER, 10.70-11.60 g

C#	Date	Year	VG	Fine	VF	XF
45	AH1270	33	15.00	25.00	35.00	50.00

DEWAS JUNIOR BRANCH

A Maratha state located in west-central India. The raja, the brother of the raja of Dewas Senior Branch had a palace in Dewas City. They descended from two brothers, Tukoji and Jiwaji who were given Dewas City in 1726 by Peshwa Baji Rao as a reward for army services.

Largely due to its geographical location Dewas suffered much at the hands of the armies of Holkar and Sindhia, and from Pindari incursions. In 1818 the State came under British protection.

LOCAL RULERS

Narayan Rao, 1864-1892

NARAYAN RAO

1864-1892AD

1/12 ANNA

COPPER

KM#	Date	Mintage	Fine	VF	XF	Unc
1	1888	.112	10.00	20.00	35.00	60.00
	1888	—	—	—	Proof	125.00

1/4 ANNA

COPPER

KM#	Date	Mintage	Fine	VF	XF	Unc
3	1888	.484	9.00	18.00	30.00	50.00
	1888	—	—	—	Proof	150.00

SILVER

KM#	Date	Mintage	Fine	VF	XF	Unc
3a	1888	(restrike)	—	—	Proof	125.00

DEWAS SENIOR BRANCH

A Maratha state located in west-central India. The raja, the brother of the raja of Dewas Junior Branch had a palace in Dewas city. They descended from two brothers Tukoji and Jiwaji who were given Dewas City in 1726 by Peshwa Baji Rao as a reward for army services.

Largely due to its geographical location Dewas suffered much at the hands of the armies of Holkar and Sindhia, and from Pindari incursions. In 1818 the State came under British protection.

LOCAL RULERS

Krishnaji Rao, 1860-1899AD
Vikrama Simha Rao, 1937-1948AD

ALLOTE MINT

PAISA

COPPER

KM#	Date	Good	VG	Fine	VF
10	ND	2.50	3.50	5.00	7.00

NOTE: Varieties exist.

REGAL ISSUES

Milled Coinage

1/12 ANNA

COPPER

KM#	Date	Mintage	Fine	VF	XF	Unc
11	1888	.112	6.00	12.00	20.00	35.00
	1888	—	—	—	Proof	125.00

SILVER

KM#	Date	Mintage	Fine	VF	XF	Unc
11a	1888	(restrike)	—	—	Proof	100.00

1/4 ANNA

COPPER

KM#	Date	Mintage	Fine	VF	XF	Unc
12	1888	.484	7.50	15.00	25.00	40.00
	1888	—	—	—	Proof	150.00

DHAR

The territory in central India in which Dhar was located had been controlled by the Paramara clan of Rajputs from the ninth century to the thirteenth, after which it passed into Muslim hands. The modern Princely State of Dhar originated in the first half of the eighteenth century when the Maratha Peshwa, Baji Rao, handed over the region as a fiefdom to Anand Rao Ponwar. Anand Rao Ponwar was of the same stock as the rulers of Dewas and a descendant of the original Paramara Rajputs. Sometimes in conflict with Holkar, sometimes with Sindhia, in 1819 Dhar came under British protection. No silver or gold coinage was ever struck at Dhar. In 1895 the British silver rupee was adopted.

LOCAL RULERS

Jaswant Rao,
AH1250-1274/1834-1857AD
Anand Rao III,
AH1276-1316/1860-1898AD
Anand Rao IV,
AH1363-1368/1943-1948AD

JASWANT RAO

AH1250-1274/1834-1857AD

PAISA

COPPER

KM#	Date	Year	Good	VG	Fine	VF
2	ND	—	2.50	4.00	6.50	10.00

Obv: Banners.

KM#	Date	Year	Good	VG	Fine	VF
1	AH1266	—	2.50	4.00	6.50	10.00

ANAND RAO III

AH1276-1316/1860-1898AD

1/2 PAISA

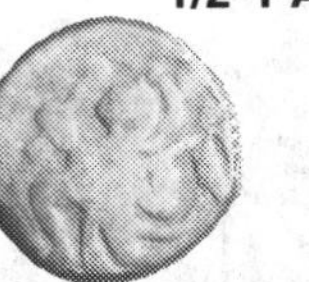

COPPER, 16mm
Obv: Hanuman w/banners.

KM#	Date	Year	Good	VG	Fine	VF
5	AH1289	—	3.00	5.00	9.00	15.00

PAISA

COPPER
Obv: Hanuman w/banners.

KM#	Date	Year	Good	VG	Fine	VF
6	AH1289	—	3.00	5.00	8.00	12.50

Milled Coinage

1/12 ANNA

COPPER

KM#	Date	Mintage	Fine	VF	XF	Unc
11	1887	—	1.35	3.50	9.00	15.00
	1887	—	—	—	Proof	125.00

SILVER

KM#	Date	Mintage	Fine	VF	XF	Unc
11a	1887	(restrike)	—	—	Proof	100.00

GOLD

KM#	Date	Mintage	Fine	VF	XF	Unc
11b	1887	(restrike)	—	—	Proof	350.00

1/2 PICE

COPPER

KM#	Date	Mintage	Fine	VF	XF	Unc
12	1887	—	2.00	5.00	12.00	20.00
	1887	—	—	—	Proof	150.00

SILVER

KM#	Date	Mintage	Fine	VF	XF	Unc
12a	1887	(restrike)	—	—	Proof	125.00

GOLD

KM#	Date	Mintage	Fine	VF	XF	Unc
12b	1887	(restrike)	—	—	Proof	450.00

1/4 ANNA

COPPER

KM#	Date	Mintage	Fine	VF	XF	Unc
13	1887	—	3.00	7.50	18.00	30.00
	1887	—	—	—	Proof	175.00

SILVER

KM#	Date	Mintage	Fine	VF	XF	Unc
13a	1887	(restrike)	—	—	Proof	150.00

GOLD

KM#	Date	Mintage	Fine	VF	XF	Unc
13b	1887	(restrike)	—	—	Proof	650.00

DHOLPUR

State located in Rajputana, northwest India.

Dholpur had a varied and turbulent history. From the eighth until the twelfth centuries it was ruled by Tonwar Rajputs. Early in the sixteenth century the entire region came under the Mughals. It was included by Akbar in Agra province. With Mughal decline after 1707, Dholpur experienced many masters until, in 1782, it fell into the hands of Sindhia. In 1803 the territory was captured by the British and in 1805 it was returned to the ranas of Gohad, Bamraolia Jats, from whom it had earlier been wrested by Sindhia. The ranas of Gohad opened the mint which operated until 1857.

RULER

Kirat Singh,
AH1203-1221/1788-1806AD, in Gohad

AH1221-1252/1806-1836AD, in Dholpur
Bhagwant Singh,
AH1252-1290/1836-1873AD

MINT

Dholpur دهولپور

Gohad گوهد

DHOLPUR MINT

Mint marks: 

On obverse

On reverse Type 1 or Type 2

In the name of Muhammad Akbar II
AH1221-1253/1806-1837AD

RUPEE

SILVER, 11.00 g

C#	Date	Year	VG	Fine	VF	XF
12.1	AH1225	4	35.00	50.00	70.00	100.00

C#	Date	Year	VG	Fine	VF	XF
12.2	AH1226	5	35.00	50.00	70.00	100.00
	1228	—	17.50	25.00	35.00	50.00
	1228	17	17.50	25.00	35.00	50.00
	—	19	17.50	25.00	35.00	50.00
	—	21	17.50	25.00	35.00	50.00
	1245	24	20.00	31.50	42.50	60.00

GOHAD MINT

Mint marks:  or 

On obverse

 reverse  or 

Pistol Star Leaf

In the name of Shah Alam II
AH1173-1221/1759-1806AD

RUPEE

SILVER, 11.00 g
Obv: Pistol.

C#	Date	Year	VG	Fine	VF	XF
5.1	AH1218	46	18.50	31.50	42.50	60.00
	1219	47	18.50	31.50	42.50	60.00
	1221	—	17.50	25.00	35.00	50.00

NOTE: Earlier dates (AH1185-1208) exist for this type.

In the name of Muhammad Akbar II
AH1221-1253/1806-1837AD

1/2 RUPEE

SILVER, 5.50 g
Rev: Pistol and star.

11 AH— — — Reported, not confirmed

RUPEE

SILVER, 11.00 g
Rev: Pistol and leaf.

C#	Date	Year	VG	Fine	VF	XF
12a.1	AH1247	26	12.50	25.00	42.00	60.00
	1249	28	12.50	25.00	42.00	60.00
	1250	29	12.50	25.00	42.00	60.00
	1251	30	12.50	25.00	42.00	60.00

SILVER, 10.90-11.10 g
Rev: Pistol and star.

C#	Date	Year	VG	Fine	VF	XF
12a.2	AH1251	30	12.50	25.00	42.00	60.00

Rev: Pistol.

C#	Date	Year	VG	Fine	VF	XF
12c	AH1252	31	12.50	25.00	42.00	60.00

***NOTE:** Actually struck in AH1274/1857AD.

NAZARANA RUPEE

SILVER, 10.90-11.10 g
Rev: Pistol and leaf.

C#	Date	Year	VG	Fine	VF	XF
12b.2	1252*	30	45.00	75.00	110.00	150.00

MOHUR

GOLD, 10.70 g

C#	Date	Year	VG	Fine	VF	XF
15	AH1252*	31	—	—	Rare	—

***NOTE:** Actually struck in AH1274/1857 AD.

DUNGARPUR

A district in northwest India which became part of Rajasthan in 1948.

The maharawals of Dungarpur were descended from the Mewar chieftains of the twelth century. In 1527 the upper Mahi basin was bifurcated to form the Princely States of Dungarpur and Banswara. Thereafter Dungarpur came successively under Mughal and Maratha control until in 1818 it came under British protection.

RULERS

Udai Singh,
VS1909-1955/1852-1898AD
Bijey Singh,
VS1955-1975/1898-1918AD
Lakshman Singh,
VS1975-2005/1918-1948AD

UDAI SINGH

VS1909-1955/1852-1898AD

1/4 PAISA

COPPER, 2.50 g

KM#	Date	Year	Good	VG	Fine	VF
1	VS1917	(1860)	6.00	10.00	16.00	25.00

1/2 PAISA

COPPER, 5.00 g
Obv: Dagger points left.

KM#	Date	Year	Good	VG	Fine	VF
4	VS1917	(1860)	—	—	—	—

PAISA

COPPER, 9.50-11.00 g
Obv: Dagger points right.

KM#	Date	Year	Good	VG	Fine	VF
2	VS1917	(1860)	3.00	5.00	8.00	12.50

Obv: Dagger points left.

KM#	Date	Year	Good	VG	Fine	VF
3	VS1917	(1860)	3.00	5.00	8.00	12.50

FARRUKHABAD

Refer to Independent Kingdoms during British rule.

GWALIOR

Sindhia

State located in central India. Capital originally was Ujjain (= Daru-l-fath), but was later transferred to Gwalior in 1810. The Gwalior ruling family, the Sindhias, were descendants of the Maratha chief Ranoji Sindhia (d.1750). His youngest son, Mahadji Sindhia (d.1794) was anxious to establish his independence from the overlordship of the Peshwas of Poona. Unable to achieve this alone, it was the Peshwa's crushing defeat by Ahmad Shah Durrani at Panipat in 1761 which helped realize his ambitions. Largely in the interests of sustaining this autonomy, but partly as a result of a defeat at East India Company hands in 1781, Mahadji concluded an alliance with the British in 1782. In 1785, he reinstalled the fallen Mughal Emperor, Shah Alam, on the throne at Dehli. Very early in the nineteenth century, Gwalior's relationship with the British began to deteriorate, a situation which culminated in the Anglo-Maratha War of 1803. Gwalior's forces under Daulat Rao were defeated. In consequence, and by the terms of the peace treaty which followed, his territory was truncated. In 1818, Gwalior suffered a further loss of land at British hands. In the years that ensued, as the East India Company's possessions became transformed into empire and as the Pax Britannica swept across the subcontinent, the Sindhia family's relationship with their British overlords steadliy improved.

RULERS

Daulat Rao,
AH1209-1243/1794-1827AD
Baija Bai, Regent,
(Widow of Daulat Rao)
AH1243-1249/1827-1833AD
Jankoji Rao,
AH1243-1259/1827-1843AD
Jayaji Rao,
AH1259-1304/1843-1886AD
Madho Rao,
VS1943-1982/1886-1925AD
Jivaji Rao,
VS1982-2005/1925-1948AD

MINTS

Mint	
Bajranggarh "Jaynagar"	जयनगर
Basoda	بسوده
Bhilsa "Alamgirpur"	عالمگیرپور
Broach	بروچ
Burhanpur	برهانپور
"Dar-as-Surar" Abode of Happiness	دار السرور
Dohad	દોહદ
Garhakota "Ravishnagar Sagar"	روش نگر ساگر
Gwalior Fort	گواليار
Isagarh	عسي گره
Jawad	
Jhansi "Balwantnagar"	بلونت نگر
Lashkar	
Mandasor	مندسور
Rajod	राजोद
Rathgarh "Daulatgarh"	

Shadorah شادهوره

Sheopur شیوپور

Sipri "Narwar" نروار

Ujjain, dar ul Fateh دارالفتح اجین

NOTE: None of the coins of Gwalior prior to the beginning of machine-struck coinage in 1889AD bears the name of the Sindhia (ruler of Gwalior), but beginning with the reign of Baija Bao, a Nagari letter is used to indicate the ruler under whom it was struck, as follows:

Sri	श्री	Baija Bao
Jo	जे	Jankoji Rao
Ji	जी	Jayaji Rao
Ma	मा	Madho Rao

However, not all the coins bear the initial of the ruler, especially the copper.

The coinage of Gwalior is extremely complicated and not fully understood. Each mint, and there were probably more than twenty in all, maintained its own styles and types, and operated fully independently of every other mint. Hence it is most logical to list the issues of each mint together, rather than attempt to list the coins by reign or denomination. The mints are best identified by the presence of special symbols on the obverse or reverse of the coins, and those symbols are noted whenever possible. Types are listed with designation of reign only when the initial of the ruler appears on the coin; others are assigned a single number for the full duration of their issuance.

Most of the coins of Gwalior are undated, or issued over long periods of time with frozen dates, in order to discourage the nefarious practice of devaluing coins of older dates (for example, one-year old coins might be devalued 1 percent, two-year olds 2 percent, and so forth). Many of the types were struck with frozen dates for several decades, and in many other cases, the dates remained frozen while the ruler's initial changed. The frozen dates may be either AH dates or regnal years, or both.

Regularly dated series often continued over long durations, such as the Ujjain rupees (C#259); the lists of such coins are probably very fragmentary, and many unlisted dates will be discovered. In general, unlisted dates are worth no more than listed dates of the same type.

BAJRANGGARH MINT

For coins issued by Jai Singh, AH1213-1233 refer to Bajranggarh State listings.

AJIT SINGH

AH1235-1274/1819-1857AD

Mint mark: 

Types of Jai Singh with added mint marks:

Lotus **Bow and arrow**

1/8 RUPEE

SILVER, 16mm, 1.34-1.45 g
Obv: Bow and arrow. Rev: Lotus.

KM#	Date	Year	VG	Fine	VF	XF
12	ND(1827-61)	NRY	10.00	15.00	21.50	30.00

1/4 RUPEE

SILVER, 2.68-2.90 g
Obv: Bow and arrow. Rev: Lotus.

KM#	Date	Year	VG	Fine	VF	XF
13	ND(1827-61)	NRY	8.50	13.50	20.00	28.50

1/2 RUPEE

SILVER, 5.35-5.80 g
Obv: Bow and arrow. Rev: Lotus.

KM#	Date	Year	VG	Fine	VF	XF
14	ND(1827-61)	NRY	7.50	12.50	18.50	27.50

RUPEE

SILVER, 10.70-11.60 g
Rev: Lotus.

KM#	Date	Year	VG	Fine	VF	XF
15	ND(1819)	21	15.00	21.50	30.00	40.00
	(1820)	22	15.00	21.50	30.00	40.00

Obv: Bow and arrow. Rev: Lotus.

KM#	Date	Year	VG	Fine	VF	XF
16	ND(1821)	23	7.00	11.00	16.50	25.00
	(1822)	24	7.00	11.00	16.50	25.00
	(1823)	25	7.00	11.00	16.50	25.00
	(1824)	26	7.00	11.00	16.50	25.00
	(1825)	27	7.00	11.00	16.50	25.00
	(1826)	28	7.00	11.00	16.50	25.00
	(1827)	29	7.00	11.00	16.50	25.00

KM#	Date	Year	VG	Fine	VF	XF
17	ND(1827-61)	NRY	6.00	9.00	13.50	20.00

BASODA MINT

Daulat Rao

AH1209-1243/1794-1827AD

In the name of Muhammad Akbar II
AH1221-1253/1806-1837AD

Mint marks:  

RUPEE

SILVER, 10.70-11.60 g

KM#	Date	Year	VG	Fine	VF	XF
18	AH124x	18	25.00	37.50	50.00	70.00

JANKOJI RAO

AH1243-1259/1833-1843AD

In the name of Muhammad Akbar II
AH1221-1253/1806-1837AD
and Jankoji Rao

With additional mint mark: 

1/4 RUPEE

SILVER

KM#	Date	Year	VG	Fine	VF	XF
A19	ND	—	—	—	—	—

RUPEE

SILVER, 10.70-11.60 g

KM#	Date	Year	VG	Fine	VF	XF
19.1	AH1252	32	25.00	37.50	50.00	70.00
	1254	32	25.00	37.50	50.00	70.00

JAYAJI RAO

AH1259-1304/1843-1886AD

In the name of Muhammad Akbar II
AH1221-1253/1806-1837AD
and Jankoji Rao

RUPEE

SILVER, 10.70-11.60 g

KM#	Date	Year	VG	Fine	VF	XF
19.2	AH1274	3x	25.00	37.50	50.00	70.00
	1274	46	25.00	37.50	50.00	70.00

BHILSA MINT

DAULAT RAO

AH1209-1243/1794-1827AD

In the name of Muhammad Akbar II
AH1221-1253/1806-1837AD

1/8 RUPEE

SILVER

KM#	Date	Year	VG	Fine	VF	XF
A20	—	—	7.50	15.00	25.00	35.00

1/4 RUPEE

 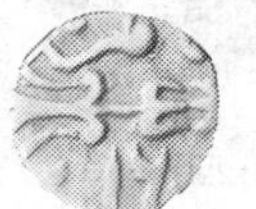

SILVER, 2.68-2.90 g

KM#	Date	Year	VG	Fine	VF	XF
20	AH—	16	8.50	17.00	28.00	40.00

1/2 RUPEE

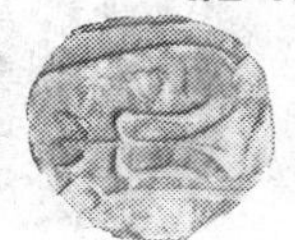 

SILVER, 5.35-5.80 g

KM#	Date	Year	VG	Fine	VF	XF
21	AH—	15	11.00	22.00	35.00	50.00

RUPEE

SILVER, 10.70-11.60 g
Obv: 3-leaf symbol. Rev: Regnal year.

KM#	Date	Year	VG	Fine	VF	XF
22	AH—	7	8.50	17.00	28.00	40.00
	—	9	8.50	17.00	28.00	40.00
	—	11	8.50	17.00	28.00	40.00
	—	13	8.50	17.00	28.00	40.00
	—	14	8.50	17.00	28.00	40.00
	—	15	8.50	17.00	28.00	40.00
	—	16	8.50	17.00	28.00	40.00
	—	17	8.50	17.00	28.00	40.00
	—	19	8.50	17.00	28.00	40.00
	—	20	8.50	17.00	28.00	40.00
	—	26	8.50	17.00	28.00	40.00
	—	51	8.50	17.00	28.00	40.00

JAYAJI RAO

AH1259-1304/1843-1886AD

NOTE: The bow & arrow and trident appear on nearly all coins of Bhilsa, Gwalior Fort, and Lashkar Mints, and cannot be used to identify any one of them.

In the name of Shah Alam II
AH1173-1221/1759-1806AD

with additional initial of Jayaji Rao जी

Frozen date AH(12)25

1/8 RUPEE

SILVER, 1.34-1.45 g
Obv: W/o sword.

KM#	Date	Year	VG	Fine	VF	XF
23.1	AH(12)25	—	7.00	11.00	16.50	25.00

Obv: W/sword.

KM#	Date	Year	VG	Fine	VF	XF
23.2	AH(12)25	—	7.00	11.00	16.50	25.00

1/4 RUPEE

SILVER, 12-14mm, 2.68-2.90 g

Obv: W/o sword.

KM#	Date	Year	VG	Fine	VF	XF
24.1	AH(12)25	—	7.00	11.00	16.50	25.00

Obv: W/sword.

KM#	Date	Year	VG	Fine	VF	XF
24.2	AH(12)25	—	7.00	11.00	16.50	25.00

1/2 RUPEE

SILVER, 5.35-5.80 g

Obv: W/o sword.

KM#	Date	Year	VG	Fine	VF	XF
25	AH(12)25	—	10.00	15.00	21.50	30.00

Obv: Sword.

KM#	Date	Year	VG	Fine	VF	XF
26	AH(12)25	—	10.00	15.00	21.50	30.00

RUPEE

SILVER, 10.70-11.60 g

Obv: W/o sword. Rev: Bow and arrow.

KM#	Date	Year	VG	Fine	VF	XF
27	AH(12)25	23	6.00	9.00	13.50	20.00

Obv: Sword. Rev: Bow and arrow.

KM#	Date	Year	VG	Fine	VF	XF
28	AH(12)25	—	5.50	8.00	12.50	18.50

With additional initial of Madho Rao II

1/8 RUPEE

SILVER, 9-10mm, 1.34-1.45 g

KM#	Date	Year	VG	Fine	VF	XF
29	AH(12)25	—	6.00	9.00	13.50	20.00

1/4 RUPEE

SILVER, 2.68-2.90 g

KM#	Date	Year	VG	Fine	VF	XF
30	AH(12)25	—	6.00	9.00	13.50	20.00

1/2 RUPEE

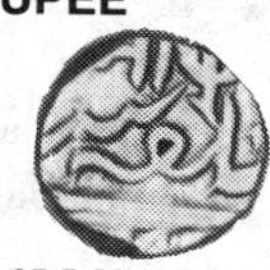

SILVER, 5.35-5.80 g

KM#	Date	Year	VG	Fine	VF	XF
31	AH(12)25	—	7.00	11.00	16.50	25.00

RUPEE

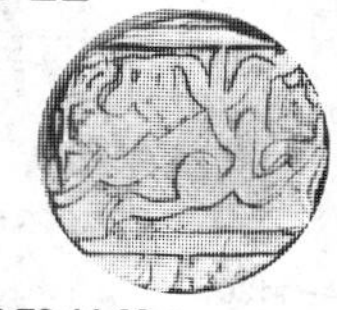

SILVER, 10.70-11.60 g

KM#	Date	Year	VG	Fine	VF	XF
32	AH(12)25	—	7.00	11.00	16.50	25.00

BROACH MINT

RUPEE

SILVER, 10.70-11.60 g

KM#	Date	Year	VG	Fine	VF	XF
34	AH—	27	5.00	10.00	17.50	25.00
	—	29	5.00	10.00	17.50	25.00
	—	32	5.00	10.00	17.50	25.00
	—	34	5.00	10.00	17.50	25.00
	—	35	5.00	10.00	17.50	25.00

BURHANPUR MINT

"Dar-as-Surar"

DAULAT RAO

AH1209-1243/1794-1827AD

In the name of Shah Alam II

AH1173-1221/1759-1806AD

PAISA

COPPER, square, 18.14 g

KM#	Date	Year	Good	VG	Fine	VF
40.1	AH1218	—	2.50	4.00	6.00	8.00

RUPEE

SILVER, 10.70-11.60 g

KM#	Date	Year	VG	Fine	VF	XF
38.2	AH1216	4x	6.00	12.00	20.00	28.00
	1217	45	6.00	12.00	20.00	28.00
	1218	—	6.00	12.00	20.00	28.00
	1219	4x	6.00	12.00	20.00	28.00
	1220	—	10.00	14.00	22.00	30.00
	1221	4x	6.00	12.00	20.00	28.00
	1221	40	6.00	12.00	20.00	28.00
	1222	—	6.00	12.00	20.00	28.00
	1223	4x	6.00	12.00	20.00	28.00
	1224	4x	6.00	12.00	20.00	28.00
	1225	—	6.00	12.00	20.00	28.00
	1227	—	6.00	12.00	20.00	28.00
	1229	—	6.00	12.00	20.00	28.00
	1230	—	6.00	12.00	20.00	28.00
	1231	—	10.00	14.00	22.00	30.00
	1232	—	6.00	12.00	20.00	28.00
	1233	—	6.00	12.00	20.00	28.00
	1234	3x	6.00	12.00	20.00	28.00
	1235	39	6.00	12.00	20.00	28.00
	1237	—	6.00	12.00	20.00	28.00
	1238	—	6.00	12.00	20.00	28.00
	1239	—	6.00	12.00	20.00	28.00
	1240	—	10.00	14.00	22.00	30.00
	1242	—	6.00	12.00	20.00	28.00
	1243	—	6.00	12.00	20.00	28.00

NOTE: Earlier dates (AH1209-1215) exist for this type.

BAIJA BAI

AH1243-1249/1827-1833AD

In the name of Shah Alam II

AH1173-1221/1759-1806AD

RUPEE

SILVER, 10.70-11.60 g

KM#	Date	Year	VG	Fine	VF	XF
38.3	AH1247	—	7.50	15.00	25.00	36.00

JANKOJI RAO

AH1243-1259/1827-1843AD

In the name of Shah Alam II

AH1173-1221/1759-1806AD

RUPEE

SILVER, 10.70-11.60 g

KM#	Date	Year	VG	Fine	VF	XF
38.4	AH1255	—	10.00	14.00	22.00	30.00

JAYAJI RAO

AH1243-1249/1827-1833AD

Mint mark:  

PAISA

COPPER, 15.23 g

KM#	Date	Year	Good	VG	Fine	VF
41	ND	—	2.50	4.50	6.50	10.00

1/4 RUPEE

SILVER, 15mm, 2.68-2.90 g

KM#	Date	Year	VG	Fine	VF	XF
42	AH1214	—	6.50	13.00	21.00	30.00

1/2 RUPEE

SILVER, 17mm, 5.35-5.70 g

KM#	Date	Year	VG	Fine	VF	XF
43	AH1214	—	10.00	20.00	32.00	45.00
	1261	—	10.00	20.00	32.00	45.00
	1274	—	10.00	20.00	32.00	45.00

RUPEE

SILVER, 10.70-11.60 g

KM#	Date	Year	VG	Fine	VF	XF
44	AH1259	—	7.50	15.00	22.00	32.00
	1260	—	7.50	15.00	22.00	32.00
	1261	—	7.50	15.00	22.00	32.00
	1262	—	7.50	15.00	22.00	32.00
	1266	—	7.50	15.00	22.00	32.00
	1267	—	7.50	15.00	22.00	32.00
	1268	—	7.50	15.00	22.00	32.00
	1271	—	7.50	15.00	22.00	32.00
	1272	—	7.50	15.00	22.00	32.00
	1273	—	7.50	15.00	22.00	32.00
	1274	—	7.50	15.00	22.00	32.00
	1275	—	7.50	15.00	22.00	32.00
	1276	—	7.50	15.00	22.00	32.00
	1277	—	7.50	15.00	22.00	32.00

In the name of Alyjah Bahadur

NOTE: Alyjah Bahadur was the hereditary title of the Sindhia rulers of Gwalior, and was used by all rulers of the dynasty.

Mint marks:

to right of date

PAISA

COPPER, 12.44-15.29 g

Rev: Leaf and snake.

KM#	Date	Year	Good	VG	Fine	VF
45	AH1260	—	4.50	8.00	12.00	17.50
	1273	—	4.50	8.00	12.00	17.50
	1274	—	4.50	8.00	12.00	17.50
	1275	—	4.50	8.00	12.00	17.50

DOHAD MINT

Mint mark: 

JAYAJI RAO

AH1259-1304/VS1900-1943/1843-1886AD

1/3 PAISA

COPPER, 1.69-1.88 g

KM#	Date	Year	Good	VG	Fine	VF
49	VS1912	(1855)	3.00	5.00	8.00	12.50

PAISA

COPPER, thick flan, 6.00-6.20 g

KM#	Date	Year	Good	VG	Fine	VF
50.1	VS1912	(1855)	5.00	9.00	13.00	20.00

Thin flan

KM#	Date	Year	Good	VG	Fine	VF
50.2	VS1912	(1855)	5.00	9.00	13.00	20.00

GARHAKOTA MINT

Mint marks: 

JAYAJI RAO

AH1259-1304/1843-1886AD

1/2 RUPEE

SILVER, 5.35-5.80 g
Similar to 1 Rupee, KM#53.

KM#	Date	Year	VG	Fine	VF	XF
51	AH—	55	7.50	12.50	20.00	32.50

RUPEE

SILVER, 10.70-11.60 g

KM#	Date	Year	VG	Fine	VF	XF
53	AH—	55	7.00	11.50	18.50	30.00

GWALIOR FORT MINT

DAULAT RAO

AH1209-1243/1794-1827AD

In the name of Shah Alam II
AH1173-1221/1759-1806AD

RUPEE

SILVER, 10.70-11.60 g

KM#	Date	Year	VG	Fine	VF	XF
57.2	AH1216	44	8.00	13.50	20.00	28.50
	1221	48	8.00	13.50	20.00	28.50

NOTE: Earlier dates (AH1210-1213) exist for this type.

In the name of Muhammad Akbar II
AH1221-1253/1806-1837AD

PAISA

COPPER

KM#	Date	Year	Good	VG	Fine	VF
59	AH1224	3	1.00	1.65	2.50	4.00
	122x	4	1.00	1.65	2.50	4.00
	1232	—	1.00	1.65	2.50	4.00
	1235	14	1.00	1.65	2.50	4.00
	1236	15	1.00	1.65	2.50	4.00
	1241	—	1.00	1.65	2.50	4.00

1/4 RUPEE

SILVER

KM#	Date	Year	VG	Fine	VF	XF
A60	AH1228	—	9.00	18.00	28.00	40.00

1/2 RUPEE

SILVER, 5.35-5.80 g
Similar to 1 Rupee, KM#61.

KM#	Date	Year	VG	Fine	VF	XF
60	AH—	—	9.00	18.00	28.00	40.00

RUPEE

Mint marks:

 on obverse

 on reverse

SILVER, 10.70-11.60 g

KM#	Date	Year	VG	Fine	VF	XF
61	AH1222	1	9.00	18.00	28.00	40.00

KM#	Date	Year	VG	Fine	VF	XF
62	AH1227	6	6.50	13.00	22.00	32.00
	1228	7	6.50	13.00	22.00	32.00
	1229	8	6.50	13.00	22.00	32.00
	1230	9	6.50	13.00	22.00	32.00
	1231	10	6.50	13.00	22.00	32.00
	1231	11	6.50	13.00	22.00	32.00
	1232	11	6.50	13.00	22.00	32.00
	1233	12	6.50	13.00	22.00	32.00
	1234	13	6.50	13.00	22.00	32.00
	1235	14	6.50	13.00	22.00	32.00
	1236	15	6.50	13.00	22.00	32.00
	1239	19	6.50	13.00	22.00	32.00
	1240	19	6.50	13.00	22.00	32.00
	1241	19	6.50	13.00	22.00	32.00

BAIJA BAO

AH1243-1249/1827-1833AD

In the name of Muhammad Shah
AH1131-1161/1719-1748AD

With Nagari *Shri* for Baija Bao

NAZARANA 1/3 MOHUR

GOLD, 18mm, 3.57-3.80 g
Nagari *Shri* for Baija Rao

KM#	Date	Year	VG	Fine	VF	XF
63	AH1130	2 (frozen)	125.00	165.00	200.00	235.00

NOTE: Struck ca.1827AD.

In the name of Muhammad Akbar II
AH1221-1253/1806-1837AD

PAISA

COPPER

KM#	Date	Year	Good	VG	Fine	VF
64	AH1244	24	3.00	5.00	8.00	12.50
	1245	25	3.00	5.00	8.00	12.50

With Nagari *Shri* for Baija Bao

RUPEE

SILVER, 10.70-11.60 g
Obv. & Rev: Five-flowered symbol.

KM#	Date	Year	VG	Fine	VF	XF
65	AH—	23	11.50	22.50	35.00	50.00

NOTE: The regnal year 23 becomes frozen with this issue on all silver coins of this mint (identified by five-flowered symbol) and of Lashkar Mint.

JANKOJI RAO

AH1243-1259/1827-1843AD

In the name of Muhammad Shah
AH1131-1161/1719-1748AD

With initial *Ja*.

NAZARANA 1/3 MOHUR

GOLD, 3.57-3.80 g
Nagari *Ja* for Jankoji

KM#	Date	Year	VG	Fine	VF	XF
66	AH1130	2 (frozen)	125.00	165.00	200.00	235.00

NOTE: Struck ca.1834AD.

In the name of Muhammad Akbar II
AH1221-1253/1806-1837AD

With additional initial of Jankoji Rao

Symbols:

 on obverse

 on rev. (points up or down)

1/8 RUPEE

SILVER, 1.34-1.45 g
Similar to Rupee, KM#72.

KM#	Date	Year	VG	Fine	VF	XF
67	AH1244	23	5.00	7.00	10.00	15.00

1/4 RUPEE

SILVER, 2.68-2.90 g
Similar to Rupee, KM#72.

KM#	Date	Year	VG	Fine	VF	XF
68	AH1244	23	6.00	10.00	14.00	20.00

Similar to Rupee, KM#73.

KM#	Date	Year	VG	Fine	VF	XF
69	AH1244	23	6.00	10.00	14.00	20.00

1/2 RUPEE

SILVER, 5.35-5.70 g

KM#	Date	Year	VG	Fine	VF	XF
70	AH1244	23	7.50	12.50	17.50	25.00

KM#	Date	Year	VG	Fine	VF	XF
71	AH1244	23	7.50	12.50	17.50	25.00

RUPEE

SILVER, 10.70-11.60 g
Rev: Bow and arrow points down.

KM#	Date	Year	VG	Fine	VF	XF
72	AH1244	23	8.50	14.00	20.00	28.00

Rev: Bow and arrow points up.

KM#	Date	Year	VG	Fine	VF	XF
73	AH1244	23	8.50	14.00	20.00	28.00

JAYAJI RAO

AH1259-1304/1843-1886

In the name of Muhammad Shah
AH1131-1161/1719-1748AD

जी

With initial *Ji*.

NAZARANA 1/3 MOHUR

GOLD, 3.57-3.80 g
Nagari *Ji* for Jayaji

KM#	Date	Year	VG	Fine	VF	XF
74	AH1130	2 (frozen)	125.00	165.00	200.00	235.00

NOTE: Struck ca.1843AD.

MOHUR

GOLD

KM#	Date	Year	VG	Fine	VF	XF
A75	AH1130	2	400.00	475.00	550.00	600.00

In the name of Muhammad Akbar II
AH1221-1253/1806-1837AD

With additional initial of Jayaji Rao

Symbols as on KM#69 and 70, but more stylized.

PAISA

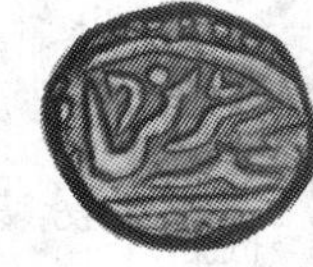

COPPER

KM#	Date	Year	Good	VG	Fine	VF
75	AH1269	—	1.25	2.00	3.00	5.00
	127x	42	1.25	2.00	3.00	5.00
	127x	45	1.25	2.00	3.00	5.00
	127x	46	1.25	2.00	3.00	5.00
	127x	47	1.25	2.00	3.00	5.00

KM#	Date	Year	Good	VG	Fine	VF
75	1277	48	1.25	2.00	3.00	5.00
	1278	49	1.25	2.00	3.00	5.00
	1279	49	1.25	2.00	3.00	5.00
	—	54	1.25	2.00	3.00	5.00
	—	56	1.25	2.00	3.00	5.00

Obv: Trisul.

KM#	Date	Year	Good	VG	Fine	VF
76	AH—	—	1.25	2.00	3.00	5.00

1/16 RUPEE

SILVER, 9mm, 0.67-0.72 g

KM#	Date	Year	VG	Fine	VF	XF
77	AH—	23	4.00	6.00	9.00	14.00

1/8 RUPEE

SILVER, 11mm, 1.34-1.45 g

KM#	Date	Year	VG	Fine	VF	XF
78	AH—	23	5.00	7.00	10.00	15.00

1/4 RUPEE

SILVER, 13mm, 2.68-2.90 g

KM#	Date	Year	VG	Fine	VF	XF
79	AH—	23	6.00	10.00	14.00	20.00

1/2 RUPEE

SILVER, 15mm, 5.35-5.70 g
Rev: Bow and arrow points down.

KM#	Date	Year	VG	Fine	VF	XF
80	AH—	23	6.00	10.00	17.50	25.00

RUPEE

SILVER, 17-19mm, 10.70-11.60 g
Rev: Bow and arrow points up.

KM#	Date	Year	VG	Fine	VF	XF
81	AH—	23	5.50	9.00	14.00	20.00

Rev: Bow and arrow points down.

KM#	Date	Year	VG	Fine	VF	XF
82	AH—	23	5.50	9.00	14.00	20.00

NAZARANA RUPEE

SILVER, 10.70-11.60 g

KM#	Date	Year	VG	Fine	VF	XF
83	AH125x	23	60.00	100.00	140.00	200.00

MADHO RAO

AH1304-1313/1886-1925AD

In the name of Muhammad Shah
AH1131-1161/1719-1748AD
With initial of Madho Rao II

1/3 MOHUR

GOLD, 21mm, 3.57-3.80 g

KM#	Date	Year	VG	Fine	VF	XF
84	AH1130	2 (frozen)	125.00	165.00	200.00	235.00

NOTE: Struck ca.1886AD.

ISAGARH MINT

DAULAT RAO

AH1209-1243/1794-1827AD

In the name of Muhammad Akbar II
AH1221-1253/1806-1837AD

Mint marks: 

PAISA

COPPER
Obv: Cannon right. Rev: Snake.

KM#	Date	Year	VG	Fine	VF	XF
89	AH—	2x	11.50	17.50	26.50	38.00

RUPEE

SILVER, 10.70-11.60 g
Rev: Cannon left.

KM#	Date	Year	VG	Fine	VF	XF
85	AH122x	8	13.50	20.00	27.50	38.00
	1230	10	13.50	20.00	27.50	38.00
	1230	11	13.50	20.00	27.50	38.00

Obv: Cannon left. Rev: Bhilsa leaf and battle axe.

KM#	Date	Year	VG	Fine	VF	XF
86	AH—	—	13.50	20.00	27.50	38.00

Obv: Cannon right.
Rev: Bhilsa leaf, battle axe and snake.

KM#	Date	Year	VG	Fine	VF	XF
87	AH1229	8	13.50	20.00	27.50	38.00
	1230	10	13.50	20.00	27.50	38.00
	1231	11	13.50	20.00	27.50	38.00
	123x	15	13.50	20.00	27.50	38.00

Obv: Cannon right and snake.
Rev: Bhilsa leaf and battle axe.

KM#	Date	Year	VG	Fine	VF	XF
88	AH—	—	13.50	20.00	27.50	38.00

JANKOJI RAO

AH1243-1259/1827-1843AD

1/4 RUPEE

SILVER, 2.67-2.90 g
Similar to 1 Rupee, KM#92.

KM#	Date	Year	VG	Fine	VF	XF
A90	AH12xx	23	8.50	13.50	20.00	28.50

1/2 RUPEE

Mint marks:

on reverse

SILVER, 5.35-5.80 g
Similar to 1 Rupee, KM#92.

KM#	Date	Year	VG	Fine	VF	XF
90	AH1243	23	8.50	13.50	20.00	28.50

Similar to 1 Rupee, KM#93.

KM#	Date	Year	VG	Fine	VF	XF
91	AH1223 (error 1243)	23	8.50	13.50	20.00	28.50

RUPEE

SILVER, 10.70-11.60 g

KM#	Date	Year	VG	Fine	VF	XF
92	AH1223 (error)	23	11.50	16.50	25.00	37.50
	1243	23	11.50	16.50	25.00	37.50

Mint mark:

on obv.

Obv: Lotus bud.

KM#	Date	Year	VG	Fine	VF	XF
93	ND	—	7.00	11.00	16.50	25.00
	AH1252	—	7.00	11.00	16.50	25.00

JAWAD MINT

JANKOJI RAO

AH1243-1259/1827-1843AD

PAISA

COPPER
Obv: Letter *Ja* and spear.

KM#	Date	Year	Good	VG	Fine	VF
103	ND	—	2.50	4.50	6.50	10.00

Obv: Letter *Ja* (retrograde) and spear.

KM#	Date	Year	Good	VG	Fine	VF
104	ND	—	2.50	4.50	6.50	10.00

Obv: Banner, letter *Ji* and snake. Rev: Trisul.

KM#	Date	Year	Good	VG	Fine	VF
105	ND	—	3.00	5.00	8.00	12.50

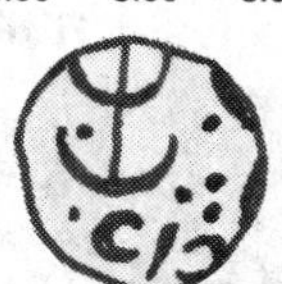

Obv: Letter *Ji*, scimitar and snake.
Rev: Trisul.

KM#	Date	Year	Good	VG	Fine	VF
106	ND	—	2.50	4.50	6.50	10.00

Obv: Letters *Ja*, *Ja*, *Ja?* and snake.
Rev: Trisul.

KM#	Date	Year	Good	VG	Fine	VF
107	ND	—	2.50	4.50	6.50	10.00

Obv: Snake between letters *S* and *ra*, scimitar.
Rev: Trisul.

KM#	Date	Year	Good	VG	Fine	VF
108	ND	—	2.50	4.50	6.50	7.50

MADHO RAO

AH1304-1313/1886-1925AD

PAISA

With initial of Madho Rao II

COPPER
Obv: Snake between letters *Ji* and *Ma*, scimitar.
Rev: Trisul.

KM#	Date	Year	Good	VG	Fine	VF
109	ND	—	3.00	5.00	8.00	12.50

Obv: Letters *Ji* and *Ma*, snake.
Rev: Trisul.

KM#	Date	Year	Good	VG	Fine	VF
110	ND	—	3.00	5.00	8.00	12.50

JHANSI MINT

To Gwalior 1865-1886AD

Regular Jhansi types (q.v.), identifiable as Sindhia issues only by date, and by Persian Ji for Jayaji. Similar to coins struck by the Maratha Governors of the Peshwa until 1853AD.

JAYAJI RAO

AH1259-1304/1843-1886AD

PAISA

COPPER, 11.15-15.55 g
Obv: Trisul. Rev: Persian *Ji* above leaf, flywhisk.

KM#	Date	Year	Good	VG	Fine	VF
111	ND	—	3.00	5.00	8.00	12.50

1/8 RUPEE

SILVER, 1.34-1.45 g
Rev: Persian *Ji*.

KM#	Date	Year	VG	Fine	VF	XF
112	ND	—	6.50	10.00	15.00	22.50

RUPEE

SILVER, 10.70-11.60 g
Rev: Persian *Ji*.

KM#	Date	Year	VG	Fine	VF	XF
113	AH—	48	7.00	11.00	16.50	25.00
	1282	5x	7.00	11.00	16.50	25.00
	1284	5x	7.00	11.00	16.50	25.00

LASHKAR MINT

In the name of Shah Alam II

AH1173-1221/1759-1806AD

NOTE: All the following coins of this mint are in the name of Shah Alam II, with initials and mint marks as shown.

Mint mark:

With regnal years of Shah Alam II

AH1173-1221/1759-1806AD

1/8 RUPEE

SILVER, 12mm, 1.34-1.45 g

KM#	Date	Year	VG	Fine	VF	XF
116	ND	(1811-21)	6.00	9.00	13.50	20.00

1/4 RUPEE

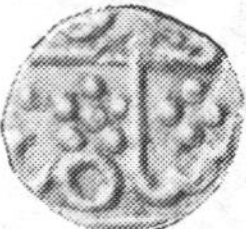

SILVER, 2.68-2.90 g

KM#	Date	Year	VG	Fine	VF	XF
117	ND	(1811-21)	6.00	9.00	13.50	20.00

1/2 RUPEE

SILVER, 16mm, 5.35-5.80 g

KM#	Date	Year	VG	Fine	VF	XF
118	ND	(1811-21)	7.00	11.00	16.50	25.00

RUPEE

SILVER, 10.70-11.60 g

KM#	Date	Year	VG	Fine	VF	XF
119	ND	(1811-21)	10.00	15.00	21.50	30.00

Mint marks:

With regnal years of Muhammad Akbar II

AH1221-1253/1806-1837AD

1/8 RUPEE

SILVER, 1.34-1.45 g

KM#	Date	Year	VG	Fine	VF	XF
120	AH—	—	4.00	6.00	9.00	14.00

1/4 RUPEE

SILVER, 2.68-2.90 g
Rev: W/dot in "*J*" of *Julus*.

KM#	Date	Year	VG	Fine	VF	XF
121.1	AH—	—	5.00	7.00	10.00	15.00

Rev: W/o dot in "*J*" of *Julus*.

KM#	Date	Year	VG	Fine	VF	XF
121.2	AH—	—	5.00	7.00	10.00	15.00

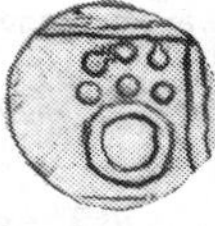

Rev: Lily in "*J*" of *Julus*.

KM#	Date	Year	VG	Fine	VF	XF
122	AH—	17	5.00	7.00	10.00	15.00

1/2 RUPEE

SILVER, 5.35-5.80 g
Rev: W/dot in "*J*" of *Julus*.

KM#	Date	Year	VG	Fine	VF	XF
123.1	AH—	—	6.00	9.00	13.50	20.00

Rev: W/o dot in "*J*" of *Julus*.

KM#	Date	Year	VG	Fine	VF	XF
123.2	AH—	—	6.00	9.00	13.50	20.00

Rev: Lily blossom in "*J*" in *Julus*.

KM#	Date	Year	VG	Fine	VF	XF
A124	AH—	17	6.00	9.00	13.50	20.00

RUPEE

SILVER, 10.70-11.60 g
Rev: W/and w/o dot in "*J*" of *Julus*.

KM#	Date	Year	VG	Fine	VF	XF
124	AH—	16	6.00	10.00	15.00	22.50
	—	17	6.00	10.00	15.00	22.50
	—	18	6.00	10.00	15.00	22.50
	—	19	6.00	10.00	15.00	22.50
	—	21	6.00	10.00	15.00	22.50
	—	22	6.00	10.00	15.00	22.50

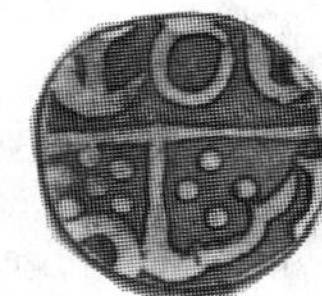

Rev: Lily in "*J*" of *Julus*.

KM#	Date	Year	VG	Fine	VF	XF
125	AH—	17	6.00	10.00	15.00	22.50
	—	19	6.00	10.00	15.00	22.50

BAIJA BAI

AH1243-1249/1827-1833AD

In the name of Muhammad Shah

AH1131-1161/1719-1748AD

MOHUR

GOLD, 10.70-11.60 g
Rev: *Shri*.

KM#	Date	Year	VG	Fine	VF	XF
126	AH1130	2	220.00	240.00	265.00	300.00

In the name of Shah Alam II

AH1173-1221/1759-1806AD

1/4 RUPEE

SILVER, 15mm, 2.68-2.90 g
Rev: *Shri* and trisul.

KM#	Date	Year	VG	Fine	VF	XF
127	AH—	23	5.00	7.00	10.00	15.00

1/2 RUPEE

SILVER, 17mm, 5.35-5.80 g
Rev: *Shri* and trisul.

KM#	Date	Year	VG	Fine	VF	XF
128	AH—	23	5.00	8.00	12.50	18.50

RUPEE

SILVER, 10.70-11.60 g
Rev: *Shri* and trisul.

KM#	Date	Year	VG	Fine	VF	XF
129	AH—	23	6.50	10.00	15.00	22.50

JANKOJI RAO

Struck by Jankoji Rao

AH1243-1259/1827-1843AD

Mint marks:

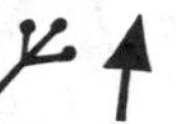

1/2 PAISA

COPPER, 5.60-6.20 g
Obv: Trisul. Rev: Flywhisk and spear.

KM#	Date	Year	Good	VG	Fine	VF
130	AH—	23	2.50	5.00	8.00	12.50

PAISA

COPPER, 13.35 g
Obv: Trisul. Rev: Flywhisk and spear.

KM#	Date	Year	Good	VG	Fine	VF
131.1	AH—	12	1.25	2.50	3.50	5.50

Obv: Trisul. Rev: Spear, r.y. off flan.

KM#	Date	Year	Good	VG	Fine	VF
131.2	AH—	22	1.25	2.50	3.50	5.50

Obv: Flower. Rev: Whisk and trident.

KM#	Date	Year	Good	VG	Fine	VF
131.3	AH—	23	1.25	2.50	3.50	5.50

Obv: Flower. Rev: Spear, trisul and whisk.

KM#	Date	Year	Good	VG	Fine	VF
131.4	AH—	31	1.25	2.50	3.50	5.50

Obv: Winged sun burst. Rev: Spear, trident and whisk.

KM#	Date	Year	Good	VG	Fine	VF
131.5	AH—	—	1.25	2.50	3.50	5.50

Obv: Double pennant. Rev: Whisk, trident and spear.

KM#	Date	Year	Good	VG	Fine	VF
131.6	AH—	—	1.25	2.50	3.50	5.50

Obv: Trident. Rev: Spear and standard.

KM#	Date	Year	Good	VG	Fine	VF
131.7	AH—	—	1.25	2.50	3.50	5.50

2 PAISA

BRONZE

KM#	Date	Year	Good	VG	Fine	VF
A132	AH—	22	—	—	—	—

In the name of Muhammad Shah

AH1131-1161/1719-1748AD

MOHUR

GOLD, 10.70-11.40 g
Rev: Bow and arrow points up, *Ja*.

KM#	Date	Year	VG	Fine	VF	XF
132	AH1130	2	220.00	240.00	265.00	300.00

Rev: Bow and arrow points down, *Ja*.

KM#	Date	Year	VG	Fine	VF	XF
133	AH1130	2	220.00	240.00	265.00	300.00

In the name of Shah Alam II

AH1173-1221/1759-1806AD

1/8 RUPEE

SILVER, 1.34-1.45 g
Rev: Bow and arrow points up, *Ja* and trisul.

KM#	Date	Year	VG	Fine	VF	XF
134	AH—	23	3.00	4.50	6.50	10.00

Rev: Bow and arrow points down, *Ja* and trisul.

KM#	Date	Year	VG	Fine	VF	XF
135	AH—	23	3.00	4.50	6.50	10.00

1/4 RUPEE

SILVER, 12mm, 2.68-2.90 g
Rev: Bow and arrow points up, *Ja* and trisul.

KM#	Date	Year	VG	Fine	VF	XF
136	AH—	23	4.00	6.00	9.00	14.00

Rev: Bow and arrow points down, *Ja* and trisul.

KM#	Date	Year	VG	Fine	VF	XF
137	AH—	23	4.00	6.00	9.00	14.00

1/2 RUPEE

SILVER, 16mm, 5.35-5.80 g
Rev: Bow and arrow points up, *Ja* and trisul.

KM#	Date	Year	VG	Fine	VF	XF
138	AH—	23	5.00	7.00	10.00	15.00

Rev: Bow and arrow points down, *Ja* and trisul.

KM#	Date	Year	VG	Fine	VF	XF
139	AH—	23	5.00	7.00	10.00	15.00

RUPEE

SILVER, 10.70-11.60 g
Rev: Bow and arrow points up, *Ja* and trisul.

KM#	Date	Year	VG	Fine	VF	XF
140	AH—	23	7.00	11.00	16.50	25.00

Rev: Bow and arrow points down, *Ja* and trisul.

KM#	Date	Year	VG	Fine	VF	XF
141	AH—	23	7.00	11.00	16.50	25.00

JAYAJI RAO

AH1259-1304/1843-1886AD

Anonymous Issues

Struck by Jayaji Rao for 30 years, 1869-1899AD.

1/2 PAISA

COPPER, 12mm, 3.00 g

KM#	Date	Year	Good	VG	Fine	VF
142	VS1926	(1869)	5.00	7.00	10.00	15.00

PAISA

COPPER, 6.00 g

KM#	Date	Year	Good	VG	Fine	VF
143	VS1926	(1869)	.35	.75	1.25	2.25

Regular Coinage

In name of Shah Alam II

AH1173-1221/1759-1806AD

With initials of Jayaji Rao

Copper coins have symbols

 or  on reverse

1/2 PAISA

COPPER, 4.80-4.95 g
Obv: Trisul. Rev: Flywhisk, *Ji* and spear.

KM#	Date	Year	Good	VG	Fine	VF
144	AH—	23	1.50	3.00	5.00	7.50

PAISA

COPPER, 9.60-9.90 g

KM#	Date	Year	Good	VG	Fine	VF
145	AH—	23	1.00	1.75	3.00	5.00

2 PAISA

COPPER, 17.00-20.00 g
Obv: *Ji*.

KM#	Date	Year	Good	VG	Fine	VF
146.1	AH—	23	2.00	3.75	6.00	10.00

Obv: W/o *Ji*.

KM#	Date	Year	Good	VG	Fine	VF
146.2	AH—	23	3.00	5.00	8.00	12.50

1/16 RUPEE

SILVER, 9mm, 0.67-0.72 g
Rev: Bow and arrow points down, *Ji*.

KM#	Date	Year	VG	Fine	VF	XF
147	AH—	23	2.50	4.50	6.50	10.00

1/8 RUPEE

SILVER, 1.34-1.45 g
Rev: Bow and arrow points down, *Ji*.

KM#	Date	Year	VG	Fine	VF	XF
148.1	AH—	23	4.00	6.00	9.00	14.00
		25	4.00	6.00	9.00	14.00

Rev: + below *Ji*.

KM#	Date	Year	VG	Fine	VF	XF
148.2	AH—	—	4.00	6.00	9.00	14.00

1/4 RUPEE

SILVER, 2.68-2.90 g
Rev: Bow and arrow points down, *Ji*.

KM#	Date	Year	VG	Fine	VF	XF
149	AH—	23	4.00	6.00	9.00	14.00
	—	24	4.00	6.00	9.00	14.00
	—	25	4.00	6.00	9.00	14.00
	—	27	4.00	6.00	9.00	14.00

1/2 RUPEE

SILVER, 5.35-5.80 g
Rev: Bow and arrow points down, *Ji*.

KM#	Date	Year	VG	Fine	VF	XF
150	AH—	23	5.00	7.00	10.00	15.00
	—	25	5.00	7.00	10.00	15.00
	—	26	5.00	7.00	10.00	15.00
	—	27	5.00	7.00	10.00	15.00

Rev: Bow and arrow points up, *Ji*.

KM#	Date	Year	VG	Fine	VF	XF
151	AH—	2x	5.00	7.00	10.00	15.00

RUPEE

SILVER, 10.70-11.60 g
Rev: Bow and arrow points down, *Ji*.

KM#	Date	Year	VG	Fine	VF	XF
152	AH—	23	6.00	9.00	13.50	20.00
	—	27	6.00	9.00	13.50	20.00
	—	29	6.00	9.00	13.50	20.00

Rev: Bow and arrow points up, *Ji*.

KM#	Date	Year	VG	Fine	VF	XF
153	AH—	2x	7.00	11.00	16.50	25.00

NAZARANA RUPEE

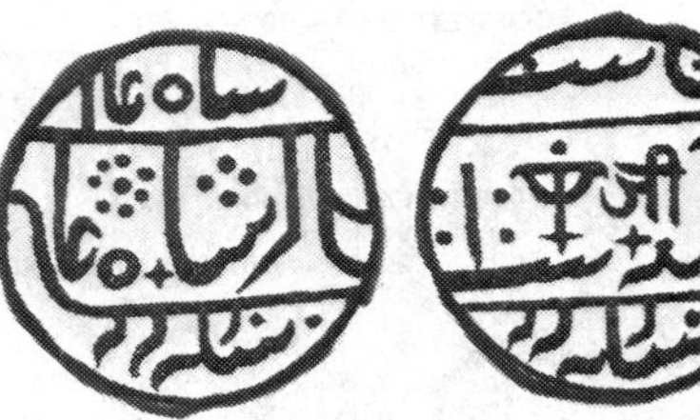

SILVER, 10.70-11.60 g
Rev: Bow and arrow points down, *Ji*, trisul.

KM#	Date	Year	VG	Fine	VF	XF
154	AH—	23	75.00	110.00	165.00	250.00

1/5 MOHUR

GOLD, 2.21 g

KM#	Date	Year	VG	Fine	VF	XF
A155	AH—	—	—	—	—	—

MOHUR

GOLD, 10.70-11.40 g
Rev: Bow and arrow points up, *Ji*.

KM#	Date	Year	VG	Fine	VF	XF
155	AH1130	2	250.00	325.00	400.00	500.00

MADHO RAO

VS1943-1982/1886-1925AD

With initial of Madho Rao II

Symbols as on previous series.

1/16 RUPEE

SILVER, 0.67-0.72 g
Rev: Bow and arrow points down *Ma*, trisul.

KM#	Date	Year	VG	Fine	VF	XF
A156	AH—	23	3.00	4.50	6.50	10.00

1/8 RUPEE

SILVER, 1.34-1.45 g
Rev: Bow and arrow points down, *Ma*, trisul.

KM#	Date	Year	VG	Fine	VF	XF
156	AH—	23	4.00	6.00	9.00	14.00

1/4 RUPEE

SILVER, 2.68-2.90 g
Rev: Bow and arrow points down, *Ma*, trisul.

KM#	Date	Year	VG	Fine	VF	XF
157	AH—	23	5.00	7.00	10.00	15.50

1/2 RUPEE

SILVER, 5.35-5.80 g
Rev: Bow and arrow points down, *Ma*, trisul.

KM#	Date	Year	VG	Fine	VF	XF
158	AH—	23	6.00	9.00	13.50	20.00

RUPEE

SILVER, 10.70-11.60 g
Rev: Bow and arrow points down, *Ma*, trisul.

KM#	Date	Year	VG	Fine	VF	XF
159	AH—	23	5.50	8.00	12.50	18.50

1/4 MOHUR

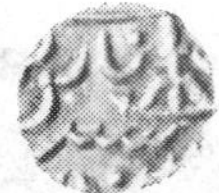

GOLD

KM#	Date	Year	VG	Fine	VF	XF
A160	ND	—	—	—	—	—

MOHUR

GOLD, 10.70-11.40 g
Rev: Bow and arrow points up, *Ma*, trisul.

KM#	Date	Year	VG	Fine	VF	XF
160	AH1130	2	250.00	325.00	400.00	500.00

MILLED COINAGE

PIE

COPPER

KM#	Date	Year	VG	Fine	VF	XF
A161	VS1946	(1889)	—	—	Rare	—

KM#	Date	Year	VG	Fine	VF	XF
161	VS(19)55	(1898)	—	—	Rare	—

1/2 PICE

COPPER, 20mm

KM#	Date	Year	VG	Fine	VF	XF
162	VS1946	(1889)	75.00	125.00	250.00	350.00

Punched from 1/4 Anna, KM#168.

KM#	Date	Year	VG	Fine	VF	XF
163	VS1946	(1889)	75.00	125.00	200.00	—

KM#	Date	Year	Fine	VF	XF	Unc
164	VS1956	(1899)	.65	2.00	4.00	10.00
	1957	(1900)	.65	2.00	4.00	10.00

NOTE: Later date (VS1958) exists for this type.

1/4 ANNA

COPPER
Obv: 16 point star, wide nose on sun.

KM#	Date	Year	VG	Fine	VF	XF
165	VS1944	(1887)	100.00	175.00	275.00	400.00

Obv: 18 point star, wide nose on sun.

KM#	Date	Year	VG	Fine	VF	XF
166	VS1944	(1887)	100.00	175.00	275.00	400.00

Obv: 17 point star, wide nose on sun.

KM#	Date	Year	VG	Fine	VF	XF
167	VS1945	(1888)	100.00	150.00	250.00	475.00

Obv: 16 point star, narrow nose on sun.

KM#	Date	Year	VG	Fine	VF	XF
168	VS1946	(1889)	62.50	87.50	140.00	200.00

KM#	Date	Year	Fine	VF	XF	Unc
169	VS1953	(1896)	.75	2.25	4.50	11.00
	1954	(1897)	.75	2.25	4.50	11.00
	1956	(1899)	.75	2.25	4.50	11.00
	1957	(1900)	.75	2.25	4.50	11.00

NOTE: Later date (VS1958) exists for this type.

1/2 ANNA

COPPER

KM#	Date	Year	VG	Fine	VF	XF
173	VS1946	(1889)	75.00	135.00	200.00	300.00

RUPEE

SILVER, 32mm

KM#	Date	Year	VG	Fine	VF	XF
174	VS1954	(1897)	75.00	135.00	200.00	300.00

NARWAR MINT

To Gwalior from 1805AD

Coins continued to be struck in the types of Narwar state with dates after AH1221/1806AD. The AH1230 date was retained for several years.

Daulat Rao

AH1209-1243/1794-1827AD

In the name of Shah Alam II
AH1173-1221/1759-1806AD

Mint marks:

Katar 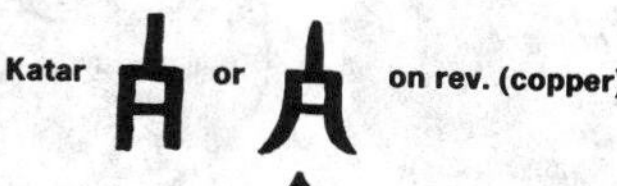 **on rev. (copper)**

Bhilsa leaf  **on rev. (silver)**

1/2 PAISA

COPPER, 3.37 g
Rev: Vertical katar.

KM#	Date	Year	Good	VG	Fine	VF
184	AH1230	7	—	—	—	—
(184.1)	1230	21	1.75	3.00	5.00	8.00

NOTE: For previously listed earlier dates see Narwar.

PAISA

COPPER

KM#	Date	Year	Good	VG	Fine	VF
185	AH1228	7	2.00	3.50	5.00	7.50
	1230	12	2.00	3.50	5.00	7.50
	1230	21	2.00	3.50	5.00	7.50

1/16 RUPEE

SILVER, 0.67-0.72 g

KM#	Date	Year	VG	Fine	VF	XF
186	AH1230	—	3.00	4.50	6.50	10.00

1/8 RUPEE

SILVER, 1.34-1.45 g

KM#	Date	Year	VG	Fine	VF	XF
187	AH1230	—	4.00	6.00	9.00	13.50

1/4 RUPEE

SILVER, 2.68-2.90 g

KM#	Date	Year	Good	VG	Fine	VF
188	AH1230	15	6.50	10.00	15.00	22.50

NOTE: For previously listed earlier date (AH1207) see Narwar.

1/2 RUPEE

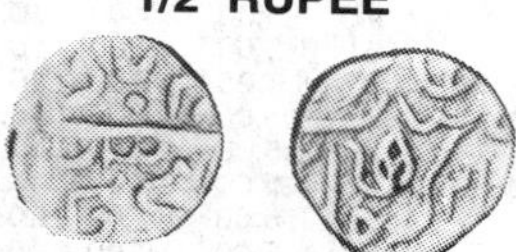

SILVER, 5.35-5.80 g

KM#	Date	Year	VG	Fine	VF	XF
189	AH1230	12	6.50	10.00	15.00	22.50
	1230	21	6.50	10.00	15.00	22.50

RUPEE

SILVER, 10.70-11.60 g

KM#	Date	Year	VG	Fine	VF	XF
190	AH1228	7	7.50	12.50	18.50	27.50
	1230	9	7.50	12.50	18.50	27.50
	1230	11	7.50	12.50	18.50	27.50
	1230	12	7.50	12.50	18.50	27.50
	1230	15	7.50	12.50	18.50	27.50
	1230	21	7.50	12.50	18.50	27.50
	—	35	7.50	12.50	18.50	27.50

RAJOD MINT

Symbol: Figure of Hanuman.

1/2 PAISA

COPPER, 7.71 g
Obv: Lingam at right.

KM#	Date	Year	Good	VG	Fine	VF
191	VS1936	(1879)	4.00	7.50	12.50	20.00

PAISA

COPPER, 17.10 g

KM#	Date	Year	Good	VG	Fine	VF
192.1	VS1930	(1873)	7.50	12.00	20.00	35.00

Reduced weight, 11.50-12.30 g
Obv: Hanuman. Rev: 9 of date in Sanskrit.

KM#	Date	Year	Good	VG	Fine	VF
192.2	VS1930	(1873)	7.50	12.00	20.00	35.00

Obv: Hanuman. Rev: 9 of date in Gujarati.

KM#	Date	Year	Good	VG	Fine	VF
193	VS1930	(1873)	7.50	12.00	20.00	35.00

Obv: Lingam at right.
Rev: 9 of date in sanskrit.

KM#	Date	Year	Good	VG	Fine	VF
194	VS1936	(1879)	7.50	12.00	20.00	35.00

Rev: 9 of date in Gujarati.

KM#	Date	Year	Good	VG	Fine	VF
195	VS1936	(1879)	7.50	12.00	20.00	35.00

Obv: Snake at right.

KM#	Date	Year	Good	VG	Fine	VF
196	VS1940	(1883)	7.50	12.00	20.00	35.00

RATHGARH MINT

RUPEE

SILVER, 10.70-11.60 g

Obv: Snake

KM#	Date	Year	VG	Fine	VF	XF
197	AH1221	1	15.00	21.00	30.00	40.00
	12xx	3	15.00	21.00	30.00	40.00
	12xx	4	15.00	21.00	30.00	40.00
	12xx	6	15.00	21.00	30.00	40.00
	12xx	7	15.00	21.00	30.00	40.00
	1232	8	15.00	21.00	30.00	40.00
	12xx	13	15.00	21.00	30.00	40.00
	123x	15	15.00	21.00	30.00	40.00
	12xx	18	15.00	21.00	30.00	40.00
	12xx	22	15.00	21.00	30.00	40.00

SHADORAH MINT

NOTE: Formerly listed as Seondha.

In the name of Muhammad Akbar II
AH1221-1253/1806-1837AD

Mint marks:

KM#199 on rev.

also has  on rev.

KM#200 obv.

on rev.

DAULAT RAO

AH1209-1243/1794-1827AD

RUPEE

SILVER, 10.70-11.60 g
Rev: Cannon left, mintname at bottom.

KM#	Date	Year	VG	Fine	VF	XF
199	AH1228	—	—	—	Rare	—

Obv: Cannon right, mintname at top.

KM#	Date	Year	VG	Fine	VF	XF
200	ND	—	—	—	Rare	—

SHEOPUR MINT

In the name of Muhammad Akbar II
AH1221-1253/1806-1837AD

Mint mark:

on rev.

DAULAT RAO

AH1209-1243/1794-1827AD

RUPEE

SILVER, 10.70-11.60 g
Rev: Cannon left.

KM#	Date	Year	VG	Fine	VF	XF
201	AH1228	7	6.50	13.00	22.00	32.00
	1228	8	6.50	13.00	22.00	32.00
	1228	9	6.50	13.00	22.00	32.00
	1228	10	6.50	13.00	22.00	32.00
	1228	11	6.50	13.00	22.00	32.00
	1228	12	6.50	13.00	22.00	32.00
	1228	13	6.50	13.00	22.00	32.00
	1228	15	6.50	13.00	22.00	32.00
	1228	16	6.50	13.00	22.00	32.00
	1228	17	6.50	13.00	22.00	32.00
	1228	18	6.50	13.00	22.00	32.00
	1228	19	6.50	13.00	22.00	32.00
	1228	20	6.50	13.00	22.00	32.00
	1228	21	6.50	13.00	22.00	32.00
	1228	22	6.50	13.00	22.00	32.00
	1228	27	6.50	13.00	22.00	32.00
	1228	28	6.50	13.00	22.00	32.00
	1230	—	6.50	13.00	22.00	32.00

BAIJA BAO

AH1243-1249/1827-1833AD

RUPEE

SILVER, 10.70-11.60 g
Rev: Cannon left.

KM#	Date	Year	VG	Fine	VF	XF
202	AH1248	27	9.00	18.00	28.00	40.00
	1248	28	9.00	18.00	28.00	40.00

JAYAJI RAO

AH1259-1304/1843-1886AD

1/8 RUPEE

SILVER, 1.34-1.45 g
Rev: Cannon left. *Ji*.

KM#	Date	Year	VG	Fine	VF	XF
A203	AH12xx	1	10.00	20.00	35.00	50.00

RUPEE

SILVER, 10.70-11.60 g
Rev: Cannon left, *Ji*.

KM#	Date	Year	VG	Fine	VF	XF
203	AH1270	1	9.00	18.00	28.00	40.00
	1271	1	9.00	18.00	28.00	40.00
	1272	1	9.00	18.00	28.00	40.00
	1273	1	9.00	18.00	28.00	40.00
	1274	1	9.00	18.00	28.00	40.00
	1276	1	9.00	18.00	28.00	40.00

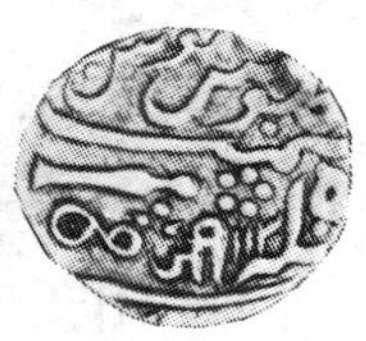

Obv: 113. Rev: 113 and *Ji*.

KM#	Date	Year	VG	Fine	VF	XF
204	AH—	13	9.00	18.00	27.00	38.00
	—	15	9.00	18.00	27.00	38.00

SIPRI MINT

Mintname: Narwar

In the name of Shah Alam II

AH1173-1221/1759-1806AD

1/2 RUPEE

SILVER, 5.35-5.80 g

KM#	Date	Year	VG	Fine	VF	XF
A205	AH1106	47	9.00	18.00	28.00	40.00

RUPEE

SILVER, 10.70-11.60 g

KM#	Date	Year	VG	Fine	VF	XF
205	AH1106	44	7.00	14.00	24.00	35.00
	1106	46	7.00	14.00	24.00	35.00
	1106	47	7.00	14.00	24.00	35.00

NOTE: The above were struck by the Kachwaha Raja of Narwar as tributary to Sindhia.

DAULAT RAO

AH1209-1243/1794-1827AD

RUPEE

SILVER, 10.70-11.60 g
Flower in outline.

KM#	Date	Year	VG	Fine	VF	XF
206	AH1106	47	10.00	20.00	32.00	45.00

Solid flower.

KM#	Date	Year	VG	Fine	VF	XF
207	AH1106	47	10.00	20.00	32.00	45.00

With regnal years of Muhammad Akbar II

AH1221-1253/1806-1837AD

KM#	Date	Year	VG	Fine	VF	XF
208	AH1106	9	13.50	27.00	45.00	65.00

BAIJA BAI

AH1243-1249/1827-1833AD

RUPEE

SILVER, 10.70-11.60 g
Rev: *Shri*.

KM#	Date	Year	VG	Fine	VF	XF
209	AH1106	17	18.00	36.00	60.00	85.00

JANKOJI RAO

AH1243-1259/1833-1843AD

RUPEE

SILVER, 10.70-11.60 g
Rev: *Ja*.

KM#	Date	Year	VG	Fine	VF	XF
210	AH—	9	11.00	22.00	35.00	50.00

With regnal years of Muhammad Akbar II

AH1221-1253/1806-1837AD

KM#	Date	Year	VG	Fine	VF	XF
211	AH—	35	9.00	18.00	30.00	42.00

UJJAIN MINT

Mint marks:

on most issues

on many copper issues

DAULAT RAO

AH1209-1243/1794-1827

PAISA

COPPER, 12.83-14.00 g

KM#	Date	Year	Good	VG	Fine	VF
219	AH12xx	—	1.50	3.00	5.00	7.50

KM#	Date	Year	Good	VG	Fine	VF
220	AH—	—	1.50	3.00	5.00	7.50

KM#	Date	Year	Good	VG	Fine	VF
221	AH—	—	1.50	3.00	5.00	7.50

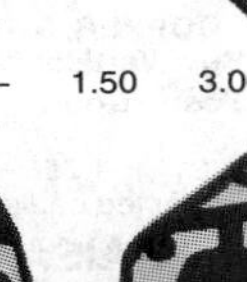

KM#	Date	Year	Good	VG	Fine	VF
222	AH1220	—	1.50	3.00	5.00	7.50

1/4 RUPEE

SILVER, 2.67-2.90 g
Obv: AH date below.

KM#	Date	Year	VG	Fine	VF	XF
A223	AH—	62	5.00	7.00	10.00	15.00
	—	64	5.00	7.00	10.00	15.00

1/2 RUPEE

SILVER, 5.35-5.80 g
Obv: AH date below.

KM#	Date	Year	VG	Fine	VF	XF
B223	AH—	64	5.50	8.00	12.50	18.50

RUPEE

SILVER, 10.70-11.60 g
Obv: AH date below.

KM#	Date	Year	VG	Fine	VF	XF
224	AH1216	44	5.00	7.00	10.00	15.00
	12xx	44	5.00	7.00	10.00	15.00
	—	45	5.00	7.00	10.00	15.00
	—	46	5.00	7.00	10.00	15.00
	—	48	5.00	7.00	10.00	15.00
	—	51	5.00	7.00	10.00	15.00
	—	52	5.00	7.00	10.00	15.00
	1225	53	5.00	7.00	10.00	15.00
	—	55	5.00	7.00	10.00	15.00
	122x	57	5.00	7.00	10.00	15.00
	—	58	5.00	7.00	10.00	15.00
	—	59	5.00	7.00	10.00	15.00
	—	60	5.00	7.00	10.00	15.00
	—	61	5.00	7.00	10.00	15.00
	—	62	5.00	7.00	10.00	15.00
	—	63	5.00	7.00	10.00	15.00
	123x	64	5.00	7.00	10.00	15.00
	—	67	5.00	7.00	10.00	15.00
	—	68	5.00	7.00	10.00	15.00
	—	69	5.00	7.00	10.00	15.00

BAIJA BAI

AH1243-1249/1827-1833AD

1/2 RUPEE

SILVER, 5.35-5.80 g

KM#	Date	Year	VG	Fine	VF	XF
226	AH—	73	7.00	11.00	16.50	25.00

RUPEE

SILVER, 10.70-11.60 g

KM#	Date	Year	VG	Fine	VF	XF
227	AH—	71	6.00	9.00	13.50	20.00
	—	73	6.00	9.00	13.50	20.00

With regnal years of Mohammad Akbar

Rev: *Shri.*

KM#	Date	Year	VG	Fine	VF	XF
228	AH—	23	—	—	Rare	—

JANKOJI RAO

AH1243-1259/1827-1843AD

With regnal years of Shah Alam II

AH1173-1221/1759-1806AD

1/4 RUPEE

SILVER, 2.67-2.90 g

KM#	Date	Year	VG	Fine	VF	XF
A229	AH—	80	5.00	7.00	10.00	15.00

1/2 RUPEE

SILVER, 5.35-5.80 g

KM#	Date	Year	VG	Fine	VF	XF
229	AH—	77	6.00	9.00	12.50	18.50
	—	80	6.00	9.00	12.50	18.50

RUPEE

SILVER, 10.70-11.60 g

KM#	Date	Year	VG	Fine	VF	XF
230	AH—	77	6.00	9.00	13.50	20.00
	—	78	6.00	9.00	13.50	20.00
	—	79	6.00	9.00	13.50	20.00
	—	80	6.00	9.00	13.50	20.00
	—	83	6.00	9.00	13.50	20.00
	—	84	6.00	9.00	13.50	20.00
	—	85	6.00	9.00	13.50	20.00

JAYAJI RAO

AH1259-1304/1843-1886AD

PAISA

COPPER, round or square

KM#	Date	Year	Good	VG	Fine	VF
231	AH1262	—	2.00	3.25	5.00	8.50
	1263	—	2.00	3.25	5.00	8.50
	1266	—	2.00	3.25	5.00	8.50
	1267	—	2.00	3.25	5.00	8.50

Obv: Arrow added.

KM#	Date	Year	Good	VG	Fine	VF
232	AH1278	—	2.00	3.25	5.00	8.50
	1281	—	2.00	3.25	5.00	8.50
	1292	—	2.00	3.25	5.00	8.50
	1295	—	2.00	3.25	5.00	8.50

Obv: *Shri.*

KM#	Date	Year	Good	VG	Fine	VF
233	AH1272	—	2.00	3.25	5.00	8.50
	1278	—	2.00	3.25	5.00	8.50
	1287	—	2.00	3.25	5.00	8.50
	1292	—	2.00	3.25	5.00	8.50
	1295	—	2.00	3.25	5.00	8.50

1/8 RUPEE

SILVER, 1.34-1.45 g

KM#	Date	Year	VG	Fine	VF	XF
234	AH—	—	4.00	6.00	9.00	13.50

1/4 RUPEE

SILVER, 2.68-2.90 g
Regnal year of Shah Alam II

KM#	Date	Year	VG	Fine	VF	XF
235	AH—	92	5.00	7.00	10.00	15.00

1/2 RUPEE

SILVER, 5.35-5.80 g
Regnal year of Shah Alam II

KM#	Date	Year	VG	Fine	VF	XF
236	AH—	98	5.50	8.00	12.50-	18.50

RUPEE

SILVER, 10.70-11.60 g

KM#	Date	Year	VG	Fine	VF	XF
237	AH—	89	6.00	9.00	13.50	20.00
	—	92	6.00	9.00	13.50	20.00
	—	93	6.00	9.00	13.50	20.00
	—	94	6.00	9.00	13.50	20.00
	—	95	6.00	9.00	13.50	20.00
	—	98	6.00	9.00	13.50	20.00
	—	99	6.00	9.00	13.50	20.00
	—	100	6.00	9.00	13.50	20.00

With regnal years of the British "Raj"

These are a continuation of the thick cruder fabric rupees similar to those issued in the later period with Shah Alam II's regnal years.

1/8 RUPEE

SILVER, 1.34-1.45 g

KM#	Date	Year	VG	Fine	VF	XF
A238	AH—	26	5.00	7.00	10.00	15.00

1/2 RUPEE

SILVER, 5.35-5.80 g

KM#	Date	Year	VG	Fine	VF	XF
C238	AH—	28	7.00	11.00	16.50	25.00

RUPEE

SILVER, 10.70-11.60 g

KM#	Date	Year	VG	Fine	VF	XF
238	AH—	3	6.00	10.00	15.00	22.50
	—	4	6.00	10.00	15.00	22.50
	—	8	6.00	10.00	15.00	22.50
	—	9	6.00	10.00	15.00	22.50
	—	20	6.00	10.00	15.00	22.50
	—	22	6.00	10.00	15.00	22.50
	—	25	6.00	10.00	15.00	22.50
	—	26	6.00	10.00	15.00	22.50
	—	28	6.00	10.00	15.00	22.50

MADHO RAO

AH1304-1344/1886-1925AD

With initial of Madho Rao II

With regnal years of the British "Raj" (Yr. 1 = AD1857)

1/16 RUPEE

SILVER, 0.67-0.72 g

KM#	Date	Year	VG	Fine	VF	XF
239	AH1312	—	4.00	6.00	9.00	13.50
	1313	37	4.00	6.00	9.00	13.50

1/8 RUPEE

SILVER, 1.34-1.45 g

KM#	Date	Year	VG	Fine	VF	XF
A240	AH—	31	5.00	7.00	10.00	15.00

KM#	Date	Year	VG	Fine	VF	XF
240	AH13xx	33	5.00	7.00	10.00	15.00
	1310	34	5.00	7.00	10.00	15.00
	1311	35	5.00	7.00	10.00	15.00
	1312	36	5.00	7.00	10.00	15.00
	1313	37	5.00	7.00	10.00	15.00

1/4 RUPEE

SILVER, 2.68-2.90 g

KM#	Date	Year	VG	Fine	VF	XF
241	AH1310	34	5.50	8.00	12.50	18.50
	1311	35	5.50	8.00	12.50	18.50
	1312	36	5.50	8.00	12.50	18.50
	1313	37	5.50	8.00	12.50	18.50
	1314	38	5.50	8.00	12.50	18.50

1/2 RUPEE

SILVER, 14-15mm, 5.35-5.80 g

KM#	Date	Year	VG	Fine	VF	XF
A242	AH—	29	6.00	9.00	13.50	20.00
	—	31	6.00	9.00	13.50	20.00

KM#	Date	Year	VG	Fine	VF	XF
242	AH1310	34	6.00	9.00	13.50	20.00
	1311	35	6.00	9.00	13.50	20.00
	1312	36	6.00	9.00	13.50	20.00
	1313	37	6.00	9.00	13.50	20.00
	1314	38	6.00	9.00	13.50	20.00

RUPEE

SILVER, 10.70-11.60 g

KM#	Date	Year	VG	Fine	VF	XF
243	AH—	29	6.50	10.00	15.00	22.50
	—	31	6.50	10.00	15.00	22.50
	—	32	6.50	10.00	15.00	22.50

Obv: AH date below.

KM#	Date	Year	VG	Fine	VF	XF
244	AH130x	33	6.50	10.00	15.00	22.50
	13xx	34	6.50	10.00	15.00	22.50

Obv: AH date in center.

KM#	Date	Year	VG	Fine	VF	XF
245	AH1310	34	5.50	8.00	12.50	18.50
	1310	35	5.50	8.00	12.50	18.50
	1311	34	5.50	8.00	12.50	18.50
	1311	35	5.50	8.00	12.50	18.50
	1311	36	5.50	8.00	12.50	18.50
	1312	34 (error)	6.50	10.00	15.00	22.50
	1312	36	5.50	8.00	12.50	18.50
	1313	37	5.50	8.00	12.50	18.50
	1314	38	5.50	8.00	12.50	18.50

UNCERTAIN MINT

PAISA

COPPER
Obv: Horse. Rev. leg: Retrograde.

KM#	Date	Year	Good	VG	Fine	VF
246	AH—	32	17.50	35.00	60.00	100.00

Obv: Hand.

KM#	Date	Year	Good	VG	Fine	VF
247	AH—	ND	10.00	20.00	35.00	50.00

HYDERABAD

Haidarabad

Hyderabad State, the largest Indian State and the last remnant of Mughal suzerainty in South or Central India, traced its foundation to Nizam-ul Mulk, the Mughal viceroy in the Deccan. From about 1724 the first nizam, as the rulers of Hyderabad came to be called, took advantage of Mughal decline in the North to assert an all but ceremonial independence of the emperor. The East India Company defeated Hyderabad's natural enemies, the Muslim rulers of Mysore and the Marathas, with the help of troops furnished under alliances between them and the Nizam. This formed the beginning of a relationship which persisted for a century and a half until India's Independence. Hyderabad was the premier Princely State, with a population (in 1935) of fourteen and a half million. It was not absorbed into the Indian Union until 1948. Hyderabad City is located beside Golkonda, the citadel of the Qutb Shahi sultans until they were overthrown by Aurangzeb in 1687. A beautifully located city on the bank of the Musi river, the mint epithet was appropriately Farkhanda Bunyad, "of happy foundation".

Hyderabad exercised authority over a number of feudatories or samasthans. Some of these, such as Gadwal and Shorapur, paid tribute to both the Nizam and the Marathas. These feudatories were generally in the hands of local rajas whose ancestry predated the establishment of Hyderabad State. There were also many mints in the State, both private and government. There was little or no standardization of the purity of silver coinage until the twentieth century. At least one banker, Pestonji Meherji by name, was distinguished by minting his own coins.

RULERS

Nizam Ali Khan,
AH1175-1218/1761-1803AD
Sikandar Jah,
AH1218-1244/1803-1829AD
Nasir-ad-Daula,
AH1244-1273/1829-1857AD
Afzal-ad-Daula,
AH1273-1285/1857-1869AD
Mir Mahbub Ali Khan II,
AH1285-1329/1869-1911AD

MINTS

امراوتی
Amaravati

اورنک اباد
Aurangabad
Mintname: Khujista Bunyad

دولت اباد
Daulatabad

فرخنده بنیاد
Haidarabad
Mintname: Farkhanda Bunyad

حیدراباد
Haidarabad

AMARAVATI MINT

RUPEE

SILVER

KM#	Date	Year	Good	VG	Fine	VF
1	AH1240	—	—	—	Rare	—
	1241	—	—	—	Rare	—

AURANGABAD MINT

Mint marks:

نجسته بنیاد

Mintname: Khujista Bunyad

NIZAM ALI KHAN

AH1175-1218/1761-1803AD

In the name of Shah Alam II
AH1173-1221/1759-1806AD

RUPEE

SILVER, 10.70-11.60 g

KM#	Date	Year	VG	Fine	VF	XF
5	AH1218	—	10.00	15.00	21.50	30.00

NOTE: Earlier dates (AH1176-1193) exist for this type.

In the name of Muhammad Akbar II
AH1221-1253/1806-1837AD

Obv: W/o Persian letter *S*.

KM#	Date	Year	VG	Fine	VF	XF
45	AH1227	6	7.50	12.50	18.50	27.50
	1228	6	7.50	12.50	18.50	27.50
	1230	9	7.50	12.50	18.50	27.50
	—	16	7.50	12.50	18.50	27.50
	(12)32	11	7.50	12.50	18.50	27.50
	1234	17	7.50	12.50	18.50	27.50
	1239	17	7.50	12.50	18.50	27.50
	1240	20	7.50	12.50	18.50	27.50
	1241	2x	7.50	12.50	18.50	27.50
	1242	—	7.50	12.50	18.50	27.50
	1242	21	7.50	12.50	18.50	27.50

NASIR AD-DAULA

AH1244-1273/1829-1857AD

In the name of Muhammad Akbar II
AH1221-1253/1806-1837AD

PAISA

COPPER

KM#	Date	Year	VG	Fine	VF	XF
63	AH1257	—	2.50	4.00	6.50	10.00

RUPEE

SILVER, 10.70-11.60 g

KM#	Date	Year	VG	Fine	VF	XF
66.1	AH1251	—	7.50	12.50	18.50	27.50

In the name of Bahadur Shah
AH1253-1274/1837-1858AD

Struck by Pestonji Meherji, a Bombay banker in the time of Nasir al-Daula, AD1829-57.

PAISA

COPPER, 11.7 g
Obv: Star and date.

C#	Date	Year	VG	Fine	VF	XF
62	AH(12)57	—	5.00	10.00	20.00	35.00

1/8 RUPEE

SILVER, 1.34-1.45 g

KM#	Date	Year	VG	Fine	VF	XF
63.2 (57)	AH1256	4	6.50	10.00	15.00	22.50

1/4 RUPEE

SILVER, 2.68-2.90 g

KM#	Date	Year	VG	Fine	VF	XF
64.1 (58)	AH1256	4	6.50	10.00	15.00	22.50

1/2 RUPEE

SILVER, 17mm, 5.35-5.80 g

KM#	Date	Year	VG	Fine	VF	XF
65.2 (59)	AH1256	4	10.00	15.00	21.50	30.00

RUPEE

SILVER, 10.70-11.60 g

KM#	Date	Year	VG	Fine	VF	XF
66.2	AH1254	1	7.50	12.50	18.50	27.50

C#	Date	Year	VG	Fine	VF	XF
(60)	1254	2	7.50	12.50	18.50	27.50
	1256	4	7.50	12.50	18.50	27.50
	1264	—	7.50	12.50	18.50	27.50

FARKHANDA BUNYAD MINT

Hyderabad

Mint mark:

Rev: Persian letter *N*: ن

SIKANDAR JAH

AH1218-1244/1803-1829AD

In the name of Shah Alam II
AH1173-1221/1759-1806AD

PAISA

COPPER

C#	Date	Year	Good	VG	Fine	VF
40	AH1217	—	1.25	2.00	3.00	4.50
	1218	—	1.25	2.00	3.00	4.50

RUPEE

SILVER, 20-21mm, 10.70-11.60 g

C#	Date	Year	VG	Fine	VF	XF
41	AH1218	—	12.50	18.50	25.00	35.00
	1220	—	12.50	18.50	25.00	35.00

HAIDARABAD MINT

Mint mark:

Persian letter *S*.

SIKANDAR JAH

AH1218-1244/1803-1829AD

In the name of Muhammad Akbar II
AH1221-1253/1806-1837AD

PAISA

COPPER, 17-20mm

C#	Date	Year	Good	VG	Fine	VF
44	AH1221	—	1.25	2.00	2.75	3.50
	1229	—	1.25	2.00	2.75	3.50
	1237	—	1.25	2.00	2.75	3.50

1/4 RUPEE

SILVER, 2.68-2.90 g

C#	Date	Year	VG	Fine	VF	XF
46	AH1238	—	5.50	8.00	12.50	18.50
	1239	—	5.50	8.00	12.50	18.50
	1241	—	5.50	8.00	12.50	18.50
	1242	23	5.50	8.00	12.50	18.50

1/2 RUPEE

SILVER, 5.35-5.80 g

C#	Date	Year	VG	Fine	VF	XF
47	AH1235	14	5.00	7.00	10.00	15.00
	1237	—	5.00	7.00	10.00	15.00
	1238	—	5.00	7.00	10.00	15.00

C#	Date	Year	VG	Fine	VF	XF
47	1241	—	5.00	7.00	10.00	15.00
	1242	23	5.00	7.00	10.00	15.00

RUPEE

SILVER, 10.70-11.60 g

C#	Date	Year	VG	Fine	VF	XF
48.1	AH1222	—	6.00	9.00	13.50	20.00
	1224	—	6.00	9.00	13.50	20.00
	1225	4	6.00	9.00	13.50	20.00
	1226	4	6.00	9.00	13.50	20.00
	1227	6	6.00	9.00	13.50	20.00
	1227	7	6.00	9.00	13.50	20.00
	1228	7	6.00	9.00	13.50	20.00
	1229	8	6.00	9.00	13.50	20.00
	1230	9	6.00	9.00	13.50	20.00
	1231	10	6.00	9.00	13.50	20.00
	1232	11	6.00	9.00	13.50	20.00
	1233	12	6.00	9.00	13.50	20.00
	1234	13	6.00	9.00	13.50	20.00
	1235	15	6.00	9.00	13.50	20.00
	1236	15	6.00	9.00	13.50	20.00
	1237	16	6.00	9.00	13.50	20.00
	1238	12 (error for 21)	6.00	9.00	13.50	20.00
	1239	21	6.00	9.00	13.50	20.00
	1240	21	6.00	9.00	13.50	20.00
	1240	22	6.00	9.00	13.50	20.00
	1241	22	6.00	9.00	13.50	20.00
	1242	23	6.00	9.00	13.50	20.00
	1243	24	6.00	9.00	13.50	20.00
	1244	25	6.00	9.00	13.50	20.00

Rev: *Maharaja* above mintname.

C#	Date	Year	VG	Fine	VF	XF
48.2	AH1238	—	6.00	9.00	13.50	20.00

NAZARANA RUPEE

SILVER, 10.70-11.60 g

C#	Date	Year	VG	Fine	VF	XF
48a	AH1237	16	100.00	175.00	250.00	350.00
	1238	17	100.00	175.00	250.00	350.00

1/16 MOHUR

GOLD, 0.67-0.70 g

C#	Date	Year	VG	Fine	VF	XF
56	AH123x	—	35.00	50.00	70.00	100.00

1/8 MOHUR

GOLD, 1.34-1.42 g

C#	Date	Year	VG	Fine	VF	XF
57	AH123x	—	45.00	65.00	90.00	125.00

1/4 MOHUR

GOLD, 2.68-2.85 g

C#	Date	Year	VG	Fine	VF	XF
58	AH1236	15	60.00	90.00	120.00	160.00

NAZARANA 1/4 MOHUR

GOLD, 2.68-2.85 g

C#	Date	Year	VG	Fine	VF	XF
A58	AH1236	15	—	—	Rare	—

1/2 MOHUR

GOLD, 5.35-5.70 g

C#	Date	Year	VG	Fine	VF	XF
59	AH123x	—	90.00	135.00	185.00	225.00

MOHUR

GOLD, 10.70-11.40 g

C#	Date	Year	VG	Fine	VF	XF
60	AH1226	—	185.00	235.00	285.00	325.00
	1227	—	185.00	235.00	285.00	325.00
	1228	7	185.00	235.00	285.00	325.00
	1231	—	185.00	235.00	285.00	325.00
	1234	—	185.00	235.00	285.00	325.00
	1235	—	185.00	235.00	285.00	325.00
	1236	15	185.00	235.00	285.00	325.00
	1237	16	185.00	235.00	285.00	325.00
	1238	—	185.00	235.00	285.00	325.00
	1241	—	185.00	235.00	285.00	325.00
	1242	—	185.00	235.00	285.00	325.00
	1243	24	185.00	235.00	285.00	325.00
	1244	—	185.00	235.00	285.00	325.00

NAZARANA MOHUR

GOLD, 10.70-11.40 g

C#	Date	Year	VG	Fine	VF	XF
60a	AH1236	15	—	—	Rare	—

NASIR AD-DAULA

AH1244-1273/1829-1857AD

Mint mark:

Rev: Persian letter *N*: ن

First Series

In the name of Muhammad Akbar II
AH1221-1253/1806-1837AD
With his regnal years to AH1252

PAISA

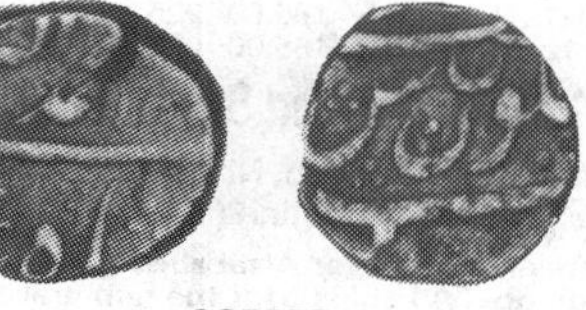

COPPER

C#	Date	Year	Good	VG	Fine	VF
61.3	AH1247	—	2.00	3.00	4.50	7.50
	1250	—	2.00	3.00	4.50	7.50
	Date off flan	—	1.00	2.00	3.50	5.00

1/4 RUPEE

SILVER, 2.68-2.90 g

C#	Date	Year	VG	Fine	VF	XF
64.3	AH1246	—	3.50	5.00	7.50	12.50
	1247	—	3.50	5.00	7.50	12.50
	1249	—	3.50	5.00	7.50	12.50
	1251	—	3.50	5.00	7.50	12.50

1/2 RUPEE

SILVER, 18mm, 5.35-5.80 g

C#	Date	Year	VG	Fine	VF	XF
65.3	AH1249	—	5.50	8.00	12.50	18.50
	1250	—	5.50	8.00	12.50	18.50
	1251	33	5.50	8.00	12.50	18.50

RUPEE

SILVER, 0.70-11.60 g

C#	Date	Year	VG	Fine	VF	XF
66.3	AH1245	26	7.50	10.00	15.00	20.00
	1246	—	7.50	10.00	15.00	20.00
	1248	29	7.50	10.00	15.00	20.00
	1249	—	7.50	10.00	15.00	20.00
	1250	31	7.50	10.00	15.00	20.00
	1251	33	7.50	10.00	15.00	20.00
	1252	34	7.50	10.00	15.00	20.00
	1253	35	7.50	10.00	15.00	20.00

1/16 MOHUR

GOLD, 0.67-0.71 g

C#	Date	Year	VG	Fine	VF	XF
68	AH—	—	25.00	35.00	45.00	60.00

1/8 MOHUR

GOLD, 1.34-1.42 g

C#	Date	Year	VG	Fine	VF	XF
69	AH—	—	35.00	50.00	70.00	100.00

1/4 MOHUR

GOLD, 2.68-2.85 g

C#	Date	Year	VG	Fine	VF	XF
70	AH—	—	50.00	85.00	120.00	150.00

1/2 MOHUR

GOLD, 5.35-5.70 g

C#	Date	Year	VG	Fine	VF	XF
71	AH—	—	90.00	125.00	165.00	200.00

MOHUR

GOLD, 22-23mm

C#	Date	Year	VG	Fine	VF	XF
72	AH1244	—	185.00	235.00	285.00	325.00
	1246	—	185.00	235.00	285.00	325.00
	1248	—	185.00	235.00	285.00	325.00
	1249	—	185.00	235.00	285.00	325.00
	1251	—	185.00	235.00	285.00	325.00

Second Series

In the name of Bahadur Shah
Years 1-22/AH1253-1274

PAISA

COPPER, round or square

C#	Date	Year	Good	VG	Fine	VF
73	AH1257	4	2.00	3.00	4.00	7.00
	1258	—	2.00	3.00	4.00	7.00
	1262	7	2.00	3.00	4.00	7.00
	1272	—	2.00	3.00	4.00	7.00
	1273	—	2.00	3.00	4.00	7.00
	Date off flan	—	1.00	2.00	3.00	4.50

1/16 RUPEE

SILVER, 9-11mm, 0.67-0.72 g

C#	Date	Year	VG	Fine	VF	XF
75	AH1272	—	4.00	7.50	10.00	15.00

1/8 RUPEE

SILVER, 11-13mm, 1.34-1.45 g

C#	Date	Year	VG	Fine	VF	XF
76	AH1272	—	4.00	7.50	10.00	15.00

1/4 RUPEE

SILVER, 14-15mm, 2.68-2.90 g

C#	Date	Year	VG	Fine	VF	XF
77	AH1257	—	7.00	11.00	16.50	25.00
	1268	—	7.00	11.00	16.50	25.00
	1272	17	7.00	11.00	16.50	25.00
	1273	18	7.00	11.00	16.50	25.00

1/2 RUPEE

SILVER, 16-19mm, 5.35-5.80 g

C#	Date	Year	VG	Fine	VF	XF
78	AH1257	5	6.50	10.00	15.00	22.50
	1260	—	6.50	10.00	15.00	22.50

RUPEE

SILVER, 10.70-11.60 g

C#	Date	Year	VG	Fine	VF	XF
79	AH1253	1	6.00	9.00	13.50	20.00
	1258	6	6.00	9.00	13.50	20.00
	1261	8	6.00	9.00	13.50	20.00
	1262	9	6.00	9.00	13.50	20.00
	1266	11	6.00	9.00	13.50	30.00
	1267	12	6.00	9.00	13.50	20.00
	1268	12	6.00	9.00	13.50	20.00
	1268	13	6.00	9.00	13.50	20.00
	1270	15	6.00	9.00	13.50	20.00
	1270	16	6.00	9.00	13.50	20.00
	1271	16	6.00	9.00	13.50	20.00
	1271	17	6.00	9.00	13.50	20.00
	1272	17	6.00	9.00	13.50	20.00
	1273	18	6.00	9.00	13.50	20.00

1/16 MOHUR

GOLD, 0.67-0.71 g

C#	Date	Year	VG	Fine	VF	XF
80	AH—	—	35.00	50.00	70.00	100.00

1/8 MOHUR

GOLD, 1.34-1.42 g

C#	Date	Year	VG	Fine	VF	XF
81	AH—	—	40.00	65.00	90.00	125.00

1/4 MOHUR

GOLD, 2.68-2.85 g

C#	Date	Year	VG	Fine	VF	XF
82	AH—	—	50.00	85.00	120.00	160.00

1/2 MOHUR

GOLD, 5.35-5.70 g

C#	Date	Year	VG	Fine	VF	XF
83	AH—	—	80.00	130.00	185.00	225.00

MOHUR

GOLD, 22mm, 10.70-11.40 gm

C#	Date	Year	VG	Fine	VF	XF
84	AH1258	6	175.00	215.00	265.00	300.00
	1260	—	175.00	215.00	265.00	300.00
	1261	8	175.00	215.00	265.00	300.00
	1263	9	175.00	215.00	265.00	300.00
	1264	—	175.00	215.00	265.00	300.00
	1265	—	175.00	215.00	265.00	300.00
	1266	11	175.00	215.00	265.00	300.00
	1267	12	175.00	215.00	265.00	300.00
	1268	—	175.00	215.00	265.00	300.00
	1269	—	175.00	215.00	265.00	300.00
	1270	—	175.00	215.00	265.00	300.00
	1271	—	175.00	215.00	265.00	300.00
	1273	17	175.00	215.00	265.00	300.00

AFZAL AD-DAULA

AH1273-1285/1857-1869AD

First Series

In the name of Bahadur Shah II

AH1253-1273/1837-1858AD

Mint marks:

#1

#2

#3

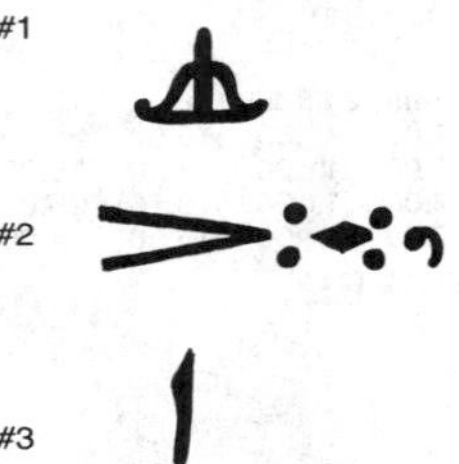

For his last two years, AH1274-75, regnal year 18 w/Persian letter *A* (symbol 3) above *Padishah* on obv. Copper coins have symbol #1, while silver and gold have #2.

1/2 PAISA

COPPER

C#	Date	Year	Good	VG	Fine	VF
85	AH1275	—	1.50	2.50	3.50	6.00
		19	1.50	2.50	3.50	6.00

PAISA

COPPER

C#	Date	Year	Good	VG	Fine	VF
86	AH1275	18	1.50	2.50	3.50	6.00
	1276	19	1.50	2.50	3.50	6.00
	1277	19	1.50	2.50	3.50	6.00
	Date off flan	—	1.25	2.25	3.00	4.50

1/8 RUPEE

SILVER, 13mm, 1.34-1.45 g

C#	Date	Year	VG	Fine	VF	XF
88	AH1275	—	4.00	7.50	10.00	15.00

1/4 RUPEE

SILVER, 14mm, 2.68-2.90 g

C#	Date	Year	VG	Fine	VF	XF
89	AH1274	—	4.00	7.50	10.00	15.00

1/2 RUPEE

SILVER, 17mm, 5.35-5.80 g

C#	Date	Year	VG	Fine	VF	XF
90	AH1274	—	6.50	10.00	15.00	22.50

RUPEE

SILVER, 10.70-11.60 g

C#	Date	Year	VG	Fine	VF	XF
91	AH1273	18	7.50	10.00	13.50	20.00
	1274	18	7.50	10.00	13.50	20.00
	1275	18	7.50	10.00	13.50	20.00

MOHUR

GOLD, 23mm

C#	Date	Year	VG	Fine	VF	XF
96	AH1274	—	185.00	225.00	275.00	325.00
	1275	—	185.00	225.00	275.00	325.00

Second Series

In the name of Asaf Jah, Nizam al-Mulk, Founder of the Nizami line (1713-1748AD)

Persian letter *A* for Afzal above *k* of *Mulk* on obv. All coins bear the numeral '92' on upper obverse.

PAISA

(Dub)

COPPER

Irregular and regular shapes, 16-30mm

Y#	Date	Year	Good	VG	Fine	VF
1	AH1282	—	1.75	2.50	3.50	5.00
	1283	—	1.75	2.50	3.50	5.00
	Date off flan		1.00	2.00	3.00	4.00

1/16 RUPEE

(Anna)

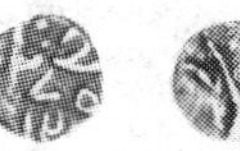

SILVER, 9mm, 0.67-0.72 g

Y#	Date	Year	VG	Fine	VF	XF
2	AH1275	—	2.50	4.00	6.50	10.00

1/8 RUPEE

SILVER, 11-13mm, 1.34-1.45 g

Y#	Date	Year	VG	Fine	VF	XF
3	AH1278	—	3.00	5.00	7.00	10.00
	1279	—	3.00	5.00	7.00	10.00

1/4 RUPEE

SILVER, 2.68-2.90 g

Y#	Date	Year	VG	Fine	VF	XF
4	AH1276	—	3.00	5.00	7.00	10.00
	1278	—	3.00	5.00	7.00	10.00
	1283	10	3.00	5.00	7.00	10.00

1/2 RUPEE

SILVER, 5.35-5.80 g

Y#	Date	Year	VG	Fine	VF	XF
5	AH1276	—	3.50	6.00	8.00	12.50
	1277	—	3.50	6.00	8.00	12.50
	128(4)	11	3.50	6.00	8.00	12.50

RUPEE

SILVER, 10.70-11.60 g

Y#	Date	Year	VG	Fine	VF	XF
6	AH1275	2	3.00	6.00	8.00	12.50
	1276	3	3.00	6.00	8.00	12.50
	1276	4	3.00	6.00	8.00	12.50
	1277	4	3.00	6.00	8.00	12.50
	1278	5	3.00	6.00	8.00	12.50
	1279	6	3.00	6.00	8.00	12.50
	1280	7	3.00	6.00	8.00	12.50
	1281	7	3.00	6.00	8.00	12.50
	1281	8	3.00	6.00	8.00	12.50
	1282	9	3.00	6.00	8.00	12.50
	1283	10	3.00	6.00	8.00	12.50
	1284	11	3.00	6.00	8.00	12.50
	1285	12	3.00	6.00	8.00	12.50

1/16 MOHUR

GOLD, 8-9mm, 0.67-0.71 g

Y#	Date	Year	VG	Fine	VF	XF
7	AH—	—	— Reported, not confirmed			

1/8 MOHUR

GOLD, 11mm, 1.34-1.42 g

Y#	Date	Year	VG	Fine	VF	XF
8	AH1279-81		40.00	55.00	70.00	90.00

1/4 MOHUR

GOLD, 14mm, 2.68-2.85 g

Y#	Date	Year	VG	Fine	VF	XF
9	AH1281	—	50.00	75.00	110.00	140.00

1/2 MOHUR

GOLD, 16mm, 5.35-5.70 g

Y#	Date	Year	VG	Fine	VF	XF
10	AH1281	—	90.00	120.00	165.00	200.00

MOHUR

GOLD, 10.70-11.40 g

Y#	Date	Year	VG	Fine	VF	XF
11	AH1275	—	160.00	185.00	220.00	265.00
	1276	—	160.00	185.00	220.00	265.00
	1277	—	160.00	185.00	220.00	265.00
	1278	—	160.00	185.00	220.00	265.00
	1279	—	160.00	185.00	220.00	265.00
	1280	—	160.00	185.00	220.00	265.00
	1281	8	160.00	185.00	220.00	265.00
	1282	—	160.00	185.00	220.00	265.00
	1283	—	160.00	185.00	220.00	265.00
	1284	—	160.00	185.00	220.00	265.00
	1285	—	160.00	185.00	220.00	265.00

MIR MAHBUB ALI KHAN II

AH1285-1329/1868-1911AD

In the name of Asaf Jah, Nizam al-Mulk, Founder of the Nizami line (1713-1748AD).

Persian letter *M* for Mahbub above *k* of *Mulk* on obv.

1/2 PAISA

COPPER

Y#	Date	Year	Good	VG	Fine	VF
A12	ND	—	—	—	—	—

PAISA (DUB)

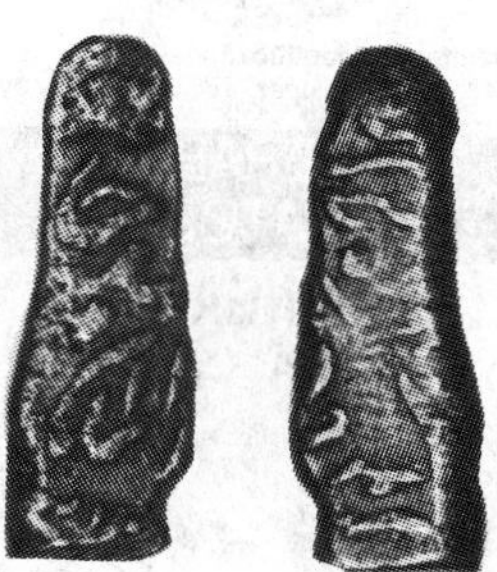

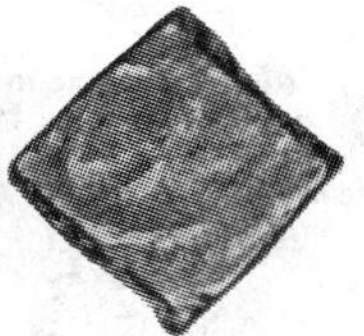

COPPER
Round, rectangular, irregular shape
Many sizes and weights

Y#	Date	Year	Good	VG	Fine	VF
12	AH1290	—	1.50	2.50	3.50	6.00
	1291	—	1.50	2.50	3.50	6.00
	1292	—	1.50	2.50	3.50	6.00
	1296	—	1.50	2.50	3.50	6.00
	1297	—	1.50	2.50	3.50	6.00
	1298	14	1.50	2.50	3.50	6.00
	1300	—	1.50	2.50	3.50	6.00
	1301	—	1.50	2.50	3.50	6.00
	1302	18	1.50	2.50	3.50	6.00
	1303	—	1.50	2.50	3.50	6.00
	1308	—	1.50	2.50	3.50	6.00
	1313	—	1.50	2.50	3.50	6.00

1/2 ANNA

COPPER

Y#	Date	Year	Good	VG	Fine	VF
A13	AH1311	27	—	—	—	—

1/16 RUPEE

.818 SILVER, 0.698 g

Y#	Date	Year	VG	Fine	VF	XF
13	AH1299	15	1.00	1.75	2.50	4.00
	1300	—	1.00	1.75	2.50	4.00
	1303	—	1.00	1.75	2.50	4.00
	1304	—	1.00	1.75	2.50	4.00
	1305	—	1.00	1.75	2.50	4.00
	1307	—	1.00	1.75	2.50	4.00
	1313	—	1.00	1.75	2.50	4.00
	1314	30	1.00	1.75	2.50	4.00

NOTE: Later date (AH1321) exists for this type.

1/8 RUPEE

.818 SILVER, 1.397 g

Y#	Date	Year	VG	Fine	VF	XF
14	AH1286	—	1.75	2.25	3.00	4.50
	1287	2	1.75	2.25	3.00	4.50
	1289	—	1.75	2.25	3.00	4.50
	1290	—	1.75	2.25	3.00	4.50
	1295	11	1.75	2.25	3.00	4.50
	1297	—	1.75	2.25	3.00	4.50
	1298	14	1.75	2.25	3.00	4.50
	1299	15	1.75	2.25	3.00	4.50
	1300	—	1.75	2.25	3.00	4.50
	1301	17	1.75	2.25	3.00	4.50
	1302	17	1.75	2.25	3.00	4.50
	1302	18	1.75	2.25	3.00	4.50
	1304	20	1.75	2.25	3.00	4.50
	1305	—	1.75	2.25	3.00	4.50
	1306	—	1.75	2.25	3.00	4.50
	1307	—	1.75	2.25	3.00	4.50
	1308	24	1.75	2.25	3.00	4.50
	1309	—	1.75	2.25	3.00	4.50
	1310	—	1.75	2.25	3.00	4.50
	1311	—	1.75	2.25	3.00	4.50
	1316	33	1.75	2.25	3.00	4.50
	1317	33	1.75	2.25	3.00	4.50
	1318	—	1.75	2.25	3.00	4.50
	Date off flan		1.00	1.50	2.00	3.00

NOTE: Later date (AH1321) exists for this type.

1/4 RUPEE

.818 SILVER, 2.794 g

Y#	Date	Year	VG	Fine	VF	XF
15	AH1286	—	2.00	2.75	4.50	7.00
	1287	—	2.00	2.75	4.50	7.00
	1288	—	2.00	2.75	4.50	7.00
	1289	—	2.00	2.75	4.50	7.00
	1290	—	2.00	2.75	4.50	7.00
	1291	7	2.00	2.75	4.50	7.00
	1294	—	2.00	2.75	4.50	7.00
	1295	—	2.00	2.75	4.50	7.00
	1297	—	2.00	2.75	4.50	7.00
	1298	14	2.00	2.75	4.50	7.00
	1299	15	2.00	2.75	4.50	7.00
	1300	16	2.00	2.75	4.50	7.00
	1301	17	2.00	2.75	4.50	7.00
	1302	—	2.00	2.75	4.50	7.00
	1304	—	2.00	2.75	4.50	7.00
	1305	22	2.00	2.75	4.50	7.00
	1306	22	2.00	2.75	4.50	7.00
	1307	23	2.00	2.75	4.50	7.00
	1307	24	2.00	2.75	4.50	7.00
	1308	—	2.00	2.75	4.50	7.00
	1309	—	2.00	2.75	4.50	7.00
	1310	—	2.00	2.75	4.50	7.00
	1313	29	2.00	2.75	4.50	7.00
	1314	—	2.00	2.75	4.50	7.00
	1315	31	2.00	2.75	4.50	7.00
	1316	32	2.00	2.75	4.50	7.00
	1316	33	2.00	2.75	4.50	7.00
	1317	33	2.00	2.75	4.50	7.00

NOTE: Later date (AH1321) exists for this type.

1/2 RUPEE

.818 SILVER, 5.589 g

Y#	Date	Year	VG	Fine	VF	XF
16	AH1286	1	3.00	4.00	6.00	12.00
	1289	—	3.00	4.00	6.00	12.00
	1290	—	3.00	4.00	6.00	12.00
	1291	7	3.00	4.00	6.00	12.00
	1292	—	3.00	4.00	6.00	12.00
	1294	10	3.00	4.00	6.00	12.00
	1295	—	3.00	4.00	6.00	12.00
	1299	15	3.00	4.00	6.00	12.00
	1301	17	3.00	4.00	6.00	12.00
	1302	18	3.00	4.00	6.00	12.00
	1304	—	3.00	4.00	6.00	12.00
	1305	22	3.00	4.00	6.00	12.00
	1306	22	3.00	4.00	6.00	12.00
	1307	23	3.00	4.00	6.00	12.00
	1308	—	3.00	4.00	6.00	12.00
	1310	—	3.00	4.00	6.00	12.00
	1316	32	3.00	4.00	6.00	12.00
	1317	—	3.00	4.00	6.00	12.00

RUPEE

.818 SILVER, 11.178 g

Y#	Date	Year	VG	Fine	VF	XF
17	AH1286	1	4.50	5.50	7.00	14.00
	1287	—	4.50	5.50	7.00	14.00
	1288	3	4.50	5.50	7.00	14.00
	1289	4	4.50	5.50	7.00	14.00
	1293	—	4.50	5.50	7.00	14.00
	1294	10	4.50	5.50	7.00	14.00
	1295	10	4.50	5.50	7.00	14.00
	1295	11	4.50	5.50	7.00	14.00
	1298	—	4.50	5.50	7.00	14.00
	1299	15	4.50	5.50	7.00	14.00
	1299	16	4.50	5.50	7.00	14.00
	1300	16	4.50	5.50	7.00	14.00
	1301	—	4.50	5.50	7.00	14.00
	1302	18	4.50	5.50	7.00	14.00
	1305	—	4.50	5.50	7.00	14.00
	1306	22	4.50	5.50	7.00	14.00
	1307	23	4.50	5.50	7.00	14.00
	1308	24	4.50	5.50	7.00	14.00
	1308	25	4.50	5.50	7.00	14.00
	1309	25	4.50	5.50	7.00	14.00
	1310	26	4.50	5.50	7.00	14.00
	1315	32	4.50	5.50	7.00	14.00
	1316	32	4.50	5.50	7.00	14.00
	1317	33	4.50	5.50	7.00	14.00
	1317	34	4.50	5.50	7.00	14.00
	1318	34	4.50	5.50	7.00	14.00

1/16 ASHRAFI

.910 GOLD, 0.698 g

Y#	Date	Year	VG	Fine	VF	XF
18	AH1305	—	20.00	30.00	40.00	60.00
	1314	—	20.00	30.00	40.00	60.00
	1315	—	20.00	30.00	40.00	60.00

NOTE: Later date (AH1321) exists for this type.

1/8 ASHRAFI

.910 GOLD, 1.397 g

Y#	Date	Year	VG	Fine	VF	XF
19	AH1293	—	25.00	40.00	60.00	75.00
	1302	—	25.00	40.00	60.00	75.00
	1306	—	25.00	40.00	60.00	75.00
	1309	—	25.00	40.00	60.00	75.00
	1313	—	25.00	40.00	60.00	75.00
	1316	—	25.00	40.00	60.00	75.00
	1317	33	25.00	40.00	60.00	75.00
	1318	—	25.00	40.00	60.00	75.00

NOTE: Later dates (AH1320-1321) exist for this type.

1/4 ASHRAFI

.910 GOLD, 2.794 g

Y#	Date	Year	VG	Fine	VF	XF
20	AH1301	—	45.00	60.00	80.00	100.00
	1304	—	45.00	60.00	80.00	100.00
	1306	—	45.00	60.00	80.00	100.00
	1309	—	45.00	60.00	80.00	100.00
	1314	30	45.00	60.00	80.00	100.00
	1315	—	45.00	60.00	80.00	100.00
	1316	—	45.00	60.00	80.00	100.00
	1318	35	45.00	60.00	80.00	100.00

NOTE: Later date (AH1319) exists for this type.

1/2 ASHRAFI

.910 GOLD, 5.589 g

Y#	Date	Year	VG	Fine	VF	XF
21	AH1316	—	75.00	90.00	110.00	140.00
	1317	—	75.00	90.00	110.00	140.00

NOTE: Later dates (AH1320-1321) exist for this type.

ASHRAFI

.910 GOLD, 11.178 g

Y#	Date	Year	VG	Fine	VF	XF
22	AH1286	1	150.00	170.00	200.00	250.00
	1287	—	150.00	170.00	200.00	250.00
	1288	—	150.00	170.00	200.00	250.00
	1289	—	150.00	170.00	200.00	250.00
	1290	—	150.00	170.00	200.00	250.00
	1292	—	150.00	170.00	200.00	250.00
	1293	—	150.00	170.00	200.00	250.00
	1294	—	150.00	170.00	200.00	250.00
	1295	—	150.00	170.00	200.00	250.00
	1296	—	150.00	170.00	200.00	250.00
	1297	—	150.00	170.00	200.00	250.00
	1298	14	150.00	170.00	200.00	250.00
	1299	—	150.00	170.00	200.00	250.00
	1300	16	150.00	170.00	200.00	250.00
	1301	—	150.00	170.00	200.00	250.00
	1302	—	150.00	170.00	200.00	250.00
	1303	—	150.00	170.00	200.00	250.00
	1304	—	150.00	170.00	200.00	250.00
	1305	—	150.00	170.00	200.00	250.00
	1306	—	150.00	170.00	200.00	250.00
	1307	—	150.00	170.00	200.00	250.00
	1308	—	150.00	170.00	200.00	250.00
	1309	—	150.00	170.00	200.00	250.00
	1310	—	150.00	170.00	200.00	250.00
	1311	—	150.00	170.00	200.00	250.00
	1312	28	150.00	170.00	200.00	250.00
	1313	—	150.00	170.00	200.00	250.00
	1314	30	150.00	170.00	200.00	250.00
	1314	31	150.00	170.00	200.00	250.00
	1315	—	150.00	170.00	200.00	250.00
	1316	—	150.00	170.00	200.00	250.00
	1317	—	150.00	170.00	200.00	250.00
	1318	—	150.00	170.00	200.00	250.00

NOTE: Later dates (AH1319-1321) exist for this type.

MILLED COINAGE

PROVISIONAL ISSUES

AH1311/27-1318/35

1/4 ANNA

COPPER

KM#	Date	Year	VG	Fine	VF	XF
27	AH1312	27	—	—	—	—
	1312	28	—	—	—	—

1/2 ANNA

COPPER

KM#	Date	Year	VG	Fine	VF	XF
28	AH1311	27	—	—	—	—

ANNA

COPPER

KM#	Date	Year	VG	Fine	VF	XF
32	AH1305	21	55.00	85.00	125.00	175.00

2 ANNAS

.818 SILVER, 1.397 g

Y#	Date	Year	VG	Fine	VF	XF
29	AH1318	35	10.00	17.50	27.50	37.50

4 ANNAS

.818 SILVER, 2.794 g

Y#	Date	Year	VG	Fine	VF	XF
30	AH1318	32	27.50	37.50	50.00	60.00
	1318	34	8.50	16.50	25.00	33.50
	1318	35	8.50	16.50	25.00	33.50

8 ANNAS

.818 SILVER, 5.589 g

Y#	Date	Year	VG	Fine	VF	XF
31	AH1312	28	10.00	20.00	30.00	40.00
	1318	34	10.00	20.00	30.00	40.00
	1318	35	10.00	20.00	30.00	40.00

RUPEE

.818 SILVER, 11.178 g

Y#	Date	Year	VG	Fine	VF	XF
32	AH1312	28	10.00	15.00	20.00	30.00
	1313	29	10.00	15.00	20.00	30.00
	1314	30	10.00	15.00	20.00	30.00
	1318	34	10.00	15.00	20.00	30.00

ASHRAFI

.910 GOLD, 24mm, 11.05-11.20 g

Y#	Date	Year	VG	Fine	VF	XF
33	AH1311	27	600.00	800.00	1000.	1250.

PATTERNS (Pn)

(Including off metal strikes)

KM#	Date	Mintage	Identification	Mkt.Val.
Pn1	AH1311	—	1 Ashrafi, Gold, 30mm,Y33a	—
Pn2	AH1312	—	1 Pai, Copper	—
PnA3	AH1312/28	—	8 Annas, Copper, Y31	—
Pn3	AH1312/29	—	2 Pai, Copper	—
Pn4	AH1312/29	—	1/2 Anna, Copper	—

TRIAL STRIKES (TS)

KM#	Date	Mintage	Identification	Mkt.Val.
TS1	AH131x	—	8 Annas, Tin, uniface, obv., yr. 2x	—

KM#	Date	Mintage	Identification	Mkt.Val.
TS2	AH131x	—	8 Annas, Tin, uniface, rev., yr. 2x	—

KM#	Date	Mintage	Identification	Mkt.Val.
TS3	AH131x	—	1 Rupee, Tin, uniface, obv.	—

KM#	Date	Mintage	Identification	Mkt.Val.
TS4	AH1311	—	1 Rupee, Tin, uniface, obv., yr. 27	—

KM#	Date	Mintage	Identification	Mkt.Val.
TS5	AH1311	—	1 Rupee, Tin, uniface, rev., yr. 27	—

HYDERABAD FEUDATORIES

AURANGABAD

'TOKA' CASH

COPPER

Rev: Battle-axe in canopy, date below.

C#	Date	Year	Good	VG	Fine	VF
28	FE1241	—	5.00	10.00	16.50	25.00

Date in Nagari numerals.

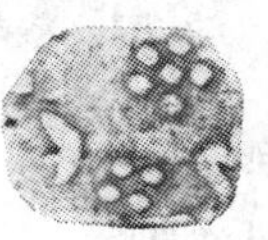

Rev: Sword at right.

C#	Date	Year	Good	VG	Fine	VF
29	AH1255	—	10.00	17.50	25.00	35.00

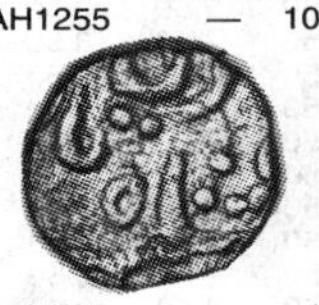

C#	Date	Year	Good	VG	Fine	VF
30	AH1273	—	4.00	8.00	12.50	20.00
	1276	—	4.00	8.00	12.50	20.00

NOTE: C#28 and #30 were named after Toka Raj who operated the Aurangabad Mint under a state license from about 1830.

ELICHPUR

ANONYMOUS COINAGE

PAISA

COPPER, 18-20mm, 11.50 g

Obv: Tiger right.

C#	Date	Year	Good	VG	Fine	VF
10	AH1250	—	4.00	6.50	10.00	15.00
	1263	—	4.00	6.50	10.00	15.00
	Date off flan	—	2.50	4.00	6.50	10.00

Obv: Tiger left.

C#	Date	Year	Good	VG	Fine	VF
10a	AH1250	—	4.00	6.50	10.00	15.00
	1263	—	4.00	6.50	10.00	15.00
	1285	—	4.00	6.50	10.00	15.00
	Date off flan	—	2.50	4.00	6.50	10.00

2 PAISA

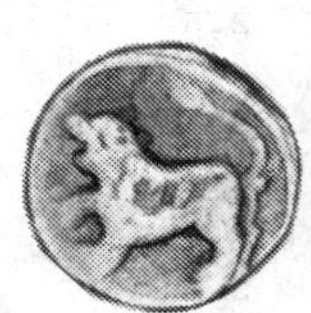

COPPER, 15.50 g

Obv: Tiger left.

C#	Date	Year	Good	VG	Fine	VF
15	AH1250	—	5.00	9.00	13.00	20.00

Obv: Tiger right.

C#	Date	Year	Good	VG	Fine	VF
15a	AH1250	—	5.00	9.00	13.00	20.00

KALAYAN

Kallian

A town located in north Mysore.

NAWAB

Mohammad Shah Khair al-Din

Mint mark:

1/8 RUPEE

SILVER, 1.34-1.45 g

KM#	Date	Year	VG	Fine	VF	XF
2	AH1226	—	7.50	12.50	18.50	27.50

RUPEE

SILVER, 10.70-11.60 g
Rev: W/o Persian *Ha* to right of tiger.

5	AH1212	—	55.00	90.00	150.00	225.00

Rev: Persian *Ha* to right of tiger.

6	AH1226	—	30.00	50.00	85.00	125.00
	ND	—	30.00	50.00	85.00	125.00

NOTE: Earlier dates (AH1212-1215) exist for this type.

NARAYANPETT

Local Rajas

Dilshadabad on coins.

MINT MARKS

Ti obv. dated AH1186/1186, C#40

क *K* rev. dated AH1186/1186, C#40

गो *Go* obv. dated AH1186/1252, C#37-40

ल *L* rev. dated AH1186/1252, C#37-40

In the name of Shah Alam II

AH1173-1221/1759-1806AD

PAISA

COPPER

C#	Date	Year	Good	VG	Fine	VF
34	AH1202	1252	3.50	5.50	8.00	12.00

1/8 RUPEE

SILVER, 1.34-1.45 g

C#	Date	Year	VG	Fine	VF	XF
37	AH1186	1252	4.50	7.50	10.00	15.00

1/4 RUPEE

SILVER, 13mm, 2.68-2.90 g

C#	Date	Year	VG	Fine	VF	XF
38	AH1186	1252	6.00	10.00	15.00	22.50

1/2 RUPEE

SILVER, 16mm, 5.35-5.80 g

39	AH1186	1252	6.50	11.50	16.50	25.00

RUPEE

SILVER, 10.70-11.60 g

40	AH1186	1186	9.00	15.00	21.50	30.00
	1186	1239	9.00	15.00	21.50	30.00
	1186	1245	9.00	15.00	21.50	30.00
	1186	1246	9.00	15.00	21.50	30.00
	1186	1251	9.00	15.00	21.50	30.00
	1186	1252	9.00	15.00	21.50	30.00
	1186	1254	9.00	15.00	21.50	30.00

SHORAPUR

Bahiri Feudatory

1/2 PAISA

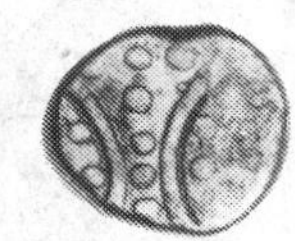

COPPER, 14mm

C#	Date	Year	Good	VG	Fine	VF
62	ND	—	3.50	5.50	8.00	12.00

COPPER, 13mm
Similar to 1 Paisa, C#66.

65	AH1262	—	2.50	4.00	6.50	10.00

PAISA

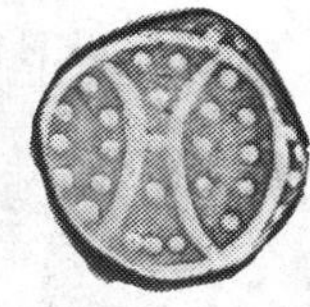

COPPER

63	ND	—	2.00	3.25	5.00	8.50

Rev: Inscribed *Bahiri*.

64	ND	—	2.50	4.00	6.50	10.00

Rev: *Bahiri*, date.

66	AH1261	—	2.50	4.00	6.50	10.00
	1262	—	2.50	4.00	6.50	10.00

Obv: Different from C#66.

67	AH1262	—	2.50	4.00	6.50	10.00

WANPARTI

Bahiri Rajas

Sagur mintname on coins is Nasirabad. The latter is honorific for the Sagur Mint copied from the rupees of Dharwar.

In the name of Muhammad Akbar II

AH1221-1253/1806-1837AD

1/4 RUPEE

SILVER, 2.67-2.90 g

C#	Date	Year	Good	VG	Fine	VF
78	AH1235	14	7.50	12.50	18.50	27.50

RUPEE

SILVER, 10.70-11.60 g
Obv: 'J'. Rev: 'A' in Nagari.

C#	Date	Year	VG	Fine	VF	XF
80	AH1235	14	7.50	12.50	18.50	27.50
	1235	15	7.50	12.50	18.50	27.50

INDORE

The Holkars were one of the three dominant Maratha powers (with the Peshwas and Sindhias), with major land holdings in Central India.

Indore State originated in 1728 with a grant of land north of the Narbada river by the Maratha Peshwa of Poona to Malhar Rao Holkar, a cavalry commander in his service. After Holkar's death (ca.1765) his daughter-in-law, Ahalya Bai, assumed the position of Queen Regent. Together with Tukoji Rao she effectively ruled the State until her death thirty years later. But it was left to Tukoji's son, Jaswant Rao, to challenge the dominance of the Poona Marathas in the Maratha Confederacy, eventually defeating the Peshwa's army in 1802. But at this point the fortunes of the Holkars suffered a serious reverse. Although Jaswant Rao had initially defeated a small British force under Col. William Monson, he was badly beaten by a contingent under Lord Lake. As a result Holkar was forced to cede a considerable portion of his territory and from this time until India's independence in 1947, the residual State of Indore was obliged to accept British protection.

For more detailed data on the Indore series, see *A Study of Holkar State Coinage,* by P.K. Sethi, S.K. Bhatt and R. Holkar (1976).

HOLKAR RULERS

Jaswant Rao,
SE1719-1734/AH1213-1226/1798-1811AD

Mulhar Rao II,
AH1226-1248/1811-1833AD

Martand Rao,
AH1249/1834AD

Hari Rao,
AH1250-1260/1834-1843AD

Khande Rao,
AH1260-1261/1843-1844AD

Tukoji Rao II,
VS1891-1943/SE1766-1808/AH1261-1304/1844-1886AD

Shivaji Rao,
VS1943-1960/FE1296-1313/1886-1903AD

HONORIFIC TITLE

Bahadur

REGNAL YEARS

In reference to:

Muhammad Akbar II, Year 1/AH1221-1222

MINTS

Indore اندور or इंदोर

Malharnagar ملہارنگر

NOTE: According to Sethi, Bhatt and Holkar, the coins of both the Maheshwar and Malharnagar Mints bear the mintname "Malharnagar" in honor of Malhar Rao I, founder of the state. They can only be distinguished by their distinctive mint marks, as noted below.

MUGHAL ISSUES

In the name of Shah Alam II

AH 1173-1221/1759-1806 AD

Until AH1296/1880AD all coinage of Indore was struck in the name of Shah Alam II, with the exception of a few rare special or nazarana issues. The coinage of the individual rulers until 1880AD cannot be told apart except by the date, as no change of type was made for more than a century.

INDORE MINT

Coins issued intermittently from 1772 to 1935 A.D.

JASWANT RAO

SE1719-1734/AH1212-1226
1797-1811AD

In the name of Mughal King of Delhi and Jaswant Rao

NAZARANA RUPEE

SILVER, 10.70-11.60 g

KM#	Date	Year	VG	Fine	VF	XF
6	SE1728	(1806)	50.00	75.00	110.00	150.00

In the name of Muhammad Akbar II
AH1221-1253/1806-1837AD
and Jaswant Rao

KM#	Date	Year	VG	Fine	VF	XF
7	SE1728	(1806)	—	—	Rare	—

KM#	Date	Year	VG	Fine	VF	XF
8	AH1222	2	25.00	35.00	50.00	75.00

Presentation Issues

These "mudra" coins appear to have been machine struck although mint machines were not introduced in Indore until 1864.

TUKOJI RAO II

VS1891-1943/SE1766-1808
AH1260-1304/1844-1886AD

COPPER 1/2 MUDRA

COPPER, 4.35-5.10 g

KM#	Date	Year	Good	VG	Fine	VF
10	SE1780	(1858)	20.00	32.50	50.00	75.00
	1788	VS1923	20.00	32.50	50.00	75.00

COPPER MUDRA

COPPER, 7.80-11.00 g

KM#	Date	Year	Good	VG	Fine	VF
11.1	SE1780	(1858)	30.00	60.00	100.00	150.00
	1788	VS1923	—	—	Rare	—

KM#	Date	Year	Good	VG	Fine	VF
11.2	AH1288	—	—	—	—	—

1/2 ANNA

COPPER, 16.60 g

KM#	Date	Year	Good	VG	Fine	VF
12	VS1942	(1885)	—	—	Rare	—

13.40 g

KM#	Date	Good	VG	Fine	VF
13	VS1942/SE1807/1885	25.00	45.00	65.00	100.00

SILVER MUDRA

SILVER, 11.20 g

KM#	Date	Year	VG	Fine	VF	XF
15	SE1780	(1858)	40.00	60.00	90.00	125.00

Obv: Blank within wreath.

KM#	Date	Year	VG	Fine	VF	XF
16	SE1780	(1858)	40.00	60.00	90.00	125.00

Obv: Two varieties of swirls.

KM#	Date	Year	VG	Fine	VF	XF
17	SE1780	(1858)	60.00	100.00	140.00	175.00

KM#	Date	Year	VG	Fine	VF	XF
18	SE1788	VS1923	75.00	110.00	150.00	200.00

KM#	Date	Year	VG	Fine	VF	XF
19	VS1934	FE1287	75.00	110.00	150.00	200.00

KM#	Date	Year	VG	Fine	VF	XF
20	VS1934	FE1287	100.00	150.00	200.00	250.00

1/2 RUPEE

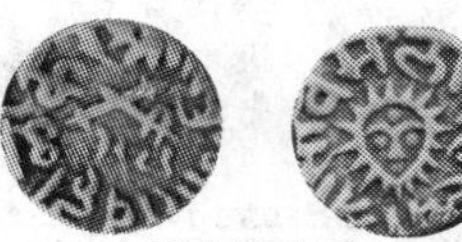

SILVER, 5.50 g

KM#	Date	Year	VG	Fine	VF	XF
21	AH1289	—	55.00	70.00	85.00	110.00
22	ND	—	55.00	70.00	85.00	110.00

RUPEE

SILVER, 11.20 g

KM#	Date	Year	VG	Fine	VF	XF
23	ND	—	25.00	35.00	45.00	60.00

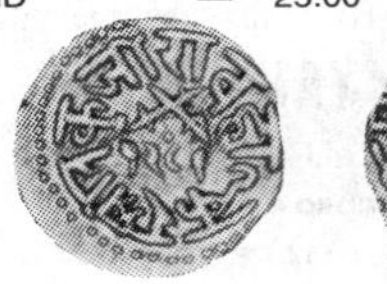

KM#	Date	Year	VG	Fine	VF	XF
24	AH1289	—	40.00	55.00	70.00	90.00

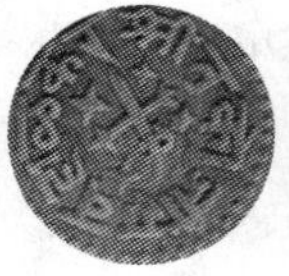

KM#	Date	Year	VG	Fine	VF	XF
25	AH1295	—	40.00	55.00	70.00	90.00

MOHUR

GOLD, 10.83 g

KM#	Date	Year	VG	Fine	VF	XF
27	VS1941	(1883)	—	—	Rare	—

Milled Coinage

SHIVAJI RAO

VS1943-1960/FE1296-1313/1886-1903AD

Without ruler's name

1/2 PAISA

COPPER

Rev: Denomination in 2 lines: *1/2 Adhela Paisa.*

KM#	Date	Year	Good	VG	Fine	VF
30.1	VS1944	(1887)	10.00	15.00	21.50	30.00

Rev: Denomination in 3 lines: *1/2 Dhaleka Paisa.*

KM#	Date	Year	Good	VG	Fine	VF
30.2	VS1944	(1887)	10.00	15.00	21.50	30.00

In the name of Shivaji Rao

Rev: Denomination in 2 lines: *Adha Paisa.*

KM#	Date	Year	Good	VG	Fine	VF
31	VS1946	(1889)	11.50	16.50	23.50	32.50

Without ruler's name

1/4 ANNA

COPPER

Obv: Date below bull.

Rev: *Indore* below denomination.

KM#	Date	Year	Good	VG	Fine	VF
32.1	VS1943	(1886)	1.50	3.00	5.00	7.50

Rev: Retrograde.

KM#	Date	Year	Good	VG	Fine	VF
32.2	VS1943	(1886)	—	—	—	—

Obv: Continuous leg. w/*Indore* below bull.

Rev: Date below denomination.

KM#	Date	Year	Good	VG	Fine	VF
32.3	VS1943	(1886)	.35	.75	1.25	2.50
	1944	(1887)	.50	1.00	1.50	3.00
	1945	(1888)	.75	1.25	2.00	4.00

Obv: Broken leg. w/*Indore* upright below bull.

KM#	Date	Year	Good	VG	Fine	VF
32.4	VS1943	(1886)	2.00	4.00	6.50	8.50
	1944	(1887)	2.00	4.00	6.50	8.50

Obv: Cross w/dot in each quadrant flanking *Indore.*

KM#	Date	Year	Good	VG	Fine	VF
32.5	VS1943	(1886)	1.00	2.00	3.00	6.00

In the name of Sivaji Rao

Obv: Continuous leg. w/ruler's name and *Indore* .

Rev: Date below denomination.

KM#	Date	Year	Good	VG	Fine	VF
33.1	VS1944	(1887)	.85	1.75	2.50	5.00
	1945	(1888)	.75	1.50	2.00	4.00
	1946	(1889)	.85	1.75	2.50	5.00
	1947	(1890)	.75	1.50	2.00	4.00

Obv. leg: Ruler's name spelled *Sayaji Rao.*

KM#	Date	Year	Good	VG	Fine	VF
33.2	VS1944	(1887)	1.00	2.00	4.00	8.00

Obv: Continuous leg. w/ruler's name and *Bahadur.*

Rev: *Indore* above denomination and date.

KM#	Date	Year	Good	VG	Fine	VF
33.3	VS1947	(1890)	.75	1.50	2.25	4.50
	1948	(1891)	.50	1.00	1.50	3.00
	1956	(1899)	.35	.75	1.25	2.50
	1957	(1900)	.65	1.25	1.75	2.50

NOTE: Later dates (VS1958-1959) exist for this type.

NOTE: Floral border varieties exist.

Rev: Date below denomination.

KM#	Date	Year	Good	VG	Fine	VF
33.4	VS1948	(1891)	1.00	2.00	4.00	6.00

Without ruler's name

1/2 ANNA

COPPER

Obv: Date below bull.

Rev: *Indore* below denomination.

KM#	Date	Year	Good	VG	Fine	VF
34.1	VS1943	(1886)	3.00	5.00	8.50	14.00

Obv: Continuous leg. w/*Indore* below bull.

KM#	Date	Year	Good	VG	Fine	VF
34.2	VS1943	(1886)	3.00	5.00	7.00	10.00
	1944	(1887)	3.00	5.00	7.00	10.00

Obv. leg: *Indore* behind bull

Rev: *Indore* above denomination and date.

KM#	Date	Year	Good	VG	Fine	VF
34.3	VS1943	(1886)	4.00	6.00	8.50	12.50

Obv: Broken leg. w/*Indore* upright below bull.

KM#	Date	Year	Good	VG	Fine	VF
34.4	VS1943	(1886)	3.00	5.00	7.00	10.00

In the name of Sivaji Rao

Obv. leg: Ruler's name and *Indore.*

Rev: Date below denomination.

KM#	Date	Year	Good	VG	Fine	VF
35.1	VS1944	(1887)	3.00	5.00	7.00	10.00
	1945	(1888)	3.00	5.00	7.00	10.00
	1947	(1890)	7.50	13.50	20.00	30.00

NOTE: Floral border varieties exist.

Obv: Broken leg. w/*Bahadur* upright below bull.

Rev: *Indore* above denomination and date.

KM#	Date	Year	Good	VG	Fine	VF
35.2	VS1943	(1886)	3.50	5.50	8.50	11.50

Obv: Continuous leg. w/ruler's name and *Bahadur.*

Rev: *Indore* above denomination and date.

KM#	Date	Year	Good	VG	Fine	VF
35.3	VS1945	(1888)	1.00	1.50	2.25	4.50
	1947	(1890)	1.00	1.50	2.00	4.00
	1948	(1891)	1.00	1.50	2.00	3.00
	1956	(1899)	1.00	1.50	2.00	3.00
	1957	(1900)	1.00	1.50	2.00	3.00

NOTE: Later dates (VS1958-1959) exist for this type.

Dump Coinage

In the name of Shah Alam II

AH 1173-1221/1759-1806 AD

First Series

Crossed scimitar and spear below sunface w/Fasli Era and Vikrama Samvat Era dating.

1/4 RUPEE

SILVER, 2.68-2.90 g

KM#	Date	Year	VG	Fine	VF	XF
37	FE1295	VS1945	17.50	25.00	35.00	50.00

1/2 RUPEE

SILVER, 5.35-5.80 g

KM#	Date	Year	VG	Fine	VF	XF
38	FE1295	VS1947	17.50	25.00	35.00	50.00
	1296	VS1947	17.50	25.00	35.00	50.00

RUPEE

SILVER, 10.70-11.60 g
Obv: Large flames.

KM#	Date	Year	VG	Fine	VF	XF
39.1	FE1294	VS1945	16.50	23.50	32.50	45.00
	1295	VS1945	16.50	23.50	32.50	45.00
	1296	VS1945	16.50	23.50	32.50	45.00

Obv: Small flames.

KM#	Date	Year	VG	Fine	VF	XF
39.2	FE1295	R.Y.122	15.00	21.50	30.00	40.00
	1296	VS1945	15.00	21.50	30.00	40.00

Obv: W/o flames.

KM#	Date	Year	VG	Fine	VF	XF
39.3	FE1295	VS1947	16.50	23.50	32.50	45.00
	1296	1947	16.50	23.50	32.50	45.00
	1297	1947	16.50	23.50	32.50	45.00

Second Series

NOTE: There are 2 minor sub-varieties, one w/U-shaped mark on forehead of sunface and the other w/dot. Vikrama Samvat Era dating.

PAISA

COPPER

KM#	Date	Year	VG	Fine	VF	XF
40	VS1947	—	—	—	Rare	—

1/8 RUPEE

SILVER, 1.34-1.45 g

KM#	Date	Year	VG	Fine	VF	XF
41	VS1947	(1890)	3.50	5.50	7.00	10.00
	1950	(1893)	3.50	5.50	7.00	10.00
	1951	(1894)	3.50	5.50	7.00	10.00

1/4 RUPEE

SILVER, 2.68-2.90 g

KM#	Date	Year	VG	Fine	VF	XF
42	VS1947	(1890)	3.50	6.00	8.50	12.50
	1951	(1893)	3.50	6.00	8.50	12.50
	1954	(1897)	3.50	6.00	8.50	12.50
	Date off flan		2.00	3.00	4.00	7.00

1/2 RUPEE

SILVER, 5.35-5.80 g

KM#	Date	Year	VG	Fine	VF	XF
43	VS1947	(1890)	4.00	7.00	10.00	15.00
	1948	(1891)	4.00	7.00	10.00	15.00
	1949	(1892)	4.00	7.00	10.00	15.00
	1950	(1893)	4.00	7.00	10.00	15.00
	1951	(1894)	4.00	7.00	10.00	15.00
	1952	(1895)	4.00	7.00	10.00	15.00
	1953	(1896)	4.00	7.00	10.00	15.00
	1954	(1897)	4.00	7.00	10.00	15.00
	Date off flan		2.50	3.50	5.00	8.00

RUPEE

SILVER, 10.70-11.60 g

KM#	Date	Year	VG	Fine	VF	XF
44	VS1947	(1890)	5.50	8.50	12.50	18.50
	1948	(1891)	5.50	8.50	12.50	18.50
	1949	(1892)	5.50	8.50	12.50	18.50
	1950	(1893)	5.50	8.50	12.50	18.50
	1951	(1894)	5.50	8.50	12.50	18.50
	1952	(1895)	5.50	8.50	12.50	18.50
	1953	(1896)	5.50	8.50	12.50	18.50
	1954	(1897)	5.50	8.50	12.50	18.50
	1955	(1898)	5.50	8.50	12.50	18.50
	Date off flan		3.00	4.50	6.00	10.00

NAZARANA RUPEE

SILVER, 11.13-11.21 g

KM#	Date	Year	VG	Fine	VF	XF
45	VS1947	(1890)	37.50	52.50	75.00	110.00

MILLED COINAGE

Third Series

This series was introduced in 1898 to counteract counterfeiting of the second series which had begun to proliferate as a result of a sharp fall in the price of silver. Idle minting machines were reactivated for this purpose, but the series was short-lived.

1/2 ANNA

COPPER, 10.03 g

KM#	Date	Year	Fine	VF	XF	Unc
46	VS1955	(1898)	—	—	Rare	—

RUPEE

SILVER, 11.20 g
Obv: Turban separates legend.

KM#	Date	Year	Fine	VF	XF	Unc
47.1	VS1956	(1899)	90.00	140.00	200.00	300.00

PATTERNS (Pn)

KM#	Date	Mintage	Identification	Mkt.Val.
Pn1	VS1955	*12 pcs.	1 Rupee, .900 Silver	650.00

TRIAL STRIKES (TS)

KM#	Date	Mintage	Identification	Mkt.Val.
TS1	VS1955	—	1 Rupee, Copper, Obv. Pn1	400.00

MAHESHWAR MINT

In operation from 1767 to 1803.

Distinctive Marks:

Bilva Leaf Silver — **Lingam - Yoni. Copper and Silver.**

NOTE: The following copper coins are illustrative of this variegated series. Many varieties and other dates exist.

1/4 RUPEE

SILVER, 2.68-2.90 g
Rev: Bilva leaf and lingam.

KM#	Date	Year	VG	Fine	VF	XF
56.2	AH1216	—	7.00	12.00	17.50	25.00
	1217	—	7.00	12.00	17.50	25.00

NOTE: Earlier dates (AH1202-1215) exist for this type.

1/2 RUPEE

SILVER, 5.35-5.80 g
Rev: Bilva leaf and lingam.

KM#	Date	Year	VG	Fine	VF	XF
57.2	AH1216	44	8.50	13.50	20.00	28.50
	1217	—	8.50	13.50	20.00	28.50

NOTE: Earlier dates (AH1202-1211) exist for this type.

RUPEE

SILVER, 10.70-11.60 g
Rev: Bilva leaf and lingam.

KM#	Date	Year	VG	Fine	VF	XF
58.2	AH1216	44	6.00	10.00	15.00	22.00
	1217	46	6.00	10.00	15.00	22.00

NOTE: Earlier dates (AH1201-1215) exist for this type.

NAZARANA RUPEE

SILVER

KM#	Date	Year	VG	Fine	VF	XF
59	AH1267	97	—	—	Rare	—

NOTE: Brief revival of this type under Tukoji Rao II for presentation.

MALHARNAGAR MINT

Located in capital, Indore City. In operation regularly from 1768 to 1878.

Mintname: Malharnagar

Distinctive Marks:

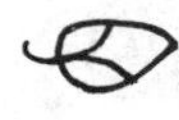 

Bilva Leaf Copper — **Sunface Copper and Silver**

In the name of Shah Alam II

AH1173-1221/1759-1806AD

PAISA

COPPER, 7.15 g
Obv: Katar. Rev: Three dots in Sunface.

KM#	Date	Year	Good	VG	Fine	VF
A61.1 (A61)	AH---	30	6.00	10.00	14.00	20.00

Rev: Four dots in sunface.

KM#	Date	Year	Good	VG	Fine	VF
A61.2	AH---	—	6.00	10.00	14.00	20.00

1/4 ANNA

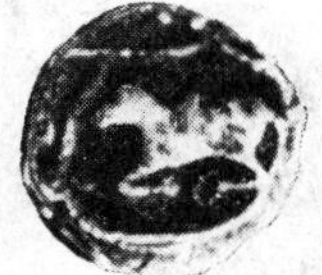

COPPER, 9.60-9.70 g

KM#	Date	Year	Good	VG	Fine	VF
61	AH1244	—	3.00	4.00	5.50	7.50
	12xx	88	3.00	4.00	5.50	7.50

COPPER, 12.20-12.40 g
Obv. leg: Hindi leg. *Pau Anna*

KM#	Date	Year	Good	VG	Fine	VF
62	AH1267	97	5.00	6.50	8.50	11.50

1/2 ANNA

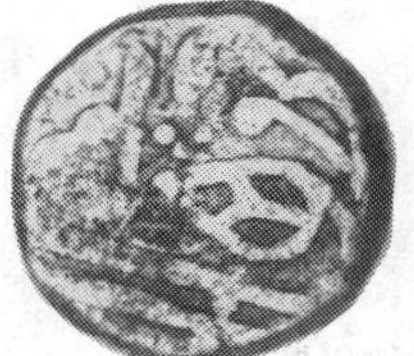

COPPER, 18.70-20.00 g
Rev: Altar before bull.

KM#	Date	Year	Good	VG	Fine	VF
63.1	AH1244	—	5.00	6.50	9.00	12.00

Rev: W/o altar.

KM#	Date	Year	Good	VG	Fine	VF
63.2	AH1243	1251	3.00	4.00	5.50	7.50
	1244	—	3.00	4.00	5.50	7.50
	12xx	88	3.00	4.00	5.50	7.50

COPPER, 12.00-17.30 g
Obv. leg: Hindi *Adha Anna*

KM#	Date	Year	Good	VG	Fine	VF
64	AH1261	—	2.50	3.25	4.00	6.00
	1266	—	2.50	3.25	4.00	6.00
	1267	97	2.75	3.50	4.50	6.50
	1268	—	2.50	3.25	4.00	6.00
	1269	99	3.00	3.50	4.50	6.50
	1271	—	2.50	3.25	4.00	6.00
	1285	—	1.75	2.50	3.50	5.50
	1286	113	2.25	3.00	4.00	6.00
	1286 dated both sides					
		—	3.00	3.50	4.00	6.00

Rev: Altar before bull.

KM#	Date	Year	Good	VG	Fine	VF
68	AH1286	—	3.00	4.00	5.00	6.50

NAZARANA 1/2 ANNA

COPPER

KM#	Date	Year	Good	VG	Fine	VF
65	AH12xx	99	—	—	—	—

1/16 RUPEE

SILVER

KM#	Date	Year	VG	Fine	VF	XF
70	AH1248	—	—	—	Rare	—
	1266	—	—	—	Rare	—

1/8 RUPEE

SILVER, 1.34-1.45 g

KM#	Date	Year	VG	Fine	VF	XF
71	AH1227	—	3.50	6.00	8.50	12.50
	1236	—	3.50	6.00	8.50	12.50
	1237	—	3.50	6.00	8.50	12.50
	1248	—	2.50	4.00	6.00	8.50
	(12)55	—	2.50	4.00	6.00	8.50
	1257	—	2.50	4.00	6.00	8.50
	1262	—	2.50	4.00	6.00	8.50
	1268	—	2.50	4.00	6.00	8.50
	1269	—	2.50	4.00	6.00	8.50
	1270	—	2.50	4.00	6.00	8.50
	1271	—	2.50	4.00	6.00	8.50
	1272	—	2.50	4.00	6.00	8.50
	1278	—	2.50	4.00	6.00	8.50
	1279	—	2.50	4.00	6.00	8.50
	1282	—	2.00	4.00	6.00	8.50
	1287	—	2.50	4.00	6.00	8.50
	1289	—	2.50	4.00	6.00	8.50
	1291	—	2.50	4.00	6.00	8.50
	1292	—	2.50	4.00	6.00	8.50
	1293	—	2.50	4.00	6.00	8.50
	1294	—	2.50	4.00	6.00	8.50
	1295	—	2.50	4.00	6.00	8.50

1/4 RUPEE

SILVER, 2.68-2.90 g

KM#	Date	Year	VG	Fine	VF	XF
72	AH1231	—	3.00	5.00	7.00	10.00
	1232	—	3.00	5.00	7.00	10.00
	1233	—	3.00	5.00	7.00	10.00
	1234	—	3.00	5.00	7.00	10.00
	1235	—	3.00	5.00	7.00	10.00
	1236	—	3.00	5.00	7.00	10.00
	1237	—	3.00	5.00	7.00	10.00
	1240	—	3.00	5.00	7.00	10.00
	1241	—	3.00	5.00	7.00	10.00
	1243	—	3.00	5.00	7.00	10.00
	1244	—	3.00	5.00	7.00	10.00
	1246	—	3.00	5.00	7.00	10.00
	1249	—	3.00	5.00	7.00	10.00
	1250	—	3.00	5.00	7.00	10.00
	1251	—	3.00	5.00	7.00	10.00
	1252	—	3.00	5.00	7.00	10.00
	1253	—	3.00	5.00	7.00	10.00
	1255	—	3.00	5.00	7.00	10.00
	1256	—	3.00	5.00	7.00	10.00
	1261	—	3.00	5.00	7.00	10.00
	1263	—	3.00	5.00	7.00	10.00
	1264	—	3.00	5.00	7.00	10.00
	1265	—	3.00	5.00	7.00	10.00
	1266	—	3.00	5.00	7.00	10.00
	1267	—	3.00	5.00	7.00	10.00
	1268	—	3.00	5.00	7.00	10.00
	1269	—	3.00	5.00	7.00	10.00
	1270	—	3.00	5.00	7.00	10.00
	1272	—	3.00	5.00	7.00	10.00
	1273	—	3.00	5.00	7.00	10.00
	1275	—	3.00	5.00	7.00	10.00
	1277	—	3.00	5.00	7.00	10.00

KM#	Date	Year	VG	Fine	VF	XF
72	1278	—	3.00	5.00	7.00	10.00
	1279	—	3.00	5.00	7.00	10.00
	1282	—	3.00	5.00	7.00	10.00
	1285	—	3.00	5.00	7.00	10.00
	1286	—	3.00	5.00	7.00	10.00
	1288	—	3.00	5.00	7.00	10.00
	1289	—	3.00	5.00	7.00	10.00
	1290	—	3.00	5.00	7.00	10.00
	1291	—	3.00	5.00	7.00	10.00
	1292	—	3.00	5.00	7.00	10.00
	1293	—	3.00	5.00	7.00	10.00
	1294	—	3.00	5.00	7.00	10.00
	1295	—	3.00	5.00	7.00	10.00

NOTE: Earlier date (AH1214) exists for this type.

25mm
Broad, thin planchet

KM#	Date	Year	VG	Fine	VF	XF
72a	AH1280	110	17.50	25.00	35.00	50.00

1/2 RUPEE

SILVER, 5.35-5.80 g

KM#	Date	Year	VG	Fine	VF	XF
73	AH(1)227	—	4.00	6.00	9.00	14.00
	1227	—	4.00	6.00	9.00	14.00
	1228	—	4.00	6.00	9.00	14.00
	1230	—	4.00	6.00	9.00	14.00
	(12)30	62	4.00	6.00	9.00	14.00
	1231	—	4.00	6.00	9.00	14.00
	1233	—	4.00	6.00	9.00	14.00
	1234	6x	4.00	6.00	9.00	14.00
	1237	—	4.00	6.00	9.00	14.00
	1238	—	4.00	6.00	9.00	14.00
	1240	—	4.00	6.00	9.00	14.00
	1242	—	4.00	6.00	9.00	14.00
	1244	72	4.00	6.00	9.00	14.00
	1245	—	4.00	6.00	9.00	14.00
	1246	—	4.00	6.00	9.00	14.00
	1247	—	4.00	6.00	9.00	14.00
	1248	—	4.00	6.00	9.00	14.00
	1250	—	4.00	6.00	9.00	14.00
	1251	—	4.00	6.00	9.00	14.00
	1253	—	4.00	6.00	9.00	14.00
	1255	—	4.00	6.00	9.00	14.00
	1258	—	4.00	6.00	9.00	14.00
	1260	—	4.00	6.00	9.00	14.00
	1262	—	4.00	6.00	9.00	14.00
	1263	—	4.00	6.00	9.00	14.00
	1264	—	4.00	6.00	9.00	14.00
	1265	—	4.00	6.00	9.00	14.00
	1266	—	4.00	6.00	9.00	14.00
	1267	—	4.00	6.00	9.00	14.00
	1268	—	4.00	6.00	9.00	14.00
	1270	—	4.00	6.00	9.00	14.00
	1272	—	4.00	6.00	9.00	14.00
	1273	—	4.00	6.00	9.00	14.00
	1274	—	4.00	6.00	9.00	14.00
	1275	—	4.00	6.00	9.00	14.00
	1276	—	4.00	6.00	9.00	14.00
	1277	—	4.00	6.00	9.00	14.00
	1278	—	4.00	6.00	9.00	14.00
	1279	—	4.00	6.00	9.00	14.00
	1280	—	4.00	6.00	9.00	14.00
	1281	—	4.00	6.00	9.00	14.00
	1283	—	4.00	6.00	9.00	14.00
	1286	—	4.00	6.00	9.00	14.00
	1288	—	4.00	6.00	9.00	14.00
	1289	—	4.00	6.00	9.00	14.00
	1291	—	4.00	6.00	9.00	14.00
	1292	—	4.00	6.00	9.00	14.00
	1293	—	4.00	6.00	9.00	14.00
	1294	120	4.00	6.00	9.00	14.00
	1285	—	4.00	6.00	9.00	14.00
	1295	—	4.00	6.00	9.00	14.00
	1296	—	4.00	6.00	9.00	14.00
	—	121	4.00	6.00	9.00	14.00

NAZARANA 1/2 RUPEE

SILVER, 5.35-5.80 g
Broad, thin planchet

KM#	Date	Year	VG	Fine	VF	XF
74	AH1236	69	25.00	37.50	50.00	70.00
	1280	110	25.00	37.50	50.00	70.00

RUPEE

SILVER, 10.70-11.60 g

KM#	Date	Year	VG	Fine	VF	XF
76	AH1216	—	5.00	7.00	10.00	15.00
	1217	44	5.00	7.00	10.00	15.00
	1224	—	5.00	7.00	10.00	15.00
	1225	59	5.00	7.00	10.00	15.00
	1226	60	5.00	7.00	10.00	15.00
	1228	62	5.00	7.00	10.00	15.00
	1230	61	5.00	7.00	10.00	15.00
	1230	62	5.00	7.00	10.00	15.00
	1231	63	5.00	7.00	10.00	15.00
	1231	64	5.00	7.00	10.00	15.00
	1232	65	5.00	7.00	10.00	15.00
	1233	66	5.00	7.00	10.00	15.00
	1234	67	5.00	7.00	10.00	15.00
	1235	68	5.00	7.00	10.00	15.00
	1237	67	5.00	7.00	10.00	15.00
	1237	70	5.00	7.00	10.00	15.00
	1238	70	5.00	7.00	10.00	15.00
	1240	—	5.00	7.00	10.00	15.00
	1241	—	5.00	7.00	10.00	15.00
	1242	75	5.00	7.00	10.00	15.00
	1243	76	5.00	7.00	10.00	15.00
	1244	72	5.00	7.00	10.00	15.00
	(12)44	74	5.00	7.00	10.00	15.00
	1246	76	5.00	7.00	10.00	15.00
	1248	77	5.00	7.00	10.00	15.00
	1249	—	5.00	7.00	10.00	15.00
	1251	81	5.00	7.00	10.00	15.00
	1250	79	5.00	7.00	10.00	15.00
	1255	85	5.00	7.00	10.00	15.00
	1257	87	5.00	7.00	10.00	15.00
	1258	88	5.00	7.00	10.00	15.00
	1260	9x	5.00	7.00	10.00	15.00
	1262	—	5.00	7.00	10.00	15.00
	1263	—	5.00	7.00	10.00	15.00
	1264	94	5.00	7.00	10.00	15.00
	1265	95	5.00	7.00	10.00	15.00
	1266	9x	5.00	7.00	10.00	15.00
	1266	96	5.00	7.00	10.00	15.00
	1267	97	5.00	7.00	10.00	15.00
	1268	98	5.00	7.00	10.00	15.00
	1269	9x	5.00	7.00	10.00	15.00
	1270	—	5.00	7.00	10.00	15.00
	1272	102	5.00	7.00	10.00	15.00
	1273	—	5.00	7.00	10.00	15.00
	1275	105	5.00	7.00	10.00	15.00
	1276	105	5.00	7.00	10.00	15.00
	1277	—	5.00	7.00	10.00	15.00
	1278	—	5.00	7.00	10.00	15.00
	1279	—	5.00	7.00	10.00	15.00
	1280	—	5.00	7.00	10.00	15.00
	1282	111	5.00	7.00	10.00	15.00
	1285	112	5.00	7.00	10.00	15.00
	1286	113	5.00	7.00	10.00	15.00
	1288	115	5.00	7.00	10.00	15.00
	1289	115	5.00	7.00	10.00	15.00
	1292	118	5.00	7.00	10.00	15.00
	1292	120	5.00	7.00	10.00	15.00
	1293	111	5.00	7.00	10.00	15.00
	1293	119	5.00	7.00	10.00	15.00
	1294	120	5.00	7.00	10.00	15.00
	1295	121	5.00	7.00	10.00	15.00
	1295	122	5.00	7.00	10.00	15.00
	1296	122	5.00	7.00	10.00	15.00

NOTE: Earlier dates(AH1180-1215) exist for this type.

NAZARANA RUPEE

SILVER, 10.70-11.60 g

KM#	Date	Year	VG	Fine	VF	XF
77	AH1225	59	—	—	Rare	—
	1280	110	—	—	Rare	—

UNCERTAIN MINTS

NOTE: 1/2 Paisa and 1 Paisa coins previously listed here now are listed in Banswara-IPS.

1/2 ANNA

Symbol Series

COPPER
Rev: Jhar.

KM#	Date	Year	Good	VG	Fine	VF
90.3 (90.2)	AH1225	—	3.50	4.50	5.50	7.50

Obv: Mace. Rev: Branch w/3 leaves.

KM#	Date	Year	Good	VG	Fine	VF
91	AH1228	—	3.50	4.50	5.50	7.50

Obv: Katar. Rev: Bilva leaf and pennant.

KM#	Date	Year	Good	VG	Fine	VF
92.1	AH1230	—	3.50	4.50	5.50	7.50

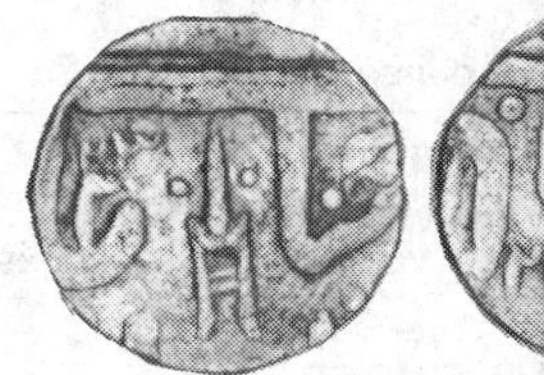

Obv: Katar. Rev: Axe and whisk.

KM#	Date	Year	Good	VG	Fine	VF
92.2	AH1230	27	3.50	4.50	5.50	7.50

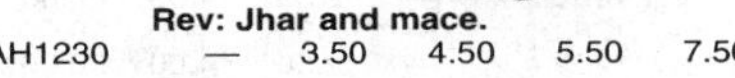

Rev: Jhar and mace.

KM#	Date	Year	Good	VG	Fine	VF
93.1	AH1230	—	3.50	4.50	5.50	7.50

Rev: Bilva leaf.

KM#	Date	Year	Good	VG	Fine	VF
93.2	AH1230	—	3.50	4.50	5.50	7.50

Rev: Flower and flag.

KM#	Date	Year	Good	VG	Fine	VF
93.3	AH1230	—	3.50	4.50	5.50	7.50

Rev: 6-petal flower and sword.

KM#	Date	Year	Good	VG	Fine	VF
93.4	AH1230	—	3.50	4.50	5.50	7.50

Obv: Katar. Rev: Broad axe.

KM#	Date	Year	Good	VG	Fine	VF
94	AH1230	—	3.50	4.50	5.50	7.50

Obv: Broad axe. Rev: Dagger.

KM#	Date	Year	Good	VG	Fine	VF
95.1	AH1233	66	3.50	4.50	5.50	7.50
	1241	—	3.50	4.50	5.50	7.50

Obv: Broad axe. Rev: Sword.

KM#	Date	Year	Good	VG	Fine	VF
95.2	AH1233	—	3.50	4.50	5.50	7.50

Obv: Halberd and date. Rev: Double pennant.

KM#	Date	Year	Good	VG	Fine	VF
95.3	AH(123)3	—	3.50	4.50	6.00	8.00

Rev: Triple banner.

KM#	Date	Year	Good	VG	Fine	VF
95.4	ND	—	3.50	4.50	5.50	7.50

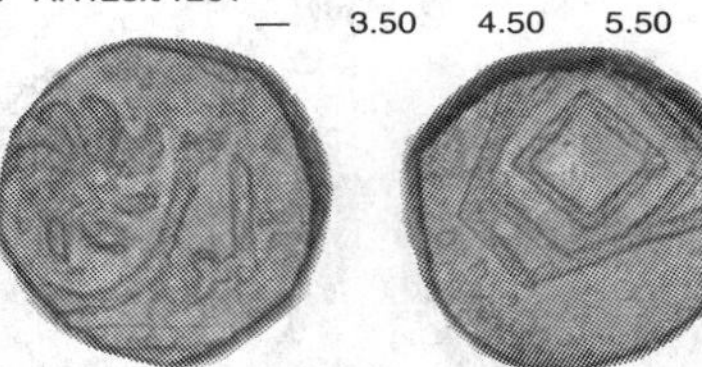

Obv: Leaf. Rev: Pennant and cannon.

KM#	Date	Year	Good	VG	Fine	VF
95.5	AH128x/1261	—	3.50	4.50	5.50	7.50

Obv: Pinwheel. Rev: Geometric design.

KM#	Date	Year	Good	VG	Fine	VF
96	ND	—	3.50	4.50	5.50	7.50

Obv: Trisul and double pennant flags.
Rev: Broad axe.

KM#	Date	Year	Good	VG	Fine	VF
97	AH1220	—	3.50	4.50	5.50	7.50

Obv: 1230. Rev: 6-petal flower and sword.

KM#	Date	Year	Good	VG	Fine	VF
98	AH1230	—	3.50	4.50	5.50	7.50

NOTE: These coins were struck AH1202-1244 with many minor varieties of symbols of which the above are only a sample.

JAFFARABAD

Jaffarabad was a tiny state of some twelve villages and fifty three square miles of territory on the southern coast of Kathiawar. The state was founded in the mideighteenth century by Sidi Hilol of the Janjira ruling house. Jaffarabad was subject to the Nawab of Janjira until 1924, after which oversight was exercised by the British Agent of the Governor-General in the Western India States Agency. The coinage is anonymous and crude, and is attributed to Jaffarabad State primarily on the basis of provenance.

Anonymous Coinage

FIRST SERIES

Obv: Persian script.

3/4 KORI

BILLON, 3.40 g

KM#	Date	Year	VG	Fine	VF	XF
1	ND	—	5.50	9.00	13.50	20.00

KORI

BILLON, 4.70 g

KM#	Date	Year	VG	Fine	VF	XF
2	ND	—	5.50	9.00	13.50	20.00

1-1/2 KORI

BILLON, 7.00 g

KM#	Date	Year	VG	Fine	VF	XF
3	ND	—	5.50	9.00	13.50	20.00

NOTE: The attribution of these coins is very tentative. The denominations are only suggested by the average weights.

SECOND SERIES

Obv: Tree between two flags.

1/2 KORI

BILLON, 2.36-3.18 g

KM#	Date	Year	VG	Fine	VF	XF
5	ND	—	5.00	7.00	10.00	15.00

KORI

BILLON, 3.46-3.82 g

KM#	Date	Year	VG	Fine	VF	XF
6	ND	—	5.00	7.00	10.00	15.00

THIRD SERIES

KORI

BILLON, 4.8-6.0 g
Obv: Incused circle over legend.
Rev: Incused circle over parallel lines.

KM#	Date	Year	VG	Fine	VF	XF
8	ND	—	6.00	9.00	14.00	22.00

JAIPUR

Tradition has it that the region of Jaipur, located in northwest India, once belonged to an ancient Kachwaha Rajput dynasty which claimed descent from Kush, one of the sons of Rama, King of Ayodhya. But the Princely State of Jaipur originated in the twelfth century. Comparatively small in size, the State remained largely unnoticed until after the sixteenth century when the Jaipur royal house became famous for its military skills and thereafter supplied the Mughals with some of their more distinguished generals. The city of Jaipur was founded about 1728 by Maharaja Jai Singh II who was also well known for his knowledge of mathematics and astronomy. The late eighteenth and early nineteenth centuries were difficult times for Jaipur. They were marked by internal rivalry, exacerbated by Maratha or Pindari incursions. In 1818 this culminated with a treaty whereby Jaipur came under British protection and oversight.

RULERS

Pratap Singh,
AH1192-1218/1778-1803AD
Jagat Singh II,
AH1218-1234/1803-1818AD
Mohan Singh,
AH1234-1235/1818-1819AD
Jai Singh III,
AH1235-1251/1819-1835AD
Ram Singh,
AH1251-1298/1835-1880AD
Madho Singh II, 1880-1922AD
Man Singh II, 1922-1949AD

All coins struck prior to AH1274/1857AD are in the name of the Mughal emperor. The corresponding AH date is listed in ( ) with each regnal year. Some overlapping of AH dates with regnal years will be found. Partial dates and recorded full dates are represented by partial ( ) or without ( ).

Beginning in 1857AD, coins were struck jointly in the names and corresponding AD dates of the British sovereign and the names and regnal years of the Maharajas of Jaipur.

The coins ordinarily bear both the AH date before 1857 or the AD date after 1857, as well as the regnal year, but as it is found only at the extreme right of the obverse die, it is almost never visible on the regular coinage but generally legible on the Nazarana coins which were struck utilizing the entire dies.

The listing of regnal years is very incomplete and many more years will turn up. In general, unlisted years are usually worth no more than years listed.

MINTNAMES

Coins were struck at two mints, which bear the following characteristic marks on the reverse:

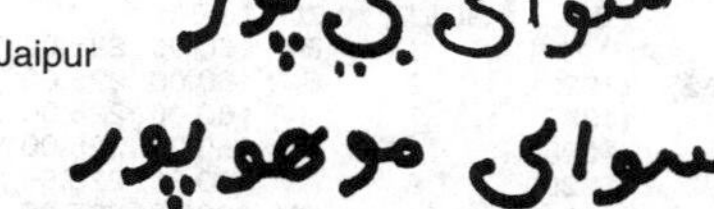

Sawai Jaipur

Sawai Madhopur

NOTE: *Sawai* is merely an honorific title accorded each of the two cities.

Mint marks:

Jhar

Leaf

Whisk

JAIPUR MINT
Mughal Issues

In the name of Shah Alam II
AH1173-1221/1759-1806AD

PAISA

COPPER
Rev: Large Jhar.

KM#	Date	Year	Good	VG	Fine	VF
39 (C35)	AH—	44	2.50	4.50	6.50	10.00
	—	45	2.50	4.50	6.50	10.00

NOTE: Earlier dates (Year 35-41) exist for this type.

NAZARANA PAISA

COPPER
Rev: Large Jhar.

KM#	Date	Year	Good	VG	Fine	VF
40 (C35a)	AH—	45	15.00	27.50	40.00	60.00
	—	46	15.00	27.50	40.00	60.00

NOTE: Earlier dates (Year 37-39) exist for this type.

NAZARANA 1/4 RUPEE

SILVER, 2.67-2.90 g

KM#	Date	Year	VG	Fine	VF	XF
46 (C-E36)	AH(1216)	44	—	—	Rare	—

RUPEE

SILVER, 10.70-11.60 g
Mint mark: Jhar

KM#	Date	Year	VG	Fine	VF	XF
50 (C36)	AH1218	44	5.50	8.00	12.50	18.50
	1218	45	5.50	8.00	12.50	18.50
	(1218)	46	5.50	8.00	12.50	18.50
	(1219)	47	5.50	8.00	12.50	18.50

NOTE: Earlier dates (AH1197-1215) exist for this type.

SILVER, 10.70-11.60 g
Large flan.

KM#	Date	Year	VG	Fine	VF	XF
51 (C36a)	AH1217	43	60.00	100.00	140.00	200.00

In the name of Muhammad Akbar II
AH1221-1253/1806-1837AD

NAZARANA PAISA

COPPER
Rev: Whisk.

KM#	Date	Year	Good	VG	Fine	VF
60 (C46)	AH—	3	20.00	32.50	50.00	75.00
	—	8	20.00	32.50	50.00	75.00
	—	11	20.00	32.50	50.00	75.00

PAISA

COPPER, 18-20mm
Similar to Nazarana Paisa, C#47a.

KM#	Date	Year	Good	VG	Fine	VF
61 (C47)	AH—	12	2.00	3.25	5.00	7.50
	—	13	2.00	3.25	5.00	7.50
	—	17	2.00	3.25	5.00	7.50
	—	22	2.00	3.25	5.00	7.50
	—	26	2.00	3.25	5.00	7.50
	—	27	2.00	3.25	5.00	7.50
	—	29	2.00	3.25	5.00	7.50
	—	35	2.00	3.25	5.00	7.50

NAZARANA PAISA

COPPER
Rev: Jhar.

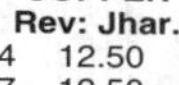

KM#	Date	Year	Good	VG	Fine	VF
62 (C47a)	AH—	4	12.50	22.00	32.50	50.00
	—	7	12.50	22.00	32.50	50.00
	—	9	12.50	22.00	32.50	50.00

KM#	Date	Year	Good	VG	Fine	VF
(C47a)	—	10	12.50	22.00	32.50	50.00
	—	11	12.50	22.00	32.50	50.00
	—	12	12.50	22.00	32.50	50.00
	—	15	12.50	22.00	32.50	50.00
	—	16	12.50	22.00	32.50	50.00
	—	22	12.50	22.00	32.50	50.00
	—	28	12.50	22.00	32.50	50.00

1/8 RUPEE

SILVER, 17-18mm, 1.34-1.45 g

KM#	Date	Year	VG	Fine	VF	XF
65	AH—	21	5.50	8.00	12.50	18.50
(C52)	(1242)	22	5.50	8.00	12.50	18.50

1/4 RUPEE

SILVER, 18-19mm, 2.68-2.90 g

KM#	Date	Year	VG	Fine	VF	XF
66	AH(1237)	17	6.00	9.00	13.50	20.00
(C53)	1238	16	6.00	9.00	13.50	20.00
	—	20	6.00	9.00	13.50	20.00
	—	24	6.00	9.00	13.50	20.00
	(1248)	28	6.00	9.00	13.50	20.00

1/2 RUPEE

SILVER, 18-20mm, 5.35-5.80 g

KM#	Date	Year	VG	Fine	VF	XF
67	AH(1236)	16	6.50	10.00	15.00	22.50
(C54)	—	23	6.50	10.00	15.00	22.50
	(1251)	31	6.50	10.00	15.00	22.50

NAZARANA 1/2 RUPEE

SILVER, 5.35-5.70 g

KM#	Date	Year	VG	Fine	VF	XF
68 (C54a)	AH—	20	—	—	—	—

RUPEE

SILVER, 10.70-11.60 g

KM#	Date	Year	VG	Fine	VF	XF
72	AH1221	1	6.00	9.00	13.50	20.00
(C55)	1222	2	6.00	9.00	13.50	20.00
	122(3)	3	6.00	9.00	13.50	20.00
	1226	4	6.00	9.00	13.50	20.00
	(1227)	7	6.00	9.00	13.50	20.00
	1228	6	6.00	9.00	13.50	20.00
	1229	9	6.00	9.00	13.50	20.00
	1230	10	6.00	9.00	13.50	20.00
	1233	11	6.00	9.00	13.50	20.00
	123x	12	6.00	9.00	13.50	20.00
	1233	13	6.00	9.00	13.50	20.00
	1234	13	6.00	9.00	13.50	20.00
	1234	14	6.00	9.00	13.50	20.00
	1235	15	6.00	9.00	13.50	20.00
	1238	18	6.00	9.00	13.50	20.00
	1240	20	6.00	9.00	13.50	20.00
	1243	22	6.00	9.00	13.50	20.00
	(1243)	23	6.00	9.00	13.50	20.00
	—	24	6.00	9.00	13.50	20.00
	1246	25	6.00	9.00	13.50	20.00
	124x	26	6.00	9.00	13.50	20.00
	1249	27	6.00	9.00	13.50	20.00
	—	28	6.00	9.00	13.50	20.00
	1250	30	6.00	9.00	13.50	20.00
	125x	31	6.00	9.00	13.50	20.00

Square

KM#	Date	Year	VG	Fine	VF	XF
74 (C55b)	AH123x	10	—	—	Rare	—

NAZARANA RUPEE

SILVER, 10.70-11.60 g

KM#	Date	Year	VG	Fine	VF	XF
73	AH1221	1	30.00	50.00	70.00	100.00
(C55a)	1230	9	30.00	50.00	70.00	100.00
	1232	11	30.00	50.00	70.00	100.00
	1237	16	30.00	50.00	70.00	100.00
	1240	20	30.00	50.00	70.00	100.00
	1240	21	30.00	50.00	70.00	100.00

KM#	Date	Year	VG	Fine	VF	XF
(C55a)	1242	22	30.00	50.00	70.00	100.00
	1243	23	30.00	50.00	70.00	100.00
	1246	25	30.00	50.00	70.00	100.00
	1248	27	30.00	50.00	70.00	100.00
	1249	27	30.00	50.00	70.00	100.00
	1249	29	30.00	50.00	70.00	100.00
	1250	28	30.00	50.00	70.00	100.00
	1251	29	30.00	50.00	70.00	100.00
	125x	30	30.00	50.00	70.00	100.00

1/2 MOHUR

GOLD, 5.35-5.80 g

KM#	Date	Year	VG	Fine	VF	XF
76 (C61)	AH124x	25	100.00	150.00	225.00	325.00

MOHUR

GOLD, 10.70-11.60 g

KM#	Date	Year	VG	Fine	VF	XF
77	AH122(1)	1	BV	160.00	225.00	300.00
(C62)	(1222)	2	BV	160.00	225.00	300.00
	(1227)	7	BV	160.00	225.00	300.00
	(1228)	8	BV	160.00	225.00	300.00
	(1229)	9	BV	160.00	225.00	300.00
	(1231)	11	BV	160.00	225.00	300.00
	(1232)	12	BV	160.00	225.00	300.00
	(1236)	16	BV	160.00	225.00	300.00
	(1239)	19	BV	160.00	225.00	300.00
	12(44)	24	BV	160.00	225.00	300.00
	(1249)	29	BV	160.00	225.00	300.00
	(1250)	30	BV	160.00	225.00	300.00

In the name of Bahadur Shah II

AH1253-1274/1837-1858AD

PAISA

COPPER

KM#	Date	Year	Good	VG	Fine	VF
80 (C85)	AH—	13	3.00	5.00	8.00	12.50

NAZARANA PAISA

COPPER

KM#	Date	Year	Good	VG	Fine	VF
81.1	AH—	1	16.00	26.50	40.00	60.00
(C85a)	—	2	16.00	26.50	40.00	60.00
	—	6	16.00	26.50	40.00	60.00
	—	10	16.00	26.50	40.00	60.00
	—	11	16.00	26.50	40.00	60.00
	—	12	16.00	26.50	40.00	60.00
	—	13	16.00	26.50	40.00	60.00
	—	14	16.00	26.50	40.00	60.00
	—	17	16.00	26.50	40.00	60.00

Square planchet.

KM#	Date	Year	Good	VG	Fine	VF
85.2	AH—	13	—	—	Rare	—

1/16 RUPEE

SILVER, 0.67-0.72 g

KM#	Date	Year	VG	Fine	VF	XF
83	AH(1259)	7	6.50	10.00	15.00	22.50
(C89)	(1261)	9	6.50	10.00	15.00	22.50
	(1270)	18	6.50	10.00	15.00	22.50

1/8 RUPEE

SILVER, 15mm, 1.34-1.45 g

KM#	Date	Year	VG	Fine	VF	XF
85 (C90)	AH(1270)	18	6.00	9.00	13.50	20.00

1/4 RUPEE

SILVER, 16-18mm, 2.68-2.90 g

Rev: *Jhar.*

KM#	Date	Year	VG	Fine	VF	XF
87	AH(1259)	7	5.50	8.00	12.50	18.50
(C91.1)	—	19	5.50	8.00	12.50	18.50
	(1272)	20	5.50	8.00	12.50	18.50

Rev: Flower.

KM#	Date	Year	VG	Fine	VF	XF
88 (C91.2)	AH(1270)	18	7.50	12.00	18.00	25.00

1/2 RUPEE

SILVER, 18-19mm, 5.35-5.80 g

KM#	Date	Year	VG	Fine	VF	XF
90	AH(1257)	5	5.50	8.00	12.50	18.50
(C92)	—	11	5.50	8.00	12.50	18.50
	(1270)	18	5.50	8.00	12.50	18.50

RUPEE

SILVER, 10.70-11.60 g

KM#	Date	Year	VG	Fine	VF	XF
93	AH1253	1	5.00	7.00	10.00	15.00
(C93)	1256	3	5.00	7.00	10.00	15.00
	1257	4	5.00	7.00	10.00	15.00
	1258	5	5.00	7.00	10.00	15.00
	1261	8	5.00	7.00	10.00	15.00
	1262	9	5.00	7.00	10.00	15.00
	1263	10	5.00	7.00	10.00	15.00
	—	11	5.00	7.00	10.00	15.00
	1265	12	5.00	7.00	10.00	15.00
	1268	14	5.00	7.00	10.00	15.00
	—	15	5.00	7.00	10.00	15.00
	1270	17	5.00	7.00	10.00	15.00
	1271	17	5.00	7.00	10.00	15.00
	—	19	5.00	7.00	10.00	15.00
	1273	20	5.00	7.00	10.00	15.00

NAZARANA RUPEE

SILVER, 32-35mm, 10.70-11.60 g

KM#	Date	Year	VG	Fine	VF	XF
95	AH1256	3	33.50	47.50	65.00	90.00
(C93a)	1258	4	33.50	47.50	65.00	90.00
	1258	5	33.50	47.50	65.00	90.00
	1262	9	33.50	47.50	65.00	90.00
	1264	11	33.50	47.50	65.00	90.00
	1268	8	(error-mule)			
			33.50	47.50	65.00	90.00
	1266	13	33.50	47.50	65.00	90.00
	1269	15	33.50	47.50	65.00	90.00
	1271	19	33.50	47.50	65.00	90.00
	1273	20	33.50	47.50	65.00	90.00

1/4 MOHUR

GOLD, 17mm, 2.68-2.85 g

KM#	Date	Year	VG	Fine	VF	XF
98 (C98)	AH(1264)	12	80.00	125.00	150.00	225.00

1/2 MOHUR

GOLD, 18mm, 5.35-5.70 g

KM#	Date	Year	VG	Fine	VF	XF
100 (C99)	AH(1264)	12	100.00	150.00	200.00	275.00

MOHUR

GOLD, 10.70-11.40 g

KM#	Date	Year	VG	Fine	VF	XF
102	AH1253	1	150.00	200.00	250.00	325.00
(C100)	(1257)	5	150.00	200.00	250.00	325.00
	12(59)	7	150.00	200.00	250.00	325.00
	1262	9	150.00	200.00	250.00	325.00
	(1262)	10	150.00	200.00	250.00	325.00
	(1263)	11	150.00	200.00	250.00	325.00
	(1264)	12	150.00	200.00	250.00	325.00
	(1265)	13	150.00	200.00	250.00	325.00
	(1266)	14	150.00	200.00	250.00	325.00
	1(267)	15	150.00	200.00	250.00	325.00
	(1271)	19	150.00	200.00	250.00	325.00
	1272	18	150.00	200.00	250.00	325.00
	(1272)	20	150.00	200.00	250.00	325.00

Regal Issues

In the names of Queen Victoria

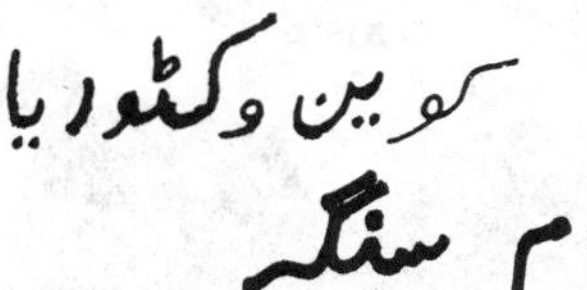

and Ram Singh

Years 22-45/1857-1880AD

NEW PAISA

COPPER

KM#	Date	Year	Good	VG	Fine	VF
105	(1871)	36	1.00	2.00	2.75	5.00
(Y1)	(1872)	37	1.00	2.00	2.75	5.00
	(1873)	38	1.00	2.00	2.75	5.00
	(1874)	39	1.00	2.00	2.75	5.00
	(1875)	40	1.00	2.00	2.75	5.00
	(1876)	41	1.00	2.00	2.75	5.00
	(1877)	42	1.00	2.00	2.75	5.00
	(1880)	45	1.25	2.25	3.25	6.00

NOTE: Years 36 and 37 are struck on broader flans.

NAZARANA OLD PAISA

COPPER, 16.00-18.50 g, 27-31mm

KM#	Date	Year	Good	VG	Fine	VF
106	1858	23	25.00	45.00	65.00	100.00
(Y1a)	1859	24	25.00	45.00	65.00	100.00
	1862	27	25.00	45.00	65.00	100.00

NAZARANA NEW PAISA

COPPER, 28mm, 6.20-6.50 g

KM#	Date	Year	Good	VG	Fine	VF
107	1862	27	12.00	18.50	30.00	45.00
(Y1b)	1864	29	12.00	18.50	30.00	45.00
	1865	30	12.00	18.50	30.00	45.00
	1872	37	12.00	18.50	30.00	45.00
	1873	38	12.00	18.50	30.00	45.00
	1875	40	12.00	18.50	30.00	45.00
	1876	41	12.00	18.50	30.00	45.00
	1877	42	12.00	18.50	30.00	45.00
	1879	44	12.00	18.50	30.00	45.00
	1880	45	12.00	18.50	30.00	45.00

1/8 RUPEE

SILVER, 14mm, 1.34-1.45 g

KM#	Date	Year	VG	Fine	VF	XF
110	(1857)	22	3.50	5.00	7.50	12.50
(Y3)	(1861)	26	3.50	5.00	7.50	12.50
	(1862)	27	3.50	5.00	7.50	12.50
	(1877)	42	3.50	5.00	7.50	12.50

1/4 RUPEE

SILVER, 2.68-2.90 g

KM#	Date	Year	VG	Fine	VF	XF
111	(1861)	26	4.00	6.00	9.00	14.00
(4)	(1862)	27	4.00	6.00	9.00	14.00
	(1863)	28	4.00	6.00	9.00	14.00
	(1864)	29	4.00	6.00	9.00	14.00
	(1867)	32	4.00	6.00	9.00	14.00
	(1868)	33	4.00	6.00	9.00	14.00
	(1876)	41	4.00	6.00	9.00	14.00
	(1878)	43	4.00	6.00	9.00	14.00
	(1879)	44	4.00	6.00	9.00	14.00

NAZARANA 1/4 RUPEE

SILVER

KM#	Date	Year	VG	Fine	VF	XF
112 (Y4a)	(1879)	44	17.50	25.00	35.00	50.00

1/2 RUPEE

SILVER, 18-21mm, 5.35-5.80 g

KM#	Date	Year	VG	Fine	VF	XF
115	(1857)	22	5.00	7.00	10.00	15.00
(Y5)	(1862)	27	5.00	7.00	10.00	15.00
	(1868)	33	5.00	7.00	10.00	15.00
	(1869)	35	5.00	7.00	10.00	15.00
	(1871)	36	5.00	7.00	10.00	15.00
	—	42	5.00	7.00	10.00	15.00
	(1879)	44	5.00	7.00	10.00	15.00
	(1880)	45	5.00	7.00	10.00	15.00

NAZARANA 1/2 RUPEE

SILVER

KM#	Date	Year	VG	Fine	VF	XF
116 (Y5a)	1865	30	17.50	25.00	35.00	50.00

RUPEE

SILVER, 10.70-11.60 g

KM#	Date	Year	VG	Fine	VF	XF
119	1858	23	5.50	8.00	12.00	18.50
(Y6)	(1860)	25	5.50	8.00	12.00	18.50
	(1861)	26	5.50	8.00	12.00	18.50
	(1862)	27	5.50	8.00	12.00	18.50
	(1863)	28	5.50	8.00	12.00	18.50
	(1864)	29	5.50	8.00	12.00	18.50
	(1865)	30	5.50	8.00	12.00	18.50
	1866	31	5.50	8.00	12.00	18.50
	1867	32	5.50	8.00	12.00	18.50

KM#	Date	Year	VG	Fine	VF	XF
(Y6)	(1868)	33	5.50	8.00	12.00	18.50
	1869	34	5.50	8.00	12.00	18.50
	(1870)	35	5.50	8.00	12.00	18.50
	(1871)	36	5.50	8.00	12.00	18.50
	(1873)	38	5.50	8.00	12.00	18.50
	(1875)	40	5.50	8.00	12.00	18.50
	(1876)	41	5.50	8.00	12.00	18.50
	(1877)	42	5.50	8.00	12.00	18.50
	(1878)	43	5.50	8.00	12.00	18.50
	(1879)	44	5.50	8.00	12.00	18.50
	(1880)	45	5.50	8.00	12.00	18.50

NAZARANA RUPEE

SILVER, 10.70-11.60 g

KM#	Date	Year	VG	Fine	VF	XF
120	1858	23	27.00	40.00	55.00	85.00
(Y6a)	1859	24	27.00	40.00	55.00	85.00
	1861	26	27.00	40.00	55.00	85.00
	1864	29	27.00	40.00	55.00	85.00
	1865	30	27.00	40.00	55.00	85.00
	1866	31	27.00	40.00	55.00	85.00
	1867	32	27.00	40.00	55.00	85.00
	1870	35	27.00	40.00	55.00	85.00
	1871	36	27.00	40.00	55.00	85.00
	1875	40	27.00	40.00	55.00	85.00

Square planchet.

KM#	Date	Year	VG	Fine	VF	XF
121 (Y6b)	1858	23	75.00	100.00	150.00	250.00

MOHUR

GOLD, 10.70-11.40 g

KM#	Date	Year	VG	Fine	VF	XF
125	(1856)	21	135.00	155.00	185.00	225.00
(Y7)	(1860)	23	135.00	155.00	185.00	225.00
	(1859)	24	135.00	155.00	185.00	225.00
	(1860)	25	135.00	155.00	185.00	225.00
	18(60)	25	135.00	155.00	185.00	225.00
	1861	26	135.00	155.00	185.00	225.00
	(1862)	27	135.00	155.00	185.00	225.00
	(1864)	29	135.00	155.00	185.00	225.00
	—	31	135.00	155.00	185.00	225.00
	—	35	135.00	155.00	185.00	225.00
	(1871)	36	135.00	155.00	185.00	225.00
	(1872)	37	135.00	155.00	185.00	225.00
	(1877)	42	135.00	155.00	185.00	225.00

In the names of Queen Victoria

کوین وکٹوریا
مادھو سنگھ

and Madho Singh II

Years 1-43/1880-1922AD

NOTE: Queen Victoria's name was retained on Madho Singh II's coinage until 1922AD. No coins were struck with Edward VII's name by Madho Singh II.

1/2 PAISA

COPPER, 2.98 g

KM#	Date	Year	Good	VG	Fine	VF
129 (Y-A8)	(1857)	22	1.00	2.00	3.50	5.50

PAISA

COPPER, 6.15-6.30 g

KM#	Date	Year	Good	VG	Fine	VF
130	(1882)	3	.60	1.00	2.00	4.00
(Y8)	(1883)	4	.60	1.00	2.00	4.00
	(1884)	5	.60	1.00	2.00	4.00
	(1887)	8	.60	1.00	2.00	4.00
	(1898)	19	.30	.65	1.35	2.00
	(1899)	20	.30	.65	1.35	2.00
	(1900)	21	.30	.65	1.35	2.00

NOTE: Later dates (Yr.22-41) exist for this type.

COPPER, 13.50-16.50 g

KM#	Date	Year	Good	VG	Fine	VF
131	1897	18	12.50	22.50	32.50	50.00
(Y8b)						

NAZARANA NEW PAISA

COPPER

KM#	Date	Year	VG	Fine	VF	XF
132	1880	1	12.50	17.50	25.00	40.00
(Y8a)	1886	7	12.50	17.50	25.00	40.00
	1891	12	12.50	17.50	25.00	40.00
	1895	16	12.50	17.50	25.00	40.00
	1897	17	12.50	17.50	25.00	40.00
	1897	18	12.50	17.50	25.00	40.00
	1899	20	12.50	17.50	25.00	40.00
	1900	21	12.50	17.50	25.00	40.00

NOTE: Later dates (1901-1917) exist for this type.

NOTE: Well-centered issues on thin planchets may be restrikes.

1/16 RUPEE

SILVER, 10mm, 0.67-0.72 g

KM#	Date	Year	VG	Fine	VF	XF
135	(1881)	2	5.00	7.00	10.00	15.00
(Y9)	(1882)	3	5.00	7.00	10.00	15.00
	(1889)	10	5.00	7.00	10.00	15.00

NOTE: Later date (1912) exists for this type.

1/8 RUPEE

SILVER, 1.34-1.45 g

KM#	Date	Year	VG	Fine	VF	XF
137	(1883)	4	2.50	3.50	5.00	8.00
(Y10)	(1885)	6	2.50	3.50	5.00	8.00
	(1886)	7	2.50	3.50	5.00	8.00
	(1888)	9	2.50	3.50	5.00	8.00
	(1890)	11	2.50	3.50	5.00	8.00
	(1891)	12	2.50	3.50	5.00	8.00
	(1897)	18	2.50	3.50	5.00	8.00
	(1898)	19	2.50	3.50	5.00	8.00
	(1900)	21	2.50	3.50	5.00	8.00

NOTE: Later dates (1901-1921) exist for this type.

1/4 RUPEE

SILVER, 2.68-2.90 g

KM#	Date	Year	VG	Fine	VF	XF
139	(1880)	1	3.00	4.50	6.50	10.00
(Y11)	(1881)	2	3.00	4.50	6.50	10.00
	(1883)	4	3.00	4.50	6.50	10.00
	(1885)	6	3.00	4.50	6.50	10.00
	(1886)	7	3.00	4.50	6.50	10.00
	(1887)	8	3.00	4.50	6.50	10.00
	(1889)	10	3.00	4.50	6.50	10.00
	(1890)	11	3.00	4.50	6.50	10.00
	(1891)	12	3.00	4.50	6.50	10.00
	(1893)	14	3.00	4.50	6.50	10.00
	(1894)	15	3.00	4.50	6.50	10.00
	(1895)	16	3.00	4.50	6.50	10.00
	(1896)	17	3.00	4.50	6.50	10.00
	(1897)	18	3.00	4.50	6.50	10.00
	(1898)	19	3.00	4.50	6.50	10.00
	(1899)	20	3.00	4.50	6.50	10.00
	1900	21	3.00	4.50	6.50	10.00

NOTE: Later dates (1901-1921) exist for this type.

1/2 RUPEE

SILVER, 5.35-5.80 g

KM#	Date	Year	VG	Fine	VF	XF
142	(1880)	1	3.50	5.00	7.50	12.50
(Y12)	(1882)	3	3.50	5.00	7.50	12.50
	(1883)	4	3.50	5.00	7.50	12.50
	(1884)	5	3.50	5.00	7.50	12.50
	(1886)	7	3.50	5.00	7.50	12.50
	(1887)	8	3.50	5.00	7.50	12.50
	(1888)	9	3.50	5.00	7.50	12.50
	(1889)	10	3.50	5.00	7.50	12.50
	(1890)	11	3.50	5.00	7.50	12.50
	(1891)	12	3.50	5.00	7.50	12.50
	(1892)	13	3.50	5.00	7.50	12.50
	(1893)	14	3.50	5.00	7.50	12.50
	(1894)	15	3.50	5.00	7.50	12.50
	(1896)	17	3.50	5.00	7.50	12.50
	(1897)	18	3.50	5.00	7.50	12.50
	(1898)	19	3.50	5.00	7.50	12.50
	(1899)	20	3.50	5.00	7.50	12.50
	190(0)	21	3.50	5.00	7.50	12.50

NOTE: Later dates (1901-1916) exist for this type.

RUPEE

SILVER, 10.70-11.60 g

KM#	Date	Year	VG	Fine	VF	XF
145	(1880)	1	4.00	6.00	9.00	14.00
(Y13)	(1881)	2	4.00	6.00	9.00	14.00
	(1882)	3	4.00	6.00	9.00	14.00
	(1883)	4	4.00	6.00	9.00	14.00
	(1884)	5	4.00	6.00	9.00	14.00
	(1885)	6	4.00	6.00	9.00	14.00
	(1886)	7	4.00	6.00	9.00	14.00
	1886	8	4.00	6.00	9.00	14.00
	1887	8	4.00	6.00	9.00	14.00
	1888	9	4.00	6.00	9.00	14.00
	(1889)	10	4.00	6.00	9.00	14.00
	(1890)	11	4.00	6.00	9.00	14.00
	(1891)	12	4.00	6.00	9.00	14.00
	(1892)	13	4.00	6.00	9.00	14.00
	(1893)	14	4.00	6.00	9.00	14.00
	(1894)	15	4.00	6.00	9.00	14.00
	(1895)	16	4.00	6.00	9.00	14.00
	(1896)	17	4.00	6.00	9.00	14.00
	(1897)	18	4.00	6.00	9.00	14.00
	(1898)	19	4.00	6.00	9.00	14.00
	(1899)	20	4.00	6.00	8.50	14.00
	(1900)	21	4.00	6.00	9.00	14.00

NOTE: Later dates (1902-1922) exist for this type.

NAZARANA RUPEE

SILVER, 30-31mm, 10.70-11.60 g

KM#	Date	Year	VG	Fine	VF	XF
146	1880	1	35.00	50.00	70.00	100.00
(Y13a)	1881	2	35.00	50.00	70.00	100.00
	1882	3	35.00	50.00	70.00	100.00
	1883	4	35.00	50.00	70.00	100.00
	1884	5	35.00	50.00	70.00	100.00

36-37mm

KM#	Date	Year	VG	Fine	VF	XF
147	1884	5	27.50	40.00	52.50	75.00
(Y13b)	1886	7	27.50	40.00	52.50	75.00
	1887	8	27.50	40.00	52.50	75.00
	1888	9	27.50	40.00	52.50	75.00
	1889	10	27.50	40.00	52.50	75.00
	1890	11	27.50	40.00	52.50	75.00
	1891	12	27.50	40.00	52.50	75.00
	1895	16	27.50	40.00	52.50	75.00
	1896	13	27.50	40.00	52.50	75.00
	1897	18	27.50	40.00	52.50	75.00
	1899	20	27.50	40.00	52.50	75.00

NOTE: Later dates (1901-1921) exist for this type.

MOHUR

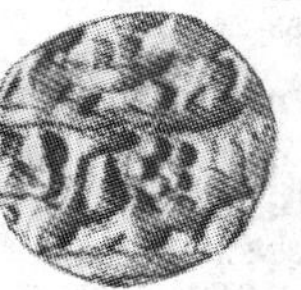

GOLD, 10.70-11.40 g

KM#	Date	Year	VG	Fine	VF	XF
150	(1881)	2	135.00	155.00	185.00	225.00
(Y14)	(1884)	5	135.00	155.00	185.00	225.00
	(1895)	16	135.00	155.00	185.00	225.00
	(1896)	17	135.00	155.00	185.00	225.00
	(1899)	20	135.00	155.00	185.00	225.00

NOTE: Later dates (1916-1920) exist for this type.

NAZARANA MOHUR

GOLD, 29-36mm, 10.70-11.40 g

KM#	Date	Year	VG	Fine	VF	XF
151	1880	1	425.00	700.00	1000.	1650.
(Y14a)	1887	8	425.00	700.00	1000.	1650.

MADHOPUR MINT

In the name of Muhammad Akbar II

AH1221-1253/1806-1837AD

PAISA

COPPER

KM#	Date	Year	Good	VG	Fine	VF
70	AH—	13	3.00	5.00	7.50	11.50
(C71)	—	14	3.00	5.00	7.50	11.50

1/2 NAZARANA RUPEE

SILVER, 5.30 g

KM#	Date	Year	VG	Fine	VF	XF
73	AH12(21)	1	—	—	—	—
(C74)						

RUPEE

SILVER, 10.70-11.60 g

KM#	Date	Year	VG	Fine	VF	XF
75	AH1221	1	6.00	9.00	13.00	20.00
(C75)	(1222)	2	6.00	9.00	13.00	20.00
	(1224)	4	6.00	9.00	13.00	20.00
	(1225)	5	6.00	9.00	13.00	20.00
	(1226)	6	6.00	9.00	13.00	20.00
	(1227)	7	6.00	9.00	13.00	20.00
	(1228)	8	6.00	9.00	13.00	20.00
	(1229)	9	6.00	9.00	13.00	20.00
	(1230)	10	6.00	9.00	13.00	20.00
	(1231)	11	6.00	9.00	13.00	20.00
	(1232)	12	6.00	9.00	13.00	20.00
	(1233)	13	6.00	9.00	13.00	20.00
	(1234)	14	6.00	9.00	13.00	20.00
	(1235)	15	6.00	9.00	13.00	20.00
	(1236)	16	6.00	9.00	13.00	20.00
	(1237)	17	6.00	9.00	13.00	20.00
	(1238)	18	6.00	9.00	13.00	20.00

KM#	Date	Year	VG	Fine	VF	XF
(C75)	(1239)	20	6.00	9.00	13.00	20.00
	(1241)	21	6.00	9.00	13.00	20.00
	(1242)	22	6.00	9.00	13.00	20.00
	(1243)	23	6.00	9.00	13.00	20.00
	(1244)	24	6.00	9.00	13.00	20.00
	(1246)	26	6.00	9.00	13.00	20.00
	(1249)	29	6.00	9.00	13.00	20.00
	(1250)	30	6.00	9.00	13.00	20.00
	(1251)	31	6.00	9.00	13.00	20.00

In the name of Bahadur Shah II

AH1253-1274/1837-1857AD

SILVER, 10.70-11.60 g

KM#	Date	Year	VG	Fine	VF	XF
76	AH(1254)	2	5.50	8.00	12.50	18.50
(C96)	1255	2	5.50	8.00	12.50	18.50
	125(5)	3	5.50	8.00	12.50	18.50
	(1256)	4	5.50	8.00	12.50	18.50
	(1257)	5	5.50	8.00	12.50	18.50
	(1258)	6	5.50	8.00	12.50	18.50
	(1259)	7	5.50	8.00	12.50	18.50
	1260	7	5.50	8.00	12.50	18.50
	(1260)	8	5.50	8.00	12.50	18.50
	(1263)	10	5.50	8.00	12.50	18.50
	(1264)	12	5.50	8.00	12.50	18.50
	(1267)	15	5.50	8.00	12.50	18.50
	(1269)	17	5.50	8.00	12.50	18.50
	(1270)	18	5.50	8.00	12.50	18.50

JAIPUR FEUDATORY STATE

Khetri

For coins previously listed here, refer to Mughal Empire, Muhammad Akbar Shah, Muzaffargarh Mint.

JAISALMIR

Although the ruling Rajputs (or rawals) of this desert territory, located in northwest India traced their ancestry back to pre-Asokan times, the State of Jaisalmir was founded by Deoraj, the first rawal, only in the tenth century. Jaisalmir city was established by Rawal Jaisal, after whom both the city and the State were named. Like Jaipur, Jaisalmir reached its zenith in Mughal times, after being forced to acknowledge the supremacy of Delhi in the time of the Emperor Shah Jahan. With Mughal disintegration, Jaisalmir also fell upon hard times and most of its outlying provinces were lost. The state came under British protection in 1818, and on March 30th, 1949 it was merged into Rajasthan.

RULERS

Mulraj Singh,
AH1176-1235/1762-1819AD
Gaj Singh,
AH1235-1263/1819-1846AD
Ranjit Singh,
AH1263-1281/1846-1864AD
Bairi Sal, 1865-1891AD

Anonymous Issues

MINT

جیسلمیر

Jaisalmir

DODIA PAISA

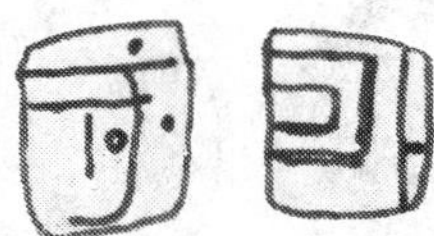

COPPER

C#	Date	Year	Good	VG	Fine	VF
4	ND		2.50	4.50	6.50	10.00

NOTE: Struck 1660-1863AD with recorded weights as low as 0.75 and as high as 2.85 g.

Mughal Issues

"Akheyshahi" Series

In the name of Muhammad Shah

AH1131-1161/1719-1748AD
Struck 1756-1860AD

1/8 RUPEE

SILVER, 11-12mm, 1.35 g

C#	Date	Year	VG	Fine	VF	XF
7	AH1153	22	5.50	8.00	10.00	15.00

1/4 RUPEE

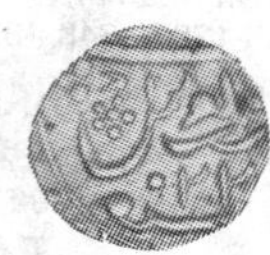

SILVER, 2.70 g

C#	Date	Year	VG	Fine	VF	XF
8	AH1153	22	4.00	6.00	9.00	14.00

1/2 RUPEE

SILVER, 5.25 g

C#	Date	Year	VG	Fine	VF	XF
9	AH1153	22	5.50	8.00	10.00	15.00

Square, 5.50 g

C#	Date	Year	VG	Fine	VF	XF
9a	AH1153	22	—	—	—	—

RUPEE

SILVER, 10.50-11.00 g

C#	Date	Year	VG	Fine	VF	XF
10	AH1152	—	12.00	20.00	30.00	45.00
	1153	22	9.00	15.00	21.50	30.00
	1155	25	—	—	—	—

Square, 11.00 g

C#	Date	Year	VG	Fine	VF	XF
10c	AH1153	22	—	—	—	—

NAZARANA RUPEE

SILVER, 11.00 g

C#	Date	Year	VG	Fine	VF	XF
10a	AH1153	22	45.00	75.00	110.00	150.00

2-1/2 RUPEE

SILVER, Square, 28.00 g

C#	Date	Year	VG	Fine	VF	XF
10b	AH1153	22	—	—	Rare	—

MOHUR

GOLD, 22mm, 10.70-10.80 g

C#	Date	Year	VG	Fine	VF	XF
15	AH1153	22	155.00	185.00	225.00	325.00

Regal Issues

In the name of Queen Victoria

First Series: Frozen regnal year 22 w/o mint marks.

1/8 RUPEE

SILVER, 1.32 g

Y#	Date	Year	VG	Fine	VF	XF
1	AH—	22	2.50	3.50	5.00	8.00

1/4 RUPEE

SILVER, 2.65 g

Y#	Date	Year	VG	Fine	VF	XF
2	AH—	22	3.00	4.50	6.50	10.00

1/2 RUPEE

SILVER, 5.30 g

Y#	Date	Year	VG	Fine	VF	XF
3	AH—	22	5.50	8.00	10.00	15.00

RUPEE

SILVER, 10.50-10.60 g

Y#	Date	Year	VG	Fine	VF	XF
4	AH—	22	8.50	13.50	20.00	28.50

NAZARANA RUPEE

SILVER, 10.60 g

Y#	Date	Year	VG	Fine	VF	XF
4a	AH—	22	45.00	75.00	110.00	150.00

Y#	Date	Year	VG	Fine	VF	XF
4b	AH—	22	90.00	150.00	220.00	300.00

NAZARANA 1-1/2 RUPEE

SILVER, 16.00 g

Y#	Date	Year	VG	Fine	VF	XF
4c	AH—	22	120.00	200.00	275.00	400.00

NAZARANA 2 RUPEE

SILVER, 21.30 g

Y#	Date	Year	VG	Fine	VF	XF
4d	AH—	22	150.00	250.00	350.00	500.00

NAZARANA 5 RUPEE

SILVER, hexagonal, 52.50 g

Y#	Date	Year	VG	Fine	VF	XF
4e	AH—	22	—	—	—	—

Second Series: Frozen regnal year 22 w/mint marks on rev.

Bird   Umbrella

1/8 RUPEE

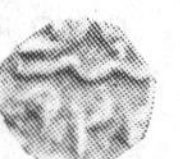

SILVER, 1.33 g

Y#	Date	Year	VG	Fine	VF	XF
5	AH—	22	2.00	3.00	4.00	7.00

1/4 RUPEE

SILVER, 2.65 g

Y#	Date	Year	VG	Fine	VF	XF
6	AH—	22	2.50	3.50	5.00	8.00

1/2 RUPEE

SILVER, 5.30 g

Y#	Date	Year	VG	Fine	VF	XF
7	AH—	22	3.00	4.50	6.50	10.00

RUPEE

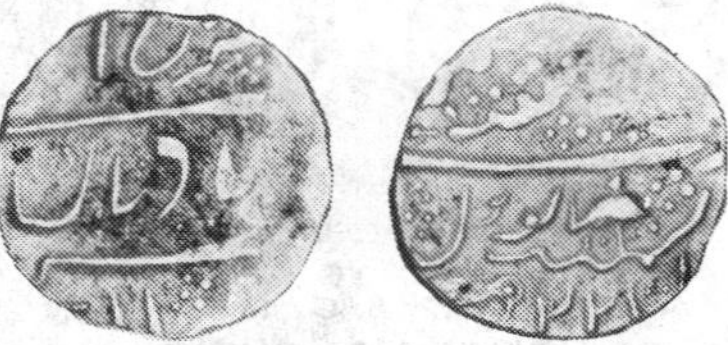

SILVER, square, 10.60 g

Y#	Date	Year	VG	Fine	VF	XF
8	AH—	22	5.00	7.00	10.00	15.00

NAZARANA RUPEE

SILVER, square, 10.60 g

Y#	Date	Year	VG	Fine	VF	XF
8a	AH—	22	60.00	80.00	100.00	150.00

Round

Y#	Date	Year	VG	Fine	VF	XF
8b	AH—	22	140.00	200.00	275.00	400.00

Octagonal, 10.55 g

Y#	Date	Year	VG	Fine	VF	XF
8d	AH—	—	—	—	—	—

NAZARANA 2 RUPEES

SILVER, 21.30 g

Y#	Date	Year	VG	Fine	VF	XF
8c	AH—	22	150.00	250.00	350.00	500.00

1/8 MOHUR

GOLD, 12mm, 1.35 g

Y#	Date	Year	VG	Fine	VF	XF
9	AH—	22	—	—	Rare	—

1/4 MOHUR

GOLD, 15mm, 2.70 g

Y#	Date	Year	VG	Fine	VF	XF
10	AH—	22	—	—	Rare	—

1/2 MOHUR

GOLD, 18mm, 5.40 g

Y#	Date	Year	VG	Fine	VF	XF
11	AH—	22	—	—	Rare	—

MOHUR

GOLD, 10.80 g

Y#	Date	Year	VG	Fine	VF	XF
12	AH—	22	165.00	210.00	300.00	425.00

JANJIRA ISLAND

Island near Bombay. Dynasty of Nawabs dates from 1489AD.

The origin of the nawabs of Janjira is obscure. They were Sidi or Abyssinian Muslims whose ancestors, serving as admirals to the Muslim rulers of the Deccan, had been granted jagirs (revenue-producing land tenures) under the Adil Shahi sultans of Bijapur. In 1870, Janjira came under direct British rule. Until 1924 the nawabs of Janjira also exercised suzerainty over Jafarabad on the Kathiawar peninsular.

RULERS

Sidi Ibrahim Khan II,
AH1204-06,19-42/1789-92,1804-26AD
Sidi Muhammad Khan,
AH1242-1265/1826-1848AD
Sidi Ibrahim Khan III,
AH1265-1297/1848-1879AD

SIDI IBRAHIM KHAN II

AH1204-1206,1219-1242
1789-1792,1804-1826AD

PAISA

COPPER

KM#	Date	Year	Good	VG	Fine	VF
5	ND	—	5.00	9.00	13.00	20.00

SIDI MUHAMMAD KHAN

AH1242-1265/1826-1848AD

PAISA

COPPER

KM#	Date	Year	Good	VG	Fine	VF
10 (15)	ND	—	4.50	8.00	12.00	17.50

SIDI IBRAHIM KHAN III

AH1265-1297/1848-1879AD

1/2 PAISA

COPPER, 2.60-3.20 g

KM#	Date	Year	Good	VG	Fine	VF
15	AH—	—	6.00	12.00	22.50	40.00

PAISA

COPPER, 6.0-7.0 g
Obv: Date.

KM#	Date	Year	Good	VG	Fine	VF
18	AH1272	—	6.00	12.00	20.00	32.50

Obv: Date

KM#	Date	Year	Good	VG	Fine	VF
25	AH1284	—	3.00	5.00	8.00	12.50

Rev: Date

KM#	Date	Year	Good	VG	Fine	VF
26	AH1284	—	2.50	4.00	6.50	10.00

Rev: Date

KM#	Date	Year	Good	VG	Fine	VF
28	AH1288	—	4.00	6.50	10.00	15.00

MOHUR

GOLD, 23 mm

KM#	Date	Year	VG	Fine	VF	XF
35	AH1283	—	1000.	1200.	1500.	1800.

JAORA

Ghafar Khan (d. 1825), the first Nawab of Jaora, was brother-in-law to Amir Khan, the Pindari leader. Jaora was subordinate to Indore, having been granted control of the territory in central India in return for the maintenance of a body of cavalry and, later, of foot soldiers which were to be made available to Indore when required. The nawabs of Jaora maintained a good relationship with the British which, after 1818, left them in control of the area independently of Indore. In August 1948 Jaora was absorbed into Madhya Pradesh.

RULERS

Muhammad Ismail,
AH1282-1313/1865-1895AD

MINT

جاورا

Jaora

PAISA

COPPER
Rev: Wheel right of flag.

KM#	Date	Year	Good	VG	Fine	VF
4	ND	—	5.00	9.00	13.00	20.00

Rev: Wheel left of flag.

KM#	Date	Year	Good	VG	Fine	VF
5	AH1282	—	5.00	9.00	13.00	20.00

KM#	Date	Year	Good	VG	Fine	VF
6	AH1284	—	4.50	8.50	12.50	18.50
	1285	—	4.50	8.50	12.50	18.50

Rev: Flag only.

KM#	Date	Year	Good	VG	Fine	VF
7	AH1295	—	2.50	4.00	6.50	10.00

Milled Coinage

PAISA

COPPER

KM#	Date	Year	VG	Fine	VF	XF
10	1893/VS1950/AH1310					
			2.50	4.00	6.50	10.00
	1893/VS1950/AH1311					
			3.00	5.00	9.00	14.00
	1894/VS1950/AH1310					
			2.50	4.00	6.50	10.00
	1894/VS1950/AH1311					
			2.50	4.00	6.50	10.00
	1894/VS1951/AH1311					

KM#	Date	Year	VG	Fine	VF	XF
10			2.50	4.00	6.50	10.00
	1895/VS1951/AH1311		2.50	4.00	6.50	10.00
	1895/VS1952/AH1311		2.50	4.00	6.50	10.00
	1895/VS1952/AH1312		3.00	5.00	9.00	14.00
	1895/VS1952/AH1313		2.50	4.00	6.50	10.00
	1895/VS1953/AH1313		3.00	5.00	9.00	14.00
	1896/VS1953/AH1313		2.50	4.00	6.50	10.00
	1896/VS1953/ AH1331 (error for 1313 w/ second 3 retrograde)		3.00	5.00	9.00	14.00
	1896/VS1953/AH1331 (error for 1313)		4.00	6.50	10.00	15.00

2 PAISA

COPPER

KM#	Date	VG	Fine	VF	XF
12	1893/VS1950/AH1310	4.50	8.00	12.00	17.50
	1894/VS1950/AH1310	5.00	9.00	13.50	20.00

JHABUA

A state located in northwest India, west of Indore.

Prior to 1818 the Raja of Jhabua was responsible for paying an annual tribute to Indore. The rajas were Rathor Rajputs who had been established in the area since the seventeenth century. They were descended from the rajas of Jodhpur. In 1818 Jhabua came under British protection and control.

RULERS

Gopal Singh,
VS1897-1952/1840-1895AD

MINT

Jhabua

1/2 PAISA

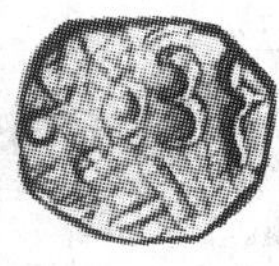

COPPER, 5.60-12.0 g
Obv: Leaf. Rev: Date.

C#	Date	Year	VG	Fine	VF	XF
A1.1	VS(19)36	(1879)	6.00	10.00	15.00	22.50

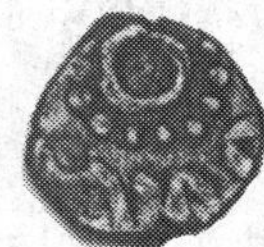

Obv: Flower. Rev: Circle w/i circle of dots.

C#	Date	Year	VG	Fine	VF	XF
A1.2	ND	—	7.50	12.00	18.00	27.50

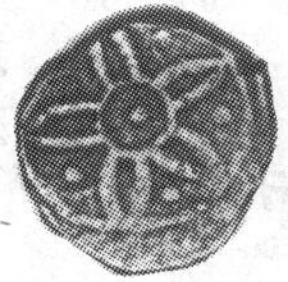
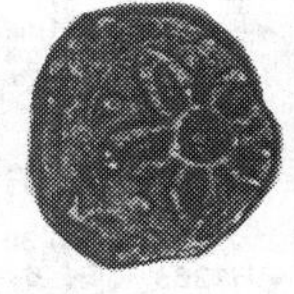

Obv. and Rev: 5-petalled flower.

C#	Date	Year	VG	Fine	VF	XF
A1.3	ND	—	7.50	12.00	18.00	27.50

PAISA

COPPER
Obv. leg: Devanagari *Jabuva*.
Rev. leg: Arabic *Jabua*.

KM#	Date	Year	Good	VG	Fine	VF
1	VS(19)29	(1872)	8.50	11.50	15.00	21.50
	(19)35	(1878)	8.50	11.50	15.00	21.50

Obv. leg: Devanagari *Sa-bu-va*. Rev: Date.

KM#	Date	Year	Good	VG	Fine	VF
2	VS(19)36	(1879)	8.50	11.50	15.00	21.50

Obv. Devanagari date: Sa(mvat) 21.

KM#	Date	Year	Good	VG	Fine	VF
3	VS(19)21	(1864)	7.00	10.00	13.50	17.50
	(19)22	(1865)	7.00	10.00	13.50	17.50

Obv: Trident. Rev: Date.

KM#	Date	Year	Good	VG	Fine	VF
4	VS(19)31	(1874)	3.50	5.00	6.50	8.50
	ND	—	3.50	5.00	6.50	8.50

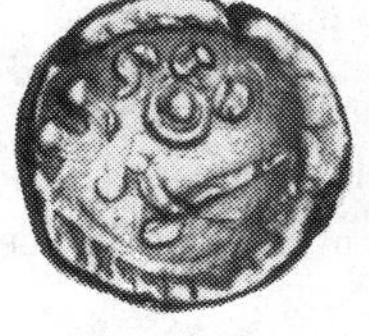
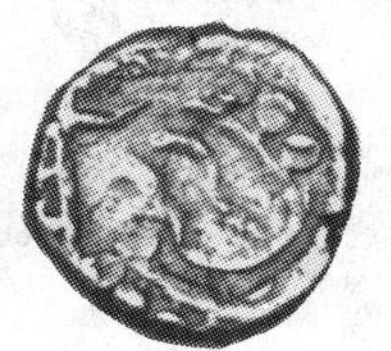

Obv: Floral design. Rev: Date.

KM#	Date	Year	Good	VG	Fine	VF
17	VS(19)32	(1875)	3.50	5.00	6.50	8.50
	(19)35	(1878)	3.50	5.00	6.50	8.50

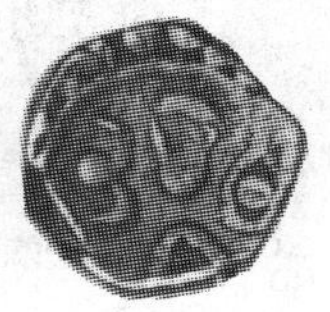

Obv: 4 lobed flower. Rev: Date.

KM#	Date	Year	Good	VG	Fine	VF
5	VS(19)34	(1877)	3.50	5.00	6.50	8.50

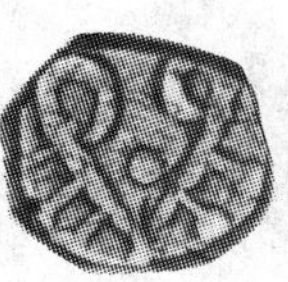

Obv: Stylized leaf.

KM#	Date	Year	Good	VG	Fine	VF
6.1	VS(19)22	(1865)	7.50	10.00	12.50	16.50
	(19)23	(1866)	5.00	7.00	10.00	14.00
	(19)24	(1867)	5.00	7.00	10.00	14.00
	(19)28	(1871)	5.00	7.00	10.00	14.00
	(19)32	(1875)	3.00	5.00	7.00	10.00
	(19)33	(1876)	3.00	5.00	7.00	10.00
	(19)35	(1878)	5.00	7.00	10.00	14.00

NOTE: Thick and thin planchets exist.

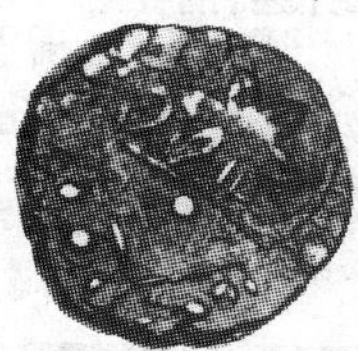
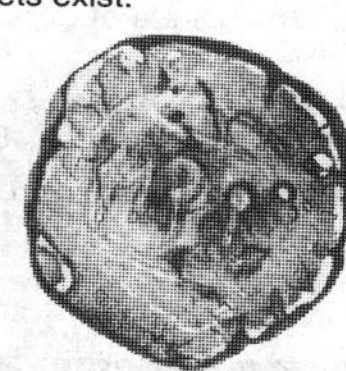

Obv: 6-petalled flower in heart-shape.
Rev: Date VS(19)21.

KM#	Date	Year	Good	VG	Fine	VF
6.2	VS(19)21	—	5.00	7.00	10.00	14.00

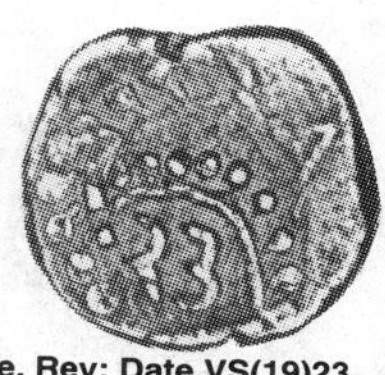

Obv: Oval in heart-shape. Rev: Date VS(19)23.

KM#	Date	Year	Good	VG	Fine	VF
6.3	VS(19)23	—	5.00	7.00	10.00	14.00

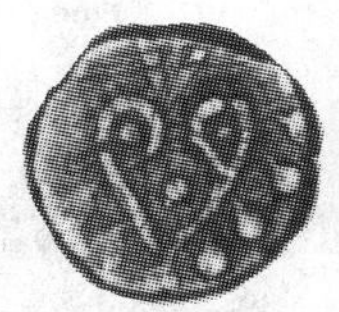
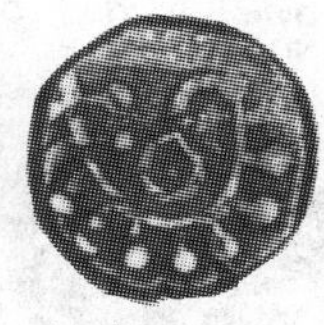

Rev: Curled branch w/berry.

KM#	Date	Year	Good	VG	Fine	VF
7	ND	—	5.00	7.00	10.00	14.00

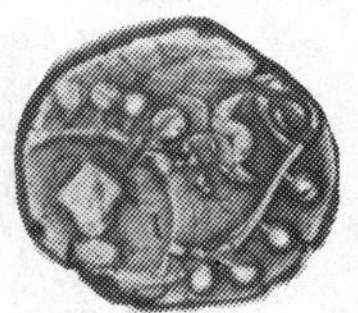

Rev: Spear point.

KM#	Date	Year	Good	VG	Fine	VF
8	ND	—	3.00	5.00	7.00	10.00

Rev: Curved dagger.

KM#	Date	Year	Good	VG	Fine	VF
9	ND	—	5.00	7.00	10.00	14.00

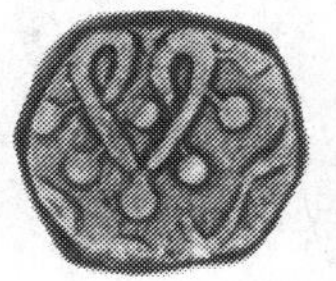
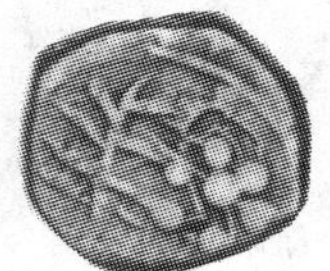

Rev: Jhar and blossom.

KM#	Date	Year	Good	VG	Fine	VF
10	ND	—	4.50	6.50	9.00	13.00

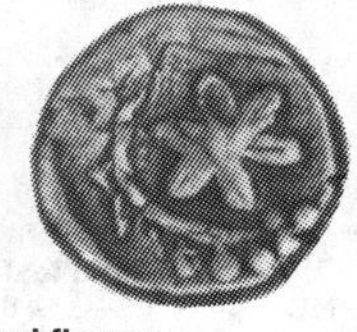

Rev: 6 lobed flower.

KM#	Date	Year	Good	VG	Fine	VF
11	ND	—	5.00	7.00	10.00	14.00

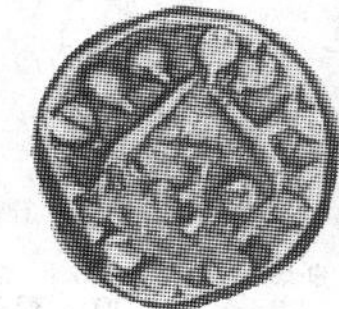
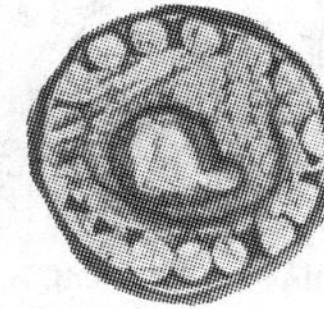

Rev: Tailed ball.

KM#	Date	Year	Good	VG	Fine	VF
12	Yr. 30	—	4.00	6.00	8.00	12.00

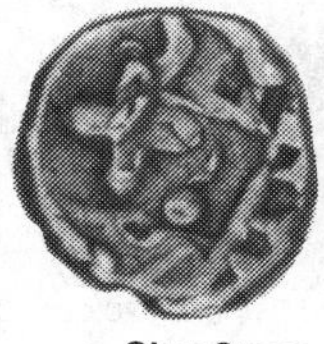
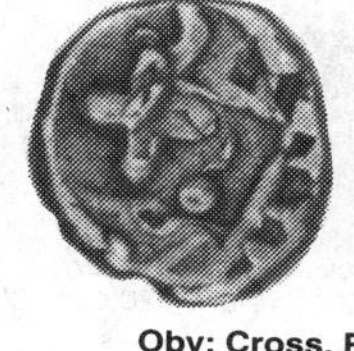

Obv: Cross. Rev: Tailed ball.

KM#	Date	Year	Good	VG	Fine	VF
13	ND	—	3.00	5.00	7.00	11.00

Obv: Square. Rev: Indistinct.

KM#	Date	Year	Good	VG	Fine	VF
14	ND	—	4.00	6.00	8.00	12.00

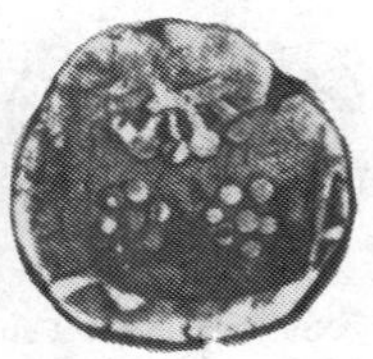

Obv: Arabic *Wa*. Rev: Groups of dots.

KM#	Date	Year	Good	VG	Fine	VF
15	ND	—	7.00	9.00	12.00	16.00

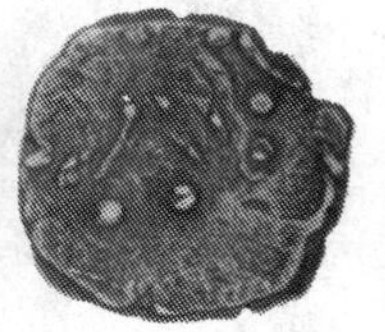

Obv: Cross and dots.

KM#	Date	Year	Good	VG	Fine	VF
16	ND	—	7.00	9.00	12.00	16.00

Obv: Date. Rev: Swastika w/i segmented circle.

KM#	Date	Year	Good	VG	Fine	VF
18.1	VS(19)29	—	8.00	12.00	20.00	30.00

Obv: Date. Rev: Swastika w/i dotted wreath.

KM#	Date	Year	Good	VG	Fine	VF
18.2	VS(19)2x	—	8.00	12.00	20.00	30.00

Obv: Stylized leaf. Rev: Swastika.

KM#	Date	Year	Good	VG	Fine	VF
18.3	ND	—	—	—	—	—

Obv: Trefoil. Rev: Swastika.

KM#	Date	Year	Good	VG	Fine	VF
19 (18.2)	ND	—	8.00	12.00	20.00	30.00

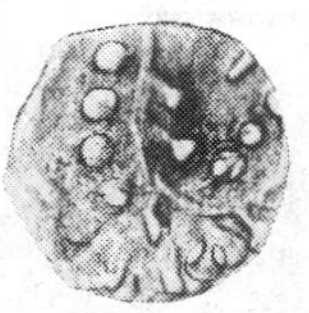

Obv: Stylized leaf. Rev: Larger leaf.

KM#	Date	Year	Good	VG	Fine	VF
20	ND	—	8.00	12.00	20.00	30.00

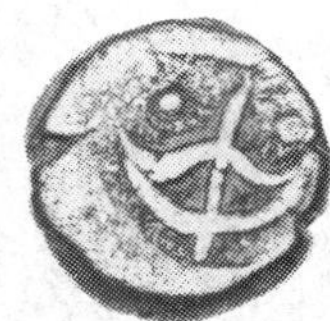

Obv: Stylized leaf. Rev: Bow and arrow.

KM#	Date	Year	Good	VG	Fine	VF
21	ND	—	8.00	12.00	20.00	30.00

Obv: Stylized leaf. Rev: 4-petal flower.

KM#	Date	Year	Good	VG	Fine	VF
22	ND	—	8.00	12.00	20.00	30.00

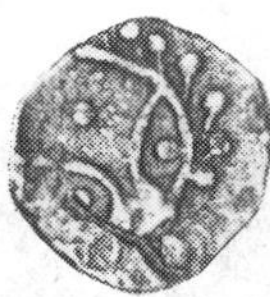

Obv: Stylized leaf. Rev: Katar.

KM#	Date	Year	Good	VG	Fine	VF
23	ND	—	8.00	12.00	20.00	30.00

Obv: 6-petal flower. Rev: Dotted circle, sword.

KM#	Date	Year	Good	VG	Fine	VF
24	ND	—	8.00	12.00	20.00	30.00

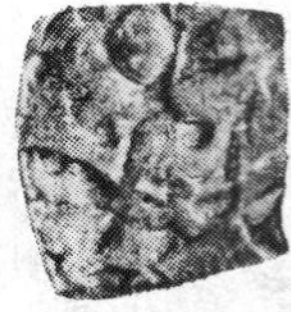

Rev: Bird walking left.

KM#	Date	Year	Good	VG	Fine	VF
25	ND	—	8.00	12.00	20.00	30.00

Obv: Tree. Rev: Date in circle.

KM#	Date	Year	Good	VG	Fine	VF
26	VS(19)3x	—	8.00	12.00	20.00	30.00

Obv: 3 dots in heart shape. Rev: 4 lobed flower.

KM#	Date	Year	Good	VG	Fine	VF
27	ND	—	8.00	12.00	20.00	30.00

Obv: 7-leaf plant left of spoke wheel.

KM#	Date	Year	Good	VG	Fine	VF
28	ND	—	8.00	12.00	20.00	30.00

Obv: Stylized flower.

KM#	Date	Year	Good	VG	Fine	VF
29	ND	—	8.00	12.00	20.00	30.00

NOTE: In addition to the above there are other symbols, and all these occur in different combinations. The crude fabric of these coins and uncommon variety of dies indicate that they were struck locally, with or without official sanction. They are commonly found overstruck on earlier types or on coins of other states.

Obv: Circle of dots. Rev: Leaf and arcs.

KM#	Date	Year	Good	VG	Fine	VF
30	ND	—	8.00	12.00	20.00	30.00

Obv: Solar symbol in leaf.

KM#	Date	Year	Good	VG	Fine	VF
31	ND	—	8.00	12.00	20.00	30.00

Obv: 16-square grid. Rev: Flower in circle.

KM#	Date	Year	Good	VG	Fine	VF
32	ND	—	10.00	15.00	25.00	37.50

Obv: 9-square grid. Rev: Plant.

KM#	Date	Year	Good	VG	Fine	VF
33	ND	—	10.00	15.00	25.00	37.50

JHALAWAR

State located in Rajputana, northwest India which was originally part of Kotah. Established in memory of services to Kotah of Zalim Singh, long-time administrator of that state. His grandson was given Jhalawar in 1837AD with the title of Raj Rana.

In 1838, at a time of great internal dissention, certain districts were removed from the territory of the Princely State of Kotah to form a principality for Madan Singh, one of the contestants for power. The new state was named Jhalawar. In 1896 the ruling maharaj-rana, Zalim Singh, was deposed by the Government of India for maladministration, and much of the area that had once been ceded to Jhalawar was returned to the sovereignty of the rulers of Kotah. Madan Singh and his successors were Jhala Rajputs from Kathiawar. The residual State of Jhalawar was incorporated into Rajasthan in 1948.

RULERS

Madan Singh,
AH1253-1261/1837-1845AD
Prithvi Singh,
AH1261-1292/1845-1875AD
Zalim Singh,
AH1294-1314/1876-1896AD
British Administration, 1896-1899

MINTNAMES

جالاوار

Jhalawar

MINT MARKS

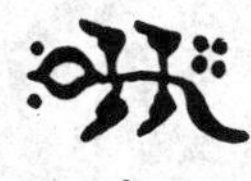

Both marks on reverse

Mughal Issues

In the name of Muhammad Akbar
AH1221-1253/1806-1837AD

RUPEE

SILVER, 11.15-11.25 g
W/*Sahib Qiran* leg.

C#	Date	Year	Good	VG	Fine	VF
8	AH—	32	40.00	62.50	85.00	120.00

In the name of Bahadur Shah II
Years 1-22/AH1253-1274/1837-1858AD

TAKKA

COPPER, square, 17.70-17.80 g

C#	Date	Year	Good	VG	Fine	VF
21	AH—	5	4.00	6.50	10.00	15.00
	—	6	4.00	6.50	10.00	15.00
	—	12	4.00	6.50	10.00	15.00
	—	21	4.00	6.50	10.00	15.00

1/8 RUPEE

SILVER, 1.40 g

C#	Date	Year	VG	Fine	VF	XF
25	AH—	11	4.00	6.00	9.00	13.50

RUPEE

SILVER, 11.15-11.25 g

C#	Date	Year	VG	Fine	VF	XF
28	AH—	1	6.50	10.00	15.00	22.50
	—	3	6.50	10.00	15.00	22.50
	1259	6	6.50	10.00	15.00	22.50
	1259	13	6.50	10.00	15.00	22.50
	—	15	6.50	10.00	15.00	22.50
	—	17	6.50	10.00	15.00	22.50
	—	18	6.50	10.00	15.00	22.50
	1259	19	6.50	10.00	15.00	22.50
	1259	20	6.50	10.00	15.00	22.50
	125x	22	6.50	10.00	15.00	22.50

NAZARANA RUPEE

SILVER, 30mm, 11.00-11.20 g

C#	Date	Year	VG	Fine	VF	XF
29	AH1259	6	35.00	60.00	85.00	120.00
	—	8	35.00	60.00	85.00	120.00
	1263	10	35.00	60.00	85.00	120.00
	—	21	35.00	60.00	85.00	120.00

Regal Issues

In the name of Queen Victoria

Regnal years 1-45 = 1857-1901AD

PAISA

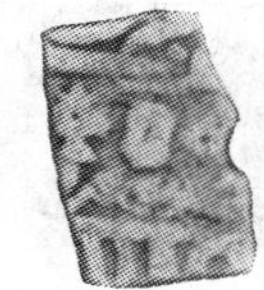

COPPER, 9.00 g

Y#	Date	Year	Good	VG	Fine	VF
1	AH—	2	2.50	4.50	7.50	12.50
	—	5	2.50	4.50	7.50	12.50

DOUBLE PAISA

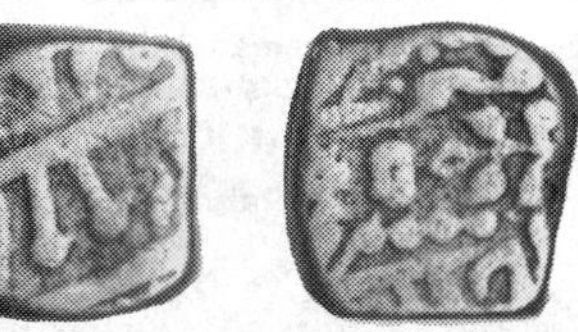

COPPER, squarish, 19-21mm, 18.00 g

Y#	Date	Year	Good	VG	Fine	VF
2	VS1915	1	1.25	2.25	4.00	6.50
	1915	4	1.25	2.25	4.00	6.50
	1915	5	1.25	2.25	4.00	6.50
	1915	6	1.25	2.25	4.00	6.50
	1915	7	1.25	2.25	4.00	6.50
	1915	8	1.25	2.25	4.00	6.50
	1915	9	1.25	2.25	4.00	6.50
	1915	10	1.25	2.25	4.00	6.50
	1915	11	1.25	2.25	4.00	6.50
	1915	12	1.25	2.25	4.00	6.50
	1915	13	1.25	2.25	4.00	6.50
	1915	16	1.25	2.25	4.00	6.50
	1915	18	1.25	2.25	4.00	6.50
	1915	21	1.25	2.25	4.00	6.50
	1915	22	1.25	2.25	4.00	6.50
	1915	23	1.25	2.25	4.00	6.50
	1915	24	1.25	2.25	4.00	6.50
	1915	27	1.25	2.25	4.00	6.50
	1915	28	1.25	2.25	4.00	6.50
	—	29	1.25	2.25	4.00	6.50

1/8 RUPEE

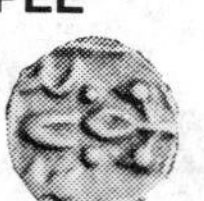

SILVER, 13mm, 1.40 g

Y#	Date	Year	VG	Fine	VF	XF
3.1	VS1915	5	5.00	7.00	10.00	15.00
	1915	17	5.00	7.00	10.00	15.00
	1915	25	5.00	7.00	10.00	15.00
	1915	27	5.00	7.00	10.00	15.00
	1915	28	5.00	7.00	10.00	15.00
3.2	AH—	37	5.00	7.00	10.00	15.00
	—	38	5.00	7.00	10.00	15.00

1/4 RUPEE

SILVER, 2.80 g

Y#	Date	Year	VG	Fine	VF	XF
4.1	VS1915	7	4.00	6.00	9.00	14.00
	1915	9	4.00	6.00	9.00	14.00
	1915	17	4.00	6.00	9.00	14.00
	1915	25	4.00	6.00	9.00	14.00
	1915	28	4.00	6.00	9.00	14.00
4.2	AH—	30	4.00	6.00	9.00	14.00
	—	33	4.00	6.00	9.00	14.00
	—	36	4.00	6.00	9.00	14.00
	—	37	4.00	6.00	9.00	14.00
	—	38	4.00	6.00	9.00	14.00

1/2 RUPEE

SILVER, 5.60-5.65 g

Y#	Date	Year	VG	Fine	VF	XF
5.1	VS1915	1	5.50	8.00	12.50	18.50
	1915	11	5.50	8.00	12.50	18.50
	1915	15	5.50	8.00	12.50	18.50
	1915	22	5.50	8.00	12.50	18.50
	1915	25	5.50	8.00	12.50	18.50
5.2	AH—	30	5.50	8.00	12.50	18.50
	—	31	5.50	8.00	12.50	18.50
5.2	—	35	5.50	8.00	12.50	18.50
	—	36	5.50	8.00	12.50	18.50

NAZARANA 1/2 RUPEE

SILVER, 5.60-5.65 g

Y#	Date	Year	VG	Fine	VF	XF
5a	AH—	38	20.00	32.50	45.00	65.00

RUPEE

SILVER, 11.20-11.30 g

Y#	Date	Year	VG	Fine	VF	XF
6.1	VS1915	1	5.50	8.00	12.50	18.50
	1915	2	5.50	8.00	12.50	18.50
	1915	3	5.50	8.00	12.50	18.50
	1915	4	5.50	8.00	12.50	18.50
	1915	5	5.50	8.00	12.50	18.50
	1915	7	5.50	8.00	12.50	18.50
	1915	9	5.50	8.00	12.50	18.50
	1915	10	5.50	8.00	12.50	18.50
	1915	11	5.50	8.00	12.50	18.50
	1915	12	5.50	8.00	12.50	18.50
	1915	13	5.50	8.00	12.50	18.50
	1915	14	5.50	8.00	12.50	18.50
	1915	15	5.50	8.00	12.50	18.50
	1915	16	5.50	8.00	12.50	18.50
	1915	17	5.50	8.00	12.50	18.50
	1915	18	5.50	8.00	12.50	18.50
	1915	19	5.50	8.00	12.50	18.50
	1915	20	5.50	8.00	12.50	18.50
	1915	21	5.50	8.00	12.50	18.50
	1915	22	5.50	8.00	12.50	18.50
	1915	24	5.50	8.00	12.50	18.50
	1915	25	5.50	8.00	12.50	18.50
	1915	26	5.50	8.00	12.50	18.50
	1915	27	5.50	8.00	12.50	18.50
	1915	28	5.50	8.00	12.50	18.50
	1915	29	5.50	8.00	12.50	18.50
	1915	30	5.50	8.00	12.50	18.50

Y#	Date	Year	VG	Fine	VF	XF
6.2	AH—	30	5.50	8.00	12.50	18.50
	—	31	5.50	8.00	12.50	18.50
	—	33	5.50	8.00	12.50	18.50
	—	34	5.50	8.00	12.50	18.50
	—	35	5.50	8.00	12.50	18.50
	—	36	5.50	8.00	12.50	18.50
	—	37	5.50	8.00	12.50	18.50
	—	38	5.50	8.00	12.50	18.50
	—	39	5.50	8.00	12.50	18.50
	—	41	5.50	8.00	12.50	18.50

NAZARANA RUPEE

SILVER, 11.20-11.25 g

Y#	Date	Year	VG	Fine	VF	XF
6a	VS1915	2	35.00	60.00	85.00	120.00
	1915	4	35.00	60.00	85.00	120.00
	1915	5	35.00	60.00	85.00	120.00
	1915	7	35.00	60.00	85.00	120.00
	1915	9	35.00	60.00	85.00	120.00
	1915	12	35.00	60.00	85.00	120.00
	1915	13	35.00	60.00	85.00	120.00
	1915	15	35.00	60.00	85.00	120.00
	1915	21	35.00	60.00	85.00	120.00
	1915	22	35.00	60.00	85.00	120.00
	1915	23	35.00	60.00	85.00	120.00
	1915	24	35.00	60.00	85.00	120.00
	1915	25	35.00	60.00	85.00	120.00
	1915	27	35.00	60.00	85.00	120.00
	1915	28	35.00	60.00	85.00	120.00

Y#	Date	Year	VG	Fine	VF	XF
6b	VS1915	3	52.50	87.50	125.00	165.00
	1915	15	52.50	87.50	125.00	165.00
6c	AH—	30	42.00	70.00	100.00	140.00
	—	31	42.00	70.00	100.00	140.00
	—	33	42.00	70.00	100.00	140.00
	—	34	42.00	70.00	100.00	140.00
	—	35	42.00	70.00	100.00	140.00
	—	36	42.00	70.00	100.00	140.00
	—	37	42.00	70.00	100.00	140.00
	—	38	42.00	70.00	100.00	140.00
	—	39	42.00	70.00	100.00	140.00
	—	40	42.00	70.00	100.00	140.00

JODHPUR

Jodhpur, or Marwar, located in northwest India was the largest Princely State in the Rajputana Agency, its population in 1941 being in excess of two and a half million. The maharajadhirajas of Jodhpur were Rathor Rajputs who claimed an extremely ancient ancestry from Rama, king of Ayodhya. With the collapse of the Rathor rulers of Kanauj in 1194 the family entered Marwar, where they laid the foundation of the new state. The city of Jodhpur was built by Rao Jodha in 1459, and the city and the state were named after him. In 1561 Akbar invaded Jodhpur, forcing its submission. In 1679 Aurangzeb sacked the city, an experience which stimulated the Rajput royal house to forge a new unity among themselves in order to extricate themselves from Mughal hegemony. Internal dissension once again asserted itself and Rajput unity, which had both benefited from and accelerated Mughal decline, fell apart before the Marathas. In 1818 Jodhpur came under British protection and control and after Indian Union the State was merged into Rajasthan. Jodhpur is best known for its particular style of riding breeches which became very popular in the West in the late nineteenth century.

RULERS

The issues of the first four rulers before 1858AD with the AH and VS dates, as well as the regnal years, are rarely actual dates and years, but were used for many years without change, and were often quite indiscriminately applied. Mismatched regnal years and dates are frequently encountered, as well as blundered dates of all sorts. Dates lying outside the reign of the rulers named on the coin (after 1858AD) were often used. Thus the date or regnal year may not represent an actual dating of the coin.

Coinage of the first four rulers (until 1858AD) is not distinguished by reign, but by type of inscription, mint, and pseudo-date.

Bhim Singh,
AH1207-1218/1792-1803AD

Man Singh,
AH1218-1259/1803-1843AD

Takhat Singh,
AH1259-1290/VS1900-1930/
1843-1873AD

Jaswant Singh,
AH1290-1313/VS1930-1952/
1873-1895AD

Sardar Singh,
VS1952-1968/1895-1911AD

MINTS

Jodhpur 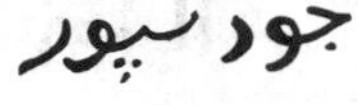

Jodhpur

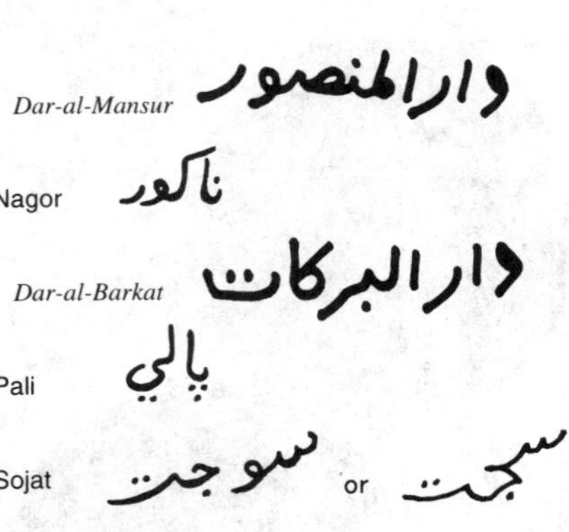

Dar-al-Mansur دارالمنصور

Nagor ناكور

Dar-al-Barkat دارالبركات

Pali پالي

Sojat سوجت or سجت

MINT MARKS
Before 1858AD

Sojat, always on reverse. (KM#226) 

Sojat, sometimes on obverse. (KM#226) 

Pali, (KM#227) 

Pali, Sojat
Usually on obverse. 

Jodhpur, on obverse. (KM#47)

Issues of 1858-1873AD

After 1858AD, the mint marks vary, and are given for each listing, wherever there is a difference.

All gold coins struck at Jodhpur Mint. All mints except Jodhpur closed by or before 1893 AD. All copper coins were probably struck at the Jodhpur Mint, but if struck elsewhere, they bear no distinguishing marks.

In addition to the mint marks indicating the mint cities, there are also the marks of the Darogas (mint overseers), which are very useful in identifying the mints, especially when the city marks are missing or off the flan. These are given by cat.# and mint: (Only one of the marks appears on any one coin, always on the obverse.)

Jodhpur (KM#46) ... रा

Sojat (KM#237) ला

Jodhpur (KM#66) गं न श्री

Jodhpur (KM#76) ग रा ... ... 卐 ...

Pali (KM#197) के

Sojat (KM#246) 

Issues of Jaswant Singh

Jodhpur (KM#76 & 81) ...

Jodhpur (KM#76) 卐 卐 ... मा मा

Pali (KM#206) ... बा बा ग ...

मा ... का। कि॥x

Pali (KM#240)

Sojat (KM#258-259) ह॥ कि कि॥

Issues of Victoria and Sardar Singh

Jodhpur all

Issues of Edward VII and George V and Sardar Singh and Sumer Singh

Jodhpur (KM#91-95, 98-100, 109, 113-115) म

Jodhpur (KM#120)

Issues of George V and Sumer Singh

Jodhpur (KM#111-112) 

Issues of George V and Umaid Singh

Jodhpur (KM#128 & 129) 

Jodhpur (KM#129) औ

Issues of Edward VIII and Umaid Singh

Jodhpur all 

Issues of George VI and Umaid Singh

Jodhpur (KM#141-143) 

Jodhpur (KM#144-147, 150-151) 

Issues of George VI and Hanwant Singh

Jodhpur all 

The Daroga's marks generally consist of a symbol or a single Nagari letter, sometimes inverted, and even lying on its side. Some letters are found on more than one series, so that the mark is not a positive identification, but taken together with the city mark and the style of the coin, will provide a correct attribution.

JODHPUR MINT

Operative between 1761AD(1175AH) and 1945AD(VS2002). There are a number of mules of late Jodhpur types struck in 1945 and later for collectors.

Anonymous Copper Issues With Regnal Years of Shah Alam II
Struck between 1792-1858AD

TAKKA

(2 Paisas)

"Bhim Shahi" Series:

COPPER, 20.00-21.00 g

KM#	Date	Year	Good	VG	Fine	VF
14.2	AH1267	—	2.00	3.00	4.50	7.50
	1227 (error for 1267)	—	—	—	Rare	—

NOTE: Some specimens portray a wide, floral border.

"Bijai Shahi" Series: From 1761AD (AH1175) to 1865AD (AH1275).
In the names of the Mughal Emperors until 1858.

In the name of Shah Alam II
AH1173-1221/1759-1806AD

RUPEE

SILVER, 11.30 g

Obv: Different kinds of swords.

KM#	Date	Year	VG	Fine	VF	XF
19	AH1218	45	6.50	10.00	15.00	22.50
	1220	—	6.50	10.00	15.00	22.50

NOTE: Earlier dates (AH1192-1215) exist for this type.

SILVER, 11.30 g
Similar to 1 Rupee, KM#19, but square.

KM#	Date	Year	VG	Fine	VF	XF
23	AH1218	45	35.00	50.00	70.00	100.00

MOHUR

GOLD, 19mm, 11.00 g

KM#	Date	Year	VG	Fine	VF	XF
26	AH1218	45	200.00	300.00	425.00	600.00

In the name of Muhammad Akbar II
AH1221-1253/1806-1837AD

TAKKA

(2 Paisas)

COPPER, 22.50-23.00 g
Obv. Mark: 31, sword. Rev. Mark: 22.

KM#	Date	Year	Good	VG	Fine	VF
32	AH—	—	2.50	3.50	5.50	8.00

1/4 RUPEE

KM#	Date	Year	VG	Fine	VF	XF
34	AH—	31/22	6.50	10.00	15.00	22.50

RUPEE

SILVER, 11.20-11.30 g

KM#	Date	Year	VG	Fine	VF	XF
35	AH1121 error for 1221		—	—	—	—

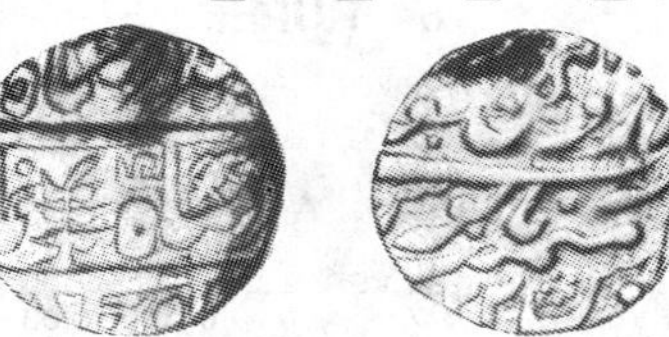

Obv: Jhar and sword.

KM#	Date	Year	VG	Fine	VF	XF
36.1	AH—	31//22	9.00	15.00	22.50	35.00

NOTE: Struck ca. 1816-1859AD.

Obv: Sword right.

KM#	Date	Year	VG	Fine	VF	XF
36.2 (37)	AH—	31//22	6.00	10.00	14.00	20.00

Obv: Small sword.

KM#	Date	Year	VG	Fine	VF	XF
36.3	AH—	—	10.00	16.00	25.00	40.00

MOHUR

GOLD, 20mm, 11.00 g
Obv: Sword.

KM#	Date	Year	VG	Fine	VF	XF
40	AH—	22	200.00	300.00	425.00	600.00

Regal Issues

In the names of Queen Victoria and Takhat Singh

First Issue

1858-1859

Actual mint names appear on this and all subsequent issues.

RUPEE

SILVER, 11.20-11.30 g
Obv: Jhar and Nagari letter. Rev: Sword, jhar and 22.

KM#	Date	Year	VG	Fine	VF	XF
46	AH—	16	7.50	12.50	18.50	27.50

MOHUR

GOLD, 20mm, 11.00 g

KM#	Date	Year	VG	Fine	VF	XF
50	AH—	16	175.00	250.00	350.00	500.00

Second Issue

1860-1869

RUPEE

SILVER, 21mm, 11.20-11.30 g
Obv: Jhar and Nagari letter.
Rev: Sword, *Jodhpur* in Persian, and 22.

KM#	Date	Year	VG	Fine	VF	XF
56	AH—	16	7.00	11.00	16.50	25.00
	—	52 & 16	7.00	11.00	16.50	25.00

In the name of Takhat Singh

Queen Victoria the exalted Queen of England and Hindustan.

Third Issue

1859-1869

Nagari legend *Sri Mataji* added on reverse of silver coins, referring to Kul Devi, patron goddess of the Rathor clan.

TAKKA

(2 Paisas)

COPPER, 20-25mm, 21.00 g

KM#	Date	Year	Good	VG	Fine	VF
71	VS1923	61	1.00	2.00	2.75	3.75
	—	30	.50	1.00	1.50	2.25
	—	61	—	—	—	—

NAZARANA TAKKA

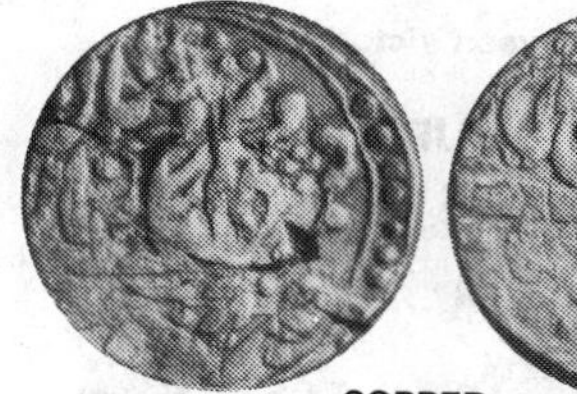

COPPER

KM#	Date	Year	Good	VG	Fine	VF
A72	VS1923	(1866)	—	—	—	—

RUPEE

SILVER, 21mm, 11.20-11.30 g
Obv: Jhar and Nagari GA.
Rev. leg: *Sri Mataji*, and sword.

KM#	Date	Year	VG	Fine	VF	XF
66	AH—	22 & 61	7.50	12.50	18.50	27.50
	—	22 only	7.50	12.50	18.50	27.50
	—	61 only	7.50	12.50	18.50	27.50

NOTE: Struck ca. 1849-1862AD.

Fourth Issue

1869-1871

RUPEE

SILVER, 11.20-11.45 g
Rev: Jhar, sword and 22.

KM#	Date	Year	VG	Fine	VF	XF
67	VS1926	(1869)	7.00	11.00	16.50	25.00

Queen Victoria referred to in title only as "Queen Ruler of India and Europe."

MOHUR

GOLD, 10.90 g

KM#	Date	Year	VG	Fine	VF	XF
70	VS1926	(1869)	—	—	Rare	—

NOTE: Struck with rupee dies.

RUPEE

SILVER
Reduced size, 11.20-11.30 g
Obv: Legend differently arranged.
Rev: Sword, Persian HA and 22.

KM#	Date	Year	VG	Fine	VF	XF
68	VS1927	(1870)	20.00	31.50	42.50	60.00
	1928	(1871)	20.00	31.50	42.50	60.00

In the name of Queen Victoria

TAKKA

(2 Paisas)

COPPER, 21.00 g

KM#	Date	Year	Good	VG	Fine	VF
72	VS1940	(1883)	1.25	2.25	3.00	4.00
	1940 inverted	1883	2.50	4.00	6.50	9.00
	1941	(1884)	1.00	2.00	2.75	3.75
	1942	(1885)	1.25	2.25	3.00	4.00
	1943	(1886)	1.25	2.25	3.00	4.00
	1944	(1887)	1.25	2.25	3.00	4.00
	1945	(1888)	1.25	2.25	3.00	4.00
	1946	(1889)	1.25	2.25	3.00	4.00
	1947	(1890)	1.25	2.25	3.00	4.00
	1948	(1891)	2.00	3.50	5.50	7.00

In the names of Queen Victoria and Jaswant Singh

1/8 RUPEE

SILVER, 1.40 g

KM#	Date	Year	VG	Fine	VF	XF
73	VS—	—	8.50	13.50	20.00	28.50

1/4 RUPEE

SILVER, 2.80 g

KM#	Date	Year	VG	Fine	VF	XF
74	VS—	—	8.50	13.50	20.00	28.50

1/2 RUPEE

SILVER, 17mm, 5.60 g

KM#	Date	Year	VG	Fine	VF	XF
75	VS1944	(1887)	15.00	25.00	35.00	50.00
	1945	(1888)	15.00	25.00	35.00	50.00

RUPEE

SILVER, 11.20-11.30 g
Obv: Jhar, Nagari letter and Persian word.
Rev: Sword and 22.

KM#	Date	Year	VG	Fine	VF	XF
76	AH1291	—	6.50	10.00	16.50	25.00
	1293	—	6.50	10.00	16.50	25.00
	1923(error for 1293)	—	6.50	11.00	16.50	25.00
	Date off flan		5.00	7.00	10.00	15.00

KM#	Date	Year	VG	Fine	VF	XF
77	VS1942	(1885)	6.50	10.00	16.50	25.00
	1924(error for 1942)	(1885)	6.50	10.00	16.50	25.00
	2491(error for 1942)	(1885)	6.50	10.00	16.50	25.00
	1943	(1886)	6.50	10.00	16.50	25.00
	1947	(1890)	6.50	10.00	16.50	25.00
	1948	(1891)	6.50	10.00	16.50	25.00
	8941(error for 1948)	(1891)	6.50	10.00	16.50	25.00
	1950	(1893)	6.50	10.00	16.50	25.00
	Date off flan		5.00	7.00	10.00	15.00

1/4 MOHUR

GOLD

KM#	Date	Year	VG	Fine	VF	XF
78	AH1293	—	—	—	—	—

1/2 MOHUR

GOLD, 5.50 g

KM#	Date	Year	VG	Fine	VF	XF
79	AH1293	—	—	—	—	—

MOHUR

GOLD, 10.10 g

KM#	Date	Year	VG	Fine	VF	XF
80	AH1293	—	—	—	—	—

GOLD, 20mm, 11.00 g

KM#	Date	Year	VG	Fine	VF	XF
81	VS1942	(1885)	175.00	250.00	350.00	500.00
	1943	(1886)	175.00	250.00	350.00	500.00
	1944	(1887)	175.00	250.00	350.00	500.00

In the names of Queen Victoria and Sardar Singh

1/8 RUPEE

SILVER, 1.40 g

KM#	Date	Year	VG	Fine	VF	XF
83	VS1955	(1898)	8.50	13.50	20.00	28.50

1/4 RUPEE

SILVER, 2.80 g

KM#	Date	Year	VG	Fine	VF	XF
84	VS1955	(1898)	7.00	11.00	16.50	25.00

1/2 RUPEE

SILVER, 5.60 g

KM#	Date	Year	VG	Fine	VF	XF
85	VS1955	(1898)	12.50	18.50	25.00	35.00

RUPEE

SILVER, 11.20 g

KM#	Date	Year	VG	Fine	VF	XF
86	VS1955	(1898)	16.00	22.50	31.50	40.00
	1956	(1899)	16.00	22.50	31.50	40.00

1/4 MOHUR

GOLD, 15mm, 2.75 g

KM#	Date	Year	VG	Fine	VF	XF
88	VS1952	(1895)	60.00	85.00	110.00	165.00

1/2 MOHUR

GOLD, 18mm, 5.50 g

KM#	Date	Year	VG	Fine	VF	XF
89	VS1952	(1895)	100.00	150.00	210.00	300.00

MOHUR

GOLD, 21mm, 11.00 g

KM#	Date	Year	VG	Fine	VF	XF
90	VS1952	(1895)	175.00	250.00	350.00	500.00

NAGOR MINT

Operative until AH1289/1872AD.

In the name of Shah Alam II
AH1173-1221/1759-1806AD

RUPEE

SILVER, 11.20-11.30 g
Rev: *Nagore* at top.

KM#	Date	Year	VG	Fine	VF	XF
177	AH1217	44	12.50	21.50	30.00	40.00
	1218	—	12.50	21.50	30.00	40.00

NOTE: Earlier dates (AH1190-1215) exist for this type.

In the name of Muhammad Akbar II
AH1221-1253/1806-1837AD

RUPEE

SILVER, 11.20-11.30 g

KM#	Date	Year	VG	Fine	VF	XF
179	AH1222	1	—	—	—	—
	1223	2	—	—	—	—
	1232	—	—	—	—	—
	1234	—	—	—	—	—

PALI MINT

Operative until VS1958/1899AD.

In the name of Shah Alam II
AH1173-1221/1759-1806AD

RUPEE

SILVER, 11.30 g
Obv: Dagger.

KM#	Date	Year	VG	Fine	VF	XF
183	AH1218	45	6.50	10.00	15.00	22.50
(185)	1128(error for 1218)	45	6.50	10.00	15.00	22.50

Obv: Sword.

KM#	Date	Year	VG	Fine	VF	XF
184	AH1228(error for 1218)	45	6.50	10.00	15.00	22.50
185	AH12x8	45	6.50	10.00	15.00	22.50

In the names of Queen Victoria and Takhat Singh

RUPEE

SILVER, 11.20-11.30 g
Obv: 2 Jhars. Rev: Sword and 54.

KM#	Date	Year	VG	Fine	VF	XF
186	—	16	11.50	17.50	23.50	32.50

Obv: Jhar and swastika or Hindu letters.
Rev: Sword and 52.

KM#	Date	Year	VG	Fine	VF	XF
187	—	16	11.50	17.50	23.50	32.50

RUPEE

SILVER, 11.20-11.30 g
Obv: 54 in Nagari.
Rev: Jhar and sword, *SRI MATAJI*

KM#	Date	Year	VG	Fine	VF	XF
196.1	VS1926	(1879)	8.50	13.50	20.00	28.50

Rev: Symbol added.

KM#	Date	Year	VG	Fine	VF	XF
196.2	VS1926	(1879)	8.50	13.50	20.00	28.50

In the names of Queen Victoria and Jaswant Singh

1/4 RUPEE

SILVER, 2.80 g

KM#	Date	Year	VG	Fine	VF	XF
204	AH—	—	7.00	11.00	16.50	25.00

1/2 RUPEE

SILVER, 5.60 g

KM#	Date	Year	VG	Fine	VF	XF
205	VS1945	(1898)	8.50	13.50	20.00	28.50

RUPEE

SILVER, 19-21mm, 11.20-11.30 g
Obv: Swastika, Persian 4 and Nagari letters.
Rev: Jhar and sword, *SRI MATAJI.*

KM#	Date	Year	VG	Fine	VF	XF
206	VS1929	(1882)	6.00	10.00	15.00	22.50
	1930	(1883)	6.00	10.00	15.00	22.50
	1931	(1884)	6.00	10.00	15.00	22.50
	1932	(1885)	6.00	10.00	15.00	22.50
	1933	(1886)	6.00	10.00	15.00	22.50
	1934	(1887)	6.00	10.00	15.00	22.50
	1935	(1888)	6.00	10.00	15.00	22.50
	1936	(1889)	6.00	10.00	15.00	22.50
	1939	(1892)	6.00	10.00	15.00	22.50
	1940	(1893)	6.00	10.00	15.00	22.50
	1941	(1894)	6.00	10.00	15.00	22.50
	1942	(1895)	6.00	10.00	15.00	22.50
	1943	(1896)	6.00	10.00	15.00	22.50
	1944	(1897)	6.00	10.00	15.00	22.50
	1945	(1898)	6.00	10.00	15.00	22.50
	1950	(1893)	6.00	10.00	15.00	22.50
	1953	(1896)	6.00	10.00	15.00	22.50
	Date off flan		3.50	5.50	9.00	15.00

NAZARANA RUPEE

SILVER
Obv: Swastika. Rev: Jhar and sword.

KM#	Date	Year	VG	Fine	VF	XF
210 (187)	(VS1929-31)	(1872-74)	20.00	31.50	42.50	60.00

In the names of Queen Victoria and Sardar Singh

RUPEE

SILVER, 11.20 g
Rev: Straight sword and jhar.

KM#	Date	Year	VG	Fine	VF	XF
216	VS1956	(1899)	15.00	25.00	35.00	50.00

SOJAT MINT

Operative until AH1306/VS1945/1888AD.

In the name of Shah Alam II
AH1173-1221/1759-1806AD

RUPEE

SILVER, 11.20-11.30 g
Fictitious mintname: Jodhpur.

KM#	Date	Year	VG	Fine	VF	XF
226	AH1204	23	7.50	12.50	18.50	27.50
	12064(sic)	23	7.50	12.50	18.50	27.50
	12x4	23	7.50	12.50	18.50	27.50

In the names of Queen Victoria and Takhat Singh

RUPEE

SILVER, 11.20-11.30 g
Obv: Jhar. Rev: Katar and 13.

KM#	Date	Year	VG	Fine	VF	XF
237	—	16	8.50	13.50	20.00	28.50

NOTE: Struck ca. 1869AD.

Anonymous Issues

TAKKA

(2 Paisa)

COPPER, 20.80-21.10 g
Obv: Frozen date AH1205 and Nagari *MA*.
Rev: Katar.

KM#	Date	Year	VG	Fine	VF	XF
240	AH1267	—	3.50	8.50	14.00	20.00
	1227 (error for 1267)	—	—	—	Rare	—

RUPEE

SILVER, 11.20-11.30 g
Obv: Persian S. Rev: Jhar, sword and *SRI MATAJI.*

KM#	Date	Year	VG	Fine	VF	XF
246	VS1926	(1869)	9.00	15.00	21.50	30.00
	1927	(1870)	9.00	15.00	21.50	30.00

In the names of Queen Victoria and Jaswant Singh

RUPEE

SILVER, 11.30-11.40 g
Obv: Devanagari *Sri Madevaji* and Jhar.
Rev: *SRI MATAJI, sword and 22.*

KM#	Date	Year	VG	Fine	VF	XF
258.1	VS193x	—	11.50	17.50	23.50	32.50

Obv: *MADEVAJI and Jhar.*

KM#	Date	Year	VG	Fine	VF	XF
258.2	VSxxxx	—	—	—	—	—

Obv: Devanagari *Sri Ragunathji.*

KM#	Date	Year	VG	Fine	VF	XF
259	—	—	13.50	20.00	27.50	37.50

JODHPUR FEUDATORY STATES

Kuchaman

Kuchaman was a semi-independent feudatory. The thakur of Kuchaman, an Udawat Rajput, was the only feudatory of Jodhpur permitted to strike his own coinage.

Refer also to Gwalior-Ajmir Mint and Maratha Confederacy-Ajmir Mint.

In the name of Queen Victoria

New series introduced in 1863AD.

1/4 RUPEE

.750 SILVER, 13mm, 2.70 g

KM#	Date	Year	VG	Fine	VF	XF
284	1863	—	11.50	18.50	25.00	35.00

1/2 RUPEE

.750 SILVER, 15-16mm, 5.40 g

KM#	Date	Year	VG	Fine	VF	XF
285	1863	—	11.50	18.50	25.00	35.00

RUPEE

.750 SILVER, 10.60-10.08 g

KM#	Date	Year	VG	Fine	VF	XF
286	1863	—	5.50	9.00	13.50	20.00

NAZARANA RUPEE

.750 SILVER, 10.90 g

KM#	Date	Year	VG	Fine	VF	XF
287	1863	—	18.50	31.50	42.50	60.00

JUNAGADH

A state located in the Kathiawar peninsula of Western India was originally a petty Rajput kingdom until conquered by the Sultan of Ahmadabad in 1472. It became a Mughal dependency under the Emperor Akbar, administered by the Ahmadabad Subah. In 1735, when the empire began to disintegrate, a Mughal officer and military adventurer, Sher Khan Babi, expelled the Mughal governor and asserted his independence. From that time until Indian independence his descendents ruled the state as nawabs. In 1947 the Nawab of Junagadh tried to acceed to the new nation of Pakistan but the Hindu majority in the state objected and Junagadh was absorbed by the Republic of India.

Junagadh first entered into treaty relations with the British in 1807 and maintained a close and friendly association with the Raj. In 1924 this relationship was formalized when Junagadh was placed under an Agent to the Governor General in the western India States. In 1935 the state comprised 3,337 square miles with a population of 545,152, four-fifths of whom were Hindus.

RULERS

Bahadur Khan,
AH1226-1256/VS1868-1897/1811-1840AD
Hamid Khan II,
AH1256-1268/VS1897-1908/1840-1851AD
Mahabat Khan II,
AH1268-1300/VS1908-1939/1851-1882AD
Bahadur Khan III,
AH1300-1309/VS1939-1948/1882-1891AD
Rasul Muhammad Khan,
AH1309-1329/VS1948-1968/1891-1911AD

Mughal Issues

In the name of Muhammad Akbar II

AH1221-1253/1806-1837AD

With title *Sri Diwana* on obverse, AH and SE dates on reverse.

DOKDO

COPPER

KM#	Date	Year	Good	VG	Fine	VF
11	AH1239					
		VS(1880)	5.00	10.00	16.00	25.00
	(1244)	1885	5.00	10.00	16.00	25.00
	1245	1886	5.00	10.00	16.00	25.00
	(1248)	1889	5.00	10.00	16.00	25.00
	Date off flan		2.50	5.00	8.00	12.50

1/2 KORI

SILVER, 2.30 g

KM#	Date	Year	VG	Fine	VF	XF
13	AH1236	VS1877	3.00	4.50	6.50	10.00
	1245	1886	3.00	4.50	6.50	10.00
	1247	1889	3.00	4.50	6.50	10.00
	1251	1892	3.00	4.50	6.50	10.00
	1267	19xx	3.00	4.50	6.50	10.00
	1268	1909	3.00	4.50	6.50	10.00
	1270	1910	3.00	4.50	6.50	10.00
	1271	1911	3.00	4.50	6.50	10.00
	1272	1912	3.00	4.50	6.50	10.00
	1273	1913	3.00	4.50	6.50	10.00
	1274	1914	3.00	4.50	6.50	10.00
	1275	1915	3.00	4.50	6.50	10.00
	1276	1916	3.00	4.50	6.50	10.00
	1277	1917	3.00	4.50	6.50	10.00
	1278	1918	3.00	4.50	6.50	10.00
	1279	1919	3.00	4.50	6.50	10.00
	1280	1920	3.00	4.50	6.50	10.00

KORI

SILVER, 4.60 g

KM#	Date	Year	VG	Fine	VF	XF
15	AH1235	VS1875	2.50	3.50	5.00	8.00
	1235	1876	2.50	3.50	5.00	8.00
	1236	1877	2.50	3.50	5.00	8.00
	1245	1885	2.50	3.50	5.00	8.00
	1245	1886	2.50	3.50	5.00	8.00
	1246	1886	2.50	3.50	5.00	8.00
	1246	1887	2.50	3.50	5.00	8.00
	1247	1887	2.50	3.50	5.00	8.00
	1247	1888	2.50	3.50	5.00	8.00
	1249	1889	2.50	3.50	5.00	8.00
	1249	1890	2.50	3.50	5.00	8.00
	1251	1892	2.50	3.50	5.00	8.00
	1561	1892	(error)			
			2.50	3.50	5.00	8.00
	1252	1892	2.50	3.50	5.00	8.00
19	AH1263	VS190x	2.50	3.50	5.00	8.00
	1267	1907	2.50	3.50	5.00	8.00
	1268	1908	2.50	3.50	5.00	8.00
23	AH1270	VS1910	2.50	3.50	5.00	8.00
	1272	1912	2.50	3.50	5.00	8.00
	1273	1913	2.50	3.50	5.00	8.00
	1273	1914	2.50	3.50	5.00	8.00
	1274	1914	2.50	3.50	5.00	8.00
	1275	1915	2.50	3.50	5.00	8.00
	1276	1915	2.50	3.50	5.00	8.00
	1277	1917	2.50	3.50	5.00	8.00
	1278	1918	2.50	3.50	5.00	8.00
	1279	1919	2.50	3.50	5.00	8.00
	1280	1920	2.50	3.50	5.00	8.00

NOTE: After the death of the Mughal Emperor Muhammad Akbar II in AH1253/1837AD, Junagadh continued to issue its coins in his name posthumously until at least AH1280/VS1920 (1863AD), well into the reign of Nawab Mahabat Khan II.

Local Issues

MAHABAT KHAN II

AH1268-1300/VS1908-1939/1851-1882AD

DOKDO

COPPER

KM#	Date	Year	Good	VG	Fine	VF
27	VS1931	(1874)	15.00	25.00	40.00	60.00
	1935	(1878)	13.50	22.50	35.00	50.00

1/2 KORI

SILVER, 2.30 g

KM#	Date	Year	VG	Fine	VF	XF
29	AH1293	VS1934	6.00	9.00	13.50	20.00
29	1299	1938	6.00	9.00	13.50	20.00

KORI

SILVER, 4.60 g

KM#	Date	Year	VG	Fine	VF	XF
30	AH1292	VS1932	2.00	3.00	4.00	7.00
	1293	1933	2.00	3.00	4.00	7.00
	1293	1934	2.00	3.00	4.00	7.00
	1297	1935	2.00	3.00	4.00	7.00
	1297	1936	2.00	3.00	4.00	7.00
	1298	1937	2.00	3.00	4.00	7.00
	1299	1938	2.00	3.00	4.00	7.00

NAZARANA KORI

SILVER, 4.60 g

KM#	Date	Year	VG	Fine	VF	XF
31	AH1297	VS1936	18.50	31.50	42.50	60.00

GOLD KORI

GOLD, 15-16mm

KM#	Date	Year	Fine	VF	XF	Unc
34	AH1292	VS1932	225.00	350.00	500.00	750.00

BAHADUR KHAN III

AH1300-1309/VS1939-1948/1882-1891AD

1/2 GOLD KORI

GOLD

KM#	Date	Year	Fine	VF	XF	Unc
39	AH1309	VS1947	150.00	225.00	375.00	550.00

GOLD KORI

GOLD, 4.61 g

KM#	Date	Year	Fine	VF	XF	Unc
41	AH1309	VS1947	225.00	350.00	500.00	750.00

KALAT

Khelat or Kelat

A state located in Baluchistan, Pakistan.

The Khanate of Kalat had originally been a feudatory of Kabul. Its ruler, the wali, later became a trusted leader in the army of Ahmad Shah Durrani, who in 1761 invaded India and crushed both Mughal and Maratha forces at the battle of Panipat. In 1839 Kalat was taken by the British, and the wali, Mehrab Khan, was killed. The victors then installed his son, Nasir Khan, as ruler and in 1854 a formal treaty was executed. From that time Kalat came under British control, with the Government of India frequently acting as referees in disputes between the wali and his chiefs. In 1893 the wali was deposed for misrule and Kalat's mint was closed.

RULERS

Mehrab Khan,
AH1232-1255/1816-1839AD
Nasir Khan,
AH1256-1274/1841-1856AD
Khudadad Khan,
AH1274-1311/1856-1893AD

MINT

Kalat

MEHRAB KHAN

AH1232-1255/1816-1839AD

FALUS

COPPER

KM#	Date	Year	Good	VG	Fine	VF
11	AH1237	—	4.00	6.00	9.00	14.00
	1238	—	4.00	6.00	9.00	14.00
	1240	—	4.00	6.00	9.00	14.00

KHUDADAD KHAN

AH1274-1311/1857-1893AD

In the name of Mahmud Khan Durrani

FALUS

COPPER
Round, irregular, or rough-cut octagonal

KM#	Date	Year	Good	VG	Fine	VF
21	AH10786 (error for 1286)					
		—	3.50	6.00	10.00	15.00
	AH1186(error for 1286?)					
		—	3.50	6.00	10.00	15.00
	1281	—	3.50	6.00	10.00	15.00
	1282	—	3.50	6.00	10.00	15.00
	1290	—	3.50	6.00	10.00	15.00
	1293	—	3.50	6.00	10.00	15.00
	1294//1293	—	3.50	6.00	10.00	15.00
	1294	—	3.50	6.00	10.00	15.00
	1295	—	2.50	4.00	7.00	10.00
	1296	—	3.50	6.00	10.00	15.00
	ND	—	2.00	3.25	5.00	8.50

KALAYANI

Refer to Hyderabad Feudatories.

KARAULI

State located in Rajputana, northwest India.

Karauli was established in the eleventh century by Jadon Rajputs, of the same stock as the royal house of Jaisalmir. They are thought to have migrated to Rajasthan from the Mathura region some years earlier. The state passed successively under Mughal and Maratha suzerainty before coming under British authority in 1817.

The Maharajas of Karauli first struck coins in the reign of Manak Pal.

RULERS

Manak Pal,
AH1186-1233/1772-1817AD
Harbaksh Pal,
AH1233-1254/1817-1838AD
Pratap Pal,
AH1255-1264/1838-1848AD
Nar Singh Pal,
AH1264-1268/1848-1852AD
Bharat Pal,
AH1268-1270/1852-1854AD
Madan Pal,
AH1270-1286/1854-1869AD
Jai Singh Pal, 1869-1875AD
Arjun Pal, 1876-1886AD
Bhanwar Pal, 1886-1927

MINT

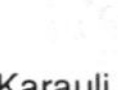
Karauli
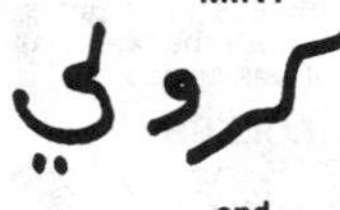
and
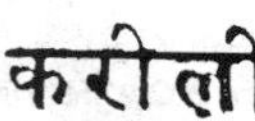

MINTNAME

Sawai Jaipur سوای جی پور

MINT MARKS

Katar

jhar on reverse

Mughal Issues

PAISA

COPPER

KM#	Date	Year	Good	VG	Fine	VF
11	AH121x	44	3.00	6.00	10.00	16.50

NOTE: Earlier dates (Yr. 25-38) exist for this type.

RUPEE

SILVER, 10.80-11.20 g

KM#	Date	Year	VG	Fine	VF	XF
16	AH1216	43	20.00	31.50	42.50	60.00
	—	44	20.00	31.50	42.50	60.00

NOTE: Earlier dates (AH1197/24-42) exist for this type.

In the name of Muhammad Akbar II

AH1221-1253/1806-1837AD

TAKKA

COPPER, 17.80-17.90 g

KM#	Date	Year	Good	VG	Fine	VF
21	AH122x	4	3.00	6.00	10.00	16.50
	—	10	3.00	6.00	10.00	16.50

RUPEE

SILVER, 10.90-11.10 g

KM#	Date	Year	VG	Fine	VF	XF
26	AH1223	2	20.00	31.50	42.50	60.00
	1227	6	20.00	31.50	42.50	60.00
	1228	7	20.00	31.50	42.50	60.00
	122x	9	20.00	31.50	42.50	60.00
	1231	10	20.00	31.50	42.50	60.00
	1232	11	20.00	31.50	42.50	60.00
	1233	12	20.00	31.50	42.50	60.00
	1233	14	20.00	31.50	42.50	60.00
	1233	15	20.00	31.50	42.50	60.00
	1237	16	20.00	31.50	42.50	60.00
	1238	16	20.00	31.50	42.50	60.00
	1239 (retrograde 9)					
		17	20.00	31.50	42.50	60.00
	1240	19	20.00	31.50	42.50	60.00
	1244	25	20.00	31.50	42.50	60.00
	1254(sic)	23	20.00	31.50	42.50	60.00

In the name of Bahadur Shah II

AH1253-1274/1837-1858AD

RUPEE

SILVER, 10.60-11.00 g

KM#	Date	Year	VG	Fine	VF	XF
31	AH12xx	9	17.50	25.00	35.00	50.00
	—	11	17.50	25.00	35.00	50.00
	—	12	17.50	25.00	35.00	50.00

With mark of Madan Pal

SILVER, 10.90-11.05 g
W/o legible AH year.

KM#	Date	Year	VG	Fine	VF	XF
33	AH—	13	17.50	25.00	35.00	50.00
	—	15	17.50	25.00	35.00	50.00

Regal Issues

In the name of Queen Victoria
Years and mark of Madan Pal

Years 1-14

NOTE: 2 types of coins exist in the name of Queen Victoria; 1859 - the year of introduction of these coins and 1852 - the official accession year of Madan Pal.

TAKKA

COPPER

KM#	Date	Year	Good	VG	Fine	VF
36	1852	12	2.50	5.00	7.50	12.00
	1852	13	2.50	5.00	7.50	12.00

1/4 RUPEE

SILVER, 13mm, 2.68-2.90 g

KM#	Date	Year	VG	Fine	VF	XF
42.1	1859	7	12.50	18.50	25.00	35.00
42.2	1852	13	12.50	18.50	25.00	35.00
	1852	14	12.50	18.50	25.00	35.00

1/2 RUPEE

SILVER, 18mm, 5.35-5.80 g

KM#	Date	Year	VG	Fine	VF	XF
43.1	1859	—	15.00	21.50	30.00	40.00
43.2	1852	—	15.00	21.50	30.00	40.00

RUPEE

SILVER, 10.90-11.00 g

KM#	Date	Year	VG	Fine	VF	XF
44.1	1859	7	15.00	21.50	30.00	40.00
	1859	9	15.00	21.50	30.00	40.00
44.2	1852	9	15.00	21.50	30.00	40.00
	1852	10	15.00	21.50	30.00	40.00
	1852	11	15.00	21.50	30.00	40.00
	1852	12	15.00	21.50	30.00	40.00
	1852	13	15.00	21.50	30.00	40.00
	1852	14	15.00	21.50	30.00	40.00
	1856(error for 1852)					
		14	15.00	21.50	30.00	40.00

In the name of the Exalted Queen, the Emperor of India
Years and mark of Arjun Pal

Years 1-11

1/2 PAISA

COPPER, 13mm, 4.50 g

KM#	Date	Year	Good	VG	Fine	VF
49	1886	11	4.50	6.00	10.00	15.00

PAISA

COPPER, 9.00 g

KM#	Date	Year	Good	VG	Fine	VF
50	1886	11	1.75	2.75	4.50	8.00

TAKKA

COPPER, 18.00 g
Rev: Katar upper right.

KM#	Date	Year	Good	VG	Fine	VF
51	1881	—	1.75	2.75	4.50	8.00
	1882 (error for 1886)					
		11	1.75	2.75	4.50	8.00
	1883	—	1.75	2.75	4.50	8.00
	1885	9	1.75	2.75	4.50	8.00
	1885	10	1.75	2.75	4.50	8.00
	1886	11	1.75	2.75	4.50	8.00

RUPEE

SILVER, 10.90-11.10 g

KM#	Date	Year	VG	Fine	VF	XF
56	1882	7	15.00	21.50	30.00	40.00
	1883	8	15.00	21.50	30.00	40.00
	1884	9	15.00	21.50	30.00	40.00
	1885	10	15.00	21.50	30.00	40.00
	1886	11	15.00	21.50	30.00	40.00

MOHUR

GOLD
Similar to 1 Rupee, KM#56.

KM#	Date	Year				
57	—	3	—	—	—	—

In the name of the Exalted Queen, the Emperor of India
Years and mark of Bhanwar Pal
Years 1-11

PAISA

COPPER, 9.00 g

KM#	Date	Year	Good	VG	Fine	VF
61	1886	1	1.75	3.00	5.00	9.00
	1887	2	1.75	3.00	5.00	9.00
	1891	5	1.75	3.00	5.00	9.00

TAKKA

COPPER, 17.80-18.30 g

KM#	Date	Year	Good	VG	Fine	VF
62	1886	1	1.75	2.75	4.50	8.00
	1887	2	1.75	2.75	4.50	8.00
	1891	5	1.75	2.75	4.50	8.00
	1891	6	1.75	2.75	4.50	8.00
	1893	8	1.75	2.75	4.50	8.00

1/8 RUPEE

SILVER, 1.35 g

KM#	Date	Year	VG	Fine	VF	XF
66	—	5	—	—	—	—

1/4 RUPEE

SILVER, 2.75 g

KM#	Date	Year	VG	Fine	VF	XF
68	1891	5	10.00	15.00	21.50	30.00
	1892	6	10.00	15.00	21.50	30.00
	1893	8	10.00	15.00	21.50	30.00
	1896	11	10.00	15.00	21.50	30.00

1/2 RUPEE

SILVER, 18mm, 5.45-5.60 g

KM#	Date	Year	VG	Fine	VF	XF
69	—	4	—	—	—	—
	1891	5	—	—	—	—
	1893	8	12.50	18.50	25.00	35.00
	1896	10	12.50	18.50	25.00	35.00

RUPEE

SILVER, 10.90-11.15 g

KM#	Date	Year	VG	Fine	VF	XF
70	1886	1	10.00	15.00	21.50	30.00
	1882(error for 1886)	2	10.00	15.00	21.50	30.00
	1886	2	10.00	15.00	21.50	30.00
	1887	2	10.00	15.00	21.50	30.00
	1888	2	10.00	15.00	21.50	30.00
	1888	3	10.00	15.00	21.50	30.00
	1889	4	10.00	15.00	21.50	30.00
	1890	4	10.00	15.00	21.50	30.00
	1890	—	10.00	15.00	21.50	30.00
	1891	5	10.00	15.00	21.50	30.00
	1891	6	10.00	15.00	21.50	30.00
	1892	8	10.00	15.00	21.50	30.00
	1893	8	10.00	15.00	21.50	30.00
	1894	8	10.00	15.00	21.50	30.00
	1894	9	10.00	15.00	21.50	30.00
	1895	10	10.00	15.00	21.50	30.00
70	1896	11	10.00	15.00	21.50	30.00
	1897	11	10.00	15.00	21.50	30.00

MEDALLIC ISSUES

1/2 MOHUR

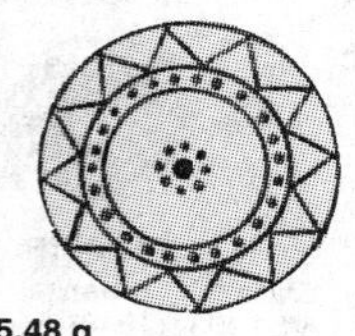

GOLD, 5.48 g

KM#	Date	Year	Fine	VF	XF	Unc
M1 (75)	ND	2	—	—	Rare	—

MOHUR

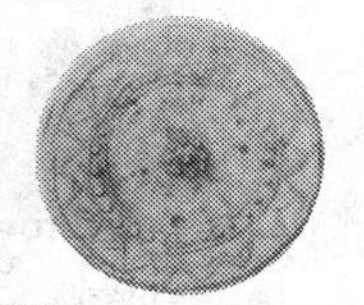

GOLD, 10.95 g

KM#	Date	Year	Fine	VF	XF	Unc
M2 (76)	ND	2	—	—	Rare	—

KASHMIR

State located in extreme northern India. Part of Afghanistan Durrani Empire 1752-1819AD, under Sikhs of Punjab 1819-1846AD, locally ruled by Dogra Rajas thereafter. For earlier coinage refer to Afghanistan and Sikh Empire.

RULERS

Dogra Rajas

Gulab Singh,
VS1903-1913/1846-1856AD

Ranbir Singh,
VS1914-1942/1857-1885AD

Pertab Singh,
VS1942-1979/1885-1925AD

MINTS

Jammu جموں

Ladakh لداخ

Srinagar سرینگر

JAMMU MINT

Dogra Issues

Anonymous Issues

1/2 PAISA

COPPER, 3.40-3.50 g
Rev: Takari leg.
Machine-punched planchets.

Y#	Date	Year	Good	VG	Fine	VF
2	VS1935	(1876)	5.00	9.00	12.00	20.00
	1936	(1877)	5.00	9.00	12.00	20.00

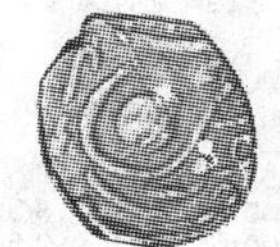
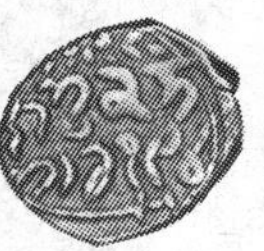

Dump style, uneven planchets.

Y#	Date	Year	Good	VG	Fine	VF
2a	VS1935	(1876)	1.00	1.75	2.50	4.00
	1936	(1877)	1.00	1.75	2.50	4.00
	1937	(1878)	1.00	1.75	2.50	4.00
	1938	(1879)	1.00	1.75	2.50	4.00
	1939	(1880)	1.00	1.75	2.50	4.00
	1940	(1881)	1.00	1.75	2.50	4.00
	1941	(1882)	1.00	1.75	2.50	4.00
	1942	(1883)	1.00	1.75	2.50	4.00
	1943	(1884)	1.00	1.75	2.50	4.00
	1946	(1887)	1.00	1.75	2.50	4.00
	1947	(1888)	1.00	1.75	2.50	4.00
	1948	(1889)	1.00	1.75	2.50	4.00
	1949	(1890)	1.00	1.75	2.50	4.00

PAISA

COPPER, 6.80-7.00 g
Obv: Persian leg. Rev: Gurmukhi leg.

Y#	Date	Year	Good	VG	Fine	VF
1	VS1914	(1857)	1.00	1.75	2.50	4.00
	1915	(1858)	1.00	1.75	2.50	4.00
	1917	(1860)	1.00	1.75	2.50	4.00
	1918	(1861)	1.00	1.75	2.50	4.00
	1919	(1862)	1.00	1.75	2.50	4.00
	1921	(1864)	1.00	1.75	2.50	4.00
	1922	(1865)	1.00	1.75	2.50	4.00
	ND	—	—	—	—	—

NOTE: Sword on reverse below top line VS1914-1919; below middle line VS1921-1922.

Anonymous Issue

1/3 MOHUR

GOLD, 3.57-3.80 g

Y#	Date	Year	VG	Fine	VF	XF
3	VS1921	(1864)	185.00	300.00	425.00	600.00

LADAKH MINT

NOTE: For coins struck at the Ladakh Mint refer to Indian Princely State, Ladakh.

SRINAGAR MINT

First Copper Series

Many varieties exist.

PAISA

COPPER
Obv: Fancy leaf.

Y#	Date	Year	Good	VG	Fine	VF
1.1	VS1904	(1847)	2.50	4.00	6.50	10.00

Obv: Trident. Rev: Scimitar through circle.

Y#	Date	Year	Good	VG	Fine	VF
1.2	VS1908	(1851)	2.50	4.00	6.50	10.00

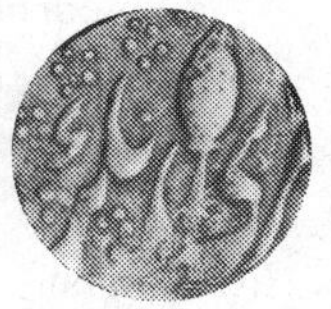

Rev: Fancy leaf.

Y#	Date	Year	Good	VG	Fine	VF
1.3	—	—	2.50	4.00	6.50	10.00

Second Copper Series

Obv: Fancy leaf. Rev: Scimitar through circle.

1/2 ANNA

COPPER

Y#	Date	Year	Good	VG	Fine	VF
8	VS1920	(1863)	5.00	9.00	13.00	20.00

ANNA

COPPER

Y#	Date	Year	Good	VG	Fine	VF
9	VS1920	(1863)	6.00	10.00	16.00	30.00
	1092 (error for 1920)		6.00	10.00	16.00	30.00
	1924	(1867)	6.00	10.00	16.00	30.00

Third Copper Series

Obv: Date in cartouche.

1/2 PAISA

COPPER, 2.50-3.00 g

Y#	Date	Year	Good	VG	Fine	VF
6	VS1922	(1865)	2.00	3.25	5.00	8.50
	1924	(1867)	2.00	3.25	5.00	8.50

PAISA

COPPER, 5.50-6.00 g

Y#	Date	Year	Good	VG	Fine	VF
7	VS1920	(1863)	.85	1.35	2.00	3.50
	1921	(1864)	.85	1.35	2.00	3.50
	1922	(1865)	.85	1.35	2.00	3.50
	1923	(1866)	1.00	1.75	2.50	4.00
	1926	(1869)	1.00	1.75	2.50	4.00
	1927	(1870)	.85	1.35	2.00	3.50
	1928	(1871)	.85	1.35	2.00	3.50
	1930	(1873)	1.00	1.75	2.50	4.00
	1931	(1874)	1.00	1.75	2.50	4.00

Fourth Copper Series

Obv: *JHS.* Rev: Takari leg.

1/4 PAISA

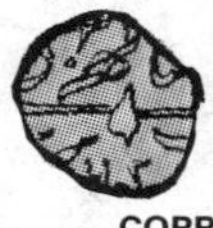

COPPER, 1.50 g

Y#	Date	Year	Good	VG	Fine	VF
17	VS1935	(1878)	3.00	5.00	8.00	12.50
	1941	(1884)	3.00	5.00	8.00	12.50
	Date off flan		1.75	2.75	4.00	7.00

1/2 PAISA

COPPER, 3.00 g

Y#	Date	Year	Good	VG	Fine	VF
18	VS1927	(1870)	1.50	2.50	4.00	6.00
	1928	(1871)	1.50	2.50	4.00	6.00
	1932	(1875)	1.00	1.75	2.50	4.00
	1933	(1876)	1.00	1.75	2.50	4.00
	1933 on obv/1934 on rev.	(1875/76)	1.25	2.25	3.50	5.50
	1934	(1877)	1.00	1.75	2.50	4.00
	1936	(1879)	1.00	1.75	2.50	4.00
	1937	(1880)	1.00	1.75	2.50	4.00
	1938	(1881)	1.00	1.75	2.50	4.00
	1939	(1882)	1.00	1.75	2.50	4.00
	1940	(1883)	1.00	1.75	2.50	4.00
	1941	(1884)	1.00	1.75	2.50	4.00

PAISA

COPPER, 6.00 g

Y#	Date	Year	Good	VG	Fine	VF
19	VS1937	(1880)	2.00	3.25	5.00	8.50
	1938	(1881)	2.00	3.25	5.00	8.50
	1939	(1882)	2.00	3.25	5.00	8.50
	1940	(1883)	2.00	3.25	5.00	8.50

First Silver Series

Rev: Leaf and date, w/o *JHS.*

NOTE: The dot for 'O' in 1903, 1904, 1905 is sometimes omitted.

1/8 RUPEE

SILVER, 1.28-1.35 g

Y#	Date	Year	VG	Fine	VF	XF
2	VS1903	(1846)	7.00	11.00	16.50	30.00
	1904	(1847)	7.00	11.00	16.50	30.00
	1905	(1848)	7.00	11.00	16.50	30.00

1/4 RUPEE

SILVER, 2.57-2.70 g

Y#	Date	Year	VG	Fine	VF	XF
3	VS1903	(1846)	6.50	10.00	15.00	27.50
	1904	(1847)	6.50	10.00	15.00	27.50

1/2 RUPEE

SILVER, 5.15-5.40 g

Y#	Date	Year	VG	Fine	VF	XF
4	VS1903	(1846)	7.50	12.50	18.50	32.50
	1904	(1847)	7.50	12.50	18.50	32.50
	1905	(1848)	7.50	12.50	18.50	32.50
	1906	(1849)	7.50	12.50	18.50	32.50

RUPEE

SILVER, 10.30-10.80 g

Y#	Date	Year	VG	Fine	VF	XF
5	VS1903	(1846)	7.00	11.00	16.50	30.00
	1904	(1847)	7.00	11.00	16.50	30.00
	1905	(1848)	7.50	12.50	18.50	32.50
	1906	(1849)	7.50	12.50	18.50	32.50

Second Silver Series

Obv. and rev: Persian leg. w/*JHS* added to rev.

1/16 RUPEE

SILVER, 0.64-0.67 g

Y#	Date	Year	VG	Fine	VF	XF
9	VS—	—	5.50	8.00	12.50	22.50

1/8 RUPEE

SILVER, 1.28-1.35 g

Y#	Date	Year	VG	Fine	VF	XF
10	VS1914	(1857)	5.50	8.00	12.50	22.50
	1925	(1868)	5.50	8.00	12.50	22.50

1/4 RUPEE

SILVER, 2.57-2.70 g

Y#	Date	Year	VG	Fine	VF	XF
11	VS1914	(1857)	6.00	9.00	13.50	25.00
	1922	(1865)	6.00	9.00	13.50	25.00
	1925	(1868)	6.00	9.00	13.50	25.00

1/2 RUPEE

SILVER, 5.15-5.40 g

Y#	Date	Year	VG	Fine	VF	XF
12	VS1914	(1857)	6.50	10.00	15.00	27.50
	1922	(1865)	6.50	10.00	15.00	27.50

"KHAM" RUPEE

SILVER, 10.30-10.80 g

Y#	Date	Year	VG	Fine	VF	XF
13	VS1906	(1849)	7.00	11.00	16.50	30.00
	1907	(1850)	7.00	11.00	16.50	30.00
	1908	(1851)	7.00	11.00	16.50	30.00
	1909	(1852)	7.00	11.00	16.50	30.00
	1910	(1853)	7.00	11.00	16.50	30.00
	1911	(1854)	7.00	11.00	16.50	30.00
	1912	(1855)	7.00	11.00	16.50	30.00
	1913	(1856)	7.00	11.00	16.50	30.00
	1914	(1857)	7.00	11.00	16.50	30.00
	1915	(1858)	7.00	11.00	16.50	30.00
	1916	(1859)	7.00	11.00	16.50	30.00
	1917	(1860)	7.00	11.00	16.50	30.00
	1918	(1861)	7.00	11.00	16.50	30.00
	1919	(1862)	7.00	11.00	16.50	30.00
	1920	(1863)	7.00	11.00	16.50	30.00
	1921	(1864)	7.00	11.00	16.50	30.00
	1922	(1865)	7.00	11.00	16.50	30.00
	1923	(1866)	7.00	11.00	16.50	30.00
	1924	(1867)	7.00	11.00	16.50	30.00
	1925	(1868)	7.00	11.00	16.50	30.00
	1926	(1869)	7.00	11.00	16.50	30.00
	1927	(1870)	7.00	11.00	16.50	30.00

Third Silver Series

Obv: Persian leg. w/*JHS.* Rev: Takari leg. Rupee weight Rupee weight reduced to 6.80 g from 10.30-10.80 g.

1/4 RUPEE

SILVER, 15mm, 1.65-1.70 g

Y#	Date	Year	VG	Fine	VF	XF
14	VS1928	(1871)	15.00	21.50	30.00	45.00

1/2 RUPEE

SILVER, 17mm, 3.30-3.40 g

Y#	Date	Year	VG	Fine	VF	XF
15	VS1928	(1871)	15.00	21.00	30.00	45.00

RUPEE

SILVER, 6.60-6.80 g
Machine-struck in collar.

Y#	Date	Year	VG	Fine	VF	XF
16	VS1927	(1870)	27.50	45.00	62.50	95.00
	1928	(1871)	27.50	45.00	62.50	95.00

Struck on machine punched planchets.

Y#	Date	Year	VG	Fine	VF	XF
16a	VS1927	(1870)	7.00	11.00	16.50	30.00
	1928	(1871)	7.00	11.00	16.50	30.00
	1929	(1872)	9.00	15.00	21.50	35.00

Struck on dump planchets.

Y#	Date	Year	VG	Fine	VF	XF
16b	VS1929	(1872)	7.50	12.50	18.50	32.50
	1930	(1873)	7.50	12.50	18.50	32.50
	1931	(1874)	7.50	12.50	18.50	32.50
	1932	(1875)	7.50	12.50	18.50	32.50

Fourth Silver Series ("Chilki")

Obv: Persian date in second line. Rev: Davanagari date in second line.

1/2 RUPEE

SILVER, 3.30 g

Y#	Date	Year	VG	Fine	VF	XF
20	VS1946	(1889)	7.00	11.00	16.50	30.00
	1948	(1891)	7.00	11.00	16.50	30.00
	1950	(1893)	7.00	11.00	16.50	30.00
	1951	(1894)	7.00	11.00	16.50	30.00

RUPEE

SILVER, 6.80 g

Y#	Date	Year	VG	Fine	VF	XF
21	VS1931	(1874)	12.50	18.50	25.00	40.00
	1932	(1875)	12.50	18.50	25.00	40.00
	1933	(1876)	12.50	18.50	25.00	40.00

6.65 g

Y#	Date	Year	VG	Fine	VF	XF
21a	VS1934	(1877)	5.50	8.00	12.50	22.50
	1935	(1878)	5.50	8.00	12.50	22.50
	1936	(1879)	5.50	8.00	12.50	22.50
	1937	(1880)	5.50	8.00	12.50	22.50
	1938	(1881)	5.50	8.00	12.50	22.50
	1939	(1882)	5.50	8.00	12.50	22.50
	1940	(1883)	5.50	8.00	12.50	22.50
	1941	(1884)	5.50	8.00	12.50	22.50
	1942	(1885)	5.50	8.00	12.50	22.50
	1943	(1886)	5.50	8.00	12.50	22.50
	1944	(1887)	5.50	8.00	12.50	22.50
	1945	(1888)	5.50	8.00	12.50	22.50
	1946	(1889)	5.50	8.00	12.50	22.50
	1947	(1890)	5.50	8.00	12.50	22.50
	1948	(1891)	5.50	8.00	12.50	22.50
	1949	(1892)	5.50	8.00	12.50	22.50
	1950	(1893)	5.50	8.00	12.50	22.50
	1951	(1894)	5.50	8.00	12.50	22.50
	1952	(1895)	5.50	8.00	12.50	22.50

NAZARANA 1/4 MOHUR

GOLD, 14-15mm, 2.30 g

Y#	Date	Year	VG	Fine	VF	XF
22	VS193x	—	—	500.00	700.00	1000.

KISHANGARH

The maharajas of Kishangarh, a small state in northwest India, in the vicinity of Ajmer, belonged to the Rathor Rajputs. The town of Kishangarh, which gave its name to the state, was founded in 1611 and was itself named after Kishen Singh, the first ruler. The maharajas succeeded in reaching terms with Akbar in the late sixteenth century, and again in 1818 with the British. In 1949 the state was merged into Rajasthan.

RULERS

Kalyan Singh,
VS1854-1889/1797-1832AD

Kalyan Singh,
VS1854-1889/1797-1832AD
Mokham Singh,
VS1889-1898/1832-1841AD
Prithvi Singh,
VS1898-1936/1841-1879AD
Sardul Singh,
VS1936-1957/1879-1900AD
Madan Singh,
VS1957-1983/1900-1926AD
Yaghyanarayan Singh,
VS1983-1995/1926-1938AD
Sumer Singh,
VS1995-2000/1938-1949AD

MINT

Kishangarh 

Mint mark:

On reverse

Mughal Issues

In the name of Muhammad Akbar II

AH1221-1253/1806-1837AD

PAISA

COPPER

C#	Date	Year	Good	VG	Fine	VF
24	ND			—	—	—

1/2 TAKKA

COPPER, 17.25-17.50 g
Crude copy of Jaipur C#47

C#	Date	Year	Good	VG	Fine	VF
25	ND	—	1.00	1.50	2.50	5.00

COPPER, 17.25-17.50 g
Crude copy of Jaipur, C#35

C#	Date	Year	Good	VG	Fine	VF
5	AH—	—	1.25	1.75	2.50	5.00
	—	7	1.25	1.75	2.50	5.00

Regal Issues

In the names of Queen Victoria and Prithvi Singh

1858-1879AD
Frozen regnal year 24 of Shah Alam II.

RUPEE

SILVER, 10.70-10.85 g

Y#	Date	Year	VG	Fine	VF	XF
1.1	1858	24	11.50	17.50	23.50	32.50

Different arrangement of inscription.

Y#	Date	Year	VG	Fine	VF	XF
1.2	1859	24	11.50	17.50	23.50	32.50

NOTE: A full size multiple rupee special strike weighing 24.33 g is known to exist.

MOHUR

GOLD, 10.9 g

Y#	Date	Year	VG	Fine	VF	XF
A1	1858	24	—	—	—	—

In the names of Queen Victoria and Sardul Singh

1879-1900AD

1/2 RUPEE

SILVER, 5.40 g

Y#	Date	Year	VG	Fine	VF	XF
A2	1880	—	11.50	18.50	25.00	35.00

RUPEE

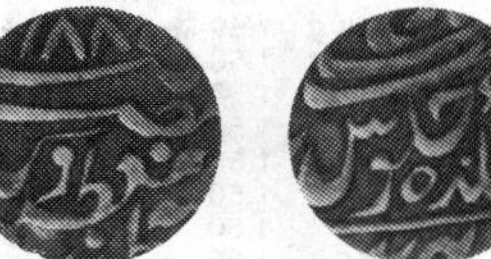

SILVER, 10.80 g

Y#	Date	Year	VG	Fine	VF	XF
2	1880	24	15.00	25.00	35.00	50.00

In the names of Empress Victoria and Madan Singh

1/2 RUPEE

SILVER, 5.40 g

Y#	Date	Year	VG	Fine	VF	XF
A3	ND	—	12.50	21.00	28.50	40.00

RUPEE

SILVER, 10.80 g

Y#	Date	Year	VG	Fine	VF	XF
C3	ND	—	—	—	—	—

MOHUR

GOLD, 10.90 g

Y#	Date	Year	VG	Fine	VF	XF
D3	ND	—	185.00	300.00	425.00	600.00

Anonymous Issues

First Series

Obv. Nagari leg: *Chadi* (= silver).

1/8 RUPEE

SILVER, 1.35 g

KM#	Date	Year	VG	Fine	VF	XF
M7 (Y9)	—	24	11.50	18.50	25.00	35.00

1/4 RUPEE

SILVER, 2.70 g

KM#	Date	Year	VG	Fine	VF	XF
M8 (Y10)	—	24	11.50	18.50	25.00	35.00

1/2 RUPEE

SILVER, 5.40 g

KM#	Date	Year	VG	Fine	VF	XF
M9 (Y11)	—	24	11.00	17.50	23.50	32.50

RUPEE

SILVER, 10.85-11.05 g

KM#	Date	Year	VG	Fine	VF	XF
M10 (Y12)	—	24	14.00	23.50	32.50	45.00

Second Series

Obv: Denominations in Nagari, Persian and "merchants numerals", in Annas.

2 ANNAS

SILVER, 1.32 g

KM#	Date	Year	VG	Fine	VF	XF
M11 (Y13)	—	24	12.50	21.00	28.50	40.00

4 ANNAS

SILVER, 2.62 g

KM#	Date	Year	VG	Fine	VF	XF
M12 (Y14)	—	24	6.00	10.00	15.00	22.50

8 ANNAS

SILVER, 5.35 g

KM#	Date	Year	VG	Fine	VF	XF
M13 (Y15)	—	24	6.50	11.00	16.50	25.00

KOLHAPUR

Maratha state in southwest India between Goa and Bombay.

The maharajas of Kolhapur traced their origins and ancestry to Raja Ram, son of Shivaji, the founder of the Maratha kingdom, and to his courageous wife Tarabai who officiated as regent on behalf of her son after Raja Ram's death in 1698. Kolhapur's existence as a separate state dates from about 1730 when a family quarrel left Sambaji, the great-grandson of Sivaji, as the first raja of Kolhapur. In recognition of their special eminence among the Maratha chieftains the rulers of Kolhapur bore the honorific title of "Chhatrapati Maharaja". Between 1811 and 1862 Kolhapur concluded a series of treaties and agreements with the British whereby the state came increasingly under British protection and control.

The mint closed ca. 1850AD.

MINT

عظم نكر كوكاك

Mintname: A'zamnagar Gokak, Pseudo*

Mughal Issues

In the name of Muhammad Shah
(struck until ca. 1850AD)

1/4 RUPEE

SILVER, 12mm, 2.68-2.90 g

C#	Date	Year	VG	Fine	VF	XF
14	ND	—	13.50	20.00	27.50	37.50

1/2 RUPEE

SILVER, 15mm, 5.35-5.80 g

C#	Date	Year	VG	Fine	VF	XF
15	ND	—	13.50	20.00	27.50	37.50

RUPEE

SILVER, 10.70-11.60 g

C#	Date	Year	VG	Fine	VF	XF
16	ND	—	6.50	11.00	16.50	25.00
	AH1132	6	6.50	11.00	16.50	25.00

Fine calligraphy

C#	Date	Year	VG	Fine	VF	XF
25	1821	—	12.50	21.00	28.50	40.00

Regal Issues

EAST INDIA COMPANY

Local issue from Shahupur.

1/2 RUPEE

SILVER, 5.35-5.80 g

C#	Date	Year	VG	Fine	VF	XF
29	1821	—	16.50	26.50	37.50	55.00

RUPEE

SILVER, 10.70-11.60 g

C#	Date	Year	VG	Fine	VF	XF
30	1821	—	16.50	26.50	37.50	55.00

KOTAH

Kotah State, located in northwest India was subdivided out of Bundi early in the seventeenth century when it was given to a younger son of the Bundi raja by the Mughal emperor. The ruler, or maharao, was a Chauhan Rajput. During the years of Maratha ascendancy Kotah fell on hard times, especially from the depredations of Holkar. In 1817 the State came under treaty with the British.

RULERS

Ram Singh II,
VS1885-1923/1828-1866AD
Chattar Singh,
VS1923-1946/1866-1889AD
Umed Singh II,
VS1946-1992/1889-1935AD

MINT

نندكاون

Mintname: *Nandgaon*

كوته عرف نندكاون

Kotah urf Nandgaon
or Nandgaon urf Kotah on earliest issues.

MINT MARKS

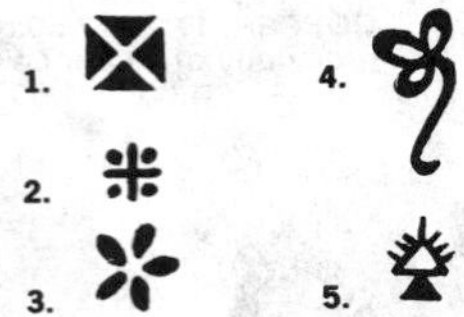

Mint mark #1 appears beneath #4 on most Kotah coins, and serves to distinguish coins of Kotah from similar issues of Bundi in the pre-Victoria period.

C#28 has mint mark #2 on obv., #1, 3 and 4 on rev. All later issues have #1 on obv., #1, 5 and 4 on rev.

Mughal Issues

In the name of Shah Alam II
AH1173-1221/1759-1806AD

TAKKA

COPPER, 17.50-18.50 g

C#	Date	Year	VG	Fine	VF	XF
20	AH—	46	3.00	4.00	5.50	8.00

NOTE: Earlier dates (Year 23-41) exist for this type.

RUPEE

SILVER, 11.05-11.20 g
Mint: *Kotah Nandgaon*
Rev: Flower mint mark in front of regnal year.

C#	Date	Year	VG	Fine	VF	XF
28.3	AH—	46	8.50	13.50	20.00	28.50
	—	47	8.50	13.50	20.00	28.50

NOTE: Earlier dates (Year 24-45) exist for this type.

NAZARANA RUPEE

SILVER, 11.20 g
Mint: Kotah Nandgaon

C#	Date	Year	VG	Fine	VF	XF
A28	AH1215	41	—	—	—	—

MOHUR

GOLD, 10.67 g
Mint: Kotah Nandgaon

C#	Date	Year	VG	Fine	VF	XF
B28	AH—	32	—	—	—	—

In the name of Muhammad Akbar II
AH1221-1253/1806-1837AD

TAKKA

COPPER, square, 17.00-18.00 g
Rev: W/mint marks #4 and #5.

C#	Date	Year	Good	VG	Fine	VF
29	AH—	4	1.50	2.50	4.50	7.00
	—	5	1.50	2.50	4.50	7.00
	—	6	1.50	2.50	4.50	7.00
	—	7	1.50	2.50	4.50	7.00
	—	8	1.50	2.50	4.50	7.00
	—	10	1.50	2.50	4.50	7.00
	—	11	1.50	2.50	4.50	7.00
	—	12	1.50	2.50	4.50	7.00
	—	13	1.50	2.50	4.50	7.00
	—	14	1.50	2.50	4.50	7.00
	—	15	1.50	2.50	4.50	7.00
	—	16	1.50	2.50	4.50	7.00
	—	17	1.50	2.50	4.50	7.00
	—	18	1.50	2.50	4.50	7.00
	—	24	1.50	2.50	4.50	7.00
	—	25	1.50	2.50	4.50	7.00
	—	26	1.50	2.50	4.50	7.00
	—	27	1.50	2.50	4.50	7.00
	—	28	1.50	2.50	4.50	7.00
	—	29	1.50	2.50	4.50	7.00
	—	30	1.50	2.50	4.50	7.00
	—	33	1.50	2.50	4.50	7.00

1/4 RUPEE

SILVER, 2.80 g
Obv: W/#1 mint mark.

C#	Date	Year	Good	VG	Fine	VF
29c	AH—	23	—	—	—	—

RUPEE

SILVER, 11.20-11.25 g
Obv: W/o mint mark #1.

C#	Date	Year	VG	Fine	VF	XF
30	AH—	1	6.50	10.00	15.00	22.50
	—	3	6.50	10.00	15.00	22.50

Obv: W/o mint mark #1.

C#	Date	Year	VG	Fine	VF	XF
30c	AH—	12	6.50	10.00	15.00	22.50
	—	15	6.50	10.00	15.00	22.50
	—	16	6.50	10.00	15.00	22.50
	—	18	6.50	10.00	15.00	22.50
	—	20	6.50	10.00	15.00	22.50
	—	22	6.50	10.00	15.00	22.50
	—	23	6.50	10.00	15.00	22.50
	—	24	6.50	10.00	15.00	22.50
	—	28	6.50	10.00	15.00	22.50
	1252	29	6.50	10.00	15.00	22.50
	—	30	6.50	10.00	15.00	22.50
	—	31	6.50	10.00	15.00	22.50
	—	32	6.50	10.00	15.00	22.50

NAZARANA RUPEE

SILVER, square, 11.20-11.30 g
Obv: W/o mint mark #1.

C#	Date	Year	VG	Fine	VF	XF
30a	AH—	5	37.50	62.50	85.00	120.00

Obv: W/o mint mark #1.

C#	Date	Year	VG	Fine	VF	XF
30d	AH—	11	37.50	62.50	85.00	120.00
	—	16	37.50	62.50	85.00	120.00
	—	18	37.50	62.50	85.00	120.00
	—	19	37.50	62.50	85.00	120.00
	—	22	37.50	62.50	85.00	120.00
	—	23	37.50	62.50	85.00	120.00
	—	24	37.50	62.50	85.00	120.00
	—	27	37.50	62.50	85.00	120.00
	—	30	37.50	62.50	85.00	120.00
	—	32	37.50	62.50	85.00	120.00

Round, 27-31mm

C#	Date	Year	VG	Fine	VF	XF
30b	AH1237	16	37.50	62.50	85.00	120.00
	1239	18	37.50	62.50	85.00	120.00
	1240	19	37.50	62.50	85.00	120.00
	1242	22	37.50	62.50	85.00	120.00
	1245	24	37.50	62.50	85.00	120.00
	124x	30	37.50	62.50	85.00	120.00
	125x	32	37.50	62.50	85.00	120.00

NOTE: Formerly listed under Bundi State.

MOHUR

GOLD, 10.70 g
Obv: W/o mint mark # 1.

C#	Date	Year	VG	Fine	VF	XF
30e	AH—	2	—	—	—	—

Obv: W/o mint mark #1.

C#	Date	Year	VG	Fine	VF	XF
30f	AH—	19	—	—	—	—

In the name of Bahadur Shah II
AH1253-1274/1837-1857AD

1/4 RUPEE

SILVER, 12mm, 2.80 g

C#	Date	Year	VG	Fine	VF	XF
A31	AH—	4	7.00	11.00	16.50	25.00
	—	16	7.00	11.00	16.50	25.00

RUPEE

SILVER, 11.00-11.25 g

C#	Date	Year	VG	Fine	VF	XF
32	AH—	4	6.00	9.00	13.50	20.00
	—	5	6.00	9.00	13.50	20.00
	—	6	6.00	9.00	13.50	20.00
	—	7	6.00	9.00	13.50	20.00
	—	8	6.00	9.00	13.50	20.00
	—	9	6.00	9.00	13.50	20.00
	—	11	6.00	9.00	13.50	20.00
	—	12	6.00	9.00	13.50	20.00
	—	13	6.00	9.00	13.50	20.00
	—	15	6.00	9.00	13.50	20.00
	—	16	6.00	9.00	13.50	20.00
	—	17	6.00	9.00	13.50	20.00
	—	18	6.00	9.00	13.50	20.00
	—	19	6.00	9.00	13.50	20.00
	—	20	6.00	9.00	13.50	20.00
	—	21	6.00	9.00	13.50	20.00

NAZARANA RUPEE

SILVER, round, 11.20 g

C#	Date	Year	VG	Fine	VF	XF
32a	AH—	1	27.50	45.00	62.50	85.00
	—	2	27.50	45.00	62.50	85.00
	—	3	27.50	45.00	62.50	85.00
	—	4	27.50	45.00	62.50	85.00
	—	5	27.50	45.00	62.50	85.00
	1205	6	27.50	45.00	62.50	85.00
	—	7	27.50	45.00	62.50	85.00
	—	8	27.50	45.00	62.50	85.00
	—	9	27.50	45.00	62.50	85.00
	—	10	27.50	45.00	62.50	85.00
	—	11	27.50	45.00	62.50	85.00
	—	12	27.50	45.00	62.50	85.00
	—	13	27.50	45.00	62.50	85.00
	—	14	27.50	45.00	62.50	85.00
	—	15	27.50	45.00	62.50	85.00
	—	16	27.50	45.00	62.50	85.00
	—	17	27.50	45.00	62.50	85.00
	—	18	27.50	45.00	62.50	85.00
	—	19	27.50	45.00	62.50	85.00
	—	20	27.50	45.00	62.50	85.00
	—	21	27.50	45.00	62.50	85.00
	—	22	27.50	45.00	62.50	85.00

Square

C#	Date	Year	VG	Fine	VF	XF
32b	AH—	11	40.00	70.00	100.00	145.00

NOTE: All specimens show rudimentary traces of AH dates on obverse.

MOHUR

GOLD, 19mm, 10.70-11.40 g

C#	Date	Year	VG	Fine	VF	XF
33	AH—	1	185.00	300.00	425.00	600.00
	—	19	185.00	300.00	425.00	600.00
	—	20	185.00	300.00	425.00	600.00
	—	21	185.00	300.00	425.00	600.00

Regal Issues

In the name of the Queen of England

From 1858AD

PAISA

COPPER, 12-16mm, 9.00-12.00 g

Y#	Date	Year	Good	VG	Fine	VF
1	AH—	37	1.50	2.50	3.75	6.00
	—	38	1.50	2.50	3.75	6.00
	—	39	1.50	2.50	3.75	6.00
	—	40	1.50	2.50	3.75	6.00

TAKKA

COPPER, 15-20mm, 16.80-18.00 g

Y#	Date	Year	Good	VG	Fine	VF
2	AH—	1	1.25	2.00	3.25	5.00
	—	2	1.25	2.00	3.25	5.00
	—	6	1.25	2.00	3.25	5.00
	—	8	1.25	2.00	3.25	5.00
	—	24	1.25	2.00	3.25	5.00
	—	27	1.25	2.00	3.25	5.00
	—	28	1.25	2.00	3.25	5.00
	—	29	1.25	2.00	3.25	5.00
	—	30	1.25	2.00	3.25	5.00
	—	31	1.25	2.00	3.25	5.00
	—	32	1.25	2.00	3.25	5.00
	—	35	1.25	2.00	3.25	5.00
	—	37	1.25	2.00	3.25	5.00
	—	38	1.25	2.00	3.25	5.00
	—	39	1.25	2.00	3.25	5.00
	—	40	1.25	2.00	3.25	5.00
	—	41	1.25	2.00	3.25	5.00

NAZARANA TAKKA

COPPER, square, 18.00 g

Y#	Date	Year	Good	VG	Fine	VF
2a	AH—	15	—	—	—	—

1/8 RUPEE

SILVER, 1.40 g

Y#	Date	Year	VG	Fine	VF	XF
3	AH—	22	5.00	7.00	10.00	15.00
	—	27	5.00	7.00	10.00	15.00
	—	20	5.00	7.00	10.00	15.00
	—	29	5.00	7.00	10.00	15.00
	—	30	5.00	7.00	10.00	15.00
	—	31	5.00	7.00	10.00	15.00
	—	32	5.00	7.00	10.00	15.00
	—	33	5.00	7.00	10.00	15.00
	—	34	5.00	7.00	10.00	15.00
	—	36	5.00	7.00	10.00	15.00
	—	37	5.00	7.00	10.00	15.00
	—	38	5.00	7.00	10.00	15.00

1/4 RUPEE

SILVER, 2.80 g

Y#	Date	Year	VG	Fine	VF	XF
4	AH—	1	4.00	6.00	9.00	14.00
	—	2	4.00	6.00	9.00	14.00
	—	5	4.00	6.00	9.00	14.00
	—	8	4.00	6.00	9.00	14.00
	—	10	4.00	6.00	9.00	14.00
	—	22	4.00	6.00	9.00	14.00
	—	23	4.00	6.00	9.00	14.00
	—	26	4.00	6.00	9.00	14.00
	—	27	4.00	6.00	9.00	14.00
	—	29	4.00	6.00	9.00	14.00
	—	30	4.00	6.00	9.00	14.00
	—	31	4.00	6.00	9.00	14.00
	—	32	4.00	6.00	9.00	14.00
	—	33	4.00	6.00	9.00	14.00
	—	35	4.00	6.00	9.00	14.00
	—	37	4.00	6.00	9.00	14.00
	—	38	4.00	6.00	9.00	14.00

1/2 RUPEE

SILVER, 5.60 g

Y#	Date	Year	VG	Fine	VF	XF
5	AH—	1	5.50	8.00	12.50	18.50
	—	4	5.50	8.00	12.50	18.50
	—	8	5.50	8.00	12.50	18.50
	—	18	5.50	8.00	12.50	18.50
	—	22	5.50	8.00	12.50	18.50
	—	24	5.50	8.00	12.50	18.50
	—	25	5.50	8.00	12.50	18.50
	—	27	5.50	8.00	12.50	18.50
	—	28	5.50	8.00	12.50	18.50
	—	29	5.50	8.00	12.50	18.50
	—	30	5.50	8.00	12.50	18.50

Y#	Date	Year	VG	Fine	VF	XF
5	—	31	5.50	8.00	12.50	18.50
	—	32	5.50	8.00	12.50	18.50
	—	33	5.50	8.00	12.50	18.50
	—	34	5.50	8.00	12.50	18.50
	—	35	5.50	8.00	12.50	18.50
	—	36	5.50	8.00	12.50	18.50
	—	37	5.50	8.00	12.50	18.50
	—	38	5.50	8.00	12.50	18.50

RUPEE

SILVER, 11.20 g

Y#	Date	Year	VG	Fine	VF	XF
6	AH—	1	5.50	8.00	10.00	15.00
	—	2	5.50	8.00	10.00	15.00
	—	4	5.50	8.00	10.00	15.00
	—	5	5.50	8.00	10.00	15.00
	—	6	5.50	8.00	10.00	15.00
	—	7	5.50	8.00	10.00	15.00
	—	8	5.50	8.00	10.00	15.00
	—	9	5.50	8.00	10.00	15.00
	—	10	5.50	8.00	10.00	15.00
	—	11	5.50	8.00	10.00	15.00
	—	12	5.50	8.00	10.00	15.00
	—	13	5.50	8.00	10.00	15.00
	—	14	5.50	8.00	10.00	15.00
	—	15	5.50	8.00	10.00	15.00
	—	16	5.50	8.00	10.00	15.00
	—	17	5.50	8.00	10.00	15.00
	—	18	5.50	8.00	10.00	15.00
	—	19	5.50	8.00	10.00	15.00
	—	20	5.50	8.00	10.00	15.00
	—	21	5.50	8.00	10.00	15.00
	—	22	5.50	8.00	10.00	15.00
	—	24	5.50	8.00	10.00	15.00
	—	25	5.50	8.00	10.00	15.00
	—	26	5.50	8.00	10.00	15.00
	—	28	5.50	8.00	10.00	15.00
	—	29	5.50	8.00	10.00	15.00
	—	31	5.50	8.00	10.00	15.00
	—	32	5.50	8.00	10.00	15.00
	—	34	5.50	8.00	10.00	15.00
	—	35	5.50	8.00	10.00	15.00
	—	37	5.50	8.00	10.00	15.00
	—	38	5.50	8.00	10.00	15.00
	—	39	5.50	8.00	10.00	15.00
	—	40	5.50	8.00	10.00	15.00
	—	41	5.50	8.00	10.00	15.00
	—	43	5.50	8.00	10.00	15.00
	—	44	5.50	8.00	10.00	15.00

10th Anniversary of Reign of Umed Singh II and 80th Birthday of Queen Victoria
Rev: Full year.

Y#	Date	Year	VG	Fine	VF	XF
7	VS1956	(1899)	17.50	25.00	35.00	50.00

NAZARANA RUPEE

SILVER, 11.20 g

Y#	Date	Year	VG	Fine	VF	XF
6a	AH—	1	32.50	45.00	62.50	85.00
	—	2	32.50	45.00	62.50	85.00
	—	3	32.50	45.00	62.50	85.00
	—	4	32.50	45.00	62.50	85.00
	—	5	32.50	45.00	62.50	85.00
	—	6	32.50	45.00	62.50	85.00
	—	7	32.50	45.00	62.50	85.00
	—	8	32.50	45.00	62.50	85.00
	—	9	32.50	45.00	62.50	85.00
	—	10	32.50	45.00	62.50	85.00
	—	11	32.50	45.00	62.50	85.00
	—	12	32.50	45.00	62.50	85.00
	—	13	32.50	45.00	62.50	85.00
	—	14	32.50	45.00	62.50	85.00
	—	15	32.50	45.00	62.50	85.00
	—	16	32.50	45.00	62.50	85.00
	—	17	32.50	45.00	62.50	85.00
	—	18	32.50	45.00	62.50	85.00
	—	19	32.50	45.00	62.50	85.00
	—	20	32.50	45.00	62.50	85.00
	—	21	32.50	45.00	62.50	85.00
	—	22	32.50	45.00	62.50	85.00

Y#	Date	Year	VG	Fine	VF	XF
6a	—	23	32.50	45.00	62.50	85.00
	—	24	32.50	45.00	62.50	85.00
	—	25	32.50	45.00	62.50	85.00
	—	26	32.50	45.00	62.50	85.00
	—	27	32.50	45.00	62.50	85.00
	—	28	32.50	45.00	62.50	85.00
	—	29	32.50	45.00	62.50	85.00
	—	30	32.50	45.00	62.50	85.00
	—	31	32.50	45.00	62.50	85.00
	—	32	32.50	45.00	62.50	85.00
	—	39	32.50	45.00	62.50	85.00
	—	43	32.50	45.00	62.50	85.00
	—	44	32.50	45.00	62.50	85.00
		Square				
6b	AH—	15	—	—	—	—
	—	16	—	—	—	—
7a	VS1956	(1899)	40.00	62.50	85.00	120.00

1/8 MOHUR

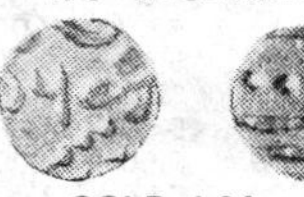

GOLD, 1.34 g

Y#	Date	VG	Fine	VF	XF
A8a	VS(19)56(1899)	185.00	300.00	425.00	600.00

1/2 MOHUR

GOLD, 5.35 g

Y#	Date	Year	VG	Fine	VF	XF
C8	AH—	42	125.00	200.00	300.00	450.00

MOHUR

GOLD, 10.70 g

Y#	Date	Year	VG	Fine	VF	XF
8	AH—	1	175.00	250.00	350.00	500.00
	—	6	175.00	250.00	350.00	500.00
	—	8	175.00	250.00	350.00	500.00
	—	9	175.00	250.00	350.00	500.00
	—	15	175.00	250.00	350.00	500.00
	—	31	175.00	250.00	350.00	500.00
	—	32	175.00	250.00	350.00	500.00
	—	44	175.00	250.00	350.00	500.00

KUTCH

State located in northwest India, consisting of a peninsula north of the Gulf of Kutch.

The rulers of Kutch were Jareja Rajputs who, coming from Tatta in Sind, conquered Kutch in the fourteenth or fifteenth centuries. The capital city of Bhuj is thought to date from the mid-sixteenth century. In 1617, after Akbar's conquest of Gujerat and the fall of the Gujerat sultans, the Kutch ruler, Rao Bharmal I (1586-1632) visited Jahangir and established a relationship which was sufficiently warm as to leave Kutch virtually independent throughout the Mughal period. Early in the nineteenth century internal disorder and the existence of rival claimants to the throne resulted in British intrusion into the state's affairs. Rao Bharmalji II was deposed in favor of Rao Desalji II who proved much more amenable to the Government of India's wishes. He and his successors continued to rule in a manner considered by the British to be most enlightened and, as a result, Maharao Khengarji III was created a Knight Grand Commander of the Indian Empire. In view of its geographical isolation Kutch came under the direct control of the Central Government at India's independence.

First coinage was struck in 1617AD.

RULERS

Rayadhanji II
AH1192-1230/1778-1814AD

राउ श्री रायधणजी

Ra-o Sri Ra-y(a)-dh(a)-n-ji

Bharmalji II
AH1230-1235/1814-1819AD

राउ श्री भारमलजी

Ra-o Sri Bha-r-m(a)-l-ji

Desalji II
AH1235-1277/VS1876-1917/1819-1860AD

राउ श्री देसलजी

Ra-o Sri De-s(a)-l-ji

राउ श्री देशलजी

Ra-o Sri De-sa-l-ji

Pragmalji II
VS1917-1932/1860-1875AD

राउ श्री प्रागमलजी

Ra-o Sri Pra-g-m(a)-l-ji

महाराउ श्री प्रागमलजी

M(a)-ha-ra-o Sri Pra-g-m(a)-l-ji

महाराजाधिराज मिरजा महाराउ श्री

Ma-ha-ra-ja Dhi-ra-j Mi-r-ja M(a)-ha-ra-o Sri

प्रागमलजी बहादुर

Pra-g-m(a)-l-ji B(a)-ha-du-r

Khengarji III
VS1932-1999/1875-1942AD

महाराओ श्री खेंगारजी

M(a)-ha-ra-o Sri Khen-ga-r-ji

महाराउ खेंगारजी

Ma-ha-ra-o Khen-ga-r-ji

महाराजाधिराज मिरजा महाराओ श्री

Ma-ha-ra-ja Dhi-ra-j Mi-r-ja M(a)-ha-ra-o Sri

खेंगारजी बहादुर कछभुज

Khen-ga-r-ji B(a)-ha-du-r K(a)-chh-bhu-j

मिरजा महाराओ श्री खेंगारजी

Mi-r-jan M(a)-ha-ra-o Sri Khen-ga-r-ji

महाराओ श्री खेंगारजी

M(a)-ha-ra-o Sri Khen-ga-r-ji

महाराजाधिराज मिरजा महाराउ

M(a)-ha-ra-ja Dhi-ra-j Mi-r-jan M(a)-ha-ra-o

श्री खेंगारजी बहादुर

Sri-Khen-ga-r-ji B(a)-ha-du-r

श्री खेंगारजी सवाई बहादुर

Sri Khen-ga-r-ji Sa-va-i B(a)-ha-du-r

महाराउ श्री खेंगारजी कछभुज

M(a)-ha-ra-o Sri Khen-ga-r-ji K(a)-chchh-bhu-j

MINT

भुज or بهوج

Bhuj (Devanagari) (Persian)

MONETARY SYSTEM

1/2 Trambiyo = 1 Babukiya
2 Trambiyo = 1 Dokda
3 Trambiyo = 1 Dhinglo
2 Dhinglo = 1 Dhabu
2 Dhabu = 1 Payalo
2 Payalo = 1 Adlinao
2 Adlina = 1 Kori

NOTE: All coins through Bharmalji II bear a common type, derived from the Gujarati coinage of Muzaffar III (late 16th century AD), and bear a stylized form of the date AH978 (1570AD). The silver issues of Bharmalji II also have the fictitious date AH1165. The rulers name appears in the Devanagri script on the obverse.

RAYADHANJI II

AH1192-1230/1778-1814AD

1/2 TRAMBIYO

COPPER, 4.70 g

C#	Date	Good	VG	Fine	VF
24	ND	—	—	—	—

TRAMBIYO

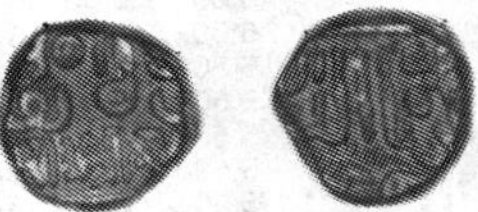

COPPER, 4.10 g

C#	Date	Good	VG	Fine	VF
25	ND	1.50	2.50	3.50	5.50

DOKDA

COPPER, 7.10 g

C#	Date	Good	VG	Fine	VF
26	ND	1.50	2.50	3.50	5.50

DHINGLO

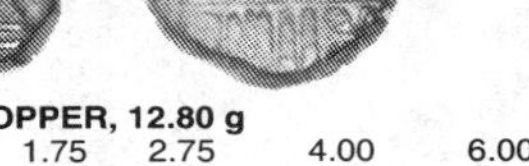

COPPER, 12.80 g

C#	Date	Good	VG	Fine	VF
27	ND	1.75	2.75	4.00	6.00

1/4 KORI

SILVER, 7-8mm, 1.30 g

C#	Date	VG	Fine	VF	XF
28	ND	5.50	8.00	12.50	18.50

1/2 KORI

SILVER, 2.35 g

C#	Date	VG	Fine	VF	XF
29	ND	5.00	7.00	10.00	15.00

KORI

SILVER, 4.50 g

C#	Date	VG	Fine	VF	XF
30	ND	5.00	7.00	10.00	15.00
		Perso-Arabic legends			
30a	ND	—	—	—	—

BHARMALJI II

AH1230-1235/1814-1819AD

TRAMBIYO

COPPER, 4.00 g

C#	Date	Good	VG	Fine	VF
31	ND	2.50	4.00	5.50	8.00

DOKDA

COPPER, 16mm, 7.50 g

C#	Date	Good	VG	Fine	VF
32	ND	2.50	4.00	5.50	8.00

DHINGLO

COPPER, 17mm, 12.50 g

C#	Date	Good	VG	Fine	VF
33	ND	3.00	4.50	6.00	9.00

1/2 KORI

SILVER, 2.10 g

C#	Date	VG	Fine	VF	XF
35.1	AH1165 (fictitious)	3.50	5.00	7.50	12.00

KORI

SILVER, 4.40 g

C#	Date	VG	Fine	VF	XF
36	AH1165 (fictitious)	3.00	4.50	6.50	10.00

DESALJI II

AH1234-1277/VS1875-1917/1818-1860AD

The coins of Desalji II may be divided into four basic series, which may be differentiated as follows:

FIRST SERIES: Similar to coins of Bharmalji, but w/Desalji's name in Devanagari on rev.

SECOND SERIES: In the name of the Mughal Emperor Akbar II and of Desalji in Devanagari on obv., mint and both dates in Persian leg. on rev. but actual SE date in Devanagari numerals. AH date is frozen (12)34, SE dates 1875-1887.

THIRD SERIES: Obv: Persian leg., rev: in Devanagari script Dates: AH1250-1266, VS1892-1904. Many sub-varieties of type, some w/only AH dates, some w/only SE dates, some w/both. In the name of Muhammad Akbar II.

FOURTH SERIES: Same as third series, but in the name of Bahadur II. VS1909-1916 on silver and gold issues and AH1267-1274 on copper.

NOTE: Although Muhammad Akbar II was succeeded by Bahadur II on the Mughal throne in AH1253, the change is not acknowledged on Kutch coinage until AH1263 and Bahadur Shah is honored until VS1916/1859AD, the year after he was deposed by the British following the mutiny.

First Series

TRAMBIYO

COPPER, 3.80-4.20 g

C#	Date	Good	VG	Fine	VF
38	ND	1.00	1.50	2.50	4.50

DOKDA

COPPER, 8.00-8.30 g

C#	Date	Good	VG	Fine	VF
39	ND	1.00	1.50	2.50	4.50

DHINGLO

COPPER, 18mm, 12.00-12.60 g

C#	Date	Good	VG	Fine	VF
40	ND	1.25	2.00	3.00	5.00

Second Series

Obv: Persian leg. w/Devanagari name below. Rev: Persian leg.

In the name of Muhammad Akbar II
AH1221-1253/1806-1837AD

NOTE: The frozen date AH1234 on this series is the accession date of Desalji II.

TRAMBIYO

COPPER, 4.00 g

C#	Date	Year	Good	VG	Fine	VF
41	AH1234	VS1880	2.50	3.50	5.00	7.50

DOKDA

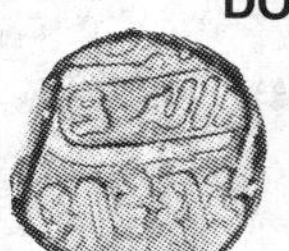

COPPER, 7.90-8.20 g

C#	Date	Year	Good	VG	Fine	VF
42	AH1234	VS1880	2.50	3.50	5.00	7.50

DHINGLO

COPPER, 12.10-12.40 g

C#	Date	Year	Good	VG	Fine	VF
43	AH1234	VS1880	2.75	4.00	5.50	8.00

1/2 KORI

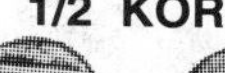

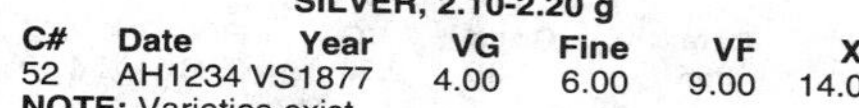

SILVER, 2.10-2.20 g

C#	Date	Year	VG	Fine	VF	XF
52	AH1234	VS1877	4.00	6.00	9.00	14.00

NOTE: Varieties exist.

KORI

SILVER, 4.60-4.70 g

C#	Date	Year	VG	Fine	VF	XF
53	AH1234	VS1875	3.00	4.50	6.50	10.00
	1234	1876	3.00	4.50	6.50	10.00
	1234	1877	3.00	4.50	6.50	10.00
	1234	1879	3.00	4.50	6.50	10.00
	1234	1880	3.00	4.50	6.50	10.00
	1234	1881	3.00	4.50	6.50	10.00
	1234	1882	3.00	4.50	6.50	10.00
	1234	1884	3.00	4.50	6.50	10.00
	1234	1885	3.00	4.50	6.50	10.00
	1234	1887	3.00	4.50	6.50	10.00

Third Series

Obv: Persian leg. Rev: Devanagari leg. below Persian mintname on copper, date below Devanagari leg. on silver.

In the name of Muhammad Akbar II
AH1221-1253/1806-1837AD

TRAMBIYO

COPPER, 4.10 g

C#	Date	Good	VG	Fine	VF
45	AH—	1.00	1.50	2.50	4.50

DOKDA

COPPER, 8.10 g

C#	Date	Good	VG	Fine	VF
46	AH1259	1.00	1.50	2.50	4.50
	1261	1.00	1.50	2.50	4.50
	1262	1.00	1.50	2.50	4.50

DHINGLO

COPPER, 12.00-12.50 g

C#	Date	Good	VG	Fine	VF
47	AH1255	1.75	3.00	4.00	6.00
	1257	1.25	2.00	3.00	5.00
	1258	1.25	2.00	3.00	5.00
	1259	1.25	2.00	3.00	5.00
	1261	1.25	2.00	3.00	5.00
	1262	1.25	2.00	3.00	5.00
	1263	—	—	—	—
	1266	1.50	2.50	3.50	5.50

1/2 KORI

SILVER, 2.10-2.20 g
Rev: Katar below Devanagari date w/Kutch *9*.

C#	Date	Year	VG	Fine	VF	XF
55	VS1891	(1834)	4.00	6.00	9.00	14.00
	1892	(1835)	3.50	5.00	7.50	12.00

Rev: Katar below date.

C#	Date	Year	VG	Fine	VF	XF
55a	AH1252	VS1893	4.00	6.00	9.00	14.00

Rev: Katar at right of Devanagari date.

C#	Date	Year	VG	Fine	VF	XF
55b	AH1252	VS1894	4.00	6.00	9.00	14.00
	1253	1895	4.00	6.00	9.00	14.00
	1258	1899	4.00	6.00	9.00	14.00
	1259	1900	4.00	6.00	9.00	14.00
	1260	1901	4.00	6.00	9.00	14.00
	1261	1902	4.00	6.00	9.00	14.00

Rev: Katar below Kutch date.

C#	Date	Year	VG	Fine	VF	XF
58	VS1895	(1838)	3.00	4.50	6.50	10.00

Obv: AH date at left in middle leg.

C#	Date	Year	VG	Fine	VF	XF
58a	AH1260	VS1901	3.50	5.00	7.50	12.00
	1263	1904	3.50	5.00	7.50	12.00

KORI

SILVER, 4.40-4.50 g
Rev: Katar below Devanagari date w/Kutch *9*.

C#	Date	Year	VG	Fine	VF	XF
56	AH1250	VS1892	4.00	6.00	9.00	14.00
	1251	1892	3.00	4.50	6.50	10.00
	1252	1893	3.00	4.50	6.50	10.00

Rev: Katar at right of Devanagari date.

C#	Date	Year	VG	Fine	VF	XF
56a	AH1252	VS1894	3.50	5.00	7.50	12.00
59	VS1895	(1838)	3.50	5.00	7.50	12.00

Rev: Katar at right of Devanagari date.

C#	Date	Year	VG	Fine	VF	XF
59b	VS1899	(1842)	3.00	4.50	6.50	10.00
	1901	(1844)	3.00	4.50	6.50	10.00
	1902	(1845)	3.00	4.50	6.50	10.00

Obv: AH date at left in middle leg.

C#	Date	Year	VG	Fine	VF	XF
59a	AH1262	VS1903	2.50	3.50	5.00	8.00

Fourth Series

In name of Bahadur Shah II
AH1253-1274/1837-1858AD

TRAMBIYO

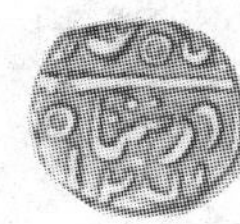

COPPER, 14mm, 3.80-4.20 g

C#	Date	Good	VG	Fine	VF
61	AH1261	2.00	3.50	5.50	8.00
	1263	1.75	2.75	4.00	5.50
	1266	1.75	2.75	4.00	5.50
	ND	1.75	2.75	4.00	5.50

C#	Date	Good	VG	Fine	VF
61a	AH1267	1.00	1.50	2.00	3.50
	1269	1.00	1.50	2.00	3.50
	1274	1.00	1.50	2.00	3.50

DOKDO

COPPER, 17-19mm, 8.10 g

C#	Date	Good	VG	Fine	VF
62	AH1263	1.50	2.50	4.00	5.50
	1266	1.50	2.50	4.00	5.50

C#	Date	Good	VG	Fine	VF
62a	AH1267	1.50	2.50	4.00	5.50
	1269	1.00	1.50	2.00	3.00
	1274	—	Reported, not confirmed		

DHINGLO

COPPER, 18-21mm, 12.00-12.50 g

C#	Date	Good	VG	Fine	VF
63	AH1263	2.50	4.00	5.25	7.00
	1266	2.00	3.50	4.50	6.00

C#	Date	Good	VG	Fine	VF
63a	AH1267	1.25	2.00	2.50	3.50
	1268	1.25	2.00	2.50	3.50
	1269	1.25	2.00	2.50	3.50
	1270	1.50	2.75	3.25	4.50
	1271	1.50	2.75	3.25	4.50
	1272	1.25	2.00	2.50	3.50
	1273	1.50	2.75	3.25	4.50
	1274	1.50	2.75	3.25	4.50

1/2 KORI

SILVER, 2.20 g

C#	Date	Year	VG	Fine	VF	XF
65	VS1909	(1852)	2.50	3.50	5.00	8.00
	1910	(1853)	2.50	3.50	5.00	8.00
	1911	(1854)	3.00	4.50	6.50	10.00
	1912	(1855)	2.50	3.50	5.00	8.00
	1913	(1856)	2.50	3.50	5.00	8.00
	1914	(1857)	2.50	3.50	5.00	8.00

KORI

SILVER, 4.40-4.50 g

C#	Date	Year	VG	Fine	VF	XF
66	VS1909	(1852)	2.50	3.50	5.00	8.00
	1910	(1853)	2.50	3.50	5.00	8.00
	1911	(1854)	3.00	4.50	6.50	10.00
	1912	(1855)	2.50	3.50	5.00	8.00
	1913	(1856)	2.50	3.50	5.00	8.00
	1914	(1857)	2.50	3.50	5.00	8.00
	1915	(1858)	5.00	7.00	10.00	15.00
	1916	(1859)	5.50	8.00	12.50	18.50

25 KORI

.999 GOLD, 4.68 g

C#	Date	Year	Fine	VF	XF	Unc
67	VS1911	(1854)	70.00	100.00	120.00	150.00
	1912	(1855)	70.00	100.00	120.00	150.00
	1913	(1856)	70.00	100.00	120.00	150.00
	1914	(1857)	70.00	100.00	120.00	150.00
	1915	(1858)	70.00	100.00	120.00	150.00

MILLED COINAGE

Regal Issues

PRAGMALJI II

VS1917-1932/1860-1875AD

Pragmalji II is the first ruler of Kutch to pay homage to Queen Victoria. He experimented with a joint formulation his first year, VS1917/1860AD, see the rare coin type Y#A14. In VS1919/1862AD he settled on a standard type acknowledging "Queen Victoria, Mighty Queen" and himself as "Rao" or "Maharao", see types Y#13, 14 and 17.

TRAMBIYO

COPPER, 3.00-3.40 g

Y#	Date	Good	VG	Fine	VF
1	1865	1.25	2.00	3.00	4.50

Rev: 2 characters right of trident.

Y#	Date	Good	VG	Fine	VF
5	1865	.50	.85	1.50	2.50
	1866	1.50	2.50	3.50	5.00

Rev: Trident above leg.

Y#	Date	Good	VG	Fine	VF
5.1	1865	.75	1.25	1.75	2.50
	1866	.50	.85	1.50	2.50
	1867	1.25	2.00	3.00	4.50
	1767 (error)	.50	.85	1.50	2.50
	1868	.50	.85	1.50	2.50

Obv: Persian leg. w/*Victoria* at bottom.

Y#	Date	Year	Good	VG	Fine	VF
9	1869	VS1925	1.00	1.50	2.50	3.75
	1869	1926	1.50	2.50	3.50	4.50

Obv: Persian leg. w/*Victoria* at top.

Y#	Date	Year	Good	VG	Fine	VF
9.1	1869	VS1926	.50	1.00	2.00	3.00
	1873	1930	.50	1.00	2.00	3.00
	1874	1930	.50	1.00	2.00	3.00

DOKDO

COPPER, 6.30-6.60 g

Y#	Date	Good	VG	Fine	VF
6	1865	1.25	2.00	2.50	3.50
	1866	1.00	1.75	2.25	3.00
	1867	.90	1.50	1.75	2.50
	1868	.60	1.00	1.50	2.75
	1869 (retrograde 9)				
		1.50	2.50	3.75	5.00
	1869	1.00	1.75	2.25	3.00

Obv: Persian leg. w/*Victoria* at top.

Y#	Date	Year	Good	VG	Fine	VF
10	1869	VS1925	1.25	2.00	3.00	4.50

Obv: Persian leg. w/*Victoria* at bottom.

Y#	Date	Year	Good	VG	Fine	VF
10.1	1869	VS1925	.60	1.00	1.50	2.50
	1869	1926	1.00	1.50	2.00	3.00
	1869	1927	1.50	2.50	3.50	5.00

Obv: Persian leg. w/*Victoria* right.

Y#	Date	Year	Good	VG	Fine	VF
10.2	1873	VS1930	1.00	1.50	2.00	3.00
	1874	1930	.60	1.00	1.50	2.50

1-1/2 DOKDA

COPPER, 9.00-10.00 g
Obv: Persian leg. w/*Victoria* at top.

Y#	Date	Year	Good	VG	Fine	VF
11	1869	VS1926	.75	1.25	1.75	2.25
	1780	1925	(error)			
			1.75	3.00	3.50	4.25
	1780	1926	(error)			
			.90	1.50	2.00	2.50

Y#	Date	Year	Good	VG	Fine	VF
11	1870	1927	.60	1.00	1.50	2.00
	1870	1928	.60	1.00	1.50	2.00
	1780	1928	(error)			
			.75	1.25	1.75	2.25
	1871	1928	.60	1.00	1.50	2.00
	1872	1928	.75	1.25	1.75	2.25

Obv: Persian leg. w/*Victoria* at right.

Y#	Date	Year	Good	VG	Fine	VF
11.1	1871	VS1928	.90	1.50	2.00	2.50
	1872	1928	.90	1.50	2.00	2.50
	1872	1929	.75	1.25	1.75	2.25
	1873	1929	.60	1.00	1.50	2.25
	1879	1929	(error)			
			.75	1.25	1.75	2.25
	1873	1930	.60	1.00	1.50	2.25
	1783	1930	(error)			
			.75	1.25	1.75	2.50
	1874	1930	.60	1.00	1.50	2.00
	1874	1931	.60	1.00	1.50	2.00
	1875	1931	1.25	2.00	2.75	3.50
	1875	1932	1.00	1.75	2.50	3.50

Obv: Persian leg. on top written differently, w/*Victoria* at right.

Y#	Date	Year	Good	VG	Fine	VF
11.2	1875	VS1932	.75	1.25	1.75	2.25
	1876	1933	.75	1.25	1.75	2.25

Obv: Persian leg. w/*Victoria* at left.

Y#	Date	Year	Good	VG	Fine	VF
11.3	1872	VS1928	1.50	2.50	3.75	5.00
	1872	1929	1.50	2.50	3.75	5.00

3 DOKDA

COPPER, 18.80-19.60 g
Rev: *Sa(m)vat* at upper left, date at right.

Y#	Date	Year	Good	VG	Fine	VF
8	1868	VS1925	2.50	4.00	6.00	8.00

Obv: Similar to Y#8.2.
Rev: *Sa(m)vat* and date at top.

Y#	Date	Year	Good	VG	Fine	VF
8.1	1868	VS1925	2.50	4.00	6.00	8.00

Rev: *Sa(m)vat* at top, date at right.

Y#	Date	Year	Good	VG	Fine	VF
8.2	1868	VS1925	2.50	4.00	6.00	8.00

Y#	Date	Year	Good	VG	Fine	VF
12	1868	VS1925	2.50	4.00	6.00	8.00
	1869	1925	2.00	3.50	5.00	7.50
	1869	1926	2.00	3.50	5.00	7.50

1/2 KORI

2.3500 g, .610 SILVER, .0460 oz ASW

Y#	Date	Year	VG	Fine	VF	XF
13	1862	VS1919	2.50	3.50	5.00	9.00
	1862	1920	2.00	3.00	4.00	8.00
	1863	1920	2.50	3.50	5.00	9.00
	1763	1920	(error)			
			2.50	3.50	5.00	9.00
	1863	1921	2.00	3.00	4.00	8.00

KORI

4.7000 g, .610 SILVER, .0921 oz ASW
Rev: Rosette at end of third line, Katar after date.

Y#	Date	Year	VG	Fine	VF	XF
A14	1860	VS1917	—	—	Rare	—

Y#	Date	Year	VG	Fine	VF	XF
14	1862	VS1918	2.00	3.00	4.00	8.00
	1862	1919	2.50	3.50	5.00	9.00
	1862	1920	2.00	3.00	4.00	8.00
	1863	1920	2.00	3.00	4.00	8.00
	1863	1921	2.00	3.00	4.00	8.00

2-1/2 KORI

6.9350 g, .937 SILVER, .2089 oz ASW

Y#	Date	Year	VG	Fine	VF	XF
15	1875	VS1931	4.00	6.00	9.00	13.50
	1785	1931	5.50	8.00	12.50	18.50
	1875	1932	4.00	6.00	9.00	13.50

5 KORI

13.8700 g, .937 SILVER, .4178 oz ASW

Y#	Date	Year	VG	Fine	VF	XF
16	1863	VS1921	20.00	31.50	42.50	60.00

Obv: Leg. rearranged.

Y#	Date	Year	VG	Fine	VF	XF
16.1	1865	VS1921	8.50	13.50	20.00	28.50
	1865	1922	7.00	11.00	16.50	25.00
	1866	1922	6.50	10.00	15.00	22.50
	1866	1923	6.50	10.00	15.00	22.50
	1870	1927	7.00	11.00	16.50	25.00
	1874	1931	6.00	9.00	13.50	20.00
	1875	1931	6.00	9.00	13.50	20.00
	1875	1932	6.00	9.00	13.50	20.00

25 KORI

4.6750 g, .999 GOLD, .1501 oz AGW

Y#	Date	Year	Fine	VF	XF	Unc
17	1862	VS1919	70.00	100.00	120.00	150.00
	1863	1920	70.00	100.00	120.00	150.00
	1863	1921	70.00	100.00	120.00	150.00

Y#	Date	Year	Fine	VF	XF	Unc
17a	1870	VS1926	70.00	100.00	120.00	150.00
	1870	1927	70.00	100.00	120.00	150.00

50 KORI

9.3500 g, .906 GOLD, .2723 oz AGW

Y#	Date	Year	Fine	VF	XF	Unc
18	1668 (sic - error for 1866)					
		VS1923	130.00	185.00	230.00	275.00
	1866	1923	110.00	150.00	180.00	225.00
	1873	1930	110.00	150.00	180.00	225.00
	1874	1930	110.00	150.00	180.00	225.00
	1874	1931	110.00	150.00	180.00	225.00

100 KORI

18.7000 g, .906 GOLD, .5446 oz AGW

Y#	Date	Year	Fine	VF	XF	Unc
19	1866	VS1922	225.00	285.00	375.00	500.00
	1866	1923	225.00	285.00	375.00	500.00

KHENGARJI III

VS1932-1998/1875-1942AD

First Series

Obv. leg: *Queen Victoria, Mighty Queen.*

DOKDO

COPPER, 8.00 g

Y#	Date	Year	Good	VG	Fine	VF
22	1878	VS1934	10.00	17.50	20.00	25.00
	1878	1935	13.50	22.50	25.00	30.00
	(1)878	1935	15.00	25.00	27.50	32.50

1-1/2 DOKDA

COPPER, 12.00 g

Y#	Date	Year	Good	VG	Fine	VF
23	1876	VS1933	.90	1.50	2.00	2.75
	1877	1933	.90	1.50	2.00	2.75
23	1877	1934	.90	1.50	2.00	2.75
	1877	1922	(error)			
			.90	1.50	2.00	2.75
	1878	1934	.90	1.50	2.00	2.75
	1878	1935	1.25	2.00	2.50	3.25

Obv: Similar to 1 1/2 Dokda, Y#11.

Y#	Date	Year	Good	VG	Fine	VF
23.1	1876	VS1933	1.25	2.00	2.50	3.50

KORI

2.3500 g, .610 SILVER, .0460 oz ASW

Y#	Date	Year	VG	Fine	VF	XF
26	1876	VS1932	50.00	75.00	110.00	150.00
	1876	1933	50.00	75.00	110.00	150.00

5 KORI

13.8700 g, .937 SILVER, .4178 oz ASW

Y#	Date	Year	VG	Fine	VF	XF
28	1876	VS1933	20.00	31.50	42.50	60.00

NOTE: Edge varieties exist.

Second Series

Obv. leg: *Victoria, Empress of India.*

TRAMBIYO

COPPER, 4.00 g

Y#	Date	Year	Good	VG	Fine	VF
30	1881	VS1938	.50	.75	1.00	1.50
	1882	1938	.30	.50	.75	1.25
	1883	1939	.30	.50	.75	1.25
	1883	1940	.50	.75	1.00	1.50

Rev: *Kutch* added below date.

Y#	Date	Year	Good	VG	Fine	VF
30.1	1883	VS1940	.50	.75	1.00	1.50

DOKDO

COPPER, 8.00 g

Y#	Date	Year	Good	VG	Fine	VF
31	1882	VS1938	.50	.75	1.00	1.50
	1882	1939	.90	1.50	2.00	2.50
	1883	1939	.50	.75	1.00	1.50

Rev: *Kutch* added below date.

Y#	Date	Year	Good	VG	Fine	VF
31.1	1883	VS1940	.50	.75	1.00	1.50
	1884	1940	.50	.75	1.00	1.50

Obv: Leg. similar to Y#31.1 but spaced

similar to Y#31.3.

Y#	Date	Year	Good	VG	Fine	VF
31.2	1892	VS1948	2.50	4.00	6.00	9.00

Obv: Urdu leg. *Victoria* written differently.

Y#	Date	Year	Good	VG	Fine	VF
31.3	1899	VS1956	.90	1.50	2.00	3.00

1-1/2 DOKDA

COPPER, 12.00 g

Y#	Date	Year	Good	VG	Fine	VF
32	1882	VS1938	.60	1.00	1.25	1.75
	1882	1939	.60	1.00	1.25	1.75
	1883	1939	.60	1.00	1.25	1.75
	1883	1940	.60	1.00	1.25	1.75

Rev: *Kutch* added below date.

Y#	Date	Year	Good	VG	Fine	VF
32.1	1883	VS1940	.60	1.00	1.25	1.75
	1884	1940	.60	1.00	1.25	1.75
	1884	1941	.60	1.00	1.25	1.75

Finer style

Y#	Date	Year	Good	VG	Fine	VF
32.2	1885	VS1943	.75	1.25	1.50	2.00
	1887	1944	.75	1.25	1.50	2.00
	1888	1944	.75	1.25	1.50	2.00
32.3	1892	VS1948	.75	1.25	1.50	2.00
	1894	1950	.75	1.25	1.50	2.00

Y#	Date	Year	Good	VG	Fine	VF
32.4	1899	VS1955	1.25	2.00	2.50	3.00
	1899	1956	1.25	2.00	2.75	3.50

3 DOKDA

COPPER, 24.00 g

Y#	Date	Year	Good	VG	Fine	VF
33	1883	VS1940	1.25	2.00	2.50	3.25
	1885	1942	.90	1.50	2.00	2.75
	1886	1942	1.35	2.25	3.00	4.25
	1887	1944	.90	1.50	2.00	2.75
	1888	1944	1.25	2.00	2.50	3.25

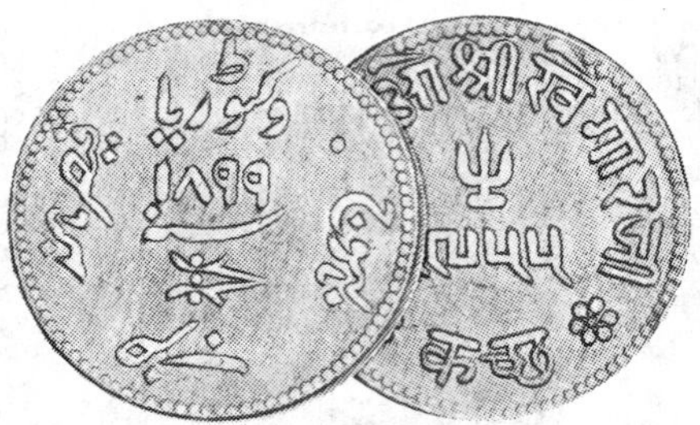

Y#	Date	Year	Good	VG	Fine	VF
33.1	1894	VS1951	1.50	2.50	3.00	3.75
	1899	1955	1.50	2.50	3.00	3.75

1/2 KORI

2.3500 g, .610 SILVER, .0460 oz ASW

Y#	Date	Year	VG	Fine	VF	XF
34	1898	VS1954	2.50	3.50	5.00	8.00
	1899	1955	2.50	3.50	5.00	8.00
	1899	1956	2.50	3.50	5.00	8.00
	1900	1956	2.50	3.50	5.00	8.00
	1900	1957	3.00	4.50	6.50	10.00

KORI

4.7000 g, .610 SILVER, .0921 oz ASW
Rev: Closed crescent.

Y#	Date	Year	VG	Fine	VF	XF
35	1881	VS1938	2.50	3.50	5.00	8.00
	1882	1938	2.50	3.50	5.00	8.00
	1882	1939	2.00	3.00	4.00	7.00
	1883	1939	2.00	3.00	4.00	7.00
	1883	1940	2.00	3.00	4.00	7.00
	1884	1941	2.50	3.50	5.00	8.00
	1885	1941	2.00	3.00	4.00	7.00

Rev: Open crescent.

Y#	Date	Year	VG	Fine	VF	XF
35.1	1894	VS1950	2.50	3.50	5.00	8.00
	1896	1952	2.50	3.50	5.00	8.00
	1897	1953	2.00	3.00	4.00	7.00
	1897	1954	2.00	3.00	4.00	7.00
	1898	1954	2.00	3.00	4.00	7.00
	1898	1955	2.00	3.00	4.00	7.00
	1899	1955	2.00	3.00	4.00	7.00
	1899	1956	2.00	3.00	4.00	7.00
	1900	1956	2.00	3.00	4.00	7.00
	1900	1957	2.00	3.00	4.00	7.00

2-1/2 KORI

6.9350 g, .937 SILVER, .2089 oz ASW
Rev: Closed crescent.

Y#	Date	Year	VG	Fine	VF	XF
36	1881	VS1938	5.00	7.00	10.00	15.00
	1882	1938	4.00	6.00	9.00	13.50

Rev: Open crescent.

Y#	Date	Year	VG	Fine	VF	XF
36.1	1894	VS1951	4.00	6.00	9.00	13.50
	1895	1951	3.50	5.00	7.00	12.00
	1897	1953	3.50	5.00	7.00	12.00
	1897	1954	3.50	5.00	7.00	12.00
	1898	1954	4.00	6.00	9.00	13.50
	1898	1955	4.00	6.00	9.00	13.50
	1899	1955	4.00	6.00	9.00	13.50

Y#	Date	Year	VG	Fine	VF	XF
36.2	1899	VS1955	4.00	6.00	9.00	13.50
	1899	1956	3.50	5.00	7.50	12.00

5 KORI

13.8700 g, .937 SILVER, .4178 oz ASW
Obv: Leaves of wreath point counter-clockwise.
Rev: W/o bars.

Y#	Date	Year	VG	Fine	VF	XF
37	1881	VS1937	6.50	10.00	15.00	22.50
	1881	1938	6.50	10.00	15.00	22.50

Obv: Similar to Y#37. Rev: Similar to Y#37.1.

Y#	Date	Year	VG	Fine	VF	XF
37.7	1881	VS1938	7.50	12.00	20.00	30.00

Obv: Leaves of wreath point clockwise.
Rev: W/o bars.

Y#	Date	Year	VG	Fine	VF	XF
37.1	1881	VS1937	6.50	10.00	15.00	22.50
	1881	1938	6.50	10.00	15.00	22.50

Obv: Similar to Y#37.
Rev: Bars to left and right of center leg.

Y#	Date	Year	VG	Fine	VF	XF
37.2	1880	VS1937	7.00	11.00	16.50	25.00
	1881	VS1937	6.50	10.00	15.00	22.50

Obv: Similar to Y#37.1. Rev: Similar to Y#37.2.

Y#	Date	Year	VG	Fine	VF	XF
37.3	1880	VS1937	6.50	10.00	15.00	22.50

Obv: Changed wreath. Rev: Closed crescent.

Y#	Date	Year	VG	Fine	VF	XF
37.4	1881	VS1938	6.50	10.00	15.00	22.50
	1882	1938	6.50	10.00	15.00	22.50
	1882	1939	6.50	10.00	15.00	22.50
	1883	1939	6.50	10.00	15.00	22.50

Y#	Date	Year	VG	Fine	VF	XF
37.4	1883	1940	6.50	10.00	15.00	22.50
	1884	1939	(error)			
			—	—	—	—
	1884	1940	6.50	10.00	15.00	22.50
	1884	1941	6.50	10.00	15.00	22.50
	1885	1941	6.50	10.00	15.00	22.50
	1885	1942	15.00	21.50	30.00	40.00
	1886	1943	15.00	21.50	30.00	40.00

Rev: Open crescent.

Y#	Date	Year	VG	Fine	VF	XF
37.5	1890	VS1947	13.50	20.00	27.50	37.50
	1893	1950	10.00	15.00	21.50	30.00
	1894	1950	6.50	10.00	15.00	22.50
	1894	1951	6.50	10.00	15.00	22.50
	1895	1951	6.50	10.00	15.00	22.50
	1895	1952	6.50	10.00	15.00	22.50
	1896	1952	6.50	10.00	15.00	22.50
	1896	1953	6.50	10.00	15.00	22.50
	1896	1954	(error)			
			13.50	20.00	27.50	37.50
	1897	1951	(error)			
			7.00	11.00	16.50	25.00
	1897	1953	6.50	10.00	15.00	22.50
	1897	1954	6.50	10.00	15.00	22.50
	1898	1951	(error)			
			12.50	18.50	25.00	35.00
	1898	1953	6.50	10.00	15.00	22.50
	1898	1954	6.50	10.00	15.00	22.50
	1898	1955	6.50	10.00	15.00	22.50
	1899	1955	7.00	11.00	16.50	25.00

Y#	Date	Year	VG	Fine	VF	XF
37.6	1899	VS1955	6.50	10.00	15.00	22.50
	1899	1956	6.50	10.00	15.00	22.50

LADAKH

Ladakh, a district in northern India, contained the western Himalayas and the valley of the upper Indus river. Area: 45,762 sq. mi. Capital: Leh.

In 1639, the Moghuls marched on Ladakh and defeated them near Karpu. The King Sen-ge-rnam-rgyal promised to pay tribute, if allowed to return home, but never did. In 1665, the Moghul governor of Kashmir demanded the acceptance of Moghul suzerainty under threat of invasion. Knowing the strength of Aurangzeb, King Deb-Idan-rnamrgyal sent a tribute of gold ashraphis, rupees and other precious objects. It is probable that coins were struck for this occasion in the name of Aurangzeb but no such coins have yet been discovered.

For the next century no further mention is made of coins until in 1781 it is recorded that a Muslim goldsmith from Leh was hired to strike Ladakhi coins called ja'u.

The obverse of the first Ladakhi timashas or ja'u is a close copy of the Farrukhsiyar inscription of the early Garhwali timashas even including the regnal year at the bottom. The reverse has a clearly written Zarb Tibet at the bottom and dots at the top. At the center are crescents and an illegible inscription.

On some of the early Ladakh coins Hejira dates appear which coincide with the period when the Garhwal mint was closed and trade was diverted from Garhwal to Ladakh. No other Ladakh coins of this first issue have been discovered with a literate date. Between 1781 and 1803 it is likely that a considerable number of ja'u were struck. Most specimens were of good silver but later issues were very debased because of the scarcity of silver.

The next type of coin has a different obverse with the Muslim title of the King of Ladakh clearly inscribed as well as the number 14 at the lower left. This issue may have been prompted to demonstrate Ladakhi independence and is the only ja'u to bear a date.

The most remarkable of all Ladakhi coins has a fully legible inscription on the obverse in smaller writing and is enclosed in a circle with no regnal year. The reverse legend refers to the prime minister as well as the title of the king and is the only Ladakhi coin to do so and is very rare.

The appearance of Mahmud Shah on the obverse of the next type coin is thought to acknowledge suzerainty of the ruler of Kashmir. There is a plain circle surrounded by a a border of dots. The reverse reverts to the earlier designs but has a finer style with thicker writing.

The next change in type took place after the conquest of Ladakh by Gulab Singh and the Dogra army in 1835. After a crushing defeat of the Dogra army in Tibet, the Ladakhis tried to shake off the Dogra supremacy but the rebellion was crushed. Ladakh was now firmly incorporated within the Empire of Jammu and the monarchy was abolished. Until 1845, Gulab Singh acknowledged Sikh suzerainty but ruled Ladakh as a part of Jammu.

After the defeat of the Sikhs by the British, Gulab Singh offered to pay the war indemnities to the British in exchange for being made independent ruler of Jammu and Kashmir.

Two types of ja'u were struck during the period of the Dogra domination. One combined the tiger knife and Mahmud Shah design and the other the tiger knife and Raja Gulab Singh in Nagari script.

Between 1867 and 1870 an issue of copper coins was made for Ladakh for local use and in 1871 a small issue of ja'u was made. Neither of these coins seemed to have much commercial impact in Ladakh and their issue was suspended after 1871. No special currency was struck in or for Ladakh after this.

RULERS

Tshe Pal Namgyal,
1802-1830AD
Tshe Wan Rabtan Namgyal,
1830-1837AD
Tshe Pal Namgyal, restored,
1839-1840AD
Kunda Namgyal,
1840-1842AD

JA'U

1815AD

SILVER
Obv: Square around *Siyar* of Furrukhsiyar.

KM#	Date	Year	Good	VG	Fine	VF
2	ND	—	6.00	10.00	17.50	25.00

1815-1816AD

In the name of Mahmud Khan

Obv. leg: *Aqibat Mahmud Khan.*

KM#	Date	Year	Good	VG	Fine	VF
3	ND	—	8.50	15.00	25.00	35.00

Obv. leg: *Aqibat Mahmud Khan* within circle.
Rev. leg: *Qalon Seban Tondub, Tibet.*

KM#	Date	Year	Good	VG	Fine	VF
4	ND	—	50.00	75.00	100.00	150.00

1816-1842AD

In the name of Mahmud Shah

Obv. and rev: Plain border.
Obv. leg: *Mahmud Shah.*

KM#	Date	Year	Good	VG	Fine	VF
5.1	ND	—	10.00	14.00	18.50	25.00

Obv. and rev: Dotted border.

KM#	Date	Year	Good	VG	Fine	VF
5.2	ND	—	10.00	14.00	18.50	25.00

Obv: Dotted border. Rev: Plain border.

KM#	Date	Year	Good	VG	Fine	VF
5.3	ND	—	10.00	14.00	18.50	25.00

KM#	Date	Year	Good	VG	Fine	VF
5.4	ND	—	10.00	14.00	18.50	25.00

Obv: Retrograde.

KM#	Date	Year	Good	VG	Fine	VF
5.5	ND	—	10.00	14.00	18.50	25.00

KM#	Date	Year	Good	VG	Fine	VF
5.6	ND	—	10.00	14.00	18.50	25.00

1841AD

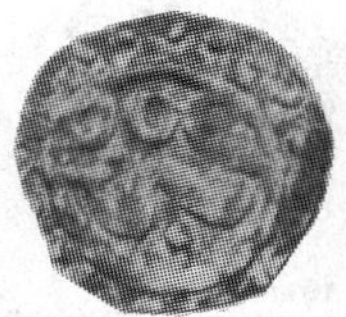

Obv. leg: *Mahmud Shah* within circle, dotted border. Rev: Katar pointing right, *Zarb Butan* above and below.

KM#	Date	Year	Good	VG	Fine	VF
6	ND	—	10.00	14.00	18.50	25.00

1842-1850AD

In the name of Gulab Singh

Obv. leg: *Raja Gulab Singh* in Nagari in 3 lines.

KM#	Date	Year	Good	VG	Fine	VF
7.1 (Y1)	ND	—	6.00	10.00	12.50	15.00

Rev: Dot on blade of Katar.

KM#	Date	Year	Good	VG	Fine	VF
7.2 (Y1)	ND	—	6.00	10.00	12.50	15.00

Rev: Figure 8 on its side on blade of Katar.

KM#	Date	Year	Good	VG	Fine	VF
7.3	ND	—	6.00	10.00	12.50	15.00

Obv. leg: Error, *Raja Galab Bing*.
Rev: Figure 8 on its side on blade of Katar.

KM#	Date	Year	Good	VG	Fine	VF
7.4	ND	—	6.00	10.00	12.50	15.00

Rev: Legend blundered.

KM#	Date	Year	Good	VG	Fine	VF
7.5	ND	—	6.00	10.00	12.50	15.00

1871AD

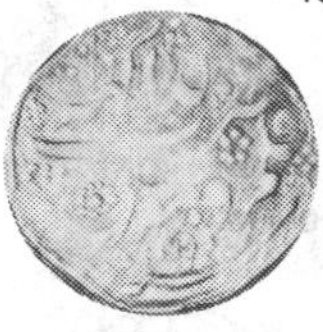

Obv. leg: *1928 Jam-bu'i Par* in Tibetan script.
Rev. leg: *Zarb Ladakh, Qilimrao Jamun, Sanah 1928* in Arabic script.

KM#	Date	Year	Good	VG	Fine	VF
8	ND	—	15.00	25.00	32.50	40.00

UNDER DOGRA RULE

After 1834AD

PAISA

COPPER, 19mm

KM#	Date	Year	Good	VG	Fine	VF
9	VS1923	(1866)	4.00	6.00	9.00	12.00
	1924	(1867)	2.50	4.00	6.50	10.00
	1925	(1868)	2.50	4.00	6.50	10.00
	1926	(1869)	2.50	4.00	6.50	10.00
	1927	(1870)	2.50	4.00	6.50	10.00

LUNAVADA

This small state in the Panch Mahal district of western India was ruled by Solanki Rajputs who claimed descent from Sidraj Jaisingh, the ruler of Anhalwara Patan and Gujerat. The rulers, or maharanas, traced their sovereignty to the early decades of the fifteenth century. At different times the State was feudatory to either Baroda or Sindhia.

WAKHAT SINGHJI

VS1924-1986/1867-1929AD

1/2 PAISA

NOTE: Struck with paisa dies, either on small planchets, or paisas cut in half.

COPPER, rectangular or round, 3.50-4.00 g
Obv: Open hand.
Rev. leg: Mughal style Persian.

KM#	Date	Year	Good	VG	Fine	VF
2.1	ND	—	2.75	4.50	6.00	9.00

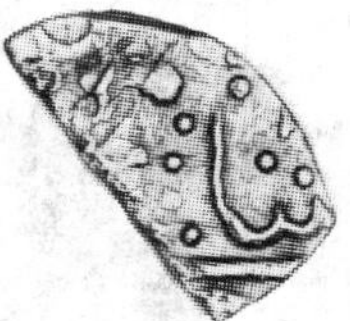

Obv: Crescent left and star right of hand.

KM#	Date	Year	Good	VG	Fine	VF
2.2	ND	—	3.00	6.00	8.50	12.50

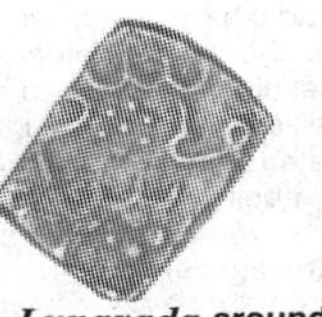

Obv: Open hand in square, *Lunavada* around clockwise. Rev: Date & Devanagari leg.

KM#	Date	Year	Good	VG	Fine	VF
3	VS1942	(1885)	3.00	5.00	7.50	10.00

Obv: Lion right *Lunavada* and date.
Rev: Devanagari leg. w/ruler's name.

KM#	Date	Year	Good	VG	Fine	VF
4	VS1949	(1892)	2.75	4.50	6.00	9.00

PAISA

COPPER, round or rectangular, 6.50-8.30 g
Obv: Two sabres.

KM#	Date	Year	Good	VG	Fine	VF
5	ND	—	3.50	6.00	8.50	12.50

Obv: Cannon barrel.

KM#	Date	Year	Good	VG	Fine	VF
6	ND	—	3.50	6.00	8.50	12.50

Obv: Open hand in square, on square planchet.

KM#	Date	Year	Good	VG	Fine	VF
9.1	VS1942	(1885)	2.50	4.00	5.50	8.50
	1249 (error)	(1885)	2.50	4.00	5.50	8.50

Similar to KM9.1 but round planchet.

KM#	Date	Year	Good	VG	Fine	VF
9.2	VS1942	(1885)	2.50	4.00	5.50	8.50

Obv: Lion, *Lunavada* and date.

KM#	Date	Year	Good	VG	Fine	VF
10	VS1949	(1892)	2.50	4.00	5.50	8.50

NOTE: Coins of Lunavada are frequently found overstruck over earlier types, and over other coins of Rampur.

MAKRAI

The rajas of Makrai belong to a very ancient Gond family whose title, Raja Hatiyarai, had been conferred upon them by the emperors of Delhi. This small state of some forty-five villages struggled with varying degrees of success against the Poona Peshwa, Sindhia and the Pindaris before passing under British protection in the nineteenth century.

RULER

Raja Bharat Shah,
1886-1920AD

PAISA

COPPER, 9-11 g
Obv: Katar. Rev: Hindi legend *Shri/Mak/Rai*

KM#	Date	Year	Good	VG	Fine	VF
1	ND	—	2.50	4.00	6.00	9.00

Square planchet.

KM#	Date	Year	Good	VG	Fine	VF
2	ND	—	—	—	—	—

MARATHA CONFEDERACY

Refer to Independent Kingdoms during British rule.

MEWAR

State located in Rajputana, northwest India. Capital: Udaipur.

The rulers of Mewar were universally regarded as the highest ranking Rajput house in India. The maharana of Mewar was looked upon as the representative of Rama, the ancient king of Ayodhya - and the family who were Sesodia Rajputs of the Gehlot clan, traced its descent through Rama to Kanak Sen who ruled in the second century. The clan is believed to have migrated to Chitor from Gujarat sometime in the eighth century.

None of the indigenous rulers of India resisted the Muslim invasions into India with greater tenacity than the Rajputs of Mewar. It was their proud boast that they had never permitted a daughter to go into the Mughal harem. Three times the fortress and town of Chitor had fallen to Muslim invaders, to Alauddin Khilji (1303), to Bahadur Shah of Gujarat (1534) and to Akbar (1568). Each time Chitor gradually recovered but the last was the most traumatic experience of all. Rather than to submit to the Mughal onslaught, the women burned themselves on funeral pyres in a fearful rite called jauhar, and the men fell on the swords of the invaders.

After the sacking of Chitor the rana, Udai Singh, retired to the Aravali hills where he founded Udaipur, the capital after 1570. Udai Singh's son, Partab, refused to submit to the Mughal and recovered most of the territory lost in 1568. In the early nineteenth century Mewar suffered much at the hands of Marathas - Holkar, Sindhia and the Pindaris - until, in 1818, the State came under British supervision. In April 1948 Mewar was merged into Rajasthan and the maharana became governor Maharajpramukh of the new province.

RULERS

Bhim Singh,
AH1192-1244/1777-1828AD
Jawan Singh,
AH1244-1254/1828-1838AD
Sirdar Singh,
AH1254-1258/1838-1842AD
Swarup Singh,
AH1258-1278/1842-1861AD
Shambhu Singh,
AH1278-1291/1861-1874AD
Sajjan Singh,
AH1291-1302/1874-1884AD
Fatteh Singh,
VS1941-1986/1884-1929AD

MINTS

Bhilwara بھیلوارا

Chitor चितोड़

Chitarkot चित्रकूट

Udaipur उदयपुर

NOTE: All Mewar coinage is struck without ruler's name, and is largely undated. Certain types were generally struck over several reigns.

BHILWARA MINT

Bhilwari Series

In the name of Alamgir II
AH1167-1173/1754-1759AD

Struck at Bhilwara Mint between ca. 1760 to the middle of the 19th century w/fictitious mint epithet: *Dar al-Khilafat Shahjahanabad*.

Mint mark:

jhar

RUPEE

SILVER, 10.70-11.10 g

C#	Date	Year	VG	Fine	VF	XF
38	ND	1	10.00	20.00	30.00	45.00
		2	10.00	20.00	30.00	45.00
		3	10.00	20.00	30.00	45.00
		4	10.00	20.00	30.00	45.00
		5	10.00	20.00	30.00	45.00
		6	10.00	20.00	30.00	45.00
		7	10.00	20.00	30.00	45.00
		8	10.00	20.00	30.00	45.00

CHITOR MINT

Chitori Series

In the name of Alamgir II AH1167-1173/1754-1759AD

Struck at Chitor Mint between ca. 1760 to the middle of the 19th century w/fictitious mint epithet: *Dar al-Khilafat Shahjahanabad.*

Mint marks: 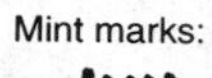  and flag  on obverse.

1/16 RUPEE

C#	Date	Year	VG	Fine	VF	XF
		SILVER, 0.70 g				
22	ND	—	3.50	9.00	12.50	18.50

1/8 RUPEE

C#	Date	Year	VG	Fine	VF	XF
		SILVER, 1.30 g				
23	ND	—	3.50	7.00	10.00	15.00

1/4 RUPEE

C#	Date	Year	VG	Fine	VF	XF
		SILVER, 2.60-2.70 g				
24	ND	—	3.00	6.00	9.00	14.00

1/2 RUPEE

C#	Date	Year	VG	Fine	VF	XF
		SILVER, 5.30-5.40 g				
25	ND	—	2.50	5.00	7.50	12.00

RUPEE

C#	Date	Year	VG	Fine	VF	XF
		SILVER, 10.70-11.10 g				
26	AH1180	—	10.00	20.00	30.00	45.00
	ND	—	3.50	7.00	10.00	15.00

UDAIPUR MINT

Udaipuri Series

In the name of Alamgir II AH1167-1173/1754-1759AD

Struck at the Udaipur mint between ca. 1780 to the middle of the 19th century w/fictitious mint epithet: *Dar al-Khilafat Shahjahanabad.*

Mint mark:

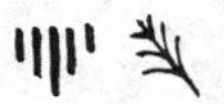  and  on obverse.

PAISA

C#	Date	Year	VG	Fine	VF	XF
		COPPER, 10.00-10.20 g				
27	ND	—	—	—	—	—

1/4 RUPEE

C#	Date	Year	VG	Fine	VF	XF
		SILVER, 2.70 g				
30	ND	—	3.50	7.00	10.00	15.00

1/2 RUPEE

C#	Date	Year	VG	Fine	VF	XF
		SILVER, 5.40 g				
31	ND	—	3.50	7.00	10.00	15.00

RUPEE

C#	Date	Year	VG	Fine	VF	XF
		SILVER, 11.80 g				
32	ND	—	4.00	8.00	12.50	18.50

Chandori Series

Ordered by Bhim Singh, and struck at the Udaipur Mint until 1842AD. Recalled by Swarup Shah.

Mint mark: 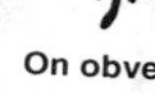

On obverse

On reverse

1/2 RUPEE

C#	Date	Year	VG	Fine	VF	XF
		SILVER, 5.35-5.80 g				
43	ND	—	7.00	11.00	16.50	25.00

RUPEE

C#	Date	Year	VG	Fine	VF	XF
		SILVER, 10.90-11.00 g				
44	ND	—	7.00	11.00	16.50	25.00

New Chandori Series

Struck at the Udaipur Mint between 1842-1890AD. Many die varieties exist.

Mint mark:

On obverse

1/16 RUPEE

Y#	Date	Year	VG	Fine	VF	XF
		SILVER, 9mm, 0.65 g				
1	ND	—	3.00	4.50	6.50	10.00

1/8 RUPEE

Y#	Date	Year	VG	Fine	VF	XF
		SILVER, 1.35 g				
2	ND	—	2.50	3.50	5.00	8.00

1/4 RUPEE

Y#	Date	Year	VG	Fine	VF	XF
		SILVER, 2.70 g				
3	ND	—	2.50	3.50	5.00	8.00

1/2 RUPEE

Y#	Date	Year	VG	Fine	VF	XF
		SILVER, 5.40 g				
4	ND	—	3.00	4.50	6.50	10.00

RUPEE

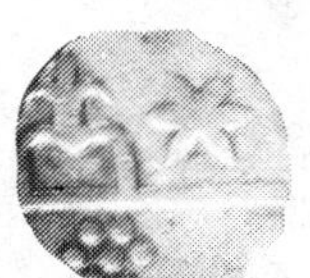 

Y#	Date	Year	VG	Fine	VF	XF
		SILVER, 10.80-10.90 g				
5	ND	—	5.00	7.00	10.00	15.00

MOHUR

Y#	Date	Year	VG	Fine	VF	XF
		GOLD, 7.52 g				
6	ND	—	150.00	185.00	350.00	325.00

Swarupshahi Series

Leg: *Dosti Landhan* "Friendship with London".

Struck at the Udaipur Mint between ca.1858-1920AD. Many die varieties exist.

1/16 RUPEE

Y#	Date	Year	VG	Fine	VF	XF
		SILVER, round, 0.65 g				
7.1	ND	—	2.50	3.50	5.00	8.00

Y#	Date	Year	VG	Fine	VF	XF
		Irregular shape, 8-10mm.				
7.2	ND	—	3.00	4.50	6.50	10.00

1/8 RUPEE

Y#	Date	Year	VG	Fine	VF	XF
		SILVER, 11-12mm, 1.30 g				
8	ND	—	3.00	4.50	6.50	10.00

1/4 RUPEE

Y#	Date	Year	VG	Fine	VF	XF
		SILVER, 2.60 g				
9	ND	—	2.50	3.50	5.00	8.00

1/2 RUPEE

Y#	Date	Year	VG	Fine	VF	XF
		SILVER, 5.20-5.40 g				
10	ND	—	3.00	4.50	6.50	10.00

RUPEE

Y#	Date	Year	VG	Fine	VF	XF
		SILVER, 10.75-10.85 g				
11	ND	—	4.00	6.00	9.00	14.00

1/4 MOHUR

Y#	Date	Year	VG	Fine	VF	XF
		GOLD, 2.70-2.75 g				
A12	ND	—	55.00	60.00	75.00	100.00

1/2 MOHUR

Y#	Date	Year	VG	Fine	VF	XF
		GOLD				
C12	ND	—	—	—	—	—

MOHUR

GOLD, 10.95 g

Y#	Date	Year	VG	Fine	VF	XF
12	ND	—	160.00	185.00	225.00	300.00

LOCAL ISSUES

Bhilwara

In the name of Shah Alam II

AH1173-1221/1759-1806AD

Symbol:

On obverse

PAISA

COPPER

Obv: Symbol vertical.

C#	Date	Year	Good	VG	Fine	VF
2.5	ND	4	3.00	5.00	7.00	9.00

NOTE: Known as the old Bhilwari Paisa, struck between 1780 and 1800AD.

Obv: Symbol oblique.

C#	Date	Year	Good	VG	Fine	VF
3	ND	5	1.50	2.50	3.50	5.00
	ND	12	1.50	2.50	3.50	5.00

NOTE: Known as the new Bhilwari Paisa, struck between about 1795 and 1845.

Chitor

2 PIES (?)

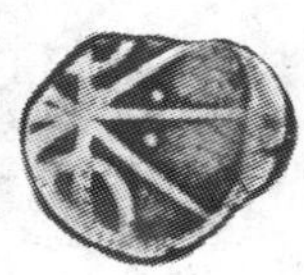

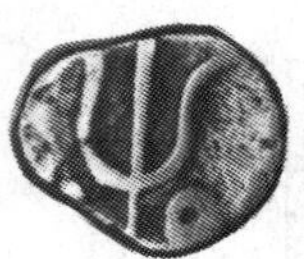

COPPER

C#	Date	Year	Good	VG	Fine	VF
2.1	ND	—	.45	.75	1.25	1.75

C#	Date	Year	Good	VG	Fine	VF
2.2	ND	—	.60	1.00	1.40	2.00

NOTE: Struck by local coppersmiths.

Jawad

Early 19th century.

PAISA

COPPER

C#	Date	Year	Good	VG	Fine	VF
4	ND	—	3.50	6.00	7.50	10.00

NOTE: For later issues, see Gwalior.

Umarda

1/2 PAISA

COPPER

Y#	Date	Year	Good	VG	Fine	VF
23	ND	6	.45	.75	1.00	1.50

NOTE: Varieties exist.

FEUDATORY STATES

Bhinda

ZURAWAR SINGH

AH1214-1243/1799-1827AD

PAISA

COPPER

C#	Date	Year	Good	VG	Fine	VF
1	ND	—	3.00	5.00	7.50	12.50

Salumba

2 PIES

COPPER

C#	Date	Year	Good	VG	Fine	VF
1	ND(1815-34)	—	3.00	5.00	7.00	12.00
	ND(1835-70)	—	3.00	5.00	7.00	12.00

Shahpura

RULERS

Jagat Singh,
AH1261-1270/1845-1853AD
Lachman Singh,
AH1270-1287/1853-1870AD
Nahat Singh,
AH1287-1351/1870-1932AD

PAISA

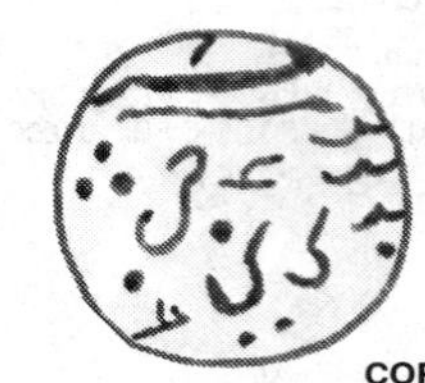

COPPER

C#	Date	Year	Good	VG	Fine	VF
10	ND(1827-70)	—	20.00	30.00	45.00	60.00

In the name of Alamgir II

AH1167-1173/1754-1759AD

Copy of his Dehli coin with Yr. 12 as a frozen fictitious year. Distinguished by the addition of a small trisul to lower obv. and is extremely rare.

1/4 RUPEE

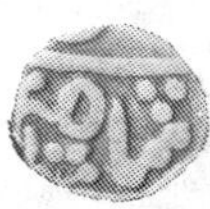

SILVER, 14mm, 2.60 g

C#	Date	Year	VG	Fine	VF	XF
20	AHxxx8	12	7.00	10.00	16.50	25.00

1/2 RUPEE

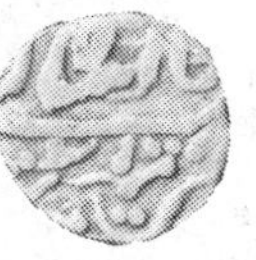

SILVER, 17mm, 5.31 g

C#	Date	Year	VG	Fine	VF	XF
21	AHxxx8	12	10.00	15.00	21.50	30.00

RUPEE

SILVER, 10.60 g

C#	Date	Year	VG	Fine	VF	XF
22	AHxxx8	12	12.50	18.50	25.00	35.00

MOHUR

GOLD, 18mm, 10.30-10.50 g

C#	Date	Year	VG	Fine	VF	XF
29	AHxxx8	12	180.00	225.00	275.00	325.00

MYSORE

Large state in Southern India. Governed until 1761AD by various Hindu dynasties, then by Haider Ali and Tipu Sultan.

In 1831, Krishnaraja being deposed for mal-administration and pensioned off, the administration of Mysore State then came directly under the British. The coinage of Mysoree ceased in 1843. After thee Great Revolt of 1857, the policy of eliminating Indian princes was discontinued and as a result, Mysore was returned in 1881 to the control of an adopted son of Krishnaraja Wodeyar. The Wodeyars continued to hold the State until 1947 although they did not issue coins. In November 1956 modern Mysore was inaugurated as a linguistic state within the Indian Union.

NOTE: For earlier issues see Mysore, Independent Kingdoms under British rule.

RULERS

Dewan Purnaiya, regent,
AH1214-1225/1799-1810AD
Krishna Raja Wodeyar,
AH1225-1285/1810-1868AD

MINTS

Mysore

Nagar

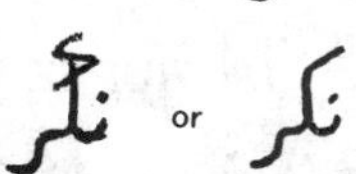

MONETARY SYSTEM

2 Fanams = 1 Anna
4 Annas = 1 Pavali
4 Pavalis = 1 Rupee

MYSORE MINT

Anonymous Issues

1/6 PAVALI

SILVER, 0.45-0.48 g

C#	Date	VG	Fine	VF	XF
199	ND	5.50	11.00	18.00	25.00

1/3 PAVALI

SILVER, 0.89-0.96 g

Obv: Dancing figure (Chamundi).

C#	Date	Year	VG	Fine	VF	XF
200	ND	—	12.50	25.00	42.00	70.00

2/3 PAVALI

SILVER, 1.78-1.92 g

Obv: Dancing figure (Chamundi).

C#	Date	Year	VG	Fine	VF	XF
201	ND	—	12.50	25.00	42.00	70.00

In the name of Shah Alam II

AH1173-1221/1759-1806AD

1/4 RUPEE (PAVALI)

SILVER, 2.68-2.90 g

Obv: Dancing figure (Chamundi).

C#	Date	Year	VG	Fine	VF	XF
202	AH1220	—	7.50	15.00	25.00	35.00
	1221	—	7.50	15.00	25.00	35.00
	1223	—	7.50	15.00	25.00	35.00
	1226	—	7.50	15.00	25.00	35.00
	1229	—	7.50	15.00	25.00	35.00
	1243	—	7.50	15.00	25.00	35.00
	1244	—	7.50	15.00	25.00	35.00
	1245	—	7.50	15.00	25.00	35.00
	1246	—	7.50	15.00	25.00	35.00
	1247	—	7.50	15.00	25.00	35.00
	1248	—	7.50	15.00	25.00	35.00
	3421	—	7.50	15.00	25.00	35.00
	4421	—	7.50	15.00	25.00	35.00

NOTE: Earlier date (AH1214) exists for this type.

C#	Date	Year	VG	Fine	VF	XF
205	AH1220	44	6.50	13.00	22.00	32.00
	1220	45	6.50	13.00	22.00	32.00
	1221	45	6.50	13.00	22.00	32.00
	—	76	6.50	13.00	22.00	32.00
	—	84	6.50	13.00	22.00	32.00

NOTE: Similar coins were issued by the Arcot Mint of French India.

1/2 RUPEE

SILVER, 5.35-5.80 g

C#	Date	Year	VG	Fine	VF	XF
206	—	35	7.50	15.00	25.00	35.00
	—	39	7.50	15.00	25.00	35.00
	—	76	7.50	15.00	25.00	35.00

RUPEE

SILVER, 10.70-11.60 g

C#	Date	Year	VG	Fine	VF	XF
207	AH1219	44	10.00	20.00	32.50	45.00
	1221	25	10.00	20.00	32.50	45.00
	1221	45	10.00	20.00	32.50	45.00
	1222	46	10.00	20.00	32.50	45.00
	1221	47	10.00	20.00	32.50	45.00
	1221	48	10.00	20.00	32.50	45.00
	1222	64	10.00	20.00	32.50	45.00
	12xx	48	10.00	20.00	32.50	45.00
	1223	64	10.00	20.00	32.50	45.00
	1224	64	10.00	20.00	32.50	45.00
	1224	74	10.00	20.00	32.50	45.00
	1225	74	10.00	20.00	32.50	45.00
	1225	94	10.00	20.00	32.50	45.00
	1226	94	10.00	20.00	32.50	45.00
	1227	95	10.00	20.00	32.50	45.00
	1228	95	10.00	20.00	32.50	45.00
	1229	96	10.00	20.00	32.50	45.00
	1230	97	10.00	20.00	32.50	45.00
	1231	98	10.00	20.00	32.50	45.00
	1232	99	10.00	20.00	32.50	45.00
	1234	98	10.00	20.00	32.50	45.00
	1234	99	10.00	20.00	32.50	45.00
	1235	98	10.00	20.00	32.50	45.00
	1236	98	10.00	20.00	32.50	45.00
	1237	37	10.00	20.00	32.50	45.00
	1238	37	10.00	20.00	32.50	45.00
	1239	3x	10.00	20.00	32.50	45.00
	1240	98	10.00	20.00	32.50	45.00
	1242	37	10.00	20.00	32.50	45.00
	1243	98	10.00	20.00	32.50	45.00
	1247	47	10.00	20.00	32.50	45.00
	1248	48	10.00	20.00	32.50	45.00
	x421	45	10.00	20.00	32.50	45.00
	x421	47	10.00	20.00	32.50	45.00

NOTE: Earlier dates (AH1214-1215) exist for this type.

FANAM

GOLD, 0.33-0.40 g
Narasimha

C#	Date	Year	VG	Fine	VF	XF
212	ND	—	7.50	10.00	13.50	20.00

PAGODA

GOLD, 3.40 g
Shiva and Parvati

C#	Date	Year	VG	Fine	VF	XF
210	ND	—	45.00	60.00	75.00	100.00

NOTE: Fanams and 1/2 Pagodas of this type are recent fabrications.

1/4 MOHUR

GOLD, 2.68-2.85 g
Mughal type

C#	Date	Year	VG	Fine	VF	XF
215	—	45	—	—	Rare	—

DEWAN PURNAIYA

Regent for Krishnaraja Wodeyar
AH1214-1225/1799-1810AD

A Sardula (mythical tiger) is illustrated on all of Dewan Purnaiya's coins.

6-1/4 CASH

COPPER

W/o value, w/*Mysore*.

C#	Date	Good	VG	Fine	VF
185	ND	4.00	6.50	10.00	16.00

W/o value or *Mysore*.

C#	Date	Good	VG	Fine	VF
185a	ND	2.50	4.50	7.00	12.00

Rev: Value in English, w/*Mysore*.

C#	Date	Good	VG	Fine	VF
185b	ND	3.00	5.50	9.00	14.00
	ND(CASH retrograde)	4.00	6.50	10.00	16.00

12-1/2 CASH

COPPER

C#	Date	Good	VG	Fine	VF
186	ND	7.00	12.00	18.00	28.00

25 CASH

COPPER
English leg. often blundered.

C#	Date	Good	VG	Fine	VF
187	ND	3.50	6.00	9.50	15.00

75 CASH

COPPER, 23.59 g

C#	Date	Good	VG	Fine	VF
189	ND(1799-1868)	—	—	—	—

NOTE: Silver coinage of Dewan Purnaiya is identical to that of Krishna Raja Wodeyar and they are all listed together following his copper issues.

KRISHNA RAJA WODEYAR

AH1225-1285/1810-1868AD
British control after 1831

(Types I-IV struck 1811-1833)

***SRI* VARIETIES**

Variety I:   

Variety II:

Type I, ca. 1811

Obv: Elephant left below sun and moon. Rev: 3 line Nagari leg.

6-1/4 CASH

COPPER

C#	Date	Good	VG	Fine	VF
170	ND	5.00	9.00	13.00	20.00

Type II

Obv: Elephant below Kanarese, *Sri* between sun and moon. Rev: 2 lines of Kanarese, denomination in English at the top on the 5 and 10 Cash, at the bottom on the 20 and 40 Cash. The English denomination is often encountered blundered.

5 CASH

COPPER
Obv. leg: *Sri* var. I.

C#	Date	Good	VG	Fine	VF
171	ND	2.00	3.25	5.00	8.50
	ND (X CASH in error)	2.50	4.50	7.00	11.50
	ND yr.2	9.00	16.00	24.00	35.00

10 CASH

COPPER
Obv. leg: *Sri* var. I.

C#	Date	Good	VG	Fine	VF
174	ND	4.50	8.00	12.00	18.00

20 CASH

COPPER
Obv. leg: *Sri* var. I.

C#	Date	VG	Fine	VF	XF
177	ND	1.25	2.25	3.50	5.50

40 CASH

COPPER
Obv. leg: *Sri* var. I.

C#	Date	VG	Fine	VF	XF
180	ND	12.50	20.00	32.50	50.00

Type III

Obv: Elephant below Kanarese, *Sri* between sun and moon. Rev: 3 line Kanarese leg., denomination in English at the bottom. The English denomination is often encountered blundered or retrograde.

5 CASH

COPPER
Obv. leg: *Sri* var. I.

C#	Date	Good	VG	Fine	VF
171a.1	ND	4.00	6.50	10.00	15.00

Obv. leg: *Sri* var. II.

C#	Date	Good	VG	Fine	VF
171a.2	ND	4.00	6.50	10.00	15.00

10 CASH

COPPER
Obv. leg: *Sri* var. II.

C#	Date	Good	VG	Fine	VF
174a	ND	3.00	5.00	8.00	12.50
	ND (X CASH retrograde)	4.00	6.50	10.00	15.00

20 CASH

COPPER
Obv. leg: *Sri* var. II.

C#	Date	Good	VG	Fine	VF
177a	ND	1.00	1.75	2.50	4.00

Type IV

Obv: Elephant below Kanarese leg. *Sri* between sun

and moon/*Chamuni*. Rev: Similar to Type III.

5 CASH

COPPER
Obv. leg: *Sri* var. I.

C#	Date	Good	VG	Fine	VF
171b	ND	2.50	4.00	6.50	10.00

10 CASH

COPPER
Obv. leg: *Sri* var. I.

C#	Date	Good	VG	Fine	VF
174b	ND	4.00	6.50	10.00	15.00

20 CASH

COPPER
Obv. leg: *Sri* var. I.

C#	Date	Good	VG	Fine	VF
177b	ND	3.00	5.00	8.00	12.50

25 CASH

COPPER, 11.20-11.40 g
Obv. leg: *Sri* var. I.

C#	Date	Good	VG	Fine	VF
179	ND	—	—	—	—

Type V

Obv: Sardula (mythical lion) below Kanarese leg. *Sri* between sun and moon/*Chamundi*. Rev. Kanarese leg. *Krishna* in center surrounded by mintname and denomination.

2-1/2 CASH

COPPER

C#	Date	Good	VG	Fine	VF
190.1	1833	4.00	6.00	9.00	13.50

5 CASH

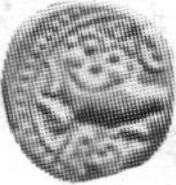

COPPER

C#	Date	Good	VG	Fine	VF
191.1	1833	2.00	3.25	5.00	8.50
	1834	2.00	3.25	5.00	8.50
	1838	2.00	3.25	5.00	8.50

10 CASH

COPPER

C#	Date	Good	VG	Fine	VF
192.1	1833	2.50	4.00	6.50	10.00
	1834/3	2.50	4.00	6.50	10.00
	1834	2.50	4.00	6.50	10.00

20 CASH

COPPER

C#	Date	Good	VG	Fine	VF
193.1	1833	2.00	3.25	5.00	8.50
	1834	2.00	3.25	5.00	8.50
	1835	2.00	3.25	5.00	8.50
	1836	2.00	3.25	5.00	8.50
	1837	2.00	3.25	5.00	8.50
	1838	2.00	3.25	5.00	8.50

NOTE: The 1833 has 2 varieties: W/palm frond before Sardula and w/frond before and above.

Type VI

Obv: Lion, date below. Struck at the Bangalore subsidary mint facility.

2-1/2 CASH

COPPER

C#	Date	Good	VG	Fine	VF
190.2	1834	3.00	5.00	8.00	12.50
	1836	3.00	5.00	8.00	12.50
	1839	2.50	4.00	6.50	10.00
	1840	2.50	4.00	6.50	10.00
	1841	2.50	4.00	6.50	10.00
	1842	2.00	3.25	5.00	8.50
	1843	2.00	3.25	5.00	8.50

5 CASH

COPPER

C#	Date	Good	VG	Fine	VF
191.2	1834	1.75	2.75	4.00	7.00
	1835	1.75	2.75	4.00	7.00
	1836	1.75	2.75	4.00	7.00
	1837	1.75	2.75	4.00	7.00
	1838	1.75	2.75	4.00	7.00
	1839	1.75	2.75	4.00	7.00
	1840	1.75	2.75	4.00	7.00
	1841	1.75	2.75	4.00	7.00
	1842	1.75	2.75	4.00	7.00
	1843	1.75	2.75	4.00	7.00

10 CASH

COPPER

C#	Date	Good	VG	Fine	VF
192.2	1834/3	4.00	6.50	11.00	17.00
	1834	4.00	6.50	10.00	15.00
	1835	3.00	5.00	8.00	12.50
	1836	3.00	5.00	8.00	12.50
	1837	3.00	5.00	8.00	12.50
	1838	3.00	5.00	8.00	12.50
	1839	3.00	5.00	8.00	12.50
	1840	3.00	5.00	8.00	12.50
	1841	3.00	5.00	8.00	12.50
	1842	3.00	5.00	8.00	12.50
	1843	3.00	5.00	8.00	12.50
	1848(sic)	2.00	3.25	5.50	8.50
	1848(sic) rev. leg: MEILLEE XX CASH. . .				
	retrograde	2.00	3.25	5.50	8.50

20 CASH

COPPER

C#	Date	Good	VG	Fine	VF
193.2	1833	3.00	5.00	8.00	12.50
	1834	3.00	5.00	8.00	12.50
	1835	2.50	4.00	6.50	10.00
	1836	2.50	4.00	6.50	10.00
	1837/5	2.00	3.25	5.50	8.50
	1837	2.00	3.25	5.50	8.50
	1838	2.00	3.25	5.50	8.50
	1839	2.00	3.25	5.50	8.50
	1840	2.00	3.25	5.50	8.50

C#	Date	Good	VG	Fine	VF
193.2	1841	2.00	3.25	5.50	8.50
	1843	2.00	3.25	5.50	8.50

NOTE: All dates have MEILEE on rev.; some 1834 have MILAY, and some 1837 have MILEE. Some numerals are distorted.

NAGAR MINT

KRISHNA RAJA WODEYAR

AH1225-1285/1810-1868AD

1/2 RUPEE

SILVER, 5.35-5.80 g

C#	Date	Year	VG	Fine	VF	XF
206a	AH—	74	13.50	22.50	31.50	42.50
	—	84	13.50	22.50	31.50	42.50

RUPEE

SILVER, 10.70-11.60 g

C#	Date	Year	VG	Fine	VF	XF
207a	AH—	46	27.50	45.00	62.50	85.00
	1225	84	27.50	45.00	62.50	85.00

NARWAR

Narwar was a tiny state in western Malwa with a population of about four thousand (ca.1900). The ruling chiefs were Jhala Rajputs. In AH1220/1805AD it came under Gwalior.

For later issues see Gwalior - Narwar Mint listings.

DAULAT RAO

AH1209-1243/1794-1827AD

In the name of Shah Alam II
AH1173-1221/1759-1806AD

Mint marks:

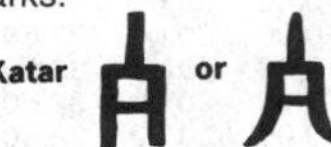

1/2 PAISA

Rev: Vertical katar.

KM#	Date	Year	Good	VG	Fine	VF
22	AH1216	43	1.75	3.00	5.00	8.00
(184.2)	1216	44	1.75	3.00	5.00	8.00
	1216	45	1.75	3.00	5.00	8.00
	1217	44	1.75	3.00	5.00	8.00
	1217	45	1.75	3.00	5.00	8.00
	1217	46	1.75	3.00	5.00	8.00
	1219	46	1.75	3.00	5.00	8.00

NOTE: Previously listed in Gwalior.

RUPEE

SILVER, 10.70-11.60 g
Rev: Katar and floral spray.

KM#	Date	Year	VG	Fine	VF	XF
26	AH1216	44	15.00	25.00	35.00	50.00
	1216	45	15.00	25.00	35.00	50.00
	1217	44	15.00	25.00	35.00	50.00
	1217	48	15.00	25.00	35.00	50.00

NAWANAGAR

(Navanagar)

State located on the Kathiawar peninsula, west-central India.

The rulers, or jams, of Kutch were Jareja Rajputs who had entered the Kathiawar peninsular from Kutch and dispossessed the ancient family of Jathwas. Nawanagar was founded about 1535 by Jam Raval, who was possibly the elder brother of the Jam of Kutch. The great fort of Nawanagar was built by Jam Jasaji (d. 1814). The state became tributary to the Gaekwar family and, in the nineteenth century, also to the British. In 1948 the state was merged into Saurashtra.

RULERS

Vibhaji,
VS1909-1951/1852-1894AD
Jaswant Singh,
VS1951-1964/1894-1907AD

MONETARY SYSTEM

2 Trambiyo = 1 Dokda
3 Trambiyo = 1 Dhinglo
8 Dokda = 1 Kori

Early Types: Stylized imitations of the coins of Muzaffar III of Gujarat (156-173AD), dated AH978 (= 1570AD), were struck from the end of the 16th century until the early part of the reign of Vibhaji. These show a steady degradation of style over the nearly 300 years of issue, but no types can be dated to specific rulers. The former attribution of these coins to Ranmalji II (1820-1852AD) is incorrect. All are inscribed Sri Jamji, title of all rulers of Nawanager.

Varieties in this series are the rule, not the exception. These include legend style, small marks in the field such as a crescent, Katar (dagger), etc., and weight ranges.

DUMP COINAGE

Crude style; ca. 1570-1850AD

TRAMBIYO

COPPER, 3.20-4.00 g

KM#	Date	Good	VG	Fine	VF
1	AH(9)78 (frozen)	1.25	2.00	3.00	4.50

DOKDO

COPPER, 7.00-8.00 g

KM#	Date	Good	VG	Fine	VF
2	AH(9)78 (frozen)	.40	.75	1.00	1.50

NOTE: Earlier issues weigh up to 9.30 g.

DHINGLO

(1 1/2 Dokda)

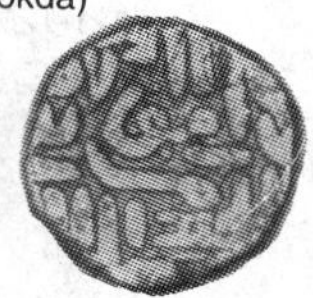

COPPER, 10.50-12.50 g

KM#	Date	Good	VG	Fine	VF
3	AH(9)78 (frozen)	1.25	2.00	3.00	4.00

1/2 KORI

SILVER, 2.30-2.40 g

KM#	Date	Good	VG	Fine	VF
4	AH(9)78 (frozen)	1.75	3.00	4.50	6.00

KORI

SILVER, 4.60-4.80 g

KM#	Date	Good	VG	Fine	VF
5	AH(9)78 (frozen)	1.50	2.50	3.50	5.00

Finer style from ca. 1850AD.

TRAMBIYO

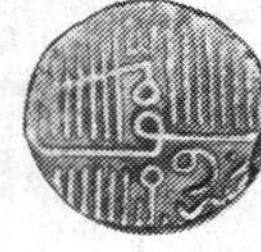

COPPER, 3.10-3.30 g

KM#	Date	Good	VG	Fine	VF
6	AH(9)78 (frozen)	1.00	2.00	3.25	4.50

DOKDO

COPPER, 6.20-6.60 g

KM#	Date	Good	VG	Fine	VF
7	AH(9)78 (frozen)	.65	1.15	1.75	2.50

DHINGLO

(1 1/2 Dokda)

COPPER, 9.30-9.90 g

KM#	Date	Good	VG	Fine	VF
8	AH(9)78 (frozen)	1.00	1.75	2.50	3.50

1/2 KORI

SILVER, 2.30-2.40 g

KM#	Date	Good	VG	Fine	VF
9	AH(9)78 (frozen)	2.50	3.50	5.00	8.00

KORI

SILVER, 4.60-4.80 g

KM#	Date	Good	VG	Fine	VF
10	AH(9)78 (frozen)	2.00	3.00	4.00	7.00

VIBHAJI

VS1909-1951/1852-1894AD

TRAMBIYO

COPPER, 3.10-3.20 g

KM#	Date	Good	VG	Fine	VF
13	AH(9)78 (frozen)	1.00	1.75	3.00	4.00

3.30-3.50 g
Similar to Dokdo, KM#16.

KM#	Date	Good	VG	Fine	VF
15	VS1919 (1862)	3.50	6.00	7.50	10.00

DOKDO

COPPER, 6.20-6.40 g

KM#	Date	Good	VG	Fine	VF
14	AH(9)78 (frozen)	.90	1.40	2.25	3.00

6.60-7.00 g

KM#	Date	Year	Good	VG	Fine
16	VS1909	(1852)	3.50	6.00	7.50
	1917	(1860)	3.50	6.00	7.50
	1919	(1862)	3.50	6.00	7.50

2 DOKDA

COPPER, 12.40-12.80 g

KM#	Date	Year	Good	VG	Fine	VF
18	VS1943	(1886)	4.00	7.00	10.00	

3 DOKDA

COPPER, 18.00-19.60 g

KM#	Date	Year	Good	VG	Fine
17	VS1928	(1871)	3.50	5.50	7.00

KM#	Date	Year	Good	VG	Fine
19	VS1942	(1885)	3.00	4.50	6.50

KORI

SILVER, 4.60-4.80 g
Plain edge

KM#	Date	Year	VG	Fine	VF	XF
20	VS1934	(1877)	5.00	7.00	12.00	20.00
	1935	(1878)	5.00	7.00	12.00	20.00
	1936	(1879)	3.00	5.00	9.00	18.00

2-1/2 KORI

SILVER, 6.80-7.20 g
Reduced weight, milled edge

KM#	Date	Year	VG	Fine	VF	XF
21	VS1948	(1891)	6.50	10.00	15.00	22.50
	1949	(1892)	6.50	10.00	15.00	22.50
	1950	(1893)	6.50	10.00	15.00	22.50

5 KORI

SILVER, 13.60-14.40 g
Reduced weight.
Obv. and rev: Large inner circle, milled edge.

KM#	Date	Year	Fine	VF	XF	Unc
22	VS1945	(1888)	7.50	12.50	18.50	27.50
	1946	(1889)	7.50	12.50	18.50	27.50
	1947	(1890)	7.50	12.50	18.50	27.50

Obv. and rev. leg: Smaller characters.

KM#	Date	Year	Fine	VF	XF	Unc
23	VS1948	(1891)	7.50	12.50	18.50	27.50
	1949	(1892)	7.50	12.50	18.50	27.50
	1950	(1893)	7.50	12.50	18.50	27.50

1/2 GOLD KORI

GOLD, 3.20-3.30 g

KM#	Date	VG	Fine	VF	XF
11	AH978 (frozen)	60.00	85.00	125.00	165.00

GOLD KORI

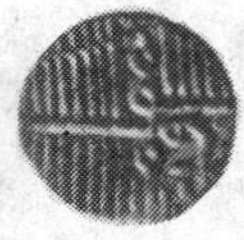

GOLD, 6.40-6.60 g

KM#	Date	VG	Fine	VF	XF
12	AH(9)78 (frozen)	85.00	125.00	185.00	250.00

JASWANT SINGH

VS1951-1964/1894-1907AD

TRAMBIYO

COPPER, 3.10-3.20 g

KM#	Date	Year	Good	VG	Fine	VF
24	VS1956(1899)		10.00	16.50	25.00	40.00

DOKDO

COPPER, 6.20-6.40 g

KM#	Date	Good	VG	Fine	VF
25	VS1956(1899)	9.00	15.00	22.50	36.50

DHINGLO

(1 1/2 Dokda)

COPPER, 9.30-9.60 g

KM#	Date	Good	VG	Fine	VF
26	VS1956(1899)	7.50	12.50	20.00	30.00

2 DOKDA

COPPER, 12.40-13.20 g

KM#	Date	Good	VG	Fine	VF
27	VS1956(1899)	12.50	20.00	33.50	45.00

3 DOKDA

COPPER, 18.60-19.80 g

KM#	Date	Good	VG	Fine	VF
28	VS1956(1899)	12.50	22.50	35.00	50.00

ORCHHA

State located in north-central India.

Orchha, the oldest and highest ranking of all the Bundela States, was founded by Rudra Pratap, a Garhwar Rajput, early in the sixteenth century. During the years of Mughal expansion, Orchha came under the supervision of Delhi. A few years later Jujhar Singh (1626-1635) rebelled but was defeated and dispossessed. Shah Jahan installed his brother as ruler in 1641. In the eighteenth century, as the Marathas took control of the region, only Orchha from among the Bundela States was not totally subjugated by the Peshwa. In the nineteenth century Orchha came under British protection.

The Orchha coinage was called Gaja Shahi because of the gaja or mace which was its symbol.

RULERS

Vikramajit Mahendra,
AH1211-1233/1796-1817AD
Dharam Pal,
AH1233-1250/1817-1834AD
Taj Singh,
AH1250-1258/1834-1842AD
Surjain Singh,
AH1258-1265/1842-1848AD
Hamir Singh,
AH1265-1291/1848-1874AD
Pratap Singh,
AH1291-1349/1874-1930AD

MINT MARKS

1 Reverse. (This is the symbol most characteristic of Orchha's coinage and is copied on the Datia imitations)

2 Obverse, most common.

3 Obverse, less common.

4 Reverse

5 Reverse

6 Reverse

7 Reverse

8 Reverse

9 Reverse

10 Reverse

Marks #4 through #10 are found in addition to Mark #1.

The Datia copies can only be distinguished by the mint marks, other than #1, which is common to both series for the list of Datia marks, see listings under that state.

There seems to be no correspondence between AH dates on the obverse and regnal years on the reverse!

In the name of Shah Alam II

AH1173-1221/1759-1806AD

1/2 PAISA

COPPER, 16mm

C#	Date	Year	Good	VG	Fine	VF
24	AH(12)32	—	1.75	3.00	5.00	8.00
	(12)33	—	1.75	3.00	5.00	8.00

PAISA

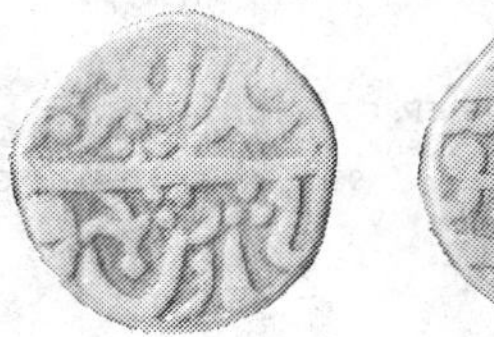

COPPER

C#	Date	Year	Good	VG	Fine	VF
25	AH1216	4x	1.00	2.00	3.25	4.50
	1232	46	1.00	2.00	3.25	4.50
	1237	16	1.00	2.00	3.25	4.50
	1278	45	1.00	2.00	3.25	4.50
	1282	42	1.00	2.00	3.25	4.50

NOTE: Earlier dates (AH120x-1214) exist for this type.

1/8 RUPEE

SILVER, 1.34-1.45 g

C#	Date	Year	VG	Fine	VF	XF
29	(AH1233)	45	4.00	7.00	10.00	16.00

NOTE: Earlier date (AH1211) exists for this type.

1/4 RUPEE

SILVER, 12mm, 2.68-2.90 g

C#	Date	Year	VG	Fine	VF	XF
30	AH1228	40	3.50	6.00	9.00	14.00
	1233	45	3.50	6.00	9.00	14.00
	1232	46	3.50	6.00	9.00	14.00
	1233	5x	3.50	6.00	9.00	14.00
	1251	3x	3.50	6.00	9.00	14.00

NOTE: Earlier date (AH1211) exists for this type.

RUPEE

SILVER, 10.70-11.60 g

C#	Date	Year	VG	Fine	VF	XF
32	AH1216	44	6.00	10.00	14.00	20.00
	1216	46	6.00	10.00	14.00	20.00
	1217	45	6.00	10.00	14.00	20.00
	1218	46	6.00	10.00	14.00	20.00
	1218	47	6.00	10.00	14.00	20.00
	121x	47	6.00	10.00	14.00	20.00
	1219	48	6.00	10.00	14.00	20.00
	1221	40	6.00	10.00	14.00	20.00
	1232	40	6.00	10.00	14.00	20.00
	1233	40	6.00	10.00	14.00	20.00
	1233	42	6.00	10.00	14.00	20.00
	1234	—	6.00	10.00	14.00	20.00
	1235	11	6.00	10.00	14.00	20.00
	1236	15	6.00	10.00	14.00	20.00
	1238	17	6.00	10.00	14.00	20.00
	1240	—	6.00	10.00	14.00	20.00
	1245	43	6.00	10.00	14.00	20.00
	1251	31	6.00	10.00	14.00	20.00
	1252	32	6.00	10.00	14.00	20.00
	1253	35	6.00	10.00	14.00	20.00
	1257	39	6.00	10.00	14.00	20.00
	1258	38	6.00	10.00	14.00	20.00

NOTE: Earlier dates (AH1211-1215) exist for this type.
NOTE: Varieties exist with different variations of obverse and reverse symbols.

In the name of Muhammad Akbar II

AH1221-1253/1806-1837AD

1/2 PAISA

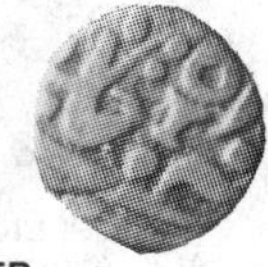

COPPER

C#	Date	Year	Good	VG	Fine	VF
37	AH(12)	33	—	—	—	—

PAISA

COPPER

C#	Date	Year	Good	VG	Fine	VF
38	AH12xx	3x	2.00	4.00	6.00	9.00
	1231	4x	—	—	—	—

RUPEE

SILVER, 20mm, 10.70-11.60 g

C#	Date	Year	VG	Fine	VF	XF
42	AH1219	2	6.00	10.00	14.00	20.00
	1321 (error for 1231)	9	7.00	11.00	16.50	25.00

C#	Date	Year	VG	Fine	VF	XF
42	1232	10	6.00	10.00	14.00	20.00
	1257	48	6.00	10.00	14.00	20.00
	1258	38	6.00	10.00	14.00	20.00
	1270	33	6.00	10.00	14.00	20.00
	1271	—	6.00	10.00	14.00	20.00
	1273	39	6.00	10.00	14.00	20.00
	127x	41	6.00	10.00	14.00	20.00
	1275	4X	6.00	10.00	14.00	20.00
	1278	45	6.00	10.00	14.00	20.00

PARTABGARH

Pratapgarh

The rulers of Partabgarh, a state located in northwest India, the maharawals, were Sesodia Rajputs who are believed to have migrated in 1553 from Mewar, where their ancestors once ruled. Arriving in the area they seized control from the local Bhil chieftains but it was not until the early eighteenth century that Partabgarh town was founded by Maharawal Partab Singh. Partabgarh was tributary to Holkar until 1818 when, with the collapse of the Maratha states, the state came under British protection. The state was then managed through the Rajputana Agency until, in April 1948, it was merged into Rajasthan.

RULERS

Salim Singh
AH1167-1189/1753-1775 AD
Sawant Singh
AH1189-1241/1775-1825AD
Dulep Singh
AH1241-1281/1825-1864AD
Udaya Singh
VS1921-1947/1864-1890AD
Raganath Singh
VS1947-1986/1890-1929AD

MINT

دیوکره

Deogarh

SAWANT SINGH

AH1189-1241/1775-1825AD

Third Type

Frozen date AH1199/Yr. 29. The meaning of Yr. 29 is the 29th regnal year of Sawant Singh, 1804 and were struck until ca. 1823.

1/8 RUPEE

SILVER, 11mm, 1.30 g

KM#	Date	Year	VG	Fine	VF	XF
10	AH1199	29	3.50	6.00	9.00	14.00

1/4 RUPEE

SILVER, 2.65 g

KM#	Date	Year	VG	Fine	VF	XF
11	AH1199	29	5.00	7.00	10.00	16.00

1/2 RUPEE

SILVER, 5.30 g

KM#	Date	Year	VG	Fine	VF	XF
12	AH1199	29	3.50	6.00	9.00	14.00

RUPEE

SILVER, 19-20mm, 10.70 g

KM#	Date	Year	VG	Fine	VF	XF
13	AH1199	29	5.00	7.00	10.00	16.00

NAZARANA RUPEE

SILVER, square, 10.85 g

KM#	Date	Year	VG	Fine	VF	XF
14	AH1199	29	35.00	60.00	85.00	125.00

DULEP SINGH

AH1241-1281/1825-1864AD

In the name of Shah Alam II

Frozen date AH1236/Yr. 45. The meaning of Yr. 45 is not known. Struck ca. 1823-1858.

1/8 RUPEE

SILVER, 1.35 g

KM#	Date	Year	VG	Fine	VF	XF
20	AH1236	45	3.50	5.50	8.00	12.50

1/4 RUPEE

SILVER, 2.70 g

KM#	Date	Year	VG	Fine	VF	XF
21	AH1236	45	3.50	6.00	9.00	14.00

1/2 RUPEE

SILVER, 5.40 g

KM#	Date	Year	VG	Fine	VF	XF
22	AH1236	45	3.50	5.50	8.50	12.50

RUPEE

SILVER, 10.90 g

KM#	Date	Year	VG	Fine	VF	XF
23	AH1236	45	4.00	6.00	9.00	14.00

NAZARANA RUPEE

SILVER, square, 10.70-10.90 g

KM#	Date	Year	VG	Fine	VF	XF
25	AH1236	45	35.00	60.00	85.00	125.00

NAZARANA 2-1/2 RUPEES

SILVER, 27.20-27.45 g

KM#	Date	Year	VG	Fine	VF	XF
26	AH1236	45	75.00	125.00	175.00	250.00

UDAYA SINGH

VS1921-1947/1864-1890AD

PAISA

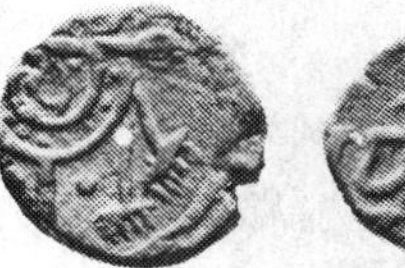

COPPER, 8.00 g

KM#	Date	Year	Good	VG	Fine	VF
30	VS1935	(1878)	1.25	2.25	3.25	5.00

NOTE: Varieties exist.

Obv: Rayed oval sunface, dot on forehead.

KM#	Date	Year	Good	VG	Fine	VF
31.1	VS1943	(1886)	1.00	1.75	2.50	4.00
(32)	1947	(1890)	.50	1.00	1.50	2.50

NOTE: Varieties exist.

Obv: Round sunface w/o dot on forehead; two knives.

KM#	Date	Year	Good	VG	Fine	VF
31.2	VS1943	(1886)	2.50	5.00	16.00	20.00

In the name of the 'Shah of London' (= Queen Victoria)

Frozen date AH1236/Yr. 45, struck from 1859 to ca. 1900. Easily distinguished from the KM#21-23 series by the word London directly below the date AH1236.

1/8 RUPEE

SILVER, 1.36 g

KM#	Date	Year	VG	Fine	VF	XF
33	AH1236	45	3.00	4.50	6.50	10.00

1/4 RUPEE

SILVER, 2.68 g

KM#	Date	Year	VG	Fine	VF	XF
34	AH1236	45	3.50	5.50	8.50	12.50

1/2 RUPEE

SILVER, 5.45 g

KM#	Date	Year	VG	Fine	VF	XF
35	AH1236	45	3.00	4.50	6.50	10.00

NAZARANA 1/2 RUPEE

SILVER, 5.40 g, Square

KM#	Date	Year	VG	Fine	VF	XF
39a	AH1236	45	—	—	Rare	—

RUPEE

SILVER, 10.90 g

KM#	Date	Year	VG	Fine	VF	XF
36	AH1236	45	4.00	6.00	9.00	14.00

NAZARANA RUPEE

SILVER, square, 10.90 g

KM#	Date	Year	VG	Fine	VF	XF
37	AH1236	45	37.50	62.50	85.00	120.00

Large flan, 11.0 g

KM#	Date	Year	VG	Fine	VF	XF
38	AH1236	45	—	—	Rare	—

RAGANATH SINGH

VS1947-1986/1890-1929AD

PAISA

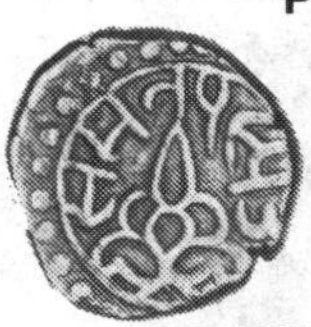

COPPER, 7.50-8.40 g

KM#	Date	Year	Good	VG	Fine	VF
40	VS1953	(1896)	1.50	2.50	3.50	5.00

PORBANDAR

State located on the Kathiawar peninsula in western India. The rulers, or ranas, of Porbandar were Jethwa Rajputs of ancient Rajput lineage. They are believed to have arrived from the north and settled the area as early as the tenth century. Their seat of government was transferred to Porbandar from Chaya, the ancient capital, in 1785. The Rana of Porbandar paid an annual tribute of 30,000 rupees to the Gaekwar of Baroda. In 1807 Porbandar acceded to British control, and in February 1948 became part of Saurashtra State. The coins of Porbandar are similar to the coins of Kutch and Navanagar and derive from a prototype struck in AH978/1570AD by Muzaffar Shah III of Gujarat. They have, in Nagari, the additional inscription, *Sri Rana.*

श्रीराणा

All are dated AH(9)78. They were struck until about 1890AD, and cannot be assigned to any specific ruler.

MONETARY SYSTEM

2 Trambiyo = 1 Dokda
3 Trambiyo = 1 Dhingla
8 Dokda = 1 Kori

1/2 TRAMBIYO

COPPER

C#	Date	Year	Good	VG	Fine	VF
30	AH(9)78 (frozen)		2.00	4.00	7.50	11.50

TRAMBIYO

COPPER

C#	Date	Year	Good	VG	Fine	VF
31	AH(9)78 (frozen)		2.00	3.25	5.00	8.50

DOKDO

COPPER

C#	Date	Year	Good	VG	Fine	VF
32	AH(9)78 (frozen)		1.00	1.75	2.50	4.50

DHINGLA

COPPER, 18-19mm

C#	Date	Year	Good	VG	Fine	VF
33	AH(9)78 (frozen)		3.00	5.00	8.00	12.50

Rectangular, 20x15mm
Cruder calligraphy

C#	Date	Year	Good	VG	Fine	VF
34	AH(9)78 (frozen)		4.50	8.50	12.50	17.50

NOTE: Said to have been struck by Khimji (1813-1831AD).

1/4 KORI

SILVER, 8-9mm

C#	Date	Year	VG	Fine	VF	XF
36	AH(9)78 (frozen)		6.50	10.00	15.00	22.50

1/2 KORI

SILVER

C#	Date	Year	VG	Fine	VF	XF
37	AH(9)78 (frozen)		4.00	6.50	10.00	15.00

KORI

SILVER

C#	Date	Year	VG	Fine	VF	XF
38	AH(9)78 (frozen)		2.50	4.00	6.50	10.00

PUDUKKOTTAI

Refer to Independent Kingdoms under British rule.

RADHANPUR

State located on the Kathiawar peninsula.

The nawabs of Radhanpur were Pathans of the Babi family who rose to high office in the service of Shah Jahan and Murad Bakhsh in Gujarat. Sometime in the late seventeenth or early eighteenth centuries one of the family was appointed faujdar of Radhanpur and the surrounding area. After Aurangzeb's death, Kamal-ud-din Khan Babi seized the governorship of Ahmadabad, but this was relinquished in 1753 to the forces of the Peshwa of Poona and the Gaekwar of Baroda. Radhanpur, however, remained in Babi control as a Maratha Jagir until 1820 when the State came under British protection.

All silver coins of Radhanpur appear to be nazarana issues.

RULERS

Zorawar Khan,
AH1241-1291/1825-1874AD
Bismilla Khan,
AH1291-1313/1874-1895AD

MINT

Radhanpur 

ZORAWAR KHAN

AH1241-1291/1825-1874AD

In the name of Queen Victoria

and Zorawar Khan

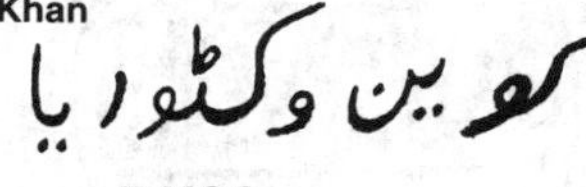

PAISA

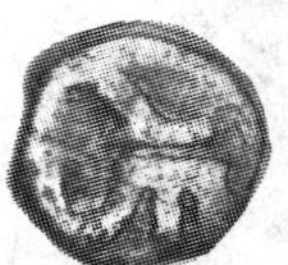

Jo 

COPPER or BRONZE, uniface

KM#	Date	Year	Good	VG	Fine	VF
3	ND	—	1.00	1.75	2.50	4.00

2 ANNAS

SILVER, 1.34-1.45 g

KM#	Date	Year	VG	Fine	VF	XF
8	AH1288	1871	15.00	25.00	35.00	50.00

4 ANNAS

SILVER, 2.68-2.90 g

KM#	Date	Year	VG	Fine	VF	XF
9	AH1287	1869	14.00	23.50	32.50	45.00
	1287	1871	14.00	23.50	32.50	45.00
	1288	1871	14.00	23.50	32.50	45.00
	1288	1872	14.00	23.50	32.50	45.00

8 ANNAS

SILVER, 5.35-5.80 g

KM#	Date	Year	VG	Fine	VF	XF
10	AH1284	1869	15.00	25.00	35.00	50.00
	1286	1867	15.00	25.00	35.00	50.00
	1286	1869	15.00	25.00	35.00	50.00
	1287	1869	15.00	25.00	35.00	50.00
	1287	1870	15.00	25.00	35.00	50.00
	1288	1871	15.00	25.00	35.00	50.00
	1289	1871	15.00	25.00	35.00	50.00

50 FALUS

SILVER

KM#	Date	Year	VG	Fine	VF	XF
5	AH1284	1867	18.50	31.50	42.50	60.00

RUPEE

SILVER, 10.70-11.60 g

KM#	Date	Year	VG	Fine	VF	XF
11	AH1286	1869	16.50	27.50	40.00	55.00
	1287	1870	14.00	23.50	32.50	45.00
	1287	1871	14.00	23.50	32.50	45.00
	1288	1871	14.00	23.50	32.50	45.00
	1288	1872	14.00	23.50	32.50	45.00
	1289	1871	14.00	23.50	32.50	45.00
	1289	1872	14.00	23.50	32.50	45.00

100 FALUS

SILVER

KM#	Date	Year	VG	Fine	VF	XF
6	AH1284	1867	18.00	30.00	45.00	65.00
	1286	1868	18.00	30.00	45.00	65.00
	1286	1869	18.00	30.00	45.00	65.00
	1287	1870	18.00	30.00	45.00	65.00
	1287	18771(error for 1871)	18.00	30.00	45.00	65.00

MOHUR

GOLD, 27mm, 10.70-11.40 g

KM#	Date	Year	VG	Fine	VF	XF
15	AH1277	1860	175.00	225.00	275.00	400.00

BISMILLA KHAN

AH1291-1313/1874-1895AD

In the name of Queen Victoria

کوئن وکٹوریا

and Bismillah Khan

PAISA

Ji जी

COPPER or BRONZE, uniface, 8.39 g

KM#	Date	Year	Good	VG	Fine	VF
16	ND	—	1.75	2.25	3.00	4.50

2 ANNAS

SILVER, 15mm, 1.34-1.45 g

KM#	Date	Year	VG	Fine	VF	XF
18	AH—	1880	18.00	30.00	42.50	60.00

4 ANNAS

SILVER, 2.68-2.90 g
Obv. leg: Field divided twice, Nawab's name at top. Rev. leg: Field divided once, Queen's name upper left.

KM#	Date	Year	VG	Fine	VF	XF
19	AH—	1880	15.00	25.00	35.00	50.00

In the name of Empress Victoria and Bismillah Khan

8 ANNAS

SILVER, 5.35-5.80 g

KM#	Date	Year	VG	Fine	VF	XF
21	AH1291	1875	12.00	20.00	30.00	45.00

In the name of Queen Victoria and Bismillah Khan

Obv. leg: Field divided twice, Nawab's name at top. Rev. leg: 2 field dividers, Queen's name center left, center line three words.

KM#	Date	Year	VG	Fine	VF	XF
22	AH1297	1880	12.00	20.00	30.00	45.00

Rev. leg: W/o field dividers, Queen's name lower left.

KM#	Date	Year	VG	Fine	VF	XF
23	AH1297	1881	12.00	20.00	30.00	45.00

Rev. leg: 2 field dividers, Queen's name center left, center line 3 words.

KM#	Date	Year	VG	Fine	VF	XF
24	AH1299	1881	12.00	20.00	30.00	45.00

Obv. leg: 2 field dividers, Nawab's name center in one line. Rev. leg: W/o field dividers, Queen's name lower left.

KM#	Date	Year	VG	Fine	VF	XF
25	AH1299	1881	12.00	20.00	30.00	45.00

RUPEE

SILVER, 10.70-11.60 g
Obv. leg: 2 field dividers, Nawab's name center in one line. Rev. leg: Field divided once above *Dak*.

KM#	Date	Year	VG	Fine	VF	XF
27	AH1297	1880	18.00	30.00	42.50	60.00
	1298	1880	18.00	30.00	45.00	65.00

Obv. leg: Field divided twice, Nawab's name at top. Rev. leg: 2 field dividers, Queen's name center left, center line 3 words.

KM#	Date	Year	VG	Fine	VF	XF
28	AH1299	1881	16.50	26.50	37.50	55.00

Obv. leg: 2 field dividers, Nawab's name center in one line. Rev. leg: Field divided once w/Queen's titles in different order.

KM#	Date	Year	VG	Fine	VF	XF
29	AH1297	1881	18.00	30.00	45.00	65.00
	1298	1881	16.50	26.50	37.50	55.00

Rev. leg: 1 field divider, w/o Queen's name, mint name above.

KM#	Date	Year	VG	Fine	VF	XF
30	AH1311	1894	18.00	30.00	42.50	60.00

Obv. leg: 1 field divider, Nawab's name above. Rev. leg: W/o Queen's name, mint name below.

KM#	Date	Year	VG	Fine	VF	XF
31	AH1311	1894	18.00	30.00	42.50	60.00

RAMPUR

This tiny estate of four and a half square miles was held by Chauda Rajputs in the old Gujerat States Agency Area. It was feudatory to Lunavada and the estate was controlled by a thakur or, latterly, by four shareholders.

Anonymous Issues

The following listings may be from Lunavada or from Rampur. They are often found overstruck on coins of Lunavada, and over other states, including Sailana.

1/2 PAISA

COPPER, 3.00-4.00 g
Obv: Open hand in square. Rev. leg: *Rampar*.

KM#	Date	Year	Good	VG	Fine	VF
1	ND	—	4.00	6.50	10.00	15.00

Obv: Sunbursts. Rev. leg: *Rampar*.

KM#	Date	Year	Good	VG	Fine	VF
2	ND	—	5.00	9.00	13.00	20.00

PAISA

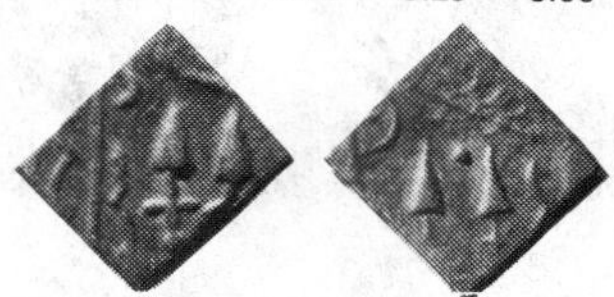

COPPER, 1.90-4.30 g
Obv: Sunbursts. Rev. leg: *Rampar*.

KM#	Date	Year	Good	VG	Fine	VF
3	ND	—	2.00	3.25	5.00	8.50

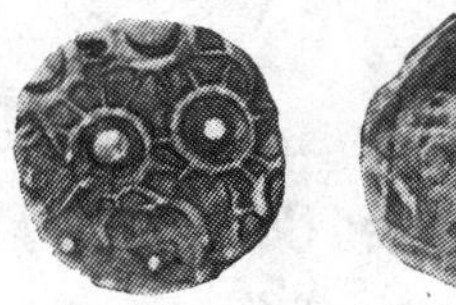

Obv: Spears. Rev: Spears.

KM#	Date	Year	Good	VG	Fine	VF
4	ND	—	2.00	3.25	5.00	8.50

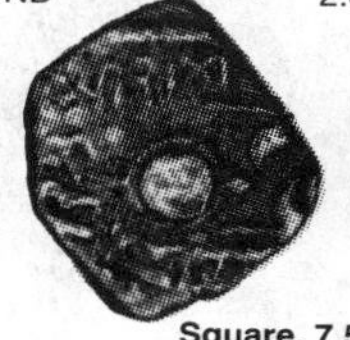

Round or square, 8.50 g
Obv: Spears. Rev: *Rampar*.

KM#	Date	Year	Good	VG	Fine	VF
5	ND	—	2.00	3.25	5.00	8.50

Round or square, 7.50-8.30 g
Obv: Sunbursts. Rev. leg: *Rampar*.

KM#	Date	Year	Good	VG	Fine	VF
6	ND	—	2.00	3.25	5.00	8.50

Square, 7.50-8.30 g
Obv: Solar symbol. Rev. leg: *Rampar*.

KM#	Date	Year	Good	VG	Fine	VF
7	ND	—	4.00	6.00	9.00	14.00

Obv: Spears. Rev: Persian legend.

KM#	Date	Year	Good	VG	Fine	VF
8	ND	—	2.00	3.25	5.00	8.50

PIE

COPPER, 2.30 g

KM#	Date	Year	Good	VG	Fine	VF
12	ND	—	—	—	—	—

RATLAM

State located northwest of Indore in Madhya Pradesh.

The rajas of Ratlam were Rathor Rajputs, descendants of the younger branch of the Jodhpur ruling family. Ratlam became the premier Rajput state in western Malwa. The founder, Ratan Singh, received the territory as a grant from Shah Jahan in 1631. Before Maratha collapse some fifteen percent of the state's annual revenue went to Sindhia as tribute. Under British protection it was supervised by the Central India Agency and in 1948 Ratlam became a district of Madhya Bharat.

RULERS

Ranjit Singh,
VS1921-1950/1864-1893AD

NOTE: For 1 Paisa previously listed here refer to Banswara-IPS.

UNCERTAIN RULER

PAISA

COPPER

Obv: Katar. Rev: Sword.

KM#	Date	Year	Good	VG	Fine	VF
15	—	—	5.00	10.00	18.00	25.00

RANJIT SINGH

VS1921-1950/1864-1893AD

PAISA

COPPER, 22mm

KM#	Date	Year	Good	VG	Fine	VF
21	VS1921	(1864)	6.00	9.00	12.50	18.50

Obv: Katar and spray. Rev: Sword.

KM#	Date	Year	Good	VG	Fine	VF
22.1	VS1927	(1870)	3.00	5.00	8.00	12.50

Obv: Katar. Rev: Flower and spray.

KM#	Date	Year	Good	VG	Fine	VF
22.2	VS1928	(1871)	2.00	3.25	5.00	8.50

KM#	Date	Year	Good	VG	Fine	VF
23	1885	—	3.00	5.00	8.00	12.50

Milled Coinage

PAISA

COPPER
Obv: Hanuman.
Thick planchet

KM#	Date	Year	Fine	VF	XF	Unc
24	VS1947	(1890)	3.50	6.00	10.00	17.50

NOTE: Restruck ca.1942-1945AD.

REWA

State located in eastern north-central India.

The rulers of Rewa were Baghela Rajputs of the Solanki clan who probably migrated from Anhilwara Patan in Gujarat about the eleventh century. Arriving in Bundelkhand they carved out for themselves a substantial kingdom which remained independent until 1597, when they were obliged to become Mughal tributaries under Akbar. With Mughal decline Rewa began to move once more towards independence, this time under the nominal suzerainty of the Peshwa. In 1812 the raja of Rewa, Jai Singh Deo was coerced into a treaty with the British and, failing to observe its conditions, was forced to yield to British control in 1813-1814. In 1948 Rewa was merged into Vindhya Pradesh.

RULERS

Jai Singh Deo,
VS1866-1892/1809-1835AD
Vishvanath Singh,
VS1892-1900/1835-1843AD
Raghuraj Singh,
VS1900-1937/1843-1880AD
Venkat Raman Singh,
VS1937-1975/1880-1918AD

JAI SINGH DEO

VS1866-1892/1809-1835AD

PAISA

COPPER, 6.80 g

KM#	Date	Year	Good	VG	Fine	VF
11	VS1890	(1823)	2.00	3.00	4.50	7.00

8.80-12.60 g

KM#	Date	Year	Good	VG	Fine	VF
12	ND	—	1.75	2.75	4.00	6.00

2 PAISA

COPPER
Obv: *Sikka Rewa* in center.

KM#	Date	Year	Good	VG	Fine	VF
14	ND	—	2.50	4.00	7.00	11.00

VISHVANATH SINGH

VS1892-1900/1835-1843AD

PAISA

COPPER, 7.80 g

KM#	Date	Year	Good	VG	Fine	VF
16	ND	—	2.50	3.50	5.00	8.50

COPPER, 7.40-7.60 g
Obv: *Sikka Rewa* in center.

KM#	Date	Year	Good	VG	Fine	VF
17	ND	—	3.00	5.00	10.00	18.00

2 PAISA

COPPER, 16.80 g

KM#	Date	Year	Good	VG	Fine	VF
18	ND	—	2.50	3.50	5.00	8.50

MOHUR

GOLD, 9.75 g

KM#	Date	Year	VG	Fine	VF	XF
22	ND	—	250.00	425.00	600.00	850.00

RAGHURAJ SINGH

VS1900-1937/1843-1880AD

In the name of Agent Bushby Saheb

PAISA

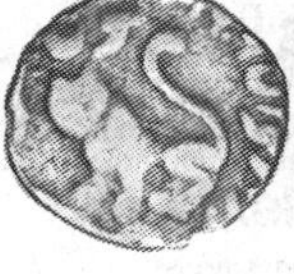

COPPER

KM#	Date	Year	Good	VG	Fine	VF
24	VS1906	(1849)	2.75	4.50	6.50	10.00

2 PAISE

COPPER
Obv: Lion left.

KM#	Date	Year	Good	VG	Fine	VF
26	VS1906	(1849)	2.75	4.50	6.50	10.00

Obv: Lion right.

KM#	Date	Year	Good	VG	Fine	VF
27	VS1906	(1849)	5.00	7.00	9.00	13.50

ROHILKHAND

Refer to Independent Kingdoms during British rule.

SAILANA

This small state in west-central India, of slightly over one hundred square miles had once been part of Ratlam, but about 1709 it asserted its independence under the leadership of Pratab Singh, the second son of Chhatrasal. The town of Sailana was founded in 1730 by Jai Singh's successor, and from that date the state was named after it. Due to its small size and vulnerability, Sailana was obliged to become tributary to Sindhia to ensure its survival. In 1819 this payment was limited to one-third of the state's revenues. Later, under agreements of 1840 and 1860, the tribute went to the British for the support of British Indian troops in the region. Barmawal was feudatory to Sailana.

LOCAL RULERS

Dule Singh,
VS1907-1952/1850-1895AD
Jaswant Singh, 1895-1919AD

ANONYMOUS COINAGE

KM#4-6 are believed to be 1 Paisa struck to progressively lighter weights in later periods.

(1/2) PAISA

COPPER, 4.80-5.80 g
Obv: Pennant points either up or down.

KM#	Date	Year	Good	VG	Fine	VF
4	ND	—	1.50	2.25	3.50	5.00

PAISA

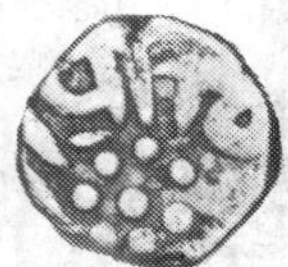

COPPER, 7.50-9.70 g
Obv: Pennant points either up or down.

KM#	Date	Year	Good	VG	Fine	VF
5	ND	—	.50	.85	1.25	2.00

NOTE: KM#5 is known struck over an Egyptian 20 Para KM#244 or #246, cut down to an irregular shape. Other combinations could exist.

(2) PAISA

COPPER, 11.60-12.30 g

KM#	Date	Year	Good	VG	Fine	VF
6	ND	—	2.00	3.25	5.00	8.50

DULE SINGH

VS1907-1952/1850-1895AD

1/2 PAISA

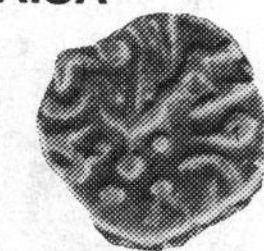

COPPER, 5.20 g
Obv: Pennant points up or down.

KM#	Date	Year	Good	VG	Fine	VF
10	VS1944	(1887)	2.00	3.25	5.00	8.00

KM#	Date	Year	Good	VG	Fine	VF
11	VS1937	(1880)	1.25	2.25	3.50	5.50
	7391 (retrograde)	(1880)	1.25	2.25	3.50	5.50

11.80 g
Rev: Sprig, Nagari date.

KM#	Date	Year	Good	VG	Fine	VF
12	VS1940	(1883)	1.75	2.75	4.00	7.00

10.90 g
Rev: Arabic numerals in Samvat date.

KM#	Date	Year	Good	VG	Fine	VF
13	1921	(1884)	1.75	2.75	4.00	7.00

PAISA

COPPER, 10.80-11.00 g
Obv: Pennant points right.
Rev: Trident.

KM#	Date	Year	Good	VG	Fine	VF
14	VS1944	(1887)	1.75	2.75	4.00	7.00

SAILANA FEUDATORY STATE

BARMAWAL

RULER

Raja Handa Singh

PAISA

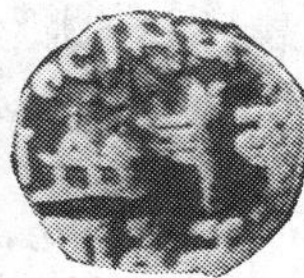

COPPER
Obv: Hanuman.

KM#	Date	Year	Good	VG	Fine	VF
1	ND	—	6.00	10.00	14.00	20.00

NOTE: KM#1 was struck prior to 1881AD.

SIKHS

Refer to Sikh Empire, Independent Kingdom during British rule.

SIKKIM

Refer to Independent Kingdom during British rule.

SIND

Refer to Independent Kingdom during British rule.

SIRMUR

Sirmur Nahan

The ruling Rajput family of this Himalayan principality claimed descent from the Jaisalmir royal house and had ruled the region, located in north India, since the end of the eleventh century. From 1803 to 1815, Sirmur came under Gurkha control but on their expulsion by the British during the Nepal War, the original Rajput family was restored to their ancestral dominions as a British feudatory.

NOTE: For earlier issues, see Gurkhas Kingdom.

RULERS

Gurkha Control from Nepal,
AH1218-1232/1803-1815AD
Fath Prakash, restored,
VS1872-1890/1815-1833AD

MINTS

Nahan

PAISA

COPPER, 17-18 g

KM#	Date	Year	Good	VG	Fine	VF
11	VS1877	(1820)	6.50	11.50	18.50	30.00

SIROHI

Formerly Rajputana States Agency; merged in Rajasthan State, except for the tehsils (districts) of Abu Road and Dilawara which were merged with Bombay. Bordered on the north, northeast and west by Jodhpur, on the south by Palanpur, Danta and Idar; and on the east by Mewar.

While the ruling family claims descent from Prithwiraj, the Chauhan King of Delhi, the actual founder of the Sirohi house was one Deoraj, a 13th century figure who was the progenitor of the Deora clan of Rajputs. The present capital, Sirohi, was founded in 1425, about which time the Rana of Chitor is said to have taken refuge at Mount Abu from the army of Kutb-ud-din of Gujarat. The British entered by treaty in 1823, disallowed the claims of Jodhpur to Sirohi lands, ultimately bringing the Minas to submission and the straying thakurs back into line.

RULER

Sheo Singh, VS1873-1919/1816-1862AD

1/4 ANNA

COPPER, 9.75-10.90 g
Rev. leg: *Zarb Raj Sirohi*, scimitar.

KM#	Date	Year	Good	VG	Fine	VF
11	VS1910	(1853)	3.50	5.50	8.50	12.50

NOTE: Previously listed under Jodhpur State.

SITAMAU

Sitamau, in western Malwa, was founded in 1695 by Raja Kesho Das, a scion of the Rathor rulers of Ratlam. Sitamau was tributary to Sindhia before passing under British protection and control in the nineteenth century.

RULERS

Fateh Singh,
VS1859-1924/1802-1867AD
Bhawani Singh,
VS1924-1942/1867-1885AD
Bahadur Singh,
VS1942-1956/1885-1899AD
Shadul Singh,
VS1956-1957/1899-1900AD
Ram Singh,
VS1957-2004/1900-1947AD

BAHADUR SINGH

VS1942-1956/1885-1899AD

1/4 PAISA

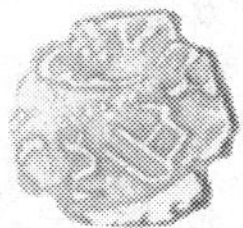

COPPER, 2.2 g
Obv: Trident, VS date.
Rev: Mintname in Devanagari and Persian.

KM#	Date	Year	Good	VG	Fine	VF
5	VS1944	(1887)	5.00	10.00	18.00	30.00

PAISA

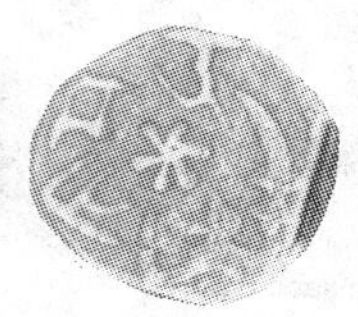

COPPER, 10.7 g
Obv: Trident, VS date. Rev: Mintname in Devanagari, 6-pointed star and sword.

KM#	Date	Year	Good	VG	Fine	VF
10	VS1944	(1887)	5.00	10.00	18.00	30.00

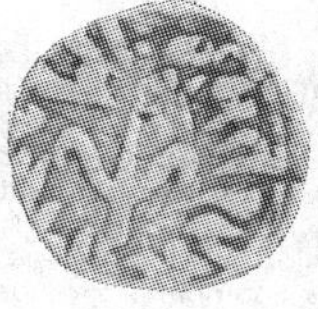
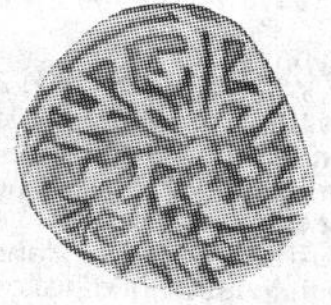

9.8 g
Obv: Trident, VS date. Rev: Ruler's name, mintname in Devanagari and Persian.

KM#	Date	Year	Good	VG	Fine	VF
12	VS1948	(1891)	4.00	8.00	15.00	25.00

9.60-9.80 g
Obv: Trident, 2 stars above, AD date.
Rev: Similar to KM#12.

KM#	Date	Year	Good	VG	Fine	VF
15	AD1892	—	7.00	15.00	25.00	40.00

NOTE: The date is expressed by the word *San* followed by Devanagari numerals and "I", the abbreviation for *Isvi* denoting the Christian calendar, and *Samvat*.

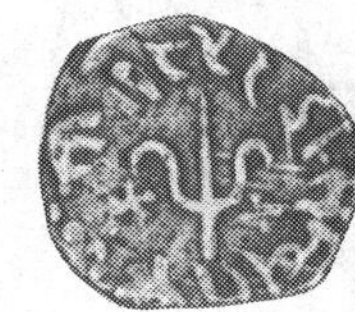

10.35 g
Obv: Trident, 2 stars below, AD date.
Rev: Similar to KM#12.

KM#	Date	Year	Good	VG	Fine	VF
18	AD1896	—	10.00	20.00	35.00	55.00

NOTE: Same as KM#15.

SHADUL SINGH

VS1956-1957/1899-1900AD

1/2 PAISA

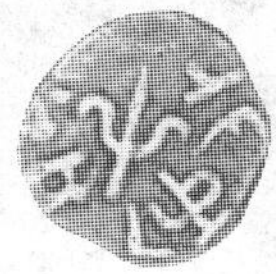
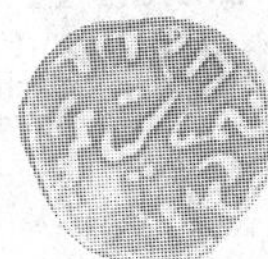

COPPER, 4.75 g
Obv: Trident, VS date.
Rev: Ruler's name, mintname in Persian.

KM#	Date	Year	Good	VG	Fine	VF
25	VS1956	(1899)	5.00	10.00	20.00	35.00

TONK

Tunk

State located partially in Rajputana and in central India. Tonk was founded in 1806 by Amir Khan (d. 1834), the Pathan Pindari leader, who received the territory from Holkar. Amir Khan caused great havoc in Central India by his lightning raids into neighboring states. In 1817 he was forced into submission by the East India Company and remained under British control until India's independence. In March 1948 Tonk was incorporated into Rajasthan.

RULERS

Amir Khan,
AH1213-1250/1798-1834AD
Wazir Muhammad Khan,
AH1250-1281/1834-1864AD
Muhammad Ali Khan,
AH1280-1284/1864-1867AD
Muhammad Ibrahim Ali Khan,
AH1284-1349/1868-1930AD

MINT MARKS

Sironj سرونج

Tonk تونک

Necklace (on C#50 only)

Flower (on all)

Leaf (several forms)

Beginning with the reign of Muhammad Ibrahim Ali Khan, most coins have both AD and AH dates. Circulation with both dates fully legible are worth about 20 per cent more than listed prices. Coins with one date fully legible are worth prices shown. Coins with both dates off are of little value.

There are many minor and major variations of type, varying with location of date, orientation of leaf, arrangement of legend. Although these fall into easily distinguished patterns, they are strictly for the specialist and are omitted here.

The Tonk rupee was known as the "Chanwarshahi".

SIRONJ MINT

Mughal Issues

In the name of Muhammad Akbar II

AH1221-1253/1806-1837AD

PAISA

COPPER, 23mm
Rev: Jhar.

C#	Date	Year	Good	VG	Fine	VF
45	AH1225	—	4.00	10.00	15.00	25.00

Rev: Horse.

C#	Date	Year	Good	VG	Fine	VF
45a	AH1226	—	5.00	12.50	20.00	30.00

Rev: Uncertain symbols.

C#	Date	Year	Good	VG	Fine	VF
45c	AH1247	—	3.50	7.00	12.00	20.00

Rev: Rosette & katar.

C#	Date	Year	Good	VG	Fine	VF
45d	AH1250	—	4.00	10.00	15.00	25.00

20-21mm
Rev: Rosette & necklace.

C#	Date	Year	Good	VG	Fine	VF
50	AH1252	—	3.00	7.00	12.00	20.00
	1253	—	3.00	7.00	12.00	20.00
	1254	—	3.00	7.00	12.00	20.00
	1269	—	3.00	7.00	12.00	20.00

1/4 RUPEE

SILVER, 13mm, 2.68-2.90 g

C#	Date	Year	VG	Fine	VF	XF
58	AH1253	—	7.50	13.00	22.00	32.00

1/2 RUPEE

SILVER, 5.35-5.80 g

C#	Date	Year	VG	Fine	VF	XF
59	AH1253	—	6.50	13.00	22.00	32.00
	1256	—	6.50	13.00	22.00	32.00
	1267	—	6.50	13.00	22.00	32.00

RUPEE

SILVER, 10.70-11.60 g

C#	Date	Year	VG	Fine	VF	XF
60	AH1219	—	6.50	13.00	21.00	30.00
	1221	—	6.50	13.00	21.00	30.00
	1228	—	6.50	13.00	21.00	30.00
	1233	—	6.50	13.00	21.00	30.00
	1235	—	6.50	13.00	21.00	30.00
	1243	—	6.50	13.00	21.00	30.00
	1245	—	6.50	13.00	21.00	30.00
	1252	—	6.50	13.00	21.00	30.00
	1253	31	6.50	13.00	21.00	30.00
	1264	—	6.50	13.00	21.00	30.00
	1269	—	6.50	13.00	21.00	30.00

Regal Issues

In the names of Queen Victoria and Wazir Muhammad Khan

AH1250-1281/1834-1864AD

PAISA

COPPER, 18-20mm

Y#	Date	Year	Good	VG	Fine	VF
1	AH1278	—	4.00	6.25	10.00	16.50

RUPEE

SILVER, 10.70-11.60 g

Y#	Date	Year	VG	Fine	VF	XF
2	AH1276	—	12.50	18.50	25.00	35.00
	1277	—	12.50	18.50	25.00	35.00
	1280	—	12.50	18.50	25.00	35.00

In the names of Queen Victoria and Muhammad Ali Khan

AH1281-1285/1864-1867AD

PAISA

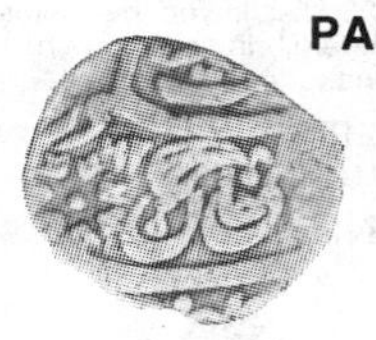
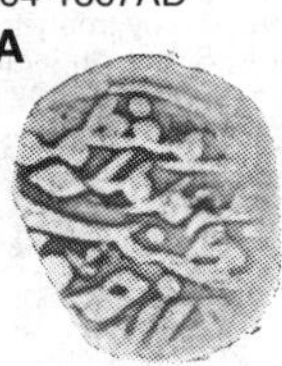

COPPER, 23-24mm

Y#	Date	Year	Good	VG	Fine	VF
3	AH1283	—	3.00	5.00	7.50	12.50
	1285	—	3.00	5.00	7.50	12.50
	1286	—	3.00	5.00	7.50	12.50
	1288	—	3.00	5.00	7.50	12.50
	1289	—	3.00	5.00	7.50	12.50

1/8 RUPEE

SILVER, 12mm, 1.34-1.45 g

Y#	Date	Year	VG	Fine	VF	XF
4	ND (off flan)	—	6.50	13.00	22.00	32.00
	AH(12)8x	—	6.50	13.00	22.00	32.00

1/4 RUPEE

SILVER, 15mm, 2.68-2.90 g

Y#	Date	Year	VG	Fine	VF	XF
5	AH1289	—	6.00	12.00	21.00	30.00

1/2 RUPEE

SILVER, 16-17mm, 5.35-5.80 g

Y#	Date	Year	VG	Fine	VF	XF
6	AH1289	—	6.50	13.00	22.00	32.00

RUPEE

SILVER, 10.70-11.60 g

Y#	Date	Year	VG	Fine	VF	XF
7	AH1282	—	9.00	18.00	28.00	40.00
	1286	—	9.00	18.00	28.00	40.00
	1288	—	9.00	18.00	28.00	40.00
	1289	—	9.00	18.00	28.00	40.00
	1292	—	9.00	18.00	28.00	40.00
	1296	—	9.00	18.00	28.00	40.00
	—	1891	9.00	18.00	28.00	40.00

In the names of Victoria Empress and Muhammad Ibrahim Ali Khan

AH1285-1348/1867-1930AD

PIE

COPPER, 16mm

Y#	Date	Year	Good	VG	Fine	VF
11	AH1314	—	4.50	8.00	12.00	17.50

PAISA

COPPER, 23mm

Y#	Date	Year	Good	VG	Fine	VF
12	AH1298	—	4.00	6.50	10.00	15.00
	1299	—	4.00	6.50	10.00	15.00
	1302	—	4.00	6.50	10.00	15.00
	1308	—	4.00	6.50	10.00	15.00

1/8 RUPEE

SILVER, 1.34-1.45 g

Y#	Date	Year	VG	Fine	VF	XF
A13	AH(13)10					
		(1893)	9.00	18.00	28.00	40.00

1/4 RUPEE

SILVER, about 12mm, 2.68-2.90 g

Y#	Date	Year	VG	Fine	VF	XF
13	AH(13)10					
		(1893)	7.50	15.00	25.00	35.00
	(13)14	(1896)	7.50	15.00	25.00	35.00

1/2 RUPEE

SILVER, 5.35-5.80 g

Y#	Date	Year	VG	Fine	VF	XF
14	AH1306	—	7.50	15.00	25.00	35.00
	1310	1893	7.50	15.00	25.00	35.00
	1314	.1896	7.50	15.00	25.00	35.00

RUPEE

SILVER, 10.70-11.60 g

Y#	Date	Year	VG	Fine	VF	XF
15	AH1299	—	9.00	18.00	28.00	40.00
	1303	—	9.00	18.00	28.00	40.00
	1304	23	9.00	18.00	28.00	40.00
	1306	—	9.00	18.00	28.00	40.00
	1309	1892	9.00	18.00	28.00	40.00
	1310	1893	9.00	18.00	28.00	40.00

In the name of Queen Victoria and Muhammad Ibrahim Ali Khan

TONK MINT

NOTE: All coins with both AH and AD dates clearly readable command about a 50 per cent premium.

1/4 PAISA

COPPER, 2.00-3.00 g
Uniface. Mint name *Tonk*.

C#	Date	Year	Good	VG	Fine	VF
15	ND	—	10.00	15.00	22.50	32.00

PAISA

COPPER

Y#	Date	Year	Good	VG	Fine	VF
8	AH1290	—	3.50	6.00	10.00	17.50

1/8 RUPEE

SILVER, 1.34-1.45 g

Y#	Date	Year	VG	Fine	VF	XF
9	AH	—	10.00	15.00	21.50	30.00

RUPEE

SILVER, 10.70-11.60 g

Y#	Date	Year	VG	Fine	VF	XF
10	AH—	1873	10.00	15.00	21.50	30.00
	1290	1873	10.00	15.00	21.50	30.00
	1290	187x	10.00	15.00	21.50	30.00
	1291	187x	10.00	15.00	21.50	30.00
	1292	187x	10.00	15.00	21.50	30.00
	1293	187x	10.00	15.00	21.50	30.00
	1294	187x	10.00	15.00	21.50	30.00
	1293	1876	10.00	15.00	21.50	30.00
	1294	1877	10.00	15.00	21.50	30.00

NOTE: Var. 1, illustrated above, has no leaf, but a branch on obverse. All others have the leaf, as on the 1 Paisa, Y#8. Six varieties are known.

In the names of Victoria Empress and Muhammad Ibrahim Ali Khan

PAISA

COPPER
Obv: AH date in exergue.

Y#	Date	Year	Good	VG	Fine	VF
16	AH1290	187x	1.75	3.25	5.00	8.00
	1292	1876	1.75	3.25	5.00	8.00
	1294	1877	1.75	3.25	5.00	8.00
	1295	187x	1.50	3.00	4.00	6.50
	1298	1880	1.50	3.00	4.00	6.50
	1298	1881	1.50	3.00	4.00	6.50
	1302	1885	1.00	2.50	3.50	5.50
	1303	1885	1.00	2.50	3.50	5.50
	1303	1886	1.00	2.50	3.50	5.50

NOTE: 4 varieties are known.

1/8 RUPEE

SILVER, 1.34-1.45 g

Y#	Date	Year	VG	Fine	VF	XF
17	AH1309	1892	6.00	9.00	13.50	20.00
	1317	1899	6.00	9.00	13.50	20.00

1/4 RUPEE

SILVER, 14-15mm, 2.68-2.90 g

Y#	Date	Year	VG	Fine	VF	XF
18	AH1305	1888	6.00	9.00	13.50	20.00
	1309	1892	6.00	9.00	13.50	20.00
	1316	189x	6.00	9.00	13.50	20.00
	1317	1899	6.00	9.00	13.50	20.00
	1318	1xxx	6.00	9.00	13.50	20.00

1/2 RUPEE

SILVER, 5.35-5.80 g

Y#	Date	Year	VG	Fine	VF	XF
19	AH129x	1882	6.50	10.00	15.00	22.50
	1305	1888	6.50	10.00	15.00	22.50
	1209	1892	6.50	10.00	15.00	22.50
	1309	1892	6.50	10.00	15.00	22.50
	1317	1899	6.50	10.00	15.00	22.50

RUPEE

SILVER, 10.70-11.60 g

Y#	Date	Year	VG	Fine	VF	XF
20	AH1292	187x	6.50	10.00	15.00	22.50
	1293	1876	6.50	10.00	15.00	22.50
	1294	187x	6.50	10.00	15.00	22.50
	1295	187x	6.50	10.00	15.00	22.50
	1295	1878	6.50	10.00	15.00	22.50
	1296	1877	6.50	10.00	15.00	22.50
	1296	1879	6.50	10.00	15.00	22.50
	1297	1879	6.50	10.00	15.00	22.50
	1297	1880	6.50	10.00	15.00	22.50
	1298	1881	6.50	10.00	15.00	22.50
	1299	1879	6.50	10.00	15.00	22.50
	1301	1884	6.50	10.00	15.00	22.50
	1302	1884	6.50	10.00	15.00	22.50
	1304	1887	6.50	10.00	15.00	22.50
	1305	1888	6.50	10.00	15.00	22.50
	1307	18xx	6.50	10.00	15.00	22.50
	1308	1890	6.50	10.00	15.00	22.50
	1308	1891	6.50	10.00	15.00	22.50
	1309	1891	6.50	10.00	15.00	22.50
	1309	1892	6.50	10.00	15.00	22.50
	1310	1893	6.50	10.00	15.00	22.50
	1311	—	6.50	10.00	15.00	22.50
	1312	189x	6.50	10.00	15.00	22.50
	1313	1895	6.50	10.00	15.00	22.50
	1315	1897	6.50	10.00	15.00	22.50

NAZARANA RUPEE

SILVER, 10.70-11.60 g

Y#	Date	Year	VG	Fine	VF	XF
20a	AH1297	1880	—	—	Rare	—

NAZARANA 2 RUPEES

SILVER, 32mm, 21.40-23.20 g

Y#	Date	Year	VG	Fine	VF	XF
21	AH1297	1880	125.00	150.00	225.00	300.00
	1298	1881	125.00	150.00	225.00	300.00

MOHUR

GOLD, 19mm, 10.70-11.40 g

Y#	Date	Year	VG	Fine	VF	XF
22	AH1297	1880	200.00	250.00	325.00	400.00
	1298	188x	200.00	250.00	325.00	400.00

NAZARANA 2 MOHURS

GOLD, 21.40-22.80 g

Y#	Date	Year	VG	Fine	VF	XF
23	AH1297	1880	350.00	600.00	800.00	1000.

TRAVANCORE

State located in extreme southwest India. A mint was established in ME965/1789-1790AD.

The region of Travancore had a lengthy history before being annexed by the Vijayanagar kingdom. With Vijayanagar's defeat at the battle of Talikota in 1565, Travancore passed under Muslim control until the late eighteenth century, when it merged as a state in its own right under Raja Martanda Varma. At this time the raja allied himself with British interests as a protection against the Muslim dynasty of Mysore. In 1795 the raja of Travancore officially accepted a subsidiary alliance with the East India Company, and remained within the orbit of British influence from then until India's independence.

RULERS

Bala Rama Varma I,
ME973-986/1798-1810AD
Rani Parvathi Bai, regent,
ME990-1004/1815-1829AD
Rama Varma III,
ME1004-1022/1829-1847AD
Martanda Varma II,
ME1022-1035/1847-1860AD
Rama Varma IV,
ME1035-1055/1860-1880AD
Rama Varma V,
ME1057-1062/1880-1885AD
Rama Varma VI,
ME1062-1101/1885-1924AD

MONETARY SYSTEM

16 Cash (Kasu) = 1 Chuckram
4 Chuckram = 1 Fanam
2 Fanams = 1 Anantaraya
7 Fanams = 1 Rupee
52-1/2 Fanam = 1 Pagoda

DATING

ME dates are of the Malabar Era. Add 824 or 825 to the ME date for the AD date. (e.g., ME1112 plus 824-825 = 1936-1937AD).

BALA RAMA VARMA I

ME973-986/1798-1810AD

1/2 CHUCKRAM

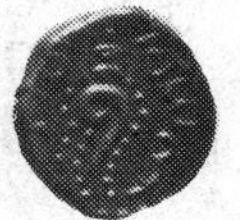

COPPER

KM#	Date	Year	VG	Fine	VF	XF
5	ND	—	4.00	7.50	12.00	20.00

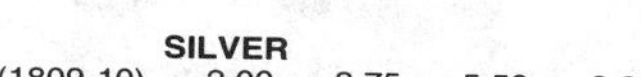

SILVER

KM#	Date	Year	VG	Fine	VF	XF
7	ND	(1809-10)	2.00	3.75	5.50	9.00

CHUCKRAM

SILVER

KM#	Date	Year	VG	Fine	VF	XF
1	ND	(1600-1860)	.60	1.00	1.50	2.00

2 CHUCKRAMS

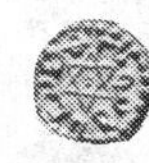
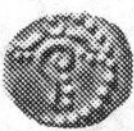

SILVER

KM#	Date	Year	VG	Fine	VF	XF
8	ND	(1809-10)	5.00	8.50	12.50	18.50

1/2 ANANTARAYA

(Fanam)

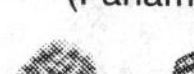

GOLD

KM#	Date	Year	VG	Fine	VF	XF
2	ND	(1790-1830)	6.00	9.00	14.00	22.00

ANANTARAYA

(2 Fanam)

GOLD

KM#	Date	Year	VG	Fine	VF	XF
3	ND	(1790-1860)	10.00	15.00	21.50	32.50

NOTE: For similar coins with leaf sprays on the obverse see KM#23, 19th century edition.

RANI PARVATHI BAI

Regent, ME990-1004/1815-1829AD

CASH

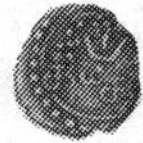

COPPER

KM#	Date	Year	VG	Fine	VF	XF
9	ME991-7	(1815-21)	3.00	5.00	8.50	12.50

2 CASH

COPPER

KM#	Date	Year	VG	Fine	VF	XF
10	ME991	(1815)	4.00	7.00	10.00	15.00
	ME997	(1821)	4.00	7.00	10.00	15.00

4 CASH

COPPER

KM#	Date	Year	VG	Fine	VF	XF
11	ME991	(1815)	6.00	10.00	14.00	20.00

8 CASH

COPPER

KM#	Date	Year	VG	Fine	VF	XF
12	ME991	(1814)	10.00	17.50	25.00	35.00

RAMA VARMA III

ME1004-1022/1829-1847AD

CASH

COPPER

KM#	Date	Year	VG	Fine	VF	XF
14	ME1005	(1830)	2.25	3.50	5.00	7.50

KM#	Date	Year	VG	Fine	VF	XF
15	ND	(1830-39)	1.50	2.25	3.50	5.00

MARTANDA VARMA II

ME1004-1022/1847-1860AD

CASH

COPPER

KM#	Date	Year	VG	Fine	VF	XF
16	ND	(1848-60)	1.00	1.75	2.50	3.50

2 CASH

COPPER

KM#	Date	Year	VG	Fine	VF	XF
17	ND	(1848-49)	3.00	5.00	7.00	10.00

4 CASH

COPPER

KM#	Date	Year	VG	Fine	VF	XF
18	ND		4.00	7.00	10.00	15.00

8 CASH

COPPER

KM#	Date	Year	VG	Fine	VF	XF
19	ND		7.50	12.50	17.50	25.00

RAMA VARMA IV

ME1035-1055/1860-1880AD

CASH

COPPER, 8-10mm

KM#	Date	Year	VG	Fine	VF	XF
20	ND	(1860-85)	.60	.1.00	1.50	2.00

CHUCKRAM

SILVER

KM#	Date	Year	VG	Fine	VF	XF
21	ND	(1860-1901)	.85	1.40	2.00	3.00

VELLI FANAM

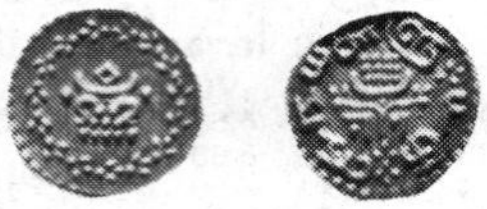

DUMP SILVER

KM#	Date	Year	VG	Fine	VF	XF
22	ND	(1860-61)	3.00	5.00	17.00	10.00

Machine-struck

KM#	Date	Year	VG	Fine	VF	XF
24.1	ND	(1864)	1.00	1.75	2.75	4.00

Rev: W/o 2 upper dots.

KM#	Date	Year	VG	Fine	VF	XF
24.2	ND	(1864)	1.00	1.75	2.75	4.00

ANATARAYA

(Fanam)

GOLD

KM#	Date	Year	Fine	VF	XF	Unc
23	ND	(1860-90)	7.50	12.50	18.50	28.50

1/2 PAGODA

GOLD, 1.28 g
Similar to 1 Pagoda, KM#16.

KM#	Date	Year	Fine	VF	XF	Unc
25	1877		65.00	100.00	140.00	200.00

PAGODA

GOLD, 2.55 g

KM#	Date	Year	Fine	VF	XF	Unc
26	1877		110.00	175.00	250.00	350.00

2 PAGODA

GOLD, 5.10 g

KM#	Date	Year	Fine	VF	XF	Unc
27	1877		160.00	265.00	375.00	550.00

RAMA VARMA V

ME1057-1062/1880-1885AD

VIRARAYA FANAM

SILVER

KM#	Date	Year	VG	Fine	VF	XF
29	ND	(1881)	1.00	1.75	2.50	3.50

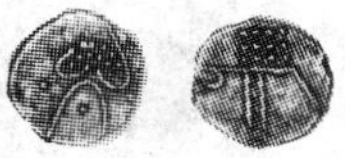

GOLD

KM#	Date	Year	Fine	VF	XF	Unc
30	ND	(1881)	6.00	10.00	15.00	22.50

1/2 SOVEREIGN

3.9940 g, .917 GOLD, .1177 oz AGW

KM#	Date	Mintage	Fine	VF	XF	Unc
31	ME1057//1881	2,000	300.00	500.00	700.00	1000.

SOVEREIGN

7.9881 g, .917 GOLD, .2354 oz AGW

KM#	Date	Mintage	Fine	VF	XF	Unc
32	ME1057//1881	1,000	200.00	350.00	500.00	700.00

RAMA VARMA VI

ME1062-1101/1885-1924AD

Dump Coinage

CASH

COPPER

KM#	Date	Year	VG	Fine	VF	XF
34	ND	(1885-95)	.60	1.00	1.50	2.25

NOTE: KM#34 is a rather degenerated copy of KM#16.

1/4 CHUCKRAM

COPPER

KM#	Date	Year	VG	Fine	VF	XF
35	ND	(1888-89)	3.00	5.00	7.00	10.00

1/2 CHUCKRAM

COPPER

KM#	Date	Year	VG	Fine	VF	XF
36	ND	(1888-89)	4.00	6.50	9.00	15.00

KALI FANAM

GOLD

KM#	Date	Year	Fine	VF	XF	Unc
39	ND	(1890-95)	5.00	8.50	12.50	17.50

1/4 RUPEE

SILVER, 2.72 g

KM#	Date	Mintage	Fine	VF	XF	Unc
37	1889	—	7.50	12.50	17.50	25.00

1/2 RUPEE

SILVER, 5.44 g

KM#	Date	Mintage	Fine	VF	XF	Unc
38	1889	—	12.00	20.00	28.00	40.00

TULABHARAM MEDALLIC ISSUES (M)

These presentation coins were struck prior to the weighing in ceremony of the Maharajah. The balance of his weight in these gold coins were distributed amongst the learned Brahmins and are referred to as Tulabhara Kasu. The legend reads *Sri Patmanabha*, the National Deity.

1/4 PAGODA

GOLD, uniface, 8.8mm, 0.63 g
Tamil leg. in 3 lines.

KM#	Date	Year	Fine	VF	XF	Unc
M1	ND	(1829,47)	50.00	70.00	100.00	150.00

Uniface, 12.7mm, 0.63 g
Tamil leg. in 3 lines.

KM#	Date	Year	Fine	VF	XF	Unc
M5	ND	(1850,55)	50.00	70.00	100.00	150.00

10.9-12.7mm, 0.64 g
Obv: Conch shell within wreath.
Rev: Tamil leg. in 3 lines within wreath.

KM#	Date	Year	Fine	VF	XF	Unc
M9	ND	(1870-1931)	45.00	65.00	90.00	135.00

1/2 PAGODA

GOLD, uniface, 10.9mm, 1.27 g
Tamil leg. in 3 lines.

KM#	Date	Year	Fine	VF	XF	Unc
M2	ND	(1829,47)	60.00	80.00	110.00	165.00

Uniface, 14.5mm, 1.27 g
Tamil leg. in 3 lines.

KM#	Date	Year	Fine	VF	XF	Unc
M6	ND	(1850,55)	60.00	80.00	110.00	165.00

1.28 g

KM#	Date	Year	Fine	VF	XF	Unc
M10	ND	(1870-1931)	55.00	85.00	120.00	175.00

PAGODA

GOLD, uniface, 13mm, 2.54 g
Tamil leg. in 3 lines.

KM#	Date	Year	Fine	VF	XF	Unc
M3	ND	(1829,47)	100.00	135.00	175.00	250.00

Uniface, 17mm, 2.54 g
Tamil leg. in 3 lines.

KM#	Date	Year	Fine	VF	XF	Unc
M7	ND	(1850,55)	100.00	135.00	175.00	250.00

2.54 g

KM#	Date	Year	Fine	VF	XF	Unc
M11	ND	(1870-1931)	85.00	140.00	200.00	285.00

2 PAGODAS

GOLD, uniface, 15.4mm, 5.06 g
Tamil leg. in 3 lines.

KM#	Date	Year	Fine	VF	XF	Unc
M4	ND	(1829,47)	120.00	200.00	275.00	400.00

Uniface, 20.3mm, 5.06 g
Tamil leg. in 3 lines.

KM#	Date	Year	Fine	VF	XF	Unc
M8	ND	(1850,55)	120.00	200.00	275.00	400.00

20.0-23.9mm, 5.09 g
Obv: Conch shell within wreath.
Rev: Tamil leg. in 3 lines within wreath.

KM#	Date	Year	Fine	VF	XF	Unc
M12	ND	(1870-1931)	125.00	210.00	300.00	425.00

PATTERNS (Pn)

(Including off metal strikes)

KM#	Date	Mintage	Identification	Mkt.Val.
Pn1	1881	—	1/2 Sovereign, White metal, KM31	210.00
Pn2	1881	—	1 Sovereign, White metal, KM32	250.00

TRIPURA

Hill Tipperah

Tripura was a Hindu Kingdom consisting of a strip of the fertile plains east of Bengal, and a large tract of hill territory beyond, which had a reputation for providing wild elephants.

At times when Bengal was weak, Tripura rose to prominence and extended its rule into the plains, but when Bengal was strong the kingdom consisted purely of the hill area, which was virtually impregnable and not of enough economic worth to encourage the Muslims to conquer it. In this way Tripura was able to maintain its full independence until the 19th century.

The origins of the Kingdom are veiled in legend, but the first coins were struck during the reign of Ratna Manikya (1464-89) and copied the weight and fabric of the contemporary issues of the Sultans of Bengal. He also copied the lion design that had appeared on certain rare tangkas of Nasir-ud-din Mahmud Shah I dated AH849 (1445AD). In other respects the designs were purely Hindu, and the lion was retained on most of the later issues as a national emblem.

Tripura rose to a political zenith during the 16th century, while Muslim rule in Bengal was weak, and several coins were struck to commemorate successful military campaigns from Chittagong in the south to Sylhet in the north. These conquests were not sustained, and in the early 17th century the Mughal army was able to inflict severe defeats on Tripura, which was forced to pay tribute.

In about 1733AD all the territory in the plains was annexed by the Mughals, and the Raja merely managed his estate there as a zemindar, although he still retained control as independent King of his hill territory.

The situation remained unchanged when the British took over the administration of Bengal in 1765, and it was only in 1871 that the British appointed an agent in the hills, and began to assist the Maharaja in the administration of his hill territory, which became known as the State of Hill Tipperah.

After the middle of the 18th century, coins were not struck for monetary reasons, but merely for ceremonial use at coronations and other ceremonies, and to keep up the treasured right of coinage.

The coins of Tripura are unusual in that the majority have the name of the King together with that of his Queen, and is the only coinage in the world where this was done consistently.

In common with most other Hindu coinages of northeast India, the coins bear fixed dates. Usually the date used was that of the coronation ceremony, but during the 16th century, coins which were struck with a design commemorating a particular event, bore the date of that event, which can be useful as a historical source, where other written evidence is virtually non-existent.

All modern Tripura coins were presentation pieces, more medallic than monetary in nature. They were struck in very limited numbers and although not intended for local circulation, they are often found in worn condition.

RULERS

Rajadhara Manikya
SE1707-1726/1785-1804AD

Rama Ganga Manikya
রাম গঙ্গা মাণিক্য
SE1728-1731,1735-1748/
1806-1809,1813-1826AD

Queens of Rama Ganga Manikya
Queen Tara
Queen Chandra Tara
চন্দ্র তারা

Durga Manikya
দুর্গা মাণিক্য
SE1731-1735/1809-1813AD

Queen of Durga Manikya
Queen Sumitra
সুমিত্রা

Kashi Chandra Manikya
SE1748-1752/1826-1830AD

Queens of Kashi Chandra Manikya
Queen Chandraveth
Queen Kirti Lakshmi

Krishna Kishore Manikya
কৃষ্ণ কিশোর মাণিক্য
SE1752-1772/1830-1850AD

Queens of Krishna Kishore
Queen Bidumukhi
Queen Ratna Mala
রত্ন মালা
Queen Purnakala
Queen Sudhakshina

Ishana Chandra Manikya
SE1772-1784/1850-1862AD

Queens of Ishana Chandra Manikya
Queen Chandresvari
Queen Muktabani
Queen Rajalakshmi

Vira Chandra Manikya
বীর চন্দ্র মাণিক্য
SE1784-1818/TE1272-1306/1862-1896AD

Queens of Vira Chandra Manikya
Queen Bhanumati
ভানুমতী
Queen Rajesvari
রাজেশ্বরী
Queen Manmohini

Radha Kishore Manikya
TE1306-1319/1896-1909AD

Queens of Radha Kishore
Queen Ratnaman Zari
Queen Tulsivati

DATING

While the early coinage is dated in the Saka Era (SE) the later issues are dated in the Tripurabda era (TE). To convert, TE date plus 590 = AD date. The dates appear to be accession years.

RAMA GANGA MANIKYA

SE1728-1731/1806-1809AD

RUPEE

SILVER, plain edge, 10.30-10.70 g
Rev. leg: W/*Queen Tara.*

KM#	Date	Year	VG	Fine	VF	XF
259	SE1728	(1806)	40.00	65.00	90.00	200.00

Oblique edge milling

KM#	Date	Year	VG	Fine	VF	XF
260	SE1728	(1806)	60.00	90.00	125.00	240.00

MOHUR

GOLD

KM#	Date	Year	VG	Fine	VF	XF
265	SE1728	(1806)	300.00	500.00	700.00	1000.

DURGA MANIKYA

SE1731-1735/1809-1813AD

RUPEE

SILVER, 10.30-10.70 g
Rev. leg: W/*Srimati Sumitra Maha Devah.*

KM#	Date	Year	VG	Fine	VF	XF
275	SE1731	(1809)	40.00	65.00	90.00	200.00

MOHUR

GOLD, 10.94 g

KM#	Date	Year	VG	Fine	VF	XF
280	SE1731	(1809)	300.00	500.00	700.00	1000.

RAMA GANGA MANIKYA

SE1735-1748/1813-1826AD

RUPEE

SILVER, 10.30-10.70 g
Rev. leg: W/*Sri Srimati Chandra Tara Maha Devi.*

KM#	Date	Year	VG	Fine	VF	XF
290	SE1743	(1821)	40.00	65.00	90.00	200.00

MOHUR

GOLD

KM#	Date	Year	VG	Fine	VF	XF
295	SE1743	(1821)	300.00	500.00	700.00	1000.

KASHI CHANDRA MANIKYA

SE1748-1752/1826-1830AD

RUPEE

SILVER, 10.30-10.70 g
Rev. leg: W/*Queen Chandravethi.*

KM#	Date	Year	VG	Fine	VF	XF
305	SE1748	(1826)	60.00	90.00	125.00	200.00

Rev. leg: W/*Queen Kirti Lakshmi.*

KM#	Date	Year	VG	Fine	VF	XF
306	SE1748	(1826)	60.00	90.00	125.00	200.00

MOHUR

GOLD
Rev. leg: W/*Queen Kirti Lakshimi.*

KM#	Date	Year	VG	Fine	VF	XF
308	SE1748	(1826)	70.00	100.00	150.00	250.00

KRISHNA KISHORA MANIKYA

SE1752-1772/1830-1850AD

RUPEE

SILVER, 10.30-10.70 g
Rev. leg: W/*Queen Bidhukala.*

KM#	Date	Year	VG	Fine	VF	XF
315	SE1752	(1830)	60.00	90.00	135.00	225.00

Rev. leg: W/*Queen Bidumukhi* added.

KM#	Date	Year	VG	Fine	VF	XF
316	SE1752	(1830)	60.00	90.00	135.00	225.00

Rev. leg: W/*Queen Purnakala* added.

KM#	Date	Year	VG	Fine	VF	XF
317	SE1752	(1830)	60.00	90.00	135.00	225.00

Rev. leg: W/*Sri Srimati Ratna Mala Maha Deva.*

KM#	Date	Year	VG	Fine	VF	XF
318	SE1752	(1830)	45.00	70.00	100.00	175.00

MOHUR

GOLD, 11.59 g
Rev. leg: W/*Queen Akhilesvari.*

KM#	Date	Year	VG	Fine	VF	XF
323	SE1752	(1830)	300.00	500.00	700.00	1000.

Rev. leg: W/*Sri Srimati Ratna Mala Maha Deva.*

KM#	Date	Year	VG	Fine	VF	XF
324	SE1752	(1830)	300.00	500.00	700.00	1000.

Rev. leg: W/*Queen Sudakshina* added.

KM#	Date	Year	VG	Fine	VF	XF
325	SE1752	(1830)	300.00	500.00	700.00	1000.

ISHANA CHANDRA MANIKYA

SE1772-1784/1850-1862AD

RUPEE

SILVER, 10.30-10.70 g
Rev. leg: W/*Queen Chandresvari.*

KM#	Date	Year	VG	Fine	VF	XF
335	SE1771	(1849)	45.00	70.00	100.00	165.00

Rev. leg: W/*Queen Muktavali.*

KM#	Date	Year	VG	Fine	VF	XF
336	SE1771	(1849)	45.00	70.00	100.00	165.00

Rev. leg: W/*Queen Raja Lakshmi.*

KM#	Date	Year	VG	Fine	VF	XF
337	SE1771	(1849)	45.00	70.00	100.00	165.00

MOHUR

GOLD
Rev. leg: W/*Queen Chandresvari.*

KM#	Date	Year	VG	Fine	VF	XF
342	SE1771	(1849)	250.00	400.00	550.00	800.00

Rev. leg: W/*Queen Muktauali.*

KM#	Date	Year	VG	Fine	VF	XF
343	SE1771	(1849)	275.00	450.00	650.00	1000.

Rev. leg: W/*Queen Raja Lakshmi.*

KM#	Date	Year	VG	Fine	VF	XF
344	SE1771	(1849)	275.00	450.00	650.00	1000.

VIRA CHANDRA MANIKYA

SE1784-1818/TE1272-1306/1862-1896AD

RUPEE

SILVER, plain edge, 10.30-10.70 g
Rev. leg: W/*Sri Srimati Bhanumati Maha Devi.*

KM#	Date	Year	VG	Fine	VF	XF
354	SE1791	(1869)	40.00	65.00	90.00	160.00

Machine struck, milled edge

KM#	Date	Year	VG	Fine	VF	XF
355	TE1279	(1869)	40.00	65.00	90.00	160.00

Rev. leg: W/*Queen Manamohini.*

KM#	Date	Year	VG	Fine	VF	XF
356	TE1279	(1869)	40.00	65.00	90.00	160.00

Rev. leg: W/*Sri Srimati Rajesvari Maha Devi.*
Hand struck

KM#	Date	Year	VG	Fine	VF	XF
357	SE1791	(1869)	50.00	80.00	120.00	200.00

Machine struck

KM#	Date	Year	VG	Fine	VF	XF
358	TE1279	(1869)	40.00	65.00	90.00	160.00

MOHUR

GOLD
Similar to 1 Rupee, KM#354.

KM#	Date	Year	VG	Fine	VF	XF
360	SE1791	(1869)	225.00	385.00	550.00	800.00

Similar to 1 Rupee, KM#356.

KM#	Date	Year	VG	Fine	VF	XF
363	TE1279	(1869)	225.00	385.00	550.00	800.00

Similar to 1 Rupee, KM#357.
Rev. leg: W/*Srimati Rajesvari Maha Devah.*

KM#	Date	Year	VG	Fine	VF	XF
364	SE1791	(1869)	250.00	425.00	600.00	850.00

RADHA KISHORE MANIKYA

TE1306-1319/1896-1909AD

1/2 RUPEE

SILVER
Rev. leg: W/*Queen Tulsiwati*

KM#	Date	Year	VG	Fine	VF	XF
373	TE1306	(1896)	50.00	80.00	120.00	200.00

RUPEE

SILVER, 11.30-11.90 g
Mule. Obv: KM#375. Rev: KM#356.

KM#	Date	Year	VG	Fine	VF	XF
374	TE1306	(1896)	60.00	90.00	125.00	200.00

Rev. leg: W/*Queen Ratna Manjari.*

KM#	Date	Year	VG	Fine	VF	XF
375	TE1306	(1896)	45.00	70.00	100.00	165.00

8.80 g
Rev. leg: W/*Queen Tulsiwati.*

KM#	Date	Year	VG	Fine	VF	XF
376	TE1306	(1896)	40.00	65.00	90.00	160.00

MOHUR

GOLD

Rev. leg: W/*Queen Ratna Manjari.*

KM#	Date	Year	VG	Fine	VF	XF
381	TE1306	(1896)	250.00	425.00	600.00	850.00

INDIA-DANISH

TRANQUEBAR

Danish India or Tranquebar is a town and former Danish colony on the southeast coast of India. In Danish times, 1620-1845, it was a factory site and seaport operated by the Danish Asiatic Company. Tranquebar and the other Danish settlements in India were sold to the British East India Company in 1845.

RULERS

Danish, until 1845

MONETARY SYSTEM

80 Kas (Cash) = Royaliner (Fano or Fanam)
8 Royaliner=1 Rupee
18 Royaliner=1 Speciesdaler

DANISH ROYAL COLONY

KAS

COPPER, 0.60 g
Obv: Crowned FVIR monogram.
Rev: Value, date below.

KM#	Date	Mintage	Good	VG	Fine	VF
151	1816	—	—	—	Rare	—
	1819	—	15.00	25.00	60.00	130.00

IV KAS

COPPER, 2.40 g
Obv: Crowned C7 monogram.

KM#	Date	Mintage	Good	VG	Fine	VF
155	1807	—	7.00	10.00	25.00	50.00

NOTE: Earlier dates (1782-1797) exist for this type.

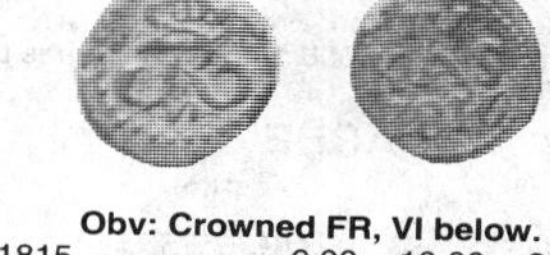
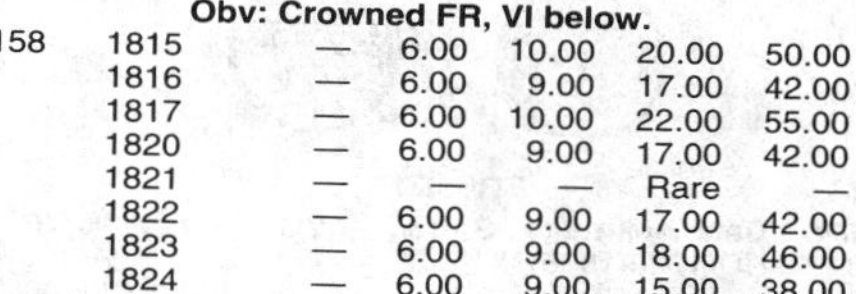

Obv: Crowned FR, VI below.

KM#	Date	Mintage	Good	VG	Fine	VF
158	1815	—	6.00	10.00	20.00	50.00
	1816	—	6.00	9.00	17.00	42.00
	1817	—	6.00	10.00	22.00	55.00
	1820	—	6.00	9.00	17.00	42.00
	1821	—	—	—	Rare	—
	1822	—	6.00	9.00	17.00	42.00
	1823	—	6.00	9.00	18.00	46.00
	1824	—	6.00	9.00	15.00	38.00

Obv: Crown design standardized.

KM#	Date	Mintage	Good	VG	Fine	VF
159.1	1824	—	6.00	9.00	18.00	45.00
	1825	—	20.00	30.00	60.00	150.00
	1830	—	6.00	10.00	20.00	50.00
	1831	—	4.50	7.00	15.00	35.00
	1832	—	4.50	7.00	15.00	35.00
	1833	—	6.00	9.00	17.00	42.00
	1834	—	6.00	10.00	20.00	50.00
	1837	—	6.00	10.00	20.00	50.00
	1838	—	6.00	10.00	18.00	45.00
	1839	—	4.00	6.00	14.00	35.00

Rev: Retrograde S in KAS.

KM#	Date	Mintage	Good	VG	Fine	VF
159.2	1817	—	8.00	10.00	20.00	50.00
	1831	—	—	—	Rare	—

Obv: Value VI (error) for IV.

KM#	Date	Mintage	Good	VG	Fine	VF
160	1824	—	—	—	Rare	—

Obv: Crowned C VIII R monogram.

KM#	Date	Mintage	Good	VG	Fine	VF
161	1840	—	7.00	11.00	22.00	55.00
	1841	—	6.00	9.00	20.00	48.00
	1841 (error, crowned C VIIII R monogram)	—	20.00	30.00	50.00	100.00
	1842	—	6.00	9.00	20.00	48.00
	1843	—	6.00	9.00	20.00	48.00
	1844	—	6.00	11.00	22.00	50.00
	1844 w/o VIII	—	7.00	12.00	25.00	60.00
	1845 w/o VIII	—	7.00	11.00	22.00	55.00

10 KAS

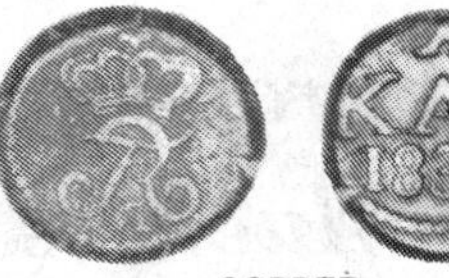

COPPER
Obv: Crowned FR, VI between and below.

KM#	Date	Mintage	Good	VG	Fine	VF
166	1816	—	10.00	16.00	50.00	130.00
	1822	—	17.00	28.00	80.00	160.00
	1838	—	12.00	18.00	65.00	130.00
	1839	—	10.00	16.00	50.00	100.00

Obv: Crowned CR, VIII between and below.

KM#	Date	Mintage	Good	VG	Fine	VF
167	1842	—	60.00	100.00	200.00	375.00

ROYALIN

SILVER
Obv: Crowned C7 monogram.
Rev: Value, arms w/lion between date.

KM#	Date	Mintage	VG	Fine	VF	XF
168	1807	—	20.00	30.00	80.00	155.00

NOTE: Earlier dates (1767-1799) exist for this type.

FANO

(Royalin, Fanam)

SILVER
Obv: Crowned FR, VI between and below.

KM#	Date	Mintage	VG	Fine	VF	XF
170	1816	—	75.00	115.00	250.00	450.00
	1818	—	100.00	150.00	325.00	600.00

2 ROYALINER

SILVER
Obv: Crowned C7 monogram.

KM#	Date	Mintage	VG	Fine	VF	XF
171	1807	—	27.00	38.00	105.00	190.00

NOTE: Earlier dates (1767-1799) exist for this type.

2 FANO

(2 Royaliner, 2 Fanams)

SILVER
Obv: Crowned FR, VI between and below.

KM#	Date	Mintage	VG	Fine	VF	XF
173	1816	—	85.00	135.00	310.00	550.00
	1818	—	125.00	200.00	450.00	800.00

INDIA-FRENCH

It was not until 1664, during the reign of Louis XIV, that the Compagnie des Indes Orientales was formed for the purpose of obtaining holdings on the subcontinent of India. Between 1666 and 1721, French settlements were established at Arcot, Mahe, Surat, Pondichery, Masulipatam, Karikal, Yanam, Murshidabad, Chandernagore, Balasore and Calicut. War with Britain reduced the French holdings to Chandernagore, Pondichery, Karikal, Yanam and Mahe. Chandernagore voted in 1949 to join India and became part of the Republic of India in 1950. Pondichery, Karikal, Yanam and Mahe formed the Pondichery union territory and joined the republic of India in 1954.

RULERS

French, until 1945

MINTS

Arcot (Arkat) اركات

Pondichery پهلجري

Surat سورت

MONETARY SYSTEM

Cache Kas or Cash
Doudou = 4 Caches
Biche = 1 Pice
2 Royalins = 1 Fanon Pondichery
5 Heavy Fanons = 1 Rupee Mahe
64 Biches = 1 Rupee

NOTE: The undated coinage was struck ca. 1720 well into the early 19th century.

ARCOT MINT

(Arkat)

Mint mark:

Crescent

A crescent moon mint mark is found to left of the regnal year for those struck at the Pondichery Mint. For listings of similar coins with lotus mint mark refer to India-British-Madras Presidency.

In the name of Shah Alam II

AH1173-1221/1759-1806AD

1/4 RUPEE

SILVER, 2.80 g

KM#	Date	Year	VG	Fine	VF	XF
13	AH1221	49	21.50	42.00	85.00	120.00
	1222	49	35.00	70.00	100.00	160.00

NOTE: Earlier date (AH1184) exists for this type.

NOTE: Similar coins with crescent mint mark were also issued by Mysore State, using the latter mint name.

1/2 RUPEE

SILVER, 5.70 g

KM#	Date	Year	VG	Fine	VF	XF
14	AH1221	49	31.50	63.00	90.00	130.00

NOTE: Earlier dates (AH1184-1205) exist for this type.

RUPEE

SILVER, 11.40 g

KM#	Date	Year	VG	Fine	VF	XF
15	AH1218	43	12.50	20.00	30.00	50.00
	1218	44	12.50	20.00	30.00	50.00
	1219/8	44	12.50	20.00	30.00	50.00
	1219	44	12.50	20.00	30.00	50.00
	1219	45	12.50	20.00	30.00	50.00
	1220	43(sic)	12.50	20.00	30.00	50.00
	1220	45	12.50	20.00	30.00	50.00
	1221	43(sic)	12.50	20.00	30.00	50.00
	1221	45	12.50	20.00	30.00	50.00
	1222	43(sic)	12.50	20.00	30.00	50.00

NOTE: Earlier dates (AH1177-1208) exist for this type.

NAZARANA RUPEE

SILVER, 32-33mm, 11.40 g

KM#	Date	Year	VG	Fine	VF	XF
16	AH1218	43(sic)	—	250.00	450.00	750.00
	1218	58	—	250.00	450.00	750.00
	1233	58(sic)	—	250.00	450.00	750.00

PONDICHERY MINT

A city south of Madras on the southeast coast which became the site of the French Mint from 1700 to 1841. Pondichery was settled by the French in 1683. It became their main Indian possession even though it was occupied by the Dutch in 1693-1698 and several times by the British from 1761-1816.

CACHE

BRONZE

KM#	Date	Mintage	Good	VG	Fine	VF
33	ND(1720-1835)	—	3.50	6.50	13.50	25.00

1/2 DOUDOU

COPPER, 2.10 g

KM#	Date	Mintage	Good	VG	Fine	VF
34	ND(1720-1835)	—	2.00	3.00	6.00	15.00

DOUDOU

COPPER, 4.20 g

KM#	Date	Mintage	Good	VG	Fine	VF
35	ND(1720-1835)	—	2.00	3.00	5.00	12.00

KM#	Date	Mintage	Good	VG	Fine	VF
52	1836	—	3.50	6.50	13.50	25.00
	1837	—	3.50	6.50	13.50	25.00

1/2 FANON

SILVER, 0.50-0.70 g

KM#	Date	Mintage	VG	Fine	VF	XF
39	ND(1720-1837)	—	10.00	15.00	25.00	40.00

KM#	Date	Mintage	VG	Fine	VF	XF
53	1837	—	16.50	28.50	45.00	75.00

FANON

SILVER, 1.500-1.593 g
Similar to 2 Fanon, KM#49.

KM#	Date	Mintage	VG	Fine	VF	XF
45	ND	—	12.50	20.00	35.00	60.00

KM#	Date	Mintage	VG	Fine	VF	XF
54	1837	—	16.50	28.50	45.00	75.00

2 FANON

SILVER, 2.20-2.76 g
Obv: Pearled crown.

KM#	Date	Mintage	VG	Fine	VF	XF
48	ND(1720-1837)	—	16.50	28.50	45.00	75.00

Obv: Flowered crown.

KM#	Date	Mintage	VG	Fine	VF	XF
49	ND(1720-1837)	—	16.50	28.50	45.00	75.00

KM#	Date	Mintage	VG	Fine	VF	XF
55	1837	—	20.00	32.50	55.00	90.00

PAGODA

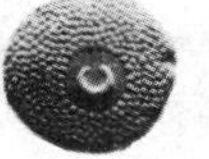

GOLD, 3.40 g
Obv: Flowered crown.

KM#	Date	Mintage	VG	Fine	VF	XF
51	ND(1830-48)	—	—	—	450.00	600.00

SURAT MINT

The French silver coins struck similar to late Mughal issues in two different periods. See also India-British,

Bombay Presidency.

1/8 RUPEE

In the name of Shah Alam II (posthumous)

SILVER, 1.42 g

KM#	Date	Year	VG	Fine	VF	XF
73	AHxxxx	4x	40.00	70.00	100.00	150.00

1/2 RUPEE

SILVER, 5.70g

KM#	Date	Year	VG	Fine	VF	XF
75	AHxxxx	49	25.00	50.00	100.00	150.00
	122(5)	52	25.00	50.00	100.00	150.00
	Mintname off flan		20.00	35.00	65.00	100.00

NOTE: For listings w/regnal year 46 see India-British, Bombay Presidency.

RUPEE

In the name of Shah Alam II (posthumous)

SILVER, 11.40g

KM#	Date	Year	VG	Fine	VF	XF
76	AH122(4)	51	20.00	30.00	60.00	100.00
	122(5)	52	20.00	30.00	60.00	100.00
	122(6)	53	20.00	30.00	60.00	100.00
	1227	54	20.00	30.00	60.00	100.00
	Mintname off flan		10.00	15.00	25.00	45.00

NOTE: For listings w/regnal year 46 see India-British, Bombay Presidency.

Rev: W/symbol.

KM#	Date	Year	VG	Fine	VF	XF
77	AH122x	5x	25.00	40.00	75.00	125.00
(76.2)	xxxx	6x	25.00	40.00	75.00	125.00

2/3 MOHUR

GOLD, 7.80 g

KM#	Date	Year	VG	Fine	VF	XF
78	AHxxxx	5x	—	—	—	—

INDIA - PORTUGUESE

Vasco da Gama, the Portuguese explorer, first visited India in 1498. Portugal seized control of a number of islands and small enclaves on the west coast of India, and for the next hundred years enjoyed a monopoly on trade. With the arrival of powerful Dutch and English fleets in the first half of the 17th century, Portuguese power in the area declined until virtually all of India that remained under Portuguese control were the west coast enclaves of Goa, Damao and Diu. They were forcibly annexed by India in 1962.

RULERS

Portuguese, until 1961

IDENTIFICATION

The undated coppers are best identified by the shape of the coat of arms.

Maria I-Somewhat triangular shield (baroque style)
Joao VI, as Regent: oval shield
Joao VI, as King: square shield superimposed on globe
Maria II: square shield on plain background

DENOMINATION

The denomination of most copper coins appears in numerals on the reverse, though 30 Reis is often given as "1/2 T", and 60 Reis as "T" (T = Tanga). The silver coins have the denomination in words, usually on the obverse until 1850, then on the reverse.

DAMAO

(Daman)

A city located 100 miles north of Bombay. It was captured by the Portuguese in 1559. A mint was opened in Damao in 1611. This mint continued in operation until 1854. While important to early Portuguese trade, Damao dwindled as time passed. It was annexed to India in 1962.

MONETARY SYSTEM

375 Bazacucos = 300 Reis
300 Reis = 1 Pardao
60 Reis = 1 Tanga
2 Pardao (Xerafins) = 1 Rupia

15 REIS

COPPER
Maria II

KM#	Date	Mintage	Good	VG	Fine	VF
25	1843	—	8.50	16.50	30.00	60.00

Pedro V

KM#	Date	Mintage	Good	VG	Fine	VF
26	1854	—	7.00	15.00	25.00	50.00

30 REIS

COPPER
Maria II

KM#	Date	Mintage	Good	VG	Fine	VF
23	1840	—	6.00	12.00	20.00	40.00

Pedro V
Similar to KM#23.

KM#	Date	Mintage	Good	VG	Fine	VF
27	1854	—	7.00	15.00	22.00	45.00

60 REIS

COPPER
Maria II

KM#	Date	Mintage	Good	VG	Fine	VF
24	1840	—	10.00	20.00	35.00	70.00

Pedro V
Similar to KM#24.

KM#	Date	Mintage	Good	VG	Fine	VF
28	1854	—	15.00	30.00	50.00	100.00

DIU

A district in Western India formerly belonging to Portugal. It is 170 miles northwest of Bombay on the Kathiawar peninsula. The Portuguese settled here and built a fort in 1535. A mint was opened in 1685 and was closed in 1859. As with Damao, the importance of Diu diminished with the passage of time. It was annexed to India in 1962.

MONETARY SYSTEM

750 Bazarucos = 600 Reis
40 Atia = 10 Tanga = 1 Rupia

5 BAZARUCOS

LEAD or TIN, 20-23mm
Joao
Obv: Crude crowned arms.
Rev: Date in angles of cross.

KM#	Date	Mintage	Good	VG	Fine	VF
44	1801	—	5.00	10.00	20.00	35.00

NOTE: Earlier dates (1799-1800) exist for this type.

21mm
Similar to 20 Bazarucos, KM#47.

KM#	Date	Mintage	Good	VG	Fine	VF
52	1807	—	7.00	15.00	30.00	55.00

Pedro IV
20-22mm

KM#	Date	Mintage	Good	VG	Fine	VF
56	1827	—	5.00	10.00	15.00	28.00
	1828	—	5.00	10.00	15.00	28.00

10 BAZARUCOS

LEAD or TIN, 27mm
Pedro IV

KM#	Date	Mintage	Good	VG	Fine	VF
57	1827	—	5.00	10.00	18.00	32.00
	1828	—	5.00	10.00	18.00	32.00

20 BAZARUCOS

TIN, 14.00-16.50 g
Joao

KM#	Date	Mintage	Good	VG	Fine	VF
47	1801	—	6.00	12.00	25.00	45.00

NOTE: Earlier dates (1799-1800) exist for this type.

33-36mm
Similar to KM#47.

KM#	Date	Mintage	Good	VG	Fine	VF
53	1807	—	15.00	27.50	40.00	70.00

Pedro IV

KM#	Date	Mintage	Good	VG	Fine	VF
58	1827	—	6.00	12.00	22.00	40.00
	1828	—	6.00	12.00	22.00	40.00

30 REIS

COPPER
Joao

KM#	Date	Mintage	Good	VG	Fine	VF
54	1818	—	6.00	12.00	22.00	42.00

60 REIS

COPPER
Joao
Similar to 30 Reis, KM#54.

KM#	Date	Mintage	Good	VG	Fine	VF
55	1818	—	7.50	15.00	28.00	55.00

150 REIS

SILVER
Joao
Obv: Crowned arms. Rev: Date in angles of cross.

KM#	Date	Mintage	Good	VG	Fine	VF
50	1806	—	30.00	50.00	110.00	225.00

Pedro V

KM#	Date	Mintage	Good	VG	Fine	VF
60	1859	—	20.00	35.00	70.00	150.00

300 REIS

SILVER
Joao

KM#	Date	Mintage	Good	VG	Fine	VF
51	1806	—	25.00	40.00	100.00	200.00

Pedro V

KM#	Date	Mintage	Good	VG	Fine	VF
61	1859	—	25.00	40.00	100.00	200.00

RUPIA

(600 Reis)

SILVER, 10.63 g
Joao
Obv: Crowned arms.
Rev: Date in angles of cross.

KM#	Date	Mintage	Good	VG	Fine	VF
49	1804	—	75.00	125.00	250.00	500.00
	1805	—	75.00	125.00	250.00	500.00
	1806	—	75.00	125.00	250.00	500.00

Maria II

KM#	Date	Mintage	Good	VG	Fine	VF
59	1841	—	100.00	150.00	300.00	600.00

PATTERNS (Pn)

(Including off metal strikes)

KM#	Date	Mintage	Identification	Mkt.Val.
Pn1	1851	—	1/4 Attia, Copper, 2.13 g	Rare

KM#	Date	Mintage	Identification	Mkt.Val.
Pn2	1851	—	1/2 Attia, Copper, 3.80 g	Rare
Pn3	1851	—	Attia, Copper, 7.60 g	Rare

GOA

Goa was the capitol of Portuguese India and is located 250 miles south of Bombay on the west coast of India. It was taken by Albuquerque in 1510. A mint was established immediately and operated until closed by the British in 1869. Later coins were struck at Calcutta and Bombay. Goa was annexed by India in 1962.

MONETARY SYSTEM

375 Bazarucos = 300 Reis
240 Reis = 1 Pardao
2 Xerafim = 1 Rupia

NOTE: The silver Xerafim was equal to the silver Pardao, but the gold Xerafim varied according to fluctuations in the gold/silver ratio.

3 REIS

COPPER
Joao
Similar to 6 Reis, KM#211.

KM#	Date	Mintage	Good	VG	Fine	VF
209	ND	—	6.00	12.00	25.00	45.00

Similar to 4-1/2 Reis, KM#225.

KM#	Date	Mintage	Good	VG	Fine	VF
224	ND	—	6.00	12.00	25.00	45.00

Maria II

KM#	Date	Mintage	Good	VG	Fine	VF
257	ND	—	5.00	8.00	15.00	28.00
	1842	—	5.00	8.00	15.00	28.00
	1844	—	5.00	8.00	15.00	28.00
	1845	—	5.00	8.00	15.00	28.00
	1846	—	5.00	8.00	15.00	28.00
	1848	—	5.00	8.00	15.00	28.00

4-1/2 REIS

COPPER
Joao
Similar to 6 Reis, KM#211.

KM#	Date	Mintage	Good	VG	Fine	VF
210	ND	—	6.00	10.00	22.00	40.00

KM#	Date	Mintage	Good	VG	Fine	VF
225	ND	—	6.00	10.00	22.00	40.00

Maria II

KM#	Date	Mintage	Good	VG	Fine	VF
258	ND	—	4.00	6.00	10.00	20.00
	1845	—	4.00	7.00	12.00	25.00
	1846	—	4.00	7.00	12.00	25.00
	1847	—	4.00	7.00	12.00	25.00
	1848	—	4.00	7.00	12.00	25.00

6 REIS

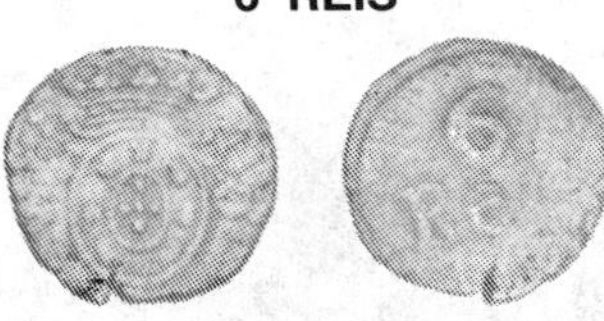

COPPER, 3.70-4.30 g
Joao

KM#	Date	Mintage	Good	VG	Fine	VF
211	ND	—	6.00	12.00	20.00	40.00

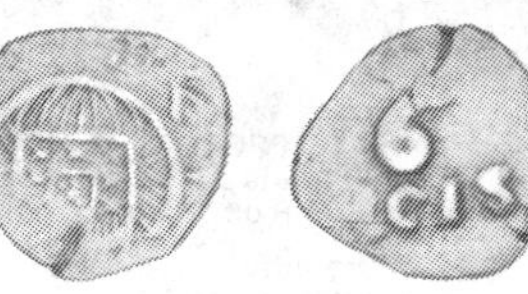

KM#	Date	Mintage	Good	VG	Fine	VF
226	ND	—	5.00	10.00	18.00	30.00

Maria II

KM#	Date	Mintage	Good	VG	Fine	VF
259	ND	—	4.00	7.00	14.00	30.00
	1845	—	4.00	7.00	14.00	30.00
	1846	—	4.00	7.00	14.00	30.00
	1847	—	4.00	7.00	14.00	30.00
	1848	—	4.00	7.00	14.00	30.00

7-1/2 REIS

COPPER, 4.80 g
Joao
Obv: Similar to 6 Reis, KM#211.
Rev. denomination: 7-1/2 REIS

KM#	Date	Mintage	Good	VG	Fine	VF
212	ND	—	8.00	16.00	35.00	65.00

Rev. denomination: 7-2/4 REIS

KM#	Date	Mintage	Good	VG	Fine	VF
213	ND	—	12.50	25.00	40.00	85.00

Obv: Similar to 6 Reis, KM#226.
Rev. denomination: 7-1/2 REIS

KM#	Date	Mintage	Good	VG	Fine	VF
227	ND	—	6.50	12.00	20.00	40.00

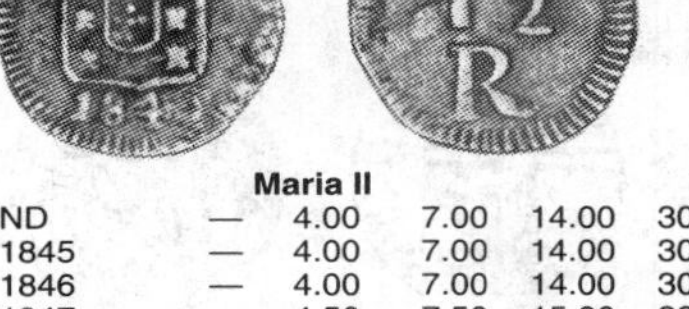

Maria II

KM#	Date	Mintage	Good	VG	Fine	VF
260	ND	—	4.00	7.00	14.00	30.00
	1845	—	4.00	7.00	14.00	30.00
	1846	—	4.00	7.00	14.00	30.00
	1847	—	4.50	7.50	15.00	32.00
	1848	—	4.50	7.50	15.00	32.00
	1849	—	4.50	7.50	15.00	32.00

9 REIS

COPPER
Joao
Obv: Similar to 6 Reis, KM#226.
Rev. denomination: 9 REIS

KM#	Date	Mintage	Good	VG	Fine	VF
228	ND	—	10.00	15.00	28.00	50.00

Rev. denomination: NOVE REIS

KM#	Date	Mintage	Good	VG	Fine	VF
229	ND	—	7.50	12.50	25.00	50.00

10 REIS

COPPER
Joao
Rev: Retrograde S.

KM#	Date	Mintage	Good	VG	Fine	VF
214	ND	—	6.00	12.00	22.00	45.00

Similar to 6 Reis, KM#226.

KM#	Date	Mintage	Good	VG	Fine	VF
230	ND	—	5.00	10.00	18.00	35.00

Maria II

KM#	Date	Mintage	Good	VG	Fine	VF
261	ND	—	3.00	6.00	12.00	25.00
	1845	—	2.00	4.00	9.00	20.00

12 REIS

COPPER
Joao

KM#	Date	Mintage	Good	VG	Fine	VF
215	ND	—	7.00	12.50	22.00	45.00

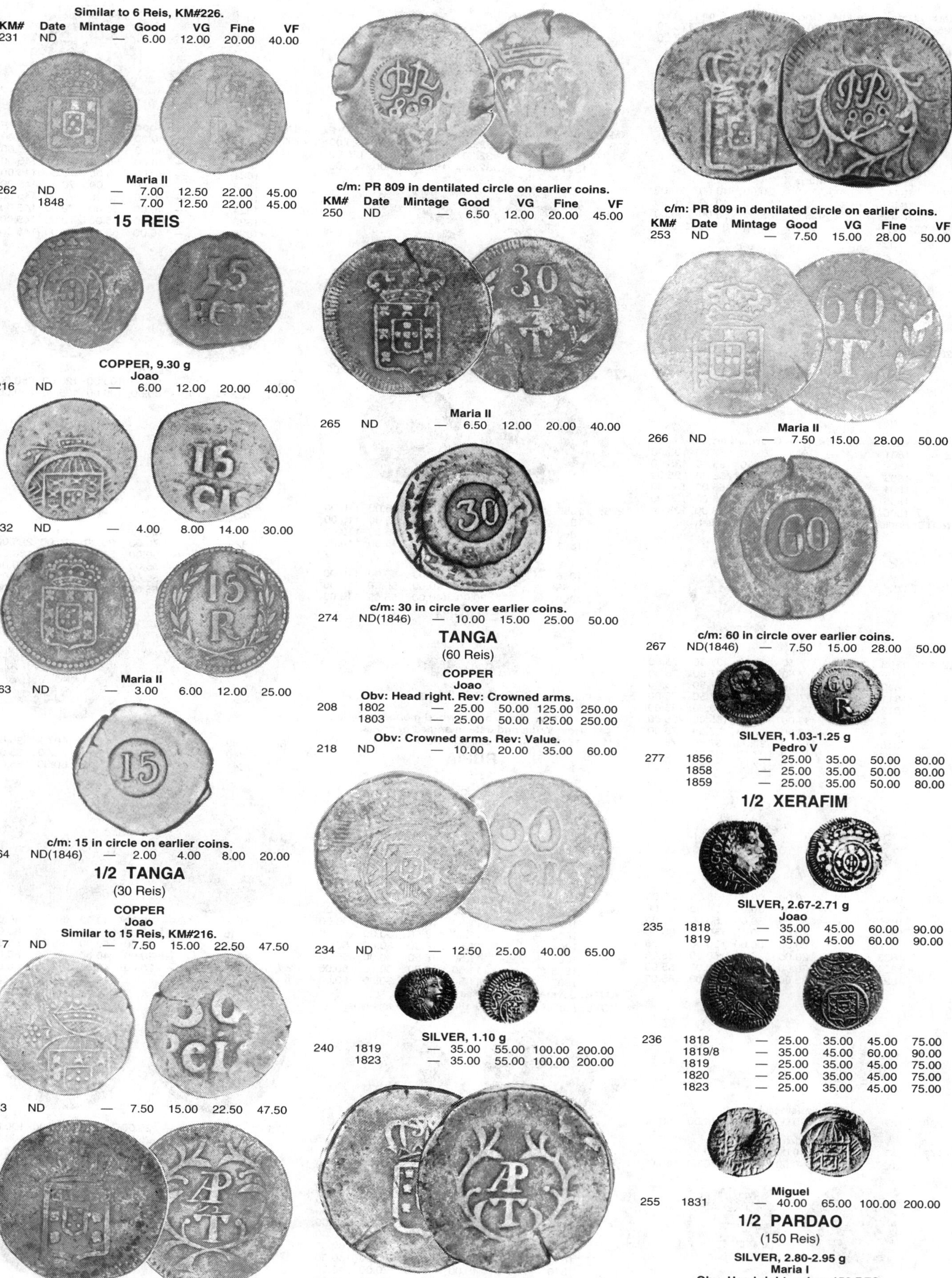

Similar to 6 Reis, KM#226.

KM#	Date	Mintage	Good	VG	Fine	VF
231	ND	—	6.00	12.00	20.00	40.00

Maria II

KM#	Date	Mintage	Good	VG	Fine	VF
262	ND	—	7.00	12.50	22.00	45.00
	1848	—	7.00	12.50	22.00	45.00

15 REIS

COPPER, 9.30 g
Joao

KM#	Date	Mintage	Good	VG	Fine	VF
216	ND	—	6.00	12.00	20.00	40.00
232	ND	—	4.00	8.00	14.00	30.00

Maria II

KM#	Date	Mintage	Good	VG	Fine	VF
263	ND	—	3.00	6.00	12.00	25.00

c/m: 15 in circle on earlier coins.

KM#	Date	Mintage	Good	VG	Fine	VF
264	ND(1846)	—	2.00	4.00	8.00	20.00

1/2 TANGA

(30 Reis)

COPPER
Joao
Similar to 15 Reis, KM#216.

KM#	Date	Mintage	Good	VG	Fine	VF
217	ND	—	7.50	15.00	22.50	47.50
233	ND	—	7.50	15.00	22.50	47.50

Miguel

KM#	Date	Mintage	Good	VG	Fine	VF
249	ND	—	6.50	12.00	20.00	45.00

c/m: PR 809 in dentilated circle on earlier coins.

KM#	Date	Mintage	Good	VG	Fine	VF
250	ND	—	6.50	12.00	20.00	45.00

Maria II

KM#	Date	Mintage	Good	VG	Fine	VF
265	ND	—	6.50	12.00	20.00	40.00

c/m: 30 in circle over earlier coins.

KM#	Date	Mintage	Good	VG	Fine	VF
274	ND(1846)	—	10.00	15.00	25.00	50.00

TANGA

(60 Reis)

COPPER
Joao
Obv: Head right. Rev: Crowned arms.

KM#	Date	Mintage	Good	VG	Fine	VF
208	1802	—	25.00	50.00	125.00	250.00
	1803	—	25.00	50.00	125.00	250.00

Obv: Crowned arms. Rev: Value.

KM#	Date	Mintage	Good	VG	Fine	VF
218	ND	—	10.00	20.00	35.00	60.00
234	ND	—	12.50	25.00	40.00	65.00

SILVER, 1.10 g

KM#	Date	Mintage	Good	VG	Fine	VF
240	1819	—	35.00	55.00	100.00	200.00
	1823	—	35.00	55.00	100.00	200.00

COPPER
Miguel

KM#	Date	Mintage	Good	VG	Fine	VF
251	ND	—	8.50	16.50	30.00	55.00

c/m: PR 809 in dentilated circle on earlier coins.

KM#	Date	Mintage	Good	VG	Fine	VF
253	ND	—	7.50	15.00	28.00	50.00

Maria II

KM#	Date	Mintage	Good	VG	Fine	VF
266	ND	—	7.50	15.00	28.00	50.00

c/m: 60 in circle over earlier coins.

KM#	Date	Mintage	Good	VG	Fine	VF
267	ND(1846)	—	7.50	15.00	28.00	50.00

SILVER, 1.03-1.25 g
Pedro V

KM#	Date	Mintage	Good	VG	Fine	VF
277	1856	—	25.00	35.00	50.00	80.00
	1858	—	25.00	35.00	50.00	80.00
	1859	—	25.00	35.00	50.00	80.00

1/2 XERAFIM

SILVER, 2.67-2.71 g
Joao

KM#	Date	Mintage	Good	VG	Fine	VF
235	1818	—	35.00	45.00	60.00	90.00
	1819	—	35.00	45.00	60.00	90.00
236	1818	—	25.00	35.00	45.00	75.00
	1819/8	—	35.00	45.00	60.00	90.00
	1819	—	25.00	35.00	45.00	75.00
	1820	—	25.00	35.00	45.00	75.00
	1823	—	25.00	35.00	45.00	75.00

Miguel

KM#	Date	Mintage	Good	VG	Fine	VF
255	1831	—	40.00	65.00	100.00	200.00

1/2 PARDAO

(150 Reis)

SILVER, 2.80-2.95 g
Maria I
Obv: Head right, value: 150 RES.
Rev: Crowned arms.

KM#	Date	Mintage	Good	VG	Fine	VF
206	1802	—	20.00	40.00	85.00	175.00
	1803	—	20.00	40.00	85.00	175.00

KM#	Date	Mintage	Good	VG	Fine	VF
206	1804	—	20.00	40.00	85.00	175.00
	1806	—	20.00	40.00	85.00	175.00

NOTE: Earlier dates (1798-1799) exist for this type.

Maria II

KM#	Date	Mintage	Good	VG	Fine	VF
271	1845	—	20.00	30.00	40.00	70.00
	1846	—	20.00	30.00	40.00	70.00
	1846/5	—	25.00	35.00	50.00	90.00
	1849	—	30.00	50.00	85.00	175.00

Pedro V

KM#	Date	Mintage	Good	VG	Fine	VF
280	1857	—	25.00	35.00	50.00	90.00
	1860	—	25.00	35.00	50.00	90.00
	1861	—	25.00	35.00	50.00	90.00

PARDAO

(300 Reis)

SILVER, 5.84-5.95 g

Obv: Head right. Rev: Crowned arms.

KM#	Date	Mintage	Good	VG	Fine	VF
204	1801	—	10.00	20.00	55.00	135.00
	1802	—	10.00	20.00	55.00	135.00
	1803	—	10.00	20.00	55.00	135.00
	1804	—	10.00	20.00	55.00	135.00
	1805	—	10.00	20.00	55.00	135.00
	1806	—	10.00	20.00	55.00	135.00

NOTE: Earlier dates (1796-1800) exist for this type.

Joao

KM#	Date	Mintage	Good	VG	Fine	VF
221	1808	—	17.50	27.50	37.50	75.00
	1809	—	17.50	27.50	37.50	75.00
	1810	—	17.50	27.50	37.50	75.00
	1811	—	17.50	27.50	37.50	75.00
	1812/09	—	35.00	60.00	100.00	225.00
	1815/09	—	35.00	60.00	100.00	225.00
	1815	—	17.50	27.50	37.50	75.00
	1816	—	17.50	27.50	37.50	75.00
	1817	—	17.50	27.50	37.50	75.00
	1818	—	17.50	27.50	37.50	75.00

KM#	Date	Mintage	Good	VG	Fine	VF
237	1818	—	20.00	30.00	50.00	85.00
	1819	—	20.00	30.00	50.00	85.00
	1820	—	20.00	30.00	50.00	85.00
	1821	—	20.00	30.00	50.00	85.00
	1822	—	20.00	30.00	50.00	85.00
	1823	—	20.00	30.00	50.00	85.00
	1824	—	20.00	30.00	50.00	85.00
	1825	—	20.00	30.00	50.00	85.00

Obv: Diademed head.

KM#	Date	Mintage	Good	VG	Fine	VF
238	ND	—	20.00	30.00	40.00	80.00

Pedro IV

KM#	Date	Mintage	Good	VG	Fine	VF
247	ND	—	40.00	55.00	70.00	145.00
	1827	—	40.00	55.00	70.00	145.00

Miguel

KM#	Date	Mintage	Good	VG	Fine	VF
256	1831	—	35.00	50.00	65.00	135.00
	1833	—	35.00	50.00	65.00	135.00

Maria II

KM#	Date	Mintage	Good	VG	Fine	VF
268	1839	—	32.50	45.00	60.00	125.00
	1840	—	32.50	45.00	60.00	125.00
	1841	—	32.50	45.00	60.00	125.00

KM#	Date	Mintage	Good	VG	Fine	VF
272	1845	—	20.00	30.00	45.00	85.00
	1846	—	20.00	30.00	45.00	85.00
	1847	—	20.00	30.00	45.00	85.00
	1848	—	20.00	30.00	45.00	85.00

Rev: Value and arms.

KM#	Date	Mintage	Good	VG	Fine	VF
276	1851	—	30.00	37.50	50.00	100.00

Pedro V

KM#	Date	Mintage	Good	VG	Fine	VF
278	1856	—	30.00	40.00	55.00	110.00
	1857	—	30.00	40.00	55.00	110.00
	1860	—	30.00	40.00	55.00	110.00
	1861	—	30.00	40.00	55.00	110.00

Luis I

KM#	Date	Mintage	Good	VG	Fine	VF
281	1866	—	30.00	40.00	55.00	110.00
	1868	—	30.00	40.00	55.00	110.00
	1869	—	30.00	40.00	55.00	110.00

XERAFIM

GOLD, 0.40-0.41 g

Joao

Obv: Arms on crowned globe.

Rev: Value and date in angles of cross.

KM#	Date	Mintage	Good	VG	Fine	VF
241	1819	—	350.00	750.00	1250.	2000.

RUPIA

SILVER, 11.80 g

KM#	Date	Mintage	Good	VG	Fine	VF
205	1801	—	11.50	18.50	30.00	50.00
	1802	—	11.50	18.50	30.00	50.00
	1803	—	11.50	18.50	30.00	50.00
	1804	—	11.50	18.50	30.00	50.00
	1805	—	11.50	18.50	30.00	50.00
	1806	—	11.50	18.50	30.00	50.00
	1807	—	11.50	18.50	30.00	50.00

NOTE: Several varieties exist.

NOTE: Earlier dates (1796-1800) exist for this type.

Joao

KM#	Date	Mintage	Good	VG	Fine	VF
219	1807 inverted "A" for "V" in "Rupia"	—	40.00	55.00	70.00	145.00
	1808	—	40.00	55.00	70.00	145.00
	1809	—	40.00	55.00	70.00	145.00
	1810	—	40.00	55.00	70.00	145.00
	1811	—	40.00	55.00	70.00	145.00
	1812	—	40.00	55.00	70.00	145.00
	1813	—	40.00	60.00	80.00	160.00
	1814	—	40.00	60.00	80.00	160.00
	1815	—	40.00	60.00	80.00	160.00
	1816	—	40.00	55.00	70.00	145.00
	1817	—	40.00	55.00	70.00	145.00

Mule. Obv: KM#219. Rev: KM#205.

KM#	Date	Mintage	Good	VG	Fine	VF
220	1807	—	40.00	55.00	70.00	145.00

KM#	Date	Mintage	Good	VG	Fine	VF
239	1818	—	40.00	55.00	70.00	145.00
	1819	—	40.00	55.00	70.00	145.00
	1820	—	40.00	55.00	70.00	145.00
	1821	—	40.00	55.00	70.00	145.00
	1822	—	40.00	55.00	70.00	145.00
	1823	—	40.00	55.00	70.00	145.00
	1824	—	40.00	55.00	70.00	145.00
	1825	—	40.00	55.00	70.00	145.00
	1826	—	40.00	55.00	70.00	145.00

Pedro IV

KM#	Date	Mintage	Good	VG	Fine	VF
248	1827	—	80.00	100.00	125.00	250.00
	1828	—	80.00	100.00	125.00	250.00

Miguel

KM#	Date	Mintage	Good	VG	Fine	VF
254	1829	—	70.00	85.00	110.00	225.00
	1830	—	60.00	75.00	90.00	180.00
	1831	—	55.00	65.00	80.00	160.00
	1832	—	55.00	65.00	80.00	160.00
	1833	—	55.00	65.00	80.00	160.00

Maria II

KM#	Date	Mintage	Good	VG	Fine	VF
269	1839	—	22.50	45.00	60.00	85.00
	1840	—	22.50	45.00	60.00	85.00
	1841	—	22.50	45.00	60.00	85.00

KM#	Date	Mintage	Good	VG	Fine	VF
273	1845	—	20.00	40.00	55.00	80.00
	1846	—	20.00	40.00	55.00	80.00
	1847	—	20.00	40.00	55.00	80.00
	1848	—	20.00	40.00	55.00	80.00
	1849	—	20.00	40.00	55.00	80.00

KM#	Date	Mintage	Good	VG	Fine	VF
275	1850	—	25.00	50.00	70.00	100.00
	1851	—	25.00	50.00	70.00	100.00

Pedro V

KM#	Date	Mintage	Good	VG	Fine	VF
279	1856	—	20.00	40.00	55.00	80.00

KM#	Date	Mintage	Good	VG	Fine	VF
279	1857	—	20.00	40.00	55.00	80.00
	1858	—	20.00	40.00	55.00	80.00
	1859	—	20.00	40.00	55.00	80.00
	1860	—	20.00	40.00	55.00	80.00
	1861	—	20.00	40.00	55.00	80.00

Luiz I

KM#	Date	Mintage	Good	VG	Fine	VF
282	1866	—	25.00	50.00	65.00	90.00
	1867	—	25.00	50.00	65.00	90.00
	1868	—	25.00	50.00	65.00	90.00
	1869	—	25.00	50.00	65.00	90.00

2 XERAFINS

GOLD, 0.81 g

Joao

KM#	Date	Mintage	Good	VG	Fine	VF
223	1815	—	—	Reported, not confirmed		
242	1819	—	—	Reported, not confirmed		

4 XERAFINS

GOLD, 1.63 g

Maria I

KM#	Date	Mintage	Good	VG	Fine	VF
202	1803	—	275.00	500.00	850.00	1400.

NOTE: Earlier dates (1791-1795) exist for this type.

Joao

KM#	Date	Mintage	Good	VG	Fine	VF
243	1819	—	450.00	900.00	1500.	2500.

8 XERAFINS

GOLD, 3.25 g

Maria I

KM#	Date	Mintage	Good	VG	Fine	VF
192	1804	—	500.00	850.00	1250.	1850.
	1805	—	500.00	850.00	1250.	1850.

NOTE: Earlier dates (1782-1795) exist for this type.

Joao

Obv: Crowned oval arms.

KM#	Date	Mintage	Good	VG	Fine	VF
244	1819	—	600.00	1000.	1650.	2750.

Obv: Similar to 1 Rupia, KM#239.

KM#	Date	Mintage	Good	VG	Fine	VF
245	1819	—	—	Reported, not confirmed		

12 XERAFINS

GOLD, 4.87 g

Maria I

KM#	Date	Mintage	Good	VG	Fine	VF
187	1801	—	250.00	500.00	850.00	1450.
	1802	—	250.00	500.00	850.00	1450.
	1803	—	250.00	450.00	750.00	1250.
	1804	—	250.00	450.00	750.00	1250.
	1806	—	250.00	450.00	750.00	1250.
	1809	—	250.00	450.00	750.00	1250.

NOTE: Earlier dates (1781-1800) exist for this type.

Joao

KM#	Date	Mintage	Good	VG	Fine	VF
222	1808	—	450.00	750.00	1250.	1850.
	1811	—	450.00	750.00	1250.	1850.
	1812	—	450.00	750.00	1250.	1850.
	1813	—	450.00	750.00	1250.	1850.
	1814	—	450.00	750.00	1250.	1850.
	1815	—	450.00	750.00	1250.	1850.
	1816	—	450.00	750 00	1250.	1850.

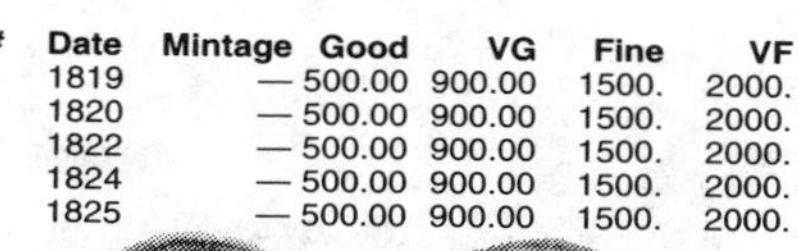

KM#	Date	Mintage	Good	VG	Fine	VF
246	1819	—	500.00	900.00	1500.	2000.
	1820	—	500.00	900.00	1500.	2000.
	1822	—	500.00	900.00	1500.	2000.
	1824	—	500.00	900.00	1500.	2000.
	1825	—	500.00	900.00	1500.	2000.

Maria II

KM#	Date	Mintage	Good	VG	Fine	VF
270	1840	—	550.00	1000.	1650.	2250.
	1841	—	550.00	1000.	1650.	2250.

COLONIAL COINAGE

MONETARY SYSTEM

960 Reis = 16 Tanga = 1 Rupia

3 REIS

COPPER

KM#	Date	Mintage	Fine	VF	XF	Unc
1	1871	.052	5.00	10.00	25.00	50.00

5 REIS

COPPER

KM#	Date	Mintage	Fine	VF	XF	Unc
2	1871	.051	6.00	12.00	28.00	60.00

OITAVO (1/8) TANGA

COPPER

Luiz I

KM#	Date	Mintage	Fine	VF	XF	Unc
7	1881	12.397	1.50	3.50	9.00	25.00
	1884	Inc. Ab.	1.50	3.50	10.00	28.00
	1886	Inc. Ab.	2.00	4.00	12.00	30.00

10 REIS

COPPER

KM#	Date	Mintage	Fine	VF	XF	Unc
3	1871	.051	7.00	14.00	30.00	65.00

QUARTO (1/4) TANGA

(15 Reis)

COPPER

KM#	Date	Mintage	Fine	VF	XF	Unc
4	1871	.051	15.00	25.00	50.00	100.00

Luiz I

KM#	Date	Mintage	Fine	VF	XF	Unc
8	1881	7.242	3.00	6.00	15.00	40.00
	1884	Inc. Ab.	3.50	7.00	17.00	45.00
	1886	Inc. Ab.	2.50	5.00	12.00	35.00
	1888	Inc. Ab.	—	—	Rare	—

1/2 TANGA

(30 Reis)

COPPER

KM#	Date	Mintage	Fine	VF	XF	Unc
5	1871	.050	18.00	28.00	55.00	120.00

TANGA

(60 Reis)

COPPER

KM#	Date	Mintage	Fine	VF	XF	Unc
6	1871	.050	25.00	40.00	85.00	190.00

OITAVO DE (1/8) RUPIA

1.4600 g, .917 SILVER, .0430 oz ASW

Luiz I

KM#	Date	Mintage	Fine	VF	XF	Unc
9	1881	.902	3.00	6.00	15.00	40.00

QUARTO DE (1/4) RUPIA

2.9200 g, .917 SILVER, .0860 oz ASW

Luiz I

KM#	Date	Mintage	Fine	VF	XF	Unc
10	1881	.471	5.00	8.00	18.00	45.00
	1885	—	—	—	Proof	650.00

MEIA (1/2) RUPIA

5.8300 g, .917 SILVER, .1719 oz ASW

Luiz I

KM#	Date	Mintage	Fine	VF	XF	Unc
11	1881	.357	4.00	8.00	18.00	55.00
	1882	Inc. Ab.	5.00	10.00	25.00	65.00
	1885	—	—	—	Proof	850.00

UMA (1) RUPIA

11.6600 g, .917 SILVER, .3438 oz ASW

Luiz I

KM#	Date	Mintage	Fine	VF	XF	Unc
12	1881	1.763	4.50	9.00	22.00	60.00
	1882	Inc. Ab.	5.00	10.00	28.00	70.00
	1885	—	—	—	Proof	1150.

PATTERNS (Pn)

(Including off metal strikes)

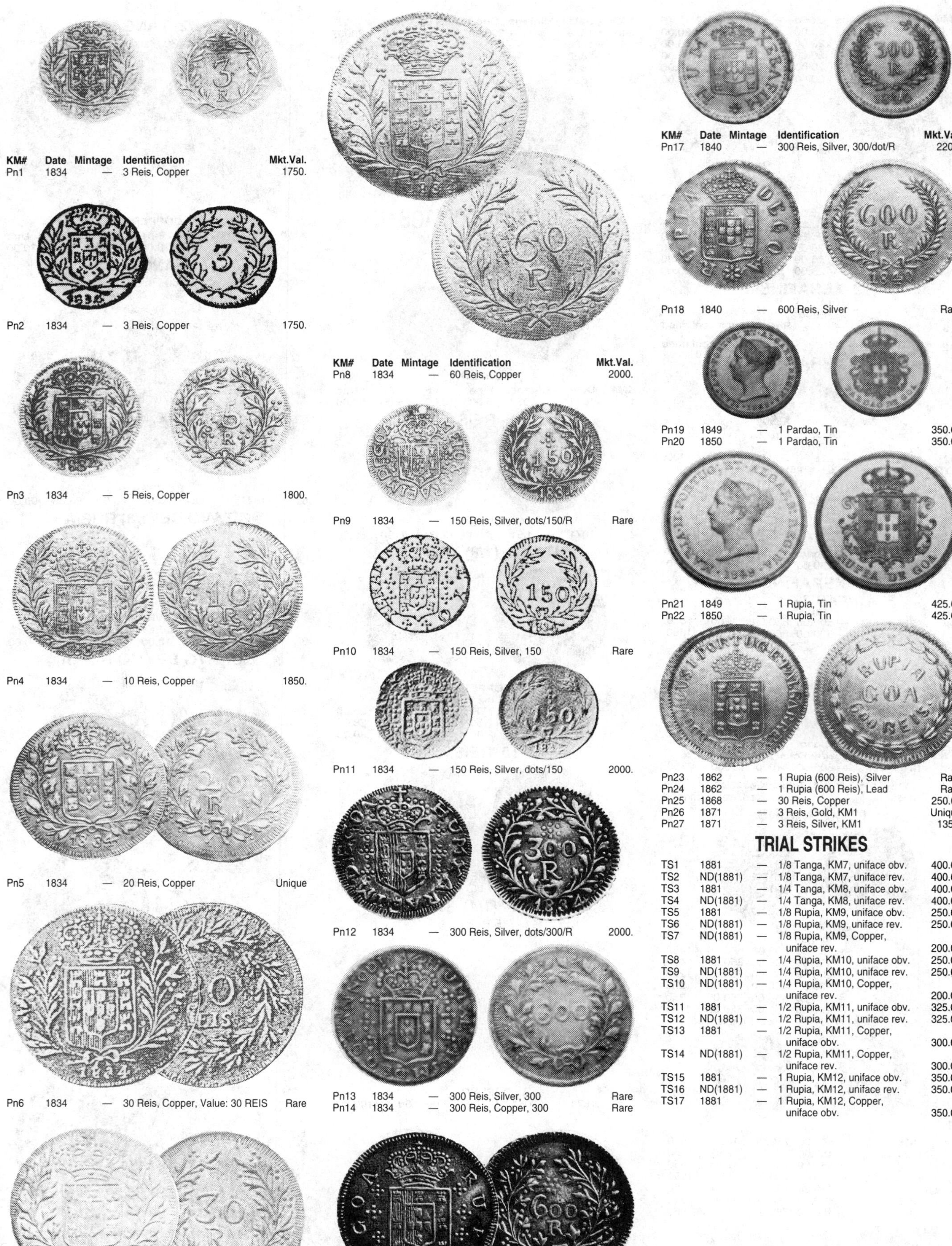

KM#	Date	Mintage	Identification	Mkt.Val.
Pn1	1834	—	3 Reis, Copper	1750.
Pn2	1834	—	3 Reis, Copper	1750.
Pn3	1834	—	5 Reis, Copper	1800.
Pn4	1834	—	10 Reis, Copper	1850.
Pn5	1834	—	20 Reis, Copper	Unique
Pn6	1834	—	30 Reis, Copper, Value: 30 REIS	Rare
Pn7	1834	—	30 Reis, Copper	1850.

KM#	Date	Mintage	Identification	Mkt.Val.
Pn8	1834	—	60 Reis, Copper	2000.
Pn9	1834	—	150 Reis, Silver, dots/150/R	Rare
Pn10	1834	—	150 Reis, Silver, 150	Rare
Pn11	1834	—	150 Reis, Silver, dots/150	2000.
Pn12	1834	—	300 Reis, Silver, dots/300/R	2000.
Pn13	1834	—	300 Reis, Silver, 300	Rare
Pn14	1834	—	300 Reis, Copper, 300	Rare
Pn15	1834	—	600 Reis, Silver	1600.
Pn16	1834	—	600 Reis, Copper	1200.

KM#	Date	Mintage	Identification	Mkt.Val.
Pn17	1840	—	300 Reis, Silver, 300/dot/R	2200.
Pn18	1840	—	600 Reis, Silver	Rare
Pn19	1849	—	1 Pardao, Tin	350.00
Pn20	1850	—	1 Pardao, Tin	350.00
Pn21	1849	—	1 Rupia, Tin	425.00
Pn22	1850	—	1 Rupia, Tin	425.00
Pn23	1862	—	1 Rupia (600 Reis), Silver	Rare
Pn24	1862	—	1 Rupia (600 Reis), Lead	Rare
Pn25	1868	—	30 Reis, Copper	250.00
Pn26	1871	—	3 Reis, Gold, KM1	Unique
Pn27	1871	—	3 Reis, Silver, KM1	1350.

TRIAL STRIKES

KM#	Date	Mintage	Identification	Mkt.Val.
TS1	1881	—	1/8 Tanga, KM7, uniface obv.	400.00
TS2	ND(1881)	—	1/8 Tanga, KM7, uniface rev.	400.00
TS3	1881	—	1/4 Tanga, KM8, uniface obv.	400.00
TS4	ND(1881)	—	1/4 Tanga, KM8, uniface rev.	400.00
TS5	1881	—	1/8 Rupia, KM9, uniface obv.	250.00
TS6	ND(1881)	—	1/8 Rupia, KM9, uniface rev.	250.00
TS7	ND(1881)	—	1/8 Rupia, KM9, Copper, uniface rev.	200.00
TS8	1881	—	1/4 Rupia, KM10, uniface obv.	250.00
TS9	ND(1881)	—	1/4 Rupia, KM10, uniface rev.	250.00
TS10	ND(1881)	—	1/4 Rupia, KM10, Copper, uniface rev.	200.00
TS11	1881	—	1/2 Rupia, KM11, uniface obv.	325.00
TS12	ND(1881)	—	1/2 Rupia, KM11, uniface rev.	325.00
TS13	1881	—	1/2 Rupia, KM11, Copper, uniface obv.	300.00
TS14	ND(1881)	—	1/2 Rupia, KM11, Copper, uniface rev.	300.00
TS15	1881	—	1 Rupia, KM12, uniface obv.	350.00
TS16	ND(1881)	—	1 Rupia, KM12, uniface rev.	350.00
TS17	1881	—	1 Rupia, KM12, Copper, uniface obv.	350.00

INDIA-BRITISH

The civilization of India, which began about 2500 B.C., flourished under a succession of empires - notably those of Chandragupta, Asoka and the Mughals - until undermined in the 18th and 19th centuries by European Colonial powers.

The Portuguese were the first to arrive, off Calicut in May 1498. It wasn't until 1612, after the Portuguese and Spanish power had begun to wane, that the British East India Company established its initial settlement at Surat. Britain could not have chosen a more propitious time as the central girdle of petty states, and the southern Vijayanagar Empire were crumbling and ripe for foreign exploitation. By the end of the century, English traders were firmly established in Bombay, Madras, Calcutta and lesser places elsewhere, and Britain was implementing its announced policy to create such civil and military institutions 'as may be the foundation of secure English domination for all time'. By 1757, following the successful conclusion of a war of colonial rivalry with France during which the military victories of Robert Clive, a young officer with the British East India Company, made him a powerful man in India, the British were firmly settled in India as not only traders but as conquerors. During the next 60 years, the British East India Company acquired dominion over most of India by bribery and force, and governed it directly or through puppet princelings.

Because of the Sepoy Mutiny of 1857-58, a large scale mutiny among Indian soldiers of the Bengal army, control of the government of India was transferred from the East India Company to the British Crown. At this point in world history, India was the brightest jewel in the imperial diadem of the British lords of the earth, but even then a movement for greater Indian representation in government presaged the Indian Empire's twilight hour less than a century hence - it would pass into history on Aug. 15, 1947.

BENGAL PRESIDENCY

East India Company

(Until 1835)

In 1633 a group of 8 Englishmen obtained a permit to trade in Bengal from the Nawab of Orissa. Shortly thereafter trading factories were established at Balasore and Hariharpur. Although greater trading privileges were granted to the East India Company by the Emperor Shah Jahan in 1634, by 1642 the 2 original factories were abandoned.

In 1651, through an English surgeon named Broughton, a permit was acquired to trade at Bengal. Hugli was the first location, followed by Kasimbazar, Balasore and Patna (the last 3 in 1653). Calcutta became of increasing importance in this area and on December 20, 1699 Calcutta was declared a presidency and renamed Fort William.

During these times there were many conflicts with the Nawab, both diplomatic and military, and the ultimate outcome was the intervention of Clive and the restoration of Calcutta as an important trading center.

During the earlier trading times in Bengal most of the monies used were imported rupees from the Madras factory. These were primarily of the Arcot type. After Clive's victory one of the concessions in the peace treaty was the right to make Mughal type coinage. The Nawab gave specific details as to what form the coinage should take.

In 1765 Emperor Shah Alam gave the East India Company possessions in Bengal, Orissa and Bihar. This made the company nominally responsible only to the Emperor.

In 1777 the "Frozen Year 19" (of Shah Alam) rupees were made at Calcutta and were continued until 1835. The Arcot rupees were discontinued at Calcutta about 1777.

MINTS

علي نكر كلكته
Alinagar Kalkatah (Calcutta)

Banaras بنارس

Calcutta (Kalkatah) كلكته

Farrukhabad فرخ اباد

Murshidabad مرشد اباد

Sagar ساكر

BANARAS

(Banares, Varanasi)

NOTE: Coins of similar dates with different legends are listed in Indian Princely States, Awadh under Lucknow Mint, with fixed regnal year 26.

In the name of Shah Alam II

AH1174-1221/1759-1806AD

PICE

COPPER, dump, 11.40 g
Mint: Banares
Obv. and rev: Trisul (trident) symbols added.

KM#	Date	Year	Good	VG	Fine	VF
16	(1802-3)	45	2.00	5.00	10.00	20.00
	(1806-7)	49	2.00	5.00	10.00	20.00

NOTE: Earlier dates (Year 28-42) exist for this type.

COPPER, 22-26mm, 6.23 g
Thick letters.

KM#	Date	Year	VG	Fine	VF	XF
27	(1815-21)	37	2.00	3.00	6.00	10.00

NOTE: Varieties exist.

Reduced weight, 19-23mm, 6.15 g
Obv. and rev. in plain circles.

KM#	Date	Year	VG	Fine	VF	XF
28	(1821-7)	37	1.75	3.75	7.50	12.50

Large flan, 24.5-26.5mm, 5.8 g

KM#	Date	Year	VG	Fine	VF	XF
29	(1827-9)	37	3.00	6.00	10.00	16.00

Obv. and rev: Crossbar on trisuls, 21-24.5mm.

KM#	Date	Year	VG	Fine	VF	XF
30	(1827-9)	37	2.50	4.50	8.50	13.50
	(1827-9)	37	—	—	Proof	80.00

1/16 RUPEE

SILVER, dump, 0.67-0.73 g
Mint: Banaras

KM#	Date	Year	VG	Fine	VF	XF
32	AH1226	17/49	12.50	25.00	50.00	100.00

NOTE: Earlier dates (AH1193-1215) exist for this type.

1/8 RUPEE

SILVER, dump, 1.34-1.45 g
Mint: Banaras

KM#	Date	Year	VG	Fine	VF	XF
33	AH1221	17/48	7.50	15.00	37.50	75.00
	122x	17/48	7.50	15.00	37.50	75.00
	1225	17/49	7.50	15.00	37.50	75.00
	1226	17/49	7.50	15.00	37.50	75.00

NOTE: Earlier dates (AH1193-1215) exist for this type.

1/4 RUPEE

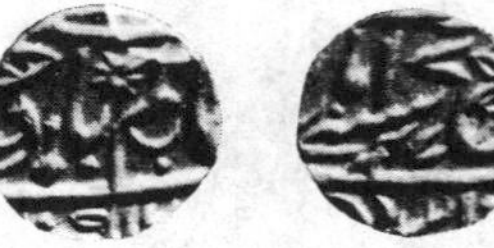

SILVER, dump, 2.68-2.91 g
Mint: Banaras

KM#	Date	Year	VG	Fine	VF	XF
34	AH122x	17/46	12.50	25.00	50.00	100.00
	1225	17/49	12.50	25.00	50.00	100.00
	1226	17/49	12.50	25.00	50.00	100.00

NOTE: Earlier dates (AH1193-1215) exist for this type.

Struck w/o Darogah's marks

KM#	Date	Year	VG	Fine	VF	XF
35	AH1229	17/49	8.00	20.00	45.00	75.00

Machine struck, broad flan, w/oblique milling.

KM#	Date	Year	VG	Fine	VF	XF
36	AH1229	17/49	—	—	Proof	—

1/2 RUPEE

SILVER, dump, 5.35-5.82 g
Mint: Banaras

KM#	Date	Year	VG	Fine	VF	XF
37	AH1225	17/49	75.00	150.00	225.00	300.00
	1226	17/49	75.00	150.00	225.00	300.00

NOTE: Earlier date (AH1193) exists for this type.

Struck w/o Darogah's marks.

KM#	Date	Year	VG	Fine	VF	XF
38	AH1229	17/49	20.00	45.00	100.00	150.00

Machine struck, broad flan w/oblique milling.

KM#	Date	Year	Fine	VF	XF	Unc
39	AH1229	17/49	15.00	37.50	75.00	150.00

RUPEE

SILVER, dump, 10.70-11.60 g
Mint: Banaras

KM#	Date	Year	VG	Fine	VF	XF
40	AH1216	17/43	14.00	23.50	25.00	45.00
	1216	17/44	14.00	23.50	25.00	45.00
	1217	17/44	14.00	23.50	25.00	45.00
	1217	17/45	14.00	23.50	25.00	45.00
	1218	17/45	14.00	23.50	25.00	45.00
	1218	17/46	14.00	23.50	25.00	45.00
	1219	17/46	14.00	23.50	25.00	45.00
	1219	17/47	14.00	23.50	25.00	45.00
	1220	17/47	14.00	23.50	25.00	45.00
	1220	17/48	14.00	23.50	25.00	45.00
	1221	17/48	14.00	23.50	25.00	45.00
	1221	17/49	14.00	23.50	25.00	45.00
	1222	17/49	14.00	23.50	25.00	45.00
	1223	17/49	14.00	23.50	25.00	45.00
	1224	17/49	14.00	23.50	25.00	45.00
	1225	17/49	14.00	23.50	25.00	45.00
	1226	17/49	14.00	23.50	25.00	45.00
	1227	17/49	25.00	40.00	52.50	75.00

NOTE: Earlier dates (AH1190-1215) exist for this type.

W/o Darogah's marks.

KM#	Date	Year	VG	Fine	VF	XF
41	AH1228	17/49	25.00	40.00	52.50	75.00
	1229	17/49	25.00	40.00	52.50	75.00

Machine struck, broad flan w/oblique milling.

KM#	Date	Year	Fine	VF	XF	Unc
42	AH1229	17/49	32.00	53.00	75.00	110.00

NAZARANA RUPEE

SILVER, 11.64 g
Mint: Banaras
Large flan

KM#	Date	Year	VG	Fine	VF	XF
44	AH1217	17/45	85.00	165.00	275.00	450.00

Large full flan

KM#	Date	Year	VG	Fine	VF	XF
45	AH1219	17/47	—	—	500.00	850.00

PATTERNS (Pn)

(Including off metal strikes)

KM#	Date	Mintage	Identification	Mkt.Val.
Pn1	AH1229/49	—	1/4 Rupee, PR293	—

KM#	Date	Mintage	Identification	Mkt.Val.
Pn2	AH1229/17/49		1/2 Rupee, PR292	—

KM#	Date	Mintage	Identification	Mkt.Val.
Pn3	AH1229/17/49		Rupee, PR291	600.00

CALCUTTA

PIE

COPPER

KM#	Date	Year	Fine	VF	XF	Unc
58	(1831)	—	.35	1.00	8.00	20.00
	(1831)	—	—	—	Proof	85.00

1/2 PICE

COPPER, 3.11 g
Mint: Calcutta

KM#	Date	Year	VG	Fine	VF	XF
A54	(1809)	37	2.50	5.00	10.00	15.00
(24)	(ca.1820)	37	(restrike)		Proof	65.00

PICE

COPPER, 6.54 g.

KM#	Date	Year	VG	Fine	VF	XF
54	(1809)	37	.40	1.00	8.00	45.00
	(ca.1820)	37	(restrike)		Proof	80.00

Reduced weight, 6.46 g, 27.2mm

KM#	Date	Year	VG	Fine	VF	XF
55	(1817)	37	.40	1.00	8.00	45.00

26mm

KM#	Date	Year	VG	Fine	VF	XF
56	(1829)	37	1.25	3.00	6.00	35.00
	(1829)	37	—	—	Proof	200.00

Reduced weight, 6.13 g, 23mm

KM#	Date	Year	VG	Fine	VF	XF
57	(1831)	37	.50	1.50	3.00	25.00
	(1831)	37	—	—	Proof	200.00

In the name of Shah Alam II
AH1174-1221/1759-1806AD

2 PICE

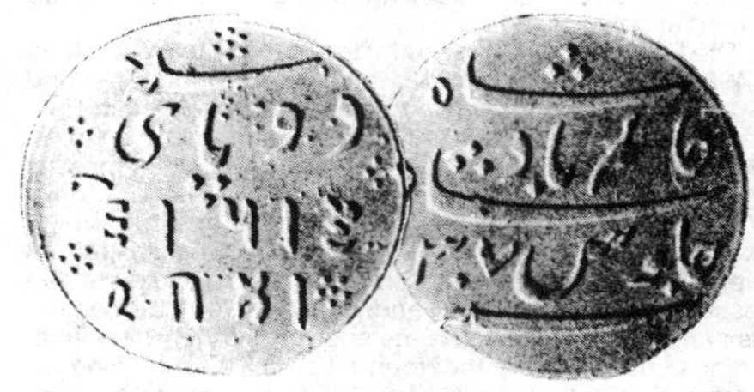

COPPER, 29.5mm, 12.33 g
Mint: Calcutta, struck for Banaras

KM#	Date	Year	VG	Fine	VF	XF
A55	(1807-10)	37	10.00	20.00	35.00	50.00
(26)	(ca.1820)	37	(restrike)		Proof	100.00

1/2 ANNA

COPPER, 27mm, 12.96 g

KM#	Date	Year	Fine	VF	XF	Unc
59	(1831-35)	—	1.00	3.00	15.00	40.00
	(1831-35)	—	—	—	Proof	150.00

FARRUKHABAD

1/2 PICE

COPPER, 2.45 g

KM#	Date	Year	VG	Fine	VF	XF
63	—	(45)	3.00	6.00	12.00	20.00

PICE

COPPER

KM#	Date	Year	Good	VG	Fine	VF
64	—	45	35.00	75.00	120.00	200.00

TRISUL 1/2 PICE

COPPER, 2.45 g

KM#	Date	Year	Good	VG	Fine	VF
464	—	—	—	Rare	—	—

TRISUL PICE

COPPER, 6.20 g
Mint: Farrukhabad
Obv: 6-pointed stars.

KM#	Date	Year	VG	Fine	VF	XF
A65	—	45	—	—	—	—

Obv: Trident replaces stars.

KM#	Date	Year	VG	Fine	VF	XF
65	(1820)	45	1.50	3.00	10.00	45.00

Mint: Sagar
Obv. & rev: Trident

KM#	Date	Year	VG	Fine	VF	XF
71	(1826)	45	1.50	3.00	10.00	45.00

Obv: 6-petalled rosette replaces trident

KM#	Date	Year	VG	Fine	VF	XF
72	(1833)	45	1.50	3.00	10.00	45.00

2 PICE

COPPER
Similar to 1 Pice, KM#64.

KM#	Date	Year	Good	VG	Fine	VF
63	—	45	—	—	—	—

1/4 RUPEE

.955 SILVER, 2.80 g
Mint: Farrukhabad
Oblique milling (1806-1819)

KM#	Date	Year	Fine	VF	XF	Unc
66	AH—	45	4.00	8.00	20.00	50.00

.909 SILVER, 2.92 g
Vertical milling (1820-1831)

KM#	Date	Year	Fine	VF	XF	Unc
67	AH—	45	4.00	8.00	20.00	50.00

Mints: Calcutta and Banaras

KM#	Date	Year	Fine	VF	XF	Unc
73	AH1204	45	4.00	8.00	20.00	50.00

Mint: Calcutta
Plain edge (1831-1833)

KM#	Date	Year	Fine	VF	XF	Unc
75	AH1204	45	3.00	6.00	15.00	35.00
	1204	45	—	—	Proof	250.00

1/2 RUPEE

.955 SILVER, 5.60 g
Mint: Farrukhabad
Oblique milling (1806-1819)

KM#	Date	Year	Fine	VF	XF	Unc
68	—	45	7.50	15.00	35.00	75.00

.909 SILVER, 5.80 g
Mints: Calcutta and Banaras
Vertical milling (1820-1831)

KM#	Date	Year	Fine	VF	XF	Unc
74	—	45	7.50	15.00	35.00	75.00

Mint: Calcutta
Plain edge (1831-1833)

KM#	Date	Year	Fine	VF	XF	Unc
76	—	45	5.00	10.00	25.00	50.00
	—	45	—	—	Proof	300.00

RUPEE

.955 SILVER, 11.21 g
Mints: Farrukhabad and Calcutta
Oblique milling (1806-1819)

KM#	Date	Year	Fine	VF	XF	Unc
69	—	45	5.00	10.00	30.00	75.00

.909 SILVER, 11.68 g
Mints: Farrukhabad, Calcutta, Banaras, Sagar
Vertical milling (1820-1831)

KM#	Date	Year	Fine	VF	XF	Unc
70	—	45	5.00	10.00	30.00	75.00

Mint: Calcutta, mm: Crescent.
Obv. and rev: Thin rim; plain edge (1831-1833).

KM#	Date	Year	Fine	VF	XF	Unc
77	—	45	4.00	8.00	25.00	50.00
	—	45	—	—	Proof	400.00

W/o mint mark.
Obv. and rev: Broad rim; plain edge (1833-1835).

KM#	Date	Year	Fine	VF	XF	Unc
78	—	45	4.00	8.00	25.00	50.00
	—	45	—	—	Proof	400.00

MURSHIDABAD

Mintname: Murshidabad (1777-1793)

1/4 RUPEE

SILVER, 2.90 g
Mints: Calcutta, Dacca, Patna
Oblique milling (1793-1818).

KM#	Date	Year	Fine	VF	XF	Unc
96	AH1204	19	1.50	5.00	15.00	25.00
	1204	19	—	—	Proof	300.00

Vertical milling (1819-1829)

KM#	Date	Year	Fine	VF	XF	Unc
104	AH1204	19	1.50	5.00	15.00	25.00

Mint: New Calcutta
Plain edge (1830-1833)

KM#	Date	Year	Fine	VF	XF	Unc
115	AH1204	19	1.50	5.00	15.00	25.00

1/2 RUPEE

SILVER, 5.80 g
Mints: Calcutta, Dacca, Murshidabad, Patna
Oblique milling (1793-1818)

KM#	Date	Year	Fine	VF	XF	Unc
97	—	19	2.50	8.50	25.00	50.00
	—	19	—	—	Proof	400.00

Vertical milling (1819-1829)

KM#	Date	Year	Fine	VF	XF	Unc
105	—	19	3.50	10.00	30.00	50.00
	—	19	—	—	Proof	300.00

Mint: New Calcutta
Plain edge (1830-1833)
Rev: Crescent at upper left.

KM#	Date	Year	Fine	VF	XF	Unc
116	—	19	3.50	10.00	30.00	50.00
	—	19	—	—	Proof	300.00

RUPEE

SILVER, 11.60 g
Mints: Calcutta, Dacca, Murshidabad, Patna
Machine struck, oblique milling (1793-1797, from 1798-1813, at Calcutta only)

KM#	Date	Year	Fine	VF	XF	Unc
99	—	19	5.00	8.50	15.00	30.00

Obv: Star added.
Vertical milling (1819-1832)

KM#	Date	Year	Fine	VF	XF	Unc
108	—	19	5.00	8.50	15.00	25.00

Rev: Privy mark 'S' at upper left.

KM#	Date	Year	Fine	VF	XF	Unc
109	—	19	15.00	25.00	60.00	100.00

Mint: New Calcutta
Plain edge (1830-1833)
Rev: Crescent at upper left.

KM#	Date	Year	Fine	VF	XF	Unc
117	—	19	5.50	11.50	22.50	45.00
	—	19	—	—	Proof	350.00

1/4 MOHUR

.996 GOLD, 3.09 g
Mints: Calcutta, Murshidabad
Mintname: Murshidabad
Oblique milling (1793-1818)

KM#	Date	Year	VG	Fine	VF	XF
100	AH1204	19	BV	45.00	75.00	150.00

.917 GOLD, 3.31 g
Vertical milling (1819-1832)

KM#	Date	Year	VG	Fine	VF	XF
110	AH1204	19	BV	50.00	100.00	175.00
	1204	19	—	—	Proof	1250.

1/2 MOHUR

.996 GOLD, 6.18 g
Mint: Calcutta
Machine struck, oblique milling (1793-1818)

KM#	Date	Year	VG	Fine	VF	XF
101	AH1202	19	BV	100.00	200.00	350.00

.917 GOLD, 6.63 gm.
Vertical milling (1819-1832)

KM#	Date	Year	VG	Fine	VF	XF
111	AH1202	19	BV	100.00	200.00	350.00
	1202	19	—	—	Proof	1500.

MOHUR

.996 GOLD, 12.36 g
Mints: Calcutta, Murshidabad
Machine struck, oblique milling (1793-1818)

KM#	Date	Year	VG	Fine	VF	XF
103	AH1202	19	BV	150.00	200.00	300.00

.917 GOLD, 13.26 g
Mint: Calcutta
Vertical milling (1819-1825)

KM#	Date	Year	VG	Fine	VF	XF
112	AH1202	19	BV	175.00	250.00	350.00
	1202	19	—	—	Proof	1650.

.996 GOLD, 12.36 g
Low relief, oblique left milling (1825)

KM#	Date	Year	VG	Fine	VF	XF
113	AH1202	19	BV	150.00	200.00	350.00

Similar to KM#113 w/crescent added (1830) on rev.

KM#	Date	Year	VG	Fine	VF	XF
114	AH1202	19	BV	175.00	300.00	400.00
	1202	19	—	—	Proof	1750.

PATTERNS (Pn)

(Including off metal strikes)

NOTE: Due to extensive revisions and new information the following section in part is listed by Pridmore (PR#) numbers. These are in reference to *The Coins of the Commonwealth of Nations,* Part 4, India - Volume I: *East India Company Presidency Series ca.1642-1835* by F. Pridmore (Spink & Son Ltd.).

KM#	Date	Mintage	Identification	Mkt.Val.
Pn20	(AH1221)/48	—	1/4 Pice, Copper, PR302	—

KM#	Date	Mintage	Identification	Mkt.Val.
Pn21	AH1221/48	—	2 Pice, Copper, PR303	—

KM#	Date	Mintage	Identification	Mkt.Val.
Pn22	1809	—	1/2 Pie, Copper, PR395	200.00
Pn22a	1809	—	1/2 Pie, Copper Gilt, PR394	—
Pn22b	1809	—	1/2 Pie, Silver, PR393	—
Pn22c	1809	—	1/2 Pie, Gold, PR392	—

KM#	Date	Mintage	Identification	Mkt.Val.
Pn23	1809	—	1 Pice, Copper, PR384	300.00

KM#	Date	Mintage	Identification	Mkt.Val.
Pn24	1809	—	1 Pie, Pewter, no motto on scroll, PR390	—
Pn24a	1809	—	1 Pie, Copper, thick planchet, PR389	300.00
Pn24b	1809	—	1 Pie, Copper, thin planchet, PR389a	—
Pn24c	1809	—	1 Pie, Copper Gilt, PR388	—
Pn24d	1809	—	1 Pie, Silver, PR387	—
Pn24e	1809	—	1 Pie, Gold, PR386	—

KM#	Date	Mintage	Identification	Mkt.Val.
Pn25	AH1228/49	—	1 Pice, Copper, PR308A	—

KM#	Date	Mintage	Identification	Mkt.Val.
Pn26	ND(1818)	—	1 Rupee, Silver, PR361	3000.

TRIAL STRIKES (TS)

1/2 PIE

COPPER
Uniface, PR#396

KM#	Date	Fine	VF	XF	Unc
TS1	1809	—	—	—	—

PICE

COPPER
Uniface, PR#385

KM#	Date	Fine	VF	XF	Unc
TS4	1809	—	—	—	—

BOMBAY PRESIDENCY

Following a naval victory over the Portuguese on December 24, 1612 negotiations were started that developed into the opening of the first East India Company factory in Surat in 1613. Silver coins for the New World as well as various other foreign coins were used in early trade. Within the decade the Mughal mint at Surat was melting all of these foreign coins and re-minting them as various denominations of Mughal coinage.

Bombay became an English holding as part of the dowry of Catherine of Braganza, Princess of Portugal when she was betrothed to Charles II of England. Also included in the dowry was Tangier and $500,000. With this acquisition the trading center of the Indian West Coast moved from Surat to Bombay.

Possession of Bombay Island took place on February 8, 1665 and by 1672 the East India Company had a mint in Bombay to serve their trading interests. European designed coins were struck here until 1717. Experimental issues of Mughal style rupees with regnal years pertaining to the reigns of James II and William and Mary were made in 1693-94.

From 1717 to 1778 the Mughal style Bombay rupee was the principal coin of the West India trade, although bulk foreign coins were used for striking rupees at Surat.

After the East India Company took over the city of Surat in 1800 they slowed the mint production and finally transferred all activity to Bombay in 1815.

MINTS

Ahmadabad احمد اباد

Bombay (Mumbai) منبى

COPPER COINAGE

1/4 PICE

COPPER, dump, 2.65 g

KM#	Date	Year	Good	VG	Fine	VF
219	1816	—	6.00	15.00	45.00	75.00
	1821	—	6.00	15.00	45.00	75.00
	1825	—	6.00	15.00	45.00	75.00

PIE

COPPER, 2.16 g
Mint: Bombay
Obv: Center lion on helmet above shield.

KM#	Date	Year	Fine	VF	XF	Unc
230	AH1246	1830	—	—	Proof	300.00
	1246	1831	.75	2.00	25.00	60.00
	1246	1831	—	—	Proof	175.00

Mint: Calcutta
Obv: Lion above shield.
Rev: Tall "PIE", tall Persian "L".

KM#	Date	Year	Fine	VF	XF	Unc
261	AH1248	1833	.40	1.00	12.00	45.00
	1248	1833	—	—	Proof	100.00

Rev: Short Persian legend.

KM#	Date	Year	Fine	VF	XF	Unc
262	AH1248	1833	.40	1.00	12.00	45.00

Mule. Obv: KM#261. Rev: KM#230.

KM#	Date	Year	Fine	VF	XF	Unc
263	AH1246	1833	—	—	—	—

Mule. Obv: KM#230. Rev: KM#261.

KM#	Date	Year	Fine	VF	XF	Unc
264	AH1248	1831	—	—	—	—

1/2 PICE

COPPER, dump, 5.31 g

KM#	Date	Year	Good	VG	Fine	VF
197	1802	—	3.00	10.00	30.00	75.00
	1803	—	— Reported, not confirmed			
	1808	—	3.00	10.00	30.00	75.00
	1810	—	3.00	10.00	30.00	75.00
	1813	—	3.00	10.00	30.00	75.00
	1815	—	3.00	10.00	30.00	75.00
	1816	—	3.00	10.00	30.00	75.00
	1818	—	3.00	10.00	30.00	75.00
	1819	—	3.00	10.00	30.00	75.00
	1825	—	3.00	10.00	30.00	75.00
	1826	—	3.00	10.00	30.00	75.00
	1827	—	3.00	10.00	30.00	75.00
	1829	—	3.00	10.00	30.00	75.00

COPPER, 9mm, 0.90-1.20 g
Obv: Bale mark. Rev: Date.

KM#	Date	Year	Good	VG	Fine	VF
202	(1)803	—	3.00	10.00	30.00	75.00

3.23 g
Obv: Center lion on helmet above shield.

KM#	Date	Year	VG	Fine	VF	XF
204	AH1219	1804	.40	1.00	8.00	40.00
	1219	1804	—	—	Proof	50.00

COPPER, machine struck, 3.83 g
Mint: Ahmadabad
Similar to 1 Pice, KM#226.

KM#	Date	Year	VG	Fine	VF	XF
255	AH1234	13	—	—	—	—

COPPER, dump, 17-18mm, 3.76 g
Mint: Local Southern Concan

KM#	Date	Year	Good	VG	Fine	VF
225	1820	—	3.00	10.00	35.00	100.00
	1821	—	3.00	10.00	35.00	100.00

PICE

COPPER, dump, 10.62 g

KM#	Date	Year	Good	VG	Fine	VF
198	1802	—	2.00	5.00	12.00	40.00
198	1803	—	2.00	5.00	12.00	40.00
	1804	—	2.00	5.00	12.00	40.00
	1808	—	2.00	5.00	12.00	40.00
	1809	—	2.00	5.00	12.00	40.00
	1810	—	2.00	5.00	12.00	40.00
	1813	—	2.00	5.00	12.00	40.00
	1815	—	2.00	5.00	12.00	40.00
	1816	—	2.00	5.00	12.00	40.00
	1818	—	2.00	5.00	12.00	40.00
	1819	—	2.00	5.00	12.00	40.00
	1825	—	2.00	5.00	12.00	40.00
	1826	—	2.00	5.00	12.00	40.00
	1827	—	2.00	5.00	12.00	40.00
	1828	—	2.00	5.00	12.00	40.00
	1829	—	2.00	5.00	12.00	40.00

COPPER, 2.20-2.85 g

KM#	Date	Year	Good	VG	Fine	VF
203	1803	—	3.00	10.00	30.00	75.00
	1807	—	3.00	10.00	30.00	75.00

6.47 g

KM#	Date	Year	VG	Fine	VF	XF
205	AH1219	1804	.40	1.00	10.00	50.00
	1219	1804	—	—	Proof	65.00

COPPER, dump, 20-22 mm, 7.00-7.55 g
Mint: Local Southern Concan

KM#	Date	Year	Good	VG	Fine	VF
226	1820	—	5.00	20.00	60.00	125.00
	1821	—	5.00	20.00	60.00	125.00

Mint: Ahmadabad
19-20mm, 7.53 g

KM#	Date	Year	Good	VG	Fine	VF
256	AH1232	—	—	—	—	—
	1233	12	—	—	—	—
	1234	12	—	—	Rare	—
	1236	(14)	5.00	15.00	45.00	125.00

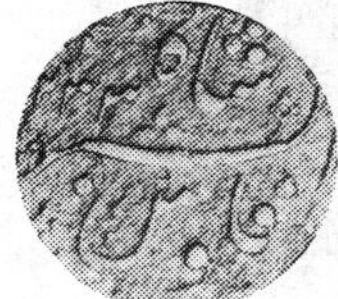

20mm, 6.70 g

KM#	Date	Year	Good	VG	Fine	VF
227	1829	—	5.00	15.00	45.00	125.00

1/4 ANNA

(Paisa)

COPPER, 6.47 g
Mint: Bombay
Obv. leg: EAST INDIA COMPANY

KM#	Date	Year	Fine	VF	XF	Unc
231.1	AH1246	1830	1.25	3.00	35.00	75.00
	1246	1830	—	—	Proof	250.00
	1246	1832	1.25	3.00	35.00	75.00

Rev: Arabic in different style, medium English letters.

KM#	Date	Year	Fine	VF	XF	Unc
231.2	AH1247	1832	1.25	3.00	35.00	75.00

Mint: Calcutta
Obv: Flat shield, w/o E.I.C. leg.
Rev: Large English letters.

KM#	Date	Year	Fine	VF	XF	Unc
232	AH1249	1833	.75	2.00	30.00	75.00
	1249	1833	—	—	Proof	200.00

Mule. Obv: KM#232. Rev: KM#231.2.

KM#	Date	Year	Fine	VF	XF	Unc
233	AH1247	1833	15.00	50.00	150.00	350.00

Obv. Convex shield w/o E.I.C. leg.
Rev: Small English letters

KM#	Date	Year	Fine	VF	XF	Unc
234	AH1249	1833	.75	2.00	30.00	75.00
	1249	1833	—	—	Proof	200.00

Mule. Obv: KM#231. Rev: KM#232.

KM#	Date	Year	Fine	VF	XF	Unc
235	AH1249	1832	9.00	27.50	80.00	200.00

2 PICE

COPPER, dump, 21.25 g
Rev: Value '2' above *Adil*.

KM#	Date	Year	Good	VG	Fine	VF
199	1802	—	1.50	4.00	7.50	15.00
	1803	—	1.50	4.00	7.50	15.00
	1804	—	1.50	4.00	7.50	15.00
	1808	—	2.00	5.50	10.00	20.00

Rev: W/o value '2' above *Adil*.

KM#	Date	Year	Good	VG	Fine	VF
200	1808	—	1.00	3.00	15.00	45.00
	1809	—	1.00	3.00	15.00	45.00
	1810	—	1.00	3.00	15.00	45.00
	1812	—	— Reported, not confirmed			
	1813	—	1.00	3.00	15.00	45.00
	1816	—	1.00	3.00	15.00	45.00
	1818	—	1.00	3.00	15.00	45.00
	1819	—	1.00	3.00	15.00	45.00
	1825	—	1.00	3.00	15.00	45.00
	1826	—	1.00	3.00	15.00	45.00
	1827	—	— Reported, not confirmed			
	1828	—	1.00	3.00	15.00	45.00
	1829	—	1.00	3.00	15.00	45.00

COPPER, 12.95 g

KM#	Date	Year	VG	Fine	VF	XF
206	AH1219	1804	.40	1.00	10.00	50.00
	1219	1804	—	—	Proof	120.00

Mule. Obv: KM#206. Rev: Madras 20 Cash, KM#321.

KM#	Date	Year	VG	Fine	VF	XF
207	—	1804	—	—	Proof	175.00

1/2 ANNA

COPPER, 30.5mm, 12.95 g

KM#	Date	Year	Fine	VF	XF	Unc
250	AH1246	1832	—	—	Proof	500.00

Rev: English letters, 2mm.

KM#	Date	Year	Fine	VF	XF	Unc
251	AH1249	1834	2.00	5.00	65.00	125.00
	1249	1834	—	—	Proof	350.00

Rev: English letters, 2.5mm.

KM#	Date	Year	Fine	VF	XF	Unc
252	AH1249	1834	2.00	5.00	65.00	125.00

Rev: English letters, 1mm.

KM#	Date	Year	Fine	VF	XF	Unc
253	AH1249	1834	2.00	5.00	65.00	125.00

COPPER, dump, 23-24mm, 15.60 gm.
Mint: Local Southern Concan
Rev: W/Nagari value and date.

KM#	Date	Year	VG	Fine	VF	XF
228	1820	—	5.00	10.00	35.00	100.00
	1821	—	5.00	10.00	35.00	100.00

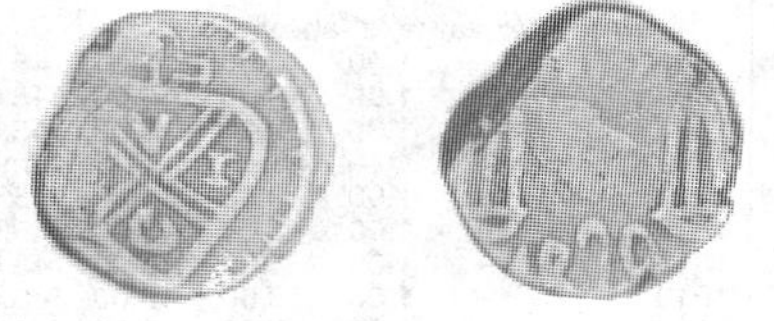

22.5mm, 13.60 gm.
Rev: Western date.

KM#	Date	Year	VG	Fine	VF	XF
229	1828	—	7.50	15.00	45.00	125.00
	1829	—	7.50	15.00	45.00	125.00

4 PICE

COPPER, 42.51 gm.
Rev: Value '4' above *Adil.*

KM#	Date	Year	VG	Fine	VF	XF
201	1802	—	10.00	20.00	60.00	150.00
	1803	—	10.00	20.00	60.00	150.00
	1804	—	10.00	20.00	60.00	150.00
	1816	—	15.00	30.00	90.00	225.00

SILVER COINAGE

PRIVY MARKS

Mint privy marks on dump issues often were intended to be "secret" (= privy marks), indicating changes in standards as well as mint of origin. The following chart is derived from IV Pridmore:

Privy marks involve the 3 diamonds and 4 dots in center line of obverse.

1		Surat 1800-15
2		Bombay 1801-02
3		Bombay 1802
4*		Bombay 1803-24
4b		Bombay 1803-24
5*		Bombay 1825-31
5b		Bombay 1825-31
6		Bombay 1800-24
7		and 1825 Bombay 1825
8		on rev. Bombay 1825-31
9		Unknown

***NOTE:** Crown also may be inverted.

1/16 RUPEE

In the name of Shah Alam II

SILVER, 0.72 g
Mint: Surat

KM#	Date	Year	VG	Fine	VF	XF
208	(1800-1815)	46	8.50	20.00	50.00	100.00

In the name of Muhammad Akbar II

Mint: Ahmadabad

KM#	Date	Year	VG	Fine	VF	XF
256	AH1234	12	4.50	6.50	9.00	12.50

See note after Rupee, KM#260.

1/8 RUPEE

In the name of Shah Alam II

SILVER, dump, 1.44 g
Mint: Surat, privy mark #1

KM#	Date	Year	VG	Fine	VF	XF
209.1	(1800-1815)	46	1.50	5.00	12.50	30.00

Mint: Bombay, privy mark #6

KM#	Date	Year	VG	Fine	VF	XF
209.2	(1800-1824)	46	1.50	5.00	12.50	30.00

1.46 g
Mint: Bombay, privy mark #8

KM#	Date	Year	VG	Fine	VF	XF
215	1825	46	1.50	5.00	12.50	30.00

Mint: Bombay, privy mark #9

KM#	Date	Year	VG	Fine	VF	XF
A215	—	—	— Reported, not confirmed			

In the name of Muhammad Akbar II

11-14mm
Mint: Ahmadabad

KM#	Date	Year	VG	Fine	VF	XF
257	AH1234	12	3.00	4.50	6.50	8.50
	1248	—	3.00	4.50	6.50	8.50

See note after Rupee, KM#260.

1/4 RUPEE

In the name of Shah Alam II

SILVER, dump, 2.88 g
Mint: Surat, privy mark #1

KM#	Date	Year	VG	Fine	VF	XF
210.1	(1800-1815)	46	1.50	5.00	10.00	15.00

Mint: Bombay, privy mark #6

KM#	Date	Year	VG	Fine	VF	XF
210.2	(1800-1824)	46	1.50	5.00	10.00	15.00

Mint: Bombay, privy mark #7

KM#	Date	Year	VG	Fine	VF	XF
210.3	(1825)	46	—	—	—	—

2.91 g
Mint: Bombay, privy mark #8

KM#	Date	Year	VG	Fine	VF	XF
216	1825	46	7.50	12.50	20.00	35.00

SILVER, 2.91 g
Mint: New Bombay (1832-35)
Machine struck, plain edge.

KM#	Date	Year	Fine	VF	XF	Unc
220	AH1215	46	1.25	3.00	15.00	25.00
	1215	46	—	—	Proof	275.00

In the name of Muhammad Akbar II

Mint: Ahmadabad

KM#	Date	Year	VG	Fine	VF	XF
258	AH1234	12	2.50	4.00	6.00	10.00

See note after Rupee, KM#260.

1/2 RUPEE

In the name of Shah Alam II

SILVER, dump, 5.76 g
Mint: Surat, privy mark #1

KM#	Date	Year	VG	Fine	VF	XF
211.1	(1800-1815)	46	3.50	7.50	15.00	25.00

Mint: Bombay, privy mark #6

KM#	Date	Year	VG	Fine	VF	XF
211.2	(1800-1824)	46	3.50	7.50	15.00	25.00

NOTE: For listings of coins w/regnal year 52 see India-French.

5.83 g
Mint: Bombay, privy mark #7

KM#	Date	Year	VG	Fine	VF	XF
217.1	1825	46	5.00	10.00	20.00	35.00

Mint: Bombay, privy mark #8

KM#	Date	Year	VG	Fine	VF	XF
217.2	1825-1831	46	5.00	10.00	20.00	35.00

Mint: Bombay, privy mark #9

KM#	Date	Year	VG	Fine	VF	XF
217.3	—	46	10.00	20.00	45.00	—

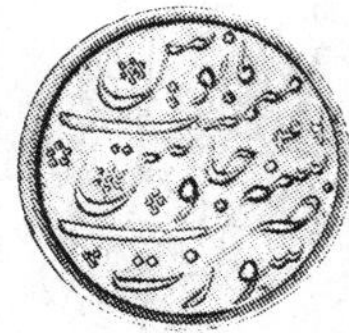

Mint: New Bombay (1832-35)
Machine struck, plain edge.

KM#	Date	Year	Fine	VF	XF	Unc
221	AH1215	46	2.50	7.50	20.00	35.00
	1215	46	—	—	Proof	350.00

In the name of Muhammad Akbar II

Mint: Ahmadabad

KM#	Date	Year	VG	Fine	VF	XF
259	AH1239	15	3.50	5.50	12.00	20.00
	1242	—	3.50	5.50	12.00	20.00
	1243	—	3.50	5.50	12.00	20.00
	1248	—	3.50	5.50	12.00	20.00

NOTE: See note after Rupee, KM#260.

RUPEE

In the name of Shah Alam II

SILVER, dump, 11.59 g
Mint: Calcutta, 1810-1813
Obv: Inverted crescent privy mark.
Machine struck, plain edge.

KM#	Date	Mintage	VG	Fine	VF	XF
224	—	2.037	15.00	35.00	75.00	125.00

Mint: Surat, privy mark #1

KM#	Date	Year	VG	Fine	VF	XF
212.1	(1800-1815)	46	7.00	10.00	15.00	25.00

Mint: Surat, privy mark #56

212.3	—	Yr.46	—	—	—	—

Mint: Bombay, privy mark #4

212.4	—	Yr.7	—	—	—	—

Mint: Bombay, privy mark #6

212.2	(1800-1824)	46	7.00	10.00	15.00	25.00

NOTE: For listings of coins w/regnal years 51-54 see India-French.

11.66 g
Mint: Bombay, privy mark #7

218.1	1825	46	7.50	12.50	20.00	35.00

Mint: Bombay, privy mark #8

218.2	1825-1831	—	7.50	12.50	20.00	35.00

Mint: Bombay, privy mark #9

218.3	—	46	—	—	Rare	—

Mint: Calcutta
Machine struck, vertical milling.

KM#	Date	Year	Fine	VF	XF	Unc
222	AH1215	46	10.00	25.00	60.00	100.00
	1215	46	—	—	Proof	400.00

Mint: Bombay
Plain edge

223	AH1215	46	3.00	5.00	20.00	50.00
	1215	46	—	—	Proof	400.00

In the name of Muhammad Akbar II

Mint: Ahmadabad

KM#	Date	Year	VG	Fine	VF	XF
260	AH1233	11	6.00	10.00	13.50	20.00
	1233	12	6.00	10.00	13.50	20.00
	1234	12	6.00	10.00	13.50	20.00
	1234	13	6.00	10.00	13.50	20.00
	1235	13	6.00	10.00	13.50	20.00
	1235	14	6.00	10.00	13.50	20.00
	1236	13	6.00	10.00	13.50	20.00
	1236	14	6.00	10.00	13.50	20.00
	1239	15	6.00	10.00	13.50	20.00
	1241	16	6.00	10.00	13.50	20.00
	1242	—	6.00	10.00	13.50	20.00
	1243	—	6.00	10.00	13.50	20.00
	1244	—	6.00	10.00	13.50	20.00
	1248	—	6.00	10.00	13.50	20.00
	1249	—	6.00	10.00	13.50	20.00
	1250	—	6.00	10.00	13.50	20.00
	1251	—	6.00	10.00	13.50	20.00

NOTE: Ahmadabad Mint was acquired by the British in 1818AD/AH1233 and finally closed in 1835AD. For other issues, see Mughals, Baroda, and Ahmadabad. Symbols as on Ahmadabad State Issues (q.v.), struck in the name of Muhammad Akbar II.

GOLD COINAGE

1/15 MOHUR

In the name of Shah Alam II

GOLD, dump, 7-8mm, 0.77 g
Mint: Surat (1800-1815)

213	—	46	27.50	45.00	75.00	125.00

Mint: Bombay
Privy mark: Crescent.

236	ND(1801-2)	46	60.00	100.00	250.00	350.00

Privy mark #4b

237.1	ND(1803-24)	46	27.50	45.00	75.00	125.00

Privy mark #5b

237.2	ND(1803-24)	46	27.50	45.00	75.00	125.00

PANCHIA

(1/3 Mohur)

GOLD, dump, 3.86 g
Mint: Surat

239	—	46	45.00	75.00	125.00	250.00

Privy mark: Crescent.

KM#	Date	Year	VG	Fine	VF	XF
240	ND(1801-2)	46	90.00	150.00	250.00	375.00

Privy mark: Inverted date.

241	1802	46	120.00	200.00	350.00	500.00

Privy mark: Normal crown.

243	ND(1803-24)	46	45.00	75.00	125.00	250.00

Privy mark: Inverted crown.

245	—	46	45.00	75.00	125.00	250.00

Privy marks: Normal crown and 6 petal rosette.

247	ND(1825-31)	46	45.00	75.00	125.00	250.00

Privy marks: Inverted crown and 6 petal rosette.

249	—	46	45.00	75.00	125.00	250.00

MOHUR

(15 Rupees)

In the name of Shah Alam II

GOLD, dump, 16-19mm, 11.59 g
Mint: Surat

214	ND(1801-15)	46	BV	175.00	250.00	350.00

Mint: Bombay
Privy mark: Crescent.

242	ND(1801-02)	46	150.00	250.00	450.00	650.00

Privy mark: Normal crown.

244	ND(1803-24)	46	BV	175.00	250.00	350.00

Privy mark: Inverted crown.

246	ND(1803-24)	46	BV	175.00	250.00	350.00

Privy marks: Normal crown and 6 petal rosette.

248	ND(1825-31)	46	BV	175.00	250.00	350.00

MALABAR COAST

Tellicherry

MINT

Mintname: Mumbai (Bombay)

1/5 RUPEE

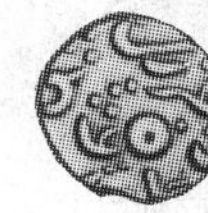

SILVER, dump, 2.32 g

277	1805	—	1.00	2.00	5.00	15.00

PAGODA

GOLD, dump, 3.00 g

KM#	Date	Year	VG	Fine	VF	XF
278	1809	—	75.00	100.00	250.00	400.00

PATTERNS (Pn)

(Including off metal strikes)

NOTE: Due to extensive revisions and new information the following section in part is listed by Pridmore (P#) numbers. These are in reference to *"The Coins of the Commonwealth of Nations", Part 4, India - Volume I: East India Company Presidency Series ca.1642-1835,* by F. Pridmore (Spink & Son Ltd.).

KM#	Date	Mintage	Identification	Mkt.Val.
PnA5	1820	—	Pie, Copper	850.00

PnB5	1820	—	1/2 Pice, Copper, KM225	350.00

PnC5	1820	—	Pice, Copper, KM226	600.00

PnD5	1820	—	1/4 Anna, Copper, KM205	500.00

PnE5	1820	—	1/2 Anna, Copper, KM228	950.00

PnF5	1821	—	Pie, Copper	850.00

Pn5	1821	—	1/4 Anna, Copper, PR335	600.00
PnA6	1821	—	1/2 Anna, Copper. Rev: ONE HALF ANNA	1200.

KM#	Date	Mintage	Identification	Mkt.Val.
Pn6	1821	—	1/2 Anna, Copper, PR334	1500.

PnA7	1821	—	Anna, Copper	2250.

Pn7	1828	—	1 Mohur, Copper, PR336	500.00

Pn8	1828/46	—	1 Mohur, Copper, PR337	—

Pn9	ND(1828)	—	1 Mohur, Copper, PR338	600.00

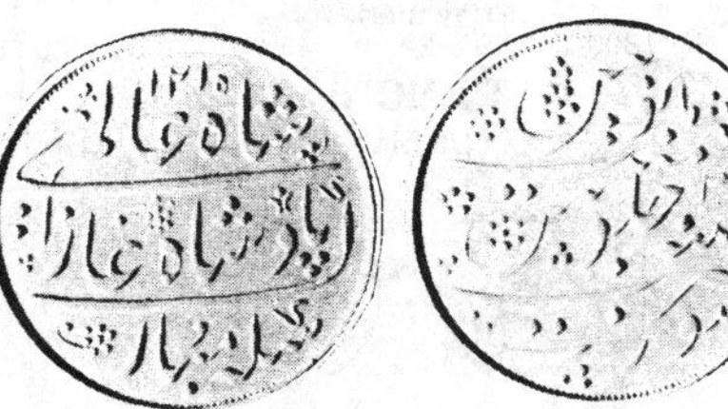

Pn10	AH1215/46	—	1 Rupee, Silver, PR332	—

KM#	Date	Mintage	Identification	Mkt.Val.
Pn11	AH1215/46	—	1 Mohur, Silver, PR333	—
Pn12	AH1249	—	1/2 Anna, Silver, KM253	1000.

MADRAS PRESIDENCY

English trade was begun on the east coast of India in 1611. The first factory was at Mazulipatam and was maintained intermittently until modern times.

Madras was founded in 1639 and Fort St. George was made the chief factory on the east coast in 1641. A mint was established at Fort St. George where coins of the style of Vijayanagar were struck.

The Madras mint began minting copper coins after the renovation. In 1689 silver fanams were authorized to be struck by the new Board of Directors.

In 1692 the Mughal Emperor Aurangzeb gave permission for Mughal type rupees to be struck at Madras. These circulated locally and were also sent to Bengal. The chief competition for the Madras coins were the Arcot rupees. Some of the bulk coins from Madras were sent to the Nawabs mint to be made into Arcot rupees. In 1742 the East India Company applied for and received permission to make their own Arcot rupees. Coining operations ceased in Madras in 1869.

MONETARY SYSTEM

1 Dudu = 10 Cash
8 Dudu = 1 Fanam
36 Fanam = 1 Pagoda (1688-1802)
3-1/2 Rupees = 1 Pagoda

MINTS

Arcot ارکات

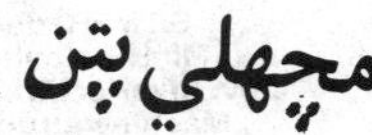

Masulipatnam (Machilipatnam)

Pagoda Series

CASH

COPPER, 1.10 g
Obv: Bale mark. Rev: Date.

KM#	Date	Mintage	Good	VG	Fine	VF
314	1803	—	1.75	3.00	12.00	50.00

Machine struck, 11.5mm, 0.64 g

KM#	Date	Mintage	Fine	VF	XF	Unc
315	1803	—	.50	2.00	10.00	25.00
	1803	—	—	—	Proof	35.00

NOTE: Similar pieces weighing 1.27 g are modern fantasies. Refer to *Unusual World Coins,* 3rd edition, ca.1992.

SILVER

315a	1803	—	—	—	Proof	75.00

GILT GOLD

315b	1803	—	—	—	Proof	350.00

GOLD

315c	1803	—	—	—	Proof	—

1/2 DUDU

(5 Cash)

COPPER, 4.43 g

KM#	Date	Mintage	Good	VG	Fine	VF
305	1802	—	— Reported, not confirmed			
	1804	—	— Reported, not confirmed			

NOTE: Earlier dates (1755-1791) exist for this type.

V (5) CASH

COPPER, 16mm, 1.21 g
Obv: Line of dots above denomination.

KM#	Date	Mintage	VG	Fine	VF	XF
324	ND(1807)	—	4.00	15.00	50.00	175.00

21mm, 3.23 g
Obv: Large lettering.

KM#	Date	Mintage	Fine	VF	XF	Unc
316	1803	—	2.00	4.00	35.00	175.00

Obv: Small lettering.

KM#	Date	Mintage	Fine	VF	XF	Unc
317	1803	—	2.00	4.00	35.00	175.00
Modified design						
318	1803	—	—	—	Proof	70.00
SILVER						
318a	1803	—	—	—	Proof	125.00
GILT GOLD						
318b	1803	—	—	—	Proof	—
GOLD						
318c	1803	—	—	—	Proof	—

1/4 DUB

(5 Cash)

COPPER, 16.5mm, 2.57 g

325 ND(1807) — 25.00 75.00 150.00 250.00

DUDU

COPPER, 6.30 g

KM#	Date	Mintage	Good	VG	Fine	VF
306	1801	—	2.00	5.00	15.00	70.00
	1805	—	2.00	5.00	15.00	70.00
	1806	—	—	Reported, not confirmed		

NOTE: Earlier dates (1755-1800) exist for this type.

X (10) CASH

COPPER, 23.5mm, 4.83 g

KM#	Date	Mintage	VG	Fine	VF	XF
326	ND(1807)	—	5.00	20.00	100.00	250.00

NOTE: Seven varieties exist; i.e. dividing lines, dots and star, etc. Also exists struck on a XX Cash planchet.

Heavy issue, 25.8mm, 6.47 g

KM#	Date	Mintage	Fine	VF	XF	Unc
319	1803	—	1.75	6.00	45.00	250.00
	1803	—	—	—	Proof	90.00
	1808	—	1.75	6.00	45.00	250.00
	1808	—	—	—	Proof	90.00
SILVER						
319a	1808	—	—	—	Proof	150.00
GILT GOLD						
319b	1808	—	—	—	Proof	600.00
GOLD						
319c	1808	—	—	—	Proof	—
COPPER, 25.8mm, 4.66 g						
320	1808	—	1.75	6.00	45.00	250.00
	1808	—	—	—	Proof	90.00

NOTE: Nice salvaged (and cleaned) examples from the Admiral Gardner are very common.

1/2 DUB

(10 Cash)

COPPER, 22.7mm, 5.15 g

327 1807 — 35.00 100.00 175.00 300.00

26mm, 4.75 g

KM#	Date	Mintage	Good	VG	Fine	VF
345	1808	—	5.00	10.00	20.00	50.00

XX (20) CASH

COPPER, 26.5mm, 9.65 g

KM#	Date	Mintage	VG	Fine	VF	XF
328	ND(1807)	—	6.50	25.00	125.00	350.00

NOTE: Five varieties exist; i.e. dividing lines, dots and star.

Heavy issue, 30.7mm, 12.95 g

KM#	Date	Mintage	Fine	VF	XF	Unc
321	1803	—	2.50	8.00	60.00	300.00
	1803	—	—	—	Proof	120.00
	1808	—	2.50	8.00	60.00	300.00
	1808	—	—	—	Proof	120.00

NOTE: For 1804 date see Bombay 2 Pice Mule, KM#207.

KM#	Date	Mintage	Fine	VF	XF	Unc
GILT COPPER						
321d	1803	—	—	—	Proof	175.00
SILVER						
321a	1808	—	—	—	Proof	150.00
GILT GOLD						
321b	1808	—	—	—	Proof	750.00
GOLD						
321c	1808	—	—	—	Proof	—
COPPER, 30.7mm, 9.33 g						
322	1808	—	2.00	8.00	60.00	300.00
	1808	—	—	—	Proof	120.00

NOTE: Nice salvaged (and cleaned) examples from the Admiral Gardner exist, trading near XF.

Mule. Obv: KM#321. Rev: 1/48 Rupee, KM#394.

KM#	Date	Mintage	Fine	VF	XF	Unc
323	180x	—	—	—	—	—

DUB

(20 Cash)

COPPER, 27.2mm, 7.56 g

KM#	Date	Mintage	VG	Fine	VF	XF
329	1807	—	15.00	75.00	150.00	200.00
	1808	—	15.00	75.00	150.00	200.00

NOTE: An unusual issue referred to as a 'Regulating Dub'. The translation is 'This and three new Dubs are one small Fanam'.

26.5mm, 10.31 g

KM#	Date	Mintage	Fine	VF	XF	Unc
330	(1807)	—	50.00	125.00	200.00	350.00

26.8mm, 10.00 g

KM#	Date	Mintage	Good	VG	Fine	VF
346	1808	—	7.50	15.00	35.00	75.00
24.3mm, 9.90 g						
347	1808	—	7.50	15.00	35.00	75.00

XL (40) CASH

COPPER, 36mm, 19.31 g
Obv: Large Persian legend.
Rev: Large legends.

KM#	Date	Mintage	VG	Fine	VF	XF
331	ND(1807)	—	12.50	50.00	200.00	500.00

Obv: Small Persian legend.
Rev: Small legends.

KM#	Date	Mintage	VG	Fine	VF	XF
332	ND(1807)	—	12.50	50.00	200.00	500.00

Obv: Dots below "XL CASH".

333	ND(1807)	—	12.50	50.00	200.00	500.00

2 DUBS
(40 Cash)

COPPER, 39.2mm, 20.61 g

334	ND(1807)	—	50.00	150.00	250.00	600.00

36mm, 19.69 gm.

KM#	Date	Mintage	Good	VG	Fine	VF
348	ND(1808)	—	8.00	20.00	75.00	150.00

FANAM

SILVER
Reduced weight, 0.91 g
Rev: W/o bead at left and right.

KM#	Date	Mintage	VG	Fine	VF	XF
307	ND(1765-1807)		3.25	8.00	20.00	40.00

10mm, 0.92 g
Obv. and rev: Center circle

335	ND(1807)	.386	4.00	10.00	25.00	45.00

Obv: W/o center circle.

336	ND(1807)	I.A.	4.00	10.00	25.00	45.00

Obv: W/o branches below star.

337	ND(1807)	I.A.	4.00	10.00	25.00	45.00

11-11.5mm

349	ND(1808)	1.545	1.00	2.00	5.00	12.00

NOTE: Two varieties exist of the buckle at the bottom of the obverse.

DOUBLE (2) FANAM

SILVER
Reduced weight, 1.83 g

308	ND(1765-1807)		4.00	10.00	25.00	50.00

12.5mm, 1.85 g
Obv: Center circle. Rev: W/o center circle.

338	ND(1807)	1.511	2.00	5.00	15.00	35.00

Obv. and rev: W/o center circle.

339	ND(1807)	I.A.	2.00	5.00	15.00	35.00

Obv. and rev: Center circles.

340	ND(1807)	I.A.	2.00	5.00	15.00	35.00

Obv: W/o center circle. Rev: W/center circle.

341	ND(1807)	I.A.	2.00	5.00	15.00	35.00

350	ND(1808)	6.044	1.50	3.00	9.00	15.00

NOTE: Four varieties exist of the buckle at the bottom of the obverse.

5 FANAMS

SILVER, 17.3mm, 4.65 g

342	ND(1807)	.988	4.00	10.00	25.00	75.00

21-22mm

KM#	Date	Mintage	VG	Fine	VF	XF
351	ND(1808)	3.954	2.00	5.00	15.00	35.00

NOTE: Eight varieties exist of the buckle at lower left of the obverse.

1/4 PAGODA

GOLD, 0.837 g
Obv: Single diety.

A280	ND(c.1800)	—	—	—	—	—

SILVER, 27.2mm, 10.58 g

343	ND(1807)	1.773	13.50	35.00	125.00	300.00

NOTE: Two varieties exist, one with 9 stars to each side of the Gopuram, the other having 13 stars.

25.5mm

352.1	ND(1808)	7.092	4.00	10.00	25.00	75.00

Obv: Small English lettering.

352.2	ND(1808)	I.A.	4.00	10.00	25.00	75.00

NOTE: Five varieties exist of the buckle at lower left of the obverse.

1/2 PAGODA

.903 SILVER, 36.5mm, 21.17 g

Dav.# 246

344	ND(1807)	.501	100.00	225.00	550.00	1000.

NOTE: Four varieties exist; 12, 14, 15 or 18 stars in the field at left and right of the Gopuram. KM#344 can be found overstruck on large plugs made from Spanish or Spanish Colonial 8 reales.

35.5mm
Obv: Large English lettering.

Dav.# 247

KM#	Date	Mintage	VG	Fine	VF	XF
353	ND(1808-11)	2.000	35.00	85.00	225.00	400.00

NOTE: KM#353 can be found overstruck on large plugs made from Spanish or Spanish Colonial 8 reales.

Obv: Small English lettering.

Dav.# 247

354	ND(1808-11)	Inc. Ab.	35.00	85.00	225.00	400.00

NOTE: KM#353 can be found overstruck on large plugs made from Spanish or Spanish Colonial 8 reales.

Obv: "HALF PGODA" (error).

Dav.# 247

355	ND(1808-11)	Inc. Ab.	35.00	85.00	225.00	400.00

NOTE: KM#353 can be found overstruck on large plugs made from Spanish or Spanish Colonial 8 reales.

PAGODA

GOLD, 10-11mm
Star Pagoda

303	ND(1740-1807)	—	50.00	125.00	175.00	275.00

12-14mm, 3.43 g
Obv: Three Swami Pagoda

304	ND(1740-1807)	—	50.00	125.00	175.00	275.00

16.9-17.5mm, 2.97 g

KM#	Date	Mintage	Fine	VF	XF	Unc
356	ND(1808-15)	1.382	50.00	125.00	175.00	275.00

2 PAGODAS

GOLD, 20.5-22.0mm, 5.94 g
Obv: 14 stars.

KM#	Date	Mintage	Fine	VF	XF	Unc
357	ND(1808-15)	1.064	100.00	250.00	425.00	550.00

21.0-22.2mm
Obv: 18 stars.

358.1	ND (1808-15)	Inc. Ab.	100.00	250.00	425.00	550.00

Obv: Small letters.

358.2	ND(1808-15)	Inc. Ab.	100.00	250.00	425.00	550.00

TEGNAPATAM

Fort St. David

Rupee Series

1/2 DUB

COPPER, dump, 16mm, 6.60-6.90 g
Obv: Persian "Struck at Machhlipatanbandar".
Rev: Date, legend.

KM#	Date	Mintage	Good	VG	Fine	VF
385	AH1175-1222	—	5.00	9.00	13.50	20.00

PIE

COPPER

KM#	Date	Year	Mintage	VF	XF	Unc
428	AH1240	1825	4.741	1.00	4.00	15.00
	1240	1825	Inc. Ab.	—	Proof	80.00
	1248	1833	—	10.00	20.00	50.00

DUB

COPPER, dump, 20mm, 13.00-14.00 g
Obv: Persian "Struck at Machhlipatanbandar".
Rev: Date, legend.

KM#	Date	Mintage	Good	VG	Fine	VF
386	AH1175-1222	—	5.50	11.50	21.50	35.00

Similar to KM#386 but w/English M on rev.

387	AH1218	—	7.50	15.00	22.50	40.00

2 PIES

COPPER

KM#	Date	Year	Mintage	VF	XF	Unc
429	AH1240	1825	7.126	2.00	6.00	20.00
	1240	1825	Inc. Ab.	—	Proof	100.00

4 PIES

COPPER
Rev: Right wreath tip points up.

KM#	Date	Year	Mintage	VF	XF	Unc
430	AH1240	1824	7.136	3.00	8.00	25.00
	1240	1824	Inc. Ab.	—	Proof	150.00

Rev: Right wreath tip points down.

431	AH1240	1825	Inc. Ab.	3.00	8.00	25.00
	1240	1825	Inc. Ab.	—	Proof	150.00

Rev: Right wreath tip points up.

432	AH1240	1825	Inc. Ab.	3.00	8.00	25.00

Rev: Right wreath tip in straight line.

433	AH1240	1825	Inc. Ab.	3.00	8.00	25.00

1/16 RUPEE

In the name of Alamgir II

SILVER, 10.5mm
Mint: Madras
(mm: Lotus, 1817-1835)
Oblique milling.

KM#	Date	Year	Fine	VF	XF	Unc
411	AH1172	6	1.00	2.00	10.00	20.00

Mint: Calcutta
(mm: Rose 1823-1825)
Oblique milling

423	AH1172	6	1.00	2.00	8.00	15.00

2 ANNAS

SILVER, 16.4mm, 1.48 g

KM#	Date	Mintage	VG	Fine	VF	XF
405	ND(1808)	.065	100.00	250.00	500.00	650.00

Rev: W/o star.

406	ND(1808)	I. A.	100.00	250.00	500.00	650.00

1/8 RUPEE

In the name of Alamgir II

SILVER, 16.5mm, 1.51 g
Mint: Calcutta
(mm: Lotus 1807)
Oblique milling

KM#	Date	Mintage	Fine	VF	XF	Unc
399	AH1172//6	.020	15.00	45.00	100.00	175.00

13.5mm, 1.46 g
Mint: Madras
(mm: Lotus 1812-1817)
Oblique milling

408	AH1172//6	.104	1.20	2.00	8.00	20.00

(mm: Closed form lotus 1817-1835)
Oblique milling

412	AH1172//6	10.790	1.20	2.00	8.00	20.00

Mint: Calcutta
(mm: Rose 1823-1825)
Oblique milling

KM#	Date	Mintage	Fine	VF	XF	Unc
424	AH1172//6	—	1.20	2.00	10.00	20.00

4 ANNAS

SILVER, 17mm, 2.97 g

KM#	Date	Mintage	VG	Fine	VF	XF
407	ND(1808)	.044	125.00	300.00	600.00	750.00

1/4 RUPEE

In the name of Alamgir II

SILVER, 15.5mm, 2.81-2.86 g
Mint: Calcutta
(mm: Lotus 1807)
16.5mm, 3.02 g
Oblique milling.

KM#	Date	Year	Mintage	VF	XF	Unc
400	AH1172	6	.018	25.00	100.00	175.00

17.4mm, 2.91 g
Mint: Madras
(mm: Lotus 1812-1817)
Indented cord milling

KM#	Date	Mintage	Fine	VF	XF	Unc
409	AH1172//6	.784	1.75	3.00	10.00	25.00
	1176//6	Inc. Ab.	1.75	3.00	10.00	25.00

(mm: Closed form lotus 1817-1835)
Indented cord milling.

KM#	Date	Mintage	Fine	VF	XF	Unc
413	AH1172//6	5.227	3.00	5.00	15.00	35.00

Mint: Calcutta
(mm: Rose 1823-1825)
Vertical milling.

KM#	Date	Mintage	Fine	VF	XF	Unc
425	AH1172//6	—	2.50	4.00	10.00	20.00

(mm: Rose, crescent added 1830-1835)
Vertical milling.

KM#	Date	Mintage	Fine	VF	XF	Unc
434	AH1172//6	—	3.00	5.00	25.00	50.00
	1172//6	—	—	—	Proof	300.00

1/2 RUPEE

In the name of Alamgir II

SILVER, 22mm, 6.05 g
Mint: Calcutta
(mm: Lotus 1807). Oblique milling.

KM#	Date	Mintage	Fine	VF	XF	Unc
401	AH1172//6	.108	17.50	30.00	75.00	150.00

Mint: Madras
21.7mm, 5.83 g
Indented cord milling.

KM#	Date	Mintage	Fine	VF	XF	Unc
402	AH1172//6	3.392	3.00	5.00	15.00	30.00
	1176//6	Inc. Ab.	3.00	5.00	15.00	30.00

(mm: Closed formed lotus 1817-1835)
Indented cord milling.

KM#	Date	Mintage	Fine	VF	XF	Unc
414	AH1172//6	10.674	1.75	3.00	15.00	25.00

Mint: Calcutta
(mm: Rose 1823-1825)
Vertical milling

KM#	Date	Mintage	Fine	VF	XF	Unc
426	AH1172//6	—	3.00	5.00	25.00	50.00
	1172//6	—	—	—	Proof	—

(mm: Rose, crescent added 1830-1835)
Vertical milling.

KM#	Date	Mintage	Fine	VF	XF	Unc
435	AH1172//6	—	6.00	10.00	35.00	65.00
	1172//6	—	—	—	Proof	350.00

RUPEE

SILVER, 28mm, 12.1 g
Mint: Calcutta. (mm: Lotus 1807).
Oblique milling

KM#	Date	Mintage	Fine	VF	XF	Unc
403	AH1172//6	2.145	9.00	15.00	50.00	100.00

27.8mm, 11.66 g
Mint: Madras
(mm: Lotus 1812-1817)
Indented cord milling

KM#	Date	Mintage	Fine	VF	XF	Unc
410	AH1172//6	10.939	1.75	3.00	10.00	25.00
	1176//6	Inc. Ab.	1.75	3.00	10.00	25.00

(mm: Closed form lotus 1817-1835)
Indented cord milling

KM#	Date	Mintage	Fine	VF	XF	Unc
415.1	AH1172//6	63.116	1.75	3.00	15.00	25.00

28.4mm
(mm: Open lotus, center graining left)

KM#	Date	Mintage	Fine	VF	XF	Unc
415.2	AH1172//6	—	1.75	3.00	15.00	25.00

Mint: Calcutta
(mm: Rose 1823-1825)
Vertical milling

KM#	Date	Mintage	Fine	VF	XF	Unc
427	AH1172//6	—	1.75	3.00	20.00	35.00

(mm: Rose, crescent added 1830-1835)
Vertical milling.

KM#	Date	Mintage	Fine	VF	XF	Unc
436	AH1172//6	—	1.75	3.00	20.00	35.00
	1172//6	—	—	—	Proof	400.00

NOTE: Dump rupees in the name of Alamgir, with a small crescent to left of regnal year and mint name *Arcot*, were struck by the French (see India-French) as were Arcot rupees in the names of other Mughal emperors.

2 RUPEES

SILVER, 39.5mm, 24.19 g
Mint: Madras. (mm: Lotus 1807).

KM#	Date	Mintage	VG	Fine	VF	XF
404.1	AH1172//2	.165	120.00	200.00	350.00	550.00

KM#	Date	Mintage	VG	Fine	VF	XF
404.2	AH1172//6	Inc. Ab.	120.00	200.00	350.00	550.00

NOTE: Struck over Spanish or Spanish Colonial 8 Reales.

1/4 MOHUR

GOLD, 17.4mm, 2.91 g
Mint: Madras. (mm: Lotus 1817).

KM#	Date	Mintage				
416	AH1172//6	2,000	300.00	500.00	850.00	1250.

17mm
Mint: Madras.

KM#	Date	Mintage	Fine	VF	XF	Unc
419	ND(1819)	.092	125.00	250.00	350.00	600.00

5 RUPEES

GOLD, 19.5mm, 3.88 g

KM#	Date	Mintage				
422	ND(1820)	2.180	45.00	75.00	125.00	175.00

1/2 MOHUR

GOLD, 21.7mm, 5.83 g
Mint: Madras. (mm: Lotus 1817).

KM#	Date	Mintage				
417	AH1172//6	7,500	450.00	750.00	1250.	2000.

21.2mm

KM#	Date	Mintage				
420	ND(1819)	.213	150.00	350.00	550.00	750.00

MOHUR

GOLD, 27.8mm, 11.66 g
Mint: Madras. (mm: Lotus 1817).

KM#	Date	Mintage	VG	Fine	VF	XF
418	AH1172//6	.059	200.00	350.00	750.00	1000.

KM#	Date	Mintage	Fine	VF	XF	Unc
421.1	ND(1819)	1.118	175.00	200.00	425.00	600.00

Obv: Large letters.

KM#	Date	Mintage	Fine	VF	XF	Unc
421.2	ND(1819)	I.A.	175.00	200.00	425.00	600.00

PATTERNS (Pn)

(Including off metal strikes)

KM#	Date	Mintage	Identification	Mkt.Val.
Pn2	1807(?)	—	20 Cash, Copper, PR342	—

KM#	Date	Mintage	Identification	Mkt.Val.
Pn3	1824	—	4 Pice, Copper, PR343	—

KM#	Date	Mintage	Identification	Mkt.Val.
Pn4	AH1172/6	—	1 Rupee, Silver, PR339	—

COLONIAL COINAGE

This section lists the coins of British India from reign of William IV (1835) to the reign of George VI (1947). The issues are divided into two main parts:

1. Coins struck under the authority of the East India Com-pany (E.I.C.) from 1835 until the trading monopoly of the E.I.C. was abolished in 1853. From August 2, 1858 the property and powers of the Company were transferred to the British Crown. From November 1, 1858 to November 1, 1862 the coins continued to bear the design and inscription of the Company.

2. Coins struck under the authority of the Crown (Regal issues) from 1862 until 1947.

The first regal issues bear the date 1862 and were struck with the date 1862 unchanged until 1874. From then onward all coins bear the year date. The copper coins dated 1862 have been tentatively attributed by their size to the mint of issue.

In 1877 Queen Victoria was proclaimed Empress of India and the title of the obverse legend was changed accordingly.

For a detailed account of the work of the various mints and the numerous die varieties the general collector and specialist should refer to *"The Coins of the British Commonwealth of Nations* to the end of the reign of King George VI - 1952", Part 4, India, Vol. 1 and 2, by F. Pridmore, Spink, 1980.

RULERS

British until 1947

MINT MARKS

The coins of British India were struck at the following mints, indicated in the catalogue by either capital letters after the date when the actual letter appears on the coins or small letters in ( ) designating the mint of issue. Plain dates indicate Royal Mint strikes.

B-Bombay, 1835-1947
C or CM-Calcutta, 1835-1947
H - Ralph Heaton & Sons, Birmingham (1857-1858)
M-Madras, 1869 (closed Sept. 1869)
W - J. Watt & Sons, Birmingham (1860)

MONETARY SYSTEM

3 Pies = 1 Pice (Paisa)
4 Pice = 1 Anna
16 Annas = 1 Rupee
15 Rupees = 1 Mohur

The transition from the coins of the Moslem monetary system began with the silver pattern Rupees of William IV, 1834, issued by the East India Company, with the value on the reverse, given in English, Bengali, Persian and Nagari characters. This coinage was struck for several years, as dated, except for the currency Rupee which was struck from 1835 to 1840, all dated 1835.

The portrait coins issued by the East India Company for Victoria show two different head designs on the obverse, which are called Type I and Type II. The coins with Type I head have a continuous obverse legend and were struck from 1840 to 1851. The coins with the Type II head have a divided obverse legend and were struck from 1850 (Calcutta) until 1862. The date on the coins remained unchanged: the Rupee, 1/2 Rupee and 1/4 Rupee are dated 1840, the 2 Annas and the Mohur are dated 1841. Both issues were struck at the Calcutta, Bombay and Madras Mints. Numerous varieties exist in the rupee series of 1840. Noticable differences in the ribbon designs of the English vs. Indian obverses exist.

Type I coins have on the reverse a dot after the date, those of Type II have no dot, except for some rare 1/4 Rupees and 2 Annas. The latter are mules, struck from reverse dies of the preceding issue.

ENGRAVER INITIALS

The following initials appear on the obverse on the truncation:

F - William N. Forbes, Calcutta, 1836-1855
R.S. - Robert Saunders, Calcutta, 1826-1836
S Incuse (Type I)
WW raised or incuse (Type II)
WWS or SWW (Type II)
WWB raised (Type II)

On both issues, the "S" is the initial of Major, later Lt. Col. J. T. Smith, mintmaster at Madras from February 1840 to September 1855.

The 'B' which occurs only on Rupees of Type II, is the initial of Major, later Lt. Col. J. H. Bell (mintmaster at Madras, 1855-1859).

The initials WW which appear on all coins of Type II, are those of William Wyon, Chief Engraver of the Royal Mint, London, who prepared this obverse design in 1849.

East India Company

1/12 ANNA

(1 Pie)

COPPER
Calcutta: 17.5mm; Bombay: 18.0mm; Madras: 17.7-17.9mm

KM#	Date	Mintage	Fine	VF	XF	Unc
445	1835(b)	72.313	1.00	2.50	4.00	8.00
	1835(m)	133.788	.75	2.00	3.00	6.00
	1835(c)	—	—	—	Proof	75.00
	1848(c)	14.380	1.25	3.00	5.00	10.00

1/2 PICE

COPPER

KM#	Date	Mintage	Fine	VF	XF	Unc
464	1853(c)	62.408	1.75	3.50	8.00	20.00
	1853(c)	—	—	—	Proof	100.00
	1853(c) (restrike)	—	—	—	P/L	25.00

1/4 ANNA

COPPER
Obv: Small shield.
Rev. large leg: ONE QUARTER ANNA.

KM#	Date	Mintage	Fine	VF	XF	Unc
446.1	1833(b)	—	—	—	Proof	175.00
	1835(b)	36.767	1.00	2.00	4.00	10.00
	1835(m)	186.530	1.00	2.00	4.00	10.00

NOTE: The 1835 dated coins exist in both medal and coin rotations.

Obv: Small shield.
Rev. small leg: ONE QUARTER ANNA.
Calcutta: 26.2mm; Bombay: 25.2mm; Madras: 25.5mm.

KM#	Date	Mintage	Fine	VF	XF	Unc
446.2	1835(b)	I.A.	1.00	2.00	4.00	10.00
	1835(c)	755.059	1.00	2.00	4.00	10.00
	1835(c)	—	—	—	Proof	75.00
	1835(m)	I.A.	1.00	2.00	4.00	10.00
	1849	—	—	—	Proof	250.00

NOTE: 6 varieties for Madras, 2 varieties for Calcutta.

Obv: Large shield.
Rev: Wreath tips are single leaves.

KM#	Date	Mintage	Fine	VF	XF	Unc
463.1	1857(h)	47.040	1.00	2.00	10.00	45.00
	1858(w)	62.720	.85	1.50	2.50	10.00
	1858(w)	—	—	—	Proof	125.00

Rev: Wreath tips are double leaves.

KM#	Date	Mintage	Fine	VF	XF	Unc
463.2	1857(h)	Inc. Ab.	.85	2.00	10.00	45.00
	1857(h)	—	—	—	Proof	125.00
	1858(h)	172.480	1.00	2.00	4.00	10.00
	1858(h)	—	—	—	Proof	125.00

1/2 ANNA

COPPER
Mule. Obv. Bombay KM#251. Rev: KM#447.

KM#	Date	Mintage	Fine	VF	XF	Unc
A447	1834	—	—	—	275.00	450.00

Bombay: 29.7mm; Madras: 30.8mm.

KM#	Date	Mintage	Fine	VF	XF	Unc
447.1	1835(b)	8.658	2.00	4.00	10.00	50.00
	1835(b)	—	—	—	Proof	100.00
	1835(b) (restrike)	—	—	—	P/L	35.00
	1835(m)	95.203	2.00	4.00	10.00	50.00
	1835(m)	—	—	—	Proof	100.00
	1845C	17.160	2.00	4.00	12.50	65.00

Beaded rim w/milled edge.

KM#	Date	Mintage	Fine	VF	XF	Unc
447.2	1835(c)	—	—	—	Proof	300.00

SILVER

KM#	Date	Mintage	Fine	VF	XF	Unc
447.2a	1835(c)	—	—	—	Proof	550.00

2 ANNAS

1.4600 g, .917 SILVER, .0430 oz ASW
Type I: Obv. leg. continuous.

Mint: Bombay, 15.8mm

KM#	Date	Mintage	Fine	VF	XF	Unc
459.1	1841.(b)	11.431	2.00	4.00	8.50	20.00

Mint: Calcutta, 15.3mm
Rev: W/crescent on left ribbon bow.

KM#	Date	Mintage	Fine	VF	XF	Unc
459.2	1841.(c)	8.385	2.00	4.00	8.50	20.00
	1841.(c) (restrike)	—	—	—	P/L	25.00
	1841.(c)	—	—	—	Proof	50.00

Obv: S incuse on truncation, small "v" on right bow of wreath.

KM#	Date	Mintage	Fine	VF	XF	Unc
459.3	1841.(m)	10.503	3.50	6.50	12.50	25.00
	1841.(b) (restrike)		—	—	P/L	25.00

NOTE: "(m)" strikes exist w/ and w/o small "v".

Type II: Obv. leg. divided.
Mint: Calcutta, 15.3mm
Rev: KM#459.2, dot after date.

KM#	Date	Mintage	Fine	VF	XF	Unc
460.1	1841.(c)	43.002	7.50	12.50	25.00	50.00
	1841.(c) (early restrike)			—	Proof	150.00

Obv: W.W. raised on truncation.

KM#	Date	Mintage	Fine	VF	XF	Unc
460.2	1841(c)	Inc. Ab.	1.50	3.00	7.50	15.00
	1841(c)	—	—	—	Proof	150.00

Mint: Bombay, 15.7mm
Obv: .W.W raised on truncation.

KM#	Date	Mintage	Fine	VF	XF	Unc
460.3	1841(b)	8.427	1.50	3.00	7.50	15.00

Obv: S incuse, W.W raised.
Mint: Madras, 15.7mm

KM#	Date	Mintage	Fine	VF	XF	Unc
460.4	1841(m)	26.930	2.00	4.00	8.50	17.50
	1841(m)	—	—	—	Proof	150.00

Obv: WW raised.

KM#	Date	Mintage	Fine	VF	XF	Unc
460.5	1849 (early restrike)			—	Proof	250.00
	1849 (restrike)		—	—	P/L	25.00

1/4 RUPEE

2.9200 g, .917 SILVER, .0860 oz ASW

آنا

Rev. I: Small Rupee, "ana" in Hindi.

آنہ

Rev II: Small Rupee, "ana" in Persian.

Rev. III: Large Rupee, "ana" in Persian.

Rev. I w/20 berries.

KM#	Date	Mintage	Fine	VF	XF	Unc
448.1	1835(c)	.922	11.50	22.50	45.00	90.00
(448.5)	1835(c)	—	—	—	Proof	500.00

Obv: RS incuse on truncation.
Rev. II w/20 berries.

KM#	Date	Mintage	Fine	VF	XF	Unc
448.2 (448.4)	1835(c)	Inc. Ab.	5.00	10.00	20.00	40.00

NOTE: Robert Saunders was Calcutta Mint Director from 1826-Jan. 1836.

Obv: W/o initials on truncation.
Rev. II w/20 berries.

KM#	Date	Mintage	Fine	VF	XF	Unc
448.3	1835(b)	5.760	5.00	10.00	20.00	40.00
	1835(b)	—	—	—	Proof	500.00
	1835(b) (restrike)	—	—	—	P/L	30.00

Obv: F incuse on truncation.
Rev. II w/20 berries.

KM#	Date	Mintage	Fine	VF	XF	Unc
448.4 (448.2)	1835(c)	9.842	4.50	7.50	15.00	40.00

Obv: F incuse on truncation. Rev. III.

KM#	Date	Mintage	Fine	VF	XF	Unc
448.5 (448.2)	1835(c) w/19 berries	Inc. Ab.	4.50	7.50	15.00	40.00
	1835.(c) w/18 berries	Inc. Ab.	4.50	7.50	15.00	40.00

Obv: F in relief in truncation.
Rev. III w/18 berries.

KM#	Date	Mintage	Fine	VF	XF	Unc
448.6	1835.(c)	Inc. Ab.	4.50	7.50	15.00	40.00
(448.1)	1835.(c)	—	—	—	Proof	500.00
	1835.(c) (restrike)	—	—	—	P/L	30.00

GOLD

KM#	Date	Mintage	Fine	VF	XF	Unc
448a	1835(c)	—	—	—	—	—

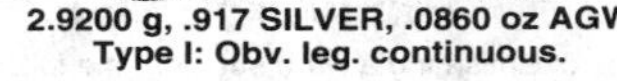

2.9200 g, .917 SILVER, .0860 oz AGW
Type I: Obv. leg. continuous.

Mint: Bombay, 19.5mm
Obv: English head.

KM#	Date	Mintage	Fine	VF	XF	Unc
453.1	1840.(b)	10.617	2.50	5.00	10.00	25.00
	1840.(b) (restrike)	—	—	—	P/L	30.00

Mint: Calcutta, 19.3mm.
Rev: W/crescent on left ribbon bow, 20 berries.

KM#	Date	Mintage	Fine	VF	XF	Unc
453.2	1840.(c)	12.994	2.50	5.00	10.00	20.00
	1840.(c)	—	—	—	Proof	200.00

Mint: Madras, 19.6mm
Obv: S incuse on truncation.
Rev: W/v on right ribbon bow, 20 berries.

KM#	Date	Mintage	Fine	VF	XF	Unc
453.3	1840.(m)	6.450	3.75	7.50	15.00	30.00

Obv: "Indian" head w/thinner features.
Rev: 34 berries.

KM#	Date	Mintage	Fine	VF	XF	Unc
453.4	1840.(c)	Inc. Ab.	2.50	5.00	10.00	20.00
	1840.(c)	—	—	—	Proof	200.00

Type II. Obv. leg. divided.
Mule. Rev. KM#453.4.

KM#	Date	Mintage	Fine	VF	XF	Unc
454.1	1840.(b & c)	40.532	10.00	20.00	40.00	80.00
	1840.(c)	—	—	—	Proof	200.00

Obv: W.W. raised on truncation.

KM#	Date	Mintage	Fine	VF	XF	Unc
454.2	1840(b & c) plain 4	Inc. Ab.	2.50	5.00	10.00	20.00
	1840(b & c) crosslet 4	Inc. Ab.	3.00	6.00	12.00	25.00
	1840(c)	—	—	—	Proof	200.00

Obv: W.W. and B raised on truncation.

KM#	Date	Mintage	Fine	VF	XF	Unc
454.3	1840(m)	13.664	4.00	6.00	12.00	30.00

Obv: W.W. S raised on truncation.

KM#	Date	Mintage	Fine	VF	XF	Unc
454.4	1840(m)	Inc. Ab.	4.00	8.00	15.00	30.00

Obv: W.W. on truncation. Plain edge.

KM#	Date	Mintage	Fine	VF	XF	Unc
454.5	1849 (early restrike)			—	Proof	300.00
	1849 (restrike)		—	—	P/L	45.00

Milled edge.

KM#	Date	Mintage	Fine	VF	XF	Unc
454.6	1849 (early restrike)			—	Proof	300.00
	1849 (restrike)		—	—	P/L	45.00

1/2 RUPEE

5.8300 g, .917 SILVER, .1719 oz ASW
Obv: W/o initial on truncation.

KM#	Date	Mintage	Fine	VF	XF	Unc
449.1	1835.(b)	3.573	7.50	15.00	30.00	60.00
	1835.(b)(restrike)		—	—	P/L	60.00

Obv: F raised on truncation.

KM#	Date	Mintage	Fine	VF	XF	Unc
449.2	1835.(c)	6.700	7.50	15.00	30.00	60.00
	1835(c) (restrike)		—	—	P/L	60.00

Obv: F incuse.

KM#	Date	Mintage	Fine	VF	XF	Unc
449.3	1835.(c)	—	7.50	15.00	30.00	60.00
	1835.(c) (early restrike)			—	Proof	250.00

Obv: RS incuse.

KM#	Date	Mintage	Fine	VF	XF	Unc
449.4	1835.(c)	.521	10.00	20.00	40.00	80.00
	1835.(c)	—	—	—	Proof	700.00

GOLD

KM#	Date	Mintage	Fine	VF	XF	Unc
449a	1835(c)	—	—	—	—	—

5.8300 g, .917 SILVER, .1719 oz ASW
Type I: Obv. leg. continuous.
Mint: Bombay, 24.5-24.6mm
Obv: "Plump" head.

KM#	Date	Mintage	Fine	VF	XF	Unc
455.1	1840.(b)	9.844	5.00	10.00	20.00	45.00
	1840.(b) (restrike)		—	—	P/L	35.00

Mint: Calcutta: 24.2-24.4mm
Rev: W/crescent on left ribbon bow.

KM#	Date	Mintage	Fine	VF	XF	Unc
455.2	1840.(c)	8.049	5.00	10.00	20.00	45.00
	1840.(c)	—	—	—	Proof	250.00
	1840.(c)(restrike)		—	—	P/L	35.00

Obv: S incuse on truncation.

KM#	Date	Mintage	Fine	VF	XF	Unc
455.3	1840.(m)	1.874	—	—	Rare	—

Obv: "Indian" head w/thinner features.
Rev: W/mm, crescent, on left ribbon bow.

KM#	Date	Mintage	Fine	VF	XF	Unc
455.4	1840.(c)	I.A.	5.00	10.00	20.00	45.00
	1840.(c)	I.A.	—	—	Proof	250.00
	1840.(c) (restrike)		—	—	P/L	35.00

Mule. Obv: KM#455.1. Rev: KM#456.1.

KM#	Date	Mintage	Fine	VF	XF	Unc
A455	1840(c)	—	4.50	8.50	17.50	40.00

Type II: Obv. leg. divided.
Obv: .W.W incuse.

KM#	Date	Mintage	Fine	VF	XF	Unc
456.1	1840(b & c)	18.551	4.00	8.00	15.00	35.00

Obv: W.W. incuse and S.

KM#	Date	Mintage	Fine	VF	XF	Unc
456.2	1840(m)	2.507	5.00	10.00	20.00	40.00

Obv:. W.W incuse. Milled edge.

KM#	Date	Mintage	Fine	VF	XF	Unc
456.3	1849 (early restrike)			—	Proof	400.00
	1849 (restrike)		—	—	P/L	50.00

Plain edge.

KM#	Date	Mintage	Fine	VF	XF	Unc
456.4	1849 (early restrike)			—	Proof	400.00
	1849 (restrike)		—	—	P/L	50.00

Mule. Obv: KM#456.1. Rev: KM#455.4.

KM#	Date	Mintage	Fine	VF	XF	Unc
A456	1840.	—	4.50	8.50	17.50	40.00

RUPEE

11.6600 g, .917 SILVER, .3438 oz ASW
Obv. leg: Thick lettering. W/o initial on truncation.

KM#	Date	Mintage	Fine	VF	XF	Unc
450.1	1835.(b)	53.713	8.50	12.50	25.00	50.00
	1835.(b)	—	—	—	Proof	500.00
	1835.(b) (restrike)		—	—	P/L	40.00

Obv: F raised on truncation.

KM#	Date	Mintage	Fine	VF	XF	Unc
450.2	1835.(c)	—	8.50	15.00	30.00	60.00
	1835.(c)	—	—	—	Proof	500.00
	1835.(c)	—	—	—	P/L	60.00

Obv: F incuse on truncation.

KM#	Date	Mintage	Fine	VF	XF	Unc
450.3	1835.(c)	—	8.50	15.00	30.00	60.00
	1835.(c)	—	—	—	Proof	750.00
	1835.(c) (restrike)		—	—	P/L	60.00

Obv: RS incuse on truncation.

KM#	Date	Mintage	Fine	VF	XF	Unc
450.4	1835.(c)	15.759	10.00	20.00	40.00	85.00
	1835.(c)	—	—	—	Proof	750.00

KM#	Date	Mintage	Fine	VF	XF	Unc
450.5	1840/35.(c)	—	90.00	175.00	300.00	600.00
450.6	1840.(c)	—	—	—	Rare	—

Obv. leg: Thin lettering. RS incuse on truncation.

KM#	Date	Mintage	Fine	VF	XF	Unc
450.7	1835.(c)	—	35.00	60.00	100.00	250.00

GOLD

KM#	Date	Mintage	Fine	VF	XF	Unc
450a	1835.(c)	—	—	—	—	—

11.6600 g, .917 SILVER, .3438 oz ASW
Type I: Obv. leg. continuous.

The major reverse varieties occur on the Type I Rupees of all three mints. The first reverse has 19 berries in the wreath, the second reverse has 34 and 35 berries (Calcutta) and 35 berries (Bombay and Madras). There are several minor varieties of the first reverse, but these are not listed. Madras specimens of Type I with the 1st reverse also have a small, raised "V" on the lower part of the right ribbon bow.

Mint: Calcutta, 1st rev. 31.5mm,
2nd rev. 31.1-31.3mm
Obv: "Plump" head.
Rev: 19 berries w/crescent on left ribbon bow.

KM#	Date	Mintage	Fine	VF	XF	Unc
457.1	1840.(c)	179.935	6.00	10.00	17.50	40.00
	1840.(c)	—	—	—	Proof	325.00

Mint: Bombay, 31.6-31.8mm
Rev: 35 berries.

KM#	Date	Mintage	Fine	VF	XF	Unc
457.2	1840.(b)	109.838	7.00	10.00	17.50	40.00

Rev: 19 berries, small diamonds.

KM#	Date	Mintage	Fine	VF	XF	Unc
457.3	1840.(b)	I.A.	7.00	10.00	17.50	40.00

Rev: 19 berries, large diamonds.

KM#	Date	Mintage	Fine	VF	XF	Unc
457.4	1840.(b)	I.A.	7.00	10.00	17.50	40.00

Mint: Madras, 31.9-32.2mm
Obv: S incuse on truncation. Rev: 19 berries, small diamonds, w/V on right ribbon bow.

KM#	Date	Mintage	Fine	VF	XF	Unc
457.5	1840.(m)	21.898	9.00	18.50	37.50	75.00

Rev: 19 berries, large diamonds.

KM#	Date	Mintage	Fine	VF	XF	Unc
457.6	1840.(m)	I.A.	9.00	18.50	37.50	75.00

Obv: W/o S.
Rev: 19 berries, w/v on right ribbon bow.

KM#	Date	Mintage	Fine	VF	XF	Unc
457.7	1840.(m)	I.A.	9.00	18.50	37.50	75.00

Obv: S incuse. Rev: 20 berries, w/o small v.

KM#	Date	Mintage	Fine	VF	XF	Unc
457.8	1840.(m)	I.A.	8.00	12.50	20.00	40.00

Obv: S incuse. Rev: 35 berries, w/o small v.

KM#	Date	Mintage	Fine	VF	XF	Unc
457.9	1840.(m)	I.A.	10.00	15.00	30.00	60.00

Obv: "Indian" head w/thinner features.
Rev: 35 berries w/crescent on left ribbon bow.

KM#	Date	Mintage	Fine	VF	XF	Unc
457.10	1840.(c)	I.A.	9.00	18.50	37.50	75.00
	1840.(c)	—	—	—	Proof	350.00

Rev: 34 berries , small "m" on left ribbon end, dot after date.

KM#	Date	Mintage	Fine	VF	XF	Unc
457.11	1840.(c)	—	—	—	Proof	350.00
457.12	1840.(m)	—	—	—	225.00	350.00

Type II: Obv. leg. divided.
Mint: Calcutta, 30.5mm.
Obv: W.W. raised. Rev: 28 berries, small diamonds.

KM#	Date	Mintage	Fine	VF	XF	Unc
458.1	1840(c)	398.554	3.00	6.00	12.00	25.00

Obv: W.W. raised. Rev: 28 berries, large diamonds.

KM#	Date	Mintage	Fine	VF	XF	Unc
458.2	1840(c)	Inc. Ab.	3.00	6.00	12.00	25.00

Mint: Bombay, 30.8mm
Obv: W.W. raised. Rev: 27 berries.

KM#	Date	Mintage	Fine	VF	XF	Unc
458.3	1840(b)	312.598	3.00	6.00	12.00	25.00
	1840(b)	—	—	—	Proof	325.00

Obv: W.W.B raised, small B. Rev: 28 berries.

KM#	Date	Mintage	Fine	VF	XF	Unc
458.4	1840(m)	55.049	3.00	6.00	12.00	25.00

Obv: W.W.B raised, large B. Rev: 28 berries.

KM#	Date	Mintage	Fine	VF	XF	Unc
458.5	1840(m)	I.A.	3.00	6.00	12.00	25.00

Obv: W.W.B raised, small letters. Rev: 28 berries.

KM#	Date	Mintage	Fine	VF	XF	Unc
458.6	1840(m)	I.A.	3.00	6.00	12.00	25.00

Obv: W.W.S raised. Rev: 28 berries.

KM#	Date	Mintage	Fine	VF	XF	Unc
458.7	1840(m)	—	3.00	6.00	12.00	25.00

Obv: W.W. Rev: 25 berries.
Milled edge.

KM#	Date	Mintage	Fine	VF	XF	Unc
458.8	1849 (early restrike)			—	Proof	500.00
	1849 (restrike)		—	—	P/L	100.00

Plain edge

KM#	Date	Mintage	Fine	VF	XF	Unc
458.9	1849 (early restrike)			—	Proof	500.00
	1849 (restrike)		—	—	P/L	100.00

Mule. Obv: KM#458.1. Rev: 25 berries.

KM#	Date	Mintage	Fine	VF	XF	Unc
458.10	1840	—	—	—	Rare	—

COPPER
Obv: W.W.B

KM#	Date	Mintage	Fine	VF	XF	Unc
458a	1840(m)	—	—	—	Rare	—

MOHUR

11.6600 g, .917 GOLD, .3437 oz AGW
Obv: W/o initials.
Milled edge.

KM#	Date	Mintage	Fine	VF	XF	Unc
451.1	1835(b)	—	200.00	350.00	500.00	850.00
	1835(b) (restrike)		—	—	P/L	275.00

Obv: RS incuse on truncation.

KM#	Date	Mintage	Fine	VF	XF	Unc
451.2	1835.(c)	.029	275.00	450.00	650.00	1000.
	1835.(c)	—	—	—	Proof	—
	1835.(c) (restrike)		—	—	P/L	400.00

Obv: F incuse on truncation.

KM#	Date	Mintage	Fine	VF	XF	Unc
451.3	1835.(c)	.111	250.00	375.00	500.00	800.00
	1835.(c) (restrike)		—	—	P/L	500.00

Plain edge.
Obv: RS incuse on truncation.

KM#	Date	Mintage	Fine	VF	XF	Unc
451.4	1835.(c)	—	—	—	Proof	Rare

Obv: F incuse on truncation.

KM#	Date	Mintage	Fine	VF	XF	Unc
451.5	1835.(c)	—	—	—	Proof	Rare

SILVER

KM#	Date	Mintage	Fine	VF	XF	Unc
451a	1835.(c)	—	—	—	Proof	Rare

COPPER

KM#	Date	Mintage	Fine	VF	XF	Unc
451b	1835.(c)	—	—	—	Proof	650.00

11.6600 g, .917 GOLD, .3437 oz AGW
Type I: Obv. leg. continuous.
Obv: Dot on truncation.

KM#	Date	Mintage	Fine	VF	XF	Unc
461.1	1841.(b)	5,960	—	—	650.00	1000.
461.2	1841.(c)	.601	175.00	225.00	300.00	400.00
	1841.(c)	—	—	—	Proof	1500.

Obv: S incuse on truncation.

KM#	Date	Mintage	Fine	VF	XF	Unc
461.3	1841.(m)	.032	250.00	325.00	450.00	600.00
	1841.(m)	—	—	—	Proof	1500.

Type II. Obv. leg. divided.

Lg. date normal 4 Lg. date crosslet 4

Obv: W.W. incuse; lg. leg. and lg. date w/normal 4.

KM#	Date	Mintage	Fine	VF	XF	Unc
462.1	1841.(c)	.442	150.00	200.00	300.00	400.00
	1841.(c) (restrike)		—	—	P/L	450.00

Obv: W.W. incuse; lg. leg. and lg. date w/crosslet 4.

KM#	Date	Mintage	Fine	VF	XF	Unc
462.2	1841.(c)	—	175.00	225.00	300.00	400.00

Small date

Obv: .W.W incuse; sm. leg. and sm. date w/normal 4.

KM#	Date	Mintage	Fine	VF	XF	Unc
462.3	1841.	—	200.00	325.00	450.00	600.00

Mule. Obv: KM#462. Rev: KM#451.

KM#	Date	Mintage	Fine	VF	XF	Unc
A462	1841.(c) (restrike)		—	—	P/L	450.00

2 MOHURS

23.3200 g, .917 GOLD, .6873 oz AGW
RS incuse on truncation.
Milled edge.

KM#	Date	Mintage	Fine	VF	XF	Unc
452.1	1835.(c)	1,170	850.00	1250.	1750.	3000.
	1835.(c)	—	—	—	Proof	3500.
	1835.(c) (restrike)		—	—	P/L	1350.

Plain edge.

KM#	Date	Mintage	Fine	VF	XF	Unc
452.2	1835.(c)	—	—	—	Rare	—

SILVER

KM#	Date	Mintage	Fine	VF	XF	Unc
452a	1835.(c)	—	—	—	Proof	1500.

COPPER

KM#	Date	Mintage	Fine	VF	XF	Unc
452b	1835.(c)	—	—	—	Proof	750.00

REGAL COINAGE

1/12 ANNA

NOTE: 1/12 Anna dated 1862 were minted at Calcutta, Bombay, and Madres using Bust A. They may be attributed according to size Bust A was used on all issues except 1877 and subsequent Calcutta issues which used Bust B.

Distinguishing Features

BUST A - Front of dress has 4-1/3 panels with a flower at center on bottom panel.

BUST B - Front of dress has 4 panels with a flower at right on bottom panel.

CALCUTTA - Issues of 1874-76 are 17.5mm in in diameter. From 1877 Bust B was used and the legend at lower right is distant from the bust. 1882-86 issues have a tiny incuse "C" on a bead of the inner circle below the date.

BOMBAY - Issues of 1874-76 are 18.0mm in diameter. From 1877 Bust A was used and the legend at lower right is close to the bust.

NOTE: Proofs and restrikes dated 1862 occur struck from pattern dies with 4-3/4 panels and a different dress floral design on obverse, and a wreath with 5 small 6-pointed stars on reverse.

COPPER

KM#	Date	Mintage	Fine	VF	XF	Unc
465	1862(c) 17.4-17.5mm					
		2.502	1.25	2.50	5.00	10.00
	1862(b) 17.9-18.0mm					
		2.999	1.25	2.50	5.00	10.00
	1862(m) 17.6-17.7mm					
		40.487	.75	1.25	2.50	7.50
	1862(c)	—	—	—	Proof	50.00
	1862(c) (restrike)		—	—	P/L	35.00
	1874(c)	4.819	1.25	2.50	5.00	10.00
	1874(b)	2.960	1.25	2.50	5.00	10.00
	1875(c)	4.646	1.25	2.50	5.00	10.00
	1875(c)	—	—	—	Proof	65.00
	1875(b)	3.068	1.25	2.50	5.00	10.00
	1876(c)	20.318	1.00	1.50	2.50	7.50
	1876(b)					
		Inc. 1875(b)	1.25	2.50	5.00	10.00

GOLD

KM#	Date	Mintage	Fine	VF	XF	Unc
465b	1862(c) (restrike)		—	—	P/L	250.00

COPPER

KM#	Date	Mintage	Fine	VF	XF	Unc
483	1877(c)	5.880	.50	1.00	2.50	6.00
	1877(c)	—	—	—	Proof	50.00
	1877(c) (restrike)		—	—	P/L	25.00
	1877(b)	1.551	.50	1.00	2.50	6.00
	1877(b)	—	—	—	Proof	50.00
	1878(c)	5.525	.50	1.00	2.50	6.00
	1878(c)	—	—	—	Proof	50.00
	1881(b)	2.954	.50	1.00	2.50	6.00
	1882(c)	4.344	.50	1.00	2.00	5.00
	1883(c)	9.840	.50	1.00	2.00	5.00
	1883(b)	4.794	.35	.75	1.75	4.00
	1883(b)	—	—	—	Proof	50.00
	1884(b)	8.074	.50	1.00	2.50	6.00
	1884(b)	—	—	—	Proof	50.00
	1885(c)	4.783	.50	1.00	2.00	5.00
	1886(c)	18.663	.35	.75	1.75	4.00
	1886(b)	5.783	.50	1.00	2.50	6.00
	1886(b)	—	—	—	Proof	50.00
	1887(c)	8.724	.50	1.00	2.00	5.00
	1887(b)	8.242	.50	1.00	2.50	6.00
	1888(c)	4.662	.50	1.00	2.00	5.00
	1888(b)	2.143	.50	1.00	2.50	6.00
	1889(c)	7.602	.50	1.00	2.00	5.00
	1889(b)	5.660	.50	1.00	2.50	6.00
	1890(c)	21.732	.35	.75	1.75	4.00
	1890(b)	—	—	—	Proof	50.00
	1890 (restrike)		—	—	P/L	20.00
	1891(c)	17.306	.35	.75	1.75	4.00
	1891(c)	—	—	—	Proof	50.00
	1891(c) (restrike)		—	—	P/L	20.00
	1892(c)	13.793	.35	.75	1.75	4.00
	1892(c)	—	—	—	Proof	50.00
	1892(c) (restrike)		—	—	P/L	20.00
	1893(c)	10.034	.35	.75	1.75	4.00
	1893(c)	—	—	—	Proof	50.00
	1893(c) (restrike)		—	—	P/L	20.00
	1894(c)	18.392	.35	.75	1.75	4.00
	1894(c)	—	—	—	Proof	50.00
	1894(c) (restrike)		—	—	P/L	20.00
	1895(c)	15.208	.35	.75	1.75	4.00
	1895(c)	—	—	—	Proof	50.00
	1896(c)	.922	.50	1.25	2.50	6.00
	1896(c)	—	—	—	Proof	50.00
	1896(c) (restrike)		—	—	P/L	20.00
	1897(c)	20.822	.35	.75	1.75	4.00
	1897(c)	—	—	—	Proof	50.00
	1897(c) (restrike)		—	—	P/L	20.00
	1898(c)	13.882	.35	.75	1.75	4.00
	1898(c)	—	—	—	Proof	50.00
	1898(c) (restrike)		—	—	P/L	20.00
	1899(c)	10.056	.35	.75	1.75	4.50
	1899(c)	—	—	—	Proof	50.00
	1899(c) (restrike)		—	—	P/L	20.00

NOTE: Later date (1901) exists for this type.

ALUMINUM

KM#	Date	Mintage	Fine	VF	XF	Unc
483a	1891(b)	—	—	—	Proof	100.00

SILVER

KM#	Date	Mintage	Fine	VF	XF	Unc
483b	1892(c) (restrike)		—	—	P/L	75.00
	1893(c) (restrike)		—	—	P/L	75.00
	1894(c) (restrike)		—	—	P/L	75.00
	1895(c) (restrike)		—	—	P/L	75.00
	1896(c) (restrike)		—	—	P/L	75.00
	1897(c) (restrike)		—	—	P/L	75.00
	1898(c) (restrike)		—	—	P/L	75.00
	1899(c) (restrike)		—	—	P/L	75.00

NOTE: Later date (1901) exists for this type.

GOLD

KM#	Date	Mintage	Fine	VF	XF	Unc
483c	1891(c) (restrike)		—	—	P/L	250.00
	1892(c) (restrike)		—	—	P/L	250.00
	1893(c) (restrike)		—	—	P/L	250.00
	1895(c) (restrike)		—	—	P/L	250.00
483c	1896(c) (restrike)		—	—	P/L	250.00
	1897(c) (restrike)		—	—	P/L	250.00
	1898(c) (restrike)		—	—	P/L	250.00
	1899(c) (restrike)		—	—	P/L	250.00

NOTE: Later date (1901) exists for this type.

1/2 PICE

NOTE: The 1/2 Pice dated 1862 was struck at Indian Government Mints i.e. Calcutta and Madras. Tentative attribution to the mint of issue has been determined by their size.

Proofs and restrikes dated 1862 were struck from pattern dies with 4-3/4 panels, a different floral dress design on obverse and counter clockwise leaves on reverse.

COPPER

KM#	Date	Mintage	Fine	VF	XF	Unc
466	1862(c) (21.20-21.25mm)					
		96.843	1.25	2.50	5.00	15.00
	1862(m) (21.4mm)					
		6.400	1.50	3.50	6.50	20.00
	1862(c)	—	—	—	Proof	50.00
	1862(c) (restrike)		—	—	P/L	25.00
	1875(c)	—	—	—	Proof	75.00
	1875(c) (restrike)		—	—	P/L	25.00

GOLD

KM#	Date	Mintage	Fine	VF	XF	Unc
466b	1862(c)	—	—	—	Proof	250.00

COPPER

KM#	Date	Mintage	Fine	VF	XF	Unc
484	1877(c)	—	—	—	Proof	75.00
	1877(c) (restrike)		—	—	P/L	25.00
	1878(c)	—	—	—	Proof	75.00
	1885(c)	6.206	1.25	2.50	4.00	10.00
	1886(c)	7.733	1.25	2.50	4.00	10.00
	1887(c)	6.464	1.25	2.50	4.00	10.00
	1888(c)	3.190	1.25	2.50	4.00	10.00
	1889(c)	7.587	1.25	2.50	4.00	10.00
	1890(c)	3.504	1.25	2.50	4.00	10.00
	1890(c)	—	—	—	Proof	50.00
	1890(c) (restrike)		—	—	P/L	20.00
	1891(c)	5.139	1.25	2.50	4.00	10.00
	1891(c)	—	—	—	Proof	50.00
	1891(c) (restrike)		—	—	P/L	20.00
	1892(c)	4.774	1.25	2.50	4.00	10.00
	1892(c)	—	—	—	Proof	50.00
	1892(c) (restrike)		—	—	P/L	20.00
	1893(c)	7.005	1.25	2.50	4.00	10.00
	1893(c)	—	—	—	Proof	50.00
	1893(c) (restrike)		—	—	P/L	20.00
	1894(c)	7.777	1.25	2.50	4.00	10.00
	1894(c)	—	—	—	Proof	50.00
	1894(c) (restrike)		—	—	P/L	20.00
	1895(c)	9.874	1.00	1.75	3.50	8.50
	1895(c)	—	—	—	Proof	50.00
	1896(c)	6.113	1.25	2.50	4.00	10.00
	1896(c)	—	—	—	Proof	50.00
	1897(c)	8.484	1.25	2.50	4.00	10.00
	1897(c)	—	—	—	Proof	35.00
	1897(c) (restrike)		—	—	P/L	20.00
	1898(c)	12.940	1.00	1.75	3.50	8.50
	1898(c)	—	—	—	Proof	50.00
	1898(c) (restrike)		—	—	P/L	20.00
	1899(c)	7.936	1.25	2.50	4.00	10.00
	1899(c)	—	—	—	Proof	50.00
	1899(c) (restrike)		—	—	P/L	20.00
	1900(c)	5.219	1.25	2.50	4.00	10.00
	1900(c) (restrike)		—	—	P/L	20.00

NOTE: Later date (1901) exists for this type.

ALUMINUM

KM#	Date	Mintage	Fine	VF	XF	Unc
484a	1891(b)	—	—	—	Proof	85.00

SILVER

KM#	Date	Mintage	Fine	VF	XF	Unc
484b	1892(c) (restrike)		—	—	P/L	75.00
	1893(c) (restrike)		—	—	P/L	75.00
	1894(c) (restrike)		—	—	P/L	75.00
	1895(c) (restrike)		—	—	P/L	75.00
	1896(c) (restrike)		—	—	P/L	75.00
	1897(c) (restrike)		—	—	P/L	75.00
	1898(c) (restrike)		—	—	P/L	75.00
	1899(c) (restrike)		—	—	P/L	75.00
	1900(c) (restrike)		—	—	P/L	75.00

NOTE: Later date (1901) exists for this type.

GOLD

KM#	Date	Mintage	Fine	VF	XF	Unc
484c	1891(c) (restrike)		—	—	P/L	450.00
	1892(c) (restrike)		—	—	P/L	450.00
	1893(c) (restrike)		—	—	P/L	450.00
	1895(c) (restrike)		—	—	P/L	450.00
	1896(c) (restrike)		—	—	P/L	450.00
	1897(c) (restrike)		—	—	P/L	450.00
	1898(c) (restrike)		—	—	P/L	450.00
	1899(c) (restrike)		—	—	P/L	450.00

NOTE: Later date (1901) exists for this type.

1/4 ANNA

NOTE: The initial 1862 dated Calcutta 1/4 Annas were struck with a diameter of 26.2-26.3mm (Type A/I). With the opening of the new Calcutta copper mint in 1865 the 1/4 Annas were struck with a diameter of 25.3-25.4mm and a tiny raised v on the bottom center of the bust. Probably only a month or so later Calcutta began to strike coins with a new obverse and reverse (Type B/II). This type was used by Calcutta for the remainder of the Victorian period.

Distinguishing Features

BUST A - Front of dress has 4 panels with a single flower at right on bottom panel.
BUST B - Front of dress has 4 panels with flowers at left and right on bottom panel. Tiny raised v on bottom center of bust. Floral design of dress differs.
REVERSE I - Leaf below first and last digit of date.
REVERSE II - Leaf below center of date.
CALCUTTA - Issues from 1874 onward are Type B/II. Most 1879-1887 issues have a tiny incuse "C" on a bead of the inner circle below the center of the date.
BOMBAY - Issues of 1875-76 have Bust A and Rev. I (A/I) and from 1877 onward are Type B/I.

NOTE: Proofs and restrikes dated 1862 occur struck from pattern dies with 4-3/4 panels and a different dress floral design.

COPPER

KM#	Date	Mintage	Fine	VF	XF	Unc
467	1862(c) A/I 26.2-26.3mm	99.504	.75	1.50	3.00	9.00
	1862(c) A/I V raised on bottom center of bust	10.654	1.25	2.50	5.00	15.00
	1862(c) B/II 25.3-25.4mm	178.731	.75	1.50	3.00	9.00
	1862(c) B/II	—	—	—	Proof	90.00
	1862(c) (restrike)		—	—	P/L	30.00
	1862(b) A/I V incuse on point of shoulder 25.5mm	32.149	1.00	2.00	4.00	12.00
	1862(b) A/I dot below date 25.5mm	2.366	2.50	5.00	10.00	25.00
	1862(b) (restrike)		—	—	P/L	30.00
	1862(m) A/I 25.5mm	186.227	.75	1.50	3.00	9.00
	1874(c)	44.678	2.00	4.00	8.00	20.00
	1875(c)	36.237	2.50	5.00	10.00	25.00
	1875(c)	—	—	—	Proof	65.00
	1875(b)	14.494	3.00	6.00	12.00	35.00
	1876(b)	3.360	3.00	6.00	12.00	35.00
	1876(c)	43.581	2.50	5.00	10.00	25.00
	1876	—	—	—	Proof	65.00

GOLD, 12.85 g

KM#	Date	Mintage	Fine	VF	XF	Unc
467b	1862(c) (restrike)	—	—	—	Proof	350.00

COPPER
Mule. Obv: KM#467. Rev: KM#486.

KM#	Date	Mintage	Fine	VF	XF	Unc
485	1875(c) (restrike)		—	—	P/L	40.00

KM#	Date	Mintage	Fine	VF	XF	Unc
486	1877(c)	65.210	.75	1.50	3.00	9.00
	1877(c)	—	—	—	Proof	65.00
	1877(c) (restrike)		—	—	P/L	25.00
	1877(b)	9.320	.75	1.50	3.00	9.00
	1877(b) (restrike)		—	—	P/L	25.00
	1878(c)	40.813	.75	1.50	3.00	9.00
	1878(c)	—	—	—	Proof	65.00
	1878(c) (restrike)		—	—	P/L	25.00
	1879(c)	43.072	.50	1.00	2.00	6.00
	1879(c)	—	—	—	Proof	65.00
	1880(c)	10.278	.35	.75	1.50	4.50
	1882(c)	52.291	.40	1.00	2.00	6.00
	1882(b)	12.409	.75	1.50	2.50	7.50
	1883(c)	57.571	.75	1.50	2.50	7.50
	1883(b)	12.443	.75	1.50	2.50	7.50
	1884(c)	43.196	.50	1.00	2.00	6.00
	1884(c)	—	—	—	Proof	65.00
	1884(b)	16.845	.75	1.50	2.50	7.50
	1885(c)	36.699	.50	1.00	2.00	6.00
	1886(c)	36.121	.50	1.00	2.00	6.00
	1886(b)	14.390	.75	1.50	2.50	7.50
	1887(c)	59.060	.50	1.00	2.00	6.00
	1887(b)	26.205	.75	1.50	2.50	7.50
	1888(c)	34.531	.75	1.50	2.50	7.50
	1888(b)	8.293	1.50	2.50	3.50	10.00
	1889(c)	88.559	.35	.75	1.50	4.50
	1889(b)	19.110	.50	1.00	2.00	6.00
	1890(c)	82.909	.35	.75	1.50	4.50
	1890(c)	—	—	—	Proof	65.00
	1891(c)	86.076	.35	.75	1.50	4.50
	1891(c)	—	—	—	Proof	65.00
	1891(c) (restrike)		—	—	P/L	25.00
	1892(c)	68.131	.35	.75	1.50	4.50
	1892(c)	—	—	—	Proof	65.00
	1892(c) (restrike)		—	—	P/L	25.00
	1893(c)	76.039	.35	.75	1.50	4.50
	1893(c)	—	—	—	Proof	65.00
	1893(c) (restrike)		—	—	P/L	25.00
	1894(c)	45.744	.35	.75	1.50	4.50
	1894(c)	—	—	—	Proof	65.00
	1894(c) (restrike)		—	—	P/L	25.00
	1895(c)	35.744	.35	.75	1.50	4.50
	1895(c)	—	—	—	Proof	65.00
	1896(c)	109.853	.35	.75	1.50	4.50
	1896(c)	—	—	—	Proof	65.00
	1897(c)	82.288	.35	.75	1.50	4.50
	1897(c)	—	—	—	Proof	65.00
	1897(c) (restrike)		—	—	P/L	25.00
	1898(c)	12.118	.35	.75	1.50	4.50
	1898(c)	—	—	—	Proof	65.00
	1898(c) (restrike)		—	—	P/L	25.00
	1899(c)	36.896	.35	.75	1.50	4.50
	1899(c)	Inc. Ab.	—	—	Proof	65.00
	1899(c) (restrike)		—	—	P/L	25.00
	1900(c)	30.534	.35	.75	1.50	4.50
	1900(c)	—	—	—	Proof	65.00
	1900(c) (restrike)		—	—	P/L	25.00

NOTE: Later date (1901) exists for this type.

ALUMINUM

KM#	Date	Mintage	Fine	VF	XF	Unc
486a	1891(b)	—	—	—	Proof	150.00

SILVER

KM#	Date	Mintage	Fine	VF	XF	Unc
486b	1891(c) (restrike)		—	—	P/L	75.00
	1892(c) (restrike)		—	—	P/L	75.00
	1893(c) (restrike)		—	—	P/L	75.00
	1894(c) (restrike)		—	—	P/L	75.00
	1895(c) (restrike)		—	—	P/L	75.00
	1896(c) (restrike)		—	—	P/L	75.00
	1897(c) (restrike)		—	—	P/L	75.00
	1898(c) (restrike)		—	—	P/L	75.00
	1899(c) (restrike)		—	—	P/L	75.00
	1900(c) (restrike)		—	—	P/L	75.00

NOTE: Later date (1901) exists for this type.

GOLD

KM#	Date	Mintage	Fine	VF	XF	Unc
486c	1891(c) (restrike)		—	—	P/L	400.00
	1892(c) (restrike)		—	—	P/L	400.00
	1893(c) (restrike)		—	—	P/L	400.00
	1895(c) (restrike)		—	—	P/L	400.00
	1896(c) (restrike)		—	—	P/L	400.00
	1897(c) (restrike)		—	—	P/L	400.00
	1898(c) (restrike)		—	—	P/L	400.00
	1899(c) (restrike)		—	—	P/L	400.00
	1900(c) (restrike)		—	—	P/L	400.00

NOTE: Later date (1901) exists for this type.

1/2 ANNA

NOTE: 1862 dated issues were struck at all three mints using Obverse A and Reverse I (A/I). They may be attributed according to size. Later 1862 dated Calcutta issues use Bust B and Reverse II (B/II).

Distinguishing Features

BUST A - Front of dress has 4-1/2 panels with no flowers on bottom incomplete panel.
BUST B - Front of dress has 4 panels with a small flower at upper left and large flower at right on bottom panel. Floral design of dress differs from Bust A. Tiny raised v on bottom left of bust.
BUST C - Front of dress has 4-3/4 panels with a single flower in center of bottom incomplete panel. An enlarged bust with floral design similar to Bust B.
REVERSE I - Slant top 1 in date and narrow spaced "ANNA".
REVERSE II - Flat top 1 in date and wide spaced "ANNA".
CALCUTTA - Issues from 1877 onward are Type C/II. 1877 Calcutta isues also have short, wide 7's in date. 1879 Calcutta issues have a tiny incuse "C" on a bead of the inner circle below the center of the date.
BOMBAY - Issues from 1877 onward are Type B/II. 1877 Bombay issues also have tall, narrow 7's in date. This type 7 appears on most Bombay issues but not on any denomination of the Calcutta Mint.

NOTE: The designations of Bust A, B and C have been changed to correspond with designations in *"Coins of the British Commonwealth of Nations Part 4, Vol. 2"* by F. Pridmore.

COPPER

KM#	Date	Mintage	Fine	VF	XF	Unc
468	1862(c) A/I 31.3mm	7.236	10.00	20.00	30.00	75.00
	1862(c) B/II 31.3mm	7.399	10.00	20.00	30.00	75.00
	1862(c) B/II	—	—	—	Proof	125.00
	1862(b) A/I 30.5mm	4.802	10.00	20.00	30.00	75.00
	1862(m) A/I 30.7mm	66.515	5.00	10.00	18.50	60.00
	1862(b) (restrike)		—	—	P/L	35.00
	1875(c) B/II	1.146	12.50	25.00	50.00	100.00
	1875(c)	—	—	—	Proof	150.00
	1875(c) (restrike)		—	—	P/L	50.00
	1876(c) B/II	2.291	12.50	25.00	50.00	100.00

GOLD

KM#	Date	Mintage	Fine	VF	XF	Unc
468b	1862(c)	—	—	—	Proof	650.00

COPPER

KM#	Date	Mintage	Fine	VF	XF	Unc
487	1877(c) C/II	3.584	10.00	20.00	40.00	100.00
	1877(c)	Inc. Ab.	—	—	Proof	100.00
	1877(c) (restrike)		—	—	P/L	40.00
	1877(b) B/II	3.454	12.00	20.00	40.00	100.00
	1878(c)	—	—	—	Proof	100.00
	1878(c) (restrike)		—	—	P/L	65.00
	1879(c)	—	—	—	Proof	100.00
	1879(c) (restrike)		—	—	P/L	75.00
	1884(b)	—	—	—	Proof	100.00
	1884(b) (restrike)		—	—	P/L	75.00
	1890(c)	—	—	—	Proof	100.00
	1890(c) (restrike)		—	—	P/L	65.00
	1891(c)	—	—	—	Proof	100.00
	1891(c) (restrike)		—	—	P/L	65.00
	1892(c)	—	—	—	Proof	100.00
	1892(c) (restrike)		—	—	P/L	65.00
	1893(c)	—	—	—	Proof	100.00
	1893(c) (restrike)		—	—	P/L	65.00
	1894	—	—	— Reported, not confirmed		

ALUMINUM

KM#	Date	Mintage	Fine	VF	XF	Unc
487a	1891(b)	—	—	—	Proof	100.00

SILVER

KM#	Date	Mintage	Fine	VF	XF	Unc
487b	1892(c) (restrike)		—	—	P/L	150.00
	1893(c) (restrike)		—	—	P/L	150.00

GOLD

KM#	Date	Mintage	Fine	VF	XF	Unc
487c	1891(c) (restrike)		—	—	P/L	500.00
	1892(c) (restrike)		—	—	P/L	500.00
	1893(c) (restrike)		—	—	P/L	500.00

2 ANNAS

Distinguishing Features

BUST A - Front of dress has 4 panels. The bottom panel has 3 leaves at left and a small flower at upper right.
BUST B - Front of dress has 3-1/2 panels. The bottom incomplete panel has only 3 leaf tops.
REVERSE I - Large top flower; 2 large petals above the base of the top flower are long and curved downward.
REVERSE II - Small top flower; 2 large petals above the base of the top flower are short and horizontal.
CALCUTTA - Issues dated 1862-1878 are 15.3-15.4mm in diameter and have no mint mark. From 1879 the mint mark is a tiny incuse "C" on the whorl below the center of the bottom flower. The 1877 issue with a bead in the tip of the top flower is attributed to Calcutta based on its diameter of 15.4 mm.
BOMBAY - Issues dated 1862-1876 are 15.7-15.9mm in diameter and until 1876 have no mint mark. From 1876-1884 the mint mark is a raised dot above the bottom flower. From 1884 the mint mark is a small "B" incuse or raised on the stem of the top flower.
MADRAS - Issues dated 1862 are 16mm in diameter.

1.4600 g, .917 SILVER, .0430 oz ASW
Obv: Bust "A".

KM#	Date	Mintage	Fine	VF	XF	Unc
469	1862(c) 15.3-15.4mm					
		29.653	1.75	3.50	7.50	15.00
	1862(c)	—	—	—	Proof	100.00
	1862(b) 15.7-15.9mm					
		21.037	2.50	5.00	10.00	20.00
	1862(b) (restrike)	—		—	P/L	35.00
	1862(m) 16.0mm					
		4.202	2.75	5.50	11.00	22.00
	1874(c)	5.690	1.75	3.50	7.50	15.00
	1874(b)	9.508	1.50	3.00	6.00	12.00
	1874(b) dot I.A.	2.50	5.00	10.00	20.00	
	1875(c)	6.512	1.50	3.00	6.00	12.00
	1875(c)	—	—	—	Proof	100.00
	1875(b)	1.712	2.50	5.00	10.00	20.00
	1876(c)	10.504	1.00	2.00	4.00	8.00
	1876(b)	3.911	2.00	4.00	8.00	16.00

GOLD

KM#	Date	Mintage	Fine	VF	XF	Unc
469a	1862	—	—	—	Proof	350.00

1.4600 g, .917 SILVER, .0430 oz ASW

KM#	Date	Mintage	Fine	VF	XF	Unc
488	1877(c)A/I, w/o mm.					
		3.575	1.25	2.50	5.00	10.00
	1877(c) A/I, dot below					
		Inc. Ab.	1.75	3.50	7.00	14.00
	1877(c)	—	—	—	Proof	100.00
	1877(c)B/II, w/o mm.					
		Inc. Ab	1.75	3.50	7.00	14.00
	1877(c) (restrike)	—	—	—	P/L	30.00
	1877(c) B/II, dot in top flower					
		Inc. Ab.	1.25	2.50	5.00	10.00
	1877(b) A/I dot above lower flower					
		2.215	1.25	2.50	5.00	10.00
	1878B A.I, dot					
		2.215	1.25	2.50	5.00	10.00
	1878B	—	—	—	Proof	100.00
	1878B (restrike)	—	—	—	P/L	30.00
	1878(c) B/II w/o mm.					
		3.994	1.25	2.50	5.00	10.00
	1879C B/II, "C" incuse					
		3.541	1.25	2.50	5.00	10.00
	1880C B/II, "C" incuse					
		2.539	1.25	2.50	5.00	10.00
	1881C B/II, "C" incuse					
		4.400	1.25	2.50	5.00	10.00
	1881C	—	—	—	Proof	100.00
	1881(b) A/I, dot					
		2.449	1.25	2.50	5.00	10.00
	1881(b) A/II, dot					
		Inc. Ab.	1.75	3.50	7.00	14.00
	1881(b) B/II, dot					
		Inc. Ab.	1.25	2.50	5.00	10.00
	1882C B/II, "C" incuse					
		14.360	1.25	2.50	5.00	10.00
	1882(b) A/I, dot					
		2.629	1.25	2.50	5.00	10.00
	1882(b) B/II, dot					
		Inc. Ab.	1.25	2.50	5.00	10.00
	1882	—	—	—	Proof	100.00
	1883C B/II, "C" incuse					
		2.736	1.25	2.50	5.00	10.00
	1883(b)A/I, w/o mm.					
		Inc. Ab.	1.25	2.50	5.00	10.00
	1883(b) A/I, dot					
		4.416	1.25	2.50	5.00	10.00
	1883(b) B/II, dot					
		Inc. Ab.	1.25	2.50	5.00	10.00
	1884C B/II, "C" incuse					
		7.200	1.25	2.50	5.00	10.00
	1884(b) A/I, w/o mm.					
		1.638	1.25	2.50	5.00	10.00
	1884(b) A/I, dot					
		Inc. Ab.	1.25	2.50	5.00	10.00
	1884B A/I, "B" raised					
		Inc. Ab.	1.25	2.50	5.00	10.00
	1884B A/I, dot, "B" raised					
		Inc. Ab.	1.25	2.50	5.00	10.00
	1884B B/II, "B" incuse					
		Inc. Ab.	1.25	2.50	5.00	10.00
	1885C B/II, "C" incuse					
		1.335	1.75	3.50	7.00	14.00
	1885B A/I, w/o mm					
		2.262	1.75	3.50	7.00	14.00
	1885B A/I, "B" raised					
		Inc. Ab.	1.75	3.50	7.00	14.00
	1885B B/II, "B" raised					
		Inc. Ab.	1.25	2.50	5.00	10.00
	1886C B/II, "C" incuse					
		10.346	1.25	2.50	5.00	10.00
	1886B B/II, "B" incuse					
		3.155	1.25	2.50	5.00	10.00
	1887C B/II, "C" incuse					
		13.927	1.25	2.50	5.00	10.00
	1887B B/II, "B" incuse					

KM#	Date	Mintage	Fine	VF	XF	Unc
488		3.283	1.25	2.50	5.00	10.00
	1888(c) B/II, w/o mm.					
		9.307	1.25	2.50	5.00	10.00
	1888B B/II, "B" incuse					
		8.039	1.25	2.50	5.00	10.00
	1888B	—	—	—	Proof	100.00
	1889C B/II, "C" incuse					
		.135	1.75	3.50	7.00	14.00
	1889B B/II, "B" incuse					
		5.895	1.25	2.50	5.00	10.00
	1890C B/II, "C" incuse					
		9.836	1.25	2.50	5.00	10.00
	1890C	—	—	—	Proof	100.00
	1890B B/II, "B" raised					
		7.790	1.25	2.50	5.00	10.00
	1890B B/II, "B" incuse					
		Inc. Ab.	1.25	2.50	5.00	10.00
	1890B (restrike)	—	—	—	P/L	30.00
	1891C B/II, "C" incuse					
		8.621	1.25	2.50	5.00	10.00
	1891C	—	—	—	Proof	100.00
	1891B B/II, "B" incuse					
		4.230	1.25	2.50	5.00	10.00
	1891B (restrike)	—	—	—	P/L	30.00
	1892C B/II, "C" incuse					
		6.971	1.25	2.50	5.00	10.00
	1892C	—	—	—	Proof	100.00
	1892B B/II, "B" incuse					
		9.347	1.25	2.50	5.00	10.00
	1892B (restrike)	—	—	—	P/L	30.00
	1893C B/II, "C" incuse					
		8.003	1.25	2.50	5.00	10.00
	1893C	—	—	—	Proof	100.00
	1893/2(b) BII, "B" incuse					
		—	20.00	40.00	85.00	100.00
	1893B B/II, "B" incuse					
		10.716	1.25	2.50	5.00	10.00
	1893B (restrike)	—	—	—	P/L	30.00
	1894C B/II, "C" incuse					
		2.461	1.25	2.50	5.00	10.00
	1894C	—	—	—	Proof	100.00
	1894B B/II, "B" incuse					
		Inc. Ab.	1.25	2.50	5.00	10.00
	1894B (restrike)	—	—	—	P/L	30.00
	1895C B/II, "C" incuse					
		9.668	1.25	2.50	5.00	10.00
	1896C B/II, "C" incuse					
		6.616	1.25	2.50	5.00	10.00
	1896C	—	—	—	Proof	100.00
	1896B B/II, "B" incuse					
		8.235	1.25	2.50	5.00	10.00
	1897C B/II, "C" incuse					
		12.103	1.25	2.50	5.00	10.00
	1897C	—	—	—	Proof	100.00
	1897B B/II, "B" incuse					
		8.041	1.25	2.50	5.00	10.00
	1897B	—	—	—	Proof	100.00
	1897B (restrike)	—	—	—	P/L	30.00
	1898C B/II, "C" incuse					
		4.011	1.25	2.50	5.00	10.00
	1898B B/II, "B" incuse					
		3.250	1.25	2.50	5.00	10.00
	1898B	—	—	—	Proof	100.00
	1898B (restrike)	—	—	—	P/L	30.00
	1899	—	—	—	Proof	100.00
	1900C B/II, "C" incuse					
		1.705	1.25	2.50	5.00	10.00
	1900	—	—	—	Proof	—
	1900B B/I "B" raised					
		—	2.50	5.00	10.00	20.00
	1900B B/II, "B" raised					
		4.439	1.25	2.50	5.00	10.00
	1900B	—	—	—	Proof	100.00
	1900B (restrike)	—	—	—	P/L	30.00

NOTE: Later date (1901) exists for this type.

COPPER OR BRONZE

KM#	Date	Mintage	Fine	VF	XF	Unc
488b	1884	—	—	—	Proof	75.00
	1891	—	—	—	Proof	75.00
	1892	—	—	—	Proof	75.00

GOLD

KM#	Date	Mintage	Fine	VF	XF	Unc
488c	1891 (restrike)	—	—	—	P/L	250.00
	1892 (restrike)	—	—	—	P/L	250.00
	1893 (restrike)	—	—	—	P/L	250.00
	1896 (restrike)	—	—	—	P/L	250.00
	1897 (restrike)	—	—	—	P/L	250.00
	1898 (restrike)	—	—	—	P/L	250.00
	1900 (restrike)	—	—	—	P/L	250.00

1.4600 g, .917 SILVER, .0430 oz ASW
Mule. Obv: KM#469. Rev: KM#488.

KM#	Date	Mintage	Fine	VF	XF	Unc
489	1877 (restrike)	—	—	—	P/L	20.00

1/4 RUPEE

NOTE: The distinguishing features of the 3 busts and 2 reverses are as following:
BUST A - The front of dress has 4 panels w/flower at right on bottom panel.
BUST B - Front of dress has 3-3/4 panels w/flower at center on incomplete bottom panel.
BUST C - Front of dress has 3 panels w/flower at left on bottom panel.

REVERSE I - The 2 large petals above the base of the top flower are long and curved downward; long stroke between "1/4".
REVERSE II - The 2 large petals above the base of the top flower are short and horizontal; short stroke between "1/4".

CALCUTTA - Issues dated 1862-1878 have no mint mark. The diameter of the coins is 19.3-19.4mm and the milling is coarse. From 1879 the mint mark is a tiny incuse "C" on the whorl below the center of the bottom flower.

BOMBAY - Issues dated 1862, 1875 and 1876 have no mint mark. These have a diameter of 19.7-19.8mm and the milling is narrow. The coins dated 1874, 1877-1883 have as mint mark a small bead directly above the bottom flower. From 1884 the mint mark is a small "B" raised or incuse on the stem of the top flower.

MADRAS - Issues dated 1862 have a diameter of 19.9-20.0mm and coarse milling.

2.9200 g, .917 SILVER, .0860 oz ASW
Obv: Bust A. Rev: I.

KM#	Date	Mintage	Fine	VF	XF	Unc
470	1862(c) 19.3-19.4mm					
		19.412	2.50	5.00	10.00	20.00
	1862(c)	—	—	—	Proof	125.00
	1862(b) 19.7-19.8mm					
		11.390	2.50	5.00	10.00	20.00
	1862(b) (restrike)	—		—	P/L	35.00
	1862(m) 19.9-20.0mm					
		5.049	5.00	10.00	20.00	40.00
	1862(m) V1(I)CTORIA (error)					
		Inc. Ab.	5.00	10.00	20.00	40.00
	1874(c)	5.444	3.00	6.00	12.00	24.00
	1874(b)	1.612	3.50	7.50	15.00	30.00
	1875(c)	2.797	3.00	6.00	12.00	24.00
	1875(c)	—	—	—	Proof	125.00
	1875(b)	5.239	3.00	6.00	12.00	24.00
	1876(c)	6.457	3.00	6.00	12.00	24.00
	1876(b)	1.427	3.50	7.50	15.00	30.00

GOLD

KM#	Date	Mintage	Fine	VF	XF	Unc
470a	1862(c) (restrike)	—		—	P/L	500.00

2.9200 g, .917 SILVER, .0860 oz ASW.
Mule. Obv: 5 Rupee, KM#476.
Rev: 1/4 Rupee, KM#470.

KM#	Date	Mintage	Fine	VF	XF	Unc
471	1862(c) (restrike)	—		—	P/L	50.00

KM#	Date	Mintage	Fine	VF	XF	Unc
490	1877(c) B/I, no mm.					
		3.440	2.50	5.00	10.00	20.00
	1877(c)	.044	—	—	Proof	125.00
	1877(b) A/I, dot					
		.884	3.50	7.50	15.00	30.00
	1877(b) B/I, dot					
		Inc. Ab.	3.50	7.50	15.00	30.00
	1877(b)	—	—	—	Proof	125.00
	1877(b) (restrike)	—	—	—	P/L	30.00
	1878C	.044	2.00	3.50	7.50	15.00
	1878(c) C/II, w/o mm.					
		Inc. Ab.	2.00	3.50	8.00	20.00
	1878(c)	—	—	—	Proof	125.00
	1878(c) (restrike)	—	—	—	P/L	30.00
	1879C C/II, "C" incuse					
		2.463	2.00	3.50	8.00	20.00
	1879(b)	—	—	—	Proof	125.00
	1880C C/II, "C" incuse					
		.821	2.00	3.50	8.00	20.00
	1881C C/II, "C" incuse					
		3.244	2.00	3.75	8.00	20.00
	1881C	—	—	—	Proof	125.00
	1881(b) A/II, dot					
		1.444	2.00	3.75	8.00	20.00
	1881(b) B/I, dot					
		Inc. Ab.	4.00	7.50	15.00	30.00
	1882C C/II, "C" incuse					
		.612	2.00	3.50	8.00	20.00
	1882C	—	—	—	Proof	125.00
	1882(b) A/II, dot					
		2.775	2.00	3.75	8.00	20.00
	1882(b) B/I, dot					
		Inc. Ab.	3.00	6.00	12.00	25.00
	1882(b) C/II, dot					
		Inc. Ab.	2.25	4.00	8.00	20.00
	1883C C/II, "C" incuse					
		2.871	4.00	7.50	15.00	30.00
	1883(b) B/I, dot					
		.184	5.00	10.00	20.00	35.00
	1884C C/II "C" incuse					
		3.596	3.75	7.50	15.00	30.00
	1884B B/I, "B" raised					
		1.709	3.75	7.50	15.00	30.00
	1884B C/II, "B" raised					
		Inc. Ab.	3.75	7.50	15.00	30.00
	1884B	—	—	—	Proof	125.00
	1885C C/II, "C" incuse					
		1.024	3.75	7.50	15.00	30.00
	1885B B/I, "B" raised					
		1.118	3.75	7.50	15.00	30.00
	1886C C/II, "C" incuse					
		7.087	2.25	4.00	8.00	20.00
	1886B C/II, "B" raised					
		1.684	3.75	7.50	15.00	30.00

KM#	Date	Mintage	Fine	VF	XF	Unc
490	1886B C/II w/o mm	Inc. Ab.	5.00	10.00	20.00	40.00
	1887C C/II, "C" incuse	6.494	2.25	4.00	8.00	20.00
	1887B C/II, "B" raised	4.422	2.50	5.00	10.00	20.00
	1888(c) C/II, no mm.	4.945	2.50	5.00	10.00	20.00
	1888B C/II, "B" raised	2.278	3.00	6.00	12.00	25.00
	1888B C/II, "B" incuse	Inc. Ab.	3.75	7.50	15.00	30.00
	1889C C/II, "C" incuse	6.056	2.25	4.00	8.00	20.00
	1889B C/II, "B" incuse	4.298	2.50	5.00	10.00	20.00
	1889	—	—	—	Proof	125.00
	1890C C/II, "C" incuse	2.019	2.50	5.00	10.00	20.00
	1890C	—	—	—	Proof	125.00
	1890B C/I, "B" incuse	.459	4.00	7.50	15.00	30.00
	1890B C/II, "B" incuse	Inc. Ab.	4.50	8.50	16.50	32.50
	1890B (restrike)		—	—	P/L	30.00
	1891C C/II, "C" incuse	7.287	2.25	4.00	8.00	20.00
	1891B C/I, "B" incuse	.883	3.75	7.50	15.00	30.00
	1892(C) C/II, "C" incuse	—	2.50	5.00	10.00	20.00
	1892(C) C/II, "C" incuse	—	—	—	Proof	125.00
	1892B C/I, "B" incuse	4.059	2.00	3.00	6.00	15.00
	1892B	—	—	—	Proof	125.00
	1893C C/II, "C" incuse	6.435	2.00	3.00	6.00	15.00
	1893C	—	—	—	Proof	125.00
	1893B C/I, "B" incuse	4.603	2.00	3.00	6.00	15.00
	1893B (restrike)		—	—	P/L	30.00
	1894C C/II, "C" incuse	6.435	2.00	3.00	6.00	15.00
	1894C	—	—	—	Proof	125.00
	1894B C/I, "B" incuse	1.534	2.00	3.00	6.00	15.00
	1894B	—	—	—	Proof	125.00
	1894B (restrike)		—	—	P/L	30.00
	1896C C/II, "C" incuse	9.464	2.00	3.00	6.00	15.00
	1896C	—	—	—	Proof	125.00
	1897C C/II, "C" incuse	5.884	2.00	3.00	6.00	15.00
	1897C	—	—	—	Proof	125.00
	1897B C/I, "B" incuse	2.385	2.00	3.00	6.00	15.00
	1897B	—	—	—	Proof	125.00
	1897B (restrike)		—	—	P/L	30.00
	1898C C/II, "C" incuse	1.330	2.00	3.00	6.00	15.00
	1898C	—	—	—	Proof	125.00
	1898B C/I, "B" incuse	4.949	2.00	3.00	6.00	15.00
	1898B	—	—	—	Proof	125.00
	1898B (restrike)		—	—	P/L	30.00
	1900C C/II, "C" incuse	1.606	2.00	3.00	6.00	15.00
	1900C	—	—	—	Proof	125.00
	1900C (restrike)		—	—	P/L	30.00

NOTE: Later date (1901) exists for this type.

COPPER OR BRONZE

KM#	Date	Mintage	Fine	VF	XF	Unc
490b	1884	—	—	—	Proof	100.00
	1891	—	—	—	Proof	100.00
	1892	—	—	—	Proof	100.00

GOLD

KM#	Date	Mintage	Fine	VF	XF	Unc
490c	1891 (restrike)		—	—	P/L	350.00
	1892 (restrike)		—	—	P/L	350.00
	1893 (restrike)		—	—	P/L	350.00
	1896 (restrike)		—	—	P/L	350.00
	1897 (restrike)		—	—	P/L	350.00
	1898 (restrike)		—	—	P/L	350.00
	1900 (restrike)		—	—	P/L	350.00

1/2 RUPEE

Distinguishing Features

BUST A - Front of dress has 4 panels w/a flower at left and right on bottom panel. Tiny raised v on bottom center of bust.

BUST B - Front of dress has 4-1/2 or 4-2/3 panels. The incomplete bottom panel has a flower at left of center.

BUST C - Front of dress similar to Bust B but with 4-3/4 panels floral design of dress differs.

Bust B   Bust C

REVERSE I - The top flower is open and the 2 large petals above the base of the top flower are short and horizontal, flat top 1 in date.

REVERSE II - The top flower is closed and the 2 large petals above the base of the top flower are long and curved downward, slant top 1 in date.

CALCUTTA - Issues have Bust A/Reverse I and Bust C/Reverse II, dated 1862-1878, and have no mint mark. From 1879 the mint mark is a small incuse "C" below the center of the bottom flower.

BOMBAY - Issues dated 1862 have no mint mark. From 1874-1884 the mint mark is a small dot above the center of the bottom flower. From 1885 the mint mark is a small "B" raised or incuse, on the stem of the top flower.

MADRAS - Issues dated 1862 have no mint mark and cannot be distinguished from the Bombay issues.

5.8300 g, .917 SILVER, .1719 oz ASW

KM#	Date	Mintage	Fine	VF	XF	Unc
472	1862(c) C/II	1.623	5.00	10.00	20.00	40.00
	1862(c) A/I	7.649	5.00	10.00	20.00	50.00
	1862(c)	—	—	—	Proof	175.00
	1862(c) A/II	.736	7.50	15.00	30.00	60.00
	1862(c)	—	—	—	Proof	175.00
	1862(b & m) B/II	7.122	5.00	10.00	20.00	40.00
	1862(b) (restrike)		—	—	P/L	35.00
	1874(b) B/II, dot	1.654	7.50	15.00	30.00	65.00
	1875(c) A/I	2.257	5.00	10.00	20.00	50.00
	1875(c)	—	—	—	Proof	175.00
	1875(b) B/II, dot	1.023	7.50	15.00	30.00	65.00
	1876(b) B/II, dot	.966	7.50	15.00	30.00	65.00

GOLD

KM#	Date	Mintage	Fine	VF	XF	Unc
472a	1862(c) (restrike)		—	—	P/L	600.00

5.8300 g, .917 SILVER, .1719 oz ASW

KM#	Date	Mintage	Fine	VF	XF	Unc
491	1877(c) A/I	.858	5.00	10.00	20.00	45.00
	1877(c)	—	—	—	Proof	175.00
	1877(b) B/II, dot	.214	7.50	15.00	30.00	60.00
	1887(b) (restrike)		—	—	P/L	30.00
	1878(c) A/I	1.390	5.00	10.00	20.00	45.00
	1878(c)	—	—	—	Proof	175.00
	1878(c) (restrike)		—	—	P/L	30.00
	1879C A/I, "C" incuse	1.008	5.00	10.00	20.00	45.00
	1879(b)	—	—	—	Proof	175.00
	1880C A/I, "C" incuse	.180	7.50	15.00	30.00	60.00
	1881C A/I, "C" incuse	.921	5.00	10.00	20.00	45.00
	1881C	—	—	—	Proof	175.00
	1881(b) B/II, dot	1.591	5.00	10.00	20.00	45.00
	1882C A/I, "C" incuse	1.161	5.00	10.00	20.00	45.00
	1882C	—	—	—	Proof	175.00
	1882(b) B/II, dot	.308	8.00	17.50	35.00	70.00
	1882(b) A/II, dot	Inc. Ab.	8.00	17.50	35.00	70.00
	1883C A/I, "C" incuse	1.036	5.00	10.00	20.00	45.00
	1884C A/I, "C" incuse	—	5.00	10.00	20.00	45.00
	1884(b) A/II, dot	1.110	5.00	10.00	20.00	45.00
	1884(b) A/II, no mm.	Inc. Ab.	5.00	10.00	20.00	45.00
	1884	—	—	—	Proof	175.00
	1885C A/I, "C" incuse	1.408	3.75	7.50	15.00	40.00
	1885B A/II, "B" raised	.390	5.00	10.00	20.00	45.00
	1886C A/I, "C" incuse	2.645	3.75	7.50	15.00	40.00
	1886B A/II, "B" raised	1.116	3.75	7.50	15.00	40.00
	1887C A/I, "C" incuse	2.275	3.75	7.50	15.00	40.00
	1887B A/II, "B" raised	.407	5.00	10.00	20.00	45.00
	1888C A/I, "C" incuse	1.100	3.75	7.50	15.00	40.00
	1888B A/II, "B" raised	1.748	5.00	10.00	20.00	45.00
491	1888(b) A/II, no mm.	Inc. Ab.	5.00	10.00	20.00	45.00
	1889C A/I, "C" incuse	2.331	3.75	7.50	15.00	40.00
	1889B A/II, "B" raised	1.083	3.75	7.50	15.00	40.00
	1889B A/I, "B" incuse	Inc. Ab.	3.75	7.50	15.00	40.00
	1890C	—	—	—	Proof	175.00
	1890C (restrike)		—	—	P/L	30.00
	1891C	—	—	—	Proof	175.00
	1891B A/I, "B" incuse	—	—	—	Proof	175.00
	1891B	—	—	—	Proof	175.00
	1891 (restrike)		—	—	P/L	30.00
	1892C A/I, "C" incuse	1.761	3.75	7.50	15.00	40.00
	1892C	—	—	—	Proof	175.00
	1892B A/I, "B" incuse	1.104	3.75	7.50	15.00	40.00
	1892B	—	—	—	Proof	175.00
	1893C A/I, "C" incuse	—	3.75	7.50	15.00	40.00
	1893C	—	—	—	Proof	175.00
	1893B A/I, "B" incuse	2.462	3.75	7.50	15.00	40.00
	1893B (restrike)		—	—	P/L	40.00
	1894C A/I, "C" incuse	1.277	3.75	7.50	15.00	40.00
	1894C	—	—	—	Proof	175.00
	1894B A/I, "B" incuse	—	4.00	10.00	20.00	50.00
	1894B (restrike)		—	—	P/L	40.00
	1896C A/I, "C" incuse	2.114	3.75	7.50	15.00	40.00
	1896C	—	—	—	Proof	175.00
	1897C A/I, "C" incuse	—	3.75	7.50	15.00	40.00
	1897C	—	—	—	Proof	175.00
	1897B A/I, "B" incuse	.560	3.75	7.50	15.00	40.00
	1897B	—	—	—	Proof	175.00
	1897B (restrike)		—	—	P/L	35.00
	1898C A/I, "C" incuse	2.057	3.75	7.50	15.00	40.00
	1898C	—	—	—	Proof	175.00
	1898B A/I, "B" incuse	.458	5.00	10.00	20.00	45.00
	1898B	—	—	—	Proof	175.00
	1898B (restrike)		—	—	P/L	35.00
	1899C A/I, "C" incuse	6.893	3.75	7.50	15.00	40.00
	1899C	—	—	—	Proof	175.00
	1899B A/I, "B" incuse	11.174	2.50	5.00	10.00	30.00
	1899B A/I, "B" incuse, inverted B	—	2.50	5.00	10.00	30.00
	1899B	Inc. Ab.	—	—	Proof	175.00
	1899B (restrike)		—	—	P/L	35.00
	1900C A/I (restrike)		—	—	P/L	35.00

ALUMINUM

KM#	Date	Mintage	Fine	VF	XF	Unc
491a	1891	—	—	—	Proof	—

COPPER OR BRONZE

KM#	Date	Mintage	Fine	VF	XF	Unc
491b	1884	—	—	—	Proof	100.00
	1891	—	—	—	Proof	100.00
	1892	—	—	—	Proof	100.00

GOLD

KM#	Date	Mintage	Fine	VF	XF	Unc
491c	1891 (restrike)		—	—	P/L	450.00
	1892 (restrike)		—	—	P/L	450.00
	1893 (restrike)		—	—	P/L	450.00
	1896 (restrike)		—	—	P/L	450.00
	1897 (restrike)		—	—	P/L	450.00
	1898 (restrike)		—	—	P/L	450.00
	1899 (restrike)		—	—	P/L	450.00

RUPEE

Distinguishing Features

NOTE: The Rupees dated 1862 were struck with the date unchanged until 1874. However, in 1863 Bombay Mint adopted a method of adding dots or beads to its dies to indicate the exact year of minting.

The beads occur in the following positions:

1. Below the base or whorl of the top flower.
2. Above or around the top of the bottom flower.
3. In both positions together.

The different busts are identified as follows:

BUST A - Front of dress has 3-3/4 panels with a small flower at left on bottom incomplete panel.
BUST B - Front of dress has 4-1/4 panels with a small flower right on bottom panel, floral design of dress differs.
BUST C - Similar to Bust A, but shorter at the bottom. Front of dress has 3-1/3 or 3-1/2 panels.

REVERSE I - The top of flower is open, flat top 1 in date.
REVERSE II - The top flower is closed, slant top 1 in

date.

REVERSE IIa - Similar to Reverse II but flower buds above "E" of "ONE" and above right of second "E" of "RUPEE" have a "pineapple-like" pattern.

REVERSE III - The top flower is half open, flat 1 in date.

NOTE: The top flowers on reverse vary as illustrated below.

I II III

NOTE: In the listing of 1862 Rupees, the date column indicates the year in which the coins are believed to have been struck. The variety column lists the Obverse/reverse combination and the bead position. For example, A/I 0/0 means Bust A, Reverse I and no beads. A/II 1/2 means Bust A, Reverse II, and 1 bead at the top and 2 beads at the bottom.

Mintage for 1862 Rupees

Calcutta	**269,427,222**
Bombay	**408,003,034**
Madras	**29,481,923**

NOTE: The B/II 0/0 coins are attributed to the mint of issues as follows:

CALCUTTA - 30.7mm or smaller, round pearls in crown arch.

BOMBAY - 30.7-30.9mm, elongated pearls in crown arch. The scroll-like floral design of the dress is in flat relief and is retouched with incuse lines.

MADRAS - 30.9-31.0mm, elongated pearls in crown arch. The floral design is in high relief and is not retouched.

11.6600 g, .917 SILVER, .3438 oz ASW
Common date: 1862

KM#	Date	Year	Fine	VF	XF	Unc
473.1	A/I, 0/0					
		1862-63(m)	5.00	7.50	12.50	25.00
	A/II, 0/0 (30.7mm)					
		1862-63(b)	12.50	20.00	32.50	60.00
	A/IIa, 0/0					
		1862-63(c)	7.50	12.50	16.50	35.00
	B/II, 0/0					
		1862-63(c)	6.50	11.50	15.00	30.00
	B/II, 0/0					
		1862-63(b)	5.00	7.50	12.50	25.00
	B/II, 0/0					
		1862-63(m)	5.00	7.50	12.50	25.00
	B/IIa, 0/0					
	1862-63(b) or (m)					
			12.50	20.00	30.00	60.00
	A/III, 0/0					
		1862-63(c)	12.50	20.00	30.00	60.00
	B/III, 0/0					
		1862-63(c)	12.50	20.00	30.00	60.00
	B/II, 1/0	1863(b)	.50	12.50	16.50	35.00
	A/II, 0/2	1864(b)	12.50	20.00	40.00	80.00
	B/II, 2/0	1864(b)	12.50	20.00	40.00	80.00
	B/II, 3/0	1864(b)	12.50	20.00	40.00	80.00
	A/II, 2/0	1864(b)	—	—	Rare	—
	B/II, 0/3	1865(b)	5.00	7.50	12.50	30.00
	B/II, 2/3	1865(b)	12.50	20.00	40.00	80.00
	A/I, 0/4	1866(b)	12.50	20.00	40.00	80.00
	B/I, 0/4	1866(b)	12.50	20.00	40.00	80.00
	A/II, 0/4	1866(b)	8.00	15.00	30.00	60.00
	A/II, 2/4	1866(b)	15.00	30.00	50.00	90.00
	B/II, 0/4	1866(b)	8.00	15.00	30.00	60.00
	A/II, 0/5	1867(b)	5.00	7.50	13.50	30.00
	A/II, 0/6	1868(b)	5.00	7.50	13.50	30.00
	A/II, 0/7	1869(b)	5.00	7.50	13.50	30.00
	B/II, 0/6	1869(b)	—	—	Rare	—
	B/II, 0/7	1869(b)	12.50	20.00	32.50	60.00
	A/II, 1/7 (top dot in top flower)					
		1869-70(b)	—	—	Rare	—
	A/II, 1/7 (top dot in normal position)					
		1872(b)	12.50	20.00	40.00	80.00
	A/II, 0/8	1870(b)	12.50	20.00	40.00	80.00
	A/II, 0/9	1871(b)	12.50	20.00	40.00	80.00
	A/II, 0/10					
		1872(b)	7.50	12.50	16.50	35.00
	A/II, 1/10 (top dot in top flower)					
		1872-73(b)	12.50	20.00	40.00	80.00
	A/II, 1/10 (top dot in normal position)					
		1873(b)	12.50	20.00	40.00	80.00
	A/I, 1/11					
		1873(b)	7.50	12.50	16.50	35.00
	A/II, 0/1	1873(b)	12.50	20.00	40.00	80.00
473.1	A/II, 1/1	1873(b)	12.50	20.00	40.00	80.00
	A/II, 0/12					
		1874(b)	12.50	20.00	40.00	80.00
	A/II, 1/2	1874(b)	10.00	17.50	27.50	50.00
	A/I, 1/2	1874(b)	12.50	20.00	40.00	80.00
	C/I, 1/2	1874(b)	12.50	20.00	40.00	80.00
	C/II, 1/2	1874(b)	10.00	17.50	27.50	50.00
		1862(c)	—	—	Proof	200.00
		1862(c) (restrike)	—	—	P/L	60.00

GOLD

KM#	Date	Mintage	Fine	VF	XF	Unc
473.1a	1862(c) (restrike)		—	—	P/L	—

From 1874 onward the coins show the year date. The designs are similar to those on the 1862 Rupees but only Busts "A" and "C" and Reverse I and II were used.

CALCUTTA - Mint issues dated 1874-78 have no mint mark. From 1879 the mint mark is a small incuse "C" on the whorl below the center of the bottom lotus flower on the reverse. All Calcutta issues have Reverse I.

BOMBAY - Mint issues dated 1874-83 usually have as mint mark a small dot directly above the bottom lotus flower. From 1883 the mint mark is a small "B" raised or incuse on the stem of the top flower. Some issues dated 1874-84 have no mint mark but except for an 1883 issue have Reverse II. Issues dated 1874-76 have Reverse II only, those dated 1877-85 have both Reverses I and II, and from 1886 only Reverse I.

NOTE: There are reverse varieties in most of the following Rupees. Reverse II flowers are found in various sizes. Two bottom rosettes are found rotated, i.e., 1 petal up or down.

11.6600 g, .917 SILVER, .3438 oz ASW

KM#	Date	Mintage	Fine	VF	XF	Unc
473.2	1874(c) A/I					
		15.014	5.00	8.00	12.00	25.00
	1874(b) A/II, w/o mm					
		28.509	5.00	8.00	12.00	25.00
	1874(b) A/II, dot					
		Inc. Ab.	7.00	10.00	15.00	30.00
	1874(b)	—	—	—	Proof	175.00
	1874(b) (restrike)	—	—	—	P/L	35.00
	1875(c) A/I					
		11.632	5.00	8.00	12.00	25.00
	1875(c)	—	—	—	Proof	175.00
	1875(b) A/II, w/o mm					
		19.360	5.00	8.00	12.00	25.00
	1875(b) A/II, dot below					
		Inc. Ab.	5.00	8.00	12.00	25.00
	1875(b)	—	—	—	Proof	175.00
	1875(b) (restrike)	—	—	—	P/L	35.00
	1875(b) C/II, dot below					
		Inc. Ab.	—	—	—	—
	1876(c) A/I					
		12.001	5.00	8.00	12.00	25.00
	1876(c)A/I	—	—	—	Proof	—
	1876(b) A/II, dot					
		28.950	5.00	8.00	12.00	25.00
	1876(b)	—	—	—	Proof	175.00
	1876(b) (restrike)	—	—	—	P/L	35.00
	1876(c) (restrike)	—	—	—	Proof	75.00

KM#	Date	Mintage	Fine	VF	XF	Unc
492	1877(c) A/I					
		39.252	5.00	8.00	12.00	25.00
	1877(c)	—	—	—	Proof	175.00
	1877(b) A/I, dot					
		95.554	5.00	8.00	12.00	25.00
	1877(b) A/II, dot					
		Inc. Ab.	5.00	8.00	12.00	25.00
	1877(b)	—	—	—	Proof	175.00
	1877(b) (restrike)	—	—	—	P/L	75.00
	1878(c) A/I					
		32.658	5.00	8.00	12.00	25.00
	1878(c)	—	—	—	Proof	175.00
	1878(b) A/I, dot					
		63.927	5.00	8.00	12.00	25.00
	1878(b) A/II, dot					
		Inc. Ab.	5.00	8.00	12.00	25.00
	1878(b)	—	—	—	Proof	175.00
	1878(b) (restrike)	—	—	—	P/L	35.00
	1879C A/I, "C" incuse					
		15.928	5.00	8.00	12.00	25.00
492	1879(b) A/I, dot					
		72.800	9.00	17.50	27.50	50.00
	1879(b) A/II, dot					
		Inc. Ab.	5.00	8.00	12.00	25.00
	1879(b) A/II, dot (rosette var.)					
		Inc. Ab.	5.00	8.00	12.00	25.00
	1879(b)	—	—	—	Proof	175.00
	1879(b) (restrike)	—	—	—	P/L	35.00
	1880C A/I, "C" incuse					
		18.400	7.00	10.00	15.00	30.00
	1880(b) A/I, dot					
		53.786	5.00	8.00	12.00	25.00
	1880(b) A/II, dot					
		Inc. Ab.	5.00	8.00	12.00	25.00
	1880(b) (restrike)	—	—	—	P/L	35.00
	1881C A/I, "C" incuse					
		2.436	7.00	10.00	15.00	35.00
	1881C	—	—	—	Proof	175.00
	1881(b) A/I, dot					
		3.162	9.00	17.50	27.50	50.00
	1881(b) A/II, dot					
		Inc. Ab.	9.00	17.50	27.50	50.00
	1881(b) (restrike)	—	—	—	P/L	35.00
	1882C A/I, "C" incuse					
		15.090	5.00	8.00	12.00	25.00
	1882C	—	—	—	Proof	175.00
	1882(b) A/I, dot					
		56.397	5.00	8.00	12.00	25.00
	1882(b) (restrike)	—	—	—	P/L	35.00
	1882(b) A/II, dot					
		Inc. Ab.	5.00	8.00	12.00	25.00
	1883C A/I, "C" incuse					
		5.123	7.00	10.00	15.00	30.00
	1883(b) A/I, no mm					
		18.023	10.00	20.00	37.50	70.00
	1883(b) A/I, dot					
		Inc. Ab.	9.00	17.50	27.50	50.00
	1883B A/I, "B" raised					
		Inc. Ab.	9.00	17.50	27.50	50.00
	1883B A/I, dot, "B" raised					
		Inc. Ab.	10.00	20.00	37.50	70.00
	1883B (restrike)	—	—	—	P/L	35.00
	1884C A/I, "C" incuse					
		11.642	5.00	8.00	12.00	25.00
	1884B A/I, "B" raised					
		36.847	7.00	10.00	17.50	35.00
	1884B A/II, "B" raised on whorl below bottom flower					
		Inc. Ab.	9.00	17.50	27.50	50.00
	1884B (restrike)	—	—	—	P/L	35.00
	1885C A/I, "C" incuse					
		34.152	5.00	8.00	12.00	25.00
	1885C	—	—	—	Proof	175.00
	1885B A/I, "B" raised					
		64.878	5.00	8.00	12.00	25.00
	1885B A/II, "B" raised					
		Inc. Ab.	5.00	8.00	12.00	25.00
	1885B C/I, "B" incuse					
		Inc. Ab	5.00	8.00	12.00	25.00
	1885B A/II, "B" incuse					
		Inc. Ab.	9.00	17.50	27.50	50.00
	1885B (restrike)	—	—	—	P/L	35.00
	1886C A/I, "C" incuse					
		10.878	5.00	8.00	12.00	25.00
	1886C	—	—	—	Proof	175.00
	1886B C/I, "B" incuse					
		41.146	5.00	8.00	12.00	25.00
	1886B (restrike)	—	—	—	P/L	35.00
	1887C C/I, "C" incuse					
		40.200	5.00	8.00	12.00	25.00
	1887B C/I, "B" raised					
		48.400	5.00	8.00	12.00	25.00
	1887B Rev.I, "B" incuse					
		Inc. Ab.	5.00	8.00	12.00	25.00
	1887B A/I, "B" incuse, inverted B					
		Inc. Ab.	5.00	8.00	12.00	25.00
	1887B C/I, "B" incuse, inverted B					
		Inc. Ab.	5.00	8.00	12.00	25.00
	1887B (restrike)	—	—	—	P/L	35.00
	1888C C/I, "C" incuse					
		7.568	5.00	8.00	12.00	25.00
	1888B C/I, "B" raised					
		63.200	5.00	8.00	12.00	25.00
	1888B C/I, "B" incuse					
		Inc. Ab.	5.00	8.00	12.00	25.00
	1888B C/I, "B" incuse, inverted B					
		Inc. Ab.	7.00	10.00	17.50	35.00
	1888B (restrike)	—	—	—	P/L	35.00
	1889C C/I, "C" incuse					
		9.368	5.00	8.00	12.00	25.00
	1889B C/I, "B" raised					
		65.300	5.00	8.00	12.00	30.00
	1889B C/I, "B" incuse					
		Inc. Ab.	5.00	8.00	12.00	25.00
	1889B (restrike)	—	—	—	P/L	35.00
	1890C C/I, "C" incuse					
		24.742	5.00	8.00	12.00	25.00
	1890C	—	—	—	Proof	175.00
	1890B C/I, "B" incuse					
		92.900	5.00	8.00	12.00	25.00
	1890B (restrike)	—	—	—	P/L	35.00
	1891C C/I, "C" incuse					
		14.670	5.00	8.00	12.00	25.00
	1891C	—	—	—	Proof	175.00
	1891B C/I, "B" incuse					
		49.500	5.00	8.00	12.00	25.00
	1891B	—	—	—	Proof	175.00
	1892C C/I, "C" incuse					
		32.455	5.00	8.00	12.00	25.00
	1892C	—	—	—	Proof	175.00

KM#	Date	Mintage	Fine	VF	XF	Unc
492	1892B C/I, "B" raised					
		72.200	5.00	8.00	12.00	25.00
	1892B C/I, "B" incuse					
		Inc. Ab.	5.00	8.00	12.00	25.00
	1892B	—	—	—	Proof	175.00
	1892B (restrike)	—	—	—	P/L	35.00
	1893C C/I, "C" incuse					
		9.140	5.00	8.00	12.00	25.00
	1893C	—	—	—	Proof	175.00
	1893B C/I, "B" incuse					
		69.590	5.00	8.00	12.00	25.00
	1893B	—	—	—	Proof	175.00
	1893B (restrike)	—	—	—	P/L	35.00
	1894C C/I	—	—	—	Proof	200.00
	1897C C/I, "C" incuse					
		.470	20.00	35.00	70.00	175.00
	1897C	—	—	—	Proof	225.00
	1897B C/I, "B" incuse					
		1.055	9.00	17.50	27.50	50.00
	1897B	—	—	—	Proof	175.00
	1897B (restrike)	—	—	—	P/L	35.00
	1898C C/I, "C" incuse					
		1.251	8.00	12.50	22.50	40.00
	1898C	—	—	—	Proof	175.00
	1898B C/I, "B" incuse					
		6.268	5.00	8.00	12.00	25.00
	1898B A/I	—	—	—	Proof	175.00
	1898B (restrike)	—	—	—	P/L	35.00
	1900C C/I, "C" incuse					
		5.291	5.00	8.00	12.00	25.00
	1900C	—	—	—	Proof	175.00
	1900B A/I, "B" incuse					
		65.237	5.00	8.00	12.00	25.00
	1900B	—	—	—	Proof	175.00
	1900B (restrike)	—	—	—	P/L	35.00

NOTE: Later date (1901) exists for this type.

ALUMINUM

KM#	Date	Mintage	Fine	VF	XF	Unc
492a	1891B	—	—	—	Proof	—

COPPER OR BRONZE

KM#	Date	Mintage	Fine	VF	XF	Unc
492b	1884	—	—	—	Proof	100.00
	1885	—	—	—	Proof	100.00
	1887	—	—	—	Proof	100.00
	1891	—	—	—	Proof	100.00
	1892	—	—	—	Proof	100.00

GOLD

KM#	Date	Mintage	Fine	VF	XF	Unc
492c	1891 (restrike)	—	—		P/L	500.00
	1892 (restrike)	—	—		P/L	500.00
	1893 (restrike)	—	—		P/L	500.00
	1898 (restrike)	—	—		P/L	500.00
	1900B (restrike)	—	—		P/L	500.00

5 RUPEES

3.8870 g, .917 GOLD, .1146 oz AGW
Obv: Young bust.
Reeded edge

KM#	Date	Year	Fine	VF	XF	Unc
474	1870CM	—	125.00	175.00	300.00	400.00
	1875	—	—	—	Proof	850.00

Plain edge

KM#	Date	Year	Fine	VF	XF	Unc
475	1870	—	—	—	Proof	850.00

SILVER

KM#	Date	Year	Fine	VF	XF	Unc
475a	1870	—	—	—	Proof	—

3.8870 g, .917 GOLD, .1146 oz AGW
Obv: Mature bust.
Reeded edge

KM#	Date	Mintage	Fine	VF	XF	Unc
476	1870(c)	.013	125.00	175.00	300.00	400.00
	1870(c)	—	—	—	Proof	450.00
	1870(c) (restrike)	—	—	—	P/L	400.00

Mule. Obv: 1/4 Rupee, Bust A, KM#490.
Rev: KM#476.
Obv: Young bust.

KM#	Date	Mintage	Fine	VF	XF	Unc
493.1	1879(b) (restrike)		—	—	P/L	400.00

Mule. Obv: 1/4 Rupee, Bust B. Rev: KM#476.

KM#	Date	Mintage	Fine	VF	XF	Unc
493.2	1879(b) (restrike)		—	—	P/L	400.00

Mule. Obv: 1/4 Rupee, Bust C. Rev: KM#476.

KM#	Date	Mintage	Fine	VF	XF	Unc
493.3	1879(b) (restrike)		—	—	P/L	400.00

Obv: Mature bust.

KM#	Date	Mintage	Fine	VF	XF	Unc
494	1879(b) (restrike)		—	—	P/L	275.00

10 RUPEES

7.7740 g, .917 GOLD, .2292 oz AGW
Obv: Young bust.
Reeded edge

KM#	Date	Mintage	Fine	VF	XF	Unc
477	1870CM	—	—	—	Proof	500.00
	1870CM (restrike)		—	—	P/L	500.00
	1875	—	—	—	Proof	1250.

Plain edge

KM#	Date	Mintage	Fine	VF	XF	Unc
478	1870	—	—	—	Proof	1250.

SILVER

KM#	Date	Mintage	Fine	VF	XF	Unc
478a	1870	—	—	—	Proof	—

7.7740 g, .917 GOLD, .2292 oz AGW
Obv: Mature bust.
Reeded edge

KM#	Date	Mintage	Fine	VF	XF	Unc
479	1870(c)	7,932	150.00	275.00	400.00	500.00
	1870(c)	—	—	—	Proof	500.00
	1870(c) (restrike)		—	—	P/L	500.00
495	1878(b)	—	—	—	Proof	1250.
	1878(b) (restrike)		—	—	P/L	500.00
	1879(b)	—	—	—	Proof	1250.
	1879(b) (restrike)		—	—	P/L	500.00

MOHUR

11.6600 g, .917 GOLD, .3437 oz AGW
Obv: Young bust.

KM#	Date	Mintage	Fine	VF	XF	Unc
480	1862(c)	.153	200.00	275.00	350.00	450.00
	1862(c)	Inc. Ab.	—	—	Proof	850.00
	1862(c) (restrike)		—	—	P/L	350.00
	1862(c) w/V on bust					
		Inc. Ab.	200.00	275.00	350.00	450.00
	1862(c) w/V on rev. in design below date					
		Inc. Ab.	200.00	275.00	350.00	450.00
	1862(c) w/V on bust and on rev.					
		—	200.00	275.00	350.00	450.00
	1862(c) w/V on bust and 2 flowers in bottom panel	I.A.	200.00	275.00	350.00	450.00
	1870(c)		—	—	Proof	750.00
	1870(c) (restrike)		—	—	P/L	400.00
	1875(c) w/V on bust					
		.011	225.00	300.00	500.00	750.00
	1875(c)		—	—	Proof	2500.
	1875(c) (restrike)		—	—	P/L	400.00

COPPER OR BRONZE

KM#	Date	Mintage	Fine	VF	XF	Unc
480a	1862(c)	—	—	—	350.00	—

Mule. Obv: KM#481. Rev: KM#480.

KM#	Date	Mintage	Fine	VF	XF	Unc
A481	1862(c)	—	—	—	P/L	400.00

11.6600 g, .917 GOLD, .3437 oz AGW
Obv: Mature bust.

KM#	Date	Mintage	Fine	VF	XF	Unc
481	1870(c)	—	—	—	Proof	2500.
	1870(c) (restrike)		—	—	P/L	400.00

Mule. Obv: KM#496. Rev: KM#481.

KM#	Date	Mintage	Fine	VF	XF	Unc
482	1870(c)	—	—	—	P/L	650.00

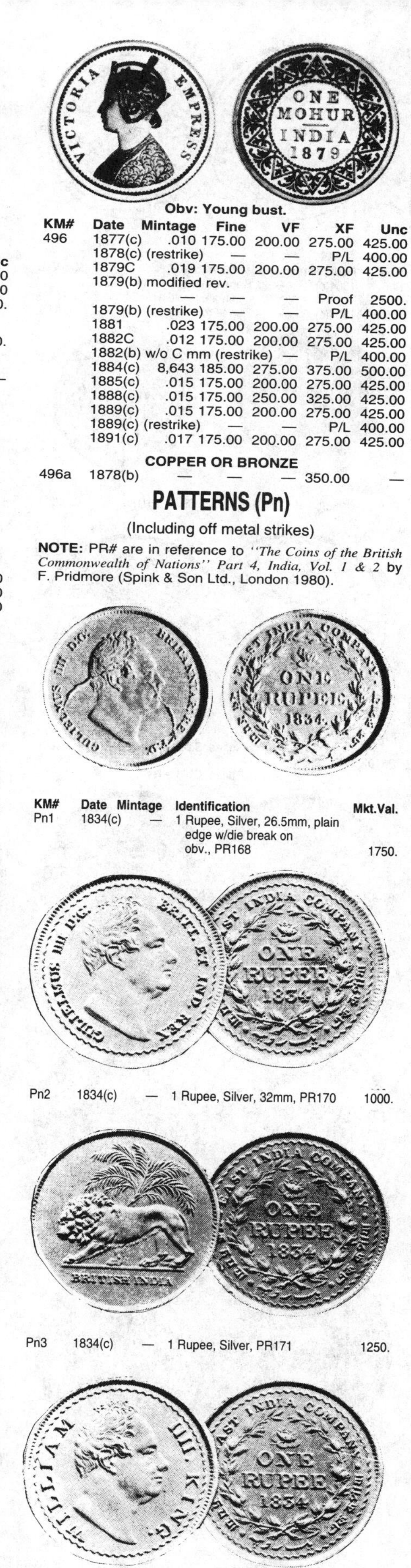

Obv: Young bust.

KM#	Date	Mintage	Fine	VF	XF	Unc
496	1877(c)	.010	175.00	200.00	275.00	425.00
	1878(c) (restrike)		—	—	P/L	400.00
	1879C	.019	175.00	200.00	275.00	425.00
	1879(b) modified rev.					
		—	—	—	Proof	2500.
	1879(b) (restrike)		—	—	P/L	400.00
	1881	.023	175.00	200.00	275.00	425.00
	1882C	.012	175.00	200.00	275.00	425.00
	1882(b) w/o C mm (restrike)			—	P/L	400.00
	1884(c)	8,643	185.00	275.00	375.00	500.00
	1885(c)	.015	175.00	200.00	275.00	425.00
	1888(c)	.015	175.00	250.00	325.00	425.00
	1889(c)	.015	175.00	200.00	275.00	425.00
	1889(c) (restrike)		—	—	P/L	400.00
	1891(c)	.017	175.00	200.00	275.00	425.00

COPPER OR BRONZE

KM#	Date	Mintage	Fine	VF	XF	Unc
496a	1878(b)		—	—	350.00	—

PATTERNS (Pn)

(Including off metal strikes)

NOTE: PR# are in reference to *"The Coins of the British Commonwealth of Nations" Part 4, India, Vol. 1 & 2* by F. Pridmore (Spink & Son Ltd., London 1980).

KM#	Date	Mintage	Identification	Mkt.Val.
Pn1	1834(c)	—	1 Rupee, Silver, 26.5mm, plain edge w/die break on obv., PR168	1750.
Pn2	1834(c)	—	1 Rupee, Silver, 32mm, PR170	1000.
Pn3	1834(c)	—	1 Rupee, Silver, PR171	1250.
Pn4	1834(c)	—	1 Rupee, Silver, milled edge, PR172	500.00
Pn5	1834(c)	—	1 Rupee, Silver, plain edge, PR173	500.00

KM#	Date	Mintage	Identification	Mkt.Val.
Pn6	1834(c)	—	1 Rupee, Silver, 31.7mm, comma after IIII, PR174	1500.
Pn7	1834(c)	—	1 Rupee (restrike)	450.00
Pn8	1835(b)	—	1/2 Rupee, Silver, PR180	1000.
Pn9	ND(1835)(c)	—	1 Rupee, Silver, PR176	1000.
Pn10	ND(1835)(c)	—	1 Rupee, Gold, PR177	—

KM#	Date	Mintage	Identification	Mkt.Val.
Pn11	1835(c)	—	1 Rupee, Silver, PR178	1000.
Pn12	1835(b)	—	1 Rupee, Silver, PR179	1250.
Pn13	1839(b)	—	1 Rupee, Silver, PR181	—

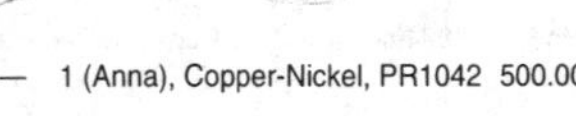

KM#	Date	Mintage	Identification	Mkt.Val.
Pn14	ND(b)	—	1 (Anna), Copper-Nickel, PR1042	500.00

KM#	Date	Mintage	Identification	Mkt.Val.
Pn15	ND(b)	—	2 (Annas), Copper-Nickel, PR1041	500.00
Pn16	1854	—	5 Rupees, Silver, plain edge, PR31	1250.
Pn17	1854	—	5 Rupees, Gold, plain edge, PR30	3000.
Pn18	1854	—	10 Rupees, Silver, plain edge, PR28	2000.
Pn19	1854	—	10 Rupees, Gold, plain edge, PR27	4000.
Pn20	1854	—	1 Mohur, Silver, plain edge, PR26	2000.
Pn21	1854	—	1 Mohur, Gold, plain edge, PR25	4500.
Pn22	1854	—	2 Mohurs, Silver, plain edge, PR7	4500.
Pn23	1854	—	2 Mohurs, Gold, plain edge, PR6	7500.
Pn24	1854	—	2 Mohurs, Gold, plain edge, (restrike)	—
Pn25	186—	—	1 Rupee, Copper, PR46	—
Pn26	1860	—	1 Rupee, Silver, PR47	700.00
Pn27	1860	—	1 Rupee, Silver piefort, PR48	800.00
Pn28	1861(c)	—	1/12 Anna, Copper, PR775	—

KM#	Date	Mintage	Identification	Mkt.Val.
Pn29	1861	—	1/2 Pice, Copper piedfort, PR707	—
Pn30	1861	—	1/4 Anna, Copper, PR596	—

KM#	Date	Mintage	Identification	Mkt.Val.
Pn31	1861	—	1/4 Anna, Copper, last digit Roman numeral I, PR597	—
Pn32	1861	—	1/2 Pice, Copper, PR708	50.00
Pn33	1861	—	1/2 Anna, Copper, PR575	—
Pn34	1861	—	2 Annas, Silver, PR480	125.00
Pn35	1861(c)	—	2 Annas, Silver, PR481	100.00
Pn36	1861(c)	—	2 Annas, Silver, (restrike)	35.00
Pn37	1861	—	1/4 Rupee, Silver, PR371	125.00
Pn38	1861	—	1/4 Rupee, Silver, piedfort, PR370	—
Pn39	1861(c)	—	1/2 Rupee, Silver, pearled center jewel on crown, PR251	175.00
Pn40	1861	—	1/2 Rupee, Silver, far "6-1", PR250	—
Pn41	1861	—	1/2 Rupee, Silver piefort, close "6-1", PR249	200.00
Pn42	1861	—	1 Rupee, Silver, Royal Mint, PR49	200.00
Pn43	1861	—	1 Rupee, Copper, PR53	250.00
Pn44	1861(c)	—	1 Rupee, Silver, w/L.C.Wyon, PR51	200.00
Pn45	1861(c)	—	1 Rupee, Silver, PR52	200.00
Pn46	1862(c)	—	1/12 Anna, Copper, PR776	60.00
Pn47	1862(c)	—	1/12 Anna, Copper, (restrike)	—
Pn48	1862(c)	—	1/12 Anna, Silver, PR777	125.00
Pn49	1862	—	1/2 Pice, Copper, PR709	50.00
Pn50	1862	—	1/2 Pice, Silver, PR709A	125.00
Pn51	1862(c)	—	1/2 Pice, Copper, PR710	50.00
Pn52	1862(c)	—	1/4 Anna, Copper, PR598	—
Pn53	1862(c)	—	1/4 Anna, Copper, (restrike)	—
Pn54	1862(c)	—	1/4 Anna, Silver, PR599	150.00
Pn55	1862	—	1/2 Anna, Copper, PR575A	100.00
Pn56	1862(c)	—	1/2 Anna, Copper, w/V in bottom of bust, PR579.	100.00
Pn57	1862(c)	—	1/2 Anna, Silver, PR580	200.00
Pn58	1862(c)	—	2 Annas, Silver, PR482	100.00
Pn59	1862(c)	—	1/4 Rupee, Silver, w/inverted V on bust, PR372	125.00
Pn60	1863	—	1 Rupee, Silver, PR106	1000.
Pn61	1864	—	1 Rupee, Silver, PR107	1000.
Pn62	1867	—	1 Rupee, Silver, plain edge, PR108	1000.
Pn63	1867	—	1 Rupee, Silver, plain edge, w/o L.C.W., PR109	1000.
Pn64	1867(c)	—	1 Rupee, Silver, milled edge, PR110	1000.
Pn65	1870	—	1 Rupee, Silver, PR9	—
PnA66	1891(b)	—	2 Annas, Aluminum, KM488a	—
PnB66	1891B	—	1/4 Rupee, Aluminum, KM490a	100.00

TOKEN ISSUES (Tn)

The British Indian Government introduced a special series of tokens for use by Famine Relief officials as part of a policy to deal with great famine disasters in Bengal in 1874 and in Southern India in 1876.

1/2 SEER

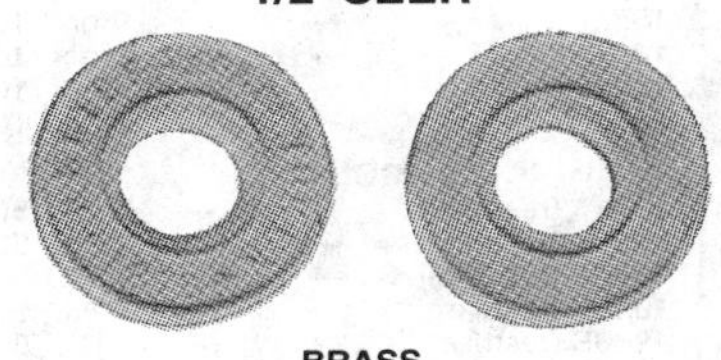

BRASS
Famine Relief

KM#	Date	Mintage	Fine	VF	XF	Unc
Tn3	1876	—	125.00	200.00	275.00	—

NOTE: 1/2 Seer = 1.028 lbs.

1/2 RUPEE

COPPER
Famine Relief

KM#	Date	Mintage	Fine	VF	XF	Unc
Tn1	ND	—	35.00	60.00	90.00	150.00

RUPEE

BRASS
Famine Relief

KM#	Date	Mintage	Fine	VF	XF	Unc
Tn2	1874(c)	—	50.00	75.00	120.00	175.00
	1874(c)	—	—	—	Proof	400.00

GOLD

KM#	Date	Mintage	Fine	VF	XF	Unc
Tn2a	1874(c)	1 known	—	—	Rare	—

TRIAL STRIKES (TS)

KM#	Date	Mintage	Identification	Mkt.Val.
TS1	ND(1840)	—	1/4 Rupee, obv. KM453, Pewter, PR184	225.00
TS2	ND(1840)	—	1/2 Rupee, obv. KM455, Pewter,	

KM#	Date	Mintage	Identification	Mkt.Val.
TS2			PR183	275.00
TS3	ND(1840)	—	1 Rupee, obv. KM457	300.00
TS4	1858	—	1/4 Anna, Copper, w/"J.W./& Co." PR158	—

KM#	Date	Mintage	Identification	Mkt.Val.
TS5	ND(1854)	—	10 Rupees, Copper, rev., PR29	Rare
TS6	ND(1854)	—	2 Mohurs, Copper, rev., PR8	Rare
TS7	(1867)	—	1 Rupee, Tin, obv., PR111A	—
TS8	1867	—	1 Rupee, Tin, rev., PR111B	—

MINT SETS (MS)

KM#	Date	Mintage	Identification	Mkt.Val.
MS1	1835c(3)	—	KM448a-450a	—

PROOF SETS (PS)

KM#	Date	Mintage	Identification	Mkt.Val.
PS1	1835c(3)	—	KM445-447	500.00
PS2	1875(3)	—	KM474,477,480	4500.

ANDAMAN ISLANDS

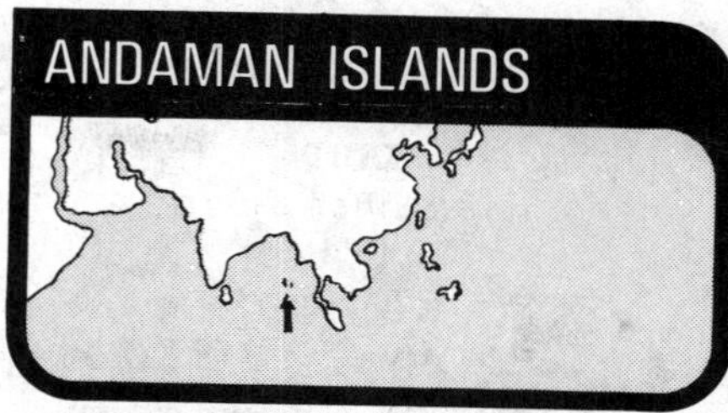

The Andaman Islands are the northern group of 204 volcanic and coral isles in the east part of the Bay of Bengal about 400 miles directly west of the coast of lower Burma has an area of 2,508 sq. mi. and a population of 65,000. Capital: Port Blair. Chief exports are timber and coconut.

In 1789 the first British settlement was established at Port Blair. It was relocated at Port Cornwallis on North Andaman in 1791 and abandoned in 1796. A penal colony on South Andaman was re-established at the place now known as Port Blair. In 1872 the islands were merged with the nearby Nicobar Islands to form a single administrative unit. No prisoners were sent here after 1921 and the penal colony was closed just after World War II. These islands were occupied by the Japanese in World War II and were for a time handed over to the "Provisional Government of Azad Hind" (Free India) to administer until August 1947. Although the islands are geographically remote from India, and their people ethnically distinct, their previous association with British India resulted in their incorporation into the Indian Republic at Independence in 1947.

RULERS

British, until 1947

TOKEN ISSUES (Tn)

RUPEE

COPPER

KM#	Date	Mintage	VG	Fine	VF	XF
Tn1	1861	*.020	1250.	1750.	2250.	3500.
W/o center hole.						
Tn1a	1861	—	—	—	Unc.	3750.
Mule w/o center hole. Obv: KM#Tn2. Rev: KM#Tn1.						
Tn1b	1861	—	—	—	Proof	Rare
Mule w/center hole. Obv: KM#Tn2. Rev: KM#Tn1.						
Tn1c	1861	—	1500.	2000.	2500.	3750.

KM#	Date	Mintage	VG	Fine	VF	XF
Tn2	1866	*.021	1750.	2250.	2750.	4250.

***NOTE:** Recalled from circulation in 1870 with 17,788 pcs. outstanding for both types.

INDONESIA

The Republic of Indonesia, the world's largest archipelago, extends for more than 3,000 miles (4,827 km.) along the equator from the mainland of southeast Asia to Australia. The 17,508 islands comprising the archipelago have a combined area of 788,425 sq. mi. (1,919,440 sq. km.) and a population of 200 million, including East Timor. Capital: Jakarta. Petroleum, timber, rubber, and coffee are exported.

Had Columbus succeeded in reaching the fabled Spice Islands, he would have found advanced civilizations a millennium old, and temples still ranked among the finest examples of ancient art. During the opening centuries of the Christian era, the islands were influenced by Hindu priests and traders who spread their culture and religion. Moslem invasions began in the 13th century, fragmenting the island kingdoms into small states which were unable to resist Western colonial infiltration. Portuguese traders established posts in the 16th century, but they were soon outnumbered by the Dutch who arrived in 1596 and gradually asserted control over the islands comprising present-day Indonesia. Dutch dominance, interrupted by British incursions during the Napoleonic Wars, established the Netherlands East Indies as one of the richest colonial possessions in the world.

The Indonesian independence movement, which began between the two world wars, was encouraged by the Japanese during their 3 1/2-year occupation during World War II. Indonesia proclaimed its independence on Aug. 17, 1945, three days after the surrender of Japan and full sovereignty. On Dec. 27, 1949, after four years of guerilla warfare including two large scale campaigns by the Dutch in an effort to reassert control, complete independence was established. Rebellions in Bandung and on the Molluccan Islands occurred in 1950. Through the efforts of President Mohammad Achmad Sukarno (1950-67) the new Republic not only held together but developed within intellectually. West Irian, formerly Netherlands New Guinea, came under the administration of Indonesia on May 1, 1963. In 1965, the army staged an anti-communist coup in which thousands perished.

On November 28, 1975 the Portuguese Province of Timor, an overseas province occupying the eastern half of the East Indian island of Timor, attained independence as the People's Democratic Republic of East Timor. On December 5, 1975 the government of the People's Democratic Republic was seized by a guerrilla faction sympathetic to the Indonesian territorial claim to East Timor which ousted the constitutional government and replaced it with the Provisional Government of East Timor. On July 17, 1976, the Provisional Government enacted a law that dissolved the free republic and made East Timor the 27th province of Indonesia.

Coinage for the Indonesian Archipelago is varied and extensive. The Dutch struck coins for the islands at various mints in the Netherlands and the islands under the auspices of the VOC (United East India Company), the Batavian Republic and the Kingdom of the Netherlands. The British issued a coinage during the various occupations by the British East Indian Company, 1811-24. Modern coinage issued by the Republic of Indonesia includes separate series for West Irian and for the Riau Archipelago, an area of small islands between Singapore and Sumatra.

NETHERLANDS EAST INDIES

RULERS

Batavian Republic, 1799-1806
Louis Napoleon, King of Holland, 1806-1811
Dutch, 1816-1942

MINT MARKS

H - Amsterdam (H)
Hk - Harderwijk (star, rosette, cock, cross, (Z)
Hn - Hoorn (star)
E - Enkhuizen (star)
Dt - Dordrecht (rosette)
K - Kampen (eagle)
S - Utrecht
Sa - Soerabaja (Za)

MONETARY SYSTEM

120 Duits = 120 Cents
1 Gulden = 1 Java Rupee
16 Silver Rupees = 1 Gold Mohur

BONKS: Because of the slow delivery of coins from the Netherlands, the government in the East Indies often resorted to the manufacture of "Bonks". These were simply lumps cut from the copper (or tin) rods used for coining. This eliminated the problems inherent in casting round coins and allowed the production of large quantities of legal tender very quickly. The thicker rods were used for the 2 and 8 Stuiver Bonks and the thinner rod for the smaller denominations.

DUITS: On many of the Duit and 1/2 Duit coins of the East Indies dated 1802-1826, the value appears as 5-1/32-G (1/2 Duit) and 5-1/16-G (Duit). This is interpreted as; 5 of the pieces equal 1/16 Guilder or 5 equal 1/32 Guilder. However, in 1802 the rate of exchange was set so that 6 Duiten should equal 1/16 Guilder which would mean the Duit actually equaled 1/96 Guilder and the 1/2 Duit equaled 1/192 Guilder, but because of the perennial shortage of small coins, the error was ignored and the coins released to circulation.

CENTS: Although some coins in 1833-1841 appear with value as 1 CT (1 Cent) and 2 CT (2 Cent) they are considered Duiten and Double Duiten and were exchanged at the rate of 1 Duit = 1/96 Guilder, not on a decimal system.

COLONIAL COINAGE

GELDERLAND

MINTMASTER PRIVY MARKS

Privy Mark	Date	Name
Ear of corn	1782-1809	Martin Hendrik Lohse

MONETARY SYSTEM

4 Duits = 1 Stuiver
20 Stuivers = 1 Gulden

DUIT

COPPER
Obv: Crowned arms of Gelderland, leg: IN DEO-SP.NOS.

KM#	Date	Mintage	VG	Fine	VF	XF
50.2	1802	—	2.75	4.50	7.50	12.50
	1803	—	2.75	4.50	7.50	12.50
	1804	—	3.50	6.00	11.50	20.00
	1805	—	3.00	5.00	8.50	14.50
	1085 (error)	—	—	—	—	—
	1806	—	2.75	4.50	7.50	12.50

NOTE: Varieties exist.
NOTE: Earlier dates (1771-1794) exist for this type.

HOLLAND

MINT MARKS

H - Heus, Amsterdam
Rosette - Dordrecht, 1601-1806
Star - Enkhuizen, 1796-1803
Star - Hoorn, 1803-1809

DUIT

COPPER
Obv: Crowned arms of Holland.
Rev: VOC monogram above date.

KM#	Date	Mintage	VG	Fine	VF	XF
70	1802 star	—	7.50	15.00	25.00	40.00
	1802 rosette	—	7.50	15.00	25.00	40.00
	1803	—	7.50	15.00	25.00	40.00
	1804	—	10.00	18.00	28.00	45.00

NOTE: 3 varieties exist.
NOTE: Earlier dates (1726-1793) exist for this type.

Batavian Republic

1799-1806

1/2 DUIT

(1/) 5 (of) 1/32 G = 1/160 G

COPPER

KM#	Date	Mintage	VG	Fine	VF	XF
75	1802	.157	2.75	4.50	7.50	12.50
	1803	—	4.00	9.00	15.00	25.00
	1804	—	4.00	9.00	15.00	25.00
	1805	—	2.75	4.50	7.50	12.50
	1806	—	1.75	3.00	5.00	8.50
	1807	—	1.00	1.75	3.00	5.00
75	1808	—	1.00	1.75	3.00	5.00
	1809	—	1.00	1.75	3.00	5.00

NOTE: Many varieties exist.

DUIT

(1/) 5 (of) 1/16 G = 1/80 G

COPPER
Obv: Holland Arms.

KM#	Date	Mintage	VG	Fine	VF	XF
76	1802	.358	2.25	3.50	5.50	10.00
	1803	—	2.25	3.50	5.50	10.00
	1804	—	2.25	3.50	5.50	10.00
	1805	—	2.25	3.50	5.50	10.00
	1806	—	2.25	3.50	5.50	10.00
	1807	—	.75	1.25	2.00	3.50
	1808/6	—	12.00	20.00	32.00	55.00
	1808	—	.75	1.25	2.00	3.50
	1809/6	—	15.00	22.50	37.50	65.00
	1809/8	—	10.00	15.00	25.00	45.00
	1809	—	2.25	3.50	5.50	10.00

NOTE: Varieties exist.

BRASS

KM#	Date	Mintage	VG	Fine	VF	XF
76a	1808	—	—	—	—	—

SILVER

KM#	Date	Mintage	VG	Fine	VF	XF
76b	1802	—	15.00	25.00	40.00	75.00

NOTE: Special presentation strikes produced by the mintmaster on demand.

1/16 GULDEN

0.6600 g, .916 SILVER, .0194 oz ASW, 15mm

KM#	Date	Mintage	Fine	VF	XF	Unc
77	1802	—	17.50	30.00	50.00	70.00

NOTE: 4 varieties exist.

16mm
Rev: W/o inner circle.

KM#	Date	Mintage	Fine	VF	XF	Unc
78	1802	—	17.50	30.00	50.00	70.00

NOTE: 3 varieties exist.

1/8 GULDEN

1.3250 g, .916 SILVER, .0390 oz ASW, 19mm

KM#	Date	Mintage	Fine	VF	XF	Unc
79	1802	—	17.50	30.00	50.00	70.00

NOTE: 4 varieties exist.

18mm
Rev: W/o inner circle.

KM#	Date	Mintage	Fine	VF	XF	Unc
80	1802	—	17.50	30.00	50.00	70.00

NOTE: 3 varieties exist.

1/4 GULDEN

2.6500 g, .916 SILVER, .0781 oz ASW

KM#	Date	Mintage	Fine	VF	XF	Unc
81	1802	—	22.50	35.00	60.00	100.00

NOTE: 6 varieties exist.

GOLD

KM#	Date	Mintage	Fine	VF	XF	Unc
81a	1802	—	—	—	Proof	Rare

1/2 GULDEN

5.3800 g, .916 SILVER, .1561 oz ASW
Rev: Ship w/INDIAE BATAV, date around.

KM#	Date	Mintage	Fine	VF	XF	Unc
82	1802	—	30.00	50.00	85.00	125.00

NOTE: 2 varieties exist.

GOLD

KM#	Date	Mintage	Fine	VF	XF	Unc
82a	1802	—	—	—	Proof	2000.

GULDEN

10.6160 g, .916 SILVER, .3127 oz ASW

KM#	Date	Mintage	Fine	VF	XF	Unc
83	1802	—	45.00	70.00	120.00	200.00

NOTE: 5 varieties exist.

GOLD

KM#	Date	Mintage	Fine	VF	XF	Unc
83a	1802	—	—	—	Proof	Rare

OVERYSSEL

MINTMASTER PRIVY MARKS

Privy Mark	Date	Name
Heraldic eagle	1763-1807	Nicolaas Wonneman

Batavian Republic

1799-1806

DUIT

COPPER
Obv: Overyssel arms.

KM#	Date	Mintage	VG	Fine	VF	XF
100	1803	—	2.75	4.00	6.00	10.00
	1804	—	2.75	4.00	6.00	10.00
	1805	—	2.75	4.00	6.00	10.00
	1806	—	4.50	8.00	13.50	23.50
	1807	—	4.50	11.00	18.00	30.00

NOTE: Varieties exist.

SILVER

KM#	Date	Mintage	VG	Fine	VF	XF
100a	1804	—	—	—	Proof	Unique
	1807 plain edge	—	—	—	Proof	—
	1807 milled edge	—	—	—	Proof	—

DUIT

COPPER
Mint mark: Child in swaddling clothes.

KM#	Date	Mintage	VG	Fine	VF	XF
111.2	1790	—	3.50	6.00	10.00	15.00

NOTE: Struck in 1827, 1834 and 1835.

Mint mark: Star between dots.

KM#	Date	Mintage	VG	Fine	VF	XF
111.3	1790	—	2.25	4.00	6.00	10.00

NOTE: Struck in 1827, 1834 and 1835.

SILVER

KM#	Date	Mintage	VG	Fine	VF	XF
111.3a	1790	—	—	—	Proof	150.00

NOTE: Struck in 1827.

COPPER
Mint mark: Star

KM#	Date	Mintage	VG	Fine	VF	XF
111.4	1790	—	2.50	5.00	8.00	13.00

NOTE: Struck in 1840-43. Mintage included in KM#290

1840 dates.

SILVER

KM#	Date	Mintage	VG	Fine	VF	XF
111.4a	1790	—	—	—	—	85.00

NOTE: Special presentation strikes produced by the mintmaster on demand in 1839-43. Mintage in KM#290 1839-40 dates.

COPPER
Mint mark: Star above child.

KM#	Date	Mintage	VG	Fine	VF	XF
111.5	1790	—	6.00	12.50	18.50	25.00

NOTE: Struck in 1840-43. Mintage included in KM#290 1840 dates.

2 DUITS

COPPER
Mint mark: Star.
Obv: Crowned arms supported by lions.
Rev: VOC monogram above date.

KM#	Date	Mintage	VG	Fine	VF	XF
118	1790	—	1.50	2.75	4.50	7.50

NOTE: Struck in 1840-43.

SILVER

KM#	Date	Mintage	VG	Fine	VF	XF
118a	1790	—	—	—	—	100.00

NOTE: Special presentation strikes produced by the mintmaster on demand. Mintage included in KM#291 1840-41 dates.

KINGDOM OF THE NETHERLANDS

MINT MARKS

D - Denver, U.S.A.
P - Philadelphia, U.S.A.
S - San Francisco, U.S.A.
(U) - Caduceus, Utrecht

PRIVY MARKS

Date	Privy Mark
1818-1840	Torch
1839-1846	Fleur de lis
1846-1874	Sword
1874	Sword in scabbard
1875-1887	Broad axe
1887	Broad axe and star
1888-1909	Halberd

MONETARY SYSTEM

100 Cents = 1 Gulden

1/2 CENT

COPPER

KM#	Date	Mintage	Fine	VF	XF	Unc
306	1855(u)	—	—	—	Proof	165.00
	1856(u)	10.800	12.50	20.00	35.00	60.00
	1857(u)	36.800	10.00	15.00	25.00	40.00
	1858(u)	53.588	3.50	6.00	12.50	25.00
	1859(u)	219.600	2.50	4.00	10.00	20.00
	1860(u)	107.124	2.50	4.00	10.00	20.00

NOTE: Later dates (1902-1909) exist for this type.

CENT

COPPER
Obv: Legend begins and ends above date.

KM#	Date	Mintage	Fine	VF	XF	Unc
307.1	1855(u)	.100	30.00	50.00	80.00	140.00
	1855(u)	—	—	—	Proof	80.00
	1856(u)	67.900	3.50	6.00	10.00	17.50
	1856(u)	—	—	—	Proof	65.00

Obv: Legend begins and ends beside date.

KM#	Date	Mintage	Fine	VF	XF	Unc
307.2	1856(u)	Inc. Ab.	3.50	6.00	10.00	17.50
	1856(u)	—	—	—	Proof	50.00
	1857(u)	162.000	2.00	4.00	10.00	15.00
	1858(u)	119.431	2.00	4.00	10.00	15.00
	1859(u)	40.800	3.50	6.00	10.00	17.50
	1860(u)	14.455	4.00	8.00	15.00	30.00
	1896(u)	60.400	3.50	6.00	10.00	17.50
	1896(u)	—	—	—	Proof	65.00
	1897(u)	69.600	5.00	10.00	20.00	35.00
	1897(u)	—	—	—	Proof	100.00
	1898(u)	36.600	3.50	6.00	10.00	17.50
	1899(u)	18.400	6.00	12.50	25.00	60.00
	1899(u)	—	—	—	Proof	65.00

NOTE: Later dates (1901-1912) exist for this type.

2-1/2 CENTS

COPPER

KM#	Date	Mintage	Fine	VF	XF	Unc
308	1856(u)	2.480	30.00	50.00	85.00	140.00
	1856(u)	—	—	—	Proof	130.00
	1857(u)	36.560	10.00	15.00	25.00	40.00
	1857(u)	—	—	—	Proof	130.00
	1858(u)	40.990	8.00	12.50	20.00	35.00
	1896(u)	1.120	25.00	40.00	65.00	100.00
	1897(u)	18.105	6.00	10.00	17.50	30.00
	1898(u)	7.600	8.00	12.50	20.00	35.00
	1899(u)	10.400	6.00	10.00	17.50	30.00

NOTE: Later dates (1902-1913) exist for this type.

1/20 GULDEN

.6100 g, .720 SILVER, .0141 oz ASW

KM#	Date	Mintage	Fine	VF	XF	Unc
303	1854(u)	—	30.00	50.00	100.00	175.00
	1854(u)	—	—	—	Proof	200.00
	1855(u)	.492	3.00	5.00	12.50	20.00
	1855(u)	—	—	—	Proof	300.00

1/10 GULDEN

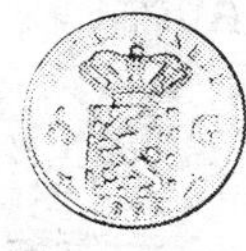

1.2500 g, .720 SILVER, .0289 oz ASW

KM#	Date	Mintage	Fine	VF	XF	Unc
304	1854(u)	3.550	2.00	4.00	7.50	15.00
	1854(u)	—	—	—	Proof	75.00
	1855(u)	6.452	2.00	4.00	7.50	15.00
	1855(u)	—	—	—	Proof	—
	1856(u)	3.000	2.50	5.00	10.00	20.00
	1857(u)	11.000	1.50	3.00	6.00	10.00
	1857(u)	—	—	—	Proof	50.00
	1858(u)	14.000	1.50	3.00	6.00	10.00
	1882(u)	7.500	2.00	4.00	7.50	15.00
	1884(u)	3.550	2.00	4.00	7.50	15.00
	1884(u)	—	—	—	Proof	100.00
	1885(u)	.825	10.00	20.00	40.00	75.00
	1891(u)	5.000	2.00	4.00	7.50	15.00
	1891(u)	—	—	—	Proof	85.00
	1893(u)	5.000	2.00	4.00	7.50	15.00
	1893(u)	—	—	—	Proof	85.00
	1896(u)	3.075	2.00	4.00	7.50	15.00
	1896(u)	—	—	—	Proof	100.00
	1898(u)	2.500	4.00	8.00	15.00	25.00
	1898(u)	—	—	—	Proof	120.00
	1900(u)	6.850	2.00	4.00	7.50	15.00

NOTE: Later date (1901) exists for this type.

1/4 GULDEN

4.0610 g, .568 SILVER, .0742 oz ASW

KM#	Date	Mintage	Fine	VF	XF	Unc
301.1	1826(u)	1.238	17.50	27.50	45.00	75.00
	1826(u)	—	—	—	Proof	120.00
	1827(u)	1.003	17.50	27.50	45.00	75.00
	1834/27(u)	1.002	17.50	27.50	45.00	75.00
	1834(u)	Inc. Ab.	17.50	27.50	45.00	75.00
	1840(u)	.973	17.50	27.50	45.00	75.00

Coarse milling

KM#	Date	Mintage	Fine	VF	XF	Unc
301.2	1826(u)	Inc. Ab.	17.50	27.50	45.00	75.00

3.1800 g, .720 SILVER, .0736 oz ASW

KM#	Date	Mintage	Fine	VF	XF	Unc
305	1854(u)	11.460	10.00	15.00	25.00	40.00
	1854(u)	—	—	—	Proof	100.00
	1855(u)	4.541	6.00	10.00	17.50	30.00
	1855(u)	—	—	—	Proof	100.00
	1857(u)	2.400	10.00	15.00	27.50	45.00
	1858(u)	4.800	6.00	10.00	17.50	30.00
	1858(u)	—	—	—	Proof	80.00
	1882(u)	2.200	10.00	15.00	27.50	45.00
	1883(u)	.800	30.00	50.00	85.00	140.00
	1883(u)	—	—	—	Proof	175.00
	1885(u)	1.750	12.50	20.00	35.00	60.00
	1890(u)	1.140	12.50	20.00	35.00	60.00
	1891(u)	.860	30.00	60.00	120.00	200.00
	1893(u)	2.000	10.00	15.00	27.50	45.00
	1893(u)	—	—	—	Proof	175.00
	1896(u)	1.230	12.50	20.00	35.00	60.00
	1898(u)	3.000	10.00	15.00	27.50	45.00
	1898(u)	—	—	—	Proof	120.00
	1900(u)	2.800	10.00	15.00	27.50	45.00

NOTE: Later date (1901) exists for this type.

1/2 GULDEN

5.3830 g, .893 SILVER
Similar to 1/4 Gulden, KM#301.1.

KM#	Date	Mintage	Fine	VF	XF	Unc
302	1826(u)	.517	20.00	35.00	60.00	100.00
	1827(u)	.037	125.00	225.00	375.00	625.00
	1834/27(u)	.501	50.00	90.00	150.00	250.00
	1834(u)	Inc. Ab.	20.00	35.00	60.00	100.00

GULDEN

10.7700 g, .893 SILVER, .3092 oz ASW

KM#	Date	Mintage	Fine	VF	XF	Unc
300	1821(u)	.099	75.00	120.00	200.00	325.00

10.0000 g, .945 SILVER, .3038 oz ASW

KM#	Date	Mintage	Fine	VF	XF	Unc
300a	1839(u)	2.217	25.00	40.00	60.00	100.00
	1840(u)	1.981	25.00	40.00	60.00	100.00

PATTERNS (Pn)

(Including off metal strikes)

KM#	Date	Mintage	Identification	Mkt.Val.
Pn1	1826(u)	—	1/2 Gulden, Gold, KM302	—
Pn2	1834(u)	—	1/2 Gulden, Gold, KM302	—
Pn3	1854(u)	—	1/10 Gulden, Gold, KM304	—
Pn4	1855(u)	—	1/20 Gulden, Gold, KM303	—
Pn5	1858(u)	—	2-1/2 Cents, Gold, KM308	—
Pn6	1860(u)	—	1/2 Cent, Gold, KM306	—
Pn7	1860(u)	—	1 Cent, Gold, KM307	—
Pn8	1885(u)	—	1/10 Gulden, Gold, KM304	—
Pn9	1885(u)	—	1/4 Gulden, Gold, KM305	—
Pn10	1898(u)	—	1 Cent, Yellow Bronze, KM307	—

PIEFORTS (P)

KM#	Date	Mintage	Identification	Mkt.Val.
P2	1834	—	1/4 Gulden, Silver	Rare
P3	1856	—	1 Cent, KM307	400.00

PROOF SETS (PS)

KM#	Date	Mintage	Identification	Issue Price	Mkt. Val.
PS1	1854/58(12)	—	KM303 (2 pcs. 1854), KM304 (2 pcs. 1855), KM305 (1855 & 1858), KM306 (2 pcs. 1855), KM307 (2 pcs. 1856), KM308 (2 pcs. 1857)	—	—

Batavian Republic

1799-1806

MINTMASTERS INITIALS

Z - J.A. Zwekkert

1/2 STUIVER

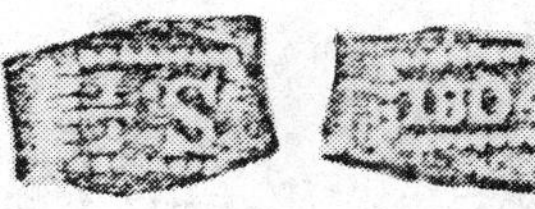

COPPER BONK, 7.72 g
Value and date each in pearled rectangle.

KM#	Date	Mintage	Good	VG	Fine	VF
213	1804	—	20.00	30.00	50.00	150.00
	1805	*.545	—	—	Rare	—

NOTE: 3 varieties exist for 1804 while most of 1805 dated coins were recalled and melted down.

STUIVER

COPPER BONK, 23.16 g

KM#	Date	Mintage	Good	VG	Fine	VF
206	1801	—	8.50	15.00	25.00	45.00
	1802	—	6.00	10.00	20.00	35.00
	1803	—	8.50	15.00	25.00	45.00

NOTE: Roman I in date of 1802 issues.
NOTE: Earlier date (1800) exists for this type.

Reduced weight, 19.30 g
Value and date each in pearl rectangle.

KM#	Date	Mintage	Good	VG	Fine	VF
210	1803	—	5.00	10.00	15.00	25.00
	1804	—	10.00	15.00	25.00	40.00
	1805	—	5.00	10.00	15.00	25.00
	1806	—	10.00	15.00	25.00	40.00

NOTE: Varieties exist.

2 STUIVER

COPPER BONK, 46.32 g

KM#	Date	Mintage	Good	VG	Fine	VF
207	1801	—	15.00	27.50	45.00	75.00
	1802	—	10.00	18.00	30.00	50.00
	1803	—	10.00	18.00	30.00	50.00

NOTE: Roman I in date of 1802 issues.
NOTE: Earlier date (1800) exists for this type.

Reduced weight, 38.60 g

KM#	Date	Mintage	Good	VG	Fine	VF
211	1803	—	10.00	15.00	22.50	40.00
	1804	—	10.00	15.00	22.50	40.00
	1805	—	10.00	15.00	22.50	40.00
	1806	—	10.00	15.00	22.50	40.00

NOTE: Varieties exist.

8 STUIVER

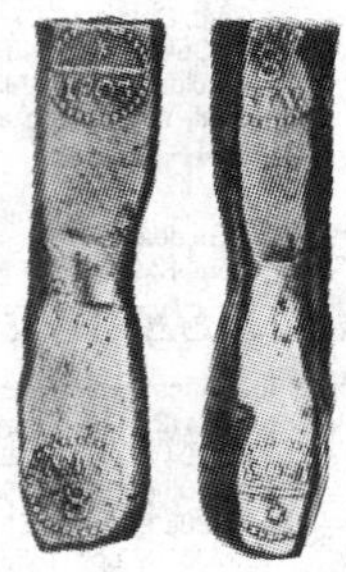

COPPER BONK, 154.40 g
Illustration reduced. Actual size: 74 mm.
Value and date in pearl circles.

KM#	Date	Mintage	VG	Fine	VF	XF
212	1803	.395	550.00	850.00	1200.	1600.

1/2 RUPEE

6.5750 g, .792 SILVER, .1674 oz ASW

KM#	Date	Mintage	VG	Fine	VF	XF
215	1805 Z	—	25.00	45.00	75.00	125.00
	1806 Z	—	25.00	45.00	75.00	125.00

NOTE: 12 varieties exist.

RUPEE

13.1500 g, .792 SILVER, .3349 oz ASW
Thick planchet.

KM#	Date	Mintage	VG	Fine	VF	XF
208	1801 Z	—	20.00	40.00	60.00	100.00
	1802 Z	—	20.00	40.00	60.00	100.00
	1803 Z	—	20.00	40.00	60.00	100.00

NOTE: Varieties exist.
NOTE: Earlier date (1800) exists for this type.

Thin planchet.

KM#	Date	Mintage	VG	Fine	VF	XF
214	1804 Z	—	17.50	30.00	50.00	80.00
	1805 Z	—	17.50	30.00	50.00	80.00
	1806 Z	—	17.50	30.00	50.00	80.00
	1808 Z	—	17.50	30.00	50.00	80.00

NOTE: Varieties exist.

1/2 GOLD RUPEE

8.0000 g, .750 GOLD, .1929 oz AGW
Obv. Arabic leg., AD date.

KM#	Date	Mintage	VG	Fine	VF	XF
209	1801 Z	—	300.00	500.00	750.00	1250.
	1802 Z	—	300.00	500.00	750.00	1250.
	1803 Z	—	—	—	Unique	—
	1807 Z	—	600.00	1100.	1600.	2400.

NOTE: Earlier date (1800) exists for this type.

Kingdom of Holland

DUIT

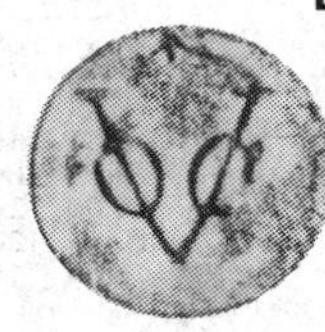

COPPER
Obv: VOC and star above. Rev: JAVA/date.

KM#	Date	Mintage	VG	Fine	VF	XF
220	1806	—	10.00	15.00	25.00	50.00
	1807	—	4.50	7.50	15.00	25.00
	1808	—	4.50	7.50	15.00	25.00
	1809	—	2.50	4.00	8.00	15.00
	1810	—	—	—	Rare	—

NOTE: Varieties exist.

Obv: Block LN. Rev: JAVA/date.

KM#	Date	Mintage	VG	Fine	VF	XF
223	1808	—	3.00	5.00	10.00	20.00
	1809	—	2.25	3.50	6.00	10.00
	1810	—	2.25	3.50	6.00	10.00

NOTE: Varieties exist.

KM#	Date	Mintage	VG	Fine	VF	XF
225	1810 Z	—	2.25	3.50	6.00	10.00
	1811 Z	—	2.25	3.50	6.00	10.00

NOTE: Several varieties of above 2 coins exist.

Obv. and rev: Ornate borders.

KM#	Date	Mintage	VG	Fine	VF	XF
226	1810 Z	—	15.00	25.00	40.00	70.00

1/2 STUIVER

COPPER
Obv: Ornate LN below value.

KM#	Date	Mintage	VG	Fine	VF	XF
227	1810 Z	—	100.00	155.00	250.00	400.00

NOTE: 3 varieties exist.

KM#	Date	Mintage	VG	Fine	VF	XF
228	1810 Z	—	2.50	4.00	6.00	10.00
	1811 Z	—	3.50	6.00	10.00	15.00

NOTE: Several varieties exist.

STUIVER

COPPER BONK, 19.30 g

KM#	Date	Mintage	Good	VG	Fine	VF
221	1807	—	15.00	25.00	45.00	75.00
	1808	—	—	—	Rare	—
	1809	—	7.50	15.00	25.00	40.00
	1810	—	6.00	10.00	17.50	30.00

NOTE: Varieties exist. Considerable depreciation in weight as dates progressed.

11.58 g., retrograde S.

KM#	Date	Mintage	Good	VG	Fine	VF
229	1809	—	22.50	45.00	65.00	90.00
	1810	—	22.50	45.00	65.00	90.00

COPPER
Obv: Ornate LN, value. Rev: JAVA/date.

KM#	Date	Mintage	VG	Fine	VF	XF
230	1810 Z	—	80.00	200.00	300.00	450.00

NOTE: 2 varieties exist.

2 STUIVER

COPPER BONK, 38.60 g

KM#	Date	Mintage	Good	VG	Fine	VF
222	1807	—	12.00	25.00	45.00	90.00
	1808	—	12.00	25.00	45.00	90.00

Reduced weight, 23.16 g

KM#	Date	Mintage	Good	VG	Fine	VF
224.1	1809	—	6.00	10.00	17.50	30.00
	1810	—	6.00	10.00	17.50	30.00

NOTE: Varieties exist.

15.0-25.0 g
Obv: Retrograde S.

KM#	Date	Mintage	Good	VG	Fine	VF
224.2	1809	—	—	—	—	—
	1810	—	3.50	7.50	12.50	20.00

Obv: Retrograde 2S.

KM#	Date	Mintage	Good	VG	Fine	VF
224.3	1807	—	60.00	90.00	135.00	175.00
	1810	—	60.00	90.00	135.00	175.00

NOTE: Varieties exist. Light weight coins (6.0-10 g) are contemporary forgeries.

Kingdom of the Netherlands

1/2 STUIVER

COPPER BONK, 7.72 g
Value and date in lined rectangle.

KM#	Date	Mintage	Good	VG	Fine	VF
216	1818	—	30.00	50.00	80.00	160.00

STUIVER

COPPER BONK, 15.44 g
Value and date each in rectangle.

KM#	Date	Mintage	VG	Fine	VF	XF
235	1818	—	15.00	25.00	35.00	60.00

NOTE: Varieties exist.

2 STUIVER

COPPER BONK, 30.88 g
Value and date each in rectangle.

KM#	Date	Mintage	VG	Fine	VF	XF
236	1818	—	15.00	25.00	45.00	75.00
	1819	—	15.00	25.00	45.00	80.00

NOTE: Varieties exist.

BRITISH OCCUPATION

1811-1816

DUIT

COPPER

KM#	Date	Mintage	VG	Fine	VF	XF
240	1811	—	4.50	7.50	12.50	20.00
	1812	—	4.50	7.50	12.50	20.00

NOTE: At least 5 varieties exist of each date.

BRASS

KM#	Date	Mintage	VG	Fine	VF	XF
240a	1812	—	7.50	15.00	25.00	45.00

TIN

KM#	Date	Mintage	VG	Fine	VF	XF
244	1813	16.747	17.50	30.00	50.00	85.00
	1814	33.656	17.50	30.00	50.00	85.00

1/2 STIVER

COPPER

KM#	Date	Mintage	VG	Fine	VF	XF
241	1811 Z	—	6.50	10.00	18.00	30.00
	1812 Z	—	4.50	7.50	12.50	20.00
	1813 Z	—	4.50	7.50	12.50	20.00
	1814 Z	—	7.50	12.50	20.00	35.00
	1815 Z	—	7.50	12.50	25.00	45.00

NOTE: At least 3 varieties exist of each date.

STIVER

COPPER

KM#	Date	Mintage	VG	Fine	VF	XF
243	1812 Z	—	—	—	Rare	—
	1814 Z	—	12.50	37.50	65.00	115.00
	1815 Z	—	45.00	90.00	140.00	250.00

NOTE: 3 varieties exist of 1814.

1/2 RUPEE

6.5700 g, .792 SILVER, .1673 oz ASW
Obv: Javanese leg. and date.
Rev: Arabic leg. and date.

KM#	Date	Year		VG	Fine	VF	XF
246	AH1668	AS1740	(1813)(error = AH1228) 3 or 4 known	—	—	Rare	—
	1229	1741	(1814)	175.00	225.00	300.00	400.00

NOTE: The 1/2 Rupee struck in silver is similar to the 1/2 Mohur struck in gold except a 5-petaled flower replaces the Christian date on the silver coins.

RUPEE

13.1500 g, .792 SILVER, .3349 oz ASW
Error date AH1668

KM#	Date	Year		VG	Fine	VF	XF
247	AH1668	AS1740	(error = AH1228) 3 var.	22.50	40.00	60.00	100.00
	1228	1740	(error w/Y's for Arabic 2's)	22.50	40.00	60.00	100.00
	1229	1741		150.00	225.00	325.00	475.00
	1230	1743	w/OZ	35.00	60.00	100.00	160.00
	1230	1743	w/.Z	35.00	60.00	100.00	160.00
	1231	1743		—	—	Unique	—
	1232	1743		45.00	75.00	125.00	200.00
	1232	1744/3		40.00	80.00	135.00	225.00
	1232	1744		35.00	60.00	100.00	160.00

NOTE: Many varieties and overstrikes exist of the above.

1/2 MOHUR

8.0060 g, .750 GOLD, .1931 oz AGW

KM#	Date	Year		VG	Fine	VF	XF
248	AH1668	AS1740	1813 (error = AH1228)	—	—	Rare	—
	1229	1743	1814	—	2000.	2250.	2750.

NOTE: Varieties exist.

8.0060 g, .833 GOLD, .2144 oz AGW

KM#	Date	Year		VG	Fine	VF	XF
248a	AH1230	AS1743	1815 w/OZ	1750.	2250.	2500.	3000.
	1230	1743	1815 w/Z	1750.	2250.	2500.	3000.
	1230	1743	1816 (error = AH1231)	1250.	1750.	2000.	2500.
	1231/0	1743	1816	1250.	1750.	2000.	2500.
	1231	1743	1816	1250.	1750.	2000.	2500.

Obv: Numerals in date reversed. Rev: M added.

KM#	Date	Year		VG	Fine	VF	XF
249	1231	1743	1816		—	Rare	—

MADURA ISLAND

SUMENEP

Sumenep is a sultanate on the island of Madura.

TITLES

سمنف

Sumenep

RULERS

Sultan Paku Nata Ningrat, 1811-1854

COUNTERMARKED COINAGE

Madura Star Series

RUPEE

SILVER

c/m: 'Madura Star' on Java 1 Rupee, KM#175.

KM#	Date	Year	Good	VG	Fine	VF
191.1	ND	(1764-89)	30.00	40.00	60.00	100.00

c/m: 'Madura Star' on Java 1 Rupee, KM#175a.

KM#	Date	Year	Good	VG	Fine	VF
191.2	ND	(1795-99)	30.00	50.00	80.00	125.00

c/m: 'Madura Star' on Java 1 Rupee, KM#214.

KM#	Date	Year	Good	VG	Fine	VF
191.3	ND	(1804-08)	35.00	55.00	90.00	150.00

c/m: 'Madura Star' on Java 1 Rupee, KM#247.

KM#	Date	Year	Good	VG	Fine	VF
191.4 (191.3)	ND	(AS1740-44)	30.00	50.00	80.00	125.00

c/m: 'Madura Star' on India-Bombay 1 Rupee, KM#224.

191.5	ND	(1810-13)	35.00	55.00	80.00	125.00

GULDEN

SILVER
c/m: 'Madura Star' on Netherlands Gelderland 1 Gulden, KM#100.1.

193.1	ND	(1760-95)	25.00	35.00	55.00	90.00

c/m: 'Madura Star' on Netherlands Holland 1 Gulden, KM#73.

193.2	ND	(1734-94)	20.00	30.00	50.00	85.00

c/m: 'Madura Star' on Netherlands Utrecht 1 Gulden, KM#102.

193.3	ND	(1748-94)	20.00	22.50	35.00	55.00

c/m: 'Madura Star' on Holland 1 Gulden, KM#83.

193.4	ND	(1802)	20.00	27.50	45.00	75.00

DUCATON

(Thaler, Daalder)

SILVER
c/m: 'Madura Star' in shield on Austria Burgau Thaler, KM#15.

KM#	Date	Year	Good	VG	Fine	VF
199.1	ND	(1764-65)	40.00	55.00	95.00	160.00

c/m: 'Madura Star' in shield on Austria Tyrol Thaler, KM#745.

199.2	ND	(1754-65)	95.00	160.00	270.00	450.00

c/m: 'Madura Star' in shield on Mexico City Mint 8 Reales, KM#104.1.

201.1	ND	(1747-60)	100.00	180.00	300.00	500.00

c/m: 'Madura Star' in shield on Mexico City Mint 8 Reales, KM#105.

201.5	ND	1771	100.00	200.00	325.00	500.00

c/m: 'Madura Star' in shield on Mexico City Mint 8 Reales, KM#106.2.

KM#	Date	Year	Good	VG	Fine	VF
201.6	ND	(1773-89)	100.00	200.00	325.00	500.00

c/m: 'Madura Star' in shield on Mexico City Mint 8 Reales, KM#107.

201.2	ND	1789	70.00	100.00	150.00	250.00
		1790	60.00	90.00	130.00	200.00

c/m: 'Madura Star' in shield on Mexico City Mint 8 Reales, KM#109.

201.3	ND	(1790-1808)	40.00	60.00	90.00	150.00

c/m: 'Madura Star' in shield on Potosi Mint 8 Reales, KM#73.1.

201.4	ND	(1791-1808)	50.00	70.00	100.00	160.00

c/m: 'Madura star' in shield on Netherlands West Friesland Ducation, KM#127.

203.1	ND	(1742-93)	55.00	90.00	135.00	200.00

c/m: 'Madura Star' in shield on Netherlands Holland Ducaton, KM#90.

203.2	ND	(1734-93)	60.00	100.00	140.00	210.00

Sumenep AH(1)230 Series

1/2 REAL BATU

SILVER
c/m: *Sumenep* and 5-petaled flower on

Mexico City Mint 'cob' 4 Reales, KM#40.

KM#	Date	Year	Good	VG	Fine	VF
196.1	ND or AH(1)230					
		17xx J	150.00	175.00	275.00	450.00

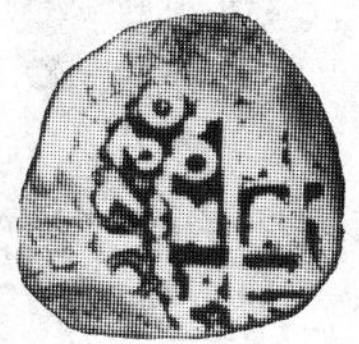

c/m: *Sumenep* and 5-petaled flower on Mexico City Mint 'cob' 4 Reales, KM#40a.

KM#	Date	Year	Good	VG	Fine	VF
196.2	ND or AH(1)230					
		1730 R	85.00	150.00	220.00	350.00
		1731 F	85.00	150.00	220.00	350.00
		1732/1 MF	100.00	175.00	250.00	400.00

NOTE: Also known w/an additional c/m 5-pointed star w/circular center.

REAL BATU

SILVER

c/m: *Sumenep* and *(1)230* in Arabic on Mexico City Mint 'cob' 8 Reales, KM#47a.

KM#	Date	Year	Good	VG	Fine	VF
197	ND or AH(1)230					
		1729 R	35.00	50.00	90.00	175.00
		1730 R	35.00	50.00	90.00	175.00
		1731 F	35.00	50.00	90.00	175.00
		1732 F	35.00	50.00	90.00	175.00

NOTE: Also known w/an additional c/m 5-pointed star w/circular center.

GOLD RUPEE

GOLD

c/m: *Sumenep* and *(1)230* in Arabic on Spanish Colonial 2 Escudos.

KM#	Date	Year	Good	VG	Fine	VF
204	AH(1)230	—	—	—	Rare	—

SUMATRA, Island of

An island, south of the Malay peninsula, was first reached by Europeans for trade in 1599. Competition between European powers for trading rights continued until 1824 at which time it became a Dutch possession. British coins for the island were struck at the Birmingham Mint by Matthew Boulton in 1786 and other issues were struck at Indian mints.

TITLES

Pulu Percha 

MONETARY SYSTEM

100 Kepings = 1 Suku
4 Suku = 1 Dollar (Spanish)

DENOMINATIONS

The following Arabic legends appear for the denomination with an Arabic number above.

(1) Keping

Sakeping

Satu Keping

دوکثغ
(2) Dua Keping

تیک کفغ
(3) Tiga Keping

امثت کثغ
(4) Ampat Keping

EAST INDIA COMPANY

1685 - 1824

KEPING

COPPER

Thick planchet, 3.476 g

KM#	Date	Year	Fine	VF	XF	Unc
262	AH1219	1804	2.00	3.50	6.00	10.00
	1219	1804	—	—	Proof	75.00
	1219	1804	—		Gilt Proof	85.00

Thin planchet, 2.050 g

KM#	Date	Year	Fine	VF	XF	Unc
263	AH1219	1804	2.50	5.00	10.00	20.00

2 KEPINGS

COPPER

Thick planchet, 6.47 g

KM#	Date	Year	Fine	VF	XF	Unc
264	AH1219	1804	3.00	6.00	15.00	25.00
		1804	—	—	Proof	75.00
		1804	—		Gilt Proof	125.00

Thin planchet, 4.40 g

KM#	Date	Year	Fine	VF	XF	Unc
265	AH1219	1804	2.50	4.50	7.50	12.50

4 KEPINGS

COPPER

Thick planchet, 12.80 g

KM#	Date	Year	Fine	VF	XF	Unc
266	AH1219	1804	5.00	10.00	20.00	45.00
	1219	1804	—	—	Proof	85.00
	1219	1804	—		Gilt Proof	200.00

Thin planchet, 8.50 g

KM#	Date	Year	Fine	VF	XF	Unc
267	AH1219	1804	10.00	15.00	25.00	45.00

PATTERNS (Pn)

KM#	Date	Mintage	Identification	Mkt.Val.
Pn15	1804	—	1 Keping, Lead, KM262	250.00
Pn16	1804	—	2 Kepings, Lead, KM264	250.00

KINGDOM OF THE NETHERLANDS

MINTMASTER INITIALS

D - Demmenie
H - H. de Heus (Amsterdam)
J - L.J. Jeekel
S - J.D.C. Suermondt (Utrecht)
V - K.J. de Vogel
W - C.H. Williams

1/2 DUIT

(1/) 5 (of) 1/32 G. = 1/160 G.

COPPER

Mint: Amsterdam

KM#	Date	Mintage	VG	Fine	VF	XF
280.3 (85)	1814 H	—	—	—	Rare	—
	1815 H	—	1.00	2.00	5.00	12.50
	1816 H	—	1.00	2.00	5.00	12.50

NOTE: Varieties exist.

Mint: Utrecht

KM#	Date	Mintage	VG	Fine	VF	XF
280.1	1816 S	23.818	2.00	4.00	7.50	12.50

NOTE: Actually minted 1820-22.

Mint: Sourabaya

KM#	Date	Mintage	VG	Fine	VF	XF
280.2	1816	—	2.00	5.00	10.00	18.50
	1818	—	1.50	3.00	7.00	12.50
	1821	—	1.50	3.00	7.00	12.50
	1822	—	2.00	5.00	10.00	17.50

NOTE: Varieties exist.

1/8 STUIVER

(1/2 Duit)

COPPER

Mint: Utrecht

KM#	Date	Mintage	VG	Fine	VF	XF
286	1822 S	1.300	2.00	5.00	10.00	20.00
	1823 S	33.000	1.00	2.75	5.50	11.50
	1824 S	21.000	1.25	3.50	6.00	11.50
	1825 S	44.000	1.25	3.50	6.00	11.50
	1826 S	69.000	1.00	2.75	5.00	10.00

NOTE: Varieties exist. Date 1826 with lion of 1822-1825 with a thick, bushy tail are very rare.

DUIT

(1/) 5 (of) 1/16 G. = 1/80 G.

COPPER

Mint: Amsterdam

KM#	Date	Mintage	VG	Fine	VF	XF
279	1814 H	—	—	—	Rare	—
(86)	1814 w/o H	—	—	—	—	—
	1815 H	—	3.00	5.00	8.50	15.00
	1816 H	—	3.00	5.00	8.50	15.00

NOTE: Varieties exist. 1814 dated coins were struck on larger planchets.

Mint: Utrecht

KM#	Date	Mintage	VG	Fine	VF	XF
281	1816 S	64.562	1.25	3.00	6.50	11.50

NOTE: Actually minted 1820-22.

Mint: Sourabaya

Obv: Double lined shield.

KM#	Date	Mintage	VG	Fine	VF	XF
282.1	1816	—	5.00	10.00	25.00	35.00
	1818	—	1.75	3.00	5.00	8.50
	1819	—	2.50	5.00	10.00	17.50
	1820	—	1.75	3.00	5.00	8.50
	1821	—	1.75	3.00	5.00	8.50
	1822	—	3.50	6.00	12.00	20.00

NOTE: 1816 dated coins were actually struck in 1820.

Obv: Single lined shield.

KM#	Date	Mintage	VG	Fine	VF	XF
282.2	1821	—	1.75	3.00	5.00	8.50
	1822	—	1.75	3.00	5.00	8.50
	1823	—	1.75	3.00	5.00	8.50
	1824	—	3.00	5.00	10.00	17.50
	1825	—	1.75	3.00	5.00	8.50
	1826	—	4.00	6.50	12.50	35.00

1/4 STUIVER

(Duit)

COPPER

Mint: Utrecht

KM#	Date	Mintage	VG	Fine	VF	XF
287	1822 S	30.000	1.75	3.00	5.00	8.50
	1823 S	29.000	1.75	3.00	5.00	8.50
	1824 S	26.000	1.75	3.00	5.00	8.50
	1825 S	125.000	1.00	1.50	2.50	4.00
	1826 S	208.000	1.00	1.50	2.50	4.00
	1836/1828 S	—	25.00	50.00	100.00	175.00
	1836 S	33.453	1.50	2.50	4.00	6.50

NOTE: 2 varieties known.

1/2 STUIVER

COPPER
Obv: G. below shield.

KM#	Date	Mintage	VG	Fine	VF	XF
283	1818	—	2.25	4.00	6.00	10.00
	1819	—	2.25	4.00	6.00	10.00
	1820	—	2.25	4.00	6.00	10.00

NOTE: Varieties exist.

Obv: G. removed, double lined shield.

KM#	Date	Mintage	VG	Fine	VF	XF
284.1	1820	—	2.50	4.50	6.50	11.50
	1821	—	2.50	4.50	6.50	11.50

Obv: Single lined shield.

KM#	Date	Mintage	VG	Fine	VF	XF
284.2	1821	—	2.00	4.00	7.50	20.00
	1822	—	1.75	3.00	5.00	8.50
	1823	—	1.75	3.00	5.00	8.50
	1824	—	1.75	3.00	5.00	8.50
	1825	—	1.75	3.00	5.00	8.50
	1826	—	2.00	4.00	7.50	20.00

KM#	Date	Mintage	VG	Fine	VF	XF
285	1821S	10.000	3.50	6.00	10.00	15.00
	1822S	7.000	3.00	5.50	9.00	15.00
	1823S	19.000	1.75	3.00	5.00	8.50
	1824S	5.500	3.00	5.50	9.00	15.00
	1825S	42.000	1.75	3.00	5.00	8.50
	1826S	66.000	1.75	3.00	5.00	8.50

DECIMAL COINAGE

100 Cents = 1 Gulden

CENT
(Duit)

COPPER

KM#	Date	Mintage	VG	Fine	VF	XF
290	1833D	21.778	15.00	30.00	50.00	100.00
	1833V	Inc. Ab.	2.50	4.25	6.50	15.00
	1834V	66.237	1.75	3.00	5.00	8.50
	1835V	48.674	1.75	3.00	5.00	8.50
	1836V	94.825	1.75	3.00	5.00	8.50
	1837V	182.888	1.75	3.00	5.00	8.50
	1837C	Inc. Ab.	—	—	Rare	—
	1837J	Inc. Ab.	1.50	2.50	4.25	7.00
	1838J	235.524	1.50	2.50	4.25	7.00
	1839J	314.953	1.50	2.50	4.25	7.00
	1839W	Inc. Ab.	1.50	2.50	4.25	7.00
	1840W	461.726	1.50	2.50	4.25	7.00

NOTE: Varieties exist. Mintage figures for 1839 and 1840 include KM#111.4 and KM#111.5.

2 CENTS
(Double Duit)

COPPER

KM#	Date	Mintage	VG	Fine	VF	XF
291	1833D	11.305*	12.50	22.50	37.50	65.00
	1833V	Inc. Ab.	2.50	4.00	6.50	11.50
	1834V	32.997	1.75	3.00	5.00	8.50
	1835V	24.627	1.75	3.00	5.00	8.50
	1836V	48.612	1.75	3.00	5.00	8.50
	1837J	54.812	1.75	3.00	5.00	8.50
	1837V	Inc. Ab.	1.75	3.00	5.00	8.50
	1838J	93.809	1.50	2.50	4.00	6.50
	1839J	90.964	1.50	2.50	4.00	6.50
	1839W	Inc. Ab.	2.50	4.00	6.50	11.50
	1840W	98.086	2.50	4.00	6.50	11.50
	1841W	115.321	2.50	4.00	6.50	11.50

NOTE: Varieties exist. Mintage figures for 1840 and 1841 include KM#118.

TOKENS (Tn)

1/4 STUIVER
(Duit)

COPPER
Mint: Birmingham
Similar to 1/4 Stuiver, KM#287, thin planchet, border of dots.

KM#	Date	Mintage	VG	Fine	VF	XF
Tn1	1826	—	1.25	2.00	3.50	6.00

PATTERNS (Pn)

(Including off metal strikes)

KM#	Date	Mintage	Identification	Mkt.Val.
Pn1	1833	—	1 Cent, Silver, KM290	—
Pn2	1834	—	1 Cent, Silver, KM290	—
Pn3	1835	—	1 Cent, Silver, KM290	—

KM#	Date	Mintage	Identification	Mkt.Val.
PnA4	1836	—	Swan Duit	45.00

KM#	Date	Mintage	Identification	Mkt.Val.
PnB4	1836	—	1 Duit	—
Pn4	1836	—	1 Cent, Silver, KM290	—
Pn5	1836	—	2 Cents, Silver, KM291	—
Pn6	1837	—	1 Cent, Silver, KM290	—
Pn7	1837	—	2 Cents, Silver, KM291	—
Pn8	1838	—	1 Cent, Silver, KM290	—
Pn9	1838	—	2 Cents, Silver, KM291	—

LOCAL ISSUES

MONETARY SYSTEM

10 Pitis = 1 Keping
900-4,000 Pitis = 1 Ringgit (Dollar)
1280 Trah = 1 Ringgit
100 Pice (Cents) = 1 Ringgit

DENOMINATIONS

The following Arabic legends appear for the denomination with an Arabic number above.

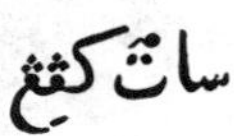

(1)Keping **Sakeping** **Satu Keping**

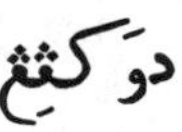

(2) Dua Keping

NOTE: Many local merchant tokens, inscribed mainly in Chinese, exist for most of the Malay states. These have not been listed.

ATCHEH

Kingdom in northwest Sumatra.

TITLES

اجه

Negeri Atcheh

RULERS

S. Alauddin Jauhar al-Alam Syah, 1795-1815,1818-1824
S. Alauddin Muh Daud Syah, 1824-1839

KEPING

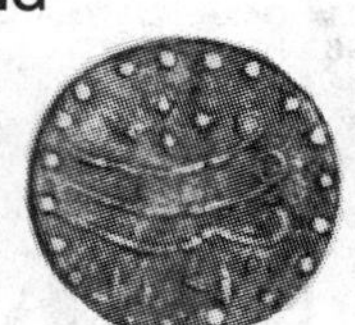

TIN
Obv. leg: Arabic *BANDAR ATJEH DAR ES SALAAM* (city of Atcheh, abode of Peace).

KM#	Date	Mintage	Good	VG	Fine	VF
1 (Tn1)	AH1260	—	4.25	7.50	12.00	20.00

TOKEN ISSUES

2 KEPINGS

COPPER
Obv. leg: Arabic *Negeri Atcheh* (State of Atcheh).

KM#	Date	Year	Fine	VF	XF	Unc
Tn2	AH1247	—	22.50	37.50	62.50	100.00
	1247	—	—	—	Proof	125.00
	1251	—	—	—	Proof	125.00

BANJARMASIN

Kingdom in South Borneo.

TITLES

Banjarmasin بنجرمسن

RULERS

S. Tamjid Illah III, 1785-1808

KEPING

COPPER
Obv. leg: Arabic *Banjarmasin*.
Rev: Date and value.

KM#	Date	Mintage	VG	Fine	VF	XF
1 (Tn1)	AH1221	—	7.50	15.00	25.00	45.00

1/4 RUPEE

SILVER
c/m: *Banjar* in Malay on Dutch West Indies (Utrecht) 1/4 Gulden, 1794, KM#2.

KM#	Date	Mintage	VG	Fine	VF	XF
62	ND	—	—	—	—	—

RUPEE

SILVER
c/m: *Banjar* in Malay on Dutch West Indies (Utrecht) Gulden, 1794, KM#3.

KM#	Date	Mintage	VG	Fine	VF	XF
3	ND	—	—	—	—	—

NOTE: A unique example of a *Banjar* countermark on a Spanish Cuarta de Onza (4 Pesos) gold coin is known to exist.

CELEBES

Actually refers to South Celebes.

TITLES

Tanah Ugi تانه اغيسى

TOKEN ISSUES

KEPING

COPPER
Obv. leg: Buginese *Tanah Ugi* (Land of the Bugis-Celebes).

Rev. leg: ***Seuwa Duwi*** **(One Doit).**

KM#	Date	Year	Fine	VF	XF	Unc
Tn1	AH1250	—	10.00	17.50	30.00	50.00
	1250	—	—	—	Proof	100.00

DELI

State in north Sumatra.

TITLES

دلي

Negeri Deli

RULERS

S. Amaluddin I, 1805-1850

TOKEN ISSUES

KEPING

COPPER

Obv. leg: Arabic ***Negeri Deli*** **(State of Deli).**

KM#	Date	Year	Fine	VF	XF	Unc
Tn1	AH1251	—	12.50	20.00	30.00	50.00
	1251	—	—	—	Proof	125.00

MALUKA

A private state in southern Borneo founded by the Englishman, Alexander Hare in 1812 acquired through a grant from the local sultan. The state existed from 1812 to 1818. The coins were made at a mint in the state in 1812 and 1813. The state ceased to exist when the area was repossessed by the Dutch in 1818.

TITLE

Maluka

DUIT

COPPER

KM#	Date	Year	VG	Fine	VF	XF
1 (Tn1)	ND	—	—	—	Rare	—

KM#	Date	Year	VG	Fine	VF	XF
13 (Tn13)	AH1227	—	9.00	18.00	35.00	75.00

NOTE: 8 varieties exist.

KM#	Date	Year	VG	Fine	VF	XF
5 (Tn5)	AH1228	1813	9.00	18.00	35.00	75.00

Rev: Floral design

KM#	Date	Year	VG	Fine	VF	XF
7 (Tn7)	AH1228	—	12.50	25.00	45.00	85.00

Crude design, similar to KM#Tn7.

KM#	Date	Year	VG	Fine	VF	XF
9 (Tn9)	AH1228	—	10.00	20.00	40.00	80.00

Rev: Date within wreath.

KM#	Date	Year	VG	Fine	VF	XF
11 (Tn11)	AH1228	—	—	—	Rare	—

COUNTERMARKED COINAGE

KEPING

COPPER

KM#	Date	Year	VG	Fine	VF	XF
c/m: Buddhist "Wheel of Law" on KM#Tn1.						
2 (Tn2)	ND	—	—	—	Rare	—
c/m: Buddhist "Wheel of Law" on KM#Tn3.						
4 (Tn4)	AH1227	—	7.00	15.00	30.00	65.00
c/m: Buddhist "Wheel of Law" on KM#Tn5.						
6 (Tn6)	AH1228	1813	7.00	15.00	30.00	65.00
c/m: Buddhist "Wheel of Law" on KM#Tn7.						
8 (Tn8)	AH1228	—	12.50	25.00	45.00	85.00
c/m: Buddhist "Wheel of Law" on KM#Tn9.						
10 (Tn10)	AH1228	—	10.00	20.00	40.00	80.00
c/m: Buddhist "Wheel of Law" on KM#Tn11.						
12 (Tn12)	AH1228	—	—	—	Rare	—

MINANGKABAU

State in west Sumatra.

TITLES

منفكابو

Minangkabau

RULERS

S. Alam Bagagar Syah, 1819-33
Tuanku Gadih Reno Sumpu (puppet) 1833-1912

KEPING

COPPER

Obv. leg: Arabic ***Minangkabau.***

KM#	Date	Year	Fine	VF	XF	Unc
Tn1	AH1251	—	12.50	20.00	30.00	50.00
	1251	—	—	—	Proof	100.00

2 KEPING

COPPER

KM#	Date	Year	Fine	VF	XF	Unc
Tn2	AH1247	—	—	Proof only		125.00
	1251	—	20.00	35.00	60.00	100.00
	1251	—	—	—	Proof	125.00

PALEMBANG

State in south Sumatra.

TITLES

فلمبغ

Palembang

RULERS

S. Mahmud Badaruddin II, 1803-1814, 1818-1821,1825

PITIS

TIN

Octagonal shape, 14mm. Obv: Arabic leg. Rev: Blank.

KM#	Date	Mintage	Good	VG	Fine	VF
1 (Tn1)	AH1219	—	6.00	10.00	16.50	25.00

Hole in center

KM#	Date	Mintage	Good	VG	Fine	VF
2 (Tn2)	AH1219	—	6.00	10.00	20.00	35.00

PONTIANAK

Sultanate in South Borneo.

RULERS

S. Syarif Kasim Alkadrie, 1808-1819

KEPING

COPPER

Obv: Crowned shield. Rev: OVC, date below.

KM#	Date	Mintage	VG	Fine	VF	XF
1	1790-1817	—	12.00	25.00	50.00	100.00

NOTE: Varieties exist.

Obv: Inscription. Rev: Scales.

KM#	Date	Mintage	VG	Fine	VF	XF
2	1790-1817	—	10.00	20.00	40.00	85.00

NOTE: Varieties exist.

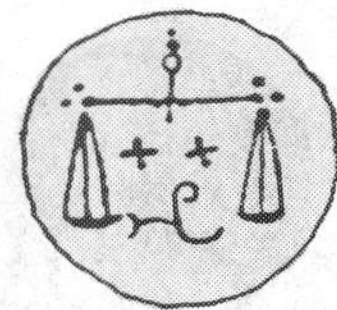

Obv: Crowned shield. Rev: Scales.

KM#	Date	Mintage	VG	Fine	VF	XF
3	1790-1817	—	10.00	20.00	40.00	85.00

NOTE: Varieties exist.

Rev: Numerals inscription.

KM#	Date	Mintage	VG	Fine	VF	XF
4	1790-1817	—	15.00	30.00	60.00	125.00

NOTE: Varieties exist.

Rev: CIVI in sections of heart-shaped shield.

KM#	Date	Mintage	VG	Fine	VF	XF
5	1790-1817	—	12.00	25.00	50.00	100.00

NOTE: Varieties exist.

NOTE: Some specimens have *Banjar *t5In Malay within the obverse shield. Combinations of obverse and reverse of all types exist.*

SIAK

State in East Sumatra.

TITLES

نكري سيك

Negeri Siak

RULERS

S. Syarif Ismail, 1827-1864

KEPING

COPPER

Obv. leg: Arabic ***Negeri Siak*** **(State of Siak).**

KM#	Date	Year	Fine	VF	XF	Unc
Tn1	AH1251	—	12.50	20.00	30.00	50.00
	1251	—	—	—	Proof	125.00

SULTANA, Island of

Although it was once thought that Island of Sultana referred to the Island of Labuan, it now appears to be a fictitious name used for the Island of Sumatra by the Singapore merchants so they could circulate these issues without alarming the Dutch Government.

KEPING

COPPER
Obv. leg: ISLAND OF SULTANA.
Rev: Arabic 1 for denomination.

KM#	Date	Year	Fine	VF	XF	Unc
Tn1	AH1411	1804	4.50	7.50	15.00	30.00

Rev: P for denomination.

KM#	Date	Year	Fine	VF	XF	Unc
Tn2	AH1219	1804	2.50	5.00	12.50	25.00

BRASS

KM#	Date	Year	Fine	VF	XF	Unc
Tn2a	AH1219	1804	—	—	Rare	—

Obv: Similar to KM#Tn1.
Rev: Similar to Sumatra, 1 Keping, KM#Tn3.

KM#	Date	Year	Fine	VF	XF	Unc
Tn3	AH1247	1804	2.50	5.00	12.50	25.00

KM#	Date	Year	Fine	VF	XF	Unc
Tn4	AH1250	1804	7.00	14.00	28.00	50.00

Obv. leg: ISLAND OF SULTANA, horses supporting shield w/2 flags. Rev: Meaningless legends.

KM#	Date	Year	Fine	VF	XF	Unc
Tn5	AH1411	1835	7.00	14.00	28.00	50.00

Obv: Similar to KM#Tn5 w/1 flag above arms, flying right, no legend.

KM#	Date	Year	Fine	VF	XF	Unc
Tn6	AH1411	1835	8.00	15.00	30.00	55.00

Obv: 1 flag above arms, flying left.

KM#	Date	Year	Fine	VF	XF	Unc
Tn7	AH1411	1835	8.00	15.00	30.00	55.00

Obv: W/o leg. Rev: Similar to KM#Tn5.

KM#	Date	Year	Fine	VF	XF	Unc
Tn8	AH1411	1835	7.00	14.00	28.00	50.00

SUMATRA

NOTE: The tokens listed below were produced for merchants of Singapore.

TOKEN ISSUES

KEPING

COPPER
Rev. value: P for Arabic 1, date.

KM#	Date	Year	Fine	VF	XF	Unc
Tn1	AH1219	1804	3.00	6.00	15.00	30.00

Rev: Q for Arabic 1.

KM#	Date	Year	Fine	VF	XF	Unc
Tn2	AH1219	1804	5.00	10.00	25.00	50.00

Rev: 1 for Arabic 1.

KM#	Date	Year	Fine	VF	XF	Unc
Tn3	AH1247	—	2.50	5.00	12.50	25.00

COPPER
Obv. leg: Arabic *Pulu Percha* (Island of Sumatra).

KM#	Date	Year	Fine	VF	XF	Unc
Tn5	AH1251	—	6.00	12.00	30.00	60.00
	1251	—	—	—	Proof	125.00

2 KEPINGS

COPPER
Obv. leg: Arabic *Pulau Percha* (Island of Sumatra).

KM#	Date	Year	Fine	VF	XF	Unc
Tn4	AH1247	—	10.00	17.50	30.00	50.00
	1247	—	—	—	Proof	100.00
	1251	—	10.00	17.50	30.00	50.00
	1251	—	—	—	Proof	100.00

TRUMON

State in northwest Sumatra.

TITLES

Negeri Trumon نكري ترومن

RULERS

Raja Bujang, 1829-r.1841

2 KEPINGS

COPPER
Obv. leg: Arabic *Negeri Trumon* (State of Trumon).

KM#	Date	Year	Fine	VF	XF	Unc
Tn1	AH1247	—	8.00	16.00	40.00	80.00
	1251	—	10.00	20.00	50.00	100.00
	1251	—	—	—	Proof	125.00

ANONYMOUS ISSUES

Issues struck for circulation.

TITLES

Tanah Malayu تانه ملايو

Pulu Malayu فولو ملايو

TOKEN ISSUES

KEPING

COPPER
Obv. leg: Arabic *Tanah Malayu* (Land of the Malays).

KM#	Date	Year	Fine	VF	XF	Unc
Tn1	AH1251	—	7.00	15.00	30.00	50.00
	1251	—	—	—	Proof	125.00

Obv: Date misformed, leg: Arabic *Tatah Malayu Satu Keping* (Land of the Malays - One Keping). C.R.READ under rooster. Rev. leg: Bugis *Wanuwa Tana Ugi Sedi Keping* (Land of the Bugis - One Keping) around 16-petal rosette.

KM#	Date	Year	Fine	VF	XF	Unc
Tn2	AH1250	—	4.50	7.50	15.00	32.00
	1250	—	—	—	Proof	125.00

NICKEL

KM#	Date	Year	Fine	VF	XF	Unc
Tn2a	AH1250	—	—	—	Proof	—

Obv. leg: Arabic *Pulu Malayu* (Island of the Malays).

KM#	Date	Year	Fine	VF	XF	Unc
Tn3	AH1411	—	5.00	10.00	18.00	40.00

Obv. leg: Arabic *Tanah Malayu* (Land of the Malays).

KM#	Date	Year	Fine	VF	XF	Unc
Tn4	AH1250	—	4.00	8.00	16.50	35.00

TIMOR

(East Timor)

An island in the Lesser Sunda group, presently part of Indonesia but a treaty of 1859 fixed the division between Portugal and the Netherlands. Portugal discovered and owned the eastern half of the island since 1524 and made coins for this colony. From 1865-1896, Timor was under the jurisdiction of Macao but was made a province in 1896 and became a colony in 1926. All of Timor fell under Japanese occupation from 1942-1945. In 1951 they became an overseas province.

MONETARY SYSTEM
100 Avos = 1 Pataca

COUNTERMARKED COINAGE

June 13, 1900

(8 REALES)

SILVER
c/m: Maltese cross on Mexico, Chihuahua 8 Reales, KM#377.2.

KM#	Date	Mintage	Fine	VF	XF	Unc
8	1890 MM	—	50.00	75.00	125.00	200.00

NOTE: Other dates, 1886, 1891, 1892, 1893, 1894, 1895 1896 are reported but mints are unknown.

IRAN

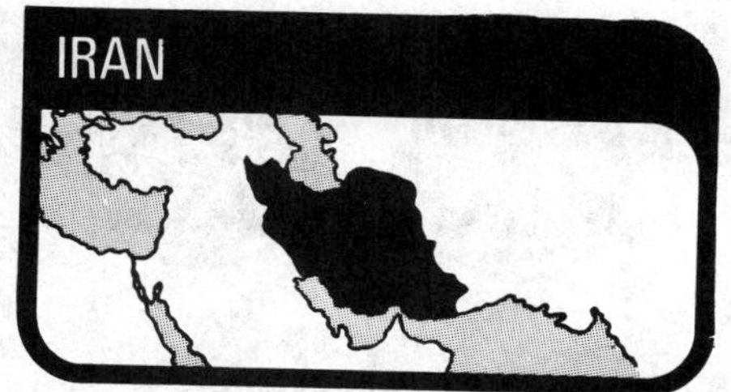

The Islamic Republic of Iran, located between the Caspian Sea and the Persian Gulf in southwestern Asia, has an area of 636,296 sq. mi. (1,648,000 sq. km.) and a population of 40 million. Capital: Tehran. Although predominantly an agricultural state, Iran depends heavily on oil for foreign exchange. Crude oil, carpets and agricultural products are exported.

Iran (historically known as Persia until 1931AD) is one of the world's most ancient and resilient nations. Strategically astride the lower land gate to Asia, it has been conqueror and conquered, sovereign nation and vassal state, ever emerging from its periods of glory or travail with its culture and political individuality intact. Iran (Persia) was a powerful empire under Cyrus the Great (600-529 B.C.), its borders extending from the Indus to the Nile. It has also been conquered by the predatory empires of antique and recent times - Assyrian, Medean, Macedonian, Seljuq, Turk, Mongol - and more recently been coveted by Russia, the Third Reich and Great Britain. Revolts against the absolute power of the Persian shahs resulted in the establishment of a constitutional monarchy in 1906.

With 4,000 troops, Reza Khan marched on the capital arriving in Tehran in the early morning of Feb. 22, 1921. The government was taken over with hardly a shot and Zia ad-Din was set up as premier, but the real power was with Reza Khan, although he was officially only the minister of war. In 1923, Reza Khan appointed himself prime minister and summoned the "majlis." Who eventually gave him military powers and he became independent of the shah's authority. In 1925 Reza Khan Pahlavi was elected Shah of Persia. A few weeks later his eldest son, Shahpur Mohammed Reza was appointed Crown Prince and was crowned on April 25, 1926.

In 1931 the Kingdom of Persia became known as the Kingdom of Iran. In 1979 the monarchy was toppled and an Islamic Republic proclaimed.

TITLES

Dar al-Khilafat	دار الخلافة

RULERS

Qajar Dynasty

Fath'ali Shah, AH1212-1250/1797-1834AD	فتحعلى
Sultan Ali Shah, in Tehran AH1250/1834AD (30 days)	سلطان على
Husayn Ali Shah, AH1250/1834AD (6 months) (in Southern Iran only)	حسين على
Muhammad Shah, AH1250-1264/1834-1848AD	شاهنشه انبيا محمد
Nasir al-Din Shah, AH1264-1313/1848-1896AD	ناصر الدين
Muzaffar al-Din Shah, AH1313-1324/1896-1907AD	مظفر الدين

NOTE: Used "Shahansha-i Anbiga Muhammad", (The Emperor of the Prophets is Muhammad).

MINTNAMES

Abu Shahr (Bushire)	ابو شهر
Ardebil	اردبيل
Astarabad (located in Iran)	استراباد
Bandar Abbas	بندر عباس
Bandar Abu Shahr	بندرابو شهر
Basra (al-Basrah, Iraq)	البصره
Behbahan	بهبهان
Bahkar (see Afghanistan map)	بهكر
Borujerd	بروجرد
Darband	دربند
Dezful	دزفول
Eravan (Iravan, Armenia)	ايروان
Fouman	فومان
Ganjeh (Ganja, Azerbaijan)	گنجه
Gilan	گيلان
Hamadan	همدان
Herat, (Afghanistan)	هرات
Huwayza	حويزه
Isfahan (Esfahan)	اصفهان
Jelou (Army Mint)	جلو
Kashan	كاشان
Kirman (Kerman)	كرمان
Kirmanshahan (Kermanshah)	كرمانشاهان
Khoy (Khoi)	خوى
Lahijan	لاهيجان
Lahore (Pakistan, see Afghanistan map)	لاهور
Maragheh	مراغه
Mashhad	مشهد
Mazandaran	مازندران
Nahawand	نهاوند
Nakhjawan (Azerbaijan)	نخجوان
Naseri	ناصرى
Nukhwi	نخوى
Panahabad	پناه آباد
Peshawar (Pakistan, see Afghanistan map)	پشاور
Qandahar (Kandahar, Afghanistan)	قندهار
Qazvin	قزوين
Qomm (Kumm)	قم
Ra'nash	رعنش
Rasht	رشت
Rekab (Rikab)	ركاب
Reza'iyeh (Army Mint)	رضائيه
Sarakhs	سرخس
Sari	سارى

Mint	
Sawuj Balagh	ساوج بلاق
Shamakha (Shemakhi, Azerbaijan)	شماخه
Shiraz	شیراز
Shirwan (Azerbaijan)	شروان
Shushtar	شوشتر
Simnan (Semnan)	سمنان
Sind (see Afghanistan map)	سند
Sultanabad	سلطان آباد
Tabaristan (also Tabarestan, region N.W. of Iran)	طبرستان
Tabriz	تبریز
Tehran	طهران
Tiflis (Georgia)	تفلیس
Tuyserkan	توی سرکان
Urumi (Reza'iyeh)	ارومی
Yazd	یزد
Zanjan	زنجان

MONETARY SYSTEM

1797-98 (AH 1211-12)

50 Dinars = 1 Shahi
15 Shahis = 1 Rupee (?)
12 Rupees and 2 Shahis = 1 Toman
200 Dinars = 1 Abbasi

NOTE: The Shahi was a fixed unit, first coined in AD1501, equal to 50 Dinars. The Toman, introduced as a unit of account about AH1240 (1824AD), was always fixed at 10,000 Dinars. The value of the Rupee for this period is not known with certainty.

1798-1825 (AH 1212-1241)

1250 Dinars = 1 Riyal
8 Riyals = 1 Toman

1825-1931
(AH1241-1344, SH1304-09)

50 Dinars = 1 Shahi
20 Shahis = 1 Kran (Qiran)
10 Krans = 1 Toman

NOTE: From AD1830-34 (AH1245-50) the gold Toman was known as a 'Keshwarsetan.'

KINGDOM

HAMMERED 'DUMP' COINAGE

Copper Coinage

During the nineteenth century, copper coins (falus, flus) were issued at some 40 or more local mints, each of which coined falus for local use only. Copper coins did not circulate generally, but were restricted to the city of their origin and its immediate environs. The local mint-master, often in collaboration with the local governor, determined the type, design, and weight of the coinage, and regulated its circulation.

In theory, copper coins were recalled and changed about every year, with a substantial fee payable to the mint-master for the exchange of old coin for new. To discourage further use the old coin was either demonetized or tariffed at a lower value, usually about half its original.

In order to facilitate the recognition of new and old coin, the type was changed annually, the type being the obverse pictorial design, so that illiterate shopkeepers could tell the difference and not be deceived by obsolete coins. However, after a number of years, the same types would be reinstated for another year. In practice, the system worked more informally, and surviving coins show that at some mints, identical types were struck for several years running and were not recalled annually.

The metrology of the copper Falus is uncertain. While it seems that Falus were intended to follow an assigned weight standard, great tolerance was permitted. The weight standard was frequently changed (or the mint-master issued lighter coins and pocketed the difference), and each mint city maintained its own standard and copper currency policies.

As a result of the frequent recoinage of copper and its frequent demonetization, copper coins were not hoarded or saved, and are consequently quite scarce today. Annual change meant that each mint had a multiplicity of types and varieties, most of which are uncommon today. The following listings are not an attempt at completeness, but give a representative selection of the products of each mint.

IMPORTANT: Most types were used at many different mints. The type can therefore not be used to attribute a coin to the mint of its issue. The ONLY certain way of attributing the coin is to read the mint name on the reverse. Well struck copper falus with clear mintname and date are worth a premium.

Abu Shahr Mint

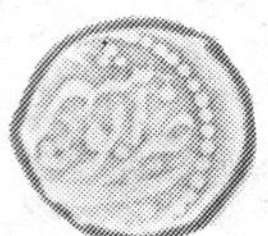

Obv: Lion.

KM#	Date	Good	VG	Fine	VF
2	AH1270	9.00	15.00	25.00	40.00

Obv: 2 lions facing.

KM#	Date	Good	VG	Fine	VF
56	AHxxxx	7.50	12.50	20.00	32.50

Obv: Bale mark.

KM#	Date	Good	VG	Fine	VF
3	AH1234	11.50	18.50	30.00	50.00

Obv: Peacock.

KM#	Date	Good	VG	Fine	VF
4	AH1239	9.00	15.00	25.00	40.00

Obv: 2 peacocks facing left and right.

KM#	Date	Good	VG	Fine	VF
57	AH1257	11.50	18.50	30.00	50.00

Obv: Fish.

KM#	Date	Good	VG	Fine	VF
5	AH1221	9.00	15.00	25.00	40.00
	1231	9.00	15.00	25.00	40.00

Ardebil Mint

Obv: Peacock holding snake in beak.

KM#	Date	Good	VG	Fine	VF
6	AH1232	9.00	15.00	25.00	40.00

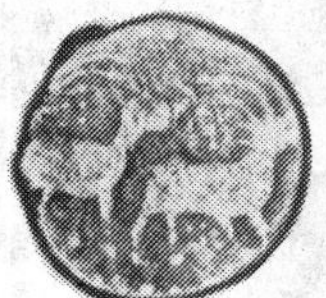
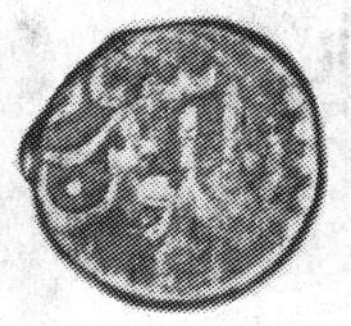

Astarabad Mint

Obv: 2 Ibexes.

KM#	Date	Good	VG	Fine	VF
7	ND	9.00	15.00	25.00	40.00

Obv: Man on horseback.

KM#	Date	Good	VG	Fine	VF
A7	AH1259	9.00	15.00	25.00	40.00

Obv: Sun above lion facing right.

KM#	Date	Good	VG	Fine	VF
58	ND	9.00	15.00	25.00	40.00

Borujerd Mint

Obv: Soldier leaning on his rifle.

KM#	Date	Good	VG	Fine	VF
10	AH124x	11.50	18.50	30.00	50.00
	1261	—	—	—	—

Obv: Small bird.

KM#	Date	Good	VG	Fine	VF
11	ND	9.00	15.00	25.00	40.00

Darband Mint

Obv: Peacock right.

KM#	Date	Good	VG	Fine	VF
59	AH1228	11.50	18.50	30.00	50.00

Ganjeh Mint

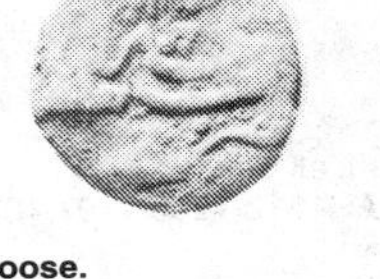

Obv: Goose.

KM#	Date	Good	VG	Fine	VF
15	AH1257	11.50	18.50	30.00	50.00

Obv: Horse.

KM#	Date	Good	VG	Fine	VF
60	AH1220	—	—	—	—

Hamadan Mint

KM#	Date	Good	VG	Fine	VF
18	AH1254	9.00	15.00	25.00	40.00

Eravan Mint

Obv: Camel.

KM#	Date	Good	VG	Fine	VF
19	AH1223	11.50	18.50	30.00	50.00

Isfahan Mint

Obv: Scales.

KM#	Date	Good	VG	Fine	VF
21	AH1242	9.00	15.00	25.00	40.00

Kashan Mint

Obv: Lion and sun in wreath.
Denomination: 50 Dinars

KM#	Date	Good	VG	Fine	VF
24	AH1293	11.50	18.50	30.00	50.00

NOTE: This type was an attempt to reform the copper coinage by Nasir al-Din Shah, and was also struck at Isfahan, Tehran, Tabriz and Shiraz in AH1293 and 1294. Kashan is the rarest mint, Tehran and Isfahan the most plentiful.

Kerman Mint

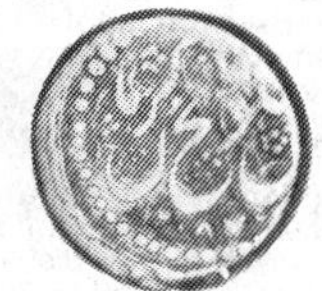

Obv: Lion in wreath.

KM#	Date	Good	VG	Fine	VF
27	AH1287	6.50	11.50	18.50	30.00

Kermanshahan Mint

Obv: Sunface.

KM#	Date	Good	VG	Fine	VF
28	AH1245	6.50	11.50	18.50	30.00

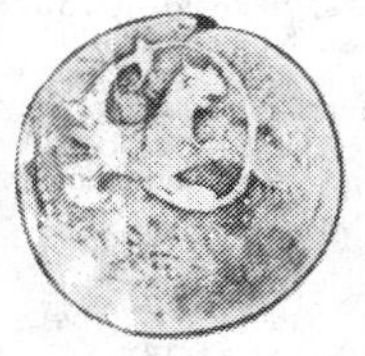
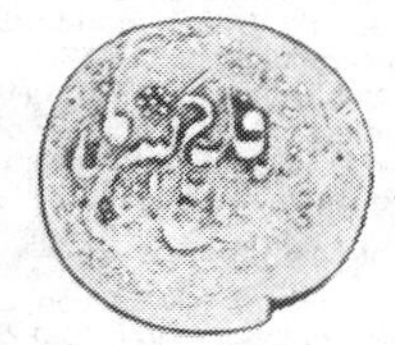

Obv: Lion.

KM#	Date	Good	VG	Fine	VF
29	ND	9.00	15.00	25.00	40.00

Obv: Camel and rider.

KM#	Date	Good	VG	Fine	VF
16	AH1244	11.50	18.50	30.00	50.00

Obv: Horseman riding left. Rev: Lion and sun.

KM#	Date	Good	VG	Fine	VF
62	AH1231	—	—	—	—

Obv: Rider on elephant standing to left, date backwards in field in front and in back of rider. Rev: Legend and mintname.

KM#	Date	Good	VG	Fine	VF
A63	AH1258	15.00	25.00	40.00	65.00

Khoy Mint

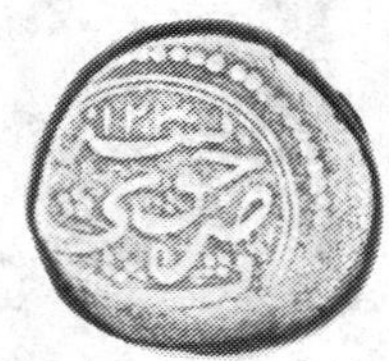

Obv: Gazelle.

KM#	Date	Good	VG	Fine	VF
26	AH1230	9.00	15.00	25.00	40.00

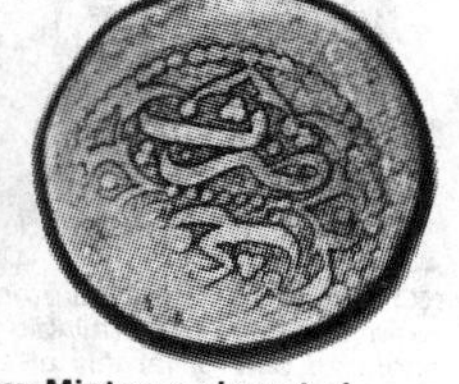

Obv: Peacock (?). Rev: Mintname inverted.

KM#	Date	Good	VG	Fine	VF
B26	AH1241	11.50	18.50	30.00	50.00

Lenjeh - Bandar Lengeh Mint

KM#	Date	Good	VG	Fine	VF
B30	AH1247	27.50	45.00	75.00	125.00
	1259	32.50	55.00	90.00	150.00

Maragheh Mint

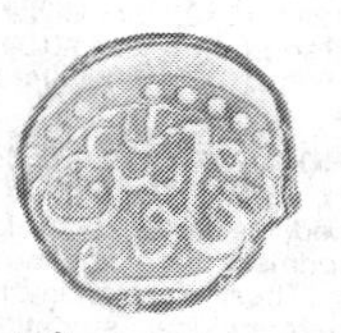

Obv: Peacock.

KM#	Date	Good	VG	Fine	VF
31	AH1270	11.50	18.50	30.00	50.00

Mashhad Mint

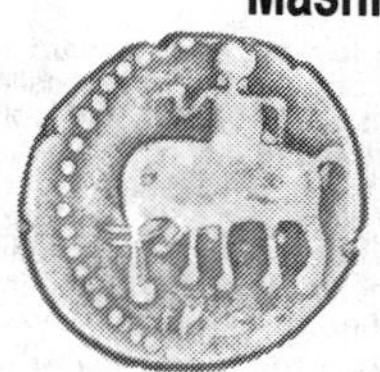

Obv: Elephant and rider.

KM#	Date	Good	VG	Fine	VF
32	AH1246	11.50	18.50	30.00	50.00

Obv: Sunface.

KM#	Date	Good	VG	Fine	VF
63	AH1237	7.50	12.50	20.00	35.00

Obv: Lion and sun.

KM#	Date	Good	VG	Fine	VF
64	AH1258	6.50	11.50	18.50	30.00
	1261	6.50	11.50	18.50	30.00

Nahawand Mint

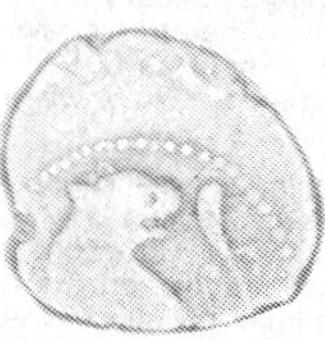

Obv: Lion sitting.

KM#	Date	Good	VG	Fine	VF
34	AH1240	9.00	15.00	25.00	40.00

Qazwin Mint

Obv: Lion and sun.

KM#	Date	Good	VG	Fine	VF
35	ND	7.50	12.50	20.00	35.00

Obv: Lion and sun in wreath.

KM#	Date	Good	VG	Fine	VF
A35	AH129x	7.50	12.50	20.00	35.00

Rasht Mint

Obv: Lion and sun.

KM#	Date	Good	VG	Fine	VF
36	AH1246	7.50	12.50	20.00	35.00

Obv: Lion.

KM#	Date	Good	VG	Fine	VF
37	AH1233	7.50	12.50	20.00	35.00

Obv: Sunface.

KM#	Date	Good	VG	Fine	VF
A37	AH1247	7.50	12.50	20.00	35.00

Sawuj Balagh Mint

Obv: 2 Guinea hens.

KM#	Date	Good	VG	Fine	VF
39	ND	11.50	18.50	30.00	50.00

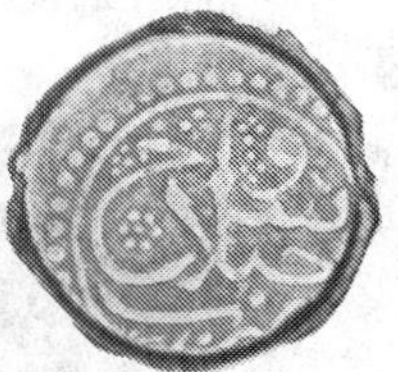

Obv: Lion and sun, stylized.

KM#	Date	Good	VG	Fine	VF
40	AH1230	6.50	11.50	18.50	30.00

Shiraz Mint

Obv: Scales.

KM#	Date	Good	VG	Fine	VF
41	AH126x	7.50	12.50	20.00	35.00

Tabriz Mint

Obv: Lion left and sun.

KM#	Date	Good	VG	Fine	VF
114	AH1224	9.00	15.00	25.00	40.00

Oblique edge milling
Obv: Radiant sunface within wreath.

KM#	Date	Good	VG	Fine	VF
115	AH1229	11.50	18.50	30.00	50.00
(A47)	1230	11.50	18.50	30.00	50.00
	1238	11.50	18.50	30.00	50.00
	1239	11.50	18.50	30.00	50.00
	1240	11.50	18.50	30.00	50.00

Mint: Tabriz
Obv: Lion right and sun.

A116	AH1235	3.50	6.00	10.00	16.50
	1236	3.50	6.00	10.00	16.50

Obv: Lion recumbent left and sun.
Rev: Arabesque border.

116 (45)	AH1235	9.00	15.00	25.00	40.00

Rev: Quatrefoil border.

117 (45)	AH1236	9.00	15.00	25.00	40.00

Obv: Rayed sun within wreath border.
Rev: Ornament, flower above, branches below.

118	AH1239	9.00	15.00	25.00	40.00

NOTE: Varieties exist.

Rev: 2 leaves added.

119	AH124x	9.00	15.00	25.00	40.00

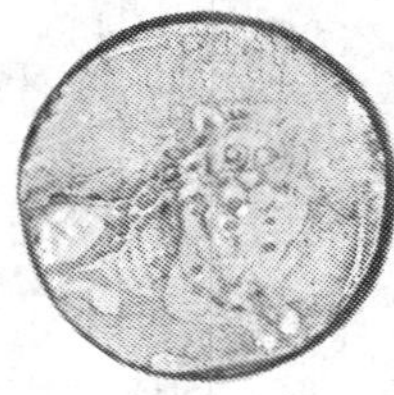

Obv: Lion passant right, facing.

120 (47)	AH1256	9.00	15.00	25.00	40.00

Tehran Mint

Obv: Peacock.

48	AH1222	7.50	12.50	20.00	35.00

Obv: Lion. Rev: "Minted in Iran".

B49	AH1255	5.00	8.00	15.00	25.00

Obv: Russian eagle.

KM#	Date	Good	VG	Fine	VF
49	ND	7.50	12.50	20.00	35.00

Obv: Lion and sun in wreath.

A49	AH1293	4.50	7.50	12.50	20.00

NOTE: Other mints also produced local Falus, for which examples were not available to illustrate. Still other mints operated only or largely at earlier dates. These include Damavand, Damghan, Darabjird, Ja'farafad, Kangan, Ra'nash, Semnan, Tus, Tuy and others.

SILVER AND GOLD COINAGE

The precious metal monetary system of Qajar Persia prior to the reforms of 1878 was the direct descendant of the Mongol system introduced by Ghazan Mahmud in 1297AD, and was the last example of a medieval Islamic coinage. It is not a modern system, and cannot be understood as such. It is not possible to list types, dates, and mints as for other countries, both because of the nature of the coinage, and because very little research has been done on the series. The following comments should help elucidate its nature.

STANDARDS: The weight of the primary silver and gold coins was set by law and was expressed in terms of the Mesqal (about 4.61 g) and the Nokhod (24 Nokhod = 1 Mesqal). The primary silver coin was the Rupee from AH1211-1212, the Riyal from AH1212-1241, and the Gheran from AH1241-1344. The standard gold coin was the Toman. Currently the price of gold is quoted in Mesqals.

DENOMINATIONS: In addition to the primary denominations, noted in the last paragraph, fractional pieces were coined, valued at one-eighth, one-fourth, and one-half the primary denomination, usually in much smaller quantities. These were ordinarily struck from the same dies as the larger pieces, sometimes on broad, thin flans, sometimes on thick, dumpy flans. On the smaller coins, the denomination can best be determined only by weighing the coin. The denomination is almost never expressed on the coin!

DEVALUATIONS: From time to time, the standard for silver and gold was reduced, and the old coin recalled and replaced with lighter coin, the difference going to the government coffers. The effect was that of a devaluation of the primary silver and gold coins, or inversely regarded, an increase in the price of silver and gold. The durations of each standard varied from about 2 to 20 years. The standards are given for each ruler, as the denomination can only be determined when the standard is known.

LIGHTWEIGHT AND ALLOYED PIECES: Most of the smaller denomination coins were issued at lighter weights than those prescribed by law, with the difference going to the pockets of the mintmasters. Other mints, notably Hamadan, added excessive amounts of alloy to the coins, and some mintmasters lost their heads as a result. Discrepancies in weight of as much as 15 percent and more are observed, with the result that it is often quite impossible to determine the denomination of a coin!

OVERSIZE COINS: Occasionally, multiples of the primary denominations were produced, usually on special occasions for presentation by the Shah to his favorites. These 'coins' did not circulate (except as bullion), and were usually worn as ornaments. They were the 'NCLT's' of their day.

MINTS & EPITHETS: Qajar coinage was struck at 34 mints (plus at least a dozen others striking only copper Falus), which are listed previously, with drawings of the mint names in Persian, as they appear on the coins. However, the Persian script admits of infinite variation and stylistic whimsy, so the forms given are only guides, and not absolute. Only a knowledge of the script will assure correct reading. In addition to the city name, most mint names were given identifying epithets, which occasionally appear in lieu of the mint name, particularly at Iravan and Mashhad.

TYPES: There were no types in the modern sense, but the arrangement of the legends and the ornamental borders were frequently changed. These changes do not coincide with changes in standards, and cannot be used to determine the mint, which must be found by actually reading the reverse inscriptions.

ARRANGEMENT

The following listings are arranged first by ruler, with various standards explained. Then, the coins are listed by denomination within each reign. For each denomination, one or more pieces, when available, are illustrated, with the mint and date noted beneath each photo. For each type, a date range is given, but this range indicates the years during which the particular type was current, and does not imply that every year of the interval is known on actual coins. Because dates were carelessly engraved, and old dies were used until they wore out or broke, we occasionally find coins of a particular type dated before or after the indicated interval. Such coins command no premium. No attempt has been made to determine which mints actually exist for which types.

FATH'ALI SHAH

AH1212-1250/1797-1834AD

Fath Ali Khan succeeded his uncle, Agha Muhammad Shah, upon the latter's death on 16 June 1797, striking coins with the nickname Baba Khan. His formal enthronement took place three months later, on 15 or 16 September 1797, at which time he received the name Fath Ali Shah. His coin types are distinguished both by inscription, calligraphy, and weight standard. As the silver and gold weight standards were not altered simultaneously, the type sequences for silver and gold differ. Note: All coins of this and succeeding reigns for hammered coinage bear the mint & date on the reverse, the mint usually with its distinguishing epithet. Only the obverse is noted in the type descriptions.

Coinage Standards of Fath 'Ali Shah

NOTE: Prices for silver coins are for average strikes, with some weakness or unevenness. Poorly struck coins are worth less, well-struck and well-centered coins can be worth from 25-100% more, depending on eye appeal and ornateness of design. Gold coins are generally better struck, but really attractive strikes or fancy designs also command a premium.

NOTE: Coins without legible date are worth about half the price of the cheapest date of the mint & type. Coins without legible mint are of little value. This and the previous note apply to coins of the later rulers Muhammad Shah and Nasir al-Din Shah as well as those of Fath Ali Shah.

Silver Types:

CO (Coronation Type). Obverse, double legend: *Amadeh az Fath-e 'Ali sekke be-zar-e shahi,* "From Fath Ali came the die to the royal precious metals." Standard for the rial (=1250 dinars) was 11.52 g.

A. Obverse, name of ruler with title *al-sultan.* Standard for the rial was 10.36 g.

B. Obverse, name of ruler with the expanded title *al-sultan, ibn al-sulan,* "Sultan, son of the sultan." Plain backgrounds with rather thick calligraphy. Same standard as Type A.

C. Obverse, as Type B, but with floriated backgrounds and finer calligraphy. Same standard as Types A and B.

D. Obverse, as Type C, similar backgrounds & calligraphy, but standard reduced to 9.21 g for the rial.

E. Obverse, new form of the royal protocol, *Fath 'Ali Shah Qajar Khusro-ve Sahebqeran,* "Fath Ali Shah Qajar, Caesar, Sahebqeran (i.e., possessor of an auspicious conjunction)." The rial was abandoned except at Mashhad and replaced by a qiran (kran) of 1000 dinars weighing 6.91 g.

F. Obverse, as Type E but the final portion of the protocol is *Khosro-ve Keshvarsetan,* "World-conquering Caesar." Same standard as type, with which it is contemporary (1246-1250). All Type F silver coins are probably mules with obverse dies intended for the gold.

There are also a number of local types, which have not been assigned type letters and are listed following the regular imperial types.

Gold Types:

R. Same as silver Type CO (Coronation Type). Standard for the toman (=10,000 dinars) is 6.14 g.

S. Inscriptions as Type A (Type S.1) or as Type B (Type S.2) same standard as Type R.

T. Inscriptions as Type B (Type T.1) or as Type C (Type T.2), based on a toman of 5.76 g. (No examples of Type T.2 with mint & date are confirmed at the present time.)

U. Inscriptions as Type C, based on a toman of 5.37 g.

V. Inscriptions as Type C, based on a toman of 4.80 g.

W. Inscriptions as Type C or D, based on a toman of 4.61 g (one mithqal weight).

X. Inscriptions as Type E *(sahebqeran* type), based on a toman of 4.61 g.

Y. Inscriptions as Type F *(keshvarsetan* type), based on a toman of 3.45 g.

Riyal Standard

1/12 RIAL

Type C

SILVER

KM#	Date	Mint	Fine	VF	XF
681	AH1230	Isfahan	40.00	60.00	80.00

Type D

SILVER, 0.86 g

691	AHxxxx	Mazandaran	35.00	50.00	65.00

1/8 RIAL

Type A

SILVER, 1.30 g

KM#	Date	Mint	Fine	VF	XF
669	AH1217	Isfahan	40.00	55.00	75.00

Type B

KM#	Date	Mint	Fine	VF	XF
682	AH1223	Isfahan	17.50	25.00	35.00
(C191b)	1223	Tabriz	25.00	35.00	55.00
	1225	Isfahan	17.50	25.00	35.00
	1226	Isfahan	17.50	25.00	35.00
	1226	Khuy	50.00	65.00	90.00
	1226	Qazvin	30.00	45.00	65.00
	1227	Borujerd	50.00	65.00	90.00
	1227	Iravan	50.00	65.00	90.00
	1227	Isfahan	17.50	25.00	35.00
	1227	Shiraz	30.00	45.00	65.00
	1228	Isfahan	17.50	25.00	35.00

Type D

SILVER, 1.15 g

KM#	Date	Mint	Fine	VF	XF
692	AH1239	Isfahan	30.00	40.00	50.00
(C192c)	1232	Shiraz	20.00	30.00	40.00
	1232	Tabriz	15.00	22.50	30.00
	xxxx	Borujerd	25.00	33.50	42.50

1/5 RIAL

Type A

SILVER, 2.07 g

KM#	Date	Mint	Fine	VF	XF
671	AHxxxx	Yazd	20.00	27.50	35.00

NOTE: Not yet attested with legible date. Such a spe-- cimen would be worth about double the price shown.

Type C

Mint: Yazd

KM#	Date	Mint	Fine	VF	XF
683	AH1224	Isfahan	20.00	27.50	40.00
	1225	Iravan	Reported, not confirmed		
	1225	Yazd	20.00	27.50	40.00
	1228	Isfahan	20.00	27.50	40.00
	1228	Yazd	17.50	25.00	35.00
	1229	Yazd	17.50	25.00	35.00
	1230	Yazd	17.50	25.00	35.00
	1231	Yazd	17.50	25.00	35.00

Type D

SILVER, 1.84 g

KM#	Date	Mint	Fine	VF	XF
693	AH1232	Yazd	17.50	25.00	35.00
(C190)	1233	Yazd	17.50	25.00	35.00
	1234	Yazd	17.50	25.00	35.00
(C189)	1235	Yazd	17.50	25.00	35.00

Type C

Normal hammered strike.

KM#	Date	Mint	Fine	VF	XF
684	AH1224	Kirman	30.00	45.00	60.00
(C192b)	1225	Kirmanshahan	20.00	30.00	45.00
	1228	Tabriz	15.00	22.50	32.50
	1229	Borujerd	30.00	45.00	60.00
	1229	Kirman	30.00	45.00	60.00
	1229	Tabriz	15.00	22.50	32.50
	1231	Mazandaran	25.00	35.00	50.00

Struck on specially prepared flan, milled edge.

KM#	Date	Mint	Fine	VF	XF
685	AH1224	Tabriz	25.00	45.00	70.00
	1225	Tabriz	25.00	45.00	70.00

Type D

SILVER, 2.30 g
Mint: Tabriz

KM#	Date	Mint	Fine	VF	XF
694	AH1232	Iravan	50.00	70.00	95.00

1/3 RIAL

Type C

SILVER, 3.45 g
Struck on rectangular flan.

KM#	Date	Mint	Fine	VF	XF
686	AHxxxx	Isfahan	60.00	75.00	100.00

Type D

SILVER, 3.07 g

KM#	Date	Mint	Fine	VF	XF
695	AH1236	Isfahan	25.00	40.00	60.00

NOTE: Uncertain denomination, may be 2/5 qiran (see KM#701).

1/2 RIAL

Type A

KM#	Date	Mint	Fine	VF	XF
673	AH1216	Kashan	30.00	40.00	55.00
	1217	Rasht	30.00	40.00	55.00
	ND	Lahijan	50.00	70.00	90.00

NOTE: Earlier dates (AH1213-1214) exist for this type.

Type B

KM#	Date	Mint	Fine	VF	XF
677	AH1217	Rasht	25.00	37.50	55.00
(C193a)	1217	Simnan	50.00	75.00	100.00
	1219	Kirmanshahan	30.00	42.50	65.00
	1219	Tabriz	25.00	37.50	55.00
	1219	Tehran	25.00	37.50	55.00
	1220	Isfahan	25.00	37.50	55.00
	1220	Shiraz	25.00	37.50	55.00
	1222	Shiraz	25.00	37.50	55.00
	1222	Urumi	45.00	65.00	85.00

Type C

KM#	Date	Mint	Fine	VF	XF
687	AH1222	Tabriz	17.50	27.50	40.00
	1224	Isfahan	17.50	27.50	40.00
	1224	Tabriz	17.50	27.50	40.00
	1225	Kashan	20.00	30.00	45.00
	1228	Mashhad	22.50	35.00	50.00
	1228	Qazvin	20.00	30.00	45.00
	1229	Qazvin	20.00	30.00	45.00
	1230	Kashan	20.00	30.00	45.00
	1230	Kirmanshahan	20.00	30.00	45.00
	1230	Qazvin	20.00	30.00	45.00

Type D

SILVER, 4.61 g

KM#	Date	Mint	Fine	VF	XF
696	AH1232	Astarabad	25.00	35.00	47.50
(C193c3)					
	1232	Kirmanshahan	15.00	22.50	32.50
	1232	Mazandaran	20.00	30.00	40.00
	1232	Urumi	30.00	40.00	55.00
	1233	Borujerd	25.00	37.50	50.00
	1233	Mazandaran	20.00	30.00	40.00
	1234	Astarabad	25.00	35.00	47.50
	1234	Kirmanshahan	15.00	22.50	32.50
	1235	Kirmanshahan	15.00	22.50	32.50
	1239	Kashan	25.00	35.00	47.50

Type E

KM#	Date	Mint	Fine	VF	XF
711	AH1242	Mashhad	50.00	70.00	90.00

RIAL

SILVER, 11.52 g

Type A

KM#	Date	Mint	Fine	VF	XF
674	AH1216	Astarabad	12.50	20.00	30.00
(C194)	1216	Iravan	25.00	45.00	65.00
	1216	Ishfahan	10.00	15.00	25.00
	1216	Kashan	12.50	20.00	30.00
	1216	Khuy	17.50	27.50	40.00
	1216	Kirman	22.50	35.00	50.00
	1216	Kirmanshahan	15.00	25.00	35.00
	1216	Lahijan	40.00	60.00	90.00
	1216	Mazandaran	12.50	20.00	30.00
	1216	Qazvin	10.00	15.00	25.00
	1216	Rasht	10.00	15.00	25.00
	1216	Shiraz	10.00	15.00	25.00
	1216	Tabriz	10.00	15.00	25.00
	1216	Tehran	10.00	15.00	25.00
	1216	Yazd	10.00	15.00	25.00
	1217	Iravan	25.00	45.00	65.00
	1217	Khuy	17.50	27.50	40.00
	1217	Rasht	12.50	18.50	26.50
	1217	Tabriz	10.00	15.00	25.00
	1218	Tabriz	12.50	20.00	30.00
	1219	Tabriz	12.50	20.00	30.00

NOTE: Earlier dates (AH1213-1215) exist for this type.

Type B

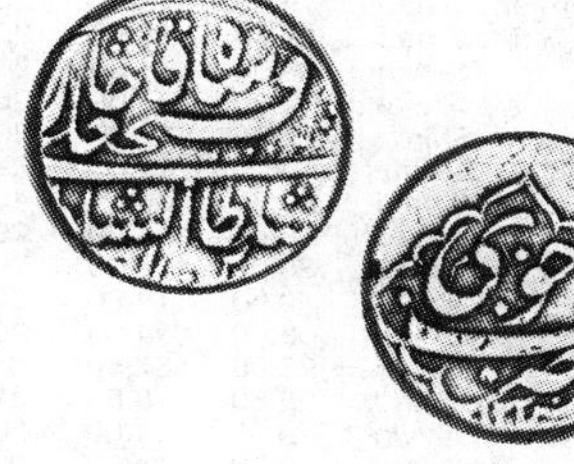

KM#	Date	Mint	Fine	VF	XF
678	AH1217	Isfahan	9.00	14.00	25.00
(C194a)	1217	Khuy	17.50	27.50	40.00
	1217	Qazvin	11.00	16.50	27.50
	1217	Tehran	9.00	14.00	25.00
	1218	Iravan	30.00	45.00	65.00
	1218	Kashan	9.00	14.00	25.00
	1218	Kirmanshahan	9.00	14.00	25.00
	1218	Mashhad	25.00	40.00	60.00
	1218	Mazandaran	12.50	20.00	30.00
	1218	Rasht	9.00	14.00	25.00
	1218, month of Rajab	Rasht	20.00	28.00	40.00
	1218	Shiraz	9.00	14.00	25.00
	1218	Yazd	9.00	14.00	25.00
	1219	Kashan	9.00	14.00	25.00
	1219	Khuy	17.50	27.50	40.00
	1219	Kirmanshahan	9.00	14.00	25.00
	1219	Lahijan	35.00	55.00	85.00
	1219	Rasht	9.00	14.00	25.00
	1219	Tabriz	10.00	15.00	25.00
	1219	Yazd	9.00	14.00	25.00
	1220	Kashan	9.00	14.00	25.00
	1220	Khuy	17.50	27.50	40.00
	1220	Kirmanshahan	9.00	14.00	25.00
	1220	Mashhad	13.50	20.00	30.00
	1220	Rasht	9.00	14.00	25.00
	1220	Shiraz	9.00	14.00	25.00
	1220	Tabriz	9.00	14.00	25.00
	1220	Yazd	9.00	14.00	25.00
	1221	Kashan	9.00	14.00	25.00
	1221	Kirman	25.00	35.00	55.00
	1221	Kirmanshahan	9.00	14.00	25.00
	1221	Rasht	9.00	14.00	25.00
	1221	Tabriz	9.00	14.00	25.00
	1221	Urumi	20.00	30.00	45.00
	1221	Yazd	9.00	14.00	25.00
	1222	Isfahan	11.50	16.50	27.50
	1222	Lahijan	40.00	60.00	90.00
	1222	Mashhad	13.50	20.00	30.00
	1222	Rasht	9.00	14.00	25.00
	1222	Tabriz	9.00	14.00	25.00
	1222	Urumi	20.00	30.00	45.00
	1222	Yazd	9.00	14.00	25.00

Type C

KM#	Date	Mint	Fine	VF	XF
688	AH1222	Kashan	9.00	14.00	20.00
(C194b)	1222	Kirman	20.00	30.00	45.00
	1222	Kirmanshahan	9.00	14.00	20.00
	1222	Qazvin	9.00	14.00	20.00
	1222	Rasht	9.00	14.00	20.00
	1222	Shiraz	9.00	14.00	20.00
	1222	Tabriz	10.00	15.00	22.50
	1222	Tehran	9.00	14.00	20.00
	1222	Yazd	10.00	15.00	22.50
	1223	Astarabad	17.50	26.00	37.50
	1223	Iravan	30.00	45.00	70.00
	1223	Isfahan	9.00	14.00	20.00
	1223	Kashan	9.00	14.00	20.00
	1223	Mashhad	12.50	18.50	27.50
	1223	Qazvin	9.00	14.00	20.00
	1223	Rasht	9.00	14.00	20.00
	1223	Shiraz	9.00	14.00	20.00
	1223	Tabriz	10.00	15.00	22.50
	1223	Urumi	20.00	30.00	45.00
	1224	Isfahan	9.00	14.00	20.00
	1224	Kashan	9.00	14.00	20.00
	1224	Khuy	16.50	25.00	40.00
	1224	Kirman	20.00	30.00	45.00
	1224	Kirmanshahan	9.00	14.00	20.00
	1224	Lahijan	40.00	65.00	100.00
	1224	Mashhad	12.50	18.50	27.50
	1224	Qazvin	9.00	14.00	20.00
	1224	Rasht	9.00	14.00	20.00
	1224	Tabriz	10.00	15.00	22.50
	1224	Tehran	9.00	14.00	20.00
	1224	Urumi	20.00	30.00	45.00
	1224	Yazd	9.00	14.00	20.00
	1225	Astarabad	17.50	26.00	37.50
	1225	Iravan	30.00	45.00	70.00
	1225	Isfahan	9.00	14.00	20.00
	1225	Kashan	9.00	14.00	20.00
	1225	Khuy	16.50	25.00	40.00
	1225	Kirmanshahan	9.00	14.00	20.00
	1225	Mashhad	12.50	18.50	27.50
	1225	Qazvin	9.00	14.00	20.00
	1225	Rasht	9.00	14.00	20.00
	1225	Shiraz	9.00	14.00	20.00
	1225	Tabriz	10.00	15.00	22.50
	1225	Urumi	20.00	30.00	45.00
	1225	Yazd	9.00	14.00	20.00
	1226	Iravan	30.00	45.00	70.00
	1226	Isfahan	9.00	14.00	20.00
	1226	Kashan	9.00	14.00	20.00
	1226	Kirman	25.00	37.50	55.00
	1226	Mashhad	12.50	18.50	27.50
	1226	Qazvin	9.00	14.00	20.00
	1226	Rasht	9.00	14.00	20.00
	1226	Shiraz	9.00	14.00	20.00
	1226	Tabriz	10.00	15.00	22.50
	1226	Tehran	10.00	15.00	22.50
	1226	Zanjan	25.00	37.50	55.00
	1227	Isfahan	9.00	14.00	20.00
	1227	Kashan	9.00	14.00	20.00
	1227	Khuy	16.50	25.00	40.00
	1227	Kirman	25.00	37.50	55.00
	1227	Kirmanshahan	9.00	14.00	20.00
	1227	Mashhad	12.50	18.50	27.50
	1227	Mazandaran	11.50	17.50	25.00
	1227	Qazvin	9.00	14.00	20.00
	1227	Rasht	9.00	14.00	20.00
	1227	Shiraz	9.00	14.00	20.00
	1228	Kashan	9.00	14.00	20.00
	1228	Kirmanshahan	9.00	14.00	20.00
	1228	Mashhad	12.50	18.50	27.50
	1228	Mazandaran	12.50	18.50	27.50
	1228	Qazvin	9.00	14.00	20.00
	1228	Rasht	9.00	14.00	20.00
	1228	Shiraz	9.00	14.00	20.00
	1228	Tabriz	9.00	14.00	20.00
	1228	Urumi	20.00	30.00	45.00
	1228	Zanjan	25.00	37.50	55.00
	1229	Kashan	9.00	14.00	20.00
	1229	Khuy	16.50	25.00	40.00
	1229	Mashhad	12.50	18.50	27.50
	1229	Mazandaran	11.50	16.50	25.00
	1229	Qazvin	9.00	14.00	20.00
	1229	Shiraz	9.00	14.00	20.00
	1229	Tehran	10.00	15.00	22.50
	1229	Urumi	20.00	30.00	45.00
	1229	Zanjan	25.00	37.50	55.00
	1230	Astarabad	15.00	22.50	35.00
	1230	Khuy	16.50	25.00	40.00
	1230	Mashhad	12.50	18.50	27.50
	1230	Rasht	9.00	14.00	20.00
	1230	Yazd	11.50	16.50	25.00
	1231	Khuy	16.50	25.00	40.00
	1231	Mashhad	14.00	20.00	30.00
	1231	Tehran	11.50	16.50	25.00
	1231	Yazd	11.50	16.50	25.00
	1232	Yazd	12.50	18.50	30.00

NOTE: Coins of AH1232 of types C and D can only be distinguished by weight.

Special strike on full even flan, milled edge.

KM#	Date	Mint	Fine	VF	XF
689	AH1221(sic)	Tabriz	65.00	100.00	175.00
	1222	Tabriz	65.00	100.00	175.00
	Common date, holed		—	—	45.00	75.00

Type D

SILVER, 9.21 g

KM#	Date	Mint	Fine	VF	XF
697	AH1232	Astarabad	8.00	12.50	18.50
(C194c)	1232	Borujerd	20.00	32.50	45.00
	1232	Isfahan	8.00	12.50	18.50
	1232	Kashan	8.00	12.50	18.50
	1232	Kirmanshahan	8.00	12.50	18.50
	1232	Mashhad	10.00	16.50	25.00
	1232	Mazandaran	8.00	12.50	18.50
	1232	Qazvin	8.00	12.50	18.50
	1232	Rasht	8.00	12.50	18.50
	1232	Shiraz	8.00	12.50	18.50
	1232	Tabriz	8.00	12.50	18.50
	1232	Tehran	8.00	12.50	18.50
	1232	Yazd	8.00	12.50	18.50
	1232	Zanjan	20.00	32.50	45.00
	1233	Ardabil	50.00	75.00	100.00
	1233	Borujerd	20.00	32.50	45.00
	1233	Isfahan	8.00	12.50	18.50
	1233	Kashan	8.00	12.50	18.50
	1233	Khuy	15.00	22.50	32.50
	1233	Kirmanshahan	8.00	12.50	18.50
	1233	Mashhad	10.00	16.50	25.00
	1233	Mazandaran	8.00	12.50	18.50
	1233	Qazvin	8.00	12.50	18.50
	1233	Rasht	8.00	12.50	18.50
	1233	Shiraz	8.00	12.50	18.50
	1233	Shushtar	40.00	60.00	80.00
	1233	Tabriz	8.00	12.50	18.50
	1233	Tehran	8.00	12.50	18.50
	1233	Urumi	25.00	35.00	55.00
	1233	Yazd	8.00	12.50	18.50
	1233	Zanjan	20.00	32.50	45.00
	1234	Arz-e Aqdas (=Mashhad)	15.00	22.50	32.50
	1234	Borujerd	20.00	32.50	45.00
	1234	Isfahan	9.00	14.00	20.00
	1234	Kashan	9.00	14.00	20.00
	1234	Khuy	15.00	22.50	32.50
	1234	Kirmanshahan	9.00	14.00	20.00
	1234	Qazvin	10.00	16.00	22.50
	1234	Rasht	9.00	14.00	20.00
	1234	Shiraz	9.00	14.00	20.00
	1234	Tehran	10.00	16.00	22.50
	1234	Zanjan	20.00	32.50	45.00
	1235	Ardabil	50.00	75.00	100.00
	1235	Arz-e Aqdas (=Mashhad)	17.50	25.00	37.50
	1235	Astarabad	14.00	20.00	30.00
	1235	Khuy	15.00	22.50	32.50
	1235	Kirmanshahan	9.00	14.00	20.00
	1235	Qazvin	9.00	14.00	20.00
	1236	Astarabad	14.00	20.00	30.00
	1236	Isfahan	10.00	16.00	22.50
	1236	Kashan	10.00	16.00	22.50
	1236	Kirmanshahan	9.00	14.00	20.00
	1236	Qazvin	10.00	16.00	22.50
	1236	Shiraz	10.00	16.00	22.50
	1236	Tabaristan	30.00	40.00	55.00
	1237	Iravan	60.00	85.00	115.00
	1237	Mashhad	20.00	32.50	40.00
	1238	Astarabad	14.00	20.00	30.00
	1238	Isdfahan	10.00	16.00	22.50
	1238	Kashan	10.00	16.00	22.50
	1238	Khuy	16.50	25.00	35.00
	1238	Kirmanshahan	9.00	14.00	20.00
	1238	Tabaristan	14.00	20.00	30.00
	1238	Tabriz	10.00	16.00	22.50
	1238	Tehran	10.00	16.00	22.50
	1238	Yazd	10.00	16.00	22.50
	1239	Isfahan	10.00	16.00	22.50
	1239	Khuy	20.00	30.00	45.00
	1239	Kirmanshahan	10.00	16.00	22.50
	1239	Mashhad	14.00	20.00	30.00
	1239	Qazvin	10.00	16.00	22.50
	1239	Rasht	10.00	16.00	22.50
	1239	Tabriz	10.00	16.00	22.50
	1239	Tehran	10.00	16.00	22.50
	1239	Yazd	10.00	16.00	22.50
	1240	Khuy	20.00	30.00	45.00
	1240	Kirmanshahan	14.00	20.00	30.00
	1240	Rasht	10.00	16.00	22.50
	1240	Tabaristan	14.00	20.00	30.00
	1240	Tabriz	14.00	20.00	30.00
	1241	Mashhad	20.00	30.00	45.00

Special strike on full even flan, milled edge.

KM#	Date	Mint	Fine	VF	XF
698	AH1238	Tabriz	100.00	135.00	185.00

Type E

KM#	Date	Mint	Fine	VF	XF
712	AH1242	Mashhad	25.00	35.00	50.00
	1243	Mashhad	25.00	35.00	50.00
	1244	Mashhad	25.00	35.00	50.00
	1246	Mashhad	25.00	35.00	50.00

2 RIALS

Type C

SILVER, 20.72 g

KM#	Date	Mint	Fine	VF	XF
690	AH1226	Tabriz	125.00	175.00	250.00

Type D

SILVER, 18.42 g

KM#	Date	Mint	Fine	VF	XF
699	AH1234	Zanjan	—	Rare	—

3 RIALS

Kran Standard

1/8 KRAN

Type E

SILVER, 0.86 g

KM#	Date	Mint	Fine	VF	XF
705 (C200)	AH1243	Khuy	35.00	50.00	70.00

1/4 KRAN

Type D

SILVER, 1.72 g

KM#	Date	Mint	Fine	VF	XF
700	AH1236	Tehran	25.00	35.00	45.00
	1237	Tabriz	22.50	30.00	40.00
	1238	Tabriz	22.50	30.00	40.00

Type E

KM#	Date	Mint	Fine	VF	XF
706	AH1242	Tabriz	20.00	30.00	40.00

Special Type

Obv: Shah seated on throne.

KM#	Date	Mint	Fine	VF	XF
719	AH1247	Isfahan	100.00	150.00	200.00

2/5 KRAN

Type D

SILVER, 2.76 g

KM#	Date	Mint	Fine	VF	XF
701 (C193c.2)	AH1245	Kirmanshahan	25.00	35.00	45.00
	1246	Kirmanshahan	25.00	35.00	45.00
	1249	Kirman	25.00	35.00	45.00

NOTE: All 2/5 Kran coins were struck during the Type E period, but with obverse dies with Type D inscriptions (probably old dies).

Type E

KM#	Date	Mint	Fine	VF	XF
707	AH1242	Kirman	25.00	35.00	45.00
	1244	Kirman	25.00	35.00	45.00

Type F

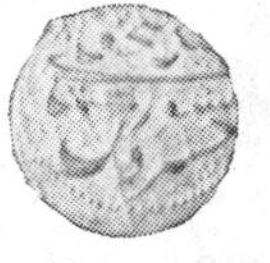

KM#	Date	Mint	Fine	VF	XF
716	AH1247	Kirman	30.00	40.00	55.00
	1250	Kirman	30.00	40.00	55.00

1/2 KRAN

Type D

SILVER, 3.45 g

KM#	Date	Mint	Fine	VF	XF
702	AH1237	Qazvin	25.00	35.00	45.00
	1237	Tehran	20.00	30.00	40.00
	1238	Kirman	30.00	40.00	55.00
	1238	Shiraz	12.50	18.50	27.50
	1238	Tehran	20.00	30.00	40.00
	1239	Shiraz	12.50	18.50	27.50
	1240	Tehran	20.00	30.00	40.00
	1245	Isfahan	15.00	22.50	32.50
	1246	Isfahan	15.00	22.50	32.50

NOTE: Dates after AH1240 are presumed struck with old obverse dies.

Type E

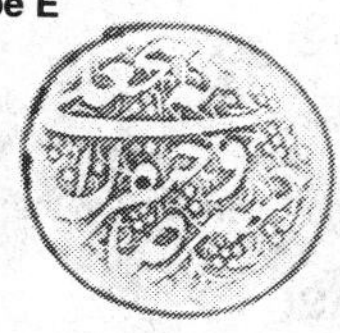

Mint: Kashan

KM#	Date	Mint	Fine	VF	XF
709 (C202)	AH1241	Hamadan	20.00	30.00	40.00
	1241	Kashan	18.50	27.50	37.50
	1241	Qumm	50.00	70.00	100.00
	1241	Rasht	17.50	25.00	35.00
	1241	Tabaristan	20.00	30.00	40.00
	1243	Kashan	18.50	27.50	37.50
	1244	Rasht	18.50	27.50	37.50
	1246	Astarabad	30.00	42.50	55.00
	1246	Shiraz	10.00	16.50	25.00
	1247	Shiraz	10.00	16.50	25.00
	1248	Mashhad	20.00	30.00	40.00
	1248	Shiraz	10.00	16.50	25.00
	1249	Shiraz	10.00	16.50	25.00

KRAN

Type E

SILVER, 6.91 g

KM#	Date	Mint	Fine	VF	XF
710 (C203)	AH1235	Rasht	25.00	35.00	47.50
	1240	Ardabil	40.00	60.00	85.00
	1240	Hamadan	15.00	22.50	32.50
	1240	Kashan	15.00	22.50	32.50
	1240	Rasht	12.50	18.50	27.50
	1241	Astarabad	10.00	16.00	25.00
	1241	Borujerd	15.00	22.50	30.00
	1241	Hamadan	8.00	12.50	18.50
	1241	Iravan	35.00	50.00	75.00
	1241	Isfahan	8.00	12.50	18.50
	1241	Kashan	8.00	12.50	18.50
	1241	Khuy	10.00	16.00	25.00
	1241	Kirman	25.00	37.50	55.00
	1241	Kirmanshahan	8.00	12.50	18.50
	1241	Qazvin	8.00	12.50	18.50
	1241	Qumm	25.00	37.50	55.00
	1241	Rasht	8.00	12.50	18.50
	1241	Rikab	25.00	37.50	55.00
	1241	Shiraz	8.00	12.50	18.50
	1241	Tabaristan	10.00	16.00	25.00
	1241	Tabriz	8.00	12.50	18.50
	1241	Tehran	8.00	12.50	18.50
	1241	Tuyserkan	30.00	45.00	65.00
	1241	Urumi	25.00	37.50	55.00
	1241	Yazd	8.00	12.50	18.50
	1241	Zanjan	16.50	25.00	35.00
	1242	Astarabad	10.00	16.00	25.00
	1242	Borujerd	15.00	22.50	30.00
	1242	Hamadan	8.00	12.50	18.50
	1242	Isfahan	8.00	12.50	18.50
	1242	Kashan	8.00	12.50	18.50
	1242	Khuy	10.00	16.00	25.00
	1242	Kirmanshahan	8.00	12.50	18.50
	1242	Nihavand	50.00	75.00	100.00
	1242	Qazvin	8.00	12.50	18.50
	1242	Qumm	25.00	37.50	55.00
	1242	Rasht	8.00	12.50	18.50
	1242	Rikab	25.00	37.50	55.00
	1242	Shiraz	8.00	12.50	18.50
	1242	Simnan	40.00	60.00	85.00
	1242	Tabaristan	10.00	16.00	25.00
	1242	Tabriz	8.00	12.50	18.50
	1242	Tehran	8.00	12.50	18.50
	1242	Tuyserkan	30.00	45.00	65.00
	1242	Yazd	8.00	12.50	18.50
	1242	Zanjan	16.50	25.00	35.00
	1243	Ardabil	40.00	60.00	85.00
	1243	Borujerd	15.00	22.50	30.00
	1243	Hamadan	8.00	12.50	18.50
	1243	Isfahan	8.00	12.50	18.50
	1243	Khuy	10.00	16.00	25.00
	1243	Kirmanshahan	8.00	12.50	18.50
	1243	Qazvin	8.00	12.50	18.50
	1243	Qumm	25.00	37.50	55.00
	1243	Rasht	8.00	12.50	18.50
	1243	Shiraz	8.00	12.50	18.50
	1243	Shushtar	40.00	55.00	75.00

KM#	Date	Mint	Fine	VF	XF
(C203)	1243	Tabaristan	10.00	16.00	25.00
	1243	Tehran	8.00	12.50	18.50
	1243	Tuyserkan	30.00	45.00	65.00
	1243	Yazd	8.00	12.50	18.50
	1243	Zanjan	16.50	25.00	35.00
	1244	Ardabil	40.00	60.00	85.00
	1244	Astarabad	10.00	16.00	25.00
	1244	Borujerd	15.00	22.50	30.00
	1244	Hamadan	8.00	12.50	18.50
	1244	Isfahan	8.00	12.50	18.50
	1244	Kirmanshahan	8.00	12.50	18.50
	1244	Qazvin	8.00	12.50	18.50
	1244	Qumm	25.00	37.50	55.00
	1244	Rasht	8.00	12.50	18.50
	1244	Shiraz	8.00	12.50	18.50
	1244	Tabaristan	10.00	16.00	25.00
	1244	Tehran	8.00	12.50	18.50
	1244	Yazd	8.00	12.50	18.50
	1244	Zanjan	16.50	25.00	35.00
	1245	Ardabil	40.00	60.00	85.00
	1245	Astarabad	10.00	16.00	25.00
	1245	Borujerd	15.00	22.50	30.00
	1245	Hamadan	9.00	13.50	20.00
	1245	Isfahan	9.00	13.50	20.00
	1245	Kirman	25.00	37.50	55.00
	1245	Qazvin	9.00	13.50	20.00
	1245	Rasht	8.00	12.50	18.50
	1245	Shiraz	9.00	13.50	20.00
	1245	Simnan	40.00	60.00	85.00
	1245	Tabriz	12.50	18.50	27.50
	1245	Yazd	9.00	13.50	20.00
(C203a)	1246	Astarabad	9.00	13.50	20.00
	1246	Borujerd	15.00	22.50	30.00
	1246	Hamadan	9.00	13.50	20.00
	1246	Isfahan	10.00	16.00	25.00
	1246	Khuy	15.00	22.50	30.00
	1246	Kirmanshahan	9.00	13.50	20.00
	1246	Qazvin	11.50	17.50	25.00
	1246	Qumm	25.00	37.50	55.00
	1246	Rasht	9.00	13.50	20.00
	1246	Shiraz	10.00	16.00	25.00
	1246	Simnan	40.00	60.00	85.00
	1246	Tabaristan	12.50	18.50	27.50
	1246	Tabriz	12.50	18.50	27.50
	1246	Tehran	9.00	13.50	20.00
	1246	Zanjan	20.00	30.00	42.50
	1247	Borujerd	15.00	22.50	30.00
	1247	Hamadan	9.00	13.50	20.00
	1247	Isfahan	10.00	16.00	25.00
	1247	Kirmanshahan	10.00	16.00	25.00
	1247	Mashhad	12.50	18.50	27.50
	1247	Qumm	25.00	37.50	55.00
	1247	Yazd	10.00	16.00	25.00
	1248	Borujerd	15.00	22.50	30.00
	1248	Hamadan	9.00	13.50	20.00
	1248	Isfahan	10.00	16.00	25.00
	1248	Kirmanshahan	10.00	16.00	25.00
	1248	Mashhad	12.50	18.50	27.50
	1248	Nihavand	50.00	75.00	100.00
	1248	Qumm	25.00	37.50	55.00
	1248	Tehran	15.00	24.00	32.50
	1248	Yazd	10.00	16.00	25.00
	1249	Isfahan	12.50	20.00	30.00
	1249	Khuy	20.00	30.00	45.00
	1249	Mashhad	12.50	20.00	30.00
	1250	Hamadan	20.00	30.00	45.00
	1250	Mashhad	20.00	30.00	45.00
	1250	Yazd	20.00	30.00	45.00

Type F

KM#	Date	Mint	Fine	VF	XF
717	AH1246	Tabaristan	40.00	55.00	75.00

1/4 TOMAN

Type V

GOLD, 1.20 g

KM#	Date	Mint	Fine	VF	XF
747	AH1228	Isfahan	150.00	200.00	260.00

Type W

GOLD, 1.15 g

KM#	Date	Mint	Fine	VF	XF
751	AH1234	Isfahan	150.00	180.00	225.00
	1236	Borujerd	125.00	160.00	200.00

1/2 TOMAN

Type T

GOLD, 2.88 g

KM#	Date	Mint	Fine	VF	XF
740	AH1220	Tabriz	200.00	275.00	350.00

Type U

GOLD, 2.68 g

KM#	Date	Mint	Fine	VF	XF
744	AH1224	Tabriz	175.00	240.00	300.00

Type V

GOLD, 2.40 g

KM#	Date	Mint	Fine	VF	XF
748	AH1228	Tabriz	150.00	200.00	250.00

Type W

GOLD, 2.30 g
Mint: Tabriz

KM#	Date	Mint	Fine	VF	XF
752 (C205d.1)	AH1233	Kirmanshahan	120.00	145.00	180.00
	1238	Tabriz	120.00	145.00	180.00

Type X

KM#	Date	Mint	Fine	VF	XF
756	AH1242	Tabriz	120.00	145.00	180.00

TOMAN

Type S

KM#	Date	Mint	Fine	VF	XF
739 (C206.2)	AH1216	Tehran	175.00	225.00	275.00
	1217	Isfahan	200.00	250.00	325.00
	1219	Yazd	200.00	250.00	325.00
	xxxx	Qazvin	150.00	185.00	225.00

NOTE: Earlier dates (AH1213-1215) exist for this type.

Type T

GOLD, 5.76 g

KM#	Date	Mint	Fine	VF	XF
741	AH1221	Yazd	200.00	275.00	350.00

NOTE: Only coins with Type B calligraphy are confirmed for Type T.

Type U

GOLD, 5.37 g

KM#	Date	Mint	Fine	VF	XF
745	AH1224	Tabriz	125.00	160.00	225.00
	1224	Tehran	125.00	160.00	225.00
	1225	Astarabad	135.00	175.00	250.00
	1225	Isfahan	125.00	160.00	225.00
	1225	Yazd	125.00	160.00	225.00

Type V

GOLD, 4.80 g

KM#	Date	Mint	Fine	VF	XF
749 (C206c)	AH1227	Kashan	100.00	125.00	175.00
	1228	Isfahan	90.00	110.00	150.00
	1228	Kashan	100.00	125.00	175.00
	1228	Mazandaran	100.00	125.00	175.00
	1228	Shiraz	90.00	110.00	150.00
	1228	Tehran	90.00	110.00	150.00
	1228	Yazd	100.00	125.00	175.00
	1229	Isfahan	110.00	140.00	200.00
	1229	Shiraz	110.00	140.00	200.00
	1229	Tehran	110.00	140.00	200.00
	1230	Yazd	110.00	140.00	200.00
	1231	Kashan	110.00	140.00	200.00
	1231	Rasht	110.00	140.00	200.00
	1231	Yazd	110.00	140.00	200.00
	1232	Mashhad	125.00	150.00	200.00
	1234(sic)	Tehran	125.00	150.00	200.00

Type W

GOLD, 4.61 g

KM#	Date	Mint	Fine	VF	XF
753 (C206d.2)	AH1230	Rasht	100.00	125.00	165.00
	1231	Qazvin	80.00	100.00	130.00
	1231	Rasht	80.00	100.00	130.00
	1231	Yazd	80.00	100.00	130.00
	1232	Isfahan	80.00	100.00	130.00
	1232	Kashan	80.00	100.00	130.00
	1232	Khuy	130.00	175.00	225.00
	1232	Qazvin	80.00	100.00	130.00
	1232	Rasht	80.00	100.00	130.00
	1232	Shiraz	80.00	100.00	130.00
	1232	Tehran	80.00	100.00	130.00
	1232	Yazd	70.00	90.00	120.00
	1233	Borujerd	140.00	180.00	225.00
	1233	Iravan	140.00	180.00	225.00

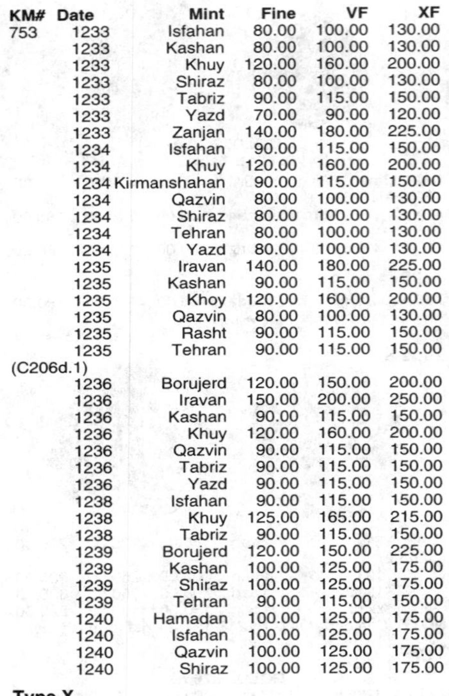

KM#	Date	Mint	Fine	VF	XF
753	1233	Isfahan	80.00	100.00	130.00
	1233	Kashan	80.00	100.00	130.00
	1233	Khuy	120.00	160.00	200.00
	1233	Shiraz	80.00	100.00	130.00
	1233	Tabriz	90.00	115.00	150.00
	1233	Yazd	70.00	90.00	120.00
	1233	Zanjan	140.00	180.00	225.00
	1234	Isfahan	90.00	115.00	150.00
	1234	Khuy	120.00	160.00	200.00
	1234	Kirmanshahan	90.00	115.00	150.00
	1234	Qazvin	80.00	100.00	130.00
	1234	Shiraz	80.00	100.00	130.00
	1234	Tehran	80.00	100.00	130.00
	1234	Yazd	80.00	100.00	130.00
	1235	Iravan	140.00	180.00	225.00
	1235	Kashan	90.00	115.00	150.00
	1235	Khoy	120.00	160.00	200.00
	1235	Qazvin	80.00	100.00	130.00
	1235	Rasht	90.00	115.00	150.00
	1235	Tehran	90.00	115.00	150.00
(C206d.1)					
	1236	Borujerd	120.00	150.00	200.00
	1236	Iravan	150.00	200.00	250.00
	1236	Kashan	90.00	115.00	150.00
	1236	Khuy	120.00	160.00	200.00
	1236	Qazvin	90.00	115.00	150.00
	1236	Tabriz	90.00	115.00	150.00
	1236	Yazd	90.00	115.00	150.00
	1238	Isfahan	90.00	115.00	150.00
	1238	Khuy	125.00	165.00	215.00
	1238	Tabriz	90.00	115.00	150.00
	1239	Borujerd	120.00	150.00	225.00
	1239	Kashan	100.00	125.00	175.00
	1239	Shiraz	100.00	125.00	175.00
	1239	Tehran	90.00	115.00	150.00
	1240	Hamadan	100.00	125.00	175.00
	1240	Isfahan	100.00	125.00	175.00
	1240	Qazvin	100.00	125.00	175.00
	1240	Shiraz	100.00	125.00	175.00

Type X

Obv: ***Sahebqeran.***

KM#	Date	Mint	Fine	VF	XF
757	AH1241	Kirmanshahan	100.00	125.00	175.00
	1241	Urumi	125.00	175.00	250.00
	1242	Hamadan	100.00	125.00	175.00
	1242	Isfahan	100.00	125.00	175.00
	1242	Tabriz	100.00	125.00	175.00
	1242	Tehran	100.00	125.00	175.00
	1243	Rasht	100.00	125.00	175.00
	1243	Tabriz	100.00	125.00	175.00
	1244	Tabriz	100.00	125.00	175.00

Type Y

GOLD, 3.45 g
Obv: ***Keshvarsetan.***

KM#	Date	Mint	Fine	VF	XF
759	AH1246	Ardabil	250.00	300.00	375.00
(C206e)	1246	Hamadan	100.00	125.00	175.00
	1246	Kashan	100.00	125.00	175.00
	1246	Khuy	100.00	125.00	175.00
	1246	Kirmanshahan	100.00	125.00	175.00
	1246	Qazvin	100.00	125.00	175.00
	1246	Rasht	90.00	115.00	160.00
	1246	Simnan	250.00	300.00	375.00
	1246	Tabriz	90.00	115.00	160.00
	1248	Hamadan	90.00	115.00	160.00
	1248	Kirman	150.00	215.00	275.00
	1248	Kirmanshahan	100.00	125.00	175.00
	1248	Qazvin	100.00	125.00	175.00
	1248	Shiraz	100.00	125.00	175.00
	1248	Tehran	100.00	125.00	175.00
	1249	Hamadan	90.00	115.00	160.00
	1249	Isfahan	100.00	125.00	175.00
	1249	Kirman	150.00	215.00	275.00
	1249	Qazvin	100.00	125.00	175.00
	1249	Rasht	100.00	125.00	175.00
	1249	Shiraz	100.00	125.00	175.00
	1249	Tehran	100.00	125.00	175.00
	1250	Hamadan	100.00	125.00	175.00
	1250	Rasht	100.00	125.00	175.00

Special Types

GOLD, 4.61 g
Obv: Shah on horseback.

KM#	Date	Mint	Fine	VF	XF
761	AH1236	Zanjan	—	1250.	2000.
(C207)					

GOLD, 3.45 g
Obv: Shah seated on throne, facing right.
Rev: Mint & date in central circle.

KM#	Date	Mint	Fine	VF	XF
763	AH1245	Isfahan	—	1100.	1600.
(C208.1)					

Obv: Shah seated on throne, facing left.
Rev: Mint & date in central square.

KM#	Date	Mint	Fine	VF	XF
764	AH1245	Isfahan	—	1100.	1600.
(C208.2)					

Rev: Mint & date in 8-pointed star.

KM#	Date	Mint	Fine	VF	XF
765	AH1248/1250	Isfahan	—	1000.	1400.
(C208.3)					

NOTE: All known pieces are dated 1248 on obverse, 1250 on reverse.

Rev: Mint & date in elongated lozenge.

KM#	Date	Mint	Fine	VF	XF
766	AH1249	Isfahan	—	1000.	1600.
(C208.4)					

3 TOMANS

Type W

GOLD, 13.82 g

KM#	Date	Mint	Fine	VF	XF
754	AH1233	Kirmanshahan	—	—	4000.

Special Type

Obv: Shah on horseback.

KM#	Date	Mint	Fine	VF	XF
762	AH1239	Zanjan	—	Rare	—

5 TOMANS

Type T

GOLD, 28.80 g

KM#	Date	Mint	Fine	VF	XF
742	AH1221	Tehran	—	Rare	—

Type U

GOLD, 26.85 g

KM#	Date	Mint	Fine	VF	XF
746	AH1226	Tabriz	—	—	5000.
	1227	Tabriz	—	—	5000.
	1227	Tehran	—	—	5000.

LOCAL COINAGES

Issues of the Khanate of Ganja in the name of Fath Ali Shah. The names of the denominations are tentative.

1/2 ABBASI

SILVER, 1.5 g
Rectangular flan.

KM#	Date	Mint	Fine	VF	XF
722	AH1216	Ganja	—	Rare	—

ABBASI

SILVER, 3 g
Round flan.

KM#	Date	Mint	Fine	VF	XF
723	AH1217	Ganja	—	Rare	—

Issues of Ibrahim Khalil Khan of Karabakh in the name of Fath Ali Shah.

ABBASI

SILVER, about 4.5 g

KM#	Date	Mint	Fine	VF	XF
728	AH1216	Panahabad	50.00	75.00	120.00

NOTE: Generally found holed or looped.
NOTE: Earlier date (AH1214) exists for this type.

Issues of the Khanate of Sheki in the name of Fath Ali Shah.

ABBASI

SILVER, about 1.8 g

KM#	Date	Mint	Fine	VF	XF
726	AH1241	Sheki	50.00	75.00	100.00
	1242	Sheki	50.00	75.00	100.00

COUNTERMARKED COINAGE

RIAL

SILVER, 10.36 g
c/m: ***Zarb Tehran 1229*** **on various rials of same ruler.**

KM#	Date	Mint	Fine	VF	XF
730	AH1229	Tehran	30.00	40.00	55.00

NADIR MIRZA AFSHAR

In Mashhad AH1210-1218/1795-1803AD

Type A Coinage

Name of ruler within central cartouche with blank margins around, *al-Sultan Nadir*. Reverse, mint and date below, benediction above, *Edama Allah Daulatahu*, "may God prolong his reign."

SHAHI

SILVER, 11.50 g

KM#	Date	Mint	Fine	VF	XF
768	AH1216	Mashhad	75.00	125.00	200.00
(671)					

RUPI

SILVER, 11.50 g

KM#	Date	Mint	Fine	VF	XF
769	AH1216	Mashhad	100.00	160.00	250.00
(672)					

HUSAIN QULI KHAN OAJAR

Rebel in Isfahan, AH1216/1801AD

Description not available.

RIYAL

SILVER, 10.40 g

KM#	Date	Mint	Fine	VF	XF
770 (676)	AH1216	Isfahan	125.00	200.00	300.00

SULTAN ALI SHAH

AH1250/1834AD

Ruled only 30 days

There is only one type for this reign. Obverse: *al-sultan ibn al-sultan Sultan 'Ali Shah Qajar.* Reverse: Mint & date as on the coins of Fath 'Ali Shah.

KRAN

SILVER, 6.90 g

KM#	Date	Mint	Fine	VF	XF
771 (C215)	AH1250	Tehran	250.00	300.00	400.00

NOTE: Holed or mounted coins are worth about half the listed price.

TOMAN

GOLD, 3.50 g

KM#	Date	Mint	Fine	VF	XF
772 (C216)	AH1250	Tehran	—	650.00	850.00

HUSAIN ALI SHAH

AH1250/1834AD

For six months in southern Iran

There is only one type for this reign. Obverse: *al-sultan ibn al-sultan Husayn Ali Shah Qajar.* Reverse: Mint and date.

KRAN

SILVER, 6.90 g

KM#	Date	Mint	Fine	VF	XF
774 (C219)	AH1250	Shiraz	350.00	425.00	500.00

TOMAN

(Ashrafi)

GOLD, 3.45 g

KM#	Date	Mint	Fine	VF	XF
775	AHxxxx	(Shiraz)?	Reported, not confirmed		

MUHAMMAD SHAH

AH1250-1264/1834-1848AD

Silver Types:

All purely inscriptional coins of Muhammad Shah share a common obverse legend, *Mohammad Shahansha-e Anbiyja*, "Muhammad, King of the Prophets," a word-play on the name of the ruler. All have mint & date on reverse, as in previous reigns. The types differ only in their weight standards:

A. Based on a kran of 6.91 g.
B. Based on a kran of 6.33 g.
C. Based on a kran of 5.76 g.
D. Based on a kran of 5.37 g.
E. Obverse: Lion & sun within wreath. Reverse: The normal Muhammad Shah legend, together with mint & date, all within a square. Same standards as type D, with which it was contemporary.

Gold Types:

R. Based on a toman of 3.84 g.
S. Based on a toman of 3.45 g.

1/8 KRAN

Type C

SILVER, 0.67 g

KM#	Date	Mint	Fine	VF	XF
788	AH1252	Shiraz	30.00	40.00	60.50
(C224a)	1253	Kirmanshahan	30.00	40.00	60.00
	1253	Shiraz	30.00	40.00	60.50

Type D

SILVER, 0.67 g
Sometimes uniface, obverse or reverse.

KM#	Date	Mint	Fine	VF	XF
792	AH1255	Shiraz	15.00	20.00	27.50
(C224b)	1260	Mashhad	15.00	20.00	27.50
	1263	Tabriz (uniface)	15.00	20.00	27.50
	ND (uniface impression of obverse)		12.50	17.50	25.00

1/5 KRAN

Type D

SILVER, 1.07 g

KM#	Date	Mint	Fine	VF	XF
793	AH1260	Yazd	25.00	35.00	50.00

1/4 KRAN

Type A

SILVER, 1.72 g

KM#	Date	Mint	Fine	VF	XF
781 (C225)	AH1250	Tabriz	30.00	40.00	60.00

Type C

SILVER, 1.44 g

KM#	Date	Mint	Fine	VF	XF
789 (C225a)	AH1252	Tabriz	40.00	55.00	75.00

1/3 KRAN

Type D

SILVER, 1.79 g

KM#	Date	Mint	Fine	VF	XF
795	AH1255	Kirman	30.00	40.00	55.00

2/5 KRAN

Type B

SILVER, 2.53 g

KM#	Date	Mint	Fine	VF	XF
785 (C225b)	AH1252	Kirman	40.00	50.00	65.00

1/2 KRAN

Type A

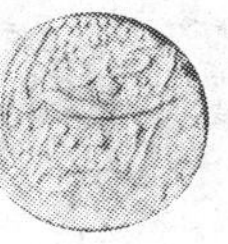

SILVER, 3.45 g

KM#	Date	Mint	Fine	VF	XF
782	AH1250	Shiraz	25.00	35.00	55.00
	1251	Shiraz	25.00	35.00	55.00

Type C

SILVER, 2.88 g

KM#	Date	Mint	Fine	VF	XF
790	AH1251	Tabriz	20.00	30.00	47.50
(C226)	1251	Tehran	20.00	30.00	47.50
(C226a)	1252	Tabriz	20.00	30.00	47.50
	1254	Isfahan	20.00	30.00	47.50

NOTE: Coins of Isfahan dated AH1254 may belong to the following standard, KM#796.

Type D

SILVER, 2.68 g

KM#	Date	Mint	Fine	VF	XF
796	AH1255	Tabaristan	12.50	18.50	27.50
(C226b)	1257	Isfahan	10.00	15.00	22.50
	1258	Isfahan	10.00	15.00	22.50
	1258	Tabaristan	12.50	18.50	27.50
	1259	Shiraz	12.50	18.50	27.50
	1260	Isfahan	10.00	15.00	22.50
	1261	Isfahan	10.00	15.00	22.50
	1261	Tabaristan	12.50	18.50	27.50
	1262	Shiraz	12.50	18.50	27.50
	1263	Isfahan	10.00	15.00	22.50
	1264	Mashhad	15.00	20.00	27.50
	1264	Tabaristan	15.00	20.00	27.50
	xxxx	Tabriz	12.50	18.50	27.50

Type E

KM#	Date	Mint	Fine	VF	XF
798	AH1263	Tehran	30.00	40.00	55.00
	1264	Tehran	30.00	40.00	55.00

KRAN

Type A

SILVER, 6.91 g

KM#	Date	Mint	Fine	VF	XF
783	AH1250	Mashhad	45.00	70.00	100.00
	1251	Mashhad	45.00	70.00	100.00

Type B

SILVER, 6.33 g

KM#	Date	Mint	Fine	VF	XF
787	AH1251	Hamadan	12.50	20.00	30.00
(C227)	1251	Isfahan	12.50	20.00	30.00
	1251	Rasht	12.50	20.00	30.00
	1251	Tabriz	12.50	20.00	30.00
	1251	Tehran	12.50	20.00	30.00
	1251	Yazd	12.50	20.00	30.00

Type C

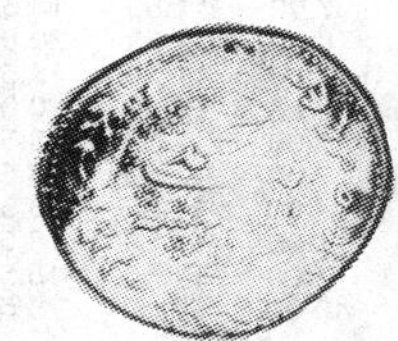

SILVER, 5.76 g
Mint: Mashhad

KM#	Date	Mint	Fine	VF	XF
791	AH1251	Rasht	10.00	15.00	22.50
(C227a)	1251	Tehran	10.00	15.00	22.50
	1252	Isfahan	7.00	11.00	17.50
	1252	Kirmanshahan	7.00	11.00	17.50
	1252	Mashhad	7.00	11.00	17.50
	1252	Rasht	7.00	11.00	17.50
	1252	Shiraz	8.00	12.50	20.00
	1252	Tabriz	7.00	11.00	17.50
	1252	Tehran	7.00	11.00	17.50
	1252	Yazd	8.00	12.50	20.00
	1253	Isfahan	7.00	11.00	17.50
	1253	Kirmanshahan	7.00	11.00	17.50
	1253	Mashhad	7.00	11.00	17.50
	1253	Rasht	7.00	11.00	17.50
	1253	Tabriz	7.00	11.00	17.50
	1253	Tehran	7.00	11.00	17.50
	1253	Yazd	8.00	12.50	20.00
	1254	Isfahan	10.00	15.00	22.50
	1254	Kirmanshahan	10.00	15.00	22.50
	1254	Mashhad	10.00	15.00	22.50
	1254	Shiraz	10.00	15.00	22.50
	1254	Tabriz	10.00	15.00	22.50

NOTE: Coins of Isfahan dated AH1254 may belong to the following standard, KM#797.

Type D

SILVER, 5.37 g

KM#	Date	Mint	Fine	VF	XF
797	AH1254(sic)	Tabriz	20.00	27.50	37.50
(C227b)	1255	Astarabad	6.00	10.00	17.50
	1255	Isfahan	6.00	10.00	17.50
	1255	Kirmanshahan	6.00	10.00	17.50
	1255	Mashhad	6.00	10.00	17.50
	1255	Rasht	6.00	10.00	17.50
	1255	Shiraz	6.00	10.00	17.50
	1255	Tabriz	6.00	10.00	17.50
	1255	Tehran	6.00	10.00	17.50
	1255	Yazd	6.00	10.00	17.50
	1256	Astarabad	7.00	11.50	20.00
	1256	Isfahan	6.00	10.00	17.50
	1256	Kirman	15.00	22.50	35.00
	1256	Kirmanshahan	6.00	10.00	17.50
	1256	Mashhad	6.00	10.00	17.50
	1256	Rasht	6.00	10.00	17.50
	1256	Shiraz	6.00	10.00	17.50
	1256	Tabaristan	6.00	10.00	17.50
	1256	Tabriz	6.00	10.00	17.50
	1256	Yazd	6.00	10.00	17.50
	1257	Isfahan	6.00	10.00	17.50
	1257	Kirmanshahan	6.00	10.00	17.50
	1257	Mashhad	6.00	10.00	17.50
	1257	Rasht	6.00	10.00	17.50
	1257	Tabaristan	6.00	10.00	17.50
	1257	Tabriz	6.00	10.00	17.50
	1257	Tehran	6.00	10.00	17.50
	1257	Yazd	6.00	10.00	17.50
	1258	Isfahan	6.00	10.00	17.50
	1258	Kirman	15.00	22.50	35.00
	1258	Kirmanshahan	6.00	10.00	17.50
	1258	Mashhad	6.00	10.00	17.50
	1258	Rasht	6.00	10.00	17.50

KM#	Date	Mint	Fine	VF	XF
(C227b)	1258	Tabaristan	6.00	10.00	17.50
	1258	Tehran	7.00	11.50	20.00
	1259	Isfahan	6.00	10.00	17.50
	1259	Kirmanshahan	6.00	10.00	17.50
	1259	Mashhad	6.00	10.00	17.50
	1259	Rasht	6.00	10.00	17.50
	1259	Shiraz	8.00	12.50	20.00
	1259	Yazd	6.00	10.00	17.50
	1260	Isfahan	6.00	10.00	17.50
	1260	Kirmanshahan	6.00	10.00	17.50
	1260	Mashhad	6.00	10.00	17.50
	1260	Rasht	6.00	10.00	17.50
	1260	Shiraz	8.00	12.50	20.00
	1260	Tabaristan	6.00	10.00	17.50
	1260	Tabriz	7.00	11.50	18.50
	1260	Yazd	6.00	10.00	17.50
	1261	Isfahan	6.00	10.00	17.50
	1261	Kirmanshahan	7.00	11.50	18.50
	1261	Mashhad	6.00	10.00	17.50
	1261	Rasht	6.00	10.00	17.50
	1261	Tabaristan	6.00	10.00	17.50
	1261	Tabriz	7.00	11.50	18.50
	1261	Yazd	6.00	10.00	17.50
	1262	Kirmanshahan	8.00	12.50	20.00
	1262	Mashhad	6.00	10.00	17.50
	1262	Rasht	6.00	10.00	17.50
	1262	Tabaristan	6.00	10.00	17.50
	1262	Yazd	6.00	10.00	17.50
	1263	Isfahan	7.00	11.50	18.50
	1263	Kirmanshahan	8.00	12.50	20.00
	1263	Rasht	7.00	11.50	18.50
	1263	Shiraz	8.00	12.50	20.00
	1263	Tabaristan	7.00	11.50	18.50
	1264	Kirmanshahan	7.00	11.50	18.50
	1264	Mashhad	7.00	11.50	18.50
	1264	Tabaristan	7.00	11.50	18.50
	1264	Yazd	7.00	11.50	18.50
	1265	Mashhad	40.00	55.00	75.00
	1266 (1265 on obv.)	Mashhad	50.00	65.00	90.00

NOTE: Coins of AH1265 and AH1266 are issues of the rebellion of Hasan Khan Salar in Mashhad (AH1264-1266).

Type E

KM#	Date	Mint	Fine	VF	XF
799	AH1258	Tehran	20.00	30.00	50.00
(C228)	1259	Tehran	25.00	37.50	60.00
	1260	Tehran	25.00	37.50	60.00
	1261	Tehran	20.00	30.00	50.00
	1262	Tehran	20.00	30.00	50.00
	1263	Tehran	20.00	30.00	50.00
	1264	Tehran	Reported, not confirmed		

2 KRANS

Type A

SILVER, 13.82 g

KM#	Date	Mint	Fine	VF	XF
784	AH1251	Tehran	125.00	150.00	200.00

Type E

SILVER, 12.74 g

KM#	Date	Mint	Fine	VF	XF
800 (C229)	AH1263	Tehran	60.00	85.00	125.00

1/2 TOMAN

Type R

GOLD, 1.92 g

KM#	Date	Mint	Fine	VF	XF
805 (C232)	AH1252	Tabriz	125.00	160.00	200.00

Lion & Sun Type

GOLD, 1.72 g
Similar to 1 Kran, KM#799.

KM#	Date	Mint	Fine	VF	XF
811	AH1258	Tehran	200.00	250.00	350.00

TOMAN

Type R

GOLD, 3.84 g

KM#	Date	Mint	Fine	VF	XF
806	AH1250	Hamadan	60.00	80.00	100.00
(C233)	1250	Isfahan	50.00	70.00	90.00
	1250	Kirmanshahan	60.00	80.00	100.00
	1250	Tabriz	50.00	70.00	90.00
	1251	Rasht	50.00	70.00	90.00
	1251	Tehran	50.00	70.00	90.00
	1252	Isfahan	50.00	70.00	90.00
	1252	Rasht	50.00	70.00	90.00
	1252	Shiraz	50.00	70.00	90.00
	1252	Tehran	50.00	70.00	90.00
	1253	Isfahan	50.00	70.00	90.00
	1253	Shiraz	50.00	70.00	90.00
	1254	Mashhad	70.00	90.00	125.00
	1254	Tabriz	50.00	70.00	90.00

Type S

Mint: Mashhad

KM#	Date	Mint	Fine	VF	XF
809	AH1255	Rasht	50.00	70.00	90.00
(C233)	1255	Shiraz	50.00	70.00	90.00
	1255	Tabriz	50.00	70.00	90.00
	1255	Tehran	50.00	70.00	90.00
	1256	Mashhad	50.00	70.00	90.00
	1256	Tabriz	50.00	70.00	90.00
	1256	Tehran	50.00	70.00	90.00
	1257	Mashhad	50.00	70.00	90.00
	1257	Rasht	50.00	70.00	90.00
	1257	Tabriz	50.00	70.00	90.00
	1257	Tehran	50.00	70.00	90.00
	1258	Rasht	50.00	70.00	90.00
	1259	Isfahan	50.00	70.00	90.00
	1259	Mashhad	50.00	70.00	90.00
	1259	Rasht	50.00	70.00	90.00
	1259	Tabriz	50.00	70.00	90.00
	1260	Mashhad	50.00	70.00	90.00
	1261	Mashhad	50.00	70.00	90.00
	1261	Tabriz	50.00	70.00	90.00
	1262	Rasht	50.00	70.00	90.00
	1263	Mashhad	50.00	70.00	90.00
	1264	Mashhad	50.00	70.00	90.00
	1265(sic)	Isfahan	50.00	70.00	90.00
	1265* (dated both sides)	Mashhad	200.00	275.00	375.00

NOTE: Coins of Mashhad struck in AH1265 (and dated on both sides) are issues of the rebel Hasan Khan Salar after Muhammad Shah's death.

Lion & Sun Type

Similar to 1 Kran, KM#799.

KM#	Date	Mint	Fine	VF	XF
812	AH1258	Tehran	200.00	300.00	400.00
(C234)	1261	Tehran	200.00	300.00	400.00
	1262	Tehran	200.00	300.00	400.00
	1263	Tehran	200.00	300.00	400.00

2 TOMANS

Special Type

GOLD, 6.90 g
Obv: Crowned ruler on throne.

KM#	Date	Mint	Fine	VF	XF
814	AH1254	Isfahan	—	—	3000.

6 TOMANS

Type R

Gold, about 23 g

KM#	Date	Mint	Fine	VF	XF
807	AH1251	Tehran	—	—	5000.

Countermarked Coinage

TOMAN

GOLD, 3.45 g
c/m: On Fath Ali Shah, type KM#759.

KM#	Date	Mint	Fine	VF	XF
816	AH1250	Tehran	300.00	375.00	475.00

NOTE: Anonymous type, could be an issue of either Sultan Ali Shah or Muhammad Shah.

HASAN KHAN SALAR

Rebel, AH1264-1266/1848-1850AD

Coins of this rebellion were struck at Mashhad in the name of Muhammad Shah. See types KM#797 & 809, dates AH1265 and 1266.

NASIR AL-DIN SHAH

AH1264-1313/1848-1896AD

The hammered silver coinage of this reign comprises two standards, one based on a kran of 5.37 g, the second based on a kran of 4.99 g. The first was inherited from the previous reign and maintained for the kran until AH1273 or 1274 (AH1276 at Tabriz). The second standard was introduced for the half kran as early as AH1269 or 1270, and seems to have been in general use for the half kran as early as AH1269 or 1270, and seems to have been in general use for the half kran by AH1271. Unfortunately, not enough information is currently available to separate all issues. For that reason, the two standards are lumped together as a single type, but will be separated in a future edition of this catalog. The 5.37 g standard will be types KM#821-824, those on the 4.99 g standard will be KM#821a-824a.

The eighth kran was intended largely for ceremonial purposes, and varies considerably in weight. It is the ancestor of the Shahi Sefid of the machine-struck period.

Machine-struck coinage was introduced in AH1293 and became general by AH1296. The latest known hammered coins are dated AH1297. All of the provincial markets were closed when hammered coinage ceased.

All of Nasir al-Din's hammered gold was struck to the 3.45 g toman standard.

All normal hammered silver and gold coinage of this reign bears on the obverse the inscription *al-sultan ibn al-sultan Nasir al-Din Shah Qajar,* occasionally somewhat shortened. The reverse bears the mint & the date, though the date occasionally appears on the obverse or on both sides.

There is great variety of design for both obverse and reverse during this reign, with many attractive and elegant cartouches and calligraphic styles. The more attractive and ornate designs command a significant premium over listed prices, from 25% to at least 200%, depending on attractiveness and rarity.

1/8 KRAN

(Shahi Safid)

SILVER, uniface, 0.62 & 0.67 g

KM#	Date	Mint	Fine	VF	XF
821	AH1267	Qazvin	12.50	20.00	30.00
(C260)	1271	Isfahan	7.50	12.50	17.50
	1272	Rasht	12.50	20.00	30.00
	1273	Isfahan	7.50	12.50	17.50
	1274	Rasht	12.50	20.00	30.00
	1274	Sistan	75.00	115.00	175.00
	1275	Tabriz	10.00	16.00	25.00
	1281	Hamadan	15.00	22.50	32.50
	1286	Isfahan	10.00	16.00	25.00
	1288	Shiraz	15.00	22.50	32.50
	1293	Tehran	15.00	22.50	32.50

1/4 KRAN

SILVER, 1.34 & 1.25 g

KM#	Date	Mint	Fine	VF	XF
822	AH1274	Tehran	10.00	14.00	22.50
(C261)	1276	Tehran	10.00	14.00	22.50
	1280	Tehran	10.00	14.00	22.50
	1284	Mashhad	12.50	17.50	26.00
	1288	Tehran	10.00	14.00	22.50
	1289	Tehran	10.00	14.00	22.50
	1292	Tehran	10.00	14.00	22.50
	1293	Tehran	10.00	14.00	22.50
	1294	Tabriz	15.00	25.00	40.00

Portrait Type

SILVER, 1.25 g
Obv: Portrait left, name & accession date (1264) in field.

KM#	Date	Mint	Fine	VF	XF
827	AH1274	Tehran	50.00	75.00	115.00

Toughra Type

SILVER, 1.25 g
Obv: Ruler's name in toughra form.

KM#	Date	Mint	Fine	VF	XF
831	AH1284	Mashhad	50.00	75.00	100.00

Special Types

SILVER, 1.25 g ?
Obv: Shah seated facing, holding sabre.

KM#	Date	Mint	Fine	VF	XF
838	AH1274	Isfahan	200.00	250.00	300.00

1/2 KRAN

SILVER, 2.68 & 2.49 g

KM#	Date	Mint	Fine	VF	XF
823	AH1264	Kashan	10.00	14.00	22.50
(C262)	1264	Tabriz	10.00	14.00	22.50
	1265	Astarabad	12.00	16.50	25.00
	1265	Isfahan	8.00	12.50	17.50
	1265	Kashan	8.00	12.50	17.50
	1265	Rasht	8.00	12.50	17.50
	1266	Hamadan	8.00	12.50	17.50
	1266	Khuy	20.00	27.50	40.00
	1266	Tabriz	8.00	12.50	17.50
	1267	Hamadan	8.00	12.50	17.50

KM#	Date	Mint	Fine	VF	XF
(C262)	1267	Isfahan	8.00	12.50	17.50
	1267	Shiraz	13.50	20.00	27.50
	1268	Tabaristan	8.00	12.50	17.50
	1269	Astarabad	10.00	14.00	22.50
	1269	Hamadan	8.00	12.50	17.50
	1269	Tabaristan	8.00	12.50	17.50
	1270	Tehran	8.00	12.50	17.50
	1271	Hamadan	8.00	12.50	17.50
	1271	Khuy	20.00	27.50	40.00
	1271	Tabriz	6.00	9.50	15.00
	1271	Tehran	6.00	9.50	15.00
	1272	Kashan	6.00	9.50	15.00
	1272	Tabaristan	6.00	9.50	15.00
	1272	Yazd	8.00	12.50	17.50
	1273	Kashan	6.00	9.50	15.00
	1273	Qazvin	6.00	9.50	15.00
	1274	Hamadan	6.00	9.50	15.00
	1274	Kashan	5.00	8.00	13.50
	1274	Kirmanshahan	6.00	9.50	15.00
	1274	Qazvin	5.00	8.00	13.50
	1274	Tabaristan	6.00	9.50	15.00
	1274	Yazd	5.00	8.00	13.50
	1275	Astarabad	6.00	9.50	15.00
	1275	Hamadan	5.00	8.00	13.50
	1275	Isfahan	5.00	8.00	13.50
	1275	Kashan	5.00	8.00	13.50
	1275	Kirmanshahan	5.00	8.00	13.50
	1275	Qazvin	5.00	8.00	13.50
	1275	Shiraz	6.00	9.50	15.00
	1275	Tabaristan	5.00	8.00	13.50
	1275	Tabriz	4.00	7.50	13.50
	1275	Tehran	5.00	8.00	13.50
	1275	Yazd	5.00	8.00	13.50
	1276	Astarabad	6.00	9.50	15.00
	1276	Isfahan	5.00	8.00	13.50
	1276	Kirman	10.00	17.50	27.50
	1276	Qazvin	5.00	8.00	13.50
	1276	Shiraz	6.00	9.50	15.00
	1276	Tabaristan	5.00	8.00	13.50
	1276	Tabriz	4.00	7.50	13.50
	1276	Tehran	5.00	8.00	13.50
	1276	Yazd	5.00	8.00	13.50
	1277	Astarabad	6.00	9.50	15.00
	1277	Kirman	10.00	17.50	27.50
	1277	Tabriz	6.00	9.50	15.00
	1277	Tehran	6.00	9.50	15.00
	1278	Tabriz	6.00	9.50	15.00
	1278	Tehran	6.00	9.50	15.00
	1278	Yazd	7.00	11.00	17.50
	1279	Kashan	7.00	11.00	17.50
	1280	Qazvin	7.00	11.00	17.50
	1282	Kirman	10.00	17.50	27.50
	1283	Qazvin	7.00	11.00	17.50

Portrait Type

SILVER, 2.50 g
Obv: Portrait left, name & accession date (1264) in field.

KM#	Date	Mint	Fine	VF	XF
828	AH1271	Tehran	10.00	16.00	25.00
(C265)	1272	Isfahan	15.00	22.50	35.00
	1272	Tehran	10.00	16.00	25.00
	1273	Isfahan	15.00	22.50	35.00
	1273	Tehran	10.00	16.00	25.00
	1274	Isfahan	15.00	22.50	35.00
	1274	Qazvin	16.50	24.00	37.50
	1274	Tehran	10.00	16.00	25.00
	1275	Qazvin	16.50	24.00	37.50
	1275	Tehran	10.00	16.00	25.00

NOTE: Prices are for well-struck examples. Weak or flat strikes are worth about half as much as shown.

KRAN

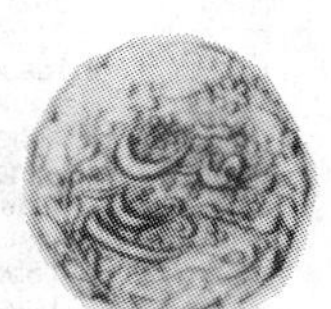

SILVER, 5.37 & 4.99 g

KM#	Date	Mint	Fine	VF	XF
824	AH1264	Kirmanshaban	20.00	27.50	35.00
(C263)	1264	Tabaristan	10.00	17.50	27.50
	1264	Tehran	10.00	17.50	27.50
	1264	Yazd	10.00	17.50	27.50
	1265	Astarabad	12.50	18.50	30.00
	1265	Kirman	12.50	18.50	30.00
	1265	Rasht	6.50	10.00	16.00
	1265	Tabaristan	6.50	10.00	16.00
	1265	Tabriz	6.50	10.00	16.00
	1265	Tehran	6.50	10.00	16.00
	1265	Yazd	6.50	10.00	16.00
	1266	Astarabad	9.00	14.00	22.50
	1266	Khuy	15.00	23.50	32.50
	1266	Kirman	12.50	18.50	30.00
	1266	Mashhad	6.50	10.00	16.00
	1266	Rasht	6.50	10.00	16.00

KM#	Date	Mint	Fine	VF	XF
(C263)	1266	Tabaristan	6.50	10.00	16.00
	1266	Tabriz	6.50	10.00	16.00
	1266	Tehran	6.50	10.00	16.00
	1266	Yazd	6.50	10.00	16.00
	1267	Astarabad	9.00	14.00	22.50
	1267	Isfahan	10.00	17.50	27.50
	1267	Mashhad	6.50	10.00	16.00
	1267	Tabaristan	6.50	10.00	16.00
	1267	Tabriz	6.50	10.00	16.00
	1268	Hamadan	10.00	17.50	27.50
	1268	Mashhad	6.50	10.00	16.00
	1268	Rasht	6.50	10.00	16.00
	1268	Tabriz	6.50	10.00	16.00
	1268	Tehran	6.50	10.00	16.00
	1269	Astarabad	12.50	18.50	30.00
	1269	Herat	50.00	75.00	100.00
	1269	Khuy	15.00	23.50	32.50
	1269	Kirman	10.00	16.00	25.00
	1269	Mashhad	6.50	10.00	16.00
	1269	Tabaristan	6.50	10.00	16.00
	1269	Tabriz	6.50	10.00	16.00
	1270	Astarabad	10.00	16.00	25.00
	1270	Khuy	15.00	23.50	32.50
	1270	Kirman	10.00	16.00	25.00
	1270	Mashhad	6.50	10.00	16.00
	1270	Rasht	7.50	11.50	18.50
	1270	Tabaristan	6.50	10.00	16.00
	1270	Tabriz	6.50	10.00	16.00
	1270	Yazd	6.50	10.00	16.00
	1271	Astarabad	10.00	16.00	25.00
	1271	Hamadan	8.00	12.50	20.00
	1271	Khuy	15.00	23.50	32.50
	1271	Kirman	10.00	16.00	25.00
	1271	Kirmanshahan	10.00	16.00	25.00
	1271	Mashhad	6.50	10.00	16.00
	1271	Tabaristan	6.50	10.00	16.00
	1271	Tabriz	6.50	10.00	16.00
	1271	Tehran	6.50	10.00	16.00
	1272	Astarabad	8.50	12.50	20.00
	1272	Kirman	10.00	16.00	25.00
	1272	Kirmanshahan	10.00	16.00	25.00
	1272	Mashhad	6.50	10.00	16.00
	1272	Qazvin	6.50	10.00	16.00
	1272	Tabaristan	6.50	10.00	16.00
	1272	Tabriz	6.50	10.00	16.00
	1273	Astarabad	10.00	16.00	25.00
	1273	Hamadan	6.50	10.00	16.00
	1273	Herat	20.00	30.00	45.00
	1273	Kashan	6.50	10.00	16.00
	1273	Mashhad	6.50	10.00	16.00
	1273	Qazvin	6.50	10.00	16.00
	1273	Tabaristan	6.50	10.00	16.00
	1273	Tabriz	6.50	10.00	16.00
	1274	Hamadan	8.00	12.50	20.00
	1274	Mashhad	6.50	10.00	16.00
	1274	Tabaristan	6.50	10.00	16.00
	1274	Tabriz	7.50	11.50	18.50
	1274	Yazd	7.50	11.50	18.50
	1275	Hamadan	8.00	12.50	20.00
	1275	Herat	20.00	30.00	45.00
	1276	Astarabad	10.00	16.00	25.00
	1276	Hamadan	8.00	12.50	20.00
	1276	Mashhad	6.50	10.00	16.00
	1276	Sarakhs	65.00	100.00	150.00
	1276	Tabriz	7.50	11.50	18.50
	1276	Yazd	7.50	11.50	18.50
	1277	Astarabad	8.50	12.50	20.00
	1277	Hamadan	6.50	10.00	16.00
	1277	Herat	20.00	30.00	45.00
	1277	Kashan	6.50	10.00	16.00
	1277	Kirman	10.00	16.00	25.00
	1277	Kirmanshahan	10.00	16.00	25.00
	1277	Mashhad	6.50	10.00	16.00
	1277	Shiraz	6.50	10.00	16.00
	1277	Tabaristan	6.50	10.00	16.00
	1277	Tabriz	6.50	10.00	16.00
	1277	Tehran	6.50	10.00	16.00
	1278	Astarabad (see KM#836)			
	1278	Hamadan	6.50	10.00	16.00
	1278	Herat	20.00	30.00	45.00
	1278	Isfahan	6.50	10.00	16.00
	1278	Kashan	6.50	10.00	16.00
	1278	Mashhad	5.50	8.50	14.50
	1278	Shiraz	6.50	10.00	16.00
	1278	Tabaristan	6.50	10.00	16.00
	1278	Tabriz	6.50	10.00	16.00
	1278	Tehran	6.50	10.00	16.00
	1278	Yazd	7.00	11.50	17.50
	1279	Astarabad	8.50	12.50	20.00
	1279	Hamadan	6.50	10.00	16.00
	1279	Herat	20.00	30.00	45.00
	1279	Isfahan	6.50	10.00	16.00
	1279	Kirmanshahan	6.50	10.00	16.00
	1279	Mashhad	5.50	8.50	14.50
	1279	Shiraz	6.50	10.00	16.00
	1279	Tabriz	6.50	10.00	16.00
	1279	Tehran	6.50	10.00	16.00
	1280	Astarabad	6.50	10.00	16.00
	1280	Hamadan	6.50	10.00	16.00
	1280	Isfahan	6.50	10.00	16.00
	1280	Kashan	7.50	11.50	18.50
	1280	Kirman	7.50	11.50	18.50
	1280	Mashhad	6.50	10.00	16.00
	1280	Qazvin	6.50	10.00	16.00
	1280	Rasht	6.50	10.00	16.00
	1280	Shiraz	6.50	10.00	16.00
	1280	Tabaristan	6.50	10.00	16.00
	1280	Tabriz	6.50	10.00	16.00
	1280	Tehran	6.50	10.00	16.00
	1280	Yazd	9.00	15.00	22.50

KM#	Date	Mint	Fine	VF	XF
(C263)	1281	Arz-e Aqdas (= Mashhad)	10.00	17.50	27.50
	1281	Astarabad	6.50	10.00	16.00
	1281	Hamadan	6.50	10.00	16.00
	1281	Isfahan	6.50	10.00	16.00
	1281	Kashan	7.50	11.50	18.50
	1281	Kirman	7.50	11.50	18.50
	1281	Kirmanshahan	8.50	13.50	20.00
	1281	Mashhad	6.50	10.00	16.00
	1281	Qazvin	6.50	10.00	16.00
	1281	Rasht	6.50	10.00	16.00
	1281	Shiraz	6.50	10.00	16.00
	1281	Tabaristan	6.50	10.00	16.00
	1281	Tabriz	6.50	10.00	16.00
	1281	Tehran	6.50	10.00	16.00
	1282	Arz-e Aqdas (=Mashhad)	10.00	17.50	27.50
	1282	Astarabad	6.50	10.00	16.00
	1282	Hamadan	6.50	10.00	16.00
	1282	Isfahan	6.50	10.00	16.00
	1282	Kashan	6.50	10.00	16.00
	1282	Kirman	6.50	10.00	16.00
	1282	Kirmanshahan	6.50	10.00	16.00
	1282	Mashhad	6.50	10.00	16.00
	1282	Qazvin	7.50	11.50	18.50
	1282	Rasht	6.50	10.00	16.00
	1282	Tabaristan	6.50	10.00	16.00
	1282	Tabriz	6.50	10.00	16.00
	1282	Tehran	6.50	10.00	16.00
	1283	Astarabad	7.50	11.50	18.50
	1283	Kashan	7.50	11.50	18.50
	1283	Kirman	7.50	11.50	18.50
	1283	Mashhad	6.50	10.00	16.00
	1283	Tabaristan	6.50	10.00	16.00
	1283	Tabriz	6.50	10.00	16.00
	1284	Arz-e Moqaddas (=Mashhad)	12.50	20.00	35.00
	1284	Astarabad	7.50	11.50	18.50
	1284	Hamadan	6.50	10.00	16.00
	1284	Isfahan	6.50	10.00	16.00
	1284	Kirman	8.00	12.50	20.00
	1284	Kirmanshahan	8.00	12.50	20.00
	1285	Hamadan	6.50	10.00	16.00
	1285	Mashhad	6.50	10.00	16.00
	1285	Shiraz	9.00	14.00	22.50
	1286	Hamadan	6.50	10.00	16.00
	1286	Isfahan	7.50	11.50	18.50
	1286	Kirman	7.50	11.50	18.50
	1286	Tehran	7.50	11.50	18.50
	1287	Astarabad	7.50	11.50	18.50
	1287	Hamadan	6.50	10.00	16.00
	1287	Herat (error for 1278)	22.50	35.00	55.00
	1287	Isfahan	6.50	10.00	16.00
	1287	Kashan	8.00	12.50	20.00
	1287	Kirman	8.00	12.50	20.00
	1287	Kirmanshahan	10.00	16.00	25.00
	1287	Tabaristan	7.50	11.50	18.50
	1288	Hamadan	6.50	10.00	16.00
	1288	Isfahan	7.50	11.50	18.50
	1288	Mashhad	7.50	11.50	18.50
	1288	Rasht	7.50	11.50	18.50
	1288	Tabaristan	7.50	11.50	18.50
	1288	Tabriz	7.50	11.50	18.50
	1288	Tehran	7.50	11.50	18.50
	1289	Hamadan	6.50	10.00	16.50
	1289	Isfahan	6.50	10.00	16.50
	1289	Kirmanshahan	8.00	12.50	20.00
	1289	Mashhad	7.50	11.50	18.50
	1289	Rasht	7.50	11.50	18.50
	1289	Shiraz	7.50	11.50	18.50
	1289	Tehran	7.50	11.50	18.50
	1290	Astarabad	7.50	11.50	18.50
	1290	Hamadan	6.50	10.00	16.50
	1290	Kirman	8.00	12.50	20.00
	1290	Mashhad	7.50	11.50	18.50
	1290	Rasht	7.50	11.50	18.50
	1290	Tabriz	7.50	11.50	18.50
	1291	Astarabad	10.00	16.00	25.00
	1291	Isfahan	7.50	11.50	18.50
	1291	Rasht (see KM#834)			
	1291	Tabriz	7.50	11.50	18.50
	1291	Tehran	7.50	11.50	18.50
	1292	Astarabad	10.00	16.00	25.00
	1292	Hamadan	8.00	12.50	20.00
	1292	Kashan	12.50	18.50	27.50
	1292	Kirman	10.00	16.00	25.00
	1292	Mashhad	7.50	11.50	18.50
	1292	Tehran	7.50	11.50	18.50
	1292	Yazd	10.00	16.00	25.00
	1293	Hamadan	8.00	12.50	20.00
	1293	Isfahan	8.00	12.50	20.00
	1293	Kirman	10.00	16.00	25.00
	1293	Mashhad	8.00	12.50	20.00
	1293	Shiraz	10.00	16.00	25.00
	1293	Tabriz	8.00	12.50	20.00
	1294	Hamadan	8.00	12.50	20.00
	1294	Mashhad	10.00	16.00	25.00
	1294	Tabriz	10.00	16.00	25.00
	1295	Mashhad	10.00	16.00	25.00
	1295	Tehran	10.00	16.00	25.00

Struck on broad-rimmed planchets, possibly machine-punched.

KM#	Date	Mint	Fine	VF	XF
825 (C266.3)	AH1279	Tabriz	40.00	60.00	100.00
	1280	Tabriz	40.00	60.00	100.00
	1294	Kermanshahan (struck on machine-punched planchet)	50.00	75.00	115.00

Portrait Type

SILVER, 5.37 g
Obv: Portrait left, name & accession date (1264) in field.

KM#	Date	Mint	Fine	VF	XF
829 (C-A265)	AH1271	Tehran	85.00	140.00	200.00
	1272	Tehran	85.00	140.00	200.00
	1279	Astarabad	100.00	175.00	250.00

Toughra Type

SILVER, 5.37 g
Obv: Ruler's name in toughra form.

KM#	Date	Mint	Fine	VF	XF
832 (C264)	AH1286	Mashhad	30.00	50.00	75.00
	1287	Mashhad	30.00	50.00	75.00
	1295	Mashhad	42.50	65.00	100.00

Rev: Mint & date in toughra form.

KM#	Date	Mint	Fine	VF	XF
834	AH1291	Mashhad	35.00	55.00	85.00
	1291	Rasht	45.00	70.00	115.00
	1292(sic)	Rasht	—	—	—

Special Types

Obv: Kalima. Rev: Mint & date.

KM#	Date	Mint	Fine	VF	XF
839	AH1269	Rasht	25.00	40.00	70.00

NOTE: Possibly a privately produced souvenir or jewelry piece.

SILVER, 4.99 g
Rev: Mint & date inscribed upon breast or a double-headed (Russian style) eagle.

KM#	Date	Mint	Fine	VF	XF
836	AH1277	Astarabad	45.00	60.00	90.00
	1278	Astarabad	45.00	60.00	90.00

Obv: Name & titles in legend, mint epithet & date in central circle.
Rev: Persian lion in crowned wreath.

KM#	Date	Mint	Fine	VF	XF
843	AH1292	Dar al-Khilafa-yi Nasiri (=Tehran)	75.00	125.00	200.00

NOTE: This type and types KM#844, 845, 846 are regarded as transitional types between the hammered and machine-struck coinage. All four types are struck on machine-punched planchets.

Obv: Royal title *khosrov-e sahebqeran-e ghazi*.

KM#	Date	Mint	Fine	VF	XF
840 (C267)	AH1293	Tabriz	80.00	125.00	200.00

Obv: Royal title *sahebqeran* only.

KM#	Date	Mint	Fine	VF	XF
841	AH1294	Yazd	80.00	125.00	200.00

NOTE: Reverse dated 1289 (muling with old die).

Obv: Ruler's name in crowned wreath.
Rev: Mint, epithet & date in crowned wreath.

KM#	Date	Mint	Fine	VF	XF
844 (C268.1)	AH1295	Tehran	35.00	50.00	70.00

Obv: Date within wreath.
Rev: Persian lion in crowned wreath.

KM#	Date	Mint	Fine	VF	XF
845.1 (C268.5)	AH1295	Tehran	30.00	45.00	65.00

Rev: Date below lion.

KM#	Date	Mint	Fine	VF	XF
845.2 (C268.2)	AH1295	Tehran	30.00	45.00	65.00

Obv: Date below wreath.

KM#	Date	Mint	Fine	VF	XF
845.3 (C268.3)	AH1295	Tehran	35.00	50.00	75.00

Obv: Shortened titles of ruler in circle.
Rev: Mint & date in crowned wreath.

KM#	Date	Mint	Fine	VF	XF
845.4 (C268.4)	AH1296	Tehran	35.00	50.00	75.00

2 KRANS

SILVER, 9.98 g
Obv: Royal title *khosrov-e sahebqeran-e ghazi*.

KM#	Date	Mint	Fine	VF	XF
842	AH1294	Tabriz	225.00	275.00	325.00

NOTE: A number of broad silver coins or medals exist with lion & sun on obverse (usually in crowned wreath), mint, date, and a couplet on reverse. The couplet states that the "coin" is a medal for service to the Shah. These are decorations and not coins, even though most of them conform to weights of 2, 3, 4, or 5 krans. Similar pieces exist in gold as well.

1/5 TOMAN

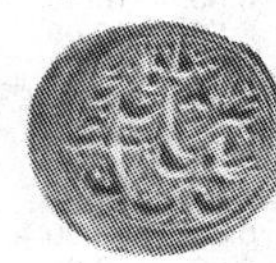

GOLD, 0.69 g

KM#	Date	Mint	Fine	VF	XF
851 (C270)	AH1270	Tehran	100.00	125.00	160.00
	1277	Tehran	100.00	125.00	160.00
	1283	Rasht	120.00	150.00	200.00
	1294	Tehran	100.00	125.00	160.00
	ND	Shiraz	120.00	150.00	200.00

1/2 TOMAN

GOLD, 1.72 g

KM#	Date	Mint	Fine	VF	XF
852 (C271)	AH1265	Tehran	85.00	100.00	140.00
	1268	Tehran	85.00	100.00	140.00
	1271	Isfahan	85.00	100.00	140.00
	1271	Qazvin	100.00	125.00	160.00
	1273	Isfahan	85.00	100.00	140.00
	1274	Mashhad	120.00	150.00	200.00
	1275	Tabriz	85.00	100.00	140.00
	1276	Herat	300.00	375.00	475.00
	1276	Sarakhs	350.00	425.00	525.00
	1276	Tehran	85.00	100.00	140.00
	1279	Mashhad	120.00	150.00	200.00
	1280	Mashhad	120.00	150.00	200.00
	1280	Tehran	85.00	100.00	140.00
	1282	Tabriz	85.00	100.00	140.00
	1282	Tehran	85.00	100.00	140.00
	1285	Tehran	85.00	100.00	140.00
	1288	Mashhad	120.00	150.00	200.00
	1294	Tabriz	150.00	185.00	240.00

Special Types

Obv: Profile bust of shah.

KM#	Date	Mint	Fine	VF	XF
860	AH1272	Tehran	250.00	325.00	400.00

Obv: Inscription in form of toughra.

KM#	Date	Mint	Fine	VF	XF
862	AH1283	Arz-e Aqdas (=Mashhad)	175.00	215.00	260.00

TOMAN

GOLD, 3.45 g

KM#	Date	Mint	Fine	VF	XF
853 (C272)	AH1265	Rasht	60.00	75.00	100.00
	1265	Tabriz	60.00	75.00	100.00
	1265	Tehran	60.00	75.00	100.00
	1266	Khuy	150.00	200.00	250.00
	1266	Mashhad	60.00	75.00	100.00
	1266	Rasht	60.00	75.00	100.00
	1267	Hamadan	60.00	75.00	100.00
	1267	Khuy	150.00	200.00	250.00
	1267	Mashhad	60.00	75.00	100.00
	1267	Qazvin	60.00	75.00	100.00
	1267	Rasht	60.00	75.00	100.00
	1268	Hamadan	60.00	75.00	100.00
	1268	Mashhad	60.00	75.00	100.00
	1268	Qazvin	60.00	75.00	100.00
	1268	Rasht	60.00	75.00	100.00
	1268	Tabriz	70.00	85.00	115.00
	1269	Hamadan	60.00	75.00	100.00
	1269	Qazvin	60.00	75.00	100.00
	1269	Rasht	60.00	75.00	100.00
	1271	Qazvin	60.00	75.00	100.00
	1271	Rasht	55.00	70.00	90.00
	1271	Tabaristan	60.00	75.00	100.00
	1271	Tabriz	60.00	75.00	100.00
	1272	Hamadan	60.00	75.00	100.00
	1272	Qazvin	60.00	75.00	100.00
	1272	Rasht	55.00	70.00	90.00
	1272	Tabaristan	60.00	75.00	100.00
	1272	Tabriz	60.00	75.00	100.00
	1273	Kirmanshahan	80.00	100.00	140.00
	1273	Mashhad	60.00	75.00	100.00
	1273	Qazvin	60.00	75.00	100.00
	1273	Rasht	55.00	70.00	90.00
	1273	Tabaristan	60.00	75.00	100.00
	1274	Astarabad	100.00	140.00	175.00
	1274	Kirmanshahan	80.00	100.00	140.00
	1274	Mashhad	60.00	75.00	100.00
	1274	Rasht	60.00	75.00	100.00
	1274	Tabaristan	60.00	75.00	100.00
	1274	Tabriz	60.00	75.00	100.00
	1275	Rasht	60.00	75.00	100.00
	1275	Tabaristan	60.00	75.00	100.00
	1275	Tehran	60.00	75.00	100.00
	1276	Mashhad	65.00	85.00	115.00
	1276	Rasht	60.00	75.00	100.00
	1276	Saraks	350.00	450.00	550.00
	1276	Tabaristan	60.00	75.00	100.00
	1277	Astarabad	100.00	140.00	175.00
	1277	Rasht	60.00	75.00	100.00
	1277	Tabaristan	60.00	75.00	100.00
	1277	Tehran	60.00	75.00	100.00
	1278	Hamadan	70.00	90.00	115.00
	1278	Tabriz	60.00	75.00	100.00
	1279	Astarabad	100.00	140.00	175.00
	1280	Hamadan	70.00	90.00	115.00
	1280	Mashhad	60.00	75.00	100.00
	1280	Qazvin	60.00	75.00	100.00
	1280	Rasht	55.00	70.00	90.00
	1280	Tabaristan	60.00	75.00	100.00
	1280	Tabriz	60.00	75.00	100.00
	1281	Rasht	55.00	70.00	90.00

KM#	Date	Mint	Fine	VF	XF
(C272)	1281	Tehran	60.00	75.00	100.00
	1284	Tabriz	60.00	75.00	100.00
	1286	Mashhad	70.00	90.00	115.00
	1287	Mashhad	70.00	90.00	115.00
	1288	Hamadan	60.00	75.00	100.00
	1288	Isfahan	60.00	75.00	100.00
	1288	Mashhad	70.00	90.00	115.00
	1288	Tabaristan	70.00	90.00	115.00

Special Types

Obv: Facing portrait of the shah.

KM#	Date	Mint	Fine	VF	XF
858 (C275)	AH1271	Tehran	500.00	700.00	900.00

Obv: Profile portrait of the shah.

KM#	Date	Mint	Fine	VF	XF
861	AH1272	Rasht	250.00	325.00	425.00
(C275)	1273	Tehran	225.00	275.00	350.00
	1274	Tehran	225.00	275.00	350.00
	1274	Tehran	225.00	275.00	350.00
	1279	Astarabad	300.00	400.00	500.00
	1291	Tehran	300.00	400.00	500.00

Obv: Inscription in toughra form.
Similar to 1 Kran, KM#832.

KM#	Date	Mint	Fine	VF	XF
863	AH1286	Mashhad	200.00	250.00	325.00

2 TOMANS

GOLD, 6.90 g

KM#	Date	Mint	Fine	VF	XF
854	AH1280	Tabriz	600.00	750.00	950.00

Special Types

Obv: Facing portrait of the shah.

KM#	Date	Mint	Fine	VF	XF
859 (C276)	AH1271	Kirmanshahan	350.00	550.00	750.00

Obv: Inscriptions in toughra form.

KM#	Date	Mint	Fine	VF	XF
864	AH1281	Mashhad	225.00	350.00	500.00
(C273)	1284	Mashhad	Reported, not confirmed		

3 TOMANS

GOLD, 10.35 g

KM#	Date	Mint	Fine	VF	XF
855	AH1280	Tabriz	—	1250.	1500.
	1292	Tabriz	—	1250.	1500.

Milled Coinage

KRAN STANDARD

AH1293-1344, SH1304-1309,
1876-1931AD

50 Dinars = 1 Shahi
1000 Dinars = 20 Shahis = 1 Kran (Qiron)
10 Krans = 1 Toman

NOTE: Dated reverse dies lacking the ruler's name were not discarded at the end of a reign (especially from Nasir al-Din to Muzaffar al-Din), but remained in use until broken or worn out. Sometimes the old date was scratched out or changed, but often the die was used with the old date unaltered. Some dies with date below wreath retained the old date but had the new date engraved among the lion's legs.

12 DINARS

(1/4 Shahi)

COPPER

KM#	Date	Mintage	Good	VG	Fine	VF
881.1	AH1301	—	20.00	30.00	65.00	85.00
(Y1.1)	1303	—	30.00	40.00	75.00	100.00
	130x	—	15.00	25.00	35.00	60.00
	ND	—	15.00	25.00	35.00	60.00

Obv. and rev: Beaded circle.

KM#	Date	Mintage	Good	VG	Fine	VF
881.2 (Y1.2)	AH1310 (error for 1301)	—	25.00	35.00	75.00	100.00

25 DINARS

(1/2 Shahi)

COPPER

KM#	Date	Mintage	VG	Fine	VF	XF
882	AH1294 FP	—	10.00	15.00	30.00	50.00
(Y2)	1294 w/o FP on rev.	—	—	25.00	40.00	75.00
	1295 FP	—	4.00	7.50	20.00	42.00
	1296	—	5.00	10.00	25.00	50.00
	1297	—	7.50	15.00	30.00	60.00
	1298	—	7.50	15.00	30.00	60.00
	1299	—	5.00	10.00	25.00	50.00
	129x	—	3.00	7.00	18.00	40.00
	1300	—	5.00	10.00	25.00	50.00
	1303	—	10.00	20.00	35.00	75.00
	ND	—	3.00	7.00	18.00	40.00

NOTE: FP are initials of the Austrian mint official, F. Pechan.

50 DINARS

(1 Shahi)

۵۰ دینار

COPPER

KM#	Date	Mintage	VG	Fine	VF	XF
883	AH1293	—	30.00	45.00	70.00	125.00
(Y4)	1294 FP	—	4.00	15.00	25.00	75.00
	1295 FP	—	2.00	6.00	15.00	40.00
	1296	—	2.00	6.00	15.00	40.00
	1297	—	2.00	6.00	18.00	50.00
	1298	—	8.00	15.00	35.00	75.00
	1299	—	7.00	12.00	30.00	65.00
	1300	—	2.00	6.00	15.00	40.00
	1301	—	2.00	6.00	15.00	40.00
	1302	—	8.00	15.00	35.00	75.00
	1303	—	2.00	6.00	15.00	40.00
	1304	—	8.00	15.00	35.00	75.00
	1305	—	6.00	10.00	25.00	65.00
	3301 (error) for 1303	—	6.00	10.00	25.00	65.00
	1330 (error) for 1303	—	10.00	20.00	35.00	75.00
	1792 (error) for 1297	—	15.00	25.00	50.00	100.00
	ND	—	4.00	10.00	25.00	50.00

NOTE: AH1293 is probably a mispunched date.

SHAHI

یکشاهی

COPPER

KM#	Date	Mintage	Good	VG	Fine	VF
884	AH1305	—	40.00	60.00	75.00	145.00
(Y4a)	ND	—	30.00	45.00	60.00	100.00

100 DINARS

(2 Shahis)

صد دینار

COPPER

KM#	Date	Mintage	VG	Fine	VF	XF
885	AH1297	—	10.00	20.00	40.00	85.00
(Y5)	1298	—	15.00	30.00	50.00	100.00
	1299	—	15.00	30.00	50.00	100.00
	1300	—	10.00	20.00	40.00	80.00
	1301	—	10.00	20.00	40.00	80.00
	1302	—	20.00	40.00	60.00	125.00
	1303	—	7.50	15.00	40.00	70.00
	1304	—	20.00	40.00	60.00	125.00
	1305	—	10.00	20.00	35.00	75.00
	1307	—	30.00	50.00	75.00	150.00
	1308	—	30.00	50.00	75.00	150.00
	1313	—	50.00	100.00	200.00	300.00
	1330 (error) for 1303	—	20.00	40.00	60.00	125.00
	3100 (error) for 1300	—	—	—	—	—
	ND	—	7.50	15.00	30.00	60.00

2 SHAHIS

دو شاهی

COPPER

KM#	Date	Mintage	Good	VG	Fine	VF
886	AH1305	—	40.00	80.00	150.00	300.00
(Y5a)	ND	—	20.00	35.00	75.00	150.00

200 DINARS

۲۰۰ دینار

COPPER

KM#	Date	Mintage	VG	Fine	VF	XF
887	AH1300	—	50.00	125.00	200.00	350.00
(Y6)	1301	—	20.00	35.00	90.00	140.00

SHAHI SEFID

(White Shahi)

Called the White (i.e., silver) Shahi to distinguish it from the Black or Copper Shahi, the Shahi Sefid was actually worth 3 Shahis (150 Dinars) or 3-1/8 Shahis (156-1/4 Dinars). It was used primarily for distribution on New Year's day (Now-Ruz) as good-luck gifts. Since 1926 special privately struck tokens, having no monetary value, have been used instead of coins.

The Shahi Sefid, worth 150 or 156-1/4 Dinars, was broader, but much thinner, than the 1/4 Kran (Rob'i), worth 250 Dinars.

شاهی

0.6908 g, .900 SILVER, .0200 oz ASW

KM#	Date	Mintage	VG	Fine	VF	XF
888 (Y7)	AH1296	—	25.00	40.00	75.00	160.00

NOTE: Date below lion instead of denomination, which is omitted.

Rev: Date below wreath.

KM#	Date	Mintage	VG	Fine	VF	XF
889	AH1297	—	3.00	7.50	15.00	28.00
(Y7a)	1298	—	3.00	6.00	12.50	25.00
	1299	—	4.00	8.00	15.00	35.00
	1300	—	3.00	6.00	12.50	25.00
	1301	—	2.00	4.50	9.00	15.00
	1302	—	7.50	12.50	25.00	50.00
	1303	—	2.00	4.50	9.00	15.00
	1304	—	10.00	15.00	30.00	65.00
	1305	—	3.00	6.00	15.00	30.00
	1307/1	—	7.50	15.00	30.00	60.00
	1307	—	7.50	15.00	30.00	60.00
	1308	—	10.00	15.00	30.00	60.00
	1309/01	—	6.00	15.00	30.00	60.00
	1309	—	6.00	15.00	30.00	60.00
	'13' only	—	10.00	20.00	40.00	90.00
	ND	—	2.00	5.00	10.00	30.00

Rev: Date amidst lion's legs.
(Variations exist)

KM#	Date	Mintage	VG	Fine	VF	XF
890	AH1313	—	20.00	35.00	60.00	100.00
(Y7b)	1--3 (error for 1313)					
		—	20.00	35.00	60.00	100.00

Obv. leg: *Nasir al-din* (KM#889).
Rev. leg: *Sahib al-zaman* (Obv. of KM#1007).

KM#	Date	Mintage	VG	Fine	VF	XF
891	ND	—	25.00	50.00	75.00	125.00
(Y8)						

Obv. leg: *Muzaffar al-din Shah.*

KM#	Date	Mintage	VG	Fine	VF	XF
965	AH1313	—	—	—	Rare	—
(Y25)	1314	—	10.00	20.00	40.00	75.00
	1315	—	10.00	20.00	40.00	75.00
	1316	—	10.00	20.00	40.00	75.00
	1317	—	15.00	25.00	50.00	100.00
	1318	—	8.00	15.00	30.00	60.00

NOTE: Some undated issues show traces of an old date (usually 1301 or 1303) below wreath on reverse. These are worth slightly more than other undated issues.

NOTE: Later dates (AH1319-1320) exist for this type.

NOTE: A number of varieties and mulings of KM#965 and KM#966 with other denominations, esp. 1/4 Krans and 500 Dinar pieces, are reported. These command a premium over others of the same types.

NOTE: A total of 58,000 pieces were reported struck in AH1322, 1323 and 1324, but none are known with those dates. The specimens were either struck from old dies or were undated types.

1/4 KRAN

(Rob'i = 5 Shahis)

ربعی

1.1513 g, .900 SILVER, 15mm, .0333 oz ASW
Rev: Date below wreath.

KM#	Date	Mintage	VG	Fine	VF	XF
892	AH1294	—	30.00	50.00	100.00	175.00
(Y9)	1296	—	4.00	7.00	15.00	30.00
	1297	—	10.00	20.00	40.00	75.00
	1298	—	10.00	20.00	30.00	50.00
	1299	—	5.00	8.00	20.00	40.00
	1300	—	4.00	7.00	15.00	30.00
	1301	—	3.00	6.00	14.00	30.00
	1303	—	3.00	6.00	14.00	30.00
	1304	—	20.00	40.00	60.00	125.00
	1305	—	8.00	15.00	25.00	50.00
	1306	—	7.00	12.50	20.00	50.00
	1307	—	20.00	40.00	60.00	135.00
	1308	—	20.00	40.00	60.00	135.00
	1309	—	15.00	25.00	50.00	100.00
	1310	—	— Reported, not confirmed			
	1311	—	20.00	40.00	60.00	135.00
	ND	—	3.00	6.00	15.00	25.00

NOTE: Many examples of KM#892 bear broken or partial dates. These command no premium.

Rev: Date amidst legs.

KM#	Date	Mintage	VG	Fine	VF	XF
893	AH1311	—	20.00	40.00	75.00	160.00
(Y9d)	1312	—	20.00	40.00	75.00	160.00
	1313	—	25.00	50.00	100.00	185.00

Obv. leg: *Muzaffar al-din Shah.*

KM#	Date	Mintage	VG	Fine	VF	XF
968	AH1314	—	30.00	50.00	100.00	200.00
(Y26)	1316	—	6.00	12.50	20.00	35.00
	1318	—	15.00	25.00	50.00	85.00

NOTE: Later date (AH1319) exists for this type.

500 DINARS

(10 Shahis = 1/2 Kran)

First Nasir al-din legend **Second Nasir al-din legend with *Sahibairan* added**

Forms of the denomination:

500 DINARS: ۵۰۰ دینار

or

پانصد دینار

10 SHAHIS: ده شاهی

2.3025 g, .900 SILVER, .0666 oz ASW
First leg. Rev: *500 Dinars*.

KM#	Date	Mintage	VG	Fine	VF	XF
894	AH1296	—	— Reported, not confirmed			
(Y10)	1297	—	8.00	15.00	30.00	70.00
	1298	—	8.00	15.00	30.00	70.00
	1299	—	— Reported, not confirmed			
	1301	—	7.00	25.00	55.00	120.00
	1306	—	7.00	15.00	35.00	100.00
	1307	—	50.00	85.00	175.00	350.00
	1311	—	25.00	40.00	75.00	140.00
	ND	—	4.00	7.50	15.00	30.00

NOTE: The undated issue is often found in higher grades than dated coins.

Nasir al-din's Return From Europe

KM#	Date	Mintage	VG	Fine	VF	XF
895	AH1307	—	50.00	100.00	215.00	325.00
(Y-A15)	1307 w/1306 on rev.					
		—	100.00	200.00	300.00	525.00

Obv: First leg. No crown.
Rev: *10 Shahis*, date amidst legs.

KM#	Date	Mintage	VG	Fine	VF	XF
896	AH1310	—	40.00	75.00	150.00	275.00
(Y10b)						

Obv: Second leg. Crown added above leg.
Rev: *10 Shahis, date amidst legs*.

KM#	Date	Mintage	VG	Fine	VF	XF
897	AH1310	—	30.00	60.00	125.00	200.00
(Y10c)	1311	—	30.00	60.00	125.00	200.00

First leg, no crown.
Rev: *500 Dinars*, date amidst legs.

KM#	Date	Mintage	VG	Fine	VF	XF
898	AH1311	—	25.00	50.00	80.00	160.00
(Y10d)	1312	—	20.00	40.00	65.00	110.00
	1313	—	25.00	50.00	80.00	160.00

Obv. leg: *Muzaffar al-din, 500 Dinars*
Rev: Date amidst legs, arranged variously.

KM#	Date	Mintage	VG	Fine	VF	XF
969	AH1298(sic)	—	50.00	100.00	150.00	250.00
(Y27.1)	1313	—	25.00	40.00	75.00	150.00
	1314	—	10.00	20.00	40.00	100.00
	1315	—	25.00	40.00	75.00	150.00
	1316	—	25.00	40.00	75.00	150.00
	1317	—	— Reported, not confirmed			
	1318	—	15.00	30.00	50.00	125.00

NOTE: Later dates (AH1319-1322) exist for this type.

NOTE: Some reverse dies were previously used under Nasir al-Din and show traces of old date beneath wreath on reverse. The 1298 is an "undated" variety showing 1298 of the dies previous user.

1000 DINARS

(Kran, Qiran)

Forms of the denomination:

1000 DINARS: یکهزار دینار

1 KRAN: یکقران

4.6050 g, .900 SILVER, .1332 oz ASW
Obv. leg: *Nasir al-din Shah*, first leg.
Rev: *1000 Dinars*.

KM#	Date	Mintage	Fine	VF	XF	Unc
899	AH1294	—	—	—	300.00	400.00
(Y11)	1295	—	—	—	300.00	400.00
	1296	—	4.00	8.00	20.00	55.00
	1297	—	5.00	10.00	25.00	60.00
	1298/7	—	10.00	20.00	40.00	80.00
	1298	—	10.00	20.00	40.00	80.00
	ND	—	4.00	10.00	25.00	60.00

Obv: Second leg. Rev: *1000 Dinars*.

KM#	Date	Mintage	Fine	VF	XF	Unc
900	AH1298	—	5.00	10.00	25.00	60.00
(Y11a)	1299	—	10.00	20.00	50.00	90.00
	129x	—	10.00	20.00	50.00	90.00
	1301	—	—	—	—	—
	1303	—	150.00	250.00	500.00	600.00
	ND	—	5.00	10.00	25.00	45.00

Obv: Second leg, crown above. Rev: *1 Kran*.

KM#	Date	Mintage	Fine	VF	XF	Unc
901	AH1310	—	100.00	150.00	250.00	425.00
(Y11c)	1311	—	60.00	125.00	225.00	375.00

Obv: Second leg, w/o crown. Rev: *1 Kran*.

KM#	Date	Mintage	Fine	VF	XF	Unc
902 (Y11b)	AH1311	—	100.00	150.00	250.00	—

Obv: Second leg., w/o crown. Rev: *1000 Dinars*.

KM#	Date	Mintage	Fine	VF	XF	Unc
903	AH1311	—	90.00	135.00	225.00	—
(Y11d)	1312	—	100.00	150.00	250.00	—

Obv. leg: *Muzaffar al-din Shah*, w/o crown.

KM#	Date	Mintage	Fine	VF	XF	Unc
970 (Y-A27)	AH1314	—	125.00	200.00	400.00	—

Obv: Crown added above leg. Rev: Date amidst lion's legs.

KM#	Date	Mintage	Fine	VF	XF	Unc
972	AH1317	—	100.00	175.00	250.00	—
(Y-A27a)	1318	—	100.00	175.00	250.00	—

NOTE: Later dates (AH1319-1322) exist for this type.

Rev: Date below wreath.

KM#	Date	Mintage	Fine	VF	XF	Unc
971 (Y-B27a)	AH1303	—	200.00	300.00	400.00	—
(Y-B27b)	1312	—	200.00	300.00	400.00	—

2000 DINARS

(2 Krans)

Forms of the denomination:

2 KRANS: دو قران

2000 DINARS: دو هزار دینار

9.2100 g, .900 SILVER, .2665 oz ASW
Obv. leg: *Nasir al-din Shah*, first leg.
Rev: *2000 Dinars*.

KM#	Date	Mintage	Fine	VF	XF	Unc
904	AH1296	—	8.00	12.00	30.00	80.00
(Y12)	1297	—	7.50	11.00	25.00	70.00
	1298/7	—	12.50	20.00	45.00	100.00
	1298	—	12.50	20.00	45.00	100.00
	ND	—	6.00	11.00	25.00	80.00

Obv: Second leg. Rev: *2000 Dinars*.

KM#	Date	Mintage	Fine	VF	XF	Unc
905	AH1298	—	10.00	15.00	35.00	80.00
(Y12a)	1299	—	10.00	15.00	35.00	80.00
	1299 B on rev.	—	25.00	50.00	100.00	175.00
	1300	—	10.00	15.00	35.00	90.00
	1301	—	10.00	15.00	35.00	100.00
	1302	—	22.50	35.00	75.00	140.00
	1303	—	20.00	30.00	75.00	140.00
	1304	—	22.50	35.00	75.00	140.00
	1305	—	10.00	15.00	35.00	100.00
	1306	—	22.50	35.00	75.00	140.00
	1307	—	22.50	35.00	75.00	140.00
	1308	—	20.00	30.00	65.00	140.00
	ND	—	10.00	15.00	35.00	90.00

NOTE: All dates after AH1301 were struck from worn dies and hence incomplete even in high grades.

NOTE: Coins dated AH1300-1305 show a 'b' to the lower left obv., often missing on poorly struck specimens or specimens from filled dies.

Rev: Crown above date below wreath.

KM#	Date	Mintage	Fine	VF	XF	Unc
908 (Y12b.1)	AH1310 (in blundered form as 13010)	—	100.00	150.00	300.00	—

Obv: Second leg., w/o crown.

KM#	Date	Mintage	Fine	VF	XF	Unc
910 (Y12c.1)	AH1311	—	100.00	150.00	300.00	—

Obv: Second leg., crown above wreath. Rev: *2 Krans*, date amidst legs.

KM#	Date	Mintage	Fine	VF	XF	Unc
909	AH1310	—	40.00	75.00	125.00	—
(Y12c.2)	1311	—	30.00	60.00	100.00	—

Obv: Second leg., w/o crown above. Rev: *2 Krans, date below wreath*.

KM#	Date	Mintage	Fine	VF	XF	Unc
907 (Y12b.2)	AH1310 (in blundered form as 13010)	—	100.00	150.00	300.00	—

Obv: Second leg., w/o crown. Rev: *2000 Dinars*.

KM#	Date	Mintage	Fine	VF	XF	Unc
911	AH1311	—	40.00	75.00	150.00	—
(Y12d)	1312	—	40.00	75.00	150.00	—

50th Year of Reign
Special leg: *Dhu'l-Qarneyn*.
Mule. Obv: Y#C15. Rev: Y#12d.

KM#	Date	Mintage	Fine	VF	XF	Unc
912	AH1313/1312					
(Y12e)	3 or 4 known	—	2500.	—	—	

NOTE: This coin was struck in quantity and was due to be released at Nasir's 50th anniversary as a largesse piece. A number of specimens were passed out to persons close to the royal court before the celebration which accounts for the few known today. Nasir al-din was assassinated just before the fiftieth year of his reign began and the balance of the issue was probably melted.

KM#	Date	Mintage	Fine	VF	XF	Unc
913 (Y-C15)	AH1313	—	1150.	2250.	5000.	—

Obv. leg: *Muzaffar al-din Shah*, w/o crown, leg: *2000 Dinars*.

KM#	Date	Mintage	Fine	VF	XF	Unc
973	AH1313	—	100.00	150.00	250.00	—
(Y28)	1314	—	75.00	125.00	225.00	—

Obv: Crown added. Rev. leg: *2000 Dinars*, position of date amidst legs varies.

KM#	Date	Mintage	Fine	VF	XF	Unc
974	AH1312	—	75.00	100.00	200.00	—
(Y28a)	1314	—	25.00	40.00	100.00	200.00
	1315	—	18.50	27.50	65.00	150.00
	1316	—	15.00	25.00	50.00	110.00
	1317	—	15.00	25.00	50.00	110.00
	1318	—	10.00	20.00	35.00	90.00

NOTE: Later dates (AH1319-1320) exist for this type.
NOTE: Blundered dates exist.

5000 DINARS

(5 Krans)

23.0251 g, .900 SILVER, .6662 oz ASW
100th Anniversary - Qajar Regime

KM#	Date	Mintage	Fine	VF	XF	Unc
A914	AH1293	—	175.00	275.00	450.00	700.00

Nasir al-Din Shah

Dav.#285

KM#	Date	Mintage	Fine	VF	XF	Unc
914	AH1296	—	100.00	150.00	275.00	425.00
(Y13)	1297	—	75.00	100.00	200.00	325.00

Obv: Crown above leg. Rev. value: *5 Krans*.

KM#	Date	Mintage	Fine	VF	XF	Unc
915 (Y13c)	AH1311	—	1300.	2000.	3500.	—

GOLD COINAGE

NOTE: Modern imitations exist of many types, particularly the small 1/5, 1/2 and 1 Toman coins. These are usually underweight (or rarely overweight), and are sold in the bazaars at a small premium over bullion. They are usually crude and probably not intended to deceive collectors, but some are sold for jewelry and some are dated outside the reign of the ruler whose name or portrait they bear.

A few deceptive counterfeits are known of the large 10 Toman pieces.

2000 DINARS

(1/5 Toman)

.6520 g, .900 GOLD, .0188 oz AGW
Obv. leg: First Nasir type. Rev: Lion and sun.

KM#	Date	Mintage	Fine	VF	XF	Unc
923 (Y-A16)	AH1295	—	125.00	175.00	350.00	425.00

Mule. Rev: KM#923. Rev: KM#991.

KM#	Date	Mintage	Fine	VF	XF	Unc
922 (Y-E16)	AH1295	—	—	—	—	—

.5749 g, .900 GOLD, .0166 oz AGW
Obv: Bust of Nasir al-din Shah.

KM#	Date	Mintage	Fine	VF	XF	Unc
924	AH1297	—	20.00	40.00	75.00	125.00
(Y16)	1298	—	22.50	45.00	100.00	150.00
	1299	—	20.00	40.00	75.00	125.00
	1300	—	20.00	40.00	75.00	135.00
	1301	—	20.00	40.00	75.00	135.00

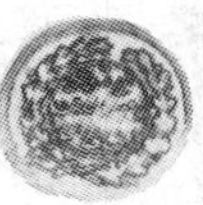

KM#	Date	Mintage	Fine	VF	XF	Unc
925 (Y-F16)	AH1309	—	—	—	Rare	—

Obv. leg: *Muzaffar-al-din Shah.*
Rev: Lion and sun.

KM#	Date	Mintage	Fine	VF	XF	Unc
986	AH9301 (error for 1319)					
(Y-A38)			125.00	175.00	275.00	400.00

5000 DINARS

(1/2 Toman)

1.6300 g, .900 GOLD, .0472 oz AGW
Obv: Nasir al-din Shah.

KM#	Date	Mintage	Fine	VF	XF	Unc
926 (Y-C16)	AH1294	—	200.00	400.00	750.00	1250.

1.4372 g, .900 GOLD, .0416 oz AGW

KM#	Date	Mintage	Fine	VF	XF	Unc
921	AH1296	—	100.00	200.00	300.00	400.00
(C16a)	1298	—	—	Reported, not confirmed		
	1309	—	200.00	400.00	750.00	1250.

Obv: First Nasir portrait type.

KM#	Date	Mintage	Fine	VF	XF	Unc
927	AH1297	—	50.00	70.00	120.00	200.00
(Y17)	1299	—	50.00	70.00	120.00	200.00
	1300	—	—	—	—	—
	1301	—	65.00	120.00	200.00	380.00
	1303	—	65.00	120.00	200.00	380.00
	1305	—	65.00	120.00	200.00	380.00
	13(0)5	—	65.00	120.00	200.00	380.00
	1307	—	125.00	275.00	400.00	600.00
	1213 (error) for 1312					
		—	100.00	150.00	275.00	350.00
	1313	—	150.00	275.00	400.00	600.00

Obv. leg: *Nasir Dhu'l Qarnayn.*

KM#	Date	Mintage	Fine	VF	XF	Unc
928 (Y-K16)	AH1313	—	—	—	Rare	—

Obv. leg: *Muzaffar al-din Shah.*

KM#	Date	Mintage	Fine	VF	XF	Unc
987	AH1314	—	115.00	225.00	325.00	450.00
(Y38)	1315	—	135.00	275.00	450.00	675.00

NOTE: AH1314 has 13 left of front legs and 14 between front and back legs.

Obv: Portrait left.

KM#	Date	Mintage	Fine	VF	XF	Unc
993	ND	—	175.00	275.00	400.00	550.00

KM#	Date	Mintage	Fine	VF	XF	Unc
994	AH1316	—	25.00	50.00	70.00	135.00
(Y35)	1318	—	25.00	50.00	75.00	150.00

NOTE: Later dates (AH1319-1324) exist for this type.

TOMAN

3.4525 g, .900 GOLD, .0988 oz AGW
30th Year of Reign
Obv: Leg. Rev: Lion and sun.

KM#	Date	Mintage	Fine	VF	XF	Unc
930 (Y-G16)	AH1293	—	400.00	500.00	700.00	1000.

3.2570 g, .900 GOLD, .0943 oz AGW
Obv. leg: First Nasir type. Rev: Lion and sun.

KM#	Date	Mintage	Fine	VF	XF	Unc
931 (Y-B16)	AH1294	—	500.00	800.00	1150.	1750.

NOTE: Coins of this type dated AH1296 and of reduced weight, 2.87 g, .900 Gold, have been reported to exist.

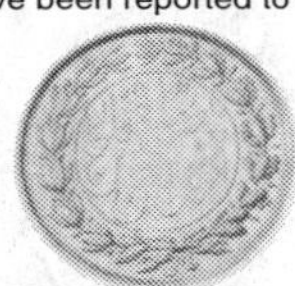

Obv: First portrait, w/o leg.
Rev. leg: First Nasir type.

KM#	Date	Mintage	Fine	VF	XF	Unc
932	ND	—	100.00	185.00	250.00	350.00
(Y-A18)	AH1297	—	110.00	200.00	300.00	450.00

Accession date: AH1264
Rev. leg: First Nasir type.

KM#	Date	Mintage	Fine	VF	XF	Unc
933	AH1297 (w/error accession date AH1294)					
(Y18)		—	150.00	300.00	500.00	750.00
	1297	—	40.00	70.00	100.00	200.00
	1298	—	100.00	200.00	300.00	500.00
	1299	—	40.00	60.00	100.00	175.00
	1300	—	80.00	165.00	250.00	425.00
	1301	—	45.00	80.00	140.00	200.00
	1303	—	50.00	100.00	150.00	225.00
	1304	—	85.00	150.00	250.00	425.00
	1305	—	45.00	80.00	140.00	200.00
	1306	—	100.00	150.00	250.00	425.00
	1307	—	80.00	125.00	200.00	325.00
	1309	—	85.00	125.00	200.00	325.00
	1311	—	100.00	150.00	250.00	375.00
	1312	—	150.00	200.00	275.00	500.00
	1313	—	—	Reported, not confirmed		

NOTE: Many of these coins have carelessly written dates, especially 1303 onward.

NOTE: Naseredin Shah coins have two dates surrounding the Shah's head. The date to the left is date of the coin, the date to the right is the accession date.

Shah's return from Europe, AH1307.

KM#	Date	Mintage	Fine	VF	XF	Unc
934 (Y-D15)	AH1307	—	400.00	750.00	1250.	1750.

Obv: Second portrait, actual date right.
Rev. leg: First Nasir type, date added.

KM#	Date	Mintage	Fine	VF	XF	Unc
936 (Y22)	AH1310	—	250.00	400.00	600.00	1000.

Rev. leg: Second Nasir type.

KM#	Date	Mintage	Fine	VF	XF	Unc
937 (Y22a)	AH1311	—	100.00	150.00	250.00	375.00

Mule. Obv. KM#933. Rev: KM#936.

KM#	Date	Mintage	Fine	VF	XF	Unc
938	AH1313//1310					
(Y-A22)		—	225.00	350.00	525.00	750.00

Obv. leg: *Muzaffar al-din Shah,*
AH1313-1314. Rev: Lion and sun.

KM#	Date	Mintage	Fine	VF	XF	Unc
988 (Y39)	AH1314	—	150.00	200.00	300.00	550.00

Rev: Lion and sun.

KM#	Date	Mintage	Fine	VF	XF	Unc
989 (Y-A39)	AH1311	—	550.00	900.00	1500.	2500.

NOTE: Although inscribed *Two Tomans,* this type is known only on 1 Toman planchets.

2 TOMANS

6.5150 g, .900 GOLD, .1885 oz AGW
Discovery of Gold in Khurason
Obv: Leg. within wreath, crown above.
Rev: Leg. within wreath.

KM#	Date	Mintage	Fine	VF	XF	Unc
940 (Y-H16)	AH1295	—	—	—	Rare	—

8th Emam Commemorative
Obv: First Nasir portrait.
Rev: Legend within wreath, crown above.

KM#	Date	Mintage	Fine	VF	XF	Unc
941 (Y-J16)	AH1295	—	—	—	Rare	—

5.7488 g, .900 GOLD, .1663 oz AGW
Accession date: AH1264
Obv: First Nasir portrait. Rev. leg: First Nasir type.

KM#	Date	Mintage	Fine	VF	XF	Unc
942	AH1297	—	125.00	200.00	275.00	450.00
(Y19)	1298	—	250.00	400.00	750.00	1250.
	1299	—	100.00	150.00	200.00	375.00
	1309	—	—	Reported, not confirmed		

Shah's Return From Europe

KM#	Date	Mintage	Fine	VF	XF	Unc
943 (Y-B15)	AH1299//1307	—	525.00	850.00	1400.	2350.

Shah's Visit To Tehran Mint

KM#	Date	Mintage	Fine	VF	XF	Unc
944 (Y-E15)	AH1308	—	—	—	Rare	—

10 TOMANS

28.7440 g, .900 GOLD, .8317 oz AGW
Obv: First portrait of Nasir al-din Shah, AH1296-97.

KM#	Date	Mintage	Fine	VF	XF	Unc
945	AH1297 H	—	1250.	1500.	2250.	3500.
(Y21)	1311 H	—	—	—	7000.	10,000.

Obv: Second portrait of Nasir al-din Shah, w/medals on chest, AH1311.

KM#	Date	Mintage	Fine	VF	XF	Unc
946 (Y-A23)	AH1311	—	2000.	3000.	5000.	7500.

KM#	Date	Mintage	Fine	VF	XF	Unc
947 (Y-B23)	AH1311	—	1500.	2500.	3500.	6000.

50th Anniversary - Reign of Nasir al-Din

KM#	Date	Mintage	Fine	VF	XF	Unc
950 (M12)	AH1313		1500.	2250.	3000.	5000.

Rev: Denomination at bottom.

KM#	Date	Mintage	Fine	VF	XF	Unc
998 (Y-B34.1)	AH1314	—	2500.	3500.	5500.	8000.

Rev: Second date replaces denomination at bottom.

KM#	Date	Mintage	Fine	VF	XF	Unc
999 (Y-B34.2)	AH1314	—	2500.	3250.	5000.	7000.

Obv: Date stamped. Rev: W/denomination.

KM#	Date	Mintage	Fine	VF	XF	Unc
1000 (Y-B34.3)	AH1314	—	2500.	3250.	5000.	7000.

25 TOMANS

.900 GOLD, 50mm.

KM#	Date	Mintage	Fine	VF	XF	Unc
951 (M5)	AH1301B		—	—	15,000.	—

Shah's Return From Europe

KM#	Date	Mintage	Fine	VF	XF	Unc
952 (M6)	AH1307		—	—	*Rare	—

***NOTE:** Stack's Hammel sale 9-82 AU realized $17,000.

MEDALLIC ISSUES (M)

10 TOMANS

28.7440 g, .900 GOLD, .8317 oz AGW
Obv. leg: First Nasir type. Rev: Lion and sun.

KM#	Date	Fine	VF	XF	Unc
M8	AH1293	—	—	Rare	—

PATTERNS (Pn)

KM#	Date	Mintage	Identification	Mkt.Val.
Pn1	ND	—	1 Kran, Silver, Brussels Mint	600.00
Pn2	AH1281	—	25 Dinars, Bronze	650.00

KM#	Date	Mintage	Identification	Mkt.Val.
Pn3	AH1281	—	50 Dinars, Bronze	1000.
Pn4	AH1281	—	1/4 Kran, Copper	550.00
Pn5	AH1281	—	1/4 Kran, Silver	550.00
Pn6	AH1281	—	500 Dinars, Copper	525.00
Pn7	AH1281	—	500 Dinars, Silver	575.00

KM#	Date	Mintage	Identification	Mkt.Val.
Pn8	AH1281	—	1000 Dinars, Copper	450.00
Pn9	AH1281	—	1000 Dinars, Silver, 11.02 g	550.00

KM#	Date	Mintage	Identification	Mkt.Val.
Pn10	AH1281	—	2000 Dinars, Copper	450.00
Pn11	AH1281	—	2000 Dinars, Silver	700.00

KM#	Date	Mintage	Identification	Mkt.Val.
Pn12	AH1281	—	2 Tomans, Gold	1850.

KM#	Date	Mintage	Identification	Mkt.Val.
Pn14	AH1293	—	500 Dinars, Silver	500.00

KM#	Date	Mintage	Identification	Mkt.Val.
Pn15	AH1294	—	25 Dinars, Copper, PF flanking date	225.00

KM#	Date	Mintage	Identification	Mkt.Val.
Pn16	AH1294	—	1/2 Toman, Gold, 1.60 g, KM926, obv. leg: first Nazir type	1000.
Pn17	AH1295	—	1/4 Toman, KM931, Obv. leg: First Nasir type	500.00

KM#	Date	Mintage	Identification	Mkt.Val.
Pn18	AH1297	—	5000 Dinars, Silver, 22.85 g, plain edge, KM914	550.00
Pn19	AH1297	—	1/4 Toman, KM931, Obv. leg: First Nasir type	500.00
Pn20	AH1297	—	1/4 Toman, Obv: First bust of Nasir	500.00
Pn21	ND	—	1000 Dinars, KM899	—

KM#	Date	Mintage	Identification	Mkt.Val.
Pn22	AH1316	—	1/2 Toman, Gilt Bronze, KM994	600.00

KM#	Date	Mintage	Identification	Mkt.Val.
Pn23	AH1316	—	1 Toman, Gilt Bronze, KM995	800.00

KM#	Date	Mintage	Identification	Mkt.Val.
Pn24	ND	—	5 Krans, Silver	1000.

KM#	Date	Mintage	Identification	Mkt.Val.
Pn25	AH1318	—	5 Krans, Silver, Paris Mint	1750.

IRAQ

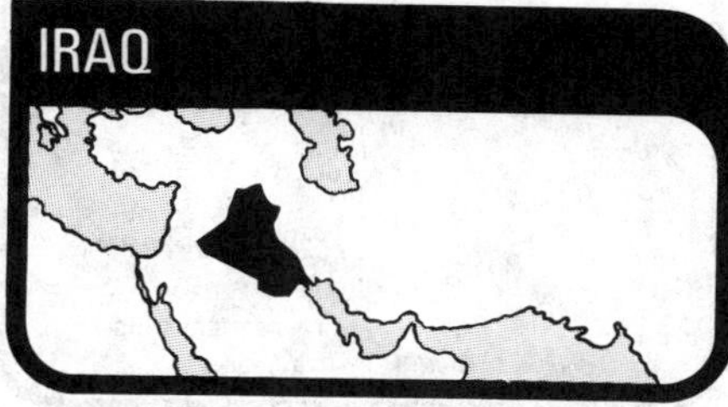

The Republic of Iraq, historically known as Mesopotamia, is located in the Near East and is bordered by Kuwait, Iran, Turkey, Syria, Jordan and Saudi Arabia. It has an area of 167,925 sq. mi. (434,920 sq. km.) and a population of 14 million. Capital: Baghdad. The economy of Iraq is based on agriculture and petroleum. Crude oil accounted for 94 percent of the exports before the war with Iran began in 1980.

Mesopotamia was the site of a number of flourishing civilizations of antiquity - Sumeria, Assyria, Babylonia, Parthia, Persia - and of the Biblical cities of Ur, Nineveh and Babylon. Desired because of its favored location which embraced the fertile alluvial plains of the Tigris and Euphrates Rivers, Mesopotamia - 'land between the rivers' - was conquered by Cyrus the Great of Persia, Alexander of Macedonia and by Arabs who made the legendary city of Baghdad the capital of the ruling caliphate. Suleiman the Magnificent conquered Mesopotamia for Turkey in 1534, and it formed part of the Ottoman Empire until 1623, and from 1638 to 1917. Great Britain, given a League of Nations mandate over the territory in 1920, recognized Iraq as a kingdom in 1922. Iraq became an independent constitutional monarchy presided over by the Hashemite family, direct descendants of the prophet Mohammed, in 1932. In 1958, the army-led revolution of July 14 overthrew the monarchy and proclaimed a republic.

RULERS

Ottoman, until 1917

MESOPOTAMIA

MONETARY SYSTEM

40 Para = 1 Piastre (Kurus)

MINTNAME

Baghdad بغداد

al-Basrah (Basra) البصره

al-Hille الحله

MAHMUD II

AH1223-1255/1808-1839AD

NOTE: The denominations of the following coins are tentative, and all authorities are not in agreement of the classification. Until a better system is available, that of C. Olcer will be followed. Most types are similar to Turkish coins, but with mintname Baghdad.

PARA

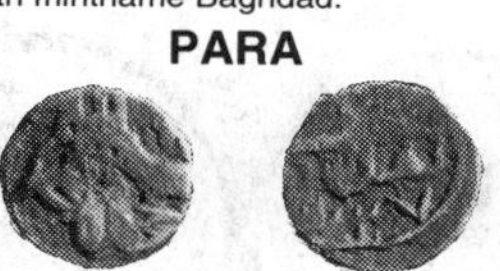

COPPER

KM#	Date	Year	Good	VG	Fine	VF
75	AH1223	—	—	—	—	—

2 PARA

COPPER, 16-19mm

KM#	Date	Year	Good	VG	Fine	VF
80	AH1239	—	—	—	—	—
	1240	—	—	—	—	—
	1241	16	— Reported, not confirmed			

5 PARA

BILLON

KM#	Date	Year	Good	VG	Fine	VF
50	AH1223	12	12.00	20.00	35.00	50.00

COPPER, 1.24 g

KM#	Date	Year	Good	VG	Fine	VF
54	AH1238	—	10.00	17.00	28.00	40.00
	1240	—	10.00	17.00	28.00	40.00
	1241	—	10.00	17.00	28.00	40.00
	1244	—	10.00	17.00	28.00	40.00

Obv. and rev: Narrow floral borders.

KM#	Date	Year	Good	VG	Fine	VF
58	AH1240	—	8.00	13.00	22.50	33.50

Rev: Year above mintname.

KM#	Date	Year	Good	VG	Fine	VF
63	AH1223	18	—	—	—	—

17-25mm

KM#	Date	Year	Good	VG	Fine	VF
69	AH1223	23	12.00	20.00	35.00	50.00
	1223	25	12.00	20.00	35.00	50.00

Obv: Similar to KM#69. Rev: *Duriba fi Bagdad 1349* in dotted circle.

KM#	Date	Year	Good	VG	Fine	VF
A70	AH—	—	—	—	—	—

Rev: Regnal year above mintname.

KM#	Date	Year	Good	VG	Fine	VF
70	AH1223	25	—	—	—	—

Obv: Star of David only. Rev: Similar to KM#70.

KM#	Date	Year	Good	VG	Fine	VF
71	AH1223	25	—	—	—	—

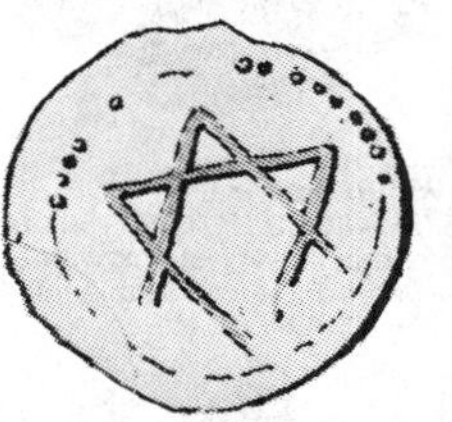

Obv: Star of David only, 29mm.

KM#	Date	Year	Good	VG	Fine	VF
72	AH1248	—	15.00	25.00	42.00	60.00

Obv: Star and crescent only, 21-25mm.

KM#	Date	Year	Good	VG	Fine	VF
73	AH1223	25	12.00	20.00	35.00	50.00
	1223	26	10.00	18.50	32.00	45.00

20-22mm

KM#	Date	Year	Good	VG	Fine	VF
79	AH1223	28	10.00	16.50	28.00	40.00
	1223	29	Reported, not confirmed			

BILLON, 0.80 g, 18mm

KM#	Date	Year	Good	VG	Fine	VF
59	AH1223	17	16.00	27.00	45.00	65.00

10 PARA

BILLON, 24mm, 2.10 g
Obv: Toughra. Rev: Mint and date within beaded borders.

KM#	Date	Year	Good	VG	Fine	VF
51	AH1223	13	50.00	85.00	140.00	200.00
	1223	15	—	—	Rare	—

26mm, 1.60-1.80 g
Obv: Toughra, mint and date. Rev. leg: 4 lines.

KM#	Date	Year	Good	VG	Fine	VF
55	AH1223	15	50.00	85.00	140.00	200.00
	1223	17	50.00	85.00	140.00	200.00

Similar to KM#55 w/ornamental borders added.

KM#	Date	Year	Good	VG	Fine	VF
60	AH1223	17	30.00	50.00	85.00	125.00

22mm, 1.40 g
Similar to KM#51, but floral borders.

KM#	Date	Year	Good	VG	Fine	VF
61	AH1223	17	30.00	50.00	85.00	125.00

20 PARA

BILLON, 28mm, 3.50-4.20 g

KM#	Date	Year	Good	VG	Fine	VF
52	AH1223	13	50.00	85.00	140.00	200.00

27mm, 3.20 g
Obv: Toughra, mint and date. Rev: 4-line leg.

KM#	Date	Year	Good	VG	Fine	VF
56	AH1223	15	50.00	85.00	140.00	200.00
	1223	17	50.00	85.00	140.00	200.00

28mm, 2.933-3.00 g
Obv. and rev: Ornamental design in margin.

KM#	Date	Year	Good	VG	Fine	VF
62	AH1223	17	45.00	75.00	125.00	175.00
	1223	21	—	—	Rare	—

Obv. and rev: Legend in margin.

KM#	Date	Year	Good	VG	Fine	VF
A63	AH1223	21	—	—	—	—

Reduced weight; 22mm, 1.20-1.60 g

KM#	Date	Year	Good	VG	Fine	VF
64	AH1223	21	32.00	55.00	90.00	130.00

22mm, 1.80-2.00 g
Similar to KM#52, but extra leg. around central design.

KM#	Date	Year	Good	VG	Fine	VF
65	AH1223	21	32.00	55.00	90.00	130.00

Similar to KM#56, 26mm, 2.00 g.

KM#	Date	Year	Good	VG	Fine	VF
68	AH1223	17	32.00	55.00	90.00	130.00
	1223	22	32.00	55.00	90.00	130.00

22-24mm
Similar to 5 Para, KM#59.

KM#	Date	Year	Good	VG	Fine	VF
75	AH1223	26	15.00	25.00	35.00	50.00
	1223	28	15.00	25.00	35.00	50.00
	1223	29	15.00	25.00	35.00	50.00

30 PARA

(Zolota)

BILLON, 31mm, 4.50 g

KM#	Date	Year	Good	VG	Fine	VF
57	AH1223	15	50.00	85.00	140.00	200.00

PIASTRE

(40 Para)

BILLON, 31mm, 3.20-4.00 g

KM#	Date	Year	Good	VG	Fine	VF
53	AH1223	13	75.00	125.00	200.00	300.00

29mm

KM#	Date	Year	Good	VG	Fine	VF
66	AH1223	21	50.00	85.00	140.00	200.00

Extra leg. added around central device.

KM#	Date	Year	Good	VG	Fine	VF
67	AH1223	21	50.00	85.00	140.00	200.00

100 PARA

BILLON, 31mm, 3.00-3.20 g

KM#	Date	Year	Good	VG	Fine	VF
76	AH1223	26	50.00	85.00	140.00	200.00

Rev: Arabic legend.

KM#	Date	Year	Good	VG	Fine	VF
77	AH1223	26	—	—	—	—
	1223	27	—	—	—	—

5 PIASTRES

BILLON, 36mm, 5.50-6.90 g

KM#	Date	Year	Good	VG	Fine	VF
78	21 (date error)			—	Rare	—
	AH1223	26	18.00	30.00	50.00	75.00
	—	27	18.00	30.00	50.00	75.00

HAYRIYE ALTIN

GOLD, 20-21mm, 1.40 g

KM#	Date	Year	VG	Fine	VF	XF
74	AH1223	25	120.00	200.00	275.00	400.00

GOVERNOR SAIT PASA

Coins without name or toughra of Mahmud II

2 PARA

COPPER, 15-18mm

KM#	Date	Year	Good	VG	Fine	VF
82	AH1230	—	20.00	32.00	55.00	80.00

5 PARA

COPPER, 27mm
Obv: *Sait Pasa* within octagram.

KM#	Date	Year	Good	VG	Fine	VF
85	AH1231	—	35.00	60.00	100.00	150.00

NOTE: This is the only Ottoman coin ever struck with a governor's name. Sait Pasa was beheaded for this infringement of tradition.

Obv: *Tamgha* within octagram.
Rev: Similar to KM#85.

KM#	Date	Year	Good	VG	Fine	VF
88	AH1231	—	25.00	42.00	70.00	100.00

NOTE: The Tamgha was originally a sheep and cattle brand, later seal or brand. Each Turkish clan formerly kept its own Tamgha, to use both as a brand and as a seal on documents.

ABDUL MEJID

AH1255-1277/1839-1861AD

5 PARA

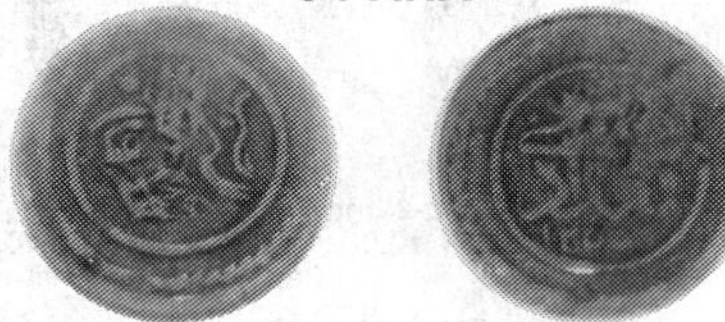

BILLON, 19-21mm

KM#	Date	Year	Good	VG	Fine	VF
91	AH1255	1	100.00	150.00	250.00	350.00

IRELAND

Ireland, the island located in the Atlantic Ocean west of Great Britain, was settled by a race of tall, red-haired Celts from Gaul about 400 BC. They assimilated the native Erainn and Picts and established a Gaelic civilization. After the arrival of St. Patrick in 432 AD, Ireland evolved into a center of Latin learning which sent missionaries to Europe and possibly North America. In 1154, Pope Adrian IV gave all of Ireland to English King Henry II to administer as a Papal fief. Because of the enactment of anti-Catholic laws and the awarding of vast tracts of Irish land to Protestant absentee land-owners, English control did not become reasonably absolute until 1800 when England and Ireland became the "United Kingdom of Great Britain and Ireland". Religious freedom was restored to the Irish in 1829, but agitation for political autonomy continued until the Irish Free State was established as a Dominion on Dec. 6, 1921 while Northern Ireland remained under the British rule.

RULERS

British to 1921

MONETARY SYSTEM

4 Farthings = 1 Penny
12 Pence = 1 Shilling
5 Shillings = 1 Crown

FARTHING

KM#	Date	Mintage	Fine	VF	XF	Unc
	COPPER					
146	1806	—	4.00	9.00	40.00	120.00
	1806	—	—	—	Proof	150.00
	COPPER GILT					
146a	1806	—	—	—	Proof	250.00
	COPPER BRONZED					
146b	1806	—	—	—	Proof	175.00
	SILVER					
146c	1806	—	—	—	Proof	1500.
	GOLD					
146d	1806	—	—	—	Proof	Rare

1/2 PENNY

KM#	Date	Mintage	Fine	VF	XF	Unc
	COPPER					
147	1805	—	6.00	12.00	60.00	150.00
	1805	—	—	—	Proof	225.00
	COPPER GILT					
147a	1805	—	—	—	Proof	285.00
	COPPER BRONZED					
147b	1805	—	—	—	Proof	185.00
	SILVER					
147c	1805	—	—	—	Proof	1500.

KM#	Date	Mintage	Fine	VF	XF	Unc
	COPPER					
150	1822	—	8.00	22.00	85.00	225.00
	1822	—	—	—	Proof	350.00

KM#	Date	Mintage	Fine	VF	XF	Unc
150	1823	—	8.00	22.00	85.00	225.00
	1823	—	—	—	Proof	350.00

PENNY

COPPER

KM#	Date	Mintage	Fine	VF	XF	Unc
148	1805	—	10.00	20.00	75.00	200.00
	1805	—	—	—	Proof	300.00

COPPER GILT

KM#	Date	Mintage	Fine	VF	XF	Unc
148a	1805	—	—	—	Proof	450.00

COPPER BRONZED

KM#	Date	Mintage	Fine	VF	XF	Unc
148b	1805	—	—	—	Proof	285.00

SILVER

KM#	Date	Mintage	Fine	VF	XF	Unc
148c	1805	—	—	—	Proof	1650.

GOLD

KM#	Date	Mintage	Fine	VF	XF	Unc
148d	1805	—	—	—	Proof	3500.

COPPER

KM#	Date	Mintage	Fine	VF	XF	Unc
151	1822	—	10.00	28.00	100.00	250.00
	1822	—	—	—	Proof	450.00
	1823	—	10.00	28.00	100.00	250.00
	1823	—	—	—	Proof	450.00

NOTE: For mule obv. KM#151 and rev. Ionian Islands 2 Oboli, KM#33 refer to Greece pattern listings.

COUNTERMARKED COINAGE

MERCHANT ISSUES

5 SHILLINGS 5 PENCE

.903 SILVER
c/m: PAYABLE AT CASTLE COMER COLLIERY, 5s. 5d. on Spanish or Spanish Colonial 8 Reales.

KM#	Date	Mintage	Good	VG	Fine	VF
145	ND(1804)	16 known	225.00	450.00	800.00	1500.

NOTE: 3 false punches have been applied to genuine Spanish Colonial coins.

MEDALLIC ISSUES (M)

1900 Reginald Huth Series

Commemorating the visit of Queen Victoria to Ireland. Struck by John Pinches, London, England.

3 SHILLINGS

SILVER

KM#	Date	Mintage	Fine	VF	XF	Unc
M2	1900	—	—	—	Proof	450.00

GOLD

KM#	Date	Mintage	Fine	VF	XF	Unc
M2a	1900	—	—	—	Rare	—

SILVER
Rev: W/III above and Oct: below crown.

KM#	Date	Mintage	Fine	VF	XF	Unc
M3	1900	—	—	—	Proof	800.00

GOLD

KM#	Date	Mintage	Fine	VF	XF	Unc
M3a	1900	—	—	—	Rare	—

SILVER
Rev: W/III above and Sep: below crown.

KM#	Date	Mintage	Fine	VF	XF	Unc
M4	1900	—	—	—	Proof	800.00

GOLD

KM#	Date	Mintage	Fine	VF	XF	Unc
M4a	1900	—	—	—	Rare	—

40 PENCE

SILVER, 18.81 g
Rev: W/XL above and Sep: below crown.

KM#	Date	Mintage	Fine	VF	XF	Unc
M1	1900	—	—	—	Proof	750.00

(2 FLORIN)

SILVER, 19.25-22.60 g

KM#	Date	Mintage	Fine	VF	XF	Unc
M5	1900	—	—	—	Proof	550.00

GOLD, 31.82 g

KM#	Date	Mintage	Fine	VF	XF	Unc
M5a	1900	—	—	—	Rare	—

NOTE: Each of the above listed medallic types is suspected to be unique.

NOTE: Similar pieces exist as 3 Shillings and 40 Pence. Refer to *Unusual World Coins,* 3rd edition, Krause Publications, Inc., c.1992.

TOKEN ISSUES (Tn)

Bank of Ireland

5 PENCE TOKEN

SILVER

KM#	Date	Mintage	Fine	VF	XF	Unc
Tn2	1805	—	7.50	25.00	50.00	150.00
	1806	—	15.00	50.00	125.00	225.00
	1806/5	5 known	50.00	150.00	350.00	750.00

10 PENCE TOKEN

SILVER

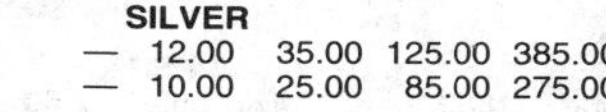

KM#	Date	Mintage	Fine	VF	XF	Unc
Tn3	1805	—	12.00	35.00	125.00	385.00
	1806	—	10.00	25.00	85.00	275.00

KM#	Date	Mintage	Fine	VF	XF	Unc
Tn5	1813	—	7.50	25.00	50.00	165.00
	1813	—	—	—	Proof	450.00

30 PENCE TOKEN

SILVER

KM#	Date	Mintage	Fine	VF	XF	Unc
Tn4	1808	—	17.50	85.00	275.00	575.00

6 SHILLINGS TOKEN

SILVER

KM#	Date	Mintage	Fine	VF	XF	Unc
Tn1	1804	—	125.00	250.00	600.00	1200.
	1804	—	—	—	Proof	1550.

NOTE: The silver proofs were struck on specially prepared plain edge polished planchets while circulation strikes were struck over Spanish and Spanish Colonial 8 Reales, that had been planed (removing 15 grains).

TRADESMENS' TOKENS

Various token issues exist which include the following: "VOCE POPULI" with HIBERNIA reverse of the 1760's, many varieties of imitation regal harp Halfpennies of the 18th century, genuine trade tokens issued by various merchants between 1789-1804, lead tokens ca. 1780-1820, silver issues including countermarked foreign coins ca 1804, copper tokens ca 1805-1830 followed by the Farthing tokens of 1830-1856. These are found listed in Seaby's *COINS AND TOKENS OF IRELAND,* 1970 edition.

1/2 PENNY

1789-1804

COPPER
Dublin 1/2 Penny token of 1795

PENNY

1805-1830

COPPER
Stephen's Dublin Penny token of 1816

PATTERNS (Pn)

KM#	Date	Mintage	Identification	Mkt.Val.
Pn33	1804	—	6 Shillings, Copper, KM-Tn1	775.00
Pn34	1804	—	6 Shillings, Copper Gilt, KM-Tn1	1650.
Pn35	1804	—	6 Shillings, Copper, head left	1900.
Pn36	1804	—	6 Shillings, Silver	1500.
Pn37	1805	—	1/2 Penny, Copper. Obv: Laureate, draped bust right. Rev: Crowned harp.	Rare
Pn38	1806	—	1 Farthing, Copper. Obv & rev: Large lettering, KM#18.	500.00
Pn39	1806	—	1 Farthing, Copper. Obv: Small lettering. Rev: Large lettering, KM#18.	500.00
Pn40	1813	—	1 Penny, Copper. Obv: Large laureated, draped bust right. Rev: Small crowned harp.	Rare
Pn41	1813	—	1 Penny, Copper. Obv. leg: GEORGIUS III.D.G. BRITANNIARUM REX.	Rare

KM#	Date	Mintage	Identification	Mkt.Val.
Pn42	1822	10-12	1 Farthing, Copper, thick and thin planchets, KM152	1750.

KM#	Date	Mintage	Identification	Mkt.Val.
Pn43	1822	—	1 Penny, Copper, KM22.	1500.

ISLE OF MAN

The Isle of Man, a dependency of the British Crown located in the Irish Sea equidistant from Ireland, Scotland and England, has an area of 227 sq. mi. (588 sq. km.) and a population of 68,000. Capital: Douglas. Agriculture, dairy farming, fishing and tourism are the chief industries.

The prevalence of prehistoric artifacts and monuments on the island give evidence that its mild, almost subtropical climate was enjoyed by mankind before the dawn of history. Vikings came to the Isle of Man during the 9th century and remained until ejected by Scotland in 1266. The island came under the protection of the British Crown in 1288, and in 1406 was granted, in perpetuity, to the earls of Derby, from whom it was inherited, 1736, by the Duke of Atholl. Rights and title were purchased from the Duke of Atholl in 1765 by the British Crown; the remaining privileges of the Atholl family were transferred to the crown in 1829. The Isle of Man is ruled by its own legislative council and the House of Keys, one of the oldest legislative assemblies in the world. Acts of Parliament passed in London do not affect the island unless it is specifically mentioned.

RULERS
(Commencing 1765)

British

MONETARY SYSTEM

14 Pence (Manx) = 1 Shilling (Br.)
5 Shillings = 1 Crown
20 Shillings = 1 Pound

FARTHING

COPPER

KM#	Date	Mintage	Fine	VF	XF	Unc
12	1839	.213	3.00	9.00	30.00	65.00
	1839	—	—	—	Proof	225.00
	1841	2 known	—	—	Proof	Rare
	1860	6 known	—	—	Proof	1900.
	1864	3 known	—	—	Proof	Rare

COPPER-GILT

KM#	Date	Mintage	Fine	VF	XF	Unc
12a	1839	—	—	—	Proof	Rare
	1860	—	—	—	Proof	Rare

1/2 PENNY

COPPER

KM#	Date	Mintage	Fine	VF	XF	Unc
10	1813	—	10.00	35.00	80.00	200.00
	1813	—	—	—	Proof	300.00

NOTE: Earlier date (1798) exists for this type.

COPPER-GILT

KM#	Date	Mintage	Fine	VF	XF	Unc
10a	1813	—	—	—	Proof	Rare

NOTE: Earlier date (1798) exists for this type.

BRONZE

KM#	Date	Mintage	Fine	VF	XF	Unc
10b	1813	—	—	—	Proof	350.00

NOTE: Earlier date (1798) exists for this type.

COPPER

KM#	Date	Mintage	Fine	VF	XF	Unc
13	1839	.214	2.50	7.50	35.00	90.00
13	1839	—	—	—	Proof	Rare
	1841	2 known	—	—	Proof	Rare
	1860	7 known	—	—	Proof	2500.

PENNY

COPPER

KM#	Date	Mintage	Fine	VF	XF	Unc
11	1813	—	8.00	35.00	100.00	225.00
	1813	—	—	—	Proof	350.00

NOTE: Earlier date (1798) exists for this type.

BRONZE GILT

KM#	Date	Mintage	Fine	VF	XF	Unc
11a	1813	—	—	—	Proof	Rare

NOTE: Earlier date (1798) exists for this type.

COPPER

KM#	Date	Mintage	Fine	VF	XF	Unc
14	1839	.081	10.00	25.00	70.00	150.00
	1839	—	—	—	Proof	Rare
	1841	2 known	—	—	Proof	Rare
	1859	7 known	—	—	Proof	1750.

BANK TOKEN ISSUES (Tn)

1/2 PENNY

COPPER
Obv: Peel Castle.
Rev. large leg: DOUGLAS BANK TOKEN.

KM#	Date	Mintage	Fine	VF	XF	Unc
Tn1	1811	—	25.00	75.00	200.00	400.00

Rev. small leg: DOUGLAS BANK TOKEN.

KM#	Date	Mintage	Fine	VF	XF	Unc
Tn2	1811	—	30.00	100.00	325.00	500.00
	1811	—	—	—	Proof	650.00

KM#	Date	Mintage	Fine	VF	XF	Unc
Tn3	1811	—	4.00	10.00	40.00	75.00

BRONZE

KM#	Date	Mintage	Fine	VF	XF	Unc
Tn3a	1811	—	—	—	Proof	—

BRASS

KM#	Date	Mintage	Fine	VF	XF	Unc
Tn3b	1811	—	10.00	25.00	100.00	175.00

COPPER
Obv: Similar to KM#Tn5 w/OFFICE DOUGLAS below Atlas.

KM#	Date	Mintage	Fine	VF	XF	Unc
Tn4	1811	—	7.50	20.00	75.00	175.00

Obv: DOUGLAS below Atlas.

KM#	Date	Mintage	Fine	VF	XF	Unc
Tn5	1811	—	350.00	600.00	—	—

Obv: Roman numeral I and flat top 3 in date.

KM#	Date	Mintage	Fine	VF	XF	Unc
Tn16	I830	—	10.00	30.00	80.00	—
	1830	—	—	—	Proof	—

NOTE: KM#Tn16 was issued by John Caine, a miller and baker of Castletown.

BRASS

KM#	Date	Mintage	Fine	VF	XF	Unc
Tn15	1815	—	200.00	325.00	—	—

NOTE: KM#Tn15 is a mule w/obv. of Canadian token.

Obv: Arabic numeral 1 and round 3 in date.

KM#	Date	Mintage	Fine	VF	XF	Unc
Tn17	1830	—	8.50	25.00	45.00	—

KM#	Date	Mintage	Fine	VF	XF	Unc
Tn21	1831	—	10.00	25.00	75.00	—
Tn21a	1831	—	—	—	Rare	—

PENNY

COPPER, normal flan
Rev. leg: DOUGLAS BANK TOKEN. . .

KM#	Date	Mintage	Fine	VF	XF	Unc
Tn6	1811	—	20.00	65.00	200.00	450.00
	1811	—	—	—	Proof	650.00

Thin flan.

KM#	Date	Mintage	Fine	VF	XF	Unc
Tn7	1811	—	—	—	Proof	850.00

Normal flan.
Obv: Similar to KM#Tn6.
Rev. leg: DOUGLAS TOKEN. . .

KM#	Date	Mintage	Fine	VF	XF	Unc
Tn8	1811	—	20.00	60.00	200.00	400.00
	1811	—	—	—	Proof	600.00

Thin flan.

KM#	Date	Mintage	Fine	VF	XF	Unc
Tn9	1811	—	—	—	Proof	—

KM#	Date	Mintage	Fine	VF	XF	Unc
Tn10	1811	—	5.00	15.00	65.00	100.00
	1811	—	—	—	Proof	—
Tn11	1811	—	4.00	8.00	20.00	200.00
	1811	—	—	—	Proof	—

Obv: Arabic 1 and round top 3 in date.

KM#	Date	Mintage	Fine	VF	XF	Unc
Tn18	1830	—	6.50	20.00	70.00	—

BRASS
Similar to KM#Tn18 w/I and flat top 3 in date.
Rev: W/quatrefoils.

KM#	Date	Mintage	Fine	VF	XF	Unc
Tn19	I830	—	6.50	20.00	60.00	—

Similar to KM#Tn19 w/pellet in quatrefoils.

KM#	Date	Mintage	Fine	VF	XF	Unc
Tn20	1830	—	15.00	35.00	125.00	—

NOTE: KM#Tn18 and 19 were issued by John Caine, a miller and baker of Castletown.

SHILLING

SILVER

KM#	Date	Mintage	Fine	VF	XF	Unc
Tn12	1811	—	175.00	375.00	750.00	1200.
	1811	—	—	—	Proof	1500.

2 SHILLINGS 6 PENCE

SILVER

KM#	Date	Mintage	Fine	VF	XF	Unc
Tn13	1811	—	300.00	600.00	1200.	2000.

COPPER

KM#	Date	Mintage	Fine	VF	XF	Unc
Tn13a	1811	—	—	—	Proof	Rare

5 SHILLINGS

SILVER

KM#	Date	Mintage	Fine	VF	XF	Unc
Tn14	1811	—	350.00	700.00	1500.	2500.
	1811	—	—	—	Proof	3000.

TRIAL STRIKES (TS)

KM#	Date	Mintage	Identification	Mkt.Val.
TS1	1813	—	1 Penny, Tin, uniface obv., KM11	115.00

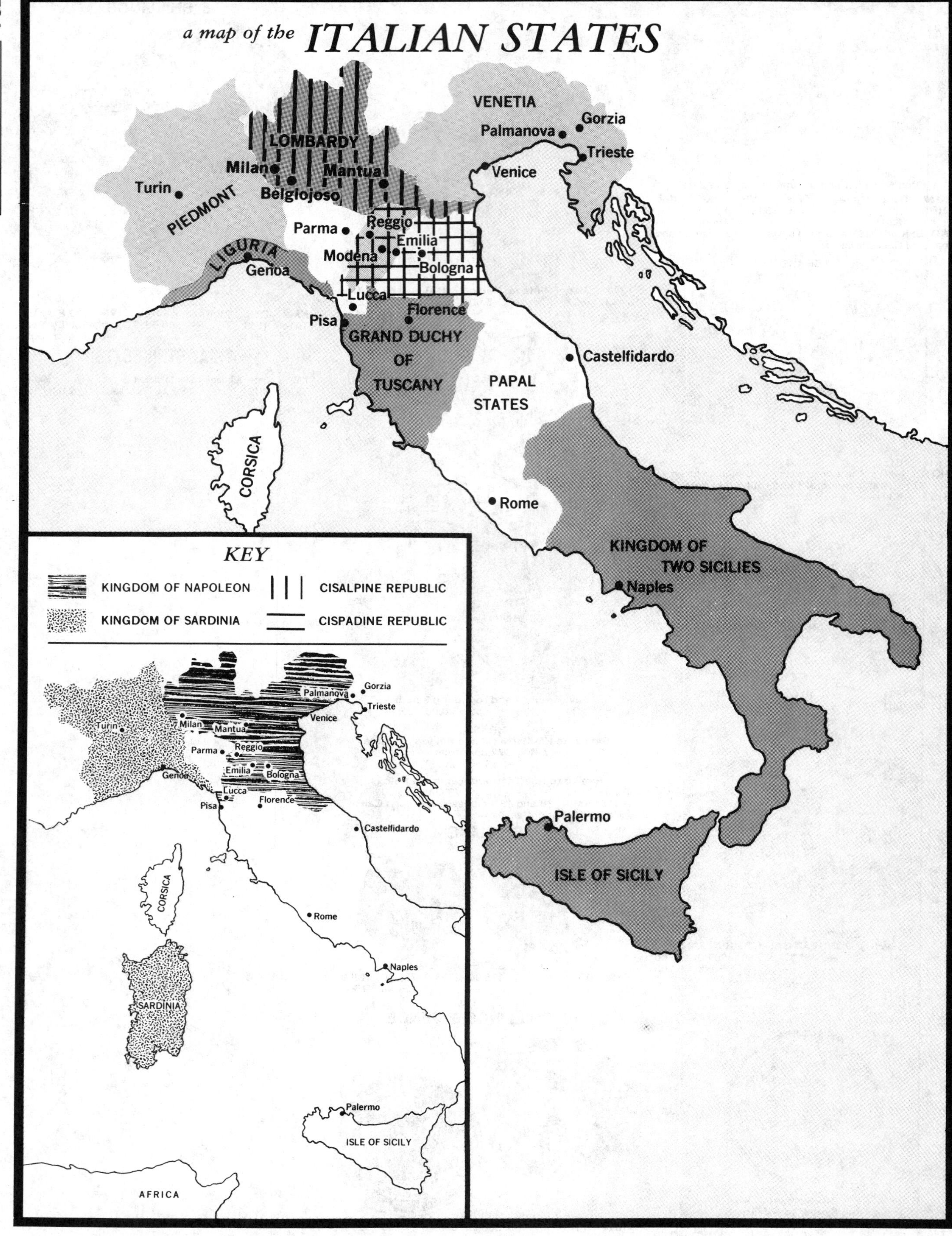
a map of the ITALIAN STATES
VENETIA
Gorzia
Palmanova
Trieste
Venice
LOMBARDY
Milan
Mantua
Belgiojoso
Turin
PIEDMONT
LIGURIA
Genoa
Parma
Reggio
Emilia
Modena
Bologna
Lucca
Florence
Pisa
GRAND DUCHY OF TUSCANY
PAPAL STATES
Castelfidardo
CORSICA
Rome
KINGDOM OF TWO SICILIES
Naples
Palermo
ISLE OF SICILY
KEY
KINGDOM OF NAPOLEON
CISALPINE REPUBLIC
KINGDOM OF SARDINIA
CISPADINE REPUBLIC
Gorzia
Palmanova
Trieste
Venice
Turin
Milan
Mantua
Parma
Reggio
Emilia
Bologna
Genoa
Lucca
Pisa
Florence
Castelfidardo
CORSICA
Rome
Naples
SARDINIA
Palermo
ISLE OF SICILY
AFRICA

ITALIAN STATES

CISALPINE REPUBLIC

Transpadane Republic

A revolutionary state founded in northern Italy by Napoleon, came into being at Milan, Lombardy, in July 1797. It was subsequently enlarged by the addition of the Cispadine Republic and territory from the Venetian hinterlands and the Swiss Cantons of the Valtellina. It collapsed upon the conquest of Italy by an Austro-Russian army, but was restored by Napoleon in 1800.

MONETARY SYSTEM

20 Soldi = 1 Lira
6 Lire = 1 Scudo

30 SOLDI

7.3300 g, .684 SILVER, .1612 oz ASW

C#	Date	Mintage	VG	Fine	VF	XF
1	(1801) yr. IX				75.00	150.00
		.300	20.00	40.00	60.00	125.00

NOTE: For KM#1, 2 and 3 with anchor and eagle head mint marks see Sardinia C#98, 99 and 100.

EMILIA

Emilia-Romagna

A northern division of Italy, came under nominal control of the papacy in 755. In 1796-1814 it was incorporated in the Italian Republic and the Kingdom of Napoleon, returning to the papacy in 1815.

MONETARY SYSTEM

100 Centesimi = 1 Lira

MINT MARKS

B - Bologna
(none) - Birmingham

1 CENTESIMO

COPPER
Obv: Crowned arms in branches.
Rev: Value and date in wreath.

KM#	Date	Mintage	Fine	VF	XF	Unc
1	1826(1860)	—	3.00	5.00	12.00	25.00

3 CENTESIMI

COPPER
Obv: Crowned arms in branches.
Rev: Value and date in wreath.

KM#	Date	Mintage	Fine	VF	XF	Unc
2	1826(1860)	—	3.00	5.00	14.00	30.00

5 CENTESIMI

COPPER
Obv: Crowned arms in branches.
Rev.: Value and date in wreath.

KM#	Date	Mintage	Fine	VF	XF	Unc
3	1826(1860)	—	3.00	5.00	16.00	35.00

NOTE: For KM#1, 2, and 3 w/anchor and eagle head mint marks see Sardinia C#98, 99, and 100.

50 CENTESIMI

2.5000 g, .900 SILVER, .0723 oz ASW
Similar to 1 Lira, C#2.

C#	Date	Mintage	Fine	VF	XF	Unc
1	1859B	—	25.00	50.00	100.00	250.00

LIRA

5.0000 g, .900 SILVER, .1446 oz ASW

C#	Date	Mintage	Fine	VF	XF	Unc
2	1859B	—	30.00	65.00	150.00	500.00

2 LIRE

10.0000 g, .900 SILVER, .2892 oz ASW
Similar to 1 Lira, C#2.

C#	Date	Mintage	Fine	VF	XF	Unc
3	1859B	—	200.00	350.00	450.00	1100.
	1860B	.013	150.00	250.00	400.00	1100.

5 LIRE

25.0000 g, .900 SILVER, .7320 oz ASW
Rev: Similar to 1 Lira, C#2.

C#	Date	Mintage	Fine	VF	XF	Unc
4	1859	—	150.00	250.00	500.00	2500.
	1860	—	150.00	200.00	400.00	2000.

10 LIRE

3.2200 g, .900 GOLD, .0931 oz AGW

C#	Date	Mintage	Fine	VF	XF	Unc
5	1860B	1,145	400.00	850.00	2000.	4000.

20 LIRE

6.4500 g, .900 GOLD, .1866 oz AGW

C#	Date	Mintage	Fine	VF	XF	Unc
6	1860B	150 pcs.	—	—	*Rare	—

***NOTE:** Stack's Hammel sale 9-82 XF realized $24,000. Stack's International sale 3-88 Gem BU realized $16,500.

NOTE: For similar coins of Vittorio Emanuele II, see Sardinia and Tuscany listings.

GENOA

A seaport in Liguria, Genoa was a dominant republic and colonial power in the Middle Ages. In 1798 Napoleon remodeled it into the Ligurian Republic, and in 1805 it was incorporated in the Kingdom of Napoleon. Following a brief restoration of the republic, it was absorbed by the Kingdom of Sardinia, 1815.

MINT MARKS

During the occupation by the French forces regular French coins, 1/2, 1, 2, 5, 20 and 40 Francs were struck between 1813 and 1814 with the mint mark C.L.

After Sardinia absorbed Genoa in 1815, regular Sardinian coins were struck until 1860 with a fouled anchor mint mark.

MONETARY SYSTEM

12 Denari = 1 Soldo
20 Soldi = 10 Parpagliola =
5 Cavallotti = 1 Lira (Madonnina)

LIGURIAN REPUBLIC

1798-1805

3 DENARI

COPPER
Obv: R.L.A.V. 1802 around D. 3, Rev: Cross.

C#	Date	Year	VG	Fine	VF	XF
25	ND(1802)	V	10.00	20.00	35.00	70.00

4 LIRE

16.6400 g, .889 SILVER, .4756 oz ASW

C#	Date	Year	VG	Fine	VF	XF
29	1804	VII	25.00	50.00	100.00	200.00

NOTE: Earlier dates (1798-1799) exist for this type.

8 LIRE

33.2700 g, .889 SILVER, .9510 oz ASW

C#	Date	Year	VG	Fine	VF	XF
30.2	1804	VII	70.00	120.00	220.00	400.00

48 LIRE

12.6070 g, .909 GOLD, .3684 oz AGW

C#	Date	Year	Fine	VF	XF	Unc
33	1801	IV	400.00	575.00	1000.	2500.
	1804	VII	400.00	575.00	1000.	2500.

NOTE: Earlier date (1798) exists for this type.

96 LIRE

25.2140 g, .917 GOLD, .7435 oz AGW

C#	Date	Year	Fine	VF	XF	Unc
34	1801	IV	450.00	750.00	1400.	3500.
	1803	VI	450.00	750.00	1400.	3500.
	1804	VII	450.00	750.00	1400.	3500.
	1805	VIII	450.00	750.00	1400.	3500.

NOTE: Earlier date (1798) exists for this type.

REPUBLIC

1814

QUATTRO (4) DENARI

COPPER

C#	Date	Mintage	VG	Fine	VF	XF
35	1814	—	2.50	5.00	9.00	20.00

2 SOLDI

BILLON
Rev. leg: . . . PRESIDIUM.

C#	Date	Mintage	VG	Fine	VF	XF
36.1	1814	—	3.50	7.50	12.00	28.00

Rev. leg: . . . PRAESIDIUM.

C#	Date	Mintage	VG	Fine	VF	XF
36.2	1814	—	4.00	8.00	15.00	32.00

4 SOLDI

BILLON

C#	Date	Mintage	VG	Fine	VF	XF
37	1814	—	5.00	10.00	16.50	35.00

10 SOLDI

2.1000 g, .889 SILVER, .0600 oz ASW
Obv: Crowned shield,
leg: GENUENSIS.
Rev: John The Baptist standing.

C#	Date	Mintage	VG	Fine	VF	XF
38	1814	—	5.50	11.50	18.50	40.00

Obv. leg: JANUENSIS

C#	Date	Mintage	VG	Fine	VF	XF
38a	1814	—	5.50	11.50	18.50	40.00

GORIZIA

Goricia, Gorz

A city in Venetia, passed to Maximilian I of Austria in 1500, and became the holding of Charles, son of Austrian emperor Ferdinand I in 1564.

RULERS

Franz II (Austria) 1792-1835

MINT MARKS

A, W - Wien - Vienna
F, H, HA - Hall
G - Graz
G - Nagybanya
H - Gunzburg
K - Kremnitz
O - Oravitza
S - Schmollnitz

MONETARY SYSTEM

20 Soldi = 1 Lira

SOLDO

COPPER
Mint mark: F
Obv: Crowned arms. Rev: Value, date.

C#	Date	Mintage	VG	Fine	VF	XF
8.1	1801	—	4.00	8.00	16.00	35.00

NOTE: Earlier dates (1792-1800) exist for this type.

Mint mark: H

C#	Date	Mintage	VG	Fine	VF	XF
8.4	1801	—	3.00	6.00	12.50	30.00
	1802	—	4.00	8.00	16.00	35.00

NOTE: Earlier dates (1798-1800) exist for this type.

2 SOLDI

COPPER
Mint mark: F
Obv: Crowned arms. Rev: Value, date.

C#	Date	Mintage	VG	Fine	VF	XF
9.2	1801	—	5.00	10.00	20.00	40.00

NOTE: Earlier date (1799) exists for this type.

Mint mark: H

C#	Date	Mintage	VG	Fine	VF	XF
9.3	1801	—	2.50	5.00	15.00	30.00
	1802	—	2.50	5.00	15.00	30.00

NOTE: Earlier date (1799) exists for this type.

15 SOLDI

(8-1/2 Kreuzer)

BILLON
Mint mark: A

C#	Date	Mintage	VG	Fine	VF	XF
10.1	1802	—	4.00	8.00	16.00	45.00

Mint mark: F

C#	Date	Mintage	VG	Fine	VF	XF
10.2	1802	—	5.00	10.00	20.00	50.00

Mint mark: H

C#	Date	Mintage	VG	Fine	VF	XF
10.3	1802	—	8.00	16.00	35.00	85.00

ITALIAN REPUBLIC

Repubblica Italiana

Created in 1802 out of the Cisalpine Republic (q.v.) with some additions. Converted into the Kingdom of Italy in 1805. Capital: Milan. Years 1-4 of the republic = 1802-1805.

RULERS

Napoleon, 1802-1805

MONETARY SYSTEM

(1803)

10 Denari = 1 Soldo
20 Soldi = 1 Lira

PATTERNS (Pn)

(Including off metal strikes)

KM#	Date	Mintage	Identification	Mkt.Val.
Pn1	A.II(1803)M	—	1 Denaro, Copper	225.00

KM#	Date	Mintage	Identification	Mkt.Val.
Pn2	A.II(1803)M	—	2 Denari, Copper	300.00

KM#	Date	Mintage	Identification	Mkt.Val.
Pn3	A.II(1803)M	—	Soldo da 5 Denari, Copper	500.00

KM#	Date	Mintage	Identification	Mkt.Val.
Pn4	A.II(1803)M	—	5 Soldi, .900 Silver	1700.

KM#	Date	Mintage	Identification	Mkt.Val.
Pn5	A.II(1803)M	—	10 Soldi, .900 Silver	2250.

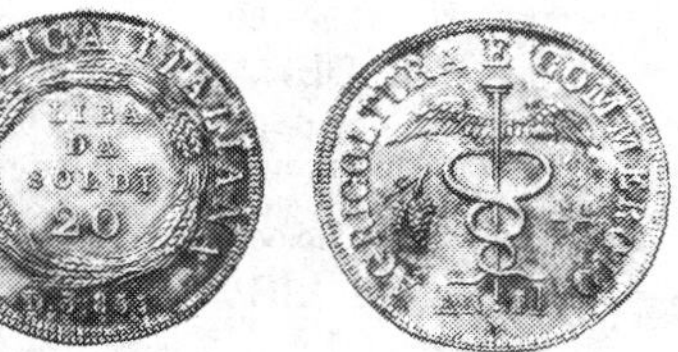

KM#	Date	Mintage	Identification	Mkt.Val.
Pn6	A.II(1803)M	—	Lira da 20 Soldi, .900 Silver	3250.

KM#	Date	Mintage	Identification	Mkt.Val.
Pn7	A.II(1803)M	—	30 Soldi, .900 Silver	4000.

KM#	Date	Mintage	Identification	Mkt.Val.
Pn8	A.II(1803)M	—	Scudo da 5 Lire, .900 Silver	12,500.
Pn9	A.II(1803)M	—	Mezzo (1/2) Doppia, .900 Gold	Rare
Pn10	A.II(1803)M	—	Mezzo (1/2) Doppia (in wreath) .900 Gold	Rare
Pn11	A.II(1803)M	—	1 Doppia, .900 Gold	Rare
Pn12	A.II(1803)M	—	1 Doppia (in wreath), .900 Gold	Rare

KM#	Date	Mintage	Identification	Mkt.Val.
Pn13	1804M	—	1/100 (Centesimo), Copper	250.00

KM#	Date	Mintage	Identification	Mkt.Val.
Pn14	1804M	—	1 Centesimo, Copper	300.00

KM#	Date	Mintage	Identification	Mkt.Val.
Pn15	1804M	—	1/2 Soldo, Copper	300.00

KM#	Date	Mintage	Identification	Mkt.Val.
Pn16	1804M	—	Mezzo (1/2) Soldo, Copper	450.00

KM#	Date	Mintage	Identification	Mkt.Val.
Pn17	1804M	—	1 Soldo, Copper	500.00

KM#	Date	Mintage	Identification	Mkt.Val.
Pn18	1804M	—	5 Soldi, .900 Silver	1100.

KM#	Date	Mintage	Identification	Mkt.Val.
Pn19	1804M	—	10 Soldi, .900 Silver	1700.

KM#	Date	Mintage	Identification	Mkt.Val.
Pn20	1804M	—	1 Lira, .900 Silver	3200.

KM#	Date	Mintage	Identification	Mkt.Val.
Pn21	1804M	—	2 Lire, .900 Silver, 8.00 g	4500.
Pn21a	1804M	—	2 Lire, .900 Silver, 8.21 g	4500.

KM#	Date	Mintage	Identification	Mkt.Val.
Pn22	1804M	—	5 Lire, .900 Silver	16,000.

KM#	Date	Mintage	Identification	Mkt.Val.
Pn23	1804M	—	(Venti-20 Lire) Denari 8, .900 Gold	42,500.
Pn24	1804M	—	(Venti-20 Lire) Denari 8, Copper	1250.

KINGDOM OF NAPOLEON

Came into being shortly after the first French empire was proclaimed on May 18, 1804; Napoleon's Italian coronation took place at Naples on May 26, 1805.

RULERS

Napoleon I, 1804-1814

MINT MARKS

B - Bologna
M - Milan
V - Venice

MONETARY SYSTEM

100 Centesimi = 20 Soldi
20 Soldi = 1 Lira

CENTESIMO

COPPER
Mint mark: B

C#	Date	Mintage	VG	Fine	VF	XF
1.1	1807	.092	2.00	4.00	7.50	16.50
	1808	2.270	2.00	4.00	7.50	16.50
	1809	4.413	2.00	4.00	7.50	16.50
	1810	3.813	2.00	4.00	7.50	16.50
	1811	1.335	2.00	4.00	7.50	16.50
	1812	4.813	2.00	4.00	7.50	16.50

Mint mark: M

C#	Date	Mintage	VG	Fine	VF	XF
1.2	1807	.097	3.75	7.50	12.50	32.50
	1808	3.372	2.00	4.00	7.50	16.50
	1808 (error) IMPERAPORE	.020	6.50	12.50	20.00	47.50
	1809	2.244	2.00	4.00	7.50	16.50
	1810/09	2.244	2.50	5.00	10.00	27.50
	1810	Inc. Ab.	2.00	4.00	7.50	16.50
	1811	1.944	2.00	4.00	7.50	16.50
	1812	2.744	2.00	4.00	7.50	16.50
	1813	3.724	2.00	4.00	7.50	16.50

NOTE: Varieties exist.

Mint mark: V

C#	Date	Mintage	VG	Fine	VF	XF
1.3	1807	.124	3.75	7.50	12.50	30.00
	1808V/M	.347	3.75	7.50	12.50	30.00
	1808	Inc. Ab.	3.75	7.50	12.50	30.00
	1809	3.017	3.00	6.00	7.50	16.50
	1810	.267	3.75	7.50	12.50	27.50
	1811	7.873	2.00	4.00	7.50	16.50
	1812	1.424	2.00	4.00	7.50	16.50
	1813	4.424	2.00	4.00	7.50	16.50

NOTE: Varieties exist.

3 CENTESIMI

COPPER
Mint mark: B

C#	Date	Mintage	VG	Fine	VF	XF
2.1	1807	.063	3.00	8.00	15.00	27.50
	1808	.215	2.00	4.00	7.50	16.50
	1810/9	1.845	4.00	8.00	15.00	32.50
	1810	Inc. Ab.	2.00	4.00	7.50	16.50
	1813/08	.845	2.50	5.00	10.00	22.00
	1813	Inc. Ab.	2.00	4.00	7.50	16.50

Mint mark: M

C#	Date	Mintage	VG	Fine	VF	XF
2.2	1807	.212	2.00	4.00	7.50	16.50
	1808	1.878	2.00	4.00	7.50	16.50
	1809	2.098	2.00	4.00	7.50	16.50
	1810/09	2.798	2.50	5.00	10.00	20.00
	1810	Inc. Ab.	2.00	4.00	7.50	16.50
	1811	2.798	2.00	4.00	7.50	16.50
	1812	3.012	2.00	4.00	7.50	16.50
	1813	2.598	2.00	4.00	7.50	16.50

NOTE: Varieties exist.

Mint mark: V

C#	Date	Mintage	VG	Fine	VF	XF
2.3	1807	.117	7.50	12.50	20.00	32.50
	1808	.527	2.00	4.00	8.00	17.50
	1809	.127	2.00	4.00	8.00	17.50
	1810/00	—	2.50	5.00	10.00	22.00
	1810	—	2.00	4.00	8.00	17.50

SOLDO

COPPER
Mint mark: B

C#	Date	Mintage	VG	Fine	VF	XF
3.1	1807	.345	5.00	10.00	20.00	40.00
	1808	.300	2.00	4.00	7.50	16.50
	1809	1.340	2.00	4.00	7.50	16.50

Mint mark: M

C#	Date	Mintage	VG	Fine	VF	XF
3.2	1807	.105	2.50	6.00	12.50	22.00
	1808	1.454	2.00	4.00	7.50	16.50
	1809	1.350	2.00	4.00	7.50	16.50
	1810	1.450	2.00	4.00	7.50	16.50
	1811	2.390	2.00	4.00	7.50	16.50
	1812	2.260	2.00	4.00	7.50	16.50
	1813	2.897	2.00	4.00	7.50	16.50

NOTE: Varieties exist.

Mint mark: V

C#	Date	Mintage	VG	Fine	VF	XF
3.3	1807	.265	2.50	5.00	15.00	37.50
	1808	.300	2.50	5.00	10.00	22.00
	1812	1.196	2.50	5.00	15.00	27.50

10 CENTESIMI

2.0000 g, .200 SILVER, .0128 oz ASW
Mint mark: M

C#	Date	Mintage	VG	Fine	VF	XF
4	1808	.012	10.00	20.00	30.00	65.00
	1809	.875	2.00	4.00	7.50	16.50
	1810	.760	2.00	4.00	7.50	16.50
	1811	1.540	2.00	4.00	7.50	16.50
	1812	.740	2.00	4.00	7.50	16.50
	1813	2.670	2.00	4.00	7.50	16.50

5 SOLDI

1.2500 g, .900 SILVER, .0361 oz ASW
Mint mark: M

C#	Date	Mintage	VG	Fine	VF	XF
5.1	1808 stars in relief on edge	.130	15.00	30.00	60.00	100.00
	1808 stars incuse on edge	Inc. Ab.	4.00	6.00	10.00	22.50
	1809	.600	4.00	6.00	10.00	22.50
	1810	1.050	4.00	6.00	10.00	22.50
	1811/0	3.000	4.50	7.00	13.00	27.50
	1811	Inc. Ab.	4.00	6.00	10.00	22.50
	1812	1.700	4.00	6.00	10.00	22.50
	1813	2.800	4.00	6.00	10.00	22.50
	1814	.700	4.00	6.00	10.00	22.50
	1814 (error) IMPERARORE	Inc. Ab.	17.50	35.00	65.00	100.00

NOTE: Varieties exist.

Mint mark: V

C#	Date	Mintage	VG	Fine	VF	XF
5.2	1812	.110	5.00	10.00	20.00	45.00

NOTE: Varieties exist.

Mint mark: B

C#	Date	Mintage	VG	Fine	VF	XF
5.3	1812	.330	4.50	7.00	11.00	25.00
	1812B/M	.390	4.50	7.00	11.00	25.00
	1813	2.800	4.00	6.50	10.00	22.50
	1813B/M	.320	4.50	7.00	11.00	25.00

10 SOLDI

2.5000 g, .900 SILVER, .0722 oz ASW
Mint mark: M

C#	Date	Mintage	VG	Fine	VF	XF
6.1	1808 stars in relief on edge	.175	10.00	20.00	40.00	80.00
	1808 stars incuse on edge	Inc. Ab.	4.50	6.50	10.00	22.50
	1809	.430	4.50	6.50	10.00	22.50
	1810	.550	4.50	6.50	10.00	22.50
	1811	2.050	4.50	6.50	10.00	22.50
	1812	.600	4.50	6.50	10.00	22.50
	1813	.490	4.50	6.50	10.00	22.50
	1814	.450	4.50	6.50	10.00	22.50

Mint mark: V

C#	Date	Mintage	VG	Fine	VF	XF
6.2	1811	.310	10.00	15.00	25.00	55.00
	1812	.160	4.50	7.00	12.50	27.50
	1813	.332	4.50	6.50	10.00	22.50

NOTE: Varieties exist.

Mint mark: B

C#	Date	Mintage	VG	Fine	VF	XF
6.3	1812	.018	5.00	10.00	15.00	32.50
	1812B/M	.015	5.00	10.00	15.00	32.50
	1813	.350	4.00	6.00	10.00	22.50

15 SOLDI

3.7500 g, .900 SILVER, .1083 oz ASW
Mint mark: M

C#	Date	Mintage	VG	Fine	VF	XF
7	1808	.038	22.50	40.00	65.00	150.00
	1809	.015	22.50	50.00	100.00	220.00
	1810	9,000	45.00	80.00	200.00	450.00
	1814	370 pcs.	45.00	80.00	150.00	350.00

LIRA

5.0000 g, .900 SILVER, .1444 oz ASW
Mint mark: M

C#	Date	Mintage	VG	Fine	VF	XF
8.1	1808 stars in relief on edge	.495	10.00	20.00	30.00	75.00
	1808 stars incuse on edge	Inc. Ab.	10.00	20.00	30.00	75.00
	1809	.025	5.00	10.00	20.00	45.00
	1810	.495	5.00	10.00	20.00	45.00

C#	Date	Mintage	VG	Fine	VF	XF
8.1	1810 (error) NATOLEON					
		Inc. Ab.	20.00	45.00	70.00	150.00
	1811	1.185	5.00	10.00	20.00	45.00
	1811/08	I.A.	25.00	50.00	85.00	175.00
	1812	.340	5.00	10.00	20.00	45.00
	1813	.230	5.00	10.00	20.00	45.00
	1814	.275	5.00	10.00	20.00	45.00
	1814M/V	I.A.	10.00	25.00	50.00	100.00

Mint mark: B

C#	Date	Mintage	VG	Fine	VF	XF
8.2	1808	.103	6.50	12.50	30.00	60.00
	1810 stars in relief on edge					
		.336	6.50	12.50	30.00	60.00
	1810 stars incuse on edge					
		.310	6.50	12.50	30.00	60.00
	1811	.310	6.50	12.50	30.00	60.00
	1812	.310	6.50	12.50	30.00	60.00
	1813	.220	6.50	12.50	30.00	60.00

Mint mark: V

C#	Date	Mintage	VG	Fine	VF	XF
8.3	1811	.045	13.50	22.50	35.00	80.00
	1812	.090	13.50	22.50	35.00	80.00
	1813	.310	12.50	20.00	32.50	75.00

NOTE: Varieties exist.

2 LIRE

10.0000 g, .900 SILVER, .2888 oz ASW
Mint mark: M

C#	Date	Mintage	VG	Fine	VF	XF
9.1	1807	.010	20.00	40.00	125.00	250.00
	1808 edge inscription in relief					
		—	125.00	250.00	300.00	450.00
	1808 edge inscription incuse					
		.311	17.50	35.00	70.00	125.00
	1809	.332	15.00	30.00	50.00	90.00
	1810	.370	15.00	30.00	50.00	90.00
	1811	.513	15.00	30.00	50.00	90.00
	1812	.334	15.00	30.00	50.00	90.00
	1813	.223	15.00	30.00	50.00	90.00
	1814	3,100	35.00	60.00	75.00	150.00

NOTE: Varieties exist.

Mint mark: B

C#	Date	Mintage	VG	Fine	VF	XF
9.2	1808	2,200	25.00	50.00	200.00	400.00
	1812	.044	10.00	15.00	35.00	60.00
	1813	.348	10.00	15.00	30.00	55.00

Mint mark: V

C#	Date	Mintage	VG	Fine	VF	XF
9.3	1811	.010	15.00	30.00	60.00	125.00
	1812	.239	10.00	20.00	40.00	80.00
	1813	.213	10.00	20.00	40.00	80.00

NOTE: Varieties exist.

5 LIRE

25.0000 g, .900 SILVER, .7234 oz ASW, 36mm
Mint mark: M
DIO PROTEGGE L'ITALIA on edge in relief, large.

C#	Date	Mintage	VG	Fine	VF	XF
10.1	1807	.039	60.00	90.00	185.00	400.00
	1808	3.278	25.00	40.00	60.00	140.00
	1809	2.480	30.00	50.00	70.00	165.00
	1810	.263	35.00	60.00	100.00	200.00

NOTE: Varieties exist.

Mint mark: V

C#	Date	Mintage	VG	Fine	VF	XF
10.2	1807	610 pcs.	—	—	Rare	—
	1808	204 pcs.	—	—	Rare	—

Mint mark: B

C#	Date	Mintage	VG	Fine	VF	XF
10.3	1808	.023	30.00	50.00	80.00	165.00
	1809	.221	25.00	40.00	65.00	100.00
	1810	.317	25.00	40.00	65.00	100.00
	1811	—	22.50	35.00	60.00	100.00

37.5mm

Mint mark: M
Edge inscription large, incuse.

C#	Date	Mintage	VG	Fine	VF	XF
10.4	1809	—	25.00	40.00	65.00	165.00
	1810	—	25.00	40.00	65.00	165.00
	1811	—	25.00	40.00	65.00	165.00
	1812	1.848	25.00	40.00	65.00	165.00
	1813	.772	25.00	40.00	65.00	165.00
	1814	.102	35.00	75.00	150.00	300.00

NOTE: Varieties exist.

Mint mark: B

C#	Date	Mintage	VG	Fine	VF	XF
10.5	1810	—	22.50	35.00	50.00	125.00

Mint mark: V

C#	Date	Mintage	VG	Fine	VF	XF
10.6	1810	—	—	—	—	—
	1811	.367	30.00	60.00	100.00	250.00
	1812	.207	25.00	40.00	80.00	165.00
	1813	.071	27.50	55.00	90.00	225.00

NOTE: Varieties exist.

Mint mark: M
Letters in legend smaller, edge inscription incuse, small.

C#	Date	Mintage	VG	Fine	VF	XF
10.7	1808	—	25.00	40.00	80.00	165.00
	1811	2.820	25.00	40.00	80.00	165.00
	1812	—	25.00	40.00	80.00	165.00

Mint mark: V

C#	Date	Mintage	VG	Fine	VF	XF
10.8	1810	.014	25.00	40.00	80.00	165.00
	1811	—	25.00	40.00	80.00	165.00

Mint mark: B

C#	Date	Mintage	VG	Fine	VF	XF
10.9	1811	.451	22.50	35.00	50.00	125.00
	1812	.210	22.50	35.00	50.00	125.00
	1813	.110	22.50	35.00	50.00	125.00

20 LIRE

6.4510 g, .900 GOLD, .1866 oz AGW
Mint mark: M

C#	Date	Mintage	VG	Fine	VF	XF
11	1808	.087	100.00	125.00	150.00	375.00
	1809	.053	100.00	125.00	150.00	375.00
	1810	.114	100.00	125.00	150.00	325.00
	1811	.055	100.00	125.00	150.00	325.00
	1812	.045	100.00	125.00	150.00	325.00
	1813	.039	100.00	125.00	150.00	300.00
	1814	.057	100.00	125.00	150.00	300.00

40 LIRE

12.9030 g, .900 GOLD, .3733 oz AGW
Mint mark: M

C#	Date	Mintage	VG	Fine	VF	XF
12	1807	3,430	250.00	350.00	500.00	1000.
	1808 w/o mint mark					
		.352	175.00	200.00	225.00	300.00
	1808 edge inscription in relief					
		Inc. Ab.	175.00	200.00	225.00	300.00
	1808 edge inscription incuse					
		.213	175.00	200.00	225.00	300.00
	1809	.038	175.00	200.00	250.00	450.00
	1810	.158	175.00	200.00	225.00	300.00
	1811	.106	175.00	200.00	225.00	300.00
	1812	.056	175.00	200.00	225.00	400.00
	1813	.041	175.00	200.00	250.00	450.00
	1814	.264	175.00	200.00	225.00	300.00

NOTE: Varieties exist.

PATTERNS (Pn)

(Including off metal strikes)

KM#	Date	Mintage	Identification	Mkt.Val.
Pn1	1806M	—	1 Centesimo, Copper	100.00
Pn2	1806M	—	2 Centesimi, Copper	200.00
Pn3	1806M	—	3 Centesimi, Copper	200.00

KM#	Date	Mintage	Identification	Mkt.Val.
Pn4	1806M	—	1 Soldo, Copper	100.00
Pn5	1806M	—	5 Soldi, Silver	150.00
Pn6	1806M	—	10 Soldi, Silver	150.00
Pn7	1806M	—	15 Soldi, Silver	150.00
Pn8	1806M	—	1 Lira, Silver	200.00
Pn9	1806M	—	2 Lire, Silver	200.00
Pn10	1806M	—	5 Lire, Silver	500.00
Pn11	1806M	—	20 Lire, Gold	Rare
Pn12	1806M	—	40 Lire, Gold	Rare
Pn13	1812M	—	5 Lire, Lead	220.00

LOMBARDY - VENETIA

Comprised the northern Italian duchies of Milan and Mantua and the Venetian Republic which were absorbed by the Kingdom of Napoleon in 1805. After Napoleon's fall they were awarded to Austria and incorporated in the Hapsburg monarchy as the Kingdom of Lombardy-Venetia.

The Lombard campaign of 1859 restored rule under the Kingdom of Italy for Lombard in 1859 and Venetia in 1866.

RULERS

French, until 1814
Austrian, until 1814-48, 1849-59
Italian, until 1946

MINT MARKS

A, W - Vienna
B - Kremnitz
M - Milan
S - Schmollnitz
V - Venice

MONETARY SYSTEM

(Until 1857)

100 Centesimi = 20 Soldi = 1 Lira
6 Lire = 1 Scudo
14 Lire = 1 Ducato
40 Lire = 1 Sovrano

AUSTRIAN ADMINISTRATION

CENTESIMO

COPPER
Mint mark: A

C#	Date	Mintage	Fine	VF	XF	Unc
1.1	1822	—	—	—	—	250.00

Mint mark: M

C#	Date	Mintage	Fine	VF	XF	Unc
1.2	1822	—	3.00	5.00	10.00	30.00
	1834	—	3.00	5.00	8.00	25.00

NOTE: Varieties exist.

Mint mark: V

C#	Date	Mintage	Fine	VF	XF	Unc
1.3	1822	—	3.00	5.00	10.00	30.00
	1834	—	3.00	5.00	8.00	20.00

NOTE: Varieties exist.

Mint mark: M

C#	Date	Mintage	Fine	VF	XF	Unc
12.1	1839	—	3.00	5.00	8.00	20.00
	1843	—	5.00	8.00	12.00	28.00
	1846	—	3.00	5.00	8.00	20.00

Mint mark: V

C#	Date	Mintage	Fine	VF	XF	Unc
12.2	1839	—	3.00	5.00	8.00	20.00
	1843	—	3.00	5.00	8.00	20.00
	1846	—	3.00	5.00	8.00	20.00

Mint mark: M

C#	Date	Mintage	Fine	VF	XF	Unc
25	1849	—	5.00	8.00	12.00	22.50
	1850	—	5.00	8.00	12.00	22.50
	1852	—	6.00	9.00	14.00	28.00

C#	Date	Mintage	Fine	VF	XF	Unc
29.1	1852	—	7.00	10.00	15.00	30.00

Mint mark: V

C#	Date	Mintage	Fine	VF	XF	Unc
29.2	1852	—	3.00	5.00	8.00	20.00

5/10 SOLDO

COPPER
Mint mark: A

C#	Date	Mintage	Fine	VF	XF	Unc
34.1	1862	12.495	2.00	3.50	6.00	15.00
	Mint mark: B					
34.2	1862	5.970	3.50	6.00	10.00	20.00
	Mint mark: V					
34.3	1862	1.915	3.50	6.00	12.00	25.00

3 CENTESIMI

COPPER
Mint mark: A

C#	Date	Mintage	Fine	VF	XF	Unc
2.1	1822	—	—	—	Rare	—
	Mint mark: M					
2.2	1822	—	4.00	6.00	12.00	30.00
	1834	—	6.00	10.00	18.00	40.00

NOTE: Varieties exist.

C#	Date	Mintage	Fine	VF	XF	Unc
	Mint mark: V					
2.3	1822	—	4.00	6.00	12.00	30.00
	1834	—	4.00	7.00	15.00	35.00

C#	Date	Mintage	Fine	VF	XF	Unc
	Mint mark: M					
13.1	1839	—	4.00	7.00	13.00	30.00
	1843	—	5.00	8.00	15.00	35.00
	1846	—	3.00	5.00	10.00	22.50
	Mint mark: V					
13.2	1839	—	3.00	5.00	10.00	22.50
	1843	—	3.00	5.00	10.00	22.50
	1846	—	3.00	5.00	10.00	22.50

C#	Date	Mintage	Fine	VF	XF	Unc
	Mint mark: M					
26	1849	—	3.50	6.00	12.00	25.00
	1850	—	3.50	6.00	12.00	25.00
	1852	—	4.00	7.00	14.00	30.00

C#	Date	Mintage	Fine	VF	XF	Unc
30.1	1852	—	4.00	7.00	14.00	30.00
	Mint mark: V					
30.2	1852	—	3.00	6.00	12.00	25.00

5 CENTESIMI

COPPER
Mint mark: A

C#	Date	Mintage	Fine	VF	XF	Unc
3.1	1822	—	—	—	Rare	—
	Mint mark: M					
3.2	1822	—	5.00	10.00	25.00	60.00
3.2	1823	—	—	Reported, not confirmed		
	1834	—	8.00	14.00	27.50	65.00
	Mint mark: V					
3.3	1822	—	5.00	10.00	25.00	60.00
	1834	—	5.00	10.00	25.00	60.00

C#	Date	Mintage	Fine	VF	XF	Unc
	Mint mark: M					
14.1	1839	—	4.50	9.00	17.50	40.00
	1843	—	4.00	8.00	15.00	35.00
	1846	—	4.00	8.00	15.00	35.00
	Mint mark: V					
14.2	1839	—	4.50	9.00	20.00	50.00
	1843	—	10.00	20.00	60.00	150.00
	1846	—	4.00	8.00	15.00	35.00

C#	Date	Mintage	Fine	VF	XF	Unc
	Mint mark: M					
27	1849	—	4.00	8.00	15.00	27.50
	1850	—	4.00	8.00	15.00	27.50

C#	Date	Mintage	Fine	VF	XF	Unc
31.1	1852	—	4.00	8.00	15.00	27.50
	Mint mark: V					
31.2	1852	—	3.00	7.00	12.00	25.00

SOLDO

COPPER
Mint mark: A

C#	Date	Mintage	Fine	VF	XF	Unc
35.1	1862	22.275	1.50	3.00	5.00	10.00
	Mint mark: B					
35.2	1862	8.971	2.00	3.00	6.00	12.00
	Mint mark: V					
35.3	1862	9.395	2.50	4.00	10.00	20.00

10 CENTESIMI

COPPER
Mint mark: M
Similar to 5 Centesimi, C#3.

C#	Date	Mintage	Fine	VF	XF	Unc
28	1849	—	30.00	40.00	80.00	250.00

C#	Date	Mintage	Fine	VF	XF	Unc
	Mint mark: V					
32	1852	—	8.00	15.00	30.00	75.00

15 CENTESIMI

COPPER
Similar to 10 Centesimi, C#32.
Mint mark: V

C#	Date	Mintage	Fine	VF	XF	Unc
33	1852	—	50.00	80.00	200.00	450.00

1/4 LIRA

1.6200 g, .600 SILVER, .0312 oz ASW
Mint mark: A

C#	Date	Mintage	Fine	VF	XF	Unc
4.1	1822	—	35.00	50.00	85.00	220.00
	1823	—	150.00	250.00	350.00	800.00
	Mint mark: M					
4.2	1822	—	15.00	25.00	40.00	120.00
	1823/2	—	15.00	25.00	40.00	120.00
	1823	—	15.00	25.00	40.00	120.00
	1824	—	15.00	25.00	40.00	120.00
	Mint mark: V					
4.3	1822	—	15.00	25.00	40.00	120.00
	1823	—	15.00	25.00	40.00	120.00
	1824	—	15.00	25.00	40.00	120.00
	Mint mark: A					
15.1	1835	—	—	Reported, not confirmed		
	1837	—	—	Reported, not confirmed		
	Mint mark: V					
15.2	1837	—	75.00	100.00	150.00	250.00
	1838	—	75.00	100.00	150.00	300.00
	1839	—	75.00	100.00	150.00	300.00
	1840	—	75.00	100.00	150.00	300.00
	1841	—	75.00	100.00	150.00	300.00
	1842	—	75.00	100.00	150.00	250.00
	1843	—	75.00	100.00	150.00	300.00
	1844	—	75.00	100.00	150.00	300.00

1/2 LIRA

2.1650 g, .900 SILVER, .0626 oz ASW
Mint mark: A

C#	Date	Mintage	Fine	VF	XF	Unc
5.1	1822	—	60.00	125.00	250.00	375.00
	1823	—	50.00	100.00	200.00	325.00
	1835	—	—	Reported, not confirmed		
	Mint mark: M					
5.2	1822	—	12.50	20.00	40.00	100.00
	1823	—	12.50	20.00	40.00	100.00
	1824/2	—	12.50	20.00	40.00	100.00
	1824	—	12.50	20.00	40.00	100.00
	Mint mark: V					
5.3	1821	—	—	Reported, not confirmed		
	1822	—	10.00	25.00	40.00	100.00
	1823/2	—	10.00	25.00	40.00	100.00
	1823	—	10.00	25.00	40.00	100.00
	1824	—	—	Reported, not confirmed		
	Mint mark: A					
16.1	1835	—	—	Reported, not confirmed		
	1837	—	—	Reported, not confirmed		
	Mint mark: V					
16.2	1837	—	35.00	65.00	125.00	250.00
	1838	—	35.00	65.00	125.00	250.00
	1839	—	50.00	80.00	175.00	350.00
	1840	—	50.00	80.00	175.00	350.00
	1841	—	50.00	80.00	175.00	350.00
	1842	—	50.00	80.00	175.00	350.00
	1843	—	50.00	80.00	175.00	350.00
	1844	—	50.00	80.00	175.00	350.00
36	1854	—	30.00	50.00	100.00	200.00
	1855	—	35.00	75.00	150.00	300.00

LIRA

4.3300 g, .900 SILVER, .1253 oz ASW
Mint mark: A

C#	Date	Mintage	Fine	VF	XF	Unc
6.1	1822	—	75.00	150.00	250.00	550.00
	1823	—	25.00	50.00	100.00	250.00
	1835	—	—	Reported, not confirmed		

C#	Date	Mintage	Fine	VF	XF	Unc
	Mint mark: M					
6.2	1822	—	20.00	40.00	80.00	200.00
	1823	—	20.00	40.00	80.00	200.00
	1824/3	—	20.00	40.00	80.00	200.00
	1824	—	20.00	40.00	80.00	200.00
	1825	—	20.00	50.00	90.00	220.00
	Mint mark: V					
6.3	1822	—	20.00	40.00	80.00	200.00
	1823	—	25.00	50.00	100.00	250.00
	Mint mark: A					
17.1	1835	—	—	Reported, not confirmed		
	1837	—	—	Reported, not confirmed		

Mint mark: V

C#	Date	Mintage	Fine	VF	XF	Unc
17.2	1837	—	50.00	80.00	175.00	375.00
	1838	—	50.00	80.00	175.00	400.00
	1839	—	50.00	80.00	200.00	400.00
	1840	—	50.00	80.00	200.00	450.00
	1841	—	50.00	80.00	200.00	450.00
	1842	—	50.00	80.00	200.00	450.00
	1843	—	50.00	80.00	200.00	450.00
	1844	—	50.00	80.00	200.00	450.00
37.1	1852	—	40.00	65.00	125.00	250.00

Mint mark: M

C#	Date	Mintage	Fine	VF	XF	Unc
37.2	1853	—	40.00	65.00	150.00	300.00
	1854	—	50.00	80.00	175.00	400.00
	1855	—	60.00	90.00	225.00	500.00
	1856	—	50.00	80.00	175.00	400.00
	1858	—	75.00	150.00	325.00	700.00

1/2 SCUDO

12.3450 g, .900 SILVER, .3527 oz ASW

Mint mark: A

C#	Date	Mintage	Fine	VF	XF	Unc
7.1	1822	—	35.00	65.00	125.00	350.00
	1823	—	30.00	55.00	110.00	225.00
	1825	—	—	Reported, not confirmed		
	1835	—	—	Reported, not confirmed		
	Mint mark: M					
7.2	1822	—	30.00	55.00	100.00	180.00
	1823	—	30.00	55.00	110.00	225.00
	1824	—	30.00	55.00	100.00	200.00
	1825	—	—	—	Rare	—
	1827	—	—	—	Rare	—
	Mint mark: V					
7.3	1822	—	25.00	35.00	60.00	150.00
	1823	—	60.00	90.00	150.00	400.00
	1824	—	25.00	35.00	65.00	160.00
	1825	—	25.00	35.00	65.00	160.00
	1826	—	25.00	35.00	65.00	160.00
	1827	—	30.00	55.00	100.00	200.00
	Mint mark: A					
18.1	1835	—	—	Reported, not confirmed		
	1837	—	—	Reported, not confirmed		
	Mint mark: V					
18.2	1837	—	75.00	125.00	250.00	500.00
	1838	—	75.00	125.00	250.00	500.00
	1839	—	75.00	125.00	250.00	500.00
	1840	—	75.00	125.00	250.00	500.00
	1841	—	75.00	125.00	250.00	500.00
	1842	—	75.00	125.00	250.00	500.00
	1843	—	75.00	125.00	250.00	500.00
	1844	—	75.00	125.00	250.00	500.00
	1845	—	75.00	125.00	250.00	500.00
	1846	—	75.00	125.00	250.00	500.00
	W/o value					
38	1853	—	150.00	200.00	300.00	800.00

6 LIRE

26.0000 g, .900 SILVER, .7524 oz ASW

Mint mark: M

C#	Date	Mintage	Fine	VF	XF	Unc
A1	1816	—	—	—	*Rare	—

***NOTE:** Swiss Bank sale No.19 1-88 XF-FDC realized $10,500.

SCUDO

26.0000 g, .900 SILVER, .7524 oz ASW

C#	Date	Mintage	Fine	VF	XF	Unc
8.1	1822	—	25.00	45.00	100.00	250.00
	1823	—	35.00	65.00	125.00	275.00
	1824	—	35.00	65.00	135.00	325.00
	1825	—	30.00	50.00	125.00	325.00
	1826	—	30.00	50.00	125.00	325.00
	1827	—	50.00	90.00	175.00	400.00
	1828	—	125.00	200.00	300.00	700.00
	1829	—	45.00	80.00	150.00	350.00
	1830	—	45.00	80.00	150.00	350.00
	1831	—	30.00	55.00	125.00	275.00
	Mint mark: A					
8.2	1821	—	—	—	Proof	—
	1822	—	50.00	90.00	185.00	400.00
	1823	—	50.00	80.00	175.00	350.00
	1824	—	65.00	100.00	200.00	500.00
	1825	—	—	Reported, not confirmed		
	1835	—	—	Reported, not confirmed		
	Mint mark: V					
8.3	1822	—	35.00	75.00	100.00	225.00
	1823	—	100.00	150.00	275.00	675.00
	1824	—	30.00	50.00	125.00	325.00
	1825	—	30.00	65.00	100.00	225.00
	1826	—	30.00	50.00	110.00	200.00
	1827	—	50.00	80.00	140.00	350.00
	1828	—	90.00	140.00	250.00	650.00
	1829	—	90.00	140.00	250.00	650.00
	1830	—	50.00	75.00	125.00	325.00
	1831	—	35.00	65.00	115.00	300.00
	1832	—	35.00	65.00	115.00	300.00

Mint mark: A

C#	Date	Mintage	Fine	VF	XF	Unc
19.1	1835	—	—	Reported, not confirmed		
	1837	—	—	Reported, not confirmed		
	Mint mark: M					
19.2	1837	—	100.00	175.00	400.00	1000.
	Mint mark: V					
19.3	1837	—	90.00	150.00	300.00	750.00
	1838	—	125.00	175.00	350.00	850.00
	1839	—	100.00	160.00	325.00	775.00
	1840	—	100.00	160.00	325.00	775.00
	1841	—	125.00	175.00	350.00	850.00
	1842	—	125.00	175.00	350.00	850.00
	1843	—	100.00	160.00	325.00	800.00
	1844	—	100.00	160.00	325.00	800.00
	1845	—	90.00	150.00	300.00	750.00
	1846	—	100.00	160.00	325.00	800.00
	W/o value					
39	1853	—	150.00	200.00	350.00	900.00

REVOLUTIONARY PROVISIONAL GOVERNMENT

5 LIRE

25.0000 g, .900 SILVER, .7234 oz ASW

Mint mark: M

Obv: Short stems above date.

C#	Date	Mintage	Fine	VF	XF	Unc
22.1	1848	.120	30.00	45.00	135.00	250.00
	Obv: Long stems extend beyond date.					
22.2	1848	Inc. Ab.	50.00	120.00	300.00	700.00
	Obv: Short stems end above date. Rev: Star near crown.					
22.3	1848	Inc. Ab.	30.00	45.00	135.00	250.00

20 LIRE

6.4500 g, .900 GOLD, .1866 oz AGW

Mint mark: M

C#	Date	Mintage	Fine	VF	XF	Unc
23	1848	4,593	300.00	500.00	800.00	1800.

40 LIRE

12.9000 g, .900 GOLD, .3733 oz AGW

Mint mark: M

C#	Date	Mintage	Fine	VF	XF	Unc
24	1848	5,875	400.00	600.00	1200.	2600.

TRADE COINAGE

ZECCHINO

3.5000 g, .900 GOLD, .1012 oz AGW

Obv: Doge kneeling before St. Mark, leg: FRANC. I. . .

Rev: Christ standing.

C#	Date	Mintage	Fine	VF	XF	Unc
9	ND(1815)	—	750.00	1500.	2000.	2500.

NOTE: Varieties exist.

1/2 SOVRANO

5.6700 g, .900 GOLD, .1640 oz AGW

Mint mark: M

C#	Date	Mintage	Fine	VF	XF	Unc
10.1	1820	—	275.00	450.00	950.00	1800.
	1822	—	150.00	200.00	500.00	1000.
	1831	—	125.00	200.00	450.00	900.00

Mint mark: A

C#	Date	Mintage	Fine	VF	XF	Unc
10.2	1822	—	125.00	200.00	400.00	850.00
	1823	—	125.00	200.00	400.00	900.00
	1831	—	125.00	200.00	400.00	900.00

Mint mark: V

C#	Date	Mintage	Fine	VF	XF	Unc
10.3	1822	—	250.00	450.00	700.00	1700.
	1823	—	150.00	250.00	550.00	1200.

Mint mark: A

C#	Date	Mintage	Fine	VF	XF	Unc
10a.1	1835	—	— Reported, not confirmed			

Mint mark: M

C#	Date	Mintage	Fine	VF	XF	Unc
10a.2	1835	—	150.00	225.00	550.00	1100.
	1835 (AVSIRIAE error)					
		—	—	—	—	—

NOTE: Varieties exist.

Mint mark: A

C#	Date	Mintage	Fine	VF	XF	Unc
20.1	1837	—	— Reported, not confirmed			
	1839	—	200.00	400.00	900.00	1800.

Mint mark: M

C#	Date	Mintage	Fine	VF	XF	Unc
20.2	1837	—	500.00	750.00	1350.	2250.
	1838	—	200.00	350.00	500.00	800.00
	1839	—	200.00	350.00	500.00	800.00
	1841	—	200.00	350.00	500.00	800.00
	1842	—	225.00	450.00	700.00	1100.
	1843	—	400.00	600.00	1000.	1500.
	1844	—	225.00	450.00	700.00	1200.
	1845	—	225.00	450.00	700.00	1200.
	1846	—	225.00	450.00	700.00	1200.
	1847	—	225.00	450.00	700.00	1200.
	1848	—	200.00	450.00	700.00	1100.

Mint mark: V

C#	Date	Mintage	Fine	VF	XF	Unc
20.3	1837	—	200.00	400.00	600.00	1000.
	1838	—	200.00	400.00	600.00	1000.
	1839	—	200.00	400.00	600.00	1000.
	1840	—	200.00	400.00	600.00	1000.
	1841	—	200.00	400.00	600.00	1000.
	1842	—	500.00	700.00	1250.	1800.
	1843	—	200.00	400.00	600.00	1000.
	1844	—	200.00	400.00	600.00	1000.
	1845	—	200.00	400.00	600.00	1000.
	1846	—	500.00	750.00	1500.	2200.
	1847	—	500.00	750.00	1500.	2200.

Mint mark: M

C#	Date	Mintage	Fine	VF	XF	Unc
20a	1849	—	250.00	400.00	800.00	1650.

C#	Date	Mintage	Fine	VF	XF	Unc
40.1	1854	—	350.00	550.00	1000.	2000.
	1855	—	350.00	550.00	1000.	2000.
	1856	—	350.00	550.00	1000.	2000.

Mint mark: V

C#	Date	Mintage	Fine	VF	XF	Unc
40.2	1854	—	350.00	550.00	1000.	2000.
	1855	—	350.00	550.00	1000.	2000.
	1856	—	350.00	550.00	1000.	2000.

SOVRANO

11.3300 g, .900 GOLD, .3278 oz AGW

Mint mark: M

C#	Date	Mintage	Fine	VF	XF	Unc
11.1	1820	—	700.00	1100.	2000.	5000.
	1822	—	250.00	400.00	600.00	1450.
	1823	—	250.00	400.00	600.00	1450.
	1824	—	250.00	400.00	600.00	1450.
	1826	—	400.00	600.00	900.00	1550.
	1827	—	350.00	550.00	850.00	1500.
	1828	—	350.00	550.00	850.00	1500.
	1829	—	250.00	400.00	600.00	1450.
	1830/20	—	—	—	—	—
	1830	—	250.00	400.00	600.00	1450.
	1831/21	—	350.00	550.00	850.00	1500.
	1831	—	250.00	350.00	500.00	1000.

Mint mark: A

C#	Date	Mintage	Fine	VF	XF	Unc
11.2	1822	—	250.00	350.00	500.00	1000.
	1823	—	250.00	350.00	500.00	1250.
	1831	—	200.00	300.00	450.00	900.00

Mint mark: V

C#	Date	Mintage	Fine	VF	XF	Unc
11.3	1822	—	350.00	500.00	800.00	1500.

Mint mark: A

C#	Date	Mintage	Fine	VF	XF	Unc
11a.1	1835	—	— Reported, not confirmed			

Mint mark: M

C#	Date	Mintage	Fine	VF	XF	Unc
11a.2	1835	—	500.00	850.00	1500.	3500.

Mint mark: A

C#	Date	Mintage	Fine	VF	XF	Unc
21.1	1837	—	500.00	700.00	1100.	2400.
	1838	—	—	—	Rare	—
	1839	—	500.00	700.00	1100.	2400.
	1840	—	—	—	Rare	—
	1841	—	600.00	850.00	1250.	2600.
	1842	—	—	—	Rare	—
	1843	—	—	—	Rare	—
	1845	—	—	—	Rare	—
	1847	—	850.00	1500.	2700.	5000.

Mint mark: M

C#	Date	Mintage	Fine	VF	XF	Unc
21.2	1837	—	700.00	1300.	2500.	4500.
	1838	—	350.00	500.00	1050.	2000.
	1840	—	350.00	500.00	1050.	2000.
	1841	—	700.00	1300.	2500.	4500.
	1848	—	350.00	500.00	1050.	2000.

Mint mark: V

C#	Date	Mintage	Fine	VF	XF	Unc
21.3	1837	—	300.00	450.00	950.00	2000.
	1838	—	300.00	450.00	900.00	1700.
	1839	—	400.00	650.00	1100.	2600.
	1840	—	300.00	450.00	950.00	2000.
	1841	—	300.00	450.00	900.00	1700.
	1842	—	300.00	450.00	950.00	2000.
	1843	—	400.00	650.00	1100.	2500.
	1844	—	400.00	650.00	1100.	2500.
	1845	—	400.00	650.00	1100.	2500.
	1846	—	300.00	450.00	950.00	2000.
	1847	—	300.00	450.00	950.00	2000.

Mint mark: M

C#	Date	Mintage	Fine	VF	XF	Unc
41.1	1853	—	600.00	950.00	1700.	3500.
41.1	1855	—	600.00	950.00	1700.	3500.
	1856	—	600.00	950.00	1700.	3500.

Mint mark: V

C#	Date	Mintage	Fine	VF	XF	Unc
41.2	1854	—	800.00	1200.	2200.	4500.
	1855	—	600.00	1000.	2000.	4000.
	1856	—	550.00	900.00	1800.	3750.

ESSAIS (E)

KM#	Date	Mintage	Identification	Mkt.Val.
E1	1816	—	1 Scudo, Lead, C8.1	—

PATTERNS (Pn)

(Including off metal strikes)

KM#	Date	Mintage	Identification	Mkt.Val.
Pn1	1821V	—	1/2 Lira, Silver, C5	—

KM#	Date	Mintage	Identification	Mkt.Val.
Pn2	1848M	—	1 Lira, Silver, 4.96 g	225.00
Pn3	1848M	—	1 Lira, Bronze, 5.06 g	400.00
Pn4	1848M	—	1 Lira, Tin, 5.06 g	250.00
Pn5	1848M	—	1 Lira, Tin, 4.28 g	200.00
Pn6	1848M	—	1 Lira, Tin, 2.92 g	200.00
Pn7	1848M	—	2 Lira, Silver, 10.00 g	300.00
Pn8	1848M	—	2 Lira, Bronze, 9.81 g	400.00
Pn9	1848M	—	2 Lira, Tin, 9.15 g	225.00
Pn10	1848M	—	2 Lira, Tin, 6.98 g	200.00

KM#	Date	Mintage	Identification	Mkt.Val.
Pn11	1848M	—	5 Lira, Copper, 24.10 g, C22.1	400.00
Pn12	1848M	—	5 Lira, Tin, 18.42 g, C22.1	500.00

KM#	Date	Mintage	Identification	Mkt.Val.
Pn13	1852M	—	10 Centesimi, Copper, C32	750.00
Pn14	1852M	—	15 Centesimi, Copper, C33	800.00

TRIAL STRIKES (TS)

KM#	Date	Mintage	Identification	Mkt.Val.
TS1	ND(1835M)	—	1 Soldo, Tin, uniface obv.	125.00
TS2	ND(1835M)	—	1/4 Lira, Tin, uniface obv.	125.00
TS3	ND(1835M)	—	1/2 Lira, Tin, uniface obv.	125.00
TS4	1835(M)	—	1/2 Lira, Tin, uniface rev.	125.00
TS5	ND(1835M)	—	1 Lira, Tin, uniface obv.	125.00
TS6	1835(M)	—	1 Lira, Tin, uniface rev.	125.00
TS7	ND(1835M)	—	1/4 Scudo, Tin, uniface obv.	125.00
TS8	1835(M)	—	1/4 Scudo, Tin, uniface rev.	125.00
TS9	ND(1835M)	—	1/2 Scudo, Tin, uniface obv.	125.00
TS10	1835(M)	—	1/2 Scudo, Tin, uniface rev.	125.00

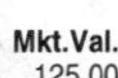

KM#	Date	Mintage	Identification	Mkt.Val.
TS11	ND(1835)M	—	1 Scudo, Tin, uniface obv.	125.00

KM#	Date	Mintage	Identification	Mkt.Val.
TS12	1835(M)	—	1 Scudo, Tin, uniface rev.	125.00

KM#	Date	Mintage	Identification	Mkt.Val.
TS13	ND(1835)M	—	1 Scudo, Tin	350.00

KM#	Date	Mintage	Identification	Mkt.Val.
TS14	1848(M)	—	1 Lira, klippe, Tin, uniface obv.	600.00

KM#	Date	Mintage	Identification	Mkt.Val.
TS15	ND(1848M)	—	1 Lira, klippe, Tin, uniface rev.	600.00
TS16	1848(M)	—	5 Lira, Tin, uniface obv., C22.1	250.00
TS17	ND(1848)M	—	5 Lira, Tin, uniface rev., C22.1	250.00

LUCCA

Luca, Lucensis
Lucca and Piombino

A town in Tuscany and the residence of a marquis, was nominally a fief but managed to maintain a de facto independence until awarded by Napoleon to his sister Elisa in 1805. In 1814 it was occupied by the Neapolitans, and from 1817 to 1847 was a duchy of the queen of Etruria, after which it became a division of Tuscany.

Principality, 1805-1814
Lucca, Duchy, 1817-1847

RULERS

Felix and Elisa (Bonaparte), 1805-1814
Maria Luisa di Borbone
Duchess, 1817-1824
Carlo Lodovico di Borbone
Duke, 1824-1847

MONETARY SYSTEM

100 Centesimi = 1 Franco

3 CENTESIMI

COPPER

KM#	Date	Mintage	VG	Fine	VF	XF
21	1806	—	6.00	15.00	25.00	60.00

5 CENTESIMI

COPPER

KM#	Date	Mintage	VG	Fine	VF	XF
22	1806	—	10.00	20.00	40.00	85.00

FRANCO

5.0000 g, .900 SILVER, .1446 oz ASW

KM#	Date	Mintage	VG	Fine	VF	XF
23	1805	—	—	—	Rare	—
	1806	—	12.50	27.50	45.00	100.00
	1807	—	12.50	27.50	45.00	100.00
	1808	—	12.50	27.50	45.00	100.00

5 FRANCHI

24.8400 g, .900 SILVER, .7188 oz ASW

KM#	Date	Mintage	VG	Fine	VF	XF
24	1805	—	30.00	50.00	100.00	250.00
	1806	—	30.00	50.00	75.00	200.00
	1807	—	30.00	50.00	75.00	200.00
	1808/7	—	30.00	50.00	75.00	200.00
	1808	—	30.00	50.00	75.00	200.00

MONETARY REFORM

4 Denari = 1 Quattrino
3 Quattrini = 1 Soldo
20 Soldi = 1 Lira

QUATTRINO

COPPER
Obv. leg: DUCATO DI LUCCA. Rev: Value, date.

KM#	Date	Mintage	VG	Fine	VF	XF
31	1826	—	3.50	7.00	15.00	35.00

MEZZO (1/2) SOLDO

COPPER
Obv. leg: DUCATO DI LUCCA, crown.
Rev: Value, date.

KM#	Date	Mintage	VG	Fine	VF	XF
32	1826	—	3.50	7.00	15.00	35.00
	1835	—	3.50	7.00	15.00	35.00

2 QUATTRINI

COPPER

KM#	Date	Mintage	VG	Fine	VF	XF
33	1826	—	4.00	8.00	16.00	40.00

SOLDO

COPPER
Obv. leg: CARLO L. D. B. I. D. S. DUCA DI LUCCA

KM#	Date	Mintage	VG	Fine	VF	XF
34	1826	—	3.50	7.00	15.00	38.00

KM#	Date	Mintage	VG	Fine	VF	XF
34a	1841	—	7.50	15.00	25.00	45.00

5 QUATTRINI

COPPER
Obv: Crowned arms. Rev: Value, date.

KM#	Date	Mintage	VG	Fine	VF	XF
35	1826	—	8.00	16.00	28.00	50.00

NOTE: Varieties exist.

2 SOLDI

1.4000 g, .200 SILVER, .0090 oz ASW
Obv: Crowned arms. Rev: Value, date.

KM#	Date	Mintage	VG	Fine	VF	XF
36	1835	—	7.50	14.00	22.00	42.00

BOLOGNINO

(2 Soldi)

3.0700 g, .200 SILVER, .0197 oz ASW
Obv: Branch w/6 leaves.

C#	Date	Year	VG	Fine	VF	XF
4a	1790	(1835)	(restrike)			
			10.00	20.00	32.00	70.00

3 SOLDI

1.6000 g, .200 SILVER, .0102 oz ASW
Obv: Crowned CL monogram.

KM#	Date	Mintage	VG	Fine	VF	XF
37	1835	—	35.00	75.00	125.00	250.00

5 SOLDI

3.0000 g, .200 SILVER, .0192 oz ASW

KM#	Date	Mintage	VG	Fine	VF	XF
38	1833 flat top 3's					
		—	7.50	14.00	22.00	50.00
	1833 round top 3's					
		—	7.50	14.00	22.00	50.00
	1838	—	7.50	14.00	22.00	50.00

10 SOLDI

2.3600 g, .666 SILVER, .0505 oz ASW

C#	Date	Mintage	Fine	VF	XF	Unc
39	1833	—	10.00	20.00	40.00	100.00
	1838	—	10.00	20.00	40.00	100.00

LIRA

4.7200 g, .666 SILVER, .1010 oz ASW

C#	Date	Mintage	Fine	VF	XF	Unc
40	1834	—	15.00	30.00	65.00	150.00
	1837	—	20.00	40.00	100.00	225.00
	1838	—	15.00	30.00	65.00	150.00

2 LIRE

9.4300 g, .666 SILVER, .2019 oz ASW

C#	Date	Mintage	Fine	VF	XF	Unc
41	1837	—	35.00	65.00	150.00	285.00

MANTUA

Mantova

A city of Lombardy, was taken by the Lombards in 568 and became a fief of the princely Italian Gonzaga family in 1328. It was stormed and sacked by the Austrians in 1630. Besieged by Napoleon in June 1796, it held until February of 1797. After forming part of the Cisalpine and Italian Republics it fell again to Austria in 1799. It was restored to the French in 1801, but reverted to Austria again as part of the Kingdom of Lombardy-Venetia, 1814-1866.

RULERS

Cisalpine Republic, 1797-1802
Italian Republic, 1802-1805
Napoleonic Kingdom of Italy, 1805-1814
Austrian, 1814-1866

MONETARY SYSTEM

6 Denari = 1 Sesino
2 Sesini = 1 Soldo
20 Soldi = 1 Lira
12 Lire = 1 Tallero

MINT

Mantua

Issues of the Austrian defenders in 1848

For Austrian 3 Kreutzer, 20 Kreutzer and 1/2 Thaler coins dated 1848 with GM mint mark see Austria KM#2192, 2209 and 2226.

NAPLES & SICILY

Two Sicilies

Consisting of Sicily and the south of Italy, Naples & Sicily came into being in 1130. It passed under Spanish control in 1502; Naples was conquered by Austria in 1707. In 1733 Don Carlos of Spain was recognized as king. From then until becoming part of the united Kingdom of Italy, Naples and Sicily, together and separately, were contested for by Spain, Austria, France, and the republican and monarchial factions of Italy.

RULERS

Ferdinando IV,
1799-1805 (2nd reign)
1815-1816 (restored in Naples)
1816-1825 (as King of the Two Sicilies)
Joseph Napoleon, 1806-1808
Joachim Murat, 1808-1815
(Gioacchino Napoleone)

Two Sicilies

Francesco I, 1825-1830
Ferdinand II, 1830-1859
Francesco II, 1859-1869

MONETARY SYSTEM

(Until 1813)

6 Cavalli = 1 Tornese
240 Tornese = 120 Grana = 12 Carlini = 6 Tari = 1 Piastra
5 Grana = 1 Cinquina
100 Grana = 1 Ducato (Tallero)

KINGDOM OF NAPLES

3 CAVALLI

COPPER

C#	Date	Mintage	VG	Fine	VF	XF
91	1804	—	4.00	10.00	20.00	50.00

4 CAVALLI

COPPER

C#	Date	Mintage	VG	Fine	VF	XF
92	1804 LD	—	4.00	10.00	20.00	50.00

TORNESE

(6 Cavalli)

COPPER
Obv: Head right. Rev: Value within wreath.

C#	Date	Mintage	VG	Fine	VF	XF
93	1804 LD	—	6.00	12.00	25.00	55.00

9 CAVALLI

COPPER
Obv: Head right. Rev: Castle.

C#	Date	Mintage	VG	Fine	VF	XF
94	1801	—	15.00	35.00	65.00	120.00
	1804	—	6.00	12.00	25.00	60.00
	1804 LD	—	6.00	12.00	25.00	60.00

2 GRANA

COPPER

C#	Date	Mintage	VG	Fine	VF	XF
101	1810	—	20.00	40.00	100.00	300.00

6 TORNESI

COPPER
Ferdinand IV

C#	Date	Mintage	VG	Fine	VF	XF
96	1801 A P	—	6.00	12.00	25.00	55.00
	1802 A P	—	6.00	12.00	28.00	60.00
	1803 A P	—	6.00	12.00	28.00	60.00
	1803 R C	—	7.50	15.00	30.00	65.00

NOTE: Earlier dates (1799-1800) exist for this type.

3 GRANA

COPPER

C#	Date	Mintage	VG	Fine	VF	XF
102	1810	—	20.00	40.00	100.00	350.00

Rev: Date below wreath.

C#	Date	Mintage	VG	Fine	VF	XF
102a	1810	—	20.00	40.00	100.00	350.00

60 GRANA

13.7500 g, .833 SILVER, .3682 oz ASW

C#	Date	Mintage	VG	Fine	VF	XF
97	1805 LD	—	35.00	75.00	175.00	350.00

120 GRANA

27.5000 g, .833 SILVER, .7365 oz ASW
Ferdinand IV

C#	Date	Mintage	VG	Fine	VF	XF
98	1802 A P	—	25.00	45.00	100.00	225.00
	1802 P-AP	—	25.00	45.00	100.00	225.00

NOTE: Earlier dates (1799-1800) exist for this type.

Obv: Head right w/smooth hair.
Rev: Crown above small shield.

C#	Date	Mintage	VG	Fine	VF	XF
99.1	1805 LD	—	30.00	60.00	125.00	275.00

Plain edge

C#	Date	Mintage	VG	Fine	VF	XF
99.2	1805 LD	—	30.00	60.00	125.00	275.00

Obv: Head right w/curly hair.

C#	Date	Mintage	VG	Fine	VF	XF
99.3	1805 LD	—	25.00	50.00	120.00	265.00

NOTE: Varieties exist.

C#	Date	Mintage	VG	Fine	VF	XF
100	1806	—	100.00	175.00	350.00	600.00
	1807/6	—	100.00	175.00	350.00	700.00
	1807	—	80.00	150.00	275.00	450.00
	1808	—	80.00	150.00	275.00	450.00

DODICI (12) CARLINI

27.5300 g, .833 SILVER, .7373 oz ASW

C#	Date	Mintage	VG	Fine	VF	XF
103	1809	—	80.00	150.00	300.00	650.00
	1810	—	80.00	150.00	325.00	700.00

NOTE: Many varieties including mulings exist.

MONETARY REFORM

100 Centesimi = 1 Franco = 1 Lira

3 CENTESIMI

BRONZE

Obv: Head left. Rev: Value.

C#	Date	Mintage	Fine	VF	XF	Unc
105	1813	1.350	500.00	1100.	1500.	3750.

5 CENTESIMI

BRONZE

C#	Date	Mintage	Fine	VF	XF	Unc
106	1813	1.280	750.00	1250.	1750.	5250.

10 CENTESIMI

BRONZE

Obv: Head left. Rev: Value.

C#	Date	Mintage	Fine	VF	XF	Unc
107	1813	.450	850.00	1350.	2000.	6000.

MEZZA (1/2) LIRA

2.5000 g, .900 SILVER, .0723 oz ASW

C#	Date	Mintage	Fine	VF	XF	Unc
108	1813	.166	50.00	75.00	175.00	475.00

LIRA

5.0000 g, .900 SILVER, .1446 oz ASW

C#	Date	Mintage	Fine	VF	XF	Unc
109	1812	.027	50.00	125.00	250.00	500.00
	1813	.199	30.00	75.00	150.00	250.00

2 LIRE

10.0000 g, .900 SILVER, .2892 oz ASW

C#	Date	Mintage	Fine	VF	XF	Unc
110	1812	.028	100.00	200.00	350.00	700.00
	1813	.220	50.00	75.00	175.00	400.00

5 LIRE

25.0000 g, .900 SILVER, .7234 oz ASW

C#	Date	Mintage	Fine	VF	XF	Unc
111	1812	2,921	600.00	1200.	2500.	5250.
	1813	.037	100.00	275.00	550.00	1200.

20 LIRE

6.4500 g, .900 GOLD, .1866 oz AGW

C#	Date	Mintage	Fine	VF	XF	Unc
112	1813	.042	200.00	350.00	550.00	1300.
	1813 N	—	1000.	2500.	3500.	—

40 FRANCHI

12.9000 g, .900 GOLD, .3732 oz AGW

C#	Date	Mintage	Fine	VF	XF	Unc
104	1810	18 pcs.	—	—	*Rare	—

NOTE: Bowers and Merena Guia sale 3-88 VF realized $19,800. Superior Pipito sale 12-87 about XF realized $30,250.

40 LIRE

12.9000 g, .900 GOLD, .3732 oz AGW

C#	Date	Mintage	Fine	VF	XF	Unc
113	1813	.024	300.00	500.00	900.00	2000.

TWO SICILIES

NOTE: Coins bearing legends FERDINANDO IV were issued for circulation in Naples while those with FERDINANDO I were struck for Two Sicilies.

MONETARY SYSTEM

6 Cavalli = 1 Tornese
240 Tornese = 120 Grana = 12 Carlini
= 6 Tari (Naples) = 1 Piastra
5 Grana = 1 Cinquina
100 Grana = 1 Ducato (Tallero)

MEZZO (1/2) TORNESE

COPPER

C#	Date	Mintage	VG	Fine	VF	XF
142	1832	—	2.00	4.00	10.00	27.50
	1833	—	2.00	4.00	10.00	27.50
	1835	—	2.00	4.00	10.00	27.50
	1836	—	2.00	4.00	10.00	27.50
	1838	—	2.00	4.00	10.00	27.50
	1839	—	2.00	4.00	10.00	27.50
	1840	—	4.00	7.00	15.00	32.50
	1844	—	2.00	4.00	8.50	22.50
	1845	—	2.00	4.00	8.50	22.50
	1846	—	2.00	4.00	8.50	22.50
	1847	—	2.00	4.00	8.50	22.50

C#	Date	Mintage	VG	Fine	VF	XF
142a	1848	—	2.00	4.00	8.50	22.50
	1849	—	2.00	4.00	8.50	22.50
	1850	—	2.00	4.00	8.50	22.50
	1851	—	2.00	4.00	8.50	22.50
	1852	—	2.00	4.00	8.50	22.50
	1853	—	2.00	4.00	8.50	22.50
	1854	—	2.00	4.00	8.50	22.50

UNO (1) TORNESE

COPPER

C#	Date	Mintage	VG	Fine	VF	XF
119	1817	—	7.50	15.00	25.00	50.00

C#	Date	Mintage	VG	Fine	VF	XF
130	1827	—	4.00	8.00	15.00	30.00

Obv: Young head w/o beard, large letters.

C#	Date	Mintage	Fine	VF	XF	Unc
143	1832	—	3.00	6.00	15.00	35.00
	1833	—	3.00	6.00	15.00	35.00
	1835	—	3.50	6.00	15.00	35.00
	1836	—	10.00	17.50	25.00	45.00

Obv: Legend w/small letters.

C#	Date	Mintage	Fine	VF	XF	Unc
143a	1838	—	3.00	6.00	15.00	35.00
	1839	—	3.00	6.00	15.00	35.00
	1840	—	3.00	6.00	15.00	35.00
	1843	—	10.00	15.00	20.00	45.00
	1844	—	3.00	6.00	12.00	30.00
	1845	—	3.00	6.00	12.50	30.00
	1846	—	3.00	6.00	12.50	30.00
	1847	—	3.00	6.00	12.50	30.00
	1848	—	10.00	15.00	20.00	45.00

Obv: Older head w/beard.

C#	Date	Mintage	Fine	VF	XF	Unc
143b	1845	—	2.00	4.00	10.00	25.00
	1849	—	2.00	4.00	10.00	25.00
	1851	—	2.00	4.00	10.00	25.00
	1852	—	2.00	4.00	10.00	25.00
	1853	—	2.00	4.00	10.00	25.00
	1854	—	2.00	4.00	10.00	25.00
	1855	—	8.00	12.50	17.50	38.00
	1857	—	2.00	4.00	10.00	25.00
	1858	—	2.00	4.00	10.00	25.00
	1859	—	2.00	4.00	10.00	25.00

UNO E MEZZO (1-1/2) TORNESE

COPPER

Obv: Young head w/o beard.

C#	Date	Mintage	Fine	VF	XF	Unc
144	1832	—	7.50	15.00	30.00	75.00
	1835	—	7.50	15.00	30.00	75.00
	1836	—	7.50	15.00	30.00	75.00
	1838	—	5.00	12.50	40.00	75.00
	1839	—	7.50	15.00	30.00	75.00
	1840	—	7.50	15.00	30.00	75.00

Obv: Young head w/beard.

C#	Date	Mintage	Fine	VF	XF	Unc
144a	1844	—	5.00	12.50	25.00	65.00
	1847	—	5.00	12.50	25.00	65.00
	1848	—	5.00	12.50	25.00	65.00

Obv: Older head w/beard.

C#	Date	Mintage	Fine	VF	XF	Unc
144b	1849	—	5.00	12.50	25.00	60.00
	1850	—	5.00	12.50	25.00	60.00
	1851	—	5.00	12.50	25.00	60.00
	1853	—	5.00	12.50	25.00	60.00
	1854	—	5.00	12.50	25.00	60.00

DUE (2) TORNESI

COPPER

C#	Date	Mintage	VG	Fine	VF	XF
131	1825	—	3.00	6.50	12.50	25.00
	1826	—	3.00	6.50	12.50	25.00

Obv: Young head w/o beard.

C#	Date	Mintage	Fine	VF	XF	Unc
145	1832	—	12.00	30.00	75.00	125.00
	1835	—	12.00	30.00	75.00	125.00

Obv: Young head w/beard.

C#	Date	Mintage	Fine	VF	XF	Unc
145a	1838	—	4.00	13.50	20.00	45.00
145a	1839	—	3.00	7.50	18.00	40.00
	1842	—	3.00	7.50	18.00	40.00
	1843	—	3.00	7.50	18.00	40.00
	1847	—	3.00	7.50	18.00	40.00
	1848	—	3.00	7.50	18.00	40.00
	1849	—	3.00	7.50	18.00	40.00
	1851	—	3.00	7.50	18.00	40.00
	1852	—	3.00	7.50	18.00	40.00
	1853	—	3.00	7.50	18.00	40.00
	1854	—	3.00	7.50	18.00	40.00
	1855	—	3.00	7.50	18.00	40.00
	1856	—	3.00	7.50	18.00	40.00

C#	Date	Mintage	Fine	VF	XF	Unc
145b	1857	—	2.50	6.00	18.00	40.00
	1858	—	2.50	6.00	18.00	40.00
	1859	—	2.50	6.00	18.00	40.00

NOTE: Many minor varieties exist such as position of the obverse legend, placement of dots in the legend, large and small dates, etc.

C#	Date	Mintage	Fine	VF	XF	Unc
158	1859	—	3.50	8.50	20.00	45.00

TRE (3) TORNESI

COPPER

Obv: Young head w/o beard.

C#	Date	Mintage	Fine	VF	XF	Unc
146	1833	—	5.00	15.00	30.00	75.00
	1835	—	5.00	15.00	30.00	75.00
	1837	—	5.00	15.00	30.00	75.00
	1838	—	5.00	15.00	30.00	75.00

Obv: Young head w/beard.

C#	Date	Mintage	Fine	VF	XF	Unc
146a	1839	—	4.00	12.50	25.00	65.00
	1842	—	4.00	12.50	25.00	65.00
	1847	—	4.00	12.50	25.00	65.00
	1848	—	4.00	12.50	25.00	50.00
	1849	—	4.00	12.50	25.00	50.00
	1851	—	4.00	12.50	25.00	50.00
	1852	—	4.00	12.50	25.00	50.00
	1854	—	4.00	12.50	25.00	50.00
	1858	—	4.00	12.50	25.00	50.00

QUATTRO (4) TORNESI

COPPER

C#	Date	Mintage	VG	Fine	VF	XF
120	1817	—	15.00	30.00	45.00	90.00

CINQUE (5) TORNESI

COPPER

Obv. leg: FERDINANDVS IV. D. G. . .

C#	Date	Mintage	VG	Fine	VF	XF
114	1816	—	10.00	25.00	35.00	70.00

Obv. leg: FERD. I.D.G. . .

C#	Date	Mintage	VG	Fine	VF	XF
121	1816	—	9.00	25.00	45.00	80.00
	1817	—	5.00	10.00	20.00	45.00
	1818	—	5.00	10.00	20.00	45.00

C#	Date	Mintage	VG	Fine	VF	XF
121a	1819	—	7.50	15.00	30.00	55.00

C#	Date	Mintage	VG	Fine	VF	XF
132	1826	—	—	—	Rare	—
	1827	—	7.50	15.00	30.00	55.00

NOTE: Many varieties exist of 1827.

Obv: Young head w/o beard.

C#	Date	Mintage	Fine	VF	XF	Unc
147	1831	—	6.00	12.50	25.00	75.00
	1832	—	6.00	12.50	25.00	75.00
	1833	—	6.00	12.50	25.00	75.00
	1838	—	6.00	12.50	25.00	75.00
	1839	—	6.00	12.50	25.00	75.00
	1840	—	6.00	12.50	25.00	75.00
	1841	—	6.00	12.50	25.00	75.00

Obv: Young head w/beard.

C#	Date	Mintage	Fine	VF	XF	Unc
147a	1841	—	5.00	10.00	25.00	75.00
	1842	—	5.00	10.00	25.00	75.00
	1843	—	5.00	10.00	25.00	75.00
	1845	—	5.00	10.00	25.00	75.00

Obv: Older head w/beard.

C#	Date	Mintage	Fine	VF	XF	Unc
147b	1846	—	4.00	8.00	22.00	65.00
	1847	—	4.00	8.00	22.00	65.00
	1848	—	8.50	17.50	42.00	150.00
	1849	—	4.00	8.00	22.00	65.00
	1851	—	4.00	8.00	22.00	65.00
	1853	—	4.00	8.00	22.00	65.00
	1854	—	4.00	8.00	22.00	65.00
	1857	—	4.00	8.00	22.00	65.00
	1858	—	6.50	12.50	25.00	70.00
	1859	—	4.00	8.00	22.00	65.00

6 TORNESI

BRONZE

NOTE: Overstruck on 10 Centesimi, 1813, C#107.

C#	Date	Mintage	Fine	VF	XF	Unc
107a	ND	—	650.00	900.00	1500.	2500.

OTTO (8) TORNESI

COPPER
Obv: FERDINANDUS IV D. G., etc.
Rev: Similar to C#122

C#	Date	Mintage	VG	Fine	VF	XF
115	1816	—	10.00	20.00	40.00	100.00

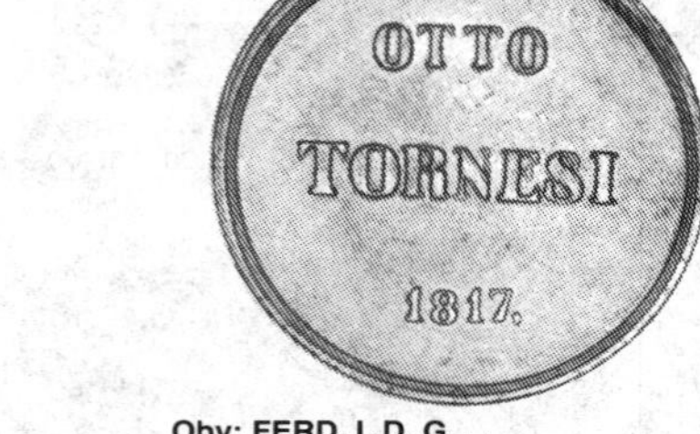

Obv: FERD. I. D. G. . .

C#	Date	Mintage	VG	Fine	VF	XF
122	1816	—	10.00	20.00	35.00	75.00
	1817	—	10.00	20.00	35.00	75.00
	1818	—	10.00	20.00	35.00	75.00

DIECI (10) TORNESI

COPPER
Rev: Similar to 5 Tornesi, C#121a.

C#	Date	Mintage	VG	Fine	VF	XF
123	1819	—	5.00	10.00	30.00	85.00

Rev: Similar to C#148.

C#	Date	Mintage	VG	Fine	VF	XF
133	1825	—	5.00	10.00	30.00	75.00

Obv: Large head w/o beard.

C#	Date	Mintage	Fine	VF	XF	Unc
148	1831	—	15.00	35.00	75.00	175.00
	1832	—	7.50	17.50	30.00	150.00
	1833	—	7.50	17.50	30.00	150.00
	1834	—	25.00	50.00	100.00	250.00
	1835	—	7.50	17.50	30.00	90.00
	1836	—	16.00	35.00	60.00	160.00
	1837	—	10.00	20.00	40.00	150.00
	1838	—	10.00	20.00	40.00	150.00
	1839	—	10.00	20.00	40.00	100.00

Obv: Medium head w/beard.

C#	Date	Mintage	Fine	VF	XF	Unc
148a	1839	—	7.50	17.50	30.00	90.00
	1840	—	12.50	25.00	40.00	95.00
	1841	—	7.50	17.50	30.00	90.00
	1844	—	7.50	17.50	30.00	90.00
	1846	—	7.50	17.50	30.00	90.00
	1847	—	10.00	25.00	50.00	150.00
	1848	—	7.50	17.50	30.00	90.00
	1849	—	7.50	17.50	30.00	90.00
	1851	—	16.00	35.00	60.00	160.00

Obv: Older head w/beard.

C#	Date	Mintage	Fine	VF	XF	Unc
148b	1851	—	6.00	12.50	27.50	75.00
	1852	—	6.00	12.50	27.50	75.00
	1853	—	6.00	12.50	27.50	75.00
	1854	—	6.00	12.50	27.50	75.00
	1855	—	6.00	12.50	27.50	75.00
	1856	—	6.00	12.50	27.50	75.00
	1857	—	9.00	18.00	45.00	135.00
	1858	—	6.00	12.50	27.50	75.00
	1859	—	6.00	12.50	27.50	75.00

NOTE: Minor varieties exist, i.e., leg. size, location.

C#	Date	Mintage	Fine	VF	XF	Unc
159	1859	—	12.50	25.00	50.00	125.00

CINQUE (5) GRANA

1.1500 g, .833 SILVER, .0308 oz ASW
Obv: Young head right w/o beard.

C#	Date	Mintage	Fine	VF	XF	Unc
149	1836	—	3.50	6.00	15.00	50.00
	1838	—	3.50	6.00	15.00	50.00
	1844	—	3.50	6.00	15.00	50.00
	1845	—	3.50	6.00	15.00	50.00
	1846	—	3.50	6.00	15.00	50.00
	1847	—	3.50	6.00	15.00	50.00

Obv: Young head w/beard.

C#	Date	Mintage	Fine	VF	XF	Unc
149a	1848	—	7.50	12.50	20.00	50.00
	1851	—	3.50	6.00	15.00	50.00
	1853	—	3.50	6.00	15.00	50.00

10 GRANA

2.2900 g, .833 SILVER, .0613 oz ASW
Obv: Head right. Rev: Arms.

C#	Date	Mintage	VG	Fine	VF	XF
116	1815	—	7.50	15.00	35.00	65.00
	1816	—	7.50	15.00	35.00	65.00

C#	Date	Mintage	VG	Fine	VF	XF
124	1818	—	5.00	10.00	20.00	50.00

Obv: Head right.

C#	Date	Mintage	VG	Fine	VF	XF
134	1826	—	5.00	10.00	15.00	35.00

Obv: Young head w/o beard, continuous leg.

C#	Date	Mintage	Fine	VF	XF	Unc
150	1832	—	7.50	15.00	30.00	60.00
	1833	—	7.50	12.50	25.00	45.00
	1834	—	7.50	15.00	30.00	60.00
	1835	—	7.50	15.00	30.00	60.00

Obv: Leg. divided over young head w/o beard.

C#	Date	Mintage	Fine	VF	XF	Unc
150a	1835	—	6.00	12.50	20.00	50.00
	1836	—	6.00	12.50	20.00	50.00
	1837	—	6.00	12.50	20.00	50.00
	1838	—	6.00	12.50	20.00	50.00
	1839	—	6.00	12.50	20.00	50.00

Obv: Young head w/beard.

C#	Date	Mintage	Fine	VF	XF	Unc
150b	1838	—	10.00	18.00	25.00	60.00
	1839	—	6.00	12.50	20.00	50.00
	1840	—	6.00	12.50	20.00	50.00
	1841	—	6.00	12.50	20.00	50.00
	1842	—	6.00	12.50	20.00	50.00
	1843	—	15.00	25.00	40.00	70.00
	1844	—	6.00	12.50	20.00	50.00
	1845	—	6.00	12.50	20.00	50.00
	1846	—	6.00	12.50	20.00	50.00

Obv: Older head w/beard.

C#	Date	Mintage	Fine	VF	XF	Unc
150c	1847	—	5.00	7.50	15.00	40.00
	1848	—	5.00	7.50	15.00	40.00
	1849	—	10.00	20.00	40.00	100.00
	1850	—	6.00	12.50	20.00	50.00
	1851	—	6.00	12.50	20.00	50.00
	1853	—	5.00	7.50	15.00	40.00
	1854	—	5.00	7.50	15.00	40.00
	1855	—	5.00	7.50	15.00	40.00
	1856	—	5.00	7.50	15.00	40.00
	1859	—	5.00	7.50	15.00	40.00

20 GRANA

4.5900 g, .833 SILVER, .1229 oz ASW

C#	Date	Mintage	VG	Fine	VF	XF
135	1826	—	10.00	20.00	40.00	80.00

Obv: Young head w/o beard.

C#	Date	Mintage	Fine	VF	XF	Unc
151	1831	—	8.50	17.50	35.00	130.00
	1832	—	8.50	17.50	35.00	130.00
	1833	—	8.50	17.50	35.00	130.00
	1834	—	8.50	17.50	35.00	130.00
	1835	—	8.50	17.50	35.00	130.00
	1836	—	8.50	17.50	35.00	130.00
	1837	—	8.50	17.50	35.00	130.00
	1838	—	8.50	17.50	35.00	130.00
	1839	—	8.50	17.50	35.00	130.00

Obv: Young head w/beard.

C#	Date	Mintage	Fine	VF	XF	Unc
151a	1839	—	8.50	17.50	35.00	130.00
	1840	—	8.50	17.50	35.00	130.00
	1841	—	8.50	17.50	35.00	130.00
	1842	—	8.50	17.50	30.00	125.00
	1843	—	8.50	17.50	35.00	130.00
	1844	—	8.50	17.50	35.00	130.00
	1845	—	8.50	17.50	35.00	130.00
	1846	—	12.50	25.00	45.00	150.00
	1847	—	8.50	17.50	35.00	130.00
	1848	—	8.50	17.50	35.00	130.00
	1850	—	8.50	17.50	35.00	130.00
	1851	—	8.50	17.50	35.00	130.00
	1852	—	8.50	17.50	35.00	130.00
	1853	—	8.50	17.50	35.00	130.00
	1854	—	8.50	17.50	35.00	130.00
	1855	—	8.50	17.50	35.00	130.00
	1856	—	8.50	17.50	35.00	130.00
	1857	—	8.50	17.50	35.00	130.00
	1858	—	8.50	17.50	35.00	130.00
	1859/8	—	10.00	22.50	45.00	150.00
	1859	—	8.50	17.50	35.00	130.00

C#	Date	Mintage	Fine	VF	XF	Unc
160	1859	—	12.50	25.00	65.00	185.00

60 GRANA

13.7500 g, .833 SILVER, .3682 oz ASW
Obv: Head right, FERD IV. D. G., etc.

C#	Date	Mintage	VG	Fine	VF	XF
117	1816	—	15.00	25.00	75.00	175.00

Obv: Crowned head right, FERD I D. G., etc.

C#	Date	Mintage	VG	Fine	VF	XF
125	1818	—	20.00	35.00	65.00	150.00

Obv: Head right. Rev: Arms within wreath.

C#	Date	Mintage	VG	Fine	VF	XF
136	1826	—	25.00	45.00	90.00	250.00

Obv: Young head w/o beard, leg. continuous.

C#	Date	Mintage	Fine	VF	XF	Unc
152	1831	—	20.00	35.00	75.00	300.00
	1832	—	20.00	35.00	75.00	300.00
	1833	—	20.00	35.00	75.00	300.00
	1834	—	20.00	35.00	75.00	300.00

Obv: Leg. divided.

C#	Date	Mintage	Fine	VF	XF	Unc
152a	1835	—	20.00	40.00	80.00	350.00
	1836	—	20.00	35.00	75.00	300.00
	1837	—	50.00	90.00	125.00	600.00
	1838	—	20.00	35.00	75.00	300.00
	1839	—	35.00	60.00	100.00	350.00

Obv: Young head w/beard.

C#	Date	Mintage	Fine	VF	XF	Unc
152b	1841	—	35.00	65.00	115.00	300.00
	1842	—	35.00	65.00	115.00	300.00
	1845	—	35.00	65.00	115.00	300.00

Obv: Older head w/beard.

C#	Date	Mintage	Fine	VF	XF	Unc
152c	1846	—	35.00	60.00	100.00	300.00
	1847	—	35.00	60.00	100.00	300.00
	1848	—	35.00	60.00	100.00	300.00
	1850	—	35.00	60.00	100.00	300.00
	1851	—	35.00	60.00	100.00	300.00
	1852	—	35.00	60.00	100.00	300.00
	1854	—	35.00	60.00	100.00	300.00
	1855	—	35.00	60.00	75.00	250.00
	1856	—	35.00	60.00	100.00	300.00
	1857	—	35.00	60.00	100.00	300.00
	1858	—	35.00	60.00	100.00	300.00
	1859	—	35.00	60.00	100.00	300.00

120 GRANA

27.5300 g, .833 SILVER, .7373 oz ASW

C#	Date	Mintage	VG	Fine	VF	XF
118	1815	—	45.00	70.00	100.00	200.00
	1816	—	50.00	80.00	125.00	225.00
	1816R	*	55.00	90.00	140.00	275.00

***NOTE:** The R(istampato) issues were struck over the coins of Joseph Napoleon and Joachim Murat.

Obv: Large crowned head.

C#	Date	Mintage	VG	Fine	VF	XF
126	1817	—	30.00	50.00	90.00	165.00
	1818	—	20.00	30.00	50.00	145.00

Obv: Small crowned head.

C#	Date	Mintage	VG	Fine	VF	XF
126a	1818	—	25.00	35.00	75.00	200.00

C#	Date	Mintage	Fine	VF	XF	Unc
137	1825	—	35.00	75.00	200.00	600.00
	1825R	—	45.00	90.00	250.00	800.00
	1826	—	35.00	75.00	200.00	600.00
	1826 R	—	45.00	90.00	250.00	800.00
	1828	—	55.00	100.00	275.00	900.00

Rev: Similar to C#153a.

C#	Date	Mintage	Fine	VF	XF	Unc
153	1831	—	22.50	30.00	75.00	200.00
	1832	—	22.50	30.00	75.00	200.00
	1833	—	30.00	50.00	90.00	225.00
	1834	—	30.00	50.00	90.00	225.00
	1835	—	22.50	30.00	75.00	200.00

C#	Date	Mintage	Fine	VF	XF	Unc
153a	1835	—	27.50	40.00	90.00	225.00
	1836	—	22.50	30.00	75.00	200.00
	1837	—	30.00	60.00	100.00	300.00

C#	Date	Mintage	Fine	VF	XF	Unc
153a	1838	—	22.50	30.00	75.00	200.00
	1839	—	30.00	60.00	100.00	300.00

Rev: Similar to C#153a.

C#	Date	Mintage	Fine	VF	XF	Unc
153b	1840	—	22.50	30.00	70.00	175.00
	1841	—	22.50	30.00	70.00	175.00
	1842	—	22.50	30.00	70.00	175.00
	1843	—	22.50	30.00	70.00	175.00
	1844	—	22.50	30.00	70.00	175.00
	1845	—	22.50	30.00	70.00	175.00
	1846	—	22.50	30.00	70.00	175.00
	1847	—	25.00	50.00	100.00	200.00
	1848	—	25.00	50.00	100.00	200.00
	1849	—	100.00	150.00	500.00	1000.
	1850	—	22.50	30.00	50.00	175.00
	1851	—	22.50	30.00	70.00	175.00

NOTE: Many varieties exist.

Rev: Similar to C#153a.

C#	Date	Mintage	Fine	VF	XF	Unc
153c	1851	—	22.50	30.00	60.00	125.00
	1852	—	22.50	30.00	60.00	125.00
	1853	—	22.50	30.00	60.00	125.00
	1854	—	22.50	30.00	60.00	125.00
	1855	—	22.50	30.00	60.00	125.00
	1856	—	22.50	30.00	60.00	125.00
	1857	—	22.50	30.00	60.00	125.00
	1858	—	22.50	30.00	60.00	125.00
	1859	—	22.50	30.00	60.00	125.00

Rev: Similar to C#153a.

C#	Date	Mintage	Fine	VF	XF	Unc
161	1859	—	30.00	50.00	125.00	250.00

3 DUCATI

3.7900 g, .996 GOLD, .1213 oz AGW

C#	Date	Mintage	VG	Fine	VF	XF
127	1818	—	150.00	225.00	350.00	700.00

Obv: Head right. Rev: Winged Genius.

C#	Date	Mintage	VG	Fine	VF	XF
138	1826	—	300.00	450.00	900.00	2000.

Obv: Young head w/o beard.

C#	Date	Mintage	Fine	VF	XF	Unc
154	1831	—	200.00	250.00	350.00	800.00
	1832	—	200.00	250.00	350.00	800.00
	1835	—	200.00	250.00	350.00	800.00
154a	1837	—	200.00	250.00	350.00	800.00

Obv: Young head w/beard.

C#	Date	Mintage	Fine	VF	XF	Unc
154b	1839	—	200.00	250.00	325.00	700.00
	1840	—	200.00	250.00	350.00	750.00

C#	Date	Mintage	Fine	VF	XF	Unc
154c	1842	—	200.00	250.00	325.00	700.00
	1845	—	200.00	250.00	325.00	700.00
	1846	—	200.00	250.00	350.00	750.00
	1848	—	200.00	250.00	325.00	700.00

Obv: Older head w/beard.

C#	Date	Mintage	Fine	VF	XF	Unc
154d	1850	—	175.00	225.00	300.00	500.00
	1851	—	175.00	225.00	300.00	500.00
	1852	—	175.00	225.00	300.00	500.00
	1854	—	125.00	175.00	250.00	450.00
	1856	—	175.00	225.00	300.00	500.00

6 DUCATI

7.5700 g, .996 GOLD, .2424 oz AGW

C#	Date	Mintage	VG	Fine	VF	XF
139	1826	—	200.00	400.00	650.00	1850.

Obv: Young head w/o beard. Rev: Winged Genius.

C#	Date	Mintage	Fine	VF	XF	Unc
155	1831	—	200.00	350.00	525.00	1300.
	1833	—	200.00	350.00	525.00	1300.
	1835	—	250.00	450.00	600.00	1650.

Obv: Young head w/beard.

C#	Date	Mintage	Fine	VF	XF	Unc
155b	1840	—	200.00	350.00	525.00	1300.

Obv: Older head w/beard.

C#	Date	Mintage	Fine	VF	XF	Unc
155c	1842	—	200.00	350.00	525.00	1300.
	1845	—	200.00	350.00	525.00	1300.
	1847	—	200.00	350.00	525.00	1300.
	1848	—	200.00	350.00	525.00	1300.
	1850	—	200.00	350.00	525.00	1300.
	1851	—	200.00	350.00	525.00	1300.
	1852	—	200.00	350.00	525.00	1300.
	1854	—	200.00	350.00	525.00	1300.
	1856	—	200.00	350.00	525.00	1300.

15 DUCATI

18.9300 g, .996 GOLD, .6062 oz AGW

C#	Date	Mintage	VG	Fine	VF	XF
128	1818	—	300.00	550.00	750.00	1400.

C#	Date	Mintage	Fine	VF	XF	Unc
140	1825	—	—	—	Rare	—

NOTE: Bowers and Merena Guia sale 3-88 XF realized $26,400.

C#	Date	Mintage	Fine	VF	XF	Unc
156	1831	—	500.00	800.00	1250.	2750.

Obv: Young head w/beard. Rev: Winged Genius.

C#	Date	Mintage	Fine	VF	XF	Unc
156c	1842	—	500.00	800.00	1250.	2750.
	1844	—	450.00	700.00	850.00	1750.
	1845	—	450.00	700.00	850.00	1750.
	1847	—	450.00	700.00	850.00	1750.

Obv: Older head w/beard.

C#	Date	Mintage	Fine	VF	XF	Unc
156d	1848	—	500.00	800.00	1250.	2750.
	1850	—	400.00	675.00	800.00	1750.
	1851	—	400.00	675.00	800.00	1750.
	1852	—	400.00	675.00	800.00	1750.
	1854	—	400.00	675.00	800.00	1750.
	1856	—	400.00	675.00	800.00	1750.

30 DUCATI

37.8700 g, .996 GOLD, 1.2128 oz AGW

C#	Date	Mintage	VG	Fine	VF	XF
129	1818	—	600.00	750.00	1400.	2200.

C#	Date	Mintage	VG	Fine	VF	XF
141	1825	—	600.00	750.00	1500.	3500.
	1826	—	600.00	750.00	1500.	3500.

C#	Date	Mintage	Fine	VF	XF	Unc
157	1831	—	500.00	800.00	1500.	2500.
	1833	—	550.00	850.00	1600.	3000.
	1835	—	550.00	850.00	1600.	3000.

C#	Date	Mintage	Fine	VF	XF	Unc
157b	1839	—	550.00	850.00	1600.	3000.
	1840	—	550.00	850.00	1600.	3000.

C#	Date	Mintage	Fine	VF	XF	Unc
157c	1842	—	—	—	Rare	—
	1844	—	550.00	850.00	1600.	3000.
	1845	—	550.00	850.00	1600.	3000.
	1847	—	550.00	850.00	1600.	3000.
	1848	—	550.00	850.00	1600.	3000.
	1851	—	550.00	850.00	1600.	3000.
	1854	—	550.00	850.00	1600.	3000.

C#	Date	Mintage	Fine	VF	XF	Unc
157e	1850	—	500.00	800.00	1500.	2500.
	1851	—	550.00	850.00	1600.	3000.
	1852	—	550.00	850.00	1600.	3000.

Obv: Small older head w/beard.

C#	Date	Mintage	Fine	VF	XF	Unc
157d	1854	—	550.00	850.00	1600.	3000.
	1856	—	550.00	850.00	1600.	3000.

PATTERNS (Pn)

(Including off metal strikes)

KM#	Date	Mintage	Identification	Mkt.Val.
Pn1	1856	—	60 Grana, Gold, C152	4400.

PARMA

A town in Emillia which was a papal possession from 1512 to 1545, was seized by France in 1796, and was attached to the Napoleonic empire in 1808. In 1814, Parma was assigned to Marie Louise, empress of Napoleon I. It was annexed to Sardinia in 1860.

RULERS

Ferdinando di Borbone, 1765-1802
Maria Luigia, Duchess, 1815-1847
Carlo II di Borbone, 1847-1849
Carlo III di Borbone, 1849-1854
Roberto di Borbone, 1854-1858

MONETARY SYSTEM

100 Centesimi = 20 Soldi = 1 Lira

CENTESIMO

COPPER
Similar to 5 Centesimi, C#25.

C#	Date	Mintage	Fine	VF	XF	Unc
23	1830	2.029	4.00	7.50	12.50	40.00

Obv: Head of Carlo III left. Rev: Oval arms.

C#	Date	Mintage	Fine	VF	XF	Unc
33	1854	—	300.00	500.00	700.00	1200.

3 CENTESIMI

COPPER
Similar to 5 Centesimi, C#25.

C#	Date	Mintage	Fine	VF	XF	Unc
24	1830	.511	20.00	30.00	50.00	100.00

Obv: Head of Carlo III left. Rev: Oval arms.

C#	Date	Mintage	Fine	VF	XF	Unc
34	1854	—	450.00	650.00	900.00	1500.

5 CENTESIMI

COPPER

C#	Date	Mintage	Fine	VF	XF	Unc
25	1830	1.506	5.00	10.00	20.00	60.00

Obv: Head of Carlo III left. Rev: Oval arms.

C#	Date	Mintage	Fine	VF	XF	Unc
35	1854	—	700.00	1000.	1500.	2200.

5 SOLDI

1.2500 g, .900 SILVER, .0361 oz ASW

C#	Date	Mintage	Fine	VF	XF	Unc
26	1815/3	.682	9.00	15.00	25.00	75.00
	1815	Inc. Ab.	7.50	12.50	20.00	50.00
	1830	—	10.00	15.00	25.00	50.00

10 SOLDI

2.5000 g, .900 SILVER, .0722 oz ASW

C#	Date	Mintage	Fine	VF	XF	Unc
27	1815	.530	12.00	20.00	30.00	85.00
	1830	—	25.00	50.00	100.00	200.00

LIRA

5.0000 g, .900 SILVER, .1444 oz ASW

C#	Date	Mintage	Fine	VF	XF	Unc
28	1815	.066	20.00	40.00	65.00	175.00

2 LIRE

10.0000 g, .900 SILVER, .2888 oz ASW

C#	Date	Mintage	Fine	VF	XF	Unc
29	1815	.022	50.00	100.00	185.00	450.00

5 LIRE

25.0000 g, .900 SILVER, .7234 oz ASW

C#	Date	Mintage	Fine	VF	XF	Unc
30	1815	.093	100.00	150.00	250.00	700.00
	1821	—	—	—	Rare	—
	1832	.044	125.00	200.00	350.00	1000.

C#	Date	Mintage	Fine	VF	XF	Unc
36	1858	1,000	350.00	500.00	900.00	1650.

20 LIRE

6.4500 g, .900 GOLD, .1866 oz AGW

C#	Date	Mintage	Fine	VF	XF	Unc
31	1815	.012	250.00	375.00	575.00	1000.
	1832	1,550	1000.	1500.	2000.	3000.

40 LIRE

12.9000 g, .900 GOLD, .3733 oz AGW

C#	Date	Mintage	Fine	VF	XF	Unc
32	1815	.220	175.00	275.00	375.00	700.00
	1821	.037	250.00	400.00	600.00	1400.

PATTERNS (Pn)

(Including off metal strikes)

KM#	Date	Mintage	Identification	Mkt.Val.
Pn1	1815	—	1 Ducato	5,500.

KM#	Date	Mintage	Identification	Mkt.Val.
Pn2	1842	—	5 Centesimi	—

PIEDMONT REPUBLIC

Established by Napoleon in 1798 in the Piedmont area of northwest Italy which was the mainland possession of the kingdom of Sardinia, the republic was overthrown by Austro-Russian forces in 1799.

SUBALPINE REPUBLIC

1800-1801

5 FRANCS

25.0000 g, .900 SILVER, .7234 oz ASW

C#	Date	Mintage	VG	Fine	VF	XF
4	L'AN 10(1801)					
		.033	40.00	60.00	90.00	200.00

NOTE: Earlier date L'AN 9 (1800) exists for this type.

20 FRANCS

6.4500 g, .900 GOLD, .1866 oz AGW

C#	Date	Mintage	VG	Fine	VF	XF
5	L'AN 10(1801)					
		1,492	275.00	475.00	750.00	1300.

NOTE: Earlier date L'AN 9 (1800) exists for this type.

SARDINIA

A Roman see in the 11th century occupied by the competitive cities of Pisa and Genoa. In 1297 it was granted to James II of Aragon, and remained under Spanish control until passing to the house of Savoy in 1720. In 1861 it became the nucleus about which the United Kingdom of Italy was formed.

RULERS

Carlo Emanuele IV 1796-1802
Vittorio Emanuele I 1802-1821
Carlo Felice 1821-1831
Carlo Alberto 1831-1849
Vittorio Emanuele II 1849-1878

M = Milan
(t) after 1802 - Eagles head = Turin (Torino)

MONETARY SYSTEM

12 Denari = 6 Cagliarese = 1 Soldo
50 Soldi = 10 Reales =
2-1/2 Lire = 1 Scudo Sardo
2 Scudi Sardi = 1 Doppietta
Commencing 1816
100 Centesimi = 1 Lira

ISLAND COINAGE

CAGLIARESE

COPPER, 17mm
Obv: Cross on Arms. Rev: Value.

C#	Date	Mintage	Fine	VF	XF	Unc
A88	ND(1813)	—	—	—	Rare	—

TRE (3) CAGLIARESE

COPPER
Obv: Cross on arms. Rev: Value.

C#	Date	Mintage	Fine	VF	XF	Unc
88	ND(1813)	—	65.00	100.00	185.00	350.00

REALE

3.1800 g, .500 SILVER, .0551 oz ASW
Obv: Head right, leg: VIC.EM.D.G.REX. SAR.CYP.ET.IER. around, date.
Rev: Eagle on shield w/head to right, crown above.

C#	Date	Mintage	Fine	VF	XF	Unc
89.1	1812	—	60.00	90.00	145.00	285.00

Rev: Eagle's head to left.

C#	Date	Mintage	Fine	VF	XF	Unc
89.2	1812	—	60.00	90.00	145.00	285.00

MONETARY REFORM

100 Centesimi = 1 Lira

CENTESIMO

COPPER
Mint mark: Eagle head.

C#	Date	Mintage	Fine	VF	XF	Unc
118	1842	1.933	40.00	60.00	75.00	140.00

3 CENTESIMI

COPPER
Mint mark: Eagle head.
Obv: Arms. Rev: Value and date.

C#	Date	Mintage	Fine	VF	XF	Unc
119	1842	2.169	10.00	20.00	40.00	75.00

5 CENTESIMI

COPPER
Mint mark: Eagle head.
Obv: Arms. Rev: Value and date.

C#	Date	Mintage	Fine	VF	XF	Unc
120	1842	1.845	10.00	25.00	50.00	90.00

MAINLAND COINAGE

2.6 SOLDI

BILLON
Obv: Head right, VICTORIVS EMANVEL around, date. Rev: Crowned displayed eagle w/arms of Savoy on breast.

C#	Date	Mintage	Fine	VF	XF	Unc
90	1814	—	4.00	8.00	20.00	50.00
	1815	—	4.00	8.00	20.00	50.00

1/2 SCUDO

17.5820 g, .905 SILVER, .5116 oz ASW

C#	Date	Mintage	Fine	VF	XF	Unc
91	1814	—	400.00	600.00	700.00	1500.
	1815	—	600.00	900.00	1250.	2500.

DOPPIA

9.1160 g, .905 GOLD, .2652 oz AGW
Obv. leg: VICTORIVS EMANVEL.
Rev. leg: D.G.REX.SAR. . .

C#	Date	Mintage	VG	Fine	VF	XF
94	1814	—	2000.	4000.	8500.	12,000.

Obv. leg: VIC.EM.D.G.REX.SAR. . .
Rev. leg: MONTISF.PR.PED.&. . .

C#	Date	Mintage	VG	Fine	VF	XF
94a	1815	—	—	—	13,000.	15,000.

NOTE: Superior Pipito sale 12-87 choice VF realized $13,750. Stack's International sale 3-88 XF realized $11,550.

MONETARY REFORM

100 Centesimi = 1 Lira

CENTESIMO

COPPER
Mint mark: Anchor

C#	Date	Mintage	Fine	VF	XF	Unc
98.1	1826 P	11.485	5.00	10.00	25.00	50.00

Mint mark: Eagle head.

C#	Date	Mintage	Fine	VF	XF	Unc
98.2	1826 L	—	3.50	6.00	15.00	45.00
	1826 P	4.812	3.50	6.00	15.00	45.00

3 CENTESIMI

COPPER
Mint mark: Anchor

C#	Date	Mintage	Fine	VF	XF	Unc
99.1	1826 P	.844	3.50	6.00	15.00	45.00

Mint mark: Eagle head

C#	Date	Mintage	Fine	VF	XF	Unc
99.2	1826 L	5.778	3.50	6.00	15.00	45.00

5 CENTESIMI

COPPER
Mint mark: Anchor

C#	Date	Mintage	Fine	VF	XF	Unc
100.1	1826 P	10.514	3.50	7.00	18.00	50.00

Mint mark: Eagle head

C#	Date	Mintage	Fine	VF	XF	Unc
100.2	1826 L	32.177	3.50	7.00	18.00	50.00
	1826 P	Inc. Ab.	3.50	7.00	18.00	50.00

NOTE: C#98, 99, 100 were struck w/o mint mark at Bologna in 1860. See Emilia KM#1, 2 and 3.

25 CENTESIMI

1.2500 g, .900 SILVER, .0361 oz ASW
Mint mark: Anchor
Obv: Head right. Rev: Arms.

C#	Date	Mintage	Fine	VF	XF	Unc
101.1	1829 P	.450	15.00	25.00	40.00	90.00
	1830 P	.135	17.50	30.00	50.00	100.00

Mint mark: Eagle head

C#	Date	Mintage	Fine	VF	XF	Unc
101.2	1829 L	.110	17.50	30.00	50.00	100.00
	1830 L	.234	15.00	25.00	40.00	90.00
	1830 P	Inc. Ab.	20.00	35.00	60.00	150.00

C#	Date	Mintage	Fine	VF	XF	Unc
109.1	1832 P	.120	75.00	150.00	300.00	600.00
	1833 P	—	20.00	35.00	60.00	150.00
	1837 P	.230	75.00	150.00	300.00	600.00

Mint mark: Anchor

C#	Date	Mintage	Fine	VF	XF	Unc
109.2	1833 P	7,921	25.00	40.00	60.00	120.00

50 CENTESIMI

2.5000 g, .900 SILVER, .0722 oz ASW
Mint mark: Eagle head

C#	Date	Mintage	Fine	VF	XF	Unc
102.1	1823 L	—	—	—	Rare	—
	1824 L	—	—	—	Rare	—
	1825 L	.492	12.50	25.00	50.00	150.00
	1826 L	.640	12.50	25.00	50.00	150.00
	1827 L	.401	12.50	25.00	50.00	150.00
	1828 L	.611	12.50	25.00	50.00	150.00
	1828 P	Inc. Ab.	12.50	25.00	50.00	150.00
	1829 P	.255	35.00	75.00	125.00	200.00
	1830 L	.456	12.50	25.00	50.00	150.00
	1830 P	Inc. Ab.	100.00	150.00	200.00	300.00
	1831 L	.143	12.50	25.00	50.00	150.00
	1831 P	Inc. Ab.	50.00	80.00	150.00	400.00

Mint mark: Anchor

C#	Date	Mintage	Fine	VF	XF	Unc
102.2	1826 P	.079	20.00	40.00	75.00	150.00
	1827 P	.143	15.00	30.00	60.00	125.00
	1828 P	.194	35.00	75.00	100.00	175.00
	1829 P	.107	15.00	30.00	60.00	125.00

Mint mark: Eagle head
Obv: Head right. Rev: Arms.

C#	Date	Mintage	Fine	VF	XF	Unc
110.1	1832 P	—	—	—	Rare	—
	1833 P	.062	20.00	40.00	75.00	200.00
	1834 P	.061	40.00	80.00	200.00	600.00
	1835 P	—	40.00	80.00	200.00	400.00
	1836 P	.022	40.00	80.00	200.00	600.00
	1837 P	.012	40.00	80.00	200.00	600.00
	1841 P	6,600	40.00	80.00	200.00	600.00
	1842 P	.010	20.00	35.00	75.00	200.00
	1843 P	.014	20.00	35.00	75.00	200.00
	1844 P	9,100	50.00	100.00	300.00	800.00
	1845 P	.016	40.00	75.00	125.00	250.00
	1846 P	.023	50.00	100.00	300.00	800.00
	1847 P	.011	50.00	100.00	200.00	400.00

Mint mark: Anchor

C#	Date	Mintage	Fine	VF	XF	Unc
110.2	1833 P	136 pcs.	50.00	100.00	200.00	400.00
	1844 P	.023	50.00	100.00	300.00	800.00

Obv: Head w/beard.

C#	Date	Mintage	Fine	VF	XF	Unc
121.1	1850 P	9,268	30.00	60.00	100.00	200.00
	1860 P	15 pcs.	—	—	Rare	—

Mint mark: Eagle head

C#	Date	Mintage	Fine	VF	XF	Unc
121.2	1850 B	—	12.50	25.00	50.00	150.00
	1852 B	.055	12.50	25.00	50.00	150.00
	1853 B	.021	12.50	25.00	50.00	150.00
	1855 B	—	30.00	60.00	150.00	300.00
	1856 B	9,754	12.50	25.00	50.00	150.00
	1857 B	.015	12.50	25.00	50.00	150.00
	1858 B	8,114	12.50	25.00	50.00	150.00
	1860 B	6,484	12.50	25.00	50.00	150.00

Mint mark: M

C#	Date	Mintage	Fine	VF	XF	Unc
121.3	1860	.982	15.00	30.00	65.00	175.00
	1861	—	50.00	100.00	200.00	500.00

LIRA

5.0000 g, .900 SILVER, .1444 oz ASW
Mint mark: Eagle head

C#	Date	Mintage	Fine	VF	XF	Unc
103.1	1823 L	—	—	—	Rare	—
	1824 L	.092	25.00	50.00	100.00	300.00
	1825 L	—	50.00	100.00	200.00	600.00
	1826 L	.547	20.00	40.00	75.00	200.00
	1827 L	.836	20.00	40.00	75.00	200.00
	1828 L	.345	20.00	40.00	75.00	200.00
	1828 P	Inc. Ab.	20.00	40.00	75.00	200.00
	1829 L	.111	20.00	50.00	100.00	400.00
	1830 P	.313	20.00	40.00	75.00	200.00

Mint mark: Anchor

C#	Date	Mintage	Fine	VF	XF	Unc
103.2	1824 P	5,670	25.00	50.00	100.00	400.00
	1825 P	—	20.00	40.00	75.00	200.00
	1826 P	.154	20.00	40.00	75.00	200.00
	1827 P	.251	20.00	40.00	75.00	200.00
	1828 P	.388	20.00	40.00	75.00	200.00
	1829 P	.159	20.00	40.00	75.00	200.00
	1830 P	.060	20.00	40.00	75.00	400.00

Obv: Head right. Rev: Arms.

C#	Date	Mintage	Fine	VF	XF	Unc
111.1	1831 P	.019	50.00	100.00	200.00	700.00
	1832 P	.035	35.00	75.00	200.00	600.00
	1833 P	7,620	50.00	100.00	200.00	700.00
	1834 P	.040	—	—	Rare	—
	1835 P	.023	25.00	50.00	100.00	300.00
	1837 P	.018	—	—	Rare	—
	1838 P	—	25.00	50.00	100.00	250.00
	1841 P	.011	—	—	Rare	—
	1844 P	.033	—	—	Rare	—

Mint mark: Eagle head

C#	Date	Mintage	Fine	VF	XF	Unc
111.2	1831 P	5,000	50.00	100.00	200.00	600.00
	1832 P	.030	50.00	100.00	200.00	600.00
	1833 P	85 pcs.	50.00	100.00	200.00	750.00
	1835 P	—	50.00	100.00	200.00	750.00
	1837 P	.028	50.00	100.00	200.00	600.00
	1838 P	.011	50.00	100.00	200.00	600.00
	1839 P	8,558	—	—	Rare	—
	1841 P	.020	—	—	Rare	—
	1842 P	5,184	—	—	Rare	—
	1843 P	.015	20.00	40.00	100.00	300.00
	1844 P	.015	—	—	Rare	—
	1845 P	.010	20.00	40.00	100.00	300.00
	1846 P	.019	—	—	Rare	—
	1847 P	.011	20.00	40.00	100.00	300.00
	1848 P	8,110	175.00	300.00	500.00	1000.
	1849 P	3,037	—	—	Rare	—

Mint mark: Anchor

C#	Date	Mintage	Fine	VF	XF	Unc
122.1	1850 P	—	50.00	75.00	125.00	400.00
	1853 P	7,051	50.00	75.00	150.00	600.00
	1859 P	.012	40.00	75.00	125.00	400.00
	1860 P	—	—	—	Rare	—

Mint mark: Eagle head

C#	Date	Mintage	Fine	VF	XF	Unc
122.2	1850 B	.092	25.00	50.00	150.00	400.00
	1851 B	—	—	—	Rare	—
	1852 B	—	—	—	Rare	—
	1853 B	.022	25.00	50.00	150.00	400.00
	1854 B	—	—	—	Rare	—
	1855 B	.016	25.00	50.00	150.00	400.00
	1856 B	.058	20.00	40.00	100.00	300.00
	1857 B	.031	20.00	40.00	100.00	300.00
	1858 B	—	—	—	Rare	—
	1859 B	5,150	20.00	40.00	100.00	250.00
	1860 B	4,752	40.00	80.00	100.00	300.00

Mint mark: M

C#	Date	Mintage	Fine	VF	XF	Unc
122.3	1859	—	50.00	100.00	200.00	600.00
	1860	.603	50.00	100.00	200.00	600.00

2 LIRE

10.0000 g, .900 SILVER, .2888 oz ASW
Mint mark: Eagle head

C#	Date	Mintage	Fine	VF	XF	Unc
104.1	1823 L	—	—	—	Rare	—
	1825 L	.261	25.00	50.00	100.00	300.00
	1826 L	.235	25.00	50.00	100.00	350.00
	1827 L	.170	25.00	50.00	100.00	350.00
	1828 L	.102	25.00	50.00	200.00	400.00
	1829 L	—	—	—	Rare	—
	1830 L	.049	25.00	50.00	100.00	350.00
	1830 P	Inc. Ab.	25.00	50.00	150.00	400.00

Mint mark: Anchor

C#	Date	Mintage	Fine	VF	XF	Unc
104.2	1825 P	—	25.00	50.00	100.00	400.00
	1826 P	.157	25.00	50.00	100.00	350.00
	1827 P	.366	25.00	50.00	100.00	350.00
	1830 P	.115	25.00	50.00	100.00	350.00
	1831 P	.072	25.00	50.00	100.00	350.00

Obv: Younger head right.

C#	Date	Mintage	Fine	VF	XF	Unc
112.1	1832 P	.035	25.00	50.00	150.00	600.00
	1833 P	187 pcs.	50.00	100.00	200.00	1000.
	1835 P	5,142	50.00	100.00	200.00	1000.
	1836 P	.030	50.00	100.00	200.00	1000.
	1844 P	.030	25.00	50.00	100.00	500.00
	1845 P	.052	50.00	100.00	200.00	750.00
	1847 P	—	50.00	100.00	200.00	750.00

Mint mark: Eagle head

C#	Date	Mintage	Fine	VF	XF	Unc
112.2	1833 P	287 pcs.	250.00	500.00	1000.	2000.
	1834 P	—	250.00	500.00	750.00	1000.
	1835 P	.024	35.00	75.00	150.00	500.00
	1836 P	—	35.00	75.00	150.00	500.00
	1838 P	.020	—	—	Rare	—
	1839 P	.014	—	—	Rare	—
	1841 P	4,259	150.00	250.00	350.00	800.00
	1842 P	.010	35.00	75.00	150.00	500.00
	1843 P	.012	35.00	75.00	150.00	500.00
	1844 P	.012	35.00	75.00	150.00	500.00
	1845 P	.015	35.00	75.00	150.00	500.00
	1846 P	.015	35.00	75.00	150.00	500.00
	1847 P	.015	—	—	Rare	—
	1848 P	.013	—	—	Rare	—
	1849 P	3,159	—	—	Rare	—

Mint mark: Anchor
Obv: Head w/beard right.

C#	Date	Mintage	Fine	VF	XF	Unc
123.1	1850 P	—	100.00	200.00	400.00	1000.
	1853 P	5,401	—	—	Rare	—
	1854 P	2,748	60.00	125.00	300.00	900.00

Mint mark: Eagle head

C#	Date	Mintage	Fine	VF	XF	Unc
123.2	1850 B	.018	60.00	125.00	300.00	900.00
	1852 B	.023	60.00	125.00	300.00	900.00
	1853 B	4,859	60.00	125.00	300.00	900.00
	1854 B	.018	60.00	125.00	300.00	900.00
	1855 B	9,414	60.00	125.00	300.00	900.00
	1856 B	.011	60.00	125.00	300.00	900.00
	1860 B	8,963	60.00	125.00	300.00	900.00

5 LIRE

25.0000 g, .900 SILVER, .7234 oz ASW
Mint mark: Eagle head
Obv: Similar to C#93.

C#	Date	Mintage	Fine	VF	XF	Unc
92	1816 L	.023	75.00	175.00	325.00	850.00
	1817 L	.044	60.00	125.00	275.00	650.00
	1818 L	.055	60.00	125.00	275.00	650.00
	1819 L	.035	60.00	125.00	275.00	650.00
	1820 L	.101	60.00	125.00	275.00	650.00

C#	Date	Mintage	Fine	VF	XF	Unc
93	1821	—	600.00	1000.	2000.	4000.

C#	Date	Mintage	Fine	VF	XF	Unc
105.1	1821 L	.035	65.00	125.00	170.00	1000.
	1822 L	.037	50.00	90.00	170.00	600.00
	1823 L	.035	50.00	90.00	170.00	425.00
	1824 L	.162	50.00	90.00	170.00	300.00
	1825 L	.395	12.50	25.00	100.00	235.00
	1826 L	.907	25.00	45.00	100.00	235.00
	1827 L	.724	12.50	25.00	100.00	235.00
	1828 L	.253	25.00	45.00	100.00	235.00
	1829 L	.312	25.00	45.00	100.00	235.00
	1830 L	.913	25.00	45.00	100.00	250.00
	1830 P	Inc. Ab.	25.00	45.00	100.00	235.00
	1831 P	.049	50.00	90.00	170.00	425.00

Mint mark: Anchor

C#	Date	Mintage	Fine	VF	XF	Unc
105.2	1824 P	.016	50.00	100.00	200.00	550.00
	1825 P	.017	65.00	125.00	250.00	675.00
	1826 P	.489	25.00	45.00	100.00	235.00
	1827 P	2.137	25.00	45.00	100.00	235.00
	1828 P	1.149	25.00	45.00	100.00	235.00
	1829 P	.597	25.00	45.00	100.00	235.00
	1830 P	1.122	25.00	45.00	100.00	235.00
	1831 P	.451	75.00	150.00	250.00	675.00

Obv: F on truncation. Rev: Arms.

C#	Date	Mintage	Fine	VF	XF	Unc
113.1	1831 P	.451	35.00	50.00	125.00	300.00

Mint mark: Eagle head

C#	Date	Mintage	Fine	VF	XF	Unc
113.2	1831 P	.049	40.00	75.00	170.00	385.00

Mint mark: Anchor
Obv: FERRARIS on truncation.

C#	Date	Mintage	Fine	VF	XF	Unc
113.3	1831 P	Inc. w/113.1	22.00	32.00	90.00	275.00
	1832 P	.317	22.00	32.00	90.00	275.00
	1833 P	.275	22.00	32.00	90.00	275.00
	1834 P	.154	22.00	32.00	90.00	275.00
	1835 P	.336	22.00	32.00	90.00	275.00
	1836 P	.595	22.00	32.00	90.00	275.00
	1837 P	.359	22.00	32.00	90.00	275.00
	1838 P	.307	22.00	32.00	90.00	275.00
	1839 P	.141	22.00	32.00	90.00	275.00
	1840 P	.193	22.00	32.00	90.00	275.00
	1841 P	.313	22.00	32.00	90.00	275.00
	1842 P	.396	22.00	32.00	90.00	275.00
	1843 P	.787	22.00	32.00	90.00	275.00
	1844 P	1.043	22.00	32.00	90.00	275.00
	1845 P	.302	22.00	32.00	90.00	275.00
	1846 P	.264	22.00	32.00	90.00	275.00
	1847 P	.142	22.00	32.00	90.00	275.00
	1848 P	.778	22.00	32.00	90.00	275.00
	1849 P	.739	22.00	32.00	90.00	275.00

Mint mark: Eagle head

C#	Date	Mintage	Fine	VF	XF	Unc
113.4	1831 P	Inc. w/113.2	45.00	80.00	175.00	400.00
	1832 P	.095	22.00	32.00	90.00	275.00
	1833 P	.060	22.00	32.00	90.00	275.00
	1834 P	.037	22.00	32.00	90.00	275.00
	1835 P	.069	22.00	32.00	90.00	275.00
	1836 P	.051	22.00	32.00	90.00	275.00
	1837 P	.036	22.00	32.00	90.00	275.00
	1838 P	.042	22.00	32.00	90.00	275.00
	1839 P	.205	22.00	32.00	90.00	275.00
	1840 P	.050	22.00	32.00	90.00	275.00
	1841 P	.015	22.00	32.00	110.00	450.00
	1842 P	.042	22.00	32.00	90.00	275.00
	1843 P	.037	22.00	32.00	90.00	275.00
	1844 P	.171	22.00	32.00	90.00	275.00
	1845 P	.042	22.00	32.00	90.00	275.00
	1846 P	.046	22.00	32.00	90.00	275.00
	1847 P	.037	22.00	32.00	90.00	275.00
	1848 P	.079	22.00	32.00	90.00	275.00
	1849 P	.104	125.00	300.00	550.00	725.00

Mint mark: Anchor

C#	Date	Mintage	Fine	VF	XF	Unc
124.1	1850 P	.721	45.00	90.00	180.00	450.00
	1851 P	.316	45.00	90.00	180.00	450.00
	1852 P	.391	45.00	90.00	180.00	450.00
	1853 P	.167	45.00	90.00	180.00	450.00
	1854 P	.284	45.00	90.00	180.00	450.00
	1855 P	.084	45.00	90.00	180.00	450.00
	1856 P	.058	45.00	90.00	180.00	450.00
	1857 P	.035	45.00	90.00	180.00	450.00
	1858 P	.030	45.00	90.00	180.00	450.00
	1859 P	.049	45.00	90.00	180.00	450.00

Mint mark: Eagle head

C#	Date	Mintage	Fine	VF	XF	Unc
124.2	1850 B	.058	45.00	90.00	180.00	450.00
	1851 B	.049	45.00	90.00	180.00	450.00
	1852 B	.097	45.00	90.00	180.00	450.00
	1854 B	.074	45.00	90.00	180.00	450.00
	1855 B	.052	45.00	90.00	180.00	450.00
	1856 B	.037	45.00	90.00	180.00	450.00
	1857 B	.019	45.00	90.00	180.00	450.00
	1858 B	.011	45.00	90.00	180.00	450.00
	1859 B	.012	45.00	90.00	180.00	450.00
	1860 B	5,044	45.00	90.00	180.00	450.00
	1861 B	.012	45.00	90.00	180.00	450.00

10 LIRE

3.2200 g, .900 GOLD, .0931 oz AGW
Mint mark: Eagle head

C#	Date	Mintage	Fine	VF	XF	Unc
114.1	1832 P	—	—	—	Rare	—
	1833 P	5,004	125.00	300.00	450.00	1000.
	1835 P	5,118	225.00	375.00	550.00	1200.
	1838 P	2,826	250.00	400.00	575.00	1250.
	1839 P	2,237	175.00	350.00	500.00	1100.
	1841 P	1,583	175.00	350.00	500.00	1100.
	1842 P	759 pcs.	250.00	475.00	650.00	1800.
	1843 P	950 pcs.	250.00	475.00	650.00	1800.
	1845 P	3,009	225.00	450.00	600.00	1500.
	1846 P	970 pcs.	250.00	475.00	650.00	1800.
	1847 P	405 pcs.	250.00	500.00	750.00	2000.

Mint mark: Anchor

C#	Date	Mintage	Fine	VF	XF	Unc
114.2	1833 P	1,550	200.00	375.00	750.00	1200.
	1835 P	—	—	—	Rare	—
	1841 P	2,809	225.00	425.00	850.00	1250.
	1843 P	4,566	225.00	425.00	850.00	1250.
	1844 P	.011	175.00	325.00	450.00	1000.
	1845 P	1,535	225.00	425.00	850.00	1250.
	1846 P	3,373	225.00	425.00	850.00	1250.
	1847 P	—	—	—	Rare	—
125.1	1850 P	4,141	300.00	750.00	1250.	1800.

Mint mark: Eagle head

C#	Date	Mintage	Fine	VF	XF	Unc
125.2	1850 B	2,326	225.00	400.00	600.00	1000.
	1852 B	—	500.00	1000.	1500.	2000.
	1853 B	—	225.00	400.00	600.00	1000.
	1854 B	1,833	225.00	400.00	600.00	1000.
	1855 B	2,566	225.00	400.00	600.00	1000.
	1856 B	2,526	225.00	400.00	600.00	1000.
	1857 B	7,193	225.00	400.00	600.00	1000.
	1858 B	2,931	225.00	400.00	600.00	1000.
	1859 B	1 known	—	—	7040.	—
	1860 B	6,036	225.00	400.00	600.00	1000.

20 LIRE

6.4500 g, .900 GOLD, .1866 oz AGW
Mint mark: Eagle head

C#	Date	Mintage	Fine	VF	XF	Unc
95	1816	.019	225.00	350.00	450.00	750.00
	1817	.040	125.00	225.00	350.00	600.00
	1818	.035	125.00	225.00	350.00	600.00
	1819	.022	125.00	225.00	350.00	600.00
	1820	.033	125.00	225.00	350.00	600.00

C#	Date	Mintage	Fine	VF	XF	Unc
96	1821	—	1500.	2500.	3750.	6000.

C#	Date	Mintage	Fine	VF	XF	Unc
106.1	1821 L	.018	175.00	225.00	300.00	475.00
	1822 L	7,460	175.00	225.00	325.00	500.00
	1823 L	.022	175.00	225.00	300.00	475.00
	1824 L	2,381	200.00	275.00	375.00	650.00
	1825 L	.028	175.00	225.00	300.00	475.00
	1826 L	.144	150.00	200.00	275.00	475.00
	1827 L	.150	150.00	200.00	275.00	475.00
	1828 L	.095	150.00	200.00	275.00	475.00
	1828 P	—	225.00	300.00	400.00	650.00
	1829 L	.061	225.00	300.00	400.00	650.00
	1829 P	—	225.00	300.00	400.00	650.00
	1830 L	—	225.00	300.00	400.00	650.00
	1830 P	.035	200.00	275.00	375.00	600.00
	1831 P	.042	125.00	200.00	300.00	475.00

Mint mark: Anchor

C#	Date	Mintage	Fine	VF	XF	Unc
106.2	1824 P	2,394	125.00	150.00	200.00	375.00
	1825 P	313 pcs.	375.00	500.00	600.00	1500.
	1827 P	1,766	225.00	300.00	400.00	500.00
	1828 P	—	—	—	Rare	—
	1829 P	—	225.00	300.00	400.00	500.00
	1830 P	3,270	375.00	500.00	600.00	800.00
	1831 P	16,189	—	—	Rare	—

C#	Date	Mintage	Fine	VF	XF	Unc
115.1	1831 P	—	100.00	125.00	150.00	275.00
	1832 P	.074	100.00	125.00	150.00	275.00
	1833 P	.080	—	—	Rare	—
	1834 P	.133	100.00	125.00	150.00	275.00
	1835 P	.052	100.00	125.00	150.00	275.00
	1836 P	.090	100.00	125.00	150.00	275.00
	1837 P	.056	—	—	Rare	—
	1838 P	.120	100.00	125.00	150.00	275.00
	1839 P	.074	—	—	Rare	—
	1840 P	.176	100.00	125.00	150.00	275.00
	1841 P	.206	125.00	175.00	250.00	375.00
	1842 P	.066	100.00	125.00	150.00	275.00
	1843 P	.045	—	—	Rare	—
	1844 P	.034	—	—	Rare	—
	1845 P	.043	100.00	125.00	150.00	275.00
	1846 P	.043	—	—	Rare	—
	1847 P	.052	100.00	125.00	150.00	275.00
	1848 P	.059	125.00	150.00	175.00	275.00
	1849 P	.111	100.00	125.00	150.00	250.00

Mint mark: Eagle head

C#	Date	Mintage	Fine	VF	XF	Unc
115.2	1831 P	—	100.00	125.00	150.00	275.00
	1832 P	.053	100.00	125.00	150.00	275.00
	1833 P	.016	100.00	125.00	150.00	275.00
	1834 P	.261	100.00	125.00	150.00	275.00
	1836 P	.014	—	—	Rare	—
	1837 P	.015	—	—	Rare	—
	1838 P	.031	100.00	125.00	150.00	275.00
	1839 P	.070	100.00	125.00	150.00	275.00
	1840 P	.028	100.00	125.00	150.00	275.00
	1841 P	.031	—	—	Rare	—
	1842 P	.026	100.00	125.00	150.00	275.00
	1843 P	.024	—	—	Rare	—
	1844 P	.030	100.00	125.00	150.00	275.00
	1845 P	.035	100.00	125.00	150.00	275.00
	1846 P	.030	100.00	125.00	150.00	275.00
	1847 P	.033	100.00	125.00	150.00	275.00

C#	Date	Mintage	Fine	VF	XF	Unc
115.2	1848 P	.059	100.00	—	Rare	—
	1849 P	.058	100.00	125.00	150.00	275.00
	Unknown Mint.					
115.3	1834	—	100.00	125.00	150.00	275.00
	1847	—	100.00	125.00	150.00	275.00

Mint mark: Anchor

C#	Date	Mintage	Fine	VF	XF	Unc
126.1	1850 B	.139	100.00	125.00	150.00	275.00
	1851 B	.296	100.00	125.00	150.00	275.00
	1852 B	.103	100.00	125.00	150.00	275.00
	1853 B	.137	100.00	125.00	150.00	275.00
	1854 B	.142	100.00	125.00	150.00	275.00
	1855 B	.148	100.00	125.00	150.00	275.00
	1856 B	.113	100.00	125.00	150.00	275.00
	1857 B	.059	100.00	125.00	150.00	275.00
	1858 B	.176	100.00	125.00	150.00	275.00
	1859 B	.436	100.00	125.00	150.00	275.00
	1860 B	.163	100.00	125.00	150.00	275.00
	Mint mark: Eagle head					
126.2	1850 P	.066	100.00	125.00	150.00	275.00
	1851 P	.163	100.00	125.00	150.00	275.00
	1852 P	.046	100.00	125.00	150.00	275.00
	1853 P	.041	—	—	Rare	—
	1855 P	.041	100.00	125.00	150.00	275.00
	1855 P (error) EMMANVEL H for II	—	100.00	125.00	150.00	275.00
	1856 P	.061	375.00	500.00	750.00	1200.
	1857 P	.067	100.00	125.00	150.00	275.00
	1858 P	.103	150.00	250.00	400.00	600.00
	1859 P	.187	100.00	125.00	150.00	275.00
	1860 P	.111	100.00	150.00	175.00	375.00
	1861 P	.156	100.00	150.00	175.00	375.00
	Mint mark: M					
126.3	1860	.023	125.00	200.00	300.00	500.00

40 LIRE

12.9000 g, .900 GOLD, .3733 oz AGW

Mint mark: Eagle head

C#	Date	Mintage	Fine	VF	XF	Unc
107.1	1822 L	5,011	300.00	400.00	600.00	1350.
	1823 L	—	—	—	Rare	—
	1825 L	.039	300.00	400.00	500.00	1150.
	1831 L	—	300.00	400.00	500.00	1150.
	1831 P	7,711	300.00	400.00	500.00	1150.
	Mint mark: Anchor					
107.2	1825 P	3,994	300.00	400.00	650.00	1650.
	1826 P	2,844	500.00	600.00	900.00	1850.

50 LIRE

16.1200 g, .900 GOLD, .4664 oz AGW

Mint mark: Eagle head

C#	Date	Mintage	Fine	VF	XF	Unc
116.1	1832 P	93 pcs.	—	—	Rare	—
	1833 P	1,773	750.00	1000.	1500.	2500.
	1834 P	657 pcs.	—	—	Rare	—
	1835 P	1,296	—	—	Rare	—
	1836 P	385 pcs.	900.00	1250.	1750.	2750.
	1838 P	992 pcs.	—	—	Rare	—
	1839 P	553 pcs.	—	—	Rare	—
	1840 P	1,402	—	—	Rare	—
	1841 P	2,753	—	—	Rare	—
	1843 P	586 pcs.	—	—	Rare	—
	Mint mark: Anchor					
116.2	1833 P	92 pcs.	4000.	5000.	6000.	8000.
	1835 P	—	—	—	Rare	—
	1841 P	562 pcs.	—	—	Rare	—

80 LIRE

25.8000 g, .900 GOLD, .7466 oz AGW

Mint mark: Eagle head

C#	Date	Mintage	Fine	VF	XF	Unc
97	1821	965 pcs.	4000.	7000.	10,000.	20,000.

C#	Date	Mintage	Fine	VF	XF	Unc
108.1	1823 L	—	—	—	Rare	—
	1824 L	5,919	450.00	550.00	650.00	1000.
	1825 L	.014	400.00	500.00	600.00	900.00
	1826 L	.076	400.00	500.00	600.00	900.00
	1827 L	.038	400.00	500.00	600.00	900.00
	1828 L	.023	400.00	500.00	600.00	900.00
	1828 P	Inc. Ab.	600.00	750.00	1000.	1500.
	1829 P	8,181	400.00	500.00	600.00	900.00
	1830 P	5,972	400.00	500.00	600.00	900.00
	1831 P	740 pcs.	800.00	1000.	1250.	2000.
	Mint mark: Anchor					
108.2	1824 P	3,904	500.00	700.00	900.00	1500.
	1825 P	8,465	400.00	550.00	725.00	1200.
	1826 P	2,305	700.00	900.00	1100.	1750.
	1827 P	.015	400.00	500.00	600.00	1100.
	1828 P	8,961	400.00	500.00	600.00	1100.
	1829 P	7,436	400.00	500.00	600.00	1100.
	1830 P	.026	400.00	500.00	600.00	1100.
	1831 P	.021	600.00	800.00	1250.	2000.

100 LIRE

32.2500 g, .900 GOLD, .9332 oz AGW

Mint mark: Anchor

C#	Date	Mintage	Fine	VF	XF	Unc
117.1	1832 P	—	500.00	600.00	850.00	1800.
	1833 P	2,587	600.00	700.00	800.00	1750.
	1834 P	.012	500.00	575.00	700.00	1400.
	1835 P	8,513	500.00	600.00	850.00	1500.
	1836 P	703 pcs.	700.00	900.00	1100.	2250.
	1837 P	250 pcs.	900.00	1100.	1350.	2750.
	1838 P	4,774	—	—	Rare	—
	1839 P	2,922	—	—	Rare	—
	1840 P	1,003	700.00	900.00	1100.	2250.
	1841 P	8,889	475.00	600.00	850.00	1750.
	1842 P	3,606	700.00	900.00	1100.	2250.
	1843 P	424 pcs.	1500.	2000.	2500.	4000.
	1844 P	2,213	1000.	1500.	2000.	3500.
	1845 P	646 pcs.	1000.	1500.	2000.	3500.
	Mint mark: Eagle head					
117.2	1832 P	—	475.00	550.00	750.00	1500.
	1833 P	6,769	475.00	550.00	750.00	1500.
	1834 P	.037	475.00	525.00	650.00	1350.
	1835 P	.026	475.00	525.00	650.00	1350.
	1836 P	6,236	475.00	525.00	650.00	1350.
	1837 P	3,885	475.00	550.00	750.00	1500.
	1838 P	3,916	—	—	Rare	—
	1840 P	2,898	475.00	550.00	750.00	1500.
	1841 P	1,207	700.00	1000.	1300.	2000.
	1842 P	864 pcs.	700.00	1000.	1300.	2000.
	1843 P	827 pcs.	700.00	900.00	1100.	2250.
	1844 P	91 pcs.	—	—	Rare	—

PATTERNS (Pn)

(Including off metal strikes)

KM#	Date	Mintage	Identification	Mkt.Val.
Pn4	1832	—	2 Lire, .900 Silver, C112.2	—

SICILY

Has a history of occupation extending back to the ancient Phoenicians. In more recent times it was part of the Kingdom of Naples and Sicily.

RULERS

Ferdinando III, 1759-1825
(became Ferdinando I in 1816
as King of Two Sicilies)
Ferdinando II, 1830-1859

MINTMASTERS INITIALS

Palermo Mint

Letter	Date	Name
JVI	1798-1807	Guiseppe Ugo
VB	1810-1816	Vicenzo Beninati

MONETARY SYSTEM

6 Cavalli = 1 Grano
20 Grani = 2 Carlini = 1 Tari
12 Tari = 1 Piastra
15 Tari = 1 Scudo
2 Scudi = 1 Oncia

MEZZO (1/2) GRANO

COPPER

Obv: Head right. Rev: Value, SICILIANO, date.

C#	Date	Mintage	VG	Fine	VF	XF
52	1836	—	40.00	90.00	180.00	325.00

UN (1) GRANO

COPPER

Obv: Eagle, leg. Rev: Value, date within wreath.

C#	Date	Mintage	VG	Fine	VF	XF
41	1801 JVI	—	6.00	10.00	20.00	45.00
	1802 JVI	—	25.00	40.00	75.00	150.00
	1803 JVI	—	20.00	30.00	50.00	100.00

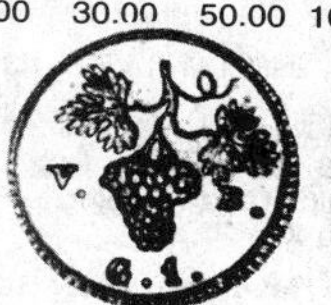

C#	Date	Mintage	VG	Fine	VF	XF
42	ND(1814) VB	—	20.00	30.00	50.00	100.00
	1814 VB	—	5.00	10.00	20.00	45.00
	1815 VB	—	5.00	10.00	20.00	45.00

NOTE: Varieties exist.

Obv: Head right. Rev: SICILIANO, value, date.

C#	Date	Mintage	VG	Fine	VF	XF
53	1836	—	50.00	100.00	200.00	350.00

DUE (2) GRANI

COPPER

Obv: Eagle, leg. Rev: Value, date within wreath.

C#	Date	Mintage	VG	Fine	VF	XF
43	1801 JVI	—	20.00	30.00	50.00	100.00
	1802 JVI	—	6.00	10.00	20.00	45.00
	1803 JVI	—	6.00	10.00	20.00	45.00
	1804 JVI	—	6.00	10.00	20.00	45.00

C#	Date	Mintage	VG	Fine	VF	XF
44	1814 VB	—	10.00	15.00	25.00	50.00
	1815 VB	—	8.00	12.00	22.00	50.00

NOTE: 1814 exists w/large and small G.2.

Obv: Head right. Rev: SICILIANI, value, date.

C#	Date	Mintage	VG	Fine	VF	XF
54	1836	—	50.00	100.00	200.00	350.00

CINQUE (5) GRANI

COPPER

Obv: Eagle, leg. Rev: Value, date within wreath.

C#	Date	Mintage	VG	Fine	VF	XF
45	1801 JVI	—	30.00	45.00	75.00	150.00
	1802 JVI	—	15.00	22.50	50.00	125.00
	1803 JVI	—	15.00	22.50	50.00	125.00
	1804 JVI	—	15.00	22.50	50.00	125.00

Obv: Large head.

C#	Date	Mintage	VG	Fine	VF	XF
46	ND(1814) VB	—	30.00	45.00	75.00	150.00
	1814 VB	—	12.00	20.00	40.00	90.00
	1815 VB	—	12.00	20.00	40.00	90.00

NOTE: Varieties exist of 1815.

Obv: Small head.

C#	Date	Mintage	VG	Fine	VF	XF
46a	1815 VB	—	12.00	20.00	40.00	90.00
	1816 VB	—	20.00	30.00	50.00	100.00

Obv: Head right. Rev: SICILIANI, crown, value, date.

C#	Date	Mintage	VG	Fine	VF	XF
55	1836	—	100.00	200.00	300.00	500.00

DIECI (10) GRANI

COPPER

Obv: Eagle, leg. Rev: Value, date within wreath.

C#	Date	Mintage	VG	Fine	VF	XF
47	1801 JVI	—	20.00	30.00	65.00	185.00
	1802 JVI	—	20.00	30.00	65.00	185.00
	1803 JVI	—	20.00	30.00	65.00	185.00
	1804 JVI	—	20.00	30.00	65.00	185.00

C#	Date	Mintage	VG	Fine	VF	XF
48	ND(1814) VB	—	30.00	50.00	100.00	200.00
	1814 VB	—	20.00	30.00	50.00	150.00
	1815 VB	—	20.00	30.00	60.00	180.00

NOTE: 1815 exists with G.10. and G.10, and w/lower right tip of bust pointing to E in REX ; also tip of bust pointing to X in REX.

Obv: Head right. Rev: SICILIANI, crown, value, date.

C#	Date	Mintage	VG	Fine	VF	XF
56	1835	—	400.00	500.00	750.00	1000.
	1836	—	150.00	250.00	400.00	650.00

6 TARI

13.6600 g, .854 SILVER, .3751 oz ASW
Obv: Head right. Rev: Eagle.

C#	Date	Mintage	VG	Fine	VF	XF
48.5	1801 JVI	—	12.50	22.50	40.00	125.00

NOTE: Earlier dates (1799-1800) exist for this type.

12 TARI

27.5330 g, .883 SILVER, .7817 oz ASW
Obv: Bust right, FERDINAN.D.G.SICIL. . .
Rev: Eagle, date.

C#	Date	Mintage	VG	Fine	VF	XF
49	1801 JVI	—	40.00	75.00	125.00	200.00
	1803 JVI	—	40.00	75.00	125.00	200.00

NOTE: 1801 exists w/REX. and REX
NOTE: Earlier dates (1799-1800) exist for this type.

Obv. leg: FERDINAN. III. D.G.SICIL. . .

C#	Date	Mintage	VG	Fine	VF	XF
49a	1801 JVI	—	40.00	75.00	125.00	200.00
	1802 JVI	—	40.00	75.00	125.00	200.00
	1803 JVI	—	40.00	75.00	125.00	200.00
	1804 JVI	—	40.00	75.00	125.00	200.00

NOTE: Earlier dates (1799-1800) exist for this type.

Rev: J.V.I. above eagle within wreath.

C#	Date	Mintage	VG	Fine	VF	XF
50	1805 JVI	—	50.00	100.00	200.00	400.00
	1806 JVI	—	50.00	100.00	200.00	400.00
	1807 JVI	—	50.00	100.00	200.00	400.00

Rev: Eagle between V. and B. within wreath.

C#	Date	Mintage	VG	Fine	VF	XF
50a	1810 VB	—	50.00	100.00	150.00	350.00

NOTE: Seven varieties exist.

2 ONCIE

8.8150 g, .906 GOLD, .2567 oz AGW
Ferdinando III

C#	Date	Mintage	Fine	VF	XF	Unc
51	1814 VB	—	3000.	5000.	8000.	15,000.

TUSCANY

Etruria

An Italian territorial division on the west-central peninsula, belonged to the Medici from 1530 to 1737, when it was given to Francis, duke of Lorraine. In 1800 the French established it as part of the Spanish dominions; from 1807 to 1809 it was a French department. After the fall of Napoleon it reverted to its pre-Napoleonic owner, Ferdinand III.

RULERS

Louis I, 1801-1803
Charles Louis, under regency of his mother Maria Louisa, 1803-1807
Annexed To France, 1807-1814
Ferdinando III, Restored, 1814-1824
Leopold II, 1824-1848, 1849-1859
Provisional Government, 1859
United to Italian Provisional Govern ment, 1859-1861

MINT MARKS

FIRENZE - Florence
LEGHORN - Livorno
PISIS - Pisa

MONETARY SYSTEM

Until 1826

12 Denari = 3 Quattrini = 1 Soldo
20 Soldi = 1 Lira
10 Lire = 1 Dena
40 Quattrini = 1 Paolo
1-1/2 Paoli = 1 Lira
10 Paoli = 1 Francescone, Scudo, Tallero
3 Zecchini = 1 Ruspone = 40 Lire

1826-1859

100 Quattrini = 1 Fiorino
4 Fiorini = 10 Paoli

1859

100 Centesimi = 1 Lira

QUATTRINO

COPPER

Obv: Square arms. Rev: Value and date.

C#	Date	Mintage	VG	Fine	VF	XF
30	1801	—	3.00	5.00	10.00	25.00

Obv: Crowned arms. Rev: Value.

C#	Date	Mintage	VG	Fine	VF	XF
40	1802	—	12.00	20.00	80.00	125.00
	1803	—	4.50	8.00	35.00	60.00
	1805 (error date)		5.00	8.50	36.50	65.00
44	1803	—	4.50	8.00	40.00	80.00
	1804	—	4.50	8.00	40.00	80.00
	1805	—	4.50	8.00	40.00	80.00
	1806	—	4.50	8.00	40.00	80.00
	1807	—	4.50	8.00	40.00	80.00

Obv: Arms, leg: FERD.III. . . Rev: Value.

C#	Date	Mintage	VG	Fine	VF	XF
53	1819	—	2.50	4.00	12.00	30.00
	1820	—	2.50	4.00	12.00	30.00
	1821	—	2.50	4.00	12.00	30.00
	1822	—	2.50	4.00	12.00	30.00
	1824	—	2.50	4.00	12.00	30.00

Obv. leg: LEOP. II A.D.'A. GRAND. DI TOSC.

C#	Date	Mintage	VG	Fine	VF	XF
62	1827	—	2.50	4.00	10.00	22.00
	1828	—	2.50	4.00	10.00	22.00
	1829	—	2.50	4.00	10.00	22.00
	1830	—	2.50	4.00	10.00	22.00
	1831	—	2.50	4.00	10.00	22.00
	1832	—	2.50	4.00	10.00	22.00
	1833	—	2.50	4.00	10.00	22.00
	1834	—	2.50	4.00	10.00	22.00
	1835	—	2.50	4.00	10.00	22.00
	1836	—	2.50	4.00	10.00	22.00
	1837	—	2.50	4.00	10.00	22.00
	1838	—	2.50	4.00	10.00	22.00
	1840	—	2.50	4.00	10.00	22.00
	1841	—	5.00	7.50	35.00	60.00
	1843	—	5.00	7.50	35.00	60.00

Obv. leg: LEOP. II A.D.'A. G-D. DI TOSC.

C#	Date	Mintage	VG	Fine	VF	XF
62a	1842	—	5.00	7.50	35.00	60.00
	1843	—	2.50	4.00	10.00	22.00
	1844	—	2.50	4.00	10.00	22.00
	1845	—	2.50	4.00	10.00	22.00
	1846	—	2.50	4.00	10.00	22.00
	1847	—	2.50	4.00	10.00	22.00
	1848	—	2.50	4.00	10.00	22.00
	1849	—	2.50	4.00	10.00	22.00
	1850	—	2.50	4.00	10.00	22.00
	1851	—	2.50	4.00	10.00	22.00
	1852	—	2.50	4.00	10.00	22.00
	1853	—	2.50	4.00	10.00	22.00
	1854	—	2.50	4.00	10.00	22.00
	1856	—	2.50	4.00	10.00	22.00
	1857	—	2.50	4.00	10.00	22.00

MEZZO (1/2) SOLDO

COPPER

C#	Date	Mintage	VG	Fine	VF	XF
45	ND(1804)	—	3.50	5.00	40.00	65.00

3 QUATTRINI

COPPER

C#	Date	Mintage	VG	Fine	VF	XF
64	1826	—	2.50	4.00	10.00	30.00
	1827	—	2.50	4.00	10.00	30.00
	1828	—	2.50	4.00	10.00	30.00
	1829	—	4.50	9.00	35.00	60.00
	1830	—	2.50	4.00	10.00	30.00
	1832	—	2.50	4.00	10.00	30.00
	1833	—	2.50	4.00	10.00	30.00
	1834	—	2.50	4.00	10.00	30.00
	1835	—	2.50	4.00	10.00	30.00
	1836	—	2.50	4.00	10.00	30.00
	1838	—	2.50	4.00	10.00	30.00
	1839	—	2.50	4.00	10.00	30.00
	1840	—	2.50	4.00	10.00	30.00
	1843	—	2.50	4.00	10.00	30.00
	1845	—	2.50	4.00	10.00	30.00
	1846	—	2.50	4.00	10.00	30.00
	1851	—	2.50	4.00	10.00	30.00
	1853	—	2.50	4.00	10.00	30.00
	1854	—	4.50	9.00	35.00	60.00

SOLDO

COPPER

Obv: Arms, leg: FERD.III. . . Rev: Value.

C#	Date	Mintage	VG	Fine	VF	XF
54	1822	—	2.00	4.00	10.00	30.00
	1823	—	2.00	4.00	10.00	30.00

Obv: Arms, leg: LEOP.II. . . Rev: Value.

C#	Date	Mintage	VG	Fine	VF	XF
63	1824	—	15.00	30.00	50.00	100.00

5 QUATTRINI

BILLON

C#	Date	Mintage	VG	Fine	VF	XF
65	1826	—	3.00	6.50	25.00	40.00
	1828	—	5.00	10.00	30.00	50.00
	1829	—	3.00	6.50	25.00	40.00
	1830	—	3.00	6.50	25.00	40.00

2 SOLDI

COPPER

Obv: Arms, leg. Rev: Value.

C#	Date	Mintage	VG	Fine	VF	XF
46	1804	—	6.00	12.00	50.00	75.00
	1805	—	6.00	12.00	50.00	75.00

Obv: Arms, leg: FERDINANDUS III. . . Rev: Value.

C#	Date	Mintage	VG	Fine	VF	XF
55	1818	—	2.00	4.00	10.00	30.00
	1822	—	2.00	4.00	10.00	30.00

DIECI (10) QUATTRINI

BILLON

C#	Date	Mintage	VG	Fine	VF	XF
32	1801	—	4.50	6.50	15.00	40.00

Obv: Squarish arms. Rev: Value.

C#	Date	Mintage	VG	Fine	VF	XF
41	1801	—	6.00	10.00	35.00	75.00
	1802	—	6.00	10.00	35.00	75.00

Obv: Arms and date. Rev: Value in field.

C#	Date	Mintage	VG	Fine	VF	XF
41a	1802	—	12.00	20.00	50.00	100.00

Obv: Arms. Rev: Value and date.

C#	Date	Mintage	VG	Fine	VF	XF
41b	1802	—	6.00	10.00	20.00	50.00

Obv: Round arms. Rev: 10 QUATTRINI.

C#	Date	Mintage	VG	Fine	VF	XF
66	1826	—	6.00	10.00	15.00	25.00
	1827	—	6.00	10.00	15.00	25.00
	1853	—	6.00	10.00	15.00	25.00
	1854	—	6.00	10.00	15.00	25.00

C#	Date	Mintage	VG	Fine	VF	XF
67	1858	—	12.00	20.00	35.00	60.00

1/2 PAOLO

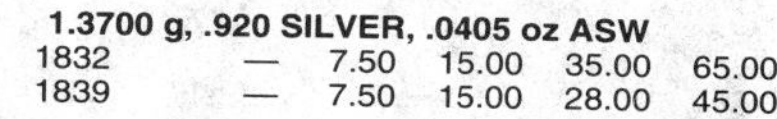

1.3700 g, .920 SILVER, .0405 oz ASW

C#	Date	Mintage	VG	Fine	VF	XF
68	1832	—	7.50	15.00	35.00	65.00
	1839	—	7.50	15.00	28.00	45.00

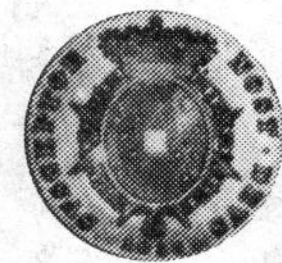

C#	Date	Mintage	VG	Fine	VF	XF
68a	1853	—	7.50	15.00	35.00	65.00
	1856	—	7.50	15.00	35.00	65.00
	1857	—	7.50	15.00	35.00	65.00
	1859	—	7.50	15.00	35.00	65.00

1/4 DI FIORINO

1.7190 g, .916 SILVER, .0506 oz ASW

Obv: Arms. Rev: Value.

C#	Date	Mintage	VG	Fine	VF	XF
69	1827	—	12.00	20.00	50.00	100.00

10 SOLDI

2.5100 g, .913 SILVER, .0736 oz ASW

Obv: Arms. Rev: Value.

C#	Date	Mintage	VG	Fine	VF	XF
56	1821	—	6.00	10.00	15.00	25.00
	1823	—	6.00	10.00	15.00	25.00

PAOLO

2.7400 g, .920 SILVER, .0810 oz ASW

C#	Date	Mintage	VG	Fine	VF	XF
70	1831	—	7.50	15.00	30.00	50.00
	1832	—	7.50	15.00	30.00	50.00
	1838	—	7.50	15.00	30.00	50.00

C#	Date	Mintage	VG	Fine	VF	XF
70a	1842	—	7.50	15.00	30.00	50.00
	1843	—	7.50	15.00	30.00	50.00
	1845	—	7.50	15.00	30.00	50.00
	1846	—	7.50	15.00	30.00	50.00
	1856	—	7.50	15.00	30.00	50.00
	1857	—	7.50	15.00	30.00	50.00
	1858	—	7.50	15.00	30.00	50.00

LIRA

3.9000 g, .920 SILVER, .1153 oz ASW

Obv: Large order collar.

Rev: W/o berries on wreath.

C#	Date	Mintage	VG	Fine	VF	XF
47.1	1803	—	10.00	15.00	40.00	85.00

Obv: Small order collar.

Rev: Berries on wreath.

C#	Date	Mintage	VG	Fine	VF	XF
47.2	1806	—	10.00	15.00	40.00	85.00

4.1030 g, .913 SILVER, .1204 oz ASW

Obv: Head right. Rev: Value.

C#	Date	Mintage	VG	Fine	VF	XF
57	1821	—	12.00	20.00	50.00	100.00
	1822	—	12.00	20.00	50.00	100.00
	1823	—	12.00	20.00	50.00	100.00

1/2 FIORINO

3.4380 g, .916 SILVER, .1012 oz ASW

Obv: Arms. Rev: Value.

C#	Date	Mintage	VG	Fine	VF	XF
71	1827	—	10.00	17.50	35.00	75.00

FIORINO

6.8760 g, .916 SILVER, .2025 oz ASW

C#	Date	Mintage	VG	Fine	VF	XF
72	1826	—	10.00	15.00	25.00	75.00
	1828	—	10.00	15.00	25.00	75.00
	1830	—	10.00	15.00	25.00	75.00
	1840	—	10.00	15.00	25.00	75.00
	1842	—	10.00	15.00	25.00	75.00

C#	Date	Mintage	VG	Fine	VF	XF
72a	1843	—	10.00	15.00	25.00	50.00
	1844	—	10.00	15.00	25.00	50.00
	1847	—	10.00	15.00	25.00	50.00
	1848	—	10.00	15.00	25.00	50.00
	1856	—	10.00	15.00	25.00	50.00
	1857	—	10.00	15.00	25.00	50.00
	1858	—	10.00	15.00	25.00	50.00

5 PAOLI

13.7500 g, .913 SILVER, .4036 oz ASW

C#	Date	Mintage	VG	Fine	VF	XF
58	1819	—	30.00	50.00	200.00	350.00
	1820	—	30.00	50.00	100.00	200.00

Obv: Longer hair.

C#	Date	Mintage	VG	Fine	VF	XF
58a	1823	—	60.00	100.00	250.00	500.00

13.7500 g, .916 SILVER, .4049 oz ASW

C#	Date	Mintage	VG	Fine	VF	XF
73	1827	—	25.00	40.00	80.00	200.00
	1828	—	25.00	40.00	80.00	200.00
	1829 PC	—	25.00	40.00	80.00	200.00

C#	Date	Mintage	VG	Fine	VF	XF
73a	1834	—	125.00	150.00	250.00	600.00

FRANCESCONE

(10 Paoli)

27.5000 g, .917 SILVER, .8108 oz ASW

Obv: Bust right. Rev: Crowned arms.

C#	Date	Mintage	VG	Fine	VF	XF
37	1801	—	25.00	50.00	100.00	200.00

NOTE: Earlier dates (1791-1800) exist for this type.

27.5000 g, .934 SILVER, .8258 oz ASW

C#	Date	Mintage	VG	Fine	VF	XF
42.1	1801	—	200.00	400.00	800.00	1500.
	1802	—	200.00	400.00	800.00	1500.

Obv. and rev: Small legends.

C#	Date	Mintage	VG	Fine	VF	XF
42.2	1803	—	65.00	100.00	150.00	300.00

Rev: Modified order chain.

C#	Date	Mintage	VG	Fine	VF	XF
42.3	1803	—	65.00	100.00	150.00	300.00

27.5000 g, .913 SILVER, .8073 oz ASW
Obv. leg: CAROLVS LVD. . .

C#	Date	Mintage	VG	Fine	VF	XF
50.1	1803	—	45.00	65.00	110.00	250.00
	1806	—	45.00	65.00	110.00	250.00
	1807	—	40.00	60.00	85.00	225.00

Obv. leg: CAROLUS LUD. . .

C#	Date	Mintage	VG	Fine	VF	XF
50.2	1806	—	45.00	65.00	110.00	250.00

C#	Date	Mintage	VG	Fine	VF	XF
59	1814	—	50.00	75.00	125.00	275.00
	1815	—	50.00	75.00	125.00	250.00
	1819	—	50.00	75.00	125.00	250.00
	1820	—	50.00	75.00	125.00	250.00
	1824	—	50.00	75.00	125.00	250.00

QUATTRO (4) FIORINI

27.5000 g, .916 SILVER, .8099 oz ASW

C#	Date	Mintage	VG	Fine	VF	XF
74	1826	—	50.00	100.00	200.00	500.00

C#	Date	Mintage	VG	Fine	VF	XF
75	1830	—	100.00	300.00	500.00	1450.

C#	Date	Mintage	VG	Fine	VF	XF
75a	1833	—	35.00	80.00	125.00	200.00
	1834	—	35.00	80.00	125.00	200.00
	1836	—	35.00	80.00	125.00	200.00
	1839	—	50.00	100.00	250.00	635.00
	1840	—	35.00	80.00	125.00	200.00
	1841	—	35.00	80.00	125.00	200.00

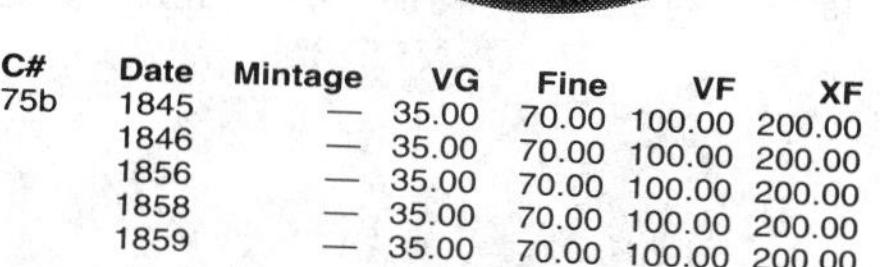

C#	Date	Mintage	VG	Fine	VF	XF
75b	1845	—	35.00	70.00	100.00	200.00
	1846	—	35.00	70.00	100.00	200.00
	1856	—	35.00	70.00	100.00	200.00
	1858	—	35.00	70.00	100.00	200.00
	1859	—	35.00	70.00	100.00	200.00

5 LIRE

19.7230 g, .958 SILVER, .6075 oz ASW

C#	Date	Mintage	VG	Fine	VF	XF
48	1803	—	25.00	40.00	125.00	250.00
	1804	—	25.00	40.00	100.00	200.00

10 LIRE

39.4470 g, .958 SILVER, 1.2151 oz ASW
Rev. leg: FLORENTIAE - date.

C#	Date	Mintage	VG	Fine	VF	XF
49.1	1803	—	50.00	90.00	150.00	350.00
	1804	—	50.00	90.00	150.00	350.00
	1805	—	50.00	90.00	150.00	350.00
	1806	—	60.00	100.00	175.00	400.00

NOTE: Legend varieties exist.

Rev. leg: FLOR - date.

C#	Date	Mintage	VG	Fine	VF	XF
49.2	1807	—	40.00	75.00	135.00	300.00

ZECCHINO

For Levant Trade

3.4900 g, .998 GOLD, .1119 oz AGW
Obv: St. Zenobio kneeling before Christ.
Rev: St. John.

C#	Date	Mintage	VG	Fine	VF	XF
51	ND(1805)	—	1500.	3000.	5000.	7000.

C#	Date	Mintage	VG	Fine	VF	XF
60	1816	—	175.00	225.00	300.00	500.00
	1821	—	175.00	225.00	300.00	500.00

3.4520 g, .998 GOLD, .1107 oz AGW

C#	Date	Mintage	VG	Fine	VF	XF
76	1824	—	100.00	150.00	200.00	400.00
	1826	—	100.00	150.00	200.00	400.00
	1829	—	100.00	150.00	200.00	400.00
	1832	—	100.00	150.00	200.00	400.00
	1853	—	100.00	150.00	200.00	400.00

RUSPONE

(3 Zecchini)

10.4610 g, .999 GOLD, .3360 oz AGW
Obv. leg: FERDINANDUS III. . .

C#	Date	Mintage	VG	Fine	VF	XF
39	1801	—	300.00	475.00	650.00	1100.

NOTE: Earlier dates (1791-1800) exist for this type.

10.4110 g, .998 GOLD, .3340 oz AGW
Obv. leg: LUD.D.G. . .

C#	Date	Mintage	VG	Fine	VF	XF
43	1801	—	500.00	800.00	1600.	3000.
	1803	—	400.00	650.00	1200.	2000.

C#	Date	Mintage	VG	Fine	VF	XF
52	1803	—	375.00	600.00	800.00	1250.
	1804	—	375.00	600.00	800.00	1250.
	1805	—	300.00	400.00	650.00	1000.
	1806	—	300.00	400.00	650.00	1000.
	1807	—	300.00	400.00	650.00	1000.

C#	Date	Mintage	VG	Fine	VF	XF
61	1815	—	350.00	550.00	800.00	1250.
	1816	—	350.00	550.00	800.00	1250.
	1818	—	350.00	550.00	800.00	1250.
	1820	—	350.00	550.00	800.00	1250.
	1823	—	350.00	550.00	800.00	1250.

C#	Date	Mintage	VG	Fine	VF	XF
77	1824	—	250.00	400.00	650.00	1000.
	1825	—	250.00	400.00	650.00	1000.
	1829	—	250.00	400.00	650.00	1000.
	1834	—	250.00	400.00	650.00	1000.
	1836	—	250.00	400.00	650.00	1000.

OTTANTA (80) FIORINI

32.6500 g, .999 GOLD, 1.0487 oz AGW

C#	Date	Mintage	VG	Fine	VF	XF
78	1827	—	400.00	550.00	1000.	2250.
	1828	—	400.00	550.00	1000.	2250.

1ST PROVISIONAL GOV'T.

(1859)

FIORINO

6.8800 g, .917 SILVER, .2028 oz ASW

C#	Date	Mintage	VG	Fine	VF	XF
79	1859	—	12.50	25.00	50.00	100.00

RUSPONE

10.4700 g, .998 GOLD, .3359 oz AGW

C#	Date	Mintage	Fine	VF	XF	Unc
80	1859	—	3000.	4000.	6000.	10,000.

2ND PROVISIONAL GOV'T.

(Italian 1859-1861)

CENTESIMO

COPPER

C#	Date	Mintage	VG	Fine	VF	XF
81	1859	25.000	4.00	8.00	17.50	40.00

2 CENTESIMI

COPPER

C#	Date	Mintage	Fine	VF	XF	Unc
82	1859	12.500	4.00	9.00	20.00	45.00

5 CENTESIMI

COPPER

C#	Date	Mintage	Fine	VF	XF	Unc
83	1859	10.000	5.00	10.00	22.00	50.00

CINQUANTA (50) CENTESIMI

2.5000 g, .900 SILVER, .0723 oz ASW
Mint mark: FIRENZE.

C#	Date	Mintage	Fine	VF	XF	Unc
84	1860	2.430	5.00	10.00	25.00	75.00
	1861	1.222	100.00	200.00	400.00	1000.

LIRA

5.0000 g, .900 SILVER, .1446 oz ASW
Mint mark: FIRENZE.
Rev: W/o dash between FIRENZE and date.

C#	Date	Mintage	Fine	VF	XF	Unc
85.1	1859	.061	15.00	30.00	75.00	200.00
	1860/59	1.655	12.50	22.50	55.00	110.00
	1860	Inc. Ab.	10.00	20.00	50.00	100.00

Rev: FIRENZE - 1860.

C#	Date	Mintage	Fine	VF	XF	Unc
85.2	1860	Inc. Ab.	7.50	15.00	30.00	80.00

2 LIRE

10.0000 g, .900 SILVER, .2892 oz ASW
Mint mark: FIRENZE.

C#	Date	Mintage	Fine	VF	XF	Unc
86	1860	.559	30.00	60.00	100.00	300.00
	1861	.164	200.00	400.00	1000.	3000.

VENICE

Venezia

A seaport of Venetia was founded by refugees from the Hun invasions. From that time until the arrival of Napoleon in 1797, it maintained an enormous foreign trade involving the possession of many islands in the Mediterranean while keeping a state of quasi-independence despite the antagonism of jealous Italian states and the Ottoman Turks. During the French Occupation Napoleon handed it over to Austria. Later, upon the defeat of the Austrians by Prussia in 1860, Venice then became a part of the United Kingdom of Italy.

RULERS

Franz II (of Austria) 1798-1806

MINT MARKS

A - Vienna
F - Hall
V - Venice
ZV - Zecca Venezia - Venice
None - Venice

AUSTRIAN OCCUPATION

MEZZA (1/2) LIRA

4.5000 g, .250 SILVER, .0361 oz ASW
Mint mark: V
Obv: Similar to 1 Lira, KM#164.1.
Rev: Value, date within ornate border.

C#	Date	Mintage	VG	Fine	VF	XF
163.1	1802	—	15.00	25.00	75.00	175.00

Mint mark: A

C#	Date	Mintage	VG	Fine	VF	XF
163.2	1802	—	— Reported, not confirmed			

Mint mark: F

C#	Date	Mintage	VG	Fine	VF	XF
163.3	1802	—	— Reported, not confirmed			

UNA (1) LIRA

11.3600 g, .250 SILVER, .0913 oz ASW

C#	Date	Mintage	VG	Fine	VF	XF
164.1	1802	—	15.00	25.00	75.00	175.00

Mint mark: A

C#	Date	Mintage	VG	Fine	VF	XF
164.2	1802	—	— Reported, not confirmed			

Mint mark: F

C#	Date	Mintage	VG	Fine	VF	XF
164.3	1802	—	— Reported, not confirmed			

1-1/2 LIRE

8.4900 g, .250 SILVER, .0682 oz ASW
Mint mark: A
Obv: Imperial eagle. Rev: Value, date within ornate border.

C#	Date	Mintage	VG	Fine	VF	XF
165.1	1802	—	10.00	15.00	35.00	75.00

Mint mark: F

C#	Date	Mintage	VG	Fine	VF	XF
165.2	1802	—	15.00	30.00	60.00	140.00

DUE (2) LIRE

.250 SILVER, 7.95-9.46 g
Mint mark: V
Obv: Large imperial eagle.
Rev: Value, date within wreath.

C#	Date	Mintage	VG	Fine	VF	XF
162	1801	—	25.00	40.00	80.00	200.00

NOTE: Three varieties exist.

Obv: Smaller imperial eagle, uncollared strike.

C#	Date	Mintage	VG	Fine	VF	XF
162a	1801	—	20.00	50.00	100.00	250.00

NOTE: Overstrikes exist.

REVOLUTIONARY ISSUES

(1848-1849)

MONETARY SYSTEM

100 Centesimi = 1 Lire

CENTESIMO

COPPER
Mint mark: ZV

C#	Date	Mintage	Fine	VF	XF	Unc
181	1849	2.761	3.00	7.00	15.00	32.00

3 CENTESIMI

COPPER
Mint mark: ZV

C#	Date	Mintage	Fine	VF	XF	Unc
182	1849	1.044	3.00	6.00	12.00	25.00

5 CENTESIMI

COPPER
Mint mark: ZV

C#	Date	Mintage	Fine	VF	XF	Unc
183	1849	1.187	3.00	7.00	15.00	32.00

15 CENTESIMI

1.2600 g, .229 SILVER, .0092 oz ASW
Mint mark: ZV

C#	Date	Mintage	Fine	VF	XF	Unc
184	1848	.155	7.50	12.50	25.00	50.00

25 CENTESIMI

1.2500 g, .900 SILVER, .0361 oz ASW
Mint mark: V

C#	Date	Mintage	Fine	VF	XF	Unc
A184	1848	—	75.00	150.00	400.00	1000.

5 LIRE

25.0000 g, .900 SILVER, .7234 oz ASW

C#	Date	Mintage	Fine	VF	XF	Unc
185	1848	6,011	75.00	125.00	200.00	375.00

Mint mark: V
Edge inscription: DIO BENEDITE L'ITALIA.

C#	Date	Mintage	Fine	VF	XF	Unc
186	1848	.011	75.00	125.00	225.00	450.00

Edge inscription error: DIO BENEDETE L'ITALIA.

C#	Date	Mintage	Fine	VF	XF	Unc
186a	1848	Inc. Ab.	100.00	200.00	325.00	650.00

20 LIRE

6.4500 g, .900 GOLD, .1866 oz AGW

C#	Date	Mintage	Fine	VF	XF	Unc
187	1848	5,210	350.00	700.00	1500.	2400.

PATTERNS (Pn)

(Including off metal strikes)

KM#	Date	Mintage	Identification	Mkt.Val.
Pn66	1802	—	1-1/2 Lire, .250 Silver, C165	—

PALMA NOVA

(In Venetia)

Was ceded to France by Austria in 1806 and was returned to Austria in 1814. In 1860 it was incorporated in the United Kingdom of Italy.

SIEGE COINAGE

Issues of French defenders in 1814

50 CENTESIMI

BILLON

C#	Date	Mintage	VG	Fine	VF	XF
2	1814	—	100.00	150.00	300.00	550.00

NOTE: Presentation pieces struck in a collar exhibit a raised rim and carry a premium.

PATTERNS (Pn)

(Including off metal strikes)

KM#	Date	Mintage	Identification	Mkt.Val.
Pn1	1814	—	25 Centesimi, Billon, C1	Rare

ITALY

The Italian Republic, a 700-mile-long peninsula extending into the heart of the Mediterranean Sea, has an area of 116,304 sq. mi. (301,230 sq. km.) and a population of 60 million. Capital: Rome. The economy centers around agriculture, manufacturing, forestry and fishing. Machinery, textiles, clothing and motor vehicles are exported.

From the fall of Rome until modern times, 'Italy' was little more than a geographical expression. Although nominally included in the Empire of Charlemagne and the Holy Roman Empire, it was in reality divided into a number of independent states and kingdoms presided over by wealthy families, soldiers of fortune or hereditary rulers. The 19th century unification movement fostered by Mazzini, Garibaldi and Cavour attained fruition in 1860-70 with the creation of the Kingdom of Italy and the installation of Victor Emmanuel, king of Sardinia, as king of Italy. Benito Mussolini came to power during the post-World War I period of economic and political unrest, and installed a Fascist dictatorship with a figurehead king as titular Head of State. Mussolini entered Italy into the German-Japanese anti comitern pact (Tri-Partite Pact) and withdrew from the League of Nations. The war did not go well for Italy and Germany was forced to assist Italy in its failed invasion of Greece. The Allied invasion of Sicily on July 10, 1943 and bombings of Rome brought the Fascist council to a no vote of confidence on July 23, 1943. Mussolini was arrested but soon escaped and set up a government in Salo. Rome fell to the Allied forces in June, 1944 and the country was allowed the status of cobelligerent against Germany. The Germans held northern Italy for another year. Mussolini was eventually captured and executed by partisans.

Following the defeat of the Axis powers, the Italian monarchy was dissolved by plebiscite, and the Italian Republic proclaimed.

KINGDOM

RULERS

Vittorio Emanuele II, 1861-1878
Umberto I, 1878-1900
Vittorio Emanuele III, 1900-1946

MINT MARKS

B - Bologna (1861)
B/I - Birmingham (1893-1894)
FIRENZE - Florence (1861)
H - Birmingham (1866-1867)
KB - Berlin (1894)
M - Milan (1861-1887)
N - Naples (1861-1867)
OM - Strasbourg (1866-1867)
R - Rome (All coins from 1878 have R except where noted).
T - Turin (1861-1867)
No MM - Paris (1862-1866)

MONETARY SYSTEM

100 Centesimi = 1 Lira

CENTESIMO

COPPER
Mint mark: M

KM#	Date	Mintage	Fine	VF	XF	Unc
1.1	1861	75.000	.75	1.50	3.00	10.00
	1861 inverted M	Inc. Ab.	15.00	30.00	60.00	200.00
	1867	72.759	.75	1.50	3.00	10.00

Mint mark: N

KM#	Date	Mintage	Fine	VF	XF	Unc
1.2	1861	48.280	3.75	8.00	15.00	30.00
1.2	1862/1	37.500	6.00	12.00	20.00	35.00
	1862	Inc. Ab.	1.25	2.00	4.00	15.00

Mint mark: T

KM#	Date	Mintage	Fine	VF	XF	Unc
1.3	1867	5.000	5.00	12.50	22.50	45.00

Mint mark: R

KM#	Date	Mintage	Fine	VF	XF	Unc
29	1895/8	13.860	1.50	3.00	7.00	22.50
	1895	Inc. Ab.	1.00	2.00	4.00	9.00
	1896	3.730	1.00	2.00	4.00	9.00
	1897	1.845	10.00	17.50	25.00	40.00
	1899	1.287	1.25	2.00	4.00	9.00
	1900	10.000	1.00	2.00	4.00	9.00

2 CENTESIMI

COPPER
Mint mark: M

KM#	Date	Mintage	Fine	VF	XF	Unc
2.1	1861	37.500	.60	1.50	4.00	15.00
	1867	54.212	.60	1.50	4.00	20.00

Mint mark: N

KM#	Date	Mintage	Fine	VF	XF	Unc
2.2	1861	23.055	.60	1.50	3.50	15.00
	1862	33.195	.60	1.50	3.50	15.00

Mint mark: T

KM#	Date	Mintage	Fine	VF	XF	Unc
2.3	1867	5.000	2.00	4.25	8.50	17.50

Mint mark: R

KM#	Date	Mintage	Fine	VF	XF	Unc
30	1895	.305	10.00	17.50	35.00	60.00
	1896	.282	25.00	50.00	100.00	150.00
	1897	4.415	.60	1.50	4.00	12.50
	1898	4.161	.60	1.50	4.00	12.50
	1900	2.735	.60	1.50	4.00	12.50

5 CENTESIMI

COPPER
Mint mark: B

KM#	Date	Mintage	Fine	VF	XF	Unc
3.1	1861	3.809	15.00	30.00	50.00	125.00

Mint mark: M

KM#	Date	Mintage	Fine	VF	XF	Unc
3.2	1861	210.000	.60	1.50	6.00	40.00
	1867	24.000	.60	1.50	5.00	30.00

Mint mark: N

KM#	Date	Mintage	Fine	VF	XF	Unc
3.3	1861	103.707	.60	1.50	7.50	45.00
	1862	106.293	.60	1.50	7.50	45.00
	1867	46.000	.60	1.50	7.50	45.00

Mint mark: R

KM#	Date	Mintage	Fine	VF	XF	Unc
31	1895	.508	12.50	25.00	35.00	80.00
	1896	.380	12.50	27.50	45.00	100.00
	1900	2,000	250.00	350.00	500.00	1000.

NOTE: 2,000 of the 1900 dated coins were struck but most were remelted and not issued.

10 CENTESIMI

COPPER

Mint mark: M

KM#	Date	Mintage	Fine	VF	XF	Unc
11.1	1862	40.000	1.50	3.50	8.00	50.00
	1866	36.000	1.50	3.50	8.00	50.00

Mint mark: None

KM#	Date	Mintage	Fine	VF	XF	Unc
11.2	1862	—	1.50	3.50	8.00	50.00
	1863	80.000	1.50	3.50	8.00	50.00
	1866	—	15.00	25.00	35.00	50.00

Mint mark: H

KM#	Date	Mintage	Fine	VF	XF	Unc
11.3	1866	40.000	1.50	3.50	8.00	50.00
	1867	50.000	1.50	3.50	8.00	50.00

Mint mark: N

KM#	Date	Mintage	Fine	VF	XF	Unc
11.4	1866	67.650	1.50	3.50	8.00	50.00
	1867	31.360	1.50	3.50	8.00	50.00

Mint mark: OM

KM#	Date	Mintage	Fine	VF	XF	Unc
11.5	1866	20.000	1.50	3.50	8.00	50.00
	1866.	Inc. Ab.	1.50	3.50	8.00	50.00
	1867	—	1.50	3.50	8.00	50.00
	1867.	—	3.00	5.00	12.50	50.00

Mint mark: T

KM#	Date	Mintage	Fine	VF	XF	Unc
11.6	1866	16.350	1.50	3.50	8.00	50.00
	1867	18.640	1.50	3.50	8.00	50.00

Mint mark: B/I

KM#	Date	Mintage	Fine	VF	XF	Unc
27.1	1893	8.547	1.50	3.50	7.00	35.00
	1894	32.000	1.50	3.50	7.00	35.00

Mint mark: R

KM#	Date	Mintage	Fine	VF	XF	Unc
27.2	1893	28.000	1.50	3.50	8.00	50.00
	1894	5.910	5.00	10.00	25.00	50.00

20 CENTESIMI

1.0000 g, .835 SILVER, .0268 oz ASW

Mint mark: T

KM#	Date	Mintage	Fine	VF	XF	Unc
12	1863 NB	461 pcs.	—	—	Rare	—

Mint mark: M

KM#	Date	Mintage	Fine	VF	XF	Unc
13.1	1863 BN	27.845	3.00	6.00	12.50	40.00

Mint mark: T

KM#	Date	Mintage	Fine	VF	XF	Unc
13.2	1863 BN	6.289	4.00	9.00	25.00	75.00
	1863 BN inverted BN	Inc. Ab.	10.00	25.00	60.00	175.00
	1867 BN	.866	20.00	50.00	100.00	300.00

COPPER-NICKEL

Mint mark: KB

KM#	Date	Mintage	Fine	VF	XF	Unc
28.1	1894	75.000	.40	1.00	3.00	9.00

Mint mark: R

KM#	Date	Mintage	Fine	VF	XF	Unc
28.2	1894	13.901	.60	1.50	4.00	12.00
	1895	11.099	.60	1.50	4.00	12.00

50 CENTESIMI

2.5000 g, .900 SILVER, .0723 oz ASW

Mint mark: FIRENZE

KM#	Date	Mintage	Fine	VF	XF	Unc
A4	1861 F	1.222	50.00	100.00	150.00	400.00

Mint mark: M

KM#	Date	Mintage	Fine	VF	XF	Unc
4.1	1861 BN	—	—	—	Rare	—

Mint mark: T

KM#	Date	Mintage	Fine	VF	XF	Unc
4.2	1861 B in shield	.045	—	—	Rare	—
	1862 BN	.185	35.00	75.00	150.00	400.00

Mint mark: N

KM#	Date	Mintage	Fine	VF	XF	Unc
4.3	1862	.630	20.00	45.00	100.00	250.00

2.5000 g, .835 SILVER, .0671 oz ASW

Mint mark: M

KM#	Date	Mintage	Fine	VF	XF	Unc
4a.1	1863 BN	4.706	4.00	7.00	12.00	40.00

Mint mark: T

KM#	Date	Mintage	Fine	VF	XF	Unc
4a.2	1863 BN	2.753	7.00	15.00	35.00	75.00

Mint mark: M

KM#	Date	Mintage	Fine	VF	XF	Unc
14.1	1863 BN	33.760	4.00	7.00	12.00	40.00
	1866 BN	19.199	12.50	20.00	30.00	60.00
	1867 BN	10.984	4.00	7.00	12.00	40.00

Mintmark: N

KM#	Date	Mintage	Fine	VF	XF	Unc
14.2	1863 BN	16.062	5.00	10.00	15.00	45.00
	1867 BN	7.838	5.00	10.00	15.00	45.00

Mint mark: T

KM#	Date	Mintage	Fine	VF	XF	Unc
14.3	1863 BN	6.301	5.00	10.00	15.00	45.00
	1867 BN	.396	35.00	85.00	175.00	400.00

Mint mark: R

KM#	Date	Mintage	Fine	VF	XF	Unc
26	1889	.635	25.00	40.00	75.00	200.00
	1892	.148	30.00	50.00	100.00	250.00

LIRA

5.0000 g, .900 SILVER, .1447 oz ASW

Mint mark: FIRENZE

KM#	Date	Mintage	Fine	VF	XF	Unc
A5	1861 F	.432	55.00	110.00	200.00	400.00

Mint mark: T

KM#	Date	Mintage	Fine	VF	XF	Unc
5.1	1861 B in shield	.019	—	—	Rare	—
	1862 BN	.105	50.00	100.00	200.00	400.00

Mint mark: N

KM#	Date	Mintage	Fine	VF	XF	Unc
5.2	1862	.497	30.00	65.00	150.00	300.00

5.0000 g, .835 SILVER, .1342 oz ASW

Mint mark: M

KM#	Date	Mintage	Fine	VF	XF	Unc
5a.1	1863 BN	24.054	2.00	5.00	10.00	40.00
	1867/3 BN	7.665	6.00	10.00	17.50	60.00
	1867 BN	I.A.	4.00	7.50	15.00	50.00

Mint mark: T

KM#	Date	Mintage	Fine	VF	XF	Unc
5a.2	1863 BN	2.270	4.00	7.50	15.00	50.00
	1867 BN	.335	25.00	50.00	150.00	300.00

Mint mark: M

KM#	Date	Mintage	Fine	VF	XF	Unc
15.1	1863 BN	29.837	2.00	5.00	12.50	50.00

Mint mark: T

KM#	Date	Mintage	Fine	VF	XF	Unc
15.2	1863 BN	3.839	60.00	125.00	200.00	375.00

Mint mark: R

KM#	Date	Mintage	Fine	VF	XF	Unc
24.1	1883	5,420	1000.	2000.	4800.	12,000.
	1884	1.995	4.00	10.00	25.00	100.00
	1886	6.095	2.50	6.00	20.00	90.00
	1892	.032	300.00	650.00	1500.	3250.
	1899	1.818	3.00	7.50	20.00	90.00
	1900	.318	5.00	12.50	35.00	150.00

Mint mark: M

KM#	Date	Mintage	Fine	VF	XF	Unc
24.2	1887	16.305	2.50	7.50	20.00	80.00

2 LIRE

10.0000 g, .900 SILVER, .2893 oz ASW

Mint mark: T

KM#	Date	Mintage	Fine	VF	XF	Unc
6.1	1861 B in shield	9,871	—	—	Rare	—

Mint mark: N

KM#	Date	Mintage	Fine	VF	XF	Unc
6.2	1862	.062	150.00	300.00	600.00	1500.

10.0000 g, .835 SILVER, .2684 oz ASW

KM#	Date	Mintage	Fine	VF	XF	Unc
6a.1	1863 BN	10.090	6.50	17.50	40.00	150.00

Mint mark: T

KM#	Date	Mintage	Fine	VF	XF	Unc
6a.2	1863 BN	4.910	7.50	20.00	50.00	175.00

Mint mark: N

KM#	Date	Mintage	Fine	VF	XF	Unc
16.1	1863 BN	—	7.50	20.00	80.00	200.00

Mint mark: T

KM#	Date	Mintage	Fine	VF	XF	Unc
16.2	1863 BN	—	7.50	25.00	100.00	250.00

Mint mark: R

KM#	Date	Mintage	Fine	VF	XF	Unc
23	1881	4.141	5.00	10.00	40.00	150.00
	1882	2.859	5.00	10.00	40.00	150.00
	1883	3.500	5.00	10.00	40.00	150.00
	1884	4.500	5.00	10.00	40.00	150.00
	1885	.598	25.00	50.00	100.00	300.00
	1886	1.902	5.00	10.00	40.00	150.00
	1887	7.500	5.00	10.00	40.00	150.00
	1897	.848	7.50	12.50	40.00	150.00
	1898	1.320	25.00	50.00	100.00	400.00
	1899	.610	7.50	12.50	35.00	150.00

5 LIRE

25.0000 g, .900 SILVER, .7234 oz ASW
Mint mark: FIRENZE
Accession to Throne of Unified Italy

KM#	Date	Mintage	Fine	VF	XF	Unc
7	1861	.021	400.00	900.00	1800.	3500.

Mint mark: T

KM#	Date	Mintage	Fine	VF	XF	Unc
8.1	1861 B in shield	.160	175.00	375.00	650.00	1200.
	1862 BN	.051	50.00	100.00	200.00	550.00
	1865 BN	.491	15.00	30.00	70.00	200.00

Mint mark: N

KM#	Date	Mintage	Fine	VF	XF	Unc
8.2	1862 BN	.142	30.00	65.00	120.00	350.00
	1864 BN	.120	20.00	40.00	90.00	225.00
	1865 BN	.312	15.00	30.00	70.00	200.00
	1866 BN	.460	1000.	1500.	2000.	4000.

Mint mark: M

KM#	Date	Mintage	Fine	VF	XF	Unc
8.3	1869 BN	3.995	10.00	17.50	40.00	175.00
	1870 BN	5.969	10.00	17.50	40.00	150.00
	1871 BN	6.697	10.00	17.50	40.00	150.00
	1872 BN	7.093	10.00	17.50	40.00	150.00
	1873 BN	8.438	10.00	17.50	40.00	150.00
	1874 BN	12.000	10.00	17.50	40.00	150.00
	1875 BN	8.982	10.00	17.50	40.00	150.00

Mint mark: R

KM#	Date	Mintage	Fine	VF	XF	Unc
8.4	1870	—	50.00	100.00	200.00	300.00
	1871	.404	65.00	135.00	250.00	400.00
	1872	.029	300.00	500.00	1000.	2500.
	1873	.017	400.00	800.00	2000.	4000.
	1875	1.018	15.00	30.00	75.00	300.00
	1876	6.390	12.00	20.00	40.00	150.00
	1877	4.410	12.00	20.00	40.00	175.00
	1878	1.700	15.00	25.00	50.00	225.00

1.6129 g, .900 GOLD, .0466 oz AGW
Mint mark: T

KM#	Date	Mintage	Fine	VF	XF	Unc
17	1863 BN	.197	75.00	100.00	175.00	275.00
	1865 BN	.408	100.00	175.00	250.00	400.00
	1865 BN	—	Proof Reported, not confirmed			

25.0000 g, .900 SILVER, .7234 oz ASW
Mint mark: R

KM#	Date	Mintage	Fine	VF	XF	Unc
20	1878	.100	200.00	400.00	800.00	2000.
	1879	4.000	20.00	40.00	125.00	600.00

10 LIRE

3.2258 g, .900 GOLD, 18mm, .0933 oz AGW
Mint mark: T

KM#	Date	Mintage	Fine	VF	XF	Unc
9.1	1861 B in shield	1,916	1500.	3000.	4500.	7500.

18.5mm

KM#	Date	Mintage	Fine	VF	XF	Unc
9.2	1863 BN	.543	75.00	100.00	150.00	250.00
	1863 BN	—	Proof Reported, not confirmed			
	1865 BN	.444	100.00	175.00	225.00	350.00

19mm

KM#	Date	Mintage	Fine	VF	XF	Unc
9.3	1863 BN	I.A.	70.00	95.00	125.00	185.00

19.5mm

KM#	Date	Mintage	Fine	VF	XF	Unc
9.4	1863 BN	I.A.	75.00	100.00	135.00	220.00

20 LIRE

6.4516 g, .900 GOLD, .1867 oz AGW
Mint mark: T

KM#	Date	Mintage	Fine	VF	XF	Unc
10.1	1861B in shield	3,267	125.00	200.00	300.00	500.00
	1861 T/F	I.A.	BV	120.00	130.00	165.00
	1862 BN	1.955	BV	100.00	110.00	140.00
	1863 BN	2.981	BV	100.00	110.00	140.00
	1864 BN	.609	BV	100.00	110.00	140.00
	1865 BN	3.109	BV	100.00	110.00	165.00
	1866 BN	.196	125.00	150.00	200.00	425.00
	1867 BN	.276	BV	100.00	110.00	165.00
	1868 BN	.340	BV	100.00	110.00	165.00
	1869 BN	.185	BV	100.00	110.00	165.00
	1870 BN	.055	125.00	200.00	400.00	850.00

Mint mark: R

KM#	Date	Mintage	Fine	VF	XF	Unc
10.2	1870	—	150.00	300.00	600.00	1450.
	1871	—	BV	125.00	200.00	425.00
	1873	2,174	400.00	800.00	1600.	3500.
	1874	.041	BV	100.00	110.00	170.00
	1875	.051	BV	100.00	110.00	170.00
	1876	.108	BV	100.00	110.00	140.00
	1877	.247	BV	100.00	110.00	140.00
	1878	.316	BV	100.00	110.00	135.00

Mint mark: M

KM#	Date	Mintage	Fine	VF	XF	Unc
10.3	1872 BN	—	100.00	150.00	250.00	500.00
	1873 BN	1.018	BV	100.00	110.00	150.00
	1874 BN	.255	BV	100.00	110.00	160.00

Mint mark: R

KM#	Date	Mintage	Fine	VF	XF	Unc
21	1879	.146	BV	100.00	110.00	125.00
	1880	.129	BV	100.00	110.00	125.00
	1881	.843	BV	100.00	110.00	125.00
	1882	6.970	BV	90.00	100.00	115.00
	1883	.182	BV	100.00	110.00	125.00
	1884	9,775	175.00	300.00	500.00	1200.
	1885	.165	BV	100.00	110.00	125.00
	1886	.059	BV	100.00	110.00	125.00
	1888	.111	BV	100.00	110.00	125.00
	1889	—	150.00	250.00	400.00	600.00
	1890	.068	BV	100.00	110.00	125.00
	1891	.032	BV	100.00	120.00	160.00
	1893	.041	BV	100.00	110.00	145.00
	1897	.038	BV	100.00	110.00	155.00

RED GOLD

KM#	Date	Mintage	Fine	VF	XF	Unc
21a	1882	Inc. Ab.	BV	110.00	125.00	175.00

50 LIRE

16.1290 g, .900 GOLD, .4667 oz AGW
Mint mark: T

KM#	Date	Mintage	Fine	VF	XF	Unc
18	1864 BN	103 pcs.	10,000.	15,000.	27,500.	35,000.

Mint mark: R

KM#	Date	Mintage	Fine	VF	XF	Unc
25	1884	2,532	900.00	1500.	2000.	3250.
	1888	2,125	1000.	2000.	2750.	3750.
	1891	414 pcs.	1500.	2500.	4000.	7500.

100 LIRE

32.2580 g, .900 GOLD, .9334 oz AGW
Mint mark: T

KM#	Date	Mintage	Fine	VF	XF	Unc
19.1	1864 BN	579 pcs.	2000.	4500.	8000.	12,000.

Mint mark: R

KM#	Date	Mintage	Fine	VF	XF	Unc
19.2	1872	661 pcs.	2000.	4500.	7500.	10,000.
	1878	294 pcs.	3500.	7000.	10,000.	17,500.

KM#	Date	Mintage	Fine	VF	XF	Unc
22	1880	145 pcs.	6000.	12,000.	16,000.	*25,000.
	1882	1,229	900.00	1500.	2500.	3750.
	1883	4,219	800.00	1250.	2250.	3500.
	1888	1,169	900.00	1500.	3000.	4500.
	1891	209 pcs.	2000.	4000.	7000.	10,000.

***NOTE:** Bowers and Merena Guia sale 3-88 Choice AU realized $24,200.

JAMAICA

Jamaica, a member of the British Commonwealth situated in the Caribbean Sea 90 miles south of Cuba, has an area of 4,244 sq. mi. (10,990 sq. km.) and a population of 2.1 million. Capital: Kingston. The economy is founded chiefly on mining, tourism and agriculture. Alumina, bauxite, sugar, rum and molasses are exported.

Jamaica was discovered by Columbus on May 3, 1494, and settled by Spain in 1509. The island was captured in 1655 by a British naval force under the command of Admiral William Penn, sent by Oliver Cromwell and ceded to Britain by the Treaty of Madrid, 1670. For more than 150 years, the Jamaican economy of sugar, slaves and piracy was one of the most prosperous in the new world. Dissension between the property-oriented island legislature and the home government prompted parliament to establish a crown colony government for Jamaica in 1866. From 1958 to 1961 Jamaica was a member of the West Indies Federation, withdrawing when Jamaican voters rejected the association. The colony attained independence on Aug. 6, 1962. Jamaica is a member of the Commonwealth of Nations. The Queen of England is Chief of State.

In 1758, the Jamaican Assembly authorized stamping a certain amount of Spanish milled coinage. Token coinage by merchants aided the island's monetary supply in the early 19th century. Sterling coinage was introduced in Jamaica in 1825, with the additional silver three halfpence under William IV and Victoria. Certain issues of three pence of William IV and Victoria were intended for colonial use, including Jamaica, as were the last dates of three pence for George VI.

There was an extensive token and work tally coinage for Jamaica in the late 19th and early 20th centuries.

A decimal standard currency system was adopted on Sept. 8, 1969.

RULERS

British, until 1962

MINT MARKS

H - Heaton

no mint mark - Royal Mint, London

MONETARY SYSTEM

4 Farthings = 1 Penny

12 Pence = 1 Shilling

8 Reales = 6 Shillings, 8 Pence

FARTHING

COPPER-NICKEL

KM#	Date	Mintage	Fine	VF	XF	Unc
15	1880	.192	1.50	2.50	12.00	35.00
	1880	—	—	—	Proof	225.00
	1882H	.384	1.00	1.75	10.00	30.00
	1882H	—	—	—	Proof	200.00
	1884	.096	2.00	4.00	20.00	50.00
	1884	—	—	—	Proof	250.00
	1885	.096	2.00	4.00	20.00	50.00
	1885	—	—	—	Proof	200.00
	1887	.192	1.50	2.50	12.00	32.50
	1887	—	—	—	Proof	200.00
	1888	.192	1.50	2.50	12.00	30.00
	1888	—	—	—	Proof	200.00
	1889	.192	1.50	2.50	12.50	32.50
	1890H	.096	2.00	4.00	20.00	50.00
	1891	.096	2.00	4.00	20.00	90.00
	1893	.096	2.00	4.00	20.00	70.00
	1894	.144	1.75	3.25	15.00	40.00
	1894	—	—	—	Proof	200.00
	1895	.144	1.75	3.25	15.00	40.00
	1897	.144	1.75	3.25	15.00	40.00
	1899	.144	1.75	3.25	15.00	40.00
	1900	.144	1.75	3.25	15.00	40.00

1/2 PENNY

COPPER-NICKEL

KM#	Date	Mintage	Fine	VF	XF	Unc
16	1869	.192	1.25	2.50	15.00	40.00
	1869	—	—	—	Proof	300.00
	1870	.240	1.25	2.50	15.00	45.00
	1870	—	—	—	Proof	500.00
	1871	.240	1.25	2.50	15.00	45.00
	1871	—	—	—	Proof	375.00
	1880	.192	2.00	4.00	20.00	55.00
	1880	—	—	—	Proof	475.00
	1882H	.096	2.00	5.00	20.00	80.00
	1882H	—	—	—	Proof	400.00
	1884	.096	2.00	5.00	20.00	55.00
	1884	—	—	—	Proof	400.00
	1885	.096	2.00	5.00	20.00	55.00
	1885	—	—	—	Proof	400.00
	1887	.072	4.00	8.00	40.00	85.00
	1888	.096	1.75	5.00	20.00	50.00
	1888	—	—	—	Proof	350.00
	1889	.096	2.00	5.00	25.00	60.00
	1890H	.120	1.75	3.25	20.00	50.00
	1891	.120	1.75	3.25	20.00	70.00
	1893	.144	1.75	3.25	20.00	50.00
	1894	.096	2.00	5.00	25.00	60.00
	1895	.096	2.00	5.00	25.00	60.00
	1897	.120	1.75	3.25	20.00	50.00
	1899	.120	1.75	3.25	20.00	50.00
	1900	.120	1.75	3.25	20.00	60.00

PENNY

COPPER-NICKEL

KM#	Date	Mintage	Fine	VF	XF	Unc
17	1869	.144	2.00	6.50	25.00	60.00
	1869	—	—	—	Proof	225.00
	1870	.120	2.00	5.00	25.00	65.00
	1870	—	—	—	Proof	775.00
	1871	.120	2.00	5.00	25.00	65.00
	1871	—	—	—	Proof	600.00
	1880	.096	4.00	12.00	50.00	100.00
	1880	—	—	—	Proof	600.00
	1882H	.048	5.00	15.00	60.00	150.00
	1882H	—	—	—	Proof	500.00
	1882	Inc. Ab.	15.00	40.00	120.00	225.00
	1882	—	—	—	Proof	1000.
	1884	.048	4.00	12.00	50.00	100.00
	1884	—	—	—	Proof	500.00
	1885	.048	4.00	12.00	50.00	100.00
	1885	—	—	—	Proof	400.00
	1887	.024	4.50	15.00	60.00	180.00
	1888	.024	4.50	15.00	60.00	180.00
	1888	—	—	—	Proof	400.00
	1889	.024	5.00	15.00	60.00	175.00
	1890	.036	4.00	12.00	50.00	120.00
	1891	.036	4.00	12.00	50.00	120.00
	1893	.024	5.00	15.00	60.00	180.00
	1894	.036	4.00	12.00	50.00	120.00
	1895	.036	4.00	12.00	50.00	120.00
	1897	.024	5.00	15.00	60.00	180.00
	1899	.024	5.00	15.00	60.00	180.00
	1900	.024	5.00	15.00	60.00	180.00

1-1/2 PENCE

.925 SILVER

From 1834 through 1870 colonial issue 1-1/2 pence were circulated in Ceylon and Jamaica. These are listed under Great Britain.

PATTERNS (Pn)

(Including off metal strikes)

KM#	Date	Mintage	Identification	Mkt.Val.
Pn1	1869	—	1/2 Penny, Brass, KM16	325.00
Pn2	1869	—	1 Penny, Bronze, KM17	325.00
Pn3	1870	—	1 Penny, Copper, KM17	325.00

JAPAN

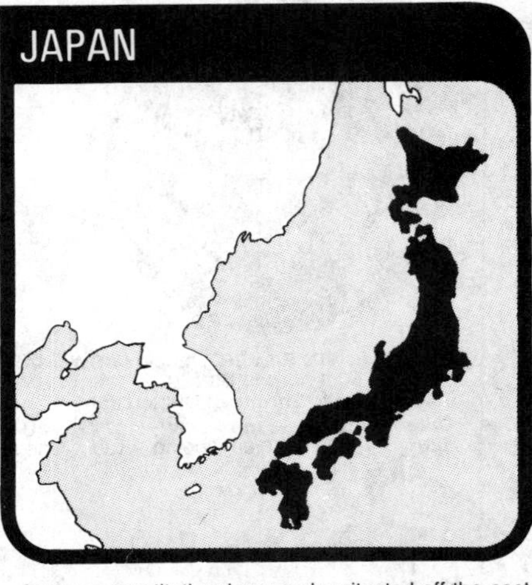

Japan, a constitutional monarchy situated off the east coast of Asia, has an area of 145,809 sq. mi. (377,835 sq. km.) and a population of 123.2 million. Capital: Tokyo. Japan, one of the major industrial nations of the world, exports machinery, motor vehicles, electronics and chemicals.

Japan, founded (so legend holds) in 660 B.C. by a direct descendant of the Sun Goddess, was first brought into contact with the west by a storm-blown Portuguese ship in 1542. European traders and missionaries proceeded to enlarge the contact until the Shogunate, sensing a military threat in the foreign presence, expelled all foreigners and restricted relations with the outside world in the 17th century. After Commodore Perry's U.S. flotilla visited in 1854, Japan rapidly industrialized, abolished the Shogunate and established a parliamentary form of government, and by the end of the 19th century achieved the status of a modern economic and military power. A series of wars with China and Russia, and participation with the Allies in World War I, enlarged Japan territorially but brought its interests into conflict with the Far Eastern interests of the United States, Britain and the Netherlands, causing it to align with the Axis Powers for the pursuit of World War II. After its defeat in World War II, General Douglas MacArthur forced Japan to renounce military aggression as a political instrument, and he instituted constitutional democratic self-government. Japan quickly gained a position as an economic world power.

Japanese coinage of concern to this catalog includes those issued for the Ryukyu Islands (also called Liuchu), a chain of islands extending southwest from Japan toward Taiwan (Formosa), before the Japanese government converted the islands into a prefecture under the name Okinawa. Many of the provinces of Japan issued their own definitive coinage under the Shogunate.

RULERS

Shoguns

Iyenari, 1787-1837

Iyeoshi, 1837-1853

Iyesada, 1853-1858

Iyemochi, 1858-1866

Yoshinobu, 1866-1867

Emperors

Komei, 1847-1866

Mutsuhito (Meiji), 1867-1912

NOTE: The personal name of the emperor is followed by the name that he chose for his regnal era.

MONETARY SYSTEM

Until 1870

Prior to the Meiji currency reform, there was no fixed exchange rate between the various silver, gold and copper "cash" coins (which previously included Chinese "cash") in circulation. Each coin exchanged on the basis of its own merits and the prevailing market conditions. The size and weight of the copper coins and the weight and fineness of the silver and gold coins varied widely. From time to time the government would declare an official exchange rate, but this was usually ignored. For gold and silver, nominal equivalents were:

16 Shu = 4 Bu = 1 Ryo

Commencing 1870

10 Rin = 1 Sen

100 Sen = 1 Yen

MONETARY UNITS

Momme 匁 Ryo 両

Bu 分 Shu 朱 Rin 厘

Sen 銭 Yen 円 or 圓 or 圓

MINT MARKS ON MON

A - Edo (Tokyo) 文
B - Sado 佐佐佐
C - Jiuman Tsubo 十
D - Koume Mura 小
E - Ichi-no-se 一
F - Onagi-gawa 川
G - Osaka 元
H - Nagasaki 長
I - Ashio 足
J - Sendai 仙
K - Sendai 千
L - Kuji (Hitachi Ohta) 久
M - Mito ト, ト
N - Aizu ノ, ノ
O - Ise イ
P - Morioka 盛
Q - Hiroshima 了
R - Yamanouchi 山

DATING

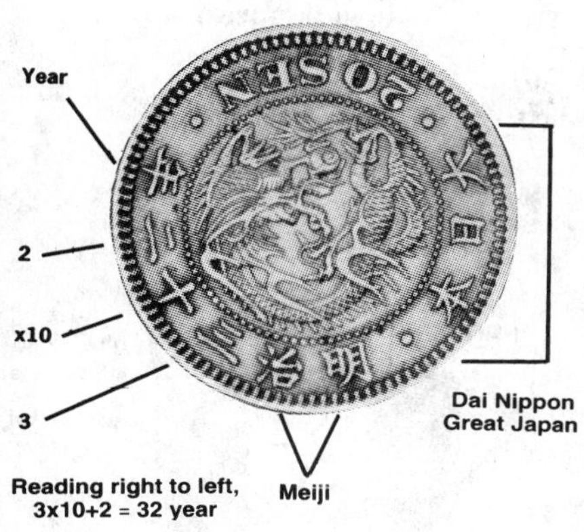

LEGENDS

Reading top-bottom, right-left.

Kanei Tsuho

EARLY COINAGE

MON

COPPER

C#	Date	Mint	VG	Fine	VF	XF
1.14	ND(1844) bosen	M	—	—	—	500.00

NOTE: C#1.14 is known only as *bosen* -seed or mother coins.

IRON
Rev: Plain.

C#	Date	Mint	VG	Fine	VF	XF
1.1a	ND(1739-1867)	—	2.00	5.00	7.50	15.00

Rev: Various mint marks.

C#	Date	Mint	VG	Fine	VF	XF
1.3a	ND(1862)	B	6.50	12.50	17.50	25.00
1.12	(1739,1838)	K	3.00	5.00	8.00	15.00

NOTE: Most copper 1 Mon pieces predate the coverage of this book. Those with mint marks B and K are *bosen* -seed or mother coins.

4 MON

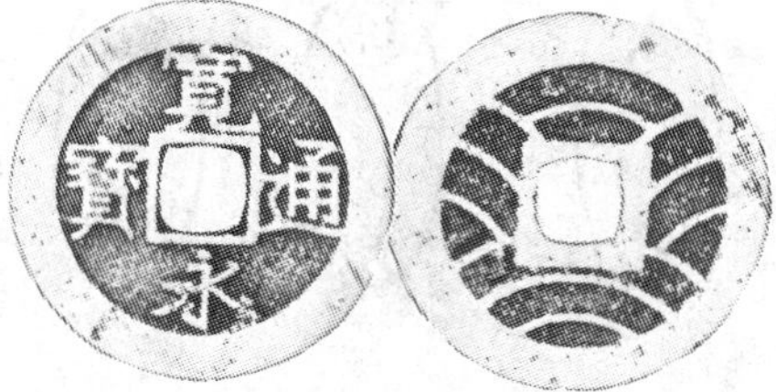

COPPER and BRASS
Rev: 11 waves.

C#	Date	Mint	VG	Fine	VF	XF
4.2	ND(1769-1860)	—	.30	.50	1.00	3.00

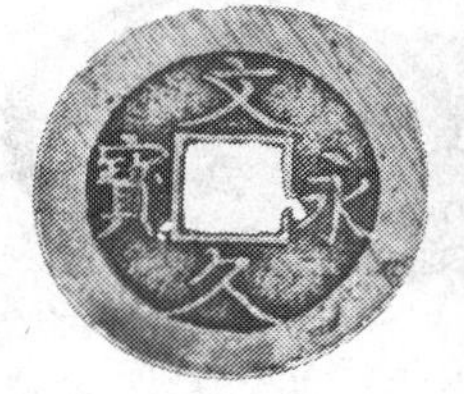

C#	Date	Mint	VG	Fine	VF	XF
6	ND(1863-67)	—	.50	1.00	1.50	3.00

Obv: Top character different style. Rev: 11 waves.

C#	Date	Mint	VG	Fine	VF	XF
6.a	ND(1863-67)	—	.50	1.00	1.50	3.00

Obv: As above but character at left abbreviated. Rev: 11 waves.

C#	Date	Mint	VG	Fine	VF	XF
6.b	ND(1863-67)	—	1.00	1.50	3.00	5.00

IRON
Rev: 11 waves; w/o mint mark.

C#	Date	Mint	VG	Fine	VF	XF
4.2a	ND(1866)	—	4.00	6.00	10.00	20.00

Rev: 11 waves and various mint marks.

C#	Date	Mint	VG	Fine	VF	XF
4.12	ND(1866)	K	3.00	6.00	12.00	20.00
4.14	(1866)	M	12.00	17.50	25.00	35.00
4.15	(1866)	N	5.00	10.00	17.50	25.00
4.16	(1866)	O	5.00	10.00	17.50	25.00
4.17	(1866)	P	5.00	10.00	17.50	25.00
4.18	(1866)	Q	250.00	300.00	400.00	500.00
4.19	(1866)	R	—	—	Rare	—

NOTE: Copper 4 Mon pieces similar to those listed only under iron issues are *bosen* -seed or mother coins.

100 MON

(Tempo Tsuho)

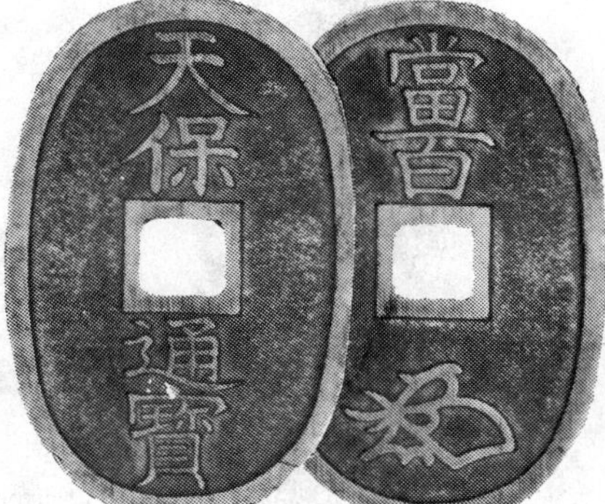

COPPER

C#	Date	Mint	VG	Fine	VF	XF
7	ND(1835-70)	—	2.50	5.00	7.00	10.00

NOTE: Varieties exist.

MAMEITAGIN 'BEAN' SILVER

God of Plenty 'Bean' Silver

KEY TO DATING MODERN MAMEITA GIN

'BUN'
GENBUN PERIOD
1736-1741
(Used 1736-1818)

文

'BUN'
BUNSEI PERIOD
1818-1830
(Used 1820-1837)

保

'HO'
TEMPO PERIOD
1830-1844
(Used 1837-1858)

'SEI'
ANSEI PERIOD
1854-1860
(Used 1859-1865)

One of the above characters is usually found on the obverse of C#8 or both sides of C#8a and C#8b. The same characters are found at both ends of chogin pieces C#9. Era designators were used continuously until the next one was introduced, regardless of intervening eras.

NOTE: Values are for pieces weighing 5-8 grams. Pieces over 10 grams may command up to twice the values shown; pieces under 5 grams somewhat less.

.460 SILVER
Obv: One or more large characters, w/o "God of Plenty". Era designator between characters.
Rev: Blank or w/chop marks.

C#	Date	Mint	VG	Fine	VF	XF
8.1a	ND(1736-1818)	—	10.00	15.00	25.00	35.00

Obv: "God of Plenty" w/other large characters. Era designator between characters and on god's belly.

C#	Date	Mint	VG	Fine	VF	XF
8.1b	ND(1736-1818)	—	20.00	30.00	45.00	60.00

.360 SILVER
Obv: One or more large characters, w/o "God of Plenty". Era designator between characters.
Bunsei

C#	Date	Mint	VG	Fine	VF	XF
8.2a	ND(1820-37)	—	10.00	20.00	30.00	40.00

Obv: "God of Plenty" w/other large characters. Era designator between characters and on god's belly.

C#	Date	Mint	VG	Fine	VF	XF
8.2b	ND(1820-37)	—	20.00	40.00	60.00	80.00

.261 SILVER
Obv: One or more large characters, w/o "God of Plenty". Era designator between characters.
Tempo

C#	Date	Mint	VG	Fine	VF	XF
8.3a	ND(1837-58)	—	10.00	15.00	22.50	30.00

Obv: "God of Plenty" w/other large characters. Era designator between characters and on god's belly.

C#	Date	Mint	VG	Fine	VF	XF
8.3b	ND(1837-58)	—	12.50	25.00	40.00	55.00

.135 SILVER
Obv: One or more large characters, w/o "God of Plenty". Era designator between characters.
Ansei

C#	Date	Mint	VG	Fine	VF	XF
8.4a	ND(1859-65)	—	6.00	10.00	17.50	25.00

Obv: "God of Plenty" w/other large characters. Era designator between characters and on god's belly.

C#	Date	Mint	VG	Fine	VF	XF
8.4b	ND(1859-65)	—	100.00	150.00	225.00	300.00

.460 SILVER
Obv. and rev: "God of Plenty" design, era designator on belly.

C#	Date	Mint	VG	Fine	VF	XF
8a.1	ND(1736-1818)	—	45.00	80.00	150.00	275.00

Obv: "God of Plenty" design. Rev: Single large *ho* or multiple small era designator.

C#	Date	Mint	VG	Fine	VF	XF
8b.1	ND(1736-1818)	—	800.00	1000.	1300.	1750.

.360 SILVER
Obv. and rev: "God of Plenty" design, era designator on belly.
Bunsei

C#	Date	Mint	VG	Fine	VF	XF
8a.2	ND(1820-37)	—	90.00	150.00	225.00	375.00

Obv: "God of Plenty" design. Rev: Single large *ho* or multiple small era designator.
Bunsei

C#	Date	Mint	VG	Fine	VF	XF
8b.2	ND(1820-37)	—	1000.	1250.	1600.	2000.

.261 SILVER
Obv. and rev: "God of Plenty" design, era designator on belly.
Tempo

C#	Date	Mint	VG	Fine	VF	XF
8a.3a	ND(1837-58)	—	50.00	100.00	150.00	250.00

Obv: "God of Plenty", era designator on belly. Rev: Character *ho* (treasure) on belly of "God of Plenty".

C#	Date	Mint	VG	Fine	VF	XF
8a.3b	ND(1837-58)	—	150.00	250.00	350.00	500.00

Obv: "God of Plenty" design. Rev: Single or multiple era designator.
Tempo

C#	Date	Mint	VG	Fine	VF	XF
8b.3a	ND(1837-58)	—	1000.	1500.	2000.	2500.

Obv: "God of Plenty". Rev: Large single character *ho* (treasure).

C#	Date	Mint	VG	Fine	VF	XF
8b.3b.	ND(1837-58)	—	1000.	1500.	2000.	2500.

.135 SILVER
Obv. and rev: "God of Plenty" design.
Ansei

C#	Date	Mint	VG	Fine	VF	XF
8a.4	ND(1859-65)	—	60.00	75.00	100.00	175.00

Obv: "God of Plenty" design. Rev: Single or multiple era designator.
Ansei

C#	Date	Mint	VG	Fine	VF	XF
8b.4a	ND(1859-65)	—	1250.	1750.	2250.	2750.

Obv: "God of Plenty". Rev: Large single character *"Ho"* (treasure).

C#	Date	Mint	VG	Fine	VF	XF
8b.4b	ND(1859-65)	—	1000.	1250.	1650.	2000.

CHO GIN

NOTE: Cho Gin illustrations are reduced by 50%.

KEY TO DATING MODERN CHO GIN (SILVER)

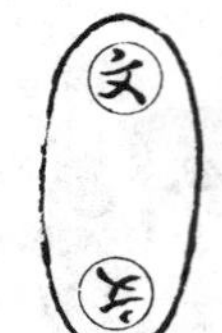
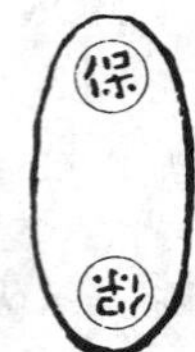
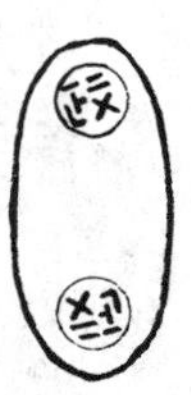

BUNSEI ERA, 1818-1830
TEMPO ERA, 1830-1844 ANSEI ERA, 1854-1860

.460 SILVER
Obv: Era marks at each end. Miscellaneous marks elsewhere. Rev: Blank except for occasional chop marks.

C#	Date	Mint	VG	Fine	VF	XF
9	ND(1736-1818)	—	125.00	225.00	375.00	500.00

.360 SILVER
Bunsei

C#	Date	Mint	VG	Fine	VF	XF
9a	ND(1820-37)	—	125.00	275.00	400.00	600.00

Illustrations Full Size

.261 SILVER
Tempo

C#	Date	Mint	VG	Fine	VF	XF
9b	ND(1837-58)	—	90.00	150.00	250.00	400.00

.135 SILVER
Ansei

C#	Date	Mint	VG	Fine	VF	XF
9c	ND(1859-65)	—	75.00	125.00	225.00	350.00

SHU

(Isshu Gin)

.989 SILVER, 2.63 g
Bunsei

C#	Date	Mintage	VG	Fine	VF	XF
11	ND(1829-37)	139.915	45.00	70.00	90.00	125.00

常 **KAEI ERA, 1848-1854 (Used 1853-1865)**

常 **MEIJI ERA, 1868-1912 (Used 1868-1869)**

.968 SILVER, 1.89 g
Kaei

C#	Date	Mintage	VG	Fine	VF	XF
12	ND(1853-65)	159.245	4.50	6.00	12.00	17.50

.880 SILVER, 1.88 g
Meiji
Rev: 3 top strokes are straight w/o curves or hooks.

C#	Date	Mintage	VG	Fine	VF	XF
12a	ND(1868-69)	18.742	10.00	15.00	22.50	30.00

NOTE: C#12 type 1 Shu are dated according to how the character illustrated is written on the reverse. Meiji 1 Shu are also known as Kaheishi 1 Shu.

2 SHU

(Nishu Gin)

.978 SILVER, 10.19 g
Meiwa-Ko-Nanryo

C#	Date	Mintage	VG	Fine	VF	XF
13	ND(1772-1824)	47.464	75.00	100.00	150.00	200.00

NOTE: Pieces struck on large planchets with full edge beads on obverse and reverse command up to three times these values.

.978 SILVER, 7.53 g
Bunsei-Shin-Nanryo

C#	Date	Mintage	VG	Fine	VF	XF
13a	ND(1824-30)	60.624	45.00	70.00	90.00	125.00

.845 SILVER, 13.62 g
Ansei

15	ND(1859)	.706	400.00	800.00	1200.	1600.

KEY TO DATING 1 BU

TEMPO ERA, 1830-1844
(Used 1837-1854)

ANSEI ERA, 1854-1860
(Used 1859-1868)

MEIJI ERA, 1868-1912
(Used 1868-1869)

NOTE: 1 Bu are dated according to how the two characters above are written on the reverse of the piece. There are other variations as well. Meiji Bu also are known as Kaheishi Bu.

BU

(Ichibu)

.991 SILVER, 8.66 g
Varieties of countermark
Tempo

16	ND(1837-54)	78.917	8.00	15.00	22.50	30.00

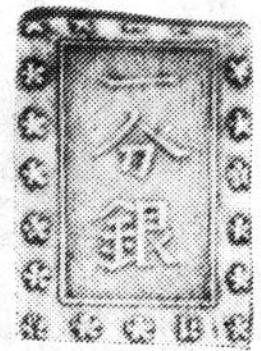

.873 SILVER, 8.63 g
Ansei

16a	ND(1859-68)	11.399	8.00	15.00	20.00	27.50

.807 SILVER, 8.66 g
Meiji

16b	ND(1868-69)	4.267	175.00	250.00	350.00	450.00

3 BU

(Sanbu)

(1859)

.903 SILVER
"Ansei Trade Dollar"
c/m: 4 characters on Mexico (Culiacan)
8 Reales, KM#377.3.

KM#	Date	Mintage	VG	Fine	VF	XF
101.1	ND(1846-58)	—	3000.	4500.	5500.	6500.

c/m: 4 characters on Mexico (Guanajuato)
8 Reales, KM#377.8.

101.2	ND(1825-58)	—	3000.	4500.	5500.	6500.

c/m: 4 characters on Mexico City
8 Reales, KM#377.10.

101.3	ND(1824-58)	—	3000.	4500.	5500.	6500.

c/m: 4 characters on Mexico (Zacatecas)
8 Reales, KM#377.13.

101.4	ND(1825-58)	—	3000.	4500.	5500.	6500.

SHU

(Isshu)

.123 GOLD/.877 SILVER, 1.39 g
Bunsei

C#	Date	Mintage	VG	Fine	VF	XF
17	ND(1824-32)	46.723	200.00	300.00	400.00	500.00

2 SHU

(Nishu)

.298 GOLD/.702 SILVER, 1.62 g

Tempo

C#	Date	Mintage	VG	Fine	VF	XF
18	ND(1832-58)	103.070	15.00	20.00	25.00	35.00

.229 GOLD/.771 SILVER, 0.75 g
Manen

18a	ND(1860-69)	25.120	17.50	22.50	30.00	40.00

KEY TO DATING 1 AND 2 BU

GENBUN PERIOD 1 BU

(Used 1736-1818)

BUNSEI PERIOD 2 BU

文 1818-1830
TYPE A DATE MARK
(Used 1818-1828)

BUNSEI PERIOD 1 BU and 2 BU

1818-1830
TYPE B DATE MARK
(Used 1819-1829 on 1 Bu)
(Used 1828-1832 on 2 Bu)

TEMPO PERIOD

保 1830-1844
(Used 1837-1858)

ANSEI PERIOD

正 1854-1859
(Used 1859)

MANEN PERIOD
1859-1860
(Without era designator)

C#21b is dated according to its weight. C#21c and C#21d can be distinguished by the character to the left on the obverse.

KEY TO DATING C#21c and C#21d

MANEN PERIOD
1860-1861
(Used 1860)

MEIJI PERIOD
1868-1912
(Used 1868-1869)

BU

(Ichi Bu)

.653 GOLD/.347 SILVER, 3.25 g
Genbun

19	ND(1736-1818)	—	55.00	70.00	100.00	150.00

.560 GOLD/.440 SILVER, 3.27 g
Bunsei
Rev: Type B mark.

20	ND(1819-29)	—	100.00	125.00	175.00	250.00

.568 GOLD/.432 SILVER, 2.80 g
Tempo

C#	Date	Mintage	VG	Fine	VF	XF
20a	ND(1837-58)	—	125.00	175.00	225.00	275.00

.570 GOLD/.430 SILVER, 2.24 g
Ansei

C#	Date	Mintage	VG	Fine	VF	XF
20b	ND(1859)	—	1000.	1500.	2000.	2750.

.574 GOLD/.426 SILVER, 0.82 g
Manen
Rev: W/o dating mark.

C#	Date	Mintage	VG	Fine	VF	XF
20c	ND(1860-67)	—	500.00	650.00	800.00	1000.

NOTE: Similar pieces without dating mark but weighing about 4 grams were made during the Kyoho era, 1716-1734.

2 BU

(Ni Bu)

.563 GOLD/.437 SILVER, 6.52 g
Bunsei
Rev: Type A mark.

C#	Date	Mintage	VG	Fine	VF	XF
21	ND(1818-28)	5.972	300.00	450.00	550.00	650.00

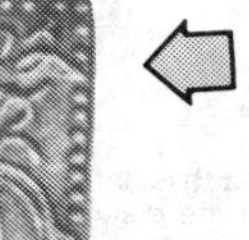

.490 GOLD/.510 SILVER, 6.56 g
Bunsei
Rev: Type B mark.

C#	Date	Mintage	VG	Fine	VF	XF
21a	ND(1828-32)	4.066	250.00	375.00	450.00	550.00

.209 GOLD/.791 SILVER, 5.62 g
Ansei
Rev: W/o mark.

C#	Date	Mintage	VG	Fine	VF	XF
21b	ND(1856-60)	7.103	75.00	100.00	150.00	200.00

A.

B.

.229 GOLD/.771 SILVER, 3.00 g
Manen
Obv: Paulownia leaf type A. Rev: W/o mark.

C#	Date	Mintage	VG	Fine	VF	XF
21c.1	ND(1860-)	100.201	300.00	450.00	600.00	800.00

Manen
Obv: Paulownia leaf type B.

C#	Date	Mintage	VG	Fine	VF	XF
21c.2	ND(1860-)	I.A.	250.00	350.00	500.00	650.00

.223 GOLD/.777 SILVER, 3.00 g
Meiji

C#	Date	Mintage	VG	Fine	VF	XF
21d	ND(1868-69)	—	30.00	40.00	50.00	60.00

KOBAN

.653 GOLD/.347 SILVER, 13.13 g
Genbun

C#	Date	Mintage	VG	Fine	VF	XF
22	ND(1736-1818)	*17.436	900.00	1200.	1600.	2000.

.559 GOLD/.441 SILVER, 13.13 g
Bunsei
Rev: Mark B.

C#	Date	Mintage	VG	Fine	VF	XF
22a	ND(1819-28)	*11.043	900.00	1400.	1800.	2250.

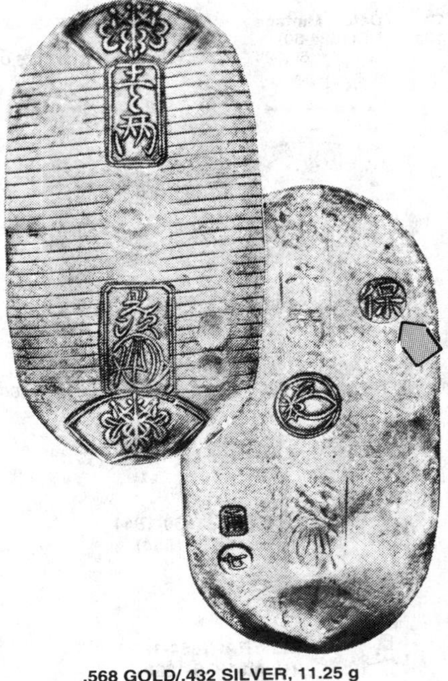

.568 GOLD/.432 SILVER, 11.25 g
Tempo

C#	Date	Mintage	VG	Fine	VF	XF
22b	ND(1837-1858)	*8.120	750.00	1000.	1250.	1750.

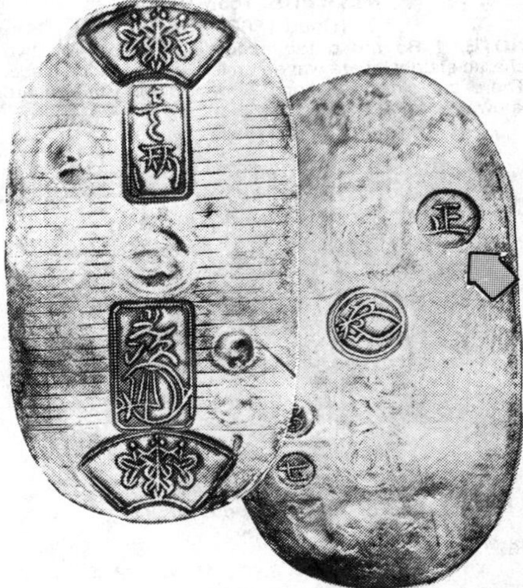

.570 GOLD/.430 SILVER, 8.97 g
Ansei

C#	Date	Mintage	VG	Fine	VF	XF
22c	ND(1859)	.351	3000.	3500.	5500.	7500.

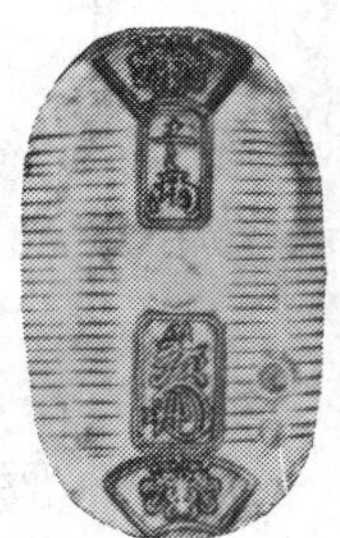
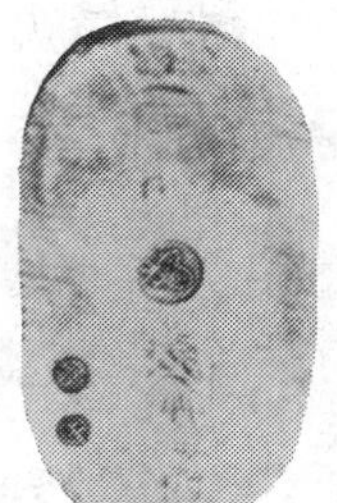

.574 GOLD/.426 SILVER, 3.30 g
Manen
Rev: W/o mark.

C#	Date	Mintage	VG	Fine	VF	XF
22d	(1860-67)	.625	550.00	850.00	1000.	1250.

***NOTE:** Koban mintage figures are in Ryo and also include Ichibu Kin.

GORYOBAN

(5 Ryo)

.842 GOLD/.158 SILVER, 33.75 g, 51x89mm
Tempo

C#	Date	Mintage	VG	Fine	VF	XF
23	ND(1837-43)	.034	5000.	8000.	12,000.	15,000.

OBAN

NOTE: Oban illustrations are reduced by 50%.

.676 GOLD/.324 SILVER, 165.38 g, 94x153mm
Kyoho

C#	Date	Mintage	VG	Fine	VF	XF
24.1	ND(1725-1837) original inking	8,515	—	—	35,000.	50,000.
	ND(1725-1837) re-inked during Tempo period	Inc. Ab.	—	—	25,000.	35,000.

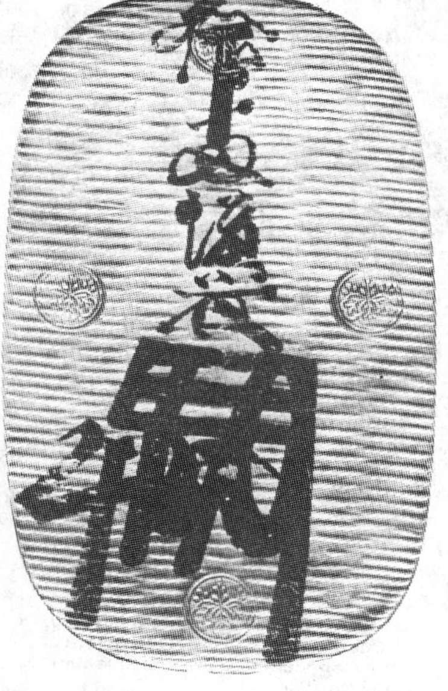

.674 GOLD/.326 SILVER, 165.38 g, 95x157mm
Tempo

C#	Date	Mintage	VG	Fine	VF	XF
24.2	ND(1838-60)	1,887	—	—	50,000.	60,000.

.344 GOLD/.639 SILVER, 112.4 g, 81x137mm

Manen
Hand made horizontal crenulations.

C#	Date	Mintage	VG	Fine	VF	XF
24a.1	ND(1860-62)	.017	—	—	17,500.	22,500.

Machine made horizontal crenulations.

C#	Date	Mintage	VG	Fine	VF	XF
24a.2	ND(1860-62)	I.A.	—	—	16,000.	20,000.

DECIMAL COINAGE

10 Rin = 1 Sen
100 Sen = 1 Yen

RIN

COPPER

Y#	Date	Mintage	Fine	VF	XF	Unc
	Meiji					
15	Yr.6(1873)	6.979	4.50	10.00	20.00	40.00
	Yr.7(1874)	I.A.	2.00	4.00	8.00	30.00
	Yr.8(1875)	3.718	4.00	9.00	20.00	50.00
	Yr.9(1876)	.023	1000.	2000.	3500.	5500.
	Yr.10(1877)	I.A.	350.00	750.00	1200.	1500.
	Yr.13(1880)	810 pcs.	1500.	2500.	4500.	7000.
	Yr.15(1882)	3.632	2.00	5.00	8.00	20.00
	Yr.16(1883)	14.128	1.00	3.00	6.00	15.00
	Yr.17(1884)	16.009	1.00	3.00	6.00	15.00
	Yr.25(1892)	—	(none struck for circulation)			

NOTE: Two varieties of year 8 exist.

1/2 SEN

COPPER
Obv: Square scales on dragon's body.

Y#	Date	Mintage	Fine	VF	XF	Unc
	Meiji					
16.1 (16)	Yr.6(1873)	16.804	3.50	15.00	65.00	300.00
	Yr.7(1874)	I.A.	3.50	15.00	65.00	350.00
	Yr.8(1875)	17.037	1.00	4.50	40.00	265.00
	Yr.9(1876)	24.292	.75	3.50	30.00	250.00
	Yr.10(1877)	29.278	75.00	150.00	275.00	2500.

NOTE: Varieties exist for Yr.7.

Obv: V scales on dragon's body.

Y#	Date	Mintage	Fine	VF	XF	Unc
16.2 (16.1)	Yr.10(1877)	I.A.	.75	2.00	10.00	45.00
	Yr.12(1879)	29.963	7.50	30.00	50.00	800.00
	Yr.13(1880)	14.090	.75	2.00	12.00	50.00
	Yr.14(1881)	17.929	.75	2.00	12.00	50.00
	Yr.15(1882)	26.458	.75	2.00	14.00	55.00
	Yr.16(1883)	38.202	.75	2.00	14.00	55.00
	Yr.17(1884)	38.480	.50	1.50	5.00	25.00
	Yr.18(1885)	31.166	.75	2.00	14.00	60.00
	Yr.19(1886)	31.831	.75	2.00	14.00	60.00
	Yr.20(1887)	35.651	.75	2.00	14.00	60.00
	Yr.21(1888)	25.744	5.00	8.00	16.00	90.00
	Yr.25(1892)	—	(none struck for circulation)			

SEN

COPPER
Obv: Square scales on dragon's body.

Y#	Date	Mintage	Fine	VF	XF	Unc
	Meiji					
17.1 (17)	Yr.6(1873)	1.301	7.00	15.00	35.00	300.00
	Yr.7(1874)	25.564	1.50	3.00	6.00	150.00
	Yr.8(1875)	32.832	1.00	2.00	4.00	125.00
	Yr.9(1876)	38.048	1.00	2.00	4.00	125.00
	Yr.10(1877)	98.041	1.00	2.00	4.00	125.00

Obv: V scales on dragon's body.

Y#	Date	Mintage	Fine	VF	XF	Unc
17.2 (17.1)	Yr.13(1880)	33.947	.75	1.50	3.00	85.00
	Yr.14(1881)	16.123	2.00	4.00	8.00	125.00
	Yr.14(1881) large 4	Inc. Ab.	25.00	50.00	100.00	225.00
	Yr.15(1882)	19.150	1.50	3.00	6.00	90.00
	Yr.16(1883)	47.613	.75	1.50	3.00	85.00
	Yr.17(1884)	53.702	.75	1.50	3.00	85.00
	Yr.18(1885)	46.846	.75	1.50	3.00	85.00
	Yr.19(1886)	26.886	.75	1.50	3.00	85.00
	Yr.20(1887)	22.249	.75	1.50	3.00	85.00
	Yr.21(1888)	25.864	.75	1.50	3.00	65.00
	Yr.25(1892)	—	(none struck for circulation)			

BRONZE

Y#	Date	Mintage	Fine	VF	XF	Unc
20	Yr.31(1898)	3.649	2.50	5.00	20.00	110.00
	Yr.32(1899)	9.764	2.00	4.50	16.00	55.00
	Yr.33(1900)	3.086	4.50	7.50	22.50	130.00

NOTE: Later dates (Yr.34-42) exist for this type.

2 SEN

BRONZE

Obv: Square scales on dragon's body.

Y#	Date	Mintage	Fine	VF	XF	Unc
	Meiji					
18.1	Yr.6(1873)	3.949	35.00	75.00	150.00	825.00
(18)	Yr.7(1874)	I.A.	3.50	7.00	15.00	450.00
	Yr.8(1875)	22.835	2.00	3.50	6.00	265.00
	Yr.9(1876)	25.817	2.00	3.50	6.00	265.00
	Yr.10(1877)	33.897	2.00	3.50	6.00	265.00

Obv: V scales on dragon's body.

Y#	Date	Mintage	Fine	VF	XF	Unc
18.2 (18.1)	Yr.10(1877)	43.290	2.00	3.50	6.00	115.00
	Yr.13(1880)	33.142	2.00	3.50	6.00	115.00
	Yr.14(1881)	38.475	2.00	3.50	6.00	115.00
	Yr.15(1882)	43.527	2.00	3.50	6.00	115.00
	Yr.16(1883)	19.476	2.00	3.50	6.00	115.00
	Yr.17(1884)	12.090	3.00	6.00	12.00	350.00
	Yr.25(1892)	—	(none struck for circulation)			

5 SEN

1.2500 g, .800 SILVER, .0321 oz ASW

Y#	Date	Mintage	Fine	VF	XF	Unc
	Meiji					
1	Yr.3(1870) shallow scales	1.501	150.00	250.00	350.00	550.00
	Yr.3(1870) deep scales	Inc. Ab.	200.00	300.00	450.00	875.00
	Yr.4(1871)	I.A.	250.00	350.00	500.00	900.00

Early variety. Rev: 66 rays, 79 beads.

Y#	Date	Mintage	Fine	VF	XF	Unc
6.1	Yr.4(1871)	1.665	50.00	125.00	250.00	400.00

Late variety. Rev: 53 rays, 65 beads.

Y#	Date	Mintage	Fine	VF	XF	Unc
6.2	Yr.4(1871)	I.A.	40.00	90.00	150.00	325.00

明 明

Type I Characters Not Connected — **Type II Characters Connected**

1.3400 g, .800 SILVER, .0344 oz ASW

Y#	Date	Mintage	Fine	VF	XF	Unc
22	Yr.6(1873) Type I	5.593	12.50	25.00	40.00	85.00
	Yr.6(1873) Type II	Inc. Ab.	50.00	75.00	125.00	250.00
	Yr.7(1874)	7.806	100.00	200.00	325.00	800.00
	Yr.8(1875)	6.396	12.50	25.00	40.00	75.00
	Yr.9(1876) Type I	5.546	12.50	25.00	40.00	85.00
	Yr.9(1876) Type II	Inc. Ab.	15.00	30.00	45.00	100.00
	Yr.10(1877) Type I	22.024	20.00	40.00	60.00	100.00
22	Yr.10(1877) Type II	Inc. Ab.	22.00	45.00	70.00	125.00
	Yr.13(1880)	79 pcs.	2500.	5000.	7500.	15,000.
	Yr.25(1892)	—	(none struck for circulation)			

NOTE: Varieties exist.

COPPER-NICKEL

Y#	Date	Mintage	Fine	VF	XF	Unc
19	Yr.22(1889)	28.841	2.00	5.00	10.00	55.00
	Yr.23(1890)	39.258	2.00	5.00	10.00	55.00
	Yr.24(1891)	15.924	2.50	6.00	15.00	100.00
	Yr.25(1892)	9.510	2.50	6.00	15.00	100.00
	Yr.26(1893)	8.531	2.50	6.00	15.00	100.00
	Yr.27(1894)	14.680	2.50	6.00	15.00	100.00
	Yr.28(1895)	1.030	50.00	100.00	200.00	1700.
	Yr.29(1896)	5.119	4.50	10.00	25.00	300.00
	Yr.30(1897)	7.857	2.50	6.00	15.00	100.00

NOTE: Varieties exist.

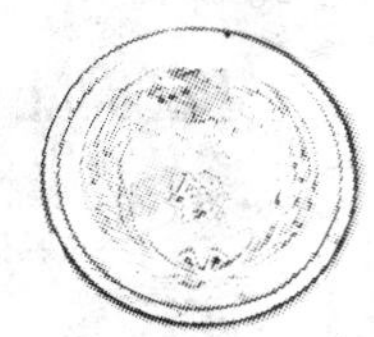

Y#	Date	Mintage	Fine	VF	XF	Unc
21	Yr.30(1897)	4.167	7.50	15.00	35.00	265.00
	Yr.31(1898)	18.197	6.00	12.00	25.00	115.00
	Yr.32(1899)	10.658	6.00	12.00	25.00	115.00
	Yr.33(1900)	2.426	10.00	20.00	35.00	235.00

NOTE: Later dates (Yr.34-39) exist for this type.

10 SEN

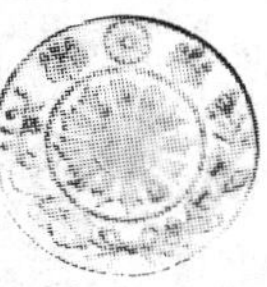

2.5000 g, .800 SILVER, .0643 oz ASW

Y#	Date	Mintage	Fine	VF	XF	Unc
	Meiji					
2	Yr.3(1870) shallow scales	6.102	15.00	30.00	45.00	155.00
	Yr.3(1870) deep scales	Inc. Ab.	20.00	35.00	55.00	175.00

2.6957 g, .800 SILVER, .0693 oz ASW

Y#	Date	Mintage	Fine	VF	XF	Unc
23	Yr.6(1873) Type I	5.109	5.00	10.00	18.00	45.00
	Yr.6(1873) Type II	Inc. Ab.	60.00	120.00	165.00	375.00

明 明

Type I Characters Not Connected — **Type II Characters Connected**

Y#	Date	Mintage	Fine	VF	XF	Unc
	Yr.7(1874)	10.221	160.00	275.00	425.00	950.00
	Yr.8(1875) Type II	8.977	15.00	30.00	50.00	135.00
	Yr.8(1875) Type I	Inc. Ab.	8.00	14.00	22.00	55.00
	Yr.9(1876)	11.890	8.00	14.00	22.00	55.00
	Yr.10(1877)	20.352	10.00	25.00	40.00	100.00
	Yr.13(1880)	77 pcs.	5000.	10,000.	20,000.	35,000.
	Yr.18(1885)	9.763	6.00	10.00	18.00	40.00
	Yr.20(1887)	10.421	6.00	10.00	18.00	40.00
	Yr.21(1888)	8.177	6.00	10.00	20.00	45.00
23	Yr.24(1891)	5.000	15.00	25.00	45.00	110.00
	Yr.25(1892)	5.000	15.00	25.00	45.00	110.00
	Yr.26(1893)	12.000	6.00	10.00	22.00	55.00
	Yr.27(1894)	11.000	6.00	10.00	25.00	100.00
	Yr.28(1895)	13.719	4.00	7.00	10.00	35.00
	Yr.29(1896)	15.080	4.00	7.00	10.00	35.00
	Yr.30(1897)	20.357	4.00	7.00	10.00	35.00
	Yr.31(1898)	13.643	5.00	9.00	18.00	40.00
	Yr.32(1899)	26.216	5.00	9.00	18.00	40.00
	Yr.33(1900)	8.183	8.50	20.00	35.00	100.00

NOTE: Later dates (Yr.34-39) exist for this type.

20 SEN

Yr.4 var.

5.0000 g, .800 SILVER, .1286 oz ASW

Y#	Date	Mintage	Fine	VF	XF	Unc
	Meiji					
3	Yr.3(1870) shallow scales	4.313	15.00	25.00	45.00	135.00
	Yr.3(1870) deep scales	Inc. Ab.	20.00	40.00	65.00	200.00
	Yr.4(1871)	I.A.	15.00	25.00	40.00	125.00
	Yr.4(1871) lower stroke in *Sen* incomplete	Inc. Ab.	75.00	100.00	150.00	300.00

明 明

Type I Character Closed — **Type II Character Open**

5.3800 g, .800 SILVER, .1383 oz ASW

Y#	Date	Mintage	Fine	VF	XF	Unc
24	Yr.6(1873) Type I	6.214	5.00	10.00	16.50	55.00
	Yr.6(1873) Type II	Inc. Ab.	65.00	125.00	250.00	650.00
	Yr.7(1874)	3.024	20.00	40.00	65.00	200.00

明 明

Type I Characters Not Connected — **Type II Characters Connected**

Y#	Date	Mintage	Fine	VF	XF	Unc
	Yr.8(1875) Type I	.612	100.00	150.00	275.00	750.00
	Yr.8(1875) Type II	Inc. Ab.	50.00	100.00	175.00	575.00
	Yr.9(1876) Type II	9.200	20.00	35.00	65.00	225.00
	Yr.9(1876) Type I	Inc. Ab.	6.00	12.00	18.00	65.00
	Yr.10(1877)	5.199	20.00	35.00	65.00	240.00
	Yr.13(1880)	96 pcs.	1750.	3250.	5500.	12,500.
	Yr.18(1885)	4.205	5.00	10.00	15.00	50.00
	Yr.20(1887)	4.794	5.00	10.00	15.00	50.00
	Yr.21(1888)	.703	60.00	125.00	200.00	1000.
	Yr.24(1891)	2.500	15.00	25.00	40.00	120.00
	Yr.25(1892)	3.054	8.50	17.50	30.00	100.00
	Yr.26(1893)	3.445	7.50	15.00	25.00	90.00
	Yr.27(1894)	4.500	6.00	12.00	18.00	140.00
	Yr.28(1895)	7.000	5.00	10.00	15.00	50.00
	Yr.29(1896)	2.599	9.00	18.00	30.00	100.00
	Yr.30(1897)	7.516	5.00	10.00	15.00	50.00
	Yr.31(1898)	17.984	5.00	10.00	15.00	50.00
	Yr.32(1899)	15.000	5.00	10.00	15.00	50.00
	Yr.33(1900)	.800	25.00	50.00	75.00	325.00

NOTE: Later dates (Yr.34-38) exist for this type.

50 SEN

12.5000 g, .800 SILVER, .3215 oz ASW

Y#	Date	Mintage	Fine	VF	XF	Unc
	Meiji					
4	Yr.3(1870)	1.806	32.50	65.00	100.00	325.00
	Yr.4(1871)	I.A.	30.00	60.00	85.00	300.00

NOTE: Varieties exist.

Type II, large dragon

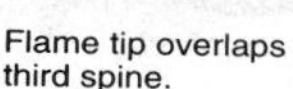

Flame tip overlaps third spine.

Type I, small dragon

Flame tip extends between third & fourth spine.

30.5mm

Type I: 19mm circle of dots around dragon.

Y#	Date	Mintage	Fine	VF	XF	Unc
4a.1 (4a)	Yr.4(1871)	2.648	50.00	100.00	150.00	300.00

Type II: 21mm circle of dots around dragon.

Y#	Date	Mintage	Fine	VF	XF	Unc
4a.2 (4a.1)	Yr.4(1871)	I.A.	400.00	800.00	1200.	3500.

13.5000 g, .800 SILVER, .3472 oz ASW

Y#	Date	Mintage	Fine	VF	XF	Unc
25	Yr.6(1873) Type I	3.447	25.00	35.00	65.00	250.00
	Yr.6(1873) Type II	Inc.Ab.	150.00	200.00	300.00	775.00
	Yr.7(1874)	.095	7500.	12,500.	20,000.	32,500.
	Yr.8(1875)	109 pcs.	8000.	11,000.	16,000.	27,500.
	Yr.9(1876)	1,251	2500.	4500.	6500.	14,000.
	Yr.10(1877)	.184	1250.	2000.	3750.	7000.
	Yr.13(1880)	179 pcs.	7500.	12,500.	20,000.	40,000.
	Yr.18(1885)	.409	125.00	175.00	275.00	900.00
	Yr.30(1897)	5.078	7.50	15.00	28.00	175.00
	Yr.31(1898)	22.797	6.50	12.50	25.00	120.00
	Yr.32(1899)	10.254	7.50	15.00	30.00	125.00
	Yr.33(1900)	3.280	10.00	18.00	35.00	220.00

NOTE: Two varieties exist for year 6 in the character *Nen* (= year). The type II has a very long lower horizontal stroke.

NOTE: Later dates (Yr.34-38) exist for this type.

YEN

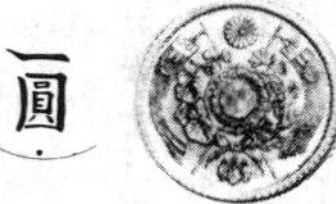

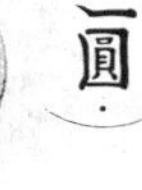

Low Dot + High Dot

1.6700 g, .900 GOLD, 13.5mm, .0482 oz AGW

Y#	Date	Mintage	Fine	VF	XF	Unc
	Meiji					
9	Yr.4(1871) low dot	1.841	175.00	300.00	400.00	650.00
	Yr.4(1871) low dot	—	—	Proof		6500.
	Yr.4(1871) high dot	Inc. Ab.	250.00	375.00	500.00	750.00

Reduced size, 12mm

Y#	Date	Mintage	Fine	VF	XF	Unc
9a	Yr.7(1874)	.116	1500.	2500.	3250.	4500.
	Yr.9(1876)	138 pcs.	4500.	7500.	12,000.	16,000.
	Yr.10(1877)	7,246	10,000.	20,000.	30,000.	45,000.
	Yr.13(1880)	112 pcs.	12,500.	22,500.	35,000.	50,000.
	Yr.25(1892)	(none struck for circulation)				

Type I Type II Type III

26.9568 g, .900 SILVER, .7800 oz ASW

Y#	Date	Mintage	Fine	VF	XF	Unc
	Meiji					
5.1 (5)	Yr.3(1870)Type 1	3.685	100.00	275.00	375.00	625.00
5.2 (5.1)	Yr.3(1870)Type 2	Inc.Ab.	125.00	300.00	400.00	675.00
5.3 (5.2)	Yr.3(1870)Type 3	Inc. Ab.	450.00	850.00	1500.	2250.

Type I, 38.6mm

Spiral on pearl held by dragon curls in counter clock-wise direction from center.

Y#	Date	Mintage	Fine	VF	XF	Unc
A25.1 (A25)	Yr.7(1874)	.942	350.00	650.00	1250.	4500.

Spiral on pearl curls clockwise from center.

Y#	Date	Mintage	Fine	VF	XF	Unc
A25.2 (A25.1)	Yr.7(1874)	I.A.	300.00	600.00	1200.	2750.
	Yr.8(1875)	.139	2000.	3000.	6000.	15,000.
	Yr.11(1878)	.856	150.00	350.00	550.00	2000.
	Yr.12(1879)	1.913	750.00	1200.	1750.	6500.
	Yr.13(1880)	5.427	50.00	125.00	200.00	1000.
	Yr.14(1881)	2.927	75.00	150.00	225.00	1250.
(A25.1)	Yr.15(1882)	5.089	45.00	75.00	125.00	850.00
	Yr.16(1883)	3.636	45.00	75.00	150.00	900.00
	Yr.17(1884)	3.599	60.00	125.00	200.00	1100.
	Yr.18(1885)	4.296	45.00	75.00	125.00	850.00
	Yr.19(1886)	9.084	45.00	75.00	125.00	875.00
	Yr.20(1887)	8.275	85.00	150.00	325.00	1350.

NOTE: Two varieties of year 7 exist. Year 11 has varieties in the bottom leaf on reverse. Year 19 edge has 198 reeds.

Type II: Reduced size, 38.1mm.

Y#	Date	Mintage	Fine	VF	XF	Unc
A25.3 (A25.2)	Yr.19(1886)	I.A.	500.00	900.00	1750.	4000.
	Yr.20(1887)	I.A.	45.00	75.00	150.00	900.00
	Yr.21(1888)	9.477	25.00	50.00	75.00	400.00
	Yr.22(1889)	9.295	25.00	45.00	65.00	225.00
	Yr.23(1890)	7.292	25.00	45.00	65.00	220.00
	Yr.24(1891)	7.518	15.00	30.00	50.00	185.00
	Yr.25(1892) flame extends between fourth and fifth spine	11.187	100.00	200.00	400.00	1350.
	Yr.25(1892) flame overlaps third spine of dragon	I.A.	20.00	35.00	55.00	210.00
	Yr.26(1893)	10.403	20.00	35.00	55.00	260.00
	Yr.27(1894)	22.118	15.00	25.00	45.00	140.00
	Yr.28(1895)	21.098	15.00	25.00	45.00	140.00
	Yr.29(1896)	11.363	15.00	25.00	45.00	140.00
	Yr.30(1897)	2.448	15.00	30.00	50.00	155.00

NOTE: Later dates (Yr.34(1901)-45(1912)) exist for this type.

NOTE: Year 19 has diameter of 38.3mm and edge has 217 reeds.

'GIN' COUNTERMARKS

c/m: *Gin* right on 1 Yen Meiji Year 3, (1870), Y#5.

c/m: *Gin* left on 1 Yen, Meiji Years 7-30, (1874-1897), Y#A25.

In 1897 Japan demonetized the silver one Yen and Trade Dollar coins, and many were melted to provide bullion from which to produce subsidiary coins. However, some 20 million Trade Dollars and one Yen coins were countermarked with the character *Gin* (meaning silver) and shipped to Taiwan, Korea and Southern Manchuria for use in circulation there. The countermark was applied to indicate that the coin was to be treated simply as bullion and to prevent the coins from returning to Japan where they could be sold to the government for gold.

The actual countermarking was done by the Tokyo and Osaka Mints; the Osaka Mint putting its *Gin* on the left side, the Tokyo Mint putting its *Gin* on the right side. Only 2,100,000 coins were countermarked at the Tokyo Mint as opposed to 18,350,000 countermarked at Osaka, making the Tokyo pieces scarcer than the Osaka pieces.

Formerly *Gin* marked coins were regarded as damaged and sold for about 80 per cent of the price of the same coin without countermark. Now, however, the *Gin* coins are being collected by date and placement of the mark, and some sell for more than a non-countermarked piece. Any additional chop marks are still considered defacement and reduce the value of a coin substantially.

Mint: Osaka
c/m: *Gin* left on 1 Yen, Y#5.

Y#	Date	Mintage	VG	Fine	VF	XF
28	Yr.3(1870)	—	125.00	250.00	350.00	600.00

Type I, 38.6mm
c/m: *Gin* left on 1 Yen, Y#A25.
Counterclockwise spiral on pearl.

Y#	Date	Mintage	VG	Fine	VF	XF
28a	Yr.7(1874)	—	250.00	400.00	800.00	1200.

Clockwise spiral on pearl.

Y#	Date	Mintage	VG	Fine	VF	XF
28a.1	Yr.7(1874)	—	200.00	350.00	700.00	1000.
	Yr.8(1875)	—	900.00	2000.	3200.	5200.
	Yr.11(1878)	—	100.00	200.00	400.00	720.00
	Yr.12(1879)	—	350.00	750.00	1200.	2000.
	Yr.13(1880)	—	30.00	60.00	120.00	200.00
	Yr.14(1881)	—	35.00	75.00	150.00	225.00
	Yr.15(1882)	—	15.00	35.00	75.00	135.00
	Yr.16(1883)	—	20.00	40.00	80.00	140.00
	Yr.17(1884)	—	35.00	75.00	150.00	225.00
	Yr.18(1885)	—	15.00	35.00	75.00	135.00
	Yr.19(1886)	—	20.00	40.00	80.00	140.00
	Yr.20(1887)	—	40.00	85.00	150.00	325.00

Type II, 38.1mm

Y#	Date	Mintage	VG	Fine	VF	XF
28a.2	Yr.19(1886)	—	300.00	500.00	800.00	1200.
	Yr.20(1887)	—	30.00	50.00	100.00	175.00
	Yr.21(1888)	—	12.00	25.00	45.00	75.00
	Yr.22(1889)	—	10.00	20.00	40.00	65.00
	Yr.23(1890)	—	10.00	20.00	40.00	65.00
	Yr.24(1891)	—	8.00	15.00	35.00	60.00
	Yr.25(1892) early variety	—	50.00	100.00	200.00	350.00
	Yr.25(1892) late variety	—	10.00	20.00	40.00	60.00
	Yr.26(1893)	—	10.00	20.00	40.00	60.00
	Yr.27(1894)	—	7.50	15.00	30.00	50.00
	Yr.28(1895)	—	7.50	15.00	30.00	50.00
	Yr.29(1896)	—	7.50	15.00	30.00	50.00
	Yr.30(1897)	—	10.00	20.00	40.00	60.00

Mint: Tokyo
c/m: *Gin* right on 1 Yen, Y#5.

Y#	Date	Mintage	VG	Fine	VF	XF
28.1	YR.3(1870)	—	125.00	250.00	350.00	650.00

Type I, 38.6mm
c/m: *Gin* right on 1 Yen, Y#A25.
Counterclockwise spiral on pearl.

Y#	Date	Mintage	VG	Fine	VF	XF
28a.3	Yr.7(1874)	—	250.00	400.00	800.00	1250.

Clockwise spiral on pearl.

Y#	Date	Mintage	VG	Fine	VF	XF
28a.4	Yr.7(1874)	—	200.00	350.00	750.00	1100.
	Yr.8(1875)	—	1000.	2200.	3250.	5400.
	Yr.11(1878)	—	100.00	200.00	350.00	750.00
	Yr.12(1879)	—	350.00	750.00	1250.	2000.
	Yr.13(1880)	—	30.00	60.00	125.00	200.00
	Yr.14(1881)	—	40.00	80.00	150.00	225.00
	Yr.15(1882)	—	20.00	40.00	75.00	145.00
	Yr.16(1883)	—	25.00	45.00	80.00	150.00
	Yr.17(1884)	—	35.00	75.00	150.00	225.00
	Yr.18(1885)	—	20.00	40.00	75.00	145.00
	Yr.19(1886)	—	25.00	45.00	80.00	150.00
	Yr.20(1887)	—	45.00	90.00	175.00	350.00

Type II, 38.1mm

Y#	Date	Mintage	VG	Fine	VF	XF
28a.5	Yr.19(1886)	—	350.00	550.00	850.00	1250.
	Yr.20(1887)	—	35.00	55.00	115.00	185.00
	Yr.21(1888)	—	15.00	30.00	50.00	85.00
	Yr.22(1889)	—	10.00	20.00	40.00	65.00
	Yr.23(1890)	—	10.00	20.00	40.00	65.00
	Yr.24(1891)	—	8.00	15.00	35.00	60.00
	Yr.25(1892) early variety	—	50.00	100.00	200.00	400.00
	Yr.25(1892) late variety	—	10.00	20.00	40.00	60.00
	Yr.26(1893)	—	10.00	20.00	40.00	60.00
	Yr.27(1894)	—	7.50	15.00	30.00	50.00
	Yr.28(1895)	—	7.50	15.00	30.00	50.00
	Yr.29(1896)	—	7.50	15.00	30.00	50.00
	Yr.30(1897)	—	10.00	20.00	40.00	60.00

REGULAR COINAGE

2 YEN

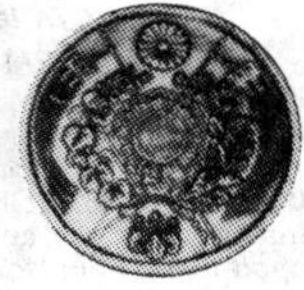

3.3333 g, .900 GOLD, 17.48mm, .0964 oz AGW

Y#	Date	Mintage	Fine	VF	XF	Unc
	Meiji					
10	Yr.3(1870)	.883	850.00	950.00	1150.	1650.
	Yr.3(1870)	—	—	—	Proof	9500.

Reduced size 16.96mm, same weight.

Y#	Date	Mintage	Fine	VF	XF	Unc
10a	Yr.7(1874)	—	Reported, not confirmed			
	Yr.9(1876)	178 pcs.	—	45,000.	60,000.	75,000.
	Yr.10(1877)	39 pcs.	—	45,000.	60,000.	75,000.
	Yr.13(1880)	87 pcs.	—	45,000.	60,000.	75,000.
	Yr.25(1892)	—	(none struck for circulation)			

5 YEN

8.3333 g, .900 GOLD, 23.8mm, .2411 oz AGW

Y#	Date	Mintage	Fine	VF	XF	Unc
	Meiji					
11	Yr.3(1870)	.273	1250.	1750.	2500.	3500.
	Yr.4(1871)	I.A.	1250.	1650.	2400.	3400.
	Yr.4(1871)	—	—	—	Proof	10,000.

Reduced size, 21.8mm, same weight.

Y#	Date	Mintage	Fine	VF	XF	Unc
11a	Yr.5(1872)	1.057	750.00	1000.	1500.	2500.
	Yr.6(1873)	3.148	750.00	1000.	1500.	2500.
	Yr.7(1874)	.728	1500.	1800.	2500.	3500.
	Yr.8(1875)	.181	1750.	2000.	2500.	3500.
	Yr.9(1876)	.146	1850.	2100.	2850.	3750.
	Yr.10(1877)	.136	1900.	2200.	3000.	4200.
	Yr.11(1878)	.101	1900.	2200.	3000.	4200.
	Yr.13(1880)	.078	1900.	2200.	3000.	4200.
	Yr.14(1881)	.149	1900.	2200.	3000.	4200.
	Yr.15(1882)	.113	1900.	2200.	3000.	4200.
	Yr.16(1883)	.108	1900.	2200.	3000.	4200.
	Yr.17(1884)	.113	1900.	2200.	3000.	4200.
	Yr.18(1885)	.200	1900.	2200.	3000.	4200.
	Yr.19(1886)	.179	1900.	2200.	3000.	4200.
	Yr.20(1887)	.179	1900.	2200.	3000.	4200.
	Yr.21(1888)	.165	1900.	2200.	3000.	4200.
	Yr.22(1889)	.353	1900.	2200.	3000.	4200.
	Yr.23(1890)	.238	1900.	2200.	3000.	4200.
	Yr.24(1891)	.216	1900.	2200.	3000.	4200.
	Yr.25(1892)	.263	1900.	2200.	3000.	4200.
	Yr.26(1893)	.260	1900.	2200.	3000.	4200.
	Yr.27(1894)	.314	1900.	2200.	3000.	4200.
	Yr.28(1895)	.320	1900.	2200.	3000.	4200.
	Yr.29(1896)	.224	1900.	2200.	3000.	4200.
	Yr.30(1897)	.107	1900.	2200.	3000.	4200.

4.1666 g, .900 GOLD, .1205 oz AGW

Y#	Date	Mintage	Fine	VF	XF	Unc
32	Yr.30(1897)	.111	850.00	950.00	1200.	2000.
	Yr.31(1898)	.055	850.00	950.00	1200.	2000.

NOTE: Later dates (Yr36-45) exist for this type.

10 YEN

16.6666 g, .900 GOLD, .4823 oz AGW

Y#	Date	Mintage	Fine	VF	XF	Unc
	Meiji					
12	Yr.4(1871)	1.867	3000.	3750.	4500.	6000.
	Yr.4(1871)	—	—	—	Proof	35,000.

Modified design

Y#	Date	Mintage	Fine	VF	XF	Unc
12a	Yr.9(1876)	1,925	15,000.	25,000.	54,000.	70,000.
	Yr.10(1877)	36 pcs.	20,000.	30,000.	70,000.	85,000.
	Yr.13(1880)	136 pcs.	20,000.	30,000.	70,000.	85,000.
	Yr.25(1892)		(none struck for circulation)			

8.3333 g, .900 GOLD, .2411 oz AGW

Y#	Date	Mintage	Fine	VF	XF	Unc
33	Yr.30(1897)	2.422	450.00	600.00	725.00	1100.
	Yr.31(1898)	3.176	450.00	600.00	725.00	1100.
	Yr.32(1899)	1.743	450.00	600.00	725.00	1100.
	Yr.33(1900)	1.114	450.00	600.00	725.00	1100.

NOTE: Later dates (Yr.34-43) exist for this type.

20 YEN

33.3332 g, .900 GOLD, .9646 oz AGW

Y#	Date	Mintage	Fine	VF	XF	Unc
	Meiji					
13	Yr.3(1870)	.046	10,000.	16,500.	25,000.	37,500.
	Yr.3(1870)	—	—	—	Proof	57,500.
	Yr.9(1876)	954 pcs.	12,500.	21,500.	44,500.	65,000.
	Yr.10(1877)	29 pcs.	18,000.	38,000.	78,000.	110,000.
	Yr.13(1880)	103 pcs.	16,500.	35,000.	74,000.	100,000.
	Yr.25(1892)	—	(none struck for circulation)			

16.6666 g, .900 GOLD, .4823 oz AGW

Y#	Date	Mintage	Fine	VF	XF	Unc
34	Yr.30(1897)	1.861	550.00	1250.	1750.	2400.

NOTE: Later dates (Yr.36-45) exist for this type.

TRADE COINAGE

TRADE DOLLAR

27.2200 g, .900 SILVER, .7876 oz ASW

Y#	Date	Mintage	Fine	VF	XF	Unc
	Meiji					
14	Yr.8(1875)	.097	300.00	650.00	1000.	2500.
	Yr.9(1876)	1.514	300.00	650.00	1000.	2500.
	Yr.10(1877)	1.125	300.00	650.00	1000.	2750.

'GIN' COUNTERMARKS

Mint: Osaka
c/m: ***Gin*** **left on Trade Dollar, Y#14.**

Y#	Date	Mintage	VG	Fine	VF	XF
28b.1	Yr.8(1875)	—	150.00	300.00	500.00	700.00
	Yr.9(1876)	—	150.00	300.00	500.00	700.00
	Yr.10(1877)	—	150.00	300.00	500.00	750.00

Mint: Tokyo
c/m: ***Gin*** **right on Trade Dollar, Y#14.**

Y#	Date	Mintage	VG	Fine	VF	XF
28b.2	Yr.8(1875)	—	175.00	350.00	550.00	750.00
	Yr.9(1876)	—	175.00	350.00	550.00	750.00
	Yr.10(1877)	—	175.00	350.00	550.00	800.00

PATTERNS (Pn)

(Including off metal strikes)

KM#	Date	Mintage	Identification	Mkt.Val.
Pn1	(1861)	—	5 Momme, Cast Bronze	—

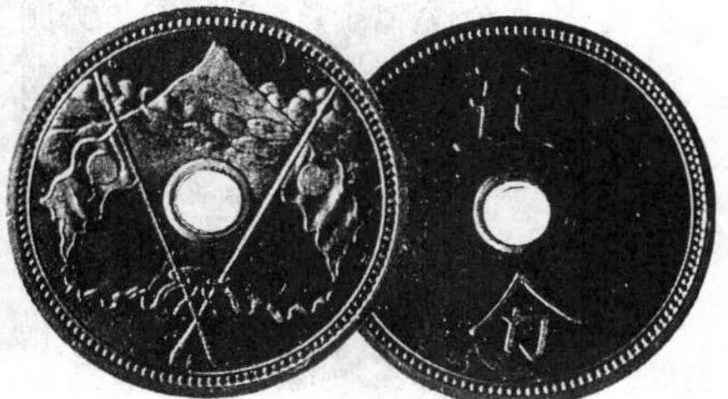

KM#	Date	Mintage	Identification	Mkt.Val.
Pn2	(1869)	—	1 Fun, Copper, crossed flags and Mt. Fuji	1000.

KM#	Date	Mintage	Identification	Mkt.Val.
Pn3	(1869)	—	5 Fun, Copper, crossed flags and Mt. Fuji	1500.

KM#	Date	Mintage	Identification	Mkt.Val.
Pn4	(1869)	—	1 Momme, Copper, crossed flags and Mt. Fuji	2500.

NOTE: Above 3 coins struck by Heaton for a proposed (rejected) coinage.

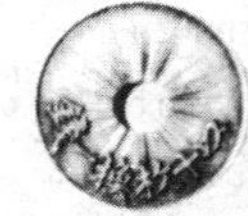

KM#	Date	Mintage	Identification	Mkt.Val.
Pn5	(1869)	—	1 Rin, Yr.2, Copper, holed	—

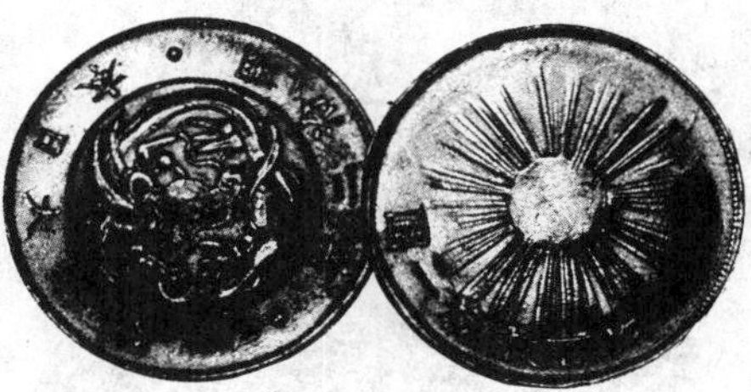

KM#	Date	Mintage	Identification	Mkt.Val.
Pn6	(1869)	—	1 Sen, Yr.2, Copper	2000.

KM#	Date	Mintage	Identification	Mkt.Val.
Pn7	(1870)	—	1 Rin, Yr.3, Copper	5000.

KM#	Date	Mintage	Identification	Mkt.Val.
Pn8	(1870)	—	1/2 Sen, Yr.3, Copper	Rare

KM#	Date	Mintage	Identification	Mkt.Val.
Pn9	(1870)	—	1 Sen, Yr.3, Copper	2750.
Pn10	(1870)	—	1/20 Yen, Yr.2, White Metal	—
Pn11	(1870)	—	1/10 Yen, Yr.3, Copper	Rare
Pn12	(1870)	—	1/10 Yen, Yr.3, White Metal	—
Pn13	(1870)	—	1/4 Yen, Yr.3, Copper	Rare
Pn14	(1870)	—	1/4 Yen, Yr.3, White Metal	—
Pn15	(1870)	—	1/2 Yen, Yr. 3, Copper	Rare

KM#	Date	Mintage	Identification	Mkt.Val.
Pn16	(1870)	—	1 Yen, Yr.3, Silver	—

NOTE: 2 subvarieties exist - 1 designed by Wyon and minted at Heaton and the other a local Japanese copy.

KM#	Date	Mintage	Identification	Mkt.Val.
Pn17	(1870)	—	2-1/2 Yen, Yr.3, Gold	Rare
Pn18	(1870)	—	5 Yen, Yr.3, Gold	—

KM#	Date	Mintage	Identification	Mkt.Val.
Pn19	(1870)	—	10 Yen, Yr.3, Gold, 32mm	Rare
Pn20	(1870)	—	10 Yen, Yr.3, Gold, Y12	—

KM#	Date	Mintage	Identification	Mkt.Val.
Pn21	(1873)	—	1 Mil/Rin, Yr.6, Copper	2750.

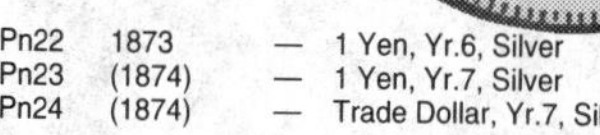

KM#	Date	Mintage	Identification	Mkt.Val.
Pn22	1873	—	1 Yen, Yr.6, Silver	Rare
Pn23	(1874)	—	1 Yen, Yr.7, Silver	—
Pn24	(1874)	—	Trade Dollar, Yr.7, Silver	—

KM#	Date	Mintage	Identification	Mkt.Val.
Pn25	(1874)	—	Trade Dollar, Yr.7, Silver	Rare

KM#	Date	Mintage	Identification	Mkt.Val.
Pn26	(1874)	—	5 Yen, Yr.7, Gold	Rare

KM#	Date	Mintage	Identification	Mkt.Val.
Pn27	(1885)	—	2 Rin, Yr.18, Copper	5000.

KM#	Date	Mintage	Identification	Mkt.Val.
Pn28	(1888)	—	5 Sen, Yr.21, Copper-Nickel	—

KM#	Date	Mintage	Identification	Mkt.Val.
Pn29	(1895)	—	5 Sen, Yr.28, Copper-Nickel	2750.
Pn30	(1899)	—	5 Rin, Yr.32, Copper	2750.

PROVINCIAL COINAGE

AKITA

Capital city of Ugo Province (now Akita Prefecture) in northwest Honshu.

50 MON

LEAD or COPPER-PLATED LEAD

KM#	Date	Mintage	Good	VG	Fine	VF
2	ND(1862)	—	50.00	80.00	120.00	150.00

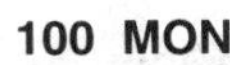

100 MON

COPPER

KM#	Date	Mintage	Good	VG	Fine	VF
4	ND(1862)	—	40.00	60.00	90.00	125.00

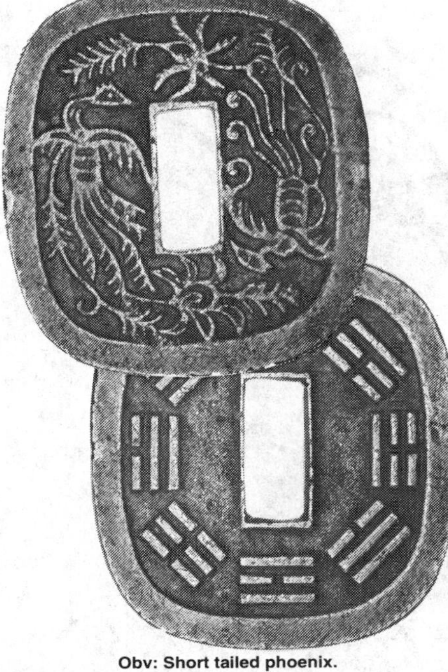

Obv: Short tailed phoenix.

KM#	Date	Mintage	VG	Fine	VF	XF
6.1	ND(1862)	—	50.00	80.00	120.00	150.00

Obv: Long tailed phoenix.

KM#	Date	Mintage	VG	Fine	VF	XF
6.2	ND(1862)	—	50.00	80.00	120.00	150.00

LEAD or COPPER-PLATED LEAD

KM#	Date	Mintage	Good	VG	Fine	VF
8	ND(1866)	—	75.00	125.00	200.00	250.00

BU

SILVER

KM#	Date	Mintage	Good	VG	Fine	VF
9	ND	—	900.00	1200.	1500.	2000.

4 MOMME 6 FUN

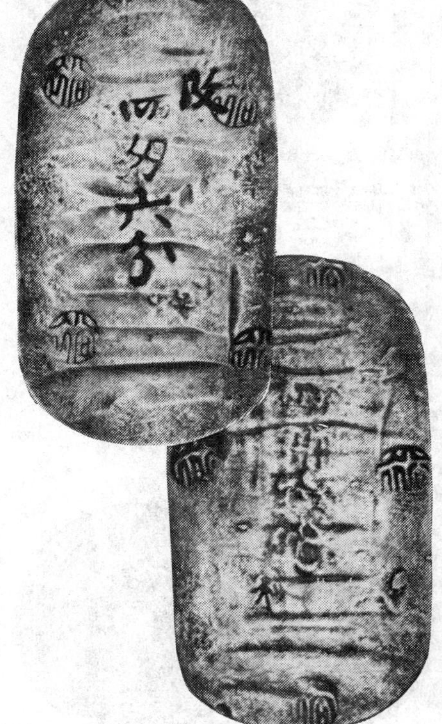

SILVER

KM#	Date	Mintage	VG	Fine	VF	XF
10	ND(1863)	—	125.00	200.00	275.00	350.00

9 MOMME 2 FUN

SILVER

KM#	Date	Mintage	VG	Fine	VF	XF
12	ND(1863)	—	400.00	550.00	650.00	750.00

HAKODATE

City on the southern end of Hokkaido. One of the ports opened by Perry's Treaty of 1854.

MON

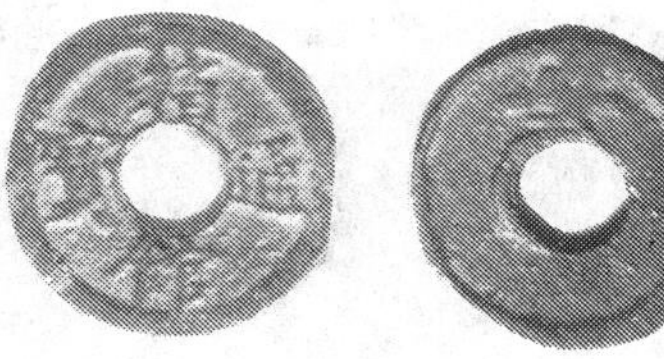

IRON
Obv: 4 characters around round hole.
Rev: 1 character above hole.

KM#	Date	Mintage	Good	VG	Fine	VF
20	ND(1856)	—	3.00	6.00	12.00	25.00
		COPPER				
20a	ND(1856)	—	—	—	100.00	175.00

NOTE: KM#20a is the *bosen* or mother coin used in manufacturing KM#20.

HOSOKURA

A lead mining district in Rikuchu Province (now Iwate Prefecture) in northern Honshu.

100 MON

LEAD

KM#	Date	Mintage	Good	VG	Fine	VF
30	ND(1863)	—	150.00	250.00	400.00	500.00

KAGA

City and province (now Ishikawa Prefecture) on the Asian side of central Honshu.

NAN RYO

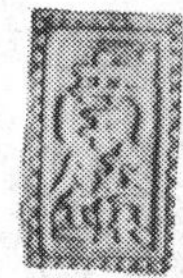

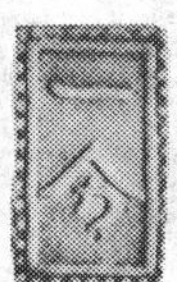

SILVER

KM#	Date	Mintage	VG	Fine	VF	XF
35	ND	—	1250.	1750.	2500.	3500.

KOSHU

A province, (formal name Kai, now Yamanashi Prefecture), located in central Honshu west of Tokyo.

The following listings are representative of a very complex series of gold coinage. Other obscure or odd denominations may exist. This series contains many varieties. The characters usually found stamped on the reverse are hall marks.

KAKU SHU-NAKA KIN
(Rectangular Half Shu Gold)

GOLD, 0.40 g, 6x8mm

KM#	Date	Mintage	VG	Fine	VF	XF
90	ND	—	800.00	1000.	1200.	1500.

SHU-NAKA KIN
(Half Shu Gold)

GOLD, 0.40-0.50 g, 8.5-9.5mm
Similar to Ichi-Bu, KM#94.

KM#	Date	Mintage	VG	Fine	VF	XF
91	ND	—	2000.	3000.	4750.	6500.

ISSHU KIN
(One Shu Gold)

GOLD, 0.90-1.00 g, 11-12mm
Similar to Ichi-Bu, KM#94.

KM#	Date	Mintage	VG	Fine	VF	XF
92	ND	—	300.00	450.00	600.00	800.00

NISSHU KIN
(Two Shu Gold)

GOLD, 1.90 g, 12-13mm
Similar to Ichi-Bu, KM#94.

KM#	Date	Mintage	VG	Fine	VF	XF
93	ND	—	325.00	500.00	750.00	1000.

ICHI-BU KIN
(One Bu Gold)

GOLD, 3.70-4.00 g, 14-17mm

KM#	Date	Mintage	VG	Fine	VF	XF
94	ND	—	300.00	450.00	600.00	800.00

ICHI-BU ISSHU KIN
(One Bu One Shu Gold)

GOLD, 4.80 g, 18mm
Similar to Ichi-bu, KM#94.

KM#	Date	Mintage	VG	Fine	VF	XF
95	ND	—	—	—	Rare	—

ICHI-BU NISSHU KIN
(One Bu Two Shu Gold)

GOLD, 5.00 g, 16mm
Similar to Ichi-Bu, KM#94.

KM#	Date	Mintage	VG	Fine	VF	XF
96	ND	—	—	—	Rare	—

NI-BU KIN
(Two Bu Gold)

GOLD, 7.00-7.50 g, 18-19mm
Similar to Ichi-Bu, KM#94.

KM#	Date	Mintage	VG	Fine	VF	XF
97	ND	—	—	—	Rare	—

NI-BU ISSHU KIN
(Two Bu One Shu Gold)

GOLD, 8.80 g, 24mm
Similar to Ichi-Bu, KM#94.

KM#	Date	Mintage	VG	Fine	VF	XF
98	ND	—	—	—	Rare	—

RYO KIN
(One Ryo Gold)

GOLD, 14.70-15.30 g, 16-19mm
Rounded "nugget" shape w/stamps, similar to Ichi-Bu, KM#94.

KM#	Date	Mintage	VG	Fine	VF	XF
99	ND	—	—	—	Rare	—

MIMASAKA

Province in western Honshu, now part of Okayama Prefecture.

BU

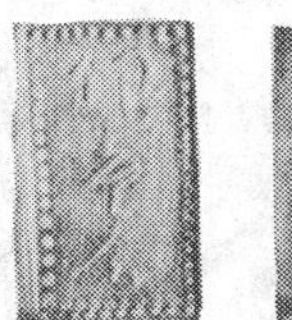

SILVER

KM#	Date	Mintage	VG	Fine	VF	XF
46	ND	—	900.00	1200.	2000.	2750.

MORIOKA

Chief city of Rikuchu Province (now Iwate Prefecture) in northern Honshu.

100 MON

COPPER

KM#	Date	Mintage	Good	VG	Fine	VF
50	ND	—	800.00	1600.	2400.	3250.

8 MOMME

SILVER

KM#	Date	Mintage	VG	Fine	VF	XF
52	(1868)	—	1000.	1500.	2000.	2500.

TAJIMA

Province, now part of Hyogo Prefecture, on the Asian side of western Honshu.

NAN RYO

SILVER

KM#	Date	Mintage	VG	Fine	VF	XF
65	ND	—	800.00	1000.	1500.	2000.

TOSA

Province encompassing most of the southern coast of Shikoku, now Kochi Prefecture.

100 MON

COPPER

KM#	Date	Mintage	VG	Fine	VF	XF
70	ND(1865)	—	—	—	Rare	—

200 MON

COPPER

KM#	Date	Mintage	VG	Fine	VF	XF
72	ND(1865)	—	—	—	Rare	—

NOTE: A total of 8 types are reported for Tosa Province.

YONEZAWA

City in Uzen Province (now in Yamagata Prefecture) in north-central Honshu.

200 MON

LEAD

KM#	Date	Mintage	Good	VG	Fine	VF
80	ND(1866)	—	80.00	125.00	200.00	300.00

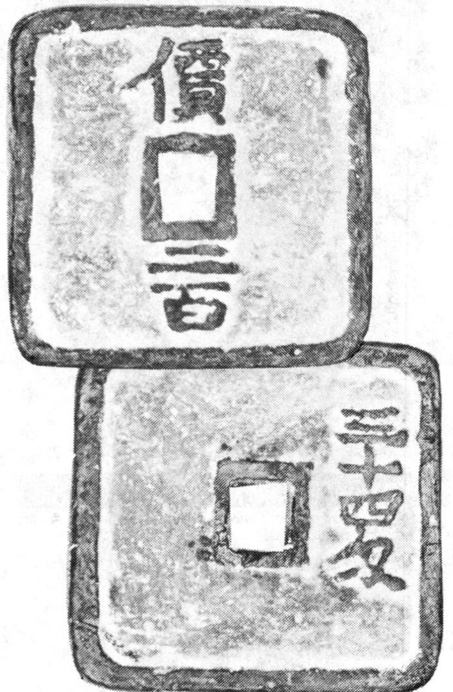

KM#	Date	Mintage	Good	VG	Fine	VF
82	ND(1866)	—	150.00	250.00	325.00	400.00

RYUKYU ISLANDS

OKINAWA

(Also called Liu-kiu and Loo-choo)

100 MON

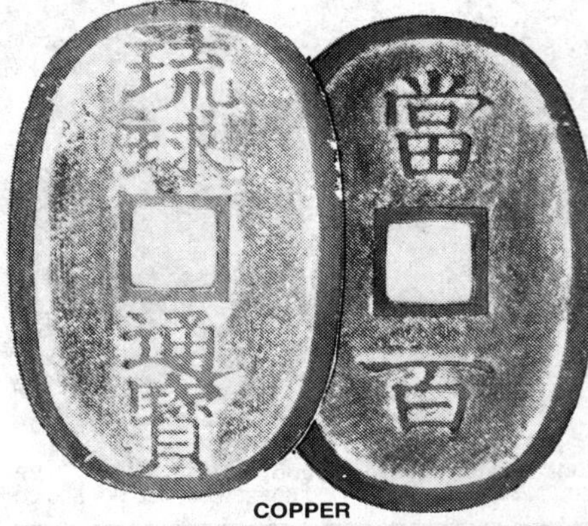

COPPER

C#	Date	Mintage	VG	Fine	VF	XF
100	ND(1862)	—	17.50	30.00	45.00	65.00

1/2 SHU

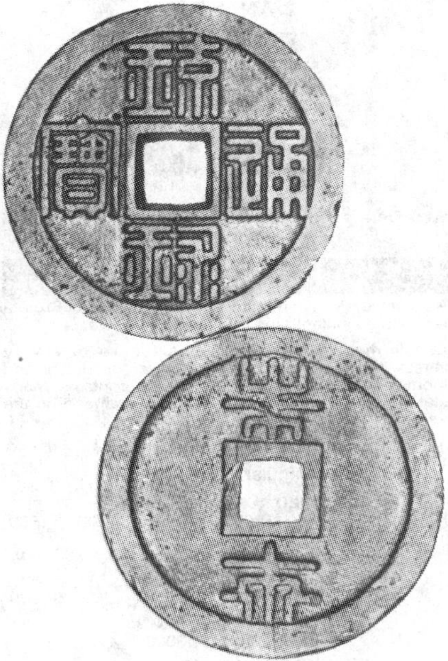

COPPER

C#	Date	Mintage	VG	Fine	VF	XF
115	ND(1862)	—	30.00	45.00	60.00	100.00

JERSEY

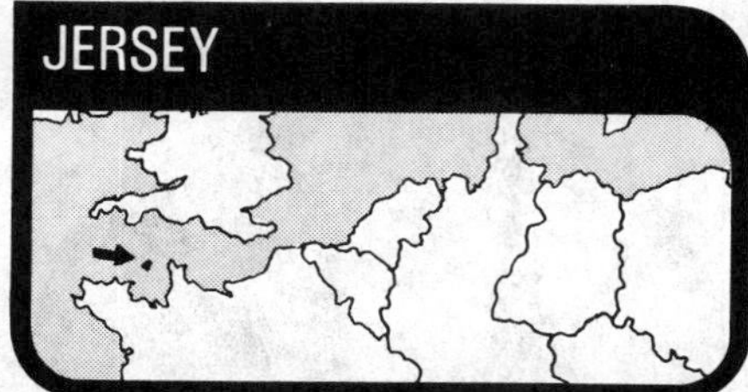

The Bailiwick of Jersey, a British Crown dependency located in the English Channel 12 miles (19 km.) west of Normandy, France, has an area of 45 sq. mi. (117 sq. km.) and a population of 74,000. Capital: St. Helier. The economy is based on agriculture and cattle breeding - the importation of cattle is prohibited to protect the purity of the island's world-famous strain of milch cows.

Jersey was occupied by Neanderthal man 100,000 B.C., and by Iberians of 2000 B.C. who left their chamber tombs in the island's granite cliffs. Roman legions almost certainly visited the island although they left no evidence of settlement. The country folk of Jersey still speak an archaic form of Norman-French, lingering evidence of the Norman annexation of the island in 933 A.D. Jersey was annexed to England in 1206, 140 years after the Norman Conquest. The dependency is administered by its own laws and customs; laws enacted by the British Parliament do not apply to Jersey unless it is specifically mentioned. During World War II, German troops occupied the island from July 1, 1940 until May 9, 1945.

Coins of pre-Roman Gaul and of Rome have been found in abundance on Jersey.

RULERS

British

MINT MARKS

H - Heaton, Birmingham

MONETARY SYSTEM

Until 1877

13 Pence (Jersey) = 1 Shilling

Commencing 1877

12 Pence = 1 Shilling

5 Shillings = 1 Crown

20 Shillings = 1 Pound

1/52 SHILLING

COPPER

KM#	Date	Mintage	Fine	VF	XF	Unc
1	1841/0	.116	10.00	30.00	80.00	160.00
	1841	—	—	—	Proof	500.00
	1861	—	—	—	Proof	650.00

BRONZE

KM#	Date	Mintage	Fine	VF	XF	Unc
1a	1861	—	—	—	Proof	Rare

1/48 SHILLING

BRONZE

KM#	Date	Mintage	Fine	VF	XF	Unc
6	1877H	*.288	10.00	20.00	55.00	120.00
	1877H	—	—	—	Proof	200.00
	1877	—	—	—	Proof	225.00

***NOTE:** Issue withdrawn except for 38,400 pieces.

1/26 SHILLING

COPPER

KM#	Date	Mintage	Fine	VF	XF	Unc
2	1841	.233	2.50	12.00	40.00	100.00
	1841	—	—	—	Proof	650.00
	1844	.233	3.00	12.00	40.00	100.00
	1851	.160	3.00	12.00	40.00	100.00
	1858	.173	3.00	12.00	40.00	100.00

KM#	Date	Mintage	Fine	VF	XF	Unc
2	1858	—	—	—	Proof	650.00
	1861	.173	3.00	12.00	40.00	100.00
	1861	—	—	—	Proof	650.00

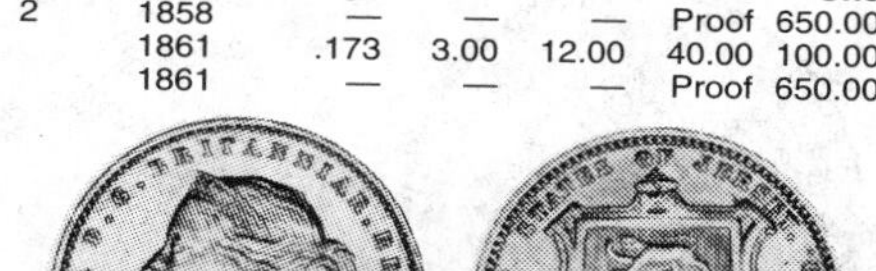

BRONZE

KM#	Date	Mintage	Fine	VF	XF	Unc
4	1866	.173	1.00	6.00	30.00	50.00
	1866	—	—	—	Proof	225.00
	1870	.160	3.00	12.00	40.00	60.00
	1870	—	—	—	Proof	350.00
	1871	.160	2.00	10.00	35.00	55.00
	1871	—	—	—	Proof	350.00

1/24 SHILLING

BRONZE

KM#	Date	Mintage	Fine	VF	XF	Unc
7	1877H	.336	1.25	4.00	12.00	30.00
	1877H	—	—	—	Proof	200.00
	1877	—	—	—	Proof	250.00
	1888	.120	1.25	4.00	12.00	30.00
	1894	.120	1.25	4.00	12.00	30.00
	1894	—	—	—	Proof	400.00

1/12 SHILLING

COPPER

KM#	Date	Mintage	Fine	VF	XF	Unc
3	1841	.116	1.00	13.50	50.00	175.00
	1841	—	—	—	Proof	800.00
	1844	.027	3.00	20.00	65.00	225.00
	1844	—	—	—	Proof	800.00
	1851	.160	1.50	13.50	50.00	160.00
	1851	—	—	—	Proof	800.00
	1858	.173	1.50	13.50	50.00	180.00
	1858	—	—	—	Proof	600.00
	1861	.173	1.50	13.50	50.00	160.00
	1861	—	—	—	Proof	600.00
	1865	—	—	—	Proof	350.00

BRONZE

KM#	Date	Mintage	Fine	VF	XF	Unc
5	1866	.173	1.00	6.50	35.00	100.00
	1866	—	—	—	Proof	225.00
	1866 w/o LCW on bust					
		—	—	—	Proof	250.00
	1870	.160	1.00	6.50	35.00	100.00
	1870	—	—	—	Proof	225.00
	1871	.160	1.00	6.50	35.00	100.00
	1871	—	—	—	Proof	325.00

1/12 SHILLING

BRONZE

KM#	Date	Mintage	Fine	VF	XF	Unc
8	1877H	.240	.50	2.00	15.00	50.00
	1877H	—	—	—	Proof	250.00
	1877	—	—	—	Proof	300.00
	1881	.075	1.00	7.00	30.00	70.00
	1888	.180	.50	2.00	15.00	50.00
	1894	.180	.50	2.00	15.00	50.00
	1894	—	—	—	Proof	400.00

TOKEN ISSUES (Tn)

1/2 PENNY

COPPER

Obv: JERSEY, GUERNSEY & ALDERNEY, value.
Rev: TO FACILITATE TRADE, date, 3 plumes

KM#	Date	Mintage	VG	Fine	VF	XF
Tn2	1813	—	30.00	50.00	100.00	350.00

PENNY

COPPER

Obv: JERSEY BANK TOKEN, bust of George III
Rev: ELIAS NEEL JERSEY, A BANK OF ENGLAND. . .

KM#	Date	Mintage	VG	Fine	VF	XF
Tn1	1812	—	—	—	Rare	—

Obv: JERSEY BANK, bust of George III
Rev: Seated female, value.

KM#	Date	Mintage	VG	Fine	VF	XF
Tn3	1813	—	250.00	450.00	600.00	1000.

KM#	Date	Mintage	VG	Fine	VF	XF
Tn4	1813	—	25.00	55.00	150.00	300.00

18 PENCE

.891 SILVER

KM#	Date	Mintage	Fine	VF	XF	Unc
Tn5	1813	*.091	50.00	80.00	200.00	350.00
	1813	—	—	—	Proof	500.00

3 SHILLINGS

.891 SILVER

Obv: Arms. Rev: Value within wreath.

KM#	Date	Mintage	Fine	VF	XF	Unc
Tn6	1813	*.045	80.00	120.00	350.00	650.00
	1813	—	—	—	Proof	950.00

COPPER

KM#	Date	Mintage	Fine	VF	XF	Unc
Tn6a	1813	—	—	—	Proof	Rare

PATTERNS (Pn)

(Including off metal strikes)

KM#	Date	Mintage	Identification	Mkt.Val.
Pn1	1866	—	1/26 Shilling, KM4	2500.
Pn2	1877 H	—	1/12 Shilling, Nickel, KM8	—
Pn3	1877	—	1/12 Shilling, Nickel, KM8	800.00
Pn4	1877	—	1/12 Shilling, Aluminum, KM8	—

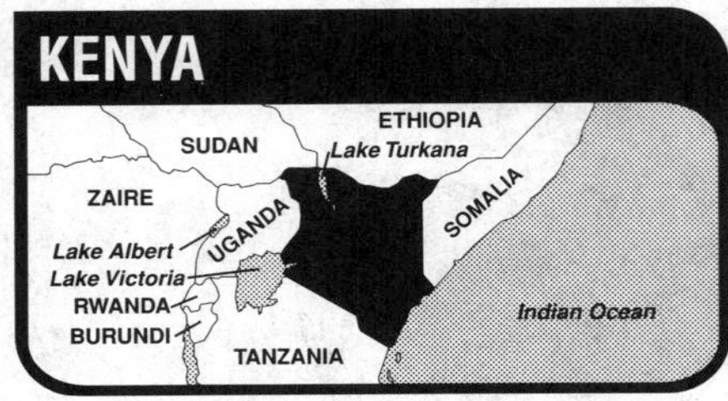

The Republic of Kenya, located on the east coast of Central Africa, has an area of 224,961 sq. mi (582,650 sq. km.) and a population of 20.1 million. Capital: Nairobi. The predominantly agricultural country exports coffee, tea and petroleum products.

The Arabs came to the coast of Kenya in the 8th century and established posts to conduct an ivory and slave trade. The Portuguese, the inveterate wanderers of the Age of Exploration, followed in the 16th century. After a lengthy and bitter struggle with the sultans of Zanzibar who controlled much of the southeastern coast of Africa, the Portuguese were driven away (late 17th century) and for many years Kenya was simply a port of call on the route to India. German and British interests in the 19th century produced agreements defining their respective spheres of influence. The British sphere was administrated by the Imperial East Africa Co. until 1895, when the British government purchased the company's rights in the East Africa Protectorate which, in 1920, was designated as Kenya Colony and protectorate - the latter being a 10-mile wide coastal strip together with Mombasa, Lamu and other small islands nominally retained by the Sultan of Zanzibar. Kenya achieved self-government in June of 1963 as a consequence of the 1952-60 Mau Mau terrorist campaign to secure land reforms and political rights for Africans. Independence was attained on Dec. 12, 1963. Kenya became a republic in 1964. It is a member of the Commonwealth of Nations. The president is Chief of State and Head of Government.

Mombasa was a thriving Arabic commercial center when first visited by Portuguese navigator Vasco da Gama in 1498. During the following two centuries Portugal made repeated efforts to capture the island stronghold but was unable to hold it against the assaults of the Muscat Arabs. In 1823 the ruling Mazuri family placed the city under British protection. Britain repudiated the protectorate and it was then seized by Seyyid Said of Oman, 1837, and annexed to Zanzibar. In 1887 the sultan of Zanzibar relinquished the port of Mombasa to British administration. It was occupied by the Imperial British East Africa Company and for the following two decades was the capital of British East Africa.

RULERS

British, until 1964

MOMBASA

TITLES

Mombasa ممباسه

MINT MARKS

H - Birmingham
C/M - Calcutta

MONETARY SYSTEM

4 Pice = 1 Anna
16 Annas = 1 Rupee

BRITISH EAST AFRICA COMPANY

PICE

BRONZE, 24.9mm
Obv. and rev: Small letters.

KM#	Date	Mintage	Fine	VF	XF	Unc
1.1	1888/AH1306C/M	.630	.75	2.50	8.00	25.00
	1888/AH1306C/M	—	—	—	Proof	150.00

NOTE: Varieties in planchet thickness exist.

25.4mm
Obv: Small letters. Rev: Medium letters.

KM#	Date	Mintage	Fine	VF	XF	Unc
1.2	1888/AH1306C/M	Inc. Ab.	.50	2.00	7.00	20.00
	1888/AH1306C/M	—	—	—	Proof	200.00

Obv. and rev: Medium letters.

KM#	Date	Mintage	Fine	VF	XF	Unc
1.5	1888/AH1306C/M	Inc. Ab.	.50	2.00	7.00	20.00

Obv. and rev: Medium letters.

KM#	Date	Mintage	Fine	VF	XF	Unc
1.3	1888/AH1306H	2.352	.35	1.25	5.00	15.00
	1888/AH1306H	—	—	—	Proof	125.00

Obv. and rev: Large letters w/o serifs, dots between words.

KM#	Date	Mintage	Fine	VF	XF	Unc
1.4	1888/AH1306H	Inc. Ab.	.25	1.00	4.00	12.50
	1888/AH1306H	—	—	—	Proof	100.00

2 ANNAS

1.4600 g, .917 SILVER, .0430 oz ASW

KM#	Date	Mintage	Fine	VF	XF	Unc
2	1890H	.016	12.00	20.00	35.00	60.00
	1890H	—	—	—	Proof	100.00

1/4 RUPEE

(4 Annas)

2.9200 g, .917 SILVER, .0860 oz ASW

KM#	Date	Mintage	Fine	VF	XF	Unc
3	1890H	.012	15.00	25.00	45.00	90.00
	1890H	—	—	—	Proof	125.00

1/2 RUPEE

(8 Annas)

5.8300 g, .917 SILVER, .1719 oz ASW

KM#	Date	Mintage	Fine	VF	XF	Unc
4	1890H	.010	20.00	40.00	70.00	125.00
	1890H	—	—	—	Proof	165.00

RUPEE

11.6600 g, .917 SILVER, .3438 oz ASW

KM#	Date	Mintage	Fine	VF	XF	Unc
5	1888H	.094	10.00	25.00	50.00	120.00
	1888H	—	—	—	Proof	225.00

PATTERNS (Pn)

(Including off metal strikes)

KM#	Date	Mintage	Identification	Mkt.Val.
Pn1	1888/AH1306H	—	1 Pice, Silver, KM1.4	300.00
Pn2	1888/AH1306H	—	1 Pice, Gold, KM1.4	Rare

PROOF SETS (PS)

KM#	Date	Mintage	Identification	Issue Price	Mkt. Val.
PS1	1888H(2)	—	KM1.4,5	—	325.00
PS2	1890H(3)	—	KM2-4	—	350.00

KOREA

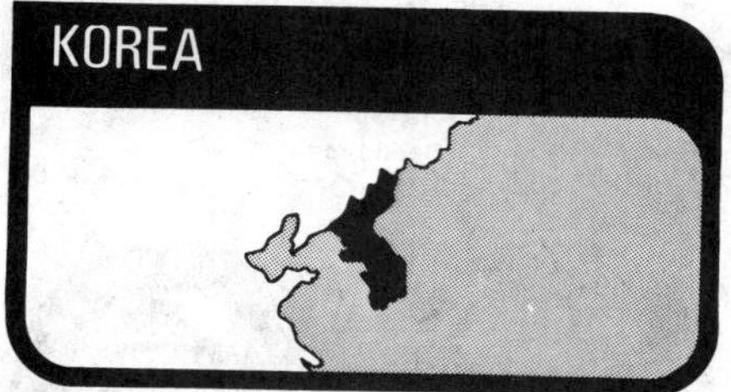

Korea, 'Land of the Morning Calm', occupies a mountainous peninsula in northeast Asia bounded by Manchuria, the Yellow Sea and the Sea of Japan.

According to legend, the first Korean dynasty, that of the House of Tangun, ruled from 2333 B.C. to 1122 B.C. It was followed by the dynasty of Kija, a Chinese scholar, which continued until 193 B.C. and brought a high civilization to Korea. The first recorded period in the history of Korea, the period of the Three Kingdoms, lasted from 57 B.C. to 935 A.D. and achieved the first political unification of the peninsula. The Kingdom of Koryo, from which Korea derived its name, was founded in 935 and continued until 1392, when it was superseded by the Yi Dynasty of King Yi. Sung Kye was to last until the Japanese annexation in 1910.

At the end of the 16th century Korea was invaded and occupied for 7 years by Japan, and from 1627 until the late 19th century it was a semi-independent tributary of China. Japan replaced China as the predominant foreign influence at the end of the Sino-Japanese War (1894-95), only to find her position threatened by Russian influence from 1896 to 1904. The Russian threat was eliminated by the Russo-Japanese War (1904-05) and in 1905 Japan established a direct protectorate over Korea. On Aug. 22, 1910, the last Korean ruler signed the treaty that annexed Korea to Japan as a government generalcy in the Japanese Empire. Japanese suzerainty was maintained until the end of World War II.

From 1633 to 1891 the monetary system of Korea employed cast coins with a square center hole. Fifty-two agencies were authorized to procure these coins from a lesser number of coin foundries. They exist in thousands of varieties. Seed, or mother coins, were used to make the impressions in the molds in which the regular cash coins were cast. Czarist-Russian Korea experimented with Korean coins when Alexiev of Russia, Korea's Financial Advisor, founded the First Asian Branch of the Russo-Korean Bank on March 1, 1898, and authorized the issuing of a set of new Korean coins with a crowned Russian-style quasi-eagle. British-Japanese opposition and the Russo-Japanese War operated to end the Russian coinage experiment in 1904.

RULERS

Yi Kwang (Sunjo Songhyo), 1801-1835
Yi Whan (Honjong Cholhyo), 1835-1850
Yi Chung (Choljong Yonghyo), 1850-1864
Yi Hyong (Kojong), 1864-1897
as Emperor Kwang Mu, 1897-1907

MONETARY UNITS

文	Mun	兩	Yang, Niang
分	Fun	圜	Hwan, Warn
錢	Chon	圓	Won Whan, Hwan

IDENTIFICATION CHART

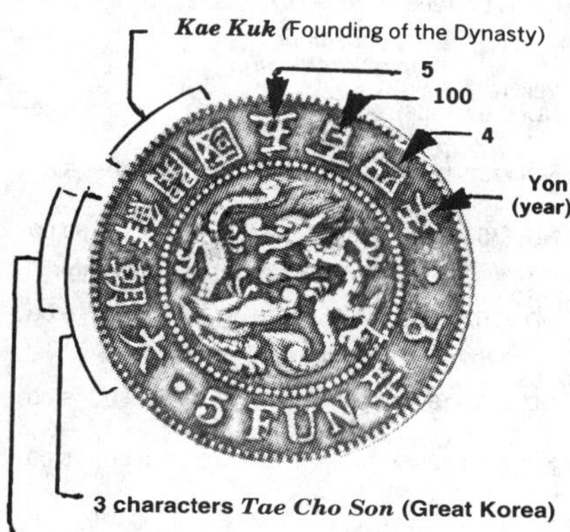

Obverse

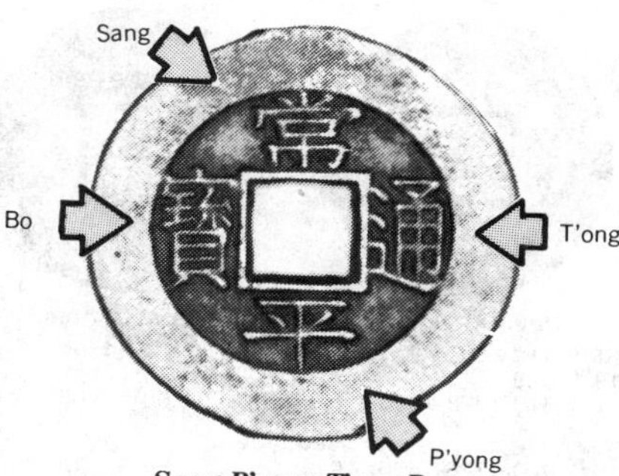

Sang P'yong T'ong Bo
"Always even currency"

Reverse

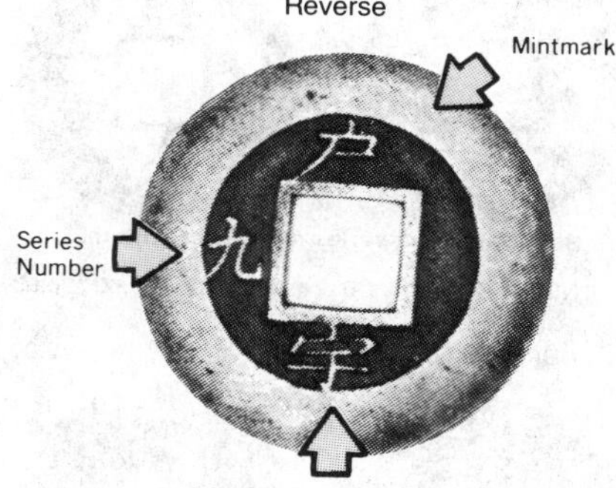

NOTE: The series number may be to the left, right or bottom of the center hole. The furnace designator may be either a numeral or a character from the THOUSAND CHARACTER CLASSIC.

SEED COINS

Seed coins are specially prepared examples, perfectly round, with sharp characters, used in the preparation of clay or sand molds.

Kyun 均
Government Tithe Office

Son 宣
Rice & Cloth Department

Chon 典
Central Government Mint

Mu 武
Palace Guard Office

Kum 禁
Court Guard Military Unit

Hun 訓 or 訓
Military Training Command

T'ong 統 or 統
T'ongyong Naval Office
Military Office in Seoul

Kyong 经
Government Office of
Pukhan Mountain Fortress

Sim 沁
Kanghwa Township Military Office

Kae 開
Kaesong Township Military Office

Song 松
Kaesong Township Military Office

I 利
Iwon Township Military Office

Ch'un 春 or 春
Ch'unch'on Township Military Office

Ch'on 川
Tanch'on Township Military Office

Ch'ang 昌
Ch'angdok Palace Mint
Ch'angwon Township Military Office

Ki 圻
Kwangju Township Military Office
in Kyonggi Province

Kyong 京
Kyonggi Provincial Office

Kyong Su 京水
Kyonggi Naval Station

P'yong 平
P'yongan Provincial Office

Ham 咸
Hamgyong Provincial Office

TREASURY DEPARTMENT

戸 or 户 or 戶 Ho (Ho Jo)

MUN

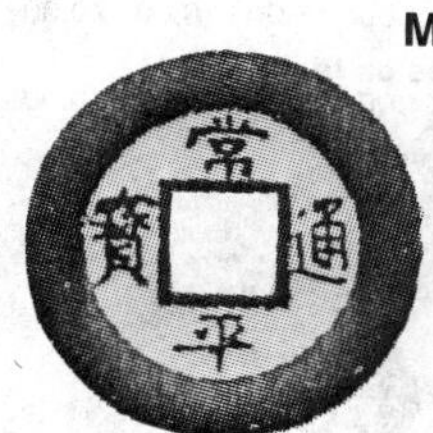
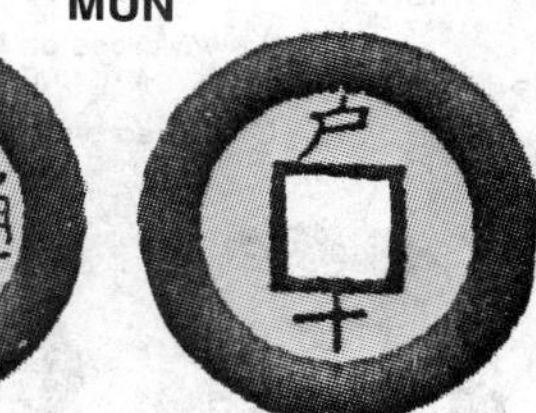

CAST COPPER or BRONZE, 26mm
Rev: *Ho* at top in different style, series number at bottom.

KM#	Date	Series	Good	VG	Fine	VF
9.1-9.10	ND(1806)	1-10	1.50	1.75	2.25	3.00
	Rev: *Ho* w/cross at top.					
9.15	ND(1806)	5	1.50	1.75	2.25	3.00
	Seed type					
9s	ND(1806)	1-10	—	—	*XF*	30.00

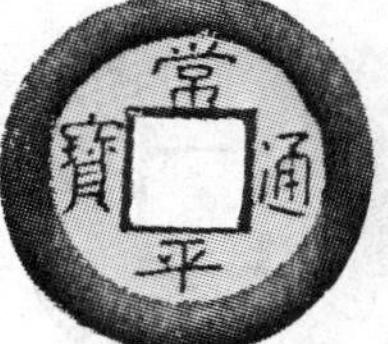
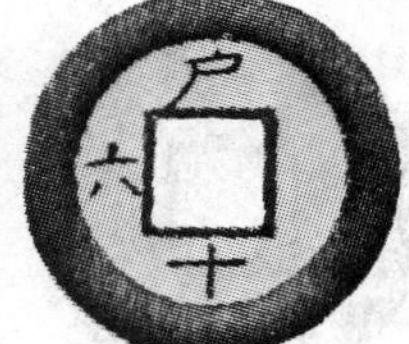

25mm
Rev: *Sip* (10) at bottom, additional series number at left.

KM#	Date	Series	Good	VG	Fine	VF
10.11-10.16	ND(1806)	11-16	1.50	1.75	2.25	3.00
	Seed type					
10s	ND(1806)	11-16	—	—	*XF*	30.00

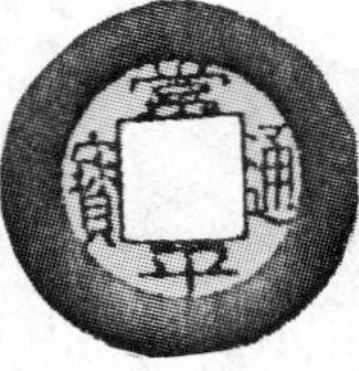
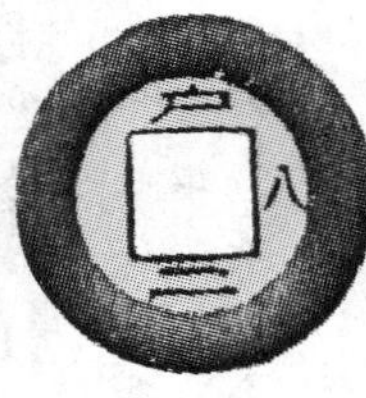

24mm
Rev: *I* (2) at bottom, series number at right.

KM#	Date	Series	Good	VG	Fine	VF
13.1-13.10	ND(1857)	1-10	2.50	3.50	5.00	10.00
	Seed type					
13s	ND(1857)	1-10	—	—	*XF*	30.00

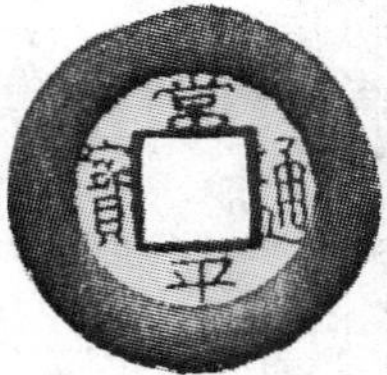

Rev: *I* (2) at bottom, series number at left.

KM#	Date	Series	Good	VG	Fine	VF
14.1-14.10	ND(1857)	1-10	3.00	4.50	7.50	15.00
	Seed type					
14s	ND(1857)	1-10	—	—	*XF*	35.00

25mm
Rev: *Sam* (3) at bottom, series number at right.

KM#	Date	Series	Good	VG	Fine	VF
15.1-15.10	ND(1832)	1-10	4.00	7.00	10.00	20.00
	Rev: *Ho* w/o cross on top.					
15.11	ND(1832)	1	4.00	7.00	10.00	20.00
	Rev: Dot in lower right field.					
15.14	ND(1832)	4	4.00	7.00	10.00	20.00
	Seed type					
15s	ND(1832)	1-10	—	—	*XF*	45.00

24mm
Rev: *Sam* (3) at bottom, series number at left.

KM#	Date	Series	Good	VG	Fine	VF
16.1-16.10	ND(1832)	1-10	4.00	7.00	10.00	20.00
	***Ho* w/o cross on top.**					
16.14	ND(1832)	4	4.00	7.00	10.00	20.00
	Seed type					
16s	ND(1832)	1-10	—	—	*XF*	45.00

23mm
Rev: *Ho* in different style, *Sam* (3) at bottom, series number at left.

KM#	Date	Series	Good	VG	Fine	VF
17.1-17.10	ND(1857)	1-10	3.50	6.00	9.00	17.50
	Seed type					
17s	ND(1857)	1-10	—	—	*XF*	40.00

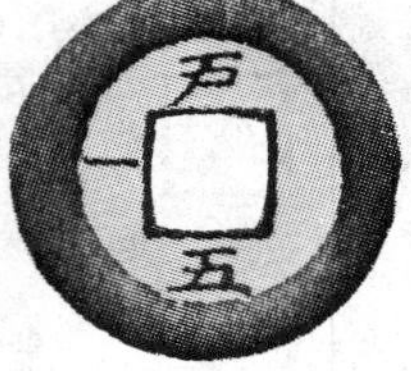

25mm
Rev: *O* (5) at bottom, series number at left.

KM#	Date	Series	Good	VG	Fine	VF
18.1	ND(1832)	1	1.50	2.50	3.50	5.00
	Seed type					
18s	ND(1832)	1	—	—	*XF*	30.00

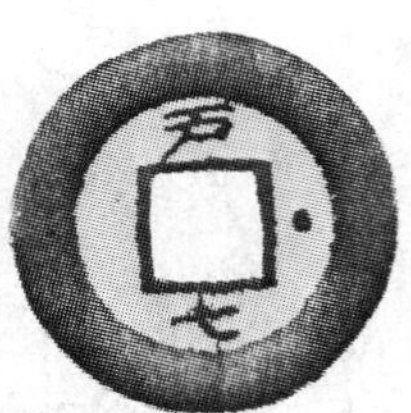

Rev: Dot at right, series number at bottom.

KM#	Date	Series	Good	VG	Fine	VF
19.1-19.9	ND(1778-1806)	1-9	2.50	3.50	5.00	7.00
	Seed type					
19s	ND(1778-1806)	4-9	—	—	*XF*	30.00

Rev: Dot at left, series number at bottom.

KM#	Date	Series	Good	VG	Fine	VF
20.1-20.6	ND(1778-1806)	1-6	4.00	7.00	10.00	20.00
	Seed type					
20s	ND(1778-1806)	5,6	—	—	*XF*	40.00

24mm
Rev: Circle at right, series number at bottom.

KM#	Date	Series	Good	VG	Fine	VF
21.1-21.10	ND(1757-1806)	1-10	1.75	2.50	3.50	5.00
	23-25mm **Obv: 2 dot *Tong*, and *P'yong* w/hooks.**					
21a.1-21a.10	ND(1757-1806)	1-10	1.75	2.50	3.50	5.00
	Seed type					
21s	ND(1757-1806)	1-10	—	—	*XF*	30.00

23mm
Rev: Circle at left, series number at bottom.

KM#	Date	Series	Good	VG	Fine	VF
22.1-22.10	ND(1757-1806)	1-10	1.75	2.50	3.50	5.00
	Obv: 2 dot *Tong* and *P'yong* w/hooks.					
22a.1-22a.10	ND(1757-1806)	1-10	1.75	2.50	3.50	5.00
	Seed type					
22s	ND(1757-1806)	1-10	—	—	*XF*	30.00

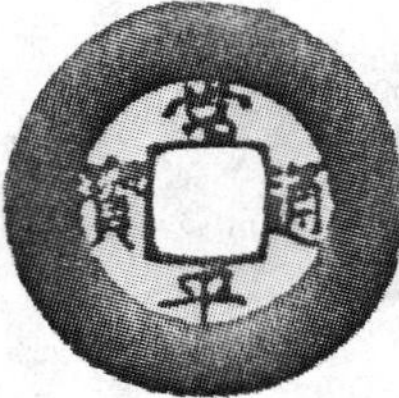

27mm
Rev: Circle at right, *Il* (1) at left, series number at bottom.

KM#	Date	Series	Good	VG	Fine	VF
23.1-23.4	ND(1814)	1-4	2.25	3.00	5.00	7.00
	Seed type					
23s	ND(1814)	1-4	—	—	*XF*	30.00

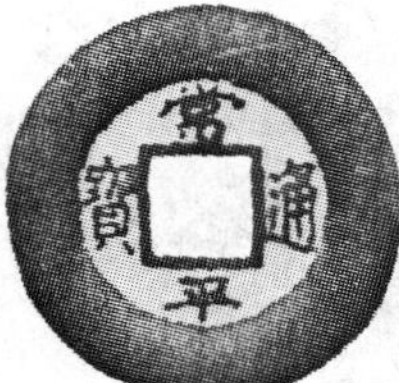

26mm
Rev: Circle at left, *Il* (1) at right, series number at bottom.

KM#	Date	Series	Good	VG	Fine	VF
24.1-24.10	ND(1840)	1-10	2.25	3.00	5.00	7.00
	Seed type					
24s	ND(1814)	1-10	—	—	*XF*	30.00

Rev: Circle at right, *I* (2)

at left, series number at bottom.

KM#	Date	Series	Good	VG	Fine	VF
25.1-25.10	ND(1814)	1-10	2.25	3.00	5.00	7.00
	Seed type					
25s	ND(1814)	1-10	—	—	*XF*	30.00

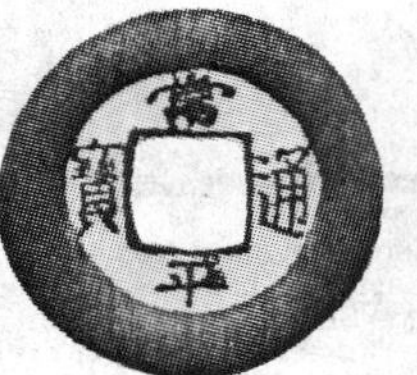
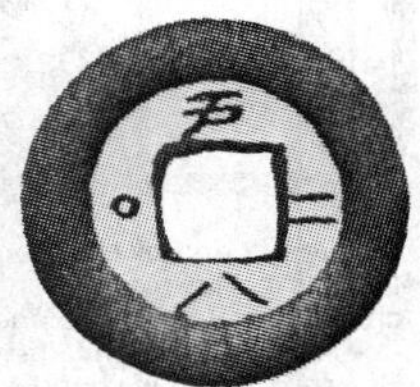

25mm
Rev: Circle at left, *I* (2) at right, series number at bottom.

KM#	Date	Series	Good	VG	Fine	VF
26.1-26.10	ND(1814)	1-10	2.25	3.50	5.00	7.00
	Seed type					
26s	ND(1814)	1-10	—	—	*XF*	30.00

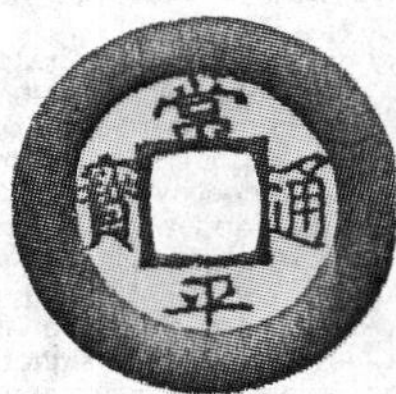

Rev: Dot at right, circle at left, series number at bottom.

KM#	Date	Series	Good	VG	Fine	VF
27.1-27.10	ND(1778-1806)	1-10	1.75	2.50	3.50	5.00
	Seed type					
27s	ND(1778-1806)	1-10	—	—	*XF*	30.00

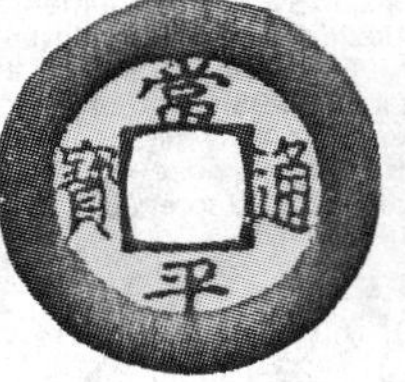
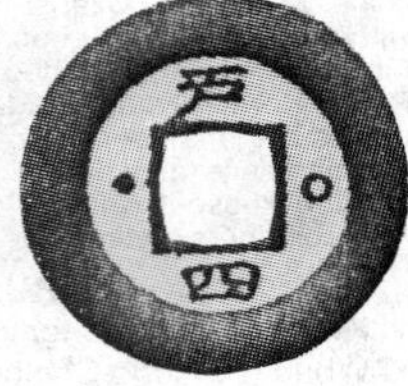

Rev: Circle at right, dot at left, series number at bottom.

KM#	Date	Series	Good	VG	Fine	VF
28.1-28.5	ND(1778-1806)	1-5	1.75	2.50	3.50	5.00
	Seed type					
28s	ND(1778-1806)	1-4	—	—	*XF*	30.00

24mm
Rev: Crescent at right, series number at bottom.

KM#	Date	Series	Good	VG	Fine	VF
29.1-29.10	ND(1757-1806)	1-10	1.75	2.25	3.50	5.00
	23-24mm **Obv: W/o *P'yong*.**					
29a.1-29a.10	ND(1757-1806)	1-10	1.75	2.50	3.50	5.00
	Rev: Star in crescent.					
29b.6	ND(1757-1806)	6	1.75	2.50	3.50	5.00
	Seed type					
29s	ND(1757-1806)	1-10	—	—	*XF*	30.00

Rev: Crescent at left, series number at bottom.

KM#	Date	Series	Good	VG	Fine	VF
30.1-30.10	ND(1757-1806)	1-10	1.75	2.50	3.50	5.00
	Obv: W/o *P'yong*, *tong* w/1 dot.					
30a.1-30a.10	ND(1757-1806)	1-10	1.75	2.50	3.50	5.00
	Obv: Star at lower left.					
30b.7	ND(1757-1806)	7	1.75	2.50	3.50	5.00
	25mm					
30c.1-30c.10	ND(1757-1806)	1-10	1.75	2.50	3.50	5.00
	Seed type					
30s	ND(1757-1806)	1-10	—	—	*XF*	25.00

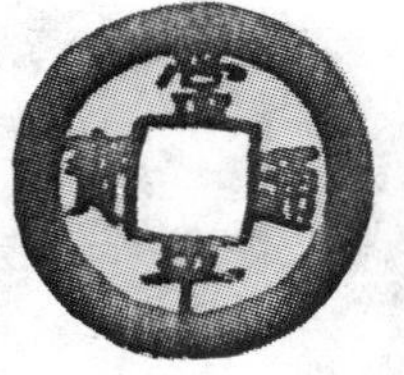

Rev: Vertical line at right, crescent at left, number 9 at bottom.

KM#	Date	Series	Good	VG	Fine	VF
31.9	ND(1778-1806)	9	1.75	2.50	3.50	5.00
	Seed type					
31s	ND(1778-1806)	1-10	—	—	*XF*	30.00

25mm
Rev: Dot at right, crescent at left, series number at bottom.

KM#	Date	Series	Good	VG	Fine	VF
32.1-32.10	ND(1778-1806)	1-10	1.75	2.50	3.50	5.00

Rev: Star in crescent.

KM#	Date	Series	Good	VG	Fine	VF
32.13	ND(1778-1806)	3	1.75	2.50	3.50	5.00
	Seed type					
32s	ND(1778-1806)	1-10	—	—	*XF*	30.00

26mm
Rev: Crescent at right, dot at left, series number at bottom.

KM#	Date	Series	Good	VG	Fine	VF
33.1-33.10	ND(1778-1806)	1-10	1.75	2.50	3.50	5.00
	Seed type					
33s	ND(1778-1806)	1-10	—	—	*XF*	30.00

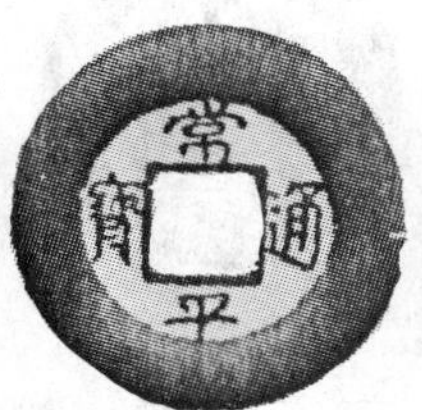

Rev: Crescent at right, *Il* (1) at left, series number at bottom.

KM#	Date	Series	Good	VG	Fine	VF
34.1-34.10	ND(1814)	1-10	2.25	3.00	5.00	7.00
	Seed type					
34s	ND(1814)	1-10	—	—	*XF*	30.00

Rev: *Il* (1) at right, crescent at left, series number at bottom.

KM#	Date	Series	Good	VG	Fine	VF
35.1-35.10	ND(1814)	1-10	2.25	3.00	5.00	7.00
	Seed type					
35s	ND(1814)	1-10	—	—	*XF*	30.00

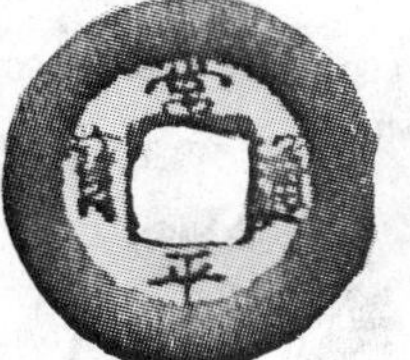
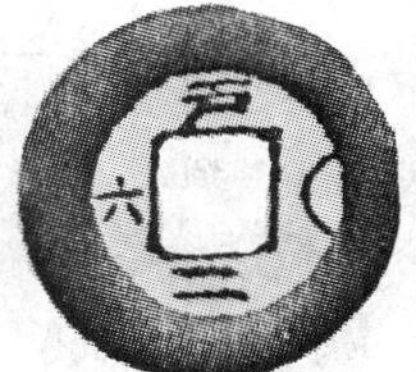

25mm
Rev: Crescent at right, *Yuk* (6) at left, series number at bottom.

KM#	Date	Series	Good	VG	Fine	VF
36.1-36.6	ND(1857)	1-10	4.00	7.00	10.00	20.00
	Seed type					
36s	ND(1857)	1-10	—	—	*XF*	45.00

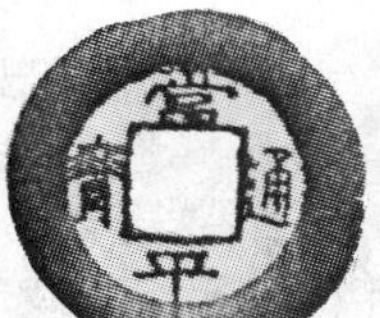

24mm
Small characters.
Rev: *Ch'on* at bottom, series number at right.

KM#	Date	Series	Good	VG	Fine	VF
37.1-37.11	ND(1832)	1-11	1.50	2.25	3.50	5.00
	Seed type					
37s	ND(1832)	1-11	—	—	*XF*	30.00

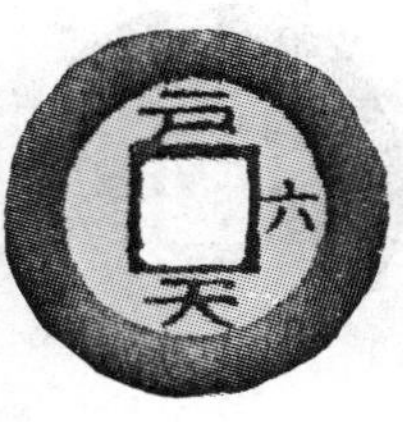

23-26mm
Large characters.

KM#	Date	Series	Good	VG	Fine	VF
38.1-38.11	ND(1852)	1-11	1.50	2.25	3.50	5.00
	Seed type					
38s	ND(1852)	1-11	—	—	*XF*	30.00

24mm
Small characters.
Rev: *Ch'on* at bottom, series number at left.

KM#	Date	Series	Good	VG	Fine	VF
39.1-39.10	ND(1832)	1-10	1.50	2.25	3.50	5.00
	Seed type					
39s	ND(1832)	1-10	—	—	*XF*	30.00

25mm
Large characters.

KM#	Date	Series	Good	VG	Fine	VF
40.1-40.11	ND(1857)	1-11	1.50	2.25	3.50	5.00
	Seed type					
40s	ND(1857)	1-11	—	—	*XF*	30.00

24mm
Rev: *Chi* at bottom, series number at left.

KM#	Date	Series	Good	VG	Fine	VF
41.1-41.10	ND(1852)	1-10	1.50	2.25	3.50	5.00
	Seed type					
41s	ND(1852)	1-10	—	—	*XF*	30.00

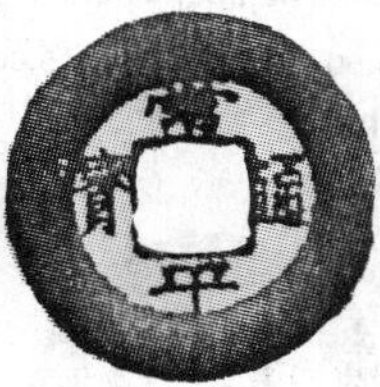
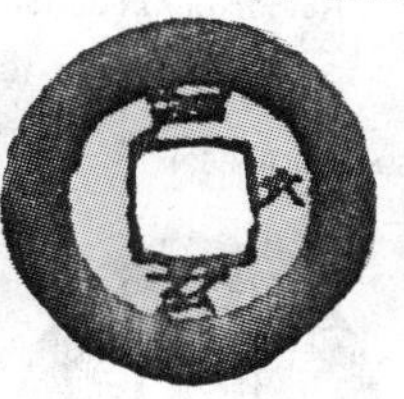

Rev: *Hyon* at bottom, series number at right.

KM#	Date	Series	Good	VG	Fine	VF
42.1-42.10	ND(1852)	1-10	1.75	2.25	3.50	5.00

Rev: Star at upper right.

KM#	Date	Series	Good	VG	Fine	VF
42.16	ND(1852)	6	1.50	2.25	3.50	5.00
	Seed type					
42s	ND(1852)	1-10	—	—	*XF*	30.00

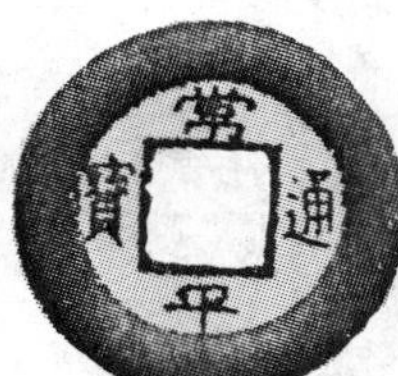
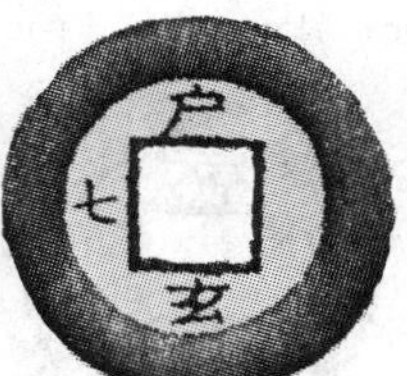

26mm
Obv. & rev: Small characters.
Rev: *Hyon* at bottom, series number at left.

KM#	Date	Series	Good	VG	Fine	VF
43.1-43.10	ND(1852)	1-10	1.50	2.25	3.50	5.00
	Seed type					
43s	ND(1852)	1-10	—	—	*XF*	30.00

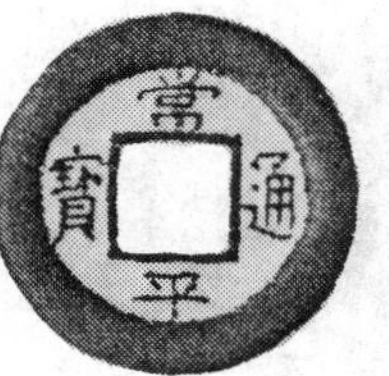
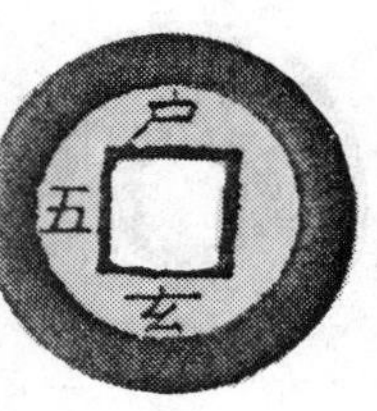

24mm
Obv. and rev: Large characters.
Rev: *Hyon* at bottom, series number at left.

KM#	Date	Series	Good	VG	Fine	VF
A43.1-A43.10	ND(1852)	1-10	1.50	2.25	3.50	5.00
	Seed type					
A43s	ND(1852)	1-10	—	—	*XF*	30.00

Rev: *Hwang* (yellow) at bottom, series number at right.

KM#	Date	Series	Good	VG	Fine	VF
44.1-44.10	ND(1832)	1-10	1.50	2.25	3.50	5.00
	Seed type					
44s	ND(1832)	1-10	—	—	*XF*	30.00

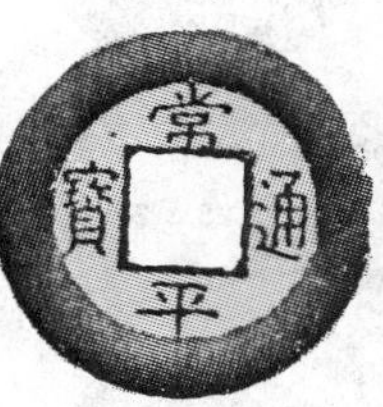
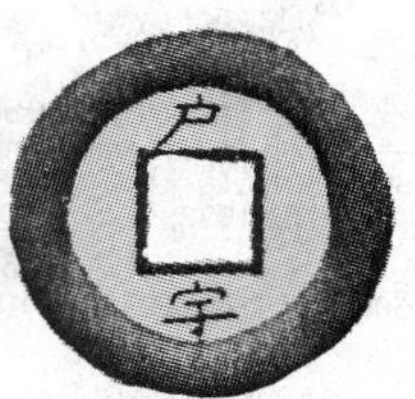

25mm
Rev: *U* at bottom.

KM#	Date	Series	Good	VG	Fine	VF
45	ND(1814)	—	1.75	2.75	4.00	6.00
	Seed type					
45s	ND(1814)	—	—	—	*XF*	30.00

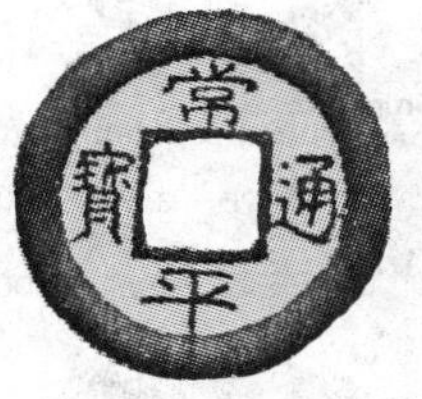
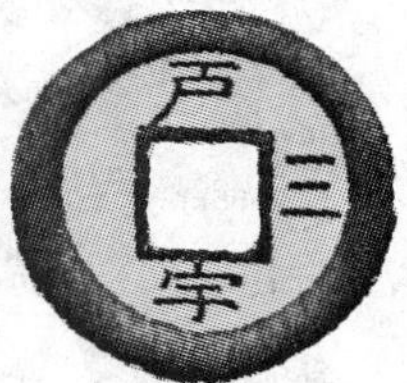

Rev: 19mm inner circle, *U* at bottom, series number at right.

KM#	Date	Series	Good	VG	Fine	VF
46.1-46.10	ND(1814)	1-10	1.50	2.25	3.50	5.00
	Seed type					
46s	ND(1814)	1-10	—	—	*XF*	30.00

23mm
Rev: 16mm inner circle, *U* at bottom, series number at right.

KM#	Date	Series	Good	VG	Fine	VF
47.1-47.10	ND(1832)	1-10	1.50	2.25	3.50	5.00
	Seed type					
47s	ND(1832)	1-10	—	—	*XF*	30.00

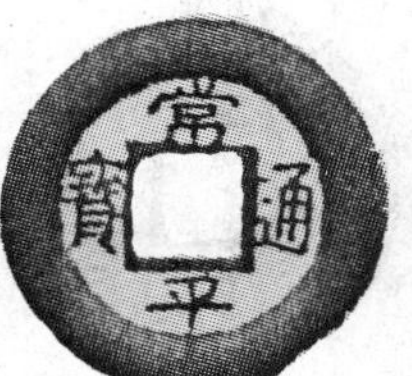
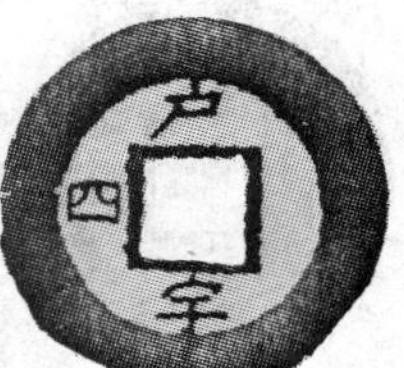

23-26mm
Rev: *U* at bottom, series number at left.

KM#	Date	Series	Good	VG	Fine	VF
48.1-48.10	ND(1814)	1-10	1.50	2.25	3.50	5.00
	Seed type					
48s	ND(1814)	1-10	—	—	*XF*	30.00

25mm
Obv: Smaller *Po* at left.

KM#	Date	Series	Good	VG	Fine	VF
A48.1-A48.10	ND(1814)	1-10	1.50	2.25	3.50	5.00

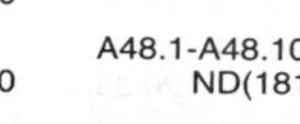

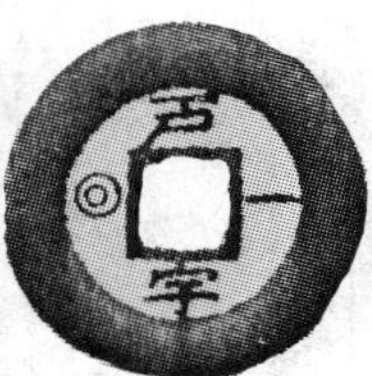

24mm
Rev: *U* at bottom, *Il* (1) at right, double circle at left.

KM#	Date	Series	Good	VG	Fine	VF
49	ND(1832)	—	1.75	2.75	4.00	6.00
	Seed type					
49s	ND(1814)	—	—	—	*XF*	30.00

Rev: *Chu* at bottom, *Chong* at left, series number at right.

KM#	Date	Series	Good	VG	Fine	VF
50.1-50.10	ND(1832)	1-10	1.50	2.25	3.50	5.00
	Seed type					
50s	ND(1832)	1-10	—	—	*XF*	30.00

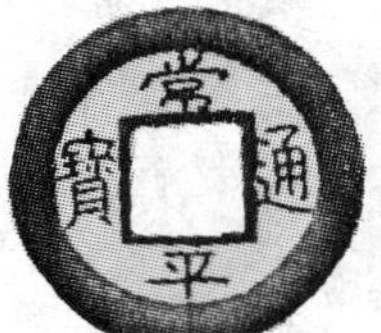

23-25mm
Rev: *Chu* at bottom, series number at left.

KM#	Date	Series	Good	VG	Fine	VF
51.1-51.10	ND(1852)	1-10	1.50	2.25	3.50	5.00
	Seed type					
51s	ND(1852)	1-10	—	—	*XF*	30.00

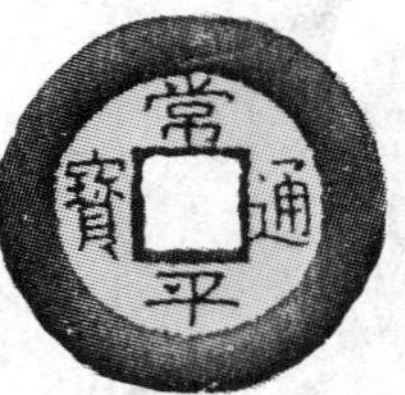
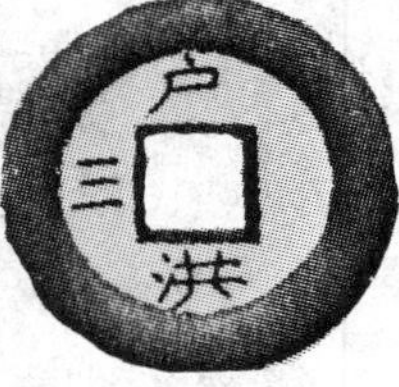

26mm
Rev: *Hong* at bottom, series number at left.

KM#	Date	Series	Good	VG	Fine	VF
52.1-52.10	ND(1852)	1-10	1.75	2.25	3.00	6.00
	Seed type					
52s	ND(1852)	1-10	—	—	*XF*	30.00
	22-24mm					
53.1-53.10	ND(1852)	1-10	1.50	2.25	3.50	5.00
	Obv: *Tong* w/1 dot.					
53a.1-53a.10	ND(1852)	1-10	1.50	2.25	3.50	5.00
	Seed type					
53s	ND(1852)	1-10	—	—	*XF*	30.00

23-25mm
Rev: *Il* (sun) at bottom, series number at left.

KM#	Date	Series	Good	VG	Fine	VF
54.1-54.10	ND(1852)	1-10	1.50	2.25	3.50	5.00
	Seed type					
54s	ND(1852)	1-10	—	—	*XF*	30.00
	Rev: *Wol* (moon) at bottom, series number at left.					
55.1-55.10	ND(1852)	1-10	1.50	2.25	3.50	5.00
	Seed type					
55s	ND(1852)	1-10	—	—	*XF*	30.00

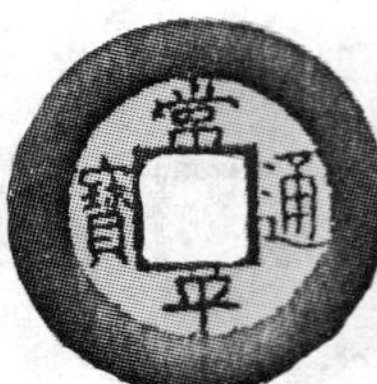
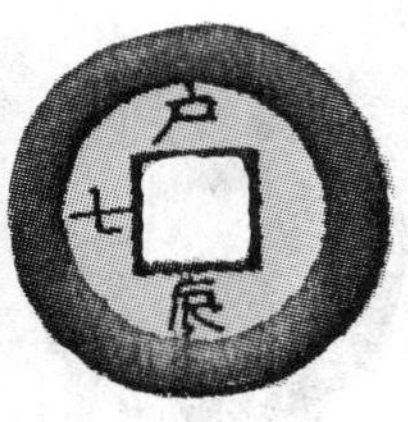

Rev: *Chin* at bottom, series number at left.

KM#	Date	Series	Good	VG	Fine	VF
56.1-56.10	ND(1852)	1-10	1.50	2.25	3.50	5.00
	Seed type					
56s	ND(1852)	1-10	—	—	*XF*	30.00

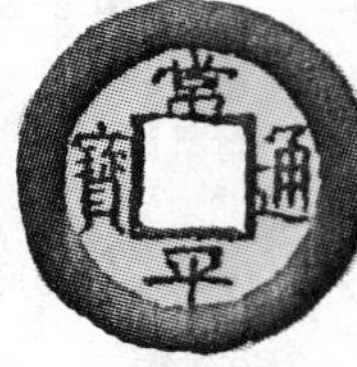

24mm
Rev: *Yol* at bottom, series number at left.

KM#	Date	Series	Good	VG	Fine	VF
57.1-57.10	ND(1852)	1-10	1.50	2.25	3.50	5.00
	Seed type					
57s	ND(1852)	1-10	—	—	*XF*	30.00

Rev: *Nae* at bottom, series number at left.

KM#	Date	Series	Good	VG	Fine	VF
58.1-58.10	ND(1852)	1-10	1.50	2.25	3.50	5.00
	Seed type					
58s	ND(1852)	1-10	—	—	*XF*	30.00

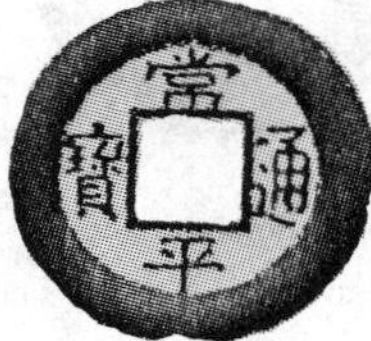
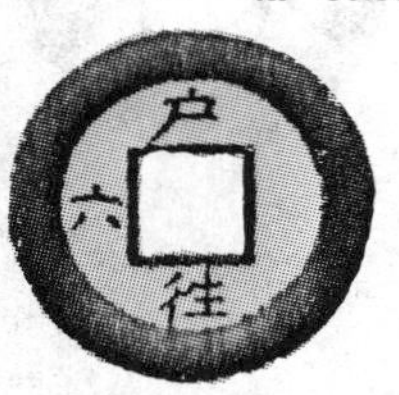

Rev: *Wang* at bottom, series number at left.

KM#	Date	Series	Good	VG	Fine	VF
59.1-59.10	ND(1852)	1-10	1.50	2.25	3.50	5.00
	Seed type					
59s	ND(1852)	1-10	—	—	*XF*	30.00

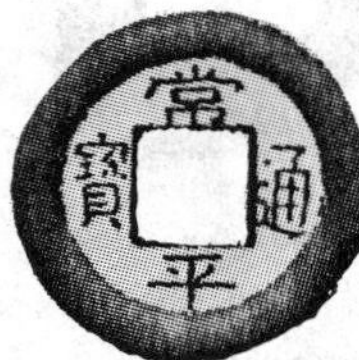

23mm
Rev: *Saeng* at bottom, series number at left.

KM#	Date	Series	Good	VG	Fine	VF
60.1-60.10	ND(1852)	1-10	1.50	2.25	3.50	5.00
	Seed type					
60s	ND(1852)	1-10	—	—	*XF*	30.00

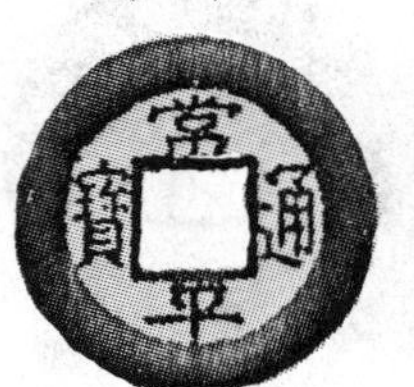
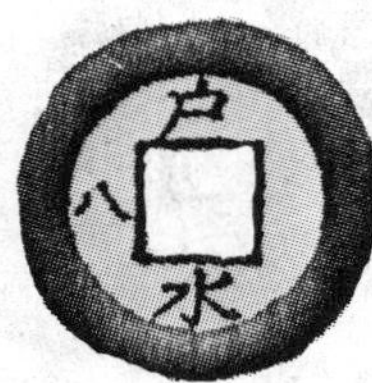

24mm
Rev: *Su* at bottom, series number at left.

KM#	Date	Series	Good	VG	Fine	VF
61.1-61.10	ND(1852)	1-10	1.50	2.25	3.50	5.00
	Seed type					
61s	ND(1852)	1-10	—	—	*XF*	30.00

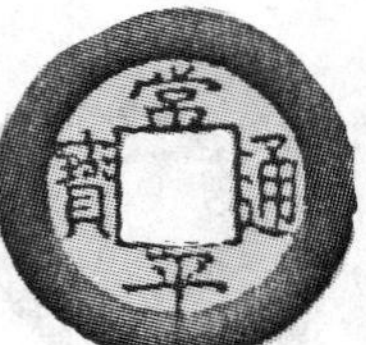
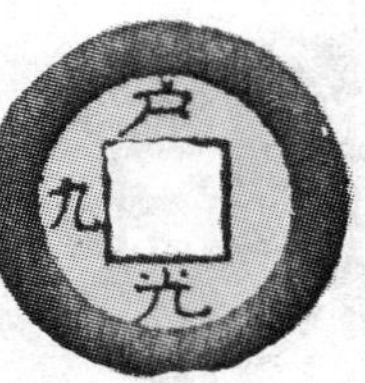

Rev: *Kwang* at bottom, series number at left.

KM#	Date	Series	Good	VG	Fine	VF
62.1-62.10	ND(1852)	1-10	1.50	2.25	3.50	5.00
	Seed type					
62s	ND(1852)	1-10	—	—	*XF*	30.00
	Rev: *Kwang* at bottom, dot at right, series number at left.					
63.6	ND(1852)	6	1.50	2.25	3.50	5.00
	Seed type					
63s	ND(1852)	6	—	—	*XF*	30.00
	25mm **Rev: *Kwang* at bottom, series number at right.**					
64.2	ND(1852)	2	1.50	2.25	3.50	5.00
	Seed type					
64s	ND(1852)	2	—	—	*XF*	30.00
	23mm **Rev: *Mun* at bottom, series number at right.**					
65.1-65.10	ND(1852)	1-10	1.50	2.25	3.50	5.00
	Seed type					
65s	ND(1832)	1-10	—	—	*XF*	30.00

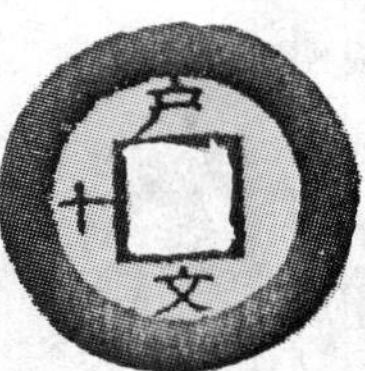

24mm
Rev: *Mun* at bottom, series number at left.

KM#	Date	Series	Good	VG	Fine	VF
66.1-66.10	ND(1832)	1-10	1.50	2.25	3.50	5.00
	Seed type					
66s	ND(1832)	1-10	—	—	*XF*	30.00

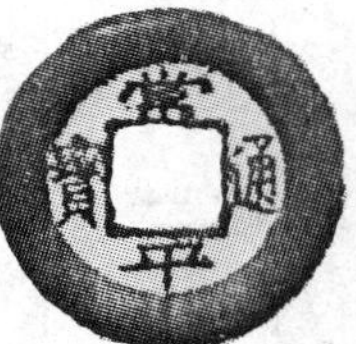

Rev: *Ho* in different style.

KM#	Date	Series	Good	VG	Fine	VF
67.1-67.10	ND(1832)	1-10	1.50	2.25	3.50	5.00
	25mm					
67.18	ND(1832)	8	1.50	2.25	3.50	5.00
	Seed type					
67s	ND(1832)	1-10	—	—	*XF*	30.00

23mm
Rev: *Mun* at bottom, circle at left, series number at right.

KM#	Date	Series	Good	VG	Fine	VF
68.1-68.10	ND(1832)	1-10	1.50	2.25	3.50	5.00
	Seed type					
68s	ND(1832)	1-10	—	—	*XF*	30.00

25mm
Rev: *Mun* at bottom, circle at right, series number at left.

KM#	Date	Series	Good	VG	Fine	VF
69.1-69.5	ND(1832)	1-5	1.75	2.75	4.00	6.00

Seed type

KM# Date Series Good VG Fine VF

69s ND(1832) 1-5 — — *XF* 30.00

24mm

Rev: *Ip* at bottom, series number at right.

70.1-70.10 ND(1814) 1-10 1.50 2.25 3.50 5.00

25mm

Rev: *Ho* w/o stem.

70a.1-70a-10 ND(1814) 1-10 1.50 2.25 3.50 5.00

Seed type

70s ND(1814) 1-10 — — *XF* 30.00

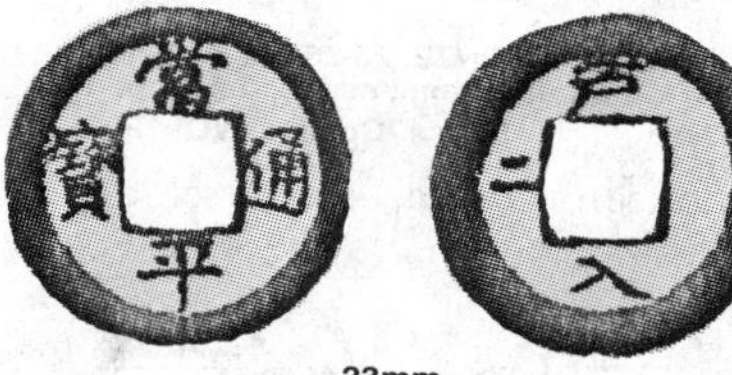

23mm

Rev: *Ip* at bottom, series number at left.

71.1-71.10 ND(1806-14) 1-10 1.50 2.25 3.50 5.00

24mm

Obv: 1 dot *Tong*, and *P'yong* w/hooks.

71a.1-71a.10 ND(1806-14) 1-10 1.50 2.25 3.50 5.00

Seed type

71s ND(1806-14) 1-10 — — *XF* 30.00

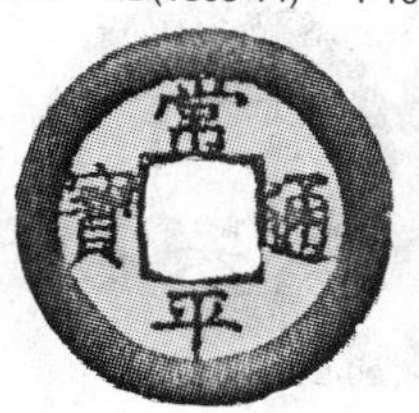

25mm

Rev: *Ip* at bottom, circle at left, series number at right.

72.1-72.10 ND(1806-14) 1-10 1.25 2.25 3.50 5.00

24mm

Wide rim.

72a.1-72a.10 ND(1806-14) 1-10 1.50 2.25 3.50 5.00

Seed type

72s ND(1806-14) 1-10 — — *XF* 30.00

Rev: *Ip* at bottom, circle at right, series number at left.

73.1-73.5 ND(1806-14) 1-5 4.00 7.00 10.00 20.00

Seed type

73s ND(1806-14) 1-5 — — *XF* 40.00

5 MUN

CAST COPPER or BRONZE

30mm

Small characters, inner circle 21-22mm.

Rev: *Tang* at right, *O* (5) at left, series number at bottom.

136.1-136.10 ND(1883) 1-10 2.00 3.00 5.00 7.00

Seed type

136s ND(1883) 1-10 — — *XF* 35.00

31mm

Medium characters, inner circle 21-22mm.

KM# Date Series Good VG Fine VF

137.1-137.11 ND(1883) 1-11 2.00 3.00 5.00 7.00

Seed type

137s ND(1883) 1-11 — — *XF* 30.00

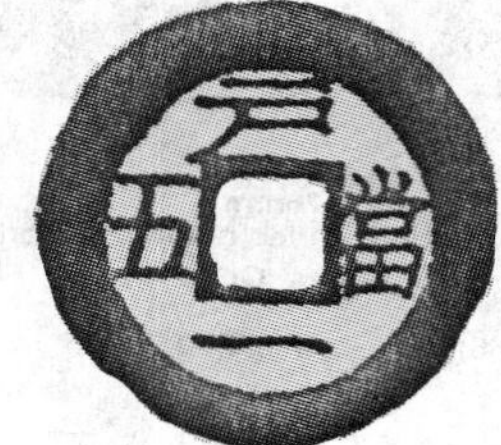

30mm

Large characters, inner circle 21-22mm.

138.1-138.11 ND(1883) 1-11 2.75 4.00 6.00 10.00

Seed type

138s ND(1883) 1-11 — — *XF* 30.00

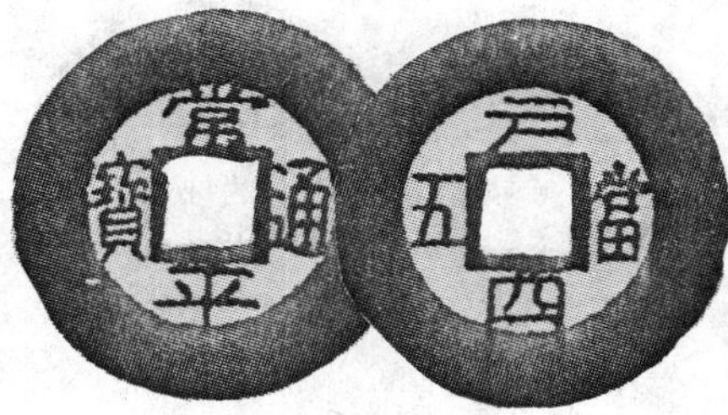

31mm

Inner circle 19mm

139.1-139.10 ND(1883) 1-10 2.75 4.00 6.00 10.00

Seed type

139s ND(1883) 1-10 — — *XF* 30.00

Rev: Small *Ho* at top, crescent under series number at bottom.

140.1-140.10 ND(1883) 1-10 2.00 3.00 5.00 7.00

Seed type

140s ND(1883) 1-10 — — *XF* 30.00

30mm

Rev: Wide *Ho* at top, crescent under series number at bottom.

141.1-141.10 ND(1883) 1-10 2.75 3.00 5.00 9.00

Seed type

141s ND(1883) 1-10 — — *XF* 30.00

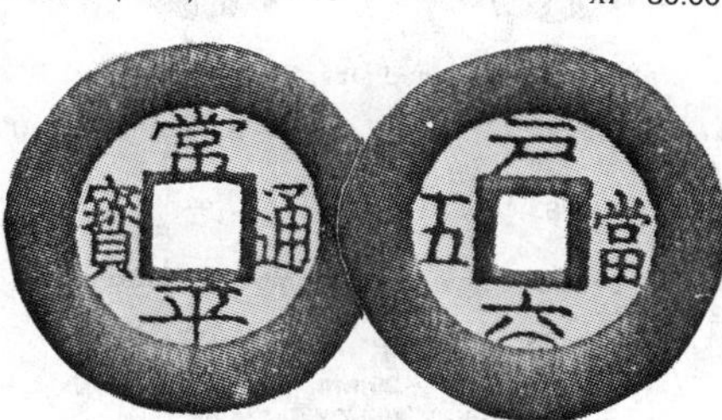

Small characters, inner circle 19mm.

Rev: Crescent under series number at bottom.

142.1-142.10 ND(1883) 1-10 2.75 4.00 6.00 10.00

Seed type

KM# Date Series Good VG Fine VF

142s ND(1883) 1-10 — — *XF* 30.00

100 MUN

CAST COPPER or BRONZE, 24.00 g, 39-40mm

143 ND(1866) — 5.50 8.00 14.00 20.00

NOTE: More than 40 varieties exist.

Seed type

143s ND(1886) — — — *XF* 45.00

GOVERNMENT TITHE OFFICE

均 Kyun (Kyun Yok Ch'ong) MUN

CAST COPPER or BRONZE, 4.00 g

24mm

Rev: *Kyun* at top, series number at bottom.

147.1-147.10 ND(1807) 1-10 1.50 2.25 3.50 5.00

Rev: Star at right.

147.18 ND(1807) 8 1.50 2.25 3.50 5.00

147.20 ND(1807) 10 1.50 2.25 3.50 5.00

Seed type

147s ND(1807) 1-10 — — *XF* 30.00

23mm

Rev: *Il* (1) at bottom, series number at right.

148.1-148.10 ND(1857) 1-10 3.50 5.50 8.00 16.00

Seed type

148s ND(1857) 1-10 — — *XF* 35.00

Rev: *Il* (1) at bottom, series number at left.

149.1-149.10 ND(1857) 1-10 3.50 5.50 8.00 16.00

Seed type

149s ND(1857) 1-10 — — *XF* 35.00

5 MUN

CAST BRONZE, 31mm

Small characters.

Rev: *Tang* at right, *O* (5) at right, series number at bottom.

150.1-150.11 ND(1883) 1-11 2.00 3.00 5.00 7.00

Seed type

150s ND(1883) 1-11 — — *XF* 30.00

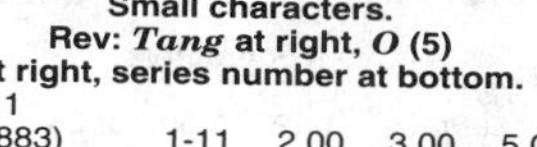

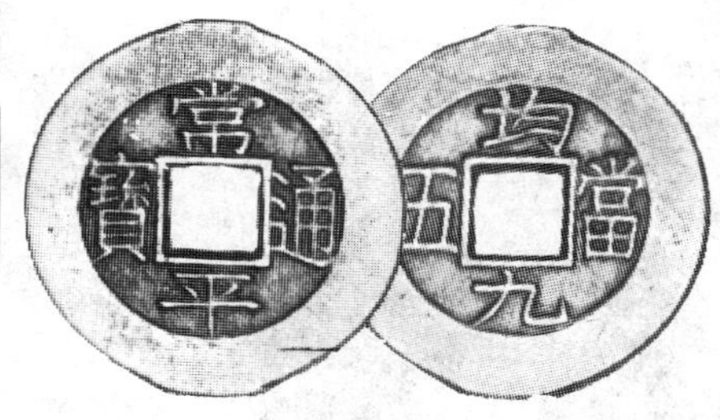

32mm
Medium characters.

KM#	Date	Series	Good	VG	Fine	VF
151.1-151.10	ND(1883)	1-10	2.25	3.00	5.00	7.00

Seed type

KM#	Date	Series	Good	VG	Fine	VF
151s	ND(1883)	1-10	—	—	*XF*	30.00

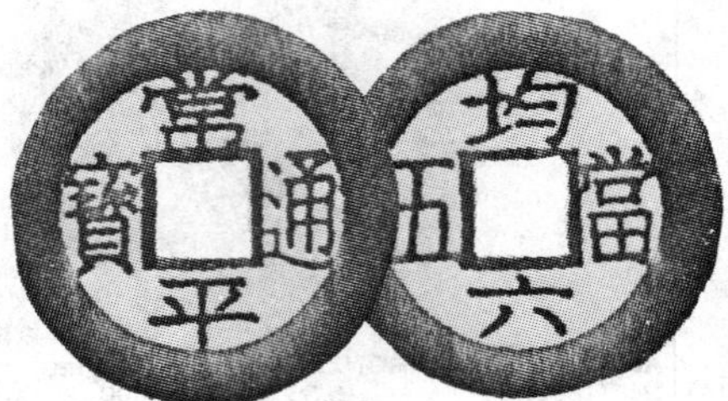

31mm
Large characters.

KM#	Date	Series	Good	VG	Fine	VF
152.1-152.10	ND(1883)	1-10	2.75	3.50	5.50	8.00

Seed type

KM#	Date	Series	Good	VG	Fine	VF
152s	ND(1883)	1-11	—	—	*XF*	30.00

30mm
Different *Kyun*

KM#	Date	Series	Good	VG	Fine	VF
153.1-153.11	ND(1883)	1-11	2.75	3.50	5.50	8.00

RICE AND CLOTH DEPARTMENT

宣 Son (Son Hye Ch'ong) 惠

MUN

CAST COPPER or BRONZE, 4.00 g
25mm
Rev: Series number at bottom.

KM#	Date	Series	Good	VG	Fine	VF
174.1-174.6	ND(1814)	1-6	1.50	2.25	3.50	5.00

Seed type

KM#	Date	Series	Good	VG	Fine	VF
174s	ND(1814)	1-6	—	—	*XF*	30.00

Large characters.
Rev: *Hye* at top, series number at bottom.

KM#	Date	Series	Good	VG	Fine	VF
175.1-175.12	ND(1806)	1-12	1.50	2.25	3.50	5.00

Seed type

KM#	Date	Series	Good	VG	Fine	VF
175s	ND(1806)	1-11	—	—	*XF*	30.00

Small characters.

KM#	Date	Series	Good	VG	Fine	VF
176.1-176.12	ND(1806)	1-12	1.50	2.25	3.50	5.00

Seed type

KM#	Date	Series	Good	VG	Fine	VF
176s	ND(1806)	1-12	—	—	*XF*	30.00

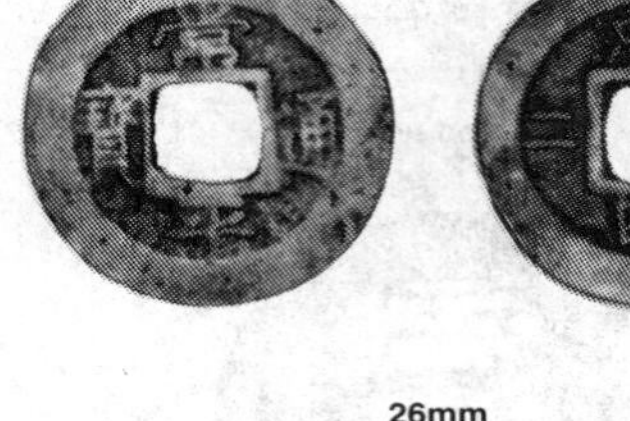

26mm
Rev: *I* (2)at left, series number at bottom.

KM#	Date	Series	Good	VG	Fine	VF
177.1-177.7	ND(1836)	1-7	1.50	2.25	3.50	5.00

Seed type

KM#	Date	Series	Good	VG	Fine	VF
177s	ND(1836)	1-7	—	—	*XF*	30.00

CENTRAL GOVERNMENT MINT

典 Chon (Chon Hwan' Guk)

5 MUN

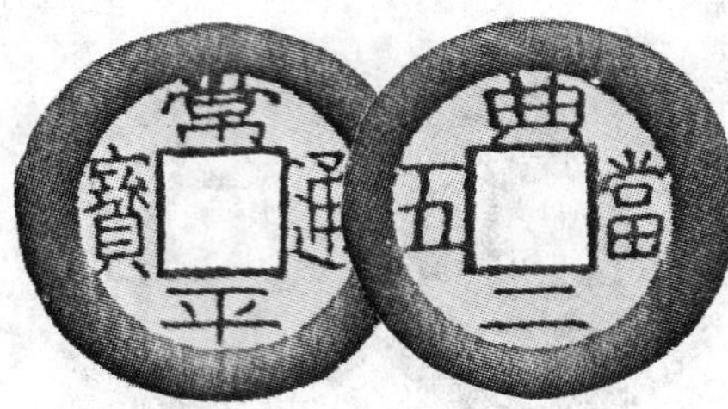

CAST BRONZE, 31mm
Large characters.
Rev: *Tang* at right, *O* (5)
at left, series number at bottom.

KM#	Date	Series	Good	VG	Fine	VF
209.1-209.12	ND(1883)	1-12	2.00	3.00	5.00	7.00

32mm
Rev: Star below *Bo.*

KM#	Date	Series	Good	VG	Fine	VF
209.21	ND(1883)	1	2.00	3.00	5.00	7.00

Seed type

KM#	Date	Series	Good	VG	Fine	VF
209s	ND(1883)	1-15	—	—	*XF*	25.00

32mm
Small characters.

KM#	Date	Series	Good	VG	Fine	VF
210.1-210.15	ND(1883)	1-15	2.00	3.00	5.00	7.00

Seed type

KM#	Date	Series	Good	VG	Fine	VF
210s	ND(1883)	1-15	—	—	*XF*	25.00

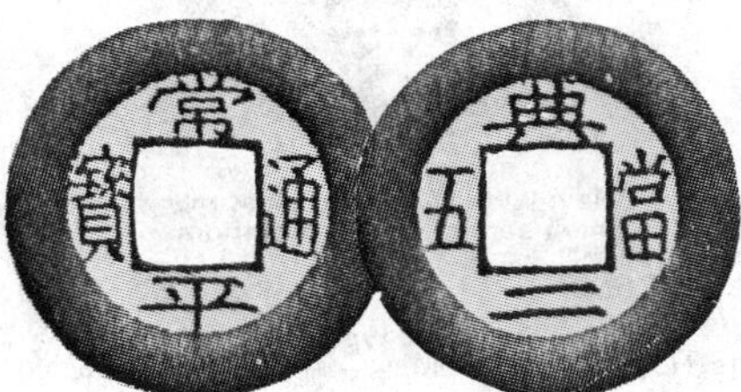

Reduced size, 29mm

KM#	Date	Series	Good	VG	Fine	VF
211.1-211.12	ND(1883)	1-12	2.00	3.00	5.00	7.00

Seed type

KM#	Date	Series	Good	VG	Fine	VF
211s	ND(1883)	1-10	—	—	*XF*	25.00

28mm
Rev: Dot below series number at bottom.

KM#	Date	Series	Good	VG	Fine	VF
212.1-212.3	ND(1883)	1-3	2.00	3.00	5.00	7.00

29mm
Obv: *P'yong* w/hooks.

KM#	Date	Series	Good	VG	Fine	VF
212.12	ND(1883)	2	2.00	3.00	5.00	7.00

Seed type

KM#	Date	Series	Good	VG	Fine	VF
212s	ND(1883)	1-3	—	—	*XF*	25.00

PALACE GUARD OFFICE

武 Mu (Mu Wi Yong)

MUN

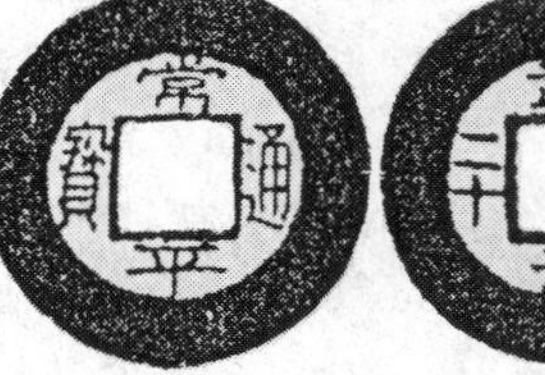

CAST BRONZE, 25-26mm, 4.00 g
Rev: *Ch'on* at bottom, series number at left.

KM#	Date	Series	Good	VG	Fine	VF
337.1-337.20	ND(1881)	1-20	1.75	2.50	3.50	5.50

Seed type

KM#	Date	Series	Good	VG	Fine	VF
337s	ND(1881)	1-20	—	—	*XF*	50.00

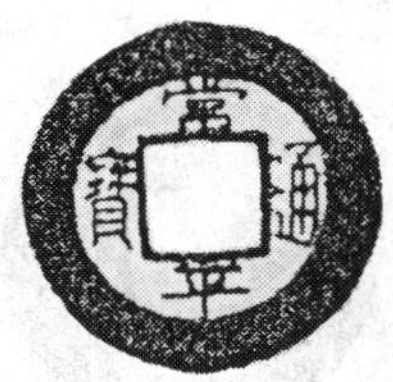

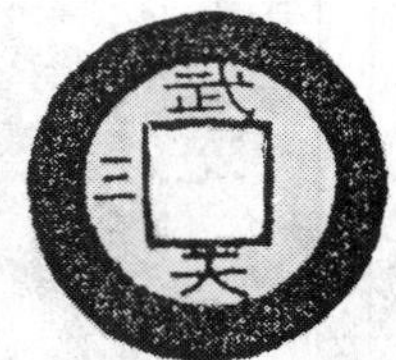

Reduced size, 23-24mm

KM#	Date	Series	Good	VG	Fine	VF
338.1-338.20	ND(1881)	1-20	1.50	2.25	3.50	5.00

Seed type

KM#	Date	Series	Good	VG	Fine	VF
338s	ND(1881)	1-20	—	—	*XF*	28.00

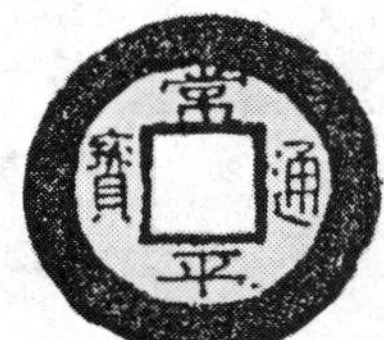

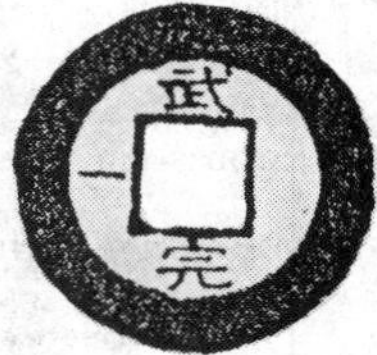

24mm
Rev: *Wan* at bottom, series number at left.

KM#	Date	Series	Good	VG	Fine	VF
339.1	ND(1881)	1	35.00	60.00	100.00	175.00

Seed type

KM#	Date	Series	Good	VG	Fine	VF
339s	ND(1881)	1	—	—	*XF*	300.00

COURT GUARD

禁 Kum (Kum Wi Yong)

MUN

CAST BRONZE, 4.00 g, 23-25mm
Large characters.
Rev: *Kum* at top, series number at bottom.

KM#	Date	Series	Good	VG	Fine	VF
340.1-340.8	ND(1823)	1-8	1.50	2.25	3.50	5.00

Seed type

KM#	Date	Series	Good	VG	Fine	VF
340s	ND(1823)	1-8	—	—	*XF*	28.00

25mm
Small characters.

KM#	Date	Series	Good	VG	Fine	VF
341.1-341.8	ND(1823)	1-8	1.50	2.25	3.50	5.00

Obv: Hooks in *P'yong.*

KM#	Date	Series	Good	VG	Fine	VF
341a.1-341a.8	ND(1823)	1-8	1.50	2.25	3.50	5.00

23mm
Obv: *P'yong* w/o hooks.

KM#	Date	Series	Good	VG	Fine	VF
341b.1-341b.8	ND(1823)	1-8	1.50	2.25	3.50	5.00

Seed type

KM#	Date	Series	Good	VG	Fine	VF
341s	ND(1823)	1-8	—	—	*XF*	28.00

MILITARY TRAINING COMMAND

訓 or 訓 Hun (Hul Ly On Do Gam)

MUN

CAST BRONZE, 4.00 g, 25mm
Rev: *Hun* at top, series number at bottom.

KM#	Date	Series	Good	VG	Fine	VF
448.1-448.6	ND(1828)	1-6	1.50	2.25	3.50	5.00

Rev: Star at upper left.

KM#	Date	Series	Good	VG	Fine	VF
448.14	ND(1828)	4	1.50	2.25	3.50	5.00

25mm
Rev: *Ch'on* at bottom, series number at left.

KM#	Date	Series	Good	VG	Fine	VF
449.1-449.10	ND(1857)	1-10	1.50	2.25	3.50	5.00
	Seed type					
449s	ND(1857)	1-10	—	—	*XF*	25.00

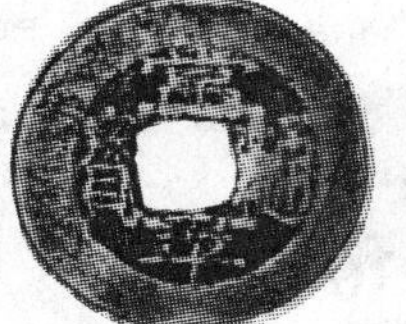

Rev: *Chong* at bottom, series number at left.

KM#	Date	Series	Good	VG	Fine	VF
450.1-450.10	ND(1857)	1-10	1.50	2.25	3.50	5.00
	Seed type					
450s	ND(1857)	1-10	—	—	*XF*	25.00

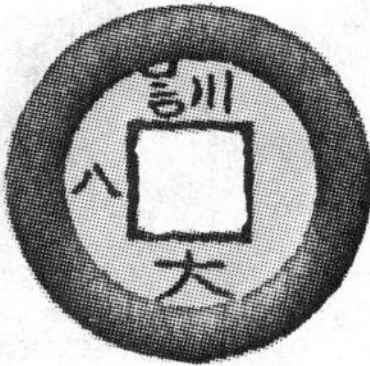

Rev: *Tae* at bottom, series number at left.

KM#	Date	Series	Good	VG	Fine	VF
451.1-451.10	ND(1857)	1-10	1.50	2.25	3.50	5.00
	Seed type					
451s	ND(1857)	1-10	—	—	*XF*	25.00

Rev: *Kong* at bottom, series number at left.

KM#	Date	Series	Good	VG	Fine	VF
452.1-452.10	ND(1857)	1-10	1.50	2.25	3.50	5.00
	Seed type					
452s	ND(1857)	1-10	—	—	*XF*	25.00

25mm
Rev: *Mun* at bottom, series number at right.

KM#	Date	Series	Good	VG	Fine	VF
453.1	ND(1857)	1	1.50	2.25	3.50	5.00
	Seed type					
453s	ND(1857)	1	—	—	*XF*	25.00

24mm

Rev: *Mun* at bottom, series number at left.

KM#	Date	Series	Good	VG	Fine	VF
454.1-454.10	ND(1857)	1-10	1.50	2.25	3.50	5.00
	Seed type					
454s	ND(1857)	1-10	—	—	*XF*	25.00

Rev: *Ch'on* (thousand) at bottom, series number at left.

KM#	Date	Series	Good	VG	Fine	VF
455.1-455.10	ND(1857)	1-10	1.50	2.25	3.50	5.00
	Seed type					
455s	ND(1857)	1-10	—	—	*XF*	25.00

25mm
Rev: *Chung* at bottom, series number at right.

KM#	Date	Series	Good	VG	Fine	VF
456.1	ND(1857)	1	1.25	1.75	2.50	3.50
	Seed type					
456s	ND(1857)	1	—	—	*XF*	25.00

24mm
Rev: *Chung* at bottom, series number at left.

KM#	Date	Series	Good	VG	Fine	VF
457.1-457.10	ND(1857)	1-10	1.50	2.25	3.50	5.00
	Rev: Star at lower right.					
457.14	ND(1857)	4	1.50	2.25	3.50	5.00
	Rev: Star at right.					
457.16	ND(1857)	6	1.50	2.25	3.50	5.00
457.17	ND(1857)	7	1.50	2.25	3.50	5.00
	Seed type					
457s	ND(1857)	1-10	—	—	*XF*	25.00

25mm
Obv: Small characters.
Rev: *T'o* at bottom, series number at right.

KM#	Date	Series	Good	VG	Fine	VF
458.1-458.10	ND(1857)	1-10	1.50	2.25	3.50	5.00
	Seed type					
458s	ND(1857)	1-10	—	—	*XF*	25.00

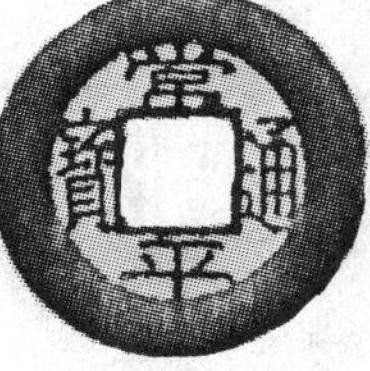
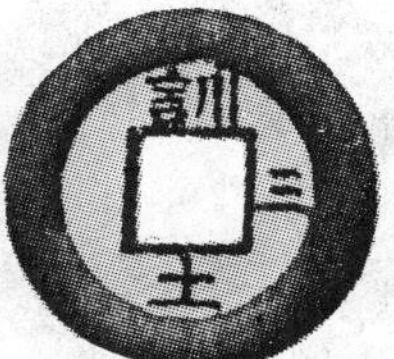

Obv: Large characters.

KM#	Date	Series	Good	VG	Fine	VF
459.1-459.10	ND(1857)	1-10	1.50	2.25	3.50	5.00
	Seed type					
459s	ND(1857)	1-10	—	—	*XF*	25.00

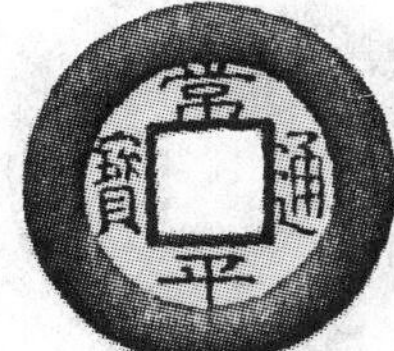

Obv: Small characters.
Rev: *T'o* at bottom, series number at left.

KM#	Date	Series	Good	VG	Fine	VF
460.1-460.10	ND(1857)	1-10	1.50	2.25	3.50	5.00
	Seed type					
460s	ND(1857)	1-10	—	—	*XF*	25.00

Obv: Large characters.

KM#	Date	Series	Good	VG	Fine	VF
461.1-461.10	ND(1857)	1-10	1.50	2.25	3.50	5.00
	Seed type					
461s	ND(1857)	1-10	—	—	*XF*	25.00

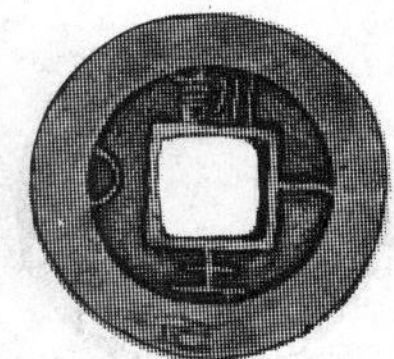

Rev: *T'o* at bottom, series number at right, crescent at left.

KM#	Date	Series	Good	VG	Fine	VF
462.1-462.5	ND(1857)	1-5	1.50	2.25	3.50	5.00
	Seed type					
462s	ND(1857)	1-5	—	—	*XF*	25.00

25mm
Obv: Small characters.
Rev: *T'o* at bottom, crescent at right, series number at left.

KM#	Date	Series	Good	VG	Fine	VF
463.1	ND(1857)	1	1.50	2.25	3.50	5.00
463.2		2	1.50	2.25	3.50	5.00
463.3		3	1.50	2.25	3.50	5.00
463.4		4	1.50	2.25	3.50	5.00
463.5		5	1.50	2.25	3.50	5.00
	Seed type					
463s	ND(1857)	1-5	—	—	*XF*	25.00

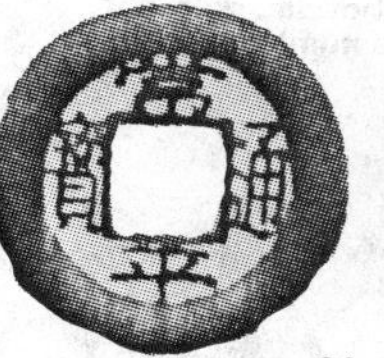

24mm
Obv: Large characters.

KM#	Date	Series	Good	VG	Fine	VF
464.1-464.5	ND(1857)	1-5	1.50	2.25	3.50	5.00
	Seed type					
464s	ND(1857)	1-5	—	—	*XF*	25.00

Rev: *Won* (first) at bottom, series number at right.

KM#	Date	Series	Good	VG	Fine	VF
465.1-465.10	ND(1857)	1-10	1.50	2.25	3.50	5.00
	Seed type					
465s	ND(1857)	1-10	—	—	*XF*	25.00

25mm
Rev: *Won* at bottom, series number at left.

KM#	Date	Series	Good	VG	Fine	VF
466.1-466.10	ND(1857)	1-10	1.50	2.25	3.50	5.00
	Seed type					
466s	ND(1857)	1-10	—	—	*XF*	25.00

Rev: *Won* at bottom, series number at right, crescent at left.

KM#	Date	Series	Good	VG	Fine	VF
467.1-467.5	ND(1857)	1-5	1.25	1.75	2.50	3.50
	Seed type					
467s	ND(1857)	1-5	—	—	*XF*	25.00

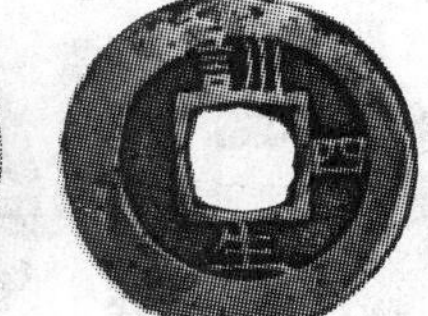

26mm

Rev: *Saeng* at bottom, series number at right.

KM#	Date	Series	Good	VG	Fine	VF
468.1-468.10	ND(1857)	1-10	1.50	2.25	3.50	5.00
	Seed type					
468s	ND(1857)	1-10	—	—	*XF*	25.00

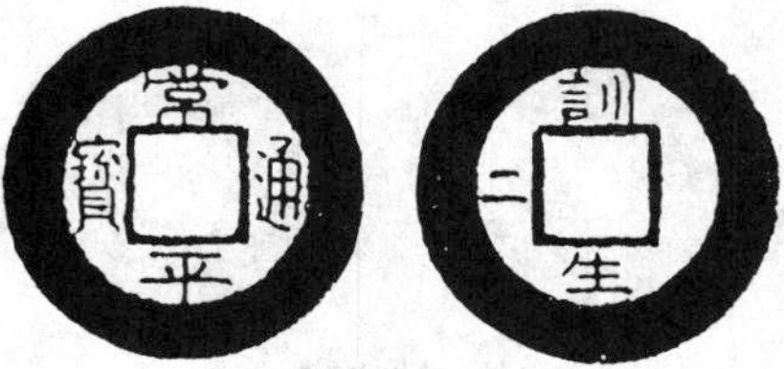

25mm
Rev: *Saeng* at bottom, series number at left.

KM#	Date	Series	Good	VG	Fine	VF
469.1-469.10	ND(1857)	1-10	1.50	2.25	3.50	5.00
	Seed type					
469s	ND(1857)	1-10	—	—	*XF*	25.00

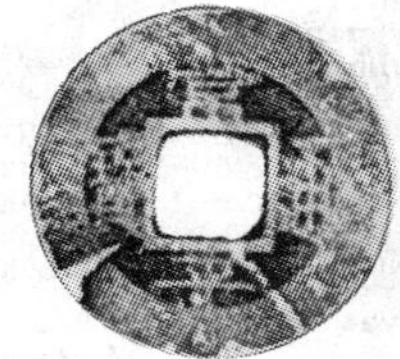

24mm
Rev: *Saeng* at bottom, crescent at right, series number at left.

KM#	Date	Series	Good	VG	Fine	VF
470.1-470.5	ND(1857)	1-5	1.50	2.25	3.50	5.00
	Seed type					
470s	ND(1857)	1-5	—	—	*XF*	25.00

25mm
Rev: *Chon* (perfect) at bottom, series number at right.

KM#	Date	Series	Good	VG	Fine	VF
471.1-471.10	ND(1857)	1-10	1.50	2.25	3.50	5.00
	Seed type					
471s	ND(1857)	1-10	—	—	*XF*	25.00

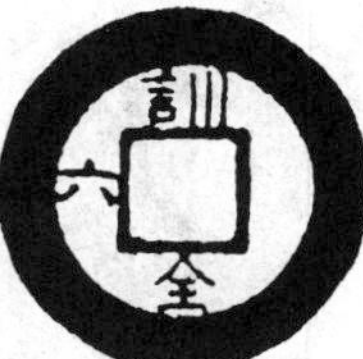

24mm
Rev: *Chon* at bottom, series number at left.

KM#	Date	Series	Good	VG	Fine	VF
472.1-472.10	ND(1857)	1-10	1.50	2.25	3.50	5.00
	Seed type					
472s	ND(1857)	1-10	—	—	*XF*	25.00

23-25mm
Rev: *Chon* at bottom, crescent at right, series number at left.

KM#	Date	Series	Good	VG	Fine	VF
473.1-473.5	ND(1857)	1-5	1.50	2.25	3.50	5.00
	Seed type					
473s	ND(1857)	1-5	—	—	*XF*	25.00

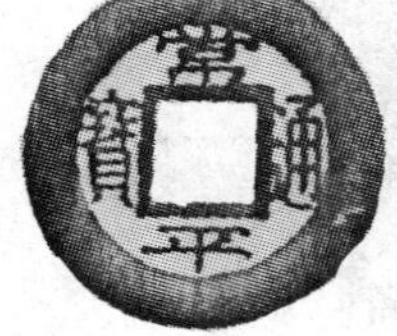

24mm
Rev: *Kil* at bottom, series number at right.

KM#	Date	Series	Good	VG	Fine	VF
474.1-474.10	ND(1857)	1-10	6.00	10.00	15.00	25.00
	Seed type					
474s	ND(1857)	1-10	—	—	*XF*	50.00

Rev: *Kil* at bottom, series number at left.

KM#	Date	Series	Good	VG	Fine	VF
475.1-475.10	ND(1857)	1-10	6.00	10.00	15.00	25.00
	Seed type					
475s	ND(1857)	1-10	—	—	*XF*	50.00

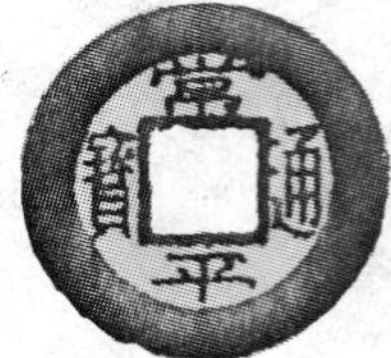

Rev: *Kil* at bottom, crescent at right, series number at left.

KM#	Date	Series	Good	VG	Fine	VF
476.1-476.5	ND(1857)	1-5	6.00	10.00	15.00	25.00
	Seed type					
476s	ND(1857)	1-5	—	—	*XF*	50.00

SEOUL MILITARY OFFICE

統 T'ong (T'ong Wi Yong)
5 MON

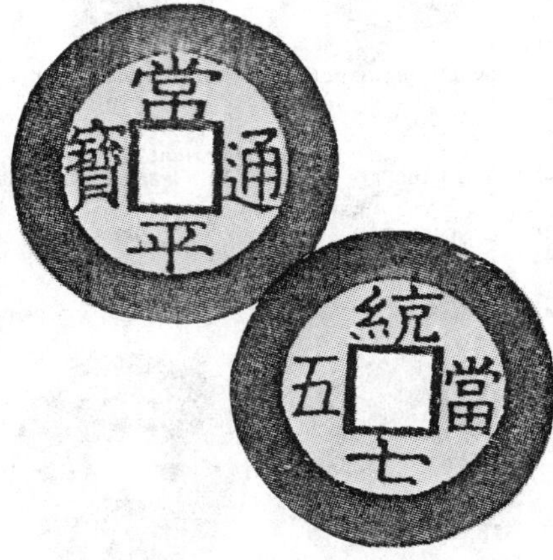

CAST BRONZE, 32mm
Inside diameter 20-22mm.
Rev: *Tang* at right, *O* (5) at left, series number at bottom.

KM#	Date	Series	Good	VG	Fine	VF
763.1-763.20	ND(1883)	1-20	2.00	3.00	5.00	7.00

KM#	Date	Series	Good	VG	Fine	VF
	Seed variety					
763s	ND(1883)	1-20	—	—	*XF*	25.00

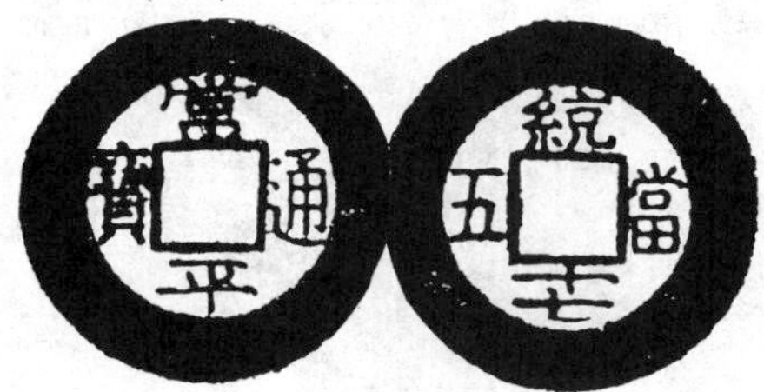

Reduced size, 29mm, inside diameter 18-19mm.

KM#	Date	Series	Good	VG	Fine	VF
764.1-764.20	ND(1883)	1-20	2.00	3.00	5.00	7.00
	Seed variety					
764s	ND(1883)	1-20	—	—	*XF*	25.00

GOVERNMENT OFFICE PUKHAN MOUNTAIN FORTRESS

经 Kyong (Kyong Ni Ch'ong)
MUN

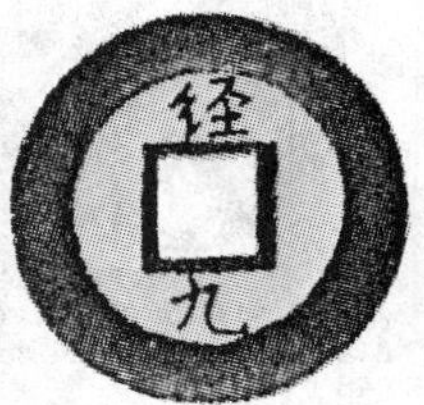

CAST BRONZE, 4.00 g, 26mm
Rev: *Kyong* at top, series number at bottom.

KM#	Date	Series	Good	VG	Fine	VF
765.1-765.10	ND(1830)	1-10	1.75	2.25	3.50	5.00
	Seed type					
765s	ND(1830)	1-10	—	—	*XF*	15.00

Rev: *Sip* (10) at bottom and additional series number at left.

KM#	Date	Series	Good	VG	Fine	VF
766.1-766.6	ND(1830)	1-6	1.75	2.25	3.50	5.00
	Rev: Star at left.					
766.11	ND(1830)	1	1.75	2.25	3.50	5.00
	Seed type					
766s	ND(1830)	1-6	—	—	*XF*	25.00

KANGWHA TOWNSHIP MILITARY OFFICE

沁 Sim (Kang Hwa Kwal Li Yong)
MUN

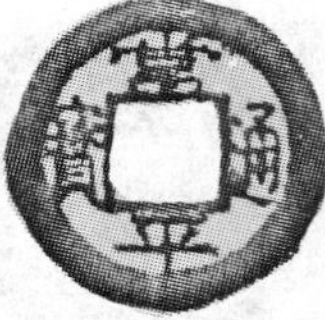

CAST BRONZE, 4.00 g, 22mm
Rev: *Sim* at top, *Won* (first) at bottom, dot at left.

KM#	Date	Series	Good	VG	Fine	VF
771	ND(1883)	—	2.75	3.00	4.00	6.00

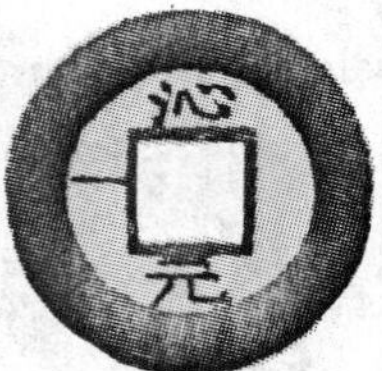

25mm
Rev: *Won* (first) at bottom, series number at left.

KM#	Date	Series	Good	VG	Fine	VF
772.1-772.10	ND(1883)	1-10	6.00	10.00	16.50	25.00

22mm
Rev: *Won* (first) at bottom, series number at right, circle at left.

KM#	Date	Series	Good	VG	Fine	VF
773	ND(1883)	1	40.00	80.00	125.00	200.00

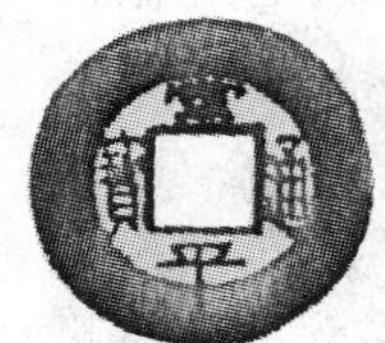

23mm
Wide rim.
Rev: *Won* (first) at bottom, series number at right, crescent at left.

KM#	Date	Series	Good	VG	Fine	VF
774.1-774.10	ND(1883)	1-10	6.00	10.00	16.50	25.00

21mm
Narrow rim.
Rev: *Won* (first) at bottom, series number at right, crescent at left.

KM#	Date	Series	Good	VG	Fine	VF
A774.1-A774.10	ND(1883)	1-10	6.00	10.00	16.50	25.00

5 MUN

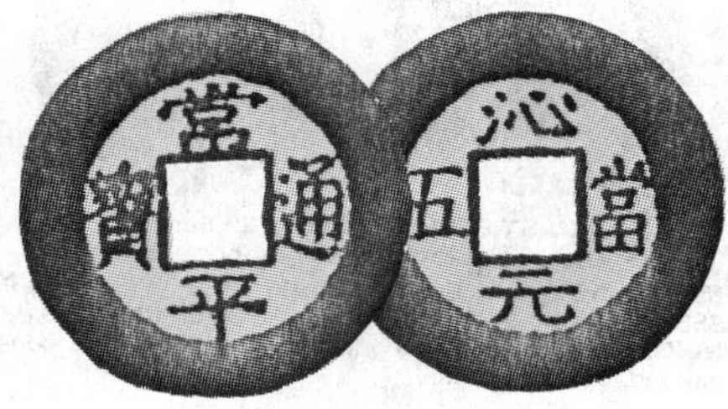

CAST BRONZE, 31mm
Rev: *Sim* at top, *Won* at bottom, *Tang* at right, *O* (5) at left.

KM#	Date	Series	Good	VG	Fine	VF
775	ND(1883)	—	4.00	6.50	10.00	15.00

30mm
Large characters.
Rev: Series number at bottom.

KM#	Date	Series	Good	VG	Fine	VF
776.1-776.11	ND(1883)	1-11	2.00	2.75	3.50	5.00

32mm
Small characters.

KM#	Date	Series	Good	VG	Fine	VF
777.1-777.10	ND(1883)	1-10	2.00	2.75	3.50	5.00

Rev: Crescent below series number.

KM#	Date	Series	Good	VG	Fine	VF
778.1-778.7	ND(1883)	1-7	8.00	12.00	20.00	30.00

Rev: Crescent at lower left.

KM#	Date	Series	Good	VG	Fine	VF
779.1-779.13	ND(1883)	1-13	3.50	5.50	8.00	12.00

KAESONG TOWNSHIP MILITARY OFFICE

開 Kae (Kae Song Kwal Li Yong)

MUN

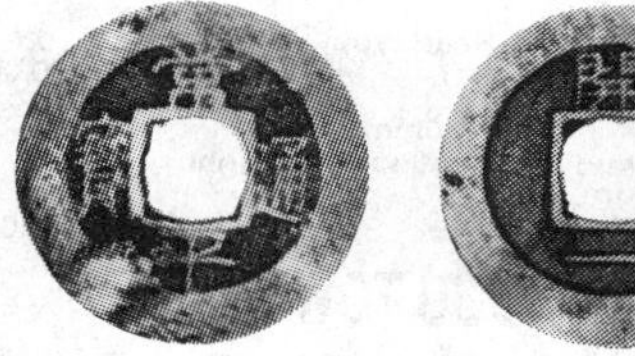

CAST BRONZE, 4.00 g, 23.5mm
Large characters.
Rev: Series number at bottom.

KM#	Date	Series	Good	VG	Fine	VF
791.1-791.5	ND(1836)	1-5	1.50	2.25	3.50	5.00

24.5mm

Rev: Circle at right, series number at bottom.

KM#	Date	Series	Good	VG	Fine	VF
793.1-793.10	ND(1816)	1-10	1.50	2.25	3.50	5.00

Rev: Star at lower left.

KM#	Date	Series	Good	VG	Fine	VF
793.11	ND(1816)	1	1.50	2.25	3.50	5.00

Rev: Star at upper left.

KM#	Date	Series	Good	VG	Fine	VF
793.17	ND(1816)	7	1.50	2.25	3.50	5.00

24mm
Rev: Circle at left, series number at bottom.

KM#	Date	Series	Good	VG	Fine	VF
794.1-794.10	ND(1816)	1-10	1.50	2.25	3.50	5.00

25mm
Rev: Crescent at right, series number at bottom.

KM#	Date	Series	Good	VG	Fine	VF
795.1-795.10	ND(1816)	1-10	1.50	2.25	3.50	5.00

25.5mm
Small characters.
Rev: Crescent at right, series number at bottom.

KM#	Date	Series	Good	VG	Fine	VF
A795.1-A795.10	ND(1836)	1-10	3.00	6.00	10.00	15.00

Rev: Star at lower left.

KM#	Date	Series	Good	VG	Fine	VF
A795.13	ND(1836)	3	3.00	6.00	10.00	15.00

25mm
Rev: Crescent at left, series number at bottom.

KM#	Date	Series	Good	VG	Fine	VF
B795.1-B795.10	ND(1816)	1-10	1.50	2.25	3.50	5.00

Small characters, wider rims.
Small crescent.

KM#	Date	Series	Good	VG	Fine	VF
C795.1-C795.10	ND(1836)	1-10	3.00	6.00	10.00	15.00

25mm
Rev: *Ch'on* at bottom, series number at right.

KM#	Date	Series	Good	VG	Fine	VF
796.1-796.10	ND(1836)	1-10	1.50	2.25	3.50	5.00

Rev: *Ch'on* at bottom, *Sip* (10) at right, additional series number at left.

KM#	Date	Series	Good	VG	Fine	VF
797.1-797.5	ND(1836)	1-5	1.50	2.25	3.50	5.00

Rev: *Ch'on* at bottom, series number at right, crescent at left.

KM#	Date	Series	Good	VG	Fine	VF
798.1-798.3	ND(1836)	1-3	1.50	2.25	3.50	5.00

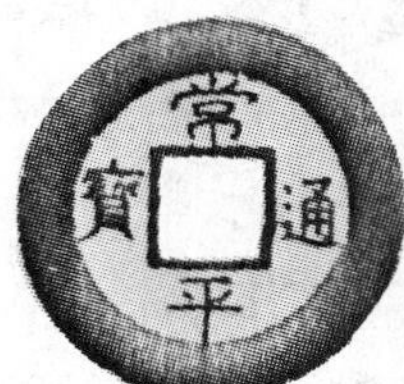
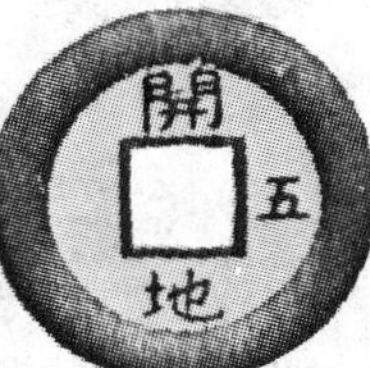

25.5mm
Rev: *Chi* at bottom, series number at right.

KM#	Date	Series	Good	VG	Fine	VF
799.1-799.10	ND(1836)	1-10	1.75	2.75	3.50	5.00

24.5mm
Rev: *Chi* at bottom, *Sip* (10) at right, additional series number at left.

KM#	Date	Series	Good	VG	Fine	VF
800.1-800.9	ND(1836)	1-9	1.75	2.75	3.50	5.00

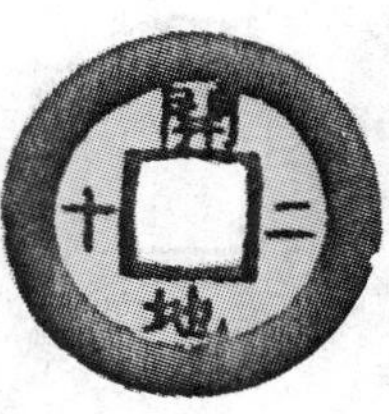

25mm
Rev: *Chi* at bottom, *I* (2) at right, *Sip* (10) at left.

KM#	Date	Series	Good	VG	Fine	VF
801.2	ND(1836)	2	1.75	2.75	3.50	5.00

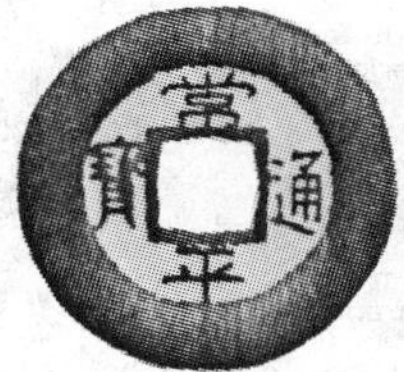

Rev: *Il* (sun) at bottom, series number at right.

KM#	Date	Series	Good	VG	Fine	VF
802.1-802.10	ND(1836)	1-10	1.75	2.75	3.50	5.00

22mm

KM#	Date	Series	Good	VG	Fine	VF
802.13	ND(1836)	3	1.75	2.75	3.50	5.00

24.5mm
Rev: *Il* (sun) at bottom, series number at left.

KM#	Date	Series	Good	VG	Fine	VF
803.1-803.10	ND(1836)	1-10	1.75	2.75	3.50	5.00

24mm
Rev: *T'o* at bottom, series number at left.

KM#	Date	Series	Good	VG	Fine	VF
804.10	ND(1836)	10	—	—	Rare	—

松 Song (Song Do Kwal Li Yong)

NOTE: *Song Do* is another name for *Kae Song*.

MUN

CAST BRONZE, 4.00 g, 25mm
Rev: *Song* at top, series number at bottom.

KM#	Date	Series	Good	VG	Fine	VF
805.1-805.10	ND(1882)	1-10	1.50	2.25	3.50	5.00

Seed type

KM#	Date	Series	Good	VG	Fine	VF
805s	ND(1882)	1-10	—	—	*XF*	25.00

IWON TOWNSHIP MILITARY OFFICE

利 I (I Won Kwal Li Yong)

MUN

CAST BRONZE, 4.00 g, 24mm
Rev: *Chon* at bottom, series number at left.

KM#	Date	Series	Good	VG	Fine	VF
834.1-834.6	ND(1882)	1-6	2.75	3.50	5.00	7.50

Seed type

KM#	Date	Series	Good	VG	Fine	VF
834s	ND(1882)	1-6	—	—	*XF*	35.00

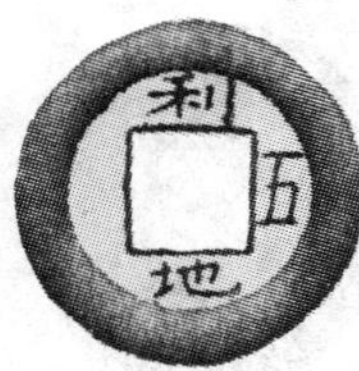

23mm
Rev: *Chi* at bottom, series number at right.

KM#	Date	Series	Good	VG	Fine	VF
835.1-835.5	ND(1882)	1-5	7.50	12.50	20.00	35.00
	Seed type					
835s	ND(1882)	1-5	—	—	*XF*	60.00

24mm
Large characters.
Rev: *Chi* at bottom, series number at left.

KM#	Date	Series	Good	VG	Fine	VF
836.1-836.5	ND(1882)	1-5	7.50	12.50	20.00	35.00
	Seed type					
836s	ND(1882)	1-5	—	—	*XF*	65.00

22mm
Small characters

KM#	Date	Series	Good	VG	Fine	VF
837.1-837.5	ND(1882)	1-5	7.50	12.50	20.00	35.00

CH'UNCH'ON TOWNSHIP MILITARY OFFICE

Ch'un (Ch'un Ch'on Kwal Li Yong)

春 or 萅 **5 MUN**

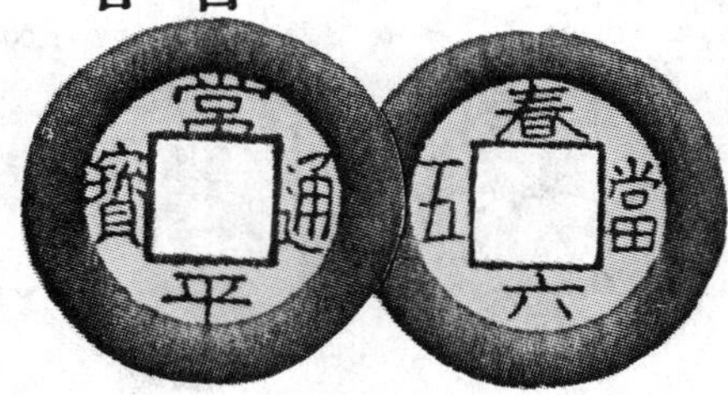

CAST BRONZE, 31mm
Large characters.
Rev: *Ch'un* at top, *Tang* at right, *O* (5) at left, series number at bottom.

KM#	Date	Series	Good	VG	Fine	VF
874.1-874.12	ND(1888)	1-12	2.00	3.00	5.00	7.00
	Seed type					
874s	ND(1888)	1-10	—	—	*XF*	35.00

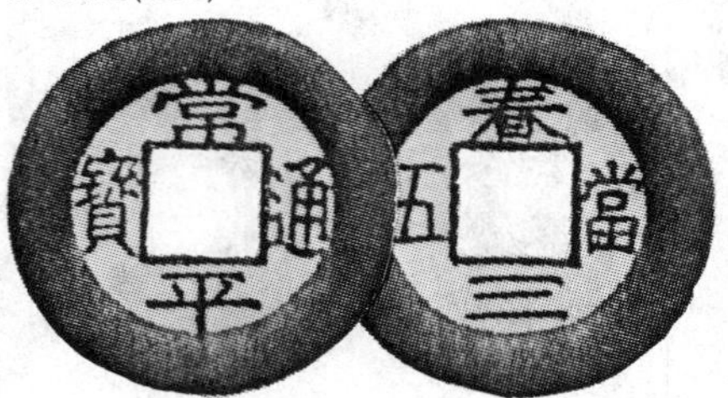

30mm
Medium characters.

KM#	Date	Series	Good	VG	Fine	VF
875.1-875.11	ND(1888)	1-11	2.00	3.00	5.00	7.00
	Seed type					
875s	ND(1888)	1-10	—	—	*XF*	35.00
	Reduced size, 27mm					
876.1-876.10	ND(1888)	1-10	2.00	3.00	5.00	7.00
	Seed type					
876s	ND(1888)	1-10	—	—	*XF*	35.00

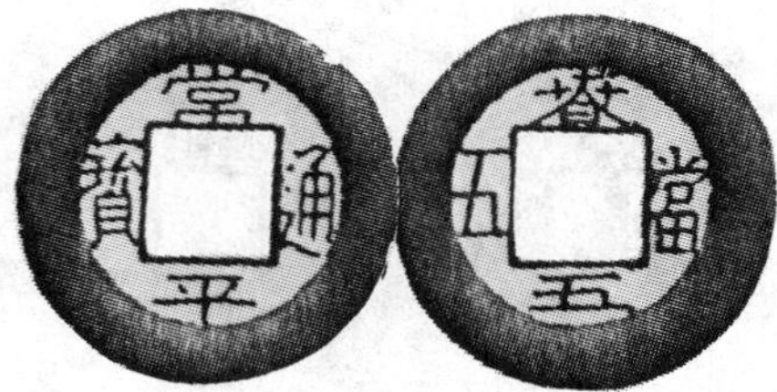

28mm
Rev: *Ch'un* at top in different style.

KM#	Date	Series	Good	VG	Fine	VF
877.1-877.20	ND(1888)	1-20	2.00	3.00	5.00	7.00
	30mm					
877a.1-877a.10	ND(1888)	1-10	2.00	3.00	5.00	7.00

Seed type

KM#	Date	Series	Good	VG	Fine	VF
877s	ND(1888)	1-20	—	—	*XF*	35.00

29mm
Rev: Crescent at bottom under series number.

KM#	Date	Series	Good	VG	Fine	VF
878.1-878.10	ND(1888)	1-10	2.75	3.50	5.00	7.00
	Seed type					
878s	ND(1888)	1-10	—	—	*XF*	35.00

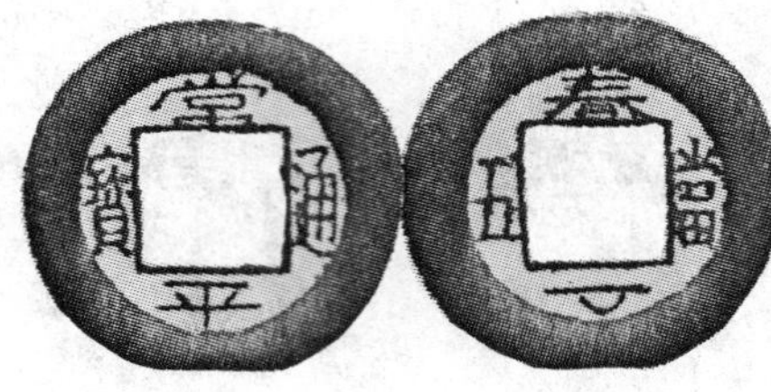

28mm
Rev: Inverted crescent at bottom under series number.

KM#	Date	Series	Good	VG	Fine	VF
879.1	ND(1888)	1	2.25	3.50	5.50	9.00
879.2-879.10		2-10	4.00	6.00	10.00	15.00
	ND(1888)	1-10	2.25	3.50	5.50	9.00
	Seed type					
879s	ND(1888)	1	—	—	*XF*	35.00

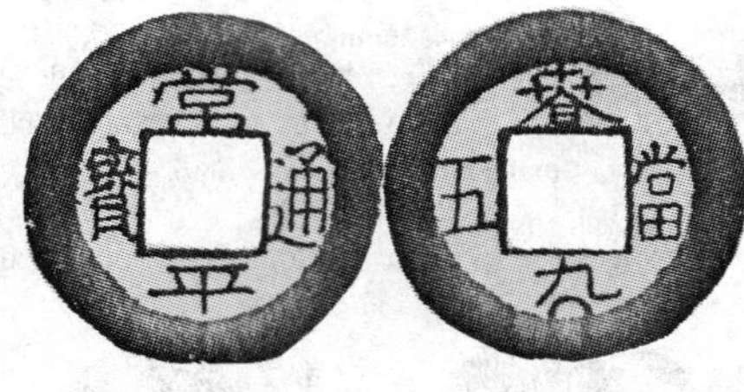

29-30mm
Rev: *Ch'un* at top in different style, crescent at bottom under series number.

KM#	Date	Series	Good	VG	Fine	VF
880.1-880.10	ND(1888)	1-10	2.75	3.50	4.50	7.00
	Seed type					
880s	ND(1888)	1-10	—	—	*XF*	27.50
	27-28mm					
A880.1-A880.20	ND(1888)	1-20	2.25	3.00	4.00	6.00

TANCH'ON TOWNSHIP MILITARY OFFICE

川 Chon (Tan Ch'on Kwal Li Yong)

5 MUN

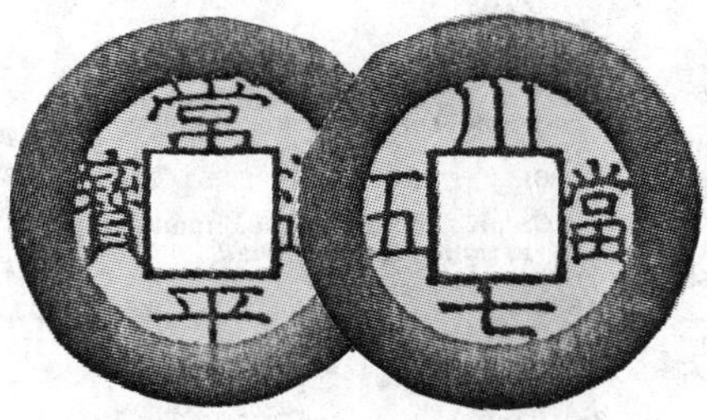

CAST BRONZE, 32mm
Inside diameter 22mm.
Rev: *Ch'on* at top, *Tang* at right, *O* (5) at left, series number at bottom.

KM#	Date	Series	Good	VG	Fine	VF
881.1-881.10	ND(1883)	1-10	3.00	4.50	6.50	9.00
	Seed type					
881s	ND(1883)	1-10	—	—	*XF*	30.00

28mm
Reduced size, inside diameter 20mm.

KM#	Date	Series	Good	VG	Fine	VF
882.1-882.10	ND(1883)	1-10	3.50	5.50	8.00	12.00
	Seed type					
882s	ND(1883)	1-10	—	—	*XF*	30.00

CH'ANG DOK PALACE MINT

昌 Ch'ang (Ch'ang Dok Kung)

MUN

CAST BRONZE, 4.00 g, 23.5mm
Rev: *Ch'ang* at top, series number at bottom.

KM#	Date	Series	Good	VG	Fine	VF
883.1	ND(1864-95)	1	4.00	6.00	10.00	16.00

NOTE Similar pieces without a series number are considered to be spurious.

Seed type

KM#	Date	Series	Good	VG	Fine	VF
883s	ND(1864-95)	1	—	—	*XF*	50.00

CH'ANG WON TOWNSHIP MILITARY OFFICE

昌 Ch'ang (Ch'ang Won Kwal Li Yong)

5 MUN

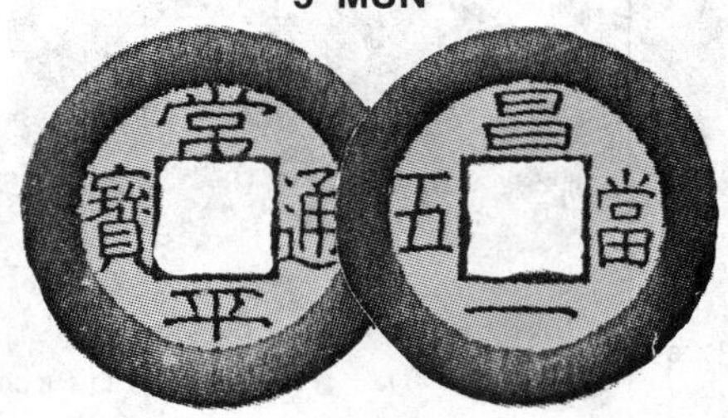

CAST BRONZE, 31mm
Large characters.
Rev: *Ch'ang* at top, *Tang* at right, *O* (5) at left, series number at bottom.

KM#	Date	Series	Good	VG	Fine	VF
884.1-884.12	ND(1887)	1-12	2.75	4.00	6.00	9.00
	Seed type					
884s	ND(1887)	1-12	—	—	*XF*	30.00
	Reduced size, 29mm **Small characters.**					
885.1-885.12	ND(1887)	1-12	2.75	4.00	6.00	9.00
	Seed type					
885s	ND(1887)	1-12	—	—	*XF*	30.00

30mm
Rev: Sun or circle at upper right.

KM#	Date	Series	Good	VG	Fine	VF
A885.1-A885.10	ND(1887)	1-10	3.00	4.50	6.50	10.00

31mm
Large characters.
Rev: Crescent at bottom under series number.

KM#	Date	Series	Good	VG	Fine	VF
886.1-886.9	ND(1887)	1-9	2.75	4.00	6.00	9.00
	Seed type					
886s	ND(1887)	1-9	—	—	*XF*	30.00

Reduced size, 29mm
Small characters.
Rev: Crescent at bottom under series number.

KM#	Date	Series	Good	VG	Fine	VF
887.1-887.10	ND(1887)	1-10	2.75	4.00	6.00	9.00
	Seed type					
887s	ND(1887)	1-10	—	—	*XF*	30.00

30mm
Rev: Crescent at upper right.

KM#	Date	Series	Good	VG	Fine	VF
A887.1-A887.10	ND(1887)	1-10	3.00	4.50	6.50	10.00

KWANG JU TOWNSHIP MILITARY OFFICE

Kyonggi Province

圻 Ki (Kwang Ju Kwal Li Yong)

MUN

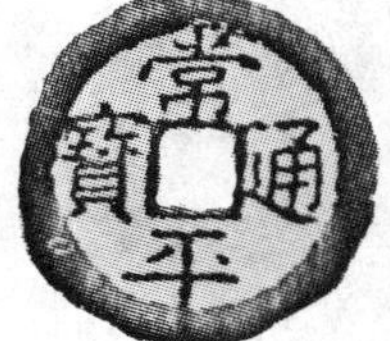

CAST COPPER, 4.50 g
Rev: *Ki* at top.

KM#	Date	Series	Good	VG	Fine	VF
888	ND(1742)	—	—	—	Rare	—

CAST BRONZE, 4.00 g, 25mm
Rev: *Ch'on* at bottom, series number at right.

KM#	Date	Series	Good	VG	Fine	VF
889.1-889.5	ND(1836)	1-5	1.75	2.25	3.00	5.00
Seed type						
889s	ND(1836)	1-5	—	—	XF	25.00

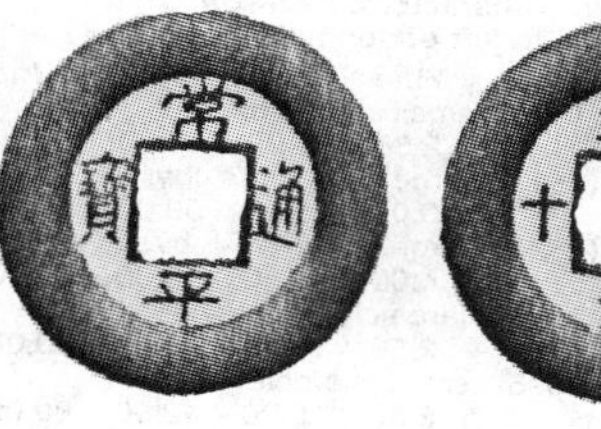
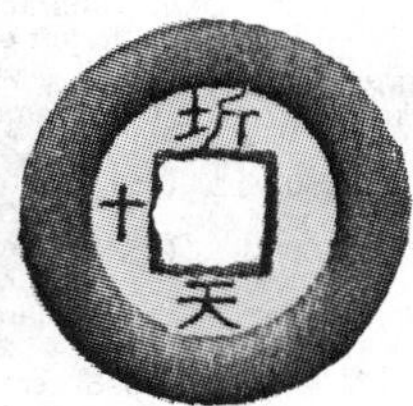

26mm
Large characters.
Rev: *Ch'on* at bottom, series number at left.

KM#	Date	Series	Good	VG	Fine	VF
890.1-890.10	ND(1836)	1-10	1.75	2.25	3.00	5.00
Seed type						
890s	ND(1836)	1-10	—	—	XF	25.00

24mm
Small characters.

KM#	Date	Series	Good	VG	Fine	VF
A890.1-A890.10	ND(1836)	1-10	1.75	2.25	3.00	5.00
Seed type						
A890s	ND(1836)	1-10	—	—	XF	25.00

27mm
Rev: *Ch'on* at bottom, series number at right, circle at left.

KM#	Date	Series	Good	VG	Fine	VF
891.1-891.5	ND(1839)	1-5	4.00	6.00	10.00	18.00
Seed type						
891s	ND(1839)	1-5	—	—	XF	35.00

Rev: Crescent at left, series number at right.

KM#	Date	Series	Good	VG	Fine	VF
892.1-892.10	ND(1836)	1-10	4.00	6.00	10.00	18.00
Seed type						
892s	ND(1836)	1-10	—	—	XF	35.00

26.5mm
Rev: Crescent at right, series number at left.

KM#	Date	Series	Good	VG	Fine	VF
893.1-893.10	ND(1839)	1-10	4.00	6.00	9.00	16.00
Seed type						
893s	ND(1839)	1-10	—	—	XF	35.00

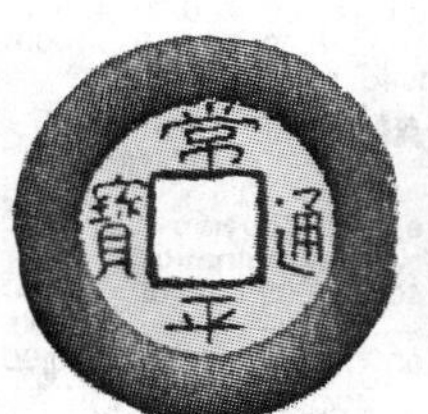

26mm
Rev: *I* (2) at bottom, series number at right.

KM#	Date	Series	Good	VG	Fine	VF
894.1-894.10	ND(1839)	1-10	5.00	8.50	13.50	20.00

KM#	Date	Series	Good	VG	Fine	VF
Seed type						
894s	ND(1839)	1-10	—	—	XF	45.00

Rev: *I* (2) at bottom, series number at left.

KM#	Date	Series	Good	VG	Fine	VF
895.1-895.10	ND(1839)	1-10	2.25	3.00	5.00	7.00
Seed type						
895s	ND(1839)	1-10	—	—	XF	35.00

Rev: *I* (2) at bottom, crescent at right, series number at left.

KM#	Date	Series	Good	VG	Fine	VF
896.1-896.10	ND(1839)	1-10	5.00	8.00	12.50	20.00
Seed type						
896s	ND(1839)	1-10	—	—	XF	45.00

KYONGGI PROVINCIAL OFFICE

京 Kyong (Kyong Gi Kam Yong)

5 MUN

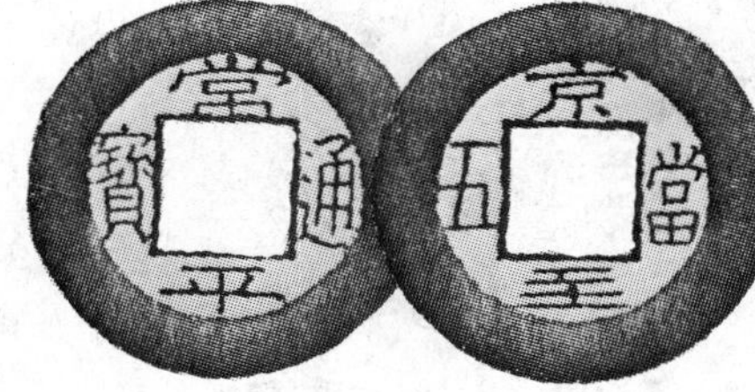

CAST BRONZE, 29-30mm
Rev: *Kyong* at top, *Tang* at right, *O* (5) at left, series number at bottom.

KM#	Date	Series	Good	VG	Fine	VF
907	ND(1888)	1-27	1.75	2.25	3.00	5.00
Seed type						
907s	ND(1888)	1-27	—	—	XF	30.00

P'YONGAN PROVINCIAL OFFICE

平 P'yong (P'yong An Kam Yong)

MUN

CAST BRONZE, 22mm, 4.00 g

KM#	Date	Series	Good	VG	Fine	VF
915.1	ND(1883)	1	1.50	2.25	3.50	5.00
915.2		2	1.50	2.25	3.50	5.00
915.3		3	1.50	2.25	3.50	5.00
915.4		4	1.50	2.25	3.50	5.00
915.5		5	1.50	2.25	3.50	5.00
915.6		6	1.50	2.25	3.50	5.00
915.7		7	1.50	2.25	3.50	5.00
915.8		8	4.00	6.00	9.00	16.00
915.9		9	4.00	6.00	9.00	16.00
915.10		10	4.00	6.00	9.00	16.00
915.11		11	4.00	6.00	9.00	16.00
Seed type						
915s	ND(1883)	1-11	—	—	XF	40.00

CAST BRONZE, 22mm, 4.00 g
Rev: Circle at left, series number at bottom.

KM#	Date	Series	Good	VG	Fine	VF
917.1-917.5	ND(1883)	1-5	1.50	2.25	3.50	5.00
Seed type						
917s	ND(1883)	1-5	—	—	XF	30.00

23mm
Rev: *Ch'on* at bottom, series number at left.

KM#	Date	Series	Good	VG	Fine	VF
918.1-918.11	ND(1891)	1-11	1.50	2.25	3.50	5.00
21mm						
918.15	ND(1891)	5	1.50	2.25	3.50	5.00
Rev: Star at upper left.						
918.17	ND(1891)	7	1.50	2.25	3.50	5.00
Seed type						
918s	ND(1891)	1-11	—	—	XF	30.00

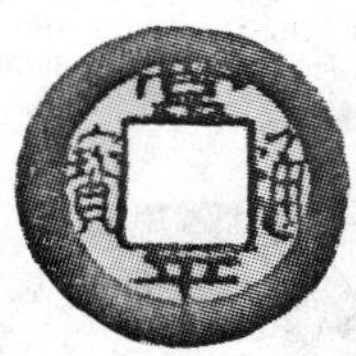

22mm
Rev: *Chi* at bottom, series number at left.

KM#	Date	Series	Good	VG	Fine	VF
919.1	ND(1891)	1	1.50	2.25	3.50	5.00
919.4		4	1.50	2.25	3.50	5.00
Seed type						
919s	ND(1891)	1,4	—	—	XF	30.00

21mm
Rev: *Il* (sun) at bottom.

KM#	Date	Series	Good	VG	Fine	VF
920	ND(1891)	—	1.75	2.25	3.00	5.00
Seed type						
920s	ND(1891)	—	—	—	XF	30.00

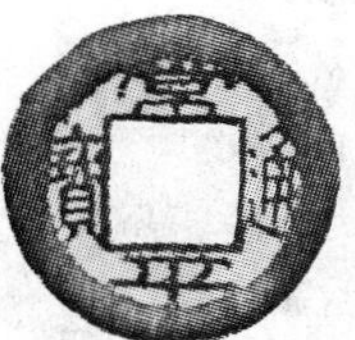
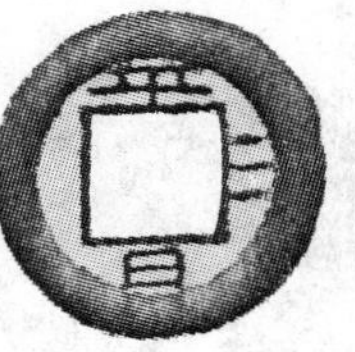

22mm
Rev: *Il* (sun) at bottom, series number at right.

KM#	Date	Series	Good	VG	Fine	VF
921.1-921.10	ND(1891)	1-10	1.50	2.25	3.50	5.00
Seed type						
921s	ND(1891)	1-10	—	—	XF	30.00

Rev: *Il* (sun) at bottom, series number at left.

KM#	Date	Series	Good	VG	Fine	VF
922.1-922.14	ND(1891)	1-14	1.50	2.25	3.50	5.00
Seed type						
922s	ND(1891)	1-14	—	—	XF	30.00

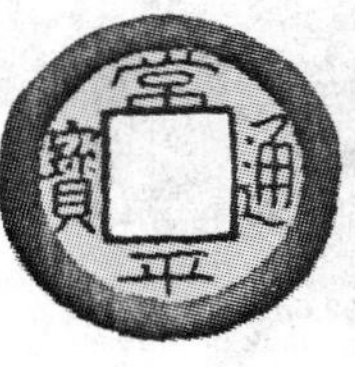

22.5mm
Rev: *Saeng* at bottom, series number at left.

KM#	Date	Series	Good	VG	Fine	VF
923.1-923.13	ND(1891)	1-13	1.50	2.25	3.50	5.00
Seed type						
923s	ND(1891)	1-13	—	—	XF	30.00

22mm
Rev: *Saeng* at bottom, series number at right, circle at left.

KM#	Date	Series	Good	VG	Fine	VF
924.1-924.10	ND(1891)	1-10	1.50	2.25	3.50	5.00
Seed type						
924s	ND(1891)	1-10	—	—	XF	30.00

5 MUN

CAST BRONZE, 31mm

KM#	Date	Series	Good	VG	Fine	VF
A970.1-A970.10	ND(1883)	1-10	1.75	2.75	3.50	5.50

HAMGYONG PROVINCIAL OFFICE

咸 Ham (Ham Gyong Kam Yong)

MUN

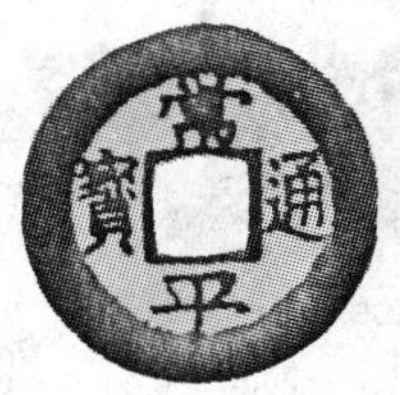

CAST BRONZE, 4.00 g, 24mm
Rev: *Ham* at top, series number at bottom.

KM#	Date	Series	Good	VG	Fine	VF
974.1-974.4	ND(1834)	1-4	1.75	2.75	3.00	5.00
Seed type						
974s	ND(1834)	1-4	—	—	XF	30.00

TAE DONG TREASURY DEPARTMENT

CHON

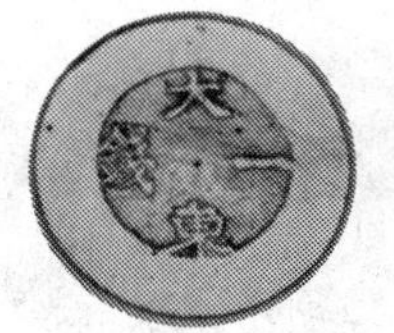
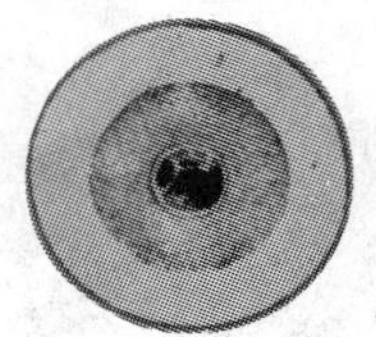

SILVER, 22mm
Rev: *Ho* in green, black or blue cloisonne enameled center circle.

KM#	Date	Mintage	VG	Fine	VF	XF
1081	ND(1882-83)	*	100.00	150.00	200.00	300.00

2 CHON

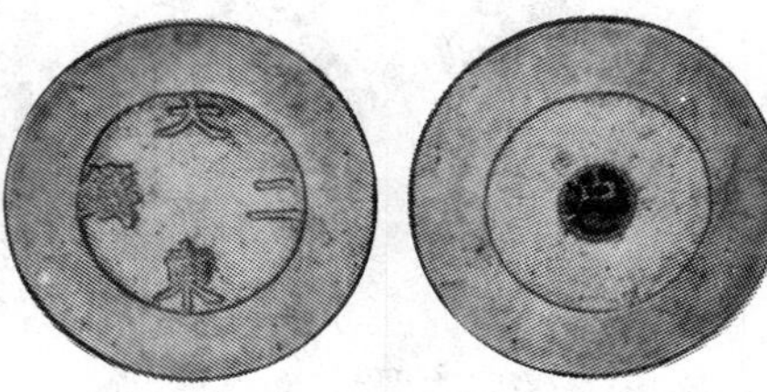

SILVER, 27mm
Rev: *Ho* in green, black or blue cloisonne enameled center circle.

KM#	Date	Mintage	VG	Fine	VF	XF
1082	ND(1882-83)	*	150.00	200.00	300.00	450.00

3 CHON

SILVER, 32.5mm
Rev: *Ho* in green, black or blue cloisonne enameled center circle.

KM#	Date	Mintage	VG	Fine	VF	XF
1083	ND(1882-83)	*	275.00	400.00	550.00	800.00

***NOTE:** Due to the added expense of adding the 'cloisonne' enamel during production the silver one, two & three Chon KM#1081-83 were discontinued in June, 1883. Examples with cloisonne missing are valued at about one half normal valuations. There are many types of trial sets of 1, 2 and 3 Chon in existence.

MILLED COINAGE

During the 1880's and 1890's, Korea experimented with several different types of machine-struck coins including a struck "Cash" coin with round center hole, KM#1100. Some pattern coins of this period exist, some of which may have actually entered circulation.

MONETARY SYSTEM
1888-1891
1000 Mun = 1 Warn

5 MUN

BRASS

KM#	Date	Mintage	Fine	VF	XF	Unc
1100	ND(1884)	—	150.00	300.00	450.00	600.00

COPPER, 3.25 g

KM#	Year	Date	Fine	VF	XF	Unc
1101	497	(1888)	60.00	120.00	200.00	400.00

10 MUN

COPPER, 6.50 g

KM#	Year	Date	Fine	VF	XF	Unc
1102	497	(1888)	125.00	265.00	400.00	700.00

WARN

26.9500 g, .900 SILVER, .7798 oz ASW

KM#	Year	Date	Fine	VF	XF	Unc
1103	497	(1888)	5500.	13,500.	15,000.	20,000.

MONETARY REFORM

1892-1902

100 Fun = 1 Yang
5 Yang = 1 Whan

FUN

BRASS, 3.50 g
Obv: 3 characters, *Tae Cho-son* (Great Korea), to left of denomination.

KM#	Year	Date	Fine	VF	XF	Unc
1104	501	(1892)	10.00	35.00	75.00	250.00
	501	(1892)	—	—	Proof	1000.
	504	(1895)	10.00	35.00	75.00	250.00
	505	(1896)	18.50	70.00	125.00	300.00

Obv: 2 characters, *Cho-son* (Korea), to left of denomination.

KM#	Year	Date	Fine	VF	XF	Unc
1105	502	(1893)	15.00	50.00	100.00	250.00
	503	(1894)	— Reported, not confirmed			
	504	(1895)	8.00	25.00	50.00	150.00
	505	(1896)	— Reported, not confirmed			

5 FUN

COPPER, 17.20 g
Obv: 3 small characters, *Tae Cho-son*, leg. above dragon divided into two parts by a dot.

KM#	Year	Date	Fine	VF	XF	Unc
1106	501	(1892)	2.50	6.00	15.00	80.00
	501	(1892)	—	—	Proof	1200.
	505	(1896)	2.50	6.00	15.00	80.00

Obv: 2 characters, *Cho-son* (Korea), to left of denomination.

KM#	Year	Date	Fine	VF	XF	Unc
1107	502	(1893) small characters obv.	2.50	6.00	15.00	90.00
	502	(1893) large characters obv.	20.00	45.00	80.00	300.00
	503	(1894) large characters obv.	4.00	8.50	18.00	100.00
	504	(1895) large characters obv.	2.50	6.00	14.00	80.00
	505	(1896) small characters obv.	2.50	5.00	12.00	80.00

Obv: 3 large characters, *Tae Cho-son* (Great Korea) to left of denomination, w/o dot in leg. above dragon.

KM#	Year	Date	Fine	VF	XF	Unc
1108	504	(1895)	2.50	5.00	12.00	80.00
	505	(1896)	3.00	8.00	18.00	100.00

KM#	Year	Date	Fine	VF	XF	Unc
	Kuang Mu					
1116	2	(1898) small characters obv.	2.00	4.00	10.00	80.00
	2	(1898) medium characters obv.	15.00	40.00	70.00	250.00
	2	(1898) large characters obv.	55.00	115.00	200.00	425.00
	3	(1899)	150.00	175.00	500.00	1000.

NOTE: Later date (Yr.6) exists for this type.

1/4 YANG

COPPER-NICKEL
Obv: 3 characters, *Tae Cho-son* (Great Korea), to left of denomination.

KM#	Year	Date	Fine	VF	XF	Unc
1109	501	(1892)	10.00	25.00	50.00	150.00
	501	(1892)	—	—	Proof	2000.
	504	(1895)	10.00	27.50	50.00	150.00

Obv: 2 characters, *Cho-son* (Korea), to left of denomination.

KM#	Year	Date	Fine	VF	XF	Unc
1110	502	(1893)	5.50	18.00	35.00	100.00
	503	(1894)	20.00	50.00	150.00	200.00
	504	(1895)	150.00	300.00	500.00	1200.
	505	(1896)	5.50	18.50	35.00	100.00

Obv: Dragon crowded by small tight circle, 11.25mm.

KM#	Year	Date	Fine	VF	XF	Unc
	Kuang Mu					
1117	1	(1897)	125.00	275.00	500.00	1000.
	2	(1898)	.95	1.50	2.75	8.00
	3	(1899) large characters obv.	115.00	250.00	500.00	1000.
	3	(1899) small characters obv.	115.00	250.00	500.00	1000.
	4	(1900)	140.00	300.00	550.00	1100.

NOTE: Later date (Yr.5) exists for this type.

NOTE: Many varieties of characters size and style exist for year 2 coins.

Obv: Larger circle around dragon.

KM#	Year	Date	Fine	VF	XF	Unc
1118	2	(1898)	5.00	8.50	17.50	100.00

NOTE: KM#1118 were counterfeits made on machinery supplied by the Japanese. These counterfeits were authorized for circulation by the Korean Government.

YANG

5.2000 g, .800 SILVER, .1338 oz ASW
Obv: 3 characters, *Tae Cho-son.*

KM#	Year	Date	Fine	VF	XF	Unc
1112	501	(1892)	65.00	100.00	150.00	400.00
	501	(1892)	—	—	Proof	5000.

Obv: 2 characters, *Cho-son.*

KM#	Year	Date	Fine	VF	XF	Unc
1113	502	(1893)	65.00	100.00	150.00	400.00

Obv: Wide spaced *Yang.*
Kuang Mu

KM#	Year	Date	Fine	VF	XF	Unc
1119	2	(1898)	80.00	150.00	250.00	450.00

Obv: Closely spaced *Yang.*

KM#	Year	Date	Fine	VF	XF	Unc
1120	2	(1898)	75.00	130.00	225.00	400.00

5 YANG

26.9500 g, .900 SILVER, .7798 oz ASW

KM#	Year	Mintage	Fine	VF	XF	Unc
1114	501(1892)	.020	700.00	1250.	2000.	3500.
	501(1892)	—	—	—	Proof	16,500.

WHAN

26.9500 g, .900 SILVER, .7798 oz ASW

KM#	Year	Mintage	Fine	VF	XF	Unc
1115	502(1893)	I.A.	2750.	5925.	10,000.	15,500.

PATTERNS (Pn)

(Including off metal strikes)

NOTE: Pn1-5 previously listed here are now listed in the Shanghai Foreign Enclave section of China.

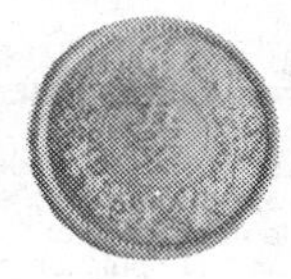

KM#	Date	Mintage	Identification	Mkt.Val.
Pn6	CD1885	—	5 Mun, White Metal (Tin alloy)	—

KM#	Date	Mintage	Identification	Mkt.Val.
Pn7	CD1885	—	1 Yang, White Metal (Tin alloy)	—
Pn8	1886,yr.495	—	1 Mun, Copper	—
Pn9	1886,yr.495	—	2 Mun, Copper	—
Pn10	1886,yr.495	—	5 Mun, Copper	—

KM#	Date	Mintage	Identification	Mkt.Val.
Pn11	1886,yr.495	—	10 Mun, Copper	1400.

KM#	Date	Mintage	Identification	Mkt.Val.
Pn12	1886,yr.495	—	20 Mun, Copper	2500.
Pn12A	1886,yr.495	—	20 Mun, Silver	4200.
Pn13	1886,yr.495	—	1/2 Niang, White Metal (Tin alloy)	—

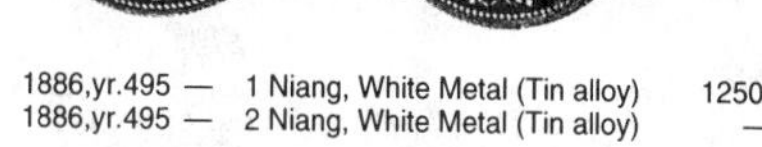

KM#	Date	Mintage	Identification	Mkt.Val.
Pn14	1886,yr.495	—	1 Niang, White Metal (Tin alloy)	1250.
Pn15	1886,yr.495	—	2 Niang, White Metal (Tin alloy)	—

KM#	Date	Mintage	Identification	Mkt.Val.
Pn16	1886,yr.495	—	5 Niang, White Metal (Tin alloy)	—
Pn17	1886,yr.495	—	1 Warn, White Metal (Tin alloy)	—
Pn18	1886,yr.495	—	1 Warn, Gilt Copper	—
Pn19	1886,yr.495	—	2 Warn, Gilt Copper	—
Pn20	1886,yr.495	—	5 Warn, Gilt Copper	—
Pn21	1886,yr.495	—	10 Warn, Gilt Copper	—
Pn22	1886,yr.495	—	20 Warn, Gilt Copper	—

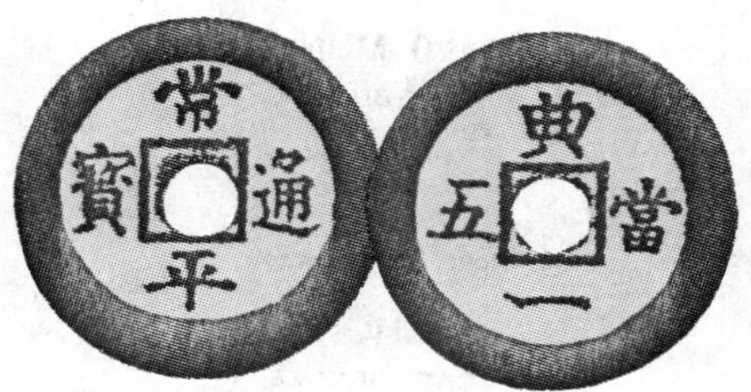

KM#	Date	Mintage	Identification	Mkt.Val.
Pn25	ND(1891)	—	5 Mun, Brass, center hole in square frame	450.00

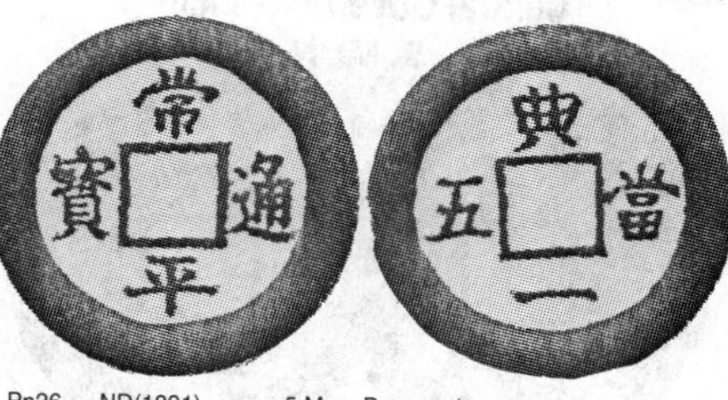

KM#	Date	Mintage	Identification	Mkt.Val.
Pn26	ND(1891)	—	5 Mun, Brass, w/o center hole in square frame	—

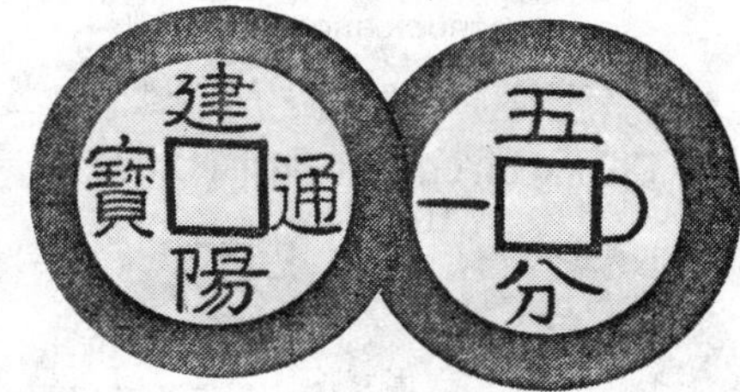

KM#	Date	Mintage	Identification	Mkt.Val.
Pn27	1896,yr.505	—	5 Fun, Bronze, cast	—

KM#	Date	Mintage	Identification	Mkt.Val.
Pn28	1896,yr.505	—	1 Chon, Copper, cast	—

KM#	Date	Mintage	Identification	Mkt.Val.
Pn29	1896,yr.505	—	5 Chon, Pewter, cast, value not circled	—

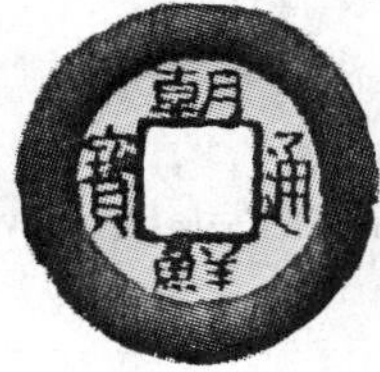

KM#	Date	Mintage	Identification	Mkt.Val.
Pn30	1896,yr.505	—	5 Chon, Bronze, cast, value circled	—
Pn31	1899,yr.3	—	1/2 Dollar, Silver	—
Pn31A	1899,yr.3	—	1/2 Won, Silver	—
Pn32	1900,yr.4	—	20 Won, Copper	—

TEST COINAGE (Tc)

Treasury Department

MUN

CAST BRONZE
Obv. leg: *Cho Son T'ong Bo.*
Rev: *Mu* at top, *Chon* at bottom.

KM#	Date	Series	Good	VG	Fine	VF
Tc1	ND(1881)	1	—	—	Rare	—

10 MUN

CAST BRONZE
Obv. leg: *Cho Son T'ong Bo.*
Rev: Blank.

KM#	Date	Series	Good	VG	Fine	VF
Tc2	ND	—	—	—	Rare	—

Rev: *Sip* (10) at top.

KM#	Date	Series	Good	VG	Fine	VF
Tc3	ND	—	—	—	Rare	—

CHON

CAST BRONZE
Obv: Similar to KM#Tc2.
Rev: *Ho* at top, *Il (1) Chon* at right.

KM#	Date	Series	Good	VG	Fine	VF
Tc4	ND(1881)	—	—	—	Rare	—

Central Government Mint

5 MUN

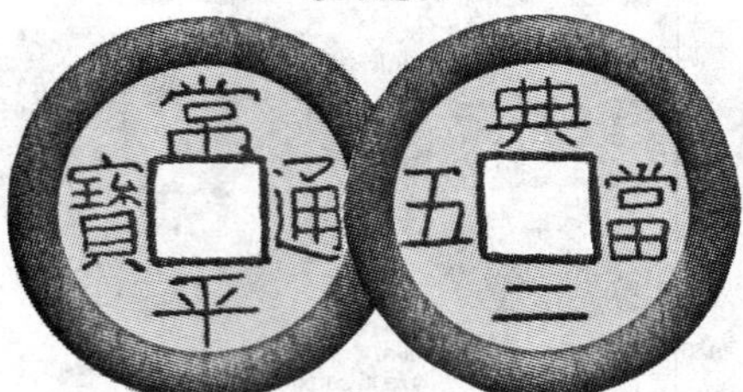

STRUCK BRONZE
Obv. leg: *Sang P'yong T'ong Bo.*
Rev: *I* at bottom, *Tang* at right, *O* (5) at left.

KM#	Date	Series	Good	VG	Fine	VF
Tc6	ND(1884)	—	—	—	Rare	—

Ch'ung Ch'ong Provincial Office

10 MUN

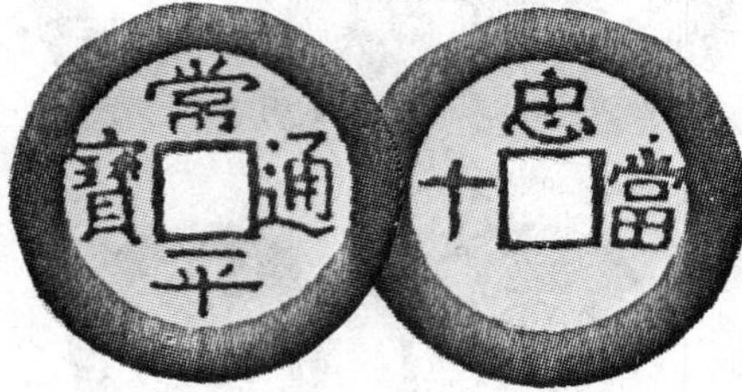

STRUCK BRASS
Obv. leg: *Sang P'yong T'ong Bo.*
Rev: *Ch'ung* at top, *Tang* at right, *Sip* (10) at left.

KM#	Date	Series	Good	VG	Fine	VF
Tc7	ND(1884)	—	—	—	Rare	—

Without Mint Mark

10 MUN

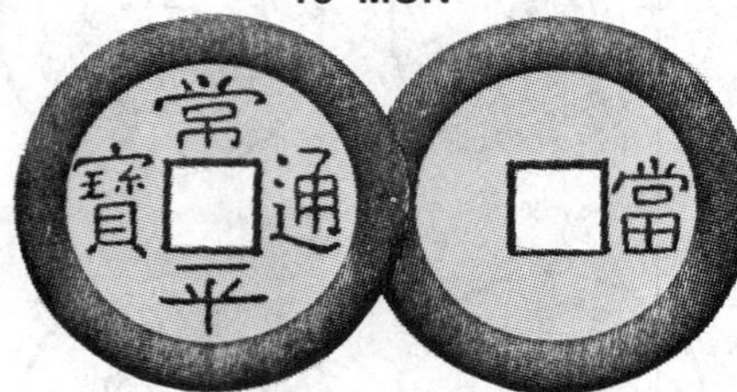

STRUCK BRASS
Obv. leg: *Sang P'yong T'ong Bo.*
Rev: *Tang* at right.

KM#	Date	Series	Good	VG	Fine	VF
Tc8	ND(1884)	—	—	—	Rare	—

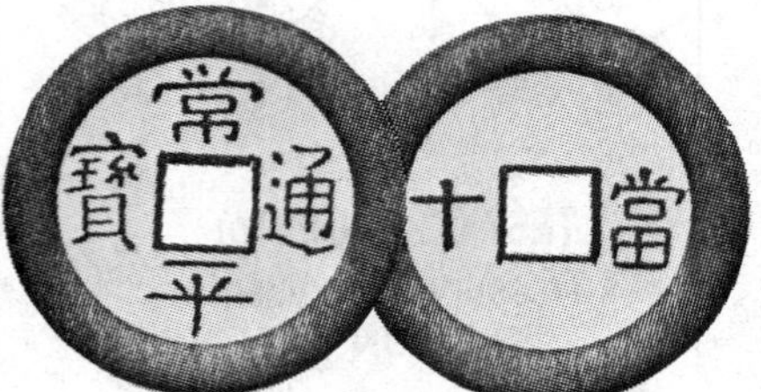

Rev: *Tang* at right, *Sip* (10) at left.

KM#	Date	Series	Good	VG	Fine	VF
Tc9	ND(1884)	—	—	—	Rare	—

PROOF SETS (PS)

KM#	Date	Mintage	Identification	Issue Price	Mkt. Val.
PS1	1892(5)	—	KM1104,1106,1109, 1112,1114	—	—

KUWAIT

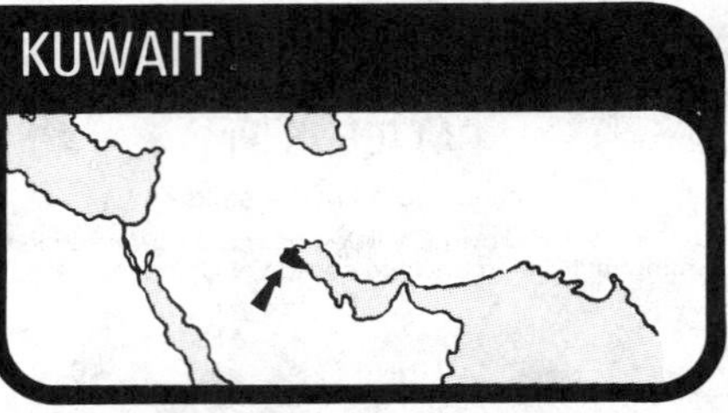

The State of Kuwait, a constitutional monarchy located on the Arabian Peninsula at the northwestern corner of the Persian Gulf, has an area of 6,880 sq. mi. (17,820 sq. km.) and a population of 1.7 million. Capital: Kuwait. Petroleum, the basis of the economy, provides 95 per cent of the exports.

The modern history of Kuwait began with the founding of the city of Kuwait, 1740, by tribesmen who wandered northward from the region of the Qatar Peninsula of eastern Arabia. Fearing that the Turks would take over the sheikhdom, Sheikh Mubarak entered into an agreement with Great Britain, 1899, placing Kuwait under the protection of Britain and empowering Britain to conduct its foreign affairs. Britain terminated the protectorate on June 19, 1961, giving Kuwait its independence (by a simple exchange of notes) but agreeing to furnish military aid on request.

Kuwait was invaded and occupied by an army from neighboring Iraq Aug. 2, 1990. Soon thereafter Iraq declared that the country would become a province of Iraq. An international coalition of military forces primarily based in Saudi Arabia led by the United States under terms set by the United Nations, attacked Iraqi military installations to liberate Kuwait. This occurred Jan. 17 1991. Kuwait City was liberated Feb. 27, and a cease-fire was declared Feb. 28. New paper currency was introduced March 24, 1991 to replace earlier notes.

TITLES

al-Kuwait

RULERS

British Protectorate, until 1961

LOCAL

Al Sabah Dynasty

Abdallah Ibn Sabah, 1762-1812
Jabir Ibn Abdallah, 1812-1859
Sabah Ibn Jabir, 1859-1866
Abdullah Ibn Sabah, 1866-1892
Muhammad Ibn Sabah, 1892-1896
Mubarak Ibn Sabah, 1896-1915

BAIZA

COPPER

KM#	Date	Year	Mintage	Good	VG	Fine
1	AH1304	(1887)	—	—	Rare	—

LIBERIA

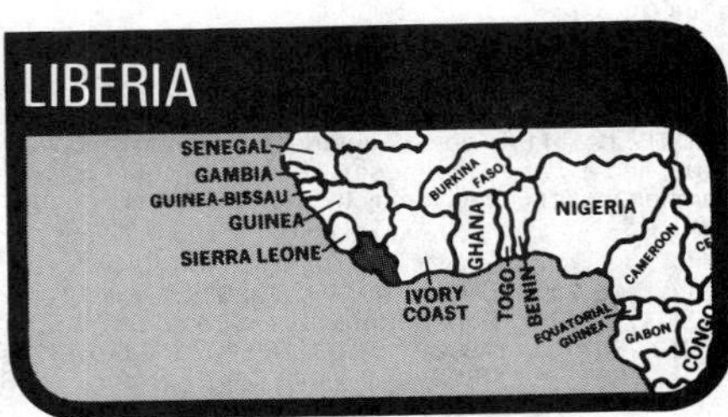

The Republic of Liberia, located on the southern side of the west African bulge between Sierra Leone and Ivory Coast, has an area of 43,000 sq. mi. (111,370 sq. km) and a population of 2.2 million. Capital: Monrovia. The major industries are agriculture, mining and lumbering. Iron ore, diamonds, rubber, coffee and coca are exported.

The Liberian coast was explored and charted by Portuguese navigator Pedro de Cintra in 1461. For the following three centuries Portuguese traders visited the area regularly to trade for gold, slaves and pepper. The modern country of Liberia, Africa's first republic, was settled in 1822 by the American Colonization Society as a homeland for American freed slaves, with the U.S. government furnishing funds and assisting in negotiations for procurement of land from the native chiefs. The various settlements united in 1839 to form the Commonwealth of Liberia, and in 1847 established the country as a republic with a constitution modeled after that of the United States.

U.S. money was declared legal tender in Liberia in 1943, replacing British West African currency.

Most of the Liberian pattern series, particularly of the 1888-90 period are acknowledged to have been 'unofficial' privately sponsored issues, but they are without exception avidly collected by most collectors of Liberian coins. The 'K' number designations on these pieces refer to a listing of Liberian patterns compiled and published by Ernst Kraus.

MINT MARKS

B - Bern, Switzerland
H - Heaton, Birmingham
(l) - London
(s) - San Francisco, U.S.

MONETARY SYSTEM

100 Cents = 1 Dollar

CENT

COPPER
Rev: 2 stars.

KM#	Date	Mintage	Fine	VF	XF	Unc
1	1847	—	6.00	14.00	25.00	60.00
	1847	—	—	—	Proof	125.00

Rev: 4 stars.

KM#	Date	Mintage	Fine	VF	XF	Unc
3	1862	—	7.00	15.00	28.00	65.00
	1862/47	—	10.00	25.00	50.00	135.00
	1862	—	—	—	Proof	125.00

BRONZE

KM#	Date	Mintage	Fine	VF	XF	Unc
5	1896H	.358	3.50	7.50	18.00	45.00
	1896H	—	—	—	Proof	135.00

NOTE: Later date (1906) exists for this type.

2 CENTS

COPPER
Rev: 2 stars.

KM#	Date	Mintage	Fine	VF	XF	Unc
2	1847	—	6.00	12.00	25.00	65.00
	1847	—	—	—	Proof	135.00

Rev: 4 stars.

KM#	Date	Mintage	Fine	VF	XF	Unc
4	1862	—	7.00	15.00	35.00	90.00
	1862	—	—	—	Proof	185.00

BRONZE

KM#	Date	Mintage	Fine	VF	XF	Unc
6	1896H	.323	3.50	7.50	18.00	50.00
	1896H	—	—	—	Proof	165.00

NOTE: Later date (1906) exists for this type.

10 CENTS

2.3200 g, .925 SILVER, .0690 oz ASW

KM#	Date	Mintage	Fine	VF	XF	Unc
7	1896H	.020	5.00	12.50	32.50	100.00
	1896H	—	—	—	Proof	250.00

NOTE: Later date (1906) exists for this type.

25 CENTS

5.8000 g, .925 SILVER, .1725 oz ASW

KM#	Date	Mintage	Fine	VF	XF	Unc
8	1896H	.015	6.00	12.50	35.00	120.00
	1896H	—	—	—	Proof	275.00

NOTE: Later date (1906) exists for this type.

50 CENTS

11.6000 g, .925 SILVER, .3450 oz ASW

KM#	Date	Mintage	Fine	VF	XF	Unc
9	1896H	5,000	10.00	20.00	50.00	265.00
	1896H	—	—	—	Proof	425.00

NOTE: Later date (1906) exists for this type.

PATTERNS (Pn)

(Including off metal strikes)

KM#	Date	Mintage	Identification	Mkt.Val.
Pn1	1847	—	1 Cent, Copper	200.00
Pn2	1847	—	2 Cents, Copper	175.00
Pn3	1847	—	10 Cents, Silver	—
Pn4	1847	—	10 Cents, Bronze	—
Pn4a	1847	—	10 Cents, Bronze, Obv: Struck on 1834 U.S. Cent	—
Pn5	1862	—	1 Cent, Copper, thick planchet	150.00
Pn6	1862	—	2 Cents, Copper, 2-1/2mm thick planchet	150.00
Pn7	1864	—	10 Cents, Silver	—
Pn8	1864	—	10 Cents, Bronze	—
Pn9	1865	—	25 Cents, Silver	750.00
Pn10	1865	—	25 Cents, Bronze	250.00
Pn11	1866	—	1 Cent, Copper	120.00
Pn12	1866	—	1 Cent, Copper	150.00
Pn13	1866	—	2 Cents, Copper	100.00
Pn14	1866	—	2 Cents, Copper	100.00
Pn15	1868	—	1 Cent, Copper	100.00
Pn16	1868	—	2 Cents, Copper	100.00
Pn17	1888	—	1 Cent, Copper, large shield	125.00
Pn18	1889	—	1 Cent, Copper, small shield	75.00
Pn19	1889	—	25 Cents, Silver	175.00
Pn20	1889	—	25 Cents, Bronze	125.00
Pn21	1889	—	25 Cents, Aluminum	120.00
Pn22	1889	—	25 Cents, Copper-Nickel	120.00

KM#	Date	Mintage	Identification	Mkt.Val.
Pn23	1889	—	25 Cents, Silver	175.00
Pn24	1889	—	25 Cents, Bronze	100.00
Pn25	1889	—	25 Cents, Aluminum	100.00
Pn26	1889	—	25 Cents, Copper-Nickel	100.00

KM#	Date	Mintage	Identification	Mkt.Val.
Pn27	1889	—	25 Cents, Silver	—
Pn28	1889	—	25 Cents, Bronze	125.00
Pn29	1889	—	25 Cents, Aluminum	120.00
Pn30	1889	—	25 Cents, Copper-Nickel	110.00

KM#	Date	Mintage	Identification	Mkt.Val.
Pn31	1889	—	50 Cents, Silver, 1-3/4mm thick	—
Pn32	1889	—	50 Cents, Silver, 2-1/2mm thick	—
Pn33	1889	—	50 Cents, Silver Plated Copper	—
Pn34	1889	—	50 Cents, Bronze	150.00
Pn35	1889	—	50 Cents, Aluminum	150.00
Pn36	1889	—	50 Cents, Copper-Nickel	150.00

KM#	Date	Mintage	Identification	Mkt.Val.
Pn37	1889	—	50 Cents, Silver, 1-3/4mm thick	—
Pn38	1889	—	50 Cents, Silver, 2-1/2mm thick	—
Pn39	1889	—	50 Cents, Bronze	140.00
Pn40	1889	—	50 Cents, Aluminum	125.00
Pn41	1889	—	50 Cents, Copper-Nickel	150.00

KM#	Date	Mintage	Identification	Mkt.Val.
Pn42	1889	—	50 Cents, Silver, 1-3/4mm thick	—
Pn43	1889	—	50 Cents, Silver, 2-1/2mm thick	—
Pn44	1889	—	50 Cents, Bronze	175.00
Pn45	1889	—	50 Cents, Aluminum	125.00
Pn46	1889	—	50 Cents, Copper-Nickel	150.00

KM#	Date	Mintage	Identification	Mkt.Val.
Pn47	1890	—	1 Cent, Copper	75.00

KM#	Date	Mintage	Identification	Mkt.Val.
Pn48	1890	—	1 Cent, Copper	65.00
Pn49	1890	—	1 Cent, Copper	65.00

KM#	Date	Mintage	Identification	Mkt.Val.
Pn50	1890	—	1 Cent, Copper	85.00

KM#	Date	Mintage	Identification	Mkt.Val.
Pn51	1890	—	2 Cents, Copper	120.00

KM#	Date	Mintage	Identification	Mkt.Val.
Pn52	1890	—	2 Cents, Copper	100.00

KM#	Date	Mintage	Identification	Mkt.Val.
Pn53	1890	—	2 Cents, Copper	85.00

KM#	Date	Mintage	Identification	Mkt.Val.
Pn54	1890	—	2 Cents, Copper	100.00

TOKEN ISSUES (Tn)

CENT

COPPER

Obv: Large ship (CH-2,3,4,6)

KM#	Date	Mintage	VG	Fine	VF	XF
Tn1	1833	—	5.00	10.00	25.00	65.00
		Obv: Small ship (CH-1,5)				
Tn2	1833	—	4.00	8.00	20.00	60.00

This piece has been attributed in six distinctive varieties by Charles G. Colver and Dan Harley, who have designated them in their order of incidence in a large hoard examined.

CH-1 **CH-2**

CH-1-Obverse; 1 in date left of tree trunk, small ship, 15 rays, 13 palm tree leaves, bush top at water line. Reverse; wide-spaced AD, single period between.

CH-2-Obverse; 1 in date under tree trunk, large ship, 14 rays, 12 palm tree leaves, bush top above water. Reverse; narrow-spaced AD, double periods between.

CH-3-Obverse; 1 in date under tree trunk, large ship, 14 rays with second touching ship, 10 palm tree leaves with leaf between LI, bush top at water line. Reverse; narrow-spaced AD, double periods between.

CH-4-Obverse; 1 in date left of tree trunk, large ship, 11 rays, 12 palm tree leaves with leaf between BE, bush top above water. Reverse; wide spaced AD, single period between, and first "N" in "COLONIZATION" tilted upward.

CH-5 Obverse; as CH-1. Reverse; very narrow AD.

CH-6 Obverse; as CH-2. Reverse; as CH-4.

PROOF SETS (PS)

KM#	Date	Mintage	Identification	Issue Price	Mkt. Val.
PS1	1896H(5)	—	KM5-9	—	1250.

LIBYA

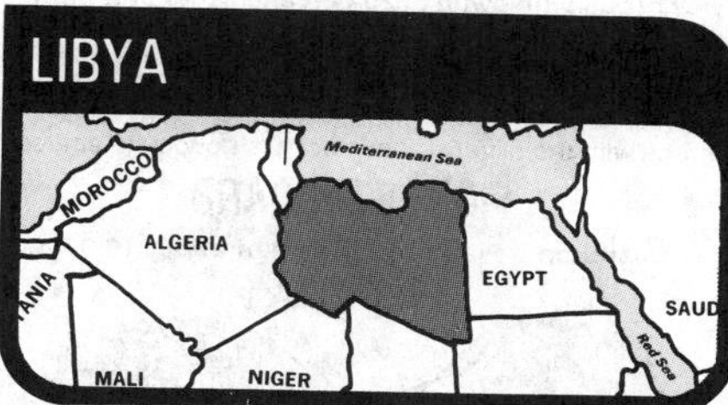

The Socialist People's Libyan Arab Jamahariya, located on the north-central coast of Africa between Tunisia and Egypt, has an area of 679,362 sq. mi. (1,759,540 sq. km.) and a population of 3.9 million. Capital: Tripoli. Crude oil, which accounts for 90 per cent of the export earnings, is the mainstay of the economy.

Libya has been subjected to foreign rule throughout most of its history, various parts of it having been ruled by the Phoenicians, Carthaginians, Vandals, Byzantines, Greeks, Romans, Egyptians, and in the following centuries the Arabs' language, culture and religion were adopted by the indigenous population. Libya was conquered by the Ottoman Turks in 1553, and remained under Turkish domination, becoming a Turkish vilayet in 1835, until it was conquered by Italy and made into a colony in 1911. The name 'Libya', the ancient Greek name for North Africa exclusive of Egypt, was given to the colony by Italy in 1934. Libya came under Allied administration after the fall of Tripoli on Jan. 23, 1943, divided into zones of British and French control. On Dec. 24, 1951, in accordance with a United Nations resolution, Libya proclaimed its independence as a constitutional monarchy, thereby becoming the first country to achieve independence through the United Nations. The monarchy was overthrown by a coup d'etat on Sept. 1, 1969, and Libya was established as a republic.

TITLES

المملكة الليبية

al-Mamlaka(t) al-Libiya(t)

الجمهورية الليبية

TRIPOLI

Tripoli (formerly Ottoman Empire Area of antique Tripolitania, 700-146 B.C.), the capital city and chief port of the Libyan Arab Jamahiriya, is situated on the North African coast on a promontory stretching out into the Mediterranean Sea. It was probably founded by Phoenicians from Sicily, but was under Roman control from 146 B.C. until 450 A.D. Invasion by Vandals and conquest by the Byzantines preceded the Arab invasions of the 11th century which, by destroying the commercial centers of Sabratha and Leptis, greatly enhanced the importance of Tripoli, an importance maintained through periods of Norman and Spanish control. Tripoli fell to the Turks, who made it the capital of the vilayet of Tripoli in 1551 and remained in their hands until 1911, when it was occupied by the Italians who made it the capital of the Italian province of Tripolitania. British forces entered the city on Jan. 23, 1943, and administered it until establishment of the independent Kingdom of Libya on Dec. 24, 1951.

RULERS

Ottoman, until 1911
refer to Turkey

LOCAL PASHAS

Yusuf Pasha Qaramanli,
AH1210-1248/1796-1833AD (resigned)
Ali Pasha Qaramanli II,
AH1248-1250/1833-1835AD

MINTNAME

طرابس

Tarabalus

طرابلس غرب

Tarabalus Gharb = (Tripoli West)

The appellation *west* serving to distinguish it from Tripoli in Lebanon, which had been an Ottoman Mint in the 16th century. On some of the copper coins, *Gharb* is omitted; several types come both with and without *Gharb.* The mint closed between the 28th and 29th year of the reign of Mahmud II.

MONETARY SYSTEM

The monetary system of Tripoli was confused and is poorly understood. Theoretically, 40 Para were equal to one Piastre, but due to the debasement of the silver coinage, later issues are virtually pure copper, though the percentage of alloy varies radically even within a given year. The 10 Para and 20 Para pieces were a little heavier than the copper Paras, with which they could easily be confounded, except that the copper Paras were generally thicker, and bear simpler inscriptions. It is not known how many of the coppers were tariffed to the debased Piastre and its fractions. Some authorities consider the copper pieces to be Beshliks (5 Para coins).

The gold coinage came in two denominations, the Zeri Mahbub (2.4-2.5 g), and the Sultani Altin (3.3-3.4 g). The ratio of the billon Piastres to the gold coins fluctuated from day to day.

OTTOMAN COINAGE

MUSTAFA IV

AH1222-1223/1807-1808AD

30 PARA

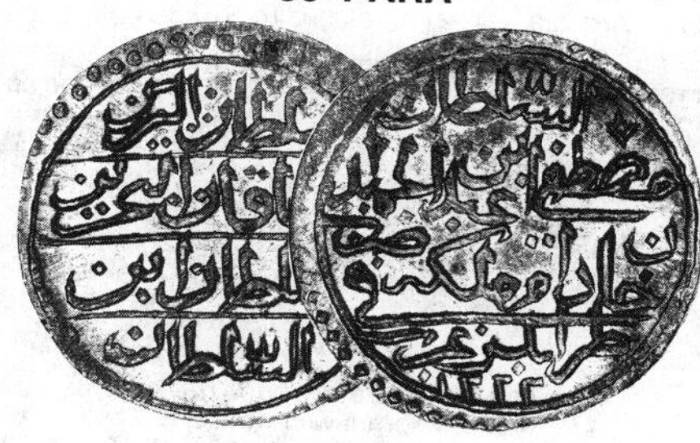

SILVER, 35mm, 12.50 g

KM#	Date	Year	VG	Fine	VF	XF
70	AH1222	—	—	—	Rare	—

ZERI MAHBUB

GOLD, 21mm, 2.45 g
Similar to Zeri Mahbub, KM#56

KM#	Date	Year	VG	Fine	VF	XF
72	AH1222	—	—	—	Rare	—

SULTANI

GOLD, 25mm, 3.33 g

KM#	Date	Year	VG	Fine	VF	XF
73	AH1222	1	—	—	Rare	—

MAHMUD II

AH1223-1255/1808-1839AD

COPPER COINAGE

Under this rubric are included all pieces intended as paras. Many of the billon coins are so debased as to be nearly pure copper, but they can be distinguished from those coins intended as paras as they are much thinner, and bear different devices and inscriptions. Some pieces are also struck in brass.

In addition to pieces bearing no regnal year, the issuance of coppers seems to be restricted to two series, the first bearing years 12 & 13, the other years 20-27. The first group is related to an anomalous billon issue in the same years (Type D below), the second issue seems to be connected to the reduced weight series of years 21-25. The undated pieces were most probably struck during one of these two periods.

All of the following pieces appear to be of one denomination, probably a para, but vary in size from about 17-23mm.

PARA

COPPER

KM#	Date	Year	Good	VG	Fine	VF
75	AH1223	—	5.00	8.00	12.50	20.00
	1223 12 obv. & 13 rev.					
		—	—	—	—	—
		12	10.00	15.00	18.50	35.00
		13	10.00	15.00	18.50	35.00
		20	10.00	15.00	17.50	30.00
	ND	—	4.00	8.00	12.00	18.00

Obv. leg: *Sultan/Mahmud Khan/ Azza Nasruhu.*

KM#	Date	Year	Good	VG	Fine	VF
77	AH1223	—	10.00	15.00	16.50	22.50
		20	10.00	15.00	17.00	25.00

Obv. leg: *Sultan/1223.* Rev. leg: *Mahmud/24.*

KM#	Date	Year	Good	VG	Fine	VF
79	AH1223	24	10.00	15.00	18.00	30.00

Obv: Toughra. Rev: Similar to KM#75, w/*Gharb.*

KM#	Date	Year	Good	VG	Fine	VF
81.1	AH1221(error)	—	8.00	12.50	20.00	45.00
	1222(error)	—	8.00	12.50	20.00	45.00
	1223	—	6.00	10.00	18.00	30.00

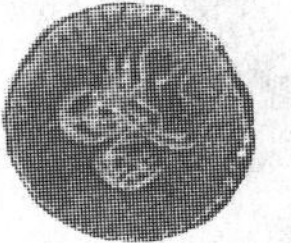

Reduced size: 17mm, 2.5 g.

KM#	Date	Year	Good	VG	Fine	VF
81.2	AH1223	24	12.00	20.00	35.00	75.00

Rev: W/o *Gharb.*

KM#	Date	Year	Good	VG	Fine	VF
83	AH1223	—	2.50	5.00	10.00	20.00

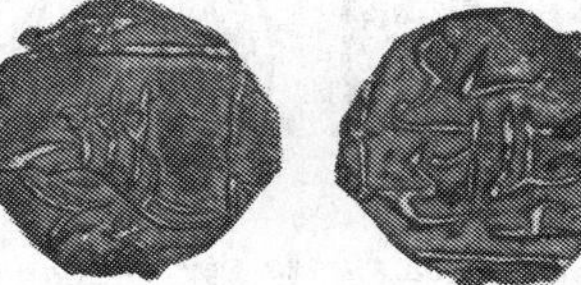

Obv. Toughra and rev. leg. within square and 8 loops.

KM#	Date	Year	Good	VG	Fine	VF
85	AH1223	2	10.00	12.00	15.00	25.00

Obv: Toughra. Rev: 6-line legend.

KM#	Date	Year	Good	VG	Fine	VF
87	AH1223	18	12.00	15.00	20.00	35.00

Obv. leg: *Sultan Mahmud Khan 1223* w/year above arabesque.

KM#	Date	Year	Good	VG	Fine	VF
89	AH1223	25	8.00	10.00	15.00	20.00
		26	8.00	10.00	15.00	25.00
		62 (error) for year 26	8.00	10.00	15.00	35.00

NOTE: Several variations are found in the arrangement of the obverse legend. Year 29 is reported, but is likely a misreading of year 26.

Similar to KM#89 but year below arabesque.

KM#	Date	Year	Good	VG	Fine	VF
90	AH1223	25	8.00	10.00	15.00	25.00

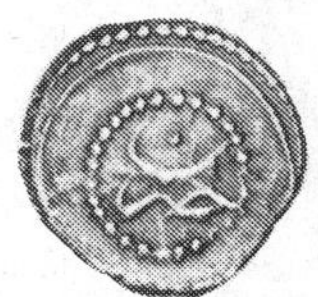

Obv: W/o dot above *B* in *DARB.*

KM#	Date	Year	Good	VG	Fine	VF
91.1	ND	—	8.00	10.00	15.00	20.00

Obv. leg: *Duriba*. Rev. leg: *Fi Trablus*.

KM#	Date	Year	Good	VG	Fine	VF
91.2	ND	—	10.00	12.00	15.00	20.00

Obv. and rev. leg. within lozenge.

93	AH1223	—	10.00	15.00	20.00	30.00

COPPER or BRASS
Obv. and rev. leg. arranged differently.

95	AH1223	23	12.00	18.00	22.00	45.00

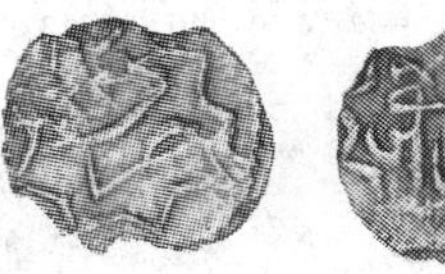

COPPER
Obv. and rev. leg. within 10-pointed stars.

97	AH1223	23	10.00	12.00	15.00	25.00

Obv. leg: *Duriba/Fi/1223*. Rev: *Tarabalus/r.y.*

99	AH1223	12	9.00	12.00	16.50	25.00
		13	9.00	12.00	16.50	25.00
		20	9.00	12.00	16.50	25.00
		21	9.00	12.00	16.50	25.00

Obv. leg: *Duriba/Fi/1223*. Rev: *Tarabalus/r.y.*

101	AH1223	13	10.00	12.50	16.50	30.00
		21	10.00	12.50	16.50	30.00

3.79g, 20mm
Rev: *Tarabalus 22* in looped star of David.

102	AH1223	22	10.00	15.00	20.00	35.00

Rev: 5 dots within wreath.

103	AH1223	20	10.00	12.50	15.00	22.50

Rev: Arabesque within garland.

105	AH1223	21	10.00	12.50	16.00	24.00

 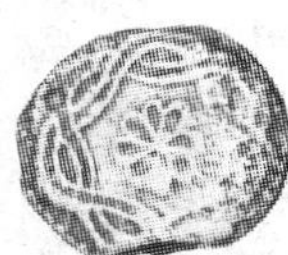

Obv: W/o *Gharb*. Rev: Rose within garland.

107	AH1223	22	10.00	12.50	15.00	22.50

 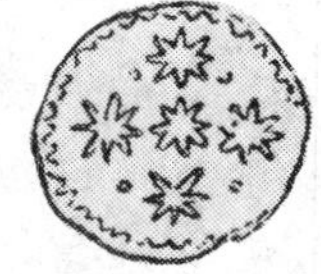

Rev: 5 stars.

109	AH1223	25	10.00	12.50	16.50	25.00

Obv. leg: *Duriba/fi/Tarabalus/1223*.
Rev: *Gharb*.

KM#	Date	Year	Good	VG	Fine	VF
111	AH1223	21	8.00	10.00	15.00	20.00

Obv: Ornament. Rev: *Gharb*.

112	AH1223	21	8.00	10.00	15.00	20.00

 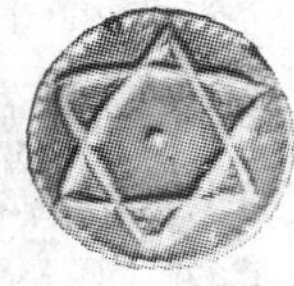

Obv. leg: *Duriba/Fi/Tarabalus/1223*.
Rev: Hexagram w/central dot.

115	AH1223	—	9.00	12.00	15.00	22.50
		25	9.00	12.00	15.00	22.50
		27	9.00	12.00	15.00	22.50

Rev: Hexagram w/4-7 dots.

117	AH1223	—	10.00	12.00	15.00	20.00

Obv: Similar to KM#111. Rev: Hexagram w/*23*.

119	AH1223	23	12.00	15.00	18.00	24.00

BILLON COINAGE

The billon coinage of Mahmud II is extremely varied, with a plethora of types deriving largely from contemporary Turkish, Egyptian, and Tunisian prototypes. There is considerable controversy over the denominations of these coins, although they seem to be based on a Piastre (40 Paras, Kuruns) of about 16 grams from yrs. 1-13, of about 12 grams from yrs. 13-21, and of 10 grams from yrs. 21-25. A new style coinage was introduced in yr. 28, but it was apparently never issued in sizable quantities and confined to the one year.

There is considerable weight variation within each denomination, in some cases up to 20 percent higher or lower than the theoretical norm. There is not yet discernible correlation between type, denomination, year, and standard. Recent evidence indicates that the net silver content was frequently and repeatedly reduced, probably in rather small increments. Thus the existence of several types for a single denomination and regnal year may indicate a multiplicity of issues with a single year, but as the full series is still not known, the complete sequence for each denomination cannot yet be reconstructed Debasements were frequent: In the 4-year period covering years 21-24, ten changes in the values of coinage are recorded, but not all changes need have referred to the denominations and designs.

Except for a few isolated miscellaneous types, all of the billon coinage can be classed into five basic types:

TYPE A: Obv: Toughra, sometimes with adjacent symbol, (i.e. flower, tamgha with arrow heads, large tamgha, crescent, letter "nun", and figures "22" and "23"). Rev: Year/mintname/*1223*.

TYPE B: Obv: Toughra/mintname/*1223*. Rev: 4-line leg. giving Sultan's titles: *Sultan al-Bahrayn Wa Khaqan al-Bahrayn al Sultan Ibn al Sultan* (sometimes with stars).

TYPE C: Obv: Sultan's name/benediction/mintname/*1223*. (4-line leg.) Rev: Same as rev. of Type B.

TYPE D: Obv: Sultan's name (sometimes with *1223*). Rev: Year/mintname/*1223* (1223 omitted when on obv.)

TYPE E: Obv: 4-line leg: *Sultan al Barrayn wa Khaqan al Bahrayn al Sultan Mahmud Khan Azza Nasruhu &* year. Rev: Mintname/*1223* (this type copied from Tunis piastre & fractions).

In addition to the variations in type, there is considerable variation in the borders. No attempt has been made in these listings to distinguish the various types of borders, though it is quite possible that such distinctions may have been monetarily important.

STANDARD COINAGE

The following listings are arranged by standard, and then by denomination within each standard. The sizes of the coins can vary considerably within each issue. The weight can vary by up to 20 percent higher or lower than the amounts shown.

All of the coins were struck in low-grade billon, tending toward pure copper on some of the later issues. Most of the coins originally were lightly silver-washed, and specimens with the silver wash intact are now quite scarce.

FIRST STANDARD

Based on a Piastre (40 Para) of about 16.00 g.

5 PARA

BILLON, 22-23mm, Type B

KM#	Date	Year	Good	VG	Fine	VF
126	AH1223	1	20.00	35.00	60.00	100.00
		2	20.00	35.00	60.00	100.00
		7	20.00	35.00	60.00	100.00
		8	25.00	40.00	75.00	125.00
		9	20.00	35.00	60.00	100.00
		10	20.00	35.00	60.00	100.00
		11	20.00	35.00	60.00	100.00
		17	20.00	35.00	60.00	100.00

10 PARA

SILVER, 1.35 g, 18mm
Rev: Ornament in circle for regnal year.

127	AH1223	—	30.00	50.00	75.00	125.00

BILLON, 22-24mm, 2.46 g, Type A

128	AH1223	—	30.00	40.00	75.00	125.00
		2	30.00	40.00	75.00	125.00

3.35 g

130	AH1223	7	30.00	50.00	75.00	125.00

131	AH1223	9	50.00	60.00	75.00	125.00

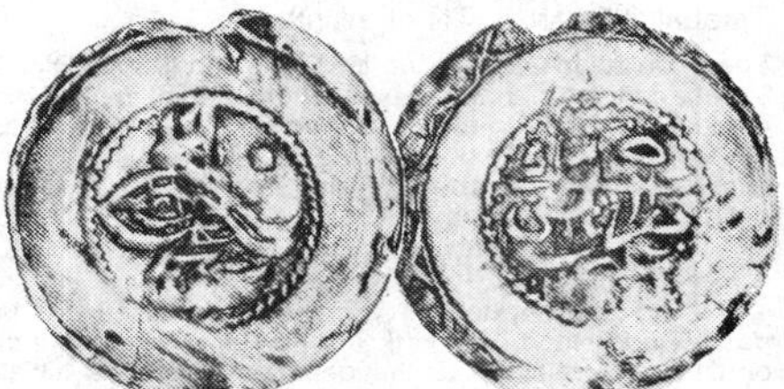

29-31mm, 3.89 g

134	AH1223	9	35.00	50.00	60.00	100.00

24mm, 1.80 g

135	AH1223	3	35.00	50.00	60.00	100.00

15 PARA

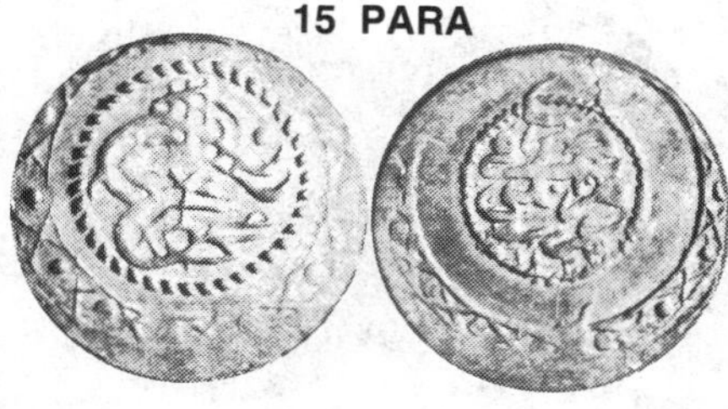

BILLON

KM#	Date	Year	Good	VG	Fine	VF
132	AH1223	7	35.00	50.00	60.00	80.00

20 PARA

BILLON, 31mm, 5.38-6.65 g, Type A

KM#	Date	Year	Good	VG	Fine	VF
136	AH1223	2	30.00	40.00	75.00	125.00
		7	30.00	40.00	75.00	125.00
137	AH1223	8	30.00	40.00	75.00	125.00

KM#	Date	Year	Good	VG	Fine	VF
138	AH1223	9	30.00	50.00	75.00	125.00
139	AH1223	10	30.00	50.00	75.00	125.00
		11	30.00	50.00	75.00	125.00

40 PARA

BILLON, 37mm, 15.68 g, Type A

KM#	Date	Year	Good	VG	Fine	VF
140	AH1223	ND	85.00	100.00	125.00	200.00

12.025 g, Type B

KM#	Date	Year	Good	VG	Fine	VF
141	AH1223	1	80.00	150.00	175.00	300.00
		2	80.00	100.00	150.00	400.00
		3	80.00	100.00	125.00	300.00
		ornament	80.00	100.00	130.00	300.00

100 PARA

BILLON, 24.68 g, 43-44mm
Ornament w/dot on either side.

KM#	Date	Year	Good	VG	Fine	VF
142	AH1223	ND	200.00	250.00	375.00	400.00

Obv: Ornament right of toughra.

KM#	Date	Year	Good	VG	Fine	VF
143	AH1223	3	—	—	Rare	—
		4	—	—	Rare	—
		5	—	—	Rare	—

Obv: Flower right of toughra.

KM#	Date	Year	Good	VG	Fine	VF
144	AH1223	4	—	—	Rare	—
		5	—	—	Rare	—
		5	special form		Rare	—
	1227(error)	4	—	—	Rare	—

SECOND STANDARD

Years 12-13
Based on a Piastre of about 14.00 g.

10 PARA

BILLON, 19mm, 2.90 g, Type D

KM#	Date	Year	Good	VG	Fine	VF
145	AH1223	12	30.00	40.00	75.00	125.00
		13	30.00	40.00	75.00	125.00

20 PARA

BILLON, 23mm, 4.41 g, Type D

KM#	Date	Year	Good	VG	Fine	VF
147	AH1223	12	30.00	50.00	60.00	100.00
		13	30.00	50.00	60.00	100.00

BILLON, 28mm, 6.35 g, Type B

KM#	Date	Year	Good	VG	Fine	VF
149	AH1223	13	35.00	60.00	100.00	150.00

40 PARA

BILLION, 35mm, Type B

KM#	Date	Year	Good	VG	Fine	VF
150	AH1223	13	100.00	125.00	150.00	200.00

THIRD STANDARD

Years 14-21
Based on a Piastre of about 12.00 g.

10 PARA

BILLON, 22-28mm, 3.09 g, Type A

KM#	Date	Year	Good	VG	Fine	VF
154	AH1223	19	30.00	50.00	70.00	100.00

Rev: Legend within square.

KM#	Date	Year	Good	VG	Fine	VF
155	AH1223	20	30.00	50.00	70.00	100.00

Type B, 22-25mm, 1.69-1.80 g

KM#	Date	Year	Good	VG	Fine	VF
156	AH1223	16	30.00	50.00	70.00	100.00
		17	30.00	50.00	70.00	100.00
		18	30.00	50.00	70.00	125.00

15 PARA

BILLON, 29mm, 3.70 g, Type E

KM#	Date	Year	Good	VG	Fine	VF
162	AH1223	17	35.00	50.00	75.00	125.00

20 PARA

BILLON, 23mm, 5.60 g, Type A

KM#	Date	Year	Good	VG	Fine	VF
164	AH1223	20	30.00	40.00	50.00	100.00

Type A, 5.59 g, 31mm

KM#	Date	Year	Good	VG	Fine	VF
166	AH1223	15	50.00	75.00	100.00	125.00
		20	50.00	75.00	100.00	125.00
		21	50.00	75.00	100.00	125.00

Type B

KM#	Date	Year	Good	VG	Fine	VF
168.1	AH1223	15	50.00	75.00	100.00	150.00

Obv: Sprig beside toughra.

KM#	Date	Year	Good	VG	Fine	VF
168.2	AH1223	15	50.00	75.00	100.00	150.00

Obv: W/o stars.

KM#	Date	Year	Good	VG	Fine	VF
168.3	AH1223	15	50.00	75.00	100.00	150.00

Type C, 6.43 g, 29mm

KM#	Date	Year	Good	VG	Fine	VF
170	AH1222	19	40.00	75.00	100.00	120.00
	1223	20	40.00	75.00	100.00	120.00

Type D, 5.10 g, 28mm

KM#	Date	Year	Good	VG	Fine	VF
172	AH1223	20	35.00	60.00	80.00	100.00

30 PARA

BILLON, 34mm, Type A

KM#	Date	Year	Good	VG	Fine	VF
174	AH1223	3	100.00	150.00	250.00	400.00

29mm, Type A

KM#	Date	Year	Good	VG	Fine	VF
176	AH1223	2	30.00	50.00	70.00	100.00

37mm, 22.13 g, Type B
Similar to 20 Para, KM#168.

KM#	Date	Year	Good	VG	Fine	VF
A178	AH1223	14	80.00	90.00	125.00	185.00

33-34mm, 7.73 g

KM#	Date	Year	Good	VG	Fine	VF
178	AH1223	17	75.00	85.00	100.00	125.00
		18	75.00	85.00	100.00	125.00

6.43 g, Type E

KM#	Date	Year	Good	VG	Fine	VF
179	AH1223	20	75.00	85.00	100.00	125.00

40 PARA

BILLON, 35mm, Type A, lozenge borders

KM#	Date	Year	Good	VG	Fine	VF
180	AH1223	21	80.00	100.00	125.00	160.00

32mm, Type A, plain borders

KM#	Date	Year	Good	VG	Fine	VF
182	AH1223	20	80.00	100.00	125.00	150.00

36-39mm, Type A, circular ornate borders

KM#	Date	Year	Good	VG	Fine	VF
184	AH1223	15	80.00	100.00	125.00	150.00
		19	80.00	100.00	125.00	150.00
		21	80.00	100.00	125.00	150.00

35-37mm, Type B

KM#	Date	Year	Good	VG	Fine	VF
186.1	AH1223	13	80.00	100.00	125.00	150.00
		14	80.00	100.00	125.00	150.00
		18	80.00	100.00	125.00	150.00
		20	80.00	100.00	125.00	150.00

Obv: W/o toughra.

KM#	Date	Year	Good	VG	Fine	VF
186.2	AH1223	20	90.00	120.00	150.00	200.00

Similar to KM#186 but letter *nun* beside toughra.
Rev: Stars on lines 1, 2 and 3.

KM#	Date	Year	Good	VG	Fine	VF
187.1	AH1223	14	100.00	150.00	185.00	250.00

Obv: Sprig beside toughra.

KM#	Date	Year	Good	VG	Fine	VF
187.2	AH1223	14	200.00	300.00	400.00	500.00

36mm, Type C

KM#	Date	Year	Good	VG	Fine	VF
188	AH1223	19	75.00	100.00	150.00	200.00
		20	75.00	100.00	150.00	200.00

34mm, Type D

KM#	Date	Year	Good	VG	Fine	VF
190.1	AH1223	18	75.00	100.00	150.00	200.00

37mm, Type E

KM#	Date	Year	Good	VG	Fine	VF
190.2	AH1223	20	75.00	100.00	150.00	200.00

33mm, 11.75 g, Type E

KM#	Date	Year	Good	VG	Fine	VF
192	AH1243	—	—	—	Rare	—

NOTE: KM#192 is dated to the actual year, as on similar coins of Tunis.

50 PARA

BILLON, 37mm, 15.44 g, Type A

KM#	Date	Year	Good	VG	Fine	VF
194	AH1243	—	—	—	Rare	—

NOTE: Refer to KM#182. The denomination of the above coin is very uncertain.

60 PARA

BILLON, 18.27 g, Type A

KM#	Date	Year	Good	VG	Fine	VF
196	AH1223	20	50.00	75.00	85.00	100.00

FOURTH STANDARD

Years 21-25

Based on a Piastre of approximately 10.00 g.

10 PARA

BILLON, 24mm, Type B

KM#	Date	Year	Good	VG	Fine	VF
201	AH1223	22	30.00	40.00	50.00	75.00
		24	30.00	40.00	50.00	75.00
		25	30.00	40.00	50.00	75.00

20 PARA

BILLION, Type B

KM#	Date	Year	Good	VG	Fine	VF
205	AH1223	22	35.00	50.00	75.00	100.00
		24	35.00	50.00	75.00	100.00
		25	35.00	50.00	75.00	100.00

29-30mm, Obv: Type D. Rev: type E.

KM#	Date	Year	Good	VG	Fine	VF
203	AH1223	22	35.00	50.00	75.00	100.00
		23	35.00	50.00	75.00	100.00

30 PARA

BILLON, 35mm, Type A

KM#	Date	Year	Good	VG	Fine	VF
206	AH1223	24	60.00	90.00	150.00	200.00

BILLON, 32mm, Type D

KM#	Date	Year	Good	VG	Fine	VF
207	AH1223	22	60.00	90.00	150.00	200.00

34mm

KM#	Date	Year	Good	VG	Fine	VF
209	AH1223	23	—	—	Rare	—

35mm
Similar to Type A, but w/large crescents at both sides similar to Turkey 10 Para, C#197 but w/o wreaths.

KM#	Date	Year	Good	VG	Fine	VF
211	AH1223	24	65.00	85.00	100.00	125.00

40 PARA

BILLON, Type A

KM#	Date	Year	Good	VG	Fine	VF
213	AH1223	21	40.00	70.00	100.00	150.00
		22	60.00	90.00	150.00	200.00
		24	40.00	70.00	100.00	125.00

Type B

KM#	Date	Year	Good	VG	Fine	VF
215	AH1223	21	85.00	100.00	150.00	225.00
		22	85.00	100.00	150.00	200.00
		24	85.00	100.00	150.00	200.00
		25	85.00	100.00	150.00	200.00

FIFTH STANDARD

Year 28 only

Uncertain metrology

MANGIR

COPPER, 0.914 g, 16mm
Obv: Toughra w/*Nuhas* (= copper) to right, year 28 to left.
Rev. leg: *Duriba/Fi/Tarabalus Gharb/1223.*

KM#	Date	Year	Good	VG	Fine	VF
217	AH1223	28	25.00	35.00	50.00	75.00

NOTE: Varieties exist.

5 PARA

BILLON, 1.855 g, 19mm
Type A, but obv. and rev. leg. within wreaths. W/*Fidda* (= Silver) to right of toughra, regnal year at left.

KM#	Date	Year	Good	VG	Fine	VF
216	AH1223	28	—	—	Rare	—

10 PARA

BILLON, 3.680 g, 21mm
Type A, but obv. and rev. leg. within wreaths.
W/*Fidda* (= Silver) to right of toughra, regnal year at left.

KM#	Date	Year	Good	VG	Fine	VF
220	AH1223	28	—	—	Rare	—

20 PARA

BILLON, 7.05-7.73 g, 25-30mm
Type A, but obv. and rev. leg. within wreaths.
W/*Fidda* (= Silver) to right of toughra, regnal year at left.

KM#	Date	Year	Good	VG	Fine	VF
218	AH1223	28	—	—	Rare	—

40 PARA

BILLON, 14.50-14.81 g, 36-38mm
Type A, but obv. and rev. leg. within wreaths.
W/*Fidda* (= Silver) to right of toughra, regnal year at left.

KM#	Date	Year	Good	VG	Fine	VF
219	AH1223	28	—	—	Rare	—

ZERI MAHBUB

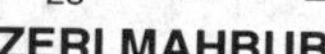

GOLD, 21-24mm, 2.30-2.50 g, Type B

KM#	Date	Year	VG	Fine	VF	XF
222	AH1223	12	150.00	175.00	250.00	350.00
		13	150.00	175.00	250.00	350.00
		14	150.00	175.00	250.00	350.00

Type E
Rev: Mintname above date.

KM#	Date	Year	VG	Fine	VF	XF
224	AH1223	18	150.00	175.00	250.00	350.00

KM#	Date	Year	VG	Fine	VF	XF
226	AH1223	20	200.00	250.00	300.00	400.00

SULTANI

GOLD, 33mm, 5.58 g
Obv: Toughra.

KM#	Date	Year	VG	Fine	VF	XF
227	AH1223	5	300.00	350.00	500.00	650.00

24-26mm, 3.20-3.40 g, Type C (variant)

KM#	Date	Year	VG	Fine	VF	XF
228	AH1223	6	150.00	200.00	250.00	350.00
		19	150.00	200.00	250.00	350.00
		ornament	150.00	200.00	250.00	350.00

Similar, but broader and thinner.

KM#	Date	Year	VG	Fine	VF	XF
230	AH1223	14	—	—	Rare	—

Rev: W/o lines dividing leg.

KM#	Date	Year	VG	Fine	VF	XF
232	AH1223	—	200.00	250.00	375.00	425.00

LIECHTENSTEIN

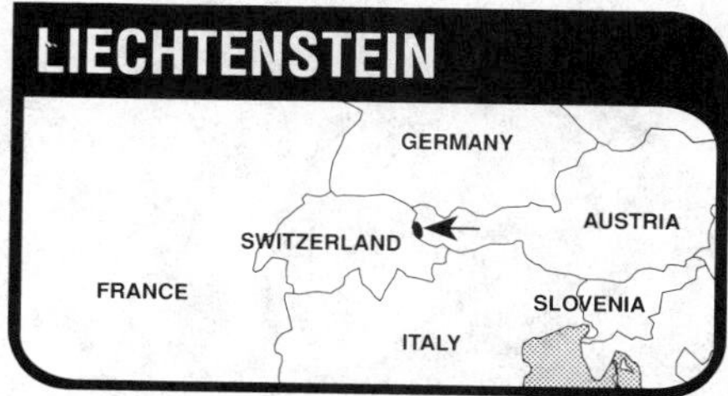

The Principality of Liechtenstein, located in central Europe on the east bank of the Rhine between Austria and Switzerland, has an area of 61 sq. mi. (160 sq. km.) and a population of 27,200. Capital: Vaduz. The economy is based on agriculture and light manufacturing. Canned goods, textiles, ceramics and precision instruments are exported.

The lordships of Schellenburg and Vaduz were merged into the principality of Liechtenstein. It was a member of the Rhine Confederation from 1806 to 1815, and of the German Confederation from 1815 to 1866 when it became independent. Liechtenstein's long and close association with Austria was terminated by World War I. In 1921 it adopted the coinage of Switzerland, and two years later entered into a customs union with the Swiss, who also operated its postal and telegraph systems and represent it in international affairs. The tiny principality abolished its army in 1868 and has avoided involvement in all European wars since that time.

RULERS

Prince John II, 1858-1929

MINT MARKS

A - Vienna
B - Bern
M - Munich (restrikes)

MONETARY SYSTEM
(1857-1868)

1-1/2 Florins = 1 Vereinsthaler

EIN (1) THALER
(Vereins)

18.5200 g, .900 SILVER, .5358 oz ASW

Y#	Date	Mintage	Fine	VF	XF	Unc
1	1862A	1,920	950.00	1500.	2750.	4000.
	1862A-M	—		(restrike)	Proof	35.00

29.5000 g, .900 GOLD, .8536 oz AGW

Y#	Date	Mintage	Fine	VF	XF	Unc
1a	1862A-M	.050		(restrike)	Proof	500.00

PLATINUM, 33.34 g

Y#	Date	Mintage	Fine	VF	XF	Unc
1b	1862A-M	—		(restrike)	Proof	1150.

MONETARY REFORM

100 Heller = 1 Krone

KRONE

5.0000 g, .835 SILVER, .1342 oz ASW

Y#	Date	Mintage	VF	XF	Unc	BU
2	1900	.050	10.00	18.00	28.00	45.00

NOTE: Later dates (1904-1915) exist for this type.

5 KRONEN

24.0000 g, .900 SILVER, .6944 oz ASW

Y#	Date	Mintage	Fine	VF	XF	Unc
4	1900	5,000	250.00	400.00	600.00	750.00

NOTE: Later dates (1904-1915) exist for this type.

10 KRONEN

3.3875 g, .900 GOLD, .0980 oz AGW

Y#	Date	Mintage	Fine	VF	XF	Unc
5	1900	1,500	—	—	5000.	7000.

20 KRONEN

6.7750 g, .900 GOLD, .1960 oz AGW

Y#	Date	Mintage	Fine	VF	XF	Unc
6	1898	1,500	—	—	4500.	5500.

ESSAIS (E)

KM#	Date	Mintage	Identification	Mkt.Val.
E1	1898	125	1 Krone, Y2	—
E2	1898	100	5 Kronen, Y4	—
E3	1898	35	10 Kronen, Y5	—
E4	1898	35	20 Kronen, Y6	—

LUXEMBOURG

The Grand Duchy of Luxembourg is located in western Europe between Belgium, Germany and France, has an area of 998 sq. mi. (2,586 sq. km.) and a population of 377,100. Capital: Luxembourg. The economy is based on steel - Luxembourg's per capita production of 16 tons is the highest in the world.

Founded about 963, Luxembourg was a prominent country of the Holy Roman Empire; one of its sovereigns became Holy Roman Emperor as Henry VII, 1308. After being made a duchy by Emperor Charles IV, 1354, Luxembourg passed under the domination of Burgundy, Spain, Austria and France, 1443-1815, regaining autonomy under the Treaty of Vienna, 1815, as a grand duchy in union with the Netherlands, though ostensibly a member of the German Confederation. When Belgium seceded from the Kingdom of the Netherlands, 1830, Luxembourg was forced to cede its greater western section to Belgium. The tiny duchy left the German Confederation in 1867 when the Treaty of London recognized it as an independent state and guaranteed its perpetual neutrality. Luxembourg was occupied by Germany and liberated by American troops in both World Wars, and is the resting place of 5,000 American soldiers, including Gen. George S. Patton.

RULERS

William III (Netherlands), 1849-1890
Adolphe, 1890-1905

MINT MARKS

A - Paris
(b) - Brussels, privy marks only
(u) - Utrecht, privy marks only

PRIVY MARKS

Angel's head, two headed eagle - Brussels
Anchor, hand - Paris, (1846-60)
Anchor, bee - Paris, (1860-79)
Sword, Caduceus - Utrecht (1846-74 although struck at Brussels until 1909)

MONETARY SYSTEM

100 Centimes = 1 Franc

2-1/2 CENTIMES

BRONZE

KM#	Date	Mintage	Fine	VF	XF	Unc
21	1854(u)	.640	1.50	3.50	8.00	30.00
	1854(u) w/o serif on E of DUCHE					
		—	3.00	9.00	20.00	55.00
	1870(u) dot above BARTH on rev.					
		.210	3.50	10.00	25.00	65.00
	1870(u) w/o dot above BARTH on rev.					
		Inc. Ab.	10.00	20.00	50.00	100.00

NOTE: Later dates (1901-1908) exist for this type.

5 CENTIMES

BRONZE

KM#	Date	Mintage	Fine	VF	XF	Unc
22.1	1854(u)	.680	3.00	9.00	20.00	55.00
	1870(u)	.304	3.50	10.00	25.00	65.00

Mint mark: A

KM#	Date	Mintage	Fine	VF	XF	Unc
22.2	1855	.600	3.00	9.00	22.00	60.00
	1860	.200	10.00	20.00	55.00	120.00

10 CENTIMES

BRONZE
Mint mark: Sword

KM#	Date	Mintage	Fine	VF	XF	Unc
23.1	1854(u)	.500	3.00	9.00	20.00	65.00
	1855(u)	—	—	—	—	—
	1870(u) dot above BARTH on rev.					
		1.313	2.00	4.00	12.50	40.00
	1870(u) w/o dot above BARTH on rev.					
		Inc. Ab.	10.00	22.00	60.00	130.00

Mint mark: A

KM#	Date	Mintage	Fine	VF	XF	Unc
23.2	1855	1.200	2.00	4.00	12.50	40.00
	1860	.900	2.50	4.50	13.50	45.00
	1865	1.000	2.00	4.00	12.50	40.00

ESSAIS (E)

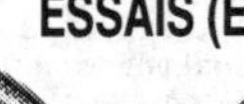

KM#	Date	Mintage	Identification	Mkt.Val.
E1	1889	100	5 Centimes, Copper	90.00
E2	1889	—	5 Centimes, Silver	375.00
E3	1889	100	10 Centimes, Copper, large arms	90.00
E4	1889	—	10 Centimes, Silver	375.00
E5	1889	50	10 Centimes, Copper, small arms	135.00

KM#	Date	Mintage	Identification	Mkt.Val.
E6	1889	—	5 Francs, Copper	650.00
E7	1889	50	5 Francs, Tin	450.00
E8	1889	50	5 Francs, Silver	1500.
E9	1889	—	5 Francs, Gold	Rare

PATTERNS (Pn)

(Including off metal strikes)

KM#	Date	Mintage	Identification	Mkt.Val.
Pn1	1854(u)	—	5 Centimes, Silver	500.00
Pn2	1854(u)	—	10 Centimes, Silver	550.00
Pn3	1870(u)	—	2-1/2 Centimes, Silver	475.00
Pn4	1870(u)	—	5 Centimes, Silver	525.00
Pn5	1870(u)	—	10 Centimes, Silver	650.00

WITH ESSAI (PE)

KM#	Date	Mintage	Identification	Mkt.Val.
PE1	1889	—	5 Francs, Tin	750.00
PE2	1889	—	10 Centimes, Silver	550.00

MADEIRA ISLANDS

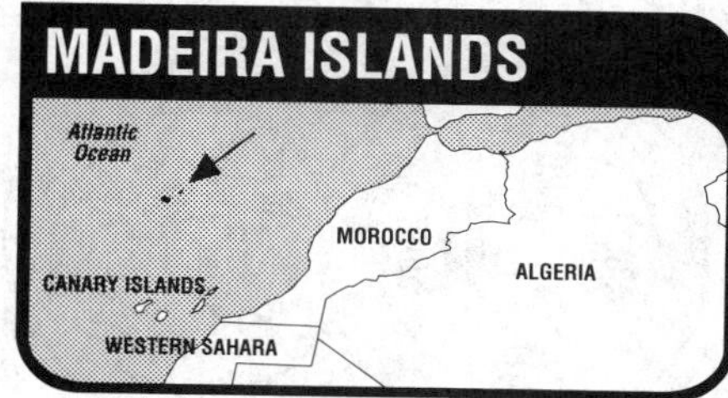

The Madeira Islands, which belong to Portugal, are located 360 miles (492 km.) off the northwest coast of Africa. They have an area of 307 sq. mi. (795 sq. km.) and a population of 270,976. The group consists of two inhabited islands named Madeira and Porto Santo and two groups of uninhabited rocks named Desertas and Selvagens. Capital: Funchal. The two staple products are wine and sugar. Bananas and pineapples are also produced for export.

Although the evidence is insufficient, it is thought that the Phoenicians visited Madeira at an early period. It is also probable that the entire archipelago was explored in early times by Genoese adventurers; an Italian map dated 1351 shows the Madeira Islands quite clearly. The Portuguese navigator Goncalvez Zarco first sighted Porto Santo in 1418, having been driven there by a storm while he was exploring the coast of West Africa. Madeira itself was discovered in 1420. The islands were uninhabited when visited by Zarco, but their colonization was immediately begun by Prince Henry the Navigator, aided by the knights of the Order of Christ. British troops occupied the islands in 1801, and again in 1807-14.

RULERS

Portuguese

V (5) REIS

COPPER

KM#	Date	Mintage	VG	Fine	VF	XF
1	1850	—	85.00	175.00	300.00	550.00

X (10) REIS

COPPER

KM#	Date	Mintage	VG	Fine	VF	XF
2	1842	—	10.00	20.00	50.00	175.00
	1850	—	—	—	Rare	—
	1852	—	10.00	20.00	45.00	150.00

XX (20) REIS

COPPER
Obv: Similar to 10 Reis, KM#2.

KM#	Date	Mintage	VG	Fine	VF	XF
3	1842	—	20.00	40.00	90.00	220.00
	1852	—	—	—	Rare	—

PATTERNS (Pn)

(Including off metal strikes)

KM#	Date	Mintage	Identification	Mkt.Val.
Pn1	1842	—	10 Reis, Silver, KM2	Rare
Pn2	1842	—	10 Reis, Gold, KM2	Rare

MALAYSIA

STRAITS SETTLEMENTS 1826-1939

MALAYA 1939-1952

MALAYA & BR. BORNEO 1952-1963

MALAYSIA 1963 –

MONETARY SYSTEM

10 Pitis = 1 Keping
900-4,000 Pitis = 1 Ringgit (Dollar)
1280 Trah = 1 Ringgit
100 Pice (cents) = 1 Ringgit

DENOMINATIONS

The following Arabic legends appear for the denomination with an Arabic number above.

(1) Keping

Sakeping

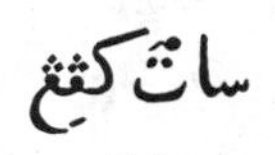
Satkeping

دو کڤيڠ
(2) Dua Keping

NOTE: Many local merchant tokens, inscribed mainly in Chinese, exist for most of the Malay states. These have not been listed.

KEDAH

A state in northwestern Malaysia. Islam introduced in 15th century. Subject to Thailand from 1821-1909. Coins issued under Governor Tengku Anum.

TITLES

Kedah كداه

SULTANS

Ahmad Taju'd-din Halim Shah, 1798-1843
Zainal Rashid al-Muazzam Shah, 1843-1854
Ahmad Taju'd-din Mukarram Shah, 1854-1879
Abdul-Hamim, 1882-1909

From 1821-1843, Kedah was actually under the control of the Siamese, and was ruled by Governor Tengku Anum.

TRA

TIN, 23mm
Obv: Arabic leg: *Tahun Alif 1224*. Rev: Arabic leg: *Balad Kedah Daru'l/Aman*. Irregular center hole.

KM#	Date	Mintage	Good	VG	Fine	VF
3	AH1224	—	25.00	40.00	55.00	80.00

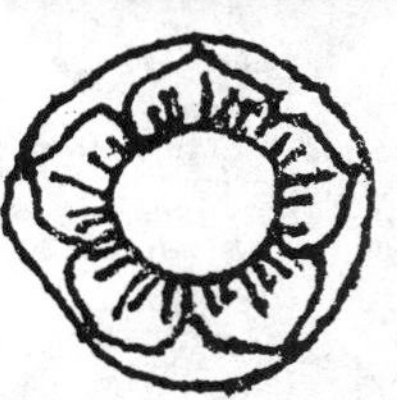

24mm
Obv: 5-petaled lotus blossom. Rev: Arabic leg: *Belanja Balad al-Perlis Kedah-Sanat 1262*. Irregular center hole.

KM#	Date	Mintage	Good	VG	Fine	VF
4	AH1262	—	25.00	40.00	55.00	80.00

18mm
Obv: Crude 12-pointed star. Rev: Arabic leg: *Belanja Balad Kedah Daru'l-Aman*. Irregular center hole.

KM#	Date	Mintage	Good	VG	Fine	VF
5	ND	—	22.00	35.00	50.00	75.00

KELANTAN

A state in northern Malaysia. Colonized by Javanese in 1300's. Subject to Thailand from 1780 to 1909.

TITLES

Kelantan كلنتن

Khalifa(t) Al-Mu'minin خليفة المؤمنين

SULTANS

Muhammed I, 1800-1835
Muhammed II, 1835-1886
Ahmad, 1886-1889
Muhammed III, 1889-1891
Mansur, 1891-1899
Interregnum, 1899-1902

PITIS

TIN, 24-29mm
Obv. Arabic leg: *Khalifat al-Mu'minin.*
Rev: Same. Many minor variations.

KM#	Date	Mintage	VG	Fine	VF	XF
1	ND	—	5.00	8.00	14.00	25.00

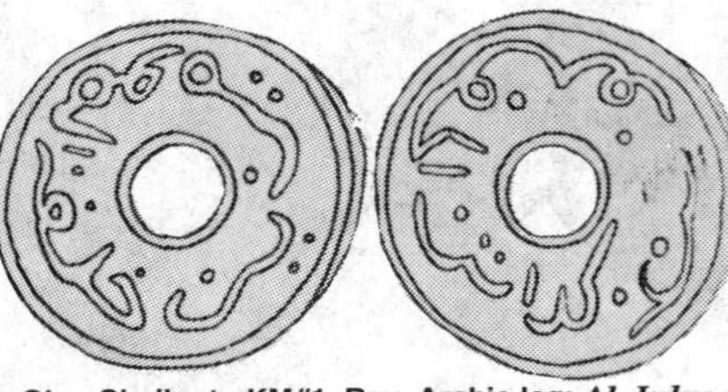

Obv: Similar to KM#1. Rev. Arabic leg: *Al-Julus Kelantan.*

KM#	Date	Mintage	VG	Fine	VF	XF
2	ND	—	10.00	15.00	30.00	50.00

28mm
Obv. Arabic leg: Similar to KM#1.
Rev: *Sanat 1256.*

KM#	Date	Mintage	VG	Fine	VF	XF
4	AH1256	—	8.00	12.00	20.00	30.00

NOTE: This type has also been attributed to Legeh.

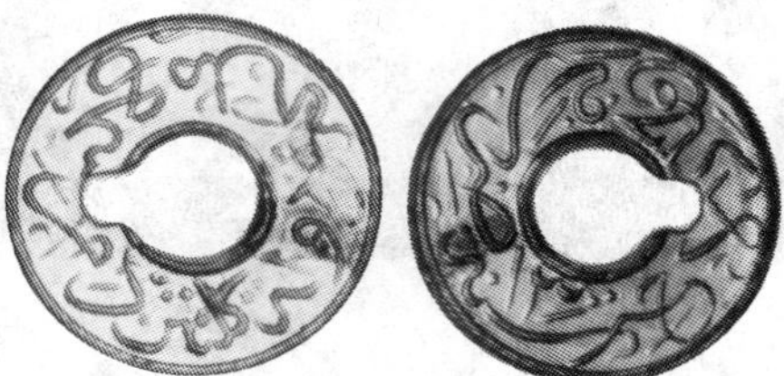

Obv. Arabic leg: *Dama Sama Mulka Daulat Kelantan.* Rev. Arabic leg: *Duriba Fi Jamadal Akhir 1300.*

KM#	Date	Mintage	VG	Fine	VF	XF
5	AH1300	—	8.00	12.00	20.00	30.00

Obv. Arabic leg: *Adim Mulkahu Belanjaan Kera Jaan Kelantan.* Rev. Arabic leg: *Sunia Fi Jumadal Ula Sanat 1314.*

KM#	Date	Mintage	VG	Fine	VF	XF
10	AH1314	—	5.00	8.00	16.00	30.00

NOTE: Legends are incuse.

LOCAL COINAGE

KEMASIN

Town in Kelantan State

TITLES

Kemasin كماسن

JOKOH

TIN, 29-30mm
Obv. Jawi leg: *Ini Pakai Di Kemasin Sanat 1300.*
Rev: Chinese inscription & 5 c/m. Two vars.

KM#	Date	Mintage	VG	Fine	VF	XF
30	AH1300	—	20.00	40.00	60.00	100.00

PATANI, PATTANI

Refer to Thailand Local Issues.

MALACCA

A state of Malaysia on the west coast. It was settled from Sumatra in the 1300's. Occupied by the Portuguese in 1511. Captured by the Dutch in 1641. Held by the British from 1795 to 1802 and 1811 to 1818. Ceded to Britain in 1824.

The attribution of the following coins to Malacca is uncertain. All were struck in England, on behalf of merchants in Singapore. All have an Arabic legend *Tanah Melayu* (Land of the Malays) above a rooster.

KEPING

COPPER
Rev: Denomination at top written like a fraction.

KM#	Date	Mintage	Fine	VF	XF	Unc
8.1	AH1247	—	2.50	5.00	10.00	30.00
	BRASS					
8.1a	AH1247	—	—	—	—	—
	COPPER					
	Rev: Denomination written simply 1.					
8.2	AH1247	—	2.00	4.00	9.00	30.00
	AH1251	—	Reported, not confirmed			
	AH1147(error)	30.00	50.00	70.00	100.00	
	AH1219(error)	3.00	6.00	15.00	40.00	
	AH1241(error)	30.00	50.00	70.00	100.00	
	AH1411(error)	3.00	6.00	15.00	45.00	

NOTE: Some of these tokens may have been restruck at a later time. Some also exist in proof.
NOTE: See Indonesia for similar tokens with differing obverses.

2 KEPING

COPPER

KM#	Date	Mintage	Fine	VF	XF	Unc
14	AH1247	—	15.00	25.00	35.00	65.00

PAHANG

A state on the east coast of Malaysia. Subject to the Suvyaya kingdom in Sumatra in the 1200's. Shuttled from native kingdom to native kingdom after 1450. Became one of the Federated Malay States in 1895.

The following coins were minted by prominent Chinese in Pahang by permission of Sultan Ahmed. They were intended for general circulation within Pahang. Many other pieces issued by merchants and gambling houses exist, but will not be listed here.

TITLES

Pahang

GOVERNORS

Bendahara Sewa Raja Tun Ali, 1806-1857
Bendahara Sewa Raja Tun Mutahir, 1857-1863

SULTANS

Ahmed Al Muazzam, 1884-1914 ruled as Governor Bendahara Sewa Raja Ahmad from 1863 to 1884

Pahang Company

1/2 CENT

TIN
Obv: 4 Chinese characters *Ch'ien Sheng T'ung Pao.* Rev. value and Arabic leg: *Pahang Company* and 1/2 C.

KM#	Date	Mintage	Good	VG	Fine	VF
6	ND	—	25.00	35.00	50.00	75.00

Minted between 1884 and 1896.

CENT

TIN
Rev: 1 C.

KM#	Date	Mintage	Good	VG	Fine	VF
9	ND	—	25.00	35.00	50.00	75.00

Minted between 1884 and 1896.

Obv: Value and Chinese *Ch'ien Sheng T'ung Pao.* Rev: Date and Arabic leg.

KM#	Date	Mintage	Good	VG	Fine	VF
11	AH1301	—	20.00	30.00	45.00	70.00

PENANG

Pulu Penang-Prince of Wales Island

An island off the west coast of Malaysia. Ceded to the British in 1791 by the sultan of Kedah and was the first British settlement in Malaya. Also known as Pulu Penang and Prince of Wales Island - which title it retained until 1867.

The currency system depended on the Spanish dollar divided into 100 pice (or cents) until 1826 when 48 pice were deemed the equivalent of one Bengal rupee until 1830. The coins are considered in three groups:

(a) The Company bale mark series, consisting of copper 1/10, 1/2 and 1 pice of 1786/1787, and silver tenth, quarter and half dollars, dated 1788;

(b) Company coat of arms issues in copper between 1810 and 1828 in denominations of 1/2, 1 and double pice pieces; and

(c) Tin issues of local mintage pice pieces of 1800-1809, which are extremely rare.

TITLES

Pulu Penang ڤولو ڤنيڠ

MONETARY SYSTEM

100 Cents (Pice) = 1 Dollar

1/2 CENT

(1/2 Pice)

COPPER
Mint: Royal

KM#	Date	Mintage	Fine	VF	XF	Unc
11	1810	1.720	15.00	30.00	60.00	125.00
	1810	—	—	—	Proof	400.00

Mint: Madras

KM#	Date	Mintage	Fine	VF	XF	Unc
12	1825	.145	40.00	70.00	150.00	300.00
	1828	.414	30.00	60.00	140.00	300.00

NOTE: Wreath varies from 21 to 26 lily cups.

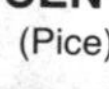

CENT
(Pice)

元

TIN, uniface, 40.35 g
Initial GL (Governor Leith) in ring.
c/m: Chinese character *Yuan*.

KM#	Date	Mintage	VG	Fine	VF	XF
8	ND(c.1800-03)	—	1250.	3000.	4500.	6000.

启

30.50 g
Initials GF (Governor Farguhar) in ring,
c/m: Chinese character *Ch'i*.

KM#	Date	Mintage	VG	Fine	VF	XF
9	ND(c.1805)	—	600.00	1150.	1850.	3000.

美

30.00-32.00 g
Native initials A & C (Anderson & Clubley)
c/m: Chinese character *Mei*.

KM#	Date	Mintage	VG	Fine	VF	XF
10	1809	—	900.00	1500.	2500.	4000.

美

English initials A & C (Anderson & Clubley)
c/m: Chinese character *Mei*.

KM#	Date	Mintage	VG	Fine	VF	XF
11	1809	—	900.00	1500.	2500.	4000.

COPPER
Royal Mint
Rev: Leaves on wreath go clockwise.

KM#	Date	Mintage	Fine	VF	XF	Unc
13	1810 small date, small shield					
		1.827	12.50	30.00	70.00	100.00
	1810	—	—	—	Proof	350.00

Madras Mint

KM#	Date	Mintage	Fine	VF	XF	Unc
14	1825	.137	30.00	70.00	140.00	240.00
	1828	.236	25.00	65.00	130.00	240.00

NOTE: Wreaths vary from 21 to 27 lily cups.

2 CENTS
(2 Pice)

COPPER
Mint: Madras

KM#	Date	Mintage	Fine	VF	XF	Unc
15	1825	.130	35.00	75.00	150.00	265.00
	1825	—	—	—	Proof	375.00
	1828	.720	15.00	40.00	120.00	200.00

NOTE: Wreaths vary from 24 to 28 lily cups.

PATTERNS (Pn)
(Including off metal strikes)

KM#	Date	Mintage	Identification	Mkt.Val.
Pn1	1810	—	1 Cent (Pice), Copper, leaves on wreath counterclockwise	550.00
Pn2	1810	—	1 Cent (Pice), Copper, leaves on wreath clockwise	550.00

PERAK

A state on the west coast of Malaysia. Important tin deposits are in this state. Part of Malay kingdoms from early times. Perak was an independent state from 1824-1874. The only coin is one made in Birmingham, England and distributed by a Singapore importer.

TITLES

Negri Peraq نكري قيرق

SULTANS

Ahmadin, 1706-1806
Abdul-Malik Mansur, 1806-1825
Abdullah Muazzam, 1825-1830
Shahabud-Din Riayat, 1831-1851
Abdullah Muhammad, 1851-1857
Jafar Muazzam, 1857-1865
Ali Al-Mukammal Inayat, 1865-1871
Ismail Muabidin, 1871-1874
Abdullah Muhammad, 1874-1877
Yusuf Sharifud-Din Mufzal, 1877-1887
Sir Idris Murshid Al-Azzam, 1887-1916

KEPING

COPPER
Obv. Arabic leg: *Negri Perak*
(State of Perak). Rev. Arabic leg:
Satu Kepang 1251
(one Keping AH 1251).

KM#	Date	Mintage	Fine	VF	XF	Unc
4	AH1251	—	10.00	15.00	25.00	50.00
	1251	—	—	—	Proof	120.00

NOTE: See Indonesia for similar tokens with differing legends.

PATTERNS (Pn)
(Including off metal strikes)

KM#	Date	Mintage	Identification	Mkt.Val.
Pn1	AH1251	—	1 Keping, Tin, KM4	—
Pn2	AH1251	—	1 Keping, Silvered, KM4	—

PERLIS

See State of Kedah

SELANGOR

A state on the west coast of Malaysia. Played a part in the trading programs of both the Dutch and the British. Signed a treaty with Britain in 1818 and Britain took control of the state in 1874.

TITLES

Negri Selangor نكري سلاغور

SULTANS

Ibrahim, 1777-1826
Muhammad, 1826-1857
Abdul-Samad, 1857-1898
Sulaiman, 1898-1938

PITIS

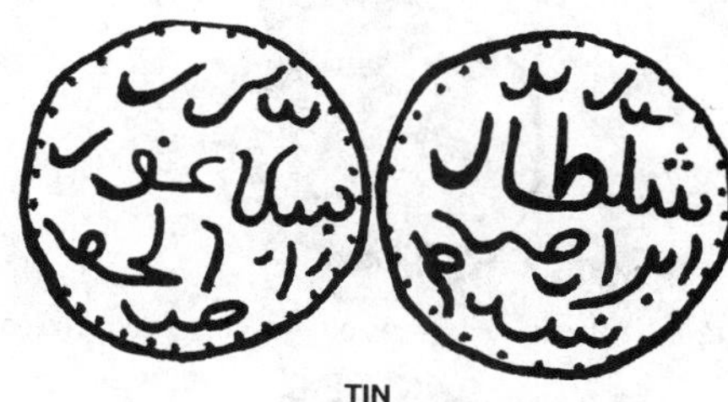

TIN
Obv. leg: Arabic
Negri Selangor Darul Ihsan.
Rev. leg: Arabic
Baginda Sultan Ibrahim Shah.

KM#	Date	Mintage	Fine	VF	XF	Unc
1	ND	—	—	—	—	—

KEPING

COPPER
Obv. Arabic leg: *Negri Selangor.*
Rev. Arabic leg: *Satu Keping 1251.*

KM#	Date	Mintage	Fine	VF	XF	Unc
3	AH1251	—	10.00	15.00	25.00	50.00

NOTE: See Indonesia for similar tokens with differing legends.

TRENGGANU

A state in eastern Malaysia on the shore of the south China Sea. Area of dispute between Malacca and Thailand with the latter emerging with possession. Trengganu became a British dependency in 1909.

TITLES

Khalifa(t) al-Mu'minin خليفة المؤمنين

Trengganu

SULTANS

Zainal Abidin II, 1793-1808
Ahmad I, 1808-1827
Abdul Rahman, 1827-1831
Daud, 1831
Mansur II, 1831-1836
Muhammed, 1836-1839
Baginda Omar, 1839-1876
Ahmad II, 1876-1881
Zainal Abidin III, 1881-1918

PITIS

TIN

KM#	Date	Mintage	VG	Fine	VF	XF
9	AH1222	—	17.50	27.50	40.00	70.00

Legend points outward instead of inward.

KM#	Date	Mintage	VG	Fine	VF	XF
10	AH1222	—	20.00	35.00	50.00	80.00

Khalifat al-Muminin 1251 Malik al-Adil.

KM#	Date	Mintage	VG	Fine	VF	XF
11	AH1251	—	30.00	50.00	75.00	120.00

KM#	Date	Mintage	VG	Fine	VF	XF
13	AH1265	—	25.00	40.00	65.00	100.00

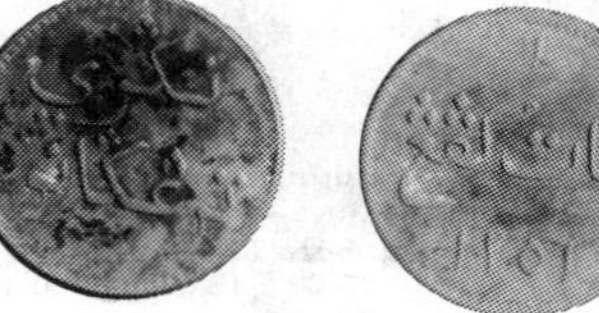

Belanja Trengganu Sanat 1299.

KM#	Date	Mintage	VG	Fine	VF	XF
14	AH1299	—	25.00	40.00	65.00	100.00

KEPING

COPPER
Obv. Arabic leg: *Negri Trengganu* (State of Trengganu). Rev. Arabic leg: *Satu Keping 1251*.

KM#	Date	Mintage	VG	Fine	VF	XF
12	AH1251	—	5.00	8.00	20.00	45.00
	AH1251	—	—	—	Proof	125.00

10 KEPING

TIN

KM#	Date	Mintage	VG	Fine	VF	XF
15	AH1310	—	10.00	20.00	30.00	60.00

STRAITS SETTLEMENTS

Straits Settlements, a former British crown colony situated on the Malay Peninsula of Asia, was formed in 1826 by combining the territories of Singapore, Penang and Malacca. The colony was administered by the East India Company until its abolition in 1853. Straits Settlements was a part of British India from 1858 to 1867 at which time it became a Crown Colony. This name was changed to Malaya in 1939.

RULERS

British

MINT MARKS

H - Heaton, Birmingham
W - Soho Mint
B - Bombay

MONETARY SYSTEM

100 Cents = 1 Dollar

EAST INDIA COMPANY

1826-1858

1/4 CENT

COPPER
Rev. leg: EAST INDIA COMPANY

KM#	Date	Mintage	Fine	VF	XF	Unc
1	1845	34.327	3.00	10.00	22.00	65.00
	1845 WW on truncation					
		—	—	—	Proof	350.00

1/2 CENT

COPPER

KM#	Date	Mintage	Fine	VF	XF	Unc
2	1845	18.737	4.00	10.00	28.00	65.00
	1845	—	—	—	Proof	350.00
	1845 WW on truncation					
		Inc. Ab.	4.00	10.00	25.00	60.00
	1845 WW on truncation					
		—	—	—	Proof	400.00

CENT

COPPER

KM#	Date	Mintage	Fine	VF	XF	Unc
3	1845	18.526	5.00	15.00	35.00	80.00
	1845 WW on truncation					
		—	—	—	Proof	450.00

BRITISH INDIA GOVERNMENT

1858-1867

1/4 CENT

COPPER
Rev. leg: INDIA STRAITS

KM#	Date	Mintage	Fine	VF	XF	Unc
4	1862	3.368	50.00	125.00	250.00	475.00
	1862	—	—	—	Proof	925.00

1/2 CENT

COPPER

KM#	Date	Mintage	Fine	VF	XF	Unc
5	1862	4.590	25.00	50.00	150.00	300.00
	1862	—	—	—	Proof	700.00

CENT

COPPER

KM#	Date	Mintage	Fine	VF	XF	Unc
6	1862	9.321	5.00	15.00	35.00	145.00
	1862	—	—	—	Proof	450.00

COLONIAL ISSUES

1867-1939

1/4 CENT

COPPER
Rev. leg: STRAITS SETTLEMENTS, plain edge.

KM#	Date	Mintage	Fine	VF	XF	Unc
7	1872	—	—	—	Proof	375.00
	1872H	9.240	6.00	12.00	35.00	100.00
	1872H	—	—	—	Proof	300.00
	1873	—	120.00	160.00	300.00	700.00
	1873	—	—	—	Proof	800.00
	1875	—	—	—	Proof	600.00
	1875W	—	—	—	Proof	600.00
	1883	.200	300.00	600.00	1100.	2000.

BRONZE

KM#	Date	Mintage	Fine	VF	XF	Unc
7a	1884	8.000	3.00	9.00	30.00	75.00
	1884	—	—	—	Proof	250.00

Reeded edge

KM#	Date	Mintage	Fine	VF	XF	Unc
14	1889	2.000	3.00	9.00	30.00	75.00
	1889	—	—	—	Proof	250.00
	1890	—	—	—	Proof	600.00
	1891	—	—	—	Proof	400.00
	1898	1.600	2.00	7.00	25.00	65.00
	1898	—	—	—	Proof	250.00
	1899	2.400	2.00	5.00	22.00	60.00

NOTE: Later date (1901) exists for this type.

1/2 CENT

COPPER
Plain edge

KM#	Date	Mintage	Fine	VF	XF	Unc
8	1872	—	—	—	Proof	350.00
	1872H	5.610	18.00	30.00	60.00	120.00
	1872H	—	—	—	Proof	350.00
	1873	—	35.00	65.00	140.00	400.00
	1874	—	—	—	Proof	400.00
	1875	—	—	—	Proof	400.00
	1875W	—	—	—	Proof	400.00
	1883	2.740	50.00	90.00	325.00	650.00

BRONZE

KM#	Date	Mintage	Fine	VF	XF	Unc
8a	1884	4.000	6.00	12.00	40.00	90.00
	1884	—	—	—	Proof	400.00

Reeded edge

KM#	Date	Mintage	Fine	VF	XF	Unc
15	1889	2.000	10.00	22.00	50.00	110.00
	1890	—	—	—	Proof	400.00
	1891	—	—	—	Proof	400.00

CENT

COPPER
Plain edge

KM#	Date	Mintage	Fine	VF	XF	Unc
9	1872	—	—	—	Proof	350.00
	1872H	5.770	3.00	12.50	35.00	75.00
	1872H	—	—	—	Proof	350.00
	1873	—	7.00	18.00	45.00	95.00
	1874	10.000	4.00	12.50	35.00	65.00
	1874H	10.000	4.00	12.50	35.00	65.00
	1874H	—	—	—	Proof	250.00
	1875	6.000	7.00	18.00	40.00	70.00
	1875	—	—	—	Proof	250.00
	1875W	—	7.00	18.00	40.00	70.00
	1875 W on truncation					
		—	—	—	Proof	250.00
	1876	—	6.00	15.00	35.00	70.00
	1877	—	6.00	15.00	35.00	70.00
	1878	—	60.00	175.00	400.00	900.00
	1883	8.640	6.00	15.00	40.00	90.00

BRONZE

KM#	Date	Mintage	Fine	VF	XF	Unc
9a	1884	6.000	1.50	6.00	20.00	50.00
	1884	—	—	—	Proof	250.00
	1885	7.412	10.00	25.00	60.00	150.00
	1886	1.512	20.00	40.00	100.00	200.00

Reeded edge

KM#	Date	Mintage	Fine	VF	XF	Unc
16	1887	8.988	2.00	6.00	25.00	60.00
	1888	10.000	2.00	6.00	25.00	60.00
	1889	6.010	2.00	6.00	25.00	60.00
	1890	11.006	2.00	6.00	25.00	60.00
	1890	—	—	—	Proof	250.00
	1891	6.004	1.50	6.00	25.00	60.00
	1894	9.034	1.50	6.00	25.00	60.00
	1895	4.466	1.50	6.00	25.00	60.00
	1897	18.040	1.50	6.00	25.00	60.00
	1898	2.086	4.00	12.00	35.00	70.00
	1898	—	—	—	Proof	220.00
	1900	2.914	1.50	5.00	20.00	50.00

NOTE: Later date (1901) exists for this type.

5 CENTS

1.3600 g, .800 SILVER, .0349 oz ASW

KM#	Date	Mintage	Fine	VF	XF	Unc
10	1871	.062	320.00	700.00	1200.	2000.
	1871	—	—	—	Proof	3000.
	1873	.060	550.00	1400.	1850.	2500.
	1874H	.060	50.00	100.00	185.00	350.00
	1876H	.040	500.00	1000.	1600.	2400.
	1877	.060	400.00	660.00	1100.	2000.
	1878	.260	15.00	35.00	90.00	200.00
	1878	—	—	—	Proof	350.00
	1879H	.100	120.00	200.00	400.00	600.00
	1880H	.090	140.00	300.00	550.00	800.00
	1881	.180	20.00	40.00	120.00	200.00
	1881	—	—	—	Proof	350.00
	1882H	.380	12.50	25.00	55.00	160.00
	1882H	—	—	—	Proof	350.00
	1883	.080	100.00	200.00	350.00	720.00
	1884	.440	5.00	12.00	35.00	90.00
	1884	—	—	—	Proof	350.00
	1885	.220	15.00	35.00	100.00	240.00
	1885	—	—	—	Proof	350.00
	1886	.340	7.50	12.50	35.00	85.00
	1887	.400	6.00	10.00	25.00	75.00
	1888	.590	5.00	10.00	20.00	65.00
	1889	1.000	2.00	4.00	15.00	55.00
	1889	—	—	—	Proof	350.00
	1890H	.400	6.00	17.50	48.00	85.00
	1890H	—	—	—	Proof	350.00
	1891	.800	2.50	5.00	15.00	55.00
	1893	.440	3.50	6.00	20.00	65.00
	1894	.340	2.50	5.00	15.00	55.00
	1895	1.480	2.00	3.00	12.50	48.00
	1896	.960	2.00	3.00	12.50	48.00

KM#	Date	Mintage	Fine	VF	XF	Unc
10	1897	.320	4.00	8.00	20.00	65.00
	1897H	.440	4.00	9.00	25.00	75.00
	1898	1.200	1.50	2.50	12.50	48.00
	1899	.078	3.00	6.00	20.00	65.00
	1900	2.720	1.50	2.50	12.50	48.00
	1900H	.400	5.00	10.00	22.00	65.00

NOTE: Later date (1901) exists for this type.

10 CENTS

2.7100 g, .800 SILVER, .0697 oz ASW

KM#	Date	Mintage	Fine	VF	XF	Unc
11	1871	.248	15.00	25.00	65.00	150.00
	1871	—	—	—	Proof	250.00
	1872H	.230	15.00	25.00	62.50	130.00
	1872H	—	—	—	Proof	250.00
	1873	.210	25.00	45.00	110.00	180.00
	1874H	.180	12.00	20.00	45.00	90.00
	1876H	.120	30.00	65.00	130.00	250.00
	1877	.160	15.00	35.00	55.00	120.00
	1878	.470	5.00	10.00	30.00	65.00
	1878	—	—	—	Proof	250.00
	1879H	.250	12.00	20.00	45.00	90.00
	1879H	—	—	—	Proof	250.00
	1880H	.235	16.50	28.00	60.00	130.00
	1881	.460	5.00	10.00	30.00	65.00
	1881	—	—	—	Proof	250.00
	1882H	.430	5.00	10.00	30.00	65.00
	1882H	—	—	—	Proof	250.00
	1883	.160	25.00	50.00	100.00	200.00
	1883H	.610	120.00	220.00	400.00	800.00
	1883H	—	—	—	Proof	1100.
	1884 crosslet 4	1.240	3.00	5.00	12.00	50.00
	1884 plain 4	Inc. Ab.	3.00	5.00	12.00	50.00
	1884	—	—	—	Proof	250.00
	1885	.400	15.00	20.00	30.00	90.00
	1885	—	—	—	Proof	250.00
	1886	.790	3.00	5.00	12.00	45.00
	1886	—	—	—	Proof	250.00
	1887	.640	3.00	5.00	12.00	45.00
	1888	1.075	2.00	4.00	12.00	45.00
	1888	—	—	—	Proof	250.00
	1889	1.500	2.00	3.00	7.50	40.00
	1889	—	—	—	Proof	250.00
	1890H	.730	3.50	6.00	15.00	50.00
	1890H	—	—	—	Proof	250.00
	1891	1.380	2.00	3.00	7.50	30.00
	1891	—	—	—	Proof	250.00
	1893	.980	2.00	3.00	7.50	30.00
	1893	—	—	—	Proof	250.00
	1894	1.640	2.00	3.00	7.50	30.00
	1895	2.324	2.00	3.00	7.50	25.00
	1896	2.256	2.00	3.00	7.50	25.00
	1897	.700	2.50	5.00	12.50	50.00
	1897H	.390	4.00	8.00	20.00	60.00
	1898	1.960	2.00	3.50	8.00	35.00
	1899	.286	2.00	3.50	8.00	35.00
	1900	2.960	2.00	3.50	8.00	35.00
	1900H	1.000	2.50	5.00	11.50	40.00
	1900H	—	—	—	Proof	250.00

NOTE: Later date (1901) exists for this type.

20 CENTS

5.4300 g, .800 SILVER, .1396 oz ASW

KM#	Date	Mintage	Fine	VF	XF	Unc
12	1871	.016	380.00	750.00	1300.	1900.
	1871	—	—	—	Proof	2800.
	1872H	.040	120.00	250.00	400.00	700.00
	1873	.030	350.00	700.00	1200.	1850.
	1874H	.045	75.00	110.00	175.00	325.00
	1876H	.030	100.00	220.00	400.00	700.00
	1877	.055	65.00	100.00	185.00	375.00
	1878	.150	12.50	18.50	55.00	145.00
	1878	—	—	—	Proof	375.00
	1879H	.050	60.00	110.00	200.00	375.00
	1879H	—	—	—	Proof	450.00
	1880H	.085	30.00	50.00	100.00	220.00
	1880H	—	—	—	Proof	375.00
	1881/71	.100	25.00	40.00	100.00	250.00
	1881	Inc. Ab.	20.00	35.00	90.00	200.00
	1882H	.245	12.00	20.00	50.00	120.00
	1882H	—	—	—	Proof	375.00
	1883	.200	15.00	22.00	55.00	130.00
	1884	.220	5.00	10.00	27.50	65.00
	1884	—	—	—	Proof	375.00
	1885	.100	20.00	35.00	90.00	200.00
	1886	.245	5.00	7.50	20.00	55.00
	1886	—	—	—	Proof	375.00
	1887	.220	5.00	7.50	15.00	48.00
	1888	.295	5.00	7.50	15.00	48.00
	1888	—	—	—	Proof	375.00

KM#	Date	Mintage	Fine	VF	XF	Unc
12	1889	.420	3.00	5.00	15.00	45.00
	1890H	.270	7.50	15.00	35.00	70.00
	1890H	—	—	—	Proof	300.00
	1891	.510	3.25	5.00	13.50	42.00
	1893	.310	3.25	5.00	13.50	42.00
	1894	.495	3.25	5.00	13.50	42.00
	1895	.580	3.25	5.00	13.50	42.00
	1896	.600	3.25	5.00	13.50	42.00
	1897	.150	8.00	15.00	30.00	80.00
	1897H	.185	8.00	15.00	30.00	80.00
	1898	.580	3.00	4.50	12.50	40.00
	1899	.204	3.00	4.50	12.50	40.00
	1900	.620	3.00	4.50	12.50	40.00
	1900H	.300	6.00	9.00	25.00	70.00
	1900H	—	—	—	Proof	375.00

NOTE: Later date (1901) exists for this type.

50 CENTS

13.5769 g, .800 SILVER, .3492 oz ASW

KM#	Date	Mintage	Fine	VF	XF	Unc
13	1886	.060	50.00	120.00	270.00	850.00
	1886	—	—	—	Proof	2200.
	1887	.094	40.00	75.00	180.00	475.00
	1887	—	—	—	Proof	2200.
	1888	.096	40.00	75.00	180.00	475.00
	1889	.032	800.00	1350.	1750.	3300.
	1890H	.042	100.00	200.00	325.00	850.00
	1891	.121	35.00	50.00	125.00	300.00
	1891	—	—	—	Proof	2200.
	1893	.024	450.00	800.00	1350.	2200.
	1893	—	—	—	Proof	2750.
	1894	.052	50.00	150.00	250.00	500.00
	1895	.056	50.00	150.00	250.00	500.00
	1896	.120	25.00	50.00	120.00	280.00
	1897	.036	100.00	200.00	320.00	800.00
	1897H	.044	85.00	150.00	250.00	600.00
	1898	.160	25.00	50.00	120.00	280.00
	1899	.136	25.00	50.00	120.00	280.00
	1900	.088	35.00	70.00	150.00	320.00
	1900H	.040	100.00	175.00	350.00	775.00

NOTE: Later date (1901) exists for this type.

PATTERNS (Pn)

(Including off metal strikes)

KM#	Date	Mintage	Identification	Mkt.Val.
Pn1	1872H	—	10 Cents, Copper, KM11	350.00
Pn2	1873	—	10 Cents, Copper, KM11	350.00
Pn3	1873	—	20 Cents, Copper, KM12, plain edge	1000.
Pn4	1890	—	1 Cent, Silver, KM16	1500.
Pn5	1891	—	1/4 Cent, Silver, KM14	1500.
Pn6	1891	—	1/4 Cent, Gold, KM14	3200.
Pn7	1891	—	1/2 Cent, Silver, KM15	1750.
Pn8	1891	—	1/2 Cent, Gold, KM15	3600.
Pn9	1891	—	1 Cent, Silver, KM16	1500.
Pn10	1891	—	1 Cent, Gold, KM16	3600.
Pn11	1898	—	1/4 Cent, Silver, KM14	1500.
Pn12	1898	—	1 Cent, Silver, KM16	1200.

SARAWAK

Sarawak is a former British colony located on the northwest coast of Borneo. The Japanese occupation during World War II so thoroughly devastated the economy that Rajah Sir Charles Vyner Brooke ceded it to Great Britain on July 1, 1946. In September, 1963 the colony joined the Federation of Malaysia.

RULERS

James Brooke, Rajah, 1841-1868
Charles J. Brooke, Rajah, 1868-1917

MINT MARKS

H Heaton, Birmingham

TOKEN ISSUES (Tn)

KEPING

COPPER
Accession Date: Sept. 24 1841

KM#	Date	Mintage	VG	Fine	VF	XF
Tn1	AH1247	—	800.00	1000.	1650.	2550.

BRASS

KM#	Date	Mintage	VG	Fine	VF	XF
Tn1a	AH1247	—	750.00	950.00	1500.	2400.

COPPER

KM#	Date	Mintage	Fine	VF	XF	Unc
4	1870	.100	8.00	20.00	50.00	120.00
	1870	—	—	—	Proof	350.00
	1896H	.283	6.00	15.00	30.00	90.00
	1896H	—	—	—	Proof	350.00

1/2 CENT

COPPER

KM#	Date	Mintage	Fine	VF	XF	Unc
2	1863	—	12.50	35.00	85.00	200.00
	1863	—	—	—	Proof	550.00

BRONZED COPPER

KM#	Date	Mintage	Fine	VF	XF	Unc
2a	1863	—	—	—	Proof	700.00

COPPER

KM#	Date	Mintage	Fine	VF	XF	Unc
5	1870	.250	5.00	16.00	40.00	95.00
	1879	.640	5.00	16.00	40.00	95.00
	1879	—	—	—	Proof	350.00
	1896H	.327	3.50	10.00	30.00	85.00
	1896H	—	—	—	Proof	350.00

CENT

COPPER

KM#	Date	Mintage	Fine	VF	XF	Unc
3	1863	—	7.00	18.00	40.00	125.00
	1863	—	—	—	Proof	450.00

BRONZED COPPER

KM#	Date	Mintage	Fine	VF	XF	Unc
3a	1863	—	—	—	Proof	650.00

COPPER

KM#	Date	Mintage	Fine	VF	XF	Unc
6	1870	—	2.50	5.00	20.00	45.00
	1870	—	—	—	Proof	200.00
	1870	—	—		Gilt Proof	200.00
	1879	.750	4.00	10.00	30.00	65.00
	1879	—	—	—	Proof	200.00
	1880	1.070	3.00	7.00	28.00	62.50
	1882	1.070	2.50	6.00	25.00	55.00
	1882	—	—	—	Proof	200.00
	1884	1.070	2.50	6.00	25.00	55.00
	1884	—	—	—	Proof	200.00
	1885	2.140	2.50	6.00	25.00	55.00
	1885	—	—	—	Proof	200.00
	1886	3.210	2.50	6.00	25.00	55.00
	1887	1.605	2.50	6.00	25.00	55.00
	1887	—	—	—	Proof	200.00
	1888	2.140	2.50	6.00	25.00	55.00
	1888	—	—	—	Proof	200.00
	1889	.535	2.50	6.00	25.00	55.00
	1889/8H	2.675	2.50	6.00	25.00	55.00
	1889H	Inc. Ab.	2.50	6.00	25.00	55.00
	1889H	—	—	—	Proof	200.00
	1890H	3.210	2.50	6.00	25.00	55.00
	1891	.535	6.00	12.00	30.00	60.00
	1891H	1.070	2.50	6.00	25.00	55.00

NOTE: Varieties exist.

KM#	Date	Mintage	Fine	VF	XF	Unc
7	1892H	2.178	2.50	5.50	20.00	50.00
	1892H	—	—	—	Proof	200.00
	1893H	1.634	2.50	5.50	20.00	50.00
	1894H	1.633	2.50	5.50	20.00	50.00
	1896H	2.178	2.50	5.50	20.00	50.00
	1896H	—	—	—	Proof	200.00
	1897H	1.089	2.50	5.50	20.00	50.00

5 CENTS

1.3500 g, .800 SILVER, .0347 oz ASW

KM#	Date	Mintage	Fine	VF	XF	Unc
8	1900H	.200	20.00	40.00	60.00	110.00
	1900H	—	—	—	Proof	350.00

NOTE: Later dates (1908-1915) exist for this type.

10 CENTS

2.7100 g, .800 SILVER, .0697 oz ASW

KM#	Date	Mintage	Fine	VF	XF	Unc
9	1900H	.150	15.00	20.00	45.00	85.00
	1900H	—	—	—	40.00	85.00

NOTE: Later dates (1906-1915) exist for this type.

20 CENTS

5.4300 g, .800 SILVER, .1396 oz ASW

KM#	Date	Mintage	Fine	VF	XF	Unc
10	1900H	.075	25.00	50.00	75.00	170.00
	1900H	—	—	—	Proof	550.00

NOTE: Later dates (1906-1915) exist for this type.

50 CENTS

13.5700 g, .800 SILVER, .3490 oz ASW

KM#	Date	Mintage	Fine	VF	XF	Unc
11	1900H	.040	70.00	120.00	220.00	350.00
	1900H	—	—	—	Proof	1350.

NOTE: Later date (1906) exists for this type.

BRITISH NORTH BORNEO

British North Borneo (now known as Sabah), a former British protectorate and crown colony, occupies the northern tip of the island of Borneo. The island of Labuan, which lies 6 miles off the northwest coast of the island of Borneo, was attached to Singapore settlement in 1907. It became an independent settlement of the Straits Colony in 1912 and was incorporated with British North Borneo in 1946. In 1963 it became part of Malaysia.

RULERS

British

MINT MARKS

H - Heaton, Birmingham

MONETARY SYSTEM

100 Cents = 1 Straits Dollar

1/2 CENT

BRONZE

KM#	Date	Mintage	Fine	VF	XF	Unc
1	1885H	.500	4.00	12.50	30.00	75.00
	1885H	—	—	—	Proof	160.00
	1886H	1.000	3.50	7.50	25.00	60.00
	1886H	—	—	—	Proof	160.00
	1887H	.500	3.50	7.50	25.00	60.00
	1891H	2.000	3.50	7.50	22.00	50.00
	1891H	—	—	—	Proof	160.00

NOTE: Later date (1907) exists for this type.

CENT

BRONZE

KM#	Date	Mintage	Fine	VF	XF	Unc
2	1882H	2.000	2.50	4.50	16.00	45.00
	1882H	—	—	—	Proof	125.00
	1884H	2.000	2.50	4.50	16.00	45.00
	1884H	—	—	—	Proof	125.00
	1885H	1.750	3.00	6.00	18.00	50.00
	1886H	5.000	2.50	4.50	16.00	45.00
	1886H	—	—	—	Proof	125.00
	1887H	6.000	2.50	4.50	16.00	45.00
	1887H	—	—	—	Proof	125.00
	1888H	6.000	2.50	4.50	16.00	45.00
	1888H	—	—	—	Proof	125.00
	1889H	9.000	2.50	4.50	16.00	45.00
	1890H	8.003	2.50	4.50	16.00	45.00
	1890H	—	—	—	Proof	125.00
	1891H	3.000	2.50	4.50	16.00	45.00
	1891H	—	—	—	Proof	125.00
	1894H	1.000	15.00	30.00	55.00	100.00
	1896H	1.000	15.00	30.00	55.00	100.00

NOTE: Later date (1907) exists for this type.

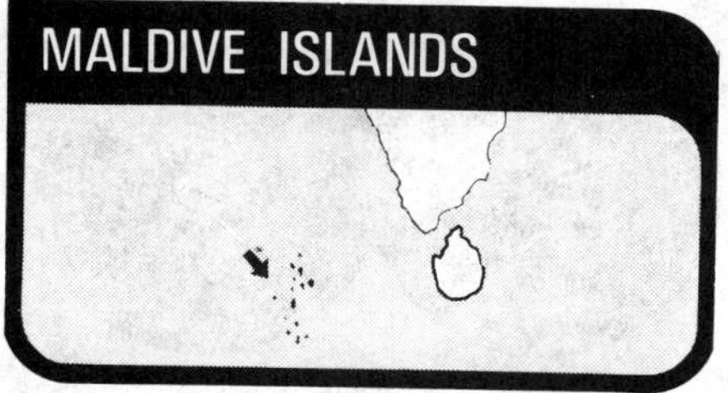

The Republic of Maldives, an archipelago of 2,000 coral islets in the northern Indian Ocean 417 miles (671 km.) west of Ceylon, has an area of 115 sq. mi. (298 sq. km.) and a population of 189,000. Capital: Male. Fishing employs 95 percent of the male work force. Dried fish, copra and coir yarn are exported.

The Maldive Islands were visited by Arab traders and converted to Islam in 1153. After being harassed in the 16th and 17th centuries by Mopla pirates of the Malabar coast and Portuguese raiders, the Maldivians voluntarily placed themselves under the suzerainty of Ceylon. In 1887 the islands became an internally self-governing British protectorate and a nominal dependency of Ceylon. Traditionally a sultanate, the Maldives became a republic in 1953 but restored the sultanate in 1954. The Sultanate of the Maldive Islands attained complete internal and external autonomy on July 26, 1965, and on Nov. 11, 1968, again became a republic.

The coins of the Maldives, issued by request of the Sultan and without direct British sponsorship, are not definitively coins of the British Commonwealth.

RULERS

Muhammad Mu'in al-Din,
AH1213-1250/1798-1835AD
Muhammad Imad al-Din IV,
AH1250-1300/1835-1882AD
Ibrahim Nur al-Din,
AH1300-1318/1882-1900AD
Muhammad Imad al-Din V,
AH1318-1322/1900-1904AD

MINTNAME

Mahle (Male)

MONETARY SYSTEM

100 Lari = 1 Rupee (Rufiyaa)

NOTE: The metrology of the early coinage is problematical. There seem to have been three denominations: a double Larin of 8-10 g, a Larin of approximately 4.8 g, and a half Larin that varied from 1.1 to 2.4 g, known as the Bodu Larin, Larin and Kuda Larin, respectively. In some years probably when copper was cheap (AH1276 & 1294), the Kuda (1/2) Larin is found with weights as high as 3.5 g. During the rule of Muhammad Imad Al-Din II Al-Muzaffar Bin Muhammad (1704-1721AD) additional denominations in the form of the 1/4, 1/8 and 1/16 Larin (1.17 g, 0.55 g and 0.29 g) were introduced on an experimental basis. This experiment was not followed by later rulers with the exception of Muhammad Imad Al-Din IV (1835-1882AD) who struck some light weight coins of about 1.1 g which can be considered 1/4 Larins.

MUHAMMAD MU'IN AL-DIN ISKANDAR

AH1213-1250/1798-1835AD

KUDA (1/2) LARIN

COPPER/BRONZE/BRASS, 1.40-2.40 g

KM#	Date	Good	VG	Fine	VF
32	AH1216	3.00	5.00	7.50	10.00
	1219	3.00	5.00	7.50	10.00
	1220	5.00	7.50	12.00	18.00
	1221	3.00	5.00	7.50	10.00
	1230	5.00	7.50	12.00	18.00
	1238	3.50	6.00	9.00	12.50
	1239	4.00	6.50	10.00	15.00
	1248	3.00	5.00	7.50	9.00

NOTE: Varieties exist. Some specimens are also struck on lightweight (1.4-1.9 g) planchets, some also being square in shape (1219, 1248). The year on the reverse occurs in 2nd, 3rd and 4th line.

MUHAMMAD IMAD AL-DIN IV ISKANDAR

AH1250-1300/1835-1882AD

1/4 LARIN

BRONZE/BRASS, 8-9mm, 0.70-1.20 g

KM#	Date	Good	VG	Fine	VF
34.1	AH1251	—	Reported, not confirmed		
	1286	5.00	7.50	12.00	17.50
	1292	5.00	7.50	12.00	17.50
	1294	5.00	7.50	12.00	17.50
	1298	4.00	6.50	10.00	15.00

NOTE: These lightweight coins are believed to have been intended as 1/4 larins since the dies with which they were struck are smaller than those for the kuda (1/2) larin, below. The issues dated AH1251 and 1298 are square or round. Varieties exist.

KUDA (1/2) LARIN

BRONZE, 1.20-2.80 g, 9-13mm

KM#	Date	Good	VG	Fine	VF
35.1	AH1252	—	Reported, not confirmed		
	1255	—	Reported, not confirmed		
	1257	2.50	3.50	6.00	9.00
	1258	2.50	3.50	6.00	9.00
	1276	2.50	3.50	6.00	9.00
	1280	2.50	3.50	6.00	9.00
	1286	2.50	3.00	5.00	8.00
	1287	—	Reported, not confirmed		
	1292	2.50	3.50	6.00	9.00
	1294	3.00	5.00	7.50	10.00
	1295	—	Reported, not confirmed		
	1298	.50	1.25	2.50	4.50

NOTE: Varieties exist. Date on second and third lines on reverse.

Rev: Date in top line.

KM#	Date	Good	VG	Fine	VF
35.2	AH1286	4.00	6.50	10.00	15.00

Obv: Leg. within border of small circles.
Rev: Leg. within quadrifoil.

KM#	Date	Good	VG	Fine	VF
35.3	AH1286	—	—	Rare	—

Square planchet.
Obv. and rev: Within circular, saw-toothed borders.

KM#	Date	Good	VG	Fine	VF
35.4	AH1276	—	—	Rare	—

LARIN

BRONZE, 3.55 g, 14.4mm

KM#	Date	Good	VG	Fine	VF
A36	AH1294	—	—	Rare	—

NOTE: Although this Larin is lightweight, it is of Larin size and its planchet was produced with a mold like the planchets of almost all other Larins and 1/2 Larins of earlier rulers. The 1/2 Larin, KM#35.1, 35.2 and 35.3 are struck on planchets cut from copper or bronze sheets.

BODU (2) LARI

BRONZE, 8.60 g
Rev: Date in third line.

KM#	Date	Good	VG	Fine	VF
36.1	AH1294	5.00	8.50	12.50	17.50
	1298	5.00	8.50	12.50	17.50

Rev: Date in second line.

KM#	Date	Good	VG	Fine	VF
36.2	AH1298	7.50	12.50	20.00	30.00

IBRAHIM NUR AL-DIN ISKANDAR

AH1300-1318/1882-1900AD

1/4 LARIN/LARIN

BRONZE, 0.70-1.40 g

KM#	Date	Fine	VF	XF	Unc
37	AH1300	2.00	3.00	4.50	6.00

NOTE: Toward the end of this reign the standard was reportedly revised by a factor of four, making this denomination officially one larin. The date occurs on second and third lines on the reverse.

MUHAMMAD IMAD AL-DIN V ISKANDAR

AH1318-1322/1900-1904AD

LARIN

COPPER/BRASS, 0.80-1.10 g

KM#	Date	Fine	VF	XF	Unc
38	AH1318	1.00	1.50	2.00	4.00

NOTE: Die varieties exist.

2 LARIAT

COPPER/BRASS, 1.40-2.20 g

KM#	Date	Fine	VF	XF	Unc
39	AH1318	1.50	3.50	5.00	7.50

NOTE: Later date (AH1319) exists for this type.

MALTA

The Republic of Malta, an independent parliamentary democracy within the British Commonwealth, is situated in the Mediterranean Sea between Sicily and North Africa. With the islands of Gozo and Comino, Malta has an area of 122 sq. mi. (320 sq. km.) and a population of 386,000. Capital: Valletta. Malta has no proven mineral resources, an agriculture insufficient to its needs, and a small, but expanding, manufacturing facility. Clothing, textile yarns and fabrics, and knitted wear are exported.

For more than 3,500 years Malta was ruled, in succession by Phoenicians, Carthaginians, Romans, Arabs, Normans, the Knights of Malta, France and Britain. Napoleon seized Malta by treachery in 1798. The French were ousted by a Maltese insurrection assisted by Britain, and in 1814 Malta, of its own free will, became a part of the British Empire. Malta obtained full independence in Sept., 1964; electing to remain within the Commonwealth with the British monarch as the nominal head of state.

Malta became a republic on Dec. 13, 1974, but remained a member of the Commonwealth of Nations. The president is Chief of State. The prime minister is the Head of Government.

RULERS

British, until 1964

BRITISH COINAGE

MONETARY SYSTEM

4 Farthings = 1 Penny

1/3 FARTHING

COPPER

NOTE: From 1827 through 1913 homeland type 1/3 Farthings along with other coinage of Great Britain circulated in Malta. The 1/3 Farthing corresponded to the copper Grano or 1/12 Penny. These are found listed under Great Britain.

MARTINIQUE

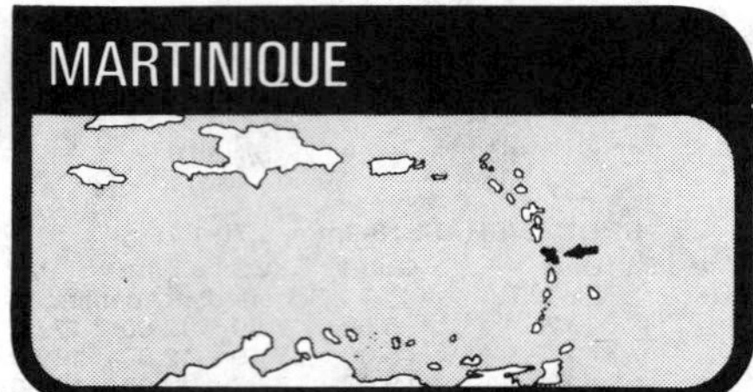

The French Overseas Department of Martinique, located in the Lesser Antilles of the West Indies between Dominica and Saint Lucia, has an area of 425 sq. mi. (1,100 sq. km.) and a population of 290,000. Capital: Fort-de-France. Agriculture and tourism are the major sources of income. Bananas, sugar, and rum are exported.

Christopher Columbus discovered Martinique, probably on June 15, 1502. France took possession on June 25, 1635, and has maintained possession since that time except for three short periods of British occupation during the Napoleonic Wars. A French department since 1946, Martinique voted a reaffirmation of that status in 1958, remaining within the new French Community. Martinique was the birthplace of Napoleon's Empress Josephine, and the site of the eruption of Mt. Pelee in 1902 that claimed 40,000 lives.

The official currency of Martinique is the French franc. The 1897-1922 coinage of the Colony of Martinique is now obsolete.

RULERS

British, 1793-1801
French, 1802-1809

MONETARY SYSTEM

15 Sols = 1 Escalin
20 Sols = 1 Livre
66 Livres = 4 Escudos = 6400 Reis

French Occupation

1802-1809

MONETARY SYSTEM

6400 Reis = 22 Livres

20 LIVRES

GOLD

c/m: 20 above eagle on false or lightweight Brazil 6400 Reis, KM#172.2.

KM#	Date	Mintage	VG	Fine	VF	XF
32	ND(1751-77)	—	1000.	1500.	2000.	3500.
	ND(1778-79)	—	700.00	1000.	1500.	2800.

c/m: 20 above eagle on false Brazil 6400 Reis, type of KM#199.

KM#	Date	Mintage	VG	Fine	VF	XF
31	ND(1777-86)	—	750.00	1150.	1650.	3000.

22 LIVRES

GOLD

c/m: 22 above eagle on Portuguese 4000 Reis, KM#184.

KM#	Date	Mintage	VG	Fine	VF	XF
38	ND(1707-22)	—	2500.	4000.	5500.	8500.

c/m: 22 above eagle on Brazil 6400 Reis, KM#151.

KM#	Date	Mintage	VG	Fine	VF	XF
39	ND(1735-50)	—	2000.	3500.	4500.	7500.

c/m: 22 above eagle on false Brazil 6400 Reis, type of KM#172.1.

KM#	Date	Mintage	VG	Fine	VF	XF
37	ND(1751-77)	—	1500.	2500.	3000.	5000.

c/m: 22 above eagle on Brazil 6400 Reis, KM#199.2.

KM#	Date	Mintage	VG	Fine	VF	XF
33	ND(1777-86)	—	1000.	1500.	1800.	3000.

c/m: 22 above eagle on Brazil 6400 Reis, KM#218.2.

KM#	Date	Mintage	VG	Fine	VF	XF
34	ND(1786-90)	—	1000.	1500.	1800.	3000.

c/m: 22 above eagle on Brazil 6400 Reis, KM#226.1.

KM#	Date	Mintage	VG	Fine	VF	XF
35	ND(1789-1805)	—	950.00	1400.	1700.	2850.

c/m: 22 above eagle on Portugal 4 Escudos, KM#240.

KM#	Date	Mintage	VG	Fine	VF	XF
36	ND(1750-76)	—	1250.	2000.	2450.	4000.

NOTE: There are many merchant c/m from Martinique during this period, but the above are probably the only official issues. There are also many counterfeits or fantasies attributed to the West Indies.

DECIMAL COINAGE

100 Centimes = 1 Franc

50 CENTIMES

COPPER-NICKEL

KM#	Date	Mintage	VG	Fine	VF	XF
40	1897	.600	10.00	20.00	35.00	80.00

NOTE: Later date (1922) exists for this type.

FRANC

COPPER-NICKEL

KM#	Date	Mintage	VG	Fine	VF	XF
41	1897	.300	12.00	22.00	45.00	90.00

NOTE: Later date (1922) exists for this type.

ESSAIS (E)

(Standard thickness)

KM#	Date	Mintage	Identification	Issue Price	Mkt. Val.
E1	1897	—	50 Centimes, KM40	—	200.00
E2	1897	—	1 Franc, KM41	—	275.00
E3	1(897)	—	50 Centimes, KM40	—	250.00
E4	1(897)	—	1 Franc, KM41	—	325.00

PIEFORTS WITH ESSAI (PE)

(Double thickness)

Standard metals unless otherwise noted

KM#	Date	Mintage	Identification	Issue Price	Mkt. Val.
PE1	1897	—	50 Centimes	—	400.00
PE2	1897	—	1 Franc	—	500.00

MAURITIUS

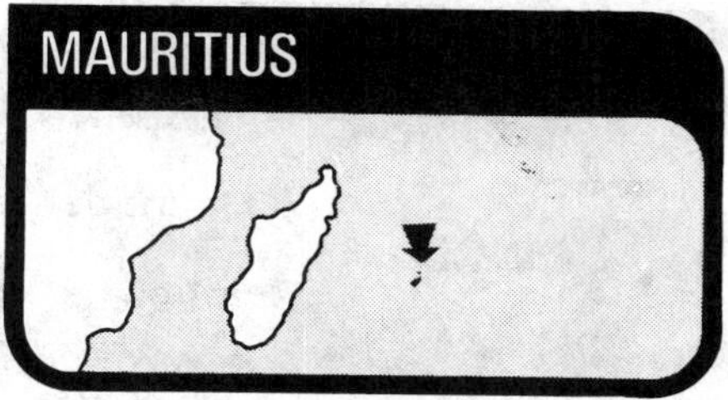

The Republic of Mauritius, a member nation of the British Commonwealth located in the Indian Ocean 500 miles (805 km.) east of Madagascar, has an area of 790 sq. mi. (1,860 sq. km.) and a population of 1 million. Capital: Port Louis. Sugar provides 90 percent of the export revenue.

Cartographic evidence indicates that Arabs and Malays arrived at Mauritius during the Middle Ages. Domingo Fernandez, a Portuguese navigator, visited the island in the early 16th century, but Portugal made no attempt at settlement. The Dutch took possession, and named the island, in 1598. Their colony failed to prosper and was abandoned in 1710. France claimed Mauritius in 1715 and developed a strong and prosperous colony that endured until the island was captured by the British, 1810, during the Napoleonic Wars. British possession was confirmed by the Treaty of Paris, 1814. Mauritius became independent on March 12, 1968. It is a member of the Commonwealth of Nations.

The first coins struck under British auspices for Mauritius were undated (1822) and bore French legends.

RULERS

British, until 1968

MINT MARKS

H - Heaton, Birmingham

SA - Pretoria Mint

MONETARY SYSTEM

20 Sols (Sous) = 1 Livre

100 Cents = 1 Rupee

25 SOUS

.500 SILVER

KM#	Date	Mintage	VG	Fine	VF	XF
1	ND(1822)	.311	15.00	30.00	50.00	150.00
	ND(1822)	—	—	—	Proof	550.00

50 SOUS

.500 SILVER

KM#	Date	Mintage	VG	Fine	VF	XF
2	ND(1822)	.286	20.00	40.00	75.00	200.00
	ND(1822)	—	—	—	Proof	700.00

ANCHOR COINAGE

(1/16, 1/8, 1/4 & 1/2 Dollar)

NOTE: Coins dated 1820 were struck for Mauritius and colonies of the British West Indies. These circulated in Mauritius until 1826 when they were shipped to the British West Indies where they will be found listed.

REGULAR COINAGE

100 Cents = 1 Rupee

CENT

BRONZE

KM#	Date	Mintage	Fine	VF	XF	Unc
7	1877	—	—	—	Proof	175.00
	1877H	.700	2.00	4.00	22.50	65.00
7	1877H	—	—	—	Proof	125.00
	1878	.250	3.00	13.00	50.00	135.00
	1878	—	—	—	Proof	350.00
	1882H	.300	1.50	5.00	30.00	80.00
	1882H	—	—	—	Proof	150.00
	1883	.500	1.25	2.50	18.50	45.00
	1883	—	—	—	Proof	175.00
	1884	.500	1.25	2.50	18.50	45.00
	1884	—	—	—	Proof	175.00
	1888	.500	1.25	2.50	18.50	45.00
	1890H	.500	1.25	2.50	18.50	45.00
	1896	.500	1.25	2.50	18.50	45.00
	1897	1.000	1.00	2.00	12.50	40.00
	1897	—	—	—	Proof	175.00

2 CENTS

BRONZE

KM#	Date	Mintage	Fine	VF	XF	Unc
8	1877	—	—	—	Proof	150.00
	1877H	.350	1.00	6.50	27.50	100.00
	1877H	—	—	—	Proof	300.00
	1878	.130	2.50	12.00	65.00	150.00
	1878	—	—	—	Proof	150.00
	1882H	.150	2.00	8.00	30.00	125.00
	1882H	—	—	—	Proof	275.00
	1883	.250	1.00	6.50	27.50	75.00
	1884	.250	1.00	6.50	27.50	75.00
	1884	—	—	—	Proof	550.00
	1888	.250	.75	4.00	20.00	50.00
	1888	—	—	—	Proof	400.00
	1890H	.250	1.00	5.00	25.00	75.00
	1896	.188	1.00	5.00	25.00	85.00
	1897	1.000	.75	4.00	20.00	50.00
	1897	—	—	—	Proof	375.00

5 CENTS

BRONZE

KM#	Date	Mintage	Fine	VF	XF	Unc
9	1877	—	—	—	Proof	375.00
	1877H	3.00	3.00	10.00	55.00	165.00
	1877H	—	—	—	Proof	900.00
	1878	.050	6.00	20.00	90.00	275.00
	1878	—	—	—	Proof	200.00
	1882H	.060	5.00	15.00	80.00	245.00
	1882H	—	—	—	Proof	375.00
	1883	.100	3.00	12.00	55.00	125.00
	1884	.100	3.00	12.00	55.00	125.00
	1884	—	—	—	Proof	250.00
	1888	.100	1.50	7.50	40.00	80.00
	1890H	.100	2.50	12.00	60.00	180.00
	1897	.600	1.50	7.50	45.00	110.00
	1897	—	—	—	Proof	185.00

10 CENTS

1.1660 g, .800 SILVER, .0300 oz ASW

KM#	Date	Mintage	Fine	VF	XF	Unc
10.1	1877	—	—	—	Proof	400.00
	1877H	.250	1.50	6.50	27.50	100.00
	1877H	—	—	—	Proof	300.00
	1878	.050	5.00	18.00	50.00	220.00
	1878	—	—	—	Proof	275.00
	1882H	.030	15.00	35.00	150.00	250.00
	1883	.100	3.00	10.00	40.00	200.00
	1883	—	—	—	Proof	275.00
	1886	.750	1.25	5.00	22.00	80.00
	1886	—	—	—	Proof	275.00
	1889H	.500	2.00	7.50	25.00	90.00
	1889	—	—	—	Proof	275.00
	1897	.500	2.00	7.50	25.00	80.00
	1897	—	—	—	Proof	400.00

Plain edge.

KM#	Date	Mintage	Fine	VF	XF	Unc
10.2	1877H	—	—	—	Proof	225.00

20 CENTS

2.3320 g, .800 SILVER, .0600 oz ASW

KM#	Date	Mintage	Fine	VF	XF	Unc
11.1	1877	—	—	—	Proof	750.00
	1877H	.375	5.00	20.00	75.00	300.00
	1877H	—	—	—	Proof	400.00
	1878	.050	10.00	30.00	150.00	400.00
	1878	—	—	—	Proof	300.00
	1882H	.015	15.00	50.00	225.00	475.00
	1883	.100	6.00	22.50	100.00	275.00
	1883	—	—	—	Proof	300.00
	1886	.750	4.00	16.00	40.00	150.00
	1886	—	—	—	Proof	300.00
	1889H	.250	5.00	20.00	60.00	200.00
	1899	.500	4.00	16.00	55.00	185.00
	1899	—	—	—	Proof	300.00

Plain edge.

KM#	Date	Mintage	Fine	VF	XF	Unc
11.2	1877H	—	—	—	Proof	750.00

PIEFORTS (P)

KM#	Date	Mintage	Identification	Issue Price	Mkt. Val.
P1	ND(1822)	—	25 Sous, Copper, KM1	—	375.00

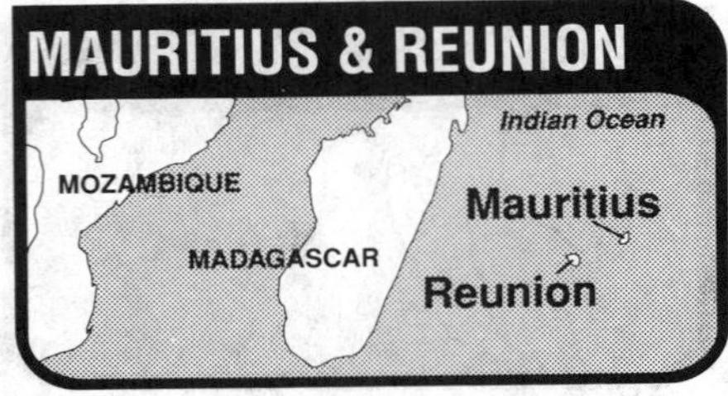

Mauritius and Reunion (Isles de France et de Bourbon), located in the Indian Ocean about 500 miles east of Madagascar, were at one time administered by France as a single colony. They utilized a common currency issue. Ownership of Mauritius passed to Great Britain in 1814. Isle de Bourbon, renamed Reunion in 1793, remained a French possession and is now an Overseas Department.

RULERS

French, until 1810

MONETARY SYSTEM

20 Sols (Sous) = 1 Livre

ISLE DE FRANCE ET BONAPARTE

Reunion had become the official name in 1792 but after the French Revolution and the beginning of the Napoleonic era (1801-1814) the name was changed to Isle de Bonaparte.

DIX (10) LIVRES

SILVER

KM#	Date	Mintage	VG	Fine	VF	XF
1	1810	—	200.00	325.00	500.00	950.00

NOTE: This coin was weakly struck on the obverse and reverse centers. Well struck examples command a premium.

MEXICO

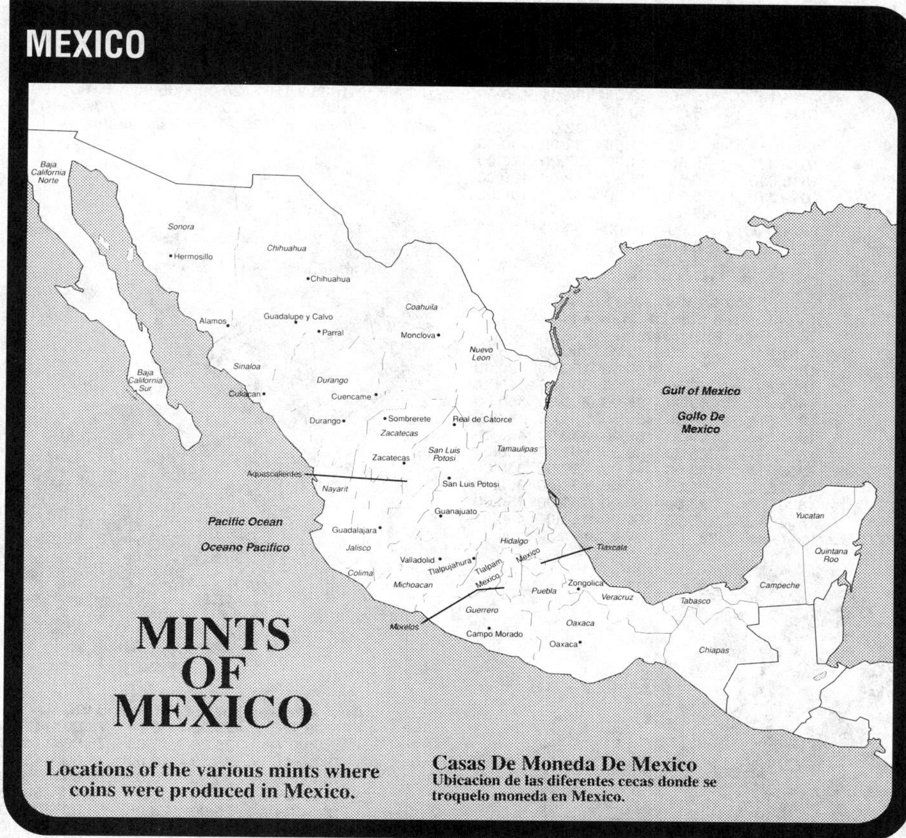

The United States of Mexico, located immediately south of the United States has an area of 759,529 sq. mi. (1,967,183 sq. km.) and an estimated population of 88 million. Capital: Mexico City. The economy is based on agriculture, manufacturing and mining. Oil, cotton, silver, coffee, and shrimp are exported.

Mexico was the site of highly advanced Indian civilizations 1,500 years before conquistador Hernando Cortes conquered the wealthy Aztec empire of Montezuma, 1519-21, and founded a Spanish colony which lasted for nearly 300 years. During the Spanish period, Mexico, then called New Spain, stretched from Guatemala to the present states of Wyoming and California, its present northern boundary having been established by the secession of Texas during 1836 and the war of 1846-48 with the United States.

Independence from Spain was declared by Father Miguel Hidalgo on Sept. 16, 1810, (Mexican Independence Day) and was achieved by General Agustin de Iturbide in 1821. Iturbide became emperor in 1822 but was deposed when a republic was established a year later. For more than half a century following the birth of the republic, the political scene of Mexico was characterized by turmoil which saw two emperors (including the unfortunate Maximilian), several dictators and an average of one new government every nine months passing swiftly from obscurity to oblivion. The land, social, economic and labor reforms promulgated by the Reform Constitution of Feb. 5, 1917 established the basis for sustained economic development and participative democracy that have made Mexico one of the most politically stable countries of modern Latin America.

COLONIAL MILLED COINAGE

RULERS

Charles IV, 1788-1808
Ferdinand VII, 1808-1821

MINT MARKS

Mo - Mexico City Mint

ASSAYERS INITIALS

Letter	Date	Name
F	1777-1803	Francisco Arance Cobos
M	1784-1801	Mariano Rodriguez
T	1801-1810	Tomas Butron Miranda
H	1803-1814	Henrique Buenaventura Azorin
J	1809-1833	Joaquin Davila Madrid
J	1812-1833	Jose Garcia Ansaldo

MONETARY SYSTEM

16 Pilones = 1 Real
8 Tlaco = 1 Real
16 Reales = 1 Escudo

1/8 (PILON)

(1/16 Real)

COPPER
Obv: Crowned F VII monogram.
Rev: Castles and lions in wreath.

KM#	Date	VG	Fine	VF	XF
59	1814	10.00	20.00	40.00	120.00
	1815	10.00	20.00	40.00	120.00

1/4 (TLACO)

(1/8 Real)

COPPER
Obv. leg: FERDIN. VII. . . around crowned F.VII.

KM#	Date	VG	Fine	VF	XF
63	1814	12.00	25.00	50.00	140.00
	1815	12.00	25.00	50.00	140.00
	1816	12.00	25.00	50.00	140.00

2/4 (2 TLACO)

(1/4 Real)

COPPER
Obv. leg: FERDIN. VII. . . around crowned F.VII.

KM#	Date	VG	Fine	VF	XF
64	1814	10.00	20.00	35.00	115.00
	1815/4	12.00	25.00	45.00	135.00
	1815	10.00	20.00	35.00	115.00
	1816	10.00	20.00	35.00	115.00
	1821	20.00	40.00	60.00	185.00

1/4 REAL

.8450 g, .903 SILVER, .0245 oz ASW

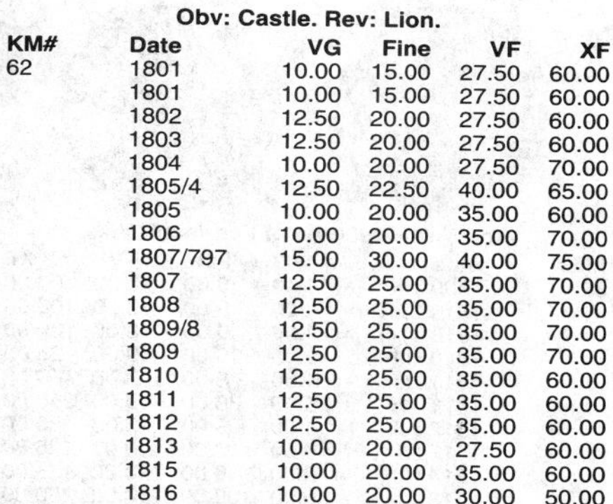

Obv: Castle. Rev: Lion.

KM#	Date	VG	Fine	VF	XF
62	1801	10.00	15.00	27.50	60.00
	1801	10.00	15.00	27.50	60.00
	1802	12.50	20.00	27.50	60.00
	1803	12.50	20.00	27.50	60.00
	1804	10.00	20.00	27.50	70.00
	1805/4	12.50	22.50	40.00	65.00
	1805	10.00	20.00	35.00	60.00
	1806	10.00	20.00	35.00	70.00
	1807/797	15.00	30.00	40.00	75.00
	1807	12.50	25.00	35.00	70.00
	1808	12.50	25.00	35.00	70.00
	1809/8	12.50	25.00	35.00	70.00
	1809	12.50	25.00	35.00	70.00
	1810	12.50	25.00	35.00	60.00
	1811	12.50	25.00	35.00	60.00
	1812	12.50	25.00	35.00	60.00
	1813	10.00	20.00	27.50	60.00
	1815	10.00	20.00	35.00	60.00
	1816	10.00	20.00	30.00	50.00

NOTE: Earlier dates (1796-1800) exist for this type.

1/2 REAL

1.6900 g, .903 SILVER, .0490 oz ASW
Obv: Armored bust of Charles IIII.
Rev: Pillars and arms.

KM#	Date	VG	Fine	VF	XF
72	1801 FM	6.50	14.00	28.00	80.00
	1801 FM	6.50	14.00	28.00	80.00
	1801 FT	4.00	10.00	20.00	45.00
	1802 FT	4.00	10.00	20.00	45.00
	1803 FT	5.00	11.50	22.00	50.00
	1804 TH	4.00	10.00	20.00	45.00
	1805 TH	4.00	10.00	20.00	45.00
	1806 TH	4.00	10.00	20.00	45.00
	1807/6 TH	5.00	11.50	22.00	50.00
	1807 TH	4.00	10.00	20.00	45.00
	1808/7 TH	5.00	11.50	22.00	50.00
	1808 TH	4.00	10.00	20.00	45.00

NOTE: Earlier dates (1792-1800) exist for this type.

Obv: Armored bust of Ferdinand VII.

KM#	Date	VG	Fine	VF	XF
73	1808 TH	3.00	7.00	15.00	30.00
	1809 TH	3.00	7.00	15.00	30.00
	1810 TH	5.00	10.00	20.00	40.00
	1810 HJ	3.00	7.00	15.00	30.00
	1811 HJ	3.00	7.00	15.00	30.00
	1812 HJ	3.00	7.00	15.00	30.00
	1812 JJ	10.00	20.00	40.00	100.00
	1813 TH	3.50	7.50	15.00	30.00
	1813 JJ	10.00	20.00	40.00	100.00
	1813 HJ	7.50	15.00	30.00	90.00
	1814 JJ	5.00	10.00	20.00	40.00

Obv: Draped bust of Ferdinand VII.

KM#	Date	VG	Fine	VF	XF
74	1814 JJ	3.00	7.00	16.50	45.00
	1815 JJ	3.00	7.00	15.00	40.00
	1816 JJ	3.00	7.00	15.00	40.00
	1817/6 JJ	—	—	—	—
	1817 JJ	3.00	7.00	16.50	45.00
	1818/7 JJ	3.00	7.00	17.50	50.00
	1818 JJ	3.00	7.00	17.50	50.00
	1819 JJ	3.00	7.00	15.00	40.00
	1820 JJ	3.00	7.00	17.50	50.00
	1821 JJ	3.00	7.00	15.00	40.00

REAL

3.3800 g, .903 SILVER, .0981 oz ASW
Obv: Armored bust of Charles IIII.

KM#	Date	VG	Fine	VF	XF
81	1801 FM	8.00	15.00	25.00	80.00
	1801 FT	3.00	8.50	16.50	60.00
	1802 FM	3.00	8.50	16.50	60.00
	1802 FT	3.00	7.50	15.00	60.00
	1803 FT	3.00	8.50	16.50	60.00
	1804 TH	3.00	7.50	15.00	60.00
	1805 TH	3.00	8.50	16.50	60.00
	1806 TH	3.00	7.50	15.00	60.00
	1807/6 TH	3.50	8.50	16.50	65.00
	1807 TH	3.00	7.50	15.00	60.00
	1808/7 TH	3.50	8.50	16.50	65.00
	1808 TH	3.00	7.50	15.00	60.00

NOTE: Earlier dates (1792-1800) exist for this type.

Obv: Armored bust of Ferdinand VII.

KM#	Date	VG	Fine	VF	XF
82	1809 TH	4.00	9.00	18.00	100.00
	1810/09 TH	4.00	9.00	18.00	100.00
	1810 TH	4.00	9.00	18.00	100.00
	1810 HJ	6.00	10.00	20.00	125.00
	1811 HJ	4.00	9.00	12.00	100.00
	1811 TH	25.00	35.00	60.00	250.00
	1812 HJ	4.00	9.00	12.00	80.00
	1812 JJ	6.00	10.00	20.00	125.00
	1813 HJ	6.00	10.00	20.00	125.00
	1813 JJ	50.00	100.00	150.00	250.00
	1814 HJ	50.00	100.00	175.00	300.00
	1814 JJ	50.00	100.00	175.00	300.00

Obv: Draped bust of Ferdinand VII.

KM#	Date	VG	Fine	VF	XF
83	1814 JJ	25.00	50.00	100.00	350.00
	1815 JJ	5.50	8.50	17.50	125.00
	1815 HJ	15.00	30.00	60.00	150.00
	1816 JJ	4.00	7.50	15.00	75.00
	1817 JJ	4.00	7.50	15.00	75.00
	1818 JJ	30.00	60.00	125.00	500.00
	1819 JJ	5.50	8.50	17.50	75.00
	1820 JJ	5.00	8.50	17.50	75.00
	1821/0 JJ	7.50	12.50	27.50	110.00
	1821 JJ	5.00	8.50	15.00	50.00

2 REALES

6.7700 g, .903 SILVER, .1965 oz ASW
Obv: Armored bust of Carolus IIII.

KM#	Date	VG	Fine	VF	XF
91	1801 FT	5.00	10.00	20.00	100.00
	1801 FM	20.00	40.00	75.00	250.00
	1802 FT	5.00	10.00	20.00	100.00
	1803 FT	5.00	10.00	20.00	100.00
	1804 TH	5.00	10.00	20.00	100.00
	1805 TH	5.00	10.00	20.00	100.00
	1806/5 TH	5.50	11.50	22.50	110.00
	1806 TH	5.00	10.00	20.00	100.00
	1807/5 TH	5.50	11.50	22.50	110.00
	1807/6 TH	15.00	30.00	60.00	200.00
	1807 TH	5.00	10.00	20.00	100.00
	1808/7 TH	5.50	11.50	22.50	110.00
	1808 TH	5.00	10.00	20.00	100.00

NOTE: Earlier dates (1792-1800) exist for this type.

Obv: Armored bust of Ferdinand VII.

KM#	Date	VG	Fine	VF	XF
92	1809 TH	6.50	12.50	45.00	150.00
	1810 TH	6.50	12.50	45.00	150.00
	1810 HJ	6.50	12.50	45.00	150.00
	1811 HJ	6.50	12.50	45.00	150.00
	1811 HJ/TH	40.00	80.00	150.00	300.00
	1811 TH	100.00	200.00	300.00	750.00

Obv: Draped bust of Ferdinand VII.

KM#	Date	VG	Fine	VF	XF
93	1812 HJ	15.00	30.00	100.00	300.00
	1812 TH	60.00	125.00	250.00	500.00
93	1812 JJ	10.00	20.00	60.00	200.00
	1813 HJ	40.00	100.00	200.00	500.00
	1813 JJ	20.00	60.00	125.00	350.00
	1813 TH	15.00	30.00	100.00	400.00
	1814/13 JJ	15.00	30.00	100.00	400.00
	1814 JJ	15.00	30.00	100.00	400.00
	1815 JJ	5.50	11.50	32.00	100.00
	1816 JJ	5.50	11.50	32.00	100.00
	1817 JJ	5.50	11.50	32.00	100.00
	1818 JJ	5.50	11.50	32.00	100.00
	1819 JJ	5.50	11.50	32.00	100.00
	1820 JJ	125.00	—	—	—
	1821/0 JJ	5.00	10.00	30.00	110.00
	1821 JJ	5.50	11.50	32.00	100.00

4 REALES

13.5400 g, .903 SILVER, .3931 oz ASW
Obv: Armored bust of Charles IIII.
Rev: Pillars, arms.

KM#	Date	VG	Fine	VF	XF
100	1801 FM	25.00	40.00	80.00	350.00
	1801 FT	60.00	100.00	150.00	500.00
	1802 FT	200.00	300.00	500.00	1000.
	1803 FT	60.00	125.00	200.00	550.00
	1803 FM	350.00	450.00	650.00	1250.
	1804 TH	25.00	50.00	150.00	450.00
	1805 TH	25.00	40.00	80.00	350.00
	1806 TH	25.00	40.00	80.00	350.00
	1807 TH	25.00	40.00	80.00	350.00
	1808/7 TH	25.00	50.00	150.00	450.00
	1808 TH	25.00	50.00	150.00	450.00

NOTE: Earlier dates (1792-1800) exist for this type.

Obv: Armored bust of Ferdinand VII.

KM#	Date	VG	Fine	VF	XF
101	1809 HJ	75.00	125.00	175.00	450.00
	1810 TH	75.00	125.00	175.00	450.00
	1810 HJ	75.00	125.00	175.00	450.00
	1811 HJ	75.00	125.00	175.00	450.00
	1812 HJ	500.00	750.00	1000.	2000.

Obv: Draped bust of Ferdinand VII.

KM#	Date	VG	Fine	VF	XF
102	1816 JJ	150.00	200.00	350.00	600.00
	1817 JJ	250.00	400.00	500.00	1000.
	1818/7 JJ	250.00	400.00	500.00	1000.
	1818 JJ	250.00	400.00	500.00	1000.
	1819 JJ	175.00	250.00	350.00	700.00
	1820 JJ	175.00	250.00	350.00	700.00
	1821 JJ	75.00	125.00	200.00	425.00

8 REALES

27.0700 g, .903 SILVER, .7859 oz ASW
Obv: Armored bust of Charles IIII.

KM#	Date	VG	Fine	VF	XF
109	1801/791 FM	35.00	60.00	100.00	250.00
	1801/0 FM	35.00	60.00	100.00	250.00
	1801/0 FT/FM	20.00	35.00	50.00	100.00
	1801 FM	20.00	40.00	100.00	250.00
	1801 FT/M	35.00	60.00	100.00	250.00
	1801 FT	20.00	35.00	50.00	100.00
	1802/1 FT	35.00	60.00	100.00	250.00
	1802 FT	20.00	35.00	50.00	100.00
	1802 FT/FM	20.00	35.00	50.00	100.00
	1803 FT	20.00	35.00	50.00	110.00
	1803 FM	600.00	900.00	—	—
	1803 FT/FM	20.00	35.00	50.00	100.00
	1803 TH	75.00	150.00	250.00	500.00
	1804/3 TH	35.00	60.00	100.00	250.00
	1804 TH	20.00	35.00	50.00	100.00
	1805/4 TH	40.00	80.00	125.00	275.00
	1805 TH	20.00	35.00	50.00	100.00
	1806 TH	20.00	35.00	50.00	100.00
109	1807/6 TH	150.00	250.00	350.00	700.00
	1807 TH	20.00	35.00	50.00	100.00
	1870 TH(error 1807)	150.00	250.00	350.00	700.00
	1808/7 TH	20.00	35.00	50.00	100.00
	1808 TH	20.00	35.00	50.00	100.00

NOTE: Earlier dates (1791-1800) exist for this type.

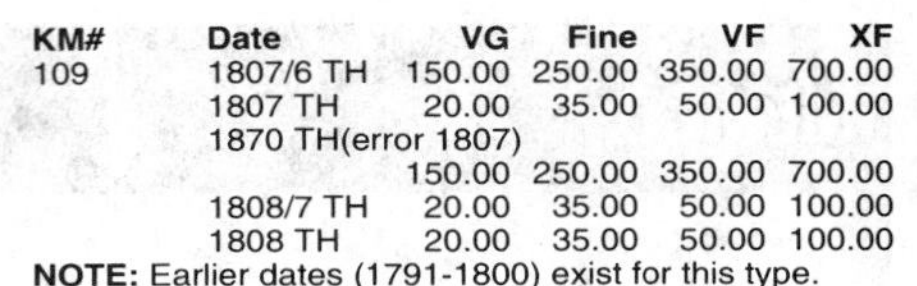

Obv: Armored bust of Ferdinand VII.

KM#	Date	VG	Fine	VF	XF
110	1808 TH	25.00	40.00	75.00	145.00
	1809/8 TH	25.00	40.00	75.00	145.00
	1809 HJ	25.00	40.00	75.00	145.00
	1809 HJ/TH	20.00	35.00	55.00	120.00
	1809 TH/JH	20.00	35.00	55.00	120.00
	1809 TH	20.00	35.00	55.00	120.00
	1810/09 HJ	25.00	40.00	75.00	145.00
	1810 HJ	25.00	40.00	75.00	145.00
	1810 HJ/TH	25.00	40.00	75.00	145.00
	1810 TH	75.00	150.00	300.00	600.00
	1811/0 HJ	20.00	35.00	55.00	120.00
	1811 HJ	20.00	35.00	55.00	120.00
	1811 HJ/TH	20.00	35.00	50.00	100.00

Obv: Draped bust of Ferdinand VII.

KM#	Date	VG	Fine	VF	XF
111	1811 HJ	20.00	40.00	60.00	125.00
	1812 HJ	50.00	75.00	125.00	250.00
	1812 JJ/HJ	20.00	35.00	50.00	90.00
	1812 JJ	20.00	35.00	50.00	90.00
	1813 HJ	50.00	75.00	125.00	250.00
	1813 JJ	20.00	35.00	50.00	90.00
	1814/3 HJ	1200.	2500.	5000.	—
	1814/3 JJ/HJ	20.00	35.00	50.00	90.00
	1814/3 JJ	20.00	35.00	50.00	90.00
	1814 JJ	20.00	35.00	50.00	90.00
	1814 HJ	500.00	800.00	1500.	3000.
	1815/4 JJ	20.00	35.00	50.00	90.00
	1815 JJ	20.00	35.00	50.00	90.00
	1816/5 JJ	20.00	35.00	50.00	85.00
	1816 JJ	20.00	35.00	50.00	85.00
	1817 JJ	20.00	35.00	50.00	85.00
	1818 JJ	20.00	35.00	50.00	85.00
	1819 JJ	20.00	35.00	50.00	85.00
	1820 JJ	20.00	35.00	50.00	85.00
	1821 JJ	20.00	35.00	50.00	85.00

1/2 ESCUDO

1.6900 g, .875 GOLD, .0475 oz AGW
Obv. leg: FERD.VII.D.G.HISP.ET IND.

KM#	Date	VG	Fine	VF	XF
112	1814 JJ	200.00	300.00	400.00	550.00
	1815/4 JJ	150.00	200.00	250.00	350.00
	1815 JJ	150.00	200.00	250.00	350.00
	1816 JJ	100.00	150.00	200.00	300.00
	1817 JJ	150.00	200.00	250.00	350.00
	1818 JJ	150.00	200.00	250.00	350.00
	1819 JJ	150.00	200.00	250.00	350.00
	1820 JJ	200.00	300.00	400.00	550.00

ESCUDO

3.3800 g, .875 GOLD, .0950 oz AGW
Obv: Armored bust of Charles IV.

KM#	Date	VG	Fine	VF	XF
120	1801 FT	125.00	165.00	235.00	375.00
	1801 FM	125.00	165.00	235.00	375.00
	1802 FT	125.00	165.00	235.00	375.00
	1803 FT	125.00	165.00	235.00	375.00
	1804/3 TH	125.00	165.00	235.00	375.00
	1804 TH	125.00	165.00	235.00	375.00
	1805 TH	125.00	165.00	235.00	375.00
	1806 TH	125.00	165.00	235.00	375.00
	1807 TH	125.00	165.00	235.00	375.00
	1808 TH	125.00	165.00	235.00	375.00

NOTE: Earlier dates (1792-1800) exist for this type.

Obv: Armored bust of Ferdinand VII.

KM#	Date	VG	Fine	VF	XF
121	1809 HJ	125.00	165.00	235.00	400.00
	1810 HJ	125.00	165.00	235.00	400.00
	1811 HJ	125.00	165.00	235.00	400.00
	1812 HJ	150.00	250.00	300.00	500.00

Obv: Undraped bust of Ferdinand VII.

KM#	Date	VG	Fine	VF	XF
122	1814 HJ	100.00	145.00	225.00	400.00
	1815 JJ	100.00	145.00	225.00	400.00
	1815 HJ	100.00	145.00	225.00	400.00
	1816 JJ	125.00	165.00	275.00	500.00
	1817 JJ	100.00	145.00	225.00	400.00
	1818 JJ	100.00	145.00	225.00	400.00
	1819 JJ	100.00	145.00	225.00	400.00
	1820 JJ	100.00	145.00	225.00	400.00

2 ESCUDOS

6.7700 g, .875 GOLD, .1904 oz AGW
Obv: Armored bust of Charles IV.

KM#	Date	VG	Fine	VF	XF
132	1801 FM	125.00	250.00	375.00	600.00
	1802 FT	125.00	250.00	375.00	600.00
	1803 FT	125.00	250.00	375.00	600.00
	1804 TH	125.00	250.00	375.00	600.00
	1805 TH	125.00	250.00	375.00	600.00
	1806 TH	125.00	250.00	375.00	600.00
	1807 TH	125.00	250.00	375.00	600.00
	1808 TH	125.00	250.00	375.00	600.00

NOTE: Earlier dates (1791-1800) exist for this type.

Obv: Undraped bust of Ferdinand VII.

KM#	Date	VG	Fine	VF	XF
134	1814 HJ	250.00	400.00	650.00	1200.
	1814 JJ	250.00	400.00	650.00	1200.
	1815 JJ	250.00	400.00	650.00	1200.
	1816 JJ	250.00	400.00	650.00	1200.
	1817 JJ	250.00	400.00	650.00	1200.
	1818 JJ	250.00	400.00	650.00	1200.
	1819 JJ	250.00	400.00	650.00	1200.
	1820 JJ	250.00	400.00	650.00	1200.

4 ESCUDOS

13.5400 g, .875 GOLD, .3809 oz AGW
Obv: Armored bust of Charles IIII.

KM#	Date	VG	Fine	VF	XF
144	1801 FM	300.00	500.00	750.00	1400.
	1801 FT	300.00	500.00	750.00	1400.
	1802 FT	300.00	500.00	750.00	1400.
	1803 FT	300.00	500.00	750.00	1400.
	1804/3 TH	300.00	500.00	750.00	1400.
	1804 TH	300.00	500.00	750.00	1400.
	1805 TH	300.00	500.00	750.00	1400.
	1806/5 TH	300.00	500.00	750.00	1400.
	1806 TH	300.00	500.00	750.00	1400.
	1807 TH	300.00	500.00	750.00	1400.
	1808/0 TH	300.00	500.00	750.00	1400.
	1808 TH	300.00	500.00	750.00	1400.

NOTE: Earlier dates (1792-1800) exist for this type.

Obv: Armored bust of Ferdinand VII.

KM#	Date	VG	Fine	VF	XF
145	1810 HJ	450.00	600.00	950.00	1600.
	1811 HJ	350.00	500.00	850.00	1400.
	1812 HJ	350.00	500.00	850.00	1400.

Obv: Undraped bust of Ferdinand VII.

KM#	Date	VG	Fine	VF	XF
146	1814 HJ	400.00	650.00	900.00	1600.
	1815 HJ	400.00	650.00	900.00	1600.
	1815 JJ	400.00	650.00	900.00	1600.
	1816 JJ	400.00	650.00	900.00	1600.
	1817 JJ	400.00	650.00	900.00	1600.
	1818 JJ	400.00	650.00	900.00	1600.
	1819 JJ	400.00	650.00	900.00	1600.
	1820 JJ	400.00	650.00	900.00	1600.

8 ESCUDOS

27.0700 g, .875 GOLD, .7616 oz AGW
Obv: Armored bust of Charles IIII.
Rev. leg: IN UTROQ. FELIX., arms, Order chain.

KM#	Date	VG	Fine	VF	XF
159	1801/0 FT	400.00	500.00	700.00	1150.
	1801 FM	375.00	475.00	650.00	900.00
	1801 FT	375.00	475.00	650.00	900.00
	1802 FT	375.00	475.00	650.00	900.00
	1803 FT	375.00	475.00	650.00	900.00
	1804/3 TH	400.00	500.00	700.00	1150.
	1804 TH	375.00	475.00	650.00	900.00
	1805 TH	375.00	475.00	650.00	900.00
	1806 TH	375.00	475.00	650.00	900.00
	1807/6 TH	400.00	500.00	700.00	1150.
	1807 TH	375.00	475.00	675.00	1000.
	1808 TH	450.00	600.00	800.00	1250.

NOTE: Earlier dates (1791-1800) exist for this type.

Obv: Armored bust of Ferdinand VII.

KM#	Date	VG	Fine	VF	XF
160	1808 TH	400.00	500.00	750.00	1000.
	1809 HJ	400.00	500.00	750.00	1150.
	1810 HJ	375.00	475.00	650.00	900.00
	1811/0 HJ	400.00	500.00	750.00	1150.
	1811 HJ	400.00	500.00	750.00	1150.
	1811 JJ	375.00	475.00	650.00	900.00
	1812 JJ	375.00	475.00	650.00	900.00

Obv: Undraped bust of Ferdinand VII.

KM#	Date	VG	Fine	VF	XF
161	1814 JJ	375.00	475.00	650.00	900.00
	1815/4 JJ	400.00	500.00	700.00	1000.
	1815/4 HJ	400.00	500.00	700.00	1000.
	1815 JJ	375.00	475.00	650.00	900.00
	1815 HJ	375.00	475.00	650.00	900.00
	1816/5 JJ	400.00	500.00	700.00	1000.
	1816 JJ	375.00	475.00	650.00	900.00
	1817 JJ	400.00	500.00	700.00	1000.
	1818/7 JJ	375.00	475.00	650.00	900.00
	1818 JJ	375.00	475.00	650.00	900.00
	1819 JJ	375.00	475.00	650.00	900.00
	1820 JJ	375.00	475.00	650.00	900.00
	1821 JJ	400.00	500.00	700.00	1000.

PROCLAMATION MEDALLIC ISSUES (Q)

The 'Q' used in the following listings refer to *Standard Catalog of Mexican Coins, Paper Money, Stocks, Bonds and Medals,* Krause Publications, Inc., copyright 1981.

Chiapa

REAL

SILVER
Obv. leg: FERNANDO VII REY DE ESPANA Y DE SUS INDIAS, crowned arms between pillars, IR below. INDIAS. Rev: Legend in 5 lines within wreath, PROCLA/MADO/ENCIUD/R.DECHIAPPA/1808.

KM#	Date	Fine	VF	XF	Unc
Q8	1808	22.50	35.00	50.00	—

2 REALES

SILVER
Obv. leg: FERNANDO VII REY DE ESPANA Y DE SUS INDIAS.

KM#	Date	Fine	VF	XF	Unc
Q10	1808	50.00	70.00	100.00	—

Queretaro

2 REALES

SILVER
Obv. leg: FERNANDO VII REY DE ESPANA.

KM#	Date	Fine	VF	XF	Unc
Q64	1808	35.00	50.00	75.00	—

4 REALES

SILVER

KM#	Date	Fine	VF	XF	Unc
Q-A66	1808	140.00	200.00	300.00	—

8 REALES

SILVER

KM#	Date	Fine	VF	XF	Unc
Q68	1808	300.00	425.00	600.00	—

WAR OF INDEPENDENCE

ROYALIST ISSUES

(1810-1821)

Provisional Mints

RULER

Ferdinand VII, 1808-1821

MINT MARKS

CA - Chihuahua
D - Durango
GA - Guadalajara
GO - Guanajuato
ZS - Zacatecas

MONETARY SYSTEM

16 Reales = 1 Escudo

CHIHUAHUA

The Chihuahua Mint was established by a decree of October 8, 1810 as a temporary mint. Their first coins were cast 8 reales using Mexico City coins as patterns and obliterating/changing the mint mark and moneyer initials. Two c/m were placed on the obverse - on the left, a T designating receipt by the Royal Treasurer, crowned pillars of Hercules on the right with pomegranate beneath, the comptroller's symbol.

In 1814 standard dies were made available, thus machine struck 8 reales were produced until 1822. Only the one denomination was made at Chihuahua.

MINT MARK: CA

8 REALES

CAST SILVER
Obv: Imaginary bust of Ferdinand VII; leg: FERDIN.VII.DEI.GRATIA. c/m: 'T' at left and pomegranate pillars at right.

KM#	Date	Good	VG	Fine	VF
123	1810 RP	—	—	Rare	—
	1811 RP	45.00	60.00	100.00	150.00
	1812 RP	30.00	40.00	60.00	90.00
	1813/2 RP	32.50	45.00	70.00	100.00
	1813 RP	30.00	40.00	60.00	90.00

27.0700 g, .903 SILVER, .7860 oz ASW
Obv: Draped bust of Ferdinand VII.
Rev: Similar to KM#123.

KM#	Date	VG	Fine	VF	XF
111.1	1813 RP	— Reported, not confirmed			
	1814 RP	— Reported, not confirmed			
	1815 RP	200.00	275.00	350.00	500.00
	1816 RP	80.00	125.00	150.00	275.00
	1817 RP	100.00	150.00	185.00	275.00
	1818 RP	100.00	150.00	185.00	275.00
	1819 RP	125.00	175.00	250.00	350.00
	1820 RP	200.00	275.00	350.00	500.00
	1821 RP	200.00	275.00	350.00	500.00
	1822 RP	400.00	600.00	800.00	1100.

NOTE: KM#111.1 is normally found counterstamped over earlier cast 8 Reales, KM#123.

DURANGO

The Durango mint was authorized as a temporary mint on the same day as the Chihuahua Mint, October 8, 1810. The mint opened in 1811 and made coins of 6 denominations between 1811 and 1822.

MINT MARK: D

1/8 REAL

COPPER
Obv: Crown above double F7 monogram.
Rev: EN DURANGO, value, date.

KM#	Date	VG	Fine	VF	XF
60	1812	32.50	75.00	125.00	250.00
	1813	—	—	Rare	—
	1814	—	—	Rare	—

Rev: Spray added above date.

KM#	Date	VG	Fine	VF	XF
61	1814	13.50	22.50	45.00	80.00
	1815	15.00	27.50	50.00	85.00
	1816	15.00	27.50	50.00	85.00
	1817	13.50	22.50	45.00	80.00
	1818	13.50	22.50	45.00	80.00
	1818 OCTAVO DD REAL (error)	40.00	75.00	—	—

1/2 REAL

1.6900 g, .903 SILVER, .0491 oz ASW
Obv: Draped bust of Ferdinand VII.

KM#	Date	VG	Fine	VF	XF
74.1	1813 RM	250.00	450.00	750.00	1800.
	1814 MZ	250.00	450.00	750.00	1850.
	1816 MZ	250.00	450.00	750.00	1850.

REAL

3.3800 g, .903 SILVER, .0981 oz ASW
Obv: Draped bust of Ferdinand VII.

KM#	Date	VG	Fine	VF	XF
83.1	1813 RM	250.00	450.00	650.00	1650.
	1814 MZ	250.00	450.00	650.00	1650.
	1815 MZ	250.00	450.00	650.00	1650.

2 REALES

6.7700 g, .903 SILVER, .1966 oz ASW
Obv: Armored bust of Ferdinand VII.

KM#	Date	VG	Fine	VF	XF
92.2	1811 RM	250.00	400.00	650.00	1650.
	1812 RM	—	—	Rare	—

Obv: Draped bust of Ferdinand VII.

KM#	Date	VG	Fine	VF	XF
93.1	1812 MZ	250.00	400.00	650.00	1650.
	1812 RM	—	—	Rare	—
	1813 MZ	300.00	600.00	1000.	2750.
	1813 RM	300.00	600.00	1000.	2750.
	1814 MZ	300.00	600.00	1000.	2750.
	1815 MZ	300.00	600.00	1000.	2750.
	1816 MZ	300.00	600.00	1000.	2750.
	1817 MZ	300.00	600.00	1000.	2750.

4 REALES

13.5400 g, .903 SILVER, .3931 oz ASW
Obv: Draped bust of Ferdinand VII.

KM#	Date	VG	Fine	VF	XF
102.1	1814 MZ	550.00	1000.	1650.	4500.
	1816 MZ	450.00	900.00	1400.	4000.
	1817 MZ	450.00	900.00	1400.	4000.

8 REALES

27.0700 g, .903 SILVER, .7860 oz ASW
Obv: Armored bust of Ferdinand VII.

KM#	Date	VG	Fine	VF	XF
110.1	1811 RM	600.00	1000.	1750.	5000.
	1812 RM	350.00	650.00	1000.	3500.
	1813 MZ	350.00	650.00	1000.	3500.
	1814 MZ	350.00	650.00	1000.	3500.

Obv: Draped bust of Ferdinand VII.

KM#	Date	VG	Fine	VF	XF
111.2	1812 MZ	350.00	500.00	800.00	1750.
	1812 RM	125.00	175.00	275.00	800.00
	1813 RM	150.00	200.00	325.00	850.00
	1813 MZ	125.00	175.00	275.00	750.00
	1814 MZ	150.00	225.00	275.00	750.00
	1815 MZ	75.00	125.00	225.00	600.00
	1816 MZ	50.00	75.00	125.00	325.00
	1817 MZ	30.00	50.00	90.00	250.00
	1818 MZ	50.00	75.00	125.00	350.00
	1818 RM	50.00	75.00	125.00	325.00
	1818 CG/RM	100.00	125.00	150.00	350.00
	1818 CG	50.00	75.00	125.00	325.00
	1819 CG/RM	50.00	100.00	150.00	300.00
	1819 CG	30.00	60.00	100.00	250.00
	1820 CG	30.00	60.00	100.00	250.00
	1821 CG	30.00	40.00	80.00	225.00
	1822 CG	30.00	50.00	90.00	240.00

NOTE: Occasionally these are found struck over Guadalajara 8 reales and are very rare in general, specimens dated prior to 1816 are rather weakly struck.

GUADALAJARA

The Guadalajara Mint made its first coins in 1812 and the mint operated until April 30, 1815. It was to reopen in 1818 and continue operations until 1822. It was the only Royalist mint to strike gold coins, both 4 and 8 escudos. In addition to these it struck the standard 5 denominations in silver.

MINT MARK: GA

1/2 REAL

1.6900 g, .903 SILVER, .0491 oz ASW
Obv: Draped bust of Ferdinand VII.

KM#	Date	VG	Fine	VF	XF
74.2	1812 MR	—	—	Rare	—
	1814 MR	40.00	100.00	200.00	300.00
	1815 MR	200.00	350.00	500.00	1000.

REAL

3.3800 g, .903 SILVER, .0981 oz ASW
Obv: Draped bust of Ferdinand VII.

KM#	Date	VG	Fine	VF	XF
83.2	1814 MR	125.00	175.00	325.00	600.00
	1815 MR	300.00	500.00	—	—

2 REALES

6.7700 g, .903 SILVER, .1966 oz ASW
Obv: Draped bust of Ferdinand VII.

KM#	Date	VG	Fine	VF	XF
93.2	1812 MR	300.00	500.00	800.00	2500.
	1814 MR	75.00	125.00	250.00	600.00
	1815/4 MR	425.00	725.00	1100.	3600.
	1815 MR	400.00	700.00	1000.	3500.
	1821 FS	200.00	250.00	350.00	900.00

4 REALES

13.5400 g, .903 SILVER, .3931 oz ASW
Obv: Draped bust of Ferdinand VII.

KM#	Date	VG	Fine	VF	XF
102.2	1814 MR	40.00	65.00	150.00	250.00
	1815 MR	80.00	150.00	300.00	500.00

Obv: Large bust.

KM#	Date	VG	Fine	VF	XF
102.3	1814 MR	50.00	100.00	200.00	400.00

Obv: Large bust w/berries in laurel.

KM#	Date	VG	Fine	VF	XF
102.4	1814 MR	—	—	Rare	—

8 REALES

27.0700 g, .903 SILVER, .7860 oz ASW
Obv: Draped bust of Ferdinand VII.

KM#	Date	VG	Fine	VF	XF
111.3	1812 MR	2000.	3500.	5000.	7000.
	1813/2 MR	60.00	100.00	150.00	400.00
	1813 MR	60.00	100.00	150.00	400.00
	1814 MR	20.00	35.00	60.00	180.00
	1815 MR	150.00	200.00	350.00	750.00
	1818 FS	30.00	50.00	75.00	200.00
	1821/18 FS	30.00	50.00	75.00	200.00
	1821 FS	25.00	35.00	60.00	165.00
	1822/1 FS	30.00	50.00	75.00	200.00
	1822 FS	30.00	50.00	75.00	200.00

NOTE: Die varieties exist. Early dates are also encountered struck over other types.

4 ESCUDOS

13.5400 g, .875 GOLD, .3809 oz ASW
Obv: Uniformed bust of Ferdinand VII.

KM#	Date	VG	Fine	VF	XF
147	1812 MR	—	—	Rare	—

8 ESCUDOS

27.0700 g, .875 GOLD, .7616 oz AGW
Obv: Large uniformed bust of Ferdinand VII.

KM#	Date	VG	Fine	VF	XF
162	1812 MR	— Reported, not confirmed			
	1813 MR	5000.	8000.	12,000.	20,000.

Obv: Small uniformed bust of Ferdinand VII.

KM#	Date	VG	Fine	VF	XF
163	1813 MR	10,000.	16,000.	30,000.	50,000.

NOTE: Spink America Gerber sale 6-96 VF or better realized $46,200.

Obv: Undraped bust of Ferdinand VII.

161.1	1821 FS	1500.	2500.	4500.	7500.

Obv: Draped bust of Ferdinand VII.

164	1821 FS	6500.	9000.	13,500.	22,500.

GUANAJUATO

The Guanajuato Mint was authorized December 24, 1812 and started production shortly thereafter; closing for unknown reasons on May 15, 1813. The mint was reopened in April, 1821 by the insurgents, who struck coins of the old royal Spanish design to pay their army, even after independence, well into 1822. Only the 2 and 8 reales coins were made.

MINT MARK: Go

2 REALES

6.7700 g, .903 SILVER, .1966 oz ASW
Obv: Draped bust of Ferdinand VII.

93.3	1821 JM	35.00	65.00	100.00	185.00
	1822 JM	30.00	50.00	75.00	145.00

8 REALES

27.0700 g, .903 SILVER, .7860 oz ASW
Obv: Draped bust of Ferdinand VII.

KM#	Date	VG	Fine	VF	XF
111.4	1812 JJ	1250.	2500.	—	—
	1813 JJ	125.00	175.00	275.00	600.00
	1821 JM	25.00	50.00	75.00	200.00
	1822/0 JM	40.00	100.00	150.00	300.00
	1822 JM	20.00	35.00	60.00	185.00

NUEVA VISCAYA

(Later became Durango State)

This 8 reales, intended for the province of Nueva Viscaya, was minted in the newly-opened Durango Mint during February and March of 1811, before the regular coinage of Durango was started.

8 REALES

.903 SILVER
Obv. leg: MON.PROV. DE NUEV.VIZCAYA, arms of Durango. Rev: Royal arms.

KM#	Date	Good	VG	Fine	VF
181	1811 RM	1000.	2250.	2850.	5500.

NOTE: Several varieties exist.

OAXACA

The city of Oaxaca was in the midst of a coin shortage when it became apparent the city would be taken by the Insurgents Royalist forces under Lt. Gen. Saravia had coins made. They were cast in a blacksmith shop. 1/2, 1 and 8 reales were made only briefly in 1812 before the Royalists surrendered the city.

1/2 REAL

.903 SILVER
Obv: Cross separating castle, lion, F,7O.
Rev. leg: OAXACA around shield.

166	1812	1000.	1500.	2500.	3500.

REAL

.903 SILVER

167	1812	300.00	600.00	1000.	2000.

8 REALES

.903 SILVER

KM#	Date	Good	VG	Fine	VF
168	1812 c/m:A	1300.	1900.	3300.	4750.
	1812 c/m:B	1300.	1900.	3300.	4750.
	1812 c/m:C	1300.	1900.	3300.	4750.
	1812 c/m:D	1300.	1900.	3300.	4750.
	1812 c/m:K	1300.	1900.	3300.	4750.
	1812 c/m:L	1300.	1900.	3300.	4750.
	1812 c/m:Mo	1300.	1900.	3300.	4750.
	1812 c/m:N	1300.	1900.	3300.	4750.
	1812 c/m:O	1300.	1900.	3300.	4750.
	1812 c/m:R	1300.	1900.	3300.	4750.
	1812 c/m:V	1300.	1900.	3300.	4750.
	1812 c/m:Z	1300.	1900.	3300.	4750.

NOTE: The above issue usually has a second c/m: O between crowned pillars.

REAL DEL CATORCE

(City in San Luis Potosi)

Real del Catorce is an important mining center in the Province of San Luis Potosi. In 1811 an 8 reales coin was issued under very primitive conditions while the city was still in Royalist hands. Few survive.

8 REALES

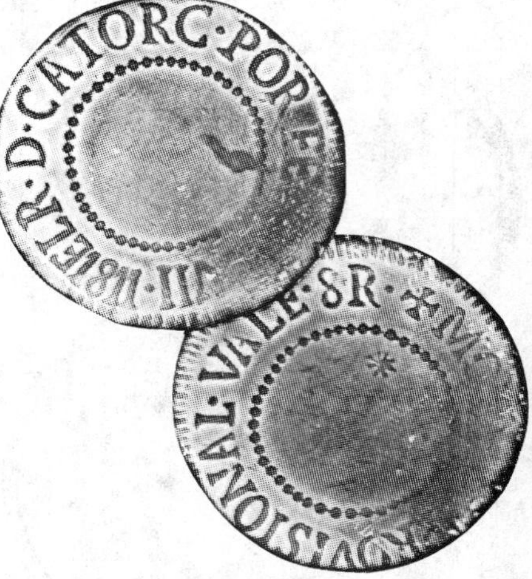

.903 SILVER
Obv. leg: EL R.D. CATORC. POR FERNA. VII.
Rev. leg: MONEDA. PROVISIONAL.VALE.8R.

KM#	Date	VG	Fine	VF	XF
169	1811	4500.	8500.	15,500.	65,000.

NOTE: Spink America Gerber Sale 6-96 VF or XF realized $63,800.

SAN FERNANDO DE BEXAR

Struck by Jose Antonio de la Garza, the 'jolas' are the only known coins issued under Spanish rule in what has become the continental United States of America.

1/8 REAL

COPPER

KM#	Date	Mintage	Good	VG	Fine	VF
170	1818	8,000	500.00	750.00	1250.	1650.

171	1818	Inc. Ab.	500.00	750.00	1250.	1650.

SAN LUIS POTOSI

Sierra De Pinos

Villa

1/4 REAL

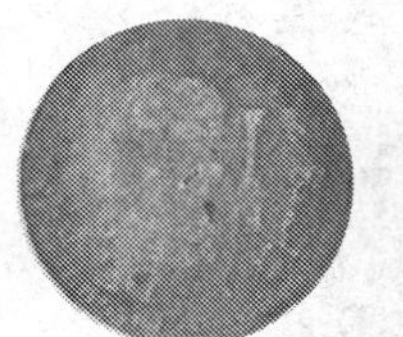

COPPER

KM#	Date	Good	VG	Fine	VF
A172	1814	75.00	125.00	200.00	300.00

SILVER

KM#	Date	Good	VG	Fine	VF
A172a	1814	—	—	Rare	—

SOMBRERETE

(Under Royalist Vargas)

The Sombrerete Mint opened on October 8, 1810 in an area that boasted some of the richest mines in Mexico. The mint operated only until July 16, 1811, only to reopen in 1812 and finally close for good at the end of the year. Mines, Administrator Fernando Vargas, was also in charge of the coining, all coins bear his name.

1/2 REAL

.903 SILVER
Obv. leg: FERDIN.VII.SOMBRERETE. . ., around crowned globes.
Rev. leg: VARGAS above lys in oval, sprays.

KM#	Date	Good	VG	Fine	VF
172	1811	45.00	70.00	150.00	250.00
	1812	50.00	90.00	175.00	275.00

REAL

.903 SILVER
Obv. leg: FERDIN.VII.SOMBRERETE. . ., around crowned globes.
Rev. leg: VARGAS above lys in oval, sprays.

KM#	Date	Good	VG	Fine	VF
173	1811	45.00	70.00	150.00	250.00
	1812	50.00	90.00	175.00	275.00

2 REALES

.903 SILVER
Obv: R.CAXA.DE.SOMBRERETE, royal arms.
Rev. c/m: VARGAS, 1811, S between crowned pillars.

KM#	Date	Good	VG	Fine	VF
174	1811 SE	100.00	250.00	450.00	700.00

4 REALES

.903 SILVER
Obv. leg: R.CAXA.DE.SOMBRERETE, royal arms.
Rev. leg: Small VARGAS/1811.

KM#	Date	Good	VG	Fine	VF
175.1	1811	75.00	150.00	300.00	650.00

Rev: Large VARGAS/1812.

KM#	Date	Good	VG	Fine	VF
175.2	1812	50.00	100.00	200.00	450.00

8 REALES

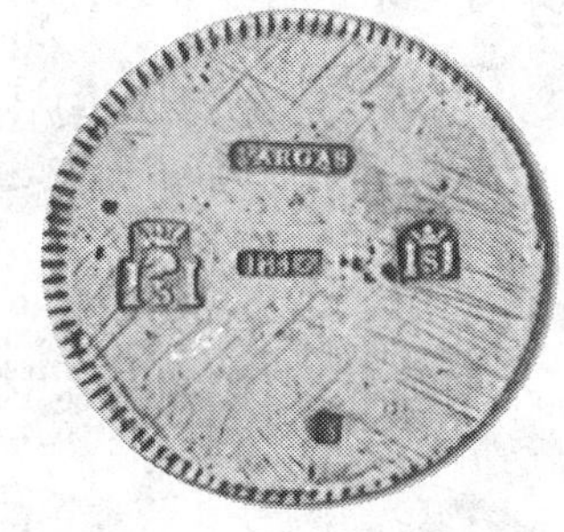

.903 SILVER
Obv. leg: R.CAXA. DE SOMBRERETE.
Rev. c/m: VARGAS, date, S between crowned pillars.

KM#	Date	Good	VG	Fine	VF
176	1810	1000.	1750.	2750.	4000.
	1811	225.00	325.00	450.00	600.00

Obv. leg: R.CAXA. DE SOMBRETE, crowned arms.
Rev. leg: VARGAS/date/3

KM#	Date	Good	VG	Fine	VF
177	1811	125.00	185.00	245.00	500.00
	1812	125.00	175.00	225.00	475.00

VALLADOLID MICHOACAN

(Now Morelia)

Valladolid, capitol of Michoacan province, was a strategically important center for military thrusts into the adjoining provinces. The Royalists made every effort to retain the position. In 1813, with the advance of the insurgent forces, it became apparent that to maintain the position would be very difficult. During 1813 it was necessary to make coins in the city due to lack of traffic with other areas. These were made only briefly before the city fell and were also used by the insurgents with appropriate countermarks.

8 REALES

.903 SILVER
Obv: Royal arms in wreath, value at sides.
Rev: PROVISIONAL/DE VALLADOLID/1813.

KM#	Date	Good	VG	Fine	VF
178	1813	—	—	Rare	—

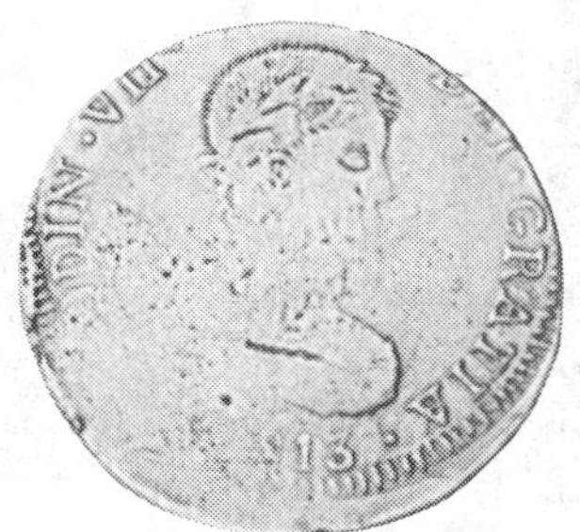

Obv: Bust, leg: FERDIN. VII.
Rev: Arms, pillars, P.D.V. in legend.

KM#	Date	Good	VG	Fine	VF
179	1813	—	—	*Rare	—

***NOTE:** Spink America Gerber sale 6-96 good realized $23,100.

ZACATECAS

The city of Zacatecas, in a rich mining region has provided silver for the world since the mid-1500's. On November 14, 1810 a mint began production for the Royalist cause. Zacatecas was the most prolific during the War of Independence. Four of the 5 "standard" silver denominations were made here, 4 Reales were not. The first, a local type showing mountains of silver on the coins were made only in 1810 and 1811. Some 1811's were made by the Insurgents who took the city on April 15, 1811, later retaken by the Royalists on May 21, 1811. Zacatecas struck the standard Ferdinand VII bust type until 1922.

MINT MARKS: Z, ZS, Zs

1/2 REAL

.903 SILVER
Obv: Local arms w/flowers and castles.

KM#	Date	Good	VG	Fine	VF
180	1810	75.00	125.00	200.00	400.00
	1181 (error 1811)	30.00	50.00	90.00	175.00

Obv: Royal arms.
Rev. leg: MONEDA PROVISIONAL DE ZACATECAS., mountain.

KM#	Date	Good	VG	Fine	VF
181	1811	30.00	50.00	90.00	175.00

Obv: Provincial bust FERDIN. VII.
Rev. leg: MONEDA PROVISIONAL DE ZACATECAS.

KM#	Date	Good	VG	Fine	VF
182	1811	30.00	40.00	65.00	135.00
	1812	25.00	35.00	60.00	120.00

1.6900 g, .903 SILVER, .0491 oz ASW
Obv: Armored bust of Ferdinand VII.

KM#	Date	Good	VG	Fine	VF
73.1	1813 FP	25.00	45.00	85.00	175.00
	1813 AG	20.00	40.00	60.00	100.00
	1814 AG	15.00	30.00	60.00	100.00
	1815 AG	12.50	25.00	40.00	60.00
	1816 AG	10.00	15.00	25.00	50.00
	1817 AG	10.00	15.00	25.00	50.00
	1818 AG	10.00	15.00	25.00	50.00
	1819 AG	10.00	15.00	25.00	50.00

Obv: Draped bust Ferdinand VII.

KM#	Date	VG	Fine	VF	XF
74.3	1819 AG	8.00	12.00	25.00	50.00
	1820 AG	8.00	12.00	25.00	50.00
	1820 RG	5.00	10.00	20.00	45.00
	1821 AG	150.00	250.00	450.00	850.00
	1821 RG	5.00	10.00	20.00	45.00

REAL

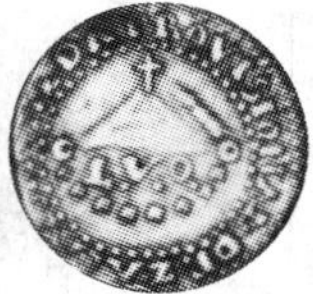

.903 SILVER
Obv: Local arms w/flowers and castles.

KM#	Date	Good	VG	Fine	VF
183	1810	100.00	150.00	300.00	500.00
	1181 (error 1811)				
		20.00	40.00	75.00	150.00

Obv: Royal arms.
Rev. leg: MONEDA PROVISIONAL DE ZACATECAS., mountain.

KM#	Date	Good	VG	Fine	VF
184	1811	15.00	30.00	55.00	125.00

Obv: Provincial bust, leg: FERDIN. VII.
Rev. leg: MONEDA PROVISIONAL DE ZACATECAS, arms, pillars.

KM#	Date	Good	VG	Fine	VF
185	1811	50.00	85.00	120.00	200.00
	1812	40.00	70.00	100.00	175.00

3.3800 g, .903 SILVER, .0981 oz ASW
Obv: Armored bust of Ferdinand VII.

KM#	Date	VG	Fine	VF	XF
82.1	1813 FP	50.00	100.00	150.00	250.00
	1814 FP	20.00	35.00	50.00	85.00
	1814 AG	20.00	35.00	50.00	85.00
	1815 AG	20.00	35.00	50.00	85.00
	1816 AG	10.00	20.00	30.00	65.00
	1817 AG	6.50	12.50	20.00	45.00
	1818 AG	6.50	12.50	20.00	45.00
	1819 AG	5.00	9.00	15.00	35.00
	1820 AG	4.00	7.50	12.50	30.00

Obv: Draped bust of Ferdinand VII.

KM#	Date	VG	Fine	VF	XF
83.3	1820 AG	5.00	10.00	17.50	42.00
	1820 RG	5.00	10.00	17.50	42.00
	1821 AG	15.00	30.00	45.00	80.00
	1821 AZ	10.00	20.00	30.00	65.00
	1821 RG	6.00	12.00	17.50	45.00
	1822 AZ	6.00	12.00	17.50	45.00
	1822 RG	15.00	30.00	45.00	80.00

2 REALES

.903 SILVER
Obv: Local arms w/flowers and castles.

KM#	Date	Good	VG	Fine	VF
186	1810	—	—	Rare	—
	1181 (error 1811)				
		25.00	40.00	60.00	100.00

Obv: Royal arms.
Rev. leg: MONEDA PROVISIONAL DE ZACATECAS., mountain above L.V.O.

KM#	Date	Good	VG	Fine	VF
187	1811	15.00	30.00	50.00	90.00

Obv: Armored bust, leg: FERDIN. VII.
Rev. leg: MONEDA PROVISIONAL DE ZACATECAS, crowned arms, pillars.

KM#	Date	Good	VG	Fine	VF
188	1811	35.00	65.00	135.00	225.00
	1812	30.00	60.00	125.00	200.00

6.7700 g, .903 SILVER, .1966 oz ASW
Obv: Large armored bust of Ferdinand VII.

KM#	Date	VG	Fine	VF	XF
92.1	1813 FP	35.00	50.00	75.00	125.00
	1814 FP	35.00	50.00	75.00	125.00
	1814 AG	35.00	50.00	75.00	125.00
	1815 AG	6.50	12.50	25.00	55.00
	1816 AG	6.50	12.50	25.00	55.00
	1817 AG	6.50	12.50	25.00	55.00
	1818 AG	6.50	12.50	25.00	55.00

Obv: Small armored bust of Ferdinand VII.

KM#	Date	VG	Fine	VF	XF
A92	1819 AG	45.00	100.00	200.00	400.00

Obv: Draped bust of Ferdinand VII.

KM#	Date	VG	Fine	VF	XF
93.4	1818 AG	6.50	12.50	25.00	50.00
	1819 AG	10.00	20.00	40.00	85.00
	1820 AG	10.00	20.00	40.00	85.00
	1820 RG	10.00	20.00	40.00	85.00
	1821 AG	10.00	20.00	40.00	85.00
	1821 AZ/RG	10.00	20.00	40.00	85.00
	1821 AZ	10.00	20.00	40.00	85.00
	1821 RG	10.00	20.00	40.00	85.00
	1822 AG	10.00	20.00	40.00	85.00
	1822 AZ	15.00	30.00	60.00	125.00
	1822 RG	10.00	20.00	40.00	85.00

8 REALES

.903 SILVER
Obv: Local arm w/flowers and castles.
Rev: Similar to KM#190.

KM#	Date	Good	VG	Fine	VF
189	1810	300.00	500.00	750.00	1250.
	1181 (error 1811)				
		100.00	150.00	225.00	350.00

NOTE: Also exists with incomplete date.

Obv. leg: FERDIN.VII.DEI. . ., royal arms.
Rev. leg: MONEDA PROVISIONAL DE ZACATECAS, mountain above L.V.O.

KM#	Date	Good	VG	Fine	VF
190	1811	65.00	100.00	135.00	220.00

Obv: Armored bust of Ferdinand VII.
Rev. leg: MONEDA PROVISIONAL DE ZACATECAS, crowned arms, pillars.

KM#	Date	Good	VG	Fine	VF
191	1811	45.00	75.00	145.00	275.00
	1812	50.00	85.00	160.00	300.00

Obv: Draped bust of Ferdinand VII.
Rev. leg: MONEDA PROVISIONAL DE ZACATECAS, crowned arms, pillars.

KM#	Date	Good	VG	Fine	VF
192	1812	75.00	150.00	275.00	450.00

27.0700 g, .903 SILVER, .7860 oz ASW
Obv: Draped bust of Ferdinand VII.

KM#	Date	VG	Fine	VF	XF
111.5	1813 AG	125.00	200.00	250.00	350.00
	1813 FP	75.00	125.00	175.00	275.00
	1814 AG	100.00	150.00	200.00	300.00
	1814 AG D over horizontal D in IND				
		125.00	175.00	225.00	325.00
	1814 AG/FP	100.00	150.00	200.00	300.00
	1814 FP	150.00	250.00	350.00	450.00
	1815 AG	50.00	100.00	150.00	250.00
	1816 AG	35.00	50.00	65.00	125.00
	1817 AG	35.00	50.00	65.00	125.00
	1818 AG	30.00	40.00	50.00	100.00
	1819 AG	30.00	40.00	50.00	100.00
	1820 AG 18/11 error				
		100.00	200.00	300.00	400.00
	1820 AG	30.00	40.00	50.00	100.00
	1820 RG	30.00	40.00	50.00	100.00
	1821/81 RG	75.00	150.00	225.00	300.00
	1821 RG	15.00	25.00	35.00	65.00
	1821 AZ	50.00	100.00	150.00	200.00
	1822 RG	40.00	60.00	100.00	175.00

Rev: Crown with lower rear arc.

KM#	Date	VG	Fine	VF	XF
111.6	1821 RG	160.00	320.00	550.00	750.00

COUNTERMARKED COINAGE

Crown and Flag

(Refer to Multiple Countermarks)

LCM - La Comandancia Militar

NOTE: This countermark exists in 15 various sizes.

2 REALES

.903 SILVER

c/m: LCM on Mexico KM#92.

KM#	Date	Year	Good	VG	Fine	VF
193.1	ND	1809 TH	75.00	150.00	200.00	300.00

c/m: LCM on Zacatecas KM#187.

KM#	Date	Year	Good	VG	Fine	VF
193.2	ND	1811	75.00	150.00	200.00	300.00

8 REALES

CAST SILVER
c/m: LCM on Chihuahua KM#123.

KM#	Date	Year	Good	VG	Fine	VF
194.1	ND	1811 RP	100.00	200.00	300.00	450.00
	ND	1812 RP	100.00	200.00	300.00	450.00

.903 SILVER
c/m: LCM on Chihuahua KM#111.1 struck over KM#123.

KM#	Date	Year	Good	VG	Fine	VF
194.2	ND	1815 RP	200.00	275.00	400.00	550.00
	ND	1817 RP	125.00	175.00	225.00	300.00
	ND	1820 RP	125.00	175.00	225.00	300.00
	ND	1821 RP	125.00	175.00	225.00	300.00

c/m: LCM on Durango KM#111.2.

KM#	Date	Year	Good	VG	Fine	VF
194.3	ND	1812 RM	70.00	125.00	190.00	250.00
	ND	1821 CG	70.00	125.00	190.00	250.00

c/m: LCM on Guadalajara KM#111.3.

KM#	Date	Year	Good	VG	Fine	VF
194.4	ND	1813 MR	150.00	225.00	300.00	475.00
	ND	1820 FS	—	—	Rare	—

c/m: LCM on Guanajuato KM#111.4.

KM#	Date	Year	Good	VG	Fine	VF
194.5	ND	1813 JM	225.00	350.00	475.00	650.00

c/m: LCM on Nueva Vizcaya KM#165.

KM#	Date	Year	Good	VG	Fine	VF
194.6	ND	1811 RM	—	—	Rare	—

c/m: LCM on Mexico KM#111.

KM#	Date	Year	Good	VG	Fine	VF
194.7	ND	1811 HJ	125.00	225.00	350.00	600.00
	ND	1812 JJ	110.00	135.00	190.00	325.00
	ND	1817 JJ	50.00	65.00	85.00	125.00
	ND	1818 JJ	50.00	65.00	85.00	125.00
	ND	1820 JJ	—	—	—	—

c/m: LCM on Sombrerete KM#176.

KM#	Date	Year	Good	VG	Fine	VF
194.8	ND	1811	—	—	Rare	—
	ND	1812	—	—	Rare	—

c/m: LCM on Zacatecas KM#190.

KM#	Date	Year	Good	VG	Fine	VF
194.9	ND	1811	225.00	350.00	450.00	—

c/m: LCM on Zacatecas KM#111.5.

KM#	Date	Year	Good	VG	Fine	VF
194.10	ND	1813 FP	—	—	—	—
	ND	1814 AG	—	—	—	—
	ND	1822 RG	—	—	—	—

LCV - Las Cajas de Veracruz

(The Royal Treasury of the City of Veracruz)

7 REALES

SILVER
c/m: LCV and 7 on underweight 8 Reales.

KM#	Date	Year	Good	VG	Fine	VF
195	ND	(-)	—	—	Rare	—

7-1/4 REALES

SILVER
c/m: LCV and 7-1/4 on underweight 8 Reales.

KM#	Date	Year	Good	VG	Fine	VF
196	ND	(-)	—	—	Rare	—

7-1/2 REALES

SILVER
c/m: LCV and 7-1/2 on underweight 8 Reales.

KM#	Date	Year	Good	VG	Fine	VF
197	ND	(-)	—	—	Rare	—

7-3/4 REALES

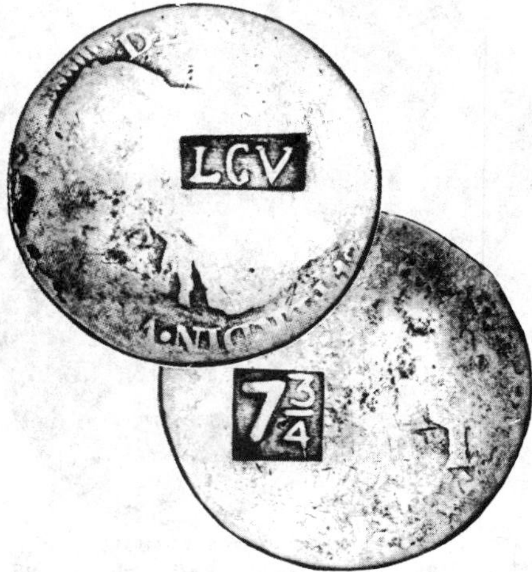

SILVER
c/m: LCV and 7-3/4 on underweight 8 Reales.

KM#	Date	Year	Good	VG	Fine	VF
198	ND	(-)	300.00	375.00	450.00	600.00

8 REALES

CAST SILVER
c/m: LCV on Chihuahua KM#123.

KM#	Date	Year	Good	VG	Fine	VF
A198	ND	1811 RP	150.00	250.00	400.00	500.00

SILVER
c/m: LCV on Zacatecas KM#191.

KM#	Date	Year	Good	VG	Fine	VF
199	ND	1811	175.00	225.00	275.00	350.00
	ND	1812	175.00	225.00	275.00	350.00

MS (Monogram) - Manuel Salcedo

8 REALES

SILVER
c/m: MS monogram on Mexico KM#110.

KM#	Date	Year	Good	VG	Fine	VF
200	ND	1809 TH	150.00	250.00	400.00	500.00
	ND	1810 HJ	150.00	250.00	400.00	500.00
	ND	1811 HJ	150.00	250.00	400.00	500.00

MVA - Monclova

8 REALES

SILVER
c/m: MVA/1811 on Chihuahua KM#111.1; struck over cast Mexico KM#110.

KM#	Date	Year	Good	VG	Fine	VF
201	ND	1809	250.00	450.00	700.00	1000.
	ND	1816 RP	250.00	450.00	700.00	1000.
	ND	1821 RP	250.00	450.00	700.00	1000.

c/m: MVA/1812 on Chihuahua KM#111.1; struck over cast Mexico KM#109.

KM#	Date	Year	Good	VG	Fine	VF
202.1	1812	1810	125.00	175.00	250.00	350.00

c/m: MVA/1812 on cast Mexico KM#109.

KM#	Date	Year	Good	VG	Fine	VF
202.2	1812	1798 FM	100.00	150.00	250.00	350.00
	1812	1802 FT	100.00	150.00	250.00	350.00

c/m: MVA/1812 on cast Mexico KM#110.

KM#	Date	Year	Good	VG	Fine	VF
202.3	1812	1809 HJ	100.00	150.00	250.00	350.00
	1812	1809 TH	100.00	150.00	250.00	350.00
	1812	1810 HJ	100.00	150.00	250.00	350.00

c/m: MVA/1812 on Zacatecas KM#189.

KM#	Date	Year	Good	VG	Fine	VF
202.5	1812	1813	300.00	350.00	450.00	550.00

PDV - Provisional de Valladolid

VTIL - (Util = useful)

(Refer to Multiple countermarks)

INSURGENT COINAGE

Supreme National Congress of America

1/2 REAL

STRUCK COPPER
Obv. leg: FERDIN. VII DEI GRATIA, eagle on bridge.
Rev. leg: S.P.CONG.NAT.IND. GUV.T., value, bow, quiver, etc.

KM#	Date	Good	VG	Fine	VF
203	1811	27.50	45.00	60.00	100.00

REAL

STRUCK SILVER
Similar to 1/2 Real, KM#203.

KM#	Date	Good	VG	Fine	VF
204	1811	45.00	75.00	125.00	200.00

2 REALES

STRUCK SILVER

KM#	Date	Good	VG	Fine	VF
205	1812	225.00	325.00	475.00	700.00

8 REALES

CAST SILVER

KM#	Date	Good	VG	Fine	VF
206	1811	150.00	250.00	350.00	500.00
	1812	150.00	250.00	350.00	500.00

STRUCK SILVER

KM#	Date	Good	VG	Fine	VF
207	1811	—	—	—	—
	1812	300.00	600.00	1000.	1500.

STRUCK COPPER
Obv. leg: FERDIN.VII. . ., eagle on bridge.
Rev. leg: PROVICIONAL POR LA SUPREMA JUNTA DE AMERICA, bow, sword and quiver.

KM#	Date	Good	VG	Fine	VF
208	1811	100.00	150.00	225.00	450.00
	1812	100.00	150.00	225.00	450.00

National Congress

1/2 REAL

STRUCK COPPER
Obv. leg: VICE FERD. VII DEI GRATIA ET, eagle on bridge.
Rev. leg: S. P. CONG. NAT. IND. GUV. T., value, bow, quiver, etc.

KM#	Date	Good	VG	Fine	VF
209	1811	45.00	85.00	150.00	200.00
	1812	27.50	60.00	100.00	150.00

KM#	Date	Good	VG	Fine	VF
209	1813	27.50	60.00	100.00	150.00
	1814	45.00	85.00	150.00	200.00

.903 SILVER

KM#	Date	Good	VG	Fine	VF
210	1812	27.50	60.00	100.00	150.00
	1813	45.00	90.00	175.00	275.00

NOTE: 1812 exists with the date reading inwards and outwards.

REAL

.903 SILVER

KM#	Date	Good	VG	Fine	VF
211	1812	22.50	45.00	65.00	100.00
	1813	22.50	45.00	65.00	100.00

NOTE: 1812 exists with the date reading either inward or outward.

2 REALES

STRUCK COPPER

KM#	Date	Good	VG	Fine	VF
212	1812	100.00	150.00	200.00	275.00
	1813	23.50	50.00	75.00	120.00
	1814	32.50	75.00	110.00	165.00

STRUCK SILVER

KM#	Date	Good	VG	Fine	VF
A213	1813	950.00	1750.	3000.	4750.

.903 SILVER

KM#	Date	Good	VG	Fine	VF
213	1813	75.00	155.00	265.00	375.00

NOTE: These dies were believed to be intended for the striking of 2 Escudos.

4 REALES

.903 SILVER
Mint: Mexico City

KM#	Date	Good	VG	Fine	VF
214	1813	600.00	1200.	2250.	3500.

8 REALES

.903 SILVER
Mint: Mexico City
Obv: Small crowned eagle.

KM#	Date	Good	VG	Fine	VF
215.1	1812	500.00	1000.	2000.	3750.

Obv: Large crowned eagle.

KM#	Date	Good	VG	Fine	VF
215.2	1813	500.00	1000.	2000.	3750.

American Congress

REAL

.903 SILVER
Obv: Eagle on cactus, leg: CONGRESO AMERICANO.
Rev: F.7 on spread mantle, leg: DEPOSIT D.L.AUCTORI J.

KM#	Date	Good	VG	Fine	VF
216	ND(1813)	35.00	65.00	100.00	175.00

Obv: Eagle on cactus, leg: CONGR.AMER.
Rev: F.7 on spread mantle, leg: DEPOS.D.L.AUT.D.

KM#	Date	Good	VG	Fine	VF
217	ND(1813)	35.00	65.00	100.00	175.00

NUEVA GALICIA

(Later became Jalisco State)

In early colonial times, Nueva Galicia was an extensive province which substantially combined later provinces of Zacatecas and Jalisco. These are states of Mexico today although the name was revived during the War of Independence. The only issue was 2 reales of rather enigmatic origin. No decrees or other authorization to strike this coin has yet been located or reported.

2 REALES

.903 SILVER
Obv. leg: PROVYCIONAL. . ., N.G. in center, date.
Rev:. . .a.juniana82R. . . in center.

KM#	Date	Good	VG	Fine	VF
218	1813	1000.	2500.	4500.	—

OAXACA

Oaxaca was the hub of Insurgent activity in the south where coinage started in July 1811 and continued until October 1814. The Oaxaca issues represent episodic strikings, usually under dire circumstances by various individuals. Coins were commonly made of copper due to urgency and were intended to be redeemed at face value in gold or silver once silver was available to the Insurgents. Some were later made in silver, but most appear to be of more recent origin, to statisfy collectors.

SUD

(Under General Morelos)

1/2 REAL

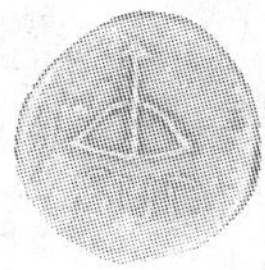

STRUCK COPPER
Obv: Bow, arrow, SUD.
Rev: Morelos monogram Mo, date.

KM#	Date	Good	VG	Fine	VF
219	1811	6.75	11.50	20.00	35.00
	1812	6.75	11.50	20.00	35.00
	1813	5.50	9.00	17.50	30.00
	1814	9.00	16.50	25.00	40.00

NOTE: Uniface strikes exist of #219.

STRUCK SILVER

KM#	Date	Good	VG	Fine	VF
220.1	1811	—	—	—	—
	1812	—	—	—	—
	1813	—	—	—	—

CAST SILVER

KM#	Date	Good	VG	Fine	VF
220.2	1811	—	—	—	—
	1812	—	—	—	—
	1813	25.00	50.00	100.00	150.00

NOTE: Use caution as most silver specimens examined appear questionable and may be considered spurious.

STRUCK SILVER
Obv. leg: PROVICIONAL DE OAXACA, bow, arrow.
Rev. leg: AMERICA MORELOS, lion.

KM#	Date	Good	VG	Fine	VF
221	1812	35.00	60.00	100.00	150.00
	1813	35.00	60.00	100.00	150.00

STRUCK COPPER

KM#	Date	Good	VG	Fine	VF
221a	1812	27.50	42.50	70.00	100.00
	1813	20.00	35.00	60.00	85.00

Obv: Similar to KM#220.
Rev: Similar to KM#221 but w/1/2 at left of lion.

KM#	Date	Good	VG	Fine	VF
A222	1813	27.50	42.50	70.00	100.00

REAL

STRUCK COPPER

KM#	Date	Good	VG	Fine	VF
222	1811	4.75	9.00	18.00	38.00
	1812	3.75	7.00	14.00	30.00
	1813	3.75	7.00	14.00	30.00

STRUCK SILVER

KM#	Date	Good	VG	Fine	VF
222a	1812	—	—	—	—
	1813	—	—	—	—

CAST SILVER

KM#	Date	Good	VG	Fine	VF
223	1812	—	—	—	—
	1813	27.50	60.00	115.00	160.00

NOTE: See note below 1/2 Real, KM#220.2

STRUCK COPPER
Obv: Bow, arrow/SUD.
Rev. leg: AMERICA MORELOS, lion.

KM#	Date	Good	VG	Fine	VF
224	1813	27.50	42.50	75.00	110.00

SILVER

KM#	Date	Good	VG	Fine	VF
225	1813	—	—	Rare	—

2 REALES

STRUCK COPPER

KM#	Date	Good	VG	Fine	VF
226.1	1811	11.00	22.50	45.00	90.00
	1812	2.50	3.75	5.00	9.00
	1813	2.50	3.75	5.00	9.00
	1814	12.50	25.00	50.00	100.00

STRUCK SILVER

KM#	Date	Good	VG	Fine	VF
226.1a	1812	175.00	300.00	500.00	750.00

Obv: 3 large stars added.

KM#	Date	Good	VG	Fine	VF
226.2	1814	10.00	20.00	40.00	60.00

Obv. leg: SUD-OXA, bow, arrow.
Rev: Morelos monogram, value, date.

KM#	Date	Good	VG	Fine	VF
227	1813	60.00	100.00	200.00	300.00
	1814	60.00	100.00	200.00	300.00

Obv. leg: SUD. OAXACA

KM#	Date	Good	VG	Fine	VF
228	1814	60.00	100.00	200.00	325.00

CAST SILVER

KM#	Date	Good	VG	Fine	VF
229	1812	60.00	100.00	150.00	225.00
	1812 filled D in SUD	60.00	100.00	150.00	225.00

NOTE: See note below 1/2 Real, KM#220.2.

4 REALES

NOTE: All known examples are modern fabrications.

CAST SILVER

KM#	Date	Good	VG	Fine	VF
230	1811	—	—	—	—
	1812				

Obv. leg: SUD-OXA, bow, arrow.
Rev: Morelos monogram.

KM#	Date	Good	VG	Fine	VF
231	1813	125.00	250.00	400.00	800.00

COPPER
Obv. leg: SUD-OXA, bow, arrow.
Rev: Morelos monogram.

KM#	Date	Good	VG	Fine	VF
232	1814	100.00	150.00	200.00	400.00

8 REALES

STRUCK COPPER
Plain fields.

KM#	Date	Good	VG	Fine	VF
233.1	1812	15.00	30.00	60.00	90.00

STRUCK SILVER

KM#	Date	Good	VG	Fine	VF
233.1a	1812	100.00	150.00	250.00	450.00

KM#	Date	Good	VG	Fine	VF
233.2	1812	6.00	8.00	12.00	15.00
	1813	6.00	8.00	12.00	15.00
	1814	10.00	12.00	15.00	20.00

Similar to KM#233.4 but lines below bow slant left.

KM#	Date	Good	VG	Fine	VF
233.3	1813	10.00	17.50	30.00	50.00

Obv: Lines below bow slant right.

KM#	Date	Good	VG	Fine	VF
233.4	1813	10.00	17.50	30.00	50.00

Ornate flowery fields.

KM#	Date	Good	VG	Fine	VF
234	1811	75.00	125.00	150.00	225.00
	1812	4.00	5.00	7.50	15.00
	1813	4.00	5.00	7.50	15.00
	1814	10.00	15.00	25.00	50.00

CAST SILVER

KM#	Date	Good	VG	Fine	VF
235	1811	—	—	—	—
	1812	75.00	125.00	200.00	350.00
	1813	60.00	100.00	175.00	300.00
	1814	—	—	—	—

NOTE: Most silver specimens available in today's market are considered spurious.

.903 SILVER, struck
Obv: PROV. D. OAXACA, M monogram.
Rev: Lion shield w/or w/o bow above.

KM#	Date	Good	VG	Fine	VF
236	1812	—	—	Rare	—

Obv: W/o leg.

KM#	Date	Good	VG	Fine	VF
237	1813	—	—	Rare	—

Obv: Bow/M/SUD. .
Rev: PROV. DE, . . ., arms.

KM#	Date	Good	VG	Fine	VF
238	1813	—	—	Rare	—

CAST SILVER
Similar to 4 Reales, KM#231.

KM#	Date	Good	VG	Fine	VF
239	1814	—	—	Rare	—

COPPER

KM#	Date	Good	VG	Fine	VF
240	1814	35.00	70.00	150.00	250.00
	OAXACA spelled out.				
241	1814	100.00	200.00	350.00	550.00

Huautla

8 REALES

COPPER
Obv. leg: MONEDA PROVI.CIONAL PS.ES. around bow, arrow/SUD.
Rev. leg: FABRICADO EN HUAUTLA.

KM#	Date	Good	VG	Fine	VF
242	1812	1000.	1500.	2000.	—

Tierra Caliente

(Hot Country)
Under General Morelos

1/2 REAL

STRUCK COPPER
Obv: Bow, T.C., SUD.
Rev: Morelos monogram, value, date.

KM#	Date	Good	VG	Fine	VF
243	1813	37.50	70.00	125.00	200.00

REAL

STRUCK COPPER
Similar to 1/2 Real, KM#243.

KM#	Date	Good	VG	Fine	VF
244	1813	13.50	25.00	50.00	80.00

2 REALES

STRUCK COPPER
Similar to 1/2 Real, KM#243.

KM#	Date	Good	VG	Fine	VF
245	1813	9.00	22.50	35.00	50.00

KM#	Date	Good	VG	Fine	VF
246	1814	22.50	50.00	100.00	175.00
	CAST SILVER				
247	1814	—	—	Rare	—

NOTE: See note below 1/2 Real, KM#220.2.

8 REALES

STRUCK COPPER

KM#	Date	Good	VG	Fine	VF
248	1813	9.00	20.00	40.00	75.00
	CAST SILVER				
249	1813	—	—	—	—

NOTE: See note below 1/2 Real, KM#220.2.

PUEBLA

The coins of Puebla emanated from Zacatlan, the headquarters of the hit-and-run Insurgent leader Osorno. The mint opened in April 1812 and operated through 1813.

Zacatlan

(Struck by General Osorno)

1/2 REAL

COPPER
Obv: Osorno monogram, ZACATLAN, date.
Rev: Crossed arrows, wreath, value.

KM#	Date	Good	VG	Fine	VF
250	1813	—	—	Rare	—

REAL

COPPER

KM#	Date	Good	VG	Fine	VF
251	1813	100.00	150.00	225.00	450.00

2 REALES

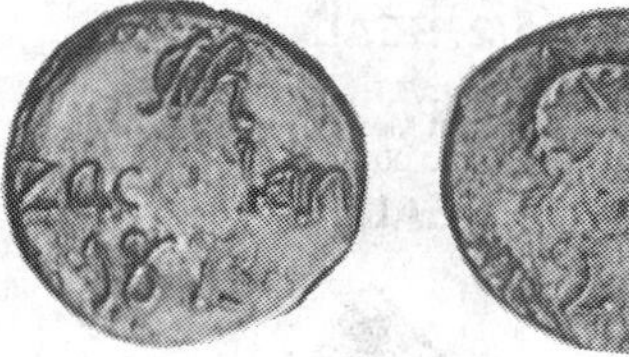

COPPER

KM#	Date	Good	VG	Fine	VF
252	1813	125.00	175.00	275.00	500.00

VERACRUZ

In Zongolica, in the province of Veracruz, 2 priests and a lawyer decided to raise an army to fight for independence. Due to isolation from other Insurgent forces, they decided to make their own coins. Records show that they intended to mint coins of 1/2, 1, 2, 4, and 8 reales, but specimens are extant of only the three higher denominations.

Zongolica

2 REALES

.903 SILVER
Obv. leg: VIVA FERNANDO VII Y AMERICA, bow and arrow.
Rev. leg: ZONGOLICA, value, crossed palm branch, sword, date.

KM#	Date	Good	VG	Fine	VF
253	1812	85.00	175.00	300.00	500.00

4 REALES

.903 SILVER
Similar to 2 Reales, KM#253.

KM#	Date	Good	VG	Fine	VF
254	1812	600.00	800.00	1200.	2000.

8 REALES

.903 SILVER

KM#	Date	Good	VG	Fine	VF
255	1812	—	—	*Rare	—

***NOTE:** Spink America Gerber sale 6-96 VF to XF realized $57,200.

COUNTERMARKED COINAGE

Congress of Chilpanzingo

Type A: Hand holding bow and arrow between quiver w/arrows, sword and bow.

Type B: Crowned eagle on bridge.

1/2 REAL

SILVER
c/m: Type A on cast Mexico City KM#72.

KM#	Date	Year	Good	VG	Fine	VF
256.1	ND	1812	42.50	70.00	90.00	120.00

c/m: Type A on Zacatecas KM#181.

KM#	Date	Year	Good	VG	Fine	VF
256.2	ND	1811	50.00	75.00	100.00	125.00

REAL

CAST SILVER
c/m: Type A on cast Mexico City KM#81.

KM#	Date	Year	Good	VG	Fine	VF
A257	ND	1803	18.50	30.00	50.00	80.00

2 REALES

SILVER

c/m: Type B on 1/4 cut of 8 Reales.

KM#	Date	Year	Good	VG	Fine	VF
257.1	ND	—	—	—	Unique	—

c/m: Type B on Zacatecas KM#186.

KM#	Date	Year	Good	VG	Fine	VF
257.2	ND	1811	—	—	Unique	—

8 REALES

SILVER

c/m: Type A on cast Mexico City KM#109.

KM#	Date	Year	Good	VG	Fine	VF
258.1	ND	1805 TH	45.00	65.00	85.00	125.00

c/m: Type A on cast Mexico City KM#110.

KM#	Date	Year	Good	VG	Fine	VF
258.2	ND	1810 HJ	50.00	75.00	100.00	150.00

c/m: Type A on cast Mexico City KM#111.

KM#	Date	Year	Good	VG	Fine	VF
258.3	ND	1811 HJ	45.00	65.00	85.00	125.00
	ND	1812 HJ	100.00	125.00	175.00	275.00

c/m: Type B on Chihuahua KM#111.1.

KM#	Date	Year	Good	VG	Fine	VF
259.1	ND	1816 RP	200.00	250.00	300.00	350.00

c/m: Type B on cast Mexico City KM#111.

KM#	Date	Year	Good	VG	Fine	VF
259.2	ND	1811 HJ	130.00	140.00	150.00	175.00

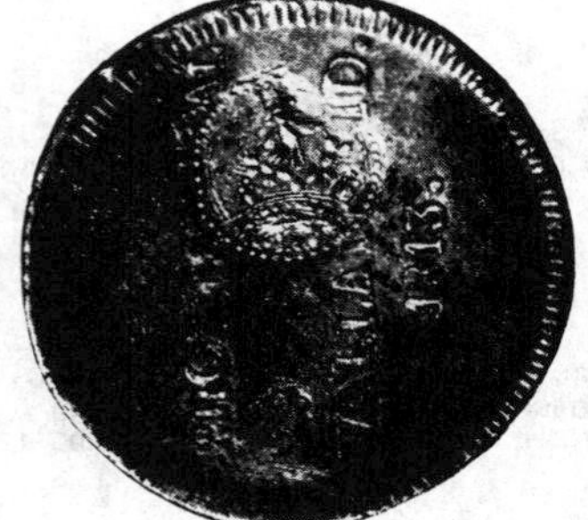

c/m: Type B on Valladolid KM#178.

KM#	Date	Year	Good	VG	Fine	VF
259.3	ND	1813	1000.	2000.	3000.	5000.

c/m: Type B on Zacatecas KM#190.

KM#	Date	Year	Good	VG	Fine	VF
259.4	ND	1810	400.00	500.00	600.00	750.00

Ensaie

8 REALES

SILVER

c/m: Eagle over ENSAIE on Mexico City KM#110.

KM#	Date	Year	Good	VG	Fine	VF
260.1	ND	1811 HJ	150.00	200.00	275.00	350.00

c/m: Eagle over ENSAIE crude sling below on Zacatecas KM#189.

KM#	Date	Year	Good	VG	Fine	VF
260.2	ND	1811	200.00	400.00	600.00	800.00

c/m: Eagle over ENSAIE, crude sling below on Zacatecas KM#190.

KM#	Date	Year	Good	VG	Fine	VF
260.3	ND	1810	—	—	—	—
	ND	1811	100.00	150.00	200.00	300.00

c/m: Eagle over ENSAIE, crude sling below on Zacatecas KM#191.

KM#	Date	Year	Good	VG	Fine	VF
260.4	ND	1810	500.00	700.00	900.00	1200.
	ND	1811	250.00	300.00	375.00	500.00
	ND	1812	200.00	250.00	285.00	400.00

Jose Maria Liceaga

J.M.L. with banner on cross, crossed olive branches. (J.M.L./V., D.s, S.M.,S.Y.S.L., Ve, A.P., s.r.a., Sea, P.G.,S.,S.M.,E.)

1/2 REAL

SILVER

c/m: JML/SM on cast Mexico City 1/2 Real.

KM#	Date	Year	Good	VG	Fine	VF
A260	ND	—	100.00	150.00	200.00	275.00

2 REALES

SILVER

c/m: J.M.L./Ve on 1/4 cut of 8 Reales.

KM#	Date	Year	Good	VG	Fine	VF
261.1	ND	—	175.00	225.00	300.00	—

c/m: J.M.L./V. on Zacatecas KM#186-187.

KM#	Date	Year	Good	VG	Fine	VF
261.2	ND	1811	200.00	225.00	250.00	300.00

c/m: J.M.L./DS on Zacatecas KM#186-187.

KM#	Date	Year	Good	VG	Fine	VF
261.3	ND	1811	200.00	235.00	275.00	325.00

c/m: J.M.L./S.M. on Zacatecas KM#186-187.

KM#	Date	Year	Good	VG	Fine	VF
261.4	ND	1811	200.00	235.00	275.00	325.00

c/m: J.M.L./S.Y. on Zacatecas KM#186-187.

KM#	Date	Year	Good	VG	Fine	VF
261.5	ND	1811	200.00	235.00	275.00	325.00

8 REALES

SILVER

c/m: J.M.L./D.S. on Zacatecas KM#189-190.

KM#	Date	Year	Good	VG	Fine	VF
262.1	ND	1811	250.00	325.00	425.00	550.00

c/m: J.M.L./E on Zacatecas KM#189-190.

KM#	Date	Year	Good	VG	Fine	VF
262.2	ND	1811	225.00	300.00	400.00	550.00

c/m: J.M.L./P.G. on Durango KM#111.2.

KM#	Date	Year	Good	VG	Fine	VF
262.3	ND	1813 RM	200.00	275.00	375.00	525.00

c/m: J.M.L./S.F. on Zacatecas KM#189-190.

KM#	Date	Year	Good	VG	Fine	VF
262.4	ND	1811	200.00	275.00	375.00	525.00

c/m: J.M.L./S.M. on Zacatecas KM#189-190.

KM#	Date	Year	Good	VG	Fine	VF
262.5	ND	1811	200.00	275.00	375.00	525.00

c/m: J.M.L./V.E. on Zacatecas KM#189-190.

KM#	Date	Year	Good	VG	Fine	VF
262.6	ND	1811	200.00	275.00	375.00	525.00

Don Jose Maria De Linares

8 REALES

SILVER

c/m: LINA/RES* on Mexico City KM#110.

KM#	Date	Year	Good	VG	Fine	VF
263.1	ND	1808 TH	250.00	300.00	375.00	500.00

c/m: LINA/RES * on Zacatecas KM#189-190.

KM#	Date	Year	Good	VG	Fine	VF
263.2	ND	1811	300.00	375.00	450.00	575.00

c/m: LINA/RES* on Zacatecas, KM#191-192.

KM#	Date	Year	Good	VG	Fine	VF
263.3	ND	1812	250.00	300.00	375.00	500.00

L.V.S. - Labor Vincit Semper

NOTE: Some authorities believe L.V.S. is for 'La Villa de Sombrerete'.

8 REALES

CAST SILVER

c/m: L.V.S. on Chihuahua KM#123.

KM#	Date	Year	Good	VG	Fine	VF
264.1	ND	1811 RP	275.00	350.00	450.00	550.00
	ND	1812 RP	200.00	250.00	300.00	375.00

c/m: L.V.S. on Chihuahua KM#111.1 overstruck on KM#123.

KM#	Date	Year	Good	VG	Fine	VF
264.2	ND	1816 RP	250.00	300.00	325.00	375.00
	ND	1817 RP	250.00	300.00	325.00	375.00
	ND	1818 RP	250.00	300.00	325.00	375.00
	ND	1819 RP	400.00	450.00	500.00	600.00
	ND	1820 RP	450.00	500.00	550.00	650.00

c/m: L.V.S. on Guadalajara KM#111.3.

KM#	Date	Year	Good	VG	Fine	VF
264.3	ND	1817	185.00	220.00	250.00	310.00

c/m: L.V.S. on Nueva Vizcaya KM#165.

KM#	Date	Year	Good	VG	Fine	VF
264.4	ND	1811 RM	1150.	3150.	5250.	8250.

c/m: L.V.S. on Sombrerete KM#177.

KM#	Date	Year	Good	VG	Fine	VF
264.5	ND	1811	300.00	350.00	450.00	550.00
	ND	1812	300.00	350.00	450.00	550.00

c/m: L.V.S. on Zacatecas KM#189-190.

KM#	Date	Year	Good	VG	Fine	VF
264.6	ND	1811	350.00	400.00	450.00	550.00

c/m: L.V.S. on Zacatecas KM#192.

KM#	Date	Year	Good	VG	Fine	VF
264.7	ND	1813	350.00	400.00	450.00	550.00

Morelos

Morelos monogram

Type A: Stars above and below monogram in circle.

Type B: Dots above and below monogram in oval.

Type C: Monogram in rectangle.

NOTE: Many specimens of Type C available in today's market are considered spurious.

2 REALES

COPPER

c/m: Type A on Oaxaca Sud, KM#226.1.

KM#	Date	Year	Good	VG	Fine	VF
A265		1812	—	—	—	—

8 REALES

SILVER

c/m: Type A on cast Mexico City KM#109.

KM#	Date	Year	Good	VG	Fine	VF
265.1	ND	1797 FM	45.00	50.00	60.00	85.00
	ND	1798 FM	45.00	50.00	60.00	85.00
	ND	1800 FM	45.00	50.00	60.00	85.00
	ND	1807 TH	45.00	50.00	60.00	85.00

c/m: Type A on Mexico City KM#110.

KM#	Date	Year	Good	VG	Fine	VF
265.2	ND	1809 TH	55.00	65.00	85.00	120.00
	ND	1811 HJ	55.00	65.00	85.00	120.00

c/m: Type A on Mexico City KM#111.

KM#	Date	Year	Good	VG	Fine	VF
265.3	ND	1812 JJ	50.00	60.00	75.00	110.00

COPPER

c/m: Type A on Oaxaca Sud KM#233.

KM#	Date	Year	Good	VG	Fine	VF
265.4	ND	1811	12.50	17.50	25.00	40.00
	ND	1812	12.50	17.50	25.00	40.00
	ND	1813	12.50	17.50	25.00	40.00
	ND	1814	12.50	17.50	25.00	40.00

CAST SILVER

c/m: Type A on Supreme National Congress KM#206.

KM#	Date	Year	Good	VG	Fine	VF
265.5	ND	1811	200.00	250.00	375.00	600.00

SILVER

c/m: Type A on Zacatecas KM#189-190.

KM#	Date	Year	Good	VG	Fine	VF
265.6	ND	1811	200.00	250.00	375.00	600.00

c/m: Type A on Zacatecas KM#191.

KM#	Date	Year	Good	VG	Fine	VF
265.7	ND	1811	200.00	250.00	375.00	600.00

c/m: Type B on Guatemala 8 Reales, C#67.

KM#	Date	Year	Good	VG	Fine	VF
266.1	ND	1810 M	—	—	Rare	—

c/m: Type B on Mexico City KM#110.

KM#	Date	Year	Good	VG	Fine	VF
266.2	ND	1809 TH	45.00	55.00	65.00	90.00

c/m: Type C on Zacatecas KM#189-190.

KM#	Date	Year	Good	VG	Fine	VF
267	ND	1811	300.00	350.00	425.00	650.00

Norte

Issued by the Supreme National Congress and the Army of the North.

c/m: Eagle on cactus; star to left; NORTE below.

1/2 REAL

SILVER
c/m: On Zacatecas KM#180.

KM#	Date	Year	Good	VG	Fine	VF
268	ND	1811	250.00	300.00	375.00	450.00

2 REALES

SILVER
c/m: On Zacatecas KM#187.

KM#	Date	Year	Good	VG	Fine	VF
269	ND	1811	225.00	275.00	325.00	400.00

c/m: On Zacatecas KM#188.

KM#	Date	Year	Good	VG	Fine	VF
A269	ND	1812	—	—	—	—

4 REALES

SILVER
c/m: On Sombrerete KM#175.

KM#	Date	Year	Good	VG	Fine	VF
B269	ND	1812	100.00	150.00	200.00	275.00

8 REALES

SILVER
c/m: On Chihuahua KM#111.1.

KM#	Date	Year	Good	VG	Fine	VF
270.1	ND	1813 RP	250.00	350.00	450.00	550.00

c/m: On Guanajuato KM#111.4.

KM#	Date	Year	Good	VG	Fine	VF
270.2	ND	1813 JM	400.00	550.00	700.00	800.00

c/m: On Zacatecas KM#189-190.

KM#	Date	Year	Good	VG	Fine	VF
270.3	ND	1811	300.00	400.00	500.00	650.00

c/m: On Zacatecas KM#191.

KM#	Date	Year	Good	VG	Fine	VF
270.4	ND	1811	200.00	300.00	400.00	550.00
	ND	1812	200.00	300.00	400.00	550.00

Osorno

c/m: Osorno monogram.
(Jose Francisco Osorno)

1/2 REAL

SILVER
c/m: On Mexico City KM#72.

KM#	Date	Year	Good	VG	Fine	VF
271.1	ND	1798 FM	65.00	100.00	150.00	200.00
	ND	1802 FT	65.00	100.00	150.00	200.00
	ND	1802 FT	65.00	100.00	150.00	200.00
	ND	1806	65.00	100.00	150.00	200.00

c/m: On Mexico City KM#73.

KM#	Date	Year	Good	VG	Fine	VF
271.2	ND	1809	65.00	100.00	150.00	200.00

REAL

SILVER
c/m: On Mexico City KM#81.

KM#	Date	Year	Good	VG	Fine	VF
272.1	ND	1803 FT	65.00	100.00	150.00	200.00
	ND	1803 FT	65.00	100.00	150.00	200.00

c/m: On Potosi Real.

KM#	Date	Year	Good	VG	Fine	VF
272.2	ND	—	75.00	115.00	175.00	250.00

c/m: On Guatemala Real, KM#54.

KM#	Date	Year	Good	VG	Fine	VF
272.3	ND	1804	75.00	115.00	175.00	250.00

2 REALES

SILVER
c/m: On Mexico City KM#88.2.

KM#	Date	Year	Good	VG	Fine	VF
A272.1	ND	1788 FM	75.00	125.00	175.00	250.00

c/m: On Mexico City KM#91.

KM#	Date	Year	Good	VG	Fine	VF
A272.2		1808 TH	75.00	125.00	175.00	250.00

c/m: On cast Mexico City KM#92.

KM#	Date	Year	Good	VG	Fine	VF
A272.3 (A272.1)	ND	1809 TH	75.00	125.00	175.00	250.00

c/m: On Zacatlan KM#252.

KM#	Date	Year	Good	VG	Fine	VF
A272.4 (A272.2)	ND	1813	150.00	200.00	300.00	400.00

4 REALES

SILVER
c/m: On Mexico City KM#97.2.

KM#	Date	Year	Good	VG	Fine	VF
273.1	ND	1782 FF	85.00	150.00	200.00	275.00

c/m: On Mexico City KM#100.

KM#	Date	Year	Good	VG	Fine	VF
273.2	ND	1799 FM	85.00	150.00	200.00	275.00

8 REALES

SILVER
c/m: On Lima 8 Reales, C#101.

KM#	Date	Year	Good	VG	Fine	VF
274.1	ND	1811 JP	200.00	225.00	250.00	300.00

c/m: On Mexico City KM#110.

KM#	Date	Year	Good	VG	Fine	VF
274.2	ND	1809 TH	125.00	150.00	225.00	300.00
	ND	1810 HJ	125.00	150.00	225.00	300.00
	ND	1811 HJ	125.00	150.00	225.00	300.00

S.J.N.G. - Suprema Junta National Gubernativa

(Refer to Multiple countermarks)

VILLA/GRAN

(Julian Villagran)

2 REALES

CAST SILVER
c/m: On cast Mexico City KM#91.

KM#	Date	Year	Good	VG	Fine	VF
298	ND	1799 FM	150.00	200.00	250.00	350.00
	ND	1802 FT	150.00	200.00	250.00	350.00

8 REALES

CAST SILVER
c/m: VILLA/GRAN on cast Mexico City KM#109.

KM#	Date	Year	Good	VG	Fine	VF
275	ND	1796 FM	200.00	250.00	300.00	400.00
	ND	1806 TH	200.00	250.00	300.00	400.00

UNCLASSIFIED COUNTERMARKS

General Vicente Guerrero

The countermark of an eagle facing left within a pearled oval has been attributed by some authors as that of General Vicente Guerrero, a leader of the insurgents in the south, 1816-1821.

1/2 REAL

SILVER
c/m: Eagle on Mexico City 1/2 Real.

KM#	Date	Year	Good	VG	Fine	VF
276	ND	—	40.00	60.00	80.00	175.00

REAL

SILVER
c/m: Eagle on Mexico City KM#78.

KM#	Date	Year	Good	VG	Fine	VF
277	ND	1772 FM	35.00	50.00	75.00	165.00

2 REALES

SILVER
c/m: Eagle on Mexico City KM#88.

KM#	Date	Year	Good	VG	Fine	VF
278.1	ND	1784 FM	40.00	60.00	100.00	225.00
		1798	40.00	60.00	100.00	220.00

c/m: Eagle on Mexico City KM#91.

KM#	Date	Year	Good	VG	Fine	VF
278.2	ND	1807 PJ	30.00	50.00	80.00	200.00

8 REALES

SILVER
c/m: Eagle on Zacatecas KM#191.

KM#	Date	Year	Good	VG	Fine	VF
279	ND	1811	100.00	150.00	200.00	350.00

ZMY

8 REALES

SILVER
c/m: ZMY on Zacatecas KM#191.

KM#	Date	Year	Good	VG	Fine	VF
286	ND	1812	100.00	150.00	210.00	275.00

MULTIPLE COUNTERMARKS

Many combinations of Royalist and Insurgent countermarks are usually found on the cast copies produced by Chihuahua and Mexico City and on the other crude provisional issues of this period. Struck Mexico City coins were used to make molds for casting necessity issues and countermarked afterwards to show issuing authority. Some were marked again by either both or separate opposing friendly forces to authorize circulation in their areas of occupation. Some countermarks are only obtainable with companion markings.

Chilpanzingo Crown and Flag

8 REALES

SILVER
c/m: Chilpanzingo Type B and crown and flag on Zacatecas KM#189-190.

KM#	Date	Year	Good	VG	Fine	VF
280	ND	1811	—	—	—	—

Chilpanzingo/ENSAIE

8 REALES

SILVER
c/m: Chilpanzingo Type B and ENSAIE on Zacatecas KM#189.

KM#	Date	Year	Good	VG	Fine	VF
A297	ND	—	175.00	250.00	350.00	—

Chilpanzingo/LVA

8 REALES

SILVER
c/m: Chilpanzingo Type A and LVA on Mexico City KM#109.

KM#	Date	Year	Good	VG	Fine	VF
297	ND	1805 TH	45.00	75.00	145.00	250.00

Chilpanzingo/LVS

8 REALES

SILVER
c/m: Chilpanzingo Type A and script LVS on cast Mexico City KM#110.

KM#	Date	Year	Good	VG	Fine	VF
281	ND	1809 HJ	45.00	65.00	135.00	250.00

Chilpanzingo/Morelos

8 REALES

SILVER
c/m: Chilpanzingo Type A and Morelos monogram Type A on cast Mexico City KM#109.

KM#	Date	Year	Good	VG	Fine	VF
284	ND	1806 TH	35.00	50.00	100.00	200.00
	ND	1807 TH	35.00	50.00	100.00	200.00

c/m: Chilpanzingo Type A and Morelos monogram Type A on struck Mexico City KM#110.

KM#	Date	Year	Good	VG	Fine	VF
285.1	ND	1809 TH	45.00	65.00	135.00	250.00

c/m: Chilpanzingo Type A and Morelos monogram Type A on cast Mexico City KM#110.

KM#	Date	Year	Good	VG	Fine	VF
285.2	ND	1810 HJ	35.00	45.00	60.00	140.00
	ND	1811 HJ	35.00	45.00	60.00	140.00

c/m: Chilpanzingo Type A and Morelos monogram Type A on cast Mexico City KM#111.

KM#	Date	Year	Good	VG	Fine	VF
285.3	ND	1811 HJ	75.00	120.00	175.00	275.00

Chilpanzingo/Morelos/LVS

8 REALES

SILVER

c/m: Chilpanzingo Type A, Morelos Type A and LVS monogram on cast Mexico City KM#110.

KM#	Date	Year	Good	VG	Fine	VF
286	ND	1809 HJ	50.00	75.00	125.00	275.00

Chilpanzingo/P.D.V.

8 REALES

SILVER

c/m: Chilpanzingo Type B and P.D.V. (Provisional De Valladolid) on Valladolid KM#178.

KM#	Date	Year	Good	VG	Fine	VF
287	ND	1813	—	—	—	—

Chilpanzingo/S.J.N.G.

8 REALES

SILVER

c/m: Chilpanzingo Type B and S.J.N.G. (Suprema Junta Nacional Gubernativa) on Zacatecas KM#189-190.

KM#	Date	Year	Good	VG	Fine	VF
288	ND	1811	—	—	—	—

C.M.S./S.C.M.

2 REALES

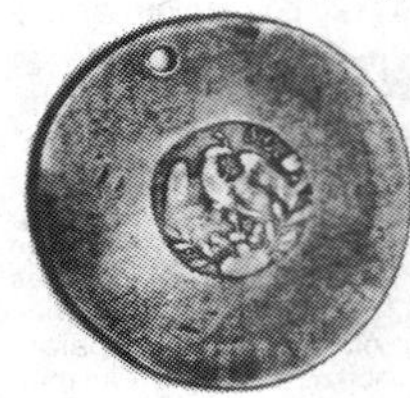

SILVER

c/m: C.M.S. (Comandancia Militar Suriana) and eagle w/S.C.M. (Soberano Congreso Mexicano) on Mexico City 2 Reales.

KM#	Date	Year	Good	VG	Fine	VF
289	ND	—	—	—	—	—

ENSAIE/J.M.L.

8 REALES

SILVER

c/m: ENSAIE and J.M.L. on Zacatecas, KM#190.

KM#	Date	Year	Good	VG	Fine	VF
A290	ND	1811	100.00	175.00	275.00	350.00

ENSAIE/VTIL

8 REALES

SILVER

c/m: ENSAIE and VTIL on Zacatecas KM#189-190.

KM#	Date	Year	Good	VG	Fine	VF
290	ND	1811	100.00	175.00	275.00	350.00

J.M.L./VTIL

2 REALES

SILVER

c/m: J.M.L./D.S. and VTIL on Zacatecas, KM#186.

KM#	Date	Year	Good	VG	Fine	VF
A286	ND	1811	75.00	125.00	175.00	250.00

c/m: J.M.L./V.E. and VTIL on Zacatecas KM#186.

KM#	Date	Year	Good	VG	Fine	VF
B286	ND	1810	75.00	125.00	175.00	250.00
	ND	1811	75.00	125.00	175.00	250.00

8 REALES

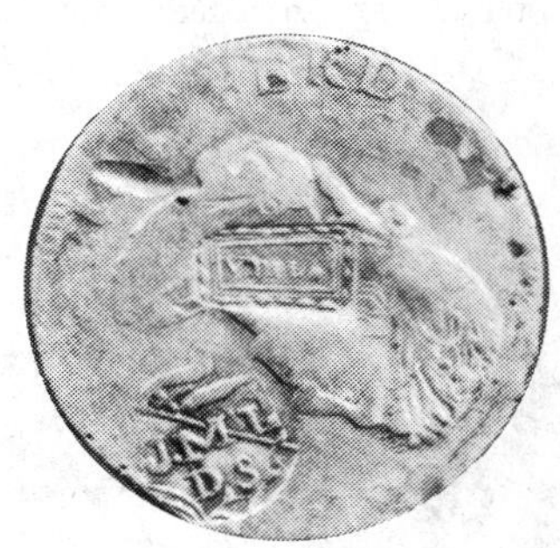

SILVER

c/m: J.M.L./D.S. and VTIL on Mexico City KM#110.

KM#	Date	Year	Good	VG	Fine	VF
291	ND	1810 HJ	85.00	150.00	250.00	400.00

L.C.M./Morelos

8 REALES

SILVER

c/m: LCM and Morelos monogram Type A on cast Mexico City KM#109.

KM#	Date	Year	Good	VG	Fine	VF
282	ND	1792 FM	—	—	—	—

Morelos/Morelos

8 REALES

SILVER

c/m: Morelos Type A and C on cast Mexico City KM#109.

KM#	Date	Year	Good	VG	Fine	VF
283	ND	1806 TH	—	—	—	—

LCM/MVA-1812
8 REALES

SILVER
c/m: LCM and MVA/1812 on Chihuahua KM#123.

KM#	Date	Year	Good	VG	Fine	VF
292	1812	1810 RP	—	—	—	—

c/m: LCM and MVA 1812 on Chihuahua KM#110.

KM#	Date	Year	Good	VG	Fine	VF
A293	1812	1810 HJ	—	—	—	—

c/m: LCM and MVA 1812 on Chihuahua KM#111.1.

KM#	Date	Year	Good	VG	Fine	VF
293	1812	(1817)	200.00	300.00	550.00	850.00
	1812	(1818)	200.00	300.00	550.00	850.00

NOTE: KM293 represents questionable issues - as the host date is later than the c/m date. However, there is no documentation existing to indicate for how long or even when these c/m's were applied.

L.V.A./Morelos
8 REALES

SILVER
c/m: Script LVA and Morelos monogram Type A on cast Mexico City KM#110.

KM#	Date	Year	Good	VG	Fine	VF
294	ND	HJ	45.00	75.00	135.00	250.00

L.V.S./MVA-1812
8 REALES

SILVER
c/m: L.V.S. and MVA/1812 on Chihuahua KM#111.1.

KM#	Date	Year	Good	VG	Fine	VF
A295	1812	(1817)	400.00	650.00	1000.	1500.

NOTE: KM#295 represents a questionable issue - as the host date is later than the c/m date. However, there is no documentation existing to indicate for how long or even when these c/m's were applied.

M.d.S./S.C.M.
2 REALES

SILVER
c/m: M.d.S. (Militar del Sur) and eagle w/S.C.M. (Soberano Congreso Mexicano) on Mexico City 2 Reales.

KM#	Date		Good	VG	Fine	VF
295	ND		—	250.00	450.00	650.00	—

OSORNO/VILLAGRAN
8 REALES

SILVER
c/m: Osorno monogram and VILLA/GRAN on cast Mexico City KM#110.

KM#	Date	Year	Good	VG	Fine	VF
296	ND	1809 TH	—	—	—	—

S.J.N.G./VTIL
8 REALES

SILVER
c/m: S.J.N.G. and VTIL on Zacatecas KM#191.

KM#	Date	Year	Good	VG	Fine	VF
298	ND	—	35.00	50.00	75.00	200.00

EMPIRE OF ITURBIDE

RULERS

Augustin I Iturbide, 1822-1823

MINT MARKS

Mo - Mexico City

ASSAYERS INITIALS

JA - Jose Garcia Ansaldo, 1812-1833
JM - Joaquin Davila Madrid, 1809-1833

1/8 REAL

COPPER
Mint: Nueva Viscaya

KM#	Date	Mintage	Good	VG	Fine	VF
299	1821	—	22.50	50.00	85.00	150.00
	1822	—	6.00	12.50	25.00	45.00
	1823	—	6.00	12.50	25.00	45.00

1/4 REAL

COPPER
Mint: Nueva Viscaya

KM#	Date	Mintage	Good	VG	Fine	VF
300	1822	—	150.00	275.00	400.00	500.00

1/2 REAL

.903 SILVER
Mint mark: Mo

KM#	Date	Mintage	Fine	VF	XF	Unc
301	1822 JM	—	17.50	30.00	60.00	300.00
	1823 JM	—	12.50	25.00	50.00	250.00

REAL

.903 SILVER
Mint mark: Mo

KM#	Date	Mintage	Fine	VF	XF	Unc
302	1822 JM	—	50.00	110.00	225.00	800.00

2 REALES

.903 SILVER
Mint mark: Mo

KM#	Date	Mintage	Fine	VF	XF	Unc
303	1822 JM	—	25.00	55.00	225.00	900.00
	1823 JM	—	20.00	45.00	175.00	800.00

8 REALES

.903 SILVER
Mint mark: Mo

KM#	Date	Mintage	Fine	VF	XF	Unc
304	1822 JM	—	45.00	95.00	250.00	900.00

Obv: Bust similar to 8 Escudos, KM#313.
Rev: Similar to KM#304.

KM#	Date	Mintage	Fine	VF	XF	Unc
305	1822 JM	—	—	—	Rare	—

Type I. Obv: Leg. divided. Rev: 8 R.J.M. at upper left of eagle.

KM#	Date	Mintage	Fine	VF	XF	Unc
306.1	1822 JM	—	60.00	145.00	350.00	1300.

Rev: Cross on crown.

KM#	Date	Mintage	Fine	VF	XF	Unc
306.2	1822 JM	—	—	—	Rare	—

Type II. Obv: Similar to KM#306.
Rev: Similar to KM#310.

KM#	Date	Mintage	Fine	VF	XF	Unc
307	1822 JM	—	135.00	325.00	550.00	2250.

Type III. Obv: Continuous leg. w/long smooth truncation. Rev: Similar to KM#306.

KM#	Date	Mintage	Fine	VF	XF	Unc
308	1822 JM	—	175.00	500.00	950.00	2000.

NOTE: Variety with long, straight truncation is valued at $5,000. in uncirculated condition.

Type IV. Obv: Similar to KM#308.
Rev: Similar to KM#310.

KM#	Date	Mintage	Fine	VF	XF	Unc
309	1822 JM	—	50.00	125.00	225.00	850.00

Type V. Obv. continuous leg. w/short irregular truncation. Rev: 8 R.J.M. below eagle.

KM#	Date	Mintage	Fine	VF	XF	Unc
310	1822 JM	—	50.00	125.00	200.00	900.00
	1823 JM	—	50.00	125.00	200.00	900.00

Type VI. Obv: Bust w/long truncation.
Rev: Similar to KM#310.

KM#	Date	Mintage	Fine	VF	XF	Unc
311	1822 JM	—	—	—	Rare	—

4 SCUDOS

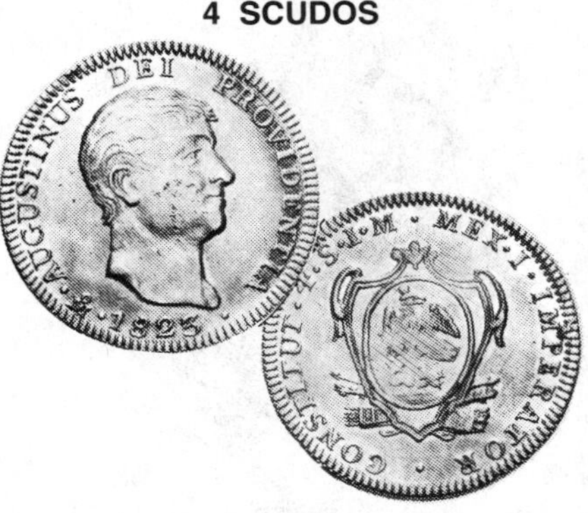

.875 GOLD
Mint mark: Mo

KM#	Date	Mintage	Fine	VF	XF	Unc
312	1823 JM	—	1000.	1750.	2750.	4500.

8 SCUDOS

.875 GOLD
Mint mark: Mo
Obv. leg: AUGUSTINUS.

KM#	Date	Mintage	Fine	VF	XF	Unc
313.1	1822 JM	—	1200.	2000.	3250.	—

NOTE: Superior Casterline sale 5-89 choice AU realized $11,000.

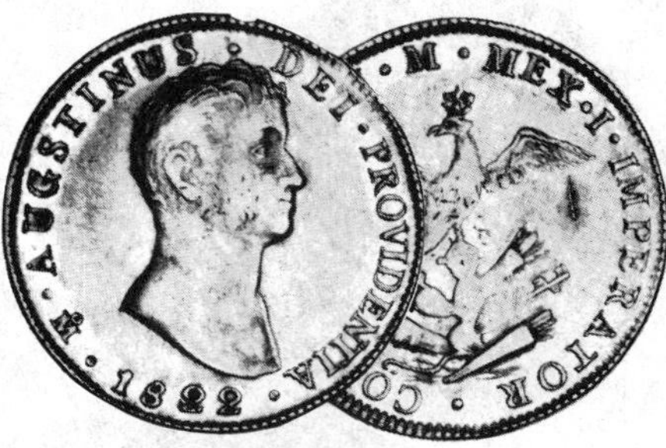

Obv. leg: AUGSTINUS (error).

KM#	Date	Mintage	Fine	VF	XF	Unc
313.2	1822 JM	—	1250.	2250.	3750.	—

KM#	Date	Mintage	Fine	VF	XF	Unc
314	1823 JM	—	1000.	1800.	3000.	4500.

REPUBLIC

MINT MARKS

A, AS - Alamos
CE - Real de Catorce
CA,CH - Chihuahua
C, Cn, Gn(error) - Culiacan
D, Do - Durango
EoMo - Estado de Mexico
Ga - Guadalajara
GC - Guadalupe y Calvo
G, Go - Guanajuato
H, Ho - Hermosillo
M, Mo - Mexico City
O, OA - Oaxaca
SLP, PI, P, I/P - San Luis Potosi
Z, Zs - Zacatecas

ASSAYERS INITIALS

ALAMOS MINT

Initials	Years	Mintmaster
PG	1862-1868	Pascual Gaxiola
DL, L	1866-1879	Domingo Larraguibel
AM	1872-1874	Antonio Moreno
ML, L	1878-1895	Manuel Larraguibel

REAL DE CATORCE MINT

Initials	Years	Mintmaster
ML	1863	Mariano Leon

CHIHUAHUA MINT

Initials	Years	Mintmaster
MR	1831-1834	Mariano Cristobal Ramirez
AM	1833-1839	Jose Antonio Mucharraz
MJ	1832	Jose Mariano Jimenez
RG	1839-1856	Rodrigo Garcia
JC	1856-1865	Joaquin Campa
BA	1858	Bruno Arriada
FP	1866	Francisco Potts
JG	1866-1868	Jose Maria Gomez del Campo
MM, M	1868-1895	Manuel Merino
AV	1873-1880	Antonio Valero
EA	1877	Eduardo Avila
JM	1877	Jacobo Mucharraz
GR	1877	Guadalupe Rocha
MG	1880-1882	Manuel Gameros

CULIACAN MINT

Initials	Years	Mintmaster
CE	1846-1870	Clemente Espinosa de los Monteros
C	1870	???
PV	1860-1861	Pablo Viruega
MP, P	1871-1876	Manuel Onofre Parodi
GP	1876	Celso Gaxiola & Manuel Onofre Parodi
CG, G	1876-1878	Celso Gaxiola
JD, D	1878-1882	Juan Dominguez
AM, M	1882-1899	Antonio Moreno
F	1870	Fernando Ferrari
JQ, Q	1899-1903	Jesus S. Quiroz

DURANGO MINT

Initials	Years	Mintmaster
RL	1825-1832	???
RM	1830-1848	Ramon Mascarenas
OMC	1840	Octavio Martinez de Castro
CM	1848-1876	Clemente Moron
JMR	1849-1852,	Jose Maria Ramirez
CP, P	1853-1864, 1867-1873	Carlos Leon de la Pena
LT	1864-1865	???
JMP, P	1877	Carlos Miguel de la Palma
PE, E	1878	Pedro Espejo
TB, B	1878-1880	Trinidad Barrera
JP	1880-1894	J. Miguel Palma
MC, C	1882-1890	Manuel M. Canseco or Melchor Calderon
JB	1885	Jacobo Blanco
ND, D	1892-1895	Norberto Dominguez

ESTADO DE MEXICO MINT

Initials	Years	Mintmaster
L	1828-1830	Luis Valazquez de la Cadena
F	1828-1830	Francisco Parodi

GUADALAJARA MINT

Initials	Years	Mintmaster
FS	1818-1835	Francisco Suarez
JM	1830-1832	???
JG	1836-1839 1842-1867	Juan de Dios Guzman
MC	1839-1846	Manuel Cueras
JM	1867-1869	Jesus P. Manzano
IC, C	1869-1877	Ignacio Canizo y Soto
MC	1874-1875	Manuel Contreras
JA, A	1877-1881	Julio Arancivia
FS, S	1880-1882	Fernando Sayago
TB, B	1883-1884	Trinidad Barrera
AH, H	1884-1885	Antonio Hernandez y Prado
JS, S	1885-1895	Jose S. Schiafino

GUADALUPE Y CALVO MINT

Initials	Years	Mintmaster
MP	1844-1852	Manuel Onofre Parodi

GUANAJUATO MINT

Initials	Years	Mintmaster
JJ	1825-1826	Jose Mariano Jimenez
MJ, MR, JM, PG, PJ, PF		???
PM	1841-1848, 1853-1861	Patrick Murphy
YF	1862-1868	Yldefonso Flores
YE	1862-1863	Ynocencio Espinoza
FR	1870-1878	Faustino Ramirez
SB, RR	???	
RS	1891-1900	Rosendo Sandoval

HERMOSILLO MINT

Initials	Years	Mintmaster
PP	1835-1836	Pedro Peimbert
FM	1871-1876	Florencio Monteverde
MP	1866	Manuel Onofre Parodi
PR	1866-1875	Pablo Rubio
R	1874-1875	Pablo Rubio
GR	1877	Guadalupe Rocha
AF, F	1876-1877	Alejandro Fourcade
JA, A	1877-1883	Jesus Acosta
FM, M	1883-1886	Fernando Mendez
FG, G	1886-1895	Fausto Gaxiola

MEXICO CITY MINT

Because of the great number of assayers for this mint (Mexico City is a much larger mint than any of the others) there is much confusion as to which initial stands for which assayer at any one time. Therefore we feel that it would be of no value to list the assayers.

OAXACA MINT

Initials	Years	Mintmaster
AE	1859-1891	Agustin Endner
E	1889-1890	Agustin Endner
FR	1861-1864	Francisco de la Rosa
EN	1890	Eduardo Navarro Luna
N	1890	Eduardo Navarro Luna

POTOSI MINT

Initials	Years	Mintmaster
JS	1827-1842	Juan Sanabria
AM	1838,1843-1849	Jose Antonio Mucharraz
PS	1842-1843,1848-1849, 1857-1861,1867-1870	Pompaso Sanabria
S	1869-1870	Pomposo Sanabria
MC	1849-1859	Mariano Catano
RO	1859-1865	Romualdo Obregon
MH, H	1870-1885	Manuel Herrera Razo
O	1870-1873	Juan R. Ochoa
CA, G	1867-1870	Carlos Aguirre Gomez
BE, E	1879-1881	Blas Escontria
LC, C	1885-1886	Luis Cuevas
MR, R	1886-1893	Mariano Reyes

ZACATECAS MINT

Initials	Years	Mintmaster
A	1825-1829	Adalco
Z	1825-1826	Mariano Zaldivar
V	1824-1831	Jose Mariano Vela
O	1829-1867	Manuel Ochoa
M	1831-1867	Manuel Miner
VL	1860-1866	Vicente Larranaga
JS	1867-1868, 1876-1886	J.S. de Santa Ana
YH	1868-1874	Ygnacio Hierro
JA	1874-1876	Juan H. Acuna
FZ	1886-1905	Francisco de P. Zarate

Die Varieties

Similar basic designs were utilized by all the Mexican mints but many variations are noticeable, particularly in the eagle, cactus and sprays.

1835 Durango, 8 Escudos

A large winged eagle was portrayed on the earlier coinage of the new republic.

1849 Mexico City, 8 Escudos

The later eagle featured undersized wings.

1844 Durango, 8 Escudos

The early renditions of the hand held Liberty cap over open book were massive in the gold escudo series.

1864 Durango, 8 Escudos

A finer more petite style was adopted later on in the gold escudo series.

State and Federal Issues

1/16 REAL

(Medio Octavo)

COPPER
Mint: Jalisco
Obv. leg: DEPARTAMENTO DE JALISCO

KM#	Date	Mintage	Good	VG	Fine	VF
316	1860	—	3.00	5.00	10.00	50.00
	Obv. leg: ESTADO LIBRE DE JALISCO					
317	1861	—	2.50	4.00	8.50	42.50

Mint: Mexico City
Obv. leg: REPUBLICA MEXICANA

KM#	Date	Mintage	VG	Fine	VF	XF
315	1831	—	10.00	15.00	35.00	100.00
	1832/1	—	12.00	17.50	35.00	125.00
	1832	—	10.00	15.00	35.00	100.00
	1833	—	8.50	15.00	35.00	100.00
	BRASS					
315a	1832	—	13.50	22.50	60.00	150.00
	1833	—	10.00	17.50	50.00	100.00
	1835	—	400.00	800.00	1250.	2500.

1/8 REAL

(Octavo Real)

COPPER
Mint: Chihuahua
Obv. leg: ESTADO SOBERANO DE CHIHUAHUA

KM#	Date	Mintage	Good	VG	Fine	VF
318	1833	—	—	—	Rare	—
	1834	—	—	—	Rare	—
	1835/3	—	—	—	Rare	—

Obv. leg: ESTADO DE CHIHUAHUA

KM#	Date	Mintage	Good	VG	Fine	VF
319	1855	—	3.50	5.00	18.00	60.00

Mint: Durango
Rev. leg: LIBERTAD

KM#	Date	Mintage	Good	VG	Fine	VF
320	1824	—	5.00	10.00	35.00	100.00
	1828	—	150.00	250.00	400.00	1000.

NOTE: These pieces were frequently struck over 1/8 Real, dated 1821-23 of Nueva Vizcaya. All known examples with these host dates are collectable contemporary counterfeits.

Rev. leg: OCTo.DE.R.DE DO., date.

KM#	Date	Mintage	Good	VG	Fine	VF
321	1828	—	6.00	15.00	35.00	100.00

Obv. leg: ESTADO DE DURANGO

KM#	Date	Mintage	Good	VG	Fine	VF
322	1833	—	—	—	Rare	—

Obv. leg: REPUBLICA MEXICANA

KM#	Date	Mintage	Good	VG	Fine	VF
323	1842/33	—	13.50	20.00	40.00	115.00
	1842	—	8.50	15.00	32.50	100.00

Obv. leg: REPUBLICA MEXICANA
Rev. leg: DEPARTAMENTO DE DURANGO

KM#	Date	Mintage	Good	VG	Fine	VF
324	1845	—	22.50	50.00	100.00	250.00
	1846	—	—	—	Rare	—
	1847	—	3.50	5.00	9.00	32.50

Obv. leg: REPUBLICA MEXICANA
Rev. leg: ESTADO DE DURANGO

KM#	Date	Mintage	Good	VG	Fine	VF
325	1851	—	3.50	6.50	10.00	30.00
	1852/1	—	3.50	6.50	10.00	30.00
	1852	—	3.00	5.00	8.00	30.00
	1854	—	6.00	10.00	17.50	65.00

 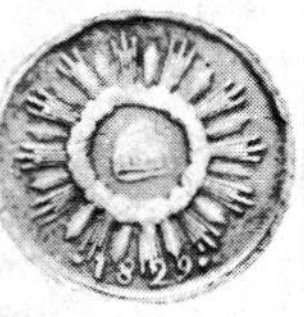

Mint: Guanajuato
Obv. leg: ESTADO LIBRE DE GUANAJUATO

KM#	Date	Mintage	Good	VG	Fine	VF
326	1829	—	3.00	5.00	10.00	25.00
	1829 error w/GUANJUATO					
		—	4.00	6.50	12.50	27.50
	1830	—	7.50	12.00	20.00	75.00

BRASS, 29mm

KM#	Date	Mintage	Good	VG	Fine	VF
327	1856	—	7.50	12.00	20.00	75.00

25mm

KM#	Date	Mintage	Good	VG	Fine	VF
328	1856	—	3.50	6.00	10.00	30.00
	1857	—	3.50	6.00	10.00	30.00

COPPER

KM#	Date	Mintage	Good	VG	Fine	VF
328a	1857	—	8.50	20.00	35.00	60.00

Mint: Jalisco
Obv. leg: ESTADO LIBRE DE JALISCO

KM#	Date	Mintage	Good	VG	Fine	VF
329	1828	—	3.00	5.00	8.00	22.50
	1831	—	100.00	200.00	300.00	400.00
	1832/28	—	3.50	5.50	9.00	25.00
	1832	—	3.50	5.50	9.00	25.00
	1833	—	3.50	5.50	9.00	25.00
	1834	—	50.00	100.00	175.00	300.00

KM#	Date	Mintage	Good	VG	Fine	VF
330	1856	—	4.00	7.00	10.00	25.00
	1857	—	4.00	7.00	10.00	25.00
	1858	—	4.00	7.00	10.00	25.00
	1861	—	100.00	200.00	300.00	400.00
	1862/1	—	4.00	7.00	10.00	25.00
	1862	—	4.00	7.00	10.00	25.00

Obv. leg: DEPARTAMENTO DE JALISCO

KM#	Date	Mintage	Good	VG	Fine	VF
331	1858	—	3.25	6.00	9.00	22.50
	1859	—	2.75	5.50	8.00	20.00
	1860/59	—	3.25	6.00	9.00	22.50
	1860	—	3.25	6.00	9.00	22.50
	1862	—	4.50	9.00	22.50	50.00

Mint: Mexico City
27mm
Obv. leg: REPUBLICA MEXICANA

KM#	Date	Mintage	VG	Fine	VF	XF
332	1829	—	450.00	900.00	1500.	2500.

21mm
Obv. leg: REPUBLICA MEXICANA

KM#	Date	Mintage	Good	VG	Fine	VF
333	1829	—	7.50	12.00	25.00	55.00
	1830	—	1.00	2.00	5.00	15.00
	1831	—	1.50	3.50	6.00	20.00
	1832	—	1.50	3.50	6.00	20.00
	1833/2	—	1.50	3.50	6.00	20.00
	1833	—	1.50	2.75	5.00	15.00
	1834	—	1.50	2.75	5.00	15.00
	1835/4	—	1.75	3.50	6.00	20.00
	1835	—	1.50	2.75	5.00	15.00

Obv. leg: LIBERTAD

KM#	Date	Mintage	Good	VG	Fine	VF
334	1841	—	6.00	15.00	30.00	75.00
	1842	—	2.50	5.00	10.00	30.00
	1850	—	12.50	20.00	30.00	80.00
	1861	—	5.00	12.00	25.00	70.00

Mint: Occidente
Obv. leg: ESTADO DE OCCIDENTE

KM#	Date	Mintage	Good	VG	Fine	VF
335	1828 reverse S					
		—	13.50	28.50	45.00	100.00
	1829	—	13.50	28.50	45.00	100.00

Mint: Potosi
Obv. leg: ESTADO LIBRE DE SAN LUIS POTOSI

KM#	Date	Mintage	Good	VG	Fine	VF
336	1829	—	6.00	9.00	15.00	50.00
	1830	—	8.00	12.00	20.00	60.00
	1831	—	5.00	8.00	12.00	40.00
	1859	—	5.00	8.00	12.00	40.00
	1865/1	—	— Reported, not confirmed			

Mint: Sonora
Obv. leg: ESTO LIBE Y SOBO DE SONORA, 28mm.

KM#	Date	Mintage	Good	VG	Fine	VF
337	1859	—	—	Rare	—	—

Mint: Zacatecas
Obv. leg: ESTo LIBe FEDo DE ZACATECAS

KM#	Date	Mintage	Good	VG	Fine	VF
338	1825	—	3.00	5.50	12.00	25.00
	1827	—	3.00	5.50	12.00	25.00
	1827 inverted A for V in OCTAVO					
		—	12.00	20.00	40.00	100.00
	1829	—	—	—	Rare	—
	1830	—	2.75	5.00	8.00	20.00
	1831	—	4.50	6.75	13.50	27.50
	1832	—	2.75	5.00	8.00	20.00
	1833	—	2.75	5.00	8.00	20.00
	1835	—	3.50	6.00	10.00	25.00
	1846	—	3.50	6.00	10.00	25.00
	1851	—	125.00	175.00	250.00	350.00
	1852	—	3.50	6.00	10.00	25.00
	1858	—	2.75	5.00	8.00	20.00
	1859	—	2.75	5.00	8.00	20.00
	1862	—	2.75	5.00	8.00	20.00
	1863 reversed 6 in date					
		—	2.75	5.00	8.00	20.00

 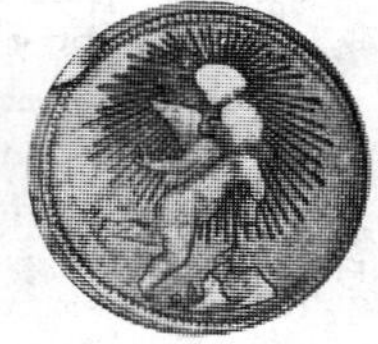

Obv. leg: DEPARTAMENTO DE ZACATECAS

KM#	Date	Mintage	Good	VG	Fine	VF
339	1836	—	4.00	8.00	15.00	40.00
	1845	—	6.00	10.00	20.00	50.00
	1846	—	5.00	9.00	18.50	45.00

1/4 REAL

(Un Quarto/Una Quartilla)
(Copper/Brass Series)

COPPER
Mint: Chihuahua
Obv. leg: ESTADO SOBERANO DE CHIHUAHUA

KM#	Date	Mintage	Good	VG	Fine	VF
340	1833	—	8.00	12.00	35.00	75.00
	1834	—	6.00	10.00	25.00	55.00
	1835	—	5.00	8.00	12.00	50.00

Obv. leg: ESTADO LIBRE DE CHIHUAHUA

KM#	Date	Mintage	Good	VG	Fine	VF
341	1846	—	3.50	6.00	12.00	50.00

NOTE: Varieties with or without fraction bar.

Obv. leg: ESTADO DE CHIHUAHUA

KM#	Date	Mintage	Good	VG	Fine	VF
342	1855	—	2.50	5.00	11.50	50.00
	1856	—	2.50	5.00	11.50	50.00

Obv. leg: DEPARTAMENTO DE CHIHUAHUA

KM#	Date	Mintage	Good	VG	Fine	VF
343	1855	—	3.00	5.00	10.00	50.00
	1855 DE (reversed D)	—	3.00	5.00	10.00	50.00

Obv. leg: E. CHIHA LIBERTAD

KM#	Date	Mintage	Good	VG	Fine	VF
344	1860	—	2.00	4.00	8.00	25.00
	1861	—	2.00	4.00	8.00	25.00
	1865/1	—	2.50	5.50	10.00	30.00
	1865	—	10.00	20.00	35.00	95.00
	1866/5	—	10.00	20.00	35.00	95.00
	1866	—	2.00	4.00	8.00	25.00

Mint: Durango
Obv. leg: REPUBLICA MEXICANA

KM#	Date	Mintage	Good	VG	Fine	VF
345	1845	—	—	—	Rare	—

Obv. leg: REPUBLICA MEXICANA
Rev: DURANGO, date, value.

KM#	Date	Mintage	Good	VG	Fine	VF
346	1858	—	—	—	Rare	—

Obv. leg: ESTADO DE DURANGO
Rev. leg: CONSTITUCION

KM#	Date	Mintage	Good	VG	Fine	VF
347	1858	—	3.00	6.50	13.50	50.00

NOTE: Variety exists in brass.

Obv. leg: DEPARTAMENTO DE DURANGO
Rev. leg: LIBERTAD EN EL ORDEN.

KM#	Date	Mintage	Good	VG	Fine	VF
348	1860	—	2.00	5.00	13.50	38.50
	1866	—	2.00	5.00	13.50	38.50

Obv. leg: ESTADO DE DURANGO
Rev. leg: INDEPENDENCIA Y LIBERTAD

KM#	Date	Mintage	Good	VG	Fine	VF
349	1866	—	2.75	6.00	15.00	45.00

Rev. leg: SUFRAGIO LIBRE

KM#	Date	Mintage	Good	VG	Fine	VF
350	1872	—	2.00	4.00	10.00	22.50

NOTE: Variety exists in brass.

Mint: Guanajuato
Obv. leg: ESTADO LIBRE DE GUANAJUATO

KM#	Date	Mintage	Good	VG	Fine	VF
351	1828	—	3.75	7.00	11.00	40.00
	1828 error w/GUANJUATO	—	3.75	7.00	11.00	40.00
	1829	—	4.50	9.00	13.50	40.00

Obv. leg: EST. LIB. DE GUANAXUATO
Rev. leg: OMNIA VINCIT LABOR

KM#	Date	Mintage	Good	VG	Fine	VF
352	1856	—	12.00	25.00	50.00	100.00
	1857	—	6.00	9.00	15.00	45.00

BRASS

KM#	Date	Mintage	Good	VG	Fine	VF
352a	1856	—	3.25	6.75	11.00	27.50
	1857	—	3.25	6.75	11.00	27.50

COPPER
Mint: Jalisco
Obv. leg: ESTADO LIBRE DE JALISCO

KM#	Date	Mintage	Good	VG	Fine	VF
353	1828	—	3.25	6.00	12.00	35.00
	1829/8	—	2.50	5.00	8.00	35.00
	1829	—	2.50	5.00	8.00	35.00
	1830/20	—	2.50	5.00	8.00	30.00
	1830/29	—	2.50	5.00	8.00	30.00
	1830	—	2.50	5.00	8.00	30.00
	1831	—	—	—	Rare	—
	1832/20	—	2.50	5.00	8.00	30.00
	1832/28	—	2.50	5.00	8.00	30.00
	1832	—	2.50	5.00	8.00	30.00
	1833/2	—	2.50	5.00	8.00	30.00
	1834	—	2.50	5.00	8.00	30.00
	1835/3	—	2.50	5.00	8.00	30.00
	1835	—	2.50	5.00	8.00	30.00
	1836	—	—	—	Rare	—

Obv. leg: DEPARTAMENTO DE JALISCO

KM#	Date	Mintage	Good	VG	Fine	VF
354	1836	—	—	—	Rare	—

Obv. leg: ESTADO LIBRE DE JALISCO

KM#	Date	Mintage	Good	VG	Fine	VF
355	1858	—	3.00	5.00	8.00	20.00
	1861	—	3.00	5.00	10.00	25.00
	1862	—	3.00	5.00	8.00	20.00

Obv. leg: DEPARTAMENTO DE JALISCO

KM#	Date	Mintage	Good	VG	Fine	VF
356	1858	—	3.00	5.00	8.00	20.00
	1859/8	—	3.00	5.00	8.00	20.00
	1859	—	3.00	5.00	8.00	20.00
	1860	—	3.00	5.00	8.00	20.00

Mint: Mexico City
Obv. leg: REPUBLICA MEXICANA.

KM#	Date	Mintage	VG	Fine	VF	XF
357	1829	—	7.00	22.50	50.00	135.00

Reduced size.

KM#	Date	Mintage	VG	Fine	VF	XF
358	1829	—	12.00	25.00	50.00	150.00
	1830	—	1.50	2.75	4.50	10.00
	1831	—	1.50	2.75	4.50	10.00
	1832	—	5.50	10.00	20.00	35.00
	1833	—	1.50	2.75	4.50	10.00
	1834/3	—	1.50	2.75	4.50	10.00

KM#	Date	Mintage	VG	Fine	VF	XF
358	1834	—	1.50	2.75	4.50	10.00
	1835	—	1.50	2.75	4.50	10.00
	1836	—	1.50	2.75	4.50	10.00
	1837	—	6.50	13.50	22.50	45.00
	BRASS **c/m: JM**					
358a.1	1831	—	8.00	15.00	35.00	75.00
	W/o countermark					
358a.2	1831	—	—	—	—	—

COPPER
Mint: Potosi
Obv. leg: ESTADO LIBRE DE SAN LUIS POTOSI
Rev. leg: MEXICO LIBRE

KM#	Date	Mintage	Good	VG	Fine	VF
359	1828	—	2.50	4.00	6.75	15.00
	1829	—	2.50	4.00	6.75	15.00
	1830	—	2.50	4.00	6.75	15.00
	1832	—	2.50	4.00	6.75	15.00
	1859 large LIBRE	—	2.50	4.00	6.75	15.00
	1859 small LIBRE	—	2.50	4.00	6.75	15.00
	1860	—	2.50	4.00	6.75	15.00

Rev. leg: REPUBLICA MEXICANA

KM#	Date	Mintage	Good	VG	Fine	VF
360	1862	1,367	2.50	4.00	6.75	13.50
	1862 LIBR	Inc. Ab.	2.50	4.00	6.75	13.50

Milled edge
Obv. leg: ESTADO LIBRE Y SOBERANO DE S.L. POTOSI
Rev. leg: LIBERTAD Y REFORMA

KM#	Date	Mintage	Good	VG	Fine	VF
361	1867	3.177	2.50	3.75	7.00	18.50
	1867 AFG	I.A.	2.50	3.75	7.00	18.50
	Plain edge					
362	1867	Inc. Ab.	2.50	3.75	7.00	18.50
	1867 AFG	I.A.	2.50	3.75	7.00	18.50

Mint: Sinaloa
Obv. leg: ESTADO LIBRE Y SOBERANO DE SINALOA

KM#	Date	Mintage	Good	VG	Fine	VF
363	1847	—	3.50	5.50	9.00	20.00
	1848	—	3.50	5.50	9.00	20.00
	1859	—	3.00	4.50	6.00	13.50
	1861	—	1.50	3.00	4.00	9.00
	1862	—	1.50	3.00	4.00	9.00
	1863	—	2.50	4.00	5.00	10.00
	1864/3	—	2.50	4.00	5.00	10.00
	1864	—	1.50	3.00	4.00	9.00
	1865	—	3.00	5.50	7.00	15.00
	1866/5	7.401	2.50	3.50	5.00	10.00
	1866	Inc. Ab.	1.50	3.00	4.00	9.00
	BRASS					
363a	1847	—	5.00	10.00	20.00	50.00

COPPER
Mint: Sonora
Obv. leg: EST.D.SONORA UNA CUART

KM#	Date	Mintage	Good	VG	Fine	VF
364	1831	—	—	—	Rare	—
	1832	—	3.00	5.00	13.50	50.00
	1833/2	—	2.00	4.00	11.00	37.50
	1833	—	2.00	4.00	11.00	37.50
	1834	—	2.00	4.00	11.00	37.50
	1835/3	—	2.00	4.00	11.00	37.50
	1835	—	2.00	4.00	11.00	37.50
	1836	—	2.00	4.00	11.00	37.50

Obv. leg: ESTO.LIBE.Y SOBO.DE SONORA

KM#	Date	Mintage	Good	VG	Fine	VF
365	1859	—	2.00	5.00	8.00	20.00
	1861/59	—	3.00	6.50	11.00	25.00
	1861	—	2.00	5.00	8.00	20.00
	1862	—	2.00	5.00	8.00	20.00
	1863/2	—	6.00	15.00	30.00	50.00

BRASS
Mint: Zacatecas
Obv. leg: ESTO LIBE FEDO DE ZACATECAS

KM#	Date	Mintage	Good	VG	Fine	VF
366	1824	—	—	—	Rare	—
	1825	—	2.50	5.00	8.00	20.00
	1826	—	100.00	150.00	200.00	300.00
	1827/17	—	2.50	5.00	8.00	20.00
	1829	—	2.50	5.00	8.00	20.00
	1830	—	2.50	5.00	8.00	20.00
	1831	—	50.00	100.00	125.00	250.00
	1832	—	2.50	5.00	8.00	20.00
	1833	—	2.50	5.00	8.00	20.00
	1834	—	—	—	Rare	—
	1835	—	2.50	5.00	8.00	20.00
	1846	—	2.50	5.00	8.00	20.00
	1847	—	2.50	5.00	8.00	20.00
	1852	—	2.50	5.00	8.00	20.00
	1853	—	2.50	5.00	8.00	20.00
	1855	—	4.50	10.00	20.00	65.00
	1858	—	2.50	5.00	8.00	20.00
	1859	—	2.50	5.00	8.00	20.00
	1860	—	100.00	150.00	200.00	300.00
	1862/57	—	2.50	5.00	8.00	20.00
	1862/59/7	—	10.00	20.00	40.00	80.00
	1862	—	2.50	5.00	8.00	20.00
	1863/2	—	2.50	5.00	8.00	20.00
	1863	—	2.50	5.00	8.00	20.00
	1864/58	—	4.00	10.00	25.00	60.00

COPPER
Obv. leg: DEPARTAMENTO DE ZACATECAS

KM#	Date	Mintage	Good	VG	Fine	VF
367	1836	—	4.00	8.50	13.50	25.00
	1845	—	—	—	Rare	—
	1846	—	3.50	6.75	9.00	20.00

SILVER SERIES

0.8450 g, .903 SILVER, .0245 oz ASW

KM#	Date	Mintage	VG	Fine	VF	XF
	Mint mark: CA					
368	1843 RG	—	75.00	125.00	300.00	500.00
	Mint mark: C					
368.1	1855 LR	—	50.00	100.00	200.00	400.00
	Mint mark: Do					
368.2	1842 LR	—	12.00	20.00	40.00	125.00
	1843 LR	—	20.00	25.00	60.00	150.00
	Mint mark: Ga					
368.3	1842 JG	—	2.50	5.50	8.00	20.00
	1843/2 JG	—	—	—	—	—
	1843 JG	—	6.00	9.00	12.50	30.00
	1843 MC	—	4.00	6.50	9.00	25.00
	1844 MC	—	4.00	6.50	9.00	25.00
	1844 LR	—	2.50	5.00	7.50	15.00
	1845 LR	—	2.50	4.50	7.50	15.00
	1846 LR	—	5.00	8.00	10.00	25.00
	1847 LR	—	4.00	6.50	9.00	25.00
	1848 LR	—	—	—	Rare	—
	1850 LR	—	—	—	Rare	—
	1851 LR	—	6.00	10.00	20.00	50.00
	1852 LR	—	50.00	100.00	135.00	200.00
	1854/3 LR	—	50.00	100.00	135.00	200.00
	1854 LR	—	5.00	10.00	12.50	30.00
	1855 LR	—	5.00	8.00	10.00	30.00
	1857 LR	—	6.50	10.00	15.00	27.50
	1862 LR	—	5.50	10.00	15.00	30.00
	Mint mark: GC					
368.4	1844 LR	—	50.00	75.00	125.00	200.00
	Mint mark: Go					
368.5	1842 PM	—	4.00	6.00	10.00	20.00
	1842 LR	—	2.00	4.00	8.00	15.00
	1843/2 LR	—	4.00	6.00	10.00	20.00
	1843 LR	—	2.00	4.00	8.00	15.00
	1844/3 LR	—	—	—	—	—
	1844 LR	—	2.00	4.00	8.00	15.00
	1845 LR	—	8.00	15.00	30.00	60.00
	1846/5 LR	—	—	—	—	—
	1846 LR	—	4.00	6.00	10.00	20.00
	1847 LR	—	2.00	4.00	8.00	15.00
	1848/7 LR	—	2.00	4.00	8.00	15.00
	1848 LR	—	2.00	4.00	8.00	15.00
	1849/7 LR	—	8.00	15.00	30.00	60.00
	1849 LR	—	2.00	4.00	8.00	15.00
	1850 LR	—	2.00	4.00	8.00	15.00
	1851 LR	—	2.00	4.00	8.00	15.00
	1852 LR	—	2.00	4.00	8.00	15.00
	1853 LR	—	2.00	4.00	8.00	15.00
	1855 LR	—	4.00	8.00	15.00	30.00
	1856/4 LR	—	—	—	—	—
	1856 LR	—	5.00	10.00	20.00	35.00
	1862/1 LR	—	3.00	5.00	10.00	20.00
	1862 LR	—	2.00	4.00	8.00	15.00
	1863 LR	—	2.00	4.00	8.00	15.00
	Mint mark: Mo					
368.6	1842 LR	—	2.00	4.00	8.00	15.00
	1843 LR	—	2.00	4.00	8.00	15.00
	1844/3 LR	—	8.00	12.00	20.00	40.00
	1844 LR	—	4.00	6.00	10.00	20.00
	1845 LR	—	4.00	6.00	10.00	20.00
	1846 LR	—	2.00	4.00	8.00	15.00
	1850 LR	—	5.00	10.00	20.00	35.00
	1858 LR	—	4.00	8.00	15.00	30.00
	1859 LR	—	4.00	6.00	10.00	20.00
	1860 LR	—	4.00	6.00	10.00	20.00
	1861 LR	—	4.00	6.00	10.00	20.00
	1862 LR	—	4.00	6.00	10.00	20.00
	1863/53 LR	—	—	—	—	—
	1863 LR	—	4.00	6.00	10.00	20.00
	Mint mark: S.L.Pi					
368.7	1842	—	2.00	4.00	8.00	15.00
	1843/2	—	4.00	6.00	10.00	20.00
	1843	—	2.00	4.00	8.00	15.00
	1844	—	2.00	4.00	8.00	15.00
	1845/3	—	4.00	6.00	10.00	25.00
	1845/4	—	4.00	6.00	10.00	25.00
	1845	—	2.00	4.00	8.00	15.00
	1847/5	—	4.00	6.00	10.00	20.00
	1847	—	2.00	4.00	8.00	15.00
	1851/47	—	4.00	8.00	15.00	30.00
	1854	—	125.00	200.00	275.00	400.00
	1856	—	4.00	8.00	15.00	30.00
	1857	—	5.00	10.00	20.00	35.00
	1862/57	—	10.00	20.00	40.00	85.00
	Mint mark: Zs					
368.8	1842/1 LR	—	4.00	8.00	15.00	30.00
	1842 LR	—	4.00	6.00	10.00	20.00

1/2 REAL

1.6900 g, .903 SILVER, .0490 oz ASW
Mint mark: Mo
Obv: Hooked-neck eagle.

KM#	Date	Mintage	Fine	VF	XF	Unc
369	1824 JM	—	40.00	60.00	125.00	500.00

Mint mark: A

KM#	Date	Mintage	Fine	VF	XF	Unc
370	1862 PG	—	—	—	Rare	—

Mint mark: Ca
Obv: Facing eagle.

KM#	Date	Mintage	Fine	VF	XF	Unc
370.1	1844 RG	—	75.00	125.00	175.00	275.00
	1845 RG	—	75.00	125.00	150.00	250.00

Mint mark: C, Co

KM#	Date	Mintage	Fine	VF	XF	Unc
370.2	1846 CE	—	30.00	50.00	75.00	150.00
	1848/7 CE	—	15.00	25.00	45.00	90.00
	1849/8 CE	—	15.00	25.00	45.00	90.00
	1849 CE	—	—	—	—	—
	1852 CE	—	12.50	20.00	40.00	80.00
	1853/1 CE	—	12.50	20.00	40.00	80.00
	1854 CE	—	20.00	35.00	50.00	100.00
	1856 CE	—	12.50	20.00	40.00	80.00
	1857/6 CE	—	20.00	35.00	50.00	100.00
	1857 CE	—	15.00	25.00	45.00	90.00
	1858 CE (error 1 for 1/2)	—	12.50	20.00	40.00	80.00
	1860/59 PV	—	20.00	35.00	50.00	100.00
	1860 PV	—	12.50	20.00	40.00	80.00
	1861 PV	—	12.50	20.00	40.00	80.00
	1863 CE (error 1 for 1/2)	—	15.00	25.00	45.00	90.00
	1867 CE	—	12.50	20.00	40.00	80.00
	1869 CE (error 1 for 1/2)	—	12.50	20.00	40.00	80.00

Mint mark: D, Do

KM#	Date	Mintage	Fine	VF	XF	Unc
370.3	1832 RM	—	125.00	225.00	350.00	600.00
	1832 RM/L	—	—	—	—	—
	1833/2 RM/L	—	75.00	100.00	150.00	225.00
	1833/1 RM/L	—	12.50	20.00	40.00	80.00
	1833 RM	—	25.00	40.00	75.00	150.00
	1834/1 RM	—	25.00	40.00	75.00	150.00
	1834 RM	—	12.50	20.00	40.00	80.00
	1837/1 RM	—	12.50	20.00	40.00	80.00
	1837/4 RM	—	12.50	20.00	40.00	80.00
	1837/6 RM	—	12.50	20.00	40.00	80.00
	1841/33 RM	—	15.00	25.00	50.00	100.00
	1842/32 RM	—	12.50	20.00	40.00	80.00
	1842 RM	—	12.50	20.00	40.00	80.00
	1842 RM 8R (error)	—	12.50	20.00	40.00	80.00
	1842 RM 1/2/8R	—	12.50	20.00	40.00	80.00
	1843/33 RM	—	15.00	25.00	50.00	100.00
	1843 RM	—	—	—	—	—
	1845/31 RM	—	12.50	20.00	40.00	80.00
	1845/34 RM	—	12.50	20.00	40.00	80.00
	1845/35 RM	—	12.50	20.00	40.00	80.00
	1845 RM	—	15.00	25.00	50.00	100.00
	1846 RM	—	30.00	50.00	80.00	200.00
	1848/5 RM	—	35.00	55.00	110.00	250.00
	1848/36 RM	—	25.00	40.00	75.00	200.00
	1849 JMR	—	25.00	40.00	75.00	200.00
	1850 RM	—	—	—	Rare	—
	1850 JMR	—	25.00	40.00	75.00	200.00
	1851 JMR	—	20.00	35.00	50.00	100.00
	1852/1 JMR	—	65.00	125.00	250.00	600.00
	1852 JMR	—	30.00	50.00	80.00	200.00
	1853 CP	—	12.50	20.00	40.00	80.00
	1854 CP	—	25.00	40.00	75.00	200.00
	1855 CP	—	25.00	40.00	60.00	150.00
	1856/5 CP	—	20.00	35.00	50.00	100.00
	1857 CP	—	20.00	35.00	50.00	100.00
	1858/7 CP	—	20.00	35.00	50.00	100.00
	1859 CP	—	20.00	35.00	50.00	100.00
	1860/59 CP	—	40.00	65.00	135.00	300.00
	1861 CP	—	125.00	200.00	300.00	600.00
	1862 CP	—	25.00	40.00	60.00	125.00
	1864 LT	—	50.00	100.00	200.00	450.00
	1869 CP	—	40.00	65.00	125.00	275.00

Mint mark: EoMo

KM#	Date	Mintage	Fine	VF	XF	Unc
370.4	1829 LF	—	175.00	300.00	500.00	1400.

Mint mark: Ga

KM#	Date	Mintage	Fine	VF	XF	Unc
370.5	1825 FS	—	25.00	40.00	75.00	150.00
	1826 FS	—	10.00	15.00	35.00	80.00
	1828/7 FS	—	12.50	20.00	40.00	90.00
	1829 FS	—	7.50	15.00	30.00	70.00
	1830/29 FS	—	40.00	60.00	100.00	200.00
	1831 LP	—	—	—	Rare	—
	1832 FS	—	10.00	20.00	35.00	80.00
	1834/3 FS	—	65.00	100.00	175.00	250.00
	1834 FS	—	10.00	20.00	35.00	80.00
	1835/4/3 FS/LP	—	15.00	25.00	40.00	90.00
	1837/6 JG	—	50.00	100.00	150.00	250.00
	1838/7 JG	—	15.00	25.00	40.00	90.00
	1839/8 JG/FS	—	35.00	75.00	150.00	250.00
	1839 MC	—	10.00	20.00	35.00	80.00
	1840/39 MC/JG	—	—	—	—	—
	1840 MC	—	15.00	25.00	40.00	90.00
	1841 MC	—	20.00	35.00	50.00	100.00
	1842/1 JG	—	15.00	25.00	40.00	90.00
	1842 JG	—	10.00	20.00	35.00	80.00

KM#	Date	Mintage	Fine	VF	XF	Unc
370.5	1843/2 JG	—	15.00	30.00	50.00	100.00
	1843 JG	—	10.00	20.00	35.00	80.00
	1843 MC/JG	—	10.00	20.00	35.00	80.00
	1843 MC	—	10.00	20.00	35.00	80.00
	1844 MC	—	10.00	20.00	35.00	80.00
	1845 MC	—	10.00	20.00	35.00	80.00
	1845 JG	—	10.00	20.00	35.00	80.00
	1846 MC	—	10.00	20.00	35.00	80.00
	1846 JG	—	10.00	20.00	35.00	80.00
	1847 JG	—	10.00	20.00	35.00	80.00
	1848/7 JG	—	10.00	20.00	35.00	80.00
	1849 JG	—	10.00	20.00	35.00	80.00
	1850/49 JG	—	—	—	—	—
	1850 JG	—	10.00	20.00	35.00	80.00
	1851/0 JG	—	10.00	20.00	35.00	80.00
	1852 JG	—	10.00	20.00	35.00	80.00
	1853 JG	—	10.00	20.00	35.00	80.00
	1854 JG	—	10.00	20.00	35.00	80.00
	1855/4 JG	—	10.00	20.00	35.00	80.00
	1855 JG	—	10.00	20.00	35.00	80.00
	1856 JG	—	10.00	20.00	35.00	80.00
	1857 JG	—	10.00	20.00	35.00	80.00
	1858/7 JG	—	10.00	20.00	35.00	80.00
	1858 JG	—	10.00	20.00	35.00	80.00
	1859/7 JG	—	10.00	20.00	35.00	80.00
	1860/59 JG	—	10.00	20.00	35.00	80.00
	1861 JG	—	5.00	12.50	25.00	60.00
	1862/1 JG	—	15.00	25.00	40.00	90.00

Mint mark: GC

KM#	Date	Mintage	Fine	VF	XF	Unc
370.6	1844 MP	—	50.00	100.00	150.00	350.00
	1845 MP	—	25.00	50.00	100.00	200.00
	1846 MP	—	25.00	50.00	100.00	200.00
	1847 MP	—	25.00	50.00	100.00	300.00
	1848 MP	—	20.00	40.00	75.00	150.00
	1849 MP	—	25.00	50.00	100.00	200.00
	1850 MP	—	30.00	60.00	125.00	250.00
	1851 MP	—	25.00	50.00	100.00	200.00

Mint mark: Go

KM#	Date	Mintage	Fine	VF	XF	Unc
370.7	1826 MJ	—	125.00	250.00	400.00	1000.
	1827/6 MJ	—	7.50	15.00	30.00	75.00
	1828/7 MJ	—	7.50	15.00	30.00	75.00
	1828 MJ denomination 2/1	—	—	—	—	—
	1828 JG	—	—	—	—	—
	1828 MR	—	50.00	100.00	150.00	250.00
	1829/8 MJ	—	5.00	10.00	25.00	50.00
	1829 MJ	—	5.00	10.00	25.00	50.00
	1829 MJ reversed N in MEXICANA	—	5.00	10.00	25.00	50.00
	1830 MJ	—	5.00	10.00	25.00	50.00
	1831/29 MJ	—	15.00	30.00	60.00	150.00
	1831 MJ	—	10.00	20.00	40.00	80.00
	1832/1 MJ	—	7.50	15.00	30.00	75.00
	1832 MJ	—	7.50	15.00	30.00	75.00
	1833 MJ round top 3	—	10.00	20.00	40.00	80.00
	1833 MJ flat top 3	—	10.00	20.00	40.00	80.00
	1834 PJ	—	5.00	10.00	25.00	50.00
	1835 PJ	—	5.00	10.00	25.00	50.00
	1836/5 PJ	—	7.50	15.00	30.00	75.00
	1836 PJ	—	5.00	10.00	25.00	50.00
	1837 PJ	—	5.00	10.00	25.00	50.00
	1838/7 PJ	—	5.00	10.00	25.00	50.00
	1839 PJ	—	5.00	10.00	25.00	50.00
	1839 PJ (error: REPUBLIGA)	—	5.00	10.00	25.00	50.00
	1840/39 PJ	—	7.50	10.00	25.00	75.00
	1840 PJ straight J	—	5.00	10.00	25.00	50.00
	1840 PJ curved J	—	5.00	10.00	25.00	50.00
	1841/31 PJ	—	5.00	10.00	25.00	50.00
	1841 PJ	—	5.00	10.00	25.00	50.00
	1842/1 PJ	—	5.00	10.00	25.00	50.00
	1842/1 PM	—	5.00	10.00	25.00	50.00
	1842 PM/J	—	5.00	10.00	25.00	50.00
	1842 PJ	—	5.00	10.00	25.00	50.00
	1842 PM	—	5.00	10.00	25.00	50.00
	1843/33 PM 1/2 over 8	—	5.00	10.00	25.00	50.00
	1843 PM convex wings	—	5.00	10.00	25.00	50.00
	1843 PM concave wings	—	5.00	10.00	25.00	50.00
	1844/3 PM	—	5.00	10.00	25.00	50.00
	1844 PM	—	10.00	20.00	40.00	90.00
	1845/4 PM	—	5.00	10.00	25.00	50.00
	1845 PM	—	5.00	10.00	25.00	50.00
	1846/4 PM	—	5.00	10.00	25.00	50.00
	1846/5 PM	—	5.00	10.00	25.00	50.00
	1846 PM	—	5.00	10.00	25.00	50.00
	1847/6 PM	—	7.50	15.00	30.00	60.00
	1847 PM	—	7.50	15.00	30.00	60.00
	1848/35 PM	—	5.00	10.00	25.00	50.00
	1848 PM	—	5.00	10.00	25.00	50.00
	1848 PF/M	—	5.00	10.00	25.00	50.00
	1849/39 PF	—	5.00	10.00	25.00	50.00
	1849 PF	—	5.00	10.00	25.00	50.00
	1849 PF (error: MEXCANA)	—	5.00	10.00	25.00	50.00
	1850 PF	—	5.00	10.00	25.00	50.00
	1851 PF	—	5.00	10.00	25.00	50.00
	1852/1 PF	—	5.00	10.00	25.00	50.00
	1852 PF	—	2.50	7.50	17.50	40.00
	1853 PF/R	—	5.00	10.00	25.00	50.00
	1853 PF	—	5.00	10.00	25.00	50.00
	1854 PF	—	5.00	10.00	25.00	50.00
	1855 PF	—	5.00	10.00	25.00	50.00

KM#	Date	Mintage	Fine	VF	XF	Unc
370.7	1856/4 PF	—	5.00	10.00	25.00	50.00
	1856/5 PF	—	5.00	10.00	25.00	50.00
	1856 PF	—	5.00	10.00	25.00	50.00
	1857/6 PF	—	5.00	10.00	25.00	50.00
	1857 PF	—	5.00	10.00	25.00	50.00
	1858/7 PF	—	7.50	15.00	30.00	60.00
	1858 PF	—	5.00	10.00	25.00	50.00
	1859 PF	—	5.00	10.00	25.00	50.00
	1860 PF small 1/2	—	5.00	10.00	25.00	50.00
	1860 PF large 1/2	—	5.00	10.00	25.00	50.00
	1860/59 PF	—	5.00	10.00	25.00	50.00
	1861 PF small 1/2	—	5.00	10.00	25.00	50.00
	1861 PF large 1/2	—	5.00	10.00	25.00	50.00
	1862/1 YE	—	5.00	10.00	25.00	50.00
	1862 YE	—	2.50	7.50	17.50	40.00
	1862 YF	—	5.00	10.00	25.00	50.00
	1867 YF	—	2.50	7.50	17.50	40.00
	1868 YF	—	2.50	7.50	17.50	40.00

NOTE: Varieties exist.

Mint mark: Ho

KM#	Date	Mintage	Fine	VF	XF	Unc
370.8	1839 PP	—	—	—	Unique	—
	1862 FM	—	500.00	650.00	1000.	—
	1867 PR/FM 6/inverted 6, & 7/1	—	100.00	175.00	250.00	500.00

Mint mark: Mo

KM#	Date	Mintage	Fine	VF	XF	Unc
370.9	1825 JM	—	10.00	20.00	40.00	80.00
	1826/5 JM	—	10.00	20.00	40.00	80.00
	1826 JM	—	5.00	10.00	20.00	60.00
	1827/6 JM	—	5.00	10.00	20.00	60.00
	1827 JM	—	5.00	10.00	20.00	60.00
	1828/7 JM	—	7.50	15.00	25.00	85.00
	1828 JM	—	10.00	20.00	40.00	90.00
	1829 JM	—	7.50	15.00	25.00	75.00
	1830 JM	—	5.00	10.00	20.00	60.00
	1831 JM	—	5.00	10.00	20.00	60.00
	1832 JM	—	7.50	12.50	27.50	60.00
	1833 MJ	—	7.50	12.50	27.50	60.00
	1834 ML	—	5.00	10.00	20.00	60.00
	1835 ML	—	5.00	10.00	20.00	60.00
	1836/5 ML/MF	—	7.50	15.00	25.00	65.00
	1836 ML	—	7.50	15.00	25.00	65.00
	1838 ML	—	5.00	10.00	20.00	60.00
	1839/8 ML	—	5.00	10.00	25.00	65.00
	1839 ML	—	5.00	10.00	20.00	50.00
	1840 ML	—	5.00	10.00	20.00	50.00
	1841 ML	—	5.00	10.00	20.00	50.00
	1842 ML	—	5.00	10.00	20.00	50.00
	1842 MM	—	5.00	10.00	20.00	50.00
	1843 MM	—	10.00	20.00	40.00	80.00
	1844 MF	—	5.00	10.00	20.00	50.00
	1845/4 MF	—	5.00	10.00	25.00	60.00
	1845 MF	—	5.00	10.00	20.00	50.00
	1846 MF	—	5.00	10.00	20.00	50.00
	1847 RC	—	10.00	20.00	40.00	80.00
	1848/7 GC/RC	—	5.00	10.00	20.00	50.00
	1849 GC	—	5.00	10.00	20.00	50.00
	1850 GC	—	5.00	10.00	20.00	50.00
	1851 GC	—	5.00	10.00	20.00	50.00
	1852 GC	—	5.00	10.00	20.00	50.00
	1853 GC	—	5.00	10.00	20.00	50.00
	1854 GC	—	5.00	10.00	20.00	50.00
	1855 GC	—	5.00	10.00	20.00	50.00
	1855 GF/GC	—	7.50	12.50	25.00	65.00
	1856/5 GF	—	7.50	12.50	25.00	65.00
	1857 GF	—	5.00	10.00	20.00	50.00
	1858 FH	—	3.00	5.00	12.50	40.00
	1858/9 FH	—	5.00	10.00	20.00	50.00
	1859 FH	—	3.00	6.00	15.00	50.00
	1860 FH/GC	—	5.00	10.00	20.00	50.00
	1860/59 FH	—	7.50	12.50	25.00	65.00
	1860 FH	—	3.00	6.00	15.00	50.00
	1860 TH	—	5.00	10.00	20.00	50.00
	1861 CH	—	3.00	6.00	15.00	45.00
	1862/52 CH	—	5.00	10.00	20.00	50.00
	1862 CH	—	3.00	6.00	15.00	45.00
	1863/55 TH/GC	—	5.00	10.00	20.00	50.00
	1863 CH/GC	—	5.00	10.00	20.00	50.00
	1863 CH	—	3.00	6.00	15.00	45.00

Mint mark: Pi

KM#	Date	Mintage	Fine	VF	XF	Unc
370.10	1831 JS	—	7.50	12.50	25.00	65.00
	1841/36 JS	—	20.00	40.00	75.00	125.00
	1842/1 PS	—	20.00	40.00	75.00	125.00
	1842/1 PS P/J	—	60.00	80.00	150.00	300.00
	1842 PS/JS	—	50.00	75.00	125.00	250.00
	1842 JS	—	20.00	40.00	75.00	125.00
	1843/2 PS	—	17.50	25.00	40.00	80.00
	1843 PS	—	15.00	25.00	35.00	70.00
	1843 AM	—	10.00	15.00	25.00	60.00
	1844 AM	—	10.00	15.00	30.00	65.00
	1845 AM	—	250.00	375.00	500.00	1500.
	1846/5 AM	—	40.00	75.00	125.00	200.00
	1847/6 AM	—	15.00	25.00	40.00	80.00
	1848 AM	—	15.00	25.00	40.00	80.00
	1849 MC/AM	—	15.00	25.00	40.00	80.00
	1849 MC	—	12.50	20.00	35.00	70.00
	1850/49 MC	—	—	—	—	—
	1850Pi MC	—	10.00	15.00	25.00	60.00
	1850P MC	—	—	—	—	—
	1851 MC	—	10.00	15.00	25.00	60.00

KM#	Date	Mintage	Fine	VF	XF	Unc
370.10	1852 MC	—	10.00	20.00	30.00	65.00
	1853 MC	—	7.50	12.50	20.00	60.00
	1854 MC	—	7.50	12.50	20.00	60.00
	1855 MC	—	15.00	20.00	35.00	70.00
	1856 MC	—	15.00	25.00	50.00	100.00
	1857 MC	—	7.50	12.50	20.00	60.00
	1857 PS	—	10.00	15.00	30.00	65.00
	1858 MC	—	12.50	20.00	35.00	70.00
	1858 PS	—	12.50	20.00	35.00	70.00
	1859 MC	—	—	—	Rare	—
	1860/59 PS	—	12.50	20.00	35.00	70.00
	1861 RO	—	10.00	15.00	30.00	60.00
	1862/1 RO	—	15.00	25.00	50.00	125.00
	1862 RO	—	15.00	25.00	50.00	125.00
	1863/2 RO	—	15.00	25.00	45.00	100.00

Mint mark: Z, Zs

KM#	Date	Mintage	Fine	VF	XF	Unc
370.11	1826 AZ	—	5.00	10.00	20.00	60.00
	1826 AO	—	5.00	10.00	20.00	60.00
	1827 AO	—	5.00	10.00	20.00	60.00
	1828/7 AO	—	5.00	10.00	20.00	60.00
	1829 AO	—	5.00	10.00	20.00	60.00
	1830 OV	—	5.00	10.00	20.00	60.00
	1831 OV	—	25.00	50.00	75.00	150.00
	1831 OM	—	5.00	10.00	20.00	60.00
	1832 OM	—	5.00	10.00	20.00	60.00
	1833 OM	—	5.00	10.00	20.00	60.00
	1834 OM	—	5.00	10.00	20.00	60.00
	1835/4 OM	—	5.00	10.00	20.00	60.00
	1835 OM	—	5.00	10.00	20.00	60.00
	1836 OM	—	5.00	10.00	20.00	60.00
	1837 OM	—	10.00	20.00	40.00	80.00
	1838 OM	—	5.00	10.00	20.00	60.00
	1839 OM	—	7.50	15.00	30.00	65.00
	1840 OM	—	10.00	25.00	45.00	90.00
	1841 OM	—	10.00	25.00	45.00	90.00
	1842/1 OM	—	5.00	10.00	20.00	60.00
	1842 OM	—	5.00	10.00	20.00	60.00
	1843 OM	—	40.00	75.00	115.00	250.00
	1844 OM	—	5.00	10.00	20.00	60.00
	1845 OM	—	5.00	10.00	20.00	60.00
	1846 OM	—	7.50	15.00	30.00	65.00
	1847 OM	—	5.00	10.00	20.00	50.00
	1848 OM	—	5.00	10.00	20.00	50.00
	1849 OM	—	5.00	10.00	20.00	50.00
	1850 OM	—	5.00	10.00	20.00	50.00
	1851 OM	—	5.00	10.00	20.00	50.00
	1852 OM	—	5.00	10.00	20.00	50.00
	1853 OM	—	5.00	10.00	20.00	50.00
	1854/3 OM	—	5.00	10.00	20.00	50.00
	1854 OM	—	5.00	10.00	20.00	50.00
	1855/3 OM	—	7.50	15.00	30.00	65.00
	1855 OM	—	5.00	10.00	20.00	50.00
	1856 OM	—	5.00	10.00	20.00	50.00
	1857 MO	—	5.00	10.00	20.00	50.00
	1858 MO	—	5.00	10.00	20.00	50.00
	1859 MO	—	6.00	8.50	17.50	35.00
	1859 VL	—	6.00	8.50	17.50	40.00
	1860/50 VL inverted A for V					
		—	5.00	10.00	20.00	50.00
	1860/59 VL inverted A for V					
			5.00	10.00	20.00	50.00
	1860 MO	—	5.00	10.00	20.00	50.00
	1860 VL	—	5.00	10.00	20.00	50.00
	1861/0 VL inverted A for V					
		—	7.50	15.00	30.00	65.00
	1861 VL inverted A for V					
		—	5.00	10.00	20.00	50.00
	1862 VL inverted A for V					
		—	5.00	10.00	20.00	50.00
	1863/1 VL inverted A for V					
		—	7.50	15.00	30.00	65.00
	1863 VL inverted A for V					
		—	5.00	10.00	20.00	50.00
	1869 YH	—	5.00	10.00	20.00	50.00

REAL

3.3800 g, .903 SILVER, .0981 oz ASW

Mint mark: Do

KM#	Date	Mintage	Fine	VF	XF	Unc
371	1824 RL	—	3250.	4000.	5250.	7500.

Mint mark: Ca

KM#	Date	Mintage	Fine	VF	XF	Unc
372	1844 RG	—	500.00	1000.	1500.	2750.
	1845 RG	—	500.00	1000.	1500.	2750.
	1855 RG	—	100.00	150.00	225.00	450.00

Mint mark: C

KM#	Date	Mintage	Fine	VF	XF	Unc
372.1	1846 CE	—	12.50	25.00	40.00	110.00
	1848 CE	—	12.50	25.00	40.00	110.00
	1850 CE	—	12.50	25.00	40.00	110.00
	1851/0 CE	—	12.50	25.00	40.00	110.00
	1852/1 CE	—	7.50	15.00	30.00	100.00
	1853/2 CE	—	7.50	15.00	30.00	100.00
	1854 CE	—	7.50	15.00	30.00	100.00
	1856 CE	—	40.00	65.00	100.00	225.00
	1857/4 CE	—	10.00	20.00	35.00	100.00
	1857/6 CE	—	10.00	20.00	35.00	100.00
	1858 CE	—	5.00	7.50	15.00	100.00
	1859 CE	—	—	—	—	—
	1860 PV	—	5.00	7.50	15.00	100.00
	1861 PV	—	5.00	7.50	15.00	100.00
	1863 CE					
	3 known		—	—	1650.	2250.
	1869 CE	—	5.00	7.50	15.00	100.00

Mint mark: Do

KM#	Date	Mintage	Fine	VF	XF	Unc
372.2	1832/1 RM	—	5.00	10.00	20.00	90.00
	1832 RM/RL	—	10.00	15.00	30.00	100.00
	1832 RM	—	5.00	10.00	20.00	100.00
	1834/24 RM/RL					
		—	15.00	25.00	50.00	150.00
	1834/3 RM/RL					
		—	15.00	25.00	50.00	150.00
	1834 RM	—	10.00	20.00	40.00	110.00
	1836/4 RM	—	5.00	7.50	15.00	100.00
	1836 RM	—	5.00	7.50	15.00	100.00
	1837 RM	—	12.50	20.00	40.00	110.00
	1841 RM	—	7.50	15.00	30.00	100.00
	1842/32 RM	—	10.00	20.00	40.00	110.00
	1842 RM	—	7.50	15.00	30.00	100.00
	1843 RM	—	5.00	7.50	15.00	100.00
	1844/34 RM	—	15.00	25.00	45.00	125.00
	1845 RM	—	5.00	7.50	15.00	100.00
	1846 RM	—	7.50	15.00	30.00	100.00
	1847 RM	—	10.00	15.00	35.00	100.00
	1848/31 RM	—	10.00	15.00	35.00	100.00
	1848/33 RM	—	10.00	15.00	35.00	100.00
	1848/5 RM	—	10.00	15.00	35.00	100.00
	1848 RM	—	7.50	12.50	20.00	100.00
	1849/8 CM	—	10.00	15.00	30.00	100.00
	1850 JMR	—	15.00	25.00	45.00	125.00
	1851 JMR	—	15.00	25.00	45.00	120.00
	1852 JMR	—	15.00	25.00	45.00	120.00
	1853 CP	—	12.50	20.00	35.00	100.00
	1854/1 CP	—	10.00	15.00	25.00	100.00
	1854 CP	—	7.50	12.50	20.00	100.00
	1855 CP	—	10.00	15.00	25.00	100.00
	1856 CP	—	12.50	20.00	35.00	100.00
	1857 CP	—	12.50	20.00	35.00	100.00
	1858 CP	—	12.50	20.00	35.00	100.00
	1859 CP	—	7.50	12.50	20.00	100.00
	1860/59 CP	—	10.00	15.00	25.00	100.00
	1861 CP	—	15.00	25.00	40.00	110.00
	1862/1 CP	—	225.00	300.00	450.00	1250.
	1864 LT	—	15.00	25.00	40.00	110.00

Mint mark: EoMo

KM#	Date	Mintage	Fine	VF	XF	Unc
372.3	1828 LF	—	200.00	300.00	450.00	1500.

Mint mark: Ga

KM#	Date	Mintage	Fine	VF	XF	Unc
372.4	1826 FS	—	15.00	30.00	50.00	125.00
	1828/7 FS	—	15.00	30.00	50.00	125.00
	1829/8/7 FS	—	—	—	—	—
	1829 FS	—	15.00	30.00	50.00	125.00
	1830 FS	—	250.00	350.00	500.00	—
	1831 LP	—	15.00	30.00	50.00	125.00
	1831 LP/FS	—	300.00	450.00	600.00	—
	1832 FS	—	250.00	350.00	500.00	—
	1833/2 G FS	—	100.00	150.00	275.00	550.00
	1833 FS	—	75.00	125.00	225.00	500.00
	1834/3 FS	—	75.00	125.00	225.00	500.00
	1835 FS	—	—	—	—	—
	1837/6 JG/FS					
		—	12.50	20.00	35.00	100.00
	1838/7 JG/FS					
		—	12.50	20.00	35.00	100.00
	1839 JG	—	250.00	350.00	500.00	—
	1840 JG	—	12.50	20.00	35.00	100.00
	1840 MC	—	7.50	12.50	25.00	70.00
	1841 MC	—	50.00	75.00	125.00	250.00
	1842/0 JG/MC					
		—	10.00	15.00	30.00	100.00
	1842 JG	—	7.50	12.50	20.00	100.00
	1843 JG	—	150.00	200.00	300.00	750.00
	1843 MC	—	5.00	7.50	15.00	100.00
	1844 MC	—	7.50	12.50	20.00	100.00
	1845 MC	—	10.00	15.00	25.00	100.00
	1845 JG	—	5.00	7.50	20.00	100.00
	1846 JG	—	12.50	20.00	35.00	100.00
	1847/6 JG	—	10.00	15.00	25.00	100.00
	1847 JG	—	10.00	15.00	25.00	100.00
	1848 JG	—	400.00	550.00	700.00	—
	1849 JG	—	7.50	12.50	20.00	100.00
	1850 JG	—	175.00	275.00	400.00	—
	1851 JG	—	10.00	15.00	25.00	100.00
	1852 JG	—	10.00	15.00	25.00	100.00
	1853/2 JG	—	10.00	15.00	25.00	100.00
	1854 JG	—	10.00	15.00	25.00	100.00
	1855 JG	—	15.00	25.00	40.00	100.00
	1856 JG	—	7.50	12.50	20.00	100.00
	1857/6 JG	—	12.50	20.00	35.00	100.00
	1858/7 JG	—	15.00	25.00	40.00	110.00
	1859/8 JG	—	25.00	50.00	75.00	150.00
	1860/59 JG	—	30.00	60.00	90.00	225.00
	1861/0 JG	—	20.00	30.00	50.00	125.00
	1861 JG	—	25.00	50.00	100.00	250.00
	1862 JG	—	7.50	12.50	20.00	100.00

Mint mark: GC

KM#	Date	Mintage	Fine	VF	XF	Unc
372.5	1844 MP	—	40.00	60.00	100.00	250.00
	1845 MP	—	40.00	60.00	100.00	250.00
	1846 MP	—	40.00	60.00	100.00	250.00
	1847 MP	—	40.00	60.00	100.00	250.00
	1848 MP	—	40.00	60.00	100.00	250.00
	1849/7 MP	—	40.00	60.00	100.00	250.00
	1849/8 MP	—	40.00	60.00	100.00	250.00
	1849 MP	—	40.00	60.00	100.00	250.00
	1850 MP	—	40.00	60.00	100.00	250.00
	1851 MP	—	40.00	60.00	100.00	250.00

Mint mark: Go

KM#	Date	Mintage	Fine	VF	XF	Unc
372.6	1826/5 JJ	—	5.00	7.50	15.00	85.00
	1826 MJ	—	4.00	6.00	15.00	85.00
	1827 MJ	—	4.00	6.00	15.00	65.00
	1827 JM	—	10.00	15.00	25.00	75.00
	1828/7 MR	—	4.00	6.00	15.00	85.00
	1828 MJ, straight J, small 8					
		—	4.00	6.00	15.00	85.00
	1828Go MJ, full J, large 8					
		—	4.00	6.00	15.00	85.00
	1828G MJ, full J, large 8					
		—	4.00	6.00	15.00	85.00
	1828 MR	—	4.00	6.00	15.00	85.00
	1829/8 MG small eagle					
		—	4.00	6.00	15.00	85.00
	1829 MJ small eagle					
		—	4.00	6.00	15.00	85.00
	1829 MJ large eagle					
		—	4.00	6.00	15.00	85.00
	1830 MJ small initials					
		—	4.00	6.00	15.00	85.00
	1830 MJ medium initials					
		—	4.00	6.00	15.00	85.00
	1830 MJ large initials					
		—	4.00	6.00	15.00	85.00
	1830 MJ reversed N in MEXICANA					
		—	4.00	6.00	15.00	85.00
	1831/0 MJ reversed N in MEXICANA					
		—	4.00	6.00	15.00	85.00
	1831 MJ	—	4.00	6.00	15.00	85.00
	1832/1 MJ	—	15.00	30.00	50.00	125.00
	1832 MJ	—	15.00	30.00	50.00	125.00
	1833 MJ top of 3 round					
		—	4.00	6.00	15.00	85.00
	1833 MJ top of 3 flat					
		—	4.00	6.00	15.00	85.00
	1834 PJ	—	4.00	6.00	15.00	85.00
	1835 PJ	—	7.50	12.50	20.00	85.00
	1836 PJ	—	4.00	6.00	15.00	85.00
	1837 PJ	—	15.00	30.00	50.00	125.00
	1838/7 PJ	—	10.00	20.00	35.00	85.00
	1839 PJ	—	4.00	6.00	15.00	85.00
	1840/39 PJ	—	4.00	6.00	15.00	85.00
	1840 PJ	—	4.00	6.00	15.00	85.00
	1841/31 PJ	—	10.00	20.00	35.00	85.00
	1841 PJ	—	4.00	6.00	15.00	85.00
	1842 PJ	—	4.00	6.00	15.00	85.00
	1842 PM	—	4.00	6.00	15.00	85.00
	1843 PM convex wings					
		—	4.00	6.00	15.00	85.00
	1843 PM concave wings					
		—	4.00	6.00	15.00	85.00
	1844 PM	—	4.00	6.00	15.00	85.00
	1845/4 PM	—	4.00	6.00	15.00	85.00
	1845 PM	—	4.00	6.00	15.00	85.00
	1846/5 PM	—	7.50	12.50	20.00	85.00
	1846 PM	—	4.00	6.00	15.00	85.00
	1847/6 PM	—	4.00	6.00	15.00	85.00
	1847 PM	—	4.00	6.00	15.00	85.00
	1848 PM	—	4.00	6.00	15.00	85.00
	1849 PF	—	10.00	20.00	35.00	85.00
	1850 PF	—	4.00	6.00	15.00	85.00
	1851 PF	—	10.00	20.00	35.00	100.00
	1853/2 PF	—	7.50	12.50	20.00	75.00
	1853 PF	—	4.00	6.00	15.00	75.00
	1854/3 PF	—	4.00	6.00	15.00	75.00
	1854 PF large eagle					
		—	4.00	6.00	15.00	75.00
	1854 PF small eagle					
		—	4.00	6.00	15.00	75.00
	1855/3 PF	—	4.00	6.00	15.00	75.00
	1855/4 PF	—	4.00	6.00	15.00	75.00
	1855 PF	—	4.00	6.00	15.00	75.00
	1856/5 PF	—	4.00	6.00	15.00	75.00
	1856 PF	—	4.00	6.00	15.00	75.00
	1857/6 PF	—	4.00	6.00	15.00	75.00
	1857 PF	—	4.00	6.00	15.00	75.00
	1858 PF	—	4.00	6.00	15.00	75.00
	1859 PF	—	4.00	6.00	15.00	75.00
	1860/50 PF	—	4.00	6.00	15.00	75.00
	1860 PF	—	4.00	6.00	15.00	75.00
	1861 PF	—	4.00	6.00	15.00	75.00
	1862 YE	—	4.00	6.00	15.00	75.00
	1862/1 YF	—	7.50	12.50	20.00	75.00
	1862 YF	—	4.00	6.00	15.00	75.00
	1867 YF	—	4.00	6.00	15.00	75.00
	1868/7 YF	—	4.00	6.00	15.00	75.00

Mint mark: Ho

KM#	Date	Mintage	Fine	VF	XF	Unc
372.7	1867 small 7/1 PR					
		—	50.00	65.00	100.00	250.00
	1867 large 7/small 7 PR					
		—	50.00	65.00	100.00	250.00
	1868 PR	—	50.00	65.00	100.00	250.00

Mint mark: Mo

KM#	Date	Mintage	Fine	VF	XF	Unc
372.8	1825 JM	—	10.00	20.00	40.00	110.00
	1826 JM	—	7.50	15.00	30.00	100.00
	1827/6 JM	—	7.50	15.00	30.00	75.00
	1827 JM	—	5.00	10.00	20.00	70.00
	1828 JM	—	7.50	15.00	30.00	100.00
	1830/29 JM	—	5.00	10.00	20.00	100.00
	1830 JM	—	5.00	12.50	25.00	100.00
	1831 JM	—	100.00	200.00	300.00	750.00

KM#	Date	Mintage	Fine	VF	XF	Unc
372.8	1832 JM	—	5.00	10.00	20.00	100.00
	1833/2 MJ	—	5.00	10.00	20.00	100.00
	1850 GC	—	5.00	10.00	20.00	100.00
	1852 GC	—	275.00	425.00	575.00	—
	1854 GC	—	10.00	20.00	40.00	100.00
	1855 GF	—	5.00	10.00	20.00	80.00
	1856 GF	—	5.00	10.00	20.00	80.00
	1857 GF	—	5.00	10.00	20.00	80.00
	1858 FH	—	5.00	10.00	20.00	80.00
	1859 FH	—	5.00	10.00	20.00	80.00
	1861 CH	—	5.00	10.00	20.00	80.00
	1862 CH	—	5.00	10.00	20.00	80.00
	1863/2 CH	—	7.50	12.50	25.00	80.00

Mint mark: Pi

KM#	Date	Mintage	Fine	VF	XF	Unc
372.9	1831 JS	—	5.00	10.00	20.00	125.00
	1837 JS	—	750.00	850.00	1000.	—
	1838/7 JS	—	250.00	300.00	375.00	—
	1838 JS	—	20.00	35.00	60.00	125.00
	1840/39 JS	—	7.50	15.00	30.00	125.00
	1840 JS	—	7.50	15.00	30.00	125.00
	1841 JS	—	7.50	15.00	30.00	125.00
	1842 JS	—	15.00	30.00	55.00	150.00
	1842 PS	—	5.00	10.00	20.00	125.00
	1843 PS	—	12.50	20.00	35.00	125.00
	1843 AM	—	40.00	60.00	80.00	150.00
	1844 AM	—	40.00	60.00	80.00	150.00
	1845 AM	—	7.50	15.00	30.00	125.00
	1846/5 AM	—	7.50	15.00	30.00	125.00
	1847/6 AM	—	7.50	15.00	30.00	125.00
	1847 AM	—	7.50	15.00	30.00	125.00
	1848/7 AM	—	7.50	15.00	30.00	125.00
	1849 PS	—	7.50	15.00	30.00	125.00
	1849/8 SP	—	60.00	100.00	150.00	—
	1849 SP	—	15.00	25.00	40.00	125.00
	1850 MC	—	5.00	10.00	20.00	125.00
	1851/0 MC	—	7.50	15.00	30.00	125.00
	1851 MC	—	7.50	15.00	30.00	125.00
	1852/1/0 MC					
		—	10.00	20.00	35.00	125.00
	1852 MC	—	7.50	15.00	30.00	125.00
	1853/1 MC	—	12.50	20.00	35.00	125.00
	1853 MC	—	10.00	20.00	35.00	125.00
	1854/3 MC	—	20.00	40.00	60.00	150.00
	1855/4 MC	—	20.00	40.00	60.00	150.00
	1855 MC	—	15.00	25.00	45.00	125.00
	1856 MC	—	15.00	25.00	45.00	125.00
	1857 PS	—	20.00	35.00	55.00	135.00
	1857 MC	—	20.00	40.00	60.00	150.00
	1858 MC	—	12.50	20.00	35.00	125.00
	1859 PS	—	10.00	15.00	30.00	125.00
	1860/59 PS	—	10.00	15.00	30.00	125.00
	1861 PS	—	7.50	12.50	20.00	125.00
	1861 RO	—	12.50	20.00	35.00	125.00
	1862/1 RO	—	12.50	20.00	35.00	90.00
	1862 RO	—	7.50	12.50	20.00	125.00

Mint mark: Zs

KM#	Date	Mintage	Fine	VF	XF	Unc
372.10	1826 AZ	—	5.00	12.50	35.00	120.00
	1826 AO	—	5.00	12.50	35.00	120.00
	1827 AO	—	5.00	12.50	35.00	120.00
	1828/7 AO	—	5.00	12.50	35.00	120.00
	1828 AO	—	5.00	12.50	35.00	120.00
	1828 AO inverted V for A					
		—	5.00	12.50	35.00	120.00
	1829 AO	—	5.00	12.50	35.00	120.00
	1830 ZsOV	—	5.00	12.50	35.00	120.00
	1830 ZOV	—	5.00	12.50	35.00	120.00
	1831 OV	—	5.00	12.50	35.00	120.00
	1831 OM	—	5.00	12.50	30.00	120.00
	1832 OM	—	5.00	12.50	30.00	120.00
	1833/2 OM	—	5.00	12.50	30.00	120.00
	1833 OM	—	5.00	12.50	30.00	120.00
	1834/3 OM	—	5.00	12.50	30.00	120.00
	1834 OM	—	5.00	12.50	30.00	120.00
	1835/4 OM	—	20.00	35.00	60.00	150.00
	1835 OM	—	4.00	8.00	20.00	65.00
	1836/5 OM	—	4.00	8.00	20.00	85.00
	1836 OM	—	4.00	8.00	20.00	85.00
	1837 OM	—	4.00	8.00	20.00	85.00
	1838 OM	—	4.00	8.00	20.00	85.00
	1839 OM	—	4.00	8.00	20.00	85.00
	1840 OM	—	4.00	8.00	20.00	85.00
	1841 OM	—	20.00	40.00	60.00	150.00
	1842/1 OM	—	4.00	8.00	20.00	85.00
	1842 OM	—	4.00	8.00	20.00	85.00
	1843 OM	—	4.00	8.00	20.00	85.00
	1844 OM	—	4.00	8.00	20.00	85.00
	1845/4 OM	—	5.00	12.50	30.00	100.00
	1845 OM	—	4.00	8.00	20.00	85.00
	1846 OM old font and obv.					
		—	4.00	8.00	20.00	85.00
	1846 OM new font and obv.					
		—	4.00	8.00	20.00	85.00
	1847 OM	—	4.00	8.00	20.00	85.00
	1848 OM	—	4.00	8.00	20.00	85.00
	1849 OM	—	10.00	25.00	50.00	125.00
	1850 OM	—	4.00	6.00	15.00	85.00
	1851 OM	—	4.00	6.00	15.00	85.00
	1852 OM	—	4.00	6.00	15.00	85.00
	1853 OM	—	4.00	6.00	15.00	85.00
	1854/2 OM	—	4.00	6.00	15.00	85.00
	1854/3 OM	—	4.00	6.00	15.00	85.00
	1854 OM	—	4.00	6.00	15.00	85.00
	1855/4 OM	—	4.00	6.00	15.00	85.00
	1855 OM	—	4.00	6.00	15.00	85.00
	1855 MO	—	4.00	6.00	15.00	85.00
	1856 MO	—	4.00	6.00	15.00	85.00
	1856 MO/OM	—	4.00	6.00	15.00	85.00
	1857 MO	—	4.00	6.00	15.00	85.00
	1858 MO	—	4.00	6.00	15.00	85.00
372.10	1859 MO	—	4.00	6.00	15.00	75.00
	1860 VL	—	4.00	6.00	15.00	75.00
	1861 VL	—	4.00	6.00	15.00	75.00
	1862 VL	—	5.00	12.50	30.00	100.00
	1868 JS	—	25.00	45.00	90.00	175.00
	1869 YH	—	4.00	8.00	20.00	75.00

2 REALES

6.7600 g, .903 SILVER, .1962 oz ASW
Mint mark: D, Do
Obv: Hooked-neck eagle.

KM#	Date	Mintage	Fine	VF	XF	Unc
373	1824 Do RL	—	50.00	125.00	300.00	850.00
	1824 D RL	—	100.00	200.00	500.00	1650.

Mint mark: Mo

KM#	Date	Mintage	Fine	VF	XF	Unc
373.1	1824 JM	—	20.00	50.00	100.00	350.00

Mint mark: A
Obv: Facing eagle, reeded edge.

KM#	Date	Mintage	Fine	VF	XF	Unc
374	1872 AM	.015	40.00	100.00	200.00	500.00

Mint mark: Ce

KM#	Date	Mintage	Fine	VF	XF	Unc
374.1	1863 ML	—	125.00	200.00	325.00	675.00

Mint mark: Ca

KM#	Date	Mintage	Fine	VF	XF	Unc
374.2	1832 MR	—	30.00	60.00	100.00	200.00
	1833 MR	—	30.00	60.00	125.00	500.00
	1834 MR	—	35.00	75.00	125.00	500.00
	1834 AM	—	35.00	75.00	125.00	500.00
	1835 AM	—	35.00	75.00	125.00	500.00
	1836 AM	—	20.00	40.00	80.00	200.00
	1844 RG	—	—	—	Unique	—
	1845 RG	—	20.00	40.00	80.00	200.00
	1855 RG	—	20.00	40.00	80.00	200.00

Mint mark: C

KM#	Date	Mintage	Fine	VF	XF	Unc
374.3	1846/1146 CE					
		—	25.00	50.00	100.00	225.00
	1847 CE	—	12.50	20.00	40.00	200.00
	1848 CE	—	12.50	20.00	40.00	200.00
	1850 CE	—	25.00	50.00	75.00	200.00
	1851 CE	—	12.50	20.00	40.00	200.00
	1852/1 CE	—	12.50	20.00	40.00	200.00
	1853/2 CE	—	12.50	20.00	40.00	200.00
	1854 CE	—	15.00	30.00	50.00	200.00
	1856 CE	—	20.00	35.00	70.00	200.00
	1857 CE	—	12.50	20.00	40.00	200.00
	1860 PV	—	12.50	20.00	40.00	200.00
	1861 PV	—	12.50	20.00	40.00	200.00
	1869 CE	—	12.50	20.00	40.00	200.00

Mint mark: Do

KM#	Date	Mintage	Fine	VF	XF	Unc
374.4	1826 RL	—	20.00	40.00	60.00	200.00
	1832 RM style of pre-1832					
		—	20.00	40.00	60.00	200.00
	1832 RM style of post-1832					
		—	20.00	40.00	60.00	200.00
	1834/2 RM	—	20.00	40.00	60.00	200.00
	1834/3 RM	—	20.00	40.00	60.00	200.00
	1835/4 RM/RL					
		—	200.00	300.00	500.00	—
	1841/31 RM	—	50.00	75.00	125.00	250.00
	1841 RM	—	50.00	75.00	125.00	250.00
	1842/32 RM	—	12.50	20.00	40.00	200.00
	1843 RM/RL	—	12.50	20.00	40.00	200.00
	1844 RM	—	35.00	50.00	80.00	200.00
	1845/34 RM/RL					
		—	12.50	20.00	40.00	200.00
	1846/36 RM	—	100.00	150.00	200.00	350.00
	1848/36 RM	—	12.50	20.00	40.00	200.00
	1848/37 RM	—	12.50	20.00	40.00	200.00
	1848/7 RM	—	12.50	20.00	40.00	200.00
	1848 RM	—	12.50	20.00	40.00	200.00
	1849 CM/RM	—	12.50	20.00	40.00	200.00
	1849 CM	—	12.50	20.00	40.00	200.00
	1851 JMR/RL					
		—	12.50	20.00	40.00	200.00
	1852 JMR	—	12.50	20.00	40.00	200.00
	1854 CP/CR	—	30.00	50.00	80.00	200.00
	1855 CP	—	250.00	350.00	500.00	—
	1856 CP	—	100.00	150.00	250.00	500.00
	1858 CP	—	12.50	20.00	40.00	200.00
	1859/8 CP	—	12.50	20.00	40.00	200.00
	1861 CP	—	12.50	20.00	40.00	200.00

Mint mark: EoMo

KM#	Date	Mintage	Fine	VF	XF	Unc
374.5	1828 LF	—	325.00	525.00	900.00	2500.

Mint mark: Ga

KM#	Date	Mintage	Fine	VF	XF	Unc
374.6	1825 FS	—	20.00	40.00	80.00	200.00
374.6	1826 FS	—	20.00	40.00	80.00	200.00
	1828/7 FS	—	100.00	150.00	225.00	400.00
	1829 FS	—	—	—	Rare	—
	1832/0 FS/LP					
		—	100.00	150.00	225.00	350.00
	1832 FS	—	12.50	20.00	40.00	200.00
	1833/2 FS/LP					
		—	12.50	20.00	40.00	200.00
	1834/27 FS	—	—	—	Rare	—
	1834 FS	—	12.50	20.00	40.00	200.00
	1835 FS	—	2100.	—	—	—
	1837 JG	—	12.50	20.00	40.00	200.00
	1838 JG	—	12.50	20.00	40.00	200.00
	1840/30 MC	—	12.50	20.00	40.00	200.00
	1841 MC	—	12.50	20.00	40.00	200.00
	1842/32 JG/MC					
		—	35.00	50.00	100.00	200.00
	1842 JG	—	20.00	40.00	80.00	200.00
	1843 JG	—	12.50	20.00	40.00	200.00
	1843 MC/JG	—	12.50	20.00	40.00	200.00
	1844 MC	—	12.50	20.00	40.00	200.00
	1845/3 MC/JG					
		—	12.50	20.00	40.00	200.00
	1845/4 MC/JG					
		—	12.50	20.00	40.00	200.00
	1845 JG	—	12.50	20.00	40.00	200.00
	1846 JG	—	12.50	20.00	40.00	200.00
	1847/6 JG	—	25.00	40.00	80.00	200.00
	1848/7 JG	—	12.50	20.00	40.00	200.00
	1849 JG	—	12.50	20.00	40.00	200.00
	1850/40 JG	—	12.50	20.00	40.00	200.00
	1851 JG	—	250.00	350.00	500.00	—
	1852 JG	—	12.50	20.00	40.00	200.00
	1853/1 JG	—	12.50	20.00	40.00	200.00
	1854/3 JG	—	250.00	350.00	500.00	—
	1855 JG	—	35.00	50.00	80.00	200.00
	1856 JG	—	12.50	20.00	40.00	200.00
	1857 JG	—	250.00	350.00	500.00	—
	1859/8 JG	—	12.50	20.00	40.00	200.00
	1859 JG	—	12.50	20.00	40.00	200.00
	1862/1 JG	—	12.50	20.00	40.00	200.00

Mint mark: GC

KM#	Date	Mintage	Fine	VF	XF	Unc
374.7	1844 MP	—	40.00	60.00	125.00	275.00
	1845 MP	—	40.00	60.00	125.00	275.00
	1846 MP	—	50.00	100.00	150.00	300.00
	1847 MP	—	35.00	50.00	100.00	250.00
	1848 MP	—	50.00	100.00	150.00	300.00
	1849 MP	—	50.00	100.00	150.00	300.00
	1850 MP	—	125.00	250.00	—	—
	1851/0 MP	—	50.00	100.00	150.00	300.00
	1851 MP	—	50.00	100.00	150.00	300.00

Mint mark: Go

KM#	Date	Mintage	Fine	VF	XF	Unc
374.8	1825 JJ	—	7.50	15.00	30.00	150.00
	1826/5 JJ	—	7.50	15.00	30.00	150.00
	1826 JJ	—	7.50	10.00	25.00	150.00
	1826 MJ	—	7.50	10.00	25.00	150.00
	1827/6 MJ	—	7.50	10.00	25.00	150.00
	1827 MJ	—	7.50	10.00	25.00	150.00
	1828/7 MR	—	7.50	15.00	30.00	150.00
	1828 MJ	—	7.50	10.00	20.00	150.00
	1828 JM	—	7.50	10.00	20.00	150.00
	1829 MJ	—	7.50	10.00	20.00	150.00
	1831 MJ	—	7.50	10.00	20.00	150.00
	1832 MJ	—	7.50	10.00	20.00	150.00
	1833 MJ	—	7.50	10.00	20.00	150.00
	1834 PJ	—	7.50	10.00	20.00	150.00
	1835/4 PJ	—	7.50	15.00	30.00	150.00
	1835 PJ	—	7.50	10.00	20.00	150.00
	1836 PJ	—	7.50	10.00	20.00	150.00
	1837/6 PJ	—	7.50	10.00	20.00	150.00
	1837 PJ	—	7.50	10.00	20.00	150.00
	1838/7 PJ	—	7.50	10.00	20.00	150.00
	1838 PJ	—	7.50	10.00	20.00	150.00
	1839/8 PJ	—	7.50	15.00	30.00	150.00
	1839 PJ	—	7.50	10.00	20.00	150.00
	1840 PJ	—	7.50	10.00	20.00	150.00
	1841 PJ	—	7.50	10.00	20.00	150.00
	1842 PJ	—	7.50	10.00	20.00	150.00
	1842 PM/PJ	—	7.50	10.00	20.00	150.00
	1842 PM	—	7.50	10.00	20.00	150.00
	1843/2 PM concave wings, thin rays, sm. letters					
		—	7.50	10.00	20.00	150.00
	1843 PM convex wings, thick rays, lg. letters					
		—	7.50	10.00	20.00	150.00
	1844 PM	—	7.50	10.00	20.00	150.00
	1845/4 PM	—	7.50	10.00	20.00	150.00
	1845 PM	—	7.50	10.00	20.00	150.00
	1846/5 PM	—	10.00	15.00	35.00	150.00
	1846 PM	—	7.50	10.00	20.00	150.00
	1847 PM	—	7.50	10.00	20.00	150.00
	1848/7 PM	—	7.50	15.00	30.00	150.00
	1848 PM	—	7.50	15.00	30.00	150.00
	1848 PF	—	100.00	150.00	250.00	500.00
	1849/8 PF/PM					
		—	7.50	10.00	20.00	150.00
	1849 PF	—	7.50	10.00	20.00	150.00
	1850/40 PF	—	7.50	10.00	20.00	150.00
	1850 PF	—	7.50	10.00	20.00	150.00
	1851 PF	—	7.50	10.00	20.00	150.00
	1852/1 PF	—	7.50	10.00	20.00	150.00
	1852 PF	—	7.50	10.00	20.00	150.00
	1853 PF	—	7.50	10.00	20.00	150.00
	1854/3 PF	—	7.50	10.00	20.00	150.00
	1854 PF old font and obv.					
		—	7.50	10.00	20.00	150.00
	1854 PF new font and obv.					
		—	7.50	10.00	20.00	150.00
	1855 PF	—	7.50	10.00	20.00	150.00
	1855 PF star in G of mint mark					

KM#	Date	Mintage	Fine	VF	XF	Unc
374.8		—	7.50	10.00	20.00	150.00
	1856/5 PF	—	10.00	15.00	35.00	150.00
	1856 PF	—	10.00	15.00	25.00	150.00
	1857/6 PF	—	7.50	10.00	20.00	150.00
	1857 PF	—	7.50	10.00	20.00	150.00
	1858/7 PF	—	7.50	10.00	20.00	150.00
	1858 PF	—	7.50	10.00	20.00	150.00
	1859/7 PF	—	7.50	10.00	20.00	150.00
	1859 PF	—	7.50	10.00	20.00	150.00
	1860/50 PF	—	7.50	10.00	20.00	150.00
	1860/59 PF	—	7.50	10.00	20.00	150.00
	1860 PF	—	7.50	10.00	20.00	150.00
	1861/51 PF	—	7.50	10.00	20.00	150.00
	1861/57 PF	—	7.50	10.00	20.00	150.00
	1861/0 PF	—	7.50	10.00	20.00	150.00
	1861 PF	—	7.50	10.00	20.00	150.00
	1862/1 YE	—	7.50	10.00	20.00	125.00
	1862 YE	—	7.50	10.00	20.00	125.00
	1862/57 YE	—	7.50	10.00	20.00	125.00
	1862 YE/PF	—	7.50	10.00	20.00	125.00
	1862 YF	—	7.50	10.00	20.00	125.00
	1863/52 YF	—	7.50	10.00	20.00	125.00
	1863 YF	—	7.50	10.00	20.00	125.00
	1867/57 YF	—	7.50	10.00	20.00	125.00
	1868/57 YF	—	10.00	15.00	25.00	125.00

NOTE: Varieties exist.

Mint mark: Ho

KM#	Date	Mintage	Fine	VF	XF	Unc
374.9	1861 FM	—	200.00	300.00	400.00	650.00
	1862/52 Ho FM/C. CE					
		—	250.00	350.00	500.00	—
	1867/1 PR/FM					
		—	75.00	150.00	250.00	500.00

Mint mark: Mo

KM#	Date	Mintage	Fine	VF	XF	Unc
374.10	1825 JM	—	10.00	15.00	30.00	175.00
	1826 JM	—	10.00	15.00	30.00	175.00
	1827 JM	—	10.00	15.00	30.00	175.00
	1828 JM	—	10.00	15.00	30.00	175.00
	1829/8 JM	—	10.00	15.00	30.00	175.00
	1829 JM	—	10.00	15.00	30.00	175.00
	1830 JM	—	40.00	60.00	125.00	250.00
	1831 JM	—	10.00	15.00	30.00	175.00
	1832 JM	—	100.00	200.00	400.00	—
	1833/2 MJ/JM					
		—	10.00	15.00	30.00	175.00
	1834 ML	—	50.00	100.00	200.00	400.00
	1836 ML	—	—	Reported, not confirmed		
	1836 MF	—	10.00	15.00	30.00	175.00
	1837 ML	—	10.00	15.00	30.00	175.00
	1840 ML	—	150.00	225.00	350.00	—
	1841 ML	—	10.00	15.00	30.00	175.00
	1842 ML	—	—	—	Rare	—
	1847 RC	—	10.00	15.00	30.00	175.00
	1848 GC	—	10.00	15.00	30.00	175.00
	1849 GC	—	10.00	15.00	30.00	175.00
	1850 GC	—	10.00	15.00	30.00	175.00
	1851 GC	—	40.00	60.00	125.00	250.00
	1852 GC	—	10.00	15.00	30.00	175.00
	1853 GC	—	10.00	15.00	30.00	175.00
	1854/44 GC	—	10.00	15.00	30.00	175.00
	1855 GC	—	10.00	15.00	30.00	175.00
	1855 GF/GC	—	10.00	15.00	30.00	175.00
	1855 GF	—	10.00	15.00	30.00	175.00
	1856/5 GF/GC					
		—	10.00	15.00	30.00	175.00
	1857 GF	—	10.00	15.00	30.00	175.00
	1858 FH	—	7.50	12.50	25.00	150.00
	1858 FH/GF	—	7.50	12.50	25.00	150.00
	1859 FH	—	7.50	12.50	25.00	150.00
	1860 FH	—	7.50	12.50	25.00	150.00
	1860 TH	—	7.50	12.50	25.00	150.00
	1861 TH	—	—	Reported, not confirmed		
	1861 CH	—	7.50	12.50	25.00	150.00
	1862 CH	—	7.50	12.50	25.00	150.00
	1863 CH	—	7.50	12.50	25.00	150.00
	1863 TH	—	7.50	12.50	25.00	150.00
	1867 CH	—	7.50	12.50	25.00	150.00
	1868 CH	—	10.00	15.00	30.00	150.00
	1868 PH	—	7.50	12.50	25.00	150.00

NOTE: Varieties exist.

Mint mark: Pi

KM#	Date	Mintage	Fine	VF	XF	Unc
374.11	1829 JS	—	10.00	15.00	30.00	200.00
	1830/20 JS	—	20.00	30.00	60.00	200.00
	1837 JS	—	10.00	15.00	30.00	200.00
	1841 JS	—	10.00	15.00	30.00	200.00
	1842/1 JS	—	10.00	15.00	30.00	200.00
	1842 JS	—	10.00	15.00	30.00	200.00
	1842 PS	—	20.00	35.00	60.00	200.00
	1843 PS	—	12.50	20.00	40.00	200.00
	1843 AM	—	10.00	15.00	30.00	200.00
	1844 AM	—	10.00	15.00	30.00	200.00
	1845 AM	—	10.00	15.00	30.00	200.00
	1846 AM	—	10.00	15.00	30.00	200.00
	1849 MC	—	10.00	15.00	30.00	200.00
	1850 MC	—	10.00	15.00	30.00	200.00
	1856 MC	—	40.00	60.00	125.00	250.00
	1857 MC	—	—	—	—	—
	1858 MC	—	12.50	20.00	40.00	200.00
	1859 MC	—	50.00	70.00	100.00	200.00
	1861 PS	—	10.00	15.00	30.00	200.00
	1862 RO	—	12.50	20.00	40.00	200.00
	1863 RO	—	100.00	250.00	350.00	500.00
	1868 PS	—	10.00	15.00	30.00	200.00
	1869/8 PS	—	10.00	15.00	30.00	200.00
	1869 PS	—	10.00	15.00	30.00	200.00

Mint mark: Zs

KM#	Date	Mintage	Fine	VF	XF	Unc
374.12	1825 AZ	—	10.00	15.00	30.00	150.00
	1826 AV (A is inverted V)					
374.12		—	7.50	10.00	25.00	150.00
	1826 AZ (A is inverted V)					
		—	7.50	10.00	25.00	150.00
	1826 AO	—	10.00	15.00	30.00	150.00
	1827 AO (A is inverted V)					
		—	6.00	8.00	12.00	150.00
	1828/7 AO	—	15.00	30.00	60.00	175.00
	1828 AO	—	7.50	10.00	25.00	100.00
	1828 AO (A is inverted V)					
		—	7.50	10.00	25.00	150.00
	1829 AO	—	7.50	10.00	25.00	150.00
	1829 OV	—	7.50	10.00	25.00	150.00
	1830 OV	—	7.50	10.00	25.00	150.00
	1831 OV	—	7.50	10.00	25.00	150.00
	1831 OM/OV	—	7.50	10.00	25.00	150.00
	1831 OM	—	7.50	10.00	25.00	150.00
	1832/1 OM	—	15.00	30.00	60.00	150.00
	1832 OM	—	7.50	10.00	25.00	150.00
	1833/27 OM	—	7.50	10.00	25.00	150.00
	1833/2 OM	—	7.50	10.00	25.00	150.00
	1833 OM	—	7.50	10.00	25.00	150.00
	1834 OM	—	40.00	60.00	125.00	200.00
	1835 OM	—	7.50	10.00	25.00	150.00
	1836 OM	—	7.50	10.00	25.00	150.00
	1837 OM	—	7.50	10.00	25.00	150.00
	1838 OM	—	15.00	30.00	60.00	150.00
	1839 OM	—	7.50	10.00	20.00	150.00
	1840 OM	—	7.50	10.00	20.00	150.00
	1841/0 OM	—	7.50	10.00	20.00	150.00
	1841 OM	—	7.50	10.00	20.00	150.00
	1842 OM	—	7.50	10.00	20.00	150.00
	1843 OM	—	7.50	10.00	20.00	150.00
	1844 OM	—	7.50	10.00	20.00	150.00
	1845 OM small letters and leaves					
		—	7.50	10.00	20.00	150.00
	1845 OM large letters and leaves					
		—	7.50	10.00	20.00	150.00
	1846 OM	—	7.50	10.00	20.00	150.00
	1847 OM	—	7.50	10.00	20.00	150.00
	1848 OM	—	7.50	10.00	20.00	150.00
	1849 OM	—	7.50	10.00	20.00	150.00
	1850 OM	—	7.50	10.00	20.00	150.00
	1851 OM	—	7.50	10.00	20.00	150.00
	1852 OM	—	7.50	10.00	20.00	150.00
	1853 OM	—	7.50	10.00	20.00	150.00
	1854/3 OM	—	7.50	10.00	20.00	150.00
	1854 OM	—	7.50	10.00	20.00	150.00
	1855/4 OM	—	7.50	10.00	20.00	150.00
	1855 OM	—	7.50	10.00	20.00	150.00
	1855 MO	—	7.50	10.00	20.00	150.00
	1856/5 MO	—	7.50	10.00	20.00	150.00
	1856 MO	—	7.50	10.00	20.00	150.00
	1857 MO	—	7.50	10.00	20.00	150.00
	1858 MO	—	7.50	10.00	20.00	150.00
	1859 MO	—	7.50	10.00	20.00	150.00
	1860/59 MO	—	7.50	10.00	20.00	150.00
	1860 MO	—	7.50	10.00	20.00	100.00
	1860 VL	—	7.50	10.00	20.00	150.00
	1861 VL	—	7.50	10.00	20.00	150.00
	1862 VL	—	7.50	10.00	20.00	100.00
	1863 MO	—	12.50	20.00	40.00	150.00
	1863 VL	—	7.50	10.00	20.00	150.00
	1864 MO	—	7.50	10.00	20.00	150.00
	1864 VL	—	7.50	10.00	20.00	150.00
	1865 MO	—	7.50	10.00	20.00	150.00
	1867 JS	—	7.50	10.00	20.00	150.00
	1868 JS	—	10.00	15.00	35.00	150.00
	1868 YH	—	7.50	10.00	20.00	150.00
	1869 YH	—	7.50	10.00	20.00	150.00
	1870 YH	—	7.50	10.00	20.00	150.00

NOTE: Varieties exist.

4 REALES

13.5400 g, .903 SILVER, .3925 oz ASW
Mint mark: Ce
Obv: Facing eagle.

KM#	Date	Mintage	Fine	VF	XF	Unc
375	1863 ML large C					
		—	200.00	500.00	850.00	4000.
	1863 ML small C					
		—	350.00	650.00	1250.	4750.

Mint mark: C

KM#	Date	Mintage	Fine	VF	XF	Unc
375.1	1846 CE	—	400.00	550.00	900.00	—
	1850 CE	—	75.00	125.00	250.00	600.00
	1852 CE	—	200.00	300.00	500.00	1250.
	1857 CE	—	—	—	Rare	—
	1858 CE	—	100.00	200.00	350.00	1000.
	1860 PV	—	25.00	50.00	125.00	600.00

Mint mark: Ga

KM#	Date	Mintage	Fine	VF	XF	Unc
375.2	1842/1 JG	—	—	Reported, not confirmed		
	1842 JG	—	—	Reported, not confirmed		
	1843 MC	—	20.00	40.00	80.00	400.00
	1844/3 MC	—	30.00	60.00	125.00	400.00
	1844 MC	—	20.00	40.00	80.00	400.00
	1845 MC	—	20.00	40.00	80.00	400.00
375.2	1845 JG	—	20.00	40.00	80.00	400.00
	1846 JG	—	20.00	40.00	80.00	400.00
	1847 JG	—	40.00	80.00	150.00	400.00
	1848/7 JG	—	40.00	80.00	150.00	400.00
	1849 JG	—	40.00	80.00	150.00	400.00
	1850 JG	—	65.00	125.00	250.00	550.00
	1852 JG	—	—	—	Rare	—
	1854 JG	—	—	—	Rare	—
	1855 JG	—	100.00	200.00	400.00	1250.
	1856 JG	—	—	—	Rare	—
	1857/6 JG	—	65.00	125.00	250.00	550.00
	1858 JG	—	125.00	250.00	450.00	1250.
	1859/8 JG	—	125.00	250.00	450.00	1250.
	1860 JG	—	—	—	Rare	—
	1863/2 JG	—	150.00	300.00	1250.	6000.
	1863 JG	—	150.00	300.00	1250.	6000.

Mint mark: GC

KM#	Date	Mintage	Fine	VF	XF	Unc
375.3	1844 MP	—	1000.	2000.	3000.	—
	1845 MP	—	3000.	4000.	5000.	9000.
	1846 MP	—	1700.	2800.	—	—
	1847 MP	—	1500.	2500.	—	—
	1849 MP	—	2000.	3000.	—	—
	1850 MP	—	500.00	1000.	—	—

Mint mark: Go

KM#	Date	Mintage	Fine	VF	XF	Unc
375.4	1835 PJ	—	12.50	25.00	60.00	350.00
	1836/5 PJ	—	15.00	30.00	75.00	350.00
	1836 PJ	—	15.00	30.00	75.00	350.00
	1837 PJ	—	12.50	25.00	60.00	350.00
	1838/7 PJ	—	15.00	30.00	75.00	350.00
	1838 PJ	—	12.50	30.00	75.00	350.00
	1839 PJ	—	12.50	25.00	60.00	350.00
	1840/30 PJ	—	20.00	50.00	100.00	350.00
	1841/31 PJ	—	150.00	250.00	450.00	1250.
	1842 PJ	—	—	—	Rare	—
	1842 PM	—	15.00	30.00	75.00	350.00
	1843/2 PM eagle w/convex wings, thick rays					
		—	12.50	25.00	60.00	350.00
	1843 PM eagle w/concave wings, thin rays					
		—	12.50	25.00	60.00	350.00
	1844/3 PM	—	15.00	30.00	75.00	350.00
	1844 PM	—	20.00	50.00	100.00	350.00
	1845/4 PM	—	20.00	50.00	100.00	350.00
	1845 PM	—	20.00	50.00	100.00	350.00
	1846/5 PM	—	15.00	30.00	75.00	350.00
	1846 PM	—	15.00	30.00	75.00	350.00
	1847/6 PM	—	15.00	30.00	75.00	350.00
	1847 PM	—	15.00	30.00	75.00	350.00
	1848/7 PM	—	20.00	50.00	100.00	350.00
	1848 PM	—	20.00	50.00	100.00	350.00
	1849 PF	—	20.00	50.00	100.00	350.00
	1850 PF	—	12.50	25.00	60.00	350.00
	1851 PF	—	12.50	25.00	60.00	350.00
	1852 PF	—	15.00	30.00	75.00	350.00
	1853 PF	—	15.00	30.00	75.00	350.00
	1854 PF large eagle					
		—	15.00	30.00	75.00	350.00
	1854 PF small eagle					
		—	15.00	30.00	75.00	350.00
	1855/4 PF	—	15.00	30.00	75.00	350.00
	1855 PF	—	12.50	25.00	60.00	350.00
	1856 PF	—	12.50	25.00	60.00	350.00
	1857 PF	—	20.00	50.00	100.00	350.00
	1858 PF	—	20.00	50.00	100.00	350.00
	1859 PF	—	20.00	50.00	100.00	350.00
	1860/59 PF	—	15.00	30.00	75.00	350.00
	1860 PF	—	15.00	30.00	75.00	350.00
	1861/51 PF	—	15.00	30.00	75.00	350.00
	1861 PF	—	20.00	50.00	100.00	350.00
	1862/1 YE	—	15.00	30.00	75.00	350.00
	1862/1 YF	—	15.00	30.00	75.00	350.00
	1862 YE/PF	—	15.00	30.00	75.00	350.00
	1862 YE	—	15.00	30.00	75.00	350.00
	1862 YF	—	15.00	30.00	75.00	350.00
	1863/53 YF	—	15.00	30.00	75.00	350.00
	1863 YF/PF	—	15.00	30.00	75.00	350.00
	1863 YF	—	15.00	30.00	75.00	350.00
	1867/57 YF/PF					
		—	15.00	30.00	75.00	350.00
	1868/58 YF/PF					
		—	15.00	30.00	75.00	350.00
	1870 FR	—	15.00	30.00	75.00	350.00

NOTE: Varieties exist. Some 1862 dates appear to be 1869 because of weak dies.

Mint mark: Ho

KM#	Date	Mintage	Fine	VF	XF	Unc
375.5	1861 FM	—	200.00	350.00	500.00	1850.
	1867/1 PR/FM					
		—	150.00	275.00	400.00	1750.

Mint mark: Mo

KM#	Date	Mintage	Fine	VF	XF	Unc
375.6	1827/6 JM	—	200.00	400.00	—	—
	1850 GC	—	—	—	Rare	—
	1852 GC	—	—	—	Rare	—
	1854 GC	—	—	—	Rare	—
	1855 GF/GC	—	50.00	100.00	200.00	500.00
	1855 GF	—	100.00	200.00	350.00	800.00
	1856 GF/GC	—	20.00	50.00	100.00	350.00
	1856 GF	—	—	—	Rare	—
	1859 FH	—	20.00	50.00	100.00	350.00
	1861 CH	—	15.00	30.00	75.00	300.00
	1862 CH	—	20.00	50.00	100.00	350.00
	1863/2 CH	—	20.00	50.00	100.00	350.00
	1863 CH	—	75.00	150.00	300.00	650.00
	1867 CH	—	20.00	50.00	100.00	350.00
	1868 CH/PH	—	30.00	75.00	150.00	400.00
	1868 CH	—	20.00	50.00	100.00	350.00
	1868 PH	—	30.00	75.00	150.00	400.00

Mint mark: O

KM#	Date	Mintage	Fine	VF	XF	Unc
375.7	1861 FR ornamental edge					

KM#	Date	Mintage	Fine	VF	XF	Unc
375.7		—	225.00	450.00	750.00	2750.
	1861 FR herringbone edge					
		—	300.00	550.00	850.00	2850.
	1861 FR obliquely reeded edge					
		—	200.00	400.00	700.00	—
	Mint mark: Pi					
375.8	1837 JS	—	200.00	350.00	—	—
	1838 JS	—	150.00	250.00	400.00	850.00
	1842 PS	—	50.00	100.00	200.00	450.00
	1843/2 PS	—	50.00	100.00	200.00	450.00
	1843/2 PS 3 cut from 8 punch					
		—	50.00	100.00	200.00	450.00
	1843 AM	—	30.00	75.00	150.00	450.00
	1843 PS	—	50.00	100.00	200.00	450.00
	1844 AM	—	30.00	75.00	150.00	450.00
	1845/4 AM	—	20.00	50.00	100.00	450.00
	1845 AM	—	20.00	50.00	100.00	450.00
	1846 AM	—	20.00	50.00	100.00	450.00
	1847 AM	—	75.00	150.00	250.00	550.00
	1848 AM	—	—	—	Rare	—
	1849 MC/AM	—	20.00	50.00	100.00	450.00
	1849 MC	—	20.00	50.00	100.00	450.00
	1849 PS	—	20.00	50.00	100.00	450.00
	1850 MC	—	20.00	50.00	100.00	450.00
	1851 MC	—	20.00	50.00	100.00	450.00
	1852 MC	—	20.00	50.00	100.00	450.00
	1853 MC	—	20.00	50.00	100.00	450.00
	1854 MC	—	100.00	200.00	400.00	1100.
	1855 MC	—	175.00	300.00	500.00	1500.
	1856 MC	—	250.00	400.00	700.00	—
	1857 MC	—	—	—	Rare	—
	1857 PS	—	—	—	Rare	—
	1858 MC	—	100.00	200.00	400.00	1000.
	1859 MC	—	2000.	3000.	—	—
	1860 PS	—	300.00	450.00	700.00	—
	1861 PS	—	30.00	75.00	150.00	450.00
	1861 RO/PS	—	30.00	75.00	150.00	450.00
	1861 RO	—	50.00	100.00	200.00	450.00
	1862 RO	—	30.00	75.00	150.00	450.00
	1863 RO	—	30.00	75.00	150.00	450.00
	1864 RO	—	1600.	2600.	—	—
	1868 PS	—	30.00	75.00	150.00	450.00
	1869/8 PS	—	30.00	75.00	150.00	450.00
	1869 PS	—	30.00	75.00	150.00	450.00
	Mint mark: Zs					
375.9	1830 OM	—	20.00	50.00	100.00	350.00
	1831 OM	—	15.00	30.00	75.00	350.00
	1832/1 OM	—	20.00	50.00	100.00	350.00
	1832 OM	—	20.00	50.00	100.00	350.00
	1833/2 OM	—	20.00	50.00	100.00	350.00
	1833/27 OM	—	15.00	30.00	75.00	350.00
	1833 OM	—	15.00	30.00	75.00	350.00
	1834/3 OM	—	20.00	50.00	100.00	350.00
	1834 OM	—	15.00	30.00	75.00	350.00
	1835 OM	—	15.00	30.00	75.00	350.00
	1836 OM	—	15.00	30.00	75.00	350.00
	1837/5 OM	—	20.00	50.00	100.00	350.00
	1837/6 OM	—	20.00	50.00	100.00	350.00
	1837 OM	—	20.00	50.00	100.00	350.00
	1838/7 OM	—	15.00	30.00	75.00	350.00
	1839 OM	—	250.00	375.00	500.00	—
	1840 OM	—	—	—	Rare	—
	1841 OM	—	15.00	30.00	75.00	350.00
	1842 OM small letters					
		—	75.00	150.00	300.00	800.00
	1842 OM large letters					
		—	15.00	30.00	75.00	350.00
	1843 OM	—	15.00	30.00	75.00	350.00
	1844 OM	—	20.00	50.00	100.00	350.00
	1845 OM	—	20.00	50.00	100.00	350.00
	1846/5 OM	—	25.00	60.00	125.00	350.00
	1846 OM	—	20.00	50.00	100.00	350.00
	1847 OM	—	15.00	30.00	75.00	350.00
	1848/6 OM	—	50.00	75.00	125.00	350.00
	1848 OM	—	20.00	50.00	100.00	350.00
	1849 OM	—	20.00	50.00	100.00	350.00
	1850 OM	—	20.00	50.00	100.00	350.00
	1851 OM	—	15.00	30.00	75.00	350.00
	1852 OM	—	15.00	30.00	75.00	350.00
	1853 OM	—	20.00	50.00	100.00	350.00
	1854/3 OM	—	30.00	75.00	150.00	350.00
	1855/4 OM	—	20.00	50.00	100.00	350.00
	1855 OM	—	15.00	30.00	75.00	350.00
	1856 OM	—	15.00	30.00	75.00	350.00
	1856 MO	—	20.00	50.00	100.00	350.00
	1857/5 MO	—	20.00	50.00	100.00	350.00
	1857 O/M	—	20.00	50.00	100.00	350.00
	1857 MO	—	15.00	30.00	75.00	350.00
	1858 MO	—	20.00	50.00	100.00	350.00
	1859 MO	—	15.00	30.00	75.00	350.00
	1860/59 MO	—	20.00	50.00	100.00	350.00
	1860 MO	—	15.00	30.00	75.00	350.00
	1860 VL	—	20.00	50.00	100.00	350.00
	1861/0 VL	—	20.00	50.00	100.00	350.00
	1861 VL	—	15.00	30.00	75.00	350.00
	1862/1 VL	—	20.00	50.00	100.00	350.00
	1862 VL	—	20.00	50.00	100.00	350.00
	1863 VL	—	20.00	50.00	100.00	350.00
	1863 MO	—	20.00	50.00	100.00	350.00
	1864 VL	—	15.00	30.00	75.00	350.00
	1868 JS	—	20.00	50.00	100.00	350.00
	1868 YH	—	15.00	30.00	75.00	350.00
	1869 YH	—	15.00	30.00	75.00	350.00
	1870 YH	—	15.00	30.00	75.00	350.00

8 REALES

27.0700 g, .903 SILVER, .7859 oz ASW
Mint mark: Do
Obv: Hooked-neck eagle.

KM#	Date	Mintage	Fine	VF	XF	Unc
376	1824 RL	—	250.00	400.00	1000.	2750.

NOTE: Varieties exist.

KM#	Date	Mintage	Fine	VF	XF	Unc
	Mint mark: Go					
376.1	1824 JM	—	250.00	400.00	1000.	3500.
	1825/4 JJ	—	550.00	800.00	1500.	6000.
	1825 JJ	—	500.00	750.00	1400.	5500.

KM#	Date	Mintage	Fine	VF	XF	Unc
	Mint mark: Mo					
376.2	1823 JM edge: circle and rectangle pattern					
		—	—	—	Rare	—
	1823 JM edge: laurel leaves					
		—	150.00	275.00	600.00	2250.
	1824 JM	—	125.00	225.00	450.00	1850.
	1824 JM (error) REPULICA					
		—	7000.	9000.	—	—

NOTE: These are rarely found with detail on the eagles breast and bring a premium if even slight feather detail is present there.

KM#	Date	Mintage	Fine	VF	XF	Unc
	Mint mark: A, As					
377	1864 PG	—	750.00	1250.	2000.	—
	1865/4 PG	—	—	—	Rare	—
	1865 PG	—	500.00	750.00	1000.	—
	1866/5 PG	—	—	—	Rare	—
	1866 PG	—	1250.	2250.	—	—
	1866 DL	—	—	—	Rare	—
	1867 DL	—	1150.	2150.	—	—

KM#	Date	Mintage	Fine	VF	XF	Unc
377	1868 DL	—	50.00	90.00	150.00	300.00
	1869/8 DL	—	50.00	90.00	150.00	—
	1869 DL	—	50.00	80.00	120.00	300.00
	1870 DL	—	30.00	60.00	120.00	300.00
	1871 DL	—	20.00	35.00	75.00	200.00
	1872 AM/DL	—	25.00	50.00	100.00	300.00
	1872 AM	—	25.00	50.00	100.00	250.00
	1873 AM	.509	15.00	25.00	50.00	150.00
	1874 DL	—	15.00	25.00	50.00	150.00
	1875A DL 7/7	—	40.00	80.00	120.00	300.00
	1875A DL	—	15.00	25.00	50.00	150.00
	1875AsDL	—	30.00	60.00	110.00	250.00
	1876 DL	—	15.00	25.00	50.00	150.00
	1877 DL	.515	15.00	25.00	50.00	150.00
	1878 DL	.513	15.00	25.00	50.00	150.00
	1879 DL	—	20.00	35.00	75.00	175.00
	1879 ML	—	30.00	60.00	125.00	350.00
	1880 ML	—	12.00	15.00	30.00	140.00
	1881 ML	.966	12.00	15.00	30.00	140.00
	1882 ML	.480	12.00	15.00	30.00	140.00
	1883 ML	.464	12.00	15.00	30.00	140.00
	1884 ML	—	12.00	15.00	30.00	140.00
	1885 ML	.280	12.00	15.00	30.00	140.00
	1886 ML	.857	12.00	15.00	25.00	110.00
	1886/0 As/Cn ML/JD					
		I.A.	15.00	20.00	35.00	160.00
	1887 ML	.650	12.00	15.00	25.00	110.00
	1888/7 ML	.508	30.00	60.00	100.00	400.00
	1888 ML	I.A.	12.00	15.00	25.00	110.00
	1889 ML	.427	12.00	15.00	25.00	110.00
	1890 ML	.450	12.00	15.00	25.00	110.00
	1891 ML	.533	12.00	15.00	25.00	110.00
	1892 ML	.465	12.00	15.00	25.00	110.00
	1893 ML	.734	10.00	12.00	22.00	85.00
	1894 ML	.725	10.00	12.00	22.00	85.00
	1895 ML	.477	10.00	12.00	22.00	85.00

NOTE: Varieties exist.

KM#	Date	Mintage	Fine	VF	XF	Unc
	Mint mark: Ce					
377.1	1863 ML	—	425.00	700.00	1350.	3000.
	1863 CeML/PiMC					
		—	425.00	750.00	1500.	3250.

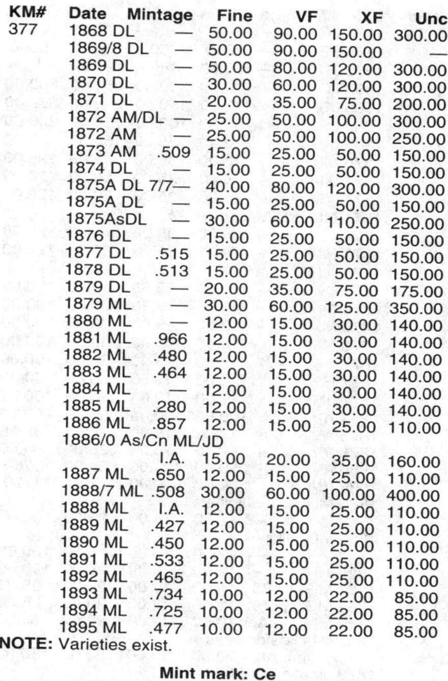

KM#	Date	Mintage	Fine	VF	XF	Unc
	Mint mark: Ca					
377.2	1831 MR	—	1000.	1750.	2250.	3250.
	1832 MR	—	125.00	200.00	300.00	600.00
	1833 MR	—	350.00	650.00	1250.	—
	1834 MR	—	—	—	Rare	—
	1834 AM	—	350.00	650.00	—	—
	1835 AM	—	150.00	250.00	400.00	800.00
	1836 AM	—	100.00	150.00	225.00	450.00
	1837 AM	—	450.00	850.00	—	—
	1838 AM	—	100.00	200.00	300.00	600.00
	1839 RG	—	1250.	2500.	3500.	—
	1840 RG 1 dot after date					
		—	300.00	500.00	800.00	1500.
	1840 RG 3 dots after date					
		—	300.00	500.00	800.00	1500.
	1841 RG	—	50.00	100.00	150.00	300.00
	1842 RG	—	25.00	40.00	75.00	150.00
	1843 RG	—	40.00	80.00	125.00	250.00
	1844/1 RG	—	35.00	70.00	100.00	200.00
	1844 RG	—	25.00	40.00	75.00	150.00
	1845 RG	—	25.00	40.00	75.00	150.00
	1846 RG	—	30.00	60.00	100.00	250.00
	1847 RG	—	40.00	80.00	125.00	250.00
	1848 RG	—	30.00	60.00	100.00	200.00
	1849 RG	—	30.00	60.00	100.00	200.00
	1850/40 RG	—	40.00	80.00	125.00	250.00
	1850 RG	—	30.00	60.00	100.00	200.00
	1851/41 RG	—	100.00	200.00	300.00	500.00
	1851 RG	—	150.00	250.00	400.00	750.00
	1852/42 RG	—	150.00	250.00	400.00	750.00
	1852 RG	—	150.00	250.00	400.00	750.00
	1853/43 RG	—	150.00	250.00	400.00	750.00
	1853 RG	—	150.00	250.00	400.00	750.00
	1854/44 RG	—	100.00	200.00	300.00	500.00
	1854 RG	—	50.00	100.00	150.00	300.00
	1855/45 RG	—	100.00	200.00	350.00	650.00
	1855 RG	—	75.00	125.00	200.00	400.00
	1856/45 RG	—	300.00	550.00	1000.	1750.
	1856/5 JC	—	400.00	650.00	1150.	2000.
	1857 JC/RG	—	40.00	80.00	125.00	250.00
	1857 JC	—	50.00	100.00	150.00	250.00
	1858 JC	—	20.00	35.00	75.00	150.00
	1858 BA	—	2000.	3500.	—	—
	1859 JC	—	40.00	80.00	125.00	250.00
	1860 JC	—	20.00	40.00	90.00	175.00
	1861 JC	—	15.00	25.00	50.00	125.00
	1862 JC	—	15.00	25.00	50.00	125.00
	1863 JC	—	20.00	35.00	75.00	150.00
	1864 JC	—	20.00	35.00	75.00	150.00
	1865 JC	—	100.00	200.00	350.00	600.00
	1865 FP	—	1350.	—	—	—

KM#	Date	Mintage	Fine	VF	XF	Unc
377.2	1866 JC	—	—	—	Rare	—
	1866 FP	—	1000.	2000.	3250.	5000.
	1866 JG	—	850.00	1650.	2750.	—
	1867 JG	—	100.00	200.00	350.00	600.00
	1868 JG	—	75.00	150.00	200.00	350.00
	1868 MM	—	50.00	100.00	150.00	300.00
	1869 MM	—	20.00	35.00	65.00	125.00
	1870 MM	—	20.00	35.00	65.00	125.00
	1871/0 MM	—	15.00	25.00	50.00	120.00
	1871 MM	—	15.00	25.00	50.00	120.00
	1871 MM first M/inverted M	—	20.00	35.00	65.00	125.00
	1873 MM	—	20.00	35.00	65.00	125.00
	1873 MM/T	—	15.00	25.00	50.00	120.00
	1874 MM	—	12.00	15.00	30.00	100.00
	1875 MM	—	12.00	15.00	30.00	100.00
	1876 MM	—	12.00	15.00	30.00	100.00
	1877 EA	.472	12.00	15.00	30.00	100.00
	1877 GR	I.A.	25.00	45.00	65.00	150.00
	1877 JM	I.A.	12.00	15.00	30.00	100.00
	1877 AV	I.A.	100.00	200.00	350.00	750.00
	1878 AV	.439	12.00	15.00	25.00	80.00
	1879 AV	—	12.00	15.00	25.00	80.00
	1880 AV	—	250.00	400.00	650.00	1250.
	1880 PM	—	500.00	800.00	1150.	1750.
	1880 MG normal initials	—	12.00	15.00	25.00	100.00
	1880 MG tall initials	—	12.00	15.00	25.00	100.00
	1880 MM	—	12.00	15.00	25.00	100.00
	1881 MG	1.085	10.00	12.00	20.00	65.00
	1882 MG	.779	10.00	12.00	20.00	65.00
	1882 MM	I.A.	10.00	12.00	20.00	65.00
	1882 MM M sideways	Inc. Ab.	20.00	40.00	90.00	150.00
	1883 sideways M MM	.818	—	—	—	—
	1883 MM	I.A.	10.00	12.00	20.00	65.00
	1884/3 MM	—	12.00	15.00	30.00	80.00
	1884 MM	—	10.00	12.00	20.00	65.00
	1885/4 MM	1.345	15.00	25.00	50.00	120.00
	1885/6 MM	I.A.	15.00	25.00	50.00	120.00
	1885 MM	I.A.	10.00	12.00	20.00	65.00
	1886 MM	2.483	10.00	12.00	20.00	65.00
	1887 MM	2.625	10.00	12.00	20.00	65.00
	1888/7 MM	2.434	15.00	25.00	50.00	120.00
	1888 MM	I.A.	10.00	12.00	20.00	65.00
	1889 MM	2.681	10.00	12.00	20.00	65.00
	1890 MM	2.137	10.00	12.00	20.00	65.00
	1891/0 MM	2.268	15.00	25.00	50.00	120.00
	1891 MM	I.A.	10.00	12.00	20.00	80.00
	1892 MM	2.527	10.00	12.00	20.00	65.00
	1893 MM	2.632	10.00	12.00	20.00	65.00
	1894 MM	2.642	10.00	12.00	20.00	65.00
	1895 MM	1.112	10.00	12.00	20.00	65.00

NOTE: Varieties exist.

Mint mark: C, Cn

KM#	Date	Mintage	Fine	VF	XF	Unc
377.3	1846 CE	—	150.00	300.00	800.00	1500.
	1847 CE	—	600.00	1000.	1500.	—
	1848 CE	—	150.00	300.00	600.00	1000.
	1849 CE	—	75.00	125.00	200.00	400.00
	1850 CE	—	75.00	125.00	200.00	400.00
	1851 CE	—	125.00	250.00	450.00	1000.
	1852/1 CE	—	100.00	150.00	250.00	500.00
	1852 CE	—	100.00	200.00	350.00	650.00
	1853/0 CE	—	200.00	350.00	700.00	1300.
	1853/2/0	—	200.00	400.00	750.00	1400.
	1853 CE thick rays	—	100.00	175.00	300.00	600.00
	1853 CE (error:) MEXIGANA	—	200.00	350.00	650.00	—
	1854 CE	—	—	—	Rare	—
	1854 CE large eagle & hat	—	175.00	350.00	750.00	1200.
	1855/6 CE	—	40.00	60.00	100.00	200.00
	1855 CE	—	25.00	40.00	75.00	150.00
	1856 CE	—	50.00	100.00	175.00	350.00
	1857 CE	—	20.00	35.00	75.00	150.00
	1858 CE	—	30.00	40.00	75.00	150.00
	1859 CE	—	20.00	35.00	75.00	150.00
	1860/9 PV/CV	—	50.00	70.00	100.00	200.00
	1860/9 PV/E	—	50.00	70.00	100.00	200.00
	1860 CE	—	25.00	40.00	75.00	150.00
	1860 PV	—	40.00	60.00	90.00	175.00
	1861/0 CE	—	40.00	60.00	100.00	250.00
	1861 PV/CE	—	75.00	125.00	200.00	350.00
	1861 CE	—	20.00	35.00	60.00	150.00
	1862 CE	—	20.00	35.00	60.00	150.00
	1863/2 CE	—	30.00	50.00	75.00	200.00
	1863 CE	—	20.00	30.00	60.00	150.00
	1864 CE	—	30.00	60.00	100.00	300.00
	1865 CE	—	125.00	200.00	325.00	650.00
	1866 CE	—	—	—	Rare	—
	1867 CE	—	125.00	200.00	375.00	750.00
	1868/7 CE	—	30.00	40.00	75.00	150.00
	1868/8	—	50.00	100.00	150.00	300.00
	1868 CE	—	30.00	40.00	75.00	150.00
	1869 CE	—	30.00	40.00	75.00	175.00
	1870 CE	—	35.00	50.00	90.00	200.00
	1873 MP	—	50.00	100.00	150.00	300.00
	1874C MP	—	20.00	30.00	45.00	100.00
	1874CN MP	—	125.00	200.00	300.00	600.00
	1875 MP	—	12.00	15.00	22.00	80.00
	1876 GP	—	12.00	15.00	30.00	90.00

KM#	Date	Mintage	Fine	VF	XF	Unc
377.3	1876 CG	—	12.00	15.00	22.00	80.00
	1877 CG	.339	12.00	15.00	22.00	80.00
	1877 Gn CG (error)	—	65.00	125.00	200.00	400.00
	1877 JA	I.A.	35.00	75.00	125.00	250.00
	1878/7 CG	.483	35.00	75.00	125.00	250.00
	1878 CG	I.A.	15.00	25.00	35.00	125.00
	1878 JD	I.A.	15.00	20.00	30.00	125.00
	1878 JD D/retrograde D	I.A.	20.00	30.00	40.00	150.00
	1879 JD	—	12.00	15.00	30.00	90.00
	1880/70 JD	—	15.00	20.00	30.00	90.00
	1880 JD	—	12.00	15.00	22.00	80.00
	1881/0 JD	1.032	15.00	20.00	30.00	90.00
	1881C JD	I.A.	12.00	15.00	22.00	80.00
	1881CnJD	I.A.	40.00	60.00	90.00	150.00
	1882 JD	.397	12.00	15.00	22.00	80.00
	1882 AM	I.A.	12.00	15.00	22.00	80.00
	1883 AM	.333	12.00	15.00	22.00	125.00
	1884 AM	—	12.00	15.00	22.00	80.00
	1885/6 AM	.227	20.00	30.00	45.00	110.00
	1885C AM	I.A.	75.00	125.00	250.00	500.00
	1885CnAM	I.A.	12.00	15.00	22.00	80.00
	1885GnAM (error)	Inc. Ab.	60.00	100.00	150.00	300.00
	1886 AM	.571	12.00	15.00	22.00	80.00
	1887 AM	.732	12.00	15.00	22.00	80.00
	1888 AM	.768	12.00	15.00	22.00	80.00
	1889 AM	1.075	12.00	15.00	22.00	80.00
	1890 AM	.874	10.00	12.00	20.00	65.00
	1891 AM	.777	10.00	12.00	20.00	65.00
	1892 AM	.681	10.00	12.00	20.00	65.00
	1893 AM	1.144	10.00	12.00	20.00	65.00
	1894 AM	2.118	10.00	12.00	20.00	65.00
	1895 AM	1.834	10.00	12.00	20.00	65.00
	1896 AM	2.134	10.00	12.00	20.00	65.00
	1897 AM	1.580	10.00	12.00	20.00	65.00

NOTE: Varieties exist.

Mint mark: Do

KM#	Date	Mintage	Fine	VF	XF	Unc
377.4	1825 RL	—	30.00	55.00	90.00	200.00
	1826 RL	—	40.00	100.00	250.00	500.00
	1827/6 RL	—	35.00	60.00	85.00	200.00
	1827 RL	—	30.00	50.00	80.00	175.00
	1828/7 RL	—	35.00	60.00	90.00	200.00
	1828 RL	—	25.00	50.00	80.00	175.00
	1829 RL	—	25.00	50.00	80.00	175.00
	1830 RM B on eagles claw	—	25.00	50.00	80.00	175.00
	1831 RM B on eagles claw	—	20.00	30.00	60.00	150.00
	1832 RM Mexican dies, B on eagles claw	—	25.00	50.00	100.00	200.00
	1832/1 RM/RL French dies	—	25.00	35.00	75.00	165.00
	1833/2 RM/RL	—	20.00	35.00	75.00	165.00
	1833 RM	—	15.00	30.00	60.00	150.00
	1834/3/2 RM/RL	—	20.00	35.00	75.00	165.00
	1834 RM	—	15.00	25.00	50.00	150.00
	1835/4 RM/RL	—	25.00	40.00	80.00	175.00
	1835 RM	—	20.00	35.00	65.00	150.00
	1836/1 RM	—	20.00	35.00	65.00	150.00
	1836/4 RM	—	20.00	35.00	65.00	150.00
	1836/5/4 RM/RL	—	75.00	150.00	250.00	500.00
	1836 RM	—	20.00	30.00	55.00	150.00
	1836 RM M on snake	—	20.00	30.00	55.00	150.00
	1837/1 RM	—	20.00	30.00	55.00	150.00
	1837 RM	—	20.00	30.00	55.00	150.00
	1838/1 RM	—	20.00	30.00	55.00	150.00
	1838/7 RM	—	20.00	30.00	55.00	150.00
	1838 RM	—	20.00	30.00	55.00	150.00
	1839/1 RM/RL	—	20.00	30.00	55.00	150.00
	1839/1 RM	—	20.00	30.00	55.00	150.00
	1839 RM	—	20.00	30.00	55.00	150.00
	1840/38/31 RM	—	20.00	30.00	55.00	150.00
	1840/39 RM	—	20.00	30.00	55.00	150.00
	1840 RM	—	20.00	30.00	55.00	150.00
	1841/31 RM	—	25.00	50.00	85.00	200.00
	1842/31 RM B below cactus	—	125.00	250.00	400.00	750.00
	1842/31 RM	—	40.00	80.00	125.00	250.00
	1842/32 RM	—	40.00	80.00	125.00	250.00
	1842 RM eagle of 1832-41	—	20.00	30.00	55.00	150.00
	1842 RM pre 1832 eagle resumed	—	20.00	30.00	55.00	150.00
	1842 RM	—	40.00	80.00	125.00	250.00
	1843/33 RM	—	50.00	90.00	150.00	250.00
	1844/34 RM	—	100.00	200.00	300.00	500.00
	1844/35 RM	—	100.00	200.00	300.00	500.00
	1845/31 RM	—	35.00	75.00	125.00	250.00
	1845/34 RM	—	35.00	75.00	125.00	250.00
	1845/35 RM	—	35.00	75.00	125.00	250.00
	1845 RM	—	20.00	30.00	55.00	150.00
	1846/31 RM	—	20.00	30.00	55.00	150.00
	1846/36 RM	—	20.00	30.00	55.00	150.00
	1846 RM	—	20.00	30.00	55.00	150.00
	1847 RM	—	25.00	50.00	80.00	185.00
	1848/7 RM	—	125.00	250.00	400.00	750.00
	1848/7 CM/RM	—	100.00	200.00	350.00	700.00
	1848 CM/RM	—	100.00	200.00	350.00	700.00
	1848 RM	—	100.00	200.00	300.00	600.00

KM#	Date	Mintage	Fine	VF	XF	Unc
377.4	1848 CM	—	50.00	100.00	200.00	400.00
	1849/39 CM	—	100.00	200.00	350.00	700.00
	1849 CM	—	100.00	200.00	350.00	700.00
	1849 JMR/CM oval 0	—	200.00	325.00	450.00	800.00
	1849 DoJMR oval O	—	200.00	400.00	600.00	1000.
	1849 DoJMR round O	—	200.00	400.00	600.00	1000.
	1850 JMR	—	100.00	150.00	250.00	500.00
	1851/0 JMR	—	100.00	150.00	250.00	500.00
	1851 JMR	—	100.00	150.00	250.00	500.00
	1852 CP/JMR	—	—	—	Rare	—
	1852 CP	—	—	—	Rare	—
	1852 JMR	—	175.00	250.00	375.00	650.00
	1853 CP/JMR	—	175.00	275.00	400.00	700.00
	1853 CP	—	200.00	350.00	600.00	1200.
	1854 CP	—	25.00	35.00	65.00	300.00
	1855 CP eagle type of 1854	—	50.00	100.00	175.00	350.00
	1855 CP eagle type of 1856	—	50.00	100.00	175.00	350.00
	1856 CP	—	50.00	100.00	175.00	350.00
	1857 CP	—	35.00	75.00	175.00	350.00
	1858/7 CP	—	25.00	35.00	70.00	165.00
	1858 CP	—	20.00	30.00	60.00	165.00
	1859 CP	—	20.00	30.00	60.00	165.00
	1860/59 CP	—	30.00	50.00	100.00	200.00
	1860 CP	—	20.00	30.00	60.00	165.00
	1861/0 CP	—	30.00	50.00	100.00	200.00
	1861 CP	—	20.00	30.00	50.00	125.00
	1862/1 CP	—	25.00	35.00	60.00	125.00
	1862 CP	—	20.00	30.00	55.00	100.00
	1863/2 CP	—	25.00	50.00	75.00	175.00
	1863/53 CP	—	30.00	60.00	90.00	200.00
	1863 CP	—	25.00	50.00	75.00	175.00
	1864 CP	—	100.00	150.00	250.00	500.00
	1864 LT	—	25.00	40.00	80.00	175.00
	1865 LT	—	—	—	Rare	—
	1866 CM	—	1750.	3250.	5500.	8000.
	1867 CM	—	—	—	Rare	—
	1867/6 CP	—	200.00	400.00	600.00	1200.
	1867 CP	—	175.00	300.00	500.00	1000.
	1867 CP/CM	—	175.00	300.00	500.00	1000.
	1867 CP/LT	—	175.00	300.00	500.00	1000.
	1868 CP	—	25.00	40.00	80.00	175.00
	1869 CP	—	20.00	30.00	50.00	125.00
	1870/69 CP	—	20.00	30.00	50.00	125.00
	1870/9 CP	—	20.00	30.00	50.00	125.00
	1870 CP	—	20.00	30.00	50.00	125.00
	1873 CP	—	125.00	225.00	325.00	600.00
	1873 CM	—	30.00	50.00	100.00	200.00
	1874/3 CM	—	12.00	15.00	22.00	100.00
	1874 CM	—	10.00	15.00	22.00	75.00
	1874 JH	—	1500.	2500.	—	—
	1875 CM	—	10.00	15.00	22.00	80.00
	1875 JH	—	100.00	175.00	275.00	500.00
	1876 CM	—	10.00	15.00	22.00	80.00
	1877 CM	.431	1650.	2750.	—	—
	1877 CP	I.A.	10.00	15.00	22.00	80.00
	1877 JMP	I.A.	—	—	Rare	—
	1878 PE	.409	15.00	25.00	40.00	100.00
	1878 TB	I.A.	10.00	15.00	22.00	80.00
	1879 TB	—	10.00	15.00	22.00	80.00
	1880/70 TB	—	150.00	250.00	375.00	650.00
	1880/70 TB/JP	—	150.00	250.00	375.00	650.00
	1880/70 JP	—	15.00	25.00	40.00	100.00
	1880 TB	—	150.00	250.00	375.00	650.00
	1880 JP	—	10.00	15.00	22.00	80.00
	1881 JP	.928	10.00	15.00	22.00	80.00
	1882 JP	.414	10.00	15.00	22.00	80.00
	1882 MC/JP	Inc. Ab.	30.00	60.00	100.00	200.00
	1882 MC	I.A.	25.00	50.00	75.00	150.00
	1883/73 MC	.452	15.00	25.00	40.00	90.00
	1883 MC	I.A.	10.00	15.00	22.00	80.00
	1884/3 MC	—	20.00	30.00	60.00	110.00
	1884 MC	—	10.00	15.00	22.00	80.00
	1885 MC	.547	10.00	12.00	20.00	70.00
	1885 JB	I.A.	25.00	35.00	50.00	125.00
	1886/3 MC	.955	15.00	25.00	40.00	100.00
	1886 MC	I.A.	10.00	12.00	20.00	70.00
	1887 MC	1.004	10.00	12.00	20.00	70.00
	1888 MC	.996	10.00	12.00	20.00	70.00
	1889 MC	.874	10.00	12.00	20.00	70.00
	1890 MC	1.119	10.00	12.00	20.00	70.00
	1890 JP	I.A.	10.00	12.00	20.00	70.00
	1891 JP	1.487	10.00	12.00	20.00	70.00
	1892 JP	1.597	10.00	12.00	20.00	70.00
	1892 ND	I.A.	25.00	50.00	100.00	200.00
	1893 ND	1.617	10.00	12.00	20.00	70.00
	1894 ND	1.537	10.00	12.00	20.00	70.00
	1895/3 ND	.761	15.00	25.00	40.00	100.00
	1895 ND	I.A.	10.00	12.00	20.00	70.00

NOTE: Varieties exist.

Mint mark: EoMo

KM#	Date	Mintage	Fine	VF	XF	Unc
377.5	1828 LF/LP	—	350.00	850.00	2000.	—
	1828 LF	—	350.00	850.00	2000.	—
	1829 LF	—	300.00	750.00	1850.	—
	1830/20 LF	—	—	—	Rare	—
	1830 LF	—	1000.	2000.	3250.	—

Mint mark: Ga

KM#	Date	Mintage	Fine	VF	XF	Unc
377.6	1825 FS	—	150.00	275.00	425.00	850.00
	1826/5 FS	—	125.00	250.00	400.00	800.00
	1827/87 FS	—	125.00	250.00	400.00	800.00
	1827 FS	—	225.00	350.00	500.00	1000.
	1287 FS (error)		8500.	9500.	—	—
	1828 FS	—	200.00	375.00	550.00	1200.
	1829/8 FS	—	200.00	375.00	550.00	1200.
	1829 FS	—	175.00	325.00	475.00	950.00
	1830/29 FS	—	175.00	300.00	450.00	900.00
	1830 FS	—	100.00	175.00	300.00	600.00
	1830 LP/FS	—	—	—	Rare	—
	1831 LP	—	200.00	400.00	600.00	1200.
	1831 FS/LP	—	300.00	500.00	750.00	1500.
	1831 FS	—	150.00	350.00	—	—
	1832/1 FS	—	50.00	100.00	175.00	300.00
	1832/1 FS/LP	—	60.00	125.00	200.00	350.00
	1832 FS	—	25.00	50.00	100.00	225.00
	1833/2/1 FS/LP	—	45.00	75.00	125.00	250.00
	1833/2 FS	—	25.00	50.00	100.00	225.00
	1834/2 FS	—	60.00	125.00	200.00	350.00
	1834/3 FS	—	60.00	125.00	200.00	350.00
	1834/0 FS	—	60.00	125.00	200.00	350.00
	1834 FS	—	50.00	100.00	150.00	300.00
	1835 FS	—	25.00	50.00	100.00	225.00
	1836/1 JG/FS	—	40.00	80.00	125.00	250.00
	1836 FS	—	400.00	750.00	—	—
	1836 JG/FS	—	25.00	50.00	100.00	225.00
	1836 JG	—	25.00	50.00	100.00	225.00
	1837/6 JG/FS	—	50.00	100.00	175.00	300.00
	1837 JG	—	40.00	80.00	125.00	250.00
	1838/7 JG	—	100.00	175.00	300.00	550.00
	1838 JG	—	100.00	150.00	275.00	500.00
	1839 MC	—	100.00	200.00	300.00	550.00
	1839 MC/JG	—	100.00	200.00	300.00	550.00
	1839 JG	—	60.00	125.00	200.00	350.00
	1840/30 MC	—	50.00	75.00	150.00	275.00
	1840 MC	—	30.00	60.00	125.00	250.00
	1841 MC	—	30.00	60.00	125.00	250.00
	1842/1 JG/MG	—	100.00	150.00	250.00	450.00
	1842/1 JG/MC	—	100.00	150.00	250.00	450.00
	1842 JG	—	25.00	50.00	100.00	225.00
	1842 JG/MG	—	25.00	50.00	100.00	225.00
	1843/2 MC/JG	—	25.00	50.00	100.00	225.00
	1843 MC/JG	—	25.00	50.00	100.00	225.00
	1843 JG	—	400.00	600.00	800.00	1500.
	1843 MC	—	50.00	100.00	150.00	300.00
	1844 MC	—	50.00	100.00	150.00	300.00
	1845 MC	—	75.00	150.00	250.00	450.00
	1845 JG	—	650.00	1150.	1750.	—
	1846 JG	—	40.00	80.00	150.00	300.00
	1847 JG	—	100.00	150.00	225.00	400.00
	1848/7 JG	—	55.00	85.00	125.00	250.00
	1848 JG	—	50.00	75.00	100.00	225.00
	1849 JG	—	90.00	125.00	175.00	325.00
	1850 JG	—	50.00	100.00	150.00	300.00
	1851 JG	—	125.00	200.00	350.00	650.00
	1852 JG	—	100.00	150.00	250.00	450.00
	1853/2 JG	—	125.00	175.00	250.00	475.00
	1853 JG	—	90.00	125.00	175.00	300.00
	1854/3 JG	—	65.00	90.00	125.00	250.00

KM#	Date	Mintage	Fine	VF	XF	Unc
377.6	1854 JG	—	50.00	75.00	125.00	250.00
	1855/4 JG	—	50.00	100.00	150.00	275.00
	1855 JG	—	25.00	50.00	100.00	225.00
	1856/4 JG	—	60.00	125.00	175.00	300.00
	1856/5 56	—	60.00	125.00	175.00	300.00
	1856 JG	—	50.00	100.00	150.00	275.00
	1857 JG	—	50.00	100.00	225.00	400.00
	1858 JG	—	100.00	150.00	300.00	500.00
	1859/7 JG	—	25.00	50.00	100.00	200.00
	1859/8 JG	—	25.00	50.00	100.00	200.00
	1859 JG	—	20.00	40.00	80.00	175.00
	1860 JG w/o dot	—	350.00	750.00	1200.	2250.
	1860 JG dot in loop of snakes tail (base alloy)	—	2000.	3250.	—	—
	1861 JG	—	—	—	Rare	—
	1862 JG	—	—	—	Rare	—
	1863/52 JG	—	—	—	—	—
	1863/59 JG	—	45.00	50.00	85.00	145.00
	1863/2 JG	—	30.00	50.00	90.00	175.00
	1863/4 JG	—	40.00	60.00	125.00	200.00
	1863 JG	—	25.00	45.00	75.00	150.00
	1863 FV	—	—	—	Rare	—
	1867 JM	—	—	—	Rare	—
	1868/7 JM	—	50.00	75.00	125.00	200.00
	1868 JM	—	50.00	75.00	125.00	200.00
	1869 JM	—	50.00	75.00	125.00	200.00
	1869 IC	—	75.00	125.00	200.00	375.00
	1870/60 IC	—	60.00	90.00	150.00	275.00
	1870 IC	—	60.00	90.00	150.00	275.00
	1873 IC	—	15.00	25.00	50.00	125.00
	1874 IC	—	10.00	15.00	22.00	90.00
	1874 MC	—	25.00	50.00	100.00	200.00
	1875 IC	—	15.00	30.00	60.00	125.00
	1875 MC	—	10.00	15.00	22.00	90.00
	1876 IC	.559	15.00	30.00	50.00	100.00
	1876 MC	I.A.	125.00	175.00	250.00	375.00
	1877 IC	.928	10.00	15.00	22.00	90.00
	1877 JA	I.A.	10.00	15.00	22.00	90.00
	1878 JA	.764	10.00	15.00	22.00	90.00
	1879 JA	—	10.00	15.00	22.00	90.00
	1880/70 FS	—	15.00	25.00	50.00	125.00
	1880 JA	—	10.00	15.00	22.00	90.00
	1880 FS	—	10.00	15.00	22.00	90.00
	1881 FS	1.300	10.00	15.00	22.00	90.00
	1882/1 FS	.537	15.00	25.00	50.00	125.00
	1882 FS	I.A.	10.00	15.00	22.00	90.00
	1882 TB/FS	I.A.	75.00	150.00	250.00	450.00
	1882 TB	I.A.	50.00	100.00	175.00	300.00
	1883 TB	.561	15.00	25.00	40.00	125.00
	1884 TB	—	10.00	12.00	20.00	85.00
	1884 AH	—	10.00	12.00	20.00	85.00
	1885 AH	.443	10.00	12.00	20.00	85.00
	1885 JS	I.A.	30.00	60.00	100.00	200.00
	1886 JS	1.039	10.00	12.00	20.00	85.00
	1887 JS	.878	10.00	12.00	20.00	85.00
	1888 JS	1.159	10.00	12.00	20.00	85.00
	1889 JS	1.583	10.00	12.00	20.00	85.00
	1890 JS	1.658	10.00	12.00	20.00	85.00
	1891 JS	1.507	10.00	12.00	20.00	85.00
	1892/1 JS	1.627	15.00	25.00	50.00	125.00
	1892 JS	I.A.	10.00	12.00	20.00	80.00
	1893 JS	1.952	10.00	12.00	20.00	80.00
	1894 JS	2.046	10.00	12.00	20.00	80.00
	1895 JS	1.146	10.00	12.00	20.00	65.00

NOTE: Varieties exist. The 1830 LP/FS is currently only known with a Philippine countermark.

Mint mark: GC

KM#	Date	Mintage	Fine	VF	XF	Unc
377.7	1844 MP	—	350.00	500.00	1000.	2000.
	1844 MP (error) reversed S in Ds, Gs	—	400.00	600.00	1200.	2250.
	1845 MP eagle's tail square	—	125.00	200.00	325.00	700.00
	1845 MP eagle's tail round	—	175.00	350.00	650.00	1200.
	1846 MP eagle's tail square	—	125.00	200.00	350.00	750.00
	1846 MP eagle's tail round	—	125.00	200.00	350.00	750.00
	1847 MP	—	150.00	250.00	400.00	800.00
	1848 MP	—	175.00	300.00	500.00	900.00
	1849 MP	—	175.00	300.00	525.00	1000.
	1850 MP	—	175.00	300.00	575.00	1100.
	1851 MP	—	300.00	500.00	900.00	1600.
	1852 MP	—	350.00	600.00	1150.	2250.

Mint mark: Go

KM#	Date	Mintage	Fine	VF	XF	Unc
377.8	1825 JJ	—	40.00	70.00	150.00	300.00
	1825 JJ error mint mark G	—	1250.	1650.	—	—
	1826 JJ straight J's	—	40.00	80.00	175.00	350.00
	1826 JJ full J's	—	30.00	60.00	125.00	250.00
	1826 MJ	—	250.00	450.00	850.00	—
	1827 MJ	—	40.00	75.00	125.00	250.00
	1827 MJ/JJ	—	40.00	75.00	125.00	250.00
	1827 MR	—	100.00	200.00	350.00	600.00
	1828 MJ	—	30.00	60.00	125.00	250.00
	1828/7 MR	—	200.00	400.00	600.00	1200.
	1828 MR	—	200.00	400.00	600.00	1200.
	1829 MJ	—	20.00	35.00	55.00	165.00
	1830 MJ oblong beading and narrow J	—	20.00	30.00	55.00	165.00
	1830 MJ regular beading and wide J	—	20.00	30.00	55.00	165.00
	1831 MJ colon after date	—	12.00	20.00	40.00	150.00
	1831 MJ 2 stars after date	—	12.00	20.00	40.00	150.00
	1832 MJ	—	12.00	20.00	40.00	150.00
	1832 MJ 1 of date over inverted 1	—	20.00	35.00	65.00	175.00
	1833 MJ	—	12.00	20.00	40.00	150.00
	1833 JM	—	900.00	1400.	2000.	2500.
	1834 PJ	—	12.00	20.00	40.00	150.00
	1835 PJ star on cap	—	12.00	20.00	40.00	150.00
	1835 PJ dot on cap	—	12.00	20.00	40.00	150.00
	1836 PJ	—	12.00	20.00	40.00	150.00
	1837 PJ	—	12.00	20.00	40.00	150.00
	1838 PJ	—	12.00	20.00	40.00	150.00
	1839 PJ/JJ	—	12.00	20.00	40.00	150.00
	1839 PJ	—	12.00	20.00	40.00	150.00
	1840/30 PJ	—	20.00	30.00	50.00	150.00
	1840 PJ	—	12.00	20.00	35.00	125.00
	1841/31 PJ	—	12.00	20.00	35.00	125.00
	1841 PJ	—	12.00	20.00	35.00	125.00
	1842/31 PM/PJ	—	25.00	35.00	60.00	150.00
	1842 PJ	—	20.00	30.00	50.00	125.00
	1842 PM/PJ	—	12.00	20.00	35.00	125.00
	1842 PM	—	12.00	20.00	35.00	125.00
	1843 PM dot after date	—	12.00	20.00	35.00	125.00
	1843 PM triangle of dots after date	—	12.00	20.00	35.00	125.00
	1844 PM	—	12.00	20.00	35.00	125.00
	1845 PM	—	12.00	20.00	35.00	125.00
	1846/5 PM eagle type of 1845	—	20.00	30.00	50.00	150.00
	1846 PM early type of 1847	—	15.00	25.00	40.00	135.00
	1847 PM	—	12.00	20.00	35.00	125.00
	1848/7 PM	—	20.00	35.00	65.00	150.00
	1848 PM	—	20.00	35.00	65.00	150.00
	1848 PF	—	12.00	20.00	35.00	125.00
	1849 PF	—	12.00	20.00	35.00	125.00
	1850 PF	—	12.00	20.00	35.00	125.00
	1851/0 PF	—	20.00	30.00	50.00	150.00
	1851 PF	—	12.00	20.00	35.00	125.00
	1852/1 PF	—	20.00	30.00	50.00	150.00
	1852 PF	—	12.00	20.00	35.00	125.00
	1853/2 PF	—	20.00	30.00	50.00	150.00
	1853 PF	—	12.00	20.00	35.00	125.00
	1854 PF	—	12.00	20.00	35.00	125.00
	1855 PF large letters	—	12.00	20.00	35.00	125.00
	1855 PF small letters	—	12.00	20.00	35.00	125.00
	1856/5 PF	—	20.00	30.00	50.00	150.00
	1856 PF	—	12.00	20.00	35.00	125.00
	1857/5 PF	—	20.00	30.00	50.00	150.00
	1857/6 PF	—	20.00	30.00	50.00	150.00
	1857 PF	—	12.00	20.00	35.00	125.00
	1858 PF	—	12.00	20.00	35.00	125.00
	1859/7 PF	—	20.00	30.00	50.00	150.00
	1859/8 PF	—	20.00	30.00	50.00	150.00
	1859 PF	—	12.00	20.00	35.00	125.00
	1860/50 PF	—	20.00	30.00	50.00	150.00
	1860/59 PF	—	12.00	18.00	25.00	85.00
	1860 PF	—	12.00	15.00	20.00	75.00
	1861/51 PF	—	15.00	20.00	30.00	100.00
	1861/0 PF	—	12.00	15.00	20.00	75.00
	1861 PF	—	12.00	15.00	20.00	75.00
	1862 YE/PF	—	12.00	15.00	20.00	75.00
	1862 YE	—	12.00	15.00	20.00	75.00

KM#	Date	Mintage	Fine	VF	XF	Unc
377.8	1862 YF	—	12.00	15.00	20.00	75.00
	1862 YF/PF	—	12.00	15.00	20.00	75.00
	1863/53 YF	—	12.00	18.00	25.00	75.00
	1863/54 YF	—	15.00	20.00	30.00	100.00
	1863 YE	—	—	—	Rare	—
	1863 YF	—	12.00	15.00	20.00	75.00
	1867/57 YF	—	15.00	20.00	30.00	100.00
	1867 YF	—	12.00	15.00	20.00	75.00
	1868/58 YF	—	15.00	20.00	30.00	100.00
	1868 YF	—	12.00	15.00	20.00	75.00
	1870/60 FR	—	20.00	30.00	50.00	150.00
	1870 YF	—	—	—	Rare	—
	1870 FR/YF	—	12.00	18.00	25.00	85.00
	1870 FR	—	12.00	15.00	20.00	75.00
	1873 FR	—	12.00	15.00	20.00	75.00
	1874/3 FR	—	15.00	20.00	30.00	85.00
	1874 FR	—	15.00	25.00	35.00	100.00
	1875/6 FR	—	15.00	20.00	30.00	85.00
	1875 FR small circle w/dot on eagle					
		—	12.00	15.00	20.00	75.00
	1876/5 FR	—	15.00	20.00	30.00	85.00
	1876 FR	—	12.00	15.00	20.00	60.00
	1877 FR	2.477	12.00	15.00	20.00	60.00
	1878/7 FR					
		2.273	15.00	20.00	30.00	75.00
	1878/7 SM	—	15.00	20.00	30.00	75.00
	1878 FR	I.A.	12.00	15.00	20.00	65.00
	1878 SM,S/F	—	15.00	20.00	25.00	70.00
	1878 SM	—	12.00	15.00	20.00	65.00
	1879/7 SM	—	15.00	20.00	30.00	75.00
	1879/8 SM	—	15.00	20.00	30.00	75.00
	1879/8 SM/FR					
		—	15.00	20.00	30.00	75.00
	1879 SM	—	12.00	15.00	20.00	65.00
	1879 SM/FR	—	15.00	20.00	30.00	75.00
	1880/70 SB	—	15.00	20.00	30.00	75.00
	1880 SB/SM	—	12.00	15.00	20.00	65.00
	1881/71 SB	—				
		3.974	15.00	20.00	30.00	75.00
	1881/0 SB	I.A.	15.00	20.00	30.00	75.00
	1881 SB	I.A.	12.00	15.00	20.00	65.00
	1882 SB	2.015	12.00	15.00	20.00	75.00
	1883 SB	2.100	35.00	75.00	125.00	250.00
	1883 BR	I.A.	12.00	15.00	20.00	65.00
	1883 BR/SR	—	12.00	15.00	20.00	65.00
	1883 BR/SB					
		Inc. Ab.	12.00	15.00	20.00	65.00
	1884/73 BR	—	20.00	30.00	40.00	100.00
	1884/74 BR	—	20.00	30.00	40.00	100.00
	1884/3 BR	—	20.00	30.00	40.00	100.00
	1884 BR	—	12.00	15.00	20.00	65.00
	1884/74 RR	—	50.00	100.00	175.00	350.00
	1884 RR	—	50.00	100.00	175.00	350.00
	1885/75 RR					
		2.363	15.00	20.00	30.00	75.00
	1885 RR	I.A.	12.00	15.00	20.00	65.00
	1886/75 RR					
		4.127	15.00	20.00	25.00	70.00
	1886/76 RR					
		Inc. Ab.	12.00	15.00	20.00	65.00
	1886/5 RR/BR					
		Inc. Ab.	12.00	15.00	20.00	65.00
	1886 RR	I.A.	12.00	15.00	20.00	65.00
	1887 RR	4.205	10.00	15.00	20.00	65.00
	1888 RR	3.985	10.00	15.00	20.00	65.00
	1889 RR	3.646	10.00	15.00	20.00	65.00
	1890 RR	3.615	10.00	15.00	20.00	65.00
	1891 RS	3.197	10.00	15.00	20.00	65.00
	1891 RR	—	Contemporary counterfeit			
	1892 RS	3.672	10.00	15.00	20.00	65.00
	1893 RS	3.854	10.00	15.00	20.00	65.00
	1894 RS	4.127	10.00	15.00	20.00	65.00
	1895/1 RS					
		3.768	15.00	20.00	25.00	75.00
	1895/3 RS	I.A.	15.00	20.00	25.00	75.00
	1895 RS	I.A.	10.00	15.00	20.00	65.00
	1896/1 Go/As RS/ML					
		5.229	15.00	20.00	25.00	75.00
	1896/1 RS	I.A.	12.00	15.00	20.00	65.00
	1896 Go/Ga RS					
		Inc. Ab.	—	—	—	—
	1896 RS	I.A.	10.00	12.00	18.00	60.00
	1897 RS	4.344	10.00	12.00	18.00	60.00

NOTE: Varieties exist.

Mint mark: Ho

KM#	Date	Mintage	Fine	VF	XF	Unc
377.9	1835 PP	—	—	—	Rare	—
	1836 PP	—	—	—	Rare	—
	1839 PR	—	—	—	Unique	—
	1861 FM reeded edge					
		—	4500.	7500.	—	—
	1862 FM plain edge, snakes tail left, long ray over *8R					
		—	—	—	Rare	—
	1862 FM plain edge, snakes tail left					
		—	1550.	2700.	—	—
	1862 FM reeded edge, snakes tail right					
		—	1650.	2750.	—	—
	1863 FM	—	150.00	300.00	800.00	—
	1864 FM	—	—	—	Rare	—
	1864 PR	—	650.00	1250.	2150.	3350.
	1865 FM	—	250.00	500.00	950.00	—
	1866 FM	—	1150.	2150.	3500.	5500.
	1866 MP	—	950.00	1750.	3000.	4650.
	1867 PR	—	100.00	175.00	275.00	500.00
	1868 PR	—	20.00	35.00	65.00	175.00
	1869 PR	—	40.00	60.00	125.00	250.00
	1870 PR	—	50.00	80.00	150.00	300.00
	1871/0 PR	—	50.00	75.00	125.00	250.00
	1871 PR	—	30.00	50.00	90.00	200.00
	1872/1 PR	—	35.00	60.00	90.00	200.00
	1872 PR	—	30.00	50.00	75.00	175.00
	1873 PR	.351	30.00	50.00	85.00	150.00
	1874 PR	—	15.00	20.00	40.00	125.00
	1875 PR	—	15.00	20.00	40.00	125.00
	1876 AF	—	15.00	20.00	40.00	125.00
	1877 AF	.410	20.00	30.00	50.00	150.00
	1877 GR	I.A.	100.00	150.00	225.00	400.00
	1877 JA	I.A.	25.00	50.00	85.00	175.00
	1878 JA	.451	15.00	20.00	40.00	120.00
	1879 JA	—	15.00	20.00	40.00	120.00
	1880 JA	—	15.00	20.00	40.00	120.00
	1881 JA	.586	15.00	20.00	40.00	120.00
	1882 HoJA O above H					
		.240	25.00	40.00	65.00	125.00
	1882 HoJA O after H					
		I.A.	25.00	40.00	65.00	125.00
	1883/2 JA	.204	225.00	375.00	550.00	1000.
	1883/2 FM/JA					
		I.A.	25.00	40.00	75.00	150.00
	1883 FM	I.A.	20.00	30.00	60.00	125.00
	1883 JA	I.A.	275.00	450.00	800.00	1500.
	1884/3 FM	—	20.00	25.00	50.00	125.00
	1884 FM	—	15.00	20.00	40.00	120.00
	1885 FM	.132	15.00	20.00	40.00	120.00
	1886 FM	.225	20.00	30.00	45.00	125.00
	1886 FG	I.A.	20.00	30.00	45.00	125.00
	1887 FG	.150	20.00	35.00	65.00	150.00
	1888 FG	.364	12.00	18.00	25.00	100.00
	1889 FG	.490	12.00	18.00	25.00	100.00
	1890 FG	.565	12.00	18.00	25.00	100.00
	1891 FG	.738	12.00	18.00	25.00	100.00
	1892 FG	.643	12.00	18.00	25.00	100.00
	1893 FG	.518	12.00	18.00	25.00	100.00
	1894 FG	.504	12.00	18.00	25.00	100.00
	1895 FG	.320	12.00	18.00	25.00	100.00

NOTE: Varieties exist.

Mint mark: Mo

KM#	Date	Mintage	Fine	VF	XF	Unc
377.10	1824 JM round tail					
		—	75.00	125.00	250.00	500.00
	1824 JM square tail					
		—	75.00	125.00	250.00	500.00
	1825 JM	—	25.00	35.00	60.00	175.00
	1826/5 JM	—	25.00	40.00	75.00	190.00
	1826 JM	—	20.00	30.00	55.00	165.00
	1827 JM medal alignment					
		—	25.00	35.00	60.00	175.00
	1827 JM coin alignment					
		—	25.00	35.00	60.00	175.00
	1828 JM	—	30.00	60.00	100.00	240.00
	1829 JM	—	20.00	30.00	60.00	175.00
	1830/20 JM	—	35.00	55.00	100.00	240.00
	1830 JM	—	30.00	50.00	90.00	220.00
	1831 JM	—	30.00	50.00	100.00	240.00
	1832/1 JM	—	25.00	40.00	65.00	180.00
	1832 JM	—	20.00	30.00	55.00	165.00
	1833 MJ	—	25.00	40.00	80.00	200.00
	1833 ML	—	500.00	750.00	950.00	2000.
	1834/3 ML	—	25.00	35.00	60.00	175.00
	1834 ML	—	20.00	30.00	55.00	165.00
	1835 ML	—	20.00	30.00	55.00	165.00
	1836 ML	—	50.00	100.00	150.00	325.00
	1836 ML/MF	—	50.00	100.00	150.00	325.00
	1836 MF	—	30.00	50.00	90.00	220.00
	1836 MF/ML	—	35.00	60.00	100.00	240.00
	1837/6 ML	—	30.00	50.00	80.00	200.00
	1837/6 MM	—	30.00	50.00	80.00	200.00
	1837/6 MM/ML					
		—	30.00	50.00	80.00	200.00
	1837/6 MM/MF					
		—	30.00	50.00	80.00	200.00
	1837 ML	—	30.00	50.00	80.00	200.00
	1837 MM	—	75.00	125.00	175.00	325.00
	1838 MM	—	30.00	50.00	80.00	200.00
	1838 ML	—	20.00	35.00	60.00	180.00
	1838 ML/MM	—	20.00	35.00	60.00	180.00
377.10	1839 ML	—	15.00	25.00	50.00	165.00
	1840 ML	—	15.00	25.00	50.00	165.00
	1841 ML	—	15.00	25.00	45.00	150.00
	1842 ML	—	15.00	25.00	45.00	150.00
	1842 MM	—	15.00	25.00	45.00	150.00
	1843 MM	—	15.00	25.00	45.00	150.00
	1844 MF/MM	—	—	—	—	—
	1844 MF	—	15.00	25.00	45.00	150.00
	1845/4 MF	—	15.00	25.00	45.00	150.00
	1845 MF	—	15.00	25.00	45.00	150.00
	1846/5 MF	—	15.00	25.00	50.00	165.00
	1846 MF	—	15.00	25.00	50.00	165.00
	1847/6 MF	—	—	—	Rare	—
	1847 MF	—	1650.	3000.	5000.	7500.
	1847 RC	—	20.00	30.00	55.00	165.00
	1847 RC/MF	—	15.00	25.00	45.00	150.00
	1848 GC	—	15.00	25.00	45.00	150.00
	1849/8 GC	—	20.00	35.00	60.00	180.00
	1849 GC	—	15.00	25.00	45.00	150.00
	1850/40 GC	—	25.00	50.00	100.00	240.00
	1850/49 GC	—	25.00	50.00	100.00	240.00
	1850 GC	—	20.00	40.00	75.00	190.00
	1851 GC	—	20.00	40.00	60.00	175.00
	1852 GC	—	15.00	30.00	55.00	160.00
	1853 GC	—	15.00	25.00	50.00	160.00
	1854 GC	—	15.00	25.00	50.00	160.00
	1855 GC	—	20.00	35.00	65.00	180.00
	1855 GF	—	12.00	15.00	30.00	125.00
	1855 GF/GC	—	12.00	15.00	30.00	125.00
	1856/4 GF	—	15.00	25.00	45.00	145.00
	1856/5 GF	—	15.00	25.00	45.00	145.00
	1856 GF	—	12.00	15.00	30.00	125.00
	1857 GF	—	10.00	15.00	30.00	125.00
	1858/7 FH/GF					
		—	10.00	15.00	30.00	125.00
	1858 FH	—	10.00	15.00	30.00	125.00
	1859 FH	—	10.00	15.00	30.00	125.00
	1860/59 FH	—	15.00	20.00	30.00	125.00
	1860 FH	—	10.00	15.00	30.00	125.00
	1860 TH	—	12.00	18.00	40.00	145.00
	1861 TH	—	10.00	15.00	20.00	75.00
	1861 CH	—	10.00	15.00	20.00	75.00
	1862 CH	—	10.00	15.00	20.00	75.00
	1863 CH	—	10.00	15.00	20.00	75.00
	1863 CH/TH	—	10.00	15.00	20.00	75.00
	1863 TH	—	10.00	15.00	20.00	75.00
	1867 CH	—	10.00	15.00	20.00	65.00
	1868 CH	—	10.00	15.00	20.00	65.00
	1868 CH/PH	—	10.00	15.00	20.00	65.00
	1868 PH	—	10.00	15.00	20.00	65.00
	1869 CH	—	10.00	15.00	20.00	65.00
	1873 MH	—	10.00	15.00	20.00	65.00
	1873 MH/HH	—	12.00	18.00	25.00	75.00
	1874/69 MH	—	15.00	25.00	45.00	100.00
	1874 MH	—	12.00	18.00	25.00	75.00
	1874 BH/MH	—	12.00	15.00	20.00	65.00
	1874 BH	—	10.00	15.00	20.00	65.00
	1875 BH	—	10.00	15.00	20.00	65.00
	1876/4 BH	—	12.00	18.00	25.00	75.00
	1876/5 BH	—	12.00	18.00	25.00	75.00
	1876 BH	—	10.00	15.00	20.00	65.00
	1877 MH	.898	10.00	15.00	20.00	65.00
	1877 MH/BH					
		Inc. Ab.	12.00	18.00	25.00	75.00
	1878 MH	2.154	10.00	15.00	20.00	65.00
	1879/8 MH	—	10.00	15.00	20.00	75.00
	1879 MH	—	10.00	15.00	20.00	65.00
	1880/79 MH	—	15.00	20.00	30.00	75.00
	1880 MH	—	10.00	15.00	20.00	75.00
	1881 MH	5.712	10.00	15.00	20.00	65.00
	1882/1 MH					
		2.746	12.00	15.00	20.00	75.00
	1882 MH	I.A.	10.00	15.00	20.00	65.00
	1883/2 MH					
		2.726	12.00	18.00	25.00	85.00
	1883 MH	I.A.	10.00	15.00	20.00	65.00
	1884/3 MH	—	15.00	20.00	30.00	75.00
	1884 MH	—	10.00	15.00	20.00	65.00
	1885 MH	3.649	10.00	15.00	20.00	65.00
	1886 MH	7.558	10.00	12.00	18.00	60.00
	1887 MH	7.681	10.00	12.00	18.00	60.00
	1888 MH	7.179	10.00	12.00	18.00	60.00
	1889 MH	7.332	10.00	15.00	20.00	65.00
	1890 MH	7.412	10.00	12.00	18.00	60.00
	1890 AM	I.A.	10.00	12.00	18.00	60.00
	1891 AM	8.076	10.00	12.00	18.00	60.00
	1892 AM	9.392	10.00	12.00	18.00	60.00
	1893 AM	10.773	10.00	12.00	18.00	55.00
	1894 AM	12.394	10.00	12.00	18.00	45.00
	1895 AM	10.474	10.00	12.00	18.00	45.00
	1895 AB	I.A.	10.00	12.00	18.00	60.00
	1896 AB	9.327	10.00	12.00	18.00	60.00
	1896 AM	I.A.	10.00	12.00	18.00	60.00
	1897 AM	8.621	10.00	12.00	18.00	60.00

NOTE: Varieties exist. 1874 CP is a die struck counterfeit.

Mint mark: O, Oa

KM#	Date	Mintage	Fine	VF	XF	Unc
377.11	1858O AE	—	5500.	—	—	—
	1858OaAE	—	—	—	Unique	—
	1859 AE A in O of mm					
		—	300.00	650.00	1150.	—
	1860 AE A in O of mm					
		—	200.00	450.00	750.00	—
	1861 O FR	—	125.00	250.00	500.00	1100.
	1861OaFR	—	150.00	350.00	600.00	—
	1862O FR	—	40.00	80.00	200.00	375.00
	1862OaFR	—	65.00	125.00	250.00	450.00
	1863O FR	—	30.00	60.00	100.00	250.00
	1863O AE	—	30.00	60.00	100.00	250.00
	1863OaAE A in O of mm					
		—	100.00	150.00	250.00	450.00
	1863OaAE A above O in mm					
		—	1650.	2750.	—	—
	1864 FR	—	25.00	50.00	75.00	200.00
	1865 AE	—	1850.	3000.	—	—
	1867 AE	—	40.00	80.00	150.00	400.00
	1868 AE	—	25.00	50.00	100.00	250.00
	1869 AE	—	30.00	60.00	100.00	250.00
	1873 AE	—	200.00	300.00	600.00	1350.
	1874 AE	.142	15.00	30.00	50.00	200.00
	1875/4 AE	.131	25.00	50.00	75.00	200.00
	1875 AE	I.A.	15.00	30.00	40.00	135.00
	1876 AE	.140	20.00	35.00	55.00	200.00
	1877 AE	.139	20.00	30.00	50.00	200.00
	1878 AE	.125	15.00	25.00	50.00	200.00
	1879 AE	.153	15.00	30.00	45.00	150.00
	1880 AE	.143	15.00	30.00	45.00	150.00
	1881 AE	.134	20.00	35.00	60.00	150.00
	1882 AE	.100	20.00	35.00	60.00	150.00
	1883 AE	.122	15.00	30.00	45.00	150.00
	1884 AE	.142	15.00	30.00	50.00	150.00
	1885 AE	.158	15.00	25.00	40.00	135.00
	1886 AE	.120	15.00	30.00	45.00	150.00
	1887/6 AE	.115	25.00	50.00	80.00	200.00
	1887 AE	I.A.	15.00	25.00	40.00	135.00
	1888 AE	.145	15.00	25.00	40.00	135.00
	1889 AE	.150	20.00	30.00	60.00	175.00
	1890 AE	.181	20.00	30.00	60.00	175.00
	1891 EN	.160	15.00	25.00	40.00	135.00
	1892 EN	.120	15.00	25.00	40.00	135.00
	1893 EN	.066	45.00	75.00	115.00	225.00

NOTE: Varieties exist.

Mint mark: Pi

KM#	Date	Mintage	Fine	VF	XF	Unc
377.12	1827 JS	—	—	—	Rare	—
	1828/7 JS	—	275.00	425.00	650.00	1250.
	1828 JS	—	225.00	375.00	550.00	1100.
	1829 JS	—	35.00	65.00	125.00	250.00
	1830 JS	—	30.00	50.00	100.00	200.00
	1831/0 JS	—	30.00	60.00	125.00	250.00
	1831 JS	—	25.00	35.00	75.00	200.00
	1832/22 JS	—	25.00	35.00	65.00	165.00
	1832 JS	—	25.00	35.00	65.00	165.00
	1833/2 JS	—	30.00	40.00	70.00	175.00
	1833 JS	—	20.00	30.00	50.00	150.00
	1834/3 JS	—	25.00	35.00	60.00	150.00
	1834 JS	—	15.00	25.00	50.00	150.00
	1835 JS denomination 8R					
		—	20.00	30.00	65.00	175.00
	1835 JS denomination 8Rs					
		—	15.00	25.00	50.00	150.00
	1836 JS	—	20.00	30.00	55.00	150.00
	1837 JS	—	30.00	50.00	85.00	200.00
	1838 JS	—	20.00	30.00	55.00	150.00
	1839 JS	—	20.00	40.00	70.00	150.00
	1840 JS	—	20.00	30.00	60.00	150.00
	1841PiJS	—	25.00	40.00	85.00	200.00
	1841iPJS (error)					
		—	50.00	100.00	200.00	400.00
	1842/1 JS	—	40.00	60.00	100.00	200.00
	1842/1 PS/JS					
377.12		—	35.00	55.00	90.00	200.00
	1842 JS eagle type of 1843					
		—	30.00	50.00	80.00	175.00
	1842 PS	—	30.00	50.00	80.00	175.00
	1842 PS/JS eagle type of 1841					
		—	30.00	50.00	80.00	175.00
	1843/2 PS round top 3					
		—	50.00	75.00	150.00	250.00
	1843 PS flat top 3					
		—	30.00	60.00	125.00	225.00
	1843 AM round top 3					
		—	20.00	30.00	55.00	150.00
	1843 AM flat top 3					
		—	20.00	30.00	55.00	150.00
	1844 AM	—	20.00	30.00	55.00	150.00
	1845/4 AM	—	25.00	50.00	100.00	225.00
	1845 AM	—	25.00	50.00	100.00	225.00
	1846/5 AM	—	25.00	35.00	55.00	150.00
	1846 AM	—	15.00	25.00	50.00	150.00
	1847 AM	—	30.00	50.00	85.00	175.00
	1848/7 AM	—	30.00	60.00	100.00	200.00
	1848 AM	—	30.00	50.00	85.00	175.00
	1849/8 PS/AM					
		—	1750.	3000.	—	—
	1849 PS	—	2250.	3750.	—	—
	1849 MC/PS	—	60.00	125.00	250.00	500.00
	1849 AM	—	1250.	2250.	4000.	—
	1849 MC	—	60.00	125.00	250.00	500.00
	1850 MC	—	40.00	80.00	150.00	300.00
	1851 MC	—	150.00	300.00	450.00	900.00
	1852 MC	—	75.00	125.00	200.00	400.00
	1853 MC	—	150.00	275.00	400.00	850.00
	1854 MC	—	100.00	150.00	250.00	500.00
	1855 MC	—	100.00	150.00	250.00	500.00
	1856 MC	—	65.00	100.00	200.00	400.00
	1857 MC	—	500.00	900.00	1500.	—
	1857 PS/MC	—	150.00	225.00	375.00	700.00
	1857 PS	—	125.00	200.00	350.00	650.00
	1858 MC/PS	—	250.00	400.00	650.00	1200.
	1858 MC	—	250.00	400.00	650.00	1200.
	1858 PS	—	—	—	Rare	—
	1859/8 MC/PS					
		—	3650.	5750.	—	—
	1859 MC	—	3500.	5500.	—	—
	1859 PS/MC	—	3500.	5500.	—	—
	1860 FC	—	2000.	4000.	6500.	—
	1860 FE	—	—	—	Rare	—
	1860 MC	—	2000.	4000.	6500.	—
	1860 PS	—	400.00	600.00	900.00	1750.
	1860 RO	—	—	—	*Rare	—
	1861 PS	—	30.00	60.00	90.00	175.00
	1861 RO	—	25.00	35.00	55.00	125.00
	1862/1 RO	—	20.00	25.00	50.00	125.00
	1862 RO	—	15.00	20.00	40.00	100.00
	1862 RO oval O in RO					
		—	15.00	20.00	40.00	100.00
	1862 RO round O in RO, 6 is inverted 9					
		—	20.00	30.00	50.00	125.00
	1863/2 RO	—	25.00	35.00	65.00	150.00
	1863 RO	—	15.00	20.00	40.00	125.00
	1863 6/inverted 6					
		—	25.00	35.00	55.00	125.00
	1863 FC	—	—	—	Rare	—
	1864 RO	—	—	—	Rare	—
	1867 CA	—	650.00	950.00	—	—
	1867 LR	—	525.00	850.00	—	—
	1867 PS/CA	—	—	—	Rare	—
	1867 PS	—	30.00	60.00	125.00	275.00
	1868/7 PS	—	30.00	60.00	125.00	250.00
	1868 PS	—	20.00	30.00	50.00	125.00
	1869/8 PS	—	20.00	25.00	45.00	125.00
	1869 PS	—	15.00	20.00	40.00	125.00
	1870/69 PS	—	1150.	2250.	4000.	—
	1870 PS	—	1000.	2000.	3500.	—
	1873 MH	—	18.00	25.00	45.00	150.00
	1874/3 MH	—	15.00	20.00	30.00	135.00
	1874 MH	—	10.00	12.00	22.00	120.00
	1875 MH	—	10.00	12.00	22.00	100.00
	1876/5 MH	—	18.00	25.00	45.00	150.00
	1876 MH	—	10.00	12.00	22.00	100.00
	1877 MH	1.018	10.00	12.00	22.00	120.00
	1878 MH	1.046	12.00	15.00	25.00	125.00
	1879/8 MH	—	15.00	20.00	30.00	125.00
	1879 MH	—	10.00	12.00	22.00	100.00
	1879 BE	—	25.00	50.00	75.00	150.00
	1879 MR	—	30.00	50.00	100.00	200.00
	1880 MR	—	250.00	400.00	800.00	—
	1880 MH	—	10.00	12.00	22.00	100.00
	1881 MH	2.100	10.00	12.00	22.00	100.00
	1882/1 MH					
		1.602	15.00	20.00	30.00	125.00
	1882 MH	I.A.	10.00	12.00	22.00	100.00
	1883 MH	1.545	10.00	12.00	22.00	100.00
	1884/3 MH	—	15.00	20.00	30.00	125.00
	1884 MH/MM					
		—	12.00	15.00	22.00	90.00
	1884 MH	—	10.00	12.00	20.00	80.00
	1885/4 MH					
		1.736	15.00	20.00	30.00	125.00
	1885/8 MH	I.A.	15.00	20.00	30.00	125.00
	1885 MH	I.A.	10.00	12.00	20.00	80.00
	1885 LC	I.A.	12.00	18.00	25.00	100.00
	1886 LC	3.347	10.00	12.00	20.00	80.00
	1886 MR	I.A.	10.00	12.00	20.00	80.00
	1887 MR	2.922	10.00	12.00	20.00	80.00
	1888 MR	2.438	10.00	12.00	20.00	80.00
	1889 MR	2.103	10.00	12.00	20.00	80.00
	1890 MR	1.562	10.00	12.00	20.00	70.00
	1891 MR	1.184	10.00	12.00	20.00	70.00
	1892 MR	1.336	10.00	12.00	20.00	70.00
	1893 MR	.530	10.00	12.00	20.00	80.00

NOTE: Varieties exist.

***NOTE:** Spink America Gerber sale 6-96 cleaned VF or better realized $33,000.

Mint mark: Zs

KM#	Date	Mintage	Fine	VF	XF	Unc
377.13	1825 AZ	—	25.00	35.00	65.00	175.00
	1826/5 AZ	—	25.00	45.00	85.00	200.00
	1826 AZ	—	20.00	35.00	65.00	175.00
	1826 AV	—	200.00	400.00	700.00	1500.
	1826 AO	—	300.00	600.00	1000.	2000.
	1827 AO/AZ	—	35.00	50.00	125.00	250.00
	1827 AO	—	25.00	45.00	85.00	200.00
	1828 AO	—	15.00	20.00	45.00	165.00
	1829 AO	—	15.00	20.00	45.00	165.00
	1829 OV	—	50.00	90.00	150.00	300.00
	1830 OV	—	15.00	20.00	45.00	165.00
	1831 OV	—	25.00	50.00	90.00	200.00
	1831 OM	—	15.00	25.00	55.00	165.00
	1832/1 OM	—	20.00	25.00	45.00	165.00
	1832 OM	—	15.00	20.00	40.00	150.00
	1833/2 OM	—	20.00	30.00	45.00	165.00
	1833 OM/MM					
		—	15.00	25.00	40.00	150.00
	1833 OM	—	15.00	20.00	35.00	150.00
	1834 OM	—	15.00	20.00	35.00	150.00
	1835 OM	—	15.00	20.00	40.00	150.00
	1836/4 OM	—	20.00	30.00	50.00	165.00
	1836/5 OM	—	20.00	30.00	50.00	165.00
	1836 OM	—	15.00	20.00	35.00	150.00
	1837 OM	—	15.00	20.00	35.00	150.00
	1838/7 OM	—	20.00	30.00	45.00	165.00
	1838 OM	—	15.00	20.00	35.00	150.00
	1839 OM	—	15.00	20.00	35.00	150.00
	1840 OM	—	15.00	20.00	35.00	150.00
	1841 OM	—	15.00	20.00	35.00	150.00
	1842 OM eagle type of 1841					
		—	15.00	20.00	35.00	150.00
	1842 OM eagle type of 1843					
		—	15.00	20.00	35.00	150.00
	1843 OM	—	15.00	20.00	35.00	150.00
	1844 OM	—	15.00	20.00	35.00	150.00
	1845 OM	—	15.00	20.00	35.00	150.00
	1846 OM	—	15.00	20.00	35.00	150.00
	1847 OM	—	15.00	20.00	35.00	150.00
	1848/7 OM	—	20.00	30.00	45.00	165.00
	1848 OM	—	15.00	20.00	35.00	150.00
	1849 OM	—	15.00	20.00	35.00	150.00
	1850 OM	—	15.00	20.00	35.00	150.00
	1851 OM	—	15.00	20.00	35.00	150.00
	1852 OM	—	15.00	20.00	35.00	150.00
	1853 OM	—	30.00	45.00	75.00	200.00
	1854/3 OM	—	20.00	30.00	60.00	175.00
	1854 OM	—	15.00	25.00	45.00	165.00
	1855 OM	—	20.00	30.00	60.00	175.00
	1855 MO	—	30.00	60.00	90.00	200.00
	1856/5 MO	—	20.00	30.00	45.00	165.00
	1856 MO	—	15.00	20.00	35.00	150.00
	1857/5 MO	—	20.00	30.00	45.00	165.00
	1857 MO	—	15.00	20.00	35.00	150.00
	1858/7 MO	—	15.00	20.00	35.00	150.00
	1858 MO	—	15.00	20.00	35.00	150.00
	1859/8 MO	—	15.00	20.00	35.00	150.00
	1859 MO	—	15.00	20.00	35.00	150.00
	1859 VL/MO	—	25.00	50.00	75.00	175.00
	1859 VL	—	20.00	40.00	60.00	165.00
	1860/50 MO	—	10.00	12.00	20.00	80.00
	1860/59 MO	—	10.00	12.00	20.00	80.00
	1860 MO	—	10.00	12.00	20.00	80.00
	1860 VL/MO	—	10.00	12.00	20.00	80.00
	1860 VL	—	10.00	12.00	20.00	80.00
	1861/0 VL/MO					
		—	10.00	12.00	20.00	80.00
	1861/0 VL	—	10.00	12.00	20.00	80.00
	1861 VL	—	10.00	12.00	20.00	80.00
	1862/1 VL	—	15.00	20.00	35.00	100.00
	1862 VL	—	10.00	12.00	20.00	80.00
	1863 VL	—	10.00	12.00	20.00	80.00
	1863 MO	—	10.00	12.00	20.00	80.00
	1864/3 VL	—	15.00	20.00	35.00	100.00
	1864 VL	—	10.00	12.00	20.00	80.00
	1864 MO	—	15.00	20.00	35.00	100.00
	1865/4 MO	—	200.00	450.00	800.00	1550.
	1865 MO	—	150.00	300.00	600.00	1250.
	1866 VL	—	Contemporary counterfeit			
	1867 JS	—	—	—	Rare	—
	1868 JS	—	10.00	12.00	20.00	80.00
	1868 YH	—	10.00	12.00	20.00	80.00
	1869 YH	—	10.00	12.00	20.00	80.00
	1870 YH	—	—	—	Rare	—
	1873 YH	—	10.00	12.00	20.00	80.00
	1874 YH	—	10.00	12.00	20.00	80.00
	1874 JA/YA	—	10.00	12.00	20.00	80.00

KM#	Date	Mintage	Fine	VF	XF	Unc
377.13	1874 JA	—	10.00	12.00	20.00	80.00
	1875 JA	—	10.00	12.00	20.00	80.00
	1876 JA	—	10.00	12.00	20.00	80.00
	1876 JS	—	10.00	12.00	20.00	80.00
	1877 JS	2.700	10.00	12.00	20.00	80.00
	1878 JS	2.310	10.00	12.00	20.00	80.00
	1879/8 JS	—	15.00	20.00	35.00	100.00
	1879 JS	—	10.00	12.00	20.00	80.00
	1880 JS	—	10.00	12.00	20.00	80.00
	1881 JS	5.592	10.00	12.00	20.00	80.00
	1882/1 JS	2.485	15.00	20.00	35.00	100.00
	1882 JS straight J	Inc. Ab.	10.00	12.00	20.00	65.00
	1882 JS full J	Inc. Ab.	10.00	12.00	20.00	65.00
	1883/2 JS	2.563	15.00	20.00	35.00	100.00
	1883 JS	I.A.	10.00	12.00	20.00	80.00
	1884 JS	—	10.00	12.00	20.00	80.00
	1885 JS	2.252	10.00	12.00	20.00	65.00
	1886/5 JS	5.303	15.00	20.00	35.00	100.00
	1886/8 JS	I.A.	15.00	20.00	35.00	100.00
	1886 JS	I.A.	10.00	12.00	20.00	65.00
	1886 FZ	I.A.	10.00	12.00	20.00	65.00
	1887ZsFZ	4.733	10.00	12.00	20.00	65.00
	1887Z FZ	I.A.	20.00	30.00	50.00	100.00
	1888/7 FZ	5.132	12.00	15.00	25.00	80.00
	1888 FZ	I.A.	10.00	12.00	20.00	65.00
	1889 FZ	4.344	10.00	12.00	20.00	65.00
	1890 FZ	3.887	10.00	12.00	20.00	65.00
	1891 FZ	4.114	10.00	12.00	20.00	65.00
	1892/1 FZ	4.238	12.00	15.00	25.00	80.00
	1892 FZ	I.A.	10.00	12.00	20.00	65.00
	1893 FZ	3.872	10.00	12.00	20.00	65.00
	1894 FZ	3.081	10.00	12.00	20.00	65.00
	1895 FZ	4.718	10.00	12.00	20.00	65.00
	1896 FZ	4.226	10.00	12.00	20.00	55.00
	1897 FZ	4.877	10.00	12.00	20.00	55.00

NOTE: Varieties exist.

1/2 ESCUDO

1.6900 g, .875 GOLD, .0475 oz AGW
Mint mark: C
Obv: Facing eagle.

KM#	Date	Mintage	VG	Fine	VF	XF
378	1848 CE	—	35.00	50.00	75.00	150.00
	1853 CE	—	35.00	50.00	75.00	150.00
	1854 CE	—	35.00	50.00	75.00	150.00
	1856 CE	—	50.00	100.00	150.00	250.00
	1857 CE	—	35.00	50.00	75.00	150.00
	1859 CE	—	35.00	50.00	75.00	150.00
	1860 CE	—	35.00	50.00	75.00	150.00
	1862 CE	—	35.00	50.00	75.00	125.00
	1863 CE	—	35.00	50.00	75.00	125.00
	1866 CE	—	35.00	50.00	75.00	125.00
	1867 CE	—	35.00	50.00	75.00	125.00
	1870 CE	—	—	—	—	—

Mint mark: Do

KM#	Date	Mintage	VG	Fine	VF	XF
378.1	1833 RM/RL	—	35.00	50.00	75.00	150.00
	1834/3 RM	—	35.00	50.00	75.00	150.00
	1835/3 RM	—	35.00	50.00	75.00	150.00
	1836/4 RM	—	35.00	50.00	75.00	150.00
	1837 RM	—	35.00	50.00	75.00	150.00
	1838 RM	—	40.00	60.00	100.00	175.00
	1843 RM	—	40.00	60.00	100.00	175.00
	1844/33 RM	—	40.00	60.00	100.00	175.00
	1844/33 RM/RL	—	65.00	125.00	275.00	450.00
	1846 RM	—	40.00	60.00	100.00	175.00
	1848 RM	—	40.00	60.00	100.00	175.00
	1850/33 JMR	—	40.00	60.00	100.00	175.00
	1851 JMR	—	40.00	60.00	100.00	200.00
	1852 JMR	—	40.00	60.00	100.00	175.00
	1853/33 CP	—	75.00	150.00	300.00	500.00
	1853 CP	—	35.00	50.00	75.00	150.00
	1854 CP	—	35.00	50.00	75.00	150.00
	1855 CP	—	35.00	50.00	75.00	150.00
	1859 CP	—	35.00	50.00	75.00	150.00
	1861 CP	—	35.00	50.00	75.00	150.00
	1864 LT	—	75.00	125.00	250.00	400.00

Mint mark: Ga

KM#	Date	Mintage	VG	Fine	VF	XF
378.2	1825 FS	—	40.00	60.00	100.00	175.00
	1829 FS	—	40.00	60.00	100.00	175.00
	1831 FS	—	40.00	60.00	100.00	175.00
	1834 FS	—	40.00	60.00	100.00	175.00
	1835 FS	—	40.00	60.00	100.00	175.00
	1837 JG	—	40.00	60.00	100.00	175.00
	1838 JG	—	40.00	60.00	100.00	175.00
	1839 JG	—	40.00	60.00	100.00	175.00
	1842 JG	—	40.00	60.00	100.00	175.00
	1847 JG	—	40.00	60.00	100.00	175.00
	1850 JG	—	35.00	50.00	75.00	150.00
	1852 JG	—	35.00	50.00	75.00	150.00
	1859 JG	—	40.00	60.00	100.00	175.00
	1861 JG	—	35.00	50.00	75.00	150.00

Mint mark: GC

KM#	Date	Mintage	VG	Fine	VF	XF
378.3	1846 MP	—	50.00	75.00	100.00	175.00
	1847 MP	—	50.00	75.00	100.00	175.00
	1848/7 MP	—	50.00	75.00	100.00	200.00
	1850 MP	—	50.00	75.00	100.00	175.00
	1851 MP	—	50.00	75.00	100.00	175.00

Mint mark: Go

KM#	Date	Mintage	VG	Fine	VF	XF
378.4	1845 PM	—	30.00	40.00	65.00	125.00
	1849 PF	—	30.00	40.00	65.00	125.00
	1851/41 PF	—	30.00	40.00	65.00	125.00
	1851 PF	—	30.00	40.00	65.00	125.00
	1852 PF	—	30.00	40.00	65.00	125.00
	1853 PF	—	30.00	40.00	65.00	125.00
	1855 PF	—	30.00	50.00	80.00	150.00
	1857 PF	—	30.00	40.00	65.00	125.00
	1858/7 PF	—	30.00	40.00	65.00	125.00
	1859 PF	—	30.00	40.00	65.00	125.00
	1860 PF	—	30.00	40.00	65.00	125.00
	1861 PF	—	30.00	40.00	65.00	125.00
	1862/1 YE	—	30.00	40.00	65.00	125.00
	1863 PF	—	30.00	50.00	80.00	150.00
	1863 YF	—	30.00	40.00	65.00	125.00

Mint mark: Mo

KM#	Date	Mintage	VG	Fine	VF	XF
378.5	1825/1 JM	—	50.00	75.00	125.00	200.00
	1825/4 JM	—	50.00	75.00	125.00	200.00
	1825 JM	—	30.00	40.00	80.00	150.00
	1827/6 JM	—	30.00	40.00	80.00	150.00
	1827 JM	—	30.00	40.00	80.00	150.00
	1829 JM	—	30.00	40.00	80.00	150.00
	1831/0 JM	—	30.00	40.00	80.00	150.00
	1831 JM	—	30.00	40.00	60.00	125.00
	1832 JM	—	30.00	40.00	60.00	125.00
	1833 MJ olive & oak branches reversed	—	30.00	50.00	90.00	175.00
	1834 ML	—	30.00	40.00	60.00	125.00
	1835 ML	—	30.00	40.00	80.00	150.00
	1838 ML	—	30.00	50.00	90.00	175.00
	1839 ML	—	30.00	50.00	90.00	175.00
	1840 ML	—	30.00	40.00	60.00	125.00
	1841 ML	—	30.00	40.00	60.00	125.00
	1842 ML	—	30.00	40.00	80.00	150.00
	1842 MM	—	30.00	40.00	80.00	150.00
	1843 MM	—	30.00	40.00	60.00	125.00
	1844 MF	—	30.00	40.00	60.00	125.00
	1845 MF	—	30.00	40.00	60.00	125.00
	1846/5 MF	—	30.00	40.00	60.00	125.00
	1846 MF	—	30.00	40.00	60.00	125.00
	1848 GC	—	30.00	40.00	60.00	125.00
	1850 GC	—	30.00	40.00	60.00	125.00
	1851 GC	—	30.00	40.00	60.00	125.00
	1852 GC	—	30.00	40.00	60.00	125.00
	1853 GC	—	30.00	40.00	60.00	125.00
	1854 GC	—	30.00	40.00	60.00	125.00
	1855 GF	—	30.00	40.00	60.00	125.00
	1856/4 GF	—	30.00	40.00	60.00	125.00
	1857 GF	—	30.00	40.00	60.00	125.00
	1858/7 FH/GF	—	35.00	50.00	75.00	150.00
	1858 FH	—	30.00	40.00	60.00	125.00
	1859 FH	—	30.00	40.00	60.00	125.00
	1860/59 FH	—	30.00	40.00	60.00	125.00
	1861 CH/FH	—	30.00	40.00	80.00	150.00
	1862 CH	—	30.00	40.00	60.00	125.00
	1863/57 CH/GF	—	30.00	40.00	60.00	125.00
	1868/58 PH	—	30.00	40.00	80.00	150.00
	1869/59 CH	—	30.00	40.00	80.00	150.00

Mint mark: Zs

KM#	Date	Mintage	VG	Fine	VF	XF
378.6	1860 VL	—	35.00	50.00	75.00	150.00
	1862/1 VL	—	35.00	50.00	75.00	150.00
	1862 VL	—	30.00	40.00	65.00	125.00

ESCUDO

3.3800 g, .875 GOLD, .0950 oz AGW
Mint mark: C
Obv: Facing eagle.

KM#	Date	Mintage	VG	Fine	VF	XF
379	1846 CE	—	75.00	100.00	200.00	350.00
	1847 CE	—	50.00	75.00	125.00	175.00
	1848 CE	—	50.00	75.00	125.00	175.00
	1849/8 CE	—	60.00	100.00	150.00	225.00
	1850 CE	—	50.00	75.00	125.00	175.00
	1851 CE	—	60.00	100.00	150.00	225.00
	1853/1 CE	—	60.00	100.00	150.00	225.00
	1854 CE	—	50.00	75.00	125.00	175.00
	1856/5/4 CE	—	60.00	100.00	150.00	225.00
	1856 CE	—	50.00	75.00	125.00	175.00
	1857/1 CE	—	60.00	100.00	150.00	225.00
	1857 CE	—	50.00	75.00	125.00	175.00
	1861 PV	—	50.00	75.00	125.00	175.00
	1862 CE	—	50.00	75.00	125.00	175.00
	1863 CE	—	50.00	75.00	125.00	175.00
	1866 CE	—	50.00	75.00	125.00	175.00
	1870 CE	—	50.00	75.00	125.00	175.00

Mint mark: Do

KM#	Date	Mintage	VG	Fine	VF	XF
379.1	1833/2 RM/RL	—	75.00	125.00	200.00	300.00
	1834 RM	—	60.00	100.00	150.00	200.00
	1835 RM	—	—	—	—	—
	1836 RM/RL	—	60.00	100.00	150.00	200.00
	1838 RM	—	60.00	100.00	150.00	200.00
	1846/38 RM	—	75.00	125.00	200.00	300.00
	1850 JMR	—	75.00	125.00	175.00	225.00
	1851/31 JMR	—	75.00	125.00	200.00	300.00
	1851 JMR	—	75.00	125.00	175.00	225.00
	1853 CP	—	75.00	125.00	175.00	225.00
	1854/34 CP	—	75.00	125.00	175.00	225.00
	1854/44 CP/RP	—	75.00	125.00	175.00	225.00
	1855 CP	—	75.00	125.00	175.00	225.00
	1859 CP	—	75.00	125.00	175.00	225.00
	1861 CP	—	75.00	125.00	175.00	225.00
	1864 LT/CP	—	75.00	125.00	175.00	225.00

Mint mark: Ga

KM#	Date	Mintage	VG	Fine	VF	XF
379.2	1825 FS	—	60.00	90.00	125.00	200.00
	1826 FS	—	60.00	90.00	125.00	200.00
	1829 FS	—	—	—	—	—
	1831 FS	—	60.00	90.00	125.00	200.00
	1834 FS	—	60.00	90.00	125.00	200.00
	1835 JG	—	60.00	90.00	125.00	200.00
	1842 JG/MC	—	60.00	90.00	125.00	200.00
	1843 MC	—	60.00	90.00	125.00	200.00
	1847 JG	—	60.00	90.00	125.00	200.00
	1848/7 JG	—	60.00	90.00	125.00	200.00
	1849 JG	—	60.00	90.00	125.00	200.00
	1850/40 JG	—	65.00	125.00	225.00	325.00
	1850 JG	—	60.00	90.00	125.00	200.00
	1852/1 JG	—	60.00	90.00	125.00	200.00
	1856 JG	—	60.00	90.00	125.00	200.00
	1857 JG	—	60.00	90.00	125.00	200.00
	1859/7 JG	—	60.00	90.00	125.00	200.00
	1860/59 JG	—	65.00	100.00	175.00	275.00
	1860 JG	—	60.00	90.00	125.00	200.00

Mint mark: GC

KM#	Date	Mintage	VG	Fine	VF	XF
379.3	1844 MP	—	75.00	100.00	175.00	250.00
	1845 MP	—	75.00	100.00	175.00	250.00
	1846 MP	—	75.00	100.00	175.00	250.00
	1847 MP	—	75.00	100.00	175.00	250.00
	1848 MP	—	75.00	100.00	175.00	250.00
	1849 MP	—	75.00	100.00	175.00	250.00
	1850 MP	—	75.00	100.00	175.00	250.00
	1851 MP	—	75.00	100.00	175.00	250.00

Mint mark: Go

KM#	Date	Mintage	VG	Fine	VF	XF
379.4	1845 PM	—	60.00	75.00	125.00	200.00
	1849 PF	—	60.00	75.00	125.00	200.00
	1851 PF	—	60.00	75.00	125.00	200.00
	1853 PF	—	60.00	75.00	125.00	200.00
	1860 PF	—	75.00	125.00	200.00	300.00
	1862 YE	—	60.00	75.00	125.00	200.00

Mint mark: Mo

KM#	Date	Mintage	VG	Fine	VF	XF
379.5	1825 JM	—	50.00	70.00	100.00	150.00
	1827/6 JM	—	50.00	70.00	100.00	150.00
	1827 JM	—	50.00	70.00	100.00	150.00
	1830/29 JM	—	50.00	70.00	100.00	150.00
	1831 JM	—	50.00	70.00	100.00	150.00
	1832 JM	—	50.00	70.00	125.00	175.00
	1833 MJ	—	50.00	70.00	100.00	150.00
	1834 ML	—	50.00	70.00	125.00	175.00
	1841 ML	—	50.00	70.00	125.00	175.00
	1843 MM	—	50.00	70.00	100.00	150.00
	1845 MF	—	50.00	70.00	100.00	150.00
	1846/5 MF	—	50.00	70.00	100.00	150.00
	1848 GC	—	50.00	70.00	125.00	175.00
	1850 GC	—	50.00	70.00	125.00	175.00
	1856/4 GF	—	50.00	70.00	100.00	150.00
	1856/5 GF	—	50.00	70.00	100.00	150.00
	1856 GF	—	50.00	70.00	100.00	150.00
	1858 FH	—	50.00	70.00	125.00	175.00
	1859 FH	—	50.00	70.00	100.00	150.00
	1860 TH	—	50.00	70.00	125.00	175.00
	1861 CH	—	50.00	70.00	100.00	150.00
	1862 CH	—	50.00	70.00	125.00	175.00
	1863 TH	—	50.00	70.00	100.00	150.00
	1869 CH	—	50.00	70.00	100.00	150.00

Mint mark: Zs

KM#	Date	Mintage	VG	Fine	VF	XF
379.6	1853 OM	—	100.00	125.00	200.00	300.00
	1860/59 VL V is inverted A	—	75.00	100.00	200.00	350.00
	1860 VL	—	75.00	100.00	150.00	200.00
	1862 VL	—	75.00	100.00	150.00	200.00

2 ESCUDOS

6.7700 g, .875 GOLD, .1904 oz AGW
Mint mark: C
Obv: Facing eagle.

KM#	Date	Mintage	VG	Fine	VF	XF
380	1846 CE	—	100.00	150.00	225.00	325.00
	1847 CE	—	100.00	150.00	225.00	325.00
	1848 CE	—	100.00	150.00	225.00	325.00
	1852 CE	—	100.00	150.00	225.00	325.00
	1854 CE	—	100.00	175.00	250.00	375.00
	1856/4 CE	—	100.00	175.00	250.00	375.00
	1857 CE	—	100.00	150.00	225.00	325.00

Mint mark: Do

KM#	Date	Mintage	VG	Fine	VF	XF
380.1	1833 RM	—	300.00	450.00	700.00	1200.
	1837/4 RM	—	—	—	—	—

KM#	Date	Mintage	VG	Fine	VF	XF
380.1	1837 RM	—	—	—	—	—
	1844 RM	—	275.00	400.00	600.00	1000.

Mint mark: EoMo

KM#	Date	Mintage	VG	Fine	VF	XF
380.2	1828 LF	—	700.00	1000.	1750.	2500.

Mint mark: Ga

KM#	Date	Mintage	VG	Fine	VF	XF
380.3	1835 FS	—	100.00	150.00	225.00	325.00
	1836/5 JG	—	100.00	150.00	225.00	300.00
	1839/5 JG	—	—	—	—	—
	1839 JG	—	100.00	150.00	200.00	275.00
	1840 MC	—	100.00	150.00	200.00	275.00
	1841 MC	—	100.00	150.00	250.00	400.00
	1847/6 JG	—	100.00	150.00	225.00	300.00
	1848/7 JG	—	100.00	150.00	225.00	300.00
	1850/40 JG	—	100.00	150.00	200.00	250.00
	1851 JG	—	100.00	150.00	200.00	275.00
	1852 JG	—	100.00	150.00	225.00	325.00
	1853 JG	—	100.00	150.00	200.00	275.00
	1854/2 JG	—	—	—	—	—
	1858 JG	—	100.00	150.00	200.00	275.00
	1859/8 JG	—	100.00	150.00	225.00	300.00
	1859 JG	—	100.00	150.00	200.00	275.00
	1860/50 JG	—	100.00	150.00	225.00	300.00
	1860 JG	—	100.00	150.00	225.00	300.00
	1861/59 JG	—	100.00	150.00	200.00	275.00
	1861/0 JG	—	100.00	150.00	200.00	275.00
	1863/1 JG	—	100.00	150.00	200.00	275.00
	1870 IC	—	100.00	150.00	200.00	275.00

Mint mark: GC

KM#	Date	Mintage	VG	Fine	VF	XF
380.4	1844 MP	—	150.00	200.00	275.00	400.00
	1845 MP	—	750.00	1250.	2000.	3000.
	1846 MP	—	750.00	1250.	2000.	3000.
	1847 MP	—	125.00	175.00	350.00	500.00
	1848 MP	—	150.00	200.00	350.00	450.00
	1849 MP	—	150.00	200.00	300.00	400.00
	1850 MP	—	150.00	200.00	300.00	400.00

Mint mark: Go

KM#	Date	Mintage	VG	Fine	VF	XF
380.5	1845 PM	—	100.00	150.00	250.00	400.00
	1849 PF	—	100.00	150.00	250.00	400.00
	1853 PF	—	100.00	150.00	250.00	400.00
	1856 PF	—	100.00	150.00	250.00	400.00
	1859 PF	—	100.00	150.00	250.00	400.00
	1860/59 PF	—	100.00	150.00	250.00	400.00
	1860 PF	—	100.00	150.00	250.00	400.00
	1862 YE	—	100.00	150.00	250.00	400.00

Mint mark: Ho

KM#	Date	Mintage	VG	Fine	VF	XF
380.6	1861 FM	—	500.00	1000.	1500.	2000.

Mint mark: Mo

KM#	Date	Mintage	VG	Fine	VF	XF
380.7	1825 JM	—	100.00	150.00	200.00	275.00
	1827/6 JM	—	100.00	150.00	200.00	275.00
	1827 JM	—	100.00	150.00	200.00	275.00
	1830/29 JM	—	100.00	150.00	200.00	275.00
	1831 JM	—	100.00	150.00	200.00	275.00
	1833 ML	—	100.00	150.00	200.00	275.00
	1841 ML	—	100.00	150.00	200.00	275.00
	1844 MF	—	100.00	150.00	200.00	275.00
	1845 MF	—	100.00	150.00	200.00	275.00
	1846 MF	—	125.00	200.00	400.00	600.00
	1848 GC	—	100.00	150.00	200.00	275.00
	1850 GC	—	100.00	150.00	200.00	275.00
	1856/5 GF	—	100.00	150.00	200.00	275.00
	1856 GF	—	100.00	150.00	200.00	275.00
	1858 FH	—	100.00	150.00	200.00	275.00
	1859 FH	—	100.00	150.00	200.00	275.00
	1861 TH	—	100.00	150.00	200.00	275.00
	1861 CH	—	100.00	150.00	200.00	300.00
	1862 CH	—	100.00	150.00	200.00	300.00
	1863 TH	—	100.00	150.00	200.00	300.00
	1868 PH	—	100.00	150.00	200.00	300.00
	1869 CH	—	100.00	150.00	200.00	300.00

Mint mark: Zs

KM#	Date	Mintage	VG	Fine	VF	XF
380.8	1860 VL	—	150.00	300.00	600.00	1200.
	1862 VL	—	250.00	500.00	800.00	1200.
	1864 MO	—	150.00	300.00	600.00	1200.

4 ESCUDOS

13.5400 g, .875 GOLD, .3809 oz AGW
Mint mark: C
Facing eagle

KM#	Date	Mintage	VG	Fine	VF	XF
381	1846 CE	—	1200.	1700.	—	—
	1847 CE	—	400.00	650.00	850.00	1250.
	1848 CE	—	600.00	900.00	1250.	1750.

Mint mark: Do

KM#	Date	Mintage	VG	Fine	VF	XF
381.1	1832 RM/LR	—	—	—	Rare	—
	1832 RM	—	600.00	900.00	1250.	1750.
	1833 RM/RL	—	—	—	Rare	—
	1852 JMR	—	—	—	Rare	—

Mint mark: Ga

KM#	Date	Mintage	VG	Fine	VF	XF
381.2	1844 MC	—	500.00	750.00	1000.	1500.
	1844 JG	—	400.00	650.00	850.00	1250.

Mint mark: GC

KM#	Date	Mintage	VG	Fine	VF	XF
381.3	1844 MP	—	400.00	650.00	850.00	1250.
	1845 MP	—	350.00	500.00	700.00	1000.
	1846 MP	—	400.00	650.00	850.00	1250.
	1848 MP	—	400.00	650.00	850.00	1250.
	1850 MP	—	500.00	750.00	1000.	1500.

Mint mark: Go

KM#	Date	Mintage	VG	Fine	VF	XF
381.4	1829/8 MJ	—	200.00	300.00	450.00	700.00
	1829 JM	—	200.00	300.00	450.00	700.00
	1829 MJ	—	200.00	300.00	450.00	700.00
	1831 MJ	—	200.00	300.00	450.00	700.00
	1832 MJ	—	200.00	300.00	450.00	700.00
	1833 MJ	—	200.00	300.00	500.00	800.00
	1834 PJ	—	250.00	450.00	650.00	1000.
	1835 PJ	—	250.00	450.00	650.00	1000.
	1836 PJ	—	200.00	300.00	500.00	800.00
	1837 PJ	—	200.00	300.00	500.00	800.00
	1838 PJ	—	200.00	300.00	500.00	800.00
	1839 PJ	—	250.00	450.00	650.00	1000.
	1840 PJ	—	200.00	300.00	500.00	800.00
	1841 PJ	—	250.00	450.00	650.00	1000.
	1845 PM	—	200.00	300.00	500.00	800.00
	1847/5 YE	—	250.00	450.00	650.00	1000.
	1847 PM	—	250.00	450.00	650.00	1000.
	1849 PF	—	250.00	450.00	650.00	1000.
	1851 PF	—	250.00	450.00	650.00	1000.
	1852 PF	—	200.00	300.00	500.00	800.00
	1855 PF	—	200.00	300.00	500.00	800.00
	1857/5 PF	—	200.00	300.00	500.00	800.00
	1858/7 PF	—	200.00	300.00	500.00	800.00
	1858 PF	—	200.00	300.00	500.00	800.00
	1859/7 PF	—	250.00	450.00	650.00	1000.
	1860 PF	—	275.00	475.00	750.00	1200.
	1862 YE	—	200.00	300.00	500.00	800.00
	1863 YF	—	200.00	300.00	500.00	800.00

Mint mark: Ho

KM#	Date	Mintage	VG	Fine	VF	XF
381.5	1861 FM	—	1000.	1500.	2500.	3750.

Mint mark: Mo

KM#	Date	Mintage	VG	Fine	VF	XF
381.6	1825 JM	—	200.00	300.00	500.00	850.00
	1827/6 JM	—	200.00	300.00	500.00	800.00
	1829 JM	—	200.00	350.00	650.00	1000.
	1831 JM	—	200.00	350.00	650.00	1000.
	1832 JM	—	275.00	475.00	750.00	1200.
	1844 MF	—	200.00	350.00	650.00	1000.
	1850 GC	—	200.00	350.00	650.00	1000.
	1856 GF	—	200.00	300.00	500.00	800.00
	1857/6 GF	—	200.00	300.00	500.00	800.00
	1857 GF	—	200.00	300.00	500.00	800.00
	1858 FH	—	200.00	350.00	650.00	1000.
	1859/8 FH	—	200.00	350.00	650.00	1000.
	1861 CH	—	400.00	800.00	1200.	1600.
	1863 CH	—	200.00	350.00	650.00	1000.
	1868 PH	—	200.00	300.00	500.00	800.00
	1869 CH	—	200.00	300.00	500.00	800.00

Mint mark: O, Oa

KM#	Date	Mintage	VG	Fine	VF	XF
381.7	1861 FR	—	1500.	2500.	4000.	6500.

Mint mark: Zs

KM#	Date	Mintage	VG	Fine	VF	XF
381.8	1862 VL	—	750.00	1250.	2250.	3500.

8 ESCUDOS

27.0700 g, .875 GOLD, .7616 oz AGW
Mint mark: Mo
Obv: Hooked-neck eagle.

KM#	Date	Mintage	Fine	VF	XF	Unc
382.1	1823 JM snake's tail curved	—	3750.	7000.	11,000.	—

NOTE: Superior Casterline sale 5-89 choice AU realized $18,700.

KM#	Date	Mintage	Fine	VF	XF	Unc
382.2	1823 JM snake's tail looped	—	3750.	7000.	11,000.	—

Mint mark: A
Obv: Facing eagle.

KM#	Date	Mintage	Fine	VF	XF	Unc
383	1864 PG	—	650.00	1250.	2250.	—
	1866 DL	—	—	—	7500.	—
	1868/7 DL	—	1500.	2250.	3250.	—
	1869 DL	—	650.00	1250.	2250.	—
	1870 DL	—	1500.	2250.	3250.	—
	1872 AM	—	—	—	Rare	—

Mint mark: Ca

KM#	Date	Mintage	Fine	VF	XF	Unc
383.1	1841 RG	—	400.00	750.00	1250.	1750.
	1842 RG	—	375.00	500.00	1000.	1500.
	1843 RG	—	375.00	500.00	1000.	1500.
	1844 RG	—	350.00	500.00	1000.	1500.
	1845 RG	—	350.00	500.00	1000.	1500.
	1846 RG	—	500.00	1250.	1500.	2000.
	1847 RG	—	1000.	2500.	—	—
	1848 RG	—	350.00	500.00	1000.	1500.
	1849 RG	—	350.00	500.00	1000.	1500.
	1850/40 RG	—	350.00	500.00	1000.	1500.
	1851/41 RG	—	350.00	500.00	1000.	1500.
	1852/42 RG	—	350.00	500.00	1000.	1500.
	1853/43 RG	—	350.00	500.00	1000.	1500.
	1854/44 RG	—	350.00	500.00	1000.	1500.
	1855/43 RG	—	400.00	650.00	1250.	1750.
	1856/46 RG	—	350.00	500.00	750.00	1250.
	1857 JC/RG	—	350.00	500.00	750.00	1250.
	1858 JC	—	350.00	500.00	750.00	1250.
	1858 BA/RG	—	350.00	500.00	750.00	1250.
	1859 JC/RG	—	350.00	500.00	750.00	1250.
	1860 JC/RG	—	350.00	500.00	1000.	1500.
	1861 JC	—	375.00	500.00	750.00	1250.
	1862 JC	—	375.00	500.00	750.00	1250.
	1863 JC	—	500.00	1000.	1750.	2250.
	1864 JC	—	400.00	750.00	1250.	1750.
	1865 JC	—	750.00	1500.	2500.	3500.
	1866 JC	—	375.00	500.00	1000.	1500.
	1866 FP	—	600.00	1250.	2000.	2500.
	1866 JG	—	375.00	500.00	1000.	1500.
	1867 JG	—	375.00	500.00	750.00	1250.
	1868 JG concave wings	—	375.00	500.00	750.00	1250.
	1869 MM regular eagle	—	375.00	500.00	750.00	1250.
	1870/60 MM	—	375.00	500.00	750.00	1250.
	1871/61 MM	—	375.00	500.00	750.00	1250.

Mint mark: C

KM#	Date	Mintage	Fine	VF	XF	Unc
383.2	1846 CE	—	375.00	500.00	1000.	1750.
	1847 CE	—	375.00	500.00	800.00	1250.
	1848 CE	—	375.00	500.00	1000.	1750.
	1849 CE	—	375.00	450.00	700.00	1250.
	1850 CE	—	375.00	450.00	700.00	1250.
	1851 CE	—	375.00	500.00	800.00	1250.
	1852 CE	—	375.00	500.00	800.00	1250.
	1853/1 CE	—	375.00	450.00	700.00	1250.
	1854 CE	—	375.00	450.00	700.00	1250.
	1855/4 CE	—	375.00	500.00	1000.	1750.
	1855 CE	—	375.00	500.00	800.00	1250.
	1856 CE	—	375.00	450.00	700.00	1250.
	1857 CE	—	375.00	450.00	700.00	1250.
	1857 CE w/o periods after C's	—	—	—	—	—
	1858 CE	—	375.00	450.00	700.00	1250.
	1859 CE	—	375.00	450.00	700.00	1250.
	1860/58 CE	—	375.00	500.00	800.00	1250.
	1860 CE	—	375.00	500.00	800.00	1250.
	1860 PV	—	375.00	450.00	700.00	1250.
	1861 PV	—	375.00	500.00	800.00	1250.
	1861 CE	—	375.00	500.00	800.00	1250.
	1862 CE	—	375.00	500.00	800.00	1250.
	1863 CE	—	375.00	500.00	800.00	1250.
	1864 CE	—	375.00	450.00	700.00	1250.
	1865 CE	—	375.00	500.00	800.00	1250.
	1866/5 CE	—	375.00	450.00	700.00	1250.
	1866 CE	—	375.00	450.00	700.00	1250.
	1867 CB (error)	—	375.00	450.00	700.00	1250.
	1867 CE/CB	—	375.00	450.00	700.00	1250.
	1868 CB (error)	—	375.00	500.00	800.00	1250.
	1869 CE	—	375.00	500.00	800.00	1250.
	1870 CE	—	375.00	500.00	800.00	1250.

Mint mark: Do

KM#	Date	Mintage	Fine	VF	XF	Unc
383.3	1832 RM	—	850.00	1750.	2000.	3000.
	1833 RM/RL	—	375.00	500.00	800.00	1250.
	1834 RM	—	375.00	500.00	800.00	1250.
	1835 RM	—	375.00	500.00	800.00	1250.
	1836 RM/RL	—	375.00	500.00	800.00	1250.
	1836 RM M on snake	—	375.00	500.00	800.00	1250.
	1837 RM	—	375.00	500.00	800.00	1250.
	1838/6 RM	—	375.00	500.00	800.00	1250.
	1838 RM	—	375.00	500.00	800.00	1250.
	1839 RM	—	375.00	450.00	700.00	1250.
	1840/30 RM/RL	—	400.00	600.00	1000.	1750.
	1841/30 RM	—	550.00	750.00	1250.	2000.
	1841/31 RM	—	375.00	500.00	800.00	1250.
	1841/34 RM	—	375.00	500.00	800.00	1250.
	1841 RM/RL	—	375.00	500.00	800.00	1250.
	1842/32 RM	—	375.00	500.00	800.00	1250.
	1843/33 RM	—	550.00	750.00	1250.	2000.
	1843/1 RM	—	375.00	500.00	800.00	1250.
	1843 RM	—	375.00	500.00	800.00	1250.
	1844/34 RM/RL	—	500.00	1000.	1500.	2500.
	1844 RM	—	450.00	800.00	1250.	2000.
	1845/36 RM	—	400.00	600.00	1000.	1750.
	1845 RM	—	400.00	600.00	1000.	1750.
	1846 RM	—	375.00	500.00	800.00	1250.
	1847/37 RM	—	375.00	500.00	800.00	1250.
	1848/37 RM	—	—	—	—	—
	1848/38 CM	—	375.00	500.00	800.00	1250.
	1849/39 CM	—	375.00	500.00	800.00	1250.
	1849 JMR	—	400.00	750.00	1250.	2000.
	1850 JMR	—	400.00	750.00	1250.	2000.
	1851 JMR	—	400.00	750.00	1250.	2000.
	1852/1 JMR	—	450.00	800.00	1250.	2000.
	1852 CP	—	450.00	800.00	1250.	2000.
	1853 CP	—	450.00	800.00	1250.	2000.
	1854 CP	—	400.00	600.00	1000.	1750.
	1855/4 CP	—	375.00	500.00	800.00	1250.
	1855 CP	—	375.00	500.00	800.00	1250.
	1856 CP	—	400.00	600.00	1000.	1750.
	1857 CP French style eagle, 1832-57	—	375.00	500.00	800.00	1250.
	1857 CP Mexican style eagle	—	375.00	500.00	800.00	1250.
	1858 CP	—	375.00	500.00	800.00	1250.
	1859 CP	—	375.00	500.00	800.00	1250.
	1860/59 CP	—	450.00	700.00	1250.	2200.
	1861/0 CP	—	400.00	600.00	1000.	1750.
	1862/52 CP	—	375.00	500.00	800.00	1250.
	1862/1 CP	—	375.00	500.00	800.00	1250.
	1862 CP	—	375.00	500.00	800.00	1250.
	1863/53 CP	—	375.00	500.00	800.00	1250.
	1864 LT	—	375.00	500.00	800.00	1250.
	1865/4 LT	—	500.00	1000.	1650.	2750.

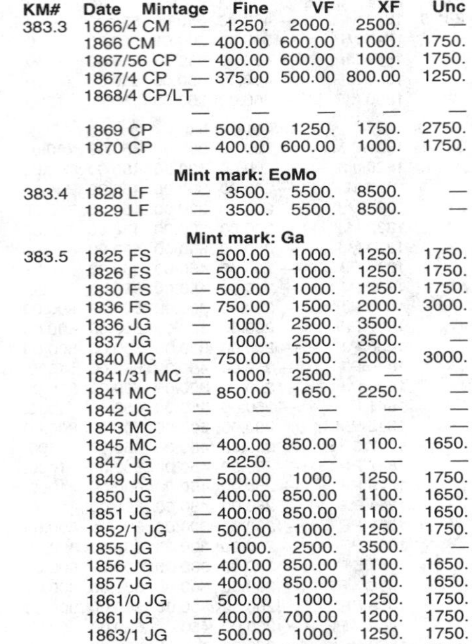

KM#	Date	Mintage	Fine	VF	XF	Unc
383.3	1866/4 CM	—	1250.	2000.	2500.	—
	1866 CM	—	400.00	600.00	1000.	1750.
	1867/56 CP	—	400.00	600.00	1000.	1750.
	1867/4 CP	—	375.00	500.00	800.00	1250.
	1868/4 CP/LT	—	—	—	—	—
	1869 CP	—	500.00	1250.	1750.	2750.
	1870 CP	—	400.00	600.00	1000.	1750.

Mint mark: EoMo

KM#	Date	Mintage	Fine	VF	XF	Unc
383.4	1828 LF	—	3500.	5500.	8500.	—
	1829 LF	—	3500.	5500.	8500.	—

Mint mark: Ga

KM#	Date	Mintage	Fine	VF	XF	Unc
383.5	1825 FS	—	500.00	1000.	1250.	1750.
	1826 FS	—	500.00	1000.	1250.	1750.
	1830 FS	—	500.00	1000.	1250.	1750.
	1836 FS	—	750.00	1500.	2000.	3000.
	1836 JG	—	1000.	2500.	3500.	—
	1837 JG	—	1000.	2500.	3500.	—
	1840 MC	—	750.00	1500.	2000.	3000.
	1841/31 MC	—	1000.	2500.	—	—
	1841 MC	—	850.00	1650.	2250.	—
	1842 JG	—	—	—	—	—
	1843 MC	—	—	—	—	—
	1845 MC	—	400.00	850.00	1100.	1650.
	1847 JG	—	2250.	—	—	—
	1849 JG	—	500.00	1000.	1250.	1750.
	1850 JG	—	400.00	850.00	1100.	1650.
	1851 JG	—	400.00	850.00	1100.	1650.
	1852/1 JG	—	500.00	1000.	1250.	1750.
	1855 JG	—	1000.	2500.	3500.	—
	1856 JG	—	400.00	850.00	1100.	1650.
	1857 JG	—	400.00	850.00	1100.	1650.
	1861/0 JG	—	500.00	1000.	1250.	1750.
	1861 JG	—	400.00	700.00	1200.	1750.
	1863/1 JG	—	500.00	1000.	1250.	1750.
	1866 JG	—	400.00	850.00	1100.	1650.

Mint mark: GC

KM#	Date	Mintage	Fine	VF	XF	Unc
383.6	1844 MP	—	550.00	750.00	1250.	2000.
	1845 MP eagle's tail square	—	550.00	750.00	1250.	2000.
	1845 MP eagle's tail round	—	550.00	750.00	1250.	2000.
	1846 MP eagle's tail square	—	450.00	650.00	1000.	1750.
	1846 MP eagle's tail round	—	450.00	650.00	1000.	1750.
	1847 MP	—	450.00	650.00	1000.	1750.
	1848 MP	—	550.00	750.00	1250.	2000.
	1849 MP	—	550.00	750.00	1250.	2000.
	1850 MP	—	450.00	650.00	1000.	1750.
	1851 MP	—	450.00	650.00	1000.	1750.
	1852 MP	—	550.00	750.00	1250.	2000.

Mint mark: Go

KM#	Date	Mintage	Fine	VF	XF	Unc
383.7	1828 MJ	—	700.00	1750.	2250.	3000.
	1829 MJ	—	600.00	1500.	2000.	2750.
	1830 MJ	—	375.00	500.00	750.00	1000.
	1831 MJ	—	600.00	1500.	2000.	2750.
	1832 MJ	—	500.00	1250.	1750.	2500.
	1833 MJ	—	375.00	500.00	700.00	700.00
	1834 PJ	—	375.00	500.00	700.00	700.00
	1835 PJ	—	375.00	500.00	700.00	700.00
	1836 PJ	—	400.00	650.00	900.00	1250.
	1837 PJ	—	400.00	650.00	900.00	1250.
	1838/7 PJ	—	375.00	500.00	700.00	1000.
	1838 PJ	—	375.00	500.00	800.00	1200.
	1839/8 PJ	—	375.00	500.00	700.00	1000.
	1839 PJ regular eagle	—	375.00	500.00	800.00	1200.
	1840 PJ concave wings	—	375.00	500.00	700.00	1000.
	1841 PJ	—	375.00	500.00	700.00	1000.
	1842 PJ	—	375.00	475.00	650.00	1000.
	1842 PM	—	375.00	500.00	700.00	1000.
	1843 PM small eagle					

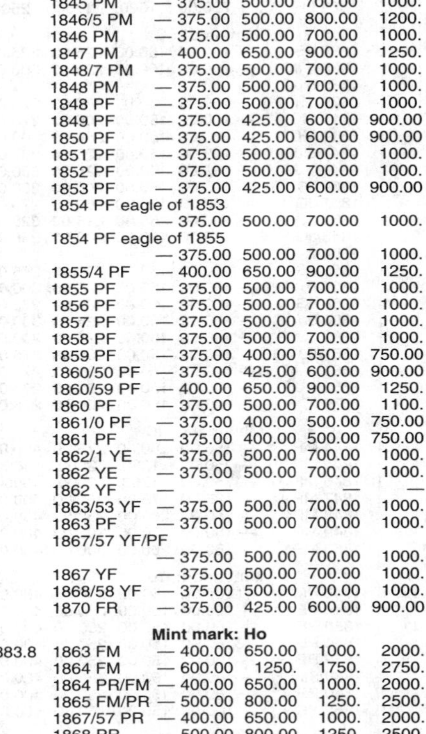

KM#	Date	Mintage	Fine	VF	XF	Unc
383.7		—	375.00	500.00	700.00	1000.
	1844/3 PM	—	400.00	650.00	900.00	1250.
	1844 PM	—	375.00	500.00	700.00	1000.
	1845 PM	—	375.00	500.00	700.00	1000.
	1846/5 PM	—	375.00	500.00	800.00	1200.
	1846 PM	—	375.00	500.00	700.00	1000.
	1847 PM	—	400.00	650.00	900.00	1250.
	1848/7 PM	—	375.00	500.00	700.00	1000.
	1848 PM	—	375.00	500.00	700.00	1000.
	1848 PF	—	375.00	500.00	700.00	1000.
	1849 PF	—	375.00	425.00	600.00	900.00
	1850 PF	—	375.00	425.00	600.00	900.00
	1851 PF	—	375.00	500.00	700.00	1000.
	1852 PF	—	375.00	500.00	700.00	1000.
	1853 PF	—	375.00	425.00	600.00	900.00
	1854 PF eagle of 1853	—	375.00	500.00	700.00	1000.
	1854 PF eagle of 1855	—	375.00	500.00	700.00	1000.
	1855/4 PF	—	400.00	650.00	900.00	1250.
	1855 PF	—	375.00	500.00	700.00	1000.
	1856 PF	—	375.00	500.00	700.00	1000.
	1857 PF	—	375.00	500.00	700.00	1000.
	1858 PF	—	375.00	500.00	700.00	1000.
	1859 PF	—	375.00	400.00	550.00	750.00
	1860/50 PF	—	375.00	425.00	600.00	900.00
	1860/59 PF	—	400.00	650.00	900.00	1250.
	1860 PF	—	375.00	500.00	700.00	1100.
	1861/0 PF	—	375.00	400.00	500.00	750.00
	1861 PF	—	375.00	400.00	500.00	750.00
	1862/1 YE	—	375.00	500.00	700.00	1000.
	1862 YE	—	375.00	500.00	700.00	1000.
	1862 YF	—	—	—	—	—
	1863/53 YF	—	375.00	500.00	700.00	1000.
	1863 PF	—	375.00	500.00	700.00	1000.
	1867/57 YF/PF	—	375.00	500.00	700.00	1000.
	1867 YF	—	375.00	500.00	700.00	1000.
	1868/58 YF	—	375.00	500.00	700.00	1000.
	1870 FR	—	375.00	425.00	600.00	900.00

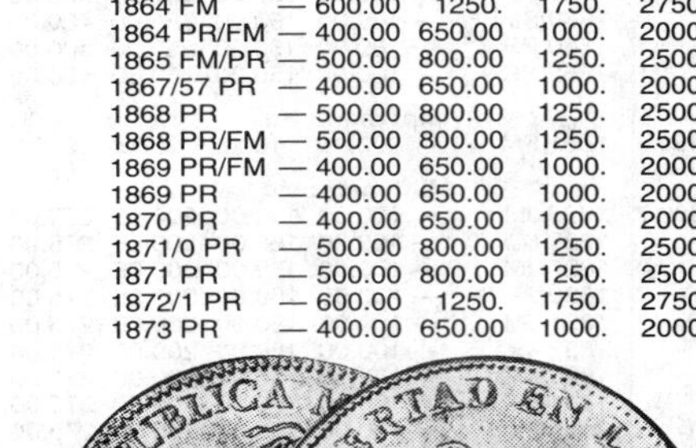

Mint mark: Ho

KM#	Date	Mintage	Fine	VF	XF	Unc
383.8	1863 FM	—	400.00	650.00	1000.	2000.
	1864 FM	—	600.00	1250.	1750.	2750.
	1864 PR/FM	—	400.00	650.00	1000.	2000.
	1865 FM/PR	—	500.00	800.00	1250.	2500.
	1867/57 PR	—	400.00	650.00	1000.	2000.
	1868 PR	—	500.00	800.00	1250.	2500.
	1868 PR/FM	—	500.00	800.00	1250.	2500.
	1869 PR/FM	—	400.00	650.00	1000.	2000.
	1869 PR	—	400.00	650.00	1000.	2000.
	1870 PR	—	400.00	650.00	1000.	2000.
	1871/0 PR	—	500.00	800.00	1250.	2500.
	1871 PR	—	500.00	800.00	1250.	2500.
	1872/1 PR	—	600.00	1250.	1750.	2750.
	1873 PR	—	400.00	650.00	1000.	2000.

Large book.

Small book.

Mint mark: Mo

KM#	Date	Mintage	Fine	VF	XF	Unc
383.9	1824 JM lg. book reverse	—	500.00	1000.	1250.	2000.
	1825 JM sm. book reverse	—	375.00	450.00	600.00	1000.
	1826/5 JM	—	700.00	1750.	2250.	3000.
	1827 JM	—	375.00	600.00	725.00	1000.
	1828 JM	—	375.00	600.00	725.00	1000.
	1829 JM	—	375.00	600.00	725.00	1000.
	1830 JM	—	375.00	600.00	725.00	1000.
	1831 JM	—	375.00	600.00	725.00	1000.
	1832/1 JM	—	375.00	600.00	725.00	1000.
	1832 JM	—	375.00	600.00	725.00	1000.
	1833 MJ	—	400.00	750.00	1000.	1500.
	1833 ML	—	375.00	450.00	600.00	900.00
	1834 ML	—	400.00	750.00	1000.	1500.
	1835/4 ML	—	500.00	1000.	1250.	2000.
	1836 ML	—	375.00	450.00	600.00	900.00

KM#	Date	Mintage	Fine	VF	XF	Unc
383.9	1836 MF	—	500.00	700.00	1200.	2000.
	1837/6 ML	—	375.00	450.00	600.00	900.00
	1838 ML	—	375.00	450.00	600.00	900.00
	1839 ML	—	375.00	450.00	600.00	900.00
	1840 ML	—	375.00	450.00	600.00	900.00
	1841 ML	—	375.00	450.00	600.00	900.00
	1842/1 ML	—	—	—	—	—
	1842 ML	—	375.00	450.00	600.00	900.00
	1842 MM	—	—	—	—	—
	1843 MM	—	375.00	450.00	600.00	900.00
	1844 MF	—	375.00	450.00	600.00	900.00
	1845 MF	—	375.00	450.00	600.00	900.00
	1846 MF	—	500.00	1000.	1250.	2000.
	1847 MF	—	950.00	2250.	—	—
	1847 RC	—	375.00	500.00	800.00	1250.
	1848 GC	—	375.00	450.00	600.00	900.00
	1849 GC	—	375.00	450.00	600.00	900.00
	1850 GC	—	375.00	450.00	600.00	900.00
	1851 GC	—	375.00	450.00	600.00	900.00
	1852 GC	—	375.00	450.00	600.00	900.00
	1853 GC	—	375.00	450.00	600.00	900.00
	1854/44 GC	—	375.00	450.00	600.00	900.00
	1854/3 GC	—	375.00	450.00	600.00	900.00
	1855 GF	—	375.00	450.00	600.00	900.00
	1856/5 GF	—	375.00	450.00	600.00	900.00
	1856 GF	—	375.00	450.00	600.00	900.00
	1857 GF	—	375.00	450.00	600.00	900.00
	1858 FH	—	375.00	450.00	600.00	900.00
	1859 FH	—	400.00	750.00	1000.	1500.
	1860 FH	—	375.00	450.00	600.00	900.00
	1860 TH	—	375.00	450.00	600.00	900.00
	1861/51 CH	—	375.00	450.00	600.00	900.00
	1862 CH	—	375.00	450.00	600.00	900.00
	1863/53 CH	—	375.00	450.00	600.00	900.00
	1863/53 TH	—	375.00	450.00	600.00	900.00
	1867 CH	—	375.00	450.00	600.00	900.00
	1868 CH	—	375.00	450.00	600.00	900.00
	1868 PH	—	375.00	450.00	600.00	900.00
	1869 CH	—	375.00	450.00	600.00	900.00

NOTE: Formerly reported 1825/3 JM is merely a reworked 5.

Mint mark: O

KM#	Date	Mintage	Fine	VF	XF	Unc
383.10	1858 AE	—	2000.	3000.	4000.	6000.
	1859 AE	—	1000.	2500.	3750.	5500.
	1860 AE	—	1000.	2500.	3750.	5500.
	1861 FR	—	450.00	850.00	1250.	2750.
	1862 FR	—	450.00	850.00	1250.	2750.
	1863 FR	—	450.00	850.00	1250.	2750.
	1864 FR	—	450.00	850.00	1250.	2750.
	1867 AE	—	450.00	850.00	1250.	2750.
	1868 AE	—	450.00	850.00	1250.	2750.
	1869 AE	—	450.00	850.00	1250.	2750.

Mint mark: Zs

KM#	Date	Mintage	Fine	VF	XF	Unc
383.11	1858 MO	—	400.00	750.00	1000.	2000.
	1859 MO	—	375.00	475.00	650.00	900.00
	1860/59 VL/MO	—	2000.	3000.	4000.	—
	1860/9 MO	—	400.00	750.00	1000.	2000.
	1860 MO	—	375.00	500.00	700.00	1000.
	1861/0 VL	—	375.00	500.00	700.00	1000.
	1861 VL	—	375.00	500.00	700.00	1000.
	1862 VL	—	375.00	500.00	700.00	1100.
	1863 VL	—	375.00	525.00	750.00	1150.
	1863 MO	—	375.00	500.00	700.00	1000.
	1864 MO	—	750.00	1000.	1500.	3000.
	1865 MO	—	375.00	500.00	700.00	1000.
	1865 MP	—	Contemporary counterfeit			
	1868 JS	—	400.00	600.00	800.00	1250.
	1868 YH	—	400.00	600.00	800.00	1250.
	1869 YH	—	400.00	600.00	800.00	1250.
	1870 YH	—	400.00	600.00	800.00	1250.
	1871 YH	—	400.00	600.00	800.00	1250.

EMPIRE OF MAXIMILIAN

RULER

Maximilian, Emperor, 1864-1867

MINT MARKS

Refer To Republic Coinage

MONETARY SYSTEM

100 Centavos = 1 Peso (8 Reales)

CENTAVO

COPPER
Mint mark: M

KM#	Date	Mintage	Fine	VF	XF	Unc
384	1864	—	35.00	60.00	150.00	1000.

5 CENTAVOS

1.3537 g, .903 SILVER, .0393 oz ASW
Mint mark: G

KM#	Date	Mintage	Fine	VF	XF	Unc
385	1864	.090	17.50	35.00	75.00	300.00
	1865	—	20.00	30.00	55.00	275.00
	1866	—	75.00	150.00	300.00	1800.

Mint mark: M

KM#	Date	Mintage	Fine	VF	XF	Unc
385.1	1864	—	12.50	20.00	55.00	275.00
	1866/4	—	25.00	40.00	75.00	385.00
	1866	—	20.00	35.00	65.00	375.00

Mint mark: P

KM#	Date	Mintage	Fine	VF	XF	Unc
385.2	1864	—	100.00	215.00	950.00	2300.

Mint mark: Z

KM#	Date	Mintage	Fine	VF	XF	Unc
385.3	1865	—	25.00	45.00	150.00	425.00

10 CENTAVOS

2.7073 g, .903 SILVER, .0786 oz ASW
Mint mark: G

KM#	Date	Mintage	Fine	VF	XF	Unc
386	1864	.045	20.00	40.00	80.00	300.00
	1865	—	25.00	45.00	85.00	325.00

Mint mark: M

KM#	Date	Mintage	Fine	VF	XF	Unc
386.1	1864	—	15.00	25.00	55.00	275.00
	1866/4	—	25.00	35.00	60.00	300.00
	1866/5	—	25.00	35.00	75.00	375.00
	1866	—	25.00	35.00	75.00	375.00

Mint mark: P

KM#	Date	Mintage	Fine	VF	XF	Unc
386.2	1864	—	70.00	150.00	300.00	600.00

Mint mark: Z

KM#	Date	Mintage	Fine	VF	XF	Unc
386.3	1865	—	25.00	55.00	145.00	475.00

50 CENTAVOS

13.5365 g, .903 SILVER, .3929 oz ASW
Mint mark: Mo

KM#	Date	Mintage	Fine	VF	XF	Unc
387	1866	.031	40.00	95.00	200.00	600.00

PESO

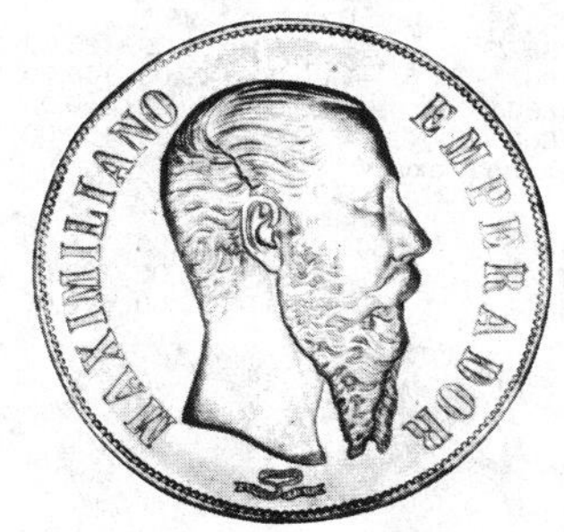

27.0700 g, .903 SILVER, .7857 oz ASW
Mint mark: Go

KM#	Date	Mintage	Fine	VF	XF	Unc
388	1866	—	300.00	500.00	800.00	2150.

Mint mark: Mo

KM#	Date	Mintage	Fine	VF	XF	Unc
388.1	1866	2.148	30.00	45.00	150.00	375.00
	1867	1.238	40.00	65.00	175.00	400.00

Mint mark: Pi

KM#	Date	Mintage	Fine	VF	XF	Unc
388.2	1866	—	55.00	125.00	275.00	725.00

20 PESOS

33.8400 g, .875 GOLD, .9520 oz AGW
Mint mark: Mo

KM#	Date	Mintage	Fine	VF	XF	Unc
389	1866	8,274	500.00	800.00	1200.	2400.

REPUBLIC DECIMAL COINAGE

100 Centavos = 1 Peso

UN (1) CENTAVO

COPPER
Mint mark: Mo
Obv: Seated Liberty.

KM#	Date	Mintage	Fine	VF	XF	Unc
390	1863 round top 3, reeded edge	—	12.00	20.00	40.00	165.00
	1863 round top 3, plain edge	—	12.00	20.00	40.00	165.00
	1863 flat top 3	—	10.00	18.00	35.00	160.00

Mint mark: SLP

KM#	Date	Mintage	Fine	VF	XF	Unc
390.1	1863	1.025	15.00	30.00	60.00	300.00

Mint mark: As
Obv: Standing eagle.

KM#	Date	Mintage	Fine	VF	XF	Unc
391	1875	—	—	—	Rare	—
	1876	.050	100.00	200.00	300.00	650.00
	1880	—	25.00	50.00	100.00	400.00
	1881	—	30.00	60.00	125.00	250.00

Mint mark: Cn

KM#	Date	Mintage	Fine	VF	XF	Unc
391.1	1874	.266	12.50	17.50	35.00	150.00
	1875/4	.153	15.00	20.00	45.00	150.00
	1875	Inc. Ab.	10.00	15.00	25.00	150.00

KM#	Date	Mintage	Fine	VF	XF	Unc
391.1	1876	.154	5.00	8.00	15.00	150.00
	1877/6	.993	7.50	11.50	17.50	175.00
	1877	Inc. Ab.	6.00	9.00	15.00	150.00
	1880	.142	7.50	10.00	12.50	150.00
	1881	.167	7.50	10.00	25.00	175.00
	1897 large N in mm.	.300	2.50	5.00	12.00	50.00
	1897 small N in mm.	Inc. Ab.	2.50	5.00	9.00	45.00

Mint mark: Do

KM#	Date	Mintage	Fine	VF	XF	Unc
391.2	1879	.110	10.00	17.50	35.00	150.00
	1880	.069	40.00	90.00	175.00	500.00
	1891	—	8.00	11.00	30.00	150.00
	1891 Do/Mo	—	8.00	11.00	30.00	150.00

Mint mark: Ga

KM#	Date	Mintage	Fine	VF	XF	Unc
391.3	1872	.263	15.00	30.00	60.00	200.00
	1873	.333	6.00	9.00	25.00	150.00
	1874	.076	15.00	25.00	50.00	175.00
	1875	—	10.00	15.00	30.00	150.00
	1876	.303	3.00	6.00	17.50	150.00
	1877	.108	4.00	6.00	20.00	150.00
	1878	.543	4.00	6.00	15.00	150.00
	1881/71	.975	7.00	9.00	20.00	175.00
	1881	Inc. Ab.	7.00	9.00	20.00	175.00
	1889 Ga/Mo	—	3.50	5.00	25.00	125.00
	1890	—	4.00	7.50	20.00	100.00

Mint mark: Go

KM#	Date	Mintage	Fine	VF	XF	Unc
391.4	1874	—	20.00	40.00	80.00	250.00
	1875	.190	11.50	20.00	60.00	200.00
	1876	—	125.00	200.00	350.00	750.00
	1877	—	—	—	Rare	—
	1878	.576	8.00	11.00	30.00	175.00
	1880	.890	6.00	10.00	25.00	175.00

Mint mark: Ho

KM#	Date	Mintage	Fine	VF	XF	Unc
391.5	1875	3,500	450.00	—	—	—
	1876	8,508	50.00	100.00	225.00	500.00
	1880 short H, round O	.102	7.50	15.00	35.00	150.00
	1880 tall H, oval O	Inc. Ab.	7.50	15.00	35.00	150.00
	1881	.459	5.00	10.00	25.00	150.00

Mint mark: Mo

KM#	Date	Mintage	Fine	VF	XF	Unc
391.6	1869	1.874	7.50	25.00	60.00	200.00
	1870/69	1.200	10.00	25.00	60.00	225.00
	1870	Inc. Ab.	8.00	20.00	50.00	200.00
	1871	.918	8.00	15.00	40.00	200.00
	1872/1	1.625	6.50	10.00	30.00	200.00
	1872	Inc. Ab.	6.00	9.00	25.00	200.00
	1873	1.605	4.00	7.50	20.00	200.00
	1874/3	1.700	5.00	7.00	15.00	100.00
	1874	Inc. Ab.	3.00	5.50	15.00	100.00
	1874.	Inc. Ab.	5.00	10.00	25.00	200.00
	1875	1.495	6.00	8.00	30.00	100.00
	1876	1.600	3.00	5.50	12.50	100.00
	1877	1.270	3.00	5.50	13.50	100.00
	1878/5	1.900	7.50	11.00	22.50	125.00
	1878/6	Inc. Ab.	7.50	11.00	22.50	125.00
	1878/7	Inc. Ab.	7.50	11.00	20.00	125.00
	1878	Inc. Ab.	6.00	9.00	13.50	100.00
	1879/8	1.505	4.50	6.50	13.50	100.00
	1879	Inc. Ab.	3.00	5.50	11.50	75.00
	1880/70	1.130	5.50	7.50	15.00	100.00
	1880/72	I.A.	20.00	50.00	100.00	250.00
	1880/79	I.A.	15.00	35.00	75.00	175.00
	1880	Inc. Ab.	4.25	6.00	12.50	75.00
	1881	1.060	4.50	7.00	15.00	75.00
	1886	12.687	1.50	2.00	8.50	40.00
	1887	7.292	1.50	2.00	5.00	35.00
	1888/78	9.984	2.50	3.00	10.00	30.00
	1888/7	Inc. Ab.	2.50	3.00	10.00	30.00
	1888	Inc. Ab.	1.50	2.00	8.50	30.00
	1889	19.970	2.00	3.00	8.00	30.00
	1890/89	18.726	2.50	3.00	10.00	40.00
	1890/990	I.A.	2.50	3.00	10.00	40.00
	1890	Inc. Ab.	1.50	2.00	8.50	30.00
	1891	14.544	1.50	2.00	8.50	30.00
	1892	12.908	1.50	2.00	8.50	30.00
	1893/2	5.078	2.50	3.00	10.00	35.00
	1893	Inc. Ab.	1.50	2.00	8.50	30.00
	1894/3	1.896	3.00	6.00	15.00	50.00
	1894	Inc. Ab.	2.00	3.00	10.00	35.00
	1895/3	3.453	3.00	4.50	12.50	35.00
	1895/85	I.A.	3.00	6.00	15.00	50.00
	1895	Inc. Ab.	2.00	3.00	8.50	25.00
	1896	3.075	2.00	3.00	8.50	25.00
	1897	4.150	1.50	2.00	8.50	25.00

NOTE: Varieties exist.

Mint mark: Oa

KM#	Date	Mintage	Fine	VF	XF	Unc
391.7	1872	.016	300.00	500.00	1200.	—
	1873	.011	350.00	600.00	—	—
	1874	4,835	450.00	—	—	—
	1875	2,860	500.00	—	—	—

Mint mark: Pi

KM#	Date	Mintage	Fine	VF	XF	Unc
391.8	1871	—	—	—	Rare	—
	1877	.249	—	—	Rare	—
	1878	.751	12.50	25.00	50.00	200.00
	1891 Pi/Mo	—	10.00	17.50	35.00	150.00
	1891	—	8.00	15.00	30.00	150.00

Mint mark: Zs

KM#	Date	Mintage	Fine	VF	XF	Unc
391.9	1872	.055	22.50	30.00	100.00	300.00
	1873	1.460	4.00	8.00	25.00	150.00
	1874/3	.685	5.50	11.00	30.00	250.00
	1874	Inc. Ab.	4.00	8.00	25.00	200.00
	1875/4	.200	8.50	17.00	45.00	250.00

KM#	Date	Mintage	Fine	VF	XF	Unc
391.9	1875	Inc. Ab.	7.00	14.00	35.00	200.00
	1876	—	5.00	10.00	25.00	200.00
	1877	—	50.00	125.00	300.00	750.00
	1878	—	4.50	9.00	25.00	200.00
	1880	.100	5.00	10.00	30.00	200.00
	1881	1.200	4.25	8.00	25.00	150.00

COPPER-NICKEL
Mint: Mexico City

KM#	Date	Mintage	Fine	VF	XF	Unc
392	1882	99.955	7.50	12.50	17.50	35.00
	1883	Inc. Ab.	.50	.75	1.00	1.50

COPPER
Obv: Restyled eagle.

KM#	Date	Mintage	Fine	VF	XF	Unc
393	1898	1.529	4.00	6.00	15.00	40.00

NOTE: Varieties exist.

Mint mark: M,Mo

KM#	Date	Mintage	Fine	VF	XF	Unc
394.1	1899	.051	150.00	175.00	300.00	800.00
	1900 wide date	4.010	2.50	4.00	7.50	25.00
	1900 narrow date	Inc. Ab.	2.50	4.00	7.50	25.00

NOTE: Later dates (1901-1905) exist for this type.

2 CENTAVOS

COPPER-NICKEL
Mint: Mexico City

KM#	Date	Mintage	Fine	VF	XF	Unc
395	1882	50.023	2.00	3.00	7.50	15.00
	1883/2	Inc. Ab.	2.00	3.00	7.50	15.00
	1883	Inc. Ab.	.50	.75	1.00	2.50

5 CENTAVOS

1.3530 g, .903 SILVER, .0392 oz ASW
Mint mark: Ca
Obv: Facing eagle. Rev: Denomination in wreath.

KM#	Date	Mintage	Fine	VF	XF	Unc
396	1868	—	40.00	65.00	125.00	400.00
	1869	*.030	25.00	40.00	100.00	350.00
	1870	.035	30.00	50.00	100.00	350.00

Mint mark: SLP

KM#	Date	Mintage	Fine	VF	XF	Unc
396.1	1863	—	75.00	125.00	350.00	1200.

Mint mark: Mo
Rev: Cap and rays.

KM#	Date	Mintage	Fine	VF	XF	Unc
397	1867/3	—	25.00	50.00	125.00	275.00
	1867	—	20.00	40.00	100.00	250.00
	1868/7	—	25.00	50.00	150.00	325.00
	1868	—	20.00	40.00	100.00	250.00

NOTE: Varieties exist.

Mint mark: P

KM#	Date	Mintage	Fine	VF	XF	Unc
397.1	1868/7	.034	25.00	50.00	125.00	300.00
	1868	Inc. Ab.	20.00	45.00	100.00	250.00
	1869	.014	200.00	300.00	600.00	—

Mint mark: As
Obv: Standing eagle.

KM#	Date	Mintage	Fine	VF	XF	Unc
398	1874 DL	—	10.00	20.00	40.00	150.00
	1875 DL	—	10.00	20.00	40.00	150.00
	1876 L	—	22.00	45.00	70.00	160.00
	1878 L mule, gold peso obverse	—	250.00	350.00	650.00	—
	1879 L mule, gold peso obverse	—	40.00	65.00	120.00	275.00
	1880 L mule, gold peso obverse	.012	55.00	85.00	165.00	325.00
	1886 L	.043	12.00	25.00	50.00	165.00
	1886 L mule, gold peso obverse	Inc. Ab.	55.00	85.00	165.00	300.00
	1887 L	.020	25.00	50.00	75.00	165.00
	1888 L	.032	12.00	25.00	50.00	125.00
	1889 L	.016	25.00	50.00	100.00	200.00
	1890 L	.030	25.00	50.00	85.00	175.00
	1891 L	8,000	65.00	125.00	200.00	400.00
	1892 L	.013	20.00	40.00	60.00	125.00
	1893 L	.024	10.00	20.00	45.00	90.00
	1895 L	.020	10.00	20.00	45.00	90.00

Mint mark: CH, Ca

KM#	Date	Mintage	Fine	VF	XF	Unc
398.1	1871 M	.014	20.00	40.00	100.00	250.00
	1873 M crude date	—	100.00	150.00	250.00	500.00
	1874 M crude date	—	25.00	50.00	75.00	150.00
	1886 M	.025	7.50	15.00	30.00	100.00
	1887 M	.037	7.50	15.00	30.00	100.00
	1887 Ca/MoM	Inc. Ab.	10.00	20.00	40.00	125.00
	1888 M	.145	1.50	3.00	6.00	25.00
	1889 M	.044	5.00	10.00	20.00	50.00
	1890 M	.102	1.50	3.00	6.00	25.00
	1891 M	.164	1.50	3.00	6.00	25.00
	1892 M	.085	1.50	3.00	6.00	25.00
	1892 M 9/inverted 9	Inc. Ab.	2.00	4.00	7.50	30.00
	1893 M	.133	1.50	3.00	6.00	25.00
	1894 M	.108	1.50	3.00	6.00	25.00
	1895 M	.074	2.00	4.00	7.50	30.00

Mint mark: Cn

KM#	Date	Mintage	Fine	VF	XF	Unc
398.2	1871 P	—	125.00	200.00	350.00	—
	1873 P	4,992	50.00	100.00	200.00	400.00
	1874 P	—	25.00	50.00	100.00	200.00
	1875 P	—	—	—	Rare	—
	1876 P	—	25.00	50.00	100.00	200.00
	1886 M	.010	25.00	50.00	100.00	200.00
	1887 M	.010	25.00	50.00	100.00	200.00
	1888 M	.119	1.50	3.00	6.00	30.00
	1889 M	.066	4.00	7.50	15.00	50.00
	1890 M	.180	1.50	3.00	6.00	25.00
	1890 D (error)	Inc. Ab.	125.00	175.00	250.00	—
	1891 M	.087	2.00	4.00	7.50	25.00
	1894 M	.024	4.00	7.50	15.00	40.00
	1896 M	.016	7.50	12.50	25.00	75.00
	1897 M	.223	1.50	2.50	5.00	20.00

Mint mark: Do

KM#	Date	Mintage	Fine	VF	XF	Unc
398.3	1874 M	—	100.00	150.00	225.00	500.00
	1877 P	4,795	75.00	125.00	225.00	450.00
	1878/7 E/P	4,300	200.00	300.00	450.00	—
	1879 B	—	125.00	200.00	350.00	—
	1880 B	—	—	—	Rare	—
	1881 P	3,020	300.00	500.00	800.00	—
	1887 C	.042	5.00	8.00	17.50	60.00
	1888/9 C	.091	6.00	10.00	20.00	70.00
	1888 C	Inc. Ab.	4.00	7.50	15.00	55.00
	1889 C	.049	3.50	6.00	12.50	50.00
	1890 C	.136	4.00	7.50	15.00	55.00
	1890 P	Inc. Ab.	5.00	8.00	17.50	60.00
	1891/0 P	.048	3.50	6.00	12.50	50.00
	1891 P	Inc. Ab.	3.00	5.00	10.00	45.00
	1894 D	.038	3.50	6.00	12.50	50.00

Mint mark: Ga

KM#	Date	Mintage	Fine	VF	XF	Unc
398.4	1877 A	—	15.00	30.00	60.00	150.00
	1881 S	.156	4.00	7.50	15.00	60.00
	1886 S	.087	2.00	4.00	7.50	25.00
	1888 S lg.G	.262	2.00	4.00	10.00	30.00
	1888 S sm.g	Inc. Ab.	2.00	4.00	10.00	30.00
	1889 S	.178	1.50	3.00	7.50	25.00
	1890 S	.068	4.00	7.50	12.50	35.00
	1891 S	.050	4.00	6.50	10.00	35.00
	1892 S	.078	2.00	4.00	7.50	25.00
	1893 S	.044	4.00	7.50	15.00	45.00

Mint mark: Go

KM#	Date	Mintage	Fine	VF	XF	Unc
398.5	1869 S	.080	15.00	30.00	75.00	175.00
	1871 S	.100	5.00	10.00	25.00	75.00
	1872 S	.030	30.00	60.00	125.00	250.00
	1873 S	.040	30.00	60.00	125.00	250.00
	1874 S	—	7.00	12.00	25.00	75.00
	1875 S	—	8.00	15.00	30.00	75.00
	1876 S	—	8.00	15.00	30.00	75.00
	1877 S	—	7.00	12.00	20.00	75.00
	1878/7 S	.020	8.00	15.00	25.00	75.00
	1879 S	—	8.00	15.00	25.00	75.00
	1880 S	.055	15.00	30.00	60.00	200.00
	1881/0 S	.160	5.00	8.00	17.50	60.00
	1881 S	Inc. Ab.	4.00	6.00	12.00	45.00
	1886 R	.230	1.50	3.00	6.00	30.00
	1887 R	.230	1.50	2.50	5.00	30.00
	1888 R	.320	1.50	2.50	5.00	20.00

KM#	Date	Mintage	Fine	VF	XF	Unc
398.5	1889 R	.060	4.00	6.00	12.00	45.00
	1890 R	.250	1.50	2.50	5.00	20.00
	1891/0 R	.168	1.80	3.00	6.00	30.00
	1891 R	Inc. Ab.	1.50	2.50	5.00	20.00
	1892 R	.138	1.50	3.00	6.00	25.00
	1893 R	.200	1.25	2.50	5.00	20.00
	1894 R	.200	1.25	2.50	5.00	20.00
	1896 R	.525	1.25	2.00	4.00	15.00
	1897 R	.596	1.50	2.00	4.00	15.00

Mint mark: Ho

KM#	Date	Mintage	Fine	VF	XF	Unc
398.6	1874/69 R	—	125.00	225.00	350.00	—
	1874 R	—	100.00	200.00	325.00	—
	1878/7 A	.022	—	—	Rare	—
	1878 A	Inc. Ab.	20.00	40.00	80.00	175.00
	1878 A mule, gold peso obverse	Inc. Ab.	40.00	80.00	150.00	300.00
	1880 A	.043	7.50	15.00	30.00	75.00
	1886 G	.044	5.00	10.00	20.00	75.00
	1887 G	.020	5.00	10.00	20.00	75.00
	1888 G	.012	7.50	15.00	30.00	85.00
	1889 G	.067	3.00	6.00	12.50	40.00
	1890 G	.050	3.00	6.00	12.50	40.00
	1891 G	.046	3.00	6.00	12.50	40.00
	1893 G	.084	2.50	5.00	10.00	30.00
	1894 G	.068	2.00	4.00	10.00	30.00

Mint mark: Mo

KM#	Date	Mintage	Fine	VF	XF	Unc
398.7	1869/8 C	.040	8.00	15.00	40.00	120.00
	1870 C	.140	4.00	7.00	20.00	60.00
	1871 C	.103	9.00	20.00	40.00	100.00
	1871 M	Inc. Ab.	7.50	12.50	25.00	60.00
	1872 M	.266	5.00	8.00	20.00	55.00
	1873 M	.020	40.00	60.00	100.00	225.00
	1874/69 M	—	7.50	15.00	30.00	75.00
	1874 M	—	4.00	7.00	17.50	50.00
	1874/3 B	—	5.00	8.00	22.50	55.00
	1874 B	—	5.00	8.00	22.50	55.00
	1875 B	—	4.00	7.00	15.00	50.00
	1875 B/M	—	6.00	9.00	17.50	60.00
	1876/5 B	—	4.00	7.00	15.00	50.00
	1876 B	—	4.00	7.00	12.50	50.00
	1877/6 M	.080	4.00	7.00	15.00	60.00
	1877 M	Inc. Ab.	4.00	7.00	12.50	60.00
	1878/7 M	.100	4.00	7.00	15.00	55.00
	1878 M	Inc. Ab.	2.50	5.00	12.50	45.00
	1879/8 M	—	8.00	12.50	22.50	55.00
	1879 M	—	4.50	7.00	15.00	50.00
	1879 M 9/inverted 9	—	10.00	15.00	25.00	75.00
	1880/76 M/B	—	5.00	7.50	15.00	50.00
	1880/76 M	—	5.00	7.50	15.00	50.00
	1880 M	—	4.00	6.00	12.00	40.00
	1881/0 M	.180	4.00	6.00	10.00	35.00
	1881 M	Inc. Ab.	3.00	4.50	9.00	35.00
	1886/0 M	.398	2.00	2.75	7.50	25.00
	1886/1 M	I.A.	2.00	2.75	7.50	25.00
	1886 M	Inc. Ab.	1.75	2.25	6.00	20.00
	1887 m	.720	1.75	2.00	5.00	20.00
	1887 M/m	I.A.	1.75	2.00	6.00	20.00
	1888/7 M	1.360	2.25	2.50	6.00	20.00
	1888 M	Inc. Ab.	1.75	2.00	5.00	20.00
	1889/8 M	1.242	2.25	2.50	6.00	20.00
	1889 M	Inc. Ab.	1.75	2.00	5.00	20.00
	1890/00 M	1.694	1.75	2.75	6.00	20.00
	1890 M	Inc. Ab.	1.50	2.00	5.00	20.00
	1891 M	1.030	1.75	2.00	5.00	20.00
	1892 M	1.400	1.75	2.00	5.00	20.00
	1892 M 9/inverted 9	Inc. Ab.	2.00	2.75	7.50	20.00
	1893 M	.220	1.75	2.00	5.00	15.00
	1894 M	.320	1.75	2.00	5.00	15.00
	1895 M	.078	3.00	5.00	8.00	25.00
	1896 B	.080	1.75	2.00	5.00	20.00
	1897 M	.160	1.75	2.00	5.00	15.00

NOTE: Varieties exist.

Mint mark: Oa

KM#	Date	Mintage	Fine	VF	XF	Unc
398.8	1890 E	.048	—	—	Rare	—
	1890 N	Inc. Ab.	65.00	125.00	200.00	350.00

Mint mark: Pi

KM#	Date	Mintage	Fine	VF	XF	Unc
398.9	1869 S	—	300.00	400.00	500.00	—
	1870 G/MoC	.020	—	—	Rare	—
	1870 O	Inc. Ab.	200.00	300.00	400.00	—
	1871 O	5,400	—	—	Rare	—
	1872 O	—	75.00	100.00	175.00	400.00
	1873	5,000	—	—	Rare	—
	1874 H	—	30.00	50.00	100.00	225.00
	1875 H	—	7.50	12.50	30.00	75.00
	1876 H	—	10.00	20.00	45.00	100.00
	1877 H	—	7.50	12.50	20.00	60.00
	1878/7 H	—	—	—	Rare	—
	1878 H	—	60.00	90.00	150.00	300.00
	1880 H	6,200	—	—	Rare	—
	1881 H	4,500	—	—	Rare	—
	1886 R	.033	12.50	25.00	50.00	125.00
	1887/0 R	.169	4.00	7.50	15.00	45.00
	1887 R	Inc. Ab.	3.00	5.00	10.00	32.00
	1888 R	.210	2.00	4.00	9.00	30.00
	1889/7 R	.197	2.50	5.00	10.00	32.00
	1889 R	Inc. Ab.	2.00	4.00	9.00	30.00
	1890 R	.221	2.00	3.00	6.00	25.00
	1891/89 R/B	.176	2.00	4.00	8.00	25.00
	1891 R	Inc. Ab.	2.00	3.00	6.00	20.00
	1892/89 R	.182	2.00	4.00	8.00	25.00
	1892/0 R	I.A.	2.00	4.00	8.00	25.00

KM#	Date	Mintage	Fine	VF	XF	Unc
398.9	1892 R	Inc. Ab.	2.00	3.00	6.00	20.00
	1893 R	.041	5.00	10.00	20.00	60.00

NOTE: Varieties exist.

Mint mark: Zs

KM#	Date	Mintage	Fine	VF	XF	Unc
398.10	1870 H	.040	12.50	25.00	50.00	125.00
	1871 H	.040	12.50	25.00	50.00	125.00
	1872 H	.040	12.50	25.00	50.00	125.00
	1873/2 H	.020	35.00	65.00	125.00	275.00
	1873 H	Inc. Ab.	25.00	50.00	100.00	250.00
	1874 H	—	7.50	12.50	25.00	75.00
	1874 A	—	40.00	75.00	150.00	300.00
	1875 A	—	7.50	12.50	25.00	75.00
	1876 A	—	50.00	75.00	100.00	200.00
	1876 S	—	12.50	25.00	50.00	125.00
	1877 S	—	3.00	6.00	12.00	40.00
	1878 S	.060	3.00	6.00	12.00	40.00
	1879/8 S	—	3.00	6.00	15.00	50.00
	1879 S	—	3.00	6.00	12.00	40.00
	1880/79 S	.130	6.00	10.00	20.00	60.00
	1880 S	Inc. Ab.	5.00	8.00	16.00	45.00
	1881 S	.210	2.50	5.00	10.00	35.00
	1886/4 S	.360	6.00	10.00	20.00	60.00
	1886 S	Inc. Ab.	2.00	3.00	6.00	20.00
	1886 Z	Inc. Ab.	5.00	10.00	25.00	65.00
	1887 Z	.400	2.00	3.00	6.00	25.00
	1888/7 Z	.500	2.00	3.00	6.00	25.00
	1888 Z	Inc. Ab.	2.00	3.00	6.00	25.00
	1889 Z	.520	2.00	3.00	6.00	25.00
	1889 Z 9/inverted 9	Inc. Ab.	2.00	3.00	6.00	25.00
	1889 ZsZ/MoM	Inc. Ab.	2.00	3.00	6.00	25.00
	1890 Z	.580	1.75	2.50	5.00	20.00
	1890 ZsZ/MoM	Inc. Ab.	2.00	3.00	6.00	25.00
	1891 Z	.420	1.75	2.50	5.00	20.00
	1892 Z	.346	1.75	2.50	5.00	20.00
	1893 Z	.258	1.75	2.50	5.00	20.00
	1894 Z	.228	1.75	2.50	5.00	20.00
	1894 ZoZ (error)	Inc. Ab.	2.00	4.00	8.00	30.00
	1895 Z	.260	1.75	2.50	5.00	20.00
	1896 Z	.200	1.75	2.50	5.00	20.00
	1896 6/inverted 6	Inc. Ab.	2.00	3.00	6.00	25.00
	1897/6 Z	.200	2.00	3.00	6.00	25.00
	1897 Z	Inc. Ab.	1.75	2.50	5.00	20.00

COPPER-NICKEL
Mint: Mexico City

KM#	Date	Mintage	Fine	VF	XF	Unc
399	1882	Inc. Ab.	.50	1.00	2.50	7.50
	1883	Inc. Ab.	25.00	50.00	80.00	250.00

.903 SILVER
Mint mark: Cn
Obv: Restyled eagle.

KM#	Date	Mintage	Fine	VF	XF	Unc
400	1898 M	.044	1.75	4.00	8.00	20.00
	1899 M	.111	5.50	8.50	20.00	50.00
	1899 Q	Inc. Ab.	1.75	2.25	4.50	12.50
	1900/800 Q	.239	3.50	5.00	12.50	30.00
	1900 Q round Q, single tail	Inc. Ab.	1.75	2.50	6.00	15.00
	1900 Q narrow C, oval Q	Inc. Ab.	1.75	2.50	6.00	15.00
	1900 Q wide C, oval Q	Inc. Ab.	1.75	2.50	6.00	15.00

NOTE: Later dates (1901-1904) exist for this type.

Mint mark: Go

KM#	Date	Mintage	Fine	VF	XF	Unc
400.1	1898 R mule, gold peso obverse	.180	7.50	15.00	30.00	75.00
	1899 R	.260	1.75	2.25	4.50	12.50
	1900 R	.200	1.75	2.25	4.50	12.50

NOTE: Varieties exist.

Mint mark: Mo

KM#	Date	Mintage	Fine	VF	XF	Unc
400.2	1898 M	.080	2.00	4.00	7.00	25.00
	1899 M	.168	1.75	2.25	4.50	12.50
	1900/800 M	.300	4.50	6.50	10.00	30.00
	1900 M	Inc. Ab.	1.75	2.25	4.50	12.50

NOTE: Later dates (1901-1905) exist for this type.

Mint mark: Zs

KM#	Date	Mintage	Fine	VF	XF	Unc
400.3	1898 Z	.100	1.75	2.25	4.50	12.50
	1899 Z	.050	2.00	3.00	7.00	20.00
	1900 Z	.055	1.75	2.50	5.00	15.00

NOTE: Later dates (1901-1905) exist for this type.

10 CENTAVOS

2.7070 g, .903 SILVER, .0785 oz ASW
Mint mark: Ca
Obv: Eagle. Rev: Value within wreath.

KM#	Date	Mintage	Fine	VF	XF	Unc
401	1868/7	—	30.00	60.00	150.00	550.00
	1868	—	30.00	60.00	150.00	550.00
	1869	.015	25.00	50.00	125.00	600.00
	1870	.017	22.50	45.00	100.00	550.00

Mint mark: SLP

KM#	Date	Mintage	Fine	VF	XF	Unc
401.2	1863	—	75.00	150.00	275.00	900.00

Mint mark: Mo

KM#	Date	Mintage	Fine	VF	XF	Unc
402	1867/3	—	50.00	100.00	150.00	450.00
	1867	—	20.00	40.00	60.00	250.00
	1868/7	—	20.00	40.00	80.00	275.00
	1868	—	20.00	45.00	75.00	250.00

Mint mark: P

KM#	Date	Mintage	Fine	VF	XF	Unc
402.1	1868/7	.038	45.00	90.00	175.00	650.00
	1868	Inc. Ab.	20.00	40.00	100.00	550.00
	1869/7	4,900	55.00	125.00	250.00	800.00

Mint mark: As

KM#	Date	Mintage	Fine	VF	XF	Unc
403	1874 DL	—	20.00	40.00	80.00	175.00
	1875 L	—	5.00	10.00	25.00	90.00
	1876 L	—	10.00	18.00	40.00	110.00
	1878/7 L	—	10.00	18.00	45.00	120.00
	1878 L	—	5.00	10.00	30.00	100.00
	1879 L	—	10.00	18.00	40.00	110.00
	1880 L	.013	10.00	18.00	40.00	110.00
	1882 L	.022	10.00	18.00	40.00	110.00
	1883 L	8,520	25.00	50.00	100.00	225.00
	1884 L	—	7.50	12.50	35.00	100.00
	1885 L	.015	7.50	12.50	35.00	100.00
	1886 L	.045	7.50	12.50	35.00	100.00
	1887 L	.015	7.50	12.50	35.00	100.00
	1888 L	.038	7.50	12.50	35.00	100.00
	1889 L	.020	7.50	12.50	35.00	100.00
	1890 L	.040	7.50	12.50	35.00	100.00
	1891 L	.038	7.50	12.50	35.00	100.00
	1892 L	.057	5.00	10.00	25.00	90.00
	1893 L	.070	10.00	18.00	40.00	110.00

NOTE: Varieties exist. An 1891 As L over 1889 HoG exists which was evidently produced at the Alamos Mint using dies sent from the Hermosillo Mint.

Mint mark: CH, Ca

KM#	Date	Mintage	Fine	VF	XF	Unc
403.1	1871 M	8,150	15.00	30.00	60.00	150.00
	1873 M crude date	—	35.00	75.00	125.00	175.00
	1874 M	—	10.00	17.50	35.00	100.00
	1880/70 G	7,620	20.00	40.00	80.00	175.00
	1880 G/g	I.A.	15.00	25.00	50.00	125.00
	1881	340 pcs.	—	—	Rare	—
	1883 M	9,000	10.00	20.00	40.00	125.00
	1884 M	—	10.00	20.00	40.00	125.00
	1886 M	.045	7.50	12.50	30.00	100.00
	1887/3 M/G	.096	5.00	10.00	20.00	75.00
	1887 M	Inc. Ab.	2.00	4.00	8.00	75.00
	1888 M	.299	1.50	2.50	5.00	75.00
	1888 Ca/Mo	Inc. Ab.	1.50	2.50	5.00	75.00
	1889/8 M	.115	2.00	4.00	8.00	75.00
	1889 M small 89 (5 Centavo font)	Inc. Ab.	2.00	4.00	8.00	75.00
	1890/80 M	.140	2.00	4.00	8.00	75.00
	1890/89 M	I.A.	2.00	4.00	8.00	75.00
	1890 M	Inc. Ab.	1.50	3.00	7.00	75.00
	1891 M	.163	1.50	3.00	7.00	75.00
	1892 M	.169	1.50	3.00	7.00	75.00
	1892 M 9/inverted 9	Inc. Ab.	2.00	4.00	8.00	75.00
	1893 M	.246	1.50	3.00	7.00	75.00
	1894 M	.163	1.50	3.00	7.00	75.00
	1895 M	.127	1.50	3.00	7.00	75.00

NOTE: Varieties exist.

Mint mark: Cn

KM#	Date	Mintage	Fine	VF	XF	Unc
403.2	1871 P	—	—	—	Rare	—
	1873 P	8,732	20.00	50.00	100.00	225.00
	1881 D	9,440	75.00	175.00	325.00	500.00
	1882 D	.012	75.00	125.00	200.00	400.00
	1885 M mule gold 2-1/2 Peso obv.	.018	25.00	50.00	100.00	200.00

KM#	Date	Mintage	Fine	VF	XF	Unc
403.2	1886 M mule, gold 2-1/2 Peso obv.					
		.013	50.00	100.00	150.00	300.00
	1887 M	.011	20.00	40.00	75.00	175.00
	1888 M	.056	5.00	10.00	25.00	125.00
	1889 M	.042	5.00	10.00	20.00	75.00
	1890 M	.132	2.00	4.00	7.50	75.00
	1891 M	.084	5.00	10.00	20.00	75.00
	1892/1 M	.037	4.00	8.00	15.00	75.00
	1892 M	Inc. Ab.	2.50	5.00	10.00	75.00
	1894 M	.043	2.50	5.00	10.00	75.00
	1895 M	.023	2.50	5.00	10.00	60.00
	1896 M	.121	1.50	2.50	5.00	50.00

Mint mark: Do

KM#	Date	Mintage	Fine	VF	XF	Unc
403.3	1878 E	2,500	100.00	175.00	300.00	600.00
	1879 B	—	—	—	Rare	—
	1880/70 B	—	—	—	Rare	—
	1880/79 B	—	—	—	Rare	—
	1884 C	—	30.00	60.00	100.00	225.00
	1886 C	.013	75.00	150.00	300.00	500.00
	1887 C	.081	4.00	8.00	15.00	100.00
	1888 C	.031	6.00	12.00	30.00	100.00
	1889 C	.055	4.00	8.00	15.00	100.00
	1890 C	.050	4.00	8.00	15.00	100.00
	1891 P	.139	2.00	4.00	8.00	80.00
	1892 P	.212	2.00	4.00	8.00	80.00
	1892 D	Inc. Ab.	2.00	4.00	8.00	80.00
	1893 D	.258	2.00	4.00	8.00	80.00
	1893 D/C	I.A.	2.50	5.00	10.00	80.00
	1894 D	.184	1.50	3.00	6.00	80.00
	1894 D/C	I.A.	2.00	4.00	8.00	80.00
	1895 D	.142	1.50	3.00	6.00	80.00

Mint mark: Ga

KM#	Date	Mintage	Fine	VF	XF	Unc
403.4	1871 C	4,734	75.00	125.00	200.00	500.00
	1873/1 C	.025	10.00	15.00	35.00	150.00
	1873 C	Inc.Ab.	10.00	15.00	35.00	150.00
	1874 C	—	10.00	15.00	35.00	150.00
	1877 A	—	10.00	15.00	30.00	150.00
	1881 S	.115	5.00	10.00	25.00	150.00
	1883 B	.090	4.00	8.00	15.00	90.00
	1884 B	—	5.00	10.00	20.00	90.00
	1884 B/S	—	6.00	12.50	25.00	90.00
	1884 H	—	3.00	5.00	10.00	90.00
	1885 H	.093	3.00	5.00	10.00	90.00
	1886 S	.151	2.50	4.00	9.00	90.00
	1887 S	.162	1.50	3.00	6.00	90.00
	1888 S	.225	1.50	3.00	6.00	90.00
	1888 GaS/HoG					
		Inc. Ab.	1.50	3.00	6.00	90.00
	1889 S	.310	1.50	3.00	6.00	40.00
	1890 S	.303	1.50	3.00	6.00	40.00
	1891 S	.199	5.00	10.00	20.00	45.00
	1892 S	.329	1.50	3.00	6.00	40.00
	1893 S	.225	1.50	3.00	6.00	40.00
	1894 S	.243	3.00	6.00	12.00	40.00
	1895 S	.080	1.50	3.00	6.00	40.00

NOTE: Varieties exist.

Mint mark: Go

KM#	Date	Mintage	Fine	VF	XF	Unc
403.5	1869 S	7,000	20.00	40.00	80.00	200.00
	1871/0 S	.060	15.00	25.00	50.00	125.00
	1872 S	.060	15.00	25.00	50.00	125.00
	1873 S	.050	15.00	25.00	50.00	125.00
	1874 S	—	15.00	25.00	50.00	125.00
	1875 S	—	250.00	350.00	500.00	800.00
	1876 S	—	10.00	20.00	40.00	100.00
	1877 S	—	80.00	120.00	200.00	400.00
	1878/7 S	.010	10.00	20.00	45.00	110.00
	1878 S	Inc. Ab.	7.50	12.00	20.00	75.00
	1879 S	—	7.50	12.00	20.00	75.00
	1880 S	—	100.00	200.00	300.00	450.00
	1881/71 S	.100	3.00	5.00	10.00	75.00
	1881/0 S	I.A.	3.50	5.00	10.00	75.00
	1881 S	Inc. Ab.	3.00	5.00	10.00	75.00
	1882/1 S	.040	3.00	6.00	12.00	75.00
	1883 B	—	3.00	5.00	10.00	75.00
	1884 B	—	1.50	3.00	6.00	75.00
	1884 S	—	6.00	12.50	25.00	90.00
	1885 R	.100	1.50	3.00	6.00	75.00
	1886 R	.095	3.00	5.00	10.00	75.00
	1887 R	.330	2.50	5.00	10.00	75.00
	1888 R	.270	1.50	3.00	6.00	75.00
	1889 R	.205	2.00	4.00	8.00	75.00
	1889 GoR/HoG					
		Inc. Ab.	3.00	5.00	10.00	75.00
	1890 R	.270	1.50	3.00	6.00	35.00
	1890 GoR/Cn M					
		Inc. Ab.	1.50	3.00	6.00	35.00
	1891 R	.523	1.50	3.00	6.00	35.00
	1891 GoR/HoG					
		Inc. Ab.	1.50	3.00	6.00	35.00
	1892 R	.440	1.50	3.00	6.00	35.00
	1893/1 R	.389	3.00	5.00	10.00	35.00
	1893 R	Inc. Ab.	1.50	3.00	6.00	35.00
	1894 R	.400	1.50	2.50	5.00	35.00
	1895 R	.355	1.50	2.50	5.00	35.00
	1896 R	.190	1.50	2.50	5.00	35.00
	1897 R	.205	1.50	2.50	5.00	35.00

NOTE: Varieties exist.

Mint mark: Ho

KM#	Date	Mintage	Fine	VF	XF	Unc
403.6	1874 R	—	30.00	60.00	100.00	200.00
	1876 F	3,140	200.00	300.00	450.00	750.00
	1878 A	—	5.00	10.00	15.00	85.00
	1879 A	—	25.00	50.00	90.00	175.00
	1880 A	—	3.00	6.00	12.50	85.00
	1881 A	.028	4.00	7.00	15.00	85.00
	1882/1 A	.025	5.00	10.00	20.00	85.00
	1882/1 a	I.A.	6.00	12.50	25.00	85.00
	1882 A	Inc. Ab.	4.00	7.00	15.00	85.00

KM#	Date	Mintage	Fine	VF	XF	Unc
403.6	1883	7,000	65.00	100.00	200.00	400.00
	1884 A	—	35.00	75.00	150.00	300.00
	1884 M	—	7.50	15.00	30.00	85.00
	1885 M	.021	12.50	25.00	50.00	100.00
	1886 M	.010	—	—	Rare	—
	1886 G	Inc. Ab.	7.50	12.50	25.00	85.00
	1887 G	—	25.00	50.00	75.00	150.00
	1888 G	.025	6.00	12.50	25.00	85.00
	1889 G	.042	3.00	6.00	10.00	85.00
	1890 G	.048	3.00	6.00	10.00	85.00
	1891/80 G	.136	3.00	6.00	10.00	85.00
	1891/0 G	I.A.	3.00	6.00	10.00	85.00
	1891 G	Inc. Ab.	3.00	6.00	10.00	85.00
	1892 G	.067	3.00	6.00	10.00	85.00
	1893 G	.067	3.00	6.00	10.00	85.00

Mint mark: Mo

KM#	Date	Mintage	Fine	VF	XF	Unc
403.7	1869/8 C	.030	10.00	20.00	40.00	100.00
	1869 C	Inc. Ab.	8.00	17.50	35.00	90.00
	1870 C	.110	3.00	7.50	15.00	50.00
	1871 C	.084	50.00	75.00	125.00	250.00
	1871 M	Inc. Ab.	12.00	17.50	45.00	125.00
	1872/69 M	.198	10.00	20.00	35.00	100.00
	1872 M	Inc. Ab.	3.00	7.50	15.00	65.00
	1873 M	.040	10.00	15.00	30.00	75.00
	1874 M	—	5.00	10.00	20.00	65.00
	1874/64 B	—	5.00	10.00	20.00	65.00
	1874 B/M	—	20.00	40.00	60.00	125.00
	1874 B	—	5.00	10.00	15.00	65.00
	1875 B	—	20.00	40.00	60.00	125.00
	1876/5 B	—	3.00	5.00	9.00	65.00
	1876/5 B/M	—	3.00	5.00	9.00	65.00
	1877/6 M	—	3.00	5.00	9.00	65.00
	1877/6 M/B	—	3.00	5.00	9.00	65.00
	1877 M	—	3.00	5.00	9.00	65.00
	1878/7 M	.100	3.00	5.00	9.00	65.00
	1878 M	Inc. Ab.	3.00	5.00	9.00	65.00
	1879/69 M	—	3.00	5.00	9.00	65.00
	1879 M/C	—	3.00	5.00	9.00	65.00
	1880/79 M	—	3.00	5.00	9.00	65.00
	1881/0 M	.510	3.00	5.00	9.00	35.00
	1881 M	Inc. Ab.	3.00	5.00	9.00	35.00
	1882/1 M	.550	3.00	5.00	9.00	35.00
	1882 M	Inc. Ab.	3.00	5.00	9.00	35.00
	1883/2 M	.250	3.00	5.00	9.00	35.00
	1884 M	—	3.00	5.00	9.00	35.00
	1885 M	.470	3.00	5.00	9.00	35.00
	1886 M	.603	3.00	5.00	9.00	35.00
	1887 M	.580	3.00	5.00	9.00	35.00
	1888/7 MoM					
		.710	3.00	5.00	9.00	35.00
	1888 MoM	I.A.	3.00	5.00	9.00	35.00
	1888 MOM	I.A.	3.00	5.00	9.00	35.00
	1889/8 M	.622	3.00	5.00	9.00	35.00
	1889 M	Inc. Ab.	3.00	5.00	9.00	35.00
	1890/89 M	.815	3.00	5.00	9.00	35.00
	1890 M	Inc. Ab.	3.00	5.00	9.00	35.00
	1891 M	.859	1.50	2.50	7.00	25.00
	1892 M	1.030	1.50	2.50	7.00	25.00
	1893 M	.310	1.50	2.50	7.00	25.00
	1893 M/C	I.A.	1.50	2.50	7.00	25.00
	1894 M	.350	5.00	10.00	20.00	60.00
	1895 M	.320	1.50	2.50	7.00	25.00
	1896 B/G	.340	1.50	2.50	7.00	25.00
	1896 M	Inc. Ab.	35.00	70.00	100.00	150.00
	1897 M	.170	1.50	2.50	5.00	20.00

NOTE: Varieties exist.

Mint mark: Oa

KM#	Date	Mintage	Fine	VF	XF	Unc
403.8	1889 E	.021	200.00	400.00	600.00	—
	1890 E	.031	100.00	150.00	250.00	500.00
	1890 N	Inc. Ab.	—	—	Rare	—

Mint mark: Pi

KM#	Date	Mintage	Fine	VF	XF	Unc
403.9	1869/8 S	4,000	—	—	Rare	—
	1870/69 O	.018	—	—	Rare	—
	1870 G	Inc. Ab.	125.00	200.00	325.00	600.00
	1871 O	.021	50.00	100.00	150.00	300.00
	1872 O	.016	150.00	225.00	350.00	650.00
	1873 O	4,750	—	—	Rare	—
	1874 H	—	25.00	50.00	100.00	200.00
	1875 H	—	75.00	125.00	200.00	400.00
	1876 H	—	75.00	125.00	200.00	400.00
	1877 H	—	75.00	125.00	200.00	400.00
	1878 H	—	250.00	500.00	750.00	—
	1879 H	—	—	—	—	—
	1880 H	—	150.00	250.00	350.00	—
	1881 H	7,600	250.00	350.00	500.00	—
	1882 H	4,000	—	—	Rare	—
	1883 H	—	125.00	200.00	300.00	500.00
	1884 H	—	25.00	50.00	100.00	200.00
	1885 H	.051	25.00	50.00	100.00	200.00
	1885 C	Inc. Ab.	—	—	Rare	—
	1886 C	.052	15.00	30.00	60.00	150.00
	1886 R	Inc. Ab.	5.00	10.00	20.00	65.00
	1887 R	.118	2.50	5.00	10.00	50.00
	1888 R	.136	2.50	5.00	10.00	50.00
	1889/7 R	.131	7.50	12.50	20.00	60.00
	1890 R	.204	1.50	3.00	7.50	40.00
	1891/89 R	.163	2.50	5.00	10.00	40.00
	1891 R	Inc. Ab.	1.50	3.50	6.00	30.00
	1892/0 R	.200	2.00	4.00	8.00	40.00
	1892 R	Inc. Ab.	1.50	2.50	5.00	40.00
	1893 R	.048	7.50	10.00	17.50	60.00

NOTE: Varieties exist.

Mint mark: Zs

KM#	Date	Mintage	Fine	VF	XF	Unc
403.10	1870 H	.020	100.00	150.00	200.00	400.00
	1871/0 H	.010	—	—	—	—
	1871 H	Inc. Ab.	—	—	—	—
	1872 H	.010	150.00	200.00	275.00	500.00

KM#	Date	Mintage	Fine	VF	XF	Unc
403.10	1873 H	.010	250.00	350.00	600.00	—
	1874/3 H	—	50.00	75.00	150.00	300.00
	1874 A	—	200.00	300.00	500.00	—
	1875 A	—	5.00	10.00	25.00	100.00
	1876 A	—	5.00	10.00	25.00	100.00
	1876 S	—	100.00	200.00	300.00	500.00
	1877 S small S					
		—	7.50	12.50	25.00	100.00
	1877 S regular S					
		—	7.50	12.50	25.00	100.00
	1878/7 S	.030	5.00	10.00	20.00	80.00
	1878 S	Inc. Ab.	5.00	10.00	20.00	80.00
	1879 S	—	5.00	10.00	20.00	80.00
	1880 S	—	5.00	10.00	20.00	80.00
	1881/0 S	.120	3.00	6.00	12.50	50.00
	1881 S	Inc. Ab.	3.00	6.00	12.50	50.00
	1882/1 S	.064	12.50	25.00	50.00	125.00
	1882 S	Inc. Ab.	12.50	25.00	50.00	125.00
	1883/73 S	.102	2.00	4.00	8.00	50.00
	1883 S	Inc. Ab.	2.00	4.00	8.00	50.00
	1884/3 S	—	2.00	4.00	8.00	50.00
	1884 S	—	2.00	4.00	8.00	50.00
	1885 S	.297	1.50	2.50	5.00	50.00
	1885 S small S in mint mark					
		Inc. Ab.	2.50	4.00	8.00	50.00
	1885 Z w/o assayers initial (error)					
		Inc. Ab.	3.50	7.50	15.00	65.00
	1886 S	.274	1.50	2.50	5.00	30.00
	1886 Z	I.A.	12.50	25.00	50.00	125.00
	1887 ZsZ	.233	1.50	2.50	5.00	30.00
	1887 Z Z (error)					
		Inc. Ab.	3.50	7.50	15.00	50.00
	1888 ZsZ	.270	1.50	2.50	5.00	30.00
	1888 Z Z (error)					
		Inc. Ab.	3.50	7.50	15.00	40.00
	1889/7 Z/S					
		.240	4.00	8.00	12.50	40.00
	1889 Z/S	I.A.	1.50	4.00	8.00	30.00
	1889 Z	Inc. Ab.	1.50	2.50	5.00	30.00
	1890 ZsZ	.410	1.50	2.50	5.00	30.00
	1890 Z Z (error)					
		Inc. Ab.	3.75	7.50	15.00	40.00
	1891 Z	1.105	1.50	2.50	5.00	30.00
	1891 ZsZ double s					
		Inc. Ab.	2.00	4.00	7.00	30.00
	1892 Z	1.102	1.50	2.50	5.00	30.00
	1893 Z	1.011	1.50	2.50	5.00	25.00
	1894 Z	.892	1.50	2.50	5.00	30.00
	1895 Z	.920	1.50	2.50	5.00	30.00
	1896/5 ZsZ	.700	1.50	2.50	5.00	30.00
	1896 ZsZ	I.A.	1.50	2.50	5.00	30.00
	1896 Z Z (error)					
		Inc. Ab.	3.75	7.50	15.00	40.00
	1897/6 ZsZ	.900	2.00	5.00	10.00	30.00
	1897/6 Z Z (error)					
		Inc. Ab.	3.75	7.50	15.00	40.00
	1897 Z	Inc. Ab.	1.50	2.50	5.00	30.00

NOTE: Varieties exist.

Mint mark: Cn
Obv: Restyled eagle.

KM#	Date	Mintage	Fine	VF	XF	Unc
404	1898 M	9,870	50.00	100.00	150.00	300.00
	1899 Q round Q, single tail					
		.080	5.00	7.50	15.00	40.00
	1899 Q oval Q, double tail					
		Inc. Ab.	5.00	7.50	15.00	40.00
	1900 Q	.160	1.50	2.50	5.00	20.00

NOTE: Later dates (1901-1904) exist for this type.

Mint mark: Go

KM#	Date	Mintage	Fine	VF	XF	Unc
404.1	1898 R	.435	1.50	2.50	5.00	20.00
	1899 R	.270	1.50	2.50	5.00	25.00
	1900 R	.130	7.50	12.50	25.00	60.00

Mint mark: Mo

KM#	Date	Mintage	Fine	VF	XF	Unc
404.2	1898 M	.130	1.50	2.50	5.00	17.50
	1899 M	.190	1.50	2.50	5.00	17.50
	1900 M	.311	1.50	2.50	5.00	17.50

NOTE: Later dates (1901-1905) exist for this type.

Mint mark: Zs

KM#	Date	Mintage	Fine	VF	XF	Unc
404.3	1898 Z	.240	1.50	2.50	7.50	20.00
	1899 Z	.105	1.50	3.00	10.00	22.00
	1900 Z	.219	7.50	10.00	20.00	45.00

NOTE: Later dates (1901-1905) exist for this type.

20 CENTAVOS

5.4150 g, .903 SILVER, .1572 oz ASW
Mint mark: Cn
Obv: Restyled eagle.

KM#	Date	Mintage	Fine	VF	XF	Unc
405	1898 M	.114	5.00	12.50	35.00	140.00
	1899 M	.044	12.00	20.00	45.00	225.00
	1899 Q	Inc. Ab.	20.00	35.00	100.00	250.00
	1900 Q	.068	6.50	12.50	35.00	140.00

NOTE: Later dates (1901-1904) exist for this type.

Mint mark: Go

KM#	Date	Mintage	Fine	VF	XF	Unc
405.1	1898 R	.135	4.00	8.00	20.00	100.00
	1899 R	.215	4.00	8.00	20.00	100.00
	1900/800 R	.038	10.00	20.00	50.00	150.00

Mint mark: Mo

KM#	Date	Mintage	Fine	VF	XF	Unc
405.2	1898 M	.150	4.00	8.00	20.00	85.00
	1899 M	.425	4.00	8.00	20.00	85.00
	1900/800 M	.295	4.00	8.00	20.00	85.00

NOTE: Later dates (1901-1905) exist for this type.

Mint mark: Zs

KM#	Date	Mintage	Fine	VF	XF	Unc
405.3	1898 Z	.195	5.00	10.00	20.00	100.00
	1899 Z	.210	5.00	10.00	20.00	100.00
	1900/800 Z	.097	5.00	10.00	20.00	100.00

NOTE: Later dates (1901-1905) exist for this type.

25 CENTAVOS

6.7680 g, .903 SILVER, .1965 oz ASW

Mint mark: A, As

KM#	Date	Mintage	Fine	VF	XF	Unc
406	1874 L	—	20.00	40.00	90.00	200.00
	1875 L	—	15.00	30.00	70.00	200.00
	1876 L	—	30.00	50.00	100.00	200.00
	1877 L	.011	200.00	300.00	500.00	—
	1877.	Inc. Ab.	10.00	25.00	60.00	200.00
	1878 L	.025	10.00	25.00	60.00	200.00
	1879 L	—	10.00	25.00	60.00	200.00
	1880 L	—	10.00	25.00	60.00	200.00
	1880.L	—	10.00	25.00	60.00	200.00
	1881 L	8,800	500.00	700.00	—	—
	1882 L	7,777	15.00	35.00	80.00	200.00
	1883 L	.028	10.00	25.00	60.00	200.00
	1884 L	—	10.00	25.00	60.00	200.00
	1885 L	—	20.00	40.00	90.00	200.00
	1886 L	.046	15.00	30.00	70.00	200.00
	1887 L	.012	12.50	27.50	65.00	200.00
	1888 L	.020	12.50	27.50	65.00	200.00
	1889 L	.014	12.50	27.50	65.00	200.00
	1890 L	.023	10.00	25.00	60.00	200.00

Mint mark: CA, CH, Ca

KM#	Date	Mintage	Fine	VF	XF	Unc
406.1	1871 M	.018	25.00	50.00	100.00	200.00
	1872 M very crude date	.024	50.00	100.00	150.00	300.00
	1883 M	.012	10.00	25.00	50.00	175.00
	1885/3 M	.035	10.00	25.00	50.00	175.00
	1885 M	Inc.Ab.	10.00	25.00	50.00	175.00
	1886 M	.022	10.00	25.00	50.00	175.00
	1887/6 M	.026	10.00	15.00	30.00	175.00
	1887 M	Inc. Ab.	10.00	15.00	30.00	175.00
	1888 M	.014	10.00	25.00	50.00	175.00
	1889 M	.050	10.00	15.00	30.00	175.00

Mint mark: Cn

KM#	Date	Mintage	Fine	VF	XF	Unc
406.2	1871 P	—	250.00	500.00	750.00	—
	1872 P	2,780	300.00	550.00	800.00	—
	1873 P	.020	100.00	150.00	250.00	500.00
	1874 P	—	20.00	50.00	125.00	250.00
	1875 P	—	250.00	500.00	750.00	—
	1876 P	—	—	—	Rare	—
	1878/7 D/S	—	100.00	150.00	250.00	500.00
	1878 D	—	100.00	150.00	250.00	500.00
	1879 D	—	15.00	35.00	70.00	175.00
	1880 D	—	250.00	500.00	750.00	—
	1881/0 D	.018	15.00	30.00	60.00	175.00
	1882 D	—	200.00	350.00	600.00	—
	1882 M	—	—	—	Rare	—
	1883 M	.015	50.00	100.00	150.00	300.00
	1884 M	—	20.00	40.00	80.00	175.00
	1885/4 M	.019	20.00	40.00	80.00	175.00
	1886 M	.022	12.50	20.00	50.00	175.00
	1887 M	.032	12.50	20.00	50.00	175.00
	1888 M	.086	7.50	15.00	30.00	175.00
	1889 M	.050	10.00	25.00	50.00	175.00
	1890 M	.091	7.50	17.50	40.00	175.00
	1892/0 M	.016	20.00	40.00	80.00	200.00
	1892 M	Inc. Ab.	20.00	40.00	80.00	200.00

Mint mark: Do

KM#	Date	Mintage	Fine	VF	XF	Unc
406.3	1873 P	892 pcs.	—	—	Rare	—
	1877 P	—	25.00	50.00	100.00	200.00
	1878/7 E	—	250.00	500.00	750.00	—
	1878 B	—	—	—	Rare	—
	1879 B	—	50.00	75.00	125.00	250.00
	1880 B	—	—	—	Rare	—
	1882 C	.017	25.00	50.00	100.00	225.00
	1884/3 C	—	25.00	50.00	100.00	200.00
	1885 C	.015	20.00	40.00	80.00	200.00
	1886 C	.033	15.00	30.00	60.00	200.00
	1887 C	.027	10.00	20.00	50.00	200.00
	1888 C	.025	10.00	20.00	50.00	200.00
	1889 C	.029	10.00	20.00	50.00	200.00
	1890 C	.068	7.50	15.00	40.00	200.00

Mint mark: Ga

KM#	Date	Mintage	Fine	VF	XF	Unc
406.4	1880 A	.038	25.00	50.00	100.00	200.00
406.4	1881/0 S	.039	25.00	50.00	100.00	200.00
	1881 S	Inc. Ab.	25.00	50.00	100.00	200.00
	1882 S	.018	25.00	50.00	100.00	200.00
	1883/2 B/S	—	50.00	100.00	150.00	300.00
	1884 B	—	20.00	40.00	80.00	150.00
	1889 S	.030	20.00	40.00	80.00	150.00

Mint mark: Go

KM#	Date	Mintage	Fine	VF	XF	Unc
406.5	1870 S	.128	10.00	20.00	50.00	125.00
	1871 S	.172	10.00	20.00	50.00	125.00
	1872/1 S	.178	10.00	20.00	50.00	125.00
	1872 S	Inc. Ab.	10.00	20.00	50.00	125.00
	1873 S	.120	10.00	20.00	50.00	125.00
	1874 S	—	15.00	30.00	60.00	150.00
	1875/4 S	—	15.00	30.00	60.00	150.00
	1875 S	—	10.00	20.00	50.00	125.00
	1876 S	—	20.00	40.00	80.00	175.00
	1877 S	.124	10.00	20.00	50.00	125.00
	1878 S	.146	10.00	20.00	50.00	125.00
	1879 S	—	10.00	20.00	50.00	125.00
	1880 S	—	20.00	40.00	80.00	175.00
	1881 S	.408	7.50	17.50	45.00	125.00
	1882 S	.204	7.50	17.50	45.00	125.00
	1883 B	.168	7.50	17.50	45.00	125.00
	1884/69 B	—	7.50	17.50	45.00	125.00
	1884/3 B	—	7.50	17.50	45.00	125.00
	1884 B	—	7.50	17.50	45.00	125.00
	1885/65 R	.300	7.50	17.50	45.00	125.00
	1885/69 R	I.A.	7.50	17.50	45.00	125.00
	1885 R	Inc. Ab.	7.50	17.50	45.00	125.00
	1886/66 R	.322	7.50	17.50	45.00	125.00
	1886/69 R/S	Inc. Ab.	7.50	17.50	45.00	125.00
	1886/5/69R	Inc. Ab.	7.50	15.00	45.00	125.00
	1886 R	Inc. Ab.	7.50	15.00	45.00	125.00
	1887 R	.254	7.50	15.00	45.00	125.00
	1887 Go/Cn R/D	Inc. Ab.	7.50	15.00	45.00	125.00
	1888 R	.312	7.50	15.00	45.00	125.00
	1889/8 R	.304	7.50	15.00	45.00	125.00
	1889/8 Go/Cn R/D	Inc. Ab.	7.50	15.00	45.00	125.00
	1889 R	Inc. Ab.	7.50	15.00	45.00	125.00
	1890 R	.236	7.50	15.00	45.00	125.00

NOTE: Varieties exist.

Mint mark: Ho

KM#	Date	Mintage	Fine	VF	XF	Unc
406.6	1874 R	.023	10.00	20.00	40.00	125.00
	1874/64 R	I.A.	10.00	20.00	40.00	125.00
	1875 R	—	—	—	Rare	—
	1876/4 F/R	.034	10.00	20.00	50.00	150.00
	1876 F/R	I.A.	10.00	25.00	60.00	150.00
	1876 F	Inc. Ab.	10.00	25.00	55.00	135.00
	1877 F	—	10.00	20.00	50.00	125.00
	1878 A	.023	10.00	20.00	50.00	125.00
	1879 A	—	10.00	20.00	50.00	125.00
	1880 A	—	15.00	30.00	60.00	125.00
	1881 A	.019	15.00	30.00	60.00	125.00
	1882 A	8,120	20.00	40.00	80.00	150.00
	1883 M	2,000	100.00	200.00	300.00	600.00
	1884 M	—	12.50	25.00	50.00	150.00
	1885 M	—	10.00	20.00	50.00	125.00
	1886 G	6,400	30.00	60.00	125.00	250.00
	1887 G	.012	10.00	20.00	40.00	125.00
	1888 G	.020	10.00	20.00	40.00	125.00
	1889 G	.028	10.00	20.00	40.00	125.00
	1890/80 G	.018	25.00	50.00	100.00	125.00
	1890 G	Inc. Ab.	25.00	50.00	100.00	125.00

NOTE: Varieties exist.

Mint mark: Mo

KM#	Date	Mintage	Fine	VF	XF	Unc
406.7	1869 C	.076	10.00	25.00	50.00	125.00
	1870/9 C	.136	6.00	12.00	30.00	125.00
	1870 C	Inc. Ab.	6.00	12.00	30.00	125.00
	1871 M	.138	6.00	12.00	30.00	125.00
	1872 M	.220	6.00	12.00	30.00	125.00
	1873/1 M	.048	10.00	25.00	50.00	125.00
	1873 M	Inc. Ab.	10.00	25.00	50.00	125.00
	1874/69 B/M	—	10.00	25.00	50.00	125.00
	1874/3 M	—	10.00	25.00	50.00	125.00
	1874/3 B	—	10.00	25.00	50.00	125.00
	1874 M	—	6.00	12.00	30.00	125.00
	1874 B/M	—	10.00	25.00	50.00	125.00
	1875 B	—	6.00	12.00	30.00	125.00
	1876/5 B	—	7.50	15.00	40.00	125.00
	1876 B	—	6.00	12.00	30.00	125.00
	1877 M	.056	10.00	25.00	50.00	125.00
	1878/1 M	.120	10.00	25.00	50.00	125.00
	1878/7 M	I.A.	10.00	25.00	50.00	125.00
	1878 M	Inc. Ab.	6.00	12.00	30.00	125.00
	1879 M	—	10.00	20.00	40.00	125.00
	1880 M	—	7.50	15.00	35.00	125.00
	1881/0 M	.300	10.00	25.00	50.00	125.00
	1881 M	Inc. Ab.	10.00	25.00	50.00	125.00
	1882 M	.212	7.50	15.00	35.00	125.00
	1883 M	.108	7.50	15.00	35.00	125.00
	1884 M	—	10.00	20.00	40.00	125.00
	1885 M	.216	10.00	20.00	40.00	125.00
	1886/5 M	.436	7.50	15.00	35.00	125.00
	1886 M	Inc. Ab.	7.50	15.00	35.00	125.00
	1887 M	.376	7.50	15.00	35.00	125.00
	1888 M	.192	7.50	15.00	35.00	125.00
	1889 M	.132	7.50	15.00	35.00	125.00
	1890 M	.060	10.00	20.00	40.00	125.00

NOTE: Varieties exist.

Mint mark: Pi

KM#	Date	Mintage	Fine	VF	XF	Unc
406.8	1869 S	—	25.00	75.00	150.00	300.00
406.8	1870 G	.050	10.00	30.00	75.00	150.00
	1870 O	Inc. Ab.	15.00	35.00	85.00	175.00
	1871 O	.030	10.00	30.00	75.00	150.00
	1872 O	.046	10.00	30.00	75.00	150.00
	1873 O	.013	15.00	40.00	90.00	175.00
	1874 H	—	15.00	40.00	90.00	200.00
	1875 H	—	10.00	20.00	60.00	150.00
	1876/5 H	—	15.00	30.00	80.00	175.00
	1876 H	—	10.00	25.00	65.00	150.00
	1877 H	.019	10.00	25.00	65.00	150.00
	1878 H	—	15.00	30.00	60.00	150.00
	1879/8 H	—	10.00	25.00	60.00	150.00
	1879 H	—	10.00	25.00	60.00	150.00
	1879 E	—	100.00	200.00	300.00	600.00
	1880 H	—	20.00	40.00	100.00	200.00
	1881 H	.050	20.00	40.00	80.00	175.00
	1881 E	Inc. Ab.	—	—	Rare	—
	1882 H	.020	10.00	20.00	60.00	150.00
	1883 H	.017	10.00	25.00	65.00	150.00
	1884 H	—	10.00	25.00	65.00	150.00
	1885 H	.043	10.00	20.00	60.00	150.00
	1886 C	.078	10.00	25.00	65.00	150.00
	1886 R	Inc. Ab.	7.50	20.00	50.00	150.00
	1886 R 6/inverted 6	Inc. Ab.	7.50	20.00	50.00	150.00
	1887 Pi/ZsR	.092	7.50	20.00	50.00	150.00
	1887 Pi/ZsB	Inc. Ab.	100.00	150.00	300.00	500.00
	1888 R	.106	7.50	20.00	50.00	150.00
	1888 Pi/ZsR	Inc. Ab.	10.00	20.00	50.00	150.00
	1888 R/B	I.A.	10.00	20.00	50.00	150.00
	1889 R	.115	7.50	15.00	40.00	150.00
	1889 Pi/ZsR	Inc. Ab.	10.00	20.00	50.00	150.00
	1889 R/B	I.A.	10.00	20.00	50.00	150.00
	1890 R	.064	10.00	20.00	50.00	150.00
	1890 Pi/ZsR/B	Inc. Ab.	7.50	15.00	40.00	150.00
	1890 R/B	I.A.	10.00	20.00	50.00	150.00

NOTE: Varieties exist.

Mint mark: Zs

KM#	Date	Mintage	Fine	VF	XF	Unc
406.9	1870 H	.152	6.00	15.00	50.00	125.00
	1871 H	.250	6.00	15.00	50.00	125.00
	1872 H	.260	6.00	15.00	50.00	125.00
	1873 H	.132	6.00	15.00	50.00	125.00
	1874 H	—	10.00	20.00	60.00	125.00
	1874 A	—	10.00	20.00	60.00	125.00
	1875 A	—	7.00	20.00	60.00	125.00
	1876 A	—	6.00	15.00	50.00	125.00
	1876 S	—	6.00	15.00	50.00	125.00
	1877 S	.350	6.00	15.00	50.00	125.00
	1878 S	.252	6.00	15.00	50.00	125.00
	1879 S	—	6.00	15.00	50.00	125.00
	1880 S	—	6.00	15.00	50.00	125.00
	1881/0 S	.570	6.00	15.00	50.00	125.00
	1881 S	Inc. Ab.	6.00	15.00	50.00	125.00
	1882/1 S	.300	10.00	17.50	55.00	125.00
	1882 S	Inc. Ab.	6.00	15.00	50.00	125.00
	1883/2 S	.193	10.00	17.50	55.00	125.00
	1883 S	Inc. Ab.	6.00	15.00	50.00	125.00
	1884/3 S	—	10.00	17.50	55.00	125.00
	1884 S	—	6.00	15.00	50.00	125.00
	1885 S	.309	6.00	15.00	50.00	125.00
	1886/5 S	.613	6.00	15.00	50.00	125.00
	1886 S	Inc. Ab.	6.00	15.00	50.00	125.00
	1886 Z	Inc. Ab.	6.00	15.00	55.00	125.00
	1887 Z	.389	6.00	15.00	50.00	125.00
	1888 Z	.408	6.00	15.00	50.00	125.00
	1889 Z	.400	6.00	15.00	50.00	125.00
	1890 Z	.269	6.00	15.00	50.00	125.00

NOTE: Varieties exist.

50 CENTAVOS

13.5360 g, .903 SILVER, .3930 oz ASW

Mint mark: A, As

Rev: Balance scale.

KM#	Date	Mintage	Fine	VF	XF	Unc
407	1875 L	—	12.00	25.00	70.00	400.00
	1876/5 L	—	25.00	50.00	120.00	450.00
	1876 L	—	12.00	25.00	70.00	400.00
	1876.L	—	—	—	—	—
	1877 L	.026	15.00	30.00	85.00	450.00
	1878 L	—	12.00	25.00	70.00	400.00
	1879 L	—	25.00	50.00	120.00	450.00
	1880 L	.057	12.00	25.00	70.00	400.00
	1881 L	.018	15.00	30.00	80.00	450.00
	1884 L	6,286	65.00	120.00	250.00	650.00
	1885 As/HoL	.021	15.00	35.00	90.00	450.00
	1888 L	—	Contemporary counterfeits			

Mint mark: Ca, CHa

KM#	Date	Mintage	Fine	VF	XF	Unc
407.1	1883 M	.012	30.00	60.00	125.00	500.00
	1884 M	—	25.00	50.00	125.00	500.00
	1885 M	.013	15.00	35.00	90.00	400.00
	1886 M	.018	20.00	40.00	100.00	450.00
	1887 M	.026	25.00	65.00	150.00	500.00

Mint mark: Cn

KM#	Date	Mintage	Fine	VF	XF	Unc
407.2	1871 P	—	400.00	550.00	750.00	1500.
	1873 P	—	400.00	550.00	750.00	1500.
	1874 P	—	200.00	300.00	500.00	1000.
	1875/4 P	—	20.00	40.00	75.00	450.00
	1875 P	—	12.00	25.00	50.00	450.00
	1876 P	—	15.00	30.00	60.00	450.00
	1877/6 G	—	15.00	30.00	60.00	450.00
	1877 G	—	12.00	25.00	50.00	450.00
	1878 G	.018	20.00	40.00	75.00	450.00
	1878 D Cn/Mo	Inc. Ab.	30.00	60.00	100.00	450.00
	1878 D	Inc. Ab.	15.00	35.00	75.00	450.00
	1879 D	—	12.00	25.00	50.00	450.00
	1879 D/G	—	12.00	25.00	50.00	450.00
	1880 D	—	15.00	30.00	60.00	450.00
	1881/0 D	.188	15.00	30.00	60.00	450.00
	1881 D	Inc. Ab.	15.00	30.00	60.00	450.00
	1881 G	Inc. Ab.	125.00	175.00	275.00	550.00
	1882 D	—	175.00	225.00	325.00	1000.
	1882 G	—	100.00	250.00	300.00	1000.
	1883 D	.019	25.00	50.00	100.00	500.00
	1885/3 CN/Pi M/H	9,254	30.00	60.00	100.00	500.00
	1886 M/G	7,030	50.00	100.00	150.00	800.00
	1886 M	Inc. Ab.	40.00	80.00	150.00	800.00
	1887 M	.076	20.00	40.00	100.00	450.00
	1888 M	—	Contemporary counterfeits			
	1892 M	8,200	40.00	80.00	150.00	800.00

Mint mark: Do

KM#	Date	Mintage	Fine	VF	XF	Unc
407.3	1871 P	591 pcs.	—	—	Rare	—
	1873 P	4,010	150.00	250.00	500.00	1250.
	1873 M/P	I.A.	150.00	250.00	500.00	1250.
	1874 M	—	20.00	40.00	175.00	750.00
	1875 M	—	20.00	40.00	80.00	350.00
	1875 H	—	150.00	250.00	450.00	1000.
	1876/5 M	—	35.00	70.00	150.00	500.00
	1876 M	—	35.00	70.00	150.00	500.00
	1877 P	2,000	30.00	45.00	150.00	1250.
	1878 B	—	—	—	Rare	—
	1879 B	—	—	—	Rare	—
	1880 P	—	30.00	60.00	125.00	500.00
	1881 P	.010	40.00	80.00	150.00	550.00
	1882 C	8,957	30.00	75.00	200.00	800.00
	1884/2 C	—	20.00	50.00	125.00	600.00
	1884 C	—	—	—	—	—
	1885 B	—	15.00	40.00	100.00	500.00
	1886 C	.016	15.00	40.00	100.00	500.00
	1887 Do/MoC	.028	15.00	40.00	100.00	500.00

Mint mark: Go

KM#	Date	Mintage	Fine	VF	XF	Unc
407.4	1869 S	—	15.00	35.00	75.00	550.00
	1870 S	.166	12.00	25.00	50.00	450.00
	1871 S	.148	12.00	25.00	50.00	450.00
	1872/1 S	.144	15.00	30.00	60.00	500.00
	1872 S	Inc. Ab.	12.00	25.00	50.00	450.00
	1873 S	.050	12.00	25.00	50.00	450.00
	1874 S	—	12.00	25.00	50.00	450.00
	1875 S	—	15.00	35.00	75.00	450.00
	1876/5 S	—	12.00	25.00	50.00	450.00
	1877 S	.076	12.00	25.00	60.00	450.00
	1878 S	.037	15.00	30.00	75.00	550.00
	1879 S	—	12.00	25.00	50.00	450.00
	1880 S	—	12.00	25.00	50.00	450.00
	1881/79 S	.032	15.00	30.00	60.00	500.00
	1881 S	Inc. Ab.	12.00	25.00	50.00	450.00
	1882 S	.018	12.00	25.00	50.00	450.00
	1883/2 B/S	—	15.00	30.00	60.00	500.00
	1883 B	—	12.00	25.00	50.00	450.00
	1883 S	—	—	—	Rare	—
	1884 B/S	—	15.00	30.00	75.00	500.00
	1885 R	.053	12.00	25.00	50.00	450.00
	1886/5 R/B	.059	15.00	30.00	60.00	500.00
	1886/5 R/S	Inc. Ab.	20.00	40.00	75.00	500.00
	1886 R	Inc. Ab.	20.00	40.00	75.00	450.00
	1887 R	.018	20.00	40.00	75.00	550.00
	1888 R	—	Contemporary counterfeits			

NOTE: Varieties exist.

Mint mark: Ho

KM#	Date	Mintage	Fine	VF	XF	Unc
407.5	1874 R	—	20.00	40.00	100.00	600.00
	1875/4 R	—	20.00	50.00	125.00	600.00
	1875 R	—	20.00	50.00	125.00	600.00
	1876/5 F/R	—	15.00	35.00	100.00	550.00
	1876 F	—	15.00	35.00	100.00	550.00
	1877 F	—	50.00	75.00	150.00	650.00
	1880/70 A	—	15.00	35.00	100.00	550.00
	1880 A	—	15.00	35.00	100.00	550.00
	1881 A	.013	15.00	35.00	100.00	550.00
	1882 A	—	75.00	150.00	250.00	750.00
	1888 G	—	Contemporary counterfeits			
	1894 G	.059	15.00	30.00	100.00	450.00
	1895 G	8,000	250.00	350.00	500.00	1250.

NOTE: Varieties exist.

Mint mark: Mo

KM#	Date	Mintage	Fine	VF	XF	Unc
407.6	1869 C	.046	15.00	35.00	95.00	600.00
	1870 C	.052	15.00	30.00	90.00	550.00
	1871 C	.014	40.00	75.00	150.00	650.00
	1871 M/C	I.A.	35.00	75.00	150.00	600.00
	1872/1 M	.060	35.00	75.00	150.00	550.00
	1872 M	Inc. Ab.	35.00	75.00	150.00	550.00
	1873 M	6,000	35.00	75.00	150.00	600.00
	1874/3 M	—	200.00	400.00	600.00	1250.
	1874/2 B	—	15.00	30.00	75.00	500.00
	1874/3 B/M	—	15.00	30.00	75.00	500.00
	1874 B	—	15.00	30.00	75.00	500.00

KM#	Date	Mintage	Fine	VF	XF	Unc
407.6	1875 B	—	15.00	30.00	75.00	550.00
	1876/5 B	—	15.00	30.00	75.00	500.00
	1876 B	—	12.00	25.00	75.00	500.00
	1877/2 M	—	20.00	40.00	100.00	550.00
	1877 M	—	15.00	30.00	90.00	500.00
	1878/7 M	8,000	25.00	50.00	125.00	600.00
	1878 M	Inc. Ab.	15.00	35.00	100.00	550.00
	1879 M	—	25.00	50.00	125.00	550.00
	1880 M	—	100.00	150.00	250.00	750.00
	1881 M	.016	25.00	50.00	125.00	600.00
	1882/1 M	2,000	30.00	60.00	150.00	750.00
	1883/2 M	4,000	150.00	225.00	350.00	1000.
	1884 M	—	150.00	225.00	350.00	1000.
	1885 M	.012	30.00	60.00	150.00	600.00
	1886/5 M	.066	15.00	35.00	90.00	450.00
	1886 M	Inc. Ab.	12.00	25.00	75.00	400.00
	1887/6 M	.088	15.00	35.00	90.00	450.00
	1887 M	Inc. Ab.	15.00	35.00	75.00	450.00
	1888 M	—	Contemporary counterfeits			

Mint mark: Pi

KM#	Date	Mintage	Fine	VF	XF	Unc
407.7	1870/780 G	.050	25.00	45.00	110.00	500.00
	1870 G	Inc. Ab.	20.00	40.00	100.00	450.00
	1870 O	Inc. Ab.	20.00	40.00	100.00	450.00
	1871 O/G	.064	15.00	30.00	80.00	400.00
	1872 O	.052	15.00	30.00	80.00	400.00
	1872 O/G	I.A.	15.00	30.00	80.00	400.00
	1873 O	.032	20.00	40.00	100.00	450.00
	1873 H	Inc. Ab.	25.00	50.00	125.00	550.00
	1874 H/O	—	15.00	30.00	80.00	400.00
	1875 H	—	15.00	30.00	80.00	400.00
	1876 H	—	30.00	60.00	150.00	700.00
	1877 H	.034	20.00	40.00	100.00	450.00
	1878 H	9,700	20.00	40.00	100.00	450.00
	1879/7 H	—	15.00	35.00	90.00	450.00
	1879 H	—	15.00	35.00	90.00	400.00
	1880 H	—	20.00	40.00	100.00	450.00
	1881 H	.028	20.00	40.00	100.00	450.00
	1882 H	.022	15.00	30.00	80.00	400.00
	1883 H 8/8	.029	50.00	100.00	200.00	750.00
	1883 H	Inc. Ab.	15.00	30.00	80.00	400.00
	1884 H	—	50.00	100.00	175.00	600.00
	1885/0 H	.045	20.00	40.00	100.00	450.00
	1885/4 H	I.A.	20.00	40.00	100.00	450.00
	1885 H	Inc. Ab.	25.00	50.00	125.00	450.00
	1885 C	Inc. Ab.	15.00	30.00	80.00	400.00
	1886/1 R	.092	50.00	100.00	175.00	600.00
	1886 C	Inc. Ab.	15.00	30.00	80.00	400.00
	1886 R	Inc. Ab.	15.00	30.00	80.00	400.00
	1887 R	.032	15.00	30.00	90.00	450.00
	1888 R	—	Contemporary counterfeits			

Mint mark: Zs

KM#	Date	Mintage	Fine	VF	XF	Unc
407.8	1870 H	.086	12.00	25.00	60.00	450.00
	1871 H	.146	12.00	25.00	50.00	400.00
	1872 H	.132	12.00	25.00	50.00	400.00
	1873 H	.056	12.00	25.00	50.00	400.00
	1874 H	—	12.00	25.00	50.00	400.00
	1874 A	—	—	—	Rare	—
	1875 A	—	12.00	25.00	50.00	400.00
	1876/5 A	—	15.00	30.00	60.00	450.00
	1876 A	—	12.00	25.00	50.00	400.00
	1876 S	—	100.00	200.00	350.00	750.00
	1877 S	.100	12.00	25.00	50.00	400.00
	1878/7 S	.254	15.00	30.00	60.00	450.00
	1878 S	Inc. Ab.	15.00	30.00	60.00	400.00
	1879 S	—	12.00	25.00	50.00	400.00
	1880 S	—	12.00	25.00	50.00	400.00
	1881 S	.201	12.00	25.00	50.00	400.00
	1882/1 S	2,000	50.00	100.00	250.00	650.00
	1882 S	Inc. Ab.	50.00	100.00	250.00	650.00
	1883 Zs/Za S	.031	30.00	60.00	100.00	450.00
	1883 S	Inc. Ab.	25.00	50.00	100.00	450.00
	1884/3 S	—	15.00	30.00	60.00	450.00
	1884 S	—	12.00	25.00	50.00	400.00
	1885/4 S	2,000	25.00	50.00	125.00	450.00
	1885 S	Inc. Ab.	25.00	50.00	125.00	450.00
	1886 Z	2,000	150.00	275.00	400.00	1000.
	1887 Z	.063	30.00	60.00	125.00	450.00

NOTE: Varieties exist.

PESO

27.0730 g, .903 SILVER, .7860 oz ASW
Mint mark: CH
Rev: Balance scale.

KM#	Date	Mintage	Fine	VF	XF	Unc
408	1872 P/M	.747	750.00	1500.	3500.	—
	1872 P	Inc. Ab.	350.00	700.00	1500.	—
	1872/1 M	I.A.	25.00	40.00	75.00	400.00
	1872 M	Inc. Ab.	17.50	25.00	50.00	250.00
	1873 M	.320	20.00	30.00	60.00	265.00
	1873 M/P	I.A.	25.00	40.00	75.00	350.00

Mint mark: Cn

KM#	Date	Mintage	Fine	VF	XF	Unc
408.1	1870 E	—	40.00	80.00	150.00	500.00
	1871/11 P	.478	25.00	45.00	90.00	350.00
	1871 P	Inc. Ab.	20.00	40.00	75.00	300.00
	1872 P	.209	20.00	40.00	75.00	300.00
	1873 P	.527	20.00	40.00	75.00	300.00

Mint mark: Do

KM#	Date	Mintage	Fine	VF	XF	Unc
408.2	1870 P	—	50.00	100.00	175.00	450.00
	1871 P	.427	25.00	50.00	75.00	300.00
	1872 P	.296	20.00	40.00	75.00	350.00
	1872 PT	I.A.	100.00	175.00	250.00	675.00
	1873 P	.203	25.00	45.00	85.00	350.00

Mint mark: Ga

KM#	Date	Mintage	Fine	VF	XF	Unc
408.3	1870 C	—	650.00	850.00	—	—
	1871 C	.829	25.00	65.00	135.00	600.00
	1872 C	.485	40.00	90.00	175.00	650.00
	1873/2 C	.277	40.00	90.00	175.00	700.00
	1873 C	Inc. Ab.	25.00	65.00	135.00	600.00

Mint mark: Go

KM#	Date	Mintage	Fine	VF	XF	Unc
408.4	1871/0 S	3.946	30.00	50.00	90.00	350.00
	1871/3 S	I.A.	20.00	35.00	70.00	275.00
	1871 S	Inc. Ab.	12.00	20.00	40.00	220.00
	1872 S	4.067	12.00	20.00	40.00	250.00
	1873/2 S	1.560	15.00	25.00	50.00	250.00
	1873 S	Inc. Ab.	12.00	20.00	45.00	250.00
	1873/Go/Mo/S/M	Inc. Ab.	12.00	20.00	45.00	250.00

Mint mark: Mo

KM#	Date	Mintage	Fine	VF	XF	Unc
408.5	1869 C	—	35.00	65.00	135.00	450.00
	1870/69 C	5.115	15.00	25.00	55.00	275.00
	1870 C	Inc. Ab.	12.00	20.00	40.00	250.00
	1870 M/C	I.A.	18.00	30.00	60.00	275.00
	1870 M	Inc. Ab.	18.00	30.00	60.00	275.00
	1871/0 M	6.974	15.00	25.00	55.00	275.00
	1871 M	Inc. Ab.	12.00	20.00	40.00	250.00
	1872/1 M/C	4.801	15.00	25.00	50.00	275.00
	1872 M	Inc. Ab.	12.00	20.00	40.00	250.00
	1873 M	1.765	12.00	20.00	40.00	250.00

NOTE: The 1869 C with large LEY on the scroll is a pattern.

Mint mark: Oa

KM#	Date	Mintage	Fine	VF	XF	Unc
408.6	1869 E	—	275.00	400.00	600.00	2000.
	1870 OAE small A	Inc. Ab.	15.00	30.00	75.00	400.00
	1870 OA E large A	Inc. Ab.	100.00	150.00	300.00	900.00
	1871/69 E	.140	30.00	50.00	125.00	550.00
	1871 OaE small A	Inc. Ab.	15.00	30.00	60.00	300.00
	1871 OA E large A	Inc. Ab.	15.00	30.00	75.00	400.00
	1872 OaE small A	.180	15.00	30.00	75.00	400.00
	1872 OA E large A	Inc. Ab.	50.00	100.00	200.00	450.00
	1873 E	.105	15.00	30.00	75.00	350.00

Mint mark: Pi

KM#	Date	Mintage	Fine	VF	XF	Unc
408.7	1870 S	1.967	200.00	350.00	500.00	1000.
	1870 S/A	I.A.	200.00	350.00	500.00	1000.
	1870 G	Inc. Ab.	25.00	50.00	125.00	450.00
	1870 H	Inc. Ab.	Contemporary counterfeit			
	1870 O/G	I.A.	25.00	35.00	125.00	450.00
	1870 O	Inc. Ab.	20.00	30.00	100.00	350.00
	1871/69 O	2.103	75.00	150.00	250.00	500.00
	1871 O/G	I.A.	15.00	30.00	60.00	300.00
	1872 O	1.873	15.00	30.00	60.00	300.00
	1873 O	.893	15.00	30.00	60.00	300.00
	1873 H	Inc. Ab.	15.00	30.00	60.00	300.00

NOTE: Varieties exist.

Mint mark: Zs

KM#	Date	Mintage	Fine	VF	XF	Unc
408.8	1870 H	4.519	12.00	30.00	40.00	220.00
	1871 H	4.459	12.00	20.00	40.00	220.00
	1872 H	4.039	12.00	20.00	40.00	220.00
	1873 H	1.782	12.00	20.00	40.00	220.00

NOTE: Varieties exist.

Mint mark: Cn
Liberty cap

KM#	Date	Mintage	Fine	VF	XF	Unc
409	1898 AM	1.720	10.00	15.00	30.00	65.00
	1898 Cn/MoAM	I.A.	15.00	30.00	90.00	150.00
	1899 AM	1.722	25.00	50.00	90.00	175.00
	1899 JQ	I.A.	10.00	15.00	50.00	125.00
	1900 JQ	1.804	10.00	15.00	30.00	80.00

NOTE: Later dates (1901-1905) exist for this type.

Mint mark: Go

KM#	Date	Mintage	Fine	VF	XF	Unc
409.1	1898 RS	4.256	10.00	15.00	35.00	75.00
	1898 Go/MoRS	Inc. Ab.	20.00	30.00	60.00	125.00
	1899 RS	3.207	10.00	15.00	30.00	75.00
	1900 RS	1.489	25.00	50.00	100.00	250.00

NOTE: Varieties exist.

Mint mark: Mo

KM#	Date	Mintage	Fine	VF	XF	Unc
409.2	1898 AM original strike - rev. w/139 Beads	10.156	7.50	10.00	17.50	60.00
	1898 AM restrike (1949) - rev. w/134 Beads	10.250	7.50	10.00	15.00	40.00
	1899 AM	7.930	10.00	12.50	20.00	70.00
	1900 AM	8.226	10.00	12.50	20.00	70.00

NOTE: Later dates (1901-1909) exist for this type.

Mint mark: Zs

KM#	Date	Mintage	Fine	VF	XF	Unc
409.3	1898 FZ	5.714	10.00	12.50	20.00	60.00
	1899 FZ	5.618	10.00	12.50	20.00	65.00
	1900 FZ	5.357	10.00	12.50	20.00	65.00

NOTE: Later dates (1901-1905) exist for this type.

1.6920 g, .875 GOLD, .0476 oz AGW

Mint mark: As

KM#	Date	Mintage	Fine	VF	XF	Unc
410	1888 L	—	—	—	Rare	—
	1888 AsL/MoM	—	—	—	Rare	—

Mint mark: Ca

KM#	Date	Mintage	Fine	VF	XF	Unc
410.1	1888 Ca/MoM	104 pcs.	—	—	Rare	—

Mint mark: Cn

KM#	Date	Mintage	Fine	VF	XF	Unc
410.2	1873 P	1,221	75.00	100.00	150.00	250.00
	1875 P	—	85.00	125.00	150.00	250.00
	1878 G	248 pcs.	100.00	175.00	225.00	450.00
	1879 D	—	100.00	150.00	175.00	275.00
	1881/0 D	338 pcs.	100.00	150.00	175.00	275.00
	1882 D	340 pcs.	100.00	150.00	175.00	275.00
	1883 D	—	100.00	150.00	175.00	275.00
	1884 M	—	100.00	150.00	175.00	275.00
	1886/4 M	277 pcs.	100.00	150.00	225.00	450.00
	1888/7 M	2,586	100.00	175.00	225.00	450.00
	1888 M	Inc. Ab.	65.00	100.00	150.00	250.00
	1889 M	—	—	—	Rare	—
	1891/89 M	969 pcs.	75.00	100.00	150.00	250.00
	1892 M	780 pcs.	75.00	100.00	150.00	250.00
	1893 M	498 pcs.	85.00	125.00	150.00	250.00
	1894 M	493 pcs.	80.00	125.00	150.00	250.00
	1895 M	1,143	65.00	100.00	150.00	250.00
	1896/5 M	1,028	65.00	100.00	150.00	250.00
	1897 M	785 pcs.	65.00	100.00	150.00	250.00
	1898 M	3,521	65.00	100.00	150.00	225.00
410.2	1898 Cn/MoM	Inc. Ab.	65.00	100.00	150.00	250.00
	1899 Q	2,000	65.00	100.00	150.00	225.00

NOTE: Later dates (1901-1905) exist for this type.

Mint mark: Go

KM#	Date	Mintage	Fine	VF	XF	Unc
410.3	1870 S	—	100.00	125.00	150.00	250.00
	1871 S	500 pcs.	100.00	175.00	225.00	450.00
	1888 R	210 pcs.	125.00	200.00	250.00	500.00
	1890 R	1,916	75.00	100.00	150.00	250.00
	1892 R	533 pcs.	100.00	150.00	175.00	325.00
	1894 R	180 pcs.	150.00	200.00	250.00	500.00
	1895 R	676 pcs.	100.00	150.00	175.00	300.00
	1896/5 R	4,671	65.00	100.00	150.00	250.00
	1897/6 R	4,280	65.00	100.00	150.00	250.00
	1897 R	Inc. Ab.	65.00	100.00	150.00	250.00
	1898 R regular obv.	5,193	65.00	100.00	150.00	250.00
	1898 R mule, 5 Centavos obv., normal rev.	Inc. Ab.	75.00	100.00	150.00	250.00
	1899 R	2,748	65.00	100.00	150.00	250.00
	1900/800 R	864 pcs.	75.00	125.00	150.00	275.00

Mint mark: Ho

KM#	Date	Mintage	Fine	VF	XF	Unc
410.4	1875 R	310 pcs.	—	—	Rare	—
	1876 F	—	—	—	Rare	—
	1888 G/MoM	—	—	—	Rare	—

Mint mark: Mo

KM#	Date	Mintage	Fine	VF	XF	Unc
410.5	1870 C	2,540	40.00	60.00	80.00	175.00
	1871 M/C	1,000	50.00	100.00	150.00	225.00
	1872 M/C	3,000	40.00	60.00	80.00	175.00
	1873/1 M	2,900	40.00	60.00	80.00	175.00
	1873 M	Inc. Ab.	40.00	60.00	80.00	175.00
	1874 M	—	40.00	60.00	80.00	175.00
	1875 B/M	—	40.00	60.00	80.00	175.00
	1876/5 B/M	—	40.00	60.00	80.00	175.00
	1877 M	—	40.00	60.00	80.00	175.00
	1878 M	2,000	40.00	60.00	80.00	175.00
	1879 M	—	40.00	60.00	80.00	175.00
	1880/70 M	—	40.00	60.00	80.00	175.00
	1881/71 M	1,000	40.00	60.00	80.00	175.00
	1882/72 M	—	40.00	60.00	80.00	175.00
		—	40.00	60.00	80.00	175.00
	1883/72 M	1,000	40.00	60.00	80.00	175.00
	1884 M	—	40.00	60.00	80.00	175.00
	1885/71 M	—	40.00	60.00	80.00	175.00
	1885 M	—	40.00	60.00	80.00	175.00
	1886 M	1,700	40.00	60.00	80.00	175.00
	1887 M	2,200	40.00	60.00	80.00	175.00
	1888 M	1,000	40.00	60.00	80.00	175.00
	1889 M	500 pcs.	100.00	150.00	200.00	275.00
	1890 M	570 pcs.	100.00	150.00	200.00	275.00
	1891 M	746 pcs.	100.00	150.00	200.00	275.00
	1892/0 M	2,895	40.00	60.00	80.00	175.00
	1893 M	5,917	40.00	60.00	80.00	175.00
	1894 M	6,244	40.00	60.00	80.00	175.00
	1895 M	8,994	40.00	60.00	80.00	175.00
	1895 B	Inc. Ab.	40.00	60.00	80.00	175.00
	1896 B	7,166	40.00	60.00	80.00	175.00
	1896 M	Inc. Ab.	40.00	60.00	80.00	175.00
	1897 M	5,131	40.00	60.00	80.00	175.00
	1898/7 M	5,368	40.00	60.00	80.00	175.00
	1899 M	9,515	40.00	60.00	80.00	175.00
	1900/800 M	9,301	40.00	60.00	80.00	175.00
	1900/880 M	Inc. Ab.	40.00	60.00	80.00	175.00
	1900/890 M	Inc. Ab.	40.00	60.00	80.00	175.00
	1900 M	Inc. Ab.	40.00	60.00	80.00	175.00

NOTE: Later dates (1901-1905) exist for this type.

Mint mark: Zs

KM#	Date	Mintage	Fine	VF	XF	Unc
410.6	1872 H	2,024	125.00	150.00	175.00	250.00
	1875/3 A	—	125.00	150.00	200.00	300.00
	1878 S	—	125.00	150.00	175.00	250.00
	1888 Z	280 pcs.	175.00	225.00	300.00	650.00
	1889 Z	492 pcs.	150.00	175.00	225.00	425.00
	1890 Z	738 pcs.	150.00	175.00	225.00	425.00

2-1/2 PESOS

4.2300 g, .875 GOLD, .1190 oz AGW

Mint mark: As

KM#	Date	Mintage	Fine	VF	XF	Unc
411	1888 As/MoL	—	—	—	Rare	—

Mint mark: Cn

KM#	Date	Mintage	Fine	VF	XF	Unc
411.1	1893 M	141 pcs.	1500.	2000.	2500.	3500.

Mint mark: Do

KM#	Date	Mintage	Fine	VF	XF	Unc
411.2	1888 C	—	—	—	Rare	—

Mint mark: Go

KM#	Date	Mintage	Fine	VF	XF	Unc
411.3	1871 S	600 pcs.	1250.	2000.	2500.	3250.
	1888 Go/MoR	110 pcs.	1750.	2250.	2750.	3500.

Mint mark: Ho

KM#	Date	Mintage	Fine	VF	XF	Unc
411.4	1874 R	—	—	—	Rare	—
	1888 G	—	—	—	Rare	—

Mint mark: Mo

KM#	Date	Mintage	Fine	VF	XF	Unc
411.5	1870 C	820 pcs.	150.00	250.00	350.00	650.00
	1872 M/C	800 pcs.	150.00	250.00	350.00	650.00
	1873/2 M	—	200.00	350.00	750.00	1250.
	1874 M	—	200.00	350.00	750.00	1250.
	1874 B/M	—	200.00	350.00	750.00	1250.
	1875 B	—	200.00	350.00	750.00	1250.
	1876 B	—	250.00	500.00	1000.	1500.
	1877 M	—	200.00	350.00	750.00	1250.
	1878 M	400 pcs.	200.00	350.00	750.00	1250.
	1879 M	—	200.00	350.00	750.00	1250.
	1880/79 M	—	200.00	350.00	750.00	1250.
	1881 M	400 pcs.	200.00	350.00	750.00	1250.
	1882 M	—	200.00	350.00	750.00	1250.
	1883/73 M	400 pcs.	200.00	350.00	750.00	1250.
	1884 M	—	250.00	500.00	1000.	1500.
	1885 M	—	200.00	350.00	750.00	1250.
	1886 M	400 pcs.	200.00	350.00	750.00	1250.
	1887 M	400 pcs.	200.00	350.00	750.00	1250.
	1888 M	540 pcs.	200.00	350.00	750.00	1250.
	1889 M	240 pcs.	150.00	300.00	525.00	850.00
	1890 M	420 pcs.	200.00	350.00	750.00	1250.
	1891 M	188 pcs.	200.00	350.00	750.00	1250.
	1892 M	240 pcs.	200.00	350.00	750.00	1250.

Mint mark: Zs

KM#	Date	Mintage	Fine	VF	XF	Unc
411.6	1872 H	1,300	200.00	350.00	500.00	1000.
	1873 H	—	175.00	325.00	450.00	700.00
	1875/3 A	—	200.00	350.00	750.00	1250.
	1877 S	—	200.00	350.00	750.00	1250.
	1878 S	300 pcs.	200.00	350.00	750.00	1250.
	1888 Zs/MoS	80 pcs.	300.00	500.00	1000.	1750.
	1889 Zs/MoZ	184 pcs.	250.00	450.00	950.00	1500.
	1890 Z	326 pcs.	200.00	350.00	750.00	1250.

CINCO (5) PESOS

8.4600 g, .875 GOLD, .2380 oz AGW

Mint mark: As

KM#	Date	Mintage	Fine	VF	XF	Unc
412	1875 L	—	—	—	—	—
	1878 L	383 pcs.	900.00	1700.	3000.	4500.

Mint mark: Ca

KM#	Date	Mintage	Fine	VF	XF	Unc
412.1	1888 M	120 pcs.	—	—	Rare	—

Mint mark: Cn

KM#	Date	Mintage	Fine	VF	XF	Unc
412.2	1873 P	—	300.00	600.00	1000.	1500.
	1874 P	—	—	—	—	—
	1875 P	—	300.00	500.00	700.00	1250.
	1876 P	—	300.00	500.00	700.00	1250.
	1877 G	—	300.00	500.00	700.00	1250.
	1882	174 pcs.	—	—	Rare	—
	1888 M	—	500.00	1000.	1350.	2000.
	1890 M	435 pcs.	250.00	500.00	750.00	1250.
	1891 M	1,390	250.00	400.00	500.00	1000.
	1894 M	484 pcs.	250.00	500.00	750.00	1600.
	1895 M	142 pcs.	500.00	750.00	1500.	2500.
	1900 Q	1,536	200.00	300.00	400.00	950.00

NOTE: Later date (1903) exists for this type.

Mintmark: Do

KM#	Date	Mintage	Fine	VF	XF	Unc
412.3	1873/2 P	—	700.00	1250.	1800.	3000.
	1877 P	—	700.00	1250.	1800.	3000.
	1878 E	—	700.00	1250.	1800.	3000.
	1879/7 B	—	700.00	1250.	1800.	3000.
	1879 B	—	700.00	1250.	1800.	3000.

Mint mark: Go

KM#	Date	Mintage	Fine	VF	XF	Unc
412.4	1871 S	1,600	400.00	800.00	1250.	2500.
	1887 R	140 pcs.	600.00	1200.	1500.	2750.
	1888 R	65 pcs.	—	—	Rare	—
	1893 R	16 pcs.	—	—	Rare	—

Mint mark: Ho

KM#	Date	Mintage	Fine	VF	XF	Unc
412.5	1874 R	—	1750.	2500.	3000.	4500.
	1877 R					

KM#	Date	Mintage	Fine	VF	XF	Unc
412.5		990 pcs.	750.00	1250.	2000.	3000.
	1877 A	Inc. Ab.	650.00	1100.	1750.	2750.
	1888G	—	—	—	Rare	—

Mint mark: Mo

KM#	Date	Mintage	Fine	VF	XF	Unc
412.6	1870 C	550 pcs.	200.00	400.00	550.00	900.00
	1871/69 M	1,600	175.00	350.00	475.00	750.00
	1871 M	Inc. Ab.	175.00	350.00	475.00	750.00
	1872 M	1,600	175.00	350.00	475.00	750.00
	1873/2 M	—	200.00	400.00	550.00	850.00
	1874 M	—	200.00	400.00	550.00	850.00
	1875/3 B/M	—	200.00	400.00	550.00	950.00
	1875 B	—	200.00	400.00	550.00	950.00
	1876/5 B/M	—	200.00	400.00	550.00	1000.
	1877 M	—	250.00	450.00	750.00	1250.
	1878/7 M	400 pcs.	200.00	400.00	550.00	1250.
	1878 M	Inc. Ab.	200.00	400.00	550.00	1250.
	1879/8 M	—	200.00	400.00	550.00	1250.
	1880 M	—	200.00	400.00	550.00	1250.
	1881 M	—	200.00	400.00	550.00	1250.
	1882 M	200 pcs.	250.00	450.00	750.00	1250.
	1883 M	200 pcs.	250.00	450.00	750.00	1250.
	1884 M	—	250.00	450.00	750.00	1250.
	1886 M	200 pcs.	250.00	450.00	750.00	1250.
	1887 M	200 pcs.	250.00	450.00	750.00	1250.
	1888 M	250 pcs.	200.00	400.00	550.00	1250.
	1889 M	190 pcs.	250.00	450.00	750.00	1250.
	1890 M	149 pcs.	250.00	450.00	750.00	1250.
	1891 M	156 pcs.	250.00	450.00	750.00	1250.
	1892 M	214 pcs.	250.00	450.00	750.00	1250.
	1893 M	1,058	200.00	400.00	500.00	800.00
	1897 M	370 pcs.	200.00	400.00	550.00	1000.
	1898 M	376 pcs.	200.00	400.00	550.00	1000.
	1900 M	1,014	175.00	350.00	450.00	750.00

NOTE: Later dates (1901-1905) exist for this type.

Mint mark: Zs

KM#	Date	Mintage	Fine	VF	XF	Unc
412.7	1874 A	—	250.00	500.00	750.00	1500.
	1875 A	—	200.00	400.00	500.00	1000.
	1877 S/A	—	200.00	400.00	550.00	1000.
	1878/7 S/A	—	200.00	400.00	550.00	1000.
	1883 S	—	175.00	375.00	500.00	750.00
	1888 Z	70 pcs.	1000.	1500.	2000.	3000.
	1889 Z	373 pcs.	200.00	300.00	500.00	850.00
	1892 Z	1,229	200.00	300.00	450.00	750.00

DIEZ (10) PESOS

16.9200 g, .875 GOLD, .4760 oz AGW
Mint mark: As
Rev: Balance scale.

KM#	Date	Mintage	Fine	VF	XF	Unc
413	1874 DL	—	—	—	Rare	—
	1875 L	642 pcs.	600.00	1250.	2500.	3500.
	1878 L	977 pcs.	500.00	1000.	2000.	3000.
	1879 L	1,078	500.00	1000.	2000.	3000.
	1880 L	2,629	500.00	1000.	2000.	3000.
	1881 L	2,574	500.00	1000.	2000.	3000.
	1882 L	3,403	500.00	1000.	2000.	3000.
	1883 L	3,597	500.00	1000.	2000.	3000.
	1884 L	—	—	—	Rare	—
	1885 L	4,562	500.00	1000.	2000.	3000.
	1886 L	4,643	500.00	1000.	2000.	3000.
	1887 L	3,667	500.00	1000.	2000.	3000.
	1888 L	4,521	500.00	1000.	2000.	3000.
	1889 L	5,615	500.00	1000.	2000.	3000.
	1890 L	4,920	500.00	1000.	2000.	3000.
	1891 L	568 pcs.	500.00	1000.	2000.	3000.
	1892 L		—	—	—	—
	1893 L	817 pcs.	500.00	1000.	2000.	3000.
	1894/3 L	1,658	—	—	—	—
	1894 L	Inc. Ab.	500.00	1000.	2000.	3000.
	1895 L	1,237	500.00	1000.	2000.	3000.

Mint mark: Ca

KM#	Date	Mintage	Fine	VF	XF	Unc
413.1	1888 M	175 pcs.	—	—	7500.	—

Mint mark: Cn

KM#	Date	Mintage	Fine	VF	XF	Unc
413.2	1881 D	—	400.00	600.00	1000.	1750.
	1882 D	874 pcs.	400.00	600.00	1000.	1750.
	1882 E	Inc. Ab.	400.00	600.00	1000.	1750.
	1883 D	221 pcs.	—	—	—	—
	1883 M	Inc. Ab.	400.00	600.00	1000.	1750.
	1884 D	—	400.00	600.00	1000.	1750.
413.2	1884 M	—	400.00	600.00	1000.	1750.
	1885 M	1,235	400.00	600.00	1000.	1750.
	1886 M	981 pcs.	400.00	600.00	1000.	1750.
	1887 M	2,289	400.00	600.00	1000.	1750.
	1888 M	767 pcs.	400.00	600.00	1000.	1750.
	1889 M	859 pcs.	400.00	600.00	1000.	1750.
	1890 M	1,427	400.00	600.00	1000.	1750.
	1891 M	670 pcs.	400.00	600.00	1000.	1750.
	1892 M	379 pcs.	400.00	600.00	1000.	1750.
	1893 M	1,806	400.00	600.00	1000.	1750.
	1895 M	179 pcs.	500.00	1000.	1500.	2500.

NOTE: Later date (1903) exists for this type.

Mint mark: Do

KM#	Date	Mintage	Fine	VF	XF	Unc
413.3	1872 P	1,755	350.00	550.00	850.00	1250.
	1873/2 P	1,091	350.00	550.00	900.00	1500.
	1873/2 M/P	Inc. Ab.	350.00	550.00	900.00	1500.
	1874 M	—	350.00	550.00	900.00	1500.
	1875 M	—	350.00	550.00	900.00	1500.
	1876 M	—	450.00	750.00	1250.	2000.
	1877 P	—	350.00	550.00	900.00	1500.
	1878 E	582 pcs.	350.00	550.00	900.00	1500.
	1879/8 B	—	350.00	550.00	900.00	1500.
	1879 B	—	350.00	550.00	900.00	1500.
	1880 P	2,030	350.00	550.00	900.00	1500.
	1881/79 P	2,617	350.00	550.00	900.00	1500.
	1882 P	1,528	—	—	Rare	—
	1882 C	Inc. Ab.	350.00	550.00	900.00	1500.
	1883 C	793 pcs.	450.00	750.00	1250.	2000.
	1884 C	108 pcs.	450.00	750.00	1250.	2000.

Mint mark: Ga

KM#	Date	Mintage	Fine	VF	XF	Unc
413.4	1870 C	490 pcs.	500.00	800.00	1000.	1500.
	1871 C	1,910	400.00	800.00	1500.	2250.
	1872 C	780 pcs.	500.00	1000.	2000.	2500.
	1873 C	422 pcs.	500.00	1000.	2000.	3000.
	1874/3 C	477 pcs.	500.00	1000.	2000.	3000.
	1875 C	710 pcs.	500.00	1000.	2000.	3000.
	1878 A	183 pcs.	600.00	1200.	2500.	3500.
	1879 A	200 pcs.	600.00	1200.	2500.	3500.
	1880 S	404 pcs.	500.00	1000.	2000.	3000.
	1881 S	239 pcs.	600.00	1200.	2500.	3500.
	1891 S	196 pcs.	600.00	1200.	2500.	3500.

Mint mark: Go

KM#	Date	Mintage	Fine	VF	XF	Unc
413.5	1872 S	1,400	2000.	4000.	6500.	10,000.
	1887 R	80 pcs.	—	—	*Rare	—
	1888 R	68 pcs.	—	—	Rare	—

***NOTE:** Stack's Rio Grande Sale 6-93, P/L AU realized, $12,650.

Mint mark: Ho

KM#	Date	Mintage	Fine	VF	XF	Unc
413.6	1874 R	—	—	—	Rare	—
	1876 F	357 pcs.	—	—	Rare	—
	1878 A	814 pcs.	1750.	3000.	3500.	5500.
	1879 A	—	1000.	2000.	2500.	4000.
	1880 A	—	1000.	2000.	2500.	4000.
	1881 A	—	—	—	Rare	—

Mint mark: Mo

KM#	Date	Mintage	Fine	VF	XF	Unc
413.7	1870 C	480 pcs.	500.00	900.00	1200.	2000.
	1872/1 M/C	2,100	350.00	550.00	900.00	1400.
	1873 M	—	400.00	600.00	950.00	1500.
	1874/3 M	—	400.00	600.00	950.00	1500.
	1875 B/M	—	400.00	600.00	950.00	1500.
	1876 B	—	—	—	Rare	—
	1878 M	300 pcs.	400.00	600.00	950.00	1500.
	1879 M		—	—	—	—
	1881 M	100 pcs.	500.00	1000.	1600.	2500.
	1882 M	—	400.00	600.00	950.00	1500.
	1883 M	100 pcs.	600.00	1000.	1600.	2500.
	1884 M	—	600.00	1000.	1600.	2500.
	1885 M	—	400.00	600.00	950.00	1500.
	1886 M	100 pcs.	600.00	1000.	1600.	2500.
	1887 M	100 pcs.	600.00	1000.	1625.	2750.
	1888 M	144 pcs.	450.00	750.00	1200.	2000.
	1889 M	88 pcs.	600.00	1000.	1600.	2500.
	1890 M	137 pcs.	600.00	1000.	1600.	2500.
	1891 M	133 pcs.	600.00	1000.	1600.	2500.
413.7	1892 M	45 pcs.	600.00	1000.	1600.	2500.
	1893 M	1,361	350.00	550.00	900.00	1400.
	1897 M	239 pcs.	400.00	600.00	950.00	1500.
	1898/7 M	244 pcs.	425.00	625.00	1000.	1750.
	1900 M	733 pcs.	400.00	600.00	950.00	1500.

NOTE: Later dates (1901-1905) exist for this type.

Mint mark: Oa

KM#	Date	Mintage	Fine	VF	XF	Unc
413.8	1870 E	4,614	400.00	600.00	900.00	1350.
	1871 E	2,705	400.00	600.00	900.00	1350.
	1872 E	5,897	400.00	600.00	900.00	1350.
	1873 E	3,537	400.00	600.00	950.00	1500.
	1874 E	2,205	400.00	600.00	1200.	1800.
	1875 E	312 pcs.	450.00	750.00	1400.	2250.
	1876 E	766 pcs.	450.00	750.00	1400.	2250.
	1877 E	463 pcs.	450.00	750.00	1400.	2250.
	1878 E	229 pcs.	450.00	750.00	1400.	2250.
	1879 E	210 pcs.	450.00	750.00	1400.	2250.
	1880 E	238 pcs.	450.00	750.00	1400.	2250.
	1881 E	961 pcs.	400.00	600.00	1200.	2000.
	1882 E	170 pcs.	600.00	1000.	1500.	2500.
	1883 E	111 pcs.	600.00	1000.	1500.	2500.
	1884 E	325 pcs.	450.00	750.00	1400.	2250.
	1885 E	370 pcs.	450.00	750.00	1400.	2250.
	1886 E	400 pcs.	450.00	750.00	1400.	2250.
	1887 E	—	700.00	1250.	2250.	4000.
	1888 E	—	—	—	—	—
413.9	1871 H	2,000	350.00	550.00	850.00	1200.
	1872 H	3,092	300.00	500.00	700.00	1000.
	1873 H	936 pcs.	400.00	600.00	950.00	1500.
	1874 H	—	400.00	600.00	950.00	1500.
	1875/3 A	—	400.00	600.00	1000.	1750.
	1876/5 S	—	400.00	600.00	1000.	1750.
	1877 S/H	506 pcs.	400.00	600.00	1000.	1750.
	1878 S	711 pcs.	400.00	600.00	1000.	1750.
	1879/8 S	—	450.00	750.00	1400.	2250.
	1879 S	—	450.00	750.00	1400.	2250.
	1880 S	2,089	350.00	550.00	950.00	1500.
	1881 S	736 pcs.	400.00	600.00	1000.	1750.
	1882 S	1,599	350.00	550.00	950.00	1500.
	1883/2 S	256 pcs.	400.00	600.00	1000.	1750.
	1884/3 S	—	350.00	550.00	950.00	1600.
	1884 S	—	350.00	550.00	950.00	1600.
	1885 S	1,588	350.00	550.00	950.00	1500.
	1886 S	5,364	350.00	550.00	950.00	1500.
	1887 Z	2,330	350.00	550.00	950.00	1500.
	1888 Z	4,810	350.00	550.00	950.00	1500.
	1889 Z	6,154	300.00	500.00	750.00	1350.
	1890 Z	1,321	350.00	550.00	950.00	1500.
	1891 Z	1,930	350.00	550.00	950.00	1500.
	1892 Z	1,882	350.00	550.00	950.00	1500.
	1893 Z	2,899	350.00	550.00	950.00	1500.
	1894 Z	2,501	350.00	550.00	950.00	1500.
	1895 Z	1,217	350.00	550.00	950.00	1500.

VEINTE (20) PESOS

33.8400 g, .875 GOLD, .9520 oz AGW
Mint mark: As
Rev: Balance scale.

KM#	Date	Mintage	Fine	VF	XF	Unc
414	1876 L	276 pcs.	—	—	Rare	—
	1877 L	166 pcs.	—	—	Rare	—
	1878 L		—	—	—	—
	1888 L	—	—	—	Rare	—

Mint mark: CH, Ca

KM#	Date	Mintage	Fine	VF	XF	Unc
414.1	1872 M	995 pcs.	500.00	650.00	950.00	2500.
	1873 M	950 pcs.	500.00	650.00	950.00	2500.
	1874 M	1,116	500.00	650.00	950.00	2500.
	1875 M	750 pcs.	500.00	650.00	950.00	2500.
	1876 M	600 pcs.	500.00	800.00	1250.	2750.
	1877	55 pcs.	—	—	Rare	—
	1882 M	1,758	500.00	650.00	950.00	2500.

KM#	Date	Mintage	Fine	VF	XF	Unc
414.1	1883 M	161 pcs.	600.00	1000.	1500.	3000.
	1884 M	496 pcs.	500.00	650.00	950.00	2500.
	1885 M	122 pcs.	600.00	1000.	1500.	3000.
	1887 M	550 pcs.	500.00	650.00	950.00	2500.
	1888 M	351 pcs.	500.00	650.00	950.00	2500.
	1889 M	464 pcs.	500.00	650.00	950.00	2500.
	1890 M	1,209	500.00	650.00	950.00	2500.
	1891 M	2,004	500.00	600.00	900.00	2250.
	1893 M	418 pcs.	500.00	650.00	950.00	2500.
	1895 M	133 pcs.	600.00	1000.	1500.	3000.
	Mint mark: Cn					
414.2	1870 E	3,749	500.00	650.00	950.00	2000.
	1871 P	3,046	500.00	650.00	950.00	2000.
	1872 P	972 pcs.	500.00	650.00	950.00	2000.
	1873 P	1,317	500.00	650.00	950.00	2000.
	1874 P	—	500.00	650.00	950.00	2000.
	1875 P	—	600.00	1200.	1800.	2500.
	1876 P	—	500.00	650.00	950.00	2000.
	1876 G	—	500.00	650.00	950.00	2000.
	1877 G	167 pcs.	600.00	1000.	1500.	3000.
	1878	842 pcs.	—	—	Rare	—
	1881/0 D	2,039	—	—	—	—
	1881 D	Inc. Ab.	500.00	650.00	950.00	2000.
	1882/1 D	736 pcs.	500.00	650.00	950.00	2000.
	1883 M	1,836	500.00	650.00	950.00	2000.
	1884 M	—	500.00	650.00	950.00	2000.
	1885 M	544 pcs.	500.00	650.00	950.00	2000.
	1886 M	882 pcs.	500.00	650.00	950.00	2000.
	1887 M	837 pcs.	500.00	650.00	950.00	2000.
	1888 M	473 pcs.	500.00	650.00	950.00	2000.
	1889 M	1,376	500.00	650.00	950.00	2000.
	1890 M	—	500.00	650.00	950.00	2000.
	1891 M	237 pcs.	500.00	900.00	1200.	2250.
	1892 M	526 pcs.	500.00	650.00	950.00	2000.
	1893 M	2,062	500.00	650.00	950.00	2000.
	1894 M	4,516	500.00	650.00	950.00	2000.
	1895 M	3,193	500.00	650.00	950.00	2000.
	1896 M	4,072	500.00	650.00	950.00	2000.
	1897/6 M	959 pcs.	500.00	650.00	950.00	2000.
	1897 M	Inc. Ab.	500.00	650.00	950.00	2000.
	1898 M	1,660	500.00	650.00	950.00	2000.
	1899 M	1,243	500.00	650.00	950.00	2000.
	1899 Q	Inc. Ab.	500.00	900.00	1200.	2250.
	1900 Q	1,558	500.00	650.00	950.00	2000.

NOTE: Later dates (1901-1905) exist for this type.

KM#	Date	Mintage	Fine	VF	XF	Unc
	Mint mark: Do					
414.3	1870 P	416 pcs.	1000.	1500.	2000.	2500.
	1871/0 P	1,073	1000.	1750.	2250.	2750.
	1871 P	Inc. Ab.	1000.	1500.	2000.	2500.
	1872/1 PT	—	1500.	3000.	4500.	7000.
	1876 M	—	1000.	1500.	2000.	2500.
	1877 P	94 pcs.	1500.	2250.	2750.	3250.
	1878	258 pcs.	—	—	Rare	—
	Mint mark: Go					
414.4	1870 S	3,250	500.00	650.00	900.00	1250.
	1871 S	.020	500.00	650.00	900.00	1250.
	1872 S	.018	500.00	650.00	900.00	1250.
	1873 S	7,000	500.00	650.00	900.00	1250.
	1874 S	—	500.00	650.00	900.00	1250.
	1875 S	—	500.00	650.00	900.00	1250.
	1876 S	—	500.00	650.00	900.00	1250.
	1876 M/S	—	—	—	—	—
	1877 M/S	.015	—	—	Rare	—
	1877 R	Inc. Ab.	500.00	650.00	900.00	1250.
	1877 S	Inc. Ab.	—	—	Rare	—
	1878/7 M/S	.013	650.00	1250.	2000.	2800.
	1878 M	Inc. Ab.	650.00	1250.	2000.	2800.
	1878 S	Inc. Ab.	500.00	650.00	900.00	1250.
	1879 S	8,202	500.00	800.00	1200.	2300.
	1880 S	7,375	500.00	650.00	900.00	1250.
	1881 S	4,909	500.00	650.00	900.00	1250.
	1882 S	4,020	500.00	650.00	900.00	1250.
	1883/2 B	3,705	550.00	750.00	1150.	2250.
	1883 B	Inc. Ab.	500.00	650.00	900.00	1250.
	1884 B	1,798	500.00	650.00	900.00	1250.
	1885 R	2,660	500.00	650.00	900.00	1250.
	1886 R	1,090	550.00	800.00	1250.	2500.
	1887 R	1,009	550.00	800.00	1250.	2500.
	1888 R	1,011	550.00	800.00	1250.	2500.
	1889 R	956 pcs.	550.00	800.00	1250.	2500.
	1890 R	879 pcs.	550.00	800.00	1250.	2500.
	1891 R	818 pcs.	550.00	800.00	1250.	2500.
	1892 R	730 pcs.	550.00	800.00	1250.	2500.
	1893 R	3,343	500.00	650.00	1000.	2000.
	1894/3 R	6,734	500.00	650.00	900.00	1250.

KM#	Date	Mintage	Fine	VF	XF	Unc
414.4	1894 R	I.A.	500.00	650.00	900.00	1250.
	1895/3 R	7,118	500.00	650.00	900.00	1250.
	1895 R	I.A.	500.00	650.00	900.00	1250.
	1896 R	9,219	500.00	650.00	900.00	1250.
	1897/6 R	6,781	500.00	650.00	900.00	1250.
	1897 R	I.A.	500.00	650.00	900.00	1250.
	1898 R	7,710	500.00	650.00	900.00	1250.
	1899 R	8,527	500.00	650.00	900.00	1250.
	1900 R	4,512	550.00	800.00	1250.	2350.
	Mint mark: Ho					
414.5	1874 R	—	—	—	Rare	—
	1875 R	—	—	—	Rare	—
	1876 F	—	—	—	Rare	—
	1888 G	—	—	—	Rare	—
	Mint mark: Mo					
414.6	1870 C	.014	500.00	600.00	800.00	1300.
	1871 M	.021	500.00	600.00	800.00	1300.
	1872/1 M	.011	500.00	600.00	800.00	1600.
	1872 M	I.A.	500.00	600.00	800.00	1300.
	1873 M	5,600	500.00	600.00	800.00	1300.
	1874/2 M	—	500.00	600.00	800.00	1350.
	1874/2 B	—	500.00	700.00	1000.	1600.
	1875 B	—	500.00	650.00	900.00	1500.
	1876 B	—	500.00	650.00	900.00	1500.
	1876 M	—	—	Reported, not confirmed		
	1877 M	2,000	500.00	700.00	1100.	2000.
	1878 M	7,000	500.00	650.00	900.00	1500.
	1879 M	—	500.00	650.00	900.00	1750.
	1880 M	—	500.00	650.00	900.00	1750.
	1881/0 M	.011	500.00	600.00	800.00	1350.
	1881 M	I.A.	500.00	600.00	800.00	1350.
	1882/1 M	5,800	500.00	600.00	800.00	1350.
	1882 M	I.A.	500.00	600.00	800.00	1350.
	1883/1 M	4,000	500.00	600.00	800.00	1350.
	1883 M	I.A.	500.00	600.00	800.00	1250.
	1884/3 M	—	500.00	650.00	900.00	1400.
	1884 M	—	500.00	650.00	900.00	1400.
	1885 M	6,000	500.00	650.00	900.00	1750.
	1886 M	.010	500.00	600.00	800.00	1500.
	1887 M	.012	600.00	800.00	1500.	2500.
	1888 M	7,300	500.00	600.00	800.00	1500.
	1889 M	6,477	500.00	600.00	900.00	1650.
	1890 M	7,852	500.00	600.00	800.00	1500.
	1891/0 M	8,725	500.00	600.00	800.00	1500.
	1891 M	I.A.	500.00	600.00	800.00	1500.
	1892 M	.011	500.00	600.00	800.00	1300.
	1893 M	.015	500.00	600.00	800.00	1300.
	1894 M	.014	500.00	600.00	800.00	1300.
	1895 M	.013	500.00	600.00	800.00	1300.
	1896 B	.014	500.00	600.00	800.00	1300.
	1897/6 M	.012	500.00	600.00	800.00	1300.
	1897 M	I.A.	500.00	600.00	800.00	1300.
	1898 M	.020	500.00	600.00	800.00	1300.
	1899 M	.023	500.00	600.00	800.00	1300.
	1900 M	.021	500.00	600.00	800.00	1300.

NOTE: Later dates (1901-1905) exist for this type.

KM#	Date	Mintage	Fine	VF	XF	Unc
	Mint mark: Oa					
414.7	1870 E	1,131	750.00	1500.	2500.	5000.
	1871 E	1,591	750.00	1500.	2500.	5000.
	1872 E	255 pcs.	1000.	1750.	3000.	7000.
	1888 E	170 pcs.	2000.	3000.	5000.	—
	Mint mark: Zs					
414.8	1871 H	1,000	3500.	6500.	7000.	9000.
	1875 A	—	4000.	6000.	7500.	9500.
	1878 S	441 pcs.	4000.	6000.	7500.	9500.
	1888 Z	50 pcs.	—	—	Rare	—
	1889 Z	640 pcs.	3500.	5500.	7000.	9000.

LOCAL COINAGE

This listing of local coinage is hardly complete. Localities, type and varieties omitted cannot automatically be presumed to be scarcer than those included below. Much research remains to be done. Our editorial staff welcomes correspondence on any new varieties.

Ahualulco

OCTAVO - 1/8 REAL

COPPER, uniface
AHUALULCO and 1813 around 1/8 in circle.

KM#	Date	Good	VG	Fine	VF
L1	1813	15.00	25.00	35.00	50.00
	Script AHO, 1/8 below.				
L2	ND	10.00	17.50	25.00	35.00

Ameca

OCTAVO - 1/8 REAL

COPPER, uniface
Church flanked by trees.

KM#	Date	Good	VG	Fine	VF
L6	1824	10.00	17.50	25.00	35.00

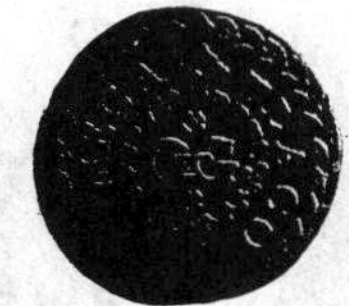

TLACO DE AMECA around QTG monogram in circle.

KM#	Date	Good	VG	Fine	VF
L7	ND	10.00	17.50	25.00	35.00
	AME/CA 1811 in circle.				
L8	1811	15.00	25.00	35.00	50.00
	Octagonal planchet.				
L9	1811	15.00	25.00	35.00	50.00
	F 1/8 Z within wavy circle.				
L10	ND	15.00	25.00	35.00	50.00

T.Z. AMECA 1833 around value.

KM#	Date	Good	VG	Fine	VF
L11	1833	10.00	15.00	22.50	30.00

V.F AMECA 1858 below value.

KM#	Date	Good	VG	Fine	VF
L12	1858	12.50	17.50	25.00	35.00

Amescua

OCTAVO - 1/8 REAL

COPPER, uniface
Mexican Eagle

KM#	Date	Good	VG	Fine	VF
L15	1828	10.00	15.00	22.50	32.50

Date below eagle.

KM#	Date	Good	VG	Fine	VF
L16	1838	13.50	20.00	28.50	40.00

Atencinco

OCTAVO - 1/8 REAL

COPPER, uniface
ATENCINCO in outer border, 8-leaved rosette above branch in center.

KM#	Date	Good	VG	Fine	VF
L19	ND	13.50	20.00	28.00	40.00

Atotonilco

OCTAVO - 1/8 REAL

COPPER, uniface
ATOTONILCO ANO DE 1808 in outer border, L.S.S./JUSU/ESES in circle.

KM#	Date	Good	VG	Fine	VF
L22	1808	25.00	37.50	52.50	75.00
	Obv. leg: ATOTONILCO ANO DE in outer border, 1821 in center. Rev. leg: E T P D Z around outer border.				
L23	1821	15.00	25.00	35.00	50.00
	Obv. leg: VILL ATOTONILCO in outer border, 1826 in center. Rev. leg: 1/8 in center, stars in outer border.				
L24	1826	15.00	25.00	35.00	50.00

Campeche

CENTAVO

BRASS

KM#	Date	Good	VG	Fine	VF
L27	1861	7.00	10.00	17.50	22.50

Catorce

1/4 REAL

COPPER
Obv. leg: FONDOS PUBLICO around border, 1/4 below flower and raised rectangle. Rev. leg: DE CATORCE 1822 around border, eagle on cactus.

KM#	Date	Good	VG	Fine	VF
L30	1822	12.00	18.50	30.00	40.00

Celaya

OCTAVO - 1/8 REAL

COPPER
Obv. leg: EN/CELAYA/DE/1803. Rev. leg: LUIS/VASQUE/S, branches below, flower above.

KM#	Date	Good	VG	Fine	VF
L33	1803	25.00	37.50	52.50	75.00

COPPER, uniface
VINDERI/QUE/CELALLA/1808

KM#	Date	Good	VG	Fine	VF
L34	1808	25.00	37.50	52.50	75.00

VISCARA/CELAYA/1814 w/ornament above.

KM#	Date	Good	VG	Fine	VF
L35	1814	17.50	25.00	35.00	50.00

Chilchota

OCTAVO - 1/8 REAL

COPPER
Obv: Head to right, leg: CHILCHOTA UN OCTAVO, date below. Rev: Wreath in center, leg: RESPONSAVIDAD DE MURGVIA.

KM#	Date	Good	VG	Fine	VF
L38	1858	15.00	25.00	35.00	50.00

Colima

OCTAVO - 1/8 REAL

COPPER
Obv. leg: VILLA DE COLIMA around border as continuous leg. Rev: Blank.

KM#	Date	Good	VG	Fine	VF
L41	1813	12.50	17.50	25.00	37.50

Obv. leg: VILLA DE COLIMA and date in 3 lines. Rev: Blank.

KM#	Date	Good	VG	Fine	VF
L42	1814	12.50	17.50	25.00	37.50

Obv. leg: OCT. DE COLI. Rev: Date.

KM#	Date	Good	VG	Fine	VF
L44	1819	15.00	22.50	30.00	45.00

Obv. leg: OCTO DE COLIMA around border, date in center circle. Rev. leg: OCTAVO within wreath, pellet in center.

KM#	Date	Good	VG	Fine	VF
L46	1824	13.50	17.50	25.00	37.50

Obv. leg: OCTO DE COLA in 3 lines.

KM#	Date	Good	VG	Fine	VF
L47	1824	13.50	17.50	25.00	37.50
	1828	13.50	17.50	25.00	37.50

Obv. leg: OCTO DE COLIMA in 3 lines. Rev. leg: ANO DE 1830 in 3 lines.

KM#	Date	Good	VG	Fine	VF
L48	1830	13.50	17.50	25.00	37.50

QUARTO - 1/4 REAL

COPPER
Obv. leg: QUART COLIMA 1816 in 3 lines in wreath. Rev: Colima monogram in wreath.

KM#	Date	Good	VG	Fine	VF
L43	1816	10.00	16.50	22.50	35.00

Obv. leg: QUARTo DE COLIMA around border; date in center circle. Rev: Colima monogram in wreath.

KM#	Date	Good	VG	Fine	VF
L45	1824	12.50	16.50	22.50	35.00

Cotija

OCTAVO - 1/8 REAL

COPPER
Obv: Seated Liberty w/staff and liberty cap, leg: DE.D.JOSE NUNES. Rev: Value and date in wreath, leg: COMMERCIO. D. COTIJA.

KM#	Date	Good	VG	Fine	VF
L51	ND	12.50	18.50	25.00	37.50

Cuido

OCTAVO - 1/8 REAL

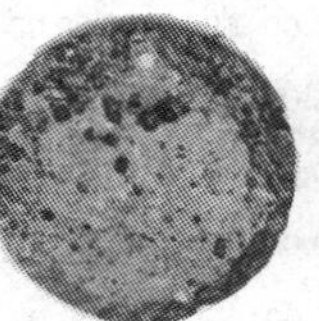

COPPER, uniface
"CUIDO" above "1/8" in spray.

KM#	Date	Good	VG	Fine	VF
L52	ND	12.50	20.00	28.50	40.00

Guadalajara

OCTAVO - 1/8 REAL

COPPER, uniface
Eagle w/wings spread, leg: GUADALAXARA.

KM#	Date	Good	VG	Fine	VF
L57	ND	27.50	37.50	52.50	75.00

Lagos

1/4 REAL

BRONZE
Obv: 2 globes w/crown above, wreath and 1/4 below. Rev: Coat of arms of Lagos.

KM#	Date	Good	VG	Fine	VF
L59	ND	60.00	75.00	115.00	175.00

SILVER

KM#	Date	Good	VG	Fine	VF
L59a	ND	150.00	200.00	300.00	500.00

Merida

1/2 GRANO

LEAD
Obv. leg: PART/DE LA SO/CIED in center. MERIDADE YUCATAN around border, 1859 below. Rev. leg: 1/2/GRANO/DE PESO/FUERTE.

KM#	Date	Good	VG	Fine	VF
L60	1859	10.00	16.00	32.50	50.00

Pazcuaro

OCTAVO - 1/8 REAL

COPPER
Obv: Town at base of mountains, lake in foreground, value 1/8 above. Rev: Woman walking right, carrying bag, fish net and fish.

KM#	Date	Good	VG	Fine	VF
L63	ND	11.00	16.50	22.50	30.00

NOTE: Also in brass and cast in bronze; minor die varieties have been observed.

Obv: 1/8 PAZCUARO. Rev: Crude portrait?.

KM#	Date	Good	VG	Fine	VF
L64	ND	12.50	17.50	25.00	35.00

Progreso

OCTAVO - 1/8 REAL

COPPER
Obv: Radiant star above open book.
Rev: Value 1/8 in double wreath.

KM#	Date	Good	VG	Fine	VF
L66	1858	15.00	22.50	32.50	42.50

CENTAVO

LEAD
Obv. leg: MUNICIPALIDAD DE PROGRESSO
UN CENT, 1873 in center.
Rev: Flank in oval band.

KM#	Date	Good	VG	Fine	VF
L67	1873	12.50	20.00	30.00	42.50

Quitupan

OCTAVO - 1/8 REAL

COPPER
Obv: Bow and 2 arrows in center,
leg: QUITUPAN. . .1854. Rev: 1/8 in center,
leg: IGNACIO BUENROSTO, monogram c/m.

KM#	Date	Good	VG	Fine	VF
L69	1854	15.00	22.50	32.50	42.50

Tacambaro

OCTAVO - 1/8 REAL

COPPER
Obv: Winged caduceus in sprays.
Rev: Value 1/8 in sprays.

KM#	Date	Good	VG	Fine	VF
L72	ND	12.50	18.50	25.00	35.00

Taretan

OCTAVO - 1/8 REAL

COPPER
Obv: Head of man right. Rev: Tree.

KM#	Date	Good	VG	Fine	VF
L75	1858	15.00	25.00	37.50	50.00

Tlazasalca

OCTAVO - 1/8 REAL

COPPER
Obv: 2 mountains, date below.
Rev: Value 1/8 in wreath.

KM#	Date	Good	VG	Fine	VF
L78	1853	16.50	25.00	35.00	50.00

Xalostotitlan

OCTAVO - 1/8 REAL

COPPER
Obv: Crown in center,
leg: AYVNTAMIENTO ILVSTRE.
Rev: 4 in center, leg: DE XALOSTOTITLAN. 1820.

KM#	Date	Good	VG	Fine	VF
L54	1820	22.50	35.00	50.00	75.00

Zamora

OCTAVO - 1/8 REAL

COPPER

KM#	Date	Good	VG	Fine	VF
L80	1842	6.00	12.50	22.50	37.50
	1848	6.00	12.50	22.50	37.50
	1854	6.00	12.50	22.50	37.50
	1858	6.00	12.50	22.50	37.50

COPPER or BRONZE
Obv: Eagle on cactus above sprays.
Rev: Liberty cap, bow and arrows above
sprays. W/or w/o various c/m.

KM#	Date	Good	VG	Fine	VF
L81	1852	6.00	12.50	22.50	37.50
	1853	6.00	12.50	22.50	37.50
	1856	6.00	12.50	22.50	37.50
	1857	6.00	12.50	22.50	37.50
	1858	6.00	12.50	22.50	37.50

NOTE: These pieces are also found with various countermarks. "Za" in a dentilated circle is the most common. "1/8" in a circular c/m is also encountered.

Zapotlan

OCTAVO - 1/8 REAL

COPPER, uniface
ZAPO/TLAN/1813

KM#	Date	Good	VG	Fine	VF
L84	1813	17.50	27.50	40.00	55.00

PATTERNS (Pn)

(Including off metal strikes)

KM#	Date	Mintage	Identification	Mkt.Val.
Pn1	1822Mo	—	8 Reales, Lead, Iturbide	—

KM#	Date	Mintage	Identification	Mkt.Val.
Pn2	1823Mo JM	—	8 Reales, Lead	Rare

KM#	Date	Mintage	Identification	Mkt.Val.
Pn3	1823Mo JM	—	8 Reales, Lead	Rare
Pn4	1823Mo JM	—	8 Escudos, Silver	—
Pn5	1824Do	—	1/8 Real, Silver	—
Pn6	1825Zs	—	1/8 Real, Silver	—
Pn7	1826Go WW	—	8 Reales, Sterling Silver	9000.
Pn8	1826Go WW	—	8 Escudos, Gold	Rare

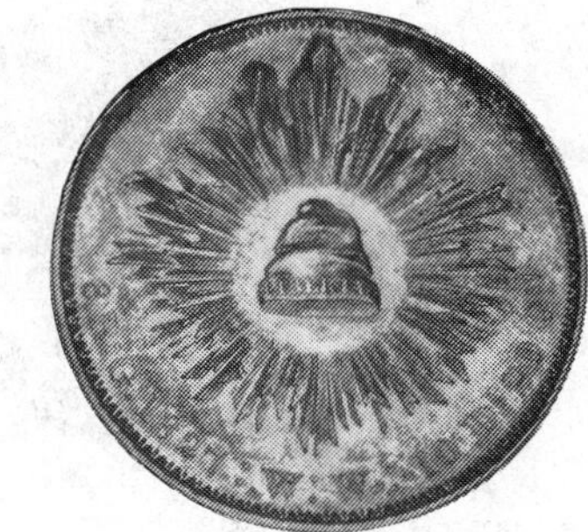

KM#	Date	Mintage	Identification	Mkt.Val.
Pn9	1827Go WW	—	8 Reales, Sterling Silver	9000.

KM#	Date	Mintage	Identification	Mkt.Val.
Pn10	1827Pi SA	—	8 Reales, Silver	Rare
Pn11	1828	—	1/8 Real, Gold, Occidente Mint	—
Pn12	1828Go	—	1/4 Real, Silver	—
Pn13	1828Pi	—	1/4 Real, Silver	—

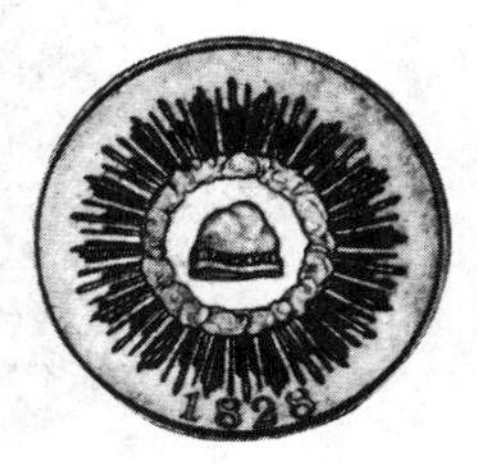

KM#	Date	Mintage	Identification	Mkt.Val.
Pn14	1828Go	—	1/4 Real, Copper	400.00
Pn14a	1828Go	—	1/4 Real, Silver	2650.
Pn15	1829Go	—	1/8 Real, Silver	—

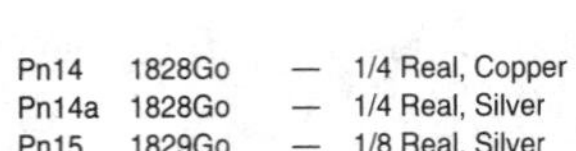

KM#	Date	Mintage	Identification	Mkt.Val.
Pn16	1829Pi JS	—	8 Reales, Silver	3000.
Pn16a	1829Pi JS	—	8 Reales, Bronze	1150.

KM#	Date	Mintage	Identification	Mkt.Val.
Pn17	183xG	—	8 Reales, Silver	2000.
Pn18	183xG PJ	—	8 Reales, Silver	—
Pn18a	183xG PJ	—	8 Reales, Copper	1250.

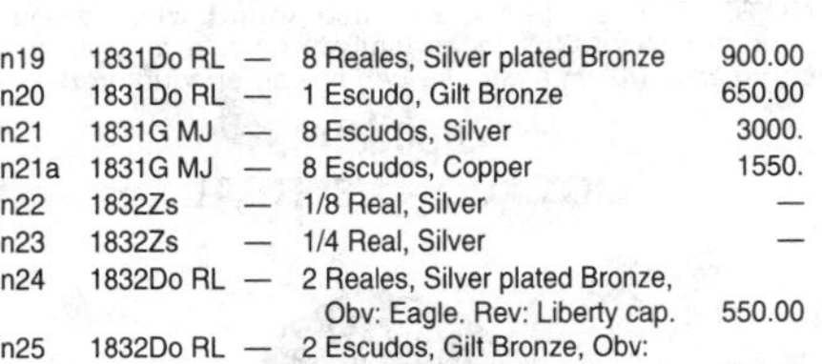

KM#	Date	Mintage	Identification	Mkt.Val.
Pn19	1831Do RL	—	8 Reales, Silver plated Bronze	900.00
Pn20	1831Do RL	—	1 Escudo, Gilt Bronze	650.00
Pn21	1831G MJ	—	8 Escudos, Silver	3000.
Pn21a	1831G MJ	—	8 Escudos, Copper	1550.
Pn22	1832Zs	—	1/8 Real, Silver	—
Pn23	1832Zs	—	1/4 Real, Silver	—
Pn24	1832Do RL	—	2 Reales, Silver plated Bronze, Obv: Eagle. Rev: Liberty cap.	550.00
Pn25	1832Do RL	—	2 Escudos, Gilt Bronze, Obv: Eagle. Rev: Liberty cap.	550.00

KM#	Date	Mintage	Identification	Mkt.Val.
Pn25a	1832Do RL	—	2 Escudos, Brass	650.00

KM#	Date	Mintage	Identification	Mkt.Val.
Pn26	1832Do LR	—	4 Escudos, Gilt Bronze	1550.
Pn26a	1832Do LR	—	4 Escudos, Brass	1550.

KM#	Date	Mintage	Identification	Mkt.Val.
Pn27	1832Do RL	—	8 Escudos, Gilt Bronze	750.00
Pn27a	1832Do RL	—	8 Escudos, Brass	750.00
Pn27b	1832Do RL	—	8 Escudos, Bronze	750.00
Pn27c	1832Do RL	—	8 Escudos, Copper	750.00
Pn28	1833Zs	—	1/8 Real, Silver	—
Pn29	1833Zs	—	1/4 Real, Silver	—

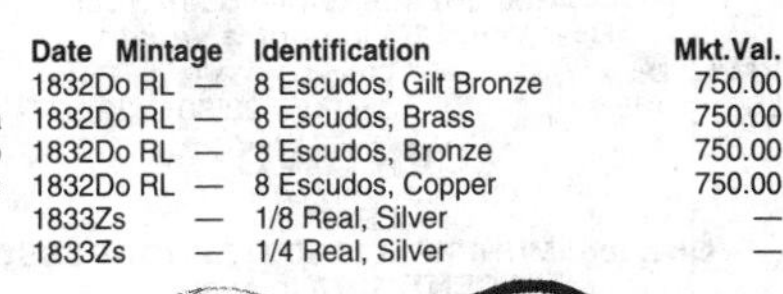

KM#	Date	Mintage	Identification	Mkt.Val.
Pn30	1833Do RL	—	1/2 Real, Silver plated Bronze	350.00
Pn30a	1833Do RL	—	1/2 Real, Silver	500.00

KM#	Date	Mintage	Identification	Mkt.Val.
Pn31	1833Do RL	—	1 Real, Silver plated Bronze	500.00
PnA32	1833Do RL	—	1 Real, White Metal	500.00
Pn32	1833/2Do RL	—	1/2 Escudo, Gilt Bronze, Obv: Eagle. Rev: Hand holding Liberty cap.	700.00

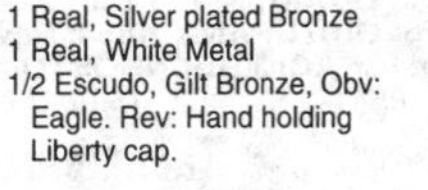

KM#	Date	Mintage	Identification	Mkt.Val.
Pn32a	1833Do RL	—	1/2 Escudo, Brass	675.00
Pn33	1834Mo	—	1/4 Real, Silver	—

KM#	Date	Mintage	Identification	Mkt.Val.
Pn34	1834Zs OM	—	1 Real, Silver	1500.

KM#	Date	Mintage	Identification	Mkt.Val.
Pn35	1834Zs OM	—	8 Reales, Copper	3500.
Pn36	1834Zs OM	—	8 Reales, Silver, reeded edge	12,500.
Pn37	1835/4Mo ML	—	4 Escudos, Copper	—

KM#	Date	Mintage	Identification	Mkt.Val.
PnA38	1836	—	1/4 Real, Copper	350.00
Pn38.1	1836Do RL	—	1/2 Real, Silver, thick planchet	250.00
Pn38.2	1836Do RL	—	1/2 Real, Silver, thin planchet	250.00
Pn39	1836G MJ	—	8 Reales, Copper	—

KM#	Date	Mintage	Identification	Mkt.Val.
Pn40	1840Do OMC	—	8 Reales, Silver	1500.
Pn40a	1840Do OMC	—	8 Reales, White Metal	1250.
Pn40b	1840Do OMC	—	8 Reales, Silver plated Bronze	700.00

KM#	Date	Mintage	Identification	Mkt.Val.
Pn41	1841Mo	—	1 Centavo, Copper	1000.
Pn42	1842Mo ML	—	1 Peso, Silver, Obv: Eagle. Rev: Liberty cap on pole.	Rare

KM#	Date	Mintage	Identification	Mkt.Val.
Pn43	1843Go PM	—	8 Reales, Copper	3550.
Pn44.1	1843Mo MM	—	8 Reales, Silver	1350.
Pn44.1a	1843Mo MM	—	8 Reales, Copper, plain edge	1250.
Pn44.2a	1843Mo MM	—	8 Reales, Copper, reeded edge	1350.
Pn45	1843Zs OM	—	8 Reales, Silver, eagle on cactus	3000.
Pn46	1844Go PM	—	8 Reales, Copper	1250.
Pn47	1844Mo MM	—	8 Reales, Copper, Obv: Eagle on cactus. Rev: Radiant Liberty cap.	1250.
Pn48	1844Zs OM	—	8 Reales, Copper, eagle on cactus	1250.

KM#	Date	Mintage	Identification	Mkt.Val.
Pn49	184x	—	8 Reales, Copper	1000.
Pn50	1846Zs	—	1/8 Real, Silver	—
Pn51	1846Zs	—	1/4 Real, Silver	—
Pn52	1848Mo GC	—	2 Escudos, Copper	—

KM#	Date	Mintage	Identification	Mkt.Val.
PnA53	1851C CE	—	8 Reales, Copper	1250.
Pn53	1854C CE	—	8 Escudos, Copper	—
Pn54	1856Go	—	1/8 Real, White Metal	—
Pn55	1856	—	1/8 Real, Silver, Jalisco Mint	—
Pn56	1856Mo GF	—	1/2 Escudo, Silver	450.00
Pn57	1857	—	1/8 Real, Silver, Jalisco Mint	650.00
Pn58	1857Zs OM	—	1 Escudo, Silver	—
Pn59	1860Mo FH	—	1/2 Escudo, Copper	—

KM#	Date	Mintage	Identification	Mkt.Val.
Pn60	1861C	—	1/4 Real, Copper	900.00
Pn61	1861Mo CH	—	8 Escudos, Silver	500.00
Pn62	1862Zs	—	1/8 Real, Silver	—
Pn63	1862Pi	—	1/4 Real, Silver	800.00

KM#	Date	Mintage	Identification	Mkt.Val.
Pn64	1862Mo	—	1 Centavo, Copper	1000.
Pn64a	1862Mo	—	1 Centavo, Silver	1500.
Pn64b	1862Mo	—	1 Centavo, Silver plated Copper	1000.
Pn65	1863Mo	—	1/8 Real, Silver, overstruck on 1801 2 Reales	—
Pn66	1863Mo	—	1 Centavo, Lead, round 3 in date	350.00
Pn66a	1863Mo	—	1 Centavo, White Metal	—
Pn66b	1863Mo	—	1 Centavo, Silver	—
Pn66c	1863Mo	—	1 Centavo, Copper, plain edge	—
Pn67	1863Mo	—	5 Centavos, Silver, Obv: Eagle on cactus. Rev: Liberty cap.	2000.

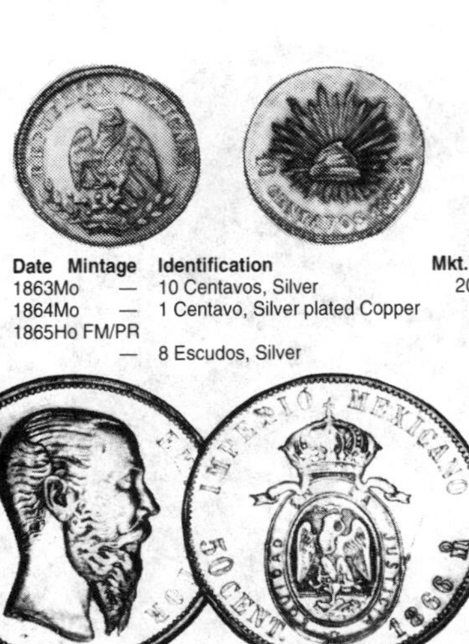

KM#	Date	Mintage	Identification	Mkt.Val.
Pn68	1863Mo	—	10 Centavos, Silver	2000.
Pn69	1864Mo	—	1 Centavo, Silver plated Copper	—
Pn70	1865Ho FM/PR	—	8 Escudos, Silver	—
Pn71	1866Mo	—	50 Centavos, White Metal	Rare
Pn71a	1866Mo	—	50 Centavos, Silver	2500.

KM#	Date	Mintage	Identification	Mkt.Val.
Pn72	1866Mo	—	1 Peso, Silver, Obv: Small letters.	2000.
Pn72a	1866Mo	—	1 Peso, Silver plated Copper	900.00
Pn72b	1866Mo	—	1 Peso, Copper-Nickel	1500.
Pn72c	1866Mo	—	1 Peso, Copper	1250.
Pn73	1866Mo	—	1 Peso, Copper, KM388.1	1250.
Pn73a	1866Mo	—	1 Peso, Lead	—

KM#	Date	Mintage	Identification	Mkt.Val.
Pn74	1866Mo	—	20 Pesos, Gilt Copper	—

KM#	Date	Mintage	Identification	Mkt.Val.
Pn75	1868Mo	—	1 Centavo, Copper	1500.
Pn76	1868Mo C	—	5 Centavos, Silver, Rev: Value in branches.	250.00
Pn77	1868Mo C	—	10 Centavos, Silver, Rev: Value in branches.	1800.

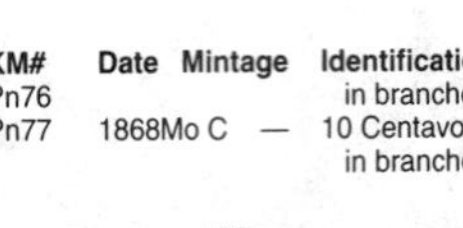

KM#	Date	Mintage	Identification	Mkt.Val.
Pn78	1868Mo CH	—	20 Pesos, Gold, XF	30,000.
PnA79	1869Mo CH	—	1/2 Escudo, Copper	350.00
PnB79	1869Mo CH	—	1 Escudo, Copper	350.00
Pn79	1869Mo CH	—	8 Escudos, Copper	—
Pn80	1869Mo C	—	5 Centavos, Copper	—
PnA81	1869Mo C	—	10 Centavos, Copper	100.00
Pn81	1869Mo C	—	25 Centavos, Copper	600.00
Pn82	1869Mo C	—	50 Centavos, Copper	—
PnA83	1869Mo C	—	1 Peso, Copper	1250.

KM#	Date	Mintage	Identification	Mkt.Val.
Pn83	1869Mo C	—	1 Peso, Silver, Rev: Large LEY.	Rare

KM#	Date	Mintage	Identification	Mkt.Val.
Pn84	1869Mo C	—	10 Pesos, Copper	300.00
Pn85	1870Mo C	—	50 Centavos, Copper	1000.
PnA86	1870Mo C	—	2-1/2 Pesos, Copper	750.00
Pn86	1870Mo C	—	20 Pesos, Copper	200.00
Pn86a	1870Mo C	—	20 Pesos, Silver	—
Pn86b	1870Mo C	—	20 Pesos, White Metal	—
Pn87	1871Mo M	—	10 Centavos, Copper	300.00
Pn88	1871Mo M	—	25 Centavos, Copper	300.00
Pn89	1871Mo M	—	1 Peso, Copper	275.00
Pn90	1872Mo M	—	1 Peso, Silver	—
Pn91	1873Mo M	—	1 Peso, Silver	Rare
Pn92	1873Mo M	—	5 Pesos, Copper	—
Pn93	1875Mo B	—	20 Pesos, Copper	475.00
PnA93	1877Mo M	—	1 Peso, Copper	125.00
Pn94	1879As L	—	10 Pesos, Silver	—

KM#	Date	Mintage	Identification	Mkt.Val.
Pn95	1880Mo M	—	10 Centavos, Copper	150.00

KM#	Date	Mintage	Identification	Mkt.Val.
Pn96	1882Ho JA	—	8 Reales, Copper	6750.
Pn97	1883Mo	—	1 Centavo, Bronze	—
Pn98	1883Mo	—	5 Centavos, Bronze	—
Pn99	1884CH M	—	20 Pesos, Copper	—
PnA100	1886Oa E	—	10 Pesos, Copper	750.00
Pn100	1888Pi R	—	1 Peso, Silver	—
Pn101	1888Pi R	—	2-1/2 Pesos, Silver	—
Pn102	1888Pi R	—	5 Pesos, Silver	—
Pn103	1888Pi R	—	10 Pesos, Bronze	—
Pn103a	1888Pi R	—	10 Pesos, Silver	500.00
Pn103b	1888Pi R	—	10 Pesos, Gold	—
Pn104	1888Pi R	—	20 Pesos, Silver	—

KM#	Date	Mintage	Identification	Mkt.Val.
Pn105	1889Mo	—	1 Centavo, White Metal	750.00
Pn106	1889Mo AM	—	5 Centavos, White Metal	—
Pn107	1889Mo AM	—	20 Centavos, White Metal	700.00
Pn108	1889Mo AM	—	50 Centavos, White Metal	650.00
Pn109	1889Mo AM	—	1 Peso, White Metal	1250.
Pn110	1889Mo AM	—	2-1/2 Pesos, White Metal	1350.
Pn111	1889Mo AM	—	10 Pesos, White Metal	800.00

KM#	Date	Mintage	Identification	Mkt.Val.
Pn112	1889Mo AM	—	20 Pesos, White Metal	1250.

KM#	Date	Mintage	Identification	Mkt.Val.
Pn113	1892Mo AM	—	20 Centavos, Silver	1000.
Pn114	1892Mo AM	—	10 Pesos, Gold, XF	30,000.

KM#	Date	Mintage	Identification	Mkt.Val.
Pn115	1892Mo AM	—	20 Pesos, Gold, XF	30,000.
PnA116	1896Go R	—	1 Peso, Silver	500.00
Pn116	1896Mo M	—	1 Peso, Silver	500.00
Pn117	1897Mo M	—	5 Centavos, Silver	2000.
Pn118	1897Mo M	—	10 Centavos, Silver	2000.
Pn119	1897Mo M	—	20 Centavos, Silver	2750.
Pn120	1897Cn	—	1 Peso, Silver	—
Pn121	1897Mo AM	—	1 Peso, Silver	19,800.

KM#	Date	Mintage	Identification	Mkt.Val.
Pn122	1898Mo	—	1 Peso, Bronze	3000.
Pn122a	1898Mo	—	1 Peso, Silver	Rare
Pn123	1898Cn M	—	20 Pesos, Silver	—

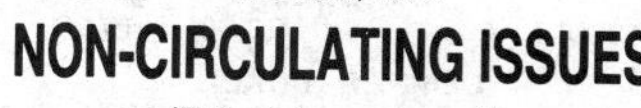

NON-CIRCULATING ISSUES

(Privately produced)

1838 Liberty Head Series

REPUBLIC OF MEXICO

UNA QUARTILLA
(1/4) REAL

CHIHUAHUA

KM#	Date	Mintage	VF	XF	Unc
		BRASS			
NC1	1838	—	250.00	500.00	850.00
		SILVER			
NC1a	1838	—	500.00	1000.	1500.

KM#	Date	Mintage	VF	XF	Unc
		COPPER			
NC2	1838	—	250.00	500.00	850.00
		BRASS			
NC2a	1838	—	250.00	500.00	850.00

DURANGO

KM#	Date	Mintage	VF	XF	Unc
		BRASS			
NC3	1838	—	250.00	500.00	850.00

GUADALAJARA

KM#	Date	Mintage	VF	XF	Unc
		BRASS			
NC4	1838	—	250.00	500.00	850.00

GUANAJUATO

KM#	Date	Mintage	VF	XF	Unc
		BRASS			
NC5	1838	—	250.00	500.00	850.00

MEXICO

KM#	Date	Mintage	VF	XF	Unc
		BRASS			
NC6	1838	—	175.00	375.00	750.00

KM#	Date	Mintage	VF	XF	Unc
NC7	1838	—	175.00	375.00	750.00

Rev: Column w/flying eagle above in wreath.

KM#	Date	Mintage	VF	XF	Unc
NC8	1838	—	250.00	500.00	850.00

POTOSI

KM#	Date	Mintage	VF	XF	Unc
		BRASS			
NC9	1838	—	250.00	500.00	850.00

TUXTLA

KM#	Date	Mintage	VF	XF	Unc
		COPPER			
NC10	1838	—	30.00	60.00	100.00

ZACATECAS

KM#	Date	Mintage	VF	XF	Unc
		BRASS			
NC11	1838	—	250.00	500.00	850.00
		SILVER			
NC11a	1838	—	500.00	1000.	1500.

1890 Liberty Head Series

Struck by the firm of L. Chr. Lauer, Nurnberg, Germany.

2 CENTAVOS

CAMPECHE

KM#	Date	Mintage	VF	XF	Unc
		BRONZE			
NC12	1890	—	20.00	40.00	70.00
		COPPER-NICKEL			
NC12a	1890	—	50.00	100.00	150.00

COAHUILA

KM#	Date	Mintage	VF	XF	Unc
		BRONZE Similar to NC15.			
NC13	1890	—	20.00	40.00	70.00
		COPPER-NICKEL			
NC13a	1890	—	50.00	100.00	150.00

MEXICO

KM#	Date	Mintage	VF	XF	Unc
		BRONZE Similar to NC15.			
NC14	1890	—	20.00	40.00	70.00
		COPPER-NICKEL			
NC14a	1890	—	50.00	100.00	150.00

NUEVO LEON

KM#	Date	Mintage	VF	XF	Unc
		BRONZE			
NC15	1890	—	20.00	40.00	70.00
		COPPER-NICKEL			
NC15a	1890	—	50.00	100.00	150.00

PUEBLA

KM#	Date	Mintage	VF	XF	Unc
		BRONZE			
NC16	1890	—	20.00	40.00	70.00
		COPPER-NICKEL			
NC16a	1890	—	50.00	100.00	150.00

QUERETARO

KM#	Date	Mintage	VF	XF	Unc
		BRONZE Similar to NC15.			
NC17	1890	—	20.00	40.00	70.00
		COPPER-NICKEL			
NC17a	1890	—	50.00	100.00	150.00

SAN LUIS POTOSI

KM#	Date	Mintage	VF	XF	Unc
		BRONZE			
NC18	1890	—	20.00	40.00	70.00
		COPPER-NICKEL			
NC18a	1890	—	50.00	100.00	150.00

TLAXCALA

KM#	Date	Mintage	VF	XF	Unc
		BRONZE			
NC19	1890	—	20.00	40.00	70.00
		COPPER-NICKEL			
NC19a	1890	—	50.00	100.00	150.00

ZACATECAS

KM#	Date	Mintage	VF	XF	Unc
		BRONZE Similar to NC19.			
NC20	1890	—	20.00	40.00	70.00
		COPPER-NICKEL			
NC20a	1890	—	50.00	100.00	150.00

MEDALLIC ISSUES
(2 CENTAVOS)

KM#	Date	Mintage	VF	XF	Unc
		BRONZE 80th Anniversary of Independence			
NC21	1890	—	40.00	80.00	120.00
		SILVERED BRONZE			
NC21a	1890	—	65.00	125.00	180.00
		COPPER-NICKEL			
NC21b	1890	—	100.00	200.00	250.00

REPUBLIC OF NORTH MEXICO
2 CENTS

KM#	Date	Mintage	VF	XF	Unc
		BRONZE			
NC22	1890	—	75.00	150.00	225.00

REPUBLIC OF THE RIO GRANDE
2 CENTS

KM#	Date	Mintage	VF	XF	Unc
		BRONZE Similar to NC22			
NC23	1890	—	100.00	200.00	300.00

TRIAL STRIKES (TS)

KM#	Date	Mintage	Identification	Mkt.Val.
TS1	1823 JM	—	8 Escudos, Silver, uniface reverse	Rare
TS2	1824 JM	—	8 Reales, Copper, uniface obverse	Rare

KM#	Date	Mintage	Identification	Mkt.Val.
TS3	1824 JM	—	8 Reales, Copper, uniface reverse	Rare
TS4	1825 JM	—	8 Reales, White Metal, hooked neck eagle	Rare
TS5	1825 JM	—	8 Reales, White Metal, radiant Liberty cap	Rare
TS6	1869 M	—	1 Centavos, Bronze	—
TS7	1883	—	1 Centavos, Bronze, uniface obverse	—
TS8	1883	—	1 Centavos, Bronze, uniface reverse	—
TS9	1883	—	2 Centavos, Bronze, uniface obverse	125.00
TS10	1883	—	2 Centavos, Bronze, uniface obverse	125.00
TS11	1883	—	5 Centavos, Bronze, uniface reverse	225.00
TS12	1883	—	5 Centavos, Bronze, uniface obverse	225.00
TS13	1883	—	5 Centavos, White Metal, uniface obverse	—
TS14	190—	—	8 Reales, Bronze plated Lead, Liberty on horseback	—

MOLDAVIA & WALLACHIA

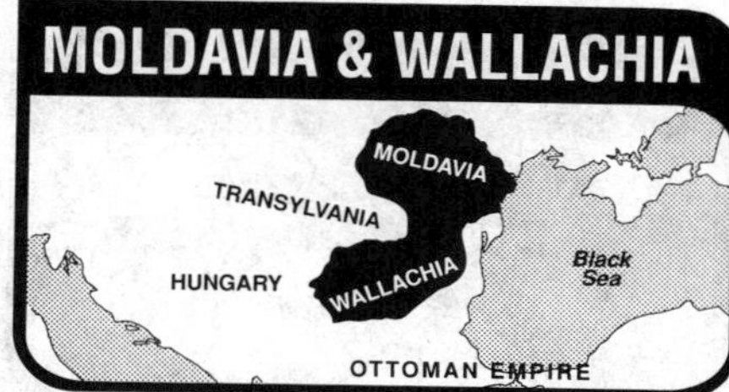

The 2 principalities that constitute most of modern Romania. A vassal state of the Turks for 300 years. As a Russian-Turkish buffer state it was occupied by Russia from 1768 to 1774.

Union of the principalities was voted for unanimously in 1848 and the two assemblies elected a prince in the person of Alexander Cuza on Jan. 17, 1859, accomplishing the de facto union of Romania. The prince, through lack of agrarian reform, was compelled to abdicate in Feb. 1866, and was succeeded by Prince Carol I who later became King in 1881.

PATTERNS (Pn)

(Including off metal strikes)

KM#	Date	Mintage	Identification	Mkt.Val.
Pn11	1860	*100	5 Parale, Bronze, obv: mantled arms	Rare
Pn12	1864	*100	5 Satimi, Bronze, obv: head of Ion Cuza	Rare
Pn13	1864	—	10 Satimi, Bronze	Rare

MONACO

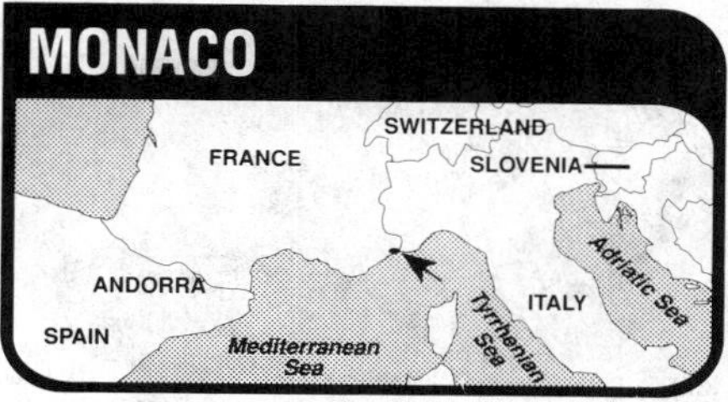

The Principality of Monaco, located on the Mediterranean coast nine miles from Nice, has an area of 0.58 sq. mi. (1.9 sq. km.) and a population of 26,000. Capital: MonacoVille. The economy is based on tourism and the manufacture of cosmetics, gourmet foods and highly specialized electronics. Monaco also derives its revenue from a tobacco monopoly and the sale of postage stamps for philatelic purpose. Gambling in Monte Carlo accounts for only a small fraction of the country's revenue.

Monaco derives its name from 'Monoikos', the Greek surname for Hercules, the mythological strong man who, according to legend, formed the Monacan headland during one of his twelve labors. Monaco has been ruled by the Grimaldi dynasty since 1297 - Prince Rainier III, the present and 31st monarch of Monaco, is still of that line - except for a period during the French Revolution until Napoleon's downfall when the Principality was annexed to France. Since 1865, Monaco has maintained a customs union with France which guarantees its privileged position as long as the royal line remains intact. Under the new constitution proclaimed on December 17, 1962, the Prince shares his power with an 18-member unicameral National Council.

RULERS

Honore IV, 1795-1819
Honore V, 1819-1841
Florestan I, 1841-1856
Charles III, 1856-1889
Albert I, 1889-1922

MINT MARKS

M - Monaco
A - Paris

PRIVY MARKS

(a) - Paris (privy marks only)
C and clasped hands - Francois Cabinas, mint director, 1837-1838
(p) - Thunderbolt - Poissy

MONETARY SYSTEM

10 Centimes = 1 Decime
10 Decimes = 1 Franc

CINQ (5) CENTIMES

CAST BRASS
Mint mark: M
Obv: Large head, BORREL F. below.

KM#	Date	Mintage	VG	Fine	VF	XF
95.1	1837 C	—	5.00	12.00	25.00	60.00
	COPPER, struck					
95.1a	1837 C	—	3.50	7.00	15.00	50.00

CAST BRASS
Obv: Small head, BORREL F. below.

KM#	Date	Mintage	VG	Fine	VF	XF
95.2	1837 C	—	4.00	10.00	35.00	75.00
	1838 C	—	— Reported, not confirmed			
	COPPER, struck					
95.2a	1837 C	—	3.50	7.00	15.00	45.00
	1838 C	—	12.00	25.00	50.00	125.00

UN (1) DECIME

COPPER, struck
Mint mark: M
Obv: BORREL F. below head.
Rev: Knot of wreath tied.

KM#	Date	Mintage	VG	Fine	VF	XF
97.1	1838 C	—	10.00	15.00	50.00	110.00
	BRASS, cast					
97.1a	1838 C	—	7.50	12.00	60.00	115.00

COPPER, struck
Obv: Smaller head, BORREL F. below.
Rev: Knot of wreath untied.

KM#	Date	Mintage	VG	Fine	VF	XF
97.2	1838 C	—	35.00	75.00	175.00	350.00
	BRASS, struck					
97.2a	1838 C	—	50.00	150.00	250.00	400.00

5 FRANCS

25.0000 g, .900 SILVER, .7234 oz ASW
Mint mark: M

KM#	Date	Mintage	Fine	VF	XF	Unc
96	1837	—	350.00	750.00	1250.	3500.

VINGT (20) FRANCS

6.4516 g, .900 GOLD, .1867 oz AGW

KM#	Date	Mintage	Fine	VF	XF	Unc
98	1878A	.025	120.00	200.00	300.00	600.00
	1879A	.050	80.00	150.00	200.00	500.00

CENT (100) FRANCS

32.2580 g, .900 GOLD, .9335 oz AGW

KM#	Date	Mintage	Fine	VF	XF	Unc
99	1882A	5,000	400.00	600.00	800.00	1200.
	1884A	.015	BV	450.00	550.00	750.00
	1886A	.015	BV	450.00	550.00	750.00

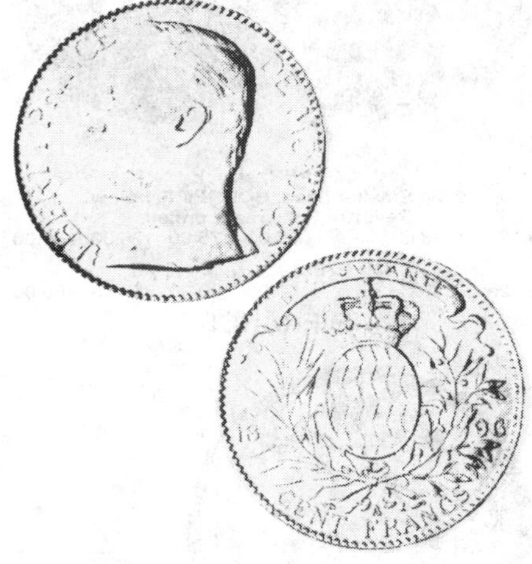

KM#	Date	Mintage	Fine	VF	XF	Unc
105	1891A	.020	BV	450.00	525.00	725.00
	1895A	.020	BV	450.00	525.00	725.00
	1896A	.020	BV	450.00	525.00	725.00

NOTE: Later dates (1901-1904) exist for this type.

PATTERNS (Pn)

(Including off metal strikes)

KM#	Date	Mintage	Identification	Mkt.Val.
Pn1	1837	—	5 Francs, .900 Silver	3500.
Pn2	1837	3 known	10 Centimes, Tin, E. Roger	—

KM#	Date	Mintage	Identification	Mkt.Val.
Pn3	1838	—	5 Centimes, Copper, E.Rogat below bust	275.00
Pn4	1838	—	5 Centimes, Copper and Tin alloy	275.00

KM#	Date	Mintage	Identification	Mkt.Val.
Pn5	1838	—	1 Decime, Copper	250.00
Pn6	1838	—	1 Decime, Copper and Tin alloy	250.00
Pn7	1838	—	1/4 Franc, .900 Silver	275.00
Pn8	1838	—	1/2 Franc, .900 Silver	350.00
Pn9	1838	—	1 Franc, .900 Silver	450.00

KM#	Date	Mintage	Identification	Mkt.Val.
Pn10	1838	—	2 Francs, .900 Silver	550.00
Pn11	1838	—	10 Francs, Tin	500.00

KM#	Date	Mintage	Identification	Mkt.Val.
Pn12	1838	—	20 Francs, Gold	—
Pn13	1838	—	40 Francs, Gold	—
Pn14	1892A	—	20 Francs, .900 Gold	3000.

TRIAL STRIKES (TS)

KM#	Date	Mintage	Identification	Mkt.Val.
TS1	1837	—	5 Francs, .900 Silver, Pn1 obv.	—
TS2	1837	—	5 Francs, .900 Silver, Pn1 rev.	—
TS3	1838	—	5 Centimes, Copper, Pn2 obv.	—
TS4	1838	—	5 Centimes, Copper, Pn2 rev.	—
TS5	1838	—	5 Centimes, Copper and Tin alloy, Pn3 obv.	—
TS6	1838	—	5 Centimes, Copper and Tin Alloy, Pn3 rev.	—
TS7	1838	—	1 Decime, Copper, Pn4 obv.	—
TS8	1838	—	1 Decime, Copper, Pn4 rev.	—
TS9	1838	—	1 Decime, Copper and Tin alloy, Pn5 obv.	—
TS10	1838	—	1 Decime, Copper and tin alloy, Pn5 rev.	—
TS11	1838	—	1/4 Franc, .900 Silver, Pn6 obv.	—
TS12	1838	—	1/4 Franc, .900 Silver, Pn6 rev.	—
TS13	1838	—	1/2 Franc, .900 Silver, Pn7 obv.	—
TS14	1838	—	1/2 Franc, .900 Silver, Pn7 rev.	—
TS15	1838	—	1 Franc, .900 Silver, Pn8 obv.	—
TS16	1838	—	1 Franc, .900 Silver, Pn8 rev.	—
TS17	1838	—	2 Francs, .900 Silver, Pn9 obv.	—
TS18	1838	—	2 Francs, .900 Silver, Pn9 rev.	—
TS19	1838	—	20 Francs, Gold, Pn10 obv.	—
TS20	1838	—	20 Francs, Gold, Pn10 rev.	—
TS21	1838	—	40 Francs, Gold, Pn11 obv.	—
TS22	1838	—	40 Francs, Gold, Pn11 rev.	—

MOROCCO

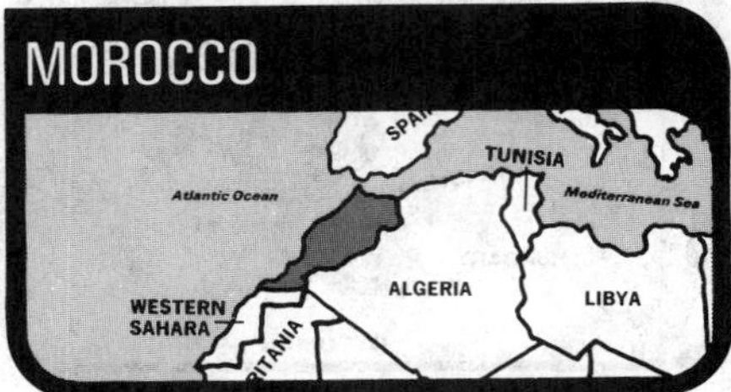

The Kingdom of Morocco, situated on the northwest corner of Africa, has an area of 275,117 sq. mi. (446,550 sq. km.) and a population of 22.5 million. Capital: Rabat. The economy is essentially agricultural. Phosphates, fresh and preserved vegetables, canned fish, and raw materials are exported.

Morocco's strategic position at the gateway to western Europe has been the principal determinant of its violent, frequently unfortunate history. Time and again the fertile plain between the rugged Atlas Mountains and the sea has echoed the battle's trumpet as Phoenicians, Romans, Vandals, Visigoths, Byzantine Greeks and Islamic Arabs successively conquered and occupied the land. Modern Morocco is a remnant of an early empire formed by the Arabs at the close of the 7th century which encompassed all of northwest Africa and most of the Iberian Peninsula. During the 17th and 18th centuries, while under the control of native dynasties, it was the headquarters of the famous Sale pirates. Morocco's strategic position involved it in the competition of 19th century European powers for political influence in Africa, and resulted in the division of Morocco into French and Spanish spheres of interest which were established as protectorates in 1912. Morocco became independent on March 2, 1956, after France agreed to end its protectorate. Spain signed similar agreements on April 7 of the same year.

TITLES

المغربية

Al-Maghribiya(t)

المملكة المغربية

Al-Mamlaka(t) al-Maghribiya(t)

المحمدية الشريفة

Al-Mohammediya(t) esh-Sherifiya(t)

RULERS

Filali Sharifs

Suleiman II,
AH1206-1238/1792-1822AD
'Abd al-Rahman II,
AH1238-1276/1822-1859AD
Mohammed IV,
AH1276-1290/1859-1873AD
Al-Hasan I (Moulai Hasan),
AH1290-1311/1873-1894AD
'Abd al-Aziz,
AH1311-1326/1894-1908AD

EARLY COINAGE

Prior to the introduction of modern machine-struck coinage in Morocco in AH1299 (= 1882AD), a variety of primitive cast bronze coins and crudely hammered silver and gold were in circulation, together with considerable quantities of foreign coins.

The cast bronze were produced in several denominations, multiples of the basic unit. the Falus. The size of the coins is variable, and the distinction of the various denominations is not always clear, particularly on the issues of Sulaiman. The early types are varied, but beginning about AH1218, the reverse bears the seal of Solomon, and the obverse contains the date and/or mint. Several early varieties with the seal of Solomon on both sides exist. The date is inscribed in European numerals, the mint, when present, is written out in Arabic script. Many of the issues are quite barbarous, with illegible dates and mints, and occasionally light in weight. These barbarous issues may have been contemporary counterfeits, and are of little numismatic value. The bronze pieces were cast in "trees", and occasionally, entire or partial 'trees' are found on the market.

The silver and gold coins usually have the mintname on one side and the date on the other. The silver unit was the dirham of about 2.7 grams (but only about 2.0 grams from circa AH 1266-78), and the gold unit was the benduqi of about 3.25 grams. There were no fixed rates of exchange between coins of different metals.

Prices are for specimens with clearly legible dates and mintnames (if any). Illegible, barbarous, and defectively produced pieces are worth much less.

MINTS

(a) - Paris privy marks only

Bi - Angland (Birmingham) بانكلند

Ln = bi-Angland (London) بانكلند

Lr = al-'Araish (Larache) العرايش

Lr = al-'Araisah (Larache) العرايشة

As = Asfi (Safi) اسفي

Pa = bi-Bariz (Paris) بباريز

Be = Berlin برلين

EM = Essaouir (Mogador) الصويرة - الصوير

Fs = Fes (Fas, Fez) فاس

FH = Fes Hazrat فاس حضرة

KH = al-Kitaoua Hazrat حضرة الكتوة

Ma = Madrid مدريد

MH = Marakesh Hazrat مراكش

Mr = Marrakesh (Marakesh) مراكش

Mk = Miknas (Meknes) مكناس

Miknasah مكناسة

MB = Moulay-Ibrahim مولاي ابراهيم

Py - Poissy Inscribed "Paris" but with thunderbolt privy mark.

Rb = Rabat رباط

RF = Rabat al-Fath رباط الفتح

Si = Sijilmasah سجلماسه

Sus سوس

Sr = al-Suwair الصوير

Sh = al-Suwairah الصويرة

Tg = Tanjah (Tangier) طنجة

Te = Tetuan تطوان

(NM) = No mint name on coin.

NOTE: Some of the above forms of the mintnames are shown as they appear on the coins, not in regular Arabic script.

The following coins are divided by reign. However, all of the coins are anonymous, and the distinction by reign is purely artificial. There is much variation within each type, and several of the subtypes overlap more than one reign. The coinage of Sulaiman II and Abd al-Rahman II are listed only by type (dates through AH1276 inclusive); those of Muhammad IV (beginning AH1277 inclusive) and those of Al Hasan I (Moulai Hasan) are broken down by mint and date. The date listings for these two rulers, however, are believed to be very incomplete.

Suleiman II

AH1206-1238/1792-1822AD

FALUS

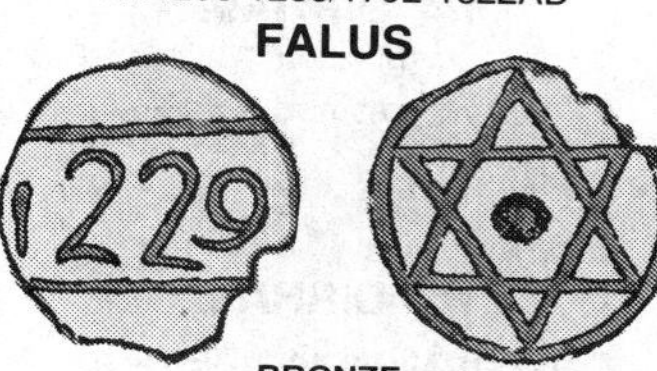

BRONZE

C#	Date	Good	VG	Fine	VF
95	AH1216-38	1.50	2.50	6.00	15.00

NOTE: Earlier dates (AH1209-15) exist for this type.

2 FALUS

BRONZE

C#	Date	Good	VG	Fine	VF
96	AH1216-38	2.00	3.00	6.00	15.00

NOTE: Earlier dates (AH1209-15) exist for this type.

4 FALUS

BRONZE

C#	Date	Good	VG	Fine	VF
98	AH1216	6.00	10.00	15.00	25.00
	1217	6.00	10.00	15.00	25.00

NOTE: Earlier dates (AH1212-15) exist for this type.

1/4 DIRHAM

SILVER, 15-18mm

KM#	Date	Mintage	Good	VG	Fine	VF
105	AH1216	—	5.00	8.50	15.00	25.00
	1217	—	5.00	8.50	15.00	25.00
	1218	—	5.00	8.50	15.00	25.00

NOTE: Earlier dates (AH1211-15) exist for this type.

DIRHAM

SILVER, 17-20mm, 2.44-2.70 g

KM#	Date	Mintage	Good	VG	Fine	VF
108	AH1216-38	—	4.00	7.00	12.50	20.00

NOTE: Earlier dates (AH1211-15) exist for this type.

1/2 BENDUQI

GOLD, 1.76 g
Mintname: Hadrat Fes

C#	Date	VG	Fine	VF	XF
114	AH1232	90.00	150.00	250.00	375.00
	1233	—	Reported, not confirmed		
	1236	90.00	150.00	250.00	375.00

BENDUQI

GOLD, 3.52 g
Mintname: Hadrat Fes

C#	Date	VG	Fine	VF	XF
115	AH1216	70.00	100.00	150.00	225.00
	1217	70.00	100.00	150.00	225.00
	1218	70.00	100.00	150.00	225.00
	1219	70.00	100.00	150.00	225.00
	1220	70.00	100.00	150.00	225.00
	1224	70.00	100.00	150.00	225.00
	1234	70.00	100.00	150.00	225.00
	1235	70.00	100.00	150.00	225.00
	1238	70.00	100.00	150.00	225.00

NOTE: Earlier dates (AH1209-14) exist for this type.

'Abd al-Rahman

AH1238-1276/1822-1859AD

1/2 FALUS

(Zelagh)

BRONZE, 13-14mm
Rev: Flower design.

C#	Date	Good	VG	Fine	VF
120	ND	2.00	3.50	6.00	10.00

NOTE: May possibly be issued by Suleiman II.

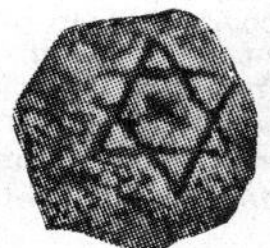

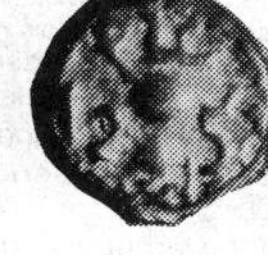

Rev: Date.

C#	Date	Good	VG	Fine	VF
121	AH1245	5.00	10.00	20.00	40.00
	1263	5.00	10.00	20.00	40.00
	1268	5.00	10.00	20.00	40.00
	1270	5.00	10.00	20.00	40.00
	1271	5.00	10.00	20.00	40.00

FALUS

BRONZE, 17-20mm

C#	Date	Good	VG	Fine	VF
122	AH1240-76	1.00	3.00	5.00	8.00

NOTE: Many varieties exist.

2 FALUS

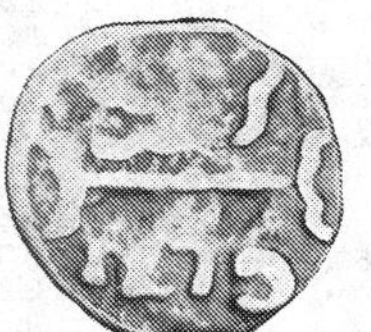

BRONZE, 22mm

C#	Date	Good	VG	Fine	VF
126	AH1240-76	1.00	2.00	4.00	6.00

NOTE: Many varieties exist.

3 FALUS

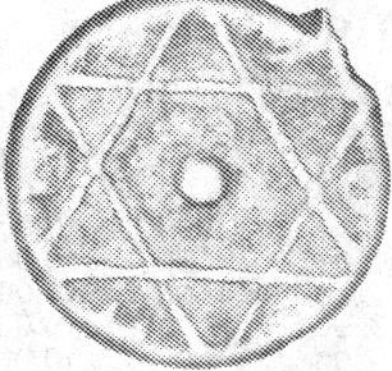

BRONZE, 25-28mm

C#	Date	Good	VG	Fine	VF
128	AH1264-69	2.50	4.50	7.50	12.50

NOTE: Many varieties exist.

DIRHAM

SILVER, 17-20mm, 2.70 g

C#	Date	Good	VG	Fine	VF
140	AH1240-52	4.00	7.00	11.00	22.50

Reduced standard, 2.00 g.

C#	Date	Good	VG	Fine	VF
140a	AH1266-76	3.25	6.00	10.00	20.00

1/2 BENDUQI

GOLD, 1.76 g
Mintname: Hadrat Fes

C#	Date	VG	Fine	VF	XF
145	AH1240	75.00	125.00	175.00	250.00
	1247	75.00	125.00	175.00	250.00
	1248	75.00	125.00	175.00	250.00
	1252	75.00	125.00	175.00	250.00

BENDUQI

GOLD, 3.52 g
Mintname: Hadrat Fes

C#	Date	VG	Fine	VF	XF
150.1	AH1241	75.00	125.00	175.00	250.00
	1242	60.00	90.00	135.00	185.00
	1243	60.00	90.00	135.00	185.00
	1244	60.00	90.00	135.00	185.00
	1245	60.00	90.00	135.00	185.00
	1246	60.00	90.00	135.00	185.00
	1247	60.00	90.00	135.00	185.00
	1248	60.00	90.00	135.00	185.00
	1249	60.00	90.00	135.00	185.00
	1250	60.00	90.00	135.00	185.00
	1251	60.00	90.00	135.00	185.00
	1252	60.00	90.00	135.00	185.00
	1253	60.00	90.00	135.00	185.00
	1254	60.00	90.00	135.00	185.00
	1255	60.00	90.00	135.00	185.00
	1256	60.00	90.00	135.00	185.00
	1257	60.00	90.00	135.00	185.00
	1258	60.00	90.00	135.00	185.00
	1259	60.00	90.00	135.00	185.00
	1266	60.00	90.00	135.00	185.00
	1267	60.00	90.00	135.00	185.00
	1269	60.00	90.00	135.00	185.00
	1270	60.00	90.00	135.00	185.00
	1271	60.00	90.00	135.00	185.00
	1272	60.00	90.00	135.00	185.00
	1273	60.00	90.00	135.00	185.00
	1274	60.00	90.00	135.00	185.00
	1275	60.00	90.00	135.00	185.00

Mintname: Meknes

C#	Date	VG	Fine	VF	XF
150.2	AH1247	—	—	—	—

Mohammed IV

AH1276-1290/1859-1873AD

FALUS

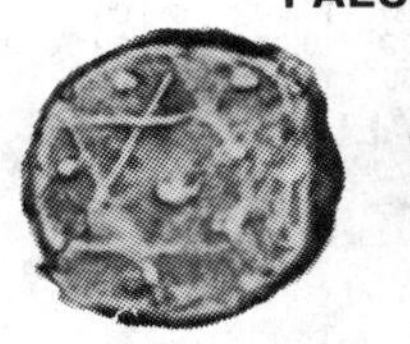

BRONZE, 17mm
Early types.

C#	Date	Good	VG	Fine	VF
160	AH1277(NM)	1.00	2.00	4.00	10.00
	1277Fs	1.00	2.00	4.00	10.00
	1278(NM)	1.00	2.00	4.00	10.00
	1278Te	2.00	3.00	6.00	15.00
	1278Fs	1.00	2.00	4.00	10.00
	1279Te	2.00	3.00	6.00	15.00
	1280	1.00	2.00	4.00	10.00
	1281Te	2.00	3.00	6.00	15.00
	1281(NM)	1.00	2.00	4.00	10.00

NOTE: Varieties exist.

Reform type
Similar to 2 Falus, C#163a.

C#	Date	Good	VG	Fine	VF
160a	AH1283Fs	2.00	3.00	10.00	20.00
	1283Mr	2.00	3.00	10.00	20.00
	1284Fs	2.00	3.00	10.00	20.00
	1285Fs	2.00	3.00	10.00	20.00
	1286Fs	2.00	3.00	10.00	20.00
	1287Fs	2.00	3.00	10.00	20.00
	1288Fs	2.00	3.00	10.00	20.00
	1289Fs	2.00	3.00	10.00	20.00

NOTE: Varieties exist.

2 FALUS

BRONZE, 21-24mm
Early types.

C#	Date	Good	VG	Fine	VF
163	AH1277Te	1.25	2.50	6.00	15.00
	1277Fs	1.00	2.00	4.00	10.00
	1277Mr	1.00	2.00	4.00	10.00
	1277(NM)	1.00	2.00	4.00	10.00
	1278Fs	1.00	2.00	4.00	10.00
	1278Te	1.25	2.50	6.00	15.00
	1278(NM)	1.00	2.00	4.00	10.00
	1279Fs	1.00	2.00	4.00	10.00
	1279(NM)	1.00	2.00	4.00	10.00
	1280(NM)	1.00	2.00	4.00	10.00
	1281Fs	1.00	2.00	4.00	10.00
	1281Te	1.25	2.50	6.00	15.00
	1281(NM)	1.00	2.00	4.00	10.00

NOTE: 1281 Fz found also with retrograde '2' in date. Varieties exist.

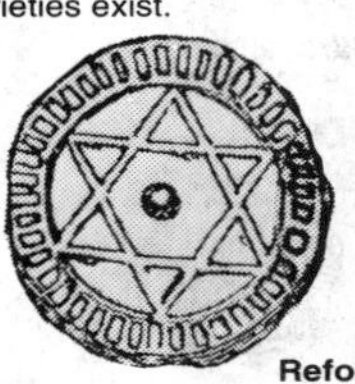

Reform type

C#	Date	Good	VG	Fine	VF
163a	AH1283Fs	2.50	4.50	6.50	11.00
	1283Mr	2.00	3.00	5.00	10.00
	1284Fs	2.00	3.00	5.00	10.00
	1285Fs	2.00	3.00	5.00	10.00
	1285Mr	2.00	3.00	5.00	10.00
	1286Fs	2.00	3.00	5.00	10.00
	1287Fs	2.00	3.00	5.00	10.00
	1288Fs	2.00	3.00	5.00	10.00
	1288Mr	2.00	3.00	5.00	10.00
	1289Fs	2.00	3.00	5.00	10.00
	1290Fs	2.00	3.00	5.00	10.00

NOTE: Varieties exist.

4 FALUS

BRONZE, 26-29mm
Reform types.

C#	Date	Good	VG	Fine	VF
166	AH1283Fs	1.75	3.25	5.00	8.00
	1283Mr	2.00	3.50	5.50	9.00
	1284Fs	1.50	3.00	4.50	7.50
	1284Mr	1.25	2.25	3.50	6.00
	1285Fs	1.25	2.25	3.50	6.50
	1285Mr	1.25	2.25	3.50	6.50
	1286/5Mr	1.75	3.25	5.00	8.00
	1286Fs	2.25	4.00	6.00	10.00
	1286Mr	1.00	1.75	2.75	4.50
	1287Fs	2.00	3.00	5.00	9.00
	1287Mr	2.00	3.00	5.00	9.00
	1288/7Fs	2.25	4.00	6.00	10.00

C#	Date	Good	VG	Fine	VF
166	1288Fs	.75	1.50	2.50	4.00
	1288Mr	1.00	1.75	3.00	5.00
	1289/79Mr	1.20	2.00	3.50	6.00
	1289/8Mr	1.20	2.00	3.50	6.00
	1289Fs	1.00	1.75	3.00	5.00
	1289Mr	1.50	2.75	4.00	6.50
	1290Fs	1.00	1.75	3.00	5.00

NOTE: Some AH1280 Fs are a poorly engraved 1284 Fs. Varieties exist.

1/4 DIRHAM

(Mazuna)

SILVER, 0.65-0.73 g, 13mm

C#	Date	Good	VG	Fine	VF
170	AH1284Fs	4.00	6.50	12.50	20.00
	1284Mr	4.00	6.50	12.50	20.00
	1286Fs	4.00	6.50	12.50	20.00
	1288Fs	4.00	6.50	12.50	20.00

1/2 DIRHAM

SILVER, 15-18mm, 1.30-1.40 g

C#	Date	Good	VG	Fine	VF
175	AH1283Fs	3.00	5.50	10.00	17.50
	1284Fs	3.00	5.50	10.00	17.50
	1284Mr	4.00	7.00	12.00	22.50
	1284Rb	4.25	8.00	15.00	27.50
	1286Fs	3.00	5.50	10.00	17.50
	1288Fs	3.00	5.50	10.00	17.50

DIRHAM

SILVER, 17-20mm
Light standard, 2.00 g.

C#	Date	Good	VG	Fine	VF
176	AH1277Fs	4.50	8.00	15.00	22.50
	1278Fs	4.50	8.00	15.00	22.50

Heavy standard, 2.70-2.93 g.

C#	Date	Good	VG	Fine	VF
176a	AH1283Fs	4.00	8.00	15.00	22.50
	1284Fs	4.00	8.00	15.00	22.50
	1284Mr	4.00	8.00	15.00	22.50
	1284Rb	4.00	8.00	15.00	22.50
	1285Fs	4.00	8.00	15.00	22.50
	1286Fs	4.00	8.00	15.00	22.50
	1288Rb	4.00	8.00	15.00	22.50

Al-Hasan I

(Moulai Hasan)

AH1290-1311/1873-1894AD

2 FALUS

BRONZE

C#	Date	Good	VG	Fine	VF
182	AH1295 uncertain mint	—	—	—	—

NOTE: All known specimens appear to be counterfeits or misread dates having inverted 6.

4 FALUS

BRONZE

C#	Date	Good	VG	Fine	VF
183	AH1291Mr	—	—	—	—
	1291Fs	5.00	8.00	12.50	22.50
	1295Mr	3.50	6.50	10.00	16.50
	1295Fs	3.50	6.50	10.00	16.50

DIRHAM

SILVER

C#	Date	Good	VG	Fine	VF
187	AH1291Fs	15.00	20.00	45.00	70.00

MONETARY REFORM

MONETARY SYSTEM

Until 1921

50 Mazunas = 1 Dirham

10 Dirhams = 1 Rial

NOTES

Various copper and silver coins dated AH1297-1311 are believed to be patterns. Copper coins similar to Y#14-17, but without denomination on reverse, are patterns.

On the silver coins the denominations are written in words and each series has its own characteristic names:

Y#4-8 (1299-1314) Denomination in Shar'i Dirhams.

Y#9-13 (1313-1319) Denomination in 'Preferred' Dirhams.

On most of the larger denominations, the denomination is given in the form of a rhymed couplet.

1/2 MAZUNA

BRONZE

Y#	Date	Mintage	Fine	VF	XF	Unc
C1	AH1310Fs	—	200.00	350.00	600.00	1000.

NOTE: Some authorities consider Y#C1 to be a Mazuna.

MAZUNA

BRONZE

Y#	Date	Mintage	Fine	VF	XF	Unc
B1	AH1310Fs	—	150.00	300.00	550.00	900.00

NOTE: Some authorities consider Y#B1 to be a 2 Mazuna.

2-1/2 MAZUNAS

BRONZE

Y#	Date	Mintage	Fine	VF	XF	Unc
1	AH1310Fs	—	125.00	250.00	500.00	800.00

NOTE: Some authorities consider Y#1 to be a 3 Mazuna.

5 MAZUNAS

BRONZE

Y#	Date	Mintage	Fine	VF	XF	Unc
2	AH1310Fs	—	60.00	100.00	200.00	500.00

10 MAZUNAS

BRONZE

Y#	Date	Mintage	Fine	VF	XF	Unc
3	AH1310Fs	—	65.00	125.00	250.00	600.00

1/2 DIRHAM

(1/20 Rial)

1.4558 g, .835 SILVER, .0391 oz ASW

Y#	Date	Mintage	Fine	VF	XF	Unc
4	AH1299Pa	2.200	1.50	3.00	6.00	18.00
	1299Pa	—	—	—	Proof	200.00
	1309Pa	1.700	2.25	5.00	12.00	25.00
	1310Pa	1.700	2.00	4.00	9.00	20.00
	1311Pa	1.700	2.00	4.00	9.00	20.00
	1312Pa	1.700	2.00	4.00	9.00	20.00
	1313Pa	1.700	2.00	4.00	9.00	20.00
	1314Pa	1.700	5.00	12.50	25.00	45.00

DIRHAM

(1/10 Rial)

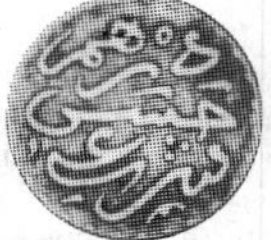

2.9116 g, .835 SILVER, .0782 oz ASW

Y#	Date	Mintage	Fine	VF	XF	Unc
5	AH1299Pa	6.800	2.00	4.00	8.00	20.00
	1309Pa	1.700	2.75	8.00	20.00	35.00
	1310Pa	1.800	2.75	7.00	15.00	30.00
	1311Pa	.800	2.75	7.50	17.00	35.00
	1312Pa	.800	2.75	7.50	17.00	35.00
	1313Pa	.800	3.00	8.00	22.50	35.00
	1314Pa	Inc. Y10	10.00	22.00	38.00	80.00

2-1/2 DIRHAMS

(1/4 Rial)

7.2790 g, .835 SILVER, .1954 oz ASW

Y#	Date	Mintage	Fine	VF	XF	Unc
6	AH1299Pa	2.100	3.00	10.00	20.00	30.00
	1299Pa	—	—	—	Proof	250.00
	1309Pa	.700	4.00	12.00	30.00	60.00
	1310Pa	.400	4.00	12.00	30.00	60.00
	1311Pa	.800	4.00	12.00	30.00	60.00
	1312Pa	.300	4.00	12.00	32.00	65.00
	1313Pa	.300	4.00	12.00	32.00	65.00
	1314Pa	—	30.00	75.00	150.00	300.00

5 DIRHAMS

(1/2 Rial)

14.5580 g, .835 SILVER, .3908 oz ASW

Y#	Date	Mintage	Fine	VF	XF	Unc
7	AH1299Pa	1.400	8.00	15.00	30.00	65.00
	1299Pa	—	—	—	Proof	350.00
	1309Pa	.280	8.00	20.00	35.00	100.00
	1310Pa	.170	8.00	20.00	35.00	90.00
	1311Pa	.170	8.00	20.00	35.00	90.00
	1312Pa	.170	8.00	20.00	35.00	90.00
	1313Pa	.170	15.00	30.00	55.00	150.00
	1314Pa	Inc. Y12	150.00	250.00	500.00	850.00

10 DIRHAMS

(Rial)

29.1160 g, .900 SILVER, .8425 oz ASW

Y#	Date	Mintage	Fine	VF	XF	Unc
8	AH1299Pa	.870	15.00	30.00	50.00	120.00

'Abd al-Aziz

AH1311-1326/1894-1908AD

1/2 DIRHAM

1.4558 g, .835 SILVER, .0391 oz ASW

Rev: Arrow heads point outward.

Y#	Date	Mintage	Fine	VF	XF	Unc
9.1	AH1313Be	.560	15.00	17.50	22.50	40.00

Rev: Arrow heads point inward.

Y#	Date	Mintage	Fine	VF	XF	Unc
9.2	AH1314Pa	2.200	7.50	12.50	17.50	35.00
	1315Pa	1.190	2.50	4.00	7.50	20.00
	1316Pa	2.280	2.50	5.00	10.00	25.00
	1317Pa	1.700	2.00	4.00	7.50	25.00
	1318Pa	1.715	4.00	8.00	12.00	25.00

NOTE: Later date (AH1319) exists for this type.

DIRHAM

2.9116 g, .835 SILVER, .0782 oz AGW

Rev: Arrow heads point outward.

Y#	Date	Mintage	Fine	VF	XF	Unc
10.1	AH1313Be	.430	6.00	12.50	22.00	45.00

Rev: Arrow heads point inward.

Y#	Date	Mintage	Fine	VF	XF	Unc
10.2	AH1314Pa	1.400	3.00	7.00	15.00	30.00
	1315Pa	.860	3.00	7.00	15.00	30.00
	1316Pa	.860	3.00	7.00	15.00	30.00
	1317Pa	.860	3.00	7.00	15.00	30.00
	1318Pa	.858	3.00	7.00	15.00	30.00

2-1/2 DIRHAMS

7.2790 g, .835 SILVER, .1954 oz ASW

Rev: Arrow heads point outward.

Y#	Date	Mintage	Fine	VF	XF	Unc
11.1	AH1313Be	.220	7.50	15.00	25.00	80.00
	1315Be	.640	5.00	10.00	15.00	55.00
	1318Be	.146	10.00	40.00	75.00	140.00

Rev: Arrow heads point inward.

Y#	Date	Mintage	Fine	VF	XF	Unc
11.2	AH1314Pa	1.036	5.00	8.00	10.00	22.00
	1315Pa	.340	5.00	10.00	15.00	55.00
	1316Pa	.400	5.00	15.00	50.00	80.00
	1317Pa	.340	5.00	15.00	50.00	80.00
	1318Pa	.340	10.00	35.00	60.00	115.00

5 DIRHAMS

14.5580 g, .835 SILVER, .3908 oz ASW

Y#	Date	Mintage	Fine	VF	XF	Unc
12.1	AH1313Be	.110	15.00	30.00	60.00	125.00
	1315Be	.360	10.00	16.00	35.00	85.00
	1318Be	.073	20.00	50.00	75.00	130.00

Y#	Date	Mintage	Fine	VF	XF	Unc
12.2	AH1314Pa	.517	10.00	20.00	60.00	120.00
	1315Pa	.160	10.00	16.00	35.00	80.00
	1316Pa	.220	10.00	20.00	35.00	100.00
	1317Pa	.170	10.00	20.00	35.00	100.00
	1318Pa	.177	12.50	25.00	50.00	120.00

10 DIRHAMS

29.1160 g, .900 SILVER, .8425 oz ASW

Y#	Date	Mintage	Fine	VF	XF	Unc
13	AH1313Be	.050	75.00	150.00	250.00	500.00
	1313Be	—	—	—	Proof	800.00

PATTERNS (Pn)

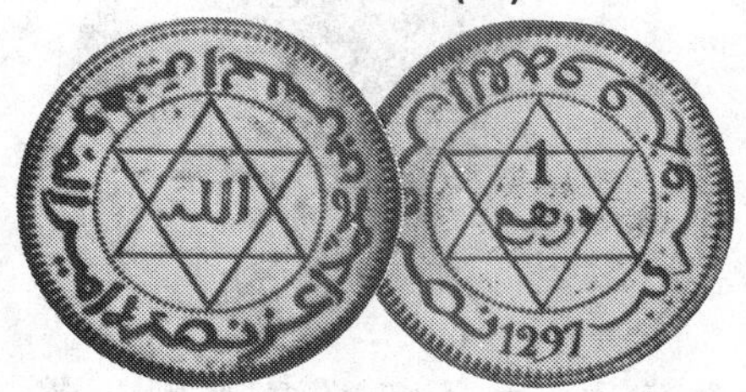

KM#	Date	Mintage	Identification	Mkt.Val.
Pn3	AH1297	—	1 Dirhem, Bronze	—

KM#	Date	Mintage	Identification	Mkt.Val.
Pn4	AH1297	—	5 Miscals	—
Pn5	AH1297	—	10 Miscals, Silver	2000.
Pn6	AH1297	—	4 Ryals, Gold	5500.

KM#	Date	Mintage	Identification	Mkt.Val.
PnA7	ND(1880-90AD)			

KM#	Date	Mintage	Identification	Mkt.Val.
PnA7		—	1 Dirham(?), Silver, Heaton Mint, in name of Marrakush Mint	—

KM#	Date	Mintage	Identification	Mkt.Val.
Pn7	AH1298	—	5 Dirhems, Silver, Paris Mint	1500.

KM#	Date	Mintage	Identification	Mkt.Val.
Pn8	AH1298	—	10 Dirhems, Silver, Paris Mint	2000.
Pn9	AH1301Fs	—	2-1/2 Mazunas, Bronze, octagonal central designs	—
Pn10	AH1301Fs	—	2-1/2 Mazunas, Bronze, stars in borders	—
Pn11	AH1301Fs	—	2-1/2 Mazunas, Bronze, floral and leaf borders	—

KM#	Date	Mintage	Identification	Mkt.Val.
Pn12	AH1301Fs	—	5 Mazunas, Bronze	—
Pn13	AH1301Fs	—	5 Mazunas, Bronze, 27.5mm	—
Pn14	AH1301Fs	—	10 Mazunas, Bronze, 28mm	—
Pn15	AH1301Fs	—	10 Mazunas, Bronze, 33mm	—
Pn16	AH1306Fs	—	1/2 Mazuna, Bronze, Y-C1	1000.
Pn17	AH1306Fs	—	1 Mazuna, Bronze, Y-B1	1000.
Pn18	AH1306Fs	—	2-1/2 Mazunas, Bronze, Y1	1000.

KM#	Date	Mintage	Identification	Mkt.Val.
Pn19	AH1306Fs	—	5 Mazunas, Bronze, Y2	1000.

KM#	Date	Mintage	Identification	Mkt.Val.
Pn20	AH1306Fs	—	10 Mazunas, Bronze, Y3	1000.

KM#	Date	Mintage	Identification	Mkt.Val.
Pn21	AH1311Fs	—	2 Falus, Bronze, 5.77 g	Rare

KM#	Date	Mintage	Identification	Mkt.Val.
Pn22	AH1311Fs	—	4 Falus, Bronze, 11.55 g	Rare
Pn23	AH1311Fs	—	6 Falus, Bronze, 17.32 g	Rare

KM#	Date	Mintage	Identification	Mkt.Val.
Pn24	AH1311Fs	—	8 Falus, Bronze, 23.09	Rare

MOZAMBIQUE

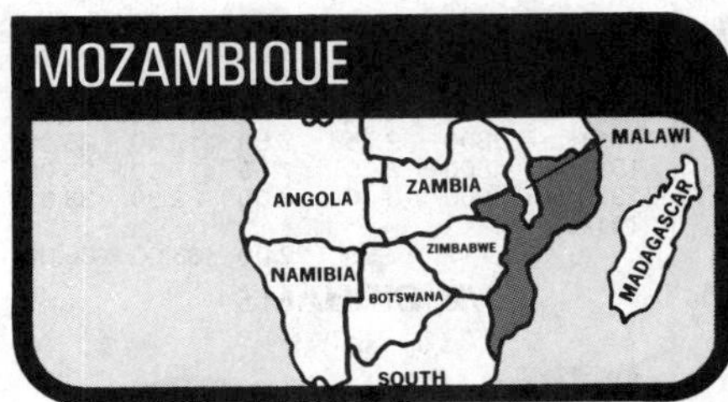

The Republic of Mozambique, a former overseas province of Portugal stretching for 1,430 miles (2,301 km.) along the southeast coast of Africa, has an area of 302,330 sq. mi. (801,590 sq. km.) and a population of 14.1 million, 99 percent of whom are native Africans of the Bantu tribes. Capital: Maputo. Agriculture is the chief industry. Cashew nuts, cotton, sugar, copra and tea are exported.

Vasco de Gama explored all the coast of Mozambique in 1498 and found Arab trading posts already established along the coast. Portuguese settlement dates from the establishment of the trading post of Mozambique in 1505. Within five years Portugal absorbed all the former Arab sultanates along the east African coast. The area was organized as a colony in 1907 and became an overseas province in 1952. In Sept. of 1974, after more than a decade of guerrilla warfare with the forces of the Mozambique Liberation Front, Portugal agreed to the independence of Mozambique, effective June 25, 1975. The Socialist party, led by President Joaquim Chissano was in power until the 2nd of November, 1990 when they became a republic.

RULERS

Portuguese, until 1975

MONETARY SYSTEM

2880 Reis = 6 Cruzados = 1 Onca

COLONIAL COINAGE

REAL

COPPER

KM#	Date	Mintage	Fine	VF	XF	Unc
24	1853	.100	10.00	20.00	40.00	70.00

II (2) REIS

COPPER

KM#	Date	Mintage	Fine	VF	XF	Unc
25	1853	.100	10.00	20.00	35.00	60.00

NOTE: The V Reis, X Reis and XX Reis pieces dated 1853 were issued primarily for circulation in Mozambique. These are also attributed to Portugal and will be found under their appropriate listings.

20 REIS

COPPER

KM#	Date	Mintage	Fine	VF	XF	Unc
18	1820	—	12.00	25.00	55.00	140.00

NOTE: For coins with c/m '10' refer to Brazil listings. Some 20 Reis coins previously listed here are now listed in St. Thomas and Prince Islands.

Similar to 40 Reis, KM#22.

KM#	Date	Mintage	Fine	VF	XF	Unc
21	1840	.040	15.00	30.00	65.00	160.00

40 REIS

COPPER

KM#	Date	Mintage	Fine	VF	XF	Unc
19	1820	—	15.00	30.00	60.00	150.00

NOTE: For coins with c/m '20' refer to Brazil listings. Some 40 Reis coins previously listed here are now listed in St. Thomas and Prince Islands.

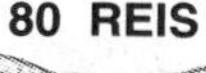

KM#	Date	Mintage	Fine	VF	XF	Unc
22	1840	.020	20.00	40.00	85.00	180.00

80 REIS

COPPER

KM#	Date	Mintage	Fine	VF	XF	Unc
20	1820	—	20.00	35.00	75.00	170.00

NOTE: Other 80 Reis coins previously listed here are now listed in St. Thomas and Prince Islands.

Similar to 40 Reis, KM#22.

KM#	Date	Mintage	Fine	VF	XF	Unc
23	1840	.010	25.00	45.00	100.00	200.00

ONCA

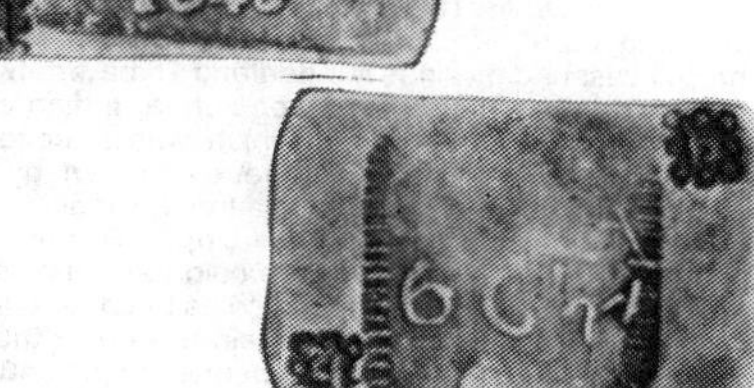

SILVER

Obv: Small date, lettering.

KM#	Date	Mintage	VG	Fine	VF	XF
26.1	1843	—	50.00	150.00	300.00	—

Obv: Large date, lettering.

KM#	Date	Mintage	VG	Fine	VF	XF
26.2	1845	—	70.00	165.00	350.00	—
	1847	—	50.00	150.00	300.00	—

NOTE: Varieties of reverse exist.

1-1/4 MATICAES

7.20 g, GOLD, Rectangular, 11x17mm

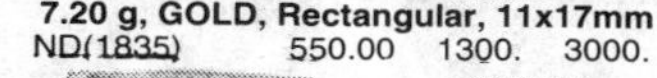

KM#	Date	Mintage	VG	Fine	VF	XF
31	ND(1835)		550.00	1300.	3000.	—

c/m: Rosette on KM#31.

KM#	Date	Mintage	VG	Fine	VF	XF
32	ND(1851)	—	300.00	700.00	1500.	—

2-1/2 MATICAES

14.50 g, GOLD

KM#	Date	Mintage	VG	Fine	VF	XF
33	ND(1835)	—	700.00	1000.	2000.	—

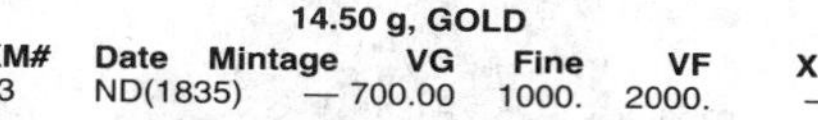

c/m: Rosette on KM#33.

KM#	Date	Mintage	VG	Fine	VF	XF
34	ND(1851)	—	250.00	450.00	750.00	—

COUNTERMARKED COINAGE

Decree of January 5, 1889

This decree ordained that all foreign silver coinage circulating in Mozambique was to be countermarked with a crowned PM within a circle. These coins were eventually to be replaced or exchanged by current Portuguese coinage upon their entry into the public treasury. The following list is a basic guide. Caution should be exercised as counterfeits exist. Grades noted are for the basic coin as the countermark is normally found in better condition than the coin bearing it.

6 PENCE

.925 SILVER

c/m: Crowned PM on Great Britain 6 Pence, KM#751.

KM#	Date	Year	Good	VG	Fine	VF
35	ND	1870	25.00	40.00	65.00	100.00

SHILLING

.925 SILVER

c/m: Crowned PM on Great Britain 1 Shilling, KM#734.

KM#	Date	Year	Good	VG	Fine	VF
36	ND	1860	25.00	40.00	65.00	100.00

1/2 RUPEE

.917 SILVER

KM#	Date	Year	Good	VG	Fine	VF
	c/m: Crowned PM on India 1/2 Rupee, KM#455.					
A37	ND	1840	12.50	20.00	35.00	60.00
	c/m: Crowned PM on India 1/2 Rupee, KM#456.					
37	ND	1840	12.50	20.00	35.00	60.00
	c/m: Crowned PM on India 1/2 Rupee, KM#472.					
A38	ND	(1862-76)	10.00	15.00	28.00	45.00
	c/m: Crowned PM on India 1/2 Rupee, KM#491.					
38	ND	(1877-88)	10.00	15.00	28.00	45.00

RUPEE

.917 SILVER

KM#	Date	Year	Good	VG	Fine	VF
	c/m: Crowned PM on India Rupee, KM#450.					
39	ND	1835	35.00	60.00	100.00	150.00
	c/m: Crowned PM on India Rupee, KM#457.					
A40	ND	1840	20.00	30.00	50.00	85.00
	c/m: Crowned PM on India Rupee, KM#458.					
40	ND	1840	20.00	30.00	50.00	85.00
	c/m: Crowned PM on India Rupee, KM#473.					
A41	ND	(1862-76)	10.00	15.00	28.00	45.00

KM#	Date	Year	Good	VG	Fine	VF
	c/m: Crowned PM on India Rupee, KM#492.					
41	ND	(1877-88)	10.00	15.00	28.00	45.00
	c/m: Crowned PM on India-Portuguese Rupia, KM#12.					
42	ND	1881-82	20.00	30.00	50.00	85.00
	c/m: Crowned PM on Mombasa Rupee, KM#5.					
43	ND	1888	25.00	37.50	62.50	100.00

8 REALES

SILVER

c/m: Crowned PM on Mexico 8 Reales, KM#377.

KM#	Date	Year	Good	VG	Fine	VF
44	ND	(1825-88)	40.00	75.00	125.00	200.00

THALER

SILVER

KM#	Date	Year	Good	VG	Fine	VF
	c/m: Crowned PM on Austria Maria Theresa Thaler, KM#T1.					
45	ND	1780	25.00	40.00	65.00	125.00
	c/m: Crowned PM on Austria-Graz Thaler, KM#464.					
AA46	ND	(1806-10)	30.00	50.00	80.00	160.00
	c/m: Crowned PM on Austria Thaler, KM#473.					
A46	ND	(1811-15)	30.00	50.00	80.00	160.00

KM#	Date	Year	Good	VG	Fine	VF
	c/m: Crowned PM on Austria Thaler, KM#493.					
46	ND	(1817-24)	30.00	50.00	80.00	160.00
	c/m: Crowned PM on Austria Thaler, KM#494.					
47	ND	(1824-30)	30.00	50.00	80.00	160.00

Decree of January 19, 1889

1889-1895

During the reign of D. Carlos I, a substitution of an indented PM (Provincia de Mocambique) which replaced the crowned PM of D. Luis I, was countermarked on all foreign silver coinage circulating in Mozambique. These coins were to be replaced or exchanged by Portuguese coinage on their entry into the public treasury.

1/4 RUPEE

.917 SILVER

KM#	Date	Year	Good	VG	Fine	VF
	c/m: PM on India 1/4 Rupee, KM#470.					
A48	ND	(1862-76)	15.00	22.50	37.50	65.00
	c/m: PM on India 1/4 Rupee, KM#490.					
48	ND	(1877-88)	15.00	22.50	37.50	65.00

1/2 RUPEE

.917 SILVER

KM#	Date	Year	Good	VG	Fine	VF
	c/m: PM on India 1/2 Rupee, KM#455.					
A49	ND	1840	12.50	20.00	35.00	60.00

KM#	Date	Year	Good	VG	Fine	VF
	c/m: PM on India 1/2 Rupee, KM#456.					
49	ND	1840	12.50	20.00	35.00	60.00
	c/m: PM on India 1/2 Rupee, KM#472.					
50	ND	(1862-76)	10.00	15.00	28.00	45.00
	c/m: PM on German East Africa 1/2 Rupie, KM#4.					
51	ND	1891	40.00	75.00	125.00	200.00

RUPEE

.917 SILVER

c/m: PM on India Rupee, KM#450.

KM#	Date	Year	Good	VG	Fine	VF
52	ND	1835	35.00	60.00	100.00	150.00

c/m: PM on India Rupee, KM#457.

KM#	Date	Year	Good	VG	Fine	VF
A53	ND	1840	20.00	30.00	50.00	85.00

c/m: PM on India Rupee, KM#458.

KM#	Date	Year	Good	VG	Fine	VF
53	ND	1840	20.00	30.00	50.00	85.00

c/m: PM on India Rupee, KM#473.

KM#	Date	Good	VG	Fine	VF
A54	ND (1862-76)	20.00	30.00	50.00	85.00

c/m: PM on India Rupee, KM#492.

KM#	Date	Good	VG	Fine	VF
54	ND (1877-88)	20.00	30.00	50.00	85.00

c/m: PM on India-Portuguese Rupia, KM#12.

KM#	Date	Year	Good	VG	Fine	VF
55	ND	1881	20.00	30.00	50.00	85.00

c/m: PM on Mombasa Rupee, KM#5.

KM#	Date	Year	Good	VG	Fine	VF
56	ND	1888	25.00	37.50	62.50	100.00

c/m: PM on German East Africa Rupie, KM#2.

KM#	Date	Good	VG	Fine	VF
57	ND (1890-94)	40.00	75.00	125.00	200.00

THALER

SILVER

c/m: PM on Austria Maria Theresa Thaler, KM#T1.

KM#	Date	Year	Good	VG	Fine	VF
58	ND	1780	25.00	40.00	65.00	125.00

c/m: PM on Austria Thaler, KM#473.

KM#	Date	Good	VG	Fine	VF
59	ND (1817-24)	30.00	50.00	80.00	160.00

c/m: PM on Austria Thaler, KM#494.

KM#	Date	Good	VG	Fine	VF
60	ND (1824-30)	30.00	50.00	80.00	160.00

PRIVATE TOKEN ISSUES

Companhia Do Nyassa

10 REIS

COPPER

KM#	Date	Mintage	Fine	VF	XF	Unc
Tn1	1894H	.508	—	—	250.00	450.00

20 REIS

COPPER

KM#	Date	Mintage	Fine	VF	XF	Unc
Tn2	1894H	.423	—	—	200.00	400.00

500 REIS

SILVER

KM#	Date	Mintage	Fine	VF	XF	Unc
Tn3	1894H	—	—	—	2000.	3500.

1000 REIS

SILVER

KM#	Date	Mintage	Fine	VF	XF	Unc
Tn4	1894H	—	—	—	6000.	—

BRONZE

KM#	Date	Mintage	Fine	VF	XF	Unc
Tn4a	1894H	—	—	—	—	—

NOTE: The above issues were produced at the Birmingham Mint to match the standards of the coins circulating in Portugal.

Listings For

MUKALLA: refer to Yemen Democratic Republic

MYANMAR

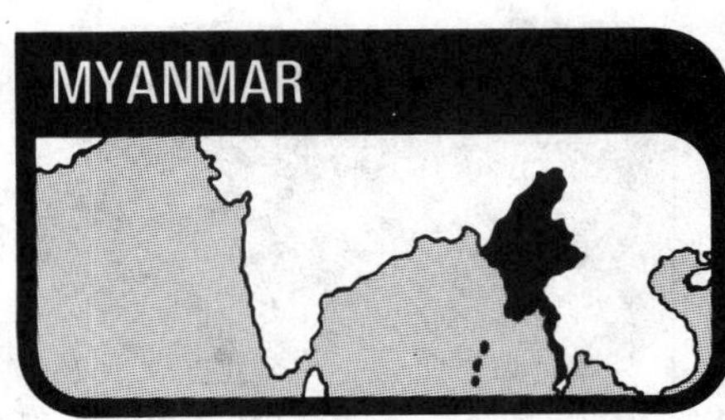

The Union of Myanmar, formerly Burma, a country of Southeast Asia fronting on the Bay of Bengal and the Andaman Sea, has an area of 261,218 sq. mi. (678,500 sq. km.) and a population of 38.8 million. Capital: Yangon (Rangoon). Myanmar is an agricultural country heavily dependent on its leading product (rice) which occupies two-thirds of the cultivated area and accounts for 40 per cent of the value of exports. Mineral resources are extensive, but production is low. Petroleum, lead, tin, silver, zinc, nickel cobalt, and precious stones are exported.

The first European to reach Burma, about 1435, was Nicolo Di Conti, a merchant of Venice. During the beginning of the reign of Bodawpaya (1781-1819AD) the kingdom comprised most of the same area as it does today including Arakan which was taken over in 1784-85. The British East India Company, while unsuccessful in its 1612 effort to establish posts along the Bay of Bengal, was enabled by the Anglo-Burmese Wars of 1824-86 to expand to the whole of Burma and to secure its annexation to British India. In 1937, Burma was separated from India, becoming a separate British colony with limited self-government. Burma became an independent nation outside the British Commonwealth on Jan. 4, 1948, the constitution of 1948 providing for a parliamentary democracy and the nationalization of certain industries. However, political and economic problems persisted, and on March 2, 1962, Gen. Ne Win took over the government, suspended the constitution, installed himself as chief of state, and pursued a socialistic program with nationalization of nearly all industry and trade. On Jan. 4, 1974, a new constitution adopted by referendum established Burma as a 'socialist republic' under one-party rule. The country name was changed to Myanmar in 1989.

The coins issued by kings Mindon and Thibaw between 1852 and 1885 circulated in Upper Burma. Indian coins were current in Lower Burma, which was annexed in 1852. Burmese coins are frequently known by the equivalent Indian denominations, although their values are inscribed in Burmese units. Upper Burma was annexed in 1885 and the Burmese coinage remained in circulation until 1889, when Indian coins became current throughout Burma. Coins were again issued in the old Burmese denominations after independence in 1948, but these were replaced by decimal issues in 1952. The Chula-Sakarat (CS) dating is sometimes referred to as BE-Burmese Era and began in 638AD.

RULERS

Bodawpaya, CS1143-1181/1782-1819AD

Bagyidaw, CS1181-1198/1819-1837AD

Tharawaddy, CS1198-1207/1837-46AD

Pagan, CS1207-1214/1846-53AD

Mindon, CS1214-1240/1853-78AD

Thibaw, CS1240-1248/1880-85AD

British, 1886-1948

MONETARY SYSTEM

(Until 1952)

4 Pyas = 1 Pe
2 Pe = 1 Mu
2 Mu = 1 Mat
5 Mat = 1 Kyat

NOTE: Originally 10 light Mu = 1 Kyat, eventually 8 heavy Mu = 1 Kyat.

Indian Equivalents

1 Silver Kyat = 1 Rupee = 16 Annas
1 Gold Kyat = 1 Mohur = 16 Rupees

1/8 PYA

LEAD

KM#	Date	Year	Good	VG	Fine	VF
22.1	BE1230	(1868)	—	—	Rare	—

Obv: Legend closer together.

KM#	Date	Year	Good	VG	Fine	VF
22.2	BE1231	(1869)	30.00	50.00	75.00	125.00

1/4 PYA

LEAD, 21-22mm
Obv: Hare crouching left. Rev: Leg. in wreath.

KM#	Date	Year	Good	VG	Fine	VF
23	CS1231	(1869)	25.00	40.00	60.00	100.00

1/4 PE

(Pice)

COPPER

KM#	Date	Year	Good	VG	Fine	VF
17	CS1227	(1865)	2.50	4.50	7.50	13.50

Rev: W/o stars above and below leg.

KM#	Date	Year	Good	VG	Fine	VF
18	CS1227	(1865)	2.50	4.50	7.50	15.00

IRON

KM#	Date	Year	Good	VG	Fine	VF
18a	CS1227	(1865)	22.50	35.00	55.00	85.00

COPPER
Rev: Flower petals at top of wreath upright.

KM#	Date	Year	Good	VG	Fine	VF
25.1	CS1240	(1878)	2.50	4.50	10.00	25.00

Rev: Flower petals at top of wreath diagonal.

KM#	Date	Year	Good	VG	Fine	VF
25.2	CS1240	(1878)	2.50	4.50	10.00	25.00

BRASS

KM#	Date	Year	Good	VG	Fine	VF
25a	CS1240	(1878)	7.50	12.50	22.50	35.00

TIN

KM#	Date	Year	Good	VG	Fine	VF
25b	CS1240	(1878)	—	—	—	—

2 PYAS

COPPER, 31mm, 10.94 g

KM#	Date	Year	Good	VG	Fine	VF
24	CS1231	(1869)	17.50	30.00	50.00	75.00

PE

0.7300 g, .917 SILVER, .0215 oz ASW

KM#	Date	Year	Fine	VF	XF	Unc
6.1	CS1214	(1852)	12.50	27.50	60.00	100.00

Accent mark omitted from value.

KM#	Date	Year	Fine	VF	XF	Unc
6.2	CS1214	(1852)	12.50	27.50	60.00	100.00

Figure J omitted from date.

KM#	Date	Year	Fine	VF	XF	Unc
6.3	CS1214	(1852)	12.50	27.50	60.00	100.00

2 dots omitted from value.

KM#	Date	Year	Fine	VF	XF	Unc
6.4	CS1214	(1852)	12.50	27.50	60.00	100.00

Accent marks and 2 dots omitted.

KM#	Date	Year	Fine	VF	XF	Unc
6.5	CS1214	(1852)	12.50	27.50	60.00	100.00

MU

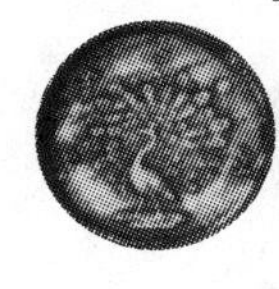

1.4580 g, .917 SILVER, .0430 oz ASW

KM#	Date	Year	Fine	VF	XF	Unc
7.1	CS1214	(1852)	5.00	10.00	17.50	90.00

Rev: Dot above top left character in denomination.

KM#	Date	Year	Fine	VF	XF	Unc
7.2	CS1214	(1852)	—	—	Proof	450.00

MAT

2.9160 g, .917 SILVER, .0860 oz ASW

KM#	Date	Year	Fine	VF	XF	Unc
8.1	CS1214	(1852)	7.50	12.50	50.00	100.00
	1214	(1852)	—	—	Proof	—

Tail omitted from last digit of date.

KM#	Date	Year	Fine	VF	XF	Unc
8.2	CS1214	(1852)	7.50	12.50	50.00	100.00

5 MU

(1/2 Rupee)

5.8319 g, .917 SILVER, .1718 oz ASW

KM#	Date	Year	Fine	VF	XF	Unc
9	CS1214	(1852)	12.50	22.50	70.00	150.00
	CS1214	(1852)	—	—	Proof	—

KYAT

(Rupee)

11.6638 g, .917 SILVER, .3436 oz ASW

KM#	Date	Year	Fine	VF	XF	Unc
10	CS1214	(1852)	7.50	12.50	35.00	150.00
	CS1214	(1852)	—	—	Proof	—

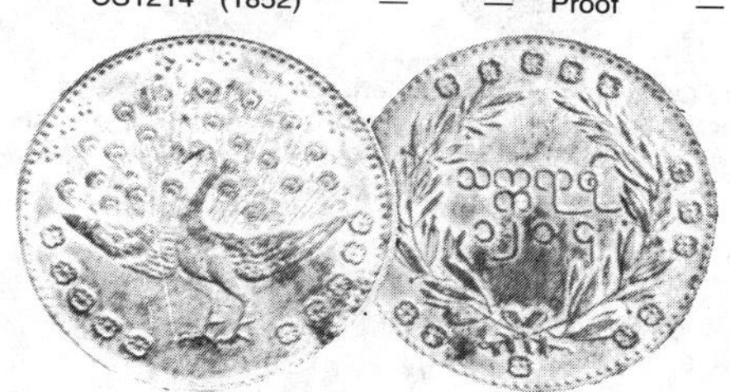

SILVER, 16.23 g
Obv: Peacock w/spread tail, flanked by two groups of 5 rosettes.

KM#	Date	Year	Good	VG	Fine	VF
11	CS1214	(1852)	150.00	350.00	500.00	850.00

Obv: Peacock in full display w/circular feather ends.

KM#	Date	Year	Good	VG	Fine	VF
12	CS1214	(1852)	250.00	500.00	1000.	1500.

SILVER, 39mm, 16.45 g
Obv: Shwepyizoe bird. Rev: Leg. above date.

KM#	Date	Year	Good	VG	Fine	VF
15	BE2396	(1853)	—	—	—	—

SILVER, 32mm, 15.75 g
Obv: Peacock w/folded tail flanked by floral garlands.

KM#	Date	Year	Good	VG	Fine	VF
16	CS1222	(1860)	—	—	—	—

PE

.900 GOLD
Obv: Facing peacock. Rev: Value in sprays.

KM#	Date	Year	Good	VG	Fine	VF
13	CS1214	(1852)	35.00	60.00	85.00	135.00

GOLD, 0.67 g

KM#	Date	Year	Good	VG	Fine	VF
19	CS1228	(1866)	35.00	60.00	95.00	175.00

MU

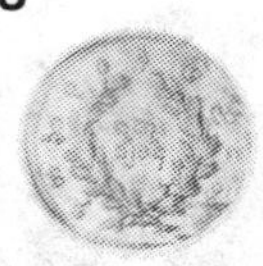

.900 GOLD
Obv: Facing peacock. Rev: Value in wreath.

KM#	Date	Year	Good	VG	Fine	VF
14	CS1214	(1852)	60.00	100.00	150.00	200.00

14mm, 1.26 g
Obv: Chinze standing left. Rev: Value in sprays.

KM#	Date	Year	VG	Fine	VF	XF
A20	CS1228	(1866)	1000.	1500.	2000.	—

2 MU 1 PE

GOLD, 2.75 g
Obv: Chinze.

KM#	Date	Year	VG	Fine	VF	XF
20	CS1228	(1866)	125.00	175.00	250.00	450.00

5 MU

(1/2 Mohur)

GOLD, 5.85 g
Obv: Chinze.

KM#	Date	Year	VG	Fine	VF	XF
26	CS1240	(1878)	—	—	Rare	—

KYAT

(Mohur)

GOLD, 11.94 g
Obv: Chinze.

KM#	Date	Year	VG	Fine	VF	XF
21	CS1228	(1866)	—	—	Rare	—

REPUBLIC

PATTERNS (Pn)

(Including off metal strikes)

KM#	Date	Mintage	Identification	Mkt.Val.
Pn1	CS1214	—	Pe, Silver, obv. stippled field	500.00

KM#	Date	Mintage	Identification	Mkt.Val.
Pn2	CS1214	—	Mu, Silver, obv. stippled field	400.00
Pn3	CS1214	—	Mat, Silver, obv. stippled field	450.00

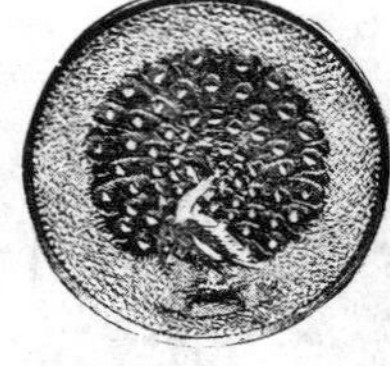

KM#	Date	Mintage	Identification	Mkt.Val.
Pn4	CS1214	—	5 Mu, Silver, obv. stippled field	650.00
Pn5	CS1214	—	5 Mu, Copper, KM9	—

KM#	Date	Mintage	Identification	Mkt.Val.
Pn6	CS1214	—	Kyat, Silver, obv. stippled field	750.00
Pn7	CS1214	—	Kyat, Gold, KM10, restrike	—

KM#	Date	Mintage	Identification	Mkt.Val.
Pn8	CS1214	*3 pcs.	Kyat, Silver	1000.
Pn9	CS1214	—	Kyat, Copper	800.00

NEPAL

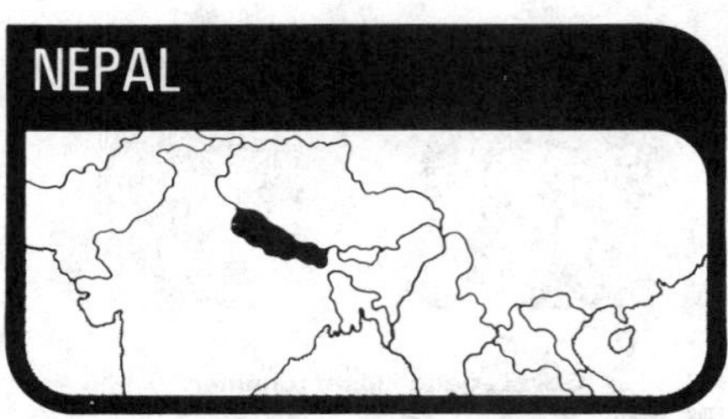

The Kingdom of Nepal, the world's only surviving Hindu kingdom, is a landlocked country occupying the southern slopes of the Himalayas. It has an area of 56,136 sq. mi. (140,800 sq. km.) and a population of 18 million. Capital: Kathmandu. Nepal has deposits of coal, copper, iron and cobalt, but they are largely unexploited. Agriculture is the principal economic activity. Rice, timber and jute are exported, with tourism being the other major foreign exchange earner.

Apart from a brief Muslim invasion in the 14th century, Nepal was able to avoid the mainstream of Northern Indian politics, due to its impregnable position in the mountains. It is therefore a unique survivor of the medieval Hindu and Buddhist culture of Northern India which was largely destroyed by the successive waves of Muslim invasions.

Prior to the late 18th century, Nepal, as we know it today, was divided among a number of small states. Unless otherwise stated, the term "Nepal" applies to the small fertile valley, about 4,500 ft. above sea level, in which the three main cities of Kathmandu, Patan and Bhatgaon are situated.

During the reign of King Yaksha Malla (1428-1482AD), the Nepalese kingdom, with capital at Bhatgaon, was extended northwards into Tibet, and also controlled a considerable area to the south of the hills. After Yaksha Malla's death, the Kingdom was divided among his sons, so four kingdoms were established with capitals at Bhatgaon, Patan, Kathmandu and Banepa, all situated within the small valley, less than 20 miles square. Banepa was quickly absorbed within the territory of Bhatgaon, but the other 3 kingdoms remained until 1769. The internecine strife between the 3 kings effectively stopped Nepal from becoming a major military force during this period, although with its fertile land and strategic position, it was by far the wealthiest and most powerful of the Himalayan states.

Apart from agriculture, Nepal owed its prosperity to its position on one of the easiest trade routes between the great monasteries of central Tibet, and India. Nepal made full use of this, and a trading community was set up in Lhasa during the 16th century, and Nepalese coins became the accepted currency medium in Tibet.

The seeds of discord between Nepal and Tibet were sown during the first half of the 18th century, when the Nepalese debased the coinage, and the fate of the Malla kings of Nepal was sealed when Prithvi Narayan Shah, King of the small state of Gorkha, to the west of Kathmandu, was able to gain control of the transhimalayan trade routes during the years after 1750.

Prithvi Narayan spent several years consolidating his position in hill areas before he finally succeeded in conquering the Kathmandu Valley in 1768, where he established the Shah dynasty, and moved his capital to Kathmandu.

After Prithvi Narayan's death a period of political instability ensued which lasted until the 1840's when the Rana family reduced the monarch to a figurehead and established the post of hereditary Prime Minister. A popular revolution in 1950 toppled the Rana family and reconstituted power in the throne. In 1959 King Mahendra declared Nepal a constitutional monarchy, and in 1962 a new constitution set up a system of panchayat (village council) democracy.

DATING

Nepal Samvat Era (NS)

All coins of the Malla kings of Nepal are dated in the Nepal Samvat era (NS). Year 1 NS began in 881, so to arrive at the AD date add 880 to the NS date. This era was exclusive to Nepal, except for one gold coin of Prana Narayan of Cooch Behar.

Saka Era (SE)

Up until 1888AD all coins of the Gorkha Dynasty were dated in the Saka era (SE). To convert from Saka to AD take Saka date + 78 = AD date. Coins dated with this era have SE before the date in the following listing.

Vikrama Samvat Era (VS)

From 1888AD most copper coins were dated in the Vikram Samvat (VS) era. To convert take VS date - 57 = AD date. Coins with this era have VS before the year in the listing. With the exception of a few gold coins struck in 1890 & 1892, silver and gold coins only changed to the VS era in 1911AD, but now this era is used for all coins struck in Nepal.

RULERS

SHAH DYNASTY

Girvan Yuddha Vikrama

गीर्वाण युद्ध विक्रम सा

SE1720-1738/1799-1816AD

Queens of Girvan Yuddha Vikrama: Siddhi Lakshmi

सिद्धि लक्ष्मी

Goraksha Rajya Lakshmi

गोरक्ष राज्य लक्ष्मी

Rajendra Vikrama

राजेन्द्र विक्रम

SE1738-1769/1816-1847AD

Queens of Rajendra Vikrama: Samrajya Lakshmi

साम्राज्य लक्ष्मी

Rajya Lakshmi

राज्य लक्ष्मी

Surendra Vikrama

सुरेन्द्र विक्रम सा

SE1769-1803/1847-1881AD

Queens of Surendra Vikrama: Trailokya Raja Lakshmi

त्रैलोक्य राज्य लक्ष्मी

Sura Raja Lakshmi

सुर राज लक्ष्मी

Deva Raja Lakshmi

देवराज लक्ष्मी

Punyakumari Raja Lakshmi

पुण्यकुमारी राज्य लक्ष्मी

Prithvi Vira Vikrama

पृथ्वी वीर विक्रम

SE1803-1833/1881-1911AD
VS1938-1968/

Queen of Prithvi Vira Vikrama: Lakshmi Divyeswari

लक्ष्मी दिव्येश्वरी

MONETARY SYSTEM

COPPER

Initially the copper paisa was not fixed in value relative to the silver coins, and generally fluctuated in value from 1/32 mohar in 1865AD to around 1/50 mohar after c1880AD, and was fixed at that value in 1903AD.

4 Dam = 1 Paisa
2 Paisa = 1 Dyak, Adhani

GOLD COINAGE

Nepalese gold coinage until recently did not carry any denominations and was traded for silver, etc. at the local bullion exchange rate. The three basic weight standards used in the following listing are distinguished for convenience, although all were known as Asarphi (gold coin) locally as follows:

GOLD MOHAR

5.60 g multiples and fractions

TOLA

12.48 g multiples and fractions

GOLD RUPEE or ASARPHI

11.66 g multiples and fractions
(Reduced to 10.00 g in 1966)

NOTE: In some instances the gold and silver issues were struck from the same dies.

NUMERALS

Nepal has used more variations of numerals on their coins than any other nation. The most common are illustrated in the numeral chart in the introduction. The chart below illustrates some variations encompassing the last four centuries.

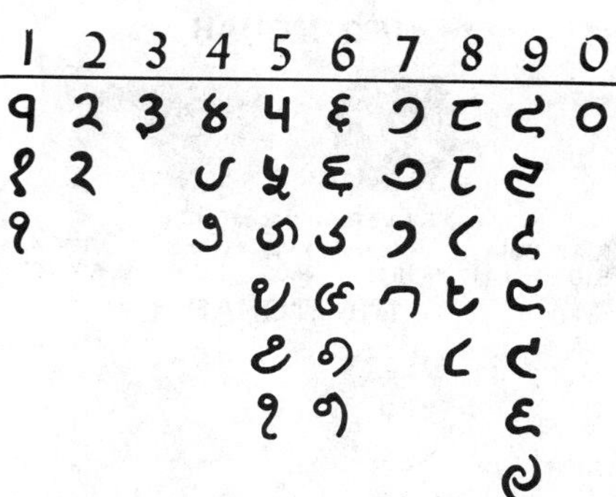

NUMERICS

Half	आधा
One	एक
Two	दुइ
Four	चार
Five	पाच
Ten	दस
Twenty	विस
Twenty-five	पचीस
Fifty	पचास
Hundred	शय

DENOMINATIONS

Paisa	पैसा
Dam	दाम
Mohar	मोहर
Rupee	रुपैयाँ
Ashrapi	असार्फी
Asarfi	अश्रफी

DIE VARIETIES

Although the same dies were usually used both for silver and gold minor denominations, the gold Mohar is easily recognized being less ornate. The following illustrations are of a silver Mohar, KM#602 and a gold Mohar KM#615 issued by Surendra Vikrama Saha Deva in the period SE1769-1803/ 1847-1881AD. Note the similar reverse legend. The obverse usually will start with the character for the word Shri either in single or multiples, the latter as Shri Shri Shri or Shri 3.

OBVERSE

SILVER SE1791 — GOLD SE1793

LEGEND

श्री श्री श्री सुरेन्द्र विक्रम साह देव

Shri Shri Shri Surendra Vikrama Saha Deva (date).

REVERSE

SILVER — GOLD

LEGEND (in center)

श्री ३ भवानी

Shri 3 Bhavani (around outer circle)

श्री श्री श्री गोरषनाथ

Shri Shri Shri Gorakhanatha

SHAH DYNASTY

RANA BAHADUR

SE1699-1720/1777-1799AD

Silver Coinage

1/4 MOHAR

In the name of Queen Raja Rajesvari

SILVER, 1.40 g

KM#	Date	Year	VG	Fine	VF	XF
496	SE1723	(1801)	7.00	10.00	15.00	22.50
	1724	(1802)	7.00	10.00	15.00	22.50

NOTE: Earlier dates (1789-1800) exist for this type.

In the name of Queen Amara Rajesvari

KM#	Date	Year	VG	Fine	VF	XF
497	SE1725	(1802)	50.00	75.00	85.00	100.00

In the name of Queen Suvarna Prabha

KM#	Date	Year	VG	Fine	VF	XF
498	SE1723	(1801)	5.50	9.00	13.50	20.00

In the name of Queen Mahamahesvari

KM#	Date	Year	VG	Fine	VF	XF
499	SE1725	(1803)	65.00	75.00	85.00	100.00

In the name of Queen Lalita Tripura Sundari

KM#	Date	Year	VG	Fine	VF	XF
500	SE1728	(1806)	10.00	13.50	18.50	25.00
	1729	(1807)	10.00	13.50	18.50	25.00
	1738	(1816)	7.00	10.00	15.00	22.50
	1741	(1819)	5.00	8.50	12.50	18.50
	1744	(1822)	10.00	13.50	18.50	25.00

In the name of Queen Lalita Tripura Sundari

3/8 MOHAR

SILVER

KM#	Date	Year	VG	Fine	VF	XF
A501	SE1726	(1804)	250.00	320.00	400.00	500.00

Gold Coinage

1/4 MOHAR

In the name of Queen Raja Rajesvari

GOLD, 1.40 g

KM#	Date	Year	Good	VG	Fine	VF
509	SE1723	(1801)	40.00	50.00	70.00	90.00
	1724	(1802)	40.00	50.00	70.00	90.00

NOTE: Earlier date (1794) exists for this type.

In the name of Queen Amara Rajesvari

KM#	Date	Year	Good	VG	Fine	VF
510	SE1724	(1802)	85.00	100.00	125.00	150.00

In the name of Queen Suvarna Prabha

KM#	Date	Year	Good	VG	Fine	VF
511.1	SE1723	(1801)	40.00	50.00	70.00	90.00

In the name of Queen Mahamahesvari

KM#	Date	Year	Good	VG	Fine	VF
511.2	SE1725	(1803)	150.00	250.00	350.00	500.00

In the name of Queen Lalita Tripura Sundari

KM#	Date	Year	VG	Fine	VF	XF
512	SE1728	(1806)	40.00	50.00	65.00	85.00
	1729	(1807)	40.00	50.00	65.00	85.00
	1741	(1819)	40.00	50.00	65.00	85.00

GIRVAN YUDDHA VIKRAMA

SE1720-1738/1799-1816AD

Copper Coinage

DAM

COPPER, 1.00 g

KM#	Date	Year	VG	Fine	VF	XF
517	VS1861	(1804)	.75	1.25	2.25	3.50

2 DAM

COPPER, 2.00 g

KM#	Date	Year	VG	Fine	VF	XF
A517	VS1861	(1804)	1.50	2.00	4.00	8.00

PAISA

COPPER, 7.60 g

KM#	Date	Year	VG	Fine	VF	XF
C517	VS1859	(1801)	—	7.00	15.00	20.00

2 PAISA

(Dhyak)

COPPER, 20.00 g

KM#	Date	Year	VG	Fine	VF	XF
B517	ND	—	3.00	5.00	10.00	15.00

4 PAISA

(Ganda)

COPPER, 40.00 g

KM#	Date	Year	VG	Fine	VF	XF
D517	ND	—	4.00	6.00	10.00	15.00

Silver Coinage

DAM

Actual Size **2 x Actual Size**

SILVER, uniface, 0.04 g

KM#	Date	Year	VG	Fine	VF	XF
518	ND	(1799-1816)	4.00	8.00	11.50	16.00

1/32 MOHAR

SILVER, uniface, 0.18 g

KM#	Date	Year	VG	Fine	VF	XF
519	ND	(1799-1816)	8.00	13.50	18.50	25.00

1/16 MOHAR

SILVER, 0.35 g

KM#	Date	Year	VG	Fine	VF	XF
520	ND	(1799-1816)	7.50	11.50	16.50	22.50

NOTE: Varieties exist.

1/8 MOHAR

SILVER, 0.70 g
Obv: Shri above sword.

KM#	Date	Year	VG	Fine	VF	XF
521	ND	(1799-1816)	6.00	10.00	13.50	18.50

Obv: Umbrella above sword.

KM#	Date	Year	VG	Fine	VF	XF
522	ND	(1799-1816)	6.00	10.00	13.50	18.50

Obv: Wreath above sword.

KM#	Date	Year	VG	Fine	VF	XF
523	ND	(1799-1816)	6.00	10.00	13.50	18.50

In the name of Queen Siddhi Lakshmi

1/4 MOHAR

SILVER,1.40 g

KM#	Date	Year	VG	Fine	VF	XF
524	SE1730	(1808)	10.00	13.50	18.50	25.00
	1733	(1811)	10.00	13.50	18.50	25.00
	1735	(1813)	10.00	13.50	18.50	25.00

In the name of Queen Goraksha Rajya Lakshmi

KM#	Date	Year	VG	Fine	VF	XF
525	SE1738	(1816)	65.00	75.00	85.00	100.00

1/2 MOHAR

SILVER, 2.77 g

KM#	Date	Year	VG	Fine	VF	XF
526	1728	(1806)	7.50	12.50	20.00	30.00
	1729	(1807)	7.50	12.50	20.00	30.00
	1730	(1808)	5.00	8.50	15.00	22.50
	1733	(1811)	7.50	12.50	20.00	30.00

NOTE: Earlier date (1799) exists for this type.

3/4 MOHAR

SILVER, 4.20 g

KM#	Date	Year	VG	Fine	VF	XF
527	SE1727	(1805)	100.00	200.00	250.00	300.00

MOHAR

SILVER, 5.60 g
Obv: 3 *Shri's* above square.

KM#	Date	Year	VG	Fine	VF	XF
529	SE1723	(1801)	4.50	6.50	9.00	11.50
	1724	(1802)	4.50	6.50	9.00	11.50
	1725	(1803)	4.50	6.50	9.00	11.50
	1728	(1806)	4.50	6.50	9.00	11.50
	1729	(1807)	4.50	6.50	9.00	11.50
	1730	(1808)	4.50	6.50	9.00	11.50
	1731	(1809)	4.50	6.50	9.00	11.50
	1732	(1810)	4.50	6.50	9.00	11.50
	1733	(1811)	4.50	6.50	9.00	11.50
	1734	(1812)	4.50	6.50	9.00	11.50
	1735	(1813)	4.50	6.50	9.00	11.50
	1736	(1814)	4.50	6.50	9.00	11.50
	1737	(1815)	4.50	6.50	9.00	11.50
	1738	(1816)	4.50	6.50	9.00	11.50

NOTE: Earlier dates (1799-1800) exist for this type.

Mule. Obv: KM#547. Rev: KM#529.

KM#	Date	Year	VG	Fine	VF	XF
530	SE1728	(1806)	50.00	80.00	100.00	125.00
	1729	(1807)	50.00	80.00	100.00	125.00

1-1/2 MOHARS

SILVER, 8.40 g

KM#	Date	Year	VG	Fine	VF	XF
531	SE1725	(1803)	25.00	35.00	50.00	75.00
	1726	(1804)	25.00	35.00	50.00	75.00

KM#	Date	Year	VG	Fine	VF	XF
532	SE1727	(1805)	75.00	125.00	175.00	250.00

3 MOHARS

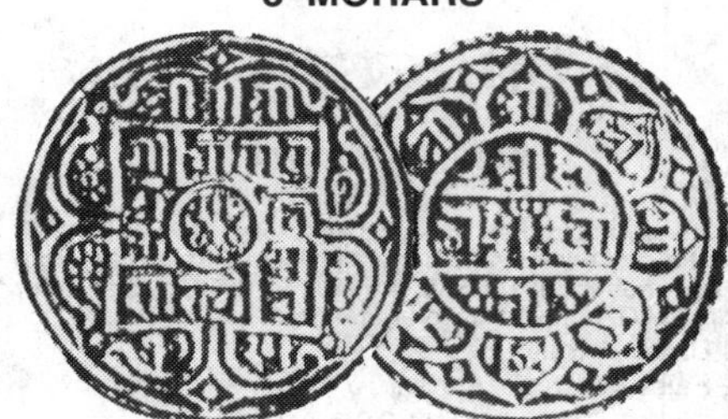

SILVER, 16.80 g
Obv: Flourishes outside central legend.

KM#	Date	Year	VG	Fine	VF	XF
A533	SE1725	(1803)	—	150.00	200.00	250.00

Obv: W/o flourishes outside central legend.

KM#	Date	Year	VG	Fine	VF	XF
533	SE1725	(1803)	—	150.00	200.00	250.00

Similar to 1-1/2 Mohars, KM#532.

KM#	Date	Year	VG	Fine	VF	XF
534	SE1726	(1804)	—	200.00	300.00	400.00

Gold Coinage

DAM

GOLD, uniface, 0.044 g

KM#	Date	Year	VG	Fine	VF	XF
535	ND	(1799-1816)	10.00	14.00	20.00	30.00

1/32 MOHAR

GOLD, uniface, 0.175 g

KM#	Date	Year	VG	Fine	VF	XF
536	ND	(1799-1816)	14.00	20.00	25.00	40.00

1/16 MOHAR

GOLD, 0.35 g

KM#	Date	Year	VG	Fine	VF	XF
537	ND	(1799-1816)	14.00	20.00	25.00	40.00

NOTE: Three varieties exist.

1/8 MOHAR

GOLD, 0.70 g
Obv: *Shri* above sword.

KM#	Date	Year	VG	Fine	VF	XF
538	ND	(1799-1816)	22.50	27.50	40.00	60.00

Obv: Umbrella above sword.

KM#	Date	Year	VG	Fine	VF	XF
539	ND	(1799-1816)	22.50	27.50	40.00	60.00

In the name of Queen Siddhi Lakshmi

1/4 MOHAR

GOLD, 1.40 g

KM#	Date	Year	VG	Fine	VF	XF
540.1	SE1730	(1808)	40.00	50.00	65.00	85.00

KM#	Date	Year	VG	Fine	VF	XF
540.3	SE1732	(1810)	40.00	50.00	65.00	85.00
	1733	(1811)	40.00	50.00	65.00	85.00

KM#	Date	Year	VG	Fine	VF	XF
540.4	SE1736	(1814)	40.00	50.00	65.00	85.00

In the name of Queen Goraksha Rajyalakshmi

KM#	Date	Year	VG	Fine	VF	XF
540.2	SE1738	(1816)	120.00	150.00	170.00	200.00

1/2 MOHAR

GOLD, 2.80 g

KM#	Date	Year	VG	Fine	VF	XF
541	SE1728	(1806)	70.00	80.00	100.00	125.00
	1729	(1807)	70.00	80.00	100.00	125.00
	1730	(1808)	70.00	80.00	100.00	125.00

NOTE: Earlier date (1799) exists for this type.

KM#	Date	Year	VG	Fine	VF	XF
542	SE1732	(1810)	150.00	200.00	250.00	300.00
	1733	(1811)	150.00	200.00	250.00	300.00
543	SE1736	(1814)	150.00	200.00	250.00	300.00

MOHAR

GOLD, 5.60 g
Similar to KM#529.

KM#	Date	Year	VG	Fine	VF	XF
544	SE1723	(1801)	125.00	150.00	175.00	200.00
	1724	(1802)	125.00	150.00	175.00	200.00
	1728	(1806)	125.00	150.00	175.00	200.00

NOTE: Earlier date (1799) exists for this type.

Obv: Square in center.

KM#	Date	Year	VG	Fine	VF	XF
546	SE1733	(1811)	150.00	175.00	225.00	250.00

1-1/2 MOHARS

GOLD, 8.40 g

KM#	Date	Year	VG	Fine	VF	XF
547	SE1726	(1804)	185.00	225.00	275.00	350.00
	1728	(1806)	185.00	225.00	275.00	350.00
	1729	(1807)	185.00	225.00	275.00	350.00

Rev: Hexagon.

KM#	Date	Year	VG	Fine	VF	XF
548	SE1736	(1814)	185.00	225.00	275.00	350.00

2 MOHARS

GOLD, 11.20 g
Obv: Square in center.

KM#	Date	Year	VG	Fine	VF	XF
550	SE1733	(1811)	250.00	275.00	325.00	375.00

PRESENTATION ISSUES

In the name of Queen Goraksha Rajya Lakshmi

RUPEE

GOLD, 11.66 g

KM#	Date	Year	VG	Fine	VF	XF
551	SE1735	(1813)	400.00	500.00	550.00	600.00

RAJENDRA VIKRAMA

SE1738-1769/1816-1847AD

Silver Coinage

DAM

Actual Size 2 x Actual Size

SILVER, uniface, 0.04 g

KM#	Date	Year	VG	Fine	VF	XF
553	ND	(1816-47)	4.00	6.00	8.00	12.50

1/32 MOHAR

SILVER, uniface, 0.18 g

KM#	Date	Year	VG	Fine	VF	XF
554	ND	(1816-47)	5.50	9.00	12.50	17.50

1/16 MOHAR

SILVER, 0.35 g

KM#	Date	Year	VG	Fine	VF	XF
555	ND	(1816-47)	5.00	8.50	12.00	17.00

1/8 MOHAR

SILVER, 0.70 g
Obv: *Shri* above sword.

KM#	Date	Year	VG	Fine	VF	XF
556	ND	(1816-47)	3.00	5.00	8.50	15.00

Obv: Umbrella above sword.

KM#	Date	Year	VG	Fine	VF	XF
557	ND	(1816-47)	3.00	5.00	8.50	15.00

In the name of Queen Samrajya Lakshmi

1/4 MOHAR

SILVER, 1.40 g

KM#	Date	Year	VG	Fine	VF	XF
558	SE1745	(1823)	8.50	12.50	18.50	25.00
	1746	(1824)	5.00	8.50	12.50	18.50
	1753	(1831)	5.00	8.50	12.50	18.50
	1755	(1833)	5.00	8.50	12.50	18.50

KM#	Date	Year	VG	Fine	VF	XF
559	SE1746	(1824)	5.00	8.50	12.50	18.50
	1759	(1837)	5.00	8.50	12.50	18.50

Obv: Wreath above vase.

KM#	Date	Year	VG	Fine	VF	XF
560	SE1746	(1824)	5.00	8.50	12.50	18.50
	1753	(1831)	5.00	8.50	12.50	18.50
	1759	(1837)	5.00	8.50	12.50	18.50

In the name of Queen Rajya Lakshmi

KM#	Date	Year	VG	Fine	VF	XF
561.1	SE1764	(1842)	8.50	12.50	18.50	25.00
	1766	(1844)	8.50	12.50	18.50	25.00
	1767	(1845)	8.50	12.50	18.50	25.00

Struck w/gold dies. Rev: Circle.

KM#	Date	Year	VG	Fine	VF	XF
561.2	SE1764	(1842)	30.00	40.00	55.00	75.00

1/2 MOHAR

SILVER, 2.80 g
Mule. Obv: KM#563. Rev: KM#526.

KM#	Date	Year	VG	Fine	VF	XF
562	SE1730	(1808)	15.00	25.00	40.00	60.00

KM#	Date	Year	VG	Fine	VF	XF
563	SE1738	(1816)	3.50	6.50	10.00	15.00
	1744	(1822)	7.50	12.50	20.00	30.00
	1746	(1824)	4.50	7.50	12.50	17.50

KM#	Date	Year	VG	Fine	VF	XF
564	SE1746	(1824)	3.50	6.50	10.00	15.00
	1753	(1831)	3.50	6.50	10.00	15.00
	1755	(1833)	3.50	6.50	10.00	15.00
	1757	(1835)	3.50	6.50	10.00	15.00

KM#	Date	Year	VG	Fine	VF	XF
564	1759	(1837)	3.50	6.50	10.00	15.00
	1762	(1840)	3.50	7.50	12.50	16.50
	1764	(1842)	3.50	7.50	12.00	16.50
	1765	(1843)	3.50	7.50	12.00	16.50
	1766	(1844)	3.50	7.50	12.00	16.50

MOHAR

SILVER, 5.60 g
Rev: Moon and sun.

KM#	Date	Year	VG	Fine	VF	XF
565.1	SE1738	(1816)	50.00	90.00	120.00	150.00

KM#	Date	Year	VG	Fine	VF	XF
565.2	SE1738	(1816)	4.50	6.50	9.00	11.50
	1739	(1817)	4.50	6.50	9.00	11.50
	1740	(1818)	4.50	6.50	9.00	11.50
	1741	(1819)	4.50	6.50	9.00	11.50
	1742	(1820)	4.50	6.50	9.00	11.50
	1743	(1821)	4.50	6.50	9.00	11.50
	1744	(1822)	4.50	6.50	9.00	11.50
	1745	(1823)	4.50	6.50	9.00	11.50
	1746	(1824)	4.50	6.50	9.00	11.50
	1747	(1825)	4.50	6.50	9.00	11.50
	1748	(1826)	4.50	6.50	9.00	11.50
	1749	(1827)	4.50	6.50	9.00	11.50
	1750	(1828)	4.50	6.50	9.00	11.50
	1751	(1829)	4.50	6.50	9.00	11.50
	1752	(1830)	4.50	6.50	9.00	11.50
	1753	(1831)	4.50	6.50	9.00	11.50
	1754	(1832)	4.50	6.50	9.00	11.50
	1755	(1833)	4.50	6.50	9.00	11.50
	1756	(1834)	4.50	6.50	9.00	11.50
	1757	(1835)	4.50	6.50	9.00	11.50
	1758	(1836)	4.50	6.50	9.00	11.50
	1759	(1837)	4.50	6.50	9.00	11.50
	1760	(1838)	4.50	6.50	9.00	11.50
	1761	(1839)	7.00	10.00	13.50	17.50
	1762	(1840)	7.00	10.00	13.50	17.50
	1764	(1842)	4.50	6.50	9.00	11.50
	1765	(1843)	7.00	10.00	13.50	17.50
	1766	(1844)	4.50	6.50	9.00	11.50
	1767	(1845)	4.50	6.50	9.00	11.50
	1768	(1846)	4.50	7.50	12.50	16.50
	1769	(1847)	7.00	10.00	13.50	17.50

Obv: ***Sri 3*** **at top.**

KM#	Date	Year	VG	Fine	VF	XF
566	SE1740	(1818)	7.00	10.00	13.50	17.50

Obv: Ornamentation reversed.

KM#	Date	Year	VG	Fine	VF	XF
567	SE1762	(1840)	7.00	10.00	13.50	17.50

2 MOHARS

SILVER, 11.20 g

KM#	Date	Year	VG	Fine	VF	XF
568	SE1738	(1816)	25.00	35.00	50.00	75.00
	1740	(1818)	25.00	35.00	50.00	75.00
	1742	(1820)	25.00	35.00	50.00	75.00
	1743	(1821)	25.00	35.00	50.00	75.00
	1744	(1822)	25.00	35.00	50.00	75.00
	1753	(1831)	25.00	35.00	50.00	75.00
	1757	(1835)	25.00	35.00	50.00	75.00
	1764	(1842)	25.00	35.00	50.00	75.00

Gold Coinage

DAM

GOLD, uniface, 0.04 g

KM#	Date	Year	VG	Fine	VF	XF
569	ND	(1816-47)	10.00	14.00	20.00	30.00

1/32 MOHAR

GOLD, uniface, 0.18 g

KM#	Date	Year	VG	Fine	VF	XF
570	ND	(1816-47)	14.00	20.00	25.00	40.00

1/16 MOHAR

GOLD, 0.35 g

KM#	Date	Year	VG	Fine	VF	XF
571	ND	(1816-47)	14.00	20.00	25.00	40.00

1/8 MOHAR

GOLD, 0.70 g

KM#	Date	Year	VG	Fine	VF	XF
572	ND	(1816-47)	22.50	27.50	35.00	50.00

In the name of Queen Samrajya Lakshmi

1/4 MOHAR

GOLD, 1.40 g

KM#	Date	Year	VG	Fine	VF	XF
573.1	SE1746	(1824)	40.00	50.00	65.00	85.00
	1757	(1835)	40.00	50.00	65.00	85.00
	1758	(1836)	40.00	50.00	65.00	85.00
	1759	(1837)	40.00	50.00	65.00	85.00

NOTE: Varieties exist.

KM#	Date	Year	VG	Fine	VF	XF
573.2	SE1757	(1835)	40.00	50.00	65.00	85.00

In the name of Queen Rajya Lakshmi

KM#	Date	Year	VG	Fine	VF	XF
574	SE1764	(1842)	40.00	50.00	65.00	85.00

1/2 MOHAR

GOLD, 2.80 g

KM#	Date	Year	VG	Fine	VF	XF
575	SE1741	(1819)	150.00	200.00	250.00	300.00

KM#	Date	Year	VG	Fine	VF	XF
576	SE1744	(1822)	65.00	75.00	85.00	100.00
	1746	(1824)	65.00	75.00	85.00	100.00
	1753	(1831)	65.00	75.00	85.00	100.00

KM#	Date	Year	VG	Fine	VF	XF
577	SE1757	(1835)	65.00	75.00	85.00	100.00

KM#	Date	Year	VG	Fine	VF	XF
578	SE1757	(1835)	65.00	75.00	85.00	100.00
	1758	(1836)	65.00	75.00	85.00	100.00
	1762	(1840)	65.00	75.00	85.00	100.00
	1764	(1842)	65.00	75.00	85.00	100.00
	1766	(1844)	65.00	75.00	85.00	100.00

MOHAR

GOLD, 24mm, 5.60 g
Obv: Square in center.

KM#	Date	Year	VG	Fine	VF	XF
579	SE1738	(1816)	125.00	150.00	175.00	200.00

27mm
Obv: Circle in center.

KM#	Date	Year	VG	Fine	VF	XF
580	SE1741	(1819)	125.00	150.00	175.00	200.00
	1758	(1836)	125.00	150.00	175.00	200.00
	1760	(1838)	125.00	150.00	175.00	200.00
	1764	(1842)	125.00	150.00	175.00	200.00
	1766	(1844)	125.00	150.00	175.00	200.00
	1768	(1846)	125.00	150.00	175.00	200.00

27mm
Obv: Square in center.

KM#	Date	Year	VG	Fine	VF	XF
581	SE1746	(1824)	135.00	160.00	200.00	250.00
	1757	(1835)	135.00	160.00	200.00	250.00

2 MOHARS

GOLD, 11.20 g

KM#	Date	Year	VG	Fine	VF	XF
582	SE1738	(1816)	250.00	275.00	325.00	375.00
	1741	(1819)	250.00	275.00	325.00	375.00
	1768	(1846)	250.00	275.00	325.00	375.00

Obv: Square in center.

KM#	Date	Year	VG	Fine	VF	XF
583	SE1746	(1824)	250.00	275.00	325.00	375.00
	1757	(1835)	— Reported, not confirmed			

PRESENTATION ISSUES

In the name of Rajendra Vikrama

RUPEE

GOLD, 11.66 g

KM#	Date	Year	VG	Fine	VF	XF
584	SE1759	(1837)	400.00	500.00	550.00	600.00

2 RUPEES

GOLD, 23.32 g

KM#	Date	Year	VG	Fine	VF	XF
585	SE1762	(1840)	750.00	1000.	1250.	1500.

SURENDRA VIKRAMA

SE1769-1803/1847-1881AD

Copper Coinage

DAM

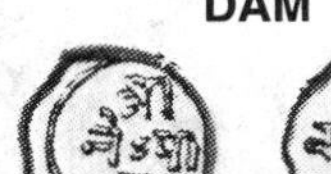

COPPER

KM#	Date	Year	Good	VG	Fine	VF
586	SE(17)88	(1866)	2.00	3.50	5.00	7.50
	(17)90	(1868)	.75	1.25	2.25	3.50
	(17)91	(1869)	.75	1.25	2.25	3.50
	(17)92	(1870)	.75	1.25	2.25	3.50
	(17)93	(1871)	.75	1.25	2.25	3.50

KM#	Date	Year	Good	VG	Fine	VF
586	(17)94	(1872)	.75	1.25	2.25	3.50
	(17)96	(1874)	.75	1.25	2.25	3.50
	(17)97	(1875)	.75	1.25	2.25	3.50
	(17)98	(1876)	.75	1.25	2.25	3.50
	(17)99	(1877)	.75	1.25	2.25	3.50
	(18)02	(1880)	— Reported, not confirmed			

Machine struck

KM#	Date	Year	Good	VG	Fine	VF
586.1	SE(17)90	(1868)	30.00	45.00	85.00	175.00

1/2 PAISA

COPPER

KM#	Date	Year	Good	VG	Fine	VF
587	SE1802	(1880)	20.00	30.00	35.00	50.00

PAISA

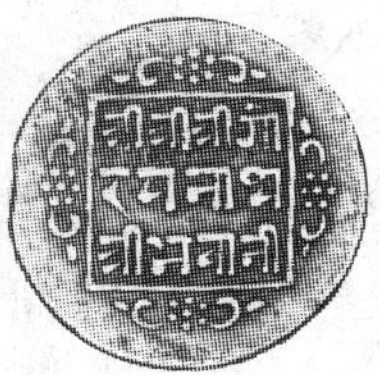

COPPER
Rev. leg: 12 characters.

KM#	Date	Year	Good	VG	Fine	VF
588	SE1787	(1865)	1.75	3.00	5.00	8.00

Obv. and rev: Border of dots.

KM#	Date	Year	Good	VG	Fine	VF
589	SE1787	(1865)	3.00	5.00	7.50	10.00

Rev. leg: 9 characters.

KM#	Date	Year	Good	VG	Fine	VF
590	SE1787	(1865)	1.50	2.00	3.50	5.00
	1788	(1866)	1.50	2.00	3.50	5.00
	1789	(1867)	1.50	2.00	3.50	5.00
	1790	(1868)	1.50	2.00	3.50	5.00
	1791	(1869)	1.50	2.00	3.50	5.00
	1792	(1870)	1.50	2.00	3.50	5.00
	1793	(1871)	1.50	2.00	3.50	5.00
	1794	(1872)	1.50	2.00	3.50	5.00
	1796	(1874)	1.50	2.00	3.50	5.00
	1797	(1875)	1.50	2.00	3.50	5.00
	1798	(1876)	1.50	2.00	3.50	5.00
	1799	(1877)	1.50	2.00	3.50	5.00
	1802	(1880)	15.00	20.00	25.00	35.00

2 PAISA

(Dak)

COPPER
Rev. leg: 12 characters.

KM#	Date	Year	Good	VG	Fine	VF
591	SE1787	(1865)	30.00	40.00	50.00	75.00

Rev. leg: 9 characters.

KM#	Date	Year	Good	VG	Fine	VF
592	SE1788	(1866)	2.00	3.50	5.00	10.00
	1790	(1868)	1.50	2.50	3.50	6.00
	1791	(1869)	1.50	2.50	3.50	6.00
	1796	(1874)	1.75	3.00	4.00	8.00
	1798	(1876)	1.75	3.00	4.00	8.00
	1802	(1880)	30.00	40.00	50.00	75.00

NOTE: Varieties exist.

Silver Coinage

DAM

SILVER, uniface, 0.04 g

KM#	Date	Year	VG	Fine	VF	XF
593	ND	(1847-81)	5.00	7.50	10.00	15.00

1/32 MOHAR

SILVER, uniface, 0.18 g

KM#	Date	Year	VG	Fine	VF	XF
594	ND	(1847-81)	6.00	10.00	13.50	18.50

1/16 MOHAR

SILVER, 0.35 g

KM#	Date	Year	VG	Fine	VF	XF
595	ND	(1847-81)	6.00	10.00	13.50	18.50

1/8 MOHAR

SILVER, 0.70 g

KM#	Date	Year	VG	Fine	VF	XF
596	ND	(1847-81)	5.00	8.50	12.50	17.50

In the name of Queen Trailokya Raja Lakshmi

1/4 MOHAR

SILVER, 1.40 g

KM#	Date	Year	VG	Fine	VF	XF
597	SE1769	(1847)	15.00	20.00	30.00	40.00
	1770	(1848)	15.00	20.00	30.00	40.00
	1772	(1850)	15.00	20.00	30.00	40.00

In the name of Queen Sura Raja Lakshmi

KM#	Date	Year	VG	Fine	VF	XF
598.1	SE1769	(1847)	15.00	25.00	35.00	45.00
	1770	(1848)	15.00	25.00	35.00	45.00
	1772	(1850)	15.00	25.00	35.00	45.00
	1775	(1853)	15.00	25.00	35.00	45.00
	1776	(1854)	15.00	25.00	35.00	45.00
	1782	(1860)	15.00	25.00	35.00	45.00
	1787	(1865)	15.00	25.00	35.00	45.00
	1788	(1866)	15.00	25.00	35.00	45.00

Struck with gold dies.

KM#	Date	Year	VG	Fine	VF	XF
598.2	SE1777	(1855)	40.00	50.00	75.00	100.00

In the name of Queen Deva Raja Lakshmi

KM#	Date	Year	VG	Fine	VF	XF
599	SE1769	(1847)	9.00	13.50	20.00	30.00
	1770	(1848)	9.00	13.50	20.00	30.00
	1772	(1850)	9.00	13.50	20.00	30.00
	1773	(1851)	9.00	13.50	20.00	30.00
	1775	(1853)	9.00	13.50	20.00	30.00
	1776	(1854)	9.00	13.50	20.00	30.00

In the name of Queen Punyakumari Raja Lakshmi

KM#	Date	Year	VG	Fine	VF	XF
600	SE1802	(1880)	40.00	50.00	75.00	100.00

1/2 MOHAR

SILVER, 2.80 g

KM#	Date	Year	VG	Fine	VF	XF
601	SE1769	(1847)	5.00	8.50	13.50	20.00
	1770	(1848)	5.00	8.50	13.50	20.00
	1771	(1849)	5.00	8.50	13.50	20.00
	1772	(1850)	5.00	8.50	13.50	20.00
	1773	(1851)	15.00	20.00	25.00	30.00
	1775	(1853)	15.00	20.00	25.00	30.00
	1776	(1854)	15.00	20.00	25.00	30.00
	1787	(1865)	15.00	20.00	25.00	30.00
	1802	(1880)	15.00	20.00	25.00	30.00

MOHAR

SILVER, 5.60 g

KM#	Date	Year	VG	Fine	VF	XF
602	SE1769	(1847)	4.50	6.50	9.00	11.50
	1770	(1848)	4.50	6.50	9.00	11.50
	1771	(1849)	4.50	6.50	9.00	11.50
	1772	(1850)	4.50	6.50	9.00	11.50
	1773	(1851)	4.50	6.50	9.00	11.50
	1774	(1852)	7.00	10.00	13.50	17.50
	1775	(1853)	4.50	6.50	9.00	11.50
	1776	(1854)	4.50	6.50	9.00	11.50
	1777	(1855)	4.50	6.50	9.00	11.50
	1778	(1856)	4.50	6.50	9.00	11.50
	1779	(1857)	4.50	6.50	9.00	11.50
	1780	(1858)	4.50	6.50	9.00	11.50
	1781	(1859)	4.50	6.50	9.00	11.50
	1782	(1860)	4.50	7.50	12.50	16.50
	1785	(1863)	7.00	10.00	13.50	17.50
	1786	(1864)	4.50	6.50	9.00	11.50
	1787	(1865)	4.50	6.50	9.00	11.50
	1788	(1866)	4.50	6.50	9.00	11.50
	1789	(1867)	4.50	6.50	9.00	11.50
	1790	(1868)	4.50	6.50	9.00	11.50
	1791	(1869)	4.50	6.50	9.00	11.50
	1792	(1870)	4.50	6.50	9.00	11.50
	1793	(1871)	4.50	6.50	9.00	11.50
	1794	(1872)	4.50	6.50	9.00	11.50
	1796	(1874)	4.50	6.50	9.00	11.50
	1797	(1875)	4.50	6.50	9.00	11.50
	1800	(1878)	4.50	6.50	9.00	11.50
	1801	(1879)	4.50	6.50	9.00	11.50
	1802	(1880)	4.50	6.50	9.00	11.50
	1803	(1881)	4.50	6.50	9.00	11.50

Machine struck, plain edge.

KM#	Date	Year	VG	Fine	VF	XF
602.1	SE1786	(1864)	12.50	15.00	20.00	27.50
	1787	(1865)	7.50	10.00	15.00	22.50
	1788	(1866)	12.50	15.00	20.00	27.50
	1789	(1867)	12.50	15.00	20.00	27.50

Struck using gold dies.

KM#	Date	Year	VG	Fine	VF	XF
602.2	SE1801	(1879)	12.50	15.00	20.00	27.50

2 MOHARS

SILVER, 11.20 g

KM#	Date	Year	VG	Fine	VF	XF
603	SE1769	(1847)	22.50	30.00	40.00	55.00
	1770	(1848)	22.50	30.00	40.00	55.00
	1771	(1849)	22.50	30.00	40.00	55.00
	1772	(1850)	22.50	30.00	40.00	55.00
	1777	(1855)	22.50	30.00	40.00	55.00
	1782	(1860)	22.50	30.00	40.00	55.00
	1796	(1874)	22.50	30.00	40.00	55.00
	1797	(1875)	22.50	30.00	40.00	55.00
	1801	(1879)	17.50	20.00	25.00	40.00
	1802	(1880)	22.50	30.00	40.00	55.00

Machine struck, milled edge.

KM#	Date	Year	VG	Fine	VF	XF
603.1	SE1786	(1864)	—	—	Rare	—

26-28mm
Struck w/regular gold dies.

KM#	Date	Year	VG	Fine	VF	XF
603.2	SE1801	(1879)	11.50	20.00	28.50	50.00
	1802	(1880)	22.50	30.00	40.00	55.00

Gold Coinage

DAM

Actual Size 2 x Actual Size
GOLD, uniface, 0.04 g
Legend in 2 lines.

KM#	Date	Year	VG	Fine	VF	XF
604	ND	(1847-81)	7.50	10.00	12.50	15.00

Actual Size 2 x Actual Size
Legend in 3 lines.

KM#	Date	Year	VG	Fine	VF	XF
A604	ND	(1847-81)	15.00	20.00	25.00	30.00

1/32 MOHAR

GOLD, uniface, 0.18 g

KM#	Date	Year	VG	Fine	VF	XF
605	ND	(1847-81)	14.00	20.00	25.00	32.50

1/16 MOHAR

GOLD, 0.35 g

KM#	Date	Year	VG	Fine	VF	XF
606	ND	(1847-81)	14.00	20.00	25.00	32.50

1/8 MOHAR

GOLD, 0.70 g

KM#	Date	Year	VG	Fine	VF	XF
607	ND	(1847-81)	22.50	27.50	35.00	45.00

In the name of Queen Trailokya Raja Lakshmi

1/4 MOHAR

GOLD, 1.40 g

KM#	Date	Year	VG	Fine	VF	XF
A608	SE1769	(1847)	40.00	50.00	65.00	85.00
	1770	(1848)	40.00	50.00	65.00	85.00

In the name of Queen Sura Raja Lakshmi

KM#	Date	Year	VG	Fine	VF	XF
608	SE1769	(1847)	40.00	50.00	65.00	85.00
608	1787	(1865)	40.00	50.00	65.00	85.00
	1790	(1868)	40.00	50.00	65.00	85.00

In the name of Queen Deva Raja Lakshmi

KM#	Date	Year	VG	Fine	VF	XF
609	SE1770	(1848)	40.00	50.00	65.00	85.00

In the name of Queen Punyakumari Raja Lakshmi

KM#	Date	Year	VG	Fine	VF	XF
610	SE1802	(1880)	55.00	75.00	100.00	135.00

1/2 MOHAR

GOLD, 2.80 g

KM#	Date	Year	VG	Fine	VF	XF
611	SE1769	(1847)	65.00	75.00	85.00	100.00
	1770	(1848)	65.00	75.00	85.00	100.00
	1802	(1880)	65.00	75.00	85.00	100.00

Rev: W/o horizontal lines.

KM#	Date	Year	VG	Fine	VF	XF
612	SE1790	(1868)	65.00	75.00	85.00	100.00

In the name of Queen Deva Raja Lakshmi

MOHAR

GOLD, 5.60 g

KM#	Date	Year	VG	Fine	VF	XF
613	SE1769	(1847)	115.00	125.00	145.00	175.00
	1791	(1869)	115.00	125.00	145.00	175.00
	1794	(1872)	115.00	125.00	145.00	175.00
	1802	(1880)	115.00	125.00	145.00	175.00

1/2 TOLA

GOLD, 21.5mm, 6.24 g

KM#	Date	Year	VG	Fine	VF	XF
614.1	SE1773	(1851)	125.00	135.00	160.00	200.00

Larger size, 26.5mm.

KM#	Date	Year	VG	Fine	VF	XF
614.2	SE1786	(1864)	125.00	135.00	160.00	200.00
	1787	(1865)	125.00	135.00	160.00	200.00

TOLA

GOLD, 12.48 g

KM#	Date	Year	VG	Fine	VF	XF
615	SE1769	(1847)	265.00	285.00	310.00	350.00
	1773	(1851)	265.00	285.00	310.00	350.00
	1774	(1852)	265.00	285.00	310.00	350.00
	1778	(1856)	265.00	285.00	310.00	350.00
	1780	(1858)	265.00	285.00	310.00	350.00
	1786	(1864)	265.00	285.00	310.00	350.00
	1787	(1865)	265.00	285.00	310.00	350.00
	1791	(1869)	265.00	285.00	310.00	350.00
	1793	(1871)	265.00	285.00	310.00	350.00
	1794	(1872)	265.00	285.00	310.00	350.00
	1802	(1880)	265.00	285.00	310.00	350.00

2 RUPEES

GOLD
Similar to 1 Tola, KM#615.

KM#	Date	Year	VG	Fine	VF	XF
616	SE1794	(1872)	450.00	525.00	650.00	800.00

PRESENTATION ISSUES

In the name of Queen Trailokyaraja Lakshmi

RUPEE

GOLD, 11.66 g

KM#	Date	Year	VG	Fine	VF	XF
617.1	SE1769	(1847)	400.00	500.00	550.00	600.00

KM#	Date	Year	VG	Fine	VF	XF
617.2	SE1771	(1849)	285.00	350.00	425.00	500.00

2 RUPEES

SILVER

KM#	Date	Year	VG	Fine	VF	XF
618	SE1769	(1847)	— Reported, not confirmed			

GOLD, 23.32 g

KM#	Date	Year	VG	Fine	VF	XF
619	SE1769	(1847)	750.00	1000.	1250.	1500.
	1771	(1849)	750.00	1000.	1250.	1500.

PRITHVI VIRA VIKRAMA

SE1803-1833/VS1938-1968
1881-1911AD

Copper Coinage

DAM

COPPER

KM#	Date	Year	Fine	VF	XF	Unc
620.1	SE(18)18	(1896)	7.50	12.00	15.00	20.00
	(18)19	(1897)	7.50	12.00	15.00	20.00

PAISA

COPPER
Obv: Trident. Rev. leg: 4 lines.

KM#	Date	Year	Good	VG	Fine	VF
623	SE1810	(1888)	30.00	50.00	75.00	100.00

Obv: Crossed khukris, circular legend border of flowers.

KM#	Date	Year	Good	VG	Fine	VF
624	VS1945	(1888)	30.00	50.00	75.00	100.00

Obv: 2 footprints above khukris.

KM#	Date	Year	Good	VG	Fine	VF
625	VS1945	(1888)	3.00	5.00	8.50	13.50
	1948	(1891)	9.00	15.00	22.50	35.00

Obv. and rev: Border of XXX's.

KM#	Date	Year	Good	VG	Fine	VF
626	VS1948	(1891)	1.00	1.50	3.00	5.00
	1949	(1892)	2.00	3.00	5.00	8.00

Obv. and rev: Border of crescents.

KM#	Date	Year	Good	VG	Fine	VF
627	VS1949	(1892)	1.00	1.50	3.00	5.00
	1950	(1893)	1.00	1.50	3.00	5.00
	1951	(1894)	1.25	1.75	3.50	6.00

Obv. and rev: Leg. within wreaths.

KM#	Date	Year	Good	VG	Fine	VF
628	VS1949	(1892)	1.00	1.50	3.00	5.00
	1950	(1893)	1.00	1.50	3.00	5.00
	1951	(1894)	1.00	1.50	3.00	5.00
	1952	(1895)	1.00	1.50	3.00	5.00
	1953	(1896)	1.00	1.50	3.00	5.00
	1954	(1897)	1.00	1.50	3.00	5.00
	1955	(1898)	1.00	1.50	3.00	5.00
	1956	(1899)	1.00	1.50	3.00	5.00
	1957	(1900)	1.00	1.50	3.00	5.00

NOTE: Later dates (VS1959-1964) exist for this type.
NOTE: Varieties in wreaths exist.

2 PAISA

(Dak)

COPPER
Obv. and rev: Circular legends.

KM#	Date	Year	Good	VG	Fine	VF
632	VS1948	(1891)	2.00	3.00	5.00	8.00
	1949	(1892)	2.50	3.50	5.00	8.00
	1950	(1893)	2.50	3.50	5.00	8.00

Silver Coinage

DAM

SILVER, uniface, 0.04 g
5 characters around sword.

KM#	Date	Year	Fine	VF	XF	Unc
635	ND	(1881-1911)	8.00	10.00	15.00	25.00

4 characters around sword.

KM#	Date	Year	Fine	VF	XF	Unc
636	ND	(1881-1911)	15.00	25.00	30.00	40.00

1/32 MOHAR

SILVER, uniface, 0.18 g
Sun and moon.

KM#	Date	Year	VG	Fine	VF	XF
637	ND	(1881-1911)	5.00	8.50	12.50	16.50

W/o sun and moon.

KM#	Date	Year	VG	Fine	VF	XF
638	ND	(1881-1911)	5.00	8.50	12.50	16.50

1/16 MOHAR

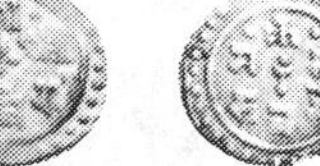 

SILVER, 0.35 g

KM#	Date	Year	Fine	VF	XF	Unc
639	ND	(1881-1911)	6.00	10.00	13.50	20.00

NOTE: Varieties exist.

1/8 MOHAR

SILVER, 0.70 g

KM#	Date	Year	Fine	VF	XF	Unc
640	ND	(1881-1911)	7.50	12.50	18.50	27.50

NOTE: Varieties exist.

1/4 MOHAR

SILVER, 1.40 g
Rev: 2 moons.

KM#	Date	Year	VG	Fine	VF	XF
641	SE1804	(1882)	15.00	17.50	25.00	35.00
	1806	(1884)	20.00	25.00	35.00	45.00
	1808	(1886)	15.00	17.50	25.00	35.00
	1811	(1889)	20.00	25.00	35.00	45.00

Rev: Moon and spiral sun.

KM#	Date	Year	VG	Fine	VF	XF
642	SE1816	(1894)	1.75	3.00	5.00	7.00
	1817	(1895)	1.75	3.00	5.00	7.00

1/2 MOHAR

SILVER, 2.77 g

KM#	Date	Year	VG	Fine	VF	XF
645	SE1803	(1881)	15.00	20.00	25.00	30.00
	1804	(1882)	15.00	20.00	25.00	30.00

Obv: Leg. modified.

KM#	Date	Year	VG	Fine	VF	XF
646	SE1805	(1883)	15.00	20.00	25.00	30.00

Machine struck, plain edge.

KM#	Date	Year	Fine	VF	XF	Unc
647	SE1816	(1894)	3.00	5.00	7.00	10.00
	1817	(1895)	3.00	5.00	7.00	10.00

NOTE: Later date (SE1824) exists for this type.
NOTE: Varieties exist.

MOHAR

SILVER, 5.60 g
Handstruck

KM#	Date	Year	VG	Fine	VF	XF
650	SE1803	(1881)	4.50	6.50	9.00	11.50
	1804	(1882)	4.50	6.50	9.00	11.50

Machine struck, plain edge.

KM#	Date	Year	Fine	VF	XF	Unc
651.1	SE1803	(1881)	15.00	25.00	35.00	50.00
	1804	(1882)	4.50	6.50	8.00	10.00
	1805	(1883)	4.50	6.50	8.00	10.00
	1806	(1884)	4.50	6.50	8.00	10.00
	1807	(1885)	4.50	6.50	8.00	10.00
	1808	(1886)	4.50	6.50	8.00	10.00
	1809	(1887)	4.50	6.50	8.00	10.00
	1810	(1888)	4.50	6.50	8.00	10.00
	1811	(1889)	15.00	25.00	35.00	50.00
	1816	(1894)	4.50	6.50	8.00	10.00
	1817	(1895)	4.50	6.50	8.00	10.00
	1818	(1896)	4.50	6.50	8.00	10.00
	1819	(1897)	4.50	6.50	8.00	10.00
	1820	(1898)	4.50	6.50	8.00	10.00
	1821	(1899)	4.50	6.50	8.00	10.00
	1822	(1900)	4.50	6.50	8.00	10.00

NOTE: Later dates (SE1823-1827) exist for this type.

2 MOHARS

SILVER, 27mm, 11.20 g
Hand struck using gold dies.

KM#	Date	Year	Fine	VF	XF	Unc
A653	SE1803	(1881)	40.00	60.00	80.00	100.00

Machine struck, plain edge.

KM#	Date	Year	Fine	VF	XF	Unc
653	SE1804	(1882)	40.00	60.00	80.00	100.00
	1811	(1889)	40.00	60.00	80.00	100.00
	1817	(1895)	8.00	12.50	17.50	25.00

Machine struck using gold dies, plain edge, 29mm.

KM#	Date	Year	Fine	VF	XF	Unc
654	SE1821	(1899)	10.00	15.00	25.00	45.00

4 MOHARS

SILVER, 22.40 g
Plain edge.

KM#	Date	Year	Fine	VF	XF	Unc
657	SE1817	(1895)	60.00	100.00	140.00	200.00

Gold Coinage

DAM

GOLD, uniface, 0.04 g
5 characters around sword.
Similar to 1/64 Mohar, KM#664.

KM#	Date	Year	Fine	VF	XF	Unc
659	ND	(1881-1911)	10.00	14.00	20.00	27.50

4 characters around sword.
Similar to 1/64 Mohar, KM#663.

KM#	Date	Year	Fine	VF	XF	Unc
660	ND	(1881-1911)	10.00	14.00	20.00	27.50

Actual Size **2 x Actual Size**
Circle around characters.

KM#	Date	Year	Fine	VF	XF	Unc
661	ND	(1881-1911)	10.00	14.00	20.00	27.50

Actual Size 2 x Actual Size

2 characters below sword.

KM#	Date	Year	Fine	VF	XF	Unc
662	ND	(1881-1911)	10.00	14.00	20.00	27.50

1/64 MOHAR

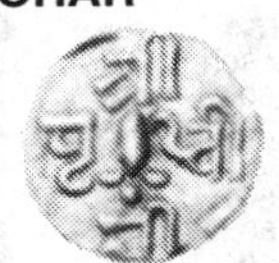

Actual Size 2 x Actual Size

GOLD, uniface, 0.09 g

Obv: 4 characters around sword.

KM#	Date	Year	Fine	VF	XF	Unc
663	ND	(1881-1911)	12.50	17.50	22.50	30.00

Actual Size 2 x Actual Size

Obv: 5 characters around sword.

KM#	Date	Year	Fine	VF	XF	Unc
664	ND	(1881-1911)	12.50	17.50	22.50	30.00

1/32 MOHAR

GOLD, uniface, 0.18 g

5 characters around sword.

KM#	Date	Year	Fine	VF	XF	Unc
665	ND	(1881-1911)	20.00	40.00	75.00	100.00

4 characters around sword.

KM#	Date	Year	Fine	VF	XF	Unc
666	ND	(1881-1911)	15.00	30.00	75.00	100.00

1/16 MOHAR

GOLD, 0.35 g

KM#	Date	Year	Fine	VF	XF	Unc
667	ND	(1881-1911)	15.00	40.00	75.00	100.00

KM#	Date	Year	Fine	VF	XF	Unc
668	SE(18)33	(1911)	15.00	30.00	75.00	100.00

1/8 MOHAR

GOLD, 0.70 g

Obv: 6 characters.

KM#	Date	Year	Fine	VF	XF	Unc
669.1	ND	(1881-1911)	22.50	40.00	75.00	100.00

Obv: 5 characters.

KM#	Date	Year	Fine	VF	XF	Unc
669.2	ND	(1881-1911)	22.50	40.00	75.00	100.00

NOTE: Varieties exist.

KM#	Date	Year	Fine	VF	XF	Unc
670	SE(18)33	(1911)	22.50	40.00	75.00	100.00

1/4 MOHAR

GOLD, 1.40 g

KM#	Date	Year	Fine	VF	XF	Unc
671.1	SE1808	(1886)	45.00	60.00	80.00	100.00
	1811	(1889)	45.00	60.00	80.00	100.00
	1817	(1895)	40.00	50.00	60.00	75.00

NOTE: Later dates (SE1823-1829) exist for this type.

1/2 MOHAR

GOLD, 2.80 g

KM#	Date	Year	Fine	VF	XF	Unc
672.1	SE1805	(1883)	65.00	75.00	85.00	100.00

KM#	Date	Year	Fine	VF	XF	Unc
672.2	SE1817	(1895)	65.00	75.00	85.00	100.00

MOHAR

GOLD, 5.60 g

KM#	Date	Year	Fine	VF	XF	Unc
673.1	SE1804	(1882)	115.00	125.00	145.00	175.00
	1805	(1883)	115.00	125.00	145.00	175.00
	1809	(1887)	115.00	125.00	145.00	175.00
	1817	(1895)	115.00	125.00	145.00	175.00
	1820	(1898)	115.00	125.00	140.00	165.00

NOTE: Later dates (SE1823-1827) exist for this type.

KM#	Date	Year	Fine	VF	XF	Unc
673.3	VS1949	(1892)	115.00	125.00	145.00	175.00

TOLA

GOLD, 12.48 g

Oblique edge milling.

KM#	Date	Year	Fine	VF	XF	Unc
674.1	SE1803	(1881)	235.00	255.00	285.00	325.00
	1805	(1883)	235.00	255.00	285.00	325.00
	1810	(1888)	235.00	255.00	285.00	325.00
	1811	(1889)	235.00	255.00	285.00	325.00

Vertical edge milling.

KM#	Date	Year	Fine	VF	XF	Unc
674.2	SE1803	(1881)	235.00	255.00	285.00	325.00
	1804	(1882)	235.00	255.00	285.00	325.00

Plain edge.

KM#	Date	Year	Fine	VF	XF	Unc
674.3	SE1807	(1885)	235.00	255.00	275.00	300.00
	1817	(1895)	235.00	255.00	275.00	300.00
	1820	(1898)	235.00	255.00	275.00	300.00

NOTE: Later dates (SE1823-1826) exist for this type.

Plain edge.

KM#	Date	Year	Fine	VF	XF	Unc
675.2	VS1947	(1890)	235.00	255.00	275.00	300.00

Oblique edge milling.

KM#	Date	Year	Fine	VF	XF	Unc
675.3	VS1949	(1892)	235.00	255.00	275.00	300.00

DUITOLA ASARPHI

GOLD, 23.32 g

KM#	Date	Year	Fine	VF	XF	Unc
676	SE1811	(1889)	600.00	700.00	800.00	1000.

Rev: Die of 4 Mohars, KM#657.

KM#	Date	Year	Fine	VF	XF	Unc
677	SE1817	(1895)	600.00	700.00	800.00	1000.

Plain edge.

KM#	Date	Year	Fine	VF	XF	Unc
678	SE1817	(1895)	600.00	700.00	800.00	1000.

NOTE: Later date (SE1825) exists for this type.

PATTERNS (Pn)

(Including off metal strikes)

KM#	Date	Mintage	Identification	Mkt.Val.
Pn1	SE1810(1888)	—	1 Paisa	Rare

KM#	Date	Mintage	Identification	Mkt.Val.
Pn2	ND(ca.1888)	—	1 Paisa	Rare

NETHERLANDS

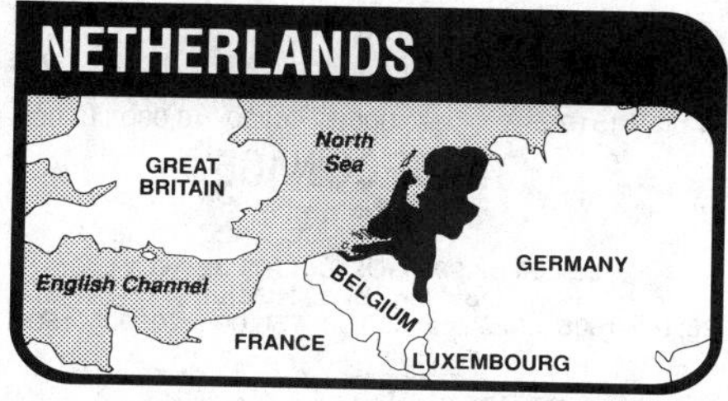

The Kingdom of the Netherlands, a country of western Europe fronting on the North Sea and bordered by Belgium and Germany, has an area of 15,770 sq. mi. (41,500 sq. km.) and a population of 15.5 million. Capital: Amsterdam, but the seat of government is at The Hague. The economy is based on dairy farming and a variety of industrial activities. Chemicals, yarns and fabrics, and meat products are exported.

After being a part of Charlemagne's empire in the 8th and 9th centuries, the Netherlands came under control of Burgundy and the Austrian Hapsburgs, and finally was subjected to Spanish dominion in the 16th century. Led by William of Orange, the Dutch revolted against Spain in 1568. The seven northern provinces formed the Union of Utrecht and declared their independence in 1581, becoming the Republic of the United Netherlands. In the following century, the 'Golden Age' of Dutch history, the Netherlands became a great sea and colonial power, a patron of the arts and a refuge for the persecuted. The United Dutch Republic ended in 1795 when the French formed the Batavian Republic. Napoleon made his brother Louis, the King of Holland in 1806, however he abdicated in 1810 when Napoleon annexed Holland. The French were expelled in 1813, and all the provinces of Holland and Belgium were merged into the Kingdom of the United Netherlands under William I, in 1814. The Belgians withdrew in 1830 to form their own kingdom, the last substantial change in the configuration of European Netherlands. German forces invaded in 1940 as the royal family fled with cargos of wealth to England where a government-in-exile was formed. A German High Commissioner, Arthur Seyss-Inquart, was placed in command until 1945 and the arrival of Allied military forces.

RULERS

BATAVIAN REPUBLIC

French domination, 1795-1806

KINGDOM OF HOLLAND

French Protectorate

Louis Napoleon, 1806-1810

FRENCH ANNEXATION

Napoleon I, 1810-1814

KINGDOM OF THE NETHERLANDS

William I, 1815-1840
William II, 1840-1849
William III, 1849-1890
Wilhelmina I, 1890-1948

MINT MARKS

B - Brussels (Belgium), 1821-1830

MINT PRIVY MARKS

Date	Privy Mark
	Harderwijk (Gelderland)
1782-1806	Ear of corn
	Dordrecht (Holland)
1600-1806	Rosette
1795-1806	None
	Enkhuizen (West Friesland)
1796-1803	Star
	Hoorn (West Friesland)
1803-1809	Star
	Kampen (Overyssel)
1763-1764,1795-1807	
	Utrecht (Utrecht)
1738-1805	Shield
	Utrecht
1806-present	Caduceus

MINTMASTERS PRIVY MARKS

Date	Privy Mark
	Brussels Mint
1821-1830	Palm branch
	Utrecht Mint
1806-1810	Bee
1810-1813	Mast
1815-1816	Cloverleaf
1817	Child in swaddling clothes
1818-1840	Torch
1839-1846	Fleur de lis
1846-1874	Sword
1874	Sword in scabbard
1875-1887	Broadaxe
1887	Broadaxe and star
1888-1909	Halberd

MONETARY SYSTEM

8 Duits = 1 Stuiver (Stiver)
6 Stuivers = 1 Schelling
20 Stuivers = 1 Gulden (Guilder or Florin)
50 Stuivers = 1 Rijksdaalder (Silver Ducat)
60 Stuivers = 1 Ducaton (Silver Rider)
14 Gulden = 1 Golden Rider

Commencing 1815

100 Cents = 1 Gulden
2-1/2 Gulden = 1 Rijksdaalder

BATAVIAN REPUBLIC

From 1796 to 1806, the Netherlands was a confederation of seven provinces, each producing coins similar in design but differing in the coat of arms or inscription. Generally the coins of each province contained an abbreviation of the name of the province somewhere in the inscription. Under the Batavian Republic, the following abbreviations were used.

PROVINCE ABBREVIATIONS

G, GEL - Gelderland
HOL, HOLL - Holland
TRANSI - Overijsel
TRA, TRAI, TRAIECTUM - Utrecht
WESTF, WESTRI - Westfriesland
ZEL, ZEELANDIA - Zeeland

RIJKSDAALDER

(2-1/2 Gulden)

.868 SILVER
Obv. leg. ends: . . . G, GEL.

KM#	Date	Mintage	Fine	VF	XF	Unc
10.1	1801	—	300.00	450.00	600.00	850.00
	1802	Inc. Ab.	300.00	450.00	600.00	850.00

NOTE: Earlier dates (1795-1800) exist for this type.

Obv. leg. ends: . . . HOL, HOLL •

KM#	Date	Mintage	Fine	VF	XF	Unc
10.2	1801/0	—	100.00	175.00	275.00	450.00
	1801	Inc. Ab.	75.00	150.00	250.00	350.00
	1802	Inc. Ab.	75.00	150.00	250.00	350.00
	1806	Inc. Ab.	950.00	1400.	2000.	2500.

NOTE: Earlier dates (1796-1800) exist for this type.

Obv. leg. ends: . . . TRA, TRAI.

KM#	Date	Mintage	Fine	VF	XF	Unc
10.4	1801	—	65.00	100.00	150.00	200.00
	1801 small 8-0	Inc. Ab.	65.00	100.00	150.00	200.00
	1802	Inc. Ab.	65.00	100.00	150.00	200.00
	1803 long sword	Inc. Ab.	65.00	100.00	150.00	200.00
	1803 short sword	Inc. Ab.	65.00	100.00	150.00	200.00
	1804	Inc. Ab.	65.00	100.00	150.00	200.00
	1805/797	I.A.	65.00	100.00	150.00	200.00
	1805	Inc. Ab.	65.00	100.00	150.00	200.00

NOTE: Earlier dates (1795-1800) exist for this type.

3 GULDEN

.915 SILVER
Obv. leg. ends: . . . HOL, HOLL.

KM#	Date	Mintage	Fine	VF	XF	Unc
9.2	1801	—	90.00	160.00	240.00	350.00

NOTE: Earlier dates (1795-1800) exist for this type.

TRADE COINAGE

DUCAT

3.5000 g, .986 GOLD, .1109 oz AGW
Obv. leg. ends:. . . G, GEL.

KM#	Date	Mintage	Fine	VF	XF	Unc
11.1	1801	—	150.00	250.00	350.00	500.00
	1802	Inc. Ab.	150.00	250.00	350.00	500.00
	1803	—	650.00	1300.	2000.	2500.

NOTE: Earlier dates (1795-1800) exist for this type.

Obv. leg. ends: . . . HOL.

KM#	Date	Mintage	Fine	VF	XF	Unc
11.2	1801 w/o star	—	90.00	150.00	200.00	200.00
	1801 star	—	220.00	475.00	700.00	1000.
	1802 w/o star	—	90.00	155.00	200.00	300.00
	1802 star	—	200.00	375.00	500.00	700.00
	1803 w/o star	—	100.00	220.00	275.00	500.00
	1804 w/o star	—	100.00	220.00	275.00	500.00
	1805 w/o star	—	200.00	375.00	600.00	850.00

NOTE: Coins with the star were struck at the Enkhuizen Mint with a total mintage of 630,455. Coins without the star were struck at the Dordrecht Mint with a total mintage of 2,861,825.
NOTE: Earlier dates (1795-1800) exist for this type.

Obv. leg. ends: . . . CRES:TRA •

KM#	Date	Mintage	Fine	VF	XF	Unc
11.3	1801	.960	70.00	130.00	200.00	300.00
	1802	1.705	70.00	130.00	200.00	300.00
	1803	2.089	70.00	130.00	200.00	275.00
	1804/3	.870	80.00	170.00	250.00	325.00
	1804	Inc. Ab.	80.00	170.00	250.00	325.00
	1805	1.300	70.00	130.00	200.00	275.00

NOTE: Earlier dates (1795-1800) exist for this type.

2 DUCAT

7.0000 g, .986 GOLD, .2219 oz AGW
Obv. leg. ends: . . . HOL, HOLL.
Similar to 1 Ducat KM#11.2.

KM#	Date	Mintage	Fine	VF	XF	Unc
12.1	1802	—	700.00	1300.	2000.	2500.

NOTE: Earlier date (1795) exists for this type.

Obv. leg. ends: . . . CRES:TRA.
Similar to 1 Ducat, KM#11.3.

KM#	Date	Mintage	Fine	VF	XF	Unc
12.2	1801	.215	350.00	700.00	1000.	1250.
	1802	.115	500.00	1000.	1500.	2000.
	1803	.365	350.00	700.00	1000.	1250.
	1804	.250	350.00	700.00	1000.	1250.
	1805	.301	350.00	700.00	1000.	1250.

NOTE: Earlier dates (1795-1800)) exist for this type.

PATTERNS (Pn)

(Including off metal strikes)

KM#	Date	Mintage	Identification	Mkt.Val.
Pn7	1801	—	1 Ducat, Copper, over 1796 Zeeland Duit, KM11.2	—
Pn8	1801	—	2 Ducat, Copper, c/s: DD, KM12.2	—
Pn9	1804	—	1 Silver Ducat, Bronze, KM10.4	—
Pn10	1806	—	1 Silver Ducat, Copper, KM10.2	—

KINGDOM OF HOLLAND

10 STUIVERS

SILVER
Mint: Utrecht

KM#	Date	Mintage	Fine	VF	XF	Unc
30	1808	—	—	—	Rare	—
	1809	—	300.00	700.00	1200.	1500.

FLORIN

SILVER
Mint: Utrecht

KM#	Date	Mintage	Fine	VF	XF	Unc
29	1807	—	550.00	1200.	1750.	2500.

GULDEN

SILVER
Mint: Utrecht

KM#	Date	Mintage	Fine	VF	XF	Unc
31	1808	—	300.00	700.00	1200.	1500.
	1809	—	300.00	700.00	1200.	1500.
	1810	—	300.00	700.00	1200.	1500.

RIJKSDAALDER

.868 SILVER
Mint: Utrecht
Obv. leg: . . . TRAI.

KM#	Date	Mintage	Fine	VF	XF	Unc
25	1806	.580	125.00	220.00	300.00	350.00
	1807	.151	150.00	250.00	325.00	400.00
	1808	.343	125.00	220.00	300.00	350.00

SILVER

KM#	Date	Mintage	Fine	VF	XF	Unc
36	1809	—	900.00	1600.	2100.	3000.

KM#	Date	Mintage	Fine	VF	XF	Unc
37	1809	—	1200.	1900.	3000.	3500.

50 STUIVERS

SILVER
Mint: Utrecht

KM#	Date	Mintage	Fine	VF	XF	Unc
28	1807	300 pcs.	900.00	1650.	2250.	2800.
	1808	2.466	100.00	175.00	250.00	325.00

2-1/2 GULDEN

SILVER
Mint: Utrecht

KM#	Date	Mintage	Fine	VF	XF	Unc
32	1808	—	1000.	2000.	2500.	3000.

10 GULDEN

6.8250 g, .917 GOLD, .2012 oz AGW
Mint: Utrecht

KM#	Date	Mintage	Fine	VF	XF	Unc
33	1808	—	1500.	3000.	4500.	6000.
	1810	—	1500.	3000.	4500.	6000.

20 GULDEN

13.6500 g, .917 GOLD, .4024 oz AGW
Mint: Utrecht

KM#	Date	Mintage	Fine	VF	XF	Unc
34	1808	—	3000.	6000.	10,000.	12,000.
	1810	—	3000.	6000.	10,000.	12,000.

TRADE COINAGE

DUCAT

3.5000 g, .986 GOLD, .1109 oz AGW
Obv. leg: HOL, HOLL

KM#	Date	Mintage	Fine	VF	XF	Unc
26.1	1806	526 pcs.	500.00	750.00	1000.	1500.

Obv. leg: TRAIECTUM, TRA, TRAI
Mint: Utrecht

KM#	Date	Mintage	Fine	VF	XF	Unc
26.2	1806 sm.dt.	.794	110.00	190.00	260.00	350.00
	1807 small date, straight 7	.622	110.00	190.00	260.00	350.00
	1808/7	.037	175.00	300.00	350.00	450.00
	1808	Inc. Ab.	140.00	250.00	325.00	375.00

Mint: St. Petersburg

KM#	Date	Mintage	Fine	VF	XF	Unc
26.3	1806 lg.dt.	1.300	110.00	190.00	260.00	350.00
	1807 large date, curved 7	1.940	110.00	190.00	260.00	350.00

KM#	Date	Mintage	Fine	VF	XF	Unc
35	1808	.283	200.00	375.00	525.00	700.00
	1809	Inc. Ab.	200.00	375.00	525.00	700.00

KM#	Date	Mintage	Fine	VF	XF	Unc
38	1809	2.371	200.00	375.00	525.00	700.00
	1810	Inc. Ab.	200.00	375.00	525.00	700.00

2 DUCAT

7.0000 g, .986 GOLD, .2218 oz AGW
Mint: Utrecht
Obv. leg: TRAIECTUM, TRA, TRAI

KM#	Date	Mintage	Fine	VF	XF	Unc
27	1806	.199	500.00	800.00	1200.	1500.
	1807	.156	500.00	800.00	1200.	1500.
	1808	—	500.00	800.00	1200.	1500.

PATTERNS (Pn)

(Including off metal strikes)

KM#	Date	Mintage	Identification	Mkt.Val.
Pn6	1807	—	10 Stuiver, Silver	2500.
Pn7	1807	—	20 Stuiver, Silver	—
Pn8	1807	—	50 Stuivers, Gold, KM28	—
Pn9	1807	—	1 Florin, Bronze, KM29	—
Pn10	1807	—	1 Gulden, Gold, KM31	—
Pn11	1808	—	10 Stuivers, Bronze, KM30	—
Pn12	1808	—	1 Gulden, Bronze, KM31	—

KM#	Date	Mintage	Identification	Mkt.Val.
Pn13	1808	—	20 Gulden, Bronze, w/o value	1500.
Pn14	1808	—	1 Rijksdaalder, Bronze, KM36	—
Pn15	1809	—	10 Stuivers, Bronze, KM30	—
Pn16	1809	—	1 Gulden, Bronze, KM31	—
Pn17	1809	—	2-1/2 Gulden, Lead	2750.
Pn18	1809	—	1 Rijksdaalder, Bronze, KM37	—
Pn19	1809	—	1 Rijksdaalder, Copper, KM37	—
Pn20	1810	—	10 Gulden, Silver, KM33	—
Pn21	1810	—	10 Gulden, Tin, KM33	350.00

FRENCH ANNEXATION

From 1810 to 1814, the Netherlands were a part of France. During this period, homeland type coins were not minted. Regular French coins were struck at the Utrecht Mint at this time, and are identified by the fish and mast privy marks. These coins are listed under France.

KINGDOM OF THE NETHERLANDS

1/2 CENT

COPPER

KM#	Date	Mintage	Fine	VF	XF	Unc
51	1818	—	650.00	1500.	3000.	5000.
	1818	—	—	—	Proof	—
	1819	.144	150.00	450.00	800.00	2500.
	1821	1.648	28.00	65.00	125.00	200.00
	1821B	.261	75.00	150.00	300.00	600.00
	1821B	—	—	—	Proof	1000.
	1822	11.240	15.00	28.00	75.00	110.00
	1822B	4.066	28.00	65.00	125.00	200.00
	1823	9.850	12.00	28.00	75.00	100.00
	1823B	14.093	12.00	28.00	75.00	100.00
	1824	2.552	28.00	75.00	150.00	225.00
	1824B	3.430	28.00	75.00	150.00	225.00
	1826	—	700.00	1750.	3500.	5500.
	1826	—	—	—	Proof	—
	1826B	1.561	28.00	75.00	150.00	225.00
	1827	5.376	15.00	28.00	75.00	100.00
	1827B	2.347	15.00	28.00	75.00	100.00
	1828	1.700	50.00	125.00	250.00	500.00
	1828B	4.234	15.00	28.00	75.00	100.00
	1829	2.947	16.50	32.50	85.00	115.00
	1831	3.850	16.50	32.50	85.00	115.00
	1832	10.328	15.00	28.00	75.00	100.00
	1833	.150	150.00	300.00	500.00	1100.
	1837	2.602	12.00	25.00	70.00	100.00
68	1841	2.600	17.50	35.00	90.00	150.00
	1843	3.120	17.50	35.00	90.00	150.00
	1846	.600	20.00	50.00	110.00	175.00
	1847	2.000	20.00	40.00	100.00	150.00

KM#	Date	Mintage	Fine	VF	XF	Unc
90	1850	2.000	10.00	25.00	50.00	85.00
	1851	2.051	10.00	25.00	50.00	85.00
	1852	2.028	40.00	80.00	120.00	240.00
	1853	2.000	10.00	25.00	50.00	85.00
	1854	3.000	8.00	18.00	35.00	60.00
	1855	.999	80.00	200.00	350.00	800.00
	1857	4.155	5.00	15.00	30.00	55.00
	1859	4.052	5.00	15.00	30.00	55.00
	1861	1.446	15.00	35.00	65.00	90.00
	1862	2.026	5.00	15.00	30.00	60.00
	1863	2.428	5.00	15.00	30.00	60.00
	1864	2.016	5.00	15.00	30.00	60.00
	1865	2.006	5.00	15.00	30.00	60.00
	1867	2.008	5.00	15.00	30.00	60.00
	1869	2.014	5.00	15.00	30.00	60.00
	1870	2.004	5.00	15.00	30.00	60.00
	1872	2.026	5.00	15.00	30.00	60.00
	1873	2.026	5.00	15.00	30.00	60.00
	1875	2.026	5.00	15.00	30.00	60.00
	1876	2.020	5.00	15.00	30.00	60.00
	1877	1.400	15.00	35.00	65.00	90.00

BRONZE
Obv: 17 small shields in field, leg: KONINGRIJK. . .

KM#	Date	Mintage	Fine	VF	XF	Unc
109	1878	4.000	4.00	8.00	15.00	35.00
	1883	.800	40.00	80.00	120.00	200.00
	1884	17.200	1.50	4.00	10.00	25.00
	1885	7.800	2.00	6.00	12.00	30.00
	1886	2.200	20.00	50.00	90.00	140.00
	1891	5.000	4.00	8.00	15.00	35.00
109	1894	5.000	4.00	8.00	15.00	35.00
	1898	2.000	10.00	30.00	60.00	120.00
	1900	3.000	8.00	15.00	40.00	70.00

NOTE: Later date (1901) exists for this type.

CENT

COPPER

KM#	Date	Mintage	Fine	VF	XF	Unc
47	1817	—	700.00	2250.	3750.	7000.
	1818	—	700.00	2250.	3750.	7000.
	1819	.165	220.00	700.00	1500.	2250.
	1821	6.435	9.00	18.00	50.00	100.00
	1821B	.113	220.00	600.00	1150.	2000.
	1822	20.462	9.00	18.00	50.00	100.00
	1822B	5.739	10.00	28.00	80.00	150.00
	1823	22.300	9.00	18.00	50.00	100.00
	1823B	11.591	10.00	25.00	80.00	150.00
	1824	3.456	30.00	80.00	145.00	250.00
	1824B	.144	175.00	450.00	1000.	2000.
	1826	8.400	10.00	28.00	80.00	150.00
	1826B	5.331	10.00	28.00	80.00	150.00
	1827	25.650	9.00	18.00	50.00	100.00
	1827B	20.026	9.00	18.00	50.00	100.00
	1828	7.343	9.00	18.00	50.00	100.00
	1828B	8.909	10.00	28.00	80.00	150.00
	1830	.850	30.00	60.00	125.00	200.00
	1831	4.861	10.00	28.00	80.00	150.00
	1837	5.202	8.00	16.00	45.00	100.00

KM#	Date	Mintage	Fine	VF	XF	Unc
100	1860	2.032	6.00	12.00	32.00	65.00
	1861	2.050	6.00	12.00	32.00	65.00
	1862	2.026	6.00	12.00	32.00	65.00
	1863	10.246	2.50	5.50	12.50	28.00
	1864	2.026	6.00	12.00	32.00	65.00
	1870	4.010	4.00	9.00	24.00	45.00
	1873	3.026	5.00	10.00	28.00	55.00
	1875	3.015	5.00	10.00	28.00	55.00
	1876	13.047	2.50	5.50	12.50	28.00
	1877	11.026	2.50	5.50	12.50	28.00

BRONZE
Obv: 17 small shields in field, leg: KONINGRIJK

KM#	Date	Mintage	Fine	VF	XF	Unc
107	1877	6.100	3.50	8.00	20.00	50.00
	1878	53.900	.50	2.00	6.00	15.00
	1880	20.000	1.50	4.00	10.00	30.00
	1881	10.000	1.50	4.00	10.00	30.00
	1882/1	—	4.00	9.00	25.00	70.00
	1882	5.000	3.00	6.00	15.00	45.00
	1883	15.000	1.50	4.00	10.00	30.00
	1884	10.000	1.50	4.00	10.00	30.00
	1892	5.000	3.50	8.00	20.00	60.00
	1896	3.000	5.00	15.00	35.00	85.00
	1897	2.500	6.00	17.00	40.00	90.00
	1898	5.000	2.50	5.00	12.00	50.00
	1899	5.100	2.50	5.00	12.00	50.00
	1900 large date					
		12.400	2.00	4.00	10.00	45.00
	1900 small date					
		Inc. Ab.	2.00	4.00	10.00	45.00
	1900	—	—	—	Proof	185.00

2-1/2 CENTS

BRONZE
Obv: 17 small shields in field, leg: KONINGRIJK.

KM#	Date	Mintage	Fine	VF	XF	Unc
108	1877	4.000	2.50	5.00	15.00	45.00
	1880	4.000	2.50	5.00	15.00	45.00
	1881	4.000	2.50	5.00	15.00	45.00
	1883	.400	15.00	25.00	50.00	125.00
	1884	3.600	3.50	7.00	18.00	50.00
	1886	2.000	4.00	10.00	20.00	55.00
	1890	2.000	4.00	10.00	20.00	55.00
	1894	1.000	15.00	25.00	50.00	185.00
	1898	1.600	10.00	20.00	40.00	100.00

5 CENTS

.8200 g, .569 SILVER, .0150 oz ASW

KM#	Date	Mintage	Fine	VF	XF	Unc
52	1818	2,500	450.00	800.00	1600.	2000.
	1818	—	—	—	Proof	3000.
	1819	3,000	300.00	600.00	1200.	1800.
	1819	—	—	—	Proof	2650.
	1822	.047	220.00	440.00	650.00	1000.
	1825B	.900	32.50	60.00	120.00	200.00
	1826B	1.021	32.50	60.00	120.00	200.00
	1827	.534	25.00	50.00	75.00	125.00
	1827B	.284	40.00	80.00	130.00	235.00
	1828B	.397	35.00	70.00	120.00	220.00

.6850 g, .640 SILVER, .0141 oz ASW

KM#	Date	Mintage	Fine	VF	XF	Unc
74	1848	100 pcs.	500.00	800.00	1200.	3000.
	1848	—	—	—	Proof	2500.

KM#	Date	Mintage	Fine	VF	XF	Unc
91	1850. dot after date					
		3.037	2.00	5.00	12.00	35.00
	1850 w/o dot after date					
		Inc. Ab.	—	—	—	—
	1853	.011	150.00	400.00	500.00	1000.
	1853	2 pcs.	—	—	Proof	2500.
	1855	.515	5.00	12.00	20.00	40.00
	1859	.400	5.00	12.00	20.00	40.00
	1862. dot after date					
		.400	5.00	12.00	20.00	40.00
	1862 w/o dot after date					
		Inc. Ab.	5.00	12.00	20.00	40.00
	1863	.640	5.00	12.00	20.00	40.00
	1868	.200	35.00	65.00	130.00	200.00
	1869	.500	5.00	12.00	20.00	40.00
	1876	.200	7.00	20.00	35.00	55.00
	1879	.200	7.00	20.00	35.00	55.00
	1879	—	—	—	Proof	160.00
	1887	.100	20.00	35.00	75.00	100.00

10 CENTS

1.6900 g, .569 SILVER, .0309 oz ASW

KM#	Date	Mintage	Fine	VF	XF	Unc
53	1818	48 pcs.	—	—	Proof	9000.
	1819	.025	275.00	600.00	1000.	2000.
	1822	.113	200.00	400.00	700.00	1500.
	1823B	.178	110.00	220.00	375.00	1000.
	1825	.972	22.00	45.00	90.00	140.00
	1825B	1.727	22.00	45.00	90.00	140.00
	1826	2.138	18.00	40.00	85.00	130.00
	1826B	1.430	22.00	50.00	100.00	180.00
	1827	5.895	10.00	25.00	50.00	100.00
	1827B	1.711	18.00	40.00	85.00	130.00
	1828	2.036	18.00	40.00	85.00	130.00
	1828B	1.168	22.00	45.00	90.00	145.00

1.4000 g, .640 SILVER, .0288 oz ASW

KM#	Date	Mintage	Fine	VF	XF	Unc
75	1848	6.859	10.00	35.00	80.00	160.00
	1848	—	—	—	Proof	375.00
	1849. dot after date					
		4.051	10.00	30.00	70.00	110.00
	1849 w/o dot after date					
		Inc. Ab.	25.00	80.00	175.00	425.00

KM#	Date	Mintage	Fine	VF	XF	Unc
80	1849	6.204	10.00	35.00	70.00	140.00
	1850	7.270	10.00	35.00	70.00	165.00
	1853	1.104	50.00	100.00	150.00	250.00
	1855	.745	60.00	120.00	160.00	280.00
	1855 low 5					
		Inc. Ab.	60.00	120.00	160.00	280.00
	1856	1.000	10.00	35.00	70.00	150.00
	1859	1.000	10.00	35.00	70.00	150.00
	1862	.800	35.00	80.00	140.00	220.00
	1863	1.240	10.00	35.00	70.00	125.00
	1868	.200	80.00	250.00	400.00	800.00
	1869	1.000	10.00	35.00	70.00	125.00

KM#	Date	Mintage	Fine	VF	XF	Unc
80	1871	1.000	10.00	35.00	70.00	125.00
	1873	1.000	10.00	35.00	70.00	125.00
	1874 sword privy mark					
		.800	50.00	200.00	350.00	850.00
	1874 sword in scabbard privy mark					
		2.000	30.00	80.00	125.00	200.00
	1876	1.000	8.00	25.00	60.00	100.00
	1877	1.000	8.00	25.00	60.00	100.00
	1878	1.000	8.00	25.00	60.00	100.00
	1879	1.000	8.00	25.00	60.00	100.00
	1880	1.000	8.00	25.00	60.00	100.00
	1881. dot after date					
		2.000	8.00	25.00	60.00	100.00
	1881 w/o dot after date					
		Inc. Ab.	8.00	25.00	60.00	100.00
	1882	2.000	8.00	25.00	60.00	100.00
	1884	1.000	8.00	25.00	60.00	100.00
	1885	2.000	8.00	25.00	60.00	100.00
	1887	1.600	8.00	25.00	60.00	100.00
	1889	2.800	5.00	20.00	50.00	90.00
	1890	2.600	5.00	20.00	50.00	90.00

KM#	Date	Mintage	Fine	VF	XF	Unc
116	1892 thin head					
		2.000	5.00	20.00	50.00	100.00
	1893	2.000	5.00	20.00	50.00	100.00
	1894	1.500	5.00	20.00	50.00	100.00
	1895	1.000	10.00	30.00	70.00	135.00
	1896	2.000	5.00	20.00	50.00	100.00
	1897	7.850	3.00	12.00	30.00	65.00

1.4000 g, .640 SILVER, .0288 oz ASW
Obv: Small head, divided legend.

KM#	Date	Mintage	Fine	VF	XF	Unc
119	1898	2.000	10.00	35.00	80.00	185.00

NOTE: Later date (1901) exists for this type.

25 CENTS

4.2300 g, .569 SILVER, .0773 oz ASW

KM#	Date	Mintage	Fine	VF	XF	Unc
48	1817	—	525.00	1500.	3000.	4500.
	1817	—	—	—	Proof	9000.
	1818	—	750.00	2500.	4000.	6500.
	1818	—	—	—	Proof	—
	1819	.013	300.00	600.00	1000.	1750.
	1819	—	—	—	Proof	3000.
	1822	.116	220.00	400.00	750.00	1000.
	1823/22B	1.334	75.00	200.00	400.00	600.00
	1823B	Inc. Ab.	20.00	45.00	100.00	150.00
	1824B	6.033	15.00	30.00	65.00	120.00
	1825	10.311	15.00	30.00	65.00	120.00
	1825B	2.608	20.00	45.00	100.00	150.00
	1826	12.282	15.00	28.00	60.00	110.00
	1826B	7.299	15.00	28.00	60.00	110.00
	1827B	2.022	20.00	45.00	100.00	150.00
	1828B	.334	150.00	300.00	650.00	900.00
	1829	.106	150.00	450.00	850.00	1400.
	1829B	1.256	28.00	55.00	145.00	250.00
	1830	1.534	28.00	55.00	145.00	250.00
	1830B	.902	30.00	55.00	145.00	250.00

3.5750 g, .640 SILVER, .0736 oz ASW

KM#	Date	Mintage	Fine	VF	XF	Unc
76	1848. dot after date					
		10.730	10.00	25.00	75.00	150.00
	1848.	—	—	—	Proof	300.00
	1848 w/o dot after date					
		Inc. Ab.	12.00	40.00	100.00	200.00
	1849/89	8.059	150.00	330.00	500.00	625.00
	1849	Inc. Ab.	7.00	20.00	60.00	135.00

KM#	Date	Mintage	Fine	VF	XF	Unc
81	1849	Inc.KM76	135.00	275.00	450.00	900.00
	1850	2.207	125.00	250.00	375.00	650.00
	1853	7,974	200.00	400.00	850.00	1500.
	1853	—	—	—	Proof	3000.
	1887	.100	135.00	275.00	450.00	850.00
	1889	.200	100.00	250.00	325.00	600.00
	1890. dot after date					
		.600	60.00	150.00	250.00	450.00
	1890 w/o dot after date					
		Inc. Ab.	90.00	200.00	335.00	475.00

KM#	Date	Mintage	Fine	VF	XF	Unc
115	1891	2 pcs.	—	—	—	—
	1892	.800	8.00	30.00	90.00	150.00
	1893	.800	8.00	30.00	90.00	150.00
	1894	1.000	7.00	30.00	90.00	150.00
	1895	1.200	7.00	30.00	90.00	150.00
	1895 slanted mintmasters mark					
		Inc. Ab.	80.00	150.00	300.00	500.00
	1896	.600	30.00	85.00	200.00	350.00
	1897	3.100	6.00	25.00	50.00	125.00

Obv: Bust w/wide truncation.

KM#	Date	Mintage	Fine	VF	XF	Unc
120.1	1898	.400	80.00	180.00	325.00	700.00

NOTE: Later date (1901) exists for this type.

1/2 GULDEN

(50 Cents)

5.3800 g, .893 SILVER, .1544 oz ASW

KM#	Date	Mintage	Fine	VF	XF	Unc
54	1818	.051	150.00	280.00	650.00	1000.
	1819	.043	150.00	280.00	650.00	1000.
	1819	—	—	—	Proof	1400.
	1822 engraver's name below bust					
		.119	150.00	280.00	500.00	800.00
	1822 w/o engraver's name					
		Inc. Ab.	250.00	475.00	750.00	1150.
	1829B	.180	150.00	300.00	600.00	800.00
	1830B/1820	—	150.00	300.00	650.00	900.00
	1830B	.100	150.00	300.00	650.00	900.00

5.0000 g, .945 SILVER, .1519 oz ASW
Reeded edge.

KM#	Date	Mintage	Fine	VF	XF	Unc
73.1	1846	—	500.00	1250.	2500.	4000.
	1846	—	—	—	Proof	3000.
	1847	1.111	22.00	60.00	200.00	450.00
	1847	—	—	—	Proof	700.00
	1848	4.050	10.00	40.00	125.00	300.00

Lettered edge.

KM#	Date	Mintage	Fine	VF	XF	Unc
73.2	1846	—	—	—	Proof	3500.

KM#	Date	Mintage	Fine	VF	XF	Unc
92	1850	—	600.00	1500.	2200.	3500.
	1850	—	—	—	Proof	4000.
	1853/43	1,711	550.00	1250.	2250.	3200.
	1857	3.606	10.00	28.00	60.00	165.00
	1858	7.604	8.00	25.00	50.00	125.00
	1859	3.001	10.00	28.00	60.00	165.00
	1860	6.603	8.00	25.00	50.00	135.00
	1861	6.001	8.00	25.00	50.00	135.00
	1862	4.002	8.00	25.00	50.00	135.00
	1863	5.152	8.00	25.00	50.00	135.00
	1864	4.001	8.00	25.00	50.00	135.00
	1866	1.402	15.00	50.00	150.00	300.00
	1868 open 8					
		4.004	8.00	25.00	50.00	125.00
	1868 closed 8					
		Inc. Ab.	8.00	25.00	50.00	120.00

KM#	Date	Mintage	Fine	VF	XF	Unc
121.1	1898	2.000	15.00	40.00	110.00	200.00
	1898	—	—	—	Proof	600.00

GULDEN

(100 Cents)

10.7600 g, .893 SILVER, .3089 oz ASW

KM#	Date	Mintage	Fine	VF	XF	Unc
55	1818	.043	400.00	750.00	1500.	2000.
	1818	—	—	—	Proof	2250.
	1819	.252	200.00	450.00	750.00	1250.
	1820	.543	70.00	150.00	325.00	650.00
	1821	1.145	70.00	150.00	325.00	650.00
	1822	.080	300.00	700.00	1500.	2000.
	1823	.743	70.00	150.00	325.00	650.00
	1823	—	—	—	Proof	900.00
	1823B	.025	650.00	1500.	2000.	2500.
	1824	1.096	70.00	150.00	325.00	650.00
	1824 dash between crown & shield					
		Inc. Ab.	60.00	125.00	225.00	475.00
	1828	.062	300.00	600.00	1250.	1700.
	1829B	.383	200.00	400.00	750.00	1200.
	1831/21	.120	200.00	400.00	750.00	1200.
	1831	Inc. Ab.	200.00	400.00	750.00	1200.
	1832/21	1.362	65.00	135.00	325.00	650.00
	1832/23	I.A.	65.00	135.00	325.00	650.00
	1832/24	I.A.	65.00	135.00	325.00	650.00
	1832/24 dash between crown & shield					
		Inc. Ab.	65.00	135.00	325.00	650.00
	1832/28	I.A.	65.00	135.00	325.00	650.00
	1832	Inc. Ab.	65.00	135.00	325.00	650.00
	1837	.383	65.00	135.00	325.00	650.00

10.0000 g, .945 SILVER, .3038 oz ASW

KM#	Date	Mintage	Fine	VF	XF	Unc
65	1840	.099	50.00	110.00	300.00	650.00
	1840	—	—	—	Proof	2000.

KM#	Date	Mintage	Fine	VF	XF	Unc
66	1840	2 pcs.	—	—	Rare	—
	1842	.661	50.00	175.00	400.00	750.00
	1842	—	—	—	Proof	900.00
	1842 shorter bust					
		Inc. Ab.	125.00	275.00	600.00	1150.
	1842	—	—	—	Proof	1250.
	1843	1.720	35.00	80.00	160.00	400.00
	1844	1.575	35.00	80.00	160.00	400.00
	1845	3.803	12.00	35.00	75.00	150.00
	1845 dash between crown & shield					
		.221	35.00	80.00	160.00	400.00
	1846 fleur de lis privy mark					
		.901	20.00	50.00	100.00	200.00
	1846 sword privy mark					
		3.772	10.00	30.00	80.00	150.00
	1847	8.280	8.00	25.00	50.00	125.00
	1848	13.615	8.00	25.00	50.00	125.00
	1849	.650	35.00	80.00	160.00	400.00

KM#	Date	Mintage	Fine	VF	XF	Unc
93	1850	10 pcs.	—	—	Rare	—
	1850	—	—	—	Proof	4750.
	1850 reeded edge					
		—	—	—	Rare	—
	1851	2.125	15.00	40.00	100.00	175.00
	1853/0	.652	200.00	300.00	550.00	850.00
	1853/1	Inc. Ab.	200.00	300.00	550.00	850.00
	1853	Inc. Ab.	100.00	200.00	350.00	650.00
	1854	4.511	12.00	25.00	45.00	110.00
	1855	5.133	12.00	25.00	45.00	110.00
	1856	4.955	12.00	25.00	45.00	110.00
	1857	2.125	15.00	30.00	60.00	130.00
	1858	4.199	12.00	25.00	55.00	120.00
	1859	2.717	12.00	25.00	55.00	130.00
	1860	4.036	10.00	20.00	40.00	120.00
	1861	5.079	10.00	20.00	40.00	120.00
	1863	7.986	10.00	20.00	40.00	120.00
	1864	3.600	10.00	20.00	40.00	120.00
	1865	6.402	10.00	20.00	40.00	120.00
	1866	1.002	20.00	45.00	100.00	200.00
	1867	*4 pcs.	—	—	Proof	20,000.

KM#	Date	Mintage	Fine	VF	XF	Unc
117	1892	3.500	6.00	20.00	60.00	150.00
	1896	.100	80.00	225.00	500.00	1000.
	1896	—	—	—	Proof	1500.
	1897	2.500	10.00	22.00	80.00	175.00
122.1	1898	2.000	22.00	50.00	125.00	325.00

NOTE: Later date (1901) exists for this type.

RIJKSDAALDER

Mint: Utrecht

28.0780 g, .868 SILVER, .7836 ASW

KM#	Date	Mintage	Fine	VF	XF	Unc
46	1815	12 pcs.	—	—	Proof	10,000.
	1816	.174	450.00	750.00	1000.	1800.
	1816	—	—	—	Proof	2000.

2-1/2 GULDEN

25.0000 g, .945 SILVER, .7596 oz ASW

KM#	Date	Mintage	Fine	VF	XF	Unc
67	1840	.044	125.00	250.00	500.00	1100.
	1840	—	—	—	Proof	1600.

KM#	Date	Mintage	Fine	VF	XF	Unc
69	1841	.054	175.00	450.00	1000.	2000.
	1841	—	—	—	Proof	2200.
	1842	1.010	40.00	80.00	200.00	500.00
	1843	.643	50.00	110.00	225.00	600.00
	1843	—	—	—	Proof	900.00
	1844	.279	80.00	175.00	300.00	700.00
	1845	3.270	20.00	40.00	125.00	300.00
	1845 dash between crown & shield					
		.504	30.00	60.00	125.00	350.00
	1845 dot on band of privy mark					
		.154	30.00	60.00	125.00	350.00
	1846 Fleur de lis privy mark					
		3.630	18.00	40.00	110.00	300.00
	1846	—	—	—	Proof	850.00
	1846 sword privy mark					
		—	18.00	40.00	110.00	250.00
	1847	9.465	10.00	20.00	70.00	200.00
	1848	8.333	10.00	20.00	70.00	200.00
	1849	2.049	20.00	60.00	140.00	300.00

KM#	Date	Mintage	Fine	VF	XF	Unc
82	1849	.439	50.00	150.00	250.00	500.00
	1849	—	—	—	Proof	950.00
	1850	5.008	12.00	25.00	70.00	200.00
	1851	3.647	12.00	25.00	70.00	200.00
	1852	4.547	12.00	25.00	70.00	200.00
	1853/2	.234	100.00	300.00	400.00	750.00
	1853	Inc. Ab.	60.00	160.00	300.00	525.00
	1854/2	4.335	50.00	125.00	250.00	500.00
	1854	Inc. Ab.	12.00	25.00	70.00	200.00
	1855	2.082	12.00	25.00	70.00	200.00
	1856	.909	40.00	90.00	150.00	350.00
	1857	3.353	12.00	25.00	70.00	200.00
	1858	8.357	12.00	25.00	70.00	150.00
	1859	4.307	12.00	25.00	80.00	175.00
	1860	.847	40.00	80.00	150.00	350.00
	1861	.876	30.00	80.00	150.00	350.00

KM#	Date	Mintage	Fine	VF	XF	Unc
82	1862	3.304	12.00	25.00	80.00	175.00
	1863	.051	250.00	500.00	1000.	1800.
	1864	2.034	12.00	20.00	50.00	150.00
	1865	2.288	12.00	20.00	50.00	150.00
	1866	3.563	12.00	20.00	50.00	150.00
	1867	4.949	10.00	18.00	50.00	125.00
	1868	4.040	10.00	18.00	50.00	125.00
	1869	5.046	10.00	18.00	50.00	125.00
	1870	6.640	8.00	15.00	40.00	100.00
	1871	6.875	8.00	15.00	40.00	100.00
	1872	13.416	8.00	15.00	40.00	100.00
	1873	5.515	8.00	15.00	40.00	100.00
	1874 sword privy mark					
		3.040	8.00	15.00	40.00	100.00
	1874 sword in scabbard privy mark					
		9.756	8.00	15.00	40.00	100.00

KM#	Date	Mintage	Fine	VF	XF	Unc
123	1898	.100	150.00	275.00	500.00	1000.
	1898	—	—	—	Proof	3000.

GOLD

KM#	Date	Mintage	Fine	VF	XF	Unc
123a	1898	—	—	—	Rare	—

3 GULDEN

39.2900 g, .893 SILVER, .9270 oz ASW

KM#	Date	Mintage	Fine	VF	XF	Unc
49	1817	12 pcs.	—	—	Proof	12,500.
	1818	.116	250.00	450.00	800.00	1200.
	1819/8	.151	600.00	1000.	1400.	2000.
	1819	Inc. Ab.	250.00	450.00	800.00	1250.
	1820	.713	250.00	450.00	800.00	1250.
	1821	.277	250.00	450.00	800.00	1250.
	1821 w/o engraver's name					
		Inc. Ab.	400.00	750.00	1000.	1500.
	1821 medal rotation					
		—	600.00	1000.	1400.	2000.
	1822	.296	400.00	750.00	1000.	1700.
	1822 w/o engraver's name					
		Inc. Ab.	400.00	750.00	1000.	1700.
	1823	.235	400.00	750.00	850.00	1250.
	1823B	.014	1200.	3000.	7000.	10,000.
	1824	.644	250.00	450.00	800.00	1250.
	1824 dash between crown & shield					
		Inc. Ab.	250.00	450.00	800.00	1250.
	1830/20	.246	250.00	450.00	800.00	1250.
	1830/24	I.A.	250.00	450.00	800.00	1250.
	1830/24 dash between crown & shield					
		Inc. Ab.	275.00	500.00	900.00	1500.
	1830	Inc. Ab.	250.00	450.00	800.00	1250.
	1831/24	.117	250.00	450.00	800.00	1250.
	1831/24 dash between crown & shield					
		Inc. Ab.	250.00	450.00	800.00	1250.
	1831	Inc. Ab.	250.00	450.00	800.00	1250.
	1832/21	.371	250.00	450.00	800.00	1250.
	1832/22	I.A.	250.00	450.00	800.00	1250.
	1832/23	I.A.	250.00	450.00	800.00	1250.
	1832/24	I.A.	250.00	450.00	800.00	1250.
	1832/24 dash between crown & shield					
		Inc. Ab.	250.00	450.00	800.00	1250.
	1832	Inc. Ab.	250.00	450.00	800.00	1250.

5 GULDEN

3.3645 g, .900 GOLD, .0973 oz AGW

KM#	Date	Mintage	Fine	VF	XF	Unc
60	1826B	.843	80.00	200.00	300.00	550.00
	1827	.518	175.00	275.00	375.00	850.00
	1827B	1.629	80.00	200.00	300.00	500.00

KM#	Date	Mintage	Fine	VF	XF	Unc
72	1843	1,595	300.00	900.00	1500.	2000.

Obv: Bust right.
Rev: Crowned arms within branches.

KM#	Date	Mintage	Fine	VF	XF	Unc
77	1848	50 pcs.	700.00	1750.	2500.	3250.
	1848	—	—	—	Proof	3250.

KM#	Date	Mintage	Fine	VF	XF	Unc
94	1850	—	600.00	1500.	2000.	2500.
	1850	—	—	—	Proof	2250.
	1851	.010	300.00	1000.	1500.	2000.

10 GULDEN

6.7290 g, .900 GOLD, .1947 oz AGW

KM#	Date	Mintage	Fine	VF	XF	Unc
56	1818	—	1000.	1500.	2250.	4750.
	1819	.107	650.00	1000.	1350.	2500.
	1820	.033	650.00	1000.	1350.	2500.
	1822	.048	650.00	1000.	1500.	3250.
	1823	.266	150.00	275.00	350.00	800.00
	1824	.336	150.00	275.00	350.00	800.00
	1824B	3.735	150.00	275.00	350.00	800.00
	1825	.228	150.00	275.00	350.00	800.00
	1825B	3.821	150.00	275.00	350.00	800.00
	1826	—	1000.	1500.	2000.	4000.
	1826B	.079	600.00	850.00	1200.	2000.
	1827B	.134	600.00	850.00	1200.	2000.
	1828	.015	900.00	1400.	1800.	3500.
	1828B	.562	150.00	275.00	350.00	800.00
	1829	9,484	650.00	1000.	1350.	2250.
	1829B	.084	650.00	1000.	1350.	2250.
	1830/20	—	—	—	—	800.00
	1830/28	.568	1000.	1200.	1500.	3000.
	1830	Inc.Ab.	150.00	275.00	350.00	800.00
	1831/0	.099	600.00	850.00	1200.	2000.
	1831	Inc. Ab.	150.00	275.00	350.00	800.00
	1832/1	1.372	600.00	850.00	1200.	2000.
	1832	Inc. Ab.	150.00	275.00	350.00	800.00
	1833	.721	150.00	275.00	350.00	800.00
	1837	.458	150.00	275.00	350.00	800.00
	1839	.326	150.00	275.00	350.00	800.00
	1840	2.760	150.00	275.00	350.00	600.00

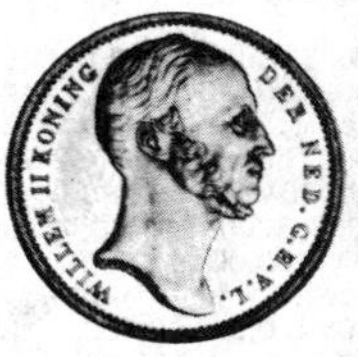

KM#	Date	Mintage	Fine	VF	XF	Unc
71	1842	860 pcs.	1100.	2000.	3000.	4000.

KM#	Date	Mintage	Fine	VF	XF	Unc
78	1848	*50 pcs.	1500.	2500.	3750.	5000.
	1848	—	—	—	Proof	6000.

KM#	Date	Mintage	Fine	VF	XF	Unc
95	1850	—	900.00	1800.	2500.	3250.
	1850	—	—	—	Proof	4000.
	1851	.010	500.00	1000.	1750.	2500.

KM#	Date	Mintage	Fine	VF	XF	Unc
105	1875	4.110	—	BV	80.00	100.00

KM#	Date	Mintage	Fine	VF	XF	Unc
106	1876	1.581	—	BV	80.00	100.00
	1877	1.108	—	BV	100.00	120.00
	1879/7	.581	125.00	175.00	250.00	350.00
	1879	Inc. Ab.	—	BV	100.00	120.00
	1880	.050	BV	110.00	145.00	175.00
	1885	.067	BV	110.00	145.00	175.00
	1886	.054	100.00	125.00	165.00	200.00
	1887	.041	100.00	125.00	165.00	200.00
	1888	.036	125.00	250.00	350.00	450.00
	1889	.205	—	BV	100.00	120.00

KM#	Date	Mintage	Fine	VF	XF	Unc
118	1892	61 pcs.	1500.	3500.	7000.	8000.
	1892	—	—	—	Proof	10,000.
	1895/1	149 pcs.	1400.	2500.	4500.	6000.
	1895/1	—	—	—	Proof	6500.
	1895	Inc. Ab.	900.00	2000.	3500.	5500.
	1897	.454	—	BV	100.00	150.00

KM#	Date	Mintage	Fine	VF	XF	Unc
124	1898	.099	125.00	175.00	225.00	350.00

20 GULDEN

13.4580 g, .900 GOLD, .3894 oz AGW
Obv: Bust right.
Rev: Crowned arms within branches.

KM#	Date	Mintage	Fine	VF	XF	Unc
79	1848	*50 pcs.	1250.	3000.	4500.	6000.

KM#	Date	Mintage	Fine	VF	XF	Unc
96	1850	—	1250.	2500.	3500.	4500.
96	1850	—	—	—	Proof	4500.
	1851	2,500	600.00	1500.	2500.	3000.
	1853	136 pcs.	1000.	2250.	3000.	4000.

TRADE COINAGE

DUCAT

3.5000 g, .983 GOLD, .1106 oz AGW
Mint: Utrecht

KM#	Date	Mintage	Fine	VF	XF	Unc
45	1814	2.930	100.00	175.00	275.00	400.00
	1815	.673	100.00	175.00	275.00	400.00
	1815 cloverleaf					
		.614	100.00	175.00	275.00	400.00
	1816	.221	110.00	225.00	325.00	500.00

KM#	Date	Mintage	Fine	VF	XF	Unc
50.1	1817	.495	200.00	350.00	600.00	750.00
	1818	1.572	75.00	125.00	200.00	300.00
	1819	.111	100.00	175.00	275.00	400.00
	1820	.010	175.00	300.00	500.00	700.00
	1821	.015	175.00	300.00	500.00	700.00
	1822	.012	175.00	300.00	500.00	700.00
	1824B	8,000	300.00	600.00	1000.	1500.
	1825	.119	100.00	175.00	275.00	400.00
	1825B	.056	175.00	300.00	500.00	700.00
	1827	.138	110.00	225.00	325.00	450.00
	1827B	.027	200.00	350.00	500.00	700.00
	1828/7	.622	100.00	175.00	275.00	400.00
	1828	Inc. Ab.	100.00	175.00	275.00	400.00
	1828B	.534	100.00	175.00	275.00	400.00
	1829/8B	.247	175.00	300.00	500.00	700.00
	1829B	Inc. Ab.	175.00	300.00	500.00	700.00
	1829	1.153	75.00	125.00	175.00	250.00
	1830B	.011	250.00	375.00	650.00	850.00
	1831	.411	75.00	125.00	175.00	250.00
	1833	.247	100.00	175.00	275.00	400.00
	1836/5	.236	125.00	275.00	500.00	850.00
	1836	Inc. Ab.	100.00	175.00	275.00	500.00
	1839	.118	100.00	200.00	300.00	450.00
	1840 Fleur de lis privy mark					
		.103	100.00	200.00	300.00	450.00

Mint: St. Petersburg

KM#	Date	Mintage	Fine	VF	XF	Unc
50.2	1818	1.350	80.00	130.00	175.00	250.00
	1827	.350	130.00	250.00	325.00	450.00
	1828	1.300	120.00	225.00	275.00	375.00
	1829	.150	80.00	130.00	175.00	200.00
	1830	2.000	80.00	130.00	175.00	200.00
	1831	1.000	80.00	130.00	175.00	200.00
	1832	1.000	100.00	200.00	275.00	350.00
	1833	.350	100.00	200.00	275.00	350.00
	1834	.150	200.00	350.00	500.00	700.00
	1835	.650	110.00	225.00	325.00	425.00
	1836	.300	110.00	225.00	325.00	450.00
	1837	1.400	80.00	170.00	250.00	350.00
	1838	1.200	80.00	170.00	250.00	350.00
	1839	1.350	80.00	170.00	250.00	350.00
	1840 torch privy mark					
		—	80.00	175.00	250.00	350.00
70.1	1841 torch privy mark					
		3.904	80.00	150.00	200.00	300.00

Mint: Utrecht

KM#	Date	Mintage	Fine	VF	XF	Unc
70.2	1841 Fleur de lis privy mark					
		.096	100.00	200.00	300.00	450.00

KM#	Date	Mintage	Fine	VF	XF	Unc
83.1	1849	.014	70.00	140.00	200.00	300.00
	1872	.030	200.00	500.00	800.00	1400.
	1873	.040	200.00	500.00	800.00	1400.
	1874	.044	200.00	500.00	800.00	1400.
	1876	.044	200.00	500.00	800.00	1400.
	1877	.015	200.00	500.00	800.00	1400.
	1878	.087	200.00	500.00	800.00	1400.
	1879	.020	200.00	500.00	800.00	1400.
	1880	.025	200.00	500.00	800.00	1400.
	1885	.081	125.00	350.00	600.00	1000.
	1894	.030	110.00	225.00	300.00	450.00
	1895/55	.058	125.00	250.00	350.00	800.00
	1895/59	I.A.	110.00	225.00	300.00	450.00
	1895	Inc. Ab.	90.00	175.00	270.00	350.00
	1899	.061	90.00	175.00	270.00	350.00

NOTE: Later dates (1901-1937) exist for this type.

BRONZE

KM#	Date	Mintage	Fine	VF	XF	Unc
83.1a	1868	—	—	—	Rare	—

3.5000 g, .983 GOLD, .1106 oz AGW
Mint: St. Petersburg

KM#	Date	Mintage	Fine	VF	XF	Unc
83.2	1849	4.750	70.00	140.00	200.00	300.00

2 DUCAT

6.9880 g, .983 GOLD, .2209 oz AGW

Mint: Utrecht

KM#	Date	Mintage	Fine	VF	XF	Unc
97	1854	—	—	—	10,000.	12,000.
	1854	—	—	—	Proof	9000.
	1867	—	—	—	—	20,000.

PATTERNS (Pn)

(Including off metal strikes)

KM#	Date	Mintage	Identification	Mkt.Val.
Pn20	1814	—	1 Rijksdaalder, Gold, KM46	Rare
Pn21	1816	—	1 Rijksdaalder, Gold, KM46	Rare
Pn22	1817	—	25 Cents, Bronze, KM48	—
Pn23	1817	—	3 Gulden, Tin, KM49	—
Pn24	1818	—	1/2 Cent, Silver, KM51	Rare

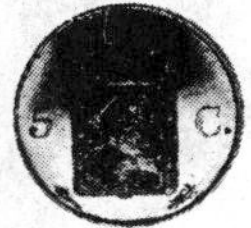

KM#	Date	Mintage	Identification	Mkt.Val.
Pn25	1818	—	5 Cents, Gold, KM52	4500.
Pn26	1818	—	5 Cents, Bronze, KM52	—
Pn27	1818	—	1/2 Gulden, Bronze, KM54	—
Pn28	1818	—	1 Gulden, Bronze, KM55	—
Pn29	1818	—	3 Gulden, Bronze, KM49	—
Pn30	1818	—	10 Gulden, Bronze, KM56	500.00
Pn31	1819	—	1/2 Cent, Gold, KM51	Rare
Pn32	1819	—	1/2 Gulden, Bronze, KM54	—
Pn33	1819	—	1 Gulden, Bronze, KM55	—
Pn34	1819/8	—	3 Gulden, Bronze, KM49	600.00
Pn35	1819	—	10 Gulden, Bronze, KM56	500.00
Pn36	1820	—	1 Gulden, Gold, KM55	Rare
Pn37	1820	—	1 Gulden, Silver, KM55	—
Pn38	1820	—	3 Gulden, Bronze, KM49	—
Pn39	1821	—	1 Gulden, Gold, KM55	Rare
Pn40	1821	—	1 Gulden, Silver, KM55	—
Pn41	1822	—	1/2 Cent, Gold, KM51	Rare
Pn42	1822	—	5 Cents, Gold, KM52	3000.
Pn43	1822	—	10 Cents, Gold, KM53	3500.
Pn44	1822	—	3 Gulden, Bronze, KM49	—
Pn45	1823	—	1 Cent, Silver, KM47	Rare
Pn46	1823	—	1 Cent, Gold, KM47	Rare
Pn47	1823	—	3 Gulden, Gold, KM49	Rare
Pn48	1824	—	1/2 Cent, Gold, KM51	Rare
Pn49	1826	—	1 Cent, Gold, KM47	Rare
Pn50	1826	—	5 Gulden, Bronze, KM60	—
Pn51	1827	—	1 Cent, Gold, KM47	Rare
Pn52	1840	2	2-1/2 Gulden, Gold, KM46	Rare

KM#	Date	Mintage	Identification	Mkt.Val.
Pn53	1843	—	10 Cents, Gold	1250.
Pn54	1843	—	10 Cents, Silver	—
Pn55	1843	—	10 Cents, Bronze	—
Pn56	1848	—	5 Cents, Gold, KM74	Rare
Pn57	1848	—	10 Cents, Gold, KM74	—
Pn58	1849	—	25 Cents, Gold, KM81	Rare
Pn59	1849	—	1 Ducat, Copper, KM83.1	—

KM#	Date	Mintage	Identification	Mkt.Val.
Pn60	1850	—	5 Gulden, .900 Gold, KM94	2250.
Pn61	1850	—	10 Gulden, .900 Gold, KM95	3750.

KM#	Date	Mintage	Identification	Mkt.Val.
Pn62	1850	—	20 Gulden, .900 Gold, KM96	5000.

KM#	Date	Mintage	Identification	Mkt.Val.
Pn63	1851	—	5 Cents, Bronze	—
Pn64	1851	—	5 Cents, Bronze	—
Pn65	1853	—	5 Cents, .718 Silver, c/m: 718, KM91	Rare
Pn66	1853	—	10 Cents, .718 Silver, c/m: 718, KM80	Rare
Pn67	1853	—	25 Cents, .718 Silver, c/m: 718, KM81	Rare

KM#	Date	Mintage	Identification	Mkt.Val.
PnA68	1860	—	1 Cent, Bronze	—
Pn68	1866	—	1/2 Gulden, Bronze, KM92	—
Pn69	1867	—	1 Gulden, Gold, KM93	Rare
Pn70	1868/58	—	1/2 Gulden, Gold, KM92	Rare
PnA71	1868	—	2 Ducat, Bronze, KM97	500.00
Pn71	1872	—	1/2 Cent, Silver, KM90	Rare
Pn72	1872	—	1/2 Cent, Gold, KM90	Rare
Pn73	1873	—	1/2 Cent, Gold, KM90	—
Pn74	1874	—	2-1/2 Gulden, Gold, sword in scabbard privy mark, KM82	Rare
Pn75	1875	—	1 Cent, Gold, KM100	Rare
Pn76	1875	—	1 Cent, Silver, KM100	Rare
Pn77	1876	—	1 Cent, Gold, KM100	Rare
Pn78	1876	—	1 Cent, Silver, KM100	Rare
Pn79	1877	—	1 Cent, Gold, KM100	Rare
Pn80	1879	—	5 Cents, Gold, KM91	Rare
Pn81	1884	—	1/2 Cent, Gold, KM109	Rare
Pn82	1884	—	1 Cent, Gold, KM107	Rare
Pn83	1884	—	2-1/2 Cents, Gold, KM108	Rare
Pn84	1884	—	10 Cents, Gold, KM80	Rare
Pn85	1885	—	10 Cents, Gold, KM80	Rare
Pn86	1887	—	5 Cents, Gold, KM91	—
Pn87	1888	—	10 Gulden, Bronze, KM106	—
Pn88	1891	—	10 Gulden, Gold, KM118	—
Pn89	1891	—	10 Gulden, Silver, KM118	—
Pn90	1892	—	10 Cents, Bronze, KM116	—
Pn91	1892	—	1 Gulden, Bronze, KM117	—
Pn92	1898	—	1/2 Gulden, Gold, KM121.1	Rare
Pn93	1898	2	1 Gulden, Gold, KM122.1	Rare
Pn94	1898	—	2-1/2 Gulden, Gold, KM123	Rare

PIEFORTS (P)

KM#	Date	Mintage	Identification	Mkt.Val.
P2	1808	—	50 Stuivers, Gold	Rare
P3	1820	—	1 Gulden, .893 Silver	Rare
P4	1822	—	1 Cent, Copper, KM47	Rare
P5	1822B	—	3 Gulden, Gold, KM49	3000.
P6	1822	—	3 Gulden, Silver, KM49	Rare
P7	1823	—	1/2 Cent, Copper, Utrecht Mint, KM51	Rare
P8	1823	—	1/2 Cent, Copper, Brussel Mint, KM51	Rare
P9	1823	—	1 Cent, Gold, KM47	Rare
P10	1827	—	1/2 Cent, Copper, KM51	Rare
P11	1827	—	1 Cent, Copper, KM47	Rare
P12	1828	—	1 Cent, Copper, KM47	Rare
P13	1837	—	1 Cent, Copper, KM47	Rare
P14	1840	—	2-1/2 Gulden, Silver, KM46	Rare
P15	1848	—	10 Cents, Silver, KM74	Rare
P16	1868/58	—	1/2 Gulden, .945 Silver	Rare
P17	1876	—	1 Cent, Silver	Rare
P18	1898	—	2-1/2 Gulden, .945 Silver	Rare

SELECT SETS (SS)

Fleur de Coin

KM#	Date	Mintage	Identification	Issue Price	Mkt. Val.
SS1	1819(9)	1 set	KM47-49,51-56	—	45,000.

NETHERLANDS ANTILLES

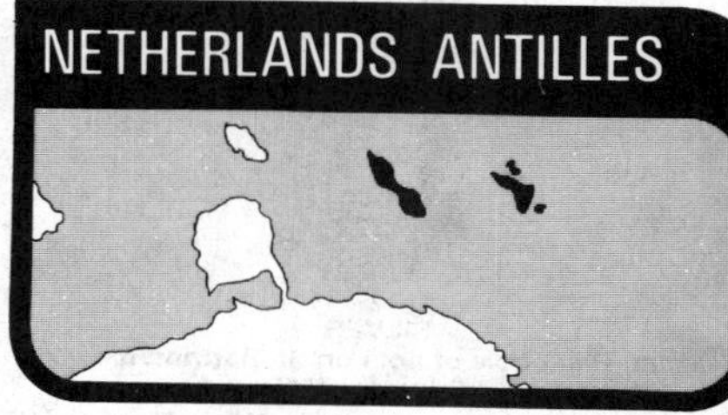

The Netherlands Antilles, comprises two groups of islands in the West Indies: Aruba (until 1986), Bonaire and Curacao and their dependencies near the Venezuelan coast and St. Eustatius, Saba, and the southern part of St. Martin (St. Maarten) southeast of Puerto Rico. The island group has an area of 371 sq. mi. (960 sq. km.) and a population of 225,000. Capital: Willemstad. Chief industries are the refining of crude oil and tourism. Petroleum products and phosphates are exported.

On Dec. 15, 1954, the Netherlands Antilles were given complete domestic autonomy and granted equality within the Kingdom with Surinam and the Netherlands. On Jan. l, 1986, Aruba achieved "status aparte" as the fourth part of the Dutch realm which was a step towards total independence.

ST. EUSTATIUS

St. Eustatius (Sint Eustatius, Statia), a Netherlands West Indian island located in the Leeward Islands of the Lesser Antilles nine miles northwest of St. Kitts, has an area of 12 sq. mi. (21 sq. km.) and a population of about 2,000. It is part of the Netherlands Antilles. The island's capital is Oranjestad. The chief industries are farming, fishing, and tourism.

Between 1630 and 1640 the Dutch seized Curacao, Saba, St. Martin and St. Eustatius, all valuable as piloting and smuggling depots. The territorial acquisitions were confirmed to the Dutch by the Treaty of Munster in 1648. Under the guidance of merchants from Flushing, St. Eustatius became a prosperous entrepot of neutral trade. On Feb. 3, 1781, British Admiral George Rodney, acting under orders, captured the island and confiscated much valuable booty. Before passing permanently into Dutch hands, St. Eustatius was attacked or captured several times by the French and English, and was in English hands during the Napoleonic Wars from 1810 to 1814.

RULERS

Dutch

MONETARY SYSTEM

6 Stuivers = 1 Reaal

COUNTERMARKED COINAGE

SE incuse countermark on French Guiana 2 Sous coins was official.

These were followed by raised SE countermarks (on a variety of worn billon & silver coins) generally thought to be forgeries.

From 1809 all coins had to be revalidated with a P countermark, which stood for Pierre dit Flamand, the artisan who designed the mark. Both raised and incuse SE varieties as well as unmarked coins were revalidated.

STUIVER

COPPER
c/m: Raised SE.

KM#	Date	Year	Good	VG	Fine	VF
1.2	ND(1797-1809)		35.00	60.00	90.00	165.00
	BILLON					
1.2a	ND(1797-1809)		40.00	65.00	100.00	175.00
	SILVER					
1.2b	ND(1797-1809)		100.00	150.00	200.00	250.00

BRITISH OCCUPATION

STUIVER

VARIOUS METALS
c/m: P revalidation on older SE.

KM#	Date	Mintage	Good	VG	Fine	VF
4	ND(1809-12)		45.00	75.00	125.00	200.00

1/2 REAL

SILVER
c/m: P in circle of dots on St. Bartholomew 4 Stivers, KM#5.

KM#	Date	Mintage	Good	VG	Fine	VF
5	ND(1810-12)	—	—	—	Rare	—

1 REAL

SILVER
c/m: P in circle of dots on St. Bartholomew 7 Stivers, KM#7.

KM#	Date	Mintage	Good	VG	Fine	VF
6.1	ND(1810-12)	—	—	—	Rare	—

c/m: P in circle of dots on St. Bartholomew 9 Stivers, KM#8.

KM#	Date	Mintage	Good	VG	Fine	VF
6.2	ND(1810-12)	—	—	—	Rare	—

2 REALES

SILVER
c/m: P in circle of dots.

KM#	Date	Mintage	Good	VG	Fine	VF
7.1	ND(1810-12)		27.50	45.00	75.00	125.00

c/m: P in circle of dots on St. Bartholomew 14 Stivers, KM#11.

KM#	Date	Mintage	Good	VG	Fine	VF
7.2	ND(1810-12)		—	—	Rare	—

ST. MARTIN

St. Martin (Sint Maarten), the only island in the Antilles owned by two European powers (France and the Netherlands), is located in the Leeward Islands of the Lesser Antilles five miles south of the British island of Anguilla. The French northern section of the island (St. Martin) is a dependency of the French Department of Guadeloupe. It has an area of 20 sq. mi. (51 sq. km.) and a population of about 4,500. Capital: Le Marigot. The Dutch southern section of the island (Sint Maarten) has an area of 17 sq. mi. (34 sq. km.) and a population of about 8,000. Capital: Philipsburg. The chief industries are farming, fishing, and tourism. Salt, horses, and mules are exported.

Although nominally a Spanish possession at the time, St. Martin was occupied by French freebooters in 1638, but when Spain relinquished claim to the island in 1648 it was peaceably divided between France and Holland in recognition of the merchant communities already established on the island by nationals of both powers. St. Martin has remained under dual French-Dutch ownership to the present time, except for a period during the Napoleonic Wars when the British seized and occupied it.

The northern section of the island uses the coins and currency of France.

MONETARY SYSTEM

6 Stuivers = 1 Reaal
20 Stuivers = 1 Gulden
12 (later 15) Reaals = 1 Peso

COUNTERMARKED COINAGE

2 STUIVERS

BILLON
c/m: StM in beaded circle plus incuse M on French Guiana 2 Sous.

KM#	Date	Mintage	Good	VG	Fine	VF
3	ND(1820)	—	70.00	110.00	140.00	175.00

c/m: Incuse Fleur-de-Lys on French Guiana 2 Sous.

KM#	Date	Mintage	Good	VG	Fine	VF
4	ND(1805)	—	100.00	150.00	200.00	250.00

SILVER
c/m: Raised Fleur-de-Lis.

KM#	Date	Mintage	Good	VG	Fine	VF
5	ND(1805)	—	30.00	50.00	75.00	100.00

c/m: Incuse Fleur-de-Lys plus S t M in beaded circle.

KM#	Date	Mintage	Good	VG	Fine	VF
6	ND(1805)	—	55.00	75.00	125.00	200.00

18 STUIVERS

SILVER
c/m: ST. MARTIN and arrows on 1/5 cut of Spanish or Spanish Colonial 8 Reales.

KM#	Date	Mintage	Good	VG	Fine	VF
12	ND(1817-20)	—	75.00	150.00	225.00	400.00

CURACAO

The island of Curacao, the largest of the Netherlands Antilles, which is an autonomous part of the Kingdom of the Netherlands located in the Caribbean Sea 40 miles off the coast of Venezuela, has an area of 173 sq. mi. (472 sq. km.) and a population of 127,900. Capital: Willemstad. The chief industries are banking and tourism. Salt, phosphates and cattle are exported.

Curacao was discovered by Spanish navigator Alonso de Ojeda in 1499 and was settled by Spain in 1527. The Dutch West India Company took the island from Spain in 1634 and administered it until 1787, when it was surrendered to the United Netherlands. The Dutch held it thereafter except for two periods during the Napoleonic Wars, 1800-1803 and 1807-16, when it was occupied by the British. During World War II, Curacao refined 60 percent of the oil used by the Allies; the refineries were protected by U.S. troops after Germany invaded the Netherlands in 1940.

During the second occupation of the Napoleonic period, the British created an emergency coinage for Curacao by cutting the Spanish dollar into 5 equal segments and countermarking each piece with a rosette indent.

MINT MARKS

D - Denver
P - Philadelphia
(u) - Utrecht

BATAVIAN REPUBLIC

MONETARY SYSTEM

1 Cent (U.S.) = 2-1/2 Stuivers
6 Stuivers = 1 Reaal
8 Realen = 1 Peso, 1793-1801
12 Realen = 1 Peso, 1801-18
6 Pesos = 1 Johannes (unmarked), 1799-1815
8 Pesos = 1 Johannes (c/m), 1799-1815
7-1/2 Pesos = 1 Johannes (c/m), 1815-27

9 STUIVERS

SILVER
c/m: 9 in oval indent on Spanish Colonial 1 Real.

KM#	Date	Mintage	Good	VG	Fine	VF
4	ND 1801	—	150.00	200.00	250.00	325.00

NOTE: The above coins along with similar coins bearing the numbers 3, 5, 14-18 are of questionable origin. Thus, they are not listed in Craig. Pridmore states these as unattributable.

3 REAAL

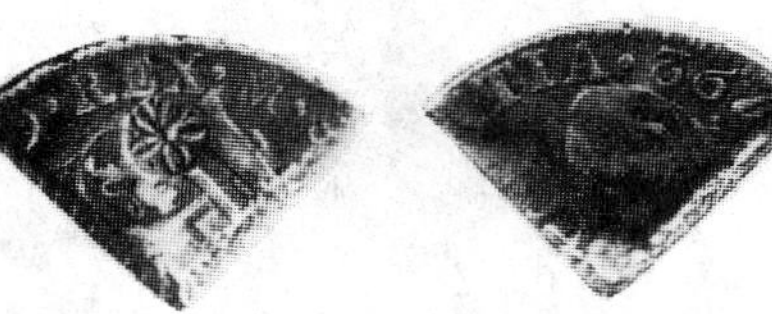

SILVER
c/m: 5-petalled rosace in circle on 1/4 cut of Spanish or Spanish Colonial 8 Reales

KM#	Date	Mintage	VG	Fine	VF	XF
7	ND(c.1810)	.030	600.00	1200.	1800.	2200.

BRITISH OCCUPATION

1807-1816

3 REAAL

SILVER
Partial reconstruction, 4 out of 5 segments
c/m: 5-petalled rosace in circle on 1/5 cut of Spanish or Spanish Colonial 8 reales

KM#	Date	Mintage	VG	Fine	VF	XF
13	ND(1815)	.040	60.00	100.00	175.00	275.00

3-1/2 REAAL

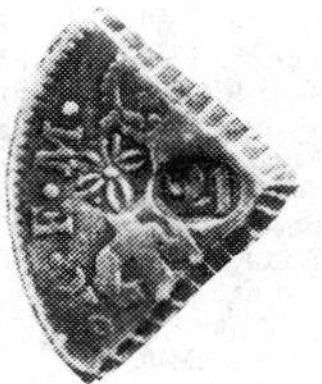

SILVER
c/m: Additional 21 in oval indent on KM#13.

KM#	Date	Mintage	VG	Fine	VF	XF
16	ND(1814)	—	900.00	1500.	2000.	4250.

6 PESOS

GOLD
Obv. c/m: GI, L, MH and B at edges, GH in center on false Brazil 6400 Reis type of KM#172.2
Rev. c/m: W.

KM#	Date	Mintage	VG	Fine	VF	XF
19	ND(1815)	—	—	—	Unique	—

Obv. c/m: GI, L, MH and B at edges, GH in center on Brazil 6400 Reis, KM#199.1.
Rev. c/m: W.

KM#	Date	Mintage	VG	Fine	VF	XF
20	ND(1815)	—	—	—	Unique	—

NETHERLANDS RESTORED

1816

MONETARY REFORM

15 Realen = 1 Peso, 1818-22
7 Stuivers = 1 Reaal, 1822-27
10 Stuivers = 1 Franc, 1822-27
5 Francs = 1 Dollar
20 Stuivers = 1 Gulden, 1827-99
2/5 Peso = 1 Gulden, 1827-96
5/7 Peso = 1 Gulden, 1896-97
1 Peso = 1 Gulden, 1897-99

STUIVER

.300 SILVER

KM#	Date	Mintage	Fine	VF	XF	Unc
24	1822	.529	50.00	75.00	125.00	220.00

NOTE: Struck also in 1840-41, circulating at that time as a 2 Cent piece.

1/4 REAAL

SILVER

25	1821	Unique?	—	—	—	—

REAAL

SILVER

Rev: 4 acorns.

26.1	1821	.121	60.00	100.00	175.00	280.00

Rev: 7 acorns.

26.2	1821	Inc. Ab.	60.00	100.00	175.00	280.00

Rev: 8 acorns.

26.3	1821	Inc. Ab.	60.00	100.00	175.00	280.00

Rev: 9 acorns.

26.4	1821	Inc. Ab.	60.00	100.00	175.00	280.00

Rev: 12 acorns.

26.5	1821	Inc. Ab.	60.00	100.00	175.00	280.00

1/4 GUILDER

SILVER
Reconstructed 4 segments
c/m: C in oval indent on 1/4 cut of Netherlands 1 Gulden.

KM#	Date	Mintage	VG	Fine	VF	XF
27	ND(1838)	.024	75.00	125.00	225.00	350.00

3 REAAL

SILVER
Reconstructed 5 segments
c/m: 3 in circle on 1/5 cut of Spanish or Spanish Colonial 8 Reales.

28	ND(1818)	.078	60.00	95.00	165.00	270.00

c/m: 3 in dentilated circle on 1/5 cut of Spanish or Spanish Colonial 8 Reales.

29	ND(1819-25)	—	50.00	85.00	150.00	245.00

5 REAAL

SILVER
c/m: 5 in circle on 1/3 cut of Spanish or Spanish Colonial 8 Reales.

KM#	Date	Mintage	VG	Fine	VF	XF
30	ND(1818)	3,000	2500.	5000.	8500.	14,500.

1/4 GULDEN

3.5800 g, .640 SILVER, .0736 oz ASW

KM#	Date	Mintage	Fine	VF	XF	Unc
35	1900(u)	.480	12.00	20.00	40.00	80.00
	1900(u)	40 pcs.	—	—	Proof	200.00

TOKEN ISSUES (Tn)

All of these tokens are known with the counterstamp of a letter C and were used by the S.E.L. Maduro Co. as coal loading tokens.

STUIVER

Jesurun and Co.

COPPER-NICKEL-ZINC
Obv: 1 STUIVER in 2 lines. Rev: J x Co.

Tn1	ND(ca.1880)	—	15.00	25.00	40.00	70.00

J.J. Naar

Rev: J.J.N.

Tn2	ND(ca.1880)	—	15.00	25.00	40.00	70.00

Leyba and Co.

Rev: L x C.

Tn3	ND(ca. 1880)	—	20.00	35.00	65.00	150.00

Listings For

NEW BRUNSWICK: refer to Canada

New Zealand, a parliamentary state located in the Southwest Pacific 1,250 miles (2,011 km.) east of Australia, has an area of 103,883 sq. mi. (268,680 sq. km.) and a population of *3.4 million. Capital: Wellington. Wool, meat, dairy products and some manufactured items are exported.

The first European to sight New Zealand was the Dutch navigator Abel Tasman in 1642. The islands were explored by British navigator Capt. James Cook who surveyed it in 1769 and annexed the land to Great Britain. The British government disavowed the annexation and for the next 70 years the only white settlers to arrive were adventurers attracted by the prospects of lumbering, sealing and whaling. Great Britain annexed the land in 1840 by treaty with the native chiefs and made it a dependency of New South Wales. The colony was granted self-government in 1852, a ministerial form of government in 1856, and full dominion status on Sept. 26, 1907. Full internal and external autonomy, which New Zealand had in effect possessed for many years, was formally extended in 1947. New Zealand is a member of the Commonwealth of Nations. The Queen of England is Chief of State.

Prior to 1933 English coins were the official legal tender but Australian coins were accepted in small transactions. Currency fluctuations caused a distintive New Zealand coinage to be introduced in 1933. The 1935 Waitangi crown and proof set were originally intended to mark the introduction but delays caused their date to be changed to 1935. The 1940 halfcrown marked the centennial of British rule, the 1949 and 1953 crowns commemorated Royal visits and the 1953 proof set marked the coronation of Queen Elizabeth.

Decimal Currency was introduced in 1967 with special sets commemorating the last issued of pound sterling (1965) and the first of the decimal issues. Since then dollars and set of coins have been issued nearly every year.

RULERS

British

MONETARY SYSTEM

12 Pence = 1 Shilling
2 Shillings = 1 Florin
2 Shillings & 6 Pence = Half Crown
5 Shillings = 1 Crown
20 Shillings = 1 Pound
2 Dollars = 1 Pound

PATTERNS (Pn)

(Including off metal strikes)

KM#	Date	Mintage	Identification	Mkt.Val.
Pn1	1879	—	Penny, Bronze, 30mm	1500.

TRADESMEN'S TOKENS

Because of a shortage of British money, New Zealand merchant tokens were issued beginning in 1857. There were some 147 varieties issued in ten cities, although the majority were issued in Auckland, Christchurch, Wellington and Dunedin. Issuance was discontinued in 1881, but they continued to circulate until 1897 when British copper and silver and Australian gold became plentiful. Almost all tokens bear the name of the city and the issuing merchant, but few have a stated value so the user had to rely on size and weight - a very irregular standard to determine value. Most tokens are of copper, a few are bronze.

Alliance Tea Co.

PENNY

COPPER, 34mm
Obv: "Y" of "COMPANY" level with "D" of "ZEALAND".

KM#	Date	Mintage	VG	Fine	VF	XF
Tn1.1	1866	—	3.00	7.50	60.00	200.00

Obv: "Y" of "COMPANY" below "D" of "ZEALAND".

KM#	Date	Mintage	VG	Fine	VF	XF
Tn1.2	1866	—	10.00	50.00	200.00	500.00

D. Andersons

Wellington

1/2 PENNY

COPPER, 27.5mm

KM#	Date	Mintage	VG	Fine	VF	XF
Tn2	ND	—	2.75	6.50	75.00	350.00

PENNY

COPPER, 34mm

KM#	Date	Mintage	VG	Fine	VF	XF
Tn3	ND	—	2.75	6.50	75.00	350.00

H. Ashton

Auckland

1/2 PENNY

COPPER, 27.5mm
Obv. leg: "NEW ZEALAND" above seated Justice.
Rev. leg: "H. ASHTON"...

KM#	Date	Mintage	VG	Fine	VF	XF
Tn4	1858	—	2.75	6.50	15.00	150.00
	1859	—	3.25	7.50	22.50	225.00

PENNY

COPPER, 34mm
Obv. leg: "NEW ZEALAND" above standing Justice.
Rev: Similar to 1/2 Penny, KM#Tn4.

KM#	Date	Mintage	VG	Fine	VF	XF
Tn5	1862	—	2.75	6.50	15.00	150.00
	1863	—	2.75	6.50	15.00	150.00

NOTE: 3 varieties of 1863 exist.

Auckland Licensed Victuallers Association

Auckland

PENNY

BRONZE, 31mm

KM#	Date	Mintage	VG	Fine	VF	XF
Tn6	ND	—	2.50	6.00	12.00	75.00

NOTE: 4 varieties exist.

Charles C. Barley

Auckland

PENNY

COPPER, 34mm
Obv. leg: "CHARLES C. BARLEY..." Rev. leg: "GOD SAVE THE QUEEN" above seated Justice.

KM#	Date	Mintage	VG	Fine	VF	XF
Tn7	1858	—	2.75	6.50	15.00	150.00

G. L. Beath & Co.

Christchurch

PENNY

BRONZE, 31mm
Obv. leg: "G. L. BEATH & CO..." Rev. leg: "ARGYE HOUSE" above facing rampant lions.

KM#	Date	Mintage	VG	Fine	VF	XF
Tn8	ND(1858)	—	5.00	12.50	30.00	150.00

NOTE: 8 varieties exist. A uniface obv. die trial sold at Spinks Australia for U.S. $600 in 1979.

S. Beaven

Invercargill

PENNY

BRONZE, 31mm

KM#	Date	Mintage	VG	Fine	VF	XF
Tn9	1863	—	25.00	50.00	125.00	225.00

Brown & Duthie

New Plymouth

PENNY

COPPER, 31mm

KM#	Date	Mintage	VG	Fine	VF	XF
Tn10	1866	—	2.75	6.50	15.00	150.00

J. Caro & Co.

Christchurch

PENNY

COPPER, 34mm

KM#	Date	Mintage	VG	Fine	VF	XF
Tn11	ND	—	2.75	6.50	15.00	150.00

Archibald Clark

Auckland

PENNY

COPPER, 34mm

KM#	Date	Mintage	VG	Fine	VF	XF
Tn12	1857	—	3.50	10.00	30.00	200.00

S. Clarkson

Christchurch

PENNY

COPPER, 34mm
Obv. leg: "S. CLARKSON..."
Rev: Similar to KM#Tn12.

KM#	Date	Mintage	VG	Fine	VF	XF
Tn13	1875	—	3.00	8.00	30.00	225.00

NOTE: 4 varieties exist.

Clarkson & Turnbull

Timaru

PENNY

COPPER, 34mm

KM#	Date	Mintage	VG	Fine	VF	XF
Tn14	1865	—	3.50	11.50	32.50	200.00

NOTE: 3 varieties exist.

Samuel Coombes

Auckland

PENNY

COPPER, 34mm

KM#	Date	Mintage	VG	Fine	VF	XF
Tn15	ND	—	3.00	7.50	20.00	150.00

NOTE: 3 varieties exist.

Day & Mieville

Dunedin

PENNY

COPPER, 34mm
Obv. leg: "DAY & MIEVILLE. . ."
Rev: Similar to KM#Tn12.

KM#	Date	Mintage	VG	Fine	VF	XF
Tn16	1857	—	2.75	6.50	15.00	75.00

E. De Carle & Co.

Dunedin

PENNY

BRONZE

KM#	Date	Mintage	VG	Fine	VF	XF
Tn17	1862	—	5.00	12.50	30.00	100.00

NOTE: 3 varieties exist.

T. S. Forsaith

Auckland

1/2 PENNY

COPPER, 28mm

KM#	Date	Mintage	VG	Fine	VF	XF
Tn18	1858	—	8.00	15.00	40.00	150.00

PENNY

COPPER, 34mm
Similar to 1/2 Penny, KM#Tn18.

KM#	Date	Mintage	VG	Fine	VF	XF
Tn19	1858	—	8.00	15.00	40.00	150.00

Gaisford & Edmonds

Christchurch

PENNY

COPPER, 34mm
Obv. leg: "GAISFORD & EDMONDS. . ."

KM#	Date	Mintage	VG	Fine	VF	XF
Tn20	1875	—	3.00	10.00	50.00	250.00

John Gilmour

New Plymouth

PENNY

COPPER, 31mm
Obv. leg: "JOHN GILMOUR. . ."
Rev: Kiwi bird below Mt. Egmont.

KM#	Date	Mintage	VG	Fine	VF	XF
Tn21	ND	—	3.00	8.50	20.00	175.00

NOTE: 2 varieties exist.

B. Gittos

Auckland

PENNY

COPPER, 34mm
Obv. leg: "B. GITTOS. . ."
Rev. leg: "WHOLESALE & RETAIL. . ."

KM#	Date	Mintage	VG	Fine	VF	XF
Tn22	1864	—	2.75	6.50	15.00	150.00

T. W. Gourlay & Co.

Christchurch

PENNY

COPPER, 34mm

KM#	Date	Mintage	VG	Fine	VF	XF
Tn23	ND	—	10.00	50.00	100.00	300.00

NOTE: 2 varieties exist.

R. Gratten

Auckland

PENNY

COPPER, 32mm
Obv. leg: "THAMES HOTEL/R. GRATTEN. . ."
Rev: Indian paddling boat within sprays.

KM#	Date	Mintage	VG	Fine	VF	XF
Tn24	1872	—	3.00	8.50	20.00	175.00

Henry J. Hall

Christchurch

1/2 PENNY

COPPER, 28mm
Obv. leg: "HENRY J. HALL. . ."
Rev. leg: "FAMILY GROCER. . ."

KM#	Date	Mintage	VG	Fine	VF	XF
Tn25	ND	—	3.00	8.50	20.00	175.00

Mule. Rev. of KM#Tn25 & rev. of E. F. Dease (Australian) 1/2 Penny, KM#Tn50.

KM#	Date	Mintage	VG	Fine	VF	XF
Tn26	ND	—	—	—	250.00	1000.

Mule. Obv. of KM#Tn25 & rev. of Lipman Levy 1/2 Penny KM#Tn38.

KM#	Date	Mintage	VG	Fine	VF	XF
Tn27	ND	—	—	—	250.00	800.00

PENNY

COPPER, 34mm

KM#	Date	Mintage	VG	Fine	VF	XF
Tn28	ND	—	3.00	8.50	20.00	150.00

NOTE: 5varieties exist.

KM#	Date	Mintage	VG	Fine	VF	XF
Tn28A	ND	—	2.75	6.50	15.00	135.00

NOTE: 6 varieties exist.

Obv. KM#Tn30. Rev: Similar to obv. KM#Tn28A.

KM#	Date	Mintage	VG	Fine	VF	XF
Tn29	ND	—	2.75	6.50	15.00	130.00

Mule. Obv. of KM#Tn29 & rev. of Emu and kangaroo (Australian) Penny.

KM#	Date	Mintage	VG	Fine	VF	XF
Tn30	ND	—	75.00	175.00	350.00	1000.

Hobday & Jobberns

Christchurch

PENNY

COPPER, 33.5mm
Obv. leg: "HOBDAY & JOBBERNS. . ."
Rev. leg: "ADVANCE CANTERBURY" below shield.

KM#	Date	Mintage	VG	Fine	VF	XF
Tn31	ND	—	3.00	8.50	20.00	125.00

NOTE: 2 major varieties exist.

Holland & Butler

Auckland

PENNY

COPPER, 34mm
Obv. leg: "HOLLAND & BUTLER. . ."
Rev. leg: "IMPORTERS OF. . ."

KM#	Date	Mintage	VG	Fine	VF	XF
Tn32	ND	—	2.75	6.50	15.00	130.00

J. Hurley & Co.

Wanganui

1/2 PENNY

COPPER, 25mm

KM#	Date	Mintage	VG	Fine	VF	XF
Tn33	ND	—	2.75	6.50	15.00	150.00

PENNY

COPPER, 31mm
Similar to 1/2 Penny, KM#Tn33.

KM#	Date	Mintage	VG	Fine	VF	XF
Tn34	ND	—	2.75	6.50	15.00	150.00

Jones & Williamson

Dunedin

PENNY

COPPER, 34mm

KM#	Date	Mintage	VG	Fine	VF	XF
Tn35	1858	—	3.00	8.50	20.00	175.00

Kirkcaldie & Stains

Wellington

1/2 PENNY

BRONZE, 25mm
Obv. leg: "KIRKCALDIE & STAINS. . ."
Rev. leg: "KIRKCALDIE & STAINS" above helmeted shield.

KM#	Date	Mintage	VG	Fine	VF	XF
Tn36	ND	—	3.00	8.50	22.00	175.00

PENNY

BRONZE, 31mm
Similar to 1/2 Penny, KM#Tn36.

KM#	Date	Mintage	VG	Fine	VF	XF
Tn37	ND	—	2.75	6.50	15.00	150.00

Lipman Levy

Wellington

1/2 PENNY

COPPER, 28mm

KM#	Date	Mintage	VG	Fine	VF	XF
Tn38	ND	—	3.00	8.50	20.00	175.00

PENNY

COPPER, 34mm
Similar to 1/2 Penny, KM#Tn38, normal die alignment.

KM#	Date	Mintage	VG	Fine	VF	XF
Tn39.1	ND	—	3.00	25.00	75.00	300.00

Die rotated 180 degrees.

KM#	Date	Mintage	VG	Fine	VF	XF
Tn39.2	ND	—	—	—	—	200.00

Mule. Obv. of KM#Tn39 and rev: "WELLINGTON & ERIN GOBRACH" around laureate head of Wellington.

KM#	Date	Mintage	Fine	VF	XF	Unc
Tn40	ND	—	—	—	500.00	750.00

Mule. Obv. of KM#Tn39 and rev. of AUSTRALIA above seated woman penny token.

KM#	Date	Mintage	Fine	VF	XF	Unc
Tn41	ND	—	—	—	600.00	800.00

Morris Marks

Auckland

PENNY

BRASS, 30mm

KM#	Date	Mintage	VG	Fine	VF	XF
Tn42	ND	—	8.00	25.00	100.00	300.00

Mason Struthers & Co.

Christchurch

PENNY

BRONZE, 31mm
Obv. leg: "MASON STRUTHERS & CO. . ."
Rev. leg: "ONE PENNY TOKEN" around Maori head right.

KM#	Date	Mintage	VG	Fine	VF	XF
Tn43	ND	—	3.00	8.50	37.50	130.00

NOTE: 2 varieties exist.

George McCaul

Grahamstown

PENNY

COPPER, 34mm
Obv. leg: "GEORGE MCCAUL. . ."
Rev: Poppet head of gold mine.

KM#	Date	Mintage	VG	Fine	VF	XF
Tn44	1874	—	2.75	6.50	15.00	100.00

J. W. Mears

Wellington

1/2 PENNY

COPPER, 29mm

KM#	Date	Mintage	VG	Fine	VF	XF
Tn45	ND	—	50.00	100.00	200.00	350.00

J. M. Merrington & Co.

Nelson

PENNY

COPPER, 34mm
Obv. leg: "J. M. MERRINGTON & CO. . ."
Rev. leg: "ADVANCE NEW ZEALAND" above standing Justice.

KM#	Date	Mintage	VG	Fine	VF	XF
Tn46	ND	—	3.00	8.50	20.00	175.00

Milner & Thompson

Christchurch

PENNY

COPPER, 34mm
Obv. leg: "MILNER & THOMPSON. . ." around winged head of angel above musical instruments.
Rev: Scene.

KM#	Date	Mintage	VG	Fine	VF	XF
Tn47	1881	—	—	—	10.00	60.00

Obv: Similar to KM#Tn47.
Rev: Similar to KM#Tn49.

KM#	Date	Mintage	VG	Fine	VF	XF
Tn48	1881	—	—	—	10.00	60.00

KM#	Date	Mintage	VG	Fine	VF	XF
Tn49	ND	—	—	—	10.00	60.00

BRONZE, 32mm
Reduced size.
Similar to KM#Tn47.

KM#	Date	Mintage	VG	Fine	VF	XF
Tn50	1881	—	—	—	10.00	60.00

Similar to KM#Tn48.

KM#	Date	Mintage	VG	Fine	VF	XF
Tn51	1881	—	—	—	10.00	60.00

NOTE: 2 other varieties exist.

Obv: Similar to obv. of KM#Tn48.
Rev: Similar to rev. of KM#Tn54.

KM#	Date	Mintage	VG	Fine	VF	XF
Tn52	1881	—	—	—	10.00	60.00

Obv: Similar to rev. of KM#Tn49.
Rev: Similar to rev. of KM#Tn54.

KM#	Date	Mintage	VG	Fine	VF	XF
Tn53	ND	—	—	—	10.00	60.00

Obv: Scene. Rev: Inscription.

KM#	Date	Mintage	VG	Fine	VF	XF
Tn54	ND	—	—	—	10.00	60.00

Obv. similar to rev. of KM#Tn49.
Rev. similar to obv. of KM#Tn54.

KM#	Date	Mintage	Fine	VF	XF	Unc
Tn55	ND	2 known	—	—	—	1800.

Morrin & Co.

Auckland

PENNY

COPPER, 34mm
Obv: Left hand palm branch lower.
Rev: Head of Justice below "A" of "AUCKLAND."

KM#	Date	Mintage	VG	Fine	VF	XF
Tn56.1	ND	—	2.75	6.50	15.00	150.00

Obv: Palm branches even.

KM#	Date	Mintage	VG	Fine	VF	XF
Tn56.2	ND	—	2.75	6.50	15.00	150.00

Obv: Last "T" of "STREET" points to "S" of "MERCHANTS."
Rev: Head of Justice below "AU" of "AUCKLAND."

KM#	Date	Mintage	VG	Fine	VF	XF
Tn56.3	ND	—	100.00	250.00	400.00	1000.

Obv: Right hand palm branch lower, last "T" of "STREET" points to "TS" of "MERCHANTS."

KM#	Date	Mintage	VG	Fine	VF	XF
Tn56.4	ND	—	75.00	175.00	300.00	600.00

Perkins & Co.

Dunedin

1/2 PENNY

BRONZE, 25mm

KM#	Date	Mintage	VG	Fine	VF	XF
Tn57	ND	—	8.00	20.00	75.00	300.00

PENNY

BRONZE, 30mm

KM#	Date	Mintage	VG	Fine	VF	XF
Tn58	ND	—	5.00	15.00	50.00	200.00

W. Peterson

Christchurch

PENNY

COPPER, 34mm

KM#	Date	Mintage	VG	Fine	VF	XF
Tn59	ND	—	10.00	30.00	70.00	280.00

William Pratt

Christchurch

PENNY

COPPER, 34mm
Obv. leg: "WILLIAM PRATT. . ."
Rev. leg: "DUNSTABLE HOUSE. . ."

KM#	Date	Mintage	VG	Fine	VF	XF
Tn60	ND	—	5.00	15.00	50.00	150.00

NOTE: 4 varieties exist.

Edward Reece

Christchurch

1/2 PENNY

COPPER, 28mm
Rev: Legends, large letters.

KM#	Date	Mintage	VG	Fine	VF	XF
Tn61.1	ND	—	8.00	20.00	75.00	175.00

NOTE: 2 varieties exist.

Rev: Legends, small letters.

KM#	Date	Mintage	VG	Fine	VF	XF
Tn61.2	ND	—	75.00	135.00	250.00	500.00

PENNY

COPPER, 34mm

KM#	Date	Mintage	VG	Fine	VF	XF
Tn62	ND	—	—	5.00	20.00	175.00

S. Hague Smith

Auckland

PENNY

COPPER, 34mm

KM#	Date	Mintage	VG	Fine	VF	XF
Tn63	ND	—	2.50	6.00	12.00	75.00

NOTE: 8 varieties exist.

M. Somerville

Auckland

PENNY

COPPER, 34mm

KM#	Date	Mintage	VG	Fine	VF	XF
Tn64	1857	—	2.75	6.50	15.00	100.00

NOTE: 4 varieties exist.

Union Bakery Co.

Christchurch

PENNY

BRONZE, 30mm

KM#	Date	Mintage	VG	Fine	VF	XF
Tn65	ND	—	3.00	10.00	22.00	100.00

KM#	Date	Mintage	VG	Fine	VF	XF
Tn72	ND	2 known	—	—	—	12,000.

United Service Hotel

Auckland

PENNY

COPPER, 34mm
Obv: Similar to KM#Tn67.
Rev: Similar to KM#Tn67 but "UNITED HOTEL" in straight line.

KM#	Date	Mintage	VG	Fine	VF	XF
Tn66	1874	—	2.50	6.00	12.00	75.00

KM#	Date	Mintage	VG	Fine	VF	XF
Tn67	ND(1874)	—	2.50	6.00	12.00	75.00

James Wallace

Wellington

1/2 PENNY

COPPER, 28mm

KM#	Date	Mintage	VG	Fine	VF	XF
Tn68	1859	—	7.50	35.00	100.00	250.00

PENNY

COPPER, 34mm
Obv. & rev: Similar to 1/2 Penny, KM#Tn68.

KM#	Date	Mintage	VG	Fine	VF	XF
Tn69	1859	—	5.00	20.00	60.00	200.00

Edward Waters

Auckland

PENNY

COPPER, 33mm
Obv. leg: "WHOLESALE & RETAIL. . . QUEEN ST." 23mm. Rev. leg: "ONE PENNY TOKEN" around Maori head right.

KM#	Date	Mintage	VG	Fine	VF	XF
Tn70.1	ND	—	7.50	35.00	100.00	250.00

Obv. leg: ". . .QUEEN ST." 19mm.

KM#	Date	Mintage	VG	Fine	VF	XF
Tn70.2	ND	—	3.50	10.00	20.00	75.00

A. S. Wilson

Dunedin

PENNY

COPPER, 34mm

KM#	Date	Mintage	VG	Fine	VF	XF
Tn71	1857	—	50.00	100.00	200.00	500.00

NICARAGUA

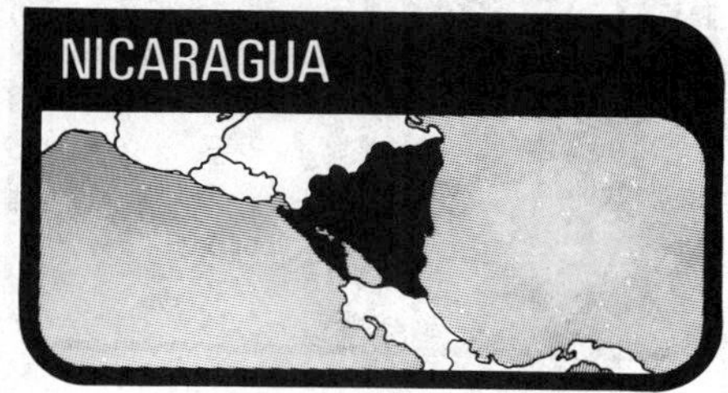

The Republic of Nicaragua, situated in Central America between Honduras and Costa Rica, has an area of 50,193 sq. mi. (129,494 sq. km.) and a population of *3.7 million. Capital: Managua. Agriculture, mining (gold and silver) and hardwood logging are the principal industries. Cotton, meat, coffee and sugar are exported.

Columbus sighted the coast of Nicaragua on Sept. 12, 1502 during the course of his last voyage of discovery. It was first visited in 1522 by conquistadores from Panama, under the command of Gil Gonzalez. The first settlements were established in 1524 at Granada and Leon by Francisco Hernandez de Cordoba. Nicaragua was incorporated, for administrative purpose, in the Captaincy General of Guatemala, which included every Central American state but Panama. On September 15, 1821 the Captaincy General of Guatemala declared itself and all the Central American provinces independent of Spain. The next year Nicaragua united with the Mexican Empire of Augustin de Iturbide, only to join in 1823 the federation of the Central American Republic. Within Nicaragua rival cities or juntas such as Leon, Granada and El Viejo vied for power, wealth and influence, often attacking each other at will. To further prove their legitimacy as well as provide an acceptable circulating coinage in those turbulent times (1821-1825), provisional mints functioned intermittantly at Granada, Leon and El Viejo. The early coinage reflected traditional but crude Spanish colonial cob-style designs. Nicaragua's first governor was Pedro Arias Davila, appointed on June 1, 1827. When the federation was dissolved, Nicaragua declared itself an independent republic on April 30, 1838.

Dissension between the Liberals and Conservatives of the contending cities kept Nicaragua in turmoil, which made it possible for William Walker to make himself President in 1855. The two major political parties finally united to drive him out and in 1857 he was expelled. A relative peace followed, but by 1912, Nicaragua had requested the U.S. Marines to restore order which began a U.S. involvement which lasted until the Good Neighbor Policy was adopted in 1933. Anastasio Somoza Garcia assumed the Presidency in 1936. This family dynasty dominated Nicaragua until its overthrow in 1979. Formal elections in 1990 renewed a democratic government in power.

MINT MARKS

H - Heaton, Birmingham
HF - Huguenin Freres, Le Locle
Mo - Mexico City
- Philadelphia, Pa.
- Sherritt
- Waterbury, Ct.

MONETARY SYSTEM

100 Centavos = 1 Peso

NOTE: Former listing for 1823 IL 1/2 Real of Leon has been identified by recognized authorities as a Honduras issue 1823 TL 1/2 Real cataloged there as KM#9.

GRANADA

1/2 REAL

SILVER
Rev: J G/1823.

KM#	Date	Good	VG	Fine	VF
5	1823	800.00	1800.	3000.	5000.

1 REAL

SILVER
Rev: D/24/G.

KM#	Date	Good	VG	Fine	VF
6	(18)24	800.00	1800.	3000.	5000.

2 REALS

SILVER
Rev: D/24/G.

KM#	Date	Good	VG	Fine	VF
7	(18)24	1000.	2000.	3500.	5250.

4 REALS

SILVER
Obv: J Cross G. Rev: D/24/G.

KM#	Date	Good	VG	Fine	VF
8	(18)24	—	—	Rare	—

EL VIEJO

2 REALS

SILVER
Type I
Obv: V/IE/JO P/24 V.

KM#	Date	Good	VG	Fine	VF
5	(18)24	1150.	2250.	4000.	6000.

Type II - Sun Over Mountains
Obv: V/IE/JO P/24/V.
Rev: P. L. 1824.

KM#	Date	Good	VG	Fine	VF
6	1824	1250.	2450.	4250.	6500.

4 REALS

SILVER
Type I
Obv: V/IE/JO P/24/V.

KM#	Date	Good	VG	Fine	VF
7	(18)24	—	—	Rare	—

NICARAGUA

CENTAVO

COPPER-NICKEL

KM#	Date	Mintage	Fine	VF	XF	Unc
1	1878	.500	3.00	6.00	20.00	85.00
	1878	—	—	—	Proof	650.00

5 CENTAVOS

1.2500 g, .800 SILVER, .0322 oz ASW

KM#	Date	Mintage	Fine	VF	XF	Unc
2	1880H	.256	2.50	5.00	15.00	125.00
	1880H	—	—	—	Proof	450.00

KM#	Date	Mintage	Fine	VF	XF	Unc
5	1887H	1.000	2.00	4.00	10.00	50.00
	1887H	—	—	—	Proof	500.00

COPPER-NICKEL

KM#	Date	Mintage	Fine	VF	XF	Unc
8	1898	2.000	.75	2.00	8.00	35.00

KM#	Date	Mintage	Fine	VF	XF	Unc
9	1899	2.000	.50	1.50	7.00	25.00

10 CENTAVOS

2.5000 g, .800 SILVER, .0643 oz ASW

KM#	Date	Mintage	Fine	VF	XF	Unc
3	1880H	.552	4.00	8.00	25.00	80.00
	1880H	—	—	—	Proof	500.00

KM#	Date	Mintage	Fine	VF	XF	Unc
6	1887H	1.500	1.00	2.50	10.00	60.00
	1887H	—	—	—	Proof	550.00

20 CENTAVOS

5.0000 g, .800 SILVER, .1286 oz ASW

KM#	Date	Mintage	Fine	VF	XF	Unc
4	1880H	.288	3.00	7.50	35.00	140.00
	1880H	—	—	—	Proof	600.00

KM#	Date	Mintage	Fine	VF	XF	Unc
7	1887H	1.000	2.00	5.00	20.00	70.00
	1887H	—	—	—	Proof	700.00

MEDALLIC ISSUES (M)

Vice-Royalty of New Spain

Leon de Nicaragua

A proclamation issue was struck for Ferdinand VII as the new King of Spain while he was under Napoleonic French guard.

(REAL)

SILVER
Ferdinand VII

KM#	Date	Mintage	Fine	VF	XF	Unc
M1	1808	1,600	85.00	135.00	200.00	350.00

PATTERNS (Pn)

(Including off metal strikes)

KM#	Date	Mintage	Identification	Mkt.Val.
Pn1	1860	—	1 Centavo	1500.

KM#	Date	Mintage	Identification	Mkt.Val.
Pn2	1878	—	1 Centavo, Copper	400.00
PnA3	1880H	—	5 Centavos, KM2, plain edge proof	500.00
PnB3	1880H	—	10 Centavos, KM3, plain edge proof	550.00
PnC3	1880H	—	20 Centavos, KM4, plain edge proof	650.00

KM#	Date	Mintage	Identification	Mkt.Val.
Pn3	1887E	—	2 Centavos, Copper	450.00

KM#	Date	Mintage	Identification	Mkt.Val.
Pn4	1892	—	1 Centavo, Copper-Nickel	325.00
Pn5	1892	—	1 Centavo, Copper	325.00
Pn6	1892	—	1 Centavo, Aluminum	375.00

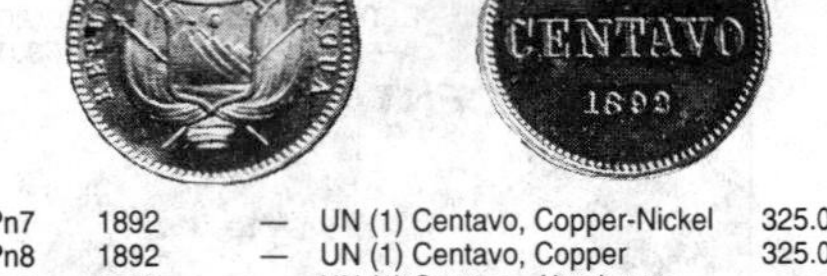

KM#	Date	Mintage	Identification	Mkt.Val.
Pn7	1892	—	UN (1) Centavo, Copper-Nickel	325.00
Pn8	1892	—	UN (1) Centavo, Copper	325.00
Pn9	1892	—	UN (1) Centavo, Aluminum	—

PIEFORTS (P)

KM#	Date	Mintage	Identification	Mkt.Val.
P1	1892	—	1 Centavo, Copper-Nickel	325.00
P2	1892	—	1 Centavo, Copper	325.00
P3	1892	—	1 Centavo, Aluminum	375.00
P4	1892	—	UN (1) Centavo, Copper-Nickel	325.00
P5	1892	—	UN (1) Centavo, Copper	325.00
P6	1892	—	UN (1) Centavo, Aluminum	—

COINS OF RESTRICTED CIRCULATION

STATE ISSUES

MERCADO DE LEON

By executive decree, the government of Nicaragua on September 12, 1859, authorized the municipality of Leon to mint between 100 and 200 Pesos in copper cents and half cents. The first known documentation of this right being exercised came in 1877 when the Heaton Mint was contracted to strike the following pieces. The 1/12 Dime and 1/24 Dime were valued at a fraction of the United States dime as both the U.S. half dime and dime were authorized as legal tender and circulated heavily in Nicaragua during this period.

1/24 DIME

COPPER

KM#	Date	Mintage	Fine	VF	XF	Unc
S1	ND(1877)	.013	75.00	150.00	300.00	500.00

1/12 DIME

COPPER

KM#	Date	Mintage	Fine	VF	XF	Unc
S2	ND(1877)	6,600	100.00	200.00	400.00	650.00

NIGERIA

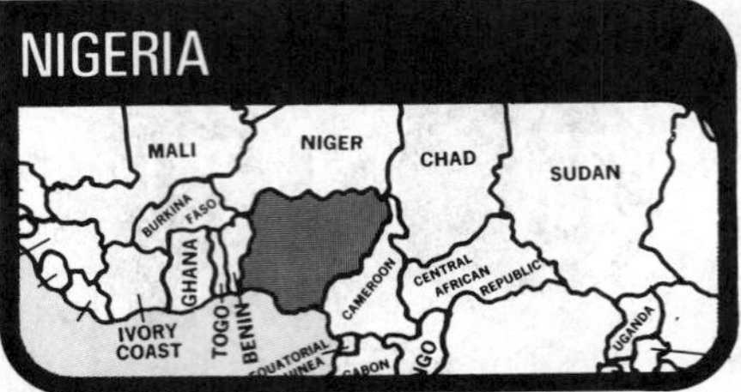

The Federal Republic of Nigeria, situated on the Atlantic coast of West Africa has an area of 356,669 sq. mi. (923,770 sq. km.) and a population of *115.2 million. Capital: Lagos. The economy is based on petroleum and agriculture. Crude oil, cocoa, tobacco and tin are exported.

Following the Napoleonic Wars, the British expanded their trade with the interior of Nigeria. British claims to a sphere of influence in that area were recognized by the Berlin Conference of 1885, and in the following year the Royal Niger Company was chartered. Direct British control of the territory was initiated in 1900, and in 1914 the amalgamation of Northern and Southern Nigeria into the Colony and Protectorate of Nigeria was effected. In 1960, following a number of territorial and constitutional changes, Nigeria was granted independence within the British Commonwealth as a federation of the Northern, Western and Eastern regions. Nigeria altered its political relationship with Great Britain on Oct. 1, 1963, by proclaiming itself a republic. It did, however, elect to remain a member of the Commonwealth of Nations. The Supreme Commander of Armed Forces is the Head of the Federal Military Government.

On May 30, 1967, the Eastern Region of the republic - an area occupied principally by the proud and resourceful Ibo tribe - seceded from Nigeria and proclaimed itself the independent Republic of Biafra with Odumegwu Ojukwu as Chief of State. Civil war erupted and raged for 31 months. Casualties, including civilian, were about two million, the majority succumbing to malnutrition and disease. Biafra surrendered to the federal government on January 15, 1970.

TOKEN ISSUES (Tn)

Mac Gregor

LAIRD

(1/8 Penny)

COPPER

KM#	Date	Mintage	Fine	VF	XF	Unc
Tn2	AH1274	1858	50.00	100.00	180.00	300.00

NOTE: Three die varieties exist.

NOTE: Variously attributed to Guinea, Gold Coast, Sierra Leone and West Africa, this token, struck in 1858, was intended to circulate at the MacGregor Laird trading posts located along the Niger and Benue rivers. In 1885 this region became the British Protectorate of Nigeria.

NORWAY

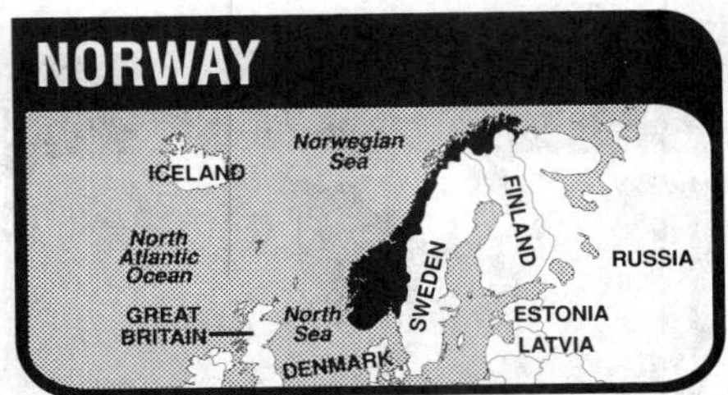

The Kingdom of Norway, a constitutional monarchy located in northwestern Europe, has an area of 150,000 sq. mi. (324,220 sq. km.), including the island territories of Spitzbergen (Svalbard) and Jan Mayen, and a population of *4.2 million. Capital: Oslo. The diversified economic base of Norway includes shipping, fishing, forestry, agriculture, and manufacturing. Nonferrous metals, paper and paperboard, paper pulp, iron, steel and oil are exported.

A united Norwegian kingdom was established in the 9th century, the era of the indomitable Norse Vikings who ranged far and wide, visiting the coasts of northwestern Europe, the Mediterranean, Greenland and North America. In the 13th century the Norse kingdom was united briefly with Sweden, then passed through inheritance in 1380 to the rule of Denmark which was maintained until 1814. In 1814 Norway fell again under the rule of Sweden. The union lasted until 1905 when the Norwegian Parliament arranged a peaceful separation and invited a Danish prince (King Haakon VII) to ascend the throne of an independent Kingdom of Norway. His son Olav V became King in 1957. Just prior to his death on Jan. 17, 1991, King Olav committed 10,000 troops to the Persian Gulf.

RULERS

Danish, until 1814
Swedish, until 1905

MINT MARKS

(h) - Crossed hammers - Kongsberg

MINTMASTERS INITIALS

Letter	Date	Name
B	1861	Brynjulf Bergslien
CHL,star(s)	1836-1888	Caspar Herman Langberg, in Kongsberg
I,IT	1880-1918	Ivar Trondsen, engraver
IAR	—	Angrid Austlid Rise, engraver
IGM	1797-1806	Johan Georg Madelung, in Altona
IGP	1807-1824	Johan Georg Prahm, in Kongsberg
JMK	1825-1836	Johan Michael Kruse, in Kongsberg
M	1815-1830	Gregorius Middelthun

MONETARY SYSTEM

1794-1873

120 Skilling = 1 Speciedaler

1/2 SKILLING

COPPER

KM#	Date	Mintage	VG	Fine	VF	XF
305.1	1839	.613	2.50	5.00	10.00	30.00
	1840	2.558	2.00	4.00	7.50	25.00
	1841	1.683	2.00	4.00	7.50	25.00
	Rev: Star below hammers.					
305.2	1841	Inc. Ab.	1.00	2.50	6.00	15.00

KM#	Date	Mintage	Fine	VF	XF	Unc
324	1863	.480	5.00	12.50	35.00	90.00

KM#	Date	Mintage	Fine	VF	XF	Unc
329	1867	3.600	1.00	2.00	7.00	20.00

SKILLING

COPPER, 25mm

Obv: Crowned FR monogram.
Rev: 5-petalled rosettes, by 1 and below date.

KM#	Date	Mintage	VG	Fine	VF	XF
274.1	1809	.346	7.50	12.50	20.00	50.00

Rev: 8-petalled rosettes, by 1 and below date.

KM#	Date	Mintage	VG	Fine	VF	XF
274.2	1809	Inc. Ab.	7.50	12.50	20.00	50.00

Rev: Ovals by 1 and below date.

KM#	Date	Mintage	VG	Fine	VF	XF
274.3	1809	Inc. Ab.	7.50	12.50	20.00	50.00

KM#	Date	Mintage	VG	Fine	VF	XF
281	1812	5.453	1.00	2.50	5.00	10.00
	*1812 w/o crossed hammers below date	Inc. Ab.	15.00	35.00	65.00	120.00

*Beware of removed mint mark or altered coin.

KM#	Date	Mintage	VG	Fine	VF	XF
284	1816	1.659	4.00	10.00	25.00	75.00

KM#	Date	Mintage	VG	Fine	VF	XF
286	1819	3.817	4.00	10.00	25.00	60.00
	1820	Inc. Ab.	3.00	7.00	17.50	45.00
	1824	6,000	30.00	50.00	110.00	250.00
	1825	—	250.00	500.00	750.00	1500.
	1827	.034	25.00	40.00	85.00	200.00
	1828	.038	550.00	1250.	2000.	—
	1831/28	1.440	35.00	60.00	135.00	265.00
	1831	Inc. Ab.	35.00	60.00	135.00	265.00
	1832	Inc. Ab.	20.00	35.00	75.00	160.00
	1833	.126	20.00	35.00	75.00	160.00
	1834	—	1250.	—	—	—

KM#	Date	Mintage	Fine	VF	XF	Unc
335	1870	1.200	2.00	7.00	15.00	60.00

2 SKILLING

1.5000 g, .250 SILVER, .0120 oz ASW

KM#	Date	Mintage	VG	Fine	VF	XF
270	1801 IGM	1.109	2.00	5.00	10.00	20.00
	1802 IGM	2.854	2.00	5.00	10.00	20.00
	1803 IGM	2.410	2.00	5.00	10.00	20.00
	1804 IGM	3.634	4.00	10.00	18.00	35.00
	1805 IGM	2.412	3.00	8.00	15.00	30.00
	1807 IGP	3.507	2.00	5.00	10.00	18.00

NOTE: Earlier date (1800) exists for this type.

COPPER
Rev: 8-petalled rosettes by 2 and below date.

KM#	Date	Mintage	VG	Fine	VF	XF
280.1	1810	3.449	2.00	4.00	8.00	20.00

Rev: Cross.

KM#	Date	Mintage	VG	Fine	VF	XF
280.2	1810	Inc. Ab.	2.00	4.00	8.00	20.00
	1811	1.190	2.50	6.00	12.00	25.00

Rev: 5-petalled rosettes by 2 and below date.

KM#	Date	Mintage	VG	Fine	VF	XF
280.3	1811	—	2.50	6.00	12.00	25.00

KM#	Date	Mintage	VG	Fine	VF	XF
295	1822	.963	7.00	15.00	35.00	90.00
	1824	.549	7.00	15.00	35.00	90.00
	1825	.510	10.00	30.00	75.00	175.00
	1827	.288	10.00	25.00	60.00	140.00
	1828	.453	10.00	25.00	60.00	140.00
	1831/28	.723	7.00	17.50	40.00	100.00
	1831	Inc. Ab.	7.00	17.50	40.00	100.00
	1832	Inc. Ab.	7.00	17.50	40.00	100.00
	1833	.060	8.00	20.00	45.00	110.00
	1834	.880	40.00	80.00	140.00	300.00

1.5000 g, .250 SILVER, .0120 oz ASW, 17mm

KM#	Date	Mintage	VG	Fine	VF	XF
297	1825	.240	5.00	12.00	25.00	60.00

KM#	Date	Mintage	VG	Fine	VF	XF
310	1842	1.500	2.00	4.00	10.00	20.00
	1843	Inc. Ab.	3.00	7.50	15.00	30.00

Rev: Rosettes.

KM#	Date	Mintage	Fine	VF	XF	Unc
336.1	1870	.900	3.00	5.00	10.00	25.00
	1871	.900	3.00	5.00	10.00	25.00

Rev: Stars.

KM#	Date	Mintage	Fine	VF	XF	Unc
336.2	1871	1.140	3.00	5.00	10.00	25.00

3 SKILLING

2.2500 g, .250 SILVER, .0181 oz ASW
Rev: Rosettes.

KM#	Date	Mintage	Fine	VF	XF	Unc
330.1	1868	.499	5.00	8.00	16.00	45.00
	1869	.103	10.00	16.00	32.50	85.00

Rev: Stars.

KM#	Date	Mintage	Fine	VF	XF	Unc
330.2	1869	.600	5.00	8.00	16.00	45.00

Rev: Rosettes.

KM#	Date	Mintage	Fine	VF	XF	Unc
338.1	1872	.504	5.00	8.00	16.00	45.00

Rev: Stars.

KM#	Date	Mintage	Fine	VF	XF	Unc
338.2	1872	.576	5.00	8.00	16.00	45.00
	1873	.600	5.00	8.00	16.00	45.00

4 SKILLING

COPPER
Rev: Rosettes by 4 and below date.

KM#	Date	Mintage	VG	Fine	VF	XF
275.1	1809	.251	12.50	30.00	70.00	150.00

Rev: Stars by 4 and below date.

KM#	Date	Mintage	VG	Fine	VF	XF
275.2	1809	Inc. Ab.	17.50	40.00	85.00	190.00
	1810	2 pcs. known	—	—	Rare	—

2.0500 g, .250 SILVER, .0165 oz ASW

KM#	Date	Mintage	VG	Fine	VF	XF
276.1	1809 IGP rev. leg: SKILLE:	2.228	3.00	6.00	14.00	32.50
276.2	1809 IGP rev. leg: SKILLE =	Inc. Ab.	3.00	6.00	14.00	32.50

3.0000 g, .250 SILVER, .0241 oz ASW

KM#	Date	Mintage	VG	Fine	VF	XF
298	1825 JMK	.333	5.00	10.00	25.00	60.00

KM#	Date	Mintage	VG	Fine	VF	XF
311	1842	.750	3.00	7.00	20.00	50.00

KM#	Date	Mintage	Fine	VF	XF	Unc
337	1871	.559	5.00	10.00	20.00	55.00

6 SKILLING

COPPER
Obv: Crowned shield. Rev: Dot after value.

KM#	Date	Mintage	VG	Fine	VF	XF
282	1813	.109	3.00	6.00	15.00	32.50

8 SKILLING

2.7300 g, .375 SILVER, .0329 oz ASW

KM#	Date	Mintage	VG	Fine	VF	XF
277	1809 IGP	1.350	5.00	10.00	20.00	50.00

3.3700 g, .500 SILVER, .0542 oz ASW

KM#	Date	Mintage	VG	Fine	VF	XF
285	1817 IGP	.241	10.00	20.00	50.00	140.00

KM#	Date	Mintage	VG	Fine	VF	XF
287	1819 IGP	.101	12.00	25.00	75.00	150.00

1.9300 g, .875 SILVER, .0543 oz ASW

KM#	Date	Mintage	VG	Fine	VF	XF
299	1825	.016	10.00	20.00	40.00	100.00
	1827/5	.014	10.00	20.00	40.00	100.00

12 SKILLING

COPPER
Obv: Crowned shield. Rev: Damaged 3 in value.

KM#	Date	Mintage	VG	Fine	VF	XF
283	1813	.739	3.00	6.00	12.50	30.00

2.8900 g, .875 SILVER, .0813 oz ASW
Plain border.

KM#	Date	Mintage	VG	Fine	VF	XF
314.1	1845	.631	5.00	10.00	22.50	50.00
	1846	.250	5.00	10.00	25.00	55.00
	1847	.256	5.00	10.00	25.00	55.00
	1848	.316	5.00	10.00	25.00	55.00

Beaded border.

KM#	Date	Mintage	VG	Fine	VF	XF
314.2	1850 leg: V KONGE					
		.287	5.00	10.00	25.00	55.00
	1850 leg: V.KONGE					
		Inc. Ab.	5.00	10.00	25.00	55.00
	1852	.313	5.00	10.00	22.50	50.00
	1853	.360	5.00	10.00	22.50	50.00
	1854	.301	5.00	10.00	22.50	50.00
	1855	.450	5.00	10.00	22.50	50.00
	1856/5	.812	4.50	9.00	20.00	40.00
	1856	Inc. Ab.	4.00	7.00	18.00	35.00

Obv: Small head.

KM#	Date	Mintage	Fine	VF	XF	Unc
320	1861	2,500	450.00	800.00	1400.	2500.
	1862	2.500	450.00	800.00	1400.	2500.

Obv: Large head.

KM#	Date	Mintage	Fine	VF	XF	Unc
326	1865	.152	40.00	90.00	200.00	375.00

KM#	Date	Mintage	Fine	VF	XF	Unc
339	1873	.490	25.00	45.00	85.00	175.00

24 SKILLING

7.3100 g, .687 SILVER, .1615 oz ASW

KM#	Date	Mintage	VG	Fine	VF	XF
288	1819 IGP	.050	20.00	40.00	80.00	150.00

5.7300 g, .875 SILVER, .1612 oz ASW

KM#	Date	Mintage	VG	Fine	VF	XF
296	1823 IGP	.125	30.00	65.00	130.00	275.00
	1824 JMK					
		7,800	35.00	75.00	150.00	300.00

KM#	Date	Mintage	VG	Fine	VF	XF
300	1825	4,600	45.00	90.00	200.00	320.00
	1827/5	.027	30.00	65.00	135.00	250.00
	1827	Inc. Ab.	30.00	65.00	135.00	250.00
	1830	5,800	55.00	110.00	225.00	425.00
	1831/0	2,400	—	—	Rare	—
	1833	—	100.00	185.00	350.00	625.00
	1834	—	100.00	185.00	350.00	625.00
	1835	2,500	75.00	165.00	300.00	575.00
	1836	2,500	90.00	175.00	325.00	600.00

5.7800 g, .875 SILVER, .1626 oz ASW
Plain border.

KM#	Date	Mintage	VG	Fine	VF	XF
315.1	1845	.357	6.00	15.00	30.00	60.00
	1846	.383	6.00	15.00	30.00	60.00
	1847	.217	9.00	20.00	40.00	85.00
	1848	.150	11.00	25.00	45.00	95.00

Beaded border.

KM#	Date	Mintage	VG	Fine	VF	XF
315.2	1850	.102	9.00	20.00	45.00	100.00
	1852	.254	9.00	20.00	45.00	85.00
	1853	.327	9.00	20.00	45.00	85.00
	1854	.212	11.00	25.00	50.00	100.00
	1855	.204	8.00	17.50	40.00	80.00

Obv: Small head.

KM#	Date	Mintage	Fine	VF	XF	Unc
321	1861	13 pcs.	—	—	*Rare	—
	1862	1,200	500.00	900.00	2000.	3500.

***NOTE:** Heritage Long Beach sale 10-88 P/L BU realized $11,275.

Obv: Large head.

KM#	Date	Mintage	Fine	VF	XF	Unc
327	1865	.079	75.00	125.00	275.00	500.00

1/15 SPECIE DALER

3.3700 g, .500 SILVER, .0542 oz ASW

Obv: Value, crowned oval arms. Rev: Value, date.

KM#	Date	Mintage	VG	Fine	VF	XF
271	1801 IGM	.382	5.00	10.00	18.00	55.00
	1802 IGM	.149	5.00	10.00	18.00	55.00

NOTE: Earlier dates (1795-1800) exist for this type.

1/5 SPECIE DALER

7.3100 g, .687 SILVER, .1615 oz ASW

KM#	Date	Mintage	VG	Fine	VF	XF
272	1801 IGM	.163	15.00	30.00	65.00	120.00
	1803 IGM	.092	15.00	30.00	65.00	120.00

NOTE: Earlier dates (1796-1800) exist for this type.

1/3 SPECIE DALER

9.6300 g, .875 SILVER, .2709 oz ASW
Similar to KM#273.

KM#	Date	Mintage	VG	Fine	VF	XF
266	1801 IGM	.108	25.00	55.00	110.00	250.00
	1802 IGM	.065	30.00	60.00	120.00	275.00
	1803 IGM	.024	35.00	65.00	125.00	285.00

NOTE: Earlier dates (1795-1800) exist for this type.

Obv: Bust right w/o bow, P.G. below portrait.

KM#	Date	Mintage	VG	Fine	VF	XF
273	1803 IGM	I.A.	125.00	250.00	500.00	1250.

1/2 SPECIE DALER

14.4500 g, .875 SILVER, .4065 oz ASW

KM#	Date	Mintage	VG	Fine	VF	XF
289	1819	.302	50.00	90.00	200.00	425.00
	1821	.069	30.00	50.00	100.00	200.00
	1823/1	6,100	75.00	150.00	300.00	650.00
	1824/1	.033	30.00	60.00	125.00	225.00
	1824	Inc. Ab.	30.00	60.00	125.00	225.00

KM#	Date	Mintage	VG	Fine	VF	XF
302	1827 SKI:	.070	30.00	60.00	125.00	250.00
	1827. SKI.	I.A.	30.00	60.00	125.00	250.00
	1829	5,100	150.00	300.00	600.00	850.00
	1830	8,000	80.00	150.00	300.00	550.00
	1831	9,000	80.00	150.00	300.00	550.00
	1832	4,700	80.00	150.00	300.00	550.00
	1833	1,500	125.00	250.00	500.00	700.00
	1834/29	.018	35.00	75.00	150.00	300.00
	1834	Inc. Ab.	35.00	75.00	150.00	300.00
	1835	9,000	35.00	75.00	150.00	300.00
	1835 star below mint mark					
		Inc. Ab.	—	—	Rare	—
	1836	4,000	50.00	100.00	225.00	350.00

KM#	Date	Mintage	VG	Fine	VF	XF
312	1844	.231	25.00	50.00	100.00	200.00

KM#	Date	Mintage	VG	Fine	VF	XF
316	1846	.146	30.00	50.00	100.00	200.00
	1847	.047	30.00	50.00	100.00	200.00
	1848	.015	30.00	50.00	100.00	250.00
	1849	.142	20.00	40.00	100.00	200.00
	1850	Inc. Ab.	20.00	40.00	100.00	200.00
	1855	.010	100.00	200.00	450.00	700.00

KM#	Date	Mintage	Fine	VF	XF	Unc
322	1861	500 pcs.	—	—	Rare	—
	1861 B below bust					
		13 pcs.	—	—	*Rare	—
	1862	.064	135.00	225.00	385.00	1100.

***NOTE:** Heritage Long Beach sale 10-88 P/L BU realized $14,575.

Obv: Larger head.

KM#	Date	Mintage	Fine	VF	XF	Unc
328	1865	700 pcs.	—	—	*Rare	—

***NOTE:** Oslo Mynthandel sale 10-89 VF realized $12,750.

KM#	Date	Mintage	Fine	VF	XF	Unc
340	1873	4,200	4500.	6000.	8500.	12,000.

SPECIE DALER

28.8900 g, .875 SILVER, .8127 oz ASW

KM#	Date	Mintage	VG	Fine	VF	XF
290	1819 IGP	.024	110.00	225.00	500.00	900.00
	1821 IGP	.101	75.00	120.00	250.00	550.00
	1823 IGP	.016	175.00	400.00	750.00	1600.
	1824/1 JMK					
		.121	60.00	100.00	225.00	550.00
	1824 JMK	I.A.	60.00	100.00	225.00	550.00

KM#	Date	Mintage	VG	Fine	VF	XF
301	1826	.025	70.00	125.00	275.00	500.00
	1826 initial M					
		Inc. Ab.	750.00	1500.	3000.	4500.
	1827/6	.132	50.00	100.00	200.00	350.00
	1827	Inc. Ab.	50.00	100.00	200.00	350.00
	1829/7	.016	75.00	170.00	350.00	600.00
	1829	Inc. Ab.	75.00	170.00	350.00	600.00
	1830	.026	50.00	100.00	275.00	500.00
	1831	.031	80.00	175.00	400.00	650.00
	1832	.024	80.00	175.00	400.00	650.00
	1833	2,732	400.00	800.00	1500.	2500.
	1834	.103	50.00	90.00	190.00	375.00
	1835	.040	50.00	90.00	190.00	375.00
	1835 star below mint mark					
		Inc. Ab.	200.00	500.00	900.00	1500.
	1836	.052	65.00	150.00	275.00	500.00

KM#	Date	Mintage	VG	Fine	VF	XF
313	1844	.302	50.00	100.00	200.00	435.00

KM#	Date	Mintage	VG	Fine	VF	XF
317	1846	.067	45.00	95.00	175.00	320.00
	1847	.140	45.00	95.00	175.00	320.00
	1848	.081	45.00	95.00	175.00	320.00
	1849	.114	45.00	95.00	175.00	320.00
	1850	.124	45.00	95.00	175.00	320.00
	1855	.148	45.00	95.00	175.00	320.00
	1856	.114	45.00	100.00	190.00	320.00
	1857	.160	45.00	100.00	190.00	320.00

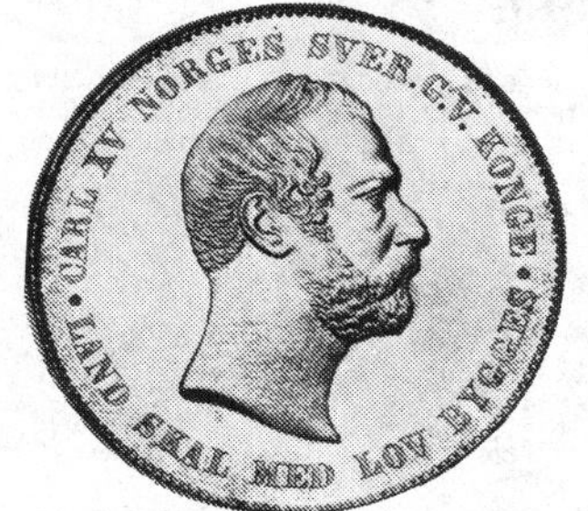

Rev: Similar to KM#313.

KM#	Date	Mintage	Fine	VF	XF	Unc
323	1861	.044	225.00	450.00	800.00	1750.
	1861 B below bust					
		13 pcs.	—	—	Rare	—
	1862	.062	225.00	450.00	800.00	1750.

Rev: Similar to KM#313.

KM#	Date	Mintage	Fine	VF	XF	Unc
325	1864	.130	175.00	325.00	500.00	1000.
	1865	.086	175.00	325.00	500.00	1000.
	1867	.030	400.00	750.00	1250.	2750.
	1868	.114	200.00	400.00	750.00	1750.
	1869	.057	200.00	350.00	600.00	1250.

DECIMAL COINAGE

100 Ore = 1 Krone (30 Skilling)

ORE

BRONZE

KM#	Date	Mintage	Fine	VF	XF	BU
352	1876	8.000	4.00	8.00	15.00	80.00
	1877	2.166	15.00	25.00	45.00	150.00
	1878	1.834	22.50	37.50	60.00	200.00
	1884	3.378	6.00	8.00	15.00	80.00
	1885	.622	50.00	100.00	150.00	300.00
	1889	3.000	4.00	7.00	15.00	45.00
	1891	3.000	5.00	8.00	17.50	50.00
	1893	3.000	5.00	8.00	17.50	50.00
	1897	3.000	5.00	8.00	17.50	50.00
	1899	4.500	2.00	4.00	10.00	35.00

NOTE: Later date (1902) exists for this type.

2 ORE

BRONZE

KM#	Date	Mintage	Fine	VF	XF	BU
353	1876	1.774	4.00	7.00	17.50	90.00
	1877	1.976	3.00	6.00	15.00	70.00
	1884	1.000	5.00	9.00	20.00	85.00
	1889	1.000	3.00	6.00	12.50	65.00
	1891	1.000	2.00	5.00	10.00	60.00
	1893	1.000	2.00	5.00	10.00	60.00
	1897	1.000	2.00	5.00	10.00	60.00
	1899	1.000	2.00	5.00	10.00	60.00

NOTE: Later date (1902) exists for this type.

5 ORE

BRONZE

KM#	Date	Mintage	Fine	VF	XF	BU
349	1875	.354	22.00	35.00	120.00	550.00
	1876	1.647	3.50	8.00	40.00	185.00
	1878	.500	6.00	20.00	60.00	300.00
	1896	1.000	2.50	6.00	35.00	175.00
	1899	.700	2.50	6.00	35.00	175.00

NOTE: Later date (1902) exists for this type.

10 ORE

(3 Skilling)

1.5000 g, .400 SILVER, .0192 oz ASW

KM#	Date	Mintage	Fine	VF	XF	BU
345	1874	2.000	10.00	20.00	60.00	200.00
	1875	.996	25.00	40.00	90.00	250.00

KM#	Date	Mintage	Fine	VF	XF	BU
350	1875	1.008	45.00	65.00	135.00	465.00
	1876	1.992	10.00	20.00	40.00	100.00
	1877	.588	50.00	100.00	185.00	525.00
	1878	.612	30.00	50.00	100.00	365.00
	1880	.600	25.00	40.00	70.00	165.00
	1882	.760	17.50	30.00	45.00	90.00
	1883	1.250	12.50	20.00	40.00	70.00
	1888	.500	18.00	35.00	55.00	125.00
	1889	.750	12.50	17.50	32.50	70.00
	1890	1.000	10.00	15.00	32.50	60.00
	1892	2.000	8.00	12.50	27.50	60.00
	1894	1.500	8.00	12.50	27.50	60.00
	1897	1.500	5.00	7.50	22.50	50.00
	1898	2.000	5.00	7.50	22.50	50.00
	1899	2.500	5.00	7.50	22.50	50.00

NOTE: Later dates (1901-1903) exist for this type.

25 ORE

2.4000 g, .600 SILVER, .0463 oz ASW

KM#	Date	Mintage	Fine	VF	XF	BU
354	1876	3.200	8.00	15.00	45.00	135.00

KM#	Date	Mintage	Fine	VF	XF	BU
360	1896	.400	15.00	30.00	90.00	275.00
	1898	.400	15.00	30.00	90.00	275.00
	1899	.600	10.00	16.00	50.00	125.00
	1900	.400	15.00	30.00	85.00	265.00

NOTE: Later dates (1901-1904) exist for this type.

50 ORE

(15 Skilling)

5.0000 g, .600 SILVER, .0964 oz ASW

KM#	Date	Mintage	Fine	VF	XF	BU
346	1874	.160	60.00	90.00	190.00	550.00
	1875	.640	70.00	100.00	225.00	650.00

Rev: W/o 15 SK.

KM#	Date	Mintage	Fine	VF	XF	BU
356	1877	.800	12.50	35.00	125.00	450.00
	1880	.120	75.00	165.00	325.00	750.00
	1885	.100	75.00	150.00	300.00	750.00
	1887	.200	30.00	55.00	100.00	300.00
	1888	.100	50.00	85.00	200.00	525.00
	1889	.200	17.50	35.00	75.00	200.00
	1891	.400	10.00	25.00	55.00	160.00
	1893	.600	7.50	22.00	55.00	160.00
	1895	.200	12.50	25.00	55.00	165.00
	1896	.500	12.50	25.00	60.00	170.00
	1897	.200	22.50	40.00	75.00	250.00
	1898	.300	12.50	25.00	60.00	160.00
	1899	.200	15.00	30.00	65.00	250.00
	1900	.300	7.50	22.00	55.00	165.00

NOTE: Later dates (1901-1904) exist for this type.

KRONE

(30 Skilling)

7.5000 g, .800 SILVER, .1929 oz ASW

KM#	Date	Mintage	Fine	VF	XF	BU
351	1875	.600	100.00	170.00	325.00	1350.

Rev: W/o 30 SK.

KM#	Date	Mintage	Fine	VF	XF	BU
357	1877	1.000	12.50	50.00	150.00	500.00
	1878	.060	450.00	900.00	1850.	5500.
	1879	.140	50.00	125.00	375.00	900.00
	1881	.080	70.00	125.00	400.00	1200.
	1882	.120	50.00	100.00	350.00	850.00
	1885	.100	40.00	75.00	240.00	600.00
	1887	.100	40.00	75.00	225.00	580.00
	1888	.075	75.00	200.00	450.00	1650.
	1889	.200	25.00	45.00	100.00	400.00
	1890	.200	25.00	45.00	100.00	400.00
	1892	.150	30.00	50.00	110.00	400.00
	1893	.100	30.00	50.00	110.00	400.00
	1894	.100	30.00	50.00	125.00	500.00
	1895/4	.100	32.50	55.00	125.00	325.00
	1895	Inc. Ab.	35.00	60.00	135.00	400.00
	1897	.250	30.00	45.00	85.00	275.00
	1898	.150	32.50	50.00	125.00	400.00
	1900	.250	20.00	45.00	85.00	250.00

NOTE: Later dates (1901-1904) exist for this type.

2 KRONER

15.0000 g, .800 SILVER, .3858 oz ASW

KM#	Date	Mintage	Fine	VF	XF	BU
359	1878	.300	25.00	90.00	285.00	800.00
	1885	.025	250.00	450.00	1000.	2750.
	1887*	.025	250.00	450.00	1000.	2750.
	1888	.025	275.00	475.00	1200.	3250.
	1890	.100	35.00	60.00	150.00	475.00
	1892	.050	60.00	120.00	285.00	1000.
	1893	.075	40.00	85.00	200.00	750.00
	1894	.075	40.00	85.00	200.00	750.00
	1897	.050	60.00	120.00	285.00	1000.
	1898	.050	60.00	120.00	285.00	1000.
	1900	.125	30.00	55.00	120.00	365.00

NOTE: Later dates (1902-1904) exist for this type.
NOTE: Restrikes are made by the Royal Mint, Norway in gold, silver and bronze.

10 KRONER

(2-1/2 Speciedaler)

4.4803 g, .900 GOLD, .1296 oz AGW

KM#	Date	Mintage	Fine	VF	XF	Unc
347	1874	.024	200.00	450.00	700.00	1000.

KM#	Date	Mintage	Fine	VF	XF	Unc
358	1877	.020	250.00	450.00	650.00	900.00

NOTE: Later date (1902) exists for this type.

20 KRONER

(5 Speciedaler)

8.9606 g, .900 GOLD, .2593 oz AGW

KM#	Date	Mintage	Fine	VF	XF	Unc
348	1874	.198	150.00	250.00	400.00	600.00
	1875	.105	150.00	250.00	400.00	600.00

KM#	Date	Mintage	Fine	VF	XF	Unc
355	1876	.109	150.00	200.00	300.00	450.00
	1877	.038	150.00	250.00	450.00	700.00
	1878	.139	150.00	200.00	300.00	450.00
	1879	.046	150.00	200.00	300.00	450.00
	1883	.036	3000.	6000.	9000.	12,500.
	1886	.101	150.00	200.00	300.00	450.00

NOTE: Later date (1902) exists for this type.

PATTERNS (Pn)

(Including off metal strikes)

KM#	Date	Mintage	Identification	Mkt.Val.
PnA39	1813	2 known	1 Skilling	Rare

KM#	Date	Mintage	Identification	Mkt.Val.
Pn39	1837	—	1/2 Skilling	—

The Sultanate of Oman (formerly Muscat and Oman), an independent monarchy located in the southeastern part of the Arabian Peninsula, has an area of 82,030 sq. mi. (212,460 sq. km.) and a population of *1.3 million. Capital: Muscat. The economy is based on agriculture, herding and petroleum. Petroleum products, dates, fish and hides are exported.

The first European contact with Muscat and Oman was made by the Portuguese who captured Muscat, the capital and chief port, in 1508. They occupied the city, utilizing it as a naval base and factory and holding it against land and sea attacks by Arabs and Persians until finally ejected by local Arabs in 1650. It was next occupied by the Persians who maintained control until 1741, when it was taken by Ahmed ibn Sa'id of the present ruling family. Muscat and Oman was the most powerful state in Arabia during the first half of the 19th century, until weakened by the persistent attack of interior nomadic tribes. British influence, initiated by the signing of a treaty of friendship with the Sultanate in 1798, remains a dominant fact of the civil and military phases of the government, although Britain recognizes the Sultanate as a sovereign state.

Sultan Sa'id bin Taimur was overthrown by his son, Qabus bin Sa'id, on July 23, 1970. The new sultan changed the nation's name to Sultanate of Oman.

TITLES

Muscat مسقط

Oman عمان

MUSCAT & OMAN

RULERS

Sultan bin Sultan,
AH1219-1273/1804-1856AD
Thuwaini bin Sa'id,
AH1273-1283/1856-1866AD
Salim bin Thuwaini,
AH1283-1285/1866-1868AD
Azzan bin Quais,
AH1285-1288/1868-1871AD
Turkee bin Sa'id,
AH1288-1306/1871-1888AD
Faisal bin Turkee,
AH1306-1332/1888-1913AD

MONETARY SYSTEM

Until 1972

4 Baisa = 1 Anna
64 Baisa = 1 Rupee
200 Baisa = 1 Saidi/Dasin Dog Dhofari Rial

1/12 ANNA

COPPER

KM#	Date	Mintage	VG	Fine	VF	XF
1	AH1311	—	25.00	35.00	60.00	125.00

1/4 ANNA

COPPER

KM#	Date	Mintage	Good	VG	Fine	VF
2	AH1311	—	6.00	10.00	18.00	40.00

COPPER or BRASS
Heaton Mint, Birmingham
Level 5

KM#	Date	Mintage	Good	VG	Fine	VF
3.1	AH1315	19.110	.50	1.00	2.00	4.00

Small, angeled 5

KM#	Date	Mintage	Good	VG	Fine	VF
3.2	AH1315	I.A.	.75	1.50	3.00	6.00

NOTE: A KM#3.2 is a much cruder issue with many die varieties known. Perhaps struck at Bombay, India.

LOCAL COINAGE

1/4 ANNA

COPPER
Obv. leg: . . . IMAM.MUSCAT.

KM#	Date	Mintage	Good	VG	Fine	VF
4.1	AH1312	—	2.00	3.25	5.00	8.50

Obv: W/o inner circle.

KM#	Date	Mintage	Good	VG	Fine	VF
4.2	AH1312	—	2.00	3.25	5.00	8.50

Rev: KM#2.
Obv. leg: . . . IMAM.MUSCAT.OMAN.

KM#	Date	Mintage	Good	VG	Fine	VF
5	AH1312//1311	—	2.50	4.25	6.00	10.00

KM#	Date	Mintage	Good	VG	Fine	VF
6	AH1312	—	2.00	3.00	5.00	8.00
	1313	—	2.50	4.25	6.00	10.00

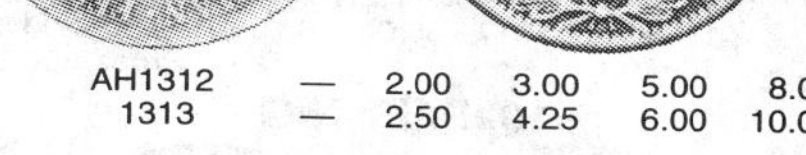

Mule. Obv: KM#6. Rev: KM#2.

KM#	Date	Mintage	Good	VG	Fine	VF
7	AH1313//1311	—	—	—	—	—

KM#	Date	Mintage	Good	VG	Fine	VF
8.1	AH1312	—	2.50	4.25	6.00	10.00

Rev: Long dentilated borders.

KM#	Date	Mintage	Good	VG	Fine	VF
8.2	AH1312	—	2.50	4.25	6.00	10.00

KM#	Date	Mintage	Good	VG	Fine	VF
9.1	AH1313	—	2.50	4.25	6.00	10.00

Obv: Legend begins at top w/o star or dot.
Rev: 5-line inscription within denticled border.

KM#	Date	Mintage	Good	VG	Fine	VF
9.2	AH1313	—	—	—	—	—

KM#	Date	Mintage	Good	VG	Fine	VF
10.1	AH1314	—	3.00	5.00	7.00	12.50

Obv: Large date, value on 1 line.

KM#	Date	Mintage	Good	VG	Fine	VF
10.2	AH1314	—	3.00	5.00	7.00	12.50

KM#	Date	Mintage	Good	VG	Fine	VF
11	AH1314	—	3.00	5.00	7.00	12.50

KM#	Date	Mintage	Good	VG	Fine	VF
12.1	AH1315	—	2.00	3.25	5.00	8.50

NOTE: Varieties exist.

Rev: Legend style varies.

KM#	Date	Mintage	Good	VG	Fine	VF
12.2	AH1315	—	2.00	3.25	5.00	8.50

Obv: Legend style varies.

KM#	Date	Mintage	Good	VG	Fine	VF
12.3	AH1315	—	2.00	3.25	5.00	8.50

KM#	Date	Mintage	Good	VG	Fine	VF
13	AH5131 (error) date retrograde	—	4.00	6.50	10.00	17.50

Rev: W/o star.

KM#	Date	Mintage	Good	VG	Fine	VF
14	AH1316	—	2.50	4.00	6.00	10.00

Rev: Star between wreath points.

KM#	Date	Mintage	Good	VG	Fine	VF
15	AH1316	—	12.50	20.00	30.00	50.00

NOTE: There are numerous varieties of each year of the native issues, varying in both obverse and reverse legends distribution, in the presence or absence of wreath borders, etc.

KM#	Date	Mintage	Good	VG	Fine	VF
16	AH1318/5	—	12.50	20.00	30.00	50.00

NOTE: Doubts in reading date.

PAPUA NEW GUINEA

Papua New Guinea, an independent member of the British Commonwealth, occupies the eastern half of the island of New Guinea. It lies north of Australia near the equator and borders on West Irian. The country, which includes nearby Bismark archipelago, Buka and Bougainville, has an area of 178,260 sq. mi. (461,690 sq. km.) and a population of *3.7 million who are divided into more than 1,000 seperate tribes speaking more than 700 mutually unintelligible languages. Capital: Port Moresby. The economy is agricultural, and exports copra, rubber, cocoa, coffee, tea, gold and copper.

In 1884 Germany annexed the area known as German New Guinea (also Neu Guinea or Kaiser Wilhelmsland) comprising the northern section of eastern New Guinea, and granted its administration and development to the Neu-Guinea Compagnie. Administration reverted to Germany in 1889 following the failure of the company to exercise adequate administration. While a German protectorate, German New Guinea had an area of 92,159 sq. mi. (238,692 sq. km.) and a population of about 250,000. Capital: Herbertshohe, 1 of 4 capitals of German New Guinea. The seat of government was transferred to Rabaul in 1910. Copra was the chief crop. Australian troops occupied German New Guinea in Aug. 1914, shortly after Great Britain declared war on Germany. It was mandated to Australia by the Leage of Nations in 1920, known as the Territory of New Guinea. The territory was invaded and most of it was occupied by Japan in 1942. Following the Japanese surrender, it came under U.N. trusteeship, Dec. 13, 1946, with Australia as the administering power.

The Papua and New Guinea act, 1949, provided for the government of Papua and New Guinea as one administrative unit. On Dec. 1, 1973, Papua New Guinea became selfgoverning with Australia retaining responsibility for defense and foreign affairs. Full independence was achieved on Sept. 16, 1975. Papua New Guinea is a member of the Commonwealth of Nations. The Queen of England is Chief of State.

GERMAN NEW GUINEA

RULERS

German, 1884-1914

MINT MARKS

A - Berlin

MONETARY SYSTEM

100 Pfennig = 1 Mark

PFENNIG

COPPER

KM#	Date	Mintage	Fine	VF	XF	Unc
1	1894A	.033	20.00	40.00	90.00	150.00
	1894A	—	—	—	Proof	400.00

2 PFENNIG

COPPER

KM#	Date	Mintage	Fine	VF	XF	Unc
2	1894A	.017	35.00	65.00	120.00	200.00
	1894A	—	—	—	Proof	550.00

10 PFENNIG

COPPER

KM#	Date	Mintage	Fine	VF	XF	Unc
3	1894A	.024	30.00	60.00	140.00	300.00
	1894A	—	—	—	Proof	1250.

1/2 MARK

2.7780 g, .900 SILVER, .0804 oz ASW

KM#	Date	Mintage	Fine	VF	XF	Unc
4	1894A	.016	50.00	100.00	200.00	350.00
	1894A	—	—	—	Proof	550.00

MARK

5.5560 g, .900 SILVER, .1608 oz ASW

KM#	Date	Mintage	Fine	VF	XF	Unc
5	1894A	.033	50.00	100.00	200.00	400.00
	1894A	—	—	—	Proof	700.00

2 MARK

11.1110 g, .900 SILVER, .3215 oz ASW

KM#	Date	Mintage	Fine	VF	XF	Unc
6	1894A	.013	125.00	225.00	465.00	875.00
	1894A	—	—	—	Proof	1250.

5 MARK

27.7780 g, .900 SILVER, .8039 oz ASW

KM#	Date	Mintage	Fine	VF	XF	Unc
7	1894A	.019	—	850.00	1250.	2150.
	1894A	—	—	—	Proof	3750.

10 MARK

3.9820 g, .900 GOLD, .1152 oz AGW

KM#	Date	Mintage	Fine	VF	XF	Unc
8	1895A	2,000	—	4000.	8250.	11,500.
	1895A	—	—	—	Proof	14,500.

20 MARK

7.9650 g, .900 GOLD, .2305 oz AGW

KM#	Date	Mintage	Fine	VF	XF	Unc
9	1895A	1,500	—	4250.	8750.	12,500.
	1895A	—	—	—	Proof	16,500.

PROOF SETS (PS)

KM#	Date	Mintage	Identification	Issue Price	Mkt. Val.
PS1	1894(7)	—	KM1-7	—	8450.

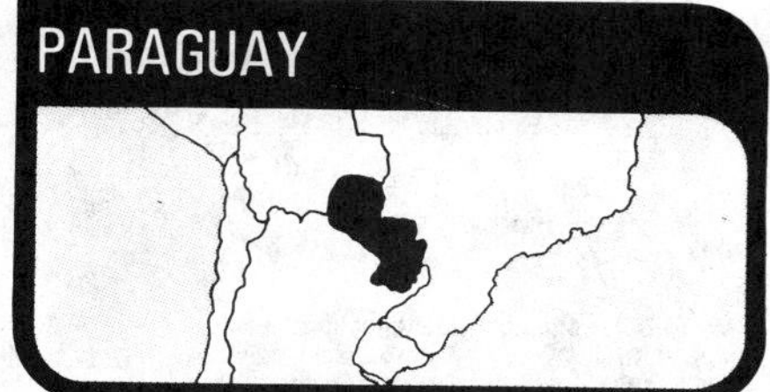

The Republic of Paraguay, a landlocked country in the heart of South America surrounded by Argentina, Bolivia and Brazil, has an area of 157,048 sq. mi. (406,750 sq. km.) and a population of *4.5 million, 95 percent of whom are of mixed Spanish and Indian descent. Capital: Asuncion. The country is predominantly agrarian, with no important mineral deposits or oil reserves. Meat, timber, hides, oilseeds, tobacco and cotton account for 70 percent of Paraguay's export revenue.

Paraguay was first visited by Alejo Garcia, a shipwrecked Spaniard, in 1524. The interior was explored by Sebastian Cabot in 1527 and 1528, when he sailed up the Parana and Paraguay rivers. Asuncion, which would become the center of a Spanish colonial province embracing much of southern South America, was established by the Spanish explorer Juan de Salazar on Aug. 15, 1537. For a century and a half the history of Paraguay was largely the history of the agricultural colonies established by the Jesuits in the south and east to Christianize the Indians. In 1811, following the outbreak of the South American wars of independence, Paraguayan patriots overthrew the local Spanish authorities and proclaimed their country's independence.

During the Triple Alliance War (1864-1870) in which Paraguay faced Argentina, Brazil and Uruguay, Asuncion's ladies gathered in an Assembly on Feb. 24, 1867 and decided to give up their jewelry in order to help the national defense. The President of the Republic, Francisco Solano Lopez accepted the offering and ordered one twentieth of it be used to mint the first Paraguayan gold coins according to the Decree of the 11th of Sept., 1867.

Two dies were made, one by Bouvet, and another by an American, Leonard Charles, while only the die made by Bouvet was eventually used.

MINT MARKS

HF - LeLocle

CONTRACTORS

(Chas. J.) SHAW - for Ralph Heaton, Birmingham Mint

MONETARY SYSTEM

100 Centesimos = 1 Peso

1/12 REAL

COPPER

KM#	Date	Mintage	Fine	VF	XF	Unc
1.1*	1845 Birmingham	2.880	7.00	20.00	65.00	175.00

Crude issue struck at Asuncion Mint.

KM#	Date	Mintage	Fine	VF	XF	Unc
1.2*	1845	.288	15.00	45.00	125.00	285.00

***NOTE:** Struck with medal die alignment. Coin strike varieties exist. After 1847 they were revalued at 1/24th Real.

4 PESOS FUERTES

6.5700 g, .900 GOLD, .1901 oz AGW
First Paraguayan Gold Coin

KM#	Date	Mintage	Fine	VF	XF	Unc
A2	1867	—	5500.	7500.	10,000.	—

DECIMAL COINAGE

100 Centavos (Centesimos) = 1 Peso

CENTESIMO

COPPER
Rev: SHAW to right of date.

KM#	Date	Mintage	Fine	VF	XF	Unc
2	1870	—	2.00	5.00	20.00	40.00

2 CENTESIMOS

COPPER
Rev: SHAW to right of date.

KM#	Date	Mintage	Fine	VF	XF	Unc
3	1870	—	3.00	8.00	30.00	60.00

4 CENTESIMOS

COPPER
Rev: SHAW to right of date.

KM#	Date	Mintage	Fine	VF	XF	Unc
4.1	1870	—	4.00	12.00	40.00	85.00

Crude issue struck at Asuncion.
Obv: W/o ribbon bow on sprays.
Rev: W/o SHAW to right of date.

KM#	Date	Mintage	VG	Fine	VF	XF
4.2	1870	—	50.00	100.00	200.00	500.00

Rev: SAEZ to right of date.

KM#	Date	Mintage	VG	Fine	VF	XF
4.3	1870	—	50.00	75.00	150.00	300.00

NOTE: Varieties exist.

5 CENTAVOS

COPPER-NICKEL

KM#	Date	Mintage	Fine	VF	XF	Unc
6	1900	.400	1.00	2.00	10.00	25.00

NOTE: Later date (1903) exists for this type.

10 CENTAVOS

COPPER-NICKEL

KM#	Date	Mintage	Fine	VF	XF	Unc
7	1900	.800	1.00	2.50	10.00	22.50

NOTE: Later date (1903) exists for this type.

20 CENTAVOS

COPPER-NICKEL

KM#	Date	Mintage	Fine	VF	XF	Unc
8	1900	.500	1.00	3.00	10.00	30.00

NOTE: Later date (1903) exists for this type.

PESO

25.0000 g, .900 SILVER, .7233 oz ASW

KM#	Date	Mintage	Fine	VF	XF	Unc
5	1889	.600*	50.00	90.00	135.00	350.00

***NOTE:** Unknown quantity melted.

PATTERNS (Pn)

(Including off metal strikes)

KM#	Date	Mintage	Identification	Mkt.Val.
Pn1	1854	—	10 Reales, Silver shell, Lead center, medal rotation	3500.
Pn2	1854	—	10 Reales, Silver shell, lead center, coin rotation	3500.
Pn3	1855	—	4 Pesos, Gold	—
Pn4	1855	—	4 Pesos, Silver	—
Pn5	1855	—	4 Pesos, Gilt Silver	—
Pn6	1855	—	4 Pesos, Copper	—

KM#	Date	Mintage	Identification	Mkt.Val.
Pn7	1855	—	10 Reales, Silver, reeded edge, medal rotation	6500.
Pn8	1855	—	10 Reales, Silver, reeded edge, coin rotation	6500.
Pn9	1855	—	10 Reales, Silver, plain edge, coin rotation	6500.
Pn10	1855	—	10 Reales, Pewter	6000.

KM#	Date	Mintage	Identification	Mkt.Val.
Pn11	1864	—	10 Reales, Silver, coarse reeded edge	6750.
Pn12	1864	—	10 Reales, Silver, fine reeded edge	6750.
Pn13	1864	—	10 Reales, Pewter, plain edge	6750.

KM#	Date	Mintage	Identification	Mkt.Val.
Pn14	1866	—	10 Reales, Silver, reeded edge, medal rotation	6750.
Pn15	1867	—	10 Reales, Silver, reeded edge, small 7	5500.
Pn16	1867	—	10 Reales, Silver, reeded edge, large 7	5500.
Pn17	1867	—	10 Reales, Copper, reeded edge, small 7	5000.

KM#	Date	Mintage	Identification	Mkt.Val.
Pn18	1867	—	4 Pesos, Gold	15,000.
Pn19	1867	1 known	4 Pesos, Copper	—
PnA19	1867	—	4 Pesos, Silver	—
Pn20	1867	1 known	CUATRO (1/4 Real) Fuertes, Gold, Charles	—

KM#	Date	Mintage	Identification	Mkt.Val.
Pn21	1868	—	2 Centimos, Brass	200.00
Pn22	1868	—	2 Centimes, German Silver	300.00

KM#	Date	Mintage	Identification	Mkt.Val.
Pn23	1868	—	2 Reales, Copper, thick planchet	—
Pn24	1868	—	2 Reales, Copper, thin planchet	—
Pn26	1868	—	2 Reales, Silver, 24mm, large date, reeded edge	1250.
Pn27	1868	—	2 Reales, Silver, 22mm	850.00
Pn29	1869	—	2 Reales, Silver, 25mm, thin planchet, broad flan	1850.

KM#	Date	Mintage	Identification	Mkt.Val.
Pn30	1869	—	2 Reales, Silver, 24mm, thick planchet, small flan	1750.
Pn31	1869	—	2 Reales, Copper, thick planchet	—
Pn32	1869	—	2 Reales, Copper, thin planchet	—
Pn33	1870	—	2 Centesimos, Silvered Copper, KM3	—
Pn34	1870	—	4 Centesimos, Silvered Copper, KM4.1	—

KM#	Date	Mintage	Identification	Mkt.Val.
Pn35	1873	—	5 Pesos, Gold	7500.
Pn36	1873	—	5 Pesos, Silver	—
Pn37	1888	—	1 Peso, Silver	1650.
Pn38	1888	—	1 Peso, Aluminum	1650.
Pn39	1888	—	1 Peso, Copper	1650.

PIEFORTS (P)

KM#	Date	Mintage	Identification	Mkt.Val.
P1	1888	—	1 Peso, Silver	3500.

TRIAL STRIKES (TS)

KM#	Date	Mintage	Identification	Mkt.Val.
TS1	1854	—	10 Reales, Silver shell, Lead center, reverse	—
TS2	1854	—	10 Reales, Silvered Copper, reverse	—
TS3	1855	—	10 Reales, Silver shell, lead center, reverse	—

Listings For

PERSIA: refer to Iran

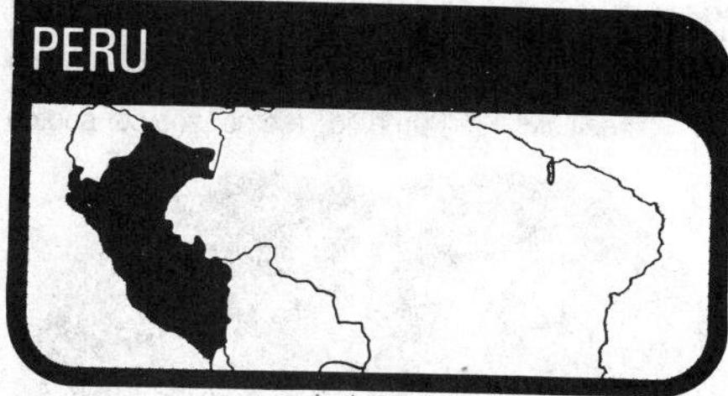

The Republic of Peru, located on the Pacific coast of South America, has an area of 496,225 sq. mi. (1,285,220 sq. km.) and a population of *21.4 million. Capital: Lima. The diversified economy includes mining, fishing and agriculture. Fish meal, copper, sugar, zinc and iron ore are exported.

Once part of the great Inca Empire that reached from northern Ecuador to central Chile, the conquest of Peru by Francisco Pizarro began in 1531. Desirable as the richest of the Spanish viceroyalties, it was torn by warfare between avaricious Spaniards until the arrival in 1569 of Francisco de Toledo, who initiated 2-1/2 centuries of efficient colonial rule which made Lima the most aristocratic colonial capital and the stronghold of Spain's American possessions. Jose de San Martin of Argentina proclaimed Peru's independence on July 28, 1821; Simon Bolivar of Venezuela secured it in December, 1824 when he defeated the last Spanish army in South America. After several futile attempts to re-establish its South American empire, Spain recognized Peru's independence in 1879.

Andres de Santa Cruz, whose mother was a high-ranking Inca, was the best of Bolivia's early presidents, and temporarily united Peru and Bolivia 1836-39, thus realizing his dream of a Peruvian/Bolivian confederation. This prompted the separate coinages of North and South Peru. Peruvian resistance and Chilean intervention finally broke up the confederation, sending Santa Cruz into exile. A succession of military strongman presidents ruled Peru until Marshall Castilla revitalized Peruvian politics in the mid-19th century and repulsed Spain's attempt to reclaim its one-time colony. Subsequent loss of southern territory to Chile in the War of the Pacific, 1879-81, and gradually increasing rejection of foreign economic domination, combined with recent serious inflation, affected the country numismatically.

As a result of the discovery of silver at Potosi in 1545, a mint was eventually authorized in 1565 with the first coinage taking place in 1568. The mint had an uneven life span during the Spanish Colonial period from 1568-1572. It was closed from 1573-1576, reopened from 1577-1588. It remained closed until 1659-1660 when an unauthorized coinage in both silver and gold were struck. After being closed in 1660, it remained closed until 1684 when it struck cob style coins until 1752.

RULERS

Spanish, until 1822

MINT MARKS

AREQUIPA, AREQ = Arequipa
AYACUCHO = Ayacucho
(B) = Brussels
CUZCO (monogram), Cuzco, Co. Cuzco
L, LIMAE (monogram), Lima (monogram), LIMA = Lima
(L) = London
PASCO (monogram), Pasco, Paz, Po = Pasco
P,(P) = Philadelphia
S = San Francisco
(W) = Waterbury, CT, USA

NOTE: The LIMAE monogram appears in three forms. The early LM monogram form looks like a dotted L with M. The later LIMAE monogram has all the letters of LIMAE more readily distinguishable. The third form appears as an M monogram during early Republican issues.

MINT ASSAYERS INITIALS

The letter(s) following the dates of Peruvian coins are the assayer's initials appearing on the coins. They generally appear at the 11 o'clock position on the Colonial coinage and at the 5 o'clock position along the rim on the obverse or reverse on the Republican coinage.

MONETARY SYSTEM

16 Reales = 2 Pesos = 1 Escudo

MILLED COINAGE

1/4 REAL

.8500 g, .903 SILVER, .0247 oz ASW
Mint mark: L
Obv: Castle, L at left, 1/4 at right.

KM#	Date	Mintage	VG	Fine	VF	XF
102.2	1801	—	9.00	15.00	25.00	50.00
	1802	—	12.50	18.50	37.50	75.00
	1803	—	12.50	18.50	37.50	75.00
	1804	—	12.50	18.50	37.50	75.00
	1805	—	12.50	18.50	37.50	75.00
	1806	—	9.00	15.00	25.00	50.00
	1807	—	9.00	15.00	25.00	50.00
	1808	—	9.00	15.00	25.00	50.00

NOTE: Earlier dates (1796-1800) exist for this type.

KM#	Date	Mintage	VG	Fine	VF	XF
108	1809	—	30.00	55.00	80.00	100.00
	1810	—	7.00	12.00	22.50	45.00
	1811	—	10.00	16.50	32.50	55.00
	1812	—	10.00	16.50	32.50	55.00
	1813	—	7.00	12.00	22.50	45.00
	1814	—	7.00	12.00	22.50	45.00
	1815	—	10.00	16.50	32.50	55.00
	1816	—	7.00	12.00	22.50	45.00
	1817	—	7.00	12.00	22.50	45.00
	1818	—	7.00	12.00	22.50	45.00
	1819	—	7.00	12.00	22.50	45.00
	1820	—	7.00	12.00	22.50	45.00
	1821	—	7.00	12.00	22.50	45.00
	1823	—	35.00	60.00	85.00	125.00
	1825	—	55.00	90.00	120.00	185.00

NOTE: Most 1809 dates found are actually dated 1802, where the base of the 2 is weakly struck.

1/2 REAL

1.6500 g, .903 SILVER, .0479 oz ASW
Mint mark: LIMAE (monogram)
Obv. leg: CAROLUS IIII, bust. Rev: Arms, pillars.

KM#	Date	Mintage	VG	Fine	VF	XF
93	1801 IJ	—	4.00	8.00	14.00	32.00
	1802 IJ	—	4.00	8.00	14.00	32.00
	1803 IJ	—	6.00	12.50	20.00	42.00
	1803 JP	—	4.00	8.00	12.50	28.00
	1804 JP	—	4.00	8.00	12.50	28.00
	1805 JP	—	4.00	8.00	14.00	32.00
	1805 IJ	—	14.00	25.00	50.00	70.00
	1806 JP	—	4.00	8.00	14.00	32.00
	1807 JP	—	4.00	8.00	12.50	28.00
	1808 JP	—	4.00	8.00	12.50	28.00

NOTE: Earlier dates (1791-1800) exist for this type.

Obv. leg: FERDND. VII. . ., Lima bust.
Rev: Arms, pillars.

KM#	Date	Mintage	VG	Fine	VF	XF
103.1	1808 JP	—	55.00	90.00	140.00	210.00

Obv. leg: FERDIN. VII.

KM#	Date	Mintage	VG	Fine	VF	XF
103.2	1809 JP	—	18.50	32.00	52.00	120.00
	1810 JP	—	10.00	17.50	32.00	90.00
	1811 JP	—	10.00	17.50	32.00	90.00

Obv: Standard bust.

KM#	Date	Mintage	VG	Fine	VF	XF
113	1811 JP	—	8.00	14.00	28.00	65.00
	1812 JP	—	3.75	7.00	14.00	28.00
	1813 JP	—	3.75	7.00	14.00	28.00
	1814 JP	—	5.00	10.00	18.50	42.00
	1815 JP	—	3.75	7.00	14.00	28.00
	1816 JP	—	3.75	7.00	14.00	28.00
	1817 JP	—	3.75	7.00	14.00	28.00
	1818 JP	—	3.75	7.00	14.00	28.00
	1819 JP	—	3.75	7.00	14.00	28.00
	1820 JP	—	3.75	7.00	14.00	28.00
	1821 JP	—	3.75	7.00	14.00	28.00

REAL

3.2500 g, .903 SILVER, .0944 oz ASW
Obv. leg: CAROLUS IIII. . ., bust of Charles IV.
Rev: Similar to KM#109.

KM#	Date	Mintage	VG	Fine	VF	XF
94	1801 IJ	—	7.50	12.50	25.00	50.00
	1802 IJ	—	18.50	32.00	50.00	80.00
	1803 IJ	—	15.00	25.00	50.00	125.00
	1803 JP	—	11.00	18.50	45.00	125.00
	1804 IJ	—	15.00	25.00	60.00	125.00
	1804 JP	—	15.00	25.00	60.00	125.00
	1805 JP	—	11.00	18.50	45.00	125.00
	1806 JP	—	7.50	12.50	25.00	60.00
	1807 JP	—	7.50	12.50	25.00	50.00
	1808 JP	—	32.00	50.00	125.00	175.00

NOTE: Earlier dates (1791-1800) exist for this type.

Obv. leg: FERDIN VII. . ., Lima bust.

KM#	Date	Mintage	VG	Fine	VF	XF
109	1808 JP	—	—	—	Rare	—
	1809 JP	—		Reported, not confirmed		
	1810 JP	—	18.50	32.00	55.00	275.00
	1811 JP	—	18.50	32.00	55.00	275.00

Obv. leg: FERDIN. VII. . ., standard bust.

KM#	Date	Mintage	VG	Fine	VF	XF
114.1	1811 JP	—	30.00	50.00	85.00	150.00
	1812 JP	—	6.00	11.00	18.00	37.50
	1813 JP	—	6.00	11.00	18.00	42.50
	1814 JP	—	4.00	8.00	15.00	35.00
	1815 JP	—	7.00	12.00	20.00	45.00
	1816 JP	—	4.50	9.00	15.00	35.00
	1817 JP	—	4.50	9.00	15.00	35.00
	1818 JP	—	4.50	9.00	15.00	35.00
	1819 JP	—	4.50	9.00	15.00	35.00
	1820 JP	—	4.50	9.00	15.00	35.00
	1821 JP	—	4.50	9.00	15.00	35.00
	1823 JP	—	17.50	30.00	70.00	135.00

Mint mark: CUZCO (monogram)

KM#	Date	Mintage	VG	Fine	VF	XF
114.2	1824/3 T	—	45.00	80.00	175.00	300.00
	1824 T	—	60.00	120.00	200.00	400.00

2 REALES

6.5000 g, .903 SILVER, .1887 oz ASW
Mint mark: LIMAE (monogram)
Obv. leg: CAROLUS IIII, bust of Charles IV.
Rev: Similar to KM#104.2.

KM#	Date	Mintage	VG	Fine	VF	XF
95	1801 IJ	—	7.00	11.50	17.50	35.00
	1802 IJ	—	7.00	11.50	17.50	30.00
	1803/2 IJ	—	13.50	22.50	40.00	80.00
	1803 IJ	—	13.50	22.50	40.00	80.00
	1803 JP	—	7.00	11.50	17.50	35.00
	1804 IJ	—	10.00	17.50	28.00	55.00
	1804 JP	—	7.00	11.50	17.50	30.00
	1805 JP	—	6.00	10.00	14.50	27.50
	1806 JP	—	7.00	11.50	17.50	30.00
	1807/0 JP	—	7.00	11.50	17.50	35.00
	1807 JP	—	7.00	11.50	17.50	35.00
	1808 JP	—	7.00	11.50	17.50	35.00

NOTE: Earlier dates (1791-1800) exist for this type.

Obv. leg: FERDND. VII. . ., Lima bust.
Rev: Arms, pillars.

KM#	Date	Mintage	VG	Fine	VF	XF
104.1	1808 JP	—	40.00	70.00	175.00	285.00
	1809 JP	—	—	—	Rare	—

Obv. leg: FERDIN. VII. . ., Lima bust.

KM#	Date	Mintage	VG	Fine	VF	XF
104.2	1808 JP	—	100.00	170.00	280.00	450.00
	1809 JP	—	—	—	Rare	—
	1810 JP	—	7.00	11.50	17.50	35.00
	1811 JP	—	17.50	27.50	50.00	85.00

Obv. leg: FERDIN. VII. . ., standard bust.

KM#	Date	Mintage	VG	Fine	VF	XF
115.1	1811 JP	—	13.50	22.50	40.00	100.00
	1812 JP	—	5.50	9.50	14.50	22.00
	1813 JP	—	5.50	9.50	14.50	22.00
	1814 JP	—	7.00	11.50	17.50	30.00
	1815 JP	—	7.00	11.50	17.50	30.00
	1816 JP	—	5.50	9.50	14.50	22.00
	1817 JP	—	5.50	9.50	14.50	22.00
	1818 JP	—	5.50	9.50	14.50	22.00
	1819 JP	—	5.50	9.50	14.50	22.00
	1820 JP	—	5.50	9.50	14.50	22.00
	1821 JP	—	5.50	9.50	14.50	22.00
	1823 JP	—	7.00	11.50	17.50	30.00

Mint mark: CUZCO (monogram)

KM#	Date	Mintage	VG	Fine	VF	XF
115.2	1824 T	—	145.00	225.00	345.00	575.00

Mint mark: LIMAE (monogram)

KM#	Date	Mintage	VG	Fine	VF	XF
115.3	1826 IR	—	85.00	145.00	285.00	425.00

NOTE: KM#115.3 was struck in Callao by Royalists prior to final capitulation on January 22, 1826.

4 REALES

13.0000 g, .903 SILVER, .3774 oz ASW
Mint: Lima
Obv. leg: CAROLUS IIII. . .

KM#	Date	Mintage	VG	Fine	VF	XF
96	1801 IJ	—	25.00	45.00	90.00	150.00
	1802 IJ	—	30.00	50.00	100.00	175.00
	1803 IJ	—	75.00	125.00	200.00	350.00
	1803 JP	—	45.00	75.00	125.00	250.00
	1804 JP	—	25.00	45.00	100.00	175.00
	1805 JP	—	25.00	40.00	100.00	175.00
	1806 JP	—	25.00	40.00	100.00	175.00
	1807 JP	—	25.00	45.00	100.00	175.00
	1808 JP	—	45.00	75.00	125.00	250.00

NOTE: Earlier dates (1791-1800) exist for this type.

Obv. leg: FERDND. VII. . ., Lima bust.
Rev: Arms, pillars.

KM#	Date	Mintage	VG	Fine	VF	XF
105.1	1808 JP	—	75.00	125.00	250.00	475.00

Obv. leg: FERDIN. VII. . ., Lima bust.

KM#	Date	Mintage	VG	Fine	VF	XF
105.2	1810 JP	—	65.00	125.00	250.00	500.00
	1811 JP	—	65.00	125.00	250.00	500.00

Obv. leg: FERDIN. VII. . ., standard bust.

KM#	Date	Mintage	VG	Fine	VF	XF
116	1811 JP	—	—	—	Rare	—
	1812 JP	—	25.00	40.00	100.00	150.00
	1813 JP	—	75.00	125.00	200.00	350.00
	1814 JP	—	75.00	125.00	200.00	350.00
	1815 JP	—	60.00	100.00	175.00	250.00
	1816 JP	—	20.00	30.00	100.00	150.00
	1817 JP	—	20.00	30.00	100.00	150.00
	1818 JP	—	20.00	30.00	100.00	150.00
	1819 JP	—	20.00	30.00	100.00	150.00
	1820 JP	—	20.00	30.00	75.00	100.00
	1821 JP	—	20.00	30.00	75.00	150.00

8 REALES

25.0000 g, .903 SILVER, .7259 oz ASW
Mint mark: LIMAE (monogram)
Rev: Similar to KM#117.2.

KM#	Date	Mintage	VG	Fine	VF	XF
97	1801 IJ	4.223	25.00	32.50	50.00	85.00
	1802 IJ	3.875	25.00	32.50	50.00	85.00
	1803 IJ	—	35.00	60.00	100.00	125.00
	1803 JP	—	25.00	32.50	50.00	85.00
	1804 JP	3.979	25.00	32.50	50.00	85.00
	1805 JP	4.030	25.00	32.50	50.00	85.00
	1806 JP	4.199	25.00	32.50	50.00	85.00
	1807 JP	3.562	25.00	32.50	50.00	85.00
	1808 JP	4.017	25.00	32.50	50.00	85.00

NOTE: Earlier dates (1791-1800) exist for this type.

Obv. leg: FERDND. VII. . ., imaginary bust.
Rev: Arms, pillars.

KM#	Date	Mintage	VG	Fine	VF	XF
106.1	1808 JP	I.A.	150.00	250.00	425.00	800.00
	1809 JP	4.197	100.00	200.00	280.00	450.00

Obv. leg: FERDIN. VII. . ., imaginary bust.

KM#	Date	Mintage	VG	Fine	VF	XF
106.2	1809 JP	I.A.	30.00	60.00	100.00	225.00
	1810 JP	4.380	30.00	60.00	100.00	225.00
	1811 JP	4.412	30.00	50.00	75.00	150.00

Obv. leg: FERDIN. VII. . ., standard bust.

KM#	Date	Mintage	VG	Fine	VF	XF
117.1	1811 JP	I.A.	50.00	90.00	140.00	225.00
	1812 JP	3.800	25.00	32.50	45.00	75.00
	1813 JP	4.033	25.00	32.50	45.00	75.00
	1814 JP	3.599	25.00	32.50	45.00	75.00
	1815/4 JP	3.642	25.00	32.50	45.00	75.00
	1815 JP	Inc. Ab.	25.00	32.50	45.00	75.00
	1816 JP	—	25.00	32.50	45.00	75.00
	1817 JP wide date	—	25.00	32.50	45.00	75.00
	1817 JP narrow date	—	25.00	32.50	45.00	75.00
	1818 JP	—	25.00	32.50	45.00	75.00
	1819 JP	3.139	25.00	32.50	45.00	75.00
	1820 JP	—	25.00	32.50	45.00	75.00
	1821 JP	—	25.00	32.50	45.00	75.00

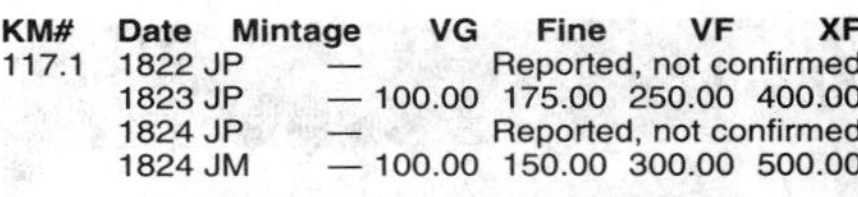

KM#	Date	Mintage	VG	Fine	VF	XF
117.1	1822 JP	—	Reported, not confirmed			
	1823 JP	—	100.00	175.00	250.00	400.00
	1824 JP	—	Reported, not confirmed			
	1824 JM	—	100.00	150.00	300.00	500.00

Mint mark: CUZCO (monogram)

KM#	Date	Mintage	VG	Fine	VF	XF
117.2	1824 T	—	60.00	100.00	175.00	350.00
	1824 G	—	90.00	150.00	250.00	550.00
	1824 G/T	—	—	—	Rare	—

1/2 ESCUDO

1.6875 g, .875 GOLD, .0475 oz AGW
Mint mark: LIMAE (monogram)

KM#	Date	Mintage	VG	Fine	VF	XF
125	1814 JP	—	225.00	450.00	800.00	1400.
	1815 JP	—	225.00	450.00	800.00	1400.
	1816 JP	—	225.00	450.00	800.00	1400.
	1817 JP	—	225.00	450.00	800.00	1400.
	1818 JP	—	225.00	450.00	800.00	1400.
	1819 JP	—	225.00	450.00	800.00	1400.
	1820 JP	—	225.00	450.00	800.00	1400.
	1821 JP	—	225.00	450.00	800.00	1400.

ESCUDO

3.3750 g, .875 GOLD, .0949 oz AGW
Mint mark: LIMAE (monogram)
Obv. leg: CAROL. IIII. . ., bust of Charles IV.
Rev: Similar to KM#126.

KM#	Date	Mintage	VG	Fine	VF	XF
89	1801 IJ	—	100.00	150.00	250.00	350.00
	1802 IJ	—	100.00	150.00	250.00	350.00
	1803 IJ	—	100.00	150.00	250.00	350.00
	1803 JP	—	100.00	150.00	250.00	350.00
	1804 JP	—	100.00	150.00	250.00	350.00
	1805 JP	—	100.00	150.00	250.00	350.00
	1806 JP	—	100.00	150.00	250.00	350.00
	1807 JP	—	100.00	150.00	250.00	350.00
	1808 JP	—	100.00	150.00	250.00	350.00

NOTE: Earlier dates (1789-1800) exist for this type.

Obv. leg: FERDIN. VII. . ., uniformed Lima bust.

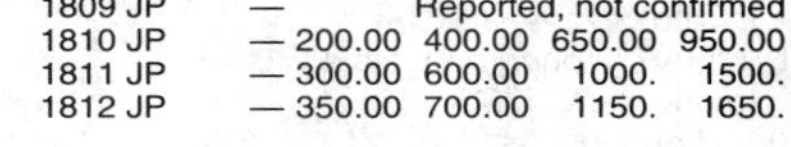

KM#	Date	Mintage	VG	Fine	VF	XF
110	1809 JP	—	Reported, not confirmed			
	1810 JP	—	200.00	400.00	650.00	950.00
	1811 JP	—	300.00	600.00	1000.	1500.
	1812 JP	—	350.00	700.00	1150.	1650.

Obv. leg: FERDIN. VII. . ., standard bust.

KM#	Date	Mintage	VG	Fine	VF	XF
119	1812 JP	—	150.00	300.00	500.00	700.00
	1813 JP	—	125.00	250.00	400.00	600.00
	1814 JP	—	150.00	300.00	500.00	700.00

Obv. leg: FERDIN. VII. . ., laureate undraped bust.

KM#	Date	Mintage	VG	Fine	VF	XF
126	1814 JP	—	150.00	225.00	350.00	450.00
	1815 JP	—	100.00	150.00	250.00	350.00
	1816 JP	—	100.00	150.00	250.00	350.00
	1817 JP	—	100.00	150.00	250.00	350.00
	1818 JP	—	100.00	150.00	250.00	350.00
	1819 JP	—	150.00	225.00	350.00	450.00
	1820 JP	—	100.00	150.00	250.00	350.00
	1821 JP	—	125.00	200.00	300.00	400.00

2 ESCUDOS

6.7500 g, .875 GOLD, .1899 oz AGW
Obv. leg: CAROL IIII, bust of Charles IV.

KM#	Date	Mintage	VG	Fine	VF	XF
100	1804 JP	—	125.00	225.00	400.00	600.00
	1805 JP	—	175.00	275.00	500.00	800.00
	1806 JP	—	175.00	275.00	500.00	800.00
	1808 PJ	—	225.00	325.00	600.00	900.00

NOTE: Earlier dates (1792-1800) exist for this type.

Obv. leg: FERDIN. VII. . ., uniformed Lima bust.
Rev: Crowned arms, Order chain.

KM#	Date	Mintage	VG	Fine	VF	XF
111	1809 JP	—	300.00	550.00	1000.	1500.
	1810 JP	—	300.00	550.00	1000.	1500.
	1811 JP	—	300.00	550.00	1000.	1500.

Obv. leg: FERDIN. VII. . ., standard bust.

KM#	Date	Mintage	VG	Fine	VF	XF
120	1812 JP	—	225.00	450.00	700.00	1100.
	1813 JP	—	225.00	450.00	700.00	1100.

Obv. leg: FERDIN. VII. . ., laureate undraped bust

KM#	Date	Mintage	VG	Fine	VF	XF
127	1814 JP	—	200.00	350.00	550.00	900.00
	1815 JP	—	200.00	350.00	550.00	900.00
	1816 JP	—	200.00	350.00	550.00	900.00
	1817 JP	—	200.00	350.00	550.00	900.00
	1818 JP	—	200.00	350.00	550.00	900.00
	1819 JP	—	200.00	350.00	550.00	900.00
	1820 JP	—	200.00	350.00	550.00	900.00
	1821 JP	—	200.00	350.00	550.00	900.00

4 ESCUDOS

13.5000 g, .875 GOLD, .3798 oz AGW
Mint mark: LIMAE monogram
Obv. leg: CAROL. IV. . .

KM#	Date	Mintage	VG	Fine	VF	XF
98	1801 IJ	—	500.00	750.00	1300.	2000.
	1804 JP	—	500.00	750.00	1300.	2000.
	1805 JP	—	500.00	750.00	1300.	2000.
	1806 JP	—	500.00	750.00	1300.	2000.
	1807 JP	—	500.00	750.00	1300.	2000.

NOTE: Earlier dates (1791-1800) exist for this type.

Obv. leg: FERDIN. VII. . ., uniformed Lima bust.

KM#	Date	Mintage	VG	Fine	VF	XF
112	1809 JP	—	1250.	1750.	2500.	4000.
	1810 JP	—	1000.	1500.	2250.	3500.

Obv: Large laureate draped bust of Ferdinand VII.

KM#	Date	Mintage	VG	Fine	VF	XF
121	1812 JP	—	1250.	1750.	2250.	3500.

Obv: Small laureate draped bust of Ferdinand VII.

KM#	Date	Mintage	VG	Fine	VF	XF
122	1812 JP	—	800.00	1250.	1750.	2500.
	1813 JP	—	800.00	1250.	1750.	2500.

Obv: Laureate, undraped bust of Ferdinand VII.

KM#	Date	Mintage	VG	Fine	VF	XF
128	1814 JP	—	600.00	1000.	1500.	2250.
	1815 JP	—	500.00	750.00	1250.	2000.
	1816 JP	—	600.00	1000.	1500.	2250.
	1817 JP	—	1200.	1750.	2250.	3500.
	1818 JP	—	600.00	1000.	1500.	2250.
	1819 JP	—	800.00	1200.	1750.	2500.
	1820 JP	—	800.00	1200.	1750.	2500.
	1821 JP	—	800.00	1200.	1750.	2500.

8 ESCUDOS

27.0000 g, .875 GOLD, .7596 oz AGW
Mint mark: LIMAE (monogram)
Obv. leg: CAROL. IIII, bust of Charles IV.

KM#	Date	Mintage	VG	Fine	VF	XF
101	1801 IJ	—	400.00	500.00	800.00	1100.
	1802 IJ	—	400.00	500.00	800.00	1100.
	1803 IJ	—	400.00	500.00	800.00	1100.
	1803 JP	—	400.00	500.00	900.00	1300.
	1804 IJ	—	600.00	900.00	1800.	3000.
	1804 JP	—	400.00	500.00	900.00	1300.
	1805 JP	—	400.00	500.00	800.00	1100.
	1806 JP	—	400.00	500.00	800.00	1100.
	1807 JP	—	400.00	500.00	800.00	1100.
	1808 JP	—	400.00	500.00	800.00	1100.

NOTE: Earlier dates (1792-1800) exist for this type.

Obv. leg: FERDIN. VII. . ., uniformed Lima bust.
Rev: Crowned arms, Order chain.

KM#	Date	Mintage	VG	Fine	VF	XF
107	1808 JP	—	900.00	1800.	3000.	4500.
	1809 JP	—	600.00	1000.	1750.	2500.
	1810 JP	—	600.00	1000.	1750.	2500.
	1811 JP	—	600.00	1000.	1750.	2500.
	1812 JP	—	800.00	1250.	2500.	3500.

Obv: Large laureate draped bust of Ferdinand VII.

KM#	Date	Mintage	VG	Fine	VF	XF
118	1811 JP	—	900.00	1750.	3000.	5000.
	1812 JP	—	600.00	1000.	1750.	2500.

Obv: Small laureate draped bust of Ferdinand VII.

KM#	Date	Mintage	VG	Fine	VF	XF
124	1812 JP	—	750.00	1250.	2000.	2500.
	1813 JP	—	750.00	1250.	2000.	2500.

KM#	Date	Mintage	VG	Fine	VF	XF
129.1	1814 JP	—	400.00	500.00	800.00	1100.
	1815 JP	—	400.00	500.00	800.00	1100.
	1816 JP	—	400.00	500.00	900.00	1300.
	1817 JP	—	400.00	500.00	800.00	1100.
	1818 JP	—	400.00	500.00	800.00	1100.
	1819 JP	—	400.00	500.00	800.00	1100.
	1820 JP	—	400.00	500.00	800.00	1100.
	1821 JP	—	400.00	500.00	900.00	1300.

Mint mark: Co
Obv: Similar to KM#129.1.

KM#	Date	Mintage	VG	Fine	VF	XF
129.2	1824 G	—	800.00	1250.	2500.	4000.

PROVISIONAL COINAGE

(Republican)

1/4 REAL

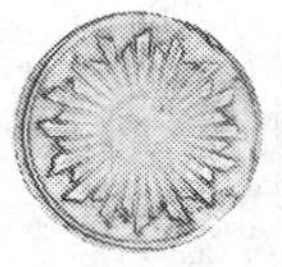

COPPER

KM#	Date	Mintage	VG	Fine	VF	XF
135	1822	—	6.00	13.50	28.00	65.00

OCTAVO DE (1/8) PESO

(1 Real)

COPPER
Mint mark: LIMA (monogram)

KM#	Date	Mintage	VG	Fine	VF	XF
137	1823	—	3.75	8.50	16.50	45.00
	1823 V	—	15.00	35.00	50.00	120.00

QUARTO DE (1/4) PESO

(2 Reales)

COPPER
Mint mark: LIMA (monogram)

KM#	Date	Mintage	VG	Fine	VF	XF
138	1823	—	2.75	6.00	14.00	42.00
	1823 V	—	9.00	18.00	35.00	75.00

NOTE: Official restrikes of KM#137 and 138 were issued in 1921, using the original dies, to commemorate the centennial of Independence.

8 REALES

25.0000 g, .903 SILVER, .7259 oz ASW
Mint mark: LIMA (monogram)
"Peru Libre" Type

KM#	Date	Mintage	VG	Fine	VF	XF
136	1822 JP	—	50.00	80.00	150.00	350.00
	1823 JP	—	50.00	75.00	135.00	300.00

COUNTERMARKED COINAGE

(Royalist)

8 REALES

SILVER
c/m: Crown above 1824 on KM#136.

KM#	Date	Year	VG	Fine	VF	XF
130	1824	1822 JP	75.00	125.00	200.00	550.00
	1824	1823 JP	50.00	90.00	165.00	350.00

NOTE: The crown/1824 countermark appears to have been applied without any discretion to obverse or reverse. Although being very collectable neither variety carries a premium over the other.

REPUBLIC

1/4 REAL

.8400 g, .903 SILVER, .0243 oz ASW
Mint: Lima

KM#	Date	Mintage	VG	Fine	VF	XF
143.1	1826	—	3.50	6.50	14.00	27.50
	1827	—	2.50	4.75	10.00	17.50
	1828	—	3.50	6.50	14.00	27.50
	1829/8	—	4.75	8.50	17.50	37.50
	1830/28	—	3.00	6.00	14.00	27.50
	1831/0	—	2.50	4.75	10.00	17.50
	1831	—	3.50	6.00	13.00	25.00
	1832	—	5.25	11.00	22.50	45.00
	1833	—	3.00	5.75	12.00	25.00
	1834/3	—	5.00	7.50	15.00	30.00
	1834	—	3.50	6.00	13.00	27.50
	1835	—	6.50	13.50	26.00	55.00
	1836/5	—	10.00	15.00	30.00	50.00
	1836	—	5.00	10.00	22.50	45.00
	1837	—	5.00	10.00	22.50	45.00
	1839/8	—	5.00	10.00	22.50	45.00
	1839	—	4.25	8.50	17.00	35.00
	1840	—	4.25	8.50	17.00	35.00
	1841/0	—	3.50	6.00	13.00	25.00
	1841	—	4.00	8.00	16.00	35.00
	1842/32	—	4.00	8.00	16.00	35.00
	1842	—	2.50	4.75	10.00	17.50
	1843/33	—	4.00	8.00	16.00	35.00
	1843	—	2.50	4.75	10.00	17.50
	1845	—	3.00	5.75	12.00	22.50
	1846	—	2.50	4.75	10.00	17.50
	1846/3	—	3.00	6.00	15.00	25.00
	1847/6	—	5.00	12.50	25.00	50.00
	1847	—	3.50	7.00	16.00	30.00
	1848/38	—	4.25	8.50	20.00	40.00
	1848	—	4.25	8.50	20.00	40.00
	1849/38	—	4.25	8.50	20.00	40.00
	1849/8	—	4.25	8.50	20.00	40.00
	1849	—	3.50	7.00	16.00	30.00
	1850	—	2.50	5.00	12.00	20.00
	1851/21	—	3.00	6.00	15.00	25.00
	1851/31	—	3.00	6.00	15.00	25.00
	1853/31	—	2.00	4.00	10.00	18.00
	1853/1	—	2.50	5.00	12.00	20.00
	1855/35	—	2.50	5.00	12.00	20.00
	1855/3	—	2.50	5.00	12.00	20.00
	1855	—	1.50	3.00	5.00	15.00
	1856/26	—	2.50	5.00	12.00	20.00
	1856/36	—	2.50	5.00	12.00	20.00
	1856/45	—	2.50	5.00	12.00	20.00
	1856	—	1.50	3.00	5.00	15.00

Mint: Arequipa

KM#	Date	Mintage	VG	Fine	VF	XF
143.2	1839	—	100.00	175.00	350.00	500.00

1/2 REAL

1.6900 g, .903 SILVER, .0490 oz ASW
Mint mark: LIMAE (monogram)
Obv. leg: REPUB.PERUANA.

KM#	Date	Mintage	VG	Fine	VF	XF
144.1	1826 JM	—	5.00	10.00	17.50	30.00
	1827/6 JM/J	—	20.00	40.00	60.00	90.00
	1827 JM	—	5.50	12.50	25.00	40.00
	1828 JM	—	3.50	7.50	15.00	25.00
	1829/8 JM	—	7.00	15.00	35.00	60.00
	1830 JM	—	7.00	15.00	35.00	60.00
	1831 MM	—	4.00	7.50	17.50	30.00
	1832 MM	—	4.00	7.50	17.50	30.00
	1833/2	—	4.00	7.50	17.50	30.00
	1833 MM	—	2.50	6.00	12.50	20.00
	1834 MM	—	3.00	7.50	15.00	30.00
	1835/3 MM	—	4.50	9.00	18.50	32.00
	1835 MM	—	4.50	9.00	18.50	32.00
	1835 MT/M	—	7.00	15.00	35.00	60.00
	1836/5 MT	—	5.00	10.00	20.00	40.00
	1836 MT	—	3.50	7.50	17.50	30.00
	1839 MB	—	3.00	6.50	15.00	25.00
	1840 MB	—	3.00	6.50	15.00	25.00

Mint mark: CUZCO (monogram)

KM#	Date	Mintage	VG	Fine	VF	XF
144.2	1827 GM	—	12.50	25.00	50.00	95.00
	1828 G	—	12.50	25.00	50.00	95.00
	1829/8 G	—	10.00	20.00	40.00	80.00
	1829 G	—	12.50	25.00	50.00	95.00
	1830/28 G	—	10.00	20.00	40.00	80.00
	1830 G	—	7.50	15.00	25.00	50.00
	1831 G	—	7.50	15.00	25.00	50.00
	1835 B	—	7.50	15.00	25.00	50.00

Mint mark: CUZCO

KM#	Date	Mintage	VG	Fine	VF	XF
144.3	1833 B	—	5.00	10.00	20.00	40.00
	1834 B	—	5.00	10.00	20.00	45.00

1.6500 g, .667 SILVER, .0354 oz ASW
Mint mark: AREQ
Obv. leg: REPUB. PERUANA

KM#	Date	Mintage	VG	Fine	VF	XF
144.4	1836 M	—	10.00	20.00	40.00	85.00

1.6500 g, .903 SILVER, .0479 oz ASW
Mint mark: LIMA (monogram)

KM#	Date	Mintage	VG	Fine	VF	XF
144.5	1840 MMB	—	10.00	20.00	35.00	65.00
	1841/0 MMB	—	15.00	30.00	50.00	85.00

Obv. leg: REP. PERUANA 10D. 20G

KM#	Date	Mintage	VG	Fine	VF	XF
144.7	1840 MB	—	5.50	12.00	25.00	55.00
	1841 MB	—	5.50	12.00	25.00	45.00
	1842 MB	—	5.50	12.00	25.00	45.00
	1843 MB	—	4.00	8.00	16.00	32.00
	1845 MB	—	4.00	8.00	15.00	25.00
	1846 MB	—	4.00	8.00	17.50	30.00
	1847 MB	—	9.00	15.00	28.00	65.00
	1849 MB	—	6.00	12.00	25.00	55.00
	1850 MB	—	5.00	10.00	20.00	45.00
	1851 MB	—	5.00	10.00	20.00	45.00
	1852 MB	—	5.00	10.00	20.00	45.00
	1853/1 MB	—	15.00	20.00	30.00	75.00
	1853/2 MB	—	Reported, not confirmed			
	1853 MB	—	15.00	20.00	30.00	75.00
	1854 MB	—	4.00	7.50	15.00	30.00
	1855 MB	—	3.50	6.50	12.50	25.00
	1856 MB	—	3.50	6.50	12.50	25.00

NOTE: Varieties exist.

REAL

3.3800 g, .903 SILVER, .0981 oz ASW
Mint mark: LIMAE (monogram)
Obv. leg: REPUB. PERUANA

KM#	Date	Mintage	VG	Fine	VF	XF
145.1	1826 JM	—	17.50	35.00	55.00	100.00
	1827 JM	—	5.00	10.00	17.50	35.00
	1828 JM	—	5.00	10.00	17.50	35.00
	1829 JM	—	Reported, not confirmed			
	1830 JM	—	8.50	17.50	35.00	60.00
	1831 JM	—	10.00	20.00	42.50	80.00
	1831 MM	—	—	—	—	—
	1832 MM	—	7.50	15.00	27.50	50.00
	1833/2 MM	—	10.00	20.00	40.00	75.00
	1834 MM	—	5.00	10.00	17.50	35.00
	1835/3	—	Reported, not confirmed			
	1836 MT	—	10.00	20.00	40.00	75.00
	1839 MB	—	7.50	15.00	27.50	50.00
	1840 MB	—	5.00	10.00	17.50	35.00

Mint mark: CUZco (monogram)
Obv. leg: REPUB. PERUANA

KM#	Date	Mintage	VG	Fine	VF	XF
145.2	1827 GM	—	17.50	35.00	60.00	100.00
	1828 G	—	17.50	35.00	60.00	100.00
	1829/8 G	—	20.00	40.00	75.00	125.00
	1829 G	—	20.00	40.00	75.00	125.00
	1830 G	—	20.00	40.00	75.00	125.00
	1831/21 G	—	20.00	40.00	75.00	125.00
	1831/0 G	—	20.00	40.00	75.00	125.00
	1831 G	—	20.00	40.00	75.00	125.00

Mint mark: CUZCO

KM#	Date	Mintage	VG	Fine	VF	XF
145.3	1834 B	—	45.00	80.00	150.00	225.00

Obv. leg: REP. PERUANA 10D 20G
Mint mark: LIMAE: (monogram)

KM#	Date	Mintage	VG	Fine	VF	XF
145.4	1841 MB	—	—	—	—	—
	1842 MB	—	10.00	20.00	40.00	75.00
	1843 MB	—	10.00	20.00	40.00	75.00
	1846 MB	—	10.00	20.00	40.00	75.00
	1847/6 MB	—	12.00	25.00	47.50	90.00
	1849 MB	—	5.50	10.00	18.00	35.00
	1850 MB (PBRUANA)	—	3.50	7.00	12.50	20.00
	1851 MB	—	4.00	8.00	14.00	25.00
	1855 MB	—	4.50	9.00	16.00	30.00
	1856/5 MB	—	3.50	7.00	12.50	20.00

2 REALES

6.7700 g, .903 SILVER, .1965 oz ASW
Mint mark: LIMA (monogram)
Obv. leg: REPUB. PERUANA

KM#	Date	Mintage	VG	Fine	VF	XF
141.1	1825 JM	—	30.00	65.00	100.00	—
	1826 JM	—	5.00	10.00	18.00	40.00
	1827 JM	—	5.00	10.00	18.00	40.00
	1828/27 JM	—	5.00	10.00	18.00	40.00
	1828 JM	—	4.00	10.00	18.00	40.00
	1828 JM inverted reverse	—	6.00	12.00	25.00	50.00
	1829 JM	—	16.00	35.00	65.00	125.00
	1830/29 JM	—	9.00	17.50	35.00	75.00
	1830 JM	—	9.00	17.50	35.00	75.00
	1831 MM	—	15.00	35.00	60.00	—
	1832/1 MM	—	9.00	17.50	35.00	75.00
	1832 MM	—	5.00	10.00	18.00	40.00
	1833 MM	—	8.00	15.00	25.00	50.00
	1834/3 MM	—	10.00	20.00	40.00	80.00
	1834 MM	—	8.00	15.00	25.00	50.00
	1835 MM	—	150.00	300.00	—	—
	1836 MT	—	150.00	350.00	—	—
	1839 MB	—	8.00	15.00	25.00	50.00
	1840 MB	—	5.00	10.00	18.00	40.00

Mint mark: CUZco (monogram)
Obv. leg: REPUB. PERUANA

KM#	Date	Mintage	VG	Fine	VF	XF
141.2	1827 GM	—	35.00	65.00	100.00	165.00
	1828 G	—	25.00	55.00	80.00	145.00
	1829 G	—	25.00	55.00	80.00	145.00
	1830 G	—	30.00	60.00	85.00	150.00
	1831 G	—	35.00	65.00	100.00	165.00

6.7700 g, .667 SILVER, .1452 oz ASW

KM#	Date	Mintage	VG	Fine	VF	XF
141.2a	1835 B	—	10.00	20.00	35.00	70.00

Mint mark: LIMAE (monogram)
Obv. leg: REP. PERUANA 10D 20G

KM#	Date	Mintage	VG	Fine	VF	XF
141.3	1840 MB	—	12.00	25.00	40.00	80.00
	1841/0 MB	—	10.00	22.00	35.00	65.00
	1841 MB	—	4.50	10.00	20.00	45.00
	1842 MB (inverted V's in PERUANA)	—	4.50	10.00	20.00	45.00
	1843 MB (inverted V's in PERUANA)	—	10.00	20.00	45.00	90.00
	1845 MB	—	10.00	20.00	40.00	80.00
	1846 MB	—	15.00	30.00	50.00	100.00
	1848/6 MB	—	5.00	12.00	22.00	50.00
	1848 MB	—	5.00	12.00	22.00	50.00
	1849 MB	—	4.00	8.00	15.00	30.00
	1850 MB	—	4.00	8.00	15.00	30.00
	1851 MB	—	4.50	10.00	20.00	45.00
	1854 MB	—	8.00	15.00	25.00	60.00
	1855 MB	—	10.00	20.00	40.00	80.00
	1856 MB	—	8.00	15.00	25.00	60.00

NOTE: Varieties exist.

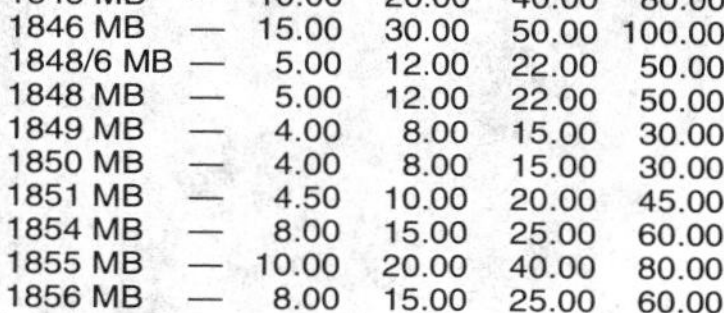

Mint: Pasco
Obv. leg: REPUB. PERUANA

KM#	Date	Mintage	VG	Fine	VF	XF
141.4	1843 M	—	400.00	750.00	—	—

4 REALES

13.0000 g, .667 SILVER, .2788 oz ASW
Mint mark: CUZco (monogram)

KM#	Date	Mintage	VG	Fine	VF	XF
151.1	1835 B	—	5.00	10.00	20.00	60.00
	1836 B	—	4.00	9.00	17.50	45.00

NOTE: Many die varieties.

Mint mark: AREQ
Obv. leg: REPUB PERUANA

KM#	Date	Mintage	VG	Fine	VF	XF
151.2	1836/26 M	—	40.00	75.00	150.00	300.00
	1836 M	—	30.00	60.00	125.00	250.00
	1839 MV	—	30.00	60.00	125.00	250.00
	1840 MV	—	30.00	60.00	125.00	250.00

13.5400 g, .903 SILVER, .3931 oz ASW
Mint mark: LIMA (monogram)
Obv. leg: REP. PERUANA

KM#	Date	Mintage	VG	Fine	VF	XF
151.3	1842 MB	—	20.00	35.00	70.00	150.00
	1843/2 MB	—	10.00	17.50	35.00	85.00
	1843 MB	—	10.00	17.50	35.00	85.00
	1845 MB	—	15.00	25.00	50.00	125.00
	1846 MB	—	20.00	35.00	70.00	150.00
	1848 MB	—	7.00	15.00	30.00	50.00
	1849 MB	—	15.00	25.00	50.00	125.00
	1850 MB	—	9.00	20.00	35.00	75.00
	1851 MB	—	8.00	17.50	32.50	70.00
	1854 MB	—	6.00	12.00	25.00	45.00
	1855/4 MB	—	6.00	12.00	25.00	45.00
	1855 MB	—	10.00	15.00	30.00	65.00
	1856 MB	—	40.00	75.00	125.00	250.00

Mint mark: PAZCO (monogram)
Obv. leg: REPUB. PERUANA, 10Ds20Gs.

KM#	Date	Mintage	VG	Fine	VF	XF
151.4	1843 M	—	25.00	50.00	120.00	250.00

Mint mark: PASCO
Obv. leg: REPUB. PERUANA 10Ds20Gs.

KM#	Date	Mintage	VG	Fine	VF	XF
151.5	1844 M	—	10.00	20.00	50.00	150.00

Obv. leg: REPUBLICA PERUANA, w/o fineness.

KM#	Date	Mintage	VG	Fine	VF	XF
151.6	1844 M	—	25.00	50.00	120.00	250.00
	1845 M	4 known	140.00	180.00	—	—

Mint mark: PASCO (monogram)
Obv. leg: REP. PERUANA 10Ds20Gs.

KM#	Date	Mintage	VG	Fine	VF	XF
151.7	1844 M	—	Reported, not confirmed			
	1855 N.S.	—	—	—	Rare	—

Mint mark: PASCO
Obv. leg: REPUB. PERUANA. 10Ds20Gs.

KM#	Date	Mintage	VG	Fine	VF	XF
151.8	1855	—	25.00	55.00	120.00	275.00

Obv. leg: REP. PERUANA 10D 20G

KM#	Date	Mintage	VG	Fine	VF	XF
151.9	1855 M	—	12.00	25.00	55.00	145.00

NOTE: Most coins of this variety have small engravers initial B in wreath above arms. At least one example is known with JB in relief.

Obv. leg: REP. PERUANA.

KM#	Date	Mintage	VG	Fine	VF	XF
151.10	1856 Z in 0	—	75.00	175.00	300.00	—
	1857 Z in 0	—	25.00	50.00	100.00	200.00
	1857 AF	—	85.00	190.00	325.00	—
	1857	—	150.00	350.00	750.00	—

8 REALES

27.0700 g, .903 SILVER, .7859 oz ASW
Mint mark: LIMA (monogram)
Obv. leg: REPUB. PERUANA
Rev: Small figure of Liberty.

KM#	Date	Mintage	VG	Fine	VF	XF
142.1	1825 JM	—	30.00	60.00	125.00	250.00
	1826 JM	—	15.00	25.00	45.00	125.00
	1827 JM	—	15.00	25.00	45.00	125.00
	1828 JM	—	75.00	150.00	250.00	500.00

NOTE: Varieties exist.

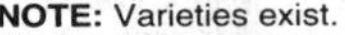

Mint mark: CUZco (monogram)

KM#	Date	Mintage	VG	Fine	VF	XF
142.2	1826 GM	—	35.00	55.00	100.00	225.00
	1826 G	—	15.00	30.00	60.00	120.00
	1827 GM	—	15.00	30.00	60.00	120.00
	1827 G	—	35.00	55.00	100.00	225.00
	1828/7 G	—	15.00	30.00	60.00	120.00
	1828 G	—	15.00	30.00	60.00	120.00
	1829 G	—	35.00	55.00	100.00	225.00
	1829 G REPMB (error)	—	—	—	Rare	—

Mint mark: LIMAE (monogram)
Rev: Large figure of Liberty.

KM#	Date	Mintage	VG	Fine	VF	XF
142.3	1828 JM	—	10.00	15.00	25.00	65.00
	1829 JM	—	11.00	17.00	30.00	75.00
	1830 JM	—	11.00	17.00	30.00	75.00
	1831 JM	—	50.00	100.00	200.00	420.00
	1831 MM	—	11.00	17.00	30.00	75.00
	1832 MM	—	10.00	15.00	25.00	60.00
	1833 MM	—	10.00	15.00	25.00	60.00
	1833 MM POR AL UNION (error)	—	—	—	Rare	—
	1834 MM	—	10.00	15.00	25.00	60.00
	1835 MM	—	11.00	17.00	30.00	75.00
	1835 MM POR AL UNION (error)	—	—	—	Rare	—
	1835 MT	—	11.00	17.00	30.00	75.00
	1836 MT	—	10.00	15.00	25.00	60.00
	1836 TM	—	30.00	50.00	100.00	250.00
	1838 MB	—	20.00	30.00	55.00	125.00
	1839 MB	—	12.00	20.00	40.00	90.00
	1840 MB	—	10.00	15.00	25.00	60.00

Mint mark: CUZCO

KM#	Date	Mintage	VG	Fine	VF	XF
142.4	1830 G	—	12.00	20.00	35.00	80.00
	1831 G	—	12.00	20.00	35.00	80.00
	1832 B	—	12.50	22.50	40.00	90.00
	1833 B	—	15.00	25.00	45.00	100.00
	1833 BoAr	—	15.00	25.00	45.00	100.00
	1834 BoAr	—	15.00	25.00	45.00	100.00

Mint mark: CUZco (monogram)

KM#	Date	Mintage	VG	Fine	VF	XF
142.5	1835/4 B	—	30.00	50.00	100.00	200.00
	1835 B	—	30.00	50.00	100.00	200.00

Mint mark: AREQ

KM#	Date	Mintage	VG	Fine	VF	XF
142.7	1839 MV	—	800.00	1500.	3500.	7000.
	1840 MV	—	600.00	1200.	3000.	6000.

Mint mark: LIMAE (monogram)
Obv. leg: REP. PERUANA 10DS 20GS
Rev: Similar to KM#142.3.

KM#	Date	Mintage	VG	Fine	VF	XF
142.8	1840 MB	—	30.00	55.00	100.00	200.00
	1841/0 MB	—	25.00	50.00	85.00	100.00
	1841 MB	—	12.00	22.00	32.00	75.00

Mint mark: CUZco (monogram)
Obv. leg: 10Ds20Gs.

KM#	Date	Mintage	VG	Fine	VF	XF
142.9	1840 A	—	15.00	30.00	60.00	125.00

Mint mark: LIMAE (monogram)
Obv. leg: REPUB. PERUANA 10Ds 20Gs.

KM#	Date	Mintage	VG	Fine	VF	XF
142.10	1841 MB	—	3000.	5000.	8000.	—
	1842 MB	—	15.00	30.00	75.00	200.00
	1843 MB	—	10.00	17.50	50.00	140.00
	1843 MB POR AL UNION (error)	—	120.00	150.00	175.00	350.00
	1843 MB inverted V in LA	—	125.00	150.00	175.00	350.00
	1844 MB	—	20.00	35.00	85.00	250.00
	1845 MB	—	10.00	17.50	50.00	140.00
	1846 MB	—	10.00	25.00	75.00	200.00
	1847/6 MB	—	25.00	50.00	100.00	325.00
	1847 MB	—	25.00	50.00	100.00	325.00
	1848/7 MB	—	10.00	25.00	75.00	200.00
	1848 MB	—	10.00	25.00	75.00	200.00
	1849/8/7 MB	—	50.00	125.00	300.00	600.00
	1849 MB	—	50.00	125.00	300.00	600.00
	1850/49 MB	—	50.00	100.00	200.00	300.00
	1850 MB ornamented edge	—	10.00	25.00	75.00	200.00
	1850 MB roped edge	—	30.00	60.00	150.00	450.00
	1851 MB	—	15.00	35.00	95.00	250.00
	1852 MB	—	20.00	45.00	120.00	300.00

23.9734 g, .903 SILVER, .6960 oz ASW
Reeded edge.

KM#	Date	Mintage	VG	Fine	VF	XF
142.10a	1855 MB	—	10.00	20.00	50.00	100.00

27.0700 g, .903 SILVER, .7859 oz ASW
Mint mark: AREQ
Obv. leg: REPUB. PERUANA. . . 10Ds20Gs.

KM#	Date	Mintage	VG	Fine	VF	XF
142.11	1841 M	—	2500.	4500.	7500.	12,000.

Mint: Pasco
Obv. leg: REPUB. PERUANA

KM#	Date	Mintage	VG	Fine	VF	XF
142.6	1836 MO	—	—	—	Rare	—

NOTE: Swiss Bank Corp. sale 20 9-88 holed fine realized $10,500.

Mint mark: LIMAE (monogram)
Obv. leg: Small REPUBLICA PERUANA, small date.
Rev: Small letters in legend.

KM#	Date	Mintage	VG	Fine	VF	XF
142.12	1853 MB	—	40.00	90.00	200.00	500.00

Mint: Pasco
Obv. leg: REPUB PERUANA. 10Ds20Gs.

KM#	Date	Mintage	VG	Fine	VF	XF
142.13	1857 Z in 0	—	—	—	10,000.	20,000.
	1857 Z in 0 PRO LA UNION (error)	—	—	—	*Rare	—

***NOTE:** Superior December Sale 12-90 VF realized $20,900.

1/2 ESCUDO

1.6875 g, .875 GOLD, .0475 oz AGW
Mint mark: LIMAE (monogram)

KM#	Date	Mintage	VG	Fine	VF	XF
146.1	1826 JM	—	45.00	90.00	150.00	200.00
	1827 JM	—	60.00	125.00	225.00	300.00
	1828 JM	—	35.00	70.00	115.00	150.00
	1829 JM	—	30.00	50.00	80.00	100.00
	1833 MM	—	35.00	70.00	115.00	150.00
	1836 TM	—	35.00	70.00	115.00	150.00
	1836 MM	—	—	—	—	—
	1839 MB	—	60.00	125.00	225.00	300.00
	1840 MB	—	30.00	50.00	80.00	100.00
	1841 MB	—	35.00	70.00	115.00	150.00
	1842 MB	—	60.00	125.00	225.00	300.00
	1850 MB	—	35.00	70.00	115.00	150.00
	1851 MB	—	75.00	150.00	300.00	425.00
	1856 MB	—	45.00	90.00	150.00	200.00

NOTE: For coins of this type dated 1838 M, see North Peru.

Mint mark: CUZCO

KM#	Date	Mintage	VG	Fine	VF	XF
146.2	1826 GM	—	35.00	60.00	95.00	125.00

ESCUDO

3.3750 g, .875 GOLD, .0949 oz AGW
Mint mark: LIMAE (monogram)
Obv. leg: REPUBLICA PERUANA

KM#	Date	Mintage	VG	Fine	VF	XF
147.1	1826 JM	—	70.00	120.00	200.00	300.00
	1827 JM	—	95.00	165.00	265.00	350.00
	1828/7 JM	—	70.00	120.00	200.00	300.00
	1828 JM	—	70.00	120.00	200.00	300.00
	1829 JM	—	55.00	85.00	135.00	200.00
	1833 MM	—	Reported, not confirmed			

Mint mark: CUZCO

KM#	Date	Mintage	VG	Fine	VF	XF
147.2	1826 GM	—	100.00	160.00	240.00	400.00
	1830 G	—	100.00	160.00	240.00	400.00

Mint mark: CUZco (monogram)

KM#	Date	Mintage	VG	Fine	VF	XF
147.3	1840 A	—	55.00	85.00	135.00	200.00
	1845 A	—	55.00	70.00	95.00	150.00
	1846 A	—	55.00	85.00	135.00	200.00

Mint mark: LIMAE (monogram)
Obv. leg: REPUB. PERUANA

KM#	Date	Mintage	VG	Fine	VF	XF
147.4	1855 MB	—	70.00	120.00	200.00	300.00

2 ESCUDOS

6.7500 g, .875 GOLD, .1899 oz AGW
Mint mark: LIMAE (monogram)
Obv. leg: REPUBLICA PERUANA

KM#	Date	Mintage	VG	Fine	VF	XF
149.1	1828 JM	—	150.00	200.00	275.00	500.00
	1829 JM	—	100.00	130.00	175.00	250.00

Obv. leg: REPUB. PERUANA

KM#	Date	Mintage	VG	Fine	VF	XF
149.2	1850 MB	—	125.00	175.00	250.00	400.00
	1851 MB	—	110.00	150.00	200.00	300.00
	1853 MB	—	95.00	115.00	140.00	200.00
	1854 MB	—	125.00	175.00	250.00	400.00
	1855 MB	—	125.00	175.00	250.00	400.00

4 ESCUDOS

13.5000 g, .875 GOLD, .3798 oz AGW
Mint mark: LIMA

KM#	Date	Mintage	VG	Fine	VF	XF
150.1	1828 JM	—	—	—	Rare	—

Mint mark: LIMAE (monogram)

KM#	Date	Mintage	VG	Fine	VF	XF
150.2	1850 MB	—	225.00	350.00	500.00	750.00
	1853 MB	—	300.00	475.00	650.00	1000.

Obv. leg: Small lettering.
Rev: Flat base below Liberty.

KM#	Date	Mintage	VG	Fine	VF	XF
150.3	1854 MB	—	200.00	300.00	450.00	650.00

Obv. leg: REPUB. PERUANA

KM#	Date	Mintage	VG	Fine	VF	XF
150.4	1855 MB	—	185.00	210.00	300.00	450.00

8 ESCUDOS

27.0000 g, .875 GOLD, .7596 oz AGW
Mint mark: LIMAE (monogram)
Obv. leg: REPUBLICA PERUANA

KM#	Date	Mintage	VG	Fine	VF	XF
148.1	1826 JM	—	350.00	375.00	500.00	800.00
	1827 JM	—	350.00	400.00	550.00	1000.
	1828 JM	—	350.00	500.00	800.00	1500.
	1829/8 JM	—	350.00	400.00	550.00	1000.
	1829 JM	—	350.00	400.00	550.00	1000.
	1833 MM	—	350.00	375.00	500.00	800.00
	1840 MB	—	350.00	500.00	800.00	1500.

Mint mark: CUZCO

KM#	Date	Mintage	VG	Fine	VF	XF
148.2	1826 GM	—	350.00	550.00	750.00	1400.
	1827 G	—	350.00	550.00	750.00	1400.
	1828/7 G	—	350.00	450.00	600.00	1100.
	1828 G	—	350.00	450.00	600.00	1100.
	1829 G	—	350.00	550.00	750.00	1400.
	1830 G	—	350.00	450.00	600.00	1100.
	1831 G	—	350.00	375.00	550.00	900.00
	1832 VOARSH	—	350.00	400.00	600.00	1000.
	1833 BoAr	—	350.00	375.00	550.00	900.00
	1834 BoAr	—	350.00	400.00	600.00	1000.

Mint mark: CUZco (monogram)

KM#	Date	Mintage	VG	Fine	VF	XF
148.3	1835 B	—	350.00	450.00	650.00	1200.
	1836 B	—	350.00	500.00	800.00	1500.
	1839 A	—	350.00	500.00	800.00	1500.
	1840 A	—	350.00	400.00	600.00	1000.
	1843 A	—	350.00	450.00	650.00	1200.
	1844 A	—	350.00	500.00	800.00	1500.
	1845 A	—	350.00	375.00	550.00	900.00

Mint mark: LIMA (monogram)
Obv. and rev: Large letters in legends.

KM#	Date	Mintage	VG	Fine	VF	XF
148.6	1850 MB	—	350.00	375.00	500.00	900.00

Obv. and rev: Small letters in legends.

KM#	Date	Mintage	VG	Fine	VF	XF
148.4	1853 MB	—	400.00	600.00	900.00	1500.
	1854 MB	—	350.00	375.00	450.00	750.00
	1855 MB	—	350.00	375.00	500.00	850.00

Obv. leg: REPUB. PERUANA

KM#	Date	Mintage	VG	Fine	VF	XF
148.5	1855 MB	—	350.00	375.00	450.00	750.00

NORTH PERU

STATE COINAGE

Estado Nor-Peruano

1/2 REAL

1.6900 g, .903 SILVER, .0490 oz ASW
Mint: Lima

KM#	Date	Mintage	VG	Fine	VF	XF
154	1836 TM	—	13.50	32.50	85.00	225.00
	1837 TM	—	9.00	20.00	50.00	100.00
	1837 M	—	10.00	25.00	60.00	100.00
	1838 M	—	10.00	25.00	60.00	100.00
	1838 MB	—	10.00	25.00	60.00	100.00
	1838 MT	—	Reported, not confirmed			

REAL

3.3800 g, .903 SILVER, .0981 oz ASW

KM#	Date	Mintage	VG	Fine	VF	XF
158	1838 MB	—	85.00	180.00	300.00	450.00

2 REALES

6.7700 g, .903 SILVER, .1965 oz ASW

KM#	Date	Mintage	VG	Fine	VF	XF
157	1837 JM	—	—	—	Rare	—
	1838 MB	—	—	—	Rare	—

8 REALES

27.0700 g, .903 SILVER, .7859 oz ASW

KM#	Date	Mintage	VG	Fine	VF	XF
155	1836 TM	—	12.00	20.00	35.00	125.00
	1837 TM	—	11.00	18.50	32.00	100.00
	1837 M	—	12.00	20.00	35.00	100.00
	1838 M	—	12.00	20.00	35.00	100.00
	1838 MB	—	11.00	18.50	32.00	100.00
	1839 MB	—	12.00	20.00	35.00	100.00

1/2 ESCUDO

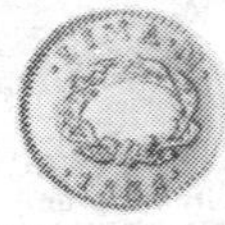 

1.6875 g, .875 GOLD, .0475 oz AGW

KM#	Date	Mintage	VG	Fine	VF	XF
159	1838 M	—	100.00	200.00	350.00	500.00

NOTE: This coin is identical to the Republic type, KM#146.1 and can only be identified by the date.

ESCUDO

3.3750 g, .875 GOLD, .0949 oz AGW

KM#	Date	Mintage	VG	Fine	VF	XF
160	1838 M	—	500.00	1000.	1500.	2000.

2 ESCUDOS

6.7500 g, .875 GOLD, .1899 oz AGW

KM#	Date	Mintage	VG	Fine	VF	XF
161	1838 M	—	1500.	2000.	2500.	3000.

4 ESCUDOS

13.5000 g, .875 GOLD, .3798 oz AGW

KM#	Date	Mintage	VG	Fine	VF	XF
162	1838 M	—	2000.	3000.	5000.	10,000.

8 ESCUDOS

27.0000 g, .875 GOLD, .7596 oz AGW

KM#	Date	Mintage	VG	Fine	VF	XF
156	1836 TM	—	—	—	Rare	—
	1838 M	—	1500.	2500.	3500.	6000.

REPUBLIC COINAGE

Rep. Nor-Peruano

1/2 REAL

1.6900 g, .903 SILVER, .0490 oz ASW

KM#	Date	Mintage	VG	Fine	VF	XF
163	1839 MB	—	42.50	100.00	175.00	300.00

8 REALES

27.0700 g, .903 SILVER, .7859 oz ASW

KM#	Date	Mintage	VG	Fine	VF	XF
164	1839 MB	—	350.00	650.00	1150.	2000.

SOUTH PERU

STATE COINAGE

Estado Sud Peruano

1/2 REAL

1.6900 g, .667 SILVER, .0362 oz ASW
Mint: Cuzco

KM#	Date	Mintage	VG	Fine	VF	XF
166	1837 B	—	10.00	25.00	50.00	175.00

8 ESCUDOS

27.0000 g, .875 GOLD, .7596 oz AGW

KM#	Date	Mintage	VG	Fine	VF	XF
167	1837 BA	—	400.00	600.00	900.00	1650.

REPUBLIC COINAGE

Repub. Sud Peruano

1/2 REAL

1.6500 g, .667 SILVER, .0354 oz ASW
Mint mark: AREQ(uipa)

KM#	Date	Mintage	VG	Fine	VF	XF
168	1837	—	10.00	20.00	45.00	125.00
	1838/7	—	—	—	—	—

2 REALES

6.5000 g, .667 SILVER, .1391 oz ASW
Mint: Cuzco

KM#	Date	Mintage	VG	Fine	VF	XF
169.1	1837 BA	—	4.00	12.00	25.00	75.00

Mint mark: AREQ(uipa)

KM#	Date	Mintage	VG	Fine	VF	XF
169.2	1838	—	5.00	15.00	35.00	90.00

4 REALES

13.5400 g, .667 SILVER, .2899 oz ASW
Mint mark: AREQ (uipa).

KM#	Date	Mintage	VG	Fine	VF	XF
172	1838 MV	—	10.00	25.00	50.00	150.00

8 REALES

27.0700 g, .903 SILVER, .7859 oz ASW
Mint mark: CUZCO
Rev. leg: FEDERACION

KM#	Date	Mintage	VG	Fine	VF	XF
170.1	1837 BA incuse edge lettering					
		—	20.00	45.00	80.00	175.00
	1837 BA raised edge lettering					
		5 known	200.00	350.00	500.00	—

Rev. leg: Small letters,
CONFEDERACION • B • A • .

KM#	Date	Mintage	VG	Fine	VF	XF
170.2	1837 BA	—	25.00	55.00	120.00	300.00

Rev. leg: Large letters,
CONFEDERACION • B • A • .

KM#	Date	Mintage	VG	Fine	VF	XF
170.4	1837 MS	—	45.00	70.00	140.00	350.00
	1838 BA	—	20.00	45.00	75.00	125.00
	1838 MS	—	20.00	45.00	75.00	125.00
	1839 MS	—	50.00	100.00	225.00	375.00

Mint mark: AREQ(uipa)

KM#	Date	Mintage	VG	Fine	VF	XF
170.3	1838 MV	—	600.00	1200.	2500.	5500.
	1839 MV	—	1650.	3250.	5250.	—

1/2 ESCUDO

1.6875 g, .875 GOLD, .0475 oz AGW
Mint mark: CUZCO (monogram)

KM#	Date	Mintage	VG	Fine	VF	XF
173	1838 MS	—	75.00	140.00	220.00	450.00

ESCUDO

3.3750 g, .875 GOLD, .0949 oz AGW

KM#	Date	Mintage	VG	Fine	VF	XF
174	1838 MS	—	90.00	160.00	280.00	525.00

8 ESCUDOS

27.0000 g, .875 GOLD, .7596 oz AGW

KM#	Date	Mintage	VG	Fine	VF	XF
171	1837 BA	—	400.00	600.00	900.00	1900.
	1838 MS	—	400.00	550.00	800.00	1750.

TRANSITIONAL COINAGE

Issued during the changeover to the decimal system.

MEDIO (1/2) REAL

1.2500 g, .900 SILVER, .0361 oz ASW
Mint: Lima

KM#	Date	Mintage	Fine	VF	XF	Unc
177	1858/68 MB	—	5.00	12.50	35.00	100.00
	1858 MB	—	4.75	11.00	27.50	60.00

KM#	Date	Mintage	Fine	VF	XF	Unc
180	1859 YB	—	4.00	9.50	22.50	50.00
	1859 Y.B	—	4.50	10.00	30.00	75.00
	1860/59 YB	—	4.00	9.50	22.50	50.00
	1860 YB/YO	—	4.00	9.50	22.50	50.00
	1860 YB	—	3.00	8.00	17.50	40.00
	1861 YB	—	4.00	9.50	22.50	50.00

NOTE: Die and date varieties exist.

REAL

2.5000 g, .900 SILVER, .0723 oz ASW

KM#	Date	Mintage	Fine	VF	XF	Unc
181	1859 Y.B	—	4.50	11.00	25.00	55.00
	1860 Y.B	—	2.75	6.00	12.50	30.00
	1861 Y.B	—	5.00	13.50	30.00	65.00

NOTE: Die varieties exist.

25 CENTAVOS

6.2500 g, .900 SILVER, .1808 oz ASW
Obv: RB below shield.

KM#	Date	Mintage	Fine	VF	XF	Unc
182	1859/8 YB	—	22.50	47.50	110.00	250.00
	1859 YB	—	40.00	75.00	165.00	350.00

NOTE: Die varieties exist.

50 CENTIMOS

12.1000 g, .900 SILVER, .3501 oz ASW

KM#	Date	Mintage	Fine	VF	XF	Unc
178	1858 MB	—	15.00	28.00	65.00	150.00
	1858 MB	—	—	—	Proof	—

50 CENTAVOS

12.1000 g, .900 SILVER, .3501 oz ASW
Rev: Liberty w/short hair.

KM#	Date	Mintage	Fine	VF	XF	Unc
179.1	1858 MB	—	15.00	30.00	75.00	250.00
	1858 YB	—	12.00	25.00	65.00	185.00
	1859 YB/Y	—	13.50	37.50	100.00	265.00

Rev: Liberty w/long hair.

KM#	Date	Mintage	Fine	VF	XF	Unc
179.2	1858 YB	—	10.00	22.50	48.00	145.00
	1859/8 YB/Y	—	10.00	22.50	48.00	145.00
	1859 YB/Y	—	9.00	20.00	40.00	125.00

NOTE: Die varieties exist.

4 ESCUDOS

13.5000 g, .875 GOLD, .3798 oz AGW

KM#	Date	Mintage	Fine	VF	XF	Unc
184	1863 YB	—	—	—	Rare	—

8 ESCUDOS

27.0000 g, .875 GOLD, .7596 oz AGW

KM#	Date	Mintage	Fine	VF	XF	Unc
183	1862 YB	—	400.00	500.00	700.00	1250.
	1863/2 YB	—	350.00	450.00	550.00	900.00
	1863 YB	—	350.00	450.00	550.00	900.00

DECIMAL COINAGE

100 Centavos (10 Dineros) = 1 Sol
10 Soles = 1 Libra

CENTAVO

COPPER-NICKEL
Obv: Date at top. Rev: Straight CENTAVO.

KM#	Date	Mintage	Fine	VF	XF	Unc
187.1	1863	1.000	1.00	2.50	6.00	22.50
	1863	—	—	—	Proof	—
	1864	Inc. Ab.	1.25	3.50	7.50	25.00

NOTE: Wreath varieties exist.

BRONZE

KM#	Date	Mintage	Fine	VF	XF	Unc
187.1a	1875	—	1.50	3.50	8.00	22.00
	1876	—	1.50	3.50	9.00	22.00
	1877	—	2.00	5.00	10.00	30.00
	1878	—	10.00	15.00	25.00	65.00

NOTE: Date varieties exist.

2 CENTAVOS

COPPER-NICKEL

Obv: Date at top.

KM#	Date	Mintage	Fine	VF	XF	Unc
188.1	1863	1.000	1.50	4.00	12.50	27.50
	1863	—	—	—	Proof	—
	1864	Inc. Ab.	1.50	4.00	12.50	27.50

COPPER or BRONZE

KM#	Date	Mintage	Fine	VF	XF	Unc
188.1a	1876	—	1.00	3.00	6.00	17.50
	1877	—	1.00	4.00	8.50	25.00
	1878	—	1.00	3.00	7.00	20.00
	1879	*	1.00	3.00	7.00	20.00
	1879 B	—	—	—	—	—

***NOTE:** Coin and medal rotations exist.

Modified dies.

KM#	Date	Mintage	Fine	VF	XF	Unc
188.2	1895 (W)	—	.75	1.75	4.00	9.50

1/2 DINERO

1.2500 g, .900 SILVER, .0362 oz ASW
Mint: Lima
Obv: Small wreath.
Rev: Denomination in curved line.

KM#	Date	Mintage	Fine	VF	XF	Unc
189	1863 YB	—	1.00	2.00	5.00	15.00
	1864 YB	—	1.50	3.00	7.50	25.00

NOTE: Engraver's initials RB appear left of shield on reverse. Roman numeral I in 1/2 on 1863 dated coins.

Mint: Cuzco

KM#	Date	Mintage	VG	Fine	VF	XF
189a	1885 JM	—	65.00	150.00	300.00	600.00

NOTE: S in wreath on obverse and engravers initials left of shield, Roman numeral I in 1/2 on reverse.

Mint: Lima
Obv: Large wreath, JR incuse on stems.
Rev: Denomination in straight line.

KM#	Date	Mintage	Fine	VF	XF	Unc
206.1	1890 TF	.870	1.50	3.00	6.00	15.00
	1891 TF	.160	2.00	3.50	8.00	20.00
	1892 TF	.228	1.00	2.00	4.50	12.00

Obv: W/o JR on stems.

KM#	Date	Mintage	Fine	VF	XF	Unc
206.2	1893 TF	—	25.00	50.00	95.00	165.00
	1895 TF	.422	1.00	2.00	5.00	14.00
	1896 TF	.456	2.00	4.00	9.00	22.50
	1896 F.	Inc. Ab.	1.00	2.00	4.50	12.00
	1896.F.	Inc. Ab.	1.00	2.00	4.50	12.00
	1896,F.(error) PBRUANA	Inc. Ab.	—	—	—	—
	1897 JF	.320	.75	1.25	2.50	6.00
	1897 VN	I.A.	3.50	7.00	16.00	37.50
	1898/7 VN	.600	1.00	2.00	5.00	14.00
	1898 VN	I.A.	.75	1.50	3.50	10.00
	1898 JF	I.A.	.60	1.25	2.50	6.00
	1899/8 JF	.500	1.00	1.75	4.00	11.00
	1899 JF	I.A.	.60	1.25	2.50	6.00
	1900/890 JF	.400	.60	1.25	2.50	6.00
	1900/899 JF	Inc. Ab.	1.00	2.00	5.00	14.00

NOTE: Later dates (1901-1917) exist for this type.

DINERO

2.5000 g, .900 SILVER, .0723 oz ASW
Mint: Lima
Obv: Small wreath.
Rev: Denomination in curved line.

KM#	Date	Mintage	Fine	VF	XF	Unc
190	1863 YB	—	1.25	2.25	4.50	20.00
	1864/3 YB	—	1.25	2.25	4.00	15.00
	1864 YB	—	1.50	2.50	5.00	22.00
	1865/3 YB	—	3.50	7.50	15.00	45.00
	1865 YB	—	2.00	5.00	10.00	45.00
	1866/5 YB	—	1.25	2.25	4.00	15.00
	1866 YB	—	1.00	1.75	3.50	12.50
	1867 YB	—	—	Reported, not confirmed		
	1870/60 YJ	—	3.00	6.00	15.00	45.00
	1870/60 YJ/YB	—	—	—	—	—
	1870/69 YJ/YB	—	1.25	2.25	4.00	15.00
	1870 YJ	—	1.25	2.25	4.50	17.50
	1870 YJ/B	—	1.25	2.25	4.00	15.00
	1872/62 YJ/B	—	65.00	125.00	200.00	325.00
	1872 YJ	—	35.00	75.00	125.00	200.00

KM#	Date	Mintage	Fine	VF	XF	Unc
190	1874 YJ	—	1.25	2.25	4.50	17.50
	1875 YJ	—	1.00	1.75	3.50	12.50
	1877 YJ.	—	2.00	5.00	10.00	35.00
	1877 Y.J.	—	3.00	5.00	15.00	50.00

NOTE: Engravers initials R.B. at left of shield on reverse of 1863-77. Varieties exist.

Mint: Cuzco

KM#	Date	Mintage	VG	Fine	VF	XF
190a	1886 JM	—	15.00	32.50	67.50	150.00

NOTE: Engravers initials FB left of shield on reverse.

Mint: Lima
Obv: Large wreath.
Rev: Denomination in straight line.

KM#	Date	Mintage	Fine	VF	XF	Unc
204.1	1888 TF	.010	50.00	90.00	150.00	250.00
	1890 TF	.400	1.25	2.25	5.00	20.00
	1891 TF	.060	3.00	8.00	20.00	42.00
	1892 TF	.069	3.00	8.00	20.00	42.00

Rev: Denomination in curved line.

KM#	Date	Mintage	Fine	VF	XF	Unc
204.2	1893 TF	.023	4.00	8.00	17.50	60.00
	1894/3 TF	—	15.00	30.00	60.00	100.00
	1895/3 TF	.090	5.00	15.00	25.00	45.00
	1895 TF	I.A.	4.00	8.00	17.50	70.00
	1896/5 TF	.534	2.50	6.00	12.50	25.00
	1896 TF	I.A.	3.00	6.00	12.00	30.00
	1896/5 F	I.A.	1.00	1.75	3.50	10.00
	1896 F	I.A.	3.00	6.00	12.00	28.00
	1897 JF	.511	1.00	1.75	3.50	10.00
	1897 VN	I.A.	1.00	1.75	3.50	10.00
	1898/7 JF	.200	3.00	6.00	12.00	28.00
	1898 JF	I.A.	1.25	2.25	4.00	12.50
	1900/90 JF	.550	1.00	2.00	3.25	10.00
	1900/98 JF	I.A.	1.25	2.25	4.00	12.50
	1900/890 JF	Inc. Ab.	1.00	2.00	3.50	10.00
	1900/898 JF	Inc. Ab.	1.00	2.00	3.50	10.00
	1900/897 JF	Inc. Ab.	1.00	2.00	3.50	10.00
	1900/89 JF	Inc. Ab.	1.00	2.00	3.50	10.00
	1900 JF	I.A.	1.25	2.25	4.00	12.50

NOTE: Later dates (1902-1916) exist for this type.
NOTE: Varieties exist.

1/5 SOL

5.0000 g, .900 SILVER, .1447 oz ASW
Mint: Lima
Obv: Small wreath.
Rev: Denomination in curved line.

KM#	Date	Mintage	Fine	VF	XF	Unc
191	1863 YB	—	1.75	4.00	8.00	45.00
	1864/3 YB	—	2.00	5.00	10.00	55.00
	1864/3 YB-DD	—	—	25.00	55.00	225.00
	1864 YB	—	1.50	3.50	7.00	35.00
	1864 YB-DD	—	20.00	40.00	65.00	225.00
	1865/4 YB	—	2.00	5.00	10.00	55.00
	1865 YB	—	1.50	3.50	7.00	45.00
	1866/5 YB	—	2.00	4.50	8.50	40.00
	1866 YB	—	1.50	3.00	6.00	30.00
	1867 YB	—	1.50	3.50	7.00	35.00
	1869 YB	—	8.00	15.00	25.00	85.00
	1874 YJ	—	1.75	4.00	7.50	40.00
	1874 YJ/YB	—	—	—	—	—
	1875 YB	—	—	—	—	—
	1875/65 YJ	—	2.50	5.00	10.00	55.00
	1875 YJ	—	1.75	4.00	7.50	40.00

NOTE: Engraver's initials RB appear left of shield on reverse. Varieties exist.

Mint: Arequipa

KM#	Date	Mintage	Fine	VF	XF	Unc
191a	1885 A.C.	—	450.00	850.00	1250.	1850.

Mint: Lima
Obv: Large wreath.
Rev: Denomination in straight line,
Libertad in relief.

KM#	Date	Mintage	Fine	VF	XF	Unc
205.1	1888 TF	.550	1.75	3.50	6.00	17.50
	1889 TF	—	—	—	Rare	—
	1890/88 TF	.085	4.50	9.00	18.00	45.00
	1890 TF	I.A.	3.50	7.00	15.00	40.00
	1891 TF	.064	5.00	10.00	20.00	60.00
	1892 TF	.128	1.75	3.50	7.00	20.00

Rev: Libertad incuse.

KM#	Date	Mintage	Fine	VF	XF	Unc
205.2	1893 TF-JR	.049	5.00	10.00	20.00	60.00
	1895 TF-JR	I.A.	7.00	15.00	30.00	75.00
	1896 TF-JR	.586	1.50	3.00	5.50	14.00
	1896 F-JR	I.A.	1.75	3.50	7.00	20.00
	1897 JF	.745	1.50	3.00	5.50	14.00
	1897 JF-JR	I.A.	1.50	3.00	5.50	14.00
	1897 VN	I.A.	1.75	3.50	6.00	15.00
	1898 JF	.350	1.50	3.00	5.50	14.00
	1899/88 JF	.700	1.50	3.00	5.50	12.50
	1899/8	I.A.	1.50	3.00	5.50	12.50
	1899 JF	I.A.	1.50	3.00	5.50	12.00
	1899 JF-JR	I.A.	1.50	3.00	5.50	12.00
	1900/800 JF	.750	2.00	4.00	8.00	17.50
	1900/800 JF-JR	I.A.	2.00	4.00	8.00	17.50
	1900/890 JF	I.A.	1.75	3.50	6.00	15.00
	1900 JF	I.A.	1.50	3.00	5.50	12.00

NOTE: Later dates (1901-1917) exist for this type.
NOTE: Some coins 1893-1900 have engravers initials JR left of shield tip on reverse and some 1911-17 have R in same location. Die varieties exist.

1/2 SOL

12.5000 g, .900 SILVER, .3617 oz ASW
Mint: Lima
Obv: Small wreath.
Rev: Denomination in curved line.

KM#	Date	Mintage	Fine	VF	XF	Unc
195	1864 YB	—	5.00	10.00	20.00	60.00
	1864 YB-D*	—	100.00	150.00	250.00	400.00
	1865 YB	—	4.00	8.50	15.00	55.00

NOTE: Engraver's initials RB appear left of shield on reverse. Date varieties exist.
***NOTE:** See 1 Sol, KM#196.2.

SOL

25.0000 g, .900 SILVER, .7234 oz ASW
Mint: Lima
Type I
Obv: Small wreath above shield has ribbon ties.
Rev: Shield below liberty's hand is tilted.
Santiago issues have LIMA on the coin.

KM#	Date	Mintage	Fine	VF	XF	Unc
196.1	1864/54 YB	—	6.00	8.50	15.00	55.00
	1864/54 Y.B	—	6.00	8.50	15.00	55.00
	1864/54 Y.B Roman I in date	—	6.00	8.50	15.00	55.00
	1864/54 Y.B w/Y.B inverted	—	6.00	8.50	15.00	55.00
	1864/54 Y.B R-B on stems/ribbon by date	—	9.00	16.00	30.00	90.00
	1865/55 YB	—	6.00	9.00	17.50	65.00
	1865/55 Y.B	—	6.00	9.00	14.00	65.00
	1865/55 Y.B/B.B	—	6.00	9.00	17.50	65.00
	1866/56 YB	—	6.00	8.00	12.00	40.00
	1866/55 Y.B	—	6.00	9.00	17.50	65.00
	1866/56 Y.B	—	6.00	8.00	12.00	40.00
	1867/57 Y.B	—	6.00	8.00	12.00	40.00
	1868/58 Y.B	—	6.00	8.00	12.00	40.00
	1868/58 Y.B BP on rev., left side	—	6.00	9.00	17.50	65.00

NOTE: Many minor die varieties, all coins are overdates.

Obv: DERTEANO on bottom row of coins falling from cornucopia.

KM#	Date	Mintage	Fine	VF	XF	Unc
196.2	1864/54 Y.B Arabic date	—	60.00	150.00	400.00	1500.
	1864/54 Y.B Roman I in date	—	100.00	175.00	500.00	1700.
	1864 Y.B Arabic date	—	—	—	Rare	—

NOTE: There are numerous minor die varieties such as D's in the denticles around the border on the obv.

Type II

KM#	Date	Mintage	Fine	VF	XF	Unc
196.3	1868 YB Roman I	—	6.00	9.00	17.50	65.00
	1868 YB Arabic 1/Roman I	—	10.00	20.00	35.00	100.00
	1868 YB Arabic 1	—	10.00	20.00	35.00	100.00
	1868 YB Arabic 1 BP on rev., left side	—	6.00	8.00	12.00	40.00
	1868 YB Arabic 1 Llama has 5 legs	—	6.00	9.00	17.50	70.00
	1869 YB Arabic 1	—	6.00	7.50	11.00	30.00
	1869 YB Arabic 1 BP on rev., left side	—	6.00	7.50	12.00	40.00
	1869 YB Roman I	—	6.00	8.00	12.00	40.00
	1870 YB	—	Reported, not confirmed			
	1870 YJ	—	6.00	7.50	12.00	40.00
	1870 YJ dot below 7 in date	—	6.00	7.50	12.00	40.00
	1871 YJ	—	6.00	7.50	11.00	30.00
	1871 YJ dot above 1 in date	—	6.00	7.50	11.00	30.00
	1871 YJ dot below 1 in date	—	6.00	7.50	11.00	30.00
	1871 YJ dot below 7 in date	—	6.00	7.50	11.00	30.00
	1872 YJ	—	6.00	7.50	11.00	30.00
	1872 YJ dot below 7 in date	—	7.00	10.00	15.00	35.00
	1873 YJ	—	10.00	20.00	40.00	135.00
	1874 YJ	—	6.00	7.50	11.00	30.00
	1875 YJ	—	6.00	7.50	11.00	35.00
	1876 YJ	—	Reported, not confirmed			

NOTE: Many minor die varieties exist.

Mint: Santiago

KM#	Date	Mintage	Fine	VF	XF	Unc
196.4	1873 LD Arabic 1	.445	7.50	15.00	25.00	75.00
	1873 LD/backwards D, Arabic 1	—	12.00	20.00	35.00	100.00
	1873 LD Arabic 1/Roman I	—	12.00	20.00	35.00	100.00
	1873 LD Roman I	—	9.00	17.50	30.00	90.00

NOTE: Many minor die varieties exist.

Type III
Letters R.B. on stems flanking date.

KM#	Date	Mintage	Fine	VF	XF	Unc
196.5	1879 YJ	—	6.00	8.50	15.00	55.00
	1880/70 YJ	—	17.50	37.50	75.00	250.00
	1880/8 YJ	—	12.00	25.00	50.00	200.00
	1880 YJ	—	12.00	25.00	50.00	150.00

Letters R.B. on ribbon of wreath, 3 berries in bunch.

KM#	Date	Mintage	Fine	VF	XF	Unc
196.6	1880 YJ	—	20.00	45.00	85.00	350.00

W/o extra letters on stem, 3 berries

KM#	Date	Mintage	Fine	VF	XF	Unc
196.29	1880 YJ	—	12.00	25.00	50.00	150.00

2 berries in bunch.

KM#	Date	Mintage	Fine	VF	XF	Unc
196.7	1880 YJ	—	15.00	35.00	75.00	200.00

W/o extra letters, 2 berries in bunch.

KM#	Date	Mintage	Fine	VF	XF	Unc
196.8	1880 YJ	—	12.00	25.00	50.00	200.00

NOTE: Many minor die varieties exist.

Type IV

KM#	Date	Mintage	Fine	VF	XF	Unc
196.9	1881 BF	—	6.00	12.00	20.00	60.00

Rev: Letters R.L. on base of column.

KM#	Date	Mintage	Fine	VF	XF	Unc
196.10	1881 BF	—	6.00	12.00	20.00	60.00

NOTE: Many minor die varieties exist.

Type V
B.F. on rev., left side.

KM#	Date	Mintage	Fine	VF	XF	Unc
196.11	1881 BF	—	6.00	9.00	17.50	65.00

R.B. on rev., left side.

KM#	Date	Mintage	Fine	VF	XF	Unc
196.12	1881 BF	—	6.00	9.00	17.50	65.00
	1882 BF	—	6.00	8.50	15.00	55.00

F.D. on rev., left side.

KM#	Date	Mintage	Fine	VF	XF	Unc
196.13	1882 BF	—	6.00	8.50	15.00	55.00

FD on rev. at base of column.

KM#	Date	Mintage	Fine	VF	XF	Unc
196.14	1882 BF	—	6.00	10.00	20.00	75.00
	1882 FN	—	6.00	12.00	25.00	80.00

NOTE: Many minor die varieties exist.

Type VI
F.D. on rev., left side.

KM#	Date	Mintage	Fine	VF	XF	Unc
196.15	1882 FN	—	6.00	9.00	17.50	65.00
	1882 FN/BN	—	—	—	—	—

FD on rev. at base of column.

KM#	Date	Mintage	Fine	VF	XF	Unc
196.16	1882 FN	—	6.00	9.00	17.50	65.00

FD on rev., RB at base of column.

KM#	Date	Mintage	Fine	VF	XF	Unc
196.17	1882 FN	—	6.00	9.00	17.50	65.00

NOTE: Many minor die varieties exist.

Type VII
B.F. on rev., left side.

KM#	Date	Mintage	Fine	VF	XF	Unc
196.18	1883 FN	—	6.00	8.50	15.00	55.00

F.D. on rev., left side, Libertad in relief.

KM#	Date	Mintage	Fine	VF	XF	Unc
196.19	1883 FN	—	6.00	8.50	15.00	55.00
	1884 BD	—	6.00	7.50	11.00	35.00
	1884 RD	—	6.00	7.50	11.00	35.00

NOTE: Many minor die varieties exist.

Type VIII
F.D. on rev., left side.

KM#	Date	Mintage	Fine	VF	XF	Unc
196.20	1884 BD	—	6.00	7.50	11.00	35.00
	1884 BD/BF	—	6.00	8.00	12.00	40.00
	1884 RD	—	6.00	7.50	11.00	35.00

Type IX
W/o extra initials.

KM#	Date	Mintage	Fine	VF	XF	Unc
196.21	1884 RD	—	7.00	9.00	15.00	50.00

Type X
Rev: Libertad incuse.

KM#	Date	Mintage	Fine	VF	XF	Unc
196.22	1885 RD	—	6.00	7.50	15.00	30.00
	1885 RD/BD	—	6.00	7.50	15.00	30.00
	1885 RD/BF	—	6.00	7.50	15.00	30.00
	1885 TD	—	6.00	7.50	15.00	30.00
	1885 TD/BD	—	6.00	7.50	15.00	30.00
	1885 TD/BF	—	6.00	7.50	15.00	30.00
	1885 TD/TF	—	6.00	7.50	15.00	30.00
	1886/5 TF	—	17.50	37.50	75.00	300.00
	1886/5 TF/BR	—	17.50	37.50	100.00	200.00
	1886 TF	—	6.00	8.50	15.00	55.00
	1887/6 TF	—	6.00	7.50	11.00	30.00
	1887/6 TF/BF	—	6.00	7.50	11.00	30.00
	1887 TF	—	6.00	7.00	10.00	27.50
	1887 TF/BF	—	6.00	7.00	10.00	27.50

NOTE: Many minor die varieties exist.

Rev: R on base of column.

KM#	Date	Mintage	Fine	VF	XF	Unc
196.23	1885 RD	—	6.00	8.50	15.00	50.00

Type XI
Rev: Shield below Liberty's hand is tilted.
UN SOL is in a straight line, Libertad in relief.

KM#	Date	Mintage	Fine	VF	XF	Unc
196.24	1888 TF	3.147	6.00	7.00	11.00	30.00
	1888 TF/BF	I.A.	6.00	7.00	11.00	30.00
	1889 TF	2.842	6.00	7.00	10.00	27.50
	1889 TF/BF	I.A.	6.00	7.00	10.00	27.50
	1890/80 TF/BF	2.304	6.00	9.00	15.00	55.00
	1890 TF/BF	Inc. Ab.	6.00	7.00	10.00	27.50
	1890 TF	I.A.	6.00	7.00	10.00	27.50
	1891/81 TF	2.981	6.00	8.00	12.00	32.50
	1891/81 TF/BF	Inc. Ab.	6.00	8.00	12.00	32.50
	1891 TF/BF	Inc. Ab.	6.00	7.00	10.00	27.50
	1891 TF	I.A.	6.00	7.00	10.00	27.50
	1892 TF	2.270	6.00	7.00	10.00	27.50
	1892 TF/BF	Inc. Ab.	6.00	7.00	10.00	27.50

NOTE: Date varieties exist.

Rev. leg: Inverted V for A in LA.

KM#	Date	Mintage	Fine	VF	XF	Unc
196.25	1889 TF/BF	I.A.	15.00	30.00	60.00	100.00

NOTE: Many minor die varieties exist, especially for the 1888 issues.

Type XII
Legends have smaller lettering, 37mm.
Rev: Libertad incuse.

KM#	Date	Mintage	Fine	VF	XF	Unc
196.26	1393/893 TF (error date)					
		—	30.00	45.00	90.00	200.00
	1893 TF	—	6.00	7.00	10.00	27.50
	1894 TF	4.358	6.00	7.00	10.00	27.50
	1895 TF	4.111	6.00	7.00	10.00	27.50
	1896 TF	2.511	6.00	8.00	12.00	40.00
	1896 F	I.A.	6.00	7.00	10.00	27.50
	1897 JF	.234	7.00	12.00	20.00	90.00

NOTE: Later dates (1914-1915) exist for this type.
NOTE: Varieties exist.

5 SOLES

8.0645 g, .900 GOLD, .2334 oz AGW
Mint mark: LIMA

KM#	Date	Mintage	Fine	VF	XF	Unc
192	1863 YB	—	125.00	150.00	225.00	375.00

10 SOLES

16.1290 g, .900 GOLD, .4667 oz AGW
Mint mark: LIMA

KM#	Date	Mintage	Fine	VF	XF	Unc
193	1863 YB	—	225.00	250.00	300.00	500.00

20 SOLES

32.2581 g, .900 GOLD, .9334 oz AGW
Mint mark: LIMA

KM#	Date	Mintage	Fine	VF	XF	Unc
194	1863 YB	—	450.00	475.00	500.00	650.00

PROVISIONAL COINAGE

5 CENTAVOS

COPPER-NICKEL

KM#	Date	Mintage	Fine	VF	XF	Unc
197	1879	12.000	1.00	1.75	3.50	6.00
	1880	2.000	1.50	3.00	6.00	10.00

10 CENTAVOS

COPPER-NICKEL

KM#	Date	Mintage	Fine	VF	XF	Unc
198	1879	3.005	1.00	2.00	6.00	10.00
	1880	4.000	1.00	1.50	2.50	5.00

20 CENTAVOS

COPPER-NICKEL

KM#	Date	Mintage	Fine	VF	XF	Unc
199	1879	.498	4.50	8.50	20.00	75.00

PESETA COINAGE

1/2 REAL

1.2500 g, .900 SILVER, .0362 oz ASW
Mint: Ayacucho

KM#	Date	Mintage	Fine	VF	XF	Unc
202	1882 LM	—	225.00	500.00	850.00	1800.

NOTE: Most specimens have been holed or soldered (and sometimes repaired) and are worth less than half of market valuations shown.

PESETA

5.0000 g, .900 SILVER, .1447 oz ASW
Mint: LIMA
Obv: B below wreath.

KM#	Date	Mintage	Fine	VF	XF	Unc
200.1	1880 BF	—	3.00	5.00	12.50	45.00

Obv: W/dot after B below wreath.

KM#	Date	Mintage	Fine	VF	XF	Unc
200.2	1880 BF	—	3.00	5.00	12.50	45.00

NOTE: Die varieties exist.

5 PESETAS

25.0000 g, .900 SILVER, .7234 oz ASW
Mint: Lima
Obv: B below wreath.

KM#	Date	Mintage	Fine	VF	XF	Unc
201.1	1880 BF	—	15.00	25.00	60.00	225.00

Obv: W/dot after B below wreath.

KM#	Date	Mintage	Fine	VF	XF	Unc
201.2	1880 BF	—	12.00	20.00	45.00	185.00

Mint: Ayacucho
Rev: Similar to KM#201.1.

KM#	Date	Mintage	Fine	VF	XF	Unc
201.3	1881 B	—	90.00	220.00	500.00	1000.
	1882 LM	—	45.00	100.00	200.00	500.00

TRADE COINAGE

LIBRA (POUND)

7.9881 g, .917 GOLD, .2354 oz AGW

KM#	Date	Mintage	Fine	VF	XF	Unc
207	1898 ROZF	—	—	BV	100.00	150.00
	1899 ROZF	—	—	BV	100.00	150.00
	1900 ROZF					
		.064	—	BV	100.00	140.00

NOTE: Later dates (1901-1969) exist for this type.

PATTERNS (Pn)

(Including off metal strikes)

KM#	Date	Mintage	Identification	Mkt.Val.
PnB1	1823	3 known	1/4 Peso	2250.

KM#	Date	Mintage	Identification	Mkt.Val.
Pn1	1825 JM	—	8 Reales, Silver, plain edge	19,500.
Pn2	1826 JM	—	8 Reales, Silver, plain edge	13,000.
Pn3	1833 MB	—	1/2 Real, Silver	—
PnA4	1836 MO	—	8 Reales, Silver, Pasco Mint	—
Pn4	1837 B	—	8 Reales, Bronze	500.00
Pn5	1837 B	—	8 Reales, Silver	—
Pn6	1855	—	1/2 Centimo, Copper, 5.5 g	220.00

KM#	Date	Mintage	Identification	Mkt.Val.
Pn7	1855	—	1 Centimo, Copper, 10.7 g	300.00
Pn9	1855 MB	—	5 Centimos, Silver	1000.
Pn10	1855 MB	—	10 Centimos, Silver	1000.
Pn11	1855 MB	—	20 Centimos, Silver	800.00
PnA11	1855 MB	—	50 Centimes, Silver, 12.5 g	2000.
Pn12	1855 MB	—	1 Peso, Silver	9000.
Pn13	1855 MB	—	2 Pesos, .900 Gold	—
Pn14	1855 MB	—	5 Pesos, .900 Gold	—
Pn15	1855 MB	—	10 Pesos, .900 Gold	—

KM#	Date	Mintage	Identification	Mkt.Val.
Pn16	1855 MB	—	20 Pesos, .900 Gold	—

NOTE: KM#Pn6-16 were the first foreign coins struck at the United States Philadelphia Mint.

KM#	Date	Mintage	Identification	Mkt.Val.
Pn17	1860	—	1 Real, Obv. bust w/o leg.	—
Pn18	1860 JP	—	2 Reales	—
Pn19	1860 BA	—	1 Peseta	—
Pn20	1863	—	1/2 Sol, .900 Silver	—
Pn21	1863	—	1 Sol, .900 Silver	—

KM#	Date	Mintage	Identification	Mkt.Val.
Pn23	1875	—	1/2 Centimo	1700.
PnA24	1876	—	1 Sol	400.00
PnA25	1886	—	1 Centavo, Bronze, KM187.1a	—
Pn25	1886	—	2 Centavos, Copper or Bronze, KM188.1a	—
PnA26	1886	6	1/2 Dinero, .900 Silver, KM206.1	750.00
PnB26	1886	6	1 Dinero, .900 Silver, KM204.1	950.00
PnC26	1886	6	1/5 Sol, .900 Silver, KM205	1250.
PnD26	1886	—	1/2 Sol, .900 Silver, KM203	1750.

KM#	Date	Mintage	Identification	Mkt.Val.
PnE26	1886	—	1 Sol, .900 Silver, KM196.22	2500.

TRIAL STRIKES (TS)

KM#	Date	Mintage	Identification	Mkt.Val.
TS1	1836 MO	—	8 Reales, Silver, KM142	—
TS2	1864	—	1 Centavo, Bronze, KM187.1a	—
TS3	1864	—	2 Centavos, Copper or Bronze, KM188.1a	—
TS4	1935	—	1 Sol, obv. KM218.2, rev. alloy percentage, N.3/25 PLT/ 10 NKL/10 ZNC/55 CRE	—
TS5	1935	—	1 Sol, obv. KM218.2, rev. alloy percentage, N.4/20 PLT/ 15 NKL/10 ZNC/55 CRE	—

PROOF SETS (PS)

KM#	Date	Mintage	Identification	Issue Price	Mkt. Val.
PS1	1886(7)	6 known	KM-PnA25,25,A26-E26		—

PHILIPPINES

The Republic of the Philippines, an archipelago in the western Pacific 500 miles (805 km.) from the southeast coast of Asia, has an area of 115,830 sq. mi. (300,000 sq. km.) and a population of *64.9 million. Capital: Manila. The economy of the 7,000-island group is based on agriculture, forestry and fishing. Timber, coconut products, sugar and hemp are exported.

Migration to the Philippines began about 30,000 years ago when land bridges connected the islands with Borneo and Sumatra. Ferdinand Magellan claimed the islands for Spain in 1521. The first permanent settlement was established by Miguel de Legazpi at Cebu in April of 1565; Manila was established in 1572. A British expedition captured Manila and occupied the Spanish colony in October 1762, but returned it to Spain by the treaty of Paris, 1763. Spain held the Philippines despite growing Filipino nationalism until 1898 when they were ceded to the United States at the end of the Spanish-American War. The Philippines became a self-governing commonwealth under the United States in 1935, and attained independence as the Republic of the Philippines on July 4, 1946.

RULERS

Spanish, until 1898

MINT MARKS

(b) Brussels, privy marks only
BSP - Bangko Sentral Pilipinas
(Lt) - Llantrisant
M, MA - Manila
SGV - Madrid
(Sh) - Sherritt
(VDM) - Vereinigte Deutsche Metall Werks; Altona, Germany
Star - Manila (Spanish)

= Manila

MONETARY SYSTEM

8 Octavos = 4 Quartos = 1 Real
8 Reales = 1 Peso

COLONIAL COINAGE

NOTE: For copper issues until 1833, minor variations in die work, planchet size and weight are relatively commonplace, compared to later issues from the up-graded Manila Mint (ca.1860).

OCTAVO

COPPER
Mint mark: M

KM#	Date	Mintage	Good	VG	Fine	VF
5	1805F	—	12.50	27.50	55.00	100.00
	1806F	—	12.50	27.50	55.00	100.00

NOTE: Earlier date (1798) exists for this type.

KM#	Date	Mintage	Fine	VF	XF	Unc
8	1820F	—	10.00	20.00	45.00	120.00
	1829F	—	50.00	75.00	250.00	550.00
	1830F	—	12.50	27.50	55.00	235.00

QUARTO

COPPER
Mint mark: M
Similar to KM#7.

KM#	Date	Mintage	Good	VG	Fine	VF
6	1805F	—	8.50	15.00	30.00	55.00
	1806F	—	8.50	15.00	30.00	55.00
	1807F	—	8.50	15.00	30.00	55.00

NOTE: Earlier dates (1798-1800) exist for this type.

KM#	Date	Mintage	VG	Fine	VF	XF
7	1817F	—	45.00	80.00	125.00	200.00
	1819F (error) 9181 w/retrograde 9					
		—	100.00	160.00	325.00	500.00
	1820F	—	8.50	18.50	40.00	60.00
	1821F	—	8.50	18.50	40.00	60.00
	1822F	—	—	—	Rare	—
	1822F (error) 2281 w/retrograde 2's					
		—	35.00	57.50	85.00	160.00
	1823F	—	12.50	25.00	45.00	100.00
	1824F	—	—	—	Rare	—
	1826F	—	8.50	18.50	40.00	60.00
	1827F	—	—	—	Rare	—
	1828F	—	8.50	18.50	45.00	80.00
	1829F	—	8.50	18.50	40.00	65.00
	1830F	—	8.50	18.50	40.00	65.00
	1831F	—	40.00	70.00	90.00	165.00
	1833F	—	40.00	70.00	90.00	165.00

NOTE: Varieties exist.

KM#	Date	Mintage	Good	VG	Fine	VF
9	1822F	—	22.50	40.00	60.00	150.00
	1823F	—	13.50	27.50	45.00	90.00
	1824F	—	27.50	50.00	80.00	200.00

Mint mark: MA

KM#	Date	Mintage	Good	VG	Fine	VF
10	1834F	—	12.00	20.00	40.00	60.00

KM#	Date	Mintage	Good	VG	Fine	VF
13	1835F	—	27.50	50.00	80.00	150.00

2 QUARTOS

COPPER
Mint mark: MA

KM#	Date	Mintage	Good	VG	Fine	VF
11	1834F	—	60.00	120.00	200.00	350.00

KM#	Date	Mintage	Good	VG	Fine	VF
14	1835F	—	45.00	80.00	150.00	250.00

4 QUARTOS

COPPER
Mint mark: MA

KM#	Date	Mintage	Good	VG	Fine	VF
12	1834F	—	100.00	150.00	225.00	500.00

KM#	Date	Mintage	Good	VG	Fine	VF
15	1835F	—	75.00	120.00	180.00	350.00

COUNTERSTAMPED COINAGE

(8 REALES)

MANILA/1828

Type I
Obv. c/s: MANILA/1828 within serrated circle.
Rev. leg: HABILITADO POR EL REY N.S.D. FERN. VII. around crowned Spanish royal arms.

This counterstamp was inaugurated on October 13, 1828 by the Captain-General of the Philippines. The outer border and reverse legend of the Type I counterstamp were intended to obliterate the legends on the foreign dollars being overstruck. This failed to work satisfactorily due to inadequate pressure by the Manila Mint coin presses, thus this counterstamp was soon discontinued and replaced by Type II.

SILVER

KM#	Date	Year	Good	VG	Fine	VF
	c/s: Type I on Bolivia 8 Soles, KM#97.					
16	1828	(1827 JM)	125.00	200.00	300.00	500.00
	c/s: Type I on Bolivia 8 Reales, KM#84.					
17	1828	(1808-25)	125.00	200.00	225.00	300.00
	c/s: Type I on Mexico 8 Reales, KM#376.					
18	1828	(1823-5)	125.00	200.00	250.00	400.00
	c/s: Type I on Mexico City 8 Reales, KM#309.					
19	1828	(1822 JM)	—	—	Rare	—
	c/s: Type I on Mexico City 8 Reales, KM#310.					
20	1828	(1822-23 JM)	225.00	400.00	600.00	800.00
	c/s: Type I on Mexico 8 Reales, KM#376.					
38	1828	(1823-24)	100.00	175.00	200.00	300.00
	c/s: Type I on Mexico 8 Reales, KM#377.					
21	1828	(1824-8)	100.00	175.00	200.00	300.00
	c/s: Type I on Peru (Lima) 8 Reales, KM#117.1.					
22	1828	(1810-24)	100.00	160.00	200.00	300.00

c/s: Type I on Peru (Lima) 8 Reales, KM#136.

KM#	Date	Year	Good	VG	Fine	VF
23	1828	(1822-3)	100.00	160.00	200.00	300.00

c/s: Type I on Peru (Lima) 8 Reales, KM#142.1.

24	1828	(1825-8)	80.00	150.00	200.00	350.00

c/s: Type I on Peru (Lima) 8 Reales, KM#142.3.

25	1828	(1828)	65.00	125.00	175.00	300.00

c/s: Type I on Peru (Cuzco) 8 Reales, KM#142.2.

26	1828	(1826-28)	80.00	150.00	200.00	300.00

NOTE: Other coin types may exist with this particular counterstamp.

MANILA/1828

Type II
Obv. c/s: MANILA/1828. Rev: Crowned Spanish royal arms without legends and serrated circles.

SILVER

c/s: Type II on Bolivia 8 Reales, KM#84.

27	1828	(1808-25)	90.00	160.00	200.00	300.00

c/s: Type II on Mexico 8 Reales, KM#376.

28	1828	(1823-25)	100.00	175.00	200.00	300.00

c/s: Type II on Mexico 8 Reales, KM#377.

29	1828	(1824-28)	90.00	160.00	200.00	300.00

c/s: Type II on Peru (Lima) 8 Reales, KM#117.1.

30	1828	(1810-24)	70.00	130.00	200.00	300.00

c/s: Type II on Peru (Lima) 8 Reales, KM#136.

31	1828	(1822-23)	70.00	130.00	200.00	300.00

c/s: Type II on Peru (Lima) 8 Reales, KM#142.1.

32	1828	(1825-28)	80.00	150.00	200.00	325.00

c/s: Type II on Peru (Lima) 8 Reales, KM#142.3.

33	1828	(1828)	60.00	90.00	130.00	200.00

NOTE: Other coin types may exist with this particular counterstamp.

(8 ESCUDOS)

MANILA/1829

Type III
c/s: MANILA/1829. Rev: Crowned Spanish royal arms.

GOLD

c/s: Type III on Mexico City 8 Escudos, KM#383.

34	1829	(1825JM)	—	—	—	—

NOTE: The above is in the collection of Fabrica Nacional de Moneda y Timbre de Madrid (Spain).

(8 REALES)

MANILA/1830

Type IV
c/s: MANILA/1830 within serrated circle . Rev. leg. HABILITADO POR EL REY N.S.D.FERN.VII. around crowned Spanish royal arms.

SILVER

Type IV on Bolivia 8 Soles, KM#97.

KM#	Date	Year	Good	VG	Fine	VF
35	1830	(1827-30)	1500.	1800.	2200.	3000.

NOTE: Rare double stamped obverse coin illustrated, Bank Leu Bostonian sale 10-90 VF realized $16,380.

c/s: Type IV on Mexico 8 Reales, KM#376.

36	1830	(1823-25)	1500.	1800.	2200.	3000.

c/s: Type IV on Mexico 8 Reales, KM#377.

37	1830	(1824-30)	1500.	1800.	2200.	3000.

NOTE: Other coin types may exist with this particular counterstamp.

COUNTERMARKED COINAGE

(8 REALES)

FERDINAND VII

SILVER

Oval Type V Round Type V
Round Type V
Actual size 9-10mm

These countermarks were introduced by decree of October 27, 1832 due to the problems encountered with the larger countermarks of 1828-1830. Pierced or holed coins were declared not valid but later were countermarked directly over the hole with Type V or Type VI countermarks and circulated freely. The latter types exist countermarked on both sides directly over the hole and are very scarce. These countermarks were retired in 1834 after the death of Ferdinand VII and replaced with a similar design showing "Y II" for Isabel II, Type VI.-Coins dated 1835 and later with either Type V countermark should be considered counterfeit.

(REAL)

SILVER

c/m: F.7.o on Mexico 1 Real.

40	ND	—	—	—	Rare	—

(2 REALES)

SILVER

c/m: F.7.o on Mexico 2 Reales, KM#372.

41	ND	(1825-34)	75.00	100.00	200.00	300.00

c/m: F.7.o on Peru 2 Reales, KM#141.

42	ND	(1825-34)	75.00	100.00	200.00	300.00

(4 REALES)

SILVER

c/m: F.7.o on Mexico 4 Reales.

43	ND	—	200.00	300.00	400.00	700.00

(8 REALES)

SILVER

c/m: F.7.o on Argentina 8 Reales, KM#5.

44.1	ND	(1813)	50.00	80.00	150.00	250.00

c/m: F.7.o on Argentina 8 Reales, KM#14.

44.2	ND	(1815)	50.00	80.00	150.00	250.00

c/m: F.7.o on Argentina 8 Soles, KM#15.

KM#	Date	Year	Good	VG	Fine	VF
45	ND	(1815)	50.00	80.00	150.00	250.00

c/m: F.7.o on Argentina 8 Reales, KM#20.

46	ND	(1826-34)	60.00	100.00	175.00	275.00

c/m: F.7.o on Bolivia 8 Reales, KM#55.

47	ND	(1773-89)	75.00	110.00	200.00	300.00

c/m: F.7.o on Bolivia 8 Reales, KM#64.

48	ND	(1789-91)	60.00	100.00	190.00	275.00

c/m: F.7.o on Bolivia 8 Reales, KM#73.

49	ND	(1791-1808)	60.00	100.00	160.00	250.00

c/m: F.7.o on Bolivia 8 Reales, KM#84.

50	ND	(1808-25)	60.00	100.00	160.00	250.00

c/m: F.7.o on Bolivia 8 Soles, KM#97.

51	ND	(1827-34)	25.00	35.00	50.00	80.00

c/m: F.7.o on Brazil 960 Reis, KM#307.

52	ND	(1809-18)	125.00	175.00	300.00	500.00

c/m: F.7.o on Brazil 960 Reis, KM#326.

53	ND	(1818-22)	125.00	175.00	400.00	600.00

c/m: F.7.o on Brazil 960 Reis, KM#368.

54	ND	(1823-7)	125.00	175.00	300.00	500.00

c/m: F.7.o on Central American Republic (Guatemala) 8 Reales, KM#4.

55	ND	(1824-34)	75.00	120.00	180.00	250.00

c/m: F.7.o on Chile 1 Peso, KM#82.

56	ND	(1817-34)	50.00	75.00	100.00	150.00

c/m: F.7.O on Columbia, Cundinamarca Province 8 Reales, KM#6.

KM#	Date	Year	Good	VG	Fine	VF
57	ND	(1820-21)	50.00	75.00	100.00	150.00
c/m: F.7.o on France 5 Francs, C#189.						
A58	1826D	—	350.00	500.00	800.00	1200.

c/m. in oval: F.7.o on Kingdom of Italy 5 Lire, C#10.1.

KM#	Date	Year	Good	VG	Fine	VF
58	1809	—	—	—	Rare	—
c/m: F.7.o on Mexico City 8 Reales, KM#105.						
59	ND	(1760-71)	—	—	Rare	—

c/m: F.7.o on Mexico City 8 Reales, KM#106.

KM#	Date	Year	Good	VG	Fine	VF
60	ND	(1772-89)	80.00	100.00	175.00	225.00
c/m: F.7.o on Mexico City 8 Reales, KM#107.						
61	ND	(1789-90FM)	60.00	100.00	175.00	225.00
c/m: F.7.o on Mexico City 8 Reales, KM#108.						
62	ND	(1790FM)	60.00	100.00	175.00	225.00

c/m: F.7.o on Mexico City 8 Reales, KM#109.

KM#	Date	Year	Good	VG	Fine	VF
63	ND	(1791-1808)	50.00	90.00	150.00	215.00

c/m: F.7.o on Mexico City 8 Reales, KM#110.

KM#	Date	Year	Good	VG	Fine	VF
64	ND	(1808-11)	60.00	100.00	175.00	220.00
c/m: F.7.o on Mexico City 8 Reales, KM#111.						
65	ND	(1811-21)	60.00	110.00	150.00	220.00
c/m: F.7.o on Mexico City 8 Reales, KM#304.						
66	ND	(1822JM)	50.00	100.00	150.00	250.00
c/m: F.7.o on Mexico City 8 Reales, KM#305.						
67	ND	(1822JM)	50.00	100.00	150.00	250.00
c/m: F.7.o on Mexico City 8 Reales, KM#306.						
68	ND	(1822JM)	50.00	100.00	150.00	250.00
c/m: F.7.o on Mexico City 8 Reales, KM#307.						
69	ND	(1822JM)	75.00	150.00	250.00	450.00
c/m: F.7.o on Mexico City 8 Reales, KM#308.						
70	ND	(1822JM)	70.00	140.00	200.00	350.00

c/m: F.7.o on Mexico City 8 Reales, KM#309.

KM#	Date	Year	Good	VG	Fine	VF
71	ND	(1822JM)	—	—	Rare	—

c/m: F.7.o on Mexico City 8 Reales, KM#310.

KM#	Date	Year	Good	VG	Fine	VF
72	ND	(1822-3JM)	50.00	100.00	150.00	250.00

c/m: F.7.o on Mexico (Guanajuato) 8 Reales, KM#376.1.

KM#	Date	Year	Good	VG	Fine	VF
73	ND	(1823-5)	45.00	80.00	125.00	200.00
c/m: F.7.o on Mexico 8 Reales, KM#377.						
74	ND	(1824-34)	30.00	50.00	60.00	80.00

c/m: F.7.o on Peru (Lima) 8 Reales, KM#78.

KM#	Date	Year	Good	VG	Fine	VF
75	ND	(1772-89)	60.00	100.00	150.00	250.00
c/m: F.7.o on Peru (Lima) 8 Reales, KM#87.						
76	ND	(1789-91)	60.00	100.00	150.00	250.00

c/m: F.7.o on Peru (Lima) 8 Reales, KM#97.

KM#	Date	Year	Good	VG	Fine	VF
77	ND	(1791-1808)	60.00	80.00	125.00	200.00
c/m: F.7.o on Peru (Lima) 8 Reales, KM#106.						
78	ND	(1808-11)	60.00	85.00	130.00	200.00
c/m: F.7.o on Peru (Lima) 8 Reales, KM#117.1.						
79	ND	(1810-24)	60.00	80.00	125.00	175.00

c/m: F.7.o on Peru (Lima) 8 Reales, KM#136.

KM#	Date	Year	Good	VG	Fine	VF
80	ND	(1822-3)	35.00	60.00	90.00	125.00

c/m: F.7.o on Peru (Lima) 8 Reales, KM#130.

KM#	Date	Year	Good	VG	Fine	VF
81	ND	(1824)	60.00	90.00	150.00	200.00

c/m. in oval: F.7.o on Peru (Lima) 8 Reales, KM#142.1.

KM#	Date	Year	Good	VG	Fine	VF
82	ND	(1825-8)	—	—	Rare	—

c/m: F.7.o on Peru (Lima) 8 Reales, KM#142.3.

KM#	Date	Year	Good	VG	Fine	VF
83	ND	(1828-34)	30.00	45.00	60.00	75.00

c/m: F.7.O on Peru (Cuzco) 8 Reales, KM#142.4.

KM#	Date	Year	Good	VG	Fine	VF
84	ND	(1830-34)	75.00	100.00	175.00	300.00

8 ESCUDOS

GOLD

c/m: F.7.o on Chile 8 Escudos, KM#84.

KM#	Date	Year	Good	VG	Fine	VF
85	ND	1822FD	3000.	3500.	4000.	5000.
		1825I	—	—	Unique	—
		1826I	—	—	Unique	—

c/m: F.7.o on Colombia 8 Escudos, KM#82.2.

KM#	Date	Year	Good	VG	Fine	VF
A86	ND	1825	—	—	Rare	*—

***NOTE:** Superior Ebsen sale 6-87 VF realized $13,750.

c/m: F.7.o on Mexico - Estado 8 Escudos, KM#383.4.

KM#	Date	Year	Good	VG	Fine	VF
86	ND	1829LF	—	—	Unique	—

NOTE: Other coin types may exist with this particular countermark.

ISABEL II

SILVER

Type VI

This countermark was introduced after the death of Ferdinand VII on December 20, 1834. It exists with several varieties of crowns. Countermarking of foreign coins was halted in Manila by the edict of March 31, 1837 after Spain had recognized the independence of Mexico, Peru, Colombia, Bolivia, Chile and other former colonies in Central and South America. Coins bearing the Type VI countermark dated 1838 or later should be considered counterfeit.

(REAL)

SILVER

c/m: Y • II • on Mexico - Zacatecas Real, KM#372.10.

KM#	Date	Year	Good	VG	Fine	VF
87	ND	(1826-37)	75.00	125.00	175.00	300.00

(2 REALES)

SILVER

c/m: Y • II • on Mexico - Zacatecas 2 Reales, KM#374.12.

KM#	Date	Year	Good	VG	Fine	VF
88	ND	(1825-37)	60.00	100.00	150.00	250.00

c/m: Y • II • on Peru (Lima) 2 Reales, KM#104.2.

KM#	Date	Year	Good	VG	Fine	VF
A90	ND	(1808-1811)	90.00	160.00	250.00	400.00

c/m: Y • II • on Peru (Lima) 2 Reales, KM#141.

KM#	Date	Year	Good	VG	Fine	VF
90	ND	(1825-37)	60.00	100.00	150.00	200.00

(GULDEN)

.920 SILVER

c/m: Y • II • on Netherlands-Holland 1 Gulden, Cr#C13.

KM#	Date	Year	Good	VG	Fine	VF
89	ND	(1793)	120.00	150.00	200.00	300.00

(4 REALES)

SILVER

c/m: Y • II • on Bolivia 4 Reales, KM#54.

KM#	Date	Year	Good	VG	Fine	VF
91	ND	(1788)	250.00	400.00	600.00	900.00

c/m: Y • II • on Mexico - Zacatecas 4 Reales, KM#375.9.

KM#	Date	Year	Good	VG	Fine	VF
92	ND	(1832)	200.00	300.00	450.00	750.00

(8 REALES)

SILVER

KM#	Date	Year	Good	VG	Fine	VF
	c/m: Y • II • on Argentina 8 Reales, KM#5.					
93.1	ND	(1813)	60.00	100.00	150.00	200.00
	c/m: Y • II • on Argentina 8 Reales, KM#14.					
93.2	ND	(1815)	60.00	100.00	150.00	200.00
	c/m: Y • II • on Argentina 8 Soles, KM#15.					
94	ND	(1815)	60.00	100.00	150.00	350.00
	c/m: Y • II • on Argentina 8 Reales, KM#20.					
95	ND	(1826-37)	60.00	100.00	150.00	250.00
	c/m: Y • II • on Bolivia 8 Reales, KM#55.					
96	ND	(1773-89)	65.00	110.00	160.00	250.00
	c/m: Y • II • on Bolivia 8 Reales, KM#64.					
97	ND	(1789-91)	65.00	110.00	160.00	250.00
	c/m: Y • II • on Bolivia 8 Reales, KM#73.					
98	ND	(1791-1808)	65.00	100.00	150.00	200.00
	c/m: Y • II • on Bolivia 8 Reales, KM#84.					
99	ND	(1808-25)	60.00	90.00	140.00	190.00

KM#	Date	Year	Good	VG	Fine	VF
	c/m: Y • II • on Bolivia 8 Sueldos, KM#97.					
100	ND	(1827-37)	25.00	35.00	45.00	80.00
	c/m: Y • II • on Brazil 960 Reis, KM#307.					
101	ND	(1809-18)	125.00	175.00	250.00	375.00
	c/m: Y • II • on Brazil 960 Reis, KM#326.					
102	ND	(1818-22)	125.00	175.00	250.00	375.00
	c/m: Y • II • on Brazil 960 Reis, KM#368.					
103	ND	(1823-30)	125.00	175.00	250.00	375.00
	c/m: Y • II • on Brazil 960 Reis, KM#385.					
104	ND	(1832-4)	—	—	Rare	—
	c/m: Y • II • on Brazil 1200 Reis, KM#454.					
105	ND	(1834-7)	150.00	300.00	400.00	600.00

c/m: Y • II • on Central American Republic - Guatemala 8 Reales, KM#4.

KM#	Date	Year	Good	VG	Fine	VF
106.1	ND	(1824-37)	100.00	200.00	300.00	500.00

c/m: Y • II • on obv. and rev. of Central American Republic - Guatemala 8 Reales, KM#4.

KM#	Date	Year	Good	VG	Fine	VF
106.2	ND	(1824 NG)	100.00	200.00	300.00	500.00

c/m: Y • II • on Central American Republic - Costa Rica 8 Reales, KM#22.

KM#	Date	Year	Good	VG	Fine	VF
107	ND	(1831)	150.00	300.00	400.00	600.00

c/m: Y • II • on Chile 1 Peso, KM#82.

KM#	Date	Year	Good	VG	Fine	VF
108	ND	(1817-34)	50.00	75.00	100.00	125.00

c/m: Y • II • on Colombia 8 Reales, KM#89.

KM#	Date	Year	Good	VG	Fine	VF
109	ND	(1834-6)	40.00	60.00	80.00	120.00

c/m: Y • II • on Mexico City 8 Reales, KM#104.

KM#	Date	Year	Good	VG	Fine	VF
110	ND	(1747-60)	—	—	Rare	—

c/m: Y • II • on Mexico City 8 Reales, KM#105.

KM#	Date	Year	Good	VG	Fine	VF
111	ND	(1760-71)	—	—	Rare	—

c/m: Y • II • on Mexico City 8 Reales, KM#106.

KM#	Date	Year	Good	VG	Fine	VF
112	ND	(1772-89)	60.00	120.00	160.00	250.00

c/m: Y • II • on Mexico City 8 Reales, KM#107.

KM#	Date	Year	Good	VG	Fine	VF
113	ND	(1789-90FM)	60.00	120.00	150.00	200.00

c/m: Y • II • on Mexico City 8 Reales, KM#108.

KM#	Date	Year	Good	VG	Fine	VF
114	ND	(1790FM)	60.00	120.00	170.00	250.00

c/m: Y • II • on Mexico City 8 Reales, KM#109.

KM#	Date	Year	Good	VG	Fine	VF
115	ND	(1791-1808)	50.00	100.00	150.00	200.00

c/m: Y • II • on Mexico City 8 Reales, KM#110.

KM#	Date	Year	Good	VG	Fine	VF
116	ND	(1808-11)	50.00	100.00	150.00	200.00

c/m: Y • 11 • on Mexico - Chihuahua 8 Reales, KM#111.1.

KM#	Date	Year	Good	VG	Fine	VF
117.1	ND	(1815-22)	100.00	150.00	220.00	300.00

c/m: Y • II • on Mexico - Durango 8 Reales, KM#111.2.

KM#	Date	Year	Good	VG	Fine	VF
117.2	ND	(1811-21)	50.00	100.00	150.00	200.00

c/m: Y • II • on Mexico City 8 Reales, KM#111.

KM#	Date	Year	Good	VG	Fine	VF
119	ND	(1811-21)	50.00	100.00	150.00	200.00

c/m: Y • II • on Mexico - Zacatecas 8 Reales, KM#111.5.

KM#	Date	Year	Good	VG	Fine	VF
118	ND	(1813-22)	50.00	100.00	150.00	200.00

c/m: Y • II • on Mexico - Zacatecas 8 Reales, KM#189.

KM#	Date	Year	Good	VG	Fine	VF
120	ND	(1811)	100.00	150.00	220.00	300.00

c/m: Y • II • on Mexico City 8 Reales, KM#304.

KM#	Date	Year	Good	VG	Fine	VF
121	ND	(1822JM)	50.00	85.00	135.00	175.00

c/m: Y • II • on Mexico City 8 Reales, KM#305.

KM#	Date	Year	Good	VG	Fine	VF
122	ND	(1822JM)	50.00	100.00	140.00	200.00

c/m: Y • II • on Mexico City 8 Reales, KM#306.

KM#	Date	Year	Good	VG	Fine	VF
123	ND	(1822JM)	50.00	100.00	140.00	200.00

c/m: Y • II • on Mexico City 8 Reales, KM#307.

KM#	Date	Year	Good	VG	Fine	VF
124	ND	(1822JM)	50.00	100.00	140.00	180.00

c/m: Y • II • on Mexico City 8 Reales, KM#308.

KM#	Date	Year	Good	VG	Fine	VF
125	ND	(1822JM)	50.00	100.00	140.00	180.00

c/m: Y • II • on Mexico City 8 Reales, KM#309.

KM#	Date	Year	Good	VG	Fine	VF
126	ND	(1822JM)	—	—	Rare	—

c/m: Y • II • on Mexico City 8 Reales, KM#310.

KM#	Date	Year	Good	VG	Fine	VF
127	ND	(1822-3JM)	40.00	80.00	125.00	180.00

c/m: Y • II • on Mexico 8 Reales, KM#376.

KM#	Date	Year	Good	VG	Fine	VF
128	ND	(1823-4)	50.00	100.00	140.00	200.00

c/m: Y • II • on Mexico 8 Reales, KM#377.

KM#	Date	Year	Good	VG	Fine	VF
129	ND	(1824-37)	30.00	50.00	75.00	125.00

c/m: Y • II • on Peru (Lima) 8 Reales, KM#64.

KM#	Date	Year	Good	VG	Fine	VF
130	ND	(1760-72)	50.00	100.00	150.00	200.00

c/m: Y • II • on Peru (Lima) 8 Reales, KM#78.

KM#	Date	Year	Good	VG	Fine	VF
131	ND	(1772-89)	50.00	100.00	150.00	200.00

c/m: Y • II • on Peru (Lima) 8 Reales, KM#87.

KM#	Date	Year	Good	VG	Fine	VF
132	ND	(1789-91)	60.00	110.00	175.00	200.00

c/m: Y • II • on Peru (Lima) 8 Reales, KM#97.

KM#	Date	Year	Good	VG	Fine	VF
133	ND	(1791-1808)	50.00	100.00	150.00	200.00

c/m: Y • II • on Peru (Lima) 8 Reales, KM#106.

KM#	Date	Year	Good	VG	Fine	VF
134	ND	(1808-11)	50.00	100.00	150.00	200.00

c/m: Y • II • on Peru (Lima) 8 Reales, KM#117.1

KM#	Date	Year	Good	VG	Fine	VF
135	ND	(1810-24)	45.00	65.00	85.00	125.00

c/m: Y • II • on Peru (Lima) 8 Reales, KM#136.

KM#	Date	Year	Good	VG	Fine	VF
136	ND	(1822-3)	30.00	40.00	65.00	90.00

c/m: Y • II • on Peru (Lima) 8 Reales, KM#130.

KM#	Date	Year	Good	VG	Fine	VF
137	ND	(1824)	100.00	150.00	215.00	325.00

c/m: Y • II • on Peru (Lima) 8 Reales, KM#142.1.

KM#	Date	Year	Good	VG	Fine	VF
138.1	ND	(1825-8)	20.00	30.00	40.00	55.00

c/m: Y • II • on Peru (Lima) 8 Reales, KM#142.3.

KM#	Date	Year	Good	VG	Fine	VF
138.2	ND	(1828-37)	20.00	30.00	40.00	55.00

c/m: Y • II • on Peru (Cuzco)
8 Reales, KM#142.4.

KM#	Date	Year	Good	VG	Fine	VF
138.4	ND	(1830-34)	40.00	65.00	100.00	165.00

c/m: Y • II • on Philippines, KM#80.

KM#	Date	Year	Good	VG	Fine	VF
139	ND	(1822-3)	75.00	115.00	200.00	275.00

NOTE: Coins bearing both Type V or Type VI countermarks with other countermarks are very scarce. Certain holed or pierced coins are sometimes found with an additional set of countermarks usually struck on both sides over the hole to approve it for normal circulation. These are very scarce.

ESCUDO

GOLD
c/m: Y • II • on Colombia 1 Escudo, KM#81.2.

KM#	Date	Year	Good	VG	Fine	VF
140	ND	(1827FM)	—	—	Unique	—

8 ESCUDO

GOLD
c/m: Y • II • on Colombia
8 Escudos, KM#82.1.

KM#	Date	Year	Good	VG	Fine	VF
141.1	ND	(1826JF)	3000.	3500.	4000.	6500.
	ND	(1831RS)	4000.	5000.	6000.	10,000.
	ND	(1832RS)	—	—	—	*12,800.
	ND	(1835RS)	—	—	—	*16,500.

c/m: Y • II • on Colombia
8 Escudos, KM#82.2.

KM#	Date	Year	Good	VG	Fine	VF
141.2	ND	(1833UR)	3000.	3500.	4000.	6500.

c/m: Y • II • on Mexico City Iturbide
8 Scudos, KM#313.1.

KM#	Date	Year	Good	VG	Fine	VF
141.3	ND	(1822)	—	—	—	*16,500.

c/m: Y • II • on Mexico City
8 Escudos, KM#383.9.

KM#	Date	Year	Good	VG	Fine	VF
141.4	ND	(1834ML)	—	—	—	**13,200.

c/m: Y • II • on Argentina-Provincias Del Rio
De La Plata 8 Escudos, KM#21.

KM#	Date	Year	Good	VG	Fine	VF
141.5	ND	(1828P)	3000.	3500.	4000.	6500.

***NOTE:** Glendining's John J. Ford Jr. sale 10-89.
****NOTE:** Sotheby's Geneva gold coins of the Hispanic world sale 5-90.
NOTE: The above countermarks have been reported on other coins, (i.e. U.S. 1/2 Dollar, Dollar, and Spanish 20 Reales).

DECIMAL COINAGE

1861-1897
100 Centavos = 1 Peso

10 CENTIMOS

2.5960 g, .900 SILVER, .0751 oz ASW

KM#	Date	Mintage	Fine	VF	XF	Unc
145	1864	4,586	85.00	165.00	450.00	1600.
	1865	.082	25.00	60.00	150.00	1000.
	1866	.039	35.00	70.00	175.00	1200.
	1867/6	.124	25.00	60.00	150.00	1000.
	1867	Inc. Ab.	25.00	50.00	125.00	950.00
	1868	*.139	6.00	12.00	25.00	125.00

NOTE: An additional 450,000 pieces were struck between 1870-74, all dated 1868.

2.5960 g, .835 SILVER, .0697 oz ASW

KM#	Date	Mintage	Fine	VF	XF	Unc
148	1880	.015	200.00	325.00	750.00	2500.
	1881/0	.624	25.00	45.00	125.00	400.00
148	1881	Inc. Ab.	20.00	40.00	95.00	400.00
	1882/1	.525	20.00	40.00	125.00	400.00
	1882	Inc. Ab.	17.00	30.00	90.00	350.00
	1883/1	.983	15.00	30.00	85.00	350.00
	1883/2	Inc. Ab.	15.00	30.00	85.00	350.00
	1883	Inc. Ab.	10.00	20.00	80.00	300.00
	1884	.010	200.00	275.00	600.00	2400.
	1885/3	—	7.50	12.00	22.00	65.00
	1885	Inc. Ab.	5.00	8.00	18.00	50.00

***NOTE:** An additional 5,432,614 pieces were struck between 1886-1898, all dated 1885.

20 CENTIMOS

5.1920 g, .900 SILVER, .1502 oz ASW

KM#	Date	Mintage	Fine	VF	XF	Unc
146	1864	.067	35.00	65.00	150.00	1600.
	1865	.239	15.00	30.00	75.00	1000.
	1866/5	.134	20.00	45.00	120.00	1200.
	1866	Inc. Ab.	25.00	50.00	135.00	1250.
	1867	.138	20.00	40.00	100.00	1200.
	1868	*.418	5.00	8.00	15.00	150.00

***NOTE:** An additional 708,400 pieces were struck between 1869-1874, all dated 1868.

5.1920 g, .835 SILVER, .1394 oz ASW

KM#	Date	Mintage	Fine	VF	XF	Unc
149	1880	.070	45.00	75.00	150.00	1250.
	1881/0	1.029	10.00	20.00	40.00	300.00
	1881	Inc. Ab.	10.00	18.00	50.00	300.00
	1882/1	.968	12.00	25.00	55.00	500.00
	1882	Inc. Ab.	12.00	25.00	55.00	500.00
	1883/2	1.972	12.00	22.00	45.00	350.00
	1883/horizontal 8	Inc. Ab.	12.00	22.00	45.00	300.00
	1883	Inc. Ab.	10.00	20.00	40.00	300.00
	1884	.859	25.00	45.00	100.00	600.00
	1885	*1.344	5.00	8.00	12.50	70.00

***NOTE:** An additional 4,092,205 pieces were struck between 1886-1898, all dated 1885.

50 CENTIMOS

12.9800 g, .900 SILVER, .3756 oz ASW

KM#	Date	Mintage	Fine	VF	XF	Unc
147	1865	.081	35.00	70.00	175.00	1500.
	1866	7,442	325.00	500.00	800.00	5000.
	1867	6,870	275.00	450.00	700.00	4000.
	1868/58	*.423	10.00	18.00	50.00	200.00
	1868/7	Inc. Ab.	10.00	18.00	50.00	200.00
	1868	Inc. Ab.	7.50	15.00	45.00	200.00

***NOTE:** An additional 200,800 pieces were struck between 1869-1874, all dated 1868.

12.9800 g, .835 SILVER, .3485 oz ASW

KM#	Date	Mintage	Fine	VF	XF	Unc
150	1880	.127	150.00	250.00	400.00	2500.
	1881	2.480	10.00	20.00	40.00	500.00
	1882/0	1.890	12.50	35.00	65.00	650.00
	1882/1	Inc. Ab.	12.50	35.00	65.00	650.00
	1882	Inc. Ab.	10.00	25.00	45.00	650.00
	1883	2.221	10.00	25.00	45.00	500.00
	1884	.023	140.00	185.00	325.00	2000.
	1885/3	*22.700	5.00	10.00	24.00	85.00
	1885	I.A.	3.50	7.50	18.00	65.00

***NOTE:** An additional 22,649,115 pieces were struck between 1886-1898, all dated 1885.

PESO

1.6915 g, .875 GOLD, .0476 oz AGW

KM#	Date	Mintage	Fine	VF	XF	Unc
142	1861/0	.237	45.00	60.00	100.00	250.00
	1861	Inc. Ab.	45.00	60.00	100.00	250.00
	1862/1	.143	45.00	60.00	100.00	250.00
	1862	Inc. Ab.	45.00	75.00	130.00	300.00
	1863/2	.236	45.00	60.00	100.00	250.00
	1863	Inc. Ab.	45.00	60.00	100.00	250.00
	1864/0	.274	45.00	60.00	100.00	250.00
	1864	Inc. Ab.	45.00	65.00	100.00	250.00
	1865/0	.189	45.00	75.00	125.00	300.00
	1865	Inc. Ab.	45.00	75.00	125.00	300.00
	1866/5	.077	150.00	250.00	400.00	1000.
	1866	Inc. Ab.	150.00	250.00	400.00	1000.
	1867	.012	350.00	700.00	1250.	3500.
	1868/6	*.028	45.00	60.00	100.00	250.00
	1868/7	Inc. Ab.	45.00	60.00	100.00	250.00
	1868	Inc. Ab.	40.00	50.00	80.00	150.00

***NOTE:** An additional 372,724 pieces were struck between 1869-1874, all dated 1868.

25.0000 g, .900 SILVER, .7234 oz ASW

KM#	Date	Mintage	Fine	VF	XF	Unc
154	1897 SGV	6.000	20.00	30.00	70.00	300.00

2 PESOS

3.3830 g, .875 GOLD, .0952 oz AGW

KM#	Date	Mintage	Fine	VF	XF	Unc
143	1861/0	.265	60.00	80.00	125.00	325.00
	1861	Inc. Ab.	60.00	80.00	125.00	325.00
	1862/1	.237	60.00	80.00	125.00	325.00
	1862	Inc. Ab.	60.00	80.00	125.00	325.00
	1863/2	.176	60.00	80.00	125.00	325.00
	1863	Inc. Ab.	60.00	80.00	125.00	325.00
	1864/0	.181	60.00	80.00	125.00	325.00
	1864/3	Inc. Ab.	60.00	80.00	125.00	325.00
	1864	Inc. Ab.	70.00	100.00	150.00	400.00
	1865	.034	150.00	225.00	400.00	750.00
	1866/5	.016	400.00	600.00	1250.	3000.
	1866	Inc. Ab.	400.00	600.00	1250.	3000.
	1868/6	*.048	55.00	70.00	115.00	250.00
	1868	Inc. Ab.	50.00	65.00	100.00	200.00

NOTE: An additional 304,691 pieces were struck between 1869-1873, all dated 1868.

4 PESOS

6.7661 g, .875 GOLD, .1903 oz AGW

KM#	Date	Mintage	Fine	VF	XF	Unc
144	1861	.183	120.00	150.00	225.00	475.00
	1862/1	.507	120.00	150.00	200.00	450.00
	1862	Inc. Ab.	120.00	150.00	200.00	450.00
	1863	.475	120.00	150.00	200.00	450.00
	1864	.461	120.00	150.00	225.00	500.00
	1865	.241	120.00	175.00	300.00	600.00
	1866/65	.044	400.00	600.00	1500.	3000.
	1866	Inc. Ab.	400.00	600.00	1500.	3000.
	1867	1,530	1200.	1800.	3000.	8000.
	1868	*.036	100.00	120.00	185.00	325.00

***NOTE:** 1,521,505 were struck between 1869-1873, all dated 1868.

KM#	Date	Mintage	Fine	VF	XF	Unc
151	1880	—	—	—	Rare	—
	1881	—	2500.	3500.	6000.	8000.
	1882	—	500.00	750.00	1100.	1600.
	1883	—	—	Reported, not confirmed		
	1884	—	—	Reported, not confirmed		
	1885	—	1500.	2000.	3000.	5500.

REVOLUTIONARY COINAGE

Island of Panay

CENTAVO

COPPER
Obv: Helmeted head right, leg.
Rev: Sun in triangle, leg.

KM#	Date	Mintage	VG	Fine	VF	XF
156	1899	—	—	—	5000.	7500.

Obv. c/m: M behind head.
Rev: NACIONAL LIBERTAD at sides of triangle.

KM#	Date	Mintage	VG	Fine	VF	XF
157	1899	—	—	—	5500.	8000.

Town of Malolos

2 CENTAVOS

COPPER
Obv: Large date.

KM#	Date	Mintage	VG	Fine	VF	XF
158.1	1899	—	—	—	4500.	7000.

Obv: Small date.

KM#	Date	Mintage	VG	Fine	VF	XF
158.2	1899	—	—	—	4750.	7250.

KM#	Date	Mintage	VG	Fine	VF	XF
159	1899	—	—	—	6000.	9000.

PRETENDER COINAGE (PT)

Charles VII of Spain

5 PESETAS

COPPER
Obv: Laureated head of Charles right; date below.
Rev: Value in branches.

KM#	Date	Mintage	Fine	VF	XF	Unc
PT1	1874(b)	—	—	—	Unique	—

PATTERNS (Pn)

(Including off metal strikes)

KM#	Date	Mintage	Identification	Mkt.Val.
Pn9	1855	—	5 Pesetas, Silver	6000.
Pn10	1857	—	1 Real, Silver	4000.
Pn11	1857	—	1 Real, Copper	3200.

KM#	Date	Mintage	Identification	Mkt.Val.
Pn12	1859	—	2 Centavos, Copper	350.00
Pn13	1859	—	2 Centavos, Copper, Proof	400.00

KM#	Date	Mintage	Identification	Mkt.Val.
Pn14	1859	—	20 Reaux (Reales), Copper	500.00

KM#	Date	Mintage	Identification	Mkt.Val.
Pn15	1859	—	40 Reaux (Reales), Copper	600.00

KM#	Date	Mintage	Identification	Mkt.Val.
Pn16	1859	—	80 Reaux (Reales), Copper	700.00

KM#	Date	Mintage	Identification	Mkt.Val.
Pn17	1880	—	50 Centimos, Bronze	3500.
Pn18	1894	—	1 Centavo, Copper	5000.

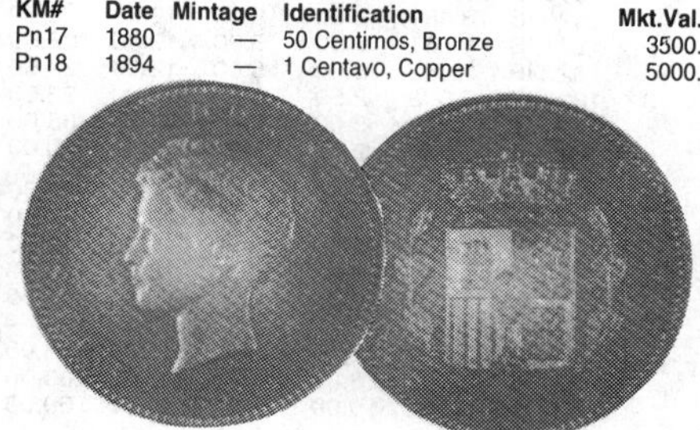

KM#	Date	Mintage	Identification	Mkt.Val.
Pn19	1894	—	2 Centavos, Copper	7000.

TRIAL STRIKES (TS)

KM#	Date	Mintage	Identification	Mkt.Val.
TS1	1859	—	4 Pesos, Gold-Plated Bronze, obv.	Unique
TS2	1859	—	4 Pesos, Gold-Plated Bronze, rev.	Unique
TS3	1861	—	1 Peso, Gold-Plated Bronze, obv.	Unique
TS4	1861	—	1 Peso, Gold-Plated Bronze, rev.	Unique
TS5	1861	—	2 Pesos, Gold-Plated Bronze, obv.	Unique
TS6	1861	—	2 Pesos, Gold-Plated Bronze, rev.	Unique
TS7	ND(1874)(b)	—	5 Pesetas, Bronze, rev.	Unique

POLAND

The Republic of Poland, located in central Europe, has an area of 120,725 sq. mi. (312,680 sq. km.) and a population of *38.2 million. Capital: Warsaw. The economy is essentially agricultural, but industrial activity provides the products for foreign trade. Machinery, coal, coke, iron, steel and transport equipment are exported.

Poland, which began as a Slavic duchy in the 10th century and reached its peak of power between the 14th and 16th centuries, has had a turbulent history of invasion, occupation or partition by Mongols, Turkey, Hungary, Sweden, Austria, Prussia and Russia.

The first partition took place in 1772. Prussia took Polish Pomerania. Russia took part of the eastern provinces. Austria took Galicia, in which lay the fortress city of Kracow (Crakow). The second partition occurred in 1793 when Russia took another slice of the eastern provinces and Prussia took what remained of western Poland. The third partition, 1795, literally removed Poland from the map. Russia took what was left of the eastern provinces. Prussia seized most of central Poland, including Warsaw. Austria took what was left of the south. Napoleon restored to Poland much of the territory lost to Prussia and Austria, but after his defeat another partition returned the Duchy of Warsaw to Prussia, made Kracow into a tiny republic, and declared what remained to be the Kingdom of Poland under the czar and in permanent union with Russia.

Poland re-emerged as an independent state recognized by the Treaty of Versailles on June 28, 1919, and maintained its independence until 1939 when it was invaded by, and partitioned between, Germany and Russia. Poland's present boundaries were determined by the U.S.-British-Russian agreement of Aug. 16, 1945. The Government of National Unity was replaced when the Polish Comunist-Socialist faction won a decisive victory at the polls in 1947 and established a 'Peoples Democratic Republic' of the Soviet type in 1952. On December 29, 1989 Poland was proclaimed as the Republic of Poland.

RULERS

Friedrich August I, King of Saxony,
As Grand Duke, 1807-1814
Alexander I, Czar of Russia,
As King, 1815-1825
Nicholas (Mikolay) I, Czar of Russia,
As King, 1825-1855

MINT MARKS

Other letters appearing with date denote the Mint Master at the time the coin was struck.

MINTMASTERS INITIALS

Mintmasters initials usually appear flanking the shield or by the date.

WARSAW MINT

Letter	Date	Name
FA	1815-1827	Friedrich Hunger
IB	1811-27	Jakub Benik
IP	1834-35	Jerzy (George) Pusch
JS	1810-11	John Stockmann
KG	1829-34	Carl Gronau

MONETARY SYSTEM

Until 1815

1 Solidus = 1 Schilling
3 Solidi = 2 Poltura = 1 Grosz
3 Poltura = 1-1/2 Grosze = 1 Polturak
6 Groszy = 1 Szostak
18 Groszy = 1 Tympf
30 Groszy = 4 Silbergroschen = 1 Zloty
1 Talar = 1 Zloty
6 Zlotych = 1 Reichsthaler
8 Zlotych = 1 Speciesthaler
5 Speciesthaler = 1 August D'or
3 Ducats = 1 Stanislaus D'or

GRAND DUCHY OF WARSAW

GROSZ

COPPER

C#	Date	Mintage	VG	Fine	VF	XF
81	1810 IS	.742	1.75	3.50	6.50	12.50
	1811 IS	4.358	1.75	3.00	5.50	10.00
	1811 IB	Inc. Ab.	1.75	3.00	5.50	10.00
	1812 IB	6.377	1.75	3.00	5.50	10.00
	1814 IB	3.072	1.75	3.00	5.50	10.00

3 GROSZE

COPPER

C#	Date	Mintage	VG	Fine	VF	XF
82	1810 IS	1.008	2.00	4.50	10.00	20.00
	1811 IS	5.479	2.00	3.50	8.00	16.00
	1811 IB	Inc. Ab.	2.00	3.50	8.00	16.00
	1812 IB	6.816	2.00	3.50	8.00	16.00
	1813 IB	1.139	2.00	4.50	10.00	20.00
	1814 IB	3.427	2.00	3.50	8.00	16.00

5 GROSZY

2.2000 g, .210 SILVER, .0148 oz ASW

C#	Date	Mintage	VG	Fine	VF	XF
83	1811 IS	11.595	4.00	7.00	15.00	28.00
	1811 IB	Inc. Ab.	4.00	7.00	15.00	28.00
	1812 IB	3.405	4.00	7.00	15.00	28.00

10 GROSZY

2.9900 g, .245 SILVER, .0235 oz ASW

C#	Date	Mintage	VG	Fine	VF	XF
84	1810 IS	—	25.00	45.00	—	—
	1812 IB	.951	5.00	10.00	17.50	36.00
	1813 IB	3.549	5.00	10.00	16.00	32.00

1/6 TALARA

4.9800 g, .535 SILVER, .0856 oz ASW

C#	Date	Mintage	VG	Fine	VF	XF
85	1811 IS	.113	9.00	15.00	45.00	95.00
	1812 IB	.223	9.00	15.00	45.00	95.00
	1813 IB	.106	15.00	25.00	50.00	160.00
	1814 IB	1.492	9.00	15.00	40.00	80.00

1/3 TALARA

8.6600 g, .625 SILVER, .1740 oz ASW

C#	Date	Mintage	VG	Fine	VF	XF
86	1810 IS	.123	10.00	18.00	50.00	100.00
	1811 IS	.993	10.00	15.00	30.00	75.00
	1812 IB	2.804	10.00	15.00	30.00	75.00
	1813 IB	1.916	10.00	15.00	30.00	75.00
	1814 IB	4.611	10.00	15.00	30.00	75.00

TALAR

22.9200 g, .720 SILVER, .5305 oz ASW

C#	Date	Mintage	VG	Fine	VF	XF
87	1811 IB	4,488	50.00	150.00	300.00	650.00
	1812 IB	.036	50.00	100.00	200.00	400.00
	1814 IB	.014	50.00	100.00	250.00	550.00

TRADE COINAGE

DUCAT

3.5000 g, .986 GOLD, .1109 oz AGW

C#	Date	Mintage	VG	Fine	VF	XF
88	1811 IB	8,546	250.00	400.00	600.00	950.00
	1813 IB	3,000	450.00	800.00	1400.	2000.

CONGRESS KINGDOM OF POLAND

MONETARY SYSTEM

30 Groszy = 15 Russian Kopeks = 1 Zloty
10 Zlotych = 1-1/2 Rubles

GROSZ

COPPER

C#	Date	Mintage	VG	Fine	VF	XF
93	1816 IB	1.873	1.00	2.00	4.00	8.00
	1817 IB	3.092	1.00	2.00	4.00	8.00
	1818 IB	4.035	1.00	2.00	4.00	8.00
	1818	Inc. Ab.	7.50	15.00	25.00	60.00
	1819 IB	Inc. Be.	1.00	2.50	5.00	10.00
	1820 IB	.372	1.00	2.50	5.00	8.00
	1821 IB	.571	1.00	2.50	5.00	8.00
	1822 IB	Inc.C#94	6.00	10.00	17.50	35.00

NOTE: Varieties of eagles exist.

(Mining)

Rev. leg: Z MIEDZI KRALOWEY.

C#	Date	Mintage	VG	Fine	VF	XF
94	1822 IB	2.721	1.75	2.50	5.00	12.00
	1823 IB	5.046	1.75	2.50	5.00	12.00
	1824 IB	5.413	1.75	2.50	5.00	12.00
	1825 IB	2.108	1.75	2.50	5.00	12.00
	1826 IB	1.096	—	—	—	12.00

C#	Date	Mintage	VG	Fine	VF	XF
105	1828 FH	1.190	1.00	2.00	4.00	8.00
	1829 FH	.931	1.00	2.00	4.00	8.00
	1830 FH	1.569	1.00	2.00	4.00	8.00
	1830 KG	I.A.	1.00	2.00	4.00	8.00
	1831 KG	1.777	1.00	2.00	4.00	8.00
	1832 KG	1.559	1.00	2.00	4.00	8.00
	1833 KG	.375	1.00	2.00	4.00	8.00
	1834 KG	.427	1.00	2.00	4.00	8.00
	1834 IP	I.A.	1.00	2.00	4.00	8.00
	1835 IP	.542	1.00	2.00	4.00	8.00

C#	Date	Mintage	VG	Fine	VF	XF
106	1835MW	I.A.	2.00	4.00	8.00	15.00
	1836MW	.839	2.00	4.00	8.00	15.00
	1837MW	1.016	1.00	2.00	4.00	8.00
	1837WM	I.A.	—	—	Rare	—
	1838MW	.488	1.00	2.00	4.00	8.00
	1839MW	.670	1.00	2.00	4.00	8.00
	1840MW	.243	1.00	2.00	4.00	8.00

NOTE: Varieties exist.

Rev: W/o wreath, pearl rim.

C#	Date	Mintage	VG	Fine	VF	XF
106a	1840MW	I.A.	7.50	12.50	17.50	32.00

Rev: JEDEN or IEDEN above value.

C#	Date	Mintage	VG	Fine	VF	XF
107	1840MW	Inc. C106	—	—	Rare	—
	1841MW	.372	—	—	Rare	—

3 GROSZE

COPPER

Plain edge, struck w/o collar.

C#	Date	Mintage	VG	Fine	VF	XF
95.1	1817 IB	.843	2.00	4.00	8.00	16.00
	1818 IB	.157	4.00	8.00	17.50	25.00

NOTE: Varieties of eagles exist.

Reeded edge, struck in collar.

C#	Date	Mintage	VG	Fine	VF	XF
95.2	1818 IB	—	—	—	Rare	—
	1819 IB	.187	2.00	4.00	8.00	16.00
	1820 IB	.089	2.00	5.00	10.00	20.00

(Mining)

Rev. leg: Z MIEDZI KRAIOWEY.

C#	Date	Mintage	VG	Fine	VF	XF
108	1826 IB	.570	7.00	10.00	15.00	28.00
	1827 IB	Inc. Ab.	7.00	10.00	15.00	28.00

Rev. leg: 3/GROSZE/POLSKI.

C#	Date	Mintage	VG	Fine	VF	XF
109	1827 FH	.495	2.50	5.00	10.00	20.00
	1828 FH	1.159	2.00	4.00	8.00	16.00
	1829 FH	1.057	2.00	4.00	8.00	16.00
	1829	—	7.00	10.00	15.00	25.00
	1830 FH	.891	2.00	4.00	8.00	16.00
	1830 KG	I.A.	12.50	20.00	35.00	75.00
	1831 FH	1.773	—	—	Rare	—
	1831 KG	1.343	2.00	4.00	8.00	16.00
	1832 FH	.030	—	—	Rare	—
	1832 KG	7,117	2.00	4.00	8.00	16.00
	1833 KG	.515	2.00	4.00	8.00	16.00
	1834 KG	.346	2.50	5.00	10.00	20.00
	1834 IP	I.A.	2.50	5.00	10.00	20.00
	1835 IP	.185	4.00	8.00	16.00	30.00

Rev: Wreath surrounds value.

C#	Date	Mintage	VG	Fine	VF	XF
110.1	1835MW	I.A.	2.00	4.00	8.00	16.00
	1836MW	.244	2.00	4.00	8.00	16.00
	1837MW	.398	2.00	4.00	8.00	16.00
	1838MW	.288	2.00	4.00	8.00	16.00
	1839MW	.333	2.00	4.00	8.00	16.00

NOTE: Varieties exist.

Obv: Eagle's heads larger, shield smaller.

C#	Date	Mintage	VG	Fine	VF	XF
110.2	1839MW	I.A.	2.00	4.00	8.00	16.00
	1840MW	.118	2.00	4.00	8.00	16.00
	1840WW	I.A.	7.00	10.00	15.00	25.00
	1841MW	.242	4.00	7.50	15.00	25.00

5 GROSZY

1.4500 g, .192 SILVER, .0090 oz ASW
Obv: Eagle's wings smaller. Rev. value: 5 GROSZY.
Smooth edge.

C#	Date	Mintage	VG	Fine	VF	XF
96.1	1816 IB	2.700	6.00	8.50	12.00	22.50

Reeded edge.

C#	Date	Mintage	VG	Fine	VF	XF
96.2	1817 IB	Inc. Ab.		—	Rare	—

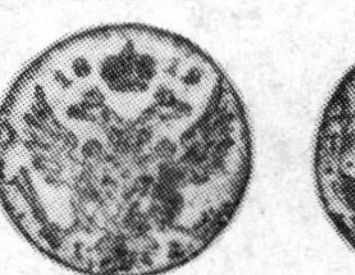

Obv: Redesigned shield.

C#	Date	Mintage	VG	Fine	VF	XF
96.3	1818 IB	3.056	2.50	5.00	12.00	22.50
	1819 IB	5.532	2.50	5.00	12.00	22.50
	1820 IB	3.481	2.50	5.00	12.00	22.50
	1821 IB	1.651	2.50	5.00	12.00	22.50
	1822 IB	1.282	2.50	5.00	12.00	22.50
	1823 IB	2.098	2.50	5.00	12.00	22.50
	1824 IB	.235	5.00	7.50	17.50	35.00
	1825 IB	.350	2.50	6.00	15.00	30.00
111	1826 IB	2.079	2.50	5.00	12.00	22.50
	1827 IB	1.904	2.50	5.00	12.00	22.50
	1827 FH	I.A.	2.50	5.00	15.00	25.00
	1828 FH	.403	2.50	5.00	15.00	25.00
	1829 FH	.714	2.50	5.00	15.00	25.00
	1829 KG	I.A.	—	—	Rare	—
	1830 FH	.571	2.50	5.00	15.00	25.00
	1831 KG	I.A.	3.00	8.00	17.50	30.00
	1832 KG	.154	10.00	15.00	30.00	60.00

C#	Date	Mintage	VG	Fine	VF	XF
111a	1836MW	.159	2.50	5.00	15.00	25.00
	1838MW	.173	2.50	5.00	15.00	25.00
	1839MW	.380	2.50	5.00	15.00	25.00
	1840MW	.127	2.50	5.00	17.50	20.00

Obv: Similar to 25 Zlotych, C#118.

C#	Date	Mintage	VG	Fine	VF	XF
112	1841	—	—	—	Proof	Rare

10 GROSZY

2.9000 g, .192 SILVER, .0180 oz ASW
Obv: Eagle.

C#	Date	Mintage	VG	Fine	VF	XF
97	1816 IB	.750	5.00	10.00	15.00	25.00
	1820 IB	.793	8.00	12.00	17.50	35.00
	1821 IB	.707	5.00	10.00	15.00	25.00
	1822 IB	1.238	5.00	10.00	15.00	25.00
	1823 IB	.262	10.00	15.00	20.00	40.00
	1825 IB	.750	7.50	10.00	15.00	30.00
113	1826 IB	.750	4.00	7.50	12.50	25.00
	1827 IB	.737	4.00	7.50	12.50	25.00
	1827 FH	I.A.	8.00	12.50	20.00	40.00
	1828 FH	.529	4.00	7.50	12.50	25.00
	1830 FH	.145	6.00	10.00	15.00	30.00
	1830 KG	I.A.	4.00	7.50	12.50	25.00
	1831 KG	16.604	6.00	10.00	15.00	30.00
	1832 KG	—	—	—	Rare	—
	1833 KG	—	—	—	Rare	—

C#	Date	Mintage	VG	Fine	VF	XF
113a	1835MW	.869	4.00	7.50	12.50	25.00
	1836MW	1.736	4.00	7.50	12.50	25.00
	1837MW	.767	4.00	7.50	12.50	25.00
	1838MW	1.735	4.00	7.50	12.50	25.00
	1839MW	.060	4.00	7.50	12.50	25.00
	1840MW	63.349	3.00	6.00	10.00	15.00
	1840WW	I.A.	6.00	12.00	15.00	30.00

ZLOTY

4.5500 g, .593 SILVER, .0872 oz ASW
Obv: Large head. Rev: Eagle, lettered edge.

C#	Date	Mintage	VG	Fine	VF	XF
98	1818 IB	2.253	6.00	10.00	20.00	40.00
	1818 IB struck in collar	—	—	—	Rare	—
	1819 IB	1.208	6.00	10.00	20.00	40.00
	1819 IB struck in collar	—	—	—	Rare	—

Obv: Smaller head.

C#	Date	Mintage	VG	Fine	VF	XF
98a	1818 IB	Inc. Ab.	—	—	Rare	—
	1822 IB	.287	6.00	10.00	20.00	40.00
	1823 IB	.052	6.00	10.00	20.00	40.00
	1824 IB	.119	6.00	10.00	20.00	40.00
	1825 IB	.084	6.00	10.00	20.00	40.00

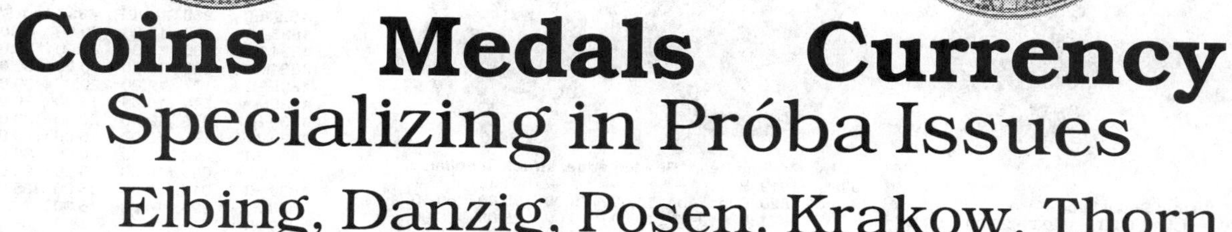

Specializing in Próba Issues

Elbing, Danzig, Posen, Krakow, Thorn

Medieval to Modern

Building Collections for over 20 years.

Acquiring Reference Books, Libraries to single volumes

Thinking of Selling? Thinking of Buying?

Call Tel: (708) 805-0706 • Fax: (708) 687-7380

Numismatics • Syngraphics

THE CUSTOM GALLERY LTD.

FINE JEWELRY ★ RARE COINS ★ EXPERT GOLDSMITHS

ANA Life Member

P.O. Box 740 • Oak Forest, IL 60452

Obv: Large head.

C#	Date	Mintage	VG	Fine	VF	XF
114.1	1827 IB	.106	6.00	10.00	20.00	38.00
	1828 FH	.092	6.00	10.00	20.00	38.00
	1829 FH	.124	6.00	10.00	20.00	38.00
	1830 FH	.614	6.00	10.00	20.00	38.00
	1831 KG	—	6.00	10.00	20.00	38.00
	1832 KG	1.112	6.00	10.00	20.00	38.00

NOTE: Varieties exist.

Obv: Small head.

C#	Date	Mintage	VG	Fine	VF	XF
114.2	1832 KG	I.A.	6.00	10.00	20.00	38.00
	1833 KG	.041	6.50	11.00	25.00	45.00
	1834 IP	.201	6.00	10.00	20.00	38.00

ZLOTY-15 KOPEKS

3.0700 g, .868 SILVER, .0857 oz ASW

C#	Date	Mintage	VG	Fine	VF	XF
129	1832 HГ	.049	6.50	10.00	15.00	30.00
	1833 HГ	.655	6.50	10.00	15.00	30.00
	1834 HГ	.030	7.50	12.50	20.00	40.00
	1834MW	.042	15.00	30.00	60.00	100.00
	1835 HГ	.150	6.50	10.00	15.00	30.00
	1835MW	2.192	5.00	7.50	10.00	25.00
	1836 HГ	1.450	6.50	10.00	15.00	30.00
	1836MW	3.331	5.00	7.50	10.00	25.00
	1837 HГ	.080	6.50	10.00	15.00	30.00
	1837MW	3.028	5.00	7.50	10.00	25.00
	1838 HГ	1.410	10.00	20.00	40.00	80.00
	1838MW	3.617	5.00	7.50	10.00	25.00
	1839 HГ	1.510	6.50	10.00	15.00	30.00
	1839 HГ	I.A.	—	—	Proof	Rare
	1839MW	3.586	5.00	7.50	10.00	25.00
	1840 HГ	1.060	6.50	10.00	15.00	30.00
	1840MW	.487	6.50	10.00	15.00	30.00
	1841 HГ	1.060	—	—	Proof	Rare
	1841MW	1.320	10.00	17.50	30.00	60.00

NOTE: Varieties exist.

40 GROSZY-20 KOPEKS

4.1000 g, .868 SILVER, .1144 oz ASW

C#	Date	Mintage	VG	Fine	VF	XF
130	1842MW	.051	10.00	15.00	20.00	35.00
	1843MW	.037	10.00	15.00	20.00	35.00
	1844MW	—	10.00	15.00	20.00	35.00
	1845MW	.062	10.00	15.00	20.00	35.00
	1846MW	—	—	—	Rare	—
	1848MW	.027	10.00	15.00	20.00	35.00
	1850MW	.038	10.00	15.00	20.00	35.00

50 GROSZY-25 KOPEKS

5.1800 g, .868 SILVER, .1445 oz ASW

C#	Date	Mintage	VG	Fine	VF	XF
131	1842MW	.057	10.00	15.00	25.00	50.00
	1843MW	.028	10.00	15.00	25.00	40.00
	1844MW	—	10.00	20.00	45.00	90.00
	1845MW	.052	10.00	15.00	25.00	40.00
	1846MW	.561	10.00	15.00	25.00	40.00
	1847MW	.485	10.00	15.00	25.00	40.00
	1848MW	.168	10.00	15.00	25.00	40.00
	1850MW	1.489	10.00	15.00	25.00	40.00

2 ZLOTE

9.0900 g, .593 SILVER, .1733 oz ASW
Lettered edge.

C#	Date	Mintage	VG	Fine	VF	XF
99	1816 IB	1.393	10.00	15.00	25.00	50.00
	1817 IB	1.084	10.00	15.00	25.00	50.00
	1818 IB	1.321	10.00	15.00	25.00	50.00
	1819 IB	1.241	10.00	15.00	25.00	50.00
	1820 IB	1.970	10.00	20.00	40.00	80.00

Obv: Medium head. Reeded edge, struck in collar.

C#	Date	Mintage	VG	Fine	VF	XF
99a	1819 IB	—	—	—	Rare	—
	1820 IB	Inc. Ab.	10.00	15.00	25.00	60.00
	1821 IB	.997	10.00	15.00	25.00	50.00
	1822 IB	.093	10.00	15.00	25.00	60.00
	1823 IB	.446	10.00	15.00	25.00	50.00
	1824 IB	.348	10.00	15.00	25.00	50.00
	1825 IB	.229	10.00	15.00	25.00	50.00

Obv: Laureated head.

C#	Date	Mintage	VG	Fine	VF	XF
115	1826 IB	.065	10.00	15.00	30.00	60.00
	1828 FH	.119	10.00	15.00	25.00	50.00
	1830 FH	.306	10.00	15.00	25.00	50.00

2 ZLOTE-30 KOPEKS

6.2100 g, .868 SILVER, .1733 oz ASW

C#	Date	Mintage	VG	Fine	VF	XF
132	1834MW	.024	12.00	20.00	35.00	65.00
	1835MW	2.229	7.50	10.00	20.00	40.00
	1836MW	2.589	7.50	10.00	20.00	40.00
	1837MW	1,544	10.00	15.00	25.00	50.00
	1838MW	1,978	10.00	15.00	25.00	50.00
	1839MW	2,037	10.00	15.00	25.00	50.00
	1840MW	.306	10.00	15.00	25.00	50.00
	1841MW	1,261	10.00	15.00	25.00	50.00

5 ZLOTYCH

15.5900 g, .868 SILVER, .4351 oz ASW

C#	Date	Mintage	VG	Fine	VF	XF
100	1816 IB	.971	30.00	60.00	125.00	265.00
	1817 IB	2.585	25.00	45.00	90.00	220.00
	1818 IB	.201	30.00	65.00	135.00	285.00

NOTE: Large and small crown varieties exist.

C#	Date	Mintage	VG	Fine	VF	XF
116	1829 FH	1.234	15.00	25.00	45.00	80.00
	1830 FH	.287	22.50	32.50	55.00	100.00
	1830 KG	I.A.	22.50	32.50	55.00	100.00
	1831 KG	.023	22.50	32.50	55.00	100.00
	1832 KG	.639	15.00	25.00	45.00	80.00
	1833 KG	.445	15.00	25.00	45.00	80.00
	1834 KG	.414	22.50	32.50	60.00	120.00
	1834 IP	—	22.50	32.50	55.00	100.00

NOTE: Large and small bust varieties exist.

Obv. leg. w/retrograde 'S'

C#	Date	Mintage	VG	Fine	VF	XF
116a	1833 KG	I.A.	22.50	32.50	55.00	100.00

5 ZLOTYCH-3/4 RUBLE

15.5400 g, .868 SILVER, .4337 oz ASW

C#	Date	Mintage	VG	Fine	VF	XF
133	1833 HГ	.258	12.00	20.00	30.00	50.00
	1834 HГ	.206	12.00	20.00	30.00	50.00
	1834MW	.086	12.00	20.00	30.00	50.00
	1835 HГ	.107	12.00	20.00	30.00	50.00
	1835MW	.540	10.00	15.00	20.00	40.00
	1836 HГ	.078	12.00	20.00	30.00	50.00
	1836MW	1.196	10.00	15.00	20.00	40.00
	1837 HГ	.262	12.00	20.00	30.00	50.00
	1837MW	1.000	10.00	15.00	20.00	40.00
	1838 HГ	.012	50.00	85.00	135.00	225.00
	1838MW	1.996	10.00	15.00	20.00	40.00
	1839 HГ	—	—	—	Rare	—
	1839 HГ	—	—	—	Proof	Rare
	1839MW	2.689	10.00	15.00	20.00	40.00
	1840 HГ	2,001	—	—	Rare	—
	1840MW	2.482	10.00	15.00	20.00	40.00
	1841 HГ	—	—	—	Rare	—
	1841MW	1.274	10.00	15.00	20.00	40.00

10 ZLOTYCH

31.1000 g, .868 SILVER, .8679 oz ASW

C#	Date	Mintage	VG	Fine	VF	XF
101.1	1820 IB	534 pcs.	—	—	Rare	—
	1821 IB	1,195	150.00	250.00	400.00	550.00
	1822 IB	233 pcs.	—	—	Rare	—

C#	Date	Mintage	VG	Fine	VF	XF
101.2	1823 IB	1,124	150.00	250.00	400.00	550.00
	1824 IB	513 pcs.	400.00	1000.	2000.	3500.
	1825 IB	—	—	—	Rare	—

Obv: Laureate head.

C#	Date	Mintage	VG	Fine	VF	XF
117	1827 IB					
		123 pcs.	—	—	Rare	—
	1827 FH	I.A.	—	—	Rare	—

10 ZLOTYCH - 1-1/2 RUBLES

31.1000 g, .868 SILVER, .8679 oz ASW

134	1833 НГ	.127	20.00	30.00	60.00	100.00
	1834 НГ	.064	25.00	40.00	80.00	150.00
	1835 НГ	.262	20.00	35.00	60.00	100.00
	1835MW	3,081	40.00	80.00	120.00	200.00
	1836 НГ	.134	20.00	35.00	60.00	100.00
	1836MW	.220	20.00	35.00	60.00	100.00
	1837 НГ	.036	40.00	80.00	120.00	200.00
	1837MW	.194	20.00	35.00	60.00	100.00
	1838 НГ	13 pcs.	—	—	Rare	—
	1838MW	.010	100.00	200.00	325.00	475.00
	1839 НГ	7,006	125.00	275.00	450.00	750.00
	1839 НГ	I.A.	—	—	Proof	Rare
	1839MW	2,295	40.00	80.00	150.00	350.00
	1840 НГ	2,001	—	—	Rare	—
	1840MW	2,747	40.00	80.00	150.00	350.00
	1841 НГ	—	—	—	Rare	—
	1841MW	.037	40.00	80.00	120.00	200.00

20 ZLOTYCH-3 RUBLES

3.8900 g, .917 GOLD, .1147 oz AGW

C#	Date	Mintage	Fine	VF	XF	Unc
136.1	1834MW					
		243 pcs.	250.00	500.00	1000.	2000.
	1835MW					
		350 pcs.	250.00	500.00	1000.	2000.
	1836MW					
		307 pcs.	250.00	500.00	1000.	2000.
	1837MW					
		423 pcs.	250.00	500.00	1000.	2000.
	1838MW					
		66 pcs.	500.00	900.00	1500.	3000.
	1839MW					
		57 pcs.	500.00	900.00	1500.	3000.
	1840MW					
		—	800.00	1500.	2000.	3500.

Mintmark: St. Petersburg СПБ

C#	Date	Mintage	Fine	VF	XF	Unc
136.2	1834 ПД	.077	150.00	225.00	300.00	425.00
	1835 ПД	.052	150.00	225.00	300.00	425.00
	1836 ПД	.010	175.00	275.00	350.00	450.00
	1837 ПД	.030	150.00	225.00	300.00	425.00
	1838 ПД	.017	175.00	275.00	350.00	450.00
	1839 ПД	.011	175.00	300.00	375.00	475.00

136.3	1840 ПД	5.473	225.00	375.00	450.00	525.00
	1841 ПД	Unique	—	Proof	—	

*NOTE: Superior Pipito sale 12-87 Proof realized $12,100.

25 ZLOTYCH

4.8900 g, .917 GOLD, .1442 oz AGW

102	1817 IB	.096	175.00	350.00	475.00	700.00
	1818 IB	.055	150.00	250.00	375.00	550.00
	1819 IB	1,124	150.00	250.00	375.00	550.00

Struck in collar.

102a	1818 IB	.086	—	—	Rare	—
	1822 IB					
		479 pcs.	300.00	550.00	1000.	1500.
	1823 IB					
		612 pcs.	500.00	900.00	1500.	2000.
	1824 IB					
		636 pcs.	400.00	600.00	1200.	1800.
	1825 IB					
		134 pcs.	400.00	600.00	1200.	1800.
	1828 IB					
		385 pcs.	400.00	600.00	1200.	1800.

118	1828 FH					
		241 pcs.	500.00	900.00	1500.	2000.
	1829 FH					
		66 pcs.	600.00	1000.	1600.	2200.
	1830 FH					
		618 pcs.	500.00	900.00	1500.	2000.
	1832 KG					
		152 pcs.	500.00	900.00	1500.	2000.
	1833 KG					
		424 pcs.	500.00	900.00	1500.	2000.

50 ZLOTYCH

9.7800 g, .917 GOLD, .2884 oz AGW

103	1817 IB	.017	250.00	400.00	600.00	1000.
	1818 IB	.050	250.00	500.00	700.00	1150.
	1819 IB	.020	250.00	500.00	750.00	1250.

9.7367 g, .917 GOLD, .2871 oz AGW

103.1	1817 IB	—	—	—	Proof	—

9.7800 g, .917 GOLD, .2884 oz AGW
Obv: Small head.

C#	Date	Mintage	Fine	VF	XF	Unc
103a	1819 IB	Inc. Ab.	250.00	400.00	600.00	1000.
	1820 IB	7,098	250.00	400.00	650.00	1000.
	1821 IB	2,638	250.00	500.00	750.00	1250.
	1822 IB	1,610	250.00	500.00	750.00	1250.
	1823 IB					
		181 pcs.	450.00	800.00	1500.	2500.
	1827 IB					
		70 pcs.	650.00	1150.	1650.	2650.

119	1827 FH					
		62 pcs.	700.00	1200.	1700.	2800.
	1829 FH					
		238 pcs.	500.00	1100.	1500.	2500.

9.7367 g, .917 GOLD, .2871 oz AGW

119.1	1829 FH					
		237 pcs.	—	—	Proof	—

REVOLUTIONARY COINAGE

1830-1831

3 GROSZE

COPPER

C#	Date	Mintage	VG	Fine	VF	XF
120	1831 KG	1.112	3.50	7.50	18.00	40.00

NOTE: Varieties in eagle exist.

10 GROSZY

2.8000 g, .192 SILVER, .0173 oz ASW

121	1831 KG	6.038	5.00	10.00	20.00	50.00

NOTE: Varieties in eagle exist.

2 ZLOTE

8.9800 g, .593 SILVER, .1712 oz ASW

123	1831 KG	.171	15.00	25.00	45.00	70.00

NOTE: Varieties exist.

5 ZLOTYCH

15.4900 g, .868 SILVER, .4323 oz ASW

C#	Date	Mintage	VG	Fine	VF	XF
124	1831 KG	.023	25.00	45.00	85.00	140.00

NOTE: Varieties in fraction numerator fineness exist.

TRADE COINAGE

DUCAT

3.5000 g, .986 GOLD, .1109 oz AGW
Obv: Eagle in legend at 1 o'clock.

C#	Date	Mintage	Fine	VF	XF	Unc
125	1831	.163	125.00	200.00	300.00	500.00

PATTERNS (Pn)

(Including off metal strikes)

KM#	Date	Mintage	Identification	Mkt.Val.
Pn122	1811 IS	—	1 Grosz, Silver, C81	—
Pn123	1813 IB	—	1 Ducat, Copper	—
Pn124	1815 IB	—	1 Grosz, Copper. Obv: Wing feathers close together	—
Pn125	1815 IB	—	1 Grosz, Copper. Obv: Wing feathers spread	—
Pn126	1815 IB	—	3 Grosze, Copper, plain edge	—
Pn127	1815 IB	—	3 Groschen, Copper	—
Pn128	1815 IB	—	3 Groschen, Copper	—
Pn129	1816 IB	—	1 Grosze, Copper, plain edge	—
Pn130	1816 IB	—	3 Grose, Copper	—
Pn131	1817 IB	—	1 Groschen, Copper	—
Pn132	1817 IB	—	1 Groschen, Copper	175.00
Pn133	1817 IB	—	3 Groschen, Copper	—
Pn134	1818 IB	—	1 Groschen, Copper	—
Pn135	1818 IB	—	3 Groschen, Copper	—
Pn136	1818 IB	—	3 Groschen, Copper	—
Pn137	1818 IB	—	3 Groschen, Copper, plain rim	—
Pn138	1818 IB	—	5 Groszy, Silver	—
Pn139	1818 IB	—	1 Zlotych, Silver	—

KM#	Date	Mintage	Identification	Mkt.Val.
Pn140	1818 IB	—	2 Zlotych, Silver	—
Pn141	1818 IB	—	25 Zlotych, Gold	—
Pn142	1819 IB	—	1 Groschen, Copper	—
Pn143	1819 IB	—	3 Groschen, Copper	—
Pn144	1819 IB	—	1 Zlotych, Silver	—
Pn145	1819 IB	—	1 Zlotych, Copper	—
Pn146	1820 IB	—	1 Groschen, Copper	—
Pn147	1820 IB	—	3 Groschen, Copper	—
Pn148	1821 IB	—	1 Groschen, Copper	—
Pn149	1822 IB	—	1 Mining Groschen, Copper	—
Pn150	1823 IB	—	1 Mining Groschen, Copper	—
Pn151	1824 IB	—	1 Groschen, Copper	—
Pn152	1824 IB	—	1 Mining Groschen, Copper	—
Pn153	1824 IB	—	3 Groschen	—
Pn154	1825 IB	—	1 Mining Groschen, Copper	—
Pn155	1826 IB	—	1 Mining Groschen, Copper	—
Pn156	1826 IB	—	3 Mining Groschen, Copper	—
Pn157	1827 IB	—	3 Mining Groschen, Copper	—
Pn158	1827 FH	—	3 Mining Groschen, Copper	—
Pn159	1827 FH	—	3 Mining Groschen, Copper	—
Pn160	1827 IB	—	10 Zlotych, Silver	—
Pn161	1828 FH	—	1 Groschen, Copper	—
Pn162	1828 FH	—	3 Groschen, Copper	—
Pn163	1829 FH	—	1 Groschen, Copper	—
Pn164	1829 FH	—	3 Groschen, Copper	—
Pn165	1829 KG	—	5 Groszy, Silver	—
Pn166	1830 FH	—	1 Groschen, Copper	—
Pn167	1830 KG	—	1 Groschen, Copper	—
Pn168	1830 FH	—	3 Groschen, Copper	—
Pn169	1831 KG	—	1 Groschen, Copper	—
Pn170	1831 KG	—	3 Groschen, Copper	200.00
Pn171	1831 KG	—	5 Groszy	—
Pn172	1831 KG	—	10 Groszy, Silver	—
Pn173	1831 IC	—	10 Groszy, Copper	—
Pn174	1831 KG	—	1 Zloty	—
Pn175	1831 KG	—	2 Zloty, Silver	200.00
Pn176	1832 KG	—	1 Groschen, Copper	—
Pn177	1832 KG	—	3 Groschen, Copper	—
Pn178	1832 KG	—	5 Groszy, Silver	—
Pn179	1832 KG	—	10 Groszy, Silver, C113	—
Pn180	1833 KG	—	1 Groschen, Copper	—
Pn181	1833 KG	—	3 Groschen, Copper	—
Pn182	1833 KG	—	10 Groszy, Silver, C113	—
Pn183	1834 KG	—	1 Groschen, Copper	175.00
Pn184	1834 IP	—	1 Groschen, Copper	—
Pn185	1834 KG	—	3 Groschen, Copper	—
Pn186	1834 IP	—	3 Groschen, Copper	—
Pn187	1835 IP	—	1 Groschen, Copper	—
Pn188	1835 IP	—	3 Groschen, Copper	—
Pn189	1835	—	10 Zlotych/1-1/2 Rubles, Silver	—
Pn190	1836MW	—	1 Grosz, Copper	—
Pn191	1836MW	—	3 Grosze, Copper	—
Pn192	1836 РП	—	10 Zlotych/1-1/2 Rubles, Silver	—
Pn193	1836 ПУ	—	10 Zlotych/1-1/2 Rubles, Silver	—
Pn194	1837MW	—	1 Grosz, Copper	—
Pn195	1837MW	—	3 Grosze, Copper	—
Pn196	1838MW	—	1 Grosz, Copper	—
Pn197	1838MW	—	3 Grosze, Copper	—
Pn198	1838 НГ	—	10 Zlotych/11/2 Rubles, Silver	—
Pn199	1839MW	—	1 Grosz, Copper	—
Pn200	1839MW	—	3 Grosze, Copper	—
Pn201	1839 НГ	—	3/4 Ruble/5 Zlotych, Silver	—
Pn202	1840MW	—	1 Grosz, Copper. Rev: Large date, value in wreath	—
Pn203	1840MW	—	1 Grosz, Copper. Rev: Small date, value in wreath	—
Pn204	1840MW	—	1 Grosz, Copper. Obv: Large date and value	—
Pn205	1840MW	—	1 Grosz, Copper. Obv: Small eagle. Rev: Large date and value	—
Pn206	1840MW	—	1 Grosz, Silver	—
Pn207	1840MW	—	1 Jeden Grosz, Copper, Obv: Small eagle	—
Pn208	1840MW	—	1 Jeden Grosz, Copper Obv: Large eagle	—
Pn209	1840MW	—	3 Grosze, Copper	—
Pn210	1840MW	—	10 Groszy, Copper. Obv: Large eagle	—
Pn211	1840MW	—	10 Groszy, Silver	—
Pn212	1840MW	—	10 Groszy, Tin	—
Pn213	1840MW	—	10 Groszy, Silver	—
Pn214	1840MW	—	10 Groszy, Silver. Rev: w/o wreath	—
Pn215	1840MW	—	3 Rubles/20 Zlotych, Gold	—
Pn216	1841MW	—	1 Grosz, Copper	—
Pn217	1841MW	—	1 Jeden Groschen, Copper	—
Pn218	1841MW	—	1 Ieden Grosz, Copper. Obv. Large eagle	—
Pn219	1841MW	—	1 Ieden Grosz, Copper. Obv. Small eagle	—
Pn220	1841MW	—	3 Grosze, Copper	—
Pn221	1841MW	—	5 Groszy, Silver. Obv: Eagle	—
Pn222	1841MW	—	5 Groszy, Silver. Obv: Head	—
Pn223	1841MW	—	10 Groszy, Silver	—
Pn224	1841 НГ	—	15 Kopecks/1 Zlotych, Silver	—
Pn225	1841 НГ	—	3/4 Ruble/5 Zlotych, Silver	—
Pn226	1841 НГ	—	11/2 Rubles/10 Zlotych, Silver	—
Pn227	1840 АЧ	—	3 Rubles/20 Zlotych, Gold	—
Pn228	1842 Mw	—	5 Kopecks/10 Groszy, Silver	—
Pn229	1842MW	—	10 Kopecks/20 Groszy, Silver	—
Pn230	1846MW	—	20 Kopecks/40 Groszy, Silver	—
Pn231	1848	—	2 Zlote, Silver	—

SPECIMEN SETS (SS)

KM#	Date	Mintage	Identification	Issue Price	Mkt. Val.
SS1	1831(5)	—	C120,121,123-125, including 1 Zloty banknote	—	1500.

DANZIG

A seaport on the northern coast of Poland giving access to the Baltic Sea. An important port from early times. Has at different times belonged to the Teutonic Knights, Pomerania, Russia, and Prussia. Danzig was a free city from 1919 to 1939 during which most of its modern coinage was made.

RULERS

Friedrich Wilhelm III (of Prussia), 1797-1840
Marshal Lefebvre (as Duke), 1807-1814

MINT MARKS

A - Berlin

MINTMASTERS INITIALS

Letter	Date	Name
M	1808-12	Johann Ludwig Meyer

MONETARY SYSTEM

3 Schilling = 1 Groschen

SCHILLING

COPPER

KM#	Date	Mintage	VG	Fine	VF	XF
135	1801A	—	6.00	12.00	28.00	65.00

KM#	Date	Mintage	VG	Fine	VF	XF
136	1808 M	—	7.50	15.00	35.00	85.00
	1812 M	—	7.50	15.00	35.00	85.00

EIN (1) GROSCHEN

COPPER

KM#	Date	Mintage	VG	Fine	VF	XF
137	1809 M	—	7.50	15.00	32.00	75.00
	1812 M	—	7.50	15.00	32.00	75.00

PATTERNS (Pn)

(Including off metal strikes)

KM#	Date	Mintage	Identification	Mkt.Val.
Pn34	1808	—	1 Schilling, Copper, KM136	—
Pn35	1808	—	1 Schilling, Silver, KM136	225.00
Pn36	1808	—	1 Schilling, Gold, KM136	3500.
Pn37	1808	—	1/5 Gulden, Silver	700.00
Pn38	1809M	—	1 Groschen, Silver, KM137	275.00
Pn39	1809M	—	1/5 Gulden, Silver	500.00
Pn40	1812M	—	1 Schilling, Silver, KM136	200.00
Pn41	1812M	—	1 Groschen, Silver, KM137	275.00
Pn42	1812M	—	1 Groschen, Gold, KM137	4500.

EAST PRUSSIA

An area on the southeastern coast of the Baltic Sea. Part of the area is in present day Poland and part in the U.S.S.R. A possession of Prussia from 1525 until 1945. Coinage for the area made by the Prussian kings except for brief occupation by Russia from 1756-1762 when Russia produced special coin types for the area.

RULERS

Friedrich Wilhelm III (of Prussia)
1797-1840

MINT MARKS

A - Berlin
E - Konigsberg
G - Glatz, Silesia

NOTE: For gold listings refer to Konigsberg Mint under Brandenburg and Prussia (German States).

PRUSSIAN COINAGE

SCHILLING

COPPER

C#	Date	Mintage	VG	Fine	VF	XF
53	1804A	—	2.50	5.00	10.00	20.00
	1805A	—	2.50	5.00	10.00	20.00
	1806A	—	2.50	5.00	10.00	20.00

C#	Date	Mintage	VG	Fine	VF	XF
54	1810A	—	2.00	4.00	9.00	18.00

1/2 GROSCHEN

COPPER

C#	Date	Mintage	VG	Fine	VF	XF
56	1811A	—	5.00	10.00	20.00	35.00

GROSCHEN

COPPER

C#	Date	Mintage	VG	Fine	VF	XF
58	1810	—	2.50	5.00	10.00	20.00
	1811A	—	2.50	5.00	10.00	20.00

3 GROSCHEN

BILLON

C#	Date	Mintage	VG	Fine	VF	XF
60	1801A	—	3.50	9.00	16.00	28.00
	1802A	—	3.50	9.00	16.00	28.00
	1803A	—	3.50	9.00	16.00	28.00
	1805A	—	3.50	9.00	16.00	28.00
	1806A	—	3.50	9.00	16.00	28.00
	1807A	—	3.50	9.00	16.00	28.00

NOTE: Earlier date (1800) exists for this type.

C#	Date	Mintage	VG	Fine	VF	XF
60a	1807G	—	3.50	9.00	16.00	28.00
	1808G	—	3.50	9.00	16.00	28.00

KRAKOW

A city in southern Poland, the third largest in the country. Formed an independent republic in 1815 that lasted until 1846 at which time the city reverted to Austria. Coins made for the republic in 1835.

MONETARY SYSTEM

30 Groszy = 1 Zloty

5 GROSZY

BILLON

KM#	Date	Mintage	VG	Fine	VF	XF
11	1835	—	10.00	20.00	35.00	60.00

10 GROSZY

SILVER

KM#	Date	Mintage	VG	Fine	VF	XF
12	1835	—	10.00	20.00	35.00	60.00

ZLOTY

SILVER

KM#	Date	Mintage	VG	Fine	VF	XF
13	1835	—	15.00	30.00	50.00	90.00

PATTERNS (Pn)

(Including off metal strikes)

KM#	Date	Mintage	Identification	Mkt.Val.
Pn1	1835	—	3 Groszy, Copper. Rev: Value and date in wreath	500.00
Pn2	1835	—	3 Groszy, Copper. Rev: Value and date	—
Pn3	1835	—	2 Zlote, Silver	—
Pn4	1835	—	2 Zlote, Lead	—

POSEN

A province of Prussia from 1793-1918. Became part of the Grand Duchy of Warsaw. Returned to Prussia after the Congress of Vienna (1815). A special coin issue was made as a provincial issue for the Grand Duchy of Posen by Prussia immediately after repossession.

RULERS

Friedrich Wilhelm III (of Prussia), 1797-1840

MINT MARKS

A - Berlin
B - Breslau

GROSCHEN

COPPER

KM#	Date	Mintage	VG	Fine	VF	XF
30	1816A	—	5.00	10.00	20.00	45.00
	1816B	—	5.00	10.00	20.00	45.00
	1817A	—	5.00	10.00	20.00	45.00

3 GROSCHEN

COPPER

KM#	Date	Mintage	VG	Fine	VF	XF
31	1816A	—	—	—	Rare	—
	1816B	—	7.00	15.00	30.00	65.00
	1817A	—	7.00	15.00	32.00	75.00

ZAMOSC

A Fortress commune in south-eastern Poland twice besieged by Russians.

MONETARY SYSTEM

30 Groszy = 1 Zloty

SIEGE COINAGE

Issued by the Saxon-Polish garrison under General Hauke.

MINT MARK

(b) - flaming bomb

6 GROSZY

COPPER

KM#	Date	Mintage	VG	Fine	VF	XF
1	1813	1,330	150.00	275.00	500.00	800.00

Rev: W/o outer leg.

KM#	Date	Mintage	VG	Fine	VF	XF
2	1813	Inc. Ab.	200.00	350.00	600.00	1000.

Rev: W/o palm fronds.

KM#	Date	Mintage	VG	Fine	VF	XF
3	1813	Inc. Ab.	—	—	Rare	—

2 ZLOTY

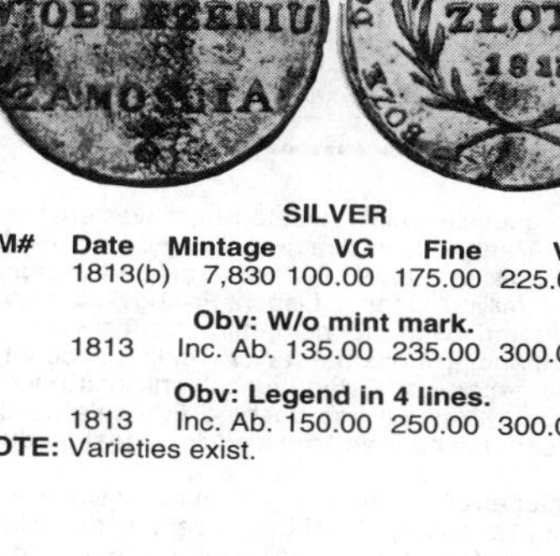

SILVER

KM#	Date	Mintage	VG	Fine	VF	XF
5	1813(b)	7,830	100.00	175.00	225.00	375.00

Obv: W/o mint mark.

KM#	Date	Mintage	VG	Fine	VF	XF
6	1813	Inc. Ab.	135.00	235.00	300.00	500.00

Obv: Legend in 4 lines.

KM#	Date	Mintage	VG	Fine	VF	XF
7	1813	Inc. Ab.	150.00	250.00	300.00	500.00

NOTE: Varieties exist.

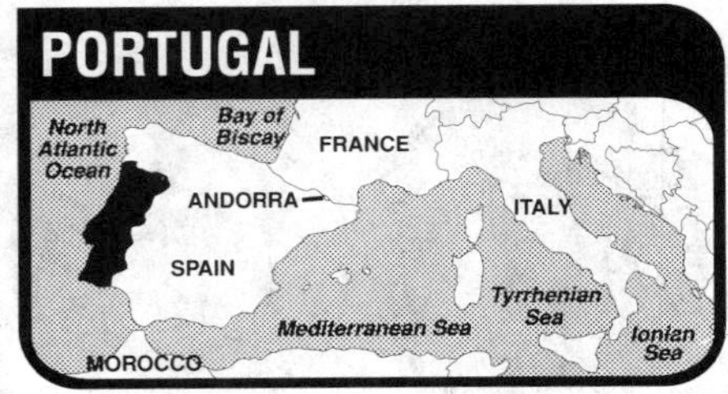

The Portuguese Republic, located in the western part of the Iberian Peninsula in southwestern Europe, has an area of 35,553 sq. mi. (92,080 sq. km.) and a population of *10.5 million. Capital: Lisbon. Portugal's economy is based on agriculture, tourism, minerals, fisheries and a rapidly expanding industrial sector. Textiles account for 33% of the exports and Portuguese wine has become world famous. Portugal has become Europe's number one producer of copper and the world's largest producer of cork.

After centuries of domination by Romans, Visigoths and Moors, Portugal emerged in the 12th century as an independent kingdom financially and philosophically prepared for the great period of exploration that would follow. Attuned to the inspiration of Prince Henry the Navigator (1394-1460), Portugal's daring explorers of the 15th and 16th centuries roamed the world's oceans from Brazil to Japan in an unprecedented burst of energy and endeavor that culminated in 1494 with Portugal laying claim to half the transoceanic world. Unfortunately for the fortunes of the tiny kingdom, the Portuguese population was too small to colonize this vast territory. Less than a century after Portugal laid claim to half the world, English, French and Dutch trading companies had seized the lion's share of the world's colonies and commerce, and Portugal's place as an imperial power was lost forever. The monarchy was overthrown in 1910 and a republic established.

On April 25, 1974, the government of Portugal was seized by a military junta which reached agreements providing for independence for the Portuguese overseas provinces of Portuguese Guinea (Guinea-Bissau), Mozambique, Cape Verde Islands, Angola, and St. Thomas and Prince Islands (Sao Tome and Principe).

On January 1, 1986, Portugal became the eleventh member of the European Economic Community and in the first half of 1992 held its first EEC Presidency.

RULERS

Joao, As Prince Regent, 1799-1816
Joao, As King (Joao VI), 1816-1826
Pedro IV, 1826-1828
Miguel, 1828-1834
Maria II, 1834-1853
Pedro V, 1853-1861
Luiz I, 1861-1889
Carlos I, 1889-1908

MINT MARKS

A - Paris (1891-1892, Copper only)
E - Evora
L - Lisbon
P - Porto
No Mint mark - Lisbon

MONETARY SYSTEM

Until 1825

20 Reis = 1 Vintem
100 Reis = 1 Tostao
480 Reis = 24 Vintens = 1 Cruzado
1600 Reis = 1 Escudo
6400 Reis = 4 Escudos = 1 Peca

1826-1836

7500 Reis = 1 Peca

Beginning in 1836 all coins were expressed in terms of Reis and arranged in a decimal sequence (until 1910).

NOTE: The primary denomination was the Peca, weighing 14.34 g, tariffed at 6400 Reis until 1825, and at 7500 Reis after 1826. The weight was not changed.

MILLED COINAGE

III (3) REIS

COPPER

Obv: JOANNES. . ., around shield. Rev: Leg. around wreath, date and denomination within.

KM#	Date	Mintage	VG	Fine	VF	XF
334	1804	.123	4.50	9.00	20.00	50.00

Obv: Crowned arms.
Rev: Value and date in branches.

KM#	Date	Mintage	VG	Fine	VF	XF
354	1818	—	20.00	40.00	80.00	175.00

V (5) REIS

COPPER

Obv. leg: JOANNES. . ., arms.
Rev. leg. ends: . . . PRINCEPS.

KM#	Date	Mintage	VG	Fine	VF	XF
325	1801	—	25.00	45.00	90.00	200.00

NOTE: Earlier date (1800) exists for this type.

Rev. leg. ends: REGENS.

KM#	Date	Mintage	VG	Fine	VF	XF
335	1804	—	Reported, not confirmed			

KM#	Date	Mintage	VG	Fine	VF	XF
346	1812	.399	1.50	2.50	7.00	15.00
	1813	.539	2.00	3.50	8.00	16.00
	1814	.448	2.25	4.50	10.00	28.00

Mule. Obv: KM#305. Rev: KM#346.

KM#	Date	Mintage	VG	Fine	VF	XF
347	1812	—	6.00	12.00	25.00	50.00

Obv: Arms, JOANNES VI.
Rev: PORTUGALIAE. . . REX, value in wreath.

KM#	Date	Mintage	VG	Fine	VF	XF
355	1818	—	50.00	110.00	225.00	450.00
	1819	.011	4.00	8.00	17.50	40.00
	1820	—	3.50	7.00	15.00	35.00
	1823	.032	4.00	8.00	17.50	40.00
	1824	.098	2.00	4.00	8.00	20.00

Obv. leg: MICHAEL I DEI GRATIA, crowned arms.
Rev: Leg. around wreath, value within, date below.

KM#	Date	Mintage	VG	Fine	VF	XF
389	1829	.401	1.50	3.00	6.00	18.00

NOTE: For similar coins dated 1830 but w/titles of Maria II, see Azores/Terceira Islands.

Titles of Maria II
Obv: Square shield.

KM#	Date	Mintage	VG	Fine	VF	XF
398	1833	—	65.00	125.00	250.00	400.00

(Struck at Porto.)

KM#	Date	Mintage	VG	Fine	VF	XF
408	1836	5,593	15.00	25.00	40.00	80.00

X (10) REIS

COPPER

Obv. leg: JOANNES. . ., arms.
Rev. leg. ends: . . . PRINCEPS.

KM#	Date	Mintage	VG	Fine	VF	XF
327	1801	—	—	—	Rare	—

NOTE: Earlier date (1800) exists for this type.

Rev. leg. ends: REGENS.

KM#	Date	Mintage	VG	Fine	VF	XF
333	1803	—	— Reported, not confirmed			

KM#	Date	Mintage	VG	Fine	VF	XF
348	1812	.332	2.00	4.00	12.00	28.00
	1813	.276	2.00	4.00	12.00	28.00

Obv. leg: JOANNES VI. . ., arms.
Rev. leg: PORTUGALIAE. . . REX, value in wreath.

KM#	Date	Mintage	VG	Fine	VF	XF
356	1818	—	20.00	40.00	80.00	150.00
	1819	.806	2.00	4.00	12.00	25.00
	1820	6,773	10.00	22.50	45.00	90.00
	1822	.021	10.00	20.00	40.00	80.00
	1823	.044	3.00	6.00	18.00	35.00
	1824	.064	3.00	5.00	15.00	30.00
	1825	—	Reported, not confirmed			

Obv. leg: MICHAEL I DEI GRATIA. . .

KM#	Date	Mintage	VG	Fine	VF	XF
390	1829	.056	2.00	3.50	6.00	15.00
(C89)	1831	.345	1.00	4.25	10.00	25.00
	1833	.070	5.50	11.50	22.50	45.00

NOTE: For similar coins dated 1830 but with titles of Maria II see Azores/Terceira Islands.

Similar to 5 Reis, KM#408.

KM#	Date	Mintage	VG	Fine	VF	XF
399	1833	—	50.00	100.00	175.00	300.00

(Struck at Porto.)

Obv: Large crowned shield.

KM#	Date	Mintage	VG	Fine	VF	XF
406	1835	.287	2.50	6.00	12.00	25.00
	1836	.227	2.00	4.00	9.00	18.00
	1837	.360	6.00	10.00	17.50	35.00

Obv: Small crowned shield.

KM#	Date	Mintage	VG	Fine	VF	XF
409	1837	Inc. Ab.	2.25	4.50	10.00	20.00
	1838	.645	2.00	3.50	7.50	16.00
	1839	.469	2.00	3.50	7.50	16.00

20 REIS

(Vintem)

COPPER, 34mm

Obv. leg: JOANNES. . ., arms. Rev. leg: PORTUGALIAE. . ., date, value within wreath.

KM#	Date	Mintage	VG	Fine	VF	XF
328	1801	—	Reported, not confirmed			

NOTE: Earlier date (1800) exists for this type.

SILVER

Obv: Globe. Rev: Cross w/rosettes in angles.

KM#	Date	Mintage	VG	Fine	VF	XF
330	ND(1799-1816)		2.50	5.00	10.00	25.00

BRONZE

Titles of Maria II

KM#	Date	Mintage	VG	Fine	VF	XF
400	1833	—	35.00	60.00	100.00	225.00

(Struck at Porto.)

40 REIS

(Pataco)

BRONZE
Plain edge

KM#	Date	Mintage	VG	Fine	VF	XF
345.1	1811	.163	6.25	12.50	20.00	50.00
	1812	1.384	4.00	8.00	16.00	45.00
	1813	1.762	3.00	6.00	12.00	40.00
	1814	.542	3.00	6.00	12.00	40.00
	1815	.118	12.00	25.00	45.00	90.00
	1817	—	Reported, not confirmed			

NOTE: There are 5 additional edge varieties of 1811 date which are found listed in the pattern section.

Milled edge

KM#	Date	Mintage	VG	Fine	VF	XF
345.2	1814	Inc. Ab.	10.00	20.00	45.00	90.00
365	1819	.422	4.00	8.00	16.00	40.00

KM#	Date	Mintage	VG	Fine	VF	XF
370	1820	1.579	3.00	5.00	12.00	38.00
	1821	1.575	3.00	5.00	12.00	38.00
	1822	2.370	3.00	5.00	12.00	38.00
	1823	2.621	3.00	5.00	12.00	38.00
	1824	3.051	3.00	5.00	12.00	38.00
	1825	1.124	3.00	6.00	14.00	40.00

Similar to KM#345.1.

KM#	Date	Mintage	VG	Fine	VF	XF
371	1821	—	50.00	90.00	200.00	450.00
	1823	—	50.00	90.00	200.00	450.00

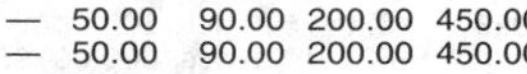

Rev: Similar to KM#345.1.

KM#	Date	Mintage	VG	Fine	VF	XF
373	1826	1.253	5.00	10.00	20.00	60.00
	1827	1.447	4.00	8.00	18.00	55.00
	1828	1.378	4.00	8.00	18.00	55.00

Obv: Large high crown.

KM#	Date	Mintage	VG	Fine	VF	XF
380	1828	1.378	6.00	12.00	22.00	65.00
	1829	1.678	5.00	10.00	20.00	60.00

Obv: Small lower crown.

KM#	Date	Mintage	VG	Fine	VF	XF
391	1829	Inc. KM380	3.00	5.00	10.00	35.00
	1830	1.783	3.00	5.00	10.00	35.00
	1831	1.391	3.00	5.00	10.00	35.00
	1832	1.780	3.00	5.00	10.00	35.00
	1833	1.631	3.00	5.00	10.00	35.00
	1834	—	Reported, not confirmed			

Titles of Maria II
Similar to 20 Reis, KM#400, shield flared outward at upper corners, value in wreath.

KM#	Date	Mintage	VG	Fine	VF	XF
401	1833	—	6.25	12.50	25.00	70.00

(Struck at Porto.)

Shield w/right-angle upper corners.

KM#	Date	Mintage	VG	Fine	VF	XF
402	1833	—	3.00	6.50	12.50	45.00
	1834	—	3.00	6.50	12.50	45.00
	1847	—	3.50	7.50	17.50	50.00

The 1833-34 coins were struck at Lisbon, the 1847 at Porto. Varieties of the 1833 and 1834 coins have a vertical axis instead of horizontal. Values are 1833 $50.00 in XF, 1834 $60.00 in XF.

50 REIS

(1/2 Tostao)

SILVER
Obv. leg: JOANNES. . . ET ALG. . .
Rev. leg: IN HOC . . ., cross.

KM#	Date	Mintage	VG	Fine	VF	XF
310	ND(1799-1816)	—	10.00	25.00	55.00	150.00

SILVER
Obv. leg. ends: . . . P. REGENS.

KM#	Date	Mintage	VG	Fine	VF	XF
311	ND(1799-1816)	—	10.00	25.00	55.00	150.00

 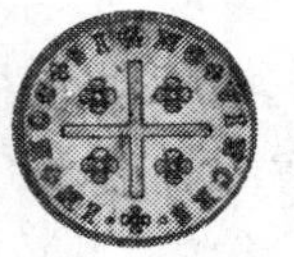

KM#	Date	Mintage	VG	Fine	VF	XF
350	ND(1799-1816)	.010	8.00	17.50	45.00	100.00

Obv. leg: MICHAEL I. . . REX, crowned value.
Rev. leg: IN HOC. . ., cross.

KM#	Date	Mintage	VG	Fine	VF	XF
381	ND(1828-34)	—	12.00	25.00	50.00	135.00

60 REIS

(3 Vintens)

SILVER, 1.83 g
Obv. leg: JOANNES. . . ET ALG., arms.
Rev. leg: IN HOC. . ., cross.

KM#	Date	Mintage	VG	Fine	VF	XF
312	ND(1799-1816)	—	3.00	5.00	12.00	35.00

SILVER, 1.83 g
Obv. leg. ends: . . . P. REGENS.

KM#	Date	Mintage	VG	Fine	VF	XF
313	ND(1799-1816)	—	2.50	4.50	10.00	28.00

Obv: Crowned arms above globe.

KM#	Date	Mintage	VG	Fine	VF	XF
351	ND(1799-1816)	—	3.50	6.50	15.00	45.00

Obv. leg: PETRUS IV. . . REX, arms.

KM#	Date	Mintage	VG	Fine	VF	XF
374	ND(1816-26)	.036	85.00	175.00	385.00	925.00

Obv. leg: MICHAEL I. . ., crowned arms.

KM#	Date	Mintage	VG	Fine	VF	XF
382	ND(1828-34)	—	3.50	6.50	15.00	45.00

LXXX (80) REIS

Tostao

NOTE: Worth 100 Reis, though marked LXXX = 80 Reis.

SILVER
Mint: Lisbon
Obv. leg: JOANNES. . . ET. ALG.
Rev. leg: IN HOC. . ., cross.

KM#	Date	Mintage	VG	Fine	VF	XF
314	ND(1799-1816)	—	5.00	10.00	25.00	65.00

Obv. leg. ends: . . . P. REGENS

KM#	Date	Mintage	VG	Fine	VF	XF
315	ND(1799-1816)	—	4.50	8.00	20.00	55.00

KM#	Date	Mintage	VG	Fine	VF	XF
352	ND(1799-1816)	—	5.00	10.00	22.50	60.00

Obv. leg: PETRUS IV. . . REX, crowned value.

KM#	Date	Mintage	VG	Fine	VF	XF
375	ND(1816-26)	9,986	300.00	600.00	1250.	3000.

Obv. leg: MICHAEL I. . ., crowned value, large high crown.

KM#	Date	Mintage	VG	Fine	VF	XF
383	ND(1828-34)	—	15.00	25.00	50.00	115.00

Obv: Small lower crown.

KM#	Date	Mintage	VG	Fine	VF	XF
384	ND(1828-34)	—	300.00	600.00	1000.	1650.

120 REIS

(6 Vintens)

SILVER
Mint: Lisbon
Obv. leg: JOANNES. . . ET ALG, arms.
Rev. leg: IN HOC. . ., cross.

KM#	Date	Mintage	VG	Fine	VF	XF
316	ND(1799-1816)	—	6.00	12.00	30.00	85.00

Obv. leg. ends: . . . P. REGENS.

KM#	Date	Mintage	VG	Fine	VF	XF
317	ND(1799-1816)	—	4.50	8.00	20.00	55.00

KM#	Date	Mintage	VG	Fine	VF	XF
353	ND(1799-1816)	—	6.50	12.00	30.00	85.00

Obv. leg: PETRUS IV. . . REX, crowned arms.

KM#	Date	Mintage	VG	Fine	VF	XF
376	ND(1816-26)	.018	175.00	350.00	800.00	2000.

Obv. leg: MICHAEL I. . ., crowned arms.

KM#	Date	Mintage	VG	Fine	VF	XF
385	ND(1828-34)	—	5.00	10.00	20.00	55.00

200 REIS

SILVER
Mint: Porto
Obv. leg: JOANNES. . . P. REGENS., arms.

KM#	Date	Mintage	VG	Fine	VF	XF
340	1806	—	60.00	100.00	170.00	325.00
	1807	—	—	—	Rare	—
	1808	—	20.00	35.00	60.00	125.00
	1809	.022	35.00	60.00	100.00	200.00
	1816	—	50.00	90.00	150.00	300.00

KM#	Date	Mintage	VG	Fine	VF	XF
357	1818	.021	30.00	60.00	120.00	225.00
	1819	.024	30.00	65.00	135.00	250.00
	1820	2,818	30.00	60.00	125.00	225.00
	1821	2,293	80.00	175.00	350.00	650.00
	1822	6,483	40.00	85.00	175.00	325.00

Obv. leg: MICHAEL I. . ., crowned arms.

KM#	Date	Mintage	VG	Fine	VF	XF
392	1829	3,584	17.50	30.00	50.00	100.00
	1830	6,594	22.50	40.00	65.00	125.00

400 REIS

SILVER
Obv. leg. ends: . . . ET. ALG.
Rev: Similar to KM#331.

KM#	Date	Mintage	VG	Fine	VF	XF
318	1801	.196	50.00	90.00	150.00	350.00
	1802	—	—	—	Rare	—

NOTE: Earlier dates (1799-1800) exist for this type.

Obv. leg. ends: P.REGENS

KM#	Date	Mintage	VG	Fine	VF	XF
331	1802	—	25.00	40.00	65.00	140.00
	1805	—	15.00	25.00	40.00	90.00
	1807	—	9.00	15.00	25.00	60.00
	1808	—	9.00	15.00	25.00	60.00
	1809	—	9.00	15.00	25.00	60.00
	1810	—	9.00	15.00	25.00	60.00
	1811	—	9.00	17.50	30.00	70.00
	1812	—	9.00	15.00	25.00	60.00
	1813	—	9.00	15.00	25.00	60.00
	1814	—	8.00	12.50	20.00	60.00

KM#	Date	Mintage	VG	Fine	VF	XF
331	1815	—	8.00	12.50	20.00	60.00
	1816	—	8.00	12.50	20.00	60.00
	1816 VINECS (error for VINCES)	—	50.00	100.00	175.00	375.00

1.0720 g, .917 GOLD, .0316 oz AGW
Obv. leg: JOANNES P.R. in crowned wreath.

KM#	Date	Mintage	VG	Fine	VF	XF
341	1807	8,857	65.00	125.00	225.00	375.00

SILVER

KM#	Date	Mintage	VG	Fine	VF	XF
358	1818	2.337	9.00	15.00	30.00	65.00
	1819	1.432	9.00	15.00	30.00	65.00
	1820	1.845	9.00	15.00	30.00	65.00
	1821	1.937	9.00	15.00	30.00	65.00
	1822	.568	10.00	20.00	40.00	90.00
	1823	.667	15.00	30.00	60.00	135.00
	1825	.028	60.00	120.00	250.00	500.00

1.0720 g, .917 GOLD, .0316 oz AGW
Obv. leg: JOAN VI in crowned wreath.

KM#	Date	Mintage	VG	Fine	VF	XF
359	1818	4,401	85.00	150.00	200.00	325.00
	1819	1,387	100.00	175.00	250.00	400.00
	1820	200 pcs.	250.00	350.00	550.00	825.00
	1821	266 pcs.	200.00	300.00	450.00	675.00

SILVER
Obv. leg: PETRUS IV. . . REX., arms.

KM#	Date	Mintage	VG	Fine	VF	XF
377	1826	.259	32.50	55.00	90.00	175.00
	1827	—	None known to have survived			

.906 SILVER
Similar to KM#331.

KM#	Date	Mintage	VG	Fine	VF	XF
386	1828	.135	50.00	90.00	150.00	300.00
	1829	.022	250.00	500.00	1000.	2000.
	1830	.029	40.00	65.00	115.00	225.00
	1831	.065	35.00	60.00	100.00	200.00
	1832	.108	35.00	60.00	100.00	200.00
	1833	.708	35.00	60.00	100.00	200.00
	1834	.705	—	—	Rare	—

Obv. leg: *MARIA II. . . REGINA*, arms.

KM#	Date	Mintage	VG	Fine	VF	XF
403.1	1833	—	500.00	1000.	1750.	3000.

(Struck in Porto.)

Obv. leg: Stars removed (Lisbon issues).

KM#	Date	Mintage	VG	Fine	VF	XF
403.2	1833	.798	10.00	17.50	30.00	75.00
	1834	1.864	9.00	15.00	25.00	50.00
	1835	3.433	9.00	15.00	25.00	45.00
	1836	.829	9.00	15.00	25.00	55.00
	1837	.194	100.00	200.00	350.00	650.00

1000 REIS

(Quartinho)

(1200 Reis)

2.6800 g, .917 GOLD, .0790 oz AGW

KM#	Date	Mintage	VG	Fine	VF	XF
360	1818	3,144	125.00	250.00	375.00	600.00
	1819	1,247	150.00	300.00	475.00	700.00
	1820	270 pcs.	250.00	425.00	600.00	1000.
	1821	275 pcs.	250.00	425.00	600.00	1000.

1/2 ESCUDO

(800 Reis)

1.7920 g, .917 GOLD, .0528 oz AGW
Obv. leg: JOANNES D.G. PORT. ET ALG. P. REGENS.

KM#	Date	Mintage	VG	Fine	VF	XF
337	1805	3,278	75.00	150.00	275.00	450.00
	1806	—	100.00	200.00	375.00	600.00
	1807	5,253	75.00	150.00	275.00	450.00

Obv. leg: JOANNES VI D.G. PORT. . .

KM#	Date	Mintage	VG	Fine	VF	XF
361	1818	270 pcs.	200.00	350.00	500.00	1000.
	1819	5,536	100.00	250.00	400.00	600.00
	1820	82 pcs.	—	—	Rare	—
	1821	286 pcs.	200.00	350.00	500.00	1000.

ESCUDO

(1600 Reis)

3.5850 g, .917 GOLD, .1057 oz AGW
Obv. leg: JOANNES D.G. PORT ET ALG. P. REGENS.

KM#	Date	Mintage	VG	Fine	VF	XF
338	1805	—	—	—	Rare	—
	1807	800 pcs.	200.00	450.00	750.00	1200.

Obv. leg: JOANNES VI D.G. PORT. . . REX, bust.

KM#	Date	Mintage	VG	Fine	VF	XF
362	1818	1,804	200.00	350.00	550.00	850.00
	1819	1,523	200.00	350.00	550.00	850.00
	1821	270 pcs.	300.00	500.00	700.00	1000.

1/2 PECA

(3200 Reis)

Revalued to 3750 Reis in 1826.

7.1500 g, .917 GOLD, .2107 oz AGW
Obv. leg: JOANNES D.G. PORT ET ALG. P. REGENS, bust.

KM#	Date	Mintage	VG	Fine	VF	XF
339	1805	74 pcs.	—	—	Rare	—

KM#	Date	Mintage	VG	Fine	VF	XF
342	1807	483 pcs.	250.00	400.00	600.00	1000.

KM#	Date	Mintage	VG	Fine	VF	XF
363	1818	100 pcs.	300.00	500.00	750.00	1200.
	1819	1,700	200.00	350.00	500.00	1000.
	1820	242 pcs.	—	—	Rare	—
	1821	196 pcs.	—	—	Rare	—
	1822	.014	150.00	250.00	375.00	600.00
	1823	—	—	—	Rare	—

KM#	Date	Mintage	VG	Fine	VF	XF
379	1827	1,713	300.00	500.00	750.00	1200.

KM#	Date	Mintage	VG	Fine	VF	XF
387	1828	242 pcs.	450.00	750.00	1250.	2000.

KM#	Date	Mintage	VG	Fine	VF	XF
396	1830	525 pcs.	500.00	800.00	1250.	2500.
	1831	225 pcs.	600.00	900.00	1500.	3000.

PECA

(6400 Reis)

Revalued to 7500 Reis in 1826.

14.3420 g, .917 GOLD, .4228 oz AGW

KM#	Date	Mintage	VG	Fine	VF	XF
332	1802	.030	500.00	1000.	1500.	2250.

KM#	Date	Mintage	VG	Fine	VF	XF
336	1804	476 pcs.	500.00	1000.	2000.	4000.
	1805	.027	225.00	375.00	550.00	900.00
	1806	.041	225.00	350.00	500.00	750.00
	1807	.036	250.00	425.00	750.00	1100.
	1808	.027	250.00	425.00	750.00	1100.
	1809	.013	250.00	425.00	750.00	1100.
	1812	.025	250.00	425.00	750.00	1100.
	1813	5,590	275.00	500.00	900.00	1400.
	1814	21 pcs.	—	—	Rare	—
	1815	305 pcs.	500.00	1000.	2000.	4000.
	1816	—	—	—	Rare	—
	1817	620 pcs.	Reported, not confirmed			

NOTE: Similar pieces with "R" after date were struck in Rio de Janeiro and are found listed under Brazil.

KM#	Date	Mintage	VG	Fine	VF	XF
364	1818	291 pcs.	400.00	800.00	1250.	2000.
	1819	1,727	250.00	500.00	750.00	1400.
	1820	1,687	225.00	450.00	650.00	1200.
	1821	391 pcs.	400.00	800.00	1250.	2000.

KM#	Date	Mintage	VG	Fine	VF	XF
364	1822	.030	225.00	300.00	425.00	600.00
	1823	.027	225.00	300.00	425.00	600.00
	1824	1,553	300.00	400.00	500.00	600.00

NOTE: Similar pieces with "R" after date were struck in Rio de Janeiro and are listed under Brazil.

KM#	Date	Mintage	VG	Fine	VF	XF
378	1826	10,883	350.00	650.00	1100.	1800.
	1828	1,255	500.00	1000.	1500.	2500.

NOTE: Similar pieces dated 1826 with square shield on reverse are patterns.

KM#	Date	Mintage	VG	Fine	VF	XF
388	1828	Inc. KM378	500.00	1000.	1500.	2750.

Modified design

KM#	Date	Mintage	VG	Fine	VF	XF
397	1830	2,274	300.00	600.00	900.00	1500.
	1831	1,618	400.00	800.00	1250.	2000.

Obv: Bare head of queen.

KM#	Date	Mintage	VG	Fine	VF	XF
404	1833	1,265	600.00	1250.	2500.	5000.

KM#	Date	Mintage	VG	Fine	VF	XF
405	1833	—	500.00	1000.	1500.	2750.
	1834	.032	250.00	450.00	700.00	1000.

Obv. leg. continuous.

KM#	Date	Mintage	VG	Fine	VF	XF
407	1835	2,989	350.00	600.00	850.00	1400.

COUNTERMARKED COINAGE

40 REIS

COPPER

c/m: GCP in a circle on 40 Reis, KM#402.

C#	Date	Mintage	Good	VG	Fine	VF
415.1	1833	—	5.00	15.00	30.00	65.00
	1847	.218	3.00	7.00	15.00	35.00

c/m: Dot added below GCP on 40 Reis, KM#402.

C#	Date	Mintage	Good	VG	Fine	VF
415.2	1847	Inc. Ab.	4.00	10.00	20.00	45.00

(870 REIS)

In 1834, the Portuguese government ordered that the countermarking of all Spanish and Spanish colonial 8 Reales in circulation with the crowned arms of Portugal, to indicate a revaluation to 870 Reis.

SILVER

c/m: On Bolivia (Potosi) 8 Reales, KM#55.

KM#	Date	Year	Good	VG	Fine	VF
440.1	ND	(1773-89)	50.00	100.00	150.00	200.00

c/m: On Bolivia (Potosi) 8 Reales, KM#74.

KM#	Date	Year	Good	VG	Fine	VF
440.2	ND	(1789-91)	60.00	125.00	175.00	250.00

c/m: On Bolivia (Potosi) 8 Reales, KM#73.

KM#	Date	Year	Good	VG	Fine	VF
440.3	ND	(1791-1808)	40.00	75.00	110.00	150.00

c/m: On Bolivia (Potosi) 8 Reales, KM#84.

KM#	Date	Year	Good	VG	Fine	VF
404.4	ND	(1808-25)	35.00	70.00	100.00	135.00

c/m: On Brazil 960 Reis, KM#326.

KM#	Date	Year	Good	VG	Fine	VF
440.5	ND	(1818-22)	65.00	125.00	200.00	250.00

c/m: On Chile (Santiago) 8 Reales, KM#51.

KM#	Date	Year	Good	VG	Fine	VF
440.6	ND	(1791-1808)	125.00	225.00	350.00	500.00

c/m: On Guatemala 8 Reales, KM#69.

KM#	Date	Year	Good	VG	Fine	VF
440.7	ND	(1808-22)	125.00	200.00	250.00	400.00

c/m: On Mexico 8 Reales, KM#103.

KM#	Date	Year	Good	VG	Fine	VF
440.8	ND	(1732-47)	100.00	175.00	225.00	300.00

c/m: On Mexico 8 Reales, KM#104.

KM#	Date	Year	Good	VG	Fine	VF
440.9	ND	(1747-60)	80.00	135.00	200.00	300.00

c/m: On Mexico 8 Reales, KM#105.

KM#	Date	Year	Good	VG	Fine	VF
440.10	ND	(1760-72)	100.00	150.00	200.00	350.00

c/m: On Mexico 8 Reales, KM#106.

KM#	Date	Year	Good	VG	Fine	VF
440.11	ND	(1772-89)	25.00	50.00	75.00	100.00

c/m: On Mexico 8 Reales, KM#107.

KM#	Date	Year	Good	VG	Fine	VF
440.12	ND	(1789-90)	35.00	65.00	85.00	125.00

c/m: On Mexico 8 Reales, KM#109.

KM#	Date	Year	Good	VG	Fine	VF
440.13	ND	(1791-1808)	25.00	50.00	75.00	100.00

c/m: On Mexico 8 Reales, KM#110.

KM#	Date	Year	Good	VG	Fine	VF
440.14	ND	(1808-11)	25.00	50.00	75.00	100.00

c/m: On Mexico 8 Reales, KM#111.

KM#	Date	Year	Good	VG	Fine	VF
440.15	ND	(1811-21)	25.00	50.00	75.00	100.00

c/m: On Mexico (Durango) 8 Reales, KM#111.2.

KM#	Date	Year	Good	VG	Fine	VF
440.16	ND	(1812-22)	125.00	225.00	350.00	500.00

c/m: On Mexico (Guadalajara) 8 Reales, KM#111.3.

KM#	Date	Year	Good	VG	Fine	VF
440.17	ND	(1812-22)	60.00	125.00	150.00	250.00

c/m: On Mexico (Guanajuato) 8 Reales, KM#111.4.

KM#	Date	Year	Good	VG	Fine	VF
440.18	ND	(1812-22)	60.00	125.00	150.00	250.00

c/m: On Mexico (Zacatecas) 8 Reales, KM#111.5.

KM#	Date	Year	Good	VG	Fine	VF
440.19	ND	(1813-22)	35.00	75.00	100.00	150.00

c/m: On Peru (Lima) 8 Reales, KM#87.

KM#	Date	Year	Good	VG	Fine	VF
440.20	ND	(1789-91)	40.00	75.00	100.00	150.00

c/m: On Peru (Lima) 8 Reales, KM#97.

KM#	Date	Year	Good	VG	Fine	VF
440.21	ND	(1791-1808)	35.00	65.00	95.00	125.00

c/m: On Peru (Lima) 8 Reales, KM#106.

KM#	Date	Year	Good	VG	Fine	VF
440.22	ND	(1808-11)	35.00	65.00	95.00	125.00

c/m: On Peru (Lima) 8 Reales, KM#117.

KM#	Date	Year	Good	VG	Fine	VF
440.33	ND	(1810-24)	30.00	60.00	90.00	125.00

c/m: On Spain (Cadiz) 8 Reales, C#136.

KM#	Date	Year	Good	VG	Fine	VF
440.34	ND	(1810-15)	60.00	100.00	150.00	250.00

c/m: On Spain (Madrid) 8 Reales, C#71.

KM#	Date	Year	Good	VG	Fine	VF
440.35	ND	(1789-1808)	65.00	125.00	175.00	275.00

c/m: On Spain (Madrid) 20 Reales, C#92.

KM#	Date	Year	Good	VG	Fine	VF
440.36	ND	(1808-13)	65.00	125.00	175.00	275.00

c/m: On Spain (Madrid) 8 Reales, C#136.

KM#	Date	Year	Good	VG	Fine	VF
440.37	ND	(1812-33)	35.00	65.00	95.00	125.00

c/m: On Spain (Seville) 8 Reales, C#40.

KM#	Date	Year	Good	VG	Fine	VF
440.38	ND	(1772-88)	125.00	250.00	350.00	500.00

c/m: On Spain (Seville) 8 Reales, C#71.

KM#	Date	Year	Good	VG	Fine	VF
440.39	ND	(1788-1808)	85.00	150.00	225.00	300.00

c/m: On Spain (Seville) 8 Reales, C#136.

KM#	Date	Year	Good	VG	Fine	VF
440.40	ND	(1809-30)	45.00	75.00	110.00	150.00

c/m: On Spain (Valencia) 8 Reales, C#136a.

KM#	Date	Year	Good	VG	Fine	VF
440.41	ND	(1809-11)	125.00	175.00	250.00	500.00

c/m: On Mozambique "8 Reales" KM#28.

KM#	Date	Year	Good	VG	Fine	VF
440.42	ND	(1834)	100.00	175.00	250.00	375.00

(30,000 REIS)

In 1847, the crowned arms countermark was applied to the Dobrao of John V. Value was raised 50%.

GOLD

c/m: Crowned arms on Brazil 20,000 Reis, KM#117.

KM#	Date	Year	Good	VG	Fine	VF
499 (467)	ND(1847)	1724-27	1500.	2500.	4000.	5500.

DECIMAL COINAGE

New denominations, all expressed in terms of Reis, were introduced by Maria II in 1836, to bring Portugal's currency into decimal form. Some of the coins retained old names, as follows:

1000 Reis Silver - Coroa
100 Reis Silver - Tostao

The diameter of the new copper coins, first minted by Maria II in 1837, was smaller than the earlier coinage, but the weight was unaltered. However, in 1882, Luis I reduced the size and weight of the copper currency.

The Real and 2 Reis pieces dated 1853 were issued for circulation in Mozambique and will be found in those listings.

3 REIS

COPPER

KM#	Date	Mintage	Fine	VF	XF	Unc
517	1868	.100	2.00	4.00	8.00	18.00
	1874	.280	2.00	4.00	8.00	18.00
	1875	1.200	2.00	4.00	9.00	20.00

5 REIS

COPPER

KM#	Date	Mintage	VG	Fine	VF	XF
480	1840	.174	2.50	5.00	10.00	25.00
	1843	3,621	5.00	8.00	17.00	45.00
	1848	.147	2.50	5.00	10.00	30.00
	1850	.180	2.50	5.00	10.00	30.00
	1852	.292	2.50	5.00	10.00	30.00
	1853	*.097	3.50	7.00	15.00	35.00

***NOTE:** Struck for circulation primarily in Mozambique.

KM#	Date	Mintage	Fine	VF	XF	Unc
513	1867	.737	1.50	3.00	7.00	15.00
	1868	.740	1.50	3.00	7.00	15.00
	1871	.240	10.00	20.00	40.00	70.00
	1872	.700	1.50	3.00	7.00	15.00
	1873	.600	8.00	15.00	27.50	50.00
	1874	1.080	1.00	2.00	5.00	12.00
	1875	2.200	1.00	2.00	5.00	12.00
	1876	.320	8.00	15.00	35.00	60.00
	1877	.620	8.00	15.00	30.00	50.00
	1878	Inc. Ab.	2.00	4.00	10.00	20.00
	1879	.332	2.00	4.00	10.00	20.00
	1882	—	Reported, not confirmed			

BRONZE

KM#	Date	Mintage	Fine	VF	XF	Unc
525	1882	5.200	.75	1.50	3.50	12.00
	1883	4.700	.75	1.50	3.50	12.00
	1884	1.730	1.00	2.00	4.00	15.00
	1885	3.200	.75	1.50	3.50	12.00
	1886	4.170	1.00	2.25	5.00	18.00

KM#	Date	Mintage	Fine	VF	XF	Unc
530	1890	.430	.75	1.50	2.00	5.00
	1891	Inc. Ab.	.50	1.00	2.00	5.00
	1892/1	1.510	.50	1.50	3.00	10.00
	1892	Inc. Ab.	.25	.75	1.50	5.00
	1893	3.280	.25	.75	1.50	6.00
	1896	.567	.25	.75	1.50	6.00
	1897	1.120	1.00	3.00	5.00	12.00
	1898	.700	.25	.75	1.50	6.00
	1899	1.220	.25	.75	1.50	5.00
	1900	1.110	1.00	3.00	5.00	12.00

NOTE: Later dates (1901-1906) exist for this type.

10 REIS

COPPER

Obv: Plain shield, struck in collared dies.

KM#	Date	Mintage	VG	Fine	VF	XF
470	1837	—	2.00	5.00	12.00	30.00
	1838	—	2.00	5.00	12.00	30.00
	1839	—	2.00	5.00	12.00	30.00

Obv: Ornate shield.

KM#	Date	Mintage	VG	Fine	VF	XF
481	1840	.392	2.00	3.00	7.00	20.00
	1841	.476	2.00	3.00	7.00	20.00
	1842	1.131	2.00	3.00	7.00	20.00
	1843	.837	2.00	3.00	7.00	20.00
	1844	.620	2.00	3.00	7.00	20.00
	1845	.545	2.00	3.00	7.00	20.00
	1846	1.166	2.00	3.00	7.00	20.00
	1847	.057	5.00	10.00	20.00	45.00
	1850	.443	2.00	3.00	7.00	20.00
	1851	1.236	2.00	3.00	7.00	20.00
	1852	.558	2.00	3.00	7.00	20.00
	1853	*.046	2.00	3.00	7.00	20.00

***NOTE:** Struck for circulation primarily in Mozambique.

KM#	Date	Mintage	VG	Fine	VF	XF
514	1867	.300	1.00	2.50	6.00	15.00
	1868	.450	2.50	5.00	12.00	28.00
	1870	Inc. Ab.	15.00	30.00	60.00	175.00
	1871	.360	2.50	5.00	10.00	20.00
	1873	2.000	.75	1.50	4.50	12.00
	1874	.220	5.00	10.00	20.00	40.00
	1878	—	Reported, not confirmed			

BRONZE

KM#	Date	Mintage	Fine	VF	XF	Unc
526	1882	14.795	1.25	2.50	5.00	12.00
	1883	Inc. Ab.	1.25	2.50	5.00	12.00
	1884	10.190	1.25	2.50	5.00	12.00
	1885	8.100	1.25	2.50	5.00	12.00
	1886	3.915	1.50	3.00	8.00	20.00

KM#	Date	Mintage	Fine	VF	XF	Unc
532	1891	3.445	1.25	2.50	5.50	12.50
	1891A	.895	2.50	6.00	15.00	35.00
	1892	9.298	1.25	2.50	5.50	12.50
	1892A	5.769	1.25	2.50	5.50	12.50

20 REIS

COPPER

KM#	Date	Mintage	VG	Fine	VF	XF
482	1847	2.484	4.00	9.00	18.00	35.00
	1848	.801	4.00	9.00	18.00	35.00
	1849	2.269	4.00	9.00	18.00	35.00
	1850	1.803	4.00	9.00	18.00	35.00
	1851	.842	4.00	9.00	18.00	35.00
	1852	1.215	4.00	9.00	18.00	35.00
	1853	*.946	4.00	9.00	18.00	35.00

***NOTE:** Struck for circulation primarily in Mozambique.

KM#	Date	Mintage	VG	Fine	VF	XF
515	1867	.745	2.00	4.00	10.00	22.00
	1870	—	20.00	40.00	70.00	150.00
	1871	.360	4.00	8.00	18.00	35.00
	1872	.050	Reported, not confirmed			
	1873	2.500	1.50	3.50	9.00	20.00
	1874	1.575	1.50	3.50	9.00	22.00

BRONZE

KM#	Date	Mintage	Fine	VF	XF	Unc
527	1882	17.235	1.00	2.00	5.00	18.00
	1883	Inc. Ab.	1.00	2.00	5.00	18.00
	1884	17.200	1.00	2.00	5.00	18.00
	1885	18.493	1.00	2.00	5.00	18.00
	1886	4.573	1.00	2.00	6.00	20.00

KM#	Date	Mintage	Fine	VF	XF	Unc
533	1891	3.282	1.00	2.00	4.00	16.00
	1891A	6.016	1.00	2.00	5.00	18.00
	1892/1	15.411	1.25	2.50	5.00	18.00
	1892	Inc. Ab.	1.00	2.00	4.00	16.00
	1892A	.658	1.50	4.00	10.00	30.00

40 REIS

Refer to earlier listings for 40 Reis of Maria II dated 1847 (KM#402).

50 REIS

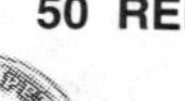

1.2500 g, .917 SILVER, .0368 oz ASW

KM#	Date	Mintage	VG	Fine	VF	XF
493	1855	.048	4.00	10.00	15.00	35.00
	1861	.800	1.00	2.00	5.00	12.00

KM#	Date	Mintage	VG	Fine	VF	XF
506	1862	.017	2.00	6.00	10.00	22.00
	1863	.215	1.00	3.00	6.00	14.00
	1864	.050	4.00	7.00	12.00	32.00
	1868	—	Reported, not confirmed			
	1874	.060	2.00	6.00	10.00	22.00
	1875	Inc. Ab.	10.00	20.00	30.00	65.00
	1876	.100	1.00	3.00	5.00	12.00
	1877	.100	1.00	3.00	5.00	12.00
	1879	.080	1.00	3.00	5.00	12.00
	1880	.320	1.00	3.00	5.00	12.00
	1886	.060	3.00	7.00	16.00	50.00
	1887	.040	10.00	25.00	60.00	175.00
	1888	Inc. Be.	—	—	Rare	—
	1889	1.000	1.00	2.00	3.50	10.00

KM#	Date	Mintage	VG	Fine	VF	XF
536	1893	.620	2.00	4.00	7.00	15.00

COPPER-NICKEL

KM#	Date	Mintage	Fine	VF	XF	Unc
545	1900	8.000	.50	1.00	2.00	7.00

100 REIS

2.9600 g, .917 SILVER, .0873 oz ASW
Obv: Young head
Reeded edge

KM#	Date	Mintage	VG	Fine	VF	XF
473	1838	2,505	35.00	65.00	135.00	285.00
	1842	—	Reported, not confirmed			
	1843	—	12.00	25.00	45.00	150.00
	1848	—	Reported, not confirmed			

Obv: Mature head.

KM#	Date	Mintage	VG	Fine	VF	XF
485	1851	9,205	6.00	12.00	25.00	75.00

Obv: Older head.

KM#	Date	Mintage	VG	Fine	VF	XF
488	1853	.066	4.50	9.00	18.00	50.00

2.5000 g, .917 SILVER, .0737 oz ASW

KM#	Date	Mintage	VG	Fine	VF	XF
490	1854	.535	3.00	6.00	12.50	40.00

Obv: Young head.

KM#	Date	Mintage	VG	Fine	VF	XF
497	1857	.043	20.00	40.00	80.00	175.00
	1858	—	20.00	40.00	80.00	175.00
	1859	.455	2.00	5.00	10.00	35.00
	1860	—	Reported, not confirmed			
	1861	.762	2.00	5.00	10.00	35.00

KM#	Date	Mintage	VG	Fine	VF	XF
510	1864	.198	4.00	8.00	16.00	40.00
	1865	.100	4.00	8.00	16.00	40.00
	1866	.010	25.00	40.00	120.00	250.00
	1869	.010	25.00	40.00	90.00	200.00
	1871	.060	4.50	9.00	18.00	45.00
	1872	.060	4.00	8.00	16.00	40.00
	1873	—		Reported, not confirmed		
	1874	.170	2.50	5.00	10.00	30.00
	1875	.130	2.25	4.50	10.00	27.50
	1876	.220	2.00	4.00	10.00	27.50
	1877	.120	2.25	4.50	10.00	27.50
	1878	.030	5.00	10.00	20.00	45.00
	1879	.560	1.50	2.00	6.00	14.00
	1880	.440	1.50	2.00	6.00	14.00
	1881	Inc. Ab.	17.50	37.50	75.00	180.00
	1886	.750	1.50	2.00	6.00	14.00
	1888	.500	1.50	2.00	6.00	14.00
	1889	1.500	1.50	2.00	5.00	12.00

KM#	Date	Mintage	VG	Fine	VF	XF
531	1890	.700	1.25	2.50	7.00	16.00
	1891	.270	2.00	5.00	10.00	22.00
	1893	1.050	1.00	2.00	6.00	15.00
	1894	Inc. Ab.	15.00	30.00	60.00	125.00
	1895	—		Reported, not confirmed		
	1898	.655	1.50	3.00	8.00	18.00

COPPER-NICKEL

KM#	Date	Mintage	Fine	VF	XF	Unc
546	1900	16.000	.25	.75	2.00	7.00

200 REIS

5.9200 g, .917 SILVER, 1746 oz ASW
Obv: Young head.
Reeded edge

KM#	Date	Mintage	VG	Fine	VF	XF
474	1838	2,177	40.00	75.00	150.00	300.00
	1841	868 pcs.	45.00	85.00	175.00	350.00
	1842	—		Reported, not confirmed		
	1843	1,181	12.00	25.00	45.00	150.00
	1846	—		Reported, not confirmed		
	1848	—		Reported, not confirmed		

5.0000 g, .917 SILVER, .1474 oz ASW

KM#	Date	Mintage	VG	Fine	VF	XF
491	1854	.292	3.00	6.00	12.50	45.00
	1855	.793	3.00	6.00	12.50	40.00

KM#	Date	Mintage	VG	Fine	VF	XF
499	1858	—	3.00	6.00	12.50	45.00
	1859	.117		Reported, not confirmed		
	1860	—	3.00	6.00	12.50	50.00
	1861	.202	25.00	50.00	100.00	200.00

KM#	Date	Mintage	VG	Fine	VF	XF
507	1862	.696	3.50	7.00	15.00	50.00
	1863	.421	3.50	8.00	18.00	60.00
	1865	.050	7.00	15.00	30.00	75.00

Second bust

KM#	Date	Mintage	VG	Fine	VF	XF
512	1866	.010	40.00	85.00	180.00	375.00
	1867	.010	30.00	65.00	135.00	275.00
	1868	5,000	30.00	60.00	120.00	275.00
	1871	.075	10.00	20.00	45.00	100.00
	1872	.070	12.00	25.00	50.00	120.00
	1875	.070	6.00	12.00	25.00	60.00
	1876	.080	35.00	70.00	145.00	325.00
	1877	.030	10.00	20.00	45.00	100.00
	1878	.020	25.00	55.00	110.00	240.00
	1879	5,050	45.00	90.00	180.00	425.00
	1880	.150	4.00	8.00	15.00	35.00
	1886	.340	2.50	5.00	12.00	28.00
	1887	3.600	2.00	3.50	9.00	20.00
	1888	.700	2.50	5.00	12.00	28.00
534	1891	2.365	1.50	2.50	5.00	12.00
	1892	.788	1.50	2.50	6.00	15.00
	1893/2	1.205	5.00	10.00	20.00	45.00
	1893	Inc. Ab.	2.50	5.00	10.00	25.00

NOTE: Later dates (1901-1903) exist for this type.

400th Anniversary Discovery of India

KM#	Date	Mintage	VG	Fine	VF	XF
537	1898	.250	2.00	4.00	6.00	12.50
	1898	—	—	P/L	Unc	22.50

500 REIS

14.8000 g, .917 SILVER, .4364 oz ASW

KM#	Date	Mintage	VG	Fine	VF	XF
471	1837	1,266	75.00	150.00	300.00	600.00
	1838	2,645	65.00	125.00	250.00	500.00
	1839	2,084	65.00	125.00	250.00	500.00
	1841	.022	6.00	12.00	25.00	60.00
	1842	.135	7.00	7.50	18.00	45.00
	1843	.105	7.50	15.00	30.00	75.00
	1844	4,265	10.00	20.00	40.00	90.00
	1845	—	15.00	30.00	60.00	120.00
	1846	.074	5.00	10.00	22.00	50.00
	1847	.775	4.00	7.50	15.00	40.00
	1848	.024	7.50	15.00	30.00	70.00
	1849	.059	6.00	12.00	25.00	60.00
	1850	.041	7.50	15.00	30.00	70.00
	1851	.155	4.00	7.50	15.00	45.00
	1853	.022	30.00	60.00	120.00	250.00

12.5000 g, .917 SILVER, .3684 oz ASW
Obv. leg: PETRUS.V. . ., young head.

KM#	Date	Mintage	VG	Fine	VF	XF
492	1854	.592	7.00	15.00	30.00	90.00

KM#	Date	Mintage	VG	Fine	VF	XF
494	1855	1.210	4.00	8.00	20.00	65.00
	1856	1.478	4.00	8.00	20.00	60.00

KM#	Date	Mintage	VG	Fine	VF	XF
498	1857	1.949	6.00	10.00	22.50	75.00
	1858	3.091	4.00	8.00	20.00	65.00
	1859	2.660	4.00	8.00	20.00	65.00

KM#	Date	Mintage	VG	Fine	VF	XF
509	1863	.148	4.00	6.50	15.00	50.00
	1864	.341	3.50	5.50	10.00	35.00
	1865	.406	3.50	5.50	10.00	35.00
	1866	.378	3.50	5.50	10.00	25.00
	1867	.458	3.50	5.50	10.00	25.00
	1868	.388	3.50	5.50	10.00	25.00
	1870	.314	3.50	5.50	10.00	27.50
	1871	.228	3.50	5.00	9.00	22.50
	1872	.576	35.00	60.00	150.00	325.00
	1875	.140	17.50	30.00	60.00	165.00
	1876	.280	15.00	25.00	50.00	145.00
	1877	.050	12.00	20.00	35.00	75.00
	1879	.788	3.50	5.00	9.00	20.00
	1886	.300	3.50	5.00	9.00	20.00
	1887	.432	3.50	5.00	9.00	20.00
	1888	2.740	3.50	5.00	9.00	18.00
	1889	.960	3.50	5.00	9.00	18.00

KM#	Date	Mintage	VG	Fine	VF	XF
535	1891	12.476	3.50	4.50	7.50	16.50
	1892/1	4.716	5.00	8.00	12.00	27.50
	1892	Inc. Ab.	3.50	4.50	7.50	16.50
	1893	2.494	4.00	6.00	10.00	22.50
	1894	.254	50.00	100.00	150.00	375.00
	1895	.216	10.00	20.00	45.00	100.00
	1896	5.120	3.50	4.50	7.50	16.50
	1898	1.320	4.00	6.00	10.00	22.50
	1899	3.100	3.50	4.50	7.50	16.50
	1900	.200	25.00	50.00	100.00	225.00

NOTE: Later dates (1901-1908) exist for this type.

400th Anniversary Discovery of India

KM#	Date	Mintage	VG	Fine	VF	XF
538	1898	.300	5.00	7.50	10.00	20.00
	1898	—	—	P/L	Unc	35.00

1000 REIS

29.6000 g, .917 SILVER, .8727 oz ASW

KM#	Date	Mintage	VG	Fine	VF	XF
472	1837	2,295	80.00	100.00	200.00	450.00
	1838	3,959	35.00	60.00	100.00	300.00
	1842	1,515	—	—	Rare	—
	1843	—	—	Reported, not confirmed		
	1844	—	20.00	40.00	75.00	150.00
	1845	10,724	20.00	40.00	75.00	150.00

1.7900 g, .917 GOLD, .0528 oz AGW

KM#	Date	Mintage	VG	Fine	VF	XF
486	1851	.012	40.00	50.00	65.00	125.00

1.7735 g, .917 GOLD, .0523 oz AGW

KM#	Date	Mintage	VG	Fine	VF	XF
495	1855	.068	35.00	40.00	55.00	100.00

25.0000 g, .917 SILVER, .7368 oz ASW
400th Anniversary Discovery of India

KM#	Date	Mintage	VG	Fine	VF	XF
539	1898	.300	10.00	12.00	15.00	35.00
	1898	—	—	P/L	Unc	75.00

KM#	Date	Mintage	VG	Fine	VF	XF
540	1899	1.500	10.00	12.00	15.00	30.00
	1900	3 known	—	—	Proof	7500.

2000 REIS

3.5470 g, .917 GOLD, .1045 oz AGW
Obv: Boy head.

KM#	Date	Mintage	Fine	VF	XF	Unc
496	1856	.038	65.00	100.00	200.00	300.00
	1857	.044	60.00	90.00	150.00	250.00

Obv: Young head.

KM#	Date	Mintage	Fine	VF	XF	Unc
500	1858	.013	60.00	90.00	150.00	275.00
	1859	.016	60.00	90.00	150.00	275.00
	1860	.053	60.00	90.00	150.00	250.00

Rev: Arms in spray.

KM#	Date	Mintage	Fine	VF	XF	Unc
511	1864	.101	60.00	100.00	150.00	250.00
	1865	.095	60.00	100.00	150.00	250.00
	1866	.086	60.00	100.00	150.00	250.00

Rev: Mantled arms.

KM#	Date	Mintage	Fine	VF	XF	Unc
518	1868	.024	65.00	125.00	200.00	300.00
	1869	.011	65.00	125.00	200.00	300.00
	1870	500 pcs.	300.00	600.00	1000.	1500.
	1871	500 pcs.	200.00	400.00	700.00	1000.
	1872	1,000	125.00	200.00	375.00	550.00
	1874	5,000	75.00	150.00	250.00	350.00
	1875	2,000	100.00	175.00	275.00	350.00
	1876	5,000	75.00	150.00	250.00	350.00
	1877	2,250	100.00	175.00	275.00	400.00
	1878	.022	65.00	125.00	200.00	300.00
	1881	1,000	150.00	200.00	400.00	600.00
	1888	500 pcs.	200.00	400.00	750.00	1200.

2500 REIS

4.7800 g, .917 GOLD, .1410 oz AGW
Obv: Young head.

KM#	Date	Mintage	Fine	VF	XF	Unc
475	1838	1,114	300.00	500.00	800.00	1200.

4.4800 g, .917 GOLD, .1321 oz AGW

KM#	Date	Mintage	Fine	VF	XF	Unc
487	1851	.058	100.00	175.00	275.00	400.00

KM#	Date	Mintage	Fine	VF	XF	Unc
489	1853	1,010	250.00	450.00	650.00	1000.

5000 REIS

9.5600 g, .917 GOLD, .2819 oz AGW
Obv: Young head.

KM#	Date	Mintage	Fine	VF	XF	Unc
476.1	1838	2,410	200.00	250.00	500.00	800.00
	1845	401 pcs.	500.00	1000.	2000.	3000.

8.9600 g, .917 GOLD, .2642 oz AGW

KM#	Date	Mintage	Fine	VF	XF	Unc
476.2	1851	.057	175.00	225.00	325.00	500.00

8.8675 g, .917 GOLD, .2613 oz AGW
Obv: Young head.

KM#	Date	Mintage	Fine	VF	XF	Unc
505	1860	.052	150.00	175.00	200.00	350.00
	1861	.081	150.00	175.00	200.00	350.00

KM#	Date	Mintage	Fine	VF	XF	Unc
508	1862	.166	150.00	175.00	200.00	350.00
	1863	.038	150.00	175.00	200.00	350.00

Rev: Mantled arms.

KM#	Date	Mintage	Fine	VF	XF	Unc
516	1867	.045	150.00	175.00	200.00	350.00
	1868	.064	150.00	175.00	200.00	350.00
	1869	.077	150.00	175.00	200.00	350.00
	1870	.061	150.00	175.00	200.00	350.00
	1871	.047	150.00	175.00	200.00	350.00
	1872	.028	150.00	175.00	200.00	350.00
	1874	6,800	150.00	175.00	200.00	350.00
	1875	.010	150.00	175.00	200.00	350.00
	1876	.015	150.00	175.00	200.00	350.00
	1877	9,400	175.00	200.00	350.00	600.00
	1878	8,400	150.00	175.00	200.00	350.00
	1880	7,000	350.00	500.00	800.00	1200.
	1883	.023	150.00	175.00	200.00	350.00
	1886	.027	150.00	175.00	200.00	350.00
	1887	.044	150.00	175.00	200.00	350.00
	1888	4,800	150.00	175.00	200.00	350.00
	1889	9,000	150.00	175.00	200.00	350.00

10,000 REIS

17.7350 g, .917 GOLD, .5227 oz AGW

KM#	Date	Mintage	Fine	VF	XF	Unc
520	1878	.023	275.00	300.00	400.00	700.00
	1879	.036	275.00	300.00	400.00	700.00
	1880	.030	275.00	300.00	400.00	700.00
	1881	.019	275.00	300.00	425.00	750.00
	1882	.015	275.00	350.00	425.00	750.00
	1883	8,500	275.00	300.00	425.00	750.00
	1884	.013	275.00	300.00	425.00	750.00
	1885	.021	275.00	300.00	425.00	950.00
	1886	1,800	300.00	400.00	600.00	1000.
	1888	7,000	350.00	500.00	700.00	1250.
	1889	4,400	350.00	500.00	700.00	1250.

PATTERNS (Pn)

KM#	Date	Mintage	Identification	Mkt.Val.
Pn29	1803	—	1 Peca, Copper, circular wreath	1000.
Pn30	1803	—	1 Peca, Copper Gilt, circular wreath	1200.

KM#	Date	Mintage	Identification	Mkt.Val.
Pn31	1803	—	1 Peca, Copper Gilt	1200.
Pn32	1803	—	1 Peca, Copper Gilt, wreath connected to shield	1200.
Pn33	ND	—	1 Peca, Lead, royal bust	350.00
Pn34	ND	—	1 Peca, Lead, bust and leg.	350.00
Pn35	ND	—	1 Peca, Lead Gilt, bust and leg.	650.00
Pn36	1804	—	1 Peca, Lead, date incuse	400.00
Pn37	1804	—	1 Peca, Lead, date in relief	450.00
Pn38	1811	—	20 Reis, Bronze, simple shield	1000.
Pn39	1811	—	20 Reis, Bronze, reduced size	Rare
Pn40	1811	—	30 Reis, Bronze, simple shield	1250.
Pn41	1811	—	30 Reis, Bronze, thin planchet	1150.
Pn42	1811	—	30 Reis, Bronze, ornate shield	Rare
Pn43	1811	—	40 Reis, Lead	600.00
Pn44	1811	—	40 Reis, Bronze, experimental edge	1850.
Pn45	1811	—	40 Reis, Bronze, experimental edge	1850.
Pn46	1811	—	40 Reis, Bronze, experimental edge	1850.
Pn47	1811	—	40 Reis, Bronze, experimental edge	1850.
Pn48	1811	—	40 Reis, Bronze, experimental edge	1850.
Pn49	1813	—	40 Reis, Bronze, reeded edge	750.00
Pn50	1814	—	40 Reis, Bronze, reeded edge	750.00
Pn51	1820	—	10 Reis, Copper, Roman numeral	500.00
Pn52	1822	—	40 Reis, Bronze	—
Pn53	1822	—	40 Reis, Bronze, coarse reeding	900.00
Pn54	1822	—	40 Reis, Bronze, fine reeding	900.00
Pn55	1822	—	40 Reis, Bronze, laurel leaved edge	1650.
Pn56	1822	—	1 Peca, Silver, shield over wreath	1750.
Pn57	1826	—	1 Peca, Copper Gilt, square arms	Rare
Pn58	1826	—	1 Peca, Copper, square arms	Rare
Pn59	1826	—	1 Peca, Copper, oval arms, KM378	Rare
Pn60	1828	—	40 Reis, Bronze, oval shield	Rare
Pn61	1828	—	1/2 Peca, Copper Gilt, KM387	1000.

KM#	Date	Mintage	Identification	Mkt.Val.
Pn62	1828	—	1 Peca, Lead, KM388	800.00
Pn63	1828	—	1 Peca, Nickel-Silver, KM388	1000.
Pn64	1828	—	1 Peca, Copper Gilt, for royal approval,KM388	1250.
Pn65	1829	—	40 Reis, Cast Lead, crowned value in arms/wreath	1500.
Pn66	1829	—	40 Reis, Gun Metal, crowned arms/value in wreath	1750.
Pn67	1829	—	80 Reis, Copper, crowned arms/ value in wreath	4500.
Pn68	1829	—	600 Reis, Copper, crowned arms/ value in wreath	4000.
Pn69	1829	—	1 Peca, Copper, engraved by Dubois	650.00
Pn70	1830	—	1 Peca, Copper, KM397	950.00
Pn71	1830	—	1 Peca, Copper, inward palms	950.00
Pn72	1831	—	1 Peca, Copper, inward palms	—
Pn73	1833	—	5 Reis, Lead, w/o collar, Roman numerals	500.00
Pn74	1833	—	10 Reis, Copper, Roman numeral	550.00
Pn75	1833	—	20 Reis, Bronze	—
Pn76	1833	—	20 Reis, Bronze, wreath variety	450.00
Pn77	1833	—	40 Reis, Bronze	—

KM#	Date	Mintage	Identification	Mkt.Val.
Pn78	1833	—	40 Reis, Bronze, wreath variety	675.00
Pn79	1833	—	400 Reis, Silver	—

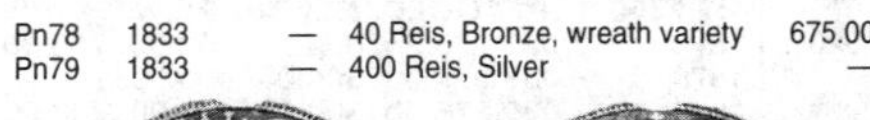

KM#	Date	Mintage	Identification	Mkt.Val.
Pn80	1833	—	1/2 Peca, Tin, Porto Mint, Maria II	1750.
Pn81	1833	—	1 Peca, Tin, Porto Mint, Maria II	2000.
Pn82	1833	—	1 Peca, Silver, high neck	Rare

KM#	Date	Mintage	Identification	Mkt.Val.
Pn83	1834	—	400 Reis, Silver, W.Wyon	2750.
Pn84	1835	—	400 Reis, Silver, W.Wyon	—
Pn85	1836	—	100 Reis, .917 Silver	350.00

KM#	Date	Mintage	Identification	Mkt.Val.
Pn86	1836	—	200 Reis, Copper, reeded edge	300.00
Pn87	1836	—	200 Reis, Copper, plain edge	300.00
Pn88	1836	—	200 Reis, .917 Silver, plain edge	500.00
Pn89	1836	—	500 Reis, Copper, plain edge	500.00
Pn90	1836	—	500 Reis, Copper, reeded edge	500.00
Pn91	1836	—	500 Reis, .917 Silver	1000.
Pn92	1836	—	1000 Reis, Copper, fine reeding	500.00
Pn93	1836	—	1000 Reis, Copper, reeded edge	500.00
Pn94	1836	—	1000 Reis, Copper, plain edge	500.00
Pn95	1836	—	1000 Reis, .917 Silver	1000.
Pn96	1836	—	2500 Reis, .917 Gold, W. Wyon	4500.
Pn97	1836	—	5000 Reis, Copper, W.Wyon	450.00
Pn98	1836	—	5000 Reis, .917 Gold, W. Wyon	5000.
Pn99	1838	—	200 Reis, Silver, plain edge	350.00
Pn100	1842	—	500 Reis, Copper, plain edge	500.00
Pn101	1842	—	500 Reis, Copper, reeded edge	500.00
Pn102	1842	—	500 Reis, Gold, plain edge	Rare
Pn103	1842	—	500 Reis, Gold, reeded edge	Rare
Pn104	1842	—	1000 Reis, Copper	600.00

KM#	Date	Mintage	Identification	Mkt.Val.
Pn105	1842	—	1000 Reis, Gold reeded edge	Unique
Pn106	1852	—	500 Reis, Copper, reeded edge	550.00
Pn107	1854	—	500 Reis, Copper	150.00
Pn108	1854	—	500 Reis, Silver	400.00
Pn109	1855	—	200 Reis, Brass	350.00
Pn110	1855	—	500 Reis, Silver	450.00
Pn111	1856	—	5000 Reis, Gold, Maria II	6500.
Pn112	1857	—	500 Reis, Silver	450.00
Pn113	1858	—	500 Reis, Copper	350.00
PnA114	1858	—	2500 Reis	—
Pn114	ND	—	10,000 Reis, Porcelain	200.00
Pn115	1858	—	10,000 Reis, Copper Gilt	1200.
Pn116	1859	—	500 Reis, Silver	500.00
Pn117	1859	—	10,000 Reis, Copper Gilt, mantled arms	1200.
Pn118	1860	—	200 Reis, Silver	450.00
Pn119	1861	—	50 Reis, Silver, crowned date	200.00
Pn120	1861	—	200 Reis, Silver, smooth hair, value between palms	200.00
Pn121	1861	—	1000 Reis, Copper	150.00
Pn122	1861	—	10,000 Reis, Gold, mantled arms	Rare
Pn123	1861	—	10,000 Reis, Copper, mantled arms	1250.
Pn124	1862	—	5 Reis, Copper	400.00
Pn125	1862	—	5 Reis, Nickel	450.00
Pn126	1862	—	10 Reis, Copper	500.00
Pn127	1862	—	10 Reis, Copper, Roman numeral	500.00
Pn128	1862	—	20 Reis, Copper	600.00
Pn129	1862	—	20 Reis, Copper, Roman numeral	600.00

KM#	Date	Mintage	Identification	Mkt.Val.
Pn130	1863	—	5 Reis, Copper, Roman numeral	400.00

KM#	Date	Mintage	Identification	Mkt.Val.
Pn131	1863	—	5 Reis, Copper, Roman numeral, large type	800.00
Pn132	1863	—	5 Reis, Nickel	750.00

KM#	Date	Mintage	Identification	Mkt.Val.
Pn133	1863	—	10 Reis, Copper, Roman numeral	200.00
Pn134	1863	—	10 Reis, Nickel	450.00

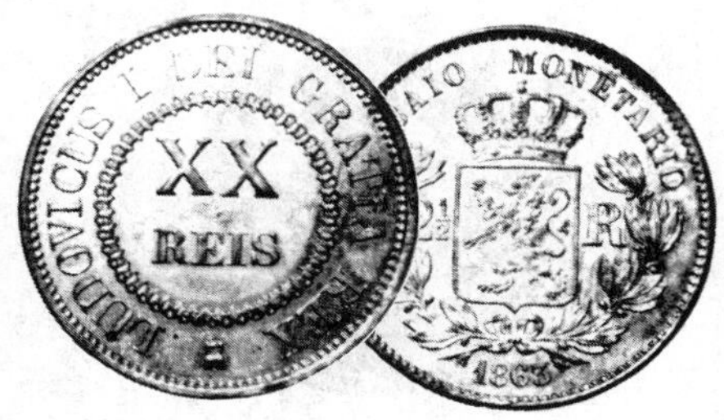

KM#	Date	Mintage	Identification	Mkt.Val.
Pn135	1863	—	20 Reis, Copper, Roman numeral	300.00
Pn136	1863	—	20 Reis, Nickel, Roman numeral	500.00
Pn137	1863	—	100 Reis, Copper, wavy hair	200.00
Pn138	1863	—	200 Reis, Copper, wavy hair	200.00
Pn139	ND	—	500 Reis, Copper, royal bust	400.00
Pn140	1863	—	500 Reis, Silver, wavy hair, shield between palms	1200.
Pn141	1863	—	500 Reis, Silver, smooth hair, shield between palms	1250.

KM#	Date	Mintage	Identification	Mkt.Val.
Pn142	ND	—	5000 Reis, Copper, Queen Victoria	1500.

KM#	Date	Mintage	Identification	Mkt.Val.
Pn143	1863	—	5000 Reis, Copper, Charles Wiener engraver	1500.
Pn144	1864	—	500 Reis, Copper, smooth hair, value between palms	—
Pn145	1865	—	200 Reis, Copper, wavy hair	200.00
Pn146	1865	—	5000 Reis, Copper, Charles Wiener engraver	500.00
Pn147	1865	—	5000 Reis, Silver	800.00
Pn148	1866	—	5000 Reis, Gold, Charles Wiener engraver	1250.
Pn149	1866	—	5000 Reis, Silver, Charles Wiener engraver	300.00

KM#	Date	Mintage	Identification	Mkt.Val.
Pn150	1866	—	5000 Reis, Copper, Charles Wiener engraver	200.00
Pn151	1866	—	5000 Reis, Copper Gilt, Charles Wiener engraver	300.00
Pn152	1866	—	5000 Reis, Tin, Charles Wiener engraver	200.00
Pn153	1866	—	5000 Reis, Lead	200.00
Pn154	1867	—	5 Reis, Brass, Roman numeral	150.00
Pn155	1874	—	3 Reis, Brass	250.00
Pn156	1877	—	5 Reis, Copper	175.00
Pn157	1877	—	100 Reis, Brass	200.00
Pn158	1877	—	200 Reis, Copper	250.00
Pn159	1878	—	10,000 Reis, Copper, shield over royal mantle	300.00
Pn160	1879	—	50 Reis, Copper, crowned date	175.00
Pn161	1879	—	500 Reis, Copper, rotated 90 degree, plain edge	200.00

KM#	Date	Mintage	Identification	Mkt.Val.
Pn162	1879	—	500 Reis, Gold, rotated 90 degree, plain edge	Rare
Pn163	1879	—	500 Reis, Copper, 'ENS' incuse	200.00
Pn164	1879	—	1000 Reis, Gold, value between palms	Rare
Pn165	1879	—	1000 Reis, Gold, crowned date	Rare

KM#	Date	Mintage	Identification	Mkt.Val.
Pn166	1879	—	1000 Reis, Copper, royal bust w/date	175.00
Pn167	1879	—	1000 Reis, Copper, crowned date, 50 Reis type	175.00
Pn168	1879	—	1000 Reis, Gold, shield over royal mantle	Rare
Pn169	1879	—	5000 Reis, Copper, shield over royal mantle	450.00
Pn170	1879	—	5000 Reis, Gold	1450.
Pn171	1880	—	200 Reis, Copper	175.00
Pn172	1880	—	2000 Reis, Copper	175.00
Pn173	1880	—	5000 Reis, Copper	185.00
Pn174	1880	—	5000 Reis, Copper, 'ENS' incuse	150.00
Pn175	1882	—	5 Reis, Brass, Roman numeral	150.00
Pn176	1883	—	1000 Reis, Gold, value inside wreath	Rare
Pn177	1886	—	200 Reis, Copper, wavy hair	—

KM#	Date	Mintage	Identification	Mkt.Val.
Pn178	1888	—	100 Reis, Silver	350.00
Pn179	1888	—	100 Reis, Nickel	200.00
Pn180	1888	—	5000 Reis, Nickel, small type, old monarch	175.00
Pn181	1888	—	5000 Reis, Copper, small type, old monarch	175.00
Pn182	1890	—	10 Reis, Copper, legend of 1891	200.00
Pn183	1890	—	20 Reis, Copper, legend of 1891	220.00
Pn184	ND	—	5 Reis, Nickel, two reverses	245.00
Pn185	1891	—	5 Reis, Copper-Nickel, royal bust, value between palms	200.00
Pn186	1891	—	20 Reis, Bronze	200.00
Pn187	1892	—	10 Reis, Copper-Nickel	200.00

KM#	Date	Mintage	Identification	Mkt.Val.
Pn188	1892	—	20 Reis, Aluminum	125.00
Pn189	1892	—	20 Reis, Copper-Nickel	165.00

KM#	Date	Mintage	Identification	Mkt.Val.
Pn190	1892	—	200 Reis, Copper-Nickel, reduced type, plain edge	350.00

KM#	Date	Mintage	Identification	Mkt.Val.
Pn191	1895	—	5000 Reis, Silver Gilt	15,000.
Pn192	1895	—	5000 Reis, Gold	Rare
Pn193	1898	—	100 Reis, Copper-Nickel, reduced type, plain edge	350.00
Pn194	1898	—	1000 Reis, Copper	450.00
Pn195	1899	—	20 Reis, Copper-Nickel	250.00
PnA196	1899	—	500 Reis, Copper, mantled arms w/o wreath	350.00
Pn196	1900	—	50 Reis, Nickel, plain edge	150.00
Pn197	1900	—	100 Reis, Copper-Nickel, plain edge	175.00
Pn198	1900	—	100 Reis, Aluminum, plain edge	175.00
Pn199	1900	3 known	10000 Reis, Gold	Rare

PROVAS (Pr)

Stamped 'PROVA' incuse in field

KM#	Date	Mintage	Identification	Mkt.Val.
PrA1	1863	—	500 Reis, Silver, PROVA above crown, KM506	300.00
PrB1	1863	—	500 Reis, Copper, PROVA above crown, KM506	250.00
PrC1	1864	—	500 Reis, Copper, PROVA above crown, KM506	250.00
Pr1	1868	—	5 Reis, Copper, Roman numeral, KM513	100.00
Pr2	1868	—	5 Reis, Copper, 1 above Roman numeral V, KM513	75.00
Pr3	1868	—	5 Reis, Copper, 2 above Roman numeral V, KM513	75.00
Pr4	1868	—	5 Reis, Copper, 3 above Roman numeral V, KM513	75.00
Pr5	1871	—	10 Reis, Copper, Roman numeral, KM514	125.00
Pr6	ND	—	500 Reis, Copper, two busts, KM535	—

TRIAL STRIKES (TS)

KM#	Date	Mintage	Identification	Mkt.Val.
TS1	1802	—	6400 Reis, Lead, obv.	850.00
TS2	1803	—	6400 Reis, Lead, obv. type of 1805	350.00
TS3	ND	—	6400 Reis, Lead, rev.	350.00
TS4	1805	—	200 Reis, Lead, obv.	250.00
TS5	ND	—	800 Reis, Lead, rev.	275.00
TS6	1805	—	1600 Reis, Lead, obv.	300.00
TS7	ND	—	1600 Reis, Lead, rev.	300.00
TS8	1805	—	3200 Reis, Lead, obv.	350.00
TS9	ND	—	3200 Reis, Lead, obv.	350.00
TS10	ND	—	3200 Reis, Lead, rev.	350.00
TS11	1817	—	400 Reis, Lead, obv.	350.00
TS12	ND	—	7500 Reis, Lead	—
TS13	ND	—	7500 Reis, Copper, obv.	—
TS14	1829	—	7500 Reis, Lead, obv., Dubois	250.00
TS15	1829	—	7500 Reis, Lead, rev., Dubois	250.00
TS16	1829	—	7500 Reis, Lead, obv., radiant field	250.00
TS17	1829	—	7500 Reis, Lead, obv., ray variety	250.00
TS18	1866	—	5000 Reis, Silver, obv., Charles Wiener	100.00
TS19	1866	—	5000 Reis, Silver, rev., Charles Wiener	100.00
TS20	1866	—	5000 Reis, Copper, obv., Charles Wiener	60.00
TS21	1866	—	5000 Reis, Copper, rev., Charles Wiener	60.00
TS22	1866	—	5000 Reis, Lead, obv. Charles Wiener	60.00
TS23	1866	—	5000 Reis, Lead, rev. Charles Wiener	60.00
TS24	1868	—	3 Reis, Copper, obv., Roman numeral	80.00
TS25	ND	—	3 Reis, Copper, rev., Roman numeral	80.00
TS26	1871	—	5 Reis, Copper, obv., Roman numeral	60.00
TS27	ND	—	10 Reis, Copper, rev., Roman numeral	70.00
TS28	ND	—	10 Reis, Copper, obv., Roman numeral	70.00
TS29	1871	—	10 Reis, Copper, rev., Roman numeral	70.00
TS30	ND	—	20 Reis, Copper, obv., Roman numeral	70.00
TS31	1871	—	20 Reis, Copper, rev., Roman numeral	70.00
TS32	ND	—	10,000 Reis, Tin, rev.	—

Listings For

PORTUGUESE INDIA: refer to Indian Enclaves

PRINCE EDWARD ISLAND: refer to Canada

PUERTO RICO

The Commonwealth of Puerto Rico, the easternmost island of the Greater Antilles in the West Indies, has an area of 3,435 sq. mi. (9,104 sq. km.) and a population of 3.3 million. Capital: San Juan. The commonwealth has its own constitution and elects its own governor. Its people are citizens of the United States, liable to the draft - but not to federal taxation. The chief industries of Puerto Rico are manufacturing, agriculture, and tourism. Manufactured goods, cement, dairy and livestock products, sugar, rum and coffee are exported, mainly to the United States.

Puerto Rico ('Rich Port') was discovered by Columbus who landed on the island and took possession for Spain on Oct. 19, 1493 - the only time Columbus set foot on the soil of what is now a possession of the United States. The first settlement, Caparra, was established by Ponce de Leon in 1508. The early years of the colony were not promising. Considerable gold was found, but the supply was soon exhausted. Efforts to enslave the Indians caused violent reprisals. Hurricanes destroyed crops and homes. French, Dutch, and English freebooters burned the towns. Puerto Rico remained a Spanish possession until 1898, when it was ceded to the United States following the SpanishAmerican War. Puerto Ricans were granted a measure of self-government and U.S. citizenship in 1917. Effective July 25, 1952, a Congressional resolution elevated Puerto Rico to the status of a free commonwealth associated with the United States.

RULERS

Spanish, until 1898

ASSAYERS INITIALS

G - Antonio Garcia Gonzalez
P - Felix Miguel Peiro Rodrigo

MONETARY SYSTEM

100 Centavos = 1 Peso

COUNTERMARKED COINAGE

In 1884 a large number of holed coins were countermarked at Puerto Rico's seven customs houses to legitimatize them with a device very similar to a fleur-de-lys. These coins were redeemed in 1894.

5 CENTIMOS

BRONZE
c/m: Lys on Spanish 5 Centimos, Y#69.

KM#	Date	Year	Good	VG	Fine	VF
1	ND	(1877-79)	75.00	125.00	175.00	275.00

10 CENTIMOS

BRONZE
c/m: Lys on Spanish 5 Centimos, Y#69.

KM#	Date	Year	Good	VG	Fine	VF
2	ND	(1877-79)	75.00	125.00	175.00	275.00

1/5 DOLLAR

SILVER
c/m: Lys on U.S. 20 Cent piece, Y#28.

KM#	Date	Year	Good	VG	Fine	VF
3	ND	(1875-78)	250.00	350.00	500.00	800.00

1/4 DOLLAR

SILVER
c/m: Lys on U.S. Bust Quarter, C#29.

KM#	Date	Year	Good	VG	Fine	VF
4	ND	(1815-28)	125.00	175.00	275.00	425.00

c/m: Lys on U.S. Seated Liberty Quarter, Y#30.

KM#	Date	Year	Good	VG	Fine	VF
5	ND	(1853)	100.00	150.00	250.00	350.00

c/m: Lys on U.S. Seated Liberty Quarter, Y#29.

KM#	Date	Year	Good	VG	Fine	VF
6	ND	(1838-65)	100.00	150.00	225.00	325.00

c/m: Lys on U.S. Seated Liberty Quarter, Y#31.

KM#	Date	Year	Good	VG	Fine	VF
7	ND	(1866-91)	100.00	150.00	225.00	325.00

c/m: Lys on Spanish or Spanish Colonial 2 Reales.

KM#	Date	Year	Good	VG	Fine	VF
8	ND	(1759-71)	75.00	125.00	200.00	300.00

1/2 DOLLAR

SILVER
c/m: Lys on U.S. Half Dollar, C#32.

KM#	Date	Year	Good	VG	Fine	VF
9	ND	(1807-36)	250.00	350.00	450.00	750.00

c/m: Lys on U.S. Half Dollar, Y#37.

KM#	Date	Year	Good	VG	Fine	VF
10	ND	(1839-66)	125.00	175.00	250.00	400.00

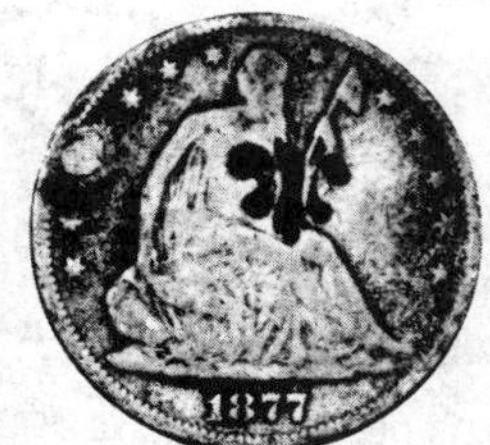

c/m: Lys on U.S. Half Dollar, Y#39.

KM#	Date	Year	Good	VG	Fine	VF
11	ND	(1866-91)	125.00	175.00	250.00	400.00

c/m: Lys on Spanish or Spanish Colonial 4 Reales.

KM#	Date	Year	Good	VG	Fine	VF
12	ND	(1791-1808)	200.00	300.00	350.00	500.00

DOLLAR

SILVER
c/m: Lys on U.S. bust type Dollar, C#34a.

KM#	Date	Year	Good	VG	Fine	VF
13	ND	(1798-1803)	500.00	600.00	800.00	1250.

c/m: Lys on U.S. Trade Dollar, Y#44.

KM#	Date	Year	Good	VG	Fine	VF
14	ND	(1873-78)	250.00	375.00	500.00	750.00

c/m: Lys on Spanish or Spanish Colonial 8 Reales.

KM#	Date	Year	Good	VG	Fine	VF
15	ND	(1772-89)	250.00	375.00	500.00	750.00

REGULAR COINAGE

5 CENTAVOS

1.2500 g, .900 SILVER, .0361 oz ASW
Alfonso XIII

KM#	Date	Mintage	Fine	VF	XF	Unc
20	1896 PGV	.600	15.00	25.00	45.00	185.00

10 CENTAVOS

2.5000 g, .900 SILVER, .0723 oz ASW

KM#	Date	Mintage	Fine	VF	XF	Unc
21	1896 PGV	.700	20.00	35.00	60.00	250.00

20 CENTAVOS

5.0000 g, .900 SILVER, .1446 oz ASW

KM#	Date	Mintage	Fine	VF	XF	Unc
22	1895 PGV	3.350	35.00	60.00	90.00	300.00

40 CENTAVOS

10.0000 g, .900 SILVER, .2893 oz ASW

KM#	Date	Mintage	Fine	VF	XF	Unc
23	1896 PGV	.725	150.00	275.00	600.00	2750.

PESO

25.0000 g, .900 SILVER, .7234 oz ASW

KM#	Date	Mintage	Fine	VF	XF	Unc
24	1895 PGV	8.500	125.00	250.00	450.00	1200.

PATTERNS (Pn)

(Including off metal strikes)

KM#	Date	Mintage	Identification	Mkt.Val.
Pn1	1890	—	10 Centimos, Copper	1750.

VIEQUES ISLAND

(Crab Island)

Vieques (Crab) Island, located to the east of Puerto Rico is the largest of the Commonwealth's offshore islands. Two-thirds of the island are leased to the U.S. navy. The neighboring island to the north, Culebra, was leased to the navy until 1974, when the naval station was closed and bombardment exercises ceased. Puerto Rico's offshore island to the west, Mona, situated between the main island and the Dominican Republic, has been unpopulated since the late 16th century, and is of no numismatic significance.

COUNTERMARKED COINAGE

Type I

c/m: 12 Rayed Sunburst

COPPER

c/m: On U.S. Nova Constellatio Cent

KM#	Date	Good	VG	Fine	VF
1	ND(1783-5)	50.00	75.00	125.00	225.00

SILVER

KM#	Date	Good	VG	Fine	VF
	c/m: On Danish West Indies 2 Skilling, KM#13.				
2	ND(1816,1837)	40.00	55.00	85.00	150.00
	c/m: On Danish West Indies 2 Skilling, KM#18.				
9	ND(1847)	—	—	—	—
	c/m: On Danish West Indies 2 Skilling, KM#19.				
3	ND(1848)	40.00	55.00	85.00	150.00
	c/m: On Danish West Indies 10 Skilling, KM#16.				
4	ND(1845)	45.00	65.00	100.00	165.00
	c/m: On Danish West Indies 10 Skilling, KM#20.1.				
10	ND(1848)	—	—	—	—
	c/m: On Danish West Indies 20 Skilling, KM#15.				
11	ND(1816)	—	—	—	—
	c/m: On Danish West Indies 20 Skilling, KM#17.				
5	ND(1840)	50.00	75.00	125.00	225.00
	c/m: On Danish West Indies 20 Skilling, KM#21.1.				
12	ND(1848)	—	—	—	—

c/m: On Danish 18th century silver coin.

KM#	Date	Good	VG	Fine	VF
6	ND	50.00	85.00	110.00	200.00

c/m: On Spanish 2 Reales, C#134.

KM#	Date	Good	VG	Fine	VF
7	ND(1825)	85.00	125.00	150.00	250.00

Type II

c/m: V in 12 Rayed Sunburst

c/m: On 1/2 cut of Spanish Colonial 2 Reales

KM#	Date	Good	VG	Fine	VF
8	ND	100.00	135.00	175.00	275.00

RAGUSA

A port city in Croatia on the Dalmatian coast of the Adriatic Sea. Upon its incorporation in Yugoslavia in 1918, its name was officially changed to Dubrovnik. Ragusa was once a great mercantile power, the merchant fleets of which sailed as far abroad as India and America. The city's present industries include oil-refining, slate mining, and the manufacture of liquers, cheese, silk, leather, and soap.

The island rock of Ragusa was colonized during the 7th century by refugees from the destroyed Latin communities of Salona and Epidaurus, and a colony of Slavs. For four centuries Ragusa successfully defended itself against attacks by foreign powers, but from 1205 to 1358 recognized Venetian suzeranity. From 1358 to 1526, Ragusa was a vassal state of Hungary. The fall of Hungary in 1526 freed Ragusa, permitting it to become one of the foremost commercial powers of the Mediterranean and a leader in the development of literature and art. After this period its importance declined, due in part to the discovery of America which reduced the importance of Mediterranean ports. A measure of its former economic importance was regained during the Napoleonic Wars when the republic, by adopting a policy of neutrality (1800-1805), became the leading carrier of the Mediterranean. This favored position was terminated by French seizure in 1805. In 1814 Ragusa was annexed by Austria, remaining a part of the Austrian Empire until its incorporation in the newly formed state of Yugoslavia in 1918. Croatia proclaimed its independence in 1991.

MONETARY SYSTEM

6 Soldi = 1 Grosetto
12 Grosetti = 1 Perpero
36 Grosetti = 1 Scudo
40 Grosetti = 1 Ducato
60 Grosetti = 1 Tallero

VI (6) GROSETTI

BILLON

Obv: St. Blaze, leg: PROT.REIP.RHAGUSIN. . . Rev: Value.

KM#	Date	Mintage	VG	Fine	VF	XF
25.1	1801	—	12.00	20.00	30.00	50.00
	Obv. leg: PROT.REIPV.RHACVSI.					
25.2	1801	—	12.00	20.00	30.00	50.00

PERPERO

BILLON

Obv: St. Blaze, leg: PROT.RAEIP. RHAGVSINAE. . . Rev: Christ.

KM#	Date	Mintage	VG	Fine	VF	XF
7	1801	—	16.50	27.50	55.00	90.00
	1802	—	16.50	27.50	55.00	90.00
	1803	—	16.50	27.50	55.00	90.00

NOTE: Earlier dates (1683-1750) exist for this type.

REUNION

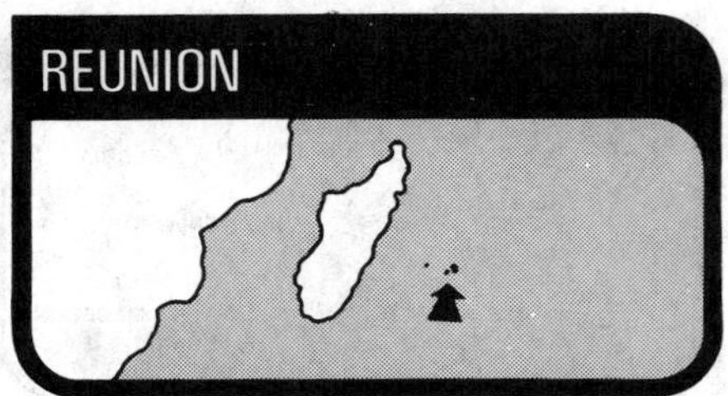

The Department of Reunion, an overseas department of France located in the Indian Ocean 400 miles (640 km.) east of Madagascar, has an area of 969 sq. mi. (2,510 sq. km.) and a population of *566,000. Capital: Saint-Denis. The island's volcanic soil is extremely fertile. Sugar, vanilla, coffee and rum are exported.

Although first visited by Portuguese navigators in the 16th century, Reunion was uninhabited when claimed for France by Capt. Goubert in 1638. It was first colonized as Isle de Bourbon by the French in 1662 as a layover station for ships rounding the Cape of Good Hope to India. It was renamed Reunion in 1793. The island remained in French possession except for the period of 1810-15, when it was occupied by the British. Reunion became an overseas department of France in 1946, and in 1958 voted to continue that status within the new French Union.

During the first half of the 19th century, Reunion was officially known as Isle de Bonaparte (1801-14) and Isle de Bourbon (1814-48). Reunion coinage of those periods is so designated.

ISLE DE BOURBON

The Restoration of the House of Bourbon in France caused the name of the Reunion Island to be changed to Isle de Bourbon from 1814-1848.

RULERS

Louis XVIII, 1814-1828

MONETARY SYSTEM

100 Centimes = 1 Franc

10 CENTIMES

BILLON

KM#	Date	Mintage	VG	Fine	VF	XF
1	1816A	.150	20.00	40.00	85.00	275.00

REUNION

MINT MARKS

(a) - Paris, privy marks only

MONETARY SYSTEM

100 Centimes = 1 Franc

50 CENTIMES

COPPER-NICKEL

KM#	Date	Mintage	Fine	VF	XF	Unc
4	1896	1.000	20.00	45.00	125.00	350.00

FRANC

COPPER-NICKEL

KM#	Date	Mintage	Fine	VF	XF	Unc
5	1896	.500	35.00	60.00	175.00	400.00

ESSAIS (E)

Standard metals unless otherwise noted

KM#	Date	Mintage	Identification	Mkt.Val.
E1	1896	—	50 Centimes, KM4	250.00
E2	1896	—	1 Franc, KM5	325.00

PIEFORTS with ESSAI (PE)

Double thickness

Standard metals unless otherwise noted

KM#	Date	Mintage	Identification	Mkt.Val.
PE1	1896	—	50 Centimes, KM4	450.00
PE1a	1896	—	50 Centimes, Bronze, KM4	600.00
PE2	1896	—	1 Franc, KM5	550.00

ROMANIA

The Republic of Romania, a country in southeast Europe, has an area of 91,699 sq. mi. (237,500 sq. km.) and a population of *23.2 million. Capital: Bucharest. Heavy industry and oil have become increasingly important to the economy since 1959. Machinery, foodstuffs, raw minerals and petroleum products are exported.

The area of Romania, generally referred to as Dacia by the ancient Romans, was subjected to wave after wave of barbarian conquest until the late 13th century. The Vlach tribes located south of the Danube river moved north, mixing in with the Slavs and Tatars, developing the two principalities of Walachia and Moldavia.

The earlier years of the principality of Walachia involved struggles with Hungary. Soon afterwards, they found themselves at war with the Turks. Final capitulation to Turkey came in 1417.

Moldavia first appeared as an independent state in 1349. Polish overlordship came about at the end of the 14th century. Stephen the Great (1457-1504) was a champion of Christendom against the Turks. When Peter Rares (1527-38 and 1541-46) came to the throne, he allied himself with the Turks as he made war on the imperial forces in Transylvania and Poland. Later he allied himself with the emperor against Poland and the sultan, but was defeated and deposed in 1538. In 1541 he returned to the throne with Turkish help.

The treaty of Kuchuk Kainarji, which ended the Russo-Turkish War in 1774, resulted in Moldavia losing its northern tip, Bukovina, to Austria. As the result of Russia's continuing interest in the area and the peace of Bucharest in 1812, southeastern Moldavia, known as Bessarabia, ceded.

Peasant uprisings in 1848 were put down by the Turks and a Russo-Turkish military intervention resumed status-quo. Russian troops did not evacuate the principalities until 1851 and during the Crimean War, were occupied in turn by Russia and Austria. The Treaty of Paris (1856) placed the principalities with their existing privileges ending the Russian protectorate.

Union of the principalities was voted for unanimously in 1848 and the two assemblies elected a prince in the person of Alexander Cuza on Jan. 17, 1859, accomplishing the de facto union of Romania. The prince, through lack of agrarian reform, was compelled to abdicate in Feb. 1866, and was succeeded by Prince Carol I who later became King in 1881.

The First Balkan War (1912) gave birth to the claim for Silistra, awarded in May 1917. The intervention and deployment of Romanian troops into Bulgaria in the Second Balkan War (1913) resulted in the acquisition of southern Dobruja.

Crossing into Transylvania on Aug. 22, Romania declared war on Austro-Hungary. They were soon expelled and the Central Powers occupied Bucharest by Dec. 6, 1916. The Treaty of Bucharest was signed on May 7, 1918, and the Central Powers disorganized the finance of the kingdom, ensuring financial ruin. On Nov. 8, 1918, when the defeat of the Central Powers was eminent, war was declared again. The King re-entered Bucharest on Nov. 30, 1918, after the German troops had evacuated Romania under the terms of the Armistice. Bessarabia was incorporated along with Transylvania and the old frontier borders were recognized by the treaties of St. Germain and Trianon.

The government was reorganized along Fascist lines between September 14, 1940 and January 23, 1941, following a military dictatorship, Marshal Ion Antonescu installed himself as Chief of State. When the Germans invaded the Soviet Union, Romania also became involved for recovering the region of Bessarabia annexed by Stalin in 1940.

On August 23, 1944, King Mihai I proclaimed the armistice with Allied Forces. Romanian Army drove out the Germans and Hungarians in North Transylvania, but the land had been subsequently occupied by the Soviet Army. That monarchy was abolished on Dec. 30, 1947, and Romania became a "People's Republic" on the Soviet pattern, which was later proclaimed a "Socialist Republic" in 1965. With the accession of N. Ceausescu to power (1965) a repressive and impoverished domestic scene worsened.

On Dec. 22, 1989 the Communist government was overthrown by organized freedom fighters in Bucharest. Ceausescu and his wife were later executed. The new government has established the republic, the official and constitutional name being Romania.

RULERS

Carol I (as Prince), 1866-81 (as King), 1881-1914

MINT MARKS

(a) - Paris, privy marks only

(b) - Brussels, privy marks only
angel head (1872-1876),

no marks (1894-1924)
B - Bucharest (1870-1900)
B - Hamburg
C - Candescu, chief engineer of the Bucharest Mint (1870)
FM - Franklin Mint
H - Heaton
HF - Huguenin, Le Locle
J - Hamburg
KN - Kings Norton
(p) - Thunderbolt - Poissy zig zag (1924)
V - Vienna
W - Watt (James Watt & Co.)
Huguenin - Le Locle
( ) - no marks, 1930 (10, 20 Lei), 1932 (100 Lei), Royal Mint - London

MONETARY SYSTEM

100 Bani = 1 Leu

BANU

COPPER

KM#	Date	Mintage	Fine	VF	XF	Unc
1	1867H	2.500	6.00	10.00	30.00	60.00
	1867H	Inc. Ab.	—	—	Proof	75.00
	1867WATT & CO.	2.500	7.00	14.00	35.00	75.00
	1867WATT & CO.	—	—	—	Proof	90.00

BAN

BRONZE

Similar to 2 Bani, KM#18.

KM#	Date	Mintage	Fine	VF	XF	Unc
A18	1883	500 pcs.	—	—	800.00	1200.

GILT BRONZE

KM#	Date	Mintage	Fine	VF	XF	Unc
A18a	1888	500 pcs.	—	—	700.00	1000.

NOTE: Presentation issues for Queen Elizabeth of Romania.

COPPER

KM#	Date	Mintage	Fine	VF	XF	Unc
26	1900B	20.007	1.50	2.25	5.50	15.00
	1900B	—	—	—	Proof	55.00

NOTE: Varieties exist.

2 BANI

COPPER

KM#	Date	Mintage	Fine	VF	XF	Unc
2	1867HEATON	5.000	2.50	6.00	12.00	30.00
	1867HEATON	Inc. Ab.	—	—	Proof	65.00
	1867WATT & CO.	5.000	5.00	12.00	20.00	40.00
	1867WATT & CO.	—	—	—	Proof	85.00

19.5mm

Obv leg: CAROL I DOMNUL (Prince)

KM#	Date	Mintage	Fine	VF	XF	Unc
11.1	1879B	.500	5.00	10.00	25.00	55.00

20mm

KM#	Date	Mintage	Fine	VF	XF	Unc
11.2	1879B	Inc. Ab.	4.00	8.00	18.00	35.00
	1880B	10.500	3.00	6.00	12.00	25.00
	1881B	1.250	15.00	25.00	50.00	120.00

Obv. leg: CAROL I REGE (King)

KM#	Date	Mintage	Fine	VF	XF	Unc
18	1882B	5.000	4.00	10.00	20.00	45.00

Rev: ROMANIA added above shield.

KM#	Date	Mintage	Fine	VF	XF	Unc
27	1900B	20.000	1.00	2.00	5.00	14.00

NOTE: Varieties exist.

5 BANI

COPPER

KM#	Date	Mintage	Fine	VF	XF	Unc
3	1867HEATON	12.500	2.50	5.00	10.00	25.00
	1867HEATON	—	—	—	Proof	80.00
	1867WATT & CO.	12.500	3.00	6.00	16.00	45.00
	1867WATT & CO.	—	—	—	Proof	100.00

Obv. leg: CAROL I REGE (King).

KM#	Date	Mintage	Fine	VF	XF	Unc
19	1882B	5.000	1.00	2.50	12.00	35.00
	1883B	2.300	1.00	2.50	12.00	36.00
	1884B	8.400	1.00	2.00	8.00	30.00
	1885B	3.600	2.00	4.00	18.00	45.00

COPPER-NICKEL

KM#	Date	Mintage	Fine	VF	XF	Unc
28	1900	20.000	1.00	2.50	7.00	18.00

10 BANI

COPPER

KM#	Date	Mintage	Fine	VF	XF	Unc
4	1867HEATON	12.500	2.00	7.00	15.00	30.00
	1867HEATON	Inc. Ab.	—	—	Proof	75.00
	1867WATT & CO.	12.500	2.00	7.00	18.00	45.00
	1867WATT & CO.	—	—	—	Proof	95.00

COPPER-NICKEL

KM#	Date	Mintage	Fine	VF	XF	Unc
29	1900	15.000	.75	2.00	5.00	15.00
	1900	—	—	—	Proof	60.00

20 BANI

COPPER-NICKEL

KM#	Date	Mintage	Fine	VF	XF	Unc
30	1900	2.500	3.00	9.00	25.00	75.00

50 BANI

2.5000 g, .835 SILVER, .0671 oz ASW

KM#	Date	Mintage	Fine	VF	XF	Unc
9	1873(b)	4.800	2.50	8.00	20.00	55.00
	1873(b) medal rotation	Inc. Ab.	4.00	10.00	25.00	65.00
	1876(b)	2.117	3.00	12.00	30.00	70.00

KM#	Date	Mintage	Fine	VF	XF	Unc
13	1881V	1.000	5.00	16.00	40.00	120.00

Rev: Large letters.

KM#	Date	Mintage	Fine	VF	XF	Unc
21.1	1884B	1.000	3.00	7.50	25.00	65.00

Obv: Different head.

KM#	Date	Mintage	Fine	VF	XF	Unc
21.2	1885B	.200	6.00	20.00	50.00	150.00

Rev: Small letters.

KM#	Date	Mintage	Fine	VF	XF	Unc
23	1894	.600	4.00	12.00	22.00	55.00
	1900	3.838	2.50	12.00	22.00	55.00

NOTE: Later date (1901) exists for this type.

LEU

5.0000 g, .835 SILVER, .1342 oz ASW

KM#	Date	Mintage	Fine	VF	XF	Unc
6	1870C	.400	20.00	45.00	125.00	375.00
	1870C medal rotation	Inc. Ab.	100.00	175.00	425.00	1000.
	1870B	Inc. Ab.	150.00	250.00	600.00	1500.
	1870 B medal rotation	Inc. Ab.	—	—	—	—

KM#	Date	Mintage	Fine	VF	XF	Unc
10	1873(b)	4.443	4.00	8.00	17.50	60.00
	1874(b)	4.511	5.00	12.00	25.00	85.00
	1876(b)	.225	400.00	600.00	1000.	2000.

NOTE: Varieties exist.

Obv. leg: CAROL I DOMNUL (Prince).

KM#	Date	Mintage	Fine	VF	XF	Unc
14	1881V	1.800	8.00	18.00	50.00	140.00
	1881V	—	—	—	Proof	—

Obv. leg: CAROL I REGE (King).

KM#	Date	Mintage	Fine	VF	XF	Unc
22	1884B	1.000	6.00	15.00	35.00	85.00
	1885B	.400	15.00	40.00	140.00	400.00
	1885B	—	—	—	Proof	—

KM#	Date	Mintage	Fine	VF	XF	Unc
24	1894	1.500	4.00	10.00	40.00	125.00
	1894	—	—	—	Proof	—
	1900	.799	4.00	9.00	25.00	75.00

NOTE: Later date (1901) exists for this type.

2 LEI

10.0000 g, .835 SILVER, .2684 oz ASW

KM#	Date	Mintage	Fine	VF	XF	Unc
8	1872(b)	.262	6.00	15.00	55.00	175.00
	1872	—	—	—	Proof	500.00
	1873(b)	1.745	4.00	10.00	30.00	80.00
	1875(b)	3.092	4.00	9.00	25.00	70.00
	1876(b)	.653	6.00	17.00	60.00	165.00

KM#	Date	Mintage	Fine	VF	XF	Unc
15	1881V	1.150	12.00	36.00	85.00	230.00

KM#	Date	Mintage	Fine	VF	XF	Unc
25	1894	.600	10.00	20.00	100.00	250.00
	1894	—	—	—	Proof	—
	1900	.087	12.00	30.00	90.00	240.00

NOTE: Later date (1901) exists for this type.

5 LEI

25.0000 g, .900 SILVER, .7234 oz ASW

KM#	Date	Mintage	Fine	VF	XF	Unc
12	1880B name near rim					
		1.800	17.50	35.00	80.00	200.00
	1880B name near truncation					
		Inc. Ab.	20.00	40.00	90.00	220.00
	1881B	2.200	15.00	30.00	55.00	175.00

KM#	Date	Mintage	Fine	VF	XF	Unc
16	1881B name near truncation					
		.570	25.00	60.00	140.00	280.00

Lettered Edge

KM#	Date	Mintage	Fine	VF	XF	Unc
17.1	1881B	1.230	15.00	35.00	85.00	265.00
	1882B	1.100	15.00	40.00	90.00	285.00
	1883B	*2.300	15.00	30.00	50.00	170.00
	1884B	.300	25.00	75.00	140.00	375.00
	1885B	.040	120.00	200.00	600.00	1500.

***NOTE:** Varieties in crown on mantle exist.

20 LEI

6.4516 g, .900 GOLD, .1867 oz AGW
Obv. leg: CAROL I DOMNULU (Prince), light beard.
Reeded edge.

KM#	Date	Mintage	Fine	VF	XF	Unc
5	1868(b)					
		200 pcs.	—	4000.	6000.	8000.

Obv. leg: CAROL I DOMNUL (Prince), heavy beard.

KM#	Date	Mintage	Fine	VF	XF	Unc
7	1870C	5,000	600.00	1000.	1800.	3000.

Obv. leg: CAROL I REGE (King).

KM#	Date	Mintage	Fine	VF	XF	Unc
20	1883B	.150	95.00	125.00	150.00	220.00
	1884	.035	— Reported, not confirmed			
	1890B	.196	100.00	150.00	175.00	240.00

PATTERNS (Pn)

(Including off metal strikes)

KM#	Date	Mintage	Identification	Mkt.Val.
Pn1	1867	—	1 Ban, Heaton	—
Pn2	1867	—	1 Ban, Watt	—
Pn3	1867	—	2 Bani, Heaton	—
Pn4	1867	—	2 Bani, Watt	—
Pn5	1867	—	5 Bani, Bronze, 1-1/2 normal thickness	—
Pn6	1867	—	5 Bani, Copper-Nickel, 1-1/2 normal thickness	400.00

KM#	Date	Mintage	Identification	Mkt.Val.
Pn7	1867	—	5 Bani, Nickel, WATT	—
Pn8	1867	—	10 Bani, Copper-Nickel, 1-1/2 normal thickness	130.00
Pn9	1867	—	10 Bani, Copper-Nickel, regular thickness	—
Pn10	1867	—	10 Bani, Nickel, WATT, plain edge	—
Pn11	1867	—	20 Lei, Gold, Berlin Mint, KM#5	5000.
Pn12	1868	—	20 Lei, Gold, plain edge	4000.

KM#	Date	Mintage	Identification	Mkt.Val.
Pn13	1869	—	50 Bani, Copper, reeded edge	—
Pn14	1869	—	50 Bani, Zinc	350.00
Pn15	1869	—	50 Bani, Brass	100.00
Pn16	1869	—	50 Bani, Bronze	100.00
Pn17	1869	—	50 Bani, White Metal	125.00
Pn18	1869	—	50 Bani, Silver	225.00

KM#	Date	Mintage	Identification	Mkt.Val.
Pn19	1869	—	1 Leu, Copper, reeded edge	—
Pn20	1869	—	1 Leu, Pewter	350.00
Pn21	1869	—	1 Leu, Bronze	125.00
Pn22	1869	—	1 Leu, White Metal	200.00
Pn23	1869	—	1 Leu, Silver	275.00

KM#	Date	Mintage	Identification	Mkt.Val.
Pn24	1869	—	2 Lei, Copper or Bronze	—
Pn25	1869	—	2 Lei, Zinc	400.00
Pn26	1869	—	2 Lei, White Metal	225.00
Pn27	1869	—	2 Lei, Silver, plain edge	350.00
Pn28	1870B	—	1 Leu, .835 Silver	150.00

KM#	Date	Mintage	Identification	Mkt.Val.
Pn29	1870	—	20 Lei, Gold	2500.
Pn30	1873	—	1 Leu,	—
Pn31	1875	—	2 Lei, Copper-Nickel	275.00
Pn32	1876	—	20 Bani, German Silver	125.00
Pn33	1876	—	50 Bani, Copper-Nickel, reeded edge	150.00
Pn34	1876	—	1 Leu, Copper-Nickel, reeded edge	175.00
Pn35	1876	—	2 Lei, Copper-Nickel, reeded edge	—
Pn36	1879	—	5 Lei, Zinc	—

KM#	Date	Mintage	Identification	Mkt.Val.
Pn37	1879	—	5 Lei, Copper	200.00
Pn38	1879	—	5 Lei, Bronze	—
Pn39	1879	—	5 Lei, Silver	—
Pn40	1881	—	1 Leu	—
Pn41	1883	500	1 Banu, Bronze	Rare
Pn42	1883	—	5 Lei, Silver	—
Pn43	1883	—	20 Lei, Gold	1000.

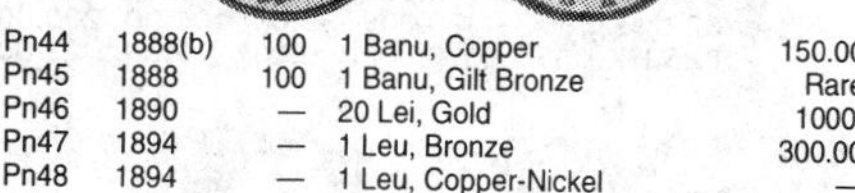

KM#	Date	Mintage	Identification	Mkt.Val.
Pn44	1888(b)	100	1 Banu, Copper	150.00
Pn45	1888	100	1 Banu, Gilt Bronze	Rare
Pn46	1890	—	20 Lei, Gold	1000.
Pn47	1894	—	1 Leu, Bronze	300.00
Pn48	1894	—	1 Leu, Copper-Nickel	—

RUSSIA

Russia, formerly the central power of the Union of Soviet Socialist Republics and now of the Commonwealth of Independent States occupies the northern part of Asia and the eastern part of Europe, in 1991 had an area of 8,649,538 sq. mi. (22,402,200 sq. km.) and a population of *288.7 million. Capital: Moscow. Exports include iron and steel, crude oil, timber, and nonferrous metals.

The first Russian dynasty was founded in Novgorod by the Viking Rurik in 862 A.D. Under Yaroslav the Wise (1019-54) the subsequent Kievan state became one of the great commercial and cultural centers of Europe before falling to the Mongols of the Batu Khan, 13th century, who were suzerains of Russia until late in the 15th century when Ivan III threw off the Mongol yoke. The Russian Empire was enlarged, solidified and Westernized during the reigns of Ivan the Terrible, Peter the Great and Catherine the Great, and by 1881 extended to the Pacific and into Central Asia. Contemporary Russian history began in March of 1917 when Tsar Nicholas II abdicated under pressure and was replaced by a provisional government composed of both radical and conservative elements. This government rapidly lost ground to the Bolshevik wing of the Socialist Democratic Labor Party which attained power following the Bolshevik Revolution which began on Nov. 7, 1917. After the Russian Civil War, the regional governments, national states and armies became federal republics of the Russian Socialist Federal Soviet Republic. These autonomous republics united to form the Union of Soviet Socialist Republics that was established as a federation under the premiership of Lenin on Dec. 30, 1922.

In the fall of 1991, events moved swiftly in the Soviet Union. Estonia, Latvia and Lithuania won their independence and were recognized by Moscow, Sept. 6. The Commonwealth of Independent States was formed Dec. 8, 1991 in Mensk by Belarus, Russia and Ukraine. It was expanded at a summit Dec. 21, 1991 to include 11 of the 12 remaining republics (excluding Georgia) of the old USSR.

EMPIRE

RULERS

Alexander I, 1801-1825
Nicholas I, 1825-1855
Alexander II, 1855-1881
Alexander III, 1881-1894
Nicholas II, 1894-1917

MINT MARKS

ЕМ - Ekaterinburg, 1763-1876
КМ - Kolpino (Izhora), 1810-1821
КМ - Kolyvan, 1767-1830 (later Suzun)
КМ - Kolpina, 1810
СМ - St. Petersburg (gold), 1796-1801
СПБ - St. Petersburg, 1724-1914
ИМ - Izhora, 1811-1821
СПМ St. Petersburg (Izhora), 1840-1843
СМ - Suzun (Kolyvan), 1831-1847
ВМ - Warsaw, 1850-1864
MW - Warsaw, 1842-1854
Star (on rim) - Paris, 1896-1899
2 Stars (on rim) - Brussels, 1897-1899

MINTMASTERS INITIALS

EKATERINBURG MINT

Initials	Years	Mintmaster
НМ	1810-21	Nicholai Mundt
ИФ	1811	Ivan Felkner
ФГ	1811-23	Franz German
ПГ	1823-25	Peter Gramatchikov
ИШ	1825	Ivan Shevkunov
ИК	1825-30	Ivan Kolobov
ФХ	1830-37	Fedor Khvochinski
КТ	1837	Konstantin Tomson
НА	1837-39	Nicholai Alexeev

IZHORA (KOLPINO) MINT

Initials	Years	Mintmaster
МК	1810-11	Mikhail Kleiner
ПС	1811-14	Paul Stupitzyn
ЯБ	1820-21	Yakov Wilson

KOLYVAN and SOUZAN MINTS

Initials	Years	Mintmaster
ПБ	1810-11	Peter Berezowski
АМ	1812-17	Alexei Maleev
ДБ	1817-18	Dmitri Bikhtov
АД	1818-21	Alexander Deichmann
АМ	1821-30	Andrei Mevius

ST. PETERSBURG MINT

Initials	Years	Mintmaster
ФЦ	1797-1801	Fedor Tsetreus
ОМ	1798-1801	Ossip Medzher
АИ	1801-03	Alexie Ivanov
ФГ	1803-17	Fedor Gelman
ХЛ	1804-05	Christopher Leo
МК	1808-09	Mikhail Kleiner
МФ	1812-22	Mikhail Fedorov
ПС	1811-25	Paul Stupitzyn
ПД	1820-38	Paul Danilov
НГ	1825-42	Nikolai Grachev
АЧ	1839-43	Alexei Chadov
КБ	1844-46	Constantine Butenev
АГ	1846-57	Alexander Gertov
ПА	1847-52	Paul Alexiev
НІ	1848-77	Nicholai Iossa
ФБ	1856-61	Fedor Blum
ПФ	1858-62	Paul Follendorf
МИ	1861-63	Mikhail Ivanov
АБ	1863	Alexander Belozerov
АС	1864-65	Aggei Svechin
НФ	1864-82	Nikolai Follendorf
СШ	1865-66	Sergei Shostak
ДС	1882-83	Dmitri Sabaneev

Initials	Years	Mintmaster
АГ	1883-99	Appolon Grasgov
ЭБ	1899-1913	Elikum Babayantz
ФЗ	1899-1901	Felix Zaleman

MONETARY SYSTEM

1/4 Kopek = Polushka ПОЛУШКА
1/2 Kopek = Denga, Denezhka ДЕНГА, ДЕНЕЖКА
Kopek КОПѢЙКА
(2, 3 & 4) Kopeks КОПѢЙКИ
(5 and up) Kopeks КОПѢЕКЪ
3 Kopeks = Altyn, Altynnik АЛТЫНЪ, АЛТЫННИКЪ
10 Kopeks = Grivna, Grivennik ГРИВНА, ГРИВЕННИКЪ
25 Kopeks = Polupoltina, Polupoltinnik ПОЛУПОЛТИНА ПОЛУПОЛТИННИКЪ
50 Kopeks = Poltina, Poltinnik ПОЛТИНА, ПОЛТИННИКЪ
100 Kopeks = Rouble, Ruble РУБЛЪ
10 Roubles = Imperial ИМПЕРІАЛЪ
10 Roubles = Chervonetz ЧЕРВОНЕЦ

NOTE: Mintage figures for years after 1885 are for fiscal years and may or may not reflect actual rarity, the commemorative silver figures being exceptions.

NOTE: For silver coins with Zlotych and Kopek or Ruble denominations see Poland.

NOTE: For gold coins with Zlotych and Ruble denominations see Poland.

POLUSHKA

(1/4 Kopek)

NOTE: Polushka dated 1801 #C92.2 previously listed here is now recognized as Novodel #N340.

COPPER, 3.00 g
Mint mark: EM

C#	Date	Mintage	VG	Fine	VF	XF
111.1	1803	.012	15.00	30.00	60.00	120.00
	1804	20 pcs.	—	—	Rare	—
	1805	.025	15.00	30.00	60.00	120.00
	1808	—	25.00	50.00	100.00	200.00
	1810/09	—	30.00	60.00	120.00	250.00
	1810	—	25.00	50.00	100.00	200.00

Mint mark: KM

C#	Date	Mintage	VG	Fine	VF	XF
111.2	1803	—	20.00	40.00	80.00	160.00
	1804	—	20.00	40.00	80.00	160.00
	1805	—	20.00	40.00	80.00	160.00
	1807	—	20.00	40.00	80.00	160.00

Mint mark: EM

C#	Date	Mintage	VG	Fine	VF	XF
142.1	1840	10.793	2.00	4.00	8.00	20.00
	1841	3.230	2.00	4.00	8.00	20.00
	1842	1.600	2.00	4.00	8.00	20.00
	1843	1.664	2.00	4.00	8.00	20.00

Mint mark: СПМ

C#	Date	Mintage	VG	Fine	VF	XF
142.2	1840	6.400	4.00	7.50	15.00	30.00
	1841	6.400	3.00	6.00	12.00	24.00
	1842	12.800	3.00	6.00	12.00	24.00

Mint mark: CM

C#	Date	Mintage	VG	Fine	VF	XF
142.3	1839	.450	12.50	25.00	50.00	100.00
	1840	2.573	4.00	7.50	15.00	30.00
	1841	3.571	4.00	7.50	15.00	30.00
	1842	3.960	4.00	7.50	15.00	30.00
	1843	2.006	4.00	7.50	15.00	30.00
	1844	3.400	4.00	7.50	15.00	30.00
	1845	3.000	4.00	7.50	15.00	30.00
	1846	3.000	4.00	7.50	15.00	30.00

Mint mark: EM

C#	Date	Mintage	VG	Fine	VF	XF
147.1	1850	5.184	1.50	3.00	5.00	10.00
	1851/0	7.776	2.00	4.00	7.00	15.00
	1851	Inc. Ab.	1.50	3.00	5.00	10.00
	1852	1.178	1.50	3.00	5.00	10.00
	1853	5.382	1.50	3.00	5.00	10.00
	1854/3	4.538	2.00	4.00	7.00	15.00
	1854	Inc. Ab.	1.50	3.00	5.00	10.00
	1855	6.442	3.00	6.00	13.00	25.00

Mint mark: BM

C#	Date	Mintage	VG	Fine	VF	XF
147.3	1850	—	7.00	12.00	25.00	50.00
147.3	1851	.080	7.00	12.00	25.00	50.00
	1852	.080	7.00	12.00	25.00	50.00
	1853	.040	7.00	12.00	25.00	50.00

Mint mark: EM
Plain border.

Y#	Date	Mintage	Fine	VF	XF	Unc
1.1	1855	6.422	2.00	4.00	8.00	20.00
	1856	6.000	2.00	4.00	8.00	20.00
	1857	6.000	2.00	4.00	8.00	20.00
	1858	6.970	2.00	4.00	8.00	20.00
	1859	3.834	2.00	4.00	8.00	20.00

Mint mark: BM

Y#	Date	Mintage	Fine	VF	XF	Unc
1.2	1855	.040	7.00	15.00	30.00	60.00
	1860	—	7.00	15.00	30.00	60.00

Mint mark: EM
Toothed border.

Y#	Date	Mintage	Fine	VF	XF	Unc
1.3	1858	—	—	—	Rare	—
	1859	—	2.00	4.00	8.00	20.00
	1860	—	60.00	120.00	200.00	300.00
	1861	.192	3.00	6.00	12.00	25.00
	1862	.992	2.00	4.00	8.00	20.00
	1863	.300	4.00	8.00	15.00	30.00
	1864	.403	4.00	8.00	15.00	30.00
	1865	.122	2.00	4.00	8.00	20.00
	1866	.326	2.00	4.00	8.00	20.00
	1867	.832	10.00	20.00	40.00	80.00

Mint mark: BM

Y#	Date	Mintage	Fine	VF	XF	Unc
1.4	1861	3.160	3.00	6.00	15.00	35.00

Mint mark: EM

Y#	Date	Mintage	Fine	VF	XF	Unc
7.1	1867	Inc.Y1.3	10.00	17.00	35.00	70.00
	1868	.700	2.00	5.00	10.00	20.00
	1869	.615	2.00	5.00	10.00	20.00
	1870	.435	2.00	5.00	10.00	20.00
	1871	.155	2.00	5.00	10.00	20.00
	1872	.540	2.00	5.00	10.00	20.00
	1873	.823	2.00	5.00	10.00	20.00
	1874	.340	2.00	5.00	10.00	20.00
	1875	.300	1.25	2.50	5.00	10.00
	1876	—	—	—	Rare	—

Mint mark: СПБ

Y#	Date	Mintage	Fine	VF	XF	Unc
7.2	1867	—	3.00	6.00	12.00	25.00
	1868	.060	3.00	6.00	12.00	25.00
	1869	.092	3.00	6.00	12.00	25.00
	1870	.020	3.50	7.50	15.00	30.00
	1871	—	—	—	Rare	—
	1876	.800	1.25	2.50	5.00	15.00
	1877	.720	1.25	2.50	5.00	15.00
	1878	1.100	1.25	2.50	5.00	15.00
	1879	.280	1.50	3.00	6.00	15.00
	1880	.180	3.00	5.00	9.00	20.00
	1881	.060	3.00	5.00	9.00	20.00

Y#	Date	Mintage	Fine	VF	XF	Unc
29	1881	.200	2.50	5.00	10.00	20.00
	1882	.060	2.50	5.00	10.00	20.00
	1883	.240	1.50	3.00	6.00	12.00
	1884	.140	2.50	4.00	8.00	20.00
	1885	.480	1.50	3.00	6.00	12.00
	1886	1.060	1.25	2.50	5.00	10.00
	1887	1.000	1.25	2.50	5.00	10.00
	1888	.200	1.50	3.00	6.00	12.00
	1889	.181	3.00	5.00	10.00	30.00
	1890	Inc. Ab.	1.50	3.00	6.00	12.00
	1891	.400	1.50	3.00	6.00	12.00
	1892	.918	1.25	2.50	5.00	12.00
	1893	.740	1.25	2.50	5.00	12.00

Y#	Date	Mintage	Fine	VF	XF	Unc
47.1	1894	—	50.00	100.00	300.00	500.00
	1895	.060	2.50	5.00	10.00	20.00
	1896	5.960	.50	1.00	2.00	7.00
	1897	3.040	.50	1.00	2.00	7.00
	1898	8.000	.50	1.00	2.00	7.00
	1899	8.000	.50	1.00	2.00	7.00
	1900	4.000	.50	1.00	2.00	7.00
	Common date	—	—	—	Proof	35.00

NOTE: Later dates (1909-1910) exist for this type.

DENGA

(1/2 Kopek)

COPPER, 6.50 g
Mint mark: EM

Obv: Monogram. Rev: Value, date.

C#	Date	Mintage	VG	Fine	VF	XF
93.2	1801	.026	7.50	15.00	30.00	60.00

NOTE: Earlier dates (1797-1800) exist for this type.

Mint mark: EM

C#	Date	Mintage	VG	Fine	VF	XF
112.1	1804	20 pcs.	—	—	Rare	—
	1805	.040	50.00	100.00	175.00	225.00
	1808	—	—	—	Rare	—
	1810	—	—	—	Rare	—

Mint mark: KM

C#	Date	Mintage	VG	Fine	VF	XF
112.2	1804	—	40.00	80.00	150.00	300.00
	1805	—	40.00	80.00	150.00	300.00
	1807	—	40.00	80.00	150.00	300.00

Obv: Type 2 eagle.

C#	Date	Mintage	VG	Fine	VF	XF
116.2	1811 ПБ	—	5.00	10.00	20.00	40.00

Mint mark: EM
Obv: Type 3 eagle.

C#	Date	Mintage	VG	Fine	VF	XF
116.3	1811 HM plain edge	.135	3.75	7.50	15.00	30.00
	1811 HM reeded edge	Inc. Ab.	3.75	7.50	15.00	30.00
	1813 HM	.024	4.00	8.00	15.00	30.00
	1815 HM	.059	4.00	8.00	15.00	30.00
	1818 HM	23.410	2.00	4.00	8.00	15.00
	1819 HM	1.360	2.00	4.00	8.00	15.00
	1822 ФГ	—	25.00	50.00	100.00	200.00
	1825 ИК	.555	3.00	6.00	12.00	25.00

Mint mark: ИМ

C#	Date	Mintage	VG	Fine	VF	XF
116.4	1810 ФГ	.026	25.00	50.00	100.00	200.00
	1810 МК	I.A.	3.50	7.00	15.00	30.00
	1811 МК	.160	2.50	5.00	10.00	20.00
	1812 ПС	.510	2.50	5.00	10.00	20.00
	1813 ПС	1.220	2.50	5.00	10.00	20.00
	1814 ПС	2.250	2.50	5.00	10.00	20.00
	1814 СП	I.A.	2.50	5.00	10.00	20.00

Mint mark: KM

C#	Date	Mintage	VG	Fine	VF	XF
116.5	1812 AM	—	4.00	8.00	15.00	30.00
	1813 AM	—	4.00	8.00	15.00	30.00
	1814 AM	—	4.00	8.00	15.00	30.00
	1815 AM	—	4.00	8.00	15.00	30.00
	1816 AM	—	4.00	8.00	15.00	30.00
	1817 AM	—	4.00	8.00	15.00	30.00

Mint mark: СПБ

C#	Date	Mintage	VG	Fine	VF	XF
116.6	1810 ФГ	—	6.00	12.00	25.00	50.00
	1811 МК	.075	3.00	6.00	12.00	25.00
	1812 ПС	—	25.00	50.00	100.00	200.00

Mint mark: EM

C#	Date	Mintage	VG	Fine	VF	XF
135.1	1827 ИК	2.165	3.00	6.00	12.00	25.00
	1828 ИК	—	3.00	6.00	12.00	25.00

Mint mark: СПБ

C#	Date	Mintage	VG	Fine	VF	XF
135.2	1828	—	25.00	50.00	100.00	200.00

COPPER, 4.00 g
Mint mark: EM

C#	Date	Mintage	VG	Fine	VF	XF
143.1	1840	10.999	2.00	4.00	8.00	15.00
	1841	3.384	2.00	4.00	8.00	15.00
	1842	3.600	2.00	4.00	8.00	15.00
	1843	2.580	2.00	4.00	8.00	15.00

Mint mark: СПБ

C#	Date	Mintage	VG	Fine	VF	XF
143.2	1840	—	6.00	12.00	25.00	50.00

Mint mark: СПМ

C#	Date	Mintage	VG	Fine	VF	XF
143.3	1840	6.400	2.00	4.00	8.00	15.00
	1841	6.400	2.00	4.00	8.00	15.00
	1842	12.800	2.00	4.00	8.00	15.00

Mint mark: СМ

C#	Date	Mintage	VG	Fine	VF	XF
143.4	1839	.454	4.00	8.00	15.00	30.00
	1840	2.560	2.00	4.00	8.00	15.00
	1841	3.542	2.00	4.00	8.00	15.00
	1842	3.960	2.00	4.00	8.00	15.00
	1843	2.006	2.00	4.00	8.00	15.00
	1844	3.400	2.00	4.00	8.00	15.00
	1845	3.000	2.00	4.00	8.00	15.00
	1846	3.000	2.00	4.00	8.00	15.00
	1847	2.532	2.00	4.00	8.00	15.00

Mint mark: MW

C#	Date	Mintage	VG	Fine	VF	XF
143.5	1848	.087	30.00	60.00	120.00	225.00

Mint mark: ЕМ

C#	Date	Mintage	VG	Fine	VF	XF
148.1	1850	3.562	1.00	2.00	4.00	8.00
	1851	6.426	1.00	2.00	4.00	8.00
	1852	14.672	1.00	2.00	4.00	8.00
	1853	12.243	1.00	2.00	4.00	8.00
	1854/3	13.754	1.25	2.50	5.00	10.00
	1854	Inc. Ab.	1.00	2.00	4.00	8.00
	1855	20.510	1.50	3.00	6.00	12.00

Mint mark: ВМ

C#	Date	Mintage	VG	Fine	VF	XF
148.3	1850	1.840	2.00	4.00	8.00	15.00
	1851	1.200	2.00	4.00	8.00	15.00
	1852	1.231	2.00	4.00	8.00	15.00
	1853	.804	2.00	4.00	8.00	15.00
	1854	.352	2.00	4.00	8.00	15.00
	1855	6.380	4.00	8.00	15.00	30.00

Mint mark: ЕМ
Plain border.

Y#	Date	Mintage	Fine	VF	XF	Unc
2.1	1855	Inc.C148.1	2.00	4.00	8.00	20.00
	1856	6.000	2.00	4.00	8.00	20.00
	1857	6.000	2.00	4.00	8.00	20.00
	1858	11.147	2.00	4.00	8.00	20.00
	1859	5.871	2.00	4.00	8.00	20.00

Mint mark: ВМ

Y#	Date	Mintage	Fine	VF	XF	Unc
2.2	1855	6.380	5.00	10.00	20.00	40.00
	1856	4.278	5.00	10.00	20.00	40.00
	1857	1.909	5.00	10.00	20.00	40.00
	1858	.311	5.00	10.00	20.00	40.00
	1859	3.719	5.00	10.00	20.00	40.00
	1860	1.861	4.00	8.00	16.00	35.00

Mint mark: ЕМ
Toothed border.

Y#	Date	Mintage	Fine	VF	XF	Unc
2.3	1859	—	2.00	4.00	8.00	20.00
	1860	2.838	2.00	5.00	10.00	20.00
	1861	2.277	2.00	5.00	10.00	20.00
	1862	3.072	2.00	5.00	10.00	20.00
	1863	1.011	2.00	5.00	10.00	20.00
	1864	1.116	3.00	6.00	12.00	30.00
	1865	.560	50.00	100.00	200.00	300.00
	1866	.333	4.00	8.00	15.00	40.00
	1867	.390	8.00	15.00	30.00	70.00

Mint mark: ВМ

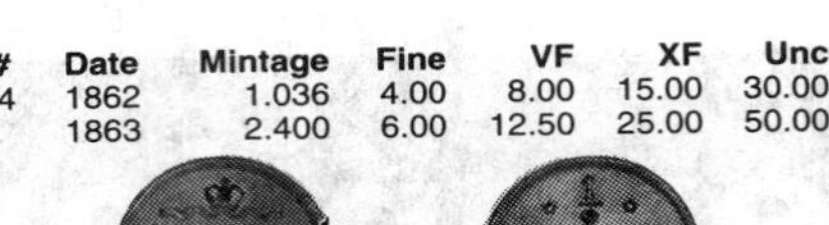

Y#	Date	Mintage	Fine	VF	XF	Unc
2.4	1861	2.819	4.00	8.00	15.00	30.00
2.4	1862	1.036	4.00	8.00	15.00	30.00
	1863	2.400	6.00	12.50	25.00	50.00

Mint mark: ЕМ

Y#	Date	Mintage	Fine	VF	XF	Unc
8.1	1867	Inc.Y2.3	7.00	15.00	30.00	60.00
	1868	1.190	1.50	3.00	6.00	12.00
	1869	.593	1.50	3.00	6.00	12.00
	1870	.510	2.00	4.00	8.00	15.00
	1871	.223	1.50	3.00	6.00	12.00
	1872	.365	1.50	3.00	6.00	12.00
	1873	.963	1.50	3.00	6.00	12.00
	1874	.300	1.50	3.00	6.00	12.00
	1875	.321	3.00	6.00	12.00	25.00
	1876	Inc. Ab.	50.00	100.00	200.00	325.00

Mint mark: СПБ

Y#	Date	Mintage	Fine	VF	XF	Unc
8.2	1867	—	5.00	10.00	20.00	40.00
	1868	.060	3.00	6.00	12.00	25.00
	1869	.145	2.00	4.50	9.00	17.50
	1870	.025	5.00	10.00	20.00	40.00
	1871	—	—	—	Rare	—
	1876	.770	1.00	2.25	4.50	9.00
	1877	1.290	1.00	2.25	4.50	9.00
	1878	1.120	1.00	2.25	4.50	9.00
	1879	.740	1.00	2.25	4.50	9.00
	1880	1.260	1.00	2.25	4.50	9.00
	1881	.420	1.00	2.25	4.50	9.00

Y#	Date	Mintage	Fine	VF	XF	Unc
30	1881	.440	1.00	2.25	4.50	15.00
	1882	.350	1.00	2.25	4.50	9.00
	1883	.540	1.00	2.25	4.50	9.00
	1884	.550	1.00	2.25	4.50	9.00
	1885	.680	1.00	2.25	4.50	9.00
	1886	.560	1.00	2.25	4.50	9.00
	1887	.600	1.00	2.25	4.50	9.00
	1888	.610	1.00	2.25	4.50	9.00
	1889	4.650	1.00	2.00	4.00	7.50
	1890	2.040	1.00	2.00	4.00	7.50
	1892	2.271	1.00	2.00	4.00	7.50
	1893	3.900	1.00	2.00	4.00	7.50
	1894	—	1.00	2.00	4.00	7.50

Y#	Date	Mintage	Fine	VF	XF	Unc
48.1	1894	—	50.00	100.00	300.00	500.00
	1895	2.992	1.00	2.00	4.00	8.00
	1896	1.340	1.00	2.00	4.00	8.00
	1897	60.000	.25	.50	1.00	5.00
	1898	76.000	.25	.50	1.00	5.00
	1899	76.000	.25	.50	1.00	5.00
	1900	36.000	.25	.50	1.00	5.00
	Common date	—	—	—	Proof	35.00

NOTE: Later dates (1908-1914) exist for this type.

KOPEK

COPPER, 4.00 g
Mint mark: ЕМ
Obv: Monogram. Rev: Value, date.

C#	Date	Mintage	VG	Fine	VF	XF
94.2	1801	1.708	3.00	6.00	12.00	25.00

NOTE: Earlier dates (1797-1800) exist for this type.

Mint mark: ЕМ

C#	Date	Mintage	VG	Fine	VF	XF
113.1	1804	20 pcs.	—	—	Rare	—
	1805	.114	20.00	40.00	80.00	150.00

Mint mark: КМ

C#	Date	Mintage	VG	Fine	VF	XF
113.2	1804	—	20.00	40.00	80.00	160.00
	1805	—	25.00	50.00	100.00	200.00
	1807	—	25.00	50.00	100.00	200.00

Obv: Type 2 eagle.

C#	Date	Mintage	VG	Fine	VF	XF
117.2	1811 ПБ	—	—	—	Rare	—

Mint mark: ЕМ
Obv: Type 3 eagle.

C#	Date	Mintage	VG	Fine	VF	XF
117.3	1810 НМ	—	—	—	Rare	—
	1811 НМ	1.926	3.00	6.00	12.00	25.00
	1811 НМ reeded edge	—	—	—	Rare	—
	1813 НМ	.030	25.00	50.00	100.00	200.00
	1815 НМ	.031	25.00	50.00	100.00	200.00
	1818 НМ	55.750	3.00	6.00	12.00	25.00
	1819 НМ	35.030	3.00	6.00	12.00	25.00
	1821 НМ	10.160	3.00	6.00	12.00	25.00
	1822 ФГ	10.265	3.00	6.00	12.00	25.00
	1823 ФГ	10.350	3.00	6.00	12.00	25.00
	1824 ПГ	—	3.00	6.00	12.00	25.00
	1825 ИК	—	3.00	6.00	12.00	25.00

NOTE: Varieties exist.

Mint mark: ИМ

C#	Date	Mintage	VG	Fine	VF	XF
117.4	1811 МК	.490	1.50	3.00	7.00	15.00
	1812 ПС	1.040	1.50	3.00	7.00	15.00
	1813 ПС	1.980	1.50	3.00	7.00	15.00
	1814 ПС	3.740	1.50	3.00	7.00	15.00
	1820 ЯВ	—	1.50	3.00	7.00	15.00
	1821 ЯВ	—	1.50	3.00	7.00	15.00

Mint mark: КМ

C#	Date	Mintage	VG	Fine	VF	XF
117.5	1812 АМ	—	2.50	5.00	10.00	20.00
	1813 АМ	—	2.50	5.00	10.00	20.00
	1814 АМ	—	2.50	5.00	10.00	20.00
	1815 АМ	—	2.50	5.00	10.00	20.00
	1816 АМ	—	2.50	5.00	10.00	20.00
	1817 АМ	—	2.50	5.00	10.00	20.00
	1818 АД	—	2.50	5.00	10.00	20.00
	1818 ДБ	—	2.50	5.00	10.00	20.00
	1819 АД	—	2.50	5.00	10.00	20.00
	1820 АД	—	2.50	5.00	10.00	20.00
	1821 АМ	—	2.50	5.00	10.00	20.00
	1822 АМ	—	2.50	5.00	10.00	20.00
	1823 АМ	—	2.50	5.00	10.00	20.00
	1824 АМ	—	2.50	5.00	10.00	20.00
	1825 АМ	—	2.50	5.00	10.00	20.00

Mint mark: СПБ

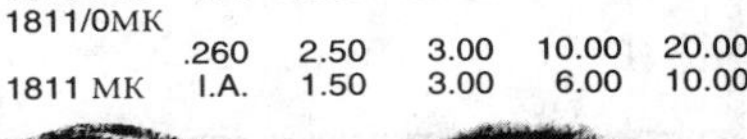

C#	Date	Mintage	VG	Fine	VF	XF
117.6	1810 ФГ	.093	25.00	50.00	100.00	200.00
	1810 МК	I.A.	25.00	50.00	100.00	200.00
	1811/0МК	.260	2.50	3.00	10.00	20.00
	1811 МК	I.A.	1.50	3.00	6.00	10.00

Mint mark: ЕМ

C#	Date	Mintage	VG	Fine	VF	XF
136.1	1827 ИК	2.646	3.00	6.00	12.00	25.00
	1828 ИК	43.015	3.00	6.00	12.00	25.00
	1829 ИК	48.215	3.00	6.00	12.00	25.00
	1830 ИК	2.100	3.00	6.00	12.00	25.00

Mint mark: КМ

C#	Date	Mintage	VG	Fine	VF	XF
136.2	1826 АМ	6.250	2.50	5.00	10.00	20.00
	1827 АМ	6.250	2.50	5.00	10.00	20.00
	1828 АМ	5.000	2.50	5.00	10.00	20.00
	1829 АМ	5.000	2.50	5.00	10.00	20.00
	1830 АМ	5.000	2.50	5.00	10.00	20.00

Mint mark: СПБ

C#	Date	Mintage	VG	Fine	VF	XF
136.3	1828	—	25.00	50.00	100.00	225.00

Mint mark: ЕМ

C#	Date	Mintage	VG	Fine	VF	XF
138.1	1831 ФХ	13.050	1.50	3.00	6.00	12.00
	1832 ФХ	3.400	1.50	3.00	6.00	12.00
	1833 ФХ	2.883	1.50	3.00	6.00	12.00
	1834/3ФХ	5.020	2.00	4.00	8.00	15.00
	1834 ФХ	I.A.	1.50	3.00	6.00	12.00
	1835 ФХ	6.570	1.50	3.00	6.00	12.00
	1836 ФХ	2.100	1.50	3.00	6.00	12.00
	1837 КТ	4.890	1.50	3.00	6.00	12.00
	1837 НА	I.A.	1.50	3.00	6.00	12.00
	1838/7НА	1.043	2.00	4.00	8.00	15.00
	1838 НА	I.A.	25.00	50.00	100.00	200.00

Mint mark: СМ

C#	Date	Mintage	VG	Fine	VF	XF
138.3	1831	2.000	2.50	5.00	10.00	20.00
	1832	2.000	2.50	5.00	10.00	20.00
	1833	.045	20.00	40.00	80.00	120.00
	1834	2.000	2.50	5.00	10.00	20.00
	1835	2.000	2.50	5.00	10.00	20.00
	1836	.100	2.50	5.00	10.00	20.00
	1837	1.000	2.50	5.00	10.00	20.00
	1838	1.800	2.50	5.00	10.00	20.00
	1839	.020	20.00	40.00	80.00	120.00

Mint mark: ЕМ

C#	Date	Mintage	VG	Fine	VF	XF
144.1	1840	20.778	1.50	3.00	7.50	22.50
	1841	19.341	1.50	3.00	7.50	22.50
	1842	13.851	1.50	3.00	7.50	22.50
	1843	12.520	1.50	3.00	7.50	22.50
	1844	—	1.50	3.00	7.50	22.50

Mint mark: СПБ

C#	Date	Mintage	VG	Fine	VF	XF
144.2	1840	11.200	7.00	15.00	30.00	60.00

Mint mark: СПМ

C#	Date	Mintage	VG	Fine	VF	XF
144.3	1840	Inc. Ab.	1.50	3.00	7.50	22.50
	1841	11.200	1.50	3.00	7.50	22.50
	1842	11.200	1.50	3.00	7.50	22.50
	1843	11.200	1.50	3.00	7.50	22.50

Mint mark: СМ

C#	Date	Mintage	VG	Fine	VF	XF
144.4	1839	.795	3.00	6.00	12.00	40.00
	1840	4.500	2.00	4.00	10.00	30.00
	1841	6.120	2.00	4.00	10.00	30.00
	1842	7.002	2.00	4.00	10.00	30.00
	1843	3.498	2.00	4.00	10.00	30.00
	1844	5.250	2.00	4.00	10.00	30.00
	1845	5.250	2.00	4.00	10.00	30.00
	1846	5.250	2.00	4.00	10.00	30.00
	1847	2.368	4.00	8.00	18.00	65.00

Mint mark: ЕМ

C#	Date	Mintage	VG	Fine	VF	XF
149.1	1850	1.843	.50	1.00	3.00	7.00
	1851	4.790	.50	1.00	3.00	7.00
	1852	14.006	.50	1.00	3.00	7.00
	1853	21.328	.50	1.00	3.00	7.00
	1854	22.397	.50	1.00	3.00	7.00
	1855	24.594	1.00	2.00	4.00	10.00

Mint mark: ВМ

C#	Date	Mintage	VG	Fine	VF	XF
149.3	1850	—	2.00	4.00	8.00	15.00
	1851	.797	2.00	4.00	8.00	15.00
	1852	.311	2.00	4.00	8.00	15.00
	1853	.391	2.00	4.00	8.00	15.00
	1855	Inc.C149.1	2.00	4.00	8.00	15.00

Mint mark: ЕМ
Obv: Crowned small A. Plain border.

Y#	Date	Mintage	Fine	VF	XF	Unc
3.1	1855	Inc.C149.1	1.00	2.00	6.00	15.00
	1856	10.641	1.00	2.00	6.00	15.00
	1857	5.659	1.00	2.00	6.00	15.00
	1858	13.731	1.00	2.00	6.00	15.00
	1859	11.059	1.00	2.00	6.00	15.00

Mint mark: ВМ
Obv: Crowned tall A. Rev: Large date.

Y#	Date	Mintage	Fine	VF	XF	Unc
3.2	1855	Inc.C149.3	2.00	4.00	12.00	25.00
	1856	3.337	2.00	4.00	12.00	25.00
	1858	1.528	2.00	4.00	12.00	25.00
	1859	3.109	2.00	4.00	12.00	25.00
	1860	3.766	2.00	4.00	12.00	25.00

Mint mark: ЕМ
Obv: Crowned small A. Toothed border.

Y#	Date	Mintage	Fine	VF	XF	Unc
3.3	1859	—	1.00	2.00	4.00	10.00
	1860	8.306	1.00	2.00	4.00	10.00
	1861	10.130	1.00	2.00	4.00	10.00
	1862	10.165	1.00	2.00	4.00	10.00
	1863	6.544	1.00	2.00	4.00	10.00
	1864/2	4.400	1.50	3.00	6.00	15.00
	1864	Inc. Ab.	1.00	2.00	4.00	10.00
	1865	14.230	1.00	2.00	4.00	10.00
	1866	12.304	1.00	2.00	4.00	10.00
	1867	5.851	5.00	10.00	20.00	40.00

Mint mark: ВМ
Obv: Crowned tall A.

Y#	Date	Mintage	Fine	VF	XF	Unc
3.4	1861	1.800	2.50	5.00	10.00	20.00
	1862	2.100	2.50	5.00	10.00	20.00
	1863	2.854	2.50	5.00	10.00	20.00
	1864	1.046	2.50	5.00	10.00	20.00

Mint mark: ЕМ

Y#	Date	Mintage	Fine	VF	XF	Unc
9.1	1867	Inc.Y3.3	3.00	6.00	12.00	25.00
	1868	6.305	.50	1.00	3.00	10.00
	1869	10.230	.50	1.00	3.00	10.00
	1870	9.875	.50	1.00	3.00	10.00
	1871	2.880	.50	1.00	3.00	10.00
	1872	5.713	.50	1.00	3.00	10.00
	1873	5.213	.50	1.00	3.00	10.00
	1874	5.013	.50	1.00	3.00	10.00
	1875	6.438	.50	1.00	3.00	10.00
	1876	1.755	4.00	8.00	15.00	30.00

Mint mark: СПБ

Y#	Date	Mintage	Fine	VF	XF	Unc
9.2	1867	Inc. Be.	2.00	4.00	8.00	20.00
	1868	.750	1.00	2.00	4.00	10.00
	1869	.739	1.00	2.00	4.00	10.00
	1870	1.143	1.00	2.00	4.00	10.00
	1871	—	—	—	Rare	—
	1876	2.930	.50	1.00	2.00	9.00
	1877	7.065	.50	1.00	2.00	9.00
	1878	8.241	.50	1.00	2.00	9.00
	1879	9.045	.50	1.00	2.00	9.00
	1880	7.730	.50	1.00	2.00	9.00
	1881	8.415	.50	1.00	2.00	9.00
	1882	5.685	.50	1.00	2.00	9.00
	1883	7.330	.50	1.00	2.00	9.00
	1884	2.500	.50	1.00	2.00	9.00
	1885	3.400	.50	1.00	2.00	9.00
	1886	3.210	.50	1.00	2.00	9.00
	1887	6.000	.25	.50	1.50	8.00
	1888	6.000	.25	.50	1.50	8.00
	1889	9.000	.25	.50	1.50	8.00
	1890	6.905	.25	.50	1.50	8.00
	1891	10.875	.25	.50	1.50	8.00
	1892	5.640	.25	.50	1.50	8.00
9.2	1893	13.395	.25	.50	1.50	8.00
	1894	15.490	.25	.50	1.50	8.00
	1895	18.200	.25	.50	1.50	8.00
	1896	22.960	.25	.50	1.50	8.00
	1897	30.000	.25	.50	1.50	8.00
	1898	50.000	.25	.50	1.50	8.00
	1899	50.000	.25	.50	1.50	8.00
	1900	30.000	.25	.50	1.50	8.00
	Common date	—	—	—	Proof	35.00

NOTE: Later dates (1901-1914) exist for this type.

2 KOPEKS

COPPER
Mint mark: ЕМ

C#	Date	Mintage	VG	Fine	VF	XF
95.3	1801	27.380	4.00	8.00	15.00	30.00

NOTE: Earlier dates (1797-1800) exist for this type.

Mint mark: КМ

C#	Date	Mintage	VG	Fine	VF	XF
95.4	1801	—	7.50	15.00	30.00	60.00

NOTE: Earlier dates (1797-1800) exist for this type.

Mint mark: ЕМ

C#	Date	Mintage	VG	Fine	VF	XF
114.1	1802	45.798	10.00	20.00	40.00	100.00
	1803	.298	25.00	50.00	100.00	200.00
	1804	—	—	—	Rare	—

Mint mark: КМ

C#	Date	Mintage	VG	Fine	VF	XF
114.2	1804	—	25.00	50.00	100.00	200.00
	1805	—	25.00	50.00	100.00	200.00
	1807	—	25.00	50.00	100.00	200.00

Mint mark: ЕМ
Obv: Type 1 eagle.

C#	Date	Mintage	VG	Fine	VF	XF
118.1	1810 НМ	79.364	1.50	2.50	5.00	10.00

NOTE: Exists with large and small date.

Mint mark: КМ
Obv: Type 2 eagle.

C#	Date	Mintage	VG	Fine	VF	XF
118.2	1810	—	4.00	8.00	15.00	30.00
	1810 ПБ	—	4.00	8.00	15.00	30.00
	1811 ПБ	—	4.00	8.00	15.00	30.00
	1812	—	4.00	8.00	15.00	30.00

Mint mark: ЕМ
Obv: Type 3 eagle.

C#	Date	Mintage	VG	Fine	VF	XF
118.3	1810 НМ	129.000	2.50	5.00	10.00	20.00
	1811 НМ plain edge	Inc. Ab.	2.50	5.00	10.00	20.00
	1811 НМ reeded edge	Inc. Ab.	2.50	5.00	10.00	20.00
	1812 НМ	132.085	2.50	5.00	10.00	20.00
	1812 НМ inverted 2	Inc. Ab.	2.50	5.00	10.00	20.00
	1813 НМ	64.980	2.50	5.00	10.00	20.00
	1814 НМ	110.000	2.50	5.00	10.00	20.00
	1815 НМ	44.970	2.50	5.00	10.00	20.00
	1816 НМ	64.150	2.50	5.00	10.00	20.00
	1817 НМ	75.000	2.50	5.00	10.00	20.00
	1818 НМ	60.625	2.50	5.00	10.00	20.00
	1818 ФГ	I.A.	2.50	5.00	10.00	20.00
	1819 НМ	100.468	2.50	5.00	10.00	20.00
	1820 НМ	75.180	2.50	5.00	10.00	20.00
	1821 НМ	55.170	2.50	5.00	10.00	20.00
	1821 ФГ	I.A.	2.50	5.00	10.00	20.00
	1822 ФГ	44.867	2.50	5.00	10.00	20.00
	1823 ФГ	44.935	2.50	5.00	10.00	20.00
	1823 ПГ	I.A.	—	—	Rare	—
	1824 ПГ	36.600	2.50	5.00	10.00	20.00
	1825 ПГ	73.856	2.50	5.00	10.00	20.00
	1825 ИШ	I.A.	2.50	5.00	10.00	20.00
	1825 ИК	I.A.	2.50	5.00	10.00	20.00
(137.1)	1826 ИК	50.450	3.00	6.00	12.00	25.00
	1827 ИК	34.065	3.00	6.00	12.00	25.00
	1828 ИК	14.475	3.00	6.00	12.00	25.00
	1829 ИК	13.790	3.00	6.00	12.00	25.00
	1830 ИК	15.450	3.00	6.00	12.00	25.00

NOTE: Varieties exist.

Mint: Kolpino

C#	Date	Mintage	VG	Fine	VF	XF
118.7	1810 МК	—	20.00	40.00	80.00	150.00

NOTE: The Kolpino mint mark was changed to **ИМ in 1910.**

Mint mark: ИМ

C#	Date	Mintage	VG	Fine	VF	XF
118.4	1810 МК	—	1.50	3.00	7.00	15.00
	1811 ПС	I.A.	1.50	3.00	7.00	15.00
	1811 МК	—	1.50	3.00	7.00	15.00
	1812 ПС	—	1.50	3.00	7.00	15.00
	1813 ПС	—	1.50	3.00	7.00	15.00
	1814 ПС	—	1.50	3.00	7.00	15.00
	1814	—	1.50	3.00	7.00	15.00

Mint mark: КМ

C#	Date	Mintage	VG	Fine	VF	XF
118.5	1812 АМ	—	1.50	2.50	5.00	10.00
	1813 АМ	—	1.50	2.50	5.00	10.00
	1814 АМ	—	1.50	2.50	5.00	10.00
	1815 АМ	—	1.50	2.50	5.00	10.00
	1816 АМ	—	1.50	2.50	5.00	10.00
	1817 АМ	—	1.50	2.50	5.00	10.00
	1817 АБ	—	1.50	2.50	5.00	10.00
	1818 ДБ	—	1.50	2.50	5.00	10.00
	1819 АД	—	1.50	2.50	5.00	10.00
	1820 АД	—	1.50	2.50	5.00	10.00
	1821 АД	—	1.50	2.50	5.00	10.00
	1821 АМ	—	1.50	2.50	5.00	10.00
	1822 АМ	—	1.50	2.50	5.00	10.00
	1823 АМ	—	1.50	2.50	5.00	10.00
	1824 АМ	—	1.50	2.50	5.00	10.00
	1825 АМ	—	1.50	2.50	5.00	10.00
(137.2)	1826 АМ	9.375	2.50	5.00	10.00	20.00
	1827 АМ	I.A.	2.50	5.00	10.00	20.00
	1828 АМ	15.000	2.50	5.00	10.00	20.00
	1829 АМ	15.000	2.50	5.00	10.00	20.00
	1830 АМ	15.000	2.50	5.00	10.00	20.00

Mint mark: СПБ

C#	Date	Mintage	VG	Fine	VF	XF
118.6	1810 ФГ	—	1.50	2.50	5.00	10.00
	1810 МК	—	1.50	2.50	5.00	10.00
	1810 ПС	—	1.50	2.50	5.00	10.00
	1811 МК	—	1.50	2.50	5.00	10.00
	1811 ПС	—	1.50	2.50	5.00	10.00
	1812 ПС	—	1.50	2.50	5.00	10.00
	1813 ПС	—	1.50	2.50	5.00	10.00
	1814 ПС	—	3.00	6.00	12.00	25.00
	1818	—	20.00	40.00	80.00	150.00
(137.3)	1828	—	25.00	50.00	100.00	200.00

Mint mark: ЕМ

C#	Date	Mintage	VG	Fine	VF	XF
139.1	1831 ФХ	—	20.00	40.00	80.00	150.00
	1833 ФХ	.261	3.00	6.00	12.00	25.00
	1837 НА	16.845	3.00	6.00	12.00	25.00
	1838/7 НА	6.623	3.50	7.00	14.00	30.00
	1838 НА	I.A.	3.00	6.00	12.00	25.00
	1839 НА	8.250	3.00	6.00	12.00	25.00

Mint mark: СМ

C#	Date	Mintage	VG	Fine	VF	XF
139.3	1831	1.500	2.50	4.50	8.00	15.00
	1832	1.500	2.50	4.50	8.00	15.00
	1833	.539	2.50	4.50	8.00	15.00
	1834	1.500	2.50	4.50	8.00	15.00
	1835	1.500	2.50	4.50	8.00	15.00
	1836	1.350	2.50	4.50	8.00	15.00
	1837	1.000	2.50	4.50	8.00	15.00
	1838	10.500	2.50	4.50	8.00	15.00
	1839	7.073	2.50	4.50	8.00	15.00

Mint mark: ЕМ

C#	Date	Mintage	VG	Fine	VF	XF
145.1	1840	20.778	2.00	4.00	8.00	25.00
	1841	14.999	2.00	4.00	8.00	25.00
	1842	12.446	2.00	4.00	8.00	25.00
	1843	11.020	2.00	4.00	8.00	25.00
	1844	5.500	2.00	4.00	8.00	25.00

Mint mark: СПБ

C#	Date	Mintage	VG	Fine	VF	XF
145.2	1840	—	6.00	12.00	25.00	75.00
	1841	—	25.00	50.00	100.00	200.00

Mint mark: СПМ

C#	Date	Mintage	VG	Fine	VF	XF
145.3	1840	4.800	2.00	4.00	8.00	20.00
	1841	Inc. Ab.	2.00	4.00	8.00	20.00
	1842	4.800	2.00	4.00	8.00	20.00
	1843	4.800	2.00	4.00	8.00	20.00

Mint mark: СМ

C#	Date	Mintage	VG	Fine	VF	XF
145.4	1839	.341	2.00	4.00	8.00	20.00
	1840	1.929	2.00	4.00	8.00	20.00
	1841	2.636	2.00	4.00	8.00	20.00
	1842	3.000	2.00	4.00	8.00	20.00
	1843	1.500	2.00	4.00	8.00	20.00
	1844	2.250	2.00	4.00	8.00	20.00
	1845	2.250	2.00	4.00	8.00	20.00
	1846	2.250	2.00	4.00	8.00	20.00
	1847	2.209	2.00	4.00	8.00	20.00

Mint mark: МШ

C#	Date	Mintage	VG	Fine	VF	XF
145.5	1848	.031	20.00	40.00	80.00	150.00

Mint mark: ЕМ

C#	Date	Mintage	VG	Fine	VF	XF
150.1	1850	2.206	1.50	3.00	6.00	12.00
	1851	8.356	1.50	3.00	6.00	12.00
	1852	6.874	1.50	3.00	6.00	12.00
	1853	7.561	1.50	3.00	6.00	12.00
	1854	4.541	1.50	3.00	6.00	12.00
(Y4.1)	1855	8.587	1.00	2.00	4.00	7.50
	1856	9.167	1.00	2.00	4.00	7.50
	1857	3.359	1.00	2.00	4.00	7.50
	1858	10.028	1.00	2.00	4.00	7.50
	1859	14.772	1.00	2.00	4.00	7.50

Mint mark: ВМ

C#	Date	Mintage	VG	Fine	VF	XF
150.3	1850	—	10.00	20.00	40.00	80.00
	1851	.298	5.00	10.00	20.00	40.00
	1852	.202	5.00	10.00	20.00	40.00
	1853	2,642	—	—	Rare	—
	1854	.148	5.00	10.00	20.00	40.00
(Y4.2)	1855	1.347	2.00	4.00	8.00	15.00
	1856	1.190	2.00	4.00	8.00	15.00
	1858	.750	2.00	4.00	8.00	15.00
	1859	1.595	2.00	4.00	8.00	15.00
	1860	1.605	—	—	Rare	—

Mint mark: ЕМ
Obv: Ribbons added to crown.

Y#	Date	Mintage	Fine	VF	XF	Unc
4a.1	1859	14.772	1.25	3.00	6.50	8.00
	1860	19.239	1.25	3.00	6.50	8.00
	1861	18.547	1.25	3.00	6.50	8.00
	1862	16.889	1.25	3.00	6.50	8.00
	1863	21.703	1.25	3.00	6.50	8.00
	1864	14.175	1.25	3.00	6.50	8.00
	1865	26.921	1.25	3.00	6.50	8.00
	1866	21.890	1.25	3.00	6.50	8.00
	1867	8.970	1.25	3.00	6.50	8.00

Mint mark: ВМ

Y#	Date	Mintage	Fine	VF	XF	Unc
4a.2	1860	1.605	3.00	6.00	12.00	25.00
	1861	.586	3.00	6.00	12.00	25.00
	1862	.966	3.00	6.00	12.00	25.00
	1863	1.739	3.00	6.00	12.00	25.00

Mint mark: ЕМ

Y#	Date	Mintage	Fine	VF	XF	Unc
10.1	1867	.150	5.00	10.00	20.00	40.00
	1868	18.200	.50	1.00	3.00	12.00
	1869	22.174	.50	1.00	3.00	12.00
	1870	21.884	.50	1.00	3.00	12.00
	1871	7.058	.50	1.00	3.00	12.00
	1872	12.734	.50	1.00	3.00	12.00
	1873	7.364	.50	1.00	3.00	12.00
	1874	8.551	.50	1.00	3.00	12.00
	1875	10.451	.50	1.00	3.00	12.00
	1876	2.905	.50	1.00	3.00	12.00

Mint mark: СПБ

Y#	Date	Mintage	Fine	VF	XF	Unc
10.2	1867	Inc. Be.	3.00	6.00	12.00	25.00
	1868	.659	1.50	3.00	6.00	15.00
	1869	.643	1.50	3.00	6.00	15.00
	1870	.231	2.00	4.00	8.00	20.00
	1871	—	—	—	Rare	—
	1876	3.240	.50	1.00	2.50	10.00
	1877	5.010	.50	1.00	2.50	10.00
	1878	8.093	.50	1.00	2.50	10.00
	1879	7.380	.50	1.00	2.50	10.00
	1880	6.525	.50	1.00	2.50	10.00
	1881	7.299	.50	1.00	2.50	10.00
	1882	4.478	.50	1.00	2.50	10.00
	1883	6.230	.50	1.00	2.50	10.00
	1884	2.625	.50	1.00	2.50	10.00
	1885	3.070	.50	1.00	2.50	10.00
	1886	3.123	.50	1.00	2.50	10.00
	1887	1.725	.50	1.00	2.50	10.00
	1888	1.823	.50	1.00	2.50	10.00
	1889	2.815	.50	1.00	2.50	10.00
	1890	2.538	.50	1.00	2.50	10.00
	1891	2.788	.50	1.00	2.50	10.00
	1892	.918	2.00	4.00	8.00	20.00
	1893	10.295	.50	1.00	2.00	8.00
	1894	8.600	.50	1.00	2.00	8.00
	1895	9.122	.50	1.00	2.00	8.00
	1896	14.675	.50	1.00	2.00	8.00
	1897	9.500	.50	1.00	2.00	8.00
	1898	17.500	.50	1.00	2.00	8.00
	1899	17.500	.50	1.00	2.00	8.00
	1900	20.500	.50	1.00	2.00	8.00
	Common date	—	—	—	Proof	35.00

NOTE: Later dates (1901-1914) exist for this type.

3 KOPEKS

(Altyn)

COPPER
Mint mark: ЕМ

C#	Date	Mintage	VG	Fine	VF	XF
146.1	1840	5.230	4.00	8.00	18.00	45.00
	1841	13.417	4.00	8.00	18.00	45.00
	1842	13.700	4.00	8.00	18.00	45.00
	1843	14.578	4.00	8.00	18.00	45.00
	1844	4.840	4.00	8.00	18.00	45.00

Mint mark: СПБ

C#	Date	Mintage	VG	Fine	VF	XF
146.2	1840	—	20.00	40.00	90.00	175.00

Mint mark: СПМ

C#	Date	Mintage	VG	Fine	VF	XF
146.3	1840	2.133	6.00	12.00	25.00	65.00
	1841	2.133	6.00	12.00	25.00	65.00
	1842	2.133	6.00	12.00	25.00	65.00
	1843	2.133	6.00	12.00	25.00	65.00

Mint mark: СМ

C#	Date	Mintage	VG	Fine	VF	XF
146.4	1839	.142	7.00	15.00	30.00	75.00
	1840	.827	5.00	10.00	22.00	55.00
	1841	1.171	5.00	10.00	22.00	55.00
	1842	1.360	5.00	10.00	22.00	55.00
	1843	.669	5.00	10.00	22.00	55.00
146.4	1844	1.000	5.00	10.00	22.00	55.00
	1845	1.000	5.00	10.00	22.00	55.00
	1846	1.000	5.00	10.00	22.00	55.00
	1847	1.000	6.00	12.00	25.00	65.00

Mint mark: MW

C#	Date	Mintage	VG	Fine	VF	XF
146.5	1848	.017	50.00	90.00	175.00	325.00

Mint mark: ЕМ
Obv: First variety - 6 coats of arms.

C#	Date	Mintage	VG	Fine	VF	XF
151.1	1850	.184	2.00	4.00	7.50	15.00
	1851	3.448	2.00	4.00	7.50	15.00
	1852	5.444	2.00	4.00	7.50	15.00
	1853	3.719	2.00	4.00	7.50	15.00
	1854	1.351	2.00	4.00	7.50	15.00
(Y5.1)	1855	2.835	1.00	2.00	5.00	10.00
	1856	6.700	1.00	2.00	5.00	10.00
	1857	4.726	1.00	2.00	5.00	10.00
	1858	10.662	1.00	2.00	5.00	10.00
	1859	15.821	1.00	2.00	5.00	10.00
	Common date		—	—	Proof	200.00

Mint mark: ВМ

C#	Date	Mintage	VG	Fine	VF	XF
151.3	1850	.050	4.00	7.50	15.00	30.00
	1851	.100	4.00	7.50	15.00	30.00
	1852	.100	4.00	7.50	15.00	30.00
	1853	.089	4.00	7.50	15.00	30.00
	1854	.161	4.00	7.50	15.00	30.00
(Y5.2)	1856	.417	2.50	5.00	10.00	20.00
	1857	.021	7.50	12.50	25.00	50.00
	1858	.712	2.50	5.00	10.00	20.00
	1859	.400	5.00	7.50	15.00	30.00

Mint mark: ЕМ
Obv: Second variety - 8 coats of arms.

Y#	Date	Mintage	Fine	VF	XF	Unc
5a.1	1859	—	2.00	4.00	8.00	25.00
	1860	14.010	2.00	4.00	8.00	25.00
	1861	7.738	2.00	4.00	8.00	25.00
	1862	10.377	2.00	4.00	8.00	25.00
	1863	3.939	2.00	4.00	8.00	25.00
	1864	6.121	4.00	8.00	15.00	30.00
	1865	5.740	40.00	80.00	150.00	250.00
	1866	6.611	2.00	4.00	8.00	25.00
	1867	1.786	4.00	8.00	15.00	30.00

Mint mark: ВМ

Y#	Date	Mintage	Fine	VF	XF	Unc
5a.2	1860	.283	7.50	15.00	30.00	75.00
	1861	.284	6.00	12.50	25.00	60.00
	1862	.200	6.00	12.50	25.00	60.00
	1863	.401	9.00	17.50	35.00	80.00

Mint mark: ЕМ
Similar to 2 Kopeks, Y#10.1

Y#	Date	Mintage	Fine	VF	XF	Unc
11.1	1867	.160	2.00	4.00	8.00	20.00
	1868	6.059	1.00	2.00	4.00	15.00
	1869	5.526	1.00	2.00	4.00	15.00
	1870	5.018	1.00	2.00	4.00	15.00
	1871	1.585	1.00	2.00	4.00	15.00
	1872	3.018	1.00	2.00	4.00	15.00
	1873	4.704	1.00	2.00	4.00	15.00
	1874	4.419	1.00	2.00	4.00	15.00
	1875	3.595	1.00	2.00	4.00	15.00
	1876	.890	1.00	2.00	4.00	15.00

COPPER
Mint mark: СПБ

Y#	Date	Mintage	Fine	VF	XF	Unc
11.2	1867	Inc. Be.	4.00	7.50	15.00	30.00
	1868	.910	2.00	4.00	8.00	20.00
	1869	.723	2.00	4.00	8.00	20.00
	1870	.080	6.00	12.00	25.00	50.00
	1871	—	—	—	Rare	—
11.2	1876	4.863	1.00	2.00	4.00	18.00
	1877	5.902	1.00	2.00	4.00	18.00
	1878	6.355	1.00	2.00	4.00	18.00
	1879	7.355	1.00	2.00	4.00	18.00
	1880	6.773	1.00	2.00	4.00	18.00
	1881	6.141	1.00	2.00	4.00	18.00
	1882	4.280	1.00	2.00	4.00	18.00
	1883	1.061	1.00	2.00	4.00	18.00
	1884	2.975	1.00	2.00	4.00	18.00
	1891	1.983	2.00	3.00	6.00	20.00
	1892	.648	2.00	3.00	6.00	20.00
	1893	6.365	.75	1.50	3.00	15.00
	1894	4.803	.75	1.50	3.00	15.00
	1895	5.417	.75	1.50	3.00	15.00
	1896	7.923	.75	1.50	3.00	15.00
	1897	6.667	.75	1.50	3.00	15.00
	1898	11.667	.75	1.50	3.00	15.00
	1899	11.667	.75	1.50	3.00	15.00
	1900	16.667	.75	1.50	3.00	15.00
	Common date	—	—	—	Proof	35.00

NOTE: Later dates (1901-1914) exist for this type.

5 KOPEKS

1.0400 g, .868 SILVER, .0290 oz ASW
Mint mark: СМ

C#	Date	Mintage	VG	Fine	VF	XF
96.1a	1801 АИ	.010	17.50	35.00	70.00	120.00
	1801 ФЧ	I.A.	—	—	Rare	—

NOTE: Earlier dates (1798-1800) exist for this type.

COPPER
Mint mark: ЕМ

C#	Date	Mintage	VG	Fine	VF	XF
115.1	1802	12.592	10.00	20.00	40.00	80.00
	1803/2	31.820	12.00	24.00	50.00	100.00
	1803	Inc. Ab.	9.00	17.50	32.50	65.00
	1804	26.268	9.00	17.50	32.50	65.00
	1805	16.519	10.00	20.00	40.00	80.00
	1806	38.416	7.50	15.00	30.00	65.00
	1807	10.667	10.00	20.00	40.00	80.00
	1808	10.001	10.00	20.00	40.00	80.00
	1809	10.140	10.00	20.00	40.00	80.00
	1810	15.802	10.00	20.00	40.00	80.00

NOTE: Varieties exist.

Mint mark: КМ

C#	Date	Mintage	VG	Fine	VF	XF
115.2	1802	4.000	12.50	25.00	50.00	100.00
	1803	3.600	12.50	25.00	50.00	100.00
	1804/3	4.000	15.00	30.00	60.00	120.00
	1804	Inc. Ab.	12.50	25.00	50.00	100.00
	1805	5.000	12.50	25.00	50.00	100.00
	1806	5.000	15.00	30.00	60.00	120.00
	1807	5.000	15.00	30.00	60.00	120.00
	1808	5.000	15.00	30.00	60.00	120.00
	1809	5.000	15.00	30.00	60.00	120.00
	1810	—	15.00	30.00	60.00	120.00

NOTE: Varieties exist.

1.0366 g, .868 SILVER, .0289 oz ASW
Mint mark: СПБ

C#	Date	Mintage	VG	Fine	VF	XF
126	1810 ФГ	—	50.00	100.00	200.00	300.00
	1811 ФГ	.080	10.00	20.00	40.00	80.00
	1811	Inc. Ab.	—	—	Rare	—
	1812 МФ	—	—	—	Rare	—
	1813 ПС	.620	3.00	6.00	12.00	25.00
	1814 ПС	1.300	3.00	6.00	12.00	25.00
	1814 МФ	I.A.	3.00	6.00	12.00	25.00
	1815 МФ	3.000	3.00	6.00	12.00	25.00
	1815	Inc. Ab.	—	—	Rare	—
	1816/5 МФ					
		1.040	3.50	7.00	14.00	30.00
	1816 МФ	I.A.	3.00	6.00	12.00	25.00
	1816 ПС	I.A.	3.00	6.00	12.00	25.00

C#	Date	Mintage	VG	Fine	VF	XF
126	1817 ПС	.120	3.00	6.00	12.00	25.00
	1818 ПС	.340	3.00	6.00	12.00	25.00
	1819 ПС	.920	3.00	6.00	12.00	25.00
	1820/19 ПС	.460	3.50	7.00	14.00	30.00
	1820 ПС	I.A.	3.00	6.00	12.00	25.00
	1820 ПД	I.A.	3.00	6.00	12.00	25.00
	1821 ПД	2.000	3.00	6.00	12.00	25.00
	1822/1 ПД	1.060	3.50	7.00	14.00	30.00
	1822 ПД	I.A.	3.00	6.00	12.00	25.00
	1823 ПД	2.300	3.00	6.00	12.00	25.00
	1824 ПД	1.740	3.00	6.00	12.00	25.00
	1825 ПД	1.160	3.00	6.00	12.00	25.00
	1825 НГ	I.A.	—	—	Rare	—
(152.3)	1826 НГ	1.340	4.00	8.00	16.00	35.00

C#	Date	Mintage	VG	Fine	VF	XF
156	1826 НГ	Inc. C152.3	3.00	6.00	12.00	25.00
	1827 НГ	1.769	3.00	6.00	12.00	25.00
	1828 НГ	.060	5.00	10.00	20.00	40.00
	1829 НГ	.080	5.00	10.00	20.00	40.00
	1830 НГ	1.500	3.00	6.00	12.00	25.00
	1831 НГ	.520	3.00	6.00	12.00	25.00

COPPER
Mint mark: ЕМ

C#	Date	Mintage	VG	Fine	VF	XF
140.1	1831 ФХ	41.120	3.50	6.50	12.50	25.00
	1831	—	4.00	8.00	15.00	30.00
	1832 ФХ	30.080	3.50	6.50	12.50	25.00
	1833 ФХ	14.332	3.50	6.50	12.50	25.00
	1834 ФХ	41.785	3.50	6.50	12.50	25.00
	1835 ФХ	41.763	3.50	6.50	12.50	25.00
	1836 ФХ	31.332	3.50	6.50	12.50	25.00
	1837/6 ФХ	19.745	4.00	8.00	15.00	30.00
	1837 ФХ	I.A.	4.00	8.00	15.00	30.00
	1837 КТ	I.A.	3.50	6.50	12.50	25.00
	1837 НА	I.A.	3.50	6.50	12.50	25.00
	1838 НА	24.430	3.50	6.50	12.50	25.00
	1839 НА	1.400	4.00	8.00	15.00	30.00

Mint mark: СМ

C#	Date	Mintage	VG	Fine	VF	XF
140.3	1831	5.900	4.00	7.50	15.00	30.00
	1832	5.900	4.00	7.50	15.00	30.00
	1833	6.295	4.00	7.50	15.00	30.00
	1834	5.900	4.00	7.50	15.00	30.00
	1835	5.000	4.00	7.50	15.00	30.00
	1836	5.240	4.00	7.50	15.00	30.00
	1837	5.200	4.00	7.50	15.00	30.00
	1838	1.420	4.00	7.50	15.00	30.00
	1839	1.400	4.00	7.50	15.00	30.00

1.0366 g, .868 SILVER, .0289 oz ASW
Mint mark: СПБ

C#	Date	Mintage	VG	Fine	VF	XF
163	1832 НГ	.224	1.50	2.75	4.00	12.00
	1833 НГ	1.026	1.50	2.75	4.00	12.00
	1834 НГ	.780	1.50	2.75	4.00	12.00
	1835 НГ	1.010	1.50	2.75	4.00	12.00
	1836 НГ	.900	1.50	2.75	4.00	12.00
	1837 НГ	1.140	1.50	2.75	4.00	12.00
	1838 НГ	2.400	1.50	2.75	4.00	12.00
	1839 НГ	1,002	20.00	40.00	80.00	150.00
	1840 НГ	.420	2.00	4.00	6.00	15.00
	1841 НГ	.100	2.00	4.00	6.00	15.00
	1842.	.100	2.00	4.00	8.00	20.00
	1842 АЧ	I.A.	2.00	4.00	6.00	15.00
	1843 АЧ	.400	2.00	4.00	6.00	15.00
	1844 КБ	.401	2.00	4.00	6.00	15.00
	1845 КБ	1.740	1.50	2.75	4.00	10.00
	1846 ПА	.280	1.50	2.75	4.00	10.00
	1847 ПА	1.010	1.50	2.75	4.00	10.00
	1848 НI	1.000	1.50	2.75	4.00	10.00
	1849 ПА	1.020	1.50	2.75	4.00	10.00
	1850 ПА	1.300	1.50	2.75	4.00	10.00
	1851 ПА	1.000	1.50	2.75	4.00	10.00
	1852 ПА	.900	1.50	2.75	4.00	10.00
	1852 НI	I.A.	—	—	Rare	—
	1853 НI	.900	1.50	2.75	7.50	20.00
	1854 НI	.500	1.50	2.75	7.50	20.00
(Y13)	1855 НI	.640	1.50	2.75	4.00	10.00

C#	Date	Mintage	VG	Fine	VF	XF
(Y13)	1856 ФБ	.680	1.50	2.75	4.00	10.00
	1857 ФБ	.080	2.00	4.00	8.00	15.00
	1858 ФБ	.040	2.50	5.00	10.00	20.00

COPPER
Mint mark: ЕМ
Obv: 6 coats of arms.

C#	Date	Mintage	Fine	VF	XF	Unc
152.1	1850	.373	4.00	7.50	15.00	40.00
	1851	2.241	4.00	7.50	15.00	40.00
	1852	3.961	4.00	7.50	15.00	40.00
	1853	1.474	30.00	60.00	120.00	200.00
	1854	.356	4.00	7.50	15.00	40.00
(Y6.1)	1855	.740	3.00	6.00	12.00	25.00
	1856	5.146	2.00	4.00	8.00	20.00
	1857	8.675	2.00	4.00	8.00	20.00
	1858	19.561	2.00	4.00	8.00	20.00
	1859	19.441	2.00	4.00	8.00	20.00

Mint mark: ВМ

C#	Date	Mintage	Fine	VF	XF	Unc
152.4	1850	—	15.00	25.00	50.00	120.00
	1851	.024	15.00	25.00	50.00	120.00
	1852	.016	15.00	25.00	50.00	120.00
	1853	.040	15.00	25.00	50.00	120.00
(Y6.2)	1856	.040	15.00	25.00	50.00	120.00

Mint mark: ЕМ
Obv: 8 coats of arms.

Y#	Date	Mintage	Fine	VF	XF	Unc
6a	1858	—	—	—	Rare	—
	1859	Inc. Ab.	2.00	4.00	8.00	20.00
	1860	25.260	2.00	4.00	8.00	20.00
	1861	28.022	2.00	4.00	8.00	20.00
	1862	22.055	2.00	4.00	8.00	20.00
	1863	22.511	2.00	4.00	8.00	20.00
	1864	26.042	2.00	4.00	8.00	20.00
	1865	38.943	2.00	4.00	8.00	20.00
	1866	24.767	2.00	4.00	8.00	20.00
	1867	11.697	4.00	8.00	16.00	40.00

1.0366 g, .750 SILVER, .0250 oz ASW
Mint mark: СПБ
Obv: Ribbons added to crown.

Y#	Date	Mintage	Fine	VF	XF	Unc
19.1	1859	.120	—	—	Rare	—
	1859 ФБ	I.A.	4.00	8.00	16.00	40.00
	1860 ФБ	.020	5.00	10.00	20.00	50.00

Obv: Redesigned eagle, engrailed edge.

Y#	Date	Mintage	Fine	VF	XF	Unc
19.2	1860 ФБ	.180	2.00	4.00	10.00	25.00
	1861 ФБ	.360	2.00	4.00	10.00	25.00
	1861 МИ	I.A.	7.50	15.00	30.00	75.00
	1861	—	—	—	Rare	—
	1862 МИ	.400	2.00	4.00	10.00	25.00
	1863 АБ	.200	2.00	4.00	10.00	25.00
	1864 НФ	.240	2.00	4.00	10.00	25.00
	1865 НФ	.240	2.00	4.00	10.00	25.00
	1866 НФ	.190	2.00	4.00	10.00	25.00
	1866 НI	I.A.	25.00	50.00	100.00	300.00

.8998 g, .500 SILVER, .0144 oz ASW
Reeded edge.

Y#	Date	Mintage	Fine	VF	XF	Unc
19a.1	1867 НI	.180	1.75	3.50	7.50	25.00
	1868 НI	.240	1.75	3.50	7.50	25.00
	1869 НI	.170	1.75	3.50	7.50	25.00
	1870 НI	.220	1.75	3.50	7.50	25.00
	1871 НI	.200	1.75	3.50	7.50	25.00
	1872 НI	.180	1.75	3.50	7.50	25.00
	1873 НI	.160	1.75	3.50	7.50	25.00
	1874 НI	.200	1.75	3.50	7.50	25.00

Y#	Date	Mintage	Fine	VF	XF	Unc
19a.1	1875 НI	.200	1.75	3.50	7.50	25.00
	1876 НI	.240	1.75	3.50	7.50	25.00
	1877 НI	.200	1.75	3.50	7.50	25.00
	1877 НФ	I.A.	5.00	10.00	20.00	50.00
	1878 НФ	.220	1.75	3.50	7.50	25.00
	1878 НI	I.A.	7.50	15.00	30.00	75.00
	1879 НФ	.140	1.75	3.50	7.50	25.00
	1880 НФ	.240	1.75	3.50	7.50	25.00
	1881 НФ	.200	1.75	3.50	7.50	25.00
	1882 НФ	1.760	1.00	2.00	4.00	10.00
	1883 ДС	1.000	1.00	2.00	4.00	10.00
	1883 АГ	I.A.	1.00	2.00	4.00	10.00
	1884 АГ	3.460	1.00	2.00	4.00	10.00
	1885 АГ	1.700	1.00	2.00	4.00	10.00
	1886 АГ	2.000	1.00	2.00	4.00	10.00
	1887 АГ	3.000	1.00	2.00	4.00	10.00
	1888 АГ	4.000	1.00	2.00	4.00	10.00
	1889 АГ	3.500	1.00	2.00	4.00	10.00
	1890 АГ	8.000	1.00	2.00	4.00	10.00
	1891 АГ	2.000	1.00	2.00	4.00	10.00
	1892 АГ	8.000	1.00	2.00	4.00	10.00
	1893 АГ	2.000	1.00	2.00	4.00	10.00
	1897 АГ	2.029	1.00	2.00	4.00	10.00
	1898 АГ	3.980	1.00	2.00	4.00	10.00
	1899 АГ	4.605	1.00	2.00	4.00	10.00
	1899 ЗБ	I.A.	1.00	2.00	4.00	10.00
	1900 ФЗ	5.205	1.00	2.00	4.00	10.00

NOTE: Later dates (1901-1914) exist for this type.

COPPER
Mint mark: ЕМ

Y#	Date	Mintage	Fine	VF	XF	Unc
12.1	1867	1.459	3.00	6.00	12.00	25.00
	1868	23.019	1.00	3.00	6.00	20.00
	1869	20.277	1.00	3.00	6.00	20.00
	1870	21.158	1.00	3.00	6.00	20.00
	1871	6.304	1.00	3.00	6.00	20.00
	1872	11.890	1.00	3.00	6.00	20.00
	1873	13.052	1.00	3.00	6.00	20.00
	1874	12.879	1.00	3.00	6.00	20.00
	1875	19.624	1.00	3.00	6.00	20.00
	1876	5.329	1.00	3.00	6.00	20.00

Mint mark: СПБ

Y#	Date	Mintage	Fine	VF	XF	Unc
12.2	1867	Inc. Be.	4.00	7.50	15.00	40.00
	1868	.821	2.00	4.00	8.00	30.00
	1869	.942	2.00	4.00	8.00	30.00
	1870	.028	5.00	10.00	20.00	40.00
	1871	—	—	—	Rare	—
	1876	4.655	1.00	3.00	6.00	20.00
	1877	7.184	1.00	3.00	6.00	20.00
	1878	12.542	1.00	3.00	6.00	20.00
	1879	14.652	1.00	3.00	6.00	20.00
	1880	6.773	1.00	3.00	6.00	20.00
	1881	13.824	1.00	3.00	6.00	20.00

NOTE: Later dates (1911-1912) exist for this type.

10 KOPEKS

(Grivennik)

2.0700 g, .868 SILVER, .0578 oz ASW

C#	Date	Mintage	VG	Fine	VF	XF
97.1a	1801 АИ	.010	25.00	50.00	100.00	200.00
	1801 ФЦ	I.A.	—	—	Rare	—

NOTE: Earlier dates (1798-1799) exist for this type.

2.0732 g, .868 SILVER, .0578 oz ASW
Mint mark: СПБ

C#	Date	Mintage	VG	Fine	VF	XF
119	1802 АИ	.190	25.00	50.00	100.00	200.00
	1803 АИ	.040	50.00	100.00	200.00	450.00
	1804/2 ФГ	.380	60.00	120.00	250.00	550.00
	1804 ФГ	I.A.	25.00	50.00	100.00	200.00
	1805/4 ФГ	.112	30.00	60.00	120.00	250.00
	1805 ФГ	I.A.	25.00	50.00	100.00	200.00

C#	Date	Mintage	VG	Fine	VF	XF
119a	1808 ФГ	—	—	—	Rare	—
	1809 МК	.035	35.00	70.00	130.00	250.00
	1810 ФГ	.077	25.00	50.00	100.00	200.00

C#	Date	Mintage	VG	Fine	VF	XF
127	1810 ФГ	—	5.00	10.00	20.00	40.00
	1811 ФГ	.930	3.50	5.00	10.00	20.00
	1812 МФ	—	—	—	Rare	—
	1813 ПС	1.010	3.50	5.00	10.00	20.00
	1814 ПС	2.120	3.50	5.00	10.00	20.00
	1814 СП	I.A.	—	—	Rare	—
	1814 МФ	I.A.	3.50	5.00	10.00	20.00

C#	Date	Mintage	VG	Fine	VF	XF
127	1815 МФ	2.000	3.50	5.00	10.00	20.00
	1816/5 ПС	.250	4.00	6.00	12.00	25.00
	1816 МФ	I.A.	3.50	5.00	10.00	20.00
	1816 ПС	I.A.	3.50	5.00	10.00	20.00
	1817 ПС	.160	3.50	5.00	10.00	20.00
	1818 ПС	.630	3.50	5.00	10.00	20.00
	1819 ПС	1.520	3.50	5.00	10.00	20.00
	1820 ПС	.520	3.50	5.00	10.00	20.00
	1820 ПД	I.A.	3.50	5.00	10.00	20.00
	1821/0 ПД	2.250	4.00	6.00	12.00	25.00
	1821 ПД	I.A.	3.50	5.00	10.00	20.00
	1822 ПД	2.070	3.50	5.00	10.00	20.00
	1823 ПД	3.850	3.50	5.00	10.00	20.00
	1824/3 ПД	1.330	4.00	6.00	12.00	25.00
	1824 ПД	I.A.	3.50	5.00	10.00	20.00
	1825 ПД	1.350	3.50	5.00	10.00	20.00
	1825 НГ	I.A.	7.50	15.00	30.00	75.00
	1826/5 НГ	2.050	9.00	18.00	40.00	100.00
(152.7)	1826 НГ	I.A.	3.50	5.00	10.00	20.00

C#	Date	Mintage	VG	Fine	VF	XF
157	1826 НГ	Inc. C152.7	3.50	5.00	10.00	20.00
	1827 НГ	1.290	3.50	5.00	10.00	20.00
	1828 НГ	.370	4.00	6.00	12.00	25.00
	1829 НГ	.040	5.00	10.00	20.00	40.00
	1830 НГ	.500	4.00	6.00	12.00	25.00
	1831 НГ	.450	4.00	6.00	12.00	25.00

COPPER
Mint mark: ЕМ

C#	Date	Mintage	VG	Fine	VF	XF
141.1	1831 ФХ	2.640	7.50	15.00	30.00	60.00
	1832 ФХ	7.620	7.50	15.00	30.00	60.00
	1833 ФХ	6.968	7.50	15.00	30.00	60.00
	1834 ФХ	9.134	7.50	15.00	30.00	60.00
	1835 ФХ	5.175	7.50	15.00	30.00	60.00
	1836 ФХ	7.240	7.50	15.00	30.00	60.00
	1837/6 КТ	9.728	9.00	18.00	35.00	70.00
	1837 ФХ	I.A.	10.00	20.00	40.00	75.00
	1837 КТ	I.A.	7.50	15.00	30.00	60.00
	1837 НА	I.A.	7.50	15.00	30.00	60.00
	1838 НА	5.468	7.50	15.00	30.00	60.00
	1839 НА	.350	8.50	17.50	35.00	70.00

Mint mark: СМ

C#	Date	Mintage	VG	Fine	VF	XF
141.3	1831	.510	15.00	25.00	50.00	125.00
	1832	.510	15.00	25.00	50.00	125.00
	1833	.700	15.00	25.00	50.00	125.00
	1834	.510	15.00	25.00	50.00	125.00
	1835	.500	15.00	25.00	50.00	125.00
	1836	.600	15.00	25.00	50.00	125.00
	1837	.500	15.00	25.00	50.00	125.00
	1838	.350	15.00	25.00	50.00	125.00
	1839	.350	20.00	35.00	60.00	140.00

2.0700 g, .868 SILVER, .0577 oz ASW
Mint mark: СПБ

C#	Date	Mintage	VG	Fine	VF	XF
164.1	1832 НГ	.104	10.00	25.00	50.00	100.00
	1833 НГ	.880	2.00	4.00	8.00	15.00
	1834/3 НГ	.400	2.50	5.00	10.00	20.00
	1834 НГ	I.A.	2.00	4.00	8.00	15.00
	1835 НГ	.940	2.00	4.00	8.00	15.00

C#	Date	Mintage	VG	Fine	VF	XF
164.1	1836 НГ	.490	2.00	4.00	8.00	15.00
	1837 НГ	2.360	2.00	4.00	8.00	15.00
	1838 НГ	.500	2.00	4.00	8.00	15.00
	1839 НГ	2.411	2.00	4.00	8.00	15.00
	1840 НГ	.190	2.00	4.00	8.00	15.00
	1841/0 НГ	.500	2.50	5.00	10.00	20.00
	1841 НГ	I.A.	2.00	4.00	8.00	15.00
	1842 НГ	—	—	—	Rare	—
	1842 АЧ	.300	2.00	4.00	8.00	15.00
	1843 АЧ	.180	2.00	4.00	8.00	15.00
	1844 КБ	.461	2.00	4.00	8.00	15.00
	1845 КБ	2.435	2.00	4.00	8.00	15.00
	1846/5 ПА	.810	2.50	5.00	10.00	20.00
	1846 ПА	I.A.	2.00	4.00	8.00	15.00
	1847 ПА	3.180	2.00	4.00	8.00	15.00
	1848 НІ	1.860	2.00	4.00	8.00	15.00
	1849 ПА	3.110	2.00	4.00	8.00	15.00
	1850 ПА	2.450	2.00	4.00	8.00	15.00
	1851 ПА	1.500	2.00	4.00	8.00	15.00
	1852 ПА	1.350	2.00	4.00	8.00	15.00
	1852 НІ	I.A.	3.00	6.00	12.00	25.00
	1853 НІ	1.350	2.00	4.00	8.00	15.00
	1854 НІ	1.000	2.00	4.00	8.00	15.00
(Y14.1)	1855 НІ	3.201	2.00	4.00	8.00	15.00
	1856 ФБ	1.940	2.00	4.00	8.00	15.00
	1857 ФБ	3.110	2.00	4.00	8.00	15.00
	1858 ФБ	2.600	2.00	4.00	8.00	15.00

Mint mark: MW

C#	Date	Mintage	VG	Fine	VF	XF
164.2	1854	—	—	—	Rare	—
(Y14.2)	1855	.103	25.00	50.00	100.00	200.00

2.0732 g, .750 SILVER, .0499 oz ASW
Mint mark: СПБ
Type 1, reticulated edge.

Y#	Date	Mintage	Fine	VF	XF	Unc
20.1	1859 ФБ	3.920	1.00	2.00	4.00	15.00
	1860 ФБ	.580	4.00	8.00	15.00	30.00

Type 2, eagle redesigned.

Y#	Date	Mintage	Fine	VF	XF	Unc
20.2	1860 ФБ	2.810	1.00	2.00	4.00	15.00
	1861 ФБ	5.660	1.00	2.00	4.00	15.00
	1861 МИ	I.A.	2.00	4.00	8.00	20.00
	1861	19.300	1.00	2.00	4.00	15.00
	1862 МИ	5.800	1.00	2.00	4.00	15.00
	1863 АБ	5.750	1.00	2.00	4.00	15.00
	1864 НФ	3.740	1.00	2.00	4.00	15.00
	1865 НФ	3.886	1.00	2.00	4.00	15.00
	1866 НФ	2.533	1.00	2.00	4.00	15.00
	1866 НІ	I.A.	1.00	2.00	4.00	15.00

1.7996 g, .500 SILVER, .0289 oz ASW
Mint mark: СПБ
Reeded edge.

Y#	Date	Mintage	Fine	VF	XF	Unc
20a.2	1867 НІ	6.445	.50	1.00	3.00	10.00
	1868 НІ	4.740	.50	1.00	3.00	10.00
	1869 НІ	3.710	.50	1.00	3.00	10.00
	1870 НІ	3.310	.50	1.00	3.00	10.00
	1871 НІ	4.195	.50	1.00	3.00	10.00
	1872 НІ	2.130	.50	1.00	3.00	10.00
	1873 НІ	2.620	.50	1.00	3.00	10.00
	1874 НІ	2.520	.50	1.00	3.00	10.00
	1875 НІ	3.590	.50	1.00	3.00	10.00
	1876 НІ	4.900	.50	1.00	3.00	10.00
	1877 НІ	2.090	.50	1.00	3.00	10.00
	1877 НФ	I.A.	3.00	6.00	12.00	25.00
	1878 НФ	6.920	.50	1.00	3.00	10.00
	1878 НІ	I.A.	5.00	10.00	20.00	50.00
	1879 НФ	6.890	.50	1.00	3.00	10.00
	1880 НФ	6.740	.50	1.00	3.00	10.00
	1881 НФ	2.950	.50	1.00	3.00	10.00
	1882 НФ	.920	.50	1.00	3.00	10.00
	1883 ДС	1.520	.50	1.00	3.00	10.00
	1883 АГ	I.A.	1.00	2.00	5.00	15.00
	1884 АГ	1.710	.50	1.00	3.00	10.00
	1885 АГ	1.300	.50	1.00	3.00	10.00
	1886 АГ	2.000	.50	1.00	3.00	10.00
	1887 АГ	4.000	.50	1.00	3.00	10.00
	1888 АГ	2.000	.50	1.00	3.00	10.00
	1889 АГ	5.000	.50	1.00	3.00	10.00
	1890 АГ	3.750	.50	1.00	3.00	10.00
	1891 АГ	3.240	.50	1.00	3.00	10.00
	1893 АГ	4.250	.50	1.00	3.00	10.00
	1894 АГ	4.000	.50	1.00	3.00	10.00
	1895 АГ	1.000	.50	1.00	3.00	10.00
	1896 АГ	2.010	.50	1.00	3.00	10.00
	1897 АГ	3.150	.50	1.00	3.00	10.00
	1898 АГ	6.610	.50	1.00	2.00	5.00
	1899 АГ	14.000	.50	1.00	2.00	5.00
	1899 ЗБ	I.A.	.50	1.00	2.00	5.00
	1900 ФЗ	2.603	.50	1.00	2.00	5.00
	Common date	—	—	—	Proof	100.00

NOTE: Later dates (1901-1914) exist for this type.

15 KOPEKS

For similar coins not listed here refer to Poland.

3.1097 g, .750 SILVER, .0750 oz ASW
Mint mark: СПБ
Reticulated edge

Y#	Date	Mintage	Fine	VF	XF	Unc
21	1860 ФБ	4.480	1.25	1.50	3.00	12.50
	1861 ФБ	10.120	1.25	1.50	3.00	12.50
	1861 МИ	I.A.	2.00	4.00	8.00	15.00
	1861	13.300	1.25	1.50	3.00	12.50
	1862 МИ	10.000	1.25	1.50	3.00	12.50
	1863 АБ	9.960	1.25	1.50	3.00	12.50
	1864 НФ	10.715	1.25	1.50	3.00	12.50
	1865 НФ	10.703	1.25	1.50	3.00	12.50
	1866 НФ	6.329	1.25	1.50	3.00	12.50
	1866 НІ	I.A.	1.25	1.50	3.00	12.50

2.6994 g, .500 SILVER, .0434 oz ASW

Y#	Date	Mintage	Fine	VF	XF	Unc
21a.2	1867 НІ	8.720	.75	1.00	3.00	10.00
	1868 НІ	7.460	.75	1.00	3.00	10.00
	1869 НІ	8.120	.75	1.00	3.00	10.00
	1870 НІ	9.380	.75	1.00	3.00	10.00
	1871 НІ	9.460	.75	1.00	3.00	10.00
	1872 НІ	5.880	.75	1.00	3.00	10.00
	1873 НІ	7.960	.75	1.00	3.00	10.00
	1874 НІ	6.960	.75	1.00	3.00	10.00
	1875 НІ	7.480	.75	1.00	3.00	10.00
	1876 НІ	9.760	.75	1.00	3.00	10.00
	1877 НІ	4.360	.75	1.00	3.00	10.00
	1877 НФ	I.A.	2.00	5.00	12.50	25.00
	1878 НФ	1.116	.75	1.00	3.00	10.00
	1879 НФ	12.504	.75	1.00	3.00	10.00
	1880 НФ	11.655	.75	1.00	3.00	10.00
	1881 НФ	4.900	.75	1.00	3.00	10.00
	1882 НФ	1.470	.75	1.00	3.00	10.00
	1882 ДС	Inc. Ab.	10.00	20.00	30.00	60.00
	1883 ДС	4.020	3.00	6.00	12.00	25.00
	1883 АГ	I.A.	.75	1.00	3.00	10.00
	1884 АГ	2.720	.75	1.00	3.00	10.00
	1885 АГ	1.420	.75	1.00	3.00	10.00
	1886 АГ	1.840	.75	1.00	3.00	10.00
	1887 АГ	3.000	.75	1.00	3.00	10.00
	1888 АГ	—	3.00	6.00	12.00	25.00
	1889 АГ	2.835	.75	1.00	2.00	6.00
	1890 АГ	3.500	.75	1.00	2.00	6.00
	1891 АГ	4.710	.75	1.00	2.00	6.00
	1893 АГ	6.500	.75	1.00	2.00	6.00
	1896 АГ	3.160	.75	1.00	2.00	6.00
	1897 АГ	I.A.	.75	1.00	2.00	6.00
	1898 АГ	3.000	.75	1.00	2.00	6.00
	1899 АГ	12.665	.75	1.00	2.00	6.00
	1899 ЗБ	I.A.	5.00	10.00	20.00	50.00
	1900 ФЗ	12.665	.75	1.00	2.00	5.00

NOTE: Later dates (1901-1914) exist for this type.

20 KOPEKS

4.1463 g, .868 SILVER, .1157 oz ASW
Mint mark: СПБ

C#	Date	Mintage	VG	Fine	VF	XF
128	1810 ФГ	.250	5.00	10.00	20.00	30.00
	1811 ФГ	1.969	3.00	5.00	10.00	20.00
	1813 ПС	1.900	3.00	5.00	10.00	20.00
	1814/3 МФ	1.850	4.00	6.00	12.00	25.00
	1814 ПС	I.A.	3.00	5.00	10.00	20.00
	1814 МФ	I.A.	3.00	5.00	10.00	20.00
	1815/4 МФ	1.025	4.00	6.00	12.00	25.00
	1815 МФ	I.A.	3.00	5.00	10.00	20.00
	1816/5 МФ	.115	4.00	6.00	12.00	25.00
	1816 МФ	I.A.	6.00	12.50	25.00	50.00
	1816 ПС	I.A.	3.00	5.00	10.00	20.00
	1817 ПС	1.545	3.00	5.00	10.00	20.00
	1818 ПС	2.000	3.00	5.00	10.00	20.00
	1819 ПС	1.705	3.00	5.00	10.00	20.00
	1820/19 ПС	1.895	4.00	6.00	12.00	25.00
	1820/19 ПД	I.A.	4.00	6.00	12.00	25.00
	1820 ПС	I.A.	4.00	6.00	12.00	25.00
	1820 ПД	I.A.	3.00	5.00	10.00	20.00
	1821/0 ПД	3.025	4.00	6.00	12.00	25.00
	1821/1 ПД	I.A.	4.00	6.00	12.00	25.00
	1821 ПД	I.A.	3.00	5.00	10.00	20.00
	1822/1 ПД	2.100	4.00	6.00	12.00	25.00
	1822 ПД	I.A.	3.00	5.00	10.00	20.00

C#	Date	Mintage	VG	Fine	VF	XF
128	1823/18 ПД	7.075	4.00	6.00	12.00	25.00
	1823/1 ПД	I.A.	4.00	6.00	12.00	25.00
	1823 ПД	I.A.	3.00	5.00	10.00	20.00
	1823	—	—	—	Rare	—
	1824 ПД	1.750	3.00	5.00	10.00	20.00
	1825/23/19 ПД	1.375	4.00	6.00	12.00	25.00
	1825 ПД	I.A.	3.00	5.00	10.00	20.00
	1825 НГ	I.A.	6.00	12.50	25.00	50.00
	1826/5 НГ	2.815	7.00	15.00	30.00	60.00
(153)	1826 НГ	I.A.	3.00	5.00	10.00	20.00

C#	Date	Mintage	VG	Fine	VF	XF
158	1826 НГ	Inc. C153	4.50	9.00	17.50	35.00
	1827 НГ	.465	4.50	9.00	17.50	35.00
	1828 НГ	.050	7.50	15.00	30.00	60.00
	1829 НГ	.250	4.50	9.00	17.50	35.00
	1830 НГ	1.175	6.00	12.00	25.00	50.00
	1831 НГ	.385	4.50	9.00	17.50	35.00

Obv: Variety I eagle.

C#	Date	Mintage	VG	Fine	VF	XF
165	1832 НГ	.097	3.00	6.00	10.00	25.00
	1833 НГ	.435	2.50	5.00	10.00	20.00
	1834 НГ	.320	2.50	5.00	10.00	20.00
	1835 НГ	.500	2.50	5.00	10.00	20.00
	1836 НГ	1.280	2.50	5.00	10.00	20.00
	1837 НГ	1.300	2.50	5.00	10.00	20.00
	1838 НГ	1.635	2.50	5.00	10.00	20.00
	1839 НГ	4.030	2.50	5.00	10.00	20.00
	1840 НГ	2.075	2.50	5.00	10.00	20.00
	1841 НГ	.025	6.00	12.00	20.00	40.00
	1842 АЧ	—	20.00	40.00	80.00	150.00
	1843 АЧ	—	20.00	40.00	80.00	150.00
	1844 КБ	—	20.00	40.00	80.00	150.00
	1845 КБ	.105	2.50	5.00	10.00	20.00
	1846 ПА	.630	2.50	5.00	10.00	20.00
	1847 ПА	3.923	2.50	5.00	10.00	20.00
	1848 НI	2.636	2.50	5.00	10.00	20.00
	1849 ПА	3.250	2.50	5.00	10.00	20.00
	1850 ПА	3.075	2.50	5.00	10.00	20.00
	1851 ПА	2.000	2.50	5.00	10.00	20.00
	1852 НI	1.800	—	—	Rare	—
	1852 ПА	I.A.	2.50	5.00	10.00	20.00
	1853 НI	1.800	2.50	5.00	10.00	20.00
	1854 НI	.990	2.50	5.00	10.00	20.00
(Y15)	1855 НI	3.090	2.50	5.00	10.00	20.00
	1856 ФБ	3.240	2.50	5.00	10.00	20.00
	1857 ФБ	4.275	2.50	5.00	10.00	20.00
	1857 MW	.027	6.00	12.50	25.00	50.00
	1858 ФБ	4.150	2.50	5.00	10.00	20.00

4.1463 g, .750 SILVER, .0999 oz ASW
Reticulated edge

Y#	Date	Mintage	Fine	VF	XF	Unc
22.1	1859 ФБ	3.960	1.50	3.00	5.00	15.00
	1860 ФБ	1.070	1.50	3.00	5.00	15.00

Obv: Eagle redesigned.

Y#	Date	Mintage	Fine	VF	XF	Unc
22.2	1860 ФБ	14.440	1.50	3.00	5.00	15.00
	1861 ФБ	19.500	1.50	3.00	5.00	15.00
	1861 МИ	I.A.	2.00	4.00	8.00	20.00
	1861	19.000	1.50	3.00	5.00	15.00
	1862 МИ	19.500	1.50	3.00	5.00	15.00
	1863 АБ	19.230	1.50	3.00	5.00	15.00
	1864 НФ	20.060	1.50	3.00	5.00	15.00
	1865 НФ	20.048	1.50	3.00	5.00	15.00
	1866 НФ	10.067	1.50	3.00	5.00	15.00
	1866 НI	Inc. Ab.	1.50	3.00	5.00	15.00

NOTE: Varieties of eagle exist for 1860 dated coins.

3.5992 g, .500 SILVER, .0579 oz ASW
Reeded edge

Y#	Date	Mintage	Fine	VF	XF	Unc
22a.1	1867 НФ	—	—	—	Rare	—
	1867 НI	15.355	1.00	2.00	3.00	12.00
	1868 НI	11.975	1.00	2.00	3.00	12.00
	1869 НI	17.017	1.00	2.00	3.00	12.00
	1870 НI	16.255	1.00	2.00	3.00	12.00
	1871 НI	18.860	1.00	2.00	3.00	12.00
	1872 НI	11.980	1.00	2.00	3.00	12.00
	1873 НI	15.185	1.00	2.00	3.00	12.00
	1874 НI	14.850	1.00	2.00	3.00	12.00
	1875 НI	15.545	1.00	2.00	3.00	12.00
	1876 НI	16.255	1.00	2.00	3.00	12.00
	1877 НI	6.950	1.00	2.00	3.00	12.00
	1877 НФ	I.A.	2.00	4.00	8.00	15.00
	1878 НФ	25.335	1.00	2.00	3.00	12.00
	1878 НI	I.A.	5.00	10.00	20.00	50.00
	1879 НФ	23.070	1.00	2.00	3.00	12.00
	1880/7 НФ	22.605	1.25	2.50	4.00	14.00
	1880 НФ	I.A.	1.00	2.00	3.00	12.00
	1881 НФ	9.350	1.00	2.00	3.00	12.00
	1882 НФ	3.535	1.00	2.00	3.00	12.00
	1883 ДС	4.270	1.00	2.00	3.00	12.00
	1883 АГ	I.A.	2.00	4.00	8.00	15.00
	1884 АГ	2.595	1.00	2.00	3.00	12.00
	1885 АГ	1.610	1.00	2.00	3.00	12.00
	1886 АГ	2.625	1.00	2.00	3.00	12.00
	1887 АГ	2.500	1.00	2.00	3.00	12.00
	1888 АГ	3.035	1.00	2.00	3.00	12.00
	1889 АГ	1.964	1.00	2.00	3.00	12.00
	1890 АГ	3.500	1.00	2.00	3.00	12.00
	1891 АГ	6.105	1.00	2.00	3.00	12.00
	1893 АГ	7.500	1.00	2.00	3.00	12.00

NOTE: Later dates (1901-1914) exist for this type.

POLUPOLTINNIK

5.1800 g, .868 SILVER, .1446 oz ASW
Mint mark: СМ

C#	Date	Mintage	VG	Fine	VF	XF
98.1a	1801 АИ	.068	35.00	70.00	150.00	300.00
	1801 ОЦ	I.A.	—	—	Rare	—

NOTE: Earlier dates (1798-1799) exist for this type.

4.1400 g, .868 SILVER, .1155 oz ASW
Mint mark: СПБ

C#	Date	Mintage	VG	Fine	VF	XF
121	1802 АИ	.324	50.00	100.00	175.00	250.00
	1803 АИ	.152	60.00	110.00	200.00	275.00
	1803 ФГ	I.A.	—	—	Rare	—
	1804 ФГ	.168	50.00	100.00	175.00	250.00
	1805 ФГ	.137	60.00	110.00	200.00	275.00

C#	Date	Mintage	VG	Fine	VF	XF
121a	1808 ФГ	—	—	—	Rare	—
	1809 МК	.040	75.00	150.00	250.00	350.00
	1809 ФГ	I.A.	—	—	Rare	—
	1810 ФГ	.066	60.00	120.00	200.00	275.00

25 KOPEKS

5.1830 g, .868 SILVER, .1446 oz ASW
Mint mark: СПБ

C#	Date	Mintage	VG	Fine	VF	XF
159	1827 НГ	1.860	5.00	10.00	25.00	50.00
	1828 НГ	.320	6.00	12.50	35.00	65.00
	1829 НГ	1.200	5.00	10.00	20.00	50.00
	1830 НГ	1.160	5.00	10.00	20.00	50.00
	1831 НГ	.484	5.00	10.00	20.00	50.00

NOTE: The 1828 with reeded edge is a rare pattern.

For similar coins not listed here refer to Poland.

Obv: Variety I eagle.

C#	Date	Mintage	VG	Fine	VF	XF
166.1	1832 НГ	.308	3.50	8.00	15.00	30.00
	1833 НГ	.260	3.50	8.00	15.00	30.00
	1834 НГ	.260	3.50	8.00	15.00	30.00
	1835 НГ	.356	3.50	8.00	15.00	30.00
	1836/5 НГ	1.072	4.00	9.00	17.00	35.00
	1836 НГ	I.A.	3.50	8.00	15.00	30.00
	1837 НГ	1.144	3.50	8.00	15.00	30.00
	1838 НГ	2.672	3.50	8.00	15.00	30.00
	1839 НГ	2.738	3.50	8.00	15.00	30.00
	1840 НГ	.604	3.50	8.00	15.00	30.00
	1841/0 НГ	.020	4.00	9.00	17.00	35.00
	1841 НГ	I.A.	20.00	40.00	80.00	150.00
	1842 АЧ	—	20.00	40.00	80.00	150.00
	1843 АЧ	—	20.00	40.00	80.00	150.00
	1844 КБ	.021	3.50	8.00	15.00	30.00
	1845 КБ	.569	3.50	8.00	15.00	30.00
	1846 ПА	.576	3.50	8.00	15.00	30.00
	1847 ПА	4.824	2.50	6.00	12.50	25.00
	1848 НI	2.636	2.50	6.00	12.50	25.00
	1849 ПА	3.440	2.50	6.00	12.50	25.00
	1850 ПА	3.740	2.50	6.00	12.50	25.00
	1851 ПА	2.400	2.50	6.00	12.50	25.00
	1852 ПА	2.160	2.50	6.00	12.50	25.00
	1852 НI	I.A.	10.00	20.00	40.00	80.00
	1853 НI	2.160	2.50	6.00	12.50	25.00
	1853	—	10.00	20.00	40.00	80.00
	1854 НI	1.148	2.50	6.00	12.50	25.00
(Y16.1)	1855 НI	10.396	2.50	5.00	7.50	12.50
	1856 ФБ	4.444	2.50	5.00	10.00	20.00
	1857 ФБ	5.420	2.50	5.00	10.00	20.00
	1858 ФБ	5.528	2.50	5.00	10.00	20.00
	1858	Inc. Ab.	5.00	10.00	20.00	40.00
	Common date		—	—	Proof	200.00

NOTE: Varieties of eagle and crown exist.

Mint mark: MW

C#	Date	Mintage	VG	Fine	VF	XF
166.2	1854	.009	12.00	25.00	50.00	100.00
(Y16.2)	1857	.033	10.00	20.00	45.00	90.00

Mint mark: СПБ
Obv: Eagle redesigned.

Y#	Date	Mintage	Fine	VF	XF	Unc
23	1859 ФБ	4.400	5.00	10.00	20.00	60.00
	1860 ФБ	1.052	7.50	15.00	30.00	80.00
	1861 ФБ	.116	12.50	25.00	50.00	125.00
	1861 МИ	Inc. Ab.	12.50	25.00	50.00	125.00
	1862 МИ	.036	20.00	40.00	85.00	175.00
	1863 АБ	.036	20.00	40.00	85.00	175.00
	1864 НФ	.068	15.00	37.50	75.00	150.00
	1865 НФ	.016	15.00	37.50	75.00	150.00
	1866 НФ	.036	15.00	37.50	75.00	150.00
	1866 НI	I.A.	15.00	37.50	75.00	150.00
	1867 НI	.048	15.00	37.50	75.00	150.00
	1868 НI	.040	15.00	37.50	75.00	150.00
	1869 НI	.020	30.00	60.00	125.00	250.00
	1870 НI	.044	15.00	37.50	75.00	150.00
	1871 НI	.024	15.00	37.50	75.00	150.00
	1872 НI	.044	15.00	37.50	75.00	150.00
	1873 НI	.036	15.00	37.50	75.00	150.00
	1874 НI	.032	15.00	37.50	75.00	150.00
	1875 НI	.024	15.00	37.50	75.00	150.00
	1876 НI	.040	15.00	37.50	75.00	150.00
	1877 НI	1.776	7.50	15.00	30.00	80.00
	1877	Inc. Ab.	—	—	Rare	—
	1877 НФ	I.A.	7.50	15.00	30.00	80.00
	1878 НФ	1.768	5.00	10.00	20.00	40.00
	1879 НФ	.032	15.00	37.50	75.00	150.00
	1880 НФ	.078	12.50	25.00	50.00	125.00
	1881 НФ	2,001	25.00	50.00	75.00	150.00
	1882 НФ	2,007	25.00	50.00	75.00	175.00
	1883 ДС	2,008	25.00	50.00	75.00	175.00
	1883 АГ	Inc. Ab.	30.00	60.00	125.00	250.00
	1884 АГ	2,004	25.00	50.00	75.00	175.00
	1885 АГ	1,011	25.00	50.00	75.00	200.00

4.9990 g, .900 SILVER, .1446 oz ASW
Mint: St. Petersburg - w/o mint mark

Y#	Date	Mintage	Fine	VF	XF	Unc
44	1886 АГ	4,058	25.00	50.00	90.00	175.00
	1887 АГ	.028	20.00	40.00	80.00	150.00
	1888 АГ	4,007	25.00	50.00	90.00	175.00
	1889 АГ	1,002	50.00	75.00	125.00	250.00
	1890 АГ	2,006	25.00	50.00	90.00	175.00
	1891 АГ	.024	25.00	50.00	90.00	175.00
	1892 АГ	4,006	25.00	50.00	90.00	175.00
	1893 АГ	8,008	25.00	50.00	90.00	175.00
	1894/3 АГ	—	17.00	34.00	66.00	110.00
	1894 АГ	—	15.00	30.00	60.00	100.00
	Common date	—	—	—	Proof	450.00

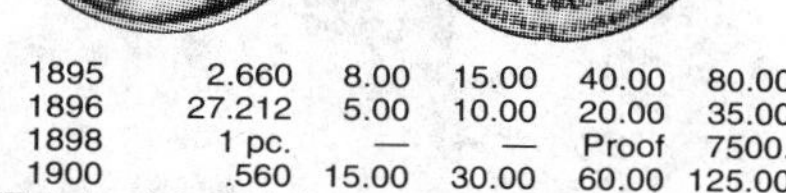

Y#	Date	Mintage	Fine	VF	XF	Unc
57	1895	2.660	8.00	15.00	40.00	80.00
	1896	27.212	5.00	10.00	20.00	35.00
	1898	1 pc.	—	—	Proof	7500.
	1900	.560	15.00	30.00	60.00	125.00

NOTE: Later date (1901) exists for this type.

30 KOPEKS

Refer to Poland

POLTINA

(1/2 Rouble)

10.3700 g, .868 SILVER, .2894 oz ASW
Mint mark: СМ
Reduced size.

C#	Date	Mintage	VG	Fine	VF	XF
99.1a	1801 ОМ	.172	40.00	75.00	150.00	275.00
	1801 ФЦ	I.A.	50.00	100.00	200.00	350.00

NOTE: Earlier dates (1797-1800) exist for this type.

10.3600 g, .868 SILVER, .2892 oz ASW
Mint mark: СПБ

C#	Date	Mintage	VG	Fine	VF	XF
123	1802 АИ	.104	25.00	50.00	100.00	250.00
	1803 АИ	.242	25.00	50.00	100.00	250.00
	1804 ФГ	.230	25.00	50.00	100.00	250.00
	1805 ФГ	.315	35.00	70.00	140.00	300.00

C#	Date	Mintage	VG	Fine	VF	XF
123a	1809 МК	.011	—	—	Rare	—
	1810 ФГ	.079	75.00	150.00	300.00	750.00

C#	Date	Mintage	VG	Fine	VF	XF
129	1810 ФГ	Inc. C123a	7.50	15.00	35.00	80.00
	1811/0 ФГ	.090	7.00	14.00	35.00	80.00
	1811 ФГ	I.A.	6.00	12.00	30.00	70.00
	1812/1 МФ	.045	7.00	14.00	35.00	80.00
	1812 МФ	I.A.	6.00	12.00	30.00	70.00
	1813 ПС	.580	6.00	12.00	30.00	70.00
	1814/3 ПС	.662	7.00	14.00	35.00	80.00
	1814 ПС	I.A.	6.00	12.00	30.00	70.00
	1814 МФ	I.A.	6.00	12.00	30.00	70.00
	1815 МФ	1.700	6.00	12.00	30.00	70.00
	1816 МФ	.270	6.00	12.00	30.00	70.00
	1816 ПС	I.A.	6.00	12.00	30.00	70.00
	1817 ПС	2.820	6.00	12.00	30.00	70.00
129	1818 ПС	4.250	6.00	12.00	30.00	70.00
	1819 ПС	2.430	6.00	12.00	30.00	70.00
	1819	Inc. Ab.	—	—	Rare	—
	1820 ПС	1.356	—	—	Rare	—
	1820 ПД	I.A.	6.00	12.00	30.00	70.00
	1821/0 ПД	.480	7.00	14.00	35.00	80.00
	1821 ПД	I.A.	6.00	12.00	30.00	70.00
	1822/1 ПД	.090	7.00	14.00	35.00	80.00
	1822/0 ПД	.090	7.00	14.00	35.00	80.00
	1822 ПД	I.A.	6.00	12.00	30.00	70.00
	1823 ПД	.200	6.00	12.00	30.00	70.00
	1824/3 ПД	.320	7.00	14.00	35.00	80.00
	1824 ПД	I.A.	6.00	12.00	30.00	70.00
	1825/4 ПД	.152	7.00	14.00	35.00	80.00
	1825 ПД	I.A.	6.00	12.00	30.00	70.00
	1826 НГ	.201	6.00	12.00	30.00	70.00

C#	Date	Mintage	VG	Fine	VF	XF
160	1826 НГ	Inc. C129	15.00	30.00	70.00	165.00
	1826 ПД	—	—	—	Rare	—
	1827 НГ	.164	15.00	30.00	70.00	165.00
	1828 НГ	.274	15.00	30.00	70.00	165.00
	1829 НГ	.880	12.50	25.00	50.00	125.00
	1830 НГ	.290	15.00	30.00	70.00	165.00
	1831 НГ	.140	15.00	30.00	70.00	165.00

Variety I eagle

C#	Date	Mintage	VG	Fine	VF	XF
167.1	1832 НГ	.050	10.00	20.00	40.00	100.00
	1833 НГ	.082	10.00	20.00	40.00	100.00
	1834 НГ	.046	10.00	20.00	40.00	100.00
	1835 НГ	.020	12.50	25.00	50.00	125.00
	1836 НГ	.140	7.50	15.00	30.00	60.00
	1837/6 НГ	.104	8.00	16.00	32.00	65.00
	1837 НГ	I.A.	7.50	15.00	30.00	60.00
	1838 НГ	.004	—	—	Rare	—
	1839/7 НГ	1.830	6.00	12.00	30.00	60.00
	1839 НГ	I.A.	5.00	10.00	25.00	45.00
	1840/3 НГ	.960	20.00	40.00	80.00	150.00
	1840 НГ	I.A.	5.00	10.00	25.00	45.00
	1841/0 НГ	.010	20.00	40.00	80.00	150.00
	1841 НГ	I.A.	15.00	30.00	60.00	125.00
	1842/39 АЧ	.214	6.00	12.00	30.00	50.00
	1842 НГ	—	—	—	Rare	—
	1842 АЧ	I.A.	5.00	10.00	25.00	40.00
	1843 АЧ	—	10.00	20.00	40.00	100.00
	1844 КБ	.348	5.00	10.00	25.00	45.00
	1845 КБ	2.009	5.00	10.00	25.00	45.00
	1846 ПА	.460	5.00	10.00	25.00	45.00
	1847 ПА	.615	5.00	10.00	25.00	45.00
	1848 НІ	1.560	5.00	10.00	25.00	45.00
	1849 ПА	.450	5.00	10.00	25.00	45.00
	1850 ПА	.530	5.00	10.00	25.00	45.00
	1851 ПА	.800	5.00	10.00	25.00	45.00
	1852 ПА	.720	5.00	10.00	25.00	45.00
	1852 НІ	I.A.	7.50	15.00	35.00	60.00
	1853 НІ	.720	5.00	10.00	25.00	45.00
	1854/0 НІ	.440	6.00	12.00	30.00	50.00
	1854 НІ	I.A.	5.00	10.00	25.00	45.00
(Y17)	1855 НІ	.714	5.00	15.00	25.00	45.00
	1856 ФБ	.450	5.00	15.00	25.00	45.00
	1857/6 ФБ	1.650	6.00	17.00	30.00	50.00
	1857 ФБ	I.A.	5.00	15.00	25.00	45.00
	1858 ФБ	1.112	5.00	15.00	25.00	50.00
	Common date		—	—	Proof	300.00

NOTE: Varieties of eagle and wreath exist.

Mint mark: MW

C#	Date	Mintage	VG	Fine	VF	XF
167.2	1842	.076	7.50	15.00	30.00	60.00
	1843	.023	10.00	20.00	40.00	80.00
	1844	.116	7.50	15.00	30.00	60.00
	1845	.138	7.50	15.00	30.00	60.00
	1846	.308	7.50	15.00	30.00	60.00
	1847	.783	7.50	15.00	30.00	60.00
	1854	.269	7.50	15.00	30.00	60.00

NOTE: Varieties of eagle exist.

Mint mark: СПБ
Variety II eagle.

Y#	Date	Mintage	Fine	VF	XF	Unc
24	1859 ФБ	1.392	10.00	20.00	40.00	100.00
	1860 ФБ	.192	20.00	40.00	85.00	175.00
	1861 ФБ	.064	25.00	50.00	100.00	200.00
	1861 МИ	I.A.	50.00	100.00	200.00	400.00
	1862 МИ	.024	30.00	60.00	125.00	250.00
	1863 АБ	.022	30.00	60.00	125.00	250.00
	1864 НФ	.034	30.00	60.00	125.00	250.00
	1865 НФ	.024	30.00	60.00	125.00	250.00
	1866 НФ	.022	30.00	60.00	125.00	250.00
	1866 НІ	I.A.	30.00	60.00	125.00	250.00
	1867 НІ	.026	30.00	60.00	125.00	250.00
	1868 НІ	.030	50.00	100.00	200.00	400.00
	1869 НІ	.020	30.00	60.00	125.00	250.00
	1870 НІ	6,000	40.00	80.00	150.00	300.00
	1871 НІ	.020	30.00	60.00	125.00	250.00
	1872 НІ	.022	30.00	60.00	125.00	250.00
	1873 НІ	.036	30.00	60.00	125.00	250.00
	1874 НІ	.016	30.00	60.00	125.00	250.00
	1875 НІ	.014	30.00	60.00	125.00	250.00
	1876 НІ	.024	30.00	60.00	125.00	250.00
	1876	Inc. Ab.	40.00	80.00	150.00	300.00
	1877 НІ	1.034	10.00	20.00	40.00	100.00
	1877 НФ	I.A.	15.00	30.00	60.00	125.00
	1878 НФ	.778	10.00	20.00	40.00	100.00
	1879 НФ	.014	30.00	60.00	125.00	250.00
	1880 НФ	.042	25.00	50.00	100.00	200.00
	1881 НФ	1,011	40.00	80.00	150.00	300.00
	1882 НФ	1,007	40.00	80.00	150.00	300.00
	1883 ДС	1,008	40.00	80.00	150.00	300.00
	1883 АГ	I.A.	50.00	100.00	200.00	400.00
	1884 АГ	1,004	40.00	80.00	150.00	300.00
	1885 АГ	511 pcs.	50.00	100.00	200.00	400.00

NOTE: Edge varieties exist.

50 KOPEKS

9.9980 g, .900 SILVER, .2893 oz ASW
Mint: St. Petersburg - w/o mint mark

Y#	Date	Mintage	Fine	VF	XF	Unc
45	1886 АГ	2,058	15.00	30.00	80.00	250.00
	1887 АГ	.026	20.00	40.00	80.00	250.00
	1888 АГ	2,007	15.00	30.00	80.00	250.00
	1889 АГ	1,002	20.00	40.00	100.00	300.00
	1890 АГ	2,006	15.00	30.00	80.00	250.00
	1891 АГ	.024	20.00	40.00	80.00	250.00
	1892 АГ	2,006	15.00	30.00	80.00	250.00
	1893 АГ	4,008	15.00	30.00	80.00	250.00
	1894 АГ	—	15.00	25.00	75.00	200.00
	Common date	—	—	—	Proof	750.00

Mint mark: Star on rim

Y#	Date	Mintage	Fine	VF	XF	Unc
58.1	1896	.245	10.00	20.00	40.00	80.00
	1897	46.755	7.50	12.50	25.00	60.00
	1899	10.000	7.50	12.50	25.00	60.00

9.9980 g, .900 SILVER, .2893 oz ASW
Mint: St. Petersburg - w/o mint mark

Y#	Date	Mintage	Fine	VF	XF	Unc
58.2	1895 АГ	5.400	5.00	10.00	25.00	65.00
	1896 АГ	17.402	5.00	8.00	15.00	55.00
	1898 АГ	—	—	—	Proof	1250.
	1899 ЗБ	15.442	5.00	10.00	25.00	65.00
	1899 ФЗ	I.A.	5.00	10.00	25.00	65.00
	1899 АГ	I.A.	5.00	10.00	25.00	65.00
	1900 ФЗ	3.360	5.00	10.00	25.00	65.00
	Common date	—	—	—	Proof	400.00

NOTE: Later dates (1901-1914) exist for this type.

ROUBLE

20.7300 g, .868 SILVER, .5785 oz ASW

Reduced size, 38mm.

C#	Date	Mintage	VG	Fine	VF	XF
101a	1801 АИ	3.143	20.00	40.00	90.00	150.00

C#	Date	Mintage	VG	Fine	VF	XF
101a	1801 ФЦ	I.A.	20.00	40.00	90.00	150.00
	1801 ОМ	I.A.	30.00	60.00	120.00	300.00

NOTE: Earlier dates (1798-1800) exist for this type.

Mint mark: СПБ
Alexander I

C#	Date	Mintage	VG	Fine	VF	XF
125	1802 АИ	5.360	20.00	40.00	80.00	150.00
	1803 АИ	2.429	20.00	40.00	80.00	150.00
	1803 ФГ	I.A.	25.00	50.00	100.00	200.00
	1804 ФГ	4.355	20.00	40.00	80.00	150.00
	1805 ФГ	2.020	20.00	40.00	80.00	150.00

C#	Date	Mintage	VG	Fine	VF	XF
125a	1807 ФГ	.533	30.00	60.00	120.00	200.00
	1808/7 ФГ	1.701	35.00	60.00	110.00	175.00
	1808 ФГ	I.A.	25.00	50.00	90.00	150.00
	1808/7 МК	I.A.	35.00	60.00	110.00	175.00
	1808 МК	I.A.	25.00	50.00	90.00	150.00
	1809 МК	2.177	25.00	50.00	90.00	150.00
	1809 ФГ	I.A.	25.00	50.00	90.00	150.00
	1810 ФГ	1.682	25.00	50.00	100.00	200.00

C#	Date	Mintage	VG	Fine	VF	XF
130	1810 ФГ	Inc. C125a	150.00	250.00	400.00	750.00
	1811 ФГ	2.675	15.00	20.00	35.00	75.00
	1812/1 МФ	4.076	16.00	22.00	40.00	85.00
	1812 МФ	I.A.	15.00	20.00	35.00	75.00
	1813/2 ПС	5.210	16.00	22.00	40.00	85.00
	1813 ПС	I.A.	15.00	20.00	35.00	75.00
	1814 МФ	3.600	15.00	20.00	35.00	75.00
	1814 ПС	I.A.	15.00	20.00	35.00	75.00
	1814	Inc. Ab.	18.00	30.00	50.00	90.00
	1815 МФ	4.750	10.00	20.00	35.00	75.00
	1816/5 МФ	1.782	16.00	22.00	40.00	85.00
	1816 МФ	I.A.	15.00	20.00	35.00	75.00
	1816 ПС	I.A.	15.00	20.00	35.00	75.00
	1817 ПС	11.775	15.00	20.00	35.00	75.00
	1818 ПС	16.275	15.00	20.00	35.00	75.00
	1818 СП	I.A.	15.00	20.00	35.00	75.00
	1818	Inc. Ab.	18.00	30.00	50.00	90.00
	1819 ПС	6.355	15.00	20.00	35.00	75.00
	1820/1 ПД					

C#	Date	Mintage	VG	Fine	VF	XF
130		1.962	11.00	22.00	40.00	85.00
	1820/19 ПД	I.A.	11.00	22.00	40.00	85.00
	1820 ПС	I.A.	75.00	150.00	250.00	400.00
	1820 ПД	I.A.	15.00	20.00	35.00	75.00
	1821/0 ПД	.840	16.00	22.00	40.00	85.00
	1821 ПД	I.A.	15.00	20.00	35.00	75.00
	1822/1 ПД	3.120	16.00	22.00	40.00	85.00
	1822 ПД	I.A.	15.00	20.00	35.00	75.00
	1823 ПД	2.955	15.00	20.00	35.00	75.00
	1824/3 ПД	2.035	16.00	22.00	40.00	85.00
	1824 ПД	I.A.	15.00	20.00	35.00	75.00
	1825/4 ПД	1.461	16.00	22.00	40.00	85.00
	1825 ПД	I.A.	15.00	20.00	35.00	75.00
	1825 НГ	I.A.	15.00	20.00	40.00	100.00
(155)	1826 НГ	.730	18.00	35.00	75.00	125.00

C#	Date	Mintage	Fine	VF	XF	Unc
161	1826 НГ	Inc.C155	35.00	75.00	125.00	275.00
	1827/6 НГ	.584	30.00	55.00	110.00	275.00
	1827 НГ	I.A.	27.50	50.00	100.00	250.00
	1828 НГ	2.530	25.00	45.00	90.00	250.00
	1829 НГ	5.510	25.00	45.00	90.00	250.00
	1830/2 НГ	6.010	27.00	50.00	100.00	275.00
	1830 НГ	I.A.	25.00	45.00	90.00	250.00
	1831/0 НГ	3.670	27.00	50.00	100.00	275.00
	1831 НГ	I.A.	25.00	45.00	90.00	250.00

NOTE: Edge varieties exist.

C#	Date	Mintage	Fine	VF	XF	Unc
168.1	1832 НГ	1.941	18.00	25.00	60.00	150.00
	1833 НГ	1.711	18.00	25.00	60.00	150.00
	1834 НГ	2.270	18.00	25.00	60.00	150.00
	1835/4 НГ	.244	27.00	45.00	85.00	200.00
	1835 НГ	I.A.	25.00	40.00	75.00	175.00
	1836/4 НГ	1.102	20.00	30.00	70.00	175.00
	1836 НГ	I.A.	18.00	25.00	60.00	150.00
	1837 НГ	1.478	18.00	25.00	60.00	150.00
	1838 НГ	.232	25.00	40.00	75.00	175.00
	1839 НГ	.036	—	—	*Rare	—
	1840/3 НГ	2.627	20.00	30.00	70.00	175.00
	1840 НГ	I.A.	18.00	25.00	60.00	150.00
	1841/0 НГ	6.155	20.00	30.00	70.00	175.00
	1841/3 НГ	I.A.	20.00	30.00	70.00	175.00
	1841 НГ	I.A.	18.00	25.00	60.00	150.00
	1842/1 АЧ	4.965	20.00	30.00	70.00	175.00
	1842 АЧ	I.A.	18.00	25.00	60.00	150.00
	1843/2 АЧ	5.320	20.00	30.00	70.00	175.00
	1843 АЧ	I.A.	18.00	25.00	60.00	150.00
	1844/3 КБ	2.933	20.00	30.00	70.00	175.00
	1844 КБ	I.A.	18.00	25.00	60.00	150.00
	1845 КБ	.683	18.00	25.00	60.00	150.00
	1846/5 ПА	3.523	20.00	30.00	70.00	175.00
	1846 ПА	I.A.	18.00	25.00	60.00	150.00
	1847 ПА	.563	20.00	30.00	70.00	165.00
	1848 НI	1.542	18.00	25.00	60.00	150.00
	1849 ПА	1.708	18.00	25.00	60.00	150.00

C#	Date	Mintage	Fine	VF	XF	Unc
168.1	1850 ПА	1.600	18.00	25.00	60.00	150.00
	1851/0 ПА	2.400	20.00	30.00	70.00	175.00
	1851 ПА	I.A.	18.00	25.00	60.00	150.00
	1852 ПА	2.560	18.00	25.00	60.00	150.00
	1852 НI	I.A.	25.00	40.00	75.00	175.00
	1853 НI	2.160	18.00	25.00	60.00	150.00
	1854 НI	3.070	18.00	25.00	60.00	150.00
(Y18)	1855 НI	1.068	18.00	25.00	60.00	150.00
	1856/5 ФБ	1.388	20.00	30.00	70.00	175.00
	1856 ФБ	I.A.	18.00	25.00	60.00	150.00
	1857 ФБ	.250	25.00	40.00	75.00	200.00
	1858 ФБ	.570	25.00	40.00	75.00	200.00
	Common date		—	—	Proof	450.00

***NOTE:** Superior Goodman sale 2-91 P/L Unc. realized, $10,450.

Mint mark: MW

C#	Date	Mintage	Fine	VF	XF	Unc
168.2	1842	.257	22.50	35.00	75.00	135.00
	1843	.267	22.50	35.00	75.00	135.00
	1844	2.364	22.50	35.00	75.00	135.00
	1845	.345	25.00	45.00	95.00	150.00
	1846	.511	22.50	35.00	75.00	135.00
	1847	.987	22.50	35.00	75.00	135.00

Mint mark: СПБ
Alexander I Monument

C#	Date	Mintage	Fine	VF	XF	Unc
169	1834	.015	75.00	150.00	325.00	500.00
	1834	—	—	—	Proof	Rare

Battle of Borodino Memorial

C#	Date	Mintage	Fine	VF	XF	Unc
170	1839 НГ	.160	65.00	125.00	250.00	485.00

NOTE: Large portion of mintage melted.
NOTE: The 1841 Marriage "Rouble" is a medal.

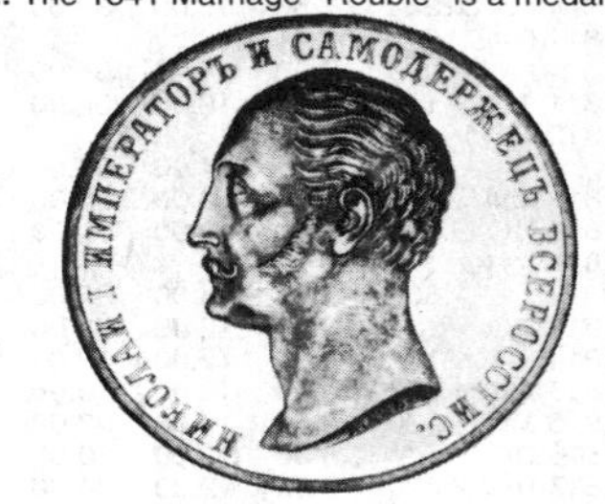

Mint: St. Petersburg - w/o mint mark
Nicholas I Memorial

Y#	Date	Mintage	Fine	VF	XF	Unc
28	1859	.050	60.00	110.00	190.00	325.00

Mint mark: СПБ

Y#	Date	Mintage	Fine	VF	XF	Unc
25	1859 ФБ	.014	75.00	150.00	300.00	500.00
	1860 ФБ	.018	75.00	150.00	400.00	750.00
	1861 ФБ	.076	50.00	100.00	150.00	350.00
	1861 МИ	I.A.	100.00	200.00	500.00	1000.
	1862 МИ	.022	50.00	100.00	150.00	350.00
	1863 АБ	.005	100.00	200.00	500.00	1000.
	1864 НФ	.114	25.00	50.00	100.00	225.00
	1865 НФ	.115	25.00	50.00	100.00	225.00
	1866 НІ	.110	25.00	50.00	100.00	225.00
	1866 НФ	I.A.	25.00	50.00	100.00	225.00
	1867 НІ	.425	17.50	25.00	50.00	135.00
	1868 НІ	.775	17.50	25.00	50.00	135.00
	1869 НІ	.285	17.50	25.00	50.00	135.00
	1870 НІ	.386	17.50	25.00	75.00	150.00
	1871 НІ	.884	17.50	25.00	50.00	135.00
	1872 НІ	.978	17.50	25.00	50.00	135.00
	1873 НІ	.673	17.50	25.00	50.00	135.00
	1874 НІ	.648	17.50	25.00	50.00	135.00
	1875 НІ	.687	17.50	25.00	50.00	135.00
	1876 НІ	.778	17.50	25.00	50.00	135.00
	1877 НІ	6.923	15.00	20.00	35.00	100.00
	1877 НФ	I.A.	15.00	20.00	35.00	100.00
	1878 НФ	8.087	15.00	20.00	35.00	100.00
	1879 НФ	.611	17.50	25.00	50.00	135.00
	1880 НФ	.521	17.50	25.00	50.00	135.00
	1881 НФ	.699	17.50	25.00	50.00	135.00
	1882 НФ	.434	17.50	25.00	50.00	135.00
	1883 ДС	.425	17.50	25.00	50.00	135.00
	1883 АГ	I.A.	100.00	200.00	500.00	1000.
	1884 АГ	.355	17.50	25.00	50.00	135.00
	1885 АГ	.500	17.50	25.00	50.00	135.00

Mint: St. Petersburg - w/o mint mark
Alexander III Coronation

Y#	Date	Mintage	Fine	VF	XF	Unc
43	1883	.279	35.00	50.00	90.00	240.00

19.9960 g, .900 SILVER, .5786 oz ASW
Mintmasters initials and stars found on edge.

Y#	Date	Mintage	Fine	VF	XF	Unc
46	1886 АГ	.488	20.00	40.00	75.00	225.00
	1887 АГ	.491	20.00	40.00	75.00	225.00
	1888 АГ	.498	20.00	40.00	75.00	225.00
	1889 АГ	1,002	125.00	250.00	500.00	1000.
	1890 АГ	.090	25.00	50.00	100.00	275.00
	1891 АГ	1.117	20.00	40.00	80.00	250.00
	1892 АГ	2.131	20.00	40.00	70.00	200.00
	1893 АГ	1.485	20.00	40.00	70.00	200.00
	1894 АГ	3,007	50.00	100.00	250.00	500.00
	Common date	—	—	—	Proof	1200.
	Mint mark: 2 stars on rim					
59.1	1897	26.000	10.00	17.50	30.00	85.00
	1898	14.000	10.00	17.50	30.00	85.00
	1899	10.000	10.00	17.50	30.00	85.00
	Mint mark: Star on rim					
59.2	1896	12.000	10.00	17.50	30.00	85.00
	1898	5.000	10.00	17.50	30.00	85.00
	Mint: St. Petersburg - w/o mint mark					
59.3	1895 АГ	1.240	12.00	20.00	35.00	100.00
	1896 АГ	12.540	10.00	17.50	30.00	85.00
	1897 АГ	18.515	10.00	17.50	30.00	85.00
	1898 АГ	18.725	10.00	17.50	30.00	85.00
	1899 ЭБ	6.503	10.00	17.50	30.00	85.00
	1899 ФЗ	I.A.	10.00	17.50	30.00	85.00
	1900 ФЗ	3.484	10.00	17.50	35.00	100.00
	Common date	—	—	—	Proof	900.00

NOTE: Later dates (1901-1915) exist for this type.

NOTE: Varieties exist with plain edge. These are mint errors and rare.

Nicholas II Coronation

Y#	Date	Mintage	Fine	VF	XF	Unc
60	1896 АГ	.191	25.00	40.00	70.00	150.00
	1896 АГ	—	—	—	Proof	500.00

Alexander II Memorial

Y#	Date	Mintage	Fine	VF	XF	Unc
61	1898 АГ	*5,000	125.00	225.00	350.00	850.00
	1898 АГ	—	—	—	Proof	1200.

1-1/2 ROUBLES/10 ZLOTYCH

For similar coins not listed here refer to Poland.

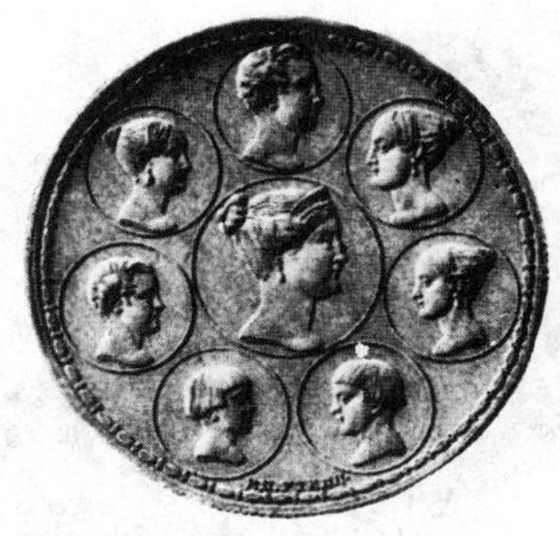

31.1000 g, .868 SILVER, .8679 oz ASW
Mint: St. Petersburg - w/o mint mark

C#	Date	Mintage	Fine	VF	XF	Unc
A172	1835	36 pcs.	—	—	5000.	10,000.

Obv: Designer's initials ПУ on truncation.

C#	Date	Mintage	Fine	VF	XF	Unc
172.1	1836	50 pcs.	—	—	5000.	7700.

C#	Date	Mintage	Fine	VF	XF	Unc
	Rev: Die break at rim lower right.					
172.2	1836	(restrike)	—	—	2500.	4000.
	Obv: Designer's name below bust.					
172.3	1836	Inc. Ab.	—	—	5000.	7500.
	Obv: W/o designer's name or initials.					
172.4	1836	Inc. Ab.	—	—	5500.	8500.

NOTE: The above coins were struck as presentation pieces.

Mint mark: СПБ
Battle of Borodino Memorial
Obv: Long rays.

C#	Date	Mintage	Fine	VF	XF	Unc
173.1	1839	6,000	400.00	800.00	1500.	2500.

Obv: Short rays.

C#	Date	Mintage	Fine	VF	XF	Unc
173.2	1839	Inc. Ab.	500.00	900.00	1500.	2500.

NOTE: Large portion of the mintage melted.

3 ROUBLES

10.3500 g, PLATINUM, .3327 oz APW
Mint mark: СПБ

C#	Date	Mintage	Fine	VF	XF	Unc
177	1828	.020	250.00	425.00	650.00	1000.
	1829	.043	225.00	350.00	525.00	750.00
	1830	.106	225.00	350.00	525.00	750.00
	1831	.087	225.00	350.00	525.00	750.00
	1832	.066	225.00	350.00	525.00	750.00
	1833	.085	250.00	400.00	600.00	850.00
	1834	.091	225.00	300.00	500.00	750.00
	1835	.139	250.00	400.00	600.00	800.00
	1836	.044	275.00	350.00	550.00	750.00
	1837	.046	275.00	350.00	550.00	750.00
	1838	.049	275.00	350.00	550.00	750.00
	1839	6 pcs.	—	—	Proof	3500.
	1840	3 pcs.	—	—	Proof	3000.
	1841	.017	250.00	400.00	600.00	850.00
	1842	.146	225.00	350.00	500.00	650.00
	1843	.172	225.00	350.00	550.00	750.00
	1844	.215	225.00	375.00	600.00	850.00
	1845	.050	250.00	425.00	650.00	900.00
	Common date	—	—	—	Proof	1450.

NOTE: The low mintage figures incorporated in the following listings of Russian platinum issues are not necessarily reflective of relative scarcity as many of the issues were restruck at later dates, using original dies in unrecorded quantities.

For similar coins not listed here refer to Poland.

3.9260 g, .917 GOLD, .1157 oz AGW

Y#	Date	Mintage	Fine	VF	XF	Unc
26	1869 НІ	.143	175.00	225.00	300.00	400.00
	1870 НІ	.200	175.00	225.00	300.00	400.00
	1871 НІ	.200	175.00	225.00	300.00	400.00
	1872 НІ	.100	175.00	225.00	300.00	400.00
	1873 НІ	.077	175.00	225.00	300.00	400.00
	1874 НІ	.270	175.00	225.00	300.00	400.00
	1875 НІ	.100	175.00	225.00	300.00	400.00
	1876 НІ	.063	175.00	225.00	300.00	400.00
	1877 НІ	.050	175.00	225.00	300.00	400.00
	1877 НФ	I.A.	175.00	225.00	300.00	400.00
	1878 НФ	.194	175.00	225.00	300.00	400.00
	1879 НФ	—	—	—	—	1900.
	1880 НФ	.100	175.00	225.00	300.00	400.00
	1881 НФ	.048	175.00	225.00	300.00	400.00
	1882 НФ	—	—	2200.	3500.	5000.
	1883 ДС	9,007	175.00	225.00	350.00	500.00
	1883 АГ	I.A.	—	—	Rare	—
	1884 АГ	.047	175.00	225.00	350.00	500.00
	1885 АГ	.029	175.00	250.00	375.00	550.00
	Common date	—	—	—	Proof	1200.

5 ROUBLES

6.0800 g, .986 GOLD, .1928 oz AGW
Mint mark: CM
Obv: Monograms of Paul I in cruciform.
Rev: Leg. in ornate square.

C#	Date	Mintage	Fine	VF	XF	Unc
104.1	1801 АИ	.180	250.00	400.00	800.00	1200.

NOTE: Earlier dates (1798-1800) exist for this type.

Mint mark: СПБ

C#	Date	Mintage	Fine	VF	XF	Unc
131	1802	15 pcs.	—	—	Rare	—
	1803 ХЛ	6 pcs.	—	—	Rare	—
	1804 ХЛ	.037	250.00	400.00	800.00	1200.
	1805 ХЛ	8,109	250.00	400.00	800.00	1200.

6.5440 g, .917 GOLD, .1929 oz AGW

C#	Date	Mintage	Fine	VF	XF	Unc
132	1817 ФГ	.710	130.00	180.00	300.00	500.00
	1818 МФ	1.520	130.00	200.00	325.00	550.00
	1819 МФ	.963	130.00	180.00	300.00	500.00
	1822 МФ	—	130.00	180.00	300.00	500.00
	1823 ПС	.440	130.00	180.00	300.00	500.00
	1824 ПС	.276	130.00	180.00	300.00	500.00
	1825 ПС	.101	400.00	700.00	1200.	2000.
	1825 ПС	—	—	—	Proof	3000.
	1825 ПД	I.A.	300.00	500.00	800.00	1400.

C#	Date	Mintage	Fine	VF	XF	Unc
174	1826 ПД	.212	130.00	180.00	300.00	500.00
	1827 ПД	—	300.00	500.00	900.00	1500.
	1828 ПД	.604	130.00	180.00	300.00	500.00
	1829 ПД	.733	130.00	180.00	300.00	500.00
	1830 ПД	.490	130.00	180.00	300.00	500.00
	1831 ПД	.846	150.00	300.00	400.00	650.00

Discovery of Gold at Kolyvan Mines

C#	Date	Mintage	Fine	VF	XF	Unc
176	1832 ПД	1,000	600.00	1200.	2200.	3500.
	1832	—	—	—	Proof	4500.

C#	Date	Mintage	Fine	VF	XF	Unc
175.1	1832 ПД	.481	100.00	120.00	150.00	220.00
	1833 ПД	.829	100.00	120.00	150.00	220.00
	1834 ПД	1.346	100.00	120.00	150.00	220.00
	1835 ПД	1.440	100.00	120.00	150.00	220.00
	1835	Inc. Ab.	—	—	Rare	—
	1836 ПД	.953	100.00	120.00	150.00	220.00
	1837 ПД	.048	150.00	200.00	250.00	400.00
	1838 ПД	.302	100.00	120.00	150.00	200.00
	1839 АЧ	1.609	100.00	120.00	150.00	200.00
	1840 АЧ	1.277	100.00	120.00	150.00	200.00
	1841 АЧ	1.668	100.00	120.00	140.00	200.00
	1842 АЧ	2.180	100.00	120.00	140.00	200.00
	1843 АЧ	1.852	100.00	120.00	140.00	200.00
	1844 КБ	2.365	100.00	120.00	140.00	200.00
	1845 КБ	2.842	100.00	120.00	140.00	200.00
	1846 АГ	3.442	100.00	120.00	140.00	200.00
	Common date	—	—	—	Proof	2000.

Mint mark: MW

C#	Date	Mintage	Fine	VF	XF	Unc
175.2	1842	695 pcs.	700.00	1000.	1500.	2500.
	1846	62 pcs.	1000.	1500.	2000.	3000.
	1848	485 pcs.	700.00	1000.	1500.	2500.
	1849	133 pcs.	700.00	1000.	1500.	2500.
	Common date	—	—	—	Proof	3000.

Mint mark: СПБ
Different eagle.

C#	Date	Mintage	Fine	VF	XF	Unc
175.3	1846 АГ	Inc. C175.1	100.00	120.00	140.00	200.00
	1847 АГ	3.900	100.00	150.00	200.00	275.00
	1848 АГ	2.900	100.00	120.00	140.00	200.00
	1849 АГ	3.100	100.00	120.00	140.00	200.00
	1850 АГ	3.900	100.00	120.00	140.00	200.00
	1851 АГ	3.400	100.00	120.00	140.00	200.00
	1852 АГ	3.900	100.00	120.00	140.00	200.00
	1853 АГ	3.900	100.00	120.00	140.00	200.00
	1854 АГ	3.900	100.00	120.00	140.00	200.00

Y#	Date	Mintage	Fine	VF	XF	Unc
A26	1855 АГ	3.400	100.00	120.00	140.00	200.00
	1856 АГ	3.800	100.00	120.00	140.00	200.00
	1857 АГ	4.500	100.00	120.00	140.00	200.00
	1858 АГ	3.500	100.00	120.00	140.00	200.00
	1858 ПФ	—	100.00	120.00	140.00	200.00
	Common date	—	—	—	Proof	2000.

Y#	Date	Mintage	Fine	VF	XF	Unc
B26	1859 ПФ	3.900	100.00	120.00	140.00	200.00
	1860 ПФ	3.600	100.00	120.00	140.00	200.00
	1861 ПФ	3.500	100.00	120.00	140.00	200.00
	1862 ПФ	6.354	100.00	120.00	140.00	200.00
	1863 МИ	7.200	100.00	120.00	140.00	200.00
	1864 АС	3.900	100.00	120.00	140.00	200.00
	1865 АС	3.902	100.00	120.00	140.00	200.00
	1865 СШ	I.A.	100.00	120.00	140.00	200.00
	1866 СШ	3.900	100.00	120.00	140.00	200.00
	1866 НІ	I.A.	100.00	120.00	140.00	200.00
	1867 НІ	3.494	100.00	120.00	140.00	200.00
	1868 НІ	3.400	100.00	120.00	140.00	200.00
	1869 НІ	3.900	100.00	120.00	140.00	200.00
	1870 НІ	5.000	100.00	120.00	140.00	200.00
	1871 НІ	.800	100.00	120.00	140.00	200.00
	1872 НІ	2.400	100.00	120.00	140.00	200.00
	1873 НІ	3.000	100.00	120.00	140.00	200.00
	1874 НІ	4.800	100.00	120.00	140.00	200.00
	1875 НІ	4.000	100.00	120.00	140.00	200.00
	1876 НІ	6.000	100.00	120.00	140.00	200.00
	1877 НІ	6.600	100.00	120.00	140.00	200.00
	1877 НФ	I.A.	100.00	120.00	140.00	200.00
	1878 НФ	6.800	100.00	120.00	140.00	200.00
	1879 НФ	7.225	100.00	120.00	140.00	200.00
	1880 НФ	6.200	100.00	120.00	140.00	200.00
	1881 НФ	5.500	100.00	120.00	140.00	200.00
	1882 НФ	4.547	100.00	120.00	140.00	200.00
	1883 ДС	5.632	100.00	120.00	140.00	200.00
	1883 АГ	I.A.	100.00	120.00	140.00	200.00
	1884 АГ	4.801	100.00	120.00	140.00	200.00
	1885 АГ	5.433	100.00	120.00	140.00	200.00
	Common date	—	—	—	140.00	200.00

6.4516 g, .900 GOLD, .1867 oz AGW
Mint: St. Petersburg - w/o mint mark

Y#	Date	Mintage	Fine	VF	XF	Unc
42	1886 АГ	.351	100.00	115.00	130.00	175.00
	1887 АГ	3.261	100.00	115.00	130.00	175.00
	1888 АГ	5.257	100.00	115.00	130.00	175.00
	1889 АГ	4.200	100.00	115.00	130.00	175.00
	1890 АГ	5.600	100.00	115.00	130.00	175.00
	1891 АГ	.541	100.00	115.00	130.00	175.00
	1892 АГ	.128	100.00	115.00	130.00	175.00
	1893 АГ	.598	100.00	115.00	130.00	175.00
	1894 АГ	.598	100.00	115.00	130.00	175.00
	Common date	—	—	—	Proof	1250.

NOTE: Edge varieties exist.

Y#	Date	Mintage	Fine	VF	XF	Unc
A61	1895 АГ	36 pcs.	—	2250.	4500.	6000.
	1896 АГ	33 pcs.	—	2250.	4500.	6000.

4.3013 g, .900 GOLD, .1244 oz AGW

62	1897 АГ	5.372	—	BV	60.00	90.00
	1898 АГ	52.378	—	BV	60.00	90.00
	1899 ЗБ	20.400	—	BV	60.00	90.00
	1899 ФЗ	I.A.	—	BV	60.00	90.00
	1900 ФЗ	.031	—	BV	70.00	95.00
	Common date	—	—	—	Proof	750.00

NOTE: Later dates (1901-1911) exist for this type.

6 ROUBLES

20.7100 g, PLATINUM, .6655 oz APW
Mint mark: СПБ

C#	Date	Mintage	Fine	VF	XF	Unc
178	1829	828 pcs.	1000.	2000.	2750.	3500.
	1830	8,610	1000.	1750.	2500.	3250.
	1831	2,784	1000.	1750.	2500.	3250.
	1832	1,502	1000.	2000.	2750.	3500.
	1833	302 pcs.	1000.	2000.	2750.	3500.
	1834	11 pcs.	1250.	2500.	3200.	5000.
	1835	107 pcs.	1000.	2000.	2500.	3250.
	1836	11 pcs.	—	—	Proof	6000.
	1837	253 pcs.	1000.	2000.	2750.	3500.
	1838	12 pcs.	—	—	Rare	—
	1839	2 pcs.	—	—	Rare	—
	1840	1 pc.	—	—	Rare	—
	1841	170 pcs.	1000.	2000.	2750.	3500.
	1842	121 pcs.	1000.	2000.	2750.	3500.
	1843	127 pcs.	1000.	2000.	2750.	3500.
	1844	4 pcs.	—	—	Rare	—
	1845	2 pcs.	—	—	Rare	—
	Common date	—	—	—	Proof	5000.

7 ROUBLES 50 KOPEKS

6.4516 g, .900 GOLD, .1867 oz AGW
Mint: St. Petersburg - w/o mint mark

Y#	Date	Mintage	Fine	VF	XF	Unc
63	1897 АГ	16.829	100.00	120.00	160.00	225.00

10 ROUBLES

12.1700 g, .986 GOLD, .3858 oz AGW
Mint mark: СПБ

C#	Date	Mintage	Fine	VF	XF	Unc
133	1802	.074	2500.	3000.	3500.	4500.
	1802 АИ	I.A.	2500.	3000.	3500.	4500.
	1804 ХЛ	.072	2500.	3000.	3500.	4500.
	1805 ХЛ	.055	1500.	2000.	2150.	4250.

12.9039 g, .900 GOLD, .3734 oz AGW

Mint: St. Petersburg - w/o mint mark

Y#	Date	Mintage	Fine	VF	XF	Unc
A42	1886 АГ	.057	200.00	300.00	500.00	800.00
	1887 АГ	.475	200.00	250.00	350.00	650.00
	1888 АГ	.023	200.00	300.00	500.00	800.00
	1889 АГ	.343	200.00	250.00	350.00	650.00
	1890 АГ	.015	200.00	300.00	500.00	800.00
	1891 АГ	3,010	250.00	400.00	600.00	850.00
	1892 АГ	8,006	250.00	400.00	600.00	850.00
	1893 АГ	1,008	250.00	400.00	600.00	850.00
	1894 АГ	1,007	200.00	250.00	350.00	600.00
	Common date	—	—	—	Proof	2800.

Rev. leg: ИМПЕРІАЛЪ (IMPERIAL).

A63	1895 АГ	125 pcs.	—	3000.	3500.	4000.
	1896 АГ	125 pcs.	—	3000.	3500.	4000.
	1897 АГ	125 pcs.	—	3000.	3500.	4000.

8.6026 g, .900 GOLD, .2489 oz AGW

64	1898 АГ	.200	—	BV	120.00	180.00
	1899 АГ	27.600	—	BV	110.00	160.00
	1899 ФЗ	I.A.	—	BV	110.00	160.00
	1899 ЗБ	I.A.	—	BV	120.00	180.00
	1900 ФЗ	6.021	—	BV	120.00	170.00
	Common date	—	—	—	Proof	1800.

NOTE: Later dates (1901-1911) exist for this type.

12 ROUBLES

41.4100 g, PLATINUM, 1.3311 oz APW
Mint mark: СПБ

C#	Date	Mintage	Fine	VF	XF	Unc
179	1830	119 pcs.	2000.	3250.	4500.	9000.
	1831	1,463	1650.	2750.	4000.	6500.
	1832	1,102	1650.	2750.	4000.	6500.
	1833	255 pcs.	2000.	3250.	4500.	9000.
	1834	11 pcs.	—	—	Proof	8000.
	1835	127 pcs.	2000.	3250.	4500.	9000.
	1836	11 pcs.	—	—	Proof	8000.
	1837	53 pcs.	2000.	3500.	5500.	10,000.
	1838	12 pcs.	—	—	Rare	—
	1839	2 pcs.	—	—	Rare	—
	1840	1 pc.	—	—	Rare	—
	1841	75 pcs.	2000.	3500.	5500.	10,000.
	1842	115 pcs.	2000.	3300.	5500.	10,000.
	1843	122 pcs.	2000.	3500.	5500.	10,000.
	1844	4 pcs.	—	—	Proof	7000.
	1845	2 pcs.	—	—	Rare	—
	Common date	—	—	—	Proof	6500.

NOTE: Varieties exist.

15 ROUBLES

12.9039 g, .900 GOLD, .3734 oz AGW
Mint: St. Petersburg - w/o mint mark

Y#	Date	Mintage	Fine	VF	XF	Unc
65	1897 АГ	11.900	BV	170.00	190.00	245.00

NOTE: Varieties exist.

25 ROUBLES

32.7200 g, .917 GOLD, .9640 oz AGW
Mint mark: СПБ

Y#	Date	Mintage	Fine	VF	XF	Unc
27	1876	100 pcs.	—	—	Proof	17,600.

NOTE: Realized in Stack's International sale 3-88.

32.2500 g, .900 GOLD, .9332 oz AGW
Mint: St. Petersburg - w/o mint mark
Rev. leg: 2-1/2 ИМПЕРІАЛА (IMPERIALS).

A65	1896	300 pcs.	—	4000.	5000.	7000.

NOTE: Later date (1908) exists for this type.

GOLD MINE INGOTS

During the late 19th and early 20th century, Russian law provided that gold mine owners who supplied gold to the mints should receive back whatever silver was recovered during refining of the gold. The silver was returned in the form of circular ingots of various weights which resembled coins. These pieces have often been erroneously described as Russian trade coins for use in Mongolia, China and Turkestan.

NOTE: Both the Doyla and the Zolotnik are weights, not denominations.

96 Dolya (Doli) = 1 Zolotnik
1 Zolotnik = 4.27 Grams

24 DOLYA

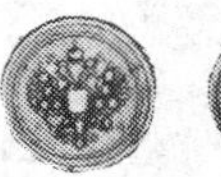

1.0664 g, .990 SILVER, .0343 oz ASW

KM#	Date	Mintage	VF	XF	Unc
1	ND	—	350.00	450.00	650.00

ZOLOTNIK

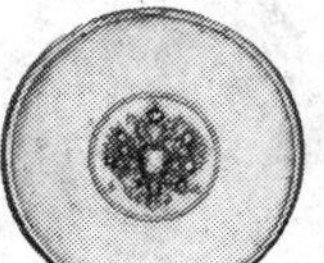

4.2656 g, .990 SILVER, .1371 oz ASW

2	ND	—	225.00	325.00	475.00

3 ZOLOTNIKS

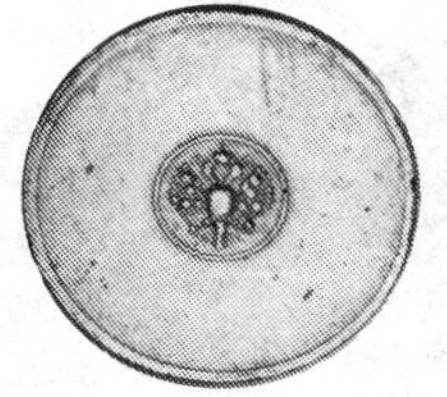

12.7969 g, .990 SILVER, .4114 oz ASW

3	ND	—	550.00	750.00	1150.

10 ZOLOTNIKS

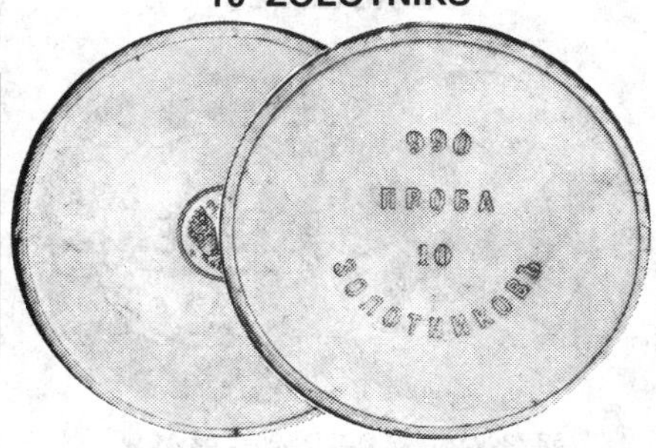

42.6563 g, .990 SILVER, 1.3714 oz ASW

KM#	Date	Mintage	VF	XF	Unc
4	ND	—	250.00	350.00	575.00

NOVODELS (N)

KM#	Date	Identification	Mkt.Val.
N340	1801КМ	1 Polushka, Copper, oblique edge milling	250.00
N341	1801КМ	1 Denga, Copper, oblique edge milling	—
N342	1801	1 Denga, Copper, oblique edge milling	Rare
N343	1801КМ	1 Kopek, Copper, reversed oblique edge milling	—
N344	1801КМ	2 Kopeks, Copper, oblique edge milling	225.00
N345	1801	2 Kopeks, Copper, oblique edge milling	Rare
N346	1801СМ	10 Kopeks, Silver, oblique edge milling	—
N347	1801СМ	1 Rouble, Silver, oblique edge milling	—

KM#	Date	Identification	Mkt.Val.
N348	1802ЕМ	1 Polushka, Copper, mm below eagle, oblique edge milling	450.00
N349	1802ЕМ	1 Polushka, Copper, mm below eagle, plain edge	325.00
N350	1802ЕМ	1 Polushka, Copper, high relief, oblique edge milling	300.00
N351	1802ЕМ	1 Polushka, Copper, mm below date, plain edge	300.00

KM#	Date	Identification	Mkt.Val.
N352	1802ЕМ	1 Polushka, Copper, low relief, oblique edge milling	275.00
N353	1802ЕМ	1 Polushka, Copper, obv. struck w/Denga die, oblique edge milling	350.00
N354	1802КМ	1 Polushka, Copper w/outer ring, oblique edge milling	300.00

KM#	Date	Identification	Mkt.Val.
N355	1802КМ	1 Polushka, Copper, w/o outer ring, oblique edge milling	300.00

KM#	Date	Identification	Mkt.Val.
N356	1802ЕМ	1 Denga, Copper, high relief, oblique edge milling	300.00
N357	1802ЕМ	1 Denga, Copper, low relief, oblique edge milling	275.00
N358	1802ЕМ	1 Denga, Copper, low relief, plain edge	275.00

KM#	Date	Identification	Mkt.Val.
N359	1802КМ	1 Denga, Copper, w/outer ring, oblique edge milling	300.00
N360	1802КМ	1 Denga, Copper, w/o outer ring, oblique edge milling	300.00
N361	1802	1 Denga, Copper, oblique edge milling	300.00

KM#	Date	Identification	Mkt.Val.
N362	1802	1 Denga, Copper, plain edge	300.00

KM#	Date	Identification	Mkt.Val.
N363	1802ЕМ	1 Kopek, Copper, high relief, oblique edge milling	350.00
N364	1802ЕМ	1 Kopek, Copper, low relief, oblique edge milling	300.00
N365	1802КМ	1 Kopek, Copper, w/outer ring, oblique edge milling	300.00

KM#	Date	Identification	Mkt.Val.
N366	1802КМ	1 Kopek, Copper, w/o outer ring, oblique edge milling	300.00
N367	1802	1 Kopek, Copper, oblique edge milling	350.00
N368	1802	1 Kopek, Copper, plain edge	300.00
N369	1802ЕМ	2 Kopeks, Copper, mm below eagle, oblique edge milling	450.00
N370	1802ЕМ	2 Kopeks, Copper, mm below eagle, plain edge	400.00
N371	1802ЕМ	2 Kopeks, Copper, high relief, oblique edge milling	350.00
N372	1802ЕМ	2 Kopeks, Copper, low relief, oblique edge milling	300.00
N373	1802ЕМ	2 Kopeks, Copper, low relief, diagonal reeded edge	300.00
N374	1802КМ	2 Kopeks, Copper, w/outer ring, oblique edge milling	300.00

KM#	Date	Identification	Mkt.Val.
N375	1802КМ	2 Kopeks, Copper, w/o outer ring, oblique edge milling	350.00
N376	1802ЕМ	5 Kopeks, Copper, mm below eagle, oblique edge milling	750.00
N377	1802ЕМ	5 Kopeks, Copper, high relief, oblique edge milling	550.00
N378	1802ЕМ	5 Kopeks, Copper, low relief, oblique edge milling	500.00
N379	1802КМ	5 Kopeks, Copper, w/outer ring, oblique edge milling	450.00
N380	1802КМ	5 Kopeks, Copper, w/o outer ring, oblique edge milling	450.00
N381	1802СПБ ФГ	10 Kopeks, Silver, oblique edge milling	—
N382	1802СПБ	1/4 Rouble, Silver, plain edge	—
N383	1802СПБ	1/4 Rouble, Copper, plain edge	—
N384	1802СПБ	1 Rouble, Silver, plain edge	—
N385	1802СПБ	1 Rouble, Silver, oblique edge milling	—
N386	1802СПБ ХЛ	10 Roubles, Gold, oblique edge milling	4000.
N387	1802СПБ АИ	10 Roubles, Gold, double weight, oblique edge milling	10,000.
N388	1803КМ	1 Polushka, Copper, oblique edge milling	300.00
N389	1803КМ	1 Denga, Copper, oblique edge milling	300.00
N390	1803КМ	1 Kopek, Copper, oblique edge milling	300.00
N391	1803КМ	2 Kopeks, Copper, oblique edge milling	350.00
N392	1803КМ	5 Kopeks, Copper, oblique edge milling	500.00
N393	1803СПБ ФГ	10 Kopeks, Silver, plain edge	—
N394	1803СПБ АИ	1/4 Rouble, Silver, plain edge	—
N395	1803СПБ ФГ	1/4 Rouble, Silver, plain edge	—
N396	1803СПБ АИ	1 Rouble, Silver, plain edge	—
N397	1803СПБ ФГ	1 Rouble, Silver, incuse edge lettering, lettered edge	—
N398	1803СПБ ХЛ	5 Roubles, Gold, oblique edge milling	6000.
N399	1803СПБ ХЛ	10 Roubles, Gold, oblique edge milling	6500.
N400	1804КМ	1 Polushka, Copper, oblique edge milling	300.00
N401	1804КМ	1 Denga, Copper, oblique edge milling	300.00
N402	1804КМ	1 Kopek, Copper, oblique edge milling	300.00
N403	1804КМ	2 Kopeks, Copper, oblique edge milling	300.00
N404	1804КМ	5 Kopeks, Copper, oblique edge milling	450.00
N405	1805КМ	1 Polushka, Copper, oblique edge milling	300.00
N406	1805КМ	1 Denga, Copper, oblique edge milling	300.00
N407	1805КМ	1 Kopek, Copper, oblique edge milling	300.00
N408	1805КМ	2 Kopeks, Copper, oblique edge milling	300.00
N409	1805КМ	5 Kopeks, Copper, oblique edge milling	450.00
N410	1806КМ	1 Polushka, Copper, w/o outer ring, oblique edge milling	300.00
N411	1806КМ	1 Denga, Copper, oblique edge milling	300.00
N412	1806КМ	1 Kopek, Copper, oblique edge milling	300.00
N413	1806КМ	2 Kopeks, Copper, oblique edge milling	300.00
N414	1806КМ	5 Kopeks, Copper, oblique edge milling	450.00
N415	1807КМ	1 Polushka, Copper, w/o outer ring, oblique edge milling	300.00
N416	1807КМ	1 Denga, Copper, oblique edge milling	300.00
N417	1807КМ	1 Kopek, Copper, oblique edge milling	300.00
N418	1807КМ	2 Kopeks, Copper, oblique edge milling	300.00
N419	1807КМ	5 Kopeks, Copper, oblique edge milling	450.00
N420	1808КМ	1 Polushka, Copper, w/o outer ring, oblique edge milling	300.00
N421	1808КМ	1 Denga, Copper, oblique edge milling	300.00
N422	1808КМ	1 Kopek, Copper, oblique edge milling	300.00
N423	1808КМ	2 Kopeks, Copper, oblique edge milling	300.00
N424	1808КМ	5 Kopeks, Copper, oblique edge milling	450.00
N425	1808СПБ ФГ	1/4 Rouble, Silver, plain edge	—
N426	1809КМ	1 Polushka, Copper, w/o outer ring, oblique edge milling	300.00
N427	1809КМ	1 Denga, Copper, oblique edge milling	300.00
N428	1809КМ	1 Kopek, Copper, oblique edge milling	300.00
N429	1809КМ	2 Kopeks, Copper, oblique edge milling	300.00
N430	1809КМ	5 Kopeks, Copper, oblique edge milling	450.00
N431	1809СПБ ФГ	10 Kopeks, Silver, plain edge	—
N432	1809СПБ	10 Kopeks, Silver, plain edge	—
N433	1809СПБ	1/2 Rouble, Silver, plain edge	—
N434	1809СПБ ХЛ	10 Roubles, Gold, oblique edge milling	10,000.

KM#	Date	Identification	Mkt.Val.
N-A435	1810КМ	1/4 Kopek, Copper, oblique edge milling	—
N435	1810КМ	1 Polushka, Copper, oblique edge milling	300.00
N436	1810КМ	1 Denga, Copper, oblique edge milling	300.00
N437	1810КМ	1 Kopek, Copper, oblique edge milling	300.00
N438	1810КМ	2 Kopeks, Copper, oblique edge milling	300.00
N439	1810КМ	5 Kopeks, Copper, oblique edge milling	450.00

New Standard

KM#	Date	Identification	Mkt.Val.
N440	1810ЕМ НМ	1 Denga, Copper, curved date, plain edge	200.00
N441	1810ЕМ	1 Denga, Copper, w/o initials, plain edge	200.00
N442	1810КМ ПБ	1 Denga, Copper, plain edge	225.00
N443	1810ЕМ НМ	1 Kopek, Copper, curved date, plain edge	200.00
N444	1810КМ ПБ	1 Kopek, Copper, w/o initials, plain edge	200.00
N445	1810ЕМ НМ	2 Kopeks, Copper, curved date, plain edge	200.00
N446	1810ЕМ НМ		

KM#	Date	Identification	Mkt.Val.
N446		2 Kopeks, Copper, small initials, plain edge	200.00
N447	1810КМ	2 Kopeks, Copper, plain edge	200.00
N448	1810КМ ПБ	2 Kopeks, Copper, small eagle, plain edge	200.00
N449	1810СПБ ФГ	2 Kopeks, Copper, plain edge	200.00
N450	1810СПБ МК	10 Kopeks, Silver, old type, plain edge	—
N451	1810СПБ ФГ	1/4 Rouble, Silver, old type, plain edge	—
N452	1810СПБ ФГ	1 Rouble, Silver, old type, plain edge	—
N453	1810СПБ ФГ	10 Kopeks, Silver, new type, plain edge	—
N454	1810СПБ	1/2 Rouble, Silver, plain edge	—
N455	1811КМ ПБ	1 Denga, Copper, wings far from rim, plain edge	175.00
N456	1811СПБ МК	1 Denga, Copper, plain edge	225.00
N457	1811КМ ПБ	1 Kopek, Copper, plain edge	200.00
N458	1811СПБ ПС	1 Kopek, Copper, plain edge	200.00
N459	1811ЕМ ИФ	2 Kopeks, Copper, oblique edge milling	450.00
N460	1811КМ ПБ	2 Kopeks, Copper, small eagle, plain edge	200.00
N461	1811СПБ ФГ	5 Kopeks, Silver, plain edge	—
N462	1811СПБ ФГ	10 Kopeks, Silver, broad crown, plain edge	—
N463	1811СПБ ФГ	1/2 Ruble, Silver, tapered crown, plain edge	—
N464	1813СПБ ПС	10 Kopeks, Silver, broad crown, plain edge	—
N465	1813СПБ	1/2 Rouble, Silver, plain edge	—
N466	1814СПБ ПС	1 Denga, Copper, plain edge	275.00
N467	1814СПБ ПС	1 Kopek, Copper, plain edge	225.00
N468	1814СПБ	5 Kopeks, Silver, tapered crown, plain edge	—
N469	1814СПБ	20 Kopeks, Silver, plain edge	—
N470	1814СПБ	1/2 Ruble, Silver, plain edge	—
N471	1815СПБ	20 Kopeks, Silver, open 2 in value, plain edge	—
N472	1815СПБ	1/2 Rouble, Silver, tapered crown, plain edge	—
N473	1815СПБ	1 Rouble, Silver, plain edge	—
N474	1816СПБ	5 Kopeks, Silver, large crown, plain edge	—
N475	1816СПБ	20 Kopeks, Silver, large crown, plain edge	—
N476	1816СПБ	1/2 Rouble, Silver, tapered crown, plain edge	—
N477	1817СПБ	1/2 Rouble, Silver, tapered crown, plain edge	—
N478	1818КМ АМ	1 Kopek, Copper, plain edge	325.00
N479	1818КМ АД	2 Kopeks, Copper, plain edge	—
N480	1818СПБ	1/2 Rouble, Silver, tapered crown, plain edge	—
N481	1819КМ АД	1 Kopek, Copper, plain edge	175.00
N482	1819КМ ДБ	2 Kopeks, Copper, plain edge	300.00
N483	1819СПБ	10 Kopeks, Silver, tapered crown, plain edge	—
N484	1819СПБ	1/2 Rouble, Silver, tapered crown, plain edge	—
N485	1819СПБ	1 Rouble, Silver, plain edge	—
N486	1820КМ АД	1 Kopek, Copper, plain edge	175.00
N487	1820СПБ	5 Kopeks, Silver, broad crown, plain edge	—
N488	1821КМ АД	1 Kopek, Copper, plain edge	200.00
N489	1821СПБ	5 Kopeks, Silver, plain edge	—
N490	1821СПБ	1 Rouble, Silver, plain edge	—
N491	1823КМ АМ	1 Denga, Copper, plain edge	Rare
N492	1825СПБ	20 Kopeks, Silver, tapered crown, plain edge	—
N493	1826СПБ	20 Kopeks, Silver, open 2 in value, plain edge	—
N494	1826СПБ	20 Kopeks, Silver, new type, large crown, plain edge	—
N495	1826СПБ ПД	1/2 Rouble, Silver, new type, lettered edge	—
N496	1830ЕМ	1 Kopek, Copper, plain edge	250.00

KM#	Date	Identification	Mkt.Val.
N497	1830ЕМ	2 Kopeks, Copper, plain edge	300.00

KM#	Date	Identification	Mkt.Val.
N498	1830ЕМ	5 Kopeks, Copper, plain edge	450.00

KM#	Date	Identification	Mkt.Val.
N499	1830ЕМ	10 Kopeks, Copper, w/o initials, plain edge	550.00
N500	1831СМ	1 Kopek, Copper, plain edge	175.00
N501	1831СМ	2 Kopeks, Copper, plain edge	200.00
N502	1831СМ	5 Kopeks, Copper, plain edge	250.00
N503	1831СМ	10 Kopeks, Copper, plain edge	425.00
N504	1832СМ	1 Kopek, Copper, plain edge	175.00
N505	1832СМ	2 Kopeks, Copper, plain edge	200.00
N506	1832СМ	5 Kopeks, Copper, plain edge	250.00
N507	1832СМ	10 Kopeks, Copper, plain edge	425.00
N508	1833СМ	1 Kopek, Copper, plain edge	175.00
N509	1833СМ	2 Kopeks, Copper, plain edge	200.00
N510	1833СМ	5 Kopeks, Copper, plain edge	250.00
N511	1833СМ	10 Kopeks, Copper, plain edge	425.00

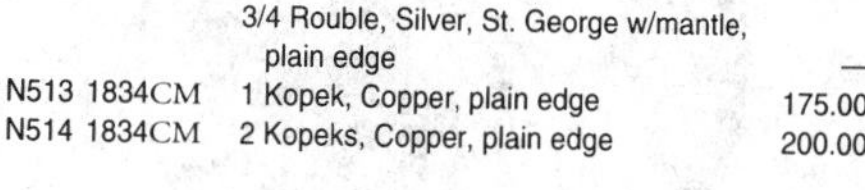

KM#	Date	Identification	Mkt.Val.
N512	1833СПБ НГ	3/4 Rouble, Silver, St. George w/mantle, plain edge	—
N513	1834СМ	1 Kopek, Copper, plain edge	175.00
N514	1834СМ	2 Kopeks, Copper, plain edge	200.00

KM#	Date	Identification	Mkt.Val.
N515	1834СМ	5 Kopeks, Copper, plain edge	250.00
N516	1834СМ	10 Kopeks, Copper, plain edge	425.00
N517	1835СМ	1 Kopek, Copper, plain edge	175.00
N518	1835СМ	2 Kopeks, Copper, plain edge	200.00

KM#	Date	Identification	Mkt.Val.
N519	1835СМ	5 Kopeks, Copper, plain edge	250.00
N520	1835СМ	10 Kopeks, Copper, plain edge	425.00
N521	1836СМ	1 Kopek, Copper, plain edge	175.00
N522	1836СМ	2 Kopeks, Copper, plain edge	200.00
N523	1836СМ	5 Kopeks, Copper, plain edge	250.00
N524	1836СМ	10 Kopeks, Copper, plain edge	425.00
N525	1837СМ	1 Kopek, Copper, plain edge	175.00
N526	1837СМ	2 Kopeks, Copper, plain edge	200.00
N527	1837СМ	5 Kopeks, Copper, plain edge	250.00
N528	1837СМ	10 Kopeks, Copper, plain edge	425.00
N529	1838СМ	1 Kopek, Copper, plain edge	175.00
N530	1838СМ	2 Kopeks, Copper, plain edge	200.00
N531	1838СМ	5 Kopeks, Copper, plain edge	250.00
N532	1838СМ	10 Kopeks, Copper, plain edge	425.00
N533	1839СМ	1 Kopek, Copper, plain edge	175.00
N534	1839СМ	2 Kopeks, Copper, plain edge	200.00
N535	1839СМ	5 Kopeks, Copper, plain edge	250.00
N536	1839СМ	10 Kopeks, Copper, plain edge	425.00

New Standard

KM#	Date	Identification	Mkt.Val.
N537	1839СМ	1 Polushka, Copper, plain edge	175.00
N538	1839СМ	1 Denga, Copper, plain edge	175.00
N539	1839СМ	1 Kopek, Copper, plain edge	200.00
N540	1839СМ	2 Kopeks, Copper, plain edge	225.00
N541	1839СМ	3 Kopeks, Copper, plain edge	275.00
N542	1840СМ	1 Polushka, Copper, plain edge	175.00
N543	1840СМ	1 Denga, Copper, plain edge	175.00
N544	1840	1 Denga, Copper, plain edge	—
N545	1840СМ	1 Kopek, Copper, plain edge	200.00
N546	1840	1 Kopek, Copper, plain edge	450.00
N547	1840СМ	2 Kopeks, Copper, plain edge	250.00
N548	1840	2 Kopeks, Copper, plain edge	—
N549	1840СМ	3 Kopeks, Copper, plain edge	250.00
N550	1840	3 Kopeks, Copper, plain edge	—
N551	1840	25 Kopeks, Silver, lis missing on scepter, plain edge	—
N552	1840	1 Rouble, Silver, St. George w/mantle, plain edge	—
N553	1841СМ	1 Polushka, Copper, plain edge	175.00
N554	1841СМ	1 Denga, Copper, plain edge	175.00
N555	1841СМ	1 Kopek, Copper, plain edge	200.00
N556	1841СМ	2 Kopeks, Copper, plain edge	225.00
N557	1841СМ	3 Kopeks, Copper, plain edge	250.00
N558	1842СМ	1 Polushka, Copper, plain edge	175.00
N559	1842СМ	1 Denga, Copper, plain edge	175.00
N560	1842СМ	1 Kopek, Copper, plain edge	200.00
N561	1842СМ	2 Kopeks, Copper, plain edge	225.00
N562	1842СМ	3 Kopeks, Copper, plain edge	250.00
N563	1842НГ	10 Kopeks, Silver, plain edge	—
N564	1842АЧ	1/2 Rouble, Silver, large center tail feather, plain edge	—
N565	1842НГ	1/2 Rouble, Silver, plain edge	—
N566	1842НГ	1 Rouble, Silver, St. George w/mantle, plain edge	—
N567	1843СМ	1 Polushka, Copper, plain edge	175.00
N568	1843СМ	1 Denga, Copper, plain edge	175.00
N569	1843СМ	1 Kopek, Copper, plain edge	200.00
N570	1843СМ	2 Kopeks, Copper, plain edge	225.00
N571	1843СМ	3 Kopeks, Copper, plain edge	250.00
N572	1844СМ	1 Polushka, Copper, plain edge	175.00
N573	1844СМ	1 Denga, Copper, plain edge	175.00
N574	1844СМ	1 Kopek, Copper, plain edge	200.00
N575	1844СМ	2 Kopeks, Copper, plain edge	225.00
N576	1844СМ	3 Kopeks, Copper, plain edge	250.00
N577	1845СМ	1 Polushka, Copper, plain edge	175.00
N578	1845СМ	1 Denga, Copper, plain edge	175.00
N579	1845СМ	1 Kopek, Copper, plain edge	200.00
N580	1845СМ	2 Kopeks, Copper, plain edge	225.00
N581	1845СМ	3 Kopeks, Copper, plain edge	250.00
N582	1846СМ	1 Polushka, Copper, plain edge	175.00
N583	1846СМ	1 Denga, Copper, plain edge	175.00
N584	1846СМ	1 Kopek, Copper, plain edge	200.00
N585	1846СМ	2 Kopeks, Copper, plain edge	225.00
N586	1846СМ	3 Kopeks, Copper, plain edge	250.00
N587	1846СПБ	1/2 Rouble, Silver, wave-shaped tail feathers, plain edge	—
N588	1847СМ	1 Denga, Copper, plain edge	175.00
N589	1847СМ	1 Kopek, Copper, plain edge	200.00
N590	1847СМ	2 Kopeks, Copper, plain edge	225.00
N591	1847СМ	3 Kopeks, Copper, plain edge	250.00

New Standard

KM#	Date	Identification	Mkt.Val.
N592	1849ЕМ	3 Kopeks, Copper, small 3, plain edge	450.00
N593	1852ПА	1 Rouble, Silver, St. George w/mantle, plain edge	—
N594	1855ЕМ	2 Kopeks, Copper, small 2, plain edge	325.00
N595	1857ЕМ	1 Denga, Copper, plain edge	Rare
N596	1859ЕМ	2 Kopeks, Copper, small 2, plain edge	250.00
N597	1859ЕМ	3 Kopeks, Copper, small 3, plain edge	250.00
N598	1859ЕМ	5 Kopeks, Copper, small 5, plain edge	300.00
N599	1860	20 Kopeks, Silver, old type large shield, plain edge	—
N600	1860	1/2 Rouble, Silver, new type short shield, lettered edge	—

KM#	Date	Identification	Mkt.Val.
N601	1860	1/2 Rouble, Silver, new type tall shield, plain edge	—
N602	1861	5 Kopeks, Silver, no mm., plain edge	—

PATTERNS (Pn)

(Including off metal strikes)

KM#	Date	Mintage	Identification	Mkt.Val.
Pn52	1801AI	—	1 Rouble, Silver, Obv: Eagle in circle. Rev: Value in wreath.	Rare

KM#	Date	Mintage	Identification	Mkt.Val.
Pn53	1801AИ	—	1 Rouble, Silver	—

KM#	Date	Mintage	Identification	Mkt.Val.
Pn54	1801AI		1 Rouble, Silver	—

KM#	Date	Mintage	Identification	Mkt.Val.
Pn55	1801AИ	—	1 Rouble, Silver	—

KM#	Date	Mintage	Identification	Mkt.Val.
Pn56	1802	—	2 Kopeks, Copper	—

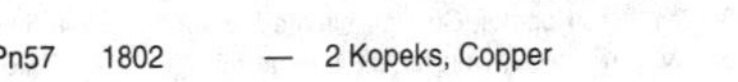

KM#	Date	Mintage	Identification	Mkt.Val.
Pn57	1802	—	2 Kopeks, Copper	—

KM#	Date	Mintage	Identification	Mkt.Val.
Pn58	1802	—	2 Kopeks, Copper	—

KM#	Date	Mintage	Identification	Mkt.Val.
Pn59	1802	—	1 Rouble, Silver	—

KM#	Date	Mintage	Identification	Mkt.Val.
Pn60	180-(1803)		5 Kopeks, Copper, C115.1.	—

KM#	Date	Mintage	Identification	Mkt.Val.
Pn61	ND(1804)	—	1/2 Rouble, Gilt	500.00
Pn62	ND(1804)	—	1/2 Rouble, Copper	—
Pn63	ND(1804)	—	1/2 Rouble, Silver	—
Pn64	ND(1804)	—	1/2 Rouble, Gold	—

NOTE: Pn61-Pn64 were struck at Birmingham Mint.

KM#	Date	Mintage	Identification	Mkt.Val.
Pn65	1804	—	1 Rouble, Copper	400.00
Pn66	1804	—	1 Rouble, Silver	—

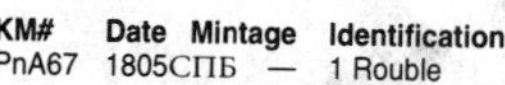

KM#	Date	Mintage	Identification	Mkt.Val.
PnA67	1805СПБ	—	1 Rouble	—

KM#	Date	Mintage	Identification	Mkt.Val.
Pn67	1806	—	1 Rouble, Silver, C125a	3250.
Pn68	180x	—	1 Rouble, Silver	—
Pn69	1806	—	1 Rouble, Silver, obv. uniformed bust of Alexander, rev. eagle in circle	3250.

KM#	Date	Mintage	Identification	Mkt.Val.
Pn70	180x	—	1 Rouble, Silver	3520.

KM#	Date	Mintage	Identification	Mkt.Val.
Pn71	1807	—	1 Rouble, Silver	2000.

KM#	Date	Mintage	Identification	Mkt.Val.
Pn72	1807	—	1 Rouble, Silver	—

KM#	Date	Mintage	Identification	Mkt.Val.
Pn73	1810EM	—	1 Denga, Copper, C116.1.	—

KM#	Date	Mintage	Identification	Mkt.Val.
Pn74	1810	—	1 Kopek, Copper	—

KM#	Date	Mintage	Identification	Mkt.Val.
Pn75	1810	—	1 Kopek, Copper, Rev: Different eagle	—

KM#	Date	Mintage	Identification	Mkt.Val.
Pn76	1810СПБ	—	1 Kopek, Copper	—

KM#	Date	Mintage	Identification	Mkt.Val.
Pn77	1810СПБ	—	1 Kopek, Copper	—

KM#	Date	Mintage	Identification	Mkt.Val.
Pn78	1810EM HM	—	1 Kopek, Copper, C117.1	—

KM#	Date	Mintage	Identification	Mkt.Val.
Pn79	1810	—	2 Kopeks, Copper	—

KM#	Date	Mintage	Identification	Mkt.Val.
Pn80	ND(1810)	—	1 Rouble, Silver	—

KM#	Date	Mintage	Identification	Mkt.Val.
Pn81	1811	—	1 Denga, Copper	—

KM#	Date	Mintage	Identification	Mkt.Val.
Pn82	1811	—	1 Denga, Copper	—

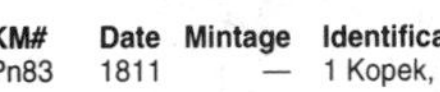

KM#	Date	Mintage	Identification	Mkt.Val.
Pn83	1811	—	1 Kopek, Copper	—
Pn84	1811	—	1 Kopek, Copper	—
Pn85	1811	—	2 Kopeks, Copper	—
Pn86	1811	—	2 Kopeks, Copper	—
Pn87	1816	—	2 Kopeks, Copper	395.00
Pn88	1825	—	1 Rouble, Silver	—
Pn89	1827СПБ	—	3 Kopeks, Copper	750.00

KM#	Date	Mintage	Identification	Mkt.Val.
Pn90	1827СПБ	—	1 Rouble, Silver	—

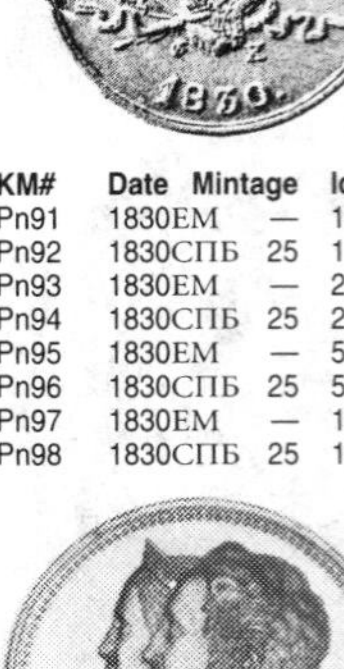
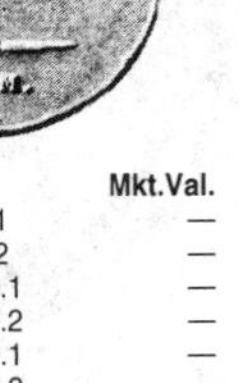

KM#	Date	Mintage	Identification	Mkt.Val.
Pn91	1830EM	—	1 Kopek, Copper, C138.1	—
Pn92	1830СПБ	25	1 Kopek, Copper, C138.2	—
Pn93	1830EM	—	2 Kopeks, Copper, C139.1	—
Pn94	1830СПБ	25	2 Kopeks, Copper, C139.2	—
Pn95	1830EM	—	5 Kopeks, Copper, C140.1	—
Pn96	1830СПБ	25	5 Kopeks, Copper, C140.2	—
Pn97	1830EM	—	10 Kopeks, Copper, C141.1	—
Pn98	1830СПБ	25	10 Kopeks, Copper, C141.2	—

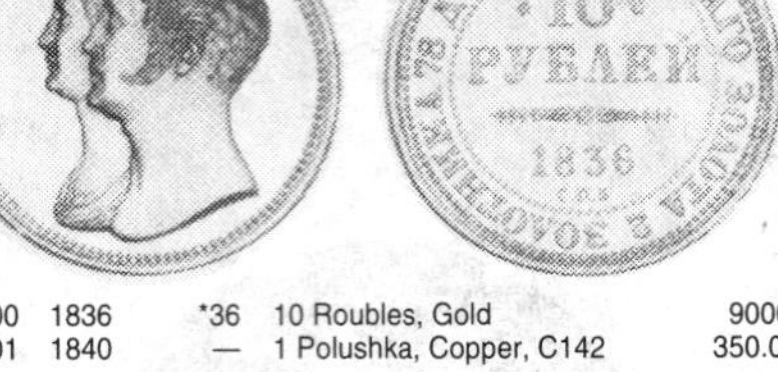

KM#	Date	Mintage	Identification	Mkt.Val.
Pn100	1836	*36	10 Roubles, Gold	9000.
Pn101	1840	—	1 Polushka, Copper, C142	350.00

KM#	Date	Mintage	Identification	Mkt.Val.
Pn102	1840	—	1/4 Kopek, Copper	—
Pn103	1840	—	1/2 Kopek, Copper, obv. crowned initial, rev. value and date	—
Pn104	1840	—	1 Kopek, Copper, C144.3	—
Pn105	1840	—	2 Kopeks, Copper, C145.2	—
Pn106	1840	—	3 Kopeks, Copper, C146.3	—

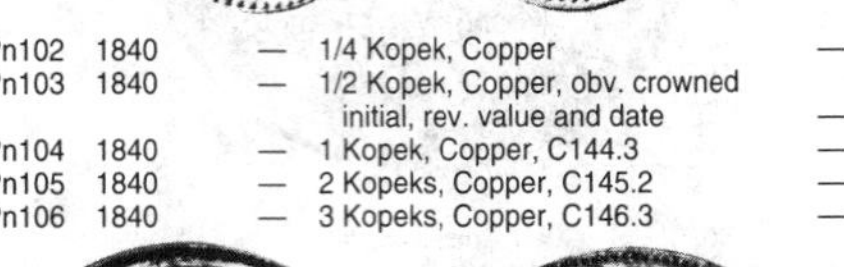

KM#	Date	Mintage	Identification	Mkt.Val.
Pn107	1845	—	1/2 Rouble, Silver	—
Pn108	1845	4 known	1 Rouble, Silver, obv. head of Nicholas, rev. eagle, date below	—

KM#	Date	Mintage	Identification	Mkt.Val.
Pn109	1848MW	—	1/2 Kopek, Copper	—
Pn110	1848MW	—	2 Kopeks, Copper	—
Pn111	1848MW	—	3 Kopeks, Copper	—
Pn112	1849EM	—	1 Polushka, Copper, C147.1	325.00

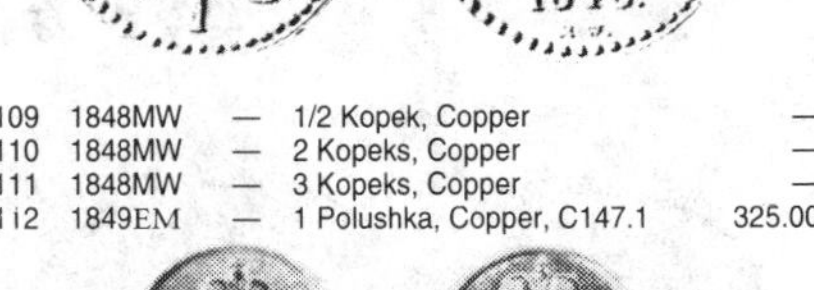

KM#	Date	Mintage	Identification	Mkt.Val.
Pn113	1849СПМ	—	1 Polushka, Copper	250.00
Pn114	1849EM	—	1 Denga, Copper, C148.1	325.00

KM#	Date	Mintage	Identification	Mkt.Val.
Pn115	1849СПМ	—	1 Denga, Copper	250.00
Pn116	1849EM	—	1 Kopek, Copper, C149.1	350.00

KM#	Date	Mintage	Identification	Mkt.Val.
Pn117	1849СПМ	—	1 Kopek, Copper	250.00

KM#	Date	Mintage	Identification	Mkt.Val.
Pn118	1849EM	—	2 Kopeks, Copper, C150.1	350.00
Pn119	1849СПМ	—	2 Kopeks, Copper, C150.2	250.00
Pn120	1849EM	—	3 Kopeks, Copper, C151.1	350.00

KM#	Date	Mintage	Identification	Mkt.Val.
Pn121	1849СПМ	—	3 Kopeks, Copper	250.00
Pn122	1849EM	—	5 Kopeks, Copper, C152.1	350.00

KM#	Date	Mintage	Identification	Mkt.Val.
Pn123	1849СПМ	—	5 Kopeks, Copper	250.00

KM#	Date	Mintage	Identification	Mkt.Val.
Pn124	1849MW	—	5 Roubles, Gold	—

KM#	Date	Mintage	Identification	Mkt.Val.
Pn125	1853BM	—	2 Kopeks, Copper	—

KM#	Date	Mintage	Identification	Mkt.Val.
Pn126	1855	—	1 Polushka, Copper	—

KM#	Date	Mintage	Identification	Mkt.Val.
Pn127	1856BM	—	1 Kopek, Copper	—

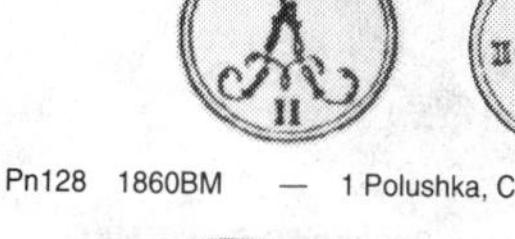

KM#	Date	Mintage	Identification	Mkt.Val.
Pn128	1860BM	—	1 Polushka, Copper	—

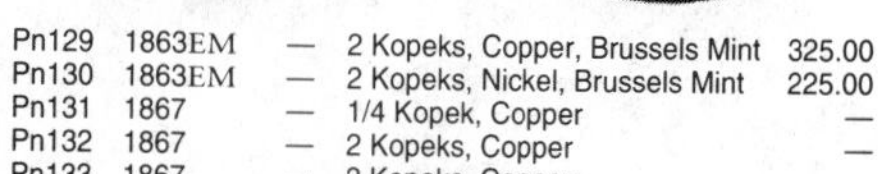

KM#	Date	Mintage	Identification	Mkt.Val.
Pn129	1863EM	—	2 Kopeks, Copper, Brussels Mint	325.00
Pn130	1863EM	—	2 Kopeks, Nickel, Brussels Mint	225.00
Pn131	1867	—	1/4 Kopek, Copper	—
Pn132	1867	—	2 Kopeks, Copper	—
Pn133	1867	—	3 Kopeks, Copper	—
Pn134	1867	—	5 Kopeks, Copper	—

KM#	Date	Mintage	Identification	Mkt.Val.
Pn135	1871	—	10 Kopeks, Copper-Nickel	825.00
Pn136	1871	—	10 Kopeks, Nickel	650.00

KM#	Date	Mintage	Identification	Mkt.Val.
Pn137	1871	—	10 Kopeks, Copper-Nickel	875.00
Pn138	1871	—	10 Kopeks, Nickel	700.00

KM#	Date	Mintage	Identification	Mkt.Val.
Pn139	1871	—	10 Kopeks, Nickel	—

KM#	Date	Mintage	Identification	Mkt.Val.
Pn140	1882	—	3 Kopeks, Nickel	—

KM#	Date	Mintage	Identification	Mkt.Val.
Pn141	1886	—	5 Roubles, Gold, plain edge	—

KM#	Date	Mintage	Identification	Mkt.Val.
Pn142	1895	36 pcs.	5 Roubles, Gold, C#A61	7150.

KM#	Date	Mintage	Identification	Mkt.Val.
Pn143	1895	125 pcs.	10 Roubles, Gold, C#A63	6000.

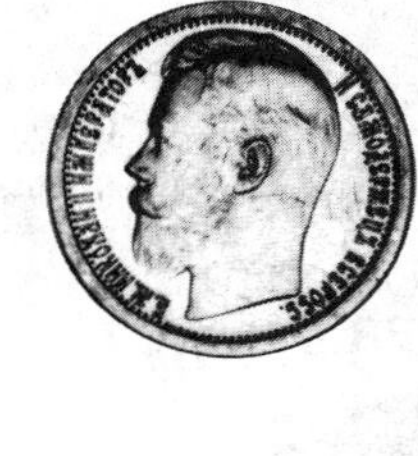

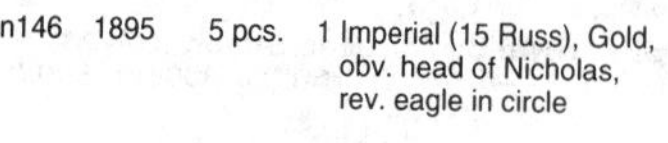

KM#	Date	Mintage	Identification	Mkt.Val.
Pn146	1895	5 pcs.	1 Imperial (15 Russ), Gold, obv. head of Nicholas, rev. eagle in circle	6000.

KM#	Date	Mintage	Identification	Mkt.Val.
Pn147	1896	5 pcs.	5 Roubles, Gold, C#A61	7000.

KM#	Date	Mintage	Identification	Mkt.Val.
Pn148	1896	125 pcs.	10 Roubles, Gold, C#A63	5775.

KM#	Date	Mintage	Identification	Mkt.Val.
Pn149	1897	—	1/2 Kopek, Copper, obv. inverted W, rev. retrograde leg., Berlin Mint	—
Pn150	1897	—	1/2 Kopek, Nickel	—

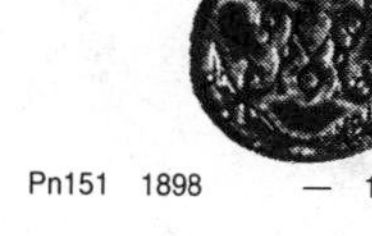

KM#	Date	Mintage	Identification	Mkt.Val.
Pn151	1898	—	1/4 Kopek, Copper, obv. inverted W, rev. retrograde leg., Berlin Mint	—
Pn152	1898	—	1/2 Kopek, Nickel Alloy	575.00

KM#	Date	Mintage	Identification	Mkt.Val.
Pn153	1898	—	1 Kopek, Copper	—
Pn154	1898	—	1 Kopek, Aluminum, Berlin Mint	—
Pn155	1898	—	1 Kopek, Nickel, Berlin Mint	—
Pn156	1898	—	2 Kopeks, Copper, Berlin Mint	—
Pn157	1898	—	3 Kopeks, Copper, Berlin Mint	—

KM#	Date	Mintage	Identification	Mkt.Val.
Pn158	1898	—	1 Rouble, Silver, Y61, no value	2500.
Pn159	1898	—	1 Rouble, Copper, Y61, no value	750.00

Listings For

Russian Caucasia-
Karabagh, Schamakhi and Sheki:
refer to Azerbaijan

Russian Turkestan-
Bukhara, Khiva and Khoqand:
refer to Uzbekistan

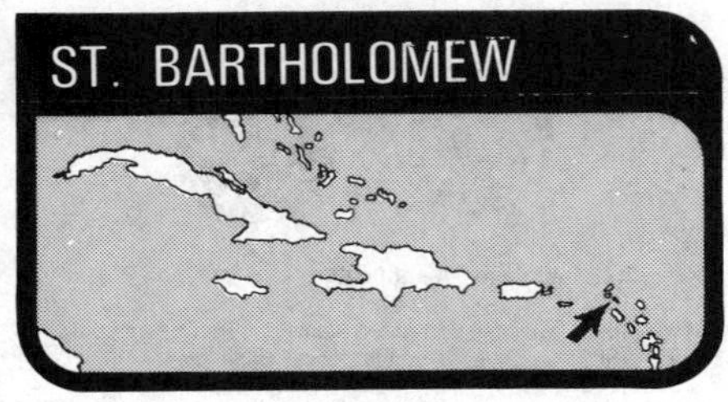

St. Bartholomew (St. Barthelemy, St. Barts), a French island possession located in the Leeward Islands of the West Indies about 15 miles northwest of Guadeloupe, of which it is a dependency, has an area of 10 sq. mi. (26 sq. km.) and a population of about 3,000. Capital: BasseTerre, on the island of that name. The treeless island produces sugar, bananas, and rum.

St. Bartholomew was occupied by France in 1648 and sold to Sweden in 1784. In 1877 it was reacquired, by purchase, by France.

The coins issued under Sweden for St. Bartholomew - crown-countermarked U.S. coins, Cayenne sous, Swedish and Polish billon - have been extensively counterfeited.

RULERS

French, until 1784, 1877-
Swedish, 1784-1877

MONETARY SYSTEM

1797-1821

6 Stivers = 1 Bit
12 Bits = 8 Spanish Reales

1821-1846
(actually used to 1864)

6 Stivers = 1 Bit (Courant)
18-3/4 Bits (Courant) = 8 Reales

1864-1878

100 Cents = 1 Dollar

COUNTERMARKED COINAGE

Proclamation of December 30, 1808

3 STIVERS

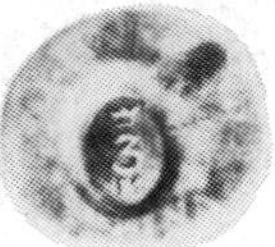

SILVER
c/m: Crowned 3/M on Spanish Colonial 1/2 Real.

KM#	Date	Mintage	Good	VG	Fine	VF
4	ND(1808)	—	150.00	250.00	500.00	950.00

4 STIVERS

SILVER
c/m: Crowned 4/M on Spanish Colonial 1/2 Real.

KM#	Date	Mintage	Good	VG	Fine	VF
5	ND(1808)	—	150.00	250.00	500.00	950.00

7 STIVERS

SILVER
c/m: Crowned 7/M on Spanish Colonial 1 Real.

KM#	Date	Mintage	Good	VG	Fine	VF
7	ND(1808)	—	150.00	250.00	500.00	950.00

9 STIVERS

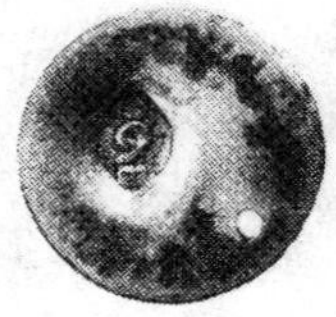
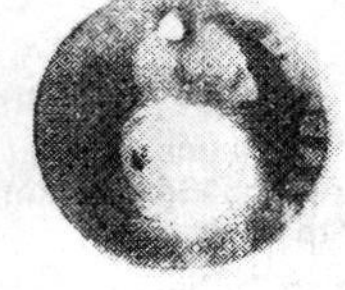

SILVER
c/m: Crowned 9/M on Spanish Colonial 1 Real.

KM#	Date	Mintage	Good	VG	Fine	VF
8	ND(1808)	—	175.00	275.00	600.00	1150.

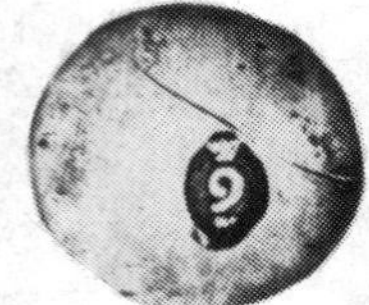

c/m: Crowned 9/M on Spanish 1 Real.

KM#	Date	Mintage	Good	VG	Fine	VF
9	ND(1808)	—	175.00	275.00	550.00	1000.

14 STIVERS

SILVER
c/m: Crowned 14/M on Spanish Colonial 2 Reales.

KM#	Date	Mintage	Good	VG	Fine	VF
11	ND(1808)	—	200.00	300.00	600.00	1200.

NOTE: For St. Bartholomew countermarked 14 Stivers with additional countermark P in circle of dots see Saint Eustatius in Netherlands Antilles.

18 STIVERS

SILVER
c/m: Crowned 18/M on Spanish Colonial 2 Reales.

KM#	Date	Mintage	Good	VG	Fine	VF
13	ND(1808)	—	350.00	550.00	1350.	2750.

NOTE: Many contemporary counterfeits of the 1808 countermarks exist.

Proclamation of July 9, 1834

STIVER

SILVER
c/m: Type I crown on Curacao Stiver, KM#24.

KM#	Date	Mintage	Good	VG	Fine	VF
3	ND(1834)	—	75.00	150.00	300.00	500.00

2 SOU

BILLON
c/m: Type II crown on Cayenne 2 Sou, KM#1.

KM#	Date	Mintage	Good	VG	Fine	VF
2.1	ND(1834-64)	—	65.00	115.00	160.00	225.00

c/m: Type III crown on Cayenne 2 Sou, KM#1.

KM#	Date	Mintage	Good	VG	Fine	VF
2.2	ND(1834-64)	—	65.00	115.00	160.00	225.00

c/m: Type IV crown on Cayenne 2 Sou, KM#1.

KM#	Date	Mintage	Good	VG	Fine	VF
2.3	ND(1834-64)	—	75.00	125.00	175.00	250.00

c/m: Type V crown on Cayenne 2 Sou, KM#1.

KM#	Date	Mintage	Good	VG	Fine	VF
2.4	ND(1834-64)	—	75.00	125.00	175.00	250.00

c/m: Type VI crown on Cayenne 2 Sou, KM#1.

KM#	Date	Mintage	Good	VG	Fine	VF
2.5	ND(1834-64)	—	85.00	135.00	190.00	275.00

c/m: Type VII crown on Cayenne 2 Sou, KM#1.

KM#	Date	Mintage	Good	VG	Fine	VF
2.6	ND(1834-64)	—	85.00	135.00	190.00	275.00

NOTE: The crown countermark of 1834 was extensively counterfeited and imitated for over a century and a half from the period of issue. Spanish and Spanish colonial hosts are almost assuredly counterfeit.

St. Helena, a British colony located about 1,150 miles (1,850 km.) from the west coast of Africa, has an area of 47 sq. mi. (410 sq. km.) and a population of *7,000. Capital: Jamestown. Flax, lace, and rope are produced for export Ascension and Tristan da Cunha are dependencies of St. Helena.

The island was discovered and named by the Portuguese navigator Joao de Nova Castella in 1502. The Portuguese imported livestock, fruit trees, and vegetables but established no permanent settlement. The Dutch occupied the island temporarily, 1645-51. The original European settlement was founded by representatives of the British East India Company sent to annex the island after the departure of the Dutch. The Dutch returned and captured St. Helena from the British on New Year's Day, 1673, but were in turn ejected by a British force under Sir Richard Munden. Thereafter St. Helena was the undisputed possession of Great Britain. The island served as the place of exile for Napoleon, several Zulu chiefs, and an ex-sultan of Zanzibar.

RULERS

British

MONETARY SYSTEM

12 Pence = 1 Shilling

BRITISH EAST INDIA COMPANY

1651-1834

HALF PENNY

COPPER

KM#	Date	Mintage	Fine	VF	XF	Unc
4	1821	—	7.00	15.00	45.00	100.00
	1821	—	—	—	Proof	150.00

BRONZE

KM#	Date	Mintage	Fine	VF	XF	Unc
4a	1821	—	—	—	Proof	150.00

GILT BRONZE

KM#	Date	Mintage	Fine	VF	XF	Unc
4b	1821	—	—	—	Proof	Rare

PATTERNS (Pn)

(Including off metal strikes)

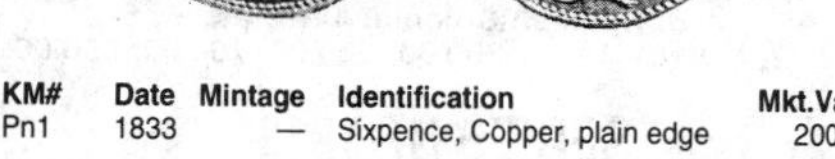

KM#	Date	Mintage	Identification	Mkt.Val.
Pn1	1833	—	Sixpence, Copper, plain edge	2000.

KM#	Date	Mintage	Identification	Mkt.Val.
Pn2	1833	—	Shilling, Copper, plain edge	3000.

KM#	Date	Mintage	Identification	Mkt.Val.
Pn3	1833	—	Half Crown, Copper, plain edge	4000.

TOKEN ISSUES (Tn)

HALF PENNY

Solomon, Dickson and Taylor

KM#	Date	Mintage	VG	Fine	VF	XF
Tn1	ND(1821)	.071	6.00	10.00	20.00	35.00

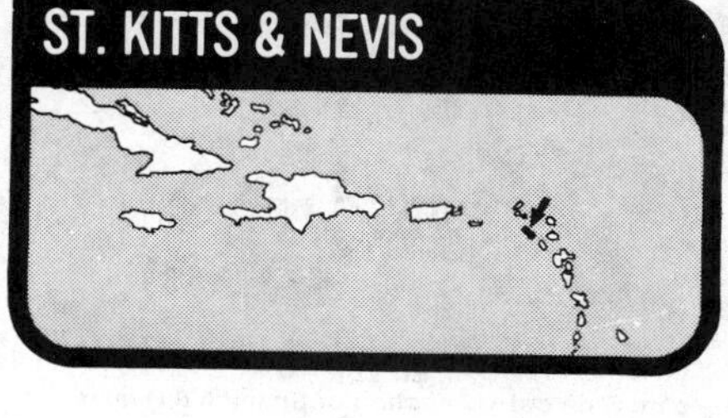

St. Kitts (St. Christopher), a West Indian island located in the Leeward Islands southeast of Puerto Rico, is the principal component of a British associated state composed of the islands of St. Kitts, Nevis, and Anguilla. The associated state has an area of 104 sq. mi. (360 sq. km.) and a population of *40,000. Capital: Basseterre, on St. Kitts. The islands export sugar, molasses, rum, cotton, and coconuts.

St. Kitts was discovered by Columbus in 1493 and was settled by Thomas Warner, an Englishman, in 1623. The island was ceded to the British by the Treaty of Utrecht, 1713. France protested British occupancy, and on three occasions between 1616 and 1782 seized the island and held it for short periods. St. Kitts used the coins and currency of the British Caribbean Territories (Eastern Group).

In early 1967 St. Kitts was united politically with Nevis and Anguilla to form a self-governing British associated state. In June 1967 Anguilla declared its independence of the federated state, and in Feb. 1969 unilaterally severed all ties with Britain and established the Republic of Anguilla. Britain refused to accept the unilateral movement and installed a commissioner to govern Anguilla, which remains a nominal part of the associated state. The political status of the three islands will be decided in the near future by a referendum.

From approximately 1750-1830, billon 2 sous of the French colony of Cayenne were countermarked 'SK' and used on St. Kitts. They were valued at 1-1/3 Pence.

RULERS

British

MONETARY SYSTEM

19th Century

108 Pence = 9 Shillings =
12 Bits = 1 Dollar

NOTE: The grades shown describe the condition of the raised countermarks, not the host coin itself, which is typically well worn.

SAINT KITTS

COUNTERMARKED COINAGE

1-1/2 PENCE

Black Dog

BILLON

c/m: S on French Colonies 24 Deniers, C#6.

KM#	Date	Year	Good	VG	Fine	VF
1	ND	(1801)	50.00	75.00	100.00	125.00

2-1/4 PENCE

BILLON

c/m: S.K. on French Guyana 2 Sous, C#1.

KM#	Date	Year	Good	VG	Fine	VF
2	ND	(1809-1812)	50.00	75.00	100.00	125.00

1/8 DOLLAR

SILVER

c/m: S on cut 1/8 section of Spanish 8 Reales.

KM#	Date	Year	Good	VG	Fine	VF
3	ND	(1801)	200.00	500.00	800.00	1000.

1/4 DOLLAR

SILVER

c/m: S on cut 1/4 section of Spanish 8 Reales.

KM#	Date	Year	Good	VG	Fine	VF
4	ND	(1801)	200.00	500.00	800.00	1000.

1/2 DOLLAR

SILVER
c/m: S on cut 1/2 section of Spanish 8 Reales.

KM#	Date	Year	Good	VG	Fine	VF
5	ND	(1801)	200.00	500.00	800.00	1000.

NEVIS

Nevis, a component of one of the West Indies Associated States, is located in the Leeward Islands and has an area of 50 sq. mi. (105 sq. km.) and a population of about 12,000. Charleston is the chief town and port. Sea-island cotton is the chief crop, and some sugar is produced.

Nevis was discovered by Columbus in 1493. It was first colonized by the English in 1628. Admiral De Grasse captured the island for France in 1782, but it was restored to Britain the following year. Alexander Hamilton, first Secretary of the Treasury, was born on Nevis in 1757.

RULERS

British

MONETARY SYSTEM

72 Black Dogs = 1 Dollar

COUNTERMARKED COINAGE

BLACK DOG

BILLON
c/m: NEVIS on French Guiana 2 Sous.

KM#	Date	Mintage	Good	VG	Fine	VF
1	ND(1801)	—	60.00	80.00	120.00	150.00

4 BLACK DOGS

SILVER
c/m: NEVIS above incuse 4.

KM#	Date	Mintage	Good	VG	Fine	VF
2	ND	—	200.00	500.00	850.00	1650.

6 BLACK DOGS

SILVER
c/m: NEVIS above incuse 6.

KM#	Date	Mintage	Good	VG	Fine	VF
3	ND	—	225.00	550.00	900.00	1750.

7 BLACK DOGS

SILVER
c/m: NEVIS above incuse 7.

KM#	Date	Mintage	Good	VG	Fine	VF
4	ND	—	200.00	500.00	850.00	1650.

9 BLACK DOGS

SILVER
c/m: NEVIS above incuse 9 on Spanish Colonial 1 Real.

KM#	Date	Mintage	Good	VG	Fine	VF
5.1	ND	—	200.00	450.00	800.00	1600.

c/m: NEVIS above incuse 9 on Potosi 1 Real.

KM#	Date	Mintage	Good	VG	Fine	VF
5.2	ND(1684)	—	450.00	900.00	1500.	—

ST. LUCIA

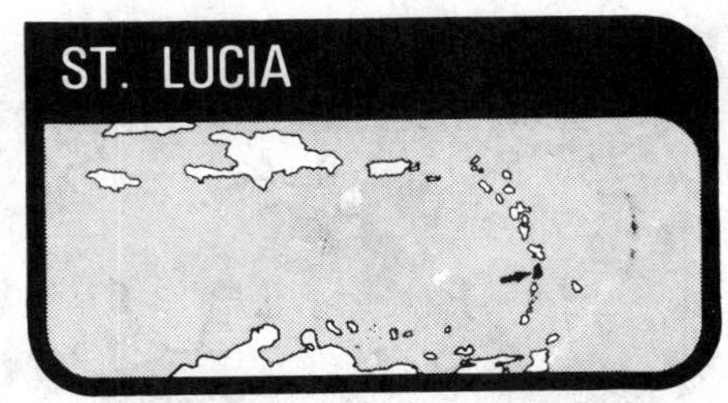

Saint Lucia, an independent island nation located in the Windward Islands of the West Indies between St. Vincent and Martinique, has an area of 238 sq. mi. (620 sq. km.) and a population of *150,000. Capital: Castries. The economy is agricultural. Bananas, copra, cocoa, sugar and logwood are exported.

Saint Lucia was discovered by Columbus in 1502. The first attempts at settlement undertaken by the British in 1605 and 1638 were frustrated by sickness and the determined hostility of the fierce Carib inhabitants. The French settled it in 1650 and made a treaty with the natives. Until 1814, when the island became a definite British possession, it was the scene of a continuous conflict between the British and French which saw the island change hands on at least 14 occasions. In 1967, under the West Indies Act, Saint Lucia was established as a British associated state, self-governing in internal affairs. Complete independence was attained on February 22, 1979. Saint Lucia is a member of the Commonwealth of Nations. The Queen of England is Chief of State.

Prior to 1950, the island used sterling, which was superseded by the currency of the British Caribbean Territories (Eastern Group) and the East Caribbean State.

RULERS

British

MONETARY SYSTEM

12 Deniers = 1 Sou
15 Sous = 1 Escalin
20 Sous = 1 Livre
6 Black Dogs = 4 Stampees
= 1 Bit = 9 Pence

COUNTERMARKED COLONIAL COINAGE

SERIES OF 1811

3 STAMPEES

SILVER
c/m: Circle w/crenalated edges on 1/4 cut of Spanish or Spanish Colonial 2 Reales.

KM#	Date	Year	Good	VG	Fine	VF
5	ND(1811)	—	—	—	—	—

ESCALIN

SILVER, 2.00 G
c/m: Circle on 1/3 cut of Spanish or Spanish Colonial 2 Reales.

KM#	Date	Year	Good	VG	Fine	VF
6	ND(1811)	—	150.00	250.00	375.00	550.00

1-1/2 ESCALINS

SILVER
c/m: Two circles on 1/4 cut of Spanish or Spanish Colonial 4 Reales.

KM#	Date	Year	Good	VG	Fine	VF
7	ND(1811)	—	250.00	400.00	600.00	850.00

2 ESCALINS

SILVER, 4.00 g
c/m: Three circles on 1/3 cut of Spanish or Spanish Colonial 4 Reales.

KM#	Date	Year	Good	VG	Fine	VF
8	ND(1811)	—	300.00	500.00	700.00	950.00

SERIES OF 1813

2 LIVRES, 5 SOUS

SILVER, 5.30 g
c/m: S:Lucie on 1/3 outer cut of Spanish or Spanish Colonial 8 Reales.

KM#	Date	Year	Good	VG	Fine	VF
9	ND(1813)	—	40.00	80.00	150.00	275.00

6 LIVRES, 15 SOUS

SILVER, 15.00 g
c/m: S:Lucie on 1/3 center cut of Spanish or Spanish Colonial 8 Reales.

KM#	Date	Year	Good	VG	Fine	VF
10	ND(1813)	—	75.00	150.00	300.00	550.00

NOTE: There are no known genuine examples existing today of any other similar varieties cut from Spanish or Spanish Colonial 2 and 4 Reales with this countermark.

ST. THOMAS & PRINCE

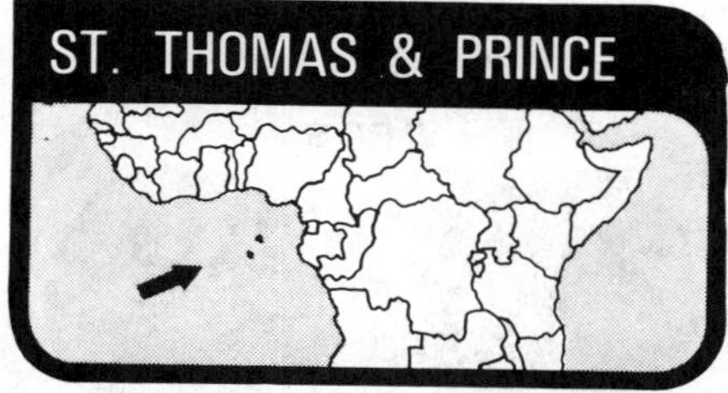

The Democratic Republic of Sao Tome and Principe (formerly the Portuguese overseas province of St. Thomas and Prince Islands) is located in the Gulf of Guinea 150 miles (241 km.) off the west African coast. It has an area of 372 sq. mi. (960 sq. km.) and a population of *121,000. Capital: Sao Tome. The economy of the islands is based on cocoa, copra and coffee.

St. Thomas and St. Prince were uninhabited when discovered by Portuguese navigators Joao de Santarem and Pedro de Escobar in 1470. After the failure of their initial settlement, 1485, the Portuguese successfully colonized St. Thomas with a colony of prisoners and exiled Jews, 1493. An initial prosperity based on the sugar trade gave way to a time of misfortune, 1567-1709, that saw the colony attacked and occupied or plundered by the French and Dutch, ravaged by the slave revolt of 1595; and finally rendered destitute by the transfer of the world sugar trade to Brazil. In the late 1800s, the colony turned from the production of sugar to cocoa, the basis of its present economy

The islands were designated a Portuguese overseas province in 1951. On April 25, 1974, the government of Portugal was seized by a military junta which reached agreements providing for independence for the Portuguese overseas provinces of Portuguese Guinea (Guinea-Bissau), Mozambique, Cape Verde Islands, Angola, and St. Thomas and Prince Islands. The Democratic Republic of Sao Tome and Principe was declared on July 12, 1975.

RULERS

Portuguese, until 1975

MINT MARKS

R = Rio

20 REIS

COPPER

KM#	Date	Mintage	VG	Fine	VF	XF
A1	1813R	.010	10.00	15.00	30.00	75.00
	1815R	—	10.00	15.00	30.00	75.00

KM#	Date	Mintage	VG	Fine	VF	XF
D1	1819 Bahia	—	2.00	4.50	12.00	35.00
	1825 Lisbon	.028	3.00	5.00	15.00	40.00

NOTE: 1820 Rio listed in Mozambique.

40 REIS

COPPER

KM#	Date	Mintage	VG	Fine	VF	XF
B1	1813 R	.015	12.00	20.00	35.00	85.00
	1815 R	—	20.00	30.00	50.00	100.00
E1	1819 Bahia	—	3.75	7.50	20.00	40.00
	1821 Bahia	—	2.00	4.50	12.00	30.00
	1822 Bahia	—	20.00	30.00	50.00	100.00
	1825 Lisbon	.024	4.00	6.00	15.00	30.00

NOTE: The difference between the Bahia and Lisbon coins is slight. The crown on the Bahia issue being rounder, approximately 2mm between the crown and rim.
NOTE: 1820 Rio listed in Mozambique.

80 REIS

COPPER

KM#	Date	Mintage	VG	Fine	VF	XF
C1	1813R	.015	10.00	15.00	25.00	70.00
F1	1819 Bahia	—	7.50	12.50	22.50	60.00
	1825 Lisbon	.014	5.00	8.00	15.00	40.00

NOTE: 1820 Rio listed in Mozambique.

St. Vincent and the Grenadines, consisting of the island of St. Vincent and the northern Grenadines (a string of islets stretching southward from St. Vincent), is located in the Windward Islands of the West Indies, West of Barbados and south of St. Lucia. The tiny nation has an area of 150 sq. mi. (340 sq. km.) and a population of *105,000. Capital: Kingstown. Arrowroot, cotton, sugar, molasses, rum and cocoa are exported. Tourism is a principal industry.

St. Vincent was discovered by Columbus on Jan. 22, 1498, but was left undisturbed for more than a century. The British began colonization early in the 18th century against bitter and prolonged Carib resistance. The island was taken by the French in 1779, but was restored to the British in 1783, at the end of the American Revolution. St. Vincent and the northern Grenadines became a British associated state in Oct. 1969. Independence under the name of St. Vincent and the Grenadines was attained at midnight of Oct. 26, 1979. The new nation chose to become a member of the Commonwealth of Nations with the Queen of England as Chief of State.

A local coinage was introduced in 1797, with the gold withdrawn in 1818 and the silver in 1823. This was replaced by sterling. From the mid-1950's, St. Vincent used the currency of the British Caribbean Territories (Eastern Group), than that of the East Caribbean States.

RULERS

British

MONETARY SYSTEM

1797-1811

8 Shillings, 3 Pence = 11 Bits
= 1 Dollar

Commencing 1811

9 Shillings = 12 Bits = 1 Dollar

COUNTERMARKED COINAGE

1811-1818

BLACK DOG

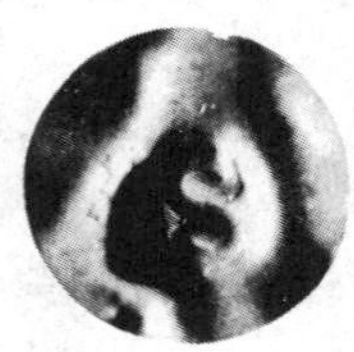

BILLON

c/m: Retrograde S within octagonal indent.

KM#	Date	Year	Good	VG	Fine	VF
7	ND(1814)	—	25.00	50.00	75.00	100.00

STAMPEE

BILLON

c/m: Retrograde S within octagonal indent on French Colonial coin bearing a crowned C c/m.

KM#	Date	Year	Good	VG	Fine	VF
8	ND(1814)	—	25.00	50.00	75.00	100.00

IV - 1/2 BITS

SILVER

c/m: S/IV 1/2/B on Mexico 2 Reales, KM#86

KM#	Date	Year	Good	VG	Fine	VF
9.1	ND	(1754 M)	300.00	500.00	750.00	1100.

c/m: S/IV 1/2/B on Mexico 2 Reales, KM#88.2

KM#	Date	Year	Good	VG	Fine	VF
9.2	ND	(1786 FM)	300.00	500.00	750.00	1100.

VI BITS

SILVER

c/m: S/VI on 23mm center disk cut from Spanish or Spanish Colonial 8 Reales.

KM#	Date	Year	Good	VG	Fine	VF
10	ND	(1811-14)	275.00	450.00	700.00	1000.

IX BITS

SILVER

c/m: S/IX on Spanish or Spanish American 4 Reales.

KM#	Date	Year	Good	VG	Fine	VF
11	ND	(1811-14)	2500.	3500.	4750.	6000.

XII BITS

SILVER

c/m: S/XII on holed Bolivia 8 Reales, KM#64.

KM#	Date	Year	Good	VG	Fine	VF
12.1	ND(1789-90 PR)		2750.	3750.	5000.	6500.

c/m: S/XII on holed Mexico 8 Reales, KM#109.

KM#	Date	Year	Good	VG	Fine	VF
12.2	ND	(1802 FT)	2750.	3750.	5000.	6500.

c/m: S/XII on holed Mexico 8 Reales, KM#110.

KM#	Date	Year	Good	VG	Fine	VF
12.3	ND	(1809 TH)	2750.	3750.	5000.	6500.

1798-1818

The countermarking of various gold coins in circulation on Saint Vincent was authorized by an Act of August 1, 1798. Standard weight for a gold "Joe" was set at 11.66 g with a denomination of 66 Shillings. Full weight gold was marked 3 times with the letter S. Underweight gold could be brought up to proper weight by plugging and marking the plug with a letter S, under the guidance of at least 1 Council member and 2 Assemblymen.

Ongoing concerns and practical implementation made this act subject to review and in all likelihood alterations were made resulting in the various plugged and full weight examples listed below. All countermarked "Joes" were recalled in 1818.

66 SHILLINGS

GOLD, 11.50-11.66 g

c/m: S (3 times) on Brazil 6400 Reis, KM#149.

KM#	Date	Year	Good	VG	Fine	VF
17	ND	17x8	1500.	2250.	3500.	5000.

c/m: S (3 times) on Brazil 6400 Reis, KM#199.2.

KM#	Date	Year	Good	VG	Fine	VF
18	ND	1786	1500.	2250.	3500.	5000.

c/m: S (3 times) on plugged Brazil 6400 Reis, KM#199.2.

KM#	Date	Year	Good	VG	Fine	VF
19	ND	1779	1500.	2500.	4000.	6000.

Obv. c/m: S (3 times). Rev. c/m: IS on the plug of a false Brazil 6400 Reis, KM#172.2.

KM#	Date	Year	Good	VG	Fine	VF
5.1	ND	1773	—	—	Rare	—

Obv. c/m: S (3 times). Rev. c/m: IS on the plug of a false Brazil 6400 Reis, KM#199.2.

KM#	Date	Year	Good	VG	Fine	VF
5.2	ND	178x	—	—	Rare	—

Obv. c/m: S (3 times) and GH on the plug of a false Brazil 6400 Reis, KM#172.2.

KM#	Date	Year	Good	VG	Fine	VF
6	ND	1767	—	—	Rare	—

6 POUNDS 12 SHILLINGS

GOLD, 23.40 g

c/m: S (3 times) on Brazil 12,800 Reis, KM#150.

KM#	Date	Year	VG	Fine	VF	XF
16	ND	1732	—	—	*Rare	—

***NOTE:** Glendining's Ford sale 9-89 VF realized $12,800.

SAN MARINO

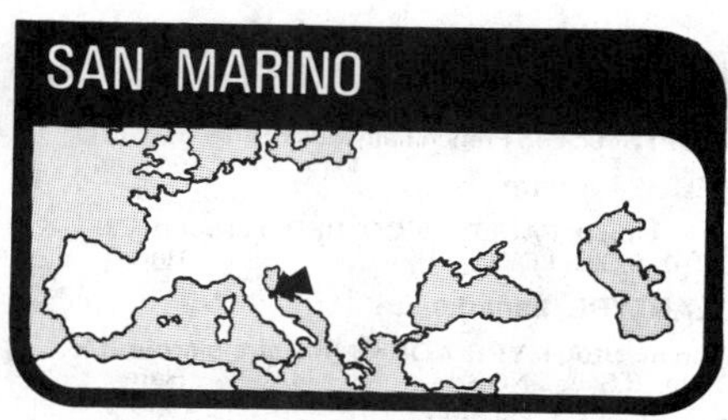

The Republic of San Marino, the oldest and smallest republic in the world is located in north central Italy entirely surrounded by the Province of Emilia-Romagna. It has an area of 24 sq. mi. (60 sq. km.) and a population of *23,000. Capital: San Marino. The principal economic activities are farming, livestock raising, cheesemaking, tourism and light manufacturing. Building stone, lime, wheat, hides and baked goods are exported. The government derives most of its revenue from the sale of postage stamps for philatelic purposes.

According to tradition, San Marino was founded about 350AD by a Christian stonecutter as a refuge against religious persecution. While gradually acquiring the institutions of an independent state, it avoided the factional fights of the Middle Ages and, except for a brief period in fief to Cesare Borgia, retained its freedom despite attacks on its sovereignty by the Papacy, the Lords of Rimini, Napoleon and Mussolini. In 1862 San Marino established a customs union with, and put itself under the protection of, Italy. A Communist-Socialist coalition controlled the Government for 12 years after World War II. The Christian Democratic Party has been the core of government since 1957. In 1978 a Communist-Socialist coalition again came into power and remained in control until 1991.

San Marino has its own coinage, but Italian and Vatican City coins and currency are also in circulation.

MINT MARKS

M - Milan
R - Rome

MONETARY SYSTEM

100 Centesimi = 1 Lira

5 CENTESIMI

COPPER

KM#	Date	Mintage	Fine	VF	XF	Unc
1	1864M	.280	4.00	8.00	35.00	150.00
	1869M	.600	3.00	7.00	20.00	42.00
	1894R	.600	3.00	6.00	17.50	35.00

10 CENTESIMI

COPPER

KM#	Date	Mintage	Fine	VF	XF	Unc
2	1875(m)	.150	4.00	8.00	30.00	80.00
	1893R	.150	4.00	7.50	25.00	50.00
	1894R	.150	4.00	7.50	25.00	50.00

50 CENTESIMI

2.5000 g, .835 SILVER, .0671 oz ASW

KM#	Date	Mintage	Fine	VF	XF	Unc
3	1898R	.040	10.00	20.00	30.00	55.00

LIRA

5.0000 g, .835 SILVER, .1342 oz ASW

KM#	Date	Mintage	Fine	VF	XF	Unc
4	1898R	.020	20.00	30.00	50.00	90.00

NOTE: Later date (1906) exists for this type.

2 LIRE

10.0000 g, .835 SILVER, .2684 oz ASW

KM#	Date	Mintage	Fine	VF	XF	Unc
5	1898R	.010	30.00	55.00	100.00	200.00

NOTE: Later date (1906) exists for this type.

5 LIRE

25.0000 g, .900 SILVER, .7234 oz ASW

KM#	Date	Mintage	Fine	VF	XF	Unc
6	1898R	.018	100.00	150.00	200.00	400.00

SAUDI ARABIA

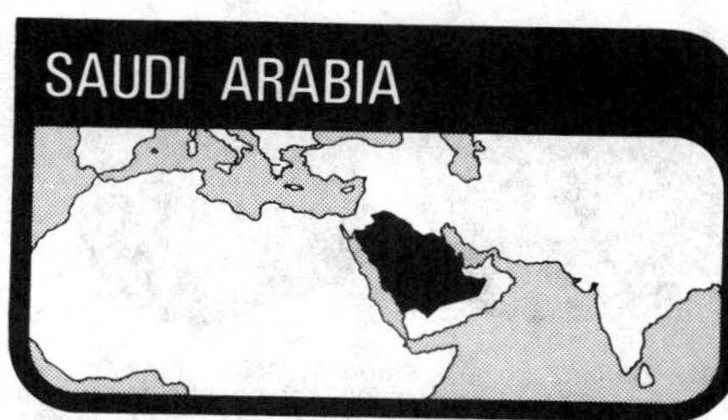

The Kingdom of Saudi Arabia, an independent and absolute hereditary monarchy comprising the former sultanate of Nejd, the old kingdom of Hejaz, Asir and Al Hasa, occupies four-fifths of the Arabian peninsula. The kingdom has an area of 830,000 sq. mi. (2,149,690 sq. km.) and a population of *16.1 million. Capital: Riyadh. The economy is based on oil, which provides 85 percent of Saudi Arabia's revenue.

Mohammed united the Arabs in the 7th century and his followers founded a great empire with its capital at Medina. The Turks established nominal rule over much of Arabia in the 16th and 17th centuries, and in the 18th century divided it into principalities.

The Kingdom of Saudi Arabia was created by King Abd Al-Aziz Bin Saud (1882-1953), a descendant of earlier Wahhabi rulers of the Arabian peninsula. In 1901 he seized Riyadh, capital of the Sultanate of Nejd, and in 1905 established himself as Sultan. In 1913 he captured the Turkish province of Al Hasa; took the Hejaz in 1925 and by 1926 most of Asir. In 1932 he combined Nejd and Hejaz into the single kingdom of Saudi Arabia. Asir was incorporated into the kingdom a year later.

TITLES

العربية السعودية

Al-Arabiya(t) as-Sa'udiya(t)

المملكة العربية السعودية

Al-Mamlaka(t) al-'Arabiya(t) as-Sa'udiya(t)

MECCA

Mecca, the metropolis of Islam and the capital of Hejaz, is located inland from the Red Sea due east of the port of Jidda. A center of non-political commercial, cultural and religious activities, Mecca remained virtually independent until 1259. Two centuries of Egyptian rule were followed by four centuries of Turkish rule which lasted until the Arab revolts which extinguished all Turkish pretensions to sovereignty over any part of the Arabian peninsula.

MINTNAME

Makkah, Mecca مكة

RULERS

Sharifs of Mecca

Ghalib b. Ma'sud, AH1219-1229
Yahya b. Surer, AH1230-1240
Abdul Muttalib and Ibn Awn, AH1240-1248

ANONYMOUS WAHHABI ISSUES

1/2 MAHMUDI

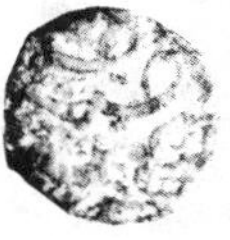 

COPPER
Mintname: *Mecca*

KM#	Date	Good	VG	Fine	VF
5	AH1240	250.00	450.00	600.00	800.00

MAHMUDI

COPPER
Mintname: *Mecca*

KM#	Date	Good	VG	Fine	VF
1	AH1219	100.00	150.00	300.00	400.00

KM#	Date	Good	VG	Fine	VF
2	AH1220	100.00	150.00	300.00	400.00
	1221	100.00	150.00	300.00	400.00
	1222	100.00	150.00	300.00	400.00

Mintname: *Mecca*
Obv: Bird. Rev: Fish.

3	AH1223	125.00	175.00	300.00	450.00

4	AH1230	125.00	175.00	300.00	450.00

SCOTLAND

Northern part of the island of Great Britain. Area of 30,414 square miles (78,772 sq. km.) and population of 5,206,200. Capital: Edinburgh. Cereal grains and potatoes are the principal farm products. Production of textiles, electrical instruments, spirits; shipbuilding and tourism are also important sources of income.

Scotland was the traditional home of the Picts in ancient times. The Romans invaded the area after 80 A.D. and Hadrian's Wall was built from 122-126 A.D. to keep the Picts from the Roman settlements to the south. In the 5th century Scotland had 4 kingdoms: Northumbria (Anglo-Saxon), Picts, Scots (of Irish extraction) and Strathclyde. St. Columba converted the Picts to Christianity in the late 6th century. Norse invasions started in the late 8th century. The Picts conquered the Scots in the 9th century and under Malcolm II (1005-1034) the Scottish kingdoms were united. The Scottish King became a vassal of the English king in 1174 (a circumstance that was to lead to many disputes). Gained independence in 1314 at Bannockburn under Robert Bruce. Ruled by Stuarts from 1371-1714. Personal union of Scotland and England when James VI succeeded Elizabeth I in 1603 as James I. Final union by Parliamentary Act in 1707.

RULERS

George III, 1760-1820
George IV, 1820-1830
William IV, 1830-1837
Victoria, 1837-1901

COMMERCIAL COUNTERMARKED COINAGE (CC)

Private issue silver tokens appeared from 1811-1812. For various reasons the Spanish "dollars" themselves were preferred in Scotland where they circulated bearing a countermark of the merchant or company responsible for its issue. Sometimes other foreign crown-sized pieces were similarly countermarked. Many pieces are found with a grill-like cancellation over the countermark and have a considerably lower market value.

VALUATIONS

Market valuations are given for the average of the condition of the parent coin as well as its countermark.

ALLOA, Clackmannanshire

SILVER
c/m: PAYABLE AT ALLOA COLLIERY in a circle around an incuse 5/.

KM#	Denomination	Good	VG	Fine
CC1	5 SHILLINGS	200.00	300.00	500.00

NOTE: This countermark is only known on counterfeit or false dollars struck in England. Specimens retaining the silver plating command a premium.

BALLINDALLOCH, Balfron, Stirlingshire

c/m: *BALLINDALLOCH*COTTON*WORKS in two circular lines around 5/.

CC7	5 SHILLINGS	275.00	850.00	1300.

c/m: BALLINDALLOCH COTTON WORK in a circle around a cotton bale.

KM#	Denomination	Good	VG	Fine
CC8	(2 SHILLINGS/6 PENCE)	—	400.00	600.00

NOTE: Struck on French half-ecus.

BEITH, Ayrshire

c/m: J. FAULDS & CO. BEITH around 5/3.

CC10	5 SHILLINGS/3 PENCE	—	Rare	—

BLANTYRE, Lanarkshire

c/m: BLANTYRE WORKS in a circle around 5/.

CC11	5 SHILLINGS	—	Rare	—

CALTON, Lanarkshire

c/m: * HENRY REID*CALTON in a circle around 5/.

CC12	5 SHILLINGS	—	Rare	—

NOTE: All known pieces are partly obliterated by cuts.

CAMPSIE, Lanarkshire

c/m: J. LECKIE CAMPSIE around 5/. in beaded circle.

CC13	5 SHILLINGS	—	Rare	—

CATRINE, Ayrshire

c/m: CATRINE.COTTON.WORKS/ No. followed by incuse number, in circle, 5/6 in center.

CC14	5 SHILLINGS/6 PENCE	—	800.00	1200.

c/m: CATRINE WORKS. No and number, in oval, 5/. in center.

CC15	5 SHILLINGS	—	Rare	—

c/m: Similar to #ST15 but value in circle.

CC16	5 SHILLINGS	—	Rare	—

c/m: Similar to #CC14, but 4/9.

CC17	4 SHILLINGS/9 PENCE	335.00	500.00	1000.

NOTE: All the Catrine c/m have an individual number stamped in, the highest known being "5067".

CULCREUCH, Stirlingshire

c/m: PAYABLE AT CULCREUCH MILL * around 5/.

CC19	5 SHILLINGS	—	Rare	—

DALRY, Ayrshire

c/m: JAMIESON & HARVIE DALRY around 5.

CC21	5 SHILLINGS	—	Rare	—

DALZELL, Lanarkshire

c/m: PAYABLE AT DALZELL FARM * w/o value.

CC22	(5 SHILLINGS)	275.00	375.00	500.00

NOTE: The Dalzell c/m are only known on French 5 Franc pieces.

c/m: ADELPHI COTTON WORK in a circle around a cotton bale.

CC23	(2 SHILLINGS/6 PENCE)	250.00	450.00	600.00

c/m: Similar to previous c/m, #CC23.

CC24	(5 SHILLINGS)	—	Rare	—

NOTE: Struck on French half-ecus.

DEANSTON, Kilmarnock, Perthshire

c/m: DEANSTON COTTON MILL in a circle around 5/' within a toothed octagon.

KM#	Denomination	Good	VG	Fine
CC28	5 SHILLINGS	—	—	1800.

DENNY, Stirlingshire

c/m: T. SHIELS & CO. (value cancelled) Rev. PAYABLE AT HERBERTSHIRE PRINT-FIELD.

CC30	5 SHILLINGS	—	Rare	—

FINTRY, Stirlingshire

c/m: *P. BY ROBERT McNEE FINTRY around 5/.

CC33	5 SHILLINGS	—	Rare	—

c/m: J. STEWART FINTRY. around 5/.

CC35	5 SHILLINGS	—	Rare	—

GALSTON, nr. Kilmarnock, Ayrshire

c/m: GALSTON above SOC.Y around 5s No. 12 all in small circular indent.

CC36	5 SHILLINGS	325.00	475.00	800.00

NOTE: This c/m is also known on a French Ecu and on a Charles II crown.

GLASGOW, Lanarkshire

(See also Port Glasgow.)

c/m: ADAMSON & LOGAN GLASGOW around FIVE SHIL.

CC37	5 SHILLINGS	—	Rare	—

c/m: T. & R. ARTHUR GLASGOW . around 5/.

CC38	5 SHILLINGS	—	Rare	—

NOTE: This c/m is usually found cancelled with a grill pattern.

c/m: W BILTON 630 ARGYLE STREET TOBACCONIST in 2 lines around 5/. Rev. c/m: A tree (the Arms of Glasgow).

CC39	5 SHILLINGS	—	Rare	—

c/m: D C above a large 12 pointed rosette w/o value.

CC40	5 SHILLINGS	300.00	400.00	650.00

NOTE: Possibly issued by D. Campbell & Co., Shuttle St., Glasgow.

c/m: +GLASGOW BANK in a circle around 5/.

within an inner circle.

KM#	Denomination	Good	VG	Fine
CC44	5 SHILLINGS	300.00	400.00	600.00

c/m: Similar to #CC44 but w/o + or inner circle, and with value 4/9.

CC45	4 SHILLINGS/9 PENCE	—	Rare	—

c/m: PAYABLE BY J. INGLIS 32´ TRONGATE GLASGOW Rev. c/m: A tree (the arms of Glasgow).

CC46	(5 SHILLINGS?)	—	Rare	—

NOTE: The only specimen now known has the c/m obliterated and the value has not been determined.

c/m: THISTLE BANK. in a circle around 6/. Rev. c/m: Thistle.

CC47	6 SHILLINGS	—	Rare	—

c/m: THISTLE BANK. in a circle around 5/: Rev. c/m: Thistle.

CC48	5 SHILLINGS	300.00	400.00	600.00

c/m: THISTLE BANK. in a circle around 4/9. Rev. c/m: Thistle.

CC49	4 SHILLINGS/9 PENCE	150.00	225.00	300.00

NOTE: This c/m is also known on counterfeit or false dollars struck in England.

c/m: Similar to #CC49 but w/o rev. c/m. thistle.

CC50	4 SHILLINGS/9 PENCE	300.00	500.00	800.00

c/m: WM. THOMSON + FLESHER +, BELL STREET GLASGOW in inner circle around 5/.

CC51	5 SHILLINGS	—	Rare	—

GREENOCK, Renfrewshire

c/m: R. & G. BLAIR.GREENOCK. in an oval around 4/6.

CC52	4 SHILLINGS/6 PENCE	—	Rare	—

c/m: GREENOCK DRAPER'S SOCIETY. around 4/6 within a triangle.

CC53	4 SHILLINGS/6 PENCE	—	Rare	—

c/m: W G & CO, 4/9 in a toothed T-shape indent.

CC54	4 SHILLINGS/9 PENCE	—	Rare	—

c/m: A.KING *GREENOCK* around 5/.

CC55	5 SHILLINGS	Reported, not confirmed		

c/m: Similar to #CC55 but value 4/6.

KM#	Denomination	Good	VG	Fine
CC56	4 SHILLINGS/6 PENCE	525.00	675.00	900.00

c/m: J. McK. & SON GREENOCK around 4/6.

CC57	4 SHILLINGS/6 PENCE	300.00	400.00	550.00

c/m: McFIE LINDSAY & COY *GREENOCK* around 4/6.

CC58	4 SHILLINGS/6 PENCE	350.00	500.00	700.00

c/m: * J & A.MUIR * GREENOCK. around 4/6.

CC59	4 SHILLINGS/6 PENCE	300.00	400.00	550.00

c/m: JOHN RODGER JUNR. * GREENOCK *, around 4/6.

CC60	4 SHILLINGS/6 PENCE	700.00	900.00	1200.

c/m: PAYABLE BY I & W SCOTT.GREENOCK. around 4/9 within a rectangle.

CC61	4 SHILLINGS/9 PENCE	—	Rare	—

c/m: J. WATT & CO. .GREENOCK. around 5/.

CC62	5 SHILLINGS	—	Rare	—

HURLET, Renfrewshire

c/m: J. & J. W. HURLET. around 5/.

KM#	Denomination	Good	VG	Fine
CC63	5 SHILLINGS	350.00	450.00	675.00

NOTE: There are 2 types of c/m, differing slightly in punctuation. Type I has an additional 3 dots punched in a triangle. A specimen of this c/m is known on a U.S. Dollar which has the 3 dots.

HUTCHESONTOWN, Renfrewshire, Purvey

c/m: FORSTER & CORBET HUTCHESONTOWN, 5/.

KM#	Denomination	Good	VG	Fine
CC64	5 SHILLINGS	600.00	800.00	1000.

JOHNSTONE, Renfrewshire

c/m: CAMPBELL HALL & WATT around JOHNSTONE 4/6.

KM#	Denomination	Good	VG	Fine
CC65	4 SHILLINGS/6 PENCE	—	Rare	—

LANARK, NEW, Lanarkshire

c/m: PAYABLE AT LANARK MILLS-, around 5/.

KM#	Denomination	Good	VG	Fine
CC66	5 SHILLINGS	150.00	200.00	275.00

c/m: Similar to #CC66 but value 4/9.

KM#	Denomination	Good	VG	Fine
CC67	4 SHILLINGS/9 PENCE	350.00	450.00	600.00

c/m: Similar to #CC66 but with value 2/6.

KM#	Denomination	Good	VG	Fine
CC68	2 SHILLINGS/6 PENCE	350.00	450.00	600.00

c/m: Similar to #CC66 but value 4/6.

KM#	Denomination	Good	VG	Fine
CC69	4 SHILLINGS/6 PENCE	350.00	450.00	600.00

NOTE: All of the 4/6 denomination and about half of the 2/6 denomination have an additional c/m of quatrefoil within a small shield. Struck on French half-ecus.

LEVERN BANK, Barrhead Renfrewshire

c/m: LEVERN.MILL.S.D & Co, around 5/6 and additional c/m: S.D in a small beaded circle.

KM#	Denomination	Good	VG	Fine
CC73	5 SHILLINGS/6 PENCE	—	Rare	—

c/m: Similar to #CC73 but value 5 and w/o the additional c/m.

KM#	Denomination	Good	VG	Fine
CC74	5 SHILLINGS	—	Rare	—

LOCHWINNOCK, Renfrewshire

c/m: N (?) ARTHUR & CO (LOCH)WINNOCH in an oval around a large 5.

KM#	Denomination	Good	VG	Fine
CC76	5 SHILLINGS	—	Rare	—

c/m: A.GIBSON. & CO. LOCHWINNOCH. within a circle around 5/.

KM#	Denomination	Good	VG	Fine
CC77	5 SHILLINGS	—	Rare	—

MUIRKIRK, Ayshire

c/m: MUIRKIRK IRON WORKS + around 5/6. Rev. c/m: View of blast furnace with smoke stack etc., dated 1809.

KM#	Denomination	Good	VG	Fine
CC78	5 SHILLINGS/6 PENCE	—	Rare	—

PAISLEY, Renfrewshire

c/m: CORCER PAISLEY around 5.

KM#	Denomination	Good	VG	Fine
CC80	5 SHILLINGS	—	—	—

NOTE: The only known specimen was reported in the 19th century but has since disappeared. A very indistinct electrotype copy exists.

c/m: McG & C. PAISLEY in a circle around 5/.

KM#	Denomination	Good	VG	Fine
CC81	5 SHILLINGS	—	Rare	—

NOTE: Presumably issued by McGavin & Clarkson.

c/m: JOHN LANG MERCHT. PAISLEY. in an oval around 5/3.

KM#	Denomination	Good	VG	Fine
CC82	5 SHILLINGS/3 PENCE	—	Rare	—

c/m: PAYABLE BY W. LANGMUIR. around Arms of Paisley. Rev. c/m: PAISLEY DOLLAR SOCIETY. around 5/3 within a wreath.

KM#	Denomination	Good	VG	Fine
CC83	5 SHILLINGS/3 PENCE	275.00	400.00	900.00

c/m: JNo. & ROBt. McKERRELL. PAISLEY in a triangle around 5/.

KM#	Denomination	Good	VG	Fine
CC84	5 SHILLINGS	—	Rare	—

c/m: J. Mc.LEAN *Cott.St.Paisley* in an oval around 5/3.

KM#	Denomination	Good	VG	Fine
CC85	5 SHILLINGS/3 PENCE	—	Rare	—

NOTE: This c/m also is known on a U.S. Dollar dated 1799. (Unique).

c/m: JOHN MORRIS . PAISLEY . in a circle around 5/3.

KM#	Denomination	Good	VG	Fine
CC86	5 SHILLINGS/3 PENCE	—	Rare	—

c/m: J. MUIR Manufr .PAISLEY. in a circle around 5/. Rev. c/m: Prince of Wales plumes.

KM#	Denomination	Good	VG	Fine
CC87	5 SHILLINGS	500.00	600.00	850.00

NOTE: The majority of specimens are cancelled with a grill pattern; these bring somewhat lower prices.

c/m: R. PEACOCK & SONS . PAISLEY. in a circle around 5/.

KM#	Denomination	Good	VG	Fine
CC88	5 SHILLINGS	500.00	600.00	850.00

NOTE: The majority of specimens are cancelled with a grill pattern; these bring somewhat lower prices.

PORT GLASGOW, Renfrewshire

c/m: ROBt. CRIGHTON Pt. GLASGOW. in a circle around 4/6.

KM#	Denomination	Good	VG	Fine
CC89	4 SHILLINGS/6 PENCE	—	Rare	—

c/m: A.STEVEN & SONS Pt GLASGOW in a circle around 4/6.

KM#	Denomination	Good	VG	Fine
CC91	4 SHILLINGS/6 PENCE	600.00	850.00	—

ROTHSAY, Buteshire

c/m: PAYABLE AT ROTHSAY MILLS + around 5/.

KM#	Denomination	Good	VG	Fine
CC92	5 SHILLINGS		Unknown	—

NOTE: The only recorded specimen was stolen and probably melted about 1920.

c/m: PAYABLE AT ROTHSAY COTTON MILLS, around a woolsack on which is stamped 5 above Sh in a rectangle w/additional 6-pointed star c/m.

KM#	Denomination	Good	VG	Fine
CC93	5 SHILLINGS	—	Rare	—

c/m: Similar to #CC92 but value 1/8 in a circle and on a cut third-dollar (or a cut third 8 reales).

KM#	Denomination	Good	VG	Fine
CC94	1 SHILLING/8 PENCE	100.00	200.00	300.00

c/m: Similar to #CC93 but value 2/4 in a rectangle on half of woolsack c/m and on a cut half-dollar (same as above).

KM#	Denomination	Good	VG	Fine
CC95	2 SHILLING/4 PENCE	—	Rare	—

c/m: Similar to #CC92 but value 2/6 in an oval and on a cut half-dollar (or a cut half 8 reales).

KM#	Denomination	Good	VG	Fine
CC96	2 SHILLINGS/ 6 PENCE	200.00	300.00	450.00

c/m: Similar to #CC93 but value 2/6 in a rectangle and on a cut half-dollar (same as above), additional w/6-pointed star c/m.

KM#	Denomination	Good	VG	Fine
CC97	2 SHILLINGS/6 PENCE	250.00	400.00	650.00

c/m: ROTHSAY COTTON WORKS. between beaded and cable circles around 4/6 above 1820.

KM#	Denomination	Good	VG	Fine
CC100	4 SHILLINGS/6 PENCE	200.00	300.00	450.00

SALTCOATS, Ayrshire

c/m: SALTCOATS *Merchants* within wreathed

border around 5/6.

KM#	Denomination	Good	VG	Fine
CC101	5 SHILLINGS/6 PENCE	—	Rare	—

STEVENSTON, Ayrshire

c/m: J.LOCKHART STEVENSON around 5 Sh within an oval.

KM#	Denomination	Good	VG	Fine
CC103	5 SHILLINGS	—	Rare	—

TOBERMORAY, Argyllshire

c/m: DUGD. McLACHLAN MERCHT. + TOBERMORY +, in circle around 5/ in center on lined background.

KM#	Denomination	Good	VG	Fine
CC102	5 SHILLINGS	—	Rare	—

NOTE: A specimen of this c/m is known on a French 5 Franc Piece.

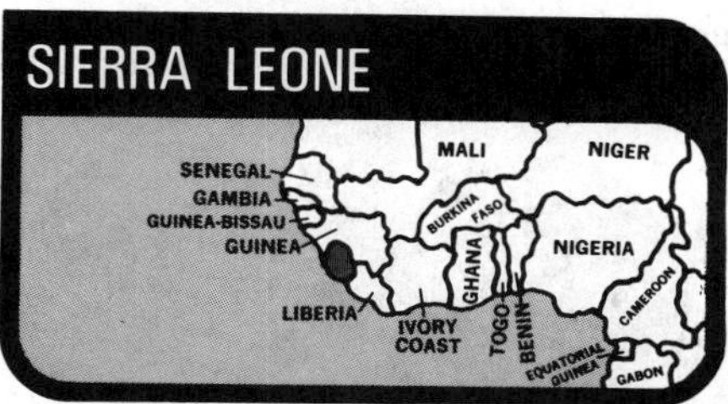

The Republic of Sierra Leone, a British Commonwealth nation located in western Africa between Guinea and Liberia, has an area of 27,699 sq. mi. (71,740 sq. km.) and a population of *4.1 million. Capital: Freetown. The economy is predominantly agricultural but mining contributes significantly to export revenues. Diamonds, iron ore, palm kernels, cocoa, and coffee are exported.

The coast of Sierra Leone was first visited by Portuguese and British slavers in the 15th and 16th centuries. The first settlement, at Freetown, 1787, was established as a refuge for freed slaves within the British Empire, runaway slaves from the United States and Negroes discharged from the British armed forces. The first settlers were virtually wiped out by tribal attacks and disease. The colony was re-established under the auspices of the Sierra Leone Company and transferred to the British Crown in 1807. The interior region was secured and established as a protectorate in 1896. Sierra Leone became independent within the Commonwealth on April 27, 1961, and adopted a republican constitution ten years later. It is a member of the Commonwealth of Nations. The president is Chief of State and Head of Government.

For similar coinage refer to British West Africa.

RULERS

British, until 1971

MONETARY SYSTEM

Until 1906

100 Cents = 50 Pence = 1 Dollar

SIERRA LEONE COMPANY

10 CENTS

.902 SILVER
Obv: Lion. Rev: Clasped hands.

KM#	Date	Mintage	Fine	VF	XF	Unc
3	1805	6,100	35.00	80.00	150.00	275.00

NOTE: Earlier dates (1791-1796) exist for this type.

COUNTERMARKED COINAGE

1/4 DOLLAR

.903 SILVER
c/m: Crowned WR on 1/4 cut of a Spanish or Colonial 8 Reales.

KM#	Date	Mintage	VG	Fine	VF	XF
10	ND(1832)	—	250.00	450.00	800.00	1250.

1/2 DOLLAR

.903 SILVER
c/m: Crowned WR on Spanish or Spanish Colonial 4 Reales.

KM#	Date	Mintage	VG	Fine	VF	XF
13	ND(1832)	—	200.00	400.00	700.00	1100.

TOKEN ISSUES (Tn)

Macaulay and Babington

PENNY

COPPER, 16.84 g
Obv. leg: SLAVE TRADE ABOLISHED/BY GREAT BRITAIN/1807. Rev. leg: Similar in Arabic.

KM#	Date	Mintage	Fine	VF	XF	Unc
Tn1.1	ND(1814) GFP	.050	7.50	15.00	45.00	120.00
	ND(1814) GFP (restrike)	—	—	Proof		200.00

NOTE: Heavier specimens weighing 24.94-26.75 g exist, probably struck later as medals.

Obv: W/o engravers initials.

KM#	Date	Mintage	Fine	VF	XF	Unc
Tn1.2	ND(1814)	—	7.50	15.00	45.00	120.00

GILT COPPER

KM#	Date	Mintage		Unc
Tn1.1a	ND(1830-32) (restrike)	—	Proof	350.00

SILVER

KM#	Date	Mintage		Unc
Tn1.1b	ND(1830-32) (restrike)	—	Proof	450.00

The Republic of South Africa, located at the southern tip of Africa, has an area, including the enclave of Walvis Bay, of 472,359 sq. mi. (1,221,040 sq. km.) and a population of *38.5 million. Capitals: Administrative, Pretoria; Legislative, Cape Town; Judicial, Bloemfontein. Manufacturing, mining and agriculture are the principal industries. Exports include wool, diamonds, gold, and metallic ores.

Portuguese navigator Bartholomew Diaz became the first European to sight the region of South Africa when he rounded the Cape of Good Hope in 1488, but throughout the 16th century the only white men to come ashore were the survivors of ships wrecked while attempting the stormy Cape passage. The first permanent settlement was established by Jan van Riebeeck of the Dutch East India Company in 1652. In subsequent decades additional Dutch and Germans and Huguenot refugees from France settled in the Cape area to form the Afrikaner segment of today's population.

Great Britain captured the Cape colony in 1795, and again in 1806, receiving permanent title in 1814. To escape British political rule and cultural dominance, many Afrikaner farmers (Boers) migrated northward (the Great Trek) beginning in 1836, and established the independent Boer Republics of the Transvaal (the South African Republic, Zuid Afrikaansche Republic) in 1852, and the Orange Free State in 1854. British political intrigues against the two republics, coupled with the discovery of diamonds and gold in the Boer-settled regions, led to the bitter Boer Wars (1880-81, 1899-1902) and the incorporation of the Boer republics into the British Empire.

RULERS

British, until 1934

MONETARY SYSTEM

Until 1961

12 Pence = 1 Shilling
2 Shillings = 1 Florin
20 Shillings = 1 Pound (Pond)

CAPE

GRIQUATOWN

Griquatown is located in the Griqualand West region of northern Cape Province, 90 miles west of Kimberley. Griqualand West occupies an area of 15,400 sq. mi. (50,500 sq. km.) north of the Orange River and west of Orange Free State. It is dry desert country, noted for its diamond fields. Chief town: Kimberley. Following the discovery of diamonds in 1867, a bitter dispute over possession erupted between the British and Orange Free State. Britain annexed the territory in 1871. It was joined to Cape Colony in 1880. Tokens for the area were commissioned by Rev. John Campbell and produced by Thomas Halliday in 1815-16, but are undated. They were eventually retired from circulation and melted. In 1890, two pattern types were struck by Otto Nolte & Co. of Berlin for advertising purposes.

RULERS

British, until 1961

Missionary Token Issues (Tn)

1/4 PENNY

COPPER

KM#	Date	Mintage	VF	XF	Unc
Tn1	ND(1815-16)	—	125.00	200.00	450.00
Tn1	ND(1815-16)	—	—	Proof	950.00

1/2 PENNY

COPPER

KM#	Date	Mintage	VF	XF	Unc
Tn2	ND(1815-16)	—	100.00	175.00	500.00
	ND(1815-16)	—	—	Proof	1100.

5 PENCE

SILVER

KM#	Date	Mintage	VF	XF	Unc
Tn4	ND(1815-16)	—	250.00	450.00	800.00
	ND(1815-16)	—	—	Proof	1250.

10 PENCE

SILVER

KM#	Date	Mintage	VF	XF	Unc
Tn5	ND(1815-16)	—	400.00	650.00	1250.
	ND(1815-16)	—	—	Proof	1500.

NOTE: Similar pieces struck in silver w/100 are modern fantasies.

PATTERNS (Pn)

(Including off metal strikes)

KM#	Date	Mintage	Identification	Mkt.Val.
Pn1	ND(1815-16)	—	1/4 Penny, Lead, KM1	400.00
Pn2	ND(1815-16)	—	1/2 Penny, Lead, KM2	450.00
Pn3	ND(1815-16)	—	5 Pence, Copper, KM4	400.00
Pn4	ND(1815-16)	—	10 Pence, Copper, KM5	400.00

KM#	Date	Mintage	Identification	Mkt.Val.
Pn5	1890	—	1 Penny, Copper	250.00

KM#	Date	Mintage	Identification	Mkt.Val.
Pn6	ND(1890)	—	1 Penny, Copper	225.00
Pn7	ND(1890)	—	1 Penny, Nickel	Rare

CAPE OF GOOD HOPE

Cape of Good Hope, the largest of the four provinces of the Republic of South Africa, has an area of 278,380 sq. mi. (721,001 sq. km.) and a population of 4.3 million. Capital: Cape Town. The colony of Cape of Good Hope was founded by the Dutch in 1652 and was occupied by the British in 1795-1803 and 1806-14. The Dutch ceded it to the British in 1814. It was united for administrative purpose with Natal, 1843-56; annexed British Kaffraria in 1865 and British Becchuanaland in 1895; and administered Basutoland (now Lesotho), 1871-84. Cape Colony attained internal self-government in 1872, and joined the Union of South Africa in 1910. An extensive token series exists. One penny patterns are known for 1889.

RULERS

British, 1814-1961

MONETARY SYSTEM

12 Pence = 1 Shilling
20 Shillings = 1 Pound

PATTERNS (Pn)

(Including off metal strikes)

KM#	Date	Mintage	Identification	Mkt.Val.
Pn1	1889	—	1 Penny, Bronze, 'I' of 'BRITANNIAR' above hair ribbon	175.00
Pn2	1889	—	1 Penny, Copper-Nickel, 'I' of 'BRITANNIAR' above hair ribbon	225.00

KM#	Date	Mintage	Identification	Mkt.Val.
Pn3	1889	—	1 Penny, Bronze	175.00
Pn4	1889	—	1 Penny, Copper-Nickel	225.00
Pn5	1889	—	1 Penny, Aluminum	500.00
Pn6	1889	—	1 Penny, Tin	500.00

KM#	Date	Mintage	Identification	Mkt.Val.
Pn7	1889	—	1 Penny (or 1/2 Crown), Silver	1400.

ORANGE FREE STATE

Orange Free State, a province of the Republic of South Africa bounded by Natal and Lesotho on the east, Cape Province on the south and west, and the Transvaal on the north, has an area of 49,866 sq. mi. (129,152 sq. km.) and a population of 1.8 million. Capital: Bloemfontein. The first settlements in the Orange region were established 1810-20, but general occupancy began with the great trek of the Boers in 1836. The British annexed it in 1848, then withdrew their sovereignty and recognized the independence of the Boer state, 1854. It joined Transvaal in the Boer War of 1899-1902, after which it was annexed by Britain and established as the Orange River Colony, May 28, 1900. It attained internal self-government in 1907 and joined the Union of South Africa in 1910. A series of patterns was struck by Otto Nolte & Co. of Berlin, but no regular-issue coins were produced. Tokens are known.

RULERS

British, 1848-1854, 1900-1961

MONETARY SYSTEM

12 Pence = 1 Shilling
20 Shillings = 1 Kroon

PATTERNS (Pn)

(Including off metal strikes)

KM#	Date	Mintage	Identification	Mkt.Val.
Pn1	1874	—	1 Penny, Bronze	175.00

KM#	Date	Mintage	Identification	Mkt.Val.
Pn2	1874	—	1 Penny, Bronze, double thickness	250.00
Pn3	1874	—	1 Penny, Bronze, triple thickness	300.00
Pn4	1874	—	1 Penny, Bronze, like Pn7	—
Pn5	1874	—	2 Pence, Bronze. Mule. Pn3 and Zuid Afrikaansche Republic, Pn5	—

KM#	Date	Mintage	Identification	Mkt.Val.
Pn6	1887	—	1 Kroon, Silver, ESSAY	6000.
Pn7	1887	—	1 Kroon, Lead, ESSAY	2500.

KM#	Date	Mintage	Identification	Mkt.Val.
Pn9	1888	—	1 Penny, Bronze, ornamental shield	175.00
Pn10	1888	—	1 Penny, Copper-Nickel	250.00
Pn11	1888	—	1 Penny, Bronze, w/"LLC" below "PENNY"	175.00

KM#	Date	Mintage	Identification	Mkt.Val.
Pn12	1888	—	1 Penny, Copper-Nickel	250.00
Pn13	1888	—	1 Penny, Bronze, plain shield	175.00
Pn14	1888	—	1 Penny, Bronze, double thickness	200.00
Pn15	1888	—	1 Penny, Bronze, triple thickness	350.00
Pn16	1888	—	1 Penny, Aluminum	600.00
Pn17	1888	—	1 Penny, Silver	700.00

ZUID-AFRIKAANSCHE REPUBLIEK

MONETARY SYSTEM

12 Pence = 1 Shilling
20 Shillings = 1 Pond

PENNY

BRONZE

KM#	Date	Mintage	Fine	VF	XF	Unc
2	1892	.083	3.00	6.00	18.00	35.00
	1892	*6 pcs.	—	—	Proof	5000.
	1893	.011	30.00	45.00	100.00	200.00
	1894	.182	5.00	10.00	30.00	120.00
	1898	.263	1.00	3.00	7.00	20.00

NOTE: In 1900, just prior to the Boer evacuation of Pretoria, blank penny planchets were released into circulation. Reasonably preserved examples have sold for about $50.00 each.

3 PENCE

1.4138 g, .925 SILVER, .0420 oz ASW

KM#	Date	Mintage	Fine	VF	XF	Unc
3	1892	.024	3.00	6.00	20.00	90.00
	1892	*35-40 pcs.	—	—	65.00	1250.
	1893	.135	3.00	10.00	55.00	145.00
	1894	.104	4.00	12.50	65.00	175.00
	1895	.113	3.00	20.00	100.00	200.00
	1896	.166	2.00	4.00	8.00	40.00
	1897	.201	2.00	4.00	8.00	35.00

6 PENCE

2.8276 g, .925 SILVER, .0841 oz ASW

KM#	Date	Mintage	Fine	VF	XF	Unc
4	1892	.028	4.00	7.50	45.00	100.00
	1892	*40-50 pcs.		—	Proof	500.00
	1893	.096	3.00	6.00	90.00	185.00
	1894	.168	3.00	6.00	60.00	215.00
	1895	.179	3.00	6.00	60.00	215.00
	1896	.205	2.00	4.00	8.00	32.00
	1896	1 known	—	—	Proof	—
	1897	.220	1.50	3.00	6.00	30.00
	1897	1 known	—	—	Proof	—

SHILLING

5.6555 g, .925 SILVER, .1682 oz ASW

KM#	Date	Mintage	Fine	VF	XF	Unc
5	1892	.130	7.50	15.00	55.00	120.00
	1892	*40-50 pcs.	—	—	Proof	600.00
	1893	.137	10.00	65.00	500.00	1200.
	1894	.366	4.00	6.00	125.00	350.00
	1895	.327	4.00	10.00	250.00	500.00
	1896	.437	4.00	10.00	90.00	250.00
	1897	.397	2.00	4.00	15.00	40.00

2 SHILLINGS

11.3100 g, .925 SILVER, .3364 oz ASW

KM#	Date	Mintage	Fine	VF	XF	Unc
6	1892	.055	10.00	25.00	65.00	150.00
	1892	*50-60 pcs.	—	—	Proof	700.00
	1893	.107	15.00	75.00	500.00	1100.
	1894	.173	6.00	28.00	275.00	600.00
	1895	.150	7.50	35.00	300.00	850.00

KM#	Date	Mintage	Fine	VF	XF	Unc
6	1896	.353	4.00	8.00	25.00	65.00
	1897	.148	3.00	6.00	20.00	60.00

2-1/2 SHILLINGS

14.1380 g, .925 SILVER, .4205 oz ASW

KM#	Date	Mintage	Fine	VF	XF	Unc
7	1892	.016	15.00	30.00	90.00	220.00
	1892	*50-60 pcs.	—	—	Proof	750.00
	1893	.135	20.00	60.00	400.00	900.00
	1894	.135	10.00	30.00	250.00	600.00
	1895	.182	10.00	40.00	350.00	700.00
	1896	.285	5.00	10.00	30.00	70.00
	1897	.149	5.00	10.00	30.00	70.00

5 SHILLINGS

28.2759 g, .925 SILVER, .8410 oz ASW
Single shaft wagon tongue.

KM#	Date	Mintage	Fine	VF	XF	Unc
8.1	1892	.014	50.00	100.00	200.00	600.00

Double shaft wagon tongue

KM#	Date	Mintage	Fine	VF	XF	Unc
8.2	1892	4,327	75.00	150.00	350.00	750.00
	1892	*25-30 pcs.	—	—	Proof	2750.

Beware of counterfeit double shafts. Aside from there being two shafts on the wagon in the coat of arms (reverse), the two wheels of the wagon must be the same size. On single shaft crowns, the rear wheel is noticeably larger than the front wheel.

Single shaft wagon tongue

Double shaft wagon tongue

1/2 POND

3.9940 g, .916 GOLD, .1176 oz AGW
Rev: Double shaft wagon tongue

KM#	Date	Mintage	Fine	VF	XF	Unc
9.1	1892	.010	100.00	150.00	200.00	350.00
	1892	*20-25 pcs.	—	—	Proof	6000.

Rev: Single shaft wagon tongue

KM#	Date	Mintage	Fine	VF	XF	Unc
9.2	1892	—	—	—	Unique	—
	1893	—	500.00	1000.	2000.	3000.
	1894	.039	65.00	80.00	150.00	400.00

KM#	Date	Mintage	Fine	VF	XF	Unc
9.2	1895	.135	75.00	100.00	200.00	500.00
	1896	.104	60.00	75.00	120.00	350.00
	1897	.075	60.00	75.00	120.00	350.00

EEN (1) POND

7.9880 g, .916 GOLD, .2353 oz AGW

Coarse beard

KM#	Date	Mintage	Fine	VF	XF	Unc
1.1	1874	142 pcs.	2250.	3000.	4000.	9000.

Fine beard

KM#	Date	Mintage	Fine	VF	XF	Unc
1.2	1874	695 pcs.	1500.	2000.	3000.	6500.

Rev: Double shaft wagon tongue

KM#	Date	Mintage	Fine	VF	XF	Unc
10.1	1892	.016	120.00	150.00	250.00	400.00
	1892	*12-15 pcs.	—	—	Proof	9000.

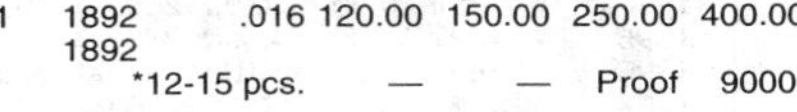

Rev: Single shaft wagon tongue

KM#	Date	Mintage	Fine	VF	XF	Unc
10.2	1892	—	300.00	500.00	1750.	4500.
	1893	.062	120.00	150.00	275.00	625.00
	1894	.318	120.00	135.00	225.00	600.00
	1895	.336	120.00	150.00	350.00	850.00
	1896	.235	120.00	135.00	225.00	600.00
	1897	.311	120.00	135.00	175.00	350.00
	1898	.137	110.00	120.00	135.00	250.00
	1898/stamped 99	130 pcs.	2500.	3000.	5000.	7500.
	1898/stamped 9	Unique	—	—	—	—
	1900	.788	120.00	135.00	160.00	275.00

PATTERNS (Pn)

(Including off metal strikes)

KM#	Date	Mintage	Identification	Mkt.Val.
Pn1	1874	—	1 Penny, Bronze, 1 PENNY	150.00
Pn2	1874	—	1 Penny, double thickness	200.00
Pn3	1874	—	1 Penny, triple thickness	400.00

KM#	Date	Mintage	Identification	Mkt.Val.
Pn4	1874	—	1 Penny, Bronze, EEN PENNY	150.00

KM#	Date	Mintage	Identification	Mkt.Val.
Pn5	1874	—	2 Pence, Bronze	150.00

KM#	Date	Mintage	Identification	Mkt.Val.
Pn6	1874	—	2-1/2 Shillings, Gilt Bronze milled edge	2500.
Pn7	1874	—	2-1/2 Shillings, Silver, milled edge	2500.
Pn8	1874	—	2-1/2 Shillings, Silver, plain edge	2500.
Pn9	1874	—	2-1/2 Shillings, Aluminum, milled edge	2000.
Pn10	1874	—	2-1/2 Shillings, Aluminum, plain edge	1500.
Pn11	1874	—	5 Shillings, Gilt Bronze, milled edge	2500.
Pn12	1874	—	5 Shillings, Gilt Bronze, plain edge	2750.
Pn13	1874	—	5 Shillings, Aluminum, milled edge	2500.

KM#	Date	Mintage	Identification	Mkt.Val.
Pn14	1874.	—	5 Shillings, Gilt Copper, milled edge	2000.
Pn15	1874.	—	5 Shillings, Gilt Copper, plain edge	2500.
Pn16	1874.	—	5 Shillings, Silver, milled edge	3500.
Pn17	1874.	—	5 Shillings, Silver, piefort, plain edge	3500.
Pn18	1874.	—	5 Shillings, Aluminum, milled edge	2000.
Pn19	1874	—	1 Pond, Bronze, short beard	1250.
Pn20	1874	—	1 Pond, Bronze, long beard	1250.

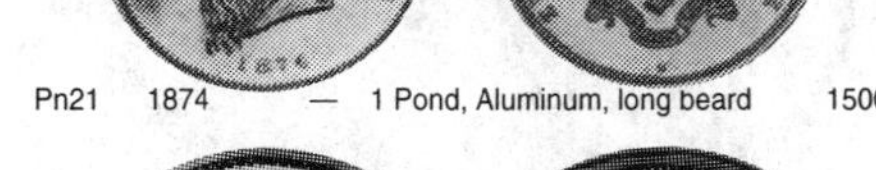

KM#	Date	Mintage	Identification	Mkt.Val.
Pn21	1874	—	1 Pond, Aluminum, long beard	1500.

KM#	Date	Mintage	Identification	Mkt.Val.
Pn22	1890	—	1 Penny, Bronze	150.00
Pn23	1898	*215	3 Pence, KM3, Gold	4000.

***NOTE:** Struck for mining magnate Sammie Marks.

SPAIN

The Spanish State, forming the greater part of the Iberian Peninsula of southwest Europe, has an area of 195,988 sq. mi. (504,714 sq. km.) and a population of 39.4 million including the Balearic and the Canary Islands. Capital: Madrid. The economy is based on agriculture, industry and tourism. Machinery, fruit, vegetables and chemicals are exported.

It isn't known when man first came to the Iberian Peninsula - the Altamira caves off the Cantabrian coast approximately 50 miles west of Santander were fashioned in Palaeolithic times. Spain was a battleground for centuries before it became a united nation, fought for by Phoenicians, Carthaginians, Greeks, Celts, Romans, Vandals, Visigoths and Moors. Ferdinand and Isabella destroyed the last Moorish stronghold in 1492, freeing the national energy and resources for the era of discovery and colonization that would make Spain the most powerful country in Europe during the 16th century. After the destruction of the Spanish Armada, 1588, Spain never again played a major role in European politics. Forcing Ferdinand to give up his throne and placing him under military guard at Valencay in 1808, Napoleonic France ruled Spain until 1814. When the monarchy was restored in 1814 it continued, only interrupted by the short-lived republic of 1873-74, until the exile of Alfonso XIII in 1931 when the Second Republic was established.

RULERS

Carlos IV, 1788-1808
Jose Napoleon, 1808-1813
Ferdinand VII, 1808-1833 (in exile until 1814)
Isabel II, 1833-1868
Carlos IV, 1833-1840 (pretender)
Provisional Government, 1868-1871
Amadeo I, 1871-1873
1st Republic, 1873-1874
Carlos VII, 1872-1875 (pretender)
Alfonso XII, 1874-1885
Regency, 1885-1886
Alfonso XIII, 1886-1931

NOTE: From 1868 to 1982, two dates may be found on most Spanish coinage. The larger date is the year of authorization and the smaller date incused on the two 6-pointed-stars found on most types is the year of issue. The latter appears in parentheses in these listings.

HOMELAND MINT MARKS

Until 1851

(b) Brussels, privy marks only
B - Burgos
B, BA - Barcelona
BGA - Berga
Bo - Bilbao
C - Catalonia

NOTE: The Catalonia Mint was located at Reus between February 1-25, 1809 and March 31, 1809 to May 20, 1810 and again from April 14 to August 15, 1810. It was then temporarily located at Tarragonia until May 9, 1811 and finally located at Palma de Mallorca from June 2, 1811 to June 20, 1814.

CA - Cuenca
G, Flower over G - Granada
J, JA - Jubia
M, MD - Madrid
P,p.P., P.L., PA - Pamplona
S, S/L - Seville
Sr - Santander
T, To, Tole - Toledo
V, VA, VAL - Valencia
Crowned C - Cadiz
Crowned M - Madrid

Aqueduct - Segovia, until 1864

1848-1980

OM - Oeschger Mesdach & Co.
3-pointed star - Segovia after 1868
4-pointed star - Jubia
6-pointed star - Madrid
7-pointed star - Seville
8-pointed star - Barcelona
Letters after date are initials of mint officials.

COLONIAL MINT MARKS

Many Spanish Colonial mints struck coins similar to regular Spanish issues until the 1820's. These issues are easily distinguished from regular Spanish issues by the following mint marks.

C, CH, Ch - Chihuahua, Mexico
D, DO, Do - Durango, Mexico
Ga - Guadalajara, Mexico
G, GG - Guatemala
G, Go - Guanajuato, Mexico
L, LIMAE, LIMA - Lima, Peru
M, MA - Manila, Philippines
M, Mo - Mexico City, Mexico
MZ - Durango, Mexico
NG - Nueva Grenada, Guatemala
NR - Nueva Reino, Colombia
PDV - Valladolid Michoacan, Mexico
P, PN, Pn - Popayan, Colombia
P, POTOSI - Potosi, Bolivia
So - Santiago, Chile
Z, Zs - Zacatecas, Mexico
5-pointed Star - Manila, Philippines

MINTMASTERS INITIALS

BARCELONA MINT

Letter	Date	Name
CC	1842-1843	
PS	1836-1841,1843-1848	Francisco Paradaltas and Simeon Sola y Roca
SM	1850	Simeon Sola y Roca and Francisco Miro
SP	1822-1823	Pablo Sala and Francisco Paradaltas

MADRID MINT

Letter	Date	Name
AF	1808	Antonio de Goycoechea
AI	1807-1808	Antonio de Goycoechea and Ildefonso de Urquiza
AI	1808-1812	Antonio Rafael Narvaez and Isidoro Ramos del Manzano
FA	1799-1808	Francisco Herrera and Antonio Goicoechea
FM	1801	Francisco Herrera and Manuel de Lamas
IA	1808	Ildefonso de Urquiza and Antonio Goycoechea
IA	1810	Isidoro Ramos del Manzano and Antonio Rafael Narvaez
IG	1808-1810	Ildefonso de Urquiza and Gregorio Lazaro Labrandero
MF	1788-1802	Manuel de Lamas and Francisco Herrera
RN	1812-1813	Antonio Rafael Narvaez
RS	1810-1812	Antonio Rafael Narvaez and Jose Sanchez Delgado

SEVILLE MINT

Letter	Date	Name
C	1790-1791,1801-1808	Carlos Tiburcio de Roxas
CJ	1815-1821	Carlos Tiburcio de Roxas and Joaquin Delgado Diaz
CN	1791-1810,1812	Carlos Tiburcio de Roxas and Nicolas Lamas
DR	1835-1838	Joaquin Delgado Diaz and Benito de Roxas
J	1823	Jose Sanchez Delgado o Joaquin Delgado
JB	1824-1833	Joaquin Delgado Diaz and Benito de Roxas
LA	1810,1812	Leonardo Carrero and Antonio de Larra
RD	1821-1823	Carlos Tiburcio de Roxas and Joaquin Delgado Diaz
RD	1835	Benito de Roxas and Joaquin Delgado Diaz
RD	1838-1852	Benito de Roxas and Vicente Delgado

VALENCIA MINT

Letter	Date	Name
GS	1811	Gregorio Lazaro Labrandero and Sixto Giber Polo
R	1821	
SG	1809-1814	Sixto Giber Polo

MONETARY SYSTEM

34 Maravedi = 1 Real (of Silver)
16 Reales = 1 Escudo

NOTE: The early coinage of Spain is listed by denomination based on a system of 16 Reales de Plata (silver) = 1 Escudo (gold). However, in the Constitutional period from 1808-1850, a concurrent system was introduced in which 20 Reales de Vellon (billon) = 8 Reales de Plata. This system does not necessarily refer to the composition of the coin itself. To avoid confusion we have listed the coins using the value as it appears on each coin, ignoring the monetary base.

KINGDOM

MARAVEDI

COPPER
Mint mark: Aqueduct
Similar to 4 Maravedis, KM#427.

KM#	Date	Mintage	VG	Fine	VF	XF
445 (C59)	1802	—	15.00	30.00	50.00	70.00

NOTE: Earlier dates (1791-1799) exist for this type.

Mint mark: J, JA
Obv: Head of Ferdinand right.
Rev: Arms in angles of cross.

KM#	Date	Mintage	VG	Fine	VF	XF
503 (C112)	1824	—	15.00	20.00	45.00	90.00

KM#	Date	Mintage	VG	Fine	VF	XF
525.1 (C167.1)	1842	—	15.00	25.00	50.00	100.00
	1843	—	75.00	150.00	300.00	425.00

Mint mark: Crowned M

KM#	Date	Mintage	VG	Fine	VF	XF
525.2 (C167.2)	1842 DG	—	100.00	200.00	300.00	400.00

Mint mark: Aqueduct

KM#	Date	Mintage	VG	Fine	VF	XF
525.3 (C167.3)	1842	—	15.00	25.00	50.00	100.00

2 MARAVEDIS

COPPER
Mint mark: Aqueduct
Similar to 4 Maravedis, KM#427.

KM#	Date	Mintage	VG	Fine	VF	XF
426 (C60)	1801	—	3.00	6.00	10.00	20.00
	1802	—	3.00	7.00	12.00	25.00
	1803	—	3.00	6.00	10.00	20.00
	1804	—	6.00	12.50	20.00	35.00
	1805	—	3.00	6.00	10.00	20.00
	1806	—	6.00	12.50	22.50	38.00
	1807	—	3.00	6.00	10.00	20.00
	1808	—	3.00	6.00	10.00	20.00

NOTE: Earlier dates (1788-1800) exist for this type.

Mint mark: J, JA

KM#	Date	Mintage	VG	Fine	VF	XF
471 (C106)	1812	—	10.00	15.00	30.00	50.00
	1813	—	5.00	11.00	20.00	35.00
	1814	—	5.00	11.00	20.00	32.00
	1815	—	5.00	11.00	20.00	32.00
	1816	—	5.00	10.00	18.00	25.00
	1817	—	5.00	11.00	20.00	38.00

Mint mark: Aqueduct

KM#	Date	Mintage	VG	Fine	VF	XF
487.1 (C116)	1816	—	4.00	8.00	12.00	25.00
	1817	—	3.00	6.00	10.00	18.00
	1818	—	3.00	6.00	10.00	18.00
	1819	—	3.00	6.00	10.00	18.00
	1820	—	3.00	6.00	10.00	18.00
	1824	—	2.00	4.00	6.00	12.00
	1825	—	2.00	4.00	6.00	12.00
	1826	—	2.00	4.00	6.00	12.00
	1827	—	2.00	4.00	6.00	12.00
	1828	—	2.00	4.00	6.00	12.00
	1829	—	2.00	4.00	6.00	12.00
	1830	—	2.00	4.00	6.00	12.00
	1831	—	2.00	4.00	6.00	12.00
	1832	—	2.00	4.00	6.00	12.00
	1833	—	2.00	4.00	6.00	12.00

Obv. leg: FERDIN. IIV. (error).

KM#	Date	Mintage	VG	Fine	VF	XF
487.2 (C116a)	1832	—	20.00	35.00	65.00	125.00

Mint mark: J, JA
Thin laureate bust

KM#	Date	Mintage	VG	Fine	VF	XF
488 (C109)	1817	—	4.00	8.00	18.00	30.00
	1818	—	4.00	7.00	15.00	28.00
	1819	—	4.00	7.00	15.00	28.00
	1820	—	4.00	7.00	15.00	28.00
	1821	—	18.00	35.00	65.00	95.00

Large bare head

KM#	Date	Mintage	VG	Fine	VF	XF
504 (C113)	1824	—	5.00	12.00	20.00	30.00
	1826	—	4.00	10.00	18.00	28.00
	1827	—	6.00	15.00	23.00	35.00

Mint mark: B, BA

KM#	Date	Mintage	VG	Fine	VF	XF
532.1 (C168.1)	1855	—	15.00	25.00	50.00	100.00
	1858	—	12.50	20.00	40.00	75.00

Mint mark: J, JA

KM#	Date	Mintage	VG	Fine	VF	XF
532.2 (C168.2)	1838	—	15.00	35.00	70.00	120.00
	1840	—	40.00	80.00	150.00	225.00
	1841	—	45.00	110.00	200.00	275.00
	1842	—	45.00	110.00	200.00	300.00
	1844	—	40.00	80.00	175.00	250.00
	1848	—	7.00	15.00	25.00	50.00
	1849	—	7.00	15.00	25.00	50.00

Mint mark: Crowned M

KM#	Date	Mintage	VG	Fine	VF	XF
532.3 (C168.3)	1837 DG	—	75.00	150.00	275.00	500.00

Mint mark: Aqueduct

KM#	Date	Mintage	VG	Fine	VF	XF
532.4 (C168.4)	1836	—	12.00	30.00	75.00	125.00
	1837	—	12.00	25.00	70.00	120.00
	1838	—	5.00	7.50	15.00	25.00
	1839	—	5.00	7.50	15.00	25.00
	1840	—	5.00	7.50	15.00	25.00
	1841	—	5.00	7.50	15.00	25.00
	1842	—	5.00	7.50	15.00	25.00
	1843	—	5.00	7.50	15.00	25.00
	1844	—	5.00	7.50	15.00	25.00
	1845	—	5.00	7.50	15.00	25.00
	1846	—	5.00	7.50	15.00	25.00
	1847	—	5.00	7.50	15.00	25.00
	1848	—	5.00	7.50	15.00	25.00
	1849	—	5.00	7.50	15.00	25.00
	1850	—	5.00	7.50	15.00	25.00

4 MARAVEDIS

COPPER
Mint mark: Aqueduct

KM#	Date	Mintage	VG	Fine	VF	XF
427 (C61)	1801	—	3.00	6.00	8.00	15.00
	1802	—	3.00	6.00	8.00	15.00
	1803	—	3.00	6.00	8.00	15.00
	1804	—	5.00	10.00	14.00	25.00
	1805	—	5.00	10.00	14.00	25.00
	1806	—	5.00	10.00	14.00	25.00
	1807	—	5.00	9.00	12.50	22.00
	1808	—	3.00	6.00	8.00	15.00

NOTE: Earlier dates (1788-1800) exist for this type.

Mint mark: J, JA
Similar to 2 Maravedis, KM#171.

KM#	Date	Mintage	VG	Fine	VF	XF
472 (C107)	1812	—	4.50	11.00	25.00	40.00
	1813	—	4.50	11.00	20.00	35.00
	1814	—	4.00	10.00	20.00	35.00
	1815	—	4.50	11.00	20.00	35.00
	1816	—	4.00	10.00	20.00	35.00
489.1 (C117.1)	1817	—	4.50	11.00	20.00	40.00
	1818	—	8.00	16.00	25.00	45.00

Mint mark: Aqueduct

KM#	Date	Mintage	VG	Fine	VF	XF
489.2 (C117.2)	1816	—	4.00	7.00	10.00	20.00
	1818	—	5.00	10.00	16.00	30.00
	1819	—	4.00	7.00	14.00	25.00
	1820	—	4.00	7.00	10.00	20.00
	1823	—	3.00	6.00	10.00	20.00
	1824	—	3.00	6.00	10.00	20.00
	1825	—	3.00	6.00	10.00	20.00
	1826	—	3.00	6.00	10.00	20.00
	1827	—	3.00	6.00	10.00	20.00
	1828	—	3.00	6.00	9.00	18.00
	1829	—	3.00	6.00	9.00	18.00
	1830	—	3.00	6.00	8.00	16.00
	1831	—	3.00	6.00	9.00	18.00
	1832	—	3.00	6.00	10.00	20.00
	1833	—	3.00	6.00	9.00	18.00

Mint mark: J, JA
Small head

Similar to 2 Maravedis, KM#171 but w/thin laureate bust.

KM#	Date	Mintage	VG	Fine	VF	XF
490.1 (C110.1)	1817	—	5.00	9.00	14.00	25.00
	1818	—	5.00	9.00	17.50	27.50
	1819	—	5.00	10.00	18.00	28.00
	1820	—	5.00	9.00	14.00	30.00

Mint mark: Aqueduct

KM#	Date	Mintage	VG	Fine	VF	XF
490.2 (C110.2)	1817	—	5.00	9.00	14.00	30.00

Mint mark: J, JA
Large head

KM#	Date	Mintage	VG	Fine	VF	XF
505 (C114)	1824	—	4.00	8.00	12.00	25.00
	1825	—	6.00	12.00	30.00	55.00
	1826	—	4.00	8.00	12.00	22.00
	1827	—	5.00	10.00	14.00	20.00
511.1 (C161.1)	1835	—	10.00	17.50	30.00	65.00
	1836	—	7.50	12.50	25.00	50.00

Mint mark: Crowned M

KM#	Date	Mintage	VG	Fine	VF	XF
511.2 (C161.2)	1836 DG	—	125.00	225.00	375.00	500.00

Mint mark: Aqueduct

KM#	Date	Mintage	VG	Fine	VF	XF
511.3 (C161.3)	1835	—	12.50	25.00	50.00	80.00
	1836	—	7.50	15.00	35.00	60.00

Mint mark: B, BA

KM#	Date	Mintage	VG	Fine	VF	XF
530.1 (C169.1)	1853	—	50.00	100.00	200.00	275.00
	1855	—	10.00	15.00	25.00	65.00

Mint mark: J, JA

KM#	Date	Mintage	VG	Fine	VF	XF
530.2 (C169.2)	1837	—	7.00	14.00	30.00	50.00
	1840	—	30.00	50.00	125.00	190.00
	1841	—	7.00	14.00	40.00	60.00
	1842	—	7.00	14.00	65.00	100.00
	1843	—	7.00	14.00	60.00	90.00
	1844	—	7.00	14.00	75.00	140.00
	1845	—	7.00	13.00	25.00	40.00
	1846	—	7.00	14.00	60.00	90.00
	1847	—	5.00	10.00	18.00	30.00
	1848	—	7.00	13.00	25.00	40.00
	1849	—	7.00	14.00	35.00	55.00
	1850	—	5.00	10.00	15.00	28.00

Mint mark: Aqueduct

KM#	Date	Mintage	VG	Fine	VF	XF
530.3 (C169.3)	1837	—	5.00	9.00	20.00	35.00
	1838	—	5.00	9.00	20.00	35.00
	1839	—	10.00	20.00	35.00	55.00
	1840	—	5.00	9.00	25.00	40.00
	1841	—	5.00	9.00	18.00	32.00
	1842	—	5.00	9.00	15.00	28.00
	1843	—	8.00	15.00	35.00	55.00
	1844	—	5.00	9.00	18.00	32.00
	1845	—	5.00	9.00	18.00	32.00
	1846	—	5.00	9.00	18.00	35.00
	1847	—	5.00	9.00	18.00	32.00
	1848	—	5.00	9.00	20.00	35.00
	1849	—	4.00	8.00	20.00	35.00
	1850	—	8.00	15.00	35.00	55.00

8 MARAVEDIS

COPPER
Mint mark: Aqueduct

KM#	Date	Mintage	VG	Fine	VF	XF
428 (C62)	1801	—	4.00	8.00	12.00	20.00
	1802	—	4.00	8.00	12.00	20.00
	1803	—	4.00	8.00	12.00	20.00
	1804	—	5.00	9.00	14.00	25.00
	1805	—	4.00	8.00	12.00	20.00
	1806	—	5.00	9.00	14.00	25.00
	1807	—	4.00	8.00	12.00	20.00
	1808	—	3.00	7.00	9.00	16.00

NOTE: Earlier dates (1788-1800) exist for this type.

KM#	Date	Mintage	VG	Fine	VF	XF
450 (C82)	1809	—	25.00	50.00	75.00	110.00
	1810	—	20.00	40.00	65.00	90.00
	1811	—	14.00	28.00	45.00	60.00
	1812	—	10.00	20.00	35.00	50.00
	1813	—	16.00	32.50	50.00	70.00

Mint mark: J, JA

KM#	Date	Mintage	VG	Fine	VF	XF
461 (C108)	1811	—	20.00	40.00	85.00	140.00
	1812	—	15.00	35.00	65.00	100.00
	1813	—	7.00	14.00	30.00	50.00
	1814	—	7.00	14.00	30.00	50.00
	1815	—	7.00	14.00	30.00	50.00
	1816	—	5.00	10.00	25.00	45.00
	1817	—	6.00	12.00	20.00	40.00

Mint mark: Aqueduct

KM#	Date	Mintage	VG	Fine	VF	XF
486.1 (C118)	1815	—	9.00	18.00	30.00	50.00
	1816	—	5.00	10.00	25.00	40.00
	1817	—	5.00	10.00	20.00	35.00
	1818	—	5.00	10.00	20.00	35.00
	1819	—	6.00	12.00	12.50	25.00
	1820	—	5.00	10.00	20.00	30.00
	1821	—	10.00	25.00	40.00	60.00
	1822	—	9.00	18.00	40.00	60.00
	1823	—	5.00	10.00	20.00	30.00
	1824	—	5.00	9.00	15.00	22.00
	1825	—	5.00	9.00	15.00	22.00
	1826	—	5.00	9.00	15.00	22.00
	1827	—	5.00	10.00	17.00	25.00
	1828	—	8.00	15.00	25.00	40.00
	1829	—	4.00	7.00	10.00	18.00
	1830	—	5.00	10.00	12.00	20.00
	1831	—	4.00	7.00	9.00	15.00
	1832	—	4.00	7.00	9.00	15.00
	1833	—	4.00	7.00	9.00	15.00

Mint mark: P, P.P., P.L., PA
Obv: Bust, leg: FERDIN.VII.D.G. HISP.REX.

KM#	Date	Mintage	VG	Fine	VF	XF
486.2 (C118a)	1823	—	12.00	25.00	45.00	65.00

Mint mark: J, JA

KM#	Date	Mintage	VG	Fine	VF	XF
491 (C111)	1817	—	4.00	8.00	10.00	25.00
	1818	—	4.00	7.00	10.00	20.00
	1819	—	4.00	7.00	10.00	20.00
	1820	—	4.00	7.00	10.00	20.00
	1821	—	3.00	6.00	10.00	20.00

Obv: Bust, leg: FERN 7o POR LA. . .

KM#	Date	Mintage	VG	Fine	VF	XF
500 (C115)	1822	—	6.00	12.00	20.00	35.00
	1823	—	5.00	10.00	17.50	32.00

Obv: Value omitted.

KM#	Date	Mintage	VG	Fine	VF	XF
501 (C115a)	1823	—	6.00	12.00	20.00	35.00

Obv: Bust, leg: FERDIN.VII D.G.HISP.REX.

KM#	Date	Mintage	VG	Fine	VF	XF
502.1 (C114.5)	1823	—	6.00	11.00	18.00	32.00
	1824	—	6.00	11.00	18.00	28.00
	1825	—	6.00	11.00	18.00	28.00
	1826	—	5.00	9.00	15.00	25.00
	1827	—	5.00	9.00	16.00	27.00

Mint mark: Aqueduct

KM#	Date	Mintage	VG	Fine	VF	XF
502.2 (C114.7)	1823	—	5.00	9.00	15.00	25.00

Mint mark: J, JA

KM#	Date	Mintage	VG	Fine	VF	XF
512.1 (C162.1)	1835	—	10.00	17.50	35.00	60.00
	1836	—	10.00	20.00	45.00	75.00

Mint mark: Crowned M

KM#	Date	Mintage	VG	Fine	VF	XF
512.2 (C162.2)	1835 DG	—	125.00	225.00	300.00	400.00

Mint mark: Aqueduct

KM#	Date	Mintage	VG	Fine	VF	XF
512.3 (C162.3)	1835	—	4.00	10.00	20.00	35.00
	1836	—	3.00	8.00	16.00	30.00

Charles V - Pretender Issue

KM#	Date	Mintage	VG	Fine	VF	XF
516 (C154)	1837	—	175.00	300.00	475.00	600.00

CAST BELL METAL
Mint mark: P, P.P., P.L., PA

C#	Date	Mintage	Good	VG	Fine	VF
517.1 (C170a.1)	1837	—	50.00	75.00	100.00	175.00

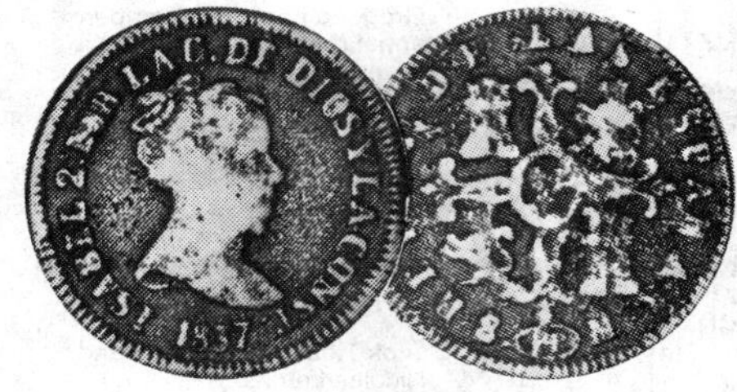

Mint mark within oval

C#	Date	Mintage	Good	VG	Fine	VF
517.2 (C170a.2)	1837	—	50.00	75.00	100.00	175.00

COPPER
Mint mark: B, BA

KM#	Date	Mintage	VG	Fine	VF	XF
531.1 (C170.1)	1853	—	35.00	60.00	100.00	235.00
	1854	*	—	—	—	—
	1855	—	50.00	80.00	150.00	275.00
	1858	—	30.00	50.00	90.00	220.00

***NOTE:** Only counterfeits seen.

Mint mark: J, JA

KM#	Date	Mintage	VG	Fine	VF	XF
531.2 (C170.2)	1837	—	5.00	10.00	22.00	35.00
	1838	—	6.00	12.00	25.00	40.00
	1839	—	10.00	25.00	55.00	80.00

KM#	Date	Mintage	VG	Fine	VF	XF
531.2	1840	—	12.00	20.00	32.50	55.00
	1841	—	6.00	12.00	20.00	35.00
	1842	—	5.00	10.00	18.00	28.00
	1843	—	5.00	10.00	18.00	28.00
	1844	—	5.00	12.00	20.00	35.00
	1845	—	5.00	10.00	15.00	25.00
	1846	—	5.00	10.00	18.00	28.00
	1847	—	5.00	10.00	18.00	28.00
	1848	—	5.00	10.00	15.00	25.00
	1849	—	10.00	15.00	20.00	35.00
	1850	—	5.00	10.00	18.00	28.00

Mint mark: Aqueduct

KM#	Date	Mintage	VG	Fine	VF	XF
531.3 (C170.3)	1837	—	5.00	10.00	20.00	40.00
	1838	—	5.00	10.00	20.00	35.00
	1839	—	5.00	9.00	17.00	28.00
	1840	—	5.00	9.00	20.00	35.00
	1841	—	5.00	9.00	17.00	28.00
	1842	—	5.00	9.00	17.00	28.00
	1843	—	5.00	9.00	17.00	28.00
	1844	—	4.00	8.00	13.00	25.00
	1845	—	4.00	8.00	15.00	28.00
	1846	—	5.00	9.00	17.00	28.00
	1847	—	5.00	11.00	17.50	28.00
	1848	—	6.00	12.50	18.50	30.00
	1849	—	5.00	10.00	12.50	28.00
	1850	—	7.00	15.00	30.00	50.00

1/2 REAL

1.6900 g, .903 SILVER, .0490 oz ASW
Mint mark: Crowned M
Obv: Bust of Charles IV right.
Rev: Crowned arms.

KM#	Date	Mintage	VG	Fine	VF	XF
438.1 (C66.1)	1802 FA	—	8.00	15.00	27.50	35.00
	1803 FA	—	5.00	10.00	18.50	30.00
	1804 FA	—	7.00	13.00	22.50	30.00
	1808 AI	—	7.00	14.00	25.00	35.00
	1808 FA	—	8.00	16.00	27.50	40.00

NOTE: Earlier dates (1789-1800) exist for this type.

Mint mark: S, S/L

KM#	Date	Mintage	VG	Fine	VF	XF
438.2 (C66.2)	1802 CN	—	8.00	16.00	32.50	40.00
	1805 CN	—	8.00	16.00	32.50	40.00
	1807 CN	—	7.00	13.00	25.00	30.00

NOTE: Earlier dates (1793-1800) exist for this type.

Mint mark: Crowned C
Obv: Laureate bust right. Rev: Crowned arms.

KM#	Date	Mintage	VG	Fine	VF	XF
482.1 (C132.1)	1814 CI	—	5.00	10.00	22.50	35.00
	1814 CJ	—	5.00	10.00	25.00	40.00

Mint mark: Crowned M

KM#	Date	Mintage	VG	Fine	VF	XF
482.2 (C132.2)	1815 GJ	—	6.00	12.50	27.50	40.00
	1816 GJ	—	6.00	12.00	18.00	30.00
	1817 GJ	—	6.00	12.00	18.00	35.00
	1818 GJ	—	6.00	12.00	16.00	30.00
	1819 GJ	—	6.00	12.00	18.00	35.00
	1820 GJ	—	6.00	12.50	18.00	30.00
	1824 AJ	—	8.00	15.00	25.00	35.00
	1826 AJ	—	6.00	12.50	25.00	30.00
	1828 AJ	—	8.00	15.00	25.00	30.00
	1830 AJ	—	6.00	12.00	17.50	35.00
	1831 AJ	—	9.00	17.50	25.00	35.00
	1832 AJ	—	6.00	12.00	20.00	30.00
	1833 AJ	—	6.00	12.00	25.00	35.00
	1833 JI	—	11.00	22.00	40.00	65.00

Mint mark: S, S/L

KM#	Date	Mintage	VG	Fine	VF	XF
482.3 (C132.3)	1825 JB	—	4.00	7.00	15.00	25.00
	1831 JB	—	4.00	7.00	15.00	25.00
	1832 JB	—	6.00	12.00	20.00	35.00
	1833 JB	—	7.00	13.00	20.00	35.00

Mint mark: C
Obv: Small draped bust.

KM#	Date	Mintage	VG	Fine	VF	XF
473.1 (C132a.1)	1812 SF	—	15.00	30.00	50.00	70.00
	1813 SF	—	15.00	30.00	50.00	70.00
	1814 SF	—	20.00	35.00	55.00	75.00

Mint mark: Crowned M

KM#	Date	Mintage	VG	Fine	VF	XF
473.2 (C132a.2)	1813 IJ	—	9.00	18.00	30.00	45.00
	1813 GJ	—	7.50	15.00	25.00	35.00
	1814 GJ	—	10.00	20.00	35.00	50.00

REAL

3.3800 g, .917 SILVER, .0995 oz ASW
Mint mark: Crowned M
Obv: Bust of Charles IV right.
Rev: Crowned arms.

KM#	Date	Mintage	VG	Fine	VF	XF
429.1 (C68.1)	1801 FA	—	5.00	10.00	16.00	25.00
	1802 FA	—	5.00	10.00	20.00	35.00
	1803 FA	—	6.00	12.00	18.00	25.00
	1805 FA	—	6.00	12.00	19.00	30.00
	1807 FA	—	6.00	12.00	18.00	25.00
	1807 AI	—	7.00	14.00	20.00	40.00
	1808 AI	—	7.00	14.00	19.00	30.00

NOTE: Earlier dates (1788-1800) exist for this type.

Mint mark: S, S/L

KM#	Date	Mintage	VG	Fine	VF	XF
429.2 (C68.2)	1802 CN	—	10.00	20.00	45.00	65.00
	1807 CN	—	9.00	18.00	35.00	50.00

NOTE: Earlier dates (1793-1800) exist for this type.

Mint mark: C
Obv: Large laureate bust.
Rev: Crowned arms.

KM#	Date	Mintage	VG	Fine	VF	XF
462.1	1811 SF	—	12.50	22.50	40.00	55.00

Mint mark: Crowned C

KM#	Date	Mintage	VG	Fine	VF	XF
462.2	1813 CJ	—	10.00	20.00	30.00	45.00

Mint mark: Crowned M

KM#	Date	Mintage	VG	Fine	VF	XF
462.3 (C133.3)	1815 GJ	—	8.00	16.50	32.50	50.00
	1816 GJ	—	8.00	16.50	30.00	50.00
	1817 GJ	—	8.00	16.50	25.00	45.00
	1819 GJ	—	10.00	20.00	27.50	45.00
	1820 GJ	—	9.00	18.50	25.00	55.00
	1824 AJ	—	15.00	30.00	55.00	80.00
	1826 AJ	—	10.00	20.00	40.00	60.00
	1828 AJ	—	10.00	20.00	40.00	60.00
	1830 AJ	—	7.00	15.00	22.00	35.00
	1831 AJ	—	8.00	17.00	30.00	45.00
	1832 AJ	—	7.00	15.00	20.00	40.00
	1833 AJ	—	10.00	20.00	30.00	50.00
	1833 JI	—	11.00	22.50	38.50	60.00
	1833 JJ	—	9.00	18.00	30.00	40.00

Mint mark: S, S/L

KM#	Date	Mintage	VG	Fine	VF	XF
462.4 (C133.4)	1830 JB	—	10.00	19.00	32.00	50.00
	1831 JB	—	6.00	12.00	25.00	35.00
	1832 JB	—	7.00	14.00	25.00	35.00
	1833 JB	—	7.00	14.00	20.00	30.00

Mint mark: C
Obv: Small draped bust.

KM#	Date	Mintage	VG	Fine	VF	XF
463.1 (C133a.1)	1811 SF	—	13.50	25.00	45.00	65.00
	1814 SF	—	22.50	40.00	80.00	130.00

Mint mark: Crowned M

KM#	Date	Mintage	VG	Fine	VF	XF
463.2 (C133a.2)	1813 IJ	—	22.50	40.00	60.00	85.00
	1814 IJ	—	15.00	30.00	45.00	75.00
	1814 GJ	—	9.00	18.50	30.00	50.00

KM#	Date	Mintage	VG	Fine	VF	XF
518.1 (C171.1)	1837 CL	—	30.00	60.00	110.00	150.00
	1838 CL	—	9.00	18.00	22.00	30.00
	1838 DG	—	50.00	90.00	170.00	230.00
	1839 CL	—	8.00	16.50	35.00	65.00
	1840 CL	—	15.00	30.00	60.00	115.00
	1841 CL	—	30.00	60.00	115.00	225.00
	1842 CL	—	35.00	70.00	140.00	180.00
	1843 CL	—	16.00	32.50	60.00	115.00
	1844 CL	—	7.00	15.00	30.00	60.00
	1845 CL	—	4.00	8.00	15.00	25.00
	1847 CL	—	4.00	8.00	15.00	25.00
	1848 CL	—	4.00	8.00	15.00	25.00
	1849 CL	—	4.00	8.00	15.00	25.00

Mint mark: S, S/L

KM#	Date	Mintage	VG	Fine	VF	XF
518.2 (C171.2)	1840 RD	—	20.00	45.00	100.00	130.00
	1844 RD	—	10.00	20.00	45.00	70.00
	1845 RD	—	15.00	30.00	70.00	100.00
	1850 RD	—	7.00	14.00	25.00	40.00
	1851 RD	—	7.00	14.00	25.00	40.00
	1852 RD	—	6.00	12.00	20.00	30.00

2 REALES

6.7700 g, .903 SILVER, .1965 oz ASW
Mint mark: Crowned M
Obv: Bust of Charles IV right.

KM#	Date	Mintage	VG	Fine	VF	XF
430.1 (C69.1)	1801 FA	—	7.00	15.00	22.00	35.00
	1802 FA	—	7.00	15.00	22.00	35.00
	1803 FA	—	7.00	15.00	22.00	35.00
	1804 FA	—	7.00	15.00	22.00	35.00
	1805 FA	—	7.00	15.00	22.00	35.00
	1806 FA	—	7.00	15.00	22.00	35.00
	1807 FA	—	7.00	15.00	22.00	35.00
	1807 AI	—	8.00	17.00	30.00	50.00
	1808 FA	—	7.00	15.00	22.00	35.00
	1808 IG	—	8.00	17.00	30.00	50.00
	1808 AI	—	7.00	15.00	25.00	40.00

NOTE: Earlier dates (1788-1800) exist for this type.

Mint mark: S, S/L

KM#	Date	Mintage	VG	Fine	VF	XF
430.2 (C69.2)	1801 CN	—	8.00	16.00	25.00	40.00
	1802 CN	—	8.00	16.00	25.00	40.00
	1803 CN	—	8.00	16.00	25.00	40.00
	1804 CN	—	8.00	16.00	25.00	40.00
	1805 CN	—	8.00	16.00	25.00	40.00
	1806 CN	—	8.00	16.00	25.00	40.00
	1807 CN	—	8.00	16.00	25.00	40.00
	1808 CN	—	8.00	16.00	25.00	40.00

NOTE: Earlier dates (1793-1800) exist for this type.

Mint mark: C

KM#	Date	Mintage	VG	Fine	VF	XF
464 (C134.1)	1811 SF	—	8.00	17.00	30.00	50.00
	1812 SF	—	40.00	70.00	125.00	175.00
	1813 SF	—	8.00	17.00	30.00	50.00
	1814 SF	—	14.00	27.50	35.00	55.00

Mint mark: Crowned C

KM#	Date	Mintage	VG	Fine	VF	XF
460.1 (C134.2)	1810 CI	—	9.00	18.00	25.00	40.00
	1810 CI w/small crowned C	—	11.00	21.00	35.00	60.00
	1811 CI	—	9.00	18.00	25.00	40.00
	1812 CI	—	9.00	18.00	25.00	40.00

Mint mark: Crowned M

KM#	Date	Mintage	VG	Fine	VF	XF
460.2 (C134.3)	1814 GJ	—	8.00	16.00	23.00	35.00
	1815 GJ	—	8.00	16.00	23.00	35.00
	1816 GJ	—	8.00	16.00	25.00	40.00
	1817 GJ	—	8.00	16.00	23.00	35.00
	1818 GJ	—	9.00	19.00	25.00	40.00
	1819 GJ	—	9.00	19.00	25.00	45.00
	1820 GJ	—	8.00	16.00	23.00	35.00
	1821 AJ	—	7.00	15.00	30.00	50.00
	1822 AJ	—	16.00	32.50	40.00	65.00
	1823 AJ	—	8.00	16.00	25.00	40.00
	1824 AJ	—	8.00	16.00	25.00	40.00
	1825 AJ	—	8.00	16.00	25.00	40.00
	1826 AJ	—	8.00	16.00	23.00	35.00
	1827 AJ	—	8.00	16.00	25.00	40.00
	1828 AJ	—	8.00	16.00	23.00	35.00
	1829 AJ	—	8.00	16.00	23.00	35.00
	1830 AJ	—	8.00	16.00	23.00	30.00
	1831 AJ	—	8.00	16.00	25.00	40.00
	1832 AJ	—	8.00	16.00	23.00	35.00
	1833 AJ	—	9.00	18.00	25.00	40.00

Mint mark: S, S/L

KM#	Date	Mintage	VG	Fine	VF	XF
460.3 (C134.4)	1815 CJ	—	10.00	20.00	30.00	50.00
	1820 CJ	—	8.00	16.00	25.00	40.00
	1821 CJ	—	7.00	14.00	20.00	30.00
	1823 CJ	—	8.00	16.00	25.00	40.00
	1824 J	—	15.00	30.00	40.00	65.00
	1824 JB	—	8.00	16.00	25.00	40.00
	1825 JB	—	8.00	16.00	25.00	40.00
	1826 JB	—	8.00	16.00	25.00	40.00
	1827 JB	—	8.00	16.00	25.00	40.00
	1828 JB	—	8.00	16.00	25.00	40.00
	1829 JB	—	8.00	16.00	25.00	40.00
	1830 JB	—	8.00	16.00	25.00	40.00
	1831 JB	—	8.00	16.00	25.00	40.00
	1832 JB	—	8.00	16.00	25.00	45.00
	1833 JB	—	9.00	18.00	27.00	50.00

Mint mark: B, BA
Obv: Bare head of Ferdinand right.
Rev: Crowned arms.

KM#	Date	Mintage	VG	Fine	VF	XF
474.1 (C134a.1)	1812 SF	—	80.00	150.00	275.00	400.00

Mint mark: C

KM#	Date	Mintage	VG	Fine	VF	XF
474.2	1810 FS	—	14.00	27.50	45.00	60.00

KM#	Date	Mintage	VG	Fine	VF	XF
(C134a.2)						
	1810 SF	—	30.00	55.00	80.00	140.00
	1811 SF	—	11.00	22.50	35.00	50.00
	1811 FS	—	15.00	30.00	45.00	60.00

Mint mark: Crowned M

KM#	Date	Mintage	VG	Fine	VF	XF
474.3	1812 IJ	—	9.00	17.50	25.00	40.00
(C134a.3)						
	1813 IJ	—	7.00	15.00	20.00	30.00
	1813 IG	—	12.00	25.00	40.00	60.00
	1813 GJ	—	7.00	15.00	20.00	30.00
	1814 GJ	—	12.00	25.00	40.00	60.00

Mint mark: V, VAL

KM#	Date	Mintage	VG	Fine	VF	XF
474.4	1811 GS	—	70.00	140.00	200.00	250.00
(C134a.4)						
	1812 GS	—	65.00	125.00	160.00	200.00

Mint mark: Crowned M
Obv: Young head of Isabella right.
Rev: Crowned arms in collar of The Golden Fleece.

KM#	Date	Mintage	VG	Fine	VF	XF
513.1	1836 CR	—	20.00	40.00	80.00	110.00
(C163.1)						
	1836 DG	—	55.00	110.00	225.00	300.00
	1837 CR	—	60.00	125.00	250.00	350.00
	1838 CR	—	60.00	115.00	230.00	300.00
	1839 CL	—	45.00	90.00	200.00	300.00
	1841 CL	—	15.00	30.00	45.00	75.00
	1842 CL	—	45.00	90.00	200.00	325.00
	1843 CL	—	17.50	35.00	75.00	110.00

Mint mark: S, S/L

KM#	Date	Mintage	VG	Fine	VF	XF
513.2	1836 DR	—	20.00	40.00	95.00	150.00
(C163.2)						
	1839 RD	—	17.00	35.00	60.00	100.00
	1840 RD	—	22.00	45.00	90.00	140.00

Charles V - Pretender Issue

KM#	Date	Mintage	VG	Fine	VF	XF
515	1838	—	225.00	375.00	450.00	600.00
(C156)						

Mint mark: Crowned M

KM#	Date	Mintage	VG	Fine	VF	XF
526.1	1844 CL	—	11.00	22.50	35.00	60.00
(C172.1)						
	1845 CL	—	11.00	22.50	35.00	50.00
	1847 CL	—	10.00	20.00	30.00	45.00
	1848 CL	—	11.00	22.50	35.00	55.00
	1849 CL	—	10.00	20.00	30.00	40.00

Mint mark: S, S/L

KM#	Date	Mintage	VG	Fine	VF	XF
526.2	1845 RD	—	22.00	45.00	100.00	165.00
(C172.2)						
	1848 RD	—	17.00	35.00	65.00	80.00
	1850/45 RD	—	30.00	60.00	100.00	150.00
	1850 RD	—	20.00	40.00	70.00	100.00
	1851 RD	—	10.00	20.00	30.00	40.00

4 REALES

13.5400 g, .917 SILVER, .3931 oz ASW
Mint mark: Crowned M
Similar to 2 Reales, KM#430.2.

KM#	Date	Mintage	VG	Fine	VF	XF
431.1	1804 FA	—	20.00	30.00	55.00	85.00
(C70.1)						
	1805 FA	—	20.00	30.00	55.00	80.00
	1806 FA	—	25.00	40.00	80.00	140.00
	1808 AI	—	30.00	50.00	70.00	120.00
	1808 FA	—	30.00	50.00	70.00	120.00

NOTE: Earlier dates (1788-1797) exist for this type.

Mint mark: S, S/L

KM#	Date	Mintage	VG	Fine	VF	XF
431.2	1803 CN	—	20.00	40.00	60.00	90.00
(C70.2)	1807 CN	—	22.00	45.00	65.00	110.00

Mint mark: C

KM#	Date	Mintage	VG	Fine	VF	XF
453.1	1809 MP	—	65.00	125.00	225.00	600.00
(C135a.1)						
	1809 SF	—	75.00	150.00	250.00	650.00
	1810 SF	—	100.00	200.00	325.00	775.00
	1814 SF	—	175.00	325.00	525.00	900.00

Mint mark: V, VAL.

KM#	Date	Mintage	VG	Fine	VF	XF
453.2	1809 SG	—	90.00	175.00	240.00	320.00
(C135a.2)						
	1810 SG	—	35.00	65.00	115.00	165.00
	1811 SG	—	40.00	70.00	135.00	185.00

Mint mark: C
Obv: Armored bust.

KM#	Date	Mintage	VG	Fine	VF	XF
465	1811 SF	—	60.00	150.00	300.00	450.00
(C135c)						

Obv: Laureate bust.

KM#	Date	Mintage	VG	Fine	VF	XF
475	1812 SF	—	100.00	225.00	450.00	650.00
(C135.1)	1813 SF	—	275.00	550.00	800.00	1000.

Mint mark: Crowned C

KM#	Date	Mintage	VG	Fine	VF	XF
476.1	1812 CJ	—	25.00	45.00	70.00	120.00
(C135.2)						
	1812 CI	—	35.00	65.00	100.00	160.00

Mint mark: Crowned M

KM#	Date	Mintage	VG	Fine	VF	XF
476.2	1814 GJ	—	90.00	175.00	300.00	400.00
(C135.3)						
	1815 GJ	—	12.00	25.00	40.00	65.00
	1816 GJ	—	20.00	40.00	65.00	110.00
	1817 GJ	—	18.00	35.00	60.00	90.00
	1818 GJ	—	18.00	35.00	60.00	100.00
	1819 GJ	—	70.00	125.00	200.00	300.00
	1822 SR	—	30.00	55.00	90.00	160.00
	1824 AJ	—	16.00	32.50	40.00	70.00
	1830 AJ	—	15.00	30.00	40.00	70.00

Mint mark: S, S/L

KM#	Date	Mintage	VG	Fine	VF	XF
476.3	1818 CJ	—	20.00	40.00	65.00	110.00
(C135.4)						
	1818 J	—	25.00	45.00	85.00	145.00
	1819 CJ	—	20.00	40.00	55.00	85.00
	1820 CJ	—	20.00	40.00	60.00	90.00
	1824 J	—	20.00	40.00	90.00	155.00
	1824 JB	—	20.00	40.00	45.00	70.00
	1825 JB	—	15.00	30.00	50.00	80.00
	1826 JB	—	20.00	35.00	55.00	90.00
	1828 JB	—	20.00	40.00	75.00	125.00
	1830 JB	—	15.00	30.00	50.00	80.00
	1832 JB	—	15.00	30.00	45.00	70.00
	1833 JB	—	20.00	35.00	55.00	90.00

Mint mark: Crowned M
Obv. leg: FERDINANDUS

KM#	Date	Mintage	VG	Fine	VF	XF
479	1813 IJ	—	75.00	150.00	300.00	450.00
(C135b)						
	1813 GJ	—	90.00	175.00	350.00	550.00
	1814 GJ	—	90.00	175.00	350.00	550.00

Obv. leg: GRACIA DE DIOS.

KM#	Date	Mintage	VG	Fine	VF	XF
510.1	1834 CR	—	60.00	125.00	210.00	350.00
(C164.1)						
	1834 DG	—	110.00	300.00	550.00	900.00
	1835 CR	—	20.00	35.00	70.00	110.00
	1836 CR	—	20.00	40.00	80.00	135.00

Mint mark: S, S/L

KM#	Date	Mintage	VG	Fine	VF	XF
510.2	1835 DR	—	20.00	35.00	70.00	110.00
(C164.2)						
	1836 DR	—	20.00	35.00	70.00	110.00

Obv. leg: GRACIA DE DIOS Y CONSTITUCION.
Mint mark: B, BA

KM#	Date	Mintage	VG	Fine	VF	XF
514	1836 PS	—	35.00	65.00	155.00	225.00
(C173a)						
	1837 PS	—	35.00	70.00	130.00	175.00
	1837 RS	—	20.00	40.00	85.00	125.00

KM#	Date	Mintage	VG	Fine	VF	XF
519.1	1837 PJ	—	15.00	25.00	50.00	70.00
(C173.1)						
	1838 PS	—	25.00	50.00	80.00	110.00
	1839 PS	—	80.00	175.00	375.00	525.00
	1840 PS	—	25.00	50.00	85.00	120.00
	1841 PS	—	15.00	25.00	45.00	65.00
	1842 CC	—	20.00	40.00	60.00	85.00
	1843 CC	—	75.00	150.00	350.00	425.00
	1843 PS	—	75.00	150.00	350.00	450.00
	1844 PS	—	20.00	40.00	70.00	100.00
	1845 PS	—	35.00	70.00	135.00	200.00
	1846 PS	—	80.00	175.00	300.00	450.00
	1847 PS	—	35.00	70.00	120.00	175.00

Mint mark: Crowned M

KM#	Date	Mintage	VG	Fine	VF	XF
519.2	1837 CR	—	25.00	45.00	65.00	90.00
(C173.2)						
	1838 CL	—	45.00	90.00	150.00	225.00
	1839 CL	—	25.00	60.00	100.00	150.00
	1840 CL	—	20.00	35.00	70.00	100.00
	1841 CL	—	20.00	35.00	70.00	100.00
	1842 CL	—	40.00	80.00	140.00	250.00
	1843 CL	—	40.00	80.00	140.00	200.00
	1844 CL	—	45.00	90.00	175.00	275.00
	1845 CL	—	40.00	80.00	160.00	250.00
	1846 CL	—	35.00	65.00	110.00	175.00
	1847 CL	—	25.00	65.00	110.00	175.00
	1848 CL	—	15.00	25.00	35.00	50.00
	1848 DG	—	125.00	200.00	475.00	750.00
	1849 CL	—	15.00	25.00	35.00	50.00

Mint mark: S, S/L

KM#	Date	Mintage	VG	Fine	VF	XF
519.3 (C173.3)	1837 DR	—	20.00	40.00	70.00	100.00
	1838 DR	—	25.00	50.00	100.00	200.00
	1838 RD	—	25.00	45.00	85.00	160.00
	1839 DR	—	35.00	70.00	180.00	300.00
	1839 RD	—	35.00	70.00	140.00	250.00
	1840 RD	—	50.00	100.00	210.00	400.00
	1841 RD	—	20.00	40.00	75.00	150.00
	1842 RD	—	20.00	40.00	70.00	150.00
	1843 RD	—	15.00	30.00	50.00	80.00
	1844 RD	—	40.00	80.00	185.00	375.00
	1845 RD	—	40.00	80.00	160.00	350.00

8 REALES

27.0700 g, .903 SILVER, .7859 oz ASW
Mint mark: Crowned M
Similar to 2 Reales, C#69.2.

KM#	Date	Mintage	VG	Fine	VF	XF
432.1	1802 MF	—	200.00	375.00	500.00	700.00
(C71.1)	1802 FA	—	100.00	185.00	265.00	400.00
	1803 FA	—	150.00	300.00	450.00	550.00
	1805 FA	—	100.00	185.00	250.00	350.00
	1808 FA	—	150.00	300.00	500.00	600.00
	1808 AI	—	140.00	280.00	425.00	650.00
	1808 IG	—	200.00	375.00	475.00	750.00

NOTE: Earlier dates (1788-1797) exist for this type.

Mint mark: S, S/L

KM#	Date	Mintage	VG	Fine	VF	XF
432.2	1802 CN	—	120.00	240.00	365.00	500.00
(C71.2)	1803 CN	—	150.00	300.00	500.00	650.00

NOTE: Earlier dates (1788-1800) exist for this type.

Mint mark: Crowned M

KM#	Date	Mintage	VG	Fine	VF	XF
454	1809 IG	—	40.00	80.00	200.00	350.00
(C93)	1810 JG	—	550.00	1100.	2500.	3250.

Mint mark: S, S/L

KM#	Date	Mintage	VG	Fine	VF	XF
451 (C136b)	1808 CN	—	50.00	100.00	185.00	275.00
	1809 CN	—	50.00	100.00	185.00	275.00

Mint mark: Crowned M

KM#	Date	Mintage	VG	Fine	VF	XF
477 (C136c)	1812 IJ	—	200.00	425.00	600.00	800.00
	1813 IJ	—	175.00	375.00	550.00	750.00
	1813 IG	—	200.00	425.00	600.00	800.00
	1813 GJ	—	225.00	475.00	700.00	900.00

Mint mark: C

KM#	Date	Mintage	VG	Fine	VF	XF
455.1 (C136a.1)	1809 MP	—	400.00	750.00	1150.	1500.
	1809 SF	—	350.00	700.00	1000.	1350.
	1810 SF	—	375.00	725.00	1150.	1500.

Mint mark: V, VAL

KM#	Date	Mintage	VG	Fine	VF	XF
455.2 (C136a.2)	1811 GS	—	300.00	700.00	1100.	1500.
	1811 SG	—	250.00	600.00	1000.	1200.

Mint mark: C

KM#	Date	Mintage	VG	Fine	VF	XF
466.1 (C136.1)	1811 SF	—	625.00	1250.	—	—
	1812 SF	—	475.00	950.00	1800.	—
	1813 SF	—	475.00	950.00	1650.	2200.
	1814 SF	—	625.00	1250.	—	—

Mint mark: Crowned C

KM#	Date	Mintage	VG	Fine	VF	XF
466.2 (C136.2)	1810 CI	—	300.00	600.00	1000.	1450.
	1811 CI	—	150.00	300.00	550.00	900.00
	1811 CJ	—	190.00	425.00	700.00	1000.
	1812 CJ	—	175.00	400.00	650.00	950.00
	1813 CJ	—	85.00	140.00	220.00	350.00
	1814 CJ	—	85.00	140.00	220.00	350.00
	1815 CJ	—	500.00	1000.	2000.	2800.

Mint mark: Crowned M

KM#	Date	Mintage	VG	Fine	VF	XF
466.3 (C136.3)	1814 GJ	—	50.00	100.00	150.00	250.00
	1815 GJ	—	50.00	100.00	150.00	250.00
	1816 GJ	—	50.00	100.00	150.00	250.00
	1817 GJ	—	65.00	125.00	200.00	325.00
466.3	1818 GJ	—	50.00	100.00	150.00	250.00
	1823 AJ	—	425.00	850.00	1400.	1700.
	1824 AJ	—	275.00	550.00	900.00	1250.
	1825 AJ	—	300.00	600.00	1100.	1600.
	1830 AJ	—	400.00	800.00	1600.	2000.

Mint mark: S, S/L

KM#	Date	Mintage	VG	Fine	VF	XF
466.4 (C136.4)	1809 CN	—	75.00	125.00	200.00	350.00
	1810 CN	—	450.00	900.00	1350.	2000.
	1812 CN	—	825.00	1650.	2400.	3600.
	1814 CJ	—	250.00	500.00	1150.	1600.
	1815 CJ	—	65.00	125.00	175.00	275.00
	1816 CJ	—	50.00	100.00	150.00	220.00
	1817 CJ	—	50.00	100.00	150.00	220.00
	1818 CJ	—	50.00	100.00	150.00	220.00
	1819 CJ	—	65.00	125.00	200.00	325.00
	1820 CJ	—	50.00	100.00	150.00	220.00

1/2 ESCUDO

1.6900 g, .875 GOLD, .0475 oz AGW
Obv: Laureate head of Ferdinand right.
Rev: Crowned oval arms.

KM#	Date	Mintage	VG	Fine	VF	XF
492 (C141)	1817 GJ	—	50.00	90.00	150.00	175.00

ESCUDO

3.3800 g, .875 GOLD, .0951 oz AGW

Mint mark: Crowned M
Obv: Bust of Charles IV right.
Rev: Crowned shield in Order chain.

KM#	Date	Mintage	VG	Fine	VF	XF
434	1801 FA	—	65.00	80.00	100.00	150.00
(C73)	1807 FA	—	65.00	80.00	100.00	150.00

NOTE: Earlier dates (1788-1799) exist for this type.

Similar to 1/2 Escudo, KM#492.

KM#	Date	Mintage	VG	Fine	VF	XF
493 (C142)	1817 GJ	—	150.00	300.00	500.00	800.00

2 ESCUDOS

6.7700 g, .875 GOLD, .1905 oz AGW
Mint mark: Crowned M

KM#	Date	Mintage	VG	Fine	VF	XF
435.1	1801 MF	—	125.00	150.00	175.00	225.00
(C74.1)	1801 FM	—	150.00	200.00	350.00	500.00
	1801 FA/MF	—	125.00	150.00	175.00	225.00
	1801 FA	—	125.00	150.00	175.00	225.00
	1802 FA	—	125.00	150.00	175.00	225.00
	1803 FA	—	125.00	150.00	175.00	225.00
	1804 FA	—	125.00	150.00	175.00	225.00
	1805 FA	—	125.00	150.00	175.00	225.00
	1806 FA	—	125.00	150.00	175.00	225.00
	1807 FA	—	125.00	150.00	175.00	225.00
	1807 AI	—	125.00	150.00	175.00	225.00
	1808 AI	—	125.00	150.00	175.00	225.00
	1808 FA	—	300.00	600.00	1000.	1500.

NOTE: Earlier dates (1788-1800) exist for this type.

Mint mark: S, S/L

KM#	Date	Mintage	VG	Fine	VF	XF
435.2	1801 CN	—	125.00	150.00	175.00	250.00
(C74.2)	1802 CN	—	125.00	150.00	175.00	250.00
	1803 CN	—	125.00	150.00	175.00	250.00
	1804 CN	—	125.00	150.00	175.00	250.00
	1805 CN	—	150.00	200.00	350.00	500.00
	1806 CN	—	125.00	150.00	175.00	250.00
	1807 CN	—	125.00	150.00	175.00	250.00
	1808 CN	—	125.00	150.00	175.00	250.00

NOTE: Earlier dates (1790-1800) exist for this type.

Mint mark: S
Obv: Wide armored, bare head of Ferdinand right.

KM#	Date	Mintage	VG	Fine	VF	XF
451 (C143a)	1808 CN	—	125.00	150.00	200.00	300.00
	1809 CN	—	135.00	175.00	250.00	350.00

Obv: Draped bust, bare head of Ferdinand right.

KM#	Date	Mintage	VG	Fine	VF	XF
456.1 (C143b.1)	1809 CN	—	150.00	250.00	400.00	650.00

Mint mark: Crowned C
Obv: Draped bust, bare head of Ferdinand right.

KM#	Date	Mintage	VG	Fine	VF	XF
456.2 (C143b.2)	1811 CI	—	250.00	450.00	750.00	1250.

Obv: Laureate armored bust of Ferdinand right.
Rev: Crowned arms in collar of The Golden Fleece.

KM#	Date	Mintage	VG	Fine	VF	XF
467 (C143c)	1811 CI	—	125.00	200.00	300.00	500.00

Mint mark: Crowned M
Obv: Large laureate military bust of Ferdinand right.

KM#	Date	Mintage	VG	Fine	VF	XF
478 (C143d)	1812 IJ	—	175.00	350.00	600.00	950.00

Obv: Small laureate military bust of Ferdinand right.

KM#	Date	Mintage	VG	Fine	VF	XF
480 (C143e)	1813 IG	—	250.00	500.00	900.00	1400.
	1813 IJ	—	150.00	275.00	400.00	600.00
	1813 GJ	—	125.00	175.00	300.00	450.00
	1814 GJ	—	125.00	225.00	350.00	500.00

Mint mark: Crowned C
Obv: Laureate bust of Ferdinand right.

KM#	Date	Mintage	VG	Fine	VF	XF
468 (C143f.1)	1811 CI	—	125.00	150.00	225.00	350.00
	1812 CI	—	125.00	150.00	225.00	350.00
	1813 CI	—	150.00	175.00	275.00	450.00
	1813 CJ	—	125.00	150.00	225.00	350.00
	1814 CJ	—	125.00	150.00	225.00	350.00

NOTE: Large and small varieties of the crowned C mint mark exist.

Mint mark: C
Obv: Laureate head of Ferdinand right.

KM#	Date	Mintage	VG	Fine	VF	XF
469 (C143f.2)	1811 SF	—	500.00	1000.	1750.	2500.
	1812 SF	—	450.00	900.00	1400.	2000.
	1813 SF	—	350.00	750.00	1200.	1750.

NOTE: Varieties in the bust design exist.

Mint mark: Crowned M

KM#	Date	Mintage	VG	Fine	VF	XF
483.1 (C143f.3)	1814 GJ	—	125.00	175.00	225.00	300.00
	1815 GJ	—	135.00	225.00	350.00	500.00
	1816 GJ	—	150.00	275.00	475.00	600.00
	1817 GJ	—	150.00	275.00	475.00	600.00
	1818 GJ	—	125.00	150.00	200.00	300.00
	1819 GJ	—	125.00	150.00	200.00	300.00
	1820 GJ	—	125.00	125.00	175.00	250.00
	1822 AJ	—	150.00	275.00	475.00	600.00
	1823 AJ	—	150.00	300.00	500.00	750.00
	1824 AJ	—	125.00	125.00	175.00	250.00
	1825 AJ	—	125.00	125.00	175.00	250.00
	1826 AJ	—	135.00	175.00	250.00	350.00
	1827 AJ	—	135.00	200.00	300.00	450.00
	1828 AJ	—	135.00	225.00	350.00	500.00
	1829 AJ	—	125.00	125.00	175.00	250.00
	1830 AJ	—	125.00	125.00	175.00	250.00
	1831 AJ	—	125.00	125.00	175.00	250.00
	1832 AJ	—	125.00	125.00	175.00	250.00
	1833 AJ	—	125.00	125.00	175.00	250.00

Mint mark: S, S/L

KM#	Date	Mintage	VG	Fine	VF	XF
483.2 (C143f.4)	1815 CJ	—	125.00	125.00	175.00	225.00
	1816 CJ	—	125.00	125.00	175.00	225.00
	1817 CJ	—	135.00	175.00	250.00	350.00
	1818 CJ	—	125.00	125.00	175.00	225.00
	1819 CJ	—	125.00	125.00	175.00	225.00
	1820 CJ	—	125.00	125.00	175.00	225.00
	1821 CJ	—	125.00	150.00	200.00	300.00
	1824 J	—	500.00	1000.	1750.	2500.
	1824 JB	—	135.00	175.00	275.00	400.00
	1825 JB	—	125.00	125.00	175.00	225.00
	1826 JB	—	125.00	125.00	175.00	225.00
	1827 JB	—	125.00	125.00	175.00	225.00
	1828 JB	—	135.00	175.00	275.00	400.00
	1829 JB	—	135.00	175.00	275.00	400.00
	1830 JB	—	135.00	225.00	350.00	500.00
	1831 JB	—	125.00	125.00	175.00	225.00
	1832 JB	—	125.00	125.00	175.00	225.00
	1833 JB	—	125.00	125.00	175.00	225.00

4 ESCUDOS

13.5400 g, .875 GOLD, .3809 oz AGW
Mint mark: Crowned M
Obv: Bust of Charles IV right.
Rev: Crowned arms in collar of The Golden Fleece.

KM#	Date	Mintage	VG	Fine	VF	XF
436.1 (C75.1)	1801 MF	—	300.00	600.00	850.00	1250.
	1801 FA	—	200.00	250.00	350.00	500.00
	1803 FA	—	225.00	300.00	425.00	600.00

NOTE: Earlier dates (1788-1796) exist for this type.

Mint mark: S, S/L

KM#	Date	Mintage	VG	Fine	VF	XF
436.2 (C75.2)	1801 C	—	1000.	2200.	3000.	4500.
	1808 C	—	1000.	2200.	3000.	4500.

Mint mark: Crowned M

KM#	Date	Mintage	VG	Fine	VF	XF
484 (C144)	1814 GJ	—	225.00	400.00	550.00	800.00
	1815 GJ	—	225.00	350.00	500.00	700.00
	1816 GJ	—	300.00	600.00	800.00	1200.
	1818 GJ	—	225.00	400.00	550.00	800.00
	1819 GJ	—	225.00	350.00	500.00	700.00
	1820 GJ	—	200.00	250.00	350.00	500.00
	1824 AI	—	750.00	1500.	2100.	3000.

8 ESCUDOS

27.0700 g, .875 GOLD, .7616 oz AGW
Mint mark: Crowned M
Obv: Bust of Charles IV right.

KM#	Date	Mintage	VG	Fine	VF	XF
437.1 (C76.1)	1802 FA	—	450.00	700.00	1100.	1700.
	1803 FA	—	900.00	1700.	2500.	4000.
	1805 FA	—	550.00	1100.	1600.	2600.

NOTE: Earlier dates (1788-1790) exist for this type.

Mint mark: Crowned C
Obv: Laureate uniformed bust of Ferdinand right.
Rev: Crowned arms.

KM#	Date	Mintage	VG	Fine	VF	XF
470 (C145)	1811 CI	—	750.00	1250.	3600.	6000.

Mint mark: C
Obv: Laureate head.

KM#	Date	Mintage	VG	Fine	VF	XF
481 (C145a.1)	1813 SF	—	3000.	7000.	10,000.	15,000.
	1814 SF	—	4000.	8000.	11,500.	*16,500.

***NOTE:** Stack's CICF Sale 4-89, XF realized $16,500.

Mint mark: Crowned M

KM#	Date	Mintage	VG	Fine	VF	XF
485 (C145a.2)	1814 GJ	—	1000.	2000.	2800.	4000.
	1816 GJ	—	1500.	3000.	4200.	6000.
	1817 GJ	—	1100.	2250.	3100.	4500.
	1819 GJ	—	1800.	3500.	5000.	7500.
	1820 GJ	—	450.00	750.00	1540.	1870.

DE VELLON COINAGE

REAL

1.3540 g, .903 SILVER, .0393 oz ASW
Mint mark: Crowned M

KM#	Date	Mintage	VG	Fine	VF	XF
553 (C88)	1812 AI	—	17.50	45.00	95.00	145.00
	1813 RN	—	25.00	60.00	120.00	180.00

2 REALES

2.7080 g, .903 SILVER, .0786 oz ASW
Mint mark: Crowned M

KM#	Date	Mintage	VG	Fine	VF	XF
550 (C89)	1811 AI	—	40.00	100.00	200.00	300.00
	1812 AI	—	35.00	80.00	160.00	240.00
	1812 RN	—	25.00	60.00	120.00	180.00
	1813 RN	—	60.00	150.00	300.00	450.00

4 REALES

5.4160 g, .903 SILVER, .1572 oz ASW
Mint mark: Crowned M

KM#	Date	Mintage	VG	Fine	VF	XF
540.1 (C90.1)	1808 AI	—	25.00	65.00	130.00	200.00
	1809 AI	—	10.00	17.50	30.00	45.00
	1810 AI	—	7.50	12.50	22.50	35.00
	1811 AI	—	6.50	10.00	20.00	30.00
	1811 RS	—	20.00	50.00	100.00	150.00
	1812 AI	—	10.00	17.50	30.00	45.00
	1812 RS	—	25.00	40.00	80.00	120.00
	1812 RN	—	10.00	17.50	30.00	45.00
	1813 RN	—	12.50	25.00	47.50	70.00

Mint mark: S, S/L

KM#	Date	Mintage	VG	Fine	VF	XF
540.2 (C90.2)	1810 LA	—	30.00	70.00	140.00	210.00
	1812 LA	—	12.50	30.00	60.00	90.00

Mint mark: B, BA

KM#	Date	Mintage	VG	Fine	VF	XF
562.1 (C137.5)	1822 SP	—	10.00	20.00	32.50	50.00
	1823 SP	—	12.50	30.00	60.00	90.00

Mint mark: Crowned M

KM#	Date	Mintage	VG	Fine	VF	XF
562.2 (C137.6)	1822 SR	—	12.50	27.50	55.00	85.00
	1823 SR	—	15.00	35.00	65.00	100.00

Mint mark: S, S/L

KM#	Date	Mintage	VG	Fine	VF	XF
562.3 (C137.7)	1823 RD	—	12.50	27.50	55.00	85.00

Mint mark: V, VAL.
Obv: Small bare head bust of Ferdinand right.

KM#	Date	Mintage	VG	Fine	VF	XF
567 (C137.1)	1823 R Spanish arms	—	10.00	20.00	35.00	55.00

10 REALES

13.5400 g, .903 SILVER, .3931 oz ASW
Mint mark: Crowned M

KM#	Date	Mintage	VG	Fine	VF	XF
541 (C91)	1809 AI	—	200.00	500.00	1000.	1500.
	1810 AI	—	120.00	300.00	600.00	900.00
	1811 AI	.058	60.00	150.00	300.00	475.00
	1812 AI	.490	35.00	80.00	160.00	250.00
	1812 RN	I.A.	35.00	80.00	160.00	250.00
	1813 RN	.135	70.00	175.00	350.00	525.00

Mint mark: Bo

KM#	Date	Mintage	VG	Fine	VF	XF
560.1 (C138.1)	1821 UG	—	15.00	35.00	70.00	100.00

Mint mark: Crowned M

KM#	Date	Mintage	VG	Fine	VF	XF
560.2 (C138.2)	1821 SR	—	10.00	17.50	30.00	45.00

Mint mark: Sr

KM#	Date	Mintage	VG	Fine	VF	XF
560.3 (C138.3)	1821 LT	—	15.00	35.00	70.00	100.00

Mint mark: S, S/L

KM#	Date	Mintage	VG	Fine	VF	XF
560.4 (C138.4)	1821 RD	—	17.50	40.00	80.00	125.00

Mint mark: Crowned M

KM#	Date	Mintage	VG	Fine	VF	XF
585.1 (C174.1)	1840 CL	—	70.00	175.00	350.00	525.00
	1840 DG	—	225.00	600.00	1200.	1800.
	1841 CL	—	65.00	165.00	325.00	500.00
	1842 CL	—	70.00	175.00	350.00	525.00
	1843 CL	—	55.00	140.00	275.00	425.00
	1844 CL	—	70.00	175.00	350.00	525.00
	1845 CL	—	100.00	250.00	500.00	750.00

Mint mark: S, S/L

KM#	Date	Mintage	VG	Fine	VF	XF
585.2 (C174.2)	1841 RD	—	75.00	150.00	300.00	600.00
	1842 RD	—	75.00	150.00	300.00	600.00
	1843 RD	—	75.00	150.00	300.00	600.00

20 REALES

27.0800 g, .903 SILVER, .7863 oz ASW
Mint mark: B, BA

KM#	Date	Mintage	VG	Fine	VF	XF
551.1 (C92.1)	1811	—	75.00	180.00	360.00	550.00
	1812	—	110.00	275.00	550.00	850.00

Mint mark: Crowned M

KM#	Date	Mintage	VG	Fine	VF	XF
551.2 (C92.2)	1808 AI	.017	100.00	250.00	500.00	750.00
	1809 AI	.700	35.00	80.00	160.00	250.00
	1810 IA	.993	400.00	1000.	2000.	3000.
	1810 AI	Inc. Ab.	30.00	75.00	150.00	225.00
	1811 AI	.460	30.00	75.00	150.00	225.00
	1812 AI	.250	65.00	140.00	275.00	425.00
	1813 RN	.068	100.00	240.00	480.00	725.00

Mint mark: S, S/L

KM#	Date	Mintage	VG	Fine	VF	XF
551.3 (C92.3)	1812 LA	.013	120.00	300.00	600.00	900.00

Mint mark: Crowned M
Smaller letters.

KM#	Date	Mintage	VG	Fine	VF	XF
561 (C139a)	1821 SR	—	400.00	1000.	2000.	3000.

KM#	Date	Mintage	VG	Fine	VF	XF
(C139a)	1822 SR	—	25.00	50.00	100.00	175.00
	1823 SR	—	60.00	125.00	200.00	300.00

Mint mark: B, BA

KM#	Date	Mintage	VG	Fine	VF	XF
563.1	1822 SP	—	120.00	250.00	400.00	850.00
(C139.1)						
	1823 SP	—	40.00	80.00	150.00	300.00

Mint mark: S, S/L

KM#	Date	Mintage	VG	Fine	VF	XF
563.2	1822 RD	—	40.00	100.00	150.00	300.00
(C139.2)						
	1823 RD	—	50.00	125.00	225.00	400.00

KM#	Date	Mintage	VG	Fine	VF	XF
575	1833 DG	—	400.00	1000.	2000.	3000.
(C140)						

Obv. leg. ends: DIOS
Rev: Similar to C#175.1.

KM#	Date	Mintage	VG	Fine	VF	XF
576	1834 DG	—	325.00	825.00	1650.	2500.
(C165)	1834 NC	4,769	200.00	500.00	1000.	1500.
	1835 CR	.013	160.00	400.00	800.00	1200.
	1836 CR	.048	125.00	300.00	600.00	1000.

KM#	Date	Mintage	VG	Fine	VF	XF
579.1	1837 CR	.115	70.00	175.00	350.00	525.00
(C175.1)						
579.1	1838 CL	.231	65.00	165.00	325.00	500.00
	1839 CL	.074	400.00	1000.	2000.	3000.
	1840 CL	6,012	650.00	1625.	3250.	5000.
	1847 DG	—	500.00	1250.	2500.	3750.
	1848 CL	.067	50.00	125.00	250.00	400.00
	1849 CL	.120	70.00	175.00	350.00	525.00
	1850 DG	—	500.00	1250.	2500.	3750.

Mint mark: S, S/L

KM#	Date	Mintage	VG	Fine	VF	XF
579.2	1842 RD	.012	225.00	500.00	1000.	1500.
(C175.2)						

80 REALES

6.7700 g, .875 GOLD, .1905 oz AGW
Mint mark: Crowned M

KM#	Date	Mintage	VG	Fine	VF	XF
542	1809 AI	—	100.00	150.00	250.00	375.00
(C94)	1810 AI	—	200.00	500.00	1000.	1500.

KM#	Date	Mintage	VG	Fine	VF	XF
552	1811 AI	.440	100.00	150.00	275.00	450.00
(C94a)	1812/1 AI	—	100.00	200.00	400.00	650.00
	1812 AI	.238	100.00	200.00	400.00	650.00
	1813 RN	.161	125.00	250.00	450.00	750.00

Mint mark: B, BA

KM#	Date	Mintage	VG	Fine	VF	XF
564.1	1822 SP	—	125.00	250.00	500.00	800.00
(C146.1)						
	1823 SP	—	100.00	125.00	200.00	300.00

Mint mark: Crowned M

KM#	Date	Mintage	VG	Fine	VF	XF
564.2	1822 SR	—	100.00	125.00	160.00	225.00
(C146.2)						
	1823 SR	—	100.00	135.00	225.00	350.00

Mint mark: S, S/L

KM#	Date	Mintage	VG	Fine	VF	XF
564.3	1823 RD	—	140.00	300.00	600.00	900.00
(C146.3)						

Mint mark: B, BA
Obv. leg. ends: DIOS

KM#	Date	Mintage	VG	Fine	VF	XF
577.1	1836 PS	—	400.00	1000.	2000.	3000.
(C166.1)						

Mint mark: Crowned M

KM#	Date	Mintage	VG	Fine	VF	XF
577.2	1834 CR	—	100.00	125.00	175.00	275.00
(C166.2)						
	1835 CR	—	100.00	125.00	160.00	250.00
	1836 CL	—	100.00	125.00	200.00	325.00
	1836 CR	—	110.00	200.00	400.00	600.00

Mint mark: S, S/L

KM#	Date	Mintage	VG	Fine	VF	XF
577.3	1835 DR	—	125.00	215.00	425.00	650.00
(C166.3)						
	1835 RD	—	110.00	175.00	350.00	525.00
	1836 DR	—	110.00	175.00	350.00	525.00
	1837 DR	—	110.00	175.00	350.00	525.00

Mint mark: B, BA

KM#	Date	Mintage	VG	Fine	VF	XF
578.1	1836 PS	—	400.00	1000.	2000.	3000.
(C176.1)						
	1838 PS CONSTITUCION					
		—	100.00	125.00	225.00	350.00
	1838 PS CONST					
		—	110.00	200.00	400.00	600.00
	1839 PS CONSTITUCION					
578.1		—	170.00	400.00	800.00	1200.
	1839 PS CONST					
		—	100.00	125.00	225.00	350.00
	1840 PS	—	100.00	125.00	150.00	225.00
	1841 PS	—	100.00	125.00	150.00	225.00
	1842 CC	—	100.00	125.00	200.00	300.00
	1842 PS	—	600.00	1500.	3000.	4500.
	1843 CC	—	450.00	1000.	2100.	3250.
	1843 PS	—	325.00	800.00	1600.	2400.
	1844 PS	—	100.00	125.00	200.00	300.00
	1845 PS	—	100.00	125.00	200.00	300.00
	1846 PS	—	100.00	125.00	180.00	275.00
	1847 PS	—	100.00	125.00	210.00	325.00
	1848 PS	—	150.00	325.00	625.00	950.00

Mint mark: Crowned M

KM#	Date	Mintage	VG	Fine	VF	XF
578.2	1834 CR	—	100.00	125.00	180.00	275.00
(C176.2)						
	1835 CR	—	100.00	125.00	160.00	250.00
	1836 CL	—	100.00	125.00	250.00	400.00
	1836 CR	—	120.00	265.00	525.00	800.00
	1837 CR	—	135.00	320.00	625.00	950.00
	1838 CL	—	130.00	300.00	600.00	900.00
	1839 CL	—	135.00	325.00	650.00	1000.
	1840 CL	—	110.00	200.00	400.00	600.00
	1841 CL	—	100.00	165.00	325.00	500.00
	1842 CL	—	175.00	400.00	800.00	1200.
	1843 CL	—	100.00	125.00	180.00	275.00
	1844 CL	—	100.00	125.00	200.00	300.00
	1845 CL	—	100.00	125.00	160.00	250.00
	1846 CL	—	100.00	150.00	300.00	450.00
	1847 CL	—	110.00	200.00	400.00	600.00
	1848 CL	—	100.00	150.00	300.00	450.00
	1849 CL	—	200.00	500.00	1000.	1500.

Mint mark: S, S/L

KM#	Date	Mintage	VG	Fine	VF	XF
578.3	1835 DR	—	110.00	220.00	425.00	650.00
(C176.3)						
	1835 RD	—	100.00	125.00	250.00	375.00
	1836 DR	—	100.00	175.00	350.00	525.00
	1837 DR	—	100.00	170.00	375.00	550.00
	1838 DR	—	130.00	300.00	600.00	900.00
	1838 RD	—	165.00	400.00	800.00	1200.
	1839 RD	—	100.00	150.00	300.00	475.00
	1840 RD	—	100.00	140.00	275.00	425.00
	1841 RD	—	100.00	150.00	300.00	450.00
	1842 RD	—	100.00	140.00	275.00	425.00
	1843 RD	—	100.00	150.00	300.00	450.00
	1844 RD	—	100.00	150.00	300.00	450.00
	1845 RD	—	100.00	125.00	225.00	350.00
	1846 RD	—	100.00	175.00	350.00	525.00
	1847 RD	—	100.00	165.00	325.00	500.00
	1848 RD	—	200.00	500.00	1000.	1600.

Mint mark: B, BA
Obv. leg. ends: CONSTITUCION

KM#	Date	Mintage	VG	Fine	VF	XF
580	1837 PS	—	110.00	250.00	500.00	750.00
(C176a)						
	1838 PS	—	100.00	125.00	225.00	350.00

160 REALES

13.5400 g, .875 GOLD, .3809 oz AGW
Mint mark: Crowned M

KM#	Date	Mintage	VG	Fine	VF	XF
565	1822 SR	—	250.00	400.00	650.00	1000.
(C147)						

320 REALES

27.0700 g, .875 GOLD, .7616 oz AGW
Mint mark: Crowned M

KM#	Date	Mintage	VG	Fine	VF	XF
545	1810 AI	.064	1500.	3250.	6500.	10,000.

KM#	Date	Mintage	VG	Fine	VF	XF
(C95)	1810 RS	I.A.	1750.	4500.	9000.	13,750.
	1812 RS	.060	1500.	3000.	6500.	9500.

KM#	Date	Mintage	VG	Fine	VF	XF
566	1822 SR	—	600.00	1300.	2750.	4250.
(C148)	1823 SR	—	1100.	2400.	5000.	7500.

DECIMAL COINAGE

10 Decimos = 1 Real
100 Centimos = 1 Real

1/20 REAL

COPPER
Mint mark: Aqueduct

KM#	Date	Mintage	VG	Fine	VF	XF
597	1852	—	5.00	12.50	22.50	38.00
(Y15)	1853	—	2.50	5.00	10.00	22.00

5 CENTIMOS

COPPER
Mint mark: Aqueduct

KM#	Date	Mintage	VG	Fine	VF	XF
602	1854	—	90.00	225.00	400.00	650.00
(Y24)	1855	—	5.00	12.50	22.50	35.00
	1856	—	2.00	4.50	7.50	12.50
	1857	—	2.25	5.50	9.00	15.00
	1858	—	10.00	25.00	40.00	70.00
	1859	—	2.00	4.50	7.50	12.50
	1860	—	2.50	6.50	12.00	20.00
	1861	—	3.50	9.00	15.00	25.00
	1862	—	3.50	9.00	15.00	25.00
	1863	—	2.50	6.50	12.00	20.00
	1864	—	5.00	12.50	22.50	35.00

1/10 REAL

COPPER
Mint mark: Aqueduct

KM#	Date	Mintage	VG	Fine	VF	XF
590	1850	—	3.00	7.50	12.50	28.00
(Y16)	1851	—	10.00	22.50	40.00	65.00
	1852	—	3.00	7.50	12.50	28.00
	1853	—	2.50	5.00	10.00	22.00

10 CENTIMOS

COPPER
Mint mark: Aqueduct

KM#	Date	Mintage	VG	Fine	VF	XF
603	1854	—	100.00	250.00	450.00	750.00
(Y25)	1855	—	5.00	12.50	21.00	35.00
	1856	—	2.75	7.00	12.00	20.00
	1857	—	2.00	4.50	7.50	12.50
	1858	—	5.00	12.50	21.00	35.00
	1859	—	2.00	4.50	7.50	12.50
	1860	—	2.00	4.50	7.50	12.50
	1861	—	2.50	6.50	11.00	18.00
	1862	—	2.75	7.00	12.00	20.00
	1863	—	3.50	9.00	15.00	25.00
	1864	—	8.50	21.00	35.00	60.00

1/5 REAL

COPPER
Mint mark: Aqueduct

KM#	Date	Mintage	VG	Fine	VF	XF
601 (Y17)	1853	—	10.00	22.50	35.00	60.00

25 CENTIMOS

COPPER
Mint mark: 8-pointed star

KM#	Date	Mintage	VG	Fine	VF	XF
615.1	1863	—	50.00	125.00	200.00	350.00
(Y26.1)	1864	—	17.50	40.00	70.00	120.00

Mint mark: Aqueduct

KM#	Date	Mintage	VG	Fine	VF	XF
615.2	1854	—	2.75	7.00	12.00	20.00
(Y26.2)	1855	—	2.00	4.50	7.50	12.50
	1856	—	2.00	4.50	7.50	12.50
	1857	—	2.25	5.50	9.00	15.00
	1858	—	2.00	4.50	7.50	12.50
	1859	—	2.00	4.50	7.50	12.50
	1860	—	2.00	4.50	7.50	12.50
	1861	—	2.00	4.50	7.50	12.50
	1862	—	2.00	4.50	7.50	12.50
	1863	—	2.00	4.50	7.50	12.50
	1864	—	2.50	6.50	11.00	18.00

1/2 REAL

COPPER
Mint mark: 4-pointed star
Similar to 1/5 Real, KM#601.

KM#	Date	Mintage	VG	Fine	VF	XF
591.1 (Y18.1)	1850	—	17.50	40.00	70.00	125.00

Mint mark: 6-pointed star

KM#	Date	Mintage	VG	Fine	VF	XF
591.2	1848 DG	—	50.00	125.00	225.00	400.00
(Y18.2)	1848	—	5.00	10.00	22.00	50.00

Mint mark: Aqueduct

KM#	Date	Mintage	VG	Fine	VF	XF
591.3	1848	—	35.00	90.00	150.00	250.00
(Y18.3)	1849	—	25.00	70.00	120.00	200.00
	1850	—	5.00	10.00	20.00	42.00
	1851	—	5.00	10.00	20.00	42.00
	1852	—	5.00	10.00	20.00	42.00
	1853	—	5.00	10.00	20.00	42.00

REAL

1.3146 g, .900 SILVER, .0380 oz ASW
Mint mark: 8-pointed star

KM#	Date	Mintage	VG	Fine	VF	XF
598.1	1852	—	7.00	16.00	27.50	45.00
(Y19.1)	1853	—	3.00	7.50	12.50	20.00
	1854	—	5.00	12.50	22.00	35.00
	1855	—	4.25	10.00	17.50	25.00

Mint mark: 6-pointed star

KM#	Date	Mintage	VG	Fine	VF	XF
598.2	1852	—	2.00	5.00	8.00	16.00
(Y19.2)	1853	—	5.00	12.50	22.00	35.00
	1854	—	14.00	35.00	60.00	85.00
	1855	—	14.00	35.00	60.00	85.00

Mint mark: 7-pointed star

KM#	Date	Mintage	VG	Fine	VF	XF
598.3	1850	—	5.00	12.50	22.00	35.00
(Y19.3)	1851	—	32.50	85.00	140.00	200.00
	1852	—	2.00	5.25	8.75	17.50
	1853	—	2.50	6.25	10.00	18.00
	1854	—	7.00	16.00	27.50	45.00
	1855	—	5.00	12.50	22.00	35.00

Mint mark: 8-pointed star

KM#	Date	Mintage	VG	Fine	VF	XF
606.1	1857	—	4.25	10.00	17.50	28.00
(Y27.1)	1858	—	5.00	12.50	22.00	35.00
	1859	—	10.00	25.00	40.00	60.00
	1860/59	—	3.25	8.50	14.00	22.00
	1860	—	3.25	8.50	14.00	22.00
	1861	—	3.25	8.50	14.00	22.00
	1862	—	6.00	15.00	25.00	38.00
	1863	—	7.00	16.00	27.50	42.00
	1864	—	10.00	25.00	40.00	60.00

Mint mark: 6-pointed star

KM#	Date	Mintage	VG	Fine	VF	XF
606.2	1857	—	4.25	10.00	17.50	28.00
(Y27.2)	1858	—	9.25	22.50	37.50	55.00
	1859	—	3.00	6.00	10.00	20.00
	1860	—	3.25	8.50	14.00	22.00
	1861	—	9.25	22.50	37.50	55.00
	1862	—	4.00	8.00	15.00	30.00
	1863	—	5.00	12.50	20.00	32.00
	1864	—	7.00	16.00	27.50	42.00

Mint mark: 7-pointed star

KM#	Date	Mintage	VG	Fine	VF	XF
606.3	1857	—	20.00	50.00	85.00	120.00
(Y27.3)	1858	—	7.50	19.00	30.00	50.00
	1859	—	10.00	25.00	40.00	60.00
	1860	—	3.25	8.50	14.00	22.50
	1861	—	18.00	45.00	75.00	110.00
	1862	—	9.25	22.50	37.50	55.00
	1863	—	3.25	8.50	14.00	22.50
	1864	—	7.00	16.00	27.50	42.00

2 REALES

2.6291 g, .900 SILVER, .0761 oz ASW
Mint mark: 8-pointed star

KM#	Date	Mintage	VG	Fine	VF	XF
599.1	1852	—	12.50	21.00	35.00	50.00
(Y20.1)	1853	—	5.00	12.50	17.50	32.00
	1854	—	18.00	45.00	75.00	110.00
	1855	—	12.50	21.00	35.00	50.00

Mint mark: 6-pointed star

KM#	Date	Mintage	VG	Fine	VF	XF
599.2	1851	—	50.00	125.00	200.00	300.00
(Y20.2)	1852	—	10.00	25.00	40.00	60.00
	1853	—	6.00	15.00	25.00	38.00
	1854	—	6.00	15.00	25.00	38.00
	1855	—	5.00	12.50	22.00	35.00

Mint mark: 7-pointed star

KM#	Date	Mintage	VG	Fine	VF	XF
599.3	1850	—	12.50	30.00	50.00	80.00
(Y20.3)	1851	—	55.00	135.00	225.00	325.00
	1852	—	5.00	12.50	22.00	35.00
	1853	—	3.00	7.50	12.50	20.00
	1854	—	5.00	12.50	22.00	35.00
	1855	—	5.00	12.50	22.00	35.00

Mint mark: 8-pointed star

KM#	Date	Mintage	VG	Fine	VF	XF
607.1	1857	—	4.25	10.00	17.50	28.00
(Y28.1)	1858	—	10.00	25.00	60.00	120.00
	1860/59	—	—	—	—	—
	1860	—	7.50	19.00	30.00	50.00
	1861	—	7.50	19.00	30.00	50.00
	1862	—	22.50	55.00	95.00	140.00
	1863	—	40.00	100.00	175.00	250.00
	1864	—	65.00	165.00	275.00	400.00

Mint mark: 6-pointed star

KM#	Date	Mintage	VG	Fine	VF	XF
607.2	1857	—	10.00	25.00	40.00	60.00
(Y28.2)	1859	—	4.50	8.50	14.00	22.00
	1860	—	16.00	40.00	70.00	100.00
	1861	—	4.25	10.00	17.50	28.00
	1862	—	4.50	8.50	14.00	22.00
	1863	—	16.00	40.00	70.00	100.00
	1864	—	30.00	70.00	120.00	175.00

Mint mark: 7-pointed star

KM#	Date	Mintage	VG	Fine	VF	XF
607.3	1857	—	20.00	40.00	80.00	120.00
(Y28.3)	1858	—	13.00	32.50	55.00	85.00
	1859	—	15.00	37.50	60.00	90.00
	1860	—	7.50	19.00	30.00	50.00
	1861	—	5.00	12.50	22.00	35.00
	1862	—	12.50	21.00	35.00	50.00
	1863	—	5.00	12.50	22.00	35.00
	1864	—	10.00	25.00	40.00	60.00

4 REALES

5.2582 g, .900 SILVER, .1521 oz ASW
Mint mark: 8-pointed star

KM#	Date	Mintage	VG	Fine	VF	XF
600.1	1852	—	7.50	15.00	35.00	55.00
(Y21.1)	1853	—	10.00	25.00	40.00	60.00
	1854	—	9.25	22.50	37.50	57.50
	1855	—	60.00	150.00	250.00	350.00

Mint mark: 6-pointed star

KM#	Date	Mintage	VG	Fine	VF	XF
600.2	1852	—	5.00	10.00	20.00	32.00
(Y21.2)	1853	—	16.00	40.00	65.00	95.00

KM#	Date	Mintage	VG	Fine	VF	XF
(Y21.2)	1854	—	7.50	19.00	30.00	50.00
	1855	—	15.00	37.50	60.00	90.00

Mint mark: 7-pointed star

KM#	Date	Mintage	VG	Fine	VF	XF
600.3	1852	—	5.00	12.50	22.00	35.00
(Y21.3)	1853	—	5.00	12.50	22.00	35.00
	1854	—	4.25	10.00	17.50	28.00
	1855	—	12.50	21.00	35.00	50.00

Mint mark: 8-pointed star

KM#	Date	Mintage	VG	Fine	VF	XF
608.1	1857	—	65.00	160.00	275.00	400.00
(Y29.1)	1858	—	15.00	37.50	60.00	90.00
	1859	—	10.00	25.00	40.00	60.00
	1860	—	10.00	25.00	40.00	60.00
	1861	—	7.50	15.00	30.00	50.00
	1862	—	60.00	150.00	250.00	350.00
	1864	—	65.00	155.00	260.00	375.00

Mint mark: 6-pointed star

KM#	Date	Mintage	VG	Fine	VF	XF
608.2	1856	—	12.50	25.00	50.00	80.00
(Y29.2)	1857	—	7.50	15.00	30.00	50.00
	1858	—	6.00	12.50	25.00	38.00
	1859	—	5.00	10.00	22.00	35.00
	1860	—	32.50	85.00	140.00	200.00
	1861	—	7.50	15.00	30.00	50.00
	1862	—	5.00	10.00	20.00	32.00
	1863	—	5.00	10.00	20.00	32.00
	1864	—	20.00	50.00	85.00	120.00

Mint mark: 7-pointed star

KM#	Date	Mintage	VG	Fine	VF	XF
608.3	1857	—	30.00	70.00	120.00	175.00
(Y29.3)	1858	—	40.00	100.00	175.00	250.00
	1859	—	30.00	70.00	120.00	175.00
	1860	—	10.00	25.00	40.00	60.00
	1861	—	12.50	30.00	50.00	80.00
	1862	—	15.00	37.50	60.00	90.00
	1863	—	12.50	21.00	35.00	50.00
	1864	—	10.00	25.00	40.00	60.00

10 REALES

13.1455 g, .900 SILVER, .3804 oz ASW
Mint mark: 8-pointed star
Similar to 4 Reales, KM#600.1.

KM#	Date	Mintage	VG	Fine	VF	XF
595.1	1851	—	150.00	375.00	625.00	900.00
(Y22.1)	1852	—	25.00	60.00	100.00	160.00
	1853	—	10.00	25.00	40.00	65.00
	1854	—	15.00	37.50	60.00	100.00
	1855	—	30.00	70.00	120.00	180.00

Mint mark: 6-pointed star

KM#	Date	Mintage	VG	Fine	VF	XF
595.2	1851	—	25.00	60.00	100.00	160.00
(Y22.2)	1852	—	10.00	20.00	40.00	65.00
	1853	—	10.00	20.00	40.00	65.00
	1854	—	14.00	35.00	60.00	85.00
	1855	—	50.00	125.00	200.00	300.00

Mint mark: 7-pointed star

KM#	Date	Mintage	VG	Fine	VF	XF
595.3	1851	—	75.00	180.00	300.00	450.00
(Y22.3)	1852	—	7.50	20.00	35.00	55.00
	1853	—	10.00	25.00	40.00	65.00
	1854	—	10.00	25.00	40.00	65.00
	1855	—	16.00	40.00	70.00	110.00
	1856	—	150.00	400.00	700.00	1000.

Mint mark: 8-pointed star

KM#	Date	Mintage	VG	Fine	VF	XF
611.1	1859	—	60.00	150.00	250.00	350.00
(Y30.1)	1860	—	60.00	150.00	250.00	350.00
	1861	—	37.50	90.00	150.00	225.00
	1862	—	50.00	125.00	200.00	300.00
	1863	—	100.00	275.00	450.00	650.00
	1864	—	55.00	135.00	225.00	325.00

Mint mark: 6-pointed star

KM#	Date	Mintage	VG	Fine	VF	XF
611.2	1857	—	32.50	85.00	140.00	200.00
(Y30.2)	1858	—	20.00	50.00	85.00	125.00
(Y30.2)	1859	—	20.00	50.00	85.00	125.00
	1860	—	15.00	30.00	45.00	90.00
	1861	—	20.00	50.00	85.00	125.00
	1862	—	12.50	21.00	35.00	55.00
	1863	—	7.50	15.00	25.00	45.00
	1864	—	20.00	50.00	85.00	125.00
	1865	—	45.00	115.00	190.00	275.00

Mint mark: 7-pointed star

KM#	Date	Mintage	VG	Fine	VF	XF
611.3	1857	—	65.00	165.00	275.00	400.00
(Y30.3)	1858	—	55.00	135.00	225.00	325.00
	1859	—	60.00	150.00	250.00	350.00
	1860	—	100.00	250.00	425.00	600.00
	1861	—	25.00	60.00	100.00	160.00
	1863	—	40.00	100.00	175.00	250.00
	1864	—	125.00	325.00	550.00	800.00

20 REALES

26.2910 g, .900 SILVER, .7607 oz ASW
Mint mark: Crowned M
Rev: Similar to 20 Reales, KM#575.

KM#	Date	Mintage	VG	Fine	VF	XF
592.1	1850 CL	.126	35.00	65.00	95.00	135.00
(Y13.1)	1850 DG	—	400.00	1000.	1750.	2500.

Mint mark: S

KM#	Date	Mintage	VG	Fine	VF	XF
592.2	1850 RD	—	200.00	500.00	750.00	1000.
(Y13.2)						

Mint mark: 8-pointed star

KM#	Date	Mintage	VG	Fine	VF	XF
593.1	1850	—	325.00	850.00	1400.	2000.
(Y23.1)	1851	1.055	150.00	300.00	400.00	600.00
	1852	1.053	250.00	625.00	1000.	1500.

Mint mark: 6-pointed star

KM#	Date	Mintage	VG	Fine	VF	XF
593.2	1850	.500	20.00	40.00	70.00	115.00
(Y23.2)	1851	Inc. Ab.	15.00	30.00	50.00	85.00
	1852	Inc. Ab.	30.00	70.00	110.00	175.00
	1854	1.355	17.50	35.00	65.00	110.00
	1855	1.229	17.50	35.00	65.00	110.00

Mint mark: 7-pointed star

KM#	Date	Mintage	VG	Fine	VF	XF
593.3	1850	—	325.00	850.00	1400.	2000.
(Y23.3)	1851	Inc. Ab.	25.00	60.00	100.00	160.00
	1852	Inc. Ab.	25.00	60.00	100.00	160.00
	1853	—	400.00	1000.	1900.	2750.
	1854	Inc. Ab.	20.00	40.00	80.00	120.00
	1855	Inc. Ab.	20.00	40.00	90.00	150.00

Mint mark: 8-pointed star

KM#	Date	Mintage	VG	Fine	VF	XF
609.1	1857	.713	200.00	475.00	850.00	1250.
(Y31.1)	1859	.880	240.00	600.00	1000.	1450.
	1862	1.594	400.00	900.00	1650.	2500.
	1863	.520	400.00	900.00	1650.	2500.

Mint mark: 6-pointed star

KM#	Date	Mintage	VG	Fine	VF	XF
609.2	1856	1.021	15.00	25.00	40.00	70.00
(Y31.2)	1857	Inc. Ab.	12.50	20.00	40.00	70.00
	1858	1.626	15.00	30.00	50.00	80.00
	1859	Inc. Ab.	17.50	37.50	60.00	100.00
	1860	.941	17.50	40.00	70.00	110.00
	1861	1.352	12.50	20.00	40.00	70.00
	1862	Inc. Ab.	25.00	60.00	100.00	160.00
	1863	Inc. Ab.	60.00	140.00	250.00	350.00
	1864	2.776	20.00	50.00	85.00	125.00

Mint mark: 7-pointed star

KM#	Date	Mintage	VG	Fine	VF	XF
609.3	1856	Inc. Ab.	70.00	175.00	300.00	425.00
(Y31.3)	1857	Inc. Ab.	30.00	70.00	120.00	175.00
	1858	Inc. Ab.	30.00	70.00	120.00	175.00
	1859	Inc. Ab.	70.00	175.00	300.00	425.00
	1860	Inc. Ab.	45.00	115.00	190.00	275.00
	1861	Inc. Ab.	50.00	125.00	225.00	375.00
	1862	Inc. Ab.	85.00	200.00	350.00	500.00
	1863	Inc. Ab.	85.00	200.00	325.00	475.00

1.6674 g, .900 GOLD, .0482 oz AGW
Mint mark: 6-pointed star

KM#	Date	Mintage	VG	Fine	VF	XF
610	1857	—	200.00	500.00	825.00	1200.
(Y32)	1861	—	40.00	85.00	140.00	200.00
	1862	—	175.00	400.00	700.00	1000.
	1863	—	425.00	1000.	1750.	2500.

40 REALES

3.3349 g, .900 GOLD, .0965 oz AGW
Mint mark: 8-pointed star

KM#	Date	Mintage	VG	Fine	VF	XF
616.1	1863	—	60.00	75.00	100.00	150.00
(Y33.1)	1864	—	400.00	900.00	1500.	2200.

Mint mark: 6-pointed star

KM#	Date	Mintage	VG	Fine	VF	XF
616.2	1861	—	100.00	225.00	400.00	600.00
(Y33.2)	1862	—	55.00	65.00	100.00	150.00
	1863	—	55.00	65.00	80.00	120.00

Obv: Draped bust of Isabel II left.
Rev: Crowned draped arms.

KM#	Date	Mintage	VG	Fine	VF	XF
618.1 (Y-A35.1)	1864	—	55.00	65.00	75.00	120.00

Mint mark: 7-pointed star

KM#	Date	Mintage	VG	Fine	VF	XF
618.2 (Y-A35.2)	1864	—	175.00	375.00	625.00	900.00

100 REALES

8.3371 g, .900 GOLD, .2412 oz AGW
Mint mark: 8-pointed star

KM#	Date	Mintage	VG	Fine	VF	XF
594.1 (Y-A23.1)	1850 SM	—	400.00	850.00	1400.	2100.

Mint mark: 6-pointed star

KM#	Date	Mintage	VG	Fine	VF	XF
594.2 (Y-A23.2)	1850 CL	—	125.00	150.00	200.00	300.00
	1850 DG	—	1500.	4000.	7000.	10,000.
	1851 CL	—	200.00	500.00	825.00	1200.

Mint mark: 7-pointed star

KM#	Date	Mintage	VG	Fine	VF	XF
594.3 (Y-A23.3)	1850 RD	—	400.00	900.00	1500.	2200.

Mint mark: 8-pointed star

KM#	Date	Mintage	VG	Fine	VF	XF
596.1 (Y-B23.1)	1851	—	700.00	1500.	2750.	4000.
	1854	—	125.00	175.00	250.00	350.00
	1855	—	125.00	150.00	200.00	300.00

Mint mark: 6-pointed star

KM#	Date	Mintage	VG	Fine	VF	XF
596.2 (Y-B23.2)	1851	—	700.00	1500.	2500.	3750.
	1852	—	550.00	1200.	2000.	3000.
	1854	—	125.00	150.00	250.00	375.00
	1855	—	125.00	150.00	175.00	275.00

Mint mark: 7-pointed star

KM#	Date	Mintage	VG	Fine	VF	XF
596.3 (Y-B23.3)	1851	—	1250.	3000.	5000.	7500.
	1852	—	600.00	1400.	2500.	3500.
	1854	—	125.00	150.00	200.00	300.00
	1855	—	125.00	140.00	160.00	225.00

Mint mark: 8-pointed star
Similar to 2 Reales, C#33.

KM#	Date	Mintage	VG	Fine	VF	XF
605.1 (Y35.1)	1856	—	250.00	600.00	1100.	1650.
	1857	—	125.00	145.00	175.00	275.00
	1858	—	125.00	165.00	275.00	400.00
	1859	—	125.00	140.00	150.00	200.00
	1860	—	125.00	140.00	150.00	200.00
	1861	—	250.00	525.00	900.00	1350.
	1862	—	175.00	350.00	475.00	350.00

Mint mark: 6-pointed star

KM#	Date	Mintage	VG	Fine	VF	XF
605.2 (Y35.2)	1856	—	125.00	140.00	150.00	175.00
	1857	—	175.00	400.00	650.00	950.00
	1858	—	125.00	175.00	300.00	450.00
	1859	—	125.00	140.00	160.00	225.00
	1860	—	125.00	135.00	145.00	175.00
	1861	—	125.00	135.00	145.00	175.00
	1862	—	125.00	135.00	145.00	175.00

Mint mark: 7-pointed star

KM#	Date	Mintage	VG	Fine	VF	XF
605.3 (Y35.3)	1856	—	250.00	600.00	1100.	1650.
	1857	—	125.00	135.00	150.00	225.00
	1858	—	125.00	150.00	250.00	375.00
	1859	—	125.00	135.00	150.00	200.00
	1860	—	125.00	135.00	150.00	200.00
	1861	—	125.00	135.00	150.00	175.00
	1862	—	125.00	135.00	150.00	175.00

Mint mark: 6-pointed star
Rev: Crowned and mantled rectangluar arms.

KM#	Date	Mintage	VG	Fine	VF	XF
617.1 (Y-B35.1)	1863	—	125.00	135.00	160.00	200.00
	1864	—	125.00	135.00	145.00	175.00

Mint mark: 7-pointed star

KM#	Date	Mintage	VG	Fine	VF	XF
617.2 (Y-B35.2)	1863	—	175.00	375.00	625.00	900.00
	1864	—	175.00	400.00	700.00	1000.

SECOND DECIMAL COINAGE

100 Centimos = 1 Escudo

NOTE: For similar coins, with denominations expressed Cs. de Peso, see Philippines.

1/2 CENTIMO

COPPER
Mint mark: 8-pointed star

KM#	Date	Mintage	VG	Fine	VF	XF
632.1 (Y36.1)	1866 OM	—	5.00	12.50	21.00	35.00
	1867 OM	—	2.25	5.50	9.00	15.00
	1868 OM	—	2.25	5.50	9.00	15.00

Mint mark: 4-pointed star

KM#	Date	Mintage	VG	Fine	VF	XF
632.2 (Y36.2)	1866 OM	—	3.50	9.00	15.00	25.00
	1867 OM	—	2.25	5.50	9.00	15.00
	1868 OM	—	1.50	3.50	6.00	10.00

Mint mark: 6-pointed star

KM#	Date	Mintage	VG	Fine	VF	XF
632.3 (Y36.3)	1865	—	45.00	115.00	200.00	325.00
	1867 OM	—	18.00	45.00	75.00	125.00

Mint mark: 3-pointed star

KM#	Date	Mintage	VG	Fine	VF	XF
632.4 (Y36.4)	1866 OM	—	2.25	5.50	9.00	15.00
	1867 OM	—	2.00	4.00	7.00	12.50
	1868 OM	—	4.00	9.00	12.50	20.00

Mint mark: 7-pointed star

KM#	Date	Mintage	VG	Fine	VF	XF
632.5 (Y36.5)	1867 OM	—	6.00	14.00	25.00	40.00
	1868 OM	—	3.50	9.00	15.00	25.00

CENTIMO

COPPER
Mint mark: 8-pointed star

KM#	Date	Mintage	VG	Fine	VF	XF
633.1 (Y37.1)	1866	—	6.00	14.00	25.00	40.00
	1866 OM	—	3.50	7.00	10.00	15.00
	1867 OM	—	3.50	7.00	10.00	15.00
	1868 OM	—	2.00	4.00	7.00	12.50

Mint mark: 4-pointed star

KM#	Date	Mintage	VG	Fine	VF	XF
633.2 (Y37.2)	1866	—	8.50	21.00	35.00	60.00
	1866 OM	—	6.00	14.00	25.00	40.00
	1867 OM	—	4.50	11.00	18.00	30.00
	1868 OM	—	1.50	3.50	6.00	10.00

Mint mark: 6-pointed star

KM#	Date	Mintage	VG	Fine	VF	XF
633.3 (Y37.3)	1865	—	55.00	150.00	250.00	400.00

Mint mark: 3-pointed star

KM#	Date	Mintage	VG	Fine	VF	XF
633.4 (Y37.4)	1866	—	6.00	14.00	25.00	40.00
	1866 OM	—	4.00	8.00	16.00	30.00
	1867	—	20.00	50.00	90.00	150.00
	1867 OM	—	2.25	5.50	9.00	15.00
	1868 OM	—	2.25	5.50	9.00	15.00

Mint mark: 7-pointed star

KM#	Date	Mintage	VG	Fine	VF	XF
633.5 (Y37.5)	1867 OM	—	2.00	5.00	9.00	15.00
	1868 OM	—	2.00	5.00	9.00	15.00

2-1/2 CENTIMOS

COPPER
Mint mark: 8-pointed star

KM#	Date	Mintage	VG	Fine	VF	XF
634.1 (Y38.1)	1866	—	2.75	7.00	12.00	20.00
	1866 OM	—	2.75	7.00	12.00	20.00
	1867 OM	—	2.00	5.00	8.00	12.50
	1868 OM	—	2.00	5.00	8.00	12.50

Mint mark: 4-pointed star

KM#	Date	Mintage	VG	Fine	VF	XF
634.2 (Y38.2)	1866 OM	—	10.00	25.00	45.00	75.00
	1867 OM	—	2.00	4.50	7.50	12.50
	1868 OM	—	2.00	4.50	7.50	12.50

Mint mark: 6-pointed star

KM#	Date	Mintage	VG	Fine	VF	XF
634.3 (Y38.3)	1865	—	65.00	175.00	275.00	475.00
	1867 OM	—	17.50	40.00	70.00	120.00

Mint mark: 3-pointed star

KM#	Date	Mintage	VG	Fine	VF	XF
634.4 (Y38.4)	1866 OM	—	25.00	60.00	100.00	175.00
	1867 OM	—	2.50	6.50	11.00	18.00
	1868 OM	—	2.00	4.50	7.50	12.50

Mint mark: 7-pointed star

KM#	Date	Mintage	VG	Fine	VF	XF
634.5 (Y38.5)	1867 OM	—	2.00	4.50	7.50	12.50
	1868 OM	—	2.75	7.00	12.00	20.00

5 CENTIMOS

COPPER
Mint mark: 8-pointed star

KM#	Date	Mintage	VG	Fine	VF	XF
635.1 (Y39.1)	1866	—	10.00	25.00	40.00	70.00
	1866 OM	—	7.00	18.00	30.00	50.00
	1867	—	75.00	175.00	300.00	525.00
	1867 OM	—	2.00	4.50	7.50	12.50
	1868 OM	—	2.00	4.50	7.50	12.50

Mint mark: 4-pointed star

KM#	Date	Mintage	VG	Fine	VF	XF
635.2 (Y39.2)	1866	—	8.50	21.00	35.00	60.00
	1867 OM	—	2.00	4.50	7.50	12.50
	1868 OM	—	3.50	9.00	15.00	25.00

Mint mark: 6-pointed star

KM#	Date	Mintage	VG	Fine	VF	XF
635.3 (Y39.3)	1865	—	80.00	200.00	325.00	550.00

Mint mark: 3-pointed star

KM#	Date	Mintage	VG	Fine	VF	XF
635.4 (Y39.4)	1866 OM	—	3.50	9.00	15.00	25.00
	1867 OM	—	3.50	9.00	15.00	25.00
	1868 OM	—	2.50	6.50	11.00	18.00

Mint mark: 7-pointed star

KM#	Date	Mintage	VG	Fine	VF	XF
635.5 (Y39.5)	1867 OM	—	4.50	11.00	18.00	30.00
	1868 OM	—	2.00	4.50	7.50	12.50

10 CENTIMOS

1.2980 g, .810 SILVER, .0338 oz ASW
Mint mark: 6-pointed star
Similar to 20 Centimos, KM#628.1.

KM#	Date	Mintage	VG	Fine	VF	XF
627.1 (Y40.1)	1865	—	5.00	12.50	21.00	30.00
	1866	—	12.00	30.00	50.00	70.00
	1867	—	100.00	250.00	425.00	600.00
	1868 (68)	—	5.00	12.50	21.00	30.00

Mint mark: 7-pointed star

KM#	Date	Mintage	VG	Fine	VF	XF
627.2 (Y40.2)	1864	—	16.00	40.00	65.00	95.00
	1865	—	5.00	12.50	20.00	30.00
	1866	—	12.50	21.00	35.00	50.00
	1868	—	60.00	150.00	275.00	400.00

20 CENTIMOS

2.5960 g, .810 SILVER, .0676 oz ASW
Mint mark: 6-pointed star

KM#	Date	Mintage	VG	Fine	VF	XF
625.1 (Y41.1)	1864	—	25.00	60.00	100.00	150.00
	1865	—	7.00	16.00	27.50	40.00
	1866	—	50.00	125.00	200.00	300.00
	1867	—	75.00	175.00	300.00	450.00
	1868 (68)	—	3.50	8.50	14.00	20.00

Mint mark: 7-pointed star

KM#	Date	Mintage	VG	Fine	VF	XF
625.2	1864	—	9.00	22.50	37.50	55.00
(Y41.2)	1865	—	10.00	25.00	40.00	60.00
	1866	—	12.00	30.00	50.00	70.00

40 CENTIMOS

5.1920 g, .810 SILVER, .1352 oz ASW
Mint mark: 8-pointed star

KM#	Date	Mintage	VG	Fine	VF	XF
628.1	1865	—	80.00	200.00	350.00	500.00
(Y42.1)						

Mint mark: 6-pointed star

KM#	Date	Mintage	VG	Fine	VF	XF
628.2	1864	—	12.50	21.00	35.00	50.00
(Y42.2)	1865	—	5.00	10.00	12.50	25.00
	1866	—	3.50	7.50	12.50	25.00
	1867	—	3.50	7.50	12.50	20.00
	1868 (68)	—	3.50	7.50	12.50	20.00

Mint mark: 7-pointed star

KM#	Date	Mintage	VG	Fine	VF	XF
628.3	1864	—	60.00	150.00	250.00	350.00
(Y42.3)	1865	—	7.50	19.00	30.00	45.00
	1866	—	6.00	12.50	22.50	35.00

ESCUDO

12.9800 g, .900 SILVER, .3756 oz ASW
Mint mark: 6-pointed star

KM#	Date	Mintage	VG	Fine	VF	XF
626.1	1864	—	20.00	50.00	85.00	120.00
(Y43.1)	1865	—	16.00	40.00	65.00	95.00
	1866	—	16.00	40.00	65.00	95.00
	1867	—	6.50	12.50	22.50	35.00
	1868 (68)	—	6.00	10.00	15.00	25.00

Mint mark: 7-pointed star

KM#	Date	Mintage	VG	Fine	VF	XF
626.2	1864	—	100.00	250.00	425.00	600.00
(Y43.2)	1866	—	75.00	175.00	300.00	450.00

2 ESCUDOS

25.9600 g, .900 SILVER, .7512 oz ASW
Mint mark: 6-pointed star
Isabel II

KM#	Date	Mintage	VG	Fine	VF	XF
629	1865	—	800.00	2000.	3750.	5500.
(Y44)	1866	—	1000.	2250.	4000.	6000.
	1867	4.234	12.50	25.00	40.00	70.00
	1868(68)	2.225	25.00	60.00	100.00	150.00

1.6774 g, .900 GOLD, .0485 oz AGW

KM#	Date	Mintage	Fine	VF	XF	Unc
630	1865	—	35.00	60.00	100.00	175.00
(Y45)	1867	—	400.00	800.00	1350.	2000.
	1868 (68)	—	300.00	600.00	1000.	1500.

4 ESCUDOS

3.3548 g, .900 GOLD, .0971 oz AGW
Mint mark: 6-pointed star

KM#	Date	Mintage	Fine	VF	XF	Unc
631.1	1865	—	55.00	70.00	90.00	140.00
(Y46.1)	1866	—	55.00	70.00	90.00	140.00
	1867	—	55.00	65.00	80.00	120.00
	1868 (68)	—	75.00	100.00	140.00	225.00

Mint mark: 7-pointed star

KM#	Date	Mintage	Fine	VF	XF	Unc
631.2	1865	—	275.00	550.00	950.00	1300.
(Y46.2)	1866	—	250.00	500.00	900.00	1200.

10 ESCUDOS

8.3870 g, .900 GOLD, .2427 oz AGW
Mint mark: 6-pointed star

KM#	Date	Mintage	Fine	VF	XF	Unc
636.1	1866	—	250.00	400.00	650.00	950.00
(Y47.1)	1867	—	125.00	200.00	325.00	450.00
	1868 (68)	—	125.00	150.00	175.00	250.00

Mint mark: 7-pointed star

KM#	Date	Mintage	Fine	VF	XF	Unc
636.2	1865	—	1500.	3500.	6000.	8500.
(Y47.2)						

Mint mark: 6-pointed star

KM#	Date	Mintage	Fine	VF	XF	Unc
636.3	1868 (73)	—	125.00	160.00	200.00	300.00
(Y47.3)						

NOTE: This coin issued during the First Republic.

PROVISIONAL COINAGE

25 MILESIMAS DE ESCUDO

BRONZE
Battle of Alcolea Bridge
Mint mark: 3-pointed star

KM#	Date	Mintage	Fine	VF	XF	Unc
645	1868	.010	60.00	120.00	250.00	500.00
(Y-A50)						

THIRD DECIMAL COINAGE

10 Milesimas = 1 Centimo
100 Centimos = 1 Peseta

CENTIMO

COPPER
Mint mark: 8-pointed star

KM#	Date	Mintage	Fine	VF	XF	Unc
660	1870OM					
(Y51)		169.891	.50	1.00	3.00	15.00

2 CENTIMOS

COPPER
Mint mark: 8-pointed star

KM#	Date	Mintage	Fine	VF	XF	Unc
661	1870OM					
(Y52)		115.869	.50	1.00	3.50	16.00

5 CENTIMOS

COPPER
Mint mark: 8-pointed star

KM#	Date	Mintage	Fine	VF	XF	Unc
662	1870OM					
(Y53)		287.381	2.00	7.50	15.00	75.00

Charles VII - Pretender Issue

KM#	Date	Mintage	Fine	VF	XF	Unc
669	1875(b)	.050	18.00	30.00	50.00	75.00
(Y66)						

BRONZE

KM#	Date	Mintage	Fine	VF	XF	Unc
674	1877OM	34.376	.75	3.50	12.00	60.00
(Y69)	1878OM	67.954	.75	3.50	12.00	60.00
	1879OM	54.994	.75	3.50	12.00	60.00

10 CENTIMOS

COPPER
Obv: Lion standing w/shield.

KM#	Date	Mintage	Fine	VF	XF	Unc
663	1870OM					
(Y54)		170.088	2.00	7.50	20.00	100.00

Charles VII - Pretender Issue

KM#	Date	Mintage	Fine	VF	XF	Unc
670	1875(b)	.100	15.00	25.00	50.00	85.00
(Y67)						

BRONZE

KM#	Date	Mintage	Fine	VF	XF	Unc
675	1877OM	29.567	.35	3.50	17.50	75.00
(Y70)	1878OM	68.740	.35	3.50	17.50	70.00
	1879OM	56.313	.35	5.00	25.00	95.00

20 CENTIMOS

1.0000 g, .835 SILVER, .0268 oz ASW
Mint mark: 6-pointed star

KM#	Date	Mintage	Fine	VF	XF	Unc
650 (Y55)	1869(69) SN-M	91 pcs.	1100.	1800.	2750.	6000.
	1870(70) SN-M	5,000	150.00	225.00	400.00	1000.

50 CENTIMOS

2.5000 g, .835 SILVER, .0671 oz ASW
Mintmark: 6-pointed star

KM#	Date	Mintage	Fine	VF	XF	Unc
651 (Y56)	1869(69) SN-M	.453	10.00	20.00	100.00	325.00
	1870(70) SN-M	.540	20.00	40.00	250.00	900.00

KM#	Date	Mintage	Fine	VF	XF	Unc
685 (Y-A76)	1880(80) MS-M	2.787	1.50	3.00	20.00	100.00
	1881(81) MS-M	5.647	1.50	3.00	25.00	115.00
	1885(85) MS-M	—	— Reported, not confirmed			
	1885/1(86) MS-M	1.468	6.00	12.00	35.00	175.00
	1885(86) MS-M	Inc. Ab.	1.50	4.00	27.50	125.00

KM#	Date	Mintage	Fine	VF	XF	Unc
690 (Y79)	1889(89) MP-M	.537	5.00	10.00	35.00	145.00
	1892/89(92) PG-M	3.954	4.00	8.00	25.00	120.00
	1892(92) PG-M	Inc. Ab.	1.00	2.50	10.00	40.00
	1892(22) PG-M	—	8.00	17.50	35.00	130.00
	1892/82(82) PG-M	—	10.00	20.00	50.00	135.00
	1892(82) PG-M	—	10.00	20.00	50.00	135.00
	1892(G2) PG-M	—	15.00	27.50	65.00	150.00
	1892(62) PG-M	—	17.50	35.00	100.00	200.00
	1892(62) PG-M/MP-M	—	—	—	—	—

NOTE: Varieties exist.

KM#	Date	Mintage	Fine	VF	XF	Unc
703 (Y83)	1894(94) PG-V	1.109	4.00	10.00	40.00	125.00

KM#	Date	Mintage	Fine	VF	XF	Unc
705 (Y87)	1896(96) PG-V	.297	15.00	32.50	100.00	250.00
	1900(00) SM-V	2.128	1.00	3.00	10.00	30.00

PESETA

5.0000 g, .835 SILVER, .1342 oz ASW
Mint mark: 6-pointed star
Obv. leg: GOBIERNO PROVISIONAL

KM#	Date	Mintage	Fine	VF	XF	Unc
652 (Y-A55)	1869(69) SN-M	7.000	3.50	15.00	90.00	300.00

Obv. leg: ESPANA

KM#	Date	Mintage	Fine	VF	XF	Unc
653 (Y58)	1869(69) SN-M	.367	30.00	220.00	850.00	2250.
	1870(70) SN-M	3.865	7.50	32.00	165.00	450.00
	1870(73) DE-M	5.165	4.00	25.00	145.00	350.00

KM#	Date	Mintage	Fine	VF	XF	Unc
672 (Y-B75)	1876(76) DE-M	4.427	3.50	30.00	160.00	450.00

KM#	Date	Mintage	Fine	VF	XF	Unc
686 (Y-B76)	1881(81) MS-M	.799	18.00	100.00	525.00	1250.
	1882/81(82) MS-M	—	10.00	75.00	325.00	750.00
	1882(82) MS-M	3.506	3.50	15.00	185.00	500.00
	1883(83) MS-M	8.440	3.00	15.00	120.00	350.00
	1884/3(84) MS-M	5,839	250.00	525.00	1650.	4500.
	1885(85) MS-M	3.336	3.50	15.00	185.00	500.00
	1885(86) MS-M	3.954	3.50	12.50	145.00	450.00

KM#	Date	Mintage	Fine	VF	XF	Unc
691 (Y80)	1889(89) MP-M	.760	35.00	85.00	265.00	1250.
	1891(91) PG-M	4.948	3.00	15.00	65.00	250.00

KM#	Date	Mintage	Fine	VF	XF	Unc
702 (Y84)	1893(93) PG-L	1.958	5.50	18.00	150.00	450.00
	1894(94) PG-V	1.044	18.00	65.00	225.00	800.00

KM#	Date	Mintage	Fine	VF	XF	Unc
706 (Y88)	1896(96) PG-V	6.412	2.50	7.00	20.00	90.00
	1899(99) SG-V	7.472	2.50	7.00	20.00	80.00
	1900(00) SM-V	18.650	2.00	5.00	15.00	70.00

NOTE: Later dates (1901-1902) exist for this type.

2 PESETAS

10.0000 g, .835 SILVER, .2685 oz ASW
Mint mark: 6-pointed star

KM#	Date	Mintage	Fine	VF	XF	Unc
654 (Y59)	1869(68) SN-M	—	17.50	50.00	165.00	600.00
	1869(69) SN-M	3.270	5.00	10.00	30.00	250.00
	1870(70) SN-M	1.504	6.50	12.50	65.00	300.00
	1870(73) DE-M	11.880	5.00	9.00	27.50	200.00
	1870(74) DE-M	14.893	5.00	9.00	27.50	175.00
	1870(75) DE-M	4.997	6.00	11.50	40.00	275.00

KM#	Date	Mintage	Fine	VF	XF	Unc
678 (Y-C76)	1879(79) EM-M	5.578	5.50	9.00	32.50	250.00
	1881(81) MS-M	3.639	5.50	9.00	32.50	250.00
	1882/1(82) MS-M	20.343	4.50	7.50	25.00	200.00
	1882(82) MS-M	Inc. Ab.	4.50	7.50	25.00	175.00
	1883(83) MS-M	3.318	5.00	9.00	28.00	200.00
	1884(84) MS-M	2.839	5.50	10.00	30.00	225.00

KM#	Date	Mintage	Fine	VF	XF	Unc
692 (Y81)	1889(89) MP-M	.559	15.00	30.00	125.00	350.00
	1891(91) PG-M	.093	75.00	150.00	475.00	1200.
	1892(92) PG-M	1.379	7.00	15.00	50.00	175.00

KM#	Date	Mintage	Fine	VF	XF	Unc
704 (Y85)	1894(94) PG-V	.279	35.00	125.00	365.00	1000.

5 PESETAS

25.0000 g, .900 SILVER, .7234 oz ASW
Mint mark: 6-pointed star

KM#	Date	Mintage	Fine	VF	XF	Unc
655 (Y60)	1869(69) SN-M	100 pcs.	3500.	5500.	7500.	12,000.
	1870(70) SN-M	5.923	12.00	25.00	65.00	285.00

KM#	Date	Mintage	Fine	VF	XF	Unc
666 (Y61)	1871(71) SD-M	13.641	10.00	20.00	45.00	200.00
	1871(73) SD-M	Inc. Ab.	20.00	40.00	135.00	250.00
	1871(73) DE-M	2.870	100.00	225.00	550.00	1500.
	1871(74) DE-M	5.075	10.00	20.00	80.00	220.00
	1871(75) DE-M	3.000	10.00	20.00	80.00	200.00

Mint mark: 6-pointed star

KM#	Date	Mintage	Fine	VF	XF	Unc
671 (Y74)	1875(75) DE-M	8.641	10.00	20.00	65.00	185.00
	1876(76) DE-M	8.548	10.00	20.00	65.00	225.00

KM#	Date	Mintage	Fine	VF	XF	Unc
676 (Y75)	1877(77) DE-M	6.987	10.00	20.00	60.00	200.00
	1878(78) DE-M	5.000	10.00	20.00	60.00	200.00
	1878(78) EM-M	4.147	10.00	20.00	65.00	225.00
	1879(79) EM-M	1.634	15.00	35.00	140.00	300.00
	1881(81) MS-M	.699	25.00	75.00	280.00	600.00

KM#	Date	Mintage	Fine	VF	XF	Unc
688 (Y76)	1882/1 MS-M	—	30.00	60.00	250.00	800.00
	1882(81) MS-M	—	10.00	22.00	100.00	350.00
	1882(82) MS-M	1.662	10.00	22.00	90.00	225.00
	1883(83) MS-M	5.507	8.00	12.00	45.00	175.00
	1884(84) MS-M	5.848	8.00	12.00	45.00	175.00
	1885(85) MS-M	3.144	8.00	12.00	45.00	175.00
	1885(86) MS-M	1.951	10.00	20.00	160.00	300.00
	1885(87) MS-M	9.000	8.00	12.00	45.00	175.00
	1885(87) MP-M	2.803	15.00	25.00	135.00	275.00

KM#	Date	Mintage	Fine	VF	XF	Unc
689 (Y82)	1888(88) MS-M	—	165.00	350.00	725.00	1600.
	1888(88) MP-M	10.644	8.00	12.00	45.00	165.00
	1889(89) MP-M	4.681	10.00	15.00	60.00	185.00
	1890(90) MP-M	4.275	10.00	15.00	60.00	185.00
	1890(90) PG-M	3.000	10.00	15.00	60.00	185.00
	1891(91) PG-M	11.660	8.00	12.00	45.00	165.00
	1892(92) PG-M	1.294	12.50	20.00	85.00	250.00

KM#	Date	Mintage	Fine	VF	XF	Unc
700 (Y86)	1892(92) PG-M	7.000	10.00	20.00	75.00	250.00
	1893(93) PG-L	2.500	12.00	20.00	85.00	325.00
	1893(93) PG-V	.518	25.00	75.00	275.00	600.00
	1894(94) PG-V	3.871	12.00	20.00	80.00	300.00

KM#	Date	Mintage	Fine	VF	XF	Unc
707 (Y89)	1896(96) PG-V	4.272	10.00	18.00	60.00	135.00
	1897(97) SG-V	6.733	8.00	15.00	50.00	120.00
	1898(98) SG-V	39.977	8.00	15.00	35.00	90.00
	1899(99) SG-V	13.930	30.00	60.00	150.00	250.00

NOTE: All other date and mintmasters or assayers initial combinations on crowns of this era are contemporary counterfeits.

10 PESETAS

3.2258 g, .900 GOLD, .0933 oz AGW
Mint mark: 6-pointed star

KM#	Date	Mintage	Fine	VF	XF	Unc
677 (Y77)	1878(78) EM-M	.091	125.00	200.00	300.00	400.00
	1879(79) EM-M	.033	400.00	800.00	1250.	1750.
	1878(61) DE-M	496 pcs.	—	—	750.00	1000.
	1878(62) DE-M	.018	—	—	75.00	85.00

NOTE: The above 2 coins were restruck by the Spanish Mint from original dies in 1961 and 1962 and are considered official restrike issues.

20 PESETAS

6.4516 g, .900 GOLD, .1867 oz AGW
Mint mark: 6-pointed star

KM#	Date	Mintage	Fine	VF	XF	Unc
693 (Y-A82)	1889(89) MP-M	.875	125.00	200.00	300.00	425.00
	1890(90) MP-M	2.344	100.00	115.00	150.00	250.00
	1887(61) PG-V	800 pcs.	—	—	550.00	850.00
	1887(62) PG-V	.011	—	—	100.00	150.00

NOTE: For above two coins dated (61) & (62) see note after 10 Pesetas, Y#77.

KM#	Date	Mintage	Fine	VF	XF	Unc
701 (Y-A86)	1892(92) PG-M	2.430	800.00	1400.	2000.	2750.

KM#	Date	Mintage	Fine	VF	XF	Unc
709 (Y-A89)	1899(99) SM-V	2.086	125.00	175.00	250.00	350.00
	1896(61) MP-M	900 pcs.	—	—	600.00	750.00
	1896(62) MP-M	.012	—	—	110.00	160.00

NOTE: For above 2 coins dated (61) & (62) see note after 10 Pesetas, KM#677.

25 PESETAS

8.0645 g, .900 GOLD, .2333 oz AGW
Mint mark: 6-pointed star

KM#	Date	Mintage	Fine	VF	XF	Unc
667 (Y-A62)	1871(75) SD-M	25 pcs.	—	—	Rare	—

KM#	Date	Mintage	Fine	VF	XF	Unc
673 (Y78)	1876(76) DE-M	1.281	120.00	135.00	150.00	200.00
	1877(77) DE-M	10.048	120.00	135.00	150.00	200.00
	1878(78) DE-M	5.192	120.00	135.00	150.00	200.00
	1878(78) EM-M	3.000	120.00	135.00	150.00	200.00
	1879(79) EM-M	3.478	120.00	135.00	150.00	200.00
	1880(80) MS-M	6.863	120.00	135.00	150.00	200.00
	1876(61) DE-M	300 pcs.	—	—	1800.	2500.
	1876(62) DE-M	6,000	—	—	300.00	400.00

NOTE: For above 2 coins dated (61) & (62) see note after 10 Pesetas, KM#677.

KM#	Date	Mintage	Fine	VF	XF	Unc
687 (Y-A78)	1881(81) MS-M	4.366	120.00	135.00	150.00	200.00
	1882(82) MS-M	.414	200.00	400.00	600.00	800.00
	1883(83) MS-M	.669	200.00	425.00	650.00	900.00
	1884(84) MS-M	1.033	150.00	250.00	450.00	600.00
	1885(85) MS-M	.503	500.00	900.00	1200.	1600.
	1885(86) MS-M	.491	750.00	1500.	2000.	2500.

100 PESETAS

32.2581 g, .900 GOLD, .9334 oz AGW
Mint mark: 6-pointed star
Provisional Government

KM#	Date	Mintage	Fine	VF	XF	Unc
664 (Y-B62)	1870(70) SD-M	12 pcs.	—	—	Rare	—

.900 YELLOW GOLD

KM#	Date	Mintage	Fine	VF	XF	Unc
668a (Y-C62)	1871(71) SD-M	25 pcs.	—	—	Rare	—

.900 RED GOLD

KM#	Date	Mintage	Fine	VF	XF	Unc
668b (Y-C62a)	1871(71) SD-M	50 pcs.	—	—	Rare	—

KM#	Date	Mintage	Fine	VF	XF	Unc
708 (Y90)	1897(97) SG-V	.150	600.00	900.00	1250.	2000.
	1897(61) SG-V	810 pcs.	—	—	1500.	2000.
	1897(62) SG-V	6,000	—	—	550.00	750.00

NOTE: The above 2 coins were restruck by the Spanish Mint from original dies in 1961 and 1962 and are considered official restrike issues.

REVOLUTIONARY COINAGE

NOTE: Former Y#62, 2 Pesetas, 1873 Cartagena Mint, Cantonal issue similar to KM#715, 10 Reales and KM#716, 5 Pesetas are all considered fantasies struck later for collectors. Refer to *Unusual World Coins*, 3rd edition, Krause Publications, Inc.

DIEZ (10) REALES

(2-1/2 Pesetas)

13.5000 g, .900 SILVER, .3907 oz ASW
Mint: Cartagena

KM#	Date	Mintage	Fine	VF	XF	Unc
715 (Y64)	1873	—	150.00	350.00	650.00	1200.

CINCO (5) PESETAS

(20 Reales)

25.0000 g, .900 SILVER, .7234 oz ASW
Mint: Cartagena

KM#	Date	Mintage	Fine	VF	XF	Unc
716 (Y63)	1873	—	75.00	150.00	225.00	450.00

NOTE: Several varieties exist.

PRETENDER COINAGE (PT)

Charles V

1835-1840

Charles V, brother of Ferdinand VII, claimed the throne upon the death of his brother, but Isabella II became the ruler. Charles V fled to Portugal and set up, what he called, the true monarchy of Spain.

NOTE: For 4 Reales issues of 1838, see regular coinage.

8 MARAVEDIS

COPPER
Mint mark: Aqueduct
c/m: CAB/BER/A on 8 Maravedi of Ferdinand VII.

C#	Date	Mintage	Fine	VF	XF
PT6 (C153)	(1833-40)	—	175.00	300.00	400.00

2 REALES

2.6291 g, .903 SILVER, .0761 oz ASW
Mint mark: Aqueduct
Obv: Mint mark above, asterisk below inscription.

C#	Date	Mintage	Good	VG	Fine	VF
PT7 (C157.1)	1837	—	225.00	375.00	450.00	600.00

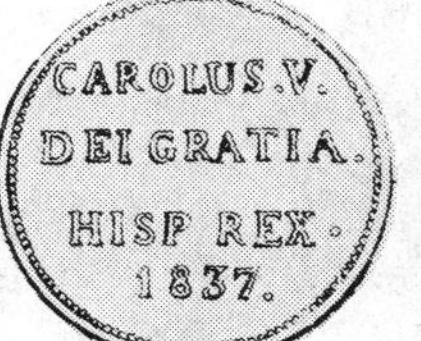

Obv: W/o mint mark and asterisk.

C#	Date	Mintage	Good	VG	Fine	VF
PT8 (C157.2)	1837	—	225.00	375.00	450.00	600.00

Charles VII

1872-75

A grandson of Charles V who claimed the throne and

maintained a court and government in exile. All Charles VII pieces were made at the Brussells Mint.

NOTE: Some pretender issues which circulated are listed in the regular coinage.

50 CENTIMOS

2.0875 g, .835 SILVER, .0671 oz ASW

KM#	Date	Mintage	VF	XF	Unc
PT13 (A67)	1876(b)	—	350.00	450.00	650.00

5 PESETAS

25.0000 g, .900 SILVER, .7234 oz ASW
Mint: Paris
Rev: Crowned arms divide value, 5-P.
Reeded edge

KM#	Date	Mintage	VF	XF	Unc
PT9.1 (68)	1874	—	—	—	2200.
	1875	—	—	—	2200.
Piedfort (double thickenss)					
PT9.2 (68a)	1874	—	—	—	3500.
Plain edge					
PT9.3 (68b)	1874	—	—	—	3500.
Triple piedfort					
PT9.4 (68c)	1874	—	—	—	4500.
BRONZE					
PT9.1a (68d)	1874	—	—	—	1200.
	1875	—	—	—	1200.

SILVER, 25.50 g
Rev: Crowned arms divide value, P-5, diamond and C below. Plain edge

KM#	Date	Mintage	VF	XF	Unc
PT10.1 (A68)	1874	—	—	—	2500.
Piedfort (double thickenss)					
PT10.2 (A68a)	1874	—	—	—	4000.
Reeded edge					
PT10.3 (A68b)	1874	—	—	—	3500.
BRONZE - Obv. only					
PT10.1a (A68c)	1874	—	—	—	1000.
BRONZE - Rev. only					
PT10.1b (A68d)	1874	—	—	—	1000.

SILVER, 25.50 g
Rev: Crowned arms divide value, 5-P, date below.

KM#	Date	Mintage	VF	XF	Unc
PT11.1 (B68)	1874	—	—	—	2500.
Piedfort (double thickness)					
PT11.2 (B68b)	1874	—	—	—	4000.
BRONZE					
PT11.1a (B68a)	1874	—	—	—	1200.
TIN					
PT11.1b (B68c)	1874	—	—	—	1200.

1.6129 g, .900 GOLD, .0467 oz AGW
Obv: Laureate head right.
Rev: Crowned arms divide value.

KM#	Date	Mintage	VF	XF	Unc
PT12 (B68d)	1874	—	—	Rare	—

SILVER, 25.50 g
Mint: Brussels

KM#	Date	Mintage	VF	XF	Unc
PT14 (C68)	1885	—	—	Proof	850.00

NOTE: The private patterns of Charles VII, were of a purely political speculative nature.

PATTERNS (Pn)

(Including off metal strikes)

KM#	Date	Mintage	Identification	Mkt.Val.
Pn10	1868	—	5 Pesetas, Copper	—

KM#	Date	Mintage	Identification	Mkt.Val.
Pn11	1869	—	10 Centimos, Copper, lion w/shield right	Rare

KM#	Date	Mintage	Identification	Mkt.Val.
Pn12	1870	—	10 Centimos, Copper, lion w/shield left	Rare
Pn13	1878	—	1 Centimo, Copper, Alfonso VII	9000.
Pn14	1878	—	2 Centimos, Copper, Alfonso XII	6000.

KM#	Date	Mintage	Identification	Mkt.Val.
Pn15	1896	—	20 Centimos, White metal	—

The following cities and provinces of Spain were coin-issuing entities.

BALEARIC ISLANDS

(Yslas Baleares)

Majorca

The Balearic Islands, an archipelago located in the Mediterranean Sea off the east coast of Spain including Majorca, Minorca, Cabrera, Ibiza, Formentera and a number of islets.

Majorca, largest of the Balearic Islands is famous for its 1,000-year-old olive trees.

RULERS

Ferdinand (Fernando) VII, 1808-1833

MONETARY SYSTEM

12 Dineros = 6 Doblers = 1 Sueldo (Sou)
30 Sueldos = 1 Duro

12 DINEROS

COPPER

C#	Date	Mintage	VG	Fine	VF	XF
L51	1811	—	40.00	75.00	125.00	275.00
	1812 DEI GRATIA, small date					
		—	5.00	8.00	15.00	35.00
	1812 DEI GRATIA, large date					
		—	5.00	8.00	15.00	35.00
	1812 DEI GRAT					
		—	12.50	20.00	35.00	85.00

30 SUELDOS

(Sous)

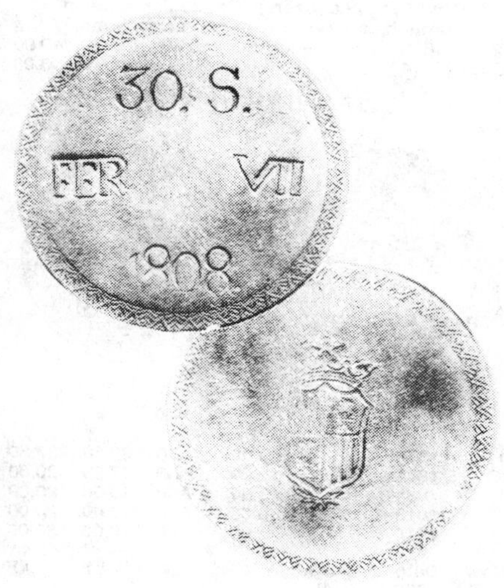

SILVER

Obv. and rev: Ornate rim.

C#	Date	Mintage	VG	Fine	VF	XF
L7.1	1808	—	50.00	85.00	120.00	240.00

Obv: FER.VII, value and date in depression.

C#	Date	Mintage	VG	Fine	VF	XF
L7.2	1808	—	40.00	60.00	110.00	200.00

Rev: Similar to C#L52.2.

C#	Date	Mintage	VG	Fine	VF	XF
L52.1	1808 FER. VII		90.00	165.00	225.00	340.00

Obv: W/o FER VII.

C#	Date	Mintage	VG	Fine	VF	XF
L52.2	1808	—	150.00	300.00	700.00	1250.

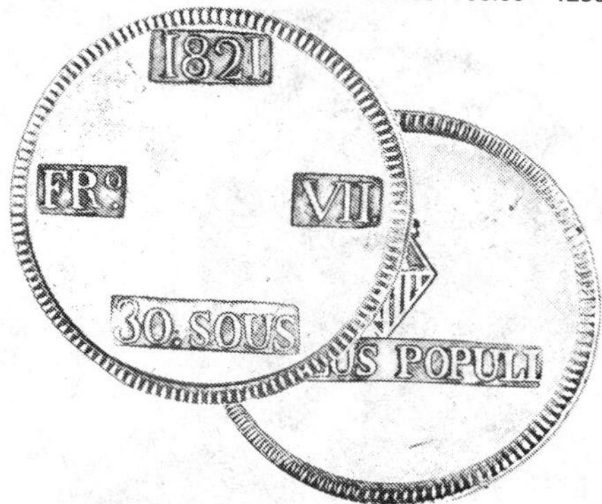

C#	Date	Mintage	VG	Fine	VF	XF
L53.1	1821 FRo. VII		40.00	60.00	110.00	200.00

Obv: (error) FRo.VII inverted.

C#	Date	Mintage	VG	Fine	VF	XF
L53.2	1821 FRo. VII		300.00	600.00	1000.	1500.

5 PESETAS

SILVER

Obv. leg. ends: . . . CONST.

C#	Date	Mintage	VG	Fine	VF	XF
L9.1	1823	—	40.00	65.00	115.00	200.00

Obv. leg. ends: . . . EYND.

C#	Date	Mintage	VG	Fine	VF	XF
L9.2	1823	—	60.00	90.00	150.00	275.00

BARCELONA

Barcelona was a maritime province located in north-east Spain. The city was the provincial capital of Barcelona. Barcelona is a major port and commercial center.

RULERS

Joseph (Jose) Napoleon, 1808-1814
Ferdinand (Fernando) VII, restored 1814-1833

MINT MARKS

Ba - Barcelona

MONETARY SYSTEM

4 Quartos = 1 Sueldo
6 Sueldos = 1 Peseta

1/2 QUARTO

COPPER
Similar to 4 Quartos, KM#67.

KM#	Date	Mintage	Good	VG	Fine	VF
75 (C-L11)	ND(1811)	—	20.00	40.00	65.00	100.00

QUARTO

COPPER
Similar to 4 Quartos, KM#67.

KM#	Date	Mintage	Good	VG	Fine	VF
65	1808	—	17.50	35.00	70.00	110.00
(C-L12)	1809	—	10.00	20.00	35.00	55.00
	1810	—	10.00	20.00	35.00	55.00
	1811	—	20.00	40.00	80.00	125.00
	1812	—	10.00	20.00	35.00	55.00
	1813	—	20.00	40.00	75.00	165.00

2 QUARTOS

COPPER
Similar to 4 Quartos, KM#67.

KM#	Date	Mintage	Good	VG	Fine	VF
66	1808	—	10.00	25.00	50.00	85.00
(C-L13)	1809	—	10.00	20.00	30.00	45.00
	1810	—	20.00	40.00	80.00	125.00
	1813	—	10.00	25.00	50.00	75.00
	1814	—	20.00	60.00	125.00	200.00

3 QUARTOS

COPPER

KM#	Date	Mintage	Good	VG	Fine	VF
80 (C-L21)	1823	—	2.00	5.00	15.00	25.00

4 QUARTOS

COPPER

KM#	Date	Mintage	Good	VG	Fine	VF
67	1808	—	10.00	30.00	60.00	90.00
(C-L14)	1809	—	5.00	10.00	20.00	35.00
	1810	—	3.00	10.00	15.00	22.00
	1811	—	4.00	10.00	15.00	22.00
	1812	—	3.00	10.00	15.00	22.00

CAST COPPER

KM#	Date	Mintage	Good	VG	Fine	VF
67a (C-L14a)	1808	—	5.00	11.50	15.00	22.00
	1809	—	3.00	9.50	15.00	22.00
	1810	—	2.00	9.50	15.00	22.00
	1811	—	4.00	10.00	17.50	28.00
	1812	—	3.00	9.50	15.00	22.00

COPPER
Obv. leg: Widely spaced.

KM#	Date	Mintage	Good	VG	Fine	VF
77 (C-L14b)	1813	—	5.00	12.50	25.00	35.00
	1814	—	7.50	15.00	30.00	45.00

CAST COPPER

KM#	Date	Mintage	Good	VG	Fine	VF
77a (C-L14c)	1813	—	5.00	11.50	15.00	22.00
	1814	—	5.00	11.50	15.00	22.00

6 QUARTOS

COPPER

KM#	Date	Mintage	Good	VG	Fine	VF
81 (C-L22)	1823	—	10.00	20.00	30.00	50.00

PESETA

SILVER

KM#	Date	Mintage	Good	VG	Fine	VF
70	1809	—	20.00	40.00	55.00	90.00
(C-L15)	1810	—	15.00	25.00	30.00	50.00
	1811	—	15.00	25.00	30.00	50.00
	1812	—	18.00	35.00	45.00	75.00
	1813	—	20.00	40.00	50.00	80.00
	1814	—	35.00	65.00	120.00	200.00

2-1/2 PESETAS

SILVER

KM#	Date	Mintage	Good	VG	Fine	VF
68	1808	—	125.00	250.00	300.00	400.00
(C-L16)	1809	—	100.00	165.00	225.00	300.00
	1810	—	200.00	400.00	500.00	650.00
	1814	—	300.00	575.00	725.00	975.00

5 PESETAS

SILVER

KM#	Date	Mintage	Good	VG	Fine	VF
69	1808	—	100.00	225.00	375.00	600.00
(C-L17)	1809	—	100.00	225.00	375.00	600.00
	1810	—	100.00	225.00	375.00	600.00
	1811	—	100.00	225.00	325.00	450.00
	1812	—	125.00	250.00	400.00	700.00
	1813	—	300.00	600.00	900.00	1250.
	1814	—	1000.	2100.	2800.	3500.

20 PESETAS

GOLD

KM#	Date	Mintage	Good	VG	Fine	VF
76	1812Ba	—	250.00	600.00	850.00	1250.
(C-L18)	1813Ba	—	350.00	750.00	1100.	1650.
	1814Ba	—	1000.	2500.	3500.	5000.

CATALONIA

Catalonia, a triangular territory forming the northeast corner of the Iberian Peninsula, was formerly a province of Spain and also formerly a principality of Aragon. In 1833 the region was divided into four provinces, Barcelona, Gerona, Lerida and Tarragona.

RULERS

Ferdinand (Fernando) VII, 1808-1833
Isabel II, 1833-1868

MINT MARKS

C - Catalonia

MONETARY SYSTEM

12 Ardites (Dineros) = 8 Ochavos =
4 Quartos = 1 Sueldo
6 Sueldos = 1 Peseta
5 Pesetas = 1 Duro

OCHAVO

COPPER

KM#	Date	Mintage	Good	VG	Fine	VF
118 (C-L34)	1813	—	10.00	20.00	30.00	45.00

QUARTO

COPPER
Obv: Crowned spade Catalonian arms.
Rev: Crowned Spanish arms.

KM#	Date	Mintage	Good	VG	Fine	VF
119 (C-L35)	1813	—	10.00	15.00	25.00	40.00

QUARTO/Y MEDIO

(1-1/2 Quartos)

COPPER
Obv: Crowned round Catalonian arms.
Rev: Crowned oval Spanish arms.

KM#	Date	Mintage	Good	VG	Fine	VF
117	1811	—	10.00	20.00	40.00	65.00
(C-L36)	1812	—	25.00	65.00	100.00	125.00
	1813	—	10.00	20.00	30.00	45.00

II QUARTOS

COPPER
Obv: Crowned lozenge Catalonian arms in branches. Rev: Crowned Spanish arms.

KM#	Date	Mintage	Good	VG	Fine	VF
120	1813	—	7.50	15.00	25.00	40.00
(C-L37)	1814	—	10.00	22.50	32.50	50.00

III QUARTOS

COPPER

KM#	Date	Mintage	Good	VG	Fine	VF
115	1810	—	9.00	17.50	22.50	37.50
(C-L38)	1811	—	7.00	12.50	17.50	30.00
	1812	—	5.00	7.50	10.00	20.00
	1813	—	5.00	7.50	10.00	20.00
	1814	—	5.00	7.50	10.00	20.00

KM#	Date	Mintage	VG	Fine	VF	XF
125 (C-L40)	1836 CATHAL	—	50.00	125.00	225.00	300.00
	1836 CATALUNA	—	40.00	80.00	120.00	150.00

KM#	Date	Mintage	VG	Fine	VF	XF
126 (C-L40a)	1836	—	12.50	25.00	32.50	40.00
	1837	—	5.00	7.50	12.50	25.00
	1838	—	6.00	10.00	15.00	30.00
	1839	—	6.00	10.00	15.00	30.00
	1840	—	12.00	25.00	40.00	65.00
	1841	—	5.00	7.50	12.50	25.00
	1842	—	20.00	40.00	80.00	110.00
	1843	—	22.00	45.00	65.00	80.00
	1844	—	10.00	15.00	20.00	30.00
	1845	—	20.00	40.00	75.00	100.00
	1846	—	10.00	20.00	25.00	35.00

VI QUARTOS

COPPER

KM#	Date	Mintage	Good	VG	Fine	VF
116	1810	—	10.00	20.00	30.00	50.00
(C-L39)	1811/0	—	12.00	25.00	40.00	60.00
	1811	—	10.00	20.00	30.00	50.00
	1812	—	7.50	12.50	20.00	35.00
	1813	—	7.50	12.50	20.00	35.00
	1814	—	12.00	25.00	40.00	60.00

KM#	Date	Mintage	VG	Fine	VF	XF
127 (C-L40.3)	1836	—	110.00	250.00	400.00	500.00

KM#	Date	Mintage	VG	Fine	VF	XF
128 (C-L40.3a)	1836	—	12.00	25.00	40.00	55.00
	1837	—	7.50	12.50	22.50	45.00
	1838	—	7.50	12.50	20.00	40.00
	1839	—	7.50	12.50	20.00	40.00
	1840	—	7.50	12.50	20.00	40.00
	1841	—	12.50	20.00	30.00	45.00
	1842	—	100.00	225.00	375.00	625.00
	1843	—	30.00	70.00	125.00	300.00
	1844	—	7.50	12.50	20.00	40.00
	1845	—	7.50	12.50	20.00	40.00
	1846	—	7.50	12.50	20.00	40.00
	1847	—	45.00	125.00	200.00	250.00
	1848	—	45.00	125.00	200.00	250.00

Charles V - Pretender Issue
Mint mark: BGA
Rev: Crowned Catalonian arms within legend.

KM#	Date	Mintage	Good	VG	Fine	VF
135 (C-A55)	1840	—	250.00	400.00	550.00	700.00

Rev: Crowned Spanish arms within legend.

KM#	Date	Mintage	Good	VG	Fine	VF
136 (C155)	1840	—	300.00	500.00	650.00	800.00

PESETA

SILVER
Mint mark: B

KM#	Date	Mintage	VG	Fine	VF	XF
129 (C-L40.7)	1836 PS	—	20.00	50.00	80.00	150.00
	1837 PS	—	25.00	65.00	110.00	175.00

GERONA

Gerona, a maritime frontier province in the extreme northeast corner of Spain and the provincial capital city of Gerona. The city of Gerona is the ancient city of Gerunda where St. Paul and St. James known as Santiago, patron saint of Spain and one of the twelve apostles, first rested when they came to Spain.

RULERS

Philipus III, 1598-1621
Ferdinand (Fernando) VII, 1808-1833

MONETARY SYSTEM

12 Ardites (Dineros) = 8 Ochavos =
4 Quartos = 1 Sueldo
6 Sueldos = 1 Peseta
5 Pesetas = 1 Duro

DURO

SILVER

10 (C-L41) 1808 — 50.00 90.00 140.00 250.00

COPPER

11 (C-L41a) 1809 — 60.00 100.00 160.00 275.00

NOTE: Rim reeding on the Duro is hand cut making each example unique.

5 PESETAS

SILVER
Rev. leg: GERONA. . .

KM#	Date	Mintage	VG	Fine	VF	XF
12 (C-L42)	1809	—	1250.	2300.	3800.	4500.

LERIDA

Lerida, a frontier province of northern Spain and the provincial capital city of Lerida. The province is bounded on the north by France and on the east by Barcelona and Gerona.

RULERS

Ferdinand VII, 1808-1833

MONETARY SYSTEM

12 Ardites (Dineros) = 8 Ochavos =
4 Quartos = 1 Sueldo
6 Sueldos = 1 Peseta
5 Pesetas = 1 Duro

5 PESETAS

SILVER

10 (C-L45) 1809 — 2000. 3000. 4500. 6000.

Rev. leg: LERIDA. . .

11 (C-L46) 1809 — 1800. 2500. 4000. 5500.

NAVARRE

Navarre, a frontier province of northern Spain and a former kingdom lies on the western end of the border between France and Spain. From the 10th through the 12th centuries Navarre was a solid power in the region.

After 1234 the kingdom fell under French dominance. In 1516 Ferdinand annexed Navarre to Spain and it was under this vice royalty that coinage was struck at the mint in Pamplona.

The Kingdom of Navarre was ultimately divided and absorbed by France and Spain.

RULERS

Carlos VII (IV in Spain), 1788-1808
Ferdinand (Fernando) III (VII in Spain), 1808-1833

MINT MARKS

P - Pamplona

1/2 MARAVEDI

COPPER
Similar to 6 Maravedi, KM#125.

KM#	Date	Mintage	VG	Fine	VF	XF
120	1818PP	—	15.00	27.50	35.00	40.00
(C-L81)	1819PP	—	20.00	40.00	50.00	60.00

KM#	Date	Mintage	VG	Fine	VF	XF
135	1831PP	—	12.00	25.00	35.00	45.00
(C-L82)	1381PP (error)		90.00	165.00	200.00	250.00
	1832PP	—	90.00	165.00	200.00	250.00

MARAVEDI

COPPER
Obv: CAR VI monogram. Rev: Arms.

KM#	Date	Mintage	VG	Fine	VF	XF
90 (C-L71)	ND P	—	10.00	20.00	27.50	35.00

COPPER

KM#	Date	Mintage	VG	Fine	VF	XF
121	1818PP	—	10.00	20.00	30.00	40.00
(C-L83)	1824Ja	—	10.00	20.00	27.50	35.00
	1825PP	—	8.00	12.50	22.50	30.00
	1826PP	—	8.00	12.50	22.50	30.00

Obv: Laureate bust. Rev: Arms.

KM#	Date	Mintage	VG	Fine	VF	XF
122 (C-L83a)	1818PP	—	9.00	17.50	22.50	30.00
	1819PP	—	9.00	17.50	22.50	30.00
	1820PP	—	10.00	20.00	27.50	35.00

Similar to 1/2 Maravedi, KM#135.

KM#	Date	Mintage	VG	Fine	VF	XF
130	1829PP	—	7.50	15.00	20.00	25.00
(C-L84)	1830/20PP	—	7.50	15.00	20.00	25.00
	1830PP	—	7.50	15.00	20.00	25.00
	1831PP	—	9.00	17.50	22.50	30.00
	1832PP	—	9.00	17.50	22.50	30.00
	1833PP	—	15.00	30.00	45.00	50.00

3 MARAVEDIS

COPPER
Similar to 6 Maravedi, KM#126.

KM#	Date	Mintage	VG	Fine	VF	XF
123	1818PP	—	25.00	45.00	65.00	85.00
(C-L89)	1819PP	—	20.00	35.00	55.00	70.00
	1820PP	—	20.00	35.00	55.00	70.00
	1825PP	—	20.00	35.00	55.00	70.00
	1826PP	—	20.00	35.00	55.00	70.00

Similar to 6 Maravedi, KM#126, but leg: FERDIN. III. . .

KM#	Date	Mintage	VG	Fine	VF	XF
124 (C-L89a)	1818PP	—	15.00	30.00	45.00	65.00
	1819PP	—	15.00	30.00	45.00	65.00

Similar to 1/2 Maravedi, KM#135.

KM#	Date	Mintage	VG	Fine	VF	XF
131	1829PP	—	12.50	25.00	40.00	60.00
(C-L90)	1830PP	—	10.00	15.00	20.00	40.00
	1831PP	—	15.00	30.00	45.00	65.00
	1832PP	—	12.50	25.00	40.00	60.00
	1833PP	—	12.50	25.00	40.00	60.00

6 MARAVEDIS

COPPER
Obv: Young bust, bare head. Rev: Arms.

KM#	Date	Mintage	VG	Fine	VF	XF
125 (C-L92)	1818PP	—	25.00	50.00	80.00	100.00

Obv: Laureate bust.

KM#	Date	Mintage	VG	Fine	VF	XF
126 (C-L92a)	1818PP	—	35.00	70.00	120.00	150.00
	1819PP	—	25.00	50.00	80.00	100.00
	1820PP	—	30.00	55.00	90.00	125.00

TARRAGONA

Tarragona, a maritime province in north east Spain, south of Barcelona and Lerida, and the provincial capital city of Tarragona. The province produces excellent wines; the city is a flourishing seaport.

RULERS

Ferdinand (Fernando) III, (VII in Spain) 1808-1833

5 PESETAS

SILVER
Obv. leg: FER/ VII/ (raised periods). Rev: Curved base crown/shield.

KM#	Date	Mintage	VG	Fine	VF	XF
5 (C-L96.1)	1809. small 0	—	50.00	85.00	125.00	200.00

Obv. leg: FER/ VII/ (raised periods). Rev: Curved base crown/shield.

KM#	Date	Mintage	VG	Fine	VF	XF
6 (C-L96.2)	1809. large 0	—	50.00	85.00	125.00	200.00

Obv. leg: FER VII. Rev: Straight base crown/shield.

KM#	Date	Mintage	VG	Fine	VF	XF
7 (C-L96.3)	1809. small 0	—	50.00	85.00	125.00	200.00

Obv. leg: FER VII. Rev: Similar to C#L96.1.

KM#	Date	Mintage	VG	Fine	VF	XF
8 (C-L96.4)	1809. small 0	—	50.00	85.00	125.00	200.00

Obv. leg: FER VII. Rev: Similar to C#L96.3.

KM#	Date	Mintage	VG	Fine	VF	XF
9 (C-L96.5)	1809. small 0, lazy 9	—	50.00	85.00	125.00	200.00

Obv. leg: FER//F.o.

KM#	Date	Mintage	VG	Fine	VF	XF
10 (C-L96.6)	1809.	—	—	—	Rare	—

TORTOSA

Tortosa, a fortified city of Spain, is in Tarragona province.

RULERS

Fernando VII, 1808-1833

DURO

(5 Pesetas)

SILVER, uniface
4 c/m: Tower, 1, DURO & TOR. raised R • SA.

KM#	Date	Mintage	VG	Fine	VF	XF
5 (C-L100)	ND(1808-9)	—	450.00	850.00	1350.	2250.

VALENCIA

Valencia, a maritime province of eastern Spain and the capital city of Valencia. Once a former kingdom, Valencia included the present provinces of Castellon de la Plana and Alicante.

RULERS

Ferdinand (Fernando) VII, 1808-1833

2 REALES DE VELLON

(1 Real)

SILVER

KM#	Date	Mintage	VG	Fine	VF	XF
80	1809LL	—	17.50	32.50	55.00	90.00

(C-L103)

4 REALES DE VELLON

(2 Reales)

SILVER

KM#	Date	Mintage	VG	Fine	VF	XF
85	1823LL	—	12.50	22.50	37.50	65.00

(C-L106)

NOTE: The 4 Reales de Vellon circulated as a regular issue 2 Reales while the 2 Reales de Vellon circulated as a regular 1 Real.

SRI (SHRI) LANKA

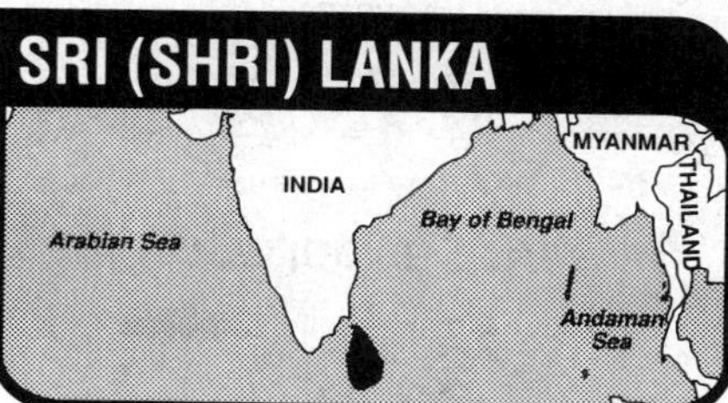

The Democratic Socialist Republic of Sri (Shri) Lanka (formerly Ceylon) situated in the Indian Ocean 18 miles (29 km.) southeast of India, has an area of 25,332 sq. mi. (65,610 sq. km.) and a population of *16.9 million. Capital: Colombo. The economy is chiefly agricultural. Tea, coconut products and rubber are exported.

The earliest known inhabitants of Ceylon, the Veddahs, were subjugated by the Sinhalese from northern India in the 6th century B.C. Sinhalese rule was maintained until 1408, after which the island was controlled by China for 30 years. The Portuguese came to Ceylon in 1505 and maintained control of the coastal area for 150 years. They were supplanted by the Dutch in 1658, who were in turn supplanted by the British who seized the Dutch colonies in 1796, and made them a Crown Colony in 1802. In 1815, the British conquered the independent Kingdom of Kandy in the central part of the island. Constitutional changes in 1931 and 1946 granted the Ceylonese a measure of autonomy and a parliamentary form of government. Britain granted Ceylon independence as a self-governing republic within the British Commonwealth on Feb. 4, 1948. On May 22, 1972, the Ceylonese adopted a new Constitution which declared Ceylon to be the Republic of Shri Lanka - 'Resplendent Island'. Shri Lanka is a member of the Commonwealth of Nations. The president is Chief of State. The prime minister is Head of Government. The present leaders of the country have reverted the country name back to Sri Lanka.

RULERS

British, 1796-1972

CEYLON

British Colonial Coinage

MINT MARKS

H - Heaton, Birmingham
B - Bombay

MONETARY SYSTEM

4 Pies = 1 Stiver
4 Stivers = 1 Fanam
12 Fanams = 1 Rixdollar = 1 Rupee = 1-1/2 Shillings
2 Rupees = 3 Shillings

DUMP COINAGE

1/4 PICE

(1/256 Rixdaler)

COPPER, dump
Obv: C.G., date. Rev: Value.

KM#	Date	Mintage	Good	VG	Fine	VF
72	1813	—	—	—	Rare	—

1/48 RIXDOLLAR

COPPER, dump
Rev: Elephant faces left.

KM#	Date	Mintage	Good	VG	Fine	VF
63	1801	—	5.00	10.00	17.50	30.00
	1802	—	5.00	10.00	17.50	30.00
	1803	—	5.00	10.00	17.50	30.00
	1811	—	6.50	12.00	22.50	40.00
	1812	—	6.50	12.00	20.00	35.00
	1813	—	8.50	15.00	22.50	40.00
	1814	—	8.50	15.00	22.50	40.00
	1815	—	8.50	15.00	22.50	40.00
	1816	—	75.00	125.00	185.00	250.00

Obv: 2 parallel lines under 48.

KM#	Date	Mintage	Good	VG	Fine	VF
66	1802	—	65.00	175.00	325.00	400.00

Rev: Elephant faces right.

KM#	Date	Mintage	Good	VG	Fine	VF
69	1803	—	—	—	Unique	—

1/24 RIXDOLLAR

COPPER, dump

KM#	Date	Mintage	Good	VG	Fine	VF
64	1801	—	10.00	22.50	35.00	55.00
	1802	—	7.00	18.50	40.00	60.00
	1803	—	6.00	17.50	30.00	50.00
	1805	—	10.00	18.50	45.00	65.00
	1811	—	7.00	16.50	30.00	50.00
	1812	—	7.00	18.50	30.00	50.00
	1813	—	7.00	18.50	35.00	55.00
	1814	—	12.50	23.50	32.50	52.00
	1815	—	12.50	21.50	45.00	65.00
	1816	—	25.00	60.00	100.00	165.00

Obv: 2 parallel lines under 24.

KM#	Date	Mintage	Good	VG	Fine	VF
67	1802	—	65.00	175.00	325.00	400.00

Rev: Elephant faces right.

KM#	Date	Mintage	Good	VG	Fine	VF
70	1803	—	60.00	140.00	225.00	325.00
	1805	—	60.00	140.00	225.00	325.00

1/12 RIXDOLLAR

COPPER, dump
Rev: Elephant faces left.

KM#	Date	Mintage	Good	VG	Fine	VF
65	1801	—	10.00	25.00	32.50	52.00
	1802	—	8.00	16.50	25.00	40.00
	1803	—	8.00	16.50	25.00	40.00
	1804	—	12.50	25.00	35.00	60.00
	1805	—	12.50	25.00	35.00	60.00
	1811	—	12.50	25.00	35.00	60.00
	1812	—	9.00	22.50	35.00	55.00
	1813	—	9.00	30.00	45.00	65.00
	1814	—	9.00	27.50	45.00	65.00
	1815	—	9.00	22.50	35.00	60.00

Obv: 2 parallel lines under 12.

KM#	Date	Mintage	Good	VG	Fine	VF
68	1802	3 known	—	—	Rare	—

Rev: Elephant faces right.

KM#	Date	Mintage	Good	VG	Fine	VF
71	1803	—	85.00	185.00	350.00	500.00

24 STIVERS

.892 SILVER

KM#	Date	Mintage	VG	Fine	VF	XF
76	1803	—	17.50	35.00	70.00	120.00
	1804	—	20.00	40.00	80.00	135.00
	1805	—	35.00	70.00	120.00	165.00
	1808	—	25.00	60.00	110.00	165.00
	1809	—	35.00	70.00	115.00	165.00

48 STIVERS

.892 SILVER

KM#	Date	Mintage	VG	Fine	VF	XF
77	1803	—	30.00	60.00	125.00	165.00
	1804	—	30.00	60.00	125.00	165.00
	1805	—	30.00	60.00	125.00	165.00
	1808	—	30.00	60.00	125.00	165.00
	1809	—	25.00	50.00	100.00	140.00
	Rev: Elephant faces right.					
78	1803	—	75.00	165.00	245.00	350.00

96 STIVERS

.833 SILVER

KM#	Date	Mintage	VG	Fine	VF	XF
79	1803	—	—	—	—	—
	1808	—	40.00	80.00	145.00	200.00
	1809	—	45.00	90.00	175.00	250.00

FANAM TOKEN

.833 SILVER, 0.58 g
Obv: Circular legends, FANAM. Rev: TOKEN.

KM#	Date	Mintage	VG	Fine	VF	XF
83	ND(1814-15)	2.095	4.00	8.00	15.00	30.00

MILLED COINAGE

1/2 STIVER

COPPER

KM#	Date	Mintage	Fine	VF	XF	Unc
80	1815	2.400	4.00	12.00	30.00	135.00
	1815	—	—	—	Proof	325.00

STIVER

COPPER

KM#	Date	Mintage	Fine	VF	XF	Unc
81	1815	2.800	3.50	10.00	30.00	135.00
	1815	—	—	—	Proof	375.00

2 STIVERS

COPPER
Obv: W/o rose below bust.

KM#	Date	Mintage	Fine	VF	XF	Unc
82.1	1815	1.920	5.00	15.00	50.00	200.00
	1815	—	—	—	Proof	500.00
	Obv: Rose below bust.					
82.2	1815	—	—	—	Proof	900.00

1/192 RIXDOLLAR

COPPER

KM#	Date	Mintage	Fine	VF	XF	Unc
73	1802	3.600	2.50	7.50	20.00	60.00
	1802	—	—	—	Proof	100.00
	1802	—	—		Gilt Proof	85.00
	1804	—	—	—	Proof	175.00
	1804	—	—		Gilt Proof	175.00

1/96 RIXDOLLAR

COPPER

KM#	Date	Mintage	Fine	VF	XF	Unc
74	1802	1.800	4.00	8.00	22.50	75.00
	1802	—	—	—	Proof	125.00
	1802	—	—		Gilt Proof	100.00

1/48 RIXDOLLAR

COPPER

KM#	Date	Mintage	Fine	VF	XF	Unc
75	1802	2.700	5.00	10.00	25.00	80.00
	1802	—	—	—	Proof	150.00
	1802	—	—		Gilt Proof	120.00
	1804	—	—	—	Proof	225.00
	1804	—	—		Gilt Proof	225.00

RIX DOLLAR

.892 SILVER

KM#	Date	Mintage	Fine	VF	XF	Unc
84	1821	.400	12.00	28.00	80.00	220.00
	1821	—	—	—	Proof	250.00

COUNTERMARKED COINAGE

1/3 RIXDOLLAR

SILVER, dump
c/m: Crown on Madras Arcot 1/4 Rupee.

KM#	Date	Mintage	VG	Fine	VF	XF
85	ND(1823)	.260	22.50	50.00	90.00	150.00

1-1/3 RIXDOLLAR

(16 Fanams)

SILVER, dump
c/m: Crown on Madras Arcot Rupee.

KM#	Date	Mintage	VG	Fine	VF	XF
86	ND(1823)	.282	80.00	160.00	240.00	360.00

PATTERNS (Pn)

(Including off metal strikes)

KM#	Date	Mintage	Identification	Mkt.Val.
Pn3	1812	—	1 Rix Dollar, Silver	5000.

KM#	Date	Mintage	Identification	Mkt.Val.
Pn4	1812	—	2 Rix Dollars, Silver	10,000.

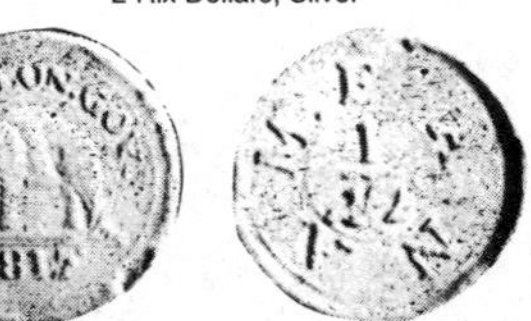

KM#	Date	Mintage	Identification	Mkt.Val.
Pn5	1815	—	Fanam (1/12 Rix Dollar), Bronze (struck over Dutch Doit)	1200.
Pn6	1815	—	Fanam (1/12 Rix Dollar), Lead	1500.

KM#	Date	Mintage	Identification	Mkt.Val.
Pn7	1815	—	1 Rix Dollar, Silver	2000.

HOMELAND COINAGE

4 Farthings = 1 Penny

1/4 FARTHING

COPPER and BRONZE

NOTE: From 1839 through 1868 homeland type 1/4 Farthings were issued by Great Britain for circulation in Ceylon. These are listed under Great Britain.

1/2 FARTHING

COPPER and BRONZE

NOTE: From 1828 through 1868 homeland type 1/2 Farthings were issued by Great Britain for circulation in Ceylon. These are listed under Great Britain.

1-1/2 PENCE

SILVER

NOTE: From 1834 through 1870 homeland type 1 1/2 Pence were issued by Great Britain for circulation in Ceylon and Jamaica. These are listed under Great Britain.

DECIMAL COINAGE

100 Cents = 1 Rupee

1/4 CENT

KM#	Date	Mintage	Fine	VF	XF	Unc
		COPPER				
90	1870	.200	1.50	3.00	5.00	12.00
	1870	—	—	—	Proof	100.00
	1890	.200	1.50	3.00	5.00	12.00
	1890	—	—	—	Proof	100.00
	1891	—	—	—	Proof	150.00
	1892	—	—	—	Proof	150.00
	1898	.160	2.50	5.00	8.00	16.00
	1898	—	—	—	Proof	100.00

NOTE: Later date (1901) exists for this type.

KM#	Date	Mintage	Fine	VF	XF	Unc
		SILVER				
90a	1870	—	—	—	Proof	250.00
	1890	—	—	—	Proof	250.00
	1891	—	—	—	Proof	250.00
	1898	—	—	—	Proof	250.00
		GOLD				
90b	1870	—	—	—	Proof	1000.

1/2 CENT

KM#	Date	Mintage	Fine	VF	XF	Unc
		COPPER				
91	1870	3.040	1.00	1.50	3.00	8.00
	1870	—	—	—	Proof	120.00
	1890	.400	1.50	3.50	8.00	16.00
	1890	—	—	—	Proof	125.00
	1891	1.000	1.25	2.75	4.00	12.00
	1891	—	—	—	Proof	125.00
	1892	—	—	—	Proof	225.00
	1895	4.040	1.00	1.75	3.00	8.00
	1895	—	—	—	Proof	120.00
	1898	4.000	1.25	2.50	4.00	10.00
	1898	—	—	—	Proof	120.00

NOTE: Later date (1901) exists for this type.

KM#	Date	Mintage	Fine	VF	XF	Unc
		SILVER				
91a	1870	—	—	—	Proof	300.00
	1890	—	—	—	Proof	300.00
	1891	—	—	—	Proof	300.00
	1895	—	—	—	Proof	300.00
	1898	—	—	—	Proof	300.00
		GOLD				
91b	1870	—	—	—	Proof	1100.
	1891	—	—	—	Proof	1100.
	1895	—	—	—	Proof	1100.

CENT

KM#	Date	Mintage	Fine	VF	XF	Unc
		COPPER				
92	1870	7.055	1.50	3.00	6.00	15.00
	1870	—	—	—	Proof	125.00
	1890	4.940	1.50	3.00	5.00	12.00
	1890	—	—	—	Proof	125.00
	1891	1.328	2.00	4.00	8.00	20.00
	1891	—	—	—	Proof	125.00
	1892	5.000	1.50	3.00	6.00	15.00
	1892	—	—	—	Proof	125.00
	1900	1.000	2.50	5.00	10.00	22.00
	1900	—	—	—	Proof	175.00

NOTE: Later date (1901) exists for this type.

KM#	Date	Mintage	Fine	VF	XF	Unc
		SILVER				
92a	1870	—	—	—	Proof	425.00
	1890	—	—	—	Proof	425.00
	1891	—	—	—	Proof	425.00
	1892	—	—	—	Proof	425.00
		GOLD				
92b	1870	—	—	—	Proof	1150.
	1891	—	—	—	Proof	1150.

5 CENTS

KM#	Date	Mintage	Fine	VF	XF	Unc
		COPPER				
93	1870	7.009	5.00	10.00	30.00	80.00
	1870	—	—	—	Proof	175.00
	1890	1.001	7.50	20.00	50.00	110.00
	1890	—	—	—	Proof	200.00
	1891	—	—	—	Proof	350.00
	1892	1.000	7.50	20.00	50.00	110.00
	1892	—	—	—	Proof	200.00
		SILVER				
93a	1890	—	—	—	Proof	500.00
	1891	—	—	—	Proof	500.00
	1892	—	—	—	Proof	500.00
		GOLD				
93b	1891	—	—	—	Proof	1200.

10 CENTS

1.1664 g, .800 SILVER, .0300 oz ASW

KM#	Date	Mintage	Fine	VF	XF	Unc
94	1892	2.500	1.50	3.50	7.00	15.00
	1892	—	—	—	Proof	150.00
	1893	2.500	1.50	3.50	7.00	15.00
	1893	—	—	—	Proof	150.00
	1894	3.000	1.50	3.50	7.00	15.00
	1894	—	—	—	Proof	150.00
	1897	1.500	1.50	3.50	9.00	20.00
	1899	1.000	1.75	4.00	10.00	25.00
	1900	1.000	1.75	4.00	10.00	25.00

25 CENTS

2.9160 g, .800 SILVER, .0750 oz ASW

KM#	Date	Mintage	Fine	VF	XF	Unc
95	1892	.500	5.00	10.00	22.00	50.00
	1892	—	—	—	Proof	150.00
	1893	1.500	3.00	7.00	15.00	35.00
	1893	—	—	—	Proof	150.00
	1895	1.200	3.00	7.00	15.00	35.00
	1899	.600	5.00	10.00	22.00	50.00
	1900	.400	6.00	12.00	25.00	60.00

50 CENTS

5.8319 g, .800 SILVER, .1500 oz ASW

KM#	Date	Mintage	Fine	VF	XF	Unc
96	1892	.250	10.00	20.00	40.00	80.00
	1892	—	—	—	Proof	200.00
	1893	.750	6.00	12.00	27.50	45.00
	1893	—	—	—	Proof	175.00
	1895	.450	5.00	8.00	30.00	60.00
	1899	.100	12.50	30.00	50.00	100.00
	1900	.200	5.00	10.00	30.00	70.00

SUDAN

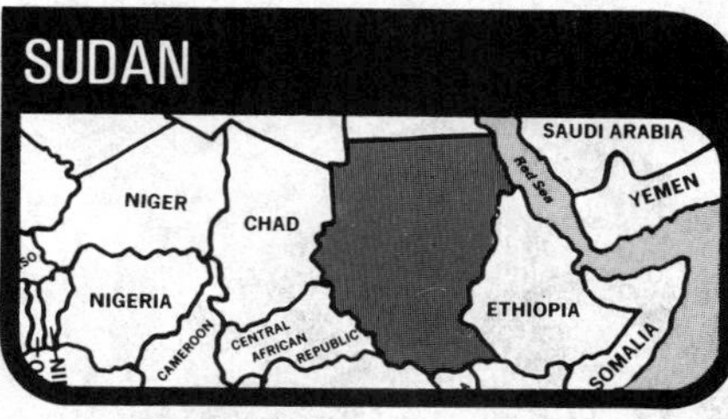

The Democratic Republic of the Sudan, located in northeast Africa on the Red Sea between Egypt and Ethiopia, has an area of 967,500 sq. mi. (2,505,810 sq. km.) and a population of *24.5 million. Capital: Khartoum. Agriculture and livestock raising are the chief occupations. Cotton, gum arabic and peanuts are exported.

The Sudan, site of the powerful Nubian kingdom of Roman times, was a collection of small independent states from the 14th century until 1820-22 when it was conquered and united by Mohammed Ali, Pasha of Egypt. Egyptian forces were driven from the area during the Mahdist revolt, 1881-98, but the Sudan was retaken by Anglo-Egyptian expeditions, 1896-98, and established as an Anglo-Egyptian condominium in 1899. Britain supplied the administrative apparatus and personnel, but the appearance of joint Anglo-Egyptian administration was continued until Jan. 9, 1954, when the first Sudanese self-government parliament was inaugurated. The Sudan achieved independence on Jan. 1, 1956 with the consent of the British and Egyptian government.

TITLES

جمهورية السودان

Jumhuriya(t) as-Sudan

الجمهورية السودان الديمقراطية

al-Jumhuriya(t) as-Sudan ad-Dimiqratiya(t)

MINTNAME

Omdurman ام درمان

RULERS

Mohammed Ahmed (the Mahdi),
AH1298-1302/1881-1885AD

Abdullah Ibn Mohammed (the Khalifa),
AH1302-1316/1885-1898AD

MONETARY SYSTEM

40 Para = 1 Ghirsh = Piastre

MOHAMMED AHMED

(the Mahdi)

AH1298-1302/1881-1885AD

Khartoum Mint

Translation of Arabic legends on Mahdi silver coinage:

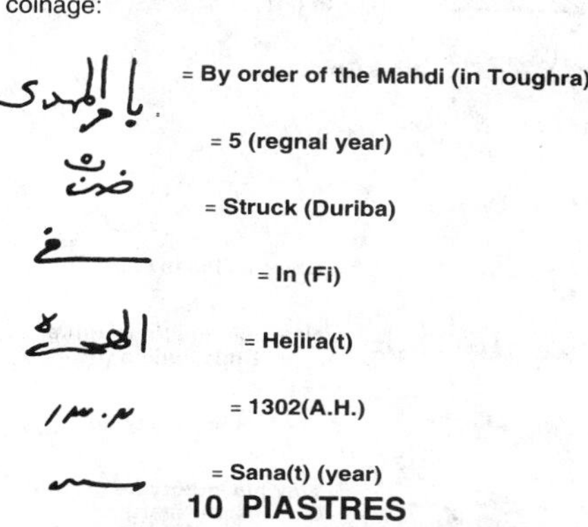

= **By order of the Mahdi (in Toughra)**

= **5 (regnal year)**

= **Struck (Duriba)**

= **In (Fi)**

= **Hejira(t)**

= **1302(A.H.)**

= **Sana(t) (year)**

10 PIASTRES

KM#	Date	Year	VG	Fine	VF	XF
		SILVER				
1	AH1302	5	—	—	Rare	—

20 PIASTRES

SILVER

KM#	Date	Year	VG	Fine	VF	XF
2	AH1302	5	225.00	325.00	500.00	700.00

100 PIASTRES

GOLD

KM#	Date	Year	VG	Fine	VF	XF
3	AH1255	2	—	—	Rare	—

NOTE: Struck by the Mahdi which is a copy of the Egyptian coin 100 Qirsh, KM#235.1 under the Ottoman Sultan. This issue is more crude than the Egyptian type and has crude edge milling. Reverse Arabic legend "Struck in Misr AH1255" (Egypt); however they were struck in the Sudan about AH1302.

ABDULLAH IBN MOHAMMED

(the Khalifa)

AH1302-1316/1885-1898AD

Omdurman Mint

مقبول = **Accepted (money) i.e., legal (in Toughra) - 'Maqbul'**

سنة = **Sana(t) (regnal year) 5**

ضرب = **Struck - 'Duriba'**

في = **In (Fi)**

امدرمان = **Omdurman**

١٣٠٤ = **1304(A.H.)**

٢٠ = **20**

قرش - ش = **Ghirsh = Piastres**

عملة جديدة = **New coinage (in toughra) - 'Umla Jadida'(t)**

جيد = **Good - 'Jayyid'**

عز نصره = **May his victory be glorified 'Azza Nasruhu'**

ش ٢٠ = **20 Piastres**

NOTE: The coins of the Khalifa have been rearranged by KM#'s rather than by metallic composition. Except for the 10 Para (KM#8), which is of copper (more or less pure), the remaining coins (KM#4-26) show the following progressive debasement:

AH Year Metallic Composition
- 1304 - Silver
- 1309 - Debased Silver
- 1310 - Debased Silver, Silver Washed Copper, Billon
- 1311 - Billon, Silver-Washed Copper, Copper
- 1312 - Billon, Silver-Washed Copper, Copper
- 1315 - Copper, Sometimes Silver-Washed

NOTE: The metal is not indicated beneath the photos, as usual, because each type occurs in a range of debasements. Different degrees of debasement do not constitute definable subtypes.

10 PARA

25mm

KM#	Date	Year	VG	Fine	VF	XF
8	AH1308	6	—	—	—	—

NOTE: Probably a pattern.

PIASTRE

(Ghirsh)

Plain borders, 18mm

KM#	Date	Year	VG	Fine	VF	XF
4	AH1304	1	60.00	100.00	150.00	250.00
	1311	9	40.00	65.00	100.00	175.00
	1311	11	40.00	65.00	100.00	175.00

2 PIASTRES

Plain borders, 18mm

KM#	Date	Year	VG	Fine	VF	XF
9	AH1310	8	65.00	100.00	250.00	325.00
	1311	9	65.00	100.00	250.00	325.00
	1311	11	65.00	100.00	250.00	325.00

Wreath borders

KM#	Date	Year	VG	Fine	VF	XF
18	AH1311	8	20.00	35.00	75.00	100.00
	1311	11	20.00	35.00	75.00	100.00

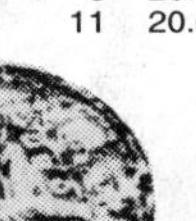

Borders of small crescents and few stars.

KM#	Date	Year	VG	Fine	VF	XF
22.1	AH1311	—	25.00	40.00	125.00	160.00

Borders of crescents, stars and roses.

KM#	Date	Year	VG	Fine	VF	XF
22.2	AH1312	—	25.00	40.00	125.00	160.00

Border of crescents and roses.

KM#	Date	Year	VG	Fine	VF	XF
22.3	AH1312	—	25.00	40.00	125.00	160.00

2-1/2 PIASTRES

Obv: *Umla Jadida* below toughra. Borders of crescents, stars, roses.

KM#	Date	Year	VG	Fine	VF	XF
23.1	AH1312	—	20.00	50.00	140.00	175.00

NOTE: KM#23.1 differs from KM#22.2 by the presence of the *Shadda* which looks like the letter W, after the numeral "2" on the reverse.

Obv: *Maqbul* below toughra.

KM#	Date	Year	VG	Fine	VF	XF
23.2	AH1312	—	30.00	85.00	275.00	350.00

Borders of crescents only.

KM#	Date	Year	VG	Fine	VF	XF
24	AH1312	—	25.00	75.00	250.00	325.00

4 PIASTRES

Plain borders, 25mm

KM#	Date	Year	VG	Fine	VF	XF
10.1	AH1310	8	175.00	250.00	450.00	625.00

Wreath borders.

KM#	Date	Year	VG	Fine	VF	XF
10.2	AH1310	8	200.00	300.00	500.00	700.00

5 PIASTRES

Borders of double crescents.

KM#	Date	Year	VG	Fine	VF	XF
5.1	AH1304	4	35.00	55.00	150.00	200.00
	1304	5	20.00	40.00	125.00	160.00
	1311	11	15.00	27.50	75.00	100.00

NOTE: Coins of AH1304/yr. 4 come in two varieties, one with numeral 1 at top on reverse and one with 4.

Obv: Denomination below toughra.

KM#	Date	Year	VG	Fine	VF	XF
5.2	AH1311	11	15.00	27.50	75.00	100.00

Plain borders, 21-22mm

KM#	Date	Year	VG	Fine	VF	XF
11	AH1310	8	45.00	75.00	250.00	300.00

Borders of crescents and stars.

KM#	Date	Year	VG	Fine	VF	XF
19	AH1311	—	20.00	40.00	80.00	100.00

Borders of crescents only

KM#	Date	Year	VG	Fine	VF	XF
20	AH1311	—	40.00	60.00	100.00	175.00

10 PIASTRES

Borders of crescents and stars.

KM#	Date	Year	VG	Fine	VF	XF
A6	AH1303	5	—	—	—	450.00

NOTE: The precise status of this coin is undetermined, possibly a restrike ca.1900.

Borders of double crescents.

KM#	Date	Year	VG	Fine	VF	XF
6	AH1304	4	75.00	150.00	250.00	350.00
	1311	11	50.00	100.00	200.00	300.00

NOTE: Edge varieties exist.

Plain borders

KM#	Date	Year	VG	Fine	VF	XF
12	AH1310	8	100.00	350.00	600.00	850.00

Wreath borders

KM#	Date	Year	VG	Fine	VF	XF
13	AH1310	8	300.00	600.00	900.00	1150.

20 PIASTRES

Borders of double crescents.

KM#	Date	Year	VG	Fine	VF	XF
7	AH1304	4	20.00	37.50	60.00	100.00
	1304 on obv. w/1 on rev.					
		5	20.00	37.50	60.00	100.00
	1306	5	40.00	60.00	90.00	200.00
	1309 on obv. w/1 on rev., normal date					
		5	20.00	37.50	60.00	100.00
	1309 on obv. w/1 on rev., 9 of date retrograde					
		5	20.00	37.50	60.00	100.00
	1309 on obv. w/o 1 on rev., normal date					
		5	40.00	60.00	90.00	200.00

NOTE: Early years have larger diameter and larger circles on obverse and reverse.

Borders of crescents, stars and roses.
Rev: *Azza Nasruhu.*

KM#	Date	Year	VG	Fine	VF	XF
14	AH1310	10	10.00	15.00	25.00	40.00
	1311	—	10.00	15.00	25.00	40.00
	1311	9	10.00	15.00	25.00	40.00
	1311	11	10.00	15.00	25.00	40.00
	1312	11	10.00	15.00	25.00	40.00
	1312	12	10.00	15.00	25.00	40.00
	1312	—	10.00	15.00	25.00	40.00

Borders of crescents only.
Rev: W/o *Azza Nasruhu.*

KM#	Date	Year	VG	Fine	VF	XF
21	AH1302	9	15.00	65.00	125.00	175.00
	1311	11	12.50	25.00	40.00	75.00
	1312	12	12.50	25.00	40.00	75.00

NOTE: The date 1302 on the year 9 is in error for 1312, and is not to be confused with the Mahdi coinage.
NOTE: Varieties exist.

Rev: W/ *Azza Nasruhu.*

KM#	Date	Year	VG	Fine	VF	XF
25	AH1311	11	10.00	20.00	30.00	55.00
	1312	12	10.00	20.00	30.00	55.00

AH1315, R.Y. 8

AH1312, R.Y. 12
Rev: Wreath borders w/spears below.

KM#	Date	Year	VG	Fine	VF	XF
15	AH1310	8	10.00	17.50	27.50	55.00
	1311	11	12.00	25.00	40.00	75.00
	1312	12	7.00	12.50	20.00	40.00
	1315	8	6.00	11.50	18.50	35.00

NOTE: Many die varieties of this type exist.

Obv. and rev: Wreath w/spears below.

KM#	Date	Year	VG	Fine	VF	XF
16	AH1310	8	20.00	50.00	100.00	150.00
	1311	12	20.00	50.00	100.00	150.00

Wreath borders. W/o spears on either side.

KM#	Date	Year	VG	Fine	VF	XF
17	AH1310	8	8.00	15.00	25.00	40.00
	1315	12	8.00	15.00	25.00	40.00

AH1312, R.Y. 12

Wreath borders. Obv: Spears below.

KM#	Date	Year	VG	Fine	VF	XF
26	AH1312	12	4.00	6.50	10.00	20.00
	1312	16	20.00	40.00	70.00	120.00
	1313	13	7.00	14.00	20.00	35.00
	1315	8	7.00	12.50	17.50	30.00
	1315	12	7.00	12.50	17.50	30.00

NOTE: Many die varieties of this type exist.

DARFUR

The province of Darfur makes up most of the western border of the Republic of Sudan. Darfur had been an independent kingdom until taken over by Egypt in 1874. While the British were involved in subduing the eastern Sudan, Ali Dinar established the sultanate of Darfur in 1898. His coins copied the type of 20 Para of Mohammed II of Egypt. The mint was located at Al Fasher (the capitol of the province) and was active from 1909 to 1914. Most of the coins bear a 1327 (1909AD) date.

TITLES

al-Fasher

RULERS

Ali Dinar, AH1316-1335/1898-1916AD

PIASTRE

BILLON

KM#	Date	Year	Good	VG	Fine	VF
2	AH1227(sic)	5	—	—	—	—
(1)	122x(sic)	(x)	—	—	—	—
	1237(sic) (w/retrograde 3)					
		71	—	—	—	—

COPPER-NICKEL-ZINC

c/s: *ALI*/1312 on KM#1.

1 Quirsh, C#133.

KM#	Date	Year	Good	VG	Fine	VF
3	AH1312					
	(AH1213/13)		—	—	Rare	—
	(AH1223)		—	—	Rare	—

NOTE: In a move to control import and circulation of KM#6, the Sultan ordered the countermarking. AH1312 is probably an error for AH1316/1898AD, the year of Ali Dinar's accession.

SWEDEN

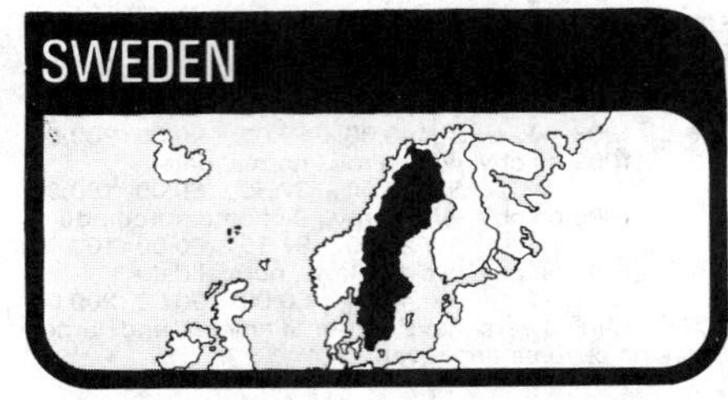

The Kingdom of Sweden, a limited constitutional monarchy located in northern Europe between Norway and Finland, has an area of 173,732 sq. mi. (449,960 sq. km.) and a population of *8.5 million. Capital: Stockholm. Mining, lumbering and a specialized machine industry dominate the economy. Machinery, paper, iron and steel, motor vehicles and wood pulp are exported.

Sweden was founded as a Christian stronghold by Olaf Skottkonung late in the 10th century. After conquering Finland late in the 13th century, Sweden, together with Norway, came under the rule of Denmark, 1397-1523, in an association known as the Union of Kalmar. Modern Sweden had its beginning in 1523 when Gustaf Vasa drove the Danes out of Sweden and was himself chosen king. Under Gustaf Adolphus II and Charles XII, Sweden was one of the great powers of 17th century Europe - until Charles invaded Russia in 1708, and was defeated at the Battle of Pultowa in June, 1709. Early in the 18th century, a coalition of Russia, Poland and Denmark took away Sweden's Baltic empire and in 1809 Sweden was forced to cede Finland to Russia. Norway was ceded to Sweden by the Treaty of Kiel in January, 1814. The Norwegians resisted for a time but later signed the Act of Union at the Convention of Moss in August, 1814.

RULERS

Gustaf IV Adolf, 1792-1809
Carl XIII, 1809-1818
Carl XIV Johan, 1818-1844
Oscar I, 1844-1859
Carl XV Adolf, 1859-1872
Oscar II, 1872-1907

MINTMASTERS INITIALS

Letter	Date	Name
AG,G	1838-1855	Alexander Grandinson
AL	1898-1916	Adolf Lindberg, engraver
CB	1821-1837	Christopher Borg
EB	1876-1908	Emil Brusewitz
G	1799-1830	Lars Grandel, engraver
G	1830-1853	Ludvig Persson Lundgren
LA	1854-1897	Lea Ahlborn, engraver
LB	1819-1821	Lars Bergencreutz
OL	1773-1819	Olof Lidijn
ST,T	1855-1876	Sebastian Tham

1798-1830

48 Skilling = 1 Riksdaler Species
2 Riksdaler (Speciesdaler) = 1 Ducat

1830-1855

32 Skilling Banco = 1 Riksdaler Riksgalds
12 Riksdaler Riksgalds = 3 Riksdaler Species

1855-1873

100 Ore = 4 Riksdaler Riksmynt
4 Riksdaler Riksmynt = 1 Riksdaler Species

Commencing 1873

100 Ore = 1 Riksdaler Riksmynt = 1 Krona

1/12 SKILLING

COPPER

KM#	Date	Mintage	VG	Fine	VF	XF
563	1802	2.039	.50	1.00	2.00	6.00
(388)	1803	1.008	.75	1.50	3.00	9.00
	1805	2.526	.50	1.00	2.00	6.00
	1808	3.476	.50	1.00	2.00	6.00

KM#	Date	Mintage	VG	Fine	VF	XF
584 (399)	1812	2.880	.75	2.00	6.00	12.00

KM#	Date	Mintage	VG	Fine	VF	XF
616	1825 reeded edge					
(417)		.576	1.50	3.00	7.00	15.00
	1825 plain edge					
		—	4.00	8.00	15.00	35.00

1/6 SKILLING

COPPER

KM#	Date	Mintage	VG	Fine	VF	XF
625	1830 reeded edge					
(425)		2.544	.50	1.50	4.00	10.00
	1830 plain edge					
		Inc. Ab.	1.00	3.00	7.00	15.00
	1831	Inc. Ab.	2.50	5.00	10.00	20.00

Draped bust w/pearl border.

KM#	Date	Mintage	VG	Fine	VF	XF
633 (433.1)	1832	.912	6.50	12.50	25.00	50.00

Plain border

KM#	Date	Mintage	VG	Fine	VF	XF
634 (433.2)	1832	Inc. Ab.	1.50	3.00	6.00	12.00

Obv: Naked bust w/pearl border.

KM#	Date	Mintage	VG	Fine	VF	XF
635 (434)	1832	Inc. Ab.	5.00	10.00	20.00	40.00

KM#	Date	Mintage	VG	Fine	VF	XF
639	1835	.538	.50	1.00	3.00	8.00
(438)	1836/5	1.498	.50	1.00	2.50	7.50
	1836	Inc. Ab.	.50	1.00	2.50	7.50
	1838	.427	1.25	3.50	6.00	17.50
	1839	.827	.50	1.00	3.00	8.00
	1840/35	.860	.60	1.30	4.00	10.00
	1840	Inc. Ab.	.50	1.00	3.00	8.00
	1843/35	.865	1.75	3.50	8.50	21.50
	1843	Inc. Ab.	1.25	2.50	6.00	15.00
	1844	.071	30.00	60.00	120.00	180.00

KM#	Date	Mintage	VG	Fine	VF	XF
656	1844/35	.291	5.00	10.00	20.00	40.00
(451)	1844	Inc. Ab.	.50	1.25	3.00	9.00
	1845	.092	2.00	4.00	10.00	30.00
	1846	.067	2.00	4.00	10.00	30.00
	1847	.823	.50	1.00	2.50	7.50
	1849	.537	.50	1.00	2.50	7.50
	1850	.407	1.00	2.00	5.00	15.00
	1851	.486	.50	1.00	2.50	7.50
	1852	.462	.50	1.00	2.50	7.50
	1853	.126	1.50	3.00	7.50	22.50
	1854	.422	.50	1.00	2.50	7.50
	1855	.311	.50	1.00	2.50	7.50

1/4 SKILLING

COPPER

KM#	Date	Mintage	VG	Fine	VF	XF
564	1802	3.383	.75	1.50	4.00	12.00
(389)	1803	3.217	.75	1.50	4.00	12.00
	1805	5.189	.75	1.50	4.00	12.00
	1806	8.141	.75	1.50	4.00	12.00
	1807	.641	1.00	2.00	5.50	17.50
	1808 narrow crown					
		7.480	1.00	2.00	5.00	15.00
	1808 wider crown					
		Inc. Ab.	.75	1.50	4.00	12.00

KM#	Date	Mintage	VG	Fine	VF	XF
592	1817	1.152	10.00	25.00	50.00	100.00
(407)						

KM#	Date	Mintage	VG	Fine	VF	XF
595	1819	2.450	.50	1.50	5.00	25.00
(410)	1820	2.610	.50	1.50	5.00	25.00
	1821	2.208	.50	1.50	5.00	25.00
	1824 space between crown & monogram					
		.768	1.00	3.00	10.00	40.00
	1824 crown touches monogram					
		Inc. Ab.	1.00	3.00	10.00	40.00
	1825 open 4 in denomination					
		2.496	.50	1.50	5.00	25.00
	1825 closed 4 in denomination					
		Inc. Ab.	.50	1.50	5.00	25.00
	1827 open 4 in denomination					
		3.200	.50	1.50	5.00	25.00
	1827 closed 4 in denomination					
		Inc. Ab.	.50	1.50	5.00	25.00
	1828	4.320	.50	1.50	5.00	25.00
	1829	4.896	.50	1.50	5.00	25.00
	1830	.256	1.00	3.00	10.00	40.00

KM#	Date	Mintage	VG	Fine	VF	XF
636	1832	.160	5.00	10.00	35.00	70.00
(435)	1833/2	.096	3.50	7.00	20.00	40.00

1/3 SKILLING

COPPER

KM#	Date	Mintage	VG	Fine	VF	XF
640	1835	.483	2.50	5.00	15.00	35.00
(439)	1836	.985	1.00	2.00	6.00	17.50
	1837	1.096	1.00	2.00	6.00	17.50
	1839/37	.921	3.00	6.00	18.00	40.00
	1839	Inc. Ab.	1.00	2.00	6.00	17.50
	1840/37	.692	4.00	8.00	22.00	50.00
	1840	Inc. Ab.	1.00	2.00	6.00	17.50
	1841	.013	25.00	50.00	100.00	150.00
	1842	.612	1.00	2.00	6.00	17.50
	1843	.593	1.00	2.00	6.00	17.50

KM#	Date	Mintage	VG	Fine	VF	XF
657	1844	.226	1.00	2.00	5.00	15.00
(452)	1845	.192	1.00	2.00	5.00	15.00
	1846	.079	2.50	5.00	10.00	30.00
	1847	.783	1.00	2.00	5.00	15.00
	1848/7	.933	1.50	2.75	7.00	21.50
	1848	Inc. Ab.	1.00	2.00	5.00	15.00
	1850 BANCO					
		.537	1.00	2.00	5.00	15.00
	1850 BANCO w/2 dots above A (error)					
		Inc. Ab.	4.00	8.00	20.00	60.00
	1851	.538	1.00	2.00	5.00	15.00
	1852	.489	1.00	2.00	5.00	15.00
	1853	.070	2.50	5.00	10.00	30.00
	1854	.495	1.00	2.00	5.00	15.00
	1855	.377	1.00	2.00	5.00	15.00

1/2 SKILLING

COPPER

Obv: 3 crowns on orb. Rev: Value, date.

KM#	Date	Mintage	VG	Fine	VF	XF
549	1801	3.203	1.00	2.50	5.00	20.00
(379)	1802	1.188	1.00	2.50	5.00	20.00

NOTE: Earlier dates (1799-1800) exist for this type.

KM#	Date	Mintage	VG	Fine	VF	XF
565	1802	*2.340	1.00	3.00	7.00	20.00
(390)	1803	*5.048	1.00	3.00	7.00	20.00
	1804	(.595)	35.00	100.00	225.00	500.00
	1805	*.173	1.25	3.00	7.00	20.00
	1807	1.950	1.25	4.00	8.00	25.00
	1809	4.845	1.25	4.00	8.00	25.00

***NOTE:** Struck over 18th century 1 ore - worth 50 per cent to 100 per cent more if earlier date visible.

KM#	Date	Mintage	VG	Fine	VF	XF
590	1815	1.421	2.00	6.00	15.00	30.00
(404)	1816	.566	2.50	9.00	18.00	37.50
	1817	Inc. Ab.	3.00	12.50	25.00	50.00

KM#	Date	Mintage	VG	Fine	VF	XF
596	1819	1.264	1.00	2.50	7.50	30.00
(411)	1820	1.296	1.00	2.50	7.50	30.00
	1821	1.840	1.00	2.50	7.50	30.00
	1822	.944	1.00	2.50	7.50	30.00
	1822 L & S reversed					
		Inc. Ab.	31.00	64.00	145.00	409.00
	1824	.640	1.00	2.50	7.50	30.00
	1825	.816	2.00	4.00	15.00	60.00
	1827 SKIL-LING					
		.800	1.00	2.50	7.50	30.00
	1827 SKIL LING					
		Inc. Ab.	5.00	10.00	25.00	75.00
	1828	1.872	1.00	2.50	7.50	30.00
	1829	2.560	1.00	2.50	7.50	30.00
	1830	.588	1.50	3.50	10.00	35.00

KM#	Date	Mintage	VG	Fine	VF	XF
637	1832	.288	3.50	7.00	20.00	40.00
(436)	1833	3 pcs.	—	—	Rare	—

2/3 SKILLING

COPPER

KM#	Date	Mintage	VG	Fine	VF	XF
641	1835	.198	3.00	6.00	20.00	60.00
(440)	1836	.928	1.50	3.00	10.00	30.00
	1837	1.026	1.50	3.00	10.00	35.00
	1839	.654	1.50	3.00	10.00	35.00
	1840	.646	1.50	3.00	10.00	35.00
	1842	.526	1.50	3.00	10.00	35.00
	1843	.626	1.50	3.00	10.00	35.00

KM#	Date	Mintage	VG	Fine	VF	XF
658	1844	.266	3.50	7.00	20.00	60.00
(453)	1845/4	.495	4.00	8.50	25.00	70.00
	1845	Inc. Ab.	3.50	7.00	20.00	60.00

Redesigned, smaller head.

KM#	Date	Mintage	VG	Fine	VF	XF
663	1845/4					
(458)		Inc. KM453	3.00	6.50	18.50	55.00
	1845					
		Inc. KM453	2.50	5.00	15.00	45.00
	1846/4	.123	1.90	3.75	12.50	37.50
	1846	Inc. Ab.	1.50	3.00	10.00	30.00
	1847	.089	1.50	3.00	10.00	30.00
	1849/4	.219	2.00	4.00	13.50	40.00
	1849	Inc. Ab.	1.50	3.00	10.00	30.00
	1850	.329	1.50	3.00	10.00	30.00
	1851	.467	1.50	3.00	10.00	30.00
	1852	.297	1.50	3.00	10.00	30.00
	1853	.052	4.00	8.00	25.00	75.00
	1854	.408	1.50	3.00	10.00	30.00
	1855	.506	1.50	3.00	10.00	30.00

SKILLING

COPPER

KM#	Date	Mintage	VG	Fine	VF	XF
566	1802	—	3.00	7.00	15.00	60.00
(391)	1803	—	6.00	14.00	30.00	100.00
	1805	—	3.00	7.00	15.00	60.00

NOTE: Struck over 18th century 2 Ore - worth 50 percent to 100 percent more if earlier date visible.

KM#	Date	Mintage	VG	Fine	VF	XF
585	1812	.480	4.00	10.00	27.50	55.00
(400)	1814	.730	4.00	12.00	30.00	60.00
	1815	Inc. Ab.	4.00	10.00	27.50	55.00
	1816	.230	4.00	10.00	27.50	55.00
	1817	.202	6.00	15.00	35.00	75.00

KM#	Date	Mintage	VG	Fine	VF	XF
597	1819	1.176	1.50	5.00	15.00	60.00
(412)	1820 oblique milling	1.376	1.50	5.00	15.00	60.00
	1820 square milling	Inc. Ab.	6.00	12.50	40.00	100.00
	1821	.704	1.50	5.00	15.00	60.00
	1822	.520	2.00	6.00	17.50	70.00
	1825	.472	1.50	5.00	15.00	50.00
	1827	.504	1.50	5.00	15.00	60.00
	1828	.664	1.50	5.00	15.00	60.00
	1829	.344	1.50	4.00	15.00	60.00
	1830	.312	2.50	6.00	17.50	70.00

KM#	Date	Mintage	VG	Fine	VF	XF
638	1832	8,000	50.00	100.00	250.00	450.00
(437)						

KM#	Date	Mintage	VG	Fine	VF	XF
642	1835 wide wreath	.186	50.00	100.00	250.00	500.00
(441)	1835 narrow wreath	Inc. Ab.	3.00	6.00	15.00	45.00
	1836/5	.651	4.00	8.00	20.00	60.00
	1836	Inc. Ab.	3.00	6.00	15.00	45.00
	1837	.628	5.00	10.00	25.00	60.00
	1838	.140	5.00	10.00	25.00	60.00
	1839	.360	5.00	10.00	25.00	60.00
	1840	.278	5.00	10.00	25.00	60.00
	1842	.499	5.00	10.00	25.00	60.00
	1843	.361	5.00	10.00	25.00	60.00

Large head of Oscar I.

KM#	Date	Mintage	VG	Fine	VF	XF
659	1844	.093	6.00	12.00	30.00	90.00
(454)	1845/4	.097	6.00	12.00	30.00	90.00

Redesigned, smaller head.

KM#	Date	Mintage	VG	Fine	VF	XF
671	1847	.150	3.00	6.00	15.00	45.00
(466)	1849	.306	3.00	6.00	15.00	45.00
	1850	.137	3.00	6.00	15.00	45.00
	1851	.151	3.00	6.00	15.00	45.00
	1852	.154	3.00	6.00	15.00	45.00
	1853	.031	6.00	12.00	30.00	90.00
	1854	.064	3.00	6.00	15.00	45.00
	1855	.040	5.00	10.00	25.00	75.00

2 SKILLING

COPPER

KM#	Date	Mintage	VG	Fine	VF	XF
643	1835	.079	10.00	20.00	60.00	200.00
(442)	1836 wide wreath	.583	120.00	250.00	500.00	1000.
	1836 narrow wreath	Inc. Ab.	3.50	7.50	22.50	70.00
	1837	.388	4.00	8.00	25.00	75.00
	1839	.270	4.00	8.00	25.00	75.00
	1840	.069	5.00	10.00	30.00	80.00
	1841	.093	5.00	10.00	30.00	80.00
	1842	.123	5.00	10.00	30.00	80.00
	1843	.162	5.00	10.00	30.00	90.00

KM#	Date	Mintage	VG	Fine	VF	XF
660	1844	.089	7.50	15.00	50.00	150.00
(455)	1845	.120	7.50	15.00	50.00	150.00

Obv: Smaller head. Rev: Similar to KM#442.

KM#	Date	Mintage	VG	Fine	VF	XF
664	1845	Inc. Ab.	7.50	15.00	45.00	135.00
(459)	1846	.056	6.00	12.00	35.00	100.00
	1847	.115	5.00	12.00	35.00	100.00
	1849	.138	5.00	12.00	35.00	100.00
	1850	.081	5.00	12.00	35.00	100.00
	1851	.083	5.00	12.00	35.00	100.00
	1852	.061	5.00	12.00	35.00	100.00
	1853	.023	8.00	15.00	50.00	150.00
	1854	.038	5.00	12.00	35.00	100.00
	1855	.011	8.00	15.00	50.00	150.00

4 SKILLING

COPPER

KM#	Date	Mintage	VG	Fine	VF	XF
672	1849	.444	4.00	8.00	30.00	90.00
(467)	1850	.170	6.00	12.00	40.00	120.00
	1851	.038	7.50	15.00	50.00	150.00
	1852	.038	7.50	15.00	50.00	150.00
	1855	.074	6.00	12.00	40.00	120.00
	1855 denomination and BANCO larger	Inc. Ab.	10.00	20.00	70.00	200.00

1/32 RIKSDALER

1.0600 g, .750 SILVER, .0255 oz ASW

KM#	Date	Mintage	VG	Fine	VF	XF
681	1851 AG	—	—	—	Rare	—
(471)	1852/1 AG	.480	1.50	3.50	7.00	25.00
	1852 AG	I.A.	1.00	2.50	5.00	15.00
	1853 AG small AG	.775	1.00	2.50	5.00	15.00
	1853 AG large AG	Inc. Ab.	1.00	2.50	5.00	15.00

1/24 RIKSDALER

.382 SILVER

KM#	Date	Mintage	VG	Fine	VF	XF
580	1810 OL	.742	3.50	7.00	20.00	60.00
(395)	1811 OL	.378	4.00	8.00	20.00	60.00
	1812 OL	.537	4.00	8.00	20.00	60.00
	1813 OL	.444	4.00	8.00	20.00	60.00
	1814 OL	.101	5.00	10.00	30.00	75.00
	1816 OL	.160	5.00	10.00	30.00	75.00

1/16 RIKSDALER

2.1300 g, .750 SILVER, .0513 oz ASW

KM#	Date	Mintage	VG	Fine	VF	XF
644	1835 CB	.433	4.00	8.00	15.00	40.00
(443)	1836/5 CB	.088	6.00	15.00	25.00	60.00

KM#	Date	Mintage	VG	Fine	VF	XF
665	1845 AG	4,185	12.50	25.00	50.00	100.00
(460)	1846/5 AG	.034	11.50	22.50	45.00	90.00
	1846 AG	I.A.	10.00	20.00	40.00	80.00
	1848/5 AG	4.173	—	—	—	—
	1848 AG	I.A.	1.50	4.00	8.00	25.00
	1849 AG	—	—	—	Rare	—
	1850 AG	1.006	2.00	5.00	10.00	30.00
	1851 AG	.847	2.00	5.00	10.00	30.00
	1852 AG	.934	2.00	5.00	10.00	30.00
	1855 AG	.830	2.00	5.00	10.00	30.00

1/12 RIKSDALER

.507 SILVER

KM#	Date	Mintage	VG	Fine	VF	XF
583 (398)	1811 OL	.735	12.00	30.00	65.00	150.00

2.8300 g, .750 SILVER, .0682 oz ASW

KM#	Date	Mintage	VG	Fine	VF	XF
630 (430)	1831 CB	.212	6.50	12.00	25.00	50.00
	1832/1 CB	1.463	6.50	13.50	25.00	40.00
	1832 CB	I.A.	5.00	10.00	20.00	40.00
	1833/1 CB	.157	7.50	15.00	32.50	60.00
	1833 CB	I.A.	6.00	12.00	25.00	50.00

1/8 RIKSDALER

4.2500 g, .750 SILVER, .1024 oz ASW

KM#	Date	Mintage	VG	Fine	VF	XF
626 (426)	1830 CB reeded edge	1.796	12.50	25.00	50.00	100.00
	1830 CB stars & flowers on edge	Inc. Ab.	37.50	75.00	150.00	300.00
	1831 CB	1.470	3.50	7.00	15.00	40.00
	1832 CB	2.829	3.00	6.00	12.00	35.00
	1833 CB	1.032	3.50	7.00	15.00	40.00
	1834 CB	.103	6.00	12.00	25.00	60.00
	1835 CB	.103	6.00	12.00	25.00	60.00
	1836 CB	9.024	15.00	30.00	60.00	100.00
	1837 CB	4,818	17.50	35.00	70.00	120.00

KM#	Date	Mintage	VG	Fine	VF	XF
682 (472)	1852 AG	.046	40.00	80.00	175.00	350.00

1/6 RIKSDALER

6.2500 g, .691 SILVER, .1388 oz ASW

KM#	Date	Mintage	VG	Fine	VF	XF
560 (385)	1801 OL	.420	10.00	25.00	50.00	100.00
	1802 OL	1.254	7.00	17.50	35.00	65.00
	1803 OL	2.341	7.00	17.50	35.00	65.00
	1804 OL	2.156	7.00	17.50	35.00	65.00
	1805 OL	.978	7.00	17.50	35.00	65.00
	1806 OL	.341	8.00	20.00	40.00	80.00
	1807 OL	.909	7.00	17.50	35.00	65.00
	1808 OL	.943	7.00	17.50	35.00	65.00
	1809 OL	.707	8.00	20.00	40.00	80.00

NOTE: Earlier date (1800) exists for this type.

KM#	Date	Mintage	VG	Fine	VF	XF
568 (393)	1809 OL	—	50.00	120.00	225.00	450.00
	1810 OL	.297	15.00	30.00	80.00	225.00
(393)	1814/0 OL	.199	20.00	45.00	90.00	225.00
	1814 OL	I.A.	20.00	45.00	90.00	225.00

Obv: NORR in legends.

KM#	Date	Mintage	VG	Fine	VF	XF
589 (405)	1815 OL	.059	60.00	135.00	300.00	550.00
	1817 OL	.091	60.00	125.00	275.00	500.00

KM#	Date	Mintage	VG	Fine	VF	XF
598 (413)	1819 OL	.052	30.00	60.00	125.00	300.00
	1826 CB	1,974	45.00	90.00	180.00	400.00

6.1900 g, .691 SILVER, .1375 oz ASW

KM#	Date	Mintage	VG	Fine	VF	XF
615 (421)	1828 CB edge inscription	1,974	—	—	Rare	—
	1828 CB w/o edge inscription	1,024	—	—	Rare	—
	1829 CB	2,039	20.00	40.00	80.00	175.00

1/4 RIKSDALER

8.5000 g, .750 SILVER, .2049 oz ASW

KM#	Date	Mintage	VG	Fine	VF	XF
627 (427)	1830 CB	.704	10.00	25.00	50.00	100.00
	1831 CB	2.470	8.00	20.00	40.00	90.00
	1832 CB	.522	10.00	25.00	50.00	100.00
	1833 CB	.063	18.00	35.00	75.00	150.00
	1834/3 CB	.953	9.00	20.00	45.00	95.00
	1834 CB	I.A.	8.00	20.00	40.00	90.00
	1836 CB	2,766	50.00	100.00	225.00	450.00

NOTE: Previously listed 1830 plain edge variety is normal but a weakly struck example.

KM#	Date	Mintage	VG	Fine	VF	XF
669 (464)	1846/4 AG	.221	20.00	45.00	90.00	200.00
	1848/4 AG	.130	20.00	45.00	90.00	200.00
	1852/44 AG	—	—	—	Rare	—
	1852 AG	—	—	—	Rare	—

1/3 RIKSDALER

.878 SILVER

KM#	Date	Mintage	VG	Fine	VF	XF
587 (402)	1813 OL	.063	115.00	235.00	400.00	800.00
	1814 OL	.033	135.00	275.00	500.00	950.00

9.7500 g, .878 SILVER, .2752 oz ASW

KM#	Date	Mintage	VG	Fine	VF	XF
612 (418)	1827 CB	—	—	—	Rare	—
	1828 CB	.061	50.00	100.00	200.00	400.00
	1829 CB	.109	50.00	100.00	200.00	425.00

NOTE: Previously listed 1828 and 1829 plain edge varieties are normal but weakly struck examples.

1/2 RIKSDALER

17.0000 g, .750 SILVER, .4099 oz ASW

KM#	Date	Mintage	VG	Fine	VF	XF
631 (431)	1831 CB	.270	45.00	90.00	150.00	335.00
	1832 CB	.142	80.00	150.00	275.00	550.00
	1833/1 CB	.191	70.00	140.00	225.00	450.00
	1833 CB	I.A.	70.00	140.00	225.00	450.00
	1836/1 CB	2,482	130.00	235.00	425.00	850.00
	1836 CB	I.A.	125.00	225.00	400.00	800.00
	1838 CB	4 pcs.	—	—	Rare	—

NOTE: Previously listed 1831 plain edge variety is normal but a weakly struck example.

KM#	Date	Mintage	VG	Fine	VF	XF
666 (461)	1845 AG	.022	75.00	150.00	300.00	650.00
	1846/5 AG	.082	65.00	125.00	275.00	550.00
	1846 AG	I.A.	55.00	110.00	250.00	500.00
	1848/7 AG	.074	40.00	80.00	175.00	400.00
	1848/5 AG	I.A.	40.00	80.00	175.00	400.00
	1848 AG	I.A.	30.00	60.00	150.00	325.00
	1852/45 AG	1,104	1000.	1500.	2650.	4600.
	1852 AG	I.A.	1000.	1500.	2650.	4500.

RIKSDALER

29.3600 g, .878 SILVER, .8287 oz ASW

KM#	Date	Mintage	VG	Fine	VF	XF
561 (386)	1801 OL	.091	80.00	175.00	360.00	725.00
	1805 OL	.150	75.00	160.00	325.00	625.00
	1806 OL	.205	70.00	150.00	300.00	550.00
	1807 OL	.037	80.00	175.00	350.00	650.00

KM#	Date	Mintage	VG	Fine	VF	XF
586	1812 OL	.043	100.00	185.00	325.00	775.00
(401)	1814/2 OL					
		Inc. Ab.	125.00	250.00	450.00	900.00
	1814 OL	6,600	125.00	250.00	450.00	900.00

Obv: NORR added to legend

KM#	Date	Mintage	VG	Fine	VF	XF
588	1814 OL	I.A.	250.00	600.00	1200.	2200.
(403)	1815 OL	.066	90.00	175.00	300.00	700.00
	1816/5 OL	.012	100.00	200.00	400.00	800.00
	1816 OL	I.A.	90.00	175.00	300.00	700.00
	1817 OL	9,895	125.00	250.00	500.00	1000.
	1818 OL	.015	165.00	325.00	650.00	1250.

29.2500 g, .878 SILVER, .8256 oz ASW

KM#	Date	Mintage	VG	Fine	VF	XF
593	1818 OL					
(408)		Inc. KM403	65.00	125.00	325.00	750.00
	1819 OL	.014	100.00	200.00	450.00	950.00
	1819 LB	I.A.	75.00	175.00	400.00	900.00
	1820 LB large bust					
		.011	150.00	250.00	500.00	1000.
	1820 LB small bust					
		Inc. Ab.	150.00	250.00	500.00	1000.
	1820 LB bust of Carl XIII					
		Inc. Ab.	—	—	Rare	—
	1821 LB	.029	50.00	100.00	300.00	550.00

KM#	Date	Mintage	VG	Fine	VF	XF
(408)	1822 CB	.034	40.00	80.00	165.00	450.00
	1823 CB large bust					
		.026	40.00	80.00	165.00	450.00
	1823 CB small bust					
		Inc. Ab.	40.00	80.00	165.00	450.00
	1824 CB	.053	40.00	80.00	165.00	450.00
	1825 CB	.020	40.00	80.00	165.00	450.00
	1826 CB	7,538	75.00	150.00	350.00	750.00
	1827 CB	.017	40.00	80.00	165.00	450.00

300 Years of Political and Religious Freedom

KM#	Date	Mintage	VG	Fine	VF	XF
610	1821 CB	7,339	60.00	125.00	250.00	450.00
(415)						

Obv: Similar to KM#614.
Rev: 7 angel heads around arms.

KM#	Date	Mintage	VG	Fine	VF	XF
613	1827 CB					
(419)		610 pcs.	250.00	500.00	1000.	1500.

Rev: 9 angel heads around arms.

KM#	Date	Mintage	VG	Fine	VF	XF
614	1827 CB	I.A.	350.00	750.00	1500.	3000.
(420)	1829 CB					
		409 pcs.	400.00	800.00	1650.	3500.

34.0000 g, .750 SILVER, .8198 oz ASW

KM#	Date	Mintage	VG	Fine	VF	XF
632	1831 CB	.047	35.00	70.00	160.00	325.00
(432)	1832/1 CB					
		2,100	175.00	350.00	750.00	1350.
	1832 CB	I.A.	150.00	300.00	650.00	1100.
	1833/1 CB	.039	40.00	80.00	185.00	400.00
	1833 CB	I.A.	35.00	70.00	160.00	325.00
	1834/1 CB	.068	30.00	60.00	135.00	300.00
	1834 CB	I.A.	30.00	60.00	135.00	300.00
	1835 CB	.331	30.00	60.00	135.00	300.00
	1836 CB	.093	35.00	70.00	160.00	350.00
	1837 CB	.177	30.00	60.00	135.00	300.00
	1837 CB-G	I.A.	60.00	125.00	300.00	600.00
	1838 AG	.834	30.00	60.00	135.00	300.00
	1838 AG-G	I.A.	70.00	150.00	350.00	700.00
	1839 AG	.212	30.00	60.00	135.00	300.00
	1840 AG	.068	45.00	90.00	220.00	500.00
	1841 AG	.549	30.00	60.00	135.00	300.00
	1842 AG	.288	35.00	70.00	160.00	325.00

NOTE: Previously listed 1834 plain edge variety is normal but a weakly struck example.

Rev: Arms w/3 crowns.

KM#	Date	Mintage	VG	Fine	VF	XF
655	1842 AG	I.A.	35.00	70.00	160.00	325.00
(450)	1843/2AG					
		3 pcs.	—	—	Rare	—

KM#	Date	Mintage	Fine	VF	XF	Unc
661	1844 AG	.088	60.00	125.00	300.00	500.00
(456)	1845 AG large head					
		.043	65.00	130.00	375.00	650.00

KM#	Date	Mintage	Fine	VF	XF	Unc
667	1845 AG small head					
(462)		Inc. KM456	75.00	150.00	350.00	700.00
	1846 AG obv. GOTH.					
		.111	45.00	100.00	285.00	500.00
	1846 AG obv. GOTH w/o period					
		Inc. Ab.	45.00	100.00	285.00	550.00
	1847 AG	.060	60.00	125.00	325.00	750.00
	1848 AG	.185	45.00	90.00	265.00	500.00
	1850 AG	.070	50.00	100.00	285.00	550.00
	1851 AG	.122	45.00	90.00	265.00	500.00
	1852 AG	.054	60.00	125.00	325.00	700.00
	1853AG GOTH, small date					
		.109	45.00	90.00	265.00	500.00
	1853 AG GOTH w/o period, small date					
		Inc. Ab.	45.00	90.00	265.00	500.00
	1853 large date					
		Inc. Ab.	50.00	100.00	300.00	575.00
	1854 AG	.034	60.00	125.00	325.00	650.00
	1855 AG small date					
		.161	45.00	90.00	265.00	500.00
	1855 AG large date					
		Inc. Ab.	60.00	125.00	325.00	650.00

MONETARY REFORM

100 Ore = 1 Riksdaler Riksmynt
4 Riksdaler Riksmynt = 1 Riksdaler Specie

1/2 ORE

BRONZE

KM#	Date	Mintage	VG	Fine	VF	XF
686	1856	.026	15.00	30.00	60.00	125.00
(476)	1857	1.312	.50	1.00	1.50	5.00
	1858/7	1.849	.75	1.50	3.00	10.00
	1858	Inc. Ab.	.50	1.00	1.50	5.00

KM#	Date	Mintage	VG	Fine	VF	XF
715	1867 lg.dt.	.064	2.50	5.00	10.00	20.00
(500)	1867 small date					
		Inc. Ab.	4.00	8.00	15.00	30.00

ORE

BRONZE

KM#	Date	Mintage	Fine	VF	XF	Unc
687	1856	.024	35.00	70.00	140.00	300.00
(477)	1857	1.596	1.50	3.00	9.00	20.00
	1858/7	6.290	2.50	5.00	15.00	30.00
	1858 L.A.	I.A.	1.00	2.50	7.50	17.50
	1858 L.A	I.A.	1.00	2.50	7.50	17.50
	1858 LA	I.A.	1.00	2.50	7.50	17.50

KM#	Date	Mintage	Fine	VF	XF	Unc
705	1860/57	.046	15.00	30.00	60.00	125.00
(490)	1860	I.A.	15.00	30.00	60.00	125.00
	1861	.300	3.00	8.00	15.00	30.00
	1862	.079	5.00	12.00	25.00	50.00
	1863	.450	5.00	12.00	25.00	50.00
	1864 L.A.	1.848	1.25	3.00	6.00	15.00
	1864 LA	I.A.	1.25	3.00	6.00	15.00
	1865/2	.561	7.00	15.00	30.00	60.00
	1865/4	I.A.	7.00	15.00	30.00	60.00
	1865	I.A.	2.50	6.00	12.00	27.50
	1866	.327	1.25	3.00	6.00	15.00
	1867	.956	1.25	3.00	6.00	15.00
	1870	1.079	1.25	3.00	6.00	15.00
	1871/61	1.063	2.50	6.00	12.00	25.00
	1871 L.A.	I.A.	1.25	3.00	6.00	15.00
	1871 LA	I.A.	1.25	3.00	6.00	15.00
	1872 L.A.	1.897	1.00	3.00	6.00	12.00
	1872 LA.	I.A.	1.00	3.00	6.00	12.00
	1872 LA	I.A.	1.00	2.50	5.00	10.00

KM#	Date	Mintage	Fine	VF	XF	Unc
728	1873 LA	1.867	3.00	6.00	12.00	25.00
(508)	1873 L.A.	I.A.	3.00	6.00	12.00	25.00
	1873 LA.	I.A.	3.00	6.00	12.00	25.00
	1873 SVFRIGES (error)					
		Inc. Ab.	20.00	40.00	60.00	125.00

2 ORE

BRONZE

KM#	Date	Mintage	Fine	VF	XF	Unc
688	1856	.022	40.00	80.00	150.00	350.00
(478)	1857 long beard					
		1.143	3.00	7.50	20.00	45.00
	1857 short beard					
		Inc. Ab.	3.00	7.50	20.00	45.00
	1858/7	2.831	5.00	10.00	30.00	60.00
	1858	Inc. Ab.	3.00	7.50	20.00	40.00

KM#	Date	Mintage	Fine	VF	XF	Unc
706	1860/57	.197	10.00	25.00	50.00	100.00
(491)	1860	Inc. Ab.	10.00	25.00	50.00	100.00
	1861	1.626	2.50	6.00	12.00	25.00
	1862	.213	6.00	15.00	30.00	60.00
	1863/2	1.621	3.00	7.50	15.00	35.00
	1863	Inc. Ab.	2.50	6.00	12.00	25.00
	1864	.600	2.50	6.00	12.00	25.00
	1865	.603	4.00	10.00	20.00	40.00
	1866/5	.400	6.00	15.00	30.00	60.00
	1866	Inc. Ab.	3.00	7.50	15.00	30.00
	1867 L.A.	.428	2.50	6.00	12.00	25.00
	1867 LA	I.A.	2.50	6.00	12.00	25.00
	1871/61	.718	3.00	7.00	13.50	25.00
	1871	Inc. Ab.	2.50	6.00	12.00	25.00
	1872/1	1.646	5.00	12.00	25.00	50.00
	1872	Inc. Ab.	2.00	5.00	10.00	20.00

KM#	Date	Mintage	Fine	VF	XF	Unc
729	1873	1.294	7.50	15.00	30.00	60.00
(509)						

NOTE: Previously dated 1873 w/o dots above "O" in GOTH is a weakly struck example.

5 ORE

BRONZE

KM#	Date	Mintage	Fine	VF	XF	Unc
690	1857 small L.A					
(480)		.731	4.00	10.00	35.00	70.00
	1857 large L.A					
		Inc. Ab.	4.00	10.00	35.00	70.00
	1857 curved top 5					
		Inc. Ab.	20.00	60.00	125.00	250.00
	1858/7	1.193	4.00	10.00	35.00	75.00
	1858	Inc. Ab.	10.00	20.00	60.00	125.00

KM#	Date	Mintage	Fine	VF	XF	Unc
707	1860/57	.068	25.00	60.00	120.00	250.00
(492)	1860	Inc. Ab.	20.00	50.00	100.00	200.00
	1861/57	.343	8.00	25.00	50.00	100.00
	1861	Inc. Ab.	6.00	15.00	30.00	60.00
	1862 star	.136	7.00	17.50	35.00	75.00
	1862 rose	I.A.	30.00	75.00	150.00	300.00
	1863/2	.633	6.50	16.50	32.50	85.00
	1863	Inc. Ab.	6.00	15.00	30.00	75.00
	1864/2	.264	6.50	16.50	32.50	85.00
	1864	Inc. Ab.	6.00	15.00	30.00	75.00
	1865	.104	7.00	17.50	35.00	75.00
	1866/5	.120	20.00	50.00	100.00	200.00
	1866	Inc. Ab.	7.00	17.50	35.00	75.00
	1867/6	.741	3.50	11.00	27.50	55.00
	1867	Inc. Ab.	3.00	10.00	25.00	50.00
	1872/66	.620	8.00	20.00	50.00	100.00
	1872	Inc. Ab.	3.00	10.00	25.00	50.00

KM#	Date	Mintage	Fine	VF	XF	Unc
730	1873/2	.783	25.00	40.00	75.00	150.00
(510)						

NOTE: Previously dated 1873 w/o dots above "O" in GOTH is a weakly struck example.

10 ORE

.8500 g, .750 SILVER, .0204 oz ASW

KM#	Date	Mintage	Fine	VF	XF	Unc
683	1855 AG small AG					
(473)		1.359	15.00	30.00	75.00	165.00
	1855 AG larger AG					
		Inc. Ab.	15.00	30.00	75.00	165.00
	1855 G long beard					
		Inc. Ab.	3.00	7.50	20.00	45.00
	1855 G shorter beard					
		Inc. Ab.	3.00	7.50	20.00	45.00
	1855 T	Inc. Ab.	3.00	7.50	20.00	45.00
	1857 ST	1.007	3.00	7.50	20.00	45.00
	1858/7 ST	.354	5.00	12.00	30.00	65.00
	1858 ST	I.A.	4.00	10.00	25.00	50.00
	1859/7 ST					
		1.684	4.00	10.00	25.00	50.00
	1859/8 ST	I.A.	4.00	10.00	25.00	50.00
	1859 ST	I.A.	3.00	7.50	20.00	45.00

KM#	Date	Mintage	Fine	VF	XF	Unc
710	1861 ST	.579	4.00	10.00	25.00	55.00
(495)	1862 ST	I.A.	300.00	600.00	900.00	1900.
	1863 ST	.449	6.00	15.00	35.00	75.00
	1864 ST	I.A.	4.00	10.00	25.00	50.00
	1865 ST	.560	4.00	10.00	25.00	50.00

KM#	Date	Mintage	Fine	VF	XF	Unc
(495)	1867 ST	.609	4.00	10.00	25.00	50.00
	1869 ST	.210	5.00	12.50	30.00	65.00
	1870 ST	.384	4.00	10.00	25.00	50.00
	1871 ST	1.162	2.00	6.00	15.00	35.00

KM#	Date	Mintage	Fine	VF	XF	Unc
727	1872 ST	.120	60.00	90.00	150.00	225.00
(507)	1873 ST	.635	50.00	75.00	100.00	175.00
	1873 ST inverted A in SVERIGE (error)					
		Inc. Ab.	65.00	130.00	200.00	350.00
	1873 ST SVF.RIGES (error)					
		Inc. Ab.	50.00	100.00	200.00	450.00

25 ORE

2.1300 g, .750 SILVER, .0513 oz ASW

KM#	Date	Mintage	Fine	VF	XF	Unc
684	1855 ST	.437	6.00	15.00	40.00	80.00
(474)	1856 ST	1.763	5.00	12.00	30.00	65.00
	1857/6 ST	.434	12.00	30.00	70.00	140.00
	1857 ST	I.A.	10.00	25.00	65.00	125.00
	1858/7 ST					
		1.183	10.00	25.00	65.00	140.00
	1858 ST	I.A.	10.00	25.00	65.00	140.00
	1859/7 ST	—	6.50	16.50	45.00	90.00
	1859/8 ST	—	6.50	16.50	45.00	90.00
	1859 ST	—	6.00	15.00	40.00	80.00

KM#	Date	Mintage	Fine	VF	XF	Unc
712	1862 ST	1,740	450.00	800.00	1200.	3000.
(497)	1864/2 ST	.266	16.50	32.50	65.00	140.00
	1864 ST	I.A.	15.00	30.00	60.00	125.00
	1865 ST	.400	15.00	30.00	60.00	125.00
	1866 ST	.039	17.50	35.00	70.00	140.00
	1867/6 ST	.198	18.00	37.50	75.00	150.00
	1867 ST	I.A.	15.00	35.00	70.00	125.00
	1871/61 ST					
		.660	12.00	22.50	50.00	100.00
	1871 ST	I.A.	11.00	20.00	45.00	90.00

50 ORE

4.2500 g, .750 SILVER, .1024 oz ASW

KM#	Date	Mintage	Fine	VF	XF	Unc
691	1857 ST	.492	50.00	100.00	200.00	400.00
(481)						

KM#	Date	Mintage	Fine	VF	XF	Unc
713	1862 ST	2,319	500.00	800.00	1250.	3000.
(498)						

RIKSDALER RIKSMYNT

8.5000 g, .750 SILVER, .2049 oz ASW
Obv: Short goatee.

KM#	Date	Mintage	Fine	VF	XF	Unc
692	1857 ST	.645	50.00	90.00	180.00	500.00
(482)						

Obv: Long goatee.

KM#	Date	Mintage	Fine	VF	XF	Unc
693	1857 ST	I.A.	35.00	75.00	140.00	350.00
(483)						

KM#	Date	Mintage	Fine	VF	XF	Unc
708	1860 ST	.125	50.00	90.00	180.00	500.00
(493)	1861/0 ST	.158	60.00	100.00	200.00	550.00
	1861 ST	I.A.	50.00	90.00	180.00	500.00
	1862 ST	—	850.00	1250.	2000.	4500.
	1864 ST	.085	60.00	100.00	200.00	550.00
	1865 ST	.059	100.00	200.00	400.00	900.00
	1867/6 ST	.106	60.00	100.00	225.00	600.00
	1867 ST	I.A.	50.00	90.00	180.00	500.00
	1871/61 ST					
		.208	60.00	100.00	225.00	600.00
	1871 ST	Inc. Ab.	40.00	80.00	160.00	450.00

NOTE: Previously listed 1864 w/o edge lettering variety is a weakly struck example.

Obv: Deepened hairlines.

KM#	Date	Mintage	Fine	VF	XF	Unc
731	1873 ST	.166	350.00	600.00	1000.	1750.
(511)						

2 RIKSDALER RIKSMYNT

17.0000 g, .750 SILVER, .4099 oz ASW

KM#	Date	Mintage	Fine	VF	XF	Unc
694	1857 ST	.288	120.00	250.00	450.00	950.00
(484)						

KM#	Date	Mintage	Fine	VF	XF	Unc
714	1862 ST					
(499)		640 pcs.	550.00	1200.	2000.	3500.
	1864/2 ST	.038	200.00	400.00	650.00	1500.
	1864 ST	I.A.	200.00	400.00	650.00	1500.
	1871 ST small date and large head					
		.019	220.00	425.00	700.00	1600.

Obv: Small head. Rev: Large date.

KM#	Date	Mintage	Fine	VF	XF	Unc
725	1871 ST	I.A.	150.00	300.00	550.00	1250.
(505)						

RIKSDALER SPECIE

(4 Riksdaler Riksmynt)

34.0061 g, .750 SILVER, .8201 oz ASW
Obv: Bust right w/short goatee. Rev: Crowned, supported arms, small mintmasters initials.

KM#	Date	Mintage	Fine	VF	XF	Unc
685	1855 ST	2,117	—	—	Rare	—
(475)	1856/5 ST	.776	250.00	500.00	750.00	1500.
	1856 ST	I.A.	100.00	200.00	400.00	1000.

Obv: Long goatee. Rev: Large mintmasters initials.

KM#	Date	Mintage	Fine	VF	XF	Unc
689	1856 ST	I.A.	50.00	100.00	250.00	475.00
(479)	1857 ST	.483	50.00	100.00	270.00	550.00
	1859 ST	.101	55.00	110.00	285.00	650.00

KM#	Date	Mintage	Fine	VF	XF	Unc
711	1861 ST	.207	55.00	110.00	220.00	450.00
(496)	1862/1 ST	.943	35.00	75.00	220.00	450.00
	1862 ST L.A., edge lettering large and small					
		Inc. Ab.	35.00	75.00	220.00	450.00
	1862 ST L A					
		Inc. Ab.	35.00	75.00	220.00	450.00
	1862 ST w/o engravers initials					
		Inc. Ab.	75.00	135.00	300.00	600.00

KM#	Date	Mintage	Fine	VF	XF	Unc
(496)	1862 ST w/o edge lettering					
		Inc. Ab.	115.00	225.00	450.00	1000.
	1863 ST	.268	55.00	110.00	265.00	525.00
	1864 ST	.535	35.00	75.00	220.00	450.00
	1865 ST	.107	55.00	110.00	265.00	525.00
	1866/5 ST	.041	70.00	130.00	285.00	650.00
	1866 ST	I.A.	65.00	120.00	275.00	550.00
	1867 ST	.064	55.00	110.00	265.00	525.00
	1868 ST	.120	55.00	110.00	265.00	525.00
	1869 ST	.314	30.00	65.00	200.00	400.00
	1870 ST	.161	55.00	110.00	265.00	525.00

NOTE: Previously listed 1862 and 1866 w/o edge lettering varieties are normal but weakly struck examples.

Obv: Larger head.

KM#	Date	Mintage	Fine	VF	XF	Unc
726	1871 ST	.260	30.00	65.00	200.00	450.00
(506)						

MONETARY REFORM

100 Ore = 1 Krona

ORE

BRONZE
Obv: Small lettering.

KM#	Date	Mintage	Fine	VF	XF	Unc
734	1874	2.370	4.00	9.00	17.50	35.00
(514)	1875/4	2.829	35.00	50.00	85.00	160.00
	1875	Inc. Ab.	4.00	9.00	17.50	35.00
	1876	1.889	17.50	25.00	40.00	85.00
	1877	1.590	9.00	17.50	30.00	65.00

Obv: Large lettering.

KM#	Date	Mintage	Fine	VF	XF	Unc
745	1877	Inc. Ab.	9.00	17.50	30.00	65.00
(523)	1878	1.570	10.00	20.00	30.00	75.00
	1879	1.630	6.00	12.50	25.00	50.00
	1880	1.713	140.00	200.00	375.00	600.00

Obv: Legend lengthened.

KM#	Date	Mintage	Fine	VF	XF	Unc
750	1879	Inc. Ab.	125.00	180.00	325.00	500.00
(528)	1880	Inc. Ab.	12.50	20.00	35.00	70.00
	1881	1.984	5.00	10.00	20.00	40.00
	1882	2.587	3.00	6.00	12.00	25.00
	1883	2.587	3.00	6.00	12.00	25.00
	1884	2.626	3.00	6.00	12.00	25.00
	1885	2.464	3.00	6.00	12.00	25.00
	1886	1.234	4.00	8.00	15.00	35.00
	1888	1.738	4.00	8.00	15.00	35.00
	1889	1.189	4.00	8.00	15.00	35.00
	1890	1.949	2.00	5.00	12.00	25.00
	1891	2.723	2.00	5.00	12.00	25.00
	1892	Inc. Ab.	45.00	65.00	110.00	225.00
	1893	2.145	2.00	5.00	12.00	25.00
	1894	.590	20.00	30.00	45.00	100.00
	1895/3	2.012	8.00	15.00	25.00	60.00
	1895	Inc. Ab.	1.00	3.00	7.00	15.00
	1896	1.463	1.00	3.00	7.00	15.00
	1897	2.544	.50	2.00	4.00	10.00
	1898	2.959	.50	2.00	4.00	10.00
	1899	2.821	.50	2.00	4.00	10.00
	1900	2.929	.50	2.00	4.00	10.00

NOTE: Later dates (1901-1905) exist for this type.

2 ORE

BRONZE
Obv: Small lettering.

KM#	Date	Mintage	Fine	VF	XF	Unc
725	1874	1.914	2.00	7.00	20.00	60.00
(515)	1875/74	2.441	30.00	55.00	100.00	225.00
	1875	Inc. Ab.	1.00	7.00	25.00	60.00
	1876/5	1.402	30.00	60.00	120.00	225.00
	1876	Inc. Ab.	3.00	12.50	35.00	90.00
	1877	1.015	3.00	12.50	35.00	90.00
	1878	.865	75.00	135.00	275.00	600.00

Obv: Large lettering.

KM#	Date	Mintage	Fine	VF	XF	Unc
746	1877	Inc. Ab.	3.00	12.50	40.00	120.00
(524)	1878	Inc. Ab.	4.00	15.00	50.00	150.00
	1879	.935	2.00	10.00	35.00	100.00
	1880	.825	3.00	15.00	50.00	140.00
	1881	1.244	1.00	4.00	12.50	60.00
	1882	1.777	1.00	4.00	12.50	60.00
	1883	1.483	1.00	4.00	12.50	60.00
	1884 open 4					
		1.316	1.00	4.00	12.50	60.00
	1884 closed 4					
		Inc. Ab.	20.00	45.00	100.00	300.00
	1885	.615	2.00	7.00	20.00	60.00
	1886	1.241	1.00	4.00	12.00	55.00
	1888	.865	1.00	4.00	12.00	55.00
	1889	.589	1.00	4.00	12.00	55.00
	1890/89	.912	40.00	80.00	250.00	500.00
	1890	Inc. Ab.	.75	2.00	7.50	30.00
	1891	.942	.75	2.00	7.50	30.00
	1892	.688	.75	2.00	7.50	35.00
	1893	.558	.75	2.00	7.50	35.00
	1894 open 4					
		.586	1.50	3.00	15.00	60.00
	1894 closed 4					
		Inc. Ab.	20.00	40.00	120.00	250.00
	1895	.781	.75	2.00	8.00	35.00
	1896	.908	.75	2.00	8.00	30.00
	1897	1.300	.50	2.00	8.00	30.00
	1898	1.527	.50	2.00	8.00	30.00
	1899	2.172	.50	2.00	8.00	30.00
	1900 oval OO					
		.688	2.00	5.00	20.00	70.00
	1900 round OO					
		Inc. Ab.	40.00	80.00	250.00	500.00

NOTE: Later dates (1901-1905) exist for this type.

5 ORE

BRONZE
Obv: Small lettering.

KM#	Date	Mintage	Fine	VF	XF	Unc
736	1874	.866	5.00	25.00	60.00	125.00
(516)	1875/4	1.234	6.00	30.00	75.00	150.00
	1875	Inc. Ab.	4.00	20.00	50.00	100.00
	1876	.609	4.00	20.00	50.00	100.00
	1877	.514	15.00	60.00	150.00	300.00
	1878	.364	4.00	20.00	50.00	100.00
	1879	.350	20.00	75.00	150.00	300.00
	1880/70	.403	15.00	50.00	125.00	250.00
	1880	Inc. Ab.	15.00	50.00	125.00	250.00
	1881	.625	4.00	20.00	50.00	100.00
	1882/1	.825	15.00	60.00	120.00	240.00
	1882	Inc. Ab.	4.00	20.00	60.00	120.00
	1883	.578	4.00	20.00	50.00	100.00
	1884	.784	4.00	20.00	50.00	100.00
	1885	.282	4.00	20.00	50.00	100.00
	1886	.269	4.50	20.00	60.00	120.00
	1887	.251	5.00	25.00	70.00	140.00
	1888	.214	5.00	25.00	70.00	140.00
	1889	.220	3.00	15.00	45.00	90.00

Obv: Large lettering.

KM#	Date	Mintage	Fine	VF	XF	Unc
757	1888	Inc. Ab.	75.00	120.00	175.00	400.00
(533)	1889	Inc. Ab.	3.00	15.00	45.00	90.00
	1890	.339	3.00	15.00	60.00	120.00
	1891/81	.374	2.00	10.00	35.00	100.00
	1891	Inc. Ab.	2.00	10.00	35.00	100.00
	1892	.586	1.00	7.00	30.00	80.00
	1895	.529	1.00	7.00	30.00	80.00
	1896	.309	2.00	10.00	35.00	95.00
	1897	.570	1.00	6.00	20.00	60.00
	1898	.721	1.00	6.00	20.00	60.00
	1899*	1.225	1.00	6.00	20.00	60.00
	1900	.365	1.00	6.00	20.00	60.00

NOTE: Later dates (1901-1905) exist for this type.
***NOTE:** Varieties exist.

10 ORE

1.4500 g, .400 SILVER, .0186 oz ASW
Obv: Small lettering.

KM#	Date	Mintage	Fine	VF	XF	Unc
737	1874 ST	2.875	12.00	20.00	45.00	100.00
(517)	1875/4 ST					
		1.503	60.00	90.00	150.00	300.00
	1875 ST	I.A.	50.00	80.00	130.00	270.00
	1876/5 ST					
		1.814	15.00	30.00	60.00	120.00
	1876 ST	I.A.	12.50	25.00	50.00	100.00

Obv: Large lettering.

KM#	Date	Mintage	Fine	VF	XF	Unc
755	1880 EB	.851	30.00	45.00	65.00	130.00
(530)	1881 EB	.763	30.00	45.00	65.00	130.00
	1882/1 EB	.735	65.00	100.00	150.00	300.00
	1882 EB	I.A.	30.00	45.00	65.00	130.00
	1883 EB	.694	20.00	35.00	55.00	100.00
	1884 EB	1.560	12.00	25.00	50.00	100.00
	1887 EB	1.513	12.00	25.00	50.00	100.00
	1890 EB	.922	12.00	25.00	50.00	100.00
	1891 EB	.827	12.00	25.00	50.00	100.00
	1892 EB	1.215	4.00	10.00	35.00	70.00
	1894 EB	1.733	2.50	7.50	25.00	45.00
	1896 EB	2.084	2.00	6.00	20.00	35.00
	1897 EB	.819	2.50	7.50	25.00	45.00
	1898 EB	2.087	1.00	4.50	20.00	35.00
	1899 EB	2.041	1.00	4.50	20.00	35.00
	1900 EB	1.173	1.50	6.00	20.00	35.00

NOTE: Later dates (1902-1904) exist for this type.

25 ORE

2.4200 g, .600 SILVER, .0467 oz ASW
Obv: Small lettering.

KM#	Date	Mintage	Fine	VF	XF	Unc
738	1874 ST	2.100	12.00	25.00	60.00	150.00
(518)	1875/4 ST					
		1.131	50.00	95.00	180.00	350.00
	1875 ST	I.A.	40.00	75.00	140.00	275.00
	1876 ST	2.225	12.00	25.00	60.00	150.00
	1877 EB	.894	15.00	30.00	75.00	175.00
	1878/7 EB	.859	70.00	150.00	300.00	700.00
	1878 EB	I.A.	60.00	125.00	250.00	650.00

Obv: Large lettering.

KM#	Date	Mintage	Fine	VF	XF	Unc
739	1874 ST	I.A.	6.00	17.50	50.00	150.00
(531)	1880 EB	1.180	6.00	17.50	50.00	150.00
	1881 EB	1.392	5.00	15.00	40.00	120.00
	1883 EB	1.100	3.00	10.00	30.00	90.00
	1885 EB	1.168	4.50	12.00	37.50	110.00
	1889 EB	.422	4.50	12.00	37.50	110.00
	1890 EB	.469	3.00	10.00	30.00	90.00
	1896 EB	.794	2.50	8.00	25.00	80.00
	1897 EB	1.097	1.50	6.00	20.00	75.00

KM#	Date	Mintage	Fine	VF	XF	Unc
(531)	1898 EB	1.458	1.50	6.00	20.00	75.00
	1899 EB	1.458	1.50	6.00	20.00	75.00

NOTE: Later dates (1902-1905) exist for this type.

50 ORE

5.0000 g, .600 SILVER, .0965 oz ASW

KM#	Date	Mintage	Fine	VF	XF	Unc
740	1875 ST	1.908	7.50	35.00	100.00	285.00
(519)	1877 EB	.149	60.00	120.00	300.00	800.00
	1878 EB	.319	10.00	50.00	125.00	400.00
	1880 EB	.188	20.00	60.00	150.00	450.00
	1881 EB	.268	15.00	50.00	125.00	400.00
	1883 EB	.770	6.00	30.00	75.00	165.00
	1898 EB	.505	6.00	30.00	75.00	165.00
	1899 EB	.720	6.00	30.00	75.00	165.00

KRONA

7.5000 g, .800 SILVER, .1929 oz ASW

KM#	Date	Mintage	Fine	VF	XF	Unc
741	1875 ST	3.531	15.00	60.00	200.00	600.00
(520)	1876/5 ST	2.510	20.00	75.00	225.00	800.00
	1876 ST	I.A.	15.00	65.00	215.00	675.00

Obv: OCH replaces O in royal title.

KM#	Date	Mintage	Fine	VF	XF	Unc
747	1877 EB	.554	20.00	85.00	300.00	950.00
(525)	1879 EB	.077	55.00	135.00	450.00	1400.
	1880 EB	.177	17.50	75.00	275.00	900.00
	1881 EB	.619	20.00	85.00	300.00	950.00
	1883 EB	.205	25.00	100.00	350.00	1000.
	1884 EB	.382	17.50	75.00	275.00	900.00
	1887 EB	.058	50.00	130.00	450.00	1500.
	1888 EB	.062	50.00	130.00	450.00	1500.
	1889 EB	.425	17.50	70.00	250.00	775.00
	1889 EB lock of hair below NO in NORGES	Inc. Ab.	125.00	450.00	1000.	3000.

Obv: W/o initials below bust.

KM#	Date	Mintage	Fine	VF	XF	Unc
760	1890 EB	.594	15.00	60.00	200.00	625.00
(535)	1897 EB	.735	10.00	40.00	125.00	400.00
	1898 EB	1.860	6.50	30.00	100.00	325.00

NOTE: Later dates (1901-1904) exist for this type.

2 KRONOR

15.0000 g, .800 SILVER, .3858 oz ASW

KM#	Date	Mintage	Fine	VF	XF	Unc
742	1876 EB wide date, 6mm wide, large E.B.	.370	700.00	1600.	3200.	—
(521)	1876 EB wide date, small E.B.	Inc. Ab.	225.00	500.00	1400.	3500.
	1876 EB smaller date, 5mm wide	Inc. Ab.	20.00	100.00	450.00	1000.
	1877 EB	.168	25.00	125.00	475.00	1250.
	1878 EB	.193	20.00	100.00	450.00	1150.
	1880 EB	.128	40.00	150.00	700.00	1850.

Obv: OCH replaces O in royal title.

KM#	Date	Mintage	Fine	VF	XF	Unc
749	1878 EB	I.A.	550.00	950.00	2000.	4000.
(527)	1880 EB	I.A.	40.00	190.00	725.00	2000.

Obv: W/o initials below bust.

KM#	Date	Mintage	Fine	VF	XF	Unc
761	1890 EB	.072	40.00	150.00	475.00	1250.
(536)	1892 EB	.087	35.00	150.00	500.00	1300.
	1893 EB	.049	45.00	175.00	550.00	1350.
	1897 EB	.207	15.00	50.00	225.00	525.00
	1898 EB	.141	15.00	50.00	250.00	550.00
	1900 EB	.131	15.00	55.00	265.00	625.00

NOTE: Later dates (1903-1904) exist for this type.

Silver Jubilee

KM#	Date	Mintage	Fine	VF	XF	Unc
762 (537)	1897 EB	.246	6.50	9.00	15.00	30.00

5 KRONOR

2.2402 g, .900 GOLD, .0648 oz AGW

KM#	Date	Mintage	Fine	VF	XF	Unc
756	1881 EB	.065	45.00	60.00	90.00	145.00
(532)	1882 EB	.030	55.00	70.00	100.00	225.00
	1883 EB	.028	60.00	90.00	120.00	250.00
	1886/3 EB	.042	45.00	60.00	90.00	135.00
	1886 EB	I.A.	45.00	60.00	90.00	135.00
	1894 EB	.051	45.00	60.00	90.00	135.00
	1899 EB	.104	40.00	50.00	70.00	100.00

10 KRONOR

4.4803 g, .900 GOLD, .1296 oz AGW

KM#	Date	Mintage	Fine	VF	XF	Unc
732	1873 ST	.200	70.00	85.00	125.00	250.00
(512.1)	1874/3 ST	.461	70.00	85.00	110.00	170.00
	1874 ST	I.A.	70.00	85.00	100.00	150.00
	1874 ST	—	—	—	Proof	1300.
	1876 ST	.133	70.00	85.00	110.00	170.00

Obv: OCH substituted for O. in royal title.

KM#	Date	Mintage	Fine	VF	XF	Unc
743	1876 EB	.037	70.00	100.00	175.00	300.00
(512.2)	1877 EB	.055	75.00	150.00	250.00	375.00
	1880 EB	.027	75.00	150.00	250.00	375.00
	1880 EB L.A.	Inc. Ab.	75.00	150.00	250.00	375.00
	1883 EB L.A.	.149	70.00	85.00	100.00	160.00
	1883 LA	I.A.	70.00	85.00	100.00	160.00
	1883 L.A. larger L.A.	Inc. Ab.	70.00	85.00	100.00	160.00

KM#	Date	Mintage	Fine	VF	XF	Unc
(512.2)	1894 EB	.036	70.00	85.00	120.00	200.00
	1895 EB	.065	70.00	85.00	120.00	200.00

20 KRONOR

8.9606 g, .900 GOLD, .2593 oz AGW

KM#	Date	Mintage	Fine	VF	XF	Unc
733	1873 ST	.115	150.00	200.00	300.00	500.00
(513)	1874 ST	.240	150.00	200.00	300.00	400.00
	1875 ST	.359	150.00	200.00	300.00	400.00
	1876/5 ST	.240	200.00	350.00	600.00	1200.
	1876 ST	I.A.	200.00	350.00	600.00	1200.

Rev: Arms wider.

KM#	Date	Mintage	Fine	VF	XF	Unc
744	1876 EB	I.A.	150.00	200.00	300.00	400.00
(522)	1877 EB	.103	150.00	200.00	300.00	400.00

Obv: OCH substituted for O. in royal title.

KM#	Date	Mintage	Fine	VF	XF	Unc
748	1877 EB	I.A.	150.00	200.00	250.00	325.00
(526)	1878/7 EB	.245	150.00	200.00	250.00	325.00
	1878 EB	I.A.	150.00	200.00	250.00	325.00
	1879 EB	.075	160.00	220.00	400.00	600.00
	1879 EB	Unique	—	—	Proof	10,000.
	1880 EB	.127	150.00	200.00	250.00	325.00
	1881 EB	.047	200.00	350.00	600.00	1000.
	1884 EB	.191	135.00	185.00	225.00	300.00
	1885 EB	6,250	500.00	800.00	1600.	2500.
	1886 EB	.173	135.00	185.00	225.00	300.00
	1887 EB	.059	200.00	350.00	600.00	1000.
	1889 EB	.202	135.00	185.00	225.00	300.00
	1890 EB	.155	135.00	185.00	225.00	300.00
	1895 EB	.135	135.00	185.00	225.00	300.00
	1898 EB	.313	125.00	175.00	220.00	285.00
	1899 EB	.261	125.00	175.00	220.00	285.00

Obv: Larger head.

KM#	Date	Mintage	Fine	VF	XF	Unc
765 (540)	1900 EB	.104	150.00	200.00	350.00	550.00

NOTE: Later dates (1901-1902) exist for this type.

TRADE COINAGE

DUCAT

3.5000 g, .976 GOLD, .1098 oz AGW

KM#	Date	Mintage	VG	Fine	VF	XF
542	1801 OL	3,100	225.00	550.00	1100.	1800.
(380)	1802 OL	4,827	175.00	375.00	750.00	1500.
	1803 OL	7,300	150.00	350.00	700.00	1200.
	1804 OL	8,700	175.00	375.00	750.00	1500.
	1805 OL	.013	150.00	350.00	700.00	1200.
	1806 OL	.014	150.00	350.00	700.00	1200.
	1807 OL	.011	150.00	350.00	700.00	1200.
	1808 OL	.033	150.00	350.00	700.00	1200.
	1809 OL	.021	150.00	350.00	700.00	1200.

NOTE: Earlier dates (1793-1800) exist for this type.

KM#	Date	Mintage	VG	Fine	VF	XF
562 (387)	1801 OL	900 pcs.	500.00	1100.	2250.	3750.

KM#	Date	Mintage	VG	Fine	VF	XF
567 (392)	1804 OL	1,254	400.00	900.00	1800.	3000.

KM#	Date	Mintage	VG	Fine	VF	XF
581 (396)	1810 OL	.014	150.00	350.00	700.00	1200.
	1811 OL	9,750	175.00	400.00	800.00	1300.
	1812 OL	.016	150.00	350.00	700.00	1200.
	1813 OL	.026	150.00	350.00	700.00	1200.
	1814 OL	.022	150.00	350.00	700.00	1200.

KM#	Date	Mintage	VG	Fine	VF	XF
591 (406)	1815 OL	8,060	185.00	400.00	800.00	1300.
	1816 OL	6,130	200.00	450.00	900.00	1400.
	1817 OL	5,673	225.00	450.00	1000.	1500.

Dalarna Mines Commemorative

KM#	Date	Mintage	VG	Fine	VF	XF
582 (397)	1810 OL	1,322	250.00	550.00	1100.	1800.

KM#	Date	Mintage	VG	Fine	VF	XF
594 (409)	1818 OL	6,389	100.00	225.00	450.00	800.00
	1819 OL	1,828	—	—	Rare	—
	1820 LB	7,248	110.00	250.00	500.00	900.00
	1821 LB	.019	100.00	225.00	450.00	800.00
	1822 CB	5,222	100.00	225.00	500.00	900.00
	1823 AG	3,155	100.00	225.00	500.00	900.00
	1824 CB	3,370	100.00	225.00	500.00	900.00
	1825 CB	8,127	100.00	225.00	450.00	800.00
	1826 CB	4,126	100.00	225.00	450.00	800.00
	1827/6 CB	4,579	110.00	250.00	500.00	875.00
	1827 CB	I.A.	100.00	225.00	450.00	800.00
	1828 CB	5,150	100.00	225.00	450.00	800.00
	1829 CB	5,642	100.00	225.00	450.00	800.00

KM#	Date	Mintage	VG	Fine	VF	XF
628 (428)	1830 CB	5,269	90.00	200.00	375.00	750.00
	1831 CB	3,917	90.00	200.00	375.00	750.00
	1832 CB	2,082	90.00	200.00	375.00	750.00
	1833 CB	2,310	90.00	200.00	375.00	750.00
	1834 CB	3,142	90.00	200.00	375.00	750.00

3.4856 g, .976 GOLD, .1094 AGW

KM#	Date	Mintage	VG	Fine	VF	XF
628a (428a)	1835 CB	7,622	90.00	200.00	375.00	750.00
	1836 CB	1,947	—	—	Rare	—
	1837 CB	.013	80.00	175.00	350.00	700.00

KM#	Date	Mintage	VG	Fine	VF	XF
(428a)	1838 AG	.015	80.00	175.00	350.00	700.00
	1839 AG	.010	80.00	175.00	350.00	700.00
	1840 AG	1,840	125.00	300.00	600.00	1200.
	1841 AG	.013	80.00	175.00	350.00	700.00
	1842 AG	.030	80.00	175.00	350.00	700.00
	1843 AG	.074	75.00	160.00	325.00	650.00

Obv: Large head of Oscar I right.

KM#	Date	Mintage	VG	Fine	VF	XF
662 (457)	1844 AG	946 pcs.	—	—	Rare	—
	1845/4 AG	.046	125.00	300.00	600.00	900.00

Obv: Smaller head.

KM#	Date	Mintage	VG	Fine	VF	XF
668 (463)	1845/4 AG	I.A.	75.00	160.00	325.00	650.00
	1845 AG	I.A.	70.00	150.00	300.00	600.00
	1846 AG	.022	70.00	150.00	300.00	600.00
	1847/4 AG	.018	80.00	165.00	350.00	675.00
	1847 AG	I.A.	70.00	150.00	300.00	600.00
	1848 AG	.037	70.00	150.00	300.00	600.00
	1849/4 AG	.014	80.00	165.00	350.00	675.00
	1849 AG	I.A.	70.00	150.00	300.00	600.00
	1850 AG	.020	70.00	150.00	300.00	600.00
	1851 AG	.016	70.00	150.00	300.00	600.00
	1852 AG	.027	70.00	150.00	300.00	600.00
	1853 AG	.013	70.00	150.00	300.00	600.00
	1854 AG small AG	.020	70.00	150.00	300.00	600.00
	1854 AG large AG	Inc. Ab.	70.00	150.00	300.00	600.00
	1855 AG	.018	70.00	150.00	300.00	600.00
	1856 ST	.012	70.00	150.00	300.00	600.00
	1857 ST small ST	.027	70.00	150.00	300.00	600.00
	1857 ST large ST	Inc. Ab.	70.00	150.00	300.00	600.00
	1858 ST	.041	70.00	150.00	300.00	600.00
	1859 ST	.031	70.00	150.00	300.00	600.00

KM#	Date	Mintage	VG	Fine	VF	XF
709 (494)	1860 ST	.058	65.00	125.00	275.00	550.00
	1861/0 ST	.038	70.00	140.00	325.00	625.00
	1861 ST	I.A.	65.00	125.00	275.00	550.00
	1862 ST	.042	65.00	125.00	275.00	550.00
	1863 ST	.037	55.00	100.00	250.00	450.00
	1864/3 ST	.038	75.00	140.00	325.00	625.00
	1864 ST small L.A.	Inc. Ab.	65.00	125.00	275.00	550.00
	1864 ST larger L.A.	Inc. Ab.	65.00	125.00	275.00	550.00
	1865 ST large year and ST	.039	65.00	125.00	275.00	550.00
	1865 ST smaller year and ST	Inc. Ab.	65.00	125.00	275.00	550.00
	1866 ST large ST	.032	65.00	125.00	275.00	550.00
	1866 ST smaller ST	Inc. Ab.	65.00	125.00	275.00	550.00
	1867 ST	.011	65.00	125.00	275.00	550.00
	1867 TS	I.A.	125.00	300.00	600.00	1000.
	1868 ST small ST	9,398	70.00	150.00	300.00	600.00
	1868 ST larger ST	Inc. Ab.	70.00	150.00	300.00	600.00

2 DUCAT

7.0000 g, .986 GOLD, .2219 oz AGW

KM#	Date	Mintage	VG	Fine	VF	XF
629 (429)	1830 CB	2 pcs.	—	—	Rare	—
	1836 CB	1,500	250.00	650.00	1300.	2000.
	1837 CB	1,989	250.00	650.00	1300.	2000.
	1838 AG	1,000	300.00	700.00	1500.	2400.
	1839 AG	2,200	250.00	650.00	1300.	2000.
	1842 AG	1,546	300.00	700.00	1500.	2400.
	1843 AG	2,159	250.00	650.00	1300.	2000.

KM#	Date	Mintage	VG	Fine	VF	XF
680 (470)	1850 AG	819 pcs.	400.00	900.00	1900.	2800.
	1852 AG	386 pcs.	—	—	Rare	—
	1857 ST	763 pcs.	350.00	800.00	1600.	2500.

4 DUCAT

13.9424 g, .976 GOLD, .4376 oz AGW

KM#	Date	Mintage	VG	Fine	VF	XF
645 (444)	1837 CB	1,625	400.00	900.00	1900.	2800.
	1838 AG	625 pcs.	450.00	1000.	2000.	3000.
	1839 AG	2,000	400.00	900.00	1900.	2800.
	1841 AG	2,084	450.00	1000.	2100.	3300.
	1843 AG	4,405	350.00	800.00	1600.	2500.

KM#	Date	Mintage	VG	Fine	VF	XF
670 (465)	1846 AG	400 pcs.	600.00	1300.	2600.	3800.
	1850 AG	507 pcs.	500.00	1000.	2100.	3200.
	1852 AG	2 pcs.	—	—	Rare	—

CAROLIN-10 FRANCS

3.2258 g, .900 GOLD, .0933 oz AGW

KM#	Date	Mintage	Fine	VF	XF	Unc
716 (501)	1868	.033	75.00	150.00	300.00	500.00
	1869	.031	75.00	150.00	300.00	550.00
	1871	5,153	125.00	250.00	500.00	800.00
	1871 larger ear	Inc. Ab.	175.00	350.00	700.00	1000.
	1872	.012	125.00	250.00	500.00	750.00
	1872 larger ear	Inc. Ab.	275.00	550.00	800.00	1250.

MEDALLIC ISSUES (M)

Largesse Money

Largesse is defined as a generous giving. The throwing of coins to the people is believed to have begun with Gustavus Vasa I (1528). It became the practice to throw coins to the people at coronations and royal funerals, while more important persons were presented with medals to commemorate the occasion.

Specially struck largesse coins of a somewhat uniform size and weight began with Carl X Adolf coronation in 1654. The coins from 1654 until and including the Coronation piece of Gustaf III (1772) are of a 2 mark denomination. The pieces after that date thru Carl XIV's funeral piece of 1844 are of a 1/3 Riksdaler denomination. It was due to the unseemly conduct of the people and the resultant deaths of some, that after this issue the practice of throwing the coins to the public was discontinued and instead they were distributed to the garrison and honored guests and carried no monetary designation. However, it may be noted that these subsequent issues with no relation to the monetary system were circulated as coin of the realm.

SILVER

Coronation of Carl XIII

KM#	Date	Mintage	VG	Fine	VF	XF
M55	1809	—	8.50	18.00	35.00	90.00

Funeral of Queen Sofia Magdalena

Obv: Large bust, E. below.

KM#	Date	Mintage	VG	Fine	VF	XF
M56.1	1813	—	12.00	25.00	50.00	100.00

Obv: Small bust, w/o E.

KM#	Date	Mintage	VG	Fine	VF	XF
M56.2	1813	—	15.00	30.00	60.00	120.00

Funeral of Carl XIII

Obv: Head right. Rev: Crowns on globe.

KM#	Date	Mintage	VG	Fine	VF	XF
M57	1818	—	—	—	Rare	—

Rev: Crowns on cushion.

KM#	Date	Mintage	VG	Fine	VF	XF
M58	1818	—	8.00	20.00	40.00	85.00

Obv: Curl on far shoulder.

KM#	Date	Mintage	VG	Fine	VF	XF
M59	1818	—	8.00	20.00	40.00	85.00

Coronation of Carl XIV John

KM#	Date	Mintage	Fine	VF	XF	Unc
M60	1818	—	20.00	40.00	90.00	150.00

Funeral of Queen Hedwig Elisabeth Charlotte

KM#	Date	Mintage	Fine	VF	XF	Unc
M61	1818	—	30.00	60.00	125.00	180.00

Funeral of Carl XIV John

KM#	Date	Mintage	Fine	VF	XF	Unc
M62	1844	—	20.00	32.50	60.00	110.00

Funeral of Oscar I

Obv: Head left. Rev: 3 towered church.

KM#	Date	Mintage	Fine	VF	XF	Unc
M63	1859	3,200	12.50	27.50	55.00	100.00

Coronation of Carl XV

KM#	Date	Mintage	Fine	VF	XF	Unc
M64	1860	3,200	12.50	27.50	55.00	100.00

Coronation of Oscar II

KM#	Date	Mintage	Fine	VF	XF	Unc
M65	1873	—	20.00	32.50	60.00	85.00

PATTERNS (Pn)

(Including off metal strikes)

KM#	Date	Mintage	Identification	Mkt.Val.
Pn1	1812	—	1 Skilling, Copper	Rare
Pn2	1818	—	1/4 Skilling, Copper, overstruck on earlier coins	—
Pn3	1818	—	1 Ducat, Tin	Rare

KM#	Date	Mintage	Identification	Mkt.Val.
Pn4	1822	—	1 Riksdaler (Specie), Copper	2000.
Pn5	1822	—	1 Riksdaler (Specie), Silver, struck in collar	6000.
Pn6	1826	—	1/2 Skilling, Copper, struck in collar	750.00
Pn7	1826	—	1/2 Skilling, Tin	500.00
Pn8	1826	—	1 Skilling, Copper, 30mm	750.00

KM#	Date	Mintage	Identification	Mkt.Val.
Pn9	1826	—	1 Skilling, Copper, 28mm	750.00
Pn10	1826	—	1 Skilling, Tin	500.00
Pn11	1827	—	1/3 Riksdaler (Specie), Copper	Rare
Pn12	1827	—	1/3 Riksdaler (Specie), Copper, lettered edge	Rare
Pn13	1829	—	1/12 Riksdaler (Specie), Copper	Rare
Pn14	1829	—	1/12 Riksdaler (Specie), Silver, thick planchet	500.00
Pn15	1829	—	1/12 Riksdaler (Specie), Silver, thin planchet	350.00
Pn16	1829 CB	—	1/6 Riksdaler (Banco), Silver	700.00

KM#	Date	Mintage	Identification	Mkt.Val.
Pn17	1829 CB	—	1/3 Riksdaler (Banco), Silver	1500.

KM#	Date	Mintage	Identification	Mkt.Val.
Pn18	1829 CB	—	1 Riksdaler (Banco), Silver	2500.
Pn19	ND(1829)	—	2/3 Riksdaler (Banco), Copper	400.00
Pn20	ND(1829)	—	2/3 Riksdaler (Banco), Silver	500.00
Pn21	1830 CB	—	12 Skilling (Banco), Silver	900.00
Pn22	1830 CB	—	1/2 Daler, Silver	650.00
Pn23	1830 CB	—	1/2 Daler, Silver, small planchet	650.00
Pn24	1830 CB	—	1 Daler, Silver	900.00
Pn25	1830 CB	—	2 Daler, Silver	900.00
Pn26	1830	—	1 Carolin/16 Skillingar, Gold	Rare
Pn27	1830	—	1 Carolin/32 Skillingar, Gold	Rare
Pn28	1830	—	2 Carolin/32 Skillingar, Gold, value changed from 1 to 2	Rare
Pn29	ND(1830)	—	1/10 Carolin, Gold	750.00
Pn30	ND(1830)	—	1/4 Carolin, Gold	750.00
Pn31	ND(1830)	—	1/2 Carolin, Gold	750.00
Pn32	ND(1830)	—	1 Carolin, Gold	1200.
Pn33	ND(1830)	—	2 Carolin, Gold	1500.

KM#	Date	Mintage	Identification	Mkt.Val.
Pn34	1831	—	1/6 Skilling (Banco), Copper	250.00
Pn35	1831 CB	—	1/3 Riksdaler, Silver	800.00
Pn36	1833	—	1/6 Skilling (Banco), Copper	600.00

KM#	Date	Mintage	Identification	Mkt.Val.
Pn37	1833	—	1 Skilling (Banco), Copper	1000.
Pn38	1834 CB	—	1/2 Riksdaler, Silver	Rare
Pn39	1834 CB	—	1 Riksdaler, Silver, plain edge	1000.
Pn40	1834 CB	—	1 Riksdaler, Silver, lettered edge	1000.
Pn41	1834 CB	—	2 Riksdaler, Silver	Rare
Pn42	1834 CB	—	4 Riksdaler, Silver, lettered edge	4500.
Pn43	ND(1834)	—	2 Skilling, Copper	1500.
Pn44	1839	—	4 Skilling (Banco), Copper	1000.

KM#	Date	Mintage	Identification	Mkt.Val.
Pn45	1843	—	2 Skilling (Banco), Copper	1000.
Pn46	1844	—	2/3 Skilling (Banco), Copper	900.00
Pn47	1844	—	4 Skilling (Banco), Copper	1000.
Pn48	ND(CXIXJ)	—	W/o denomination, Copper	900.00
Pn49	ND(CXIVJ)	—	W/o denomination, Copper	900.00
Pn50	1844	—	4 Skilling (Banco), Copper, plain edge	1800.
Pn51	1844	—	4 Skilling (Banco), Copper, reeded edge	1500.

KM#	Date	Mintage	Identification	Mkt.Val.
Pn52	1844	—	4 Skilling (Banco), Copper, plain edge	700.00
Pn53	1844	—	4 Skilling (Banco), Copper, reeded edge	800.00

KM#	Date	Mintage	Identification	Mkt.Val.
Pn54	ND(1844)	—	1/2 Cent, Copper	650.00
Pn55	ND(1844)	—	1/2 Cent, Copper, thick planchet	750.00
Pn56	ND(1844)	—	1 Cent, Copper	650.00
Pn57	ND(1844)	—	2 Cent, Copper	900.00

KM#	Date	Mintage	Identification	Mkt.Val.
Pn58	ND(1844)	—	5 Cent, Copper	900.00
Pn59	ND(1844)	—	5 Cent, Copper, thick planchet	1000.

KM#	Date	Mintage	Identification	Mkt.Val.
Pn60	ND(1844)	—	10 Cent, Copper	1250.
Pn61	1845	—	2 Skilling, Copper	Rare
Pn62	1845	—	4 Skilling, Copper	Rare
Pn63	1845	—	1/16 Riksdaler (Specie), Silver	1200.
Pn64	ND(1845)	—	1/16 Riksdaler (Specie), head on both sides	Rare
Pn65	ND(c.1848)	—	5 Pennigar, Copper	Rare
Pn66	ND(c.1848)	—	10 Pennigar, Copper	Rare

KM#	Date	Mintage	Identification	Mkt.Val.
Pn67	ND(c.1852)	—	4 Skilling (Banco), Silver	350.00
Pn68	ND(c.1852)	—	4 Skilling (Banco), Silver	350.00

KM#	Date	Mintage	Identification	Mkt.Val.
Pn69	1853	—	1 Ore, Copper	300.00
Pn70	1853	—	1 Ore, Copper	300.00

KM#	Date	Mintage	Identification	Mkt.Val.
Pn71	1853	—	2 Ore, Copper, plain edge	550.00
Pn72	1853	—	2 Ore, Copper, reeded edge	550.00
Pn73	ND(c.1854)	—	1/2 Ore, Copper	225.00

KM#	Date	Mintage	Identification	Mkt.Val.
Pn74	ND(c.1854)	—	1/2 Ore, Copper, "150 Rd"	225.00

KM#	Date	Mintage	Identification	Mkt.Val.
Pn75	ND(c.1854)	—	1/2 Ore, Copper, "125 Rd"	250.00
Pn76	ND(c.1854)	—	1/2 Ore, Copper, blank planchet w/punched value	Rare

KM#	Date	Mintage	Identification	Mkt.Val.
Pn77	ND(c.1854)	—	1 Ore, Copper, 150 Rd	150.00
Pn78	ND(c.1854)	—	1 Ore, Copper, blank planchet w/punched value	Rare
Pn79	1854	—	2 Ore, Copper, date on rev.	Rare

KM#	Date	Mintage	Identification	Mkt.Val.
Pn80	ND(c.1854)	—	2 Ore, Copper, 150 Rd	650.00
Pn81	ND(c.1854)	—	2 Ore, Copper, thick planchet	750.00

KM#	Date	Mintage	Identification	Mkt.Val.
Pn82	ND(c.1854)	—	5 Ore, Copper, "200 Rd"	650.00

KM#	Date	Mintage	Identification	Mkt.Val.
Pn83	ND(c.1854)	—	5 Ore, Copper, "250 Rd"	650.00
Pn84	ND(c.1854)	—	5 Ore, Copper, "250 Rd", thick planchet	650.00
Pn85	ND(c.1854)	—	5 Ore, Copper, blank w/punched value	Rare

KM#	Date	Mintage	Identification	Mkt.Val.
Pn86	ND(c.1854)	—	10 Ore, Copper, "200 R"	900.00

KM#	Date	Mintage	Identification	Mkt.Val.
Pn87	ND(c.1854)	—	10 Ore, Copper, "250 Rd"	900.00

KM#	Date	Mintage	Identification	Mkt.Val.
PnA88	1855 AG	—	1 Riksdaler Specie, Silver	Rare
Pn88	1880	—	2 Kronor, Silver, Gold center	Rare
Pn89	1880	—	2 Kronor, Silver, 15.10 g	Rare
Pn90	1880	—	5 Kronor, Gold, 15.5 on rev.	Rare
Pn91	1880	—	5 Kronor, Gold, 16.0 on rev.	Rare
Pn92	1880	—	5 Kronor, Gold, 16.5 on rev.	Rare
Pn93	1881	—	1 Krona, Silver, w/Gold center	Rare
Pn94	1881	—	1 Krona, Silver, 5.95 g	Rare
Pn95	ND(c.1890)	—	5 Ore, Bronze, "3" Denomination	Rare
Pn96	1892	—	2 Ore, Aluminum, KM746	—
Pn97	1892	—	2 Kronor, Aluminum, KM761	—
Pn98	1900	—	20 Kronor, Bronze, KM765	—

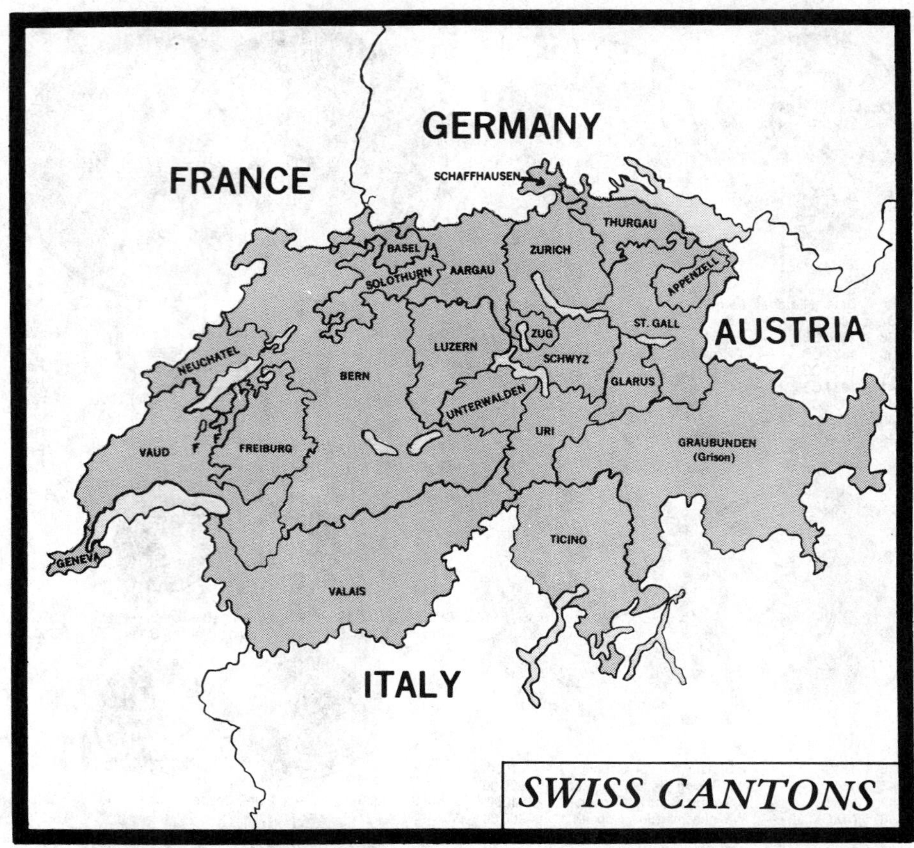

In Switzerland, canton is the name given to each of the 23 states comprising the Swiss Federation. The origin of the cantons is rooted in the liberty-loving instincts of the peasants of Helvetia.

After the Romans departed Switzerland to defend Rome against the barbarians, Switzerland became, in the Middle Ages, a federation of fiefs of the Holy Roman Empire. In 888 it was again united by Rudolf of Burgundy, a minor despot, and for 150 years Switzerland had a king. Upon the death of the last Burgundian king, the kingdom crumbled into a loose collection of feudal fiefs ruled by bishops and ducal families who made their own laws and levied their own taxes. Eventually this division of rule by arbitrary despots became more than the freedom-loving and resourceful peasants could bear. The citizens living in the remote valleys of Uri, Schwyz (from which Switzerland received its name) and Unterwalden decided to liberate themselves from all feudal obligations and become free.

On Aug. 1, 1291, the elders of these three small states met on a tiny heath known as the Rutli on the shores of the Lake of Lucerne and negotiated an 'eternal pact' which recognized their right to local self-government, and pledged one another assistance against any encroachment upon these rights. The pact was the beginning of the 'Everlasting League' and the foundation of the Swiss Confederation.

CANTONAL MINT MARKS OF SWITZERLAND

Mint mark	Canton	Mint
A.-B.	Geneva	Geneva 1847 (Auguste Bovet)
A.B.	Graubunden	Geneva 1842 (Antoine Bovy)
A-B	Graubunden	Private coiner 1836 (Antoine Bovy)
A-B	Graubunden	Geneva 1842 (Antoine Bovy)
B	Basel	Basel 1826 (Bel-Bessiere)
B	Freiburg	Freiburg 1830 (Bel-Bessiere)
B	Glarus	Unknown site 1806-1814
B	Graubunden	Bern 1820
B	Graubunden	Private coiner 1826
B	Luzern	Luzern 1807-1814 (Bruppacher)
B	Schwyz	Schwyz or Aargau 1810
B	Zurich	Zurich 1806-1813 (Bruckmann)
BEL	Basel	Basel 1826 (Bel-Bessiere)
BEL	Freiburg	Freiburg 1830-1846 (Bel-Bessiere)
BEL	Vaud	Lausanne 1826-1834 (Bel-Bessiere)
D	Zurich	Stuttgart 1842-1848
DB	Schwyz	Schwyz 1843-1846
F	Glarus	Unknown site 1806-1807
G	Geneva	Geneva An 8-13
H	Geneva	Geneva 1817 (Hoyer)
H	Schwyz	Schwyz or Aargau 1810-1811
HB	Graubunden	Private coiner 1836 (Bruppacher)
K	St. Gall	St. Gall 1807-1817 (Kukler)
M	Aargau	Aargau 1807-1808 (Meyer)
M	Schwyz	Aargau or Schwyz 1844
N	Graubunden	Bern 1825 (Nett)
SIBER	Vaud	Lausanne 1845 (Siber)
Star	Ticino	Luzern 1813

AARGAU

Argau, Argovie

Located in north central Switzerland. Was named after the river Aar. Was admitted to the Swiss Confederation in 1803.

MONETARY SYSTEM

10 Rappen = 4 Kreuzer = 1 Batzen
10 Batzen = 1 Frank

RAPPEN

BILLON

KM#	Date	Mintage	Fine	VF	XF	Unc
15	1809	.044	25.00	45.00	80.00	175.00
	1811	.039	10.00	17.50	25.00	60.00
	1816	—	10.00	17.50	25.00	60.00
	Rev: Wreath of stars and flowers.					
18	1810	.020	25.00	45.00	80.00	175.00

2 RAPPEN

BILLON

KM#	Date	Mintage	Fine	VF	XF	Unc
11	1808	.092	6.00	12.50	17.50	35.00
	1811	—	15.00	30.00	40.00	75.00
	1812	—	6.00	12.50	20.00	50.00
	1813	—	6.00	12.50	20.00	50.00
	1814	—	6.00	12.50	20.00	50.00
	1816	—	6.00	12.50	20.00	50.00

2-1/2 RAPPEN

(Ein (1) Kreuzer)

BILLON

KM#	Date	Mintage	Fine	VF	XF	Unc
25	1831	—	8.00	17.50	30.00	75.00

5 RAPPEN

BILLON

KM#	Date	Mintage	Fine	VF	XF	Unc
24	1829	1,000	12.50	22.50	60.00	150.00
	1831	—	12.50	22.50	60.00	150.00

1/2 BATZEN

BILLON

KM#	Date	Mintage	Fine	VF	XF	Unc
8.1	1807	—	15.00	50.00	80.00	200.00
	1808	—	15.00	50.00	80.00	200.00
	1809	—	12.50	22.50	60.00	175.00
	1811	—	12.50	22.50	60.00	175.00
	1815	—	12.50	22.50	60.00	175.00

NOTE: Varieties exist.

Cruder style.

KM#	Date	Mintage	Fine	VF	XF	Unc
8.2	1807	—	15.00	50.00	80.00	200.00

BATZEN

BILLON

Obv: Oval arms, leg: AARGAU. Rev: Oak branches.

KM#	Date	Mintage	Fine	VF	XF	Unc
5	1805	1,000	45.00	90.00	150.00	350.00

Obv. leg: ARGAU.

KM#	Date	Mintage	Fine	VF	XF	Unc
6	1806	—	45.00	125.00	180.00	450.00

Obv: Pointed arms w/garlands.

KM#	Date	Mintage	Fine	VF	XF	Unc
7	1806	—	45.00	125.00	180.00	400.00

KM#	Date	Mintage	Fine	VF	XF	Unc
9.1	1807	.132	15.00	27.50	50.00	150.00
	1808	.184	15.00	27.50	50.00	150.00
	1809	.350	15.00	27.50	50.00	150.00
	1810	.215	15.00	27.50	50.00	150.00
	1811	.060	15.00	27.50	50.00	150.00
	1816	—	20.00	45.00	125.00	275.00

NOTE: Varieties exist.

Cruder style.

KM#	Date	Mintage	Fine	VF	XF	Unc
9.2	1807	—	15.00	27.50	50.00	150.00

Obv. leg: ARGAU. Rev: Palm branches.

KM#	Date	Mintage	Fine	VF	XF	Unc
12	1808	—	80.00	110.00	160.00	500.00

Rev: Beaded inner circle

KM#	Date	Mintage	Fine	VF	XF	Unc
21	1826	—	10.00	25.00	37.50	100.00

Rev: W/o inner circle.

KM#	Date	Mintage	Fine	VF	XF	Unc
22	1826	—	30.00	60.00	110.00	200.00

5 BATZEN

SILVER

KM#	Date	Mintage	Fine	VF	XF	Unc
10	1807 M	250 pcs.	200.00	250.00	375.00	800.00
	1808 M	.114	25.00	45.00	90.00	225.00

KM#	Date	Mintage	Fine	VF	XF	Unc
13.1	1808	—	60.00	125.00	180.00	375.00
	1809	.084	12.50	25.00	65.00	175.00
	1810	.171	12.50	25.00	65.00	175.00

KM#	Date	Mintage	Fine	VF	XF	Unc
13.2	*1811*	.065	12.50	25.00	65.00	175.00

KM#	Date	Mintage	Fine	VF	XF	Unc
13.3	1812	.073	70.00	150.00	300.00	750.00
	1814	—	70.00	150.00	300.00	750.00
	1815	—	12.50	25.00	65.00	175.00

KM#	Date	Mintage	Fine	VF	XF	Unc
23	1826	.508	10.00	20.00	40.00	135.00

10 BATZEN

SILVER

Obv: Palm and laurel wreath flanking arms.

KM#	Date	Mintage	Fine	VF	XF	Unc
14	1808	3,884	55.00	120.00	175.00	700.00
	1809	9,842	40.00	90.00	150.00	675.00
	1818	3,223	50.00	100.00	200.00	725.00

Obv: Laurel branches both sides of arms.

KM#	Date	Mintage	Fine	VF	XF	Unc
16	1809	Inc. Ab.	50.00	100.00	200.00	750.00

20 BATZEN

SILVER

KM#	Date	Mintage	Fine	VF	XF	Unc
17	1809	.014	65.00	145.00	250.00	800.00

4 FRANK

SILVER

KM#	Date	Mintage	Fine	VF	XF	Unc
20	1812	2,527	250.00	400.00	600.00	1850.

PATTERNS (Pn)

(Including off metal strikes)

KM#	Date	Mintage	Identification	Mkt.Val.
Pn1	1809	80	20 Batzen, Silver	3500.

APPENZELL

Located in northeast Switzerland, completely surrounded by the canton of St. Gall. The name was derived from "Abbot's Cell". Achieved independence from the abbots of St. Gall in the period 1377/1411. Divided by religious differences into two half cantons, Ausser-Rhoden (Protestant) and Inner-Rhoden (Catholic). Both were joined to the Canton to Santis 1797-1803, but regained their independent status in 1803.

MONETARY SYSTEM

4 Pfenning = 1 Kreuzer
10 Rappen = 4 Kreuzer = 1 Batzen
10 Batzen = 1 Franken

AUSSER RHODEN

PFENNIG

COPPER

KM#	Date	Mintage	Fine	VF	XF	Unc
11	1816	.066	90.00	150.00	210.00	350.00

KREUZER

BILLON

KM#	Date	Mintage	Fine	VF	XF	Unc
10	1813	.086	17.50	30.00	75.00	150.00

1/2 BATZEN

BILLON

KM#	Date	Mintage	Fine	VF	XF	Unc
5	1808	.073	25.00	70.00	150.00	300.00
	1809	.060	17.50	30.00	85.00	275.00
	1816	.081	20.00	45.00	125.00	275.00

BATZEN

BILLON

KM#	Date	Mintage	Fine	VF	XF	Unc
6	1808	.266	20.00	45.00	115.00	265.00
	1816	.203	20.00	45.00	115.00	265.00

1/2 FRANKEN

SILVER

KM#	Date	Mintage	Fine	VF	XF	Unc
7	1809	6,534	100.00	250.00	450.00	1000.

2 FRANKEN

SILVER

KM#	Date	Mintage	Fine	VF	XF	Unc
8	1812	1,861	180.00	265.00	550.00	1250.

4 FRANKEN

SILVER

KM#	Date	Mintage	Fine	VF	XF	Unc
9	1812	2,357	250.00	400.00	750.00	1800.

KM#	Date	Mintage	Fine	VF	XF	Unc
12	1816	1,850	275.00	475.00	900.00	2000.

BASEL

Basilea

A bishopric in northwest Switzerland, founded in the 5th century. The first coinage was c.1000AD. During the Reformation Basel became Protestant and the bishop resided henceforth in the town of Porrentruy. The Congress of Vienna gave the territories of the Bishopric to Bern. Today they form the Canton Jura and the French speaking part of Bern.

CANTON

MONETARY SYSTEM

After 1803

10 Rappen = 1 Batzen
10 Batzen = 1 Frank

RAPPEN

BILLON

KM#	Date	Mintage	Fine	VF	XF	Unc
201	1810	—	6.00	10.00	25.00	45.00
	1818	—	6.00	10.00	25.00	45.00

2 RAPPEN

BILLON

KM#	Date	Mintage	Fine	VF	XF	Unc
202	1810	—	6.00	10.00	20.00	65.00
	1818	—	6.00	10.00	20.00	65.00

5 RAPPEN

BILLON

KM#	Date	Mintage	Fine	VF	XF	Unc
204	1826B	—	10.00	15.00	40.00	90.00

Obv: Oval shield.

KM#	Date	Mintage	Fine	VF	XF	Unc
205	1826	—	100.00	275.00	550.00	1100.

Obv: Value in exergue.

KM#	Date	Mintage	Fine	VF	XF	Unc
206	1826	—	100.00	250.00	500.00	1000.

1/2 BATZEN

BILLON

KM#	Date	Mintage	Fine	VF	XF	Unc
197	1809	—	12.50	20.00	50.00	100.00

BATZEN

BILLON

Under the Republic

KM#	Date	Mintage	Fine	VF	XF	Unc
195	1805	—	50.00	100.00	250.00	500.00

As a Canton

KM#	Date	Mintage	Fine	VF	XF	Unc
196	1805	—	37.50	80.00	125.00	275.00
	1806	—	17.50	40.00	85.00	200.00
	1809	—	9.00	17.50	40.00	150.00
	1810	—	12.00	25.00	35.00	130.00

KM#	Date	Mintage	Fine	VF	XF	Unc
207	1826	—	100.00	250.00	750.00	1500.

KM#	Date	Mintage	Fine	VF	XF	Unc
208	1826B	—	5.00	18.00	35.00	85.00

3 BATZEN

SILVER

KM#	Date	Mintage	Fine	VF	XF	Unc
198	1809	—	10.00	25.00	50.00	120.00
	1810	—	15.00	40.00	65.00	140.00

5 BATZEN

SILVER

KM#	Date	Mintage	Fine	VF	XF	Unc
199	1809	—	20.00	40.00	80.00	275.00
	1810	—	12.50	25.00	50.00	250.00

Obv: BATZEN

KM#	Date	Mintage	Fine	VF	XF	Unc
209	1826	—	12.50	25.00	45.00	225.00

Obv: BATZn

KM#	Date	Mintage	Fine	VF	XF	Unc
210	1826	—	25.00	85.00	200.00	500.00

PATTERNS (Pn)

(Including off metal strikes)

KM#	Date	Mintage	Identification	Mkt.Val.
Pn4	1826	—	5 Batzen, Silver	—

BERN

A city and canton in west central Switzerland. It was founded as a military post in 1191 and became an imperial city with the mint right in 1218. It was admitted to the Swiss Confederation as a canton in 1353.

MINTMASTERS INITIALS

DUPLONE

7.6400 g, .900 GOLD, .2210 oz AGW
Obv: Crowned pointed shield. Rev: Standing Swiss.

KM#	Date	Mintage	Fine	VF	XF	Unc
163	1819	—	500.00	1000.	1750.	3000.
	1829	—	600.00	1200.	2000.	3500.

NOTE: Earlier date (1797) exists for this type.

MONETARY REFORM

MONETARY SYSTEM
Commencing 1803
10 Rappen = 1 Batzen
10 Batzen = 1 Frank

RAPPEN

BILLON
Obv. leg: CANTON BERN

KM#	Date	Mintage	Fine	VF	XF	Unc
172	1811	—	6.00	12.50	18.00	45.00
	1829	—	12.50	22.50	37.50	80.00

Obv. leg: REPUBL. BERN

KM#	Date	Mintage	Fine	VF	XF	Unc
175	1818	—	6.00	12.50	18.00	45.00
	1819	—	6.00	12.50	18.00	45.00
	1836	—	6.00	12.50	18.00	45.00

2 RAPPEN

BILLON

KM#	Date	Mintage	Fine	VF	XF	Unc
171	1809	—	10.00	20.00	50.00	125.00

2-1/2 RAPPEN

BILLON

KM#	Date	Mintage	Fine	VF	XF	Unc
173	1811	.114	7.00	15.00	20.00	50.00
	1829	—	7.00	15.00	20.00	50.00

5 RAPPEN

BILLON
Rev: W/inner beaded circle.

KM#	Date	Mintage	Fine	VF	XF	Unc
192	1826	—	3.00	10.00	20.00	65.00

Rev: W/o inner beaded circle.

KM#	Date	Mintage	Fine	VF	XF	Unc
193	1826	—	6.00	20.00	30.00	90.00

1/2 BATZEN

BILLON

KM#	Date	Mintage	Fine	VF	XF	Unc
176	1818	—	5.00	15.00	30.00	110.00
	1824	—	5.00	15.00	30.00	110.00

BATZEN

BILLON

KM#	Date	Mintage	Fine	VF	XF	Unc
177	1818	—	5.00	12.50	30.00	90.00
	1824	—	5.00	12.50	30.00	90.00

Obv. denomination: BATZ

KM#	Date	Mintage	Fine	VF	XF	Unc
194.1	1826	—	2.50	10.00	20.00	60.00

Obv. denomination: BAZ

KM#	Date	Mintage	Fine	VF	XF	Unc
194.2	1826	—	5.00	12.50	30.00	75.00

NOTE: These are found overstruck on 1 Batzen, KM#87.

2-1/2 BATZEN

SILVER
Obv. denomination: BATZ

KM#	Date	Mintage	Fine	VF	XF	Unc
195.1	1826	—	10.00	25.00	50.00	125.00

Obv. denomination: BAZ

KM#	Date	Mintage	Fine	VF	XF	Unc
195.2	1826	—	20.00	40.00	65.00	185.00

5 BATZEN

SILVER

KM#	Date	Mintage	Fine	VF	XF	Unc
170	1808	—	17.50	40.00	60.00	175.00
	1810	—	17.50	40.00	60.00	185.00
	1811	—	80.00	110.00	275.00	750.00
	1818	—	30.00	55.00	100.00	225.00

Obv. denomination: BATZ

KM#	Date	Mintage	Fine	VF	XF	Unc
196.1	1826	—	12.50	25.00	35.00	115.00

Obv. denomination: BAZ

KM#	Date	Mintage	Fine	VF	XF	Unc
196.2	1826	—	20.00	45.00	85.00	220.00

Obv: Denomination in exergue.

KM#	Date	Mintage	Fine	VF	XF	Unc
196.3	1826	—	50.00	100.00	250.00	450.00

FRANK

SILVER

KM#	Date	Mintage	Fine	VF	XF	Unc
174	1811	.011	35.00	85.00	225.00	425.00

2 FRANKEN

SILVER

KM#	Date	Mintage	Fine	VF	XF	Unc
198	1835	—	90.00	150.00	320.00	900.00

4 FRANKEN

SILVER

KM#	Date	Mintage	Fine	VF	XF	Unc
190	1823	—	200.00	450.00	900.00	2500.

KM#	Date	Mintage	Fine	VF	XF	Unc
199	1835	—	125.00	275.00	575.00	2000.

COUNTERSTAMPED COINAGE

40 BATZEN (BZ)

During the period 1816-1819 an estimated 660,000 French Ecus of Louis XV and Louis XVI 1726-1793 and 6 Livres dated 1793-1794 along with 40 Batzen and 4 Franken of the Helvetian Republic were counterstamped with a bear and 40 BZ. on shields.

Approximately ninety percent of the counterstamped pieces were melted by 1851. It is estimated some 5,000 pieces or less still exist.

SILVER
c/s: On France Louis XV Ecu, C#42.

KM#	Date	Year	VG	Fine	VF	XF
178	ND	(1726-41)	100.00	150.00	225.00	650.00

c/s: On France Louis XV Ecu, C#47.

KM#	Date	Year	VG	Fine	VF	XF
179	ND	(1740-71)	100.00	150.00	225.00	650.00

c/s: On France Louis XV Ecu, C#47a.

KM#	Date	Year	VG	Fine	VF	XF
180	ND	(1770-74)	100.00	150.00	225.00	650.00

c/s: On France Louis XVI Ecu, C#78.

KM#	Date	Year	VG	Fine	VF	XF
181	ND	(1774-92)	100.00	150.00	225.00	650.00

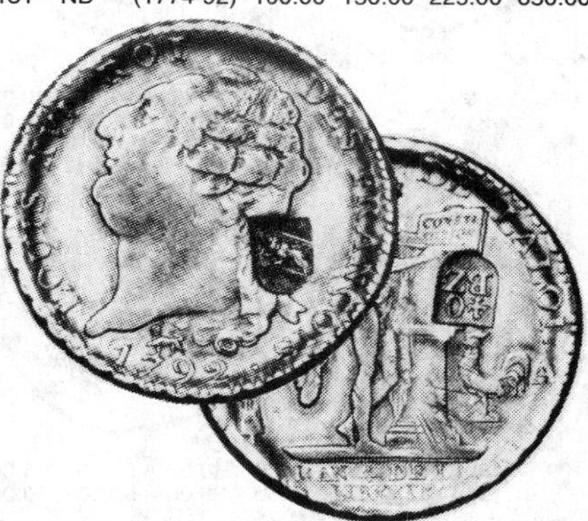

c/s: On France Louis XVI Constitutional Ecu, C#93.

KM#	Date	Year	VG	Fine	VF	XF
182	ND	(1792-93)	225.00	300.00	550.00	1500.

c/s: On France 6 Livres, C#123.

KM#	Date	Year	VG	Fine	VF	XF
183	ND	(1793-94)	400.00	750.00	1500.	2500.

c/s: On Helvetia 40 Batzen, KM#4.1.

184 ND (1798) — Reported, not confirmed

c/s: On Helvetia 40 Batzen, KM#4.2.

185 ND (1798) — Reported, not confirmed

c/s: On Helvetia 4 Franken, KM#10.

186 ND (1799-1801) — Reported, not confirmed

TRADE COINAGE

4 DUCAT

14.0000 g, .986 GOLD, .4438 oz AGW
Obv: Crowned supported arms.
Rev: Small denomination and date.

KM#	Date	Mintage	VG	Fine	VF	XF
155.1	1825	—	2500.	6000.	10,000.	13,500.

PATTERNS (Pn)

(Including off metal strikes)

KM#	Date	Mintage	Identification	Mkt.Val.
Pn20	1804	—	1 Batzen, Billon	1100.

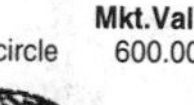

KM#	Date	Mintage	Identification	Mkt.Val.
Pn21	1825	—	1 Batzen, Billon, cross in circle	600.00

KM#	Date	Mintage	Identification	Mkt.Val.
Pn22	1825	—	1 Batzen, Silver, cross w/o circle	—

KM#	Date	Mintage	Identification	Mkt.Val.
Pn23	1825	—	5 Batzen, Silver	900.00

KM#	Date	Mintage	Identification	Mkt.Val.
Pn24	1826	—	1 Concordiataler, Silver	8500.

KM#	Date	Mintage	Identification	Mkt.Val.
Pn25	1838	100 pcs.	1 Cent, Copper w/small Silver inner plug	500.00
Pn26	1838	Inc. Ab.	1 Cent, Silvered Copper	900.00

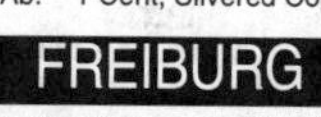

FREIBURG

Friburg, Fribourg, Freyburg

A canton and city located in western Switzerland. The city was founded in 1178 and obtained the mint right in 1422. It joined the Swiss Confederation in 1481. During the Helvetian Republic period it was known as Sarine Et Broye but changed the name back to Freiburg in 1803.

MONETARY SYSTEM

10 Rappen = 1 Batzen
10 Batzen = 1 Frank

2-1/2 RAPPEN

BILLON
Obv: Arms, value below.

KM#	Date	Mintage	Fine	VF	XF	Unc
81	1827	—	6.00	9.00	16.00	40.00

Obv: Pointed arms.

KM#	Date	Mintage	Fine	VF	XF	Unc
91	1846BEL	—	6.00	9.00	16.00	40.00

5 RAPPEN

BILLON

KM#	Date	Mintage	Fine	VF	XF	Unc
70	1806	—	15.00	25.00	50.00	200.00

Obv: Date.

KM#	Date	Mintage	Fine	VF	XF	Unc
82	1827	—	15.00	22.50	32.50	125.00
	1828	—	12.50	20.00	25.00	100.00

Rev: Date.

KM#	Date	Mintage	Fine	VF	XF	Unc
87	1830BEL	—	5.00	10.00	15.00	50.00
	1831BEL	—	4.00	9.00	12.00	48.00

1/2 BATZEN

BILLON

KM#	Date	Mintage	Fine	VF	XF	Unc
73	1810	—	12.50	20.00	32.50	125.00
	1811	—	8.00	17.50	27.50	125.00

BATZEN

BILLON

KM#	Date	Mintage	Fine	VF	XF	Unc
71	1806	—	12.00	18.00	65.00	250.00

KM#	Date	Mintage	Fine	VF	XF	Unc
74	1810	—	12.00	18.00	65.00	250.00

KM#	Date	Mintage	Fine	VF	XF	Unc
75	1811	—	7.00	12.50	27.50	70.00

Obv. value: BAZ

KM#	Date	Mintage	Fine	VF	XF	Unc
83	1827	—	7.00	12.50	27.50	70.00
	1828	—	7.00	12.50	27.50	70.00

Obv. value: BATZ.

KM#	Date	Mintage	Fine	VF	XF	Unc
85	1829	—	7.00	12.50	27.50	70.00

KM#	Date	Mintage	Fine	VF	XF	Unc
88	1830B	—	7.00	12.50	27.50	70.00

5 BATZEN

SILVER

KM#	Date	Mintage	Fine	VF	XF	Unc
76	1811	—	20.00	40.00	65.00	250.00
	1814	—	20.00	40.00	65.00	250.00

KM#	Date	Mintage	Fine	VF	XF	Unc
84	1827	—	20.00	40.00	65.00	250.00
	1828	—	20.00	45.00	75.00	285.00
	1829	—	35.00	100.00	250.00	500.00

KM#	Date	Mintage	Fine	VF	XF	Unc
89	1830	—	12.50	25.00	55.00	265.00

10 BATZEN

SILVER

KM#	Date	Mintage	Fine	VF	XF	Unc
77	1811	4,907	90.00	150.00	350.00	1000.
78	1812	Inc. Ab.	60.00	100.00	250.00	750.00

4 FRANKEN

SILVER

KM#	Date	Mintage	Fine	VF	XF	Unc
79	1813	2,429	225.00	425.00	700.00	1600.

PATTERNS (Pn)

(Including off metal strikes)

KM#	Date	Mintage	Identification	Mkt.Val.
Pn7	1811	—	1 Batzen, Silver, KM75	—

GENEVA

A canton and city in southwestern Switzerland. The city became a bishopric c.400 AD and was part of the Burgundian Kingdom for 500 years. They became completely independent in 1530. In 1798 they were occupied by France but became independent again in 1813. They joined the Swiss Confederation in 1815.

MINTMASTERS INITIALS

Letter	Date	Name
A-B	—	Auguste Bovet
H	—	Hoyer

MONETARY SYSTEM

1814-1838

12 Deniers = 4 Quarts = 1 Sol
12 Sols = 1 Florin
12 Florins, 9 Sols = 1 Thaler
35 Florins = 1 Pistole

6 DENIERS

KM#	Date	Mintage	Fine	VF	XF	Unc
		BILLON				
115	1817	—	2.50	5.00	14.00	30.00
		SILVER				
115a	1817	—	—	—	100.00	150.00

KM#	Date	Mintage	Fine	VF	XF	Unc
		BILLON				
118	1819	—	2.50	5.00	14.00	30.00
	1825	—	4.00	8.00	18.00	42.00
	1833	—	2.50	5.00	14.00	30.00
		SILVER				
118a	1819	—	—	—	100.00	150.00
	1825	—	—	—	115.00	175.00
	1833	—	—	—	100.00	150.00

SOL

KM#	Date	Mintage	Fine	VF	XF	Unc
		BILLON				
116	1817 H	—	2.00	5.00	10.00	25.00
		SILVER				
116a	1817 H	—	—	—	80.00	135.00

KM#	Date	Mintage	Fine	VF	XF	Unc
		BILLON				
119	1819	—	2.00	5.00	10.00	22.50
		SILVER				
119a	1819	—	—	—	85.00	135.00

KM#	Date	Mintage	Fine	VF	XF	Unc
		BILLON				
120	1825	—	2.00	5.00	10.00	22.50
	1833	—	2.00	5.00	10.00	22.50
		SILVER				
120a	1825	—	—	—	85.00	135.00
	1833	—	—	—	85.00	135.00

1-1/2 SOL

KM#	Date	Mintage	Fine	VF	XF	Unc
		BILLON				
117	1817 H	—	2.50	9.00	20.00	40.00

KM#	Date	Mintage	Fine	VF	XF	Unc
121	1825	—	2.50	9.00	20.00	40.00
		SILVER				
121a	1825	—	—	—	130.00	200.00

NOTE: Types KM#115a, 118a, 116a, 120, 120a and 121a struck in fine silver are presentation pieces.

DECIMAL COINAGE

100 Centimes = 1 Franc

CENTIME

KM#	Date	Mintage	Fine	VF	XF	Unc
		BILLON				
125	1839	.325	2.50	4.50	9.00	25.00
		SILVER				
125a	1839	—	—	—	80.00	125.00

KM#	Date	Mintage	Fine	VF	XF	Unc
		COPPER				
130	1840	—	2.50	4.50	9.00	25.00
	1844	—	2.50	4.50	9.00	25.00
	1846	—	3.50	6.00	9.00	25.00

KM#	Date	Mintage	Fine	VF	XF	Unc
132	1847	—	2.50	4.50	9.00	25.00
		SILVER				
132a	1847	—	—	—	80.00	125.00

2 CENTIMES

KM#	Date	Mintage	Fine	VF	XF	Unc
		BILLON				
126	1839	.078	4.00	8.00	25.00	60.00
		SILVER				
126a	1839	—	—	—	200.00	300.00

4 CENTIMES

KM#	Date	Mintage	Fine	VF	XF	Unc
		BILLON				
127	1839	.331	3.50	6.50	12.50	27.50
		SILVER				
127a	1839	—	—	—	115.00	175.00

5 CENTIMES

KM#	Date	Mintage	Fine	VF	XF	Unc
		BILLON				
131	1840	.699	3.00	8.00	9.00	15.00
		SILVER				
131a	1840	—	—	—	45.00	75.00

BILLON

Rev: Arms on shield.

KM#	Date	Mintage	Fine	VF	XF	Unc
133	1847 A.-B.	I.A.	3.00	8.00	17.50	40.00
		SILVER				
133a	1847	—	—	—	130.00	200.00

10 CENTIMES

KM#	Date	Mintage	Fine	VF	XF	Unc
		BILLON				
128	1839	—	3.00	8.00	17.50	35.00
	1844	—	3.00	7.00	12.50	27.50
		SILVER				
128a	1839	—	—	—	115.00	175.00

BILLON

KM#	Date	Mintage	Fine	VF	XF	Unc
134	1847 A.-B.	—	3.00	7.00	12.50	27.50

SILVER

KM#	Date	Mintage	Fine	VF	XF	Unc
134a	1847	—	—	—	85.00	135.00

25 CENTIMES

BILLON

KM#	Date	Mintage	Fine	VF	XF	Unc
129	1839	—	2.50	8.00	17.50	35.00
	1844	—	2.50	8.00	17.50	35.00

SILVER

KM#	Date	Mintage	Fine	VF	XF	Unc
129a	1839	—	—	—	115.00	175.00

BILLON

KM#	Date	Mintage	Fine	VF	XF	Unc
135	1847 A.-B.	—	4.00	10.00	20.00	40.00

SILVER

KM#	Date	Mintage	Fine	VF	XF	Unc
136	1847	—	—	—	115.00	175.00

NOTE: Types KM#125a-129a, 131a-134a and 136 struck in fine silver are presentation pieces.

5 FRANCS

SILVER

KM#	Date	Mintage	Fine	VF	XF	Unc
137	1848	1,176	150.00	210.00	275.00	600.00

10 FRANCS

SILVER
Obv: Similar to 5 Francs, KM#137.

KM#	Date	Mintage	Fine	VF	XF	Unc
138	1848	385 pcs.	200.00	500.00	750.00	1400.
	1851	678 pcs.	150.00	400.00	600.00	1000.

3.8000 g, .750 GOLD, .0916 oz AGW

KM#	Date	Mintage	Fine	VF	XF	Unc
139	1848	336 pcs.	600.00	1250.	1750.	2500.

20 FRANCS

7.6000 g, .750 GOLD, .1833 oz AGW

KM#	Date	Mintage	Fine	VF	XF	Unc
140	1848	3,421	400.00	750.00	1500.	2000.

PATTERNS (Pn)

(Including off metal strikes)

KM#	Date	Mintage	Identification	Mkt.Val.
Pn8	1831	—	42 Sols	1500.

KM#	Date	Mintage	Identification	Mkt.Val.
Pn9	1838	—	1 Centime	200.00

KM#	Date	Mintage	Identification	Mkt.Val.
Pn10	1838	—	2 Centimes	200.00
Pn11	1838	—	5 Centimes	200.00

KM#	Date	Mintage	Identification	Mkt.Val.
Pn12	1838	—	10 Centimes	500.00

KM#	Date	Mintage	Identification	Mkt.Val.
Pn13	1838	—	25 Centimes	500.00

KM#	Date	Mintage	Identification	Mkt.Val.
Pn14	1846	—	1 Centime	200.00

GLARUS

A canton in eastern Switzerland. Independence was gained in c.1390 but from 1798-1803 it was occupied by the French. They rejoined the Swiss Confederation in 1803.

MONETARY SYSTEM

3 Rappen = 1 Schilling
100 Rappen = 1 Frank

SCHILLING

BILLON

KM#	Date	Mintage	Fine	VF	XF	Unc
10	1806 F	--	45.00	100.00	250.00	600.00
	1807 F	—	35.00	80.00	200.00	500.00

Obv: Shield w/garlands.

KM#	Date	Mintage	Fine	VF	XF	Unc
13	1808	—	35.00	80.00	200.00	500.00
	1809	—	35.00	80.00	200.00	500.00
	1811	—	35.00	80.00	200.00	500.00
	1812	—	35.00	80.00	200.00	500.00
	1813	—	35.00	80.00	200.00	500.00

Obv: Shield in branches.

KM#	Date	Mintage	Fine	VF	XF	Unc
15	1809	—	35.00	80.00	200.00	500.00
	1810	—	250.00	500.00	1000.	2500.

3 SCHILLING

BILLON

KM#	Date	Mintage	Fine	VF	XF	Unc
11	1806	.134	85.00	200.00	350.00	1000.

KM#	Date	Mintage	Fine	VF	XF	Unc
14	1808	—	85.00	200.00	350.00	1000.
	1812	—	85.00	200.00	350.00	1000.

KM#	Date	Mintage	Fine	VF	XF	Unc
16	1809	—	85.00	200.00	350.00	1000.
	1810	—	85.00	200.00	350.00	1000.
	1814	—	85.00	200.00	350.00	1000.

15 SCHILLING

SILVER

KM#	Date	Mintage	Fine	VF	XF	Unc
12	1806 B	7,067	150.00	400.00	1000.	2000.
	1807 B	Inc. Ab.	150.00	400.00	1000.	2000.
	1811 B	Inc. Ab.	200.00	500.00	1250.	2500.
	1813 B	Inc. Ab.	200.00	500.00	1250.	2500.
	1814 B	Inc. Ab.	150.00	400.00	1000.	2000.

40 BATZEN

.900 SILVER
Glarus Shooting Festival

KM#	Date	Mintage	VF	XF	Unc	BU
20	1847	3,200	1250.	2000.	3750.	5500.
	1847	—	—	—	P/L	6000.

GRAUBUNDEN

The largest and most easterly of the Swiss cantons. The district was set up in the reign of Roman Emperor Augustus and was one of the various factions sparring for power in the 14th and 15th centuries. The name is derived from "Grey League". The first coins were issued in c. 1600. They joined the Swiss Confederation in 1803.

MINTMASTERS INITIALS

A-B - Bouey
H.B. - Bruppacher

MONETARY SYSTEM

15 Rappen = 6 Bluzger = 1 Schweizer Batzen
10 Schweizer Batzen = 1 Frank
16 Franken = 1 Duplone

1/6 BATZEN

BILLON
Rev. value: 1/6 BATZEN

KM#	Date	Mintage	Fine	VF	XF	Unc
5	1807	.058	6.00	12.50	25.00	60.00
	1820	.480	15.00	25.00	35.00	90.00

Rev. value: 1/6 BAZEN

KM#	Date	Mintage	Fine	VF	XF	Unc
16	1842 A.B.	.172	5.00	10.00	20.00	60.00

1/2 BATZEN

BILLON

KM#	Date	Mintage	Fine	VF	XF	Unc
6	1807	.075	20.00	40.00	100.00	275.00
	1820 B	.060	15.00	25.00	55.00	175.00

KM#	Date	Mintage	Fine	VF	XF	Unc
9	1812	.100	25.00	60.00	185.00	400.00

KM#	Date	Mintage	Fine	VF	XF	Unc
13	1836 A-B	.212	15.00	25.00	45.00	125.00
	1842 A-B	.162	10.00	20.00	35.00	85.00

BATZEN

BILLON

KM#	Date	Mintage	Fine	VF	XF	Unc
7	1807	.056	12.00	32.00	65.00	225.00

KM#	Date	Mintage	Fine	VF	XF	Unc
11	1820 B	.050	12.00	32.00	65.00	225.00
	1826 B	.050	20.00	50.00	115.00	325.00

Rev: Value w/short "1".

KM#	Date	Mintage	Fine	VF	XF	Unc
14	1836 HB	I.A.	75.00	150.00	350.00	800.00

Rev: Value w/tall "1".

KM#	Date	Mintage	Fine	VF	XF	Unc
15	1836	.099	15.00	25.00	50.00	200.00
	1842 A-B	.100	10.00	22.50	40.00	175.00

5 BATZEN

SILVER

KM#	Date	Mintage	Fine	VF	XF	Unc
8	1807	6,398	50.00	80.00	125.00	425.00
	1820	.016	50.00	80.00	125.00	425.00
	1826	—	80.00	170.00	210.00	525.00

10 BATZEN

SILVER

KM#	Date	Mintage	Fine	VF	XF	Unc
12	1825N	2,000	175.00	300.00	600.00	1250.

4 FRANCS

.880 SILVER
Chur in Graubunden Shooting Festival

KM#	Date	Mintage	VF	XF	Unc	BU
17	1842	6,000	425.00	625.00	1350.	2250.
	1842	—	—	—	P/L	2400.

16 FRANKEN

7.6400 g, .900 GOLD, .2211 oz AGW

KM#	Date	Mintage	Fine	VF	XF	Unc
10	1813	100 pcs.	2500.	5000.	10,000.	15,000.

LUZERN

Lucerne

A canton and city in central Switzerland. The city grew around the Benedictine Monastery which was founded in 750. They joined the Swiss Confederation as the 4th member in 1332. Few coins were issued before the 1500s.

MINTMASTERS INITIALS

Letter	Date	Name
B	1794-1807	Bruppacher

ANGSTER

COPPER
Similar to 1 Rappen, KM#96.

KM#	Date	Mintage	Fine	VF	XF	Unc
76	1804	—	25.00	75.00	150.00	275.00
	1811	—	10.00	20.00	30.00	75.00
	1823	—	6.00	12.00	18.00	30.00
	1832	—	6.00	12.00	18.00	30.00
	1834	—	6.00	12.00	18.00	30.00

NOTE: Earlier dates (1775-1791) exist for this type.

Obv. leg: CANTON LUZERN

KM#	Date	Mintage	Fine	VF	XF	Unc
117	1839	—	6.00	12.00	18.00	30.00
	1843	—	6.00	12.00	18.00	30.00

RAPPEN

COPPER
Similar to KM#96.

KM#	Date	Mintage	Fine	VF	XF	Unc
75	1804	—	6.00	12.00	18.00	35.00

NOTE: Earlier dates (1774-1796) exist for this type.

KM#	Date	Mintage	Fine	VF	XF	Unc
96	1804	—	4.00	6.50	12.50	30.00

Rev. value: 1 RAPPEN or RAPEN

KM#	Date	Mintage	Fine	VF	XF	Unc
115	1831	—	4.00	6.50	12.50	30.00
116	1834	—	4.00	6.50	12.50	30.00

Obv. leg: CANTON LUZERN, oak circle.

KM#	Date	Mintage	Fine	VF	XF	Unc
118	1839	—	4.00	6.50	12.50	30.00

Obv. leg: CANTON LUZERN, oak wreath.

KM#	Date	Mintage	Fine	VF	XF	Unc
119	1839	—	4.00	6.50	12.50	30.00
	1843	—	4.00	6.50	12.50	30.00
	1844	—	4.00	6.50	12.50	30.00
	1845	—	4.00	6.50	12.50	30.00
	1846	—	4.00	6.50	12.50	30.00

1/2 BATZEN - 5 RAPPEN

BILLON

KM#	Date	Mintage	Fine	VF	XF	Unc
106	1813	—	10.00	27.50	50.00	125.00

BATZEN - 10 RAPPEN

BILLON
Obv. value: 1 BAZ. Rev: X RAPPEN.

KM#	Date	Mintage	Fine	VF	XF	Unc
95	1803	—	15.00	35.00	50.00	200.00

KM#	Date	Mintage	Fine	VF	XF	Unc
97	1804	—	9.00	15.00	25.00	125.00
	1805	—	—	—	—	—
	1806	—	17.50	37.50	65.00	220.00

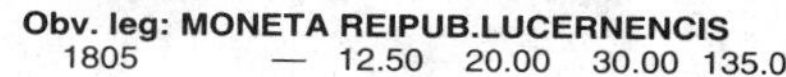

Obv. leg: MONETA REIPUB.LUCERNENCIS

KM#	Date	Mintage	Fine	VF	XF	Unc
99	1805	—	12.50	20.00	30.00	135.00

KM#	Date	Mintage	Fine	VF	XF	Unc
101	1807	—	6.50	12.50	25.00	125.00
	1808	—	6.50	12.50	25.00	125.00
	1809	—	6.50	12.50	25.00	125.00
	1810	—	6.50	12.50	25.00	125.00
	1811	—	6.50	12.50	25.00	125.00

KM#	Date	Mintage	Fine	VF	XF	Unc
107	1813	—	6.50	12.50	25.00	125.00

2-1/2 BATZEN

SILVER
Obv: Date (Republica).

KM#	Date	Mintage	Fine	VF	XF	Unc
110	1815	—	30.00	60.00	90.00	225.00

Rev: Date (Canton).

KM#	Date	Mintage	Fine	VF	XF	Unc
111	1815	—	12.50	20.00	30.00	135.00

5 BATZEN

SILVER

KM#	Date	Mintage	Fine	VF	XF	Unc
100	1806	—	30.00	60.00	150.00	350.00

KM#	Date	Mintage	Fine	VF	XF	Unc
104	1810	—	25.00	50.00	90.00	285.00

KM#	Date	Mintage	Fine	VF	XF	Unc
108	1813	—	25.00	50.00	90.00	285.00
	1814	—	25.00	50.00	90.00	285.00

KM#	Date	Mintage	Fine	VF	XF	Unc
112	1815	—	25.00	50.00	90.00	285.00
	1816	—	25.00	50.00	90.00	285.00

10 BATZEN

SILVER

KM#	Date	Mintage	Fine	VF	XF	Unc
105	1811	—	225.00	425.00	650.00	2000.
	1812	—	40.00	100.00	200.00	1000.

40 BATZEN

SILVER

KM#	Date	Mintage	Fine	VF	XF	Unc
113	1816	3,107	350.00	500.00	950.00	1750.
	1817	3,989	400.00	550.00	1100.	2000.

4 FRANKEN

SILVER

KM#	Date	Mintage	Fine	VF	XF	Unc
109	1813	—	200.00	300.00	550.00	1200.
	1814	.044	75.00	125.00	225.00	850.00

10 FRANKS

3.2258 g, .900 GOLD, .0933 oz AGW

KM#	Date	Mintage	Fine	VF	XF	Unc
98	1804	—	500.00	1000.	1400.	2500.

20 FRANKS

6.4516 g, .900 GOLD, .1867 oz AGW

KM#	Date	Mintage	Fine	VF	XF	Unc
102	1807 B	—	1400.	2500.	4250.	8000.

NEUCHATEL

A canton on the west central border of Switzerland. The first coins (bracteates) were struck in the 11th century. They were under Prussian rule from 1707 to 1806. France occupied the canton from 1806-1815. They reverted to Prussia until 1857, when they became a full member of the Swiss Confederation.

NOTE: For coins previously listed here dated 1707-1806, see German States, Prussia.

RULERS

Prussian, 1707-1806
Alexandre Berthier, Prince,
1806-1814
Prussian, 1814-1857

MONETARY SYSTEM

4 Kreuzer = 1 Batzen
7 Kreuzer = 1 Piecette
21 Batzen = 1 Gulden
2 Gulden = 1 Thaler

KREUZER

BILLON

KM#	Date	Mintage	Fine	VF	XF	Unc
66	1807	—	5.00	9.00	18.00	55.00
	1808	—	5.00	9.00	18.00	55.00

KM#	Date	Mintage	Fine	VF	XF	Unc
71	1817	.303	5.00	9.00	15.00	50.00
	1818	Inc. Ab.	7.50	10.00	15.00	60.00

1/2 BATZEN

Rev. value: DEMI BATZ

KM#	Date	Mintage	Fine	VF	XF	Unc
67	1807	—	9.00	12.50	22.50	60.00

Rev. value: 1/2 BATZ

KM#	Date	Mintage	Fine	VF	XF	Unc
68.1	1807	—	4.50	7.50	15.00	50.00
	1808	—	4.50	7.50	20.00	65.00
	1809	—	6.00	10.00	22.50	65.00

Rev. value: 2/1 BATZ

KM#	Date	Mintage	VG	Fine	VF	XF
68.2	1807	—	—	—	—	—

BATZEN

BILLON

KM#	Date	Mintage	Fine	VF	XF	Unc
65	1806	—	15.00	20.00	32.50	125.00
	1807	—	5.00	10.00	25.00	75.00
	1808	—	5.00	10.00	25.00	75.00
	1809	—	5.00	10.00	25.00	75.00
	1810	—	15.00	20.00	40.00	175.00

KM#	Date	Mintage	Fine	VF	XF	Unc
69	1807	—	5.00	10.00	25.00	75.00
	1808	—	5.00	10.00	25.00	75.00

PATTERNS (Pn)

(Including off metal strikes)

KM#	Date	Mintage	Identification	Mkt.Val.
Pn14	1814	—	2 Francs, Copper	—
Pn15	1814	—	2 Francs, Silver	850.00

KM#	Date	Mintage	Identification	Mkt.Val.
Pn16	181x.	—	5 Francs, Silver, PRIN. Edge: POIDS VINGT/CINQ GRAMMES/TI/TRE NEUF D/IXIEMES UNICUM	—
Pn17	181x.	—	5 Francs, Copper	—

KM#	Date	Mintage	Identification	Mkt.Val.
Pn18	181x.	—	5 Francs, Silver, PRINCE (Restruck at end of 19th Century)	700.00

ST. GALL

St. Gallen

Letter	Date	Name
K	1808-17	?

A canton in northeast Switzerland which completely surrounds the canton of Appenzell. It joined the Swiss Confederation in 1803.

PFENNIG

BILLON

Uniface, arms on concave planchet.

KM#	Date	Mintage	Fine	VF	XF	Unc
100	ND	.151	5.00	8.00	15.00	75.00

2 PFENNIG

BILLON

KM#	Date	Mintage	Fine	VF	XF	Unc
108	1808	—	100.00	200.00	300.00	750.00

1/2 KREUZER

BILLON

KM#	Date	Mintage	Fine	VF	XF	Unc
109	1808 K	.111	10.00	18.50	35.00	100.00
	1809 K	.118	10.00	18.50	35.00	100.00
	1810 K	.101	10.00	18.50	35.00	100.00
	1811 K	.099	10.00	18.50	35.00	100.00
	1812 K	.175	10.00	18.50	35.00	100.00
	1813 K	.149	10.00	17.50	30.00	80.00
	1814 K	.114	10.00	17.50	30.00	80.00
	1815 K	.136	10.00	17.50	30.00	80.00
	1816 K	.238	10.00	17.50	30.00	80.00
	1817 K	—	10.00	17.50	30.00	80.00

KREUZER

BILLON

KM#	Date	Mintage	Fine	VF	XF	Unc
101	1807 K	.162	10.00	25.00	50.00	175.00
	1808 K	.202	10.00	25.00	50.00	175.00

KM#	Date	Mintage	Fine	VF	XF	Unc
102	1807	Inc. KM101	100.00	180.00	350.00	600.00
	1809 K	.160	6.00	15.00	35.00	100.00
	1810 K	.146	6.00	15.00	35.00	100.00
	1811 K	.106	6.00	15.00	35.00	100.00
	1812 K	.135	6.00	15.00	35.00	100.00
	1813 K	.102	6.00	15.00	35.00	100.00
	1815 K	1.116	6.00	15.00	35.00	100.00
	1816 K	.135	6.00	15.00	35.00	100.00

1/2 BATZEN

BILLON

KM#	Date	Mintage	Fine	VF	XF	Unc
103	1807	.110	10.00	15.00	45.00	150.00
	1808 K	.209	5.00	10.00	40.00	125.00
	1809 K	.267	5.00	10.00	40.00	125.00
	1810 K	.290	5.00	10.00	40.00	165.00
	1811 K	.349	5.00	10.00	50.00	200.00
	1812 K	.252	5.00	10.00	50.00	200.00
	1813 K	.154	5.00	10.00	50.00	200.00
	1814 K	.140	5.00	10.00	50.00	200.00
	1815 K	.181	5.00	10.00	50.00	200.00
	1816 K	.134	5.00	10.00	50.00	200.00
	1817 K	—	15.00	25.00	150.00	350.00

KM#	Date	Mintage	Fine	VF	XF	Unc
104	1807 K	Inc. KM103	10.00	15.00	50.00	150.00
	1808 K	Inc. KM103	5.00	10.00	50.00	125.00
	1809 K	Inc. KM103	5.00	10.00	50.00	125.00
	1810 K	Inc. KM103	10.00	15.00	50.00	175.00

NOTE: Some varieties of KM#104 do not have the K mint mark.

BATZEN

BILLON

KM#	Date	Mintage	Fine	VF	XF	Unc
105	1807 K	.063	20.00	35.00	125.00	450.00
	1808 K	.133	10.00	20.00	75.00	250.00
	1809 K	.187	10.00	20.00	50.00	200.00

KM#	Date	Mintage	Fine	VF	XF	Unc
106	1807	Inc. KM105	15.00	25.00	90.00	300.00

Obv: Date. Rev. value: 1 BATZEN.

KM#	Date	Mintage	Fine	VF	XF	Unc
110	1810 K	.259	5.00	12.50	50.00	200.00
	1811 K	.319	5.00	12.50	50.00	200.00
	1812 K	.341	5.00	12.50	50.00	200.00
	1813 K	—	5.00	12.50	50.00	200.00
	1814 K	.229	5.00	12.50	50.00	200.00
	1815 K	1.008	5.00	12.50	50.00	200.00
	1816 K	.068	5.00	12.50	50.00	200.00
	1817 K	—	15.00	22.50	75.00	250.00

NOTE: Many varieties of KM#110 are known, including some w/o the K mint mark.

6 KREUZER

BILLON
Obv: Arms in oak branches.
Rev: Value and date in oak branches.

KM#	Date	Mintage	Fine	VF	XF	Unc
107	1807	4,510	75.00	200.00	500.00	850.00

5 BATZEN

SILVER
Obv: Date in exergue.

KM#	Date	Mintage	Fine	VF	XF	Unc
111	1810 K	—	30.00	45.00	100.00	350.00
	1811 K	—	45.00	65.00	125.00	400.00
	1812 K	—	55.00	120.00	160.00	400.00
	1813 K	—	40.00	60.00	125.00	400.00

KM#	Date	Mintage	Fine	VF	XF	Unc
113	1813 K	—	30.00	55.00	90.00	300.00
	1814 K	—	30.00	55.00	90.00	300.00
	1817 K	—	45.00	65.00	100.00	350.00

KM#	Date	Mintage	Fine	VF	XF	Unc
114	1817 K	—	45.00	65.00	100.00	350.00

1/2 FRANKEN

SILVER

KM#	Date	Mintage	Fine	VF	XF	Unc
112	1810 K	759 pcs.	1000.	2000.	4000.	—

SCHAFFHAUSEN

A canton located on the north central border of Switzerland. The first coins, which were issued in the 13th century were known as "Ram Bracteates". It joined the Swiss Confederation in 1501.

MONETARY SYSTEM

4 Kreuzer = 1 Batzen

KREUZER

BILLON

KM#	Date	Mintage	Fine	VF	XF	Unc
65	1808	.216	40.00	80.00	120.00	300.00

1/2 BATZEN

BILLON

KM#	Date	Mintage	Fine	VF	XF	Unc
66	1808	.080	20.00	30.00	75.00	300.00

KM#	Date	Mintage	Fine	VF	XF	Unc
68	1809	.030	22.00	35.00	100.00	325.00

BATZEN

BILLON

KM#	Date	Mintage	Fine	VF	XF	Unc
67	1808	.064	55.00	80.00	150.00	300.00

Rev. value: 1 BATZEN

KM#	Date	Mintage	Fine	VF	XF	Unc
69	1809	.015	27.50	45.00	90.00	275.00

SCHWYZ

Schwytz, Suitensis

A canton in central Switzerland. In 1291 it became one of the three cantons that would ultimately become the Swiss Confederation and were known as the "Everlasting League". The first coinage was issued in 1624.

MINTMASTERS INITIALS

Letter	Date	Name
DB	1843-46	?
H	1810-11	?
M	1844	?

MONETARY SYSTEM

2 Angster = 1 Rappen
10 Rappen = 1 Batzen
10 Batzen = 1 Frank
4 Franken = 1 Thaler

ANGSTER

COPPER

KM#	Date	Mintage	Fine	VF	XF	Unc
55	1810	—	5.00	9.00	18.00	30.00
	1811	—	5.00	9.00	18.00	30.00
	1812	—	5.00	9.00	18.00	30.00
	1813	—	12.50	20.00	30.00	75.00
	1814	—	7.50	15.00	25.00	50.00
	1815	—	12.50	20.00	30.00	75.00
	1816	—	5.00	9.00	18.00	30.00
	1821	—	12.50	20.00	30.00	75.00
	1827	—	12.50	20.00	30.00	75.00
	1838	—	12.50	20.00	30.00	75.00
	1843	—	5.00	9.00	15.00	30.00
	1845	—	5.00	9.00	15.00	30.00
	1846	—	5.00	9.00	15.00	30.00

RAPPEN

COPPER

KM#	Date	Mintage	Fine	VF	XF	Unc
59	1811	—	5.00	12.50	20.00	35.00
	1812	—	3.50	7.50	12.50	28.00
	1815	—	3.50	7.50	12.50	28.00
	1845	—	3.75	5.00	8.00	20.00
	1846	—	6.00	12.00	18.00	30.00

NOTE: Many varieties exist, including some w/value 1

RAPEN and mint mark B.

KM#	Date	Mintage	Fine	VF	XF	Unc
60	1811	—	5.00	12.00	18.00	30.00
	1812	—	3.00	7.00	10.00	25.00

KM#	Date	Mintage	Fine	VF	XF	Unc
65	1815	—	3.00	7.00	12.00	28.00
	1816	—	7.50	12.00	18.00	30.00
	1843	—	3.75	5.00	10.00	25.00
	1844	—	7.50	12.00	18.00	30.00
	1845	—	3.00	5.00	10.00	25.00
	1846	—	6.00	12.00	18.00	30.00

2 RAPPEN

BILLON

KM#	Date	Mintage	Fine	VF	XF	Unc
61	1811	—	6.00	10.00	16.00	40.00
	1812	—	6.00	10.00	16.00	40.00
	1813	—	6.00	10.00	16.00	40.00

NOTE: Varieties of these coins are known with value as 2 RAPEN.

KM#	Date	Mintage	Fine	VF	XF	Unc
62	1811	—	6.00	12.00	18.00	40.00
	1812	—	3.75	7.50	14.00	32.00
	1813	—	5.00	12.00	18.00	40.00
	1814	—	3.75	7.50	14.00	32.00
	1815	—	3.75	7.50	14.00	32.00
	1842	—	15.00	30.00	40.00	80.00
	1843	—	3.75	7.50	14.00	32.00
	1843 DB	—	3.75	7.50	14.00	32.00
	1844 DB	—	10.00	15.00	27.50	60.00
	1845 DB	—	3.75	7.50	14.00	32.00
	1846 DB	—	3.75	7.50	14.00	32.00

NOTE: Many varieties exist, including some w/value 2 RAPEN and mint mark B.

2/3 BATZEN

BILLON

KM#	Date	Mintage	Fine	VF	XF	Unc
56	1810	—	17.50	35.00	65.00	150.00
	1811	—	17.50	35.00	65.00	150.00

Rev. value: 2/3 BATZEN

KM#	Date	Mintage	Fine	VF	XF	Unc
63	1812	—	55.00	90.00	130.00	300.00

Rev. value: 2/3 BATZ

KM#	Date	Mintage	Fine	VF	XF	Unc
64	1812	—	60.00	150.00	180.00	400.00

2 BATZEN

BILLON

KM#	Date	Mintage	Fine	VF	XF	Unc
57	1810B	—	50.00	120.00	200.00	450.00

4 BATZEN

SILVER
Obv: Arms in laurel branches.
Rev: Value and date in wreath, leg. around border.

KM#	Date	Mintage	Fine	VF	XF	Unc
58	1810 H	—	200.00	500.00	1500.	—
	1811 H	—	80.00	150.00	275.00	900.00

NOTE: Varieties exist with value 4 BATZ.

TRADE COINAGE

DUCAT

3.5000 g, .986 GOLD, .1109 oz AGW

KM#	Date	Mintage	Fine	VF	XF	Unc
66	1844 M	50 pcs.	4000.	7000.	9000.	15,000.

SOLOTHURN

Solodornensis, Soleure

A canton in northwest Switzerland. Bracteates were struck in the 1300s even though the mint right was not officially granted until 1381. They joined the Swiss Confederation in 1481.

MONETARY SYSTEM

10 Rappen = 4 Kreuzer = 1 Batzen
10 Batzen = 1 Frank

RAPPEN

BILLON

KM#	Date	Mintage	Fine	VF	XF	Unc
71	1813	—	18.00	30.00	50.00	125.00

2-1/2 RAPPEN

BILLON

KM#	Date	Mintage	Fine	VF	XF	Unc
85	1830	—	5.00	10.00	25.00	60.00

5 RAPPEN

BILLON

KM#	Date	Mintage	Fine	VF	XF	Unc
78	1826	—	20.00	35.00	60.00	150.00

KREUZER

BILLON

KM#	Date	Mintage	Fine	VF	XF	Unc
72	1813	—	10.00	15.00	30.00	75.00

BATZEN - 10 RAPPEN

BILLON

KM#	Date	Mintage	Fine	VF	XF	Unc
65	1805	—	15.00	30.00	50.00	150.00

KM#	Date	Mintage	Fine	VF	XF	Unc
66	1807	—	60.00	100.00	200.00	500.00
	1808	—	15.00	30.00	50.00	150.00
	1809	—	15.00	30.00	50.00	150.00

KM#	Date	Mintage	Fine	VF	XF	Unc
67	1809	—	15.00	30.00	50.00	150.00
	1810	—	6.00	12.50	30.00	75.00
	1811	—	6.00	12.50	30.00	75.00

KM#	Date	Mintage	Fine	VF	XF	Unc
79	1826	—	6.00	12.50	30.00	85.00

KM#	Date	Mintage	Fine	VF	XF	Unc
80	1826	—	6.00	12.50	27.50	75.00

2-1/2 BATZEN

SILVER
Obv: Crowned oval arms in laurel branches.
Rev: Cross in quatrefoil.

KM#	Date	Mintage	Fine	VF	XF	Unc
81	1826	—	20.00	40.00	80.00	175.00

5 BATZEN

SILVER

KM#	Date	Mintage	Fine	VF	XF	Unc
68	1809	—	100.00	300.00	500.00	900.00
	1811	—	40.00	80.00	135.00	400.00

Obv. value: 5 BATZ

KM#	Date	Mintage	Fine	VF	XF	Unc
82	1826	—	25.00	35.00	65.00	200.00

Obv. value: 5 BAZ.

KM#	Date	Mintage	Fine	VF	XF	Unc
83	1826	—	30.00	40.00	75.00	275.00

FRANK

SILVER

KM#	Date	Mintage	Fine	VF	XF	Unc
70	1812	2,000	175.00	350.00	550.00	1250.

4 FRANKEN

SILVER

KM#	Date	Mintage	Fine	VF	XF	Unc
73	1813	250 pcs.	400.00	550.00	1000.	2000.

8 FRANKEN

3.8200 g, .900 GOLD, .1105 oz AGW

KM#	Date	Mintage	Fine	VF	XF	Unc
74	1813	106 pcs.	2500.	5000.	8000.	12,000.

16 FRANKEN

7.6400 g, .900 GOLD, .2211 oz AGW

KM#	Date	Mintage	Fine	VF	XF	Unc
75	1813	150 pcs.	2750.	6000.	10,000.	15,000.

32 FRANKEN

15.2800 g, .900 GOLD, .4421 oz AGW
Obv: Crowned oval arms on spade shield in branches, date below.
Rev: Standing knight holding shield, value below.

KM#	Date	Mintage	Fine	VF	XF	Unc
76	1813	—	—	—	Rare	—

THURGAU

Thurgovie

A canton in northeast Switzerland. They were ruled by the Swiss Confederates beginning c. 1460 until 1798. In 1803 they joined the Swiss Confederation.

MONETARY SYSTEM

4 Kreuzer = 1 Schweizer Batzen
10 Batzen = 1 Frank

1/2 KREUZER

BILLON

KM#	Date	Mintage	Fine	VF	XF	Unc
1	1808	.100	100.00	250.00	750.00	1250.

KREUZER

BILLON

KM#	Date	Mintage	Fine	VF	XF	Unc
2	1808	.099	20.00	40.00	65.00	150.00

1/2 BATZEN

BILLON

KM#	Date	Mintage	Fine	VF	XF	Unc
3	1808	.149	22.50	45.00	90.00	185.00

BATZEN

BILLON

KM#	Date	Mintage	Fine	VF	XF	Unc
4	1808	.232	25.00	50.00	100.00	245.00
	1809	Inc. Ab.	25.00	50.00	100.00	245.00

5 BATZEN

SILVER

KM#	Date	Mintage	Fine	VF	XF	Unc
5	1808	2,580	275.00	450.00	750.00	1750.

TICINO

Tessin

A canton in southeast Switzerland. They were previously known as the Lombard vassal state of Bellinzona. They joined the Swiss Confederation in 1803.

MONETARY SYSTEM

12 Denari = 1 Soldo
20 Soldi = 1 Franco

TRE (3) DENARI

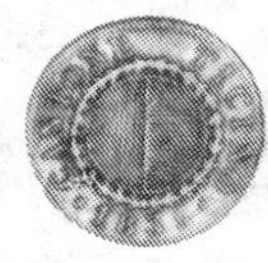

COPPER
Obv: Arms. Rev: Value above branches.

KM#	Date	Mintage	Fine	VF	XF	Unc
5	1814	.417	9.00	15.00	27.50	100.00
	1835	.598	9.00	15.00	27.50	100.00

KM#	Date	Mintage	Fine	VF	XF	Unc
9	1841	.322	9.00	15.00	27.50	100.00

SEI (6) DENARI

COPPER
Obv: Arms. Rev: Value and date within wreath.

KM#	Date	Mintage	Fine	VF	XF	Unc
1	1813	.280	9.00	15.00	32.50	100.00
	1835	.364	15.00	27.50	40.00	120.00
	1841	.241	9.00	15.00	32.50	100.00

TRE (3) SOLDI

BILLON

KM#	Date	Mintage	Fine	VF	XF	Unc
2	1813 star	1.405	15.00	35.00	60.00	200.00
	1813 w/o star	Inc. Ab.	15.00	30.00	45.00	150.00
	1835	.323	7.00	15.00	30.00	100.00
	1838	.514	7.00	15.00	30.00	100.00
	1841	.243	7.00	15.00	30.00	100.00

1/4 FRANCO

SILVER

KM#	Date	Mintage	Fine	VF	XF	Unc
7	1835	.058	40.00	75.00	200.00	400.00

1/2 FRANCO

SILVER

KM#	Date	Mintage	Fine	VF	XF	Unc
8	1835	.044	45.00	85.00	500.00	900.00

FRANCO

SILVER

KM#	Date	Mintage	Fine	VF	XF	Unc
3	1813 star	5,920	125.00	350.00	850.00	1500.
	1813 w/o star	Inc. Ab.	90.00	250.00	700.00	1250.

2 FRANCHI

SILVER

KM#	Date	Mintage	Fine	VF	XF	Unc
4	1813 star	4,150	500.00	1000.	1600.	2500.
	1813 w/o star	Inc. Ab.	350.00	650.00	1200.	2250.

4 FRANCHI

SILVER

KM#	Date	Mintage	Fine	VF	XF	Unc
6	1814 star	7,921	250.00	500.00	850.00	3000.
	1814 w/o star	Inc. Ab.	250.00	475.00	750.00	2500.

NOTE: Coins of 3 Soldi, Franco, 2 Franchi and 4 Franchi with star mint mark were struck at Luzern. Those without star were coined at Bern.

UNTERWALDEN

Subsilvania

A canton in central Switzerland which was one of the three original cantons which became the Swiss Confederation in 1291. It is made up of two half cantons - Nidwalden and Obwalden. They had their own coinage beginning in the 1500s.

MONETARY SYSTEM

4 Kreuzer = 1 Batzen
10 Batzen = 1 Frank

NIDWALDEN

1/2 BATZEN

BILLON

KM#	Date	Mintage	Fine	VF	XF	Unc
11	1811	.012	40.00	100.00	200.00	350.00

BATZEN - 10 RAPPEN

BILLON

KM#	Date	Mintage	Fine	VF	XF	Unc
12	1811	.012	40.00	100.00	200.00	350.00

5 BATZEN

SILVER

KM#	Date	Mintage	Fine	VF	XF	Unc
13	1811	3,600	150.00	300.00	450.00	1200.

OBWALDEN

1/2 BATZEN

BILLON

KM#	Date	Mintage	Fine	VF	XF	Unc
51	1812	—	30.00	70.00	150.00	400.00

BATZEN

BILLON

KM#	Date	Mintage	Fine	VF	XF	Unc
52	1812	—	30.00	70.00	150.00	400.00

5 BATZEN

SILVER

KM#	Date	Mintage	Fine	VF	XF	Unc
53	1812	—	100.00	250.00	500.00	1000.

URI

Uranie

A canton in central Switzerland. It is one of the three original cantons which became the Swiss Confederation in 1291. They had their own coinage from the early 1600s until 1811.

MONETARY SYSTEM

10 Rappen = 1 Batzen
10 Batzen = 1 Frank

RAPPEN

BILLON

KM#	Date	Mintage	Fine	VF	XF	Unc
40	1811	.019	100.00	175.00	200.00	400.00

1/2 BATZEN

BILLON

KM#	Date	Mintage	Fine	VF	XF	Unc
41	1811	.015	45.00	75.00	145.00	350.00

BATZEN - 10 RAPPEN

BILLON

KM#	Date	Mintage	Fine	VF	XF	Unc
42	1811	.020	50.00	80.00	200.00	400.00

2 BATZEN

SILVER

KM#	Date	Mintage	Fine	VF	XF	Unc
43	1811	4,995	90.00	160.00	300.00	750.00

4 BATZEN

SILVER

KM#	Date	Mintage	Fine	VF	XF	Unc
44	1811	3,510	150.00	275.00	450.00	1200.

VAUD

Waadt

A canton in southwest Switzerland. They had possession of Bern from 1536 until 1798. They joined the Swiss Confederation in 1803.

MINTMASTERS INITIALS

BEL - Bel Bessiere, 1827-1831

MONETARY SYSTEM

10 Rappen = 1 Batz
10 Batz = 1 Franc
4 Francs = 1 Thaler

RAPPEN

BILLON

KM#	Date	Mintage	Fine	VF	XF	Unc
5	1804	.211	30.00	80.00	150.00	225.00

KM#	Date	Mintage	Fine	VF	XF	Unc
12	1807	Inc. Ab.	20.00	60.00	100.00	165.00

2-1/2 RAPPEN

BILLON

KM#	Date	Mintage	Fine	VF	XF	Unc
14	1809	.230	10.00	15.00	27.50	60.00

KM#	Date	Mintage	Fine	VF	XF	Unc
18	1816	—	10.00	15.00	27.50	60.00

1/2 BATZEN - 5 RAPPEN

BILLON

KM#	Date	Mintage	Fine	VF	XF	Unc
6	1804	2.962	5.00	8.00	15.00	50.00
	1805	Inc. Ab.	7.00	10.00	25.00	75.00
	1806	Inc. Ab.	7.00	10.00	25.00	75.00
	1807	Inc. Ab.	5.00	8.00	15.00	50.00
	1808	Inc. Ab.	5.00	8.00	15.00	50.00
	1809	—	5.00	8.00	15.00	50.00
	1810	—	5.00	8.00	15.00	50.00
	1811	—	5.00	8.00	15.00	50.00
	1813	—	5.00	8.00	15.00	50.00
	1814	—	5.00	8.00	15.00	50.00
	1816	—	5.00	8.00	15.00	50.00
	1817	—	5.00	8.00	15.00	50.00
	1818	—	3.00	5.00	10.00	35.00
	1819	—	3.00	5.00	10.00	30.00

BATZEN - 10 RAPPEN

BILLON

Obv: W/o branches around shield.

KM#	Date	Mintage	Fine	VF	XF	Unc
7	1804	—	75.00	250.00	500.00	850.00

KM#	Date	Mintage	Fine	VF	XF	Unc
8	1804	—	8.00	27.50	40.00	100.00
	1805	—	6.00	12.50	25.00	65.00
	1806	—	6.00	12.50	25.00	65.00
	1807	—	6.00	12.50	25.00	65.00
	1808	—	300.00	600.00	1000.	1500.
	1809	—	15.00	25.00	40.00	100.00
	1810	—	5.00	10.00	20.00	45.00
	1811	—	5.00	10.00	20.00	45.00
	1812	—	5.00	10.00	20.00	45.00
	1813	—	5.00	10.00	20.00	45.00
	1814	—	5.00	10.00	20.00	45.00
	1815	—	5.00	10.00	20.00	45.00
	1816	—	5.00	10.00	20.00	45.00
	1817	—	5.00	10.00	20.00	45.00
	1818	—	4.00	8.00	15.00	35.00
	1819	—	5.00	8.00	15.00	35.00
	1820	—	6.00	12.50	25.00	60.00

KM#	Date	Mintage	Fine	VF	XF	Unc
20	1826	—	27.50	50.00	75.00	175.00
	1827 BEL	—	5.50	10.00	17.00	35.00
	1828 BEL	—	5.50	8.00	15.00	32.00
	1829 BEL	—	5.50	10.00	17.00	35.00
	1830 BEL	—	5.50	8.00	15.00	32.00
	1831	—	5.50	8.00	15.00	32.00
	1832 BEL	—	6.00	12.00	17.50	35.00
	1834 BEL	—	12.50	30.00	45.00	100.00

5 BATZEN

SILVER

KM#	Date	Mintage	Fine	VF	XF	Unc
9	1804	1,692	250.00	500.00	1000.	2000.

KM#	Date	Mintage	Fine	VF	XF	Unc
11	1805	—	90.00	200.00	260.00	600.00
	1806	—	90.00	200.00	260.00	600.00

KM#	Date	Mintage	Fine	VF	XF	Unc
13	1807	—	25.00	50.00	90.00	285.00
	1810	—	25.00	50.00	90.00	285.00
	1811	—	25.00	50.00	90.00	285.00
	1812	—	25.00	40.00	80.00	265.00
	1813	—	25.00	40.00	80.00	265.00
	1814	—	25.00	50.00	90.00	285.00

KM#	Date	Mintage	Fine	VF	XF	Unc
21.1	1826	—	12.50	27.50	80.00	200.00
	1827 BEL	—	10.00	20.00	45.00	140.00
	1828 BEL	—	10.00	20.00	45.00	140.00
	1829 BEL	—	12.50	27.50	80.00	200.00
	1830 BEL	—	10.00	20.00	45.00	140.00
	1831 BEL	—	10.00	20.00	45.00	140.00

Rev: Plumes in quatrefoil.

KM#	Date	Mintage	Fine	VF	XF	Unc
21.2	1827 BEL	—	10.00	30.00	45.00	150.00

10 BATZEN

SILVER

KM#	Date	Mintage	Fine	VF	XF	Unc
10	1804	1,234	250.00	500.00	1000.	2500.

KM#	Date	Mintage	Fine	VF	XF	Unc
15	1810	1,234	45.00	100.00	165.00	600.00
	1811	2,963	45.00	100.00	165.00	600.00

KM#	Date	Mintage	Fine	VF	XF	Unc
19	1823	6,198	45.00	100.00	165.00	600.00

20 BATZEN

SILVER

KM#	Date	Mintage	Fine	VF	XF	Unc
16	1810	6,590	50.00	90.00	265.00	700.00
	1811	Inc. Ab.	50.00	90.00	265.00	700.00

40 BATZEN

SILVER

KM#	Date	Mintage	Fine	VF	XF	Unc
17	1812	2,485	200.00	400.00	750.00	1700.

NOTE: 616 pieces were melted in 1851.

FRANC

SILVER

KM#	Date	Mintage	Fine	VF	XF	Unc
22	1845	8,626	20.00	35.00	75.00	150.00

NOTE: This coin was struck to commemorate a Shooting Festival held on August 10, 1845. It had legal tender status.

COUNTERSTAMPED COINAGE

39 BATZEN (BZ)

As in the canton of Bern, French Ecus dated 1726 to 1793 along with 6 Livres dated 1793-1794 were counterstamped from 1816-1819 and freely circulated. In Vaud, the counterstamp consisted of the arms of Vaud on one side and the new value 39 BZ on the other.

SILVER

c/s: On France Louis XV Ecu, C#42.

KM#	Date	Year	VG	Fine	VF	XF
23	ND	(1726-41)	600.00	1000.	1500.	—

c/s: On France Louis XV Ecu, C#47.

KM#	Date	Year	VG	Fine	VF	XF
24	ND	(1740-71)	600.00	1000.	1500.	—

c/s: On France Louis XV Ecu, C#47a.

KM#	Date	Year	VG	Fine	VF	XF
25	ND	(1770-74)	600.00	1000.	1500.	—

c/s: On France Louis XVI Ecu, C#78.

KM#	Date	Year	VG	Fine	VF	XF
26	ND	(1774-92)	600.00	1000.	1500.	—

c/s: On France Louis XVI Constitutional Ecu, C#93.

KM#	Date	Year	VG	Fine	VF	XF
27	ND	(1792-93)	750.00	2000.	3500.	—

c/s: On France 6 Livres, C#123.

KM#	Date	Year	VG	Fine	VF	XF
28	ND	(1793-94)	900.00	2500.	4000.	—

PATTERNS (Pn)

(Including off metal strikes)

KM#	Date	Mintage	Identification	Mkt.Val.
Pn1	1804	—	1/2 Batzen, Billon	—

KM#	Date	Mintage	Identification	Mkt.Val.
Pn2	1830	—	1/4 Franc, Silver	—

ZUG

Tugium, Tugiensis

A canton in central Switzerland. They joined the Swiss Confederation in 1352 and had their own coinage from 1564 to 1805.

MONETARY SYSTEM

6 Angster = 3 Rappen
= 1 Schilling = 1 Assis

ANGSTER

COPPER
Obv: Arms in branches.
Rev: Date, value in cartouche.

KM#	Date	Mintage	VG	Fine	VF	XF
61	1804	—	22.00	50.00	175.00	300.00

NOTE: Earlier dates (1778-1796) exist for this type.

RAPPEN

COPPER
Obv: Arms in branches.
Rev: Date, value in cartouche.

KM#	Date	Mintage	VG	Fine	VF	XF
63	1805	—	5.00	12.00	30.00	100.00

NOTE: Earlier dates (1782-1794) exist for this type.

ZURICH

Thicurinae, Thuricensis, Ticurinae, Turicensis

A canton in north central Switzerland. It was the mint for the dukes of Swabia in the 10th and 11th centuries. The mint right was obtained in 1238. The first coinage struck were bracteates and the last coins were struck in 1848. It joined the Swiss Confederation in 1351.

MINTMASTERS INITIALS

B - Bruckmann

MONETARY SYSTEM

Commencing 1803

3 Haller = 1 Rappen
4 Rappen = 1 Schilling
10 Schilling = 4 Batzen
160 Batzen = 1 Ducat

3 HALLER

BILLON

KM#	Date	Mintage	Fine	VF	XF	Unc
180	ND	3.518	4.50	6.00	10.00	20.00

Error: HALER

KM#	Date	Mintage	Fine	VF	XF	Unc
181	ND	Inc. Ab.	5.00	10.00	15.00	25.00

NOTE: These were struck from 1827-1841.

RAPPEN

BILLON

KM#	Date	Mintage	Fine	VF	XF	Unc
194	1842	—	4.50	9.00	20.00	45.00
	1844	—	12.00	20.00	30.00	60.00
	1845	—	4.50	9.00	20.00	45.00
	1846	—	75.00	250.00	500.00	850.00
	1848	—	4.50	9.00	16.00	35.00

2 RAPPEN

BILLON

KM#	Date	Mintage	Fine	VF	XF	Unc
195	1842D	.460	9.00	15.00	22.50	45.00

10 SCHILLING

SILVER

KM#	Date	Mintage	Fine	VF	XF	Unc
182	ND(1806)	—	25.00	50.00	100.00	250.00
	1807 B	—	50.00	75.00	175.00	400.00
	1808 B	—	12.50	27.50	50.00	125.00
	1809 B	—	12.50	27.50	50.00	125.00
	1810 B	—	12.50	27.50	50.00	125.00
	1811 B	—	12.50	27.50	50.00	125.00

8 BATZEN

SILVER

KM#	Date	Mintage	Fine	VF	XF	Unc
184	1810 B	.108	40.00	60.00	125.00	300.00
	1814 B	Inc. Ab.	50.00	90.00	150.00	350.00

10 BATZEN

SILVER

KM#	Date	Mintage	Fine	VF	XF	Unc
185	1812 B	.028	60.00	90.00	150.00	350.00

20 BATZEN

SILVER
Rev: Large date, thick stems.

KM#	Date	Mintage	Fine	VF	XF	Unc
186	1813 B	—	90.00	165.00	275.00	525.00

Rev: Small date, thin stems.

KM#	Date	Mintage	Fine	VF	XF	Unc
187	1813	—	90.00	165.00	275.00	525.00

Obv: Longer garlands. Rev: Small date, thin stems.

KM#	Date	Mintage	Fine	VF	XF	Unc
188	1813	—	100.00	175.00	285.00	550.00

Rev: Wreath separated at top.

KM#	Date	Mintage	Fine	VF	XF	Unc
192	1826	—	120.00	200.00	350.00	750.00

40 BATZEN

SILVER
Obv: Shield 18mm wide, short right hand garland.
Rev: Large date.

KM#	Date	Mintage	Fine	VF	XF	Unc
189	1813	—	80.00	120.00	250.00	500.00

Obv: Shield 19mm wide, long right hand garland.
Rev: Small date.

KM#	Date	Mintage	Fine	VF	XF	Unc
190	1813 B	—	80.00	120.00	250.00	500.00

Obv: Shield 18mm wide, short right hand garland, small wreath. Rev: Small date.

KM#	Date	Mintage	Fine	VF	XF	Unc
191	1813 B	—	80.00	120.00	250.00	500.00

TRADE COINAGE

DUCAT

3.5000 g, .986 GOLD, .1109 oz AGW

KM#	Date	Mintage	Fine	VF	XF	Unc
185	1810 B	—	600.00	900.00	1250.	3000.

MEDALLIC ISSUES (M)

(DUCAT)

3.5000 g, .986 GOLD, .1109 oz AGW
Magister Zwingli

KM#	Date	Mintage	Fine	VF	XF	Unc
M2	1819	—	—	300.00	400.00	550.00

PATTERNS (Pn)

(Including off metal strikes)

KM#	Date	Mintage	Identification	Mkt.Val.
Pn8	1811	—	1/2 Kreuzer, Billon	Rare

KM#	Date	Mintage	Identification	Mkt.Val.
Pn9	1842	—	1 Kreuzer, Billon	Rare

SWITZERLAND

The Swiss Confederation, located in central Europe north of Italy and south of Germany, has an area of 15,941 sq. mi. (41,290 sq. km.) and a population of *6.6 million. Capital: Bern. The economy centers about a well developed manufacturing industry. Machinery, chemicals, watches and clocks, and textiles are exported.

Switzerland, the habitat of lake dwellers in prehistoric times, was peopled by the Celtic Helvetians when Julius Caesar made it a part of the Roman Empire in 58 B.C. After the decline of Rome, Switzerland was invaded by Teutonic tribes, who established small temporal holdings which in the Middle Ages, became a federation of fiefs of the Holy Roman Empire. As a nation, Switzerland originated in 1291 when the districts of Nidwalden, Schwyz and Uri united to defeat Austria and attain independence as the Swiss Confederation. After acquiring new cantons in the 14th century, Switzerland was made independent from the Holy Roman Empire by the 1648 Treaty of Westphalia. The revolutionary armies of Napoleonic France occupied Switzerland and set up the Helvetian Republic, 1798-1803. After the fall of Napoleon, the Congress of Vienna, 1815, recognized the independence of Switzerland and guaranteed its neutrality. The Swiss Constitutions of 1848 and 1874 established a union modeled upon that of the United States.

MINT MARKS

A - Paris
AB - Strasbourg
B - Bern
B. - Brussels 1874
BA - Basel
BB - Strasbourg
S - Solothurn

NOTE: The coinage of Switzerland has been struck at the Bern Mint since 1853 with but a few exceptions. All coins minted there carry a 'B' mint mark through 1969, except for the 2-Centime and 2-Franc values where the mint mark was discontinued after 1968. In 1968 and 1969 some issues were struck at both Bern (B) and in London (no mint mark).

MONETARY SYSTEM

10 Rappen = 1 Batzen
10 Batzen = 1 Franc
16 Franken = 1 Duplone

HELVETIAN REPUBLIC

RAPPEN

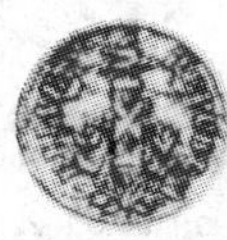

BILLON
Obv: Fasces in branches. Rev: Value in wreath.

KM#	Date	Mintage	Fine	VF	XF	Unc
11	1801	—	5.00	10.00	20.00	70.00
	1802	—	7.50	15.00	25.00	75.00

NOTE: Earlier date (1800) exists for this type.

1/2 BATZEN

BILLON

KM#	Date	Mintage	Fine	VF	XF	Unc
6	1802	—	10.00	16.00	28.00	120.00
	1803	—	12.50	25.00	45.00	140.00

NOTE: Earlier dates (1799-1800) exist for this type.

BATZEN

BILLON
Obv: HELVET.REPUBL. in wreath.
Rev: Similar to 1 Rappen, KM#11.

KM#	Date	Mintage	Fine	VF	XF	Unc
8	1801B	—	12.50	22.50	75.00	225.00
	1802B	—	12.50	22.50	75.00	225.00
	1803B	—	12.50	22.50	75.00	225.00

NOTE: Earlier dates (1799-1800) exist for this type.

5 BATZEN

SILVER
Obv: Standing Swiss holding flag.
Rev: Value within wreath.

KM#	Date	Mintage	Fine	VF	XF	Unc
9	1802B	—	200.00	275.00	425.00	900.00

NOTE: Earlier dates (1799-1800) exist for this type.

10 BATZEN

SILVER
Obv: Standing Swiss holding flag.
Rev: Value within wreath.

KM#	Date	Mintage	Fine	VF	XF	Unc
1	1801B	—	75.00	160.00	300.00	750.00

NOTE: Earlier dates (1798-1799) exist for this type.

4 FRANKEN

SILVER

Dav.#1772

KM#	Date	Mintage	Fine	VF	XF	Unc
10	1801B	—	375.00	650.00	1000.	2250.

NOTE: Earlier date (1799) exists for this type.

SWITZERLAND

Confoederatio Helvetica

MONETARY SYSTEM

100 Rappen (Centimes) = 1 Franc

RAPPEN

BRONZE

KM#	Date	Mintage	Fine	VF	XF	Unc
3	1850A	2.270	24.00	45.00	75.00	190.00
	1851A	2.730	12.00	20.00	35.00	100.00
	1853B thick cross	2.008	20.00	35.00	65.00	150.00
	1853B thin cross	Inc. Ab.	600.00	1000.	1800.	3000.
	1855B	.500	200.00	350.00	500.00	950.00
	1856B	2.500	10.00	20.00	40.00	85.00
	1857B	1.587	20.00	35.00	50.00	110.00
	1863B	.501	100.00	200.00	300.00	550.00
	1864B	.501	120.00	210.00	325.00	600.00
	1866B	1.000	40.00	75.00	125.00	250.00
	1868B	2.000	8.00	15.00	30.00	60.00
	1870B	.500	60.00	125.00	220.00	325.00
	1872B	2.080	10.00	20.00	30.00	65.00
	1875B	.975	20.00	35.00	45.00	100.00
	1876B	1.000	16.00	35.00	40.00	80.00
	1877B	.923	16.00	35.00	40.00	80.00
	1878B	.981	16.00	35.00	45.00	80.00
	1879B	.998	16.00	30.00	40.00	80.00
	1880B	.992	16.00	30.00	50.00	80.00
	1882B	1.000	12.00	25.00	35.00	55.00
	1883B	1.000	10.00	20.00	30.00	45.00
	1884B	1.000	10.00	20.00	30.00	45.00
	1887B	1.504	7.00	12.00	20.00	38.00
	1889B	.500	25.00	75.00	110.00	220.00
	1890B	1.000	8.00	16.00	25.00	40.00
	1891B thick cross	2.000	9.00	18.00	27.00	45.00
	1891B thin cross	Inc. Ab.	8.00	14.00	20.00	42.00
	1892B	1.000	8.00	16.00	25.00	40.00
	1894B	1.000	10.00	20.00	30.00	50.00
	1895B	2.000	3.50	6.00	10.00	20.00
	1896B	36 pcs.	—	—	Rare	—
	1897B	.500	12.00	25.00	40.00	60.00
	1898B	1.500	3.50	6.00	10.00	24.00
	1899B	1.500	3.50	8.00	10.00	24.00
	1900B	2.000	2.50	6.00	9.00	20.00

NOTE: Later dates (1902-1941) exist for this type.

2 RAPPEN

BRONZE

KM#	Date	Mintage	Fine	VF	XF	Unc
4	1850A	7.290	2.00	6.00	15.00	40.00
	1851A	3.720	1.50	6.00	15.00	40.00
	1866B	1.000	5.00	13.00	24.00	45.00
	1870B	.540	18.00	30.00	50.00	110.00
	1875B	.984	3.00	8.00	13.00	35.00
	1879B	.990	3.00	7.00	10.00	32.00
	1883B	1.000	2.00	5.00	9.00	32.00
	1886B	1.000	1.50	5.00	9.00	28.00
	1888B	.500	15.00	25.00	40.00	110.00
	1890B	1.000	2.50	5.00	10.00	22.00
	1893B	2.000	1.25	2.50	5.00	18.00
	1896B	20 pcs.	—	—	Rare	—
	1897B	.487	10.00	20.00	30.00	65.00
	1898B	.500	9.00	20.00	30.00	60.00
	1899B	1.000	2.00	5.00	10.00	22.00
	1900B	1.000	2.50	5.00	10.00	22.00

NOTE: Later dates (1902-1941) exist for this type.

5 RAPPEN

BILLON

KM#	Date	Mintage	Fine	VF	XF	Unc
5	1850BB	7.970	4.00	10.00	25.00	90.00
	1850AB	Inc. Ab.	25.00	120.00	400.00	1000.
	1850	Inc. Ab.	175.00	450.00	1200.	1800.
	1851BB	12.042	150.00	400.00	850.00	1600.
	1872B	1.213	12.00	25.00	50.00	100.00
	1873B	1.622	10.00	20.00	40.00	90.00
	1874B	1.700	10.00	20.00	40.00	95.00
	1876B	.989	20.00	45.00	75.00	150.00
	1877B	.978	24.00	50.00	80.00	160.00

COPPER-NICKEL

KM#	Date	Mintage	Fine	VF	XF	Unc
26	1879B	1.000	6.00	12.00	40.00	150.00
	1880B	2.000	3.25	6.00	20.00	65.00
	1881B	2.000	2.50	5.00	18.00	60.00
	1882B	3.000	1.00	2.50	12.00	54.00
	1883B	3.000	1.00	2.00	10.00	52.00
	1884B	2.000	2.50	6.00	18.00	70.00
	1885B	3.000	1.00	4.00	12.00	45.00
	1887B	.500	20.00	35.00	100.00	350.00
	1888B	1.500	3.25	6.00	20.00	60.00
	1889B	.500	15.00	30.00	90.00	350.00
	1890B	1.000	5.00	7.00	22.00	90.00
	1891B	1.000	4.50	7.00	22.00	110.00
	1892B	1.000	4.50	7.00	22.00	110.00
	1893B	2.000	.50	1.50	12.00	42.00
	1894B	2.000	.50	1.50	12.00	40.00
	1895B	2.000	.50	1.50	12.00	40.00
	1896B	16 pcs.	—	—	Rare	—
	1897B	.500	7.00	12.00	30.00	145.00
	1898B	2.500	.50	1.00	10.00	35.00
	1899B	1.500	3.50	6.00	20.00	100.00
	1900B	2.000	.75	2.50	12.00	45.00

NOTE: Later dates (1901-1980) exist for this type.

10 RAPPEN

BILLON

KM#	Date	Mintage	Fine	VF	XF	Unc
6	1850BB	8.780	6.00	15.00	40.00	120.00
	1851BB	4.530	14.00	50.00	160.00	480.00
	1871B	.844	20.00	35.00	60.00	140.00
	1873B	1.398	16.00	30.00	50.00	115.00
	1875B	.174	300.00	500.00	750.00	1350.
	1876B	1.962	16.00	25.00	45.00	115.00

COPPER-NICKEL

KM#	Date	Mintage	Fine	VF	XF	Unc
27	1879B	1.000	4.00	10.00	30.00	165.00
27	1880B	2.000	2.00	6.00	25.00	85.00
	1881B	3.000	.65	3.50	12.50	65.00
	1882B	3.000	.65	2.50	12.50	90.00
	1883B	2.000	2.00	6.00	16.00	90.00
	1884B	3.000	.65	3.00	12.50	48.00
	1885B	3.000	.50	3.00	12.50	48.00
	1894B	1.000	2.00	6.00	17.50	95.00
	1895B	2.000	.50	2.00	15.00	50.00
	1896B	16 pcs.	—	—	Rare	—
	1897B	.500	2.00	5.00	20.00	120.00
	1898B	1.000	7.00	10.00	40.00	150.00
	1899B	.500	7.00	10.00	40.00	180.00
	1900B	1.500	.75	2.50	12.00	66.00

NOTE: Later dates (1901-1995) exist for this type.

20 RAPPEN

BILLON

KM#	Date	Mintage	Fine	VF	XF	Unc
7	1850BB	5.390	6.00	15.00	40.00	150.00
	1851BB	6.160	50.00	225.00	600.00	1200.
	1858B	1.548	14.00	25.00	45.00	195.00
	1859B	2.776	7.00	10.00	25.00	110.00

NICKEL

KM#	Date	Mintage	Fine	VF	XF	Unc
29	1881B	1.000	1.50	4.00	20.00	75.00
	1883B	2.500	.35	1.50	12.00	60.00
	1884B	4.000	.25	1.00	10.00	36.00
	1885B	3.000	.25	1.00	10.00	45.00
	1887B	.500	6.00	10.00	40.00	150.00
	1891B	1.000	.75	1.50	15.00	60.00
	1893B	1.000	.75	1.50	15.00	60.00
	1894B	1.000	.75	1.50	15.00	60.00
	1896B	1.000	.75	1.50	15.00	60.00
	1897B	.500	2.75	6.00	20.00	200.00
	1898B	.500	6.00	10.00	30.00	120.00
	1899B	.500	5.00	8.00	30.00	135.00
	1900B	1.000	.75	1.50	10.00	60.00

NOTE: Later dates (1901-1938) exist for this type.

1/2 FRANC

2.5000 g, .900 SILVER, .0723 oz ASW

KM#	Date	Mintage	Fine	VF	XF	Unc
8	1850A	4.500	50.00	100.00	250.00	600.00
	1850A	—	—	—	P/L	1500.
	1851A	Inc. Ab.	45.00	90.00	225.00	550.00
	1851A	—	—	—	P/L	1500.

2.5000 g, .835 SILVER, .0671 oz ASW

KM#	Date	Mintage	Fine	VF	XF	Unc
23	1875B	1.000	15.00	60.00	175.00	500.00
	1875B	—	—	—	P/L	1500.
	1877B	1.000	15.00	60.00	185.00	600.00
	1877B	—	—	—	P/L	1800.
	1878B	1.000	20.00	70.00	200.00	650.00
	1878B	—	—	—	P/L	2400.
	1879B	1.000	12.00	30.00	125.00	350.00
	1879B	—	—	—	P/L	1500.
	1881B	1.000	4.00	12.00	125.00	350.00
	1881B	—	—	—	P/L	1500.
	1882B	1.000	6.00	20.00	125.00	420.00
	1882B	—	—	—	P/L	1500.
	1894A	.800	12.00	40.00	125.00	360.00
	1894A	—	—	—	P/L	900.00
	1896B	28 pcs.	—	—	Rare	—
	1896B	—	—	—	P/L	Rare
	1898B	1.600	1.50	4.00	15.00	120.00
	1898B	—	—	—	P/L	600.00
	1899B	.400	5.00	12.00	75.00	330.00
	1899B	—	—	—	P/L	1500.
	1900B	.400	6.00	12.00	85.00	330.00
	1900B	—	—	—	P/L	1500.

NOTE: Later dates (1901-1967) exist for this type.

FRANC

5.0000 g, .900 SILVER, .1447 oz ASW

KM#	Date	Mintage	Fine	VF	XF	Unc
9	1850A	5.750	50.00	125.00	250.00	600.00
	1850A	—	—	—	P/L	1800.
	1851A	Inc. Ab.	60.00	150.00	275.00	675.00
	1851A	—	—	—	P/L	1800.
	1857B	526 pcs.	2400.	4400.	7800.	15,000.
	1857B	—	—	—	P/L	Rare

5.0000 g, .800 SILVER, .1286 oz ASW

KM#	Date	Mintage	Fine	VF	XF	Unc
9a	1860B	.515	100.00	225.00	800.00	2400.
	1860B	—	—	—	P/L	3600.
	1861B	3.002	15.00	35.00	150.00	475.00
	1861B	—	—	—	P/L	1800.

5.0000 g, .835 SILVER, .1342 oz ASW

KM#	Date	Mintage	Fine	VF	XF	Unc
24	1875B	1.036	15.00	40.00	250.00	950.00
	1875B	—	—	—	P/L	3000.
	1876B	2.500	5.00	20.00	125.00	475.00
	1876B	—	—	—	P/L	2400.
	1877B	2.520	6.00	25.00	175.00	600.00
	1877B	—	—	—	P/L	2400.
	1880B	.944	10.00	50.00	325.00	1850.
	1880B	—	—	—	P/L	3600.
	1886B	1.000	2.50	12.00	85.00	390.00
	1886B	—	—	—	P/L	1500.
	1887B	1.000	2.50	12.00	85.00	250.00
	1887B	—	—	—	P/L	1200.
	1894A	1.200	2.50	10.00	85.00	300.00
	1894A	—	—	—	P/L	1050.
	1896B	28 pcs.	—	—	Rare	—
	1896B	—	—	—	P/L	Rare
	1898B	.400	3.00	10.00	100.00	360.00
	1898B	—	—	—	P/L	1800.
	1899B	.400	3.00	10.00	100.00	360.00
	1899B	—	—	—	P/L	1800.
	1900B	.400	6.00	12.00	125.00	500.00
	1900B	—	—	—	P/L	1800.

NOTE: Later dates (1901-1967) exist for this type.

2 FRANCS

10.0000 g, .900 SILVER, .2894 oz ASW

KM#	Date	Mintage	Fine	VF	XF	Unc
10	1850A	2.500	125.00	300.00	475.00	1000.
	1850A	—	—	—	P/L	3000.
	1857B	622 pcs.	3000.	4500.	9000.	15,000.
	1857B	—	—	—	P/L	Rare

10.0000 g, .800 SILVER, .2572 oz ASW

KM#	Date	Mintage	Fine	VF	XF	Unc
10a	1860B	2.001	30.00	65.00	250.00	1100.
	1860B	—	—	—	P/L	3000.
	1862B	1.000	35.00	80.00	325.00	1250.
	1862B	—	—	—	P/L	3000.
	1863B	.500	110.00	225.00	750.00	2700.
	1863B	—	—	—	P/L	4800.

10.0000 g, .835 SILVER, .2685 oz ASW

KM#	Date	Mintage	Fine	VF	XF	Unc
21	1874B	1.000	8.00	30.00	300.00	1200.
	1874B	—	—	—	P/L	3600.
	1875B	.982	12.00	40.00	400.00	1500.
	1875B	—	—	—	P/L	4500.
	1878B	1.500	6.00	15.00	275.00	900.00
	1878B	—	—	—	P/L	3000.
	1879B	.518	10.00	30.00	650.00	4500.
	1879B	—	—	—	P/L	12,000.

KM#	Date	Mintage	Fine	VF	XF	Unc
21	1886B	1.000	3.00	10.00	100.00	600.00
	1886B	—	—	—	P/L	3000.
	1894A	.700	3.00	10.00	185.00	725.00
	1894A	—	—	—	P/L	2400.
	1896B	20 pcs.	—	—	Rare	—
	1896B	—	—	—	P/L	Rare

NOTE: Later dates (1901-1967) exist for this type.

5 FRANCS

25.0000 g, .900 SILVER, .7234 oz ASW

KM#	Date	Mintage	Fine	VF	XF	Unc
11	1850A	.140	140.00	275.00	550.00	1200.
	1850A	—	—	—	P/L	6000.
	1851A	.360	110.00	250.00	400.00	1000.
	1851A	—	—	—	P/L	6000.
	1873B	.030	600.00	1200.	2000.	4000.
	1873B	—	—	—	P/L	9000.
	1874B.	1.400	100.00	175.00	350.00	1200.
	1874B.	—	—	—	P/L	6000.
	1874B	.196	100.00	220.00	425.00	1000.
	1874B	—	—	—	P/L	4500.

NOTE: The dot after the B is for Brussels. For coins dated 1855 see Shooting Talers.

KM#	Date	Mintage	Fine	VF	XF	Unc
34	1888B	.025	200.00	350.00	1250.	3000.
	1888B	—	—	—	P/L	7500.
	1889B	.225	75.00	125.00	350.00	1200.
	1889B	—	—	—	P/L	4500.
	1890B	.305	75.00	125.00	350.00	1200.
	1890B	—	—	—	P/L	4500.
	1891B	.150	80.00	130.00	375.00	1350.
	1891B	—	—	—	P/L	4500.
	1892B	.190	75.00	125.00	350.00	1200.
	1892B	—	—	—	P/L	4500.
	1894B	.034	300.00	750.00	2000.	6000.
	1894B	—	—	—	P/L	12,000.
	1895B	.046	200.00	500.00	1650.	4500.
	1895B	—	—	—	P/L	9000.
	1896B	2,000	—	—	Rare	—
	1896B	—	—	—	P/L	Rare
	1900B	.033	325.00	600.00	1500.	4200.
	1900B	—	—	—	P/L	9000.

NOTE: Later dates (1904-1916) exist for this type.

20 FRANCS

6.4516 g, .900 GOLD, .1867 oz AGW
Reeded edge.

KM#	Date	Mintage	VF	XF	Unc	BU
31.1	1883	.250	BV	70.00	100.00	175.00

Edge: DOMINUS XXX PROVIDEBIT XXXXXXXXXX

KM#	Date	Mintage	VF	XF	Unc	BU
31.3	1886	.250	BV	70.00	100.00	175.00
	1887B	176 pcs.	—	—	Rare	—
	1888B	4,224	4000.	5500.	7000.	10,000.
	1889B	.100	80.00	100.00	150.00	200.00
	1890B	.125	BV	75.00	100.00	165.00
	1891B	.100	BV	85.00	110.00	170.00
	1892B	.100	BV	85.00	110.00	170.00
	1893B	.100	BV	85.00	110.00	170.00
	1893B*	25 pcs.	—	—	Rare	—
	1894B	.121	BV	85.00	100.00	165.00
	1895B	.200	BV	85.00	100.00	160.00
	1895B*	19 pcs.	—	—	Rare	—
	1896B	.400	BV	85.00	100.00	150.00

***NOTE:** Struck of bright Valaisan gold from Gondo with a small cross punched in the center of the Swiss cross.

Edge: DOMINUS XXX/XXXXXXXXXX PROVIDEBIT

KM#	Date	Mintage	VF	XF	Unc	BU
31.2	1896B	Inc. Ab.	Reported, not confirmed			
35.1	1897B	.400	BV	75.00	90.00	110.00
	1897B*	29 pcs.	—	—	Rare	—
	1898B	.400	BV	75.00	90.00	110.00
	1899B	.300	BV	75.00	90.00	110.00
	1900B	.400	BV	75.00	90.00	110.00

NOTE: Later dates (1901-1935) exist for this type.

SHOOTING FESTIVAL COMMEMORATIVES

The listings which follow have traditionally been categorized in many catalogs as "Swiss Shooting Thalers". Technically, all are medallic issues, rather than "coins", excepting the Solothurn issue of 1855, which according to the Swiss Federal Finance Department was "legally equal" to the then current silver 5 Francs issue to which it was identical in design, aside from bearing an edge inscription which read, EIDGEN FREISCHIESSEN SOLOTHURN (National Shooting Fest (in) Solothurn). For subsequent issues, denominations have been indicated "with government consent (though they) were not given legal tender status". The presence of the denomination was intended to indicate these "talers were of the same weight and fineness as (prescribed for) legal tender coins". Two generally associated "Shooting Festival" coins of earlier dates - 1842 Graubunden and 1847 Glarus - will be found incorporated in the listings for these cantons, as they were issued prior to the Swiss confederation of 1848.

5 FRANCS

.835 SILVER
Solothurn
Similar to KM#11 but edge is lettered:
EIDGEN FREISCHIESEN SOLOTHURN 1855*

KM#	Date	Mintage	VF	XF	Unc	BU
S3	1855	3,000	750.00	1300.	2750.	3750.
	1855	—	—	—	P/L	9000.

Bern

KM#	Date	Mintage	VF	XF	Unc	BU
S4	1857	5,195	175.00	350.00	650.00	1000.
	1857	—	—	—	P/L	3000.

Zurich

KM#	Date	Mintage	VF	XF	Unc	BU
S5	1859	6,000	90.00	200.00	400.00	700.00
	1859	—	—	—	P/L	2400.

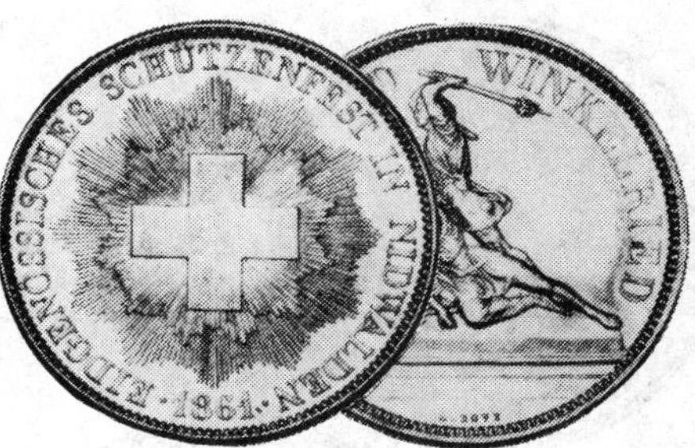

Stans in Nidwalden

KM#	Date	Mintage	VF	XF	Unc	BU
S6	1861	6,000	100.00	250.00	450.00	800.00
	1861	—	—	—	P/L	2400.

La Chaux-De-Fonds in Neuchatel

KM#	Date	Mintage	VF	XF	Unc	BU
S7	1863	6,000	100.00	300.00	550.00	900.00
	1863	—	—	—	P/L	2400.

Schaffhausen

KM#	Date	Mintage	VF	XF	Unc	BU
S8	1865	.010	60.00	125.00	245.00	450.00
	1865	—	—	—	P/L	1200.

Schwyz

KM#	Date	Mintage	VF	XF	Unc	BU
S9	1867	8,000	65.00	135.00	250.00	500.00
	1865	—	—	—	P/L	1200.

Zug

KM#	Date	Mintage	VF	XF	Unc	BU
S10	1869	6,000	100.00	175.00	400.00	700.00
	1869	—	—	—	P/L	1800.

Zurich

KM#	Date	Mintage	VF	XF	Unc	BU
S11	1872	.010	45.00	120.00	250.00	450.00
	1872	—	—	—	P/L	1050.

St. Gallen

KM#	Date	Mintage	VF	XF	Unc	BU
S12	1874	.015	45.00	90.00	150.00	300.00
	1874	—	—	—	P/L	1200.

Lausanne

KM#	Date	Mintage	VF	XF	Unc	BU
S13	1876	.020	50.00	90.00	175.00	300.00
	1876	—	—	—	P/L	900.00

Basel

KM#	Date	Mintage	VF	XF	Unc	BU
S14	1879	.030	30.00	60.00	125.00	200.00

Fribourg

KM#	Date	Mintage	VF	XF	Unc	BU
S15	1881	.030	30.00	60.00	135.00	225.00
	1881	—	—	—	P/L	900.00

Lugano

KM#	Date	Mintage	VF	XF	Unc	BU
S16	1883	.030	30.00	60.00	125.00	250.00
	1883	—	—	—	P/L	900.00

Bern

KM#	Date	Mintage	VF	XF	Unc	BU
S17	1885	.025	30.00	65.00	135.00	230.00
	1885	—	—	—	P/L	900.00

ESSAIS (E)

KM#	Date	Mintage	Identification	Mkt.Val.
E1	1851	—	2 Rappen, Copper	525.00

NOTE: Struck at Strassburg.

KM#	Date	Mintage	Identification	Mkt.Val.
E2	1851	—	2 Rappen, Brass	350.00
E3	1851	—	2 Rappen, Silver	1750.

PATTERNS (Pn)

(Including off metal strikes)

KM#	Date	Mintage	Identification	Mkt.Val.
Pn1	1850	—	10 Rappen, Billon	1000.
Pn2	1850A	—	50 Rappen, Copper	3500.
Pn3	1850A	—	1/2 Franc, Tin	3000.
Pn4	1850	—	1/2 Franc, Copper	2500.
Pn5	1850	—	1 Franc, Copper	550.00
Pn6	1850	—	2 Francs, Tin	4500.
Pn7	1850	—	5 Francs, Copper	5000.
Pn8	1850	—	10 Francs, Nickel	700.00
Pn9	1850	—	5 Francs, Tin	3500.
Pn10	1851BB	—	5 Rappen, Silver	4500.
Pn11	1851BB	—	5 Rappen, Bronze	3500.
Pn12	1851	—	20 Rappen, Copper	3000.
Pn13	1851	—	5 Francs, Copper	5250.

KM#	Date	Mintage	Identification	Mkt.Val.
Pn14	1860	—	2 Francs, Silver	1650.

KM#	Date	Mintage	Identification	Mkt.Val.
Pn15	1871B	—	20 Rappen, Nickel	3500.
Pn16	1871B	—	20 Rappen, Copper-Nickel	4250.

KM#	Date	Mintage	Identification	Mkt.Val.
Pn17	1871B	—	20 Francs, Gold. Obv: Shield.	6500.
Pn18	1871B	—	20 Francs, Tin	4000.

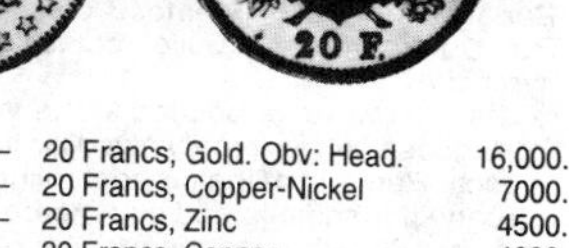

KM#	Date	Mintage	Identification	Mkt.Val.
Pn19	1871	—	20 Francs, Gold. Obv: Head.	16,000.
Pn20	1871	—	20 Francs, Copper-Nickel	7000.
Pn21	1871	—	20 Francs, Zinc	4500.
Pn22	1873	—	20 Francs, Copper	4000.
Pn23	1873	—	20 Francs, Nickel	5000.

KM#	Date	Mintage	Identification	Mkt.Val.
Pn24	1873	1,000	20 Francs, Gold, Helvetia w/head mint mark (Brussels)	4500.
Pn25	1873	—	20 Francs, Copper	4000.
Pn26	1873	—	20 Francs, Gold, Helvetia w/o head mint mark	8500.
Pn27	1874	—	5 Francs, Copper-Nickel	—
Pn28	1875B	—	20 Rappen, Billon, KM7	5000.
Pn29	1875B	—	20 Rappen, Copper-Nickel, KM7	5000.

KM#	Date	Mintage	Identification	Mkt.Val.
Pn30	ND(1875)B	—	20 Rappen, Copper-Nickel	4000.
Pn31	ND(1875)B	—	20 Rappen, Billon	4000.
Pn32	1876	—	5 Rappen, Copper-Nickel	—
Pn33	1881B	—	20 Rappen, Copper-Nickel	3000.
Pn34	1883	—	20 Francs, Gold	—
Pn35	1894A	—	1/2 Franc, Silver	6000.
Pn36	1894A	—	1 Franc, Silver	10,000.
Pn37	1894A	—	2 Francs, Silver	10,000.
Pn38	1897	—	20 Francs, Copper-Nickel	1400.

KM#	Date	Mintage	Identification	Mkt.Val.
Pn39	1897B	12 pcs.	20 Francs, Gold	*Rare

***NOTE:** Swiss Bank sale #19 1-88 FDC realized $47,580.

MINT SETS (MS)

KM#	Date	Mintage	Identification	Issue Price	Mkt. Val.
MS1	1896(9)	—	KM3-4,21,23-24,26-27, 29,34	—	Rare

The United Republic of Tanzania, located on the east coast of Africa between Kenya and Mozambique, consists of Tanganyika and the islands of Zanzibar and Pemba. It has an area of 364,900 sq. mi. (945,090 sq. km.) and a population of *25.2 million. Capital: Dar es Salaam (Haven of Peace). The chief exports are cotton, coffee, diamonds, sisal, cloves, petroleum products, and cashew nuts.

Tanzania is a member of the Commonwealth of Nations. The President is Chief of State.

GERMAN EAST AFRICA

German East Africa (Tanganyika), located on the coast of east-central Africa between British East Africa (now Kenya) and Portuguese East Africa (now Mozambique), had an area of 362,284 sq. mi. (938,216 sq. km.) and a population of about 6 million. Capital: Dar es Salaam. Chief products prior to German control were ivory and slaves; after German control, sisal, coffee, and rubber. Germany acquired control of the area by treaties with coastal chiefs in 1884, established it as a protectorate in 1891, and proclaimed it the Colony of German East Africa in 1897. After World War I, Tanganyika was entrusted to Great Britain as a League of Nations mandate, and after World War II as a United Nations trust territory. Tanganyika became an independent nation within the British Commonwealth on Dec. 9, 1961.

Coins dated up until 1901 were issued by the German East Africa Company. From 1904 onwards, coins were issued by the government.

TITLES

شراكتة المانيا

Sharaka(t) Almania

RULERS

Wilhelm II, 1888-1918

MINT MARKS

A - Berlin
J - Hamburg
T - Tabora

MONETARY SYSTEM

Until 1904

64 Pesa = 1 Rupie

Commencing 1904

100 Heller = 1 Rupie

PESA

COPPER

KM#	Date	Mintage	Fine	VF	XF	Unc
1	1890	1.000	.75	3.00	6.00	20.00
	1890	—	—	—	Proof	110.00
	1891	12.551	1.00	3.75	7.50	22.00
	1892	27.541	1.00	3.75	7.50	35.00

1/4 RUPIE

2.9160 g, .917 SILVER, .0859 oz ASW

KM#	Date	Mintage	Fine	VF	XF	Unc
3	1891	.077	5.00	12.00	35.00	85.00
	1891	—	—	—	Proof	175.00
	1898	.100	6.00	18.00	50.00	135.00

NOTE: Later date (1901) exists for this type.

1/2 RUPIE

5.8319 g, .917 SILVER, .1719 oz ASW

KM#	Date	Mintage	Fine	VF	XF	Unc
4	1891	.068	12.50	25.00	65.00	150.00
	1891	—	—	—	Proof	220.00
	1897	.075	14.00	30.00	80.00	200.00

NOTE: Later date (1901) exists for this type.

RUPIE

11.6638 g, .917 SILVER, .3437 oz ASW

KM#	Date	Mintage	Fine	VF	XF	Unc
2	1890	.154	10.00	18.00	35.00	120.00
	1890	—	—	—	Proof	300.00
	1891	.126	10.00	18.00	40.00	130.00
	1891	—	—	—	Proof	300.00
	1892	.360	10.00	18.00	35.00	125.00
	1892	—	—	—	Proof	300.00
	1893	.142	12.50	27.50	60.00	250.00
	1894	.048	20.00	125.00	250.00	500.00
	1897	.244	12.50	27.50	60.00	180.00
	1898	.357	12.50	27.50	60.00	180.00
	1899	.227	15.00	32.50	75.00	225.00
	1900	.209	12.50	27.50	60.00	200.00

NOTE: Later dates (1901-1902) exist for this type.

2 RUPIEN

23.3200 g, .917 SILVER, .6872 oz ASW

KM#	Date	Mintage	Fine	VF	XF	Unc
5	1893	.033	150.00	285.00	650.00	1800.
	1893	—	—	—	Proof	3500.
	1894	.018	200.00	350.00	750.00	2400.

ZANZIBAR

The British protectorate of Zanzibar and adjacent small islands, located in the Indian Ocean 22 miles (35 km.) off the coast of Tanganyika, comprised a portion of British East Africa. Zanzibar was also the name of a sultanate which included the Zanzibar and Kenya protectorates. Zanzibar has an area of 637 sq. mi. (1,651 sq. km.). Chief city: Zanzibar. The islands are noted for their cloves, of which Zanzibar is the world's foremost producer.

Zanzibar came under Portuguese control in 1503, was conquered by the Omani Arabs in 1698, became independent of Oman in 1860, and (with Pemba) came under British control in 1890. Britain granted the protectorate self-government in 1961, and independence within the British Commonwealth on Dec. 19, 1963. On April 26, 1964, Tanganyika and Zanzibar (with Pemba) united to form the United Republic of Tanganyika and Zanzibar. The name of the country, which remained within the British Commonwealth was changed to Tanzania on Oct. 29, 1964.

TITLES

زنجباراه

Zanjibara

RULERS

Sultan Barghash Ibn Sa' Id, 1870-1888AD
Sultan Ali Bin Hamud, 1902-1911AD

MONETARY SYSTEM

64 Pysa (Pice) = 1 Rupee
136 Pysa = 1 Ryal (to 1908)
100 Cents = 1 Rupee (to 1909)

PYSA

COPPER

KM#	Date	Mintage	Fine	VF	XF	Unc
1	AH1299	4.640	1.00	1.75	3.50	25.00
	1299	—	—	—	Proof	150.00
7	AH1304	18.680	1.25	2.00	4.50	35.00
	1304	—	—	—	Proof	175.00

1/4 RYAL

SILVER

KM#	Date	Mintage	Fine	VF	XF	Unc
2	AH1299	—	—	—	Rare	—

1/2 RYAL

SILVER

KM#	Date	Mintage	Fine	VF	XF	Unc
3	AH1299	—	—	—	Rare	—

RYAL

SILVER

KM#	Date	Mintage	Fine	VF	XF	Unc
4	AH1299	.060	125.00	175.00	275.00	500.00

21/2 RYALS

GOLD

KM#	Date	Mintage	Fine	VF	XF	Unc
5	AH1299	—	—	—	—	17,000.

5 RYALS

GOLD

KM#	Date	Mintage	Fine	VF	XF	Unc
6	AH1299	2,000	—	—	—	11,000.

PATTERNS (Pn)

(Including off metal strikes)

KM#	Date	Mintage	Identification	Mkt.Val.
Pn1	AH1299	—	1 Ryal, Copper, KM4	Unique

THAILAND

The Kingdom of Thailand (formerly Siam), a constitutional monarchy located in the center of mainland southeast Asia between Burma and Laos, has an area of 198,457 mi. (514,000 sq. km.) and a population of *55.5 million. Capital: Bangkok. The economy is based on agriculture and mining. Rubber, rice, teakwood, tin and tungsten are exported.

The history of The Kingdom of Siam, the only country in south and southeast Asia that was never colonized by an European power, dates from the 6th century A.D. when Thai people started to migrate into the area a process that accelerated with the Mongol invasion of China in the 13th century. After 400 years of sporadic warfare with the neighboring Burmese, King Taskin won the last battle in 1767. He founded a new capital, Dhonburi, on the west bank of the Chao Praya River. King Rama I moved the capital to Bangkok in 1782, thus initiating the so-called Bangkok Period of Siamese coinage characterized by Pot Duang money (bullet coins) stamped with regal symbols.

The Thai were introduced to the Western world by the Portuguese, who were followed by the Dutch, British and French. Rama III of the present ruling dynasty negotiated a treaty of friendship and commerce with Britain in 1826, and in 1896 the independence of the kingdom was guaranteed by an Anglo-French accord.

RULERS

Rama I (Phra Buddha Yodfa Chulalok), 1782-1809
Rama II (Phra Buddha Lert La Nabhalai), 1809-1824
Rama III (Phra Nang Klao), 1824-1851
Rama IV (Phra Chom Klao 'Mongkut'), 1851-1868
Rama V (Phra Maha Chulalongkorn), 1868-1910

MONETARY SYSTEM

Old currency system

2 Solos = 1 Att
2 Att = 1 Sio (Pai)
2 Sio = 1 Sik
2 Sik = 1 Fuang
2 Fuang = 1 Salung (not Sal'ung)
4 Salung = 1 Baht
4 Baht = 1 Tamlung
20 Tamlung = 1 Chang

UNITS OF OLD THAI CURRENCY

Chang -	ชั่ง	Sik -	ซีก
Tamlung -	ตำลึง	Sio (Pai) -	เสี้ยว
Baht -	บาท	Att -	อัฐ
Salung -	สลึง	Solos -	โสพส
Fuang -	เฟื้อง		

MINT MARKS

H-Heaton Birmingham

DATING

Typical BE Dating

1 2 3 8   1 2 4 4

Typical CS Dating

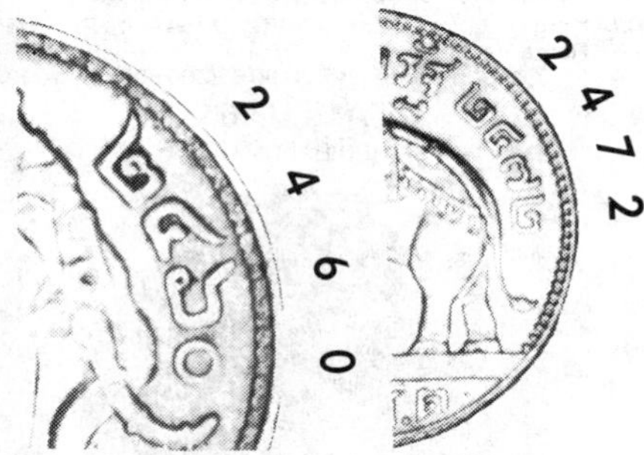

NOTE: Sometimes the era designator *BE* or *CS* will actually appear on the coin itself.

Denomination

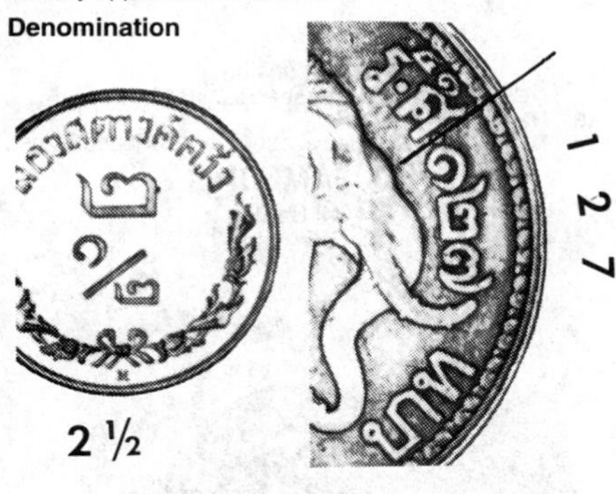

2 ½

2-1/2 (Satang)   RS Dating

DATE CONVERSION TABLES

B.E. date - 543 = A.D. date
Ex: 2516 - 543 = 1973

R.S. date + 1781 = A.D. date
Ex: 127 + 1781 = 1908

C.S. date + 638 = A.D. date
Ex 1238 + 638 = 1876

Primary denominations used were 1 Baht, 1/4 and 1/8 Baht up to the reign of Rama IV. Other denominations are much scarcer.

BULLET COINAGE

Gold and silver "bullet" coins have been a medium of exchange since medieval times. Interesting enough is the fact that a 1 Baht bullet made of gold will weigh the same as a 1 Baht bullet in silver. The reason for this is that Baht originally was a weight not a denomination. It was a coinage weight only until the time of Rama VII, (1925-1935) and now it is a weight and also a denomination (as far as standard weight coins are concerned). Usually 1 gold Baht was equal to 16 silver Baht on an exchange basis.

Bullet Weights

Grams

BAHT	1/2 BAHT	1/4 BAHT	1/8 BAHT	1/16 BAHT	1/32 BAHT	1/64 BAHT
15.40	7.70	3.85	1.92	0.96	0.48	0.24

Chopmarks exist on bullet coins as they do on many other coins that have traveled on their way through the Orient. One must be careful not to mistake a money changers chopmark for the regular dynastic marks on the bullet. Some chopmarks are rather simple in design while others appear to be rather elaborate.

DYNASTIC MARKS

Chakra

 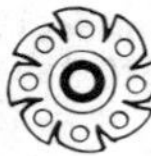 

The Chakra, symbol of the God Vishnu, is the mark of the Bangkok Dynasty. It varies slightly in design between issues, being very ornate on ceremonial issues.

RAMA I

1782-1809

Tri   Unalom

The trident, the symbol of the Hindu God, Siva, used as the first mark of Rama I. The unalom is an ornamented conch shell, used as the second mark of Rama I.

RAMA II

1809-1824

Krut

A facing Krut, half man - half bird, used as the mark of Rama II.

RAMA III

1824-1851

Krut Sio   Prasat   Dok Mai

The Krut bird to left, used as the first mark of Rama III. The Prasat, the palace used as second mark of Rama III. The Dok Mai was a flower used as third mark of Rama III.

Bai Matum   Ruang Puang   Arrow Head

The Bai Matum is a bale-fruit tree used as the fourth mark of Rama III. The Ruang Puang is a beehive used as the fifth mark of Rama III. Very similar to Dok Mai, having only 1 dot below the point used as the sixth mark of Rama III.

Chaleo

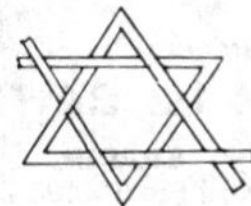

A symbol of varied meanings. In this instance it is believed to represent a charm to ward off evil spirits, found as a seventh mark on bullet coinage of Rama III.

RAMA IV

1851-1868

P'ra Tao   Mongkut

The P'ra Tao or royal water pot was used as the first mark of Rama IV. The Royal Siamese Crown was used as the second mark of Rama IV.

RAMA V

1868-1910

P'ra Kieo 1876   Cho Rampeuy 1880

The Royal Coronet worn on the top knot of the Royal Princess on ceremonial occasions. First used on the occasion of the funeral of Princess Charoenkamol Suksawadi who died in 1874. The Thai flower was on a ceremonial issue along with an ornate crown of 2 vessels in memory of Somdet Pira Deb Sirindhra, the mother of Rama V and commemorating his age, dated CS1242.

MARKET VALUATIONS

Market valuations are primarily based on the quality and condition of the countermarks found on bullet coinage.

SILVER POT DUANG

(Bullet Coins)

1/128 BAHT

SILVER, 0.12 g

C#	King	Mark	VG	Fine	VF	XF
120	Rama IV	P'ra Tao	—	—	—	—

ATT

(1/64 Baht)

SILVER, 0.24 g

C#	King	Mark	VG	Fine	VF	XF
121	Rama IV	P'ra Tao	20.00	30.00	45.00	75.00

SIO

(Pai) (1/32 Baht)

SILVER, 0.48 g

C#	King	Mark	VG	Fine	VF	XF
1	Rama I	Tri	10.00	15.00	22.00	32.00
8	Rama I	Unalom	10.00	15.00	22.00	32.00
42	Rama III	Prasat	10.00	15.00	22.00	32.00
51	Rama III	Dok Mai	10.00	15.00	22.00	32.00
61	Rama III	Bai Matum	10.00	15.00	22.00	32.00
71	Rama III	Ruang Puang	10.00	15.00	22.00	32.00
81	Rama III	Arrow Head	10.00	15.00	22.00	32.00
122	Rama IV	P'ra Tao	10.00	15.00	20.00	30.00

SIK

(1/16 Baht)

SILVER, 0.96 g

C#	King	Mark	VG	Fine	VF	XF
2	Rama I	Tri	12.00	20.00	30.00	50.00
9	Rama I	Unalom	16.00	27.00	40.00	65.00
16	Rama II	Krut	20.00	35.00	50.00	85.00
43	Rama III	Prasat	6.00	10.00	15.00	25.00
52	Rama III	Dok Mai	5.00	6.00	10.00	16.00
62	Rama III	Bai Matum	5.00	8.00	12.00	20.00
72	Rama III	Ruang Puang	5.00	8.00	12.00	20.00
82	Rama III	Arrow Head	5.00	8.00	12.00	20.00
123	Rama IV	P'ra Tao	3.00	5.00	8.50	12.50
133	Rama IV	Mongkut	6.00	10.00	14.00	20.00

FUANG

(1/8 Baht)

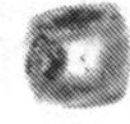 

SILVER, 1.92 g

C#	King	Mark	VG	Fine	VF	XF
3	Rama I	Tri	15.00	25.00	37.00	62.00
10	Rama I	Unalom	15.00	25.00	37.00	62.00
17	Rama II	Krut	20.00	35.00	50.00	85.00
44	Rama III	Prasat	6.00	10.00	15.00	25.00
44.1	Rama III	Prasat and Unalom	25.00	40.00	60.00	100.00
44.2	Rama III	Prasat and Krut	25.00	40.00	60.00	100.00
53	Rama III	Dok Mai	5.00	8.00	12.00	20.00

C#	King	Mark	VG	Fine	VF	XF
63	Rama III	Bai Matum	4.00	7.00	10.00	16.00
73	Rama III					
		Ruang Puang	4.00	7.00	10.00	16.00
83	Rama III	Arrow Head	4.00	7.00	11.00	17.00
124	Rama IV	P'ra Tao	3.00	5.00	8.00	13.00
134	Rama IV	Mongkut	3.00	5.00	8.00	13.00

SALU'NG

(1/4 Baht)

SILVER, 3.85 g

C#	King	Mark	VG	Fine	VF	XF
4	Rama I	Tri	11.00	18.00	27.00	45.00
11	Rama I	Unalom	15.00	25.00	37.00	65.00
18	Rama II	Krut	20.00	25.00	40.00	70.00
45	Rama III	Prasat	6.00	10.00	15.00	25.00
54	Rama III	Dok Mai	6.00	10.00	15.00	25.00
64	Rama III	Bai Matum	5.00	8.00	12.00	20.00
74	Rama III					
		Ruang Puang	5.00	9.00	13.00	22000
84	Rama III	Arrow Head	5.00	9.00	13.00	22.00
125	Rama IV	P'ra Tao	5.00	8.00	12.00	20.00
135	Rama IV	Mongkut	5.00	8.00	12.00	20.00

2 SALU'NG

(1/2 Baht)

SILVER, 7.70 g

C#	King	Mark	VG	Fine	VF	XF
5	Rama I	Tri	12.00	22.00	35.00	60.00
12	Rama I	Unalom	15.00	25.00	37.50	65.00
19	Rama II	Krut	25.00	35.00	50.00	85.00
46	Rama III	Prasat	7.00	12.00	18.00	30.00
55	Rama III	Dok Mai	18.00	30.00	45.00	75.00
65	Rama III	Bai Matum	12.00	20.00	30.00	50.00

C#	King	Mark	VG	Fine	VF	XF
136	Rama IV	Mongkut	7.00	12.00	20.00	32.00
136.1	Rama IV					
		Mongkut and Prasat	20.00	35.00	50.00	75.00

BAHT

SILVER, 15.40 g

C#	King	Mark	VG	Fine	VF	XF
1	Rama I	Tri	15.00	20.00	25.00	40.00

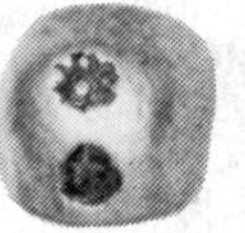

C#	King	Mark	VG	Fine	VF	XF
13	Rama I	Unalom	15.00	20.00	25.00	40.00

C#	King	Mark	VG	Fine	VF	XF
20	Rama II	Krut	15.00	20.00	25.00	40.00
39	Rama III	Chaleo	350.00	600.00	1000.	—
47	Rama III	Prasat	15.00	20.00	25.00	40.00
56	Rama III	Dok Mai	30.00	50.00	75.00	125.00
66	Rama III	Bai Matum	27.00	45.00	65.00	110.00
127	Rama IV	P'ra Tao	Reported, not confirmed			

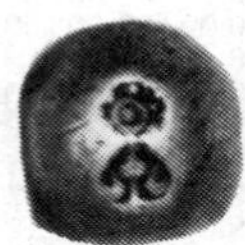

C#	King	Mark	VG	Fine	VF	XF
137.1	Rama IV	Mongkut	15.00	25.00	35.00	60.00
137.2	Rama IV					
		Mongkut and Prasat	42.50	70.00	100.00	160.00

Death of Princess Charoenkamol Suksawadi

C#	King	Mark	VG	Fine	VF	XF
177	Rama V	P'ra Kieo	—	—	Rare	—

1-1/2 BAHT

SILVER, 23.10 g

C#	King	Mark	VG	Fine	VF	XF
48	Rama III	Prasat	—	—	Rare	—

2 BAHT

SILVER, 30.80 g

C#	King	Mark	VG	Fine	VF	XF
14	Rama I	Unalom	750.00	1250.	2000.	—
21	Rama II	Krut	—	—	Rare	—
49	Rama III	Prasat	—	—	Rare	—

c/m: 8 dots in Chakra

C#	King	Mark	VG	Fine	VF	XF
138	Rama IV	Mongkut	100.00	140.00	210.00	375.00

c/m: 6 blades in Chakra

C#	King	Mark	VG	Fine	VF	XF
138.1	Rama IV	Mongkut	200.00	300.00	420.00	700.00

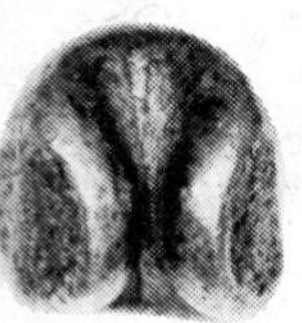

c/m: 8 blades in Chakra, elaborate design.

C#	King	Mark	VG	Fine	VF	XF
138.2	Rama IV	Mongkut	100.00	150.00	225.00	425.00

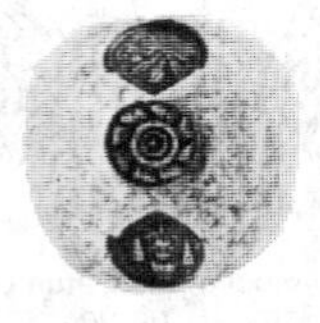

Somdet P'ra Deb Sirindhra

C#	King	Mark	VG	Fine	VF	XF
188	Rama V					
		Cho Rampeuy	225.00	335.00	450.00	750.00

2-1/2 BAHT

SILVER, 38.50 g

C#	King	Mark	VG	Fine	VF	XF
31	Rama III	Krut Sio	250.00	375.00	550.00	850.00

NOTE: Three varieties exist.

TAMLUNG

(4 Baht)

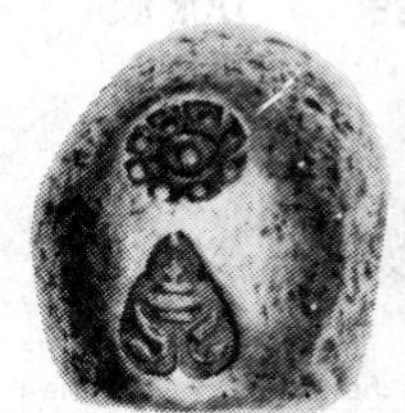
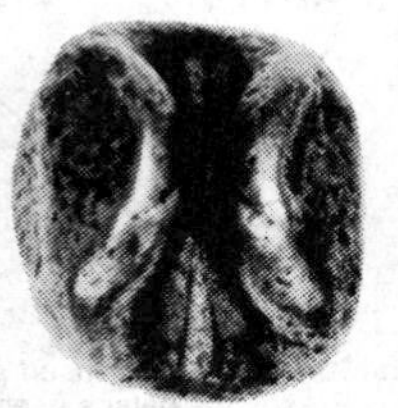

SILVER, 61.60 g

c/m: 8 dots in Chakra

C#	King	Mark	VG	Fine	VF	XF
139.1	Rama IV	Mongkut	225.00	350.00	450.00	800.00

c/m: 7 dots in Chakra

C#	King	Mark	VG	Fine	VF	XF
139.2	Rama IV	Mongkut	200.00	300.00	420.00	750.00

Cremation of Somdet P'ra Deb Sirindhra

C#	King	Mark	VG	Fine	VF	XF
189	Rama V					
		Cho Rampeuy	250.00	365.00	525.00	850.00

4-1/2 BAHT

SILVER

C#	King	Mark	VG	Fine	VF	XF
32	Rama III	Krut Sio	600.00	750.00	950.00	1200.

8 BAHT

SILVER, 123.20 g

C#	King	Mark	VG	Fine	VF	XF
33	Rama III	Krut Sio	625.00	800.00	1000.	1250.

2-1/2 TAMLUNG

(10 Baht)

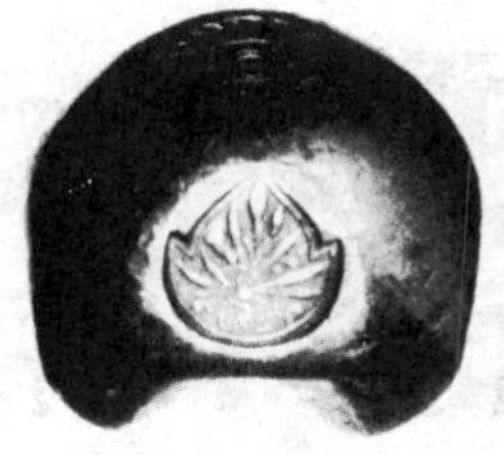

SILVER, 154.00 g

Cremation of Somdet P'ra Deb Sirindhra

C#	King	Mark	VG	Fine	VF	XF
190	Rama V					
		Cho Rampeuy	500.00	650.00	800.00	1000.

5 TAMLUNG

(20 Baht)

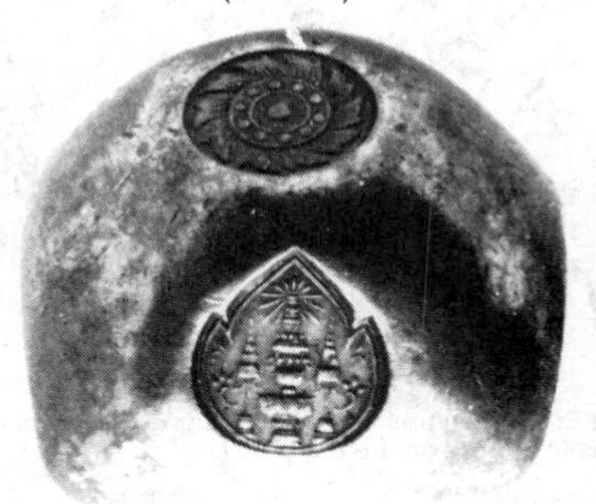

SILVER, 308.00 g

Cremation of Somdet P'ra Deb Sirindhra

C#	King	Mark	VG	Fine	VF	XF
191	Rama V					
		Cho Rampeuy	1200.	1500.	1850.	2250.

10 TAMLUNG

(40 Baht)

SILVER, 616.00 g

Cremation of Somdet P'ra Deb Sirindhra

C#	King	Mark	VG	Fine	VF	XF
192	Rama V					
		Cho Rampeuy	2250.	3000.	3750.	4500.

20 TAMLUNG

(80 Baht)

SILVER, 1185.-1232. g

Illustration reduced. Actual size: 65mm

Chakra-wheel engraved turning counterclockwise.

C#	King	Mark	VG	Fine	VF	XF
140.1	Rama IV	Mongkut	4500.	6000.	7500.	9000.

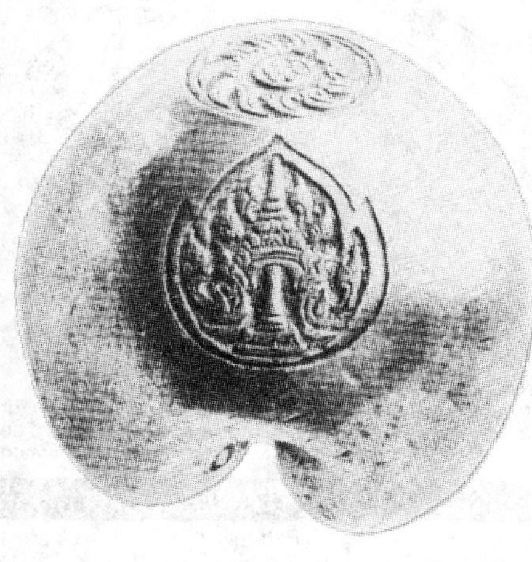

Chakra-wheel engraved turning clockwise.

C#	King	Mark	VG	Fine	VF	XF
140.2	Rama IV	Mongkut	4500.	6000.	7500.	9000.

Cremation of Somdet P'ra Deb Sirindhra

C#	King	Mark	VG	Fine	VF	XF
193	Rama V	Cho Rampeuy	4500.	6000.	7500.	9000.

GOLD POT DUANG

(Bullet Coins)

1/32 GOLD BAHT

GOLD, 0.48 g

C#	King	Mark	VG	Fine	VF	XF
152	Rama IV	P'ra Tao	60.00	90.00	115.00	175.00
162	Rama IV	Mongkut	—	—	—	—

1/16 GOLD BAHT

GOLD, 0.96 g

C#	King	Mark	VG	Fine	VF	XF
92	Rama III	Prasat	75.00	120.00	150.00	250.00
153	Rama IV	P'ra Tao	100.00	150.00	200.00	300.00
163	Rama IV	Mongkut	70.00	100.00	125.00	225.00

1/8 GOLD BAHT

GOLD, 1.96 g

C#	King	Mark	VG	Fine	VF	XF
93	Rama III	Prasat	125.00	175.00	250.00	350.00
103	Rama III	Dok Mai	150.00	200.00	300.00	400.00
113	Rama III	Bai Matum	150.00	200.00	300.00	400.00
154	Rama IV	P'ra Tao	100.00	150.00	200.00	275.00

1/4 GOLD BAHT

GOLD, 3.85 g

C#	King	Mark	VG	Fine	VF	XF
155	Rama IV	P'ra Tao	200.00	300.00	400.00	750.00
165	Rama IV	Mongkut	250.00	325.00	425.00	800.00

1/2 GOLD BAHT

GOLD, 7.70 g

C#	King	Mark	VG	Fine	VF	XF
105	Rama III	Dok Mai	—	—	Rare	—
166	Rama IV	Mongkut	250.00	400.00	700.00	1750.

GOLD BAHT

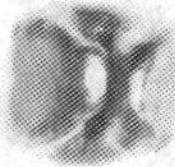

GOLD, 15.40 g

C#	King	Mark	VG	Fine	VF	XF
96	Rama III	Prasat	900.00	1750.	3250.	5500.
167	Rama IV	Mongkut	800.00	1650.	3000.	5000.

1-1/2 GOLD BAHT

(Met Kanoon)

GOLD, 23.10 g

C#	King	Mark	VG	Fine	VF	XF
167.5	Rama IV	Mongkut	—	—	Rare	—

NOTE: Unlike other bullet coins this does not have its ends hammered into the normal bullet configuration.

2 GOLD BAHT

GOLD, 30.80 g

C#	King	Mark	VG	Fine	VF	XF
168	Rama IV	Mongkut	—	—	Rare	—

4 GOLD BAHT

GOLD, 61.60 g

C#	King	Mark	VG	Fine	VF	XF
169	Rama IV	Mongkut	—	—	Rare	—

TRANSITIONAL COINAGE

A series of hammered flat coinage ordered by Rama IV to alleviate a shortage in small bullet coinage while awaiting arrival of the modern coinage presses from England.

FUANG

SILVER, 1.85 g, uniface
Obv: *Chakra* above Royal Crown and *P'ra Tao* at left and right.

C#	Date	Mintage	VG	Fine	VF	XF
170	ND(c.1856)	—	250.00	425.00	600.00	850.00

2.00 g, 15mm
Obv: Royal Crown.
Rev. leg: *Krungthep* (Bangkok).

C#	Date	Mintage	VG	Fine	VF	XF
173	ND(c.1856)	—	—	—	Rare	—

SALUNG

SILVER, 3.70 g, uniface
Obv: *Chakra* above Royal Crown and *P'ra Tao* at left and right.

C#	Date	Mintage	VG	Fine	VF	XF
171	ND(c.1856)	—	275.00	450.00	625.00	900.00

Obv: Royal Crown.
Rev. leg: *Krungthep* (Bangkok).

C#	Date	Mintage	VG	Fine	VF	XF
174	ND(c.1856)	—	—	—	Rare	—

GOLD 1/2 FUANG

GOLD, 1.00 g, uniface
Obv: *Chakra* above Royal Crown and *P'ra Tao* at left and right.

C#	Date	Mintage	VG	Fine	VF	XF
172	ND(c.1856)	—	—	—	Rare	—

GOLD FUANG

GOLD, 1.80 g
Obv: Royal Crown.
Rev. leg: *Krungthep* (Bangkok).

C#	Date	Mintage	VG	Fine	VF	XF
175	ND(c.1856)	—	—	—	*Rare	—

***NOTE:** Taisei-Baldwin-Gillio Singapore sale 3-96 AU realized $42,000.

GOLD SALUNG

GOLD, 3.80 g
Obv: Royal Crown.
Rev. leg: *Krungthep* (Bangkok).

C#	Date	Mintage	VG	Fine	VF	XF
176	ND(c.1856)	—	—	—	Rare	—

COUNTERMARKED TRADE COINAGE

Foreign trade brought in quantities of Latin American silver 8 reales which were not widely accepted by the public. As a result many were then officially countermarked with the royal marks "Chakra and "Mongkut" in the period 1858-1860 to guarantee their current exchange value.

DOLLAR

.903 SILVER
c/m: *Chakra* and *Mongkut* on Mexico-Chihuahua 8 Reales, KM#377.2.

C#	Date	Year	Good	VG	Fine	VF
141.1	ND	(1831-57)	350.00	600.00	1000.	1500.

c/m: *Chakra* and *Mongkut* on Mexico-Durango 8 Reales, KM#377.4.

C#	Date	Year	Good	VG	Fine	VF
141.4	ND	(1825-57)	400.00	700.00	1150.	1650.

c/m: *Chakra* and *Mongkut* on Mexico-Guanajanto 8 Reales, KM#377.8.

C#	Date	Year	Good	VG	Fine	VF
141.6	ND	(1825-57)	300.00	550.00	950.00	1450.

c/m: *Chakra* and *Mongkut* on Mexico City 8 Reales, KM#377.10.

C#	Date	Year	Good	VG	Fine	VF
141.8	ND	(1824-57)	300.00	550.00	950.00	1450.

c/m: *Chakra* and *Mongkut* on Mexico-Zacatecas 8 Reales, KM#377.13.

C#	Date	Year	Good	VG	Fine	VF
141.11	ND	(1825-57)	400.00	700.00	1150.	1650.

c/m: *Chakra* and *Mongkut* on Peru-Cuzco 8 Reales, KM#142.4.

C#	Date	Year	Good	VG	Fine	VF
141.14	ND	(1830-34)	450.00	800.00	1250.	1750.

NOTE: The *Mongkut* c/m illustrated is believed to be a modern fabrication.

c/m: *Chakra* and *Mongkut* on Peru-Lima 8 Reales, KM#142.10.

141.17	ND	(1841-55)	450.00	800.00	1250.	1750.

c/m: *Chakra* and *Mongkut* on Philippines countermarked 8 Reales, KM#129.

141.20	ND	(1825-57)	600.00	1000.	1750.	2500.

LOCAL COINAGE

The following tin coins were struck in 5 of the 7 districts formerly comprising the Kingdom of Patani, during the period of Thai Suzerainty (1832-1902).

JARING

(Jering)

All coins of Jaring are uniface

One of the 7 provinces cut out of Patani State after the uprising of 1830/31. It lies on the east coast of the Malay peninsula. The uniface tin coins were made from 1845 to 1894.

TITLES

Jering جريج

PITIS

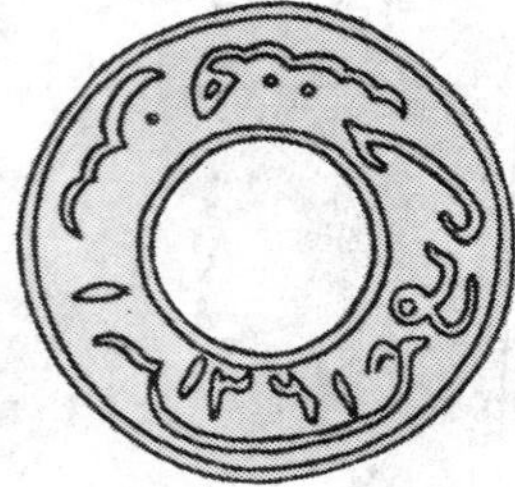

TIN

Arabic leg: *Ini Pitis Jering Sanat 1261*

KM#	Date	Good	VG	Fine	VF
1	AH1261	10.00	15.00	35.00	70.00

Arabic leg: *Ini Pitis Balad Jarin Sanat 1297*

KM#	Date	Good	VG	Fine	VF
2	AH1297	10.00	15.00	35.00	70.00

Arabic leg: *Hadha al-Diwan al-Raj al-Adil Fi Balad al-Jarin 1302*

KM#	Date	Good	VG	Fine	VF
3	AH1302	11.50	17.50	40.00	80.00
	1312	11.50	17.50	40.00	80.00

Crude imitation of KM#3

KM#	Date	Good	VG	Fine	VF
3a	ND	7.00	12.00	20.00	45.00

LEGEH

Ligeh, Ligor, Langkat

One of the inland provinces cut out of Patani State. Coins attributable to Legeh run from 1840 to 1893. Siam again assumed control in 1902.

TITLES

Dar es-Salam دار السلام

Negri Ligkeh نكري لغكه

PITIS

TIN

Obv. leg: Arabic *Pitis Negeri Langkat Dar al-Salam.* Rev. leg: Arabic *Malik al Adil Khalifat al-Mu'minin.*

KM#	Date	Good	VG	Fine	VF
1	ND	13.50	22.50	45.00	85.00

NOTE: For a piece dated 1256, sometimes attributed to Legeh, see KM#4 of Kelantan (Malaysia).

Obv. leg: Arabic *Al-Sultan al-Muzaffar Daulat Langkat Khalifat.* Rev. leg: Arabic *Al-Shamar Wal-Qamar Fi Rabi al-Awal Sanat 1307*

KM#	Date	Good	VG	Fine	VF
2	AH1307	8.00	16.00	35.00	70.00
	1313	—	Reported, not confirmed		

PATANI

Pattani

Patani (Pattani), a former Malay state in the Malay peninsula, is a small province or 'changwat' of Thailand (Siam) on the eastern side of peninsula Thailand near the border of Malaya, has an area of 777 sq. mi. (2,012 sq. km.) and a population of about 275,000. After the 1830/31 uprising it was one of 7 provinces administered by Siam through Malayan governors. Patani was the most prolific coin issuer of the Siamese period having made coins periodically from 1845 to 1891. Formerly ruled by a Moslem Rajah subject to Siam.

TITLES

Khalifa(t) al-Karam خليفة الكرم

al-Patani الفطاني

PITIS

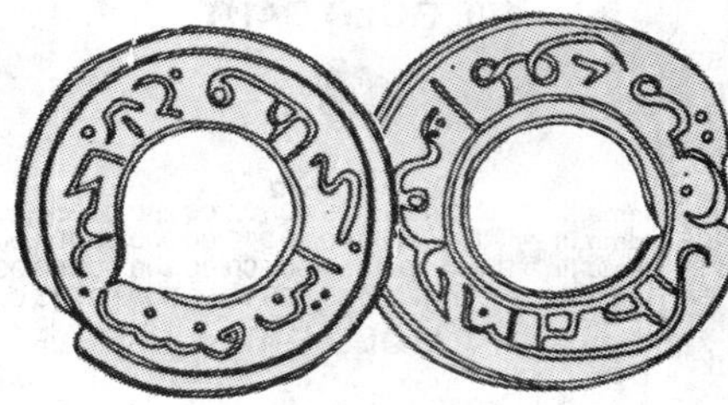

TIN

Obv. leg: Arabic *Ini Pitis Belanja Raja Patani.* Rev. leg: Arabic *Khalifat al-Mu'minin Sanat 1261.*

KM#	Date	Good	VG	Fine	VF
1	AH1261	7.50	12.50	20.00	30.00

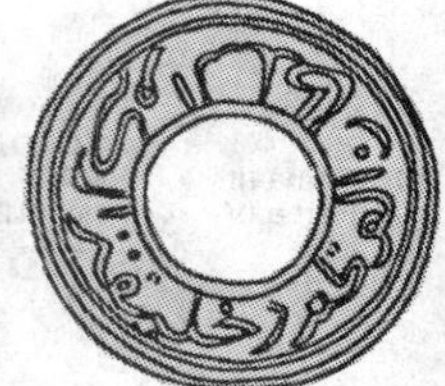

Obv. leg: Arabic *al-Sultan al-Azam Wa Khalifat al-Karam.* Rev. leg: Arabic *Al-Malik al-Balad al-Patani al-Imami 1284*

KM#	Date	Good	VG	Fine	VF
2	AH1284	7.50	12.50	20.00	30.00

Obv. leg: Arabic *al-Sultan al-Patani Sanat 1297.* Rev. leg: Arabic *Wa Khalifat al-Karam.*

KM#	Date	Good	VG	Fine	VF
3	AH1297	7.50	12.50	20.00	30.00

Obv. leg: Arabic *al-Matsaraf Fi Balad al-Patania Sanat 1301.* Rev. leg: Arabic *Zarb FI Harat al-Daulat Azza Nasrahu* incuse.

KM#	Date	Good	VG	Fine	VF
4	AH1301	12.50	17.50	27.50	40.00

Obv. leg: Arabic *al-Matsaraf Fi Balad al-Patani Sanat 1309.* Rev. leg: Arabic *Ini Pitis Belanja di-Dalam Negri Patani* in relief.

KM#	Date	Good	VG	Fine	VF
5	AH1309	7.50	12.50	20.00	30.00

KUPANG

GOLD

Obv: Bull standing to left.
Rev. leg: Arabic *Malik al-Adil* in 2 lines.

KM#	Date	Year	Fine	VF	XF	Unc
50	ND	(1800-50)	45.00	50.00	65.00	90.00

Obv: Bull standing to left.
Rev. leg: Arabic *al-Adil*

KM#	Date	Year	Fine	VF	XF	Unc
51	ND	(1800-50)	45.00	50.00	65.00	90.00

Obv: Bull standing to left.
Rev. leg: Arabic *Malik al-Adil* in 3 lines.

KM#	Date	Year	Fine	VF	XF	Unc
52	ND	(1800-50)	45.00	50.00	65.00	90.00

Obv: Bull standing to left.
Rev. leg: Arabic *Asma Adil.*

KM#	Date	Year	Fine	VF	XF	Unc
53	ND	(1800-50)	45.00	50.00	65.00	90.00

Obv: Bull standing to right.
Rev. leg: Arabic *Malik al-Adil* in 2 lines.

KM#	Date	Year	Fine	VF	XF	Unc
54	ND	(1800-50)	60.00	85.00	115.00	150.00

Obv: 8-pointed star.
Rev. leg: Arabic *Malik al-Adil.*

KM#	Date	Year	Fine	VF	XF	Unc
55	ND	(1800-50)	50.00	60.00	80.00	120.00

Obv: 6-pointed star.
Rev. leg: Arabic *Malik al-Adil.*

KM#	Date	Year	Fine	VF	XF	Unc
56	ND	(1800-50)	45.00	50.00	65.00	90.00

Obv: 4-petalled flower.
Rev. leg: Arabic *Malik al-Adil.*

KM#	Date	Year	Fine	VF	XF	Unc
57	ND	(1800-50)	50.00	60.00	75.00	100.00

Obv. leg: Arabic *Dama Shah.*
Rev. leg: Arabic *Binaqdi Sahibi.*

KM#	Date	Year	Fine	VF	XF	Unc
58	ND	(1800-50)	50.00	60.00	75.00	100.00

Obv. leg: Arabic *Shah Adil.*
Rev. leg: Arabic *Malik al-Adil.*

KM#	Date	Year	Fine	VF	XF	Unc
59	ND	(1800-50)	50.00	60.00	75.00	100.00

Obv. leg: Arabic *al-Julus Kelantan.*
Rev. leg: Arabic *al-Mutawakkilu Ala Liah.*

KM#	Date	Year	Fine	VF	XF	Unc
60	ND	(1800-50)	50.00	60.00	75.00	100.00

Obv. leg: Arabic *Aqam'u'd-Din.*
Rev. leg: Arabic *Malik al-Adil.*

KM#	Date	Year	Fine	VF	XF	Unc
61	ND	(1800-50)	50.00	60.00	75.00	100.00

Obv. leg: Arabic *Shah Alam.*
Rev. leg: Arabic *Malik al-Adil.*

KM#	Date	Year	Fine	VF	XF	Unc
62	ND	(1800-50)	50.00	60.00	75.00	100.00

Obv. leg: Arabic *Sultan.*
Rev. leg: Arabic *Mu'azzam Shah.*

KM#	Date	Year	Fine	VF	XF	Unc
63	ND	(1800-50)	60.00	70.00	90.00	130.00

Obv. leg: Arabic *Sultan Muhammad.*
Rev. leg: Arabic *Mu'azzam Shah.*

KM#	Date	Year	Fine	VF	XF	Unc
64	ND	(1800-50)	60.00	70.00	90.00	130.00

Obv. leg: Arabic *al-Julus Kelantan.*
Rev. leg: Arabic *Khalifata'r-Rahman.*

KM#	Date	Year	Good	Fine	VF	XF	Unc
65	ND(1800-50)		—	40.00	50.00	70.00	100.00

REMAN

Rhaman

Another of the inland provinces cut from Patani State. Only a single type tin coin is presently known from Reman. This piece was minted about 1890.

TITLES

رحمن

Rehman

PITIS

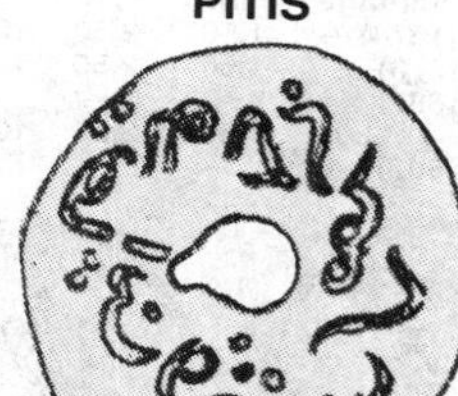

TIN

Uniface. Retrograde Arabic leg: *Ini Pitis Rahman Raja Melayu*

KM#	Date	Good	VG	Fine	VF
1	ND	12.50	22.50	45.00	85.00

SAI

Saiburi, Teluban

Sai is one of the provinces on the east coast of Malaya cut from the state of Patani. The tin Pitis of this province were made from c.1870 to 1891 and are distinctive in that they have a reverse that bears no legend. It carries only a decorative motif.

TITLES

السيوي

al-Saiwi

PITIS

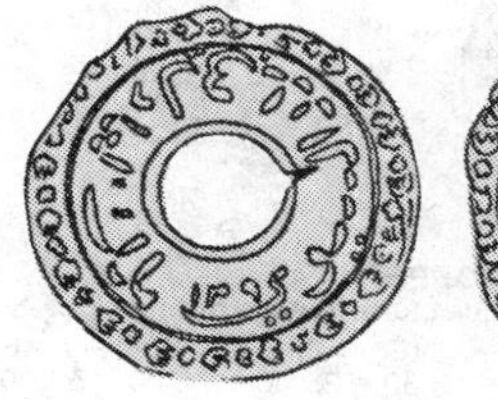

TIN

Obv. leg: Arabic *Malik al-Adil Fi Balad al-Saiwi 1290*

KM#	Date	Good	VG	Fine	VF
1	AH1290	12.50	20.00	30.00	60.00

Obv. leg: Arabic *al-Dawlat al-Khairiyat Fi Balad al-Saiwi 1307*

KM#	Date	Good	VG	Fine	VF
2	AH1307	12.50	20.00	30.00	60.00

NOTE: A number of Chinese token issues are tentatively assigned to the Patani state of Jala (Jalor).

SINGGORA

Songkhla

Singgora (modern Songkhla) was an important seaport and trading center on the Gulf of Siam on the eastern side of peninsular Thailand and just a few miles north of the border with Malaya. It borders Patani province to the southeast. Songkhla remains a key commercial center today. Its rare coinage from the early 19th century features Arabic legends on obverse and chinese characters on reverse, clearly indicating the influence of Chinese traders in its economy.

Negri Singgora

نگرى سڠگور

PITIS

TIN

Obv: Arabic leg. including mint name.
Rev: Chinese characters.

KM#	Date	Good	VG	Fine	VF
1	ND	—	—	Rare	—

Obv: Arabic leg. with mint name and date.
Rev: Chinese characters.

KM#	Date	Good	VG	Fine	VF
2	AH1241	—	—	Rare	—

THAILAND

REGULAR COINAGE

1/16 FUANG

(1 Solot)

TIN

Dark color and crude rims. Usually plain edge.

Y#	Date	Year	VG	Fine	VF	XF
5	ND	(1862)	1.00	2.50	6.00	18.00

NOTE: Rotated dies are common.

Y#	Date	Year	VG	Fine	VF	XF
16	ND	(1868)	5.00	10.00	20.00	45.00

1/2 ATT

(1 Solot)

COPPER

Y#	Date	Mintage	Fine	VF	XF	Unc
17	CS1236(1874)	—	1.00	2.00	9.00	45.00
	1244(1882)	2.560	1.00	2.00	9.00	45.00
	1244(1882)	—	—	—	Proof	200.00

COPPER-NICKEL

Y#	Date	Mintage	Fine	VF	XF	Unc
17a	CS1244(1882)	—	75.00	150.00	300.00	1000.

BRONZE

Y#	Date	Mintage	Fine	VF	XF	Unc
21	CS1249(1887)	—	2.00	5.00	18.00	165.00
	RS109(1890)	10.240	1.00	2.00	12.00	100.00
	118(1899)	—	1.00	2.00	12.00	100.00
	118(1899)	—	—	—	Proof	1250.

NOTE: Later date (1905) exists for this type.

NOTE: These coins were also minted in RS114, RS115, RS121, and RS122. The last year had a mintage of 5,120,000. Coins with these dates have not been observed and were probably additional mintings of coins dated RS109 and RS118. A nickel pattern dated RS114 does exist. Varieties in numeral size and rotated dies exist.

1/8 FUANG

(1 Att)

TIN
Dark color, reeded edge.
Obv: Large elephant. Rev: Lower row of jewels in crown between lines.

Y#	Date	Year	VG	Fine	VF	XF
6.1	ND	(1862)	2.00	5.00	10.00	25.00

Rev: Lower row of jewels in crown enclosed.

Y#	Date	Year	VG	Fine	VF	XF
6.2	ND	(1862)	1.50	4.00	9.00	18.00

Obv: Small elephant. Rev: Lower row of jewels in crown between lines.

Y#	Date	Year	VG	Fine	VF	XF
6.3	ND	(1862)	1.50	4.00	9.00	18.00

Rev: Lower row of jewels in crown enclosed.

Y#	Date	Year	VG	Fine	VF	XF
6.4	ND	(1862)	5.00	10.00	20.00	50.00

NOTE: Rotated dies are common.

ATT

(1/64 Baht)

COPPER

Y#	Date	Mintage	Fine	VF	XF	Unc
18	CS1236(1874)	—	1.50	2.50	10.00	80.00
	1238(1876)	—	1.50	2.50	10.00	80.00
	1244(1882)	15.300	1.50	2.50	10.00	80.00
	1244(1882)	—	—	—	Proof	275.00

BRONZE

Y#	Date	Mintage	Fine	VF	XF	Unc
22	CS1249(1887)	—	2.00	4.00	15.00	135.00
	RS109(1890)	10.240	1.50	2.50	8.50	100.00
	114*(1895)	5.120	1.50	3.00	10.00	115.00
	115(1896)	—	1.50	3.00	10.00	115.00
	118(1899)	—	1.50	3.00	10.00	115.00
	118(1899)	—	—	—	Proof	850.00

NOTE: Later dates (1902-1905) exist for this type.

***NOTE:** RS114 and RS122 exist with large (greater than 1mm) and small (less than 1mm) numerals.

NOTE: Full red uncirculated coins of this type carry a substantial premium.

1/4 FUANG

(1/32 Baht = 1 Sio)

COPPER
Thick (2.5mm) planchet, crude with plain edge.

Y#	Date	Year	VG	Fine	VF	XF
1	ND	(1865)	15.00	35.00	75.00	150.00

BRASS

Y#	Date	Year	VG	Fine	VF	XF
1a	ND	(1865)	15.00	40.00	80.00	150.00

Thin (1.5mm) planchet

Y#	Date	Year	VG	Fine	VF	XF
3	ND	(1865)	15.00	35.00	65.00	125.00

NOTE: Rotated dies are common.

2 ATT

(1/32 Baht = 1 Sio)

COPPER

Y#	Date	Mintage	Fine	VF	XF	Unc
19	CS1236(1874)	—	2.00	4.00	15.00	125.00
	1238(1876)	—	2.00	4.00	15.00	120.00
	1244(1882)	10.200	2.00	4.00	15.00	120.00

BRONZE

Y#	Date	Mintage	Fine	VF	XF	Unc
23	CS1249(1887)	—	3.50	7.00	25.00	275.00
	RS109(1890)	5.120	1.50	3.00	12.00	110.00
	114(1895)	—	1.50	3.00	12.00	110.00
	115(1896)	—	1.50	3.00	12.00	110.00
	118(1899)	—	1.50	3.00	12.00	110.00
	119(1900)	.735	2.50	5.00	20.00	150.00

NOTE: Later dates (1902-1905) exist for this type.

NOTE: Varieties in numeral size and rotated dies exist.

NOTE: Full red uncirculated coins of this type carry a substantial premium.

1/2 FUANG

(1/16 Baht = 1 Sik)

COPPER
Thick (3mm) planchet. Crude, plain edges.

Y#	Date	Year	VG	Fine	VF	XF
2	ND	(1865)	10.00	20.00	45.00	125.00

BRASS

Y#	Date	Year	VG	Fine	VF	XF
2a	ND	(1865)	12.00	25.00	55.00	135.00

Thin (1.5mm) planchet.

Y#	Date	Year	VG	Fine	VF	XF
4	ND	(1865)	12.00	25.00	85.00	200.00

NOTE: Rotated dies are common.

1/16 BAHT

(1 Sik)

SILVER, 1.00 g
Thick Flan

Y#	Date	Mintage	Fine	VF	XF	Unc
7.1 (Y7)	ND(1860)	—	15.00	30.00	125.00	400.00

Obv: Smaller crown, Rev: Larger elephant.

Y#	Date	Mintage	Fine	VF	XF	Unc
7.2 (Y7.1)	ND(1860)	—	20.00	35.00	150.00	475.00

.900 GOLD, 1.00 g
Reeded edge. Thin flan.

Y#	Date	Mintage	Fine	VF	XF	Unc
7a	ND(1864)	—	—	—	—	—

4 ATT

(1/16 Baht = 1 Sik)

COPPER

Y#	Date	Mintage	Fine	VF	XF	Unc
20	CS1238(1876)	—	20.00	60.00	185.00	600.00

NOTE: Frequently counterfeited.

FUANG

(1/8 Baht)

SILVER, 1.94 g
Thick flan
Denomination indicated by number of stars outside chakra; 1 star = 1/8 Baht.

Y#	Date	Mintage	Fine	VF	XF	Unc
8	ND(1860)	—	4.00	9.00	45.00	160.00

.900 GOLD, 1.94 g
Reeded edge. Thin flan.

Y#	Date	Mintage	Fine	VF	XF	Unc
8a	ND(1864)	—	800.00	1600.	3000.	5000.

SILVER, 1.89 g

Y#	Date	Mintage	Fine	VF	XF	Unc
28	ND(1868)	—	4.00	8.00	45.00	160.00

Y#	Date	Mintage	Fine	VF	XF	Unc
32	ND(1876-1900)	—	3.00	7.00	30.00	90.00
	ND(1876-1900)	—	—	—	Proof	2500.

GOLD

Y#	Date	Mintage	Fine	VF	XF	Unc
32b	ND(1876)	—	800.00	1600.	3500.	6000.

SALUNG

(1/4 Baht)

SILVER, 3.71 g
Denomination indicated by number of stars outside chakra; 2 stars = 1/4 Baht.

Y#	Date	Mintage	Fine	VF	XF	Unc
9	ND(1860)	—	12.00	25.00	120.00	375.00

GOLD, 3.71 g

Y#	Date	Mintage	Fine	VF	XF	Unc
9a	ND(1864)	—	—	—	—	—

SILVER, 3.82 g

Y#	Date	Mintage	Fine	VF	XF	Unc
29	ND(1868)	—	8.00	17.50	80.00	260.00

Y#	Date	Mintage	Fine	VF	XF	Unc
33	ND(1876-1900)	—	6.00	15.00	45.00	175.00
	ND(1876-1900)	—	—	—	Proof	2700.

2 SALUNG

(1/2 Baht)

SILVER, 7.54 g
Denomination indicated by number of stars outside chakra; 4 stars = 1/2 Baht.

Y#	Date	Mintage	Fine	VF	XF	Unc
10.1	ND(1860)	—	35.00	180.00	400.00	1000.

GOLD, 7.55 g

Y#	Date	Mintage	Fine	VF	XF	Unc
10.2a	ND(1864)	—	—	—	*Rare	—

***NOTE:** Spink-Taisei Auction #15, 9-93 Unc. realized $23,000.

Reeded edge.

Y#	Date	Mintage	Fine	VF	XF	Unc
15.5	ND(1895)	—	—	—	—	—

BAHT

15.4500 g, .900 SILVER, .4470 oz ASW
Denomination indicated by number of stars outside chakra; 8 stars = 1 Baht.

Y#	Date	Mintage	Fine	VF	XF	Unc
11	ND(1860)	—	15.00	25.00	125.00	375.00

GOLD, 15.25 g

Y#	Date	Mintage	Fine	VF	XF	Unc
11a	ND(1864)	—	—	—	*Rare	—

***NOTE:** Spink-Taisei Auction #15, 9-93 Unc. realized $34,000.

SILVER

Y#	Date	Mintage	Fine	VF	XF	Unc
31	ND(1868)	—	15.00	25.00	120.00	400.00

Y#	Date	Mintage	Fine	VF	XF	Unc
34	ND(1876-1900)	—	5.00	10.00	40.00	165.00
	ND(1876-1900)	—	—	—	Proof	6000.

Queen's Royal Mint Visit
Obv. leg: *Rong Krasab* (Royal Mint) and RS date 116 added in field.

Y#	Date	Mintage	Fine	VF	XF	Unc
B34	RS116(1897)	—	—	—	5000.	7000.

2 BAHT

30.2000 g, .900 SILVER, .8738 oz ASW

Denomination indicated by number of stars outside chakra; 16 stars = 2 Baht.

Y#	Date	Mintage	Fine	VF	XF	Unc
12	ND(ca.1863)	—	175.00	375.00	650.00	1400.

GOLD, 30.30 g

Y#	Date	Mintage	Fine	VF	XF	Unc
12a	ND(1864)	—	—	—	*Rare	—

***NOTE:** Spink-Taisei Auction #15, 9-93 Unc. realized $44,000.

POT DUENG

(2-1/2 BAHT)

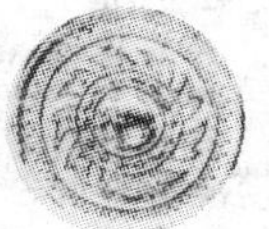

***.997 GOLD, 2.20 g**
Rev: Crude elephant.

Y#	Date	Mintage	Fine	VF	XF	Unc
13	ND(1863)	—	800.00	1500.	2500.	4000.

GOLD, 1.90-2.00 g

Y#	Date	Mintage	Fine	VF	XF	Unc
13.1	ND(1895)	—	650.00	1250.	2000.	2800.

Rev: Refined elephant.

Y#	Date	Mintage	Fine	VF	XF	Unc
13.5	ND(1895)	—	600.00	1000.	1800.	2600.

TAMLUNG

(4 Baht)

60.4000 g, .900 SILVER, 1.7477 oz ASW
60th Birthday of Rama IV
Plain edge

Y#	Date	Mintage	Fine	VF	XF	Unc
A12	ND(1864)	—	—	—	*Rare	—

***NOTE:** Spink-Taisei Auction #15, 9-93 Unc. realized $16,000.

.997 GOLD, 60.77 g

Y#	Date	Mintage	Fine	VF	XF	Unc
A12a	ND(1864)	—	—	—	Rare	—

NOTE: Spink-Taisei Auction #4, 2-88, XF specimen realized $74,800.

PIT

(4 Baht)

Reeded edge, 3.40 g.
Rev: Crude elephant.

Y#	Date	Mintage	Fine	VF	XF	Unc
14	ND(1863)	—	1000.	1500.	2300.	4000.

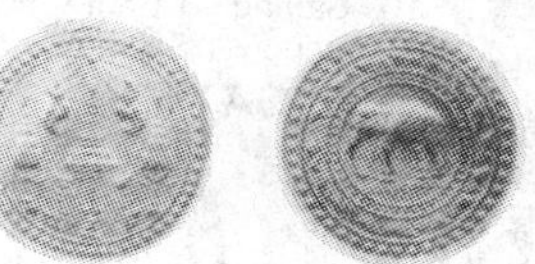

3.65-4.00 g
Rev: Refined elephant.

Y#	Date	Mintage	Fine	VF	XF	Unc
14.5	ND(1895)	—	1000.	1600.	2500.	3500.

TOT
(8 Baht)

.997 GOLD, 6.80 g
Reeded edge.
Rev: Crude elephant.

Y#	Date	Mintage	Fine	VF	XF	Unc
15	ND(1863)	—	1250.	2500.	4500.	10,000.

GOLD, 7.30-8.00 g

Y#	Date	Mintage	Fine	VF	XF	Unc
15.1	ND(1895)	—	1000.	1750.	2800.	6500.

Rev: Refined elephant.

Y#	Date	Mintage	Fine	VF	XF	Unc
15.6	ND(1895)	—	— Reported, not confirmed			

PRESENTATION COINAGE
Bannakarn (Royal Gift) Coins

FUANG
(1/8 Baht)

SILVER, 2.00 g, plain edge
Similar to 1/8 Baht, Y#8.
Obv: Larger crown.

KM#	Date	Year	Mintage	VF	XF	Unc
11	ND	(1857-58)	—	1000.	1500.	2750.

SALUNG
(1/4 Baht)

SILVER, 3.90 g
Plain edge

KM#	Date	Year	Mintage	VF	XF	Unc
12	ND	(1857-58)	—	1250.	2250.	3250.

1/2 BAHT

SILVER
Plain edge

KM#	Date	Year	Mintage	VF	XF	Unc
13	ND	(1857-58)	—	—	Rare	—

NOTE: The total mintage for KM#11-13 equalled 840 Baht.

1 BAHT

SILVER, 15.50 g
Milled edge

KM#	Date	Year	Mintage	VF	XF	Unc
14	ND	(1857-58)	2,400	1500.	2500.	3500.
	ND	(c.1868)	—	—	Rare	—

NOTE: Spink-Taisei Auction #4, Feb. 1988, realized $20,125.

POT DUENG
(2-1/2 Baht)

GOLD, 2.15 g

KM#	Date	Year	Mintage	VF	XF	Unc
10	ND	(1857-58)	—	—	Rare	—

DECIMAL COINAGE
100 Satang = 1 Baht
25 Satang = 1 Salung

2-1/2 SATANG

COPPER-NICKEL

Y#	Date	Year	Mintage	VF	XF	Unc
24	RS116H	(1897)	5.080	3.00	5.00	10.00
	116H	(1897)	—	—	Proof	25.00

NOTE: Issued in 1898 although dated RS116 (1897).

5 SATANG

COPPER-NICKEL

Y#	Date	Year	Mintage	VF	XF	Unc
25	RS116H	(1897)	5.080	10.00	15.00	40.00
	116H	(1897)	—	—	Proof	75.00

NOTE: Issued in 1898 although dated RS116 (1897).

10 SATANG

COPPER-NICKEL

Y#	Date	Year	Mintage	VF	XF	Unc
26	RS116H	(1897)	3.810	20.00	50.00	150.00
	116H	(1897)	—	—	Proof	185.00

20 SATANG

COPPER-NICKEL

Y#	Date	Year	Mintage	VF	XF	Unc
27	RS116H	(1897)	3.126	10.00	22.00	55.00

PATTERNS (Pn)
(Including off metal strikes)

KM#	Date	Mintage	Identification	Mkt.Val.
Pn1	ND(1857-58)	—	1/8 Baht, Copper, KM11	—
Pn2	ND(1860)	—	1/16 Baht, Copper, Y7	130.00
Pn3	ND(1860)	—	1/16 Baht, White Metal, Y7	200.00
Pn4	ND(1860)	—	1/8 Baht, Copper, Y8	120.00
Pn5	ND(1860)	—	1/8 Baht, White Metal, Y8	200.00
Pn6	ND(1860)	—	1/4 Baht, Copper, Y9	250.00
Pn7	ND(1860)	—	1/4 Baht, White Metal, Y9	400.00

KM#	Date	Mintage	Identification	Mkt.Val.
Pn8	ND(1860)	—	1/4 Baht(?), Copper, w/o stars	350.00
Pn9	ND(1860)	—	1/2 Baht, Copper, Y10	400.00
Pn10	ND(1860)	—	1/2 Baht, White Metal, Y10	700.00
Pn11	ND(1860)	—	1 Baht, Copper, Y11	650.00
Pn12	ND(1860)	—	1 Baht, White Metal, Y11	1250.

KM#	Date	Mintage	Identification	Mkt.Val.
Pn13	ND(1860)	—	2 Baht, Copper, lg. elephant, Y12	1000.
Pn14	ND(1860)	—	2 Baht, White Metal, Y12	1750.

KM#	Date	Mintage	Identification	Mkt.Val.
Pn15	ND(1860)	—	2 Baht, Copper, sm. elephant, plain edge	800.00
Pn16	ND(1860)	—	4 Baht, White Metal, Y12	4000.
Pn17	ND(1860)	—	4 Baht, Gold, w/single outline around Thai leg., YA12a	Rare
Pn18	ND(1868)	—	1/16 Baht, Silver	1000.
Pn19	ND(1868)	—	1/16 Baht, Copper	160.00
Pn20	ND(1868)	—	1/8 Baht, Silver	1000.
Pn21	ND(1868)	—	1/8 Baht, Copper	250.00

KM#	Date	Mintage	Identification	Mkt.Val.
Pn22	ND(1868)	—	1/4 Baht, Silver	1000.
Pn23	ND(1868)	—	1/4 Baht, Copper	350.00
Pn24	ND(1868)	—	1/2 Baht, Silver	—
Pn25	ND(1868)	—	1/2 Baht, Copper	1000.
Pn26	ND(1868)	—	1/2 Baht, Nickel	1250.

KM#	Date	Mintage	Identification	Mkt.Val.
Pn27	ND(1868)	—	1 Baht, Silver	800.00
Pn28	ND(1868)	—	1 Baht, Copper	650.00
Pn29	ND(1868)	—	1 Baht, Nickel	1250.
Pn30	ND(1868)	—	2 Baht, Copper	1750.
Pn31	ND(1868)	—	2 Baht, Nickel	1250.

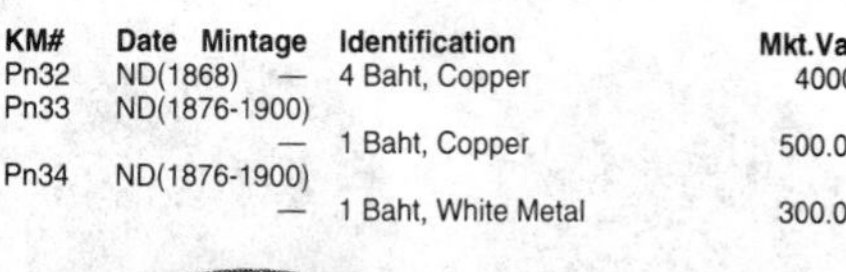

KM#	Date	Mintage	Identification	Mkt.Val.
Pn32	ND(1868)	—	4 Baht, Copper	4000.
Pn33	ND(1876-1900)	—	1 Baht, Copper	500.00
Pn34	ND(1876-1900)	—	1 Baht, White Metal	300.00

KM#	Date	Mintage	Identification	Mkt.Val.
Pn35	ND(1877)	—	2 Baht, Silver	12,500.
Pn36	ND(1877)	—	2 Baht, Copper	5000.
Pn37	ND(1877)	—	2 Baht, Bronzed Copper	5500.
Pn38	ND(1877)	—	2 Baht, White Metal	2000.

KM#	Date	Mintage	Identification	Mkt.Val.
Pn39	CS1249(1887)	—	2 Att, Nickel, Y23	375.00
Pn40	RS114(1895)	—	1/2 Att, Nickel	300.00

KM#	Date	Mintage	Identification	Mkt.Val.
Pn41	RS114(1895)	—	1 Att, Nickel	300.00
Pn42	RS114(1895)	—	2 Att, Nickel	5000.
Pn43	RS115(1896)	—	1 Att, Nickel	200.00
Pn44	RS118(1899)			

KM#	Date	Mintage	Identification	Mkt.Val.
Pn44		—	1/2 Att, Tin, Y21	—
Pn45	RS118(1899)	—	1 Att, Tin, Y22	—
Pn46	RS118(1899)	—	2 Att, Tin, Y23	—

TOKEN ISSUES (Tn)

(2 KEPING)

COPPER
Obv. leg: *Muang Thai* (Thailand).
Rev: Elephant.

KM#	Date	Year	Mintage	VF	XF	Unc
Tn1	CS1197	(1835)	500 pcs.	—	350.00	450.00
	CS1197	(1835)	—	—	Proof	350.00

GILT COPPER

KM#	Date	Year	Mintage	VF	XF	Unc
Tn1a	CS1197	(1835)	—	—	—	500.00

Rev: Lotus.

KM#	Date	Year	Mintage	VF	XF	Unc
Tn2	CS1197	(1835)	500 pcs.	—	325.00	400.00
	CS1197	(1835)	—	—	Proof	400.00

NOTE: Produced in England as samples for a medium to replace the circulating cowries. They met disfavor with Rama III and were never adopted.

MINT SETS (MS)

KM#	Date	Mintage	Identification	Issue Price	Mkt. Val.
MS1	ND(1895)(3)	—	Y13-15	—	—

TIBET

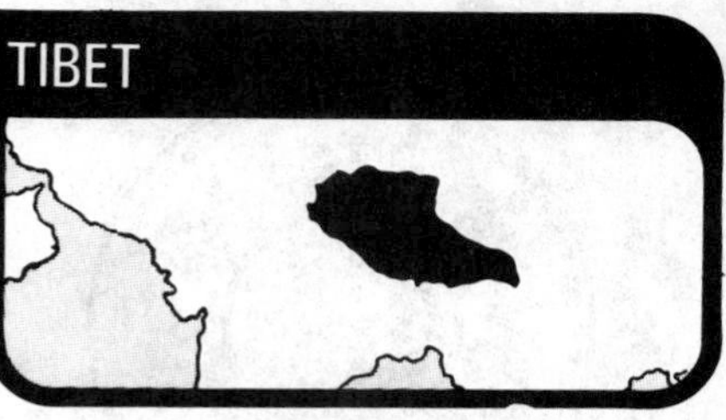

Tibet, an autonomous region of China located in central Asia between the Himalayan and Kunlun Mts. has an area of 471,660 sq. mi. (1,221,599 sq. km.) and a population of *1.9 million. Capital: Lhasa. The economy is based on agriculture and livestock raising. Wool, livestock, salt and hides are exported.

Lamaism, a form of Buddhism, developed in Tibet in the 8th century. From that time until the 1900s, the Tibetan rulers virtually isolated the country from the outside world. The British in India achieved some influence in the early 20th century, and encouraged Tibet to declare its independence from China in 1913. The Communist revolution in China marked a new era in Tibetan history. Chinese Communist troops invaded Tibet in Oct., 1950. After a token resistance, Tibet signed an agreement with China in which China recognized the spiritual and temporal leadership of the Dalai Lama, and Tibet recognized the suzerainty of China. In 1959, a nationwide revolt triggered by Communist-initiated land reform broke out. The revolt was ruthlessly crushed. The Dalai Lama fled to India, and on Sept. 1, 1965, the Chinese made Tibet an autonomous region of China.

The first coins to circulate in Tibet were those of neighboring Nepal from about 1570. Shortly after 1720, the Nepalese government began striking specific issues for use in Tibet. These coins had a lower silver content than those struck for use in Nepal and were exchanged with the Tibetans for an equal weight in silver bullion. Around 1763 the Tibetans struck their own coins for the first time in history. The number of coins struck at that time must have been very small. Larger quantities of coins were struck by the Tibetan government mint which opened in 1791 with the permission of the Chinese. Operations of this mint however were suspended two years later. The Chinese opened a second mint in Lhasa in 1792. It produced a coinage until 1836. Shortly thereafter, the Tibetan mint was reopened and the government of Tibet continued to strike coins until 1953.

DATING

Based on the Tibetan calendar, Tibetan coins are dated by the cycle which contains 60 years. To calculate the western date use the following formula: Number of cycles -1, x 60 + number of years + 1026. Example 15th cycle 25th year = 1891 AD. Example: 15th cycle, 25th year 15 - 1 x 60 + 25 + 1026 = 1891AD.

13/30 = 1776	**14/30 = 1836**	**15/30 = 1896**
13/40 = 1786	**14/40 = 1846**	**15/40 = 1906**
13/50 = 1796	**14/50 = 1856**	**15/50 = 1916**
13/60 = 1806	**14/60 = 1866**	**15/60 = 1926**
14/10 = 1816	**15/10 = 1876**	**16/10 = 1936**
14/20 = 1826	**15/20 = 1886**	**16/20 = 1946**

Certain Sino-Tibetan issues are dated in the year of reign of the Emperor of China.

MONETARY SYSTEM

15 Skar = 1-1/2 Sho = 1 Tangka
10 Sho = 1 Srang

TANGKA

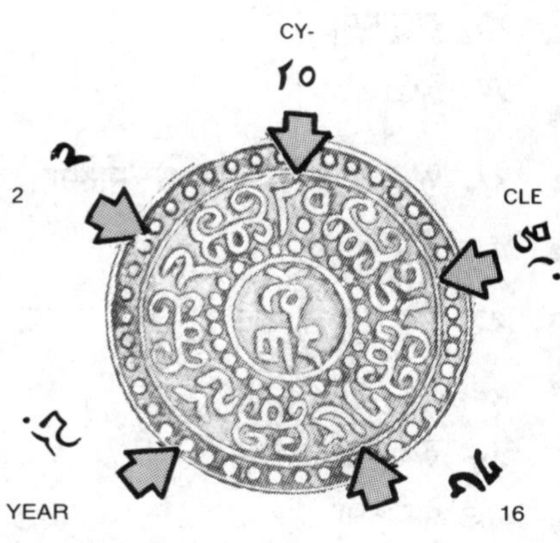

16(th)CYCLE 2(nd)YEAR = 1928AD

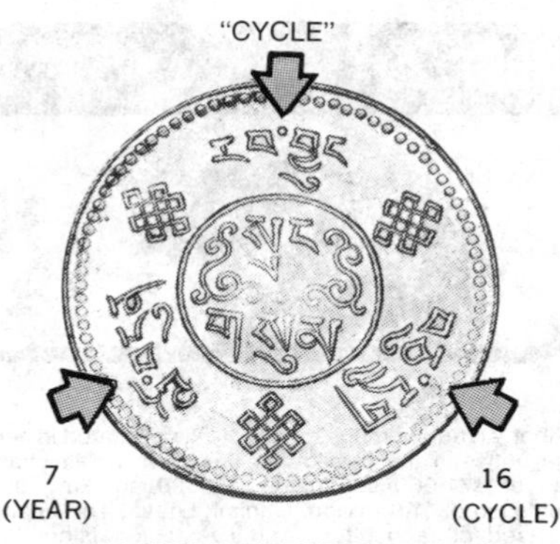

16(th) CYCLE 7(th) YEAR = 1933AD

NUMERALS

1	༡	གཅིག་		
2	༢	གཉིས་		
3	༣	གསུམ་		
4	༤	བཞི་		
5	༥	ལྔ་		
6	༦	དྲུག་		
7	༧	བདུན་		
8	༨	བརྒྱད་		
9	༩	དགུ་		
10	༡༠	བཅུ་	or	བཅུ་ཐམ་པ་
11	༡༡	བཅུག་	or	བཅུ་གཅིག་
12	༡༢	བཅུས་	or	བཅུ་གཉིས་
13	༡༣	བཅུ མ་	or	བཅུ་གསུམ་
14	༡༤	བཅུ་བཞི་		
15	༡༥	བཅོ་ལྔ་		
16	༡༦	བཅུ་དྲུག་		
17	༡༧	བཅུ་བདུན་		
18	༡༨	བཅོ་བརྒྱད་		
19	༡༩	བཅུ་དགུ་		
20	༢༠	ཉི་ཤུ		
21	༢༡	ཉི་ཤུ་ཙ་གཅིག་	or	ཉེར་གཅིག་
22	༢༢	ཉེར་གཉིས་		
23	༢༣	ཉེར་གསུམ་		
24	༢༤	ཉེར་ བཞི་		
25	༢༥	ཉེར་ ལྔ་		
26	༢༦	ཉེར་ དྲུག་		
27	༢༧	ཉེར་བདུན་		
28	༢༨	ཉེར་བརྒྱད་		

SINO-TIBETAN COINAGE

RULERS

Chia Ch'ing, 1796-1820
Tao Kuang, 1820-1851

Early Period: 1792-1836

SHO

SILVER, 3.40-3.80 g
25-29mm

C#	Date	Year	Good	VG	Fine	VF
83	8	(1803)	12.50	30.00	45.00	65.00
	9	(1804)	12.50	30.00	45.00	65.00
	24	(1819)	12.50	25.00	35.00	50.00
	25	(1820)	10.00	20.00	27.50	37.50

NOTE: Earlier dates (1-5) exist for this type.

***One Miscal* in Manchu script added, 30mm.**

C#	Date	Year	Good	VG	Fine	VF
85	6	(1801)	—	—	Rare	—

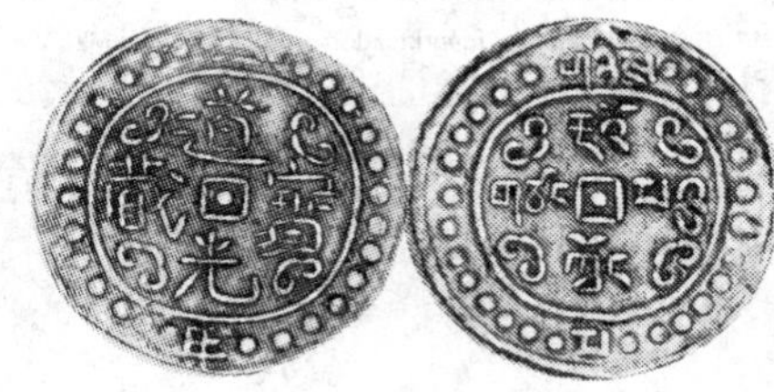

26-28mm

C#	Date	Year	Good	VG	Fine	VF
93	1	(1821)	25.00	40.00	70.00	100.00
	2	(1822)	10.00	15.00	25.00	40.00
	3	(1823)	10.00	15.00	25.00	40.00
	4	(1824)	15.00	30.00	40.00	60.00
	15	(1835)	30.00	40.00	60.00	90.00
	16	(1836)	30.00	40.00	60.00	90.00

TIBETAN COINAGE

'Kong-par' TANGKA

SILVER, 5.00-5.60 g
Rev: Sun and moon above date arch.

C#	Date	Year	Good	VG	Fine	VF
60.2	13-46	—	8.50	12.00	20.00	30.00

NOTE: It is believed that this type was struck in the 1820's. A variety w/reversed designs on the reverse exist.

4.20-5.60 g
Obv: Similar to C#60.1 but larger Buddhist characters.
Rev: Crescent and 3 dots above date arch.

C#	Date	Year	Good	VG	Fine	VF
60.3	13-46	—	3.00	4.50	7.00	10.00

NOTE: It is believed that this type was struck in the 1860's. Numerous varieties exist including 1 w/missing date.

3.60-5.20 g
Mint: Giamda

C#	Date	Year	Good	VG	Fine	VF
A13.1	15-24	(1890)	3.00	4.00	6.00	9.00
	15-25	(1891)	4.00	5.50	9.00	14.00

NOTE: Varieties of reverse exist including whirlwind at 1 o'clock in counter clockwise direction.

Rev: 2 circles around lotus.

C#	Date	Year	Good	VG	Fine	VF
A13.2	15-24	(1890)	—	—	Rare	—

NOTE: Varieties exist.

Miscellaneous TANGKAS

SILVER, ca. 5.40 g

C#	Date	Good	VG	Fine	VF
15	ND(ca.1840)	100.00	150.00	225.00	350.00

NOTE: Varieties exist. Inscription in seal script.

4.60-4.80 g

C#	Date	Year	Good	VG	Fine	VF
27	15-28	(1894)	4.00	8.00	13.00	20.00
	15-30	(1896)	15.00	23.00	30.00	40.00

NOTE: Later dates (15/40-15/46 = 1906-1912) exist for this type.

NOTE: In addition to the above meaningful (probably) dates, the following meaningless ones exist: 13-16, 13-31, 13-92, 16-16, 16-61, 16-69, 16-92, 16-93, 92-39, 96-61 (sixes may be reversed threes and nines reversed ones). These are of billon, varying from 3.9 to 4.7 g.

NOTE: The legend appears to be in ornamental Lansa script and has yet to be deciphered. The type is a copy of the Nepalese issue: 'Cho-Tang'. Although struck unofficially, it was legal tender, due to an edict issued in 1881 ordering that no distinction be made between false and genuine coins!

NOTE: This type was cut in parts of 3, 4 and 5 petals to make change and the resulting fractions are occasionally encountered.

'Ga-den' TANGKA

SILVER, 5.00-5.50 g
Obv: 5 petals around lotus center.

Y#	Date	Mintage	Good	VG	Fine	VF
13	ND(ca.1850)	—	5.00	10.00	15.00	25.00

NOTE: 2 major (lotus flower in center circle w/1 or 3 stems) and numerous minor die varieties exist.

4.00-5.20 g
Dodpal Mint
Obv: 5 dots around lotus center, North symbol.

Y#	Date	Mintage	VG	Fine	VF	XF
13.1	ND(ca1875)	—	1.00	2.00	3.00	4.50

NOTE: 5 major varieties exist, fishes swim clockwise or counter clockwise.

3.90-5.20 g
Tip Arsenal Mint
Obv: 3 elongated dots on either side of lotus center and new arrangement of 8 symbols.

13.2	ND(ca.1895-1901)	1.00	2.25	3.75	5.00

NOTE: 5 major varieties exist.

BILLON, 4.70-5.30 g
Obv: 7 dots around lotus center, uniform edge and thickness.

13.3	ND(ca.1900)	—	20.00	25.00	40.00	50.00

Listings For

TIMOR: refer to Indonesia

TRINIDAD & TOBAGO

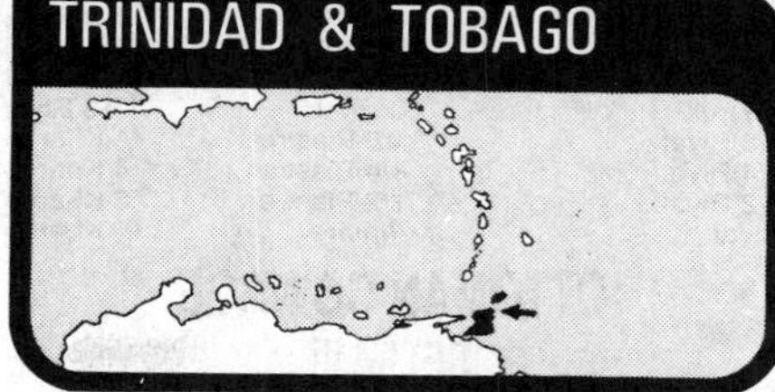

The Republic of Trinidad and Tobago, a member of the British Commonwealth situated 7 miles (11 km.) off the coast of Venezuela, has an area of 1,981 sq. mi. (5,130 sq. km.) and a population of *1.2 million. Capital: Port-of-Spain. The island of Trinidad contains the world's largest natural asphalt bog. Birds of Paradise live on little Tobago, the only place outside of their native New Guinea where they can be found in a wild state. Petroleum and petroleum products are the mainstay of the economy. Petroleum products, crude oil and sugar are exported.

Trinidad and Tobago were discovered by Columbus in 1498. Trinidad remained under Spanish rule from the time of its settlement in 1592 until its capture by the British in 1797. It was ceded to the British in 1802. Tobago was occupied at various times by the French, Dutch and English before being ceded to Britain in 1814. Trinidad and Tobago were merged into a single colony in 1888. The colony was part of the Federation of the West Indies until Aug. 31, 1962, when it became an independent member of the Commonwealth of Nations. A new constitution establishing a republican form of government was adopted on Aug. 1, 1976. Trinidad and Tobago is a member of the Commonwealth of Nations. The President is Chief of State. The Prime Minister is Head of Government.

RULERS

British, until 1976

TRINIDAD

Trinidad was discovered by Columbus in 1498. It remained under Spanish rule from the time of its settlement in 1592 until its capture by the British in 1797. It was ceded to the British in 1802.

MONETARY SYSTEM

9 Bits or Shillings = 8 Reales

CUT & COUNTERMARKED COINAGE

3 PENCE

SILVER
Cut quarter segment from Spanish Colonial 1 Real.

Kann#	Date	Mintage	Good	VG	Fine	VF
3	ND(1804)	—	18.00	25.00	50.00	80.00

6 PENCE

SILVER
Cut half segment from Spanish Colonial 1 Real.

6	ND(1804)	—	18.00	25.00	50.00	80.00

SHILLING

SILVER, 3.00-3.31 g
c/m: T on 1/8 or 1/9 cut of Spanish or Spanish Colonial 8 Reales.

9	ND(1798-1801)	—	400.00	500.00	800.00	1200.

NOTE: The attribution of this type has been questioned.

2.98 g
c/m: T on center plug cut from Spanish or Spanish Colonial 8 Reales, C#26.

10	ND(1811)	.025	120.00	150.00	260.00	425.00

9 SHILLINGS

SILVER
c/m: T on holed Spanish or Spanish Colonial 8 Reales.

Kann#	Date	Mintage	Good	VG	Fine	VF
13	ND(1811)	.025	400.00	500.00	700.00	900.00

Similar to KM#13 but w/o T c/m.

14	ND(1811)	I.A.	300.00	400.00	600.00	800.00

TOKEN ISSUES (Tn)

J. G. D'ade & Co.

FARTHING

COPPER

KM#	Date	Mintage	VG	Fine	VF	XF
Tn2	ND(1874)	.010	100.00	225.00	450.00	750.00

H. E. Rapseys

1/2 STAMPEE

COPPER

Tn3	ND(1860)	—	75.00	200.00	400.00	650.00

Francois Declos

1/2 PENNY

COPPER
c/m: FD on various types of 1/2 Penny size coins including French Colonial.

Tn1.1	ND(1854-74)	—	35.00	75.00	125.00	200.00

c/m: FD on H. E. Rapseys 1/2 Stampee, Tn3.

Tn1.2	ND(1854-74)	—	50.00	100.00	175.00	275.00

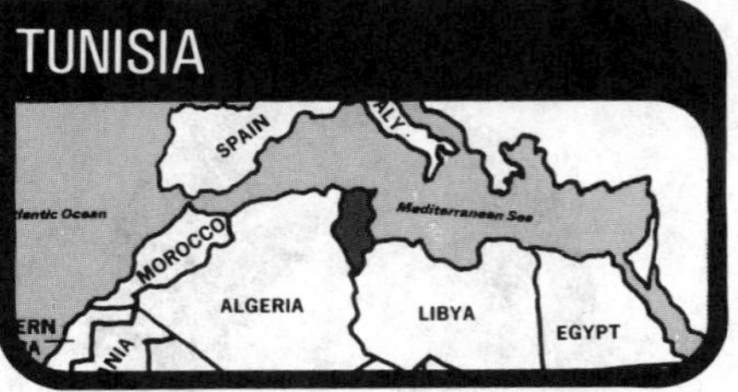

The Republic of Tunisia, located on the northern coast of Africa between Algeria and Libya, has an area of 63,170 sq. mi. (163,610 sq. km.) and a population of *7.9 million. Capital: Tunis. Agriculture is the backbone of the economy. Crude oil, phosphates, olive oil, and wine are exported.

Tunisia, settled by the Phoenicians in the 12th century B.C., was the center of the seafaring Carthaginian empire. After the total destruction of Carthage, Tunisia became part of Rome's African province. It remained a part of the Roman Empire (except for the 439-533 interval of Vandal conquest) until taken by the Arabs, 648, who administered it until the Turkish invasion of 1570. Under Turkish control, the public revenue was heavily dependent upon the piracy of Mediterranean shipping, an endeavor that wasn't abandoned until 1819 when a coalition of powers threatened appropriate reprisal. Deprived of its major source of income, Tunisia underwent a financial regression that ended in bankruptcy, enabling France to establish a protectorate over the country in 1881. National agitation and guerrilla fighting forced France to grant Tunisia internal autonomy in 1955 and to recognize Tunisian independence on March 20, 1956. Tunisia abolished the monarchy and established a republic on July 25, 1957.

MINT MARKS

A - Paris, AH1308/1891-AH1348/1928
(a) - Paris, privy marks, AH1349/1929-AH1376/1957
FM - Franklin Mint, Franklin Center, PA
- Numismatica Italiana, Arezzo, Italy

TUNIS

Tunis, the capital and major seaport of Tunisia, existed in the Carthaginian era, but its importance dates only from the Moslem conquest, following which it became a major center of Arab power and prosperity. Spain seized it in 1535, lost it in 1564, retook it in 1573 and ceded it to the Turks in 1574. Thereafter the history of Tunis merged with that of Tunisia.

RULERS

Ottoman, until 1881

LOCAL RULERS

Hammuda Pasha II, AH1196-1229/1782-1813AD
'Uthman, AH1229-1230/1813-1814AD
Mahmud Pasha, AH1230-1239/1814-1824AD
Husayn II, AH1239-1251/1824-1835AD
Mustapha, AH1251-1253/1835-1837AD
Ahmad I Pasha, AH1253-1271/1837-1855AD
Muhammad Bey, AH1271-1276/1855-1859AD
Muhammad Al-Sadiq Bey, AH1276-1299/1859-1882AD
Ali Bey, AH1299-1320/1882-1902AD

NOTE: All coins struck until AH1298/1881AD bear the name of the Ottoman Sultan; the name of the Bey of Tunis was added in AH1272/1855AD. After AH1298, when the French established their protectorate, only the Bey's name appears on the coin until AH1376/1956AD.

MINT

تونس

Tunis

With exceptions noted in their proper place, all coins were struck at Tunis prior to AH1308/1891AD. Thereafter, all coins were struck at Paris with mint mark A until 1928, symbols of the mint from 1929-1957.

MONETARY SYSTEM

Until 1891

6 Burben (Bourbine) = 1 Burbe (Bourbe)
2 Burbe (Bourbe) = 1 Nasri
13 Burbe = 1 Kharub (Caroub)
16 Kharub (Caroub) = 1 Piastre (Rial Sebili)

Arabic name	French name	Value
Qafsi of Falls Raqiq	Bourbine	1/12 Nasri
Fals	Bourbe	6 Qafsi or 1/2 Nasri
Nasri	Asper	1/52 Riyal
Kharub	Caroub	1/16 Riyal
1/8 Riyal	1/8 Piastre	1 Kharub
1/4 Riyal	1/4 Piastre	4 Kharub
1/2 Riyal	1/2 Piastre	8 Kharub
Riyal	Piastre	16 Kharub

OTTOMAN COINAGE

SELIM III

AH1203-1222/1789-1807AD

NASRI

(Asper)

BILLON, 9x9mm, square
Obv. leg: ***Sultan Selim.*** **Rev: Date and mint.**

KM#	Date	Mintage	Good	VG	Fine	VF
75	AH1216	—	30.00	60.00	100.00	150.00

4 KHARUB

BILLON, 21mm, 4.00 g

KM#	Date	Mintage	Good	VG	Fine	VF
74	AH1216	—	50.00	100.00	150.00	250.00
	1217	—	50.00	100.00	150.00	250.00

NOTE: Earlier date (AH1215) exists for this type.

8 KHARUB

BILLON, 27-28mm, 7.10-7.70 g
Similar to 1 Piastre, KM#72.

KM#	Date	Mintage	Good	VG	Fine	VF
73	AH1216	—	15.00	25.00	42.00	85.00
	1217	—	15.00	25.00	42.00	85.00
	1218	—	15.00	25.00	42.00	85.00
	1219	—	15.00	25.00	42.00	85.00
	1220	—	15.00	25.00	42.00	85.00
	1221	—	15.00	25.00	42.00	85.00
	1222	—	15.00	25.00	42.00	85.00

NOTE: Varieties of ornamentation exist.
NOTE: Earlier dates (AH1206-1215) exist for this type.

PIASTRE

BILLON, 14.90-16.00 g

KM#	Date	Mintage	Good	VG	Fine	VF
72.2	AH1216	—	18.00	30.00	50.00	95.00
	1217	—	18.00	30.00	50.00	95.00
	1218	—	18.00	30.00	50.00	95.00
	1219	—	18.00	30.00	50.00	95.00
	1220	—	18.00	30.00	50.00	95.00
	1221	—	18.00	30.00	50.00	95.00
	1222	—	18.00	30.00	50.00	95.00

NOTE: Varieties of ornamentation exist.
NOTE: Earlier dates (AH1206-1215) exist for this type.

MUSTAFA IV

AH1222-1223/1807-1808AD

4 KHARUB

BILLON, 21mm, 3.50 g
Similar To 1 Piastre, KM#72.

KM#	Date	Mintage	Good	VG	Fine	VF
78	AH1223	—	100.00	200.00	400.00	650.00

8 KHARUB

BILLON, 27mm, 7.50 g

KM#	Date	Mintage	Good	VG	Fine	VF
76	AH1222	—	125.00	225.00	450.00	750.00
	1223	—	125.00	225.00	450.00	750.00

PIASTRE

BILLON, 35mm, 16.00 g

KM#	Date	Mintage	Good	VG	Fine	VF
77	AH1222	—	100.00	175.00	300.00	500.00
	1223	—	100.00	175.00	300.00	500.00

MAHMUD II

AH1223-1255/1808-1839AD

BURBEN

COPPER, 0.80 g

KM#	Date	Mintage	Good	VG	Fine	VF
85	AH1230	—	15.00	35.00	75.00	120.00
	1231	—	15.00	35.00	75.00	120.00
	1232	—	15.00	35.00	75.00	120.00

NASRI

(Asper)

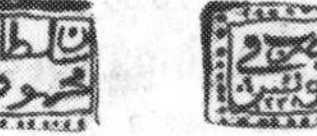

BILLON, 8mm square, 0.20 g

KM#	Date	Mintage	Good	VG	Fine	VF
83	AH1228	—	30.00	50.00	100.00	250.00
	1229	—	30.00	50.00	100.00	250.00

KHARUB

BILLON, 0.60-0.70 g

KM#	Date	Mintage	Good	VG	Fine	VF
91	AH1229	—	—	—	—	—
	1241	—	6.00	10.00	17.50	30.00
	1242	—	6.00	10.00	17.50	30.00
	1249	—	3.00	5.00	10.00	22.00
	1250	—	3.00	5.00	10.00	22.00
	1251	—	3.00	5.00	10.00	22.00
	1252	—	3.00	5.00	10.00	22.00
	1253	—	3.00	5.00	10.00	22.00
	1254	—	3.00	5.00	10.00	22.00
	1255	—	3.00	5.00	10.00	22.00

2 KHARUB

BILLON, 16mm, 1.30 g

KM#	Date	Mintage	Good	VG	Fine	VF
92	AH1243	—	20.00	30.00	60.00	85.00
	1244	—	20.00	30.00	60.00	85.00

4 KHARUB

BILLON, 21mm, 3.50 g

KM#	Date	Mintage	Good	VG	Fine	VF
81	AH1223	—	30.00	60.00	120.00	200.00
	1228	—	30.00	60.00	120.00	200.00
	1231	—	30.00	60.00	120.00	200.00

20mm, 2.50 g

KM#	Date	Mintage	Good	VG	Fine	VF
88	AH1240	—	10.00	20.00	50.00	100.00
	1241	—	10.00	20.00	50.00	100.00
	1242	—	10.00	20.00	50.00	100.00
	1243	—	10.00	20.00	50.00	100.00
	1245	—	10.00	20.00	50.00	100.00
	1246	—	10.00	20.00	50.00	100.00

KM#	Date	Mintage	Good	VG	Fine	VF
88	1249	—	10.00	20.00	50.00	100.00
	1250	—	10.00	20.00	50.00	100.00
	1252	—	10.00	20.00	50.00	100.00
	1253	—	10.00	20.00	50.00	100.00
	1254	—	10.00	20.00	50.00	100.00
	1255	—	10.00	20.00	50.00	100.00

8 KHARUB

BILLON, 27mm, 7.50 g

KM#	Date	Mintage	Good	VG	Fine	VF
84	AH1228	—	40.00	75.00	150.00	185.00
	1229	—	40.00	75.00	150.00	185.00
	1230	—	40.00	75.00	150.00	185.00
	1231	—	40.00	75.00	150.00	185.00
	1232	—	40.00	75.00	150.00	185.00
	1233	—	40.00	75.00	150.00	185.00

26mm, 5.00 g

KM#	Date	Mintage	Good	VG	Fine	VF
89	AH1240	—	10.00	20.00	50.00	100.00
	1241	—	10.00	20.00	50.00	100.00
	1242	—	10.00	20.00	50.00	100.00
	1243	—	10.00	20.00	50.00	100.00
	1244	—	10.00	20.00	50.00	100.00
	1245	—	10.00	20.00	50.00	100.00
	1246	—	10.00	20.00	50.00	100.00
	1247	—	10.00	20.00	50.00	100.00
	1248	—	10.00	20.00	50.00	100.00
	1251	—	10.00	20.00	50.00	100.00
	1252	—	10.00	20.00	50.00	100.00
	1253	—	10.00	20.00	50.00	100.00
	1254	—	10.00	20.00	50.00	100.00

PIASTRE

BILLON, 16.00 g

KM#	Date	Mintage	Good	VG	Fine	VF
82	AH1225	—	20.00	40.00	70.00	115.00
	1226	—	20.00	40.00	70.00	115.00
	1227	—	20.00	40.00	70.00	115.00
	1228	—	20.00	40.00	70.00	115.00
	1229	—	20.00	40.00	70.00	115.00
	1230	—	20.00	40.00	70.00	115.00
	1231	—	20.00	40.00	70.00	115.00
	1232	—	20.00	40.00	70.00	115.00
	1233	—	25.00	50.00	80.00	125.00
	1234	—	40.00	75.00	125.00	175.00

11.00-11.50 g

KM#	Date	Mintage	Good	VG	Fine	VF
90	AH1240	—	10.00	15.00	25.00	50.00
	1241	—	10.00	15.00	25.00	50.00
	1242	—	10.00	15.00	25.00	50.00
	1243	—	10.00	15.00	25.00	50.00
	1244	—	10.00	15.00	25.00	50.00
	1245	—	10.00	15.00	25.00	50.00
	1246	—	10.00	15.00	25.00	50.00
	1247	—	10.00	15.00	25.00	50.00
	1248	—	10.00	15.00	25.00	50.00
	1249	—	10.00	15.00	25.00	50.00
	1250	—	10.00	15.00	25.00	50.00
	1251	—	10.00	15.00	25.00	50.00
	1252	—	10.00	15.00	25.00	50.00
	1253	—	10.00	15.00	25.00	50.00
	1254	—	10.00	15.00	25.00	50.00
	1255	—	10.00	15.00	25.00	50.00

NOTE: Varieties in ornamentation exist.

2 PIASTRES

BILLON, 39mm, 27.40 g

KM#	Date	Mintage	Good	VG	Fine	VF
86	AH1232	—	Reported, not confirmed			

38mm, 23.00 g

KM#	Date	Mintage	Good	VG	Fine	VF
93	AH1244	—	45.00	75.00	150.00	200.00
	1245	—	45.00	75.00	150.00	200.00
	1246	—	45.00	75.00	150.00	200.00
	1248	—	75.00	125.00	175.00	350.00

SULTAN ABDUL MEJID

AH1255-1277/1839-1861AD

Without the name of the Bey of Tunis

PRE-REFORM COINAGE

4 KHARUB

BILLON, 20mm, 2.77 g

KM#	Date	Mintage	Good	VG	Fine	VF
97	AH1256	—	50.00	80.00	200.00	400.00

8 KHARUB

BILLON, 26mm, 5.00 g

KM#	Date	Mintage	Good	VG	Fine	VF
98	AH1256	—	50.00	80.00	200.00	400.00

PIASTRE

BILLON, 32mm, 11.00 g

KM#	Date	Mintage	Good	VG	Fine	VF
96	AH1255	—	35.00	60.00	150.00	200.00

REFORM COINAGE

After AH1263/1847AD

BURBE

COPPER, 1.00 g

KM#	Date	Mintage	Good	VG	Fine	VF
101	AH1263	—	2.00	4.00	10.00	20.00
	1264	—	2.00	4.00	10.00	20.00
	1265	—	2.00	4.00	10.00	20.00
	1266	—	2.00	4.00	10.00	20.00
	1267	—	2.00	4.00	10.00	20.00

NASRI

(Asper)

COPPER, 2.00 g

KM#	Date	Mintage	Good	VG	Fine	VF
102	AH1263	—	2.00	4.00	7.00	15.00
	1264	—	2.00	4.00	7.00	15.00
	1265	—	2.00	4.00	7.00	15.00
	1266	—	2.00	4.00	7.00	15.00
	1267	—	2.00	4.00	7.00	15.00

1/2 KHARUB

(3-1/4 Nasri)

COPPER, 5.50 g
Reeded edge.

KM#	Date	Mintage	Good	VG	Fine	VF
103.1	AH1263	—	4.00	8.00	15.00	30.00

Plain edge.

KM#	Date	Mintage	Good	VG	Fine	VF
103.2	AH1264	—	2.50	4.00	7.50	15.00
	1265	—	2.50	4.00	7.50	15.00
	1266	—	2.50	4.00	7.50	15.00
	1267	—	2.50	4.00	7.50	15.00
	1268	—	2.50	4.00	7.50	15.00
	1269	—	2.50	4.00	7.50	15.00

KHARUB

COPPER, 11.50 g
Reeded edge.

KM#	Date	Mintage	Good	VG	Fine	VF
104.1	AH1263	—	8.00	15.00	35.00	50.00

Plain edge.

KM#	Date	Mintage	Good	VG	Fine	VF
104.2	AH1263	—	4.00	8.00	15.00	25.00
	1264	—	2.00	4.00	10.00	15.00
	1265	—	2.00	4.00	10.00	15.00
	1266	—	2.00	4.00	10.00	15.00
	1267	—	2.00	4.00	10.00	15.00
	1268	—	2.00	4.00	10.00	15.00
	1269	—	1.00	2.00	5.00	10.00
	1270	—	6.00	10.00	20.00	30.00
	1271	—	6.00	10.00	20.00	30.00

c/m: Arabic '1' on KM#104.

KM#	Date	Mintage	Good	VG	Fine	VF
105	AH1263-71	—	3.00	6.00	12.00	25.00

2 PIASTRES

SILVER, 28mm, 6.50 g

KM#	Date	Mintage	VG	Fine	VF	XF
106	AH1263	—	45.00	75.00	125.00	225.00
	1264	—	45.00	75.00	125.00	225.00

Modified design

KM#	Date	Mintage	VG	Fine	VF	XF
109	AH1267	—	40.00	67.50	100.00	175.00

5 PIASTRES

SILVER, 33mm, 16.00 g

KM#	Date	Mintage	VG	Fine	VF	XF
107	AH1263	—	150.00	225.00	325.00	550.00
	1264	—	150.00	225.00	325.00	550.00

Modified design

KM#	Date	Mintage	VG	Fine	VF	XF
108	AH1265	—	50.00	80.00	140.00	250.00
	1266	—	20.00	32.50	50.00	75.00
	1267	—	20.00	32.50	50.00	75.00
	1268	—	22.50	37.50	60.00	90.00
	1269	—	50.00	80.00	140.00	250.00
	1270	—	50.00	80.00	140.00	250.00
	1271	—	20.00	32.50	50.00	75.00

SULTAN ABDUL MEJID

With Muhammad Bey
AH1272-1276/1856-1859AD

The copper coins of this series exhibit two major varieties of calligraphy, the first having thin, crude lettering, the second having thicker, more elegant lettering.

3 NASRI

(3 Asper)

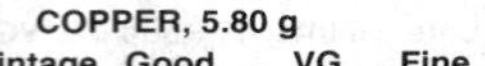

COPPER, 5.80 g

KM#	Date	Mintage	Good	VG	Fine	VF
112.1	AH1272	—	4.50	7.50	15.00	30.00
	1273	—	4.50	7.50	15.00	30.00

Thick legend.

KM#	Date	Mintage	Good	VG	Fine	VF
112.2	AH1272	—	4.50	7.50	15.00	30.00
	1274	—	4.50	7.50	15.00	30.00

6 NASRI

(6 Asper)

COPPER, 11.60 g

KM#	Date	Mintage	Good	VG	Fine	VF
113.1	AH1272	—	2.75	4.50	10.00	20.00
	1273	—	2.75	4.50	10.00	20.00

Thick legend.

KM#	Date	Mintage	Good	VG	Fine	VF
113.2	AH1272	—	2.75	4.50	10.00	20.00
	1273	—	2.75	4.50	10.00	20.00
	1274	—	2.75	4.50	10.00	20.00

KHARUB

COPPER
c/m: Arabic '1' on 6 Nasri, KM#113.1 and 113.2.

KM#	Date	Mintage	Good	VG	Fine	VF
114	AH1272-4	—	3.00	6.00	12.00	25.00

13 NASRI

(13 Asper)

COPPER, 23.00 g

KM#	Date	Mintage	Good	VG	Fine	VF
115.1	AH1272	—	5.00	8.50	12.50	25.00
	1273	—	5.00	8.50	12.50	25.00

Thick legend.

KM#	Date	Mintage	Good	VG	Fine	VF
115.2	AH1273	—	5.00	8.50	12.50	25.00
	1274	—	5.00	8.50	12.50	25.00
	1275	—	6.00	10.00	15.00	30.00

2 KHARUB

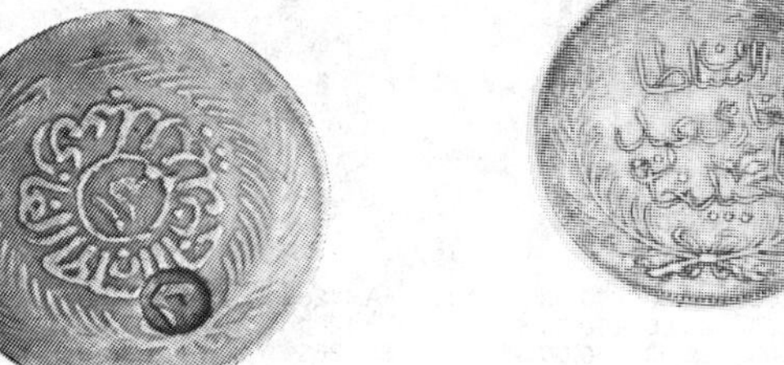

COPPER
c/m: Arabic '2' on 13 Nasri, KM#115.1.

KM#	Date	Mintage	Good	VG	Fine	VF
116	AH1272	—	3.50	6.00	10.00	25.00
	1273	—	3.50	6.00	10.00	25.00
	1274	—	3.50	6.00	10.00	25.00

c/m: Arabic '2' on 13 Nasri, KM#115.2.

KM#	Date	Mintage	Good	VG	Fine	VF
131	AH1273	—	3.50	6.00	10.00	25.00
	1274	—	3.50	6.00	10.00	25.00
	1275	—	3.50	6.00	10.00	25.00

Thick legend. 23.00 g

KM#	Date	Mintage	Good	VG	Fine	VF
134.1	AH1273	—	6.00	10.00	20.00	40.00
	1274	—	6.00	10.00	20.00	40.00
	1275	—	3.00	6.00	12.00	25.00
	1276	—	5.00	8.00	15.00	30.00

Thin legend.

KM#	Date	Mintage	Good	VG	Fine	VF
134.2	AH1276	—	12.00	18.00	28.00	45.00

SILVER, 0.40 g

KM#	Date	Mintage	Good	VG	Fine	VF
132	AH1273	—	10.00	18.00	50.00	90.00
	1274	—	10.00	18.00	50.00	90.00
	1275	—	10.00	18.00	50.00	90.00
	1276	—	10.00	18.00	50.00	90.00

4 KHARUB

SILVER, 0.80 g

KM#	Date	Mintage	VG	Fine	VF	XF
135	AH1274	—	20.00	35.00	100.00	150.00
	1275	—	20.00	35.00	100.00	150.00

8 KHARUB

SILVER, 1.60 g

KM#	Date	Mintage	VG	Fine	VF	XF
136	AH1274	—	20.00	45.00	100.00	180.00
	1275	—	20.00	45.00	100.00	180.00

PIASTRE

SILVER, 3.20 g
Thick legend.

KM#	Date	Mintage	VG	Fine	VF	XF
117.1	AH1272	—	25.00	40.00	100.00	180.00
	1273	—	25.00	40.00	100.00	180.00

Thin legend.

KM#	Date	Mintage	VG	Fine	VF	XF
117.2	AH1272	—	25.00	40.00	100.00	180.00

2 PIASTRES

SILVER, 6.40 g
Thick legend.

KM#	Date	Mintage	VG	Fine	VF	XF
118.1	AH1272	—	30.00	60.00	150.00	250.00

Thin legend.

KM#	Date	Mintage	VG	Fine	VF	XF
118.2	AH1272	—	30.00	60.00	150.00	270.00

3 PIASTRES

SILVER, 9.60 g

KM#	Date	Mintage	VG	Fine	VF	XF
119	AH1272	—	100.00	150.00	300.00	450.00

4 PIASTRES

SILVER, 31mm, 12.80 g

KM#	Date	Mintage	VG	Fine	VF	XF
120	AH1272	—	100.00	180.00	450.00	750.00

5 PIASTRES

SILVER, 33mm, 16.00 g

KM#	Date	Mintage	VG	Fine	VF	XF
121	AH1272	—	150.00	300.00	800.00	1200.
	1273	—	150.00	300.00	800.00	1200.
	1274	—	150.00	300.00	800.00	1200.

.9800 g, .900 GOLD, 12mm, .0284 oz AGW

KM#	Date	Mintage	VG	Fine	VF	XF
122	AH1272	—	22.50	30.00	75.00	130.00
	1273	—	22.50	30.00	75.00	130.00
	1274	—	22.50	30.00	75.00	130.00
	1275	—	22.50	30.00	75.00	130.00

10 PIASTRES

1.7700 g, 1.000 GOLD, .0569 oz AGW

KM#	Date	Mintage	VG	Fine	VF	XF
123	AH1272	—	40.00	60.00	100.00	160.00

1.9700 g, .900 GOLD, .0570 oz AGW

KM#	Date	Mintage	VG	Fine	VF	XF
124	AH1272	—	40.00	60.00	100.00	160.00
	1274	—	40.00	60.00	100.00	160.00

20 PIASTRES

3.5500 g, 1.000 GOLD, 21mm, .1141 oz AGW

KM#	Date	Mintage	VG	Fine	VF	XF
125	AH1272	—	100.00	125.00	200.00	400.00

25 PIASTRES

4.9200 g, .900 GOLD, 20mm, .1424 oz AGW

KM#	Date	Mintage	VG	Fine	VF	XF
133	AH1273	—	125.00	150.00	250.00	400.00
	1274	—	125.00	150.00	250.00	400.00
	1275	—	125.00	150.00	250.00	400.00

40 PIASTRES

7.1000 g, 1.000 GOLD, 26mm, .2283 oz AGW

KM#	Date	Mintage	VG	Fine	VF	XF
126	AH1272	—	135.00	175.00	300.00	525.00

50 PIASTRES

9.8400 g, .900 GOLD, .2847 oz AGW

KM#	Date	Mintage	VG	Fine	VF	XF
127	AH1272	—	175.00	200.00	300.00	500.00
	1273	—	175.00	200.00	300.00	500.00
	1274	—	175.00	200.00	300.00	500.00
	1275	—	175.00	200.00	300.00	500.00

80 PIASTRES

14.2100 g, 1.000 GOLD, 31mm, .4569 oz AGW

KM#	Date	Mintage	VG	Fine	VF	XF
128	AH1272	—	325.00	450.00	800.00	1100.

100 PIASTRES

17.7100 g, 1.000 GOLD, 33mm, .5694 oz AGW

KM#	Date	Mintage	VG	Fine	VF	XF
129	AH1272	—	400.00	600.00	800.00	1250.

19.6800 g, .900 GOLD, .5695 oz AGW

KM#	Date	Mintage	VG	Fine	VF	XF
130	AH1272	—	375.00	500.00	700.00	1150.
	1273	—	375.00	500.00	700.00	1150.
	1274	—	375.00	500.00	700.00	1150.

SULTAN ABDUL MEJID

With Muhammad al-Sadiq Bey
AH1276-1277/1859-1860AD

2 KHARUB

COPPER, 23.00 g

Thin legend.

KM#	Date	Mintage	VG	Fine	VF	XF
137.1	AH1276	—	10.00	20.00	35.00	80.00

Thick legend.

KM#	Date	Mintage	VG	Fine	VF	XF
137.2	AH1276	—	10.00	20.00	35.00	80.00

8 KHARUB

SILVER, 18mm, 1.60 g

KM#	Date	Mintage	VG	Fine	VF	XF
142	AH1276	—	60.00	100.00	250.00	450.00
	1277	—	60.00	100.00	250.00	450.00

PIASTRE

SILVER, 22mm, 3.20 g

KM#	Date	Mintage	VG	Fine	VF	XF
143	AH1278 (sic)	—	75.00	150.00	300.00	500.00

2 PIASTRES

SILVER, 6.40 g

KM#	Date	Mintage	VG	Fine	VF	XF
138	AH1276	—	—	—	Rare	—

25 PIASTRES

GOLD, 20mm, 4.90 g

KM#	Date	Mintage	VG	Fine	VF	XF
139	AH1276	—	125.00	200.00	325.00	650.00

50 PIASTRES

GOLD, 26mm, 9.80 g

KM#	Date	Mintage	VG	Fine	VF	XF
140	AH1276	—	150.00	300.00	500.00	750.00

100 PIASTRES

GOLD, 33mm, 19.70 g

KM#	Date	Mintage	VG	Fine	VF	XF
141	AH1276	—	1000.	1250.	1500.	2000.

SULTAN ABDUL AZIZ

With Muhammad al-Sadiq Bey
AH1277-1293/1860-1876AD

1/4 KHARUB

COPPER, 1.00 g

KM#	Date	Mintage	VG	Fine	VF	XF
153	AH1281	3.200	4.00	6.00	10.00	20.00

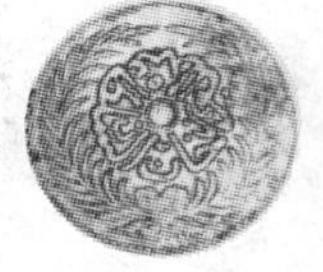

1.50 g

KM#	Date	Mintage	VG	Fine	VF	XF
171	AH1289	—	5.00	8.00	30.00	60.00

1/2 KHARUB

COPPER, 1.80 g

KM#	Date	Mintage	VG	Fine	VF	XF
154	AH1281	3.200	1.00	2.00	4.00	8.00

3.20 g

KM#	Date	Mintage	VG	Fine	VF	XF
172	AH1289	—	2.50	8.00	20.00	40.00

KHARUB

COPPER, 3.50 g

KM#	Date	Mintage	VG	Fine	VF	XF
155	AH1281	5.600	1.00	2.00	6.00	10.00

6.20 g

KM#	Date	Mintage	VG	Fine	VF	XF
173	AH1289	—	1.50	2.25	8.00	20.00
	1290	—	2.25	3.50	10.00	25.00

2 KHARUB

COPPER, 7.50 g

KM#	Date	Mintage	VG	Fine	VF	XF
156	AH1281	12.000	.75	1.25	4.00	12.00

NOTE: Thick and thin planchets exist.

12.90 g

KM#	Date	Mintage	VG	Fine	VF	XF
157	AH1281	—	—	Reported, not confirmed		
	1283	—	2.50	6.00	15.00	25.00
	1284	—	—	Reported, not confirmed		

NOTE: 3 varieties of inscription exist for AH1283. Slightly thinner planchets exist.

12.00-12.50 g

KM#	Date	Mintage	VG	Fine	VF	XF
174	AH1289	—	1.75	3.00	6.00	12.50
	1290	—	3.50	6.00	12.50	30.00

4 KHARUB

COPPER, 15.00 g

KM#	Date	Mintage	VG	Fine	VF	XF
158	AH1281	12.000	3.00	6.00	10.00	20.00
	1283	—	25.00	40.00	60.00	125.00

8 KHARUB

COPPER, 30.00 g

KM#	Date	Mintage	VG	Fine	VF	XF
159	AH1281	10.000	2.00	5.00	10.00	20.00

NOTE: KM#153-156, 158 and 159 were struck at the Heaton Mint, Birmingham, and are relatively common in higher grades

SILVER, 1.80 g

KM#	Date	Mintage	VG	Fine	VF	XF
160	AH1281	—	30.00	50.00	100.00	150.00
	1282	—	30.00	50.00	100.00	150.00
	1283	—	30.00	50.00	100.00	150.00
	1284	—	30.00	50.00	100.00	150.00
	1285	—	30.00	50.00	100.00	150.00
160	1286	—	30.00	50.00	100.00	150.00
	1287	—	30.00	50.00	100.00	150.00
	1288	—	30.00	50.00	100.00	150.00
	1289	—	15.00	25.00	50.00	100.00
	1290	—	30.00	50.00	100.00	150.00
	1291	—	30.00	50.00	100.00	150.00
	1292	—	30.00	50.00	100.00	150.00
	1293	—	30.00	50.00	100.00	150.00

PIASTRE

SILVER, 3.20 g

KM#	Date	Mintage	VG	Fine	VF	XF
145	AH1279	—	10.00	15.00	35.00	65.00
	1280	—	20.00	35.00	60.00	100.00
	1281	—	20.00	35.00	60.00	100.00
	1282	—	20.00	35.00	60.00	100.00
	1284	—	20.00	35.00	60.00	100.00
	1287	—	20.00	35.00	60.00	100.00
	1288	—	20.00	35.00	60.00	100.00
	1289	—	5.00	9.00	20.00	50.00
	1290	—	6.00	10.00	25.00	60.00
	1291	—	20.00	35.00	60.00	100.00
	1292	—	20.00	35.00	60.00	100.00
	1293	—	20.00	35.00	60.00	100.00

c/m: Star on Piastre, KM#145.

KM#	Date	Mintage	VG	Fine	VF	XF
146	AH1289	—	10.00	15.00	35.00	65.00

2 PIASTRES

SILVER, 6.27 g

KM#	Date	Mintage	VG	Fine	VF	XF
161	AH1281 Paris					
		—	—	—	Proof	375.00

NOTE: Without name of the Bey of Tunis - possibly a pattern.

6.40 g

KM#	Date	Mintage	VG	Fine	VF	XF
147	AH1279	—	30.00	60.00	100.00	150.00
	1280	—	30.00	60.00	100.00	150.00
	1282	—	30.00	60.00	100.00	150.00
	1283	—	30.00	60.00	100.00	150.00
	1284	—	30.00	60.00	100.00	150.00
	1287	—	30.00	60.00	100.00	150.00
	1288	—	30.00	60.00	100.00	150.00
	1289	—	20.00	25.00	50.00	90.00
	1290	—	20.00	25.00	50.00	90.00
	1291	—	30.00	60.00	100.00	150.00
	1292	—	30.00	60.00	100.00	150.00
	1293	—	30.00	60.00	100.00	150.00

c/m: Star on 2 Piastres, KM#147.

KM#	Date	Mintage	VG	Fine	VF	XF
165	AH1287-93	—	10.00	18.00	45.00	75.00

3 PIASTRES

SILVER, 30mm, 9.60 g

KM#	Date	Mintage	VG	Fine	VF	XF
166	AH1288	—	100.00	150.00	250.00	400.00

4 PIASTRES

SILVER, 12.80 g

KM#	Date	Mintage	VG	Fine	VF	XF
167	AH1288	—	20.00	40.00	95.00	180.00
	1290	—	12.00	25.00	50.00	100.00
	1291	—	12.00	25.00	50.00	100.00
	1292	—	15.00	30.00	80.00	150.00
	1293	—	15.00	30.00	80.00	150.00

c/m: Star on KM#167.

KM#	Date	Mintage	VG	Fine	VF	XF
168	AH1288-93	—	25.00	50.00	100.00	150.00

Mule. Obv: KM#186. Rev: KM#167.

KM#	Date	Mintage	VG	Fine	VF	XF
175	AH1292	—	35.00	65.00	120.00	210.00

5 PIASTRES

.9800 g, .900 GOLD, .0284 oz AGW

KM#	Date	Mintage	VG	Fine	VF	XF
162	AH1281	—	20.00	30.00	50.00	110.00
	1281	—	—	—	Proof	150.00

c/m: Star on KM#162.

KM#	Date	Mintage	VG	Fine	VF	XF
163	AH1281	—	20.00	30.00	50.00	110.00

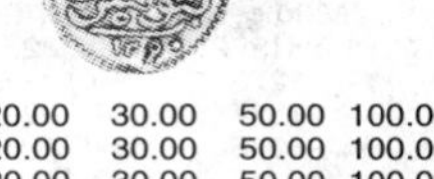

KM#	Date	Mintage	VG	Fine	VF	XF
169	AH1288	—	20.00	30.00	50.00	100.00
	1289	—	20.00	30.00	50.00	100.00
	1290	—	20.00	30.00	50.00	100.00
	1291	—	20.00	30.00	50.00	100.00
	1292	—	25.00	40.00	60.00	110.00

NOTE: Varieties exist for AH1290 dated coins.

c/m: Star on KM#169.

KM#	Date	Mintage	VG	Fine	VF	XF
170	AH1288	—	20.00	35.00	60.00	100.00
	1289	—	20.00	35.00	60.00	100.00
	1290	—	20.00	35.00	60.00	100.00
	1291	—	20.00	35.00	60.00	100.00
	1292	—	20.00	35.00	60.00	100.00

16.0000 g, .900 SILVER, 33mm, .4630 oz ASW

KM#	Date	Mintage	VG	Fine	VF	XF
164	AH1281	—	100.00	150.00	250.00	325.00
	1282	—	100.00	150.00	250.00	325.00
	1288	—	100.00	150.00	250.00	325.00
	1290	—	100.00	150.00	250.00	325.00
	1291	—	100.00	150.00	250.00	325.00
	1293	—	100.00	150.00	250.00	325.00

10 PIASTRES

1.9700 g, .900 GOLD, .0570 oz AGW

KM#	Date	Mintage	VG	Fine	VF	XF
150	AH1280	—	40.00	60.00	80.00	180.00
	1281	—	40.00	60.00	80.00	180.00
	1281	—	—	—	Proof	300.00
	1284	—	40.00	60.00	80.00	180.00
	1287	—	40.00	60.00	80.00	180.00
	1288	—	40.00	60.00	80.00	180.00

c/m: Star on KM#150.

KM#	Date	Mintage	VG	Fine	VF	XF
151	AH1280-8	—	45.00	70.00	85.00	135.00

25 PIASTRES

4.9200 g, .900 GOLD, .1424 oz AGW

KM#	Date	Mintage	VG	Fine	VF	XF
148	AH1278	—	100.00	150.00	225.00	300.00
	1279	—	100.00	150.00	225.00	300.00
	1280	—	100.00	150.00	225.00	300.00
	1281	—	100.00	150.00	225.00	300.00
	1281	—	—	—	Proof	400.00
	1282	—	—	—	Rare	—
	1283	—	100.00	150.00	225.00	300.00
	1284	—	—	—	Rare	—
	1285	—	100.00	150.00	225.00	300.00
	1286	—	—	—	Rare	—
	1287	—	100.00	150.00	225.00	300.00
	1288	—	100.00	150.00	225.00	300.00
	1289	—	100.00	125.00	165.00	250.00
	1290	—	100.00	125.00	165.00	250.00
	1291	—	100.00	125.00	165.00	250.00

50 PIASTRES

9.8400 g., .900 GOLD, .2847 oz AGW

KM#	Date	Mintage	VG	Fine	VF	XF
152	AH1280	—	200.00	225.00	285.00	500.00
	1281	—	200.00	225.00	275.00	350.00
	1281	—	—	—	Proof	550.00
	1286	—	200.00	225.00	275.00	350.00
	1288	—	200.00	225.00	275.00	350.00
	1293	—	250.00	275.00	350.00	450.00

100 PIASTRES

19.6800 g, .900 GOLD, .5695 oz AGW

KM#	Date	Mintage	VG	Fine	VF	XF
149	AH1279	—	375.00	575.00	950.00	2000.
	1280	—	375.00	575.00	950.00	2000.
	1281	—	375.00	575.00	950.00	2000.
	1281	—	—	—	Proof	3200.
	1283	—	375.00	575.00	950.00	2000.
	1285	—	375.00	575.00	950.00	2000.
	1286	—	375.00	575.00	950.00	2000.

NOTE: KM#148-150, 152, 161, 162, 164 and 166, dated AH1281, were all struck at Tunis, from dies produced at the Heaton Mint in Birmingham, hence their obvious superiority.

SULTAN MURAD V

With Muhammad al-Sadiq Bey
AH1293/1876AD

4 PIASTRES

SILVER, 12.80 g

KM#	Date	Mintage	VG	Fine	VF	XF
176	AH1293	—	—	—	Rare	—

25 PIASTRES

4.9200 g, .900 GOLD, 20mm, .1424 oz AGW

KM#	Date	Mintage	VG	Fine	VF	XF
177	AH1293	—	300.00	500.00	850.00	1600.

SULTAN ABDUL HAMID II

With Muhammad al-Sadiq Bey
AH1293-1299/1876-1882AD

2 KHARUB

COPPER, 31mm, 12.50 g

KM#	Date	Mintage	VG	Fine	VF	XF
180	AH1293	—	12.50	20.00	45.00	85.00

8 KHARUB

SILVER, 1.50 g

Obv: *al-Ghazi*

KM#	Date	Mintage	VG	Fine	VF	XF
181	AH1294	—	37.50	75.00	150.00	275.00
	1295	—	30.00	60.00	125.00	225.00
	1296	—	37.50	75.00	150.00	275.00
	1297	—	37.50	75.00	150.00	275.00
	1298	—	37.50	75.00	150.00	275.00

Obv: W/o *al-Ghazi*

KM#	Date	Mintage	VG	Fine	VF	XF
188	AH1293	—	60.00	125.00	250.00	375.00
	1294	—	60.00	125.00	250.00	375.00

PIASTRE

SILVER, 22.5mm, 3.20 g
Obv: W/o *al-Ghazi*

KM#	Date	Mintage	VG	Fine	VF	XF
182	AH1293	—	35.00	75.00	150.00	300.00
	1294	—	35.00	75.00	150.00	300.00

Obv: *al-Ghazi* added.

KM#	Date	Mintage	VG	Fine	VF	XF
189	AH1294	—	35.00	75.00	150.00	300.00
	1295	—	35.00	75.00	150.00	300.00
	1296	—	35.00	75.00	150.00	300.00
	1297	—	35.00	75.00	150.00	300.00
	1298	—	35.00	75.00	150.00	300.00

c/m: Star on KM#182.

KM#	Date	Mintage	VG	Fine	VF	XF
183	AH1293-4	—	35.00	60.00	100.00	150.00

c/m: Star on KM#189.

KM#	Date	Mintage	VG	Fine	VF	XF
190	AH1294-8	—	35.00	60.00	100.00	150.00

2 PIASTRES

SILVER, 26.5mm, 6.40 g

KM#	Date	Mintage	VG	Fine	VF	XF
184	AH1293	—	40.00	70.00	150.00	300.00
	1294	—	40.00	70.00	150.00	300.00

Obv: *al-Ghazi* added.

KM#	Date	Mintage	VG	Fine	VF	XF
191	AH1294	—	40.00	70.00	150.00	300.00
	1297	—	60.00	100.00	175.00	350.00

c/m: Star on KM#184.

KM#	Date	Mintage	VG	Fine	VF	XF
185	AH1293	—	35.00	75.00	150.00	300.00
	1294	—	35.00	75.00	150.00	300.00

c/m: Star on KM#191.

KM#	Date	Mintage	VG	Fine	VF	XF
192	AH1294	—	35.00	75.00	150.00	300.00

4 PIASTRES

SILVER, 12.8 g, 31mm
Obv: W/o *al-Ghazi*

KM#	Date	Mintage	VG	Fine	VF	XF
186	AH1293	—	20.00	60.00	125.00	250.00
	1294	—	20.00	60.00	125.00	250.00

Obv: *al-Ghazi* added.

KM#	Date	Mintage	VG	Fine	VF	XF
193	AH1294	—	20.00	60.00	125.00	250.00
	1295	—	20.00	60.00	125.00	250.00
	1296	—	20.00	60.00	125.00	250.00
	1297	—	20.00	60.00	125.00	250.00

c/m: Star on KM#186.

KM#	Date	Mintage	VG	Fine	VF	XF
187	AH1293	—	20.00	35.00	75.00	150.00
	1294	—	20.00	35.00	75.00	150.00

c/m: Star on KM#193.

KM#	Date	Mintage	VG	Fine	VF	XF
194	AH1294	—	20.00	35.00	75.00	150.00
	1295	—	20.00	35.00	75.00	150.00
	1296	—	20.00	35.00	75.00	150.00
	1297	—	20.00	35.00	75.00	150.00

5 PIASTRES

0.9800 g, .900 GOLD, 12.5mm, .0284 oz AGW

KM#	Date	Mintage	VG	Fine	VF	XF
195	AH1294	—	40.00	75.00	150.00	250.00

10 PIASTRES

1.9700 g, .900 GOLD, .0570 oz AGW

KM#	Date	Mintage	VG	Fine	VF	XF
199	AH1295	—	—	—	—	—

25 PIASTRES

4.9200 g, .900 GOLD, .1424 oz AGW

KM#	Date	Mintage	VG	Fine	VF	XF
196	AH1294	—	85.00	110.00	175.00	250.00
	1295	—	85.00	110.00	175.00	250.00
	1296	—	85.00	110.00	175.00	250.00
	1297	—	85.00	110.00	175.00	250.00
	1298	—	—	—	Rare	—

50 PIASTRES

9.8400 g, .900 GOLD, 26mm, .2847 oz AGW
Obv: W/o *al-Ghazi*.

KM#	Date	Mintage	VG	Fine	VF	XF
197	AH1294	—	—	—	Rare	—

Obv: *al-Ghazi* added.

KM#	Date	Mintage	VG	Fine	VF	XF
198	AH1295	—	—	—	Rare	—
	1297	—	150.00	200.00	250.00	350.00

100 PIASTRES

19.6800 g, .900 GOLD, 33mm, .5695 oz AGW

KM#	Date	Mintage	VG	Fine	VF	XF
A199	AH1295	—	— Reported, not confirmed			

PROOF SETS (PS)

KM#	Date	Mintage	Identification	Issue Price	Mkt. Val.
PS1	1864(AH1281) (5)	—	KM148-150,152,162	—	4500.

TUNISIA

FRENCH PROTECTORATE

MUHAMMAD AL-SADIQ BEY

Alone: AH1298-1299/1881-1882AD

8 KHARUB

SILVER, 18.5mm, 1.60 g

KM#	Date	Mintage	Fine	VF	XF	Unc
201	AH1299	—	200.00	400.00	750.00	1250.

PIASTRE

SILVER, 3.20 g

KM#	Date	Mintage	Fine	VF	XF	Unc
202	AH1299	—	200.00	400.00	750.00	1250.

2 PIASTRES

SILVER, 26.5mm, 6.40 g

KM#	Date	Mintage	Fine	VF	XF	Unc
203	AH1299	—	200.00	400.00	750.00	1250.

25 PIASTRES

4.9200 g, .900 GOLD, 20mm, .1424 oz AGW

KM#	Date	Mintage	Fine	VF	XF	Unc
200	AH1298	—	100.00	250.00	500.00	750.00
	1300	—	150.00	300.00	600.00	950.00

50 PIASTRES

9.8400 g, .900 GOLD, 26mm, .2847 oz AGW

KM#	Date	Mintage	Fine	VF	XF	Unc
204	AH1299	—	300.00	400.00	650.00	1000.

ALI BEY

AH1299-1320/AD1882-1902

8 KHARUB

SILVER, 1.60 g

KM#	Date	Mintage	Fine	VF	XF	Unc
205	AH1300	—	15.00	25.00	55.00	115.00
	1301	—	15.00	25.00	55.00	115.00
	1302	—	15.00	25.00	55.00	115.00
	1303	—	15.00	25.00	55.00	115.00
	1304	—	15.00	25.00	55.00	115.00
	1305	—	15.00	25.00	55.00	115.00
	1306	—	15.00	25.00	55.00	115.00
	1307	—	15.00	25.00	55.00	115.00
	1308	—	15.00	25.00	55.00	115.00

PIASTRE

SILVER, 3.20 g

KM#	Date	Mintage	Fine	VF	XF	Unc
206	AH1300	—	18.00	30.00	75.00	155.00
	1301	—	18.00	30.00	75.00	155.00
	1302	—	18.00	30.00	75.00	155.00
	1303	—	18.00	30.00	75.00	155.00
	1304	—	18.00	30.00	75.00	155.00
	1305	—	18.00	30.00	75.00	155.00
	1306	—	18.00	30.00	75.00	155.00
	1307	—	18.00	30.00	75.00	155.00
	1308	—	18.00	30.00	75.00	155.00

Modified design.

KM#	Date	Mintage	Fine	VF	XF	Unc
215	AH1308	—	20.00	35.00	75.00	150.00

2 PIASTRES

SILVER, 6.40 g

KM#	Date	Mintage	Fine	VF	XF	Unc
207	AH1300	—	30.00	50.00	125.00	275.00
	1301	—	30.00	50.00	125.00	275.00
	1302	—	30.00	50.00	125.00	275.00
	1303	—	30.00	50.00	125.00	275.00
	1304	—	30.00	50.00	125.00	275.00
	1305	—	30.00	50.00	125.00	275.00
	1306	—	30.00	50.00	125.00	275.00
	1307	—	30.00	50.00	125.00	275.00
	1308	—	30.00	50.00	125.00	275.00

Modified design.

KM#	Date	Mintage	Fine	VF	XF	Unc
210	AH1308	—	40.00	70.00	125.00	275.00

4 PIASTRES

SILVER, 12.80 g

KM#	Date	Mintage	Fine	VF	XF	Unc
208	AH1300	—	30.00	50.00	150.00	325.00
	1301	—	30.00	50.00	150.00	325.00
	1302	—	30.00	50.00	150.00	325.00
	1303	—	30.00	50.00	150.00	325.00
	1304	—	30.00	50.00	150.00	325.00
	1305	—	30.00	50.00	150.00	325.00
	1306	—	30.00	50.00	150.00	325.00
	1307	—	30.00	50.00	150.00	325.00
	1308	—	30.00	50.00	150.00	325.00

Modified design.

KM#	Date	Mintage	Fine	VF	XF	Unc
216	AH1308	—	40.00	70.00	180.00	350.00

25 PIASTRES

4.9200 g, .900 GOLD, .1424 oz AGW

KM#	Date	Mintage	Fine	VF	XF	Unc
209	AH1300	—	85.00	110.00	150.00	250.00
	1302	—	85.00	110.00	150.00	250.00

25 PIASTRES-15 FRANCS

4.8730 g, .900 GOLD, .1410 oz AGW

KM#	Date	Mintage	Fine	VF	XF	Unc
212	AH1304	.080	85.00	110.00	175.00	300.00
	1308	Inc. Ab.	85.00	110.00	175.00	300.00

Rev: Modified design.

KM#	Date	Mintage	Fine	VF	XF	Unc
214	AH1307A	.052	85.00	110.00	175.00	300.00
	1308A	.120	85.00	110.00	175.00	300.00
	1308A	—	—	—	Proof	2000.

50 PIASTRES

4.8730 g, .900 GOLD, .1410 oz AGW

KM#	Date	Mintage	Fine	VF	XF	Unc
213	AH1304	—	200.00	350.00	500.00	750.00

100 PIASTRES

9.7460 g, .900 GOLD, .2820 oz AGW

KM#	Date	Mintage	Fine	VF	XF	Unc
211	AH1303	—	300.00	600.00	1000.	1500.

DECIMAL SYSTEM

100 Centimes = 1 Franc

NOTE: The following coins all bear French inscriptions on one side, Arabic on the other, and usually have both AH and AD dates. They are struck in the name of the Tunisian Bey.

CENTIME

BRONZE
Obv. leg: *Ali.*

KM#	Date	Year	Mintage	VF	XF	Unc
219	AH1308	1891A	.500	6.00	10.00	23.00

2 CENTIMES

BRONZE
Obv. leg: *Ali.*

KM#	Date	Year	Mintage	VF	XF	Unc
220	AH1308	1891A	1.000	2.25	5.00	15.00

5 CENTIMES

BRONZE
Obv. leg: *Ali.*

KM#	Date	Year	Mintage	VF	XF	Unc
221	AH1308	1891A	4.300	2.00	7.00	23.00
	1308	1891A	—	—	Proof	50.00
	1309	1892A	1.192	2.50	8.00	23.00
	1310	1893A	1.008	3.00	10.00	25.00

10 CENTIMES

BRONZE
Obv. leg: *Ali.*

KM#	Date	Year	Mintage	VF	XF	Unc
222	AH1308	1891A	2.600	4.00	8.00	22.00
	1309	1892A	1.374	4.00	10.00	25.00
	1310	1892A	—	75.00	125.00	200.00
	1310	1893A	.026	75.00	125.00	200.00

50 CENTIMES

2.5000 g, .835 SILVER, .0671 oz ASW
Obv. leg: *Ali.*

KM#	Date	Year	Mintage	VF	XF	Unc
223	AH1308	1891A	1.470	15.00	25.00	50.00
	1309	1892A	1,000	—	100.00	175.00
	1310	1893A	1,000	—	100.00	175.00
	1311	1893A	—	—	100.00	175.00
	1311	1894A	1,000	—	100.00	175.00
	1313	1895A	1,000	—	100.00	175.00
	1314	1896A	1,000	—	100.00	175.00
	1315	1897A	1,000	—	100.00	175.00
	1316	1898A	1,000	—	100.00	175.00
	1317	1899A	1,000	—	100.00	175.00
	1318	1900A	1,000	—	100.00	175.00

NOTE: Later dates (AH1319-1320) exist for this type.

FRANC

5.0000 g, .835 SILVER, .1342 oz ASW
Obv. leg: *Ali.*

KM#	Date	Year	Mintage	VF	XF	Unc
224	AH1308	1891A	1.575	20.00	35.00	50.00
	1309	1892A	1.575	20.00	35.00	50.00
	1310	1893A	703 pcs.	—	135.00	225.00
	1311	1894A	703 pcs.	—	135.00	225.00
	1313	1895A	703 pcs.	—	135.00	225.00
	1314	1896A	703 pcs.	—	135.00	225.00
	1315	1897A	703 pcs.	—	135.00	225.00
	1316	1898A	703 pcs.	—	135.00	225.00
	1317	1899A	703 pcs.	—	135.00	225.00
	1318	1900A	703 pcs.	—	135.00	225.00

NOTE: Later dates (AH1319-1320) exist for this type.

2 FRANCS

10.0000 g, .835 SILVER, .2685 oz ASW
Obv. leg: *Ali.*

KM#	Date	Year	Mintage	VF	XF	Unc
225	AH1308	1891A	.595	20.00	35.00	70.00
	1309	1892A	.432	20.00	35.00	70.00
	1310	1893A	300 pcs.	—	150.00	250.00
	1311	1893A	—	—	150.00	250.00
	1311	1894A	300 pcs.	—	150.00	250.00
	1313	1895A	300 pcs.	—	150.00	250.00
	1314	1896A	300 pcs.	—	150.00	250.00
	1315	1897A	300 pcs.	—	150.00	250.00
	1316	1898A	300 pcs.	—	150.00	250.00
	1317	1899A	300 pcs.	—	150.00	250.00
	1318	1900A	300 pcs.	—	150.00	250.00

NOTE: Later dates (AH1319-1320) exist for this type.

Obv. leg: *Muhammad al-Hadi.*

10 FRANCS

3.2258 g, .900 GOLD, .0933 oz AGW
Obv. leg: *Ali.*

KM#	Date	Year	Mintage	VF	XF	Unc
226	AH1308	1891A	.400	50.00	70.00	100.00
	1308	1891A	—	—	Proof	1250.
	1309	1892A	83 pcs.	—	450.00	850.00
	1310	1893A	83 pcs.	—	450.00	850.00
	1311	1894A	83 pcs.	—	450.00	850.00
	1313	1895A	83 pcs.	—	450.00	850.00
	1314	1896A	83 pcs.	—	450.00	850.00
	1315	1897A	83 pcs.	—	450.00	850.00
	1316	1898A	83 pcs.	—	450.00	850.00
	1317	1899A	83 pcs.	—	450.00	850.00
	1318	1900A	83 pcs.	—	450.00	850.00

NOTE: Later dates (AH1319-1320) exist for this type.

20 FRANCS

6.4516 g, .900 GOLD, .1867 oz AGW
Obv. leg: *Ali.*

KM#	Date	Year	Mintage	VF	XF	Unc
227	AH1308	1891A	.400	BV	80.00	110.00
	1308	1891	—	—	Proof	1500.
	1309	1892A	.937	BV	80.00	110.00
	1310	1892A	Inc. Ab.	BV	80.00	110.00
	1310	1893A	.035	BV	80.00	110.00
	1311	1894A	20 pcs.	—	550.00	1000.
	1313	1895A	20 pcs.	—	550.00	1000.
	1314	1896A	20 pcs.	—	550.00	1000.
	1315	1897A	.164	BV	80.00	110.00
	1316	1898A	.150	BV	80.00	110.00
	1316	1899A	.150	BV	80.00	110.00
	1318	1900A	.150	BV	80.00	110.00

NOTE: Later dates (AH1319-1320) exist for this type.

TURKEY

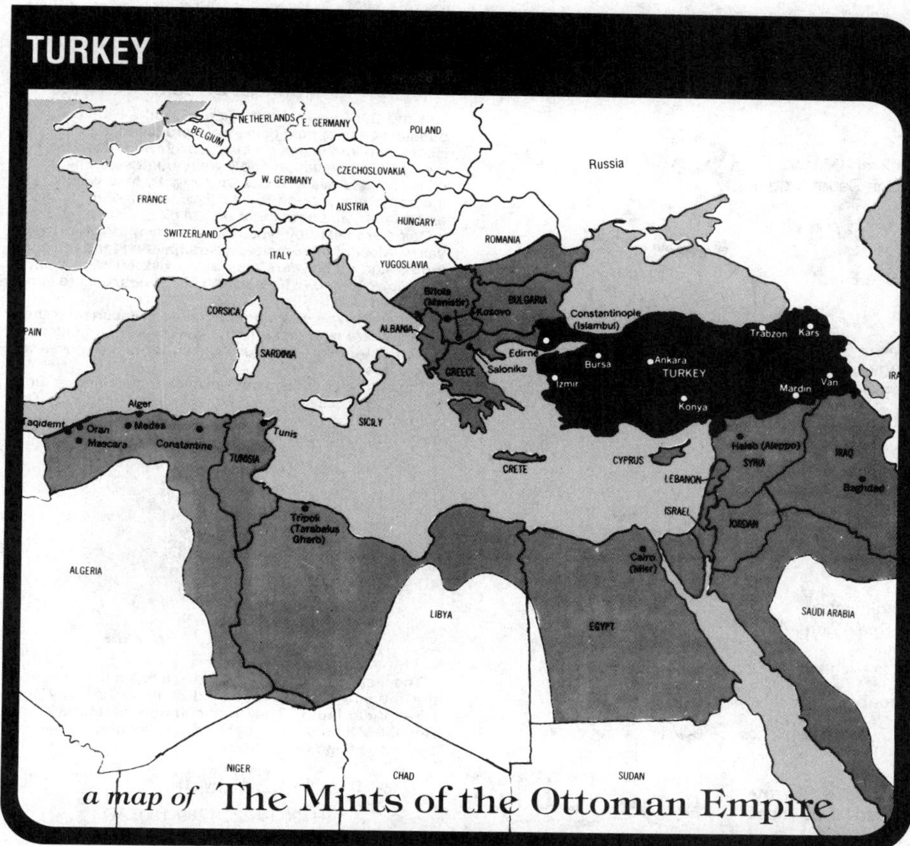

The Republic of Turkey, a parliamentary democracy of the Near East located partially in Europe and partially in Asia between the Black and the Mediterranean Seas, has an area of 301,382 sq. mi. (780,580 sq. km.) and a population of *55.4 million. Capital: Ankara. Turkey exports cotton, hazelnuts, and tobacco, and enjoys a virtual monopoly in meerschaum.

The Ottoman Turks, a tribe from Central Asia, first appeared in the early 13th century, and by the 17th century had established the Ottoman Empire which stretched from the Persian Gulf to the southern frontier of Poland, and from the Caspian Sea to the Algerian plateau. The defeat of the Turkish navy by the Holy League in 1571, and of the Turkish forces besieging Vienna in 1683, began the steady decline of the Ottoman Empire which, accelerated by the rise of nationalism, contracted its European border, and by the end of World War I deprived it of its Arab lands. The present Turkish boundaries were largely fixed by the Treaty of Lausanne in 1923. The sultanate and caliphate, the political and spiritual ruling institutions of the old empire, were separated and the sultanate abolished in 1922. On Oct. 29, 1923, Turkey formally became a republic.

RULERS

Selim III, AH1203-1222/1789-1807AD
Mustafa IV, AH1222-1223/1807-1808AD
Mahmud II, AH1223-1255/1808-1839AD
Abdul Mejid, AH1255-1277/1839-1861AD
Abdul Aziz, AH1277-1293/1861-1876AD
Murad V, AH1293/1876AD
Abdul Hamid II, AH1293-1327/1876-1909AD

MINTNAMES

Baghdad
See Iraq-Mesopotamia
بغداد

Bursa
(Brusah)
بروسة

Constantine (Constaniyah, Qusantinah) See Algeria-Algiers
قسطنتنيه

Constantinople
(Qustantiniyah)
قسطنطنية

Damascus
(Damask) See Syria
دمشق

Edirne
(Adrianople)
ادرنة

Haleb
(Aleppo)
See Syria
حلب

Islambul
Istanbul
اسلامبول or اسلامبول

Jaza'Ir
(See Algeria-Algiers)
جزاير

Kara Amid
(Amid)

Kosova
قوصوه

Manistir
مناستر

al-Mascara
See Algeria-Algiers
المعسكر

Medea مديه
See Algeria-Algiers

Makkah (Mecca) مكه
See Saudi Arabia

Misr مصر
See Egypt

Revan روان
(Erevan, now Yerevan)
See Armenia

Salonika سلانيك
(Selanik, Saloniki)

Taqidemt تاقدمت
See Algeria-Algiers

Tarabalus طرابلس
See Libya-Tripoli

Tarabalus Gharb طرابلس غرب
See Libya-Tripoli

Tiflis تفليس
See Georgia

Tunis تونس
See Tunisia-Tunis

Van وان
(Wan) - Until AH1032. AH1133-34
See Armenia

MONETARY EQUIVALENTS

3 Akche = 1 Para
5 Para = Beshlik (Beshparalik)
10 Para = Onluk
20 Para = Yirmilik
30 Para = Zolota
40 Para = Kurush (Piastre)
1-1/2 Kurush (Piastres) = Altmishlik

MONETARY SYSTEM

Silver Coinage

40 Para = 1 Kurush (Piastre)
2 Kurush (Piastres) = 1 Ikilik
2-1/2 Kurush (Piastres) = Yuzluk
3 Kurush (Piastres) = Uechlik
5 Kurush (Piastres) = Beshlik
6 Kurush (Piastres) = Altilik

Gold Coinage

100 Kurush (Piastres) = 1 Turkish Pound (Lira)

This system has remained essentially unchanged since its introduction by Ahmad III in 1688, except that the Asper and Para have long since ceased to be coined. The Piastre, established as a crown-sized silver coin approximately equal to the French Ecu of Louis XIV, has shrunk to a tiny copper coin, worth about 1/15 of a U.S. cent. Since the establishment of the Republic in 1923, the Turkish terms, Kurus and Lira, have replaced the European names Piastres and Turkish Pounds.

MINT VISIT ISSUES

From time to time, certain cities of the Ottoman Empire, such as Bursa, Edirne, Kosova, Manistir and Salonika were honored by having special coins struck at Istanbul, but with inscriptions stating that they were struck in the city of honor. These were produced on the occasion of the Sultan's visit to that city. The coins were struck in limited, but not small quantities, and were probably intended for distribution to the notables of the city and the Sultan's own followers. Because they were of the same size and type as the regular circulation issues struck at Istanbul, many specimens found their way into circulation and worn or mounted specimens are found today, al-though some have been preserved in XF or better condition. Mintage statistics are not known.

MONNAIE DE LUXE

In the 23rd year of the reign of Abdul Hamid II, two parallel series of gold coins were produced, regular mint issues and 'monnaies de luxe', which were intended primarily for presentation and jewelry purposes. The 'Monnaie de Luxe' were struck to a slightly less weight and the same fineness as regular issues, but were broader and thinner, and from more ornate dies.

Coins are listed by type, followed by a list of reported years. Most of the reported years have never been confirmed and other years may also exist. Mintage figures are known for the AH1293 and 1327 series, but are unreliable and of little utility.

Although some years are undoubtedly much rarer than others, there is at present no date collecting of Ottoman gold and therefore little justification for higher prices for rare dates.

There is no change in design in the regular series. Only the toughra, accessional date and regnal year vary. The deluxe series show ornamental changes. The standard coins generally do not bear the denomination.

HONORIFIC TITLES

El Ghazi

Reshat

The first coinage of Abdul Hamid II has a flower right of the toughra while the second coinage has *el Ghazi* (The Victorious). The first coinage of Mohammad Reshat V has *Reshat* right of the toughra while his second coinage has *el Ghazi.*

SELIM III

AH1203-1222/1789-1807AD

THIRD COINAGE

Light coinage based on a Piastre weighing approximately 12.80 g with second toughra.

PARA

.465 SILVER, 0.32 g
Mintname: *Islambul*

KM#	Date	Year	VG	Fine	VF	XF
486	AH1203	14	.75	1.25	6.00	12.00
		15	.75	1.25	6.00	12.00
		16	.75	1.25	6.00	12.00
		17	.75	1.25	6.00	12.00
		18	.75	1.25	6.00	12.00
		19	2.00	4.00	12.00	30.00

NOTE: Earlier dates (Yr.1-13) exist for this type.

5 PARA

.465 SILVER, 1.60 g
Mintname: *Islambul*

KM#	Date	Year	VG	Fine	VF	XF
489	AH1203	14	6.50	10.00	25.00	40.00
		15	6.50	10.00	25.00	40.00
		16	6.50	10.00	25.00	40.00
		17	6.50	10.00	25.00	40.00
		18	6.50	10.00	25.00	40.00
		19	10.00	15.00	35.00	75.00

NOTE: Earlier dates (Yr.1-13) exist for this type.

10 PARA

.465 SILVER, 3.05 g
Mintname: *Islambul*

KM#	Date	Year	VG	Fine	VF	XF
492	AH1203	14	4.00	8.00	17.50	35.00
		15	4.00	8.00	17.50	35.00
		16	4.00	8.00	17.50	35.00
		17	4.00	8.00	17.50	35.00
		18	4.00	8.00	17.50	35.00
		19	8.00	15.00	25.00	55.00

NOTE: Earlier dates (Yr.1-13) exist for this type.

20 PARA

.465 SILVER, 6.45 g
Mintname: *Islambul*

KM#	Date	Year	VG	Fine	VF	XF
495	AH1203	15	50.00	100.00	190.00	350.00
		16	50.00	100.00	190.00	350.00
		19	—	—	Rare	—

NOTE: Earlier dates (Yr.1-13) exist for this type.

PIASTRE

.465 SILVER, 12.62 g
Mintname: *Islambul*

KM#	Date	Year	VG	Fine	VF	XF
498	AH1203	14	20.00	30.00	60.00	125.00
		15	25.00	35.00	70.00	150.00
		16	25.00	35.00	70.00	150.00
		17	25.00	35.00	70.00	150.00
		18	25.00	35.00	70.00	150.00
		19	150.00	250.00	400.00	750.00

NOTE: Earlier dates (Yr.1-13) exist for this type.

2 PIASTRES

.465 SILVER, 25.60 g
Mintname: *Islambul*

Dav.#335

KM#	Date	Year	VG	Fine	VF	XF
504	AH1203	14	10.00	12.00	30.00	45.00
		15	10.00	12.00	30.00	45.00
		16	10.00	12.00	30.00	45.00
		17	10.00	12.00	30.00	45.00
		18	30.00	75.00	100.00	200.00
		19	75.00	150.00	250.00	400.00

NOTE: Earlier dates (Yr.1-13) exist for this type.

YUZLUK

.465 SILVER, 32.00 g
Mintname: *Islambul*

Dav.#334

KM#	Date	Year	VG	Fine	VF	XF
507	AH1203	14	10.00	12.00	25.00	40.00
		15	10.00	12.00	25.00	50.00
		16	10.00	12.00	25.00	55.00
		17	10.00	12.00	25.00	70.00
		18	30.00	40.00	60.00	110.00
		19	50.00	75.00	150.00	350.00

NOTE: Earlier dates (Yr.1-13) exist for this type.

1/4 ZERI MAHBUB

GOLD, 0.60 g
Mintname: *Islambul*

KM#	Date	Year	VG	Fine	VF	XF
510	AH1203	14	22.50	35.00	50.00	75.00
		15	22.50	35.00	50.00	75.00
		16	22.50	35.00	50.00	75.00
		17	22.50	35.00	50.00	75.00

NOTE: Earlier dates (Yr.7-13) exist for this type.
NOTE: With *Azza Nasara.*

1/4 ALTIN

(Findik)

GOLD, 15mm, 0.90 g
Mintname: *Islambul*
Plain borders

KM#	Date	Year	VG	Fine	VF	XF
514	AH1203	14	22.50	35.00	50.00	70.00
		15	22.50	35.00	50.00	70.00
		16	22.50	35.00	50.00	70.00
		17	22.50	35.00	50.00	70.00
		18	22.50	35.00	50.00	70.00
		19	30.00	50.00	75.00	125.00

NOTE: Earlier dates (Yr.1-13) exist for this type.

1/2 ZERI MAHBUB

GOLD, 1.10-1.20 g

Mintname: *Islambul*

KM#	Date	Year	VG	Fine	VF	XF
517	AH1203	14	40.00	65.00	80.00	100.00
		15	40.00	65.00	80.00	100.00
		16	40.00	65.00	80.00	100.00
		17	40.00	65.00	80.00	100.00
		18	50.00	80.00	120.00	180.00
		19	100.00	200.00	300.00	400.00

NOTE: Earlier dates (Yr.1-12) exist for this type.

1/2 ALTIN

GOLD, 1.65 g
Mintname: *Islambul*

KM#	Date	Year	VG	Fine	VF	XF
520	AH1203	18	60.00	90.00	135.00	185.00

NOTE: Earlier dates (Yr.1-13) exist for this type.

ZERI MAHBUB

GOLD
Mintname: *Islambul*

KM#	Date	Year	VG	Fine	VF	XF
523	AH1203	14	35.00	50.00	90.00	120.00
		15	35.00	50.00	90.00	120.00
		16	35.00	50.00	90.00	120.00
		17	35.00	50.00	90.00	120.00
		18	35.00	50.00	90.00	120.00
		19	35.00	50.00	90.00	120.00

NOTE: Earlier dates (Yr.10-13) exist for this type.

ALTIN

GOLD, 3.45 g
Mintname: *Islambul*

KM#	Date	Year	VG	Fine	VF	XF
527	AH1203	17	60.00	85.00	135.00	185.00
		18	60.00	85.00	135.00	185.00
		19	60.00	85.00	135.00	185.00

MUSTAFA IV

AH1222-1223/1807-1808AD

MANGHIR

COPPER, 2.70g
Mintname: *Qustantiniyah*

KM#	Date	Year	VG	Fine	VF	XF
534	AH1222	1	—	—	—	—

AKCE

.465 SILVER, 12mm, 0.12 g
Mintname: *Qustantiniyah*
Similar to Para, KM#536.

KM#	Date	Year	VG	Fine	VF	XF
535	AH1222	1	Reported, not confirmed			
		2	Reported, not confirmed			

PARA

.465 SILVER, 0.40 g
Mintname: *Qustantiniyah*

KM#	Date	Year	VG	Fine	VF	XF
536	AH1222	1	25.00	35.00	50.00	80.00
		2	35.00	50.00	70.00	100.00

5 PARA

.465 SILVER, 1.50 g
Mintname: *Qustantiniyah*

KM#	Date	Year	VG	Fine	VF	XF
537	AH1222	1	50.00	90.00	200.00	350.00
		2	60.00	140.00	350.00	500.00

10 PARA

.465 SILVER, 3.14 g
Mintname: *Qustantiniyah*

KM#	Date	Year	VG	Fine	VF	XF
538	AH1222	1	40.00	90.00	200.00	300.00
		2	50.00	100.00	350.00	500.00

PIASTRE

.465 SILVER, 12.65-12.95 g
Mintname: *Qustantiniyah*

KM#	Date	Year	VG	Fine	VF	XF
539	AH1222	1	250.00	600.00	800.00	1000.
		2	300.00	700.00	1000.	1500.

2 ZOLOTA

.465 SILVER, 18.00-19.45 g
Mintname: *Qustantiniyah*

KM#	Date	Year	VG	Fine	VF	XF
540.1	AH1222	1	600.00	1000.	2000.	3000.

Obv: Regnal year between ornaments.

KM#	Date	Year	VG	Fine	VF	XF
540.2	AH1222	1	—	—	—	—

2 PIASTRES

.465 SILVER, 24.95-26.10 g
Mintname: *Qustantiniyah*

KM#	Date	Year	VG	Fine	VF	XF
541	AH1222	1	500.00	850.00	1750.	2500.

21/2 PIASTRES

.465 SILVER, 42mm, 32.80 g
Mintname: *Qustantiniyah*

KM#	Date	Year	VG	Fine	VF	XF
542	AH1222	1	650.00	1100.	1750.	2500.

1/4 ALTIN

GOLD, 0.77 g
Mintname: *Qustantiniyah*

KM#	Date	Year	VG	Fine	VF	XF
543.1	AH1222	1	40.00	60.00	100.00	150.00
		2	45.00	65.00	120.00	175.00

Reduced size: 13.4mm.
Rev: *AZZ NASRAHUC* added at top.

KM#	Date	Year	VG	Fine	VF	XF
543.2	AH1223	14	50.00	70.00	125.00	185.00

1/2 ZERI MAHBUB

GOLD, 1.20 g
Mintname: *Qustantiniyah*

KM#	Date	Year	VG	Fine	VF	XF
544	AH1222	1	60.00	100.00	175.00	250.00
		2	60.00	100.00	200.00	300.00

ZERI MAHBUB

GOLD, 2.35 g
Mintname: *Qustantiniyah*

KM#	Date	Year	VG	Fine	VF	XF
545	AH1222	1	90.00	200.00	300.00	400.00
		2	125.00	300.00	400.00	500.00

ALTIN

GOLD, 3.20 g
Mintname: *Qustantiniyah*

KM#	Date	Year	VG	Fine	VF	XF
546	AH1222	1	70.00	100.00	120.00	170.00
		2	90.00	120.00	140.00	200.00

MAHMUD II

AH1223-1255/1808-1839AD

Silver Coinage

The silver currency of the reign of Mahmud II is characterized by frequent change of standard, so that the Piastre (Kurus), which began with 5.90 g of pure silver, had dropped to only 0.56 g in the lower denominations (token currency), and 0.94 g in the higher (actual currency). From time to time, the fineness, diameter, weight and type of the coins were changed, with the result that it is difficult, and not very meaningful, to attempt to trace individual denominations through the 32 years of his reign. For that reason, following Craig and others, the coins are grouped by standards of weight, fineness, or size. Changes in fineness, weight, and size are regularly indicated, as are distinguishing features whenever necessary for the proper identification of coins. The tolerance on Mahmud's silver coinage was considerable, particularly on the smaller denominations, and the weights listed are approximate. During the 15th-16th years of his reign, Mahmud II obtained the title *ADLI* = "Just" which was inscribed right of his toughra.

First Series

Years 1-2

AKCE

.465 SILVER, 9mm, 0.10-0.16 g
Mintname: *Qustantiniyah*

KM#	Date	Year	VG	Fine	VF	XF
550	AH1223	1	6.00	15.00	35.00	70.00
		2	6.00	15.00	35.00	70.00

PARA

.465 SILVER, 0.32 g
Mintname: *Qustantiniyah*

KM#	Date	Year	VG	Fine	VF	XF
551	AH1223	1	4.00	15.00	25.00	40.00
		2	4.00	15.00	25.00	40.00

5 PARA

.465 SILVER, 1.50-1.60 g
Mintname: *Qustantiniyah*

KM#	Date	Year	VG	Fine	VF	XF
552	AH1223	1	8.00	30.00	55.00	80.00
		2	8.00	30.00	55.00	80.00

10 PARA

.465 SILVER, 2.80-3.20 g
Mintname: *Qustantiniyah*

KM#	Date	Year	VG	Fine	VF	XF
553	AH1223	*1	10.00	30.00	60.00	90.00
		2	12.00	35.00	70.00	100.00

***NOTE:** Two obverse varieties exist.

30 PARA

SILVER, 9.53 g
Mintname: *Qustantiniyah*

KM#	Date	Year	VG	Fine	VF	XF
549	AH1223	1	Unique	—	—	—

PIASTRE

.465 SILVER, 12.00-13.18 g
Mintname: *Qustantiniyah*

KM#	Date	Year	VG	Fine	VF	XF
554	AH1223	1	100.00	300.00	550.00	800.00
		2	150.00	350.00	650.00	850.00

Second Series

Years 2-14

AKCE

.465 SILVER, 11mm, 0.10-0.12 g
Mintname: *Qustantiniyah*

KM#	Date	Year	VG	Fine	VF	XF
556	AH1223	5	2.50	10.00	30.00	50.00
		12	2.50	10.00	30.00	50.00

PARA

.465 SILVER, 0.18-0.26 g
Mintname: *Qustantiniyah*

KM#	Date	Year	VG	Fine	VF	XF
557	AH1223	3	1.00	3.00	4.00	10.00
		4	1.00	3.00	4.00	10.00
		5	1.00	3.00	4.00	10.00
		6	1.00	3.00	4.00	10.00
		7	1.00	3.00	4.00	10.00
		8	1.00	3.00	4.00	10.00
		9	1.00	3.00	4.00	10.00
		10	1.00	3.00	4.00	10.00
		11	1.00	3.00	4.00	10.00
		12	1.00	3.00	4.00	10.00
		13	1.00	3.00	4.00	10.00
		14	1.00	3.00	4.00	10.00

5 PARA

.465 SILVER, 1.01-1.20 g
Mintname: *Qustantiniyah*

KM#	Date	Year	VG	Fine	VF	XF
558	AH1223	3	5.00	10.00	30.00	45.00
		4	5.00	10.00	30.00	45.00
		5	5.00	10.00	30.00	45.00
		6	5.00	10.00	30.00	45.00
		7	5.00	10.00	30.00	45.00
		8	5.00	10.00	30.00	45.00
		9	5.00	10.00	30.00	45.00
		10	5.00	10.00	30.00	45.00
		11	5.00	10.00	30.00	45.00
		12	5.00	10.00	30.00	45.00
		13	5.00	10.00	30.00	45.00
		14	5.00	10.00	30.00	45.00

10 PARA

.465 SILVER, 2.10-2.50 g
Mintname: *Qustantiniyah*

KM#	Date	Year	VG	Fine	VF	XF
559	AH1223	3	4.00	10.00	25.00	40.00
		4	4.00	10.00	25.00	40.00
		5	4.00	10.00	25.00	40.00
		6	4.00	10.00	25.00	40.00
		7	4.00	10.00	25.00	40.00
		8	4.00	10.00	25.00	40.00
		9	4.00	10.00	25.00	40.00
		10	4.00	10.00	25.00	40.00
		11	4.00	10.00	25.00	40.00
		12	4.00	10.00	25.00	40.00
		13	4.00	10.00	25.00	40.00
		14	4.00	10.00	25.00	40.00

PIASTRE

.465 SILVER, 33mm, 9.60 g
Mintname: *Qustantiniyah*

KM#	Date	Year	VG	Fine	VF	XF
560	AH1223	3	12.00	20.00	40.00	75.00
		4	12.00	20.00	40.00	75.00
		5	12.00	20.00	40.00	75.00
		6	12.00	20.00	40.00	75.00
		7	12.00	20.00	40.00	75.00
		8	12.00	20.00	40.00	75.00
		9	12.00	20.00	40.00	75.00
		10	12.00	20.00	40.00	75.00
		11	12.00	20.00	40.00	75.00
		12	12.00	20.00	40.00	75.00
		13	12.00	20.00	40.00	75.00

Third Series - Cihadiye

(Jyhadiye)

Years 3-11

PIASTRE

.730 SILVER, 4.60-5.20 g
Mintname: *Qustantiniyah*

KM#	Date	Year	VG	Fine	VF	XF
562	AH1223	3	175.00	300.00	500.00	850.00

100 PARA

(2-1/2 Piastres)

.730 SILVER, 12.50-13.20 g
Mintname: *Qustantiniyah*

KM#	Date	Year	VG	Fine	VF	XF
563	AH1223	2	— Reported, not confirmed			
		3	100.00	175.00	350.00	600.00
		4	100.00	175.00	350.00	600.00
		5	100.00	175.00	350.00	600.00
		6	100.00	175.00	350.00	600.00
		7	100.00	175.00	350.00	600.00
		8	100.00	175.00	350.00	600.00
		9	100.00	175.00	350.00	600.00
		10	175.00	300.00	550.00	800.00
		11	350.00	600.00	850.00	1250.

5 PIASTRES

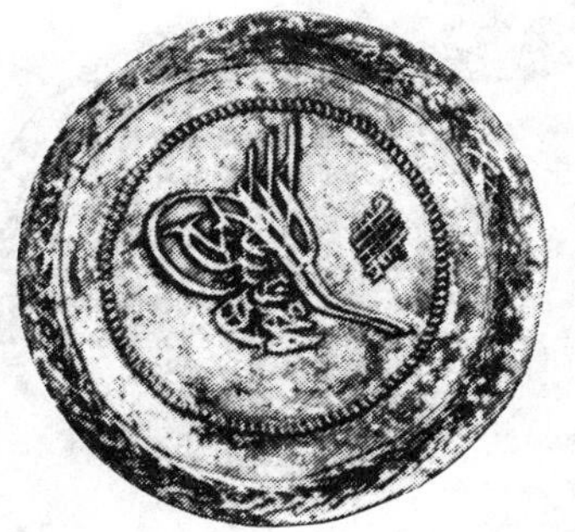

.730 SILVER, 24.00-26.00 g
Mintname: *Qustantiniyah*

KM#	Date	Year	VG	Fine	VF	XF
564	AH1223	3	20.00	30.00	55.00	90.00
		4	20.00	30.00	50.00	85.00
		5	20.00	30.00	50.00	85.00
		6	20.00	30.00	50.00	85.00
		7	20.00	30.00	50.00	85.00
		8	20.00	30.00	75.00	110.00
		9	20.00	30.00	75.00	110.00
		10	100.00	150.00	225.00	350.00
		11	275.00	400.00	650.00	1000.

Fourth Series

Years 14-15

PARA

.465 SILVER, 0.15 g
Mintname: *Qustantiniyah*
Obv: W/o flower.

KM#	Date	Year	VG	Fine	VF	XF
566	AH1223	14	1.25	2.50	6.00	12.00
		15	1.25	2.50	6.00	12.00

5 PARA

.465 SILVER, 18mm, 0.85 g
Mintname: *Qustantiniyah*

KM#	Date	Year	VG	Fine	VF	XF
567	AH1223	14	7.00	15.00	50.00	80.00

10 PARA

.465 SILVER, 22mm, 1.60-1.80 g
Mintname: *Qustantiniyah*

KM#	Date	Year	VG	Fine	VF	XF
568	AH1223	14	5.00	10.00	35.00	60.00
		15	10.00	20.00	50.00	100.00

PIASTRE

.465 SILVER, 32mm, 5.50 g
Mintname: *Qustantiniyah*

KM#	Date	Year	VG	Fine	VF	XF
569	AH1223	14	25.00	35.00	75.00	150.00
		15	45.00	60.00	100.00	175.00

2 PIASTRES

.465 SILVER, 11.50-13.40 g
Mintname: *Qustantiniyah*

KM#	Date	Year	VG	Fine	VF	XF
570	AH1223	14	25.00	50.00	100.00	200.00
		15	30.00	60.00	120.00	225.00

NOTE: Some coins have stars above and below regnal year box.

Fifth Series

Years 15-16
Reeded edge on all but Para

PARA

.730 SILVER, 0.14-0.17 g
Mintname: *Qustantiniyah*
Obv: Flower right of toughra.

KM#	Date	Year	VG	Fine	VF	XF
572	AH1223	15	1.50	3.00	6.00	15.00
		16	1.50	3.00	6.00	15.00

5 PARA

.730 SILVER, 0.80 g
Mintname: *Qustantiniyah*

KM#	Date	Year	VG	Fine	VF	XF
573	AH1223	15	8.00	17.50	40.00	60.00
		16	7.50	15.00	35.00	50.00

10 PARA

.730 SILVER, 1.60 g
Mintname: *Qustantiniyah*

KM#	Date	Year	VG	Fine	VF	XF
574	AH1223	15	7.50	15.00	20.00	35.00
		16	7.50	15.00	20.00	35.00

PIASTRE

.730 SILVER, 6.15 g
Mintname: *Qustantiniyah*

KM#	Date	Year	VG	Fine	VF	XF
575	AH1223	15	20.00	30.00	50.00	100.00
		16	20.00	30.00	50.00	100.00

2 PIASTRES

.730 SILVER, 12.00-13.00 g
Mintname: *Qustantiniyah*

KM#	Date	Year	VG	Fine	VF	XF
576	AH1223	15	10.00	18.00	40.00	70.00
		16	10.00	20.00	45.00	80.00

Sixth Series

Years 16-21

PARA

.600 SILVER, 12mm, 0.15-0.20 g
Mintname: *Qustantiniyah*

KM#	Date	Year	VG	Fine	VF	XF
578	AH1223	17	1.50	3.00	10.00	17.50
		18	1.50	3.00	10.00	17.50
		19	1.50	3.00	10.00	17.50
		20	1.50	3.00	10.00	17.50
		21	1.50	3.00	10.00	17.50

5 PARA

SILVER
Mintname: *Qustantiniyah*
Obv: Flower exists w/2 and 3 buds.

KM#	Date	Year	VG	Fine	VF	XF
A579	AH1223	18	—	—	—	—

ZOLOTA

NOTE: Formerly listed Zolota, KM#581 is considered a modern production, using the center of 60 Para, KM#580, by leading authorities.

30 PARA

SILVER, 2.98 g

KM#	Date	Year	VG	Fine	VF	XF
B579	AH1223	16	4.00	6.00	15.00	30.00

.600 SILVER, 3.00-3.40 g
Mintname: *Qustantiniyah*

KM#	Date	Year	VG	Fine	VF	XF
579	AH1223	17	4.00	6.00	15.00	30.00
		18	4.00	6.00	15.00	30.00
		19	4.00	6.00	15.00	30.00
		20	4.00	6.00	15.00	30.00
		21	4.00	6.00	15.00	35.00

NOTE: This coin occurs frequently in high grade.

60 PARA

.600 SILVER, 5.60-6.25 g
Mintname: *Qustantiniyah*

KM#	Date	Year	VG	Fine	VF	XF
580	AH1223	16	8.00	12.00	25.00	40.00
		17	5.00	8.00	16.00	25.00
		18	5.00	8.00	16.00	25.00
		19	5.00	8.00	16.00	25.00
		20	5.00	8.00	16.00	25.00
		21	5.00	8.00	16.00	25.00

NOTE: This coin occurs frequently in high grade.

Seventh Series

Years 21-22
Wavy borders

NOTE: A Para was struck in this series, in low grade silver .460, in the year 22, but is not distinguishable from yr. 22 pieces of the eighth series KM#586.

AKCE

SILVER
Mintname: *Qustantiniyah*

KM#	Date	Year	VG	Fine	VF	XF
582	AH1223	21	3.00	5.00	7.00	15.00

20 PARA

.833 SILVER, 0.80 g
Mintname: *Qustantiniyah*

KM#	Date	Year	VG	Fine	VF	XF
583	AH1223	21	4.00	6.00	9.00	15.00
		22	20.00	35.00	60.00	100.00

NOTE: This coin occurs frequently in high grade, also with open and closed rosettes on obverse and reverse.

PIASTRE

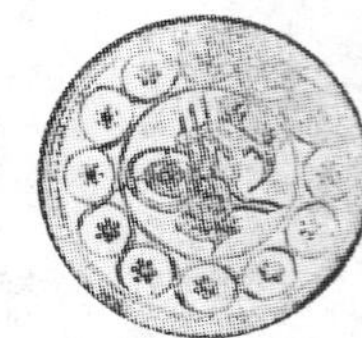
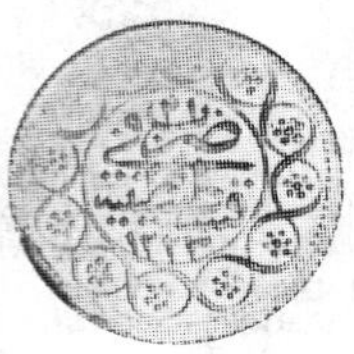

.833 SILVER, 1.40-1.60 g
Mintname: *Qustantiniyah*

KM#	Date	Year	VG	Fine	VF	XF
584	AH1223	21	5.00	6.50	11.00	20.00
		22	25.00	35.00	60.00	100.00

NOTE: This coin occurs frequently in high grade, also with open and closed rosettes on obverse and reverse.

10 PIASTRES

Two different designs exist dated year 22 and are both considered patterns.

Eighth Series - Cedid

(Jadid)

Years 22-25

NOTE: Coins of the eighth series are readily distinguished from the ninth series, as they lack the dot or rosette below the inner wreath that appears on the ninth series. In the eighth and ninth series, with the exception of the Para, all coins have the word *Adli* (the Just) right of the toughra, sometimes with vertical mark below. The Para is distinguished only by date, however. Many coins are debased with a silver wash.

PARA

.220 SILVER, 0.10 g
Mintname: *Qustantiniyah*

KM#	Date	Year	VG	Fine	VF	XF
586	AH1223	22	1.00	2.25	3.50	8.00
		23	1.00	2.25	3.50	8.00
		24	1.00	2.25	3.50	8.00
		25	2.00	3.00	4.50	10.00

10 PARA

.220 SILVER, 17mm, 0.80 g
Mintname: *Qustantiniyah*

KM#	Date	Year	VG	Fine	VF	XF
587	AH1223	22	2.00	6.00	15.00	35.00
		23	2.00	6.00	15.00	35.00
		24	2.00	6.00	15.00	35.00
		25	2.00	6.00	15.00	35.00

20 PARA

.220 SILVER, 1.40-1.80 g
Mintname: *Qustantiniyah*

KM#	Date	Year	VG	Fine	VF	XF
588	AH1223	21	—	—	Rare	—
		22	1.00	2.00	5.00	12.00
		23	1.00	2.00	5.00	12.00
		24	1.00	2.00	5.00	12.00
		25	1.00	2.00	5.00	12.00

PIASTRE

.220 SILVER, 2.60-3.00 g
Mintname: *Qustantiniyah*

KM#	Date	Year	VG	Fine	VF	XF
589	AH1223	22	2.75	3.00	6.25	15.00
		23	2.75	3.00	6.25	15.00
		24	2.75	3.00	6.25	15.00
		25	2.75	3.00	6.25	15.00

100 PARA

(2-1/2 Piastres)

.220 SILVER, 7.20-7.80 g
Mintname: *Qustantiniyah*

KM#	Date	Year	VG	Fine	VF	XF
590	AH1223	22	4.75	7.50	11.00	25.00
		23	3.50	5.00	8.00	15.00
		24	3.50	5.00	8.00	15.00
		25	3.50	5.00	8.00	15.00

5 PIASTRES

.220 SILVER, 15.00-16.00 g
Mintname: *Qustantiniyah*

KM#	Date	Year	VG	Fine	VF	XF
591	AH1223	22	3.00	5.00	12.50	25.00
		23	3.00	5.00	12.50	25.00
		24	3.00	5.00	12.50	25.00
		25	3.00	5.00	15.00	30.00

Ninth Series

Years 25-32

Rosette or dot added beneath inner wreath on obverse and reverse except on 1 Akce and 1 Para.

AKCE

.170 SILVER, 0.04-0.07 g
Mintname: *Qustantiniyah*

KM#	Date	Year	VG	Fine	VF	XF
593	AH1223	25	5.00	10.00	25.00	55.00
		26	2.50	4.00	15.00	40.00
		27	2.50	4.00	15.00	40.00

PARA

.170 SILVER, 0.08-0.15 g

Mintname: *Qustantiniyah*

KM#	Date	Year	VG	Fine	VF	XF
594	AH1223	26	1.00	1.50	2.75	7.00
		27	.75	1.25	2.00	5.00
		28	.75	1.25	2.00	5.00
		29	.75	1.25	2.00	5.00
		30	.75	1.25	2.00	5.00
		31	.75	1.25	2.00	5.00
		32	.75	1.25	2.00	5.00

10 PARA

.170 SILVER, 0.50-0.75 g
Mintname: *Qustantiniyah*

KM#	Date	Year	VG	Fine	VF	XF
595	AH1223	25	2.00	3.00	5.00	12.50
		26	5.00	7.50	10.00	18.50
		27	2.00	3.00	5.00	12.50
		28	2.00	3.00	5.00	12.50
		29	2.00	3.00	5.00	12.50
		30	2.00	3.00	5.00	12.50
		31	2.00	3.00	5.00	12.50
		32	2.00	3.00	5.00	12.50

20 PARA

.170 SILVER, 1.35-1.60 g
Mintname: *Qustantiniyah*

KM#	Date	Year	VG	Fine	VF	XF
596	AH1223	25	2.00	2.50	4.00	10.00
		26	2.00	2.50	4.00	10.00
		27	2.00	2.50	4.00	10.00
		28	2.00	2.50	4.00	10.00
		29	2.00	2.50	4.00	10.00
		30	2.00	2.50	4.00	10.00
		31	2.00	2.50	4.00	10.00
		32	2.00	2.50	4.00	10.00

NOTE: Years 26 and 31 are easily confused.

PIASTRE

.170 SILVER, 2.60-3.00 g
Mintname: *Qustantiniyah*

KM#	Date	Year	VG	Fine	VF	XF
597	AH1223	25	3.50	5.00	8.00	17.50
		26	3.50	5.00	8.00	17.50

100 PARA

(2-1/2 Piastres)

.170 SILVER, 6.40-7.80 g
Mintname: *Qustantiniyah*

KM#	Date	Year	VG	Fine	VF	XF
598	AH1223	25	3.00	4.50	9.00	18.50
		26	3.00	4.50	9.00	18.50

5 PIASTRES

.170 SILVER, 13.00-16.00 g
Mintname: *Qustantiniyah*

KM#	Date	Year	VG	Fine	VF	XF
599	AH1223	25	4.00	7.00	12.50	25.00
		26	4.00	7.00	12.50	25.00

Tenth Series

Years 26-32

1-1/2 PIASTRE

.435 SILVER, 2.60-3.00 g
Mintname: *Qustantiniyah*

KM#	Date	Year	VG	Fine	VF	XF
601	AH1223	26	4.00	6.00	12.00	25.00
		27	3.50	5.00	10.00	20.00
		28	3.50	5.00	10.00	20.00
		29	3.50	5.00	10.00	20.00
		30	3.50	5.00	10.00	20.00
		31	3.50	5.00	10.00	20.00
		32	3.50	5.00	10.00	20.00

3 PIASTRES

.435 SILVER, 5.60-6.20 g
Mintname: *Qustantiniyah*

KM#	Date	Year	VG	Fine	VF	XF
602	AH1223	26	5.00	7.50	12.00	25.00
		27	4.50	6.00	10.00	20.00
		28	4.50	6.00	10.00	20.00
		29	4.50	6.00	10.00	20.00
		30	4.50	6.00	10.00	20.00
		31	4.50	6.00	10.00	20.00
		32	4.50	6.00	10.00	20.00

6 PIASTRES

.435 SILVER, 11.00-13.00 g
Mintname: *Qustantiniyah*

KM#	Date	Year	VG	Fine	VF	XF
603	AH1223	26	6.00	8.00	15.00	40.00
		27	6.00	8.00	15.00	30.00
		28	6.00	8.00	15.00	30.00
		29	6.00	8.00	15.00	30.00
		30	6.00	8.00	15.00	30.00
		31	6.00	8.00	15.00	30.00
		32	6.50	9.00	17.50	32.50

Gold Coinage

The gold emissions of Mahmud II are characterized by several simultaneous series, each with its characteristic name. They are distinguished by weight and by special symbols, such as the ornament right of the toughra, the border, and variations in design. These are indicated for each series, along with the weights and diameters of each denomination. Each series comprises several denominations, with the basic unit known as the Altin (Gold Coin) or Tak (Single); other denominations include the Double (Clifte), Half (Yarim, or Nisfiye), and Quarter (Ceyrek, or Rubiye). Not all denominations were struck in every series. Some series can be divided into several subvarieties, which are listed separately below. Finally, a few coins were struck that do not fit into any of the series.

Zeri Mahbub Series

"Beloved Gold Series"

The obverse of all denominations consists of a toughra, with mint name and date below on the 1 and 1/2 Zeri Mahbub only. The reverse of the 1 and 1/2 bears a four-line inscription; the reverse of the 1/4, the mint and date.

FIRST TYPE

Lily on 1 and 1/2 Zeri Mahbub, branch with one rose on the 1/4 Zeri Mahbub.

1/4 ZERI MAHBUB

GOLD, 0.70-0.80 g
Mintname: *Qustantiniyah*

KM#	Date	Year	VG	Fine	VF	XF
605	AH1223	1	15.00	20.00	30.00	40.00
		2	15.00	20.00	30.00	40.00
		3	15.00	25.00	40.00	60.00
		4	15.00	20.00	30.00	40.00
		5	15.00	20.00	30.00	40.00

1/2 ZERI MAHBUB

GOLD, 1.10-1.20 g
Mintname: *Qustantiniyah*

KM#	Date	Year	VG	Fine	VF	XF
606	AH1223	1	35.00	50.00	70.00	90.00
		2	35.00	50.00	70.00	90.00
		3	35.00	50.00	70.00	90.00
		4	35.00	50.00	70.00	90.00
		5	35.00	50.00	70.00	90.00

ZERI MAHBUB

GOLD, 2.30-2.40 g
Mintname: *Qustantiniyah*

KM#	Date	Year	VG	Fine	VF	XF
607	AH1223	1	50.00	75.00	100.00	150.00
		2	50.00	75.00	100.00	150.00
		3	—	Reported, not confirmed		
		4	—	Reported, not confirmed		
		5	150.00	275.00	400.00	750.00

SECOND TYPE

Rose replaces lily on 1 and 1/2 Zeri Mahbub, branch with 2 roses replaces branch with 1 rose on the 1/4 Zeri Mahbub.

1/4 ZERI MAHBUB

GOLD, 0.75-0.79 g
Mintname: *Qustantiniyah*

KM#	Date	Year	VG	Fine	VF	XF
608	AH1223	6	15.00	20.00	30.00	45.00
		7	15.00	20.00	30.00	45.00
		8	15.00	20.00	30.00	45.00
		9	15.00	20.00	30.00	45.00
		10	15.00	20.00	30.00	45.00
		11	15.00	20.00	35.00	50.00
		12	15.00	20.00	35.00	50.00
		13	15.00	20.00	35.00	50.00
		14	15.00	20.00	35.00	50.00

1/2 ZERI MAHBUB

GOLD, 18mm, 1.10-1.20 g
Mintname: *Qustantiniyah*

KM#	Date	Year	VG	Fine	VF	XF
609	AH1223	6		Reported, not confirmed		
		7		Reported, not confirmed		
		8	40.00	60.00	80.00	100.00
		9		Reported, not confirmed		
		10		Reported, not confirmed		
		11		Reported, not confirmed		
		12	40.00	60.00	80.00	100.00

ZERI MAHBUB

GOLD, 2.30-2.40 g
Mintname: *Qustantiniyah*

KM#	Date	Year	VG	Fine	VF	XF
610	AH1223	6	40.00	75.00	85.00	125.00
		7	40.00	75.00	85.00	125.00
		8	40.00	75.00	85.00	125.00
		9	40.00	75.00	85.00	125.00
		10	40.00	75.00	85.00	125.00
		11	40.00	75.00	85.00	125.00
		12	40.00	75.00	85.00	125.00
		13		Reported, not confirmed		
		14	40.00	75.00	85.00	125.00
		15	40.00	75.00	85.00	125.00

Rumi Series

Characterized by a flower right of toughra and an ornamental border, consisting of a wavy line hexagon, on both sides.

1/2 RUMI ALTIN

GOLD, 1.20 g
Mintname: *Qustantiniyah*

KM#	Date	Year	VG	Fine	VF	XF
612	AH1223	10	75.00	100.00	125.00	175.00
		11	75.00	100.00	125.00	175.00
		12	75.00	100.00	125.00	175.00
		13	75.00	100.00	125.00	175.00

RUMI ALTIN

GOLD, 2.40 g
Mintname: *Qustantiniyah*

KM#	Date	Year	VG	Fine	VF	XF
613	AH1223	10	200.00	250.00	300.00	350.00

2 RUMI ALTIN

GOLD, 4.70-4.80 g
Mintname: *Qustantiniyah*

KM#	Date	Year	VG	Fine	VF	XF
614	AH1223	8	80.00	100.00	125.00	200.00
		9	80.00	100.00	125.00	200.00
		10	80.00	100.00	125.00	200.00
		11	80.00	100.00	125.00	200.00
		12	80.00	100.00	125.00	200.00
		13	80.00	100.00	125.00	200.00
		22	80.00	125.00	150.00	225.00

New Rumi Series

Similar to the Rumi series, except that the wavy borders are replaced by an inscription containing the name and titles of Mahmud II.

RUMI ALTIN

GOLD, 23mm, 2.40 g
Mintname: *Qustantiniyah*

KM#	Date	Year	VG	Fine	VF	XF
616	AH1223	9		Reported, not confirmed		
		10	40.00	50.00	90.00	120.00
		11	40.00	50.00	90.00	120.00
		12	40.00	50.00	90.00	120.00
		13	40.00	50.00	90.00	120.00
		14	40.00	50.00	90.00	120.00
		15	40.00	50.00	90.00	120.00

2 RUMI ALTIN

GOLD, 4.70-4.80 g
Mintname: *Qustantiniyah*

KM#	Date	Year	VG	Fine	VF	XF
617	AH1223	9	100.00	125.00	150.00	200.00
		10	100.00	125.00	150.00	200.00
		11	100.00	125.00	150.00	200.00
		12	100.00	125.00	150.00	200.00

Surre Series

'Surre' means a purse, the amount sent by the Sultan annually to the Hejaz for the holy cities. They were used by pilgrims to Mecca. They bear the mint name *Darulhilafe* in place of *Constantinople*, with either of 2 epithets, *El-Aliye* (the Lofty) or *Es-Seniye* (the Sublime) and are therefore known as Elaliye and Esseniye Altins, respectively.

El-Aliye Surre Series

1/4 SURRE ALTIN

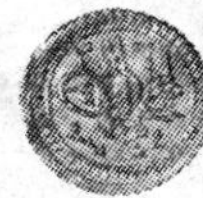

GOLD, 0.48 g
Mintname: *Darulhilafe*

KM#	Date	Year	VG	Fine	VF	XF
619	AH1223	15	30.00	50.00	100.00	150.00
		16	30.00	50.00	100.00	150.00

1/2 SURRE ALTIN

GOLD, 15-16mm, 0.78 g
Mintname: *Darulhilafe*

KM#	Date	Year	VG	Fine	VF	XF
620	AH1223	15	40.00	60.00	150.00	250.00
		16	40.00	60.00	150.00	250.00

SURRE ALTIN

GOLD, 1.56 g
Mintname: *Darulhilafe*

KM#	Date	Year	VG	Fine	VF	XF
621	AH1223	15	60.00	85.00	110.00	150.00
		16	60.00	85.00	110.00	150.00

Esseniye Surre Series

1/4 SURRE ALTIN

GOLD, 0.48 g
Mintname: *Darulhilafe*

KM#	Date	Year	VG	Fine	VF	XF
623	AH1223	15	30.00	45.00	100.00	150.00

1/2 SURRE ALTIN

GOLD, 0.78 g
Mintname: *Darulhilafe*

KM#	Date	Year	VG	Fine	VF	XF
624	AH1223	15	50.00	75.00	200.00	300.00

SURRE ALTIN

GOLD, 1.50 g
Mintname: *Darulhilafe*

KM#	Date	Year	VG	Fine	VF	XF
625	AH1223	15	60.00	90.00	150.00	225.00

Additional Series

The following type does not fit into any of the recognized series.

1/4 ALTIN

GOLD, 14mm, 0.58 g
Considered a 1/4 Zeri Mahbub.
***Azze Nasaru* above mintname:**
Qustantiniyah

KM#	Date	Year	VG	Fine	VF	XF
627	AH1223	13	15.00	20.00	40.00	60.00
		14	15.00	20.00	40.00	60.00
		15	15.00	20.00	40.00	60.00

Adli Series

Types as the Zeri Mahbub series, except that the word *Adli* replaces the flower right of toughra.

1/4 ADLI ALTIN

GOLD, 0.40-0.45 g
Mintname: *Qustantiniyah*

KM#	Date	Year	VG	Fine	VF	XF
629	AH1223	16	20.00	30.00	75.00	125.00
		17	20.00	30.00	75.00	125.00

1/2 ADLI ALTIN

GOLD, 0.75-0.85 g
Mintname: *Qustantiniyah*

KM#	Date	Year	VG	Fine	VF	XF
630	AH1223	15	45.00	60.00	75.00	90.00
		16		Reported, not confirmed		
		17	45.00	60.00	75.00	90.00

KM#	Date	Year	VG	Fine	VF	XF
630		18	45.00	60.00	75.00	90.00
		19	45.00	60.00	75.00	90.00
		20	45.00	60.00	75.00	90.00
		21	45.00	60.00	75.00	90.00
		22	45.00	60.00	75.00	90.00
		23	45.00	60.00	75.00	90.00
		24	Reported, not confirmed			
		25	45.00	60.00	75.00	90.00
		26	Reported, not confirmed			
		27	45.00	60.00	75.00	90.00
		28	Reported, not confirmed			
		29	45.00	60.00	75.00	90.00
		30	45.00	60.00	75.00	90.00
		31	45.00	60.00	75.00	90.00
		32	45.00	60.00	75.00	90.00

ADLI ALTIN

GOLD, 1.50-1.60 g
Mintname: *Qustantiniyah*

KM#	Date	Year	VG	Fine	VF	XF
631	AH1223	15	30.00	40.00	100.00	130.00
		17	30.00	40.00	100.00	130.00
		18	30.00	40.00	100.00	130.00
		19	30.00	40.00	100.00	130.00
		20	30.00	40.00	100.00	130.00

New Adli Series

Toughra on obverse, mint and date on reverse. Additional legends around, obverse and reverse. Mintname Qustantiniyah has epithet ***Al-Mahrusa*** added.

1/4 NEW ADLI ALTIN

GOLD, 0.38-0.43 g
Mintname: *Qustantiniyah*

KM#	Date	Year	VG	Fine	VF	XF
632	AH1223	17	10.00	20.00	30.00	45.00

Mintname: *Qustantiniyah*

KM#	Date	Year	VG	Fine	VF	XF
633	AH1223	15	10.00	20.00	30.00	45.00
		17	10.00	20.00	30.00	45.00
		18	10.00	20.00	30.00	45.00
		19	10.00	20.00	30.00	45.00
		20	10.00	20.00	30.00	45.00
		21	10.00	20.00	30.00	45.00
		22	10.00	20.00	30.00	45.00
		23	10.00	20.00	30.00	45.00
		24	10.00	20.00	40.00	55.00

1/2 NEW ADLI ALTIN

GOLD, 0.78 g
Mintname: *Qustantiniyah*

KM#	Date	Year	VG	Fine	VF	XF
634	AH1223	16	30.00	40.00	50.00	75.00
		17	30.00	40.00	50.00	75.00
		18	30.00	40.00	50.00	75.00
		19	30.00	40.00	50.00	75.00
		20	30.00	40.00	50.00	75.00
		21	Reported, not confirmed			

NEW ADLI ALTIN

GOLD, 1.58 g
Mintname: *Qustantiniyah*

KM#	Date	Year	VG	Fine	VF	XF
635	AH1223	16	27.50	40.00	60.00	80.00
		17	27.50	40.00	60.00	80.00
		18	27.50	40.00	60.00	80.00
		19	27.50	40.00	60.00	80.00
		20	27.50	40.00	60.00	80.00
		21	Reported, not confirmed			
		22	Reported, not confirmed			

Hayriye Series

Similar to the New Adli, but in place of the ring of legend around the edge, there are alternating ovals of inscription and branches.

1/2 HAYRIYE ALTIN

GOLD, 0.86 g
Mintname: *Qustantiniyah*

KM#	Date	Year	VG	Fine	VF	XF
637	AH1223	21	25.00	35.00	45.00	65.00
		22	25.00	35.00	45.00	65.00
		23	25.00	35.00	45.00	65.00
		24	25.00	35.00	45.00	65.00
		25	25.00	35.00	45.00	65.00
		26	25.00	35.00	45.00	65.00

HAYRIYE ALTIN

GOLD, 1.73 g
Mintname: *Qustantiniyah*

KM#	Date	Year	VG	Fine	VF	XF
638	AH1223	21	30.00	35.00	45.00	90.00
		22	30.00	35.00	45.00	90.00
		23	30.00	35.00	45.00	90.00
		24	30.00	35.00	45.00	90.00
		25	30.00	35.00	45.00	90.00
		26	Reported, not confirmed			

2 HAYRIYE ALTIN

GOLD, 3.55 g
Mintname: *Qustantiniyah*

KM#	Date	Year	VG	Fine	VF	XF
639	AH1223	21	100.00	125.00	150.00	200.00

New (Yeni) Series

The Yeni or new series comprises but 1 denomination, distinguished by starlike wavy pattern around edge.

1/4 NEW ALTIN

Yeni Rubiye

GOLD, 12mm, 0.26-0.31 g
Mintname: *Qustantiniyah*

KM#	Date	Year	VG	Fine	VF	XF
641	AH1223	24	15.00	25.00	40.00	55.00
		25	15.00	25.00	40.00	55.00
		26	15.00	25.00	40.00	55.00
		27	15.00	25.00	40.00	55.00
		28	15.00	25.00	40.00	55.00
		29	Reported, not confirmed			
		30	17.50	22.50	25.00	30.00

Cedid Mahmudiye Series

Like the Hayriye, but ovals of inscription and branches replaced by a wreath design.

1/4 CEDID MAHMUDIYE

GOLD, 0.38-0.40 g
Mintname: *Qustantiniyah*

KM#	Date	Year	VG	Fine	VF	XF
643	AH1223	26	15.00	25.00	35.00	45.00
		27	15.00	25.00	35.00	45.00
		28	15.00	25.00	35.00	45.00
		29	15.00	25.00	35.00	45.00
		30	15.00	25.00	35.00	45.00
		31	15.00	25.00	35.00	45.00
		32	15.00	25.00	35.00	45.00

1/2 CEDID MAHMUDIYE

GOLD, 0.76-0.80 g

Mintname: *Qustantiniyah*

KM#	Date	Year	VG	Fine	VF	XF
644	AH1223	26	20.00	30.00	45.00	65.00
		27	20.00	30.00	45.00	65.00
		28	20.00	30.00	45.00	65.00
		29	20.00	30.00	45.00	65.00
		30	20.00	30.00	45.00	65.00
		31	20.00	30.00	45.00	65.00
		32	20.00	30.00	45.00	65.00

CEDID MAHMUDIYE

GOLD, 1.58-1.60 g
Mintname: *Qustantiniyah*

KM#	Date	Year	VG	Fine	VF	XF
645	AH1223	26	30.00	40.00	55.00	75.00
		27	30.00	40.00	55.00	75.00
		28	30.00	40.00	55.00	75.00
		29	30.00	40.00	55.00	75.00
		30	30.00	40.00	55.00	75.00
		31	30.00	40.00	55.00	75.00
		32	30.00	40.00	55.00	75.00

Mint Visit Coinage

Mahmud II's visit to Edirne.

ادرنة

Edirne Mint mark:

1/2 HAYRIYE ALTIN

GOLD, 0.88 g
Mintname: *Edirne*

KM#	Date	Year	VG	Fine	VF	XF
647	AH1223	24	60.00	100.00	150.00	250.00

1 HAYRIYE ALTIN

GOLD, 1.80 g
Mintname: *Edirne*

KM#	Date	Year	VG	Fine	VF	XF
648	AH1223	24	100.00	120.00	150.00	200.00

2 HAYRIYE ALTIN

GOLD, 3.55 g
Mintname: *Edirne*

KM#	Date	Year	VG	Fine	VF	XF
649	AH1223	24	175.00	225.00	275.00	350.00

ABDUL MEJID

AH1255-1277/1839-1861AD

Standard, fineness, and denominations of the silver coinage similar to the ninth (for the 1, 10, and 20 Para) and tenth (for the 1-1/2, 3, and 6 Piastres) series of Mahmud II (KM#594-596, 601-603).

Pre-Reform Coinage

PARA

BILLON, 0.14-0.20 g
Mintname: *Qustantiniyah*

KM#	Date	Year	VG	Fine	VF	XF
651	AH1255	1	1.50	2.25	3.00	5.00
		2	1.50	2.25	3.00	5.00
		3	2.50	4.00	5.00	7.50
		4	1.50	2.25	3.00	5.00
		5	1.50	2.25	3.00	5.00
		6	7.50	10.00	15.00	20.00

10 PARA

BILLON, 0.60-0.80 g
Mintname: *Qustantiniyah*

KM#	Date	Year	VG	Fine	VF	XF
652	AH1255	1	2.00	3.00	4.00	7.50
		2	2.00	3.00	4.00	7.50
		3	3.00	4.00	5.00	8.00
		4	2.00	3.00	4.00	7.50
		5	2.00	3.00	4.00	7.50

20 PARA

BILLON, 1.35-1.60 g
Mintname: *Qustantiniyah*

KM#	Date	Year	VG	Fine	VF	XF
653	AH1255	1	.50	1.00	2.50	4.00
		2	1.50	2.50	4.00	7.50
		3	1.50	2.50	4.00	7.50
		4	1.00	2.00	3.50	5.00
		5	2.00	3.00	5.00	9.00

1-1/2 PIASTRES

SILVER, 2.60-3.00 g
Mintname: *Qustantiniyah*

KM#	Date	Year	VG	Fine	VF	XF
654	AH1255	1	6.00	8.50	13.00	19.00
		2	5.00	6.50	12.00	18.00
		3	7.00	9.00	14.00	20.00
		4	5.00	6.50	12.00	18.00
		5	5.00	6.50	12.00	18.00

3 PIASTRES

SILVER, 5.60-6.20 g
Mintname: *Qustantiniyah*

KM#	Date	Year	VG	Fine	VF	XF
655	AH1255	1	20.00	40.00	100.00	150.00
		2	45.00	75.00	150.00	200.00
		3	100.00	200.00	275.00	350.00
		4	100.00	200.00	275.00	350.00

6 PIASTRES

SILVER, 12.42-13.00 g
Mintname: *Qustantiniyah*

KM#	Date	Year	VG	Fine	VF	XF
656	AH1255	1	40.00	50.00	75.00	150.00
		2	80.00	120.00	200.00	325.00
		4	—	—	Rare	—

1/4 MEMDUHIYE ALTIN

GOLD, 0.38-0.40 g
Mintname: *Qustantiniyah*

KM#	Date	Year	VG	Fine	VF	XF
657	AH1255	1	17.50	25.00	35.00	55.00
		2	17.50	25.00	35.00	55.00
		3	17.50	25.00	35.00	55.00
		4	17.50	25.00	35.00	55.00
		5	17.50	25.00	35.00	55.00

1/2 MEMDUHIYE ALTIN

GOLD, 0.78-0.80 g
Mintname: *Qustantiniyah*

KM#	Date	Year	VG	Fine	VF	XF
658	AH1255	1	40.00	50.00	60.00	80.00
		2	40.00	50.00	60.00	80.00
		3	40.00	50.00	60.00	80.00
		4	40.00	50.00	60.00	80.00
		5	40.00	50.00	60.00	80.00

MEMDUHIYE ALTIN

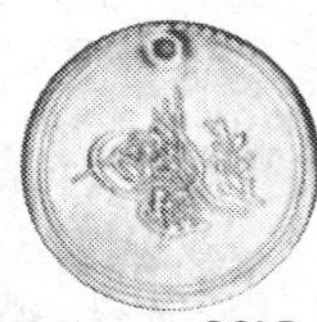

GOLD, 1.58-1.60 g
Mintname: *Qustantiniyah*

KM#	Date	Year	VG	Fine	VF	XF
659	AH1255	1	45.00	55.00	75.00	150.00
		2	45.00	55.00	75.00	150.00
		3	45.00	55.00	75.00	150.00
		4	45.00	55.00	75.00	150.00
		5	45.00	55.00	75.00	150.00

NOTE: The Memduhiye issue of Abdul Mejid was of the same fineness, weight and diameter as the Mahmudiye issue of Mahmud II. Although officially valued at 20 Piastres, the actual value of the Memduhiye Altin varied with the relative prices of gold and silver.

1/2 ZERI MAHBUB

GOLD, 0.80 g
Rev: 4-line inscription, mintname: *Qustantiniyah.*

KM#	Date	Year	VG	Fine	VF	XF
660	AH1255	1	45.00	60.00	75.00	100.00
		2	45.00	60.00	75.00	100.00
		3	45.00	60.00	75.00	100.00
		4	45.00	60.00	75.00	100.00
		5	45.00	60.00	75.00	100.00
		6	75.00	100.00	120.00	200.00

PATTERNS (Pn)

(Including off metal strikes)

KM#	Date	Mintage	Identification	Mkt.Val.
Pn1	AH1223, yr.1	—	20 Para, Silver	—
Pn2	AH1223, yr.1	—	30 Para, Silver	—
Pn3	AH1223, yr.1	—	60 Para, Silver	—
Pn4	AH1223, yr.1	—	80 Para, Silver	—
Pn5	AH1223, yr.1	—	100 Para, Silver	—

Modern Coinage

MONETARY SYSTEM

1844-1923

40 Para = 1 Kurush (Piastre)

100 Kurush (Piastre) = 1 Lira

NOTE: The 20 Kurush coin was known as a Mecidi, after the name of Abdul Mejid, who established the currency reform in 1844. The entire series is sometimes called Mejidiye coinage.

PARA

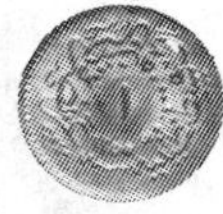

COPPER
Accession date: AH1255
Mintname: *Qustantiniyah*
Thick planchet, 1.00-1.10 g

KM#	Year	Mintage	VG	Fine	VF	XF
665.1	8	1.000	2.00	4.00	10.00	20.00
665.1	9	.375	5.00	10.00	30.00	50.00
	10	1.250	3.00	5.00	12.00	25.00
	11	.165	2.00	4.00	8.00	15.00
	12	1.600	2.00	4.00	8.00	15.00
	13	.800	2.00	3.00	6.00	12.00
	14	.300	4.00	6.00	15.00	25.00
	15	.700	3.00	6.00	12.00	20.00
	16	3.400	3.00	6.00	12.00	20.00

Medium planchet, 0.80-0.90 g

KM#	Year	Mintage	VG	Fine	VF	XF
665.2	16	Inc. Ab.	.50	1.00	1.75	5.00
	17	.800	1.00	3.00	6.00	10.00
	18	4.500	.75	1.50	2.50	5.00

Thin planchet, 0.50-0.60 g

KM#	Year	Mintage	VG	Fine	VF	XF
665.3	18	Inc. Ab.	.50	1.00	2.50	5.00
	19	2.500	.25	.50	1.25	2.50
	21	2.000	10.00	20.00	45.00	70.00

NOTE: The thin planchet coin of "year 16" is actually year 19 with broken 9.

5 PARA

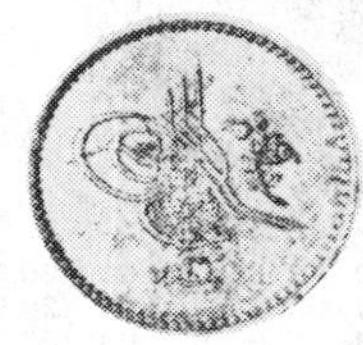
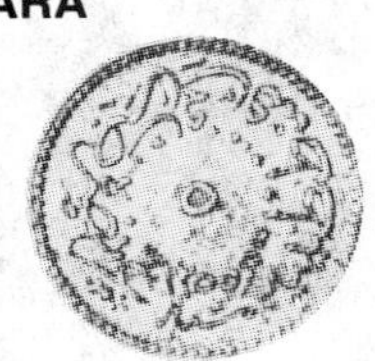

COPPER
Accession date: AH1255
Mintname: *Qustantiniyah*
Thick planchet, 4.90-6.80 g

KM#	Year	Mintage	VG	Fine	VF	XF
666.1	7	—	7.50	15.00	20.00	50.00
	8	1.000	1.00	2.00	7.50	15.00
	9	.300	10.00	20.00	50.00	100.00
	10	.800	1.50	3.00	6.00	15.00
	11	2.542	1.50	3.00	6.00	15.00
	12	3.680	.75	1.25	5.00	15.00
	13	4.640	.75	1.25	5.00	15.00
	14	3.400	.75	1.25	8.00	25.00
	15	5.060	.75	1.25	8.00	25.00

Medium planchet, 3.70-4.20 g

KM#	Year	Mintage	VG	Fine	VF	XF
666.2	15	Inc. Ab.	2.00	4.00	20.00	40.00
	16	6.300	.50	1.00	2.00	10.00
	17	6.500	.50	1.00	2.00	10.00

Thin planchet, 2.50-3.30 g

KM#	Year	Mintage	VG	Fine	VF	XF
666.3	18	2.000	1.25	2.75	15.00	25.00
	19	9.300	.50	1.00	2.00	10.00
	20	10.060	.50	1.00	2.00	10.00
	21	6.200	.50	1.00	2.00	10.00

10 PARA

COPPER
Accession date: AH1255
Mintname: *Qustantiniyah*
Thick planchet, 9.00-12.80 g

KM#	Year	Mintage	VG	Fine	VF	XF
667.1	15	.750	5.00	15.00	30.00	75.00

Medium planchet, 7.50-8.20 g

KM#	Year	Mintage	VG	Fine	VF	XF
667.2	16	9.120	.75	1.50	3.75	12.00
	17	9.110	.75	1.50	3.75	12.00
	18	1.900	1.25	2.50	5.00	15.00

Thin planchet, 4.90-5.70 g

KM#	Year	Mintage	VG	Fine	VF	XF
667.3	17	Inc. Ab.	2.50	5.00	6.50	15.00
	18	Inc. Ab.	1.25	2.50	5.00	15.00
	19	33.600	.35	.75	2.00	12.00
	20	20.800	.35	.75	2.00	12.00
	21	7.500	.35	.75	2.00	12.00

20 PARA

COPPER
Accession date: AH1255
Mintname: *Qustantiniyah*
Thick planchet, 14.00-16.00 g

KM#	Year	Mintage	VG	Fine	VF	XF
668.1	10	—	—	—	—	—
	16	4.350	1.25	2.50	5.00	15.00
	17	2.050	2.00	4.00	7.50	20.00

NOTE: Varieties exist.

Thin planchet, 10.00-11.00 g

KM#	Year	Mintage	VG	Fine	VF	XF
668.2	17	Inc. Ab.	1.00	2.00	4.50	15.00
	19	1.200	1.00	2.00	4.50	15.00
	20	3.000	1.00	2.00	4.50	15.00
	21	8.400	.50	1.00	3.00	15.00

0.6013 g, .830 SILVER, .0160 oz ASW
Mintname: *Qustantiniyah*

KM#	Year	Mintage	VG	Fine	VF	XF
669	9	.400	3.00	6.00	25.00	60.00
	10	.910	2.50	5.00	15.00	25.00
	11	.390	2.00	4.00	15.00	25.00
	12	.270	3.75	7.50	20.00	35.00
	13	.230	4.50	9.00	40.00	75.00
	14	.180	3.75	7.50	15.00	25.00
	15	.240	4.00	8.00	30.00	50.00
	16	.270	2.50	5.00	15.00	25.00
	17	.170	5.00	10.00	40.00	75.00
	18	.260	2.00	4.00	20.00	35.00
	19	.900	2.00	4.25	20.00	35.00
	20	.150	2.00	4.25	15.00	25.00
	21	.250	4.25	8.50	15.00	25.00
	22	.190	4.25	8.50	15.00	25.00
	23	.620	50.00	150.00	300.00	500.00

40 PARA

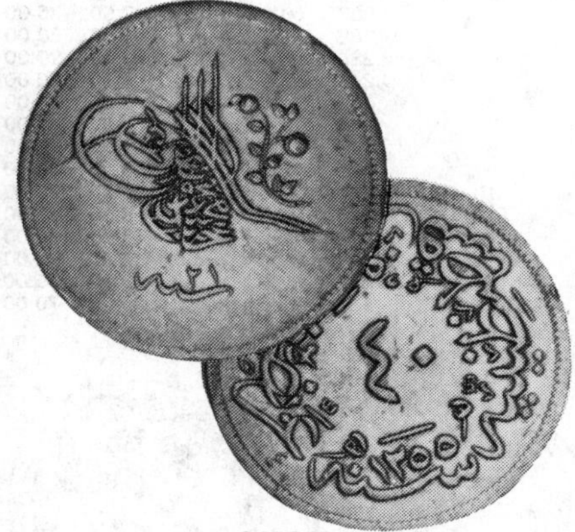

COPPER
Accession date: AH1255
Mintname: *Qustantiniyah*

KM#	Year	Mintage	VG	Fine	VF	XF
670	17	1.450	2.50	5.00	7.50	30.00
	17	—	—	—	Proof	—
	18	3.950	1.50	3.25	8.00	30.00
	19	11.3000	1.25	2.50	6.50	30.00
	20	14.030	1.25	2.50	6.50	30.00
	21	9.300	1.25	2.50	6.50	30.00
	22	4.140	2.50	5.00	10.00	35.00
	23	—	50.00	75.00	100.00	150.00

NOTE: Varieties exist in numerals.

KURUSH

1.2027 g, .830 SILVER, .0321 oz ASW
Accession date: AH1255
Mintname: *Qustantiniyah*

KM#	Year	Mintage	VG	Fine	VF	XF
671	6	—	20.00	30.00	50.00	100.00
	7	.650	1.00	2.00	6.00	12.00
	8	1.420	1.00	2.00	6.00	12.00
	9	.910	1.00	2.00	6.00	12.00
	10	.970	1.00	2.50	7.00	15.00
	11	1.040	1.00	2.50	7.00	15.00
	12	1.100	1.00	2.50	7.00	15.00
	13	.820	1.00	2.50	7.00	15.00
	14	.790	1.00	2.50	7.00	15.00
	15	.960	1.00	3.00	8.00	20.00
	16	1.220	1.00	2.50	7.00	15.00
	17	.810	7.00	15.00	30.00	75.00
	18	.720	1.50	4.00	10.00	25.00
	19	2.270	1.00	3.00	8.00	20.00
	20	1.165	1.00	3.00	8.00	20.00
	21	1.405	1.00	2.50	7.00	15.00
	22	.825	1.00	3.00	8.00	20.00
	23	.755	5.00	10.00	20.00	50.00

NOTE: Varieties exist.

2 KURUSH

2.4055 g, .830 SILVER, .0642 oz ASW
Accession date: AH1255
Mintname: *Qustantiniyah*

KM#	Year	Mintage	VG	Fine	VF	XF
672	7	1.035	1.00	2.00	6.00	12.00
	8	1.150	1.00	2.00	6.00	12.00
	9	.530	1.00	3.00	8.00	20.00
	10	.543	1.50	4.00	10.00	25.00
	11	.695	1.50	4.00	10.00	20.00
	12	.685	1.50	5.00	12.00	25.00
	13	.540	1.50	5.00	12.00	25.00
	14	.280	5.00	10.00	25.00	50.00
	15	.300	1.50	5.00	12.00	25.00
	16	.510	1.50	5.00	12.00	25.00
	19	.275	20.00	40.00	65.00	135.00
	20	.105	15.00	30.00	50.00	115.00
	21	—	—	—	Rare	—

5 KURUSH

6.0130 g, .830 SILVER, .1605 oz ASW
Accession date: AH1255
Mintname: *Qustantiniyah*

KM#	Year	Mintage	VG	Fine	VF	XF
673	6	1.347	2.00	4.00	10.00	22.50
	7	2.612	2.00	4.00	10.00	22.50
	8	.362	2.00	4.00	10.00	22.50
	9	.240	2.50	5.00	12.00	30.00
	10	.252	3.00	6.00	15.00	40.00
	11	.314	2.50	4.50	17.00	35.00
	12	.452	2.50	4.50	15.00	35.00
	13	.498	2.50	4.50	15.00	35.00
	14	.354	2.50	4.50	15.00	35.00
	15	.680	2.00	4.00	10.00	22.50
	16	.972	2.00	4.00	10.00	22.50
	17	.206	2.50	4.50	15.00	35.00
	18	.218	2.50	4.50	15.00	35.00
	19	.384	2.50	4.50	15.00	35.00
	20	.310	2.50	4.50	15.00	35.00
	21	.324	2.50	4.50	15.00	35.00
	22	.214	2.50	4.50	15.00	35.00
	23	.120	5.00	10.00	22.50	50.00

NOTE: Varieties exist.

10 KURUSH

12.0270 g, .830 SILVER, .3210 oz ASW
Accession date: AH1255
Mintname: *Qustantiniyah*

KM#	Year	Mintage	VG	Fine	VF	XF
674	6	.338	15.00	35.00	80.00	150.00
	7	.012	350.00	500.00	800.00	1100.
	9	—	—	—	Rare	—
	13	—	—	—	Rare	—

20 KURUSH

24.0550 g, .830 SILVER, .6419 oz ASW
Accession date: AH1255
Mintname: *Qustantiniyah*
Rev: Small inscription.

KM#	Year	Mintage	VG	Fine	VF	XF
675	6	2.013	9.00	15.00	20.00	45.00
	7	.740	9.00	15.00	20.00	45.00
	8	1.671	9.00	15.00	20.00	45.00
	9	3.125	8.00	12.00	18.00	40.00
	10	1.020	9.00	15.00	20.00	45.00
	11	.815	9.00	15.00	20.00	45.00
	12	.684	9.00	15.00	20.00	45.00
	13	.485	9.00	15.00	20.00	45.00
	14	.633	9.00	15.00	20.00	45.00
	15	.797	9.00	15.00	20.00	45.00

Rev: Large inscription.

KM#	Year	Mintage	VG	Fine	VF	XF
676	8	Inc. Ab.	—	—	—	—
	15	Inc. Ab.	9.00	15.00	20.00	45.00
	16	.320	9.00	15.00	20.00	45.00
	17	.410	10.00	15.00	30.00	55.00
	18	.340	12.00	20.00	35.00	70.00
	19	.201	40.00	75.00	125.00	200.00
	20	.103	12.00	20.00	35.00	75.00
	21	.513	9.00	15.00	30.00	60.00
	22	.624	9.00	15.00	30.00	60.00
	23	.317	25.00	40.00	80.00	150.00

25 KURUSH

1.8040 g, .917 GOLD, .0532 oz AGW
Accession date: AH1255
Mintname: *Qustantiniyah*

KM#	Year	Mintage	VG	Fine	VF	XF
677	17	—	25.00	35.00	70.00	110.00
	18	—	25.00	35.00	70.00	110.00
	19	—	25.00	35.00	70.00	110.00
	20	—	25.00	35.00	70.00	110.00
	21	—	25.00	35.00	70.00	110.00
	22	—	25.00	35.00	70.00	110.00
	23	—	25.00	35.00	70.00	110.00

50 KURUSH

3.6080 g, .917 GOLD, .1064 oz AGW
Accession date: AH1255
Mintname: *Qustantiniyah*

KM#	Year	Mintage	VG	Fine	VF	XF
678	6	—	BV	50.00	70.00	110.00
	7	—	BV	50.00	70.00	110.00
	8	—	BV	50.00	70.00	110.00
	9	—	BV	50.00	70.00	110.00
	10	—	BV	50.00	70.00	110.00
	11	—	BV	50.00	70.00	110.00
	12	—	BV	50.00	70.00	110.00
	13	—	BV	50.00	70.00	110.00
	15	—	BV	50.00	70.00	110.00
	16	—	BV	50.00	70.00	110.00
	17	—	BV	50.00	70.00	110.00
	20	—	1750.	2500.	3500.	5000.
	22	—	1750.	2500.	3500.	5000.

100 KURUSH

7.2160 g, .917 GOLD, .2128 oz AGW
Accession date: AH1255
Mintname: *Qustantiniyah*

KM#	Year	Mintage	VG	Fine	VF	XF
679	5	—	—	BV	100.00	115.00
	6	—	—	BV	100.00	115.00
	7	—	—	BV	100.00	115.00
	8	—	—	BV	100.00	115.00
	9	—	—	BV	100.00	115.00
	10	—	—	BV	100.00	115.00
	11	—	—	BV	100.00	115.00
	12	—	—	BV	100.00	115.00
	13	—	—	BV	100.00	115.00
	14	—	—	BV	100.00	115.00
	15	—	—	BV	100.00	115.00
	16	—	—	BV	100.00	115.00
	17	—	—	BV	100.00	115.00
	18	—	—	BV	100.00	115.00
	19	—	—	BV	100.00	115.00
	20	—	—	BV	100.00	115.00
	21	—	—	BV	100.00	115.00
	22	—	—	BV	100.00	115.00
	23	—	—	BV	100.00	115.00

250 KURUSH

18.0400 g, .917 GOLD, .5319 oz AGW
Accession date: AH1255
Mintname: *Qustantiniyah*

KM#	Year	Mintage	VG	Fine	VF	XF
680	7	—	250.00	275.00	450.00	650.00

KM#	Year	Mintage	VG	Fine	VF	XF
680	18	—	250.00	275.00	450.00	650.00
	22	—	2000.	3000.	4000.	6000.

NOTE: This is the first Ottoman coin to bear a numeral denomination, the 250 is at 6 o'clock on the obverse.

500 KURUSH

36.0800 g, .917 GOLD, 1.0638 oz AGW
Accession date: AH1255
Mintname: *Qustantiniyah*

KM#	Year	Mintage	VG	Fine	VF	XF
681	18	9,140	BV	525.00	750.00	1100.
	20	—	2000.	3000.	4000.	6000.
	22	—	2000.	3000.	4000.	6000.

Mint Visit Coinage

Abdul Mejid's visit to Edirne.

Edirne Mint mark ادرنة

50 KURUSH

3.6080 g, .917 GOLD, .1064 oz AGW
Accession date: AH1255
Mintname: *Edirne*

KM#	Year	Mintage	Fine	VF	XF	Unc
682	8	.010	250.00	375.00	550.00	1150.

100 KURUSH

7.2160 g, .917 GOLD, .2128 oz AGW
Accession date: AH1255
Mintname: *Edirne*

KM#	Year	Mintage	Fine	VF	XF	Unc
683	8	.010	300.00	525.00	700.00	1400.

ABDUL AZIZ

AH1277-1293/1861-1876AD

5 PARA

COPPER
Accession date: AH1277
Mintname: *Qustantiniyah*

KM#	Year	Mintage	VG	Fine	VF	XF
685	1	—	2.25	5.00	12.50	20.00

KM#	Year	Mintage	Fine	VF	XF	Unc
699	4	16.000	1.00	3.00	5.00	10.00

10 PARA

COPPER
Accession date: AH1277
Mintname: *Qustantiniyah*

KM#	Year	Mintage	VG	Fine	VF	XF
686	1	—	3.00	4.00	10.00	20.00

KM#	Year	Mintage	Fine	VF	XF	Unc
700	4	8.000	1.00	3.00	5.00	10.00
	4	—	—	—	Proof	125.00

20 PARA

COPPER
Accession date: AH1277
Mintname: *Qustantiniyah*

KM#	Year	Mintage	VG	Fine	VF	XF
687	1	—	4.00	5.00	12.50	25.00

KM#	Year	Mintage	Fine	VF	XF	Unc
701	4	4.000	1.00	2.50	6.00	12.00
	4	—	—	—	Proof	175.00

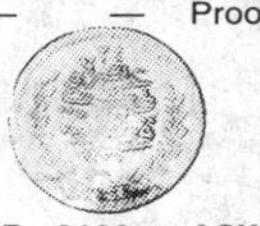

0.6013 g, .830 SILVER, .0160 oz ASW

KM#	Year	Mintage	VG	Fine	VF	XF
688	1	.420	3.50	6.00	12.00	25.00
	2	.850	3.50	6.00	12.00	25.00
	3	1.570	3.50	6.00	12.00	25.00
	4	.930	25.00	50.00	100.00	150.00
	5	.740	3.50	6.00	12.00	25.00
	6	.520	5.00	10.00	17.50	40.00
	7	.350	7.50	15.00	30.00	60.00

40 PARA

COPPER
Accession date: AH1277
Mintname: *Qustantiniyah*

KM#	Year	Mintage	Fine	VF	XF	Unc
702	4	2.000	3.00	9.00	15.00	30.00

KURUSH

1.2027 g, .830 SILVER, .0321 oz ASW
Accession date: AH1277
Mintname: *Qustantiniyah*

KM#	Year	Mintage	VG	Fine	VF	XF
689	1	.545	2.00	3.00	10.00	25.00
	2	2.245	2.00	3.00	7.50	20.00
	3	1.370	2.00	3.00	7.50	20.00
	4	.900	2.00	3.00	7.50	20.00
	5	.685	2.00	3.00	7.50	20.00
	7	.535	35.00	75.00	100.00	200.00

2 KURUSH

2.4055 g, .830 SILVER, .0642 oz ASW
Accession date: AH1277
Mintname: *Qustantiniyah*

KM#	Year	Mintage	VG	Fine	VF	XF
690	1	.055	25.00	50.00	100.00	200.00
	2	.065	45.00	90.00	200.00	400.00
	3	.235	20.00	35.00	75.00	125.00
	5	.135	40.00	75.00	125.00	250.00
	5	—	—	—	Proof	1500.

5 KURUSH

6.0130 g, .830 SILVER, .1605 oz ASW
Accession date: AH1277
Mintname: *Qustantiniyah*

KM#	Year	Mintage	VG	Fine	VF	XF
691	1	.016	2.50	4.00	8.50	20.00
	2	.280	5.00	10.00	17.50	35.00
	3	.288	2.50	4.00	8.50	20.00
	4	.280	2.50	4.00	8.50	20.00
	5	.242	2.50	4.00	8.50	20.00
	6	.342	2.50	4.00	8.50	20.00
	7	.248	2.50	4.00	8.50	20.00
	8	.020	70.00	130.00	225.00	350.00
	9	.050	2.50	4.00	8.50	20.00
	10	.230	2.50	4.00	8.50	20.00
	11	.126	2.50	4.00	8.50	20.00
	12	.186	2.50	4.00	8.50	20.00
	13	.284	2.50	4.00	8.50	20.00
	14	.202	5.00	10.00	17.50	35.00
	15	.154	10.00	20.00	35.00	70.00

10 KURUSH

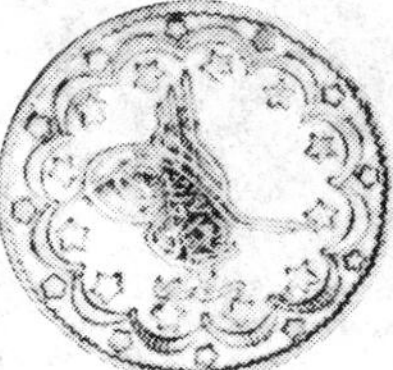

12.0270 g, .830 SILVER, .3210 oz ASW
Accession date: AH1277
Mintname: *Qustantiniyah*

KM#	Year	Mintage	VG	Fine	VF	XF
692	1	—	20.00	50.00	100.00	200.00
	2	.280	50.00	100.00	200.00	350.00
	5	—	—	—	Proof	6000.

20 KURUSH

24.0550 g, .830 SILVER, .6419 oz ASW
Accession date: AH1277
Mintname: *Qustantiniyah*
Rev: Similar to Y#22.

KM#	Year	Mintage	VG	Fine	VF	XF
693	1	1.055	9.00	15.00	20.00	40.00
	2	3.106	9.00	15.00	20.00	40.00
	3	.257	12.00	20.00	35.00	70.00
	4	.234	15.00	25.00	50.00	100.00
	5	.387	10.00	18.00	25.00	50.00
	6	.314	9.00	15.00	20.00	40.00
	7	.640	9.00	15.00	20.00	40.00
	8	1.457	9.00	15.00	20.00	40.00
	9	.859	9.00	15.00	20.00	40.00
	10	.528	9.00	15.00	20.00	40.00
	11	.530	9.00	15.00	20.00	40.00
	12	.233	9.00	15.00	20.00	40.00
	12	—	—	—	Proof	1000.
	13	.514	9.00	15.00	20.00	40.00
	14	.584	9.00	15.00	20.00	40.00
	15	4.034	9.00	15.00	20.00	40.00

NOTE: Varieties exist in size of accession date.

25 KURUSH

1.8040 g, .917 GOLD, .0532 oz AGW
Accession date: AH1277

Mintname: *Qustantiniyah*

KM#	Year	Mintage	VG	Fine	VF	XF
694	1	.052	27.50	32.50	40.00	60.00
	2	.086	27.50	32.50	40.00	60.00
	3	.089	27.50	32.50	40.00	60.00
	4	.069	27.50	32.50	40.00	60.00
	5	.067	27.50	32.50	40.00	60.00
	6	.073	27.50	32.50	40.00	60.00
	7	.116	27.50	32.50	40.00	60.00
	9	.177	27.50	32.50	40.00	60.00
	11	.065	27.50	32.50	40.00	60.00
	12	.122	27.50	32.50	40.00	60.00
	13	.152	27.50	32.50	40.00	60.00
	15	.017	32.50	45.00	60.00	100.00

50 KURUSH

3.6080 g, .917 GOLD, .1064 oz AGW
Accession date: AH1277
Mintname: *Qustantiniyah*

KM#	Year	Mintage	VG	Fine	VF	XF
695	1	5,800	65.00	125.00	250.00	350.00
	2	—	65.00	125.00	250.00	350.00
	3	—	1750.	2500.	3500.	5000.
	7	2,000	60.00	85.00	150.00	250.00
	8	2,000	Reported, not confirmed			
	9	.025	60.00	85.00	150.00	250.00

100 KURUSH

7.2160 g, .917 GOLD, .2128 oz AGW
Accession date: AH1277
Mintname: *Qustantiniyah*

KM#	Year	Mintage	VG	Fine	VF	XF
696	1	2.347	—	BV	100.00	115.00
	2	3.129	—	BV	100.00	115.00
	3	.478	—	BV	100.00	115.00
	4	.628	—	BV	100.00	115.00
	5	.561	—	BV	100.00	115.00
	6	.330	—	BV	100.00	115.00
	7	1.491	—	BV	100.00	115.00
	8	.495	—	BV	100.00	115.00
	9	1.570	—	BV	100.00	115.00
	10	.304	—	BV	100.00	115.00
	11	.866	—	BV	100.00	115.00
	12	.372	—	BV	100.00	115.00
	13	.246	—	BV	100.00	115.00
	14	.286	—	BV	100.00	115.00
	15	3,600	110.00	120.00	160.00	200.00

250 KURUSH

18.0400 g, .917 GOLD, .5319 oz AGW
Accession date: AH1277
Mintname: *Qustantiniyah*

KM#	Year	Mintage	VG	Fine	VF	XF
697	1	3,880	325.00	425.00	800.00	1250.
	5	—	375.00	525.00	900.00	1550.
	7	2,800	300.00	400.00	600.00	1000.
	8	.030	250.00	325.00	450.00	650.00
	9	8,000	250.00	350.00	500.00	700.00

500 KURUSH

36.0800 g, .917 GOLD, 1.0638 oz AGW
Accession date: AH1277
Mintname: *Qustantiniyah*

KM#	Year	Mintage	VG	Fine	VF	XF
698	1	3,180	525.00	700.00	1000.	1400.
	3	1,580	600.00	800.00	1250.	1750.
	5	—	800.00	1000.	1750.	2500.
	7	.021	BV	525.00	650.00	950.00
	8	.071	BV	525.00	650.00	950.00
	9	.074	BV	525.00	650.00	950.00
	10	.030	BV	525.00	650.00	950.00
	11	.036	BV	525.00	650.00	950.00
	13	.059	BV	525.00	650.00	950.00

Mint Visit Coinage

Abdul Aziz's visit to Bursa.

بروسة

Bursa Mint mark

KURUSH

1.2027 g, .830 SILVER, .0321 oz ASW
Accession date: AH1277
Mintname: *Bursa*

KM#	Year	Mintage	Fine	VF	XF	Unc
703	1	.040	200.00	300.00	500.00	1000.

2 KURUSH

2.4055 g, .830 SILVER, .0642 oz ASW
Accession date: AH1277
Mintname: *Bursa*

KM#	Year	Mintage	Fine	VF	XF	Unc
704	1	.040	150.00	225.00	400.00	800.00

5 KURUSH

6.0130 g, .830 SILVER, .1605 oz ASW
Accession date: AH1277
Mintname: *Bursa*

KM#	Year	Mintage	Fine	VF	XF	Unc
705	1	.018	125.00	200.00	350.00	550.00

25 KURUSH

1.8040 g, .917 GOLD, .0532 oz AGW
Accession date: AH1277
Mintname: *Bursa*

KM#	Year	Mintage	Fine	VF	XF	Unc
706	1	4,800	150.00	300.00	450.00	650.00

50 KURUSH

3.6080 g, .917 GOLD, .1064 oz AGW
Accession date: AH1277
Mintname: *Bursa*

KM#	Year	Mintage	Fine	VF	XF	Unc
707	1	2,476	200.00	400.00	650.00	1000.

100 KURUSH

7.2160 g, .917 GOLD, .2128 oz AGW
Accession date: AH1277
Mintname: *Bursa*

KM#	Year	Mintage	Fine	VF	XF	Unc
708	1	9,737	400.00	650.00	1000.	1600.

MURAD V

AH1293/1876AD

KURUSH

1.2027 g, .830 SILVER, .0321 oz ASW
Accession date: AH1293
Mintname: *Qustantiniyah*
Obv: W/o flower right of toughra.

KM#	Year	Mintage	VG	Fine	VF	XF
710	1	.280	75.00	125.00	175.00	300.00

5 KURUSH

6.0130 g, .830 SILVER, .1605 oz ASW
Accession date: AH1293
Mintname: *Qustantiniyah*
Obv: W/o flower right of toughra.

KM#	Year	Mintage	VG	Fine	VF	XF
711	1	.020	100.00	150.00	250.00	400.00

20 KURUSH

24.0550 g, .830 SILVER, .6419 oz ASW
Accession date: AH1293
Mintname: *Qustantiniyah*
Obv: W/o flower right of toughra.

KM#	Year	Mintage	VG	Fine	VF	XF
712	1	.128	25.00	45.00	60.00	100.00

NOTE: Beware of specimens of KM#722 altered to appear as a piece of Murad. The toughra is very different.

25 KURUSH

1.8040 g, .917 GOLD, .0532 oz AGW
Accession date: AH1293

Mintname: *Qustantiniyah*
Obv: Crescent above toughra.

KM#	Year	Mintage	VG	Fine	VF	XF
713	1	.014	100.00	175.00	300.00	450.00

50 KURUSH

3.6080 g, .917 GOLD, .1064 oz AGW
Accession date: AH1293
Mintname: *Qustantiniyah*
Obv: Crescent above toughra.

KM#	Year	Mintage	VG	Fine	VF	XF
714	1	4,500	300.00	500.00	750.00	1250.

100 KURUSH

7.2160 g, .917 GOLD, .2128 oz AGW
Accession date: AH1293
Mintname: *Qustantiniyah*
Obv: Crescent above toughra.

KM#	Year	Mintage	VG	Fine	VF	XF
715	1	7,700	BV	110.00	175.00	250.00

ABDUL HAMID II

AH1293-1327/1876-1909AD

5 PARA

COPPER
Accession date: AH1293
Mintname: *Qustantiniyah*

KM#	Year	Mintage	VG	Fine	VF	XF
728	2	—	—	—	Rare	—
	3	—	.25	.50	3.00	10.00
	4	—	.25	.50	3.00	10.00

20 PARA

0.6013 g, .830 SILVER, .0160 oz ASW
Mintname: *Qustantiniyah*
Accession date: AH1293
Obv: Flower right of toughra.

KM#	Year	Mintage	VG	Fine	VF	XF
717	1	.110	25.00	50.00	100.00	175.00
	4	.050	40.00	100.00	200.00	300.00

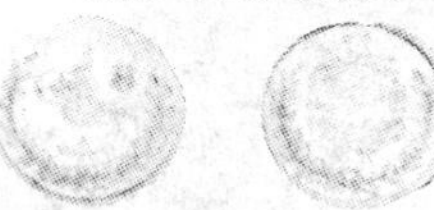

Obv: *el-Ghazi* right of toughra.

KM#	Year	Mintage	VG	Fine	VF	XF
734	8	.350	5.00	7.50	15.00	35.00

KURUSH

1.2027 g, .830 SILVER, .0321 oz ASW
Accession date: AH1293
Mintname: *Qustantiniyah*
Obv: Flower right of toughra.

KM#	Year	Mintage	VG	Fine	VF	XF
718	1	.345	40.00	75.00	150.00	250.00
	2	.020	50.00	100.00	175.00	300.00
	4	.045	40.00	75.00	150.00	250.00

Obv: *el-Ghazi* right of toughra.

KM#	Year	Mintage	VG	Fine	VF	XF
735	8	.210	1.00	1.75	3.50	7.00
	9	.600	1.00	2.00	3.00	5.00
	11	8.830	1.00	2.00	3.00	5.00
	13	.130	4.00	10.00	20.00	35.00
	16	4.000	1.00	2.00	3.00	5.00
	17	6.440	1.00	2.00	3.00	5.00

KM#	Year	Mintage	VG	Fine	VF	XF
735	18	.040	5.00	15.00	30.00	50.00
	19	3.070	1.00	2.00	3.00	5.00
	20	4.122	1.00	2.00	3.00	5.00
	21	.040	3.00	7.50	15.00	30.00
	22	3.979	1.00	2.00	3.00	5.00
	23	3.760	1.00	2.00	3.00	5.00
	24	2.041	1.00	2.00	3.00	5.00

NOTE: Later dates (Yr.25-34) exist for this type.
NOTE: Size of date & inscription varieties exist.

2 KURUSH

2.4055 g, .830 SILVER, .0642 oz ASW
Accession date: AH1293
Mintname: *Qustantiniyah*
Obv: Flower right of toughra.

KM#	Year	Mintage	VG	Fine	VF	XF
719	1	.010	250.00	500.00	800.00	1500.

Obv: *el-Ghazi* right of toughra.

KM#	Year	Mintage	VG	Fine	VF	XF
736	8	.103	2.00	2.50	5.00	10.00
	9	.605	1.75	2.75	4.50	8.00
	11	5.115	1.50	2.00	4.00	7.00
	12	.325	1.75	2.75	4.50	8.00
	13	.030	15.00	22.50	35.00	75.00
	16	.980	1.50	2.00	4.00	7.00
	17	3.736	1.50	2.00	4.00	7.00
	18	.023	15.00	25.00	35.00	75.00
	19	3.507	1.50	2.00	4.00	7.00
	20	3.370	1.50	2.00	4.00	7.00
	21	.021	15.00	25.00	35.00	75.00
	22	2.980	1.50	2.00	4.00	7.00
	23	3.139	1.50	2.00	4.00	7.00
	24	1.490	1.75	2.25	4.50	8.00

NOTE: Later dates (Yr.25-34) exist for this type.

5 KURUSH

6.0130 g, .830 SILVER, .1605 oz ASW
Accession date: AH1293
Mintname: *Qustantiniyah*
Obv: Flower right of toughra.

KM#	Year	Mintage	VG	Fine	VF	XF
720	1	.042	50.00	100.00	150.00	250.00
	2	.014	30.00	60.00	100.00	200.00
	3	.016	10.00	20.00	35.00	75.00
	4	.269	7.50	15.00	30.00	60.00

Obv: *el-Ghazi* right of toughra.

KM#	Year	Mintage	VG	Fine	VF	XF
737	8	.082	4.00	8.00	11.00	17.50
	9	.614	BV	3.50	5.00	9.50
	11	1.788	BV	3.50	5.00	9.50
	12	1.880	BV	3.50	5.00	9.50
	13	2.182	BV	3.50	5.00	9.50
	14	.380	BV	3.50	5.00	9.50
	15	.194	BV	4.00	6.00	12.00
	16	.914	BV	3.50	5.00	9.50
	17	1.337	BV	3.50	5.00	9.50
	18	.012	20.00	35.00	55.00	85.00
	19	.031	10.00	20.00	35.00	60.00
	20	.162	4.00	7.50	12.00	20.00
	21	.018	15.00	30.00	45.00	75.00
	22	.008	15.00	30.00	45.00	75.00
	23	.007	15.00	30.00	45.00	75.00
	24	.126	BV	3.75	6.50	10.00

NOTE: Later dates (Yr.25-34) exist for this type.

10 KURUSH

12.0270 g, .830 SILVER, .3210 oz ASW
Accession date: AH1293
Mintname: *Qustantiniyah*
Obv: Flower right of toughra.

KM#	Year	Mintage	VG	Fine	VF	XF
721	1	.004	125.00	200.00	300.00	500.00
	3	.005	12.50	25.00	50.00	100.00

Obv: *el-Ghazi* right of toughra.

KM#	Year	Mintage	VG	Fine	VF	XF
738	12	—	25.00	50.00	100.00	175.00
	13	.161	5.00	10.00	20.00	45.00
	20	.034	25.00	50.00	100.00	175.00

NOTE: Later dates (Yr.31-33) exist for this type.

20 KURUSH

24.0550 g, .830 SILVER, .6419 oz ASW
Accession date: AH1293
Mintname: *Qustantiniyah*
Obv: Flower right of toughra.
Rev: Similar to KM#712.

KM#	Year	Mintage	VG	Fine	VF	XF
722	1	1.402	BV	12.00	25.00	40.00
	2	1.357	BV	12.00	20.00	35.00
	3	5.940	BV	12.00	20.00	35.00

25 KURUSH

1.8040 g, .917 GOLD, .0532 oz AGW
Accession date: AH1293
Mintname: *Qustantiniyah*
Obv: Flower right of toughra.

KM#	Year	Mintage	VG	Fine	VF	XF
723	1	—	—	—	Rare	—
	2	—	—	—	Rare	—
	3	5,000	50.00	100.00	150.00	200.00
	4	3,600	50.00	100.00	150.00	200.00
	5	—	50.00	100.00	125.00	175.00
	6	—	50.00	100.00	125.00	175.00

Obv: *el-Ghazi* right of toughra.

KM#	Year	Mintage	VG	Fine	VF	XF
729	6	—	—	—	Rare	—
	7	—	BV	25.00	32.00	45.00
	8	—	BV	25.00	32.00	45.00
	9	—	BV	25.00	32.00	45.00
	10	—	BV	25.00	32.00	45.00
	11	—	BV	25.00	32.00	45.00
	12	—	BV	25.00	32.00	45.00
	13	—	BV	25.00	32.00	45.00
	14	—	BV	25.00	32.00	45.00
	15	—	BV	25.00	32.00	45.00
	16	—	BV	25.00	32.00	45.00
	17	—	BV	25.00	32.00	45.00
	18	—	BV	25.00	32.00	45.00
	19	—	BV	25.00	32.00	45.00
	20	—	BV	25.00	32.00	45.00
	21	—	BV	25.00	32.00	45.00
	22	—	BV	25.00	32.00	45.00
	23	—	BV	25.00	32.00	45.00
	24	—	BV	25.00	32.00	45.00

NOTE: Later dates (Yr.25-34) exist for this type.

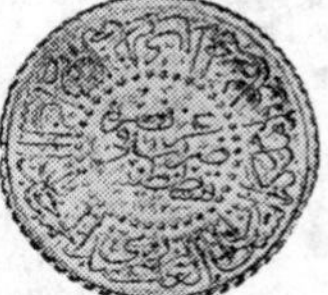

1.7540 g, .917 GOLD, .0517 oz AGW
Monnaie de Luxe

KM#	Year	Mintage	VG	Fine	VF	XF
739	18	—	—	—	Rare	—
	23	—	50.00	65.00	75.00	95.00
	24	—	50.00	65.00	75.00	95.00

NOTE: Later dates (Yr.25-34) exist for this type.

50 KURUSH

3.6080 g, .917 GOLD, .1064 oz AGW
Accession date: AH1293
Mintname: *Qustantiniyah*
Obv: Flower right of toughra.

KM#	Year	Mintage	VG	Fine	VF	XF
724	1	—	75.00	100.00	150.00	300.00
	3	—	75.00	100.00	150.00	300.00
	6	—	100.00	200.00	350.00	750.00

Obv: *el-Ghazi* right of toughra.

KM#	Year	Mintage	VG	Fine	VF	XF
731	7	—	BV	50.00	60.00	90.00
	8	—	BV	50.00	60.00	90.00
	9	—	BV	50.00	60.00	90.00
	10	—	BV	50.00	60.00	90.00
	11	—	BV	50.00	60.00	90.00
	12	—	BV	50.00	60.00	90.00
	13	—	BV	50.00	60.00	90.00
	14	—	BV	50.00	60.00	90.00
	15	—	BV	50.00	60.00	90.00
	16	—	BV	50.00	60.00	90.00
	17	—	BV	50.00	60.00	90.00
	18	—	BV	50.00	60.00	90.00
	19	—	BV	50.00	60.00	90.00
	20	—	BV	50.00	60.00	90.00
	21	—	BV	50.00	60.00	90.00
	22	—	BV	50.00	60.00	90.00
	23	—	BV	50.00	60.00	90.00
	24	—	BV	50.00	60.00	90.00

NOTE: Later dates (Yr.25-34) exist for this type.

3.5080 g, .917 GOLD, .1034 oz AGW
Monnaie de Luxe

KM#	Year	Mintage	VG	Fine	VF	XF
740	18	—	—	—	Rare	—
	23	—	50.00	75.00	90.00	140.00
	24	—	50.00	75.00	90.00	140.00

NOTE: Later dates (Yr.25-34) exist for this type.

100 KURUSH

7.2160 g, .917 GOLD, .2128 oz AGW
Accession date: AH1293
Mintname: *Qustantiniyah*
Obv: Flower right of toughra.

KM#	Year	Mintage	VG	Fine	VF	XF
725	1	—	110.00	150.00	200.00	275.00
	2	—	110.00	150.00	200.00	275.00
	3	—	110.00	150.00	200.00	275.00
	4	—	150.00	200.00	300.00	400.00
	6	—	110.00	150.00	200.00	275.00

Obv: *el-Ghazi* right of toughra.

KM#	Year	Mintage	VG	Fine	VF	XF
730	6	—	—	BV	100.00	115.00
	7	—	—	BV	100.00	115.00
	8	—	—	BV	100.00	115.00
	9	—	—	BV	100.00	115.00
	10	—	—	BV	100.00	115.00
	11	—	—	BV	100.00	115.00
	12	—	—	BV	100.00	115.00
	13	—	—	BV	100.00	115.00
	14	—	—	BV	100.00	115.00
	15	—	—	BV	100.00	115.00
	16	—	—	BV	100.00	115.00
	17	—	—	BV	100.00	115.00
	18	—	—	BV	100.00	115.00
	19	—	—	BV	100.00	115.00
	20	—	—	BV	100.00	115.00
	21	—	—	BV	100.00	115.00
	22	—	—	BV	100.00	115.00
	23	—	—	BV	100.00	115.00
	24	—	—	BV	100.00	115.00

NOTE: Later dates (Yr.25-34) exist for this type.

7.0160 g, .917 GOLD, .2068 oz AGW
Monnaie de Luxe

KM#	Year	Mintage	VG	Fine	VF	XF
741	18	—	—	—	Rare	—
	23	—	BV	100.00	135.00	190.00
	24	—	BV	100.00	135.00	190.00

NOTE: Later dates (Yr.25-34) exist for this type.

250 KURUSH

18.0400 g, .917 GOLD, .5319 oz AGW
Accession date: AH1293
Mintname: *Qustantiniyah*
Obv: Flower right of toughra.

KM#	Year	Mintage	VG	Fine	VF	XF
726	1	120 pcs.	600.00	1000.	1600.	2000.

Obv: *El Ghazi* right of toughra.

KM#	Year	Mintage	VG	Fine	VF	XF
732	11	—	BV	250.00	300.00	450.00
	12	—	BV	250.00	300.00	450.00
	13	—	BV	250.00	300.00	450.00
	14	—	BV	250.00	300.00	450.00
	15	—	BV	250.00	300.00	450.00
	16	—	BV	250.00	300.00	450.00
	17	—	BV	250.00	300.00	450.00
	18	—	BV	250.00	300.00	450.00
	19	—	BV	250.00	300.00	450.00
	20	—	BV	250.00	300.00	450.00
	21	—	BV	250.00	300.00	450.00
	22	—	BV	250.00	300.00	450.00
	23	—	BV	250.00	300.00	450.00
	24	—	BV	250.00	300.00	450.00

NOTE: Later dates (Yr.25-34) exist for this type.

17.5400 g, .917 GOLD, .5169 oz AGW
Monnaie de Luxe

KM#	Year	Mintage	VG	Fine	VF	XF
742	24	—	BV	275.00	400.00	600.00

NOTE: Later dates (Yr.25-34) exist for this type.

500 KURUSH

36.0800 g, .917 GOLD, 1.0638 oz AGW
Accession date: AH1293
Mintname: *Qustantiniyah*
Obv: Flower right of toughra.

KM#	Year	Mintage	VG	Fine	VF	XF
727	1	—	BV	500.00	650.00	900.00
	2	—	BV	500.00	650.00	900.00
	3	—	BV	500.00	650.00	900.00
	4	—	BV	500.00	650.00	900.00
	6	—	BV	500.00	650.00	900.00

Obv: *El Ghazi* right of toughra.

KM#	Year	Mintage	VG	Fine	VF	XF
733	11	—	BV	500.00	550.00	750.00
	12	—	BV	500.00	550.00	750.00
	13	—	BV	500.00	550.00	750.00
	14	—	BV	500.00	550.00	750.00
	15	—	BV	500.00	550.00	750.00
	16	—	BV	500.00	550.00	750.00
	17	—	BV	500.00	550.00	750.00
	18	—	BV	500.00	550.00	750.00
	19	—	BV	500.00	550.00	750.00
	20	—	BV	500.00	550.00	750.00
	21	—	BV	500.00	550.00	750.00
	22	—	BV	500.00	550.00	750.00
	23	—	BV	500.00	550.00	750.00
	24	—	BV	500.00	550.00	750.00

NOTE: Later dates (Yr.25-34) exist for this type.

UNITED STATES

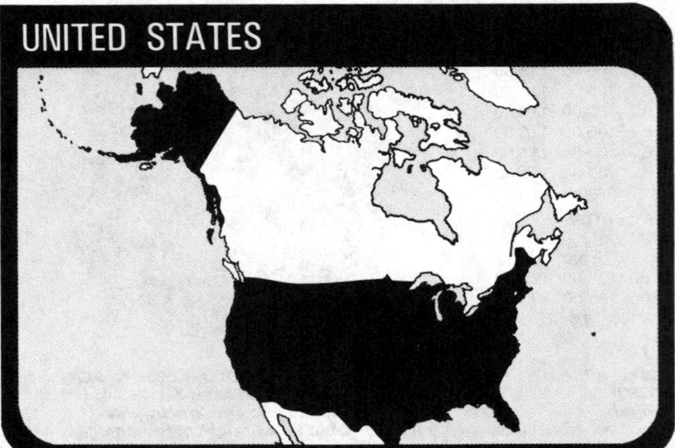

The United States of America as politically organized, under the Articles of Confederation consisted of the 13 original British-American colonies — New Hampshire, Massachusetts, Rhode Island, Connecticut, New York, New Jersey, Pennsylvania, Delaware, Virginia, North Carolina, South Carolina, Georgia and Maryland — clustered along the eastern seaboard of North American between the forests of Maine and the marshes of Georgia. Under the Article of Confederation, the United States had no national capital; Philadelphia, where the "United States in Congress Assembled" met, was the "seat of government." The population during this political phase of America's history (1781-1789) was about 3 million, most of whom lived on self-sufficient family farms. Fishing, lumbering and the production of grains for export were major economic endeavors. Rapid strides were also being made in industry and manufacturing by 1775, the (then) colonies were accounting for one-seventh of the world's production of raw iron.

On the basis of the voyage of John Cabot to the North American mainland in 1497, England claimed the entire continent. The first permanent English settlement was established at Jamestown, Virginia, in 1607. France and Spain also claimed extensive territory in North America. At the end of the French and Indian Wars (1763), England acquired all of the territory east of the Mississippi River, including East and West Florida. From 1776 to 1781, the States were governed by the Continental Congress. From 1781 to 1789, they were organized under the Articles of Confederation, during which period the individual States had the right to issue money. Independence from Great Britain was attained by the American Revolution in 1776. The Constitution which organized and governs the present United States was ratified on Nov. 21, 1788.

Half cents

Draped Bust

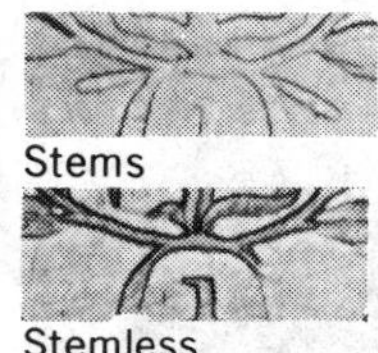

Stems

Stemless

Designer: Robert Scot. **Size:** 23.5 millimeters. **Weight:** 5.44 grams. **Composition:** 100% copper. **Notes:** The wreath on the reverse was redesigned slightly in 1802, resulting in "reverse of 1800" and "reverse of 1802" varieties. The "stems" varieties have stems extending from the wreath above and on both sides of the fraction on the reverse. On the 1804 "crosslet 4" variety, a serif appears at the far right of the crossbar on the 4 in the date. The "spiked chin" variety appears to have a spike extending from Liberty's chin, the result of a damaged die. Varieties of the 1805 strikes are distinguished by the size of the 5 **in the date.** Varieties of the 1806 strikes are distinguished by the size of the 6 in the date.

Half Cents

Date	Mintage	G-4	VG-8	F-12	VF-20	XF-40	MS-60
1802/0 rev. 1800	14,366	12,000.	19,500.	27,500.	—	—	—
1802/0 rev. 1802	Inc. Ab.	600.	975.	2350.	4750.	9800.	—
1803	97,900	33.00	48.00	100.	225.	800.	6500.
1804 plain 4, stemless wreath	1,055,312	30.00	38.00	50.00	80.00	250.	1200.
1804 plain 4, stems	Inc. Ab.	40.00	75.00	140.	250.	1500.	12,000.
1804 crosslet 4, stemless	Inc. Ab.	30.00	45.00	75.00	110.	350.	1250.
1804 crosslet 4, stems	Inc. Ab.	30.00	40.00	65.00	100.	325.	1100.
1804 spiked chin	Inc.Ab.	30.00	45.00	70.00	100.	300.	1050.
1805 small 5, stemless	814,464	30.00	42.00	65.00	105.	350.	2750.
1805 small 5, stems	Inc. Ab.	700.	1250.	2250.	4250.	12,500.	—
1805 large 5, stems	Inc. Ab.	30.00	49.00	70.00	110.	350.	2500.
1806 small 6, stems	356,000	150.	300.	450.	900.	2500.	—
1806 small 6, stemless	Inc. Ab.	29.00	40.00	50.00	70.00	195.	1250.
1806 large 6, stems	Inc. Ab.	28.00	40.00	50.00	70.00	225.	1050.
1807	476,000	28.00	45.00	65.00	110.	400.	3000.
1808/7	400,000	150.	275.	550.	1000.	5000.	25,000.
1808	Inc. Ab.	29.00	40.00	60.00	150.	750.	4500.

Classic Head

Designer: John Reich. **Size:** 23.5 millimeters. **Weight:** 5.44 grams. **Composition:** 100% copper. **Notes:** Restrikes listed were produced privately in the mid-1800s. The 1831 restrikes have two varieties with different-size berries in the wreath on the reverse. The 1828 strikes have either 12 or 13 stars on the obverse.

Date	Mintage	G-4	VG-8	F-12	VF-20	XF-40	MS-60
1809/6	1,154,572	28.00	40.00	45.00	60.00	175.	850.
1809	Inc. Ab.	28.00	40.00	50.00	75.00	200.	750.
1809 circle in 0	—	32.00	45.00	65.00	100.	350.	2000.
1810	215,000	34.00	45.00	75.00	140.	600.	3000.
1811	63,140	110.	200.	500.	1250.	3500.	—
1811 restrike, reverse of 1802, uncirculated						—	25,000.
1825	63,000	27.00	35.00	50.00	75.00	200.	850.
1826	234,000	27.00	35.00	40.00	60.00	125.	600.
1828 13 stars	606,000	27.00	30.00	35.00	50.00	85.00	300.
1828 12 stars	Inc. Ab.	30.00	33.00	40.00	60.00	225.	850.
1829	487,000	27.00	30.00	35.00	50.00	125.	475.
1831 original	2,200	—	—	4900.	5600.	7700.	—
1831 1st restrike, lg. berries, reverse of 1836, proof						—	6000.
1831 2nd restrike, sm. berries, reverse of 1840, proof						—	20,000.
1832	154,000	27.00	30.00	35.00	55.00	90.00	300.
1833	120,000	27.00	30.00	35.00	45.00	80.00	250.
1834	141,000	27.00	30.00	35.00	45.00	80.00	250.
1835	398,000	27.00	30.00	35.00	45.00	80.00	250.
1836 original	—	—		Proof only	—	—	5000.
1836 restrike, reverse of 1840, proof only						—	18,000.

Braided Hair

Designer: Christian Gobrecht. **Size:** 23 millimeters. **Weight:** 5.44 grams. **Composition:** 100% copper. **Notes:** 1840-1848 strikes, both originals and restrikes, are known in proof only; mintages are unknown. The small-date varieties of the 1849, both originals and restrikes are known in proof only. Restrikes were produced clandestinely by Philadelphia Mint personnel in the mid-1800s.

Date	G-4	VG-8	F-12	VF-20	XF-40	AU-50	MS-60	Prf-60
1840 original	—	—	—	Proof only	—	—	—	3800.
1840 1st restrike	—	—	—	Proof only	—	—	—	3500.
1840 2nd restrike	—	—	—	Proof only	—	—	—	3200.
1841 original	—	—	—	Proof only	—	—	—	3800.
1841 1st restrike	—	—	—	Proof only	—	—	—	3500.
1841 2nd restrike	—	—	—	Proof only	—	—	—	3000.
1842 original	—	—	—	Proof only	—	—	—	3800.
1842 1st restrike	—	—	—	Proof only	—	—	—	3500.
1842 2nd restrike	—	—	—	Proof only	—	—	—	3200.

Half Cent

Date	G-4	VG-8	F-12	VF-20	XF-40	AU-50	MS-60	Prf-60
1843 original	—	—	—	Proof only	—	—	—	3800.
1843 1st restrike	—	—	—	Proof only	—	—	—	3500.
1843 2nd restrike	—	—	—	Proof only	—	—	—	3200.
1844 original	—	—	—	Proof only	—	—	—	3800.
1844 1st restrike	—	—	—	Proof only	—	—	—	3500.
1844 2nd restrike	—	—	—	Proof only	—	—	—	3200.
1845 original	—	—	—	Proof only	—	—	—	3800.
1845 1st restrike	—	—	—	Proof only	—	—	—	3500.
1845 2nd restrike	—	—	—	Proof only	—	—	—	3200.
1846 original	—	—	—	Proof only	—	—	—	3800.
1846 1st restrike	—	—	—	Proof only	—	—	—	3500.
1846 2nd restrike	—	—	—	Proof only	—	—	—	3200.
1847 original	—	—	—	Proof only	—	—	—	3800.
1847 1st restrike	—	—	—	Proof only	—	—	—	10,000.
1847 2nd restrike	—	—	—	Proof only	—	—	—	3200.
1848 original	—	—	—	Proof only	—	—	—	3800.
1848 1st restrike	—	—	—	Proof only	—	—	—	3500.
1848 2nd restrike	—	—	—	Proof only	—	—	—	3200.
1849 original, small date		—	—	Proof only	—	—	—	3800.
1849 1st restrike small date		—	—	Proof only	—	—	—	3200.
1849 lg. date	39,864	35.00	40.00	45.00	60.00	150.		600.
1850	39,812	33.00	35.00	40.00	60.00	200.		750.
1851	147,672	23.00	28.00	35.00	50.00	70.00		200.
1852 original	—	—		—	Proof only	—		35,000.
1852 1st restrike	—	—		—	Proof only	—		3500.
1852 2nd restrike	—	—		—	Proof only	—		5000.
1853	129,694	24.00	29.00	35.00	45.00	65.00		195.
1854	55,358	25.00	32.00	35.00	45.00	65.00		195.
1855	56,500	25.00	32.00	35.00	45.00	65.00		195.
1856	40,430	30.00	38.00	44.00	52.00	90.00		275.
1857	35,180	42.00	48.00	60.00	75.00	140.		350.

Large cents

Draped Bust

Designer: Robert Scot. **Size:** 29 millimeters. **Weight:** 10.98 grams. **Composition:** 100% copper. **Notes:** The 1801 "3 errors" variety has the fraction on the reverse reading "1/000th" has only one stem extending from the wreath above and on both sides of the fraction on the reverse, the "United" in "United States of America" appears as "linited."

Date	Mintage	G-4	VG-8	F-12	VF-20	XF-40	MS-60
1801	1,362,837	36.00	65.00	125.	280.	1000.	—
1801 3 errors	Inc. Ab.	85.00	175.	900.	1750.	5500.	—
1802	3,435,100	34.00	55.00	110.	225.	775.	2250.
1803	2,471,353	34.00	55.00	110.	225.	775.	2250.
1804	96,500	850.	1100.	1500.	2550.	7000.	—
1805	941,116	35.00	55.00	125.	300.	875.	2450.
1806	348,000	39.00	95.00	135.	350.	1100.	4700.
1807	727,221	31.00	53.00	110.	225.	775.	2250.

Classic Head

Designer: John Reich. **Size:** 29 millimeters. **Weight:** 10.89 grams. **Composition:** 100% copper.

Date	Mintage	G-4	VG-8	F-12	VF-20	XF-40	MS-60
1808	1,109,000	35.00	75.00	175.	425.	1200.	3600.
1809	222,867	60.00	140.	350.	1300.	2650.	6300.
1810	1,458,500	36.00	75.00	210.	600.	1100.	3850.
1811	218,025	65.00	120.	315.	875.	1300.	7000.
1812	1,075,500	36.00	65.00	180.	525.	975.	2800.
1813	418,000	55.00	115.	665.	1100.	1400.	—
1814	357,830	36.00	65.00	180.	530.	975.	2800.

Large cents

Coronet

Designer: Robert Scot. **Size:** 28-29 millimeters. **Weight:** 10.89 grams. **Composition:** 100% copper. **Notes:** The 1817 strikes have either 13 or 15 stars on the obverse.

Date	Mintage	G-4	VG-8	F-12	VF-20	XF-40	MS-60
1816	2,820,982	14.00	17.00	28.00	84.00	175.	420.
1817 13 stars	3,948,400	12.50	15.00	24.00	56.00	120.	275.
1817 15 stars	Inc. Ab.	16.00	25.00	45.00	125.00	350.	1550.
1818	3,167,000	12.50	16.00	24.00	56.00	125.	250.
1819	2,671,000	12.50	14.00	23.00	63.00	120.	275.
1820	4,407,550	12.50	17.00	23.00	63.00	120.	275.
1821	389,000	28.00	49.00	185.	550.	2000.	6650.
1822	2,072,339	12.50	15.00	32.00	84.00	195.	575.
1823	Inc. 1824	60.00	110.	275.	625.	2750.	—
1823/22	Inc. 1824	49.00	95.00	240.	600.	2450.	—
1824	1,262,000	14.00	23.00	38.00	145.	350.	625.
1824/22	Inc. Ab.	17.00	25.00	56.00	225.	975.	—
1825	1,461,100	13.00	16.00	35.00	110.	300.	840.
1826	1,517,425	12.50	16.00	26.00	84.00	175.	700.
1826/25	Inc. Ab.	16.00	24.00	60.00	175.	700.	1800.
1827	2,357,732	12.50	15.00	23.00	75.00	135.	385.
1828	2,260,624	12.50	14.00	26.00	84.00	175.	425.
1829	1,414,500	12.50	14.00	22.00	100.	140.	425.
1830	1,711,500	12.50	14.00	22.00	70.00	135.	385.
1831	3,359,260	12.50	14.00	22.00	63.00	125.	315.
1832	2,362,000	12.50	14.00	22.00	63.00	125.	315.
1833	2,739,000	12.50	14.00	22.00	56.00	120.	265.
1834	1,855,100	12.50	14.00	22.00	56.00	140.	250.
1835	3,878,400	12.50	14.00	22.00	56.00	91.00	225.
1836	2,111,000	13.00	15.00	23.00	57.00	105.	250.

Braided Hair

Slanting 5s

Upright 5s

Designer: Christian Gobrecht. **Size:** 27.5 millimeters. **Weight:** 10.89 grams. **Composition:** 100% copper. **Notes:** 1840 and 1842 strikes are known with both small and large dates, with little difference in value. 1855 and 1856 strikes are known with both slanting and upright, "5s" in the date, with little difference in value. A slightly larger Liberty head and larger reverse lettering were used beginning in 1843. One 1843 variety uses the old obverse with the new reverse.

Date	Mintage	G-4	VG-8	F-12	VF-20	XF-40	MS-60
1837	5,558,300	12.50	14.00	22.00	51.00	91.00	300.
1838	6,370,200	12.50	14.00	22.00	51.00	91.00	225.
1839	3,128,661	12.50	14.00	22.00	51.00	105.	350.
1839/36	Inc. Ab.	325.	500.	840.	1850.	4750.	—
1840	2,462,700	11.00	14.00	17.00	38.00	70.00	475.
1841	1,597,367	11.00	14.00	17.00	38.00	70.00	425.
1842	2,383,390	11.00	14.00	17.00	38.00	70.00	425.
1843	2,425,342	11.00	14.00	17.00	38.00	75.00	445.
1843 obverse 1842 with reverse of 1844							
	Inc. Ab.	12.00	15.00	21.00	38.00	80.00	350.
1844	2,398,752	9.00	14.00	14.00	22.00	54.00	215.
1844/81	Inc. Ab.	14.00	25.00	40.00	65.00	200.	600.
1845	3,894,804	9.00	12.00	14.00	19.50	44.00	225.
1846	4,120,800	9.00	12.00	14.00	19.50	44.00	225.
1847	6,183,669	9.00	12.00	14.00	19.50	44.00	160.
1848	6,415,799	9.00	12.00	14.00	19.50	44.00	160.
1849	4,178,500	9.00	12.00	14.00	28.00	60.00	275.
1850	4,426,844	9.00	12.00	14.00	19.50	44.00	160.
1851	9,889,707	9.00	12.00	14.00	19.50	41.00	160.
1851/81	Inc. Ab.	15.00	19.00	35.00	60.00	175.	500.
1852	5,063,094	9.00	12.00	14.00	19.50	41.00	160.
1853	6,641,131	9.00	12.00	14.00	19.50	41.00	160.
1854	4,236,156	9.00	12.00	14.00	19.50	41.00	160.
1855	1,574,829	12.00	13.00	16.00	21.00	45.00	170.
1856	2,690,463	11.00	12.00	14.00	16.00	40.00	160.
1857	333,456	42.00	49.00	56.00	65.00	90.00	250.

Small cents

Flying Eagle

Large letters; "AM" connected

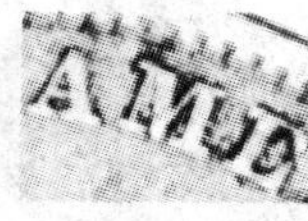
Small letters; "AM" separated

Designer: James B. Longacre. **Size:** 19 millimeters. **Weight:** 4.67 grams. **Composition:** 88% copper, 12% nickel. **Notes:** on the large-letter variety of 1858, the "A" and "M" in "America" are connected at their bases; on the small-letter variety, the two letters are separated.

Date	Mintage	G-4	VG-8	F-12	VF-20	XF-40	AU-50	MS-60	MS-65	Prf-65
1856	Est. 1,500	4000.	4250.	4550.	5250.	5750.	6150.	7500.	30,000.	18,000.
1857	17,450,000	13.00	16.00	23.00	33.00	76.00	135.	200.	2750.	27,500.
1858 LL	24,600,000	13.00	17.00	24.00	38.00	80.00	150.	225.	2750.	18,000.
1858 SL	Inc. Ab.	13.00	16.00	24.00	38.00	80.00	150.	225.	2850.	25,000.

Indian Head

1859

1860-1909

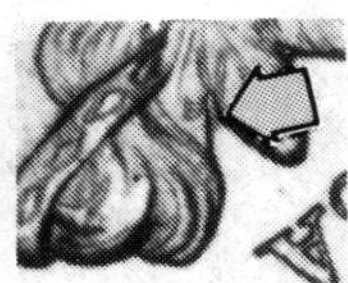
1864 "L"

Copper-nickel composition

Designer: James B. Longacre. **Size:** 19 millimeters. **Weight:** 4.67 grams. **Composition:** 88% copper, 12% nickel.

Date	Mintage	G-4	VG-8	F-12	VF-20	XF-40	AU-50	MS-60	MS-65	Prf-65
1859	36,400,000	7.00	10.00	15.00	32.00	70.00	125.	200.	2500.	5500.
1860	20,566,000	6.00	8.50	11.50	17.50	42.00	75.00	130.	850.	3500.
1861	10,100,000	14.00	18.00	24.00	30.00	75.00	120.	160.	850.	6750.
1862	28,075,000	4.25	6.50	11.00	17.50	27.50	49.00	80.00	750.	2250.
1863	49,840,000	4.00	6.00	10.00	12.50	25.00	50.00	70.00	850.	2950.
1864	13,740,000	13.00	17.00	21.00	29.00	45.00	75.00	125.	1250.	2950.

Bronze composition

Weight: 3.11 grams. **Composition:** 95% copper, 5% tin and zinc. **Notes:** The 1864 "L" variety has the designer's initial in Liberty's hair to the right of her neck.

Date	Mintage	G-4	VG-8	F-12	VF-20	XF-40	AU-50	MS-60	MS-65	Prf-65
1864	39,233,714	6.00	9.00	14.00	24.00	40.00	50.00	75.00	325.	4500.
1864 L	Inc. Ab.	35.00	52.00	80.00	115.	175.	225.	275.	1350.	60,000.
1865	35,429,286	6.00	8.00	11.00	15.00	32.00	50.00	77.00	400.	2250.
1866	9,826,500	29.00	35.00	45.00	80.00	125.	175.	225.	1100.	950.
1867	9,821,000	31.00	35.00	45.00	80.00	125.	175.	225.	1100.	950.
1868	10,266,500	28.00	32.00	47.00	80.00	125.	175.	225.	950.	950.
1869/9	6,420,000	84.00	120.	190.	225.	285.	350.	400.	1350.	—
1869	Inc. Ab.	39.00	55.00	160.	200.	260.	325.	380.	1350.	1100.
1870	5,275,000	34.00	49.00	140.	210.	260.	325.	375.	1350.	1100.
1871	3,929,500	40.00	60.00	200.	225.	300.	375.	425.	2500.	1100.
1872	4,042,000	59.00	70.00	200.	250.	325.	400.	500.	3500.	1100.
1873	11,676,500	13.00	17.00	30.00	45.00	95.00	125.	185.	1100.	800.
1874	14,187,500	12.00	16.00	27.00	41.00	80.00	120.	150.	650.	850.
1875	13,528,000	12.00	17.00	31.00	41.00	80.00	115.	150.	850.	2250.
1876	7,944,000	22.00	29.00	42.00	65.00	110.	155.	195.	1100.	800.
1877	852,500	435.	510.	675.	925.	1375.	1700.	2250.	7500.	5000.
1878	5,799,850	22.00	30.00	45.00	65.00	115.	180.	200.	950.	450.
1879	16,231,200	5.00	7.00	10.00	21.00	35.00	50.00	70.00	400.	375.
1880	38,964,955	2.50	4.00	5.50	8.50	20.00	40.00	65.00	350.	375.
1881	39,211,575	2.50	3.75	5.50	7.50	13.00	23.00	35.00	300.	375.
1882	38,581,100	2.50	3.75	5.50	7.50	13.00	23.00	35.00	300.	375.
1883	45,589,109	2.00	3.25	5.00	7.00	13.00	23.00	35.00	300.	375.
1884	23,261,742	3.00	4.00	6.00	11.00	23.00	33.00	50.00	550.	375.
1885	11,765,384	4.75	7.00	13.00	21.00	40.00	60.00	75.00	750.	375.
1886	17,654,290	3.25	6.50	16.00	25.00	55.00	75.00	100.	1100.	425.
1887	45,226,483	1.50	1.95	4.00	5.00	12.00	20.00	30.00	400.	400.
1888	37,494,414	1.50	1.95	4.00	7.00	15.50	25.00	45.00	950.	500.
1889	48,869,361	1.40	1.85	4.00	5.00	10.00	25.00	30.00	400.	400.
1890	57,182,854	1.40	1.85	2.50	5.00	10.00	24.00	30.00	400.	500.

Small cents

Date	Mintage	G-4	VG-8	F-12	VF-20	XF-40	AU-50	MS-60	MS-65	Prf-65
1891	47,072,350	1.40	1.75	2.60	5.00	10.00	24.00	30.00	400.	450.
1892	37,649,832	1.40	1.95	3.50	5.00	10.00	24.00	30.00	400.	450.
1893	46,642,195	1.40	1.75	2.60	5.00	10.00	24.00	35.00	325.	500.
1894	16,752,132	2.25	3.25	7.50	12.50	22.50	35.00	49.00	375.	500.
1895	38,343,636	1.40	1.75	2.50	4.00	12.50	22.50	35.00	225.	400.
1896	39,057,293	1.40	1.75	2.50	4.00	11.00	21.00	32.00	250.	400.
1897	50,466,330	1.35	1.75	2.50	4.00	9.00	21.00	30.00	225.	375.
1898	49,823,079	1.30	1.75	2.50	4.00	10.00	19.50	30.00	200.	375.
1899	53,600,031	1.30	1.50	2.30	4.00	10.00	17.00	30.00	135.	375.
1900	66,833,764	1.30	1.40	2.25	3.00	7.50	16.00	24.00	150.	375.

NOTE: Later dates (1901-1909) exist for this type.

Two-cent

Small motto

Large motto

Designer: James B. Longacre. **Size:** 23 millimeters. **Weight:** 6.22 grams. **Composition:** 95% copper, 5% tin and zinc. **Notes:** The motto "In God We Trust" was modified in 1864, resulting in small-motto and large-motto varieties for that year.

Date	Mintage	G-4	VG-8	F-12	VF-20	XF-40	AU-50	MS-60	MS-65	Prf-65
1864 SM	19,847,500.	60.00	75.00	100.	150.	250.	325.	500.	1350.	45,000.
1864 LM	Inc. Ab.	8.00	10.00	20.00	23.00	32.00	48.00	70.00	365.	1200.
1865	13,640,000	8.00	11.00	20.00	23.00	32.00	48.00	70.00	365.	925.
1866	3,177,000	10.00	13.00	20.00	23.00	32.00	48.00	70.00	455.	925.
1867	2,938,750	10.00	13.00	20.00	23.00	32.00	60.00	95.00	365.	925.
1868	2,803,750	10.00	13.00	20.00	24.00	36.00	65.00	145.	365.	925.
1869	1,546,000	10.00	11.00	20.00	35.00	60.00	80.00	165.	425.	925.
1870	861,250	11.00	12.00	21.00	32.50	57.00	90.00	185.	460.	925.
1871	721,250	13.00	15.00	24.00	40.00	75.00	115.	175.	470.	925.
1872	65,000	85.00	130.	170.	250.	400.	575.	775.	2750.	925.
1873	Est. 1100	Proof only		900.	925.	950.	975.	—	—	1700.

THREE CENT SILVER

Type 1 — No Outlines To Star

Designer: James B. Longacre. **Size:** 14 millimeters. **Weight:** 8 grams. **Composition:** 75% silver (.0193 ounces), 25% copper. **Notes:** The Type I design has no outline in the star.

Date	Mintage	G-4	VG-8	F-12	VF-20	XF-40	AU-50	MS-60	MS-65	Prf-65
1851	5,447,400	15.00	16.00	22.00	30.00	65.00	125.	145.	1100.	—
1851O	720,000	18.00	22.00	35.00	56.00	115.	200.	280.	1850.	—
1852	18,663,500	13.00	16.00	20.00	28.00	50.00	120.	145.	1100.	—
1853	11,400,000	13.00	16.00	22.00	30.00	54.00	125.	145.	1100.	—

Type 2 — Three Outlines To Star

Weight: .75 grams. **Composition:** 90% silver (.0218 ounces), 10% copper. **Notes:** The Type II design has three lines outlining the star.

Date	Mintage	G-4	VG-8	F-12	VF-20	XF-40	AU-50	MS-60	MS-65	Prf-65
1854	671,000	16.00	19.00	24.00	41.00	90.00	215.	315.	4100.	25,000.
1855	139,000	21.00	29.00	44.00	85.00	145.	250.	475.	8200.	15,000.
1856	1,458,000	16.00	18.00	22.00	41.00	85.00	210.	250.	5700.	14,500.
1857	1,042,000	16.00	18.00	22.00	41.00	85.00	225.	280.	3900.	9750.
1858	1,604,000	16.00	18.00	25.00	37.00	85.00	210.	230.	3900.	6400.

Silver three-cent

Type 3 — Two Outlines To Star

Notes: The Type III design has two lines outlining the star.

Date	Mintage	G-4	VG-8	F-12	VF-20	XF-40	AU-50	MS-60	MS-65	Prf-65
1859	365,000	15.00	18.00	22.00	35.00	70.00	125.	150.	1050.	2250.
1860	287,000	17.00	20.00	25.00	35.00	70.00	125.	150.	1050.	7500.
1861	498,000	15.00	18.00	24.00	35.00	70.00	125.	150.	1050.	2250.
1862	343,550	17.00	20.00	25.00	35.00	70.00	125.	150.	1050.	2500.
1863	21,460	200.	225.	280.	315.	350.	440.	625.	1925.	1500.
1864	12,470	250.	275.	325.	375.	425.	465.	565.	1600.	1350.
1865	8,500	260.	300.	350.	375.	400.	450.	595.	1750.	1250.
1866	22,725	225.	250.	280.	325.	350.	375.	565.	1700.	1175.
1867	4,625	285.	325.	350.	375.	400.	485.	625.	2300.	1175.
1868	4,100	285.	325.	350.	375.	400.	440.	625.	4800.	1350.
1869	5,100	285.	325.	350.	375.	400.	440.	625.	4400.	1350.
1870	4,000	285.	325.	350.	375.	400.	440.	750.	4600.	1150.
1871	4,360	285.	325.	350.	375.	400.	440.	580.	1650.	1150.
1872	1,950	300.	325.	375.	400.	450.	500.	650.	4700.	1275.
1873	600	Proof only		750.	850.	950.	1050.	—	—	1400.

Nickel three-cent

Designer: James B. Longacres. **Size:** 17.9 millimeters. **Weight:** 1.94 grams. **Composition:** 75% copper, 25% nickel.

Date	Mintage	G-4	VG-8	F-12	VF-20	XF-40	AU-50	MS-60	MS-65	Prf-65
1865	11,382,000	7.00	9.00	11.50	12.50	15.00	38.00	83.00	630.	1700.
1866	4,801,000	7.00	9.00	11.50	12.50	15.00	38.00	83.00	630.	1250.
1867	3,915,000	8.00	9.00	11.50	12.50	15.00	38.00	83.00	630.	1025.
1868	3,252,000	8.00	9.00	11.50	12.50	15.00	38.00	83.00	630.	1025.
1869	1,604,000	9.50	11.50	12.00	13.00	15.00	40.00	83.00	630.	900.
1870	1,335,000	9.50	11.50	12.00	13.00	16.00	42.00	100.	630.	1000.
1871	604,000	9.50	11.50	12.00	13.00	18.00	45.00	100.	725.	450.
1872	862,000	9.50	11.50	12.00	13.00	17.00	43.00	100.	1250.	875.
1873	1,173,000	9.50	11.50	12.00	13.00	16.00	42.00	100.	2400.	900.
1874	790,000	9.50	11.50	12.00	13.00	17.00	43.00	110.	2000.	875.
1875	228,000	9.50	11.50	13.00	16.00	25.00	63.00	160.	725.	1300.
1876	162,000	9.50	13.00	17.00	24.00	38.00	100.	175.	2150.	450.
1877	Est. 900	Proof only		900.	975.	1075.	1150.	—	—	1400.
1878	2,350	Proof only		375.	400.	425.	450.	—	—	700.
1879	41,200	45.00	50.00	60.00	70.00	80.00	120.	240.	725.	650.
1880	24,955	63.00	70.00	90.00	105.	130.	150.	265.	725.	650.
1881	1,080,575	9.50	11.50	12.00	13.00	17.00	40.00	90.00	725.	600.
1882	25,300	63.00	70.00	84.00	95.00	110.	145.	250.	1000.	650.
1883	10,609	125.	145.	175.	200.	240.	270.	375.	2900.	650.
1884	5,642	290.	330.	350.	380.	425.	450.	550.	4800.	650.
1885	4,790	350.	380.	425.	460.	500.	600.	725.	1950.	675.
1886	4,290	Proof only		—	275.	325.	350.	—	—	650.
1887/6	7,961	Proof only		—	325.	360.	400.	—	—	625.
1887	Inc. Ab.	240.	250.	275.	300.	325.	425.	500.	1175.	700.
1888	41,083	35.00	40.00	45.00	50.00	70.00	110.	270.	750.	650.
1889	21,561	63.00	70.00	90.00	105.	125.	150.	260.	750.	650.

Half dimes

Draped Bust

Half dimes

Heraldic-eagle reverse

Designer: Robert Scot. **Size:** 16.5 millimeters. **Weight:** 1.35 grams. **Composition:** 89.25% silver (.0388 ounces), 10.75% copper. **Notes:** Some 1800 strikes have "Liberty" spelled as "Libekty."

Notes: Some 1800 strikes have "Liberty" spelled as "Libekty."

Date	Mintage	G-4	VG-8	F-12	VF-20	XF-40	MS-60
1801	33,910	700.	800.	1075.	1500.	2650.	10,000.
1802	13,010	9500.	13,500.	20,000.	35,000.	60,000.	—
1803	37,850	625.	700.	1050.	1400.	2400.	5050.
1805	15,600	725.	825.	1125.	1550.	2750.	—

Liberty Cap

Designer; William Kneass. **Size:** 15.5 millimeters. **Weight:** 1.35 grams. **Composition:** 89.25% silver (.0388 ounces), 10.76% copper. **Notes:** Design modifications in 1835, 1836 and 1837 resulted in variety combination, with large and small dates, and large and small "5C" inscriptions on the reverse.

Date	Mintage	G-4	VG-8	F-12	VF-20	XF-40	AU-50	MS-60	MS-65
1829	1,230,000	15.00	25.00	29.00	50.00	125.	225.	270.	2850.
1830	1,240,000	15.00	25.00	29.00	50.00	125.	225.	270.	2850.
1831	1,242,700	15.00	25.00	29.00	50.00	125.	225.	270.	2850.
1832	965,000	15.00	25.00	29.00	50.00	125.	300.	450.	7000.
1833	1,370,000	15.00	25.00	29.00	50.00	125.	230.	325.	3500.
1834	1,480,000	15.00	25.00	29.00	50.00	125.	225.	270.	2850.
1835 lg.dt., lg. 5C.	2,760,000	15.00	25.00	29.00	50.00	125.	240.	270.	2850.
1835 lg.dt., sm. 5C.	Inc. Ab.	15.00	25.00	29.00	50.00	125.	220.	270.	2850.
1835 sm.dt., lg. 5C.	Inc. Ab.	15.00	25.00	29.00	50.00	125.	225.	270.	2850.
1835 sm.dt., sm. 5C.	Inc. Ab.	15.00	25.00	29.00	50.00	125.	225.	270.	2850.
1836 lg. 5C.	1,900,000	15.00	25.00	29.00	50.00	125.	225.	270.	2850.
1836 sm. 5C.	Inc. Ab.	15.00	25.00	29.00	50.00	125.	225.	270.	2850.
1837 lg. 5C.	2,276,000	15.00	25.00	29.00	50.00	125.	225.	270.	2850.
1837 sm. 5C.	Inc. Ab.	25.00	40.00	50.00	80.00	160.	350.	1250.	8500.

Seated Liberty

No stars 1837-1859 Stars Obverse legend 1860-1873

No stars around rim

Designer: Christian Gobrecht. **Size:** 15.5 millimeters. **Weight:** 1.34 grams. **Composition:** 90% silver (.0388 ounce), 10% copper. **Notes:** A design modification in 1837 resulted in small-date and large-date varieties.

Date	Mintage	G-4	VG-8	F-12	VF-20	XF-40	AU-50	MS-60	MS-65
1837 sm. dt.	Inc. Ab.	25.00	35.00	53.00	100.	210.	375.	600.	3400.
1837 lg. dt.	Inc. Ab.	25.00	35.00	53.00	100.	210.	375.	600.	3400.
1838O	70,000	70.00	110.	225.	400.	750.	1450.	—	—

Stars around rim

Notes: The two varieties of 1838 are distinguished by the size of the stars on the obverse. The 1839-O with reverse of 1838-O was struck from rusted reverse dies. The result is a bumpy surface on this variety's reverse.

Date	Mintage	G-4	VG-8	F-12	VF-20	XF-40	AU-50	MS-60	MS-65
1838 lg.stars	2,255,000	9.25	9.50	12.50	25.00	65.00	170.	240.	1900.
1838 sm.stars	Inc. Ab.	20.00	30.00	50.00	125.	225.	285.	750.	10,500.
1839	1,069,150	9.50	11.00	13.00	29.00	70.00	170.	240.	1900.

Half dimes

Date	Mintage	G-4	VG-8	F-12	VF-20	XF-40	AU-50	MS-60	MS-65
1839O	1,034,039	10.00	12.00	16.00	31.00	75.00	200.	350.	2000.
1839O rev. 1838O	—	375.	575.	750.	1200.	2250.	3500.	—	—
1840	1,344,085	9.25	9.50	13.00	21.00	65.00	125.	225.	1800.
1840O	935,000	10.00	15.00	24.00	45.00	85.00	225.	600.	10,500.

Drapery added to Liberty

Notes: In 1840 drapery was added to Liberty's left elbow. Varieties for the 1848 Philadelphia strikes are distinguished by the size of the numerals in the date.

Date	Mintage	G-4	VG-8	F-12	VF-20	XF-40	AU-50	MS-60	MS-65
1840	Inc. Ab.	20.00	32.50	50.00	75.00	150.	250.	700.	6500.
1840O	Inc. Ab.	30.00	50.00	80.00	125.	325.	950.	—	—
1841	1,150,000	9.25	9.50	12.00	22.00	55.00	90.00	130.	1050.
1841O	815,000	10.00	15.00	22.50	40.00	85.00	200.	650.	—
1842	815,000	9.25	9.50	12.00	22.00	55.00	90.00	130.	1050.
1842O	350,000	28.00	40.00	65.00	185.	600.	1500.	—	—
1843	1,165,000	9.25	9.50	12.00	18.00	41.00	95.00	130.	1050.
1844	430,000	9.50	10.00	12.00	24.00	60.00	110.	225.	2250.
1844O	220,000	60.00	95.00	175.	350.	950.	2200.	—	—
1845	1,564,000	9.25	9.50	12.00	22.00	44.00	95.00	130.	1050.
1845/1845	Inc. Ab.	12.50	17.50	25.00	45.00	75.00	200.	325.	5000.
1846	27,000	225.	325.	450.	700.	1450.	3000.	—	—
1847	1,274,000	9.25	9.50	12.00	18.00	55.00	95.00	225.	2250.
1848 med. date	668,000	9.50	10.00	12.00	32.00	60.00	125.	225.	2250.
1848 lg. date	Inc. Ab.	15.00	20.00	30.00	50.00	100.	225.	425.	2250.
1848O	600,000	12.00	17.50	25.00	42.50	90.00	225.	600.	5000.
1849/8	1,309,000	12.00	17.50	25.00	45.00	100.	180.	500.	5000.
1849/6	Inc. Ab.	10.00	14.00	20.00	35.00	75.00	175.	425.	5000.
1849	Inc. Ab.	9.25	9.50	12.00	18.00	45.00	95.00	600.	5000.
1849O	140,000	22.00	40.00	75.00	145.	450.	800.	1775.	16,000.
1850	955,000	9.25	9.50	12.00	18.00	41.00	175.	250.	2750.
1850O	690,000	11.00	16.00	22.50	50.00	100.	350.	800.	4000.
1851	781,000	9.25	9.50	12.00	18.00	50.00	110.	300.	2250.
1851O	860,000	10.00	15.00	25.00	35.00	75.00	165.	600.	2250.
1852	1,000,500	9.25	9.50	12.50	18.00	41.00	100.	130.	1050.
1852O	260,000	23.00	35.00	70.00	110.	265.	675.	1200.	—
1853	135,000	25.00	38.00	55.00	85.00	185.	350.	600.	8500.
1853O	160,000	135.	190.	275.	550.	1200.	3000.	—	—

Arrows at date

Weight: 1.24 grams. **Composition:** 90% silver (.0362 ounces), 10% copper.

Date	Mintage	G-4	VG-8	F-12	VF-20	XF-40	AU-50	MS-60	MS-65	Prf-65
1853	13,210,020	7.50	8.00	12.50	17.00	50.00	100.	160.	2000.	20,000.
1853O	2,200,000	9.25	9.50	15.00	35.00	75.00	125.	325.	—	—
1854	5,740,000	8.00	9.00	12.50	17.00	50.00	135.	250.	4550.	20,000.
1854O	1,560,000	9.50	10.00	12.50	25.00	60.00	175.	700.	—	—
1855	1,750,000	9.50	10.00	12.50	20.00	55.00	135.	250.	5000.	20,000.
1855O	600,000	15.00	20.00	25.00	55.00	125.	325.	1000.	—	—

Arrows at date removed

Notes: On the 1858/inverted date variety, the same was engraved into the die upside down and then re-engraved right side up. Another 1858 date was the date doubled.

Date	Mintage	G-4	VG-8	F-12	VF-20	XF-40	AU-50	MS-60	MS-65	Prf-65
1856	4,880,000	9.50	10.00	12.50	18.00	41.00	90.00	200.	1550.	22,500.
1856O	1,100,000	9.50	10.00	12.50	27.00	70.00	200.	600.	—	—
1857	7,280,000	8.00	9.00	12.50	15.00	45.00	90.00	200.	1550.	5000.
1857O	1,380,000	9.50	11.50	13.00	25.00	65.00	200.	450.	—	—
1858	3,500,000	9.25	9.50	12.50	18.00	45.00	75.00	145.	1550.	9000.
1858 inverted date										
	Inc. Ab.	30.00	40.00	65.00	115.	200.	325.	500.	—	—
1858 doubled date										
	Inc. Ab.	45.00	60.00	90.00	175.	285.	425.	700.	—	—
1858O	1,660,000	9.50	11.50	14.00	26.00	65.00	190.	265.	—	—
1859	340,000	9.50	12.00	15.00	33.00	85.00	175.	250.	1550.	5000.
1859O	560,000	9.25	10.00	13.00	30.00	80.00	175.	350.	—	—

Transitional patterns

Notes: These non-circulation pieces were struck as experiments in transferring the legend "United States of America" from the reverse for the obverse.

Date	Mintage	G-4	VG-8	F-12	VF-20	XF-40	AU-50	MS-60	MS-65	Prf-65
1859 obverse of 1859, reverse 1860						—	—	—	—	17,500.
1860 obverse of 1859, reverse 1860						—	—	4000.	8500.	—

Obverse legend

Notes: In 1860 the legend "United States of America" replaced the stars on the obverse.

Date	Mintage	G-4	VG-8	F-12	VF-20	XF-40	AU-50	MS-60	MS-65	Prf-65
1860	799,000	10.00	12.00	15.00	25.00	45.00	70.00	145.	1150.	2150.
1860O	1,060,000	9.00	10.00	15.00	30.00	55.00	85.00	350.	3550.	—
1861	3,361,000	8.00	9.50	12.50	14.00	28.00	57.00	145.	1150.	1650.
1861/0	Inc. Ab.	20.00	30.00	50.00	90.00	150.	275.	450.	—	—
1862	1,492,550	8.00	9.50	12.50	16.00	30.00	57.00	145.	1150.	1650.

Half dimes

Date	Mintage	G-4	VG-8	F-12	VF-20	XF-40	AU-50	MS-60	MS-65	Prf-65
1863	18,460	135.	165.	200.	260.	375.	500.	650.	1500.	1400.
1863S	100,000	18.00	25.00	35.00	65.00	125.	250.	900.	—	—
1864	48,470	275.	315.	375.	500.	625.	700.	950.	2750.	1500.
1864S	90,000	32.00	45.00	65.00	95.00	200.	425.	850.	—	—
1865	13,500	275.	300.	345.	425.	500.	700.	900.	2500.	1400.
1865S	120,000	22.00	28.00	37.00	60.00	110.	300.	900.	—	—
1866	10,725	215.	250.	295.	415.	525.	600.	1000.	2400.	1400.
1866S	120,000	19.00	24.00	29.00	50.00	115.	300.	800.	6000.	—
1867	8,625	350.	400.	475.	550.	625.	765.	975.	2750.	1500.
1867S	120,000	19.00	24.00	40.00	60.00	115.	300.	825.	—	—
1868	89,200	30.00	60.00	95.00	135.	195.	300.	475.	2400.	1400.
1868S	280,000	9.50	11.00	16.00	30.00	60.00	150.	325.	—	—
1869	208,600	10.00	15.00	30.00	40.00	75.00	125.	235.	4900.	1650.
1869S	230,000	10.00	14.00	20.00	33.00	60.00	150.	325.	—	—
1870	536,600	9.50	10.00	12.50	17.00	35.00	125.	175.	1200.	1650.
1870S		Unique, Superior Galleries, July 1986, B.U., $253,000.								
1871	1,873,960	9.25	9.50	12.50	14.00	28.00	65.00	150.	1100.	1650.
1871S	161,000	16.00	22.00	30.00	55.00	95.00	135.	350.	3200.	—
1872	2,947,950	8.00	9.00	12.50	14.00	25.00	65.00	150.	1100.	1650.
1872S mint mark in wreath										
	837,000	10.00	15.00	20.00	30.00	45.00	65.00	155.	1100.	—
1872S mint mark below wreath										
	Inc. Ab.	10.00	15.00	20.00	30.00	35.00	65.00	150.	1100.	—
1873	712,600	10.00	12.00	15.00	24.00	40.00	70.00	200.	1500.	3500.
1873S	324,000	15.00	17.00	19.00	40.00	60.00	90.00	250.	1750.	—

Nickel five-cent

Shield

With rays   Without rays

Designer: James B. Longacre. **Size:** 20.5 millimeters. **Weight:** 5 grams. **Composition:** 75% copper, 25% nickel. **Notes:** In 1867 the rays between the stars on the reverse were eliminated, resulting in varieties with and without rays for that year.

Date	Mintage	G-4	VG-8	F-12	VF-20	XF-40	AU-50	MS-60	MS-65	Prf-65
1866	14,742,500	15.00	18.00	22.00	34.00	95.00	155.	225.	2200.	3400.
1867 w/rays	2,019,000	16.00	18.00	24.00	37.00	100.	165.	235.	4200.	75,000.
1867 w/o rays	28,890,500	8.00	10.00	12.00	14.00	34.00	50.00	90.00	600.	1200.
1868	28,817,000	8.00	10.00	12.00	14.00	34.00	50.00	90.00	600.	1150.
1869	16,395,000	10.00	12.50	13.50	15.00	34.00	50.00	90.00	600.	940.
1870	4,806,000	12.00	13.00	14.00	19.00	45.00	56.00	90.00	875.	1075.
1871	561,000	30.00	40.00	60.00	75.00	120.	165.	270.	1375.	900.
1872	6,036,000	12.00	13.00	14.00	19.00	40.00	70.00	115.	780.	700.
1873	4,550,000	12.00	14.00	15.00	20.00	40.00	65.00	125.	780.	675.
1874	3,538,000	12.00	14.00	24.00	29.00	52.00	70.00	125.	1000.	950.
1875	2,097,000	14.00	16.00	28.00	40.00	65.00	85.00	150.	2100.	1500.
1876	2,530,000	12.00	14.00	24.00	34.00	55.00	75.00	125.	1000.	900.
1877	Est. 900	Proof only		—	1000.	1050.	1100.	—	—	1875.
1878	2,350	Proof only		550.	600.	630.	650.	—	—	800.
1879	29,100	245.	285.	345.	390.	440.	455.	600.	1650.	750.
1880	19,995	300.	345.	385.	440.	540.	560.	630.	4000.	800.
1881	72,375	140.	175.	225.	240.	380.	400.	540.	1250.	550.
1882	11,476,600	10.00	12.50	14.00	16.00	32.00	50.00	90.00	550.	550.
1883	1,456,919	10.00	12.00	14.00	20.00	32.50	60.00	90.00	550.	550.
1883/2	—	63.00	88.00	155.	200.	275.	345.	415.	3000.	—

Liberty

With "Cents"   Without "Cents"

Nickel five-cent

Designer: Charles E. Barber. **Size:** 21.2 millimeters. **Weight:** 5 grams. **Composition:** 75% copper, 25% nickel. **Notes:** In 1883 "Cents" was added to the reverse, resulting in varieties with "Cents" and without "Cents" for that year.

Date	Mintage	G-4	VG-8	F-12	VF-20	XF-40	AU-50	MS-60	MS-65	Prf-65
1883 NC	5,479,519	3.75	4.25	4.75	5.50	7.00	10.00	29.00	260.	1000.
1883 WC	16,032,983	8.00	9.25	14.00	20.00	37.50	60.00	85.00	475.	550.
1884	11,273,942	10.00	13.00	16.00	23.00	45.00	75.00	125.	720.	500.
1885	1,476,490	260.	280.	350.	425.	650.	695.	850.	1850.	875.
1886	3,330,290	76.00	110.	145.	205.	295.	350.	485.	2150.	550.
1887	15,263,652	7.00	8.00	17.50	20.00	37.00	65.00	90.00	540.	500.
1888	10,720,483	12.50	13.00	18.00	29.00	60.00	91.00	135.	650.	485.
1889	15,881,361	5.50	7.50	16.00	19.50	35.00	65.00	94.00	525.	500.
1890	16,259,272	5.00	7.50	15.50	20.00	35.00	66.00	100.	850.	550.
1891	16,834,350	3.50	5.00	12.00	16.00	35.00	65.00	94.00	775.	500.
1892	11,699,642	4.00	5.50	13.00	17.50	33.00	67.00	100.	750.	500.
1893	13,370,195	3.50	5.00	12.50	17.00	32.00	60.00	95.00	700.	500.
1894	5,413,132	7.00	9.00	37.00	60.00	135.	150.	185.	800.	550.
1895	9,979,884	2.75	3.50	11.00	18.00	35.00	65.00	87.00	850.	600.
1896	8,842,920	4.00	5.50	13.50	20.00	40.00	69.00	100.	1075.	550.
1897	20,428,735	1.75	2.50	5.50	9.50	22.00	50.00	80.00	740.	490.
1898	12,532,087	1.90	2.50	5.75	10.50	32.50	55.00	85.00	600.	490.
1899	26,029,031	1.35	1.75	5.50	7.50	18.00	47.50	80.00	500.	490.
1900	27,255,995	1.20	1.50	5.00	7.50	17.50	35.00	65.00	470.	490.

Dimes

Draped Bust

Heraldic eagle

Heraldic-eagle reverse

Notes: The 1805 strikes have either 4 or 5 berries on the olive branch held by the eagle.

Date	Mintage	G-4	VG-8	F-12	VF-20	XF-40	MS-60
1801	34,640	450.	560.	875.	1375.	3200.	—
1802	10,975	625.	850.	1200.	2200.	4200.	—
1803	33,040	450.	560.	750.	1125.	1975.	5500.
1804 13 stars	8,265	1000.	1400.	2100.	4400.	7500.	—
1804 14 stars	Inc. Ab.	1200.	1700.	2350.	4750.	8000.	—
1805 4 berries	120,780	375.	525.	725.	950.	1800.	4050.
1805 5 berries	Inc. Ab.	650.	800.	1000.	1500.	2500.	4200.
1807	165,000	375.	525.	725.	975.	1800.	4050.

Liberty Cap

Designer: John Reich. **Size:** 18.8 millimeters. **Weight:** 2.7 grams. **Composition:** 89.25% silver (.0775 ounces), 10.76% copper. **Notes:** Varieties of the 1814, 1821 and 1928 strikes are distinguished by the size of the numerals in the dates. The 1820 varieties are distinguished by the size of the 0 in the number. The 1823 overdates have either large "E's" or small "E's" in "United States of America" on the reverse.

Date	Mintage	G-4	VG-8	F-12	VF-20	XF-40	AU-50	MS-60	MS-65
1809	51,065	100.	200.	375.	650.	925.	2500.	4200.	22,500.
1811/9	65,180	90.00	140.	240.	425.	750.	1500.	4000.	22,500.
1814 sm. dt.	421,500	40.00	60.00	90.00	210.	450.	700.	800.	8000.
1814 lg. dt.	Inc.Ab.	17.50	26.00	44.00	115.	350.	625.	800.	8000.
1820 lg. O	942,587	17.00	24.00	35.00	105.	330.	625.	800.	8000.
1820 sm. O	Inc.Ab.	17.00	24.00	35.00	105.	330.	625.	800.	8000.
1821 lg. dt.	1,186,512	16.00	23.00	38.00	105.	330.	625.	800.	8000.
1821 sm. dt.	Inc.Ab.	18.50	25.00	45.00	125.	370.	625.	800.	8000.
1822	100,000	300.	450.	800.	1450.	2500.	4450.	6000.	—
1823/22 lg.E's	440,000	15.00	22.00	40.00	110.	300.	625.	800.	8000.
1823/22 sm.E's	Inc.Ab.	15.00	22.00	40.00	110.	300.	625.	800.	8000.
1824/22	Undetermined	30.00	48.00	90.00	325.	525.	1275.	2500.	—
1825	510,000	18.00	25.00	40.00	145.	375.	775.	1250.	8000.
1827	1,215,000	15.00	22.00	35.00	95.00	300.	775.	1000.	8000.
1828 lg.dt.	125,000	75.00	90.00	145.	260.	650.	900.	2600.	—

Dimes

Reduced size

Size: 18.5 millimeters. **Notes:** The three varieties of 1829 strikes and two varieties of 1830 strikes are distinguishable by the size of "10C" on the reverse. On the 1833 "high 3" variety, the last 3 in the date, a tougher than the first 3. The two varieties of the 1834 strikes are distinguished by the size of the date the date.

Date	Mintage	G-4	VG-8	F-12	VF-20	XF-40	AU-50	MS-60	MS-65
1828 sm.dt.	Inc. Ab.	30.00	45.00	75.00	195.	475.	775.	1750.	—
1829 lg.10C.	770,000	35.00	45.00	85.00	150.	375.	600.	1500.	—
1829 med.10C.	Inc. Ab.	17.50	25.00	35.00	85.00	265.	425.	625.	8000.
1829 sm.10C.	Inc. Ab.	14.00	17.00	22.00	60.00	185.	415.	625.	8000.
1829 curl base 2		3200.	3950.	7500.	—	—	—	—	—
1830 lg.10C.	510,000	14.00	17.00	22.00	60.00	185.	415.	625.	8000.
1830 sm.10C.	Inc. Ab.	15.00	19.00	25.00	63.00	200.	415.	625.	8000.
1830/29	Inc. Ab.	20.00	25.00	50.00	100.	240.	500.	1000.	—
1831	771,350	14.00	17.00	22.00	60.00	185.	350.	600.	5050.
1832	522,500	14.00	17.00	22.00	60.00	185.	350.	600.	5050.
1833	485,000	14.00	17.00	22.00	60.00	185.	350.	600.	5050.
1834	635,000	14.00	17.00	22.00	60.00	185.	350.	600.	5050.
1835	1,410,000	14.00	17.00	22.00	60.00	185.	350.	600.	5050.
1836	1,190,000	14.00	17.00	22.00	60.00	185.	350.	600.	5050.
1837	1,042,000	14.00	17.00	22.00	60.00	185.	350.	625.	5050.

Seated Liberty

No stars

Stars

Drapery

Arrows at date

Obverse legend

No stars

Designer: Christian Gobrecht. **Size:** 17.9 millimeters. **Weight:** 2.67 grams. **Composition:** 90% silver (.0773 ounces), 10% copper. Notes: The two 1837 varieties are distinguished by the size of the numerals in the date.

Date	Mintage	G-4	VG-8	F-12	VF-20	XF-40	AU-50	MS-60	MS-65
1837 sm.date	Inc. Ab.	29.00	40.00	75.00	275.	550.	750.	1100.	6500.
1837 lg.date	Inc. Ab.	29.00	40.00	75.00	275.	550.	750.	1100.	6500.
1838O	406,034	40.00	55.00	90.00	375.	725.	1250.	3500.	21,000.

Stars around rim

Notes: The two 1838 varieties are distinguished by the size of the stars on the obverse. The 1838 "partial drapery" variety has drapery on Liberty's left elbow. The 1839-O with reverse of 1838-O variety was struck from rusted dies. This variety has a bumpy surface on the reverse.

Date	Mintage	G-4	VG-8	F-12	VF-20	XF-40	AU-50	MS-60	MS-65
1838 sm.stars	1,992,500	20.00	30.00	45.00	75.00	175.	300.	950.	—
1838 lg.stars	Inc. Ab.	9.00	11.00	15.00	25.00	60.00	170.	575.	8500.
1838 partial drapery	Inc. Ab.	30.00	45.00	60.00	125.	195.	325.	550.	—
1839	1,053,115	9.00	15.00	17.50	35.00	70.00	170.	265.	2500.
1839O	1,323,000	8.75	12.00	20.00	40.00	85.00	300.	1250.	—
1839O rev. 1838O	—	145.	200.	350.	550.	950.	—	—	—
1840	1,358,580	9.00	15.00	20.00	30.00	60.00	170.	300.	2500.
1840O	1,175,000	12.50	22.00	40.00	70.00	125.	295.	975.	—

Drapery added to Liberty

Note: In 1840 drapery was added to Liberty's left elbow.

Date	Mintage	G-4	VG-8	F-12	VF-20	XF-40	AU-50	MS-60	MS-65
1840	Inc. Ab.	30.00	45.00	85.00	165.	275.	1250.	—	—
1841	1,622,500	10.00	13.00	16.00	25.00	45.00	175.	260.	2550.
1841O	2,007,500	9.00	11.00	15.00	28.00	60.00	250.	1500.	—
1842	1,887,500	8.75	9.50	10.00	17.00	45.00	175.	260.	2550.
1842O	2,020,000	10.00	18.00	30.00	75.00	225.	1350.	2900.	—
1843	1,370,000	8.75	9.25	10.00	17.00	45.00	175.	260.	2550.
1843/1843	—	9.00	12.00	18.00	30.00	75.00	200.	295.	—
1843O	150,000	35.00	65.00	125.	250.	700.	2000.	—	—

Dimes

Date	Mintage	G-4	VG-8	F-12	VF-20	XF-40	AU-50	MS-60	MS-65
1844	72,500	275.	350.	550.	700.	1450.	2200.	3000.	—
1845	1,755,000	8.75	9.25	10.00	19.00	45.00	120.	260.	2550.
1845O	230,000	19.00	35.00	60.00	165.	475.	1200.	—	—
1846	31,300	80.00	110.	175.	295.	850.	2000.	—	—
1847	245,000	17.50	25.00	35.00	60.00	125.	350.	950.	—
1848	451,500	12.00	15.00	22.00	40.00	75.00	185.00	750.	7050.
1849	839,000	10.00	13.00	18.00	28.00	55.00	140.00	500.	7050.
1849O	300,000	15.00	22.00	35.00	85.00	275.	950.	—	—
1850	1,931,500	8.75	9.25	10.00	25.00	60.00	120.	260.	2550.
1850O	510,000	10.00	14.00	28.00	60.00	160.	400.	1250.	—
1851	1,026,500	8.75	9.25	10.00	19.00	60.00	120.	325.	—
1851O	400,000	10.00	15.00	30.00	75.00	175.	450.	1500.	—
1852	1,535,500	8.75	9.25	10.00	15.00	50.00	120.	290.	2550.
1852O	430,000	16.00	22.00	35.00	85.00	195.	425.	1800.	—
1853	95,000	65.00	85.00	100.	180.	300.	450.	800.	—

Arrows at date

Weight: 2.49 grams. **Composition:** 90% silver (.721 ounces), 10% copper.

Date	Mintage	G-4	VG-8	F-12	VF-20	XF-40	AU-50	MS-60	MS-65	Prf-65
1853	12,078,010	8.75	9.25	10.00	14.00	45.00	125.	330.	2500.	31,500.
1853O	1,100,000	10.00	13.00	20.00	45.00	145.	400.	900.	—	—
1854	4,470,000	8.75	9.25	10.00	14.00	45.00	125.	330.	2500.	31,500.
1854O	1,770,000	9.00	9.50	11.00	25.00	75.00	175.	600.	—	—
1855	2,075,000	8.75	9.25	10.00	15.00	48.00	170.	350.	3800.	31,500.

Arrows at date removed

Notes: The two 1856 varieties are distinguished by the size of the numerals in the date.

Date	Mintage	G-4	VG-8	F-12	VF-20	XF-40	AU-50	MS-60	MS-65	Prf-65
1856 sm. dt.	5,780,000	8.75	9.25	10.00	12.50	32.00	115.	250.	7050.	38,000.
1856 lg. dt.	Inc. Ab.	10.00	12.00	15.00	25.00	65.00	175.	475.	—	—
1856O	1,180,000	9.00	15.00	20.00	35.00	85.00	200.	500.	—	—
1856S	70,000	135.	165.	250.	425.	900.	1750.	—	—	—
1857	5,580,000	8.75	9.25	11.25	13.00	32.00	100.	260.	2500.	3400.
1857O	1,540,000	9.00	10.00	12.00	25.00	65.00	200.	350.	—	—
1858	1,540,000	10.00	14.00	20.00	35.00	55.00	145.	260.	2500.	3400.
1858O	290,000	15.00	19.00	35.00	70.00	125.	275.	800.	—	—
1858S	60,000	110.	150.	200.	325.	675.	1400.	—	—	—
1859	430,000	11.00	15.00	20.00	40.00	60.00	140.	350.	—	3400.
1859O	480,000	9.00	11.00	19.00	35.00	70.00	225.	550.	—	—
1859S	60,000	125.	160.	250.	450.	1000.	2000.	—	—	—
1860S	140,000	28.00	36.00	48.00	100.	275.	800.	—	—	—

Transitional pattern

Notes: This non-circulation strike was an experiment in transferring the legend "United States of America" from the reverse to the obverse.

Date	Mintage	G-4	VG-8	F-12	VF-20	XF-40	AU-50	MS-60	MS-65	Prf-65
1859 obverse of 1859, reverse of 1860					—	—	—	—	—	25,000.

Obverse legend

Notes: In 1860 the legend "United States of America" replaced the stars on the obverse. The 1873 "closed 3" and "open 3" varieties are distinguished by the around of space between the upper left and lower left serifs of the 3 in the date.

Date	Mintage	G-4	VG-8	F-12	VF-20	XF-40	AU-50	MS-60	MS-65	Prf-65
1860	607,000	17.50	22.00	30.00	38.00	55.00	125.	275.	—	1400.
1860O	40,000	300.	425.	575.	950.	2500.	4200.	6000.	—	—
1861	1,884,000	8.75	10.00	13.00	18.00	35.00	65.00	125.	—	1400.
1861S	172,500	45.00	80.00	125.	225.	375.	900.	—	—	—
1862	847,550	10.00	13.00	19.00	25.00	45.00	65.00	150.	—	1400.
1862S	180,750	35.00	52.00	95.00	175.	300.	775.	—	—	—
1863	14,460	250.	375.	500.	600.	750.	900.	1200.	—	1400.
1863S	157,500	30.00	35.00	55.00	90.00	275.	550.	1200.	—	—
1864	11,470	250.	325.	400.	500.	600.	775.	1650.	—	1400.
1864S	230,000	24.00	30.00	40.00	80.00	225.	425.	1200.	—	—
1865	10,500	275.	350.	450.	550.	675.	1050.	1250.	—	1400.
1865S	175,000	35.00	45.00	60.00	100.	250.	700.	—	—	—
1866	8,725	300.	375.	575.	675.	800.	1200.	1800.	—	1750.
1866S	135,000	35.00	45.00	75.00	145.	325.	675.	1900.	—	—
1867	6,625	425.	575.	800.	900.	1150.	1300.	1600.	—	1750.
1867S	140,000	35.00	45.00	70.00	125.	275.	575.	1200.	—	—
1868	464,000	10.00	12.00	20.00	31.00	70.00	175.	300.	—	1400.
1868S	260,000	15.00	20.00	30.00	60.00	115.	285.	600.	—	—
1869	256,600	12.00	16.00	30.00	55.00	115.	200.	600.	—	1400.
1869S	450,000	12.00	17.00	25.00	38.00	65.00	150.	400.	—	—
1870	471,000	11.00	14.00	19.00	32.00	70.00	135.	300.	—	1400.
1870S	50,000	215.	280.	375.	450.	575.	850.	2000.	—	—

Dimes

Date	Mintage	G-4	VG-8	F-12	VF-20	XF-40	AU-50	MS-60	MS-65	Prf-65
1871	907,710	11.00	15.00	20.00	28.00	45.00	130.	300.	—	1400.
1871CC	20,100	800.	1150.	1950.	3500.	6750.	10,500.	—	—	—
1871S	320,000	35.00	45.00	55.00	90.00	175.	350.	900.	—	—
1872	2,396,450	8.75	9.50	11.00	18.00	31.00	95.00	175.	—	1400.
1872CC	35,480	350.	525.	850.	1750.	3000.	4750.	—	—	—
1872S	190,000	40.00	50.00	70.00	125.	215.	450.	1100.	—	—
1873 closed 3										
	1,568,600	9.00	11.00	14.00	27.00	50.00	100.	200.	—	1400.
1873 open 3										
	Inc. Ab.	15.00	18.00	30.00	48.00	100.	225.	650.	—	—
1873CC	12,400	Eliasberg Sale, May 1996, MS-65 $550,000								

Arrows at date

Weight: 2.5 grams. **Composition:** 90% silver (.0724 ounces), 10% copper.

Date	Mintage	G-4	VG-8	F-12	VF-20	XF-40	AU-50	MS-60	MS-65	Prf-65
1873	2,378,500	8.75	13.00	25.00	50.00	150.	350.	500.	4500.	4500.
1873CC	18,791	750.	975.	1850.	3750.	5750.	9750.	—	—	—
1873S	455,000	15.00	20.00	28.00	60.00	180.	320.	1500.	—	—
1874	2,940,700	8.75	13.00	17.50	50.00	150.	315.	500.	4500.	4500.
1874CC	10,817	2950.	4500.	6500.	9750.	17,500.	—	—	—	—
1874S	240,000	26.00	33.00	55.00	115.	250.	450.	1500.	—	—

Arrows at date removed

Notes: On the 1876-CC doubled obverse variety, doubling appears in the words "of America" in the legend.

Date	Mintage	G-4	VG-8	F-12	VF-20	XF-40	AU-50	MS-60	MS-65	Prf-65
1875	10,350,700	8.75	9.25	10.00	12.00	22.00	60.00	125.	2250.	4600.
1875CC mint mark in wreath										
	4,645,000	8.75	9.50	11.00	18.00	3750.	90.00	160.	2700.	—
1875CC mint mark under wreath										
	Inc. Ab.	8.00	15.00	22.50	37.50	65.00	165.	235.	3000.	—
1875S mint mark in wreath										
	9,070,000	12.00	17.50	28.00	43.00	65.00	125.	225.	3100.	—
1875S mint mark under wreath										
	Inc. Ab.	10.00	14.00	17.50	25.00	35.00	70.00	125.	1100.	—
1876	11,461,150	8.75	9.25	11.00	12.00	24.00	60.00	110.	1100.	1200.
1876CC	8,270,000	8.75	9.25	11.00	18.00	30.00	60.00	175.	—	—
1876CC (doubled obverse)										
	Inc. Ab.	12.00	20.00	32.00	95.00	225.	400.	700.	—	—
1876S	10,420,000	11.00	13.00	15.00	20.00	35.00	85.00	165.	1100.	—
1877	7,310,510	8.75	9.25	9.75	13.00	23.00	60.00	110.	1100.	1200.
1877CC	7,700,000	8.75	9.25	10.75	18.00	35.00	75.00	175.	—	—
1877S	2,340,000	12.00	15.00	18.00	27.00	50.00	105.	225.	—	—
1878	1,678,800	9.00	9.50	10.00	18.00	30.00	60.00	110.	1100.	1200.
1878CC	200,000	50.00	75.00	110.	165.	275.	450.	775.	3900.	—
1879	15,100	165.	200.	250.	275.	350.	475.	675.	1750.	1500.
1880	37,335	120.	140.	175.	210.	250.	325.	450.	1750.	1500.
1881	24,975	135.	160.	190.	240.	325.	425.	650.	2500.	1600.
1882	3,911,100	8.75	9.25	11.00	12.00	24.00	60.00	110.	1100.	1200.
1883	7,675,712	8.75	9.25	11.00	12.00	24.00	60.00	110.	1100.	1200.
1884	3,366,380	8.75	9.25	11.00	12.00	24.00	60.00	110.	1100.	1200.
1884S	564,969	16.00	19.00	31.00	50.00	115.	200.	500.	—	—
1885	2,533,427	8.75	9.25	10.75	12.00	24.00	60.00	110.	1100.	1200.
1885S	43,690	350.	475.	725.	1400.	2450.	2950.	3750.	—	—
1886	6,377,570	8.75	9.25	10.00	12.00	22.00	60.00	110.	1100.	1200.
1886S	206,524	40.00	55.00	85.00	135.	185.	275.	600.	—	—
1887	11,283,939	8.75	9.25	10.00	12.00	22.00	60.00	110.	1100.	1200.
1887S	4,454,450	9.00	12.00	16.00	22.00	38.00	80.00	110.	1100.	—
1888	5,496,487	8.75	9.25	10.00	12.00	22.00	60.00	110.	1100.	1200.
1888S	1,720,000	10.00	13.00	17.00	25.00	40.00	95.00	200.	—	—
1889	7,380,711	8.75	9.25	10.00	12.00	22.00	60.00	110.	1100.	1200.
1889S	972,678	14.00	18.00	25.00	35.00	70.00	150.	475.	4500.	—
1890	9,911,541	8.75	9.25	10.00	12.00	22.00	60.00	110.	1100.	1200.
1890S	1,423,076	11.00	14.00	20.00	57.50	85.00	155.	400.	4900.	—
1890S/S	Inc. Ab.	25.00	30.00	40.00	85.00	135.	250.	—	—	—
1891	15,310,600	8.75	9.25	10.00	12.00	22.00	60.00	110.	1100.	1200.
1891O	4,540,000	9.00	9.75	11.00	13.00	24.00	70.00	175.	1750.	—
1891O/horz. O										
	Inc. Ab.	65.00	95.00	125.	175.	225.	400.	—	—	—
1891S	3,196,116	10.00	12.00	18.00	35.00	55.00	135.	225.	1650.	—

Barber

Designer: Charles E. Barber. **Size:** 17.9 millimeters. **Weight:** 2.5 grams. **Composition:** 90% silver (.0724 ounces), 10% copper.

Dimes

Date	Mintage	G-4	VG-8	F-12	VF-20	XF-40	AU-50	MS-60	MS-65	Prf-65
1892	12,121,245	2.50	5.00	14.00	19.50	22.00	55.00	90.00	540.	1450.
1892O	3,841,700	5.85	11.50	27.00	38.00	45.00	72.00	145.	1200.	—
1892S	990,710	35.00	69.00	140.	170.	210.	230.	350.	2500.	—
1893	3,340,792	5.50	10.50	17.50	21.00	32.00	72.00	145.	810.	1450.
1893O	1,760,000	16.50	30.00	90.00	110.	135.	155.	260.	2900.	—
1893S	2,491,401	7.75	19.00	25.00	30.00	49.00	110.	230.	3600.	—
1894	1,330,972	10.00	24.00	84.00	110.	130.	155.	250.	1110.	1450.
1894O	720,000	39.00	78.00	160.	205.	290.	600.	1100.	8400.	—
1894S	24	Eliasberg Sale, May 1996, Prf-64 $451,000.							—	—
1895	690,880	55.00	85.00	200.	400.	450.	500.	600.	2400.	2000.
1895O	440,000	225.	300.	690.	950.	1825.	2500.	2800.	10,000.	—
1895S	1,120,000	26.00	40.00	105.	145.	175.	230.	440.	6300.	—
1896	2,000,762	8.00	19.00	44.00	58.00	74.00	100.	145.	1320.	1450.
1896O	610,000	50.00	95.00	215.	285.	380.	600.	755.	6000.	—
1896S	575,056	60.00	90.00	220.	240.	295.	440.	695.	3500.	—
1897	10,869,264	2.25	2.75	5.85	8.50	23.00	68.00	110.	700.	1450.
1897O	666,000	43.00	74.00	225.	280.	345.	505.	755.	4150.	—
1897S	1,342,844	11.00	22.00	72.00	83.00	140.	200.	390.	3500.	—
1898	16,320,735	1.45	1.95	6.50	9.00	20.00	50.00	91.00	540.	1450.
1898O	2,130,000	5.50	12.00	60.00	91.00	130.	195.	425.	3500.	—
1898S	1,702,507	4.50	8.50	22.00	31.00	52.00	110.	325.	3800.	—
1899	19,580,846	1.45	1.75	5.85	8.50	20.00	52.00	91.00	540.	1450.
1899O	2,650,000	4.50	9.75	58.00	78.00	115.	200.	360.	4800.	—
1899S	1,867,493	4.75	9.75	16.50	20.00	35.00	85.00	295.	3500.	—
1900	17,600,912	1.50	2.10	6.00	8.50	20.00	52.00	91.00	900.	1450.
1900O	2,010,000	7.00	15.00	78.00	125.	190.	325.	520.	6000.	—
1900S	5,168,270	2.75	3.60	8.50	11.00	21.00	72.00	165.	1675.	—

NOTE: Later dates (1901-1916) exist for this type.

20-cent

Mintmark

Designer: William Barber, **Size:** 22 millimeters. **Weight:** 5 grams. **Composition:** 90% silver (.1447), 10% copper.

Date	Mintage	G-4	VG-8	F-12	VF-20	XF-40	AU-50	MS-60	MS-65	Prf-65
1875	39,700	60.00	70.00	85.00	120.	180.	325.	600.	6000.	9500.
1875S	1,155,000	45.00	50.00	70.00	100.	160.	300.	475.	4900.	—
1875CC	133,290	50.00	60.00	95.00	150.	265.	475.	630.	8200.	—
1876	15,900	110.	125.	150.	200.	315.	500.	650.	6000.	7500.
1876CC	10,000	Eliasberg sale, Apr. 1997, MS-65, $148,500.							—	—
1877	510	Proof only		—	1500.	1700.	1850.	—	—	7500.
1878	600	Proof only		—	1300.	1400.	1500.	—	—	7600.

Quarters

Draped Bust

Heraldic eagle

Designer: Robert Scot. **Size:** 27.5 millimeters. **Weight:** 6.74 grams. **Composition:** 89.24% silver (.1935 ounces), 10.76% copper.

Heraldic-eagle reverse

Date	Mintage	G-4	VG-8	F-12	VF-20	XF-40	AU-50	MS-60	MS-65
1804	6,738	1000.	1475.	2750.	4750.	8250.	16,500.	22,000.	116,000.
1805	121,394	210.	300.	450.	850.	2900.	3500.	5850.	46,500.
1806	206,124	225.	285.	425.	800.	2900.	3500.	5850.	46,500.
1806/5	Inc. Ab.	235.	315.	495.	950.	2900.	4350.	5850.	46,500.
1807	220,643	210.	300.	450.	850.	2900.	3500.	5850.	46,500.

Quarters

Liberty Cap

Motto

Designer: John Reich. **Size:** 27 millimeters. **Weight:** 6.74 grams. **Composition:** 89.24% silver (.1935 ounces), 10.76% copper. **Notes:** Varieties of the 1819 strikes are distinguished by the size of the 9 in the date. Varieties of the 1820 strikes are distinguished by the size of the 0 in the date. One 1822 variety and one 1828 variety have "25" engraved over "50" in the denomination. The 1827 restrikes were produced privately using dies sold as scrap by the U.S. Mint.

Date	Mintage	G-4	VG-8	F-12	VF-20	XF-40	AU-50	MS-60	MS-65
1815	89,235	60.00	80.00	110.	335.	850.	2000.	3100.	22,000.
1818	361,174	40.00	60.00	90.00	275.	675.	1300.	1550.	12,500.
1818/15	Inc. Ab.	65.00	80.00	110.	315.	800.	2000.	3100.	22,000.
1819 sm.9	144,000	55.00	70.00	100.	300.	700.	1350.	1550.	12,500.
1819 lg.9	Inc. Ab.	55.00	70.00	100.	300.	700.	1350.	1550.	12,500.
1820 sm.O	127,444	60.00	75.00	110.	315.	700.	1500.	3000.	12,500.
1820 lg.O	Inc. Ab.	50.00	65.00	100.	275.	675.	1300.	1550.	12,500.
1821	216,851	50.00	65.00	100.	275.	675.	1300.	1550.	12,500.
1822	64,080	75.00	90.00	130.	400.	975.	1400.	1550.	12,500.
1822 25/50C.	I.A.	2500.	3500.	4750.	6500.	8750.	10,000.	15,000.	25,000.
1823/22	17,800	12,500.	17,500.	22,500.	27,500.	44,000.	—	—	—
		Superior, Aug. 1990, proof, $62,500.					—	—	—
1824/2	Unrecorded	100.	140.	200.	575.	1250.	1950.	5000.	—
1825/22	168,000	100.	165.	285.	575.	1250.	1850.	2450.	—
1825/23	Inc. Ab.	50.00	65.00	100.	275.	725.	1200.	1700.	10,500.
1825/24	Inc. Ab.	60.00	75.00	115.	325.	825.	1400.	1900.	11,500.
1827 original	4,000	Eliasberg, Apr. 1997, VF-20, $39,600.							—
1827 restrike	I.A.	Eliasberg, Apr. 1997, Prf-65, $77,000.						—	—
1828	102,000	50.00	65.00	95.00	275.	650.	1500.	1900.	12,500.
1828 25/50C.	I.A.	165.	225.	350.	650.	1350.	3000.	8000.	—

No Motto

No Motto

Designer: William Kneass. **Size:** 24.3 millimeters. **Notes:** In 1831 the motto "E Pluribus Unum" was removed from the reverse. Varieties of the 1831 strikes are distinguished by the size of the lettering on the reverse.

Date	Mintage	G-4	VG-8	F-12	VF-20	XF-40	AU-50	MS-60	MS-65
1831 sm. let.	398,000	45.00	50.00	60.00	90.00	240.	750.	900.	13,000.
1831 lg.let.	Inc. Ab.	45.00	50.00	60.00	90.00	240.	750.	900.	13,000.
1832	320,000	45.00	50.00	60.00	90.00	240.	750.	900.	13,000.
1833	156,000	48.00	60.00	80.00	120.	325.	800.	1275.	17,000.
1834	286,000	45.00	50.00	60.00	90.00	240.	750.	900.	13,000.
1835	1,952,000	45.00	50.00	60.00	90.00	240.	750.	900.	13,000.
1836	472,000	45.00	50.00	60.00	90.00	240.	750.	900.	13,000.
1837	252,400	47.00	53.00	64.00	95.00	250.	750.	900.	13,000.
1838	832,000	45.00	50.00	60.00	90.00	240.	750.	900.	13,000.

Seated Liberty

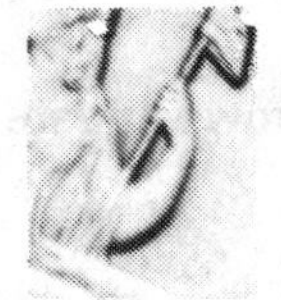

Without drapery

Arrows at date

1853 reverse rays

Motto above eagle

No drapery

Designer: Christian Gobrecht. **Size:** 24.3 millimeters. **Weight:** 6.68 grams. **Composition:** 90% silver (.1934 ounces), 10% copper.

Date	Mintage	G-4	VG-8	F-12	VF-20	XF-40	AU-50	MS-60	MS-65
1838	Inc. Ab.	15.00	22.00	27.00	55.00	195.	475.	1050.	—
1839	491,146	14.00	20.00	27.00	52.00	195.	450.	1050.	25,000.
1840O	425,200	13.00	19.00	27.00	60.00	300.	400.	1050.	25,000.

Drapery added to Liberty

Notes: In 1840 drapery was added to Liberty's left elbow. Two varieties for 1842 and 1842-O are distinguished by the size of the numerals in the date. 1852 obverse dies were used to strike the 1853 no-arrows variety, with the 2 being recut to form a 3.

Date	Mintage	G-4	VG-8	F-12	VF-20	XF-40	AU-50	MS-60	MS-65
1840	188,127	30.00	40.00	55.00	75.00	180.	350.	750.	—
1840O	Inc. Ab.	20.00	30.00	50.00	110.	185.	500.	1150.	—
1841	120,000	45.00	60.00	80.00	135.	225.	385.	800.	—
1841O	452,000	12.50	24.00	40.00	70.00	185.	300.	800.	—
1842 sm. dt.	88,000				Eliasberg, Apr. 1997, Prf-63, $66,000.				—
1842 lg. dt.	Inc. Ab.	95.00	145.	170.	275.	475.	950.	2700.	—
1842O sm. dt.	769,000	375.	500.	850.	1750.	3750.	—	—	—
1842O lg. dt.	Inc. Ab.	13.50	16.00	30.00	60.00	245.	800.	—	—
1843	645,600	12.50	16.00	25.00	45.00	80.00	175.	290.	3500.
1843O	968,000	20.00	33.00	53.00	175.	375.	1250.	—	—
1844	421,200	12.50	16.00	25.00	43.00	80.00	185.	290.	3500.
1844O	740,000	12.50	21.00	38.00	55.00	175.	375.	1200.	—
1845	922,000	12.50	15.00	25.00	40.00	75.00	185.	450.	3500.
1846	510,000	15.00	25.00	37.50	65.00	115.	245.	485.	3500.
1847	734,000	12.50	15.00	25.00	45.00	75.00	190.	425.	3500.
1847O	368,000	22.00	40.00	80.00	110.	285.	850.	—	—
1848	146,000	35.00	48.00	70.00	130.	275.	425.	1175.	—
1849	340,000	16.00	22.00	40.00	70.00	100.	375.	1000.	—
1849O	Unrecorded	325.	545.	900.	1500.	3000.	7000.	—	—
1850	190,800	30.00	45.00	55.00	95.00	175.	325.	1000.	—
1850O	412,000	17.50	30.00	45.00	85.00	225.	750.	1100.	—
1851	160,000	35.00	50.00	75.00	135.	225.	400.	1000.	—
1851O	88,000	175.	265.	325.	575.	1000.	2600.	—	—
1852	177,060	37.50	47.50	75.00	110.	185.	400.	900.	—
1852O	96,000	165.	255.	300.	550.	900.	2750.	—	—
1853 recut date	44,200	350.	475.	675.	925.	1200.	1750.	3250.	—

Arrows at date, reverse rays

Weight: 6.68 grams. **Composition:** 90% silver (.18 ounce), 10% copper.

Date	Mintage	G-4	VG-8	F-12	VF-20	XF-40	AU-50	MS-60	MS-65	Prf-65
1853 rays	15,210,020	12.50	16.00	24.00	38.00	160.	295.	900.	17,500.	—
1853/4	Inc. Ab.	30.00	47.50	75.00	165.	300.	950.	2750.	—	—
1853O rays	1,332,000	12.50	26.00	30.00	75.00	275.	1500.	3000.	—	—

Reverse rays removed

Notes: The 1854-O "huge O" variety has an oversized mintmark.

Date	Mintage	G-4	VG-8	F-12	VF-20	XF-40	AU-50	MS-60	MS-65	Prf-65
1854	12,380,000	12.50	16.00	22.00	32.00	145.	285.	410.	7100.	15,000.
1854O	1,484,000	12.50	17.00	28.00	45.00	165.	375.	1500.	—	—
1854O huge O	Inc. Ab.	100.	145.	200.	375.	650.	—	—	—	—
1855	2,857,000	12.50	16.00	22.00	24.00	70.00	285.	410.	7100.	15,000.
1855O	176,000	35.00	55.00	90.00	275.	750.	1750.	3750.	—	—
1855S	396,400	25.00	45.00	65.00	145.	325.	1250.	1750.	—	—

Arrows at date removed

Date	Mintage	G-4	VG-8	F-12	VF-20	XF-40	AU-50	MS-60	MS-65	Prf-65
1856	7,264,000	12.50	15.00	22.00	32.00	58.00	145.	325.	3500.	15,000.
1856O	968,000	13.00	16.00	26.00	40.00	110.	485.	1250.	—	—
1856S	286,000	45.00	65.00	95.00	275.	585.	1275.	—	—	—
1856S/S	Inc. Ab.	55.00	80.00	155.	325.	650.	1875.	—	—	—
1857	9,644,000	12.50	15.00	22.00	28.00	50.00	145.	290.	3000.	15,000.
1857O	1,180,000	13.00	17.00	27.00	40.00	80.00	275.	1075.	—	—
1857S	82,000	95.00	125.	165.	275.	575.	975.	3250.	—	—
1858	7,368,000	12.50	15.00	22.00	28.00	50.00	190.	290.	3000.	11,500.
1858O	520,000	18.00	25.00	45.00	65.00	135.	425.	1250.	—	—
1858S	121,000	45.00	70.00	120.	275.	675.	1650.	—	—	—
1859	1,344,000	14.00	15.00	23.00	30.00	63.00	190.	700.	—	7000.
1859O	260,000	18.00	25.00	35.00	50.00	90.00	450.	900.	—	—
1859S	80,000	90.00	125.	175.	275.	675.	7000.	—	—	—
1860	805,400	12.50	15.00	23.00	30.00	64.00	155.	900.	11,500.	4000.
1860O	388,000	14.00	19.00	35.00	50.00	95.00	225.	1450.	—	—
1860S	56,000	165.	245.	350.	625.	2750.	9000.	—	—	—

Quarters

Date	Mintage	G-4	VG-8	F-12	VF-20	XF-40	AU-50	MS-60	MS-65	Prf-65
1861	4,854,600	12.50	14.00	22.00	28.00	45.00	190.	290.	3000.	4000.
1861S	96,000	60.00	80.00	165.	295.	775.	5250.	—	—	—
1862	932,550	10.00	15.00	24.00	35.00	60.00	175.	290.	3000.	4000.
1862S	67,000	55.00	70.00	140.	245.	650.	1775.	2750.	—	—
1863	192,060	25.00	40.00	60.00	95.00	225.	325.	750.	—	7000.
1864	94,070	50.00	60.00	90.00	125.	275.	450.	925.	11,500.	7000.
1864S	20,000	250.	375.	575.	1200.	2500.	3750.	—	—	—
1865	59,300	55.00	70.00	95.00	120.	250.	375.	875.	11,500.	7000.
1865S	41,000	70.00	100.	135.	275.	575.	1250.	2000.	—	—
1866	—		Unique	—	—	—	—	—	—	—

Motto above eagle

Notes: In 1866 the motto "In God We Trust" was added to the reverse. The 1873 closed-3 and open-3 varieties are known and are distinguished by the around of space between the upper left and lower left serifs in the 3.

Date	Mintage	G-4	VG-8	F-12	VF-20	XF-40	AU-50	MS-60	MS-65	Prf-65
1866	17,525	275.	310.	375.	475.	700.	1500.	2250.	—	6750.
1866S	28,000	200.	290.	420.	650.	1250.	1800.	—	—	—
1867	20,625	175.	200.	240.	325.	475.	625.	1300.	—	6750.
1867S	48,000	145.	200.	275.	375.	750.	1750.	3000.	—	—
1868	30,000	105.	155.	200.	255.	375.	525.	1200.	—	6750.
1868S	96,000	50.00	70.00	135.	245.	575.	1250.	2300.	—	—
1869	16,600	215.	260.	325.	425.	575.	950.	1400.	—	6750.
1869S	76,000	60.00	95.00	165.	300.	625.	1575.	—	—	—
1870	87,400	40.00	48.00	80.00	135.	250.	325.	1000.	—	6550.
1870CC	8,340	3200.	4250.	5750.	9500.	15,500.	—	—	—	—
1871	119,160	30.00	40.00	55.00	115.	185.	425.	1000.	—	6550.
1871CC	10,890	1700.	2550.	3750.	6500.	11,500.	25,000.	—	—	—
1871S	30,900	240.	300.	400.	575.	925.	1750.	3000.	—	—
1872	182,950	30.00	40.00	50.00	100.	155.	445.	1250.	—	4050.
1872CC	22,850	400.	625.	1050.	2250.	3750.	7500.	—	—	—
1872S	83,000	900.	1475.	1950.	2500.	3850.	6750.	—	—	—
1873 clsd.3	212,600	175.	265.	325.	525.	775.	1250.	—	—	8000.
1873 open 3	Inc. Ab.	30.00	37.50	55.00	95.00	175.	325.	750.	—	—
1873CC	4,000			Eliasberg, Apr. 1997, MS-62, $187,000.					—	—

Closed 3, no arrows

Open 3, arrows

Arrows at date

Date	Mintage	G-4	VG-8	F-12	VF-20	XF-40	AU-50	MS-60	MS-65	Prf-65
1873	1,271,700	12.50	16.00	31.00	50.00	190.	380.	700.	3500.	5500.
1873CC	12,462	1500.	2950.	4500.	9250.	13,500.	—	—	—	—
1873S	156,000	25.00	35.00	70.00	145.	275.	600.	1100.	—	—
1874	471,900	16.00	24.00	38.00	75.00	200.	400.	750.	3500.	5500.
1874S	392,000	18.50	28.00	40.00	110.	195.	400.	725.	—	—

Arrows at date removed

Note: The 1876-CC fine-reeding variety has a more finely reeded edge.

Date	Mintage	G-4	VG-8	F-12	VF-20	XF-40	AU-50	MS-60	MS-65	Prf-65
1875	4,293,500	12.00	15.00	22.00	28.00	70.00	115.	350.	1450.	1650.
1875CC	140,000	50.00	80.00	145.	295.	575.	775.	1400.	—	—
1875S	680,000	22.00	30.00	50.00	80.00	165.	300.	575.	—	—
1876	17,817,150	12.00	15.00	22.00	28.00	70.00	115.	350.	1450.	1650.
1876CC	4,944,000	14.00	17.00	25.00	40.00	85.00	235.	425.	3900.	—
1876CC fine reeding										
	Inc. Ab.	13.00	16.00	24.00	35.00	70.00	210.	375.	—	—
1876S	8,596,000	12.00	15.00	22.00	28.00	70.00	115.	225.	1450.	—
1877	10,911,710	12.00	15.00	22.00	28.00	70.00	115.	225.	1450.	1650.
1877CC	4,192,000	12.00	16.00	25.00	35.00	70.00	200.	375.	—	—
1877S	8,996,000	12.00	15.00	22.00	28.00	70.00	115.	220.	1450.	—
1877/horz. S	Inc. Ab.	32.00	48.00	65.00	100.	225.	375.	650.	—	—
1878	2,260,800	12.00	15.00	25.00	40.00	70.00	165.	360.	4100.	1650.
1878CC	996,000	16.00	25.00	38.00	55.00	100.	215.	425.	4100.	—
1878S	140,000	75.00	140.	260.	325.	575.	800.	1500.	—	—
1879	14,700	145.	170.	215.	285.	345.	410.	525.	—	1650.
1880	14,955	155.	170.	215.	285.	345.	410.	525.	—	1650.
1881	12,975	145.	170.	215.	285.	345.	410.	525.	—	1650.
1882	16,300	160.	185.	225.	295.	355.	450.	600.	—	1650.
1883	15,439	160.	195.	225.	295.	355.	450.	600.	—	1650.
1884	8,875	200.	245.	300.	375.	475.	550.	650.	—	1650.
1885	14,530	170.	190.	245.	285.	345.	415.	600.	—	1650.
1886	5,886	325.	400.	450.	540.	675.	850.	1000.	—	1650.
1887	10,710	245.	295.	345.	400.	475.	550.	650.	—	1650.
1888	10,833	175.	205.	245.	295.	375.	475.	600.	—	1650.
1888S	1,216,000	13.00	15.00	22.00	30.00	70.00	135.	225.	1450.	—
1889	12,711	170.	200.	235.	285.	360.	450.	600.	—	1650.

Quarters

Date	Mintage	G-4	VG-8	F-12	VF-20	XF-40	AU-50	MS-60	MS-65	Prf-65
1890	80,590	50.00	55.00	80.00	110.	185.	275.	400.	—	1650.
1891	3,920,600	12.00	15.00	22.00	30.00	70.00	150.	225.	1450.	1650.
1891O	68,000	125.	165.	260.	475.	875.	—	—	—	—
1891S	2,216,000	12.00	15.00	25.00	45.00	85.00	185.	350.	4400.	—

Barber

Mintmark

Designer: Charles E. Barber. **Size:** 24.3 millimeters. **Weight:** 6.25 grams. **Composition:** 90% silver (.1809 ounces), 10% copper.

Date	Mintage	G-4	VG-8	F-12	VF-20	XF-40	AU-50	MS-60	MS-65	Prf-65
1892	8,237,245	3.75	4.50	19.50	30.00	65.00	115.	175.	1300.	1600.
1892O	2,640,000	5.75	8.50	24.00	35.00	72.00	145.	275.	1350.	—
1892S	964,079	13.00	30.00	62.00	75.00	110.	260.	390.	6300.	—
1893	5,484,838	3.50	6.50	21.00	30.00	65.00	115.	205.	1700.	1600.
1893O	3,396,000	5.00	7.50	25.00	40.00	72.00	145.	260.	1800.	—
1893S	1,454,535	8.00	13.00	34.00	55.00	100.	260.	390.	7100.	—
1894	3,432,972	4.50	5.75	23.00	32.00	75.00	120.	205.	1275.	1600.
1894O	2,852,000	5.50	9.00	33.00	39.00	75.00	180.	310.	3000.	—
1894S	2,648,821	5.75	7.50	28.00	39.00	75.00	165.	310.	4100.	—
1895	4,440,880	4.75	5.75	22.00	30.00	65.00	120.	205.	1700.	1600.
1895O	2,816,000	6.50	9.50	35.00	45.00	82.00	215.	360.	2800.	—
1895S	1,764,681	6.00	11.00	40.00	55.00	75.00	210.	345.	3500.	—
1896	3,874,762	5.00	5.75	24.00	30.00	65.00	120.	220.	1550.	1600.
1896O	1,484,000	7.50	14.00	65.00	180.	320.	620.	845.	8100.	—
1896S	188,039	260.	415.	590.	870.	1900.	2900.	4150.	15,000.	—
1897	8,140,731	3.50	6.00	22.00	35.00	65.00	115.	175.	1300.	1600.
1897O	1,414,800	7.75	15.00	75.00	175.	310.	550.	775.	3700.	—
1897S	542,229	16.00	35.00	150.	200.	325.	600.	900.	6300.	—
1898	11,100,735	3.20	5.00	19.00	30.00	65.00	110.	175.	1300.	1600.
1898O	1,868,000	6.75	15.00	55.00	75.00	155.	315.	490.	8600.	—
1898S	1,020,592	5.00	12.50	30.00	44.00	65.00	175.	345.	5200.	—
1899	12,624,846	3.20	5.00	19.00	30.00	65.00	110.	170.	1300.	2200.
1899O	2,644,000	4.75	12.00	30.00	36.00	85.00	240.	370.	5200.	—
1899S	708,000	8.50	20.00	44.00	58.00	75.00	195.	345.	3350.	—
1900	10,016,912	3.50	5.50	19.00	30.00	65.00	110.	170.	1300.	2200.
1900O	3,416,000	6.50	14.00	55.00	75.00	90.00	240.	390.	3700.	—
1900S	1,858,585	5.75	9.00	36.00	48.00	65.00	110.	300.	5800.	—

NOTE: Later dates (1901-1916) exist for this type.

Half dollars

Heraldic eagle

Heraldic-eagle reverse

Designer: Robert Scot. **Size:** 32.5 millimeters. **Weight:** 13.48 grams. **Composition:** 89.24% silver (.3869 ounces), 10.76% copper.

Notes: The two varieties of the 1803 strikes are distinguished by the size of the 3 in the date. The several varieties of the 1806 strikes are distinguished by the style of 6 in the date, size of the stars on the obverse, and whether the stem of the olive branch held by the reverse eagle extends through the claw.

Date	Mintage	G-4	VG-8	F-12	VF-20	XF-40	MS-60
1801	30,289	225.	300.	550.	825.	1850.	25,000.
1802	29,890	175.	240.	440.	775.	1700.	25,000.
1803 sm. 3	188,234	150.	170.	285.	450.	900.	7500.
1803 lg. 3	Inc. Ab.	125.	150.	200.	350.	750.	6000.
1805	211,722	125.	150.	200.	350.	800.	6500.
1805/4	Inc. Ab.	140.	200.	300.	500.	1200.	8750.
1806 round top 6, large stars							
	839,576	125.	140.	180.	350.	675.	6000.

Half dollars

Date	Mintage	G-4	VG-8	F-12	VF-20	XF-40	MS-60
1806 round top 6, small stars							
	Inc. Ab.	125.	140.	180.	375.	675.	6250.
1806 knobbed 6, stem not through claw							
	—	—	35,000.	45,000.	70,000.	95,000.	—
1806 pointed top 6, stem not through claw							
	Inc. Ab.	115.	130.	160.	290.	550.	5000.
1806 pointed top 6, stem through claw							
	Inc. Ab.	120.	135.	175.	300.	600.	5750.
1806/5	Inc. Ab.	125.	160.	210.	350.	675.	6500.
1806/inverted 6	Inc. Ab.	200.	250.	475.	750.	1500.	10,000.
1807	301,076	120.	135.	175.	300.	600.	5750.

Liberty Cap

"50 Cents" reverse

"Half Dol." reverse

Designer: John Reich. **Size:** 32.5 millimeters. **Weight:** 13.48 grams. **Composition:** 89.24% silver (.3869 ounces), 10.76% copper. **Notes:** There are three varieties of the 1807 strikes. Two are distinguished by the size of the stars on the obverse. The third was struck from a reverse die that had a 5 cut over a 2 in the "50C." denomination. Two varieties of the 1811 are distinguished by the size of the 8 in the date. A third has a period between the 8 and second 1 in the date. One variety of the 1817 has a period between the 1 and 7 in the date. Two varieties of the 1819/18 overdate are distinguished by the size of the 9 in the date. Two varieties of the 1820 are distinguished by the size of the date. On the 1823 varieties, the "broken 3" appears to be almost separated in the middle of the 3 in the date; the "patched 3" has the error repaired; the "ugly 3" has portions of its detail missing. The 1827 "curled 2" and "square 2" varieties are distinguished by the numeral's base — either curled or square. Among the 1828 varieties "knobbed 2" and "no knob" refers to whether the upper left serif of the digit is rounded. THe 1830 varieties are distinguished by the size of the 0 in the date. The four 1834 varieties are distinguished by the sizes of the stars, date and letters in the inscriptions. The 1836 "50/00" variety was struck from a reverse die that had "50" recut over "00" in the denomination.

Date	Mintage	G-4	VG-8	F-12	VF-20	XF-40	AU-50	MS-60	MS-65
1807 sm. stars	750,500	65.00	90.00	175.	325.	800.	3500.	5900.	40,000.
1807 lg. stars	Inc. Ab.	50.00	80.00	150.	300.	750.	3000.	5500.	—
1807 50/20 C.	Inc. Ab.	45.00	60.00	75.00	165.	400.	1500.	4000.	30,000.
1807 bearded goddess									
	—	275.	495.	675.	1175.	2750.	7500.	—	—
1808	1,368,600	37.50	42.50	53.00	90.00	185.	600.	1800.	11,000.
1808/7	Inc. Ab.	40.00	50.00	60.00	125.	200.	750.	1750.	15,000.
1809	1,405,810	36.00	42.50	55.00	85.00	185.	550.	1600.	15,000.
1810	1,276,276	34.50	38.00	46.00	90.00	170.	500.	1750.	15,000.
1811 sm. 8	1,203,644	32.00	37.50	45.00	60.00	110.	450.	750.	7500.
1811 lg. 8	Inc. Ab.	32.50	38.00	50.00	70.00	140.	500.	900.	8500.
1811 dt. 18.11	Inc. Ab.	40.00	47.00	72.00	135.	275.	650.	1500.	12,000.
1812	1,628,059	32.50	37.50	45.00	60.00	105.	375.	775.	7500.
1812/1 sm. 8	Inc. Ab.	42.50	50.00	75.00	110.	250.	800.	2000.	12,000.
1812/1 lg. 8	Inc. Ab.	1275.	1875.	2450.	3750.	6000.	17,500.	—	—
1813	1,241,903	32.50	37.50	45.00	70.00	125.	450.	1250.	11,000.
1813 50/UNI reverse									
	1,241,903	40.00	70.00	100.	195.	325.	775.	1750.	12,000.
1814	1,039,075	34.50	38.00	45.00	60.00	125.	500.	1350.	9000.
1814/3	Inc. Ab.	40.00	60.00	95.00	145.	295.	650.	1200.	10,000.
1815/2	47,150	700.	850.	1150.	1500.	2200.	4000.	9000.	50,000.
1817	1,215,567	31.50	33.00	40.00	60.00	100.	350.	750.	8500.
1817/3	Inc. Ab.	70.00	105.	165.	275.	500.	1350.	3150.	25,000.
1817/4		50,000.	60,000.	85,000.	145,000.	200,000.	—	—	—
1817 dt. 181.7	Inc. Ab.	37.00	47.00	60.00	100.	175.	500.	1200.	10,000.
1818	1,960,322	31.50	33.00	40.00	60.00	100.	350.	800.	8500.
1818/7	Inc. Ab.	35.00	40.00	55.00	85.00	165.	600.	1250.	11,000.
1819	2,208,000	31.50	33.00	40.00	60.00	100.	350.	800.	8500.
1819/8 sm. 9	Inc. Ab.	31.50	33.00	40.00	70.00	130.	450.	1100.	9500.
1819/8 lg. 9	Inc. Ab.	31.50	33.00	40.00	70.00	120.	400.	1000.	9000.
1820 sm. dt.	751,122	40.00	55.00	80.00	145.	250.	650.	1400.	10,000.
1820 lg. dt.	Inc. Ab.	37.00	50.00	68.00	120.	220.	500.	1200.	10,000.
1820/19	Inc. Ab.	40.00	53.00	75.00	130.	240.	700.	1400.	12,000.
1821	1,305,797	33.00	35.00	40.00	70.00	95.00	500.	950.	9750.
1822	1,559,573	32.00	34.00	40.00	55.00	85.00	300.	700.	7250.

Half dollars

Date	Mintage	G-4	VG-8	F-12	VF-20	XF-40	AU-50	MS-60	MS-65
1822/1	Inc. Ab.	40.00	49.00	60.00	125.	235.	475.	950.	11,000.
1823	1,694,200	31.50	33.00	40.00	50.00	85.00	290.	750.	7500.
1823 broken 3	Inc. Ab.	43.00	63.00	90.00	160.	275.	750.	1300.	12,000.
1823 patched 3	Inc. Ab.	38.00	53.00	78.00	125.	200.	450.	880.	8000.
1823 ugly 3	Inc. Ab.	40.00	58.00	83.00	145.	235.	650.	1200.	11,000.
1824	3,504,954	31.00	33.00	40.00	47.00	80.00	225.	575.	7500.
1824/21	Inc. Ab.	35.00	40.00	55.00	65.00	130.	380.	950.	7900.
1824/various dates	Inc. Ab.	35.00	45.00	70.00	145.	265.	475.	975.	12,000.
1825	2,943,166	31.50	33.00	40.00	50.00	77.00	210.	500.	7000.
1826	4,004,180	31.50	33.00	40.00	50.00	77.00	210.	500.	7000.
1827 curled 2	5,493,400	33.00	45.00	58.00	85.00	165.	325.	700.	7750.
1827 square 2	Inc. Ab.	31.50	33.00	40.00	45.00	77.00	250.	650.	7500.
1827/6	Inc. Ab.	35.00	40.00	43.00	60.00	125.	325.	850.	9000.
1828 curled base 2, no knob	3,075,200	33.00	36.00	40.00	55.00	90.00	275.	650.	7000.
1828 curled base 2, knobbed 2	Inc. Ab.	35.00	40.00	50.00	65.00	100.	300.	700.	7250.
1828 small 8s, square base 2, large letters	Inc. Ab.	27.50	33.00	36.00	43.00	80.00	210.	550.	6250.
1828 small 8s, square base 2, small letters	Inc. Ab.	45.00	58.00	100.	185.	275.	700.	1200.	9500.
1828 large 8s, square base 2	Inc. Ab.	33.00	37.00	43.00	55.00	95.00	325.	750.	8000.
1829	3,712,156	27.50	33.00	36.00	43.00	77.00	210.	500.	9000.
1829/7	Inc. Ab.	35.00	40.00	60.00	85.00	165.	250.	800.	—
1830 small 0 in date	4,764,800	27.50	33.00	36.00	43.00	77.00	210.	500.	6500.
1830 large 0 in date	Inc. Ab.	27.50	33.00	36.00	43.00	77.00	210.	500.	6500.
1831	5,873,660	27.50	33.00	36.00	43.00	77.00	210.	500.	6500.
1832 sm. lt.	4,797,000	27.50	33.00	36.00	43.00	77.00	210.	500.	6500.
1832 lg. let.	Inc. Ab.	30.00	45.00	58.00	85.00	145.	300.	650.	7500.
1833	5,206,000	27.50	33.00	36.00	43.00	77.00	210.	500.	6500.
1834 small date, large stars, small letters	6,412,004	27.50	33.00	36.00	43.00	77.00	210.	500.	6500.
1834 small date, small stars, small letters	Inc. Ab.	27.50	33.00	36.00	43.00	77.00	210.	500.	6500.
1834 large date, small letters	Inc. Ab.	27.50	33.00	36.00	43.00	77.00	210.	500.	6500.
1834 large date, large letters	Inc. Ab.	27.50	33.00	36.00	43.00	77.00	210.	500.	6500.
1835	5,352,006	27.50	33.00	36.00	43.00	77.00	275.	600.	9000.
1836	6,545,000	27.50	33.00	36.00	43.00	77.00	210.	500.	6500.
1836 50/00	Inc. Ab.	55.00	80.00	105.	185.	275.	600.	1300.	—

Reeded edge, "50 Cents" on reverse

Designer: Christian Gobrecht. **Size:** 30 millimeters. **Weight:** 13.36 grams. **Composition:** 90% silver (.3867 ounces), 10% copper.

Date	Mintage	G-4	VG-8	F-12	VF-20	XF-40	AU-50	MS-60	MS-65
1836	1,200	575.	675.	875.	1150.	1875.	3000.	5000.	22,500.
1837	3,629,820	32.00	38.00	43.00	60.00	115.	325.	750.	12,500.

"Half Dol." on reverse

Date	Mintage	G-4	VG-8	F-12	VF-20	XF-40	AU-50	MS-60	MS-65
1838	3,546,000	32.00	38.00	43.00	60.00	125.	475.	825.	14,000.
1838O Proof only	Est. 20	—	—	—	—	45,000.	75,000.	90,000.	200,000.
1839	1,392,976	32.00	38.00	41.00	60.00	125.	365.	900.	16,000.
1839O	178,976	115.	145.	195.	280.	500.	1200.	2500.	17,500.

Seated Liberty

Mintmark

Designer: Christian Gobrecht. **Size:** 30.6 millimeters. **Weight:** 3.36 grams. **Composition:** 90% silver (.3867 ounces), 10% copper. **Notes:** The 18939 varieties are distinguished by whether there's drapery extending from Liberty's left elbow. One variety of the 1840 strikes has smaller lettering; another used the old reverse of 1838. Varieties of 1842 and 1846 are distinguished by the size of the numerals in the date.

Date	Mintage	G-4	VG-8	F-12	VF-20	XF-40	AU-50	MS-60	MS-65
1839 no drapery from elbow	Inc. Ab.	38.00	65.00	110.	250.	725.	1500.	2350.	107 K
1839 drapery	Inc. Ab.	20.00	28.00	40.00	75.00	145.	265.	450.	—
1840 sm. let.	1,435,008	16.50	20.00	30.00	60.00	110.	350.	575.	8250.
1840 rev. 1838	Inc. Ab.	115.	165.	215.	325.	500.	1200.	2500.	—
1840O	855,100	17.00	27.50	45.00	80.00	125.	300.	585.	—

Half dollars

Date	Mintage	G-4	VG-8	F-12	VF-20	XF-40	AU-50	MS-60	MS-65
1841	310,000	35.00	45.00	80.00	140.	265.	425.	1300.	—
1841O	401,000	17.00	25.00	45.00	85.00	150.	240.	875.	—
1842 sm. date	2,012,764	27.00	37.00	55.00	95.00	165.	325.	1300.	12,000.
1842 lg. date	Inc. Ab.	16.00	21.00	33.00	50.00	75.00	120.	1250.	12,000.
1842O sm. date	957,000	575.	800.	1400.	2250.	4000.	—	—	—
1842O lg. date	Inc. Ab.	17.00	23.00	48.00	115.	225.	750.	1750.	—
1843	3,844,000	16.00	21.00	30.00	50.00	80.00	180.	350.	4500.
1843O	2,268,000	16.00	21.00	30.00	55.00	90.00	250.	550.	—
1844	1,766,000	16.00	21.00	30.00	50.00	85.00	180.	350.	4500.
1844O	2,005,000	16.00	21.00	36.00	55.00	80.00	195.	525.	—
1844/1844O	Inc. Ab.	425.	650.	1000.	1375.	2300.	4900.	—	—
1845	589,000	30.00	40.00	50.00	90.00	170.	340.	900.	—
1845O	2,094,000	16.00	21.00	35.00	45.00	100.	240.	550.	—
1845O no drapery	Inc. Ab.	25.00	35.00	65.00	115.	185.	375.	750.	—
1846 med. dt.	2,210,000	16.00	20.00	30.00	40.00	70.00	175.	500.	9000.
1846 tall dt.	Inc. Ab.	22.00	30.00	60.00	85.00	145.	250.	650.	12,000.
1846/horiz. 6	Inc. Ab.	140.	215.	250.	375.	550.	1000.	2500.	—
1846O med.dt.	2,304,000	16.00	18.00	30.00	45.00	100.	225.	550.	12,000.
1846O tall dt.	Inc. Ab.	125.	245.	325.	575.	950.	2000.	3600.	—
1847/1846	1,156,000	2000.	2750.	3200.	4250.	6500.	—	—	—
1847	Inc. Ab.	20.00	30.00	45.00	60.00	90.00	190.	480.	9000.
1847O	2,584,000	16.00	25.00	35.00	50.00	95.00	250.	640.	7000.
1848	580,000	35.00	55.00	75.00	135.	240.	475.	1400.	9000.
1848O	3,180,000	18.00	25.00	40.00	50.00	95.00	285.	750.	9000.
1849	1,252,000	22.00	35.00	50.00	85.00	150.	365.	1250.	9000.
1849O	2,310,000	16.00	25.00	40.00	60.00	115.	250.	650.	9000.
1850	227,000	200.	250.	340.	400.	575.	875.	1500.	—
1850O	2,456,000	16.00	25.00	40.00	55.00	115.	250.	650.	9000.
1851	200,750	250.	300.	375.	465.	650.	800.	1800.	—
1851O	402,000	37.00	45.00	65.00	95.00	175.	300.	610.	9000.
1852	77,130	300.	350.	425.	600.	800.	925.	1450.	—
1852O	144,000	60.00	90.00	150.	325.	525.	975.	1850.	—
1853O	Unrecorded	Eliasberg Sale, 1997, VG-8, $154,000.							

Arrows at date, reverse rays

Weight: 12.44 grams. **Composition:** 90% silver (.36 ounces), 10% copper.

Date	Mintage	G-4	VG-8	F-12	VF-20	XF-40	AU-50	MS-60	MS-65	Prf-65
1853 rays on reverse	3,532,708	16.50	27.00	40.00	90.00	250.	505.	1700.	21,500.	—
1853O rays on reverse	1,328,000	19.00	31.00	44.00	100.	290.	700.	2100.	21,500.	—

Reverse rays removed

Date	Mintage	G-4	VG-8	F-12	VF-20	XF-40	AU-50	MS-60	MS-65	Prf-65
1854	2,982,000	16.00	22.00	33.00	50.00	100.	270.	675.	8000.	—
1854O	5,240,000	16.00	22.00	33.00	50.00	100.	265.	500.	8000.	—
1855	759,500	23.00	30.00	40.00	60.00	150.	325.	1200.	8000.	22,500.
1855/4	Inc. Ab.	35.00	60.00	80.00	125.	225.	400.	1500.	—	—
1855O	3,688,000	16.00	22.00	33.00	50.00	100.	270.	650.	8000.	—
1855S	129,950	300.	425.	650.	1300.	2650.	6000.	—	—	—

Arrows at date removed

Date	Mintage	G-4	VG-8	F-12	VF-20	XF-40	AU-50	MS-60	MS-65	Prf-65
1856	938,000	19.00	25.00	32.00	47.50	90.00	150.	350.	6500.	12,500.
1856O	2,658,000	16.00	21.00	28.00	45.00	82.00	150.	450.	12,500.	—
1856S	211,000	40.00	65.00	105.	225.	450.	1250.	2500.	19,000.	—
1857	1,988,000	16.00	18.00	28.00	45.00	82.00	150.	350.	5150.	12,500.
1857O	818,000	18.00	21.00	25.00	55.00	100.	250.	850.	12,500.	—
1857S	158,000	75.00	95.00	145.	285.	575.	800.	2400.	19,000.	—
1858	4,226,000	16.00	18.00	35.00	60.00	80.00	150.	350.	6500.	12,500.
1858O	7,294,000	16.00	17.00	35.00	45.00	70.00	150.	450.	12,500.	—
1858S	476,000	20.00	30.00	48.00	90.00	175.	400.	950.	12,500.	—
1859	748,000	16.50	27.00	42.00	55.00	90.00	200.	650.	6600.	5500.
1859O	2,834,000	16.00	25.00	40.00	50.00	85.00	150.	450.	6500.	—
1859S	566,000	20.00	38.00	55.00	85.00	215.	375.	750.	12,500.	—
1860	303,700	22.00	27.50	45.00	75.00	120.	350.	1000.	6500.	5500.
1860O	1,290,000	16.00	20.00	35.00	45.00	76.00	160.	450.	5150.	—
1860S	472,000	18.00	30.00	50.00	75.00	130.	245.	850.	12,500.	—
1861	2,888,400	16.00	25.00	35.00	45.00	70.00	150.	410.	5150.	5500.
1861O	2,532,633	16.00	25.00	40.00	50.00	85.00	150.	450.	5150.	—
1861S	939,500	17.00	28.00	42.50	60.00	100.	195.	975.	9500.	—
1862	253,550	24.00	32.00	50.00	95.00	150.	265.	750.	5150.	5500.
1862S	1,352,000	16.00	27.00	35.00	60.00	90.00	175.	450.	9000.	—

Half dollars

Date	Mintage	G-4	VG-8	F-12	VF-20	XF-40	AU-50	MS-60	MS-65	Prf-65
1863	503,660	20.00	28.00	40.00	70.00	130.	250.	7[illegible]0.	5150.	5500.
1863S	916,000	16.00	25.00	35.00	50.00	80.00	150.	4[illegible]0.	9000.	—
1864	379,570	24.00	32.00	55.00	85.00	160.	200.	7[illegible]0.	5150.	5500.
1864S	658,000	16.50	20.00	45.00	60.00	115.	275.	[illegible]75.	9000.	—
1865	511,900	20.00	27.50	40.00	70.00	125.	24[illegible].	[illegible]50.	5150.	5500.
1865S	675,000	17.00	21.00	35.00	50.00	85.00	[illegible]60.	450.	9000.	—
1866	—	—	—	—	Proof, unique		—	—	—	
1866S	60,000	75.00	110.	165.	325.	79[illegible]	1500.	5000.	—	—

Motto above e[agle]

[Notes: In 1866 t]he [... W]e Trust" was added to the reverse. The "closed 3" and "open 3" varietie[s ...] by the amount of space between the upper and lower left serifs of the 3.

Date	Mintage	G-4	VG-8	F-12	VF-20	XF-40	AU-50	MS-60	MS-65	Prf-65
		[illegible]0	24.00	40.00	50.00	90.00	155.	350.	4800.	3750.
		[illegible].00	24.00	40.00	58.00	95.00	275.	650.	5000.	—
		[illegible]5.00	35.00	55.00	85.00	145.	240.	350.	4800.	3750.
		16.00	24.00	40.00	50.00	75.00	155.	350.	7000.	—
1866		35.00	45.00	75.00	120.	225.	300.	525.	7100.	3750.
	1866[illegible]0	16.00	24.00	33.00	50.00	105.	165.	350.	7000.	—
	18[illegible]00	18.00	24.00	33.00	45.00	85.00	160.	385.	4600.	3750.
	[illegible],000	16.00	27.00	35.00	50.00	100.	175.	600.	7000.	—
	[illegible]4,900	18.00	27.00	35.00	60.00	100.	160.	475.	7000.	3750.
	54,617	500.	800.	1300.	2650.	4500.	—	—	—	—
	[illegible],004,000	16.00	24.00	40.00	60.00	110.	275.	575.	7000.	—
	1,204,560	16.00	24.00	35.00	50.00	70.00	155.	350.	7000.	3750.
[illegible]CC	153,950	135.	180.	295.	485.	950.	2000.	3500.	9150.	—
1871S	2,178,000	16.00	24.00	35.00	50.00	69.00	155.	400.	7000.	—
1872	881,550	16.00	24.00	39.00	55.00	75.00	160.	430.	2850.	3750.
1872CC	272,000	50.00	85.00	190.	300.	650.	1700.	2500.	8800.	—
1872S	580,000	23.00	28.00	55.00	85.00	170.	375.	975.	7000.	—
1873 closed 3	801,800	19.00	24.00	38.00	90.00	125.	235.	500.	4500.	3750.
1873 open 3	Inc. Ab.	2200.	2700.	4100.	5500.	7500.	—	—	—	—
1873CC	122,500	140.	185.	275.	575.	1250.	2500.	4100.	9000.	3750.

1873S no arrows, 5,000 minted, no specimens known to survive.

Arrows at date

Weight: 12.5 grams. **Composition:** 90% silver (.3618 ounces), 10% copper.

Date	Mintage	G-4	VG-8	F-12	VF-20	XF-40	AU-50	MS-60	MS-65	Prf-65
1873	1,815,700	16.50	25.00	36.00	85.00	225.	530.	950.	15,000.	9000.
1873CC	214,560	135.	160.	250.	550.	1350.	2250.	4500.	—	—
1873S	233,000	55.00	75.00	110.	225.	475.	725.	1600.	15,000.	—
1874	2,360,300	16.50	25.00	36.00	85.00	225.	530.	950.	15,000.	9000.
1874CC	59,000	250.	350.	525.	975.	1850.	2900.	4500.	14,000.	—
1874S	394,000	25.00	35.00	55.00	135.	275.	575.	1700.	15,000.	—

Arrows at date removed

Date	Mintage	G-4	VG-8	F-12	VF-20	XF-40	AU-50	MS-60	MS-65	Prf-65
1875	6,027,500	15.00	24.00	29.00	40.00	60.00	120.	425.	3500.	3200.
1875CC	1,008,000	18.00	34.00	53.00	95.00	185.	300.	540.	5450.	—
1875S	3,200,000	15.00	24.00	29.00	42.00	60.00	120.	340.	2700.	—
1876	8,419,150	15.00	24.00	32.00	40.00	60.00	135.	340.	5300.	3200.
1876CC	1,956,000	17.00	30.00	48.00	85.00	175.	275.	560.	4200.	—
1876S	4,528,000	15.00	24.00	32.00	40.00	63.00	145.	340.	2700.	—
1877	8,304,510	15.00	24.00	29.00	40.00	65.00	145.	340.	2700.	3750.
1877CC	1,420,000	17.00	33.00	43.00	75.00	145.	275.	630.	3250.	—
1877S	5,356,000	15.00	24.00	29.00	40.00	65.00	145.	340.	2700.	—
1878	1,378,400	20.00	28.00	36.00	50.00	115.	170.	425.	3650.	3200.
1878CC	62,000	285.	365.	475.	850.	1350.	2300.	4000.	—	—
1878S	12,000	8500.	11,000.	14,000.	17,500.	21,000.	24,500.	30,000.	—	—
1879	5,900	200.	220.	290.	350.	400.	475.	700.	2900.	3250.
1880	9,755	190.	210.	240.	310.	375.	475.	700.	2900.	3250.
1881	10,975	170.	195.	240.	300.	365.	465.	700.	2900.	3250.
1882	5,500	220.	240.	300.	390.	470.	550.	850.	3600.	3250.
1883	9,039	180.	210.	240.	290.	375.	475.	750.	2900.	3250.
1884	5,275	275.	300.	365.	425.	475.	550.	800.	2900.	3250.
1885	6,130	215.	235.	300.	360.	435.	525.	800.	2900.	3250.
1886	5,886	295.	345.	410.	450.	495.	600.	850.	4800.	3250.
1887	5,710	325.	385.	450.	550.	650.	750.	900.	2900.	3250.
1888	12,833	190.	210.	250.	310.	390.	440.	700.	2900.	3250.

Half dollars

Date	Mintage	G-4	VG-8	F-12	VF-20	XF-40	AU-50	MS-60	MS-65	Prf-65
1889	12,711	175.	200.	235.	300.	375.	425.	700.	2900.	3250.
1890	12,590	175.	200.	235.	300.	375.	425.	700.	3250.	3250.
1891	200,600	40.00	50.00	60.00	90.00	140.	290.	500.	3250.	3250.

Barber

Mintmark

Designer: Charles E. Barber. **Size:** 30.6 millimeters. **Weight:** 12.5 grams. **Composition:** 90% silver (.3618 ounces), 10% copper.

Date	Mintage	G-4	VG-8	F-12	VF-20	XF-40	AU-50	MS-60	MS-65	Prf-65
1892	935,245	21.00	28.00	48.00	90.00	180.	260.	390.	2600.	3300.
1892O	390,000	165.	190.	230.	285.	405.	425.	820.	5500.	—
1892S	1,029,028	170.	195.	235.	295.	380.	565.	855.	5500.	—
1893	1,826,792	13.50	20.00	45.00	80.00	150.	310.	500.	3775.	3300.
1893O	1,389,000	23.00	34.00	70.00	125.	275.	370.	520.	9600.	—
1893S	740,000	75.00	95.00	175.	285.	400.	505.	1100.	12,500.	—
1894	1,148,972	17.50	33.00	68.00	100.	215.	350.	520.	3125.	3300.
1894O	2,138,000	13.00	19.00	63.00	95.00	235.	340.	500.	4500.	—
1894S	4,048,690	12.00	18.00	48.00	80.00	200.	340.	440.	9600.	—
1895	1,835,218	8.50	15.00	50.00	85.00	165.	310.	560.	3400.	3300.
1895O	1,766,000	12.50	22.00	55.00	100.	230.	360.	560.	6000.	—
1895S	1,108,086	18.00	31.00	68.00	125.	260.	360.	540.	7800.	—
1896	950,762	16.00	23.00	55.00	90.00	200.	325.	535.	5400.	3400.
1896O	924,000	24.00	35.00	90.00	145.	345.	620.	1150.	12,000.	—
1896S	1,140,948	65.00	80.00	125.	200.	350.	540.	1100.	10,750.	—
1897	2,480,731	8.00	10.00	30.00	75.00	130.	310.	435.	3300.	3300.
1897O	632,000	55.00	85.00	350.	650.	850.	1150.	1450.	4900.	—
1897S	933,900	110.	125.	260.	400.	630.	945.	1250.	8000.	—
1898	2,956,735	8.00	9.00	28.00	71.00	135.	300.	390.	2600.	3300.
1898O	874,000	18.00	35.00	100.	160.	360.	495.	800.	8400.	—
1898S	2,358,550	9.00	17.00	42.00	86.00	200.	350.	800.	9000.	—
1899	5,538,846	6.75	8.00	26.00	71.00	135.	300.	390.	3300.	3900.
1899O	1,724,000	8.00	13.00	45.00	90.00	210.	360.	585.	6100.	—
1899S	1,686,411	13.00	22.00	54.00	88.00	190.	340.	585.	6600.	—
1900	4,762,912	6.00	7.75	28.00	71.00	130.	300.	390.	2600.	3300.
1900O	2,744,000	7.00	10.00	40.00	90.00	250.	310.	750.	14,500.	—
1900S	2,560,322	8.00	12.00	42.00	95.00	190.	310.	625.	9600.	—

NOTE: Later dates (1901-1915) exist for this type.

Silver dollars

Draped Bust

Heraldic eagle

Designer: Robert Scot. **Size:** 39-40 millimeters. **Weight:** 26.96 grams. **Composition:** 89.24% silver (.7737 ounces), 10.76% copper.

Notes: The "close" and "wide" varieties of 1802 refer to the amount of space between the numerals in the date. The 1803 large-3 and small-3 varieties are distinguished by the size of the 3 in the date.

Date	Mintage	G-4	VG-8	F-12	VF-20	XF-40	MS-60
1801	54,454	400.	475.	600.	850.	1900.	10,000.
1801	Unrecorded		Proof restrike, rare				
1802/1 close	Inc. Ab.	360.	450.	550.	850.	1600.	9600.
1802/1 wide	Inc. Ab.	360.	450.	550.	850.	1600.	9600.

Silver dollars

Date	Mintage	G-4	VG-8	F-12	VF-20	XF-40	MS-60
1802 close, perfect date							
	Inc. Ab.	375.	450.	600.	875.	1650.	7500.
1802 wide, perfect date							
	Inc. Ab.	375.	450.	600.	875.	1650.	9600.
1802	Unrecorded	Proof restrike, rare					
1803 lg. 3	85,634	360.	440.	600.	850.	1575.	9600.
1803 sm. 3	Inc. Ab.	395.	475.	675.	975.	1850.	7500.
1803	Unrecorded	Proof restrike, rare					
1804	15 known	—	Eliasberg Sale, Apr. 1997, Prf-63, $1,825,000.				

Seated Liberty

No motto

Designer: Christian Gobrecht. **Size:** 38.1 millimeters. **Weight:** 26.73 grams. **Composition:** 90% silver (.7736 ounces), 10% copper.

Date	Mintage	G-4	VG-8	F-12	VF-20	XF-40	AU-50	MS-60	MS-65	Prf-65
1840	61,005	160.	180.	225.	300.	575.	750.	1600.	—	—
1841	173,000	100.	130.	180.	220.	375.	575.	1300.	24,000.	—
1842	184,618	100.	120.	175.	220.	300.	550.	1100.	24,000.	—
1843	165,100	100.	120.	175.	220.	300.	550.	1400.	24,000.	—
1844	20,000	175.	235.	300.	425.	575.	800.	3000.	—	—
1845	24,500	175.	235.	250.	350.	500.	750.	2000.	—	—
1846	110,600	100.	120.	175.	220.	275.	500.	1400.	24,000.	—
1846O	59,000	110.	140.	190.	285.	475.	1400.	4000.	—	—
1847	140,750	100.	120.	175.	220.	300.	650.	950.	15,000.	—
1848	15,000	250.	290.	400.	525.	700.	1400.	2050.	—	—
1849	62,600	110.	140.	190.	240.	350.	700.	1600.	—	—
1850	7,500	500.	625.	750.	900.	1100.	1975.	3500.	—	—
1850O	40,000	200.	260.	350.	650.	1400.	3200.	5000.	—	—
1851	1,300	—	—	8000.	9500.	13,500.	21,500.	—	—	—
1852	1,100	—	—	6500.	7500.	11,500.	21,500.	—	—	—
1853	46,110	175.	225.	270.	375.	575.	800.	1300.	—	—
1854	33,140	1000.	1200.	1500.	225.	3500.	4850.	7000.	—	—
1855	26,000	800.	1000.	1300.	1900.	2650.	4500.	9000.	—	—
1856	63,500	350.	450.	550.	650.	975.	1650.	2250.	—	—
1857	94,000	325.	425.	525.	900.	1500.	1500.	3000.	—	—
1858	Est. 200	Proof only		—	4200.	5500.	6250.	—	—	—
1859	256,500	200.	250.	350.	450.	700.	1000.	2500.	15,000.	13,500.
1859O	360,000	100.	110.	175.	210.	265.	500.	950.	15,000.	—
1859S	20,000	200.	275.	400.	600.	1350.	3000.	—	—	—
1860	218,930	140.	180.	230.	300.	475.	600.	1300.	15,000.	13,500.
1860O	515,000	100.	110.	175.	210.	265.	500.	900.	15,000.	—
1861	78,500	440.	500.	600.	800.	1250.	1400.	3000.	—	13,500.
1862	12,090	450.	500.	625.	850.	1250.	1750.	3200.	—	13,500.
1863	27,660	265.	325.	400.	500.	800.	1350.	2750.	—	13,500.
1864	31,170	220.	265.	315.	425.	675.	1300.	2900.	—	13,500.
1865	47,000	195.	245.	290.	400.	625.	1250.	2750.	—	13,500.
1866	2 known without motto									

Motto added to reverse

Notes: In 1866 the motto "In God We Trust" was added to the reverse above the eagle.

Silver dollars

Date	Mintage	G-4	VG-8	F-12	VF-20	XF-40	AU-50	MS-60	MS-65	Prf-65
1866	49,625	150.	200.	250.	350.	550.	900.	1600.	28,500.	7000.
1867	47,525	170.	250.	300.	415.	600.	1000.	1800.	28,500.	7000.
1868	62,700	140.	190.	225.	350.	525.	900.	2000.	28,500.	7000.
1869	424,300	115.	150.	200.	325.	500.	800.	2000.	28,500.	7000.
1870	416,000	[illegible]	135.	175.	225.	325.	600.	1500.	28,500.	7000.
1870CC	11,462	[illegible]	245.	325.	500.	975.	2250.	4250.	—	—
1870S	Unrecorded	Elia[illegible] Sale, Apr. 1997, EF-45 to AU-50, $264,000.							—	—
1871	1,074,760	100.	[illegible]	175.	210.	315.	550.	900.	24,000.	7000.
1871CC	1,376	1800.	[illegible]	3500.	5000.	8500.	18,500.	—	—	—
1872	1,106,450	85.00	[illegible]	[illegible]55.	210.	315.	550.	1250.	24,000.	7000.
1872CC	3,150	900.	125[illegible]	[illegible]	2150.	3750.	8500.	15,000.	—	—
1872S	9,000	150.	225.	[illegible]	575.	1100.	3000.	10,000.	—	—
1873	293,600	130.	150.	[illegible]	[illegible]0.	350.	600.	1350.	28,500.	7000.
1873CC	2,300	3250.	4750.	6[illegible]	[illegible]	17,500.	35,000.	47,500.	—	—
1873S	700	None known						—	—	—

Trade

Designer: William Barber. **Size:** 38.1 millimeters. **Weight:** 27.22 grams. **Composition:** [illegible] silver (.7878 ounces), 10% copper.

Date	Mintage	G-4	VG-8	F-12	VF-20	XF-40	AU-50	MS-60	MS-65	Prf-65
1873	397,500	90.00	105.	125.	165.	250.	325.	1000.	12,000.	12,000.
1873CC	124,500	150.	175.	225.	300.	425.	675.	1500.	80,000.	—
1873S	703,000	130.	145.	160.	180.	260.	350.	1200.	25,000.	—
1874	987,800	80.00	90.00	125.	165.	225.	325.	700.	15,000.	12,000.
1874CC	1,373,200	80.00	90.00	105.	165.	240.	350.	1000.	40,000.	—
1874S	2,549,000	70.00	80.00	95.00	120.	165.	250.	675.	30,000.	—
1875	218,900	295.	300.	375.	475.	625.	800.	1850.	13,000.	6500.
1875CC	1,573,700	80.00	90.00	105.	130.	200.	375.	900.	40,000.	—
1875S	4,487,000	60.00	70.00	85.00	100.	120.	210.	500.	7000.	—
1875S/CC	Inc.Ab.	275.	325.	400.	575.	825.	1000.	1500.	70,000.	—
1876	456,150	70.00	80.00	100.	125.	165.	400.	675.	7500.	6500.
1876CC	509,000	110.00	125.00	150.	200.	325.	400.	900.	75,000.	—
1876S	5,227,000	60.00	70.00	85.00	100.	120.	210.	475.	10,000.	—
1877	3,039,710	60.00	70.00	85.00	105.	130.	210.	525.	16,000.	19,000.
1877CC	534,000	120.	150.	175.	245.	350.	500.	1200.	70,000.	—
1877S	9,519,000	60.00	70.00	85.00	100.	120.	210.	475.	8000.	—
1878	900	Proof only		—	1100.	1250.	1500.	—	—	22,000.
1878CC	97,000	425.	525.	675.	850.	1750.	2100.	5500.	67,500.	—
1878S	4,162,000	60.00	70.00	85.00	100.	120.	210.	475.	7000.	—
1879	1,541	Proof only		—	900.	950.	1100.		—	22,000.
1880	1,987	Proof only		—	900.	950.	1100.		—	19,500.
1881	960	Proof only		—	950.	1000.	1250.		—	20,000.
1882	1,097	Proof only		—	950.	1000.	1250.		—	20,000.
1883	979	Proof only		—	1000.	1100.	1300.		—	20,000.
1884	10	Proof only			Eliasberg, Apr. 1997, Prf-66, $396,000.					—
1885	5	Proof only			Eliasberg, Apr. 1997, Prf-65, $907,500.					—

MORGAN DOLLARS

Designer: George T. Morgan. **Size:** 38.1 millimeters. **Weight:** 26.73 grams. **Composition:** 90% silver (.7736 ounces), 10% copper. **Notes:** "65DMPL" values are for coins grading MS-65 deep-mirror prooflike. The 1878 "8 tail feathers" and "7 tail feathers" varieties are distinguished by the number of feathers in the eagle's tail. On the "reverse of 1878" varieties, the top of the top feather in the arrows held by the eagle is straight across and the eagle's breast is concave. On the "reverse of 1879 varieties" the top feather in the arrows held by the eagle is slanted and the eagle's breast in convex. The 1890-CC "tail-bar variety" has a bar extending from the arrows features to the wreath on the reverse, the result of a die gouge.

Reverse of 1879

7 over 8 tail feathers

Date	Mintage	VG-8	F-12	VF-20	XF-40	AU-50	MS-60	MS-63	MS-64	MS-65	65DMPL	Prf-60	Prf-63	Prf-65
1878 8 tail feathers	750,000	12.50	14.00	17.50	21.00	30.00	60.00	95.00	210.	1200.	6000.	925.	1650.	6250.
1878 7 tail feathers, reverse of 1878	Inc. Ab.	12.50	14.00	15.00	16.00	20.00	32.00	45.00	175.	1100.	5000.	1000.	2400.	7900.
1878 7 tail feathers, reverse of 1879	Inc. Ab.	11.00	12.50	16.50	17.50	25.00	32.00	100.	275.	2350.	6950.	—		55,000.
1878 7 over 8 tail feathers	9,759,550	12.50	14.00	19.00	28.00	42.00	76.00	100.	275.	2350.	10,000.	—		—
1878CC	2,212,000	35.00	36.00	40.00	44.00	52.00	84.00	100.	215.	1050.	3450.	—		—
1878S	9,744,000	11.00	12.00	13.00	14.00	15.00	24.00	38.00	45.00	200.	2200.	—		—
1879	14,807,100	9.50	10.50	12.50	15.00	14.00	21.00	32.00	63.00	700.	750.	1450.	5000.	5500.
1879CC	756,000	39.00	62.00	112.	325.	790.	1300.	3000.	5050.	17,000.	50,000.	—		—
1879O	2,887,000	9.50	10.00	13.00	12.50	19.00	45.00	100.	320.	2750.	16,500.	—		—
1879S reverse of 1878	9,110,000	10.00	12.00	12.50	16.00	30.00	83.00	330.	1300.	5350.	17,500.	—		—
1879S reverse of 1879	9,110,000	9.00	10.00	12.50	15.00	14.00	20.00	25.00	45.00	110.	350.	—		—
1880	12,601,335	9.00	10.00	12.50	15.00	14.00	18.00	31.00	80.00	700.	750.	1450.	5000.	5500.
1880CC reverse of 1878	591,000	41.00	56.00	69.00	90.00	120.	195.	250.	540.	1750.	8500.	—		—
1880CC reverse of 1879	591,000	41.00	56.00	69.00	90.00	115.	195.	210.	250.	600.	2650.	—		—
1880O	5,305,000	9.50	10.00	11.00	12.50	16.00	39.00	275.	1600.	16,000.	63,000.	—		—
1880S	8,900,000	9.50	10.00	11.00	13.00	16.00	20.00	25.00	43.00	100.	290.	—		—
1881	9,163,975	9.50	10.00	11.00	12.50	15.00	18.00	29.00	70.00	650.	12,500.	750.	1450.	5500.
1881CC	296,000	81.00	105.	120.	130.	140.	180.	190.	230.	500.	1200.	—		—
1881O	5,708,000	9.50	10.00	11.00	12.50	15.00	17.00	31.00	110.	1600.	15,000.	—		—
1881S	12,760,000	9.50	10.00	11.00	13.00	16.00	18.00	25.00	43.00	100.	300.	—		—
1882	11,101,100	9.50	10.00	11.00	12.50	15.00	17.00	29.00	46.00	350.	4100.	750.	1450.	5500.
1882CC	1,133,000	35.00	36.00	40.00	50.00	52.00	83.00	90.00	100.	300.	440.	—		—
1882O	6,090,000	9.50	10.00	11.00	12.50	15.00	17.00	25.00	56.00	600.	3800.	—		—
1882S	9,250,000	9.50	10.00	11.00	12.50	15.00	18.00	29.00	45.00	110.	900.	—		—
1883	12,291,039	9.50	10.00	11.00	12.50	15.00	17.00	29.00	45.00	120.	630.	750.	1450.	5500.
1883CC	1,204,000	35.00	36.00	40.00	45.00	50.00	83.00	88.00	100.	230.	500.	—		—
1883O	8,725,000	9.00	9.50	11.00	12.50	15.00	18.00	31.00	43.00	110.	500.	—		—
1883S	6,250,000	9.50	10.50	12.50	21.00	100.	365.	1600.	5850.	28,500.	94,500.	—		—
1884	14,070,875	9.50	10.00	11.00	12.50	15.50	18.00	29.00	45.00	200.	1900.	750.	1450.	5500.
1884CC	1,136,000	40.00	42.00	45.00	49.00	51.00	84.00	88.00	100.	240.	500.	—		—
1884O	9,730,000	9.00	9.50	11.00	12.50	15.50	18.00	31.00	42.00	110.	360.	—		—
1884S	3,200,000	9.50	10.50	14.00	31.00	180.	3400.	24,000.	69,500.	150,000.	—	—		—
1885	17,787,767	9.00	9.50	11.00	12.50	15.50	18.00	27.00	45.00	110.	380.	750.	1450.	5500.
1885CC	228,000	160.	170.	175.	180.	185.	205.	230.	270.	600.	900.	—		—
1885O	9,185,000	9.00	9.50	11.00	12.50	15.00	18.00	29.00	42.00	110.	340.	—		—
1885S	1,497,000	10.00	12.50	15.00	22.00	44.00	95.00	140.	320.	1750.	8800.	—		—
1886	19,963,886	9.00	9.50	11.00	12.50	15.00	18.00	25.00	45.00	110.	500.	750.	1450.	5500.
1886O	10,710,000	9.50	10.00	11.00	15.00	62.00	250.	2750.	8300.	230,000.	—	—		—
1886S	750,000	10.00	12.50	19.00	29.00	39.00	125.	225.	550.	2750.	8800.	—		—
1887	20,290,710	9.00	9.50	11.00	12.50	15.00	18.00	28.00	45.00	110.	325.	750.	1450.	5500.
1887O	11,550,000	9.50	10.00	11.00	13.00	19.00	38.00	75.00	230.	4550.	8200.	—		—
1887S	1,771,000	10.00	10.50	11.50	15.00	31.00	63.00	135.	450.	2600.	5900.	—		—
1888	19,183,833	9.00	10.00	11.00	12.50	15.00	18.00	25.00	45.00	150.	1400.	750.	1450.	5500.
1888O	12,150,000	8.50	9.50	11.00	13.00	15.00	18.00	29.00	46.00	430.	1400.	—		—
1888S	657,000	12.00	19.00	31.00	60.00	55.00	125.	190.	500.	3700.	8800.	—		—
1889	21,726,811	9.00	9.50	11.00	12.50	15.00	18.00	27.00	48.00	280.	2250.	750.	1450.	5500.
1889CC	350,000	190.	240.	400.	900.	2650.	6550.	15,500.	26,500.	260,000.	—	—		—
1889O	11,875,000	9.50	10.00	11.00	13.50	28.00	70.00	180.	530.	4800.	13,000.	—		—
1889S	700,000	13.00	17.50	22.00	29.00	48.00	120.	150.	300.	1450.	5650.	—		—
1890	16,802,590	9.50	10.00	11.00	13.00	15.00	18.00	31.00	140.	3500.	9450.	750.	1450.	5500.
1890CC	2,309,041	35.00	36.00	37.50	50.00	88.00	225.	350.	660.	5800.	6450.	—		—
1890CC tail bar	Inc. Ab.	35.00	36.00	37.50	50.00	88.00	225.	350.	660.	5800.	6450.	—		—
1890O	10,701,000	9.50	10.00	11.00	13.00	19.00	27.00	55.00	170.	1900.	7250.	—		—
1890S	8,230,373	9.50	10.00	11.00	13.00	19.00	32.00	60.00	130.	800.	6000.	—		—
1891	8,694,206	9.50	10.00	11.00	12.50	19.00	35.00	100.	550.	7200.	11,500.	750.	1450.	5500.
1891CC	1,618,000	35.00	36.00	37.50	50.00	81.00	170.	240.	450.	2900.	16,000.	—		—
1891O	7,954,529	9.50	10.00	11.00	12.50	30.00	70.00	195.	600.	6000.	21,500.	—		—
1891S	5,296,000	9.50	10.00	11.00	12.50	19.00	35.00	66.00	180.	1400.	5650.	—		—

Silver dollars

Date	Mintage	VG-8	F-12	VF-20	XF-40	AU-50	MS-60	MS-63	MS-64	MS-65	65DMPL	Prf-60	Prf-63	Prf-65
1892	1,037,245	10.00	10.50	12.00	18.50	56.00	115.	250.	530.	3300.	12,000.	750.	1450.	5500.
1892CC	1,352,000	40.00	50.00	69.00	100.	200.	380.	650.	1300.	5150.	19,000.	—		—
1892O	2,744,000	9.50	10.00	11.50	16.00	45.00	88.00	180.	550.	5800.	27,000.	—		—
1892S	1,200,000	10.00	16.00	39.00	160.	2150.	13,000.	34,000.	48,000.	75,500.	—	—		—
1893	378,792	56.00	60.00	82.00	100.	180.	330.	810.	1300.	5800.	31,500.	750.	1450.	5500.
1893CC	677,000	69.00	94.00	175.	425.	750.	1130.	3650.	8800.	48,000.	88,000.	—		—
1893O	300,000	62.00	88.00	110.	190.	470.	1300.	6050.	12,600.	195,000.	—	—		—
1893S	100,000	700.	1025.	1550.	3550.	11,875.	29,000.	61,000.	150,000.	280,000.	—	—		—
1894	110,972	210.	250.	295.	340.	540.	900.	3100.	5800.	19,000.	—	1050.	1500.	5500.
1894O	1,723,000	16.00	22.00	31.00	46.00	125.	480.	3150.	6600.	45,500.	—	—		—
1894S	1,260,000	19.00	27.00	45.00	94.00	200.	390.	680.	1500.	4800.	12,500.	—		—
1895	12,880 Proof only		11,250.	13,750.	16,000.	17,500.	—	—	—	—	—	19,000.	24,500.	32,000.
1895O	450,000	85.00	100.	145.	200.	700.	8200.	26,000.	56,500.	210,000.	—	—		—
1895S	400,000	115.	140.	190.	390.	670.	1250.	3300.	5350.	19,000.	40,500.	—		—
1896	9,967,762	9.00	9.50	11.00	12.50	15.00	17.00	27.00	43.00	130.	550.	750.	1450.	5500.
1896O	4,900,000	9.50	10.00	11.00	15.00	100.	630.	7300.	33,000.	113,500.	—	—		—
1896S	5,000,000	10.00	20.00	41.00	125.	360.	680.	1300.	2700.	7700.	20,000.	—		—
1897	2,822,731	9.50	10.00	11.00	12.50	15.00	20.00	28.00	42.00	200.	2150.	750.	1450.	5500.
1897O	4,004,000	9.50	11.00	12.00	17.50	85.00	425.	4400.	11,350.	34,000.	45,500.	—		—
1897S	5,825,000	9.50	10.00	11.00	13.00	20.00	35.00	53.00	85.00	440.	1225.	—		—
1898	5,884,735	9.50	10.00	11.00	12.50	15.00	18.00	27.00	43.00	170.	1000.	750.	1450.	5500.
1898O	4,440,000	11.00	11.50	13.00	13.75	14.50	20.00	25.00	42.00	110.	390.	—		—
1898S	4,102,000	10.00	11.00	13.75	24.00	56.00	140.	200.	400.	1700.	7900.	—		—
1899	330,846	17.50	27.00	33.00	42.00	56.00	70.00	80.00	150.	500.	1700.	750	1450.	5500.
1899O	12,290,000	9.50	10.00	11.00	12.50	15.00	17.00	27.00	42.00	110.	675.	—		—
1899S	2,562,000	10.00	12.50	16.00	27.00	66.00	140.	225.	365.	1435.	6600.	—		—
1900	8,880,938	9.50	10.00	11.00	12.50	15.00	17.00	28.00	43.00	130.	10,000.	750.	1450.	5500.
1900O	12,590,000	9.50	10.00	11.00	13.00	15.00	20.00	27.00	43.00	110.	2850.	—		—
1900O/CC	Inc. Ab.	17.50	21.00	27.50	44.00	87.00	170.	315.	470.	1350.	14,500.	—		—
1900S	3,540,000	10.00	12.50	16.50	26.00	46.00	110.	155.	295.	925.	6300.	—		—

NOTE: Later dates (1901-1904, and 1921) exist for this type.

Type coins

Notes: Values listed for the most common dates of each design type in grades MS-64 and Proof-64. The 64 grade is relatively new. Except for Morgan dollars. Peace dollars and commemoratives, there is little history among other issues to support MS-64 and proof 64 values, other than type coins.

Description	MS-64	Proof-64
Draped Bust half cents (red & brown)	3000.	—
Classic Head half cents (red & brown)	595.	—
Braided Hair half cents (red & brown)	565.	—
Draped Bust large cents (red & brown)	8800.	—
Classic Head large cents (red & brown)	11,500.	—
Coronet large cents (red & brown)	600.	—
Braided Hair large cents (red & brown)	320.	—
Flying Eagle cents	915.	10,000.
Indian Head cents, 1859 copper-nickel	850.	3000.
Indian Head cents, 1860-1864 copper-nickel	240.	1100.
Indian Head cents, bronze (red & brown)	60.00	250.
Two-cent (red & brown)	175.	500.
Nickel three-cent	200.	350.
Silver three-cent, Type I	350.	—
Silver three-cent, Type II	1200.	4000.
Silver three-cent, Type III	350.	600.
Flowing Hair half dimes	10,000.	—
Draped Bust half dimes, small eagle	26,500.	—
Draped Bust half dimes, heraldic eagle	13,000.	—
Liberty Cap half dimes	1050.	—
Seated Liberty half dimes, no stars	1400.	—
Seated Liberty half dimes, no drapery	560.	—
Seated Liberty half dimes, stars around rim	490.	1750.
Seated Liberty half dimes, with arrows	550.	—
Seated Liberty half dimes, obverse legend	345.	600.
Shield nickels, with rays	595.	2350.
Shield nickels, no rays	225.	350.
Liberty nickels, no "Cents"	63.00	350.
Liberty nickels, with "Cents"	125.	230.
Buffalo nickels, Type I	50.00	800.
Buffalo nickels, Type II	—	—
Jefferson nickels, wartime	—	75.00
Draped Bust dimes, small eagle	20,000.	—
Draped Bust dimes, heraldic eagle	12,000.	—
Liberty Cap dimes, 1809-1827 (large size)	3450.	—
Liberty Cap dimes, 1828-1837 (reduced size)	2250.	—
Seated Liberty dimes, no stars	3400.	—
Seated Liberty dimes, no drapery	1050.	—

Description	MS-64	Proof-64
Seated Liberty dimes, stars around rim	950.	1750.
Seated Liberty dimes, 1853-1855 with arrows	1100.	14,500.
Seated Liberty dimes, obverse legend	320.	500.
Seated Liberty dimes, 1873-1874 with arrows	2150.	1650.
Barber dimes	200.	550.
Mercury dimes	—	125.
Twenty-cent	1600.	2900.
Draped Bust quarters, heraldic eagle	17,650.	—
Liberty Cap quarters, 1815-1828 (large size)	5000.	—
Liberty Cap quarters, 1831-1838 (reduced size)	4200.	—
Seated Liberty quarters, no drapery	7450.	—
Seated Liberty quarters, no motto	1050.	1700.
Seated Liberty quarters, arrows and rays	4850.	—
Seated Liberty quarters, 1854-1855, with arrows	2350.	—
Seated Liberty quarters, with motto	670.	800.
Seated Liberty quarters, 1873-1874, with arrows	1950.	2900.
Barber quarters	450.	800.
Standing Liberty quarters, Type I, full head	330.	—
Standing Liberty quarters, Type II	195.	—
Standing Liberty quarters, Type II, full head	265.	—
Flowing Hair half dollars	82,000.	—
Draped Bust half dollars, heraldic eagle	23,500.	—
Liberty Cap half dollars	2600.	—
Liberty Cap half dollars, reeded edge	4050.	—
Seated Liberty half dollars, no drapery	38,000.	—
Seated Liberty half dollars, no motto	1950.	2000.
Seated Liberty half dollars, arrows and rays	6450.	—
Seated Liberty half dollars, 1854-1855, with arrows	2700.	—
Seated Liberty half dollars, with motto	1050.	1150.
Seated Liberty half dollars, 1873-1874, with arrows	3750.	2900.
Barber half dollars	1050.	1350.
Walking Liberty half dollars	—	310.
Draped Bust dollars, small eagle	86,500.	—
Draped Bust dollars, heraldic eagle	36,500.	—
Seated Liberty dollars, no motto	5900.	5500.
Seated Liberty dollars, with motto	5750.	5000.
Morgan dollars	—	2650.
Trade dollars	2750.	3050.

Gold dollars

Liberty Head

Mintmark

Designer: James B. Longacre. **Size:** 13 millimeters. **Weight:** 1.672 grams. **Composition:** 90% gold (.0484 ounce), 10% copper. **Notes:** On the "closed wreath" varieties of 1849, the wreath on the reverse extends closer to the numeral 1.

Date	Mintage	F-12	VF-20	XF-40	AU-50	MS-60
1849 open wreath	688,567	110.	120.	165.	185.	650.
1849 closed wreath	Inc. Ab.	110.	120.	165.	175.	375.
1849C closed wreath	11,634	275.	425.	750.	1500.	4500.
1849C open wreath	Inc. Ab.			Extremely Rare		—
1849D open wreath	21,588	285.	410.	800.	1100.	3125.
1849O open wreath	215,000	135.	165.	210.	325.	700.
1850	481,953	120.	135.	150.	180.	380.
1850C	6,966	390.	585.	950.	2200.	6000.
1850D	8,382	350.	550.	1150.	1950.	6100.
1850O	14,000	195.	260.	370.	775.	2750.
1851	3,317,671	120.	135.	165.	175.	275.
1851C	41,267	275.	410.	650.	950.	2300.
1851D	9,882	275.	400.	750.	1600.	3650.
1851O	290,000	150.	175.	195.	250.	690.
1852	2,045,351	100.	120.	150.	170.	275.
1852C	9,434	275.	450.	750.	1200.	3400.
1852D	6,360	315.	600.	1150.	1400.	5500.
1852O	140,000	120.	150.	210.	295.	1000.
1853	4,076,051	115.	130.	150.	170.	275.
1853C	11,515	240.	475.	1200.	1650.	5000.
1853D	6,583	325.	675.	950.	2100.	6250.
1853O	290,000	140.	160.	195.	220.	500.
1854	736,709	115.	150.	160.	175.	280.
1854D	2,935	530.	860.	1850.	5000.	15,000.
1854S	14,632	260.	300.	440.	650.	1800.

Small Indian Head

Designer: James B. Longacre. **Size:** 15 millimeters. **Weight:** 1.672 grams. **Composition:** 90% gold (.084 ounces), 10% copper.

Date	Mintage	F-12	VF-20	XF-40	AU-50	MS-60
1854	902,736	210.	265.	370.	500.	3000.
1855	758,269	210.	265.	370.	500.	3000.
1855C	9,803	625.	950.	2650.	5000.	9000.
1855D	1,811	1400.	2300.	4500.	6900.	19,000.
1855O	55,000	350.	550.	800.	950.	5500.
1856S	24,600	390.	650.	1100.	1700.	6900.

Large Indian Head

Designer: James B. Longacre. **Size:** 15 millimeters. **Weight:** 1.672 grams. **Composition:** 90% gold (.0484 ounces), 10% copper. **Notes:** The 1856 varieties are distinguished by whether the 5 in the date is slanted or upright. The 1873 varieties are distinguished by the amount of space between the upper left and lower left serifs in the 3.

Date	Mintage	F-12	VF-20	XF-40	AU-50	MS-60	Prf-65
1856 upright 5	1,762,936	130.	160.	180.	325.	475.	—
1856 slanted 5	Inc. Ab.	120.	140.	170.	190.	300.	—
1856D	1,460	2250.	3500.	5500.	8500.	22,000.	—
1857	774,789	120.	140.	170.	190.	300.	—
1857C	13,280	350.	500.	1000.	2300.	9400.	—
1857D	3,533	275.	825.	1650.	2900.	11,000.	—
1857S	10,000	260.	500.	600.	1000.	5650.	—
1858	117,995	120.	140.	170.	190.	300.	19,000.

Gold dollars

Date	Mintage	F-12	VF-20	XF-40	AU-50	MS-60	Prf-65
1858D	3,477	375.	775.	1300.	1900.	7250.	—
1858S	10,000	280.	375.	500.	1350.	6250.	—
1859	168,244	120.	140.	160.	190.	300.	12,000.
1859C	5,235	300.	500.	1250.	2500.	10,000.	—
1859D	4,952	475.	780.	1150.	2000.	7200.	—
1859S	15,000	225.	250.	480.	1000.	5500.	—
1860	36,668	120.	140.	170.	190.	375.	16,000.
1860D	1,566	1700.	2500.	3800.	5750.	25,000.	—
1860S	13,000	200.	325.	475.	700.	2500.	—
1861	527,499	120.	140.	170.	190.	3000.	16,000.
1861D	Unrecorded	4300.	6000.	8500.	14,000.	32,500.	—
1862	1,361,390	110.	120.	155.	175.	280.	18,000.
1863	6,250	360.	450.	875.	1700.	4000.	16,500.
1864	5,950	285.	370.	475.	750.	900.	—
1865	3,725	285.	370.	585.	750.	1600.	16,500.
1866	7,130	290.	380.	450.	700.	1000.	16,500.
1867	5,250	345.	440.	550.	750.	1200.	18,000.
1868	10,525	260.	295.	400.	585.	1100.	—
1869	5,925	325.	360.	520.	800.	1100.	—
1870	6,335	260.	285.	500.	775.	1050.	19,500.
1870S	3,000	350.	475.	800.	1400.	2400.	—
1871	3,930	260.	285.	440.	525.	750.	—
1872	3,530	285.	315.	480.	575.	900.	20,500.
1873 closed 3	125,125	325.	425.	700.	1000.	2000.	—
1873 open 3	Inc. Ab.	110.	120.	155.	175.	280.	—
1874	198,820	110.	120.	155.	175.	280.	—
1875	420	1800.	2500.	3600.	4500.	5700.	45,000.
1876	3,245	220.	250.	360.	475.	890.	17,500.
1877	3,920	150.	175.	350.	480.	800.	24,000.
1878	3,020	180.	215.	365.	470.	850.	18,000.
1879	3,030	165.	190.	300.	400.	700.	18,000.
1880	1,636	145.	160.	200.	235.	450.	18,000.
1881	7,707	145.	160.	200.	235.	450.	15,500.
1882	5,125	160.	175.	210.	235.	350.	9750.
1883	11,007	145.	165.	200.	235.	300.	9750.
1884	6,236	140.	160.	190.	230.	300.	9750.
1885	12,261	145.	160.	200.	235.	300.	9750.
1886	6,016	145.	165.	200.	235.	300.	9750.
1887	8,543	145.	165.	200.	235.	300.	9750.
1888	16,580	145.	165.	200.	235.	300.	9750.
1889	30,729	145.	165.	200.	235.	300.	9750.

Gold $2.50 (Quarter eagle)

Liberty Cap

Designer: Robert Scott. **Size:** 20 millimeters. **Weight:** 4.37 grams. **Composition:** 91.67% gold (.1289 ounces), 8.33% copper. **Note:** The 1804 varieties are distinguished by the number of stars on the obverse.

Date	Mintage	F-12	VF-20	XF-40	MS-60
1802/1	3,035	3000.	4250.	5000.	20,000.
1804 13-star reverse	3,327	16,000.	25,000.	55,000.	155,000.
1804 14-star reverse	Inc. Ab.	3250.	4250.	5750.	21,000.
1805	1,781	3000.	4500.	5400.	22,500.
1806/4	1,616	3000.	4500.	5000.	22,500.
1806/5	Inc. Ab.	6500.	12,500.	22,000.	110,000.
1807	6,812	2800.	4000.	5000.	20,000.

Turban Head

Designer: John Reich. **Sizes:** 20 millimeters (1808), 18.5 millimeters (1821-1827), and 18.2 millimeters (1829-1834). **Weight:** 4.37 grams. **Composition:** 91.67% gold (.1289 ounces), 8.33% copper.

Date	Mintage	F-12	VF-20	XF-40	MS-60
1808	2,710	9000.	12,500.	22,000.	45,000.
1821	6,448	3250.	3500.	4500.	16,250.
1824/21	2,600	3000.	3600.	4250.	15,000.

Date	Mintage	F-12	VF-20	XF-40	MS-60
1825	4,434	3000.	3600.	4250.	12,500.
1826/25	760	3500.	4600.	5500.	35,000.
1827	2,800	3600.	4500.	5000.	18,500.
1829	3,403	3000.	3250.	4000.	9500.
1830	4,540	3000.	3250.	4250.	9250.
1831	4,520	3000.	3250.	4250.	9500.
1832	4,400	3000.	3250.	4250.	9500.
1833	4,160	3000.	3500.	4250.	9750.
1834	4,000	6750.	10,000.	19,500.	55,000.

Liberty Without Turban

Mintmark

Designer: William Kneass. **Size:** 18.2 millimeters. **Weight** 4.18 grams. **Composition:** 89.92% gold (.1209 ounces), 10.08% copper.

Date	Mintage	VF-20	XF-40	AU-50	MS-60	MS-65
1834	112,234	300.	550.	700.	2000.	25,000.
1835	131,402	265.	400.	700.	2000.	25,000.
1836	547,986	255.	400.	585.	1750.	25,000.
1837	45,080	265.	425.	700.	2850.	25,000.
1838	47,030	265.	425.	700.	2400.	25,000.
1838C	7,880	1000.	2500.	6500.	20,000.	—
1839	27,021	265.	600.	1800.	4000.	25,000.
1839C	18,140	775.	1800.	3000.	16,000.	—
1839D	13,674	1200.	2250.	5000.	24,000.	—
1839O	17,781	500.	1100.	1650.	5000.	—

Coronet Head

1848 "Cal."

Designer: Christian Gobecht. **Size:** 18 millimeters. **Weight:** 4.18 grams. **Composition:** 90% gold (.121 ounces), 10% copper. **Notes:** Varieties for 1843 are distinguished by the size of the numerals in the date. On 1848 variety has "Cal." inscribed on the reverse, indicating it was made from California gold. The 1873 "closed 3" and "open 3" varieties are distinguished by the amount of space between the upper left and lower left serifs in the 3 in the date.

Date	Mintage	F-12	VF-20	XF-40	AU-50	MS-60	Prf-65
1840	18,859	180.	245.	700.	1625.	7500.	—
1840C	12,822	325.	600.	1250.	5000.	15,000.	—
1840D	3,532	500.	2000.	4100.	9500.	28,000.	—
1840O	33,580	225.	250.	900.	1800.	7500.	—
1841	—	—	—	27,500.	50,000.	—	—
1841C	10,281	275.	550.	1250.	3250.	9600.	—
1841D	4,164	600.	1200.	2600.	9000.	18,750.	—
1842	2,823	350.	850.	3000.	6250.	15,500.	—
1842C	6,729	525.	1200.	2600.	7500.	11,000.	—
1842D	4,643	700.	1500.	2900.	8250.	18,500.	—
1842O	19,800	375.	375.	1500.	2900.	14,500.	—
1843	100,546	200.	225.	250.	375.	1750.	—
1843C sm. dt.	26,064	1000.	2500.	5500.	8500.	21,000.	—
1843C lg. dt.	Inc. Ab.	500.	600.	900.	3500.	8000.	—
1843D	36,209	400.	650.	1100.	2000.	7900.	—
1843O sm. dt.	288,002	200.	225.	325.	450.	1250.	—
1843O lg. dt.	76,000	250.	350.	450.	1750.	3125.	—
1844	6,784	200.	400.	850.	2500.	6800.	—
1844C	11,622	325.	675.	1550.	6500.	17,000.	—
1844D	17,332	325.	625.	1200.	2000.	7200.	—
1845	91,051	200.	250.	290.	350.	1100.	—
1845D	19,460	325.	650.	1125.	2500.	8500.	—
1845O	4,000	750.	750.	1900.	5600.	15,000.	—
1846	21,598	300.	400.	725.	1350.	6500.	—
1846C	4,808	550.	1000.	2000.	7500.	20,000.	—
1846D	19,303	450.	750.	1200.	2400.	8500.	—
1846O	66,000	200.	300.	525.	1150.	5000.	—
1847	29,814	200.	275.	400.	700.	3500.	—
1847C	23,226	300.	600.	1000.	2000.	5600.	—
1847D	15,784	300.	600.	1000.	2000.	7500.	—
1847O	124,000	200.	275.	425.	1150.	3000.	—
1848	7,497	350.	625.	1000.	1750.	8250.	—
1848 "Cal."	1,389	7000.	9500.	15,000.	22,500.	35,000.	—
1848C	16,788	400.	650.	1200.	2250.	10,000.	—
1848D	13,771	400.	600.	1200.	2000.	8750.	—
1849	23,294	175.	280.	500.	800.	2200.	—
1849C	10,220	400.	700.	1750.	4750.	20,000.	—
1849D	10,945	400.	700.	1200.	2750.	16,000.	—
1850	252,923	175.	200.	225.	300.	1250.	—
1850C	9,148	275.	600.	1400.	3250.	16,000.	—
1850D	12,148	350.	700.	1200.	2500.	14,000.	—
1850O	84,000	200.	300.	575.	1400.	5500.	—
1851	1,372,748	115.	125.	170.	200.	350.	—
1851C	14,923	375.	675.	1500.	4000.	16,500.	—
1851D	11,264	275.	650.	1300.	3450.	12,000.	—
1851O	148,000	200.	250.	350.	1000.	5000.	—
1852	1,159,681	115.	125.	170.	180.	350.	—
1852C	9,772	350.	625.	1550.	3500.	17,000.	—
1852D	4,078	450.	1000.	2750.	5250.	18,000.	—
1852O	140,000	200.	250.	300.	975.	5500.	—
1853	1,404,668	115.	125.	180.	200.	350.	—
1853D	3,178	500.	1350.	2650.	4500.	17,000.	—
1854	596,258	175.	185.	210.	250.	375.	—
1854C	7,295	250.	625.	1650.	5000.	17,500.	—
1854D	1,760	1800.	2700.	6000.	12,500.	21,000.	—
1854O	153,000	200.	250.	300.	650.	1700.	—
1854S	246	15,000.	19,000.	37,500.	62,500.	—	—
1855	235,480	175.	185.	180.	225.	400.	—
1855C	3,677	500.	1300.	2850.	5000.	19,000.	—
1855D	1,123	2000.	4000.	8000.	18,500.	31,000.	—
1856	384,240	125.	150.	180.	200.	350.	—
1856C	7,913	500.	850.	2000.	4500.	17,500.	—
1856D	874	4000.	6000.	13,000.	19,000.	42,000.	—
1856O	21,100	200.	250.	715.	1500.	7000.	—
1856S	71,120	200.	250.	435.	900.	4800.	—
1857	214,130	175.	185.	210.	250.	390.	—
1857D	2,364	565.	1000.	2000.	4000.	13,000.	—
1857O	34,000	160.	180.	350.	1500.	5600.	—
1857S	69,200	150.	180.	400.	900.	6250.	—
1858	47,377	135.	150.	225.	400.	1600.	—
1858C	9,056	350.	600.	1300.	2500.	10,000.	—
1859	39,444	150.	180.	300.	500.	1350.	—
1859D	2,244	600.	1350.	3000.	5000.	25,000.	—
1859S	15,200	200.	500.	1200.	3000.	8500.	—
1860	22,675	200.	250.	300.	600.	1250.	19,000.
1860C	7,469	350.	850.	1400.	4500.	21,000.	—
1860S	35,600	200.	300.	700.	1500.	4400.	—
1861	1,283,878	115.	125.	170.	200.	325.	20,000.
1861S	24,000	200.	350.	950.	3000.	6600.	—
1862	98,543	200.	250.	300.	550.	1250.	20,000.
1862/1	Inc. Ab.	650.	1000.	2150.	3500.	8750.	—
1862S	8,000	650.	950.	2500.	5950.	15,500.	—
1863S	10,800	400.	600.	1500.	2800.	6700.	—
1864	2,874	2500.	5400.	13,500.	26,000.	65,000.	22,500.
1865	1,545	2000.	4325.	8500.	20,000.	45,000.	32,000.
1865S	23,376	200.	225.	630.	2000.	4500.	—
1866	3,110	550.	1200.	5000.	11,000.	20,000.	29,500.
1866S	38,960	200.	300.	975.	2600.	8750.	—
1867	3,250	225.	360.	840.	1700.	5500.	29,500.
1867S	28,000	200.	250.	875.	2400.	5600.	—
1868	3,625	200.	300.	500.	1000.	2500.	—
1868S	34,000	200.	250.	500.	1500.	5000.	—
1869	4,345	200.	250.	500.	850.	2800.	24,500.
1869S	29,500	200.	250.	600.	1200.	4500.	—
1870	4,555	210.	275.	550.	1000.	3800.	32,500.
1870S	16,000	200.	285.	350.	1300.	5500.	—
1871	5,350	210.	275.	350.	900.	2400.	32,500.
1871S	22,000	225.	285.	350.	800.	3000.	—
1872	3,030	225.	360.	825.	2000.	8000.	30,000.
1872S	18,000	225.	285.	500.	1375.	4300.	—
1873 closed 3	178,025	125.	175.	200.	230.	560.	24,000.
1873 open 3	Inc. Ab.	125.	160.	225.	250.	325.	—
1873S	27,000	200.	250.	575.	1100.	2500.	—
1874	3,940	200.	250.	500.	1000.	2500.	28,000.
1875	420	1500.	3600.	5250.	9000.	16,000.	—
1875S	11,600	200.	250.	400.	800.	4500.	—
1876	4,221	175.	230.	625.	900.	3400.	24,500.
1876S	5,000	210.	250.	600.	1200.	3600.	—
1877	1,652	325.	450.	600.	900.	3000.	32,500.
1877S	35,400	125.	180.	210.	250.	650.	—
1878	286,260	125.	130.	165.	180.	300.	34,000.
1878S	178,000	125.	150.	165.	210.	425.	—
1879	88,990	125.	130.	165.	180.	300.	24,500.
1879S	43,500	125.	130.	165.	500.	1350.	—
1880	2,996	215.	250.	350.	600.	1200.	26,000.
1881	691	700.	1350.	2750.	5000.	8600.	27,500.
1882	4,067	125.	225.	300.	350.	800.	18,000.
1883	2,002	125.	225.	400.	800.	2000.	18,000.
1884	2,023	125.	225.	400.	625.	1550.	20,000.
1885	887	500.	800.	1500.	2500.	4650.	18,000.
1886	4,088	125.	210.	300.	550.	1400.	19,500.
1887	6,282	125.	190.	225.	500.	1000.	16,000.

Gold $2.50

Gold $2.50

Date	Mintage	F-12	VF-20	XF-40	AU-50	MS-60	Prf-65
1888	16,098	125.	190.	225.	260.	350.	21,000.
1889	17,648	125.	190.	250.	275.	450.	21,000.
1890	8,813	125.	190.	200.	250.	475.	16,000.
1891	11,040	125.	190.	250.	275.	450.	17,500.
1892	2,545	135.	195.	200.	450.	950.	17,000.
1893	30,106	125.	130.	200.	260.	400.	13,000.
1894	4,122	125.	130.	200.	325.	650.	13,000.
1895	6,199	125.	130.	200.	270.	325.	13,000.
1896	19,202	125.	130.	165.	180.	300.	13,000.
1897	29,904	125.	130.	165.	180.	275.	13,000.
1898	24,165	125.	130.	165.	180.	275.	13,000.
1899	27,350	125.	130.	165.	180.	275.	13,000.
1900	67,205	125.	130.	165.	180.	275.	13,000.

NOTE: Later dates (1901-1907) exist for this type.

Gold $3

Designer: James B. Longacre. **Size:** 20.5 millimeters. **Weight:** 5.015 grams. **Composition:** 90% gold (.1452 ounces), 10% copper. **Notes:** The 1873 "closed 3" and "open 3" varieties are distinguished by the amount of space between the upper left and lower left serifs of the 3 in the date.

Date	Mintage	F-12	VF-20	XF-40	AU-50	MS-60	Prf-65
1854	138,618	400.	575.	625.	730.	1750.	35,000.
1854D	1,120	4500.	7250.	13,500.	23,500.	47,000.	—
1854O	24,000	450.	425.	750.	2000.	4300.	—
1855	50,555	425.	575.	625.	730.	2200.	—
1855S	6,600	650.	1000.	1750.	4750.	20,000.	—
1856	26,010	425.	600.	690.	900.	2250.	—
1856S	34,500	500.	760.	900.	1800.	8250.	—
1857	20,891	425.	600.	690.	1100.	3000.	35,000.
1857S	14,000	650.	1000.	1800.	4000.	16,000.	—
1858	2,133	625.	800.	1050.	2000.	4900.	35,000.
1859	15,638	425.	600.	675.	730.	2250.	35,000.
1860	7,155	425.	700.	850.	1000.	2500.	35,000.
1860S	7,000	525.	760.	1800.	5000.	10,000.	—
1861	6,072	550.	760.	1000.	1500.	3000.	35,000.
1862	5,785	525.	760.	900.	1300.	3200.	35,000.
1863	5,039	550.	700.	850.	1450.	3400.	35,000.
1864	2,680	600.	760.	1150.	2400.	4000.	35,000.
1865	1,165	700.	800.	1600.	3750.	6000.	35,000.
1866	4,030	600.	700.	950.	1275.	3000.	35,000.
1867	2,650	600.	700.	950.	1275.	3000.	35,000.
1868	4,875	600.	700.	900.	1275.	3000.	35,000.
1869	2,525	600.	700.	1000.	1275.	3500.	35,000.
1870	3,535	600.	700.	1000.	1350.	3800.	35,000.
1870S	Unique	Private Sale, 1992 XF-40 $1,500,000.					
1871	1,330	600.	750.	1200.	1500.	3400.	35,000.
1872	2,030	600.	700.	1200.	1800.	2900.	35,000.
1873 open 3	25			Proof only	—		—
1873 closed 3	Unknown	—	4000.	6500.	7000.	23,000.	—
1874	41,820	400.	550.	600.	750.	1700.	35,000.
1875	20			Proof only			175,000.
1876	45			10,000.	12,000.		65,000.
1877	1,488	700.	1100.	2750.	4400.	7500.	35,000.
1878	82,324	400.	550.	625.	730.	1650.	30,000.
1879	3,030	475.	650.	850.	1250.	2250.	30,000.
1880	1,036	550.	750.	1200.	1800.	2250.	30,000.
1881	554	600.	1000.	2100.	3500.	4250.	32,000.
1882	1,576	550.	700.	1250.	1600.	2200.	30,000.
1883	989	700.	700.	1250.	1750.	2300.	32,000.
1884	1,106	550.	900.	1500.	1850.	2250.	30,000.
1885	910	550.	900.	1500.	2000.	2750.	32,000.
1886	1,142	550.	825.	1400.	2000.	3000.	30,000.
1887	6,160	525.	625.	800.	1000.	2300.	30,000.
1888	5,291	525.	625.	800.	1000.	2300.	30,000.
1889	2,429	525.	625.	800.	1000.	2300.	30,000.

Gold $5 (Half eagle)

Liberty Cap

Designer: Robert Scot. **Size:** 25 millimeters. **Weight:** 8.75 grams. **Composition:** 91.00 (.258 ounces), 8.33% copper.

Gold $5

Heraldic eagle

Date	Mintage	F-12	VF-20	XF-40	MS-60
1802/1	53,176	1150.	1550.	2450.	6000.
1803/2	33,506	1150.	1550.	2450.	6000.
1804 sm. 8	30,475	1150.	1550.	2450.	6850.
1804 lg. 8	Inc. Ab.	1150.	1550.	2450.	7300.
1805	33,183	1150.	1550.	2450.	6000.
1806 pointed 6	64,093	1150.	1550.	2600.	6250.
1806 round 6	Inc. Ab.	1150.	1550.	2450.	5000.
1807	32,488	1150.	1550.	2450.	5200.

Turban Head

Capped draped bust Capped head

Capped draped bust

Designer: John Reich. **Size:** 25 millimeters. **Weight:** 8.75 grams. **Composition:** 91.67% gold (.258 ounces), 8.33% copper. **Notes:** The 1810 varieties are distinguished by the size of the numerals in the date and the size of the 5 in the "5D" on the reverse. The 1811 varieties are distinguished by the size of the 5 in the "5D" on the reverse.

Date	Mintage	F-12	VF-20	XF-40	MS-60
1807	51,605	1250.	1650.	2150.	6000.
1808	55,578	1250.	1650.	2150.	6000.
1808/7	Inc. Ab.	1400.	1550.	2400.	9500.
1809/8	33,875	1250.	1500.	2150.	6000.
1810 sm. date, sm. 5	100,287	—	20,000.	35,000.	85,000.
1810 sm. dt., lg. 5	Inc. Ab.	1300.	1650.	2400.	6000.
1810 lg. dt., sm. 5	Inc. Ab.	14,000.	25,000.	40,000.	100,000.
1810 lg. dt., lg. 5	Inc. Ab.	1250.	1400.	2000.	5750.
1811 sm. 5	99,581	1250.	1400.	2000.	5000.
1811 lg. 5	Inc. Ab.	1150.	1350.	2000.	5000.
1812	58,087	1000.	1350.	2000.	5250.

Capped head

Notes: 1820 varieties are distinguished by whether the 2 in the date has a curved base of square base and by the size of the letters in the reverse inscriptions. 1832 varieties are distinguished by whether the 2 in the date has a curved base or square base and by the number of stars on the reverse. 1834 varieties are distinguished by whether the 4 has a serif at its far right.

Date	Mintage	F-12	VF-20	XF-40	MS-60
1813	95,428	1300.	1500.	2250.	5600.
1814/13	15,454	1600.	2000.	4000.	8000.
1815	635	Private sale Jan. 1994, MS-61, $150,000.			
1818	48,588	1500.	1900.	2850.	8500.
1819	51,723	6250.	12,500.	22,000.	37,500.
1820 curved base 2, sm. letters	263,806	1500.	1900.	3200.	9400.
1820 curved base 2, lg. letters	Inc. Ab.	1500.	1900.	4500.	40,000.
1820 sq. base 2	Inc. Ab.	1500.	1900.	3200.	9400.
1821	34,641	2200.	8000.	13,000.	30,000.
1822	(3 known) 17,796	Private Sale 1993, VF-30, $1,000,000.			
1823	14,485	1600.	2000.	3700.	14,500.
1824	17,340	4500.	8750.	13,000.	27,500.
1825/21	29,060	4500.	6750.	11,000.	26,500.
1825/24	I.A.	Bowers & Merena, Mar. 1989, XF,$148,500.			
1826	18,069	2750.	6000.	7100.	19,000.
1827	24,913	—	—	—	32,500.
1828/7	28,029	Bowers & Merena, Jun. 1989, XF, $20,900.			
1828	Inc. Ab.	4250.	6500.	12,500.	48,000.
1829 lg. plan.	57,442	Superior, July 1985, MS-65, $104,500.			
1829 sm. plan.	Inc. Ab.	Private Sale, 1992 (XF-45), $89,000.			
1830 sm. "5D."	126,351	3500.	5000.	6500.	12,000.

Date	Mintage	F-12	VF-20	XF-40	MS-60
1830 lg. "5D."	Inc. Ab.	3500.	5000.	7000.	12,500.
1831	140,594	3500.	5100.	6500.	16,000.
1832 curved base 2, 12-stars	157,487	—	Rare	—	—
1832 square base 2, 13 stars	Inc. Ab.	1800.	2000.	3000.	12,000.
1833	193,630	3500.	5000.	6250.	15,500.
1834 plain 4	50,141	3500.	5000.	6250.	17,000.
1834 crosslet 4	Inc. Ab.	4000.	6000.	7750.	20,000.

Liberty Without Turban

Designer: William Kneass. **Size:** 22.5 millimeters. **Weight:** 8.36 millimeters. **Composition:** 89.92% gold (.2418 ounces), 10.08% copper. Notes: 1834 varieties are distinguished by whether the 4 has a serif at its far right.

Date	Mintage	VF-20	XF-40	AU-50	MS-60	MS-65
1834 plain 4	658,028	300.	500.	850.	2100.	50,000.
1834 crosslet 4	Inc. Ab.	1150.	2375.	5250.	15,000.	—
1835	371,534	300.	500.	900.	2900.	62,000.
1836	553,147	300.	500.	850.	2125.	62,000.
1837	207,121	325.	525.	925.	3500.	62,000.
1838	286,588	300.	500.	900.	3250.	62,000.
1838C	17,179	1550.	4250.	9500.	30,000.	—
1838D	20,583	1450.	3500.	7000.	25,000.	—

Coronet Head

No motto

Designer: Christian Gobrecht. **Size:** 21.6 millimeters. **Weight:** 8.359 grams. **Composition:** 90% gold (.242 ounces), 10% copper. **Notes:** Varieties for the 1842 Philadelphia strikes are distinguished by the size of the letters in the reverse inscriptions. Varieties for the 1842-C and D strikes are distinguished by the size of the numerals in the date. Varieties for the 1843-O strikes are distinguished by the size of the letters in the reverse inscriptions.

Date	Mintage	F-12	VF-20	XF-40	MS-60	Prf-65
1839	118,143	200.	250.	435.	3500.	—
1839/8 curved date	Inc. Ab.	200.	300.	600.	1750.	—
1839C	17,205	450.	950.	1300.	20,000.	—
1839D	18,939	400.	800.	1700.	15,000.	—
1840	137,382	190.	225.	350.	4100.	—
1840C	18,992	400.	700.	1650.	23,000.	—
1840D	22,896	400.	700.	1500.	16,000.	—
1840O	40,120	200.	325.	700.	9500.	—
1841	15,833	200.	375.	850.	5600.	—
1841C	21,467	300.	675.	1450.	12,000.	—
1841D	30,495	325.	600.	1250.	11,000.	—
1841O	50		2 known	—	—	—
1842 sm. let.	27,578	150.	300.	1300.	12,500.	—
1842 lg. let.	Inc. Ab.	350.	700.	2000.	13,500.	—
1842C sm. dt.	28,184	2000.	6500.	25,000.	100,000.	—
1842C lg. dt.	Inc. Ab.	350.	750.	1500.	11,250.	—
1842D sm. dt.	59,608	350.	650.	1250.	14,000.	—
1842D lg. dt.	Inc. Ab.	1250.	2250.	6000.	37,500.	—
1842O	16,400	350.	1000.	5000.	24,000.	—
1843	611,205	150.	165.	195.	2200.	—
1843C	44,201	350.	600.	1400.	10,000.	—
1843D	98,452	350.	550.	1000.	8000.	—
1843O sm. let.	19,075	325.	550.	1400.	20,000.	—
1843O lg. let.	82,000	200.	325.	900.	11,250.	—
1844	340,330	150.	180.	250.	2100.	—
1844C	23,631	300.	725.	2700.	18,500.	—
1844D	88,982	375.	550.	1050.	12,000.	—
1844O	364,600	200.	225.	600.	5000.	—
1845	417,099	150.	165.	195.	2750.	—
1845D	90,629	360.	850.	1850.	12,500.	—
1845O	41,000	200.	350.	1100.	12,000.	—
1846	395,942	150.	180.	210.	3000.	—
1846C	12,995	425.	900.	2500.	22,500.	—

Date	Mintage	F-12	VF-20	XF-40	MS-60	Prf-65
1846D	80,294	400.	550.	1350.	9250.	—
1846O	58,000	200.	350.	1450.	12,750.	—
1847	915,981	150.	165.	195.	1200.	—
1847C	84,151	375.	575.	1450.	16,500.	—
1847D	64,405	400.	500.	1100.	9000.	—
1847O	12,000	475.	2300.	10,500.	29,000.	—
1848	260,775	150.	180.	250.	1200.	—
1848C	64,472	400.	650.	1600.	15,000.	—
1848D	47,465	400.	500.	1500.	13,000.	—
1849	133,070	150.	180.	300.	2700.	—
1849C	64,823	350.	500.	1100.	11,500.	—
1849D	39,036	350.	700.	1350.	14,500.	—
1850	64,491	200.	350.	550.	3500.	—
1850C	63,591	325.	550.	1100.	13,000.	—
1850D	43,984	350.	500.	1500.	20,000.	—
1851	377,505	150.	165.	200.	2800.	—
1851C	49,176	325.	600.	1100.	14,000.	—
1851D	62,710	350.	525.	1375.	15,000.	—
1851O	41,000	325.	650.	1500.	15,000.	—
1852	573,901	150.	165.	195.	1200.	—
1852C	72,574	350.	550.	1100.	8000.	—
1852D	91,584	350.	500.	1000.	8750.	—
1853	305,770	150.	180.	210.	2250.	—
1853C	65,571	350.	525.	1000.	8000.	—
1853D	89,678	350.	500.	900.	7500.	—
1854	160,675	160.	200.	500.	3000.	—
1854C	39,283	400.	600.	1600.	16,500.	—
1854D	56,413	350.	500.	1000.	10,000.	—
1854O	46,000	250.	300.	500.	6800.	—
1855	117,098	160.	200.	250.	2400.	—
1855C	39,788	350.	625.	1750.	13,500.	—
1855D	22,432	400.	600.	1500.	19,000.	—
1855O	11,100	350.	700.	2900.	20,000.	—
1855S	61,000	200.	425.	1100.	15,000.	—
1856	197,990	175.	310.	340.	2000.	—
1856C	28,457	350.	600.	1300.	11,500.	—
1856D	19,786	400.	600.	1300.	11,000.	—
1856O	10,000	400.	800.	2800.	22,000.	—
1856S	105,100	190.	300.	800.	6600.	—
1857	98,188	160.	200.	250.	3000.	—
1857C	31,360	300.	600.	1300.	13,000.	—
1857D	17,046	300.	600.	1250.	14,500.	—
1857O	13,000	300.	700.	2000.	20,000.	—
1857S	87,000	200.	300.	700.	8000.	—
1858	15,136	200.	275.	800.	5250.	70,000.
1858C	38,856	375.	800.	1250.	14,000.	—
1858D	15,362	300.	600.	1200.	12,000.	—
1858S	18,600	350.	650.	2600.	25,000.	—
1859	16,814	200.	275.	600.	6500.	—
1859C	31,847	300.	525.	1400.	15,000.	—
1859D	10,366	400.	725.	2000.	13,000.	—
1859S	13,220	450.	1250.	4750.	31,000.	—
1860	19,825	200.	300.	600.	3500.	—
1860C	14,813	350.	800.	2000.	13,500.	—
1860D	14,635	300.	800.	1800.	13,500.	—
1860S	21,200	450.	1200.	2800.	23,000.	—
1861	688,150	150.	165.	195.	1200.	—
1861C	6,879	700.	1500.	3400.	25,000.	—
1861D	1,597	2500.	4000.	7000.	34,000.	—
1861S	18,000	450.	1100.	4500.	33,000.	—
1862	4,465	450.	750.	2500.	19,000.	—
1862S	9,500	1400.	4500.	10,500.	56,000.	—
1863	2,472	500.	1150.	3450.	23,000.	—
1863S	17,000	425.	1200.	4750.	32,500.	—
1864	4,220	400.	600.	2100.	13,500.	—
1864S	3,888	2200.	6750.	15,000.	50,000.	—
1865	1,295	600.	1200.	3150.	22,000.	—
1865S	27,612	425.	1200.	3600.	15,000.	—
1866S	9,000	600.	1600.	6000.	30,000.	—

Mintmark

With motto

Notes: In 1866 the motto "In God We Trust" was added above the eagle on the reverse. The 1873 "closed 3" and "open 3" varieties are known and are distinguished by the amount of space between the upper right and lower left serifs on the 3 in the date.

Date	Mintage	VF-20	XF-40	AU-50	MS-60	MS-65	Prf-65
1866	6,730	725.	1800.	4400.	12,500.	—	35,000.
1866S	34,920	1350.	4500.	8500.	25,000.	—	—
1867	6,920	550.	2500.	4000.	8000.	—	35,000.
1867S	29,000	1600.	5000.	10,000.	25,000.	—	—
1868	5,725	650.	1800.	4000.	10,000.	—	35,000.
1868S	52,000	500.	2400.	7200.	20,000.	—	—
1869	1,785	875.	2300.	5000.	21,000.	—	35,000.
1869S	31,000	375.	2400.	8500.	24,000.	—	—
1870	4,035	700.	2800.	4500.	17,500.	—	35,000.
1870CC	7,675	4400.	9500.	20,000.	40,000.	—	—
1870S	17,000	1200.	4000.	11,500.	26,000.	—	—

Gold $5

Date	Mintage	VF-20	XF-40	AU-50	MS-60	MS-65	Prf-65
1871	3,230	875.	2150.	6500.	22,000.	—	35,000.
1871CC	20,770	975.	3000.	8000	28,000.	—	—
1871S	25,000	550.	2000.	3250.	17,500.	—	—
1872	1,690	750.	2000.	4700.	15,000.	—	35,000.
1872CC	16,980	850.	3500.	14,000.	20,000.	—	—
1872S	36,400	525.	1850.	3550.	10,000.	—	—
1873 closed 3	49,305	225.	250.	625.	1250.	—	35,000.
1873 open 3	63,200	225.	250.	625.	2800.	—	—
1873CC	7,416	2200.	6500.	15,500.	28,500.	—	—
1873S	31,000	875.	2700.	5000.	20,000.	—	—
1874	3,508	625.	2200.	5000.	16,500.	—	35,000.
1874CC	21,198	675.	1750.	5500.	12,000.	—	—
1874S	16,000	725.	3750.	9000.	20,000.	—	—
1875	220	45,000.	55,000.	96,000.	—	—	110,000.
1875CC	11,828	1500.	5400.	13,000.	31,500.	—	—
1875S	9,000	950.	3300.	7900.	23,500.	—	—
1876	1,477	1000.	2600.	5300.	11,250.	47,000.	35,000.
1876CC	6,887	1500.	5750.	9500.	20,000.	—	—
1876S	4,000	1700.	5000.	12,750.	28,000.	—	—
1877	1,152	800.	2400.	4500.	12,000.	—	35,000.
1877CC	8,680	1000.	3300.	8000.	18,000.	—	—
1877S	26,700	325.	900.	3600.	8300.	—	—
1878	131,740	140.	225.	250.	375.	—	35,000.
1878CC	9,054	3500.	9000.	20,000.	34,000.	—	—
1878S	144,700	150.	190.	250.	500.	—	—
1879	301,950	140.	175.	205.	250.	11,000.	20,000.
1879CC	17,281	350.	1300.	3000.	6250.	—	—
1879S	426,200	200.	275.	325.	975.	—	—
1880	3,166,436	140.	165.	175.	250.	—	20,000.
1880CC	51,017	350.	875.	2000.	7500.	—	—
1880S	1,348,900	140.	165.	175.	215.	—	—
1881	5,708,802	140.	165.	175.	215.	7000.	20,000.
1881/80	Inc. Ab.	350.	600.	750.	1500.	—	—
1881CC	13,886	500.	1500.	4150.	9000.	—	—
1881S	969,000	140.	165.	175.	215.	—	—
1882	2,514,568	140.	175.	195.	250.	7000.	20,000.
1882CC	82,817	375.	650.	1500.	5000.	—	—
1882S	969,000	140.	165.	175.	215.	—	—
1883	233,461	140.	175.	200.	550.	7000.	20,000.
1883CC	12,958	375.	800.	3500.	12,000.	—	—
1883S	83,200	195.	225.	330.	1150.	—	—
1884	191,078	150.	175.	260.	1250.	—	20,000.
1884CC	16,402	450.	825.	4250.	13,500.	—	—
1884S	177,000	160.	175.	200.	325.	—	—
1885	601,506	140.	165.	170.	215.	—	20,000.
1885S	1,211,500	140.	175.	190.	225.	7000.	—
1886	388,432	150.	185.	225.	375.	—	20,000.
1886S	3,268,000	130.	165.	175.	225.	—	—
1887	87		Proof only	—	—	—	140,000.
1887S	1,912,000	140.	175.	185.	240.	—	—
1888	18,296	175.	250.	300.	530.	—	20,000.
1888S	293,900	190.	275.	340.	1700.	—	—
1889	7,565	260.	440.	530.	1125.	—	20,000.
1890	4,328	250.	400.	875.	2000.	—	20,000.
1890CC	53,800	300.	400.	550.	1250.	—	—
1891	61,413	140.	235.	250.	775.	7500.	20,000.
1891CC	208,000	250.	375.	500.	850.	29,500.	—
1892	753,572	140.	165.	180.	220.	—	20,000.
1892CC	82,968	300.	600.	700.	1550.	—	—
1892O	10,000	600.	1250.	2250.	4700.	—	—
1892S	298,400	175.	225.	325.	725.	—	—
1893	1,528,197	140.	175.	195.	225.	5600.	20,000.
1893CC	60,000	300.	400.	625.	2000.	4250.	—
1893O	110,000	200.	300.	400.	2000.	—	—
1893S	224,000	170.	180.	200.	290.	7500.	—
1894	957,955	140.	175.	195.	300.	4750.	20,000.
1894O	16,600	195.	350.	475.	1125.	—	—
1894S	55,900	275.	350.	850.	3750.	7500.	—
1895	1,345,936	140.	165.	170.	215.	4750.	20,000.
1895S	112,000	190.	275.	400.	2900.	20,000.	—
1896	59,063	160.	185.	225.	350.	7500.	20,000.
1896S	155,400	225.	275.	600.	1200.	—	—
1897	867,883	140.	165.	170.	215.	4750.	20,000.
1897S	354,000	165.	190.	250.	940.	—	—
1898	633,495	140.	165.	170.	215.	4750.	20,000.
1898S	1,397,400	140.	165.	170.	215.	4750.	—
1899	1,710,729	140.	165.	170.	215.	4750.	20,000.
1899S	1,545,000	140.	165.	170.	215.	4750.	—
1900	1,405,730	140.	165.	170.	215.	4750.	20,000.
1900S	329,000	165.	200.	300.	700.	5000.	—

NOTE: Later dates (1901-1908) exist for this type.

Gold $10 (Eagle)

Liberty Cap

Designer: Robert Scot. **Size:** 33 millimeters. **Weight:** 17.5 grams. **Composition:** 91.67% gold (.5159 ounces), 8.33% copper.

Date	Mintage	F-12	VF-20	XF-40	MS-60
1801	44,344	2400.	3000.	4000.	11,000.
1803	15,017	2600.	3250.	4000.	11,000.
1804	3,757	3750.	4200.	6000.	18,000.

Gold $10

Heraldic eagle

Coronet Head

Old-style head

New-style head

Old-style head, no motto

Designer: Christian Gobrecht. **Size:** 27 millimeters. **Weight:** 16.718 grams. **Composition:** 90% gold (.4839 ounces), 10% copper.

Date	Mintage	F-12	VF-20	XF-40	MS-60	Prf-65
1838	7,200	650.	1175.	2900.	21,000.	—
1839 lg. lts.	38,248	600.	1175.	1950.	17,500.	—

New-style head, no motto

Notes: The 1842 varieties are distinguished by the size of the numerals in the date.

Date	Mintage	F-12	VF-20	XF-40	MS-60	Prf-65
1839 sm. lts.	Inc. Ab.	700.	1600.	5500.	—	—
1840	47,338	380.	425.	750.	9000.	—
1841	63,131	380.	415.	650.	8000.	—
1841O	2,500	850.	2450.	5400.	29,000.	—
1842 sm. dt.	81,507	380.	425.	1200.	35,000.	—
1842 lg. dt.	Inc. Ab.	380.	415.	750.	8750.	—
1842O	27,400	250.	285.	700.	12,500.	—
1843	75,462	380.	415.	700.	13.00	—
1843O	175,162	380.	415.	600.	8000.	—
1844	6,361	475.	1300.	2900.	16,000.	—
1844O	118,700	380.	425.	600.	11,000.	—
1845	26,153	380.	750.	950.	16,000.	—
1845O	47,500	350.	490.	625.	12,500.	—
1846	20,095	500.	900.	1275.	22,000.	—
1846O	81,780	350.	490.	975.	10,500.	—
1847	862,258	240.	280.	325.	3750.	—
1847O	571,500	250.	290.	400.	5000.	—
1848	145,484	300.	350.	400.	5500.	—
1848O	38,850	400.	600.	1400.	16,000.	—
1849	653,618	240.	280.	360.	3900.	—
1849O	23,900	500.	800.	3000.	21,000.	—
1850	291,451	240.	280.	315.	3500.	—
1850O	57,500	350.	400.	600.	11,250.	—
1851	176,328	300.	325.	525.	9500.	—
1851O	263,000	280.	300.	550.	5750.	—
1852	263,106	330.	425.	525.	3500.	—
1852O	18,000	500.	700.	1200.	22,500.	—
1853	201,253	240.	280.	800.	3500.	—
1853O	51,000	350.	400.	575.	8750.	—
1854	54,250	350.	400.	700.	6000.	—
1854O sm. dt.	52,500	225.	400.	1000.	12,000.	—
1854O lg. dt.	Inc. Ab.	375.	600.	2250.	—	—
1854S	123,826	280.	300.	575.	11,000.	—
1855	121,701	240.	280.	315.	3500.	—
1855O	18,000	350.	600.	2000.	15,000.	—
1855S	9,000	850.	1900.	4250.	31,000.	—
1856	60,490	300.	330.	360.	4800.	—
1856O	14,500	400.	600.	2000.	15,500.	—
1856S	68,000	330.	380.	625.	10,000.	—
1857	16,606	330.	380.	1000.	12,000.	—
1857O	5,500	700.	1000.	2000.	18,750.	—
1857S	26,000	380.	525.	800.	7750.	—
1858	2,521	2500.	5000.	8000.	33,000.	—
1858O	20,000	330.	380.	850.	12,000.	—
1858S	11,800	750.	2150.	3250.	31,000.	—

Gold $10

Date	Mintage	F-12	VF-20	XF-40	MS-60	Prf-65
1859	16,093	330.	380.	825.	11,500.	—
1859O	2,300	1275.	3500.	9000.	49,000.	—
1859S	7,000	900.	2000.	4500.	43,500.	—
1860	15,105	330.	380.	800.	8100.	—
1860O	11,100	400.	575.	1000.	12,500.	—
1860S	5,000	750.	2700.	6000.	43,500.	—
1861	113,233	280.	325.	375.	3000.	—
1861S	15,500	675.	1900.	2750.	34,000.	—
1862	10,995	350.	475.	1000.	11,250.	—
1862S	12,500	700.	1950.	3000.	37,500.	—
1863	1,248	2000.	3650.	9000.	50,000.	—
1863S	10,000	725.	1700.	3500.	26,000.	—
1864	3,580	800.	1900.	3000.	16,750.	—
1864S	2,500	2750.	5800.	11,500.	50,000.	—
1865	4,005	750.	2150.	3500.	34,000.	—
1865S	16,700	1450.	5000.	14,500.	48,500.	—
1865S/inverted 186	—	—	2500.	6000.	49,000.	—
1866S	8,500	1300.	3000.	3600.	47,500.	—

Reverse motto

New-style head, with motto

Notes: In 1866 the motto "In God We Trust" was added above the eagle on the reserve. The 1873 "closed 3" and "open 3" varieties are distinguished by the amount of space between the upper left and lower left serifs of the 3 in the date.

Date	Mintage	VF-20	XF-40	AU-50	MS-60	MS-65	Prf-65
1866	3,780	750.	3000.	6750.	15,500.	—	60,000.
1866S	11,500	1750.	3900.	9500.	24,000.	—	—
1867	3,140	1750.	4500.	10,500.	28,000.	—	60,000.
1867S	9,000	2600.	8500.	20,000.	43,500.	—	—
1868	10,655	600.	1800.	5750.	15,000.	—	60,000.
1868S	13,500	1250.	2000.	3500.	25,000.	—	—
1869	1,855	1750.	3000.	5600.	33,500.	—	65,000.
1869S	6,430	1800.	3200.	5400.	28,500.	—	—
1870	4,025	750.	1450.	2125.	16,500.	—	60,000.
1870CC	5,908	7000.	19,000.	32,500.	68,500.	—	—
1870S	8,000	2000.	3250.	7250.	34,000.	—	—
1871	1,820	1600.	2875.	3750.	20,000.	—	60,000.
1871CC	8,085	2250.	6000.	15,000.	43,500.	—	—
1871S	16,500	1750.	4700.	8000.	27,500.	—	—
1872	1,650	2500.	3900.	12,500.	25,000.	—	60,000.
1872CC	4,600	2500.	10,000.	25,000.	60,000.	—	—
1872S	17,300	530.	1000.	2000.	25,000.	—	—
1873 closed 3	825	4200.	14,000.	28,000.	46,500.	—	60,000.
1873CC	4,543	2700.	12,000.	27,000.	46,500.	—	—
1873S	12,000	1600.	5000.	9000.	31,250.	—	—
1874	53,160	300.	350.	550.	2450.	—	60,000.
1874CC	16,767	875.	2900.	7200.	23,500.	—	—
1874S	10,000	1700.	3375.	6900.	43,500.	—	—
1875	120	Akers, Aug. 1990, proof, $115,000.					—
1875CC	7,715	3500.	9000.	20,000.	53,000.	—	—
1876	732	3000.	6750.	12,500.	55,000.	—	50,000.
1876CC	4,696	3000.	10,000.	19,000.	50,000.	—	—
1876S	5,000	2100.	4000.	12,000.	40,000.	—	—
1877	817	3500.	9000.	16,000.	43,500.	—	40,000.
1877CC	3,332	2400.	4550.	8750.	37,500.	—	—
1877S	17,000	500.	6750.	2300.	24,000.	—	—
1878	73,800	225.	350.	450.	1000.	—	50,000.
1878CC	3,244	3500.	8000.	17,000.	40,000.	—	—
1878S	26,100	450.	715.	1625.	21,000.	—	—
1879	384,770	225.	230.	375.	850.	—	40,000.
1879CC	1,762	5000.	12,500.	26,000.	43,500.	—	—
1879O	1,500	2200.	3800.	11,000.	32,000.	—	—
1879S	224,000	310.	360.	425.	1700.	—	—
1880	1,644,876	225.	230.	245.	400.	—	40,000.
1880CC	11,190	425.	675.	2200.	7500.	—	—
1880O	9,200	400.	600.	900.	7500.	—	—
1880S	506,250	225.	230.	325.	600.	—	—
1881	3,877,260	225.	230.	245.	300.	—	40,000.
1881CC	24,015	400.	550.	1300.	7500.	—	—
1881O	8,350	400.	875.	3000.	8000.	—	—
1881S	970,000	225.	230.	245.	450.	—	—
1882	2,324,480	225.	230.	245.	290.	—	40,000.
1882CC	6,764	475.	1800.	5250.	10,000.	—	—
1882O	10,820	400.	850.	2500.	5000.	—	—
1882S	132,000	225.	230.	245.	1100.	13,500.	—
1883	208,740	225.	230.	325.	450.	6500.	40,000.
1883CC	12,000	400.	850.	3000.	9250.	—	—
1883O	800	3200.	8500.	17,000.	37,500.	—	—
1883S	38,000	295.	375.	450.	900.	13,500.	—
1884	76,905	225.	230.	325.	715.	13,500.	86,000.
1884CC	9,925	525.	1300.	4000.	10,000.	—	—
1884S	124,250	225.	230.	325.	425.	—	—
1885	253,527	225.	230.	245.	425.	6500.	40,000.
1885S	228,000	225.	230.	300.	330.	6500.	—
1886	236,160	225.	230.	300.	395.	6500.	40,000.
1886S	826,000	225.	230.	245.	290.	6500.	—

Gold $10

Date	Mintage	VF-20	XF-40	AU-50	MS-60	MS-65	Prf-65
1887	53,680	310.	300.	475.	750.	50,000.	40,000.
1887S	817,000	225.	230.	245.	425.	6500.	—
1888	132,996	300.	325.	365.	565.	50,000.	40,000.
1888O	21,335	225.	230.	350.	750.	—	—
1888S	648,700	225.	230.	245.	300.	6500.	—
1889	4,485	400.	500.	1000.	2000.	—	40,000.
1889S	425,400	225.	230.	245.	375.	6500.	—
1890	58,043	300.	315.	425.	650.	13,500.	40,000.
1890CC	17,500	375.	450.	600.	2000.	—	—
1891	91,868	225.	230.	245.	290.	13,500.	40,000.
1891CC	103,732	300.	350.	550.	650.	—	—
1892	797,552	225.	230.	245.	290.	6500.	40,000.
1892CC	40,000	375.	450.	500.	2150.	—	—
1892O	28,688	225.	230.	245.	350.	—	—
1892S	115,500	300.	310.	350.	400.	13,500.	—
1893	1,840,895	225.	230.	245.	290.	4500.	40,000.
1893CC	14,000	380.	600.	1400.	4750.	—	—
1893O	17,000	225.	230.	350.	675.	—	—
1893S	141,350	300.	310.	350.	390.	13,500.	—
1894	2,470,778	225.	230.	245.	360.	4850.	40,000.
1894O	107,500	225.	230.	375.	900.	13,500.	—
1894S	25,000	300.	475.	1200.	4500.	13,500.	—
1895	567,826	225.	300.	310.	340.	6500.	40,000.
1895O	98,000	225.	230.	245.	650.	13,500.	—
1895S	49,000	225.	400.	1250.	4000.	40,000.	—
1896	76,348	225.	230.	245.	350.	6500.	40,000.
1896S	123,750	225.	350.	1000.	2750.	—	—
1897	1,000,159	225.	230.	245.	290.	5000.	40,000.
1897O	42,500	225.	230.	375.	500.	11,000.	—
1897S	234,750	225.	325.	500.	850.	6500.	—
1898	812,197	225.	230.	245.	290.	6500.	40,000.
1898S	473,600	225.	230.	310.	360.	6500.	—
1899	1,262,305	225.	230.	245.	290.	4500.	40,000.
1899O	37,047	300.	315.	375.	950.	13,500.	—
1899S	841,000	225.	230.	325.	360.	6500.	—
1900	293,960	225.	230.	245.	290.	6500.	40,000.
1900S	81,000	300.	330.	400.	815.	12,500.	—

NOTE: Later dates (1901-1907) exist for this type.

Gold $20 (Double Eagle)

Coronet Head

"Twenty D", no motto

Reverse motto

1861 Pequet reverse

"Twenty D", no motto

Designer: James B. Longacre. **Size:** 34 millimeters. **Weight:** 33.436 grams. **Composition:** 90% gold (.9677 ounces), 10% copper. **Notes:** In 1861 the reverse was redesigned by Anthony C. Paquet, but it was withdrawn soon after is release. the letters in the inscriptions on the Paquet-reverse variety are taller than on the regular reverse.

Date	Mintage	VF-20	XF-40	AU-50	MS-60	MS-65	Prf-65
1849	1	Unique, in Smithsonian collection				—	—
1850	1,170,261	600.	625.	1000.	3125.	—	—
1850O	141,000	780.	1250.	3000.	15,000.	—	—
1851	2,087,155	600.	625.	950.	2300.	—	—
1851O	315,000	715.	810.	1825.	11,500.	—	—
1852	2,053,026	600.	625.	950.	3000.	—	—
1852O	190,000	685.	815.	1775.	12,000.	—	—
1853	1,261,326	600.	625.	950.	4850.	—	—
1853O	71,000	700.	1000.	2900.	20,000.	—	—

Gold $20

Date	Mintage	VF-20	XF-40	AU-50	MS-60	MS-65	Prf-65
1854	757,899	600.	625.	950.	5500.	—	—
1854O	3,250	17,500.	52,000.	—	—	—	—
1854S	141,468	700.	880.	1025.	1950.	34,000.	—
1855	364,666	600.	625.	1050.	6250.	34,000.	—
1855O	8,000	3000.	6000.	14,750.	54,000.	—	—
1855S	879,675	600.	625.	1000.	9100.	—	—
1856	329,878	600.	715.	1050.	8450.	—	—
1856O	2,250	19,000.	30,000.	60,000.	—	—	—
1856S	1,189,750	600.	625.	950.	3650.	—	—
1857	439,375	600.	625.	950.	3800.	—	—
1857O	30,000	1075.	1850.	3650.	14,000.	—	—
1857S	970,500	600.	625.	950.	2600.	—	—
1858	211,714	835.	1075.	1300.	4950.	—	—
1858O	35,250	1175.	1950.	6000.	15,500.	—	—
1858S	846,710	600.	625.	975.	8100.	—	—
1859	43,597	975.	2600.	4250.	37,500.	—	—
1859O	9,100	3150.	6800.	12,500.	37,500.	—	—
1859S	636,445	600.	625.	1000.	4200.	—	—
1860	577,670	600.	625.	950.	3900.	—	—
1860O	6,600	3450.	6250.	14,000.	37,500.	—	—
1860S	544,950	600.	625.	1050.	5850.	—	—
1861	2,976,453	600.	625.	950.	2750.	—	—
1861 Paquet rev.	Inc. Ab.						
		Bowers & Merena, Nov. 1988, MS-67, $660,000.					—
1861O	17,741	1500.	3550.	7000.	18,000.	—	—
1861S	768,000	600.	625.	1050.	7500.	—	—
1861S Paquet rev.	Inc. Ab.	5850.	11,000.	20,000.	59,000.	—	—
1862	92,133	910.	1600.	2750.	14,750.	—	—
1862S	854,173	600.	625.	1375.	8000.	—	—
1863	142,790	600.	750.	1625.	12,500.	—	—
1863S	966,570	600.	625.	1050.	6350.	—	—
1864	204,285	600.	950.	1650.	10,500.	—	—
1864S	793,660	600.	625.	1575.	8850.	—	—
1865	351,200	600.	700.	1050.	5750.	—	—
1865S	1,042,500	600.	700.	1125.	7150.	—	—
1866S	Inc. Below	1850.	3750.	7750.	25,000.	—	—

"Twenty D" with motto

Notes: In 1866 the motto "In God We Trust" was added to the reverse above the eagle. The 1873 "closed 3" and "open 3" varieties are known and are distinguished by the amount of space between the upper left and lower left serif in the 3 in the date.

Date	Mintage	VF-20	XF-40	AU-50	MS-60	MS-65	Prf-65
1866	698,775	685.	780.	1175.	4700.	—	—
1866S	842,250	665.	850.	1575.	11,250.	—	—
1867	251,065	625.	650.	800.	1300.	—	—
1867S	920,750	615.	650.	1500.	13,250.	—	—
1868	98,600	850.	1125.	1950.	7500.	—	—
1868S	837,500	625.	675.	975.	8450.	—	—
1869	175,155	725.	810.	875.	4950.	—	—
1869S	686,750	625.	665.	875.	3900.	—	—
1870	155,185	775.	885.	1650.	8450.	—	—
1870CC	3,789	35,000.	65,000.	80,000.	125,000.	—	—
1870S	982,000	625.	640.	835.	5200.	—	—
1871	80,150	750.	910.	1400.	3650.	—	—
1871CC	17,387	3000.	4700.	10,500.	35,000.	—	—
1871S	928,000	625.	665.	765.	3450.	—	—
1872	251,880	625.	650.	750.	2600.	—	—
1872CC	26,900	1150.	1500.	4950.	18,500.	—	—
1872S	780,000	560.	575.	615.	2750.	—	—
1873 closed 3	Est. 208,925	625.	750.	1150.	2200.	—	—
1873 open 3	Est. 1,500,900	560.	575.	615.	715.	—	—
1873CC	22,410	850.	1700.	3900.	21,500.	—	—
1873S	1,040,600	625.	650.	750.	1500.	—	—
1874	366,800	625.	650.	715.	1075.	—	—
1874CC	115,085	685.	780.	1075.	7800.	—	—
1874S	1,214,000	560.	575.	615.	1250.	—	—
1875	295,740	560.	575.	615.	715.	—	—
1875CC	111,151	665.	780.	950.	1825.	—	—
1875S	1,230,000	560.	575.	615.	715.	—	—
1876	583,905	560.	575.	615.	715.	—	—
1876CC	138,441	690.	775.	1150.	3250.	—	—
1876S	1,597,000	560.	575.	615.	715.	—	—

"Twenty Dollars"

Notes: In 1877 the denomination on the reverse was changed to read "Twenty D".

Date	Mintage	VF-20	XF-40	AU-50	MS-60	MS-65	Prf-65
1877	397,670	595.	600.	665.	700.	—	—
1877CC	42,565	730.	975.	1575.	12,500.	—	—
1877S	1,735,000	485.	595.	605.	690.	—	—
1878	543,645	585.	600.	625.	715.	—	—
1878CC	13,180	975.	1300.	3400.	18,000.	—	—
1878S	1,739,000	485.	585.	600.	690.	—	—
1879	207,630	650.	665.	685.	910.	—	—
1879CC	10,708	1050.	1650.	4500.	18,500.	—	—
1879O	2,325	3250.	4700.	13,000.	25,000.	—	—
1879S	1,223,800	485.	585.	600.	1250.	—	—
1880	51,456	485.	600.	800.	3200.	—	—
1880S	836,000	485.	625.	650.	1125.	—	—
1881	2,260	4050.	6800.	13,000.	45,000.	—	65,000.
1881S	727,000	485.	585.	650.	900.	—	—
1882	630	7800.	15,000.	24,000.	50,000.	—	75,000.
1882CC	39,140	730.	780.	1050.	6500.	—	—
1882S	1,125,000	485.	580.	600.	715.	—	—

Gold $20

Date	Mintage	VF-20	XF-40	AU-50	MS-60	MS-65	Prf-65
1883	92	—	—	—	—	—	—
1883CC	59,962	715.	775.	950.	3100.	—	—
1883S	1,189,000	485.	580.	600.	665.	—	—
1884	71		Stacks, Nov. 1989, proof, $71,500.				—
1884CC	81,139	650.	775.	975.	2600.	—	—
1884S	916,000	485.	580.	600.	650.	—	—
1885	828	7400.	9100.	11,500.	32,500.	—	—
1885CC	9,450	1025.	1600.	3800.	11,500.	—	—
1885S	683,500	485.	585.	625.	650.	—	—
1886	1,106	8800.	11,000.	20,000.	43,000.	—	65,000.
1887	121	—	—	—	—	—	65,000.
1887S	283,000	485.	585.	615.	750.	—	—
1888	226,266	485.	575.	600.	675.	—	—
1888S	859,600	485.	490.	510.	650.	—	—
1889	44,111	575.	600.	625.	750.	—	78,000.
1889CC	30,945	795.	875.	1300.	3900.	—	—
1889S	774,700	485.	490.	510.	665.	—	—
1890	75,995	540.	550.	560.	665.	—	—
1890CC	91,209	675.	775.	1050.	2600.	—	—
1890S	802,750	485.	490.	510.	665.	—	—
1891	1,442	3600.	5500.	8250.	27,000.	—	—
1891CC	5,000	1900.	2900.	5500.	14,000.	—	—
1891S	1,288,125	485.	490.	510.	535.	—	—
1892	4,523	1200.	1600.	2900.	5900.	—	—
1892CC	27,265	745.	810.	1250.	2900.	—	—
1892S	930,150	485.	490.	510.	535.	—	—
1893	344,339	485.	490.	510.	535.	—	—
1893CC	18,402	815.	875.	1175.	2100.	—	—
1893S	996,175	485.	490.	510.	535.	—	—
1894	1,368,990	485.	490.	510.	535.	—	67,500.
1894S	1,048,550	485.	490.	510.	535.	—	—
1895	1,114,656	485.	490.	510.	535.	—	—
1895S	1,143,500	485.	490.	510.	535.	7200.	—
1896	792,663	485.	490.	510.	535.	—	67,500.
1896S	1,403,925	485.	490.	510.	535.	—	—
1897	1,383,261	485.	490.	510.	535.	—	67,500.
1897S	1,470,250	485.	490.	510.	535.	—	—
1898	170,470	485.	490.	510.	650.	—	67,500.
1898S	2,575,175	485.	490.	510.	535.	7800.	—
1899	1,669,384	485.	490.	510.	535.	7800.	67,500.
1899S	2,010,300	485.	490.	510.	535.	—	—
1900	1,874,584	485.	490.	510.	535.	7100.	67,500.
1900S	2,459,500	485.	490.	510.	535.	7200.	—

NOTE: Later dates (1901-1907) exist for this type.

Commemoratives

Date	Event	Mintage	AU-50	MS-60	MS-63	MS-64	MS-65
1893	Isabella (25¢)	24,214	215.	230.	485.	900.	2650.

Date	Event	Mintage	AU-50	MS-60	MS-63	MS-64	MS-65
1892	Columbian Expo	950,000	12.00	24.00	80.00	135.	610.
1893	Columbian Expo	1,550,405	12.00	24.00	75.00	110.	670.

Date	Event	Mintage	AU-50	MS-60	MS-63	MS-64	MS-65
1900	Lafayette ($1)	36,026	270.	500.	1200.	2350.	8000.

HAWAII

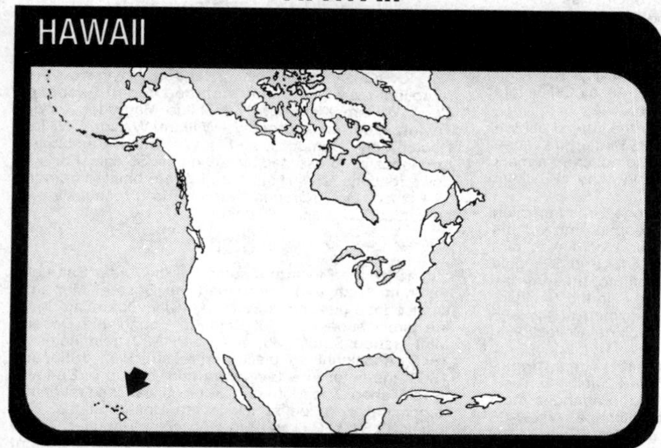

Hawaii, the 50th state, consists of eight main islands and numerous smaller islets of coral and volcanic origin. Situated in the central Pacific Ocean 2,400 miles from San Francisco, the Hawaiian archipelago has an area of 6,450 sq. mi. and a population 1,083,000. Capitol: Honolulu. The principal sources of income are, in order: tourism, defense, and agriculture.

The islands, originally populated by Polynesians from the Society Islands, were rediscovered by British navigator Capt. James Cook in 1778. He named them the Sandwich Islands. King Kamehameha I (the Great) united the islands under one kingdom which endured until 1893, when Queen Liliuokalani was deposed and a provisional government established. This was followed in 1894 by a republic which governed Hawaii until 1898, when the islands were ceded to the United States. Hawaii was organized as a territory in 1900, and attained statehood on August 21, 1959.

RULERS

Kamehameha I, 1795-1819
Kamehameha II, 1819-24
Kamehameha III, 1825-54
Kamehameha IV, 1854-63
Kamehameha V, 1863-72
Lunalilo, 1873-74
Kalakaua, 1874-91
Liliuokalani, 1891-93
Provisional Govt., 1893-94
Republic, 1894-98
Annexed to U.S., 1898-1900
Territory, 1900-59

MONETARY SYSTEM

100 Hapa Haneri — Akahi Dala
100 Cents — 1 Dollar (Dala)

CENT

COPPER

KM#	Date	Mintage	VG	Fine	VF	XF	AU	MS-60	MS-65
1a	1847 plain 4, 13 berries (6 left, 7 right)								
		.100	150.00	225.00	275.00	425.00	550.00	800.00	2500.
1b	1847 plain 4, 15 berries (8 left, 7 right)								
		Inc. Ab.	175.00	250.00	325.00	425.00	600.00	950.00	2500.
1f	1847 plain 4, 15 berries (7 left, 8 right)								
		Inc. Ab.	175.00	250.00	325.00	425.00	600.00	950.00	2500.
1c	1847 plain 4, 17 berries (8 left, 9 right)								
		Inc. Ab.	175.00	250.00	325.00	550.00	800.00	1200.	3000.
1d	1847 crosslet 4, 15 berries (7 left, 8 right)								
		Inc. Ab.	150.00	225.00	300.00	425.00	600.00	900.00	2500.
1e	1847 crosslet 4, 18 berries (9 left, 9 right)								
		Inc. Ab.	225.00	325.00	400.00	650.00	1200.	2000.	4500.

SOUVENIR CENT

Modern replicas of the 1847 cent have been produced in several varieties, struck of brass oroide since the late 1940's for sale to tourists as souvenirs of their visits to the islands.

10 CENTS (UMI KENETA)

2.5000 g, .900 SILVER, .0724 oz ASW

KM#	Date	Mintage	VG	Fine	VF	XF	AU	MS-60	MS-65
3	1883	.250	35.00	45.00	80.00	250.00	550.00	1000.	3000.
	1883	26 pcs.	—	—	—	—	Proof	7500.	15,000.

1/4 DOLLAR (HAPAHA)

6.2200 g, .900 SILVER, .1800 oz ASW

KM#	Date	Mintage	VG	Fine	VF	XF	AU	MS-60	MS-65
5	1883	.500	35.00	45.00	60.00	90.00	150.00	225.00	550.00
	1883/1383								
		Inc. Ab.	40.00	50.00	60.00	100.00	175.00	250.00	600.00
	1883	26 pcs.	—	—	—	—	Proof	7500.	15,000.

COPPER

KM#	Date	Mintage	VG	Fine	VF	XF	AU	MS-60	MS-65
5a	1883	18 pcs.	—	—	—	—	Proof	4500.	9000.

1/2 DOLLAR (HAPALUA)

12.5000 g, .900 SILVER, .3618 oz ASW

KM#	Date	Mintage	VG	Fine	VF	XF	AU	MS-60	MS-65
6	1883	.700	50.00	65.00	100.00	250.00	500.00	900.00	4500.
	1883	26 pcs.	—	—	—	—	Proof	8500.	20,000.

COPPER

KM#	Date	Mintage	VG	Fine	VF	XF	AU	MS-60	MS-65
6a	1883	18 pcs.	—	—	—	—	Proof	5000.	10,000.

DOLLAR (AKAHI DALA)

26.7300 g, .900 SILVER, .7736 oz ASW

KM#	Date	Mintage	VG	Fine	VF	XF	AU	MS-60	MS-65
7	1883	.500	170.00	250.00	300.00	600.00	1500.	5000.	15,000.
	1883	26 pcs.	—	—	—	—	Proof	10,000.	30,000.

COPPER

KM#	Date	Mintage	VG	Fine	VF	XF	AU	MS-60	MS-65
7a	1883	18 pcs.	—	—	—	—	Proof	9000.	15,000.

NOTE: Official records indicate the following quantities of the above issues were redeemed and melted: KM#1, 88,305; KM#3, 79; KM#5, 257,400; KM#6, 612,245; KM#7, 453,652. That leaves approximate net mintages of: KM#1, 11,600; KM#3, 250,000; KM#5, (regular date) 202,600, (overdate) 40,000; KM#6, 87,700; KM#7, 46,300.

TERRITORIAL GOLD

Territorial gold pieces (also referred to as "Private" and "Pioneer" gold) are those struck outside the U.S. Mint and not recognized as official issues by the federal government. The pieces so identified are of various shapes, denominations, and degrees of intrinsic value, and were locally required because of the remoteness of the early gold fields from a federal mint and/or an insufficient quantity of official coinage in frontier areas.

The legality of these privately issued pieces derives from the fact that federal law prior to 1864 prohibited a state from coining money, but did not specifically deny that right to an individual, providing that the privately issued coins did not closely resemble those of the United States.

In addition to coin-like gold pieces, the private minters of the gold rush days also issued gold in ingot and bar form. Ingots were intended for circulation and were cast in regular values and generally in large denominations. Bars represent a miner's deposit after it had been assayed, refined, cast into convenient form (generally rectangular), and stamped with the appropriate weight, fineness, and value. Although occasionally cast in even values for the convenience of banks, bars were more often of odd denomination, and when circulated were rounded off to the nearest figure. Ingots and bars are omitted from this listing.

Georgia and North Carolina

The first territorial gold pieces were struck in 1830 by **Templeton Reid**, a goldsmith and assayer who established a private mint at Gainesville, Georgia, at the time gold was being mined on a relatively large scale in Georgia and North Carolina. Reid's pieces were issued in denominations of $2.50, $5, and $10. Except for an undated variety of the $10 piece, all are dated 1830.

The southern Appalachians were also the scene of a private gold minting operation conducted by Christopher Bechtler Sr., his son August, and nephew Christopher Jr. The Bechtlers, a family of German metallurgists, established a mint at Rutherfordton, North Carolina, which produced territorial gold coins for a longer period than any other private mint in American history. Christopher Bechtler Sr. ran the Bechtler mint from July 1831 until his death in 1842, after which the mint was taken over by his son August who ran it until 1852.

The Bechtler coinage includes but 3 denominations -$1, $2.50, and $5 -but they were issued in a wide variety of weights and sizes. The coinage is undated, except for 3 varieties of the $5 piece which carry the inscription "Aug. 1, 1834" to indicate that they conform to the new weight standard adopted by the U.S. Treasury for official gold coins. **Christopher Bechtler Sr.** produced $2.50 and $5 gold coins for Georgia, and $1, $2.50, and $5 coins for North Carolina. The dollar coins have the distinction of being the first gold coins of that denomination to be produced in the United States. While under the supervision of **August Bechtler**, the Bechtler mint issued $1 and $5 coins for North Carolina.

California

Norris, Grieg & Norris produced the first territorial gold coin struck in California, a $5 piece struck in 1849 at Benicia City, though it bears the imprint of San Francisco. The coining facility was owned by Thomas H. Norris, Charles Greig, and Hiram A. Norris, members of a New York engineering firm. A unique 1850 variety of this coin has the name STOCKTON beneath the date, instead of SAN FRANCISCO.

Early in 1849, John Little Moffat, a New York assayer, established an assay office at San Francisco in association with Joseph R. Curtis, Philo H. Perry, and Samuel Ward. The first issues of the **Moffat & Co.** assay office consisted of rectangular $16 ingots and assay bars of various and irregular denominations. In early August, the firm began striking $5 and $10 gold coins which resemble those of the U.S. Mint in design, but carry the legend S.M.V. (Standard Mint Value) CALIFORNIA GOLD on the reverse. Five-dollar pieces of the same design were also issued in 1850.

On Sept. 30, 1850, Congress directed the Secretary of the Treasury to establish an official Assay Office in California. Moffat & Co. obtained a contract to perform the duties of the U.S. Assay Office. **Augustus Humbert**, a New York watchcase maker, was appointed U.S. Assayer of Gold in California. Humbert stamped the first octagonal coin-ingots of the Provisional Government Mint on Jan. 31, 1851. The $50 pieces were accepted at par with standard U.S. gold coins, but were not officially recognized as coins. Officially, they were designated as "ingots." Colloquially, they were known as slugs, quintuple eagles, or 5-eagle pieces.

The $50 ingots failed to alleviate the need of California for gold coins. The banks regarded them as disadvantageous to their interests and utilized them only when compelled to do so by public need or convenience. Being of sound value, the ingots drove the overvalued $5, $10, and $20 territorial gold coins from circulation, bringing about a return to the use of gold dust for everyday transactions. Eventually, the slugs became so great a nuisance that they were discounted 3 percent when accepted. This unexpected turn of events forced Moffat & Co. to resume the issuing of $10 and $20 gold coins in 1852. The $10 piece was first issued with the Moffat & Co. imprint on Liberty's coronet, and later with the official imprint of Augustus Humbert on reverse. The $20 piece was issued with the Humbert imprint.

On Feb. 14, 1852, John L. Moffat withdrew from Moffat & Co. to enter the diving bell business, and Moffat & Co. was reorganized as the **United States Assay Office of Gold**, composed of Joseph R. Curtis, Philo H. Perry, and Samuel Ward. The U.S. Assay Office of Gold issued gold coins in denominations of $50 and $10 in 1852, and $20 and $10 in 1853. With the exception of the $50 slugs, they carry the imprint of the Assay Office on reverse. The .900 fine issues of this facility reflect an attempt to bring the issues of the U.S. Assay Office into conformity with the U.S. Mint standard.

The last territorial gold coins to bear the imprint of Moffat & Co. are $20 pieces issued in 1853, after the retirement of John L. Moffat. These coins do not carry a mark of fineness, and generally assay below the U.S. Mint standard.

Templeton Reid, previously mentioned in connection with the private gold issues of Georgia, moved his coining equipment to California when gold was discovered there, and in 1849 issued $10 and $25 gold pieces. No specimens are available to present-day collectors. The only known $10 piece is in the Smithsonian Collection. The only known specimen of the $25 piece was stolen from the U.S. Mint Cabinet Collection in 1858 and was never recovered.

Little is known of the origin and location of the **Cincinnati Mining & Trading Co.** It is believed that the firm was organized in the East and was forced to abandon most of its equipment while enroute to California. A few $5 and $10 gold coins were struck in 1849. Base metal counterfeits exist.

The **Massachusetts & California Co.** was organized in Northampton, Mass., in May 1849 by Josiah Hayden, S. S. Wells, Miles G. Moies, and others. Coining equipment was taken to San Francisco where $5 gold pieces were struck in 1849. The few pieces extant are heavily alloyed with copper.

Wright & Co., a brokerage firm located in Portsmouth Square, San Francisco, issued an undated $10 gold piece in the autumn of 1849 under the name of **Miners' Bank**. Unlike most territorial gold pieces, the Miners' Bank eagle was alloyed with copper. The coinage proved to be unpopular because of its copper-induced color and low intrinsic value. The firm was dissolved on Jan. 14, 1850.

In 1849, Dr. **J. S. Ormsby** and Major William M. Ormsby struck gold coins of $5 and $10 denominations at Sacramento under the name of Ormsby & Co. The coinage, which is identified by the initials J. S. O., is undated. Ormsby & Co. coinage was greatly over-valued, the eagle assaying at as little as $9.37.

The **Pacific Co.** of San Francisco issued $5 and $10 gold coins in 1849. The clouded story of this coinage is based on conjecture. It is believed that the well-struck pattern coins of this type were struck in the East by the Pacific Co. that organized in Boston and set sail for California on Feb. 20, 1849, and that the crudely hand-struck pieces were made by the jewelry firm of Broderick and Kohler after the dies passed into their possession. In any event, the intrinsic value of the initial coinage exceeded face value, but by the end of 1849, when they passed out of favor, the coins had been debased so flagrantly that the eagles assayed for for as little as $7.86.

Dubosq & Co., a Philadelphia jewelry firm owned by Theodore Dubosq Sr. and Jr. and Henry Dubosq, took melting and coining equipment to San Francisco in 1849, and in 1850 issued $5 and $10 gold coins struck with dies allegedly made by U.S. Mint Engraver James B. Longacre. Dubosq & Co. coinage was immensely popular with the forty-niners because its intrinsic worth was in excess of face value.

The minting equipment of David C. Broderick and Frederick D. Kohler (see Pacific Co.) was acquired in May 1850 by San Francisco jewelers George C. Baldwin and Thomas S. Holman, who organized a private minting venture under the name of **Baldwin & Co**. The firm produced a $5 piece of Liberty Head design and a $10 piece with Horseman device in 1850. Liberty Head $10 and $20 pieces were coined in 1851. Baldwin & Co. produced the first $20 piece issued in California.

Schultz & Co. of San Francisco, a brass foundry located in the rear of the Baldwin & Co. establishment, and operated by Judge G. W. Schultz and William T. Garratt, issued $5 gold coins from early 1851 until April of that year. The inscription "SHULTS & CO." is a misspelling of SCHULTZ & CO.

Dunbar & Co. of San Francisco issued a $5 gold piece in 1851, after Edward E. Dunbar, owner of the California Bank in San Francisco, purchased the coining equipment of the defunct Baldwin & Co.

The San Francisco-based firm of **Wass, Molitor & Co.** was owned by 2 Hungarian exiles, Count S. C. Wass and A. P. Molitor, who initially founded the firm as a gold smelting and assaying plant. In response to a plea from the commercial community for small gold coins, Wass, Molitor & Co. issued $5 and $10 gold coins in 1852. The $5 piece was coined with small head and large head varieties, and the $10 piece with small head, large head, and small close-date varieties. The firm produced a second issue of gold coins in 1855, in denominations of $10, $20, and $50.

The U.S. Assay Office in California closed its doors on Dec. 14, 1853, to make way for the newly established San Francisco Branch Mint. The Mint, however, was unable to start immediate quantity production due to the lack of refining acids. During the interim, John G. Kellogg, a former employee of Moffat & Co., and John Glover Richter, a former assayer in the U.S. Assay Office, formed **Kellogg & Co.** for the purpose of supplying businessmen with urgently needed coinage. The firm produced $20 coins dated 1854 and 1855, after which Augustus Humbert replaced Richter and the enterprise reorganized as Kellogg & Humbert Melters, Assayers & Coiners. Kellogg & Humbert endured until 1860, but issued coins, $20 pieces, only in 1855.

Oregon

The Oregon Exchange Co., a private mint located at Oregon City, Oregon Territory, issued $5 and $10 pieces of local gold in 1849. The initials K., M., T., A., W. R. C. (G on the $5 piece), and S. on the obverse represent the eight founders of the **Oregon Exchange Co.** : William Kilborne, Theophilus Magruder, James Taylor, George Abernathy, William Willson, William Rector, John Campbell, and Noyes Smith. Campbell is erroneously represented by a G on the $5 coin. For unknown reasons, the initials A and W are omitted from the $10 piece. O.T. (Oregon Territory) is erroneously presented as T.O. on the $5 coin.

Utah

In 1849, the **Mormons** settled in the Great Salt Lake Valley of Utah and established the Deseret Mint in a small adobe building in Salt Lake City. Operating under the direct supervision of Brigham Young, the Deseret Mint issued $2.50, $5, $10, and $20 gold coins in 1849. Additional $5 pieces were struck in 1850 and 1860, the latter in a temporary mint set up in Barlow's jewelry shop. The Mormon $20 piece was the first of that denomination to be struck in the United States. The initials G.S.L.C.P.G. on Mormon coins denotes "Great Salt Lake City Pure Gold." It was later determined that the coinage was grossly deficient in value, mainly because no attempt was made to assay or refine the gold.

Colorado

The discovery of gold in Colorado Territory was accompanied by the inevitable need for coined money. Austin M. Clark, Milton E. Clark, and Emanuel H. Gruber, bankers of Leavenworth, Kansas, moved to Denver where they established a bank and issued $2.50, $5, $10, and $20 gold coins in 1860 and 1861. To protect the holder from loss by abrasion, **Clark, Gruber & Co.** made their coins slightly heavier than full value required. The 1860 issues carry the inscription PIKE'S PEAK GOLD on reverse. CLARK, GRUBER & CO. appears on the reverse of the 1861 issues, and PIKE'S PEAK on the coronet of Liberty. The government purchased the plant of Clark, Gruber & Co. in 1863 and operated it as a federal Assay Office until 1906.

In the summer of 1861, **John Parsons**, an assayer whose place of business was located in South Park at the Tarryall Mines, Colorado, issued undated gold coins in the denominations of $2.50 and $5. They, too, carry the inscription PIKE'S PEAK GOLD on reverse.

J. J. Conway & Co., bankers of Georgia Gulch, Colorado operated the Conway Mint for a short period in 1861. Undated gold coins in the denominations of $2.50, $5, and $10 were issued. A variety of the $5 coin does not carry the numeral 5 on reverse. The issues of the Conway Mint were highly regarded for their scrupulously maintained value.

NOTE: The above introduction is organized chronologically by geographical region. However, for ease of use the following listings appear alphabetically by state and issuer, except for small California gold.

Small California Gold

During the California gold rush, a wide variety of U.S. and foreign coins was used for small change, but their number was extremely limited. More common was the use of gold dust, though this offered the miner relatively low value for his gold.

By 1852 California jewelers had begun to manufacture 25¢, 50¢ and $1 gold pieces in round and octagonal shapes. Makers included Antonio Louis Nouizillet, Isadore Routhier, Robert B. Gray, Pierre Frontier, Eugene Diviercy, Herman J. Brand, and Herman and Jacob Levison. Reuben N. Hershfield and Noah Mitchell made their coins in Leavenworth, Kansas and most of their production was seized in August 1871. M. Deriberpie was an engraver who cut dies for Nouizillet. Only two or three of these companies were in production at any one time. Many varieties bear the maker's initials. In general, the large Liberty Head types, Eagle reverses and Washington Head types were made by Frontier and his partners. The small Liberty Head types were generally made by Nouizillet and later by Gray and then the Levison brothers and the California Jewelry Co. Coins initialed "G.G." are apparently patterns made by Frontier and Diviercy for the New York firm of Gaime, Guillemot & Co., that never went into production.

The gold rush era coins were generally struck from unrefined native gold-silver alloy. Some were hand struck from hand engraved dies. Others were pressed from high quality hubbed dies into reeded collars. After establishment of the San Francisco Mint in 1854, private coinage gradually died out. By 1857-1858, almost no private gold coins were being made. Production resumed, however, in 1859 as the small denomination gold pieces proved popular as souvenirs and for use in jewelry. By then intrinsic value was generally ignored. Planchets were thinner and were often low-grade surfaced with pure gold. New designs such as the Indian Heads were introduced and the use of polished dies to impart proof-like surfaces became common.

Though all private coinage was outlawed by the Private Coinages Act of 1864, this law was unenforced in California and production of small denominated gold continued through 1882. In the spring of 1883, Col. Henry Finnegass of the U.S. Secret Service halted production of the private gold pieces. Undenominated tokens (lacking DOLLARS, CENTS or the equivalent on reverse) were also made during this latter period, sometimes by the same manufacturing jeweler using the same obverse die as the small denomination gold coins.

Approximately 15,000 pieces of California small denomination gold are estimated to exist, in a total of 500 varieties. A few varieties are undated, mostly gold rush era pieces; and a few are back-dated. Major varieties are listed here. Individual listings may consist of several varieties; prices quoted are for the most common variety. True MS-65 coins are rare and bring substantial premiums. Walter Breen has established that Period One pieces (1852-1856) were "circulating issues", unlike those made 1859-1882 or later which were souvenirs or jewelry pieces. Public awareness to these differences will no doubt eventually place premium values on Period One coins. For further information consult W. Breen and R.J. Gillio CALIFORNIA PIONEER FRACTIONAL GOLD, 1983.

1/4 DOLLAR - OCTAGONAL

Obv: Large Liberty head.
Rev: Value and date within beaded circle.

KM#	Date	XF	AU	Unc	BU
1.1	1853	65.00	110.00	200.00	250.00
	1854	65.00	110.00	200.00	250.00
	1855	65.00	110.00	200.00	250.00
	1856	65.00	110.00	200.00	250.00

Rev: Value and date within wreath.

KM#	Date	XF	AU	Unc	BU
1.2	1859	65.00	110.00	200.00	250.00
	1864	75.00	125.00	240.00	350.00
	1866	75.00	125.00	240.00	350.00
	1867	65.00	110.00	200.00	250.00
	1868	70.00	125.00	240.00	350.00
	1869	70.00	125.00	240.00	350.00
	1870	65.00	110.00	200.00	250.00
	1871	65.00	110.00	200.00	250.00

Obv: Large Liberty head above date.
Rev: Value and CAL within wreath.

KM#	Date	XF	AU	Unc	BU
1.3	1872	65.00	110.00	200.00	250.00
	1873	50.00	85.00	160.00	200.00

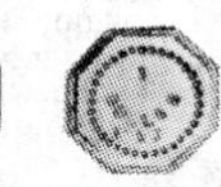

Obv: Small Liberty head.
Rev: Value and date within beaded circle.

KM#	Date	XF	AU	Unc	BU
1.4	1853	75.00	125.00	240.00	350.00

Obv: Small Liberty head above date.
Rev: Value within wreath.

KM#	Date	XF	AU	Unc	BU
1.5	1854	65.00	110.00	200.00	250.00

Obv: Small Liberty head.
Rev: Value and date within wreath.

KM#	Date	XF	AU	Unc	BU
1.6	1855	75.00	125.00	240.00	350.00
	1856	55.00	90.00	175.00	235.00
	1857*	50.00	85.00	160.00	200.00
	1860	65.00	110.00	200.00	250.00
	1870	65.00	115.00	210.00	300.00

*All are Kroll counterfeits or restrikes of Kroll counterfeits.

 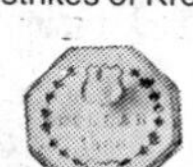

Rev: Value in shield and date within wreath.

KM#	Date	XF	AU	Unc	BU
1.7	1863	65.00	110.00	210.00	300.00
	1864	65.00	110.00	210.00	300.00
	1865/4	85.00	145.00	285.00	400.00
	1866	85.00	145.00	285.00	400.00
	1867	75.00	125.00	240.00	350.00
	1868	75.00	125.00	240.00	350.00
	1869	75.00	125.00	240.00	350.00
	1870	75.00	125.00	240.00	350.00

 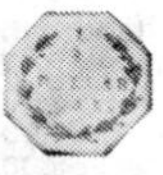

Obv: Small Liberty head above date.
Rev: Value and CAL within wreath.

KM#	Date	XF	AU	Unc	BU
1.8	1870	65.00	110.00	200.00	250.00
1.8	1871	65.00	110.00	200.00	250.00
	1873	75.00	125.00	240.00	350.00
	1874	65.00	110.00	200.00	275.00
	1875/3	75.00	125.00	240.00	350.00
	1876	65.00	110.00	200.00	275.00

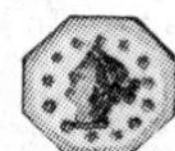 

Obv: Goofy Liberty head.
Rev: Value and date within wreath.

KM#	Date	XF	AU	Unc	BU
1.9	1870	85.00	145.00	285.00	400.00

Obv: Oriental Liberty head above date.
Rev: 1/4 CALDOLL within wreath.

KM#	Date	XF	AU	Unc	BU
1.10	1881	275.00	500.00	800.00	1150.

Obv: Large Liberty head above 1872.
Rev: Value and 1871 within wreath.

KM#	Date	XF	AU	Unc	BU
1.11	1872-71	600.00	1000.	1750.	2150.

Obv: Large Indian head above date.
Rev: Value within wreath.

KM#	Date	XF	AU	Unc	BU
2.1	1852*	125.00	225.00	375.00	500.00
	1868	145.00	260.00	425.00	600.00
	1874	135.00	240.00	400.00	550.00
	1876	125.00	225.00	375.00	500.00
	1880	75.00	125.00	240.00	350.00
	1881	75.00	125.00	240.00	350.00

*This is a back dated issue.

Rev: Value and CAL within wreath.

KM#	Date	XF	AU	Unc	BU
2.2	1872	65.00	110.00	210.00	300.00
	1873	100.00	180.00	300.00	425.00
	1874	65.00	110.00	210.00	300.00
	1875	65.00	110.00	210.00	300.00
	1876	65.00	110.00	210.00	300.00

Obv: Small Indian head above date.

KM#	Date	XF	AU	Unc	BU
2.3	1875	125.00	225.00	375.00	500.00
	1876	125.00	225.00	375.00	500.00
	1881	125.00	225.00	375.00	500.00

Obv: Aztec Indian head above date.

KM#	Date	XF	AU	Unc	BU
2.4	1880	125.00	225.00	375.00	500.00

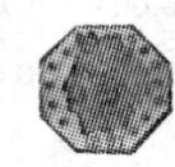 

Obv: Dumb Indian head above date.
Rev: Value and CAL within wreath.

KM#	Date	XF	AU	Unc	BU
2.6	1881	550.00	1000.	1750.	2150.

Obv: Young Indian head above date.
Rev: Value within wreath.

KM#	Date	XF	AU	Unc	BU
2.7	1881	375.00	700.00	1150.	1400.

Rev: Value and CAL within wreath.

KM#	Date	XF	AU	Unc	BU
2.8	1882	375.00	700.00	1150.	1400.

Obv: Washington head above date.

KM#	Date	XF	AU	Unc	BU
3	1872	275.00	525.00	950.00	1200.

1/4 DOLLAR - ROUND

Obv: Defiant eagle above date.
Rev: 25¢ within wreath.

KM#	Date	XF	AU	Unc	BU
4	1854	23,000.	30,000.	35,000.	45,000.

Obv: Large Liberty head.
Rev: Value and date within wreath.

KM#	Date	XF	AU	Unc	BU
5.1	1853	300.00	500.00	700.00	1000.
	1854	150.00	250.00	325.00	450.00
	1859	70.00	120.00	200.00	300.00
	1865	90.00	160.00	265.00	375.00
	1866	90.00	160.00	265.00	375.00
	1867	65.00	110.00	185.00	275.00
	1868	65.00	110.00	185.00	275.00
	1870	65.00	110.00	185.00	275.00
	1871	65.00	110.00	185.00	275.00

Obv: Large Liberty head above date.
Rev: Value and CAL within wreath.

KM#	Date	XF	AU	Unc	BU
5.2	1871	65.00	110.00	185.00	275.00
	1872	90.00	160.00	265.00	375.00
	1873	65.00	110.00	185.00	275.00

Obv: Small Liberty head.
Rev: 25¢ in wreath.

KM#	Date	XF	AU	Unc	BU
5.3	ND	1000.	1650.	2450.	3500.

Rev: 1/4 DOLL. or DOLLAR and date in wreath.

KM#	Date	XF	AU	Unc	BU
5.4	ND	90.00	150.00	200.00	275.00
	1853	350.00	600.00	750.00	1100.
	1855*	120.00	200.00	275.00	365.00
	1856	100.00	175.00	225.00	325.00
	1860	65.00	110.00	185.00	275.00
	1863/1860	250.00	450.00	650.00	1000.
	1864	100.00	180.00	265.00	350.00
	1865	65.00	110.00	185.00	275.00
	1866	125.00	210.00	285.00	400.00
	1867	65.00	110.00	185.00	275.00
	1869	65.00	110.00	185.00	275.00
	1870	125.00	210.00	285.00	400.00

*Kroll counterfeits of this date exist.

Rev: Value in shield and date within wreath.

KM#	Date	XF	AU	Unc	BU
5.5	1863	140.00	260.00	425.00	600.00

Obv: Small Liberty head above date.
Rev: Value and CAL within wreath.

KM#	Date	XF	AU	Unc	BU
5.6	ND	135.00	250.00	400.00	575.00
	1870	65.00	110.00	185.00	275.00
	1871	65.00	110.00	185.00	275.00
	1873	135.00	235.00	300.00	475.00
	1874	125.00	225.00	285.00	435.00
	1875	135.00	235.00	300.00	475.00
	1876	110.00	185.00	275.00	365.00

Obv: Goofy Liberty head.
Rev: Value and date within wreath.

KM#	Date	XF	AU	Unc	BU
5.7	1870	115.00	190.00	285.00	375.00

Obv: Liberty head with H and date below.
Rev: Value and CAL in wreath.

KM#	Date	XF	AU	Unc	BU
5.8	1871	110.00	185.00	275.00	365.00

Obv: Large Indian head above date.
Rev: Value within wreath.

KM#	Date	XF	AU	Unc	BU
6.1	1852*	130.00	220.00	400.00	600.00
	1868	140.00	250.00	425.00	650.00
	1874	140.00	250.00	425.00	650.00
	1876	60.00	100.00	200.00	300.00
	1880	60.00	100.00	200.00	300.00
	1881	60.00	100.00	200.00	300.00

*This is a back dated issue.

Rev: Value and CAL within wreath.

KM#	Date	XF	AU	Unc	BU
6.2	1872	65.00	110.00	220.00	350.00
	1873	100.00	185.00	375.00	575.00
	1874	65.00	110.00	220.00	350.00
	1875	60.00	100.00	200.00	300.00
	1876	65.00	110.00	220.00	350.00

Obv: Small Indian head above date.

KM#	Date	XF	AU	Unc	BU
6.3	1875	65.00	110.00	220.00	350.00
	1876	130.00	220.00	400.00	600.00

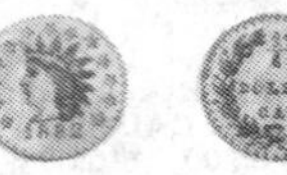

Obv: Young Indian head above date.

KM#	Date	XF	AU	Unc	BU
6.4	1882	400.00	725.00	1225.	1750.

Obv: Washington head above date.

KM#	Date	XF	AU	Unc	BU
7	1872	285.00	525.00	875.00	1250.

1/2 DOLLAR - OCTAGONAL

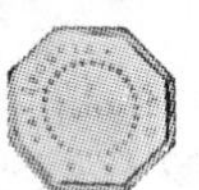

Obv: Liberty head above date.
Rev: 1/2 DOLLAR in beaded circle.
CALIFORNIA GOLD around circle.

KM#	Date	XF	AU	Unc	BU
8.1	1853	165.00	280.00	350.00	425.00
	1854	110.00	225.00	285.00	350.00
	1856	165.00	285.00	365.00	425.00

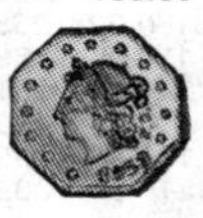

Rev: Small eagle with rays ("peacock").

KM#	Date	XF	AU	Unc	BU
8.2	1853	475.00	875.00	1450.	—

Obv: Large Liberty head.
Rev: Large eagle with date.

KM#	Date	XF	AU	Unc	BU
8.3	1853	750.00	1350.	2250.	—

Rev: Value and date within wreath.

KM#	Date	XF	AU	Unc	BU
8.4	1859	90.00	200.00	265.00	325.00
	1866	110.00	225.00	285.00	350.00
	1867	110.00	225.00	285.00	350.00
	1868	110.00	225.00	285.00	350.00
	1869	110.00	225.00	285.00	350.00
	1870	110.00	225.00	285.00	350.00
	1871	65.00	115.00	200.00	300.00

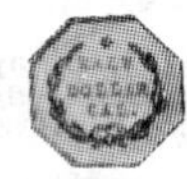

Obv: Large Liberty head above date.
Rev: Value and CAL within wreath.

KM#	Date	XF	AU	Unc	BU
8.5	1872	60.00	110.00	185.00	275.00
	1873	60.00	110.00	185.00	275.00

Obv: Liberty head.
Rev: Date in wreath, HALF DOL. CALIFORNIA GOLD around wreath.

KM#	Date	XF	AU	Unc	BU
8.6	1854	110.00	225.00	285.00	350.00
	1855	165.00	280.00	350.00	425.00
	1856*	110.00	225.00	285.00	350.00
	1868**	60.00	110.00	185.00	275.00

*Some back dated pieces were struck in 1864.
**All are Kroll counterfeits.

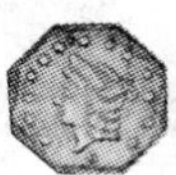
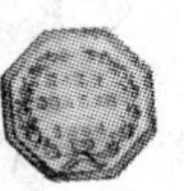

Obv: Small Liberty head.
Rev: HALF DOLLAR and date in wreath.

KM#	Date	XF	AU	Unc	BU
8.7	1864	60.00	110.00	185.00	275.00
	1870	110.00	225.00	285.00	350.00

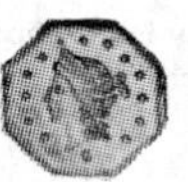

Rev: CAL.GOLD HALF DOL and date in wreath.

KM#	Date	XF	AU	Unc	BU
8.8	1869	60.00	110.00	185.00	275.00
	1870	60.00	110.00	185.00	275.00

Obv: Small Liberty head above date.
Rev: Value and CAL in wreath.

KM#	Date	XF	AU	Unc	BU
8.9	1870	55.00	110.00	185.00	275.00
	1871	55.00	110.00	185.00	275.00
	1873	110.00	225.00	285.00	350.00
	1874	110.00	225.00	285.00	350.00
	1875	250.00	475.00	800.00	1150.
	1876	110.00	225.00	285.00	350.00

Obv: Goofy Liberty head.
Rev: Value and date within wreath.

KM#	Date	XF	AU	Unc	BU
8.10	1870	100.00	200.00	285.00	350.00

Obv: Oriental Liberty head above date.
Rev: 1/2 CALDOLL within wreath.

KM#	Date	XF	AU	Unc	BU
8.11	1881	275.00	500.00	900.00	1250.

Obv: Large Indian head above date.
Rev: Value within wreath.

KM#	Date	XF	AU	Unc	BU
9.1	1852*	400.00	560.00	925.00	—
	1868	300.00	500.00	850.00	—
	1874	300.00	500.00	850.00	—
	1876	250.00	450.00	750.00	1000.
	1880	90.00	165.00	275.00	450.00
	1881	300.00	500.00	850.00	—

*This is a back dated issue.

Rev: Value and CAL within wreath.

KM#	Date	XF	AU	Unc	BU
9.2	1852*	200.00	300.00	500.00	800.00
	1868	200.00	300.00	500.00	800.00
	1872	90.00	165.00	275.00	450.00
	1873	100.00	200.00	325.00	525.00
	1874/3	90.00	165.00	275.00	450.00
	1874	115.00	210.00	350.00	550.00
	1875	90.00	165.00	275.00	450.00
	1876	90.00	165.00	275.00	450.00
	1878	115.00	210.00	350.00	550.00
	1880	115.00	210.00	350.00	550.00
	1881	115.00	210.00	350.00	550.00

*This is a back dated issue.

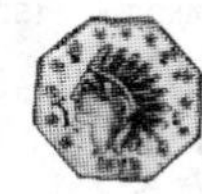

Obv: Small Indian head above date.

KM#	Date	XF	AU	Unc	BU
9.3	1875	200.00	300.00	500.00	800.00
	1876	200.00	300.00	500.00	800.00

Obv: Young Indian head above date.

KM#	Date	XF	AU	Unc	BU
9.4	1881	250.00	400.00	600.00	900.00
	1882	400.00	550.00	850.00	—

1/2 DOLLAR - ROUND

Obv: Arms of California and date.
Rev: Eagle and legends.

KM#	Date	XF	AU	Unc	BU
10	1853	1250.	2750.	6800.	—

Obv: Liberty head.
Rev: Large eagle and legends.

KM#	Date	XF	AU	Unc	BU
11.1	1854	1000.	2250.	6000.	—

Obv: Liberty head and date.
Rev: HALF DOL. CALIFORNIA GOLD around wreath.

KM#	Date	XF	AU	Unc	BU
11.2	1854	175.00	210.00	325.00	500.00

Obv: Liberty head.
Rev: Date in wreath. Value and CALIFORNIA GOLD around wreath.

KM#	Date	XF	AU	Unc	BU
11.3	1852	145.00	180.00	275.00	400.00
	1853	85.00	120.00	250.00	335.00
	1854*	350.00	450.00	750.00	1000.
	1855	175.00	210.00	325.00	500.00
	1856	125.00	180.00	275.00	400.00
	1860	125.00	180.00	275.00	400.00

*Beware of Kroll type counterfeits & restrikes which are worth only about 1/3 of originals.

Rev: Small eagle and legends.

KM#	Date	XF	AU	Unc	BU
11.4	1853	2000.	4000.	6500.	—

Rev: Value in wreath. CALIFORNIA GOLD and date around wreath.

KM#	Date	XF	AU	Unc	BU
11.5	1853	220.00	400.00	650.00	1100.

Rev: Value and date within wreath.

KM#	Date	XF	AU	Unc	BU
11.6	1854	550.00	850.00	1500.	—
	1855	155.00	210.00	325.00	475.00
	1859	115.00	165.00	250.00	350.00
	1865	150.00	250.00	450.00	750.00
	1866	150.00	250.00	450.00	750.00
	1867	125.00	180.00	275.00	400.00
	1868	125.00	180.00	275.00	400.00
	1869	150.00	250.00	450.00	750.00
	1870	115.00	165.00	250.00	350.00
	1871	115.00	165.00	250.00	350.00
	1873	150.00	250.00	450.00	750.00

Obv: Liberty head above date.
Rev: Value and CAL within wreath.

KM#	Date	XF	AU	Unc	BU
11.7	1870	100.00	150.00	225.00	325.00
	1871	100.00	150.00	225.00	325.00
	1872	150.00	250.00	450.00	750.00
	1873	125.00	185.00	300.00	450.00
	1874	125.00	180.00	275.00	400.00
	1875	125.00	180.00	275.00	400.00
	1876	125.00	180.00	275.00	400.00

Obv: Liberty head.
Rev: Value and date within wreath. CALIFORNIA GOLD outside.

KM#	Date	XF	AU	Unc	BU
11.8	1863*	265.00	425.00	675.00	950.00

*This issue is a very rare Kroll counterfeit.

Obv: Liberty head.
Rev: HALF DOLLAR and date in wreath.

KM#	Date	XF	AU	Unc	BU
11.9	1864	100.00	165.00	250.00	350.00
	1866	—	—	Rare	—
	Superior Sale Sept. 1988 Unique Unc. $2860.				
	1867	115.00	170.00	265.00	400.00
	1868	115.00	170.00	265.00	400.00
	1869	115.00	170.00	265.00	400.00
	1870	125.00	185.00	300.00	450.00

Obv: Goofy Liberty head.
Rev: Value and date within wreath.

KM#	Date	XF	AU	Unc	BU
11.11	1870	125.00	225.00	400.00	700.00

Obv: Liberty head with H and date below.
Rev: Value and CAL within wreath.

KM#	Date	XF	AU	Unc	BU
11.12	1871	125.00	225.00	400.00	700.00

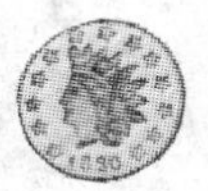

Obv: Large Indian head above date.
Rev: Value within wreath.

KM#	Date	XF	AU	Unc	BU
12.1	1852*	200.00	350.00	600.00	1200.
	1868	200.00	350.00	600.00	1200.
	1874	200.00	350.00	600.00	1200.
	1876	115.00	210.00	350.00	650.00
	1878/6	400.00	650.00	1000.	—
	1880	100.00	175.00	275.00	575.00
	1881	100.00	175.00	275.00	575.00

*This is a back dated issue.

Rev: Value and CAL within wreath.

KM#	Date	XF	AU	Unc	BU
12.2	1872	100.00	180.00	300.00	600.00
	1873	100.00	180.00	300.00	600.00
	1874/3	125.00	225.00	375.00	700.00
	1874	100.00	180.00	300.00	600.00
	1875/3	115.00	210.00	350.00	650.00
	1875	125.00	225.00	375.00	700.00
	1876/5/3	115.00	210.00	350.00	650.00
	1876	215.00	400.00	650.00	1250.

Obv: Small Indian head above date.

KM#	Date	XF	AU	Unc	BU
12.3	1875	100.00	175.00	275.00	575.00
	1876	125.00	225.00	375.00	700.00

Obv: Young Indian head above date.

KM#	Date	XF	AU	Unc	BU
12.4	1882	300.00	550.00	900.00	—

DOLLAR - OCTAGONAL

Obv: Liberty head.
Rev: Large eagle and legends.

KM#	Date	XF	AU	Unc	BU
13.1	ND	1500.	2350.	3750.	—
	1853	3000.	3500.	5500.	—
	1854	1000.	1500.	2000.	3500.

Rev: Value and date in beaded circle. CALIFORNIA GOLD initials around circle.

KM#	Date	XF	AU	Unc	BU
13.2	1853 DERI	275.00	500.00	750.00	1100.
	1853 DERIB	450.00	800.00	1100.	—
	1853 FD	350.00	650.00	900.00	—
	1853 N	275.00	500.00	750.00	1100.
	1854 DERI	450.00	800.00	1100.	—
	1854 FD	350.00	650.00	900.00	—
	1855 FD	350.00	650.00	900.00	—
	1856	2100.	3300.	5000.	—
	1863*	150.00	225.00	325.00	500.00

*All are Kroll counterfeits or restrikes of Kroll counterfeits. Restrikes have reeded edge.

Rev: Value and date inside wreath. Legends outside wreath.

KM#	Date	XF	AU	Unc	BU
13.3	1854	275.00	500.00	750.00	1100.
	1855 NR	275.00	500.00	750.00	1100.
	1858 K*	150.00	250.00	350.00	600.00
	1859 FD	1100.	1700.	2700.	—
	1860	170.00	275.00	400.00	700.00
	1868 G	240.00	375.00	525.00	850.00
	1869 G	170.00	275.00	400.00	700.00
	1870 G	300.00	450.00	650.00	1000.
	1871	300.00	450.00	650.00	1000.

*All are Kroll counterfeits.

Obv: Goofy Liberty head.
Rev: Value and date inside wreath.

KM#	Date	XF	AU	Unc	BU
13.4	1870	170.00	275.00	450.00	750.00

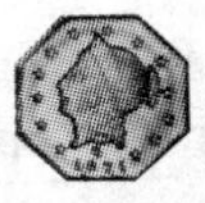

Obv: Liberty head above date.
Rev: Value and date within wreath. CALIFORNIA GOLD around wreath.

KM#	Date	XF	AU	Unc	BU
13.5	1871 G	170.00	250.00	365.00	650.00
	1874	850.00	1450.	2200.	—
	1875	850.00	1450.	2200.	—
	1876	850.00	1450.	2200.	—

Obv: Large Indian head above date.
Rev: 1 DOLLAR inside wreath. CALIFORNIA GOLD around wreath.

KM#	Date	XF	AU	Unc	BU
14.1	1872	750.00	1275.	1800.	—
	1873/2	850.00	1450.	2150.	—
	1873	500.00	750.00	1225.	2000.
	1874	350.00	450.00	775.00	1400.
	1875	350.00	450.00	775.00	1400.
	1876	350.00	450.00	775.00	1400.

Obv: Small Indian head above date.
Rev: 1 DOLLAR CAL inside wreath.

KM#	Date	XF	AU	Unc	BU
14.2	1875	750.00	1150.	1600.	—
	1876	850.00	1250.	1750.	—

Rev: 1 DOLLAR inside wreath. CALIFORNIA GOLD around wreath.

KM#	Date	XF	AU	Unc	BU
14.3	1876	800.00	1275.	2150.	—

DOLLAR - ROUND

Obv: Liberty head.
Rev: Large eagle and legends.

KM#	Date	XF	AU	Unc	BU
15.1	1853	—	—	Rare	—

Superior Sale Sept. 1987 MS63 $35,200.

Rev: Value and date inside wreath. CALIFORNIA GOLD around wreath.

KM#	Date	XF	AU	Unc	BU
15.2	1854 GL	—	—	Rare	—
	1854 FD	—	—	Rare	—
	1854	—	—	Rare	—
	Superior Sale Sept. 1988 Fine $13,200.				
	1857	—	—	Unique	—
	1870 G	800.00	1550.	2150.	—
	1871	900.00	1650.	2700.	—

Obv: Liberty head above date. Rev: Value inside wreath. CALIFORNIA GOLD around wreath.

KM#	Date	XF	AU	Unc	BU
15.3	1870 G	600.00	1400.	1950.	—
	1871 G	900.00	1650.	2700.	—

Obv: Goofy Liberty head.
Rev: Value and date inside wreath. CALIFORNIA GOLD around wreath.

KM#	Date	XF	AU	Unc	BU
15.4	1870	550.00	1100.	1600.	—

Obv: Large Indian head above date.
Rev: Value inside wreath. CALIFORNIA GOLD outside wreath.

KM#	Date	XF	AU	Unc	BU
16	1872	650.00	1450.	2150.	—

Regular Issues

CALIFORNIA

Baldwin & Company

5 DOLLARS

KM#	Date	Fine	VF	XF	Unc
17	1850	4000.	6500.	10,000.	25,000.

10 DOLLARS

KM#	Date	Fine	VF	XF	Unc
18	1850 Horseman	15,000.	27,500.	45,000.	70,000.

KM#	Date	Fine	VF	XF	Unc
19	1851	10,000.	15,500.	30,000.	—

20 DOLLARS

KM#	Date	Fine	VF	XF	Unc
20	1851	—	—	—	—

Stack's-Superior Sale Dec.1988, XF-40 $52,800.

NOTE: Beware of copies cast in base metals.

Blake & Company

20 DOLLARS

KM#	Date	Fine	VF	XF	Unc
21	1855	—	—	—	—

NOTE: Many modern copies exist.

J. H. Bowie

5 DOLLARS

KM#	Date	Fine	VF	XF	Unc
22	1849	—	—	—	—

Cincinnati Mining and Trading Company

5 DOLLARS

KM#	Date	Fine	VF	XF	Unc
23	1849	—	—	Rare	—

10 DOLLARS

KM#	Date	Fine	VF	XF	Unc
24	1849	—	—	Rare	—

Brand Sale 1984, XF $104,500.

Dubosq & Company

5 DOLLARS

KM#	Date	Fine	VF	XF	Unc
26	1850	25,000.	42,500.	Rare	—

10 DOLLARS

KM#	Date	Fine	VF	XF	Unc
27	1850	25,000.	45,000.	Rare	—

Dunbar & Company

5 DOLLARS

KM#	Date	Fine	VF	XF	Unc
28	1851	22,500.	32,500.	52,500.	—

Spink & Son Sale 1988, AU $62,000.

Augustus Humbert United States Assayer

10 DOLLARS

AUGUSTUS HUMBERT imprint

KM#	Date	Fine	VF	XF	Unc
29.1	1852/1	2000.	3500.	5500.	15,000.
	1852	1500.	2500.	4750.	11,500.

Error: IINITED.

KM#	Date	Fine	VF	XF	Unc
29.2	1852/1	—	—	Rare	—
	1852	—	—	Rare	—

20 DOLLARS

KM#	Date	Fine	VF	XF	Unc
30	1852/1	4500.	6000.	9500.	—

Garrett Sale Mar. 1980, Humberts Proof $325,000.
Private Sale May 1989, Humberts Proof (PCGS Pr-65) $1,350,000.

50 DOLLARS

Obv: 50 D C 880 THOUS, eagle.
Edge: Lettered. Rev: 50 in center.

KM#	Date	Fine	VF	XF	Unc
31.1	1851	9500.	12,000.	22,000.	—

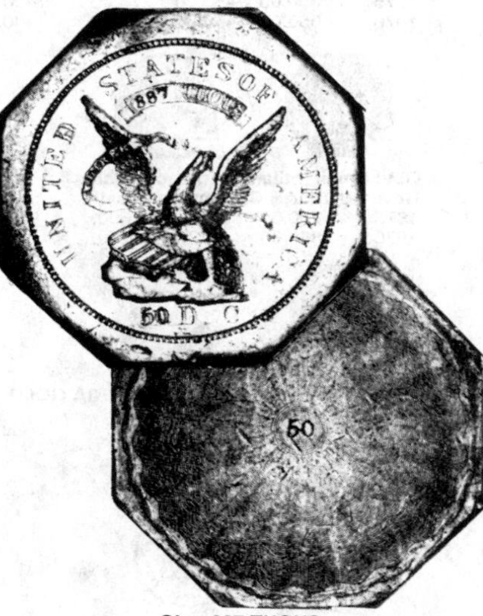

Obv: 887 THOUS.

KM#	Date	Fine	VF	XF	Unc
31.1a	1851	6500.	10,000.	18,500.	38,500.

Obv: 880 THOUS. Rev: Without 50.

KM#	Date	Fine	VF	XF	Unc
31.2	1851	5000.	9,000.	17,500.	37,500.

Obv: 887 THOUS.

KM#	Date	Fine	VF	XF	Unc
31.2a	1851	—	14,500.	25,000.	—

ASSAYER inverted

KM#	Date	Fine	VF	XF	Unc
31.3	1851	—	—	Unique	—

Obv: 880 THOUS. Rev: Rays from central star.

KM#	Date	Fine	VF	XF	Unc
31.4	1851	—	—	Unique	—

Obv: 880 THOUS. Rev: "Target".

KM#	Date	Fine	VF	XF	Unc
32.1	1851	5500.	8500.	16,500.	35,000.

Obv: 887 THOUS.

KM#	Date	Fine	VF	XF	Unc
32.1a	1851	5500.	8500.	16,500.	35,000.

Garrett Sale March 1980, Humberts Proof $500,000.

Rev: Small design.

KM#	Date	Fine	VF	XF	Unc
32.2	1851	5500.	8500.	16,500.	—
	1852	4500.	8000.	18,500.	40,000.

Bloomfield Sale December 1996, BU $159,500.

Kellogg & Company

20 DOLLARS

Obv: Thick date. Rev: Short arrows.

KM#	Date	Fine	VF	XF	Unc
33.1	1854	1250.	2250.	4350.	17,500.

Obv: Medium date.

KM#	Date	Fine	VF	XF	Unc
33.2	1854	1250.	2250.	4350.	17,500.

Obv: Thin date.

KM#	Date	Fine	VF	XF	Unc
33.3	1854	1250.	2250.	4350.	17,500.

Rev: Long arrows.

KM#	Date	Fine	VF	XF	Unc
33.4	1854	1250.	2250.	4350.	17,500.
	1855	1250.	2500.	4650.	18,500.

Garrett Sale Mar. 1980 Proof $230,000.

Rev: Medium arrows.

KM#	Date	Fine	VF	XF	Unc
33.5	1855	1250.	2500.	4650.	18,500.

Rev: Short arrows.

KM#	Date	Fine	VF	XF	Unc
33.6	1855	1250.	2500.	4650.	18,500.

50 DOLLARS

KM#	Date	Fine	VF	XF	Unc
34	1855	—	—	—	—

Heritage ANA Sale Aug. 1997, Proof $156,500.

Massachusetts and California Company

5 DOLLARS

KM#	Date	Fine	VF	XF	Unc
35	1849	35,000.	55,000.	Rare	—
				Proof	110,000.

Miners Bank

10 DOLLARS

RED GOLD

KM#	Date	Fine	VF	XF	Unc
36	ND(1849)	—	12,000.	24,500.	55,000.

Garrett Sale Mar. 1980, MS-65 $135,000.

YELLOW GOLD

KM#	Date	Fine	VF	XF	Unc
36a	ND(1849)	—	—	—	—

Rare as most specimens have heavy copper alloy.

Moffat & Co.

5 DOLLARS

KM#	Date	Fine	VF	XF	Unc
37.1	1849	850.00	1350.	4000.	12,000.

Rev: Die break at DOL.

KM#	Date	Fine	VF	XF	Unc
37.2	1849	850.00	1350.	4000.	12,000.

Rev: Die break on shield.

KM#	Date	Fine	VF	XF	Unc
37.3	1849	850.00	1350.	4000.	12,000.

Rev: Small letters.

KM#	Date	Fine	VF	XF	Unc
37.4	1850	950.00	1550.	5000.	14,000.

Rev: Large letters.

KM#	Date	Fine	VF	XF	Unc
37.5	1850	950.00	1550.	5000.	14,000.

Garrett Sale Mar. 1980, MS-60 $21,000.

10 DOLLARS

Rev. val: TEN DOL., arrow below period.

KM#	Date	Fine	VF	XF	Unc
38.1	1849	1650.	3500.	6000.	15,000.

Rev: Arrow above period.

KM#	Date	Fine	VF	XF	Unc
38.2	1849	1650.	3500.	6000.	15,000.

Rev. val: TEN D., large letters.

KM#	Date	Fine	VF	XF	Unc
38.3	1849	2250.	5000.	7500.	16,500.

Rev: Small letters.

KM#	Date	Fine	VF	XF	Unc
38.4	1849	2250.	5000.	7500.	16,500.

MOFFAT & CO. imprint, wide date.

KM#	Date	Fine	VF	XF	Unc
39.1	1852	2000.	4250.	8500.	17,500.

Close date

KM#	Date	Fine	VF	XF	Unc
39.2	1852	1800.	4000.	8500.	17,500.

NOTE: Struck by Augustus Humbert.

20 DOLLARS

KM#	Date	Fine	VF	XF	Unc
40	1853	2150.	3750.	6000.	16,500.

NOTE: Struck by Curtis, Perry & Ward.

Norris, Greig & Norris

HALF EAGLE

Obv: Period after ALLOY. Plain edge.

KM#	Date	Fine	VF	XF	Unc
41.1	1849	2250.	3750.	7500.	22,500.

Obv: W/o period after ALLOY.

KM#	Date	Fine	VF	XF	Unc
41.2	1849	2250.	3750.	7500.	22,500.

Obv: Period after ALLOY. Reeded edge.

KM#	Date	Fine	VF	XF	Unc
41.3	1849	1750.	3000.	6000.	22,500.

Obv: W/o period after ALLOY.

KM#	Date	Fine	VF	XF	Unc
41.4	1849	1750.	3000.	6000.	22,500.

Rev: STOCKTON beneath date.

KM#	Date	Fine	VF	XF	Unc
42	1850	—	—	Unique	—

J.S. Ormsby

5 DOLLARS

Plain edge

KM#	Date	Fine	VF	XF	Unc
43.1	ND(1849)	—	—	Unique	—

Reeded edge

KM#	Date	Fine	VF	XF	Unc
43.2	ND(1849)	—	—	Unique	—

Superior Auction 1989, VF $137,500.

10 DOLLARS

KM#	Date	Fine	VF	XF	Unc
44	ND(1849)	—	—	—	—

Garrett Sale March 1980, F-12 $100,000.

Pacific Company

5 DOLLARS

KM#	Date	Fine	VF	XF	Unc
45	1849	—	—	—	—

Garrett Sale March 1980, VF-30 $180,000.

10 DOLLARS

Plain edge

KM#	Date	Fine	VF	XF	Unc
46.1	1849	—	—	Rare	—

Waldorf Sale 1964, $24,000.

Reeded edge

KM#	Date	Fine	VF	XF	Unc
46.2	1849	—	—	Rare	—

Templeton Reid

10 DOLLARS

KM#	Date	Fine	VF	XF	Unc
47	1849	—	—	Unique	—

20 DOLLARS

KM#	Date	Fine	VF	XF	Unc
48	1849	—	Unknown		—

NOTE: Only known specimen of above stolen from U.S. Mint in 1858 and never recovered. Also see listings under Georgia.

Schultz & Company

5 DOLLARS

KM#	Date	Fine	VF	XF	Unc
49	1851	—	—	45,000.	—

United States Assay Office of Gold

10 DOLLARS

Obv: TEN DOLS 884 THOUS.
Rev: O of OFFICE below I of UNITED.

KM#	Date	Fine	VF	XF	Unc
50.1	1852	1750.	2500.	3850.	9500.

Garrett Sale March 1980, MS-60 $18,000.

Rev: O below N, strong beads.

KM#	Date	Fine	VF	XF	Unc
51.2	1852	1750.	2500.	3850.	9500.

Rev: Weak beads.

KM#	Date	Fine	VF	XF	Unc
51.3	1852	1750.	2500.	3850.	9500.

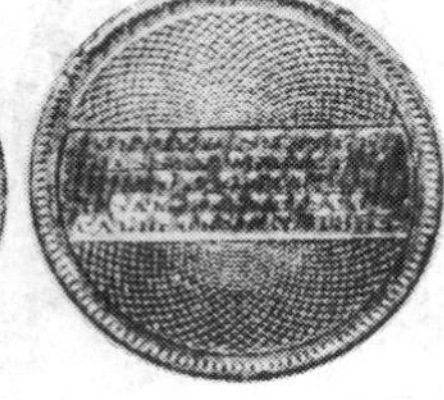

Obv: TEN D, 884 THOUS.

KM#	Date	Fine	VF	XF	Unc
52	1853	5000.	7750.	14,500.	—

Obv: 900 THOUS

KM#	Date	Fine	VF	XF	Unc
52a	1853	2700.	4200.	6500.	—

Garrett Sale March 1980, MS-60 $35,000.

20 DOLLARS

Obv: 884/880 THOUS.

KM#	Date	Fine	VF	XF	Unc
53	1853	8500.	12,500.	17,500.	23,500.

Obv: 900/880 THOUS.

KM#	Date	Fine	VF	XF	Unc
53a	1853	1550.	2750.	4250.	10,000.

NOTE: 1853 Liberty Head listed under Moffat & Co.

50 DOLLARS

Obv: 887 THOUS.

KM#	Date	Fine	VF	XF	Unc
54	1852	4000.	6500.	14,500.	26,500.

Obv: 900 THOUS.

KM#	Date	Fine	VF	XF	Unc
54a	1852	5500.	7500.	16,000.	28,500.

Wass, Molitor & Co.

5 DOLLARS

Obv: Small head, rounded bust.

KM#	Date	Fine	VF	XF	Unc
55.1	1852	2000.	4000.	6750.	16,500.

Thick planchet.

KM#	Date	Fine	VF	XF	Unc
55.2	1852	—	—	Unique	—

Obv: Large head, pointed bust.

KM#	Date	Fine	VF	XF	Unc
56	1852	2000.	4250.	7000.	17,500.

10 DOLLARS

Obv: Long neck, large date.

KM#	Date	Fine	VF	XF	Unc
57	1852	3000.	5500.	7500.	14,500.

Obv: Short neck, wide date.

KM#	Date	Fine	VF	XF	Unc
58	1852	1650.	2750.	5000.	—

Obv: Short neck, small date.

KM#	Date	Fine	VF	XF	Unc
59.1	1852	—	—	Rare	—

Eliasberg Sale May 1996, EF-45 $36,300.

Obv: Plugged date.

KM#	Date	Fine	VF	XF	Unc
59.2	1855	6000.	8000.	12,000.	—

20 DOLLARS

Obv: Large head.

KM#	Date	Fine	VF	XF	Unc
60	1855	—	—	Rare	—

Obv: Small head.

KM#	Date	Fine	VF	XF	Unc
61	1855	7000.	11,500.	20,000.	—

50 DOLLARS

KM#	Date	Fine	VF	XF	Unc
62	1855	8500.	14,500.	28,000.	—

Bloomfield Sale December 1996, BU $170,500.

COLORADO

Clark, Gruber & Co.

2-1/2 DOLLARS

KM#	Date	Fine	VF	XF	Unc
63	1860	750.00	1300.	2500.	9000.

Garrett Sale March 1980, MS-65 $12,000.

KM#	Date	Fine	VF	XF	Unc
64.1	1861	850.00	1500.	2750.	12,500.

Ex. high edge.

KM#	Date	Fine	VF	XF	Unc
64.2	1861	850.00	1750.	3500.	13,500.

5 DOLLARS

KM#	Date	Fine	VF	XF	Unc
65	1860	1200.	1950.	3350.	9250.

Garrett Sale March 1980, MS-63 $9,000.

KM#	Date	Fine	VF	XF	Unc
66	1861	1500.	2500.	4500.	14,500.

10 DOLLARS

KM#	Date	Fine	VF	XF	Unc
67	1860	2750.	3950.	9000.	23,500.

KM#	Date	Fine	VF	XF	Unc
68	1861	1500.	2500.	4500.	14,500.

20 DOLLARS

KM#	Date	Fine	VF	XF	Unc
69	1860	30,000.	60,000.	80,000.	100,000.

Eliasberg Sale May 1996, AU $90,200.
Schoonmaker Sale June 1997, VCF $62,700.

KM#	Date	Fine	VF	XF	Unc
70	1861	7000.	10,000.	20,000.	—

J.J. Conway

2-1/2 DOLLARS

KM#	Date	Fine	VF	XF	Unc
71	ND(1861)	—	45,000.	70,000.	—

5 DOLLARS

KM#	Date	Fine	VF	XF	Unc
72.1	ND(1861)	—	—	Rare	—

Brand Sale June 1984, XF-40 $44,000.

Rev: Numeral 5 omitted.

KM#	Date	Fine	VF	XF	Unc
72.2	ND(1861)	—	—	Unique	—

10 DOLLARS

KM#	Date	Fine	VF	XF	Unc
73	ND(1861)	—	60,000.	Rare	—

John Parsons

2-1/2 DOLLARS

KM#	Date	Fine	VF	XF	Unc
74	ND(1861)	—	—	Rare	—

Garrett Sale March 1980, VF-20 $85,000.

5 DOLLARS

KM#	Date	Fine	VF	XF	Unc
75	ND(1861)	—	—	Rare	—

Garrett Sale March 1980, VF-20 $100,000.

GEORGIA

Christopher Bechtler

2-1/2 DOLLARS

Rev: GEORGIA, 64 G, 22 CARATS

KM#	Date	Fine	VF	XF	Unc
76.1	ND	1650.	2650.	5000.	10,000.

Rev: GEORGIA, 64 G, 22 CARATS, even 22.

KM#	Date	Fine	VF	XF	Unc
76.2	ND	1850.	2850.	5500.	11,500.

5 DOLLARS

Obv: RUTHERF. Rev: 128 G, 22 CARATS.

KM#	Date	Fine	VF	XF	Unc
77	ND	2000.	3500.	5500.	11,500.

Obv: RUTHERFORD.

KM#	Date	Fine	VF	XF	Unc
78.1	ND	2000.	3750.	6000.	12,500.

Rev: Colon after 128 G:

KM#	Date	Fine	VF	XF	Unc
78.2	ND	—	20,000.	30,000.	—

Akers Pittman Sale October 1997, VF-EF $26,400.

Templeton Reid

2-1/2 DOLLARS

KM#	Date	Fine	VF	XF	Unc
79	1830	16,500.	39,500.	55,000.	—

5 DOLLARS

KM#	Date	Fine	VF	XF	Unc
80	1830	—	—	Rare	—

Garrett Sale Nov. 1979, XF-40 $200,000.

10 DOLLARS

Obv: With date.

KM#	Date	Fine	VF	XF	Unc
81	1830	—	—	Rare	—

Obv: Undated.

KM#	Date	Fine	VF	XF	Unc
82	ND(1830)	—	—	Rare	—

NOTE: Also see listings under California.

NORTH CAROLINA

August Bechtler

DOLLAR

Rev: CAROLINA, 27 G. 21C., plain edge.

KM#	Date	Fine	VF	XF	Unc
83.1	ND	450.00	650.00	1150.	2950.

Reeded edge

KM#	Date	Fine	VF	XF	Unc
83.2	ND	450.00	650.00	1150.	2950.

5 DOLLARS

Rev: CAROLINA, 134 G. 21 CARATS.

KM#	Date	Fine	VF	XF	Unc
84	ND	2000.	4000.	6500.	12,500.

Rev: CAROLINA, 128 G. 22 CARATS.

KM#	Date	Fine	VF	XF	Unc
85	ND	3000.	5500.	8000.	15,000.

Rev: CAROLINA, 141 G:20 CARATS.

KM#	Date	Fine	VF	XF	Unc
86	ND	3000.	5000.	7500.	14,500.

NOTE: Proof restrikes exist from original dies. In the Akers Pittman Sale Oct. 1997, an example sold for $14,300.

Christopher Bechtler

DOLLAR

Obv: CAROLINA, N reversed. Rev: 28 G.

KM#	Date	Fine	VF	XF	Unc
87	ND	900.00	1200.	1700.	3750.

Obv: N. CAROLINA. Rev: 28 G centered w/o star.

KM#	Date	Fine	VF	XF	Unc
88.1	ND	1500.	2200.	3500.	8000.

Obv: N. CAROLINA. Rev: 28 G high w/o star. . .

KM#	Date	Fine	VF	XF	Unc
88.2	ND	3000.	4500.	6500.	12,000.

Obv: N CAROLINA. Rev: 30 G.

KM#	Date	Fine	VF	XF	Unc
89	ND	850.00	1100.	2000.	4000.

2-1/2 DOLLARS

Rev: CAROLINA, 67 G. 21 CARATS.

KM#	Date	Fine	VF	XF	Unc
90.1	ND	1250.	2150.	5500.	11,500.

Rev: 64 G 22 CARATS, uneven 22.

KM#	Date	Fine	VF	XF	Unc
90.2	ND	1450.	2850.	6000.	12,000.

Rev: Even 22.

KM#	Date	Fine	VF	XF	Unc
90.3	ND	1650.	3000.	6500.	12,500.

Rev: CAROLINA, 70 G. 20 CARATS.

KM#	Date	Fine	VF	XF	Unc
91	ND	1650.	3000.	6750.	18,500.

Bowers and Merena Long Sale May, 1995 MS-63 $31,900.

Obv: NORTH CAROLINA, 20 C.75 G. Rev: RUTHERFORD in a circle. Border of large beads.

KM#	Date	Fine	VF	XF	Unc
92.1	ND	—	5500.	7500.	15,000.

Obv: NORTH CAROLINA, w/o 75 G, wide 20 C.

KM#	Date	Fine	VF	XF	Unc
92.2	ND	2800.	5000.	7000.	14,500.

Obv: Narrow 20 C.

KM#	Date	Fine	VF	XF	Unc
92.3	ND	2800.	5000.	7000.	14,500.

Obv: NORTH CAROLINA w/o 75 G, CAROLINA above 250 instead of GOLD.

KM#	Date	Fine	VF	XF	Unc
93.1	ND	—	—	Unique	—

Obv: NORTH CAROLINA, 20 C. Rev: 75 G. Border finely serrated.

KM#	Date	Fine	VF	XF	Unc
93.2	ND	4500.	7500.	10,500.	—

5 DOLLARS

Rev: CAROLINA, 134 G. star 21 CARATS.

KM#	Date	Fine	VF	XF	Unc
94	ND	1650.	3250.	6000.	11,000.

Rev: 21 above CARATS, w/o star.

KM#	Date	Fine	VF	XF	Unc
95	ND	—	—	Unique	—

Obv: RUTHERFORD. Rev: CAROLINA, 140 G. 20 CARATS. Plain edge.

KM#	Date	Fine	VF	XF	Unc
96.1	1834	1750.	3750.	6500.	11,500.

Reeded edge

KM#	Date	Fine	VF	XF	Unc
96.2	1834	2000.	4000.	7000.	12,500.

Obv: RUTHERF. Rev: CAROLINA. 140 G. 20 CARATS. 20 close to CARATS.

KM#	Date	Fine	VF	XF	Unc
97.1	1834	1800.	3850.	6750.	12,000.

Rev: 20 away from CARATS.

KM#	Date	Fine	VF	XF	Unc
97.2	1834	2250.	5500.	8250.	—

Obv: RUTHERF. Rev: CAROLINA, 141 G, 20 CARATS.

KM#	Date	Fine	VF	XF	Unc
98	ND	—	Proof restrike 15,500.		

Rev: NORTH CAROLINA, 150 G, below 20 CARATS.

KM#	Date	Fine	VF	XF	Unc
99.1	ND	2800.	4500.	8500.	18,500.

Rev: Without 150 G.

KM#	Date	Fine	VF	XF	Unc
99.2	ND	3200.	6000.	10,000.	20,000.

OREGON

Oregon Exchange Co.

5 DOLLARS

KM#	Date	Fine	VF	XF	Unc
100	1849	10,000.	17,500.	28,600.	—

10 DOLLARS

KM#	Date	Fine	VF	XF	Unc
101	1849	20,000.	35,000.	55,000.	—

UTAH

Mormon Issues

2-1/2 DOLLARS

KM#	Date	Fine	VF	XF	Unc
102	1849	3200.	5000.	7750.	20,000.

5 DOLLARS

KM#	Date	Fine	VF	XF	Unc
103	1849	3000.	4250.	6500.	13,500.

KM#	Date	Fine	VF	XF	Unc
104	1850	3750.	5500.	8500.	—

KM#	Date	Fine	VF	XF	Unc
105	1860	5500.	9000.	14,500.	27,500.

10 DOLLARS

KM#	Date	Fine	VF	XF	Unc
106	1849	—	—	Rare	—

Heritage ANA Sale July 1988, AU $93,000.

20 DOLLARS

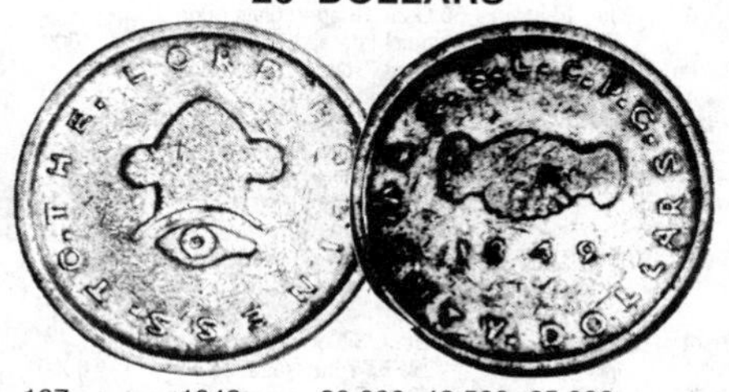

KM#	Date	Fine	VF	XF	Unc
107	1849	20,000.	42,500.	65,000.	—

PATTERNS (Pn)

The United States pattern section contains Judd cross reference numbers and selected descriptive references from the 6th edition of *United States Pattern, Experimental and Trial Pieces* edited by Abe Kosoff from the original edition by J. Hewitt Judd, M.D. Copyright 1977, 1959 Western Publishing Company, Inc. Used by permission.

Market values established in this section are based on auction results gleened from *Auction Prices Realized*, an annual compilation of U.S. auction firm sales edited by Bob Wilhite and Tom Michael and published by Krause Publications of Iola, Wisconsin. Due to the wide variance in grade amongst U.S. patterns, these values represent only an average example of the type. To determine values for patterns of greater or lesser quality the serious collector may wish to research the market trend of a given type over time by using several volumes of *Auction Prices Realized* as well as original auction catalogs.

DENOMINATION EQUIVALENTS

10 Cent = Dime
25 Cent = Quarter Dollar
50 Cent = Half Dollar
Dollar = Silver Dollar
Gold Dollar = Gold Dollar
2-1/2 Dollar = Quarter Eagle
5 Dollar = Half Eagle
10 Dollar = Eagle
20 Dollar = Double Eagle

NOTE: Photographs are representative of the type group, and not always the particular listing that it appears above.

KM#	Date	Mintage	Identification	Mkt.Val.
Pn14	1803	—	5 Dollar, Copper, reeded edge, restrikes from rusty dies, J27	—
Pn15	1804	—	1 Cent, Tin, plain edge, restrike, J28	—
Pn16	1804	—	5 Dollar, Silver, reeded edge, restrike, J29	2750.
Pn17	1804	—	5 Dollar, Silver, plain edge, restrike, J30	2500.
Pn18	1804	—	5 Dollar, Copper, reeded edge, restrike, J31	2000.
Pn19	1804	—	5 Dollar, Tin, restrike, J32	2000.
Pn20	1804	4 known	10 Dollar (Eagle), Gold, obv: plain 4 in date, rev: beaded border, J33	—
Pn21	1804	4-5 struck	10 Dollar, Silver, reeded edge, J34	13,500.
Pn22	1804	—	10 Dollar, Silver, plain edge, J34a	—
Pn23	1805	—	2-1/2 Dollar (Quarter Eagle), Copper reeded edge, restrike, J35	—
Pn24	1805	—	5 Dollar, Silver, restrike, J36	2750.
Pn25	1805	—	5 Dollar, Copper, restrike, J37	2250.
Pn26	1805	—	5 Dollar, Tin, restrike, J38	2200.
Pn27	1806	—	1 Cent, Copper, obv: die of the quarter, rev: 1807 cent, plain edge, restrike mule, J38a	—
Pn28	1808	—	5 Dollar, Silver, reeded edge, restrike, J39	—
Pn29	1808	—	5 Dollar, Silver, plain edge, restrike, J40	—
Pn30	1810	2	1 Cent, White Metal, restrike, J41	7500.
Pn31	1810	—	50 Cent, Copper, plain edge, restrike, J42	5000.
Pn32	1810	—	50 Cent, Brass, plain edge, J42a	—
Pn33	1810	—	50 Cent, Brass, plain edge, restrike, J43	5000.
Pn34	1814	3 known	50 Cent, Platinum, J44	Rare
Pn35	1818	—	1 Cent, Silver, obv: die of the quarter, restrike, J45	Unique
Pn36	1823	12	1 Cent, Silver, plain edge, restrike, J46	—
Pn37	1823	—	1 Cent, Copper, plain edge, restrike, J46a	750.00
Pn38	1823	—	50 Cent, Copper, reeded edge, restrike, J47	—
Pn39	1827	4-5 known	25 Cent, Copper, rev: die of 1819, restrike, J48	8500.
Pn40	1831	—	2-1/2 Dollar, Silver, reeded edge, J49	Unique
Pn41	1834	2 known	2-1/2 Dollar, Copper, reeded edge, J50	Rare
Pn42	1834	—	5 Dollar, Copper, plain edge, J51	3000.
Pn43	1834	—	5 Dollar, Copper, plain edge, J51a	400.00

NOTE: The authenticity of this piece has been questioned.

KM#	Date	Mintage	Identification	Mkt.Val.
Pn44	1836	—	2 Cent, Billon, plain edge, J52	3000.
Pn45	1836	—	2 Cent, Billon, reeded edge, J53	3500.
Pn46	1836	—	2 Cent, Copper, plain edge, J54	3000.
Pn47	1836	—	2 Cent, Copper, reeded edge, J55	550.00
Pn48	1836	—	2 Cent, White Metal, plain edge, J56	550.00
Pn49	1836	—	2 Cent, White Metal, reeded edge, J56a	2000.

KM#	Date	Mintage	Identification	Mkt.Val.
Pn50	1836	1,200 est.	50 Cent, Silver, reeded edge, J57	2300.
Pn51	1836	18	1 Dollar, Silver, plain edge, name above date, stars, J58	99,000.
Pn51a	1836	—	1 Dollar, Silver, restrike from cracked reverse die, J58a	10,000.
Pn52	1836	—	1 Dollar, Copper, plain edge, J59	121,000.

KM#	Date	Mintage	Identification	Mkt.Val.
Pn53	1836	1,000	1 Dollar, Silver, plain edge, coin turn, name on base, stars, J60	8000.
Pn53a	1836	600	1 Dollar, Silver, plain edge, medal turn, J60	8000.
Pn53b	1836	—	1 Dollar, Silver, plain edge, restrikes from cracked reverse, J60a	4500.
Pn54	1836	—	1 Dollar, Silver, reeded edge, restrike, J61	—
Pn55	1836	—	1 Dollar, Copper, plain edge, restrike, J62	—
Pn56	1836	—	1 Dollar, Silver, plain edge, name above date, no stars, restrike, J63	35,000.
Pn57	1836	—	1 Dollar, Copper, plain edge, restrike, J64	12,500.
Pn58	1836	—	1 Dollar, Silver, plain edge, name on base, no stars, restrike, J65	35,000.
Pn59	1836	—	1 Dollar, Copper, plain edge, restrike, J66	12,500.

KM#	Date	Mintage	Identification	Mkt.Val.
Pn60	1836	5	1 Gold Dollar, Gold, coin turn, plain edge, J67	11,500.
Pn61	1836	—	1 Gold Dollar, Gold alloyed w/Silver, medal turn, plain edge, J68	12,000.
Pn62	1836	—	1 Gold Dollar, Silver, plain edge, J69	4850.
Pn62a	1836	—	1 Gold Dollar, Silver Gilt, plain edge, J69a	4850.
Pn63	1836	—	1 Gold Dollar, Copper, plain edge, J70	4750.
Pn63a	1836	—	1 Gold Dollar, Copper Gilt, plain edge, J70a	4750.
Pn64	1836	—	1 Gold Dollar, Oroide, plain edge, J71	—
Pn65	1838	—	50 Cent, Silver, reeded edge, J72	5000.

KM#	Date	Mintage	Identification	Mkt.Val.
Pn66	1838	2-3 known	50 Cent, Silver, reeded edge, 143 reeds, J73	10,000.
Pn66a	1838	—	50 Cent, Silver, reeded edge, 152 reeds, restrike, J73a	4250.
Pn67	1838	—	50 Cent, Copper, reeded edge, restrike, J74	1500.
Pn68	1838	1 known	50 Cent, Silver, reeded edge, J75	—
Pn69	1838	1 known	50 Cent, Silver, plain edge, curved date, LIBERTY incuse, 206 gr, J76	—
Pn69a	1838	—	50 Cent, Silver, reeded edge, straight date, 192 gr, restrike, J76	5500.
Pn69b	1838	—	50 Cent, Silver, reeded edge, straight date, 192 gr, restrike, J76a	5500.
Pn70	1838	1 known	50 Cent, Copper, plain edge, straight date, J77	4000.
Pn70a	1838	—	50 Cent, Copper, plain edge, restrike from rusted die, J77a	2500.
Pn71	1838	—	50 Cent, Copper, reeded edge, straight date, rusted die, J78	4500.
Pn72	1838	2 known	50 Cent, Silver, reeded edge, curved date, LIBERTY raised, J79	—
Pn73	1838	3 known	50 Cent, Silver, reeded edge, straight date, restrike, J79a	7500.
Pn74	1838	—	50 Cent, Silver, reeded edge, LIBERTY incuse, J79a	6000.
Pn75	1838	—	50 Cent, Silver, reeded edge, straight date, restrike, J80	6500.
Pn76	1838	—	50 Cent, Copper, reeded edge, restrike, J81	5500.
Pn77	1838	2 known	50 Cent, Silver, reeded edge, curved date, J82	—
Pn77a	1838	1 known	50 Cent, Silver, plain edge, restrike, J82a	10,000.
Pn78	1838	1 known	50 Cent, Silver, reeded edge, J83	—

KM#	Date	Mintage	Identification	Mkt.Val.
Pn79	1838	—	1 Dollar, Silver, reeded edge, no name on base, J84	18,700.
Pn79a	1838	—	1 Dollar, Silver, reeded edge, restrike, rev: w/o stars, J84a	15,000.
Pn80	1838	—	1 Dollar, Silver, plain edge, restrike, J85	15,500.
Pn81	1838	—	1 Dollar, Copper, reeded edge, J86	Rare
Pn82	1838	—	1 Dollar, Copper, plain edge, restrike, J87	14,500.

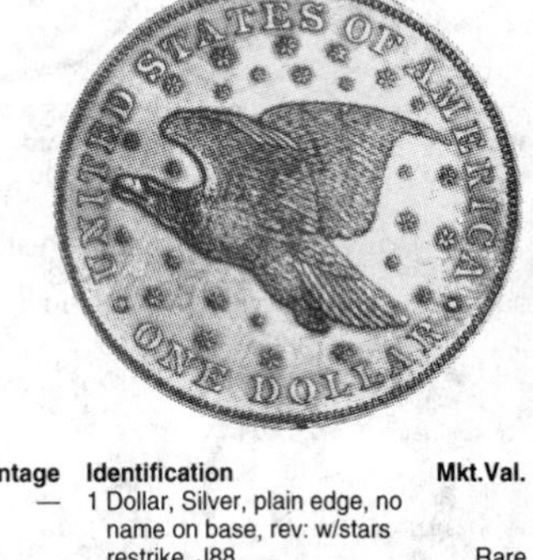

KM#	Date	Mintage	Identification	Mkt.Val.
Pn83	1838	—	1 Dollar, Silver, plain edge, no name on base, rev: w/stars restrike, J88	Rare
Pn84	1838	—	1 Dollar, Copper, plain edge, restrike, J89	Rare
Pn85	1838	—	1 Dollar, Copper, reeded edge, restrike, J90	Rare
Pn86	1839	—	50 Cent, Silver, reeded edge, restrike, J91	4500.
Pn87	1839	—	50 Cent, Silver, reeded edge, restrike, J92	—
Pn88	1839	7 known	50 Cent, Silver, reeded edge, J93	6000.
Pn89	1839	—	50 Cent, Copper, reeded edge, J94	—
Pn90	1839	—	50 Cent, Silver, reeded edge, 152 reeds, J95	12,000.
Pn91	1839	—	50 Cent, Copper, reeded edge, J96	5000.
Pn92	1839	—	50 Cent, Silver, reeded edge, restrike, 146 reeds, J97	12,000.
Pn93	1839	—	50 Cent, Copper, reeded edge, restrike, J98	11,550.
Pn94	1839	2 known	50 Cent, Silver, reeded edge, 143 reeds, J99	37,500.
Pn95	1839	2 known	50 Cent, Silver, reeded edge, restrike, J100	37,500.
Pn95a	1839	—	50 Cent, Silver, reeded edge, J100a	—
Pn96	1839	1 known	50 Cent, Silver, plain edge, J101	42,500.
Pn97	1839	—	50 Cent, Silver, reeded edge, 152 reeds, restrike, J102	5500.
Pn98	1839	—	50 Cent, Copper, reeded edge, 152 reeds, restrike, J103	5500.

KM#	Date	Mintage	Identification	Mkt.Val.
Pn99	1839	300	1 Dollar, Silver, reeded edge, no name or stars, J104	15,400.
Pn99a	1839	—	1 Dollar, Silver, restrike, medal turn, J104a	10,000.
Pn99b	1839	—	1 Dollar, Silver, restrike, coin turn, J104b	10,000.
Pn100	1839	—	1 Dollar, Silver, plain edge, J105	17,600.

KM#	Date	Mintage	Identification	Mkt.Val.
Pn101	1839	—	1 Dollar, Copper, reeded edge, J106	Rare
Pn102	1839	—	1 Dollar, Copper, plain edge, J107	Rare
Pn103	1839	—	1 Dollar, Silver, plain edge, no name, rev: w/stars, restrike, J108	Rare
Pn104	1839	—	1 Dollar, Silver, plain edge, J109	Unique
Pn105	ND(1840)	—	25 Cent, Brass, broad planchet, J110	Unique
Pn106	1846	Unique	2-1/2 Dollar, Copper, reeded edge, J110a	3650.
Pn107	1849	—	3 Cent, Silver & Copper, (50-50) reeded edge, 22 gr, J111	3000.
Pn107a	1849	—	3 Cent, Silver & Copper, (50-50) restrike, J111a	3000.
Pn108	1849	—	3 Cent, Silver & Copper, (60-40) reeded edge, 18.5 g, J112	3250.
Pn109	ND(1849)	—	3 Cent, Silver-Copper, plain edge, J113	3000.
Pn109a	ND(1849)	—	3 Cent, Silver-Copper, plain edge, restrike, J113a	3000.
Pn110	ND(1849)	—	3 Cent, Copper-Nickel, plain edge, restrike, J114	3000.
Pn111	1849	—	1 Gold Dollar, plain edge, 25.8 gr, J115	Rare
Pn112	1849	3 known	1 Gold Dollar, Silver, Gold plated, J116	5500.
Pn113	1849	1 known	20 Dollar, Gold, reeded edge, J117	Rare
Pn114	1849	—	20 Dollar, Brass Gilt, reeded edge, J118	Unique
Pn115	1850	—	1 Cent, Billon, plain edge, w/hole, J119	2500.
Pn116	1850	—	1 Cent, Billon, plain edge, w/o hole, restrike, J120	650.00
Pn117	1850	—	1 Cent, Copper, plain edge, w/hole, J121	1600.
Pn118	1850	—	1 Cent, Copper, plain edge, w/o hole, restrike, J122	1650.
Pn119	1850	—	1 Cent, Copper-Nickel, plain edge, w/hole, J123	1650.
Pn120	1850	—	1 Cent, Copper-Nickel, plain edge, w/o hole, restrike, J124	2500.
Pn121	1850	—	1 Cent, White Metal, plain edge, w/hole, J124a	3500.
Pn122	1850	—	3 Cent, Silver, plain edge, 12.75 gr, J125	2000.
Pn122a	1850	—	3 Cent, Silver, plain edge, restrike, J125a	1500.
Pn123	ND(1850)	2 known	20 Dollar, Silver, reeded edge, J126	Rare
Pn124	ND(1851)	—	1 Cent, Billon, plain edge, w/hole, J127	1650.
Pn124a	ND(1851)	—	1 Cent, Billon, plain edge, w/large hole, J127a	1650.
Pn125	ND(1851)	—	1 Cent, Billon, plain edge, w/o hole, restrike, J128	1900.
Pn125a	ND(1851)	—	1 Cent, Billon, reeded edge, w/o hole, thin, restrike, J128a	1900.
Pn125b	ND(1851)	—	1 Cent, Billon, reeded edge, w/o hole, thick, restrike, J128a	1900.
Pn126	ND(1851)	—	1 Cent, Copper, plain edge, w/hole, J129	1950.
Pn126a	ND(1851)	—	1 Cent, Copper, plain edge, w/o hole, restrike, J130	2365.
Pn127	ND(1851)	—	1 Cent, Copper-Nickel, reeded edge, w/o hole, restrike, J131	2350.
Pn127a	ND(1851)	—	1 Cent, Nickel, reeded edge, w/o hole, J131a	2400.

NOTE: Examples of Pn127 & 127a exist silver plated.

KM#	Date	Mintage	Identification	Mkt.Val.
Pn128	1851	5 known	1 Dollar, Copper, reeded edge, restrike, J132	5000.
Pn129	1852	—	1 Dollar, Nickel, reeded edge, J133	6500.
Pn130	1852	—	1 Dollar, Copper, reeded edge, restrike, J134	6000.
Pn131	1852	6 known	1 Gold Half Dollar, Gold, reeded edge, 13 gr, J135	9000.
Pn132	1852	4 known	1 Gold Dollar, Gold, reeded edge, 25.8 gr, J136	10,000.
Pn133	1852	2 known	1 Gold Dollar, Gold, plain edge, J137	17,500.
Pn134	1852	—	1 Gold Dollar, Silver, plain edge, thick planchet, J138	4000.
Pn134a	1852	—	1 Gold Dollar, Silver, plain edge, thin planchet, J138	4000.
Pn135	1852	—	1 Gold Dollar, Copper, plain edge, J139	2350.
Pn136	1852	—	1 Gold Dollar, Copper-Nickel, plain edge, J140	2750.
Pn137	1852	—	1 Gold Dollar, Nickel, plain edge, J140a	2500.
Pn138	1852	—	1 Gold Dollar, Gold, plain edge, J141	Rare
Pn139	1852	—	1 Gold Dollar, Silver, plain edge, J142	Rare
Pn140	1852	—	1 Gold Dollar, Copper, plain edge, J143	2800.
Pn141	1852	—	1 Gold Dollar, Nickel, plain edge, J144	Unique
Pn142	1852	—	1 Gold Dollar, Gold, plain edge, thick planchet, 25.8 gr, J145	15,500.
Pn142a	1852	—	1 Gold Dollar, Gold, plain edge, thin planchet, J145	11,500.
Pn143	1852	5 known	1 Gold Dollar, Silver, plain edge, J146	6000.
Pn144	1852	—	1 Gold Dollar, Copper, plain edge, J147	3750.
Pn145	1852	—	1 Gold Dollar, Copper-Nickel, plain edge, J148	3750.
Pn146	1852	—	1 Gold Dollar, Nickel, plain edge, thin planchet, J148a	2750.
Pn147	1852	—	1 Gold Dollar, Brass, plain edge, J148b	7000.

NOTE: Restrikes exist from cracked dies. Gilt examples also exist.

KM#	Date	Mintage	Identification	Mkt.Val.
Pn148	1853	—	1 Cent, German Silver (40% Nickel), reeded edge, J149	2750.
Pn148a	1853	—	1 Cent, German Silver (30% Nickel), reeded edge, thick planchet, J150	5000.
Pn148b	1853	—	1 Cent, German Silver (30% Nickel), reeded edge, thin planchet, J150	4500.
Pn149	1853	—	1 Cent, Nickel-Copper (60-40), reeded edge, J151	1500.
Pn150	1853	—	1 Cent, German Silver, plain edge, J152	850.00
Pn151	1853	—	1 Cent, Nickel, plain edge, w/o hole, thick planchet, J152a	850.00
Pn152	1853	—	1 Cent, Nickel, plain edge, w/hole, thin planchet, J152b	850.00
Pn153	1853	—	3 Cent, Silver, plain edge, J153	Unique
Pn154	1853	—	1 Dollar, Copper, reeded edge, restrike, J154	1500.
Pn155	1854	2 known	1/2 Cent, Copper-Nickel, plain edge, J155	Rare
Pn156	1854	—	1 Cent, German Silver (40% Nickel), reeded edge, J156	1650.
Pn157	1854	—	1 Cent, German Silver (30% Nickel), reeded edge, J157	1650.
Pn158	1854	—	1 Cent, Nickel-Copper (40-60), reeded edge, J158	2250.
Pn159	1854	—	1 Cent, Copper, reeded edge, J159	2500.
Pn160	1854	—	1 Cent, Copper, plain edge, 100 gr, J160	1800.
Pn161	1854	—	1 Cent, Bronze, plain edge, 96 gr, J161	1500.
Pn161a	1854	—	1 Cent, Bronze, restrike from damaged die, J161	1250.
Pn162	1854	—	1 Cent, Oroide, plain edge, J162	2750.
Pn163	1854	—	1 Cent, Copper, plain edge, 100 gr, J163	1850.
Pn164	1854	—	1 Cent, Bronze, plain edge, 96 gr, J164	3000.
Pn164a	1854	—	1 Cent, Bronze, restrike from damaged dies, J164	2200.
Pn165	1854	—	1 Cent, Copper, plain edge, restrike, J165	Rare
Pn166	1854	—	1 Cent, Copper, plain edge, 100 gr, J165a	—
Pn166a	1854	—	1 Cent, Copper, restrike from clashed dies, J165a	—
Pn167	1854	—	1 Cent, Bronze, plain edge, J165b	3000.
Pn167a	1854	—	1 Cent, Bronze, restrike from clashed dies, J165b	3000.
Pn168	1854	—	1/2 Dime, German Silver, plain edge, J166	—
Pn169	1855	—	1 Cent, Copper, plain edge, 100 gr, J167	1750.
Pn169a	1855	—	1 Cent, Copper, plain edge, 115 gr, restrike, J167	1650.
Pn170	1855	—	1 Cent, Pure Nickel, plain edge, J167a	—
Pn171	1855	—	1 Cent, Bronze, plain edge, 96 gr, J168	1350.
Pn171a	1855	—	1 Cent, Bronze, plain edge, 115 gr, restrike, J168	1200.
Pn172	1855	—	1 Cent, Oroide, plain edge, J169	—
Pn173	1855	—	1 Cent, Copper-Nickel (80-20), plain edge, J170	2450.
Pn174	1855	—	1 Cent, Copper-Nickel (60-40), plain edge, J171	1450.
Pn175	1855	—	1 Cent, Copper, plain edge, J172	2750.
Pn176	1855	—	1 Cent, Bronze, plain edge, J173	2250.
Pn177	1855	—	1 Cent, Oroide, plain edge, J174	—
Pn178	1855	—	1 Cent, Nickel, J174a	4500.
Pn179	1855	—	50 Cent, Aluminum, reeded edge, J175	Unique
Pn180	1855	—	1 Gold Dollar, White Metal, plain edge, J175a	Unique
Pn181	1855	—	10 Dollar, Copper, reeded edge, restrike, J176	Rare
Pn182	1856	—	1/2 Cent, Copper-Nickel, plain edge, J177	2850.
Pn183	1856	—	1 Cent, Copper-Nickel, plain	

KM#	Date	Mintage	Identification	Mkt.Val.
Pn183			edge, J178	3500.
Pn184	1856	—	1 Cent, Copper, plain edge, J179	5000.
Pn185	1856	—	1 Cent, Copper-Nickel, plain edge, J180	5000.
Pn186	1856	—	1 Cent, Copper, plain edge, J181	5000.
Pn187	1856	—	1 Cent, Bronze, plain edge, J182	5250.
Pn188	1856	—	1 Cent, Nickel, plain edge, J183	5250.
Pn189	1856	—	1 Cent, Copper-Nickel, plain edge, J184	6500.
Pn190	1855	—	1 Cent, Copper, plain edge, J185	5500.
Pn191	1857	—	1 Cent, Copper-Nickel, plain edge, J186	6250.
Pn192	1857	—	1 Cent, Copper, plain edge, J187	4250.
Pn193	1857	—	1 Cent, Nickel, plain edge, J187a	5000.
Pn194	1857	—	25 Cent, Copper, reeded edge, J188	2650.
Pn195	1857	—	2-1/2 Dollar, Copper, reeded edge, J189	2500.
Pn196	ND(1857)	1 known	20 Dollar, Copper, plain edge, J190	—
Pn197	1858	—	1 Cent, Copper-Nickel, plain edge, J191	2550.
Pn197a	1858	—	1 Cent, Copper-Nickel, restrike from rusty dies, J191	1250.
Pn198	1858	—	1 Cent, Copper-Nickel, plain edge, J192	2500.
Pn199	1858	—	1 Cent, Copper-Nickel, plain edge, J193	1650.
Pn200	1858	—	1 Cent, Copper-Nickel, broad planchet, plain edge, J194	Unique
Pn201	1858	—	1 Cent, Copper, plain edge, J195	Unique

KM#	Date	Mintage	Identification	Mkt.Val.
Pn202	1858	—	1 Cent, Copper-Nickel, J196	3500.
Pn203	1858	—	1 Cent, Copper-Nickel, J197	4500.
Pn204	1858	—	1 Cent, Copper-Nickel, J198	2450.
Pn205	1858	—	1 Cent, Copper-Nickel, broad planchet, plain edge, J199	4500.
Pn206	1858	—	1 Cent, Copper-Nickel, plain edge, J200	Rare
Pn207	1858	—	1 Cent, Copper-Nickel, plain edge, J201	Rare

KM#	Date	Mintage	Identification	Mkt.Val.
Pn208	1858	—	1 Cent, Copper-Nickel, plain edge, J202	1500.

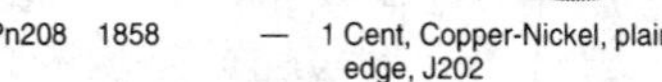

KM#	Date	Mintage	Identification	Mkt.Val.
Pn209	1858	—	1 Cent, Copper-Nickel, plain edge, J203	1500.

KM#	Date	Mintage	Identification	Mkt.Val.
Pn210	1858	—	1 Cent, Copper-Nickel, plain edge, J204	1500.
Pn211	1858	—	1 Cent, Copper, plain edge, J205	3000.
Pn212	1858	—	1 Cent, Copper-Nickel, plain edge, J206	1650.
Pn213	1858	—	1 Cent, Copper, plain edge, J207	2250.
Pn214	1858	—	1 Cent, Nickel, plain edge, J207a	3000.

KM#	Date	Mintage	Identification	Mkt.Val.
Pn215	1858	—	1 Cent, Copper-Nickel, plain edge, thick planchet, J208	1450.
Pn215a	1858	—	1 Cent, Copper-Nickel, plain edge, thin planchet, J208	950.00
Pn216	1858	—	1 Cent, Copper, plain edge, J209	4500.
Pn217	1858	—	1 Cent, Bronze, plain edge, J210	5000.

KM#	Date	Mintage	Identification	Mkt.Val.
Pn218	1858	—	1 Cent, Copper-Nickel, plain edge, J211	1250.

KM#	Date	Mintage	Identification	Mkt.Val.
Pn219	1858	—	1 Cent, Copper-Nickel, plain edge, J212	1150.
Pn220	1858	—	1 Cent, Copper-Nickel, plain edge, J213	1250.
Pn221	1858	—	1 Cent, Copper-Nickel, broad planchet, plain edge, J214	8250.
Pn222	1858	—	1 Cent, Copper, plain edge, J215	—
Pn223	1858	—	1 Cent, Copper-Nickel, broad planchet, plain edge, J216	—
Pn224	1858	—	1 Cent, Copper, plain edge, J217	—
Pn225	1858	—	1 Cent, Nickel, J217a	—
Pn226	1858	—	1 Cent, Copper, plain edge, J218	—
Pn227	1858	—	1 Cent, Nickel alloy, plain edge, J218a	—
Pn228	1858	—	1 Cent, Copper-Nickel, plain edge, J219	11,550.
Pn229	1858	—	1 Cent, Copper-Nickel, plain edge, J220	Unique
Pn230	1858	—	25 Cent, Silver, reeded edge, J221	4500.
Pn231	1858	—	50 Cent, Silver, reeded edge, J222	Rare
Pn232	1858	—	50 Cent, Copper, reeded edge, defaced, J223	Unique
Pn233	1858	—	1 Gold Dollar, Gold, reeded edge, J224	Unique
Pn234	1858	—	1 Gold Dollar, Copper, reeded edge, J225	6500.
Pn235	1859	—	1 Cent, Copper-Nickel, plain edge, J226	1150.

KM#	Date	Mintage	Identification	Mkt.Val.
Pn236	1859	—	1 Cent, Copper-Nickel, plain edge, J227	1200.

KM#	Date	Mintage	Identification	Mkt.Val.
Pn237	1859	—	1 Cent, Copper-Nickel, plain edge, J228	1000.
Pn238	1859	—	1 Cent, Copper, plain edge, J229	1250.

KM#	Date	Mintage	Identification	Mkt.Val.
Pn239	1859	—	1 Cent, Copper, plain edge, J230	1100.
Pn240	1859	—	1 Cent, Bronze, plain edge, J231	1550.
Pn241	1859	—	1 Cent, Lead, plain edge, J231a	—
Pn242	1859	—	1/2 Dime, Silver, reeded edge, J232	10,000.
Pn243	1859	—	10 Cent, Silver, reeded edge, J233	12,500.
Pn244	1859	—	25 Cent, Silver, reeded edge, J234	5000.

KM#	Date	Mintage	Identification	Mkt.Val.
Pn245	1859	—	50 Cent, Silver, reeded edge, J235	1450.
Pn246	1859	—	50 Cent, Copper, reeded edge, J236	3000.
Pn247	1859	—	50 Cent, Silver, reeded edge, J237	1650.
Pn248	1859	—	50 Cent, Copper, reeded edge, J238	1900.

KM#	Date	Mintage	Identification	Mkt.Val.
Pn249	1859	—	50 Cent, Silver, reeded edge, J239	2650.
Pn250	1859	—	50 Cent, Copper, reeded edge, J240	2750.

KM#	Date	Mintage	Identification	Mkt.Val.
Pn251	1859	—	50 Cent, Silver, reeded edge, J241	2450.
Pn252	1859	—	50 Cent, Copper, reeded edge, J242	2000.
Pn253	1859	—	50 Cent, Silver, reeded edge, J243	2000.
Pn254	1859	—	50 Cent, Copper, reeded edge, J244	1750.

KM#	Date	Mintage	Identification	Mkt.Val.
Pn255	1859	—	50 Cent, Silver, reeded edge, J245	3750.
Pn256	1859	—	50 Cent, Copper, reeded edge, J246	3650.
Pn257	1859	—	50 Cent, Silver, reeded edge,	

KM#	Date	Mintage	Identification	Mkt.Val.
Pn257			K247	2400.
Pn258	1859	—	50 Cent, Copper, reeded edge, J248	2200.
Pn259	1859	—	50 Cent, Silver, reeded edge, J249	2400.
Pn260	1859	—	50 Cent, Copper, reeded edge, J250	2200.
Pn261	1859	—	50 Cent, Silver, reeded edge, J251	2350.
Pn262	1859	—	50 Cent, Copper, reeded edge, J252	2150.
Pn263	1859	—	50 Cent, Silver, reeded edge, J253	2800.
Pn264	1838(1859)	2 known	50 Cent, Silver, reeded edge, J254	—
Pn265	1838(1859)	3 known	50 Cent, Copper, reeded edge, J255	4000.
Pn266	1859	—	1 Gold Dollar, Copper, reeded edge, J256	3500.
Pn267	1859	—	20 Dollar, Copper, reeded edge, J257	5000.
Pn267a	1859	—	20 Dollar, Copper Bronzed, reeded edge, J257	5000.
Pn267b	1859	—	20 Dollar, Copper Gilt, reeded edge, J257	5000.
Pn268	1859	—	20 Dollar, Copper, reeded edge, J258	5500.
Pn268a	1859	—	20 Dollar, Copper Gilt, reeded edge, J258	5500.
Pn269	1859	—	20 Dollar, Copper, reeded edge, J259	—
Pn270	1859	—	20 Dollar, Copper, reeded edge, J260	8000.
Pn270a	1859	—	20 Dollar, Copper Gilt, reeded edge, J260	8000.
Pn271	1859	—	20 Dollar, Copper, reeded edge, J261	—
Pn271a	1859	—	20 Dollar, Copper Gilt, reeded edge, J261	—
Pn272	1859	—	20 Dollar, Copper, reeded edge, J262	6000.
Pn272a	1859	—	20 Dollar, Copper Gilt, reeded edge, J262	6000.
Pn273	1859	—	20 Dollar, Copper, reeded edge, J263	—
Pn274	ND(1860)	—	1 Cent, Copper-Nickel, plain edge, J264	—
Pn275	1860	—	1 Cent, Copper, plain edge, J265	1000.
Pn276	1860	—	1 Cent, Copper-Nickel, plain edge, J266	—
Pn277	1860	100	1/2 Dime, Silver, reeded edge, J267	4000.
Pn278	1860	—	2-1/2 Dollar, Copper-Nickel, J268	—
Pn279	1860	—	50 Cent, Copper, reeded edge, J269	—
Pn280	1857//1860	—	2-1/2 Dollar, Copper, reeded edge, J270	4500.
Pn281	1860	—	5 Dollar, Gold, reeded edge, J271	Rare
Pn282	1860	—	5 Dollar, Copper, reeded edge, J272	4000.
Pn282a	1860	—	5 Dollar, Copper Gilt, reeded edge, J272	5000.

KM#	Date	Mintage	Identification	Mkt.Val.
Pn283	1860	—	20 Dollar, Gold, reeded edge, J272a	Unique
Pn284	1860	—	20 Dollar, Copper, reeded edge, J273	18,500.
Pn284a	1860	—	20 Dollar, Copper Gilt, reeded edge, J273	18,500.
Pn285	1861	—	1 Cent, Copper, plain edge, J274	—
Pn286	1861	—	25 Cent, Copper, reeded edge, J275	3500.
Pn287	1861	—	25 Cent, Copper-Nickel, reeded edge, J276	3500.

KM#	Date	Mintage	Identification	Mkt.Val.
Pn288	1861	—	50 Cent, Silver, reeded edge, J277	4500.
Pn289	1861	—	50 Cent, Copper, reeded edge, J278	2750.
Pn290	1861	—	50 Cent, Silver, reeded edge, J279	5000.
Pn291	1861	—	50 Cent, Copper, reeded edge, J280	4200.
Pn291a	1861	—	50 Cent, Copper Bronzed, reeded edge, J280	4000.
Pn292	1861	—	2-1/2 Dollar, Silver, reeded edge, J281	4500.
Pn293	1861	—	2-1/2 Dollar, Copper, reeded edge, J282	2500.

KM#	Date	Mintage	Identification	Mkt.Val.
Pn294	1861	—	5 Dollar, Copper, reeded edge, J283	3000.
Pn294a	1861	—	5 Dollar, Copper Bronzed, reeded edge, J283	2850.
Pn294b	1861	—	5 Dollar, Copper Gilt, reeded edge, J283	2850.
Pn295	1861	—	10 Dollar, Gold, reeded edge, J284	Rare
Pn296	1861	—	10 Dollar, Copper, reeded edge, J285	4000.
Pn297	1861	—	10 Dollar, Copper Bronzed, reeded edge, J285	3750.
Pn297a	1861	—	10 Dollar, Copper Gilt, reeded edge, J285	3750.
Pn298	1861	—	10 Dollar, Gold, reeded edge, J286	Rare
Pn299	1861	—	10 Dollar, Copper, reeded edge, J287	4250.
Pn300	1861	—	10 Dollar, Copper Bronzed, reeded edge, J287	4000.
Pn300a	1861	—	10 Dollar, Copper Gilt, reeded edge, J287	4000.
Pn301	1861	—	20 Dollar, Copper, J288	11,550.
Pn301a	1861	—	20 Dollar, Copper Gilt, J288	11,550.
Pn302	1861	—	20 Dollar, Copper, reeded edge, J289	Unique
Pn303	1862	—	1 Cent, Copper, plain edge, J290	2000.
Pn304	1862	—	1 Cent, Copper-Nickel, reeded edge, J291	2000.
Pn305	1862	—	1 Cent, Oroide, plain edge, J292	—
Pn306	1862	—	50 Cent, Silver, reeded edge, J293	2250.
Pn307	1862	—	50 Cent, Copper, reeded edge, J294	1250.
Pn308	1862	—	50 Cent, Silver, reeded edge, J295	2500.
Pn309	1862	—	50 Cent, Copper, reeded edge, J296	3550.
Pn310	1862	—	10 Dollar, Copper, reeded edge, J297	3250.
Pn310a	1862	—	10 Dollar, Copper Bronzed, reeded edge, J297	3000.

KM#	Date	Mintage	Identification	Mkt.Val.
Pn311	1862	—	10 Dollar, Copper, reeded edge, J298	2250.
Pn311a	1862	—	10 Dollar, Copper Bronzed, reeded edge, J298	2000.
Pn311b	1862	—	10 Dollar, Copper Gilt, reeded edge, J298	2000.

KM#	Date	Mintage	Identification	Mkt.Val.
Pn312	1863	—	1 Cent, Bronze, plain edge, J299	1250.
Pn313	1863	—	1 Cent, Copper-Nickel, reeded edge, J300	1650.
Pn314	1863	3 known	1 Cent, Bronze, plain edge, J301	10,450.
Pn315	1863	—	1 Cent, Copper-Nickel, plain edge, J302	20,900.
Pn316	1863	—	1 Cent, Oroide, plain edge, J303	—
Pn317	1863	2 known	1 Cent, Aluminum, plain edge, J304	—

KM#	Date	Mintage	Identification	Mkt.Val.
Pn318	1863	—	2 Cent, Bronze, thick planchet, plain edge, J305	1850.
Pn318a	1863	—	2 Cent, Bronze, thin planchet, plain edge, J305	1650.
Pn319	1863	—	2 Cent, Copper-Nickel, plain edge, J306	2000.
Pn320	1863	—	2 Cent, Oroide, plain edge, J307	—
Pn321	1863	—	2 Cent, Aluminum, plain edge, J308	—
Pn322	1863	—	2 Cent, Bronze, plain edge, J309	2500.
Pn323	1863	—	2 Cent, Copper-Nickel, plain edge, J310	2750.
Pn324	1863	—	2 Cent, Aluminum, plain edge, J311	5000.

KM#	Date	Mintage	Identification	Mkt.Val.
Pn325	1863	—	2 Cent, Bronze, plain edge, 96 gr, J312	2000.
Pn326	1863	—	2 Cent, Copper, plain edge, 106 gr, J312a	2000.
Pn327	1863	—	2 Cent, Copper-Nickel, plain edge, J313	2200.
Pn328	1863	—	2 Cent, Aluminum, plain edge, J314	—
Pn329	1863	—	2 Cent, Aluminum, plain edge, small motto, J314a	—
Pn330	1863	—	2 Cent, Bronze, plain edge, J315	4500.
Pn331	1863	—	2 Cent, Bronze, plain edge, J316	12,000.
Pn332	1863	—	2 Cent, Copper-Nickel, plain edge, J317	—
Pn333	1863	—	2 Cent, Aluminum, plain edge, J318	6500.

KM#	Date	Mintage	Identification	Mkt.Val.
Pn334	1863	—	3 Cent, Bronze, plain edge, 144 gr, J319	2000.
Pn334a	1863	—	3 Cent, Bronze, plain edge, 119 gr, restrike, J319	1850.
Pn335	1863	—	3 Cent, Aluminum, plain edge, J320	5750.

KM#	Date	Mintage	Identification	Mkt.Val.
Pn336	1863	—	3 Cent, Copper, plain edge, J321	4500.
Pn337	1863	—	3 Cent, Aluminum, plain edge, J322	3250.
Pn338	1863	—	1/2 Dime, Copper, reeded edge, J323	3750.
Pn339	1863	—	1/2 Dime, Aluminum, reeded edge, J324	2500.

KM#	Date	Mintage	Identification	Mkt.Val.
Pn340	1863	—	10 Cent, Silver, plain edge, J325	1650.
Pn341	1863	—	10 Cent, Silver, reeded edge, J325a	—
Pn342	1863	—	10 Cent, Copper-Silver (75-25), reeded edge, thin planchet, 25.25 g, J326	3750.
Pn342a	1863	—	10 Cent, Copper-Silver (75-25), reeded edge, thick planchet, 38.35 gr, J326	4000.
Pn343	1863	—	10 Cent, Copper-Silver (75-25), plain edge, J326a	2500.
Pn344	1863	—	10 Cent, Aluminum, plain edge, 11 gr, J327	2000.
Pn345	1863	—	10 Cent, Aluminum-Silver (97-3),	

KM#	Date	Mintage	Identification	Mkt.Val.
Pn345			reeded edge, 8 gr, J328	1800.
Pn346	1863	—	10 Cent, Tin, plain edge, 20.5 gr, J329	2350.
Pn347	1863	—	10 Cent, Tin-Copper (97-3), 25 gr, J330	6500.
Pn348	1863	—	10 Cent, Nickel, reeded edge, J330a	6500.
Pn349	1863	—	10 Cent, Silver-Nickel, reeded edge, J331	—
Pn350	1863	—	10 Cent, Copper, reeded edge, J331a	—
Pn351	1863	—	10 Cent, Nickel, J331b	—
Pn352	1863	—	10 Cent, Aluminum, plain edge, J332	2750.
Pn353	1863	—	10 Cent, Copper, reeded edge, J333	1600.
Pn354	1863	—	10 Cent, Aluminum, reeded edge, J334	2200.
Pn355	1863	—	25 Cent, Silver, reeded edge, J335	2450.
Pn356	1863	—	25 Cent, Copper, reeded edge, J336	3000.
Pn357	1863	—	25 Cent, Aluminum, reeded edge, J337	3500.
Pn358	1863	—	50 Cent, Silver, reeded edge, J338	1350.
Pn359	1863	—	50 Cent, Copper, reeded edge, J339	2000.
Pn360	1863	—	50 Cent, Silver, reeded edge, J340	4500.
Pn361	1863	—	50 Cent, Copper, reeded edge, J341	2450. 2200.
Pn362	1863	—	50 Cent, Silver, reeded edge, J342	2750.
Pn363	1863	—	50 Cent, Copper, reeded edge, J343	2500.
Pn364	1863	—	50 Cent, Aluminum, reeded edge, J344	2750.
Pn365	1863	—	1 Dollar, Silver, reeded edge, J345	27,500.
Pn366	1863	—	1 Dollar, Copper, reeded edge, J346	11,500.
Pn367	1863	—	1 Dollar, Aluminum, reeded edge, J347	10,850.
Pn368	1863	—	1 Dollar, Copper, reeded edge, J348	3000.
Pn369	1863	—	10 Dollar, Gold, reeded edge, J349	Rare
Pn370	1863	—	10 Dollar, Copper, reeaed edge, J350	3000.
Pn371	1863	—	10 Dollar, Gold, reeded edge, J351	Rare
Pn372	1863	—	10 Dollar, Copper, reeded edge, J352	3000.
Pn373	1864	—	1 Cent, Copper-Aluminum (13:1), plain edge, 39 gr, J353	2250.
Pn374	1864	—	1 Cent, Copper-Aluminum (19:1), plain edge, J354	4250.
Pn375	1864	—	1 Cent, Copper-Aluminum (9:1), plain edge, 40 gr, J355	1800.
Pn376	1864	—	1 Cent, Bronze, thin planchet, J355a	4150.
Pn377	1864	—	1 Cent, Copper-Tin (9:1), plain edge, 45 gr, J356	2750.
Pn378	1864	—	1 Cent, Copper, thick planchet, plain edge, J356a	1450.
Pn379	1864	—	1 Cent, Copper, plain edge, J357	2250.
Pn380	1864	—	1 Cent, Copper-Nickel, plain edge, thick planchet, J358	2250.
Pn380a	1864	—	1 Cent, Copper-Nickel, plain edge, thin planchet, J358a	2000.
Pn381	1864	—	1 Cent, Nickel, plain edge, J359	—
Pn382	1864	—	1 Cent, Oroide, plain edge, J360	—
Pn383	1864	2	1 Cent, Aluminum, plain edge, J361	2250.
Pn384	1864	—	1 Cent, Composition, plain edge, J361a	6500.
Pn385	1864	—	1 Cent, Copper-Nickel, plain edge, J362	—
Pn386	1864	—	2 Cent, Copper, plain edge, J363	2000.
Pn387	1864	—	2 Cent, Copper-Nickel, plain edge, large planchet, J364	—
Pn388	1864	—	2 Cent, Aluminum, plain edge, J365	—
Pn389	1864	—	2 Cent, Bronze, plain edge, J366	6000.
Pn390	1864	—	2 Cent, Copper, plain edge, J367	6000.
Pn391	1864	—	2 Cent, Copper-Nickel, plain edge, J368	—
Pn392	1864	—	2 Cent, Aluminum, plain edge, J369	—
Pn393	1864	—	2 Cent, Copper, plain edge, J370	3000.
Pn394	1864	—	2 Cent, Copper-Nickel, plain edge, J371	1850.
Pn395	1864	—	2 Cent, Aluminum, plain edge, J372	—
Pn396	1864	—	2 Cent, Nickel, plain edge, J372a	—
Pn397	1864	—	2 Cent, Copper, plain edge, J373	—
Pn398	1864	—	2 Cent, Copper-Nickel, plain edge, J374	—
Pn399	1864	—	3 Cent, Copper, plain edge, J375	5000.
Pn400	1864	—	3 Cent, Aluminum, plain edge, J376	5000.
Pn401	1864	—	3 Cent, Nickel, plain edge, J377	—
Pn402	1864	—	1/2 Dime, Copper, reeded edge, J378	4800.
Pn403	1864	—	1/2 Dime, Aluminum, reeded edge, J379	—
Pn404	1864	—	1/2 Dime, Nickel, reeded edge, J380	—
Pn405	1864	—	10 Cent, Copper, reeded edge, J381	3000.
Pn406	1864	—	10 Cent, Aluminum, reeded edge, J382	6000.
Pn407	1864	—	10 Cent, Nickel, reeded edge, J383	6000.
Pn408	1864	—	25 Cent, Silver, reeded edge, J384	4000.
Pn409	1864	—	25 Cent, Copper, reeded edge, J385	3500.
Pn410	1864	—	25 Cent, Silver, reeded edge, J386	4500.
Pn411	1864	—	25 Cent, Copper, reeded edge, J387	1750.
Pn412	1864	—	25 Cent, Aluminum, reeded edge, J388	3500.
Pn413	1864	—	25 Cent, Nickel, reeded edge, J389	10,000.
Pn414	1864	—	25 Cent, Copper, reeded edge, J390	—
Pn415	1864	—	50 Cent, Silver, reeded edge, J391	6875.
Pn416	1864	—	50 Cent, Copper, reeded edge, J392	4500.
Pn417	1864	—	50 Cent, Aluminum, reeded edge, J393	4500.
Pn418	1864	—	50 Cent, Nickel, reeded edge, J394	Unique
Pn419	1864	—	50 Cent, Aluminum, reeded edge, J395	3500.
Pn420	1864	—	1 Dollar, Silver, reeded edge, J396	27,500.
Pn421	1864	—	1 Dollar, Copper, reeded edge, J397	—
Pn422	1864	—	1 Dollar, Aluminum, reeded edge, J398	Rare
Pn423	1864	—	1 Dollar, Nickel, reeded edge, J399	Rare
Pn424	1864	—	3 Dollar, Copper, reeded edge, J400	—
Pn425	1864	—	3 Dollar, Copper-Nickel, reeded edge, J401	—
Pn426	1864	—	3 Dollar, Nickel, reeded edge, J402	—
Pn427	1865	—	1 Cent, Copper, plain edge, J403	2500.
Pn428	1865	—	1 Cent, Copper, reeded edge, thin planchet, J403	3000.
Pn428a	1865	—	1 Cent, Copper, reeded edge, thick planchet, J403a	3250.
Pn429	1865	—	1 Cent, Copper-Nickel, plain edge, thin planchet, J404	3250.
Pn429a	1865	—	1 Cent, Copper-Nickel, plain edge, thick planchet, J404	3500.
Pn430	1865	—	1 Cent, Copper-Nickel, reeded edge, thin planchet, J405	3750.
Pn430a	1865	—	1 Cent, Copper-Nickel, reeded edge, thick planchet, J405	4000.
Pn431	1865	—	1 Cent, Nickel, plain edge, J406	3500.
Pn432	1865	2 known	1 Cent, Nickel-Silver, plain edge, J406a	—
Pn433	1865	—	2 Cent, Copper-Silver, plain edge, J407	1750.
Pn434	1865	—	2 Cent, Copper, plain edge, J408	3250.
Pn434a	1865	—	2 Cent, Copper, Silvered, plain edge, J408	3250.
Pn435	1865	—	2 Cent, Copper-Nickel, plain edge, J409	3750.
Pn436	1865	—	2 Cent, Nickel, plain edge, J409a	—
Pn437	1865	—	2 Cent, Silver, plain edge, J409b	—
Pn438	1865	—	3 Cent, Nickel, plain edge, J410	1850.
Pn439	1865	—	3 Cent, Copper, plain edge, J411	1150.
Pn440	1865	—	3 Cent, Aluminum, plain edge, J412	—
Pn441	1865	—	3 Cent, Copper, plain edge, J413	1250.
Pn442	1865	—	3 Cent, Oroide, plain edge, J414	—
Pn443	1865	—	3 Cent, Aluminum, plain edge, J414a	2250.
Pn444	1865	—	3 Cent, Copper, plain edge, J415	2000.

KM#	Date	Mintage	Identification	Mkt.Val.
Pn445	1865	—	5 Cent, Nickel, plain edge, J416	5500.
Pn446	1865	—	5 Cent, Copper, plain edge, J417	3550.
Pn447	1865	—	5 Cent, Nickel, plain edge, J418	3550.
Pn448	1865	—	5 Cent, Copper, plain edge, J419	3550.
Pn449	1865	—	1/2 Dime, Copper, reeded edge, J420	4000.
Pn450	1865	—	10 Cent, Copper, reeded edge, J421	3250.
Pn451	1865	—	10 Cent, Nickel, reeded edge, J422	3750.
Pn452	1865	—	25 Cent, Silver, reeded edge, J423	4450.
Pn453	1865	—	25 Cent, Copper, reeded edge, J424	4000.
Pn454	1865	—	25 Cent, Silver & Copper, reeded edge, J424a	—
Pn455	1865	—	25 Cent, Silver, reeded edge, J425	4250.
Pn456	1865	—	25 Cent, Copper, reeded edge, J426	4850.
Pn457	1865	—	25 Cent, Aluminum, reeded edge, J427	4850.
Pn458	1865	—	25 Cent, Copper, J428	—
Pn459	1865	—	50 Cent, Silver, reeded edge, J429	8500.
Pn460	1865	—	50 Cent, Copper, reeded edge, J430	3250.
Pn461	1865	—	50 Cent, Aluminum, reeded edge, J431	3750.
Pn462	1865	—	50 Cent, Copper, reeded edge, J432	2750.
Pn463	1865	—	50 Cent, Aluminum, reeded edge, J433	4000.
Pn464	1865	—	1 Dollar, Silver, reeded edge, J434	12,000.
Pn465	1865	—	1 Dollar, Copper, reeded edge, J435	9000.
Pn466	1865	—	1 Dollar, Aluminum, reeded edge, J436	9000.
Pn467	1865	—	1 Dollar, Copper, reeded edge, J437	4000.
Pn468	1865	—	1 Gold Dollar, Copper, reeded edge, J438	3550.
Pn469	1865	—	2-1/2 Dollar, Copper, reeded edge, J439	3000.
Pn470	1865	2 known	3 Dollar, Gold, reeded edge, J440	Rare
Pn471	1865	—	3 Dollar, Copper, reeded edge, J441	3850.
Pn472	1865	1 known	3 Dollar, Silver, reeded edge, J441a	—
Pn473	1865	—	3 Dollar, Copper, reeded edge, J442	—
Pn474	1865	—	3 Dollar, Copper-Nickel, reeded edge, J443	—
Pn475	1865	—	3 Dollar, Nickel, reeded edge, J444	—
Pn476	1865	—	3 Dollar, Bronze, reeded edge, J444a	—

KM#	Date	Mintage	Identification	Mkt.Val.
Pn477	1865	2 known	5 Dollar, Gold, reeded edge, J445	Rare
Pn478	1865	—	5 Dollar, Copper, reeded edge, J446	5500.
Pn479	1865	—	5 Dollar, Copper, reeded edge, J447	5500.
Pn480	1865	—	5 Dollar, Aluminum, reeded edge, J448	6000.
Pn481	1865	2 known	10 Dollar, Gold, reeded edge, J449	Rare
Pn482	1865	—	10 Dollar, Copper, reeded edge, J450	4500.
Pn483	1865	—	10 Dollar, Copper, reeded edge, J451	6000.

KM#	Date	Mintage	Identification	Mkt.Val.
Pn484	1865	2 known	20 Dollar, Gold, reeded edge, J452	Rare
Pn485	1865	—	20 Dollar, Copper, reeded edge, J453	6500.
Pn486	1865	—	20 Dollar, Copper Gilt, reeded edge, J453	6000.
Pn487	1865	—	20 Dollar, Copper, reeded edge, J454	—
Pn488	1866	—	1 Cent, Copper, plain edge, J455	2150.
Pn489	1866	—	1 Cent, Copper-Nickel, plain edge, J456	2150.
Pn490	1866	—	1 Cent, Nickel, plain edge, J457	2250.
Pn491	1866	—	2 Cent, Copper-Nickel, plain edge, J458	—
Pn492	1866	—	2 Cent, Nickel, plain edge, J459	2000.
Pn493	1866	—	3 Cent, Copper, plain edge, J460	1500.

KM#	Date	Mintage	Identification	Mkt.Val.
Pn494	1866	—	5 Cent, Nickel, plain edge, J461	1800.
Pn495	1866	—	5 Cent, Copper, plain edge, J462	4000.
Pn496	1866	—	5 Cent, Copper-Nickel, plain edge, J463	3000.

KM#	Date	Mintage	Identification	Mkt.Val.
Pn497	1866	—	5 Cent, Nickel, plain edge, J464	4500.
Pn498	1866	—	5 Cent, Copper, plain edge, J465	8500.
Pn499	1866	—	5 Cent, Bronze, plain edge, J466	7150.
Pn500	1866	—	5 Cent, Silver, plain edge, J466a	—

KM#	Date	Mintage	Identification	Mkt.Val.
Pn501	1866	—	5 Cent, Nickel, plain edge, J467	4750.
Pn502	1866	—	5 Cent, Copper, plain edge, J468	4750.
Pn503	1866	—	5 Cent, Bronze, plain edge, J469	4750.

KM#	Date	Mintage	Identification	Mkt.Val.
Pn504	1866	—	5 Cent, Nickel, plain edge, J470	3200.
Pn505	1866	—	5 Cent, Copper, plain edge, J471	3000.
Pn506	1866	—	5 Cent, Bronze, plain edge, J472	3200.
Pn507	1866	—	5 Cent, Nickel, plain edge, J473	2850.
Pn508	1866	—	5 Cent, Copper, plain edge, J474	2850.
Pn509	1866	—	5 Cent, Bronze, plain edge, J475	2850.
Pn510	1866	1 known	5 Cent, Nickel, plain edge, J476	—
Pn511	1866	2 known	5 Cent, Copper, plain edge, J477	6500.
Pn512	1866	1 known	5 Cent, Brass, plain edge, J478	—
Pn513	1866	3 known	5 Cent, White Metal, plain edge, J479	6000.
Pn514	1866	—	5 Cent, Nickel, plain edge, J480	Unique
Pn515	1866	—	5 Cent, Nickel, plain edge, J481	4000.
Pn516	1866	—	5 Cent, Copper, plain edge, J482	4500.

KM#	Date	Mintage	Identification	Mkt.Val.
Pn517	1866	—	5 Cent, Nickel, plain edge, J483	5750.
Pn518	1866	—	5 Cent, Copper, plain edge, J484	5500.
Pn519	1866	—	5 Cent, Bronze, plain edge, J485	8000.
Pn520	1866	—	5 Cent, Nickel, plain edge, J486	7500.
Pn521	1866	—	5 Cent, Copper, plain edge, J487	6500.
Pn522	1866	—	5 Cent, Bronze, plain edge, J488	4850.

KM#	Date	Mintage	Identification	Mkt.Val.
Pn523	1866	—	5 Cent, Nickel, plain edge, J489	2500.
Pn524	1866	—	5 Cent, Copper, plain edge, J490	3250.
Pn525	1866	—	5 Cent, Bronze, plain edge, J491	3250.

KM#	Date	Mintage	Identification	Mkt.Val.
Pn526	1866	—	5 Cent, Nickel, plain edge, J492	4500.
Pn527	1866	—	5 Cent, Copper, plain edge, J493	4500.

KM#	Date	Mintage	Identification	Mkt.Val.
Pn528	1866	—	5 Cent, Nickel, plain edge, J494	7500.
Pn529	1866	—	5 Cent, Copper, plain edge, J495	7150.
Pn530	1866	—	5 Cent, Bronze, plain edge, J496	7150.

KM#	Date	Mintage	Identification	Mkt.Val.
Pn531	1866	—	5 Cent, Nickel, plain edge, J497	4500.
Pn532	1866	—	5 Cent, Copper, plain edge, J498	5250.
Pn533	1866	—	5 Cent, Bronze, plain edge, J499	5250.
Pn534	1866	—	5 Cent, Nickel, plain edge, J500	—
Pn535	1866	—	5 Cent, Nickel, plain edge, J501	4650.
Pn536	1866	—	5 Cent, Copper, plain edge, J502	4650.
Pn537	1866	—	5 Cent, Bronze, plain edge, J503	4650.
Pn538	1866	—	5 Cent, Nickel, plain edge, J504	3150.
Pn539	1866	—	5 Cent, Copper, plain edge, J505	2750.
Pn540	1866	—	5 Cent, Bronze, plain edge, J506	2750.

KM#	Date	Mintage	Identification	Mkt.Val.
Pn541	1866	—	5 Cent, Nickel, plain edge, J507	3150.
Pn542	1866	—	5 Cent, Copper, plain edge, J508	2500.
Pn543	1866	—	5 Cent, Bronze, plain edge, J509	2200.
Pn544	1866	—	5 Cent, White Metal, J509a	3000.
Pn545	1866	—	5 Cent, Copper, plain edge, J510	—
Pn546	1866	—	5 Cent, Bronze, plain edge, J511	—
Pn547	1866	—	5 Cent, Steel, plain edge, J512	—
Pn548	1866	—	5 Cent, Nickel, plain edge, J513	—
Pn549	1866	—	5 Cent, Copper, plain edge, J514	—
Pn550	1866	—	5 Cent, Brass, plain edge, J515	—
Pn551	1866	—	5 Cent, Nickel, plain edge, J516	2250.
Pn552	1866	—	5 Cent, Copper, plain edge, J517	2750.
Pn553	1866	—	5 Cent, Silver, plain edge, J518	4500.
Pn554	1866	—	5 Cent, Brass, plain edge, J519	3500.

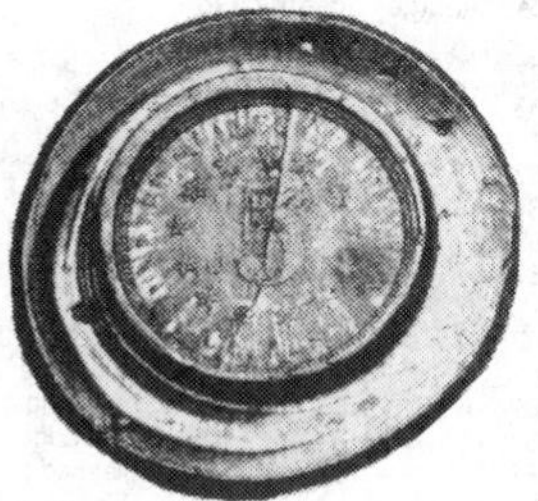

KM#	Date	Mintage	Identification	Mkt.Val.
Pn555	1866	—	5 Cent, Lead, plain edge, J520	1750.

KM#	Date	Mintage	Identification	Mkt.Val.
Pn556	1866	—	5 Cent, Silver, plain edge, J521	—
Pn557	1866	—	5 Cent, Copper, plain edge, J522	4000.
Pn558	1866	—	5 Cent, Brass, plain edge, J523	4000.
Pn559	1866	—	5 Cent, White Metal, plain edge, J524	4000.
Pn559a	1866	—	5 Cent, Nickel, plain edge, J524a	7750.
Pn560	1866	—	5 Cent, Copper, plain edge, J525	8500.
Pn561	1866	—	5 Cent, White Metal, plain edge, J526	4000.
Pn562	1866	—	5 Cent, Nickel, plain edge, J527	—
Pn563	1866	—	5 Cent, Nickel, plain edge, J528	—
Pn564	1866	—	5 Cent, Nickel, plain edge, J529	—
Pn565	1866	—	5 Cent, White Metal, plain edge, J530	5000.
Pn566	1866	—	5 Cent, Nickel, plain edge, J531	5000.
Pn567	1866	—	5 Cent, Nickel, plain edge, J531a	5000.
Pn568	1866	—	5 Cent, White Metal, plain edge, J532	7500.
Pn569	1866	—	5 Cent, Copper, plain edge, J533	—
Pn570	1866	—	10 Cent, Nickel, reeded edge, J534	3500.
Pn571	1866	—	10 Cent, Silver Nickel, reeded edge, J535	—
Pn572	1866	—	25 Cent, Silver, reeded edge, J536	Unique
Pn573	1866	—	25 Cent, Copper, reeded edge, J537	5000.
Pn574	1866	—	50 Cent, Silver, reeded edge, J538	Unique
Pn575	1866	—	50 Cent, Copper, reeded edge, J539	1750.
Pn576	1866	2 known	1 Dollar, Silver, reeded edge, J540	Rare

KM#	Date	Mintage	Identification	Mkt.Val.
Pn577	1866	—	1 Dollar, Copper, reeded edge, J541	5000.
Pn578	1866	—	2-1/2 Dollar, Nickel, reeded edge, J542	4500.
Pn579	1866	—	3 Dollar, Nickel, reeded edge, J543	4500.
Pn580	1866	—	3 Dollar, Aluminum, reeded edge, J544	—
Pn581	1866	1 known	5 Dollar, White Metal, plain edge, J545	Rare
Pn582	1866	—	5 Dollar, Copper, reeded edge, J546	3500.
Pn583	1866	1 known	5 Dollar, White Metal, plain edge, J547	4500.
Pn584	1866	—	10 Dollar, Copper, reeded edge, J548	5000.
Pn585	1866	—	20 Dollar, Copper, reeded edge, J549	7000.
Pn585a	1866	—	20 Dollar, Copper, Gilt, reeded	

KM#	Date	Mintage	Identification	Mkt.Val.
Pn585a			edge, J549	7000.
Pn586	1867	—	1 Cent, Copper, plain edge, J550	2250.
Pn587	1867	—	1 Cent, Copper-Nickel, plain edge, J551	—
Pn588	1867	—	1 Cent, Nickel, plain edge, J552	2500.
Pn589	1867	—	1 Cent, Oroide, plain edge, J553	—
Pn590	1867	—	2 Cent, Copper, plain edge, J554	2000.
Pn591	1867	—	2 Cent, Copper-Nickel, plain edge, J555	—
Pn592	1867	—	2 Cent, Nickel, plain edge, J556	2250.
Pn593	1867	—	2 Cent, Oroide, plain edge, J557	2000.
Pn594	1867	—	3 Cent, Copper, plain edge, J558	2650.
Pn595	1867	—	3 Cent, Oroide, plain edge, J559	—
Pn596	1867	—	3 Cent, Copper, plain edge, J560	2000.

KM#	Date	Mintage	Identification	Mkt.Val.
Pn597	1867	—	5 Cent, Aluminum, plain edge, J561	2150.
Pn598	1867	—	5 Cent, Aluminum, reeded edge, J562	2150.
Pn599	1867	—	5 Cent, Copper, plain edge, J563	—
Pn600	1867	—	5 Cent, Copper, reeded edge, J564	2500.
Pn601	1867	—	5 Cent, Nickel, plain edge, J565	—

KM#	Date	Mintage	Identification	Mkt.Val.
Pn602	1867	—	5 Cent, Nickel, plain edge, J566	2150.
Pn603	1867	—	5 Cent, Copper, plain edge, J567	2250.
Pn604	1867	—	5 Cent, Copper, plain edge, J568	—
Pn605	1867	1 known	5 Cent, Nickel, plain edge, J569	—
Pn606	1867	—	5 Cent, Nickel, plain edge, J570	1750.
Pn607	1867	—	5 Cent, Copper, plain edge, J571	2000.
Pn608	1867	—	5 Cent, Copper, plain edge, J572	3500.

KM#	Date	Mintage	Identification	Mkt.Val.
Pn609	1867	—	5 Cent, Copper, plain edge, J573	2650.

KM#	Date	Mintage	Identification	Mkt.Val.
Pn610	1867	2 known	5 Cent, Copper, plain edge, J573a	5000.
Pn611	1867	—	5 Cent, White Metal, plain edge, J574	—
Pn612	1867	—	5 Cent, Nickel, plain edge, J575	—
Pn613	1867	—	5 Cent, Nickel, plain edge, J576	—
Pn614	1867	—	5 Cent, Nickel, plain edge, J577	—
Pn615	1867	—	5 Cent, Nickel, plain edge, J578	—
Pn616	1867	—	5 Cent, Copper, plain edge, J578a	—
Pn617	1867	—	5 Cent, Silver, plain edge, J579	—
Pn618	1867	—	5 Cent, Nickel, plain edge, J580	—
Pn619	1867	—	5 Cent, White Metal, plain edge, J581	—
Pn620	1867	—	5 Cent, Nickel, plain edge, J582	2750.
Pn621	1867	—	5 Cent, Silver, plain edge, J583	2750.
Pn622	1867	—	5 Cent, White Metal, plain edge, J584	—
Pn622a	1867	—	5 Cent, Nickel, plain edge, J584a	9350.
Pn623	1867	—	5 Cent, White Metal, plain edge, J585	3000.
Pn624	1867	—	1/2 Dime, Copper, reeded edge, J586	2750.

KM#	Date	Mintage	Identification	Mkt.Val.
Pn625	1867	—	10 Cent, Copper, reeded edge, J587	5000.
Pn626	1867	—	10 Cent, Nickel, reeded edge, J588	4500.
Pn627	1867	—	10 Cent, Silver-Nickel, reeded edge, J589	—
Pn628	1867	—	25 Cent, Copper, reeded edge, J590	3000.
Pn629	1867	—	50 Cent, Copper, reeded edge, J591	3500.

KM#	Date	Mintage	Identification	Mkt.Val.
Pn630	1867	—	1 Dollar, Copper, reeded edge, J592	4500.
Pn631	1867	5	1 Dollar, Brass, reeded edge, J593	7000.
Pn632	1867	—	1 Gold Dollar, Copper, reeded edge, J594	—
Pn633	1867	—	2-1/2 Dollar, Copper, reeded edge, J595	5500.
Pn634	1867	—	3 Dollar, Copper, reeded edge, J596	5250.
Pn635	1867	—	3 Dollar, Nickel, reeded edge, J597	—
Pn636	1867	—	3 Dollar, Silver, reeded edge, J598	6500.
Pn637	1867	—	5 Dollar, Copper, reeded edge, J599	4000.
Pn638	1867	—	5 Dollar, Nickel, reeded edge, J600	4000.

KM#	Date	Mintage	Identification	Mkt.Val.
Pn639	1867	2 known	5 Dollar, Nickel, plain edge, J601	7150.
Pn640	1867	—	10 Dollar, Copper, reeded edge, J602	6850.
Pn641	1867	—	10 Dollar, Nickel, reeded edge, J603	7000.
Pn642	1867	—	20 Dollar, Copper, reeded edge, J604	6500.
Pn643	1868	—	1 Cent, Nickel, plain edge, J605	2000.
Pn644	1868	—	1 Cent, Copper, plain edge, J606	2500.
Pn645	1868	—	1 Cent, Aluminum, plain edge, J607	2750.

KM#	Date	Mintage	Identification	Mkt.Val.
Pn646	1868	—	1 Cent, Nickel, plain edge, J608	1550.
Pn647	1868	—	1 Cent, Copper, plain edge, J609	2000.

KM#	Date	Mintage	Identification	Mkt.Val.
Pn648	1868	—	1 Cent, Nickel, plain edge, J610	7250.

KM#	Date	Mintage	Identification	Mkt.Val.
Pn649	1868	—	1 Cent, Copper, plain edge, J611	6000.
Pn650	1868	—	1 Cent, Aluminum, plain edge, J612	3000.
Pn651	1868	—	2 Cent, Nickel, plain edge, J613	3000.
Pn652	1868	—	2 Cent, Aluminum, plain edge, J614	3000.

KM#	Date	Mintage	Identification	Mkt.Val.
Pn653	1868	—	3 Cent, Nickel, plain edge, J615	2250.
Pn654	1868	—	3 Cent, Copper-Nickel, plain edge, J615a	1750.
Pn655	1868	—	3 Cent, Copper, plain edge, J616	2600.
Pn656	1868	—	3 Cent, Aluminum, plain edge, J617	2600.
Pn657	1868	—	3 Cent, Aluminum, plain edge, J617a	—
Pn658	1868	2 known	3 Cent, Copper, plain edge, J617b	—
Pn659	1868	—	3 Cent, Copper-Nickel, plain edge, J617c	—

KM#	Date	Mintage	Identification	Mkt.Val.
Pn660	1868	—	3 Cent, Nickel, plain edge, J618	1650.
Pn661	1868	—	3 Cent, Copper, plain edge, J619	2750.
Pn662	1868	—	3 Cent, Aluminum, plain edge, J620	1750.
Pn663	1868	—	3 Cent, Aluminum, plain edge, J620a	—
Pn664	1868	—	3 Cent, Aluminum, plain edge, J621	1700.
Pn665	1868	—	3 Cent, Aluminum, plain edge, J622	1850.

KM#	Date	Mintage	Identification	Mkt.Val.
Pn666	1868	—	5 Cent, Nickel, plain edge, J623	1250.

KM#	Date	Mintage	Identification	Mkt.Val.
Pn667	1868	—	5 Cent, Nickel, broad planchet, plain edge, J624	2450.
Pn668	1868	—	5 Cent, Nickel, broad planchet, reeded edge, J625	6500.
Pn669	1868	—	5 Cent, Copper, plain edge, J626	2000.
Pn670	1868	—	5 Cent, Copper, broad planchet, plain edge, J627	2800.
Pn671	1868	—	5 Cent, Copper, broad planchet, reeded edge, J628	3000.
Pn672	1868	—	5 Cent, Aluminum, plain edge, J629	3750.
Pn673	1868	—	5 Cent, Nickel, plain edge, J630	4500.

KM#	Date	Mintage	Identification	Mkt.Val.
Pn674	1868	—	5 Cent, Copper, plain edge, J631	5500.
Pn675	1868	—	5 Cent, Copper, plain edge, J632	—
Pn676	1868	—	5 Cent, Aluminum, plain edge, J632a	Rare

KM#	Date	Mintage	Identification	Mkt.Val.
Pn677	1868	—	5 Cent, Nickel, plain edge, J633	1500.
Pn678	1868	—	5 Cent, Copper, plain edge, J634	1750.
Pn679	1868	—	5 Cent, Copper, plain edge, J635	3200.
Pn680	1868	—	5 Cent, Aluminum, plain edge, J636	3000.
Pn681	1868	—	1/2 Dime, Copper, plain edge,	

KM#	Date	Mintage	Identification	Mkt.Val.
Pn681			J637	2750.
Pn682	1868	—	1/2 Dime, Nickel, plain edge, J638	3250.
Pn683	1868	—	1/2 Dime, Aluminum, plain edge, J639	3000.
Pn684	1868	—	10 Cent, Silver, reeded edge, J640	—
Pn685	1868	—	10 Cent, Nickel, reeded edge, J641	3250.
Pn686	1868	—	10 Cent, Copper, reeded edge, J642	3500.
Pn687	1868	—	10 Cent, Silver, reeded edge, J643	3000.
Pn688	1868	—	10 Cent, Nickel, reeded edge, J644	3750.
Pn689	1868	—	10 Cent, Copper, plain edge, J645	4500.
Pn690	1868	—	10 Cent, Aluminum, plain edge, J646	2650.

KM#	Date	Mintage	Identification	Mkt.Val.
Pn691	1868	—	10 Cent, Nickel, plain edge, J647	2550.
Pn692	1868	—	10 Cent, Copper, plain edge, J648	2800.
Pn693	1868	—	10 Cent, Aluminum, reeded edge, J649	2000.
Pn694	1868	—	25 Cent, Aluminum, reeded edge, J650	2000.
Pn695	1868	—	50 Cent, Aluminum, reeded edge, J651	2200.
Pn696	1868	—	1 Dollar, Aluminum, reeded edge, J652	2500.
Pn697	1868	—	1 Gold Dollar, Aluminum, reeded edge, J653	3250.
Pn698	1868	—	2-1/2 Dollar, Aluminum, reeded edge, J654	3000.
Pn699	1868	—	3 Dollar, Aluminum, reeded edge, J655	4000.

KM#	Date	Mintage	Identification	Mkt.Val.
Pn700	1868	—	5 Dollar, Copper, reeded edge, J656	4500.
Pn700a	1868	—	5 Dollar, Copper Gilt, reeded edge, J656	4250.
Pn701	1868	—	5 Dollar, Copper, plain edge, J657	4250.
Pn702	1868	—	5 Dollar, Aluminum, reeded edge, J658	4200.
Pn703	1868	—	5 Dollar, Alluminum, plain edge, J659	4200.
Pn704	1868	—	5 Dollar, Aluminum, reeded edge, J660	4500.
Pn705	1868	4 known	10 Dollar, Gold, reeded edge, J661	Rare
Pn706	1868	—	10 Dollar, Copper, reeded edge, J662	4000.
Pn706a	1868	—	10 Dollar, Copper Gilt, reeded edge, J662	3950.
Pn707	1868	—	10 Dollar, Aluminum, reeded edge, J663	3750.
Pn708	1868	—	10 Dollar, Aluminum, reeded edge, J664	3500.
Pn709	1868	—	20 Dollar, Aluminum, reeded edge, J665	7250.

KM#	Date	Mintage	Identification	Mkt.Val.
Pn710	1869	—	1 Cent, Nickel, plain edge, J666	1650.
Pn711	1869	—	1 Cent, Copper, plain edge, J667	3000.
Pn712	1869	—	1 Cent, Copper, plain edge, J668	1650.
Pn713	1869	—	1 Cent, Copper-Nickel, plain edge, J669	3250.
Pn714	1869	—	1 Cent, Nickel, plain edge, J670	1850.
Pn715	1869	—	1 Cent, Aluminum, plain edge, J671	1650.
Pn716	1869	—	2 Cent, Copper, plain edge, J672	4000.
Pn717	1869	—	2 Cent, Nickel, plain edge, J673	—
Pn718	1869	—	2 Cent, Aluminum, plain edge, J674	4000.
Pn719	1869	—	2 Cent, Copper-Aluminum, plain edge, J674a	3950.
Pn720	1869	—	2 Cent, Silver-Copper, plain edge, J675	—
Pn721	1869	—	3 Cent, Nickel, plain edge, J676	1500.
Pn722	1869	—	3 Cent, Copper, plain edge, J677	2500.
Pn723	1869	—	3 Cent, Copper, plain edge, J678	2450.
Pn724	1869	—	3 Cent, Aluminum, plain edge, J679	2200.
Pn725	1869	—	3 Cent, Copper, plain edge, J680	2200.
Pn726	1869	—	3 Cent, Nickel, plain edge, J681	—

KM#	Date	Mintage	Identification	Mkt.Val.
Pn727	1869	—	3 Cent, Aluminum, plain edge, J682	2200.
Pn728	1869	—	5 Cent, Nickel, plain edge, J683	6650.
Pn729	1869	—	5 Cent, Nickel, plain edge, J684	2250.
Pn730	1869	—	5 Cent, Copper, plain edge, J685	2200.
Pn731	1869	—	5 Cent, Nickel, plain edge, J686	—
PnA732	1869	—	5 Cent, Nickel, obv. as Pn731, rev. bust right Washington	10,450.
Pn732	1869	—	5 Cent, Copper, plain edge, J687	6500.
Pn733	1869	—	5 Cent, Aluminum, plain edge, J688	6000.
Pn734	1869	—	5 Cent, Steel, plain edge, J689	Unique
Pn735	1869	—	5 Cent, Nickel, plain edge, J690	—
Pn736	1869	—	5 Cent, Nickel, plain edge, J691	Unique
Pn737	1869	—	1/2 Dime, Copper, reeded edge, J692	2000.
Pn738	1869	—	1/2 Dime, Aluminum, reeded edge, J693	1550.
Pn739	1869	—	1/2 Dime, Nickel, reeded edge, J694	2750.
Pn740	1869	—	1/2 Dime, Nickel, plain edge, J695	2750.

KM#	Date	Mintage	Identification	Mkt.Val.
Pn741	1869	—	10 Cent, Silver, reeded edge, J696	1500.
Pn742	1869	—	10 Cent, Silver, plain edge, J697	2000.
Pn743	1869	—	10 Cent, Copper, reeded edge, J698	1000.
Pn744	1869	—	10 Cent, Copper, plain edge, J699	2850.
Pn745	1869	—	10 Cent, Aluminum, reeded edge, J700	3750.
Pn746	1869	—	10 Cent, Aluminum, reeded edge, J701	3250.

KM#	Date	Mintage	Identification	Mkt.Val.
Pn747	1869	—	10 Cent, Silver, reeded edge, J702	1200.
Pn748	1869	—	10 Cent, Silver, plain edge, J703	2700.
Pn749	1869	—	10 Cent, Copper, reeded edge, J704	3000.
Pn750	1869	—	10 Cent, Copper, plain edge, J705	1750.
Pn751	1869	—	10 Cent, Aluminum, reeded edge, J706	1500.
Pn752	1869	—	10 Cent, Aluminum, plain edge, J707	1500.

KM#	Date	Mintage	Identification	Mkt.Val.
Pn753	1869	—	10 Cent, Silver, reeded edge, J708	1250.
Pn754	1869	—	10 Cent, Silver, plain edge, J709	1250.
Pn755	1869	—	10 Cent, Copper, reeded edge, J710	1650.
Pn756	1869	—	10 Cent, Copper, plain edge, J711	1650.
Pn757	1869	—	10 Cent, Aluminum, reeded edge, J712	1650.
Pn758	1869	—	10 Cent, Aluminum, plain edge, J713	1650.

KM#	Date	Mintage	Identification	Mkt.Val.
Pn759	1869	—	10 Cent, Silver-Nickel, reeded edge, J714	2500.
Pn760	1869	—	10 Cent, Copper, reeded edge, J715	2500.

KM#	Date	Mintage	Identification	Mkt.Val.
Pn761	1869	—	10 Cent, Silver-Nickel-Copper, reeded edge, J716	1800.
Pn762	1869	3 known	10 Cent, Silver, reeded edge, J716a	3500.
Pn763	1869	—	10 Cent, Copper, reeded edge, J717	2500.
Pn764	1869	—	10 Cent, Copper-Nickel (75-25), reeded edge, J717a	—
Pn765	1869	—	10 Cent, Copper, reeded edge, J718	4000.
Pn766	1869	—	10 Cent, Aluminum, reeded edge, J719	4000.
Pn767	1869	—	10 Cent, Nickel, reeded edge, J720	4300.

KM#	Date	Mintage	Identification	Mkt.Val.
Pn768	1869	—	25 Cent, Silver, reeded edge, J721	1250.
Pn769	1869	—	25 Cent, Silver, plain edge, J722	1500.
Pn770	1869	—	25 Cent, Copper, reeded edge, J723	2200.
Pn771	1869	—	25 Cent, Copper, plain edge, J724	2200.
Pn772	1869	—	25 Cent, Aluminum, reeded edge, J725	2200.
Pn773	1869	—	25 Cent, Aluminum, plain edge, J726	1900.

KM#	Date	Mintage	Identification	Mkt.Val.
Pn774	1869	—	25 Cent, Silver, reeded edge, J727	2750.
Pn775	1869	—	25 Cent, Silver, plain edge, J728	2850.
Pn776	1869	—	25 Cent, Copper, reeded edge, J729	2250.
Pn777	1869	—	25 Cent, Copper, plain edge, J730	2250.
Pn778	1869	—	25 Cent, Aluminum, reeded edge, J731	2800.
Pn779	1869	—	25 Cent, Aluminum, plain edge, J732	2800.

KM#	Date	Mintage	Identification	Mkt.Val.
Pn780	1869	—	25 Cent, Silver, reeded edge, J733	1450.
Pn781	1869	—	25 Cent, Silver, plain edge, J734	3650.
Pn782	1869	—	25 Cent, Copper, reeded edge, J735	1200.
Pn783	1869	—	25 Cent, Copper, plain edge, J736	1200.
Pn784	1869	—	25 Cent, Aluminum, reeded edge, J737	1000.
Pn785	1869	—	25 Cent, Aluminum, plain edge, J738	1000.
Pn786	1869	—	25 Cent, Copper, reeded edge, J739	1500.
Pn787	1869	—	25 Cent, Aluminum, reeded edge, J740	1500.
Pn788	1869	—	25 Cent, Aluminum, plain edge, J741	—

KM#	Date	Mintage	Identification	Mkt.Val.
Pn789	1869	1	50 Cent, Silver, reeded edge, J742	1825.
Pn790	1869	—	50 Cent, Silver, reeded edge, J742a	Rare
Pn791	1869	—	50 Cent, Silver, plain edge, J743	2200.
Pn792	1869	—	50 Cent, Copper, reeded edge, J744	2550.
Pn793	1869	—	50 Cent, Copper, plain edge, J745	3250.
Pn794	1869	—	50 Cent, Aluminum, reeded edge, J746	3500.
Pn795	1869	—	50 Cent, Aluminum, plain edge, J747	3650.
Pn796	1869	—	50 Cent, Silver, reeded edge, w/o "B", J747a	—

KM#	Date	Mintage	Identification	Mkt.Val.
Pn797	1869	—	50 Cent, Silver, reeded edge, J748	1650.
Pn798	1869	—	50 Cent, Silver, plain edge, J749	2650.
Pn799	1869	—	50 Cent, Copper, reeded edge, J750	2850.
Pn800	1869	—	50 Cent, Copper, reeded edge, J751	2500.
Pn801	1869	—	50 Cent, Aluminum, reeded edge, J752	6000.
Pn802	1869	—	50 Cent, Aluminum, plain edge, J753	2200.
Pn803	1869	—	50 Cent, Brass, reeded edge, J753a	Unique

KM#	Date	Mintage	Identification	Mkt.Val.
Pn804	1869	—	50 Cent, Silver, reeded edge, J754	4750.
Pn805	1869	—	50 Cent, Silver, plain edge, J755	1850.
Pn806	1869	—	50 Cent, Copper, reeded edge, J756	1500.
Pn807	1869	—	50 Cent, Copper, plain edge, J757	1500.
Pn808	1869	—	50 Cent, Aluminum, reeded edge, J758	3600.
Pn809	1869	—	50 Cent, Aluminum, plain edge, J759	3200.
Pn810	1869	—	50 Cent, Brass, reeded edge, J759a	Unique
Pn811	1869	—	50 Cent, Copper, reeded edge, J760	3650.
Pn812	1869	—	50 Cent, Aluminum, reeded edge, J761	4650.
Pn813	1869	—	50 Cent, Nickel, reeded edge, J762	6000.
Pn814	1869	—	1 Dollar, Copper, reeded edge, J763	4250.
Pn815	1869	—	1 Dollar, Aluminum, reeded edge, J764	4250.
Pn816	1869	—	1 Dollar, Nickel, reeded edge, J765	4500.
Pn817	1869	—	1 Gold Dollar, Copper, reeded edge, J766	—
Pn818	1869	—	1 Gold Dollar, Aluminum, reeded edge, J767	4500.
Pn819	1869	—	1 Gold Dollar, Nickel, reeded edge, J768	4500.
Pn820	1869	—	2-1/2 Dollar, Copper, reeded edge, J769	4500.
Pn821	1869	—	2-1/2 Dollar, Aluminum, reeded edge, J770	4500.
Pn822	1869	—	2-1/2 Dollar, Nickel, reeded edge, J771	—
Pn823	1869	—	3 Dollar, Copper, reeded edge, J772	4250.
Pn824	1869	—	3 Dollar, Aluminum, reeded edge, J773	8000.
Pn825	1869	—	3 Dollar, Nickel, reeded edge, J774	—
Pn826	1869	—	5 Dollar, Copper, reeded edge, J775	2250.
Pn827	1869	—	5 Dollar, Aluminum, reeded edge, J776	1950.
Pn828	1869	—	5 Dollar, Nickel, reeded edge, J777	—
Pn829	1869	—	5 Dollar, Brass, reeded edge, J778	Unique
Pn830	1869	—	10 Dollar, Copper, thick planchet, reeded edge, J779	5500.
Pn830a	1869	—	10 Dollar, Copper Bronzed, thick planchet, reeded edge, J779a	5000.
Pn830b	1869	—	10 Dollar, Copper, thin planchet, reeded edge, J779	5500.
Pn830c	1869	—	10 Dollar, Copper Bronzed, thin planchet, reeded edge, J779	5000.
Pn831	1869	—	10 Dollar, Aluminum, reeded edge, J780	6000.
Pn832	1869	—	10 Dollar, Copper, reeded edge, J781	5000.
Pn833	1869	—	10 Dollar, Aluminum, reeded edge, J782	5000.
Pn834	1869	—	10 Dollar, Nickel, reeded edge, J783	—
Pn835	1869	—	20 Dollar, Copper, reeded edge, J784	5000.
Pn836	1869	—	20 Dollar, Aluminum, reeded edge, J785	5000.
Pn837	1869	—	20 Dollar, Nickel, reeded edge, J786	—
Pn838	1870	—	1 Cent, Copper, plain edge, J787	3000.
Pn839	1870	—	1 Cent, Aluminum, plain edge,	

KM#	Date	Mintage	Identification	Mkt.Val.
Pn839			J788	3000.
Pn840	1870	—	1 Cent, Nickel, plain edge, J789	—
Pn841	1870	—	2 Cent, Copper, plain edge, J790	5000.
Pn842	1870	—	2 Cent, Aluminum, plain edge, J791	5000.
Pn843	1870	—	2 Cent, Nickel, plain edge, J792	—
Pn844	1870	—	2 Cent, Silver-Copper, plain edge, J793	6000.
Pn845	1870	—	3 Cent, Copper, plain edge, J794	3000.
Pn846	1870	—	3 Cent, Aluminum, plain edge, J795	3000.

KM#	Date	Mintage	Identification	Mkt.Val.
Pn847	1870	—	3 Cent, Silver, plain edge, J796	4500.
Pn848	1870	—	3 Cent, Silver, reeded edge, J797	4500.
Pn849	1870	—	3 Cent, Copper, plain edge, J798	2500.
Pn850	1870	—	3 Cent, Copper, reeded edge, J799	2750.
Pn851	1870	—	3 Cent, Aluminum, plain edge, J800	2500.
Pn852	1870	—	3 Cent, Aluminum, reeded edge, K801	2500.
Pn853	1870	—	3 Cent, Copper, plain edge, J802	3200.
Pn854	1870	—	3 Cent, Aluminum, plain edge, J803	3200.
Pn855	1870	—	3 Cent, Nickel, plain edge, J804	—
Pn856	1870	—	3 Cent, Brass, plain edge, J804a	—
Pn857	1870	—	5 Cent, Copper, plain edge, J805	3200.
Pn858	1870	—	5 Cent, Aluminum, plain edge, J806	3250.
Pn859	1870	—	5 Cent, Nickel, plain edge, J807	—
Pn860	1870	—	5 Cent, Steel, plain edge, J808	Unique

KM#	Date	Mintage	Identification	Mkt.Val.
Pn861	1870	—	1/2 Dime, Silver, reeded edge, J809	2550.
Pn862	1870	—	1/2 Dime, Silver, plain edge, J810	3200.
Pn863	1870	—	1/2 Dime, Copper, reeded edge, J811	4200.
Pn864	1870	—	1/2 Dime, Copper, plain edge, J812	1650.
Pn865	1870	—	1/2 Dime, Aluminum, reeded edge, J813	1850.
Pn866	1870	—	1/2 Dime, Aluminum, plain edge, J814	1850.

KM#	Date	Mintage	Identification	Mkt.Val.
Pn867	1870	—	1/2 Dime, Silver, reeded edge, J815	2500.
Pn868	1870	—	1/2 Dime, Silver, plain edge, J816	2000.
Pn869	1870	—	1/2 Dime, Copper, reeded edge, J817	1750.
Pn870	1870	—	1/2 Dime, Copper, plain edge, J818	2150.
Pn871	1870	—	1/2 Dime, Aluminum, reeded edge, J819	1850.
Pn872	1870	—	1/2 Dime, Aluminum, plain edge, J820	1850.
Pn873	1870	—	1/2 Dime, Copper, reeded edge, J821	3500.
Pn874	1870	—	1/2 Dime, Copper, plain edge, J822	—
Pn875	1870	—	1/2 Dime, Aluminum, reeded edge, J823	3500.
Pn876	1870	—	1/2 Dime, Nickel, reeded edge, J824	—
Pn877	1870	—	10 Cent, Silver, reeded edge, J825	3550.
Pn878	1870	—	10 Cent, Silver, plain edge, J826	2000.
Pn879	1870	—	10 Cent, Copper, reeded edge, J827	2000.
Pn880	1870	—	10 Cent, Copper, plain edge, J828	2200.
Pn881	1870	—	10 Cent, Aluminum, reeded edge, J829	3000.
Pn882	1870	—	10 Cent, Aluminum, plain edge, J830	3000.
Pn883	1870	—	10 Cent, Silver, reeded edge, J831	4000.
Pn884	1870	—	10 Cent, Silver, plain edge, J832	4000.
Pn885	1870	—	10 Cent, Copper, reeded edge, J833	2850.
Pn886	1870	—	10 Cent, Copper, plain edge, J834	2550.
Pn887	1870	—	10 Cent, Aluminum, reeded edge, J835	3500.
Pn888	1870	—	10 Cent, Aluminum, plain edge, J836	3500.

KM#	Date	Mintage	Identification	Mkt.Val.
Pn889	1870	—	10 Cent, Silver, reeded edge, J837	1250.
Pn890	1870	—	10 Cent, Silver, plain edge, J838	2000.
Pn891	1870	—	10 Cent, Copper, reeded edge, J839	4500.
Pn892	1870	—	10 Cent, Copper, plain edge, J840	5200.
Pn893	1870	—	10 Cent, Aluminum, reeded edge, J841	3000.
Pn894	1870	—	10 Cent, Aluminum, plain edge, J842	2800.
Pn895	1870	—	10 Cent, Silver, reeded edge, J843	3650.
Pn896	1870	—	10 Cent, Silver, plain edge, J844	1800.
Pn897	1870	—	10 Cent, Copper, reeded edge,	

KM#	Date	Mintage	Identification	Mkt.Val.
Pn897			J845	2000.
Pn898	1870	—	10 Cent, Copper, plain edge, J846	2000.
Pn899	1870	—	10 Cent, Aluminum, reeded edge, J847	2800.
Pn900	1870	—	10 Cent, Aluminum, plain edge, J848	2800.

KM#	Date	Mintage	Identification	Mkt.Val.
Pn901	1870	—	10 Cent, Silver, reeded edge, J849	1500.
Pn902	1870	—	10 Cent, Silver, plain edge, J850	1500.
Pn903	1870	—	10 Cent, Copper, reeded edge, J851	1500.
Pn904	1870	—	10 Cent, Copper, plain edge, J852	1500.
Pn905	1870	—	10 Cent, Aluminum, reeded edge, J853	2000.
Pn906	1870	—	10 Cent, Aluminum, plain edge, J854	2000.

KM#	Date	Mintage	Identification	Mkt.Val.
Pn907	1870	—	10 Cent, Silver, reeded edge, J855	5600.
Pn908	1870	—	10 Cent, Silver, plain edge, J856	5400.
Pn909	1870	—	10 Cent, Copper, reeded edge, J857	1950.
Pn910	1870	—	10 Cent, Copper, plain edge, J858	2000.
Pn911	1870	—	10 Cent, Aluminum, reeded edge, J859	3000.
Pn912	1870	—	10 Cent, Aluminum, plain edge, J860	3000.
Pn913	1870	—	10 Cent, Silver, reeded edge, J861	1600.
Pn914	1870	—	10 Cent, Silver, plain edge, J862	3750.
Pn915	1870	—	10 Cent, Copper, reeded edge, J863	1850.
Pn916	1870	—	10 Cent, Copper, plain edge, J864	3200.
Pn917	1870	—	10 Cent, Aluminum, reeded edge, J865	2200.
Pn918	1870	—	10 Cent, Aluminum, plain edge, J866	2550.

KM#	Date	Mintage	Identification	Mkt.Val.
Pn919	1870	—	10 Cent, Silver, reeded edge, J867	2250.
Pn920	1870	—	10 Cent, Silver, plain edge, J868	2750.
Pn921	1870	—	10 Cent, Copper, reeded edge, J869	5250.
Pn922	1870	—	10 Cent, Copper, plain edge, J870	5500.
Pn923	1870	—	10 Cent, Aluminum, reeded edge, J871	5500.
Pn924	1870	—	10 Cent, Aluminum, plain edge, J872	5500.
Pn925	1870	—	10 Cent, Copper, reeded edge, J873	4650.
Pn926	1870	—	10 Cent, Aluminum, reeded edge, J874	4750.
Pn927	1870	—	10 Cent, Nickel, reeded edge, J875	—
Pn928	1870	—	25 Cent, Silver, reeded edge, J876	3200.
Pn929	1870	—	25 Cent, Silver, plain edge, J877	3250.
Pn930	1870	—	25 Cent, Copper, reeded edge, J878	5250.
Pn931	1870	—	25 Cent, Copper, plain edge, J879	3000.
Pn932	1870	—	25 Cent, Aluminum, reeded edge, J880	5250.
Pn933	1870	—	25 Cent, Aluminum, plain edge, J881	5250.

KM#	Date	Mintage	Identification	Mkt.Val.
Pn934	1870	—	25 Cent, Silver, reeded edge, J882	3000.
Pn935	1870	—	25 Cent, Silver, plain edge, J883	3000.
Pn936	1870	—	25 Cent, Copper, reeded edge, J884	2850.
Pn937	1870	—	25 Cent, Copper, plain edge, J885	2850.
Pn938	1870	—	25 Cent, Aluminum, reeded edge, J886	3000.
Pn939	1870	—	25 Cent, Aluminum, plain edge, J887	3000.
Pn940	1870	—	25 Cent, Silver, reeded edge, J888	1850.
Pn941	1870	—	25 Cent, Silver, plain edge, J889	2000.
Pn942	1870	—	25 Cent, Copper, reeded edge, J890	2250.
Pn943	1870	—	25 Cent, Copper, plain edge, J891	2250.
Pn944	1870	—	25 Cent, Aluminum, reeded edge, J892	3300.
Pn945	1870	—	25 Cent, Aluminum, plain edge, J893	3300.

KM#	Date	Mintage	Identification	Mkt.Val.
Pn946	1870	—	25 Cent, Silver, reeded edge, J894	1850.
Pn947	1870	—	25 Cent, Silver, plain edge, J895	1750.
Pn948	1870	—	25 Cent, Copper, reeded edge, J896	3000.
Pn949	1870	—	25 Cent, Copper, plain edge, J897	3000.
Pn950	1870	—	25 Cent, Aluminum, reeded edge, J898	1200.
Pn951	1870	—	25 Cent, Aluminum, plain edge, J899	1200.
Pn952	1870	—	25 Cent, Silver, reeded edge, J900	1250.

KM#	Date	Mintage	Identification	Mkt.Val.
Pn953	1870	—	25 Cent, Silver, plain edge, J901	2850.
Pn954	1870	—	25 Cent, Copper, reeded edge, J902	3000.
Pn955	1870	—	25 Cent, Copper, plain edge, J903	3000.
Pn956	1870	—	25 Cent, Aluminum, reeded edge, J904	3250.
Pn957	1870	—	25 Cent, Aluminum, plain edge, J905	3250.
Pn958	1870	—	25 Cent, Silver, reeded edge, J906	2250.

KM#	Date	Mintage	Identification	Mkt.Val.
Pn959	1870	—	25 Cent, Silver, plain edge, J907	2250.
Pn960	1870	—	25 Cent, Copper, reeded edge, J908	2450.
Pn961	1870	—	25 Cent, Copper, plain edge, J909	2450.
Pn962	1870	—	25 Cent, Aluminum, reeded edge, J910	4000.
Pn963	1870	—	25 Cent, Aluminum, plain edge, J911	4000.

KM#	Date	Mintage	Identification	Mkt.Val.
Pn964	1870	—	25 Cent, Silver, reeded edge, J912	2000.
Pn965	1870	—	25 Cent, Silver, plain edge, J913	2000.
Pn966	1870	—	25 Cent, Copper, reeded edge, J914	2650.
Pn967	1870	—	25 Cent, Copper, plain edge, J915	4200.
Pn968	1870	—	25 Cent, Aluminum, reeded edge, J916	3000.
Pn969	1870	—	25 Cent, Aluminum, plain edge, J917	2750.
Pn970	1870	—	25 Cent, Silver, reeded edge, J918	1850.
Pn971	1870	—	25 Cent, Silver, plain edge, J919	2000.
Pn972	1870	—	25 Cent, Copper, reeded edge, J920	2650.
Pn973	1870	—	25 Cent, Copper, plain edge, J921	2650.
Pn974	1870	—	25 Cent, Aluminum, reeded edge, J922	3250.
Pn975	1870	—	25 Cent, Aluminum, plain edge, J923	3250.
Pn976	1870	—	25 Cent, Copper, reeded edge, J924	3500.
Pn977	1870	—	25 Cent, Aluminum, reeded edge, J925	3500.
Pn978	1870	—	25 Cent, Nickel, reeded edge, J926	—
Pn979	1870	—	50 Cent, Silver, reeded edge, J927	6500.
Pn980	1870	—	50 Cent, Silver, reeded edge, LIBERTY raised, J927a	—
Pn981	1870	—	50 Cent, Silver, plain edge, J928	6750.
Pn982	1870	—	50 Cent, Copper, reeded edge, J929	6000.
Pn983	1870	—	50 Cent, Copper, reeded edge, LIBERTY raised, J929a	—
Pn984	1870	—	50 Cent, Copper. plain edge, J930	6000.
Pn985	1870	—	50 Cent, Aluminum, reeded edge, J931	5500.
Pn986	1870	—	50 Cent, Aluminum, plain edge, J932	5500.

KM#	Date	Mintage	Identification	Mkt.Val.
Pn987	1870	—	50 Cent, Silver, reeded edge, J933	5300.
Pn988	1870	—	50 Cent, Silver, plain edge, J934	3500.
Pn989	1870	—	50 Cent, Copper, reeded edge, J935	3500.
Pn990	1870	—	50 Cent, Copper, plain edge, J936	3250.
Pn991	1870	—	50 Cent, Aluminum, reeded edge, J937	3500.
Pn992	1870	—	50 Cent, Aluminum, plain edge, J938	3500.

KM#	Date	Mintage	Identification	Mkt.Val.
Pn993	1870	—	50 Cent, Silver, reeded edge, J939	2000.
Pn994	1870	—	50 Cent, Silver, plain edge, J940	1550.
Pn995	1870	—	50 Cent, Copper, reeded edge, J941	3000.
Pn996	1870	—	50 Cent, Copper, plain edge, J942	3000.
Pn997	1870	—	50 Cent, Aluminum, reeded edge, J943	3250.
Pn998	1870	—	50 Cent, Aluminum, plain edge, J944	3250.
Pn999	1870	—	50 Cent, Silver, reeded edge, J945	3550.
Pn1000	1870	—	50 Cent, Silver, plain edge, J946	3650.
Pn1001	1870	—	50 Cent, Copper, reeded edge, J947	4850.
Pn1002	1870	—	50 Cent, Copper, plain edge, J948	5000.
Pn1003	1870	—	50 Cent, Aluminum, reeded edge, J949	5000.
Pn1004	1870	—	50 Cent, Aluminum, plain edge, J950	5000.
Pn1005	1870	—	50 Cent, Silver, reeded edge, J951	2200.
Pn1006	1870	—	50 Cent, Silver, plain edge, J952	2200.
Pn1007	1870	—	50 Cent, Copper, reeded edge, J953	5000.
Pn1008	1870	—	50 Cent, Copper, plain edge, J954	5000.
Pn1009	1870	—	50 Cent, Aluminum, reeded edge, J955	4500.
Pn1010	1870	—	50 Cent, Aluminum, plain edge, J956	4750.

KM#	Date	Mintage	Identification	Mkt.Val.
Pn1011	1870	—	50 Cent, Silver, reeded edge, J957	2200.
Pn1012	1870	—	50 Cent, Silver, plain edge, J958	2200.
Pn1013	1870	—	50 Cent, Copper, reeded edge, J959	3850.
Pn1014	1870	—	50 Cent, Copper, plain edge, J960	4500.
Pn1015	1870	—	50 Cent, Aluminum, reeded edge, J961	4500.
Pn1016	1870	—	50 Cent, Aluminum, plain edge, J962	4500.
Pn1017	1870	—	50 Cent, Silver, reeded edge, J963	5500.
Pn1018	1870	—	50 Cent, Silver, plain edge, J964	5500.
Pn1019	1870	—	50 Cent, Copper, reeded edge, J965	5500.
Pn1020	1870	—	50 Cent, Copper, plain edge, J966	5500.
Pn1021	1870	—	50 Cent, Aluminum, reeded edge, J967	6000.
Pn1022	1870	—	50 Cent, Aluminum, plain edge, J968	6000.
Pn1023	1870	—	50 Cent, Silver, reeded edge, J969	4500.
Pn1024	1870	—	50 Cent, Silver, plain edge, J970	4750.
Pn1025	1870	—	50 Cent, Copper, reeded edge, J971	4500.
Pn1026	1870	—	50 Cent, Copper, plain edge, J972	4750.
Pn1027	1870	—	50 Cent, Aluminum, reeded edge, J973	5000.
Pn1028	1870	—	50 Cent, Aluminum, plain edge, J974	5000.
Pn1029	1870	—	50 Cent, Silver, reeded edge, J975	5000.
Pn1030	1870	—	50 Cent, Silver, plain edge, J976	5000.
Pn1031	1870	—	50 Cent, Copper, reeded edge,	

KM#	Date	Mintage	Identification	Mkt.Val.
Pn1031			J977	4500.
Pn1032	1870	—	50 Cent, Copper, plain edge, J978	4200.
Pn1033	1870	—	50 Cent, Aluminum, reeded edge, J979	5000.
Pn1034	1870	—	50 Cent, Aluminum, plain edge, J980	5000.
Pn1035	1870	—	50 Cent, Silver, reeded edge, J981	3200.
Pn1036	1870	—	50 Cent, Silver, plain edge, J982	3800.
Pn1037	1870	—	50 Cent, Copper, reeded edge, J983	4500.
Pn1038	1870	—	50 Cent, Copper, plain edge, J984	3750.
Pn1039	1870	—	50 Cent, Aluminum, reeded edge, J985	4750.
Pn1040	1870	—	50 Cent, Aluminum, plain edge, J986	4750.

KM#	Date	Mintage	Identification	Mkt.Val.
Pn1041	1870	—	50 Cent, Silver, reeded edge, J987	4000.
Pn1042	1870	—	50 Cent, Silver, plain edge, J988	4000.
Pn1043	1870	—	50 Cent, Copper, reeded edge, J989	3500.
Pn1044	1870	—	50 Cent, Copper, plain edge, J990	6500.
Pn1045	1870	—	50 Cent, Aluminum, reeded edge, J991	5000.
Pn1046	1870	—	50 Cent, Aluminum, plain edge, J992	5300.
Pn1047	1870	—	50 Cent, Copper, reeded edge, J993	5000.
Pn1048	1870	—	50 Cent, Aluminum, reeded edge, J994	5000.
Pn1049	1870	—	50 Cent, Nickel, reeded edge, J995	—
Pn1050	1870	—	50 Cent, Copper-Nickel, J995a	—

KM#	Date	Mintage	Identification	Mkt.Val.
Pn1051	1870	—	1 Dollar, Silver, reeded edge, J996	4850.
Pn1052	1870	—	1 Dollar, Silver, plain edge, J997	4500.
Pn1053	1870	—	1 Dollar, Copper, reeded edge, J998	4000.
Pn1054	1870	—	1 Dollar, Copper, plain edge, J999	3250.
Pn1055	1870	—	1 Dollar, Aluminum, reeded edge, J1000	5000.
Pn1056	1870	—	1 Dollar, Aluminum, plain edge, J1001	5000.
Pn1057	1870	—	1 Dollar, Silver, reeded edge, J1002	6500.
Pn1058	1870	—	1 Dollar, Silver, plain edge, J1003	3500.
Pn1059	1870	—	1 Dollar, Copper, reeded edge, J1004	8500.

KM#	Date	Mintage	Identification	Mkt.Val.
Pn1060	1870	—	1 Dollar, Copper, plain edge, J1005	3500.
Pn1061	1870	—	1 Dollar, Aluminum, reeded edge, J1006	5000.
Pn1062	1870	—	1 Dollar, Aluminum, plain edge, J1007	5000.
Pn1063	1870	—	1 Dollar, Silver, reeded edge, J1008	7000.
Pn1064	1870	—	1 Dollar, Silver, plain edge, J1009	11,500.
Pn1065	1870	—	1 Dollar, Copper, reeded edge, J1010	6000.
Pn1066	1870	—	1 Dollar, Copper, plain edge, J1011	6000.
Pn1067	1870	—	1 Dollar, Aluminum, reeded edge, J1012	6000.
Pn1068	1870	—	1 Dollar, Aluminum, plain edge, J1013	6000.

KM#	Date	Mintage	Identification	Mkt.Val.
Pn1069	1870	—	1 Dollar, Silver, reeded edge, J1014	3500.
Pn1070	1870	—	1 Dollar, Silver, plain edge, J1015	4000.
Pn1071	1870	—	1 Dollar, Copper, reeded edge, J1016	4650.
Pn1072	1870	—	1 Dollar, Copper, plain edge, J1017	4250.
Pn1073	1870	—	1 Dollar, Aluminum, reeded edge, J1018	8500.
Pn1074	1870	—	1 Dollar, Aluminum, plain edge, J1019	8250.
Pn1075	1870	—	1 Dollar, Copper, reeded edge, J1020	12,100.
Pn1076	1870	—	1 Dollar, Aluminum, reeded edge, J1021	—
Pn1077	1870	—	1 Dollar, Nickel, reeded edge, J1022	17,000.
Pn1078	1870	—	1 Gold Dollar, Copper, reeded edge, J1023	—
Pn1079	1870	—	1 Gold Dollar, Aluminum, reeded edge, J1024	—
Pn1080	1870	—	1 Gold Dollar, Nickel, reeded edge, J1025	—
Pn1081	1870	—	2-1/2 Dollar, Copper, reeded edge, J1026	3750.
Pn1082	1870	—	2-1/2 Dollar, Aluminum, reeded edge, J1027	3550.
Pn1083	1870	—	2-1/2 Dollar, Nickel, reeded edge, J1028	—
Pn1084	1870	—	3 Dollar, Copper, reeded edge, J1029	6000.
Pn1085	1870	—	3 Dollar, Aluminum, reeded edge, J1030	8500.
Pn1086	1870	—	3 Dollar, Nickel, reeded edge, J1031	7500.
Pn1087	1870	—	5 Dollar, Copper, reeded edge, J1032	7200.
Pn1088	1870	—	5 Dollar, Aluminum, reeded edge, J1033	—
Pn1089	1870	—	5 Dollar, Nickel, reeded edge, J1034	—
Pn1090	1870	—	10 Dollar, Copper, reeded edge, J1035	—
Pn1091	1870	—	10 Dollar, Aluminum, reeded edge, J1036	—

KM#	Date	Mintage	Identification	Mkt.Val.
Pn1092	1870	—	10 Dollar, Nickel, reeded edge, J1037	—
Pn1093	1870	—	20 Dollar, Copper, reeded edge, J1038	16,500.
Pn1094	1870	—	20 Dollar, Aluminum, reeded edge, J1039	—
Pn1095	1870	—	20 Dollar, Nickel, reeded edge, J1040	—
Pn1096	1871	—	1 Cent, Copper, plain edge, J1041	—
Pn1097	1871	—	1 Cent, Aluminum, plain edge, J1042	—
Pn1098	1871	—	2 Cent, Copper, plain edge, J1043	1250.
Pn1099	1871	—	2 Cent, Aluminum, plain edge, J1044	7000.
Pn1100	1871	—	3 Cent, Copper, plain edge, J1045	2500.
Pn1101	1871	—	3 Cent, Aluminum, plain edge, J1046	2500.
Pn1102	1871	—	3 Cent, Copper, plain edge, J1047	3000.
Pn1103	1871	—	3 Cent, Nickel, plain edge, J1048	Unique
Pn1104	1871	—	3 Cent, Aluminum, plain edge, J1049	3000.

KM#	Date	Mintage	Identification	Mkt.Val.
Pn1105	1871	—	5 Cent, Nickel, plain edge, J1050	2750.
Pn1106	1871	—	5 Cent, Copper, plain edge, J1051	2250.
Pn1106a	1871	—	5 Cent, Copper, Silver plated, plain edge, J1051	1850.
Pn1107	1871	—	5 Cent, Aluminum, plain edge, J1052	5000.

KM#	Date	Mintage	Identification	Mkt.Val.
Pn1108	1871	—	5 Cent, Nickel, plain edge, J1053	3000.
Pn1109	1871	—	5 Cent, Copper, plain edge, J1054	2250.
Pn1110	1871	—	5 Cent, Aluminum, plain edge, J1057	5000.
Pn1111	1871	—	5 Cent, Copper, plain edge, J1056	3000.
Pn1112	1871	—	5 Cent, Aluminum, plain edge, J1057	5000.
Pn1113	1871	—	5 Cent, Steel, plain edge, J1058	Unique
Pn1114	1871	—	1/2 Dime, SIlver, reeded edge, J1059	2650.
Pn1115	1871	—	1/2 Dime, Copper, reeded edge, J1060	3750.
Pn1116	1871	—	1/2 Dime, Aluminum, reeded edge, J1061	4500.
Pn1117	1871	—	1/2 Dime, Silver, reeded edge, J1062	4500.
Pn1118	1871	—	1/2 Dime, Copper, reeded edge, J1063	6000.
Pn1119	1871	—	1/2 Dime, Aluminum, reeded edge, J1064	7500.
Pn1120	1871	—	1/2 Dime, Silver, reeded edge, J1065	4500.
Pn1121	1871	—	1/2 Dime, Copper, reeded edge, J1066	3650.
Pn1122	1871	—	1/2 Dime, Aluminum, reeded edge, J1067	7500.
Pn1123	1871	—	1/2 Dime, Silver, reeded edge, J1068	2750.
Pn1124	1871	—	1/2 Dime, Copper, reeded edge, J1069	2000.
Pn1125	1871	—	1/2 Dime, Aluminum, reeded edge, J1070	—
Pn1126	1871	—	1/2 Dime, Copper, reeded edge, J1071	1750.
Pn1127	1871	—	1/2 Dime, Aluminum, reeded edge, J1072	—
Pn1128	1871	—	1/2 Dime, Nickel, reeded edge, J1073	—
Pn1129	1871	—	10 Cent, Silver, reeded edge, J1074	6000.
Pn1130	1871	—	10 Cent, Copper, reeded edge, J1075	3000.
Pn1131	1871	—	10 Cent, Aluminum, reeded edge, J1076	7000.
Pn1132	1871	—	10 Cent, Silver, reeded edge, J1077	3500.
Pn1133	1871	—	10 Cent, Copper, reeded edge, J1078	4500.
Pn1134	1871	—	10 Cent, Aluminum, reeded edge, J1079	—

KM#	Date	Mintage	Identification	Mkt.Val.
Pn1135	1871	—	10 Cent, Silver, reeded edge, J1080	1450.
Pn1136	1871	—	10 Cent, Copper, reeded edge, J1081	4200.
Pn1137	1871	—	10 Cent, Aluminum, reeded edge, J1082	2250.

KM#	Date	Mintage	Identification	Mkt.Val.
Pn1138	1871	—	10 Cent, Nickel, reeded edge, J1083	—

KM#	Date	Mintage	Identification	Mkt.Val.
Pn1139	1871	—	10 Cent, Silver, reeded edge, J1084	4000.
Pn1140	1871	—	10 Cent, Copper, reeded edge, J1085	2250.
Pn1141	1871	—	10 Cent, Aluminum, reeded edge, J1086	—
Pn1142	1871	—	10 Cent, Copper, reeded edge, J1087	2750.
Pn1143	1871	—	10 Cent, Aluminum, reeded edge, J1088	3000.
Pn1144	1871	—	10 Cent, Nickel, reeded edge, J1089	3550.
Pn1145	1871	—	25 Cent, Silver, reeded edge, J1090	—
Pn1146	1871	—	25 Cent, Copper, reeded edge, J1091	5000.
Pn1147	1871	—	25 Cent, Aluminum, reeded edge, J1092	6000.
Pn1148	1871	—	25 Cent, Silver, reeded edge, J1093	5000.
Pn1149	1871	—	25 Cent, Copper, reeded edge, J1094	4500.
Pn1150	1871	—	25 Cent, Aluminum, reeded edge, J1095	—
Pn1151	1871	—	25 Cent, Silver, reeded edge, J1096	5000.
Pn1152	1871	—	25 Cent, Copper, reeded edge, J1097	4200.
Pn1153	1871	—	25 Cent, Aluminum, reeded edge, J1098	12,650.
Pn1154	1871	—	25 Cent, Silver, reeded edge, J1099	5000.
Pn1155	1871	—	25 Cent, Copper, reeded edge, J1100	4650.
Pn1156	1871	—	25 Cent, Aluminum, reeded edge, J1101	—
Pn1157	1871	—	25 Cent, Copper, reeded edge, J1102	3500.
Pn1158	1871	—	25 Cent, Aluminum, reeded edge, J1103	4000.
Pn1159	1871	—	25 Cent, Nickel, reeded edge, J1104	—
Pn1160	1871	—	50 Cent, Silver, reeded edge, J1105	6750.
Pn1161	1871	—	50 Cent, Copper, reeded edge, J1106	6875.
Pn1162	1871	—	50 Cent, Aluminum, reeded edge, J1107	7000.
Pn1163	1871	—	50 Cent, Silver, reeded edge, J1108	—
Pn1164	1871	—	50 Cent, Copper, reeded edge, J1109	6500.
Pn1165	1871	—	50 Cent, Aluminum, reeded edge, J1110	8500.
Pn1166	1871	—	50 Cent, Silver, reeded edge, J1111	—
Pn1167	1871	—	50 Cent, Copper, reeded edge, J1112	6000.
Pn1168	1871	—	50 Cent, Aluminum, reeded edge, J1113	7000.
Pn1169	1871	—	50 Cent, Silver, reeded edge, J1114	6000.
Pn1170	1871	—	50 Cent, Copper, reeded edge, J1115	3300.
Pn1171	1871	—	50 Cent, Aluminum, reeded edge, J1116	5000.
Pn1172	1871	—	50 Cent, Copper, reeded edge, J1117	4500.
Pn1173	1871	—	50 Cent, Aluminum, reeded edge, J1118	6500.
Pn1174	1871	—	50 Cent, Nickel, reeded edge, J1119	Unique
Pn1175	1871	—	1 Dollar, Silver, reeded edge, J1120	14,300.
Pn1176	1871	—	1 Dollar, Silver, plain edge, J1121	9000.
Pn1177	1871	—	1 Dollar, Copper, reeded edge, J1122	9650.
Pn1178	1871	—	1 Dollar, Copper, plain edge, J1123	9750.
Pn1179	1871	—	1 Dollar, Aluminum, reeded edge, J1124	15,400.
Pn1180	1871	—	1 Dollar, Aluminum, plain edge, J1125	Rare
Pn1181	1871	—	1 Dollar, Silver, reeded edge, J1126	7500.
Pn1182	1871	—	1 Dollar, Silver, plain edge, J1127	6000.
Pn1183	1871	—	1 Dollar, Copper, reeded edge, J1128	6000.
Pn1184	1871	—	1 Dollar, Copper, plain edge, J1129	6000.
Pn1185	1871	—	1 Dollar, Aluminum, reeded edge, J1130	7000.
Pn1186	1871	—	1 Dollar, Aluminum, plain edge, J1131	7000.
Pn1187	1871	—	1 Dollar, Copper, reeded edge, J1132	—
Pn1188	1871	—	1 Dollar, Copper, plain edge,	

KM#	Date	Mintage	Identification	Mkt.Val.
Pn1188			J1132a	—
Pn1189	1871	—	1 Dollar, Silver, reeded edge, J1133	5775.
Pn1190	1871	—	1 Dollar, Silver, plain edge, J1134	6000.
Pn1191	1871	—	1 Dollar, Copper, reeded edge, J1135	4650.
Pn1192	1871	—	1 Dollar, Copper, plain edge, J1136	4500.
Pn1193	1871	—	1 Dollar, Aluminum, reeded edge, J1137	6000.
Pn1194	1871	—	1 Dollar, Aluminum, plain edge, J1138	6000.
Pn1195	1871	—	1 Dollar, Silver, reeded edge, J1138a	—
Pn1196	1871	—	1 Dollar, Aluminum, reeded edge, J1138b	—
Pn1197	1871	—	1 Dollar, Silver, reeded edge, J1139	6500.
Pn1198	1871	—	1 Dollar, Silver, plain edge, J1140	6500.
Pn1199	1871	—	1 Dollar, Copper, reeded edge, J1141	7000.
Pn1200	1871	—	1 Dollar, Copper, plain edge, J1142	6000.
Pn1201	1871	—	1 Dollar, Aluminum, reeded edge, J1143	7000.
Pn1202	1871	—	1 Dollar, Aluminum, plain edge, J1144	7000.
Pn1203	1871	—	1 Dollar, Silver, reeded edge, J1145	7500.
Pn1204	1871	—	1 Dollar, Silver, plain edge, J1146	7500.
Pn1205	1871	—	1 Dollar, Copper, reeded edge, J1147	7450.

KM#	Date	Mintage	Identification	Mkt.Val.
Pn1206	1871	—	1 Dollar, Copper, plain edge, J1148	5500.
Pn1207	1871	—	1 Dollar, Aluminum, reeded edge, J1149	7150.
Pn1208	1871	—	1 Dollar, Aluminum, plain edge, J1150	4500.
Pn1209	1871	—	1 Dollar, Copper, reeded edge, J1151	4000.
Pn1210	1871	—	1 Dollar, Aluminum, reeded edge, J1152	4000.
Pn1211	1871	—	1 Dollar, Nickel, reeded edge, J1153	—
Pn1212	1871	—	Commercial Dollar, Silver, reeded edge, J1154	7500.
Pn1213	1871	—	Commercial Dollar, Silver, plain edge, J1155	8000.
Pn1214	1871	—	Commercial Dollar, Copper, reeded edge, J1156	—
Pn1215	1871	—	Commercial Dollar, Copper, plain edge, J1157	—
Pn1216	1871	—	Commercial Dollar, Silver, reeded edge, J1158	—
Pn1217	1871	—	Commercial Dollar, Copper, reeded edge, J1159	—
Pn1218	1871	—	Commercial Dollar, Silver, reeded edge, J1160	—
Pn1219	1871	—	1 Gold Dollar, Copper, reeded edge, J1161	3450.
Pn1220	1871	—	1 Gold Dollar, Aluminum, reeded edge, J1162	4000.
Pn1221	1871	—	1 Gold Dollar, Nickel, reeded edge, J1163	5000.
Pn1222	1871	—	2-1/2 Dollar, Copper, reeded edge, J1164	4000.
Pn1223	1871	—	2-1/2 Dollar, Aluminum, reeded edge, J1165	4500.
Pn1224	1871	—	2-1/2 Dollar, Nickel, reeded edge, J1166	5000.
Pn1225	1871	—	3 Dollar, Copper, reeded edge, J1167	4800.
Pn1226	1871	—	3 Dollar, Aluminum, reeded edge, J1168	5000.
Pn1227	1871	—	3 Dollar, Nickel, reeded edge, J1169	5500.
Pn1228	1871	—	5 Dollar, Copper, reeded edge, J1170	5000.
Pn1229	1871	—	5 Dollar, Aluminum, reeded edge, J1171	5750.
Pn1230	1871	—	5 Dollar, Nickel, reeded edge, J1172	5000.
Pn1231	1871	—	10 Dollar, Copper, reeded edge, J1173	5775.
Pn1232	1871	—	10 Dollar, Aluminum, reeded edge, J1174	6500.
Pn1233	1871	—	10 Dollar, Nickel, reeded edge, J1175	5000.
Pn1234	1871	—	20 Dollar, Copper, reeded edge, J1176	4000.
Pn1235	1871	—	20 Dollar, Aluminum, reeded edge, J1177	6000.
Pn1236	1871	—	20 Dollar, Nickel, reeded edge, J1178	6500.
Pn1237	1872	—	1 Cent, Copper, plain edge, J1179	3000.
Pn1238	1872	—	1 Cent, Copper-Nickel, plain edge, J1180	—
Pn1239	1872	—	1 Cent, Aluminum, plain edge, J1181	4000.
Pn1240	1872	—	1 Cent, Nickel, plain edge, J1182	—
Pn1241	1872	—	2 Cent, Copper, plain edge, J1183	3250.
Pn1242	1872	—	2 Cent, Aluminum, plain edge, J1184	3750.
Pn1243	1872	—	3 Cent, Copper, plain edge, J1185	3000.
Pn1244	1872	—	3 Cent, Aluminum, plain edge, J1186	3500.
Pn1245	1872	—	3 Cent, Copper, plain edge, J1187	3250.
Pn1246	1872	—	3 Cent, Aluminum, plain edge, J1188	3750.
Pn1247	1872	—	5 Cent, Copper, plain edge, J1189	3250.
Pn1248	1872	—	5 Cent, Aluminum, plain edge, J1190	3750.
Pn1249	1872	—	1/2 Dime, Copper, reeded edge, J1191	3250.
Pn1250	1872	—	1/2 Dime, Aluminum, reeded edge, J1192	3750.
Pn1251	1872	—	10 Cent, Copper, reeded edge, J1193	3000.
Pn1252	1872	—	10 Cent, Aluminum, reeded edge, J1194	3500.
Pn1253	1872	—	25 Cent, Silver, reeded edge, J1195	—
Pn1254	1872	—	25 Cent, Copper, reeded edge, J1196	—
Pn1255	1872	—	25 Cent, Aluminum, reeded edge, J1197	—
Pn1256	1872	—	25 Cent, Copper, reeded edge, J1198	3500.
Pn1257	1872	—	25 Cent, Aluminum, reeded edge, J1199	4000.

KM#	Date	Mintage	Identification	Mkt.Val.
Pn1258	1872	—	50 Cent, Silver, reeded edge, J1200	20,350.
Pn1259	1872	—	50 Cent, Copper, reeded edge, J1201	20,900.
Pn1260	1872	—	50 Cent, Aluminum, reeded edge, J1202	Rare
Pn1261	1872	—	50 Cent, Copper, reeded edge, J1203	4000.
Pn1262	1872	—	50 Cent, Aluminum, reeded edge, J1204	4750.
Pn1263	1872	—	1 Dollar, Silver, reeded edge, J1205	—
Pn1264	1872	—	1 Dollar, Copper, reeded edge, J1206	—
Pn1265	1872	—	1 Dollar, Aluminum, reeded edge, J1207	19,800.
Pn1266	1872	—	1 Dollar, Silver, reeded edge, J1208	Rare
Pn1267	1872	—	1 Dollar, Silver, plain edge, J1209	Rare

KM#	Date	Mintage	Identification	Mkt.Val.
Pn1268	1872	—	1 Dollar, Copper, reeded edge, J1210	7000.
Pn1269	1872	—	1 Dollar, Aluminum, reeded edge, J1211	8500.
Pn1270	1872	—	Commercial Dollar, Silver, reeded edge, J1212	5500.
Pn1271	1872	—	Commercial Dollar, Silver, plain edge, J1213	6500.

KM#	Date	Mintage	Identification	Mkt.Val.
Pn1272	1872	—	Commercial Dollar, Silver, reeded edge, J1214	7500.
Pn1273	1872	—	Commercial Dollar, Silver, plain edge, J1215	8450.
Pn1274	1872	—	Commercial Dollar, Copper, reeded edge, J1216	5500.
Pn1275	1872	—	Commercial Dollar, Copper, plain edge, J1217	5500.
Pn1276	1872	—	Commercial Dollar, Aluminum, reeded edge, J1218	—
Pn1277	1872	—	Commercial Dollar, Silver, reeded edge, J1219	11,000.
Pn1278	1872	—	Commercial Dollar, Copper, reeded edge, J1219a	Unique
Pn1279	1872	—	Trade Dollar, Silver, reeded edge, J1220	5000.
Pn1280	1872	—	Trade Dollar, Copper, reeded edge, J1221	9350.
Pn1281	1872	—	Trade Dollar, Aluminum, reeded edge, J1222	—
Pn1282	1872	—	Trade Dollar, Silver, reeded edge, J1223	—

KM#	Date	Mintage	Identification	Mkt.Val.
Pn1283	1872	—	1 Gold Dollar, Gold, reeded edge, J1224	Unique
Pn1284	1872	—	1 Gold Dollar, Copper, reeded edge, J1225	9000.
Pn1285	1872	—	1 Gold Dollar, Aluminum, reeded edge, J1226	19,000.
Pn1286	1872	—	1 Gold Dollar, Copper, reeded edge, J1227	6000.
Pn1287	1872	—	1 Gold Dollar, Aluminum, reeded edge, J1228	6500.
Pn1288	1872	—	1 Gold Dollar, Silver, reeded edge, J1229	Unique

KM#	Date	Mintage	Identification	Mkt.Val.
Pn1289	1872	—	2-1/2 Dollar, Gold, reeded edge, J1230	Unique

KM#	Date	Mintage	Identification	Mkt.Val.
Pn1290	1872	—	2-1/2 Dollar, Copper, reeded edge, J1231	11,000.
Pn1291	1872	—	2-1/2 Dollar, Aluminum, reeded edge, J1232	15,000.
Pn1292	1872	—	2-1/2 Dollar, Copper, reeded edge, J1233	5000.
Pn1293	1872	—	2-1/2 Dollar, Aluminum, reeded edge, J1234	7000.
Pn1294	1872	—	3 Dollar, Gold, reeded edge, J1235	Unique
Pn1295	1872	—	3 Dollar, Copper, reeded edge, J1236	12,000.
Pn1296	1872	—	3 Dollar, Aluminum, reeded edge, J1237	17,500.
Pn1297	1872	—	3 Dollar, Copper, reeded edge, J1238	7500.
Pn1298	1872	—	3 Dollar, Aluminum, reeded edge, J1239	6500.
Pn1299	1872	—	5 Dollar, Gold, reeded edge, J1240	Unique
Pn1300	1872	—	5 Dollar, Copper, reeded edge, J1241	7000.
Pn1301	1872	—	5 Dollar, Aluminum, reeded edge, J1242	13,500.
Pn1302	1872	—	5 Dollar, Copper, reeded edge, J1243	7500.
Pn1303	1872	—	5 Dollar, Aluminum, reeded edge, J1244	14,500.

KM#	Date	Mintage	Identification	Mkt.Val.
Pn1304	1872	—	10 Dollar, Gold, reeded edge, J1245	Unique
Pn1305	1872	—	10 Dollar, Copper, reeded edge, J1246	16,000.
Pn1306	1872	—	10 Dollar, Aluminum, reeded edge, J1247	15,000.
Pn1307	1872	—	10 Dollar, Copper, reeded edge, J1248	4650.
Pn1308	1872	—	10 Dollar, Aluminum, reeded edge, J1249	9000.

KM#	Date	Mintage	Identification	Mkt.Val.
Pn1309	1872	—	20 Dollar, Gold, reeded edge, J1250	Unique
Pn1310	1872	—	20 Dollar, Copper, reeded edge, J1251	17,600.
Pn1311	1872	—	20 Dollar, Aluminum, reeded edge, J1252	45,000.
Pn1312	1872	—	20 Dollar, Copper, reeded edge, J1253	—
Pn1313	1872	—	20 Dollar, Aluminum, reeded edge, J1254	—
Pn1314	1873	—	1 Cent, Copper, plain edge, J1255	3500.
Pn1315	1873	—	1 Cent, Aluminum, plain edge, J1256	3450.
Pn1316	1873	—	1 Cent, Nickel, plain edge, J1257	—
Pn1317	1873	—	2 Cent, Copper, plain edge, J1258	—
Pn1318	1873	—	2 Cent, Aluminum, plain edge, J1259	—
Pn1319	1873	—	3 Cent, Copper, plain edge, J1260	3500.
Pn1320	1873	—	3 Cent, Aluminum, plain edge, J1261	7000.
Pn1321	1873	—	3 Cent, Copper, plain edge, J1262	3150.
Pn1322	1873	—	3 Cent, Aluminum, plain edge, J1263	3250.
Pn1323	1873	—	5 Cent, Copper, plain edge, J1264	3150.
Pn1324	1873	—	5 Cent, Aluminum, plain edge, J1265	3250.
Pn1325	1873	—	1/2 Dime, Copper, reeded edge, J1266	3150.
Pn1326	1873	—	1/2 Dime, Aluminum, reeded edge, J1267	3250.
Pn1327	1873	—	10 Cent, Copper, reeded edge, J1268	3650.
Pn1328	1873	—	10 Cent, Aluminum, reeded edge, J1269	3250.
Pn1329	1873	—	25 Cent, Copper, reeded edge, J1270	2850.
Pn1330	1873	—	25 Cent, Aluminum, reeded edge, J1271	3250.
Pn1331	1873	—	50 Cent, Copper, reeded edge, J1272	3250.
Pn1332	1873	—	50 Cent, Aluminum, reeded edge, J1273	3500.
Pn1333	1873	—	1 Dollar, Copper, reeded edge, J1274	3650.
Pn1334	1873	—	1 Dollar, Aluminum, reeded edge, J1275	4000.

KM#	Date	Mintage	Identification	Mkt.Val.
Pn1335	1873	—	Trade Dollar, Silver, reeded edge, J1276	4500.
Pn1336	1873	—	Trade Dollar, Silver, plain edge, J1277	4000.
Pn1337	1873	—	Trade Dollar, Copper, reeded edge, J1278	5500.
Pn1338	1873	—	Trade Dollar, Aluminum, reeded edge, J1279	6500.
Pn1339	1873	—	Trade Dollar, White Metal, plain edge, J1280	6500.

KM#	Date	Mintage	Identification	Mkt.Val.
Pn1340	1873	—	Trade Dollar, Silver, reeded edge, J1281	3500.
Pn1341	1873	—	Trade Dollar, Silver, plain edge, J1282	9500.
Pn1342	1873	—	Trade Dollar, Copper, reeded edge, J1283	4000.
Pn1343	1873	—	Trade Dollar, Aluminum, reeded edge, J1284	4500.
Pn1344	1873	—	Trade Dollar, Copper, reeded edge, J1285	—
Pn1345	1873	—	Trade Dollar, Aluminum, reeded edged, J1286	—
Pn1346	1873	—	Trade Dollar, White Metal, plain edge, J1287	—
Pn1347	1873	—	Trade Dollar, Copper, reeded edge, J1288	—
Pn1348	1873	—	Trade Dollar, Copper, reeded edge, J1289	—
Pn1349	1873	—	Trade Dollar, Silver, reeded edge, J1290	—
Pn1350	1873	—	Trade Dollar, Silver, plain edge, J1291	—
Pn1351	1873	—	Trade Dollar, White Metal, plain edge, J1292	—

KM#	Date	Mintage	Identification	Mkt.Val.
Pn1352	1873	—	Trade Dollar, Silver, reeded edge, J1293	3000.
Pn1353	1873	—	Trade Dollar, Silver, plain edge, J1294	4500.
Pn1354	1873	—	Trade Dollar, Copper, reeded edge, J1295	8250.
Pn1355	1873	—	Trade Dollar, Copper, plain edge, J1296	8500.
Pn1356	1873	—	Trade Dollar, Aluminum, reeded edge, J1297	—
Pn1357	1873	—	Trade Dollar, White Metal, plain edge, J1298	—
Pn1358	1873	—	Trade Dollar, White Metal, plain edge, J1299	—
Pn1359	1873	—	Trade Dollar, Silver, reeded edge, J1300	12,500.
Pn1360	1873	—	Trade Dollar, Copper, reeded edge, J1301	11,550.
Pn1361	1873	—	Trade Dollar, Copper, plain edge, J1302	12,500.
Pn1362	1873	—	Trade Dollar, Aluminum, reeded edge, J1303	—
Pn1363	1873	—	Trade Dollar, White Metal, plain edge, J1304	—
Pn1364	1873	—	Trade Dollar, Silver, reeded edge, J1304a	Unique
Pn1365	1873	4 pcs.	Trade Dollar, Copper, reeded edge, J1305	Rare
Pn1366	1873	—	Trade Dollar, White Metal, plain edge, J1306	—
Pn1367	1873	—	Trade Dollar, White Metal, plain edge, J1307	—
Pn1368	1873	—	Trade Dollar, Silver, J1308	—
Pn1369	1873	—	Trade Dollar, White Metal, plain edge, J1309	6500.

KM#	Date	Mintage	Identification	Mkt.Val.
Pn1370	1873	—	Trade Dollar, Silver, reeded edge, J1310	4250.
Pn1371	1873	—	Trade Dollar, Silver, plain edge, J1311	5500.
Pn1372	1873	—	Trade Dollar, Copper, reeded edge, J1312	6000.
Pn1373	1873	—	Trade Dollar, Aluminum, reeded edge, J1313	—
Pn1374	1873	—	Trade Dollar, White Metal, plain edge, J1314	—

KM#	Date	Mintage	Identification	Mkt.Val.
Pn1375	1873	—	Trade Dollar, Silver, reeded edge, J1315	4200.
Pn1376	1873	—	Trade Dollar, Silver, plain edge, J1316	4650.
Pn1377	1873	—	Trade Dollar, Copper, reeded edge, J1317	5500.
Pn1378	1873	—	Trade Dollar, Aluminum, reeded edge, J1318	6500.
Pn1379	1873	—	Trade Dollar, White Metal, plain edge, J1319	6500.
Pn1380	1873	—	Trade Dollar, Silver, reeded edge, J1320	Rare
Pn1381	1873	—	Trade Dollar, Copper, reeded edge, J1321	Rare

KM#	Date	Mintage	Identification	Mkt.Val.
Pn1382	1873	—	Trade Dollar, Silver, reeded edge, J1322	3850.
Pn1383	1873	—	Trade Dollar, Silver, plain edge, J1323	4500.

KM#	Date	Mintage	Identification	Mkt.Val.
Pn1384	1873	—	Trade Dollar, Copper, reeded edge, J1324	4000.
Pn1385	1873	—	Trade Dollar, Aluminum, reeded edge, J1325	6500.
Pn1386	1873	—	Trade Dollar, White Metal, plain edge, J1326	6500.
Pn1387	1873	—	Trade Dollar, Silver, reeded edge, J1326a	Rare
Pn1388	1873	—	Trade Dollar, White Metal, plain edge, J1326b	Rare
Pn1389	1873	—	Trade Dollar, Copper, reeded edge, J1327	5500.
Pn1390	1873	—	Trade Dollar, Aluminum, reeded edge, J1328	—
Pn1391	1873	—	Trade Dollar, White Metal, plain edge, J1329	—
Pn1392	1873	—	Trade Dollar, Tin, reeded edge, J1330	—
Pn1393	1873	—	1 Gold Dollar, Copper, reeded edge, J1331	3750.
Pn1394	1873	—	1 Gold Dollar, Aluminum, reeded edge, J1332	6500.
Pn1395	1873	—	2-1/2 Dollar, Copper, reeded edge, J1333	5000.
Pn1396	1873	—	2-1/2 Dollar, Aluminum, reeded edge, J1334	5500.
Pn1397	1873	—	3 Dollar, Copper, reeded edge, J1335	6650.
Pn1397a	1873	—	3 Dollar, Copper Gilt, reeded edge, J1335	6500.
Pn1398	1873	—	3 Dollar, Aluminum, reeded edge, J1336	4750.
Pn1399	1873	2 known	5 Dollar, Gold, reeded edge, J1337	Rare
Pn1400	1873	—	5 Dollar, Copper, reeded edge, J1338	6500.
Pn1401	1873	—	5 Dollar, Aluminum, reeded edge, J1339	5000.
Pn1402	1873	—	5 Dollar, Copper, reeded edge, J1340	3000.
Pn1403	1873	—	5 Dollar, Aluminum, reeded edge, J1341	3000.
Pn1404	1873	—	10 Dollar, Copper, reeded edge, J1342	3500.
Pn1405	1873	—	10 Dollar, Aluminum, reeded edge, J1343	3500.
Pn1406	1873	—	20 Dollar, Copper, reeded edge, J1344	3500.
Pn1407	1873	—	20 Dollar, Aluminum, reeded edge, J1345	5500.
Pn1408	1874	—	1 Cent, Copper, plain edge, J1346	2250.
Pn1409	1874	—	1 Cent, Aluminum, plain edge, J1347	3250.
Pn1410	1874	—	3 Cent, Copper, plain edge, J1348	2250.
Pn1411	1874	—	3 Cent, Aluminum, plain edge, J1349	3250.
Pn1412	1874	—	5 Cent, Copper, plain edge, J1350	2250.
Pn1413	1874	—	5 Cent, Aluminum, plain edge, J1351	3250.
Pn1414	1874	—	10 Cent, Copper, reeded edge, J1352	2500.
Pn1415	1874	—	10 Cent, Aluminum, reeded edge, J1353	3750.

KM#	Date	Mintage	Identification	Mkt.Val.
Pn1416	1874	—	20 Cent, Silver, plain edge, J1354	2650.
Pn1417	1874	—	20 Cent, Copper, plain edge, J1355	3250.
Pn1418	1874	—	20 Cent, Aluminum, plain edge, J1356	3450.
Pn1419	1874	—	20 Cent, Silver, plain edge, J1357	—
Pn1420	1874	—	20 Cent, Nickel, plain edge, J1358	5000.
Pn1421	1874	—	25 Cent, Copper, reeded edge, J1359	4000.
Pn1422	1874	—	25 Cent, Aluminum, reeded edge, J1360	4500.
Pn1423	1874	—	50 Cent, Copper, reeded edge, J1361	4000.
Pn1424	1874	—	50 Cent, Aluminum, reeded edge, J1362	4750.
Pn1425	1874	—	Trade Dollar, Copper, reeded edge, J1363	11,275.
Pn1426	1874	—	Trade Dollar, Aluminum, reeded edge, J1364	4300.
Pn1427	1874	—	1 Gold Dollar, Copper, reeded edge, J1365	—
Pn1428	1874	—	1 Gold Dollar, Aluminum, reeded edge, J1366	—
Pn1429	1874	—	2-1/2 Dollar, Copper, reeded edge, J1367	4500.
Pn1430	1874	—	2-1/2 Dollar, Aluminum, reeded edge, J1368	4750.
Pn1431	1874	—	3 Dollar, Copper, reeded edge, J1369	5000.
Pn1432	1874	—	3 Dollar, Aluminum, reeded edge, J1370	5500.
Pn1433	1874	—	5 Dollar, Copper, reeded edge, J1371	5650.
Pn1434	1874	—	5 Dollar, Copper, reeded edge, J1372	4750.
Pn1435	1874	2 known	10 Dollar, Gold, reeded edge, J1373	154,000.
Pn1436	1874	—	10 Dollar, Copper, reeded edge,	

KM#	Date	Mintage	Identification	Mkt.Val.
Pn1436			J1374	5800.
Pn1437	1874	—	10 Dollar, Copper, plain edge, J1375	13,000.
Pn1438	1874	—	10 Dollar, Aluminum, reeded edge, J1376	35,000.
Pn1439	1874	—	10 Dollar, Nickel, reeded edge, J1377	8000.
Pn1440	1874	—	10 Dollar, Nickel, plain edge, J1378	8000.
Pn1441	1874	—	10 Dollar, Copper, reeded edge, J1379	4500.
Pn1442	1874	—	10 Dollar, Aluminum, reeded edge, J1380	5000.
Pn1443	1874	—	20 Dollar, Copper, reeded edge, J1381	4500.
Pn1444	1874	—	20 Dollar, Aluminum, reeded edge, J1382	5000.
Pn1445	1875	—	1 Cent, Copper, plain edge, J1383	2500.
Pn1446	1875	—	1 Cent, Aluminum, plain edge, J1384	2750.
Pn1447	1875	—	3 Cent, Copper, plain edge, J1385	2800.
Pn1448	1875	—	3 Cent, Aluminum, plain edge, J1386	5000.
Pn1449	1875	—	5 Cent, Copper, plain edge, J1387	7750.
Pn1450	1875	—	5 Cent, Aluminum, plain edge, J1388	7000.
Pn1451	1875	—	1/2 Dime, Aluminum, reeded edge, J1389	—
Pn1452	1875	—	10 Cents, Copper, reeded edge, J1390	2250.
Pn1453	1875	—	10 Cent, Aluminum, reeded edge, J1391	2500.

KM#	Date	Mintage	Identification	Mkt.Val.
Pn1454	1875	—	20 Cent, Silver, plain edge, J1392	5000.
Pn1455	1875	—	20 Cent, Copper, plain edge, J1393	4000.
Pn1456	1875	—	20 Cent, Aluminum, plain edge, J1394	7000.
Pn1457	1875	—	20 Cent, Nickel, plain edge, J1395	4750.
Pn1458	1875	—	20 Cent, Silver, Silver, plain edge, J1396	6350.
Pn1459	1875	—	20 Cent, Copper, plain edge, J1397	3750.
Pn1460	1875	—	20 Cent, Aluminum, plain edge, J1398	4000.

KM#	Date	Mintage	Identification	Mkt.Val.
Pn1461	1875	—	20 Cent, Silver, plain edge, J1399	3750.
Pn1462	1875	—	20 Cent, Copper, plain edge, J1400	4000.
Pn1463	1875	—	20 Cent, Aluminum, plain edge, J1401	—
Pn1464	1875	—	20 Cent, Nickel, plain edge, J1402	4750.

KM#	Date	Mintage	Identification	Mkt.Val.
Pn1465	1875	—	20 Cent, Silver, plain edge, J1403	4500.
Pn1466	1875	—	20 Cent, Copper, plain edge, J1404	4000.

KM#	Date	Mintage	Identification	Mkt.Val.
Pn1467	1875	—	20 Cent, Aluminum, plain edge, J1405	5750.
Pn1468	1875	—	20 Cent, White Metal, plain edge, J1406	—

KM#	Date	Mintage	Identification	Mkt.Val.
Pn1469	1875	—	20 Cent, Silver, plain edge, J1407	3850.
Pn1470	1875	—	20 Cent, Copper, plain edge, J1408	3450.
Pn1471	1875	—	20 Cent, Aluminum, plain edge, J1409	—
Pn1472	1875	—	20 Cent, Nickel, plain edge, J1410	4000.
Pn1473	1875	—	20 Cent, Silver, plain edge, J1411	3500.
Pn1474	1875	—	20 Cent, Copper, plain edge, J1412	3500.
Pn1475	1875	—	20 Cent, Aluminum, plain edge, J1413	4650.
Pn1476	1875	—	20 Cent, Copper, plain edge, J1414	3000.
Pn1477	1875	—	20 Cent, Aluminum, plain edge, J1415	3750.
Pn1478	1875	—	25 Cent, Copper, reeded edge, J1416	2000.
Pn1479	1875	—	25 Cent, Aluminum, reeded edge, J1417	2200.
Pn1480	1875	—	50 Cent, Copper, reeded edge, J1418	2000.
Pn1481	1875	—	50 Cent, Aluminum, reeded edge, J1419	2200.
Pn1482	1875	6	1 Dollar, Silver, reeded edge, J1420	8500.
Pn1483	1875	8	1 Dollar, Copper, reeded edge, J1421	6500.
Pn1484	1875	2	1 Dollar, Aluminum, reeded edge, J1422	—
Pn1485	1875	6	Trade Dollar, Silver, reeded edge, J1423	—
Pn1486	1875	8	Trade Dollar, Copper, reeded edge, J1424	8000.
Pn1487	1875	3	Trade Dollar, Aluminum, reeded edge, J1425	—
Pn1488	1875	—	Trade Dollar, Silver, reeded edge, J1426	—
Pn1489	1875	—	Trade Dollar, Copper, reeded edge, J1427	8000.
Pn1490	1875	—	Trade Dollar, Aluminum, reeded edge, J1428	—
Pn1491	1875	—	Trade Dollar, White Metal, reeded edge, J1429	—
Pn1492	1875	—	Trade Dollar, Copper, reeded edge, J1430	7000.
Pn1493	1875	—	Trade Dollar, Aluminum, reeded edge, J1431	7500.
Pn1494	1875	—	1 Gold Dollar, Copper, reeded edge, J1432	7000.
Pn1494a	1875	—	1 Gold Dollar, Copper Gilt, reeded edge, J1432	6750.
Pn1495	1875	—	1 Gold Dollar, Aluminum, reeded edge, J1433	—
Pn1496	1875	—	2-1/2 Dollar, Copper, reeded edge, J1434	7000.
Pn1496a	1875	—	2-1/2 Dollar, Copper Gilt, reeded edge, J1434	6750.
Pn1497	1875	—	2-1/2 Dollar, Aluminum, reeded edge, J1435	—
Pn1498	1875	—	3 Dollar, Copper, reeded edge, J1436	7000.
Pn1498a	1875	—	3 Dollar, Copper Gilt, reeded edge, J1436	6750.
Pn1499	1875	—	3 Dollar, Aluminum, reeded edge, J1437	10,500.

KM#	Date	Mintage	Identification	Mkt.Val.
Pn1500	1875	2 known	5 Dollar, Gold, reeded edge, J1438	Rare
Pn1501	1875	—	5 Dollar, Copper, reeded edge, J1439	8000.
Pn1502	1875	—	5 Dollar, Aluminum, reeded edge, J1440	Rare
Pn1503	1875	—	5 Dollar, White Metal, J1440a	Rare
Pn1504	1875	—	5 Dollar, Copper, reeded edge, J1441	8250.
Pn1504a	1875	—	5 Dollar, Copper Gilt, reeded edge, J1441	6750.
Pn1505	1875	—	5 Dollar, Aluminum, reeded edge, J1442	—
Pn1505a	1875	—	5 Dollar, Aluminum Gilt, reeded edge, J1442	—
Pn1506	1875	2 known	10 Dollar, Gold, reeded edge, J1443	Rare
Pn1507	1875	—	10 Dollar, Copper, reeded edge, J1444	7750.
Pn1507a	1875	—	10 Dollar, Copper Gilt, reeded edge, J1444	6750.
Pn1508	1875	—	10 Dollar, Aluminum, reeded edge, J1445	Rare
Pn1509	1875	—	10 Dollar, White Metal, J1445a	Rare

KM#	Date	Mintage	Identification	Mkt.Val.
Pn1510	1875	—	10 Dollar, Copper, reeded edge, J1446	—
Pn1511	1875	—	10 Dollar, Aluminum, reeded edge, J1447	—
Pn1512	1875	—	20 Dollar, Copper, reeded edge, J1448	7500.
Pn1513	1875	—	20 Dollar, Aluminum, reeded edge, J1449	15,400.
Pn1514	1876	—	1 Cent, Aluminum, plain edge, J1450	2000.
Pn1515	1876	3 known	1 Cent, Nickel, plain edge, J1451	2000.
Pn1516	1876	—	10 Cent, Copper, reeded edge, J1452	2000.
Pn1517	1876	—	10 Cent, Nickel, reeded edge, J1453	2000.
Pn1518	1876	—	20 Cent, Copper, plain edge, J1454	5775.
Pn1519	1876	—	25 Cent, Copper, reeded edge, J1455	4500.
Pn1520	1876	2 known	50 Cent, Copper, reeded edge, J1456	6600.
Pn1521	1876	2 known	1 Dollar, Silver, reeded edge, J1457	Rare
Pn1522	1876	—	1 Dollar, Copper, plain edge, J1458	—
Pn1523	1876	—	1 Dollar, Copper, reeded edge, J1458a	—
Pn1524	1876	2 known	1 Dollar, Silver, reeded edge, J1459	Rare
Pn1525	1876	—	1 Dollar, Copper, reeded edge, J1460	—
Pn1526	1876	—	1 Dollar, Copper, plain edge, J1461	—
Pn1527	1876	2 known	1 Dollar, Silver, reeded edge, J1462	Rare
Pn1528	1876	—	1 Dollar, Copper, reeded edge, J1463	9650.
Pn1529	1876	—	1 Dollar, Copper, plain edge, J1463a	Unique
Pn1530	1876	—	1 Dollar, Silver, reeded edge, J1464	Rare
Pn1531	1876	—	1 Dollar, Copper, reeded edge, J1465	Rare
Pn1532	1876	—	1 Dollar, Copper, plain edge, J1466	Rare
Pn1533	1876	5 known	1 Dollar, Silver, reeded edge, J1467	22,000.
Pn1534	1876	—	1 Dollar, Copper, reeded edge, J1468	Rare
Pn1535	1876	—	1 Dollar, Copper, plain edge, J1469	—
Pn1536	1876	—	1 Dollar, Silver, reeded edge, J1470	Rare
Pn1537	1876	—	1 Dollar, Copper, reeded edge, J1471	Rare
Pn1538	1876	2 known	1 Dollar, Silver, reeded edge, J1472	Rare
Pn1539	1876	4 known	1 Dollar, Copper, reeded edge, J1473	11,000.
Pn1540	1876	2 known	Trade Dollar, Silver, reeded edge, J1474	Rare
Pn1541	1876	—	Trade Dollar, Copper, reeded edge, J1475	Rare
Pn1542	1876	—	Trade Dollar, Copper, reeded edge, J1476	4750.
Pn1543	1876	—	Trade Dollar, Aluminum, reeded edge, J1477	—
Pn1544	1876	—	1 Gold Dollar, Copper, reeded edge, J1478	4250.
Pn1545	1876	—	1 Gold Dollar, Aluminum, reeded edge, J1479	—
Pn1546	1876	—	2-1/2 Dollar, Copper, reeded edge, J1480	4750.
Pn1547	1876	—	2-1/2 Dollar, Aluminum, reeded edge, J1481	—
Pn1548	1876	—	3 Dollar, Copper, reeded edge, J1482	5775.
Pn1549	1876	—	3 Dollar, Aluminum, reeded edge, J1483	—
Pn1550	1876	—	5 Dollar, Copper, reeded edge, J1484	4850.
Pn1551	1876	—	5 Dollar, Aluminum, reeded edge, J1485	—
Pn1552	1876	—	10 Dollar, Copper, reeded edge, J1486	4650.
Pn1553	1876	—	10 Dollar, Aluminum, reeded edge, J1487	—
Pn1554	1876	—	20 Dollar, Gold, reeded edge, J1488	Unique
Pn1555	1876	—	20 Dollar, Copper, reeded edge, J1489	—
Pn1556	1876	—	20 Dollar, Gold, reeded edge, J1490	Unique
Pn1557	1876	—	20 Dollar, Copper, reeded edge, J1491	8500.
Pn1558	1876	—	20 Dollar, Copper Gilt, plain edge, J1492	Unique
Pn1559	1876	—	20 Dollar, Copper, reeded edge, J1493	8500.
Pn1560	1876	—	20 Dollar, Aluminum, reeded edge, J1494	—
Pn1561	1877	—	1 Cent, Copper-Nickel, plain edge, J1495	—
Pn1562	1877	—	1 Cent, Nickel, plain edge, J1496	2750.

KM#	Date	Mintage	Identification	Mkt.Val.
Pn1563	1877	—	10 Cent, Silver, reeded edge, (may not exist), J1497	—
Pn1564	1877	—	10 Cent, Copper, reeded edge, J1498	4250.
Pn1565	1877	—	10 Cent, Copper Silvered, reeded edge, J1498	4550.
Pn1566	1877	—	25 Cent, Silver, reeded edge, J1499	—
Pn1567	1877	—	25 Cent, Copper, reeded edge, J1500	4000.
Pn1568	1877	—	25 Cent, Copper Silvered, reeded edge, J1500	4000.
Pn1569	1877	—	50 Cent, Silver, reeded edge, J1501	Rare
Pn1570	1877	—	50 Cent, Copper, reeded edge, J1502	—
Pn1571	1877	—	50 Cent, Silver, reeded edge, J1503	22,000.
Pn1572	1877	—	50 Cent, Silver, reeded edge, J1504	11,550.
Pn1573	1877	—	50 Cent, Copper, reeded edge, J1505	—
Pn1574	1877	—	50 Cent, Silver, reeded edge, J1506	23,100.
Pn1575	1877	2 known	50 Cent, Copper, reeded edge, J1507	Rare
Pn1576	1877	—	50 Cent, Silver, reeded edge, J1508	Rare
Pn1577	1877	—	50 Cent, Copper, reeded edge, J1509	10,500.
Pn1578	1877	—	50 Cent, Silver, reeded edge, J1509a	Rare
Pn1579	1877	—	50 Cent, Copper, plain edge, J1509b	—
Pn1580	1877	—	50 Cent, Silver, reeded edge, J1509c	—
Pn1581	1877	—	50 Cent, Silver, reeded edge, J1510	17,500.
Pn1582	1877	—	50 Cent, Copper, reeded edge, J1511	Rare
Pn1583	1877	—	50 Cent, Silver, reeded edge, J1512	31,900.
Pn1584	1877	—	50 Cent, Copper, reeded edge, J1513	Rare
Pn1585	1877	—	50 Cent, Silver, reeded edge, J1514	22,550.
Pn1586	1877	—	50 Cent, Copper, reeded edge, J1515	Rare
Pn1587	1877	—	50 Cent, Silver, reeded edge, J1516	25,300.
Pn1588	1877	—	50 Cent, Copper, reeded edge, J1517	10,000.
Pn1589	1877	—	50 Cent, Silver, reeded edge, (may not exist), J1518	—
Pn1590	1877	—	50 Cent, Copper Silvered, reeded edge, J1518a	Unique
Pn1591	1877	—	50 Cent, Copper, reeded edge, J1519	9500.
Pn1592	1877	—	50 Cent, Silver, reeded edge, J1520	Rare

KM#	Date	Mintage	Identification	Mkt.Val.
Pn1593	1877	—	50 Cent, Copper, reeded edge, J1521	Rare
Pn1594	1877	—	50 Cent, Silver, reeded edge, J1522	Rare
Pn1595	1877	—	50 Cent, Copper, reeded edge, J1523	17,050.
Pn1596	1877	—	50 Cent, Silver, reeded edge, J1523a	Unique
Pn1597	1877	—	50 Cent, Copper, reeded edge, J1523b	Rare
Pn1598	1877	—	50 Cent, Silver, reeded edge, J1524	8750.
Pn1599	1877	—	50 Cent, Copper, reeded edge, J1525	8000.
Pn1600	1877	—	50 Cent, Silver, reeded edge, J1526	Rare
Pn1601	1877	—	50 Cent, Copper, reeded edge, J1527	Rare
Pn1602	1877	—	50 Cent, Silver, reeded edge, J1528	Rare
Pn1603	1877	—	50 Cent, Copper, reeded edge, J1529	Rare
Pn1604	1877	—	50 Cent, Silver, reeded edge, J1530	Rare
Pn1605	1877	—	50 Cent, Copper, reeded edge, J1531	Rare
Pn1606	1877	—	50 Cent, Silver, reeded edge, (may not exist), J1532	—
Pn1607	1877	3 known	50 Cent, Copper, reeded edge, J1533	Rare
Pn1608	1877	—	50 Cent, Silver, reeded edge, J1534a	Rare
Pn1609	1877	—	50 Cent, Copper, reeded edge, J1534	Rare
Pn1610	1877	—	50 Cent, Silver, reeded edge, J1535	Rare
Pn1611	1877	—	50 Cent, Copper, reeded edge, J1536	Rare
Pn1612	1877	—	50 Cent, Silver, reeded edge, J1537	Rare
Pn1613	1877	—	50 Cent, Copper, reeded edge, J1538	Rare
Pn1614	1877	—	50 Cent, Silver, reeded edge, J1539	11,850.
Pn1615	1877	—	50 Cent, Copper, reeded edge, J1539a	Rare
Pn1616	1877	—	50 Cent, Silver, reeded edge, J1540	9500.
Pn1617	1877	—	50 Cent, Copper, reeded edge, J1541	10,000.
Pn1618	1877	—	50 Cent, Silver, reeded edge, (may not exist), J1541a	—
Pn1619	1877	3 known	50 Cent, Copper, reeded edge, J1541b	Rare
Pn1620	1877	—	1 Dollar, Copper, reeded edge, J1542	8750.
Pn1621	1877	—	1 Dollar, Copper, reeded edge, J1543	9500.
Pn1622	1877	—	1 Dollar, Copper, reeded edge, J1544	9500.
Pn1623	1877	—	1 Dollar, Copper Silvered, reeded edge, J1544	9500.
Pn1624	1877	—	10 Dollar, Copper, reeded edge, J1545	6000.
Pn1624a	1877	—	10 Dollar, Copper Gilt, reeded edge, J1545	Rare
Pn1625	1877	—	50 Dollar, Gold, reeded edge, J1546	Unique
Pn1626	1877	—	50 Dollar, Copper, reeded edge, J1547	120,000.
Pn1626a	1877	—	50 Dollar, Copper Gilt, reeded edge, J1547	Rare

KM#	Date	Mintage	Identification	Mkt.Val.
Pn1627	1877	—	50 Dollar, Gold, reeded edge, J1548	Unique
Pn1628	1877	—	50 Dollar, Copper, reeded edge, J1549	Rare
Pn1628a	1877	—	50 Dollar, Copper Gilt, reeded edge, J1549	Rare

KM#	Date	Mintage	Identification	Mkt.Val.
Pn1629	1878	—	1 Dollar, Silver, reeded edge, J1550	6000.
Pn1630	1878	—	1 Dollar, Silver, reeded edge, rev: lg. stars, J1550a	9000.
Pn1631	1878	—	1 Dollar, Copper, reeded edge, J1551	8500.
Pn1632	1878	—	1 Dollar, Silver, reeded edge, J1552	7150.
Pn1633	1878	—	1 Dollar, Copper, reeded edge, J1553	7150.

KM#	Date	Mintage	Identification	Mkt.Val.
Pn1634	1878	—	1 Dollar, Silver, reeded edge, J1554	5000.
Pn1635	1878	—	1 Dollar, Copper, reeded edge, J1555	3550.
Pn1636	1878	—	1 Dollar, Aluminum, reeded edge, J1556	—
Pn1637	1878	—	1 Dollar, White Metal, reeded edge, J1556a	—
Pn1638	1878	13 pcs.	Goloid Dollar, Goloid, reeded edge, J1557	2450.
Pn1639	1878	—	Goloid Dollar, Silver, reeded edge, J1558	8500.
Pn1639a	1878	—	Goloid Dollar, Silver, light weight reeded edge, J1558	2850.
Pn1640	1878	—	Goloid Dollar, Copper, reeded edge, J1559	4850.

KM#	Date	Mintage	Identification	Mkt.Val.
Pn1641	1878	4 known	Goloid Dollar, Goloid, reeded edge, J1560	5000.
Pn1642	1878	—	Goloid Dollar, Silver, reeded edge, J1561	—
Pn1643	1878	—	Goloid Dollar, Copper, reeded edge, J1562	4500.
Pn1644	1878	—	Goloid Metric Dollar, Goloid, reeded edge, J1563	2650.
Pn1645	1878	—	Goloid Metric Dollar, Silver, reeded edge, J1564	4200.
Pn1645a	1878	—	Goloid Metric Dollar, Silver, light weight restrike, reeded edge, J1564	2200.
Pn1646	1878	—	1 Dollar, Copper, reeded edge, J1565	Rare

KM#	Date	Mintage	Identification	Mkt.Val.
Pn1647	1878	2 known	2-1/2 Dollar, Gold, reeded edge, J1566	115,500.

KM#	Date	Mintage	Identification	Mkt.Val.
Pn1648	1878	—	2-1/2 Dollar, Copper, reeded edge, J1567	7000.
Pn1648a	1878	—	2-1/2 Dollar, Copper Gilt, reeded edge, J1567	3550.
Pn1649	1878	—	5 Dollar, Copper, reeded edge, J1568	4000.
Pn1649a	1878	—	5 Dollar, Copper Gilt, reeded edge, J1568	4000.
Pn1650	1878	—	5 Dollar, Copper, reeded edge, J1568a	4000.
Pn1651	1878	—	5 Dollar, Copper, reeded edge, J1569	5000.
Pn1651a	1878	—	5 Dollar, Copper Gilt, reeded edge, J1569	4850.
Pn1652	1878	—	5 Dollar, Gold, reeded edge, J1570	Unique

KM#	Date	Mintage	Identification	Mkt.Val.
Pn1653	1878	—	5 Dollar, Copper, reeded edge, J1571	4850.
Pn1654	1878	—	5 Dollar, Gold, reeded edge, J1572	Unique
Pn1655	1878	—	5 Dollar, Copper, reeded edge, J1573	4850.

KM#	Date	Mintage	Identification	Mkt.Val.
Pn1656	1878	—	5 Dollar, Copper, reeded edge, J1574	4500.
Pn1656a	1878	—	5 Dollar, Copper Gilt, reeded edge, J1574	4500.
Pn1657	1878	—	5 Dollar, Brass, reeded edge, J1574a	Rare
Pn1556	1878	—	5 Dollar, Gold, reeded edge, J1575	Rare
Pn1659	1878	—	5 Dollar, Copper, reeded edge, J1576	7650.
Pn1659a	1878	—	5 Dollar, Copper Gilt, reeded edge, J1576	7500.
Pn1660	1878	—	5 Dollar, Gold, reeded edge, J1577	Rare
Pn1661	1878	—	5 Dollar, Copper, reeded edge, J1578	7000.
Pn1661a	1878	—	5 Dollar, Copper Gilt, reeded edge, J1578	6500.
Pn1662	1878	—	10 Dollar, Gold, plain edge, J1579	Rare
Pn1663	1878	—	10 Dollar, Copper, thin planchet, reeded edge, J1580	6500.
Pn1663a	1878	—	10 Dollar, Copper, thick planchet, reeded edge, J1580	4650.

KM#	Date	Mintage	Identification	Mkt.Val.
Pn1664	1878	—	10 Dollar, Gold, reeded edge, J1581	Rare
Pn1665	1878	—	10 Dollar, Copper, reeded edge, J1582	6500.
Pn1666	1879	—	1 Cent, Nickel, plain edge, J1583	Rare

KM#	Date	Mintage	Identification	Mkt.Val.
Pn1667	1879	—	10 Cent, Silver, reeded edge, J1584	8000.
Pn1668	1879	—	10 Cent, Copper, reeded edge, J1585	3500.

KM#	Date	Mintage	Identification	Mkt.Val.
Pn1669	1879	—	10 Cent, Silver, reeded edge, J1586	4000.
Pn1670	1879	—	10 Cent, Copper, reeded edge, J1587	4000.
Pn1671	1879	—	10 Cent, Silver, reeded edge, J1588	8000.
Pn1672	1879	—	10 Cent, Silver, reeded edge, J1589	3750.
Pn1673	1879	—	25 Cent, Silver, reeded edge, J1590	14,300.
Pn1674	1879	—	25 Cent, Copper, reeded edge, J1591	6000.
Pn1675	1879	—	25 Cent, White Metal, reeded edge, J1592	Rare
Pn1676	1879	—	25 Cent, Silver, reeded edge, J1593	19,800.
Pn1677	1879	—	25 Cent, Copper, reeded edge, J1594	14,500.
Pn1678	1879	—	25 Cent, White Metal, reeded edge, J1594a	Rare
Pn1679	1879	—	25 Cent, White Metal, plain edge, J1595	Rare
Pn1680	1879	—	25 Cent, White Metal, plain edge, J1596	Unique

KM#	Date	Mintage	Identification	Mkt.Val.
Pn1681	1879	—	50 Cent, Silver, reeded edge, J1597	7000.
Pn1682	1879	—	50 Cent, Copper, reeded edge, J1598	7000.
Pn1683	1879	—	50 Cent, Silver, reeded edge, J1599	8500.
Pn1684	1879	—	50 Cent, Copper, reeded edge, J1600	8250.

KM#	Date	Mintage	Identification	Mkt.Val.
Pn1685	1879	—	50 Cent, Silver, reeded edge, J1601	7500.

KM#	Date	Mintage	Identification	Mkt.Val.
Pn1686	1879	—	50 Cent, Copper, reeded edge, J1602	7000.
Pn1687	1879	—	1 Dollar, Silver, reeded edge, J1603	39,600.
Pn1688	1879	—	1 Dollar, Copper, reeded edge, J1604	10,800.
Pn1689	1879	—	1 Dollar, Silver, reeded edge, J1605	—
Pn1690	1879	—	1 Dollar, Copper, reeded edge, J1606	—
Pn1691	1879	—	1 Dollar, White Metal, reeded edge, J1607	Rare
Pn1692	1879	—	1 Dollar, Silver, reeded edge, J1608	35,200.
Pn1693	1879	—	1 Dollar, Copper, reeded edge, J1609	18,975.
Pn1694	1879	—	1 Dollar, Lead, reeded edge, J1610	—
Pn1695	1879	—	1 Dollar, Silver, reeded edge, J1611	7000.
Pn1696	1879	—	1 Dollar, Copper, reeded edge, J1612	5500.
Pn1697	1879	—	1 Dollar, Silver, reeded edge, J1613	5500.
Pn1698	1879	—	1 Dollar, Copper, reeded edge, J1614	3500.
Pn1699	1879	—	1 Dollar, Silver, reeded edge, J1615	19,800.

KM#	Date	Mintage	Identification	Mkt.Val.
Pn1700	1879	—	1 Dollar, Copper, reeded edge, J1616	11,000.

KM#	Date	Mintage	Identification	Mkt.Val.
Pn1701	1879	—	Metric Dollar, Silver Alloy, 25 g, reeded edge, J1617	3000.
Pn1702	1879	—	Metric Dollar, Silver, light etching, lt. restrike, J1618	2150.
Pn1703	1879	—	Metric Dollar, Copper, reeded edge, J1619	5400.
Pn1704	1879	—	Metric Dollar, Aluminum, reeded edge, J1620	—
Pn1705	1879	—	Metric Dollar, Lead, reeded edge, J1621	—
Pn1706	1879	—	Metric Dollar, Silver Alloy, reeded edge, J1622	9750.
Pn1707	1879	—	Metric Dollar, Copper, reeded edge, J1623	10,000.
Pn1708	1879	—	Metric Dollar, Aluminum, reeded edge, J1624	—
Pn1709	1879	—	Metric Dollar, White Metal, reeded edge, J1625	—

KM#	Date	Mintage	Identification	Mkt.Val.
Pn1710	1879	—	Goloid Metric Dollar, Goloid, 14 g, reeded edge, J1626	4000.
Pn1711	1879	—	Goloid Metric Dollar, Silver, reeded edge, J1627	4000.
Pn1712	1879	—	Goloid Metric Dollar, Copper, reeded edge, J1628	4000.
Pn1713	1879	—	Goloid Metric Dollar, Aluminum, reeded edge, J1629	7500.
Pn1714	1879	—	Goloid Metric Dollar, Lead, reeded edge, J1630	—
Pn1715	1879	—	Goloid Metric Dollar, Goloid, 14 g, reeded edge, J1631	10,000.
Pn1716	1879	—	Goloid Metric Dollar, Copper, reeded edge, J1632	6500.
Pn1717	1879	—	Goloid Metric Dollar, Aluminum, reeded edge, J1633	5500.
Pn1718	1879	—	Goloid Metric Dollar, White Metal, reeded edge, J1634	—

KM#	Date	Mintage	Identification	Mkt.Val.
Pn1719	1879	415	4 Dollar Stella, Gold, 109 g, reeded edge, J1635	45,000.
Pn1720	1879	—	4 Dollar Stella, Gold, restrike, 103-109 g, worn obv. die, J1636	30,000.
Pn1721	1879	—	4 Dollar Stella, Copper, reeded edge, J1636	9000.
Pn1722	1879	—	4 Dollar Stella, Aluminum, reeded edge, J1637	—
Pn1723	1879	10	4 Dollar Stella, Gold, reeded edge, J1638	198,000.
Pn1724	1879	—	4 Dollar Stella, Copper, reeded edge, J1639	11,550.
Pn1725	1879	—	4 Dollar Stella, Aluminum, reeded edge, J1640	Rare
Pn1726	1879	—	4 Dollar Stella, White Metal, reeded edge, J1641	Rare
Pn1727	1879	—	Metric 20 Dollar, Copper, reeded edge, J1642	Unique
Pn1728	1879	4 known	Metric 20 Dollar, Gold, 540.5 g, reeded edge, J1643	187,000.
Pn1728a	1879	—	Metric 20 Dollar, Gold, restrike, 516 g, reeded edge, J1643	—
Pn1729	1879	—	Metric 20 Dollar, Copper, reeded edge, J1644	—
Pn1730	1880	—	Metric Dollar, Silver Alloy, reeded edge, J1645	5000.
Pn1731	1880	—	Metric Dollar, Copper, reeded edge, J1646	3500.
Pn1732	1880	—	Metric Dollar, Aluminum, reeded edge, J1647	10,175.

KM#	Date	Mintage	Identification	Mkt.Val.
Pn1733	1880	—	Metric Dollar, Silver Alloy, reeded edge, J1648	7250.
Pn1734	1880	—	Metric Dollar, Copper, reeded edge, J1649	7150.
Pn1735	1880	—	Metric Dollar, Aluminum, reeded edge, J1650	12,000.

KM#	Date	Mintage	Identification	Mkt.Val.
Pn1736	1880	—	Goloid Metric Dollar, Goloid, reeded edge, J1651	7500.
Pn1737	1880	—	Goloid Metric Dollar, Copper, reeded edge, J1652	12,500.
Pn1738	1880	—	Goloid Metric Dollar, Aluminum, reeded edge, J1653	3550.

KM#	Date	Mintage	Identification	Mkt.Val.
Pn1739	1880	—	Goloid Metric Dollar, Goloid, reeded edge, J1654	10,000.
Pn1740	1880	—	Goloid Metric Dollar, Copper, reeded edge, J1655	12,000.
Pn1741	1880	—	Goloid Metric Dollar, Aluminum, reeded edge, J1656	—

KM#	Date	Mintage	Identification	Mkt.Val.
Pn1742	1880	15	4 Dollar Stella, Gold, reeded edge, J1657	60,000.
Pn1743	1880	—	4 Dollar Stella, Copper, reeded edge, J1658	9000.
Pn1744	1880	—	4 Dollar Stella, Aluminum, reeded edge, J1659	15,125.
Pn1745	1880	10	4 Dollar Stella, Gold, reeded edge, J1660	264,000.
Pn1746	1880	—	4 Dollar Stella, Copper, reeded edge, J1661	12,100.
Pn1746a	1880	—	4 Dollar Stella, Copper Gilt, reeded edge, J1661	10,500.
Pn1747	1880	—	4 Dollar Stella, Aluminum, J1662	10,450.
Pn1748	1880	—	5 Dollar, Copper, reeded edge, J1663	Unique
Pn1749	1881	—	1 Cent, Nickel, plain edge, J1664	—

KM#	Date	Mintage	Identification	Mkt.Val.
Pn1750	1881	—	1 Cent, Nickel, plain edge, J1665	1850.
Pn1751	1881	—	1 Cent, Copper, plain edge, J1666	2500.
Pn1752	1881	—	1 Cent, Aluminum, plain edge, J1667	2750.

KM#	Date	Mintage	Identification	Mkt.Val.
Pn1753	1881	—	3 Cent, Nickel, plain edge, J1668	2800.
Pn1754	1881	—	3 Cent, Copper, plain edge, J1669	2200.
Pn1755	1881	—	3 Cent, Aluminum, plain edge, J1670	4000.
Pn1756	1881	—	5 Cent, Nickel, plain edge, J1671	3750.
Pn1757	1881	—	5 Cent, Copper, plain edge, J1672	3000.
Pn1758	1881	—	5 Cent, Aluminum, plain edge, J1673	4500.
Pn1759	1881	—	5 Cent, Nickel, plain edge, J1674	Unique
Pn1760	1882	—	5 Cent, Nickel, plain edge, J1675	Rare
Pn1761	1882	—	5 Cent, Copper, plain edge, J1676	Rare
Pn1762	1882	—	5 Cent, Nickel, plain edge, J1677	4000.
Pn1763	1882	—	5 Cent, Copper, plain edge, J1678	3500.
Pn1764	1882	—	5 Cent, Aluminum, plain edge, J1679	5000.

KM#	Date	Mintage	Identification	Mkt.Val.
Pn1765	1882	—	5 Cent, Nickel, plain edge, J1680	3000.
Pn1766	1882	—	5 Cent, Copper, plain edge, J1681	3250.
Pn1767	1882	—	5 Cent, Aluminum, plain edge, J1682	3750.
Pn1768	1882	—	5 Cent, Nickel, 5 equally spaced bars on edge, J1683	10,120.
Pn1769	1882	—	5 Cent, Nickel, plain edge, J1684	2000.
Pn1770	1882	—	5 Cent, Copper, plain edge, J1685	2000.
Pn1771	1882	—	5 Cent, Aluminum, plain edge, J1686	6000.
Pn1772	1882	—	5 Cent, Nickel, plain edge, J1687	2400.
Pn1773	1882	—	5 Cent, Copper, plain edge, J1688	—
Pn1774	1882	—	5 Cent, Aluminum, plain edge, J1689	2750.

KM#	Date	Mintage	Identification	Mkt.Val.
Pn1775	1882	—	5 Cent, Nickel, plain edge, J1690	6250.
Pn1776	1882	—	5 Cent, Copper, plain edge, J1691	2500.
Pn1777	1882	—	5 Cent, Aluminum, plain edge, J1692	4650.
Pn1778	1882	—	5 Cent, Nickel, plain edge, J1693	5300.
Pn1779	1882	—	5 Cent, Copper, plain edge, J1694	6000.
Pn1779a	1882	—	5 Cent, Copper, small thin planchet, plain edge, J1694a	2000.
Pn1780	1882	—	5 Cent, Aluminum, plain edge, J1695	7000.
Pn1781	1882	—	5 Cent, White Metal, plain edge, J1696	Rare
Pn1782	1882	—	5 Cent, Nickel, 5 equally spaced bars on edge, J1697	Rare
Pn1783	1882	—	25 Cent, Silver, reeded edge, J1698	14,300.
Pn1784	1882	—	25 Cent, Copper, reeded edge, J1699	Rare
Pn1785	1882	—	50 Cent, Silver, reeded edge, J1700	12,100.
Pn1786	1882	—	50 Cent, Copper, reeded edge, J1701	14,500.
Pn1787	1882	—	1 Dollar, Silver, reeded edge, J1702	27,500.
Pn1788	1882	—	1 Dollar, Copper, reeded edge, J1703	24,200.
Pn1789	1882	—	1 Dollar, Copper, reeded edge, J1703a	8750.
Pn1790	1882	—	Trade Dollar, Copper, reeded edge, J1703b	Rare

KM#	Date	Mintage	Identification	Mkt.Val.
Pn1791	1883	—	5 Cent, Pure Nickel, plain edge, J1704	2750.
Pn1792	1883	—	5 Cent, Nickel, plain edge, J1705	2750.
Pn1793	1883	—	5 Cent, Aluminum, plain edge, J1706	3000.
Pn1794	1883	—	5 Cent, Nickel, plain edge, J1706a	Unique
Pn1795	1883	—	5 Cent, Pure Nickel, plain edge, J1707	2850.
Pn1796	1883	—	5 Cent, Nickel, plain edge, J1708	—
Pn1797	1883	—	5 Cent, Aluminum, plain edge, J1709	3750.

KM#	Date	Mintage	Identification	Mkt.Val.
Pn1798	1883	—	5 Cent, Nickel, plain edge, J1710	3000.
Pn1799	1883	—	5 Cent, Aluminum, plain edge, J1711	2200.
Pn1800	1883	—	5 Cent, Nickel, plain edge, J1712	2550.
Pn1801	1883	—	5 Cent, Aluminum, plain edge, J1713	—

KM#	Date	Mintage	Identification	Mkt.Val.
Pn1802	1883	—	5 Cent, Nickel, plain edge, J1714	2650.
Pn1803	1883	—	5 Cent, Copper, plain edge, J1715	—
Pn1804	1883	—	5 Cent, Aluminum, plain edge, J1716	—
Pn1805	1883	—	5 Cent, Nickel, plain edge, J1717	2650.
Pn1806	1883	—	5 Cent, Copper, plain edge, J1718	9000.
Pn1807	1883	—	5 Cent, Aluminum, plain edge, J1719	3000.

KM#	Date	Mintage	Identification	Mkt.Val.
Pn1808	1883	—	5 Cent, Aluminum, plain edge, J1720	—
Pn1809	1883	—	Trade Dollar, Copper, reeded edge, J1720a	—

KM#	Date	Mintage	Identification	Mkt.Val.
Pn1810	1884	—	1 Cent, Nickel, plain edge, J1721	2500.
Pn1811	1884	—	1 Cent, Aluminum, plain edge, J1722	3500.
Pn1812	1884	—	1 Cent, White Metal, plain edge, J1723	Rare
Pn1813	1884	—	1 Cent, Nickel Alloy, plain edge, J1723a	Rare

KM#	Date	Mintage	Identification	Mkt.Val.
Pn1814	1884	—	5 Cent, Nickel, plain edge, J1724	3000.
Pn1815	1884	—	5 Cent, Aluminum, plain edge, J1725	3500.
Pn1816	1884	—	5 Cent, White Metal, plain edge, J1726	—
Pn1817	1884	—	5 Cent, Aluminum, plain edge, J1727	—
Pn1818	1884	—	10 Cent, Copper, reeded edge, J1728	—
Pn1819	1884	—	25 Cent, Copper, reeded edge, J1729	—
Pn1820	1884	—	50 Cent, Copper, reeded edge, J1730	—
Pn1821	1884	—	1 Dollar, Copper, reeded edge, J1731	—
Pn1822	1884	—	Trade Dollar, Copper, reeded edge, J1732	—
Pn1823	1884	—	Trade Dollar, Copper Silvered, reeded edge, J1732	—
Pn1824	1884	—	Gold Dollar, Copper, reeded edge, J1733	—
Pn1825	1884	—	2-1/2 Dollar, Copper, reeded edge, J1734	—
Pn1826	1884	—	3 Dollar, Copper, reeded edge, J1735	—
Pn1827	1884	—	5 Dollar, Copper, reeded edge, J1736	—
Pn1828	1884	—	10 Dollar, Copper, reeded edge, J1737	—
Pn1829	1884	—	20 Dollar, Copper, reeded edge, J1738	—

KM#	Date	Mintage	Identification	Mkt.Val.
Pn1830	1885/3	—	1 Cent, Silver, plain edge, J1740	5500.
Pn1830a	1885/3	—	1 Cent, Silver, w/o hole, plain edge, J1740a	Rare
Pn1831	1885	—	3 Cent, Aluminum, plain edge, J1741	6500.

KM#	Date	Mintage	Identification	Mkt.Val.
Pn1832	1885	—	5 Cent, Silver, plain edge, J1742	3200.
Pn1833	1885	—	5 Cent, Aluminum, plain edge, J1743	4000.
Pn1834	1885	—	10 Cent, Aluminum, reeded edge, J1744	4000.
Pn1835	1885	—	25 Cent, Aluminum, reeded edge, J1745	4000.
Pn1836	1885	—	50 Cent, Aluminum, reeded edge, J1746	3750.

KM#	Date	Mintage	Identification	Mkt.Val.
Pn1837	1885	—	1 Dollar, Silver, lettered edge, J1747	4500.
Pn1838	1885	—	1 Dollar, Copper, lettered edge, J1748	4500.
Pn1839	1885	—	1 Dollar, Aluminum, lettered edge, J1749	7750.
Pn1840	1885	—	1 Dollar, Aluminum, reeded edge, J1750	8000.
Pn1841	1885	—	1 Dollar, Copper, reeded edge, J1750a	8500.
Pn1842	1885	—	1 Gold Dollar, Aluminum, reeded edge, J1751	—
Pn1843	1885	—	2-1/2 Dollar, Aluminum, reeded edge, J1752	—
Pn1844	1885	—	3 Dollar, Aluminum, reeded edge, J1753	—
Pn1845	1885	—	5 Dollar, Aluminum, reeded edge, J1754	—
Pn1846	1885	—	10 Dollar, Aluminum, reeded edge, J1755	—
Pn1847	1885	—	20 Dollar, Aluminum, reeded edge, J1756	—
Pn1848	1890	—	1 Cent, Copper, plain edge, J1757	4000.
Pn1849	1890	—	1 Cent, Copper-Nickel, plain edge, J1758	4650.
Pn1850	1890	—	1 Cent, Aluminum, plain edge, J1759	5000.
Pn1851	1891	2 known	10 Cent, Silver, reeded edge, J1760	Rare
Pn1852	1891	2 known	25 Cent, Silver, reeded edge, J1761	Rare
Pn1853	1891	2 known	50 Cent, Silver, reeded edge, J1762	Rare
Pn1854	1891	2 known	50 Cent, Silver, reeded edge, J1763	Rare
Pn1855	1891	2 known	50 Cent, Silver, reeded edge, J1764	Rare
Pn1856	1891	2 known	50 Cent, Silver, reeded edge, J1765	Rare
Pn1857	1891	3 known	50 Cent, Silver, reeded edge, J1766	Rare

KM#	Date	Mintage	Identification	Mkt.Val.
Pn1858	1896	—	1 Cent, Nickel Alloy, plain edge, J1767	1500.
Pn1859	1896	—	1 Cent, Pure Nickel, plain edge, J1767a	1750.
Pn1860	1896	—	1 Cent, Bronze, plain edge, J1768	2200.
Pn1861	1896	—	1 Cent, Aluminum, plain edge, J1769	2750.

KM#	Date	Mintage	Identification	Mkt.Val.
Pn1862	1896	—	5 Cent, Nickel Alloy, plain edge, J1770	2450.
Pn1863	1896	—	5 Cent, Pure Nickel, plain edge, J1771	2200.
Pn1864	1896	—	5 Cent, Aluminum, plain edge, J1772	2000.

URUGUAY

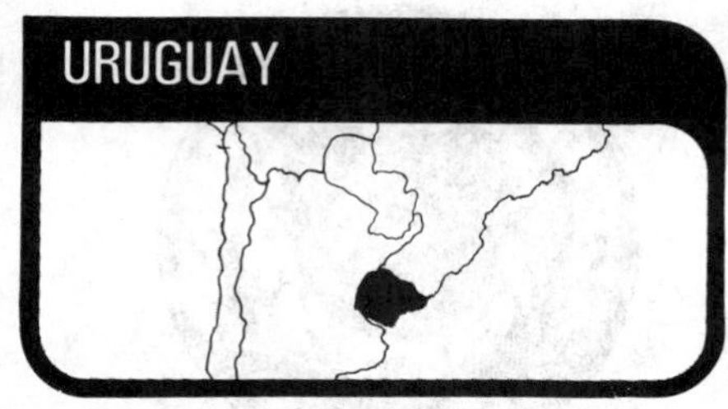

The Oriental Republic of Uruguay (so called because of its location on the east bank of the Uruguay River) is situated on the Atlantic coast of South America between Argentina and Brazil. This most advanced of South American countries has an area of 68,536 sq. mi. (176,220 sq. km.) and a population of *3 million. Capital: Montevideo. Uruguay's chief economic asset is its rich, rolling grassy plains. Meat, wool, hides and skins are exported.

Uruguay was discovered in 1516 by Juan Diaz de Solis, a Spaniard, but settled by the Portuguese who founded Colonia in 1680. Spain contested Portuguese possession and, after a long struggle, gained control of the country in 1778. During the general South American struggle for independence, Uruguay 's first attempt was led by Gaucho soldier Jose Gervasio Artigas leading the Banda Oriental which was quelled by Spanish and Portuguese forces in 1811. The armistice was soon broken and Argentine force from Buenos Aires cast off the Spanish bond in the Plata region in 1814 only to be reconquered by the Portuguese from Brazil in the struggle of 1816-20. Revolt flared anew in 1825 and independence was reasserted in 1828 with the help of Argentina. The Uruguayan Republic was established in 1830.

MINT MARKS

A - Paris, Berlin, Vienna
(a) Paris, privy marks only
D - Lyon (France)
H - Birmingham
Mx, Mo - Mexico City
(p) Poissy, France
So - Santiago (Small O above S)
(u) - Utrecht

MONETARY SYSTEM

100 Centesimo = 1 Peso

CENTESIMO

BRONZE, 5.00 g

KM#	Date	Mintage	Fine	VF	XF	Unc
11	1869A	1.000	1.00	2.00	12.00	40.00
	1869H	1.000	1.00	2.00	12.00	40.00

2 CENTESIMOS

BRONZE, 10.00 g

KM#	Date	Mintage	Fine	VF	XF	Unc
12	1869A	3.000	1.00	2.50	15.00	45.00
	1869H	2.000	1.00	2.50	15.00	45.00

4 CENTESIMOS

BRONZE, 20.00 g

KM#	Date	Mintage	Fine	VF	XF	Unc
13	1869A	2.000	2.50	6.00	18.00	75.00
	1869H	6.250	2.50	6.00	18.00	60.00
	1869H	—	—		Specimen	200.00

5 CENTESIMOS

COPPER, 4.25 g

KM#	Date	Mintage	VG	Fine	VF	XF
1	1840	1,500	125.00	250.00	400.00	650.00
	1844/0	—	95.00	190.00	325.00	475.00
	1854/40	—	20.00	30.00	50.00	100.00

4.35 g

KM#	Date	Mintage	VG	Fine	VF	XF
6	1855	—	75.00	125.00	225.00	500.00

KM#	Date	Mintage	Fine	VF	XF	Unc
8	1857D	—	6.00	12.00	28.00	65.00

10 CENTESIMOS

2.5000 g, .900 SILVER, .0723 oz ASW

KM#	Date	Mintage	Fine	VF	XF	Unc
14	1877A privy mark anchor points left					
		3.000	3.50	6.00	10.00	35.00
	1877A privy mark anchor points right					
		Inc. Ab.	50.00	75.00	150.00	400.00
	1877A	—	—	—	Proof	—
	1893/77So	—	—	—	—	—
	1893 w/o mm	—	50.00	70.00	110.00	250.00
	1893So	1.000	2.50	7.00	15.00	50.00

20 CENTESIMOS

COPPER
28.00 g, 2.75mm thick
Rev: Small design.

KM#	Date	Mintage	VG	Fine	VF	XF
2.1	1840	2,125	20.00	60.00	100.00	250.00

Reduced weight 21.00 g, 1.75mm thick.

KM#	Date	Mintage	VG	Fine	VF	XF
2.2	1843/40	—	25.00	70.00	120.00	275.00
	1844	—	35.00	85.00	165.00	325.00

Rev: Small design.

KM#	Date	Mintage	VG	Fine	VF	XF
2.3	1854	—	20.00	40.00	80.00	150.00

Rev: Large design.

KM#	Date	Mintage	VG	Fine	VF	XF
7	1854	—	22.00	50.00	100.00	265.00
	1855	—	20.00	45.00	85.00	245.00

21.30 g

KM#	Date	Mintage	Fine	VF	XF	Unc
9	1857D	—	5.00	10.00	22.00	75.00

5.0000 g, .900 SILVER, .1446 oz ASW

KM#	Date	Mintage	Fine	VF	XF	Unc
15	1877A	1.500	3.00	5.00	12.00	45.00
	1877A	—	—	—	Proof	—
	1893/73So	.750	5.00	7.50	15.00	65.00

40 CENTESIMOS

COPPER

Obv: Male sunface.

KM#	Date	Mintage	VG	Fine	VF	XF
3	1844	—	40.00	80.00	150.00	300.00

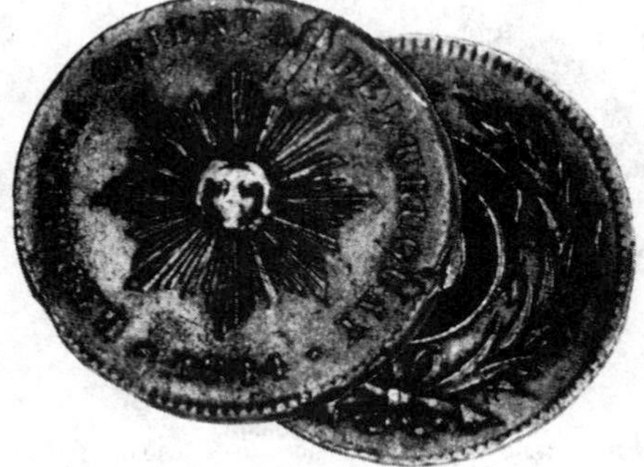

Obv: Female sunface.

KM#	Date	Mintage	VG	Fine	VF	XF
4	1844	50 est.	175.00	375.00	750.00	1250.

NOTE: There are at least 12 different obverse and reverse die varieties known for the 40 Centesimos dated 1844.

KM#	Date	Mintage	Fine	VF	XF	Unc
10	1857D	—	5.00	10.00	45.00	125.00

50 CENTESIMOS

12.5000 g, .900 SILVER, .3617 oz ASW

KM#	Date	Mintage	Fine	VF	XF	Unc
16	1877A	.400	6.00	8.00	20.00	90.00
	1877A	—	—	—	Proof	—
	1893/73So	.500	6.00	8.00	20.00	90.00
	1894	.800	6.00	8.00	20.00	90.00

NOTE: 1894 has larger letters.

PESO

27.0000 g, .875 SILVER, .7596 oz ASW

KM#	Date	Mintage	Fine	VF	XF	Unc
5	1844	1,500	200.00	350.00	750.00	1850.

NOTE: KM#5 exists both with coin and medal reverse alignments.

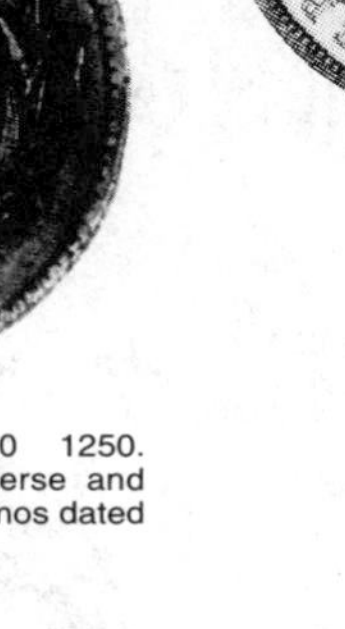

25.5000 g, .917 SILVER, .7518 oz ASW

KM#	Date	Mintage	Fine	VF	XF	Unc
17	1877A	.300	25.00	45.00	100.00	400.00
	1877A	—	—	—	Proof	1000.
	25.0000 g, .900 SILVER, .7235 oz ASW					
17a	1878A	*.100	125.00	350.00	800.00	1500.
	1893/73So	.500	25.00	50.00	100.00	400.00
	1893So	Inc. Ab.	20.00	35.00	85.00	375.00
	1893	.600	20.00	35.00	75.00	325.00
	1895	1.000	15.00	25.00	65.00	300.00

***NOTE:** 43,200 melted after they were recovered from salt water.

COUNTERSTAMPED COINAGE

PESO

SILVER

KM#	Date	Mintage	Fine	VF	XF	Unc
18	1895	—	75.00	135.00	245.00	—

NOTE: Dies were made in the Paysandu area of Uruguay, and Brazil 2,000 reis were overstruck to create an 1895 1 peso coin. These coins are considered by some to be a contemporary counterfeit and probably have no official standing.

ESSAIS (E)

KM#	Date	Mintage	Identification	Mkt.Val.
E1	1856	—	40 Centesimos, KM10	—

KM#	Date	Mintage	Identification	Mkt.Val.
E2	1869	—	100 Centesimos, Silver, Liberty head	—
E3	1869	—	100 Centesimos, Silver, Arms	—

PATTERNS (Pn)

(Including off metal strikes)

KM#	Date	Mintage	Identification	Mkt.Val.
Pn1	1844	—	1 Peso, Lead	—
Pn2	1854	—	40 Reales, Gold, 8.75 g	—
PnA3	1869	—	2 Centesimos, Bronze	—
Pn3	1869	—	4 Centesimos, Bronze	—
Pn4	1869	—	100 Centesimos, Silver	—
Pn5	1869A	—	1 Centesimo, Silver, KM11	—
Pn6	1869H	—	1 Centesimo, Silver, KM11	—
Pn7	1869A	—	1 Centesimo, Gold, KM11	—
Pn8	1869H	—	1 Centesimo, Gold, KM11	—

KM#	Date	Mintage	Identification	Mkt.Val.
PnA9	1869H	—	2 Centesimos, Bronze, KM12, w/o designer's name	—

KM#	Date	Mintage	Identification	Mkt.Val.
Pn9	1869A	—	2 Centesimos, Silver, KM12	—
Pn10	1869H	—	2 Centesimos, Silver, KM12	—
Pn11	1869A	—	2 Centesimos, Gold, KM12	—
Pn12	1869H	—	2 Centesimos, Gold, KM12	—
PnA13	1869H	—	4 Centesimos, Copper, KM13	—
Pn13	1869A	—	4 Centesimos, Silver, KM13	—
Pn14	1869H	—	4 Centesimos, Silver, KM13	—
Pn15	1869A	—	4 Centesimos, Gold, KM13	—
Pn16	1869H	—	4 Centesimos, Gold, KM13	—
PnA17	1869	—	5 Centavos, Nickel	—
PnB17	1869	—	10 Centavos, Nickel	—
PnC17	1869	—	20 Centavos, Nickel	—
Pn17	1870	—	10 Centesimos, Copper	—
Pn18	1870	—	10 Centesimos, .900 Silver, KM14	—
Pn19	1870	—	20 Centesimos, Copper,	—
Pn20	1870	—	20 Centesimos, Silver	—
Pn21	1870	—	50 Centesimos, Copper, KM16, plain or reeded edge	—
Pn22	1870	—	50 Centesimos, .900 Silver, KM16	—
Pn23	1870	—	50 Centesimos, Gold, 10mm, KM16	—
Pn24	1870	—	1 Peso, Copper, 37mm, KM17	—
Pn25	1870	—	1 Peso, .900 Silver, KM17	—
Pn26	1870	—	1 Peso, Gold, 16mm, KM17	—
Pn27	1870	—	1 Peso, Copper, 16mm, KM17	—

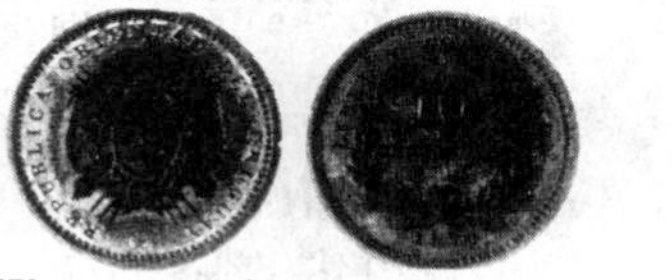

KM#	Date	Mintage	Identification	Mkt.Val.
Pn28	1870	—	2 Pesos, Copper	—
Pn29	1870	—	5 Pesos, Copper	—
Pn30	1870	—	5 Pesos, Copper, gilt	—
Pn31	1870	—	1 Doblon, Bronze, gilt	—
Pn32	1899	—	5 Centavos, Nickel, w/o value	—
Pn32a	1899	—	5 Centesimos, Copper-Nickel, w/o value	—
Pn33	1899	—	5 Centavos, Nickel, value below	125.00
PnA34	1899	—	5 Centavos, Copper-Nickel	125.00
Pn34	1899	—	10 Centavos, Nickel, w/o value	—
Pn34a	1899	—	10 Centesimos, Copper-Nickel, w/o value	—
Pn35	1899	—	10 Centavos, Nickel, value below	125.00
Pn35a	1899	—	10 Centavos, Copper-Nickel	125.00
Pn36	1899	—	20 Centavos, Nickel, w/o value	—
Pn36a	1899	—	20 Centesimos, Copper-Nickel, w/o value	—
Pn37	1899	—	20 Centavos, Nickel, value below	135.00
Pn37a	1899	—	20 Centavos, Copper-Nickel	135.00

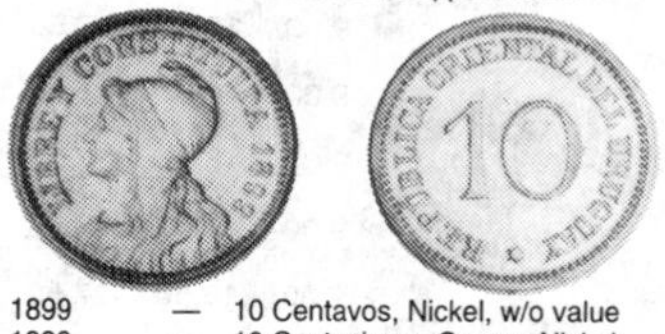

PIEFORTS (P)

(Double thickness)

KM#	Date	Mintage	Identification	Mkt.Val.
P1	1870	—	20 Centesimos, Copper	300.00

UZBEKISTAN

The Republic of Uzbekistan (formerly the Uzbek S.S.R.), is bordered on the north by Kazakhstan, to the east by Kirghizia and Tajikistan, on the south by Afghanistan and on the west by Turkmenistan. The republic is comprised of the regions of Andizhan, Bukhara, Dzhizak, Ferghana, Kashkadar, Khorezm (Khiva), Namangan, Navoi, Samarkand, Surkhan-Darya, Syr-Darya, Tashkent and the Karakalpak Autonomous Republic. It has an area of 172,741 sq. mi. (447,400 sq. km.) and a population of 20.3 million. Capital: Tashkent.

Crude oil, natural gas, coal, copper, and gold deposits make up the chief resources, while intensive farming, based on artificial irrigation, provides an abundance of cotton.

The original population was believed to be Iranian towards the north while the southern part hosted the satrapies of Sogdiana and Bactria, members of the Persian empire and once part of the empire of Alexander of Macedon. In the 2nd century B.C. they suffered an invasion by easterners referred to by the Chinese as *Yue-chi* and *Hiung-nu*. At the end of the 7th century and into the 8th century an Arab army under Emir Kotaiba ibu Muslim conquered Khiva (Khorezm) and Bukhara (Sogdiana). Persian influence developed from the Abbasid caliphs of Baghdad. About 874 the area was conquered by the Persian Saminids of Balkh.

In 999 a Turkic Karakhanid dynasty, the first to embrace Islam, supplanted the Samanids in Samarkand and Bukhara. At the beginning of the 11th century the Seljuk Turks passed through Transoxiana and appointed a hereditary governor at Khorezm. In 1141 another dynasty appeared in Transoxiana, the Kara Kitai from north China. Under the Seljuk shahs Khorezm remained a Moslem outpost.

The Mongol invasion of Jenghiz Khan in 1219-20 brought destruction and great ethnic changes among the population. The conquerors became assimilated and adopted the Turkic language "Chagatai." At the beginning of the 16th century Turkestan was conquered by another wave of Turkic nomads, the Uzbeks (Usbegs). The term "Uzbek" was used in the 15th century to indicate Moslem. In the 18th century Khokand made itself independent from the emirate of Bukhara, but was soon subject to China, which had conquered eastern Turkestan (now called Sinkiang). The khanate of Khiva, in 1688, became a vassal of Persia, but recovered its independence in 1747. While the Uzbek emirs and khans ruled central Turkestan, in the north were the Kazakhs, in the west lived the nomadic Turkmens, in the east dwelled the Kirghiz, and in the southeast was the homeland of the Persian-speaking Tajiks. In 1714-17, Peter the Great sent a military expedition against Khiva which ended in a disaster. In 1853, Ak-Mechet ("White Mosque", renamed Perovsk, later Kzyl Orda), was conquered by the Russians, and the following year the fortress of Vermoye (later Alma-Ata) was established. On July 29, 1867, Gen. C.P. Kaufmann was appointed governor general of Turkestan with headquarters in Tashkent. On July 5 Mozaffar ed-Din, emir of Bukhara, signed a treaty making his country a Russian vassal state with much-reduced territory. Khiva was conquered by Gen. N.N. Golovachev, and on Aug. 24, 1873, Khan Mohammed Rakhim Kuli had to become a vassal of Russia. Furthermore, all his possessions east of the Amu Darya were annexed to the Turkestan governor-generalship. The khanate of Khokand was suppressed and on March 3, 1876, became the Fergana province. On the eve of WW I, Khiva and Bukhara were enclaves within a Russian Turkestan divided into five provinces or oblasti. The czarist government did not attempt to Russify the indigenous Turkic or Tajik populations, preferring to keep them backward and illiterate. The revolution of March 1917 created a confused situation in the area. In Tashkent there was a Turkestan committee of the provisional government; a Communist-controlled council of workers', soldiers' and peasants' deputies; also a Moslem Turkic movement, Shuro-i-Islamiya, and a young Turkestan or Jaddidi (Renovation) party. The last named party claimed full political autonomy for Turkestan and the abolition of the emirate of Bukhara and the khanate of Khiva. After the Communist *coup d'etat* in Petrograd, the council of people's commissars on Nov. 24 (Dec. 7), 1917, published an appeal to "all toiling Moslems in Russia and in the east" proclaiming their right to build their national life "freely and unhindered". In response, the Moslem and Jaddidi organizations in Dec. 1917 convoked a national congress in Khokand which appointed a provisional government headed by Mustafa Chokayev (or Chokaigolu; 1890-1941) and resolved to elect a constituent assembly to decide whether Turkestan should remain within a Russian federal state or proclaim its independence. In the spring of 1919 a Red army group defeated Kolchak and in September its commander, M.V. Frunze, arrived in Tashkent with V.V. Kuibyshev as political commissar. The Communists were still much too weak in Turkestan to proclaim the country part of Soviet Russia. Faizullah Khojayev organized a young Bukhara movement, which on Sept. 14, 1920, proclaimed the dethronement of Emir Mir Alim. Bukhara was then made a S.S.R. In 1920 the Tashkent Communist government declared war on Junaid, who took to flight, and Khiva became another S.S.R. In Oct. 1921, Enver Pasha, the former leader of the young Turks, appeared in Bukhara and assumed command of the Basmachi movement. In Aug. 1922 he was forced to retreat into Tajikistan and died on Aug. 4, in a battle near Baljuvan. Khiva concluded a treaty of alliance with the Russian S.F.S.R. in Sept. 1920, and Bukhara followed suit in March 1921. Theoretically, a Turkestan Autonomous Soviet Socialist Republic had existed since May 1, 1918; in 1920 this "Turkrepublic", as it was called, was proclaimed part of the R.S.F.S.R. On Sept. 18, 1924, the Uzbek and Turkmen peoples were authorized to form S.S.R.'s of their own, and the Kazakhs, Kirghiz, and Tajiks to form autonomous S.S.R.'s. On Oct. 27, 1924, the Uzbek and Turkmen S.S.R. were officially constituted and the former was formally accepted on Jan. 15, 1925, as a member of the U.S.S.R. Tajikistan was an autonomous soviet republic within Uzbekistan until Dec. 5, 1929, when it became a S.S.R. On Dec. 5, 1936, Uzbekistan was territorially increased by incorporating into it the Kara-Kalpak A.S.S.R., which had belonged to Kazakhstan until 1930 and afterward had come under direct control of the R.S.F.S.R.

On June 20, 1990 the Uzbek Supreme Soviet adopted a declaration of sovereignty, and in Aug. 1991, following the unsuccessful coup, it declared itself independent as the "Republic of Uzbekistan", which was confirmed by referendum in Dec. That same month Uzbekistan became a member of the CIS.

EMIRATE OF BUKHARA

Bukhara, a city and former emirate in southern Russian Turkestan, formed part (Sogdiana) of the Seleucid empire after the conquest of Alexander the Great and remained an important regional center, sometimes city state, until the 19th century. It became virtually a Russian vassal in 1868 as a consequence of the Czarist invasion of 1866, following which it gradually became a part of Russian Turkestan and then part of Uzbekistan S.S.R., now Uzbekistan.

RULERS

Haidar Tora,
AH1215-1242/1800-1826AD
Hussain Sayyid,
AH1242/1826AD
Nasrullah,
AH1242-1277/1826-1860AD
Muzaffar al-Din,
AH1277-1284/1860-1867AD
Russian Vassal,
AH1284-1336/1868-1917AD

MINTNAME

بخارا

Bukhara

MONETARY SYSTEM

10 Falus = 1 Tenga

HAIDAR TORA

(Amir Said Mir Haidar)
AH1215-1242/1800-1826AD

FALUS

COPPER
Obv. and rev: Legends.

KM#	Date	Good	VG	Fine	VF
41 (C48)	AH1232	4.00	6.00	12.00	25.00

Obv. and rev: Legend within Greek border.

KM#	Date	Good	VG	Fine	VF
31 (C51)	AH1221	5.00	8.00	16.00	30.00
	1228	5.00	8.00	16.00	30.00
	1229	5.00	8.00	16.00	30.00
	1241	5.00	8.00	16.00	30.00
	1242	5.00	8.00	16.00	30.00

Rev: Fish.

KM#	Date	Good	VG	Fine	VF
62 (C52)	AH1241	—	10.00	20.00	35.00

2 FALUS

SILVER

KM#	Date	VG	Fine	VF	XF
33 (C54)	AH1227	8.00	15.00	25.00	50.00
	1228	8.00	15.00	25.00	50.00

TENGA

SILVER, 2.50-3.00 g

KM#	Date	VG	Fine	VF	XF
28 (C55)	AH1216	8.00	15.00	25.00	45.00
	1217	8.00	15.00	25.00	45.00
	1223//1217	9.00	16.50	27.50	50.00
	1226	8.00	15.00	25.00	45.00
	1228//1215	9.00	16.50	27.50	50.00
	1229	9.00	16.50	27.50	50.00
	1230//1229	9.00	16.50	27.50	50.00
	1230//1231	9.00	16.50	27.50	50.00
	1231//1216	9.00	16.50	27.50	50.00
	1231//1230	9.00	16.50	27.50	50.00
	1232//1231	9.00	16.50	27.50	50.00
	1233//1218	9.00	16.50	27.50	50.00
	1233//1233	9.00	16.50	27.50	50.00
	1234	8.00	15.00	25.00	45.00
	1235	8.00	15.00	25.00	45.00
	1236	8.00	15.00	25.00	45.00
	1237//1234	9.00	16.50	27.50	50.00
	1237//1236	9.00	16.50	27.50	50.00

NOTE: Border varieties exist.

In his own name

TILLA

GOLD
Obv: Teardrop. Rev: Circle.

KM#	Date	VG	Fine	VF	XF
27 (C61)	AH1217//1216	95.00	120.00	175.00	225.00
	1218	85.00	110.00	160.00	200.00
	1219	85.00	110.00	160.00	200.00
	1220//1216	95.00	120.00	175.00	225.00

NOTE: Earlier date (AH1215) exists for this type.

Rev: Octagon.

KM#	Date	VG	Fine	VF	XF
30 (C62)	AH1221	100.00	150.00	225.00	300.00
	1222	100.00	150.00	225.00	300.00
	1225	100.00	150.00	225.00	300.00
	1226	100.00	150.00	225.00	300.00
	1227	100.00	150.00	225.00	300.00
	1229	100.00	150.00	225.00	300.00

Obv: Teardrop. Rev: Circle.

KM#	Date	VG	Fine	VF	XF
32 (C63)	AH1225	75.00	100.00	150.00	175.00

In the name of Ma'sum Ibn Danyal

Obv: Teardrop border.

KM#	Date	VG	Fine	VF	XF
34 (C65)	AH1229	85.00	110.00	160.00	200.00
	1230/1229	95.00	120.00	175.00	225.00
	1230	85.00	110.00	160.00	200.00
	1231	85.00	110.00	160.00	200.00
	1233//1033(sic)	95.00	120.00	175.00	225.00
	1233//1232	95.00	120.00	175.00	225.00
	1234	85.00	110.00	160.00	200.00

KM#	Date	VG	Fine	VF	XF
43 (C65a)	AH1233	75.00	100.00	150.00	185.00
	1234	75.00	100.00	150.00	185.00
	1235	75.00	100.00	150.00	185.00

KM#	Date	VG	Fine	VF	XF
52 (C66)	AH1236//1235	75.00	100.00	150.00	185.00
	1236	75.00	100.00	150.00	185.00
	1239//1240	85.00	110.00	175.00	225.00
	1241	75.00	100.00	150.00	185.00

HUSSAIN SAYYID

AH1242/1826AD

TENGA

SILVER

KM#	Date	VG	Fine	VF	XF
61 (C70)	AH1241//1242	20.00	50.00	75.00	100.00

NASRULLAH

AH1242-1277/1826-1860AD

FALUS

BRASS

KM#	Date	Good	VG	Fine	VF
66 (C71)	AH1244	10.00	20.00	35.00	70.00

In the name of Haidar Tora

TENGA

SILVER

KM#	Date	VG	Fine	VF	XF
64 (C72)	AH1243//1242	50.00	70.00	100.00	135.00
	1244	50.00	70.00	100.00	135.00
	1247//1244	50.00	70.00	100.00	135.00
	1275//1273	50.00	70.00	100.00	135.00
	1275//1274	50.00	70.00	100.00	135.00
	1277//1276	50.00	70.00	100.00	135.00

ANONYMOUS COINAGE

FALUS

COPPER or BRASS

KM#	Date	Good	VG	Fine	VF
67 (C90)	AH1277	5.00	8.50	15.00	22.50
	1281	5.00	8.50	15.00	22.50
	1284	5.00	8.50	15.00	22.50
	1285	5.00	8.50	15.00	22.50

NOTE: Later dates (AH1322-1324) exist for this type.
NOTE: Varieties exist.

In the name of Ma'sum Ibn Danyal

TENGA

SILVER, 3.20 g

KM#	Date	VG	Fine	VF	XF
63 (C75)	AH1242	8.50	15.00	30.00	45.00
	1244	8.50	15.00	30.00	45.00
	1245	8.50	15.00	30.00	45.00
	1247	8.50	15.00	30.00	45.00
	1248	8.50	15.00	30.00	45.00
	1249	8.50	15.00	30.00	45.00
	1255	8.50	15.00	30.00	45.00
	1257	8.50	15.00	30.00	45.00
	1258	8.50	15.00	30.00	45.00

KM#	Date	VG	Fine	VF	XF
(C75)	1261	10.00	20.00	40.00	75.00
	1263	8.50	15.00	30.00	45.00
	1265	8.50	15.00	30.00	45.00
	1267	8.50	15.00	30.00	45.00
	1269	8.50	15.00	30.00	45.00
	1271	8.50	15.00	30.00	45.00
	1273	8.50	15.00	30.00	45.00
	1275	8.50	15.00	30.00	45.00
	1276	8.50	15.00	30.00	45.00
	1277	8.50	15.00	30.00	45.00
(C91)	AH1278	7.00	13.50	25.00	40.00
	1278//1279	20.00	30.00	45.00	60.00
	1279	7.00	13.50	25.00	40.00
	1280//1279	20.00	30.00	45.00	60.00
	1281//1280	20.00	30.00	45.00	60.00
	1281	7.00	13.50	25.00	40.00
	1282	7.00	13.50	25.00	40.00
	1283	7.00	13.50	25.00	40.00
	1284	7.00	13.50	25.00	40.00
	1285	7.00	13.50	25.00	40.00
	1293//1283	20.00	30.00	45.00	60.00
	1293//1284	20.00	30.00	45.00	60.00
	1293	7.00	13.50	25.00	40.00
	1294//1293	20.00	30.00	45.00	60.00
	1294//1296	20.00	30.00	45.00	60.00
	1294	7.00	13.50	25.00	40.00
	1295	20.00	30.00	45.00	60.00
	1296	7.00	13.50	25.00	40.00
	1297//1296	20.00	30.00	45.00	60.00
	1297//1298	20.00	30.00	45.00	60.00
	1297	7.00	13.50	25.00	40.00
	1298	7.00	13.50	25.00	40.00
	1299//1297	20.00	30.00	45.00	60.00
	1299//1298	20.00	30.00	45.00	60.00
	1299	7.00	13.50	25.00	40.00
	1300//1254	20.00	30.00	45.00	60.00
	1300//1299	20.00	30.00	45.00	60.00
	1300	7.00	13.50	25.00	40.00
	1301//1299	20.00	30.00	45.00	60.00
	1301//1300	20.00	30.00	45.00	60.00
	1301	7.00	13.50	25.00	40.00
	1303	7.00	13.50	25.00	40.00
	1304//1303	20.00	30.00	45.00	60.00
(Y2)	1304	6.50	12.50	20.00	30.00
	1305//1304	10.00	16.50	27.50	40.00
	1305	6.50	12.50	20.00	30.00
	1306//1299	20.00	30.00	45.00	60.00
	1306//1305	10.00	16.50	27.50	40.00
	1306//1307	10.00	16.50	27.50	40.00
	1306//1308	10.00	16.50	27.50	40.00
	1306	6.50	12.50	20.00	30.00
	1307	6.50	12.50	20.00	30.00
	1308//1307	20.00	30.00	45.00	60.00
	1308//1309	10.00	16.50	27.50	40.00
	1308	6.50	12.50	20.00	30.00
	1309//1304	20.00	30.00	45.00	60.00
	1309//1310	10.00	16.50	27.50	40.00
	1309	6.50	12.50	20.00	30.00
	1310//1308	20.00	30.00	45.00	60.00
	1310//1311	20.00	30.00	45.00	60.00
	1310//1315	10.00	16.50	27.50	40.00
	1310	6.50	12.50	20.00	30.00
	1311	6.50	12.50	20.00	30.00
	1315	6.50	12.50	20.00	30.00
	1316	6.50	12.50	20.00	30.00

NOTE: Varieties exist.

NOTE: Later dates (AH1319-1323) exist for this type.

TILLA

GOLD

KM#	Date	VG	Fine	VF	XF
65	AH1243//1242				

KM#	Date	VG	Fine	VF	XF
(C85)		85.00	110.00	165.00	200.00
	1243	75.00	100.00	150.00	185.00
	1244//1245	85.00	110.00	165.00	200.00
	1244	75.00	100.00	150.00	185.00
	1246	75.00	100.00	150.00	185.00
	1247//1244	85.00	110.00	165.00	200.00
	1247/6//1246	85.00	110.00	165.00	200.00
	1248	75.00	100.00	150.00	185.00
	1254	75.00	100.00	150.00	185.00
	1255//1254	85.00	110.00	165.00	200.00
	1255	75.00	100.00	150.00	185.00
	1256//1254	85.00	110.00	165.00	200.00
	1256//1255	85.00	110.00	165.00	200.00
	1256	75.00	100.00	150.00	185.00
	1257//1258	85.00	110.00	165.00	200.00
	1257//1261	75.00	100.00	150.00	185.00
	1264	75.00	100.00	150.00	185.00
	1265//1266	85.00	110.00	165.00	200.00
	1272//1275	85.00	110.00	165.00	200.00
	1273//1243 (sic)	85.00	110.00	165.00	200.00
	1273//1274	75.00	100.00	150.00	185.00
	1273//1275	75.00	100.00	150.00	185.00
(C95)	AH1278	70.00	90.00	115.00	150.00
	1279	70.00	90.00	115.00	150.00
	1283	70.00	90.00	115.00	150.00
	1284	70.00	90.00	115.00	150.00
	1285	70.00	90.00	115.00	150.00
	1289	70.00	90.00	115.00	150.00
	1291	60.00	85.00	115.00	150.00
	1294	60.00	85.00	115.00	150.00
	1296//1300	75.00	100.00	125.00	175.00
	1296	60.00	85.00	115.00	150.00
	1297	60.00	85.00	115.00	150.00
	1299	60.00	85.00	115.00	150.00
(Y3)	AH1303	75.00	100.00	125.00	165.00
	1306	75.00	100.00	125.00	165.00
	1309	75.00	100.00	125.00	165.00
	1315	75.00	100.00	125.00	165.00
	1316	75.00	100.00	125.00	165.00

NOTE: Later dates (AH1319-1329) exist for this type.

NOTE: The date combination of obv: AH1279 and rev: AH1285 is reported for the above coin.

KHOQAND

Khoqand, a town and former khanate in eastern Turkestan, was a powerful state in the 18th century. Russian superiority in the area was recognized following the holy war of 1875 and was annexed in 1875. It regained its independence briefly during 1918-1920 and became a Soviet Peoples Republic briefly between 1920-1924, and finally was absorbed into Uzbekistan S.S.R., now Uzbekistan.

RULERS

Muhammad Ali Khan,
AH1238-1256/1822-1840AD
Sher Ali,
AH1258-1261/1842-1845AD
Muhammad Khudayar Khan, 1st reign,
AH1261-1275/1845-1858AD
Malla Khan,
AH1275-1278/1858-1862AD
Shah Murad,
AH1278-1279/1862AD
Muhammad Khudayar Khan, 2nd reign
AH1279-1280/1862-1863AD
Sayyid Sultan,
AH1280-1282/1863-1865AD
Muhammad Khudayer Khan, 3rd reign
AH1282-1292/1865-1875AD
Independent until AH1283/1866AD
Russian Vassal AH1283-1293/
1866-1876AD
Nasir al-Din,
AH1292-1293/1875-1876AD
Annexed To Russia, 1875-1876AD
Muhammad Fulad, Rebel,
AH1292-1293/1875-1876AD

MINTNAMES

Until AH1257, the coinage of Khoqand was struck at two mints.

فرغانة

Fe - Fergana(t)

خوقند

Kd - Khoqand

Muhammad Ali Khan

AH1238-1256/1822-1840AD

PUL

COPPER

C#	Date	VG	Fine	VF	XF
60	AH1249 (Kd)	20.00	30.00	40.00	65.00

C#	Date	VG	Fine	VF	XF
63	AH1252(Fa)	35.00	60.00	100.00	150.00

TENGA

SILVER

C#	Date	VG	Fine	VF	XF
65	AH1241	15.00	30.00	60.00	90.00
	1243	15.00	30.00	60.00	90.00
	1244	15.00	30.00	60.00	90.00
	1245	15.00	30.00	60.00	90.00
	125x	15.00	30.00	60.00	90.00
	ND(Kd)	15.00	30.00	60.00	90.00

NOTE: Borders on obverse and reverse vary.

TILLA

GOLD

C#	Date	VG	Fine	VF	XF
67	AH1247(Fa)	—	—	Rare	—

C#	Date	VG	Fine	VF	XF
68	AH1252	75.00	100.00	175.00	250.00
	1254	75.00	100.00	175.00	250.00
	1255	75.00	100.00	175.00	250.00
	1256	75.00	100.00	175.00	250.00
	1257	75.00	100.00	175.00	250.00

NOTE: AH1257 dated strikes are posthumous issues.

Sher Ali

AH1258-1261/1842-1845AD

FALUS

COPPER

C#	Date	VG	Fine	VF	XF
—	AH1259	—	—	—	—

TILLA

GOLD

C#	Date	VG	Fine	VF	XF
78	AH1259/1258	100.00	125.00	225.00	300.00
	1259	80.00	100.00	225.00	300.00
	1260	80.00	100.00	225.00	300.00

Muhammad Khudayar Khan

1st Reign
AH1261-1275/1845-1858AD

PUL

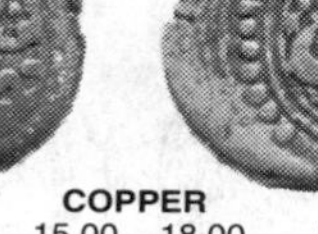

COPPER

C#	Date	VG	Fine	VF	XF
87	AH 1265	15.00	18.00	25.00	35.00
	1269	15.00	18.00	25.00	35.00

TENGA

SILVER

C#	Date	VG	Fine	VF	XF
95	AH1266//1268				
		30.00	40.00	60.00	100.00
	1266	20.00	30.00	45.00	80.00
	1269	20.00	30.00	45.00	80.00
	1270	20.00	30.00	45.00	80.00
	1271	20.00	30.00	45.00	80.00
	1272	20.00	30.00	45.00	80.00
	1273	20.00	30.00	45.00	80.00
	1274	20.00	30.00	45.00	80.00
	1275	20.00	30.00	45.00	80.00

TILLA

GOLD

C#	Date	VG	Fine	VF	XF
100	AH1260	75.00	100.00	140.00	200.00
	1261//1264				
		95.00	125.00	160.00	220.00
	1261	75.00	100.00	140.00	200.00
	1262//1261				
		95.00	125.00	160.00	220.00
	1263	75.00	100.00	140.00	200.00
	1264	75.00	100.00	140.00	200.00
	1265	75.00	100.00	140.00	200.00
	1266	75.00	100.00	140.00	200.00
	1270	75.00	100.00	140.00	200.00
	1272	75.00	100.00	140.00	200.00
	1273	75.00	100.00	140.00	200.00
	1274	75.00	100.00	140.00	200.00
	1275	75.00	100.00	140.00	200.00

Obv: New title.

C#	Date	VG	Fine	VF	XF
100.5	AH1261//1262				
		125.00	275.00	400.00	550.00
	1265	125.00	275.00	400.00	550.00

Malla Khan

AH1275-1278/1858-1862AD

PUL

COPPER

C#	Date	VG	Fine	VF	XF
112	AH1277	12.00	20.00	32.50	60.00

TENGA

SILVER

C#	Date	VG	Fine	VF	XF
115	AH1275	20.00	40.00	50.00	85.00
	1276	20.00	40.00	50.00	85.00
	1277	20.00	40.00	50.00	85.00

TILLA

GOLD

C#	Date	VG	Fine	VF	XF
118	AH1275	75.00	100.00	140.00	200.00
	1276	75.00	100.00	140.00	200.00
	1277	75.00	100.00	140.00	200.00
	1278	75.00	100.00	140.00	200.00

Shah Murad

AH1278-1279/1862AD

TILLA

GOLD

C#	Date	VG	Fine	VF	XF
128	AH1278	100.00	150.00	250.00	350.00

Muhammad Khudayar Khan

2nd Reign

AH1279-1280/1862-1863AD

TENGA

SILVER

Obv. & rev: Teardrop borders.

C#	Date	VG	Fine	VF	XF
130	AH1279	30.00	60.00	100.00	150.00

TILLA

GOLD

C#	Date	VG	Fine	VF	XF
135	AH-			Reported, not confirmed	

Sayyid Sultan

AH1280-1282/1863-1865AD

TENGA

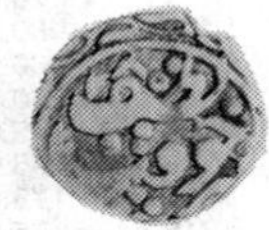

SILVER

C#	Date	VG	Fine	VF	XF
140	AH1280	30.00	45.00	75.00	150.00
	1281	30.00	45.00	75.00	150.00
	1285	30.00	45.00	75.00	150.00

NOTE: AH1285 dated strikes are posthumous issues.

TILLA

GOLD

C#	Date	VG	Fine	VF	XF
145	AH1280	100.00	120.00	160.00	225.00
	1281	100.00	120.00	160.00	225.00

Muhammad Khudayar Khan

3rd Reign

AH1282-1292/1865-1875AD

PUL

COPPER

C#	Date	VG	Fine	VF	XF
148	AH1287	15.00	20.00	30.00	45.00

TENGA

SILVER

C#	Date	VG	Fine	VF	XF
151	AH1282	20.00	30.00	45.00	80.00
	1283	20.00	30.00	45.00	80.00
	1284	20.00	30.00	45.00	80.00
	1285	20.00	30.00	45.00	80.00
	1286	20.00	30.00	45.00	80.00
	1287	20.00	30.00	45.00	80.00
	1289	20.00	30.00	45.00	80.00
	1291	20.00	30.00	45.00	80.00
	1292	20.00	30.00	45.00	80.00

In the name of Malla Khan

C#	Date	VG	Fine	VF	XF
152	AH1289	30.00	50.00	80.00	100.00

TILLA

GOLD

C#	Date	VG	Fine	VF	XF
155	AH1282	70.00	90.00	125.00	175.00
	1283	70.00	90.00	125.00	175.00
	1285	70.00	90.00	125.00	175.00
	1288	70.00	90.00	125.00	175.00

Nasir al Din

AH1292-1293/1875-1875AD

TILLA

GOLD

C#	Date	VG	Fine	VF	XF
165	AH1292			Reported, not confirmed	

Muhammad Fulad

Rebel

AH1292-1293/1875-1876AD

TENGA

SILVER

C#	Date	VG	Fine	VF	XF
105	AH1292	20.00	30.00	40.00	60.00
	1293	20.00	30.00	40.00	60.00

KHWAREZM (KHIVA)

Khwarezm (Khiva), a present town once a great kingdom under the names of Chorasmia, Khwarezm and Urgenj, is located in Russian Turkestan east of the Caspian Sea and south of the Aral Sea. Russia established relations with Khwarezm (Khiva) in the 17th century, occupied it in 1873, and annexed it in 1875. Revolution concentrated Russia's preoccupation elsewhere during 1917 and Khwarezm (Khiva) seized this opportunity to declare its independence. It was able to sustain this status for a scant two years. By 1919 the Soviet regime guished the independent state. In AH1338/1920AD it became Khwarezm Soviet People's Republic and later became part of the Uzbekistan S.S.R., now Uzbekistan.

RULERS

Muhammad Rahim,
AH1221-1241/1805-1825AD
Allah Quli,
AH1241-1258/1825-1842AD
Rahim Quli,
AH1258-1261/1842-1845AD
Muhammad Amin,
AH1261-1271/1845-1855AD
Qutlugh Muhammad,
AH1271-1272/1855-1856AD
Sayyid Muhammad Khan,
AH1272-1282/1856-1864AD
Sayyid Muhammad Rahim,
AH1282-1289/1864-1872AD
Sayid Muhammad Rahim, Russian Vassal,
AH1290-1313/1873-1896AD

MINTNAME

Khwarezm خوارزم

RUSSIAN KHANATE

Muhammad Rahim

AH122x-1241/1825AD

TENGA

SILVER, 3.00 g

C#	Date	VG	Fine	VF	XF
40	AH1232	20.00	30.00	50.00	85.00
	1235	20.00	30.00	50.00	85.00

Allah Quli

AH1241-1258/1825-1842AD

TENGA

SILVER, 3.00 g

C#	Date	VG	Fine	VF	XF
50	AH1247	20.00	30.00	50.00	85.00
	1248	20.00	30.00	50.00	85.00
	1258	20.00	30.00	50.00	85.00

NOTE: Varieties exist.

Muhammad Amin

AH1261-1271/1845-1855AD

TENGA

SILVER, 3.00 g

C#	Date	VG	Fine	VF	XF
60	AH1262	18.00	25.00	40.00	75.00
	1263	18.00	25.00	40.00	75.00
	1264	18.00	25.00	40.00	75.00
	1265	18.00	25.00	40.00	75.00
	1266	18.00	25.00	40.00	75.00
	1267	18.00	25.00	40.00	75.00
	1268	18.00	25.00	40.00	75.00
	1269	18.00	25.00	40.00	75.00

Rev: Two borders enclose legend.

C#	Date	VG	Fine	VF	XF
60a	ND	18.00	25.00	40.00	75.00

1/2 TILLA

GOLD

C#	Date	VG	Fine	VF	XF
65	AH1261	200.00	350.00	500.00	750.00
	1265	200.00	350.00	500.00	750.00

Rev. leg. in octagonal frame.

C#	Date	VG	Fine	VF	XF
65a	AH1270	200.00	350.00	500.00	750.00
	1271	200.00	350.00	500.00	750.00

Qutlugh Muhammad

AH1271-1272/1855-1856AD

1/2 TILLA

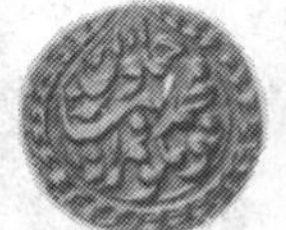

GOLD

Y#	Date	VG	Fine	VF	XF
A1	AH1271	250.00	450.00	750.00	1100.
	1272	250.00	450.00	750.00	1100.

Sayyid Muhammad Khan

AH1272-1282/1856-1864AD

FALUS

COPPER

Y#	Date	VG	Fine	VF	XF
1	AH1272	20.00	35.00	50.00	75.00
	1274	20.00	35.00	50.00	75.00
	1275	20.00	35.00	50.00	75.00
	1277	20.00	35.00	50.00	75.00
	1278	20.00	35.00	50.00	75.00
	1279	20.00	35.00	50.00	75.00
	1280	20.00	35.00	50.00	75.00

NOTE: Varieties exist.

TENGA

SILVER, 3.00 g

Obv: Date in center. Rev: Ornamented.

Y#	Date	VG	Fine	VF	XF
2	AH1273	20.00	30.00	45.00	75.00
	1274	20.00	30.00	45.00	75.00
	1275	20.00	30.00	45.00	75.00
	1276	20.00	30.00	45.00	75.00
	1277	20.00	30.00	45.00	75.00
	1278	20.00	30.00	45.00	75.00
	1279	20.00	30.00	45.00	75.00
	1280	20.00	30.00	45.00	75.00
	1281	20.00	30.00	45.00	75.00
	1288	20.00	30.00	45.00	75.00

NOTE: AH1288 dated strikes are posthumous issues.

TILLA

GOLD

Y#	Date	VG	Fine	VF	XF
A3	AH1276	275.00	450.00	700.00	1000.
	1277	275.00	450.00	700.00	1000.

Sayyid Muhammad Rahim

AH1282-1289/1864-1872AD

FALUS

COPPER

Y#	Date	VG	Fine	VF	XF
3	AH1286	12.50	25.00	50.00	75.00
	1290	12.50	25.00	50.00	75.00
	1308	12.50	25.00	50.00	75.00
	1310	12.50	25.00	50.00	75.00
	1311	12.50	25.00	50.00	75.00

NOTE: Varieties exist.

NOTE: AH1286-1311 dated strikes are posthumous issues.

TENGA

SILVER

Y#	Date	VG	Fine	VF	XF
6	AH1282	15.00	20.00	30.00	45.00
	1283	15.00	20.00	30.00	45.00
	1284//1283	20.00	28.00	40.00	60.00
	1284	15.00	20.00	30.00	45.00
	1285	15.00	20.00	30.00	45.00
	1288	15.00	20.00	30.00	45.00
	1287	18.00	25.00	42.50	70.00
	1294	18.00	25.00	42.50	70.00
	1294//1295	18.00	25.00	42.50	70.00
	1296//1297	18.00	25.00	42.50	70.00
	1298	18.00	25.00	42.50	70.00
	1301	18.00	25.00	42.50	70.00
	1303	18.00	25.00	42.50	70.00
	1305	18.00	25.00	42.50	70.00

Y#	Date	VG	Fine	VF	XF
6	1306	18.00	25.00	42.50	70.00
	1307	18.00	25.00	42.50	70.00
	1308	18.00	25.00	42.50	70.00
	1311	18.00	25.00	42.50	70.00
	1312	18.00	25.00	42.50	70.00
	1313	18.00	25.00	42.50	70.00

NOTE: AH1294-1313 dated strikes are posthumous issues.

VATICAN-PAPAL STATES

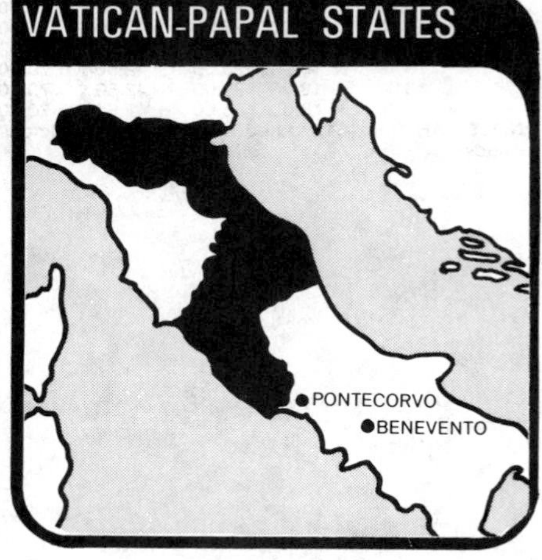

During many centuries prior to the formation of the unified Kingdom of Italy, when Italy was divided into numerous independent papal and ducal states, the Popes held temporal sovereignty over an area in central Italy comprising some 17,000 sq. mi. (44,030 sq. km.) including the city of Rome. At the time of the general unification of Italy under the Kingdom of Sardinia, 1861, the papal dominions beyond Rome were acquired by that kingdom diminishing the Pope's sovereignty to Rome and its environs. In 1870, while France's opposition to papal dispossession was neutralized by its war with Prussia, the Italian army seized weakly defended Rome and made it the capital of Italy, thereby abrogating the last vestige of papal temporal power. In 1871, the Italian Parliament enacted the Law of Guarantees, which guaranteed a special status for the Vatican area, and spiritual freedom and a generous income for the Pope. Pope Pius IX and his successors adamantly refused to acknowledge the validity of these laws and voluntarily "imprisoned" themselves in the Vatican. The impasse between State and Church lasted until the signing of the Lateran Treaty, Feb. 11, 1929, by which Italy recognized the sovereignty and independence of the new Vatican City state.

PONTIFFS

Pius VII, 1800-1823
  Sede Vacante, Aug. 20-Sept. 28, 1823
Leo XII, 1823-1829
  Sede Vacante, Feb. 10-Mar. 31, 1829
Pius VIII, 1829-1830
  Sede Vacante, Nov. 30, 1830-Feb. 2, 1831
Gregory XVI, 1831-1846
  Sede Vacante, June 1-16, 1846
Pius IX, 1846-1878
Leo XIII, 1878-1903

MINT MARKS

B - Bologna
R - Rome

MONETARY SYSTEM

(Until 1860)

5 Quattrini = 1 Baiocco
5 Baiocchi = 1 Grosso
6 Grossi = 4 Carlini = 3 Giulio = 3 Paoli = 1 Testone.
14 Carlini = 1 Piastre
100 Baiocchi = 1 Scudo
10 Testone = Doppia

QUATTRINO

COPPER

KM#	Date	Year	VG	Fine	VF	XF
1260	1801R	—	5.00	10.00	25.00	45.00
(C106)						

KM#	Date	Year	VG	Fine	VF	XF
1264	1802R	II	4.00	7.50	12.50	25.00
(C107)						

Obv. value: QVATTRINO.

KM#	Date	Year	VG	Fine	VF	XF
1276.1						
	1816B	XVI	4.00	7.50	12.50	25.00
(C107a)						
	1816R	XVI	4.00	7.50	12.50	25.00
	1816R	XVII	4.00	7.50	12.50	25.00
	1821B	XXII	5.00	8.50	14.00	28.00
	1821R	XXII	4.00	7.50	12.50	25.00
	1822B	XXII	4.00	7.50	12.50	25.00

Obv. value: VN QVATTRINO.

KM#	Date	Year	VG	Fine	VF	XF
1276.2						
	1816B	XVI	15.00	25.00	40.00	70.00
(C107.5)						

KM#	Date	Year	VG	Fine	VF	XF
1294.1						
	1824(B)	I	4.00	8.00	15.00	30.00
(C125.5)						

KM#	Date	Year	VG	Fine	VF	XF
1294.2						
	1824R	I	3.00	6.00	15.00	30.00
(C126)						
	1825R	II	3.00	6.00	15.00	30.00

KM#	Date	Year	VG	Fine	VF	XF
1298	1826R	IV	3.00	6.00	15.00	30.00
(C126a)						

KM#	Date	Year	VG	Fine	VF	XF
1299	1829R	I	4.00	9.00	17.00	35.00
(C135)						

KM#	Date	Year	VG	Fine	VF	XF
1312	1831R	I	2.00	4.00	7.50	15.00
(C144)						

NOTE: Retrograde 1's in date.

KM#	Date	Year	VG	Fine	VF	XF
1318	1835R	V	2.00	4.00	7.50	20.00
(C144a)						
	1836B	VI	2.00	4.00	7.50	20.00
	1838R	VIII	2.00	4.00	7.50	20.00
1318	1839B	IX	4.00	7.50	12.50	25.00
	1839R	IX	2.00	4.00	7.50	20.00
	1840B	X	4.00	7.50	12.50	25.00
	1841R	X	3.00	5.00	8.50	20.00
	1841R	XI	2.00	4.00	7.50	20.00
	1843B	XIII	2.00	4.00	7.50	20.00
	1843R	XIII	2.00	4.00	7.50	20.00
	1844B	XIV	2.00	4.00	7.50	20.00
	1844R	XIV	2.00	4.00	7.50	20.00

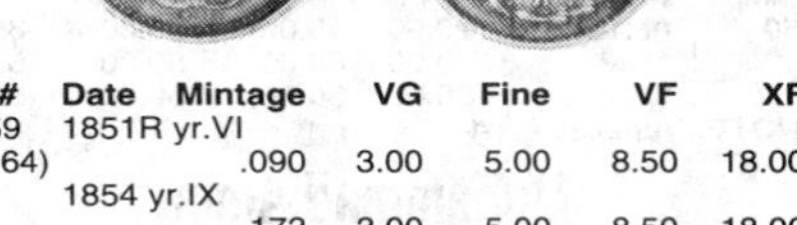

KM#	Date	Mintage	VG	Fine	VF	XF
1359	1851R yr.VI					
(C164)		.090	3.00	5.00	8.50	18.00
	1854 yr.IX					
		.173	3.00	5.00	8.50	18.00

MEZZO (1/2) BAIOCCO

COPPER

KM#	Date	Year	VG	Fine	VF	XF
1261	1801R	—	4.00	7.50	15.00	30.00
(C108)						

NOTE: Varieties exist.

KM#	Date	Year	VG	Fine	VF	XF
1265	1802R	II	3.00	5.00	12.00	25.00
(C109)						

KM#	Date	Year	VG	Fine	VF	XF
1277	1816R	XVI	6.00	10.00	15.00	35.00
(C109a)						
	1816R	XVII	6.00	10.00	15.00	35.00

KM#	Date	Year	VG	Fine	VF	XF
1278	1816B	XVI	3.00	5.00	8.50	15.00
(C109a.1)						
	1816B	XVII	3.00	5.00	8.50	15.00
	1822B	XXII	4.00	7.50	14.00	25.00
	1822R	XXII	4.00	7.50	14.00	25.00

KM#	Date	Year	VG	Fine	VF	XF
1290	1822R	XXII	10.00	20.00	35.00	50.00
(C109a.2)						

KM#	Date	Year	VG	Fine	VF	XF
1295 (C127)	1824B	I	6.00	12.50	20.00	35.00

KM#	Date	Year	VG	Fine	VF	XF
1296 (C127a)	1825R	II	4.00	9.00	18.00	35.00
	1826R	III	4.00	9.00	18.00	35.00

KM#	Date	Year	VG	Fine	VF	XF
1300 (C136)	1829B	I	6.00	15.00	30.00	55.00
	1829R	I	6.00	15.00	30.00	55.00

KM#	Date	Year	VG	Fine	VF	XF
1313 (C145)	1831R	I	2.00	4.00	7.50	20.00
	1832B	II	3.00	6.00	10.00	25.00
	1832B	III	2.00	5.00	9.00	22.00
	1833B	III	2.00	4.00	7.50	20.00
	1834B	IV	2.00	4.00	7.50	20.00

KM#	Date	Year	VG	Fine	VF	XF
1319 (C145a)	1835B	V	2.00	4.00	7.50	15.00
	1835R	V	2.00	4.00	7.50	15.00
	1836B	VI	2.00	4.00	7.50	15.00
	1836/5R	VI	2.00	4.00	7.50	15.00
	1836R	VI	2.00	4.00	7.50	15.00
	1837B	VII	2.00	4.00	7.50	15.00
	1837R	VII	3.50	6.50	12.50	17.50
	1838B	VIII	2.00	4.00	7.50	15.00
	1838R	VIII	3.50	6.50	12.50	17.50
	1839B	IX	2.00	4.00	7.50	15.00
	1839R	IX	3.50	6.50	12.50	17.50
	1840R	IX	3.50	6.50	12.50	17.50
	1840B	X	3.00	5.00	8.50	15.00
	1840R	X	2.00	4.00	7.50	15.00
	1841B	X	3.00	6.00	9.00	17.50
	1841R	XI	2.00	4.00	7.50	15.00
	1842B	XI	2.00	4.00	7.50	15.00
	1842B	XII	2.00	4.00	7.50	15.00
	1842R	XII	2.00	4.00	7.50	15.00
	1843B	XII	2.00	4.00	7.50	15.00
	1843B	XIII	2.00	4.00	7.50	15.00
	1843R	XIII	2.00	4.00	7.50	15.00
	1844B	XIII	2.00	4.00	7.50	15.00
	1844B	XIV	2.00	4.00	7.50	15.00
	1844R	XIV	2.00	4.00	7.50	15.00
	1845B	XV	2.00	4.00	7.50	15.00
	1845R	XV	2.00	4.00	7.50	15.00

KM#	Date	Mintage	VG	Fine	VF	XF
1340 (C165)	1847B yr.II	.074	2.00	4.00	7.50	22.50
	1847R yr.II	9,000	3.50	6.50	12.50	25.00
	1848/7B yr.II	.049	2.50	4.50	7.50	22.50
	1848B yr.II	I.A.	3.50	6.50	12.50	25.00
	1848R yr.II	.644	2.00	4.00	7.50	22.50
	1848R yr.III	I.A.	2.00	4.00	7.50	22.50
	1848R yr.IIII	Inc. Ab.	3.50	6.50	12.50	25.00
	1849B yr.III	.104	2.00	4.00	7.50	22.50
	1849B yr.IV	I.A.	2.00	4.00	7.50	22.50
	1849R yr.IIII	1.921	2.00	4.00	7.50	22.50
	1849R yr.IV	Inc. Ab.	2.00	4.00	7.00	22.50

KM#	Date	Mintage	VG	Fine	VF	XF
1355 (C166)	1850B yr.IV	.176	2.00	4.00	7.50	15.00
	1850R yr.IV	5.552	2.00	4.00	7.50	15.00
	1850B yr.V	Inc. Ab.	2.00	4.00	7.50	15.00
	1850R yr.V	Inc. Ab.	2.00	4.00	7.50	15.00
	1851B yr.V	1.257	2.00	4.00	7.50	15.00
	1851R yr.V	4.001	2.00	4.00	7.50	15.00
	1851B yr.VI	Inc. Ab.	2.00	4.00	7.50	15.00
	1851R yr.VI	Inc. Ab.	2.00	4.00	7.50	15.00
	1852B yr.VI	.706	2.00	4.00	7.50	15.00

BAIOCCO

COPPER

KM#	Date	Year	VG	Fine	VF	XF
1246 (C110)	1801R	I	12.00	25.00	45.00	75.00

NOTE: Earlier date (1800) exists for this type.

KM#	Date	Year	VG	Fine	VF	XF
1262 (C111)	1801R	—	5.00	12.00	20.00	38.00

KM#	Date	Year	VG	Fine	VF	XF
1263 (C111.1)	1801R	—	5.00	12.00	20.00	38.00

Rev: G. PASINATES S. C. below date.

KM#	Date	Year	VG	Fine	VF	XF
1266 (C111.2)	1801R	—	15.00	30.00	50.00	90.00

KM#	Date	Year	VG	Fine	VF	XF
1267 (C112)	1802R	II	5.00	12.00	20.00	32.00
	1815B	XVI	5.00	12.00	20.00	32.00

KM#	Date	Year	VG	Fine	VF	XF
1279 (C112.1)	1816B	XVI	5.00	12.00	20.00	32.00
	1816R	XVI	5.00	12.00	20.00	32.00
	1816B	XVII	5.00	12.00	20.00	32.00
	1816R	XVII	10.00	22.50	38.00	65.00

KM#	Date	Year	VG	Fine	VF	XF
1301	1829R	I	7.50	18.00	30.00	45.00

NOTE: Two varieties of edge inscription exist.

KM#	Date	Year	VG	Fine	VF	XF
1314 (C146)	1831R	I	5.00	10.00	15.00	25.00
	1832R	I	15.00	25.00	45.00	70.00
	1832R	II	7.50	12.50	25.00	45.00

KM#	Date	Year	VG	Fine	VF	XF
1320 (C146a)	1835B	V	2.00	5.00	8.00	22.00

KM#	Date	Year	VG	Fine	VF	XF
1320	1835R	V	2.00	5.00	8.00	22.00
	1836B	VI	2.00	5.00	8.00	22.00
	1836R	VI	2.00	5.00	8.00	22.00
	1837B	VII	2.00	5.00	8.00	22.00
	1837R	VII	2.00	5.00	8.00	22.00
	1838B	VIII	10.00	20.00	35.00	45.00
	1838R	VIII	5.00	10.00	15.00	25.00
	1839R	VIII	7.50	12.50	20.00	30.00
	1839B	IX	2.00	5.00	8.00	22.00
	1839R	IX	5.00	10.00	15.00	25.00
	1840B	X	2.00	5.00	8.00	22.00
	1840R	X	2.00	5.00	8.00	22.00
	1841B	X	5.00	10.00	15.00	25.00
	1841B	XI	10.00	20.00	35.00	50.00
	1841R	XI	3.50	6.50	12.50	17.50
	1842R	XI	3.50	6.50	12.50	17.50
	1842B	XII	2.00	5.00	8.00	22.00
	1842R	XII	3.50	6.50	12.50	17.50
	1843R	XII	3.50	6.50	12.50	17.50
	1843B	XIII	3.50	6.50	12.50	17.50
	1843R	XIII	3.50	6.50	12.50	17.50
	1844B	XIII	2.00	5.00	10.00	25.00
	1844B	XIV	2.00	5.00	10.00	25.00
	1844R	XIV	2.00	5.00	10.00	25.00
	1845B	XV	2.00	5.00	10.00	25.00
	1845R	XV	3.50	6.50	12.50	17.50

KM#	Date	Mintage	VG	Fine	VF	XF
1339.1 (C167)	1846B yr.I	—	6.00	10.00	17.50	30.00
	1846R yr.I	7,500	4.00	7.50	12.50	25.00
	1847B yr.I	.058	4.00	7.50	12.50	25.00
	1847R yr.I	.014	7.50	12.50	20.00	35.00
	1847R yr.II	I.A.	4.00	7.50	12.50	25.00
	1848R yr.II	.494	3.50	6.50	12.50	17.50
	1848R yr.III	I.A.	2.00	4.00	7.50	15.00

C#	Date	Mintage	VG	Fine	VF	XF
(C167)	1848R yr.IV	I.A.	2.00	4.00	7.50	15.00

NOTE: Varieties of date wording exist.

KM#	Date	Mintage	VG	Fine	VF	XF
1339.2 (C167.1)	1849R yr.IV	1.080	2.00	4.00	7.50	15.00

KM#	Date	Mintage	VG	Fine	VF	XF
1345 (C168)	1849B yr.IV	.061	6.00	10.00	17.50	30.00
	1850B yr.IV	.402	2.00	7.00	12.50	25.00
	1850R yr.IV	4.681	2.00	6.00	9.00	17.50
	1850B yr.V	Inc. Ab.	2.00	7.00	12.50	25.00
	1850R yr.V	Inc. Ab.	2.00	6.00	9.00	17.50
	1851B yr.V	.899	2.00	6.00	9.00	17.50
	1851R yr.V	5.706	2.00	7.00	12.50	25.00
	1851B yr.VI	Inc. Ab.	2.00	4.00	7.50	15.00
	1851R yr.VI	Inc. Ab.	2.00	7.00	12.50	25.00
	1852B yr.VI	.655	2.00	4.00	7.50	15.00
	1852R yr.VI	1.211	7.50	15.00	20.00	35.00
	1853R yr.VII	.035	7.50	15.00	20.00	35.00

2 BAIOCCHI

COPPER

KM#	Date	Mintage	VG	Fine	VF	XF
1343 (C169)	1848B yr.III	.644	3.00	8.00	14.00	22.00
	1848R yr.III	.227	3.00	8.00	14.00	22.00
	1849R yr.IV	1.117	3.00	8.00	14.00	22.00
	1849B yr.III	—	3.00	8.00	14.00	22.00
	1849B yr.IV	—	3.00	8.00	14.00	22.00

KM#	Date	Mintage	VG	Fine	VF	XF
1344 (C169a)	1850B yr.IV	—	3.00	8.00	14.00	22.00
	1850R yr.IV	3.784	3.00	8.00	14.00	22.00
	1850B yr.V	—	7.50	12.50	20.00	35.00
	1850R yr.V	I.A.	2.00	7.00	12.00	20.00
	1851B yr.V	—	2.00	7.00	12.00	20.00
	1851R yr.V	2.557	2.00	7.00	12.00	20.00
	1851B yr.VI	—	2.00	7.00	12.00	20.00
	1851R yr.VI	I.A.	2.00	7.00	12.00	20.00
	1852B yr.V	—	5.00	10.00	17.50	30.00
	1852R yr.V	1.727	4.00	9.00	15.00	25.00
	1852B yr.VI	—	2.00	7.00	12.00	20.00
	1852R yr.VI	I.A.	2.00	7.00	12.00	20.00
	1852R yr.VII	I.A.	4.00	9.00	15.00	30.00
	1853R yr.VI	1.460	4.00	9.00	15.00	30.00
	1853B yr.VII	—	3.50	8.00	12.50	22.50
	1853R yr.VII	I.A.	2.00	7.00	12.00	20.00
	1853R yr.VIII	I.A.	2.00	7.00	12.00	20.00
	1854R yr.VIII	5,000	35.00	75.00	100.00	140.00

GROSSO

1.3210 g, .917 SILVER, .0389 oz ASW

KM#	Date	Year	VG	Fine	VF	XF
1075 (C113)	1815R	XVI	7.50	15.00	22.50	40.00
	1816B	XVI	15.00	25.00	40.00	70.00
	1816B	XVII	7.50	15.00	22.50	40.00
	1817B	XVII	7.50	15.00	22.50	40.00

5 BAIOCCHI

1.3430 g, .900 SILVER, .0388 oz ASW

KM#	Date	Year	VG	Fine	VF	XF
1321 (C147)	1835R	V	3.00	7.50	15.00	25.00
	1836B	VI	3.00	7.50	15.00	25.00
	1839R	IX	5.00	10.00	17.50	30.00
	1840B	X	3.00	7.50	15.00	25.00
	1841R	X	10.00	20.00	35.00	50.00
	1841B	XI	3.00	7.50	15.00	25.00
	1841R	XI	15.00	25.00	40.00	70.00
	1842B	XI	3.00	7.50	15.00	25.00
	1842R	XI	15.00	25.00	40.00	70.00
	1842B	XII	3.00	7.50	15.00	25.00
	1842R	XII	3.00	7.50	15.00	25.00

KM#	Date	Year	VG	Fine	VF	XF
1321	1843B	XIII	3.00	7.50	15.00	25.00
	1843R	XIII	3.00	7.50	15.00	25.00
	1844B	XIII	3.00	7.50	15.00	25.00
	1844B	XIV	3.00	7.50	15.00	25.00
	1844/3R	—	3.50	8.00	17.50	32.50
	1844R	XIV	3.00	7.50	15.00	25.00
	1845B	XV	3.00	7.50	15.00	25.00
	1845R	XV	3.00	7.50	15.00	25.00
	1846R	XVI	3.00	7.50	15.00	25.00

KM#	Date	Mintage	VG	Fine	VF	XF
1341a (C171)	1847B yr.I	2.387	3.00	7.50	15.00	25.00
	1847R yr.II	1.191	3.00	7.50	15.00	25.00
	1848R yr.II	2,122	18.00	40.00	75.00	125.00
	1849R yr.IV	.021	3.00	7.50	15.00	25.00
	1850R yr.V	.010	3.00	7.50	15.00	25.00
	1851R yr.V	.011	3.00	7.50	15.00	25.00
	1851R yr.VI	Inc. Ab.	3.00	7.50	15.00	25.00
	1852R yr.VII	.020	3.00	7.50	15.00	25.00
	1853R yr.VII	.014	3.00	7.50	15.00	25.00
	1855R yr.IX	9,200	18.00	40.00	75.00	120.00
	1855R yr.X	I.A.	18.00	40.00	75.00	120.00

1.4280 g, .800 SILVER, .0367 oz ASW

KM#	Date	Mintage	VG	Fine	VF	XF
1341b (C171a)	1856R yr.X	3,440	18.00	40.00	75.00	120.00
	1857R yr.XI	.023	3.00	7.50	15.00	30.00
	1858R yr.XII	1.573	3.00	7.50	15.00	25.00
	1858B yr.XIII	.224	10.00	25.00	40.00	75.00
	1858R yr.XIII	Inc. Ab.	3.00	7.50	15.00	30.00
	1859B yr.XIII	.173	10.00	25.00	40.00	75.00
	1859R yr.XIII	.083	3.00	7.50	15.00	30.00
	1860R yr.XV	.169	3.00	7.50	15.00	25.00
	1861R yr.XVI	.147	3.00	7.50	15.00	25.00
	1862R yr.XVII	.135	3.00	7.50	15.00	25.00
	1863R yr.XVIII	.044	3.00	7.50	15.00	30.00
	1864R yr.XIX	.101	3.00	7.50	15.00	30.00

1.3330 g, .835 SILVER, .0357 oz ASW

KM#	Date	Mintage	VG	Fine	VF	XF
1341c (C171b)	1865R yr.XIX	.106	9.00	15.00	25.00	45.00
	1865R yr.XX	Inc. Ab.	3.00	7.50	15.00	30.00
	1866R yr.XX	.040	5.00	10.00	17.50	35.00

COPPER

KM#	Date	Mintage	VG	Fine	VF	XF
1346 (C170)	1849B yr.IV	—	5.00	12.00	22.50	37.50
	1849R yr.IV	.938	5.00	12.00	22.50	37.50
	1850B yr.IV	—	5.00	12.00	22.50	37.50
	1850R yr.IV	10.164	5.00	12.00	22.50	37.50

KM#	Date	Mintage	VG	Fine	VF	XF
(C170)	1850B yr.V	—	5.00	12.00	22.50	37.50
	1850R yr.V	I.A.	5.00	12.00	22.50	37.50

Rev: Similar to KM#1346.

KM#	Date	Mintage	VG	Fine	VF	XF
1356 (C170a)	1850B yr.V	—	5.00	12.00	22.50	37.50
	1850R yr.V	I.A.	5.00	12.00	22.50	37.50
	1851B yr.V	—	5.00	12.00	22.50	37.50
	1851R yr.V	7.949	5.00	12.00	22.50	37.50
	1851B yr.VI	—	4.00	12.00	22.50	37.50
	1851R yr.VI	I.A.	4.00	12.00	22.50	37.50
	1852B yr.VI	—	4.00	12.00	22.50	37.50
	1852R yr.VI	9.746	4.00	12.00	22.50	37.50
	1852B yr.VII	—	4.00	12.00	22.50	37.50
	1852R yr.VII	Inc. Ab.	4.00	12.00	22.50	37.50
	1853B yr.VII	—	4.00	12.00	22.50	37.50
	1853R yr.VII	8.428	4.00	12.00	22.50	37.50
	1853B yr.VIII	—	4.00	12.00	22.50	37.50
	1853R yr.VIII	Inc. Ab.	4.00	12.00	22.50	37.50
	1854B yr.VIII					
	1854R yr.VIII	1.977	9.00	17.50	25.00	45.00
	1854B yr.IX	—	4.00	12.00	22.50	37.50
	1854R yr.IX	I.A.	9.00	17.50	25.00	45.00

GIULIO

2.6420 g, .917 SILVER, .0779 oz ASW
Holy Year Issue
Rev: Holy Door open w/rays.

KM#	Date	Year	VG	Fine	VF	XF
1079 (C114)	1817/6B	XVIII	18.00	38.00	55.00	100.00
	1817B	XVIII	15.00	35.00	45.00	100.00

10 BAIOCCHI

2.6870 g, .900 SILVER, .0777 oz ASW

KM#	Date	Year	Good	VG	Fine	VF
1325 (C148)	1836B	VI	12.50	25.00	40.00	75.00
	1836R	VI	5.00	10.00	15.00	35.00
	1839B	IX	5.00	10.00	15.00	35.00
	1839R	IX	5.00	10.00	15.00	35.00
	1841B	XI	5.00	8.00	15.00	30.00
	1841R	XI	10.00	20.00	35.00	50.00
	1842B	XI	5.00	10.00	15.00	35.00
	1842B	XII	5.00	8.00	15.00	30.00
	1842R	XII	12.50	25.00	40.00	75.00
	1843B	XIII	5.00	10.00	15.00	35.00
	1844B	XIV	5.00	10.00	15.00	35.00
	1846R	XVI	10.00	20.00	35.00	50.00

KM#	Date	Mintage	VG	Fine	VF	XF
1342a (C172)	1847B yr.I	.011	12.50	25.00	40.00	75.00
	1847B yr.II	I.A.	12.50	25.00	40.00	75.00
	1847R yr.II	.012	5.00	10.00	15.00	35.00

KM#	Date	Mintage	VG	Fine	VF	XF
(C172)	1848/7R yr.III	.033	5.00	10.00	15.00	35.00
	1848B yr.II	.017	12.50	25.00	40.00	75.00
	1848R yr.II	I.A.	5.00	10.00	15.00	35.00
	1848B yr.III	I.A.	12.50	25.00	40.00	75.00
	1848R yr.III	I.A.	5.00	10.00	15.00	35.00
	1849R yr.IIII	1,274	25.00	45.00	75.00	125.00
	1850R yr.IIII	.089	5.00	10.00	15.00	35.00
	1850R yr.V	I.A.	5.00	10.00	15.00	35.00
	1852R yr.VII	.033	5.00	10.00	15.00	35.00
	1853R yr.VII	.041	5.00	10.00	15.00	35.00
	1854R yr.VIII	5,570	35.00	75.00	100.00	175.00
	1855R yr.IX	4,400	35.00	75.00	100.00	175.00
	1856R yr.X	1,140	45.00	80.00	100.00	175.00

2.8570 g, .800 SILVER, .0734 oz ASW

KM#	Date	Mintage	VG	Fine	VF	XF
1342b (C172a)	1858R yr.XII	2.548	3.50	7.50	15.00	25.00
	1858R yr.XIII		4.00	7.50	15.00	25.00
	1858B yr. XIII	Inc. Ab.	10.00	25.00	40.00	75.00
	1859R yr.XIII	.088	10.00	20.00	35.00	50.00
	1860R yr.XIV	.150	10.00	20.00	35.00	50.00
	1861R yr.XVI	.327	3.00	7.50	15.00	25.00
	1862R yr.XVI	7.417	3.00	7.50	15.00	25.00
	1862R yr.XVII	Inc. Ab.	3.00	7.50	15.00	25.00
	1863R yr.XVI	—	65.00	125.00	175.00	225.00
	1863R yr.XVII	1.084	3.00	7.50	15.00	25.00
	1863R yr.XVIII	Inc. Ab.	3.00	7.50	15.00	25.00
	1864R yr.XVIII	1.147	8.00	20.00	35.00	50.00
	1864R yr.XIX	Inc. Ab.	8.00	20.00	35.00	50.00

2.6660 g, .835 SILVER, .0715 oz ASW

KM#	Date	Mintage	VG	Fine	VF	XF
1342c (C172b)	1865R yr.XIX	.409	7.00	15.00	22.50	40.00
	1865R yr.XX	Inc. Ab.	7.00	15.00	22.50	40.00

DOPPIO (2) GIULIO

(1/5 Scudo)

5.2850 g, .917 SILVER, .1558 oz ASW

KM#	Date	Year	VG	Fine	VF	XF
1816 (C115)	1816B	XVII	20.00	40.00	75.00	100.00
	1816B	XVIII	20.00	40.00	75.00	100.00
	1818B	XVII	10.00	20.00	35.00	60.00
	1818B	XVIII	10.00	20.00	35.00	60.00

Sede Vacante Issue

KM#	Date	Year	VG	Fine	VF	XF
1823	1823B	—	36.00	75.00	100.00	175.00

20 BAIOCCHI

5.2850 g, .917 SILVER, .1558 oz ASW

KM#	Date	Year	VG	Fine	VF	XF
1317 (C149)	1834R	IV	15.00	25.00	45.00	70.00

5.3740 g, .900 SILVER, .1555 oz ASW

KM#	Date	Year	VG	Fine	VF	XF
1322 (C150)	1835B	V	8.00	15.00	18.00	30.00
	1835R	V	10.00	20.00	30.00	40.00
	1836R	V	80.00	125.00	200.00	350.00
	1836B	VI	8.00	15.00	18.00	30.00
	1836R	VI	40.00	75.00	100.00	175.00
	1837R	VII	20.00	40.00	75.00	120.00
	1838B	VIII	8.00	15.00	18.00	30.00
	1838R	VIII	10.00	20.00	30.00	40.00
	1839R	IX	10.00	20.00	30.00	40.00
	1840B	X	8.00	15.00	18.00	30.00
	1841B	XI	8.00	15.00	18.00	30.00
	1841R	XI	10.00	20.00	30.00	40.00
	1842B	XII	25.00	45.00	75.00	125.00
	1842R	XII	10.00	20.00	30.00	40.00
	1844B	XIII	8.00	15.00	18.00	30.00
	1844R	XIII	100.00	200.00	350.00	650.00
	1844B	XIV	8.00	15.00	18.00	30.00
	1845B	XV	8.00	15.00	18.00	30.00
	1846R	XVI	10.00	20.00	30.00	40.00

KM#	Date	Mintage	VG	Fine	VF	XF
1337 (C173)	1848R yr. II	—	8.00	20.00	35.00	50.00
	1848R yr. III	—	8.00	20.00	35.00	50.00
	1849B yr.III	—	10.00	25.00	40.00	75.00
	1849B yr.IV	—	15.00	25.00	40.00	75.00
	1849R yr.IV	—	8.00	20.00	35.00	50.00
	1850B yr.IV	—	15.00	25.00	40.00	75.00
	1850R yr.IV	—	8.00	15.00	22.50	40.00
	1850R yr.V	—	8.00	15.00	22.50	40.00
	1851B yr.V	—	15.00	25.00	40.00	75.00
	1852B yr.VII	—	30.00	60.00	90.00	125.00
	1852R yr.VII	.010	15.00	25.00	40.00	75.00
	1853R yr.VII	.126	10.00	25.00	40.00	75.00
	1854R yr.VIII	—	8.00	20.00	35.00	50.00
	1856R yr.X	—	10.00	25.00	40.00	75.00

NOTE: Two varieties of ANNO III exist.

5.7140 g, .800 SILVER, .1469 oz ASW

KM#	Date	Mintage	VG	Fine	VF	XF
1360 (C173a)	1858B yr.XII	—	10.00	25.00	40.00	75.00
	1858R yr.XII	—	6.00	15.00	22.50	40.00
	1858B yr.XIII	—	10.00	20.00	35.00	60.00
	1858R yr.XIII	—	4.00	10.00	15.00	25.00
	1859B yr.XIII	.604	8.00	20.00	35.00	60.00
	1859R yr.XIII	1.104	4.00	12.00	20.00	28.00
	1859R yr.XIV	Inc. Ab.	4.00	12.00	20.00	28.00
	1860/50R	—	4.00	10.00	15.00	25.00
	1860R yr.XIV	3.656	4.00	10.00	15.00	25.00
	1860R yr.XV	Inc. Ab.	4.00	10.00	15.00	25.00
	1861R yr.XV	2.987	4.00	12.00	20.00	28.00
	1861R yr.XVI	Inc. Ab.	4.00	12.00	20.00	28.00
	1862R yr.XVI	1.150	4.00	12.00	20.00	28.00
	1862R yr.XVII	Inc. Ab.	4.00	12.00	20.00	28.00
	1863R yr.XVII	3.155	4.00	12.00	20.00	28.00
	1863R yr.XVIII	Inc. Ab.	4.00	12.00	20.00	28.00
	1864R yr.XVIII	2.100	4.00	12.00	20.00	28.00
	1864R yr.XIX	Inc. Ab.	10.00	20.00	35.00	60.00
	1865R yr.XIX					

KM#	Date	Mintage	VG	Fine	VF	XF
(C173a)		7.346	4.00	10.00	15.00	25.00
	1865R yr.XX	Inc. Ab.	4.00	10.00	15.00	25.00
	1866R yr.XX	5.600	4.00	10.00	15.00	25.00

TESTONE

(30 Baiocchi)

7.9280 g, .917 SILVER, .2337 oz ASW

KM#	Date	Year	VG	Fine	VF	XF
1071 (C116)	1802R	III	17.50	35.00	65.00	120.00
	1803R	III	17.50	35.00	65.00	120.00

30 BAIOCCHI

7.9280 g, .917 SILVER, .2337 oz ASW

KM#	Date	Year	VG	Fine	VF	XF
1100 (C138)	1830R	II	18.00	40.00	100.00	150.00

Sede Vacante Issue

KM#	Date	Year	VG	Fine	VF	XF
1101 (C141)	1830B	—	20.00	42.50	100.00	150.00
	1830R	—	20.00	42.50	100.00	150.00

KM#	Date	Year	VG	Fine	VF	XF
1104 (C151)	1834R	IV	16.00	38.00	80.00	120.00

8.0610 g, .900 SILVER, .2332 oz ASW

KM#	Date	Year	VG	Fine	VF	XF
1109 (C152)	1836B	VI	25.00	40.00	70.00	100.00
	1836R	VI	25.00	65.00	125.00	200.00
	1837B	VII	25.00	40.00	70.00	100.00
	1837R	VII	25.00	65.00	125.00	200.00
	1838R	VIII	25.00	40.00	70.00	100.00
	1846R	XVI	25.00	40.00	70.00	100.00

50 BAIOCCHI

13.2140 g, .917 SILVER, .3896 oz ASW

KM#	Date	Year	VG	Fine	VF	XF
1316 (C153)	1832B	II	25.00	40.00	90.00	150.00
	1832R	II	28.00	45.00	90.00	150.00
	1834R	IV	28.00	45.00	90.00	150.00

NOTE: Two varieties of 1832B exist.

13.4350 g, .900 SILVER, .3887 oz ASW

KM#	Date	Year	VG	Fine	VF	XF
1323 (C154)	1835R	V	20.00	35.00	65.00	90.00
	1836B	VI	20.00	35.00	65.00	90.00
	1836R	VI	45.00	65.00	110.00	175.00
	1837B	VII	20.00	35.00	65.00	90.00
	1840B	X	45.00	65.00	110.00	175.00
	1841B	XI	20.00	35.00	65.00	90.00
	1842R	XII	45.00	65.00	110.00	175.00
	1843R	XIII	20.00	35.00	65.00	110.00
	1845R	XV	20.00	35.00	65.00	110.00
	1846R	XVI	20.00	35.00	65.00	110.00

KM#	Date	Mintage	VG	Fine	VF	XF
1357 (C174)	1850R yr.IV	.104	25.00	45.00	75.00	100.00
	1850R yr.V	I.A.	25.00	45.00	75.00	100.00
	1853R yr.VII	.684	50.00	75.00	110.00	175.00
	1853R yr.VIII	Inc. Ab.	25.00	45.00	75.00	100.00
	1854B yr.IX	2,718	25.00	45.00	75.00	100.00
	1856B yr.X	4,226	25.00	45.00	75.00	100.00
	1857B yr.XII	8,711	50.00	75.00	110.00	175.00

1/2 SCUDO

13.2500 g, .917 SILVER, .3907 oz ASW

KM#	Date	Year	VG	Fine	VF	XF
1247 (C117)	1802R	II	30.00	70.00	100.00	150.00
	1802R	III	30.00	70.00	100.00	150.00
	1803R	III	30.00	70.00	100.00	150.00
	1816B	XVII	30.00	70.00	100.00	150.00

NOTE: Earlier date (1800) exists for this type.

Sede Vacante Issue

KM#	Date	Year	VG	Fine	VF	XF
1291 (C123)	1823B	—	40.00	75.00	140.00	200.00

Sede Vacante Issue

KM#	Date	Year	VG	Fine	VF	XF
1302 (C132)	1829B	—	35.00	70.00	135.00	185.00
	1829R	—	35.00	70.00	135.00	185.00

SCUDO

26.2500 g, .917 SILVER, .7739 oz ASW

KM#	Date	Year	VG	Fine	VF	XF
1249 (C119)	1802R	II	38.00	80.00	125.00	225.00
	1802R	III	40.00	100.00	140.00	250.00
	1802R	IV	38.00	80.00	125.00	225.00
	1803R	IV	60.00	125.00	175.00	300.00
	1805R	VI	38.00	80.00	125.00	225.00
	1807R	VIII	38.00	80.00	125.00	235.00

26.4280 g, .917 SILVER, .7792 oz ASW
Rev: Similar to KM#1280.

KM#	Date	Year	VG	Fine	VF	XF
1275 (C119.1)	1815R	XVI	35.00	80.00	110.00	200.00
	1816B	XVII	35.00	75.00	110.00	200.00
	1817B	XVII	40.00	100.00	125.00	220.00
	1818B	XVIII	35.00	80.00	110.00	200.00

KM#	Date	Year	VG	Fine	VF	XF
1280 (C120)	1816R	XVII	—	—	Rare	—

Obv: Large bust.

KM#	Date	Year	VG	Fine	VF	XF
1297.1 (C128.1)	1825B	III	75.00	125.00	200.00	325.00

Sede Vacante Issue

KM#	Date	Year	VG	Fine	VF	XF
1303 (C133)	1829B	—	75.00	150.00	250.00	325.00
	1829R	—	125.00	200.00	275.00	400.00

Sede Vacante Issue

KM#	Date	Year	VG	Fine	VF	XF
1292 (C124)	1823B	—	100.00	150.00	300.00	500.00

Obv: Small bust.

KM#	Date	Year	VG	Fine	VF	XF
1297.2 (C128.2)	1825R	II	90.00	150.00	225.00	325.00
	1826R	III	90.00	150.00	225.00	325.00

KM#	Date	Year	VG	Fine	VF	XF
1310 (C139)	1830B	I	85.00	150.00	185.00	300.00
	1830ROMA	I	65.00	125.00	175.00	250.00

Rev: Large rays above.

KM#	Date	Year	VG	Fine	VF	XF
1297.3 (C128.3)	1826R	III	90.00	160.00	235.00	335.00

Sede Vacante Issue

KM#	Date	Year	VG	Fine	VF	XF
1311 (C142)	1830B	—	65.00	125.00	185.00	265.00
	1830ROMA	—	85.00	150.00	200.00	300.00

Sede Vacante Issue

KM#	Date	Year	VG	Fine	VF	XF
1293 (C124.1)	1823R	—	275.00	475.00	850.00	1500.

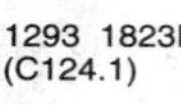

KM#	Date	Year	VG	Fine	VF	XF
1315	1831B	I	50.00	85.00	135.00	185.00
(C155)						
	1831R	I	50.00	75.00	125.00	185.00
	1833B	III	90.00	150.00	225.00	325.00
	1833R	III	50.00	85.00	135.00	185.00
	1833R	III	90.00	150.00	225.00	350.00
	1834R	IV	50.00	75.00	125.00	185.00
	1834R	IV	90.00	150.00	225.00	325.00

26.8710 g, .900 SILVER, .7776 oz ASW

KM#	Date	Year	VG	Fine	VF	XF
1324	1835B	V	45.00	75.00	110.00	175.00
(C156)						
	1835R	V	60.00	110.00	165.00	225.00
	1836R	VI	60.00	110.00	165.00	225.00
	1837R	VII	45.00	75.00	110.00	175.00
	1838B	VIII	60.00	110.00	165.00	225.00
	1838R	VIII	60.00	110.00	165.00	225.00
	1839R	VIII	60.00	110.00	165.00	225.00
	1839R	IX	60.00	110.00	165.00	225.00
	1840R	X	55.00	100.00	150.00	200.00
	1841R	XI	60.00	110.00	165.00	225.00
	1842R	XI	75.00	175.00	250.00	350.00
	1842R	XII	110.00	300.00	500.00	1000.
	1843R	XIII	45.00	75.00	110.00	175.00
	1844R	XIV	60.00	110.00	165.00	225.00
	1845R	XV	45.00	75.00	100.00	175.00
	1846R	XVI	45.00	75.00	100.00	175.00

Sede Vacante Issue

C#	Date	Year	VG	Fine	VF	XF
1335	1846R	—	90.00	175.00	250.00	350.00
(C162)						

Obv: NIC. CER. BARA below bust.

KM#	Date	Mintage	VG	Fine	VF	XF
1336.1	1846B yr.I					
(C175)		2,073	75.00	125.00	175.00	225.00
	1846R yr.I					
		1,820	125.00	200.00	275.00	400.00
	1847B yr.II	.020	60.00	100.00	150.00	200.00
	1847R yr.II	.012	75.00	125.00	175.00	225.00
	1848R yr.II	.029	60.00	100.00	150.00	200.00
	1848R yr.III	I.A.	75.00	125.00	175.00	225.00

Obv: W/o NIC. CER. BARA below bust.

KM#	Date	Mintage	VG	Fine	VF	XF
1336.2	1850R yr.IV					
(C175.1)		9,222	35.00	65.00	125.00	155.00
	1853R yr.VII					
		.527	35.00	65.00	125.00	155.00
	1853B yr.VIII					
		2,310	100.00	200.00	300.00	500.00
	1853R yr.VIII					
		Inc. Ab.	35.00	65.00	125.00	155.00
	1854B yr.IX					
		3,715	100.00	200.00	300.00	500.00
	1854R yr.IX					
		.146	35.00	65.00	125.00	155.00
	1856R yr.XI					
		1,050	100.00	200.00	300.00	500.00

1.7330 g, .900 GOLD, .0501 oz AGW, 14.4mm

KM#	Date	Year	Fine	VF	XF	Unc
1358	1853B yr.VIII					
(C176)		3,306	75.00	150.00	200.00	500.00
	1853R yr.VIII					
		.209	60.00	120.00	150.00	200.00
	1854B yr.VIII					
		5,539	75.00	150.00	200.00	500.00
	1854R yr.VIII					
		.097	60.00	120.00	150.00	200.00
	1854R yr.IX					
		Inc. Ab.	60.00	120.00	150.00	200.00
	1857R yr.XII					
		.016	75.00	125.00	175.00	300.00

16.3mm

KM#	Date	Year	Fine	VF	XF	Unc
1361	1858R yr.XII					
(C176a)		.359	60.00	110.00	150.00	200.00
	1858R yr.XIII					
		Inc. Ab.	60.00	110.00	150.00	200.00
	1859R yr.XIII					
		.103	60.00	110.00	150.00	200.00
	1861R yr.XV					
		.084	60.00	110.00	150.00	200.00
	1861R yr.XVI					
		Inc. Ab.	60.00	110.00	150.00	200.00
	1862R yr.XVI					
		.226	60.00	110.00	150.00	200.00
	1862R yr.XVII					
		Inc. Ab.	60.00	110.00	150.00	200.00
	1863R yr.XVII					
		.149	60.00	110.00	150.00	200.00
	1863R yr.XVIII					
		Inc. Ab.	60.00	110.00	150.00	200.00
	1864R yr.XIX					
		5,735	70.00	125.00	175.00	300.00
	1865R yr.XIX					
		.021	60.00	110.00	150.00	200.00

2 ZECCHINI

6.9040 g, .998 GOLD, .2215 oz AGW

KM#	Date	Year	Fine	VF	XF	Unc
1088	1825R	III	500.00	900.00	1500.	3000.
(C130)						

KM#	Date	Year	Fine	VF	XF	Unc
1089	1828R	V	500.00	900.00	1500.	3000.

2-1/2 SCUDI

4.3340 g, .900 GOLD, .1254 oz AGW

KM#	Date	Year	Fine	VF	XF	Unc
1106	1835B	V	150.00	250.00	350.00	450.00
(C 158)						
	1835R	V	150.00	250.00	350.00	450.00
	1836B	V	150.00	250.00	350.00	450.00
	1836B	VI	100.00	200.00	250.00	325.00
	1836R	VI	100.00	200.00	250.00	325.00
	1837R	VII	150.00	250.00	350.00	450.00
	1839R	IX	150.00	250.00	350.00	450.00
	1840B	X	100.00	200.00	250.00	325.00
	1841R	XI	150.00	250.00	350.00	500.00
	1842B	XII	100.00	200.00	250.00	325.00
	1842R	XII	175.00	275.00	400.00	600.00
	1843B	XIII	100.00	200.00	250.00	325.00
	1844B	XIII	150.00	250.00	350.00	450.00
	1845B	XV	175.00	275.00	400.00	600.00
	1845R	XV	150.00	250.00	350.00	500.00
	1846B	XVI	100.00	200.00	250.00	325.00

KM#	Date	Year	Fine	VF	XF	Unc
1117	1848R yr.II					
(C177)		3,197	175.00	275.00	375.00	500.00
	1853R yr.VII					
		.117	100.00	175.00	250.00	325.00
	1853R yr.VIII					
		Inc. Ab.	100.00	160.00	225.00	325.00
	1854R yr.VIII					
		.276	80.00	135.00	175.00	225.00
	1854B yr.IX					
		.032	80.00	135.00	175.00	275.00
	1854R yr.IX					
		Inc. Ab.	80.00	135.00	175.00	225.00
	1855R yr.IX					
		.059	80.00	135.00	175.00	225.00
	1855R yr.X					
		Inc. Ab.	80.00	135.00	175.00	225.00
	1856B yr.X					
		8,040	100.00	175.00	250.00	350.00
	1856R yr.X					
		.104	85.00	135.00	175.00	225.00
	1856R yr.XI					
		Inc. Ab.	85.00	135.00	175.00	225.00
	1857R yr.X	—	100.00	160.00	225.00	325.00
	1857R yr.XI	—	175.00	275.00	375.00	500.00
	1857B yr.XII					
		6,284	150.00	250.00	325.00	400.00
	1857R yr.XII	—	90.00	135.00	175.00	275.00
	1858R yr.XII	—	90.00	135.00	200.00	325.00
	1858B yr.XIII					
		2,787	175.00	275.00	375.00	500.00
	1858R yr.XIII	—	90.00	135.00	175.00	275.00
	1859B yr.XIII					
		.066	100.00	160.00	225.00	325.00
	1859R yr.XIII	—	80.00	135.00	175.00	250.00
	1859R yr.XIV	—	80.00	135.00	175.00	250.00
	1860R yr.XIV	—	80.00	135.00	175.00	250.00
	1860R yr.XV	—	80.00	135.00	175.00	250.00
	1861R yr.XV	—	80.00	135.00	175.00	250.00
	1861R yr.XVI	—	80.00	135.00	175.00	250.00
	1862R yr.XVI	—	80.00	135.00	175.00	250.00
	1862R yr.XVII	—	80.00	135.00	175.00	250.00
	1863R yr.XVII	—	80.00	135.00	175.00	250.00

5 SCUDI

8.6680 g, .900 GOLD, .2508 oz AGW

KM#	Date	Year	Fine	VF	XF	Unc
1105	1834R	IV	—	—	*Rare	—
(C159)						

***NOTE:** Bowers and Merena Guia sale 3-88 XF (cleaned) realized $12,650.

KM#	Date	Year	Fine	VF	XF	Unc
1107 (C160)	1835B	V	225.00	450.00	650.00	800.00
	1835R	V	225.00	450.00	650.00	800.00
	1836R	VI	225.00	450.00	650.00	800.00
	1837R	VI	350.00	700.00	900.00	1500.
	1837R	VII	225.00	450.00	650.00	800.00
	1838R	VII	225.00	450.00	650.00	800.00
	1838R	VIII	225.00	450.00	650.00	800.00
	1839R	VIII	300.00	600.00	800.00	1200.
	1839R	IX	300.00	600.00	800.00	1200.
	1840R	IX	300.00	600.00	800.00	1200.
	1841B	XI	350.00	550.00	750.00	1500.
	1841R	XI	225.00	450.00	650.00	800.00
	1842B	XII	225.00	450.00	650.00	800.00
	1842R	XII	225.00	450.00	650.00	800.00
	1843B	XIII	350.00	550.00	750.00	1500.
	1843R	XIII	225.00	450.00	650.00	800.00
	1845R	XV	225.00	450.00	650.00	800.00
	1846R	XVI	225.00	450.00	650.00	800.00

Sede Vacante Issue

KM#	Date	Year	Fine	VF	XF	Unc
1115 (C163)	1846R	—	725.00	1200.	1600.	2500.

KM#	Date	Mintage	Fine	VF	XF	Unc
1116 (C178)	1846B yr.I	.011	225.00	450.00	600.00	800.00
	1846R yr.I	5,755	300.00	500.00	750.00	1000.
	1847R yr.II	1,399	400.00	700.00	900.00	1250.
	1848R yr.III	1,633	325.00	575.00	800.00	1200.
	1850R yr.IV	6,473	300.00	700.00	850.00	1100.
	1854R yr.IX	.104	225.00	375.00	500.00	750.00

10 SCUDI

17.3360 g, .900 GOLD, .5016 oz AGW

KM#	Date	Year	Fine	VF	XF	Unc
1108 (C161)	1835B	V	350.00	675.00	950.00	1350.
	1835R	V	275.00	550.00	750.00	1100.
	1836R	V	275.00	550.00	750.00	1100.
	1836B	V	275.00	550.00	750.00	1100.
	1836R	VI	300.00	675.00	950.00	1400.
	1837R	VI	300.00	675.00	950.00	1400.
	1837R	VII	275.00	550.00	750.00	1100.
	1838R	VII	275.00	550.00	750.00	1250.
	1838R	VIII	275.00	550.00	750.00	1250.
	1839R	VIII	275.00	550.00	750.00	1250.
	1839R	IX	300.00	675.00	950.00	1400.
	1840B	X	300.00	675.00	950.00	1400.
	1840R	X	275.00	550.00	750.00	1250.
	1841R	X	275.00	550.00	750.00	1250.
	1841B	XI	275.00	550.00	750.00	1250.
	1841R	XI	275.00	550.00	750.00	1250.
	1842R	XI	275.00	550.00	750.00	1250.
	1842B	XII	275.00	550.00	750.00	1250.
	1842R	XII	275.00	550.00	750.00	1250.
	1843R	XIII	300.00	675.00	950.00	1400.
	1844R	XIV	300.00	675.00	950.00	1400.
	1845B	XV	275.00	550.00	750.00	1250.
	1845R	XV	300.00	675.00	950.00	1400.

KM#	Date	Year	Fine	VF	XF	Unc
1125 (C179)	1850R yr.IV	5,875	650.00	1250.	1750.	2750.
	1850R yr.V	I.A.	450.00	1000.	1500.	2000.
	1856R yr.XI	2,483	650.00	1000.	1500.	2500.

DOPPIA

5.4690 g, .917 GOLD, .1612 oz AGW
Mint: Rome

KM#	Date	Year	Fine	VF	XF	Unc
1070 (C121)	(1800-01)R	I	125.00	200.00	275.00	475.00
	(1801-02)R	II	125.00	200.00	275.00	475.00
	(1802-03)R	III	125.00	200.00	275.00	475.00
	(1803-04)R	IV	125.00	200.00	275.00	475.00
	(1804-05)R	V	125.00	200.00	275.00	475.00
	(1807-08)R	VIII	125.00	200.00	275.00	475.00
	(1809-10)R	X	125.00	200.00	275.00	475.00

Modified design.

KM#	Date	Year	Fine	VF	XF	Unc
1076 (C121.1)	(1815-16)R	XVI	125.00	200.00	275.00	475.00
	(1817-18)R	XVIII	150.00	200.00	300.00	500.00
	(1823-24)R	XXIV	125.00	200.00	275.00	475.00

Mint: Bologna

KM#	Date	Year	Fine	VF	XF	Unc
1077 (C121.2)	(1815-16)B	XVI	200.00	300.00	500.00	900.00
	(1816-17)B	XVII	175.00	275.00	450.00	800.00
	(1820-21)B	XXI	175.00	275.00	450.00	800.00
	(1821-22)B	XXII	175.00	275.00	450.00	800.00

Sede Vacante Issue

KM#	Date	Year	Fine	VF	XF	Unc
1086 (C125)	1823B	—	175.00	275.00	450.00	900.00
	1823R	—	175.00	275.00	450.00	900.00

KM#	Date	Year	Fine	VF	XF	Unc
1087 (C129)	(1823-24)R	I	150.00	250.00	350.00	700.00
	(1824-25)B	II	150.00	250.00	350.00	700.00
	(1824-25)R	II	150.00	250.00	350.00	700.00

Sede Vacante Issue

KM#	Date	Year	Fine	VF	XF	Unc
1090 (C134)	1829B	—	300.00	450.00	850.00	1400.
	1829R	—	300.00	450.00	850.00	1400.

Sede Vacante Issue

KM#	Date	Year	Fine	VF	XF	Unc
1102 (C143)	1830R	—	325.00	650.00	1000.	1650.

5.4500 g, .917 GOLD, .1606 oz AGW

KM#	Date	Year	Fine	VF	XF	Unc
1103 (C157)	1833R	III	300.00	500.00	900.00	1500.
	1834B	III	275.00	450.00	700.00	1150.

DECIMAL COINAGE

5 Centesimi = 1 Soldi
20 Soldi = 1 Lira

CENTESIMO

COPPER

KM#	Date	Mintage	Fine	VF	XF	Unc
1370 (C180)	1866R yr.XXI	.500	5.00	10.00	15.00	55.00
	1867R yr.XXII	2.900	3.00	6.00	9.00	20.00
	1868R yr.XXII	1.950	6.00	18.00	25.00	55.00

1/2 SOLDO

(2-1/2 Centesimi)

COPPER

KM#	Date	Mintage	Fine	VF	XF	Unc
1371 (C181)	1866R yr.XXI	.200	5.00	10.00	20.00	35.00
	1867R yr.XXI	2.890	2.00	5.00	12.00	25.00
	1867R yr.XXII	2.890	2.00	5.00	12.00	25.00

SOLDO

(5 Centesimi)

COPPER
Obv: Small bust.

KM#	Date	Mintage	Fine	VF	XF	Unc
1372.1 (C182)	1866R yr.XXI	1.300	2.50	6.00	15.00	35.00

Obv: Large bust.

KM#	Date	Mintage	Fine	VF	XF	Unc
1372.2						
	1866R yr.XXI large date					
(C182a)		2.850	6.00	18.00	40.00	100.00
	1866R yr. XXI small date					
		Inc. Ab.	1.75	4.00	8.00	20.00
	1867R yr.XXI large date					
		6.500	3.50	10.00	20.00	50.00
	1867R yr.XXI small date					
		Inc. Ab.	1.75	4.00	8.00	20.00

2 SOLDI

(10 Centesimi)

COPPER

KM#	Date	Mintage	Fine	VF	XF	Unc
1373	1866R yr.XXI					
(C183)		3.500	3.50	8.00	17.50	40.00
	1867R yr.XXI					
		3.500	3.50	8.00	17.50	40.00

4 SOLDI

(20 Centesimi)

COPPER

KM#	Date	Mintage	Fine	VF	XF	Unc
1374	1866R yr.XXI					
(C184)		2.470	6.00	12.00	20.00	50.00
	1867R yr.XXI					
		2.100	6.00	12.00	20.00	50.00
	1867R yr.XXII					
		2.876	6.00	12.00	20.00	50.00
	1868R yr.XXII					
		4.987	6.00	12.00	20.00	40.00
	1868R yr.XXIII					
		4.876	6.00	12.00	20.00	40.00
	1869R yr.XXIII					
		2.767	6.00	12.00	20.00	50.00
	1869R yr.XXIV					
		3.150	6.00	12.00	20.00	45.00

5 SOLDI

(25 Centesimi)

1.2500 g, .835 SILVER, .0335 oz ASW

KM#	Date	Mintage	Fine	VF	XF	Unc
1375	1866R yr.XXI					
(C186)		.100	4.00	10.00	20.00	30.00
	1867R yr.XXI					
		.915	3.00	8.00	12.00	20.00
	1867R yr.XXII					
		1.124	3.00	8.00	12.00	20.00

10 SOLDI

(50 Centesimi)

2.5000 g, .835 SILVER, .0671 oz ASW
Obv. leg: PIVS IX PON. MAX. A. . .

KM#	Date	Mintage	Fine	VF	XF	Unc
1376	1866R yr.XXI					
(C187)		.290	15.00	22.50	40.00	60.00
	1867R yr.XXI					
		3.950	2.50	5.00	9.00	20.00
	1867R yr.XXII					
		3.950	2.50	5.00	9.00	20.00
	1868R yr.XXII					
		8.200	2.50	5.00	9.00	18.00

Obv. leg: PIVS IX P.M.A. . .
Rev: Large R at wreath bottom.

KM#	Date	Mintage	Fine	VF	XF	Unc
1386.1						
	1868R yr.XXIII					
(C187a)		4.765	2.50	5.00	9.00	20.00
	1869R yr.XXIII					
		4.435	2.50	5.00	9.00	20.00
	1869R yr.XXIV					
		2.765	3.00	7.00	12.50	25.00

Rev: Wreath nearly closed at top, small R below.

KM#	Date	Mintage	Fine	VF	XF	Unc
1386.2						
	1868R yr.XXIII					
		Inc. Ab.	2.50	5.00	9.00	20.00

LIRA

5.0000 g, .835 SILVER, .1342 oz ASW
Obv: Small bust w/o ornament below.

KM#	Date	Mintage	Fine	VF	XF	Unc
1377.1						
	1866R yr.XX					
(C188)		100 pcs.	300.00	500.00	800.00	1400.

Obv: Ornament below bust.

KM#	Date	Mintage	Fine	VF	XF	Unc
1377.2						
	1866R yr.XXI					
(C188b)		1.765	15.00	25.00	30.00	75.00

Obv: Medium bust.

KM#	Date	Mintage	Fine	VF	XF	Unc
1377.3						
	1866R yr.XXI					
(C188d)		.275	30.00	100.00	135.00	200.00

Obv: Large bust, PIUS IX PON. MAX. AN. . .

KM#	Date	Mintage	Fine	VF	XF	Unc
1378	1866R yr.XXI					
(C188a)		1.675	4.00	10.00	20.00	40.00
	1867R yr.XXI					
		3.876	4.00	8.00	15.00	30.00
	1867R yr.XXII					
		3.987	4.00	8.00	15.00	30.00
	1868R yr.XXII					
		2.050	4.00	10.00	20.00	40.00

Obv. leg: PIUS IX PON.M.A. . .

KM#	Date	Mintage	Fine	VF	XF	Unc
1387	1868R yr.XXIII					
(C188c)		3.877	4.00	8.00	20.00	40.00
	1869R yr.XXIII					
		1.145	7.50	12.50	27.50	55.00
	1869R yr.XXIV					
		.346	30.00	65.00	100.00	200.00

2 LIRE

10.0000 g, .835 SILVER, .2684 oz ASW
Obv: Small small bust w/o ornament.
Leg: PIUS IX PON MAX.A. . .

KM#	Date	Mintage	Fine	VF	XF	Unc
1379.1						
	1866R yr.XX					
(C189)		610 pcs.	700.00	1250.	2500.	4000.

Obv: Ornament below large bust.

KM#	Date	Mintage	Fine	VF	XF	Unc
1379.2						
	1866R yr.XXI					
(C189a)		.987	12.50	20.00	40.00	85.00
	1867R yr.XXI					
		.224	75.00	150.00	250.00	500.00
	1867R yr.XXII					
		1.220	12.50	20.00	35.00	80.00
	1868R yr.XXII					
		.530	50.00	120.00	175.00	350.00

Obv. leg: PIUS IX PON.M.A. . .

KM#	Date	Mintage	Fine	VF	XF	Unc
1379.3						
	1868R yr.XXIII					
(C189b)		.978	12.50	20.00	40.00	85.00
	1869R yr.XXIV					
		.810	12.50	20.00	40.00	85.00
	1870R yr.XXIV					
		.179	40.00	100.00	150.00	275.00

2-1/2 LIRE

12.5000 g, .900 SILVER, .3617 oz ASW

KM#	Date	Mintage	Fine	VF	XF	Unc
1384	1867R yr.XXI					
(C190)		.257	35.00	75.00	110.00	220.00

5 LIRE

1.6120 g, .900 GOLD, .0466 oz AGW

KM#	Date	Mintage	Fine	VF	XF	Unc
1380	1866R yr.XXI					
(C192)		3,230	225.00	375.00	500.00	850.00

KM#	Date	Mintage	Fine	VF	XF	Unc
1380	1867R yr.XXII	3,787	175.00	350.00	500.00	800.00

25.0000 g, .900 SILVER, .7234 oz ASW

KM#	Date	Mintage	Fine	VF	XF	Unc
1385 (C191)	1867R yr.XXI	5,800	100.00	200.00	350.00	550.00
	1870R yr.XXIV	.099	60.00	90.00	200.00	350.00
	1870R yr.XXV	.115	50.00	80.00	175.00	325.00

10 LIRE

3.2250 g, .900 GOLD, .0933 oz AGW
Obv. leg: PIUS IX PONT. MAX.A. . .

KM#	Date	Mintage	Fine	VF	XF	Unc
1381.1 (C193)	1866R yr.XXI	8,579	150.00	300.00	400.00	600.00

Obv. leg: PIUS IX PON. MAX. A. . .

KM#	Date	Mintage	Fine	VF	XF	Unc
1381.2 (C193b)	1867R yr.XXI	8,580	150.00	300.00	400.00	600.00
	1867R yr.XXII	9,176	150.00	250.00	350.00	500.00

Obv. leg: PIUS IX P.M.A. . .

KM#	Date	Mintage	Fine	VF	XF	Unc
1381.3 (C193a)	1869R yr.XXIV	5,944	175.00	350.00	550.00	850.00

20 LIRE

6.4510 g, .900 GOLD, .1866 oz AGW
Plain edge, small bust

KM#	Date	Mintage	Fine	VF	XF	Unc
1382.1 (C194)	1866R yr.XX	945 pcs.	900.00	1500.	2500.	5500.

Reeded edge

KM#	Date	Mintage	Fine	VF	XF	Unc
1382.2 (C194.1)	1866R yr.XX	.022	350.00	650.00	950.00	1450.
	1866R yr.XXI	.102	125.00	175.00	275.00	350.00
	1867R yr.XXI	.044	150.00	225.00	350.00	550.00

Obv: Medium bust.

KM#	Date	Mintage	Fine	VF	XF	Unc
1382.3 (C194.2)	1867R yr.XXII	.057	125.00	175.00	275.00	350.00
	1868R yr.XXII	.038	150.00	225.00	350.00	550.00
	1868R yr.XXIII	Inc. Ab.	350.00	650.00	950.00	1450.

Obv: Large bust.

KM#	Date	Mintage	Fine	VF	XF	Unc
1382.4 (C194.3)	1868R yr.XXIII	.112	125.00	175.00	250.00	300.00
	1869R yr.XXIII	.054	125.00	175.00	275.00	350.00
	1869R yr.XXIV	.076	125.00	175.00	250.00	300.00
	1870R yr.XXIV	.024	200.00	275.00	350.00	550.00
	1870R yr.XXV	.027	150.00	225.00	300.00	425.00

50 LIRE

16.1290 g, .900 GOLD, .4667 oz AGW

KM#	Date	Mintage	Fine	VF	XF	Unc
1388 (C195)	1868R yr.XXII	1,172	850.00	950.00	2200.	4500.
	1868R yr.XXIII	257 pcs.	2750.	4000.	6000.	8500.
	1870R yr.XXIV	1,460	850.00	950.00	2200.	4200.

32.2580 g, .900 GOLD, .9335 oz AGW

KM#	Date	Mintage	Fine	VF	XF	Unc
1383 (C196)	1866R yr.XXI	1,117	900.00	1000.	2500.	4750.
	1868R yr.XXIII	545 pcs.	2000.	2750.	4500.	6500.
	1869R yr.XXIII	625 pcs.	2000.	2750.	4500.	6500.
	1869R yr.XXIV	450 pcs.	2500.	4250.	6000.	8500.

PATTERNS (Pn)

(Including off metal strikes)

KM#	Date	Mintage	Identification	Mkt.Val.
Pn2	1834R	—	5 Scudi, Silver, Klippe, 17.60 g	800.00

KM#	Date	Mintage	Identification	Mkt.Val.
Pn3	MDCCCXXXXVI	—	1 Scudo, Silver, 41.00 g, KM1335	1500.

KM#	Date	Mintage	Identification	Mkt.Val.
Pn4	1868 yr.XXII	—	4 Soldi, .835 Silver, reeded edge	7250.
Pn5	1868 yr.XXII	—	4 Soldi, .835 Silver, plain edge	6000.

KM#	Date	Mintage	Identification	Mkt.Val.
Pn6	1878	—	5 Lire, Leo XIII	—

VATICAN PAPAL CITY STATES

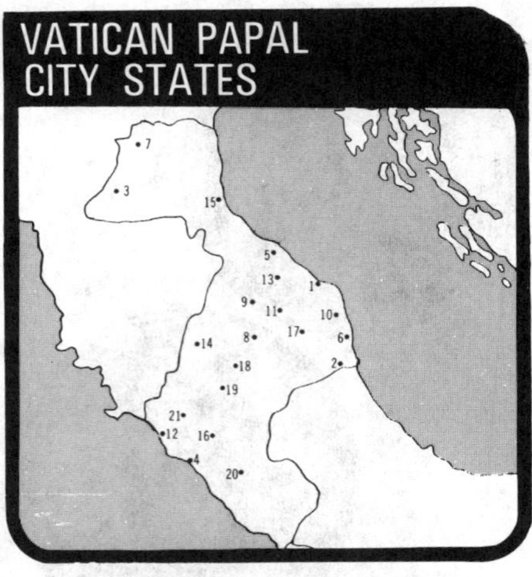

The 21 Papal City States spanned the Papal states from one end to the other. Most of the cities had been the holy see for hundreds of years. Many of them housed religious architecture and relics that were a veritable history of the church. Many had strong local families that helped administrate the city and occasionally opposed the Papal authority. Most of these cities stayed in the Papal states until 1860 when Papal territories began to crumble due to the move for unification of all Italy.

EXTRINSIC MINT

Avignon (Southern France)

PONTIFFS

Refer to Papal States.

MONETARY SYSTEM

6 Quattrini = 1 Bolognino or Baiocco
5 Baiocchi = 1 Grossi
2 Grossi = 1 Giuli = 1 Paoli
3 Giulio = 3 Paoli = 1 Testone
10 Giulio = 10 Paoli = 1 Scudo
3 Scudi = 1 Doppia

ROMAN REPUBLIC

Repubblica Romana

A short-lived Republican movement fostered by the French Revolution, submerged the Papal States in 1798-99. They reappeared in 1814, and except for the Republican movement of 1848-49, maintained their authority until 1860.

MINT MARKS

B - Bologna
R - Rome

Second Republic

1848-1849

1/2 BAIOCCO

COPPER
Rev: Eagle.

KM#	Date	Fine	VF	XF	Unc
21 (C21)	1849R	6.00	12.00	25.00	50.00

BAIOCCO

COPPER
Rev: Eagle.

KM#	Date	Fine	VF	XF	Unc
22 (C22)	1849R	8.50	16.00	32.00	65.00

3 BAIOCCHI

COPPER
Obv: Round 3. Rev: Eagle.

KM#	Date	Fine	VF	XF	Unc
23.1 (C23.1)	1849R	12.00	25.00	50.00	80.00
	Obv: Flat topped 3.				
23.2 (C23.2)	1849B	18.00	35.00	70.00	120.00
	1849R	12.00	25.00	50.00	80.00
	Obv: Small round 3.				
23.3 (C23.3)	1849R	15.00	30.00	60.00	110.00

4 BAIOCCHI

1.9500 g, .200 SILVER, .0125 oz ASW
Rev: Eagle.

KM#	Date	Fine	VF	XF	Unc
24 (C24)	1849B	7.00	14.00	35.00	80.00
	1849R	6.00	12.00	25.00	55.00

8 BAIOCCHI

3.9000 g, .200 SILVER, .0251 oz ASW
Rev: Eagle.

KM#	Date	Fine	VF	XF	Unc
25 (C25)	1849R	12.00	25.00	50.00	80.00

16 BAIOCCHI

7.8000 g, .200 SILVER, .0502 oz ASW
Rev: Eagle.

KM#	Date	Fine	VF	XF	Unc
26 (C26)	1849R	20.00	35.00	70.00	120.00

40 BAIOCCHI

20.0000 g, .200 SILVER, .1286 oz ASW
Rev: Eagle.

KM#	Date	Fine	VF	XF	Unc
27 (C27)	1849R	30.00	60.00	150.00	250.00

ANCONA

Anconna

A city in the Marches, was founded by Syracusan refugees about 390 B.C. It became a semi-independent republic under papal protection in the 14th century, and a papal state in 1532. From 1797 until the formation of the United Kingdom of Italy it was part of the Roman Republic (1798-99), a papal state (1799-1808), part of the Italian Kingdom of Napoleon (1808-14), a papal state (1814-48), a part of the Roman Republic (1848-49), and a papal state (1849-60).

MINT MARKS

A - Ancona

Second Republic

1848-1849

BAIOCCO

CAST COPPER
Rev: A below date.

KM#	Date	VG	Fine	VF	XF
12 (C12)	1849A	10.00	20.00	45.00	85.00

3 BAIOCCHI

CAST COPPER
Obv. leg: REPUBBLICA ROMANA around fasces.
Rev: Value, date, mm.

KM#	Date				
13 (C13)	1849A	—	—	Rare	—

NOTE: Some authorities consider this a contemporary counterfeit.

The Republic of Venezuela ("Little Venice"), located on the northern coast of South America between Colombia and Guyana, has an area of 352,145 sq. mi. (912,050 sq. km.) and a population of 20 million. Capital: Caracas. Petroleum and mining provide a significant portion of Venezuela's exports. Coffee, grown on 60,000 plantations, is the chief crop. Metalurgy, refining, oil, iron and steel production are the main employment industries.

Columbus discovered Venezuela on his third voyage in 1498. Initial exploration did not reveal Venezuela to be a land of great wealth. An active pearl trade operated on the off-shore islands and slavers raided the interior in search of Indians to be sold into slavery, but no significant mainland settlements were made before 1567 when Caracas was founded. Venezuela, the home of Bolivar, was among the first South American colonies to rebel against Spain in 1810. The declaration of Independence of Venezuela was signed by seven provinces which are represented by the seven stars of the Venezuelan flag. Coinage of Caracas and Margarita use the seven stars in their designs. These original provinces were: Barcelona, Barinas, Caracas, Cumana, Margarita, Merida and Trujillo. The Provinces of Coro, Guyana and Maracaibo were added to Venezuela during the Independence War. Independence was attained in 1821 but not recognized by Spain until 1845. Together with Ecuador, Panama and Colombia, Venezuela was part of "Gran Colombia" until 1830, when it became a sovereign and independent state.

RULERS

Spanish, until 1810
Spanish and Independent, 1810-1823
Republic, 1823-present

MINT MARKS

A - Paris
(a) - Paris, privy marks only
(aa) - Altena
(b) - Berlin
(bb) - Brussels
(cc) - Canada
(c) - Caracas
H, Heaton - Heaton, Birmingham

MONETARY SYSTEM

16 Reales = 1 Escudo
8 Reales = 1 Peso

PROVINCE OF BARINAS

The name of Barinas is used to identify the colonial coins minted from 1817 to 1824 by General Jose Antonio Paez in the west-central south Venezuela in different towns such as Achaguas and Caujaral which are commonly known as Yagual and Chipi-chipis, both from the province of Barinas.

ACHAGUAS

(1813-14)

2 REALES

(El Yagual)

SILVER

KM#	Date	Mintage	Good	VG	Fine	VF
1	781	—	100.00	150.00	200.00	300.00

CAUJARAL

(1813-24)

1 REAL

(Chipi-chipi)

SILVER

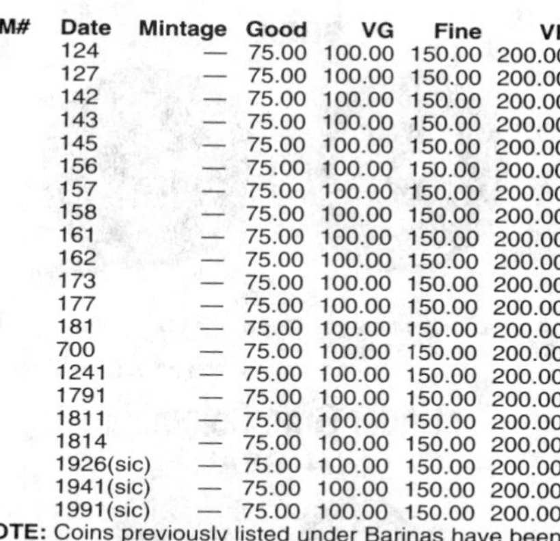

KM#	Date	Mintage	Good	VG	Fine	VF
2	124	—	75.00	100.00	150.00	200.00
	127	—	75.00	100.00	150.00	200.00
	142	—	75.00	100.00	150.00	200.00
	143	—	75.00	100.00	150.00	200.00
	145	—	75.00	100.00	150.00	200.00
	156	—	75.00	100.00	150.00	200.00
	157	—	75.00	100.00	150.00	200.00
	158	—	75.00	100.00	150.00	200.00
	161	—	75.00	100.00	150.00	200.00
	162	—	75.00	100.00	150.00	200.00
	173	—	75.00	100.00	150.00	200.00
	177	—	75.00	100.00	150.00	200.00
	181	—	75.00	100.00	150.00	200.00
	700	—	75.00	100.00	150.00	200.00
	1241	—	75.00	100.00	150.00	200.00
	1791	—	75.00	100.00	150.00	200.00
	1811	—	75.00	100.00	150.00	200.00
	1814	—	75.00	100.00	150.00	200.00
	1926(sic)	—	75.00	100.00	150.00	200.00
	1941(sic)	—	75.00	100.00	150.00	200.00
	1991(sic)	—	75.00	100.00	150.00	200.00

NOTE: Coins previously listed under Barinas have been removed from the catalog pending revised attribution.

PROVINCE OF CARACAS

This province surrounds the national capital, also named Caracas, Spain opened the first mint in Venezuela in that city in November 1802. Coins were made initially from 1802 to 1805. Caracas rebelled on April 19, 1810, and the Spanish retreated, but retook the city in July, 1812 and Royalist coinage resumed. Copper and silver coins were struck through 1821, when Bolivar's troops defeated the Spanish.

ROYALIST COINAGE

1/8 REAL

COPPER

C#	Date	Mintage	Good	VG	Fine	VF
1	1802	.059	250.00	500.00	800.00	1300.
	1804	.019	900.00	1300.	1900.	2600.
	1805	.100	250.00	450.00	650.00	1000.
	1814	.012	400.00	600.00	850.00	1200.
	1817	4,500	1200.	1600.	2200.	3200.
	1818	.094	100.00	170.00	250.00	350.00

1/4 REAL

COPPER

C#	Date	Mintage	Good	VG	Fine	VF
2	1802	.014	700.00	900.00	1300.	2200.
	1804	6,589	1500.	2000.	4000.	6000.
	1805	.070	400.00	600.00	1000.	1500.
	1813	.010	30.00	50.00	90.00	130.00
	1814/3	.040	10.00	25.00	60.00	85.00
	1814	Inc. Ab.	8.00	15.00	50.00	75.00
	1816	.750	6.00	10.00	40.00	60.00

Large date — Small date

Date	Mintage	Good	VG	Fine	VF
1817 large date	.490	3.00	5.00	10.00	20.00
1817 small date	1.640	2.00	3.50	9.00	17.50
1818	2.240	2.00	3.50	9.00	17.50
1821	.650	4.00	8.50	17.50	30.00

NOTE: Beginning around 1813, average planchet size begins to diminish.

ROYALIST and/or REPUBLICAN COINAGE

(1813-17)

REAL

(Macuquino)

SILVER, 2.4-3.0 g
Cob style - Caracas shape.

C#	Date	Mintage	Good	VG	Fine	VF
12	42(1)	—	50.00	100.00	200.00	300.00
	182	—	50.00	100.00	200.00	300.00
	721	—	50.00	100.00	200.00	300.00
	781	—	50.00	100.00	200.00	300.00
	931	—	50.00	100.00	200.00	300.00

2 REALES

(Macuquinos)

SILVER, 4.50-5.80 g
Cob style - Caracas shape.

C#	Date	Mintage	Good	VG	Fine	VF
13.1	142	—	50.00	100.00	150.00	250.00
	152	—	50.00	100.00	150.00	250.00
	172	—	50.00	100.00	150.00	250.00
	174	—	50.00	100.00	150.00	250.00
	182	—	50.00	100.00	150.00	250.00
	183	—	50.00	100.00	150.00	250.00
	184	—	50.00	100.00	150.00	250.00
	281	—	50.00	100.00	150.00	250.00
	471	—	50.00	100.00	150.00	250.00
	741	—	50.00	100.00	150.00	250.00
	751	—	50.00	100.00	150.00	250.00
	781	—	50.00	100.00	150.00	250.00

Round style.

C#	Date	Mintage	Good	VG	Fine	VF
13.2	186	—	50.00	100.00	150.00	250.00
	816	—	50.00	100.00	150.00	250.00
	817	—	50.00	100.00	150.00	250.00
	1816	—	65.00	150.00	250.00	300.00
	1817	—	65.00	150.00	250.00	300.00

NOTE: Varieties exist in the shape, placement and design of most obv. and rev. features of these coins.

ROYALIST COINAGE

REAL

SILVER, 2.45-3.25 g
Rev: Lion in upper left of cross.

C#	Date	Mintage	Good	VG	Fine	VF
5.1	1817 BS	6,500	700.00	1200.	2500.	4500.
	1818 BS	.014	200.00	350.00	450.00	900.00

Rev: Castle in upper left of cross.

C#	Date	Mintage	Good	VG	Fine	VF
5.2	1817 BS	I.A.	700.00	1200.	2500.	4500.
	1820 BS	.011	500.00	600.00	1100.	2000.
	1821 BS	8,000	600.00	700.00	1200.	2700.

2 REALES

(Morilleros)

SILVER, 23-25mm,4.3-5.3 g

Rev: Lion in upper left of cross.

C#	Date	Mintage	Good	VG	Fine	VF
6.1	1817 BS	.076	50.00	80.00	200.00	350.00
	1818 BS	.777	8.50	13.50	22.50	42.50
	1819/8 BS	1.450	8.50	13.50	22.50	42.50
	1819 BS	I.A.	8.50	13.50	22.50	42.50
	1820 BS	.755	9.00	16.50	35.00	75.00
	1821 BS	.110	12.50	27.50	50.00	87.50

Rev: Castle in upper left of cross.

C#	Date	Mintage	Good	VG	Fine	VF
6.2	1817 BS	I.A.	40.00	70.00	150.00	250.00
	1818 BS	I.A.	7.50	13.50	22.50	40.00
	1820 BS	I.A.	8.50	16.50	37.50	75.00
	1821 BS	I.A.	13.50	27.50	55.00	100.00

NOTE: Beware of contemporary counterfeits struck in German silver, (copper-nickel-zinc alloy). These are valued at roughly 25-30% of genuine silver pieces.

4 REALES

SILVER, 9.50-10.30 g

Rev: Lion in upper left of cross.

C#	Date	Mintage	Good	VG	Fine	VF
7.1	1819 BS	.018	375.00	600.00	1200.	2000.

Rev: Castle in upper left of cross.

C#	Date	Mintage	Good	VG	Fine	VF
7.2	1819 BS	I.A.	375.00	600.00	1200.	2000.
	1820 BS	.029	375.00	600.00	1200.	2000.

NOTE: Die varieties exist.

REPUBLICAN COINAGE

1812

19 refers to 19 April 1810, date of the Declaration of Independence.

1/8 REAL

COPPER

Caracas Mint

C#	Date	Mintage	Good	VG	Fine	VF
21	1812(c)	7,000	250.00	350.00	700.00	1200.

1/4 REAL

COPPER, 26-30mm

C#	Date	Mintage	Good	VG	Fine	VF
22	1812(c)	.030	45.00	75.00	125.00	185.00

1/2 REAL

SILVER

Obv: Large "1/2".

C#	Date	Mintage	Good	VG	Fine	VF
25	Ano 2(1812)(c)	.016	675.00	1000.	1700.	2700.

REAL

SILVER

C#	Date	Mintage	Good	VG	Fine	VF
26	Ano 2(1812)(c)	.020	500.00	700.00	1200.	2200.

Under Gran Colombia

1/4 REAL

SILVER

C#	Date	Mintage	Good	VG	Fine	VF
31	1821(c)	.090	150.00	225.00	600.00	1000.
	1822(c)	.540	65.00	125.00	275.00	500.00

C#	Date	Mintage	Good	VG	Fine	VF
34	1829(c)	.750	10.00	20.00	35.00	75.00
	1830(c)	.650	12.50	22.50	38.50	85.00

2 REALES

SILVER

Rev: Cross between 2 rosettes.

C#	Date	Mintage	Good	VG	Fine	VF
36	1818(1830)BS	.268	15.00	22.00	37.50	65.00

NOTE: Sometimes found struck over cut down Spanish De Vellon 4 Reales, KM#137.

PATTERNS (Pn)

(Including off metal strikes)

KM#	Date	Mintage	Identification	Mkt.Val.
Pn1	Ano 2(1812)	2 pcs. known	1/2 Real, Silver, small 1/2 above D-R	Rare

KM#	Date	Mintage	Identification	Mkt.Val.
Pn2	1829 O	—	1/2 Real, Silver	Unique

PROVINCE OF GUAYANA

Coinage for this province in eastern Venezuela was authorized by an act of October 26, 1813. This was to alleviate the coin shortage caused by the isolation of the province from other Spanish forces.

ROYALIST COINAGE

1/4 REAL

COPPER

C#	Date	Mintage	Good	VG	Fine	VF
40	1813	—	600.00	900.00	1300.	1700.

1/2 REAL

Outlined castle, variety of C#41.1.

Outlined lion, variety of C#41.1.

Solid castle and lion.

Large flan, 26.1-30mm.

COPPER

C#	Date	Mintage	Good	VG	Fine	VF
41.1	1813	—	25.00	40.00	100.00	200.00
	1814	—	5.00	10.00	25.00	60.00

Small flan, 22-26mm.

C#	Date	Mintage	Good	VG	Fine	VF
41.2	1814	—	5.00	10.00	25.00	60.00
	1815	—	5.00	10.00	25.00	60.00
	1816	—	7.00	13.50	27.50	65.00
	1817	—	5.00	10.00	25.00	60.00

NOTE: These types generally have only partial dates visible, examples with full clear dates command a premium, while examples with no traces of date showing are worth significantly less.

PROVINCE OF MARACAIBO

A province in northwestern Venezuela includes the city of Maracaibo, situated on the channel between Lake Maracaibo and the Caribbean. This crude coinage was presumably necessary because of the temporary isolation of local Royalist forces from the main Spanish armies. The coins of Maracaibo were struck by order dated March 13, 1813 by Fernando Mijares, Captain General of the Province of Maracaibo.

ROYALIST COINAGE

1/2 REAL

COPPER

KM#	Date	Mintage	Good	VG	Fine	VF
1	1813	—	135.00	250.00	385.00	550.00

2 REALES

(1813-14)

(Lanzas de Maracaibo)

SILVER

KM#	Date	Mintage	Good	VG	Fine	VF
2	38	—	125.00	225.00	375.00	550.00
	181	—	125.00	225.00	375.00	550.00
	182	—	125.00	225.00	375.00	550.00
	1813	—	135.00	250.00	385.00	550.00
	1814	—	135.00	250.00	385.00	550.00

PROVINCE OF MARGARITA

An island north of Venezuela which at the beginning of the Independence War had trade relations with the other islands of the Caribbean in which the Spanish coins of Maravedis were used. 15 days after the Declaration of Independence of Caracas, Margarita joined that declaration on the 4th of April, 1810.

REPUBLICAN COINAGE

4 MARAVEDIS

COPPER
Obv: 3 men in a boat, sun above, leg: MARGARITA PERLA PRECIOSA.
Rev: Denomination encircled w/7 stars, leg: DA FX DIA 4 DE MAIO 1810.

KM#	Date	Mintage	Good	VG	Fine	VF
1	1810	—	—	—	Rare	—

REPUBLIC OF VENEZUELA

MONETARY SYSTEM
10 Centavos = 1 Real
10 Reales = 1 Peso

1/4 CENTAVO

COPPER, 2.9-3.0 g

Y#	Date	Mintage	VG	Fine	VF	XF
1	1843(I)	3.840	2.00	7.50	22.50	55.00
	1852H	2.000	2.25	8.50	40.00	130.00

2.7 g

Y#	Date	Mintage	VG	Fine	VF	XF
4	1852(I)	4.000	2.00	7.50	22.50	55.00

1/2 CENTAVO

COPPER, 24mm, 5.7-6.0 g

Y#	Date	Mintage	VG	Fine	VF	XF
2	1843(I)	.960	2.75	9.50	25.00	100.00
	1843(I)	—	—	—	Proof	400.00
	1852H	.500	4.50	13.50	75.00	300.00

22mm, 5.4 g
Rev: 24 berries.

Y#	Date	Mintage	VG	Fine	VF	XF
5.1	1852(I)	1.000	2.75	9.50	45.00	150.00

Rev: 23 berries.

Y#	Date	Mintage	VG	Fine	VF	XF
5.2	1852(I)	Inc. Ab.	8.50	28.50	120.00	300.00

CENTAVO

COPPER, 32mm, 11.4-12.1 g
Rev: Slant top 1.

Y#	Date	Mintage	VG	Fine	VF	XF
3.1	1843(I)	.480	13.50	32.50	70.00	150.00
	1843(I)	—	—	—	Proof	600.00

Rev: Flat top 1.

Y#	Date	Mintage	VG	Fine	VF	XF
3.2	1852H	.250	6.00	20.00	60.00	140.00
	1852H	—	—	—	Proof	600.00

30mm, 10.9 g

Y#	Date	Mintage	VG	Fine	VF	XF
6	1852(I)	.500	4.00	9.50	27.50	75.00
	1852(I)	—	—	—	Proof	600.00

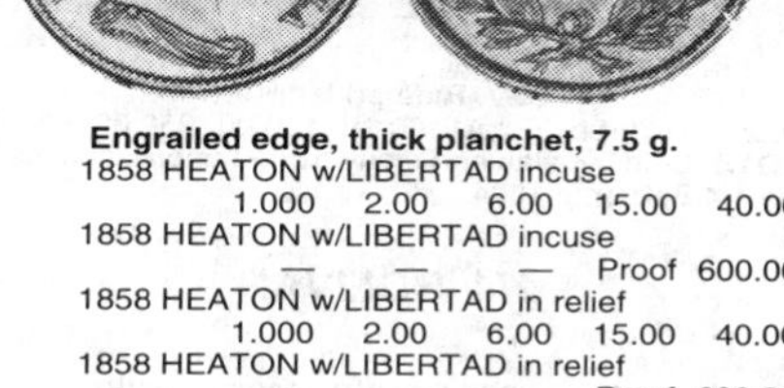

Engrailed edge, thick planchet, 7.5 g.

Y#	Date	Mintage	VG	Fine	VF	XF
7	1858 HEATON w/LIBERTAD incuse	1.000	2.00	6.00	15.00	40.00
	1858 HEATON w/LIBERTAD incuse	—	—	—	Proof	600.00
	1858 HEATON w/LIBERTAD in relief	1.000	2.00	6.00	15.00	40.00
	1858 HEATON w/LIBERTAD in relief	—	—	—	Proof	600.00
	1862HEATON	1.500	1.75	5.00	13.50	35.00
	1863HEATON	.500	3.50	9.00	25.00	70.00

1/2 REAL

1.1500 g, .900 SILVER, .0333 oz ASW
Similar to 2 Reales, Y#10 but value shown as 1-1/2 Real, erroneously.

Y#	Date	Mintage	VG	Fine	VF	XF
8	1858A	.040	80.00	175.00	350.00	800.00

REAL

2.3000 g, .900 SILVER, .0666 oz ASW
Similar to 2 Reales, Y#10.

Y#	Date	Mintage	VG	Fine	VF	XF
9	1858A	.042	60.00	150.00	365.00	850.00

2 REALES

4.6000 g, .900 SILVER, .1331 oz ASW

Y#	Date	Mintage	VG	Fine	VF	XF
10	1858A	.030	75.00	180.00	400.00	1000.

5 REALES

11.5000 g, .900 SILVER, .3328 oz ASW

Y#	Date	Mintage	VG	Fine	VF	XF
11	1858A	.026	75.00	175.00	385.00	1000.

10 REALES

SILVER

Y#	Date	Mintage	Fine	VF	XF	Unc
A11	1863A	*.300	—	—	6000.	9000.

***NOTE:** Almost entire issue melted, estimated 200 pcs. survived.

MONETARY REFORM

(1871-79)
100 Centavos = 1 Venezolano

CENTAVO

COPPER-NICKEL

Y#	Date	Mintage	VG	Fine	VF	XF
25	1876(p)	8.000	4.00	6.00	15.00	45.00
	1876(p)	—	—	—	Proof	600.00
	1877(p)	2.000	5.00	8.00	20.00	55.00
	1877(p)	—	—	—	Proof	600.00

2-1/2 CENTAVOS

COPPER-NICKEL

Y#	Date	Mintage	VG	Fine	VF	XF
26	1876(p)	1.500	6.00	15.00	30.00	100.00
	1876(p)	—	—	—	Proof	600.00
	1877(p)	.500	7.00	20.00	40.00	120.00
	1877(p)	—	—	—	Proof	600.00

5 CENTAVOS

1.2500 g, .835 SILVER, .0336 oz ASW
Rev: Serifed A.

Y#	Date	Mintage	VG	Fine	VF	XF
12.1	1874A	.800	3.50	5.00	15.00	35.00
	1874A	—	—	—	Proof	800.00
	1876A	.520	4.00	9.00	20.00	50.00
	1876A	—	—	—	Proof	800.00

Rev: Unserifed A.

Y#	Date	Mintage	VG	Fine	VF	XF
12.2	1874A	Inc. Ab.	3.50	5.00	15.00	35.00
	1876A	Inc. Ab.	4.00	9.00	20.00	50.00

10 CENTAVOS

2.5000 g, .835 SILVER, .0671 oz ASW
Rev: Serifed A.

Y#	Date	Mintage	VG	Fine	VF	XF
13.1	1874A	.800	4.50	12.00	22.00	50.00
	1874A	—	—	—	Proof	800.00
	1876A	.280	10.00	25.00	60.00	140.00

Rev: Unserifed A.

Y#	Date	Mintage	VG	Fine	VF	XF
13.2	1874A	Inc. Ab.	4.50	12.00	22.00	50.00
	1876A	Inc. Ab.	10.00	25.00	60.00	140.00

20 CENTAVOS

5.0000 g, .835 SILVER, .1342 oz ASW

Y#	Date	Mintage	VG	Fine	VF	XF
14	1874A small A					
		.400	10.00	20.00	40.00	120.00
	1874A large A					
		Inc. Ab.	10.00	20.00	40.00	120.00
	1876A	.136	20.00	45.00	100.00	300.00

50 CENTAVOS

12.5000 g, .835 SILVER, .3356 oz ASW

Y#	Date	Mintage	VG	Fine	VF	XF
15	1873A	.200	20.00	50.00	120.00	550.00
	1874A	.200	20.00	50.00	120.00	550.00
	1876A	.158	20.00	50.00	120.00	550.00

VENEZOLANO

25.0000 g, .900 SILVER, .7234 oz ASW

Y#	Date	Mintage	VG	Fine	VF	XF
16	1876A	.035	45.00	100.00	300.00	1400.
	1876A	—	—	—	Proof	8500.

5 VENEZOLANOS

8.0645 g, .900 GOLD, .2333 oz AGW

Y#	Date	Mintage	Fine	VF	XF	Unc
17	1875A	.069	115.00	200.00	300.00	600.00

MONETARY REFORM

100 Centimos = 1 Bolivar

5 CENTIMOS

COPPER-NICKEL

Y#	Date	Mintage	Fine	VF	XF	Unc
27	1896(b)	4.000	.50	2.00	15.00	65.00

NOTE: Later dates (1915-1938) exist for this type.

12-1/2 CENTIMOS

COPPER-NICKEL

Y#	Date	Mintage	Fine	VF	XF	Unc
28	1896(b)	6.000	1.00	4.00	20.00	100.00

NOTE: Later dates (1925-1938) exist for this type.

1/5 BOLIVAR

1.0000 g, .835 SILVER, .0268 oz ASW
Obv: Crude letters.

Y#	Date	Mintage	VG	Fine	VF	XF
19.1	1879(bb)	.125	100.00	150.00	250.00	600.00

Obv: Refined letters.

Y#	Date	Mintage	VG	Fine	VF	XF
19.2	1879(bb)	I.A.	100.00	150.00	250.00	600.00

NOTE: Coin recalled and many melted upon issuance of the 1/4 Bolivar in 1894.

1/4 BOLIVAR

1.2500 g, .835 SILVER, .0336 oz ASW

Y#	Date	Mintage	Fine	VF	XF	Unc
20	1894A	2.000	2.00	3.50	8.50	20.00
	1900(a)	.407	5.00	14.00	28.00	80.00

NOTE: Later dates (1901-1948) exist for this type.

1/2 BOLIVAR

2.5000 g, .835 SILVER, .0671 oz ASW

Y#	Date	Mintage	Fine	VF	XF	Unc
21	1879(bb)	.200	40.00	90.00	300.00	750.00
	1886(c) high second 8					
		.300	20.00	50.00	175.00	425.00
	1886(c) low second 8					
		Inc. Ab.	20.00	50.00	175.00	425.00
	1887(c)	.310	50.00	100.00	300.00	750.00
	1888(c)	.230	400.00	600.00	1100.	2000.
	1889(c)	.080	2000.	3000.	5000.	7000.
	1893A	.500	15.00	30.00	125.00	350.00
	1900A	.600	20.00	50.00	175.00	400.00
	1900(a)	—	35.00	55.00	220.00	500.00

NOTE: Later dates (1901-1946) exist for this type.

BOLIVAR

5.0000 g, .835 SILVER, .1342 oz ASW

Y#	Date	Mintage	Fine	VF	XF	Unc
22	1879(bb)	.375	28.00	85.00	500.00	1200.
	1886A	—	—	—	Rare	—
	1886(c) wide date					
		.600	22.00	45.00	250.00	950.00
	1886(c) narrow date					
		Inc. Ab.	22.00	45.00	250.00	950.00
	1887(c)	.280	125.00	300.00	1000.	2000.
	1888(c)	.197	150.00	400.00	1100.	2200.
	1889(c)	.118	150.00	350.00	1000.	2000.
	1893(a)	.500	12.00	28.00	120.00	400.00
	1900(a)	.380	20.00	45.00	120.00	400.00

NOTE: Later dates (1901-1936) exist for this type.

2 BOLIVARES

10.0000 g, .835 SILVER, .2685 oz ASW

Y#	Date	Mintage	Fine	VF	XF	Unc
23	1879(bb)	.375	25.00	80.00	400.00	950.00

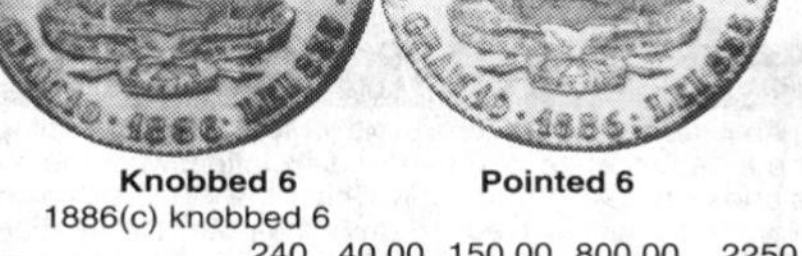

Knobbed 6 — Pointed 6

Y#	Date	Mintage	Fine	VF	XF	Unc
	1886(c) knobbed 6					
		.240	40.00	150.00	800.00	2250.
	1886(c) pointed 6					
		Inc. Ab.	40.00	150.00	800.00	2250.
	1887(c) high second 8					
		.200	11.50	50.00	200.00	500.00
	1887(c) low second 8					
		Inc. Ab.	11.50	50.00	200.00	500.00
	1888(c)	.141	55.00	200.00	650.00	1750.
	1889(c)	.050	60.00	250.00	750.00	2000.
	1894(a)	.250	16.50	45.00	300.00	800.00
	1900(a)	.350	15.00	35.00	150.00	500.00

NOTE: Later dates (1902-1936) exist for this type.

5 BOLIVARES

25.0000 g, .900 SILVER, .7234 oz ASW
Obv: Date on ribbon right of arms
28 DE MARZO DE 1864.

Y#	Date	Mintage	Fine	VF	XF	Unc
24	1879(bb)	.250	12.00	65.00	400.00	1300.
	1886(c) normal date					
		.470	12.00	35.00	200.00	700.00
	1886(c) low second 8					
		Inc. Ab.	12.00	35.00	200.00	700.00
	1886(c) tight 8's					
		Inc. Ab.	12.00	35.00	200.00	700.00
	1886(c) w/o accent on Bolivar					
		Inc. Ab.	12.00	35.00	200.00	700.00
	1887(c)	.500	12.00	40.00	300.00	1000.
	1888(c) high second 8					
		.281	12.00	40.00	300.00	1000.
	1888(c) low second 8					
		Inc. Ab.	12.00	40.00	300.00	1000.
	1889(c)	.329	12.00	40.00	300.00	1000.
	1900(a)	.270	12.00	28.00	150.00	700.00

NOTE: Later dates (1901-1936) exist for this type.

20 BOLIVARES

6.4516 g, .900 GOLD, .1867 oz AGW

Y#	Date	Mintage	Fine	VF	XF	Unc
32	1879(bb)	.041	BV	100.00	150.00	300.00
	1880(bb) 1 & 8 close					
		.084	BV	100.00	110.00	300.00
	1880(bb) 1 & 8 apart					
		Inc. Ab.	BV	100.00	110.00	300.00
	1880(bb) tight 8's					
		Inc. Ab.	BV	100.00	110.00	300.00
	1886(c) high 6					
		.023	BV	130.00	150.00	200.00
	1886(c) low 6					
		Inc. Ab.	BV	130.00	150.00	200.00
	1887(c)	.132	125.00	175.00	250.00	600.00
	1888/6(c)	.081	100.00	150.00	200.00	450.00
	1888(c)	Inc. Ab.	110.00	160.00	220.00	500.00

NOTE: Later dates (1904-1912) exist for this type.

100 BOLIVARES

32.2580 g, .900 GOLD, .9334 oz AGW

Y#	Date	Mintage	Fine	VF	XF	Unc
34	1886(c) normal date					
		4,250	BV	600.00	700.00	1000.
	1886(c) 8 & 6 close					
		Inc. Ab.	BV	600.00	700.00	1000.
	1886(c) 8 & 6 apart					
		Inc. Ab.	BV	600.00	700.00	1000.
	1887(c)	.028	BV	600.00	700.00	1000.
	1888(c)	.032	BV	600.00	700.00	1000.
	1889(c)	.023	BV	600.00	700.00	1000.

ESSAIS (E)

KM#	Date	Mintage	Identification	Mkt.Val.
E1	1863	—	1 Centavo	125.00

KM#	Date	Mintage	Identification	Mkt.Val.
E2	1863	—	2 Centavos	150.00
E3	1863	—	1/2 Real	—
E4	1863	—	1 Real	—
E5	1863	—	2 Reales	—
E6	1863	—	4 Reales	10,000.
E7	1863	—	10 Reales	7000.
E8	1863	—	10 Reales, plain edge	10,000.
E9	1873	—	5 Centavos	1000.
E10	1873	—	10 Centavos	1500.
E11	1874	—	20 Centavos	2500.

KM#	Date	Mintage	Identification	Mkt.Val.
E12	1874	—	1 Venezolano, .900 Silver	10,500.

KM#	Date	Mintage	Identification	Mkt.Val.
E13	1875	—	5 Venezolanos, .900 Gold	—
E14	1875	—	10 Venezolanos, .900 Gold	—
E16	1875	—	20 Venezolanos, .900 Gold	—
E17	1888	—	50 Bolivares, .900 Gold	—

PATTERNS (Pn)

(Including off metal strikes)

KM#	Date	Mintage	Identification	Mkt.Val.
Pn1	1858H	—	1 Centavo, Copper, Y7	100.00
Pn2	1858H	—	1 Centavo, Copper-Nickel-Zinc, Y7	175.00

KM#	Date	Mintage	Identification	Mkt.Val.
Pn3	1875	—	10 Venezolanos, .900 Gold	15,000.

TRIAL STRIKES (TS)

KM#	Date	Mintage	Identification	Mkt.Val.
TS1	1875	—	10 Venezolanos, .900 Gold, Obv:	

COINS OF RESTRICTED CIRCULATION

STATE ISSUES

ESTADO TACHIRA

2 REALES

BRONZE
With R. below 2.

KM#	Date	Mintage	VG	Fine	VF	XF
S1	1872	—	—	—	Rare	—
		With star below 2.				
S2	1872	—	—	—	Rare	—

LEPROSARIUM COINAGE (L)

The Venezuelan Government maintained a large leper colony on Providencia Island, in Lake Maracaibo, where several hundred persons suffering from Hansen's disease were cared for. To provide for monetary transactions on the island, and to prevent ordinary coins from returning to general circulation after being handled by lepers, the Venezuelan Government formerly provided a distinctive currency. They had value only on the island until 30 years ago, when the illness was almost extinguished in South America and medical research revealed that little risk was involved in handling these coins.

MARACAIBO LAZARETO NACIONAL

1/4 REAL

COPPER

KM#	Date	Mintage	VG	Fine	VF	XF
L9	1897	—	—	—	Rare	—

1/8 BOLIVAR

COPPER

KM#	Date	Mintage	VG	Fine	VF	XF
L10	1898	—	—	—	Rare	—

VIETNAM/ANNAM

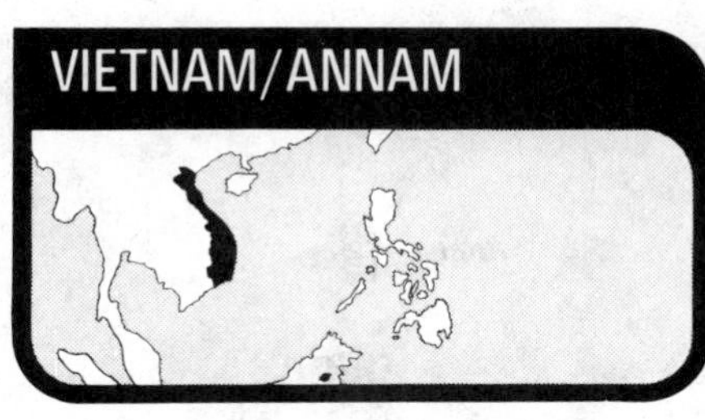

In 207 B.C. a Chinese general set up the Kingdom of Nam-Viet on the Red River. This kingdom was overthrown by the Chinese under the Han Dynasty in 111 B.C., whereupon the country became a Chinese province under the name of Giao-Chi, which was later changed to Annam or peaceful or pacified South. Chinese rule was maintained until 968, when the Vietnamese became independent until 1407 when China again invaded Viet Nam. The Chinese were driven out in 1428 and the country became independent and named Dai-Viet. Gia Long renamed the country Dai Nam in 1802.

After the French conquered Dai Nam, they split the country into three parts. The South became the Colony of Cochinchina; the North became the Protectorate of Tonkin; and the central became the Protectorate of Annam. The emperors were permitted to have their capital in Hue and to produce small quantities of their coins, presentation pieces, and bullion bars. Annam had an area of 57,840 sq. mi. (141,806 sq. km.) and a population of about 6 million. Chief products of the area are silk, cinnamon and rice. There are important mineral deposits in the mountainous inland.

United Dai Nam

EMPERORS

Gia Long, 1802-1820 嘉隆

Minh Mang, 1820-1841 明命

Thieu Tri, 1841-1847 紹治

Tu Duc, 1848-1883 嗣德

Kien Phuc, 1883-1884 建福

Ham Nghi, 1884-1885 咸宜

Protectorate of Annam

EMPERORS

Dong Khanh, 1885-1888 同慶

Thanh Thai, 1888-1907 成泰

REBELS and INVADERS

Bao Hung, 1801-1802 寶興

Tri Nguyen, 1831-1834 治元

Nguyen Long, 1832-1833 元隆

IDENTIFICATION

Khai 啓

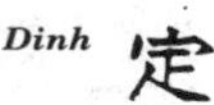 *Bao* *Thong* 通

Dinh 定

Khai Dinh Thong Bao

The square holed cash coins of Annam are easily identified by reading the characters top-bottom (emperor's name) and right-left ("Thong Bao" general currency). The character at right will change with some emperors.

CYCLICAL DATES

	庚	辛	壬	癸	甲	乙	丙	丁	戊	己
戌	1850 1910		1862 1922		1874 1934		1886 1946		1838 1898	
亥		1851 1911		1863 1923		1875 1935		1887 1947		1839 1899
子	1840 1900		1852 1912		1864 1924		1876 1936		1888 1948	
丑		1841 1901		1853 1913		1865 1925		1877 1937		1889 1949
寅	1830 1890		1842 1902		1854 1914		1866 1926		1878 1938	
卯		1831 1891		1843 1903		1855 1915		1867 1927		1879 1939
辰	1880 1940		1832 1892		1844 1904		1856 1916		1868 1928	
巳		1881 1941		1833 1893		1845 1905		1857 1917		1869 1929
午	1870 1930		1882 1942		1834 1894		1846 1906		1858 1918	
未		1871 1931		1883 1943		1835 1895		1847 1907		1859 1919
申	1860 1920		1872 1932		1884 1944		1836 1896		1848 1908	
酉		1861 1921		1873 1933		1885 1945		1837 1897		1849 1909

NOTE: This table has been adapted from *Chinese Bank Notes* by Ward Smith and Brian Matravers.

Cyclical dates consist of a pair of characters one of which indicates the animal associated with that year. Every 60 years, this pair of characters is repeated. The first character of a cyclical date corresponds to a character in the first row of the chart above. The second character is taken from the column at left. In this catalog where a cyclical date is used, the abbreviation CD appears before the A.D. date.

Annamese silver and gold coins were sometimes dated according to the year of the emperor's reign. In this case, simply add the year of reign to the year in which the reign would be 1849 (1847 plus 3 = 1850 -1 = 1849 or 1847 = 1; 1848 = 2; 1849 = 3). In this catalog the A.D. date appears in parenthesis followed by the year of reign.

NUMERALS

NUMBER	CONVENTIONAL	FORMAL	COMMERCIAL
1	一 元	壹 弌	〡
2	二	弍 貳	〢
3	三	叁 弎	〣
4	四	肆	〤
5	五	伍	〥
6	六	陸	〦
7	七	柒	〧
8	八	捌	〨
9	九	玖	〩
10	十	拾 什	十
20	十 二 or 廿	拾貳	〢十
25	五 十 二 or 五 廿	伍拾貳	〢十〥
30	十 三 or 卅	拾叁	〣十
100	百 一	佰壹	〡百
1,000	千 一	仟壹	〡千
10,000	萬 一	萬壹	〡万
100,000	萬 十 億 一	萬拾 億壹	十万
1,000,000	萬百一	萬佰壹	〡百万

NOTE: This table has been adapted from *Chinese Bank Notes* by Ward Smith and Brian Matravers.

MONETARY SYSTEM

COPPER AND ZINC

10 Dong (zinc) = 1 Dong (copper)
600 Dong (zinc) = 1 Quan (string of cash)
Approx. 2600 Dong (zinc) = 1 Piastre

NOTE: Ratios between metals changed frequently, therefore the above is given as an approximate relationship.

SILVER AND GOLD

2-1/2 Quan = 1 Lang
10 Tien (Mace) = 1 Lang (Tael)
14 to 17 Piastres (silver) = 1 Piastre (gold)
14 to 17 Lang (silver) = 1 Lang (gold)

The real currency of Dai Nam and An Nam consisted of copper and zinc coins similar to Chinese cash-style coins and were called sapeques and dongs by the French.

The smaller gold pieces saw a limited circulation, mainly among the local merchants and foreign traders. The larger gold pieces were used mainly for hoarding, while most of these were intended as rewards and gifts. Many of these gold pieces appear to have been struck from silver coin dies or vice-versa.

The fineness of the gold and silver pieces varied considerably. The silver and gold dragon coins with the streaked edges were intended to be equivalant to the Mexican and Spanish Colonial 8 Reales (Dollar/Piastre) and 8 Escudos, and their minor denominations, but the silver normally exchanged for much less because their fineness usually ranged from .500 to .700 fine. The gold and silver coins with other designs and smooth edges are generally considered as presentation pieces but some did appear in circulation when their owners came upon hard times. Their fineness usually ranges from .500 to .999. Authentic gold of all designs are rarely found below .850 fine.

Only a few Vietnamese silver and gold pieces are inscribed with their weight and fineness and therefore must be weighed and tested. It should be remembered that Phan, Tien and Lang are weights and not denominations. The pieces inscribed with Van and Quan are money of account terms but could be considered the first Vietnamese denominations. The Vietnamese ignored these terms and exchanged them and all other metalic forms at the prevailing market value of their intrinsic weight and not their inscribed or total weight. Without testing devices or a specific gravity setup, you will only be able to determine the total weight of your piece. For the pieces described in this catalog without weights or terms inscribed on them, they are classified by their total weight. The following table will assist you to determine your pieces Phan, Tien or Lang weight:

PHAN SYSTEM

1 Phan	.3778 grams
5 Phan (or 1/2 Tien)	1.8892 grams
10 Phan (or 1 Tien)	3.7783 grams

TIEN SYSTEM

1/2 Tien (or 5 Phan)	1.8892 grams
1 Tien (or 10 Phan)	3.7783 grams
1/1/2 Tien	5.6675 grams
2 Tien	7.5566 grams
2-1/2 Tien (or 1/4 Lang)	9.4458 grams
3 Tien	11.3349 grams
4 Tien	15.1132 grams
5 Tien (or 1/2 Lang)	18.8915 grams
6 Tien	22.6698 grams
7 Tien	26.4481 grams
8 Tien	30.2264 grams
9 Tien	34.0047 grams
10 Tien (or 1 Lang)	37.7830 grams

LANG SYSTEM

1/2 Lang (or 5 Tien)	18.8915 grams
1 Lang (or 10 Tien)	37.7783 grams
5 Lang	188.9150 grams
10 Lang	377.8300 grams
50 Lang	1889.15 grams
100 Lang	3778.30 grams

NOTE: The Van and Quan pieces are denominations for fiat money. A 10 Van coin was officially worth 10 full weight 1 Tien coins of copper, but, of course, weighed less and less during the inflationary times of their period of issue. The 3 Quan silver bar was officially worth 3 full weight strings of copper coins. The weight of these Van and Quan coins and bars varied considerably and are specified at their listing. The heavier weight pieces are generally the earliest issues with the lighter ones the latest.

PALACE ISSUES

C#53 "1 Mach or 60 Dong"

There are many dollar size and larger copper and brass tokens with obverses similar to the small square holed cash coins listed here with eight, four, or two characters or dragon and fish on the reverse. These were believed to have been given as gifts or bestowed as rewards and circulated to some extent although they do not carry any designation of weight or denomination. The large 130-135mm square holed circular copper pieces with the emperor's name on the obverse and an 8 character legend reverse were displayed in respect of the current emperor. They had a nominal 'trade value' of 600 sapeques as quoted by Bernard J. Permar in *"Catalogue of Annam Coins, 968-1955"*.

NOTE: Sch# are in reference to Albert Schroeder's *"Annam, Etudes Numismatiques"* or to the same numbering system used in *"Gold and Silver Coins of Annam"*, by Bernard Permar and John Novak.

CHARACTER IDENTIFICATION

The Vietnamese used Chinese-style characters for official documents and coins and bars. Some were modified to their liking and will sometimes not match the Chinese character for the same word. The above identification and this table will translate most of the Vietnamese characters (Chinese-style) on their coins and bars described herein.

Chinese/French

Vietnamese/English

An Nam = name of the French protectorate 安南

Dai Nam = name of the country under Gia Long's Nguyen dynasty 大南

Viet Nam = name used briefly during Minh Mang's reign and became the modern name of the country 越南

河內 Ha Noi = city and province in Tonkin

內帑 Noi Thang = court treasury in the capital of Hue

Nien = year 

Tao = made 造

Ngan = silver 銀

Kim = gold 金

Tien = a weight of about 3.78 grams 錢

Lang = a weight of about 37.78 grams 兩

Quan = a string of cash style coins 貫

Phan = a weight of about .38 grams 分

Van = cash-style coins 文

Trung Binh = a name of weight standard 中平

PROVINCIAL DESIGNATORS

An Giang	江安
Bac Ninh	寧北
Binh Dinh	定平
Can Than	申庚
Dinh Tuong	祥定
Gia Dinh	定嘉
Hung Yen	遠興
Lang Son	山諒
Nghe An or	安清 or 安乂
Phu Yen	燕虎
Quang Nam	南廣
Quang Yen	義廣
Son Tay	西山
Thai Nguyen	原太

COPPER, BRASS and ZINC 'CASH' COINAGE

(1 Phan)

CAST BRASS

Rev: Plain.

C#	Date	Emperor	Good	VG	Fine	VF
51.1	(1792-1801)	Canh Thinh	1.25	2.00	3.00	6.00

Rev: Crescent (left), dot (right).

C#	Date	Emperor	Good	VG	Fine	VF
51.2	(1792-1801)	Canh Thinh	3.50	5.50	9.00	16.00

Obv: Double rim.

C#	Date	Emperor	Good	VG	Fine	VF
51.3	(1792-1801)	Canh Thinh	2.25	4.00	6.50	12.00

Obv. & rev: Double rim.

C#	Date	Emperor	Good	VG	Fine	VF
51.4	(1792-1801)	Canh Thinh	3.50	5.50	9.00	16.00

Rev: 4 crescents, tips inward.

C#	Date	Emperor	Good	VG	Fine	VF
51.5	(1792-1801)	Canh Thinh	2.75	5.00	8.00	15.00

Rev: 4 bumps next to inner rim.

C#	Date	Emperor	Good	VG	Fine	VF
51.6	(1792-1801)	Canh Thinh	4.25	7.00	11.00	20.00

Rev: Numeral one (bottom).

C#	Date	Emperor	Good	VG	Fine	VF
51.7	(1792-1801)	Canh Thinh	4.25	7.00	11.00	20.00

Obv: *Dai Bao, Bao* abbreviated.

C#	Date	Emperor	Good	VG	Fine	VF
52.1	(1792-1801)	Canh Thinh	5.75	9.50	16.00	27.00

Obv: *Dai Bao, Bao* abbreviated.
Obv. & rev: Double rim.

C#	Date	Emperor	Good	VG	Fine	VF
52.2	(1792-1801)	Canh Thinh	9.00	14.00	20.00	30.00

NOTE: C#51.1 and 51.4 are reported in tin by Toda.

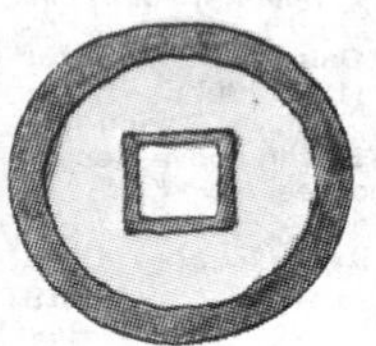

Rev: Plain.

C#	Date	Emperor	Good	VG	Fine	VF
57	(1801-02)	Bao Hung	—	—	Rare	—

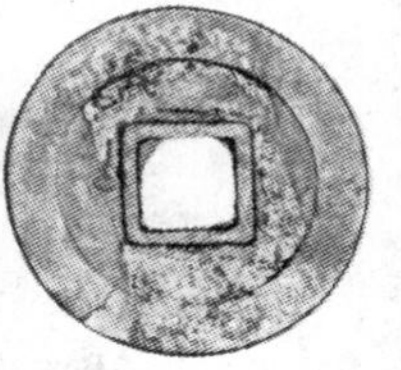

COPPER ALLOYS, 24-25mm

Rev: Plain.

C#	Date	Emperor	Good	VG	Fine	VF
61.1	(1802-20)	Gia Long	1.25	2.00	3.50	6.00

22.6-24mm

C#	Date	Emperor	Good	VG	Fine	VF
61.2	(1802-20)	Gia Long	.85	1.50	2.75	4.50

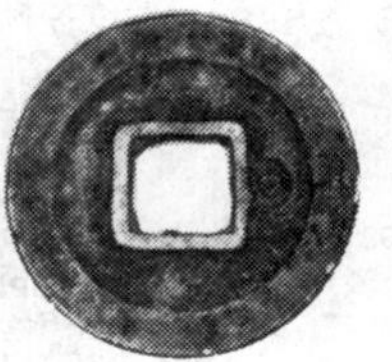

Rev: Dot.

C#	Date	Emperor	Good	VG	Fine	VF
61.3	(1802-20)	Gia Long	2.00	3.50	5.50	9.00

Rev: Circle.

C#	Date	Emperor	Good	VG	Fine	VF
61.3a	(1802-20)	Gia Long	2.00	3.50	5.50	9.00

Obv: Double rim.

C#	Date	Emperor	Good	VG	Fine	VF
61.3b	(1802-20)	Gia Long	2.00	3.50	5.50	9.00

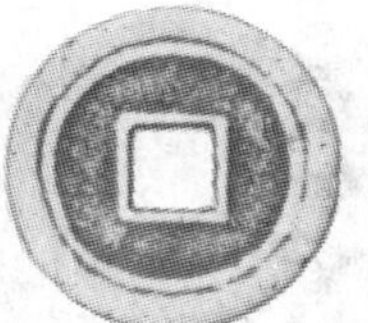

Obv. & rev: Double rim.

C#	Date	Emperor	Good	VG	Fine	VF
61.3c	(1802-20)	Gia Long	2.00	3.50	5.50	9.00

Rev: Crescent.

C#	Date	Emperor	Good	VG	Fine	VF
61.4	(1802-20)	Gia Long	2.75	4.50	7.50	12.50

CAST ZINC

Rev: Plain.

C#	Date	Emperor	Good	VG	Fine	VF
73	(1802-20)	Gia Long	4.50	7.50	12.50	20.00

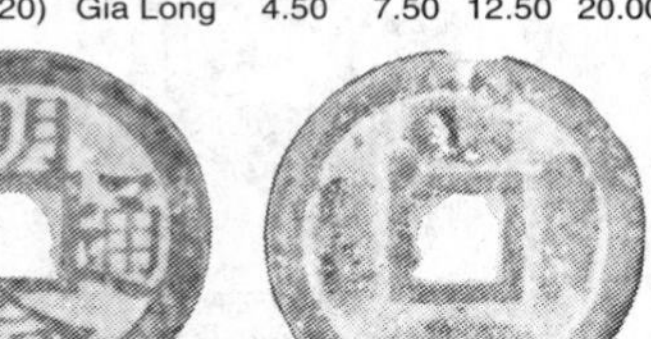

CAST COPPER ALLOYS, 24-25mm

C#	Date	Emperor	Good	VG	Fine	VF
81.1	(1820-41)	Minh Mang	1.00	1.75	2.75	4.50

22.7-24mm

C#	Date	Emperor	Good	VG	Fine	VF
81.2	(1820-41)	Minh Mang	.75	1.25	2.00	3.50

21mm

C#	Date	Emperor	Good	VG	Fine	VF
81.3	(1820-41)	Minh Mang	.75	1.25	2.00	3.50

CAST ZINC

C#	Date	Emperor	Good	VG	Fine	VF
79	(1820-41)	Minh Mang	1.25	2.00	3.50	8.00

CAST COPPER ALLOYS
Nguy Khoi Rebellion
Obv. leg: *Tri Nguyen Thong Bao.*

C#	Date	Emperor	Good	VG	Fine	VF
137	(1831-34)	Tri Nguyen	8.50	13.50	21.50	35.00

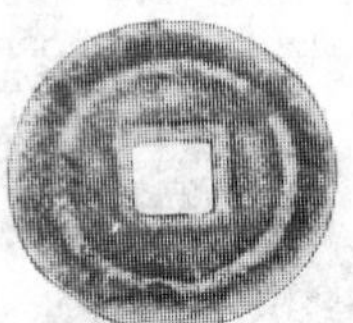

Nung Rebellion
Obv. leg: *Nguyen Long Thong Bao,* cursive *Nguyen.*

C#	Date	Emperor	Good	VG	Fine	VF
138.1	(1832-33)	Nguyen Long	8.50	13.50	21.50	35.00

Obv: Conventional *Nguyen.*

C#	Date	Emperor	Good	VG	Fine	VF
138.2	(1823-33)	Nguyen Long	10.50	18.00	30.00	45.00

Obv: Cursive *Nguyen.* Rev: Double rim.

C#	Date	Emperor	Good	VG	Fine	VF
139.1	(1832-33)	Nguygen Long	10.50	18.00	30.00	45.00

Rev: Character *Xuong.*

C#	Date	Emperor	Good	VG	Fine	VF
139.2	(1832-33)	Nguyen Long	10.50	18.00	30.00	45.00

CAST COPPER ALLOYS, 24-25mm

C#	Date	Emperor	Good	VG	Fine	VF
141.1	(1841-47)	Thieu Tri	.60	1.00	1.75	3.00

23-24mm

C#	Date	Emperor	Good	VG	Fine	VF
141.2	(1841-47)	Thieu Tri	.60	1.00	1.75	3.00

CAST ZINC

C#	Date	Emperor	Good	VG	Fine	VF
140	(1841-47)	Thieu Tri	2.75	4.50	7.50	12.50

CAST COPPER ALLOYS, 24-25mm

C#	Date	Emperor	Good	VG	Fine	VF
201.1	(1848-83)	Tu Duc	1.25	2.00	3.50	6.00

22-24mm

C#	Date	Emperor	Good	VG	Fine	VF
201.2	(1848-83)	Tu Duc	1.25	2.00	3.50	6.00

CAST ZINC
Obv: *Kien Phuc Thong Bao.*

C#	Date	Emperor	Good	VG	Fine	VF
271.1	(1883-84)	Kien Phuc	18.50	30.00	50.00	80.00

Obv: *Phuc* written differently.

C#	Date	Emperor	Good	VG	Fine	VF
271.2	(1883-84)	Kien Phuc	18.50	30.00	50.00	80.00

CAST COPPER ALLOYS
Obv: *Ham Nghi Thong Bao.*

C#	Date	Emperor	Good	VG	Fine	VF
281	(1884-85)	Ham Nghi	35.00	60.00	100.00	165.00

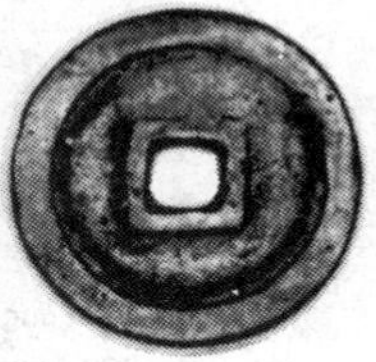

23-24mm

C#	Date	Emperor	Good	VG	Fine	VF
301.1	(1885-88)	Dong Khanh	2.75	4.50	7.50	12.50

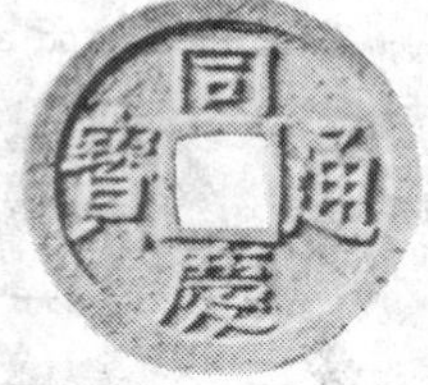

26mm

C#	Date	Emperor	Good	VG	Fine	VF
301.2	(1885-88)	Dong Khanh	11.50	18.50	30.00	50.00

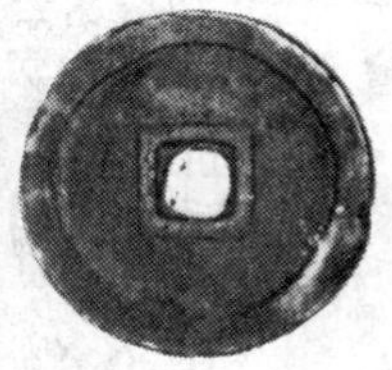

Rev: Blank.

Y#	Date	Emperor	Good	VG	Fine	VF
1	(1888-1907)	Thanh Thai	2.00	3.50	5.50	9.00

CASH
(6 Phan)

CAST COPPER ALLOYS
Rev: *Luc Phan* in seal script.

C#	Date	Emperor	Good	VG	Fine	VF
62	(1802-20)	Gia Long	2.75	4.50	7.50	12.50

CASH
(7 Phan)

CAST ZINC
Rev: *That Phan.*

C#	Date	Emperor	Good	VG	Fine	VF
63	(1802-20)	Gia Long	5.50	9.00	15.00	25.00

6 VAN

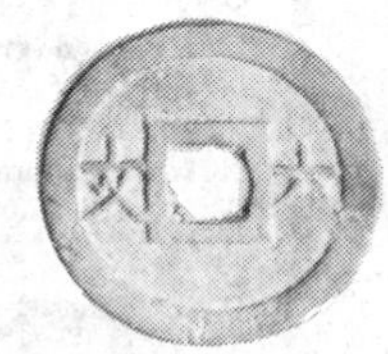

CAST COPPER ALLOYS, 24-26mm
Rev: *Luc Van.*

C#	Date	Emperor	Good	VG	Fine	VF
202	(1848-83)	Tu Duc	1.25	2.00	3.50	6.00

23mm

C#	Date	Emperor	Good	VG	Fine	VF
202.1	(1848-83)	Tu Duc	1.25	2.00	3.50	6.00

C#	Date	Emperor	Good	VG	Fine	VF
282	(1884-85)	Ham Nghi	35.00	60.00	100.00	165.00

Y#	Date	Emperor	Good	VG	Fine	VF
A2	(1888-1907)	Thanh Thai	—	—	—	—

NOTE: The above piece has been questioned by some authorities.

8 VAN

CAST ZINC
Rev: Plain.

C#	Date	Emperor	Good	VG	Fine	VF
191	(1848-83)	Tu Duc	2.00	3.50	5.50	9.00

Rev: *Ha Noi.*

C#	Date	Emperor	Good	VG	Fine	VF
192.1	(1848-83)	Tu Duc	5.00	8.50	13.50	21.50

Rev: *Son Tay.*

C#	Date	Emperor	Good	VG	Fine	VF
192.2	(1848-83)	Tu Duc	6.00	10.00	16.50	25.00

CAST COPPER ALLOYS
Obv: *Trung Bao* (heavy currency).
Rev: *Bat Van* and *An Nam.*

C#	Date	Emperor	Good	VG	Fine	VF
203	(1848-83)	Tu Duc	—	—	Rare	—

10 VAN

CAST COPPER ALLOYS
Rev: 4 Chinese characters *Tang . . . Shih Wen.*

C#	Date	Emperor	Good	VG	Fine	VF
65	(1802-20)	Gia Long	11.50	18.50	30.00	50.00

Rev: *Chuan Thap Van.*

C#	Date	Emperor	Good	VG	Fine	VF
204	(1848-83)	Tu Duc	11.50	18.50	30.00	50.00

Rev: *Chuan Nhat Thap Van.*

C#	Date	Emperor	Good	VG	Fine	VF
204a	(1848-83)	Tu Duc	11.50	18.50	30.00	50.00

Rev: *Thap Van.*

Y#	Date	Emperor	Good	VG	Fine	VF
2	(1888-1907)	Thanh Thai	.50	.75	1.25	2.50

NOTE: Later issues after the French colonial coinage was introduced in 1885 are considered awards for various services.

20 VAN

CAST COPPER or BRASS
Rev: *Chuan Nhi Thap Van.*

C#	Date	Emperor	Good	VG	Fine	VF
205	(1848-83)	Tu Duc	70.00	100.00	140.00	200.00

30 VAN

CAST COPPER or BRASS
Rev: *Chuan Tam Thap Van.*

C#	Date	Emperor	Good	VG	Fine	VF
205.5	(1848-83)	Tu Duc	85.00	120.00	170.00	240.00

40 VAN

CAST COPPER or BRASS
Rev: *Chuan Tu Thap Van.*

C#	Date	Emperor	Good	VG	Fine	VF
206	(1848-83)	Tu Duc	85.00	120.00	170.00	240.00

50 VAN

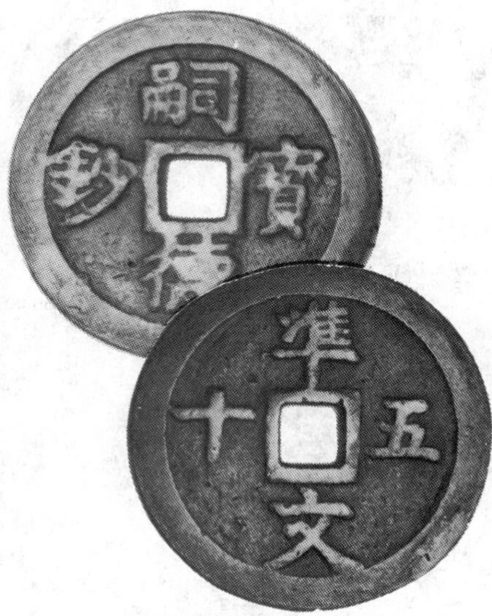

CAST COPPER or BRASS
Rev: *Chuan Ngu Thap Van*.

C#	Date	Emperor	Good	VG	Fine	VF
206.5	(1848-83)	Tu Duc	70.00	100.00	140.00	200.00

60 VAN

CAST COPPER or BRASS, 43mm
Rev: *Chuan Luc Thap Van*.

C#	Date	Emperor	Good	VG	Fine	VF
207.1	(1848-83)	Tu Duc	42.50	60.00	85.00	120.00

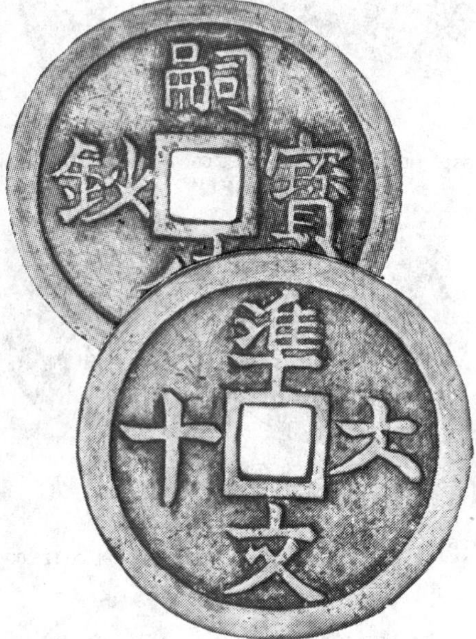

47-49mm

C#	Date	Emperor	Good	VG	Fine	VF
207.2	(1848-83)	Tu Duc	42.50	60.00	85.00	120.00

SILVER COINAGE

The silver dragon coins with crude oblique milled edges are considered to be those in imitation of the Mexican/Spanish Colonial 8 Reales (Dollar/Piastre) coins and its minor denominations. The smooth edge silver dragon coins and those with square center holes are considered presentation pieces. Each coin is compared to the Weight System table in the introduction and assigned the respective Tien or Lang designation corresponding to its actual weight in grams.

VIRTUES

Certain coins were issued in weights from 1 Tien through 1 Lang each with a different virtue.

1 Tien - Viet Tu (benignity)
2 Tien - Viet Hein (gratitude)
3 Tien - Viet Lang (kindness)
4 Tien - Viet De (respect)
5 Tien - Viet Ngai (justice)
6 Tien - Viet Thinh (obedience)
7 Tien - Viet Hue (benevolence)
8 Tien - Viet Thuan (submissiveness)
9 Tien - Viet Nhan (humanity)
1 Lang - Viet Trung (faithfulness)

"THONG BAO" SERIES

1/2 TIEN

SILVER, 1.80 g
Obv. leg: *Thieu Tri Thong Bao*. Rev: Blank.

Sch#	Date	Emperor	VG	Fine	VF	XF
257	ND(1841-47)	Thieu Tri	30.00	60.00	100.00	175.00

NOTE: Cash-style coins of silver were used as presentation pieces and were not meant for general circulation.

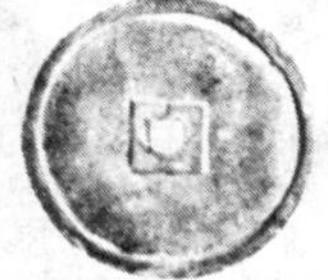

1.50 g
Obv. leg: *Tu Duc Thong Bao*.

Sch#	Date	Emperor	VG	Fine	VF	XF
367	ND(1848-83)	Tu Duc	27.50	55.00	90.00	160.00

Rev. leg: *Su Dan Phu Tho*.

Sch#	Date	Emperor	VG	Fine	VF	XF
367B	ND(1848-83)	Tu Duc	30.00	60.00	100.00	175.00

TIEN

SILVER, 4.50 g
Obv. leg: *Minh Mang Thong Bao*.

Sch#	Date	Emperor	VG	Fine	VF	XF
180	ND(1820-41)	Minh Mang	30.00	60.00	100.00	175.00

NOTE: Cash-style coins of silver were used as presentation pieces and were not meant for general circulation.

3.60 g
Obv. leg: *Thieu Tri Thong Bao*.
Rev. leg: *Nhat Nguyen*.

Sch#	Date	Emperor	VG	Fine	VF	XF
250	ND(1841-47)	Thieu Tri	30.00	60.00	100.00	175.00

3.70-4.00 g
Rev: Sun, moon and 5 planets.

Sch#	Date	Emperor	VG	Fine	VF	XF
262	ND(1841-47)	Thieu Tri	27.50	55.00	90.00	160.00

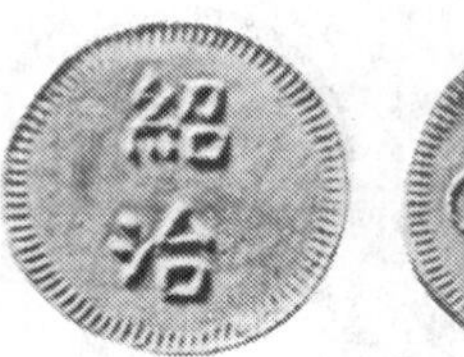

3.60-4.00 g
Obv. leg: *Thieu Tri*. Rev: Scepter and swastika.

Sch#	Date	Emperor	VG	Fine	VF	XF
264	ND(1841-47)	Thieu Tri	27.50	55.00	90.00	160.00

Rev: Mirror image of Sch#264.

Sch#	Date	Emperor	VG	Fine	VF	XF
265	ND(1841-47)	Thieu Tri	27.50	55.00	90.00	160.00

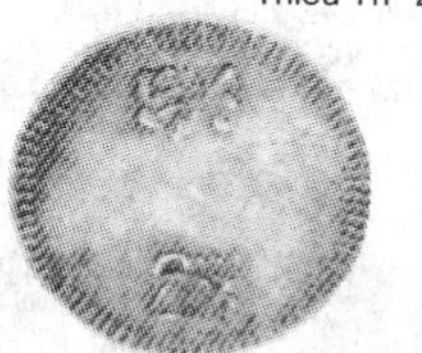
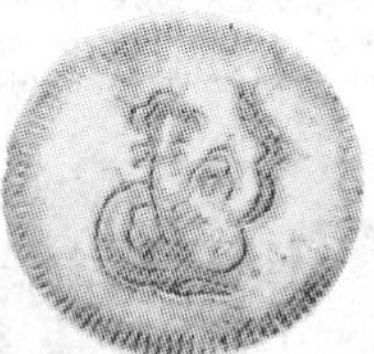

4.00 g
Obv. leg: *Thieu Tri*. Rev: Guitar.

Sch#	Date	Emperor	VG	Fine	VF	XF
266A	ND(1841-47)	Thieu Tri	35.00	70.00	120.00	200.00

3.70 g
Rev. leg: *Tam Da*, above the Three Plenties.

Sch#	Date	Emperor	VG	Fine	VF	XF
267	ND(1841-47)	Thieu Tri	30.00	60.00	100.00	170.00

Rev: Flaming sun.

Sch#	Date	Emperor	VG	Fine	VF	XF
287A	ND(1841-47)	Thieu Tri	21.50	42.50	70.00	125.00

Rev: Fan

Sch#	Date	Emperor	VG	Fine	VF	XF
291A	ND(1841-47)	Thieu Tri	35.00	70.00	120.00	200.00

Obv. leg: *Thieu Tri Thong Bao*.
Rev: Two scepters and two swastikas.

Sch#	Date	Emperor	VG	Fine	VF	XF
256	ND(1841-47)	Thieu Tri	32.50	65.00	110.00	200.00

3.50 g
Obv. leg: *Tu Duc Thong Bao*.
Rev. leg: *Nhat Nguyen* cosmic evolution.

Sch#	Date	Emperor	VG	Fine	VF	XF
353	ND(1848-83)	Tu Duc	30.00	60.00	100.00	175.00

3.70 g
Rev: Sun, moon and 5 planets.

Sch#	Date	Emperor	VG	Fine	VF	XF
352	ND(1848-83)	Tu Duc	27.50	55.00	90.00	160.00

3.74 g
Rev. leg: ***Nhat Duc*** **between 2 stylized fish.**

Sch#	Date	Emperor	VG	Fine	VF	XF
354.1	ND(1848-83)	Tu Duc	27.50	55.00	90.00	160.00

 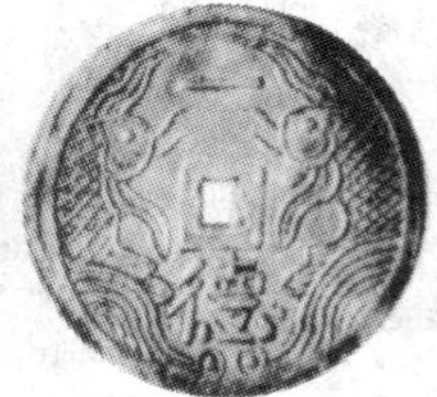

Rev. leg: ***Nhat Duc*** **between 2 goldfish.**

354.2	ND(1848-83)	Tu Duc	27.50	55.00	90.00	160.00

3.80 g
Rev. leg: ***Nhi Duc*** **between sun, moon and clouds.**

355B	ND(1848-83)	Tu Duc	30.00	60.00	100.00	175.00

Obv. and rev: Small characters.
Rev. leg: ***Tam Da*****, above the Three Plenties.**

357.1	ND(1848-83)	Tu Duc	35.00	70.00	120.00	200.00

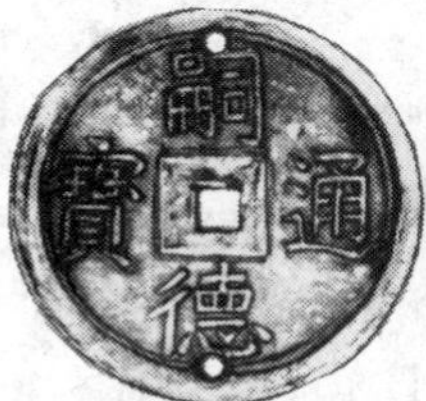 

Obv. and rev: Large characters.

357.2	ND(1848-83)	Tu Duc	35.00	70.00	120.00	200.00

3.60 g
Rev: 2 swastikas and 2 scepters which look like flowers.

361	ND(1848-83)	Tu Duc	32.50	65.00	130.00	225.00

3.70 g
Rev. leg: ***Tu Bao*****, between Four Precious Objects.**

362	ND(1848-83)	Tu Duc	35.00	70.00	120.00	200.00

3.30 g
Rev: The Five Precious Objects.

363	ND(1848-83)	Tu Duc	30.00	60.00	100.00	175.00

3.50-3.70 g
Rev: Eight Precious Objects.

364	ND(1848-83)	Tu Duc	30.00	60.00	100.00	175.00

NOTE: There are three varieties of this coin based upon the placement of the symbols.

3.80 g
Rev. leg: ***Nhat Tien Viet Tu*** **on dragon.**

Sch#	Date	Emperor	VG	Fine	VF	XF
377	ND(1848-83)	Tu Duc	30.00	60.00	100.00	175.00

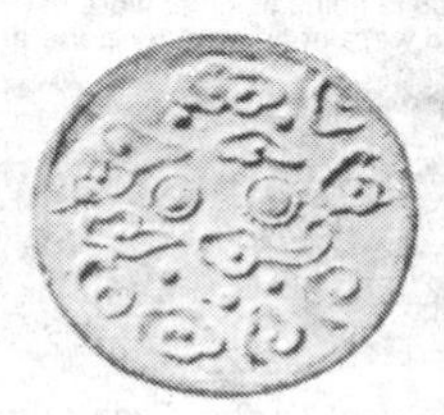

3.90 g
Rev: Sun, moon and 5 planets.

386	ND(1848-83)	Tu Duc	27.50	55.00	90.00	160.00

4.00 g
Rev. leg: ***Tam Da*****, above Three Plenties.**

387	ND(1848-83)	Tu Duc	27.50	55.00	90.00	160.00

4.10 g
Rev: Scepter and Swastika.

388	ND(1848-83)	Tu Duc	35.00	70.00	120.00	200.00

3.80 g
Rev: Horn.

389	ND(1848-83)	Tu Duc	32.50	65.00	110.00	180.00

3.50 g
Rev: Five Precious Objects.

390	ND(1848-83)	Tu Duc	27.50	55.00	90.00	160.00

1-1/2 TIEN

SILVER, 5.00-6.00 g
Obv. leg: ***Minh Mang*****.**

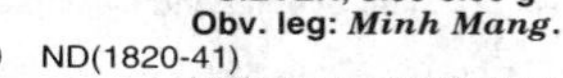

189	ND(1820-41)	Minh Mang	27.50	55.00	90.00	160.00

5.63 g
Obv. leg: ***Thieu Tri*****.**

Sch#	Date	Emperor	VG	Fine	VF	XF
266B	ND(1841-47)	Thieu Tri	32.50	65.00	110.00	180.00

5.20 g
Obv. leg: ***Tu Duc Thong Bao*****.**
Rev. leg: ***Phu Tho Da Nam*****.**

358	ND(1848-83)	Tu Duc	35.00	70.00	120.00	200.00

5.30 g
Rev. leg: ***Su Dan Phu Tho*****.**

351C	ND(1848-83)	Tu Duc	35.00	70.00	120.00	200.00

2 TIEN

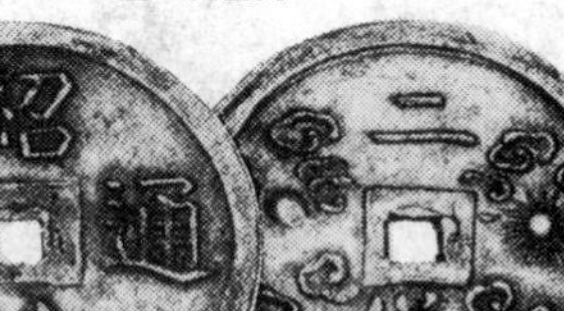

SILVER, 7.60 g
Obv. leg: ***Thieu Tri Thong Bao*****.**
Rev. leg: ***Nhi Nghi*****, between sun, moon and clouds.**

251	ND(1841-47)	Thieu Tri	30.00	60.00	100.00	175.00

7.50 g
Rev: 2 facing dragons.

240	ND(1841-47)	Thieu Tri	45.00	90.00	150.00	250.00

7.60 g
Obv. leg: ***Tu Duc Thong Bao*****.**
Rev. leg: ***Su Dan Phu Tho*****.**

351B	ND(1848-83)	Tu Duc	30.00	60.00	100.00	175.00

6.60 g
Obv. leg: ***Tu Duc Thong Bao.***
Rev. leg: ***Nhi Nghi*** **between sun, moon and clouds.**

Sch#	Date	Emperor	VG	Fine	VF	XF
355	ND(1848-83)	Tu Duc	42.50	90.00	150.00	250.00

7.30 g
Rev. leg: ***Nhi Tien Viet Hien*** **on dragon.**

Sch#	Date	Emperor	VG	Fine	VF	XF
378	ND(1848-83)	Tu Duc	45.00	90.00	150.00	250.00

Rev: 2 facing dragons.

Sch#	Date	Emperor	VG	Fine	VF	XF
—	ND(1848-83)	Tu Duc	42.50	90.00	150.00	250.00

Obv. leg: ***Dong Khanh Thong Bao.***
Rev. leg: ***Su Dan Phu Tho.***

Sch#	Date	Emperor	VG	Fine	VF	XF
420	ND(1885-89)	Dong Khanh	45.00	90.00	150.00	250.00

Rev. leg: ***Nhi Nghi*** **between sun, moon and clouds.**

Sch#	Date	Emperor	VG	Fine	VF	XF
425A	ND(1885-89)	Dong Khanh	45.00	90.00	150.00	250.00

NOTE: Later issues after the French colonial coinage was introduced in 1885 are considered awards for various services.

1/4 LANG

SILVER, 9.20 g
Obv. leg: ***Thieu Tri Thong Bao, Trieu Dan Lai Chi.*** **Rev: Dragon.**

Sch#	Date	Emperor	VG	Fine	VF	XF
249	ND(1841-47)	Thieu Tri	50.00	100.00	175.00	300.00

9.60 g
Obv. leg: ***Thieu Tri Thong Bao*** **around flaming sun.**
Rev. leg: ***Long Van Khe Hoi*** **around dragon.**

Sch#	Date	Emperor	VG	Fine	VF	XF
261	ND(1841-47)	Thieu Tri	62.50	125.00	200.00	350.00

9.40 g
Obv. leg: ***Tu Duc Thong Bao, Trieu Dan Lai Chi.*** **Rev: Simple dragon.**

Sch#	Date	Emperor	VG	Fine	VF	XF
350.1	ND(1848-83)	Tu Duc	50.00	100.00	175.00	300.00

Rev: Round faced dragon w/streamers.

Sch#	Date	Emperor	VG	Fine	VF	XF
350.2	ND(1848-83)	Tu Duc	50.00	100.00	175.00	300.00

Rev: Ornate dragon.

Sch#	Date	Emperor	VG	Fine	VF	XF
350.3	ND(1848-83)	Tu Duc	50.00	100.00	175.00	300.00

9.50-9.80 g
Obv. leg: ***Tu Duc Thong Bao*** **around flaming sun.**
Rev. leg: ***Long Van Khe Hoi*** **around dragon.**

Sch#	Date	Emperor	VG	Fine	VF	XF
375	ND(1848-83)	Tu Duc	62.50	125.00	200.00	350.00

8.80 g
Obv. leg: ***Dong Khanh Thong Bao*** **around flaming sun.**
Rev. leg: ***Long Van Khe Hoi*** **around dragon.**

Sch#	Date	Emperor	VG	Fine	VF	XF
422	ND(1885-88)	Dong Khanh	62.50	125.00	200.00	350.00

NOTE: Later issues after the French colonial coinage was introduced in 1885 are considered awards for various services.

3 TIEN

SILVER, 13.30-13.70 g
Obv. leg: ***Minh Mang Thong Bao.***
Rev: Dragon.

Sch#	Date	Emperor	VG	Fine	VF	XF
184	ND(1820-41)	Minh Mang	67.50	135.00	225.00	375.00
185	(1833) Yr.14	Minh Mang	67.50	135.00	225.00	375.00

Sch#	Date	Emperor	VG	Fine	VF	XF
186	(1834) Yr.15	Minh Mang	67.50	135.00	225.00	375.00

13.30 g
Obv. leg: ***Thieu Tri Thong Bao.***

Rev: 2 facing dragons.

Sch#	Date	Emperor	VG	Fine	VF	XF
239	ND(1841-47)	Thieu Tri	70.00	140.00	240.00	400.00

13.50 g
Obv. leg: *Thieu Tri Thong Bao*.
Rev: Small dragon.

Sch#	Date	Emperor	VG	Fine	VF	XF
260	ND(1841-47)	Thieu Tri	67.50	135.00	225.00	375.00

13.34 g
Rev: Large dragon.

Sch#	Date	Emperor	VG	Fine	VF	XF
259	ND(1841-47)	Thieu Tri	67.50	135.00	225.00	375.00

11.90 g
Rev. leg: *Tam Tho*, above Three Longevities.

Sch#	Date	Emperor	VG	Fine	VF	XF
252	ND(1841-47)	Thieu Tri	67.50	135.00	225.00	375.00

Obv. leg: *Tu Duc Thong Bao*.
Rev. leg: *Long Van* on facing dragon.

Sch#	Date	Emperor	VG	Fine	VF	XF
373	ND(1848-83)	Tu Duc	70.00	140.00	240.00	400.00

11.30 g
Rev. leg: *Tam Tien Viet Lang* on dragon.

Sch#	Date	Emperor	VG	Fine	VF	XF
379	ND(1848-83)	Tu Duc	70.00	140.00	240.00	400.00

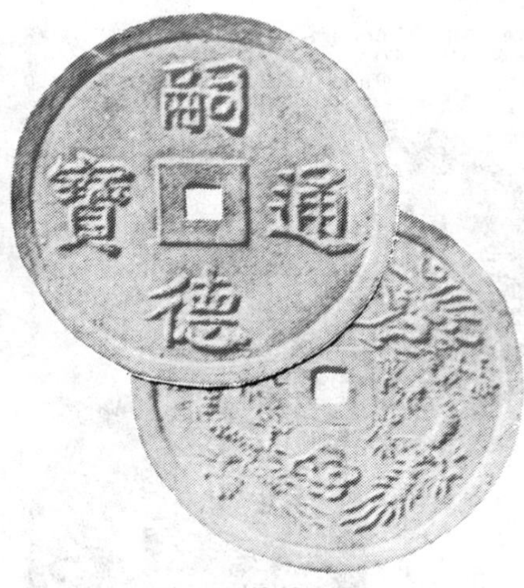

13.10 g
Rev: Flaming sun between 2 facing dragons w/long tails.

Sch#	Date	Emperor	VG	Fine	VF	XF
347.1	ND(1848-83)	Tu Duc	70.00	140.00	240.00	400.00

Rev: 2 facing dragons w/short tails.

Sch#	Date	Emperor	VG	Fine	VF	XF
347.2	ND(1848-83)	Tu Duc	70.00	140.00	240.00	400.00

Rev: Clouds below dragon's long tails.

Sch#	Date	Emperor	VG	Fine	VF	XF
347.3	ND(1848-83)	Tu Duc	70.00	140.00	240.00	400.00

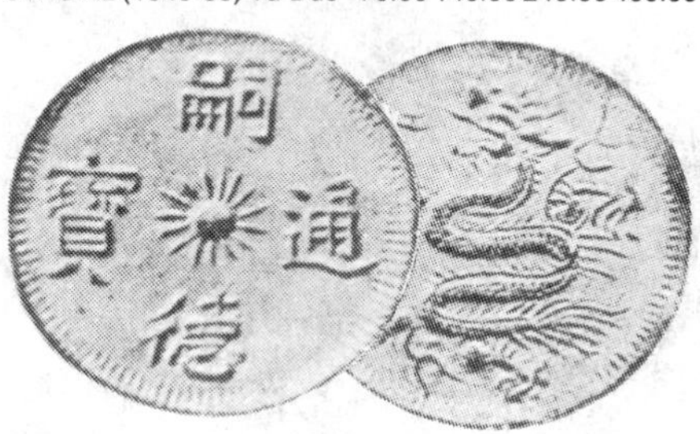

13.30 g

Sch#	Date	Emperor	VG	Fine	VF	XF
369	ND(1848-83)	Tu Duc	67.50	135.00	225.00	375.00

Plain edge, 32.2mm, 13.45 g

Sch#	Date	Emperor	VG	Fine	VF	XF
369A	ND(1848-83)	Tu Duc	45.00	90.00	150.00	250.00

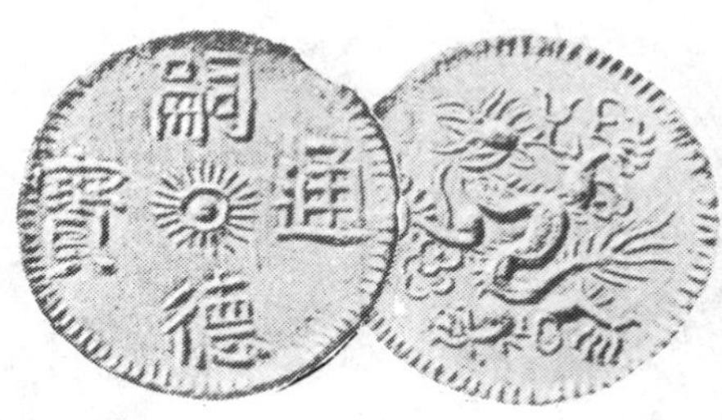

12.40 g
Obv: Dot in center of sun.

Sch#	Date	Emperor	VG	Fine	VF	XF
370	ND(1848-83)	Tu Duc	45.00	90.00	150.00	250.00

Obv. leg: Large characters.
Rev. leg: *Tam Tho* above the Three Longevities.

Sch#	Date	Emperor	VG	Fine	VF	XF
407A	ND(1848-83)	Tu Duc	50.00	100.00	175.00	300.00

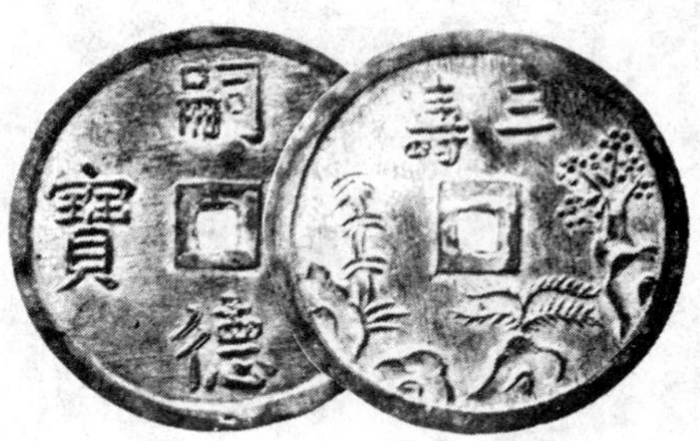

Obv. leg: Small characters. Rev: Finer style.

Sch#	Date	Emperor	VG	Fine	VF	XF
407B	ND(1848-83)	Tu Duc	50.00	100.00	175.00	300.00

Rev: 1 hill at bottom.

Sch#	Date	Emperor	VG	Fine	VF	XF
407C	ND(1848-83)	Tu Duc	50.00	100.00	175.00	300.00

Rev: Dragon.

Sch#	Date	Emperor	VG	Fine	VF	XF
414	ND(1848-83)	Tu Duc	50.00	100.00	175.00	300.00

10.20 g
Obv. leg: *Dong Khanh Thong Bao*.
Rev. leg: *Su Dan Da Nam*.

Sch#	Date	Emperor	VG	Fine	VF	XF
421	ND(1885-88)	Dong Khanh	62.50	125.00	225.00	375.00

SILVER, 15.30 g
Obv. leg: *Thanh Thai Thong Bao*.
Rev: Dragon.

Sch#	Date	Emperor	VG	Fine	VF	XF
428	ND(1888-1907)	Thanh Thai	70.00	140.00	240.00	400.00

4 TIEN

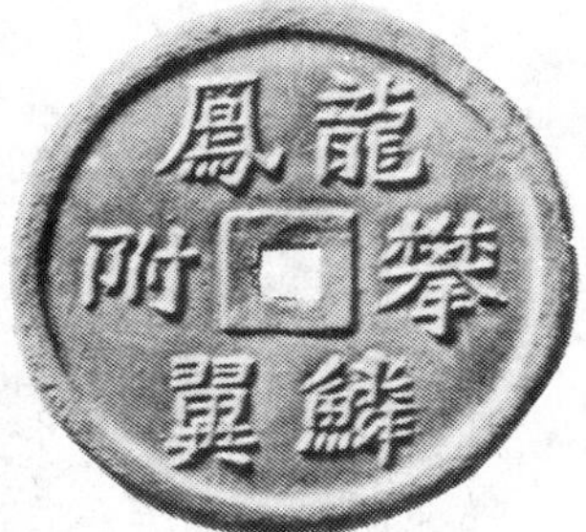

SILVER, 15.50 g
Obv. leg: *Thieu Tri* between bird and dragon.
Rev. leg: *Phan Long Lau Phu Phung Duc*.

Sch#	Date	Emperor	VG	Fine	VF	XF
246	ND(1841-47)	Thieu Tri	70.00	140.00	240.00	400.00

Obv. leg: *Thieu Tri Thong Bao*.
Rev. leg: *Tu My* between Four Perfections.

Sch#	Date	Emperor	VG	Fine	VF	XF
254	ND(1841-47)	Thieu Tri	62.50	125.00	225.00	375.00

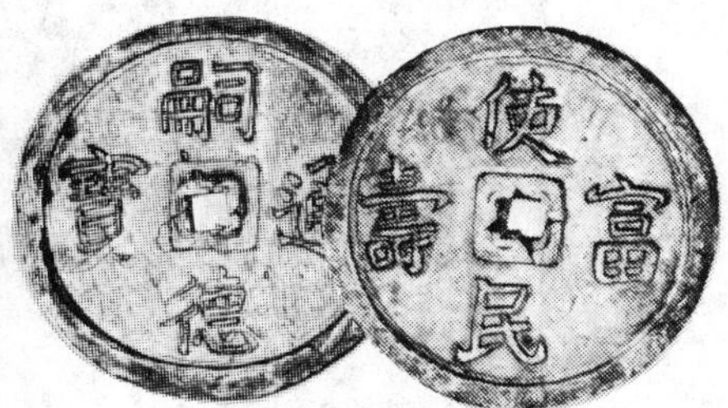

15.00-15.50 g
Obv. leg: *Tu Duc Thong Bao*.
Rev. leg: *Su Dan Phu Tho*.

Sch#	Date	Emperor	VG	Fine	VF	XF
351	ND(1848-83)	Tu Duc	62.50	125.00	225.00	375.00

15.00 g
Rev. leg: *Tu Tien Viet De* on dragon.

Sch#	Date	Emperor	VG	Fine	VF	XF
380	ND(1848-83)	Tu Duc	70.00	140.00	240.00	400.00

Rev. leg: *Tu My* between - Four Perfections.

Sch#	Date	Emperor	VG	Fine	VF	XF
—	ND(1848-83)	Tu Duc	70.00	140.00	240.00	400.00

Rev: Design finer style.

Sch#	Date	Emperor	VG	Fine	VF	XF
—	ND(1848-83)	Tu Duc	70.00	140.00	240.00	400.00

Obv. leg: *Dong Khanh Thong Bao*.
Rev. leg: *Tu My* between - Four Perfections.

Sch#	Date	Emperor	VG	Fine	VF	XF
—	ND(1885-88)	Dong Khanh	80.00	160.00	275.00	450.00

NOTE: Later issues after the French colonial coinage was introduced in 1885 are considered awards for various services.

5 TIEN

SILVER, 19.00 g
Obv. leg: *Minh Mang Thong Bao*.
Rev. leg: *Long Van* on facing dragon.

Sch#	Date	Emperor	VG	Fine	VF	XF
188	ND(1820-41)	Minh Mang	70.00	140.00	240.00	400.00

Obv. leg: *Thieu Tri Thong Bao*, *Van The Vinh Lai*.

Sch#	Date	Emperor	VG	Fine	VF	XF
242	ND(1841-47)	Thieu Tri	80.00	160.00	275.00	450.00

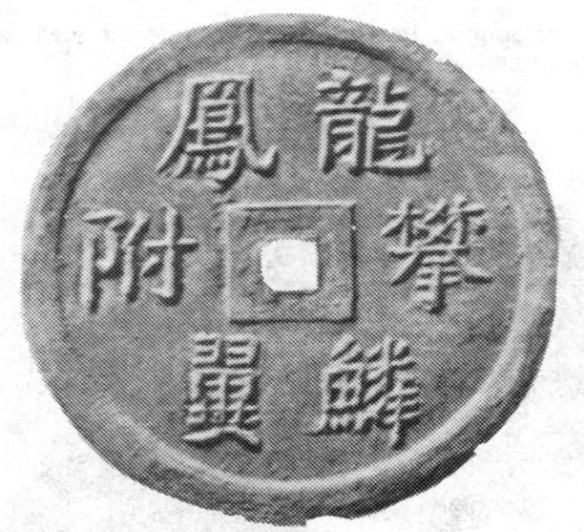

19.20 g
Obv. leg: *Thieu Tri* between bird and dragon. Rev. leg: *Phan Long Lau Phu Phung Duc*.

Sch#	Date	Emperor	VG	Fine	VF	XF
243	ND(1841-47)	Thieu Tri	80.00	160.00	275.00	450.00

18.50-19.00 g
Obv. leg: *Thieu Tri Thong Bao, Trieu Dan Lai Chi*. Rev: Facing dragon.

Sch#	Date	Emperor	VG	Fine	VF	XF
247	ND(1841-47)	Thieu Tri	70.00	140.00	240.00	400.00

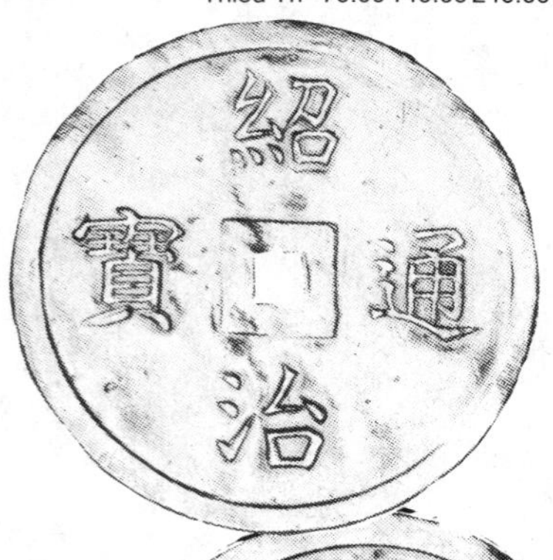

17.00-18.50 g
Obv. leg: *Thieu Tri Thong Bao*. Rev. leg: *Phu Tho Da Nam*.

Sch#	Date	Emperor	VG	Fine	VF	XF
253	ND(1841-47)	Thieu Tri	70.00	140.00	240.00	400.00

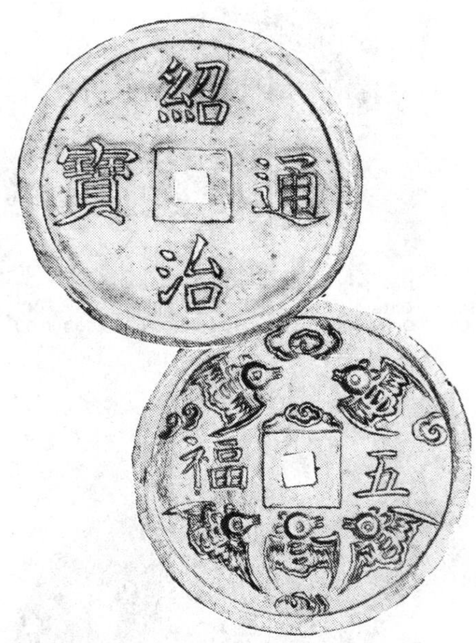

Rev. leg: *Ngu Phuc* between five bats.

Sch#	Date	Emperor	VG	Fine	VF	XF
255	ND(1841-47)	Thieu Tri	80.00	160.00	275.00	450.00

19.00 g
Rev. leg: *Long Van Khe Hoi* around facing dragon.

Sch#	Date	Emperor	VG	Fine	VF	XF
261	ND(1841-47)	Thieu Tri	80.00	160.00	275.00	450.00

43mm, 26.60 g
Obv. leg: *Tu Duc Thong Bao*. Rev: 2 facing dragons.

Sch#	Date	Emperor	VG	Fine	VF	XF
347A	ND(1848-83)	Tu Duc	100.00	200.00	325.00	550.00

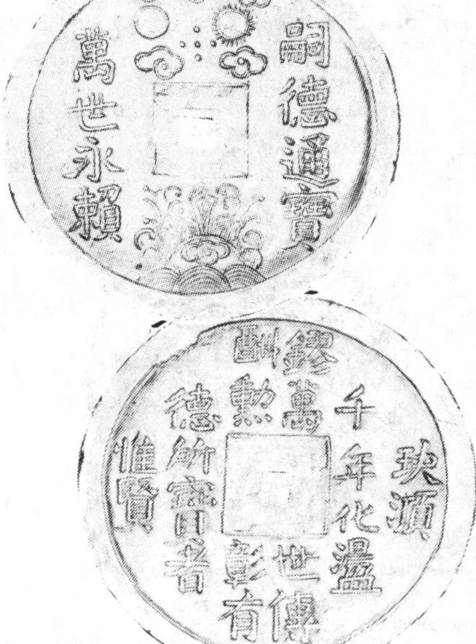

Obv. leg: *Tu Duc Thong Bao, Van The Vinh Lai*.

Sch#	Date	Emperor	VG	Fine	VF	XF
348	ND(1848-83)	Tu Duc	80.00	160.00	275.00	450.00

18.00 g
Obv. leg: *Tu Duc Thong Bao, Trieu Dan Lai Chi*.

Sch#	Date	Emperor	VG	Fine	VF	XF
349.1	ND(1848-83)	Tu Duc	70.00	140.00	240.00	400.00

Rev: Round faced dragon.

Sch#	Date	Emperor	VG	Fine	VF	XF
349.2	ND(1848-83)	Tu Duc	70.00	140.00	240.00	400.00

18.90 g
Obv. leg: *Tu Duc Thong Bao.*
Rev. leg: *Ngu Phuc* between five bats.

Sch#	Date	Emperor	VG	Fine	VF	XF
359	ND(1848-83)	Tu Duc	80.00	160.00	275.00	450.00

18.50 g
Obv. & rev: Small sun at center.
Rev. leg: *Long Van* on facing dragon.

Sch#	Date	Emperor	VG	Fine	VF	XF
372.1	ND(1848-83)	Tu Duc	80.00	160.00	275.00	450.00

Obv. & rev: Large sun at center.

Sch#	Date	Emperor	VG	Fine	VF	XF
372.2	ND(1848-83)	Tu Duc	80.00	160.00	275.00	450.00

18.90-20.00 g
Obv: Flaming sun at center.
Rev. leg: *Long Van Khe Hoi* around facing dragon.

Sch#	Date	Emperor	VG	Fine	VF	XF
374.1	ND(1848-83)	Tu Duc	80.00	160.00	275.00	450.00

Rev: Cloud below *Hoi* at left.

Sch#	Date	Emperor	VG	Fine	VF	XF
374.2	ND(1848-83)	Tu Duc	80.00	160.00	275.00	450.00

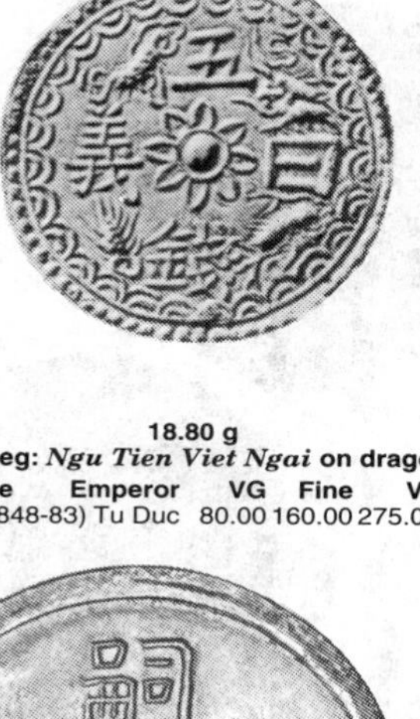

18.80 g
Rev. leg: *Ngu Tien Viet Ngai* on dragon.

Sch#	Date	Emperor	VG	Fine	VF	XF
381	ND(1848-83)	Tu Duc	80.00	160.00	275.00	450.00

17.00 g
Rev. leg: *Phu Tho Da Nam.*

Sch#	Date	Emperor	VG	Fine	VF	XF
408A	ND(1848-83)	Tu Duc	70.00	140.00	240.00	400.00

6 TIEN

SILVER, 23.00 g
Obv. leg: *Tu Duc Thong Bao.*
Rev. leg: *Luc Tien Viet Thinh* on dragon.

Sch#	Date	Emperor	VG	Fine	VF	XF
382	ND(1848-83)	Tu Duc	100.00	200.00	350.00	600.00

7 TIEN

SILVER, 35mm, 26.30-26.70 g
Obv. leg: *Minh Mang Thong Bao*, around large sun. Rev: Small dragon.

Sch#	Date	Emperor	VG	Fine	VF	XF
181A	ND(1820-48)	Minh Mang	140.00	280.00	450.00	750.00

NOTE: Plain edge silver dragon coins are considered as medallic or presentation pieces while the crude oblique milled edge versions were meant for circulation for most Emperors.

40-42mm, 26.66-27.42 g
Obv: Large sun. Rev: Large dragon.

Sch#	Date	Emperor	VG	Fine	VF	XF
181B	ND(1820-48)	Minh Mang	140.00	280.00	450.00	600.00

Sch#	Date	Emperor	VG	Fine	VF	XF
181	(1832) Yr.13	Minh Mang	90.00	180.00	300.00	500.00

Obv: Small sun. Rev: Large dragon.

Sch#	Date	Emperor	VG	Fine	VF	XF
182	(1833) Yr.14	Minh Mang	70.00	140.00	240.00	400.00
183	(1834) Yr.15	Minh Mang	40.00	80.00	150.00	250.00

Sch#	Date	Emperor	VG	Fine	VF	XF
183A	(1835) Yr.16	Minh Mang	90.00	180.00	300.00	500.00

25.80-26.40 g
Obv. leg: *Thieu Tri Thong Bao*.
Rev: 2 facing dragons.

Sch#	Date	Emperor	VG	Fine	VF	XF
238	ND(1841-47)	Thieu Tri	175.00	350.00	600.00	1000.

26.40-28.50 g
Obv. leg: *Thieu Tri* between bird and dragon.
Rev. leg: *Phan Long Lan Phu Phung Duc*.

Sch#	Date	Emperor	VG	Fine	VF	XF
244	ND(1841-47)	Thieu Tri	90.00	180.00	300.00	500.00

40.5mm, 26.50 g
Obv. large leg: *Thieu Tri Thong Bao*.
Rev: Small dragon left.

Sch#	Date	Emperor	VG	Fine	VF	XF
258.1	ND(1841-47)	Thieu Tri	70.00	140.00	240.00	400.00

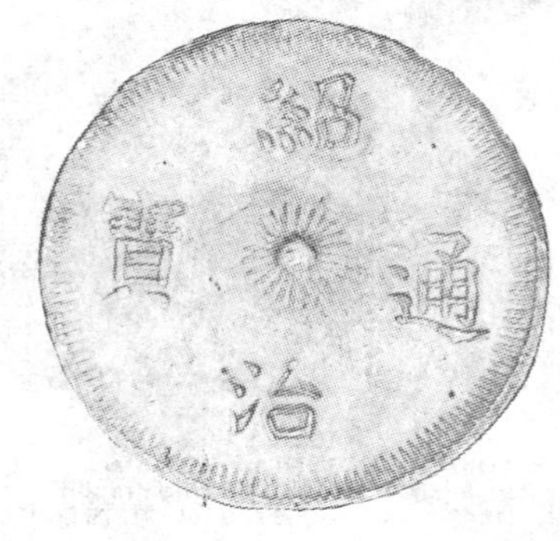

Obv: Small leg.
Rev: Large dragon left.

Sch#	Date	Emperor	VG	Fine	VF	XF
258.2	ND(1841-47)	Thieu Tri	90.00	180.00	300.00	500.00

Rev: Dragon right.

Sch#	Date	Emperor	VG	Fine	VF	XF
258A	ND(1841-47)	Thieu Tri	100.00	200.00	350.00	600.00

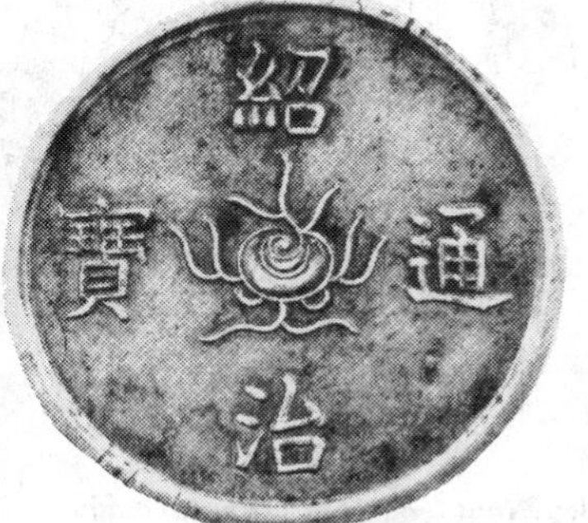

Obv: Flaming sun at center.
Rev. leg: *Long Van Khe Hoi* around facing dragon.

Sch#	Date	Emperor	VG	Fine	VF	XF
—	(1841-47)	Thieu Tri	125.00	250.00	450.00	750.00

51-53mm, 26.6 g
Obv. leg: *Tu Duc Thong Bao.*
Rev: Plain sun between 2 large facing dragons.

Sch#	Date	Emperor	VG	Fine	VF	XF
347B	ND(1848-83)	Tu Duc	150.00	300.00	500.00	850.00

Rev: Ornate sun between 2 small facing dragons.

Sch#	Date	Emperor	VG	Fine	VF	XF
347C	ND(1848-83)	Tu Duc	150.00	300.00	500.00	850.00

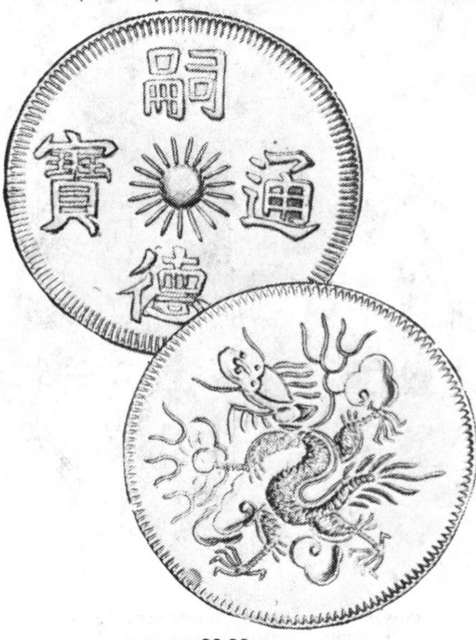

26.20 g
Rev: Dragon left.

Sch#	Date	Emperor	VG	Fine	VF	XF
368	ND(1848-83)	Tu Duc	70.00	140.00	240.00	400.00

26.50 g
Rev. leg: *Long Van* on facing dragon.

Sch#	Date	Emperor	VG	Fine	VF	XF
371	ND(1848-83)	Tu Duc	100.00	200.00	350.00	600.00

26.00 g
Rev. leg: *That Tien Viet Hue* on dragon.

Sch#	Date	Emperor	VG	Fine	VF	XF
383	ND(1848-83)	Tu Duc	150.00	300.00	500.00	850.00

7 TIEN 2 PHAN

(Dollar)

SILVER
Rev. leg: *That Tien Nhi Phan.*

Sch#	Date	Emperor	VG	Fine	VF	XF
—	ND(1848-83)	Tu Duc	90.00	180.00	300.00	500.00

NOTE: Originally considered fantasies it has now been determined these were issued for payment of the war ransom to France in April 1865.

8 TIEN

SILVER, 30.50 g
Obv. leg: *Tu Duc Thong Bao.*
Rev. leg: *Bat Tien Viet Thuan* on dragon.

Sch#	Date	Emperor	VG	Fine	VF	XF
384	ND(1848-83)	Tu Duc	150.00	300.00	500.00	850.00

9 TIEN

SILVER, 34.20 g
Obv. leg: *Tu Duc Thong Bao.*
Rev. leg: *Cuu Tien Viet Nhan* on dragon.

Sch#	Date	Emperor	VG	Fine	VF	XF
385	ND(1848-83)	Tu Duc	165.00	325.00	575.00	950.00

LANG

SILVER, 38mm, 38.00 g
Obv. leg: *Minh Mang Thong Bao* around small sun.
Rev. leg: *Long Van* on facing dragon.

Sch#	Date	Emperor	VG	Fine	VF	XF
187	ND(1820-41)	Minh Mang	120.00	240.00	400.00	650.00

40mm
Obv. & rev: Large sun at center.

Sch#	Date	Emperor	VG	Fine	VF	XF
187A	ND(1820-41)	Minh Mang	135.00	270.00	450.00	750.00

38-38.80 g
Illustration reduced. Actual size: 63mm.
Obv. leg: *Thieu Tri Thong Bao, Van The Vinh Lai.*

Sch#	Date	Emperor	VG	Fine	VF	XF
241	ND(1841-47)	Thieu Tri	165.00	325.00	575.00	950.00

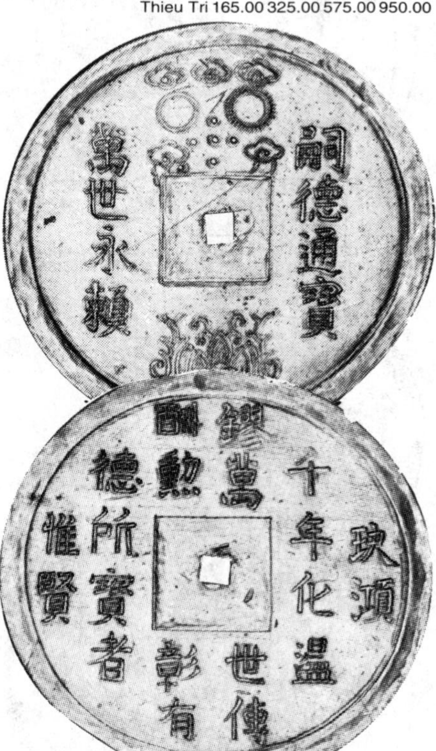

37.30 g
Illustration reduced. Actual size: 63mm.
Obv. leg: *Tu Duc Thong Bao, Van The Vinh Lai.*

Sch#	Date	Emperor	VG	Fine	VF	XF
348	ND(1848-83)	Tu Duc	165.00	325.00	575.00	950.00

37.20 g
Obv. leg: *Tu Duc Thong Bao.*
Rev. leg: *Long Van* on facing dragon.

Sch#	Date	Emperor	VG	Fine	VF	XF
371	ND(1848-83)	Tu Duc	135.00	270.00	450.00	700.00

37.40 g
Rev. leg: *Nhat Lang Viet Trung* on dragon.

Sch#	Date	Emperor	VG	Fine	VF	XF
376	ND(1848-83)	Tu Duc	225.00	450.00	750.00	1250.

SILVER BARS

All of the bars described here are inscribed with their weight, except the 10 Lang "banana bars", and many contain a date or the name of the province in which they were made.

TIEN

SILVER, 3.80-3.90 g

Sch#	Date	Emperor	VG	Fine	VF	XF
174	ND(1820-41)	Minh Mang	45.00	75.00	100.00	150.00

4.20 g

Sch#	Date	Emperor	VG	Fine	VF	XF
175	ND(1820-41)	Minh Mang	45.00	75.00	100.00	150.00

1-1/2 TIEN

SILVER, 5.00-5.20 g

Sch#	Date	Emperor	VG	Fine	VF	XF
340	ND(1848-83)	Tu Duc	45.00	75.00	100.00	150.00

2 TIEN

SILVER, 8.00 g

Sch#	Date	Emperor	VG	Fine	VF	XF
176	ND(1820-41)	Minh Mang	50.00	85.00	120.00	175.00

7.00-7.50 g
Court Treasury. Rev: 5 characters.

Sch#	Date	Emperor	VG	Fine	VF	XF
331	ND(1848-83)	Tu Duc	50.00	85.00	120.00	175.00

7.90 g
Court Treasury. Rev: Error, third and fifth characters the same.

Sch#	Date	Emperor	VG	Fine	VF	XF
337	ND(1848-83)	Tu Duc	50.00	85.00	120.00	175.00

6.80 g
Rev: 4 characters.

Sch#	Date	Emperor	VG	Fine	VF	XF
335	ND(1848-83)	Tu Duc	50.00	85.00	120.00	175.00

3 TIEN

SILVER, 11.60 g

Sch#	Date	Emperor	VG	Fine	VF	XF
177	ND(1820-41)	Minh Mang	75.00	125.00	175.00	250.00

10.20 g
Court Treasury

Sch#	Date	Emperor	VG	Fine	VF	XF
332	ND(1848-83)	Tu Duc	75.00	125.00	175.00	250.00

4 TIEN

SILVER, 15.40 g

Sch#	Date	Emperor	VG	Fine	VF	XF
178	ND(1820-41)	Minh Mang	85.00	140.00	200.00	300.00

15.50 g
Court Treasury

Sch#	Date	Emperor	VG	Fine	VF	XF
236	ND(1841-47)	Thieu Tri	85.00	140.00	200.00	300.00

15.00 g
Court Treasury

Sch#	Date	Emperor	VG	Fine	VF	XF
333	ND(1848-83)	Tu Duc	85.00	140.00	200.00	300.00

5 TIEN

SILVER, weight unknown
Rev: *Trung Binh* at top.

Sch#	Date	Emperor	VG	Fine	VF	XF
122	ND(1802-20)	Gia Long	100.00	175.00	250.00	350.00

Rev: 4 characters.

Sch#	Date	Emperor	VG	Fine	VF	XF
122A	ND(1802-20)	Gia Long	100.00	175.00	250.00	350.00

SILVER, 19.00 g
Rev: 4 characters.

Sch#	Date	Emperor	VG	Fine	VF	XF
179	ND(1820-41)	Minh Mang	100.00	175.00	250.00	350.00

19.20 g
Court Treasury. Rev: 5 characters.

Sch#	Date	Emperor	VG	Fine	VF	XF
237	ND(1841-47)	Thieu Tri	100.00	175.00	250.00	350.00

19.00 g
Court Treasury

Sch#	Date	Emperor	VG	Fine	VF	XF
334	ND(1848-83)	Tu Duc	100.00	175.00	250.00	350.00

LANG

SILVER, 37.94 g
Large characters.

Sch#	Date	Emperor	VG	Fine	VF	XF
118	ND(1802-20)	Gia Long	25.00	40.00	55.00	80.00

NOTE: Produced as a common form of bullion into the 20th century.

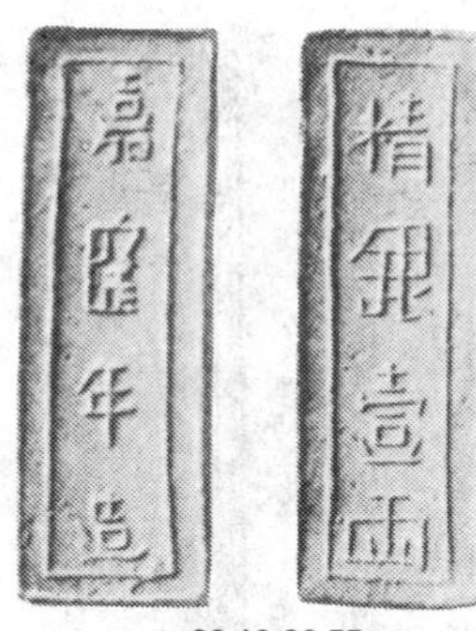

38.13-38.55 g
Small characters.

Sch#	Date	Emperor	VG	Fine	VF	XF
119	ND(1802-20)	Gia Long	60.00	100.00	140.00	200.00

NOTE: Varieties of edge inscriptions exist.

SILVER, 57.2-57.8mm, 38.16-38.57 g

Sch#	Date	Emperor	VG	Fine	VF	XF
169	ND(1820-41)	Minh Mang	75.00	125.00	175.00	250.00

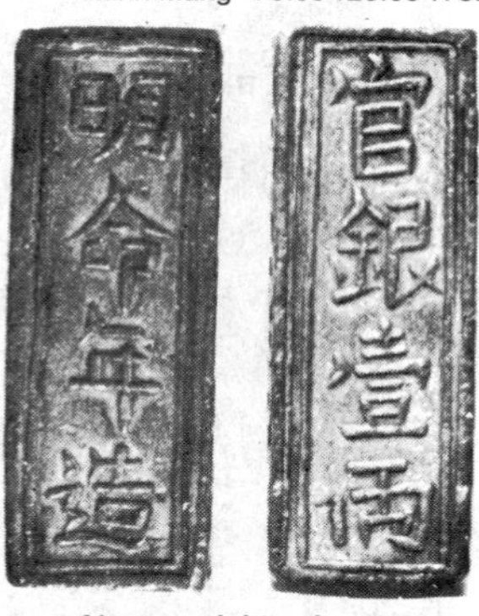

41mm, weight unknown.

Sch#	Date	Emperor	VG	Fine	VF	XF
—	ND(1820-41)	Minh Mang	60.00	100.00	140.00	200.00

38.00 g
Court Treasury

Sch#	Date	Emperor	VG	Fine	VF	XF
219	ND(1841-47)	Thieu Tri	75.00	125.00	185.00	275.00

Rev: *Gia Dinh* at top.

Sch#	Date	Emperor	VG	Fine	VF	XF
—	CD1844	Thieu Tri	100.00	175.00	250.00	350.00

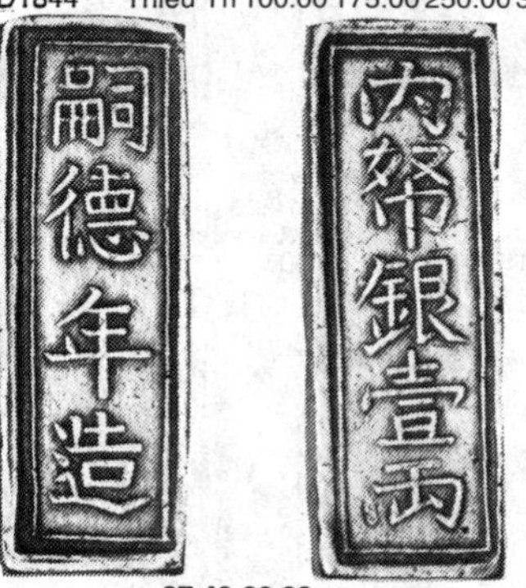

37.43-38.33 g
Court Treasury

Sch#	Date	Emperor	VG	Fine	VF	XF
324B	ND(1848-83)	Tu Duc	25.00	40.00	55.00	80.00

NOTE: Produced as a common form of bullion into the 20th century.

38.00 g
***Binh Dinh* on edge.**

Sch#	Date	Emperor	VG	Fine	VF	XF
320A	ND(1848-83)	Tu Duc	60.00	100.00	140.00	200.00

Weight unknown
***Dinh Tuong* on edge.**

Sch#	Date	Emperor	VG	Fine	VF	XF
320B	CD1859	Tu Duc	100.00	175.00	250.00	350.00

57mm, 38.29 g
***Phu Yen* on edge.**

Sch#	Date	Emperor	VG	Fine	VF	XF
320C	CD1859	Tu Duc	100.00	175.00	250.00	350.00

Canh Than

Sch#	Date	Emperor	VG	Fine	VF	XF
323	CD1860	Tu Duc	100.00	175.00	250.00	350.00

58mm, 38.69 g
Obv: Date. Rev: *Binh Dinh* at top.

Sch#	Date	Emperor	VG	Fine	VF	XF
321	CD1861	Tu Duc	100.00	175.00	250.00	350.00

Weight unknown
Rev. leg: *Phu Yen* at top.

Sch#	Date	Emperor	VG	Fine	VF	XF
322	CD1861	Tu Duc	100.00	175.00	250.00	350.00

37.00 g
Obv: Date. Rev. leg: *An Giang*.

Sch#	Date	Emperor	VG	Fine	VF	XF
324	CD1863	Tu Duc	150.00	250.00	350.00	500.00

37.70 g
Court Treasury. Very crude.
Fineness (.700) inscribed on edge.

Sch#	Date	Emperor	VG	Fine	VF	XF
423	ND(1885-88)	Dong Khanh	75.00	125.00	175.00	250.00

SILVER, 65mm, weight unknown.
Obv. leg: *Than Thai Thong Bao, Van The Vinh Lai*. Rev: Similar to Sch#241.

Sch#	Date	Emperor	VG	Fine	VF	XF
431	ND(1888-1907)	Thanh Thai	175.00	350.00	600.00	1000.

NOTE: Later issues after the French colonial coinage was introduced in 1885 are considered awards for various services.

5 LANG

SILVER, 181.00-191.00 g

Sch#	Date	Emperor	VG	Fine	VF	XF
170	ND(1820-41)	Minh Mang	200.00	350.00	500.00	700.00

40x92mm, 186.00-191.00 g

Court Treasury

Sch#	Date	Emperor	VG	Fine	VF	XF
220	ND(1841-47)	Thieu Tri	200.00	350.00	500.00	700.00

10 LANG

Curved Series

SILVER, about 385.00 g
Top: W/two 4-character rectangular markings.

Sch#	Date	Emperor	VG	Fine	VF	XF
—	ND(1802-19)	Gia Long	75.00	125.00	185.00	275.00

NOTE: Produced as a common form of bullion into the 20th century.

Court Treasury. Similar to Sch#173.

171 CD1832 Minh Mang 300.00 500.00 700.00 1000.

***Quang An*. Similar to Sch#173.**

— CD1832 Minh Mang 300.00 500.00 700.00 1000.

Court Treasury. Similar to Sch#173.

172 CD1833 Minh Mang 300.00 500.00 700.00 1000.

***Son Tay*. Similar to Sch#173.**

— CD1833 Minh Mang 300.00 500.00 700.00 1000.

***Son Tay*.**

173 CD1837 Minh Mang 300.00 500.00 700.00 1000.

383.00 g
***Son Tay*. Similar to Sch#173.**

330 CD1852 Tu Duc Reported, not confirmed

***Thai Nguyen*. Similar to Sch#173.**

325 CD1860 Tu Duc 275.00 450.00 625.00 900.00

***Binh Dinh*. Similar to Sch#173.**

326 CD1861 Tu Duc 275.00 450.00 625.00 900.00

***Son Tay*. Similar to Sch#173.**

327 CD1880 Tu Duc 275.00 450.00 625.00 900.00

***Nghe An*. Similar to Sch#173.**

328 CD1882 Tu Duc 275.00 450.00 625.00 900.00

Top: W/two 4-character rectangular markings.

— ND(1848-83) Tu Duc 75.00 125.00 185.00 275.00

NOTE: Produced as a common form of bullion into the 20th century.

NOTE: 10 Lang curved "banana bars" of these types without any characters on their top surfaces but with various markings on their ends and sides were also produced as a common form of bullion into the 20th century.

Flat Series

42x115mm
Court Treasury.

Sch#	Date	Emperor	VG	Fine	VF	XF
221	ND(1841-74)	Thieu Tri	250.00	425.00	600.00	850.00

NOTE: Illustration reduced 50% of actual size.

45x120mm. About 385.00 g
Rev. leg: *Hung Yen* at top.

222 CD1844 Thieu Tri 250.00 425.00 600.00 850.00

Rev. leg: *Binh Dinh* at top.

223 CD1844 Thieu Tri 250.00 425.00 600.00 850.00

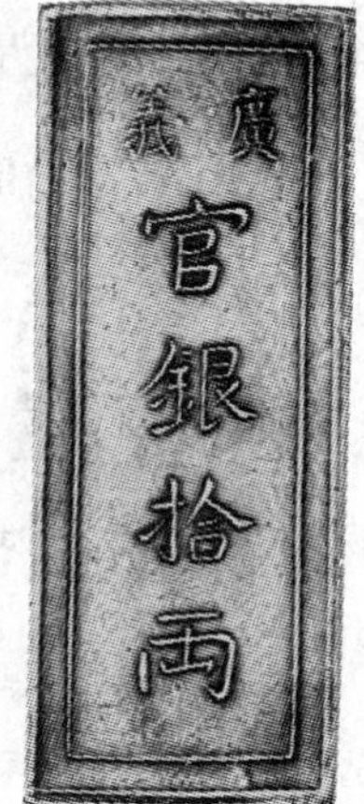

***Quang Yen*.**

— CD1844 Thieu Tri 250.00 425.00 600.00 850.00

NOTE: Illustration reduced 50% of actual size.

Rev. leg: *Son Tay* at top.

224 CD1845 Thieu Tri 250.00 425.00 600.00 850.00

48x120mm, 385.00 g
Rev. leg: *Quang Nam* at top.

225 CD1846 Thieu Tri 250.00 425.00 600.00 850.00

Rev. leg: *Son Tay* at top.

— CD1846 Thieu Tri 250.00 425.00 600.00 850.00

Rev. leg: *Din Nam* at top.

— CD1846 Thieu Tri 250.00 425.00 600.00 850.00

NOTE: Illustration reduced 50% of actual size.

46x120mm
Rev. leg: *Hung Yen* at top.

226 CD1847 Thieu Tri 250.00 425.00 600.00 850.00

Rev. leg: *Lang Son* at top.

227 CD1847 Thieu Tri 250.00 425.00 600.00 850.00

Rev. leg: *Bac Ninh* at top.

228 CD1847 Thieu Tri 250.00 425.00 600.00 850.00

Rev. leg: *Son Tay* at top.

229 CD1847 Thieu Tri 250.00 425.00 600.00 850.00

Rev. leg: *Gia Dinh* at top.

230 CD1847 Thieu Tri 250.00 425.00 600.00 850.00

Weight unknown
Rev. leg: *Hung Yen* at top.

Sch#	Date	Emperor	VG	Fine	VF	XF
—	CD1844	Thieu Tri	250.00	425.00	600.00	850.00

Rev. leg: *Son Tay* at top.

— CD1844 Thieu Tri 250.00 425.00 600.00 850.00

34x100mm, 382.50 g
Court Treasury

329 ND(1848-83) Tu Duc 250.00 425.00 600.00 850.00

NOTE: Illustration reduced 50% of actual size.

20 LANG

SILVER, 49x122mm, 765.50 g
Court Treasury. Legends both sides framed within ornate border of dragons obv. and bats rev.

231 ND(1841-47) Thieu Tri — — Rare —

30 LANG

SILVER, 55x127mm, 1149.00 g
Similar to 20 Lang, Sch #231.

232 ND(1841-47) Thieu Tri — Rare —

40 LANG

SILVER, 60x130mm, 1528.00 g
Similar to 20 Lang, Sch#231.

233 ND(1841-47) Thieu Tri — — Rare —

50 LANG

SILVER, 65x140mm, 1915.00 g
Similar to 20 Lang, Sch#231.

234 ND(1841-47) Thieu Tri — — Rare —

100 LANG

SILVER, 77x160mm, 3831.00 g
Similar to 20 Lang, Sch#231.

235 ND(1841-47) Thieu Tri — — Rare —

QUAN SYSTEM

(Silver Bars Only)

1/2 QUAN

SILVER, weight unknown

338 ND(1848-83) Tu Duc 42.50 70.00 100.00 150.00

7/10 QUAN

SILVER, 3.50 g

339 ND(1848-83) Tu Duc 60.00 100.00 140.00 200.00

QUAN

SILVER, 5.00-5.28 g

340 ND(1848-83) Tu Duc 50.00 85.00 120.00 175.00

1-1/2 QUAN

SILVER, 7.50-8.00 g

Sch#	Date	Emperor	VG	Fine	VF	XF
341	ND(1848-83)	Tu Duc	60.00	100.00	140.00	200.00

2 QUAN

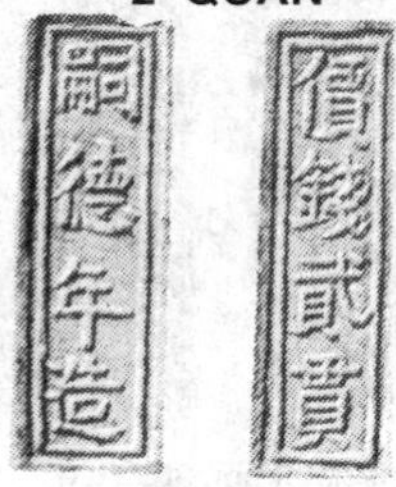

SILVER, 10.50 g

Sch#	Date	Emperor	VG	Fine	VF	XF
342	ND(1848-83)	Tu Duc	65.00	110.00	160.00	225.00

10.30-10.50 g
Similar to Sch#342, but thinner characters.

Sch#	Date	Emperor	VG	Fine	VF	XF
345	ND(1848-83)	Tu Duc	75.00	125.00	175.00	250.00

2-1/2 QUAN

SILVER, 13.00-13.50 g

Sch#	Date	Emperor	VG	Fine	VF	XF
343	ND(1848-83)	Tu Duc	85.00	140.00	200.00	275.00

3 QUAN

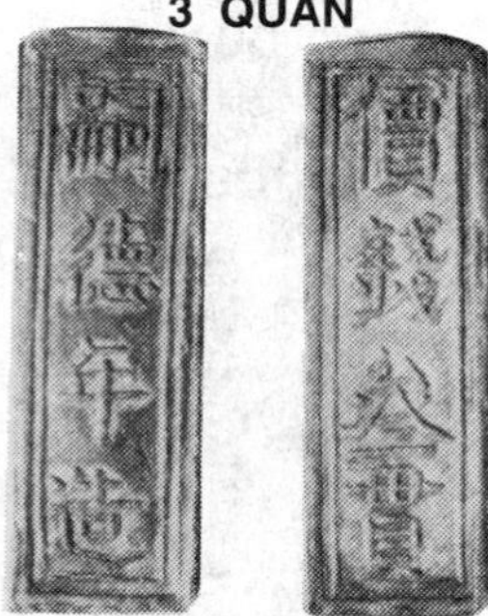

SILVER, 15.92-16.20 g
Thick characters.

Sch#	Date	Emperor	VG	Fine	VF	XF
344	ND(1848-83)	Tu Duc	90.00	150.00	210.00	300.00

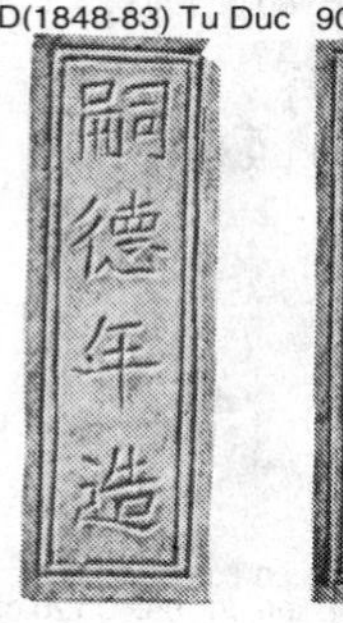

15.40 g
Thin characters.
Obv. & rev: Double borders.

Sch#	Date	Emperor	VG	Fine	VF	XF
346	ND(1848-83)	Tu Duc	90.00	150.00	210.00	300.00

GOLD COINAGE

1/2 TIEN

GOLD, 1.80 g
Obv. leg: *Thieu Tri Thong Bao.* Rev: Blank.

Sch#	Date	Emperor	VG	Fine	VF	XF
257	ND(1841-47)	Thieu Tri	150.00	275.00	450.00	700.00

Obv. leg: *Dong Khanh Thong Bao.*
Rev: Blank.

Sch#	Date	Emperor	VG	Fine	VF	XF
424	ND(1885-88)	Dong Khanh	150.00	275.00	450.00	700.00

NOTE: Later issues after the French colonial coinage was introduced in 1885 are considered awards for various services.

TIEN

GOLD, 3.65-4.00 g
Obv. leg: *Minh Mang Thong Bao.*
Rev: 5 planets.

Sch#	Date	Emperor	VG	Fine	VF	XF
209.1	ND(1820-41)	Minh Mang	300.00	600.00	900.00	1400.

Rev: Mirror image.

Sch#	Date	Emperor	VG	Fine	VF	XF
209.2	ND(1820-41)	Minh Mang	300.00	600.00	900.00	1400.

Obv. leg: *Thieu Tri Thong Bao.*
Rev. leg: *Nhat Nguyen.*

Sch#	Date	Emperor	VG	Fine	VF	XF
250B	ND(1841-47)	Thieu Tri	350.00	700.00	1150.	1800.

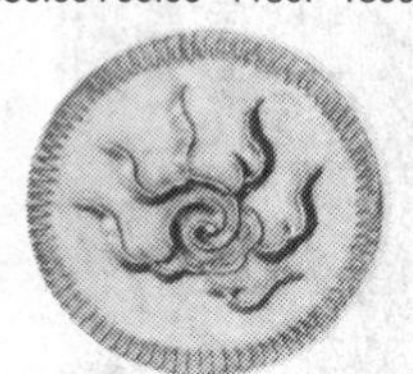

Rev: Flaming sun w/lower flames right.

Sch#	Date	Emperor	VG	Fine	VF	XF
287.1	ND(1841-47)	Thieu Tri	325.00	650.00	1000.	1500.

Rev: Flaming sun w/lower flames left.

Sch#	Date	Emperor	VG	Fine	VF	XF
287.2	ND(1841-47)	Thieu Tri	325.00	650.00	1000.	1500.

3.80 g
Rev: Scepter and swastika.

Sch#	Date	Emperor	VG	Fine	VF	XF
288	ND(1841-47)	Thieu Tri	325.00	650.00	1000.	1500.

4.00 g
Rev: Guitar.

Sch#	Date	Emperor	VG	Fine	VF	XF
289.1	ND(1841-47)	Thieu Tri	325.00	650.00	1000.	1500.

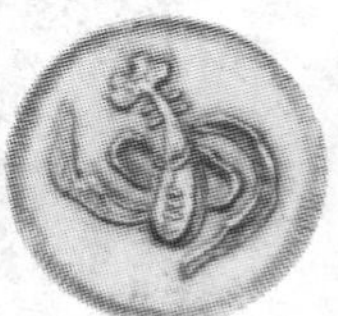

Rev: Mirror image.

Sch#	Date	Emperor	VG	Fine	VF	XF
289.2	ND(1841-47)	Thieu Tri	—	—	—	1800.

Rev: Horn.

Sch#	Date	Emperor	VG	Fine	VF	XF
290	ND(1841-47)	Thieu Tri	325.00	650.00	1000.	1500.

3.80 g
Rev: Fan.

Sch#	Date	Emperor	VG	Fine	VF	XF
291	ND(1841-47)	Thieu Tri	325.00	650.00	1000.	1500.

4.00 g
Rev: Calabash.

Sch#	Date	Emperor	VG	Fine	VF	XF
292	ND(1841-47)	Thieu Tri	325.00	650.00	1000.	1500.

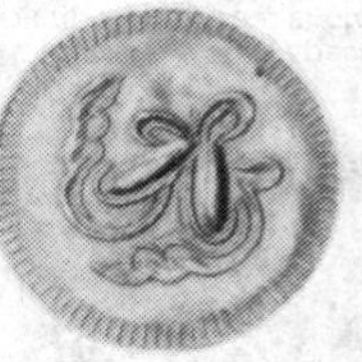

4.20 g
Rev: Clappers.

Sch#	Date	Emperor	VG	Fine	VF	XF
293	ND(1841-47)	Thieu Tri	325.00	650.00	1000.	1500.

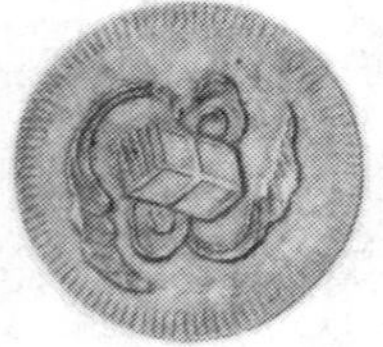

4.00 g
Rev: Books.

Sch#	Date	Emperor	VG	Fine	VF	XF
294	ND(1841-47)	Thieu Tri	325.00	650.00	1000.	1500.

3.80 g
Rev: *Tam Da*, above the Three Plenties.

Sch#	Date	Emperor	VG	Fine	VF	XF
295	ND(1841-47)	Thieu Tri	325.00	650.00	1000.	1500.

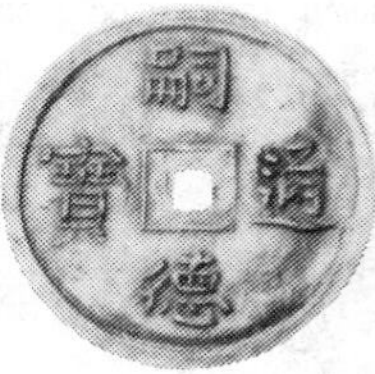

3.70 g
Rev. leg: *Nhat Nguyen*.

Sch#	Date	Emperor	VG	Fine	VF	XF
353B	ND(1848-83)	Tu Duc	—	—	—	3000.

3.80 g
Rev: *Nhat Nguyen Tien Viet Tu* on dragon.

Sch#	Date	Emperor	VG	Fine	VF	XF
377	ND(1848-83)	Tu Duc	325.00	650.00	1000.	1500.

Rev: Sun, moon and 5 planets.

Sch#	Date	Emperor	VG	Fine	VF	XF
386A	ND(1848-83)	Tu Duc	325.00	650.00	1000.	1500.

Rev: Scepter and swastika.

Sch#	Date	Emperor	VG	Fine	VF	XF
388B	ND(1848-83)	Tu Duc	—	—	—	3000.

GOLD, 3.90 g
Obv. leg: *Thanh Thai Thong Bao*.
Rev: *Nhat Nguyen*.

Sch#	Date	Emperor	VG	Fine	VF	XF
432	ND(1888-1907)	Thanh Thai	325.00	650.00	1000.	1500.

NOTE: Later issues after the French colonial coinage was introduced in 1885 are considered awards for various services.

1-1/2 TIEN

GOLD, 5.40-6.50 g
Obv. leg: *Minh Mang*.
Rev: Five Precious symbols.

Sch#	Date	Emperor	VG	Fine	VF	XF
211	ND(1820-41)	Minh Mang	350.00	700.00	1100.	1650.

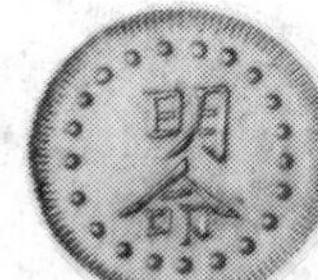

5.70 g
Rev: Eight Precious symbols.

Sch#	Date	Emperor	VG	Fine	VF	XF
212	ND(1820-41)	Minh Mang	350.00	700.00	1100.	1650.

Rev: Mirror image.

Sch#	Date	Emperor	VG	Fine	VF	XF
213	ND(1820-41)	Minh Mang	350.00	700.00	1100.	1650.

5.60 g
Obv. leg: *Tu Duc Thong Bao*.
Rev. leg: *Su Dan Phu Tho*.

Sch#	Date	Emperor	VG	Fine	VF	XF
406	ND(1848-83)	Tu Duc	350.00	700.00	1000.	1500.

6.40-6.90 g
Obv. leg: *Dong Kanh Thong Bao*.
Rev. leg: *Nhi Nghi* between moon and sun.

Sch#	Date	Emperor	VG	Fine	VF	XF
425.1	ND(1885-88)	Dong Khanh	240.00	480.00	800.00	1200.

Rev. leg: *Nhi Nghi* between sun and moon.

Sch#	Date	Emperor	VG	Fine	VF	XF
425.2	ND(1885-88)	Dong Khanh	240.00	480.00	800.00	1200.

GOLD, 6.60 g
Obv. leg: *Thanh Thai Thong Bao*.
Rev. leg: *Nhi Nghi* between moon and sun.

Sch#	Date	Emperor	VG	Fine	VF	XF
435	ND(1888-1907)	Thanh Thai	240.00	480.00	800.00	1200.

NOTE: Later issues after the French colonial coinage was introduced in 1885 are considered awards for various services.

2 TIEN

GOLD, 7.80 g
Obv. leg: *Minh Mang*.
Rev. leg: *Tam Da* above the Three Plenties.

Sch#	Date	Emperor	VG	Fine	VF	XF
210	ND(1820-41)	Minh Mang	350.00	700.00	1100.	1650.

Obv. leg: *Thieu Tri Thong Bao*.
Rev. leg: *Nhi Nghi* between moon and sun.

Sch#	Date	Emperor	VG	Fine	VF	XF
281	ND(1841-47)	Thieu Tri	350.00	700.00	1100.	1650.

7.30 g
Obv. leg: *Tu Duc Thong Bao*.
Rev. leg: *Nhi Tien Viet Hien* on dragon.

Sch#	Date	Emperor	VG	Fine	VF	XF
378	ND(1848-83)	Tu Duc	350.00	700.00	1100.	1650.

Rev: Flaming sun between facing dragons.

Sch#	Date	Emperor	VG	Fine	VF	XF
402B	ND(1848-83)	Tu Duc	400.00	800.00	1200.	1800.

2-1/2 TIEN

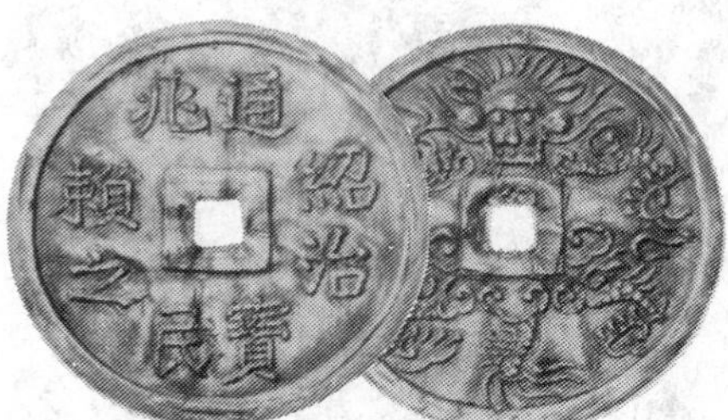

GOLD, 8.90 g
Obv. leg: *Thieu Tri Thong Bao*.
Rev: Facing dragon.

Sch#	Date	Emperor	VG	Fine	VF	XF
280B	ND(1841-47)	Thieu Tri	—	—	—	3250.

9.25-9.85 g
Obv. leg: *Thieu Tri Thong Bao*, *Trieu Dan Lai Chi*. Rev. leg: *Long Van Khe Hoi* around facing dragon.

Sch#	Date	Emperor	VG	Fine	VF	XF
375	ND(1848-83)	Tu Duc	400.00	750.00	1200.	1750.

3 TIEN

GOLD, 11.50-13.30 g
Obv. leg: *Minh Mang Thong Bao*.

Sch#	Date	Emperor	VG	Fine	VF	XF
207	ND (1820-40)	Minh Mang	550.00	1100.	1800.	2700.

Sch#	Date	Emperor	VG	Fine	VF	XF
208	(1833) Yr.14	Minh Mang	550.00	1100.	1800.	2700.

Sch#	Date	Emperor	VG	Fine	VF	XF
206C	(1834) Yr.15	Minh Mang	550.00	1100.	1800.	2700.

Sch#	Date	Emperor	VG	Fine	VF	XF
206D	(1835) Yr.16	Minh Mang	—	—	2000.	—

13.54 g
Obv. leg: *Thieu Tri Thong Bao.*
Rev: Large dragon.

Sch#	Date	Emperor	VG	Fine	VF	XF
285	ND(1841-47)	Thieu Tri	550.00	1100.	1800.	2700.

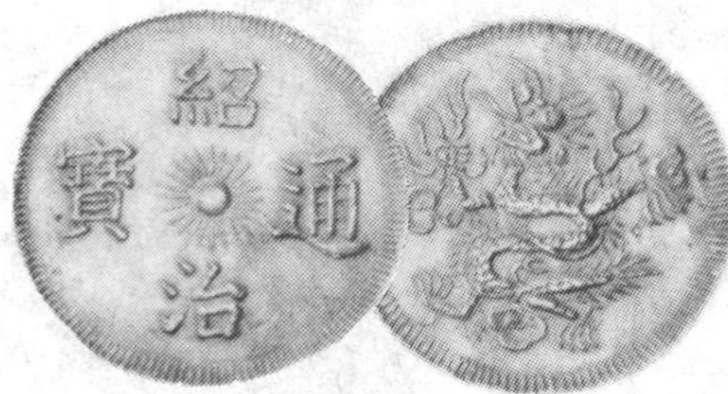

Rev: Small dragon.

Sch#	Date	Emperor	VG	Fine	VF	XF
286	ND(1841-47)	Thieu Tri	550.00	1100.	1800.	2700.

13.24 g
Obv. leg: *Tu Duc Thong Bao.*

Sch#	Date	Emperor	VG	Fine	VF	XF
413	ND(1848-83)	Tu Duc	550.00	1100.	1800.	2700.

11.00 g
Rev. leg: *Tam Thao* above Three Longevities.

Sch#	Date	Emperor	VG	Fine	VF	XF
407	ND(1848-83)	Tu Duc	600.00	1200.	2000.	3000.

11.20 g
Rev. leg: *Long Van* on facing dragon.

Sch#	Date	Emperor	VG	Fine	VF	XF
373B	ND(1848-83)	Tu Duc	600.00	1200.	2000.	3000.

11.30 g
Rev. leg: *Tam Tien Viet Lang* on dragon.

Sch#	Date	Emperor	VG	Fine	VF	XF
379B	ND(1848-83)	Tu Duc	550.00	1100.	1800.	2700.

GOLD, 10.50-12.40 g
Obv. leg: *Thanh Thai Thong Bao.*
Rev: Dragon.

Sch#	Date	Emperor	VG	Fine	VF	XF
433	ND(1888-1907)	Thanh Thai	1000.	2000.	3250.	5000.

10.00-10.50 g
Rev: *Tam Tho*, dragon above Three Longevities.

Sch#	Date	Emperor	VG	Fine	VF	XF
436	ND(1888-1907)	Thanh Thai	550.00	1100.	1800.	2700.

NOTE: Later issues after the French colonial coinage was introduced in 1885 are considered awards for various services.

4 TIEN

GOLD, 14.70 g
Obv. leg: *Tu Duc Thong Bao.*
Rev. leg: *Su Dan Phu Tho.*

Sch#	Date	Emperor	VG	Fine	VF	XF
406	ND(1848-83)	Tu Duc	650.00	1300.	2200.	3300.

14.50-15.20 g
Rev. leg: *Tu My* between the Four Perfections.

Sch#	Date	Emperor	VG	Fine	VF	XF
409.1	ND(1848-83)	Tu Duc	650.00	1300.	2200.	3300.

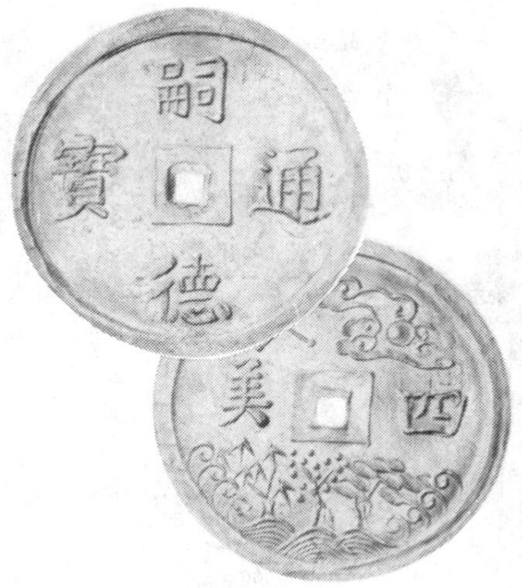

Rev: Finer style.

Sch#	Date	Emperor	VG	Fine	VF	XF
409.2	ND(1848-83)	Tu Duc	650.00	1300.	2200.	3300.

15.00 g
Rev. leg: *Tu Tien Viet De* on dragon.

Sch#	Date	Emperor	VG	Fine	VF	XF
380	ND(1848-83)	Tu Duc	650.00	1300.	2200.	3300.

13.16 g
Rev: Flaming sun between facing dragons.

Sch#	Date	Emperor	VG	Fine	VF	XF
402C	ND(1848-83)	Tu Duc	—	—	—	7000.

GOLD, 14.50 g
Obv. leg: *Thanh Thai Thong Bao.*
Rev. leg: *Tu My* between Four Perfections.

Sch#	Date	Emperor	VG	Fine	VF	XF
437	ND(1888-1907)	Thanh Thai	650.00	1300.	2200.	3300.

NOTE: Later issues after the French colonial coinage was introduced in 1885 are considered awards for various services.

5 TIEN

GOLD, 19.20 g
Obv. leg: *Minh Mang Thong Bao.*
Rev. leg: *Phu Tho Da Nam.*

Sch#	Date	Emperor	VG	Fine	VF	XF
205	ND(1820-41)	Minh Mang	1000.	2000.	3250.	5000.

17.61 g
Obv. leg: ***Thieu Tri Thong Bao.***
Rev. leg: ***Phu Tho Da Nam.***

Sch#	Date	Emperor	VG	Fine	VF	XF
253B	ND(1841-47)	Thieu Tri	1100.	2200.	3600.	5400.

19.50 g
Obv. leg: ***Thieu Tri Thong Bao, Van The Vinh Lai.***

279	ND(1841-47)	Thieu Tri	1100.	2200.	3600.	5400.

18.00-20.00 g
Obv. leg: ***Tu Duc Thong Bao.***
Rev. leg: ***Long Van Khe Hoi*** **around dragon.**

374B	ND(1848-83)	Tu Duc	1000.	2000.	3250.	5000.

18.90 g
Obv: Sun w/8 rays at center.
Rev. leg: ***Long Van*** **on facing dragon.**

414C	ND(1848-83)	Tu Duc	1000.	2000.	3250.	5000.

18.24 g
Obv: Sun w/12 rays at center.

Sch#	Date	Emperor	VG	Fine	VF	XF
414D	ND(1848-83)	Tu Duc	1000.	2000.	3250.	5000.

19.00 g
Obv. leg: ***Tu Duc Thong Bao, Trieu Dan Lai Chi.*** **Rev: Facing dragon.**

405	ND(1848-83)	Tu Duc	1000.	2000.	3250.	5000.

19.22 g
Obv. leg: ***Tu Duc Thong Bao, Van The Vinh Lai.***

404	ND(1848-83)	Tu Duc	1200.	2400.	4000.	6000.

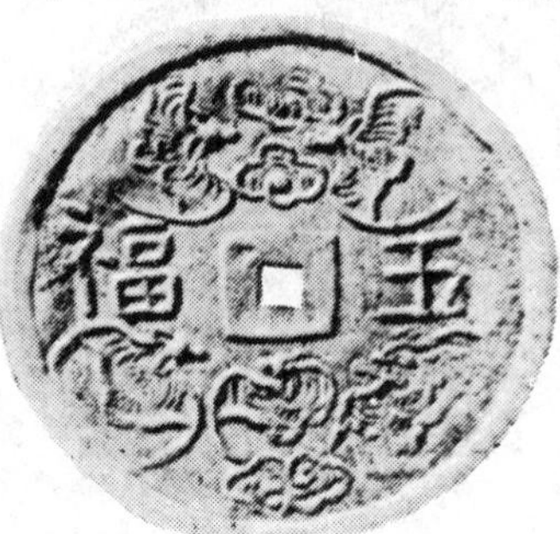

18.00 g
Obv. leg: ***Tu Duc Thong Bao.***
Rev. leg: ***Ngu Phuc*** **and 5 bats.**

410	ND(1848-83)	Tu Duc	1000.	2000.	3250.	5000.

18.80 g

Rev. leg: ***Ngu Tien Viet Ngai*** **on dragon.**

Sch#	Date	Emperor	VG	Fine	VF	XF
381	ND(1848-83)	Tu Duc	1000.	2000.	3250.	5000.

6 TIEN

GOLD, 23.00 g
Obv. leg: ***Tu Duc Thong Bao.***
Rev. leg: ***Luc Tien Viet Thinh*** **on dragon.**

382	ND(1848-83)	Tu Duc	1100.	2200.	3600.	5400.

Obv. leg: ***Than Thai Thong Bao.***
Rev: Large dragon.

382A	ND(1888-1907)	Thanh Thai	1100.	2200.	3600.	5400.

7 TIEN

GOLD, 26.50-27.50 g
Obv. leg: ***Minh Mang Thong Bao.***

—	ND(1820-40)	Minh Mang	1200.	2400.	4000.	6000.

—	(1832) Yr.13	Minh Mang	1200.	2400.	4000.	6000.
206	(1834) Yr.15	Minh Mang	1200.	2400.	4000.	6000.
206B	(1835) Yr.16	Minh Mang	1200.	2400.	4000.	6000.

26.60-27.00 g
Obv. leg: *Thieu Tri Thong Bao.*
Rev: Dragon left.

Sch#	Date	Emperor	VG	Fine	VF	XF
283	ND(1841-47)	Thieu Tri	1200.	2400.	4000.	6000.

28.15-28.20 g
Rev: Dragon right.

Sch#	Date	Emperor	VG	Fine	VF	XF
284	ND(1841-47)	Thieu Tri	1300.	2600.	4400.	6600.

26.75 g
Rev: Flaming sun between facing dragons.

Sch#	Date	Emperor	VG	Fine	VF	XF
278	ND(1841-47)	Thieu Tri	1200.	2400.	4000.	6000.

Obv. leg: *Tu Duc Thong Bao.*
Obv. and rev: Dentilated borders.
Rev: Dragon left.

Sch#	Date	Emperor	VG	Fine	VF	XF
368B	ND(1848-83)	Tu Duc	1200.	2400.	4000.	6000.

26.80 g
Obv. and rev: Pearled borders.

Sch#	Date	Emperor	VG	Fine	VF	XF
411	ND(1848-83)	Tu Duc	1200.	2400.	4000.	6000.

26.20 g
Rev. leg: *Long Van* on facing dragon.

Sch#	Date	Emperor	VG	Fine	VF	XF
414B	ND(1848-83)	Tu Duc	1200.	2400.	4000.	6000.

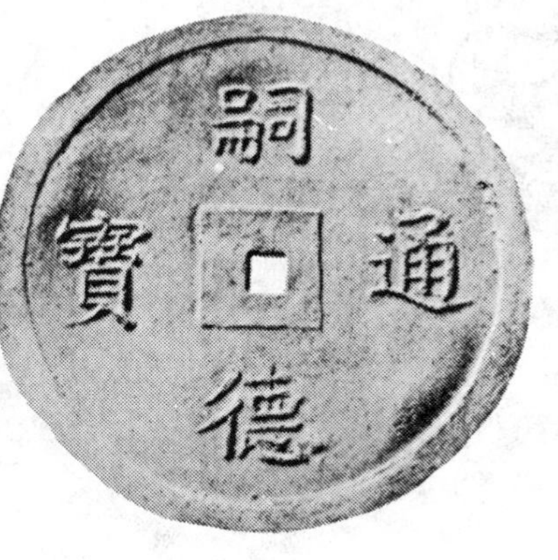

26.45-27.00 g
Obv: Small legends.
Rev: Small thin, curved facing dragons.

Sch#	Date	Emperor	VG	Fine	VF	XF
402.1	ND(1848-83)	Tu Duc	1200.	2400.	4000.	6000.

Obv: Large legends.
Rev: Large, thick facing dragons.

Sch#	Date	Emperor	VG	Fine	VF	XF
402.2	ND(1848-83)	Tu Duc	1200.	2400.	4000.	6000.

26.00 g
Rev. leg: *That Tien Viet Hue* on dragon.

Sch#	Date	Emperor	VG	Fine	VF	XF
383B	ND(1848-83)	Tu Duc	1200.	2400.	4000.	6000.

8 TIEN

GOLD, 30.50 g
Obv. leg: *Tu Duc Thong Bao.*
Rev. leg: *Bat Tien Viet Thuan* on dragon.

Sch#	Date	Emperor	VG	Fine	VF	XF
384B	ND(1848-83)	Tu Duc	1400.	2800.	4800.	7000.

9 TIEN

GOLD, 34.07-34.20 g
Obv. leg: ***Tu Duc Thong Bao.***
Rev. leg: ***Cuu Tien Viet Nhan*** **on dragon.**

Sch#	Date	Emperor	VG	Fine	VF	XF
385B	ND(1848-83)	Tu Duc	1500.	3000.	5200.	8000.

LANG

GOLD, 37.70-38.00 g
Obv. leg: ***Tu Duc Thong Bao, Van The Vinh Lai.***

Sch#	Date	Emperor	VG	Fine	VF	XF
403	ND(1848-83)	Tu Duc	2700.	5400.	9000.	14,500.

37.00-37.69 g
Obv. leg: ***Tu Duc Thong Bao.***
Rev. leg: ***Long Van*** **on facing dragon.**

Sch#	Date	Emperor	VG	Fine	VF	XF
414	ND(1848-83)	Tu Duc	2500.	5000.	8000.	12,500.

37.40 g
Rev. leg: ***Nhat Lang Viet Trung*** **on dragon.**

Sch#	Date	Emperor	VG	Fine	VF	XF
376B	ND(1848-83)	Tu Duc	2700.	5400.	9000.	13,500.

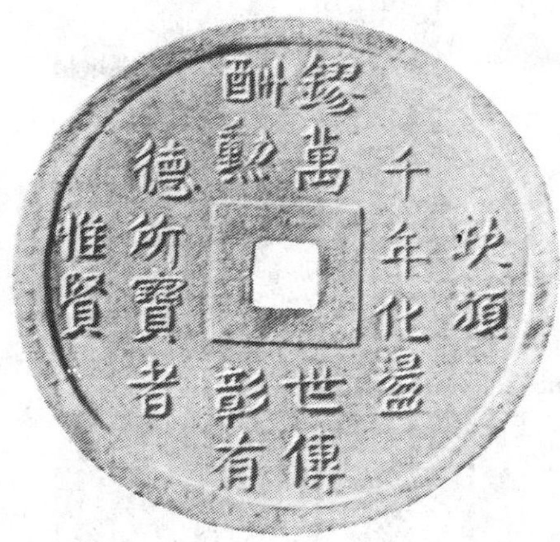

Weight unknown
Obv. leg: ***Thanh Thai Thong Bao, Van The Vinh Lai.***

Sch#	Date	Emperor	VG	Fine	VF	XF
431	ND(1888-1907)	Thanh Thai	2700.	5400.	9000.	14,500.

NOTE: Later issues after the French colonial coinage was introduced in 1885 are considered awards for various services.

GOLD BARS

All of the bars described here are inscribed with their weight, except the 10 Lang "banana bars", and many contain a date or the name of the province in which they were made.

TIEN

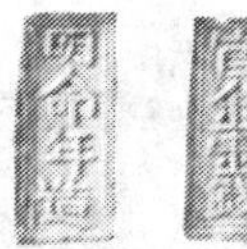

GOLD, weight unknown

Sch#	Date	Emperor	VG	Fine	VF	XF
200	ND(1820-41)	Minh Mang	325.00	650.00	1000.	1500.

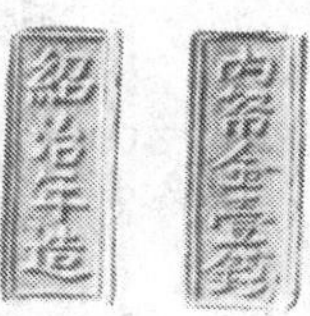

.850 GOLD, 3.90 g
Court Treasury

Sch#	Date	Emperor	VG	Fine	VF	XF
273	ND(1841-47)	Thieu Tri	325.00	650.00	1000.	1500.

NOTE: Fineness on edge.

Weight unknown
Court Treasury

Sch#	Date	Emperor	VG	Fine	VF	XF
397	ND(1848-83)	Tu Duc	325.00	650.00	1000.	1500.

2 TIEN

GOLD, weight unknown

Sch#	Date	Emperor	VG	Fine	VF	XF
201	ND(1820-41)	Minh Mang	350.00	700.00	1100.	1650.

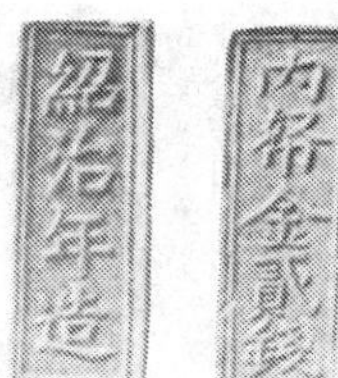

.850 GOLD, 7.50 g
Court Treasury

Sch#	Date	Emperor	VG	Fine	VF	XF
274	ND(1841-47)	Thieu Tri	360.00	720.00	1200.	2000.

NOTE: Fineness on edge.

Weight unknown
Court Treasury

Sch#	Date	Emperor	VG	Fine	VF	XF
398	ND(1848-83)	Tu Duc	360.00	720.00	1200.	2000.

NOTE: Fineness on edge.

3 TIEN

GOLD, weight unknown

Sch#	Date	Emperor	VG	Fine	VF	XF
202	ND(1820-41)	Minh Mang	550.00	1100.	1800.	2700.

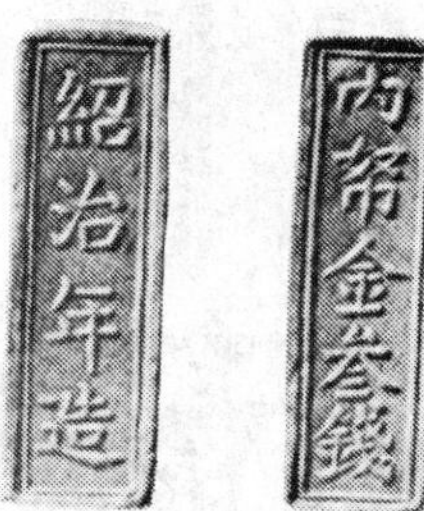

11.30 g

Sch#	Date	Emperor	VG	Fine	VF	XF
275	ND(1841-47)	Thieu Tri	550.00	1100.	1800.	2700.

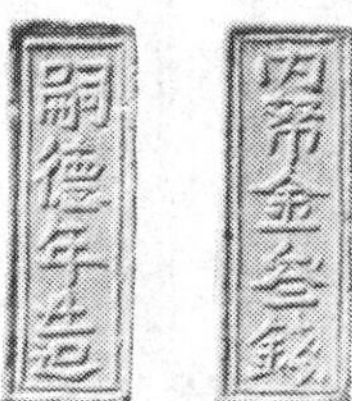

Weight unknown
Court Treasury

Sch#	Date	Emperor	VG	Fine	VF	XF
399	ND(1848-83)	Tu Duc	550.00	1100.	1800.	2700.

4 TIEN

GOLD, weight unknown

Sch#	Date	Emperor	VG	Fine	VF	XF
203	ND(1820-41)	Minh Mang	—	—	Rare	—

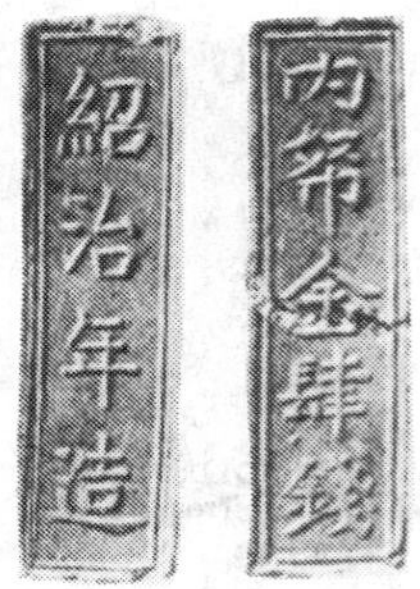

.850 GOLD, 15.25 g
Court Treasury

Sch#	Date	Emperor	VG	Fine	VF	XF
276	ND(1841-47)	Minh Mang	—	—	Rare	—

NOTE: Fineness on edge.

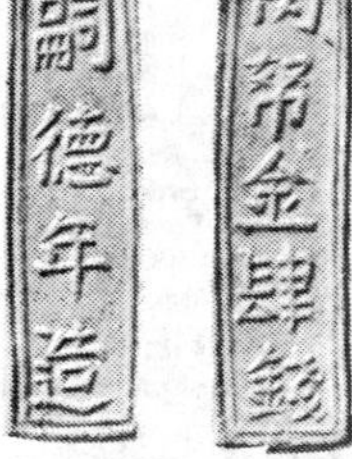

Weight unknown
Court Treasury

Sch#	Date	Emperor	VG	Fine	VF	XF
400	ND(1848-83)	Tu Duc	—	—	Rare	—

NOTE: Fineness on edge.

5 TIEN

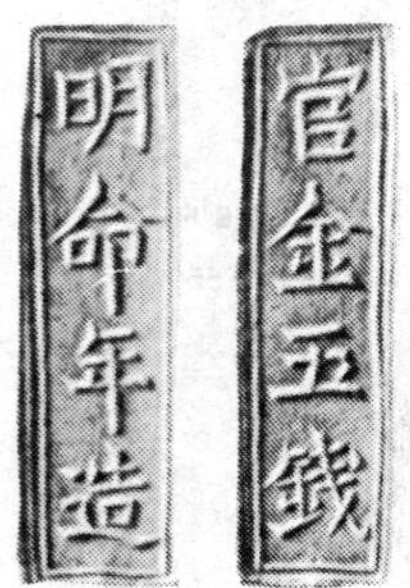

GOLD, weight unknown

Sch#	Date	Emperor	VG	Fine	VF	XF
204	ND(1820-41)	Minh Mang	—	—	Rare	—

.850 GOLD, 18.85 g
Court Treasury

Sch#	Date	Emperor	VG	Fine	VF	XF
277	ND(1841-47)	Thieu Tri	—	—	Rare	—

NOTE: Fineness on edge.

Weight unknown
Court Treasury

Sch#	Date	Emperor	VG	Fine	VF	XF
401	ND(1848-83)	Tu Duc	—	—	Rare	—

NOTE: Fineness on edge.

LANG

.850 GOLD, weight unknown
Very crude.

Sch#	Date	Emperor	VG	Fine	VF	XF
190	ND(1820-41)	Minh Mang	—	—	Rare	—

NOTE: Fineness on edge.

Court Treasury

Sch#	Date	Emperor	VG	Fine	VF	XF
268	ND(1841-47)	Thieu Tri	—	—	Rare	—

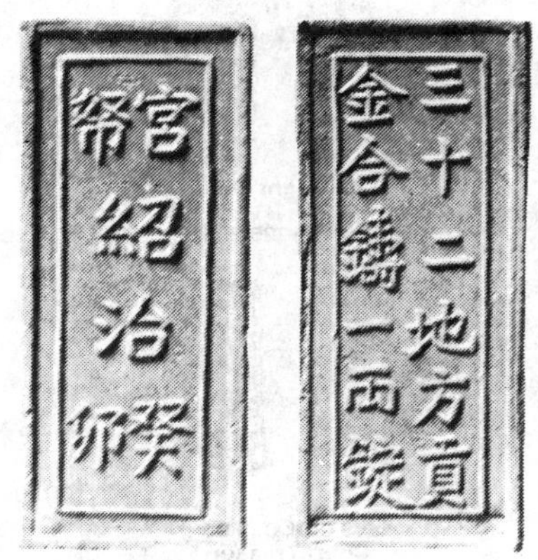

Sch#	Date	Emperor	VG	Fine	VF	XF
269	CD1843	Thieu Tri	—	—	Rare	—

NOTE: Fineness on edge.

.950 GOLD, 37.40 g
Court Treasury

Sch#	Date	Emperor	VG	Fine	VF	XF
391	ND(1848-83)	Tu Duc	—	—	Rare	—

NOTE: Fineness on edge.
NOTE: Stack's NYINC sale 12-89 virtual Unc realized $8250.

.850 GOLD
Court Treasury

Sch#	Date	Emperor	VG	Fine	VF	XF
392	ND(1848-83)	Tu Duc	—	—	Rare	—

NOTE: Fineness on edge.

Court Treasury. Crude.

Sch#	Date	Emperor	VG	Fine	VF	XF
423	ND(1885-88)	Dong Khanh	—	—	Rare	—

.850 GOLD, 36.10-36.70 g
Court Treasury

Sch#	Date	Emperor	VG	Fine	VF	XF
429	ND(1888-1907)	Thanh Thai	—	—	Rare	—

NOTE: Fineness on edge.

.800 GOLD
Court Treasury

Sch#	Date	Emperor	VG	Fine	VF	XF
430	ND(1888-1907)	Thanh Thai	—	—	Rare	—

NOTE: Fineness on edge.

5 LANG

.850 GOLD, weight unknown

Sch#	Date	Emperor	VG	Fine	VF	XF
191	ND(1820-41)	Minh Mang	—	—	Rare	—

NOTE: Fineness on edge.

190.25 g
Court Treasury

Sch#	Date	Emperor	VG	Fine	VF	XF
394	ND(1848-83)	Tu Duc	—	—	Rare	—

NOTE: Fineness on edge.

10 LANG

.850 GOLD, weight unknown
Similar to Silver 10 Lang, Sch#173.
Court Treasury

Sch#	Date	Emperor	VG	Fine	VF	XF
192	CD1837	Minh Mang	—	—	Rare	—

NOTE: Fineness on edge.

.750 GOLD, 382.40 g, 43x108mm
Court Treasury

Sch#	Date	Emperor	VG	Fine	VF	XF
270	ND(1841-47)	Thieu Tri	—	—	Rare	—

NOTE: Fineness on edge.

.900 GOLD, weight unknown. 30x100mm
Rev: 4 characters. All legends engraved.

Sch#	Date	Emperor	VG	Fine	VF	XF
396	ND(1848-83)	Tu Duc	—	—	Rare	—

NOTE: Fineness on edge.

Obv. leg: ***Bac Ninh.***

Rev: 2 characters (engraved) plus hallmark.

Sch#	Date	Emperor	VG	Fine	VF	XF
395	CD1849	Tu Duc	—	—	Rare	—

30 LANG

.750 GOLD, weight unknown, 43x101mm
Obv. leg: ***Dai Nam Nguyen Bao.***
Similar to 40 Lang, Sch#195.

193 Yr.21(1840)Thieu Tri — — Rare —

NOTE: Fineness on edge.

40 LANG

.750 GOLD, weight unknown
Illustration reduced. Actual size: 43x107mm.
Obv. leg: ***Dai Nam Nguyen Bao.***

195 Yr.21(1840) Minh Mang — — Rare —

NOTE: Fineness on edge.

.900 GOLD, 43x112mm
Obv. leg: ***Viet Nam Nguyen Bao.***

194 ND(1820-41) Minh Mang — — Rare —

NOTE: Fineness on edge.

50 LANG

.750 GOLD, weight unknown
48x118mm
Obv. leg: ***Viet Nam Nguyen Bao.***

196 Yr.18(1837) Minh Mang — — Rare —

NOTE: Fineness on edge.

.800 GOLD, 49x115mm
Obv. leg: ***Dai Nam Nguyen Bao.***
Obv. and rev. leg. framed within ornate border.

197 Yr.19(1838) Minh Mang — — Rare —

NOTE: Fineness on edge.

.700 GOLD, 1917.35 g
Court Treasury

271 CD1843 Thieu Tri — — Rare —

NOTE: Fineness on edge.

100 LANG

.850 GOLD, weight unknown, 59x138mm
Obv. leg: ***Viet Nam Nguyen Bao,***
small characters.
Obv. and rev. leg. framed within ornate border.

198 Yr.14(1833) Minh Mang — — Rare —

NOTE: Fineness on edge.

Similar to Sch#198 but large characters on obv.

199 Yr.14(1833) Minh Mang — — Rare —

.700 GOLD, 3831.00 g
Illustration reduced. Actual size: 78x146mm.
Court Treasury
Obv. and rev. leg. framed within ornate border.

272 CD1843 Thieu Tri — — Rare —

NOTE: Fineness on edge.

VIETNAM/FRENCH COCHIN CHINA

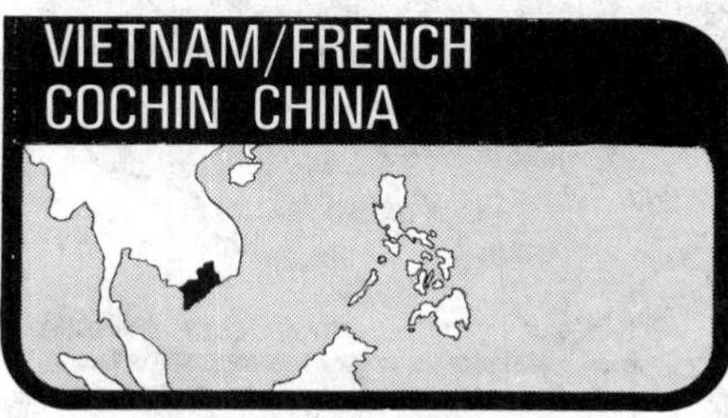

Cochin-China, a colony of France in Indo-China, now part of Viet Nam, occupied an alluvial plain of the Mekong Delta along the South China Sea. In its colonial period, Cochin-China had an area of 24,981 sq. mi. (63,701 sq. km.) and a population of about 5 million. Capital: Saigon. The region was (and is) one of Asia's chief rice-growing areas. Fishing is also an important economic activity. French Cochin-China exported rice, fish and timber.

The region, inhabited mainly by Vietnamese, was formerly part of the ancient Khmer empire and later of the Empire of Dai Viet. It was brought under French control in 1862-67 and made a colony. The Japanese occupied the area before World War II to use as a base for the invasion of Malaya. When France regained power of the area following World War II, Cochin-China was included in the Federation of Indo-China as an autonomous republic. It was attached to Viet Nam in 1949.

MINT MARKS

A - Paris
K - Bordeaux

MONETARY SYSTEM

5 Sapeques = 1 Cent
100 Cents = 1 Piastre

SAPEQUE

BRONZE
Center hole punched in France 1 Centime, Y#41.

KM#	Date	Mintage	Fine	VF	XF	Unc
1	1875K	1.000	6.00	12.00	25.00	65.00

KM#	Date	Mintage	Fine	VF	XF	Unc
2	1879A	20.000	3.00	6.00	12.50	35.00
	1879A	—	—	—	Proof	200.00
	1885A	100 pcs.	—	—	Proof	450.00

NOTE: The above coin has 2/1000 on the reverse and thus is often mistaken for a 2 Sapeque.

CENT

BRONZE

KM#	Date	Mintage	Fine	VF	XF	Unc
3	1879A	.500	5.00	15.00	50.00	200.00
	1879A	—	Proof - Reported, not confirmed			
	1884A	.444	6.00	25.00	65.00	300.00
	1885A	.255	7.00	30.00	100.00	475.00
	1885A	100 pcs.	—	—	Proof	650.00

10 CENTS

2.7216 g, .900 SILVER, .0787 oz ASW

KM#	Date	Mintage	Fine	VF	XF	Unc
4	1879A	.400	20.00	35.00	90.00	325.00
	1879A	—	—	—	Proof	575.00
	1884A	.510	25.00	60.00	125.00	375.00
	1885A	100 pcs.	—	—	Proof	800.00

20 CENTS

5.4431 g, .900 SILVER, .1575 oz ASW

KM#	Date	Mintage	Fine	VF	XF	Unc
5	1879A	.350	30.00	60.00	150.00	425.00
	1879A	—	—	—	Proof	725.00
	1884A	.320	40.00	70.00	185.00	475.00
	1885A	100 pcs.	—	—	Proof	900.00

50 CENTS

13.6078 g, .900 SILVER, .3937 oz ASW

KM#	Date	Mintage	Fine	VF	XF	Unc
6	1879A	.180	90.00	150.00	300.00	1250.
	1879A	—	—	—	Proof	2750.
	1884A	.010	400.00	600.00	900.00	3000.
	1885A	100 pcs.	—	—	Proof	1500.

PIASTRE

27.2156 g, .900 SILVER, .7875 oz ASW

KM#	Date	Mintage	Fine	VF	XF	Unc
7	1885A	100 pcs.	—	—	Proof	Rare

NOTE: Superior Goodman sale 5-95 proof w/tiny edge nick realized, $10,925.

ESSAIS (E)

Standard metals unless otherwise noted

KM#	Date	Mintage	Identification	Mkt.Val.
E1	1878	—	1 Sapeque	250.00
E2	ND	—	1 Sapeque, as above, w/o date	250.00
E3	1879	—	1 Sapeque, w/o mint mark, ESSAI on rev., filled square hole	200.00

KM#	Date	Mintage	Identification	Mkt.Val.
E4	1879	—	1 Sapeque, w/o mint mark, ESSAI on rev., open square hole	200.00
E5	1879A	—	1 Sapeque, w/mint mark, w/o	

KM#	Date	Mintage	Identification	Mkt.Val.
E5			ESSAI on rev., filled square hole	200.00
E11	1879A	—	50 Cents, mint mark between anchors, ESSAIS below CENT on rev.	2450.

KM#	Date	Mintage	Identification	Mkt.Val.
E12	1879A	—	1 Piastre, KM7	11,500.
E13	1879	—	1 Piastre, (E) KM7	10,000.
E14	1884A	—	1 Piastre, KM7	12,500.
E15	1885A	—	1 Sapeque, w/mint mark, w/o ESSAI on rev., open square hole	—

PATTERNS (Pn)

(Including off metal strikes)

KM#	Date	Mintage	Identification	Mkt.Val.
Pn1	1879 A	—	1 Sapeque, Nickel-Silver	300.00

PIEFORTS (P) WITH ESSAI (PE)

Standard metals unless otherwise noted

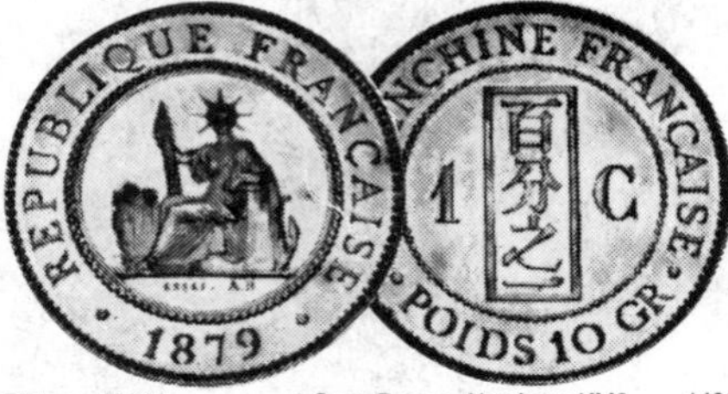

KM#	Date	Mintage	Identification	Mkt.Val.
PE1	1879A	—	1 Cent, Bronze-Aluminum,KM3	1400.
PE2	1879A	—	1 Cent, Brass, KM3	600.00

TRIAL STRIKE (TS)

KM#	Date	Mintage	Identification	Mkt.Val.
TS1	1879	—	1 Sapeque, KM2 over France 2 Centimes, Y20	250.00

KM#	Date	Mintage	Identification	Mkt.Val.
TS2	1879	—	10 Cents, KM4, obv. on 33.5mm Aluminum planchet	450.00
TS3	1879	—	50 Cents, KM6, obv., white metal	375.00

PROOF SETS (PS)

KM#	Date	Mintage	Identification	Issue Price	Mkt. Val.
PS1	1879A(5)	—	KM2-6	Reported, not confirmed	
PS2	1885A(5)	100	KM3-7	—	15,000.

YEMEN REPUBLIC

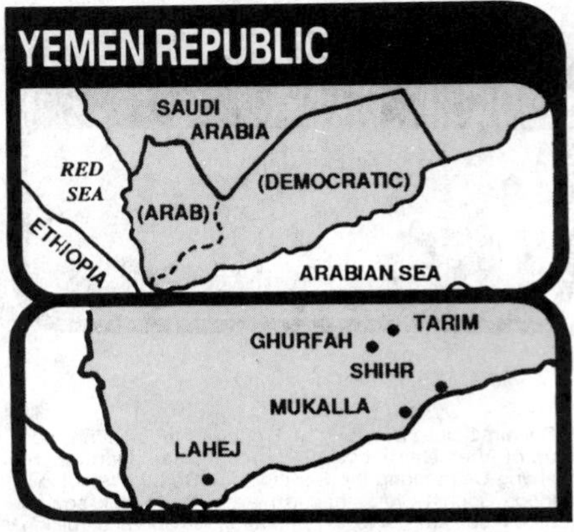

The Republic of Yemen, formerly Yemen Arab Republic and Peoples Republic of Yemen is located on the southern coast of the Arabian Peninsula. It has an area of 205,020 sq. mi. (531,000 sq. km.) and a population of 12 million. Capital: Sana'a. The port of Aden is the main commercial center and the area's most valuable natural resource. Recent oil and gas finds and a developing petroleum industry have improved their economic prospects. Agriculture and local handicrafts are the main industries. Cotton, fish, coffee, rock salt and hides are exported.

On May 22, 1990, the Yemen Arab Republic (North Yemen) and Peoples Democratic Republic of Yemen (South Yemen) merged into a unified Republic of Yemen.

TITLES

دار الخلافة

Dar al-Khilafa(t)

MUTAWAKKILITE KINGDOM

One of the oldest centers of civilization in the Middle East, Yemen was once part of the Minaean Kingdom and of the ancient Kingdom of Sheba, after which it was captured successively by Egyptians, Ethiopians and Romans. It was converted to Islam in 628 A.D. and administered as a caliphate until 1538, when it came under Ottoman occupation in 1849. The second Ottoman occupation which began in 1872 was maintained until 1918 when autonomy was achieved through revolution.

TITLES

المملكة المتوكلية اليمنية

al-Mamlaka(t) al-Mutawakkiliya(t) al-Yamaniya(t)

RULERS

Qasimid Dynasty

al-Mansur Ali I,
AH1189-1224/1775-1809AD
al-Mutawakkil Ahmad,
AH1224-1231/1809-1816AD
al-Mahdi Abdullah,
AH1231-1251/1816-1835AD
al-Mansir Ali II,
AH1251-1252/1835-1837AD and AH1259-1261/1844-1845AD and AH1266/1850AD and AH1267-1288/1851-1874AD
al-Nasir Abdullah,
AH1252-1256/1837-1840AD
al-Hadi Muhammad,
AH1256-1259/1840-1844AD
al-Mutawakkil Muhammad,
AH1261-1265/1845-1849AD
al-Mansur Ahmad,
AH1265-1269/1849-1853AD
al-Mansur Muhammad bin Yahya,
(Imam Mansur) AH1307-1322/1890-1904AD

MINTNAME

Sana'a

NOTE: ***Sana'a*** **= city,** ***Sana*** **= year.**

MONETARY SYSTEM

After AH1322/1904AD

1 Zalat = 1/160 Riyal
2 Zalat = 1 Halala = 1/80 Riyal
2 Halala = 1 Buqsha = 1/40 Riyal
40 Buqsha = 1 Riyal

NOTE: The Riyal was called an IMADI (RIYAL) during the reign of Imam Yahya "Imadi" honorific name for Yahyawi and an AHMADI (RIYAL) during the reign of Imam Ahmad. The 1 Zalat, Y#2.1, B1, A3, A4 and all Imam Yahya gold strikes except Y#F10, which bear no indication of value. All of the Mutawakkilite coins after AH1322/1904AD bear the denomination expressed as fraction of the Riyal as follows.

BRONZE and ALUMINUM

Thumn ushr = 1/80 Riyal = 1/2 Buqsha = 1 Halala
Rub ushr = 1/40 Riyal = 1 Buqsha

SILVER

Nisf ushr = 1/20 Riyal = 2 Buqsha = 1/2 Bawlah
Nisf thumn = 1/16 Riyal = 2-1/2 Buqsha
Ushr = 1/10 Riyal = 4 Buqsha = 1 Bawlah
Thumn = 1/8 Riyal = 5 Buqsha
Rub = 1/4 Riyal = 10 Buqsha
Nisf = 1/2 Riyal = 20 Buqsha
1 Riyal (Imadi, Ahmadi) = 40 Buqsha

DATING

All coins of Imam Yahya have accession date AH 1322 on obverse and actual date of issue on reverse. All coins of Imam Ahmad bear accession date AH1367 on obverse and actual date on reverse.

NOTE: If not otherwise noted, all coins of Imam Yahya and Imam Ahad as well as the early issues of the Republic (Y#20 through Y#A25 and Y#32), were struck at the mint in Sana'a. The Sana'a Mint was essentially a medieval mint, using hand-cut dies and crudely machined blanks. There is a large amount of variation from one die to the next in arrangement of legends and ornaments, form of crescents, number of stars, size of the circle, etc., and literally hundreds of subtypes could be identified. Types are divided only when there are changes in the inscriptions, or major variations in the basic type, such as the presence or absence of *Rabb al-Alamin* in the legend or the position of the word *Sana* (= year) in relation to the year.

AL-MANSUR ALI I

AH1189-1224/1775-1809AD

HARF

BILLON, 0.25-0.40 g

KM#	Date	Mintage	Good	VG	Fine	VF
300	AH1216-24	—	15.00	25.00	35.00	50.00

NOTE: Earlier dates (AH1189-1215) exist for this type.

BUQSHA

BILLON, 0.70-1.10 g

KM#	Date	Mintage	Good	VG	Fine	VF
302	AH1216-24	—	15.00	25.00	35.00	50.00

NOTE: Earlier dates (AH1189-1215) exist for this type.

Issues of Shaikhs of Abu Arisl

In the name of Hammud bin Muhammad (known as Ibn Mismar) AH1217-1232/1802-1817AD

BILLON

Obv: Hammud bin Muhammad. Rev: Duriba fi Abu Arish 1222.

KM#	Date	Mintage	Good	VG	Fine	VF
303	AH1222	—	—	—	Rare	—

Anonymous Wahhabi Issues

BILLON, 0.80 g

Obv: Al hamd Allah. Rev: Duriba fi Zabi.

KM#	Date	Mintage	Good	VG	Fine	VF
304	AH1223	—	—	—	Rare	—

AL-MUTAWAKKIL AHMAD

AH1224-1231/1809-1816AD

HARF

BILLON, 0.25-0.45 g

KM#	Date	Mintage	Good	VG	Fine	VF
305	AH1224-31	—	15.00	25.00	35.00	50.00

BUQSHA

BILLON, 0.70-1.10 g

KM#	Date	Mintage	Good	VG	Fine	VF
306	AH1224-31	—	15.00	25.00	35.00	50.00

AL-MAHDI ABDULLAH

AH1231-1251/1816-1835AD

HARF

BILLON, 0.25-0.40 g

KM#	Date	Mintage	Good	VG	Fine	VF
310 (C51)	AH1231-51	—	10.00	15.00	20.00	30.00

BUQSHA

BILLON, 0.75-1.10 g

KM#	Date	Mintage	Good	VG	Fine	VF
315	AH1231-51	—	7.00	10.00	15.00	25.00

AL-MANSUR ALI II

AH1251-1252/1835-1837AD

HARF

BILLON, 0.25-0.40 g

KM#	Date	Mintage	Good	VG	Fine	VF
320	AH1251-52	—	—	—	Rare	—

AH1259-1261/1844-1845AD

HARF

BILLON, 0.25-0.40 g

KM#	Date	Mintage	Good	VG	Fine	VF
325	AH1259-61	—	—	—	Rare	—

AH1266/1850AD

HARF

BILLON, 0.25-0.40 g

KM#	Date	Mintage	Good	VG	Fine	VF
330	AH1266	—	—	—	Rare	—

AH1267-1288/1851-1874AD

HARF

BILLON, 0.25-0.40 g

KM#	Date	Mintage	Good	VG	Fine	VF
335	AH1267-88	—	—	—	Rare	—

AL-NASIR ABDULLAH

AH1252-1256/1837-1840AD

HARF

BILLON, 0.25-0.40 g

KM#	Date	Mintage	Good	VG	Fine	VF
340	AH1252-56	—	—	—	Rare	—

AL-HADI MUHAMMAD

AH1256-1259/1840-1844AD

HARF

BILLON, 0.25-0.40 g

KM#	Date	Mintage	Good	VG	Fine	VF
345	AH1256-59	—	—	—	Rare	—

AL-MUTAWAKKIL MUHAMMAD

AH1261-1265/1845-1849AD

HARF

BILLON to COPPER, 0.25-0.40 g

KM#	Date	Mintage	Good	VG	Fine	VF
350	ND	—	12.50	20.00	20.00	40.00

AL-MANSUR AHMAD

AH1265-1269/1849-1853AD

HARF

BILLON, 0.25-0.40 g

KM#	Date	Mintage	Good	VG	Fine	VF
355	ND	—	—	—	Rare	—

IMAM MANSUR

AH1307-1322/1890-1904AD

Coins for this ruler were struck at Qaflat Idhar. Harf and Kabir strikes have similar inscriptions with varieties in position of date, legend arrangements and ornamentation. No indication of value on coins.

HARF

BRONZE, 1.2-2.1 g, 16-18mm
Obv. leg: *Billah/al-Mansur*/date/*Sana*.
Rev. leg: *Allah/Abd*.

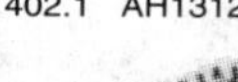

KM#	Date	Mintage	Good	VG	Fine	VF
402.1	AH1312	—	—	—	—	—

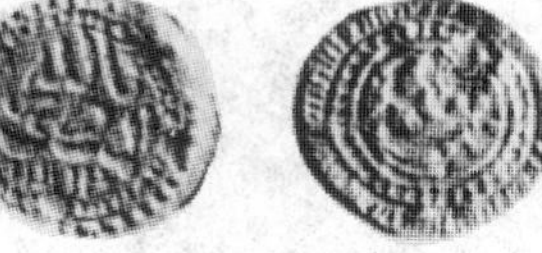

1.30 g
Similar to KM#402.1 but w/o *Sana*.

KM#	Date	Mintage	Good	VG	Fine	VF
402.2	AH1313	—	—	—	—	—

BUQSHA

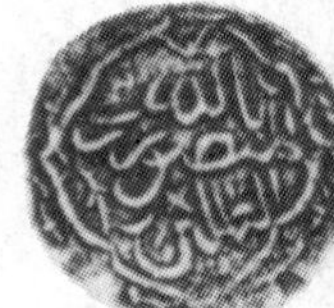 

BRONZE, 3.00 g, 23mm
Obv. leg: *Billah/al-Mansur/Rabb/al-Alamin*.
Rev. leg: *Amir/sana/al-mu'minin/1312*.

KM#	Date	Mintage	Good	VG	Fine	VF
405	AH1312	—	—	—	—	—

3.10 g, 24mm
Obv: Similar to KM#405.
Rev. leg: *Allah/Abd/Amir al-mu'/minin*/date/*sana*.

KM#	Date	Mintage	Good	VG	Fine	VF
406	AH1313	—	—	—	—	—

KABIR

(2 Buqsha)

SILVER, 0.50 g, 16mm
Obv: *Billah/al-Mansu/r*, flower below.
Rev: *Allah/Abd/1311/xxx*.

KM#	Date	Mintage	Good	VG	Fine	VF
407.1	AH1311	—	—	—	—	—

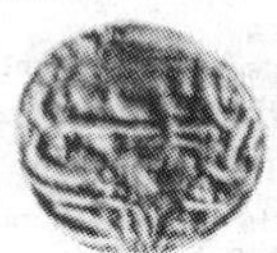 

0.60-0.70 g, 17mm
Rev: Date at bottom.

KM#	Date	Mintage	Good	VG	Fine	VF
407.2	AH1318	—	—	—	—	—

0.40-0.80 g, 15-17mm
Obv. leg: *Billah/al-Mansu/r*, ornament below.
Rev. leg: *Allah*/date, *Abd* as circle.

KM#	Date	Mintage	Good	VG	Fine	VF
408.1	AH1312	—	—	—	—	—
	1316	—	—	—	—	—
	1318	—	—	—	—	—

NOTE: Varieties of shape of ornaments exist.

0.70-0.80 g
Obv: *Billah/al-Mansur*/date.
Rev: *Allah/Abd*, ornament below.

KM#	Date	Mintage	Good	VG	Fine	VF
408.2	AH1312	—	—	—	—	—
	1314	—	—	—	—	—

NOTE: Varieties of shape of ornaments exist.

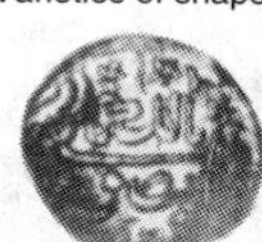 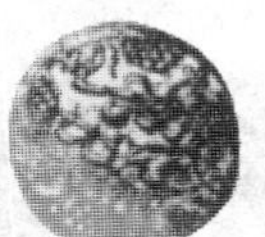

0.70-1.0g
Obv: *Billah/al-Mansu/r*.
Rev: *Allah/Abd/1315*, ornament below.

KM#	Date	Mintage	Good	VG	Fine	VF
409	AH1315	—	—	—	—	—

SILVER, 0.60-1.00 g, 15-16mm
Obv: Similar to KM#409.
Rev: *Allah/Abd*/date divided by ornament.

KM#	Date	Mintage	Good	VG	Fine	VF
410 (Y-A1)	AH1316	—	15.00	30.00	50.00	75.00

NOTE: Later dates (AH1319-1321) exist for this type.

NOTE: Varieties with 3 and 4 stars on reverse exist.

NOTE: Strikes on thin planchets (34.26 g) exist.

EASTERN ADEN PROTECTORATE

Between 1200 B.C. and the 6th century A.D., what is now the Peoples Democratic Republic of Yemen was part of the Minaean kingdom. In subsequent years it was controlled by Persians, Egyptians and Turks. Aden, one of the cities mentioned in the Bible, had been a port for trade between the East and West for 2,000 years. British rule began in 1839 when the British East India Co. seized control to put an end to the piracy threatening trade with India. To protect their foothold in Aden, the British found it necessary to extend their control into the area known historically as the Hadhramaut, and to sign protection treaties with the shaiks of the hinterland.

QUAITI STATE OF SHIHR AND MUKALLA

The Quaiti State of Shihr and Mukalla was comprised in Eastern Aden Protectorate located in southern Arabia.

KASADI of MUKALLA

A port, city sultanate and capital of the Quaiti state of Shihr and Mukalla in Eastern Aden Protectorate in southern Arabia, was a principal port servicing trade between the Middle East and India and Java.

TITLES

المكلا

al-Mukala

RULERS

Salah bin Muhammad,
AH12xx-1290/18xx-1873AD
Umar bin Salah,
AH1290-1298/1873-1881AD

1/2 KHUMSI

BRONZE

KM#	Date	Good	VG	Fine	VF
1	AH1276	25.00	45.00	75.00	120.00

KHUMSI

BRONZE

KM#	Date	Good	VG	Fine	VF
2	AH1276	20.00	40.00	65.00	100.00

QUAITI STATE

TITLES

قيطي

Qa'iti

RULERS

Munasir bin Abdullah bin Umar,
AH1246-1283/1830-1866AD
Awadh bin Umar,
AH1283-1327/1866-1909AD

COUNTERMARKED COINAGE

The counterstamps on the following coins will have one of two possible legend varieties. They are:

(KM#31)
a.) 1307 Magar/ad-Dawlah/bin 'Abd Allah/Al Qaiti (1307, seat of government, Abd Allah Al Qa'iti).

(KM#32)
b.) Magar/ad-Dawlah/1307/sana (seat of government, 1307).

1/12 ANNA

COPPER
c/m: Arabic in 10mm circle on India 1/12 Anna, KM#445.

KM#	Date	Year	Good	VG	Fine	VF
1	AH1307	(1835-48)	8.50	13.50	18.50	30.00

1/4 ANNA

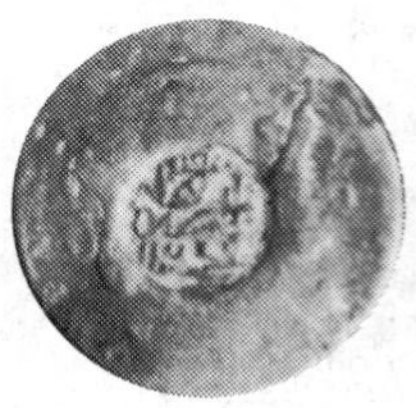

COPPER
c/m: Arabic in 10mm circle on India-Bombay Presidency 1/4 Anna, KM#231.

KM#	Date	Year	Good	VG	Fine	VF
6	AH1307	(1830-32)	4.50	7.50	12.50	22.50

c/m: Arabic in 15mm circle on India-Bombay Presidency 1/4 Anna, KM#232.

KM#	Date	Year	Good	VG	Fine	VF
5	AH1307	(1833)	8.50	13.50	18.50	30.00

c/m: Arabic in 10mm circle on India 1/4 Anna, KM#446.

KM#	Date	Year	Good	VG	Fine	VF
7	AH1307	(1833-58)	4.50	7.50	12.50	22.50

c/m: Arabic in 15mm circle on India 1/4 Anna, KM#467.

KM#	Date	Year	Good	VG	Fine	VF
8	AH1307	(1862-76)	4.50	7.50	12.50	22.50

c/m: Arabic in 10mm circle on Zanzibar Pysa, KM#1.

KM#	Date	Year	Good	VG	Fine	VF
10	AH1307	(AH1299)	7.50	12.50	17.50	27.50

c/m: Arabic in 10mm circle on Mombasa 1/4 Anna, KM#1.

KM#	Date	Year	Good	VG	Fine	VF
9	AH1307	(1888)	7.50	12.50	17.50	27.50

1/2 ANNA

COPPER
c/m: Arabic in 15mm circle on India-Bombay Presidency 1/2 Anna, KM#251.

KM#	Date	Year	Good	VG	Fine	VF
15	AH1307	(1834)	8.50	13.50	18.50	30.00

c/m: Arabic in 15mm circle on India 1/2 Anna, KM#447.

KM#	Date	Year	Good	VG	Fine	VF
16	AH1307	(1835-45)	8.50	13.50	18.50	30.00

c/m: in 15mm circle on India 1/2 Anna, KM#468.

KM#	Date	Year	Good	VG	Fine	VF
17	AH1307	(1862-76)	8.50	13.50	18.50	30.00

1/4 RUPEE

SILVER
c/m: Arabic in 10mm circle on India-Bengal Presidency 1/4 Rupee, KM#96.

KM#	Date	Year	Good	VG	Fine	VF
20	(AH1307)	AH1204	8.50	13.50	18.50	30.00

1/2 RUPEE

SILVER
c/m: Arabic in 15mm circle on Mexico 2 Reales, KM#88.

KM#	Date	Year	Good	VG	Fine	VF
28	AH1307	(1772-89)	10.00	15.00	22.50	32.50

c/m: Arabic in 15mm circle on India-Bengal Presidency 1/2 Rupee, KM#97.

KM#	Date	Year	Good	VG	Fine	VF
29	AH1307	(1793-1818,ND)	10.00	15.00	22.50	32.50

c/m: Arabic in 10mm circle on English 1 Shilling, KM#734.

KM#	Date	Year	Good	VG	Fine	VF
26	AH1307	(1838-87)	7.50	12.50	17.50	27.50

c/m: Arabic in 10mm circle on India 1/2 Rupee, KM#491.

KM#	Date	Year	Good	VG	Fine	VF
25	AH1307	(1877-99)	7.50	12.50	17.50	27.50

c/m: Arabic in 15mm circle on India 1/2 Rupee, KM#491.

KM#	Date	Year	Good	VG	Fine	VF
27	AH1307	(1877-99)	10.00	15.00	22.50	32.50

RUPEE

SILVER
c/m: Arabic in 10mm circle on India Rupee, KM#457.

KM#	Date	Year	Good	VG	Fine	VF
30	AH1307	(1840)	10.00	15.00	22.50	32.50

PRICES - Single c/m on coin. Add 15 percent for each additional c/m.

c/m: Arabic in 15mm circle on India Rupee, KM#458.

KM#	Date	Year	Good	VG	Fine	VF
31	AH1307	(1840)	11.50	17.50	25.00	35.00

c/m: Arabic in 10mm circle on India Rupee, KM#458.

KM#	Date	Year	Good	VG	Fine	VF
32	AH1307	(1840)	10.00	15.00	22.50	32.50

c/m: Arabic in 10mm circle on India Rupee, KM#473.1

KM#	Date	Year	Good	VG	Fine	VF
33	AH1307	(1862-1874)	11.50	17.50	25.00	35.00

c/m: Arabic in 10mm circle on India Rupee, KM#492.

KM#	Date	Year	Good	VG	Fine	VF
34	AH1307	(1877-1901)	11.50	17.50	25.00	35.00

RYAL

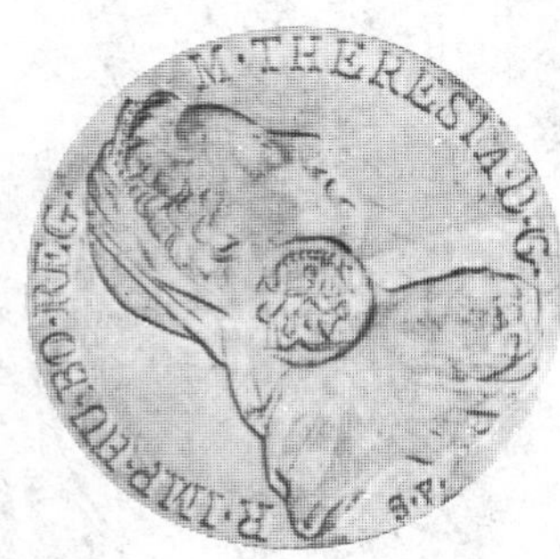

SILVER

c/m: Arabic in 10mm circle on Austria MTT, KM#T1.

KM#	Date	Year	Good	VG	Fine	VF
35	AH1307	(1780)	25.00	35.00	45.00	60.00

c/m: Arabic in 15mm circle on Austria MTT, KM#T1.

KM#	Date	Year	Good	VG	Fine	VF
36	AH1307	(1780)	30.00	40.00	50.00	70.00

SOVEREIGN

GOLD

c/m: Arabic on English Sovereign, KM#767.

KM#	Date	Year	Good	VG	Fine	VF
40	AH1307	(1887-92)	—	—	Rare	—

REGULAR COINAGE

5 KHUMSI

COPPER and BRONZE

KM#	Date	Year	Good	VG	Fine	VF
45	AH1315	1897	7.00	10.00	17.00	30.00

KM#	Date	Year	Good	VG	Fine	VF
48	AH1318	1900	6.00	8.00	14.00	25.00

NOTE: Overstrikes on East India Co. 1/4 Annas exist.

1/3 RIYAL

SILVER

KM#	Date	Good	VG	Fine	VF
46	AH1315	150.00	250.00	350.00	500.00

1/2 RIYAL

SILVER

KM#	Date	Good	VG	Fine	VF
47	AH1316	175.00	300.00	450.00	600.00

KATHIRI STATE OF SEIYUN & TARIM

Kathiri State of Seiyun and Tarim, a city sultanate in Eastern Aden Protectorate, was an important oasis settlement in the Hadhramaut Wadi region of southern Arabia. It became a British treaty protectorate in the 1880's.

TITLES

Tarim 

RULERS

Syed Hussein ibn Sahil, AH1258/1842AD

MINT MARKS

H - Heaton, Birmingham

MONETARY SYSTEM

128 Khumsi = 1 Riyal = 1 Maria Theresa Thaler

NOTE: The Arabic 128 in the obverse legend of AH1270 series indicates equivalency with the Maria Theresa Thaler. The Arabic 910 in the obverse legend of the AH1315 series probably indicates the silver fineness.

KHUMSI

COPPER, thin

KM#	Date	Year	Mintage	VG	Fine	VF
5	AH1258	(1842)	—	12.00	20.00	30.00

3 KHUMSI

COPPER, thick

KM#	Date	Year	Mintage	VG	Fine	VF
6	AH1258	(1842)	—	20.00	30.00	50.00

4 KHUMSI

.8000 g, .900 SILVER, .0231 oz ASW

KM#	Date	Year	Mintage	Fine	VF	XF
10	AH1270	(1853)	—	55.00	85.00	125.00

6 KHUMSI

.9000 g, .900 SILVER, .0260 oz ASW

KM#	Date	Year	Mintage	Fine	VF	XF
15	AH1315H	(1897)	.335	5.00	10.00	18.00
	1315H	(1897)	—	—	Proof	50.00

8 KHUMSI

1.6500 g, .900 SILVER, .0477 oz ASW

KM#	Date	Year	Mintage	Fine	VF	XF
11	AH1270	(1853)	—	55.00	85.00	125.00

12 KHUMSI

1.5000 g, .910 SILVER, .0434 oz ASW

KM#	Date	Year	Mintage	Fine	VF	XF
16	AH1315H	(1897)	.167	8.00	16.00	25.00
	1315H	(1897)	—	—	Proof	75.00

16 KHUMSI

3.3500 g, .900 SILVER, .0969 oz ASW

KM#	Date	Year	Mintage	Fine	VF	XF
12	AH1270	(1853)	—	65.00	100.00	150.00

24 KHUMSI

3.1500 g, .910 SILVER, .0911 oz ASW

KM#	Date	Year	Mintage	Fine	VF	XF
17	AH1315H	(1897)	.083	7.50	15.00	25.00
	1315H	(1897)	—	—	Proof	125.00

30 KHUMSI

7.6500 g, .900 SILVER, .2213 oz ASW

KM#	Date	Year	Mintage	Fine	VF	XF
7	AH1258	(1842)	—	100.00	150.00	250.00

WESTERN ADEN PROTECTORATE

LAHEJ

A rather small partially independent sultanate situated north of the port city of Aden. Lahej had entered into a protective treaty relationship with Britain following Britain's capture of the port of Aden in 1839.

TITLES

Lahej

LOCAL RULERS

Ali ibn Mohasan,
AH1265-1279/1849-1863AD
Fazal ibn Ali,
AH1291-1315/1874-1898AD

1/2 BAIZA

COPPER

KM#	Date	Mintage	Fine	VF	XF	Unc
1	ND(1860)	—	20.00	35.00	60.00	175.00

Accession date: AH1291

KM#	Date	Mintage	Fine	VF	XF	Unc
2	ND(1896)	.678	22.50	40.00	70.00	200.00
	ND(1896)	—	—	—	Proof	350.00

MONTENEGRO

The former independent kingdom of Montenegro, now one of the nominally autonomous federated units of Yugoslavia, was located in southeastern Europe north of Albania. As a kingdom, it had an area of 5,333 sq. mi. (13,812 sq. km.) and a population of about 250,000. Capital: Podgorica. The predominantly pastoral kingdom had few industries.

Montenegro became an independent state in 1355 following the break-up of the Serb empire. During the Turkish invasion of Albania and Herzegovina in the 15th century, the Montenegrins moved their capital to the remote mountain village of Cetinje where they maintained their independence through two centuries of intermittent attack, emerging as the only one of the Balkan states not subjugated by the Turks. When World War I began, Montenegro joined with Serbia and was subsequently invaded and occupied by the Austrians. Austria withdrew upon the defeat of the Central Powers, permitting the Serbians to move in and maintain the occupation. Montenegro then joined the kingdom of the Serbs, Croats and Slovenes, which later became Yugoslavia.

CATTARO

A seaport of Montenegro, Yugoslavia, occupies a ledge between the Montenegrin mountains and an inlet of the Adriatic Sea which forms one of the finest natural harbors in the world. It has at various times been occupied by Turks, Venetians, Spaniards, French, English and Austrians. It became a part of Yugoslavia in 1918. Cattaro was united to the French Empire during the period of 1807-13. In 1813, while the city was besieged by Montenegrins and a British fleet, the French defenders issued an emergency cast silver coinage.

FRENCH SIEGE COINAGE

FRANC

CAST SILVER, 5.50-6.30 g

KM#	Date	Mintage	Good	VG	Fine	VF
1	1813	—	80.00	125.00	200.00	300.00

5 FRANCS

CAST SILVER, 28.00-30.00 g

KM#	Date	Mintage	Good	VG	Fine	VF
2	1813	—	300.00	500.00	800.00	1250.

10 FRANCS

CAST SILVER, 59.00-59.60 g

KM#	Date	Mintage	Good	VG	Fine	VF
3	1813	—	450.00	850.00	1250.	2000.

Serbia, a former inland Balkan kingdom has an area of 34,116 sq. mi. (88,361 sq. km.). Capital: Belgrade.

Serbia emerged as a separate kingdom in the 12th century and attained its greatest expansion and political influence in the mid-14th century. After the Battle of Kosovo, 1389, Serbia became a vassal principality of Turkey and remained under Turkish suzeranity until it was re-established as an independent kingdom by the 1887 Treaty of Berlin. Following World War I, which had its immediate cause in the assassination of Austrian Archduke Francis Ferdinand by a Serbian nationalist, Serbia joined with the Croats and Slovenes to form the new Kingdom of the South Slavs with Peter I of Serbia as king. The name of the kingdom was later changed to Yugoslavia. Invaded by Germany during World War II, Serbia emerged as a constituent republic of the Socialist Federal Republic of Yugoslavia.

RULERS

Michael, Obrenovich III
as Prince, 1839-1842, 1860-1868
Milan, Obrenovich IV,
as Prince, 1868-1882
as King, 1882-1889
Alexander I, 1889-1902

MINT MARKS

A - Paris
(a) - Paris, privy mark only
H - Birmingham
V - Vienna
БП (BP) Budapest

MONETARY SYSTEM

100 Para = 1 Dinara

DENOMINATIONS

ПАРА = Para
ПАРЕ = Pare
ДИНАР = Dinar
ДИНАРА = Dinara

KINGDOM

PARA

BRONZE
SERBIA spelled: СРБСКИ

KM#	Date	Mintage	Fine	VF	XF	Unc
1.1	1868	7.500	4.00	12.50	30.00	75.00

SERBIA spelled: СРЪСКИ

KM#	Date	Mintage	Fine	VF	XF	Unc
1.2	1868	Inc. Ab.	5.00	15.00	35.00	95.00

5 PARA

BRONZE

KM#	Date	Mintage	Fine	VF	XF	Unc
2	1868	7.420	3.00	10.00	32.00	90.00
	1868	—	—	—	Proof	275.00

KM#	Date	Mintage	Fine	VF	XF	Unc
7	1879	6.000	2.00	6.00	28.00	70.00
	1879	—	—	—	Proof	200.00

COPPER-NICKEL

KM#	Date	Mintage	Fine	VF	XF	Unc
18	1883	4.000	1.00	3.00	8.00	22.00
	1884H	3.000	1.00	3.00	8.00	25.00
	1884H	—	—	—	Proof	200.00

NOTE: Later dates (1904-1917) exist for this type.

10 PARA

BRONZE

KM#	Date	Mintage	Fine	VF	XF	Unc
3	1868	6.590	4.00	12.50	35.00	90.00
	1868	—	—	—	Proof	325.00

KM#	Date	Mintage	Fine	VF	XF	Unc
8	1879	9.000	3.00	8.00	27.50	70.00
	1879	—	—	—	Proof	200.00

COPPER-NICKEL

KM#	Date	Mintage	Fine	VF	XF	Unc
19	1883	5.000	.75	1.75	5.00	16.00
	1884H	6.500	.75	1.75	4.50	12.00
	1884H	—	—	—	Proof	250.00

NOTE: Later dates (1904-1917) exist for this type.

20 PARA

COPPER-NICKEL

KM#	Date	Mintage	Fine	VF	XF	Unc
20	1883	2.500	1.00	3.50	12.00	25.00
	1884H	6.000	1.00	2.50	8.00	16.00
	1884H	—	—	—	Proof	300.00

NOTE: Later dates (1904-1917) exist for this type.

50 PARA

2.5000 g, .835 SILVER, .0671 oz ASW

KM#	Date	Mintage	Fine	VF	XF	Unc
4	1875	2.000	6.50	16.50	60.00	160.00
	1875	—	—	—	Proof	300.00

KM#	Date	Mintage	Fine	VF	XF	Unc
9	1879	.600	4.00	15.00	30.00	95.00
	1879	—	—	—	Proof	275.00

DINAR

5.0000 g, .835 SILVER, .1342 oz ASW

KM#	Date	Mintage	Fine	VF	XF	Unc
5	1875	3.000	12.50	27.50	90.00	280.00
	1875	—	—	—	Proof	450.00

KM#	Date	Mintage	Fine	VF	XF	Unc
10	1879	.800	5.00	15.00	45.00	130.00
	1879	—	—	—	Proof	300.00

KM#	Date	Mintage	Fine	VF	XF	Unc
21	1897	4.001	2.50	6.50	15.00	55.00

2 DINARA

10.0000 g, .835 SILVER, .2684 oz ASW

KM#	Date	Mintage	Fine	VF	XF	Unc
6	1875	1.000	25.00	75.00	165.00	380.00
	1875	—	—	—	Proof	525.00

KM#	Date	Mintage	Fine	VF	XF	Unc
11	1879	.750	7.00	22.00	60.00	185.00
	1879	—	—	—	Proof	475.00

KM#	Date	Mintage	Fine	VF	XF	Unc
22	1897	1.000	4.50	12.50	32.00	85.00
	1897	—	—	—	Proof	165.00

5 DINARA

25.0000 g, .900 SILVER, .7234 oz ASW
Edge Type 1: БОГ*ЧУВА*СРБИЈУ***

KM#	Date	Mintage	Fine	VF	XF	Unc
12	1879	.200	28.00	60.00	150.00	350.00
	1879	—	—	—	Proof	1200.

Edge Type 2: БОГ*СРБИЈУ*ЧУВА***

KM#	Date	Mintage	Fine	VF	XF	Unc
13	1879	Inc. Ab.	40.00	80.00	175.00	450.00

10 DINARA

3.2258 g, .900 GOLD, .0933 oz AGW

KM#	Date	Mintage	Fine	VF	XF	Unc
16	1882V	.300	75.00	125.00	175.00	320.00

20 DINARA

6.4516 g, .900 GOLD, .1867 oz AGW
Obv. leg: Full title.

KM#	Date	Mintage	Fine	VF	XF	Unc
14	1879A	.050	125.00	160.00	300.00	550.00
	1879A	—	—	—	Proof	5000.

Obv. leg: Short title.

KM#	Date	Mintage	Fine	VF	XF	Unc
17	1882V	.300	100.00	120.00	180.00	325.00

PATTERNS (Pn)

(Including off metal strikes)

KM#	Date	Mintage	Identification	Mkt.Val.
Pn1	1882V	—	20 Dinara, Copper	1250.
Pn2	1890	—	1 Dinar, Silver	5000.
Pn3	1890	—	2 Dinara, Silver	6000.
Pn4	1890	—	2 Dinara, Aluminum-Bronze	—
Pn5	1890	—	2 Dinara, Gilt Bronze	—
PnA6	1892	—	1 Dinar, Silver	7000.
PnB6	1892	—	2 Dinara, Silver	8000.

ZAIRE

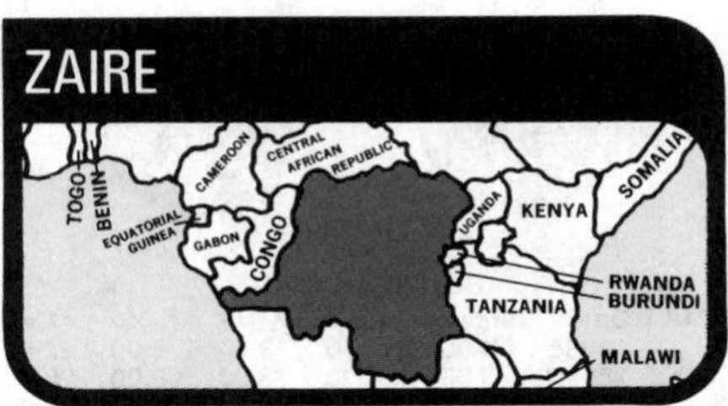

The Republic of Zaire (formerly the Belgian Congo), located in the south-central part of Africa, has an area of 905,568 sq. mi. (2,345,410 sq. km.) and a population of *34.3 million. Capital: Kinshasa. The mineral-rich country produces copper, tin, diamonds, gold, zinc, cobalt and uranium.

In ancient times the territory comprising Zaire was occupied by Negrito peoples (Pygmies) pushed into the mountains by Bantu and Nilotic invaders. The interior was first explored by the American correspondent Henry Stanley, who was subsequently commissioned by King Leopold II of Belgium to conclude development treaties with the local chiefs. The Berlin conference of 1885 awarded the area to Leopold, who administered and exploited it as his private property until it was annexed to Belgium in 1908. Belgium received the mandate for the German territory of Ruanda-Urundi as a result of the international treaties after WWI. During World War II, Belgian Congolese troops fought on the side of the Allies, notably in Ethiopia. Following the eruption of bloody independence riots in 1959, Belgium granted the Belgian Congo independence as the Republic of the Congo on June 30, 1960. The nation officially changed its name to Zaire on Oct. 27, 1971.

CONGO FREE STATE

RULER

Leopold II

CENTIME

COPPER

KM#	Date	Mintage	Fine	VF	XF	Unc
1	1887	.180	1.50	3.00	6.00	18.00
	1888	Inc. Ab.	1.00	2.00	4.00	10.00

2 CENTIMES

COPPER

KM#	Date	Mintage	Fine	VF	XF	Unc
2	1887	.130	1.50	3.00	6.00	20.00
	1888	Inc. Ab.	1.00	2.00	4.00	10.00

5 CENTIMES

COPPER

KM#	Date	Mintage	Fine	VF	XF	Unc
3	1887	.180	2.00	4.00	8.00	20.00
	1888/7	Inc. Ab.	1.50	3.00	5.00	15.00
	1888	Inc. Ab.	1.50	3.00	6.00	20.00
	1894	.150	2.00	4.00	7.00	25.00

10 CENTIMES

COPPER

KM#	Date	Mintage	Fine	VF	XF	Unc
4	1887	.040	5.00	10.00	20.00	60.00
	1888	Inc. Ab.	2.00	3.50	9.00	28.00
	1889	.100	3.00	7.00	15.00	40.00
	1894	.150	2.50	5.00	12.00	32.00

50 CENTIMES

2.5000 g .835 SILVER, .0671 oz ASW

KM#	Date	Mintage	Fine	VF	XF	Unc
5	1887	.020	7.00	15.00	30.00	70.00
	1887	—	—	—	Proof	250.00
	1891	.060	8.00	17.50	35.00	80.00
	1894	.040	8.00	20.00	40.00	100.00
	1896	.200	8.00	15.00	35.00	75.00

FRANC

5.0000 g, .835 SILVER, .1342 oz ASW

KM#	Date	Mintage	Fine	VF	XF	Unc
6	1887	.020	10.00	20.00	40.00	110.00
	1891	.070	10.00	22.00	45.00	120.00
	1894	.070	12.00	25.00	50.00	135.00
	1896	.160	9.00	18.00	35.00	100.00

2 FRANCS

10.0000 g, .835 SILVER, .2685 oz ASW

KM#	Date	Mintage	Fine	VF	XF	Unc
7	1887	.020	25.00	45.00	100.00	195.00
	1891	.030	30.00	50.00	125.00	275.00
	1894	.080	30.00	50.00	120.00	250.00
	1896	.100	30.00	50.00	100.00	200.00

5 FRANCS

25.0000 g, .900 SILVER, .7234 oz ASW
Obv. leg: LEOPOLD II R.D.BELGES. . .

KM#	Date	Mintage	Fine	VF	XF	Unc
8.1	1887	8,000	95.00	160.00	235.00	525.00
	1891	.030	100.00	175.00	250.00	550.00
	1894	.050	100.00	175.00	250.00	550.00
	1896	.110	90.00	150.00	250.00	525.00

Obv. leg: LEOPOLD II ROI DES BELGES. . .

8.2	1887	100 pcs.	1000.	2500.	4250.	6500.

PATTERNS (Pn)

(Including off metal strikes)

KM#	Date	Mintage	Identification	Mkt.Val.
Pn1	1887	—	10 Centimes, w/o dots or rays	400.00
Pn2	1887	—	50 Centimes, Brass	125.00
Pn3	1887	—	1 Franc, Brass	175.00
Pn4	1887	—	2 Franc, Brass	250.00

Pn5	1896	—	5 Francs, Lead and Tin alloy	—
Pn6	1896	—	5 Francs, .900 Silver, milled edge	1100.
Pn7	1896	—	5 Francs, .900 Silver, plain edge	1100.
Pn8	1896	—	5 Francs, .900 Silver, lettered edge	1200.

LEGEND ABBREVIATIONS

Following in alphabetical order is a listing of the Latin legends found on World coins. The legend as it appears on the coin is in bold typeface. The translation is followed by issuer.

Common Abbreviations

A.A. - Archidux Austriae. . . . . Archduke of Austria.

Arch. Aust. Dux Burg. Mar. Mor. Co. Tyr - Archidux Austriae Dux Burgundiae Marchio Moraviae Comes Tyrolis. . . . . Archduke of Austria, Duke of Burgundy, Margrave of Moravia, Count of Tyrol.

D.G. - Dei Gratia. . . . .By the grace of God.

Dan. Nor. Van. Got. Rex - Daniae, Norvegiae, Vandalorum Gothorum Rex. . . . . King of Denmark, Norway, Vandalia, Gotland.

Dux Sles. Hol. Stor. Ditm. Com. Old. & Delm. - Dux Slesvivi Holsatiae Stormariae et Ditmarsiae Comes in Oldenburg et Delmenhorst. . . . . Duke of Schleswig-Holstein, Stormarn, and Ditmarsh, Count in Oldenburg and Delmenhorst.

F.D. - Fidei Defensor. . . . . Defender of the Faith.

Ger. Hun. Boh. Rex - Germaniae Hungariae Bohemiae Rex. . . . . King of Germany, Hungary, Bohemia.

P.M. - Pontifex Maximus. . . . . Supreme Pontiff.

Rex Pol. Ma. Dux Lit. Rus. Prus. Mas. Sam. Liv. nec non Svec. Gotor. Vandal. Haere. Rex - Rex Poloniae Magnus Dux Lithuaniae Russiae Prussiae Masoviae Samgitiae Livoniae nec non Svecorum Gothorum Vandalorum Haereditarius Rex. . . . . King of Poland, Grand Duke of Lithuania, Russia, Prussia, Masovia, Semgallia, Livonia, as well as hereditary King of Sweden, Gotland, and Vandalia.

German States Prefaces

Prefaced and numbered below are abbreviations which frequently appear in German States legends. They will be referred to numerous times.

1. **ANHALT - F.A.C.A.D.S.B.I. & K.** . . . . . . Prince of Anhalt, Count of Aschersleben, Lord of Zerbst, Bernburg, Jever, and Knyphausen.

2. **BAVARIA - PFALZ - JULICH-BERG - BERG - B.I.C.& M.D.C.V.S.M.R. & M.D.I.R.** . . . . . Bavaria, Julich, Cleves, Berg, Count of Veldenz, Sponheim, Mark & Ravensberg & Moers, Lord in Ravenstein.
C.P.R.S.R.I. Archit. & El. D.B. . . . . . Count Palatine of the Rhine, Archtreasurer of the H.R.E., Duke of Bavaria. . . . . (as above)

3. **BRANDENBURG** (Legends are abbreviated in both Latin and German)
Mar. Brand. S.R.I. Arc. & Elec. Magd. Pruss, dux lvl. (Gu.) Cli. & Mont. (Ber.) (Churf. I. Pr. z. Gu. C. & B.). . . . . Margrave of Brandenburg, Arch-chamberlain and Elector of the H.R.E., Duke of Magdeburg, Prussia, Julich, Cleves, and Berg.
Stet. Pomer. Cas. (der C.) W.a.i.S. zu K. u. I. (Cro. Car. Sile.) Hert. . . . . . Stettin, Pomerania, Cassubia, Vandalia, also Duke in Silesia of Krossen and Jagerndorf.
B.N.P.R.Co. Ma. & Ra. d.i. Rav. (B.z.N.F.z.R.G.z.D.) P.H.M.C. . . . . . Burgrave of Nuremberg, Prince of Rugen, Count of Mark & Ravensberg, Lord in Ravenstein, Prince of Halberstadt, Minden, Cammin.

4. **BRUNSWICK - Dux (Hertz.) Bruns. Luneb.** . . . . . Duke of Brunswick and Luneburg.

5. **HABSBURG - D.G.R.I.S.A. Germ. Hung. Boh. Rex.** . . . . By the grace of God, Roman Emperor always august, King of Germany, Hungary, Bohemia. . . . . **also S.R.I.** . . . . . Holy Roman Empire.

6. **MANSFELD - Comes & dn. in Mansf. nob. dm. in Held. Seb. et Schrap.** Count and Lord in Mansfeld, noble Lord of Heldrungen, Seeburg, and Schraplau.

7. **SAXONY - Saxo. Iul. Cli. B. (Mon.) A. & W. Lan. Thu. Mar. Mis. Pri. Hen. C.M. & R.D.R.** . . . . . Saxony, Julich, Cleves, Berg, Angria, and Westphalia, Landgrave of Thuringia, Margrave of Meissen, Prince of Henneberg, Count of Mark & Ravensberg, Lord in Ravenstein.

8. **SCHWARZBURG - E. IV. com. imp. com. Schwartz. & Honst. dom. A.S.L.L. et Cl.** . . . . . of the four Counts of the Empire, Count of Schwarzburg and Hohnstein, Lord of Arnstein, Sondershausen, Leutenberg, Lohra, and Klettenberg.

9. **STOLBERG - Stol. Konig. Rut. (Roch.) Wer. Hon. zu Epst. Mintz. Brev. Eich. Lo. u. Cletten.** . . . . . Stolberg, Konigstein, Rochefort, Wernigerode, Hohnstein, Lord of Epstein, Munzenberg, Breuberg, Eichsfeld, Lohra, and Klettenberg.

10. **WURTTEMBERG - Dux Wirt. & Tec. (com Montp.) (in Sil. Ols.) (B.).** . . . . Duke of Wurttemberg and Teck, Count of Mompelgard, in Silesia-Oels, Bernstadt, or Berolstein.

11. **HESSE - Landg. Hass. princ. (admi.) Hersf. C.C.D.Z.E.N.S.Y.B.** . . . . Landgrave of Hesse, Prince (administrator) of Hersfeld, Katzenellenbogen, Cassel, Diez, Ziegenhayn, Nidda, and Schauenburg, Isenburg, Budingen.

A

Ad Norm(am) conv(entionis) According to the convention standard. (Baden, Furstenberg, Hohenzollern-Hechingen, Wurttemberg)

Adolph Georg Furst zu Schaumburg-Lippe Adolph George, Prince of Schaumburg-Lippe. (Schaumburg-Lippe)

Adolph Herzog zu Nassau Adolph, Duke of Nassau. (Nassau)

Agricoltura e Commercio Agriculture and Commerce. (Italian Republic)

Albert Furst zu Schwarzburg Albert, Prince of Schwarzburg. (Schwarzburg)

Albert Koenig von Sachsen Albert, King of Saxony. (Saxony)

Albert Roi des Belges Albert, King of the Belgians. (Belgium)

Alex(ander) Carl Herzog zu Anhalt Alexander Carl, Duke of Anhalt. (Anhalt)

Alexander I Ces. Ros. Wskrzesiciel Krol Pols. Alexander I, Tsar of all the Russias, King of Poland. (Poland)

Alexander I Cesarz Sa. W. Ros. Krol Polski Alexander I, Tsar of all the Russias, King of Poland. (Poland)

Alexandrine * Ludwig * Friedrich * Wilhelm und Sophie Grosherzogin von Baden Besuchen die Munzstaette den 29 Febr. 1832. Heil Ihnen Alexandrina, Ludwig, Frederick, William, and Sophie, Grand Duchess of Baden visit the mint on February 29, 1832. Prosperity to them. (Baden)

Alexius Friedrich Christian Herzog zu Anhalt Alexius Frederick Christian, Duke of Anhalt. (Anhalt)

Alfonso XII Por La G(racia) de Dios Alfonzo XII, by the grace of God. (Spain)

Alfonzo XII Rey de Espana Alfonzo XII, King of Spain. (Spain)

Alfonzo XIII Por La G(racia) de Dios Alfonzo XIII, D.G. (Spain)

Alfred Herzog von Sachsen Coburg und Gotha Alfred, Duke of Saxe-Coburg-Gotha. (Saxe-Coburg-Gotha)

Alla Naz(ione) Fran. La Rep(ubblica) Cisal. Riconoscente To the French nation, the grateful Cisalpine Republic. (Cisalpine Republic)

Alleanza Dei Populi Liberi Alliance of the free people. (Venice)

Allgemeine Ausstellung Deutscher Industrie und Gewerbs Erzeugnisse General Exhibition of German industrial and craft products. (Bavaria)

Althingi Vas Sett At Rathi Ulfliots Ok Allra Landsmanna Parliament was established by the Council of Ulfliot and by all the people. (Iceland)

Amadeo I Rey de Espana Amadeus I, King of Spain. (Spain)

Anton Koenig und Friedrich August Mitregent von Sachsen Anton, King and Frederick August, co-regent of Saxony. (Saxony)

Anton Koenig von Sachsen (cross) den 6 Iuni 1836 Anton, King of Saxony (died) on June 6, 1836. (Saxony)

Anton V.G.G. Koenig von Sachsen Anton, D.G., King of Saxony. (Saxony)

Arch. Aust. D. Burg. Loth. M. D. Het. Archduke of Austria, Duke of Burgundy, Lorraine, Grand Duke of Etruria. (Austria)

Arnold Winkelreid. (Switzerland)

Audere Semper Ever to dare. (Albania)

Auxilium de Sancto Aid from the Saint. (Papal States)

B

Bai(y)erischer Kronthaler Bavarian Kronentaler. (Bavaria)

Bayerisch-Wurtembergischer Zollverein, geschlossen 1827 Bavarian-Wurttemberg customs union, formed 1827. (Bavaria)

Bayern Errichteten die H. Ottokapelle zu Kiefersfelden zum Andenken an Koen. Otto's Abschied v. seinem Vaterlande Bavaria, erected the Otto chapel at Kiefersfelden in commemoration of King Otto's departure from his fatherland. (Bavaria)

Bayerns Treue Faithfulness of Bavarians. (Bavaria)

Berathung u. Grundung e. Deutschen Parlaments 31 Marz 1848 Deliberation over the establishment of a German parliament on March 31, 1848. (Frankfurt)

Berg. und Clevische Land Munz Legal coin of Berg and Cleves. (Berg)

Bergische Landmunz Legal coin of Berg. (Berg)

Bergsegen des Harzes Blessings of the Harz mines. (Hannover)

Bernhard Herzog zu Sachsen Meiningen Bernhard, Duke of Saxe-Meiningen. (Saxe-Meiningen)

Besucht zum Erstenmal die von Ihm erbaute Munzstatte zu Wiesbaden den 28 Dec. 1851 Visit for the first time to the mint built by himself at Wiesbaden on December 28, 1851. (Nassau)

Beytritt von Baden zum Teutschen Zollverein Joining of Baden to the German Customs Union. (Bavaria)

Bieberer Silber Silver of the Bieber (mines). (Hesse-Cassel)

Bizalmarn Az Osi Erenyben Affirmed of ancient and good quality. (Hungary)

Bog Cuva Jugoslaviju God guard Yugoslavia. (Yugoslavia)

Bonaparte Premier Consul Bonaparte, First Consul. (France)

Britanniarum Regina Fid. Def. Queen of the Britains, Defender of the Faith. (France)

C

Canton Appenzell, Argau, Bern, Freyburg, Graubunden, Luzern, Soloth, Ticino, de Vaud, Zurich. (Swiss Cantons)

Capit(ulum) Cath(edrale) Monasterien(se) Sede Vacante The Cathedral Chapter, Munster. The seat being vacant. (Munster)

Car. Albertus D.G. Rex Sard. Cyp. et Hier. Charles Albert, D.G., King of Sardinia, Cyprus, and Jerusalem. (Sardinia)

Car. Felix D.G. Rex Sar. Cyp. et Hier. Charles Felix, D.G., King of Sardinia, Cyprus, and Jerusalem. (Sardinia)

Carl Alexander Grossherzog von Sachsen Carl Alexander, Grand Duke of Saxony (Weimar). (Saxony)

Carl Anton Furst zu Hohenzollern Sigmaringen Carl Anton, Prince of Hohenzollern-Sigmaringen. (Hohenzollern-Sigmaringen)

Carl August H.Z.S. Weimar u. Eisenach Carl August, Duke of Saxe-Weimar-Eisenach. (Saxe-Weimar-Eisenach)

Carl Eduard Herzog V. Sachsen Coburg u. Gotha Carl Edward, Duke of Saxe-Coburg, and Gotha. (Saxe-Coburg-Gotha)

Carl Friedr(ich) Grossherzog z(u) Sachsen W(eim.) E(is.) Carl Frederick, Grand Duke of Saxe-Weimar-Eisenach. (Saxe-Weimar-Eisenach)

Carl Friedrich Grosherzog von Baden Carl Frederick, Grand Duke of Baden. (Baden)

Carl Furst Primas (der Rhein Confoed.) Carl, Prince Primate of the Rhine Confederation. (Rhine Confederation)

Carl Furst zu Hohenzollern Sigmaringen Carl, Prince of Hohenzollern-Sigmaringen. (Hohenzollern-Sigmaringen)

Carl Furst zu Isenburg Carl, Prince of Isenburg. (Isenburg)

Carl Kronpr. v. Wurttemb. u Olga Grosfurstin v. Russl. verm d. 13 Juli 1846 Carl, Crown Prince of Wurttemberg and Olga, Grand Duchess of Russia, married on July 13, 1846. (Wurttemberg)

Carl Ludwig Erzherzog v. Osterreich Protector D. Osterreichischen Touristen Club Charles Louis, Archduke of Austria, Sponsor of the Austrian Tourist's Club. (Austria)

Carl XIII Sv. Norr. Goth. och V. Konung Charles XIII, King of Sweden, Norway, Gothland, and Vandalia. (Sweden)

Carl XIII Sveriges Goth. och V. Konung Charles XIII, King of Sweden, Gothland, and Vandalia. (Sweden)

Carl XIV Johan, Norges, Sver. G. og V. Konge Charles XIV, John, King of Norway, Sweden, Gothland, and Vandalia. (Norway)

Carl XIV Sveriges Norr. Goth. och V. Konung Charles XIV, King of Sweden, Norway, Gothland, and Vandalia. (Sweden)

Carl XV Norges Sver. G. V. K9nge Charles XV, King of Norway, Sweden, Gothland, Vandalia. (Norway)

Carl XV Sveriges Norr. Goth. och Vend. Konung Charles XIV, King of Sweden, Gothland, and Vandalia. (Sweden)

Carlos I Rei de Portugal Carlos I, King of Portugal. (Portugal)

Carlos I Rei e Amelia Rainha de Portugal Carlos I, King and Amelia, Queen of Portugal. (Portugal)

Carol I Domnul Romaniei Carol I, Prince of Romania. (Romania)

Carol I Rege al Romaniei Carol I, King of Bohemia. (Romania)

Carola Magna Ducissa Feliciter Regnante Grand Duchess Charlotte, happily reigning. (Luxembourg)

Carolus Ioachim D.G. Princ Furstenberg Carl Ioachim, D.G., Prince of Furstenberg. (Furstenberg)

Carolus Lud. D.G. Rex Etr(uriae) & M. Aloysia R(egina) Rectrix I. I. H. H. Charles Louis, D.G., King of Etruria and Maria Luisa, Queen Regent, Prince and Princess of Spain. (Tuscany)

Carolus IIII dei G. Charles IV, D.G. (Spain)

Carolus XIV Ioh. D.G. Rex Svegiae et Norv. An Avril 1821 Charles XIV John, D.G., King of Sweden and Norway, April, 1821. (Sweden)

Cartagena Sitiada Por Los Centralistas Cartagena besieged by the Centralists. (Spain)

Cattaro en Etat de Siege Cattaro in a state of siege. (Cattaro)

Centenaire des Chemins de Fer Belges Centenary of the Belgian railways. (Belgium)

Centenario da Guerra Peninsular Centenary of the Peninsular War. (Portugal)

Charles X Roi de France Charles X, King of France. (France)

Charlotte Grande-Duchesse de Luxembourg Charlotte, Grand Duchess of Luxemburg. (Luxemburg)

Charta Magna Bavariae Magna Carta of Bavaria. (Bavaria)

Christian VIII Konge af Danmark Christian VIII, King of Denmark. (Denmark)

Christian IX Konge af Danmark Christian IX, King of Denmark. (Denmark)

Christianus VII D.G. Dan. Norv. V.G. Rex Christian VII, D.G., King of Denmark, Norway, Vandalia, and Gothland. (Denmark)

Christianus VIII D.G. Daniae V. G. Rex Christian VIII, D.G., King of Denmark, Vandalia, and Gothland. (Denmark)

Christianus IX D.G. Daniae V. G. Rex Christian IX, D.G., King of Denmark, Vandalia, and Gothland. (Denmark)

Cinque Lire Five lire. (Tuscany)

Cinque Lire Italiane Firenze, Marzo 1861 Five Italian lire, Florence, March, 1961. (Italy)

Civitas Lucemborgensis Millesimum Ovans Expletannum Completing the celebration of 1000 years of the city of Luxemburg. (Luxemburg)

Com(es) in Thengen et Sup(remus) Haer(editarius) Prov(inciae) Carn(iolae) Maresch(allus) Count in Thengen and Supreme Hereditary Marshal in the Province of Carniola. (Auersperg)

Concordia patriae Nutrix Peace, the nurse of the fatherland. (Waldeck)

Concordia Res Parvae Crescunt Little things grow through concord. (Batavian Republic)

Confederation Suisse Swiss Confederation. (Swiss Confederation)

Confederaz. Svizzera Swiss Confederation. (Swiss Confederation)

Confoederatio helvetica Helvetian Confederation. (Helvetian Confederation)

Constituirende Versammlung I.D.F. Stadt Frankfurt 18 Mai 1848 Constituting asssembly of the Imperial Diet of Frankfurt, City of Frankfurt, May 18, 1848. (Frankfurt)

Cum Deo et Iure With God and Law. (Wurttemberg)

Custos Regni Deus God the Guardian of the Realm. (Naples & Sicily)

D

D.G. Car. Frid. March. Bad. & H.S.R.I. Elect. C. Pal. Rh. & D.G., Carl Frederick, Margrave of Baden and Elector of S.R.I., Count Palatine of the Rhine. . . . . (Baden)

D.G. Henr. XIII S.L. Ruth S.R.I. Princ. Com. E. Dom. Plav. D.G., Henry XIII, senior line of Reuss, Prince of S.R.I., Count and Lord of Plauen. (Reuss-Greiz)

D.G. Max(im) Ios(eph) C.P.R.U.B.D. S.R.I.A. & El. (D.I.C. & M.) D.G., Maximilian Joseph, Count Palatine of the Rhine and also Duke of Bavaria, Archdapifer and Elector of S.R.I., Duke of Julich, Cleves, and Mark. (Bavaria)

Das Schwert zur Hand in Herzen Gott, So wird D. Schweizer nie z. Spott The sword in hand and God in the heart, so will the Swiss never become a laughing stock. (Swiss)

De Namm des Heeren zy Geloofd The name of the Lord be praised. (Netherlands)

Decus et Tutamen Anno Regni Ornament and safeguard in the year of the reign. (Great Britain)

Dem Bund zum Schutz dem Feind zum Trutz With the League for offense, against the enemy for defense. (Switzerland)

Dem Prinzen Albert Ernst Georg und der Prinzessinn Elisabeth v. Sachs. bei Ihrem Besuche in der Munze zu Dresden im Iahre 1839 For Prince Albert Ernest George and the Princess Elizabeth of Saxony on their visit to the mint at Dresden in the year 1839. (Saxony)

Dem Vaterlande For the fatherland. (Saxe-Weimar)

Dem Verdienste seine Kronen, Reichenbach-Fraunhofer Honor to whom honor is due, Reichenbach and Fraunhofer. (Bavaria)

Den Benediktinern wieder eine Lehranstalt ubergeben On the handing over of another school to the Benedictine Order. (Bavaria)

Den Siegem bei Waterloo gewidmet am 18 Juni 1865 Dedicated to the victors of Waterloo on June 18, 1865. (Hannover)

Den 29 Ianuar 1869 (Died) on January 29, 1869. (Saxe-Coburg-Gotha)

Denkm. der Trennung der Koen. Therese von Ihrem Sohne dem Koen. Otto, Errichtet bei Aibling von Bayerischen Frauen Monument on the separation of Queen Therese from her son, King Otto, erected at Aibling by Bavarian women. (Bavaria)

Denkmahl der Anhaenglichkeit Bayerns an seinen Herrschersstamm, Errichtet zu Oberwittelsbach Monument on the devotion of Bavarians to their ruling house, erected at Oberwittelsbach. (Bavaria)

Denkmahl der Dreyssig Tausend Bayern welche im Russischen Kriege den Tod Fanden Monument for the 30,000 Bavarians who died in the Russian wars. (Bavaria)

Denkmahl des Koenigs Maximilian Joseph, Errichtet von der Hauptstadt Munchen Monument for King Maximilian Joseph, erected by the capital Munich. (Bavaria)

Denkmahl des Konigs Maximilian II in Lindau, Errichtet v.d. Stadten an der Sud-Nord-Bahn Monument for King Maximilian II in Lindau, erected by the cities on the South-North railway. (Monaco)

Deo Juvante With the aid of God. (Monaco)

Der Rhein Deutschlands Strom, nicht Deutschlands Grenze The Rhine, Germany's river, not Germany's frontier. (Germany)

Der St. Michaels-Orden zum Verdienst-Orden bestimmt The Order of St. Michael appointed an order of merit. (Bavaria)

Der Se(e)gen des Bergbaues The blessings of the mines. (Saxony)

Des Bergwerks Wohfahrt ist des Harzes Gluck, Die Grube Bergwerks-Wohlfahrt bei Clausthal kam in Ausbeute 1830 The welfare of the mine is the prosperity of Harz, the pits and the prosperity of the mine at Clausthal came into production in 1830. (Hannover)

Deus et Dies God and the Day. (Parma)

Die Eintheilung d. Konigreichs auf Geschichtl Grundlage zuruckgefuhrt 1838 The divisions of the kingdom restored to their historical foundations. (Bavaria)

Die Koenigin von Bayern Stiftet den Theresien Orden The Queen of Bavaria founds the Order of Therese. (Bavaria)

Dieci Lire Ten lire.

Dieci Paoli. Quattro Fiorini Ten paoli, four florins. (Tuscany)

Dieu Protege La Belgique God protect Belgium. (Belgium)

Dieu Protege La France God protect France. (France)

Dieus Sveti Latviju God guard Latvia. (Latvia)

Dio Benedite L'Italia God bless Italy. (Italy)

Dio Premiera La Costanza God rewards constancy. (Venice)

Dio Protegge (11 Re e) Il Regno God protect the king and the realm. (Naples & Sicily)

Dio Protegge L'Italia God protect Italy. (Sardinia)

Dios Es El Rey de Los Reyes God is the King of Kings. (Spain)

Dirige Me Domine Guide me, Lord. (Parma)

Domine Conserva Nos in Pace Lord, save us in peace. (Zurich)

Domine Salvum Fac Regem Lord, save the king. (France)

Domine Spes Mea A Iuventute Mea Lord, my hope in my youth. (Tuscany)

Dominus Providebit The Lord will provide. (Bern)

Drei(y) Ein Halb Gulden XV Ein Pfund Fein 3-1/2 guldens, 15 to the fine pound. (Bavaria)

Duodecim Lustris 1848, 1908 Gloriose Peractis Twelve lustra (60 years) 1848-1908 gloriously completed. (Austria)

Durch Kampf und Sieg zum Frieden Through struggle and victory to peace. (Bavaria)

Dux Sab. Ianvae (or Genvae) et Montisf. Princ. Ped. Duke of Savoy, Genoa, Montferrat, Prince of Piedmont. (Sardinia)

E

Eala Frya Fresena Frya of all the Frisians. (Hannover)

Eccl. S. Barbarae Patronae Fodin. Kuttenbergensium Duo Flor. Arg. Puri The Church of St. Barbara, Patron of the Kuttenberg Mines, two florins of pure silver. (Austria)

Edwardus VII Dei Gra. Britt. Omn. Rex Fid. Def. Ind. Imp. Edward VII, D.G., King of all the Britains, Defender of the Faith, Emperor of India. (Britains)

Eendragt Maakt Magt Union makes strength. (Netherlands)

Ehre dem Ehre Gebuhrt Honor to whom honor is due. (Bavaria)

Ehre Ist Mein Hoechstes Ziel Honour is my highest goal. (Switzerland)

Eidgen Freischiesen Solothiurn Federal Public Shooting Match in Solothurn. (Switzerland)

Eidgenossisches Frei(y) schiessen Federal Public Shooting Match; in Zurich (KM-S5), in Chur; in Bern (KM-S4); in Glarus (KM-20). (Switzerland)

Eidgenossisches Schutzenfest in Basel (KM-S14) Federal Shooting Festival in Basel; in Bern (KM-S6); in Nidwalden (KM-S6); in St. Gallen (KM-S12); in Schaffhausen (KM-S8); in Schwyz (KM-S9); in Zug (KM-S10); in Zurich (KM-S11). (Switzerland)

Ein Gedenkthaler zu Schiller's Hundertjahriger Geburtsfeier A commemorative thaler on the hundredth anniversary of Schiller's birth. (Frankfurt)

Ein Gedenkthaler zum Deutschen Schutzenfeste Juli 1862 A commemorative thaler on the German shooting festival July, 1862. (Frankfurt)

Ein Gott-Ein Recht-Eine Wahrheit One God, one justice, one truth. (Oldenburg)

Ein Thaler zu 100 Krzr. - Im Kronen Fuss One thaler of 100 kreuzer, on the kronen standard. (Baden)

Ein Vereinsthaler xxx Ein Pfund Fein One convention thaler, 30 to the fine pound. (Liechtenstein & German States)

Einigkeit und Recht und Freiheit Unity and right and freedom. (Germany)

Eintracht Macht Stark Union makes strength. (Chur)

Elizabeth II Dei Gratia Britt. Omn. Regina Fidei Defensor Elizabeth II, D.G., Queen of Great Britain, Defender of the Faith. (Great Britain)

Emanuel II Portug. et Algarb. Rex Manuel II, King of Portugal and Algarve. (Portugal)

Emma Furstin Regent c. Vormund. zu Waldeck u. P. Emma, Princess Regent and guardian of Waldeck and Pyrmont. (Waldeck & Pyrmont)

En Barcelona In Barcelona. (Spain)

Entree de Fribourg & Soleure dans La Confederation Suisse Entry of Fribourg and Solothurn into the Swiss Confederation. (Swiss)

Er Saete Gerechtigkeit und Erntete Liebe. Hosea X. 12 He sowed justice and harvested love. (Saxony)

Ernst August Friederike Marie, Marie, Georg Ernest, August, Frederika, Marie, Marie, George. (Hannover)

Ernst August - Viktoria Luise Herzog u. Herzogin zu Braunschweig (u. Luneb.) Ernest August, Victoria Louise, Duke and Duchess of Brunswick-Luneburg. (Brunswick-Luneburg)

Ernst August V.G.G. Koenig von Hannover Ernest August, D.G., King of Hannover. (Hannover)

Ernst August Koenig von Hannover Ernest August, King of Hannover. (Hannover)

Ernst Herzog v. Sachsen Coburg u. Gotha Ernest, Duke of Saxe-Coburg-Gotha. (Saxe-Coburg-Gotha)

Ernst Herzog von Sachsen Altenburg Ernest, Duke of Saxe-Altenburg. (Saxe-Altenburg)

Ernst Herzog z. S. Coburg Saalf. F. z. Lichtenb. Ernest, Duke of Saxe-Coburg-Saalfeld, Prince of Lichtenburg. (Saxe-Coburg-Saalfeld)

Ernst Herzog z. S. Coburg u. Gotha F. z. Lichtenb. Ernest, Duke of Saxe-Coburg and Gotha, Prince of Lichtenburg. (Saxe-Coburg-Gotha)

Ernst Herzog zu Sachsen Coburg-Gotha Ernest, Duke of Saxe-Coburg-Gotha. (Saxe-Coburg-Gotha)

Ernst Herzog zu Sachsen Coburg und Saalfeld Ernest, Duke of Saxe-Coburg and Saalfeld. (Saxe-Coburg-Saalfeld)

Ernst Ludwig Grosherzog von Hessen Ernest Ludwig, Grand Duke of Hesse. (Hesse)

Eroffnung der Neuen Munze Sept. 1840 Opening of the new mint September, 1840. (Frankfurt)

Errichtung der Bayerischen Hypotheken-Bank Establishment of the Bavarian Mortgage Bank. (Bavaria)

Erste Eisenbahn in Deutschland mit Dampfwagen von Nurnberg nach Furth First railway in Germany with steam engines from Nuremberg to Furth. (Bavaria)

Erwahlt zum Kaiser der Deutschen d. 28 Marz 1849 Elected the Emperor of the Germans on March 28, 1849. (Frankfurt)

Erwahlt zum Reichsverweser uber Deutschland d 29 Iuni 1849 Elected imperial regent over Germany on June 29, 1849. (Frankfurt)

Erzherzog Johann von Oesterreich Archduke John of Austria. (Frankfurt)

Espana Spain. (Spain)

Et in Minimus Integer Faithful even in the smallest things. (Olmutz)

F

F. Berhard im Bart Prince Berhard the bearded. (Germany)

Feines Silber Fine silver. (Hannover)

Feldherrnhalle Hall of Generals. (Bavaria)

Felice ed Eliza PP. (Principes) de Lucca e Piombino Felix and Elisa, Prince and Princess of Lucca and and Piombino. (Lucca)

Ferd(inandus) D.G. H(ungariae) et B(ohemiae) Reg(ius) Pr(inceps) A. A. S(acri) R(omani) I(mperil) Pr(inceps) El(ector) Salisb(urgensis) Ferdinand, D.G., Royal Prince of Hungary and Bohemia, Archduke of Austria, Prince of S.R.I., Elector of Salzburg. (Salzburg)

Ferd(inandus) I D. G. Aust(riae) Imp(erator) Hung(ariae) B(ohemiae) Rex H(umus) N(ominis) V R(ex) L(ombardiae) I(llyriae) A.A. Ferdinand I, D.G., Emperor of Austria, King of Hungary and Bohemia, Fifth of this name, King of Lombardy, Venice, Dalmatia, Galicia, Lodomeria, Illyria, Archduke of Austria. (Hungary)

Ferd. Hu. et Bo. Reg. Pr. A.A.S.R.I.Pr. El. Salisb. Ferdinand, Royal Prince of Hungary and Bohemia, Archduke of Austria, Prince of S.R.I., Elector of Salzburg. (Salzburg)

Ferd. I D.G. Austr. Imp. Hung. Boh. R(ex) H(etruriae) N(eapolis) V(enetiae) Ferdinand I, D.G., Emperor of Austria, King of Hungary and Bohemia, Fifth of this name, King of Lombardy, Venice, Dalmatia, Galicia, Lodomeria, Illyria, Archduke of Austria. (Austria)

Ferd. I D.G. Regni Sicilarum et Hier Rex Ferdinand I, D.G., King of the Sicilies and Jerusalem. (Naples & Sicily)

Ferd. IV D.G. utr. Sic. et Hier, Rex Ferdinand IV, D.G., King of the Two Sicilies and Jerusalem. (Naples & Sicily)

Ferdin. VII Dei G. Ferdinand VII, D.G. (Spain)

Ferdinan. III D.G. Sicil. et Hier. Rex Ferdinand III, D.G., King of Sicily and Jerusalem. (Naples & Sicily)

Ferdinan. IV D. G. Siciliar, et Hie Rex Ferdinand IV, D.G., King of the Sicilies and Jerusalem. (Naples & Sicily)

Ferdinand Souv. Landgraf z. Hessen Ferdinand, sovereign landgrave of Hesse. (Hesse-Homburg)

Ferdinandus I D.G. Austriae Imperator Ferdinand I, D.G., Emperor of Austria. (Austria)

Ferdinandus II Dei Gratia Rex Ferdinand II, D.G., King. (Naples & Sicily)

Ferdinandus III D.G. P(rinceps) R(egius) H(ungariae) et B(ohemiae) A. A. M(agnus) D(ux) Etrur(iae) Ferdinand III, D.G., Royal Prince of Hungary and Bohemia, Archduke of Austria, Grand Duke of Tuscany. (Tuscany)

Ferdinandus III D.G. Rex Ferdinand III, King, D.G. (Naples & Sicily)

Ferdinandus IV D.G. Rex Ferdinand IV, King, D.G. (Naples & Sicily)

Ferdinandus VII Dei G(ratia) Ferdinand VII, D.G. (Spain)

Ferencz Jozsef I K.A.Cs. Es. M.H.S.D.O. Ap. Kir (Hungary)

Fern. 7 P. La G.D. Dios Y La Const. Ferdinand VII, D.G. and the Constitution. (Spain)

Fern. 7 P.L.G.D. Dios Rey de Espan. E Ynd. Ferdinand VII, D.G., King of Spain and the Indies. (Spain)

Fernando 7 Por La G. De Dios Ferdinand VII, D.G. (Spain)

Fernando 7 Por La Gracia De Dios Y La Constitucion Ferdinand VII, D.G. and the Constitution. (Spain)

Fernando VII Rey de Espana Ferdinand VII, King of Spain. (Spain)

Fert, Fert, Fert (A monogram) (Sardinia & Italy)

Fest Frei Schiessen von Weiner Schutzen Verein Public Shooting Festival of the Vienna Shooting Association. (Austria)

Fid. Def. Ind. Imp. Defender of the Faith, Emperor of India. (Great Britain)

Fideliter et Constanter Faithfully and steadfastly. (Saxe-Coburg-Gotha)

Folkets Karlek Min Beloning The love of the people is my compensation. (Sweden)

Folkets Kjaerlighed Min Styrke, Dod Den 20 Januar 1848 The love of the people is my strength. (Denmark)

Folkets Val Min Hogsta Lag The welfare of the people is my strength. (Denmark)

Fr. Wilh. III K.V. Preuss Frederick William III, King of Prussia. (Prussia)

Franc Ios. I D.G. Austr. Imp. et Hung. Rex Ap. Elisabetha Imp. et Reg. Francis Joseph I, D.G., Emperor of Austria and Apostolic King of Hungary, Elizabeth, Empress and Queen. (Austria)

Franc Ios. I D.G. Austr. Imp. et Hung. Rex Ap. Elisabetha Imp. et Reg. Francis Joseph I, D.G., Emperor of Austria, King of Hungary and Bohemia. (Austria)

Franc. D.G. Ep. Princ Gurc Antiq. Com de Salm Reifferscheid Francis, D.G., Prince-Bishop of Gurk, Count of Reifferscheid. (Gurk)

Franc. Ios. I D.G. Austrie Imperator Francis Joseph I, D.G., Emperor of Austria. (Austria)

Franc. Ios. I D.G. Imp. Austr. Rex Boh. Gal. Ill. etc. Ap. Rex Hung. Francis Joseph I, D.G., Emperor of Austria, King of Bohemia, Galicia and Illyria and King of Hungary. (Austria)

Franc. I D.G. Aust. Imp. Hung. B.L.V.G.L.I. Rex A.A. Francis I, D.G., Emperor of Austria, King of Hungary and Bohemia, Lombardy, Venice, Galicia, Lodomeria, Illyria, Archduke of Austria. (Hungary)

Franc. II D.G.R.I.S.A. Conservator Castri Francis II, D.G., R.I.S.A., Protector of the city. (Frankfurt)

Francisc. Ios. I D.G. Austriae Imp. et Elisabetha Max. in Bavar. Ducis Fil. Francis Joseph I, D.G., Emperor of Austria and Elizabeth, daughter of Maximilian, Duke of

Bavaria. (Austria)
Franciscus I D.G. Austriae Imperator Francis I, D.G., Emperor of Austria. (Austria)
Franciscus I Dei Gratia Rex Francis I, King, D.G. (Naples & Sicily)
Franciscus II D.G. Rom. et Haer. Aust. Imp. Francis II, D.G., Emperor of the Romans and Hereditary Emperor of Austria. (Austria)
Franciscus II D.G. Rom. Imp. Semp. Aug. Francis II, D.G., R.I.S.A. (Regensburg)
Franciscus II D.G.R. Imp. S. A. Germ. Hu. Bo. Rex Francis II, D.G., R.I.S.A., King of Germany, Hungary, Bohemia. (Austria)
Franciscus II Dei Gratia Rex Francis II, King, D.G. (Naples & Sicily)
Franz Herzog zu Sachsen Cob. Saalfeld Francis, Duke of Saxe-Coburg-Saalfeld. (Saxe-Coburg-Saalfeld)
Franz Joseph I V.G.G. Kaiser V. Oesterreich Francis Joseph I, D.G., Kaiser of Austria. (Austria)
Frederick VII Konge af Danmark Frederick VII, King of Denmark. (Denmark)
Fredericus VI D.G. Dan. V.G. Rex Frederick VI, D.G., King of Denmark, Vendalia, and Gothland. (Denmark)
Fredericus VII D.G. Daniae V.G. Rex Frederick VII, D.G., King of Denmark, Vendalia, and Gothland. (Denmark)
Frederik IX Konge af Danmark Frederik IX, King of Denmark. (Denmark)
Freie Hansestadt Bremen Free Hanseatic city of Bremen. (Bremen)
Freie Stadt Danzig Free State of Danzig. (Danzig)
Freie Stadt Frankfurt Free city of Frankfurt. (Frankfurt)
Freie und Hansestadt Hamburg Free Hanseatic city of Hamburg. (Hamburg)
Freie und Hansestadt Lubeck Free Hanseatic city of Lubeck. (Lubeck)
Frid. Aug. Rex Sax(oniae) Dux Varsov Frederick August, King of Saxony, Duke of Warsaw. (Poland)
Frid. August D.G. Dux Sax. Elector Frederick August, D.G., Duke and Elector of Saxony. (Saxony)
Frid. August D.G. Rex Saxoniae Frederick August, D.G., King of Saxony. (Saxony)
Friderich I Koenig von Wurttemberg Frederick I, King of Wurttemberg. (Wurttemberg)
Fridericus D.G. Rex Wurt. S.R.I. Ar. Vexill. et Elect Frederick, D.G., King of Wurttemberg, Archmarshal, Standard Bearer, and Elector of the S.R.I. (Wurttemberg)
Fridericus D.G. Rex Wurt(t)emberg(iae) Frederick, D.G., King of Wurttemberg. (Wurttemberg)
Fridericus Pr. Waldecciae Com. Pyr. Frederick, Prince of Waldeck, Count of Pyrmont. (Pyrmont)
Fridericus Wurtembergiae Rex Frederick, King of Wurttemberg. (Wurttemberg)
Fridericus II D.G. Dux Wurt. S.R.I. Ar. Vex. et Elector Frederick II, D.G., Duke of Wurttemberg, Archmarshal, Standard Bearer, and Elector of the S.R.I. (Wurttemberg)
Friedensschluss zu Frankfurt A.M. 10 Mai 1871 Peace of Frankfurt-on-the-Main May 10, 1871. (Bavaria)
Friedr(ich) August Koenig v(on) Sachsen Frederick August, King of Saxony. (Saxony)
Friedr. Franz. I. 1815 - Friedr. Franz. IV. 1915. Grossherzoge v. Mecklenb. Schw. Frederick Francis IV, 1915 - Grand Dukes of Mecklenburg-Schwerin. (Mecklenburg-Schwerin)
Friedr. Gunther Furst zu Schwarzburg Frederick Gunther, Prince of Schwarzburg. (Schwarzburg-Rudolstadt)
Friedr. Wilhelm I Kurfurst v. Hessen Frederick William I, Elector of Hesse. (Hesse-Cassel)
Friedr. Wilhelm III Koenig v(on) Preussen Frederick William III, King of Prussia. (Prussia)
Friedr. Wilhelm IV Koenig v. Preussen Frederick William IV, King of Prussia. (Prussia)
Friedrich August Grossherzog v. Oldenburg Frederick August, Grand Duke of Oldenburg. (Oldenburg)
Friedrich August Herzog zu Nassau Frederick August, Duke of Nassau. (Nassau)
Friedrich August Konig v. Sachsen Frederick August, King of Saxony. (Saxony)
Friedrich August V.G.G. Koenig v. Sachsen Frederick August, D.G., King of Saxony. (Saxony)
Friedrich August II Koenig von Sachsen d. 9 Aug. 1854 Frederick August II, King of Saxony, (died) on August 9, 1854. (Saxony)
Friedrich der Streitbare * Friedrich August * 1409 Universitat Leipzig 1909 Frederick the Valiant, Frederick August, 1409, the University of Leipzig 1909. (Saxony)
Friedrich Deutscher Kaiser Konig v. Preussen Frederick, Emperor of Germany, King of Prussia. (Prussia)
Friedrich Franz - Alexandra Grossherzog u. Grossherzogin v. Mecklenb. Schw. Frederick Francis, Alexandra, Grand Duke and Grand Duchess of Mecklenburg-Schwerin. (Mecklenburg-Schwerin)
Friedrich Franz Grossh. v. Mecklenb. Schw. Frederick Francis, Grand Duke of Mecklenburg-Schwerin. (Mecklenburg-Schwerin)
Friedrich Franz V.G.G. Grossh. v. Mecklenb. Schw. Frederick Francis, D.G., Grand Duke of Mecklenburg-Schwerin. (Mecklenburg-Schwerin)
Friedrich Furst zu Waldeck und Pyrmont Frederick, Prince of Waldeck and Pyrmont. (Waldeck and Pyrmont)
Friedrich Grosherzog von Vaden Frederick, Grand Duke of Baden. (Baden)
Friedrich Gunther Furst zu Schwarzburg Rudolstadt Frederick Gunther, Prince of Schwarzburg-Rudolstadt. (Schwarzburg-Rudolstadt)
Friedrich Herzog von Anhalt Frederick, Duke of Anhalt. (Anhalt)
Friedrich Prinz und Regent von Baden Frederick, Prince and Regent of Baden. (Baden)
Friedrich und Luise von Baden Frederick and Louise of Baden. (Baden)
Friedrich W. C. Furst zu Hohenz. Hech. Frederick William Constantine, Prince of Hohenzollern-Hechingen. (Hohenzollern-Hechingen)
Friedrich. Wilh. V.G.G. Grossh. v. Mecklenb. Frederick William, D.G., Grand Duke of Mecklenburg-Strelitz. (Mecklenburg-Strelitz)
Friedrich Wilhelm Furst zu Nassau Frederick William, Prince of Nassau. (Nassau)
Friedrich Wilhelm IV Koenig von Preussen Frederick William IV, King of Prussia. (Prussia)
Friedrich I. 1701. Wilhelm II. 1901 Frederick I, 1701, William II, 1901. (Prussia)
Friedrich II Grossherzog von Baden Frederick II, Grand Duke of Baden. (Baden)
Friedrich II. Marie. Herzog und Herzogin von Anhalt Frederick II, Marie, Duke and Duchess of Anhalt. (Anhalt)
Fur Freiheit und Vaterland For freedom and Fatherland. (Switzerland)
Fur Gott und Vaterland For God and Fatherland. (Bavaria)
Furchtlos und Treu Fearless and true. (Wurttemberg)
Furstentag zu Frankfurt am Main im August 1863 Assembly of Princes in Frankfurt-on-the-Main in August 1863. (Frankfurt)

G

G.N.A. 1808 un Duro Gerona 1808, one duro. (Spain)
Garantie National National Security. (France)
Gaule Subalpine Subalpine Gaul. (Subalpine Republic)
Gedenkthaler zur Eroffnungs Feier der neuen Borse in Bremen am 5 Novemb. 1864 Commemorative thaler on the opening celebration of the new Exchange in Bremen on November 5, 1864. (Bremen)
Georg Furst zu Schaumburg-Lippe George, Prince of Schaumburg-Lippe. (Schaumburg-Lippe)
Georg Furst zu Waldeck und Pyrmont & George, Prince of Waldeck and Pyrmont, ... (Waldeck and Pyrmont)
Georg Heinr(ich) Furst z(u) Waldeck u. Pyrmont George Henry, Prince of Waldeck and Pyrmont. (Waldeck and Pyrmont)
Georg Herzog zu Sachsen Altenburg George, Duke of Saxe-Altenburg. (Saxe-Altenburg)
Georg Herzog zu Sachsen Meiningen George, Duke of Saxe-Meiningen. (Saxe-Meiningen)
Georg Koenig von Sachsen George, King of Saxony. (Saxony)
Georg Kronprinz von Hannover, Marie Herzoginn v. S. Altenb. Verm. 18 Febr. 1845 George, Crown Prince of Hannover, Marie, Duchess of Saxe-Altenburg, married Feb. 18, 1845. (Hannover)
Georg Prinz z. Waldeck Furst z. Pyromont George, Prince of Waldeck, Prince of Pyrmont. (Waldeck and Pyrmont)
Georg Victor Furst zu Waldeck u Pyrmont George Victor, Prince of Waldeck and Pyrmont. (Waldeck and Pyrmont)
Georg Wilhelm Furst zu Schaumburg-Lippe George William, Prince of Schaumburg-Lippe. (Schaumburg-Lippe)
Georg II Herzog v(on) Sachsen-Meiningen George II, Duke of Saxe-Meiningen. (Saxe-Meiningen)
Georg III V.G.G. Konig und Churfurst George III, D.G., King and Elector. (Hannover)
Georg IV Konig v. Grosbritan. u. Hannover George IV, King of Great Britain and Hannover. (Hannover)
Georg V V.G.G. Koenig v. Hannover George V, D.G., King of Hannover. (Hannover)
Georgius III D.G. Britanniarum Rex F.D. George III, D.G., King of Great Britain, Defender of the Faith. (Great Britain)
Georgius III Dei Gratia Rex George III, King, D.G. (Great Britain)
Georgius IIII D.G. Britanniar. Rex F.D. George IV, D.G., King of the Britains, Defender of the Faith. (Great Britain)
Georgius V D.G. Britt. Omn. Rex F.D. Ind. Imp. George V, D.G., King of all the Britains, Defender of the Faith, Emperor of India. (Great Britain)
Georgius V Dei Gra. Britt. Omn. Rex George V, D.G., King of all the Britains. (Great Britain)
Georgius VI D.G. Br. Omn. Rex George VI, D.G., King of all the Britains. (Great Britain)
Georgius VI D.G. Br. Omn. Rex F.D. George VI, D.G., King of Great Britain, Defender of the Faith. (Great Britain)
Gepraegt in Gegenwart S.M. des Koenigs. Dresden d. 24 April 1855 Struck in the presence of His Majesty the King, Dresden on April 24, 1855. (Saxony)
Gerecht und Beharrlich Just and firm. (Bavaria)
Germ. Hun. Boh. Rex A.A.D. Loth. Ven. Sal. King of Germnay, Hungary, Bohemia, Archduke of Austria, Duke of Lorraine, Venice, Salzburg. (Austria)
Gerona Ano De 1809 Gerona, Year of 1809. (Spain)
Gioacchino Napol(eone) (Re Delle Due Sicil(ie) Joachim Napoleon, King of the Two Sicilies. (Naples & Sicily)
Glori in Excelsis Deo Glory to God in the highest. (Sweden)
Gluckauf! Clausthal in September 1839 Good luck! Clausthal in September 1839. (Hannover)
God Zy (Zij) Met ons God be with us. (Netherlands)
Goethe Goethe. (Germany)
Gott Beschirme Uns God protect us. (Hesse-Cassel)
Gott Ehre Vaterland God, Honour, Fatherland. (Hesse-Darmstadt)
Gott Mit Uns (many) God with us. (Germany)
Gott Schirme Mecklenburg God protect Mecklenburg. (Mecklenburg-Strelitz)
Gott Schutze Ihn und den Theuren Erben Seines Throns God protect him and the dear Heir to his Throne. (Prussia)
Gott Segne Anhalt God bless Anhalt. (Anhalt-Bernburg)
Gott Segne Bayern God bless Bavaria. (Bavaria)
Gott Segne Handel u. Schiffahrt God bless business and commerce. (Bremen)
Gott Segne Sachsen God bless Saxony. (Saxony)
Gott und das Vaterland God and the Fatherland. (Bavaria)
Gott und Recht God and right. (Saxe-Weimar)
Gott war mit Uns God was with us. (Bremen)
Gotth. Ephraim Lessing Gotthold Ephraim Lessing. (Germany)
Governo Provvisorio di Lombardia Provisional government of Lombardy. (Lombardy)
Graf Zeppelin Weltflug Graf Zeppelin world flight. (Germany)
Grafl. Schaumburg Lipp. Vormundschaftl. Munze County Schaumburg-Lippe, guardianship coin. (Schaumburg-Lippe)
Grand-Duche de Luxembourg Grand duchy of Luxemburg. (Luxemburg)
Gregorius XVI (Pon(tifex) M(ax)(imus) Gregory XVI, Pope. (Papal States)
Grosherzogthum Baden Grand duchy of Baden. (Papal States)
Grosherzogthum Sachsen Grand duchy of Saxe-Weimar. (Saxe-Weimar)
Gud och Folket God and the people. (Sweden)
Gunth. Fried. Carl Furst z. Schwarzb. Sondersh. Gunther Frederick Carl, Prince of Schwarzburg-Sonderhausen. (Schwarzburg-Sondershausen)
Gunther Fr. C. II Furst z. Schwarzb. Sondersh. Gunther Frederick Carl II, Prince of Schwarzburg-Sondershausen. (Schwarzburg-Sondershausen)
Gustaf IV Adolph Sv. G. och V. Konung Gustav IV, Adolph, King of Sweden, Gothland, and Vendalia. (Sweden)
Gustaf V Sveriges Konung Gustaf V., King of Sweden. (Sweden)
Gustaf VI Adolf Sveriges Konung Gustaf VI, Adolf, King of Sweden. (Sweden)

H

Hac Nitimur Hanc Tuemur With this we strive, this we will defend. (Netherlands)
Hakimiyet Milletindir Sovereignty is of the people. (Turkey)
Handel'sfreiheit durch Eintracht Free trade through agreement. (Wurttemberg)
Handelsvertrag zwischen Bayern, Preussen, Wurttemberg und Hessen Commercial treaty between Bavaria, Prussia, Wurttemberg and Hesse. (Bavaria)
Hans Landwing Retter das Panner Bei Arbedo Hans Landwing saves the standard at Arbedo. (Switzerland)
Harz-Segen Harz blessings. (Hannover)
Heinrich d. Li. lung. Linie Furst Reuss von Ebersdorf Henry of the younger line, line of the princes of Reuss-Ebersdorf. (Reuss-Ebersdorf)
Heinrich Herzog zu Anhalt Henry, Duke of Anhalt. (Anhalt-Kothen)
Heinrich XIV V.G.G. Reg. Furst Reuss I.L. Henry XIV, D.G., ruling Prince of Reuss, Younger Line. (Reuss-Younger Line)
Heinrich XX V.G.G. Aelt. L(in) Souv(erain) Furst Reuss Henry XX, D.G., Older Line, Sovereign Prince of Reuss. (Reuss-Greiz)
Heinrich XXII V.G.G. Alt. L. Souv. Furst Reuss Henry XXII, D.G., Older Line, Sovereign Prince of Reuss. (Reuss-Greiz)
Heinrich LXII lung. Lin. und Stamm. Altest Furst Reuss Henry LXII, Younger Line and oldest branch, Prince of Reuss. (Reuss-Schleiz)
Heinrich LXVII V.G.G. Reg. Furst Reuss I.L. Henry LXVII, D.G., ruling Prince of Reuss, Younger Line. (Reuss-Schleiz)
Heinrich LXXII Jung. Lin. Furst Reuss Henry LXXII, Younger Line, Prince of Reuss. (Reuss-Schleiz)
Helvetia Switzerland. (Switzerland)
Helvetische Republik Swiss Republic. (Swiss Republic)
Herman Frider. Otto D.G. Princ. de Hohenzollern Heching. Herman Frederick Otto, D.G., Prince of Hohenzollern-Hechingen. (Hohenzollern-Hechingen)
Herzogthurn Anhalt, Getheilt 1603 Vereint 1863 Duchy of Anhalt, divided 1603, united 1863. (Anhalt)
Herzogthurn Nassau Duchy of Nassau. (Nassau)
Hieronymus D.G.A. & P.S.A.S.L.N.G. Prim. Jerome, D.G., Archbishop and Prince of Salzburg. (Salzburg)
Hieronymus Napoleon Jerome Napoleon. (Westphalia)
Hindenburg Reichsprasident Hindenburg, President of Germany. (Germany)
Hispaniar(um) Infans Prince of the Spains. (Spain)
Hispaniarum et Ind. Rex King of the Spains and the Indies. (Spain)
Hispaniarum Rex King of the Spains. (Spain)
Honi Soit Qui Mal Y Pense Evil to him who thinks evil. (Great Britain)
Honore V Prince de Monaco Honore V, Prince of Monaco. (Monaco)
Hun. Boh. Gal. Rex A.A. D. Lo. Sal. Wirc. King of Hungary, Bohemia, Galicia, Archduke of Austria, Dalmatia, Lodomeria, Salzburg, and Wurzburg. (Austria)
Hun. Boh. Gal. Rex A.A. Lo Wi. et in Fr. Dux King of Hungary, Bohemia, Galicia, Archduke of Austria, Lodomeria, Wurzburg, and in Franconia, Duke. (Austria)
Hundert Jahre Bremerhaven Centennial of Bremerhaven.

(Germany)

Hundertjahrige Grundung der Hochschule zu Erlangen durch d. Markgr. Friedr. v. Brandenb. Bayr. Centenary of the foundation of the University of Erlangen by the Margrave, Frederick of Brandenburg-Bayreuth. (Bavaria)

Hun(g) Boh. Lomb. et Ven. Gal. Lod. II(l) Rex A.A. King in Hungary, Bohemia, Lombardy, and Venice, Galicia, Lodomeria, Illyria, Archduke of Austria. (Austria)

Hungar. Bohem. Gal. Lod. Ill. Rex. A.A. King in Hungary, Bohemia, Galicia, Lodomeria, Illyria, Archduke of Austria. (Austria)

I

Ich Bau auf Gott I rely on God. (Reuss-Schleiz)

Iedem Das Seinige To each his own. (Appenzell)

In Hoc Signo Vinces In this sign you will conquer. (Portugal)

In Memor. Vindicatae Libert. ac Relig. In memory of the establishment of liberty and religion. (Sweden)

In te Domine Speravi In thee have I hoped, O Lord. (Gurk)

In Terra Pax Peace in the land. (Papal States)

Indipendenza Italiana Italian Independence. (Italian)

Ioachim Grosherzog von Berg Joachim, Grand Duke of Berg. (Berg)

Ioachim Herzog zu Berg u. Cleve Joachim, Duke of Berg and Cleves. (Berg)

Iohann Koenig, Amalie Koenigin v. Sachsen John, King, Amalie, Queen of Saxony. (Saxony)

Iohann V.G.G. Koenig v. Sachsen John, D.G., King of Saxony. (Saxony)

Ioseph Herzog zu Sachsen Altenburg Joseph, Duke of Saxe-Altenburg. (Saxe-Altenburg)

Ioseph Nap. Dei Gratia Joseph Napoleon, D.G. (Spain)

Ioseph Napol. D.G. utr. Sicil. Rex Joseph Napoleon, D.G., King of the Two Sicilies. (Naples & Sicily)

Isabel 2 Por La Gracia De Dios Isabel II, D.G. (Spain)

Isabel 2 Por la Gracia de Dios y La Constitucion Isabel II, D.G., and the Constitution. (Spain)

Isti Sunt Patres Tui Verique Pastores These are your fathers and true shepherds. (Papal States)

Italia Libera Dio Lo Vuole A Free Italy, God wills it. (Lombardy)

Iustitia Regn(orum) Fundamentum Justice, the Foundation for kingdoms. (Austria)

J

Jahrhundertfeier Centennial. (Mecklenburg-Schwerin)

Jahrtausend Feier der Rheinlands Millenary Jubilee of the Rhineland. (Germany)

Jan de Blannen John, the Blind. (Luxembourg)

Joannes D.G. Port. et Alg. P. Regens John, D.G., Prince Regent of Portugal and Algarve. (Portugal)

Joannes D.G. P(rinceps) Portugaliae et Alg(arbiae) John, D.G., Prince of Portugal and Algarve. (Portugal)

Joannes VI D.G. Portug. Brasil et Algarb. Rex John VI, D.G., King of Portugal, Brazil, and Algarve. (Portugal)

Joh. Fried. d. Groszmut Kurf. v. Sachsen, Stifter d. Univ. Jena John Frederick the magnanimous, Elector of Saxony, Founder of the University of Jena. (Saxony)

Johann II Furst zu (or von) Liechtenstein John II, Prince of Liechtenstein. (Liechtenstein)

K

Kanton Schwyz Canton Schwyz. (Schwyz)

Karl Koenig von Wuerttemberg Karl, King of Wurttemberg. (Wurttemberg)

Klar und Fest Clear and firm. (Liechtenstein)

Koenig von Westphalen Fr. Pr. King of Westphalia, Prince of France. (Westphalia)

Koenigl. Wurttemb. Kronen Thaler Kingdom of Wurttemberg crown thaler. (Wurttemberg)

Kong Frederik IX Dronning Ingrid af Danmark King Frederik IX, Queen Ingrid of Denmark. (Denmark)

Koningrijk Holland Kingdom of Holland. (Holland)

Kon. Wurttemb. Kingdom of Wurttemberg. (Wurttemberg)

Kur. Hess. Land Munze Electorate of Hesse, legal money. (Hesse-Cassel)

Kurfurstenthurn Hessen Electorate of Hesse. (Hesse-Cassel)

L

L.L. Ph. M.V. Duc de Brabant M.H.A. Duchesse de Brabant 21-22 Aout 1853 Leopold Louis Philippe, Maria Victor, Duke of Brabant, Maria Henrietta, Duchess of Brabant, 21-22 August, 1853. (Belgium)

Land Skal Med Lov Bygges The country shall be built by law. (Norway)

Land Skall Med Lag Byggas The country shall be built by law. (Sweden)

Landtag Provincial legislature. (Bavaria)

Largiente Numine Diety bestowing his bounty. (Regensburg)

Latvijas Republika Latvian Republic. (Latvia)

Lege et Fide By law and faith. (Austria)

Leo XII Pon(tifex) (Max(imus) Leo XII, Pope. (Papal States)

Leopold Friedrich Herzog zu (von) Anhalt Leopold, Grand Duke of Anhalt. (Anhalt-Dessau)

Leopold Grosherzog von Baden Leopold, Grand Duke of Baden. (Baden)

Leopold Premier Roi des Belges Leopold I, King of the Belgians. (Belgians)

Leopold II Roi des Belges Leopold II, King of the Belgians. (Belgians)

Leopoldus D.G. P.I.A. P(rinceps) R(egius) H(ungariae) et B(ohemiae) A.A. Magn(us) Dux Etr(uriae) Leopold II, D.G., Prince of Imperial Austria, Prince Regent of Hungary and Bohemia, Archduke of Austria, Grand Duke of Tuscany. (Tuscany)

Lerida Ano de 1809 Lerida Year of 1809. (Spain)

Lex Tua Veritas Law is your truth. (Tuscany)

Ley Patria Rey Law, Fatherland, King. (Spain)

Ley 900 Milesimas 40 Piezas en Kilog Law 900/1000, 40 pieces per kilogram. (Spain)

Liberta Eguaglianza Liberty, Equality. (Ligurian Republic)

Libertade Inferme e de' Tiranni Agevol Preda Weak liberty is the easy prey of tyrants. (Switzerland)

Liberte, Egalite, Eridania Liberty, Equality, Eridania. (Subalpine Republic)

Liberte, Egalite, Fraternite Liberty, Equality, Fraternity. (France)

Literatur, Vetenskap, Konst Literature, Science, Art. (Sweden)

Lodew. Nap. Kon. Van Holl Louis Napoleon, King of Holland. (Holland)

Louis Philippe (I) Roi de France Louis Philippe I, King of the French. (France)

Louis XVIII Roi de France Louis XVIII, King of France. (France)

Lucilinburhuc Luxemburg. (Luxemburg)

Ludewig Grosherzog von Hessen Ludwig, Grand Duke of Hesse. (Hesse-Darmstadt)

Ludovicus I D.G. (Hisp(aniarum) Inf(ans) Rex Etruriae Par(mae) Plac(entiae) and Prince Louis I, D.G., Prince of the Spains, King of Etruria, Prince of Parma and Piacenza. (Tuscany)

Ludovicus II Bavariae Rex Ludwig II, King of Bavaria. (Bavaria)

Ludwig Erbprinz v. B. Geb. 25 August; Ludwig Koen. Prinz v. B. Geb. 7 Januar Ludwig, Crown Prince of Baden, born August 25; Ludwig, Royal Prince of Baden, born January 7. (Baden)

Ludwig Grosherzog von Baden Ludwig, Grand Duke of Baden. (Baden)

Ludwig Loenig von Bayern Ludwig, King of Bavaria. (Bavaria)

Ludwig I Giebt die Krone an seinen Sohn Maximilian am 20 Maerz 1848 Ludwig I, gives his crown to his son Maximilian on March 20, 1848. (Bavaria)

Ludwig I Koenig von Bayern Ludwig I, King of Bavaria. (Bavaria)

Ludwig II Koenig v. Bayern Ludwig II, King of Bavaria. (Bavaria)

Ludwig II Grosherzog von Hessen Ludwig II, Grand Duke of Hesse. (Hesse-Darmstadt)

Ludwig III Koenig von Bayern Ludwig III, King of Bavaria. (Bavaria)

Ludwig III Grosherzog von Hessen Ludwig III, Grand Duke of Hesse. (Hesse-Darmstadt)

Ludwig IV Grosherzog von Hessen Ludwig IV, Grand Duke of Hesse. (Hesse-Darmstadt)

Ludwigscanal Ludwig's Canal. (Bavaria)

Luitpold Prinz-Regent v. Bayern Leopold, Prince-Regent of Bavaria. (Bavaria)

Lumen ad Revelationem Gentium Light and revelation for the peoples. (Papal States)

L'Union Fait La Force Union makes strength. (Belgium)

M

Magnus ab Integro Saeclorum Nascitur Ordo The great order of the centuries is born anew. (Bavaria)

Magyar Kiralysag Hungarian Kingdom. (Hungarian)

Magyar Koztarsasag Hungarian Republic. (Hungarian)

Manibus Ne Laedar Avris Lest I be injured by greedy hands. (Sweden)

Maria Luigia Princ(ipissa) Imp. Arcid. d'Austria Marie Louise, Imperial Princess Archduchess of Austria. (Parma)

Maria II D.G. Portug. et Alg. Regina Maria II, D.G., Queen of Portugal and Algarve. (Portugal)

Maria II Portug. et Algarb Regina Maria II, Queen of Portugal and Algarve. (Portugal)

Matrimonio Coniuncti Joined in wedlock. (Austria)

Maximilian Ioseph Churfurst in Baiern Maximilian Joseph, Elector in Bavaria. (Bavaria)

Maximilian Ioseph Churfurst zu Pfalzbaiern Maximilian Joseph, Elector in the Palatinate. (Rhenish Palatinate)

Maximilian Ioseph Konig von Baiern Maximilian Joseph, King of Bavaria. (Bavaria)

Maximilian Kronpr. v. Bayern u. Marie K. Prinz. v. Preuss. verm.d. 12 Octb. 1842 Maximilian, Crown Prince of Bavaria and Marie, Crown Princess of Prussia, married on October 12, 1842. (Bavaria)

Maximilian II Koenig v. Bayern Maximilian II, King of Bavaria. (Bavaria)

Maximilianus Iosephus Bavariae Rex Maximilian Joseph, King of Bavaria. (Bavaria)

Med Folket For Fosterlandet By the people for the fatherland. (Sweden)

Med Gud for Aere og Ret. Dod Den 15 November 1863 With God, for honor and justice, Died on November 15, 1863. (Denmark)

Med Logum Skal Land Byggja By law shall the land be built. (Iceland)

Megkoronaztatasanak Negyvenedik Evfordulojara Fortieth anniversary of the coronation. (Hungary)

Meglio Vivere Un Giorno Da Leone Che Cento Anni Da Pecora Better to live one day as a lion than a hundred years as a sheep. (Italy)

Michael I D.G. Portug. et Algarb. Rex Michael I, D.G., King of Portugal and Algarve. (Portugal)

Mihai I Regele Romanilor Michael I, King of Romania. (Romania)

Mikolay I Ces. Wsz. Rossyi Krol Polski Panuiacy Nicholas I, Tsar of all the Russians and present King of Poland. (Poland)

Mit Gott durch Kampf zu Sieg und Einigung With God through struggle to victory and union. (Wurttemberg)

Mit Gottes Hulfe With God's help. (Schaumburg-Lippe)

Mit Herz und Hand Fuer's Alpenland With heart and hand for the Alpine land. (Austria)

Mit Vereinten Kraeften With united strength. (Austria)

Mo(neta) Arg(entiae) Ord. Faed. Belg(ii) Holl. Silver money of the Federated Belgian Union - Holland. (Holland)

Mo. Arg. Pro Conf(oederatiae) Belg(ii) D(ucatus) Gel(riae) and C(omitatus) Z(utphaniae) Silver money of the Confederated Belgian Provinces, Duchy of Gelderland and County of Zutphen. (Netherlands)

Mo. No. Arg. Pro. Confoe. Belg. Trai. . . . .Holl. New silver money of the confederated Belgian Provinces - Utrecht or Holland. (Netherlands)

Moldova Lui Stefan in Veci a Romaniei Moldavia, Stefan the Great, his country of Romania forever. (Romania)

Mon. Nov. Castri Imp. Friedberg New money of the free city of Friedberg. (Friedberg)

Munt van Het Koningryk Der Nederlanden Money of the Kingdom of the Netherlands. (Netherlands)

Munzvereinigung Sudteutscher Staaten Monetary union of the South German States. (Bavaria)

N

Nach Funfzig-Jahriger Regierung For the fiftieth anniversary of the reign. (Schaumburg-Lippe)

Nap. Lodew. I Kon. Van Holl. Napoleon Louis I, King of Holland. (Holland)

Napoleone Imperator E Re Napoleon, Emperor and King. (Italy)

Navigare Necesse Est It is necessary to navigate. (Germany)

Nec Aspera Terrent Nor do difficulties terrify. (Brunswick)

Nec Temere Nec Timide Neither rashly nor timidly. (Danzig)

Nicolaus Friedr. Peter Gr. H. v. Oldenburg Nicholas Frederick Peter, Grand Duke of Oldenburg. (Oldenburg)

Non Relinquam Vos Orphanos I shall not leave you as orphans. (Papal States)

Nulla Dolo Via Sub Bono Principe There is no path for guile under a good prince. (Naples & Sicily)

O

Omnia Cum Deo Everything with God. (Reuss-Greiz)

Oscar Norges Sver. G. og V. Konge Oscar, King of Norway, Sweden, Gothland, and Vendalia. (Norway)

Oscar Sveriges Norr. Goth. och Vend. Konung Oscar, King of Sweden, Norway, Gothland, and Vendalia. (Sweden)

Otto Koenig von Bayern Otto, King of Bavaria. (Bavaria)

Otto Prinz v. Bayern Griechenlands Erster Koenig Otto, Prince of Bavaria, first King of Greece. (Bavaria)

P

P.M. Sa. Sc. Cz. nec no. Sv. Go. Va. He. Rex (4336-41) Prussia, Masovia, Semgallia, Czersk as well as hereditary King of Sweden, Gothland, Vandalia. (Poland)

Palma Sub Pondere Crescit The palm grows under its weight. (Waldeck)

Patria Si Dreptul Meu The country and my right. (Romania)

Patrona Bavariae Patroness of Bavaria. (Bavaria)

Paul Alexander Leopold Furst zur Lippe. Paul Alexander Leopold, Prince of hope. (Lippe-Detmold)

Paul Friedr(ich) August Gr(oss)h(erzog) v(on) Oldenburg Paul Frederick August, Grand Duke of Oldenburg. (Oldenburg)

Paul Friedrich Emil Leopold Furst z. Lippe. Paul Friedrich Emil Leopold, Prince of Lippe. (Lippe-Detmold)

Per Aspera - Ad Astra Through difficulties to the stars. (Mecklenburg-Schwerin)

Per La Gr(acia) Di Dio Duch. di Parma Piac. E. Guast D.G., Duchess of Parma, Piacenza, and Guastalla. (Parma)

Peso Grani 1726 Bonta Oncie 10.16 Grain weight 1726, fine ounces 10.16. (Ligurian Republic)

Petrus IV D.G. Portug. Algarb. Rex Peter IV, D.G., King of Portugal and Algarve. (Ligurian Republic)

Philipp Souv. Landgraf zu Hessen Phillip, Sovereign Landgrave of Hesse. (Hesse-Darmstadt)

Philipp. Landgraf z. Hessen. Ernst Ludwig Grossherzog v. Hessen u. B. R. Phillip, Landgrave of Hesse, Ernest Ludwig, Grand Duke of Hesse. (Hesse-Darmstadt)

Piece de 5 Francs Piece of 5 francs. (France)

Pius VII Pon(tifex) M(aximus) Pius VII, Pope. (Papal States)

Pius VIII Pont. Max. Pius VIII, Pope. (Papal States)

Pius IX Pont. Max. Pius IX, Pope. (Papal States)

Post Tenebras Lux Light after darkness. (Switzerland)

Pour Etre Forts Soyons Unis Let us be united to be strong. (Switzerland)

Primitiae Fodin Kuttenb. ab Aerari. Iterum Susceptarum First results dug from the Kuttenberg mines in a renewed undertaking. (Austria)

Prin Statornicie La Izbanda Through stability to success. (Romania)

Princ Aichst. Pas. et Ber. S.R.I.P. Elector Prince of Eichstaedt, Passau, and Berchtesgaden, Prince of S.R.

I., Elector. (Salzburg)

Princ Aichst. Passau et Berchtolsgad Prince of Eichstaedt, Passau, and Berchtesgaden. (Salzburg)

Princ. Gallic Magn. Elect. Imp. Prince of France, Grand Imperial Elector. (Naples & Sicily)

Principato di Lucca E Piombino Principality of Lucca and Piombino. (Naples & Sicily)

Principe E Grand' Ammiraglio Di Francia Prince and Grand Admiral of France. (Naples & Sicily)

Prinz Jean vu Letzeburg Prince Jean of Luxemburg. (Luxemburg)

Pro Deo et Populo For God and the people. (Bavaria)

Providentia Optimi Principis With the forethought of the wisest leaders. (Naples & Sicily)

Q

Quin Matrimonii Lustrum Celebrant XXIV Aprilis MDCCCLXXIX They celebrate the 25th wedding anniversary April 24, 1879. (Austria)

Quinque Coronae 5 korona. (Austria)

R

Ratt och Sanning Justice and truth. (Sweden)

Recta Tueri (or Tveri) Defend the right. (Austria & Hungary)

Regensburg Regensburg (Ratisbon). . . . . (Regensburg)

Regni Vtr. Sic. et Hier. Of the Kingdom of the Two Sicilies and Jerusalem. (Naples & Sicily)

Regno D'Italia Kingdom of Italy. (Italy)

Regno Delle Due Sicilie Kingdom of the Two Sicilies. (Naples & Sicily)

Reitersaule Maximilian's I Churfursten v. Bayern Errichtet v. Konig Ludwig I Equestrian column of Maximilian I, Elector of Bavaria, erected by King Ludwig I. (Bavaria)

Relinquo vos Liberos ab Utroque homine I leave you as children of each man. (San Marino)

Repubblica de S(an) Marino Republic of San Marino. (San Marino)

Repubblica Italiana Italian Republic. (Italian Republic)

Repubblica Ligure Ligurian Republic. (Ligurian Republic)

Repubblica Veneta Venetian Republic. (Venetian Republic)

Republica Bernensis Republic of Bern. (Republic of Bern)

Republica Portuguesa Portugese Republic. (Portugese Republic)

Republica Portuguesa, 5 de Outubro de 1910 Portugese Republic 5 October, 1910. (Portugese)

Republik Osterreich, funfzig schilling Republic of Austria, 50 schilling. (Austria)

Republika Ceskoslovenska Republic of Czechoslovakia. (Czechoslovakia)

Republique et Canton de Geneve Republic and Canton of Geneva. (Geneve)

Respublica S. Marini Republic of San Marino. (San Marino)

Ret og Sandhed Justice and truth. (Norway)

Revolucion - Cinco Pesetas - Cantonal Revolution, 5 pesetas, Cantonal. (Spain)

Rex Lomb. et Ven. Dalm. Gal. Lod. III. A.A. King of Lombardy and Venice, Dalmatia, Galicia, Lodomeria, Illyria, Archduke of Austria. (Austria)

Rey Const. de Espana Constitutional King of Spain. (Spain)

Rey de Espana Y de Las Indias King of Spain and the Indies. (Spain)

Rey de las Espanas King of the Spains. (Spain)

Reyna de Espana Y de Las Indias Queen of Spain and the Indies. (Spain)

Rey(i)na de Las Espanas Queen of the Spains. (Spain)

Roberto I D. DI PAR. PIAC. Ecc. E Luisa M. Di. Borb. Regg. Robert I, Duke of Parma, Piacenza, ... and Luisa Maria of Bourbon, Regent. (Parma)

Royaume de Belgique Kingdom of Belgium. (Belgium)

Rudolph Joan D.G. Case. A.R. Hun. Boh. Princ. A.A. Rudolph John, D.G., Imperial and Royal Prince of Hungary and Bohemia, Archduke of Austria. (Austria)

Rzeczpospolita Polska Polish Republic. (Polish)

S

S. Carolus Magnus Fundator St. Charles the Great, Founder. (Munster)

S. Maria Mater Dei Patrona Hung. Blessed Mary, Mother of God, Patron of Hungary. (Hungary)

S.R.E. Tit. S. Petri in Mont. Aur. Card. Archiep. Olom. Cardinal Archbishop of Olmutz. (Olmutz)

Salus Populi The safety of the people. (Spain)

Salus Reipublicae Suprema Lex Supreme law is the safety of the state. (Poland)

Salvam Fac Rempublicam Tuam Your state safe in union. (San Marino)

Schweizer(tsche) Eidsgenoss(enschaft) Swiss Federal

Scudo di Lire Sei 27 Pratile Anno VIII Scudo of 6 lire, June 16, 1800. (Cisalpine Republic)

Sede Vacante The chair being vacant. (Papal States)

Segen des Anhalt Bergbaues Blessings of the Anhalt mines. (Anhalt-Bernburg)

Segen des Badischer Bergbaues Blessings of the Baden mines. (Baden)

Segen des Bergbau Blessings of the mines. (Saxony)

Segen des Himmels Blessings of heaven. (Bavaria)

Se(e)gen des Mansfelder Bergbaues Blessings of the Mansfeld mines. (Prussia)

Seinem Vater Carl Friederich dem Gesegneten To his father Caarl Frederick the Victorious. (Bavaria)

Shqipni Albania. (Albania)

Sieges Thaler Victory taler. (Prussia)

Slovenska Republica Slovakian Republic. (Slovakian)

Soberania Nacional National Sovereignty. (Spain)

Sous Le Regne du Roi Leopold III In the reign of King Leopold III. (Belgium)

Standbild A. Durer's Errichtet zu Nurnberg Statue of Albrecht Durer, erected at Nuremberg. (Bavaria)

Standbild des Canzler's Freyherrn v. Kreittmayr, Errichtet in Munchen 1845 Statue of Chancellor Baron von Kreittmayr, erected in Munich, 1845. (Bavaria)

Standbild des Furstbischof's Julius Echter v. Mespelbrunn, Errichtet zu Wurzburg 1847 Statue of Bishop-Elector Julius Echter of Mespelbrunn, erected at Wurzburg, 1847. (Bavaria)

Standbild des Johann Christoph Ritter von Gluck, Errichtet in Munchen v. Konig Ludwig I 1848 Statue of John Christopher, Knight von Gluck, erected at Munich by King Ludwig I, 1848. (Bavaria)

Standbild des Roland de Latre gen. Orlando di Lasso, Errichtet in Munchen v. Konig Ludwig I 1849 Statue of Roland de Latre called Orlando di Lasso, erected in Munich by King Ludwig I, 1849. (Bavaria)

Standbild Jean Paul Friedrich Richter's, Errichtet zu Bayreuth 1841 Statue of Jean Paul Frederick Richter, erected at Bayreuth, 1841. (Bavaria)

Stark im Recht Strong in justice. (Frankfurt)

Stato Pontificio The Papal State. (Papal States)

Stiftung des Ludwigs-Ordens Founding of the Ludwig Order. (Bavaria)

Supra Firmam Petram Upon a firm rock. (Papal States)

Susceptor Noster Deus God is our defense. (Tuscany)

Suum Cuique, Loenungs Thaler To each his own, coronation thaler. (Prussia)

Svensk. Odlings Beframjare Promoter of Swedish culture. (Swedish)

Svenska Folkets Lagbundna Frihet Freedom within the law of the Swedish people. (Swedish)

Sveriges Riksdag Swedish Parliament. (Swedish)

Szechenyi, Istvan Stephen Szechenyi. (Hungary)

Szt. Istvan St. Stephen. (Hungary)

Szuletesenek 75 Evfordulojara 75th anniversary of his birth. (Hungary)

T

Tansics, Mihaly Michael Tancsics. (Hungary)

Tausend Jahre Burg und Stadt Meissen A thousand years of the town and city of Meissen. (Germany)

(In) Terra Pax Peace in the land. (Papal States)

Tir Federal a Fribourg Federal Shooting Match at Fribourg. (Switzerland)

Tir Federal a la Chaux-de-Fonds Juillet 1863 Federal Shooting Match at Chaux-de-Fonds, July, 1863. (Switzerland)

Tir Federal de 1876 a Lausanne Federal Shooting Match of 1876 at Lausanne. (Switzerland)

Tiro Federale in Lugano Federal Shooting Match at Lugano. (Switzerland)

Tiroler Freiheit Tyrolean liberty. (Austria)

Trau - Schau Wem Trust, look, to whom. (Baden)

Treu Der Verfassung Loyal to the constitution. (Germany)

Tritt die Regierung des Landes an am 13 October 1825 Assumes the government of the country on October 13, 1825. (Bavaria)

Tueatur Unita Deus, Anno Dom 1847 May God guard these United (Kingdoms) in the year of our Lord 1847. (Great Britain)

Turkiye Cumhuriyeti Republic of Turkey. (Turkey)

U

Ueb Aug und Hand Fuer's Vaterland Train eye and hand for the fatherland. (Austria)

Umberto I Re D'Italia Humbert I, King of Italy. (Italy)

Union et Force Union and strength. (France)

Unione E Virtu' Union and strength. (Cisalpine Republic)

Unione Italiana Italian Union. (Venice)

Ut sit suo Pondere Tutus That he may be safe by his own weight. (Nassau)

U(V)tr. Sic. Hier. Hisp. Inf(ans) Of the Two Sicilies and Jerusalem, Prince of Spain. (Naples & Sicily)

V

V.G.G. Heinrich d. XIII Aelt. Reuss G.U.H.V.P. Reg. F.z. Greiz D.G., Henry the XIII, eldest line of Reuss, Count and Lord of Plauen, ruling Prince of Greiz. (Reuss-Greiz)

Veni Lumen Cordium Come light of hearts. (Papal States)

Verbum Dni. Manet in Aeternum The word of the Lord abides forever. (Hesse-Darmstadt)

Vereinsmunze (many) Convention money. (German States)

Vereinten sich mit den Getreuen Staenden zu neuer Verfassung des Staats They united themselves with the faithful supporters in the new composition of the state. (Saxony)

Verfassungssaeule, Errichtet vom Gr. v. Schoenborn, Eingeweiht 1828 Constitution column erected by Count von Schoenborn, dedicated 1828. (Bavaria)

Veritas Lex Tua The truth is your law. (Salzburg)

Verlegung der Ludwig Maximilians Hochschule von Landshut nach Munchen 1826 Removal of the Ludwig Maximilian University from Landshut to Munich, 1826. (Bavaria)

Verni Sebe-Svorne Napred Faithful to ourselves, united forward. (Slovakia)

Vic. Em. D.G. Rex Sar. Cyp. et Ier. Victor Emmanuel, D.G., King of Sardinia, Cyprus, and Jerusalem. (Sardinia)

Victoria Dei Gratia Victoria, D.G. (Great Britain)

Victoria Dei Gratia Britanniar. Reg. F.D. Victoria, D.G., Queen of the Britains, Defender of the Faith. (Great Britain)

Victoria Dei Gra. Britt. Regina Fid. Def. Ind. Imp. Victoria, D.G., Queen of Britain, Defender of the Faith, Empress of India. (Great Britain)

Victoria D.G. Britt. Reg. F.D. Victoria, D.G., Queen of Britain, Defender of the Faith. (Great Britain)

Victorius Emmanuel II D.G. Rex Sard. Cyp. et Hier. Victor Emmanuel II, D.G., King of Sardinia, Cyprus, and Jerusalem. (Great Britain)

Videant Pauperes et Laetentur Let the poor see and rejoice. (Tuscany)

Vierzehn Eine Feine Mark Fourteen to the fine mark. (Prussia)

Viribus Unitis With men united. (Austria)

Virtute et Prudentia With virtue and prudence. (Austria)

Virtute Viam Dimetiar I shall mark the way with valour. (Waldeck)

Vitez Nagybanyai Horthy Miklos Kormanyzosaganak 10 Evfordulojara 10th anniversary of the government of the great hero, Nicholas Horthy. (Hungary)

Vitez Nagybanyai Horthy Miklos Kormanyzorszog Kormanyzoja Hungarian government of the great hero Nicholas Horthy. (Hungary)

Vitt. Em. III Re Victor Emmanuel III, King. (Italy)

Vittorio Emanuele II Victor Emmanuel II; . . . . . **Re d'Italia** King of Italy. (Italy)

Vittorio Emanuele III Victor Emmanuel III; . . . . . **Re . . . .** King; **d'Italia** . . . . .of Italy; **E Imperator** . . . . . and Emperor. (Italy)

Vollendet den 5 Mai 1827, Psalm 91 V. 14-16 Completed on May 5, 1827, Psalm 91, verses 14-16. (Saxony)

Vollendung der Oesterreichischen Sudbahn Completion of the Austrian Southern Railways. (Austria)

W

W. Setna Rocznice Powstania 100th anniversary of liberation. (Poland)

Waldeckischer Kronthaler Waldeck crown thaler. (Waldeck)

Walhalla Valhalla. (Bavaria)

Wiener Munzvertrag 24 Jan. 1857 Vienna monetary convention January 24, 1857. (Schaumburg-Lippe)

Wilh. II Kurf. u. Friedr. Wilh. Kurpr. u. Mitregent William II, Elector, and Frederick William, Elector and Co-Regent. (Hesse-Cassel)

Wilh. II Kurf. u. Friedr. Wilh. Kurprinz-Mitregent William II, Elector, and Frederick William, Electoral Prince and Co-Regent. (Hesse-Cassel)

Wilhalm Ernst - Caroline Groszherzog u. Groszherzogin v. Sachsen William Ernest, Caroline, Grand Duke and Grand Duchess of Saxony (Weimar). (Saxe-Weimar)

Wilhelm Deutscher Kaiser Konig v. Preussen William, Emperor of Germany, King of Prussia. (Prussia)

Wilhelm Herzog z. Braunschweig u. L(un) William, Duke of Brunswick and Luneburg. (Brunswick-Luneburg)

Wilhelm Herzog zu Nassau William, Duke of Nassau. (Nassau)

Wilhelm Koenig. Augusta Koenigin v. Preussen William, King, Augusta, Queen of Prussia. (Prussia)

Wilhelm Koenig von Preussen William, King of Prussia. (Prussia)

Wilhelm Koenig von Wurt(t)em(berg) William, King of Wurttemberg. (Wurttemberg)

Wilhelm Konig v. Wurttemberg William, King of Wurttemberg. (Wurttemberg)

Wilhelm I Kurf. Souv. Landgr. z. Hessen. Gr. H.v. Fulda William I, Elector, Sovereign, Landgrave of Hesse, Grand Duke of Fulda. (Hesse-Cassel)

Wilhelm II Deutscher Kaiser Konig v. Preussen William II, Emperor of Germany, King of Prussia. (Prussia)

Wilhelm II Koenig von Wuerttemberg William II, King of Wurttemberg. (Wurttemberg)

Wilhelm II Kurf. Souv. Langr. z. Hessen Gr. H. v. Fulda William II, Elector, Sovereign, Landgrave of Hesse, Grand Duke of Fulda. (Hesse-Cassel)

Wilhelm IV Koenig v. Gr. Brit. u. Hannover William IV, King of Great Britain and Hannover. (Hannover)

Wilhelmina Koningin der Nederlanden Wilhelmina, Queen of the Netherlands. (Netherlands)

Wilhelmus S(acri) R(omani) I(mperii) Pr(inceps) Auersperg Dux de Gotshee William, Prince of S.R.I. and Auersperg, Duke of Gotschee. (Auersperg)

Wilhelmus I D.G. Elect. Landg. Hass. William I, D.G., Elector and Landgrave of Hesse. (Hesse-Cassel)

Wilhelmus IX D.G. Hass. Landg. Com. Han. William IX, D.G., Landgrave of Hesse, Count of Hanau. (Hesse-Cassel)

Willem Koning der Ned(erlanden) G(root) H(ertog) V(an) L(uxemburg) William, King of the Netherlands, Grand Duke of Luxembourg. (Netherlands)

Willem II Koning der Ned. G.H.V.L. William II, King of the Netherlands. . . . . (Netherlands)

Willem III Koning der Ned. G.H.V.L. William III, King of the Netherlands, ... (Netherlands)

Wir Wollen Sein Ein Einig Volk von Brudern We will be a united people of brothers. (Austria)

X

Y

Ylas Baleares Balearic Islands. (Spain)

Z

Z. Sreba Kraiowego From the nation's silver. (Poland)

Zehen Eine Feine Mark (many). 10 to the fine mark. (German States)

Zehn Eine Feine Mark (many). 10 to the fine mark. (German States)

Zehn Eine Mark Feine (many) 10 to the fine mark. (German States)

Zollverein mit Preussen, Sachsen, Hessen. U. Thuringen Customs union with Prussia, Saxony, Hesse, and Thuringia. (Bavaria)

Zu Gothe's Hundertjahriger Geburtsfeier am 28 August 1849 For the centennial of Goethe's birth on August 28, 1849. (Frankfurt)

Zu Ihrer Voelker Heil To the welfare of the peoples. (Bavaria)

Zur Dritten Sacularfeier des Religions Friedens vom 25 Sept. For the third centenary of the Religious Peace on September 25. (Frankfurt)

Zur Erinnerung an d. Wiederherstellung d. Munsters in Ulm In commemoration of the restoration of the cathedral in Ulm. (Wurttemberg)

Zur Erinnerung an den Glorreich Erkampften Frieden vom 10 Mai 1871 In commemoration of the gloriously fought for peace of May 10, 1871. (Bremen)

Zur Erinnerung an die Feier des 13 Dec. 1865 In commemoration of the celebration of December 13, 1865. (Hannover)

Zur Erinnerung an die Wiederherstellung der Mariensaule in Munchen In commemoration of the restoration of the Madonna column in Munich. (Bavaria)

Zur Erinnerung an Sr. Majestat des Konigs und Ihrer Majestat der Konigin allerhochsten Besuch d. Munze In commemoration of His Majesty the King's and Her Majesty the Queen's most gracious visit to the mint. (Hannover)

Zur Eroffnung des Carl Ludwig Hauses auf der Raxalpe Im September 1877 On the opening of the Carl Ludwig Inn on the Raxalpe in September, 1877. (Austria)

Zur Feier der 25 Jaehrigen Regierung For the of the 25th anniversary of the reign. (Brunswick)

Zur Feier Funf und Zwanzig Jahriger Regierung For the celebration of the 25th anniversary of the reign. (Reuss-Ebersdorf)

Zur Feier 25 Jahriger Regierung am 7 Marz 1867 For the celebration of the 25th anniversary of the reign on March 7, 1867. (Mecklenburg-Schwerin)

Zur Feier 25 Jaehriger Segensreicher Regierung For the celebration of the 25th anniversary of the prosperous reign. (Nassau)

Zur Feier XXV Jaehriger Regierung d. 17 April 1843 For the celebration of the 25th anniversary of the reign on April 17, 1843. (Reuss-Schleiz)

Zur Feier 50 Jaehriger Regierung d. 6 Nov. 1864 For the celebration of the 50th anniversary of the reign on November 6, 1864. (Schwarzburg-Rudolstadt)

Zurich Zurich. (Zurich)

Zur Sicherung des Gewichts On the guarantee of the weight. (Nassau)

Zur v. Sacularfeier des Munz-rechts der Stadt Frankfurt A.M. For the centenary of the minting rights of the city of Frankfurt-on-the-Main. (Frankfurt)

Zur 50 Jahrigen Jubelfeier der Befreiung Deutschlands On the 50th anniversary jubilee of the deliverance of Germany. (Bremen)

Zur 50 Jahrigen Vereinigung Ostfrieslands mit Hannover On the 50th anniversary of the union of East Friesland with Hannover. (Hannover)

Zwei Gulden XLV Ket Forint Two gulden 45 two florins. (Austria)

Zwei Vereinsthaler XV Ein Pfund Fein (many) 2 Vereinstalers, 15 to the fine pound. (German States)

Zweites Deutsches Bundesschiessen in Bremen 1865 Second German Shooting match in Bremen, 1865. (Bremen)

NUMBERS

75/100 Delar Finsilfver 75/100 dollar fine silver. (Sweden)

I Oesterreichisches Bundesschiessen First Austrian Shooting Match. (Austria)

I Thaler Hannoverisch Cassen-Geld One thaler Hannoverian Cassa money. (Hannover)

III Deutsches Bundes Schiessen Wien 1869 Third German Shooting Match at Vienna, 1868. (Austria)

4 Centenario da Descoberta da India Fourth centenary of the discovery of India. (Portugal)

IX Olympische Winterspiele Ninth Olympic Winter Games. (Austria)

32 Schillinge Hamburger Courant 32 schilling current Hamburg. (Hamburg)

60 Schilling Schlesw. Holst. Courant 60 schillings current money Schleswig-Holstein. (Schleswig-Holstein)

450 Jahre Universitat Tubingen 450th anniversary of Tubingen University. (Germany)

534 8/9 Troyska Ass Finsilfver 534 8/9 Troy ounces fine silver. (Poland)

600 Jahre Tirol Osterreich 600 years Tyrol Austria. (Austria)

MDCCCLI Civium Industria Floret Civitas By the industry of the people, the state flourishes 1851. (Great Britain)

HEJIRA DATE CONVERSION CHART

HEJIRA DATE CHART

HEJIRA (Hijra, Hegira), the name of the Muslim era (A.H. = Anno Hegirae) dates back to the Christian year 622 when Mohammed "fled" from Mecca, escaping to Medina to avoid persecution from the Koreish tribemen. Based on a lunar year the Muslim year is 11 days shorter.

*= Leap Year (Christian Calendar)

AH Hejira	AD Christian Date
1010	1601, July 2
1011	1602, June 21
1012	1603, June 11
1013	1604, May 30
1014	1605, May 19
1015	1606, May 19
1016	1607, May 9
1017	1608, April 28
1018	1609, April 6
1019	1610, March 26
1020	1611, March 16
1021	1612, March 4
1022	1613, February 21
1023	1614, February 11
1024	1615, January 31
1025	1616, January 20
1026	1617, January 9
1027	1617, December 29
1028	1618, December 19
1029	1619, December 8
1030	1620, November 26
1031	1621, November 16
1032	1622, November 5
1033	1623, October 25
1034	1624, October 14
1035	1625, October 3
1036	1626, September 22
1037	1627, September 12
1038	1628, August 31
1039	1629, August 21
1040	1630, July 10
1041	1631, July 30
1042	1632, July 19
1043	1633, July 8
1044	1634, June 27
1045	1635, June 17
1046	1636, June 5
1047	1637, May 26
1048	1638, May 15
1049	1639, May 4
1050	1640, April 23
1051	1641, April 12
1052	1642, April 1
1053	1643, March 22
1054	1644, March 10
1055	1645, February 27
1056	1646, February 17
1057	1647, February 6
1058	1648, January 27
1059	1649, January 15
1060	1650, January 4
1061	1650, December 25
1062	1651, December 14
1063	1652, December 2
1064	1653, November 22
1065	1654, November 11
1066	1655, October 31
1067	1656, October 20
1068	1657, October 9
1069	1658, September 29
1070	1659, September 18
1071	1660, September 6
1072	1661, August 27
1073	1662, August 16
1074	1663, August 5
1075	1664, July 25
1076	1665, July 14
1077	1666, July 4
1078	1667, June 23
1079	1668, June 11
1080	1669, June 1
1081	1670, May 21
1082	1671, May 10
1083	1672, April 29
1084	1673, April 18
1085	1674, April 7
1086	1675, March 28

AH Hejira	AD Christian Date	AH Hejira	AD Christian Date	AH Hejira	AD Christian Date	AH Hejira	AD Christian Date
1087	1676, March 16*	1178	1764, July 1*	1269	1852, October 15*	1360	1941, January 29
1088	1677, March 6	1179	1765, June 20	1270	1853, October 4	1361	1942, January 19
1089	1678, February 23	1180	1766, June 9	1271	1854, September 24	1362	1943, January 8
1090	1679, February 12	1181	1767, May 30	1272	1855, September 13	1363	1943, December 28
1091	1680, February 2*	1182	1768, May 18*	1273	1856, September 1*	1364	1944, December 17*
1092	1681, January 21	1183	1769, May 7	1274	1857, August 22	1365	1945, December 6
1093	1682, January 10	1184	1770, April 27	1275	1858, August 11	1366	1946, November 25
1094	1682, December 31	1185	1771, April 16	1276	1859, July 31	1367	1947, November 15
1095	1683, December 20	1186	1772, April 4*	1277	1860, July 20*	1368	1948, November 3*
1096	1684, December 8*	1187	1773, March 25	1278	1861, July 9	1369	1949, October 24
1097	1685, November 28	1188	1774, March 14	1279	1862, June 29	1370	1950, October 13
1098	1686, November 17	1189	1775, March 4	1280	1863, June 18	1371	1951, October 2
1099	1687, November 7	1190	1776, February 21*	1281	1864, June 6*	1372	1952, September 21*
1100	1688, October 26*	1191	1777, February 9	1282	1865, May 27	1373	1953, September 10
1101	1689, October 15	1192	1778, January 30	1283	1866, May 16	1374	1954, August 30
1102	1690, October 5	1193	1779, January 19	1284	1867, May 5	1375	1955, August 20
1103	1691, September 24	1194	1780, January 8*	1285	1868, April 24*	1376	1956, August 8*
1104	1692, September 12*	1195	1780, December 28*	1286	1869, April 13	1377	1957, July 29
1105	1693, September 2	1196	1781, December 17	1287	1870, April 3	1378	1958, July 18
1106	1694, August 22	1197	1782, December 7	1288	1871, March 23	1379	1959, July 7
1107	1695, August 12	1198	1783, November 26	1289	1872, March 11*	1380	1960, June 25*
1108	1696, July 31*	1199	1784, November 14*	1290	1873, March 1	1381	1961, June 14
1109	1697, July 20	1200	1785, November 4	1291	1874, February 18	1382	1962, June 4
1110	1698, July 10	1201	1786, October 24	1292	1875, February 7	1383	1963, May 25
1111	1699, June 29	1202	1787, October 13	1293	1876, January 28*	1384	1964, May 13*
1112	1700, June 18	1203	1788, October 2*	1294	1877, January 16	1385	1965, May 2
1113	1701, June 8	1204	1789, September 21	1295	1878, January 5	1386	1966, April 22
1114	1702, May 28	1205	1790, September 10	1296	1878, December 26	1387	1967, April 11
1115	1703, May 17	1206	1791, August 31	1297	1879, December 15	1388	1968, March 31*
1116	1704, May 6*	1207	1792, August 19*	1298	1880, December 4*	1389	1969, March 20
1117	1705, April 25	1208	1793, August 9	1299	1881, November 23	1390	1970, March 9
1118	1706, April 15	1209	1794, July 29	1300	1882, November 12	1391	1971, February 27
1119	1707, April 4	1210	1795, July 18	1301	1883, November 2	1392	1972, February 16*
1120	1708, March 23*	1211	1796, July 7*	1302	1884, October 21*	1393	1973, February 4
1121	1709, March 18	1212	1797, June 26	1303	1885, October 10	1394	1974, January 25
1122	1710, March 2	1213	1798, June 15	1304	1886, September 30	1395	1975, January 14
1123	1711, February 19	1214	1799, June 5	1305	1887, September 19	1396	1976, January 3*
1124	1712, February 9*	1215	1800, May 25	1306	1888, September 7*	1397	1976, December 23*
1125	1713, January 28	1216	1801, May 14	1307	1889, August 28	1398	1977, December 12
1126	1714, January 17	1217	1802, May 4	1308	1890, August 17	1399	1978, December 2
1127	1715, January 7	1218	1803, April 23	1309	1891, August 7	1400	1979, November 21
1128	1715, December 27	1219	1804, April 12*	1310	1892, July 26*	1401	1980, November 9*
1129	1716, December 16*	1220	1805, April 1	1311	1893, July 15	1402	1981, October 30
1130	1717, December 5	1221	1806, March 21	1312	1894, July 5	1403	1982, October 19
1131	1718, November 24	1222	1807, March 11	1313	1895, June 24	1404	1983, October 8
1132	1719, November 14	1223	1808, February 28*	1314	1896, June 12*	1405	1984, September 27*
1133	1720, November 2*	1224	1809, February 16	1315	1897, June 2	1406	1985, September 16
1134	1721, October 22	1225	1810, February 6	1316	1898, May 22	1407	1986, September 6
1135	1722, October 12	1226	1811, January 26	1317	1899, May 12	1408	1987, August 26
1136	1723, October 1	1227	1812, January 16*	1318	1900, May 1	1409	1988, August 14*
1137	1724, September 29*	1228	1813, January 4	1319	1901, April 20	1410	1989, August 3
1138	1725, September 9	1229	1813, December 24	1320	1902, April 10	1411	1990, July 24
1139	1726, August 29	1230	1814, December 14	1321	1903, March 30	1412	1991, July 13
1140	1727, August 19	1231	1815, December 3	1322	1904, March 18*	1413	1992, July 2*
1141	1728, August 7*	1232	1816, November 21*	1323	1905, March 8	1414	1993, June 21
1142	1729, July 27	1233	1817, November 11	1324	1906, February 25	1415	1994, June 10
1143	1730, July 17	1234	1818, October 31	1325	1907, February 14	1416	1995, May 31
1144	1731, July 6	1235	1819, October 20	1326	1908, February 4*	1417	1996, May 19*
1145	1732, June 24*	1236	1820, October 9*	1327	1909, January 23	1418	1997, May 9
1146	1733, June 14	1237	1821, September 28	1328	1910, January 13	1419	1998, April 28
1147	1734, June 3	1238	1822, September 18	1329	1911, January 2	1420	1999, April 17
1148	1735, May 24	1239	1823, September 7	1330	1911, December 22	1421	2000, April 6*
1149	1736, May 12*	1240	1824, August 26*	1331	1912, December 11*	1422	2001, March 26
1150	1737, May 1	1241	1825, August 16	1332	1913, November 30	1423	2002, March 15
1151	1738, April 21	1242	1826, August 5	1333	1914, November 19	1424	2003, March 5
1152	1739, April 10	1243	1827, July 25	1334	1915, November 9	1425	2004, February 22*
1153	1740, March 29*	1244	1828, July 14*	1335	1916, October 28*	1426	2005, February 10
1154	1741, March 19	1245	1829, July 3	1336	1917, October 17	1427	2006, January 31
1155	1742, March 8	1246	1830, June 22	1337	1918, October 7	1428	2007, January 20
1156	1743, February 25	1247	1831, June 12	1338	1919, September 26	1429	2008, January 10*
1157	1744, February 15*	1248	1832, May 31*	1339	1920, September 15*	1430	2008, December 29
1158	1745, February 3	1249	1833, May 21	1340	1921, September 4	1431	2009, December 18
1159	1746, January 24	1250	1834, May 10	1341	1922, August 24	1432	2010, December 8
1160	1747, January 13	1251	1835, April 29	1342	1923, August 14	1433	2011, November 27*
1161	1748, January 2	1252	1836, April 18*	1343	1924, August 2*	1434	2012, November 15
1162	1748, December 22*	1253	1837, April 7	1344	1925, July 22	1435	2013, November 5
1163	1749, December 11	1254	1838, March 27	1345	1926, July 12	1436	2014, October 25
1164	1750, November 30	1255	1839, March 17	1346	1927, July 1	1437	2015, October 15*
1165	1751, November 20	1256	1840, March 5*	1347	1928, June 20*	1438	2016, October 3
1166	1752, November 8*	1257	1841, February 23	1348	1929, June 9	1439	2017, September 22
1167	1753, October 29	1258	1842, February 12	1349	1930, May 29	1440	2018, September 12
1168	1754, October 18	1259	1843, February 1	1350	1931, May 19	1441	2019, September 11*
1169	1755, October 7	1260	1844, January 22*	1351	1932, May 7*	1442	2020, August 20
1170	1756, September 26*	1261	1845, January 10	1352	1933, April 26	1443	2021, August 10
1171	1757, September 15	1262	1845, December 30	1353	1934, April 16	1444	2022, July 30
1172	1758, September 4	1263	1846, December 20	1354	1935, April 5	1445	2023, July 19*
1173	1759, August 25	1264	1847, December 9	1355	1936, March 24*	1446	2024, July 8
1174	1760, August 13*	1265	1848, November 27*	1356	1937, March 14	1447	2025, June 27
1175	1761, August 2	1266	1849, November 17	1357	1938, March 3	1448	2026, June 17
1176	1762, July 28	1267	1850, November 6	1358	1939, February 21	1449	2027, June 6*
1177	1763, July 12	1268	1851, October 27	1359	1940, February 10*	1450	2028, May 25